With Supplement

# CHAMBERS TWENTIETH CENTURY DICTIONARY

Edited by A M Macdonald OBE BA(Oxon)

Chambers

W & R Chambers Ltd
11 Thistle Street Edinburgh EH2 1DG

New edition © W & R Chambers Ltd 1972
Supplement © W & R Chambers Ltd 1977

Latest Reprint 1980

| | |
|---|---|
| Standard | ISBN 0 550 10226 4 |
| Presentation | ISBN 0 550 10227 2 |
| Quarter Leather | ISBN 0 550 10228 0 |
| Full Leather | ISBN 0 550 10229 9 |
| Half Leather handbound | ISBN 0 550 10230 2 |
| Full Leather handbound | ISBN 0 550 10231 0 |

Printed in Great Britain by
Clark Constable Ltd.
Edinburgh

# Contents

# Publisher's preface

*Chambers Twentieth Century Dictionary* has always faithfully reflected changes in a living language. Now the pace of change has increased rapidly, for many diverse influences are at work, and a new version has had to be prepared.

There have been revolutionary developments in the sciences and technology, and the influence of mass media has made new scientific and technical terms no longer the monopoly of the specialist. The hitherto somewhat rigid barrier between formal and colloquial English is collapsing to such an extent that some contemporary fiction is virtually unintelligible to those without a wide colloquial vocabulary. Again, the hitherto largely artificial gulf between 'English' and 'American English' is being bridged. At the same time Britain's closer ties with Europe are increasing the number of foreign words and phrases likely to be encountered by the reader of English.

As the 1970s dawned, it became clear that our normal continuous and painstaking revision of the existing text was inadequate for modern needs. A fundamental reappraisal was begun.

This, then, is the first entirely new edition of the *Twentieth Century Dictionary* in twenty years. For many years the most comprehensive dictionary designed for general use, it has now been brought fully abreast of the 1970s in its coverage of everyday language and affairs.

The continuing aim is to provide, in convenient and easily legible form, a comprehensive vocabulary aid for the present-day reader, speaker and writer of English. We have retained all the features which have made the *Twentieth Century Dictionary* the valued companion of the literary reader and writer, but the whole work has been thoroughly re-examined. To a large extent, however, we have concentrated on recording the changes taking place in contemporary English.

This new edition is almost one-fifth longer than its predecessor. In part this is due to the increased size of type: the main reason for the greater length, however, is the vast amount of additional material.

Many of the words and phrases added such as *fibre optics, free-rider, genetic engineering, hologram, jet set, patrial, running mate, solar noise, value-added tax* and *velodrome* are new. Other, older words (and these form a very important category) have recently acquired new and highly specialised meanings which have been added in this edition: for example, *capsule, core, dish, gay, gutsy, kitsch, module, stewardship, underground,* and *viable*.

This new edition is catholic and broadminded in its noting of colloquialisms and slang terms, as these may now be considered an integral part of spoken and written English. For example, definitions are given of such words as *drop out, hang-up, switched on, turn on, uptight* and *whizz-kid*.

Examples of the large number of foreign words and phrases appearing in the main text are *actualités, antipasto, apparatchik, batterie de cuisine, gesellschaft* and *souk*. American words in current use are no longer denied full acceptance by being glossed 'U.S.' and American spellings such as the following are given as alternatives: *defence*, in U.S. *defense*; *anaesthesia*, in U.S. *anesthesia*; *manoeuvre*, in U.S. *maneuver*; *moulding*, in U.S. *molding*.

Other distinguishing features are the detailed etymologies, the pronunciation guides, the appendices, the idiomatic turns of speech and, last but not least, the literary words from the sixteenth century onwards which have for so long made *Chambers Twentieth Century Dictionary* the chosen companion of the omnivorous general reader as well as the crossword addict's favourite tool.

Many hundreds of new words and meanings from many sources have been collected by the dictionary staff, but we are indebted also to scores of users of the dictionary who have sent in words and lists of words. We value greatly the interest they have shown.

The excellence and comprehensive nature of the *Twentieth Century Dictionary* still owes much to the sure foundations laid by three former Editors: Rev. Thomas Davidson, William Geddie MA BSc and John M. Dickie MA. The immense task of preparing this new edition has been directed throughout by Miss A. M. Macdonald BA whose experience of dictionary making is probably unrivalled. Her knowledge, advice and help have always been readily given to her colleagues, among whom Mrs E. Kirkpatrick MA and Miss P. Kerr MA have been the principal assistant editors. To all of them we, the publishers, wish to express our appreciation.

## Note on this edition

Considerable revisions have been made to this edition. As well as alterations to the text, emendations have been made to several of the appendices. In particular, the list of abbreviations has been updated and extended.

## Supplement

Language is never static; alterations and additions are continually being made to it. Consequently we have added a supplement to take account of recent developments. It contains words and phrases which are new to British English, such as **access broadcasting, quadraphonics, flexitime, skateboard** and **white hole,** words which have acquired new meanings, such as **bionics, ethnic** and **tachograph,** and words which have come into greater prominence in recent years, such as **mesothelioma** and **toxocara.**

# Notes to the user of the dictionary

## The Arrangement of Entries

In order to save space, words from the same root have often been grouped together under a headword, but cross-references have been included where these seemed necessary. Thus, we have given '**patrology** (see **patristic**)', but not '**coolness** (see **cool**)'. Where elementary word-building is concerned, we have sometimes left the reader to make words for himself. Nowadays most adjectives can be used to make nouns in **-ness**, but we do not claim to have given a noun in **-ness** with every possible adjective. Similarly, we have not always noted that a present participle in **-ing** can be made from a verb and used also as an adjective or noun.

Derivatives are not listed in crude alphabetical order but in a more logical form. The direct derivatives, i.e. the headword with an inseparable suffix, come first. These are followed by compound words beginning with the headword and then by phrases containing the headword. In each of the three groups terms appear in alphabetical order.

## Labels

The position of the classifying or descriptive labels attached to words and meanings is significant. A label relating to *grammatical form* appears before the word or meaning to which it applies. A label relating to *classification* (e.g. *coll.*, *slang*, *obs.*, *chem.*, *elect.*, *psych.*) precedes the list of meanings where it applies to all the meanings given. Where a label applies to only one meaning of a word it immediately follows that meaning.

## Literary Words

In cases where the use of a word by a particular author is the main reason for its inclusion, the author is usually named. Often, however, the word is found also in other writers of the same period. Scots words have been included because they were used by eighteenth- and nineteenth-century writers who are generally regarded as being in the mainstream of English literature.

### Etymologies

The etymology is given in square brackets at the end of each article. The sign — is to be read 'derived from'. Whatever follows after a semicolon is not the source of the word but a word from the same ultimate source.

### German Nouns

A point to note is that German nouns have not been given the initial capital letter, as in an English dictionary the capital might mislead.

### Pronunciation

A detailed chart of pronunciation is given on pages viii and ix.

# Detailed chart of pronunciation

Respelling is a rough method of showing pronunciation compared with the use of phonetic symbols, but it has two merits—it is intelligible to a large number of people who do not know phonetic symbols, and it allows for more than one interpretation so that each user of the dictionary may choose a pronunciation in keeping with his speech.

## Vowels and Diphthongs in Accented Syllables

| Symbol | | Examples | Pronunciation |
|---|---|---|---|
| ā | as in | name, aid, rein, tare, wear, hair, heir | nām, ād, rān, tār, wār, hār, ār |
| ä | ,, | grass, path, palm, harm, heart | gräs, päth, päm, härm, härt |
| a | ,, | sat, bad, have | sat, bad, hav |
| ē | ,, | lean, keel, dene, chief, seize, gear, sheer, here, bier | lēn, kēl, dēn, chēf, sēz, gēr, shēr, hēr, bēr |
| e | ,, | red, thread, said, bury | red, thred, sed, ber'i, |
| ī | ,, | side, shy, dye, height, hire, byre | sīd, shī, dī, hīt, hīr, bīr |
| i | ,, | pin, busy, hymn | pin, biz'i, him |
| ō | ,, | bone, road, foe, low, dough, more, soar, floor, port | bōn, rōd, fō, lō, dō, mōr, sōr, flōr, pōrt |
| | | (For alternative pronunciation of port, more, etc., see ö) | |
| o | ,, | got, shot, shone | got, shot, shon |
| ö | ,, | haul, lawn, fall, bought, swarm, port, more | höl, lön, föl, böt, swörm, pört, mör |
| | | (For alternative pronunciation of port, more, etc., see ō) | |
| ōō | ,, | fool, sou, boor, tour | fōōl, sōō, bōōr, tōōr |
| ŏŏ | ,, | good, full, would | gŏŏd, fŏŏl, wŏŏd |
| ū | ,, | tune, due, newt, view, endure | tūn, dū, nūt, vū, in-dūr' |
| u | ,, | bud, run, love | bud, run, luv |
| û | ,, | heard, bird, world, absurd | hûrd, bûrd, wûrld, ab-sûrd' |
| ow | ,, | mount, frown, sour | mownt, frown, sowr |
| oi | ,, | toy, buoy, soil | toi, boi, soil |

## Vowels in Unaccented Syllables

Neutral vowels in unaccented syllables are usually shown by ə (schwa);
    e.g. el'ə-mənt, in'fənt, ran'dəm, pre'shəs (precious), nā'chər (nature)
In certain cases, they are more exactly represented by i;
    e.g. ē'vil, bi-hōld', bles'id, man'ij, di-ment'

## Vowels followed by r

In certain accents, for example in Scots, Irish, General American, r is pronounced wherever it occurs in the spelling and this is the form adopted in the dictionary.
In certain other accents, for example Received Pronunciation or what is sometimes called the BBC accent, it is pronounced only when it occurs before a vowel. Elsewhere the following rules apply.

| | | | |
|---|---|---|---|
| ār | is pronounced as | | eə |
| är | ,, | ,, ,, | ä |
| ēr | ,, | ,, ,, | ēə |
| er | ,, | ,, ,, | eə |
| īr | ,, | ,, ,, | īə |
| ör | ,, | ,, ,, | ö or öə |
| ōōr | ,, | ,, ,, | ōōə |
| ūr | ,, | ,, ,, | ūə |
| ûr | ,, | ,, ,, | ûə |
| owr | ,, | ,, ,, | owə |

# Consonants

| Symbol | | Examples | Pronunciation |
|---|---|---|---|
| *b* | as in | hob, rabbit | *hob, rab'it* |
| *ch* | ,, | church, much, match | *chûrch, much, mach* |
| *d* | ,, | ado, dew | *ə-dōō', dū* |
| *dh* | ,, | then, father | *dhen, fä'dhər* |
| *f* | ,, | faint, phase, rough | *fānt, fāz, ruf* |
| *g* | ,, | gold, guard, ghastly | *gold, gärd, gäst'li* |
| *gz* | ,, | exact | *igz-akt'* |
| *h* | ,, | happy, home | *hap'i, hōm* |
| *hh* | ,, | loch, leprechaun | *lohh, lep'rə-hhön* |
| *(h)w* | ,, | whale, which | *(h)wāl, (h)wich* |
| *j* | ,, | jack, gentle, ledge, region | *jak, jen'tl, lej, rē'jən* |
| *k* | ,, | keep, cat, chorus | *kēp, kat, kōr'əs (kör')* |
| *ks* | ,, | lax, vex | *laks, veks* |
| *kw* | ,, | quite, coiffeur | *kwīt, kwu-fœr'* |
| *l* | ,, | lamp, collar | *lamp, kol'ər* |
| *m* | ,, | meat, palm, stammer | *mēt, päm, stam'ər* |
| *n* | ,, | net, gnome, knee, dinner | *net, nōm, nēē, din'ər* |
| *ng* | ,, | fling, longing | *fling, long'ing* |
| *ngg* | ,, | single, longer, languor | *sing'gl, long'gər, lang'gər* |
| *ngk* | ,, | monkey, precinct | *mungk'i, prē'singkt* |
| *p* | ,, | peat, apple | *pēet, ap'l* |
| *r* | ,, | rest, wreck, arrive | *rest, rek, ə-rīv'* |
| *s* | ,, | sad, city, circuit, scene, mass, psalm | *sad, sit'i, sûr'kit, sēn, mas, säm* |
| *sh* | ,, | shine, machine, sure, militia, acacia | *shin, mə-shēn', shōōr, mi-lish'ə, ə-kā'sh(y)ə* |
| *t* | ,, | tape, nettle, thyme | *tāp, net'l, tīm* |
| *th* | ,, | thin, three | *thin, thrē* |
| *v* | ,, | valid, river | *val'id, riv'ər* |
| *y* | ,, | young, bastion | *yung, bast'yən* |
| *z* | ,, | zoo, was, roads | *zōō, woz, rōdz* |
| *zh* | ,, | azure, measure, congé, lesion | *azh'ər (or ā'zhūr), mezh'ər, kō̄-zhā, lē'zhən* |

## Additional Sounds in Foreign Words

| Symbol | | Examples | Pronunciation |
|---|---|---|---|
| *e* | as in | père, même, maître | *per, mem, metr'* |
| *ø* | ,, | deux, feu, peu | *dø, fø, pø* |
| *œ* | ,, | fleur, leur, cœur | *flœur, lœr, kœr* |
| *ü* | ,, (1) | Fr. sur, luminaire | *sür, lü-mēn-er* |
| | (2) | Ger. über, Führer (nearly *ē*) | *üb'ər, fü'rər* |

### Nasalised vowels

| | | | |
|---|---|---|---|
| *ã* | ,, | sang, temps, dent | *sã, tã, dã* |
| *ɛ̃* | ,, | faim, vin, plein | *fɛ̃, vɛ̃, plɛ̃* |
| *ɔ̃* | ,, | tomber, long, sonde | *tɔ̃-bā, lɔ̃, sɔ̃d* |
| *œ̃* | ,, | lundi, humble, un | *lœ̃-di, œ̃bl, œ̃* |

An apostrophe is used to mark such pronunciations as *t'h* (where the sound is two separate consonants). It is also used in words such as timbre (*tɛ̃br'*).

# List of abbreviations used in the dictionary

| | | | | | |
|---|---|---|---|---|---|
| *abbrev.* | abbreviation | *dial.* | dialect(al) | *med.* | medicine |
| *abl.* | ablative | *Dict.* | Dictionary | *metaph.* | metaphysics |
| *acc.* | according | *dim.* | diminutive | *meteor.* | meteorology |
| *accus.* | accusative | *dub.* | doubtful | *mil.* | military |
| *adj(s).* | adjective(s) | | | *Milt.* | Milton |
| *adv(s).* | adverb(s) | *E.* | East | *min.* | mineralogy |
| *aero.* | aeronautics | *econ.* | economics | *mod.* | modern |
| *agri.* | agriculture | *e.g.* | (L. *exempli gra-* | *mus.* | music |
| *alch.* | alchemy | | *tia*) for | *myth.* | mythology |
| *alg.* | algebra | | example | | |
| *anat.* | anatomy | *elect.* | electricity | *N.* | North |
| *anc.* | ancient(ly) | *entom.* | entomology | *n(s).* | noun(s) |
| *ant.* | antiquities | *erron.* | erroneous(ly) | *nat. hist.* | natural history |
| *anthrop.* | anthropology | *esp.* | especially | *naut.* | nautical |
| *aor.* | aorist | *ety.* | etymology | *neg.* | negative |
| *app.* | apparently | | | *neut.* | neuter |
| *approx.* | approximately | *facet.* | facetiously | *nom.* | nominative |
| *arch.* | archaic | *fam.* | familiar, | *n.pl.* | noun plural |
| *archaeol.* | archaeology | | family | *n.sing.* | noun singular |
| *archit.* | architecture | *fem.* | feminine | *N.T.* | New Testament |
| *arith.* | arithmetic | *fig.* | figurative(ly) | | (A.V.) |
| *astrol.* | astrology | *fl.* | floruit | *North.* | Northern |
| *astron.* | astronomy | *fol.* | followed, | | |
| *at. numb.* | atomic number | | following | *obs.* | obsolete |
| *attrib.* | attributive(ly) | *fort.* | fortification | *opp.* | opposed, |
| *augm.* | augmentative | *freq.* | frequentative | | opposite |
| *A.V.* | Authorised | *fut.* | future | *opt.* | optics |
| | Version | | | *org.* | organic |
| | | *gen.* | genitive | *orig.* | original(ly), |
| *B.* | Bible (A.V.) | *gen(er).* | generally | | origin |
| *biol.* | biology | *geog.* | geography | | |
| *book-k.* | book-keeping | *geol.* | geology | *O.S.* | Old Style |
| *bot.* | botany | *geom.* | geometry | *O.T.* | Old Testament |
| | | *ger.* | gerundive | | (A.V.) |
| *c.* | (L. *circa*) about | *gram.* | grammar | | |
| *cap.* | capital | | | *p.* | participle |
| *cent.* | century | *her.* | heraldry | *p.adj.* | participial |
| *cf.* | (L. *confer*) | *hist.* | history | | adjective |
| | compare | *hort.* | horticulture | *paint.* | painting |
| *chem.* | chemistry | *hyperb.* | hyperbolically | *palaeog.* | palaeography |
| *cog.* | cognate | | | *pa.p.* | past participle |
| *coll.* | colloquial(ly) | *i.e.* | (L. *id est*) that | *part.* | participle |
| *collec.* | collective(ly) | | is | *pass.* | passive |
| *comp.* | composition | *illit.* | illiterate | *pa.t.* | past tense |
| *compar.* | comparative | *imit.* | imitative | *path.* | pathology |
| *conj(s).* | conjunction(s) | *imper.* | imperative | *perf.* | perfect |
| *conn.* | connected, | *impers.* | impersonal(ly) | *perh.* | perhaps |
| | connection | *incl.* | including | *pers.* | person(al) |
| *contr.* | contracted, | *indic.* | indicative | *petr.* | petrology |
| | contraction | *infin.* | infinitive | *pfx.* | prefix |
| *cook.* | cookery | *inten(s).* | intensive | *phil(os).* | philosophy |
| *corr.* | corruption, | *interj(s).* | interjection(s) | *philol.* | philology |
| | corresponding | *interrog.* | interrogative(ly) | *phon.* | phonetics |
| *crystal.* | crystallography | *intrans.* | intransitive | *phot.* | photography |
| | | *irreg.* | irregular(ly) | *phys.* | physics |
| *dat.* | dative | | | *physiol.* | physiology |
| *demons.* | demonstrative | *lit.* | literal(ly) | *pl.* | plural |
| *der.* | derived, | *log.* | logic | *poet.* | poetical |
| | derivation | | | *pol. econ.* | political |
| *derog.* | derogatory, | *mach.* | machinery | | economy |
| | derogatorily | *masc.* | masculine | *pop.* | popular(ly) |
| | | *math.* | mathematics | *poss.* | possessive, |
| | | *mech.* | mechanics | | possibly |

| | | | | | |
|---|---|---|---|---|---|
| *Pr. Bk.* | Book of Common Prayer | *rel.* | related, relative | *term.* | termination |
| *pr.p.* | present participle | *rhet.* | rhetoric | *theat.* | theatre, theatrical |
| *prep(s).* | preposition(s) | *R.V.* | Revised Version | | |
| *pres.* | present | | | *theol.* | theology |
| *pret.* | preterite | *S.* | South | *trans.* | transitive, translation |
| *print.* | printing | *sculp.* | sculpture | | |
| *priv.* | privative | *Shak.* | Shakespeare | *trig.* | trigonometry |
| *prob.* | probably | *sig.* | signifying | *TV* | television |
| *pron(s).* | pronoun(s) | *sing.* | singular | | |
| *pron.* | pronunciation | *specif.* | specifically | *ult.* | ultimately |
| *prop.* | properly | *Spens.* | Spenser | *usu.* | usually |
| *pros.* | prosody | *subj.* | subjunctive | | |
| *psych.* | psychology | *suff.* | suffix | *vb(s).* | verb(s) |
| | | *superl(s).* | superlative(s) | *v(s).i.* | verb(s) intransitive |
| *q.v.,qq.v.(pl.)* | which see | *surg.* | surgery | | |
| | | *s.v.* | (L. *sub verba*) under the word | *voc.* | vocative |
| ® | registered trademark | | | *v(s).t.* | verb(s) transitive |
| | | | | *vulg.* | vulgar |
| *R.C.* | Roman Catholic | *telecomm.* | telecommunications | *W.* | West |
| *redup.* | reduplication | | | | |
| *refl(ex).* | reflexive | *teleg.* | telegraphy | *zool.* | zoology |

| | | | | | |
|---|---|---|---|---|---|
| *A.F.* | Anglo-French | *Heb.* | Hebrew | *O.H.G.* | Old High German |
| *Afrik.* | Afrikaans | *Hind.* | Hindustani | | |
| *Amer.* | American | *Hung.* | Hungarian | *O.Ir.* | Old Irish |
| *Angl.* | Anglian | | | *O.N.* | Old Norse |
| *Ar.* | Arabic | *Ice(l).* | Icelandic (Modern) | *O.N.Fr.* | Old Northern French |
| *Assyr.* | Assyrian | | | | |
| *Austr.* | Australian | *Ind.* | Indian | *O.Sax.* | Old Saxon |
| | | *Ir.* | Irish | | |
| *Bav.* | Bavarian | *It.* | Italian | *Pers.* | Persian |
| *Beng.* | Bengali | | | *Peruv.* | Peruvian |
| *Bohem.* | Bohemian | *Jap.* | Japanese | *Pol.* | Polish |
| *Braz.* | Brazilian | *Jav.* | Javanese | *Port.* | Portuguese |
| *Bret.* | Breton | | | *Prov.* | Provençal |
| | | *L.* | Latin | | |
| *Celt.* | Celtic | *L.G.,L.Ger.* | Low German | *Rom.* | Roman |
| *Chin.* | Chinese | *Lith.* | Lithuanian | *Russ.* | Russian |
| *Copt.* | Coptic | *L.L.* | Low or Late Latin | | |
| | | | | *S.Afr.* | South African |
| *Dan.* | Danish | | | *Sans.* | Sanskrit |
| *Du.* | Dutch | *M.Du.* | Middle Dutch | *Scand.* | Scandinavian |
| | | *M.E.* | Middle English | *Scot.* | Scottish (Broad Scots) |
| *Egypt.* | Egyptian | *Mex.* | Mexican | | |
| *Eng.* | English | *M.Flem.* | Middle Flemish | *Sinh.* | Sinhalese |
| | | *M.Fr.* | Middle French | *Slav.* | Slavonic |
| | | *M.H.G.* | Middle High German | *Sp.* | Spanish |
| *Finn.* | Finnish | | | *Sw.* | Swedish |
| *Flem.* | Flemish | *M.L.G.* | Middle Low German | | |
| *Fr.* | French | | | *Turk.* | Turkish |
| *Fris.* | Frisian | | | | |
| | | *Norm.* | Norman | *U.K.* | United Kingdom |
| *Gael.* | Gaelic | *Norw.* | Norwegian | *U.S.* | United States (often includes Canadian) |
| *Ger.* | German | | | | |
| *Gmc.* | Germanic | *O.E.* | Old English | | |
| *Goth.* | Gothic | *O.Fr.* | Old French | *W.* | Welsh |
| *Gr.* | Greek | *O.Fris.* | Old Frisian | *W.S.* | West Saxon |

# Notes on American English

American English came of age and declared its independence early in the 20th century. Since then its influence has become world-wide and it has affected the parent tongue. In 1952 we spoke of 'the virtual drying up of the Atlantic as a speech barrier'; the traffic has been from west to east, not from east to west. In this newest version of the dictionary the label '(U.S.)', formerly used to distinguish purely American English, has been dropped almost entirely.

Certain differences of spelling remain and spelling differences in a number of individual words (e.g. *maneuver*, *defense*, and *practice* as a verb) have been noted in the dictionary. Groups of words in which the spelling is different are as follows:

| Eng. | U.S. | |
|---|---|---|
| *our* | *or* | American spellings such as *color*, *humor*, have often been noted in the text. |
| *re* | *er* | *center*, *meter*, *reconnoiter*, *saltpeter*, *theater*, etc.<br>But, to show the hard sound of *c* or *g*: *acre*, *lucre*, *massacre*, *ogre*, etc. |
| *ll* | *l* | Americans have single *l* in all derivatives in *-ed*, *-ing*, *-er* (or *-or*) of words ending in an *l*: *appareled*, *-ing*, *beveled*, *-ing*, *canceled*, *-ing*, *caroled*, *-ing*, *caviled*, *-ing*, *chiseled*, *-ing*, *counseled*, *-ing*, *-or*, *disheveled*, *-ing*, *driveled*, *-ing*, *-er*, *equaled*, *-ing*, *imperiled*, *-ing*, *jeweled*, *-ing*, *-er*, *libeled*, *-ing*, *-er*, *paneled*, *-ing*, *reveled*, *-ing*, *-er*, *sniveled*, *-ing*, *-er*, *traveled*, *-ing*, *-er*, *victualed*, *-ing*, *-er*, etc. Also *woolen*. |

| Eng. | U.S. | |
|---|---|---|
| *l* or *ll* | *ll* | *enroll*, *enthrall*, *instill*, *thralldom*. |
| *l* | *ll* | In *fulfill*, *skillful*, *willful*.<br>In nouns in *-ment*: *enrollment*, *enthrallment*, *fulfillment*, *installment*. |
| *pp* | *p* | *kidnaped*, *-ing*, *-er*, *worshiped*, *-ing*, *-er*. |
| *tt* | *t* | *carbureted*, *-er*, *sulfureted*. |
| *ae*, *oe* or *e* | *e* | The tendency to replace *ae* and *oe* in words from Greek or Latin by *e* is more strongly developed in the United States than in Britain: e.g. *etiology*, *hemoglobin*, *esophagus*. |
| *ise* or *ize* | *ize* | In verbs and their derivatives that may be spelt *-ise* or *-ize*, Americans prefer *-ize*. |

American pronunciation is naturally not the same in all areas and in all classes, but generally speaking it shows differences from British English pronunciation in the following respects (not specifically noted in the dictionary):

| Eng. | U.S. |
|---|---|
| *ä* | Various shorter forms of the vowel are common in place of English *ä*. |
| *ö* | Alternative form *ä* is common in words such as *haunt*, *launch*, *saunter*, *taunt*, *vaunt*. |
| *o* | A longer vowel than the normal British one is heard in *coffee*, *long*, *officer*, *soft*, etc., and *ä* also is widely used in these words. *Block*, *pond*, *probable*, *top*, etc., always have *ä*. |
| *ū* | In British English this is a diphthong; in American English it often loses its diphthongal character, becoming *ōo*. |

*Vowels and diphthongs before r:*

| | |
|---|---|
| *ā* | Two main diphthongs are heard both in England and in America, and in one of these diphthongs the first element approaches a lengthened form of *ĕ*. In America sometimes the second element of the diphthong disappears; the usual pronunciation of *Maryland*, for instance, is *mer'i-land*. |
| *a* | Some Americans tend to make a sound approaching *e*, so that *marry*, for instance, approximates to *merry*. |

| Eng. | U.S. |
|---|---|
| *i* | The sound heard in *squirrel*, *stirrup*, and commonly also in *syrup*, approaches *ú*. |
| *u* | In English, when *ur* is followed by a vowel, the sound of the *u* is not *ú*, but Americans tend to pronounce the same vowel in *her* and *hurry*. Other examples are *furry*, *occurring*, *worry*—and also *courage*. |
| *ar* spelt *er* | In words such as *clerk* and *Derby* where English speech preserves an older pronunciation *är*, American speech follows the spelling. |
| *-ə-ri* | Americans tend to give words in *-ary* and *-ory* a stronger secondary accent and to pronounce *-er'i* and *-ōr'i*. Examples are *necessary*, *monetary*, *secondary*, *temporary*, *obligatory*, *peremptory*, *respiratory*. |
| *-il* | In the commoner words Americans pronounce *il*, as *agile* (*aj'il*), *fertile*, *fragile*, *futile*, *hostile*. In *infantile*, *juvenile*, *mercantile*, *versatile*, both *il* and *ī* are heard; *gentile* is always pronounced *il*. |

Some individual differences in the sounds of certain words are noted in the dictionary, e.g. *tomato*, *schedule*, *simultaneous*.

Some variations in meaning between British English and American English are indicated in the dictionary, e.g. *bonnet*, *hood*; *braces*, *suspenders*. A few words used only in the U.S. are likewise indicated, e.g. *sidewalk*.

# A

**A, a, ā,** *n.* the first letter in our alphabet, as in the Roman, etc. (see **aleph, alpha**); in music, the major sixth of the scale of C: of first class or order, or of a class arbitrarily designated A: see **blood-group**: designating the principal series of paper sizes, ranging from A0 (841 × 1189 mm.) to A10 (26 × 37 mm.): as a mediaeval Roman numeral A = 50 or 500; Ā = 5000.— **A1** (*ā wun*), the symbol for a first-class vessel in Lloyd's Register: hence first-rate; **A´-bomb,** atomic bomb; **A´-effect** (see **alienation**); **A´-level** (*n., adj.*), (examination at end of school course) demanding an advanced knowledge of a school subject: a pass in an A-level (advanced); **A´-road,** a trunk or a principal road.

**a,** *ə,* also (esp. emphatic) *ā, adj.* the indefinite article, a broken down form of **an** used before a consonant sound. [O.E. *ān,* one.]

**A,** *ä, ə,* (*dial.*) *pron.* a monophthongised form of **I**.

**a,** *ä, ə,* (*dial.*) *pron.* he: she: it: they. [O.E. *hē,* he, *hēo,* she, *hie,* they.]

**a´,** *ö, ä,* Scots and Northern form of **all.**—*pron.* **a´´body,** everybody.—*adv.* **a´´gate,** every way. —*pron.* **a´´thing,** everything.—*adv.* **a´´where,** everywhere.

**a,** *ə,* a reduced form of the O.E. prep. *an, on,* on, in, at, chiefly used in composition as a prefix, as *a*broad, *a*sleep, occasionally used separately as a preposition, as *once a year.*

**à,** *ə,* a form of the Latin prep. *ab,* from, of, as in Thomas à Kempis (Thomas from Kempen).

**aardvark,** *ärt´färk´* (S.Afr.), *ärd´värk, n.* the ant-bear, a South African edentate. [Du. *aarde,* earth, *vark* (now *varken*), pig.]

**aardwolf,** *ärt´volf´* (S.Afr.), *ärd´woolf, n.* the earth-wolf, a hyena-like South African carnivore. [Du. *aarde,* earth, *wolf,* wolf.]

**Aaronic, -al,** *ā-ron´ik, -l, adjs.* pertaining to Aaron, the Jewish high-priest: pontifical.—**Aaron's beard,** a saxifrage, grown dangling from pots: the great St John's wort: ivy-leaved toadflax, or other plant; **Aaron's rod,** mullein, golden-rod, or other plant, with tall straight flowering stem.

**aasvogel,** *äs´fool* (S.Afr.), *äs´fō-gəl, n.* a South African vulture. [Du. *aas,* carrion, *vogel,* bird.]

**Ab,** *ab, n.* the eleventh civil, fifth ecclesiastical month of the Jewish Calendar (parts of July and August). [Syriac.]

**ab-,** *ab-, pfx.* used to indicate a centimetre-gram-second electromagnetic unit (e.g. **abampere, abvolt,** equivalent respectively to 10 amperes, $10^{-8}$ volts). [**absolute.**]

**aba, abba,** *a´ba,* or **abaya,** *a-bä´ya, n.* a Syrian cloth, of goat's or camel's hair, usually striped: an outer garment made of it. [Ar. '*abā,* '*abāya.*]

**abaca,** *ä-bä-kä´, n.* a plantain grown in the Philippine Islands: its fibre, called Manila hemp. [Tagálog.]

**aback,** *ə-bak´, adv.* backwards: said of sails pressed backward against the mast by the wind (*naut.*)—hence (*fig.*) **taken aback,** taken by surprise. [O.E. *on bæc,* on back.]

**abactinal,** *ab-ak-tī´nəl, ab-ak´ti-nəl,* (*zool.*) *adj.* remote from the actinal area: without rays.—*adv.* **abactinally.**

**abactor,** *ab-ak´tər, n.* cattle thief. [L.L.]

**abacus,** *ab´ə-kəs, n.* a counting-frame: a level tablet on the capital of a column, supporting the entablature (*archit.*):—*pl.* **ab´aci** (*-sī*). [L. *abacus*—Gr. *abax, -akos.*]

**Abaddon,** *ə-bad´ən, n.* Apollyon: hell (*Milt.*). [Heb. *ăbaddōn,* from *ābad,* to be lost.]

**abaft,** *ə-bäft´,* (*naut.*) *adv.* and *prep.* behind. [Prep. **a** and O.E. *bæftan,* after—pfx. *be-, æftan.* See **aft.**]

**abalone,** *ab-a-lō´nā, n.* the sea-ear, especially a richly coloured kind found on the Pacific coast of North America. [Uncertain origin.]

**abandon,** *ə-ban´dən, v.t.* to give up: to desert: to yield (oneself) without restraint: to give up all claims to: to banish (*Shak.*).—*n.* (sometimes as Fr. *ä-bä-dō̃*) condition of letting oneself go: careless freedom of action.—*v.t.* **aband´,** to abandon (*Spens.*).—*adj.* **aban´doned,** completely deserted: given up, as to a vice: profligate: very wicked.—*adv.* **aban´donedly.**—*ns.* **abandonee´** (*law*), an insurer to whom a wreck has been abandoned; **aban´donment.** [O.Fr. *abandoner,* to put at one's disposal or in one's control (*àbandon*), or to the ban; see **ban.**]

**à bas,** *a bä, interj.* (Fr.) down, down with!

**abase,** *ə-bās´, v.t.* to lower: to cast down: to humble: to degrade.—*adj.* **abased´,** lowered.—*n.* **abase´ment.** [O.Fr. *abaissier,* to bring low—L. *ad,* to, L.L. *bassus,* low.]

**abash,** *ə-bash´, v.t.* to strike with shame: to put out of countenance: to astound: to confound.— *adjs.* **abashed´; abash´less,** shameless: unabashed.—*n.* **abash´ment.** [O.Fr. *esbahir*—pfx. *es-* (L. *ex,* out), *bahir,* to astound—interj. *bah.*]

**abask,** *ə-bäsk´, adv.* in genial warmth. [**bask.**]

**abate,** *ə-bāt´, v.t.* to demolish (*obs.*): to put an end to (*law*): to nullify, to bring down (*law*): to lessen: to deduct (with *of*): to mitigate: to blunt: to curtail (*Shak.*): to except (*Shak.*).— *v.i.* to grow less: to subside: to be abated (*law*). —*adjs.* **abāt´able; abāt´ed,** blunted: diminished: lowered: subdued: beaten down or cut away, as the background of relief.—*n.* **abate´ment,** the act or process of abating: the sum or quantity abated: state of being abated: the abandonment of an action, or the reduction of a legacy (*law*): a supposed mark of dishonour on a coat of arms (*her.*)—apparently never actually used. [O.Fr. *abatre,* to beat down—L. *ab,* from, and L.L. *batēre,* for L. *batuēre,* to beat.]

**abate,** *ə-bāt´, v.i.* and *v.t.* (*refl.*) to intrude on a freehold and take possession before the heir.— *ns.* **abate´ment; abat´or.** [O.Fr. *enbatre,* to thrust in.]

**abatis, abattis,** *ab´ə-tis, ə-bat´ē, -is* (*fort.*) *n.* a rampart of felled trees, branches outward:— *pl.* **abat(t)is** (*-ēz*). [Fr.; see **abate** (1).]

**abat-jour,** *a-ba-zhoor,* (Fr.) a skylight: a screen or shutter.

**abattoir,** *ab´ə-twär, n.* a public slaughterhouse. [Fr.; see **abate** (1).]

**abattu,** *a-bat-ü,* (Fr.) cast down, dejected.

**abature,** *ab´ə-chər, n.* the trail through underwood beaten down by a stag. [Fr.; see **abate** (1).]

**abat-voix,** *a-ba-vwä,* (Fr.) a sounding-board.

**abaxial,** *ab-ak´si-al,* (*bot.*) *adj.* away from the axis. [Pfx. *ab-* and **axis.**]

**abaya.** See **aba.**

**abb,** *ab, n.* properly woof- or weft-yarn, but sometimes warp-yarn. [O.E. *āb, āweb*—pfx. *ā,* out, *webb,* web.]

**abba,** *ab´a, n.* father (applied to God) (*N.T.*): a Syriac or Coptic bishop. [Aramaic word *abbā* retained in the Greek N.T. and its translations.]

**abba.** See **aba.**

**abbacy,** *ab'ə-si, n.* the office or jurisdiction of abbot: the time during which one is abbot: an abbey.—*adj.* **abbatial** (*ab-ā'shl*), pertaining to an abbey, abbot or abbess. [App. orig. Scot.: L.L. *abbātia,* abbey.]

**Abbasid(e),** *a-bas'id, -id, ab'ə-sid, -sid, n.* any member of the later (750-1543) of the two great dynasties of caliphs, descendants of *Abbas,* uncle of Mohammed.

**abbé,** *ab'ā, n.* a courtesy title for a priest, an ecclesiastic in minor orders, or for a tutor or holder of a benefice, even if a layman. [Fr., orig. abbot.]

**abbess,** *ab'es, n.* a woman who is head of an abbey. [L.L. *abbātissa,* fem. of *abbās,* abbot.]

**abbey,** *ab'i, n.* a convent under an abbot or abbess, or (*loosely*) a prior or prioress: the church now or formerly attached to it: a name often retained by an abbatial building that has become a private house:—*pl.* **abb'eys.**—**abb'ey-counter, -piece,** a pilgrim's token, evidence of a visit to an abbey; **abb'ey-laird** (*hist.*), a debtor in sanctuary in the precincts of Holyrood Abbey; **abb'ey-lubber,** a lazy monk—a term much used by the Reformers. [O.Fr. *abaïe* (Fr. *abbaye*)—L.L. *abbātia.* See **abba** (1), **abbacy.**]

**abbot,** *ab'ət, n.* a male head of an abbey:—*fem.* **abb'ess.**—*n.* **abb'otship.**—**abbot of unreason,** a lord of misrule or mock abbot in mediaeval revels. [L.L. *abbās, abbātis*—Aramaic *abbā;* see **abba** (1).]

**abbreviate,** *ə-brē'vi-āt, v.t.* to shorten: to contract: to abridge.—*adj.* shortened.—*ns.* **abbrēviā'tion,** an act of shortening: a shortened form: part of a word written or printed for the whole; **abbrē'viātor.**—*adj.* **abbrē'viatory** (*-ə-tor-i*).—*n.* **abbrē'viāture** (*obs.*), an abbreviation: an abridgment. [L. *abbreviāre, -ātum*—*ab,* intens., *brevis,* short.]

**ABC,** *ā-bē-sē',* also (*obs.*) **abcee, absey,** *ab'si, n.* the alphabet, from its first letters: a first reading-book: hence first rudiments: anything arranged alphabetically, as an acrostic, a railway guide.— **absey book** (*Shak.*), a primer or hornbook.

**Abderian,** *ab-dē'ri-ən, adj.* of Abdera, a town in Thrace, the Gotham of the ancients, and birthplace of Democritus, 'the laughing philosopher'. —Also *n.*—*n.* **Abderite** (*ab'dər-it*), a native or citizen of Abdera: a simpleton, Gothamite.

**abdicate,** *ab'di-kāt, v.t.* and *v.i.* formally to renounce or give up (office or dignity).—*adjs.* **ab'dicable; ab'dicant.**—*n.* **abdicā'tion.** [L. *ab,* from or off, *dicāre, -ātum,* to proclaim.]

**abdomen,** *ab'də-mən, ab-dō'mən, n.* the belly: in mammals, the part between diaphragm and pelvis: in arthropods, the hind-body.—*adj.* **abdominal** (*-dom'*).—*adv.* **abdom'inally.**—*adj.* **abdom'inous,** pot-bellied. [L. *abdōmen, -inis.*]

**abduce,** *ab-dūs', v.t.* an earlier form of **abduct.**— *adj.* **abdūc'ent,** drawing back: separating.— *v.t.* **abduct** (*-dukt'*), to take away by fraud or violence: to kidnap.—*ns.* **abduction** (*-duk'shən*), the carrying away, esp. of a person by fraud or force: separation of parts of the body after a wound or fracture (*surg.*): muscular action drawing one part away from another: a syllogism whose minor premise is only probable (*log.*); **abduc'tor,** one who abducts: a muscle that draws away. [L. *abducĕre*—*ab,* from, *ducĕre, ductum,* to draw, lead.]

**abeam,** *ə-bēm', (naut.) adv.* on the beam, or in a line at right angles to a vessel's length. [Prep. **a** and **beam.**]

**abear,** *ə-bār', v.t.* to bear, comport, behave (*obs.*): to endure or tolerate (*dial.*). [O.E. *āberan.*]

**abecedarian,** *ā-bi-sē-dā'ri-ən, adj.* pertaining to the ABC: rudimentary: arranged in the

manner of an acrostic.—*n.* a learner of the ABC, a beginner: a teacher of the ABC: an Anabaptist of a sect that rejected all learning. [ABC.]

**abed,** *ə-bed', adv.* in bed. [Prep. **a,** and **bed.**]

**abeigh,** *ə-bēhh', (Scot.) adv.* aloof. [Origin obscure.]

**abele,** *ə-bēl', ā'bl, n.* the white poplar-tree. [Du. *abeel*—O.Fr. *abel, aubel*—L.L. *albellus*—L. *albus,* white.]

**Aberdeen,** *ab-ər-dēn',* sometimes *ab', adj.* of or originating in *Aberdeen* or Aberdeenshire.—*n.* (in full **Aberdeen terrier**) a coarse-haired kind of Scottish terrier.—*adj.* **Aberdō'nian,** of Aberdeen: (*traditionally*) parsimonious.—Also *n.*—**Aberdeen Angus** (*ang'gəs*), a breed of polled cattle descended from Aberdeenshire humlies and Angus doddies.

**aberdevine,** *ab-ər-di-vin', n.* a bird-fancier's name for the siskin. [Ety. uncertain.]

**Aberdonian.** See **Aberdeen.**

**aberglaube,** *ab-ər-glow'bə,* (Ger.) superstition.

**Abernethy biscuit,** *ab-ər-neth'i, -nēth'i,* or *ab',* a hard biscuit, apparently originally with caraway seeds. [Poss. after Dr John *Abernethy* (1764-1831), who was interested in diet.]

**aberrate,** *ab'ər-āt, v.i.* to wander or deviate from the right way.—*ns.* **aberrance** (*-er'*), **aberr'ancy.** —*adj.* **aberr'ant,** wandering: having characteristics not strictly in accordance with type (*bot., zool.*).—*n.* **aberrā'tion** (*-ər-*), deviation from the usual, normal, or right: wandering of the intellect, mental lapse: non-convergence of rays, owing to difference in refrangibility of different colours (*chromatic aberration*) or to difference of focus of the marginal and central parts of a lens or mirror (*spherical aberration*): an apparent displacement of a star, owing to the finite ratio of the velocity of light to that of the earth (*aberration of light*). [L. *aberrāre, -ātum*—*ab,* from, *errāre,* to wander.]

**abet,** *ə-bet', v.t.* to incite by encouragement or aid (used chiefly in a bad sense): to back up (*Spens.*): to make good:—*pr.p.* **abett'ing;** *pa.p.* **abett'ed.**— *n.* (*Spens.*) **abetting.**—*ns.* **abet'ment; abett'or.** [O.Fr. *abeter*—*à* (L. *ad,* to), and *beter,* to bait; see **bait.**]

**ab extra,** *ab eks'tra,* (L.), from the outside.

**abeyance,** *ə-bā'əns, n.* state of suspension or temporary inactivity: state of being without a claimant (as a peerage).—Also **abey'ancy.** [O.Fr. *abeance*—*à* (L. *ad* to), and *beer, baer,* to gape, open wide; origin uncertain.]

**abhominable.** See **abominable.**

**abhor,** *ab-hör', v.t.* to shrink from with horror: to detest: to loathe: to protest against, to reject (*Shak.*): to fill with horror (*Shak.*):—*pr.p.* **abhorr'ing;** *pa.t.* and *pa.p.* **abhorred'.**—*ns.* **abhorr'ence** (*-hor'*), extreme hatred: a thing abhorred; **abhorr'ency** (*obs.*).—*adj.* **abhorr'ent,** detesting: repugnant: strongly opposed: out of keeping: detestable: detested.—*adv.* **abhorr'ently.** —*ns.* **abhorr'er,** one who abhors: (*cap.; hist.*) a member of the court party in England in 1679, who abhorred the Petitioners, a Tory; **abhorr'-ing,** repugnance: an object of abhorrence. [L. *abhorrēre*—*ab,* from, and *horrēre,* to bristle, shudder.]

**Abib,** *ā'bib, n.* earlier name for Nisan. [Heb. *ābib,* lit. an ear of corn.]

**abide,** *ə-bīd', v.t.* to bide or wait for: to meet, face, sustain: to endure: to tolerate.—*v.i.* to remain: to dwell or stay: to conform, adhere (with *by*):— *pa.t.* **abōde',** also **abid'ed,** *Spens.* **abid';** *pa.p.* **abōde',** **abid'ed,** also **abīdd'en.**—*n.* **abid'ance.**— *adj.* **abid'ing,** continual, permanent.—*n.* a continuance (*arch.*).—*adv.* **abid'ingly.** [O.E. *ābīdan*—pfx. *ā-,* and *bīdan,* to wait.]

**abide,** *ə-bīd',* (*Shak.*; *Milt.*) *v.t.* to aby. [aby, confounded with **abide** (1).]

à bientôt, *a byẽ-tō*, (Fr.) see you again soon.
Abies, *ăb'i-ēz, n.* the genus of the true firs. [L.]
abigail, *ab'i-gāl, n.* a lady's-maid. [From *Abigail*, in Beaumont and Fletcher's *Scornful Lady*, or 1 Sam. xxv.]
ability, *ə-bil'i-ti, n.* quality or fact of being able: power (physical and mental): strength: skill. [O.Fr. *ableté* (Fr. *habileté*), remodelled on its source, L. *habilitās*, *-ātis—habēre*, to have, hold; see **able.**]
ab initio, *ab in-ish'i-ō, -it'i-ō,* (L.) from the beginning.
ab intra, *ab in'tra,* (L.) from the inside.
abiogenesis, *ab-i-ō-jen'is-is,* or *ā-bi-, n.* the origination of living by non-living matter, spontaneous generation.—*adj.* abiogenetic (*-ji-net'ik*).—*adv.* abiogenet'ically.—*n.* abiogenist (*-oj'ə-nist*), a believer in abiogenesis. [Coined by T. H. Huxley in 1870; Gr. *a-*, neg., *bios*, life, *genesis*, birth.]
abiturient, *ab-it-ū'ri-ənt, n.* in Germany, a pupil leaving school for a university. [Mod. L. *abituriēns, -entis*, pr.p. of *abiturīre*, desiderative of L. *abīre*, to go away—*ab*, from, *īre*, to go.]
abject, *ab-jekt', v.t.* to throw or cast down or away (*obs.*).—*adj.* ab'ject, cast away: mean: worthless: grovelling: base.—*n.* an outcast: a base slave: one in more servile subjection than a subject.—*n.* abjec'tion, abjectness: casting forth: forcible expulsion of spores (*bot.*).—*adv.* ab'jectly.—*n.* ab'jectness. [L. *abjicēre*, *abjectum* —*ab*, from, *jacēre*, to throw.]
abjoint, *ab-joint',* (*bot.*) *v.t.* to cut off by forming a septum.—*n.* abjunction (*-jungk'shən*). [L. *ab*, from, joint, junction.]
abjure, *ab-jōōr', v.t.* to renounce on oath or solemnly: to recant: to repudiate.—*ns.* abjura'tion; abjur'er. [L. *ab*, from, *jurāre*, *-ātum*, to swear.]
ablactation, *ab-lak-tā'shən, n.* a weaning: grafting by inarching. [L. *ab*, *lactāre*, to suckle—*lac*, milk.]
ablation, *ab-lā'shən, n.* removal: decrease by melting, evaporation, weathering.—*adjs.* ablatitious (*-lə-tish'əs*); ab'lative (*-lə-tiv*), pertaining to ablation: in or belonging to a case which in Indo-Germanic languages originally expressed *direction from*, or *time when*, later extended to other functions (*gram.*).—*n.* the ablative case: a word in the ablative.—*adj.* ablati'val. [L. *ab*, from, *lātum*, used as supine of *ferre*, to take.]
ablaut, *äp'lowt, ab'lowt,* (*philol.*) *n.* a variation in root vowel as in sing, sang, song, sung, explained by former accentuation—also called gradation. [Ger. *ab*, off, *laut*, sound.]
ablaze, *ə-blāz', adv.* and *adj.* in a blaze, on fire: gleaming brightly. [Prep. a, and blaze.]
able, *ā'bl, adj.* having enough strength, power or means (to do a thing): skilful.—*v.t.* to enable (*obs.*): to warrant (*Shak.*).—*adj.* a'ble-bod'ied, of a strong body: free from disability, etc.: robust.—*advs.* a'bly; a(i)blins (*ā'blinz*) or yibbles (*yib'lz*), perhaps (*Scot.*).—*able seaman, able-bodied seaman* (abbrev. A.B.), one able to perform all the duties of seamanship and having a higher rating than the ordinary sailor. [See **ability.**]
-able, *-ə-bl, adj. suff.* capable of being.—Also -ible.
ablet, *ab'lit, n.* the bleak. [Fr. *ablette*—L.L. *a(l)bula*, dim, of *alba*, white.]
abloom, *ə-blōōm', adv.* and *adj.* in a blooming state. [Prep. a, on, and bloom.]
ablow, *ə-blō', adv.* and *adj.* in a blowing state. [Prep. a, and blow.]
ablush, *ə-blush', adv.* and *adj.* in a blushing state. [Prep. a, and blush.]
ablution, *ə-blōō'shən, n.* (often in *pl.*) act of washing, esp. the body: ceremonial washing: (*sing.*) the wine and water used to rinse the chalice, drunk by the officiating priest.—*adj.*

ablu'tionary. [L. *ablūtiō, -ōnis—ab*, away, *luĕre*, to wash.]
abnegate, *ab'ni-gāt, v.t.* to deny: to renounce.—*ns.* abnega'tion; ab'negātor. [L. *ab*, away, *negāre*, to deny.]
abnormal, *ab-nör'ml, adj.* not normal.—*ns.* abnor'malism; abnormality (*-nör-mal'i-ti*).—*adv.* abnor'mally.—*n.* abnor'mity.—*adj.* abnor'mous (*rare*). [Fr. *anormal*—L.L. *anormalus*—Gr. *anōmalos* (see **anomaly**); influenced by L. *norma*, rule, and *ab*, from.]
aboard, *ə-bōrd', -bōrd', adv.* or *prep.* on board: in or into a ship, railway train, etc.: alongside. [Prep. a, on, and board.]
abode, *ə-bōd', n.* a dwelling-place: stay.—*v.t.* and *v.i., pa.t.* and *pa.p.* of **abide.**
abode, *ə-bōd', n.* a presage.—*v.t.* (*Shak.*) to presage.—*n.* abode'ment (*obs.*), a foreboding: an omen. [O.E. *ābodian*, to proclaim; cf. **bode, forebode.**]
aboideau, aboiteau, *ä-bwä-dō, -tō, n.* a tide-gate. [Canadian Fr.]
a'body. See a³.
ab officio et beneficio, *ab o-fish'i-ō (-fik') et ben-e-fish'i-ō (-fik'),* (L.L.) from office and benefice of a clergyman suspended.
aboil, *ə-boil', adv.* and *adj.* in a boiling state. [Prep. a, on, and boil.]
abolish, *ə-bol'ish, v.t.* to put an end to.—*adj.* abol'ishable.—*ns.* abol'ishment (*rare*); aboli'tion.—*adjs.* aboli'tional, aboli'tionary.—*ns.* aboli'tionism; aboli'tionist, one who seeks to abolish anything, esp. slavery. [L. *abolēre, -itum*, partly through Fr. *abolir.*]
abolla, *ab-ol'ä, n.* a Roman military cloak. [L.]
abomasum, *ab-ō-mā'səm, n.* the fourth or true stomach of ruminants, lying close to the omasum. —Also abomā'sus. [L. *ab*, away from, *omāsum*, tripe, paunch (a Gallic word).]
abominate, *ə-bom'in-āt, v.t.* to abhor: to detest.— *adj.* abom'inable, hateful: detestable.—An old spelling is abhom'inable, to agree with a fancied derivation from Lat. *ab homine.*—*n.* abom'inableness.—*adv.* abom'inably.—*ns.* abomina'tion, extreme aversion: an object of detestation; abom'inator.—abominable snowman, a mythical hairy manlike creature supposed to live in the snows of Tibet. [L. *abōmināri, -ātus*, to turn from as of bad omen; see **omen.**]
à bon droit, *a bõ drwä,* (Fr.) with justice.
à bon marché, *a bõ mar-shä,* (Fr.) at a good bargain, cheap.
abonnement, *ə-bom'in-ät,* (Fr.) subscription.
aboral, *ab-ō'ral, -ō', (zool.) adj.* away from the mouth. [L. *ab*, from, and oral.]
abord, *ə-bōrd', -bōrd'* (*arch.*), *v.t.* to accost.—*n.* approach. [Fr. *aborder—à bord*, to the side.]
abord, *ə-bōrd', -bōrd' (Spens.) adv.* astray. [Perh. for **abroad.**]
ab origine, *ab ō-rij'in-ē, -rēg'-in-e,* (L.) from the very first, from the source.
aborigines, *ab-ə-rij'in-ēz, n.pl,* the original or native inhabitants of a country. A *sing.* formed by dropping *s* is used esp. of aboriginal Australians—aborigine (*ab-ə-rij'i-nē*)—also abor'igin (*-bor'*), -ine, -en.—*adj.* aborig'inal, earliest, primitive, indigenous.—*n.* one of the aborigines. —*ns.* aborig'inalism, due recognition of native peoples; aboriginality (*-al'i-ti*), fact of being aboriginal.—*adv.* aborig'inally. [L. *aboriginēs— ab*, from, *origō, -inis,* beginning.]
abort, *ə-bört', v.i.* to miscarry in birth: to be arrested in development at an early stage: to come to nothing.—*v.t.* to cause to abort: to check at an early stage: to stop (e.g. flight of rocket) in emergency before completion of mission.—*n.* an instance of abortion (esp. of rocket).—*adj.* abortifacient (*-i-fā'shənt, -shi-ənt*), causing abortion.—*n.* means of causing abortion. —*ns.* aborticide (*-i-sīd*), foeticide; abor'tion,

the premature expulsion of an embryo or a foetus, or the procuring of this, esp. in the first three months of pregnancy: arrest of development: the product of such arrest: anything that fails in course of coming into being: a misshapen being or monster; **abor′tionist,** one who procures abortion.—*adjs.* **abor′tive,** born untimely: unsuccessful: brought forth in an imperfect condition: checked in development.—*adv.* **abort′ively.**—*n.* **abort′iveness.**—**contagious abortion,** contagious bacterial infections of cattle and of horses, causing abortion. [L. *aborīrī, abortus*—pfx. *ab*-, reversing the meaning, *orīrī,* to rise.]

**abought,** *ə-böt′, pa.t.* and *pa.p.* of **aby.**

**aboulia, abulia,** *a-bōō′li-a, -bow′, -bū′, n.* loss of will-power. [Gr. *a*-, priv., *boulē,* will.]

**abound,** *ə-bownd, v.i.* to be in great plenty: to be rich (with *in*): to be filled (with *with*).—*adj.* **abound′ing.** [O.Fr. *abunder*—L. *abundāre,* to overflow—*ub,* from, *unda,* a wave.]

**about,** *ə-bowt′, prep.* round on the outside of: around: here and there in: near in place, time, size, etc.: on the person of: connected with: concerning: engaged in.—*adv.* around: halfway round, in the opposite direction (e.g. *to face about*): nearly: here and there: on the opposite tack: in motion or activity.—**about′-face,** (orig. used in U.S. as command) act of turning to face in the opposite direction: complete change of opinion, attitude, etc.—Also *v.i.*—Also **about′-turn.**—*prep.* **abouts′** (*Spens.*), about. —*v.t.* and *v.i.* **about′-ship′,** to put (the ship) on the opposite tack.—*n.* **about′-sledge,** a heavy blacksmith's hammer.—**about** to (do, etc.), on the point of (doing, etc.); **be about,** to be astir: to be on the point of (doing something; with infin.); **bring about,** to cause to take place; **come about,** to happen in the course of time; **go about,** to prepare to do; **put about** (see **put**); **turn about,** alternately: in rotation. [O.E. *onbūtan—on,* in, *būtan,* without—*be,* by, *ūtan,* orig. a locative—*ūt,* out.]

**above,** *ə-buv′, prep.* over: in or to a position higher than that of: beyond in degree, amount, number, importance, etc.: too magnanimous or proud for:—*adv.* overhead: in a higher position, order, or power: in an earlier passage: in heaven.—*adj.* mentioned, stated, or given in an earlier passage.—*adjs.* **above′-board,** open, without deception; **above′-ground,** alive: not buried; **above′-mentioned;** **above′-named.**—**above oneself,** elated: conceited. [Late O.E. *ābufan*—O.E. *ā*-, on, *bufan,* above—*be,* by, *ufan,* above.]

**ab ovo,** *ab ō′vō, -wō,* (L.; 'from the egg') from the beginning. See *Quotations from Latin.*

**abracadabra,** *ab-rə-kə-dab′rə, n.* a magic word, written in amulets: a spell or conjuring word: gibberish. [Found in a 2nd-cent. poem by Q. Serenus Sammonicus.]

**abrade,** *ə-brād′, v.t.* to wear down or off.—*adj.* and *n.* **abrā′dant,** abrasive. [L. *ab,* from, *rādēre, rāsum,* to scrape.]

**Abraham-man,** *ā′brə-həm-man′,* **Abram-man,** *ā′-brəm-man′, n.* originally a Bedlam inmate let out to beg: a sturdy beggar, esp. one shamming insanity (*arch.*).—**to sham Abraham,** to feign sickness. [Said to be from an Abraham Ward in old Bedlam, London.]

**abraid, abrade,** *ə-brād′,* or (*Spens.*) **abray,** *ə-brā′, obs. v.t.* to awake, rouse.—*v.i.* to start: to awake. [O.E. *ābregdan*—intens. pfx. *ā*-, and *bregdan;* see **braid** (1).]

**abram,** *ā′brəm,* (*Shak.*) *adj.* an obs. form of **auburn.**

**abranchiate,** *ə-brang′ki-āt, adj.* without gills. [Gr. *a*-, priv., *branchia,* gills.]

**abrasion,** *ə-brā′zhən, n.* wearing away: a worn-down or grazed place.—*adj.* **abrā′sive** (*-ziv, -siv*), tending to abrade (also *fig.*).—*n.* a substance

used to remove matter by scratching and grinding. [See **abrade.**]

**à bras ouverts,** *a brä-zōō-ver,* (Fr.) with open arms.

**abraxas,** *a-braks′as, n.* a mystic word, or a gem engraved therewith, often bearing a mystical figure of combined human and animal form, used as a charm: (*cap.*) the genus of the gooseberry or magpie moth. [Said to have been coined by the 2nd-cent. Egyptian Gnostic Basilides to express 365 by addition of the numerical values of the Greek letters.]

**abray.** See **abraid.**

**abreaction,** *ab-rē-ak′shən,* (*psych.*) *n.* resolution of a neurosis by reviving forgotten or repressed ideas of the event first causing it. [L. *ab,* from, and **reaction.**]

**abreast,** *ə-brest′, adv.* with fronts in line: side by side: keeping pace with (with *of*), e.g., *abreast of the other car, the times.* [Prep. **a,** on, and **breast.**]

**abrégé,** *a-brā-zhā,* (Fr.) abridgment.

**abricock,** *ab′ri-kok,* an obs. form of **apricot.**

**abridge,** *ə-brij′, v.t.* to shorten: to epitomise: to curtail.—*ns.* **abridg′er; abridg′ment** (sometimes **abridge′ment**), contraction: shortening: a compendium of a larger work: an epitome or synopsis: (prob.) a pastime (*Shak.*). [O.Fr. *abregier* (Fr. *abréger*)—L. *abbreviāre.*]

**abrim,** *ə-brim′, adv.* and *adj.* in a brimming state, up to the brim. [Prep. **a,** and **brim.**]

**abroach,** *ə-brōch′, adv.* and *adj.* in a condition to let the liquor run out: in a state to be diffused, afloat, astir. [Prep. **a,** and **broach.**]

**abroad,** *ə-bröd′, adv.* over a wide area: in full breadth: out of doors: at large: in the field: current: in or to another country: wide of the mark: astray. [Prep. **a,** and **broad.**]

**abrogate,** *ab′rō-gāt, v.t.* to annul.—*n.* **abroga′tion.** —*adj.* **ab′rogative.**—*n.* **ab′rogator.** [L. *ab,* away, *rogāre, -ātum,* to ask, or to propose a law.]

**Abroma,** *a-brō′ma, n.* a genus of East Indian sterculiaceous fibre-yielding trees. [Gr. *a*-, priv., *brōma,* food.]

**abrooke,** *ə-brōōk′,* (*Shak.*) *v.t.* to brook, bear, or endure. [Pfx. *a*-, intens., and **brook** (2).]

**abrupt,** *ə-brupt′, adj.* truncated: as if broken off: sudden: unexpected: precipitous: passing with sudden transitions: (of manners) short, rude.— *n.* (*Milt.*) an abyss.—*n.* **abrup′tion** (*-shən*), a breaking off.—*adv.* **abrupt′ly.**—*n.* **abrupt′ness.** [L. *abruptus*—*ab,* from, *rumpĕre, ruptum,* to break.]

**Abrus,** *a′brəs, n.* a tropical genus akin to the bean, to which crab's-eyes belong.—*n.* **a′brin,** a poisonous protein contained in its seeds. [Gr. *habros,* graceful.]

**abscess,** *ab′ses, -sis, n.* a collection of pus in a cavity. [L. *abscessus*—*abs,* from, *cēdĕre, cēssum,* to go, retreat.]

**abscind,** *ab-sind′, v.t.* to cut off.—*n.* **abscissa** (*-sis′a*), also **absciss, abscisse** (*ab′sis*) the intercept between a fixed point and the foot of an ordinate: the *x*-co-ordinate in analytical geometry:—*pl.* **abscissae** (*ab-sis′ē, -sis′i*), **absciss′as, ab′scisses.**—*n.* **abscission** (*-sizh′ən*), act of cutting off, or state of being cut off: a figure of speech in which words demanded by the sense are left unsaid, the speaker stopping short suddenly (*rhet.*): organised shedding of a part by means of an absciss layer (*bot.*): liberation of a fungal spore by breakdown of part of its stalk (*bot.*).— **absciss layer** (*bot.*), a layer of parenchymatous cells through which a leaf, branch, or bark scale separates off. [L. *abscindĕre, abscissum,* to cut off—*ab,* from, *scindĕre,* to cut.]

**abscond,** *ab-skond′, v.i.* to hide, or get out of the way, esp. to escape a legal process.—*ns.* **abscond′-ence; abscond′er.** [L. *abscondĕre*—*abs,* from or away, *condĕre,* to hide.]

**abseil,** *ap′zil, ab-sil′, v.i.* to let oneself down a rock face using a double rope.—*n.* abseil'ing. [Ger. -*ab*, down, *seil*, rope.]

absent, *ab'sant, adj.* being away: not present: inattentive.—*v.t.* (*ab-sent'*; usu. *refl.*) to keep away.—*ns.* ab'sence, the state of being away or not present: want: non-existence: abstraction, inattention; absentee', one who is absent on any occasion: one who makes a habit of living away from his estate or his office; absentee'ism, the practice of absenting oneself from duty, station, or estate.—*adv.* ab'sently.—*adj.* ab'sent-mind'ed, inattentive to surroundings: preoccupied.— *adv.* ab'sent-mind'edly.—*n.* ab'sent-mind'edness. [L. *absēns, -sentis,* pr.p. of *abesse*—*ab,* away from, *esse,* to be.]

absente reo, *ab-sent'ē rē'ō, -te rā'ō,* (L.) in absence of the accused.

absey, absey book. See ABC.

absinth(e), *ab'sinth, n.* wormwood or other species of Artemisia: a liqueur containing (orig. at all events) extract of wormwood.—*adj.* absinth'-iated, impregnated with absinth. [Fr. *absinthe*— L. *absinthium*—Gr. *apsinthion,* wormwood.]

absit, *ab'sit,* (L.) *lit.* let him be absent—leave to pass one night away from college.—absit in-vidia, *ab'sit in-vid'i-a, -wid',* may there be no ill will: no offence; absit omen, *ab'sit ō'mən,* may there be no (ill) omen (as in a word just used).

absolute, *ab'sal-ōōt, -ūt, adj.* free from limits, restrictions, or conditions: certain, positive: complete: unlimited: free from mixture: independent of relation to other things: peremptory: unrestricted by constitutional checks: out of ordinary syntactic relation (*gram*): existing in and by itself without necessary relation to anything else (*philos.*): capable of being conceived independently of anything else.—*n.* (with the; often *cap.*) that which is absolute, self-existent, uncaused.—*adv.* ab'solutely, separately, by itself: unconditionally: positively: completely—as a colourless but emphatic affirmative (-*lōōt'li, -lūt'*).—*ns.* ab'soluteness; absolu'tion, release from punishment: acquittal: remission of sins, declared officially by a priest, or the formula by which it is expressed; ab'solutism, government, and theory of government, by a ruler without restriction: adherence to the doctrine of the Absolute; ab'solutist, a supporter of absolute government, or of a philosophy of the Absolute. —Also *adj.*—*adj.* absolutory (*ab-sol'ū-tər-i*), of, or giving, absolution.—absolute alcohol, water-free alcohol; absolute magnitude, the magnitude that a star would have at a standard distance of 10 parsecs; absolute music, music which does not attempt to illustrate or describe—opp. to *programme music*; absolute pitch, the pitch of a note as determined by the number of vibrations per sec.: a sense of or memory for absolute pitch; absolute temperature, temperature measured on the Kelvin scale or Rankine scale; absolute units, those derived directly from fundamental units and not based on arbitrary numerical definitions; the internationally adopted fundamental units are the metre, kilogram, second, kelvin, ampere and candela; absolute zero, the zero of the absolute scale of temperature (approx. −273°C). [L. *absolūtus,* pa.p. of *absolvēre;* see absolve.]

absolve, *ab-zolv', -solv', v.t.* to loose or set free: to pardon: to give absolution to or for: to acquit: to discharge (with *from*): to accomplish, finish off (*Milt.*).—*ns.* absolv'er; absolv'itor (L. 3rd pers. imper. passive, let him be absolved), (*Scots law*), a decision favourable to a defender. [L. *absolvēre*—*ab,* from, *solvēre,* to loose.]

absonant, *ab'sən-ənt, adj.* discordant: abhorrent: unnatural: contrary to reason (with *to* or *from*) —opp. to consonant. [L. *ab,* from, *sonāns, -antis,* p.r.p. of *sonāre,* to sound.]

absorb, *ab-sörb', -zörb', v.t.* to suck in: to swallow up: to imbibe: to take in: to incorporate: to take up and transform (energy) instead of transmitting or reflecting: to engage wholly.—*n.* absorbabil'ity.—*adj.* absorb'able.—*adj.* absorbed', swallowed up: entirely occupied.—*adv.* absorb'-edly.—*n.* absorb'ency.—*adj.* absorb'ent, absorbing: able to absorb.—*n.* that which absorbs.— *n.* absorb'er, that which absorbs: material for capturing neutrons without generating more neutrons (*nuc.*).—*adj.* absorb'ing, engrossing the attention.—*adv.* absorbingly. —*ns.* absorptiometer (*-sörp-shi-om'i-tər*), an apparatus for determining the solubility of gases in liquids; absorp'tion, the act of absorbing: entire occupation of mind.—*adj.* absorp'tive, having power to absorb.—*ns.* absorp'tiveness, absorptiv'ity.— absorption bands, lines, dark bands, lines, interrupting a spectrum, due to absorption of light in the medium traversed; absorption spectrum, a system of such lines and bands. [L. *ab,* from, *sorbēre, sorptum,* to suck in.]

absquatulate, *ab-skwot'ū-lāt (facet.; U.S.) v.i.* to decamp: to squat.

abstain, *ab-stān', v.i.* to hold or refrain (from).— *v.t.* (*Spens.*) to restrain—*ns.* abstain'er, one who abstains, esp. from alcoholic drinks; absten'tion, [Fr. *abstenir*—L. *abs,* from, *tenēre,* to hold.]

abstemious, *ab-stē'mi-əs,* adj. temperate: sparing in food, drink, or enjoyments.—*adv.* abste'miously. —*n.* abste'miousness. [L. *abstēmius*—*abs,* from, *tēmētum,* strong wine.]

absterge, *ab-stûrj', v.t.* to wipe: to cleanse: to purge.—*adj.* absterg'ent, serving to cleanse.— *n.* a cleansing agent.—*n.* abster'sion.—*adj.* abster'sive, having the quality of cleansing: purgative.—Also *n.* [L. *abstergēre, -tersum,* to wipe away—*abs,* from, *tergēre,* to wipe.]

abstinent, *ab'stin-ənt, adj.* abstaining: temperate. —*ns.* ab'stinence, an abstaining or refraining, especially from some indulgence (with *from*); ab'stinency, the quality of being abstinent.—*adv.* ab'stinently. [L. *abstinēns, -entis,* pr.p. of *abstinēre;* see abstain.]

abstract, *ab-strakt', v.t.* to draw away: to separate: to remove quietly: to purloin: to summarise: to separate by the operation of the mind, as in forming a general concept from consideration of particular instances.—*n.* (*ab'strakt*) a summary, abridgment: in *Shak. Ant. and Cleo.* III. vi., explained by some as an abridgment of time for separation—others conjecture *obstruct:* that which represents the essence: an abstraction.— *adj.* (*ab'strakt*) abstracted: apart from actual material instances, existing only as a mental concept—opp. to *concrete:* away from practice, theoretical: (of terms) denoting a quality of a thing apart from the thing, as 'redness': representing ideas in geometric and other designs, not the forms of nature (*paint.* and *sculp.*).— *adj.* abstract'ed, drawn off (with *from*): removed: absent in mind.—*adv.* abstract'edly.—*ns.* abstract'edness; abstrac'ter, abstrac'tor, one who makes abstracts (with -or for a grade of Civil Service clerks); abstrac'tion, act of abstracting: state of being abstracted: abstract quality or character: withdrawal from worldly things: absence of mind: a purloining: the process of abstracting by the mind: a thing existing only in idea: a theory, visionary notion: an abstract term: an abstract composition (*paint.* and *sculp.*). —*adj.* abstrac'tional.—*n.* abstrac'tionist, one dealing in abstractions or unrealities.—*adj.* abstrac'tive, able or tending to abstract: formed by or pertaining to abstraction.—*n.* anything abstractive: an abstract.—*adv.* ab'stractly.—*n.* ab'stractness.—abstract of title, summary of facts concerning ownership; in the abstract, as an abstraction: in theory. [L. *abs,* away from, *trahēre, tractum,* to draw.]

Neutral vowels in unaccented syllables: *el'ə-mənt;* for certain sounds in foreign words, see p. viii

abstrict, *ab-strikt'*, (*biol.*) *v.t.* to set free (spores, etc.), esp. by constriction of the stalk.—*n.*
abstric'tion. [L. *ab*, from, *stringĕre*, *strictum*, to tie.]
abstruse, *ab-strōōs'*, *adj.* hidden (*arch.*): remote from apprehension: difficult to understand.—*adv.* abstruse'ly.—*n.* abstruse'ness. [L. *abstrūsus*, thrust away—*abs*, away, *trūdĕre*, *trūsum*, to thrust.]
absurd, *ab-sûrd'*, *adj.* opposed to reason: ridiculous.—*ns.* absurd'ity, absurd'ness.—*adv.* absurd'ly. [L. *absurdus*—*ab*, from, *surdus*, deaf, inaudible, indistinct, harsh, out of fashion, not to the purpose.]
abthane, *ab'thān*, *n.* a monastic territory of the Columban church. [L.L. *abthania*—Gael. *abdhaine*, abbacy.]
abulia. See aboulia.
abuna, *ä-bōō'na*, *n.* an Ethiopian patriarch. [Ethiopian,—Ar., our father.]
abundance, *ə-bund'əns*, *n.* ample sufficiency: great plenty: a call of nine tricks (*solo whist*).—*n.* abund'ancy.—*adj.* abund'ant.—*adv.* abund'antly. [See abound.]
abune, *ə-bün'*, a Scots form of above.
ab urbe condita, *ab ûr'be kon'di-ta, ōōr'bä kon'di-tä*, from the founding of the city (of Rome) 753 B.C.—Abbrev. A.U.C.
aburst, *ə-bûrst'*, *adv.* and *adj.* in a bursting condition. [Prep. a, and burst.]
abuse, *ə-būz'*, *v.t.* to make a bad use of: to take undue advantage of: to betray (as confidence): to misrepresent: to deceive: to revile: to maltreat: to violate.—*ns.* abuse (*ə-būs'*), wrong use: evil or corrupt practice: deceit: hurt: undue advantage: betrayal (of confidence): ill usage: violation: reviling; abuser, (*ə-bū'zər*); abū'sion (-*zhən*; *Spens.* also -*zi-ən*; now rare), misuse: deception: wrong: outrage: reviling,—*adj.* abū'sive (-*siv*) wrong: containing, giving, of the nature of, abuse: coarsely reviling: catachrestical (*arch.*).—*adv.* abū'sively.—*n.* abū'siveness. [L. *ab*, from, *ūti, ūsus*, to use.]
abut, *ə-but'*, *v.t.* to end or lean (*on, upon, against*): to border:—*pr.p.* abutt'ing; *pa.t.* and *pa.p.* abutt'ed.—*ns.* abut'ment, endwise meeting or junction: that which a limb of an arch ends or rests against (*archit.*): place of abutting; abutt'al, abutment: (in *pl.*) boundaries; abutt'er, one whose property abuts.—*adj.* abutt'ing, confronting. [O.Fr. *abouter*, to touch by an end, and O.Fr. *abuter*, to touch at the end; cf. also Fr. *aboutir*, to end at—*à*, to, *bout*, *but*, end; see butt (4).]
Abutilon, *a-bū'ti-lon*, *n.* a showy-flowered genus of the mallow family, some species yielding fibres. [Ar. *aubūtilūn*.]
abuzz, *ə-buz'*, *adv.* and *adj.* in a buzz. [Prep. a, and buzz.]
aby, abye, *ə-bī'*, (*arch.*) *v.t.* to pay the penalty for: to pay as a penalty.—*v.i.* to atone: to endure, continue:—*pa.t.* and *pa.p.* abought (*ə-böt'*). [Pfx. a-, back, and O.E. *bycgan*, to buy; merging and confused with abide.]
abysm, *ə-bizm'*, *n.* (*arch.* and *poet.*) abyss.—*adj.* abys'mal, bottomless: unfathomable: very deep: abyssal.—*adv.* abys'mally. [O.Fr. *abisme*, from a L.L. superl. of *abyssus*; see abyss.]
abyss, *ə-bis'*, *n.* a bottomless gulf: primal chaos: the supposed water-filled cavity under the earth: hell: anything very deep: the depths of the sea: a measureless or apparently measureless chasm.—*adj.* abyss'al, abysmal—esp. of ocean depths. [Gr. *abyssos*, bottomless—*a-*, priv., *byssos*, depth, bottom.]
Abyssinian cat, *ab-i-sin'i-ən*, -*sin'yən*, a small domestic cat, of African origin, greyish or brownish ticked with darker colour.
acacia, *ə-kā'sh(y)ə*, *n.* a wattle, any plant of the genus *Acacia*, akin to the sensitive plants: also

applied to the *false acacia* (of the genus Robinia). [L.—Gr. *akakiā*.]
academy, *ə-kad'ə-mi*, *n.* (orig.) Plato's school of philosophy: a higher, would-be higher, or specialised school, or a university: a riding-school: a society for the promotion of science or art: the annual exhibition of the Royal Academy or of the Royal Scottish Academy.—*n.* academe (*ak-ə-dēm'*), an academic, esp. if pedantic: an academy (*poet.*).—*adj.* academic (-*dem'*), of the philosophical school of Plato: of an academy or university: sceptical: scholarly: formal: theoretical only.—*n.* a Platonic philosopher: one studying or teaching at a university, esp. one who has scholarly tastes: (*pl.*) purely theoretical arguments.—*adj.* academ'-ical, academic.—*n.* (in *pl.*) university garb.—*n.* academ'icalism, close adherence to formal academic teaching.—*adv.* academ'ically.—*ns.* academician (*ə-kad-ə-mish'ən*), a member of an academy esp. of the French Academy or the R.A. or R.S.A.; academ'icism, academ'icalism; acad'emist, an academic: an academician. [Gr. *Akadēmeiā*, the garden, orig. outside Athens, where Plato taught.]
Acadian, *ə-kā'di-ən*, *adj.* and *n.* Nova Scotian. [Fr. *Acadie*, Nova Scotia—Micmac Ind. *ākăde*, abundance.]
acajou, *ak'ə-zhōō, -zhōō'*, *n.* the cashew tree or its fruit or gum: a kind of mahogany. [See cashew.]
acaleph(e), *ak'ə-lef*, -*lēf*, acalepha, -*lē'fa*, *ns.* old names for a jellyfish—applied to a group of varying extension of Coelenterata.—*n.* and *adj.* acalē'phan. [Gr. *akalēphē*, a nettle, sea-anemone.]
acanaceous, *ak-ə-nā'shəs*, (*bot.*) *adj.* prickly. [L. *acanos*, a kind of thistle—Gr. *akanos*—*akē*, a point.]
acanth, *ə-kanth'*, *n.* acanthus.—*n.* acanth'a, a thorn, prickle: a spinous process.—*n.pl.* Acanth'ceae (*ak-*), the acanthus family, akin to the figworts.—*adj.* acanth'ceous, prickly: of the Acanthaceae.—*n.* acanth'in, strontium sulphate in skeletons of Radiolaria.—*adj.* acanth'ine, of, like, ornamented with, acanthus.—*n.pl.* Acanthoceph'ala, a division of parasitic worms with spiny proboscis and no mouth or alimentary canal (Gr. *kephalē*, head).—*adjs.* acanth'oid, like acanthus; acanthopterygian (*ak-an-thop-tər-ij'-yən*) spiny-finned (Gr. *pteryx*, -*ygos*, wing, fin); acanth'ous, spiny.—*n.* acanth'us, any plant of the prickly-leaved genus *Acanthus*, esp. *A. spinosus* or *A. mollis*: a conventionalised representation of an acanthus leaf, as in Corinthian capitals. [Gr. *akantha*, prickle, *akanthos*, acanthus—*akē*, point.]
acapnia, *ə-kap'ni-a*, *n.* deficiency of carbon dioxide. [Gr. *a-*, priv., *kapnos*, smoke.]
a cappella, *ä käp-pel'la* (*mus.*), 'in (early) church style', *i.e.* sung without accompaniment or with accompaniment merely doubling the voice parts: alla breve.—Also al'la cappel'la. [It.]
acarpous, *a-kär'pəs, ä-*, (*bot.*) *adj.* sterile, not bearing fruit. [Gr. *a-*, priv., *karpos*, fruit.]
acarus, *ak'ə-rəs*, *n.* a mite:—*pl.* ac'ari.—*adj.* acā'rian—*ns.* acari'asis, disease due to mites; acaricide (*a-kar'i-sid*), a mite killer; ac'arid, one of the Acarida.—*n.pl.* Acar'ida, the order of Arachnida to which mites and ticks belong.—*adjs. ns.* acar'idan, acarid'ean, acarid'ian.—*n.pl.* Acari'na, Acarida.—*adj.* ac'arine.—*n.* acarodomatium, acaridomatium (-*dō-mā'shyəm*), a dwelling for mites provided by certain plants that benefit from their presence:—*pl.* -ā'tia.—*adj.* ac'aroid, mite-like.—*ns.* acarol'ogist; acarol'-ogy; acaroph'ily, symbiotic association of plants with mites.—acarine disease, a disease of bees due to mites in the spiracles. [Gr. *akari*, a mite—*akarēs*, too short to cut—*a-*, priv., *keirein*, to cut.]

**acatalectic**, *a-kat-ə-lek'tik*, (*pros.*) *adj.* having the full number of syllables.—*n.* an acatalectic verse. [Gr. *akatalēktos—a-*, priv.; see **catalectic**.]

**acatalepsy**, *a-kat-ə-lep'si*, (*Sceptic philos.*) *n.* the unknowableness to a certainty of all things.— *adj.* and *n.* **acatalep'tic**. [Gr. *akatalēpsiā—a-*, priv., *kata*, thoroughly, *lēpsis*, a seizing.]

**acates**, *ə-kāts'*, (*obs.*) *n.pl.* bought provisions.—*n.* **acāt'er**, **-our** (*obs.*), an officer who bought provisions, a caterer. [O.Fr. *acat*—L.L. *accaptāre*, to acquire—L. *ad*, to, *captāre*, to seize; see **cate**, **cater**.]

**acaulescent**, *ak-ö-les'ənt*, having a very short stem. [Gr. *a-*, priv., L. *caulis*, stem, and suff. *-escent*.]

**accablé**, *ak-a-blā*, (Fr.) depressed, overwhelmed.

**accede**, *ək-sēd'*, *v.i.* to come forward: to arrive (with *to*): to come to office or dignity: to join up, become a party, hence agree or assent (with *to*).—*ns.* **accēd'ence**; **accēd'er**. [L. *accēdĕre*, *accēssum*, to go near—*ad*, to, *cēdĕre*, to go; see **cede**.]

**accelerando**, *ak-sel-ər-an'dō*, It. *ät-chel-er-än'dō*, *adj.* and *adv.* with increasing speed. [It.]

**accelerate**, *ək-sel'ər-āt*, *v.t.* to increase the speed of: to hasten the progress or occurrence of.—*v.i.* to become faster.—*ns.* **accel'erant**, an accelerating agent (also *adj.*); **accelerā'tion**, increase of speed: rate of change of velocity: a cumulative advance ahead of the normal or theoretical: the power or means of accelerating.—*adj.* **accel'erative**, quickening.—*n.* **accel'erātor**, any person or thing that accelerates, esp. a substance that accelerates chemical action, a nerve or muscle that increases rate of action, an apparatus for changing the speed of a machine, or one for imparting high energies to atomic particles. Devices for accelerating charged particles include the **cyclotron** type (for accelerating the heavier particles, as protons), modifications of this, as the **synchrocyclotron** type and the **synchrotron** type (for accelerating electrons). Other types of accelerators are the **proton synchrotron** (of which examples are the **cosmotron** and the **bevatron**), the **betatron** (for accelerating electrons; used in medicine and industry), **linear accelerators** and **electron ring accelerators**.—*n.* **accelerom'eter**, an instrument for measuring acceleration of aircraft, etc.—*adj.* **accel'eratory**. [L. *accelerāre*, *-ātum—ad*, to, *celer*, swift.]

**accend**, *ək-send'*, (*obs.*) *v.i.* to kindle.—*n.* **accen'sion**. [L. *accendĕre*, *accēnsum*, to kindle.]

**accent**, *ak'sənt*, *n.* modulation of the voice: tone of voice: stress on a syllable, word, or note: a mark used to direct this stress: a mark over a letter to indicate differences of stress, pitch, length, or quality of sound, or for other purpose: intensity: any mode of utterance characteristic of a region, a class, or an individual: a distinguishing mark: distinctive mode of expression, as of an artist: a significant word, or words generally (*poet.*): a touch bringing out some particular effect (*paint.*): (*pl.*) speech, language. —*v.t.* (*ək-sent'*), to express or mark the accent of: to utter: to accentuate.—*adj.* **accent'ūal**, according to, characterised by, accent.—*n.* **accentūal'ity**.—*adv.* **accent'ūally**.—*v.t.* **accent'ūate**, to mark, play, or pronounce with accent: to make prominent, emphasise.—*n.* **accentūā'tion**. [L. *accentus—ad*, to, *cantus*, song.]

**Accentor**, *ak-sent'ör*, *-ər*, *n.* the hedge-sparrow genus. [L. one who sings with another—*ad*, to, *cantor*, singer.]

**accept**, *ək-sept'*, *v.t.* (old-fashioned or formal, *v.i.* with *of*) to take (something offered): to receive (with approbation, favour, consent, resignation, or passivity): to reply to, engaging more or less to comply: to promise to pay (a bill of exchange): to understand, take, in respect of meaning.— *adj.* **accept'able**, worth accepting: welcome.—*n.*

**accept'ableness**.—*adv.* **accept'ably**.—*ns.* **acceptabil'ity**; **accept'ance**, accepting: favourable reception: favour: acceptableness: an agreeing to terms: an accepted bill: acceptation; **accept'ancy**; **accept'ant**, one who accepts.—*adj.* ready to receive.—*ns.* **acceptā'tion**, a kind reception: sense in which a word, etc., is understood; **accept'er**.—*adj.* **accept'ive**, ready to receive.— *ns.* **acceptiv'ity**; **accept'or**, one who accepts, esp. a bill of exchange: an impurity in semiconductor material which increases the conductivity of the material. [L. *acceptāre—accipĕre*, *acceptum— ad*, to, *capĕre*, to take.]

**acceptilation**, *ək-sept-il-ā'shən*, *n.* the remission of a debt by fictitious payment (*Roman* and *Scots law*); Christ's atonement on the theory that only God's acceptance made his sacrifice sufficient (*theol.*). [L. *accepti lātiō*, lit. 'bringing of receipt', verbal release from debt.]

**access**, *ak'ses*, *n.* approach: admittance: way, or opportunity, of approach or entrance: addition, accession: onset or attack of illness: a fit (of illness or passion).—*n.* and *adj.* **access'ary**, accessory (esp. in legal senses).—*n.* **accessibil'ity**. —*adj.* **access'ible**, within reach: approachable.— *adv.* **access'ibly**.—*n.* **accession** (*ak-sesh'ən*), act or event of acceding: a coming, esp. to office or dignity, or as an addition or new member: that which is added: addition by nature or industry to existing property (*law*): acquisition of such addition by the owner of the existing property (*law*): assent: an access, fit (*obs.*).—*v.t.* to enter in a book as an accession to a library.—*adj.* **access'ory**, additional: subsidiary, present along with something more important: adventitious: contributing: aiding, participating in, a crime (*law*) or misdeed, but not as principal.—*n.* anything, esp. an item of equipment, that is secondary, additional, or non-essential: one who aids or gives countenance to a crime.—*adj.* **accessor'ial**.—*adv.* **access'orily**.—**accessory minerals**, those whose presence or absence is not regarded in naming a rock; **deed of accession** (*Scots law*), one by which a bankrupt's creditors accede to a settlement privately, *i.e.* by trust-deed. [See **accede**.]

**acciaccatura**, *ät-chäk-a-tōō'ra*, (*mus.*) *n.* a short appoggiatura. [It. *acciaccare*, to crush.]

**accidence**, *ak'sid-əns*, *n.* the part of grammar treating of the 'accidents', *i.e.* inflexions of words.—*n.* **ac'cident**, that which happens: an unforeseen or unexpected event: a chance: a mishap: an unessential quality or property: unevenness of surface.—*adj.* **accidental** (*-dent'*), happening by chance: not essential: a sharp, flat, or natural not in the key-signature (*mus.*): (in *pl.*) strong chance effects of light (*paint.*).— *ns.* **accident'alism**, the state or quality of being accidental: chance manner: a system based on symptoms rather than on causes (*med.*): use of accidentals (*paint.*): the theory that events happen without a cause (*philos.*); **accidental'ity**.— *adv.* **accident'ally**.—*adjs.* **accident'ed**, uneven: varied; **accident-prone**, (usu. predicatively) more than normally liable to have accidents.—**a chapter of accidents**, an unforeseen course of events: a series of accidents. [L. *accidēns*, *-entis*, pr.p. of *accidĕre*, to happen—*ad*, to, *cadĕre*, to fall.]

**accidie**, *ak'si-di*, *n.* acedia. [O.F. *accide*—L.L. *acēdia*; see **acedia**.]

**accinge**, *ak-sinj'*, (*fig.*) *v.t.* to gird. [L. *ad*, to, *cingĕre*, to gird.]

**accipitrine**, *ak-sip'i-trin*, *-trin*, *adj.* pertaining to hawks. [L. *accipiter*, a hawk.]

**accite**, *ak-sīt'*, *v.t.* to cite: to summon: to excite (*Shak.*). [L.L. *accitāre—ad*, to, *citāre*, to cite, call.]

**acclamation**, *ak-lə-mā'shən*, *n.* a shout of applause or assent.—*v.t.* **acclaim** (*ə-klām'*), to hail or

declare by acclamation.—*n.* acclamation.—*adj.* acclamatory (ə-klam'ə-tər-i). [L. *acclāmāre—ad*, to, *clāmāre*, *-ātum*, to shout; see claim.]
**acclimatise, -ize,** ə-kli'mə-tiz, *v.t.* to inure to a new climate.—Also **accli'mate** (or *ak'li-, -li-).—n.* **acclimatisā'tion.**—Also **acclimatā'tion, acclimā'tion** (*ak-li-, -li-*). [Fr. *acclimater—à*, to, *climat,* climate.]
**acclivity,** ə-kliv'i-ti, *n.* an upward slope.—*adjs.* **accliv'itous, accli'vous.** [L. *ad,* to, *clivus,* a slope.]
**accloy,** ə-kloi', (*obs.*) *v.t.* to prick or lame with a horseshoe nail: to clog, choke or encumber (*Spens.*): to sate, cloy (*Spens.*). [See cloy.]
**accoast,** ə-kōst', an older form of accost.
**accoil,** ə-koil', (*rare*) *n.* reception.—*v.i. pa.t.* (*Spens.*) **accoyld',** assembled. [O.Fr. *acoil* (Fr. *accueil*).]
**accolade,** ak-ol-ād', -äd', *n.* an embrace: the action used in conferring knighthood, formerly an embrace, a kiss, now a tap on each shoulder with the flat of a sword: high award, honour, or praise publicly given: a brace or other line connecting staves (*mus.*): a bracelike ornament. [Fr.,—L. *ad,* to, *collum,* neck.]
**accommodate,** ə-kom'ə-dāt, *v.t.* to adapt: to make suitable: to adjust: to harmonise or force into consistency: to furnish or supply (*with*): to find or afford room, etc., for: to provide with a loan: to oblige.—*v.i.* to come to terms: to make adjustment.—*adjs.* **accomm'odable; accomm'-odāting,** ready to make adjustment: obliging: pliable: easily corrupted.—*n.* **accommodā'tion,** adaptation: adjustment, esp. of the eye to change of distance: wresting of language to a sense not intended: obligingness: settlement or compromise: supplying of wants (esp. housing or refreshment): a help towards satisfaction of a want: a convenience: lodgings, quarters (sometimes *pl.*): space for what is required: adaptation of revelation by way of compromise with human ignorance or weakness (*theol.*): a loan of money.—*adj.* **accomm'odātive.**—*ns.* **accomm'-odātiveness; accomm'odātor.**—**accommodation address,** an address to which mail may be sent but which is not that of the addressee's home or office; **accommodation bill,** a bill drawn, accepted, or endorsed by one or more persons as security for a sum advanced to another by a third party, as a banker; **accommodation ladder,** a stairway outside of a ship for entering and leaving boats; **accommodation train** (*U.S.*), one stopping at all or most stations on the way. [L. *accommodāre, -ātum—ad,* to, *commodus,* fitting.]
**accompany,** ə-kum'pə-ni, *v.t.* to go or be in company with: to attend: to go along with: to perform an accompaniment to or for: to associate, join, or couple.—*ns.* **accom'panier; accom'paniment,** that which accompanies: a subsidiary part or parts supporting a solo (*mus.*); **accom'panist** (also **accom'panyist**), a player of accompaniments. [Fr. *accompagner*; see company.]
**accomplice,** ə-kom'plis, or -kum', *n.* an associate in crime (*of* or *with* a person, *in* or *of* the crime): an associate (*Shak.*). [L. *complex, -icis,* joined; pfx. unexplained.]
**accomplish,** ə-kom'plish, or -kum', *v.t.* to complete: to fulfil: to achieve: to equip: to finish off, complete, in culture and acquirements.—*adjs.* **accom'plishable; accom'plished,** complete, finished, or highly skilled in acquirements, esp. graceful acquirements: polished.—*ns.* **accom'-plisher; accom'plishment,** completion: achievement: rendering accomplished: a skilled acquirement in matters of culture or social grace, sometimes superficial or merely ornamental. [O.Fr. *acomplir*—L. *ad,* to, *complēre,* to fill up; see complete.]

**accompt, accomptable, accomptant,** obsolescent spellings of **account, accountable, accountant,** with the same pronunciation.
**accorage.** See **accourage.**
**accord,** ə-körd', *v.i.* to agree: to be in correspondence (*with*).—*v.t.* to cause to agree: to reconcile: to grant (to a person).—*n.* agreement: harmony: the set of notes to which an instrument is tuned: grant: assent.—*adj.* **accord'able.**—*ns.* **accord'ance, accord'ancy,** agreement: conformity: a granting.—*adj.* **accord'ant,** agreeing: corresponding.—*adv.* **accord'antly.**—*n.* **accord'er.**—*adj.* **accord'ing,** in accordance: agreeing: harmonious.—*adv.* **accord'ingly,** agreeably (*obs.*): suitably: in agreement (with what precedes): therefore.—**according as,** in proportion as: depending on whether; **according to,** in accordance with, or agreeably to: as asserted by; **as accords,** as may be appropriate: **of one's own accord,** of one's own spontaneous motion; **with one accord,** with spontaneous unanimity. [O.Fr. *acorder*—L. *ad,* to, *cor, cordis,* the heart.]
**accordion,** ə-kör'di-ən, *n.* a musical instrument consisting of folding bellows, keyboard, and free metal reeds.—*n.* **accord'ionist.**—**accordion-pleat-ing,** pleating with very narrow folds like the bellows of an accordion. [accord.]
**accost,** ə-kost', earlier **accoast, -kōst',** *v.t.* to approach and address: to speak first to: to solicit as a prostitute.—*v.i.* (*Spens.*) to lie alongside, border: to fly along near the ground.—*n.* address: greeting.—*adj.* **accost'able.** [O.Fr. *acoster*—L.L. *accostāre,* to be side by side—L. *ad,* to, *costa,* a rib, a side.]
**accouchement,** a-kōōsh'mä, -ment, *n.* delivery in childbed.—*ns.* **accoucheur** (*-shœr*), a man who assists women in childbirth; **accoucheuse** (*-shœz*), a midwife. [Fr.]
**account,** ə-kownt', *v.t.* to reckon: to judge, value: to recount (*obs.*).—*v.i.* to count: to reckon: to keep accounts: to give a reason or explanation: to give a statement of money dealings: to answer as one responsible: to have the responsibility or credit (of killing or otherwise disposing of anything or anybody; with *for*).—*n.* counting: reckoning: a reckoning of money or other responsibilities: a statement of money owing: advantage: value: estimation: consideration: sake: a descriptive report: a statement: a narrative.—*n.* **accountabil'ity.**—*adj.* **account'able,** liable to account, responsible: explicable.—*n.* **account'ableness.**—*adv.* **account'ably.**—*ns.* **account'ancy,** the office or work of an accountant; **account'ant,** one who keeps, or is skilled in, accounts; **account'antship,**—*n.* and *adj.* **account'-ing.**—**account'-book,** a book for keeping accounts in.—**bring, call, to account,** to demand of one an explanation or justification of what one has done: to reprimand; **find one's account,** to derive advantage; **for account of,** on behalf of; **for the account,** for settlement on the regular settling-day; **go to one's (long) account,** go to the last judgment, die; **hold to account,** hold responsible; **in account with,** in business relations requiring the keeping of an account with; **make account of,** to set value upon; **on** or **to account,** as an instalment or interim payment; **on account of,** because of: on no account, not for any reason or consideration; **take into account,** to take into consideration; **take no account of,** to overlook; **turn to (good) account,** to turn to advantage. [O.Fr. *acconter*—L. *ad,* to, *computāre,* to reckon; see compute, count (2).]
**accourage,** a-kur'ij, *accourage,* ak-or-āj', (*Spens.*) *v.t.* to encourage. [O.Fr. *acorager—à,* to, and *corage,* courage.]
**accourt,** ə-kōrt', -kört, *v.t.* to entertain. [An invention of Spenser's—court.]
**accoutre,** ə-kōō'tər, *v.t.* to dress or equip (esp. a warrior):—*pr.p.* **accoutring** (ə-kōō'tər-ing);

*pa.p.* **accou′tred** (*-tərd*).—*n.* **accou′trement** (*-təror -tra-*), also obs. **accustrement, accoustrement,** equipping: (usu. in *pl.*) dress: military equipments. [Fr. *accoutrer*, earlier *accoustrer*; origin doubtful.]

**accoy,** *ə-koi′*, (*Spens.*) *v.t.* to still: to soothe: to subdue:—*pa.p.* **accoied′, accoyed′.** [O.Fr. *acoyer*—*à*, to, and *coi*, quiet—L. *quiētus*; see **coy**.]

**accoyld.** See **accoil.**

**accredit,** *ə-kred′it*, *v.t.* to bring into credit, show to be true or correct: to accept as true: to furnish or send with credentials: to certify as meeting official requirements: to attribute (to): to ascribe to (*with* the thing attributed).—*n.* **accreditā′tion.**—*adj.* **accred′ited,** furnished with credentials: certified officially: accepted as valid: (of livestock) certified free from a particular disease, e.g. brucellosis. [Fr. *accréditer*—*à*, to, *crédit*, credit.]

**accrescent.** *ə-kres′ənt*, *adj.* growing: ever-increasing: enlarged and persistent (*bot.*).—*n.* **accresc′-ence.**—*v.i.* **accrête′,** to grow together: to become attached.—*v.t.* to unite: to form or gather round itself.—*n.* **accrē′tion,** continued growth: the growing together of parts externally, or continuous coherence: that which has grown in such a way: an extraneous addition.—*adj.* **accrē′tive.** [L. *accrēscĕre, accrētum*—*ad*, to, *crēscĕre*, to grow.]

**accrue** (*Spens.* **accrew**), *ə-krōō′*, *v.i.* to come as an accession, increment, or product: to fall (to one) by way of advantage: to fall due: to increase (*Spens.*).—*v.t.* (*Spens.*) to accumulate.—*n.* **accru′al.** [O.Fr. *acrewe*, what grows up to the profit of the owner—*acreistre*—L. *accrēscĕre*.]

**accubation,** *ak-ū-bā′shən*, *n.* a lying or reclining on a couch. [L. *ad*, to, and *cubāre*, to lie down.]

**acculturation,** *ə-kul-chər-ā′shən*, *n.* process, or result, of adopting features (artefacts, customs, beliefs) from another civilisation. [L. *ad*, and **culture.**]

**accumbent,** *ə-kumb′ənt*, *adj.* lying down or reclining on a couch: having the radicle lying along the edges of the cotyledons (*bot.*). [L. *ad*, to, *cumbĕre*, to lie.]

**accumulate,** *ə-kūm′ūl-āt*, *v.t.* to heap or pile up: to amass.—*v.i.* to increase greatly: to go on increasing: to take degrees by accumulation, to take a higher degree at the same time with a lower, or at a shorter interval than usual (also *v.t.*).—*adj.* heaped up: amassed.—*n.* **accūmŭlā′-tion,** heaping up: a heap or mass.—*adj.* **accūm′-ūlātive,** heaping up or growing by progressive addition: cumulative.—*n.* **accūm′ūlātor,** a thing or person that accumulates: a means of storing energy, esp. an electric battery that can be recharged by sending a reverse current through it: in a computer, etc., a device that performs arithmetical operations and stores the results.— **accumulator** (bet), a bet on four or more races, original stake and winnings from each race being, by previous arrangement, laid on the next race, so that the gambler either wins much or loses all. [L. *ad*, to, *cumulus*, a heap.]

**accurate,** *ak′ū-rit*, *adj.* exact.—*n.* **acc′ūracy** (*-ə-si*), correctness: exactness.—*adv.* **acc′ūrately.** —*n.* **acc′ūrateness.** [L. *accūrātus*, performed with care—*ad*, to, *cūra*, care.]

**accurse,** *ə-kûrs′*, *v.t.* to curse: to devote to misery or destruction.—*adj.* **accurs′ed** (or *-kûrst′*), subjected to a curse: doomed: worthy of a curse. [O.E. pfx. *ā-*, and *cursian*, to curse.]

**accuse,** *ə-kūz′*, *v.t.* to bring a charge against (with *of*).—*n.* (*Shak.*) accusation.—*adj.* **accūs′able.**— *ns.* **accūs′al,** accusation; **accūsā′tion,** the act of accusing: a charge brought.—*adj.* **accūs′ative,** accusing: in or belonging to a grammatical case which expresses the direct object of transitive verbs—primarily expressing destination or the goal of motion.—*n.* the accusative case: a word in the accusative.—*adjs.* **accūsati′val; accūsatō′-rial,** of an accuser; **accūs′atory,** containing accusation.—*adj.* **accused′.**—*n.* (*sing.* or *pl.*) the person or persons accused.—*ns.* **accuse′ment** (*Spens.*), a charge; **accus′er.** [L. *accūsāre, -ātum*—*ad*, to, *causa*, cause, partly through O.Fr. *accuser.* Accusative case (L. *casus accūsātivus*) is a mistranslation of Gr. *ptōsis aitiātikē*, the case indicating what is caused or effected—*aitiā*, cause (also accusation).]

**accustom,** *ə-kus′təm*, *v.t.* to make familiar by custom: to habituate.—*adj.* **accus′tomary.**—*adj.* **accus′tomed,** usual: frequent: habituated: in the habit.—*n.* **accus′tomedness.** [O.Fr. *acostumer* (Fr. *accoutumer*)—*à*, to, *costume*, *coustume*; see **custom.**]

**ace,** *ās, n.* a unit: the one in dice, cards, dominoes, etc.: a single point: a point or hole won at one stroke (*tennis, golf*): a jot: one of the highest character (*Burns*): an airman or other of distinguished achievement (*coll.*).—*adj.* of highest quality: outstanding.—**within an ace of,** within a hair's-breadth of. [Fr. *as*—L. *as*, unity— *as*, Tarentine Doric form of Gr. *heis*, one.]

**-acea,** *-ā-sē-a*, *n. pl. suff.*, used in names of zoological divisions, esp. orders, classes.

**-aceae,** *-ā-sē-ē*, *n.pl. suff.* used in names of plant families.

**acedia,** *ə-sē′di-a*, *n.* listlessness: torpor: sloth. [Gr. *akēdiā, akēdeia*—*a-*, priv., *kēdos*, care. See **accidie.**]

**acephalous,** *ə-sef′ə-ləs, adj.* headless. [Gr. *akephalos*—*a-*, priv., *kephalē* head.]

**Acer,** *ā′sər, āk′ər, n.* the maple genus, giving name to the family **Acerā′ceae** (*as-*).—*adj.* **acerā′ceous.** [L. *acer*, maple.]

**acerb,** *ə-sûrb′*, **acerbic,** *ə-sûr′bik, adjs.* bitter and sour.—*v.t.* **acerbate** (*as′ər-bāt*) to embitter: to irritate.—*n.* **acerb′ity.** [L. *acerbus.*]

**acerose,** *as′ər-ōs, adj.* chaffy: needle-pointed (*bot.*). [L. *acerōsus*—*acus, -eris*, chaff, confused with *acus, -ūs*, needle, or *acer*, sharp.]

**acerous,** *ə-sē′rəs, adj.* without horns, antennae, tentacles. [Gr. *a-*, priv. *keras*, horn.]

**acervate,** *ə-sûr′vāt, adj.* heaped.—*n.* **acervā′tion.** [L. *acervāre, -ātum*, to heap.]

**acescence,** *as-es′əns*, **acescency,** *-i, ns.* souring: turning (of milk).—*adj.* **acesc′ent.** [L. *acēscĕre,* to sour—*acēre*, to be sour.]

**acet-, aceto-,** *as′it-(ō-), a-, ə-set′-(ō-), a-sēt′-(ō-),* in composition, vinegar.—*ns.* **ac′etal,** a liquid formed by oxidation of alcohol, etc.: any of a class of compounds of which this is the type; **ac′etaldehyde,** a liquid of characteristic smell, acetic aldehyde; **ac′etamide,** the amide of acetic acid; **ac′etate,** a salt of acetic acid (**acetate rayon,** a rayon made from cellulose acetate).—*adj.* **acetic** (*-sēt′, -set′*), of, of the nature of, producing, vinegar (**acetic acid,** the sour principle in vinegar, CH₃COOH).—*n.* **acetificā′tion** (*-set-*).— *v.t.* and *v.i.* **acet′ify,** to turn into vinegar.—*n.* **ac′etone,** the simplest of the ketones: any ketone.—*adjs.* **acetose′,** acetous; **acet′ous,** like, or producing, vinegar: sour.—*ns.* **ac′etyl,** the radical (CH₃CO) of acetic acid (**ac′etyl-salicyl′ic acid,** aspirin got by heating salicylic acid with **acetyl chloride**); **acetylene** (*-set′*), *a* gas (C₂H₂), produced from calcium carbide and water, used in welding, synthesising acetic acid, illumination, etc. [L. *acētum*, vinegar.]

**acetabulum,** *as-et-ab′ū-ləm, -ēt-*, *n.* the hollow that receives the head of the thigh-bone: one of the cotyledons of the placenta of ruminants: the cavity that receives a leg in the body of insects: in various animals, a sucker:—*pl.* **acetab′ula.**— *adj.* **acetab′ular.** [L. *acētābulum*, a vinegar cup.]

**Achaean,** *ə-kē′ən,* **Achaian,** *-ki′, -kā′, adj.* belonging to *Achāïā*, in the Peloponnese or to Greece generally.—Also *n.*

achaenium, etc. See achene.

acharné, *a-shär-nā*, (Fr.) furious, desperate (esp. of battles).—avec acharnement, *a-vek a-shär-nə-mä*, obstinately, furiously, rancorously, with gusto.

Achates, *ə-kā'tēz*, *n.* an intimate and trusty comrade, from Aeneas's friend the 'fidus Achates' of the Aeneid.

achates, *ə-chāts'*, (*Spens.*). Same as acates.

ache, *āk*, *n.* a continued pain.—*v.i.* to be in continued pain.—*ns.* ach'age (*Tennyson*); ach'ing.—*adj.* ach'y. [The verb was properly *ake*, the noun *ache*, as in *speak, speech.*—O.E. *acan* (*vb.*), *æce* (*n.*).]

ache, *āch*. Same as aitch.

achene, *a-kēn'*, achaenium, achenium, *a-kē'ni-əm*, *n.* a dry, indehiscent, one-seeded fruit, formed of one carpel, the seed separate from the fruit wall, as in the buttercup.—*adj.* achē'nial.—*n.* achae'nocarp, any dry, indehiscent fruit, esp. an achene. [From Gr. *a-*, priv., and *chainein*, to gape.]

Achernar, *ā'kər-när*, *n.* a first-magnitude star in the constellation Eridanus. [Ar. *ākhir al nahr*, end of the river (Eridanus).]

Acheron, *ak'ər-on*, (Gr. *myth.*) *n.* one of the rivers of the infernal regions.—*adj.* Acheron'tic. [Gr. *Acherōn*.]

Acheulean, Acheulian, *ə-shōō'li-ən*, *adj.* belonging to an early Palaeolithic culture above the Chellean and below the Mousterian. [Saint *Acheul*, near Amiens, where implements of this period are found in river deposits.]

achieve (*obs.* atchieve), *ə-chēv'*, *v.t.* to bring to a successful issue: to end (*obs.*): to perform: to accomplish: to win.—*adj.* achiev'able.—*n.* achieve'ment, achieving: an exploit: an escutcheon or armorial shield granted in memory of some achievement: escutcheon, armour, etc., hung over a tomb: a hatchment.—achievement age, level of individual's educational achievement as determined by comparing his score in a test with the average score of others of the same age; achievement quotient, ratio of achievement age to chronological age (usu. × 100). [Fr. *achever*, from *à chief* (*venir*)—L.L. *ad caput*, to a head; see chief, hatchment.]

Achillean, *ak-il-ē'ən*, *adj.* like *Achilles*, the great Greek hero in the Trojan war, invulnerable except in the heel, by which his mother held him when she dipped him in the Styx.—Achilles' tendon, the attachment of the soleus and gastrocnemius muscles of the calf of the leg to the heel-bone.

Achitophel, Ahithophel, *ə-kit'*, or *-hit'ō-fel*, *n.* a cautious person (*Shak.*): (after Dryden's application to Shaftesbury) an able but unprincipled counsellor. [From David's counsellor who abetted the rebellion of Absalom.]

achkan, *äch'kən*, *n.* in India, a knee-length coat with a high collar, buttoned all the way down. [Hind. *ackan.*]

achlamydeous, *ak-lə-mid'i-əs*, (*bot.*) *adj.* without perianth. [Gr. *a-*, priv., *chlamys, -ydos*, a mantle.]

achondroplasia, *ak-on-drō-plā'zhi-a*, *n.* dwarfism characterised by shortness of the arms and legs.—*adj.* achondroplastic (-*plas'tik*). [Gr. *a-*, priv., *chondros*, cartilage, *plassein*, to make.]

achromatic, *ak-rō-mat'ik*, *adj.* transmitting light without much chromatic aberration.—*adv.* achromat'ically.—*ns.* achrō'matin, the part of a cell nucleus that does not stain with basic dyes; achrō'matism, the state of being achromatic.—*v.t.* achrō'matise, -ize, to render achromatic. [Gr. *a-*, priv., *chrōma, -atos*, colour.]

acicular, *as-ik'ū-lər*, *adj.* needle-shaped: slender and sharp-pointed.—*adj.* acic'ulate, marked as if with needle-scratches. [L. *acicula*, dim. of *acus*, a needle.]

acid, *as'id*, *adj.* sharp: sour: of soil, having an

acid reaction: biting, keen (*fig.*): ill-natured, morose (*fig.*): pertaining to, of the nature of, having the properties of, an acid (*chem.*): containing a large proportion of silica (*geol.*).—*n.* a substance with a sour taste: in chemistry, variously considered as:—any of a class of substances which turn vegetable blues (e.g. litmus) red, and combine with bases, certain metals, etc., to form salts; any of a class of substances that dissolve in water with the formation of hydrogen ions; any of a class of substances that can transfer a proton to another substance; etc.: something harsh, biting, sarcastic (*fig.*): L.S.D. or other hallucinogenic drug (*slang*).—*v.t.* acid'ify, to make acid: to convert into an acid.—*v.i.* to become acid:—*pr.p.* acid'ifying; *pa.t.* and *pa.p.* acid'ified.—*v.t.* acid'ulate, to make slightly acid.—*adjs.* acid'ic; acidifi'able; acid'ulous, slightly sour: subacid: containing carbonic acid, as mineral waters: caustic, sharp (*fig.*).—*ns.* acidificā'tion; acid'ity, the quality of being acid or sour: the extent to which a solution is acid (see pH-value); acidim'eter, apparatus for performing acidimetry; acidim'etry, measurement of the concentration of acids by titration with a standard solution of alkali; acidō'sis (*med.*), presence of acids in the blood beyond normal limits.—acid drop, a sweet flavoured with tartaric acid; acid dye, a dyestuff with acid properties; acid-head, (*drug-taking slang*) a head (*q.v.*); acid salt, a salt in which only part of the replaceable hydrogen is replaced by a metal; acid test, a test for gold by acid: a searching test (*fig.*). [L. *acidus*, sour—*acēre*, to be sour.]

acierate, *as'i-ər-āt*, *v.t.*, to turn into steel.—*n.* ac'ierage, the covering of a metal plate with a film of iron. [Fr. *aciérer*—*acier*, steel.—L.L. *aciārium* (*ferrum*), lit. edging (iron)—L. *aciēs*, edge.]

aciform, *as'i-förm*, *adj.* needle-shaped. [L. *acus*, needle, suff. -form.]

acinaciform, *as-in-as'i-förm*, (*bot.*) *adj.* scimitar-shaped. [Gr. *akinakēs*, a short sword (a Persian word), suff. -form.]

acinus, *as'i-nəs*, *n.* one of the small fruits that compose an aggregate fruit, as in the raspberry: an aggregate fruit: a pip: a racemose gland:—*pl.* aci'ini.—*adjs.* acinā'ceous, full of pips: berry-like: like a cluster of grapes; acin'iform, berry-like. [L. *acinus*, berry, pip.]

ack-ack, *ak-ak*, *adj.* anti-aircraft.—*adv.* ack-emm'a, ante meridiem. [Formerly signallers' names for the letters AA, AM.]

ackee. Same as akee.

acknow, *ak-nō'*, (*obs.*) *v.t.* to recognise: to acknowledge.—*adj.* acknowne' (*Shak.*), confessedly cognisant. [O.E. *on*, in, on, *cnāwan*, to know.]

acknowledge, *ək-nol'ij*, *v.t.* to own a knowledge of: to own as true, or genuine, or valid, or one's own: to confess: to own with gratitude or thanks: to admit or intimate receipt of.—*adj.* acknowl'-edgeable.—*adv.* acknowl'edgeably.—*n.* acknowl'-edgment (sometimes acknowl'edgement), recognition: admission: confession: thanks: an intimation of receipt. [From acknow; see knowledge.]

aclinic, *ak-lin'ik*, *adj.* without inclination, or magnetic dip. [Gr. *aklinēs*, horizontal—*a-*, priv., *klinein*, to tilt.]

acme, *ak'mi*, *n.* the top or highest point: the culmination or perfection in the career of anything: crisis, as of a disease (*arch.*).—*n.* ac'mite, a soda pyroxene whose crystals often show a steep pyramid. [Gr. *akmē*—*akē*, a point.]

acne, *ak'ni*, *n.* inflammation of the sebaceous follicles, as on the nose. [Perh. Gr. *akmē*, a point.]

acock, *ə-kok'*, *adv.* in a cocked manner: defiantly.—*adv.* acock-bill (*naut.*), having the end pointing upward, as an anchor ready for dropping, or yards topped up (a sign of mourning). [Prep. **a**, and **cock**.]

**acoemeti,** *a-sem′i-ti, n.pl.* an Eastern order of monks (5th-6th cent.), who by alternating choirs kept divine service going on day and night. [Latinised pl. of Gr. *akoimētos,* sleepless—*a-*, priv., and *koimaein,* to put to sleep.]

**acold,** *a-kōld′,* (*Shak.*) *adj.* chilled. [Prob. O.E. *ācōlod, pa.p.* of *ācōlian*—pfx. *ā-*, intens., and *cōlian,* to cool.]

**acolouthos,** *ak-a-loo′thos,* (*hist.*) *n.* the head of the Varangian guard of the Byzantine emperors. —*n.* **acolou′thite** (*obs.*), an acolyte—*adj.* **acol-(o)u′thic,** pertaining to an after-image or sensation following upon the immediate effect of a stimulus.—*n.* **acolyte** (*ak′a-līt*), **acolyth** (*-lith*), one in minor orders, next below subdeacon (*R.C. Church*): an inferior church officer: an attendant or assistant. [Gr. *akolouthos,* an attendant—*akoloutheein,* to follow.]

**à compte,** *a kɔt,* (Fr.), on account: in part payment.

**aconite,** *ak′a-nit, n.* wolf's-bane or monk's-hood (*Aconitum*): poison got from it, or (*poet.*) deadly poison in general (often aconi′tum).—*adj.* **aconit′ic.**—*n.* **aconitine** (*-kon′*), a poisonous alkaloid from aconite.—**winter aconite,** an early-flowering ranunculaceous plant (*Eranthis hyemalis*). [L. *aconitum*—Gr. *akoniton.*]

**à contre coeur,** *a kɔ̃-tr′ kœr,* (Fr.) reluctantly.

**acorn,** *ā′körn, n.* the fruit of the oak.—*adj.* **ā′corned.**—**ā′corn-cup′,** the woody cup-shaped involucre of an acorn; **ā′corn-shell,** a cirripede of the genus Balanus (L., acorn). [O.E. *æcern;* form influenced by confusion with **corn** and perh. **oak** (Northern *aik,* O.E. *āc*).]

**à corps perdu,** *a kor per-dü,* (Fr.) desperately, with might and main.

**Acorus,** *ak′a-ras, n.* the sweet-flag genus of the arum family. [Latinised from Gr. *akoros.*]

**acosmism,** *a-koz′mizm, n.* disbelief in the existence of an eternal world, or of a world distinct from God.—*n.* **acos′mist.** [Gr. *a-*, priv., and *kosmos,* the world.]

**acotyledon,** *a-kot-i-lē′dan, n.* a cryptogam.—*adj.* **acotylē′donous.** [Gr. *a-*, priv., and **cotyledon.**]

**acouchy,** *a-koo′shē,* a kind of agouti. [Tupí *acuchy.*]

**à coup sûr,** *a kōō sür,* (Fr.) a certainty.

**acoustic, -al,** *a-kōōs′tik, -al, adjs.* pertaining to the sense of hearing or to the theory of sounds: used in hearing, auditory: operated by sound vibrations, as an *acoustic mine.*—*adv.* **acous′tically.**—*ns.* **acousti′cian** (*-ti′shan*), one who studies or has studied the science of acoustics: one who makes or repairs acoustic instruments, etc.; **acoust′ics,** (*pl.* in form, treated as *sing.*) the science of sound: (as *pl.*) acoustic properties. [Gr. *akoustikos*—*akouein,* to hear.]

**à couvert,** *a kōō-ver,* (Fr.) under cover, protected.

**acquaint,** *a-kwānt′, v.t.* to let or make to know: to inform.—*adj.* (*Scot.* and *North.*) acquainted. —*ns.* **acquaint′ance,** knowledge, esp. falling short of intimacy: a person (sometimes persons) known slightly; **acquaint′anceship,** slight knowledge.—*adj.* **acquaint′ed,** personally known: having personal knowledge of (usu. with *with*). [O.Fr. *acointer*—L.L. *accognitāre*—L. *ad,* to, *cognitus,* known.]

**acquest,** *a-kwest′, n.* acquisition: a thing acquired. [O.Fr.; see **acquire.**]

**acquiesce,** *ak-wi-es′, v.i.* to rest satisfied or without making opposition: to assent (with *in*).—*n.* **acquiesc′ence,** quiet assent or submission.—*adj.* **acquiesc′ent,** acquiescing.—*n.* one who acquiesces.—*advs.* **acquiesc′ently, acquiesc′ingly.** [L. *acquiēscĕre*—*ad,* to, *quiēs,* rest.]

**acquire,** *a-kwir′, v.t.* to gain: to attain to.—*n.* **acquirabil′ity.**—*adjs.* **acquir′able,** that may be acquired; **acquired′.**—*ns.* acquire′ment, acquisi-

tion: something learned or got by effort, not a gift of nature; **acquisition** (*ak-wi-zish′an*), the act of acquiring: that which is acquired.—*adj.* **acquisitive** (*a-kwiz′*) able or ready to acquire.—*ns.* **acquis′itiveness,** propensity to acquire; **acquist** (*a-kwist′*; *Milt.*), acquisition.—**acquired character,** a character originating in the actual life of an organism, not inherited; **acquired taste,** a liking that comes after some experience: a thing so liked (often ironically). [L. *acquirĕre, -quisitum*—*ad,* to, *quaerĕre,* to seek.]

**acquit,** *a-kwit′,* (*obs.*) acquite, acquight, *a-kwīt′, v.t.* to free: to release: to discharge, as a debt: to discharge (oneself of a duty): hence to behave, conduct (oneself): to prove (oneself): to release from an accusation:—*pr.p.* acquitt′ing; *pa.t.* and *pa.p.* acquitt′ed, *obs.* acquit′.—*ns.* acquit′ment (*obs.*); acquitt′al, a judicial discharge from an accusation; acquitt′ance, a discharge from an obligation or debt: a receipt in evidence of such a discharge.—*v.t.* (*Shak.*) to acquit, clear. [O.Fr. *aquiter*—L. *ad,* to; *quiētāre,* to quiet, settle; see **quit.**]

**acrawl,** *a-krôl′, adv.* crawling (with *with*). [Prep. **a**, and **crawl.**]

**acre,** *ā′kar, n.* a measure of 4840 sq. yards: (Scottish acre) 6150·4 sq. yards, (Irish) 7840 sq. yards—both obsolete: (in *pl.*) lands, estates.—*n.* acreage (*ā′kar-ij*), area in acres.—*adj.* acred (*ā′kard*), landed.—*n.* ā′cre('s)-breadth, 22 yards. [O.E. *æcer,* field; Ger. *acker,* L. *ager,* Gr. *agros,* Sans. *ajra,* a plain.]

**acrid,** *ak′rid, adj.* biting: pungent.—*n.* acrid′ity. [L. *ācer, ācris,* sharp, keen; noun suffix perh. in imitation of *acid.*]

**acridin(e),** *ak′ri-dēn, -din, n.* a compound found in coal-tar, a parent substance of dyes and antibacterial drugs.—*n.* acriflavin(e) (*-flā′vēn, -vin*), an antiseptic. [acrid, n. suff. -ine, flavin(e).]

**acrimony,** *ak′ri-man-i, n.* bitterness of feeling or language.—*adj.* acrimō′nious.—*adv.* acrimō′niously. [L. *ācrimōnia*—*ācer,* sharp.]

**acro-,** *ak-rō-,* in composition, tip, point, summit. [Gr. *akron,* tip, end, *akros,* highest, outermost.] **acroamatic, -al,** *ak-rō-a-mat′ik, -al, adjs.* oral (not published): esoteric. [Gr. *akroāmatikos*—*akroāma,* anything to be listened to—*akroaesthai,* to listen.]

**acrobat,** *ak′rō-bat, n.* a rope-dancer: a tumbler: a performer of gymnastic feats.—*adj.* **acrobat′ic.** —*n.pl.* acrobat′ics, acrobatic performances (esp. *fig.*); **ac′robatism,** the art of the acrobat. [Gr. *akrobatēs,* acrobat, *akrobatos,* walking on tiptoe—*akron,* point, and the root of *bainein,* to go.]

**acrogen,** *ak′rō-jan, n.* a cryptogam with growing-point at the tip—a fern or moss.—*adj.* acrogenous (*a-kroj′i-nas*). [Gr. *akron,* -genēs, born.]

**acrolein,** *a-krō′li-in,* (*chem.*) *n.* the aldehyde of allyl alcohol, a pungent-smelling colourless liquid. [L. *ācer, ācris,* sharp, *olēre,* to smell.]

**acrolith,** *ak′rō-lith, n.* a wooden statue with stone extremities. [Gr. *akrolithos*—*akron,* point, *lithos,* stone.]

**acromegaly,** *ak-rō-meg′a-li, n.* a disease characterised by overgrowth, esp. of the face and extremities. [Gr. *akron,* point, *megas, megalos,* great.]

**acromion,** *a-krō′mi-on, n.* a process of the spine of the scapula (also **acromion process**).—*adj.* acro′mial.—*n.* akros, outermost, ōmos, shoulder.]

**acronychal,** *a-kron′ik-al, adj.* at nightfall (of the rising or setting of stars).—*adv.* acron′ychally. [Gr. *akronychos,* at nightfall—*akron,* point, *nychos, -eos,* night.]

**acronym,** *ak′rō-nim, n.* a word formed from the initial letters of other words, as *radar.* [**acro-**, and Gr. *onyma* = *onoma,* name.]

**acropetal,** *a-krop′i-tl, adj.* in the direction of the apex.—*adv.* acrop′etally. [Gr. *akron,* L. *petĕre,* to seek.]

acrophobia, *ak-rō-fō'bi-ə*, *n.* fear of heights. [Gr. *akron*, tip, *akros*, highest, *phobos*, fear.]

acrophony, *ə-krof'ən-i*, *n.* the use of a symbol (derived from an ideogram) to represent the initial sound only of the name of the object for which the ideogram stood.—*adjs.* acrophonet'ic, acrophon'ic (*-fon'*). [acro-, Gr. *phōnē*, sound.]

acropolis, *a-krop'ol-is*, *ə-krop'ə-lis*, *n.* a citadel, esp. that of Athens. [Gr. *akropolis—akros*, highest, *polis*, a city.]

acrospire, *ak'rō-spīr*, (*bot.*) *n.* the first leaf that sprouts from a germinating seed. [M.E. *akerspire*—O.E. *æhher* (see *icker*), ear, spire (1).]

across, *ə-kros'*, *prep.* from side to side of: on or to the other side of: crosswise.—Also *adv.*— come across, to alight upon, meet: to hand over information, confession, money, etc., in answer to demand or inducement (*coll.*); get or come across, to take effect (on the audience across the footlights, and so generally); get it across, to make acceptable, to bring to a successful issue; put it across (someone), to deceive (him). [Prep. a, and cross.]

acrostic, *ə-kros'tik*, *n.* a poem or puzzle in which the first (or last) letters of each line spell a word or sentence: an acronym. [Gr. *akros*, extreme, *stichos*, a line.]

acroterion, *ak-rō-tē'ri-on*, (*archit.*) *n.* a pedestal or ornament at the top or side angle of a pediment:—*pl.* acrotē'ria.—Also acroterium, acrō'-ter (or *ak'*).—*adj.* acrotē'rial. [Gr. *akrōtērion*, extremity—*akros*.]

acrotism, *ak'rot-izm*, (*med.*) *n.* absence of pulsation. [Gr. *a-*, priv., *krotos*, sound made by striking.]

acrylic acid, *ə-kril'ik as'id*, a very reactive acid belonging to the series of oleic acids, obtainable from acrolein by oxidation.—acrylic resins, thermoplastic resins formed by the polymerisation of esters, amides, etc., derived from acrylic acid. [acrolein, Gr. *hȳlē*, matter.]

acrylonitrile, *ə-kril-ō-ni'tril*, *n.* vinyl cyanide, used in making by polymerisation synthetic fibres for carpets, etc., and synthetic rubbers.

act, *akt*, *v.i.* to exert force or influence: to produce an effect: to behave oneself: to perform, as on the stage: to feign: to be suitable for performance.—*v.t.* to perform: to imitate or play the part of.—*n.* something done or doing: an exploit: the very process (of doing something): a decree: legislative enactment: written instrument in verification: short prayer (*R.C. Church*): distinct main section of a play: individual performance, as in variety: public disputation or lecture maintained for a degree.—*ns.* actabil'ity; act'ing, action: act or art of performing an assumed or a dramatic part: feigning.—*adj.* performing some duty temporarily, or for another.—*ns.* act'or, one who acts: a stage-player:—*fem.* act'ress; act'ure (*Shak.*, *Lover's Compl.*) action, performance.—act of God, a result of natural forces, unexpected and not preventable by human foresight; act of grace, a favour, esp. a pardon granted by a sovereign; act on, to exert an influence on: to act in accordance with; act up to, to come in practice up to the standard of: to fulfil. [L. *āctus, -ūs*, an action, doing, *āctum*, a thing done, *āctor*, a doer, actor; *agĕre*, *āctum*, to do, drive.]

acta, *ak'ta*, *n.pl.* official minutes of proceedings: official proceedings or acts.—acta sanctorum, *ak'ta sangk-tō'rəm, -tō'*, *-rōōm*, (L.) deeds of the saints.

Actaeon, *ak-tē'ən*, *n.* a hunter transformed into a stag by Artemis: hence one with horns implanted upon him, a cuckold.—*v.t.* to cuckold. [L. *Actaeōn*—Gr. *Aktaiōn*.]

acte gratuit, *akt gra-twē*, (Fr.) impulsive act lacking motive.

actin(o)-, *ak-tin-(o-)*, in composition, ray.—*adj.*

actinal (*ak-ti'nəl*, or *ak'ti-nəl*), belonging to the radiating bands on the body of an echinoderm where the tube-like feet are, or to the region of the mouth and tentacles in Anthozoa.—*n.*

actinia (*-tin'*), a sea-anemone (properly a particular genus).—*n.* and *adj.* actin'ian.—*adj.* actin'ic, of or showing actinism.—*ns.* ac'tinide, ac'tinoid, any element of a group from atomic number 89 (actinium) upwards; ac'tinism, the chemical action of radiant energy; actin'ium, a radioactive metal (atomic number 89) found in pitchblende; actin'olite (Gr. *lithos*, a stone), a green amphibole: actinom'eter, an instrument for measuring the heat-intensity or the actinic effect of light rays.—*adj.* actinomor'phic (Gr. *morphē*, form; *biol.*), radially symmetrical.—*ns.* Actinomyces (*-mī'sēz*; Gr. *mykēs*, fungus), the ray-fungus, a genus of minute fungi or filamentous bacteria with radiating mycelium; actinomycosis (*-kō'sis*), lumpy-jaw in cattle, etc., or other disease caused by Actinomyces; ac'tinon, actinium emanation, an isotope of radon; actinother'apy, the treatment of disease by exposure to rays, esp. ultraviolet rays.—*n.pl.* Actinozo'a, the Anthozoa.—actinic glass, glass that impedes actinic rays; actinic rays, those rays that have a marked chemical action, esp. the ultraviolet. [Gr. *aktis, aktinos*, ray.]

action, *ak'shən*, *n.* acting: activity: behaviour: a deed: operation: gesture: fighting: a battle: a lawsuit, or proceedings in a court: mode of moving the legs: the movement of events in a drama, novel, etc.: mechanism, esp. of a keyboard instrument.—*adj.* ac'tionable, giving ground for a lawsuit.—action committee, or group, members of an organisation who are chosen to take active measures; action painting, an American version of tachism concerned with the physical manipulation of paint; action radius, the distance a ship or aircraft can go without running out of fuel before reaching its base or starting-point again; action station, a post to be manned during or preparatory to battle; ac'tion-taking (*Shak.*), resorting to law instead of resorting to fighting. [Fr.,—L. *āctiō, -ōnis*.]

active, *ak'tiv*, *adj.* acting: in actual operation: given to action: brisk: busy: nimble: practical, as opp. to speculative: effective: of that voice in which the subject of the verb represents the doer of the action (*gram.*).—*v.t.* ac'tivate, to make active: to increase the energy of: to increase the capacity for adsorption in (carbon): to increase the biological activity of (sewage, etc.) by aeration: to stimulate: to make radioactive.—*ns.* activā'tion; ac'tivātor.— *adv.* ac'tively.—*ns.* ac'tivism, a philosophy of creative will, esp. the practical idealism of Rudolf Eucken (1846-1926): a policy of vigorous action; ac'tivist, a believer in the philosophy of activism: one who supports a policy of vigorous action: one who plays a special part in advancing a project or in strengthening the hold of political ideas; activ'ity, quality, state, or fact of being active: a school exercise designed to teach through practical experiment, research, and discussion: (esp. in *pl.*) doings; ac'tiveness.— activated, or active, carbon, carbon in a highly adsorbent condition, obtained from vegetable matter by carbonisation in the absence of air; active immunity, immunity due to the making of antibodies within the organism; active life (*theol.*), life devoted to good works as opposed to contemplation; active list, a list of full-pay officers engaged in or available for service; active service, service in the battle area, or (orig. *U.S.*) in army, navy or air force even in time of peace. [L. *āctīvus*.]

acton, *ak'tən*, ha(c)queton, *hak'(i)tən*, *n.* a stuffed jacket worn under a coat of mail. [O.Fr.

*auqueton*—Sp.—Ar. *al qūtun*, the cotton.]
**actor, actress.** See under **act**.
**actual,** *ak'tū-əl, ak'choŏ-əl, adj.* of the nature of an action (*Shak.*): real: existing in fact: at the time being.—*v.t.* **ac'tualise, -ize,** to make actual: to realise in action.—*ns.* **actualisā'tion, -ization; ac'tualist,** one who looks to actual facts; **actuality** (*-al'i-ti*), fact or state of being actual: realism: something that really is.—*adv.* **ac'tually,** as a matter of fact: truly, however little one might expect it. [Fr. *actuel*—L.L. *āctuālis*.]
**actualités,** *ak-tü-al-ē-tā,* (Fr.) newsreel or current affairs programme.
**actuary,** *ak'tū-ər-i, n.* a registrar or clerk (still in the Convocation of Canterbury): one who makes the calculations connected with insurance.—*adj.* **actuarial** (*-ā'ri-əl*). [L. *āctuārius* (*scriba*), an amanuensis, a clerk.]
**actuate,** *ak'tū-āt, v.t.* to put into, or incite to, action.—*v.i.* to act.—*ns.* **actuā'tion; ac'tuātor.** [L. *āctus,* action; see **act**.]
**acuity,** *ə-kū'i-ti, n.* sharpness. [L.L. *acuitās, -ātis*—L. *acus,* needle.]
**aculeate(d),** *ə-kū'li-āt(-id), adjs.* pointed: prickly: having a sting: stinging. [L. *aculeātus* —*aculeus,* a sting, goad, dim. of *acus,* needle.]
**acumen,** *ə-kū'men, ak'ū-mən, n.* sharpness: quickness of perception: penetration.—*v.t.* **acū'minate,** to sharpen: to give point to.—*v.i.* (*rare*) to taper.—*adj.* (*bot.*) tapering in long hollow curves to a point (also **acū'minated**).—*n.* **acuminā'tion.** [L. *acūmen, -inis,* a point.]
**acupressure,** *ak-ū-presh'ər, n.* arrest of haemorrhage by a needle pressing across the artery.—*n.* **avizandum.**
**acupunc'ture,** science of puncturing the skin with needles to effect anaesthesia, relieve symptoms, etc. [L. *acus.* needle. **pressure, puncture.**]
**acushla,** *ə-koŏsh'la,* (Ir.) darling.
**acute,** *ə-kūt', adj.* sharp: sharp-pointed: ending in an acute angle (*bot.*): keen: mentally penetrating: piercing: finely discriminating: keenly perceptive: shrewd: urgently pressing.—*n.* an acute accent.—*adv.* **acute'ly.**—*n.* **acute'ness.**—**acute accent,** a mark (') originally indicating a rising pitch, now used for various purposes; **acute angle,** one less than a right angle; **acute disease,** one that comes to a crisis. [L. *acūtus,* pa.p. of *acuĕre,* to sharpen.]
**acyclic,** *ā-, a-sī'klik, adj.* not periodic: not whorled (*bot.*): with open-chain structure, aliphatic (*chem.*). [Gr. *a-,* priv., *kyklos,* a wheel.]
**ad,** *ad, n.* coll. for **advertisement.**
**adage,** *ad'ij, n.* an old saying: a proverb. [Fr.,— L. *adagium*—*ad,* to, and root of *āiō,* I say.]
**adagio,** *ə-dä'j(y)ō,* (*mus.*) *adv.* slowly.—*adj.* slow.—*n.* a slow movement: a piece in adagio time:—*pl.* **ada'gios.** [It.,—*ad agio,* at ease.]
**Adam,** *ad'əm, n.* the first man according to Genesis: unregenerate human nature: a gaoler (perh. as wearing buff) (*Shak.*).—*adjs.* **Adam,** applied to a style of architecture, interior decoration and furniture, designed by Robert and James Adam in the 18th century; **Adamic, -al** (*ə-dam'ik, -əl*), of or like Adam: naked.—*n.* **Ad'amite,** a descendant of Adam: one who goes naked, esp. of a 2nd-century sect in North Africa.—*adjs.* **Adamit'ic, -al.**—*n.* **Ad'amitism.**—**Adam's ale** or **wine,** water; **Adam's apple,** the projection of the thyroid cartilage in front of the throat, fabled to be part of the forbidden fruit stuck in Adam's throat: forbidden fruit (see **forbid**); **Adam's flannel,** mullein; **Adam's needle,** a species of Yucca. [Heb. *Ādām.*]
**adamant,** *ad'-əm-ənt, -ant, n.* name applied by the ancients to various hard substances, e.g. steel: imagined rock with fabulous properties: diamond (*obs.*): lodestone (*obs.*).—*adjs.* **ad'a-mant,** unyielding; **adamantē'an** (*Milt.*), hard as adamant; **adaman'tine,** unbreakable: impregnable: impenetrable: magnetically attractive

(*obs.*).—**adamantine lustre** (*min.*), a lustre approaching the metallic but without opacity. [Gr. *adamas, -antos,* prob. orig. steel, also diamond—*a-,* priv., and *damaein,* to tame, overcome.]
**Adansonia,** *ad-an-sō'ni-a, n.* the baobab genus. [Michel *Adanson,* French botanist (1727-1806).]
**ad aperturam libri,** *ad ap-er-tūr'am lib'rī, -toor'- am lib'rē,* (L.) as the book opens.
**adapt,** *ə-dapt', v.t.* to make fit or suitable.—*n.* **adaptabil'ity.**—*adj.* **adapt'able.**—*n.* **adaptation** (*ad-əp-tā'shən*), the fact, act, process, or result of adapting: a character by which anything is adapted to conditions: adjustment.—*adjs.* **adapt'ative; adapt'ed,** modified to suit: suitable. —*ns.* **adapt'er, -or,** one who, or that which, adapts: an attachment or accessory enabling a piece of apparatus to be used for a purpose, or in conditions, other than that, or those, for which it was orig. intended; **adap'tion,** adaptation.—*adj.* **adapt'ive.**—*adv.* **adapt'ively.**—*n.* **adapt'iveness.** [Fr. *adapter*—L. *adaptāre*—*ad,* to, and *aptāre,* to fit.]
**Adar,** *ä'där,* or *ā'där, n.* the twelfth month of the Jewish ecclesiastical, the sixth of the civil, year (part of February and March).—**Adar Sheni** (*shā'nē;* 'Adar the second'), Veadar. [Heb. *adār.*]
**ad arbitrium,** *ad är-bit'ri-əm, -oŏm,* (L.) at pleasure.
**ad astra,** *ad as'tra,* (L.) to the stars.
**ad avizandum,** *ad a-viz-an'dəm, a-vēz-än'doŏm,* (*Scottish law* L.) for further consideration; see **avizandum.**
**adaw,** *ə-dö',* (*Spens.*), *v.t.* to daunt: to subdue. —*v.i.* to subside. [App. a 16th-cent. misunderstanding of the M.E. *adaw. adaw,* out of life— O.E. *of dagum,* from days (dat. pl.).]
**adaxial,** *ad-aks'i-əl, adj.* next or towards the axis. [L. *ad,* to.]
**adays,** *ə-dāz', (obs.) adv.* by day: daily (*Spens.*). [O.E. *dæges,* gen. of *dæg,* day, with prep. *a* added later.]
**ad captandum (vulgus),** *ad kap-tan'dəm (vul-gəs), -doom (wŏol'goŏs),* (L.) (used as *adv.* or *adj.*) with the intention of appealing to the emotions of, or pleasing, the crowd.
**ad clerum,** *ad kler'əm, klā'roŏm,* (L.) to the clergy.
**ad crumenam,** *ad kroŏ'mə-nam, kroŏ-mä'nam,* (L.) to the purse.
**add,** *ad, v.t.* to put, join, or annex (to something else): to sum up, compute the sum of: to say further.—*v.i.* to make an addition.—*ns.* **add'er,** one who adds: a machine for adding; **addita-ment** (*ə-dit'ə-mənt,* or *ad'),* something added; **addi'tion,** the act of adding: a thing added: the part of arithmetic or algebra that deals with adding: title, designation (*Shak.*).—*adj.* **addi'-tional,** added.—*adv.* **addi'tionally.**—*adjs.* **addi-ti'tious,** increasing; **add'itive,** of the nature of an addition: characterised by addition: to be added.—*n.* a substance added to foodstuffs, etc., for a special purpose.—**addition compound, product** (*chem.*), one formed by the direct union of two or more substances; **add-to system,** a hire-purchase arrangement by which a customer obtains a series of articles, making a down payment on the first only; **add up,** to amount on adding: to be consistent, satisfactory to the mind: to point to a reasonable conclusion; **add up to,** to come to as result or conclusion. [L. *addĕre, additum*—*ad,* to, *dăre,* to put.]
**addax,** *ad'aks, n.* a large African antelope with long slightly twisted horns. [L., from an African word.]
**addeem,** *ə-dēm' (obs.), v.t.* to adjudge: to award. [Pfx. *ad-,* and **deem**.]
**addend,** *ad'end, ə-dend', n.* a number or quantity added. [**addendum.**]

**addendum**, *ə-den'dəm*, *n.* a thing to be added:— *pl.* **adden'da.** [L. gerundive of *addĕre*; see **add.**]
**adder**, *ad'ər*, *n.* the only venomous British snake, a viper (*q.v.*).—**add'erstone**, a prehistoric spindle-whorl or bead, popularly attributed to the agency of adders; **ad'der's-tongue**, a genus (*Ophioglossum*) of ferns whose spores grow on a spike resembling a snake's tongue; **ad'der's-wort**, **add'erwort**, the bistort, or snakeweed, supposed to cure snake-bite. [O.E. *nǣdre* (an adder for a *nadder*; cf. obs. Ger. *atter* for *natter*).]
**addict**, *ə-dikt'*, *v.t.* to give up (to), devote, apply habitually (to).—*adj.* (*obs.*) addicted.—*n.* (*ad'-ikt*), a slave to a habit or vice, esp. drugs.—*adj.* **addict'ed**, inclined or given up (with *to*).—*ns.* **addict'edness**, **addic'tion.**—drug of addiction, habit-forming drug. [L. *addicĕre*, *addictum* —*ad*, to, *dicĕre*, to declare.]
**addio**, *ad-ē'o*, (It.) good-bye (**a Dio**, to God).
**Addison's disease**, *ad'i-sənz diz-ēz'*, a disease in which there is progressive destruction of the suprarenal cortex, accompanied by wasting, weakness, low blood-pressure, and pigmentation of the skin (bronzed skin). [Dr Thomas *Addison* (1793-1860), who investigated it.]
**addle**, *ad'l*, *n.* liquid filth (now *dial.*).—*adj.* putrid: bad (as an egg): barren, empty: muddled.—*v.t.* and *v.i.* to make or become addle.—*adjs.* **add'led**; **add'le-brained, -headed, -pated, muddle-headed.**—*n.* **add'lement.** [O.E. *adela*, mud.]
**addoom**, *ə-dōōm'*, (*Spens.*) *v.t.* to adjudge, award. [Pfx. *ad-*, and **doom.**]
**addorsed**, *ə-dörst'*, (*her.*) *adj.* turned back to back. [L. *ad*, to, *dorsum*, back.]
**address**, *ə-dres'* *v.t.* to arrange (*obs.*): to prepare (*obs.*): to dress (*obs.*): to don (*arch.*): to apply or devote (oneself; with *to*): to apply oneself to: to direct: to aim: to direct one's words to, speak directly to: to send: to put a written or printed direction or indication of destination upon: to woo (*arch.*).—*v.i.* to direct one's words (towards) (*Shak.*): to prepare oneself (*Shak.*).—*n.* act or mode of addressing: deportment: adroitness: preparation, a move, incipient act (*Milt.*): a formal communication in writing: a speech: direction, as of a letter: place to which letters may be directed: place where one may be found: (in *pl.*) attentions of the nature of courtship.—*adj.* **addressed'**, **addrest'**, set up (*Spens.*): ready, prepared (*Shak.*): arrayed (*obs.*): equipped (*obs.*): aimed: directed.—*ns.* **addressee'**, the person to whom a missive or communication is addressed; **address'er, -or.** [Fr. *adresser*—L.L. *addirectiāre* —L. *ad*, to, *directum*, straight; see **dress**, **direct.**]
**adduce**, *ə-dūs'*, *v.t.* to bring forward in discussion, to cite or quote.—*adj.* **adduc'ent**, drawing inward or together, as a muscle.—*n.* **adduc'er.**—*adj.* **adduc'ible.**—*v.t.* **adduct** (*ə-dukt'*), to draw inward or together.—*n.* **adduc'tion**, the act of adducing or of adducting.—*adj.* **adduc'tive**, tending to bring forward.—*n.* **adduc'tor**, an adducent muscle. [L. *addūcĕre*, *adductum*—*ad*, to, and *dūcĕre*, to bring.]
**adeem**, *ə-dēm'*, (*law*) *v.t.* to cancel (a bequest) by destruction or sale of the thing bequeathed, or otherwise.—*n.* **ademption** (*-dem'shən*). [L. *ad*, to, and *emĕre*, *emptum*, to take.]
**adelantado**, *a-de-lan-tä'dō*, *n.* a grandee: a provincial governor. [Sp.]
**à demi**, *a də-mē*, (Fr.) by halves, half.
**aden-**, in composition, gland.—*ns.* **adenec'tomy**, surgical removal of a gland; **adenine**, *ad'ən-ēn*, a substance found in all glandular tissues, one of the four bases in deoxyribo-nucleic acids, in close association with thymine; **adenitis** (*ad-ən-i'tis*) inflammation of glands.—*adj.* **ad'enoid**, glandlike: glandular.—*n.* (usu. in *pl.*) enlargement of glandular tissue at the back of the nose.

—*adj.* **adenoid'al**, of adenoids: affected by, or as if by, adenoids (as a voice).—*ns.* **adenoidec'tomy**, surgical removal of adenoids; **adenō'ma**, a glandlike tumour:—*pl.* **adenō'mata**, or **-mas.**— *adj.* **adenō'matous.** [Gr. *adēn*, gland.]
**Adeni**, *ä'di-ni*, *n.* and *adj.* (a citizen) of Aden.
**adept**, *ad'ept*, *ə-dept'*, *a-dept'*, *adj.* completely skilled.—*n.* (*ad'ept*, *ə-dept'*, *a-dept'*) a proficient: one who has attained the great secret (e.g. of the philosopher's stone). [L. *adeptus* (*artem*), having attained (an art), pa.p. of *adipiscī*, to attain.]
**adequate**, *ad'i-kwit*, *-kwāt*, *adj.* sufficient: competent.—*adv.* **ad'equately.**—*ns.* **ad'equateness**, **ad'equacy** (*-kwə-si*).—*adj.* **ad'equative.** [L. *adaequātus*, made equal—*ad*, to, and *aequus*, equal.]
**adermin**, *a-dûr'min*, *n.* former name of pyridoxin. [Gr. *a-* privative, *derma*, skin, because deprivation of this vitamin was shown to cause dermatitis in rats.]
**Ades** (*Milt.*), *n.* variant of **Hades.**
**adespota**, *ad-es'pot-a*, *n.pl.* anonymous works. [Gr. *a-*, priv., and *despotēs*, master.]
**à dessein**, *a des-ĕ*, (Fr.) on purpose.
**ad eundem gradum**, *ad ē-un'dəm grād'əm*, *ā-ōōn'- dem grād'ōōm*, (L.) to the same degree (at another university).
**à deux**, *a də*, (Fr.) of two, between two, two-handed; **à deux mains**, with both hands: for two hands.
**ad finem**, *ad fin'əm*, *fēn'em*, (L.) to the end: toward the end.
**adharma**, *ə-där'mä*, *n.* unrighteousness—opposite of **dharma.** [Sans.]
**adhere**, *əd-, ad-hēr'*, *v.i.* to stick: to remain fixed or attached: to cleave (as to a party, a leader, a doctrine): to be consistent (*Shak.*): to agree: to affirm a judgment (Scots law).—*n.* **adhēr'ence**, state of adhering: concrescence of unlike parts (*bot.*).—*adj.* **adhēr'ent**, sticking: concrescent and unlike.—*n.* one who adheres: a follower: a partisan: one who is loosely associated with a body without being a member.—*n.* **adhēr'er.** [L. *ad*, to, *haerēre*, *haesum*, to stick.]
**adhesion**, *əd-hē'zhən*, *n.* the act of adhering or sticking: steady attachment: concrescence of unlike parts (*bot.*): reunion of separated surfaces (*surg.*): abnormal union of parts that have been inflamed (*path.*): a band of fibrous tissue joining such parts.—*adj.* **adhē'sive** (*-siv*, *-ziv*), sticky: apt to adhere.—*n.* a substance used for sticking things together.—*adv.* **adhē'sively.**—*n.* **adhē'siveness.** [See **adhere.**]
**adhibit**, *əd-hib'it*, *v.t.* to apply: to attach: to admit: to administer.—*n.* **adhibi'tion.** [L. *ad-hibēre*, *-itum*—*ad*, to, *habēre*, to hold.]
**ad hoc**, *ad hok*, (L.) for this special purpose (used as *adj*).
**ad hominem**, *ad hom'in-em*, (L.) to the man, addressed to the feelings or prejudices of the hearer or reader.
**adiabatic**, *ad-i-ə-bat'ik*, *adj.* without transference of heat.—*adv.* **adiabat'ically.** [Gr. *a-*, priv., *dia*, through, *batos*, passable.]
**Adiantum**, *ad-i-an'təm*, *n.* the maidenhair genus of ferns. [Gr. *adiantos—a-*, priv., and *diantos*, capable of being wetted.]
**adiaphoron**, *ad-i-af'ə-ron*, *n.* in theology and ethics, a thing indifferent—any tenet or usage considered non-essential:—*pl.* **adiaph'ora.**—*ns.* **adiaph'orism**, tolerance or indifference in regard to non-essential points in theology: latitudinarianism; **adiaph'orist.**—*adj.* **adiaph'orous.** [Gr., from *a-*, priv., *diaphoros*, differing—*dia*, apart, *pherein*, to carry.]
**adiathermic**, *ad-i-ə-thûr'mik*, *adj.* impervious to radiant heat. [Gr. *a-*, priv., *dia*, through, *thermē*, heat.]
**adieu**, *ə-dū'*, *interj.* (I commend you) to God:

farewell.—*n.* a farewell:—*pl.* adieus or adieux (*ə-dūz'*). [Fr. *à Dieu*, to God.]

ad infinitum, *ad in-fin-it'əm, -ēt'ōōm*, (L.) to infinity.

ad inquirendum, *ad in-kwir-en'dum, in-kwēr-en'-dōōm*, (L.L.) for making inquiry—name of a writ.

ad interim, *ad in'tər-im*, (L.L.) for the meantime.

adiós, *ad-ē-os'*, (Sp; lit. 'to God') good-bye.

adipic, *ə-dip'ik, adj.* of fat (adipic acid, $C_6H_{10}O_4$, an acid got by treating fat with nitric acid).—*adj.* adipose (*ad'i-pōs*), fatty.—*n.* adiposity (*-pos'i-ti*).—adipose tissue, the vesicular structure in the animal body which contains the fat. [L. *adeps, adipis*, soft fat.]

adipocere, *ad'i-pō-sēr*, or *-sēr'*, *n.* a fatty, waxy substance resulting from the decomposition of animal bodies in moist places or under water, but not exposed to air. [L. *adeps, adipis*, soft fat, and *cēra*, wax.]

adit, *ad'it, n.* an opening or passage, esp. into a mine. [L. *aditus—ad*, to, *ire, itum*, to go.]

adjacent, *ə-jā'sənt, adj.* lying near.—*n.* adja'cency.—*adv.* adja'cently. [L. *ad*, to, *jacēns, -entis*, pr.p. of *jacēre*, to lie.]

adjective, *aj'ik-tiv, adj.* added: dependent: subsidiary: (of dyes) requiring a mordant.—*n.* a word added to a noun to qualify it, or limit its denotation by reference to quality, number, or position.—*adj.* adjectival (*-tiv'l*) of an adjective: using many adjectives: used facetiously as a euphemism (e.g. *What adjectival nonsense!*).—*advs.* adjecti'vally; ad'jectively. [L. *adjectivum* (*nōmen*), added (word)—*adjicēre, -jectum*, to add—*ad*, to, *jacēre*, to throw.]

adjoin, *ə-join', v.t.* to join on: to lie next to.—*v.i.* to be in contact:—*adj.* adjoin'ing.—*n.* adj'oint, a civil officer who assists a French maire: an assistant professor in a French college. [Through Fr. *adjoign-*, pr.p. stem, and *adjoint*, pa.p., of *adjoindre*—L. *adjungēre—ad*, to, *jungēre*, to join.]

adjourn, *ə-jûrn', v.t.* to put off to another day: to postpone: to discontinue (a meeting) in order to reconstitute it at another time or place.—*v.i.* to suspend proceedings and disperse for any time specified, or (*sine diē*) without such time being specified.—*ns.* adjourn'al (*obs.*); adjourn'ment. [O.Fr. *ajorner*—L.L. *adiurnāre*—L. *ad*, to, L.L. *jurnus*, L. *diurnus*, daily; cf. journal.]

adjudge, *ə-juj', v.t.* to decide: to assign: to award.—*n.* adjudg'ment (sometimes adjudge'ment), the act of adjudging: sentence. [O.Fr. *ajuger*—L. *adjūdicāre*; cf. judge.]

adjudicate, *ə-jōō'di-kāt, v.t.* to determine judicially: to pronounce: to award.—*v.i.* to pronounce judgment: to act as judge in a competition between amateurs in one of the arts, e.g. music.—*ns.* adjudica'tion, act or process of adjudicating: an order of the Bankruptcy Court, adjudging a debtor to be a bankrupt, and transferring his property to a trustee (*Eng. law*); adju'dicator. [L. *adjūdicāre, -ātum*.]

adjunct, *aj'ung(k)t, adj.* joined or added.—*n.* a thing joined or added, but subordinate or not essentially a part: a person (usually subordinate) joined to another in office or service: any word or clause enlarging the subject or predicate (*gram.*): any accompanying quality or non-essential attribute (*logic*).—*n.* adjunction (*ə-jungk'shən*).—*adj.* adjunct'ive, forming an adjunct.—*advs.* adjunct'ively; adjunct'ly. [L. *adjunctus* pa.p. of *adjungēre*, to join.]

adjure, *ə-jōōr', v.t.* to cause to swear (*obs.*): to charge on oath or solemnly.—*n.* adjura'tion (*aj-*).—*adj.* adjur'atory.—*adj.* adjur'ing. [L. *adjūrāre—ad*, to, *jūrāre, -ātum*, to swear.]

adjust, *ə-just', v.t.* to put into due relation: to regulate: to settle.—*adj.* adjust'able.—*ns.* adjust'er, one who adjusts: see average, loss; adjust'ment; adjust'or, an organ or faculty that determines

behaviour in response to stimuli. [Obs. Fr. *adjuster*—L.L. *adjuxtāre*, to put side by side—L. *juxtā*, near; confused by association with *jūstus*, right.]

adjutage, ajutage, *aj'ōō-tij, n.* a nozzle as for a fountain. [Fr. *ajutage*; cf. adjust.]

adjutant, *aj'ōō-tənt, n.* an officer specially appointed to assist a commanding officer: a large Indian stork or crane (from its stalking gait).—*ns.* adj'utancy, the office of an adjutant: assistance; adj'utant-gen'eral, head of a department of the general staff: the executive officer of a general. [L. *adjūtāns, -antis*, pr.p. of *adjūtāre*, freq. of *adjūvāre—ad*, to, *jūvāre*, to assist.]

adjuvant, *aj'ōō-vənt, adj.* helping.—*n.* a help: an ingredient to help the main ingredient (*med.*).—*n.* ad'juvancy. [Fr.,—L. *ad*, to, *jūvāre*, to help.]

ad lib. See ad libitum.

ad libitum, *ad lib'i-təm, -tōōm*, (L.) at pleasure.—*Abbrev.* ad lib.—ad-lib, ad-lib', (*coll.*) *v.t.* and *v.i.* to extemporise, esp. to fill up time.

ad-man. See under advertisement.

ad manum, *ad mān'um, mān'ōōm*, (L.) at hand, ready.

ad-mass, admass. See under advertisement.

admeasure, *ad-mezh'ər, v.t.* to measure: to apportion.—*n.* admeas'urement. [O.Fr. *amesurer*—L.L. *admēnsūrāre*—L. *ad*, to, *mēnsūra*, measure.]

adminicle, *əd-min'i-kl, n.* anything that aids or supports: an auxiliary: any corroboratory evidence (*law*).—*adj.* adminic'ular.—*v.t.* and *v.i.* adminic'ulate. [L. *adminiculum*, a support—*ad*, to, *manus*, hand.]

administer, *əd-min'is-tər, v.t.* to govern: to manage as a steward, substitute, or executor: to dispense (justice, rites): to tender (an oath, medicine).—*v.i.* to minister.—*adj.* admin'istrable.—*adj.* and *n.* admin'istrant.—*n.* administrā'tion, the act of administering: management: dispensation of sacraments: the government.—*v.t.* admin'istrate to administer.—*adj.* admin'istrative, concerned with administration.—*n.* admin'istrātor, one who manages or directs: the person to whom is committed, under a commission entitled letters of administration, the administration or distribution of the personal estate of a deceased person, in default of an executor: one empowered to act for a person legally incapable of acting for himself (*Scots law*):—*fem.* admin'istrātrix.—*n.* admin'istrator-ship. [L. *administrāre, -ātum—ad*, to, *ministrāre*, to minister.]

admiral, *ad'mər-əl, n.* the chief commander of a navy: a naval officer ranking with a general in the army (admiral of the fleet with field-marshal): an admiral's flagship: the chief ship in a fleet of merchantmen or fishing boats: a cone-shell: a butterfly of certain kinds (see red, white).—*ns.* ad'miralship, the office or art of an admiral; Ad'miralty, board administering navy (since 1964 under Ministry of Defence): building where it transacts business.—Lord High Admiral, office dating from 15th century, William IV (when Duke of Clarence) being last holder until office was taken over by the Crown in 1964. [O.Fr. *a(d)miral*—Ar. *amīr-al-bahr*, a lord of the sea, confused with L. *admirābilis* (see admire).]

admire, *əd-mir', v.t.* to have (or express) a high opinion of: to wonder at (*arch.*).—*v.i.* (*obs.*) to wonder.—*adj.* ad'mirable, worthy of being admired.—*n.* ad'mirableness.—*adv.* ad'mirably.—*ns.* admir'a(u)nce (*Spens.*), admiration; ad-mirā'tion, the act of admiring: wonder, together with esteem, love, or veneration: astonishment (*B., Shak.*, and *Milt.*): admirableness (*Shak.*): an object of admiration (*Shak.*): a wonder (*Shak.*).—*adj.* ad'mirātive.—*n.* admir'er, one who admires: a lover.—*adv.* admir'ingly.—Admirable Crichton (*krī'tən*), one who excels in many things, from James Crichton (1560-82),

Neutral vowels in unaccented syllables: *el'ə-mənt*; for certain sounds in foreign words, see p. viii

Scottish athlete, Latin poet, polymath. [Fr. *admirer*—L. *ad*, at, *mīrāri*, to wonder.]
**ad misericordiam**, *ad mi-zer-i-kōr'di-am*, (L.) (appealing) to pity—of an argument, etc.
**admit**, *əd-mit'*, *v.t.* to allow to enter: to let in: to concede: to acknowledge: to be capable of (also *v.i.* with *of*):—*pr.p.* **admitt'ing**; *pa.p.* **admitt'ed**.—*n.* **admissibil'ity**.—*adj.* **admiss'ible**, that may be admitted or allowed (generally, or specially as legal proof).—*n.* **admission** (-*mish'ən*), the act of admitting: anything admitted or conceded: leave to enter.—*adjs.* **admiss'ive**; **admitt'able**, that may be admitted.—*n.* **admitt'-ance**, admission: acceptability, acceptance (*Shak.*): the property of an electric circuit by virtue of which a current flows under the action of a potential difference (*elect.*).—*adj.* **admitt'ed**.—*adv.* **admitt'edly**. [Partly through Fr.,—L. *admittĕre*, *-missum*—*ad*, to, *mittĕre*, *missum*, to send.]
**admix**, *əd-*, *ad-miks'*, *v.t.* to mix with something else.—*n.* **admix'ture**, the action of mixing: what is added to the chief ingredient of a mixture. [L. *ad*, to, and **mix**.]
**ad modum**, *ad mōd'əm*, *mod'ōom*, (L.) after the manner (of).
**admonish**, *əd-mon'ish*, *v.t.* to warn: to reprove mildly.—*n.* **admon'ishment**, admonition. [O.Fr. *amonester*—L.L. *admonestāre*—L. *admonēre*—*ad*, to, *monēre*, to warn.]
**admonition**, *ad-mon-ish'ən*, or *-mən-*, *n.* reproof: counsel: advice: ecclesiastical censure.—*adjs.* **admonitive** (*-mon'*), **admon'itory**, containing admonition.—*n.* **admon'itor**. [L. *admonitiō*, *-ōnis*; cf. **admonish**.]
**adnascent**, *ad-nas'ənt*, *adj.* growing to or upon something else. [L. *adnāscēns*, *-entis*, pr.p. of *adnāsci*—*ad*, to, *nāscī*, to be born.]
**adnate**, *ad'nāt*, *ad-nāt'*, (*bot.*) *adj.* attached (esp. by the whole length) to another organ.—*n.* **adnation** (-*nā'shən*). [L. *adnātus*, usu. *agnātus*—*ad*, to, (*g*)*nātus*, born.]
**ad nauseam**, *ad nö'shi-am*, *-zi-*, *now'si-*, (L.) to the pitch of producing disgust.
**ado**, *ə-dōō'*, *n.* a to-do: bustle: trouble: difficulty: stir or fuss. [**at do**, Northern English infin. **with at** instead of **to**, borrowed from Scand.]
**adobe**, *ə-dō'bi*, *n.* a sun-dried brick: a house made of such bricks: (also **adobe clay**) a name for any kind of mud which, when mixed with straw, can be sun-dried into bricks.—Also *adj.* [Sp.,—*adobar*, to plaster.]
**adolescent**, *ad-ō-les'ənt*, *adj.* passing from childhood to maturity.—Also *n.*—*n.* **adolesc'ence**, the state or time of being adolescent. [L. *adolēscēns*, *-entis*, pr.p. of *adolēscĕre*, to grow up.]
**Adonai**, *ə-dōn'ī*, *ə-don-ā'ī*, *n.* a name of the Deity in the O.T., usu. translated by Lord. See also *Jehovah*. [Heb. *adōnāi*, my lord.]
**Adonis**, *ə-dō'nis*, *n.* a youth beloved by Aphrodite: a beautiful youth: a beau or dandy: the ranunculaceous pheasant's-eye genus.—*n.pl.* **Adō'nia**, the festival of mourning for Adonis.—*n.* **Adonic** (*ə-don'ik*) a verse of a dactyl and a spondee, said to have been used in the Adonia.—Also *adj.*—*v.t.* and *v.i.* **ad'onise**, *-ize*, to adorn (oneself). [Gr. *Adōnis*—Phoenician *adōn*, lord.]
**adoors**, *ə-dōrz'*, *-dörz'*, (*obs.*) *adv.* at doors: at the door. [Prep. **a**, at, and **door**.]
**adopt**, *ə-dopt'*, *v.t.* to take voluntarily as one's own child, with the rights of a child: to take into any relationship: to take as one's own: to take up: to take over: to take (a precaution): to choose formally (e.g. a candidate): to endorse, approve (e.g. a resolution, minutes).—*adj.* **adopt'ed**, taken by adoption.—*ns.* **Adop'tianism**, **Adoptionism** (*ə-dop'shən-izm*; often **adoptianism**), the doctrine that Christ, as man, is the adopted son of God: **adop'tianist**, **adop'tionist**; **adop'tion**.—*adjs.* **adop'tious** (*-shəs*; *Shak.*), adopted;

**adopt'ive**, that adopts or is adopted. [L. *adoptāre*—*ad*, to, *optāre*, to choose.]
**adore**, *ə-dōr'*, *-dör'*, *v.t.* to worship: to love or reverence intensely: to adorn (*Spens.*).—*adj.* **ador'able**.—*n.* **ador'ableness**.—*adv.* **ador'ably**.—*ns.* **adorā'tion**; **ador'er**.—*adv.* **ador'ingly**. [L. *ad*, to, *ōrāre*, to pray.]
**adorn**, *ə-dörn'*, *v.t.* to deck or dress: to embellish.—*n.* (*Spens.*) adornment.—*adj.* (*Milt.*) adorned, ornate.—*n.* **adorn'ment**, ornament: decoration. [O.Fr. *äorner*, *adorner*—L. *adōrnāre*—*ad*, to, *ōrnāre*, to furnish.]
**adown**, *ə-down'*, (*poet.*) *adv.* and *prep.* an older form of **down**.
**ad patres**, *ad pāt'rēz*, *pat'rās*, (L.) (gathered) to his fathers, dead.
**adpress**, *ad-pres'*, *v.t.* to press together.—*adj.* **adpressed'**, (*bot.*) closely pressed together but not united.—Also **appress'**. [L. *ad*, to, *premĕre*, *pressum*, to press.]
**adrad**, *ə-drad'*, **adred**, *ə-dred'* (*Spens.*) *adj.* afraid. [O.E. *ofdrǣd*—pfx. *of-*, *drǣdan*, to dread.]
**adread**, *ə-dred'*, (*obs.*) *v.t.* to fear.—*pa.t.* **adrad'** (*Spens.*). [O.E. *ondrǣdan*—pfx. *on-*, *on*, *and-*, to and *drǣdan*, to dread.]
**ad referendum**, *ad ref-er-en'dum*, *-dōōm*, (L.) to be further considered.
**ad rem**, *ad rem*, (L.) to the point: to the purpose.
**adren(-o)-**, *ə-dren(-ō)-*, *-drēn(-ō)-*, in composition; adrenal, adrenal glands, adrenalin.—*adj.* **adrenal** (*ə-drēn'al*), beside the kidneys.—*n.* an adrenal gland.—*n.* **adrenalin(e)** (*-ren'*, *-rēn'*) a hormone secreted by the adrenal glands, used to cause constriction of the small arteries.—*adj.* **adrenocorticotrophic** (*ad-rē'nō-kör'ti-kō-tro'fik*; cortex, and Gr. *trophē*, food), stimulating the activity of the adrenal cortex.—*n.* **adrenocorticotrophin** (*-trō'fin*), a hormone used in the treatment of rheumatoid arthritis:—abbrev. ACTH.—**adrenal glands**, the suprarenal capsules, two small ductless glands over the kidneys. [L. *ad*, to, *rēnēs*, kidneys.]
**adrift**, *ə-drift'*, *adj.* or *adv.* in a drifting condition: loose from moorings: left to one's own resources, without help, guidance, or contacts: cut loose. [Prep. **a**, and **drift**.]
**adroit**, *ə-droit'*, *adj.* dexterous: showing address.—*adv.* **adroit'ly**.—*n.* **adroit'ness**. [Fr. *à droit*, according to right—L. *directus*, straight; see **direct**.]
**à droite**, *a drwät*, (Fr.) to the right.
**adry**, *ə-dri'*, *adj.* and *adv.* in a state of thirst or dryness. [After **athirst**, **acold**, etc.]
**adscititious**, *ad-sit-ish'əs*, *adj.* added or assumed: additional. [L. *adsciscĕre*, *-scitum*, to take or assume—*ad*, to, *sciscĕre*, to inquire—*scire*, to know.]
**adscript**, *ad'skript*, *adj.* attached to the soil.—*n.* a feudal serf so attached.—*n.* **adscrip'tion**. [L. *adscriptus*—*ad*, to, *scribĕre*, to write.]
**adsorb**, *ad-sörb'*, *v.t.* of a solid, to take up a vapour on its surface (cf. **absorb**).—*ns.* **adsorb'-ate**, the vapour adsorbed; **adsorb'ent**, a solid (as charcoal) that adsorbs a vapour in contact with it; **adsorp'tion**. [L. *ad*, to, *sorbēre*, to suck in.]
**adsum**, *ad'sum*, *-sōom*, (L.) I am present: here.
**ad summum**, *ad sum'um*, *sōom'ōom*, (L.) to the highest point.
**adularia**, *ad-ū-lā'ri-a*, *n.* a transparent orthoclase feldspar. [From the *Adula* group in the Alps.]
**adulate**, *ad'ū-lāt*, *v.t.* to fawn upon, to flatter.—*ns.* **adulā'tion**; **adulā'tor**.—*adj.* **ad'ulatory**. [L. *adūlāri*, *adūlātus*, to fawn upon.]
**Adullamite**, *ə-dul'əm-it*, *n.* John Bright's name for a Whig seceder from the Liberal party (1866). [From the cave of *Adullam*, 1 Sam. xxii. 1, 2.]
**adult**, *ad'ult*, *ə-dult'*, *adj.* grown up: mature: of or for adults.—*n.* a grown-up person.—*n.*

**ad'ulthood.** [L. *adultus*, pa.p. of *adolēscĕre*, to grow up; see adolescent.]

**adulterate,** *ə-dult'ər-āt, v.t.* to debase, falsify, by mixing with something inferior or spurious: to commit adultery with (*obs.*).—*v.i.* (*Shak.*) to commit adultery.—*adj.* defiled by adultery: spurious: corrupted by base elements.—*ns.* **adult'erant,** that with which anything is adulterated; **adultera'tion,** the act of adulterating: the state of being adulterated; **adult'erator,** one who adulterates a commodity; **adult'erer,** one guilty of adultery:—*fem.* **adult'eress.**—*adj.* **adult'erine,** resulting from adultery: spurious: illegal (*hist.*).—*n.* the offspring of adultery.—*v.i.* **adult'erise, -ize** (*arch*), to commit adultery.—*adj.* **adult'erous,** pertaining to, of the nature of, guilty of, adultery.—*adv.* **adult'erously.**—*n.* **adult'ery,** violation of the marriage-bed, whether one's own or another's: unchastity generally (*B.*): applied opprobriously, esp. by theologians to marriages disapproved of: image-worship: adulteration, falsification (*obs.*). [L. *adulterāre, -ātum,* prob. from *ad* to, and *alter,* another. Some forms come from Fr., remodelled later on Latin.]

**adumbrate,** *ad'um-brāt,* or *-um', v.t.* to give a faint shadow of: to shadow forth: to foreshadow: to overshadow.—*n.* **adumbra'tion.** [L. *adumbrāre, -ātus—ad,* to, *umbra,* a shadow.]

**adunc,** *ə-dungk', adj.* hooked.—Also **adunc'ate, -d, adunc'ous.**—*n.* **aduncity** (*ə-dun'si-ti*). [L. *aduncus, aduncātus—ad,* to, *uncus,* a hook.]

**ad unguem,** *ad ung'gwem, ōong',* (L.) to the nail: to a nicety.

**ad unum omnes,** *ad ūn'um om'nēz, ōon'ōōm om'-nās,* (L.) all to a man.

**adust,** *ə-dust', v.t.* (*Milt.*) to scorch.—*adj.* burnt up or scorched (*obs.*): browned with the sun (*obs.*): sallow and atrabilious (from the old notions of dryness of body). [L. *adūstus,* pa.p. of *adūrĕre,* to burn up.]

**ad valorem,** *ad val-ör'əm, -ōr', wal-,* (L.) according, in proportion, to value.

**advance,** *əd-väns', v.t.* to put forward: to promote: to further: to raise (*Shak.*): to extol (*obs.*): to raise in price: to supply beforehand: to pay before due time: to lend, esp. on security.—*v.i.* to move or go forward: to make progress: to rise in rank or in value.—*n.* a forward move: progress: a rise in price, value, wages: payment beforehand: a loan: an approach, overture, move towards agreement, favour, etc.—*adj.* before in place: made, given, etc., ahead of time.—*adj.* **advanced',** at, appropriate to, a far-on stage (of education, thought, emancipation, life, etc.).—*n.* **advance'ment,** promotion: furthering: payment in advance.—**advance copy,** proof, one sent in advance of publication; **advance factory,** one built to encourage development, in the belief that a firm will take it over; **advance(d) guard,** a guard or party in front of the main body: **advance note,** an order for (generally) a month's wage given to a sailor on engaging. —**in advance,** beforehand: in front. **Ü.Fr.** *avancer*—L.L. *abante* (Fr. *avant*)—L. *ab ante,* from before; the prefix refashioned later as if from *ad.*]

**advantage,** *əd-vänt'ij, n.* superiority over another: a favouring condition or circumstance: gain or benefit: the first point after deuce (*tennis, lawn-tennis*).—*v.t.* and *v.i.* to benefit or profit.—*adjs.* **advan'tageable** (*rare*), profitable: convenient; **advantageous** (*ad-vən-tā'jəs*), of advantage: useful (with *to* and *for*).—*adv.* **advantā'geously.**—*n.* **advantā'geousness.**—**advantage rule,** in games, a rule under which an infringement and its penalty are overlooked when this is to the advantage of the non-offending side.—**advantage server, striker,** the first point after deuce has been gained by the server, the striker; **have the advantage**

**of,** to recognise without being recognised; **take advantage of,** to avail oneself of: to make undue use of an advantage over; **take at advantage,** to use favourable conditions against: to take by surprise; **to advantage,** so that the merits are readily perceived. [Fr. *avantage—avant,* before; see advance.]

**advection,** *ad-vek'shən,* (*meteor.*) *n.* movement horizontally of air or atmospheric conditions. [L. *advectio—ad, vehĕre,* to carry.]

**advene,** *ad-vēn', v.i.* to be superadded.—*n.* **advent** (*ad'vənt*), a coming or arrival: (*cap.*) the first or the second coming of Christ: the period immediately before the festival of the Nativity, including four Sundays.—*n.* **Ad'ventist,** one who expects a second coming of Christ: a millenarian.—*adj.* **adventitious** (*ad-vən-tish'əs*), accidental: additional: foreign: appearing casually: developed out of the usual order or place.—*adv.* **adventi'tiously.**—*adj.* **adventive** (*-vent'*), adventitious: not permanently established (*bot.*).—*n.* a thing or person coming from without.—*n.* **adven'ture,** a chance: a remarkable incident: an enterprise: trial of the issue: risk: a commercial speculation: an exciting experience: the spirit of enterprise.—*v.t.* to risk: to dare: to venture: to put forward as a venture: to venture to say or utter.—*v.i.* to risk oneself: to take a risk.—*n.* **adven'turer,** one who engages in hazardous enterprises: a soldier of fortune, or speculator: one who pushes his fortune, esp. by unscrupulous means:—*fem.* **adven'turess** (chiefly in bad sense).—*adjs.* **adven'turous, adven'turesome,** enterprising: ready to incur risk.—*adv.* **adven'turously.**—*n.* **adven'turousness.**—**adventure playground,** a playground with objects that can be used by children for building, to climb on, etc. [L. *advenire, adventum* (*ad,* to, *venire,* to come), fut.p. *adventūrus; adventus,* coming; *adventicius,* extraneous; partly through Fr.]

**adverb,** *ad'vûrb, n.* a word added to a verb, adjective, or other adverb to express some modification of the meaning or an accompanying circumstance.—*adj.* **adverb'ial** (*əd-*)—*v.t.* **adverb'ialise, -z-,** to give the character of adverb to.—*adv.* **adverb'ially.** [L. *adverbium—ad,* to, *verbum,* a word (a trans. of Gr. *epirrēma,* lit. that which is said afterwards).]

**ad verbum,** *ad vûr'bum, wer'bōōm,* (L.) to a word: word for word.

**adversaria,** *ad-vər-sā'ri-a, n.pl.* miscellaneous notes: a commonplace-book. [L. *adversāria.*]

**adversary,** *ad'vər-sər-i, n.* an opponent: the Adversary, Satan.—*adjs.* **advers'ative** (*ad-vûrs'*), denoting opposition, contrariety, or variety; **ad'verse** (*-vûrs*), contrary (with *to*): opposed: unfavourable: facing the main axis (*bot.*).—*adv.* **ad'versely.**—*ns.* **ad'verseness; advers'ity,** adverse circumstances: misfortune: perversity (*Shak.*). [L. *adversus—ad,* to, and *vertĕre, versum,* to turn.]

**advert,** *ad-vûrt', v.i.* to turn one's attention: to refer.—*ns.* **advert'ence, advert'ency,** attention: heedfulness: regard.—*adj.* **advert'ent,** attentive: heedful.—*adv.* **advert'ently.** [L. *advertĕre—ad,* to, *vertĕre,* to turn.]

**advert.** See advertise.

**advertise, -ize,** *ad'vər-tiz, -tiz',* formerly (as *Shak.*) *-vûrt'iz, v.t.* to inform, give notice to (*arch.*): to give notice of: to give public information about merits claimed for: to draw attention to: to offer for sale by public notice, printed or broadcast.—*v.i.* to issue advertisements: to ask (for) by means of public notice, e.g. in a newspaper.—*ns.* **advertisement** (*əd-vûr'tis-mənt*), the act of advertising: a public notice (*coll.* abbrev. **ad, ad'vert**): any device for obtaining public favour or notoriety: news (*obs.*): **advertiser** (*ad',* or *-tiz'*), one who advertises: often part of a newspaper's title; **advertis'ing.**—

**adj.** (*Shak.*) attentive.—**ad-man,** *ad'-man,* one who takes part in advertising, esp. advertising addressed to the admass; **ad-mass, admass,** the mass which advertisers seek to reach in commercial sound radio and television. [Fr. *avertir, avertiss-*—L. *advertĕre*; see **advert** (1).]

**advew,** *ad-vū',* (*Spens.*) *v.t.* to view. [L. *ad,* to, and **view.**]

**advice,** *əd-vīs',* *n.* counsel: information (usu. in *pl.*): formal official intelligence about anything: specially skilled opinion, as of a physician or lawyer.—*adjs.* **advice'ful** (*obs.*) (*Spens.,* **avize'-full**), watchful: attentive: skilled in advising.—**advice'-boat** (*obs.*), a swift vessel employed in conveying despatches. [O.Fr. *advis* (Fr. *avis*)—L. *ad vīsum,* according to what is seen or seems best.]

**advise,** *əd-vīz',* *v.t.* to view (*obs.*): to take thought of, consider (*obs.*): to take to avizandum: to bethink: to counsel: to recommend: to inform: to announce.—*v.i.* to reflect, deliberate (*obs.*): to consult (with).—*n.* **advisabil'ity.**—*adj.* **advis'able,** to be recommended: expedient: open to advice.—*n.* **advis'ableness.**—*adv.* **advis'ably.**—*adjs.* **advis'atory** (*rare*), advisory; **advised',** having duly considered: considered: deliberate: apprised: amenable to advice.—*adv.* **advis'edly** (*-id-li*), after consideration: intentionally: wisely, prudently.—*ns.* **advis'edness,** deliberate consideration: prudent procedure; **advise'ment** (*obs.* or *arch.*), counsel, deliberation; **advis'er,** **advis'or,** one who advises; **advis'ership;** **advis'ing** (*Shak.*), counsel, advice.—*adj.* **advis'ory,** having the attribute or function of advising. [O.Fr. *aviser,* and L.L. *advisāre*; cf. **advice.**]

**ad vivum,** *ad vī'vum,* *wē'woŏm,* (L.) to the life, lifelike.

**advocaat,** *ad'vō-kät,* *n.* a liqueur containing eggs and flavourings: a medicinal drink of eggs, rum, and lemon-juice. [Du. *advokaaten-,* advocate's dram, as a clearer of the throat.]

**advocate,** *ad'və-kit,* *ad'və-kāt,* *n.* an intercessor or defender: one who pleads the cause of another: one who is qualified to plead before the higher courts of law—the ordinary name in Scotland corresponding to barrister in England: (*cap.*; New English Bible) the Holy Spirit.—*v.t.* (*ad'vəkāt*) to plead in favour of: to recommend.—*ns.* **ad'vocacy** (*-kə-si*), the function of an advocate: a pleading for: defence; **advocā'tion;** **ad'vocātor.**—*adj.* **ad'vocātory.**—**advocate in Aberdeen,** a solicitor (in Aberdeen); **Lord Advocate,** the first law-officer of the crown and public prosecutor of crimes for Scotland. [O.Fr. *avocat* and L. *advocātus*—*advocāre, -ātum,* to call in—*ad,* to, *vocāre,* to call.]

**advoutrer,** *əd-vow'trər,* **advou'try,** forms intermediate between **avoutrer** and **adulterer,** etc.

**advowson,** *əd-vow'zən,* *n.* the right of presentation to a church benefice. [O.Fr. *avoeson*—L.L. *advocātiō, -ōnis*—L. *advocātus.*]

**adward** (*Spens.*). Same as **award.**

**adynamia,** *a-di-nā'mi-a,* *n.* helplessness, want of power accompanying a disease.—*adj.* **adynamic,** (*-am'*), without strength: characterised by the absence of force (*phys.*). [Gr. *a-,* priv., and *dynamis,* strength.]

**adytum,** *ad'i-təm,* *n.* the most sacred part of a temple: the chancel of a church:—*pl.* **ad'yta.** [Latinised from Gr. *adyton*—*a-,* priv., *dyein,* to enter.]

**adze,** *adz,* *n.* a cutting tool with an arched blade which is set at right angles to the handle. [O.E. *adesa.*]

**ae,** *ā, yā, ye, adj.* Scot. form of O.E. *ān,* one, used attributively.—*adj.* **aefa(u)ld, ā'fald,** *-fawld,* onefold, single: single-minded: faithful: simple: sincere: honest.

**aecidium,** *ə-sid'i-əm,* *n.* a cup-shaped fructification

in rust fungi:—*pl.* **aecid'ia.**—*n.* **aecid'iospore,** a spore produced in it. [Gr. *aikiā,* injury.]

**aedile,** *ē'dīl,* *n.* a magistrate in ancient Rome who had the charge of public buildings, games, markets, police, etc.—*n.* **ae'dileship.** [L. *aedīlis*—*aedēs, -is,* a building.]

**aegirine,** *ē'jir-ēn,* **ae'girite,** *-it,* *ns.* a green pleochroic pyroxene. [*Ægir,* Norse sea-god or giant.]

**aegis,** *ē'jis,* *n.* orig. a shield belonging to Zeus, or to Pallas: protection: patronage. [Gr. *aigis.*]

**aeglogue,** *ēg'log,* *n.* arch. for **eclogue.** [From the mistaken belief that the word meant goat-herd discourse—Gr. *aix, aigos,* goat, *logos,* discourse.]

**aegrotat,** *ē-grō'tat,* or *ē',* *n.* in universities, a medical certificate of illness, or a degree granted on it. [L. *aegrōtat,* is sick, 3rd pers. sing. pres. indic. of *aegrōtāre*—*aeger,* sick.]

**aemule,** *ē'mūl,* (*Spens.*) *v.t.* to emulate. [L. *aemulāri.*]

**Aeneid,** *ē'ni-id, ə-nē'id,* *n.* an epic poem written by Virgil, the hero of which is Aeneas. [L. *Aenēis, -idos.*]

**Aeneolithic,** *ā-ē-ni-ō-lith'ik,* *adj.* belonging to a transitional stage at the end of the Neolithic age, when copper was already in use. [L. *aēneus,* brazen, and Gr. *lithos,* stone.]

**aeolian,** *ē-ō'li-ən,* *adj.* pertaining to, acted on by, or due to the agency of, the wind: aerial.—**aeolian** (or with *cap.*) **harp,** a sound-box with strings tuned in unison, sounding harmonics in current of air; **aeolian rocks** (*geol.*), those deposited by wind, as desert sands. [L. *Aeolus*—Gr. *Aiolos,* god of the winds.]

**Aeolian,** *ē-ō'li-ən,* *adj.* of Aeolis or Aeolia, in north-west Asia Minor, or its Greek colonists.—*n.* an Aeolian Greek.—*adj.* **Aeolic** (*-ol'ik*), the Greek dialect of the Aeolians.—**Aeolian mode,** in ancient Greek music, the same as the Hypodorian or Hyperphrygian: in old church music, the authentic mode with A for its final.

**aeolipile, aeolipyle,** *ē'əl-i-pīl,* or *ē-ol'i-pīl,* *n.* a hollow ball turned by tangential escape of steam. [L. *Aeolus,* god of the winds, and *pila,* ball; or Gr. *Aiolou pylai,* Gates of Aeolus.]

**aeolotropy,** *ē-əl-ot'rə-pi,* *n.* variation in physical properties according to direction.—*adj.* **aeolotrop'ic.** [Gr. *aiolos,* changeful, *tropē,* a turn.]

**aeon, eon,** *ē'on,* *n.* a vast age: eternity: the largest, or a very large division of geological time: a power emanating from the supreme deity, with its share in the creation and government of the universe.—*adj.* **aeō'nian,** eternal. [L. *aeon*—Gr. *aiōn.*]

**Aepyornis,** *ē-pi-ör'nis,* *n.* a gigantic Recent fossil wingless bird of Madagascar. [Gr. *aipys,* tall, *ornis,* bird.]

**aequo animo,** *ē-, i-kwō an'i-mō,* (L.) with an equable mind.

**aerate,** *ā'ər-āt,* *v.t.* to put air into: to charge with air or with carbon dioxide or other gas (as **aerated waters**).—*ns.* **ā'erātor,** an apparatus for the purpose; **āerā'tion,** exposure to the action of air: mixing or saturating with air or other gas: oxygenation of the blood by respiration.—**aerated concrete,** lightweight concrete made by a process which traps gas bubbles in the mix; **aerating root,** a root that rises erect into the air, a breathing organ in mud plants. [L. *āēr,* air.]

**aerenchyma,** *ā-(ə)r-eng'ki-ma,* (*bot.*) *n.* respiratory tissue.—*adj.* **aerenchym'atous** (*-ki'*). [Gr. *āēr,* air, *en,* in, *chyma,* that which is poured.]

**aerial,** *ā-ē'ri-əl,* also *-er',* *adj.* of, in, belonging to: the air: airy: unreal: lofty: (*ā'(ə-)ri-əl*) atmospheric: elevated: connected with aircraft, e.g. used in, against, aircraft; using aircraft (as aerial support, reconnaissance, warfare): carried out from aircraft: growing in air (*biol.*).—*n.*

(*ā'(ə-)ri-əl*) a wire exposed to receive or emit electromagnetic waves: an antenna.—*n.* **aeriality** (*-al'i-ti*).—*adv.* **aer'ially.**—**aerial railway, ropeway,** one for overhead conveyance. [L. *āĕrius*—*āēr,* air.]

**aerie, aery, ayrie, eyrie** (now common), **eyry,** *ā'ri,* also *ē'ri, i'ri, n.* the nest of a bird of prey, esp. an eagle: a house or stronghold perched on some high or steep place: the brood in the nest, or a stock of children (*Shak.*). [O.Fr. *aire;* origin unknown.]

**aeriform,** *ā'(ə)r-i-förm, adj.* gaseous: unreal. [L. *āēr,* air, and *förma,* form.]

**aero-,** *ā'(ə)r-ō-,* in combination, air.—*n.* **aerobat'ics** (*pl.* in form, but treated as *sing.;* Gr. *batein,* to tread), the art of performing stunts in the air: aerial acrobatics.—*n.* **ā'erobe** (Gr. *bios,* life), an organism that requires free oxygen for respiration.—Also **aerō'biont.**—*adjs.* **aerobic** (*-ob'*), **aerobiotic** (*-ot'ik*), requiring free oxygen for respiration: effected by aerobes, as a biochemical change: involving the activity of aerobes.—*advs.* **aerob'ically, aerobiot'ically.**—*adj.* **aerobiolog'ical** (*-bi-ō-loj'*).—*ns.* **aerobiol'ogy,** study of airborne micro-organisms; **aerobiō'sis,** life in presence of oxygen; **ā'erobomb,** a bomb for dropping from aircraft; **ā'erobus,** a large aircraft; **ā'erodart,** an arrow-headed missile of steel dropped from aircraft in warfare; **ā'erodrome,** an area, with its buildings, etc., used for the take-off and landing of aircraft: an early flying-machine (*hist.;* Gr. *dromos,* running).—*adjs.* **aerodynam'ic, -al.**—*ns.* **aerodynam'icist,** one concerned with the movement of bodies in a flow of air or gas; **aerodynam'ics** (*pl.* in form but treated as *sing.*), the dynamics of gases; **ā'erodyne** (*-din;* Gr. *dŷnamis,* power), a heavier-than-air aircraft.—*adj.* **aeroelas'tic,** able to be deformed by aerodynamic forces.—*ns.* **aeroelastic'ian,** one who studies flutter and vibration in high-speed aircraft; **aeroem'bolism,** an airman's condition similar to caisson disease, caused by rapid ascent to high altitudes; **ā'eroengine,** an aircraft engine; **ā'erofoil,** a body (e.g. wing, tail plane) shaped so as to produce an aerodynamic reaction (lift) normal to its direction of motion, for a small resistance (drag) in that plane; **ā'erogram,** a message by wireless telegraphy: a message sent by telegram (or telephone) and aeroplane: an aerogramme: an aerograph record; **ā'erogramme, aérogramme,** an air-letter: a sheet of thin paper, with postage stamp imprinted, to be folded and sent by airmail at a special low rate; **ā'erograph,** a meteorograph: an airborne automatic recording instrument; **aerog'raphy,** meteorology; **aerohy'droplane,** a winged hydroplane or flying-boat; **ā'erolite, aerolith,** a meteoric stone or meteorite (Gr. *lithos,* a stone); **aerolithol'ogy,** the science of aerolites.—*adjs.* **aerolit'ic; aerolog'ical.**—*ns.* **aerol'ogist; aerol'ogy,** the branch of science that treats of the atmosphere; **ā'eromancy,** divination by atmospheric phenomena: weather forecasting (Gr. *manteiā,* divination); **aerom'eter,** an instrument for measuring the weight or density of air and gases; **aerom'etry,** pneumatics.—*adj.* **aeromet'ric.**—*ns.* **ā'eromotor,** an engine for aircraft; **ā'eronaut** (Gr. *nautēs,* a sailor), a balloonist or airman.—*adjs.* **aeronaut'ic, -al.**—*ns.* **aeronaut'ics** (*pl.* in form but treated as *sing.*), the science or art of aerial navigation; **ā'eroneuros'is,** flight fatigue, a nervous disorder of airmen, with emotional and physical symptoms; **aeron'omy,** the science of the earth's atmosphere; **aeron'ombi; aerophō'bia,** morbid fear of draughts (Gr. *phobos,* fear).—*adj.* **aerophōb'ic.**—*ns.* **ā'erophyte,** an epiphyte (Gr. *phyton,* a plant); **ā'eroplane,** any heavier-than-air power-driven flying-machine, with fixed wings: a small plane for aerostatic experiments (see **plane**); **aeroplank'ton,** minute

organisms carried in the air; **aerosid'erite** (Gr. *sidēros,* iron), an iron meteorite; **ā'erosol,** a colloidal system, such as a mist or a fog, in which the dispersion medium is a gas: a liquid, e.g. insecticide, in a container under pressure: the container; **ā'erospace,** the earth's atmosphere together with space beyond (*as adj.* pertaining to, or capable of operating in, air and space); **ā'erostat,** a balloon or other aircraft lighter than air: a balloonist: an air sac (*zool.*) (Gr. *statos,* standing).—*adj.* **aerostat'ic.**—*ns.* **aerostat'ics** (*pl.* in form, but treated as *sing.*), the science of the equilibrium and pressure of air and other gases: the science or art of ballooning; **aerostation** (*-stā'shən*), ballooning.—*adj.* **aerotac'tic,** pertaining to or showing aerotaxis.—*ns.* **aerotax'is** (*biol.*), movement towards or from oxygen (Gr. *taxis,* arrangement; adj. *taktikos*); **ā'erotrain,** a train driven by an aircraft engine, riding on a cushion of air.—*adj.* **aerotrop'ic** (Gr. *tropē,* turning).—*n.* **aerot'ropism** (*bot.*), curvature in response to concentration of oxygen. [Gr. *āēr,* air.]

**aeruginous,** *ē-roō'ji-nəs, i-roō'jə-, adj.* pertaining to or like copper-rust or verdigris. [L. *aerūginōsus—aerūgō,* rust of copper—*aes, aeris,* brass, copper.]

**aery, aerie,** *ā'(ə-)ri,* (*poet.*) *adj.* aerial: incorporeal: spiritual: visionary.—**aerie light** (*Milt.*), light as air. [L. *āĕrius;* see **aerial.**]

**aery.** See **aerie.**

**aes alienum,** *ēz al-i-ēn'um, is al-i-ān'ōōm,* (L.) debt, lit. another's copper or brass.

**æsc, ash,** *n.* the rune (F) for a, used in O.E. for æ: the ligature æ used in O.E. for the same sound (that of *a* in Mod. Eng. *cat*). [O.E. *æsc,* ash-tree, the name of the rune.]

**Aesculapian,** *ēs-kū-lā'pi-ən,* or *es-, adj.* pertaining to Aesculapius, and so to the art of healing.—Also **Esculapian.** [L. *Aesculāpius,* Gr. *Asklēpios,* god of healing.]

**Aesculus,** *ēs'kū-ləs, n.* the horse-chestnut genus of Hippocastanaceae.—*n.* **aes'culin,** a glucoside in horse-chestnut bark. [L. *aesculus,* a species of oak.]

**aesir.** See as (2).

**aesthesia,** in U.S. **es-, es-thēz'i-a, is-, ēs-, aesthesis,** *n.* feeling: sensitivity.—*n.* **aesthes'iogen,** something producing sensation, esp. a stimulus or suggestion producing a sensory effect on a subject under hypnosis.—*adj.* **aesthesiogen'ic.**—*adj.* **aesthetic, es-thet'ik, is-, ēs-,** **co-ang** relating to perception by the senses: generally relating to possessing, or pretending to, a sense of beauty: artistic or affecting to be artistic.—*n.* **aes'thete** (*-thēt*), a professed disciple of aestheticism: one who affects an extravagant love of art.—*adj.* **aesthet'ical,** pertaining to aesthetics.—*adv.* **aesthet'ically.**—*n.* **aesthetician** (*-tish'ən*), one devoted to or versed in aesthetics.—*v.t.* **aesthet'icise, -ize,** (*-siz*) to render aesthetic.—*ns.* **aesthet'icism,** the principles of aesthetics: the cult of the beautiful, applied esp. to a late 19th-century movement to bring art into life, which developed into affectation; **aesthet'icist; aesthet'ics** (*pl.* in form, but treated as *sing.*), the principles of taste and art: the philosophy of the fine arts. [Gr. *aisthētikos,* perceptive—*aisthanesthai,* to feel or perceive.]

**aestival,** in U.S. **es-, ēs-ti'vəl,** or **es-, adj.** of summer.—*v.i.* **aes'tivate** (*-ti-vāt*), to pass the summer.—*n.* **aestivā'tion,** a spending of the summer: manner of folding in the flower-bud (*bot.*): arrangement of foliage leaves relative to one another in the bud (*bot.*): dormancy during the dry season (*zool.* and *bot.*). [L. *aestivus, aestivālis,* relating to summer, *aestivāre,* to pass the summer—*aestās,* summer.]

**aes triplex,** *ēz tri'pleks, is trip'leks,* (L.) triple brass, a strong defence.

aetatis suae, ē-tat'is sū'ē, ī-tät'is sōō'ī, (L.) of his (or her) age.

aether, ē'thər, n. Same as ether (but not generally used in the chemical sense).

Aethiopian. See Ethiopian.

aethrioscope, ē'thri-ō-skōp, n. an instrument for measuring the minute variations of temperature due to the condition of the sky. [Gr. aithriā, the open sky, skopeein, to look at.]

aetiology, in U.S. et-, ē-ti-ol'ə-ji, n. the science or philosophy of causation: an inquiry into the origin or causes of anything, esp. a disease.—adj. aetiolog'ical. [Gr. aitiologiā—aitiā, cause, logos, discourse.]

Aetnean. See Etnean.

afar, ə-fär', adv. from a far distance (usually from afar): at or to a distance (usually afar off). [of and on, far.]

afear, affear(e), ə-fēr', (Spens.) v.t. to frighten.— adj. afeard', affeard' (Shak.), afraid. [Pfx. a-, intens., O.E. fǣran, to frighten.]

affable, af'ə-bl, adj. easy to speak to: courteous, esp. towards inferiors: pleasant, friendly.—n. affabil'ity.—adv. aff'ably. [Fr.,—L. affābilis—affāri, to speak to—ad, to, and fāri, to speak.]

affair, ə-fār', n. that which is to be done: business: any small matter: a minor battle: a matter of intimate personal concern: a thing (coll.): (pl.) transactions in general: public concerns. [O.Fr. afaire (Fr. affaire)—à and faire— L. ad, to, facēre, to do; cf. ado.]

affaire, a-fer, (Fr.) liaison, intrigue: (usu. with name of chief person involved following or preceding) an episode, incident, arousing speculation and scandal.—affaire (d'amour), a-fer (dam-ōōr), a love affair; affaire de cœur, a-fer də kœr, affair of the heart; affaire d'honneur, a-fer do-nœr, affair of honour (a duel).

affeard, affear'd. See afeard, affeared.

affect, ə-fekt', v.t. to act upon: to infect or attack as disease: to influence: to move the feelings of: (in pass. only) to assign, allot.—n. disposition of body or mind (obs.): affection, love (obs.): (af'ekt) the emotion that lies behind action (psych.): pleasantness or unpleasantness of, or complex of ideas involved in, an emotional state (psych.).—adjs. affect'ed; affect'ing, having power to move the emotions.—adv. affect'ingly, —adj. affect'ive, of, arising from, or influencing, emotion.—adv. affect'ively.—n. affectivity (af-ek-tiv'i-ti). [L. afficēre, affectum—ad, to, facēre, to do.]

affect, ə-fekt', v.t. to aim at, aspire to (obs.): to have'a liking for (arch.): to make a show of preferring: to do, wear, inhabit, by preference: to assume: to assume the character of: to make a show or pretence of.—v.i. to incline, tend.—n. affectā'tion (af-ik-), assumption of or striving after an appearance of what is not natural or real: pretence.—adjs. affect'ed, full of affectation: feigned.—adv. affect'edly.—ns. affect'edness; affect'er. [L. affectāre, -ātum, freq. of afficēre; see affect above.]

affection, ə-fek'shən, n. the act of influencing: emotion: disposition: inclination: love: attachment: affectation (Shak.): an attribute or property: a disease.—v.t. (rare) to love.—adjs. affec'tional; affec'tionate, full of affection: loving: eager, passionate, well inclined (obs.).—adv. affec'tionately.—n. affec'tionateness.— adj. affec'tioned, disposed (B.): full of affectation (Shak.). [L. affectiō, -ōnis.]

affeer, ə-fēr', v.t. to assess: to reduce to a certain fixed sum.—adj. affeered' (Shak. affear'd'), confirmed.—n. affeer'ment. [O.Fr. affeurer— L.L. afforāre—L. ad, to, forum, a market.]

affenpinscher, af'en-pinsh-ər, a small dog related to the Brussels griffon, having tufts of hair on the face. [Ger.,—affe, monkey, pinscher, terrier.]

afferent, af'ər-ənt, adj. bringing inwards, as the nerves that convey impulses to the central nervous system. [L. afferēns, -entis—ad, to, and ferre, to carry.]

affettuoso, äf-fet-tōō-ō'sō, (mus.) adj. tender.— adv. tenderly.—Also n. [It.]

affiance, ə-fi'əns, v.t. to betroth.—n. faith pledged: contract of marriage: trust: affinity (obs.).— adj. affi'anced, betrothed. [O.Fr. afiance; see affy.]

affiche, af-ēsh, (Fr.) notice, placard.

affidavit, af-i-dā'vit, n. a written declaration on oath. [L.L. affidāvit, 3rd pers. sing. perf. of affidāre, to pledge one's faith; see affy.]

affied, See affy.

affiliate, ə-fil'i-āt, v.t. to adopt or attach as a member or branch: to impute paternity of: to assign the origin of.—v.i. to become closely connected, to associate: to fraternise.—n. an affiliated person, an associate: a branch, unit, or subsidiary of an organisation.—n. affilia'tion. —adj. affil'iable. [L. affīliātus, adopted—ad, to, fīlius, a son.]

affine, a-fin', n. (obs.) a relation, esp. by marriage. —adj. preserving finiteness (affine geometry, the geometry associated with affine transformations; affine transformation, the composition of a reversible linear mapping followed by a translation).—adj. affined', related: bound by some tie.—n. affinity, ə-fin'i-ti, nearness (obs.): relationship by marriage: relation of sponsor and godchild: natural or fundamental relationship, esp. common origin: attraction, esp. chemical attraction: a spiritual attraction between two persons: a person whose attraction for another is supposed to be of this kind.—adj. affin'itive. [O.Fr. affin—L. affinis, neighbouring—ad, to, at, finis, a boundary.]

affirm, ə-fûrm', v.t. to assert confidently or positively: to ratify (a judgment): to confirm or stand by (one's own statement): to state in the affirmative (log.): to declare formally, without an oath (law).—v.i. to make an affirmation.— adj. affirm'able.—n. affirm'ance, affirmation: assertion: confirmation.—adj. and n. affirm'-ant.—n. affirmation (af-ər-mā'shən, -ûr-), assertion: that which is affirmed: a positive judgment or proposition: a solemn declaration in lieu of an oath.—adj. affirm'ative, affirming or asserting: positive, not negative: dogmatic.—n. the affirmative mode: an affirmative word, proposition or utterance.—adv. affirm'atively.— adj. affirm'atory.—n. affirm'er.—adv. affirm'-ingly. [O.Fr. afermer—L. affirmāre—ad, to, firmus, firm.]

affix, ə-fiks', v.t. to fix to something: to subjoin: to attach: to append: to add (to something).— n. (af'iks) an addition to a root, stem, or word, to modify its meaning or use, whether prefix or suffix: any appendage or addition. [L. affīgere, -fixum—ad, to, fīgere, to fix.]

afflated, ə-flā'tid, adj. inspired.—ns. afflā'tion, afflā'tus, inspiration (often divine). [L. afflāre, -flātum (vb.), afflātus, -ūs (n.)—ad, to, flāre, to breathe.]

afflict, ə-flikt', v.t. to humble (B.): to distress grievously: to harass: to vex.—adj. afflict'ed, overthrown (Milt.): humble (Spens.): harassed by disease of body or mind: suffering.—n. and adj. afflict'ing, distressing.—n. afflic'tion, state or cause of grievous distress.—adj. afflict'ive, causing distress. [L. afflīgere, -flictum, to overthrow, cast down—ad, to, flīgere, to dash to the ground.]

affluent, af'lōō-ənt adj. inflowing: abounding: wealthy.—n. an inflowing stream.—n. aff'luence, wealth: an inflowing stream.—adv. aff'luently. —ns. aff'luentness; aff'lux, affluxion (ə-fluk'-shən), an inflow, an accession.—affluent society, a society in which the ordinary person can afford many things once regarded as luxuries. [L. *affluĕre*—*ad*, to, *fluĕre*, *fluxum*, to flow.]

**afforce**, *ə-fōrs'*, *ə-förs'*, (*law*) *v.t.* to strengthen (e.g. a jury by addition of skilled persons).—*n.* **afforce'ment**. [O.Fr. *aforcer*—L.L. *exfortiāre*—L. *ex*, out, *fortis*, strong.]

**afford**, *ə-förd'*, *ə-förd'*, *v.t.* to yield, give, provide: to bear the expense, or disadvantage, of (having the necessary money or other resources or security of position): (*Spens.* **affoord**) to consent. [M.E. *aforthen*—O.E. *geforthian*, to further or cause to come forth.]

**afforest**, *a-*, *ə-for'ist*, *v.t.* to convert into huntingground: to cover with forest.—*adj.* **affor'estable**.—*n.* **afforestā'tion**. [L.L. *afforēstāre*—L. *ad*, to, and L.L. *forēsta*, forest.]

**affranchise**, *a-*, *ə-fran'chiz*, *-shiz*, *v.t.* to free from slavery, or from some obligation.—*n.* **affran'chisement** (*-chiz-*, *-shiz-*). [O.Fr. *afranchir*, *afranchiss-*—*à*, to, *franchir*, to free, *franc*, free.]

**affrap**, *a-frap'*, (*Spens.*) *v.t.* and *v.i.* to strike. [It. *affrappare*—pfx. *af-* (L. *ad*, to), and *frappare*, to strike; or directly from **frap**.]

**affray**, *ə-frā'*, *n.* a disturbance, breach of the peace: a brawl, fight, fray: fear (*Spens.*).—*v.t.* to disturb, startle: to frighten: to scare away.—*adj.* **affrayed'**, alarmed (now **afraid'**). [O.Fr. *afrayer*, *esfreer* (Fr. *effrayer*)—L.L. *exfridāre*, to break the king's peace—L. *ex*, out of, O.H.G. *fridu* (Ger. *friede*), peace.]

**affreightment**, *ə-frāt'mənt*, *n.* the hiring of a vessel. [Fr. *affrétement* (*affrètement*), remodelled upon *freight*.]

**affrended**, *a-frend'id*, (*Spens.*) *adj.* reconciled. [**friend**.]

**affret**, *a-fret'*, (*Spens.*) *n.* a furious onset. [Prob. from It. *affrettare*, to hasten.]

**affricate**, *af'ri-kit*, *-kāt n.* consonant sound beginning as a plosive and passing into the corresponding fricative (*phon.*).—*adjs.* **affric'ative**; **aff'ricāted**.—*n.* **affricā'tion**. [L. *affricāre*, *-ātum*, to rub against—*ad*, to, *fricāre*, to rub.]

**affright**, *ə-frit'*, *v.t.* to frighten —*n.* sudden terror. —*adj.* **affright'ed**.—*adv.* **affright'edly**.—*v.t.* **affright'en**.—*adj.* **affright'ened**.—*adj.* **affright'ful** (*arch.*), frightful.—*n.* **affright'ment**, sudden fear. [O.E. *āfyrhtan*—*ā-*, intens., *fyrhtan*, to frighten.]

**affront**, *ə-frunt'*, *v.t.* to meet face to face: to face: to confront: to throw oneself in the way of (*Shak.*): to insult to one's face.—*n.* a contemptuous treatment: an open insult: indignity.—*adj.* **affronté**, **affrontée**, **affrontee** (*ä-fron'tä*, *ə-frun'tē*), facing each other; also looking frontwise, or towards the beholder (*her.*).—*adj.* **affront'ed**.—*n.* and *adj.* **affront'ing**.—*adv.* **affront'ingly**.—*adj.* **affront'ive**. [O.Fr. *afronter*, to slap on the forehead—L.L. *affrontāre*—L. *ad*, to, *frōns*, *frontis*, forehead.]

**affusion**, *ə-fū'zhən*, *n.* pouring on (esp. in baptism). [L. *affūsiō*, *-ōnis*—*affundĕre*—*ad*, to, *fundĕre*, *fūsum*, to pour.]

**affy**, *ə-fi'*, (*obs.*) *v.t.* to trust: to assure on one's faith: to betroth: to repose or put (trust).—*v.i.* to trust or confide:—*pr.p.* **affy'ing**; *pa.t.* and *pa.p.* **affied'** (*Spens.* **affyde'**). [O.Fr. *afier*—L.L. *affidāre*—L. *ad*, to, *fidēs*, faith; cf. **affiance**.]

**Afghan**, *af'gan*, *n.* a native or citizen, or the language, of Afghanistan: (without *cap.*) a heavy knitted or crocheted woollen blanket or shawl.—**Afghan hound** an ancient hunting and sheep dog ... Afghanistan and northern India, kept as a ... the West.

...do, *a-fish-yo-nä'dō*, *a-fē-thyō-nä'dhō*, (Sp.) ...rdent follower, fan.

...*dv.* to, in, or on the field: to or at ...field.]

...d *adv.* on fire: in a state of ...n, fire.]

...*i.* and *adv.* in a flaming or ..., flame.]

**afloat**, *ə-flōt'*, *adv.* and *adj.* in a floating state: at sea: unfixed: in circulation. [**on**, **float**.]

**à fond**, *a fɔ̃*, (Fr.) fundamentally: thoroughly.

**afoot**, *ə-foot'*, *adv.* and *adj.* on foot: astir: actively in being. [**on**, **foot**.]

**afore**, *ə-fōr'*, *-för'*, *prep.* in front of, before.—*adv.* beforehand, previously.—*adv.* **afore'hand**, beforehand: before the regular time for accomplishment: in advance.—*adjs.* **afore'mentioned**, previously mentioned, aforesaid; **afore'said**, said or named before; **afore'thought**, thought of or meditated before: premeditated.—*n.* premeditation.—*adv.* **afore'time**, in former or past times. [O.E. *onforan*—*on*, *foran*; see **before**.]

**a fortiori**, *ā för-ti* (or *-shi*) *-ör'ī*, *ä för-ti-ör'ē*, (L.) with stronger reason.

**afoul**, *ə-fowl'*, *adj.* and *adv.* in entanglement: in collision (with *of*). [**on**, **foul**.]

**afraid**, *ə-frād'*, *adj.* struck with fear: timid: reluctantly inclined to think (that): regretfully admitting. [Pa.p. of **affray**.]

**afreet**. See **afrit**.

**afresh**, *ə-fresh'*, *adv.* anew. [Pfx. *a-*, **fresh**.]

**African**, *af'rik-ən*, *adj.* of Africa.—*n.* a native of Africa: a Negro or other person of black race, esp. one whose people live now, or lived recently in Africa.—*n.* **Af'ric** (*poet.*), Africa.—*adj.* African.—*ns.* **Afrikan'er** (formerly **African'er**, **African'der**, **Afrikan'der**), one born in South Africa of white parents (esp. of Dutch descent); **African'der**, a South African breed of cattle; **Af'ricanism**, an African characteristic; **Af'ricanist**, one learned in matters relating to Africa.—*adj.* **Af'ricanoid**, of African type.—*v.t.* **Af'ricanise**, **-ize**, to make African: to exclude people of other races from, replacing them by Africans.—Also *v.i.*—*ns.* **Africanisātion**, **-izātion**; **Afrikaans** (*af-ri-käns'*), one of two official languages of S. Africa; it developed from 17th-cent. Dutch.—**African violet**, a plant from tropical Africa (*Saintpaulia ionantha*), commonly with violet-coloured flowers but not related to the violet; **Afrikander Bond**, a South African nationalist league (1881-1911). [L. *Africānus*.]

**afrit**, **afreet**, *ä-frēt'*, *af'rēt*, *n.* an evil demon in Arabian mythology. [Ar. *'ifrit*, a demon.]

**Afro**, *af'rō*, *adj.* slang abbrev. for African (sometimes without *cap.*).—**Afro-**, in composition, African (and).—*adj.*, **Afro-American**, pertaining to American(s) of African descent.—Also *n.*—*adj.* **Afro-Asian**, *-āzh'yən*, of, consisting of, Africans and Asians: of Asian origin but African citizenship: of mixed Asian and African blood: (of language) belonging to a group spoken in southwest Asia and north Africa.

**afront**, *ə-frunt'*, *adv.* in front (*obs.*): abreast (*Shak.*). [**on**, **front**.]

**afrormosia**, *af-rör-mō'zi-a*, *n.* a very durable West African wood used as alternative to teak.

**aft**, *äft*, *adj.* or *adv.* behind: near or towards the stern of a vessel. [O.E. *æftan*.]

**after**, *äf'tər*, *prep.* and *adv.* behind in place: later in time than: following in search of: in imitation of: in proportion to, or in agreement with: concerning: subsequent to, or subsequently, afterwards: in the manner of, or in imitation of: according to: in honour of.—*adj.* behind in place: later in time: more towards the stern (in this sense as if the *comp.* of **aft**).—*conj.* later than the time when.—*ns.* **af'terbirth**, the placenta and membranes expelled from the uterus after a birth: a posthumous birth; **af'terburner**, the device used in afterburning; **af'terburning**, reheat; **af'tercare**, care subsequent to a period of treatment.—Also *adj.*—*ns.* **af'ter-clap**, an unexpected sequel, after an affair is supposed to be at an end; **af'ter-crop**, a second crop from the same land in the same year; **af'ter-damp**, chokedamp, arising in coal-mines after an explosion of fire-damp; **after-dinn'er**, the time following

---

in unaccented syllables: *el'ə-mənt*; for certain sounds in foreign words, see p. viii dinner.—*adj.* belonging to that time, esp. before leaving the table.—*n.* af'ter-effect, an effect that comes after an interval.—*v.t.* aftereye' (*Shak.*), to gaze after.—*ns.* af'tergame, a second game played in the hope of reversing the issue of the first: means employed after the first turn of affairs; af'terglow, a glow in the sky after sunset: af'tergrass, the grass that springs after mowing or reaping; af'tergrowth, a later growth: an aftermath; af'ter-guard, the men on the quarter-deck and poop who work the after sails, many of them unskilled: hence a drudge or person in a mean capacity: a merchant ship's officers; af'ter-image, an image that persists for a time after one looks at an object.— *n.pl.* af'terings, the last milk drawn in milking.— *ns.* af'ter-life, a future life: later life; af'ter-light, the light of later knowledge; af'termath, a second mowing of grass in the same season: later consequences, esp. if bad (*fig.*); afternoon', the time between noon and evening.—Also *adj.* af'ternoon.—*n.pl.* af'terpains, the pains after childbirth.—*n.* af'terpiece, minor piece after a play.—*n.pl.* af'ters (*slang*), dessert.—*ns.* af'ter-shaft, a second shaft arising from the quill of a feather; af'tersupper, time between supper and bedtime (*obs.*); prob. a dessert at the end of a supper, poss. a rere-supper (*Shak.*).—*adj.* in the time after supper.—*ns.* af'tertaste, a taste that remains or comes after eating or drinking; af'terthought, a thought or thing thought of after the occasion: a later thought or reflection or modification; af'tertime, later time.—*advs.* af'terward (*rare* except *U.S.*), afterwards, in after-time: later: subsequently.—*n.* af'terword, an epilogue.—after a fashion (see fashion). [O.E. *æfter*, in origin a comparative from *af* (*æf*), off, of which aft is orig. a superlative, but itself compared *æfter*, *æfterra*, *æftemest*, and tending to be regarded as comparative of aft; see of, off.]

aftermost, äf'tər-mōst, -məst, aftmost, äft', *adjs.* superl. of aft, nearest the stern: hindmost. [O.E. *æftemest*, a double superlative.]

aga, agha, ä'gə, ä-gä', *n.* a Turkish commander or chief officer.—Aga Khan (*kän*), the head of the Ismaili Mohammedans. [Turk. *aga*, *aghā*.]

agaçant, *a-ga-sä*, *fem.* agaçante, -*sät*, (Fr.) provoking, alluring; agacerie, -*s(ə)rē*, allurement, coquetry.

Agadah. See Haggada.

again, *ə-gen'*, also *ə-gān'*, *adv.* once more: in return: in response or consequence: back: further: on the other hand: to the same amount in addition: at some future time (*dial.*).—*prep.* against (*dial.*). [O.E. *ongēan*, *ongegn*; Ger. *entgegen*.]

against, *ə-genst'*, also *ə-gänst'*, *prep.* opposite to: in opposition or resistance to: in protection from: in or into contact or collision with or pressure upon: towards the time of (*obs.*): in anticipation of: in contrast or comparison with: in exchange for: instead of.—*conj.* in readiness for the time that. [again, with gen. ending -*es*, and -*t* as in whilst, betwixt, amongst.]

agalactia, *ag-ə-lak'shi-ä*, *n.* failure to secrete milk. [Gr. *a-*, priv., *gala*, *galaktos*, milk.]

agalloch, *ə-gal'ək*, *n.* eaglewood. [Gr. *agallochon*, a word of Eastern origin; see eaglewood.]

agalmatolite, *ag-al-mat'ə-lit*, *n.* material of various kinds (steatite, pyrophyllite, etc.) from which the Chinese cut figures. [Gr. *agalma*, -*atos*, a statue (of a god), *lithos*, stone.]

Agama, *ag'ə-mä*, *n.* an Old World genus of thick-tongued lizards giving name to the family Agamidae (*a-gam'i-dē*).—*adj.* and *n.* ag'amoid. [Carib name of another lizard.]

Agamemnon, *a-ga-mem'non*, (Gr.) leader of Greeks in Trojan war, king of Mycenae: generic name for a king.

agami, *ag'ə-mi*, *n.* the golden-breasted trumpeter,

a crane-like bird of South America. [Carib name.]

agamic, *a-gam'ik*, agamous, *ag'ə-məs*, *adjs.* a-sexual: parthenogenetic: cryptogamous (*obs.*). —*n.* agamogenesis (-*jen'*), reproduction without sex, as in lower animals and in plants. [Gr. *a-*, priv., *gamos*, marriage.]

agamid, *a'gə-mid*, *n.* an Old World lizard of the family Agamidae (*ə-gam'i-dē*), of which the type genus is A'gama. [From Carib.]

Aganippe, *ag-ə-nip'ē*, *n.* a fountain on Mt Helicon, sacred to the Muses: poetic inspiration. [Gr. *Aganippē*.]

agape, *ag'ə-pē*, *n.* a love-feast, held by the early Christians at communion time, when contributions were made for the poor: selfless Christian brotherly love: the love of God for man.—*pl.* ag'apae (-*pē*).—*n.* Agapemone (-*pēm'* or -*pem'ə-nē*) a religious community of men and women whose 'spiritual marriages' were in some cases not strictly spiritual, founded in 1849 at Spaxton, near Bridgwater: any similar community, esp. with reference to its delinquencies. [Gr. *agapē*, love, *monē*, tarrying, abode.]

agape, *ə-gāp'*, *adj.* or *adv.* with gaping mouth. [Prep. a, and gape.]

agar-agar, *ä'gär-ä'gär*, *ä'gär-ä'gär*, *n.* a jelly prepared from seaweeds of various kinds used in bacteria-culture, medicine, glue-making, silk-dressing, and cooking: any of the seaweeds concerned.—Also a'gar. [Malay.]

agaric, *ag'ər-ik*, or *əg-ar'ik*, *n.* a fungus, properly one of the mushroom family, but loosely applied. —*adj.* agar'ic. [Gr. *agarikon*.]

agate, *ag'it*, -*āt*, *n.* a banded variegated chalce-dony: a dwarfish person (as if a figure cut in agate) (*Shak.*): ruby type. [Fr., —Gr. *achātēs*, said to be so called because first found near the river *Achates* in Sicily.]

agate, *ə-gāt'*, *adv.* agoing, on the way: astir: afoot: astray. [Prep. a, and gate; a Northern word.]

agathodaimōn, *a'ga-thō-dī'mon*, (Gr.) one's good genius.

à gauche, *a gōsh*, (Fr.) to the left: on the left.

Agave, *a-gä'vē*, *n.* an aloe-like American genus of amaryllids, in Mexico usually flowering about the seventh year, in hothouse conditions requiring 40-60 (popularly a hundred) years.—Also called American aloe, maguey, century-plant. [L. *Agāvē*, Gr. *Agauē*, daughter of Cadmus, fem. of *agauos*, illustrious.]

agaze, *ə-gāz'*, *adj.* and *adv.* at gaze, gazing. [Prep. a, and gaze.]

agazed, *ə-gāzd'*, (*Shak.*) *adj.* struck with amazement. [Prob. a variant of aghast.]

age, *āj*, *n.* duration of life: the time during which a person or thing has lived or existed: time of life reached: mature years: legal maturity: the time of being old: equivalence in development to the average of an actual age: a period of time: any great division of world, human, or individual history: a generation: a century: (often *pl.*) a long time, however short (*coll.*).— *v.i.* to grow old: to develop the characteristics of old age.—*v.t.* to make to seem old or to be like the old: to mature:—*pr.p.* aging or ageing (*āj'ing*); *pa.t.* and *pa.p.* aged (*ājd*).—*adj.* aged (*āj'id*), advanced in age: (*ājd*) of the age of.—*n. pl.* (*āj'id*), old people.—*ns.* agedness (*āj'idni* condition of being aged; ag(e)'ing, proce growing old or developing qualities of th maturing: change in properties that certain metals at atmospheric tem heat treatment or cold worki less, never growing old, timeless; age'long, lasting a enough to be deemed leg respect to voting, crime, etc.); over age, too old; un not yet of age. [O.Fr. *aäge* (Fr. *âge*)—L. *aetās*, *-ātis*, for *aevitās*—L. *aevum*, age.]

**agee.** See **ajee.**

**agen** (*Milt. and other poets*). Same as **again.**

**agency.** See **agent.**

**agenda,** *ə-* or *a-jen′də*, *n.pl.* things to be done— programme of business for a meeting (sometimes treated as a *sing.*). [L. neuter pl. of *agendus*, to be done, gerundive of *agēre*, to do.]

**agent,** *ā′jənt*, *n.* a person or thing that acts or exerts power: any natural force acting on matter: one authorised or delegated to transact business for another: formerly a bank mana- ger: formerly the representative of the govern- ment in a group of Indian states: a paid political party worker: a secret agent, spy.—*v.t.* (*Scot.*), to conduct as a law agent.—*adj.* acting: of an agent.—*n.* **agency** (*ā′jən-si*), the office or business, operation or action, of an agent; instrumenta- lity: formerly a group of Indian states assigned to an agent.—*adj.* **agen′tial** (*-shəl*), pertaining to an agent or agency.—**agency shop,** a shop in which the union, usu. by agreement with the management, represents all workers whether they are members of it or not; **law agent** (*Scot.*), a solicitor—any qualified legal practitioner other than an advocate. [L. *agēns, -entis*, pr.p. of *agēre*, to do.]

**agent provocateur,** *a-zhā prō-vo-ka-tər*, (Fr.) one employed to lead others, by pretended sympathy, into acts incurring penalties.

**agger,** *aj′ər, ag′*, (*Rom. hist.*) *n.* a mound, esp. one of wood or earth for protection or other military purpose: any elevation, esp. artificial. [L.]

**aggiornamento,** *a-jör-na-men′tō*, (It.) modernis- ing.

**agglomerate,** *ə-glom′ər-āt*, *v.t.* to make into a ball: to collect into a mass.—*v.i.* to grow into a mass. —*adj.* agglomerated: clustered: gathered in a head (*bot.*).—*n.* a volcanic rock consisting of irregular fragments.—*n.* **agglomerā′tion.**—*adjs.* **agglom′erative; agglom′erated.** [L. *agglom- erāre*, *-ātum*—*ad*, to, L. *glomus, glomeris*, a ball.]

**agglutinate,** *ə-glōōt′in-āt*, *v.t.* to glue together: to cause to cohere or clump.—*v.i.* to cohere as if glued: to clump.—*adj.* agglutinated.—*adjs.* **agglut′inable; agglut′inant.**—*n.* an agglutina- ting agent.—*ns.* **agglutinā′tion,** the act of aggluti- nating: an agglutinated mass: the clumping of bacteria, blood corpuscles, protozoa, etc. (*biol.*); **agglut′inin,** an antibody causing agglutination of bacteria, blood-corpuscles, etc.—*adj.* **agglut′- inative,** tending, or having power, to agglutinate. —*n.* **agglut′inogen,** the substance in bacteria or in blood cells that stimulates the formation of, and unites with, agglutinin.—**agglutinative languages,** languages in which elements are combined without so losing their independence as to be mere inflexions. [L. *agglūtināre*—*ad*, to, *glūten, -inis*, glue.]

**aggrace,** *ə-grās′* (*Spens.*) *v.t.* to grace: to favour:— *pa.t.* **aggraced′, agraste′.**—*n.* kindness: favour. [grace, after It. *aggratiare* (now *aggraziare*).]

**aggrandise, -ize,** *ag′rən-diz, -ran-*, *v.t.* to make greater.—*n.* **aggrandisement** (*əg-ran′diz-mənt*). [Fr. *agrandir, agrandiss-*—L. *ad*, to, *grandis*, large.]

**aggrate,** *ə-grāt′*, (*obs.*) *v.t.* to gratify or please: to thank. [It. *aggratare*—L. *ad*, to, *grātus*, pleas- ing.]

**aggravate,** *ag′rə-vāt*, *v.t.* to make more grievous or worse: to irritate (*coll.*).—*adj.* **agg′ravating.**— *adv.* **agg′ravatingly.**—*n.* **aggravā′tion.** [L. *ag- gravāre, -ātus*—*ad*, to, *gravis*, heavy.]

**aggregate,** *ag′ri-gāt*, *v.t.* to collect into a mass or whole: to assemble: to add as a member to a society: to amount to (*coll.*).—*v.i.* to accumu- late.—*adj.* (*-git, -gāt*) formed of parts that com- bine to make a whole: gathered in a mass or whole: united in a colonial organism: formed

from an apocarpous gynaeceum (*bot.*).—*n.* (*-git, -gāt*) an assemblage: a mass: a total: any material mixed with cement to form concrete: a collection of elements having a common pro- perty that identifies the collection (*math.*).—*adv.* **agg′regately.**—*n.* **aggregā′tion.**—*adj.* **agg′regā- tive.** [L. *aggregāre, -ātum*, to bring together, as a flock—*ad*, to, *grex, gregis*, a flock.]

**aggress,** *ə-gres′*, *v.i.* to make a first attack: to begin a quarrel: to intrude.—*n.* **aggression** (*-gresh′ən*), a first act of hostility or injury: self- assertiveness, either as a good characteristic or as a sign of emotional instability.—*adj.* **aggress′- ive,** making the first attack, or prone to do so: discourteously hostile or self-assertive: offensive as opposed to defensive: showing energy and initiative.—*adv.* **aggress′ively.**—*ns.* **aggress′ive- ness; aggress′or,** one who attacks first. [L. *aggredi, -gressus*—*ad*, to, *gradi*, to step.]

**aggri, aggry,** *ag′ri, adj.* applied to ancient West African variegated glass beads. [Origin un- known.]

**aggrieve,** *ə-grēv′*, *v.t.* to press heavily upon: to pain or injure.—*adj.* **aggrieved′,** injured: having a grievance. [O.Fr. *agrever*—L. *ad*, to, *gravis*, heavy.]

**aggro.** Slang abbrev. of **aggravation,** meaning 'stirring up of trouble'.

**aghast,** *ə-gäst′*, earlier (as *Milt.*) **agast,** *adj.* stupe- fied with horror. [Pa.p. of obs. *agast*—O.E. intens. pfx. *ā-*, and *gǣstan*, to terrify.]

**agila,** *ag′i-lä*, *n.* eaglewood. [Port. *águila*, eagle- wood, or Sp. *águila*, eagle; see **eaglewood.**]

**agile,** *aj′il*, in U.S. *-əl*, *adj.* nimble.—*adv.* **ag′ilely.** —*n.* **agility** (*ə-jil′i-ti*), nimbleness. [Fr.,—L. *agilis*—*agēre*, to do or act.]

**agin,** *ə-gin′*, (*dial.*, esp. Ir.) *prep.* against. [**again.**]

**agio,** *aj′(i-)ō, äj′*, *n.* the sum payable for the con- venience of exchanging one kind of money for another, as silver for gold, paper for metal: the difference in exchange between worn or debased coinage and coinage of full value: the amount of deviation from the fixed par of exchange between the currencies of two countries: the discount on a foreign bill of exchange: money-changing.—*n.* **agiotage** (*aj′ə-tij*), agio: money-changing: stock- jobbing: speculative manoeuvres in stocks. [The word used in It. is *aggio*, a variant of *agio*, convenience.]

**agist,** *ə-jist′*, *v.t.* to take in to graze for payment: to charge with a public burden.—*ns.* **agist′ment,** the action of agisting: the price paid for cattle pasturing on the land: a burden or tax; **agist′or, agist′er,** an officer in charge of cattle agisted. [O.Fr. *agister—à* (L. *ad*) to, *giste*, resting-place— *gésir*, from a freq. of *jacēre*, to lie.]

**agitate,** *aj′i-tāt*, *v.t.* to keep moving: to stir violently: to disturb: to perturb: to excite: to discuss, or keep up the discussion of.—*v.i.* to stir up public feeling.—*adj.* **ag′itāted.**—*adv.* **ag′- itātedly.**—*n.* **agitā′tion.**—*adj.* **ag′itātive.**—*n.* **ag′- itātor,** an agent, esp. for the private soldiers in the Parliamentary army (*hist.*): one who excites or keeps up a social or political agitation: apparatus for stirring. [L. *agitāre*, freq. of *agēre*, to put in motion.]

**agitato,** *äj-it-ä′tō*, (*mus.*) *adj.* agitated.—*adv.* agi- tatedly. [It.,—L. *agitāre*, to agitate.]

**agitprop,** *aj′it-prop′*, *n.* (often *cap.*) (department, person, engaged in) agitation and propaganda, esp. pro-Communist.—Also *adj.*

**Aglaia,** *ä-glī′a*, *n.* one of the Graces. [Gr. *aglaiā*, splendour, triumph.]

**aglet, aiglet, aiguillette,** *ag′lit, āg′lit, ä-gwi-let′*, *n.* the metal tag of a lace or string: an ornamen- tal tag or other metal appendage: anything dan- gling: (usu. **aiguillette**) a tagged point of braid hanging from the shoulder in some uniforms.— **aglet babie** (*Shak.*), prob. a small figure form- ing the tag of a lace. [Fr. *aiguillette*, dim. of

**aiguille,** a needle—from L. *acūcula,* dim. of *acus,* a needle.]

**agley, aglee,** *ə-glē′, ə-glī′,* (*Scot.*) *adv.* askew: awry. [Prep. a, and Scot. *gley,* squint.]

**aglimmer,** *ə-glim′ər, adj.* and *adv.* in a glimmering state. [Prep. a, and glimmer.]

**aglitter,** *ə-glit′ər, adj.* and *adv.* in a glitter. [Prep. a, and glitter.]

**aglow,** *ə-glō′, adj.* and *adv.* in a glow. [Prep. a, and glow.]

**agnail,** *ag′nāl, n.* a torn shred of skin beside the nail.—Also **hang′nail.** [O.E. *angnægl,* corn—*ange, enge,* compressed, painful, *nægl,* nail (for driving in), confused with *hang, anger,* and (finger-) *nail.*]

**agname,** *ag′nām, n.* a name over and above the ordinary name and surname.—*adj.* **ag′named.** [name; after L.L. *agnōmen.*]

**agnate,** *ag′nāt, adj.* related on the father's side or (*Roman law*) through males only: allied.—*n.* a person so related.—*adjs.* **agnatic** (*-nat′*), **-al.** *adv.* **agnat′ically.**—*n.* **agnā′tion.** [L. *agnātus—ad,* to, (g)*nāscī,* to be born. See **cognate.**]

**agnise, ag-,** *əg-nīz′,* (*arch.*) *v.t.* to acknowledge, to confess. [L. *agnōscĕre—ad,* to, (g)*nōscĕre,* to know; on the model of **cognise,** etc.]

**agnomen, ag-,** *əg-nō′mən, n.* a name added to the family name, generally on account of some great exploit, as *Africanus* to Publius Cornelius Scipio. [L.,—*ad,* to, and (g)*nōmen,* a name.]

**agnostic, ag-,** *əg-nos′tik, n.* one who holds that we know nothing of things beyond material phenomena—that a First Cause and an unseen world are things unknown and (some would add) apparently unknowable.—*n.* **agnos′ticism.** [Coined by T. H. Huxley in 1869 from Gr. *a-,* priv. and *gnōstikos,* good at knowing; see **gnostic.**]

**agnus castus,** *ag′nəs kas′təs,* a species of *Vitex,* a verbenaceous tree. [Gr. *agnos,* the name of the tree, and L. *castus,* a translation of Gr. *hagnos,* chaste, with which *agnos* was confused.]

**agnus dei,** *ag′nəs dē′ī, äg′nōōs dā′ē,* a part of the mass beginning with these words: music for it: a figure of a lamb emblematic of Christ, bearing the banner of the cross: a cake of wax stamped with such a figure, and blessed by the Pope. [L. *agnus Dēī,* lamb of God.]

**ago,** *ə-gō′,* **agone,** *ə-gon′ adv.* gone: past: since. [O.E. *āgān,* pa.p. of *āgān,* to pass away—intens. pfx. *ā-,* and *gān,* to go.]

**agog,** *ə-gog′, adj.* and *adv.* in excited eagerness. [Perh. connected with O.Fr. *en gogues,* frolicsome, of unknown origin.]

**agoge, a-gō′jē, n.** in ancient Greek music, tempo: sequence in melody.—*adj.* **agogic** (*a-goj′ik*), giving the effect of accent by slightly dwelling on a note.—*n.pl.* **agog′ics.** [Gr. *agōgē,* leading.]

**à gogo,** à *go-go, a-gō-gō,* (Fr.) in abundance, to one's heart's content; used in names of discothèques, etc.—**gogo,** go-go, used loosely as *adj.,* with meaning influenced by Eng. *go:* active, alert to seize opportunities.

**agoing,** *ə-gō′ing, adj.* and *adv.* in motion. [Prep. a, and going.]

**agon.** See **agony.**

**agone.** See **ago.**

**agonic,** *ə-gon′ik, adj.* making no angle.—**agonic line,** the line of no magnetic variation, along which the magnetic needle points directly north and south. [Gr. *agōnos—a-,* priv., *gōniā,* angle.]

**agonothetes,** *a-gō-nō-thē′tēz, -thā′tāz,* (Gr.) a judge or director of public games.

**agony,** *ag′ə-ni, n.* conflict in games: a violent struggle: extreme suffering: the death struggle: Christ's anguish in Gethsemane.—*v.i.* **ag′onise, -ize,** to struggle, contend: to suffer agony.—*v.t.* to subject to agony.—*adj.* **ag′onised,** suffering or expressing anguish.—*adv.* **ag′onisedly** (*-iz-id-li*).—*adj.* **ag′onising,** causing agony.—*adv.* **ag′-**

**onisingly.**—*ns.* **ag′on,** a conflict between two protagonists: a struggle; **ag′onist,** a competitor in public games: one engaged in a struggle, whether physical or spiritual: chief character in a literary work; **agonistes,** *a-gon-is′tēz,* one in the grip of inner conflict.—*adjs.* **agonist′ic, -al,** relating to athletic contests: combative.—*adv.* **agonist′ically.**—*n.* (*pl.* in form, treated as *sing.*) **agonist′ics,** the art and theory of games and prize-fighting.—**agony column,** the part of a newspaper containing special advertisements, as for missing friends and the like. [Gr. *agōniā,* contest, agony, *agōnistēs,* competitor—*agōn,* meeting, contest.]

**agood,** *ə-gōōd′,* (*Shak.*) *adv.* in good earnest, heartily. [Prep. a, and good.]

**agora,** *ag′ə-rə, n.* an assembly, place of assembly, market-place.—*n.* **agorapho′bia,** morbid fear of (crossing) open places. [Gr. *agorā,* assembly, market-place, *phobos,* fear.]

**agouta,** *ə-gōō′tə, n.* a rat-like insectivore (*Solenodon*) of Haiti. [Taino *aguta.*]

**agouti, aguti,** *ə-gōō′tē, n.* a small South American rodent allied to the guinea-pig. [Fr.,—Sp. *aguti* —Guarani *acuti.*]

**agraffe,** *ə-graf′, n.* a hooked clasp. [Fr. *agrafe—à,* to, *grappe*—L.L. *grappa*—O.H.G. *chrapfo* (Ger. *krappen*), hook.]

**à grands frais,** *a grä fre,* (Fr.) at great expense.

**agrapha.** See **agraphon.**

**agraphia,** *a-graf′i-ə, n.* loss of power of writing, from brain disease or injury.—*adj.* **agraph′ic.** [Gr. *a-,* priv. *graphein,* to write.]

**agraphon,** *a′gra-fon, pl.* **agrapha,** *-fa,* (Gr.) a traditional utterance ascribed to Jesus, not in the canonical Gospels.

**agrarian,** *əg-rā′ri-ən, adj.* relating to land, or its management or distribution.—*n.* **agrā′rianism,** equitable division of lands: a political movement in favour of change in conditions of property in land. [L. *agrārius—ager,* a field.]

**agraste,** (*Spens.*) *pa.t.* of **aggrace.**

**agravic,** *ə-grav′ik, adj.* pertaining to a condition or place where the effect of gravity is zero.

**agree,** *ə-grē′, v.i.* to be, or come to be, of one mind: to make friends again (*obs.* or *dial.*): to suit, do well (with): to concur: to accede: to assent: to be consistent: to harmonise: to get on together: to be in grammatical concord, take the same gender, number, case, or person.—*v.t.* to please, satisfy (*obs.*): to reconcile (persons; *obs.*): to settle (a dispute or a difference; *obs.*): to arrange with consent of all (*obs.* for a time, but in recent use): to concede (that):—*pa.p.* **agreed′.**—*n.* **agreeabil′ity.**—*adj.* **agree′able,** suitable: pleasant: in harmony: conformable: willing, consenting (*coll.*).—*adv.* in accordance.—*n.* **agree′ableness.**—*adv.* **agree′ably.**—*n.* **agree′ment,** concord: conformity: harmony: a compact, contract, treaty: an embellishment (*obs.*). [O.Fr. *agréer,* to accept kindly—L. *ad,* to, and *grātus,* pleasing.]

**agrégé,** *a-grā-zhā,* (Fr.) a successful candidate in a competitive university examination for teaching posts.

**agrément,** *a-grā-mä, n.* approval by state of diplomatic representative sent to it: (*pl.*) amenities (also **agrémens**): courtesies, charms, blandishments: embellishments, as grace notes and trills (*mus.*). [Fr.]

**agrestic,** *ə-gres′tik, adj.* of the fields: rural: unpolished. [L. *agrestis—ager,* a field.]

**agribusiness,** *ag′ri-biz′nis, n.* all the operations for supplying the market with farm produce taken together, including growing, provision of farm machinery, distribution, etc. [*agri*culture and business.]

**agriculture,** *ag′ri-kul-chər, n.* the art or practice of cultivating the land.—*adj.* **agricul′tural.**—*n.* **agricul′turist,** one skilled in agriculture: a

*fāte, fär; mē, hûr* (her); *mīne, mōte, för; mūte, mōōn, fŏŏt; dhen* (then)

farmer.—Also agricult'uralist. [L. *agricultūra*— *ager*, a field, *cultūra*, cultivation.]

agrimony, ag'ri-mən-i, n. a genus (*Agrimonia*) of the rose family, with small yellow flowers and bitter taste: extended to other plants, especially hemp-agrimony (*Eupatorium cannabinum*), a composite. [L. *agrimōnia* (a blunder or misreading)—Gr. *argemōnē*, long prickly-headed poppy.]

agrin, ə-grin', adv. in the act of grinning. [Prep. a, and grin.]

agriology, ag-ri-ol'ə-ji, n. the comparative study of the customs found among primitive peoples. [Gr. *agrios*, wild—*agros*, field, and *logos*, a discourse.]

agrise, agrize, agryze, a-grīz', v.t. to terrify (*Spens.*): to horrify: to disfigure.—*adj.* agrised'. [O.E. *āgrīsan*, to dread.]

agro-, ag-rō-, in composition, pertaining to soil: agricultural.—*adj.* agrobiolog'ical.—*ns.* agrobiol'ogy, study of plant nutrition and soil yields: agrobiol'ogist.—*adjs.* agrolog'ic(al).—*ns.* agrol'-ogy, study of structure, history, etc., of soils, esp. as they affect agriculture; agrol'ogist.

agronomy, a-gron'ə-mi, n. rural economy.—*adjs.* agronomial, (-ō'miəl); agronomic (-om'ik).—*n.* agron'omist. [Gr. *agros*, field, *nemein*, to dispense, manage.]

agrostology, ag-ros-tol'ə-ji, n. the study of grasses.—*adj.* agrostological (-tə-loj'i-kl).—*n.* agrostol'ogist. [Gr. *agrōstis*, dog's-tooth grass.]

aground, ə-grownd', adv. in or to a stranded condition: on the ground. [Prep. a, and ground.]

aguacate, ä-gwä-kä'tä, n. the avocado pear. [Sp., —Nahuatl *ahuacatl*.]

aguardiente, ä-gwär-dyen'tä, n. a brandy made in Spain and Portugal: any spirituous liquor. [Sp., from *agua ardiente*, burning water.—L. *aqua*, water, *ardēns, -entis*—*ardēre*, to burn.]

ague, ā'gū, n. a burning fever (*B.*): a fever with hot and cold fits: malaria: a shivering fit.— *adjs.* agued (ā'gūd), struck with ague: shivering: cold; ā'guish.—*adv.* ā'guishly.—*a'*gue-cake, a swelling on the spleen, caused by ague; ā'gue-fit'.—*adj.* ā'gue-proof. [O.Fr. (*fièvre*) *ague*—L. (*febris*) *acūta*, sharp (fever).]

aguise, aguize, a-gīz, v.t. to dress, equip (*Spens.*): adorn: to fashion. [Pfx. a-, and guise.]

ah, ä, interj. expressing surprise, joy, pity, complaint, objection, etc. [Perh. O.Fr. *ah*.]

aha, ə-hä', interj. of exultation, pleasure, surprise, or contempt. [ah, and ha.]

à haute voix, a ōt vwä, (Fr.) aloud.

ahead, ə-hed', adv. further on: in advance: forward: headlong. [Prep. a, and head.]

aheap, ə-hēp', adv. in a heap. [Prep. a, and heap.]

aheight, ə-hīt', (*arch.*) adv. on high, aloft. [Prep. a, and height.]

ahem, ə-h(e)m', interj, a lengthened form of hem.

Ahithophel. See Achitophel.

ahigh, ə-hī', adv. on high. [Prep. a, and high.]

ahimsa, ä-him'sä, n. duty of sparing animal life: non-violence. [Sans. *ahiṁsā*.]

ahint, ə-hint', ahind, ə-hin(d)', (*Scot.*, etc.) adv. and prep. behind. [O.E. *æthindan*.]

ahold, ə-hōld', adv. at or to grips, or a condition of holding: near the wind (*i.e.* so as to hold there) (*obs. naut.*; *Shak.*). [Prep. a, and hold.]

ahorseback, ə-hörs'bak, adv. on horseback. [Prep. a.]

ahoy, ə-hoi', (*naut.*) interj. used in hailing. [ah and hoy.]

Ahriman, ä'ri-män, n. the evil spirit, opposed to Ormuzd. [Pers. *Ahriman*, Zend *anro mainyus*, dark spirit.]

à huis clos, a wē klō, (Fr.) with closed doors.

ahull, ə-hul', (*naut.*) adv. with sails furled, and helm lashed to the lee-side. [Prep. a, and hull.]

ahungered, ə-hung'gərd, ahungry, -gri, (both *arch.*) adjs. oppressed with hunger.—Also, from con-

fusion of prefixes, anhung'(e)red, an-hung'ry (or an hungry). [Prob. O.E. *of-hyngred*.]

Ahuramazda, ä'hōōr-ä-maz-dä. Same as Ormuzd.

ai, ä'ē, n. the three-toed sloth. [Tupí *ai*, representing the animal's cry.]

aia. See ayah.

aiblins. See able.

aid, ād, v.t. to help.—*n.* help: succour: assistance, as in defending an action: that which helps: an auxiliary: a helper: an apparatus, etc., that gives help, e.g. hearing-aid, navigational aid: a feudal tax for certain purposes—paying the lord's ransom, the expense of knighting his son, his daughter's marriage: subsidy or money grant to the king.—*n.* aid'ance, aid, help, support.— *adj.* aid'ant (*arch.*), aiding, helping.—*adj.* aid'ed.—*n.* aid'er.—*adjs.* aid'ful; aid'ing; aid'less.— in aid of, (*coll.*) intended to achieve. [O.Fr. *aider*—L. *adjūtāre*, freq. of *adjuvāre*—*juvāre*, *jūtum*, to help.]

aide-de-camp, ed-, ād'də-kä, n. an officer who carries the orders of a general and acts as secretary: an officer attending a king, governor, etc.: —*pl.* aides-de-camp (ed-, ād'-). [Fr., assistant on the field.]

aide-mémoire, ed-mä-mwär, (Fr.) an aid to the memory: a reminder: a memorandum-book: a written summary of a diplomatic document.

aidōs, i'dōs, (Gr.) shame, modesty.

aiery, a variant of aerie.

aiglet. Same as aglet.

aigre-doux, egr'-dōō (*fem.* -douce, -dōōs), (Fr.) bitter-sweet, sourish.

aigrette, ā'gret, ā-gret', n. an egret: an egret plume: a plume: a tuft: a pappus: a spray of jewels. [Fr.]

aiguille, ā-gwēl', n. a sharp, needle-like peak of rock: a slender boring-tool.—*n.* aiguillette' (see aglet). [Fr.]

aikido, i-kē'dō, n. a Japanese combative sport using locks and pressure against joints.

aikona, i'kon'ə, (Bantu) it is not: no.

ail, āl, v.t. (*impers.*) to trouble, afflict, be the matter with: to have the matter with one.—*v.i.* to be sickly, indisposed.—*n.* trouble: indisposition.— *adj.* ail'ing, unwell: in poor health.—*n.* ail'ment, pain: indisposition: disease, esp. if not very serious.—what ails him at? (*Scot.*), what is his objection to? [O.E. *eglan*, to trouble.]

ailanto, ā-lan'tō, n. the tree of heaven (genus *Ailantus*; family *Simarubaceae*), a lofty and beautiful Asiatic tree.—Also ailan'thus. [Amboyna (Moluccas) name *aylanto*, tree of the gods.]

aileron, āl, *el'ə-rõ, -ron*, n. a flap on an aeroplane wing-tip for lateral balancing: a half-gable, as on a penthouse.—*n.* ailette (ā-let'), a plate of armour for the shoulder. [Fr. dims. of *aile*—L. *āla*, a wing.]

ailes de pigeon, el də pē-zhõ, (Fr.) pigeon's wings— powdered side-curls of hair.

ailour(o)-, ailur(o)-, i-lōōr'(ə)-, in composition, cat. —*ns.* ail(o)ur'ophile (-*fīl*), a cat lover or fancier; ail(o)urophilia (-*fil'i-a*), love of cats; ail(o)ur'ophobe (-*fōb*), a cat hater: one with an abnormal fear of cats; ail(o)urophobia (-*fō'bi-a*). [Gr. *ailouros*, cat.]

aim, ām, v.t. to estimate, guess (*obs.*): to place: to point, level, direct, with (or as if with) a view to hitting an object: to purpose or try (to do).— *v.i.* to conjecture (*obs.*): to direct a course: to level a weapon: to direct a blow or missile: to direct an utterance with personal or special application: to direct one's intention and endeavours with a view to attainment.—*n.* a guess or estimate (*Shak.*): an act or manner of aiming: a shot (*Shak.*): an object or purpose aimed at: design: intention.—*adj.* aim'less, without fixed aim.—*adv.* aim'lessly.—*n.* aim'lessness.—cry aim (*arch.*), to encourage by calling out 'aim', hence, to applaud; give aim (*arch.*), to guide by reporting result of previous shots; take aim, to aim

deliberately. [Prob. partly O.Fr. *esmer* (Picardian *amer*)—L. *aestimāre*, partly O.Fr. *aesmer* —L. *adaestimāre*; cf. esteem, estimate.]
**ain**, *ān*, (*Scot*.), *adj*. own. [O.N. *eiginn* or O.E. *ǣgen*, a variant of *āgen*.]
**ainé** (*fem*. **ainée**), *e-nā*, (Fr.) elder, senior.
**ain't**, *ānt*, (*coll*.) contracted form of *are not*, used also for *am* or *is not*: also of *have not*.
**Ainu**, *i'nōō*, *n*. a people of Japan whose abundant body hair has been the subject of remark: their language.
**air**, *ār*, *n*. the gaseous mixture (chiefly nitrogen and oxygen) of which the atmosphere is composed: any gas (*obs*.): a light breeze: breath (*obs*.): effluvium: the aura or atmosphere that invests anything: bearing, outward appearance, manner, look: an assumed or affected manner: (in *pl*.) affectation of superiority: exposure, noising abroad: melody, tune: the chief, usually upper, part or tune.—*adj*. of, pertaining to, the air: affecting, regulating, (the) air: by means of (the) air: operated by air: of aircraft: carried out, or conveyed, by aircraft.—*v.t.* to expose to the air: to ventilate: to warm and dry: to give an airing to: to wear openly, display: to publish abroad.—*v.i.* to take an airing: to become aired. —*n.* **air'er**, one who airs: a frame on which clothes are dried.—*adv.* **air'ily**, in an airy manner: jauntily.—*ns.* **air'iness**; **air'ing**, exposure to air or heat or to general notice: a short excursion in the open air.—*adjs.* **air'less**, without air: without free communication with the outer air: without wind: stuffy; **air'y**, consisting of or relating to air: open to the air: like air: unsubstantial: sprightly: offhand.— **air'-am'bulance**, an aircraft used to take patients from remote places to hospital; **air'-arm**, the branch of the fighting services that uses aircraft; **air'-base**, a base of operations for aircraft; **air'-bath**, exposure of the body to air: apparatus for therapeutic application of compressed or rarefied air, or for drying substances in air; **air'-bed**, an inflated mattress; **air'-bell**, an airbubble; **air'-bends**, aeroembolism; **air'-bladder**, a sac containing gas, as those that buoy up certain sea-weeds: a fish's swim-bladder, serving to regulate buoyancy and in some cases acting as a lung.—*adj.* **air'borne**, carried by air: borne up in the air.—**air'-brake**, a brake worked by compressed air: a means of checking the speed of an aircraft; **air'-brick**, a block for ventilation; **air'-bridge**, a link by air transport between two points; **air'-brush**, a device for spraying paint by compressed air; **air'-bubble**, a bubble of air, specif. one causing a spot on a photograph.—*adj.* **air'-built**, built in air: having no solid foundation.—**air'-bus'**, aerobus; **air'-car**, one made to ride on a cushion of air; **air'-cavity**, **air'-cell** (*bot*.), an intercellular space containing air; **air'-chief-mar'shal**, an air-force officer ranking with an admiral or general; **air'-comm'odore**, an air-force officer ranking with a commodore or brigadier; **air'-compress'or**, a machine which draws in air at atmospheric pressure, compresses it, and delivers it at higher pressure; **air'-condi'tioning**, the bringing of air to the desired state of purity, temperature and humidity.—*v.t.* **air'-condi'tion**, to equip, e.g. a building, with devices for air-conditioning.— **air'-cooling**, cooling by means of air.—*adj.* **air'-cooled**.—**air'-corr'idor**, in an area where flying is restricted, a narrow strip along which flying is allowed; **air'-cov'er**, protection given by fighter aircraft to other forces during a military operation: the protecting aircraft; **aircraft**, *sing.* (also *pl*.) any structure or machine for navigating the air; **air'craft-carrier**, a vessel from which aircraft can take off and on which they may alight; **air'craftman**, an air force member of lowest rank. —Also **air'craftsman**; **air'craft(s)woman**, lowest

rank in the W.R.A.F.; **air'-crew'**, the crew of an aircraft; **air'-cushion**, a cushion that can be inflated: protective barrier, e.g. between a hovercraft and land or water, formed by downdriven air; **air'-drain**, a cavity in the external walls of a building to prevent damp from getting through to the interior.—*adj.* **air'-drawn**, drawn in air: visionary: imaginary (*Shak*.).—**air'drome** (chiefly *U.S.*), aerodrome; **air'-drop** (*mil*.), a landing of men or supplies by parachute; **air'-engine**, an engine driven by heated or compressed air; **air'field**, an open expanse where aircraft may land and take off; **air force**, a force organised for warfare in the air; **air'-gap**, a gap in the magnetic circuit of a piece of electrical apparatus, e.g. the gap between the rotor and stator of an electric machine; **air'-gas**, producer gas; **air'graph**, a letter photographically reduced for sending by air; **air'-grating**, a grating admitting air for ventilation; **air'-gun**, a gun that discharges missiles by compressed air: **air'hole**, a hole for the passage of air: a hole in ice where animals come up to breathe: an air-pocket; **air'-host'ess, see hostess; **air'-house'**, an inflatable building of nylon or Terylene coated with polyvinyl chloride which can be used by industrial firms for storage, etc.; **air'-jacket**, a casing containing air to reduce loss or gain of heat: a garment with airtight cavities to buoy up in water; **air'-lane'**, a route normally taken by aircraft because of steady winds; **air letter**, a letter sent by air mail; **air lift**, a transport operation carried out by air; **air line**, a route or system of traffic by aircraft: (*U.S.*) a beeline; **air'liner**, a large passenger aircraft: an aircraft plying in an air line; **air'-lock**, a small chamber in which pressure of air can be raised or lowered, through which communication is made between a caisson where the air is compressed and the outer air: a bubble in a pipe obstructing flow of liquid; **air mail**, mail conveyed by air; **air'man**, an aviator—*fem.* **air'woman**; **air'manship**, the art of handling aircraft; **air'-mar'shal**, an air-force officer ranked with a vice-admiral or a lieutenantgeneral; **air'-mechan'ic**, one who tends and repairs aircraft.—*adj.* **air'-minded**, having thought habitually and favourably directed towards flying.—**air'-miss**, a near collision between aircraft; **air'-officer**, an air-force officer of general rank; **air'plane** (chiefly *U.S.*), an aeroplane; **air'-plant**, an epiphyte; **air'-pocket**, a region of rarefied or down-flowing air, in which aircraft drop: an aerodrome with a custom-house, used as a station for international transport of passengers and cargo; **air'-power**, military power in respect of aircraft; **air'-pump**, an instrument for pumping air out or in; **air'-raid**, an attack on a place by aircraft; **air'-rail**, a rail on which a road vehicle is carried overhead for part of its course; **air'-sac**, an outgrowth of the lung in birds, helping respiration or lightening the body: in insects, a dilatation of the trachea; **air'screw**, the propeller of an aircraft; **Air Scout**, a member of a branch of the Scouts with special interest in air activities; **air'shaft**, a passage for air into a mine; **air'ship**, a mechanically driven dirigible aircraft, lighter than air; **air'-sickness**, nausea affecting travellers by air.—*adj.* **air'sick**.—**air'space**, cubic contents available for respirable air: an air-cell; **air'-splint'**, a contrivance zipped up and inflated for giving temporary support to an injured limb; **air'stop**, a stopping-place for helicopters; **air'-strike**, an attack with aircraft; **air'strip**, a temporary or emergency landing-place for aircraft: a runway; **air terminal**, a terminus to or from which passengers are conveyed from or to an airport.—*adjs.* **air'tight**, impermeable to air: impenetrable (*fig.*); **air-to-air**, from one aircraft to another.—**air'-trap**, a device to prevent escape of foul air; **air'-umbrella**, strong air-cover; **air'-vice-mar'shal**, an air-force officer ranking with a rear-admiral or major-general.—*advs.* **air'ward, air'wards**, up in the air.—**air'way**, a passage for air: an organised route for air travel: used in *pl.* to form names of airline companies; **air'worthiness**.— *adjs.* **air'worthy**, in fit condition for safe flying; **air'y-fair'y**, fanciful: delicate.—**air-sea rescue**, combined use of aircraft and high-speed launches in sea rescue; **air-traffic control**, system of regional centres and airport units which instruct aircraft exactly about route to follow, height at which to fly, etc.; **give the air**, to dismiss; **(go) up in the air**, (to become) excited or angry; **in the air**, prevalent in an indefinite form; **off the air**, not broadcasting, or being broadcast, for a period of time; **on the air**, broadcast by radio: in the act of broadcasting; **take air**, to get wind, become known; **take the air**, to have an airing. [O.Fr. (and Fr.) *air*—L. *āēr, āēris*—Gr. *āēr, āeros*, air.]

**Airedale**, *ār'dāl, n.* (in full **Airedale terrier**) a large terrier of a breed from *Airedale* in Yorkshire.

**airn**, *ārn*, a Scots form of **iron**.

**airt**, *ārt, (Scot.) n.* direction, quarter.—*v.t.* to direct. [Perh. Gael. *aird*, point (of compass).]

**aisle**, *īl, n.* a side division of the nave or other part of a church or similar building, generally separated off by pillars: (*loosely*) any division of a church, or a small building attached: (*loosely*) a passage between rows of seats: a passageway (*U.S.*): the corridor of a railway train (*U.S.*).— *adj.* **aisled** (*ild*), having aisles. [O.Fr. *ele* (Fr. *aile*)—L. *āla*, a wing; confused with **isle** and **alley**.]

**ait, eyot**, *āt, n.* a small island. [Cf. O.E. *ēgath, igeoth,* app. conn. with *īeg*, island; the phonology is obscured.]

**ait**, *āt*, Scots form of **oat**.

**aitch**, *āch, n.* the eighth letter of the alphabet (H, h). [O.Fr. *ache*, from which L.L. *ahha* is inferred.]

**aitchbone**, *āch'bōn, n.* the bone of the rump: the cut of beef over it. [*An aitchbone* is for *a nachebone*—O.Fr. *nache*—L. *natis*, buttock; and **bone**.]

**aitu**, *ī'tōō, n.* in Polynesia, a demigod.

**aizle**. See **easle**.

**Aizoon**, *ā-i-zō'on, n.* an African genus of plants giving name to the family **Aizoā'ceae**, akin to the goosefoots. [App. Gr. *āei*, ever, *zōos*, living.]

**à jamais**, a *zha-me*, (Fr.) for ever.

**ajar**, *ə-jär', adv.* and *adj.* partly open. [O.E. *on, on, cerr*, a turn.]

**Ajax**, *ā'jaks*, (L.,—Gr. *Aiās*) the Greek hero next to Achilles in the Trojan war: a privy, by a pun on *a jakes* (*obs.*).

**ajee, agee**, *ə-jē', (Scot.* and *dial.*) *adv.* off the straight: ajar. [Prep. **a**, and **gee**, to move to one side; **jee**, a call to a horse to move to one side.]

**ajowan**, *aj'ō-wən*, or **ajwan**, *aj'wən, n.* a plant of the caraway genus yielding ajowan oil and thymol. [Origin uncertain.]

**ajutage**. See **adjutage**.

**ake**, *āk*, old spelling of the verb **ache**.

**akee**, *a-kē'*, a small African sapindaceous tree, now common in the West Indies: its edible fruit. [Kru *ā-kee*.]

**akene**, *a-kēn', n.* Same as **achene**.

**akimbo**, *ə-kim'bō, adj.* and *adv.* with hand on hip and elbow out. [M.E.*in kenebow*; poss. in a keen (sharp) bow or bend; other suggestions are *canbow* (i.e. can-handle), and O.N. *kengboginn*, bent into a crook—*kengr*, kink, *boginn*, bowed.]

**akin**, *ə-kin', adv.* by kin: of nature.—*adj.* related by blood: of like nature. [Prep. **a**, and **kin**.]

**akol(o)uthos**, etc. Same as **acolouthos**, etc.

**akvavit**. Same as **aquavit**.

**à la**, *a la*, *prep.* in the manner of, e.g. *à la James*

*Joyce*; in cooking, prepared with, in the manner of (a person or place), e.g. *à la Dubarry*, with cauliflower, *à la Florentine*, with spinach, etc. [Fr.—contraction of *à la mode de.*]

**ala**, *ā'la, n.* a membranous outgrowth on a fruit (*bot.*): a side petal in the pea family (*bot.*): a large side sepal in the milkworts (*bot.*): a leafy expansion running down the stem from a leaf (*bot.*): any flat winglike process, esp. of bone (*zool.*):—*pl.* **alae** (*ā'lē*).—*adjs.* **ā'lar**, **ā'lary**, pertaining to a wing; **ā'late**, **-d**, winged, having an ala. [L. *āla*, wing.]

**alabamine**, *al-ə-bäm'ēn, n.* a name proposed for element no. 85; now called **astatine**. [*Alabama*, where its discovery in nature was claimed.]

**alabandine**. See **almandine**.—*n.* **aland'ite**, a cubic mineral, manganese sulphide.

**à l'abandon**, *a la-bā-dō,* (Fr.) neglected, uncared for: (in *Eng.*) carelessly, recklessly.

**alabaster**, *al'ə-bäs-tər*, or *bäs', (Spens., Shak., Milt.,* etc. **alablaster**) *n.* a semi-transparent massive gypsum.—*adj.* of or like alabaster.— **oriental alabaster**, stalactitic calcite. [Gr. *alabastros*, said to be from *Alabastron*, a town in Egypt.]

**à la belle étoile**, *a la be-lā-twäl,* (Fr.) in the open air.

**à la bonne heure!** *a la bo-nœr*, (Fr.) well done! that is right.

**à l'abri**, *a la-brē*, (Fr.) under shelter.

**à la campagne**, *a la kā-pan-y', (Fr.) in the country.

**à la carte**, *a la kart*, *ä lä kärt*, (Fr.) according to the bill of fare.

**alack**, *ə-lak', interj.* denoting regret.—*interj.* **alack'-a-day**, alack the day: woe be to the day. [Prob. **ah**, and **lack**.]

**alacrity**, *ə-lak'ri-ti, n.* briskness: cheerful readiness: promptitude. [L. *alacritās, -ātis—alacer, alacris*, brisk.]

**à la dérobée**, *a la dā-ro-bā*, (Fr.) by stealth.

**à la hauteur de**, *a la ō-tœr də*, (Fr.) on a level with, abreast of: able to understand, or to deal with.

**alalagmos**, *a-la-lag'mos*, (Gr.) war-cry, cry of *alalai*.

**à la lanterne**, *a la lā-tern*, (Fr.) to the lamp(-chain) —away with them and hang them (as in the French Revolution).

**alalia**, *ə-lā'li-a, n.* loss of speech. [Gr. *a-*, priv., and *laleein*, to talk.]

**à la main**, *a la mē*, (Fr.) in hand, ready: by hand.

**à la maître d'hôtel**, *a la metr' dō-tel*, (Fr.) in the style of a house-steward, of a hotel-keeper: in major-domo fashion.

**alameda**, *a-la-mā'dä, n.* a public walk, esp. between rows of poplars. [Sp. *álamo*, poplar.]

**à la mode**, *a la mod(ə)*, **alamode**, *a-lə-mōd', adv.* and *adj.* according to the fashion, fashionable; in cooking, of beef, larded and stewed with vegetables: of desserts, served with ice-cream (*U.S.*).—**alamode**, *n.* a light glossy silk. [Fr. *à la mode.*]

**alamort**, *a-lə-mort', adj.* half-dead: dejected. [Fr. *à la mort*, to the death; see also **amort**.]

**aland**, *ə-land', adv.* ashore. [Prep. **a**, and **land**.]

**alang**, *ä'läng*, or **a'lang-a'lang**. Same as **lalang**.

**alannah**, *ə-län'a, n.* in endearment, my child. [Ir. *a*, O, *leanbh*, child.]

**à la page**, *a la päzh*, (Fr.) up to date, au courant.

**alar, alary**. See **ala**.

**alarm**, *ə-lärm', n.* a call to arms: notice of danger: a mechanical contrivance for arousing, warning, or giving notice: the noise made by it: a din (*obs.*): a fear-stricken state: apprehension of danger.— *v.t.* to call to arms (*obs.*): to give notice of danger: to arouse: to strike with fear.—*adj.* **alarmed'**.—*adv.* **alarm'edly**.—*adj.* **alarm'ing**.—*adv.* **alarm'ingly**.—*n.* **alarm'ist**, a scaremonger. —Also *adj.*—*n.* and *v.t.* **alarum** (*ə-la'rəm, -lä', -lä'*), alarm (now *arch.* except of a warning mechanism or sound).—**alarm'-bell**; **alarm'-clock'**, a clock that can be set to ring an alarm at a chosen time; **alar(u)ms and excursions,** a stage direction for a sketchy conventionalised representation of skirmishing or the outskirts of a battle: hence, vague hostilities or confused activity. [O.Fr. (Fr.) *alarme*—It. *all'arme,* to (the) arms.]

**alas,** *ə-läs',* *interj.* expressive of grief.—**alas the day, alas the while,** ah! unhappy day, time. [O.Fr. *ha las, a las* (mod. Fr. *hélas*); *ha,* ah, and *las, lasse,* wretched, weary—L. *lassus,* wearied.]

**alastrim,** *ə-las'trim, n.* a mild form of smallpox or a similar disease. [Port.]

**alate,** *ə-lāt', adv.* (*arch.*) lately. [of, and **late.**]

**alate.** See **ala.**

**a latere,** *ā la'te-rē, ä la'te-re,* (L.) lit. from the side: confidential (of legate sent by the Pope).

**à la volée,** *a la vo-lā,* (Fr.) on the flight (said of any quick return).

**alay, alaiment,** old spellings of **allay, allayment.**

**alb,** *alb, n.* a long white tight-sleeved vestment. [O.E. *albe*—L.L. *alba*—L. *albus,* white.]

**albacore,** *al'bə-kōr, -kör, n.* a large tunny: a species of mackerel (*S.Afr.*).—Also written **al'bicore.** [Port. *albacor*—Ar. *al,* the, *bukr,* young camel.]

**Alban,** *al'bən,* **Albany,** *-i,* **Albion,** *-i-ən, ns.* ancient names for the island of Great Britain, now used poetically for Britain, England, or esp. Scotland. —**Alban,** the ancient kingdom of the Picts and (Celtic) Scots, which the addition of Lothian and Strathclyde transformed into Scotland; **Albany,** a Scottish dukedom first conferred in 1398.— **Albany herald,** one of the Scottish heralds. [Celtic.]

**albata,** *al-bā'ta, n.* a variety of German silver. [L. *albāta* (*fem.*), whitened—*albus,* white.]

**albatross,** *al'bə-tros, n.* a large, long-winged sea-bird of remarkable powers of flight: a hole in three below par (*golf*). [See **alcatras;** perh. influenced by L. *albus,* white.]

**albe, albee, all-be,** *ōl-bē', ōl'bē, conj.* (*arch.*) albeit. [all, and be.]

**albedo,** *al-bē'dō, n.* whiteness: the proportion of incident light reflected, as by a planet. [L. *albēdō,* whiteness—*albus,* white.]

**albeit,** *ōl-bē'it, conj.* although it be (that): even if, although. [all be it.]

**albergo,** *al-ber'gō,* (It.) an inn, auberge.

**albert,** *al'bərt, n.* a short kind of watch-chain. [After Queen Victoria's husband.]

**albertite,** *al'bər-tit, n.* a pitch-black solid bitumen. [Discovered at the *Albert* mine, New Brunswick, Canada.]

**albescent,** *al-bes'ənt, adj.* becoming white: whitish. —*n.* **albesc'ence.** [L. *albēscēns, -entis,* pr.p. of *albēscēre,* to grow white—*albus,* white.]

**albespyne, albespine,** *al'bə-spin,* (*arch.*) *n.* hawthorn. [O.Fr. *albespine* (Fr. *aubépine*)—L. *alba spina,* white thorn.]

**Albigensian,** *al-bi-jen'si-ən, adj.* of the town of *Albi* or its district (the Albigeois), in the S. of France: of a Catharist or Manichaean sect or of the 13th-century crusade (beginning in the Albigeois) by which, with the Inquisition, the Catholic Church stamped it out in blood.— Also *n.—n.pl.* **Albigen'sēs.**—*n.* **Albigen'sianism.** [L.L *Albigēnsēs.*]

**albino,** *al-bē'nō,* in U.S. *-bi', n.* a person or other animal with abnormally white skin and hair and pink pupil: a plant lacking in pigment:—*pl.* **albi'nos**—*fem.* **albiness** (*al'bin-es*).—*ns.* **al'-binism** (*-bin-*), **albinoism** (*-bē'*).—*adj.* **albinotic** (*al-bin-ot'ik*). [Port. *albino,* white Negro or albino—L. *albus,* white.]

**albite,** *al'bit, n.* a white plagioclase felspar, sodium and aluminium silicate.—*v.t.* **al'bitise, -ize,** to turn into albite. [L. *albus,* white.]

**albricias,** *al-brē-thē'as,* (Sp.) a reward to the bearer of good news.

**albugo,** *al-bū'gō, n.* leucoma.—*adj.* **albugineous,**

(*-jin'i-əs*), like the white of an egg or of the eye. [L. *albūgō, -inis,* whiteness—*albus,* white.]

**album,** *al'bəm, n.* among the Romans, a white tablet or register on which the praetor's edicts and such public notices were recorded: a blank book for the insertion of photographs, autographs, poetical extracts, scraps, postage-stamps, or the like: a printed book of selections, esp. of music: a booklike container for gramophone records: a visitors' book (*U.S.*):—*pl.* **al'bums.**—*n.* **al'bum-leaf** (trans. of Ger. *albumblatt*), a short musical composition. [L. neut. of *albus,* white.]

**albumen,** *al-bū'mən, -min,* or *al', n.* white of egg: the nutritive material surrounding the yolk in the eggs of higher animals, a mixture of proteins (*zool.*): any tissue within the seed-coat other than the embryo itself—endosperm and perisperm, a store of food for the young plant, no matter what its chemical nature (*bot.*): an albumin (*obs.*).— *v.t.* **albū'menise, albū'minise, -ize,** (*phot.*) to cover or impregnate with albumen or an albuminous solution.—*ns.* **albū'min** (or *al'*), a protein of various kinds soluble in pure water, the solution coagulable by heat; **albū'minate,** an alkali compound of an albumin.—*adj.* **albū'minoid,** like albumen.—*n.* an old name for a protein in general: any one of a class of substances including keratin and chondrin.—*adj.* **albū'minous,** like or containing albumen or albumin: insipid.—*n.* **albūminūr'ia,** presence of albumin in the urine. [L. *albūmen, -inis*—*albus,* white.]

**album Graecum,** *al'bum grē'kum, al'bōōm gri'kōōm,* (L.L.) the dried dung of dogs, once used for inflammation of the throat.

**alburnum,** *al-bûrn'əm, n.* sapwood, the soft wood between inner bark and heartwood.—*adj.* **alburn'ous.** [L. *albus,* white.]

**alcahest.** See **alkahest.**

**Alcaic,** *al-kā'ik, adj.* of or pertaining to the Greek lyric poet *Alcaeus* (*Alkaios,* fl. 600 B.C.), or of the kind of verse invented by him.—*n.* (esp. in *pl.*) Alcaic verses.—**Alcaic strophe,** a form much used by Horace, consisting of two eleven-syllable Alcaics: ‿ — ‿ — ‿ — / — ‿ ‿ — ‿ —: a nine-syllable: ‿ — ‿ — ‿ — — ‿ —, and a ten-syllable: — ‿ ‿ — ‿ ‿ — ‿ — — ‿; imitated by Tennyson in 'O mighty-mouth'd inventor of harmonies'.

**alcaicería,** *al-kī-the-rē'a,* (Sp.) a bazaar.

**alcaide, alcayde,** *al-kād', äl-kī'dhä, -dā,* (Sp.) *n.* governor of a fortress: a gaoler. [Sp. *alcaide*— Ar. *al-qā'id*—*al,* the, *qā'id,* leader—*qāda,* to lead.]

**alcalde, äl-käl'dä,** (Sp.) *n.* a judge. [Sp.,—Ar. *al-qādī*—*qada,* to judge.]

**alcarraza,** *al-ka-ra'tha,* (Sp.) a porous vessel for cooling water.

**alcatras,** *al'kə-tras, n.* a name applied to several large water birds, as the pelican, gannet, frigate-bird, albatross. [Sp. *alcatraz,* pelican.]

**alcázar,** *al-ka-zär', -kä'thär,* (Sp.) a palace, fortress, bazaar.

**alchemy, alchymy,** *al'ki-mi, n.* the infant stage of chemistry, its chief pursuits the transmutation of other metals into gold, and the elixir of life: transmuting potency (*fig.*): a gold-like substance (e.g. brass) (*obs.*): a trumpet made of it (*obs.*).—*adjs.* **alchemic** (*-kem'ik*), **-al.**—*n.* **al'-chemist.** [Ar. *al-kimiā*—*al,* the, and *kimiā*— late Gr. *chēmeiā, chȳmeiā,* variously explained as the Egyptian art (*Khēmiā,* 'black-land', Egypt, from the Egyptian name), the art of *Chȳmes* (its supposed inventor), or the art of pouring (*chȳma,* fluid; cf. *cheein,* to pour).]

**Alcides,** *al-si'dēz,* (L.,—Gr.) a patronymic of Hercules, from Alcaeus, father of Amphitryon.

**alcohol,** *al'kə-hol, n.* a fine powder, esp. a sublimate (*obs.*): hence (*obs.*) an essence, a distillate: a liquid generated by the fermentation of sugar or other saccharine matter and forming the intoxi-cating element of fermented liquors: a general term for a class of hydrocarbon compounds analogous to common (or ethyl) alcohol, in which a hydroxyl group is substituted for an atom of hydrogen.—*adj.* alcohol'ic, of, like, containing, or due to alcohol.—*n.* one addicted to excessive drinking of alcohol.—*n.* al'coholism, alcoholic poisoning: condition suffered by an alcoholic.— *v.t.* al'coholise, -ize, to convert into or saturate with alcohol: to rectify.—*n.* alcoholisā'tion, -z-.—*n.* alcoholom'eter, an instrument for measuring the proportion of alcohol in solutions; alcoholom'etry. [Ar. *al-koh'l—al*, the, *koh'l*, antimony powder used in the East to stain the eyelids.]

al conto, *al kon'tō*, (It.) à la carte.

al contrario, *al kon-trä'ri-ō*, (Sp.) on the contrary.

Alcoran, *al-ko-rän'*, (*arch.*) *n.* the Koran. [Fr.,— Arab. *al*, the, Koran.]

alcorza, *al-kör'tha*, (Sp.) a kind of sweetmeat: icing.

alcove, *al'kōv*, *n.* a recess in a room: any recess: a shady retreat. [Sp. *alcoba*, a place in a room railed off to hold a bed—Ar. *al*, the, *qobbah*, a vault.]

Alcyonium, *al-si-ō'ni-əm*, *n.* a genus of Anthozoa growing in masses of polyps called dead men's fingers.—*n.pl.* Alcyonā'ria, the order to which belong Alcyonium, sea-pens, red coral and organ-pipe coral.—*n.* and *adj.* alcyonā'rian. [Gr. *alkyoneion*, an organism said to resemble a halcyon's nest—*alkyōn*, halcyon, kingfisher.]

aldea, *al-dā'a*, (Sp.) a village, hamlet.

Aldebaran, *al-deb'ə-ran*, *n.* a first-magnitude red star of the Hyades. [Ar. *al-dabarān*, the follower (of the Pleiades).]

aldehyde, *al'di-hīd*, *n.* a volatile fluid with a suffocating smell, obtained by the oxidation of alcohol: a compound differing from an alcohol in having two atoms fewer of hydrogen. [Contr. for *alcohol dēhydrogenātum*, alcohol deprived of hydrogen.]

al dente, *al den'tā*, (It.) of pasta, firm to the teeth.

alder, *öl'dər*, *n.* any tree of the genus *Alnus*, related to the birches, usually growing in moist ground: extended to various other trees or shrubs: an artificial fishing fly.—*adj.* al'dern, made of alder.—al'der-buck'thorn, a species of buckthorn (*Rhamnus Frangula*); al'der-fly, a riverside neuropterous insect.—*adj.* al'der-leaved. [O.E. *alor*; Ger. *erle*; L. *alnus*.]

alder-liefest, *öl-dər-lēf'ist*, (*Shak.*) *adj.* most beloved of all. [O.E. *alra* (W.S. *ealra*), gen. pl. of *al* (*eal*), all, and superl. of lief.]

alderman, *öl'dər-mən*, *n.* in O.E. times a nobleman of highest rank, a governor of a shire or district, a high official: later, head of a guild: in English boroughs, a civic dignitary next in rank to the mayor, elected by fellow councillors: a superior member of an English county council: a member of the governing body of a borough or of its upper house, elected by popular vote (*U.S.*):— *pl.* al'dermen.—*adj.* aldermanic (*-man'-ik*).—*n.* alderman'ity.—*adjs.* al'dermanlike, al'dermanly, pompous and portly.—*ns.* al'dermanry; al'der-manship. [O.E. *aldorman* (W.S. *ealdorman*)— *aldor* (*ealdor*), a chief—*ald* (*eald*) old, and noun-forming suffix *-or*.]

Alderney, *öl'dər-ni*, *n.* a small dairy-cow, formerly of a breed kept in *Alderney*, now loosely including Jersey and Guernsey.

Aldine, *öl'dīn*, *adj.* from the press, or named in honour, of *Aldus* Manutius of Venice and his family (15th-16th cent.).

aldose, *al'dōs*, *n.* any of a class of monosaccharide sugars of aldehyde constitution. [aldehyde.]

ale, *āl*, *n.* a beverage made from an infusion of malt by fermentation—name applied to beers in brewing of which yeast ferments on the top of the liquid: a festival, from the liquor drunk (*arch.*).— ale'bench, a bench in or before an alehouse; ale'-berry, a beverage made from ale and bread sops with flavouring; ale'-bush, ale'-pole, ale'-stake, a bush, pole, or stake used as an alehouse sign; ale'-conner, a civic officer appointed to test the quality of ale brewed (*hist.*); ale'-cost, costmary (used in flavouring ale); ale'-draper (*obs.*), a tavern-keeper; ale'-hoof, ground-ivy (O.E. *hōfe*); ale'-house, a house in which ale is sold.—*adj.* (*Shak.*) ale'washed.—*n.* ale'wife, a woman who sells ale: a fish akin to the herring, common off the N.E. of America (perhaps from its corpulent shape, but perhaps a different word):— *pl.* ale'wives. [O.E. (Anglian) *alu* (W.S. *ealu*); O.N. *öl*.]

aleatory, *ā'li-ə-tər-i*, *adj.* depending on contingencies: in which chance influences choice of notes (*music*): also used of element of chance in poetic composition, etc. [L. *āleātōrius—āleātor*, a dicer—*ālea*, a die.]

Alecto, *a-lek'tō*, *n.* one of the Furies. [Gr. *Alēktō*, lit. unceasing.]

alectryön, *a-lek'tri-ōn*, (Gr.) a cock.

alee, *ə-lē'*, *adv.* on or toward the lee-side. [O.N. *ā*, on, *hlē*, lee.]

aleft, *ə-left'*, *adv.* on or to the left hand. [Prep. a, and left.]

alegar, *al'* or *āl'i-gər*, *n.* sour ale, or vinegar made from it. [ale, with termination as vinegar.]

alegge, aleggeaunce. See allege (1).

Alemannic, *al-i-man'ik*, *adj.* of the Alemannen (L. *Alamanni, Alemanni*), an ancient people of S.W. Germany, or their dialect.—*n.* the High German dialect of Switzerland, Alsace, etc.

alembic, *ə-lem'bik*, *n.* old distilling apparatus.— *adj.* alem'bicated, over-refined. [Ar. *al*, the, *anbīq*—Gr. *ambix*, cap of a still.]

alembroth, *ə-lem'broth*. See sal alembroth.

alength, *ə-length'*, *adv.* at full length. [Prep. a, and length.]

à l'envi, *a lä-vē*, (Fr.) emulously: in emulation.

aleph, *ä'lef, ä'lef*, *n.* the first letter of the Phoenician and Hebrew alphabets, resembling an ox's head, representing a glottal stop, but adopted by the Greeks for a vowel sound. See A, alpha. [Heb. *āleph*, ox.]

alepine, *al'i-pēn*, *n.* a mixed fabric of wool and silk or mohair and cotton. [Perh. *Aleppo*.]

alerce, *ə-lûrs'*, *ä-ler'thä*, *n.* the wood of the sandarach-tree: the Chilean arbor vitae. [Sp., larch—L. *larix, -icis*, larch, perhaps confused with Ar. *al'arza*, the cedar.]

alerion, allerion, *a-lē'ri-ən*, (*her.*) *n.* an eagle displayed, without feet or beak. [Fr.]

alert, *ə-lûrt'*, *adj.* watchful: wide-awake: brisk.— *n.* a sudden attack or surprise: a danger warning: the time for which it lasts: condition of preparedness.—*v.t.* to make alert.—*adv.* alert'ly. —*n.* alert'ness.—on, upon the alert, upon the watch: wakefully attentive. [Fr. *alerte*—It. *all'erta*, on the erect—*erto*—L. *ērēctus*, erect.]

Aleurites, *al-ū-rī'tēz*, *n.* a genus of plants of the spurge family, yielding tung oil and candlenut. [Gr. *aleuron*, flour.]

aleurone, *a-lū'rōn*, *n.* a protein found in some seeds. [Gr. *aleuron*, flour.]

alevin, *al'i-vin*, *n.* a young fish, esp. a salmonid. [Fr.,—O.Fr. *alever*, to rear—L. *ad*, to, *levāre*, to raise.]

alew, *ə-lōō'*, *-lū'*, (*Spens.*) *n.* same as halloo.

alexanders, *al-ig-zän'dərz*, *n.* an umbelliferous plant (genus *Smyrnium*) formerly used as celery is. [O.E. *alexandre*; L. *olus atrum, olusatrum, lit.* 'black herb, vegetable', has been suggested as source.]

Alexandrian, *al-ig-zän'dri-ən*, *adj.* relating to *Alexandria* in Egypt, its school of philosophy, its poetry, or the general character of its culture and taste, erudite and critical rather than original in inspiration—sometimes with a suggestion of decadence: relating to *Alexander* the Great or other of the name.—Also *n.*—*n.* and *adj.* **Alexan'drine**, Alexandrian.—*n.* **alexan'drine**, a verse of six iambs (as in English), or in French of 12 and 13 syllables in alternate couplets (perhaps from a poem on *Alexander* the Great by *Alexandre* Paris). —Also *adj.*—*n.* **alexan'drite**, a dark green chrysoberyl discovered on the day of majority of the Cesarevich later *Alexander II.*

**alexia**, *a-lek'si-a, n.* loss of power to read: word-blindness. [Gr. *a-*, priv., *legein*, to speak, confused with L. *legēre*, to read.]

**alexin**, *a-lek'sin, n.* a body present in the blood serum, which uniting with an anti-serum gives protection against disease.—*adj.* **alexipharmic** (*-si-fär'mik*), acting against poison.—*ns.* **alexiphar'mic, alexiphar'makon**, an antidote to poison. [Gr. *alexein*, to ward off, *alexipharmakos—pharmakon*, poison.]

**alfa**, *al'fa.* See **halfa**.

**alfalfa**, *al-fal'fa, n.* a kind of lucerne. [Sp. *alfalfa*—Ar. *alfaçfaçah*.]

**alfaquí**, *al-fa-kē', (Sp.)* Moslem expounder of the law.

**alférez**, *al-fā'rāth, (Sp.)* standard-bearer.

**alforja**, *al-för'hha, (Sp.)* a saddle-bag: baboon's cheek-pouch.

**alfresco**, *al-fresk'ō, adv.* and *adj.* on fresh or moist plaster: in the fresh or cool air. [It.; see **fresco, fresh.**]

**alga**, *al'ga, n.* a seaweed: any member of the Algae:—*pl.* **algae** (*al'jē*), **Algae** (*bot.*), a great group of Thallophytes, the seaweeds and allied forms.— *adj. al'gal* (*-gəl*).—*ns.* **al'gin** (*-jin*), sodium alginate, a gummy nitrogenous organic compound got from seaweeds; **al'ginate**, a salt of alginic acid. —*adjs.* **algin'ic** (as **alginic acid**, an acid obtained from certain seaweeds, used in plastics, medicine, etc.); **al'goid** (*-goid*), of the nature of, resembling, an alga; **algolog'ical.**—*ns.* **algol'ogist; algol'ogy** phycology. [L. *alga*, seaweed.]

**algarroba**, *al-ga-rō'ba, n.* the carob: the mesquite: the fruit of either.—Also **algaro'ba, algarro'bo.** [Sp. *algarroba, -o.*—Ar. *al kharrūbah*; cf. **carob.**]

**algate**, *-s, öl'gāt(s), adv.* always, at all events, nevertheless (*obs.*): altogether (*Spens.*). [all and gate; orig. *dat.*, with *-s* on analogy of *always*, etc.]

**algebra**, *al'ji-bra, n.* a method of calculating by symbols—by means of letters employed to represent quantities, and signs to represent their relations, thus forming a kind of generalised arithmetic: in modern mathematics, any of a number of systems using symbols and involving reasoning about relationships and operations.— *adjs.* **algebraic** (*-brā'ik*), **-al.**—*n.* **algebrā'ist**, one skilled in algebra. [It. and Sp.,—Ar. *al-jebr*, the resetting (of anything broken), hence combination —*jabara*, to reunite.]

**Algerine**, *al'jə-rēn, adj.* of Algeria or Algiers.—*n.* a native of Algeria: a pirate (*hist.*).—Also **Algē'rian.**

**algesia**, *al-jē'zi-a*, or *-si-, n.* sensitiveness to pain.— *n.* **algē'sis**, sensation of pain. [Mod. L.—Gr. *algēsis—algein*, to suffer.]

**algid**, *al'jid, adj.* cold, chill—esp. applied to a cold fit in disease.—*n.* **algid'ity.** [L. *algidus*, cold.]

**alginate, algology,** etc. See **alga**.

**Algol**, *al'gol, n.* a variable star in the constellation Perseus. [Ar. *al ghūl*, the ghoul.]

**Algol**, *al'gol, n.* a type of computer language. [Algo(rithmic) l(anguage).]

**algolagnia**, *al-gō-lag'ni-a, n.* sexual pleasure got from inflicting or suffering pain. [Gr. *algos*, pain, *lagneiā*, lust.]

**Algonquian, Algonkian,** *al-gong'ki-ən,* **Algonquin, Algonkin,** *-kin, n.* a member of a leading group of Indian tribes in the valley of the Ottawa and around the northern tributaries of the St Lawrence: their language.—Also *adj.* [Micmac

Indian *algoomaking*, at the place of spearing fish.]

**algorism**, *al'go-rizm, n.* the Arabic system of numeration: arithmetic.—Also **al'gorithm.** [L.L. *algorismus*—Ar. *al-Khwārazmi*, the native of Khwārazm (Khiva), i.e. the 9th-cent. mathematician Abu Ja'far Mohammed ben Musa.]

**algorithm**, *al'go-ridhm, n.* a rule for solving a mathematical problem in a finite number of steps.—*adj.* **algorith'mic.** [algorism.]

**alguazil**, *al-gwa-zil', **alguacil**, äl-gwä-thēl', n.* in Spain, an officer who makes arrests, etc. [Sp. (now) *alguacil*—Ar. *al-wazīr.* See **vizier.**]

**algum**, *al'gəm, (B.) n.* a wood imported into ancient Palestine, prob. red sandalwood.—Also **al'mug.** [Heb. *algūm.*]

**Alhagi**, *al-hā'ji, -hä'jē, n.* a papilionaceous manna-yielding genus of desert shrubs. [Ar. *al-hāj.*]

**Alhambra**, *al-ham'bra, n.* the palace of the Moorish kings of Granada in Spain.—*adj.* **Alhambresque** (*-bresk'*). [Ar. *al-hamrā'*, the red (house).]

**alias**, *ā'li-äs, L. ä'li-äs, adv.* otherwise.—*n.* an assumed name:—*pl.* **a'liases.** [L. *aliäs*, at another time, otherwise—*alius*, other.]

**alibi**, *al'i-bī, L. äl'i-bē, n.* the plea in a criminal charge of having been elsewhere at the material time: the fact of being elsewhere: an excuse for failure (*coll.*). [L. *alibī*, elsewhere, orig. locative —*alius*, other.]

**alicant**, *al-i-kant', n.* a wine made near *Alicante*, in Spain.

**alicyclic**, *al-i-sik'lik, adj.* having properties of aliphatic organic compounds but containing a ring of carbon atoms instead of an open chain. [aliphatic, cyclic.]

**alidad**, *al'i-dad*, or *-dad'*, **alidade, -dād, n.* a revolving index for reading the graduations of an astrolabe, quadrant, or similar instrument, or for taking the direction of objects. [Ar. *al 'idādah*, the revolving radius—'*adid*, humerus.]

**alien**, *ā'li-ən, -lyən, adj.* belonging to something else: extraneous: repugnant: inconsistent: incompatible: estranged.—*n.* a foreigner: a resident neither native-born nor naturalised: an outsider: a plant introduced by man but maintaining itself.—*v.t.* to alienate: to transfer: to estrange.—*n.* alienabil'ity.—*adj.* a'lienable, capable of being transferred to another.—*n.* a'lienage, state of being an alien.—*v.t.* a'lienate, to transfer: to estrange.—*adj.* withdrawn: estranged.—*ns.* ä'lienātor; aliena'tion, estrangement: insanity: the critical detachment with which, according to Bertolt Brecht, audience and actors should regard a play, considering action and dialogue and the ideas in the drama without emotional involvement.—*adj.* al'iened, made alien: estranged.— *ns.* al'ienee, one to whom property is transferred; al'ienism, the position of being a foreigner: study and treatment of mental diseases; a'lienist, one who specially studies or treats mental diseases; a'lienor (*law*), one who transfers property.—**alienation effect, A-effect,** the effect sought or produced in accordance with Brecht's theory. [L. *aliēnus—alius*, other.]

**alight**, *ə-līt', v.i.* to dismount, descend: to perch, settle: to land: to come to rest: to come by chance (upon something): to fall, strike—*pa.t.* and *pa.p.* alight'ed (or alit'). [O.E. *ālihtan.* See **light** (3).]

**alight**, *ə-līt', adj.* on fire: lighted up. [Prep. **a**, and **light** (1).]

**align, aline,** *ə-līn', v.t.* to regulate by a line: to arrange in line.—*n.* align'ment, aline'ment, a laying out by a line: setting in a line or lines: the ground-plan of a railway or road: a row, as of standing-stones: taking of side, or side taken, politically, etc.—**alignment chart,** a nomogram, esp. one comprising three scales in which a line joining values on two determines a value on the third. [Fr. *aligner*—L. *ad*, to, *lineāre*, line.]

**alike**, *ə-līk', adj.* the same in appearance or

footer *fāte, fär; mē, hûr* (her); *mīne; mōte, för; mūte; mōōn, fōōt; dhen* (then) character.—*adv.* equally. [O.E. *gelic*, combined with O.N. *ālikr*, O.E. *onlic*; see like.]

**aliment**, *al'i-mənt, n.* nourishment: food: provision for maintenance, alimony.—*v.t.* to support, sustain: to provide aliment for.—*adjs.* **alimental** (*-ment'l*), supplying food; **aliment'ary**, pertaining to aliment: nutritive.—*n.* **alimentā'tion.**—*adj.* **aliment'ative.**—*n.* **aliment'iveness**, a phrenologist's word for the instinct to seek food or drink. —**alimentary canal**, the passage from mouth to anus. [L. *alimentum—alĕre*, to nourish.]

**alimony**, *al'i-mən-i, n.* an allowance for support made by a man to a woman pending or after her divorce or legal separation from him. [L. *alimōnia—alĕre*, to nourish.]

**à l'improviste**, *a lē-prō-vēst*, (Fr.) on a sudden: unexpectedly: unawares.

**aline, alinement.** See **align.**

**alineation.** See **allineation.**

**aliped**, *al'i-ped, n.* a wing-footed animal, as the bat. —Also *adj.* wing-footed. [L. *ālipes, -pedis—āla*, wing, *pēs, pedis*, foot.]

**aliphatic**, *al-i-fat'-ik, (chem.) adj.* fatty: belonging to the open-chain class of organic compounds, or methane derivatives—opp. to *aromatic.* [Gr. *aleiphar, aleiphatos*, oil.]

**aliquant**, *al'i-kwənt, adj.* such as will not divide a number without a remainder, thus 5 is an aliquant part of 12. [L. *aliquantum*, somewhat.]

**aliquot**, *al'i-kwot, adj.* such as will divide a number without a remainder. [L. *aliquot*, some, several.]

**Alisma**, *a-liz'ma, n.* the water-plantain genus of monocotyledons, giving name to the family **Alismā'ceae.**—*adj.* **alismā'ceous.** [Gr. *alisma*, water-plantain.]

**alit.** See **alight** (1).

**alive**, *ə-liv', adj.* in life: in vigour: in being: lively: sensitive, cognisant (with *to*).—**alive with**, swarming with; **look alive**, be brisk: hurry up. [O.E. *on life* (dat. of *lif*, life), in life.]

**alizari**, *al-i-zä'rē, n.* levantine madder.—*n.* **alizarin(e)** (*a-liz'ə-rin, -rēn*), the colouring matter of madder root ($C_{14}H_8O_4$), the made synthetically. [Sp. and Fr., prob.—Ar. *al*, the, *'açārah*, juice pressed out.]

**alkahest, alcahest**, *al'kə-hest, n.* the universal solvent of the alchemists. [App. a sham Ar. coinage of Paracelsus.]

**alkali**, *al'kə-li*, or *-lī, (chem.) n.* a substance which in aqueous solution has more hydroxyl ions than hydrogen ions, and has strong basic properties:— *pl.* **al'kali(e)s.**—*adj.* of, pertaining to, containing, forming, an alkali.—*ns.* **alkalesc'ence, alkalesc'- ency.**—*adj.* **alkalesc'ent**, tending to become alkaline: slightly alkaline.—*v.t.* and *v.i.* **al'kalify.** —*adj.* **alkaline** (*-lin, -līn*), having the properties of an alkali: containing much alkali.—*n.* **alkalinity** (*-lin'*), quality of being alkaline: extent to which a solution is alkaline.—*v.t.* **al'kalise, -ize**, to render alkaline.—*n.* **al'kaloid**, any of various nitrogenous organic bases found in plants, having specific physiological action.—*adj.* pertaining to, resembling, alkali.—*ns.* **alkalim'eter**, an instrument for measuring the concentration of alkalies; **alkalim'etry**; **al'kyl** (*-kil*), general name for monovalent hydrocarbon radicals.—**alkali metals**, the univalent metals of first group of periodic system, lithium, sodium, potassium, rubidium, caesium, francium, forming strong basic hydroxides.—**alkaline earth**, an oxide of any of the alkaline earth metals: an alkaline earth metal; **alkaline earth metals**, the bivalent metals of the second group, calcium, strontium, barium, and sometimes magnesium and radium. [Ar. *alqalīy*, the calcined ashes.]

**alkanet**, *al'kə-net, n.* a Mediterranean boraginaceous plant (genus *Alkanna*): a red dye got from its root: extended to various kindred plants (*Anchusa*, etc.). [Sp. *alcaneta*, dim.—Ar. *al-henná*, the henna.]

**Alkoran**, *n.* Same as **Alcoran.**

**alkyd** (resin), *al'kid* (*rez'in*), any of a group of synthetic resins used in paints and protective coatings and in adhesives. [*alkyl* and acid.]

**all**, *öl, adj.* comprising every individual one (e.g. *all men, all roads, all instances*): comprising the whole extent, etc., of (e.g. *all winter*): any whatever: (preceding 'the') as many as there are, or as much as there is (e.g. *all the men, all the cheese*): also used following *pl. pers. pron.*, or sometimes *pl. n.* (e.g. *we all laughed, the guests all came*): the greatest possible (e.g. *with all haste, in all sincerity*): every.—*n.* the whole: everybody: everything: the totality of things—the universe: one's whole possessions (formerly often in *pl.*).—*adv.* wholly: entirely: quite: without limit, infinitely: on all sides: on each side, apiece: even, just (passing into a mere intensive, as in *all on a summer's day*, or almost into a conjunction by omission of *if* or *though*).—In composition, infinite, infinitely: universal: completely: wholly: by all: having all for object.— Possible compounds are without limit: only a selection can be given.—*adj.* **all'-Amer'ican**, representative of the whole of America, esp. in some admirable quality: chosen to represent the United States: consisting entirely of U.S. or American members.—**All Blacks**, New Zealand international rugby team.—*adj.* **all'-building** (*Shak.*), possibly, on which all is built, but prob. a misprint.—*n.* **all-chang'ing-word**, a spell that transforms everything.—*adj.* **all-cheer'ing**, giving cheerfulness to all.—*n.* **all'-clear'**, a signal that the reason for sheltering, or (*fig.*) for inactivity, is past.—*adjs.* **all'-day**, lasting all day; **all-dread'- ed**, dreaded by all; **all'-elec'tric**, using only electricity for heating and lighting; **all-end'ing.** —*n.* **All'-father**, Woden: Zeus: God.—*adj.* **all'- fired**, (*coll.* orig. *U.S.*), infernal (perh. for hell-fired).—*adv.* **all'-firedly.**—*ns.* **all-fives'**, a game of dominoes in which it is sought to make the end pips sum a multiple of five; **all-fours'**, a card game in which there are four chances that score a point (see also four); **all-giv'er** (*Milt.*), the giver of all—God; **all'-good**, the plant Good-King-Henry.—*adj.* **all-good'**, infinitely good.— *interj.* **all-hail**, a greeting, lit. all health.—*n.* a salutation of 'All hail'.—*v.t.* to greet with 'All hail'.—*adj.* (orig. gen. *pl.* of *n.*; *obs.*) **all'-hall'- own, -hall'owen, -holl'own, -hall'ond** (*Shak.* allhollown summer, a spell of fine weather about All Hallows).—*ns.* **All-hall'owmass**, the feast of All Saints; **All-Hall'ows, All Saints' Day; All-hall'owtide**, the season of All-Hallows; **all'heal**, a panacea (*obs.*): the great valerian or other plant; **all-hid'**, hide-and-seek—*adjs.* **all'-night**, lasting all night; **all-obey'ing** (*Shak.*), obeyed by all; **all'-out**, using maximum effort; **all- ō'verish**, having an indefinite sense of indisposition, discomfort, or malaise.—*n.* **all-ō'verishness.** —*adjs.* **all-pow'erful**, supremely powerful: omnipotent; **all'-red'** (*obs.*), exclusively on British territory (from the conventional colouring of maps); **all'-risks'**, (of insurance) covering all risks except a number specifically excluded (as e.g. war risks, damage due to depreciation, etc.); **all'-round'**, including, applying to, all: adequate, complete, or competent on all sides.— *ns.* **all'-round'er**, one who shows ability in many sports, or many kinds of work, etc.; **all'-round'- ness.**—*adj.* **all-rul'ing.**—*n.* **all'seed**, a weed (genus *Radiola*) of the flax family, or other many-seeded plant.—*adj.* **all-see'ing.**—*ns.* **all-sē'er** (*Shak.*), one who sees all—God; **all'spice**, pimento or Jamaica pepper, supposed to combine the flavours of cinnamon, nutmeg, and cloves (see also Calycanthus).—*adjs.* **all'-star'**, having a cast or team all of whom are stars; **all- tell'ing** (*Shak.*); **all'-time**, of all time to date.—

*adv.* **all'-thing** (*Shak.*), every way.—*n., adj.* **all'-up**, (of loaded aircraft) total (weight).—**all'-work**, all kinds of work (esp. domestic).—**after all**, when everything has been considered: in spite of all that: nevertheless; **all along**, everywhere along: all the time; **all and some** (*obs.*), one and all; **all at once**, suddenly; **all but**, everything short of, almost; **All Fools' Day**, the day of making April Fools, 1st April; **All Hallows' Day**, All Saints' Day; **all in**, exhausted; everything included; **all in all**, all things in all respects, all or everything together: that which one is wholly wrapped up in; **all-in wrestling**, wrestling with almost no holds barred as against the rules; **all out**, at full power or speed: completely exhausted; **all over**, everywhere: over the whole of: covered with (*coll.*): thoroughly, entirely: very characteristically; **all over with**, finished, done with, completely at an end with; **all right**, a coll. phrase expressing assent or approbation; **all-round camera**, a camera able to make a strip picture of the whole periphery of an object revolved before it; **All Saints' Day**, 1st November, a festival in honour of the saints collectively; **all's one**, it is just the same; **All Souls' Day**, 2nd November, a R.C. day of prayer for souls in Purgatory; **all there**, completely sane: alert; **all the same** (see **same**); **all-time record**, a record exceeding all others in all times (**all-time high**, low, a high, low, level never before reached); **all to one** (*obs.*), altogether; **all up with**, at an end with: beyond any hope for; **all-wing aeroplane**, an aeroplane with no fuselage, the cabin being in the wings; **and all**, as well as the rest; **and all that**, and all the rest of it, *et cetera*; **at all**, in the least degree: in any way: in any circumstances: used also merely to give emphasis; **be all over a person**, to irk him with too much show of friendliness; **for all**, not withstanding; **for good and all**, finally; **in all**, all told: in total: **once (and) for all**, once and once only, finally; **when all is said and done**, after all: all things considered. [O.E. (Anglian) *all*, (W.S. *eall*): Ger. *all*.]

**alla breve**, äl′lä brā′vä, (*mus.*) in quick common time. [It., according to the breve, there being orig. a breve to the bar.]

**alla cappella**, äl′lä käp-pel′lä. See **a cappella**.

**alla Franca**, äl′-lä frangk′a, (It.) in the French style.

**Allah**, al′ä, *n.* among Mohammedans, God. [Ar. *allāh*—*alilāh*, the God.]

**alla marcia**, äl′lä mär′cha, (*mus.*) in the manner of a march. [It.]

**allantois**, a-lan′tō-is, *n.* a membranous sac-like appendage for effecting oxygenation in the embryos of mammals, birds, and reptiles.—*adjs.* **allanto′ic**; **allan′toid** (-*toid*), sausage-shaped; pertaining to the allantois.—*n.* the allantois. [Irregularly formed from Gr. *allās*, -*āntos*, a sausage, *eidos*, form.]

**alla prima**, äl′lä prē′ma, (It.) a technique of painting in which only one layer of pigment is applied to the surface to complete the canvas.

**alla stoccata**, äl′lä sto-kä′ta, (It.) thrusting with a pointed weapon.

**alla Tedesca**, äl′lä te-des′kä, (It.) in the German style.

**alla vostra salute**, äl′lä vôs′tra sa-lōō′tä, (It.) to your health.

**allay**, earlier **aleye**, **alay**, etc., *ə-lā′*, *v.t.* to put down: to quell: to calm: to alleviate: to abate: to reduce: to alloy.—*v.i.* to abate.—*ns.* **allay′er**; **allay′ing**; **allay′ment**. [O.E. *ālecgan*—pfx. *ā-*, intens., *lecgan*, to lay. This vb. in M.E. became indistinguishable in form in some of its parts from **allay** (2) or **alloy**, and from **allege** (1), and the meanings also overlapped.]

**allay**, *ə-lā′*, *v.t.* to alloy: to mix with something inferior: to dilute: to debase: to abate or de-

tract from the goodness of.—*n.* alloy: alloying: dilution: abatement: impairment. [See **alloy** and the etymological note to **allay** (1).]

**all-be**. See **albe**.

**alledge**. Old spelling of **allege**.

**allée**, *a-lā*, (Fr.) an avenue, a walk or garden-path.

**allege** (*Spens.* **allegge**, **alegge**), *ə-lej′*, *v.t.* to alleviate: to allay.—*n.* **allege′ance** (*ə-lej′əns*; *Spens.* **aleggeaunce**, *a-lej′i-ans*), alleviation. [O.Fr. *aleger*—L. *alleviāre* (see **alleviate**) fused with O.E. *ālecgan* (see **allay** (1)).]

**allege**, *ə-lej′*, *v.t.* to declare in court upon oath (*obs.*): to assert with a view to subsequent proof, hence without proof: to bring forward in argument or plea: to adduce: to cite (*arch.*).—*n.* **allegation** (*al-i-gā′shən*), the act of alleging: that which is alleged: an unproved or unaccepted assertion: citation.—*adj.* **alleged** (*ə-lejd′*).—*adv.* **alleg′edly**. [O.Fr. *esligier*, to clear at law—L. *ex*, from, *litigāre*, to sue.]

**allegiance**, *ə-lē′jəns*, *n.* the relation or obligation of liegeman to liege-lord or of subject to sovereign or state: loyalty (to a person or cause).—*adj.* (*Shak.*) **alle′giant**. [L. *ad*, to, and **liege**.]

**allegory**, *al′i-gər-i*, *n.* a narrative to be understood symbolically: symbolical narration.—*adjs.* **allegoric** (-*gor′ik*), **-al**.—*adv.* **allegor′ically**.—*v.t.* **all′egorise, -ize**, to put in form of an allegory: to treat as allegory.—*v.t.* to use allegory.—*ns.* **allegorisā′tion**, **-z-**; **all′egoriser**, **-z-**; **all′egorist**. [Gr. *allēgoriā*—*allos*, other, *agoreuein*, to speak.]

**allegro**, *a-lā′grō* (It. *äl-lā′grō*), (*mus.*) *adv., adj.* with brisk movement.—*n.* an allegro piece or movement.—*adv.* and *adj.* **allegret′to**, somewhat brisk. [It.,—L. *alacer*, brisk.]

**allele**, *al-ēl′*, *n.* a shortened form of **allelomorph** (*al-ēl′ō-mörf*). either of a pair of alternative characters inherited according to Mendelian law: a gene considered as the means of transmission of an allele.—*adj.* **allelomor′phic**.—*n.* **allelomor′phism**. [Gr. *allēlōn*, of one another, *morphē*, form.]

**alleluia**, **alleluiah**, *al-i-lōō′yä*. Same as **hallelujah**.

**allemande**, *al′(i-)mand*, *al-mäd*, *n.* a smooth-running suite movement of moderate tempo, in common time, coming after the prelude (of German origin): a Swabian dance in triple time: a German dance in 2-4 time: a movement affecting change of order in a dance. [Fr. *allemande* (*fem.*), German.]

**allenarly**, *al-en′ər-li*, (*obs. except in Scots law*) *adv.* solely, only. [**all**, **anerly**.]

**allergy**, *al′ər-ji*, *n.* an altered or acquired state of sensitivity: abnormal reaction of the body to substances normally harmless: hypersensitivity to certain antigens or other exciting substances: (*coll.*) antipathy.—*n.* **all′ergen**, any substance that induces an allergic reaction.—*adj.* **allergic** (*ə-lûr′jik*). [Gr. *allos*, other, *ergon*, work.]

**allerion**. See **alerion**.

**alleviate**, *ə-lēv′i-āt*, *v.t.* to make light: to mitigate.—*ns.* **allēviā′tion**; **allēv′iātor**. [L.L. *alleviāre*, *-ātum*—L. *ad*, to, *levis*, light.]

**alley**, *al′i*, *n.* a walk in a garden or shrubbery: a passage: a narrow lane: a back-lane: a long narrow enclosure, or rink, for bowls or skittles.—*pl.* **all′eys**.—*adj.* **alleyed** (*al′id*), having alleys or the form of an alley.—*n.* **all′eyway**, a narrow passage: a corridor. [O.Fr. *alee* (Fr. *allée*), a passage, from *aller*, to go.]

**alley**, **ally**, *al′i*, *n.* a choice taw or large marble.—*n.* **all′(e)y-taw′**, **-tor′**. [Prob. originally of **alabaster**.]

**allez-vous-en**, *a-lā-vōō-zä*, (Fr.) away with you: begone.

**allheal**. See **all**.

**alliaceous**, *al-i-ā′shəs*, *adj.* garlic-like. [L. *allium*, garlic.]

**alliance**. See **ally**.

*fāte, fär; mē, hûr* (her); *mīne; mōte, för; mūte; mōōn, fŏŏt; dhen* (then)

**allice, allis,** *al'is, n.* a species of shad.—Also **allis shad.** [L. *alōsa, alausa,* shad.]
**allicholy,** *allycholly, al'i-kol-i, (Shak.) n.* and *adj.* jocularly, for melancholy.
**alligate,** *al'i-gāt, v.t.* to conjoin: to perform alligation.—*n.* **alligation** (-gā'shən), binding together: conjunction: calculation of values or properties of a mixture (*arith.*). [L. *alligāre,* -*ātum*—*ad,* to, and *ligāre,* to bind.]
**alligator,** *al'i-gā-tər,* earlier **al(l)igarta,** -*gär'tə, n.* a reptile of a mainly American family differing from crocodiles in the broader snout and other characters.—**alligator apple,** a fruit and tree of the custard-apple genus; **alligator pear** (see **avocado**). [Sp. *el,* the (L. *ille*), *lagarto,* lizard (L. *lacertus*).]
**allineation, alineation,** *a-lin-i-ā'shən, n.* position in a straight line: alignment. [L. *ad,* to, *lineāre,* -*ātum,* to draw a line—*linea,* line.]
**alliteration,** *ə-* or *a-lit-ər-ā'shən, n.* the recurrence of the same initial sound (not necessarily letter) in words in close succession, as 'Sing a Song of Sixpence': head-rhyme—the characteristic structure of versification of O.E. and other old Gmc. languages, each line having three accented syllables (two in the first half) with the same initial consonant, or with different initial vowels.—*v.i.* **allit'erate,** to begin with the same sound: to constitute alliteration: to practise alliteration.—*adj.* **allit'erative.** [L. *ad,* to, and *litera, littera,* a letter.]
**allo-,** in composition, other, as **alloch(e)iria** (-*ki'ri- a,* -*ki'*; Gr. *cheir,* hand), attribution of a sensation to the wrong part of the body, e.g. to the other hand when one is painful: denoting one of a group constituting a structural unit, as **all'omorph,** -*mörf,* one of two or more forms of the same morpheme; **all'ophone,** -*fōn,* one of two or more forms of the same phoneme; different, from outside, as **all'oplasm** (*n.*), protoplasm differentiated to perform a special function, **alloplas'tic** (*adj.*), affected by, or affecting, external factors. [Gr. *allos,* other.]
**allocarpy,** *al'ō-kär-pi, (bot.) n.* fruiting after cross-fertilisation. [Gr. *karpos,* fruit.]
**allocate,** *al'ō-kāt, al'ə-kāt, v.t.* to place: to locate: to apportion.—*n.* **alloca'tion,** act of allocating: a share allocated: allotment: apportionment: an allowance made upon an account. [L. *allocāre* —*ad,* to, *locāre,* -*ātum,* to place—*locus,* a place.]
**alloch(e)iria.** See **allo-.**
**allocution,** *al-ō-kū'shən, n.* an exhortation, esp. (*Roman hist.*) of a general to his troops: a formal address, esp. of the Pope to the cardinals. [L. *allocūtiō,* -*ōnis*—*ad,* to, and *loqui, locūtus,* to speak.]
**al(l)odium,** *a-lō'di-əm, n.* an estate not subject to a feudal superior.—Also **a(l)lod** (*al'od*).—*adj.* **al(l)ō'dial**—opp. to *feudal.* [L.L. *allōdium,* from a Gmc. word meaning complete ownership; cf. **all** and O.E. *ēad,* wealth, prosperity.]
**allogamy,** *al-og'ə-mi, (bot.) n.* cross-fertilisation.— *adj.* **allog'amous.** [Gr. *allos,* other, *gamos,* marriage.]
**allograph,** *al'ō-gräf, n.* a writing made by one person on behalf of another. [Gr. *graphē,* writing.]
**alloiostrophos,** *a-loi-os'tro-fos,* (Gr.) irregularly divided, not in alternate strophe and antistrophe.
**allomorph.** See **allo-.**
**allonge,** *al-ōzh, n.* piece of paper attached to bill of exchange for further endorsements. [Fr.]
**allons,** *a-lõ,* (Fr.) let us go: come on: come.
**allopathy,** *al-op'ə-thi, n.* orthodox medical practice, treatment of diseases by drugs, etc., whose effect on the body is the opposite of that of the disease, distinguished from *homoeopathy.*—*n.* **all'ōpath.**—*adi.* **allopathic** (*al-ō-path'ik*).—*n.* **allöp'athist.** [Ger. *allopathie,* coined by Hahne-

**mann** (1755-1843)—Gr. *allos,* other, *pathos,* suffering.]
**allophone, alloplasm, alloplastic.** See **allo-.**
**allot,** *ə-lot', v.t.* to divide as by lot: to distribute in portions: to parcel out: to assign:—*pr.p.* **allott'ing;** *pa.t.* and *pa.p.* **allott'ed.**—*ns.* **allot'-ment,** act of allotting: part or share allotted: a portion of a field assigned to a cottager to labour for himself: a piece of ground let out for spare-time cultivation under a public scheme; **allott'-ery** (*Shak.*), a share allotted. [O.Fr. *aloter*—à, to, and the Gmc. root of **lot.**]
**allotriomorphic,** *a-lot-ri-ō-mör'fik, adj.* crystalline in internal structure but not in outward form. [Gr. *allotrios,* alien, *morphē,* form.]
**allotropy,** *al-ot'rə-pi, n.* the property (esp. in chemical elements, as carbon) of existing in more than one form.—*n.* **allotrope** (*al'ə-trōp*), an allotropic form.—*adj.* **allotrop'ic.**—*n.* **allot'ro-pism.**—*adj.* **allot'ropous,** having nectar accessible to all kinds of insects (*bot.*): of insects, short-tongued, as visiting allotropous flowers. [Gr. *allos,* other, and *tropos,* turn, habit.]
**allow,** *ə-low', v.t.* to praise (*obs.*): to pass, sanction, accept (*arch.*): to concede: to conclude, hence to assert (*U.S.*): to permit: to indulge (*Shak.*): to accord as due: to assign: to grant or give, esp. periodically: to abate: to assume as an element in calculation or as something to be taken into account.—*v.i.* to admit (with *of*): to make allowance (with *for*).—*adj.* **allow'able,** that may be allowed: permissible: excusable.— *n.* **allow'ableness.**—*adv.* **allow'ably.**—*n.* **allow'-ance,** that which is allowed: approbation (*arch.*): admission, acknowledgment, permission (*Shak.*): a limited portion or amount allowed, allotted, granted: a ration or stint: money allowed to meet expenses or in consideration of special conditions: abatement: a sum periodically granted: a taking into account in calculation or excuse.— *v.t.* to put upon an allowance: to supply in limited quantities.—*adj.* **allowed',** permitted: licensed: acknowledged.—*adv.* **allow'edly.** [O. Fr. *alouer,* to praise, bestow, of double origin: (1) L. *allaudāre*—*ad,* to, *laudāre,* to praise; (2) L. *ad, locāre,* to place.]
**alloy,** *al'oi, ə-loi', n.* a mixture of metals: extended to a mixture of metal with non-metal: the baser ingredient in such a mixture (esp. in gold or silver): any admixture that impairs or debases: fineness, standard, of gold or silver.—*v.t.* to mix (metal): to mix with a less valuable metal: to impair or debase by being present: to temper, qualify.—*v.i.* to become alloyed. [Fr. *aloi* (n.), *aloyer* (vb.)—O.Fr. *alei, aleier*—L. *alligāre*—*ad,* to, *ligāre,* to bind; **allay** (2) is from the corresponding Norm. Fr. *alai,* confused with **allay** (1).]
**allspice.** See under **all.**
**all-to, alto,** also **all to,** *öl'tōō,* a spurious *adv.* and *pfx.* arising from the wrong division of **all** and a word with the pfx. *to-,* asunder, as **allto brake, all to brake** for **all tobrake:** hence, altogether, as **altoruffled** (*Milt.* **all to ruffl'd**).
**allude,** *ə-lōōd', -lūd', v.i.* to convey an indirect reference in passing: to refer without explicit mention, or with suggestion of further associations: to refer.—*n.* **allu'sion** (-*zhən*), indirect reference.—*adj.* **allu'sive** (-*siv*), alluding: hinting: referring indirectly: canting (*her.*).—*adv.* **allu'sively.**—*n.* **allu'siveness.** [L. *allūdēre*—*ad,* *lūdēre, lūsum,* to play.]
**allure,** *ə-lūr', -lōōr', v.t.* to draw on as by a lure: to entice.—*n.* **allure';** **allure'ment.**—*adj.* **allur'-ing.**—*adv.* **allur'ingly.** [O.Fr. *alurer*—à, to, *lurer,* to lure.]
**allure,** *a-lür,* (Fr.) mien, gait, air.
**allusion, etc.** See **allude.**
**alluvion,** *ə-lōō'vi-ən, -lū', n.* land gradually gained from a river or the sea by the washing up of sand

and earth: a flood: alluvium. [L. *alluviō*, *-ōnis*. See alluvium.]

alluvium, *ə-lōō'vi-əm*, *-lū'*, *n.* matter transported in suspension and deposited by rivers or floods: —*pl.* allu'via.—*adj.* allu'vial. [L. neut. of *alluvius*, washed up—*ad*, to, *luĕre*, to wash.]

ally, *ə-lī'*, *v.t.* to join in relation of marriage, friendship, treaty, co-operation, or assimilation:—*pr.p.* ally'ing; *pa.t.* and *pa.p.* allied'.—*n.* a'lly (formerly, and still by some, *ə-lī'*), a member of or party to an alliance: a state or sovereign joined in league for co-operation in a common purpose: anything that co-operates or helps: a kinsman (*Shak.*): anything near to another in classification or nature:—*pl.* a'llies (or *-līz'*).—*n.* alli'ance, state of being allied: union, or combination by marriage, treaty, etc.: kinship: a group of allies or kindred: a subclass or group of families (*bot.*).—*adj.* a'llied (or *-līd'*). [O.Fr. *alier*—L. *alligāre*; see alligate.]

ally, ally-taw. See alley (2).

allyl, *al'il*, (*chem.*) *n.* an organic radical ($C_3H_5$) whose sulphide is found in oil of garlic. [L. *allium*, garlic, and Gr. *hýlē*, matter.]

alma, almah, *al'ma*, *n.* an Egyptian dancing-girl. —Also al'me, al'meh (*-me*). [Ar. '*almah*, learned (in dancing and music)—'*alama*, to know.]

alma, *al'mä*, (It.) soul, essence.

almacantar, almucantar, *al-mə-kan'tər*, *-mū-*, *n.* a circle of altitude, parallel to the horizon: an instrument for determining a star's passage across an almacantar. [Ar. *almuqantarāt*, the sundials—*al*, the, *qantarah*, bridge.]

Almagest, *al'mə-jest*, *n.* a great treatise by the Alexandrian astronomer Ptolemy (*c.* A.D. 150): extended to other great works. [Ar. *al-majistē*—*al*, the, Gr. *megistē* (*syntaxis*), greatest (systematic treatise).]

Almain, *al'mān*, (*obs.*) *n.* and *adj.* German.—*ns.* al'main, the allemande (suite movement, or leaping dance); Al'maine, Al'many, Al'emaine, Germany. [Fr. *allemand*, German, *Allemagne*, Germany—L. *Alamanni*, a people of South-west Germany.]

alma mater, *al'ma mä'tər*, *mä'ter*, (L.) benign mother—applied by alumni to their university.

almanac, *öl'mə-nak*, *n.* a register of the days, weeks, and months of the year, with astronomical events, anniversaries, etc. [App. from an Ar. word *al-manākh*.]

almandine, *al'man-dīn*, *-dēn*, earlier alaban'dine, *n.* precious (red iron-alumina) garnet. [L.L. *alabandina*—*Alabanda*, a town in Caria, where it was found.]

alme, almeh. See alma (1).

almery. See ambry.

almighty, *öl-mīt'i*, *adj.* omnipotent: irresistible: invincible: mighty.—Also *adv.*—the Almighty, God; the almighty dollar (Washington Irving), money, esp. as all-powerful. [O.E. *ælmihtig*.]

almirah, *al-mīr'a*, *n.* a cupboard, wardrobe, cabinet. [Hindi *almārī*—Port. *almario*—L. *armārium*; see ambry.]

almond, *ä'mənd*, *n.* the fruit, and esp. the kernel, of a tree akin to the peach, with a dry husk instead of flesh: anything of the shape of an almond (an ellipse pointed at one end), as a tonsil, a rock-crystal ornament.—*adj.* al'mond-eyed', with apparently almond-shaped eyes.— al'mond-bloss'om; al'mond-oil'; al'mond-tree. [O.Fr. *almande* (Fr. *amande*)—L. *amygdala*—Gr. *amygdalē*.]

almoner, *ä'mən-ər*, *al'mən-ər*, *n.* a distributor or (*arch.*) giver of alms: a medical social worker attached to a hospital (no longer official title).— *n.* al'monry, a place of distribution of alms. [O.Fr. *aumoner*, *aumonier* (Fr. *aumônier*)—L.L. *eleēmosynārius* (adj.). See alms.]

almost, *öl'mōst*, *-məst*, *adv.* very nearly. [all, most (in sense of nearly).]

almous. Same as awmous.

alms, *ämz*, *n. sing.* and *pl.* relief given out of pity to the poor: a good or charitable deed (*obs.*).— alms'-deed, a charitable deed; alms'-dish, a dish for receiving alms; alms'-drink, leavings of drink (*Shak.*); alms'-fee, Peter's pence; alms'-folk, people supported by alms; alms'-house, a house endowed for the support and lodging of the poor; alms'-man, a man who lives by alms; alms'-woman. [O.E. *ælmysse*, through L.L. from Gr. *eleēmosynē*—*eleos*, compassion; see also awmous.]

almucantar. See almacantar.

almug, *al'mug*, (*B.*) *n.* algum. [Heb. *almūg*, prob. for *algūm*.]

alnage, *öl'nij*, *n.* measurement by the ell: inspection of cloth.—*n.* al'nager, an official inspector of cloth. [O.Fr. *aulnage*—*aulne*, ell.]

alodium, alod, alodial. Same as allodium, allod, allodial.

Aloe, *al'ō-ē*, *n.* a liliaceous genus, mainly South African, mostly trees and shrubs.—*n.* (without *cap.*; *al'ō*), any member of the genus; extended to the so-called American aloe (see Agave), also (often *pl.*) to aloes-wood or its resin: (usu. in *pl.* form but treated as *sing.*) a bitter purgative drug, the inspissated juice of the leaves of various species of Aloe.—*adj.* aloed (*al'ōd*), planted, shaded, mixed, flavoured, with aloes.—al'oes-wood, the heart-wood of eaglewood.—*adj.* aloet'ic.—*n.* a medicine containing a great proportion of aloes. [Directly and through O.E. *aluwan*, *alewan* (pl.).—L. *aloē*—Gr. *aloē*; the application to eaglewood comes from the Septuagint translation of Heb. *ahālim*, *ahālōth*, agalloch.]

aloft, *ə-loft'*, *-löft'*, *adv.* on high: overhead: above: on the top: high up: up the mast: in or to heaven.—*prep.* (*Shak.*) on the top of. [O.N. *ā lopt* (pron. *loft*), of motion; *ā lopti*, of position—*ā*, on, in, to, *lopt* (see loft).]

alogia, *ə-lōj'ē-a*, *n.* inability to speak, due to brain lesion. [Gr. *a-*, priv., and *logos*, speech.]

alogical, *a-loj'i-kl*, or *ā-*, *adj.* outside the domain of logic. [Gr. *a-*, priv., and logical.]

aloha, *ä-lō'a*, *-lō'hä*, *n.* love: kindness.—*interj.* greetings: farewell. [Hawaiian.]

alone, *ə-lōn'*, *adj.* single: solitary: unaccompanied: without any other: by oneself: unique. —*adv.* singly.—*adv.* alone'ly (*obs.* or *arch.*).—*n.* alone'ness. [all and one.]

along, *ə-long'*, *adv.* by or through the length: lengthwise: at full length: throughout: onward: together, in company or conjunction.— *prep.* lengthwise by, through, or over: by the side of.—*adj.* alongshore' (see longshore).—*n.* alongshore'man.—*prep.* and *adv.* along'side, beside: side by side (with): close to the side (of). [O.E. *andlang*—pfx. *and-*, against, and *lang*, long.]

along, *ə-long'*, (*arch.* and *dial.*) *adj.* on account (of, on). [O.E. *gelang*; see long (1).]

alongst, *ə-longst'*, (*obs.* and *dial.*) *adv.* and *prep.* along: by the length (of). [O.E. *andlanges*— *andlang*, along, with adv. gen. ending *-es* and *-t* as in amidst, betwixt, etc.]

aloof, *ə-lōōf'*, *adv.* to windward (*obs.*): some way off (from): apart: with avoidance or detachment: without participation: with reserve suggesting consciousness of superiority.—*adj.* distant, withdrawn.—*prep.* (*Milt.*) aloof from. —*adv.* aloof'ly.—*n.* aloof'ness. [Prep. a, and loof (luff).]

alopecia, *al-ō-pē'si-a*, *-sh*(*y*)*a*, *n.* baldness.—*adj.* alopecoid (*al-ō-pē'koid*, *al-op'i-koid*), fox-like.— alopecia areata (*ar-ē-ā'ta*, *ar-ē-ä'ta*), baldness occurring in patches on the scalp, possibly caused by a nervous disturbance. [Gr. *alōpekiā*,

fox-mange, a bald spot, *alōpekoeidēs*, fox-like—
*alōpēx*, fox.]
**aloud**, *ə-lowd'*, *adv.* loudly: audibly. [Prep. a,
and loud.]
**à l'outrance**, *a lōo-träs*, erroneously for **à outrance** (Fr.).
**alow**, *ə-lō'*, (*naut.*) *adv.* to a lower position: in
the lower part of a ship. [Prep. a, and low.]
**alow(e)**, *ə-low'*, (*Scot.*) *adv.* ablaze. [Prep. a, and
low (flame).]
**alp**, *alp*, *n.* a high mountain: a mountain pasture:
—(*pl.*; *cap.*) specially applied to the lofty ranges
of Switzerland and neighbouring countries.—*ns.*
**alp'enhorn**, **alp'horn**, a long powerful horn, of
wood and bark, used chiefly by Alpine cowherds;
**alp'enstock**, a mountain traveller's long spiked
staff.—*adj.* **Alp'ine**, **alp'ine** (-*in*), of the Alps or
other mountains: growing on mountain tops.—
*n.* an alpine plant: a member of the Alpine
race.—*ns.* **alp'inism** (-*in*-), the art or practice of
mountain climbing; **alp'inist**.—**Alpine race**, one
of the principal races of white men, characterised
by broad head, sallow skin, moderate stature.
[L. *Alpēs*, the Alps; perh. Celtic.]
**alpaca**, *al-pak'ə*, *n.* a domesticated animal akin
to the llama: cloth made of its long silken wool.
[Sp., prob. from Quichua.]
**alpargata**, *äl-pär-gä'tä*, *n.* a light sandal with rope
or hemp sole. [Sp.]
**al pasto**, *al päs'tō*, (It.) according to a fixed rate
(said of meals in a restaurant).
**alpeen**, *al'pēn*, *n.* a cudgel. [Ir. *ailpín*.]
**alpha**, *al'fə*, *n.* the first letter of the Greek alphabet
(A, α): the first or brightest star of a constellation: the beginning: as an ancient Greek
numeral α′ = 1, ,α = 1000.—*adjs.* **alpha(nu)-
meric**, **-al**, consisting of, or (of a machine)
using, both letters and numbers; **alpha particle**,
a helium nucleus given off by radioactive substances; **alpha rays**, streams of alpha particles.
—**alpha and omega**, beginning and end. [Gr.
*alpha*—Heb. *āleph*. See aleph, A.]
**alphabet**, *al'fə-bit*, *-bet*, *n.* a system of letters, esp.
arranged in conventional order: first elements:
an index (*obs.*).—*v.t.* (*U.S.*) to arrange alphabetically.—*n.* **alphabetä'rian**, one learning his
alphabet, a beginner: a student of alphabets.—
*adjs.* **alphabet'ic**, **-al**, relating to or in the order
of an alphabet; **alphabet'iform**, shaped like
letters.—*adv.* **alphabet'ically**.—*v.t.* **al'phabetise**,
**-ize**, to arrange alphabetically. [Gr. *alphabētos*
—*alpha*, *bēta*, the first two Greek letters.]
**Alphonsine**, *al-fon'sin*, *-zin*, *adj.* of Alphonso X
(the Wise), king of Castile, or his planetary
tables, completed in 1252.
**Alpini**, *äl-pē'nē*, *n.pl.* Italian troops for mountain
warfare:—*sing.* **Alpi'no**. [It., Alpine.]
**al più**, *al pū*, (It.) at most.
**already**, *öl-red'i*, *adv.* previously, or by the time
in question. [all, ready.]
**alright**, an unaccepted spelling of **all right**.
**als**, *äls*, *öls*, an old form of **also, as**.
**Alsatia**, *al-sā'sh(y)ə*, *n.* a district long disputed by
Germany and France—Alsace or Elsass: cant
name for the sanctuary (till 1697) for debtors
and criminals at Whitefriars, London.—*adj.*
**Alsa'tian**, of Alsatia in either sense: officially
chosen to apply to a German sheep-dog of wolf-
like breed, often used by police and security
officers because of its strength and fierceness (in
U.S. German Shepherd dog, German Police dog).
—Also *n.*
**alsike**, *al'sik*, *n.* a white or pink-flowered clover.
[From *Alsike*, near Uppsala, a habitat.]
**also**, *öl'sō*, *adv.* likewise: further.—*n.* **al'so-ran**,
a horse that *also ran* in a race but did not get a
'place': a person of like degree of importance.
[O.E. *all* (W.S. *eall*) *swā*, all so.]
**alsoon(e)**, *al-sōōn'*, (*Spens.*) *adv.* as soon. [as,
soon.]

**Alstroemeria**, *al-strə-mē'ri-a*, *n.* a South American
genus of amaryllids with inverted leaves. [C.
*Alströmer*, 18th-cent. Swedish botanist.]
**alt**, *alt*, *n.* a high tone, in voice or instrument.—
**in alt**, in the octave above the treble stave beginning with G: in an exalted and high-flown mood
(*fig.*). [L. *altus*, high.]
**alt**, *alt*, (*Milt.*) *n.* halt, rest. [Fr. *alte* or Sp. *alto*—
Ger. *halt*.]
**Altair**, *äl-tä'ir*, *n.* a first-magnitude star in the
constellation Aquila. [Ar. *al ta'ir*, the bird.]
**altaltissimo**, *alt-al-tis'i-mō*, *n.* the very highest
summit. [Reduplicated compound of It. *alto*,
high, and *altissimo*, highest.]
**alta moda**, *al'ta mo'da*, (It.) high fashion, the art
of designing and making exclusive, fashionable
clothes.
**altar**, *ölt'ər*, *n.* block or table for making sacrifices
on: table used for mass or the eucharist (by
those who regard it as a sacrifice): sometimes,
without such implication, the communion table:
a scene of worship or marriage ceremony (*fig.*):
a ledge on a dry-dock wall.—*ns.* **alt'arage**,
offerings made upon the altar during the offertory, provided for the maintenance of the priest;
**alt'ar-cloth**, the covering of the altar, often used
as including the frontal and the superfrontal;
**al'tarpiece**, a work of art placed above and
behind an altar:—*n.pl.* **alt'ar-rails**, rails separating the sacrarium from the rest of the chancel.—
*ns.* **alt'ar-stone**, a stone serving as an altar: a
consecrated slab forming, or inserted in, the top
of an altar; **al'tar-tomb**, a monumental memorial, in form like an altar, often with a canopy.—
*adv.* **alt'arwise**, in the position of an altar—
north and south, at the upper end of the chancel.
—**family altar**, the symbol or place of family
worship; **high altar**, the principal altar; **lead to
the altar**, to marry (a woman). [L. *altāre—altus*,
high.]
**altazimuth**, *alt-az'i-məth*, *n.* an instrument devised
by Airy for determining *alt*itude and *azimuth*.
**alter**, *öl'tər*, *v.t.* to make different: to modify: to
castrate.—*v.i.* to become different.—*n.* **alter-
abil'ity**.—*adjs.* **al'terable**; **al'terant**, altering:
having the power of producing changes.—*n.* an
alterative.—*n.* **alterä'tion**.—*adj.* **al'terātive**,
having power to alter.—*n.* a medicine that makes
a change in the vital functions.—*p.adj.* **al'tered**,
(of a rock) changed in mineral composition by
natural forces.—*n.* **alterity** (*öl-*, *al-ter'i-ti*),
otherness. [L. *alter*, one of two, the other of
two, from the root of *alius*, other, and the old
comp. suff. *-ter*.]
**alter**, *al'tər*, *öl'*, *n.* another person as a conception
in one's mind.—**alter ego**, *al'ter eg'ō*, *öl'tər
ē'gō*, one's second self (see second). [L., other.]
**altercate**, *öl'tər-kät*, *v.i.* to bandy words, wrangle.
—*n.* **alterca'tion**.—*adj.* **tercātive**. [L. *alter-
cārī*, *-ātus—alter*, other.]
**altern**, *öl-*, *al-tûrn'*, *adj.* alternate.—*adv.* **alternately**. [L. *alternus*.]
**alternat**, *al-ter-na*, (Fr.) the diplomatic practice of
determining precedence among powers of equal
rank by lot or of otherwise avoiding the difficulty.
**alternate**, *öl'tər-nāt*, also *al'*, formerly (as *Milt.*)
*-tûr'*, *v.t.* to cause to follow by turns or one after
the other (prop. of two things).—*v.i.* to follow or
interchange with each other (prop. of two
things): to happen by turns, change by turns.—
*n.* deputy, substitute: alternative.—*adj.* **alter'-
nate** (-*tûr'*; in U.S. *öl'*), arranged or coming one
after the other by turns: every other or second:
of leaves, placed singly with change of side at
each node: (of floral whorls, each occupying, in
ground plan, the spaces of the next.—*adv.*
**alter'nately**.—*ns.* **alter'nance** (or *al'*-) alternation; **alter'nant** (or *al'*-), a spelling or sound
variant that does not affect meaning (allomorph
or allophone): a type of determinant (*math.*).—

*adj.* **al′ternāting.**—*ns.* **alternā′tion,** the act of alternating: alternate succession: interchange: reading or singing antiphonally; **alter′native** (*-nə-tiv*), a pair (loosely a set) of possibilities (esp. of choice) excluding all others: a choice between them: one of them, esp. other than the one in question.—*adj.* possible as an alternative: disjunctive: alternate (*obs.*).—*adv.* **alter′natively,** with an alternative: by way of alternative.—*n.* **alt′ernātor,** a generator of alternating current.— **alternating current,** an electric current that periodically reverses its direction; **alternative vote,** a system of voting whereby, if an elector's favourite candidate is out of the running, his vote is transferred to the candidate he has marked next in order of preference.—**alternation of generations** (*biol.*), the occurrence in a life-cycle of two or more different forms in successive generations, the offspring being unlike the parents, and commonly reproducing by a different method. [L. *alternāre, -ātum*—*alter,* one or other of two.]

**alternatim,** *öl-tər-nā′təm,* (*mus.*) *adv.* alternately. [L. *alternātim.*]

**alterne,** *al-tûrn′, n.* one of two or more plant communities adjoining but differing greatly. [Fr. *alterne,* alternate—L. *alternus.*]

**alternis vicibus,** *al′tûr′nis vi′si-bus, al-ter′nēs vē′ki-boōs, wē′,* (L.) alternately.

**alterum tantum,** *al′tə-rum tan′tum, al′te-roōm tan′toōm,* (L.) as much more.

**altesse,** *al-tes,* (Fr.), **alteza,** *al-tā′tha,* (Sp.) **altezza,** *al-tet′sa,* (It.) highness.

**Althaea,** *al-thē′ə, n.* the marsh-mallow and hollyhock genus. [Gr. *althaiā,* marsh-mallow.]

**Althing,** *öl′thing, n.* the Icelandic parliament. [O.N. and Icel.]

**althorn,** *alt′hörn, n.* a tenor saxhorn. [alt (1).]

**although,** *öl-dhō′, conj.* though (esp., but not necessarily, in stating matter of fact). [all, though.]

**altimeter,** *al-tim′i-tər, n.* instrument for measuring heights, by means of differences in atmospheric pressure, or (*radio altimeter*) by means of time taken for radio wave from an aircraft to be reflected back, calculation of height being also made by noting change in frequency using the Doppler effect. [L. *altus,* high, and **meter.**]

**altisonant,** *al-tis′ən-ənt, adj.* high-sounding. [L. *altus,* high, *sonāns, -antis,* pr.p. *sonāre,* sound.]

**altissimo,** *al-tis′(s)i-mō, (mus.) adj.* very high.—in **altissimo,** in second octave above treble stave, beginning with G. [It., superl. of *alto,* high.]

**altitonant,** *al-tit′ən-ənt, adj.* thundering on high or loudly. [L. *altus,* high, *tonāns, -antis,* pr.p. of *tonāre,* to thunder.]

**altitude,** *al′ti-tūd, n.* height: angle of elevation above the horizon: perpendicular from vertex upon base: high rank or eminence: a high point or position: (in *pl.*) exalted mood, passion, or manner.—*adj.* **altitūd′inal,** pertaining to altitude: found at high level.—*n.* **altitūdinā′rian,** one given to loftiness in doctrine or belief.—Also *adj.*—*adj.* **altitūd′inous,** high. [L. *altitūdō, -inis,* —*altus,* high.]

**alto,** *al′tō, (mus.) n.* prop. counter-tenor, the highest male voice: extended to contralto, the lowest female voice: the part sung by a counter-tenor or contralto: the possessor of a counter-tenor or contralto voice: a viola:—*pl.* **al′tos.**—Also *adj.* [It.,—L. *altus,* high.]

**altogether,** *öl-too-gedh′ər,* or *-tə-, adv.* all together (*obs.* or by confusion): wholly: completely: without exception: in total: all things considered.—**for altogether,** for all time, for good and all; **the altogether** (*coll.*), the nude. [all and together.]

**alto-rilievo,** *äl′tō-rēl-yä′vō, n.* high relief: figures projected by at least half their thickness from the background on which they are sculptured.—

Partly anglicised as **al′to-relie′vo** (*al-tō-ri-lē′vō*). [It. See **relief.**]

**altrices,** *al-trī′sēz, n.pl.* birds whose young are hatched very immature and have to be fed in the nest by the parents.—*adj.* **altricial** (*-trish′l*). [L. *altricēs* (pl. of *altrix*), feeders, nurses.]

**altruism,** *al′troō-izm, n.* the principle of living and acting for the interest of others.—*n.* **al′truist.**— *adj.* **altruist′ic.**—*adv.* **altruist′ically.** [Fr. *altruisme,* formed by Comte from It. *altrui,* someone else—L. *alteri huic,* to this other.]

**altum silentium,** *al′tum si-len′sh(y)um, al′toōm si-len′ti-oōm,* (L.) profound silence.

**aludel,** *al′oō-dəl, -ū-, n.* a pear-shaped pot used in sublimation. [Sp.,—Ar. *al-uthāl.*]

**alula,** *al′ū-la, n.* the bastard-wing. [L. dim. of *āla,* wing.]

**alum,** *al′əm, n.* double sulphate of aluminium and potassium, with 24 molecules of water, crystallising in transparent octahedra: any like compound of a trivalent metal (especially aluminium) and a univalent metal or radical.—*ns.* **alumina** (*ə-lū′* or *ə-loō′mi-na*), oxide of aluminium; **alu′minate,** a salt whose acid is aluminium hydroxide.—*adj.* **aluminif′erous,** alum-bearing.— *v.t.* **alum′inise, -ize,** to treat (a metal) so as to form an aluminium alloy on its surface: to coat (e.g. glass) with aluminium.—*n.* **alumin′ium** (*al-ū-* or *al-oō-*), a remarkably light silvery metal (at. numb. 13), first named (though not then isolated) by Sir Humphry Davy **alu′mium,** then (as still *U.S.*) **alum′inum.**—*adj.* **alu′minous,** of the nature of, or containing, alum or alumina; **al′umish,** having the character or taste of alum.— **aluminium bronze,** an alloy of aluminium and copper, of lighter weight than gold, but like it in colour; **al′um-root,** an American plant of the saxifrage family with astringent root; **al′um-shale, -slate,** a slate consisting mainly of clay, iron pyrites, and coaly matter, from which alum is obtained: **al′um-stone,** alunite. [L. *alūmen, -inis,* alum.]

**alumnus,** *al-um′nəs, n.* a former pupil or student:—*pl.* **alum′ni:**—*fem.* **alum′na** (*pl.* **alum′nae, -nē**). [L., foster-son, pupil—*alēre,* to nourish.]

**alunite,** *al′ū-nit, -oō-, n.* alum-stone, a hydrous sulphate of aluminium and potassium. [Fr. *alun,* alum.]

**alure,** *al′yər, (obs.) n.* a walk behind battlements: a gallery: a passage. [O.Fr. *aleure*—*aller,* to go.]

**alveary,** *al′vi-ər-i, n.* a beehive: a name given to an early dictionary of English, French, Greek and Latin: the hollow of the external ear, where wax collects (*anat.*).—*adj.* **al′veated,** vaulted, like a beehive. [L. *alveārium,* beehive—*alveus,* a hollow.]

**alveolus,** *al-vē′ə-las, al′vi-, n.* a pit or small depression; a tooth-socket: a cell, as in the lungs:—*pl.* **alveoli.**—*adjs.* **alve′olar** (*-ōl′, al′*), of an alveolus: produced with tongue against the roots of the upper teeth (*phon.*): pitted; **alvē′-olate** (or *al′vi-*), pitted: honeycombed: inserted in an alveolus.—*n.* **al′veole,** an alveolus.— **alveolar arch,** part of the jaw in which the teeth are inserted. [L. *alveolus,* dim. of *alveus,* a hollow.]

**alvine,** *al′vin, adj.* of the belly. [L. *alvīnus*—*alvus,* belly.]

**alway,** *öl′wā,* (*arch.*) through all time: always.—*adv.* **al′ways,** every time: ever: continually: in any case: (*Scot.*) still. [all and way.]—O.E. *ealne weg* (*accus.*) and M.E. *alles weis* (gen.).]

**alycompaine.** Same as **elecampane.**

**Alyssum,** *al′is-əm, ə-lis′, n.* a genus of cruciferous plants with white or yellow flowers, grown in rock-gardens.—**sweet alyssum,** a white scented perennial of a related genus. [Gr. *alysson,* a plant reputed to cure madness—*a-,* priv., and *lyssa,* madness.]

am, *am*, *əm*, used as 1st person sing. of the verb *to be*. [O.E. (Anglian) *am*, *eam* (W.S. *eom*), a relic of the verbs in -*mi*, from the root *es*-; cf. Gr. *eimi* (for *esmi*), L. *sum*, Sans. *asmi*.]

amadavat, *am-ə-də-vat'*, *n.* an Indian songbird akin to the weaver-birds.—Also avadavat'. [From *Ahmadabad*, whence they were sent to Europe.]

amadou, *am'ə-dōō*, *n.* tinder made from fungi (genus *Polyporus*) growing on trees, used also as a styptic. [Fr., of doubtful origin.]

amah, *ä'ma*, *n.* (*Oriental*) a native maidservant or child's nurse, esp. wet-nurse. [Port.]

amain, *ə-mān'*, *adv.* with main force: violently: at full speed: exceedingly. [Prep. a, and main.]

à main armée. *a mē-när-mā*, (Fr.) by force of arms, with mailed fist.

a majori (ad minus), *ā mə-jö'rī* (*ad mī'nus*), *ä mī-ōr'ē* (*ad mī'nōōs*), (L.) from the greater (to the less).

amalgam, *ə-mal'gəm*, *n.* a mixture of mercury with other metal: any soft mixture: an intimate mixture: an ingredient.—*v.t.* amal'gamate, to mix with mercury: to merge.—*v.i.* to unite in an amalgam: to come together as one: to blend.— *n.* amalgamā'tion, a blending or merging: a union of diverse elements.—*adj.* amal'gamātive. [L.L. *amalgama*, perh.—Gr. *malagma*, an emollient.]

amandine, *am-an'din*, -*din*, -*dēn*, or *am'*, *n.* a protein in sweet almonds: a candle or a cosmetic which is prepared from them. [Fr. *amande*, almond.]

Amanita, *am-an-i'ta*, *n.* a genus of toadstools, near akin to the mushroom, including the fly agaric (*q.v.*) and other poisonous kinds. [Gr. *amānitai* (pl.), a kind of fungus.]

amanuensis, *ə-man-ū-en'sis*, *n.* one who writes to dictation: a copying secretary:—*pl.* amanuen'-sēs. [L. *āmanuēnsis*—*ā*, from, *manus*, hand.]

amaracus, *ə-mar'ə-kəs*, *n.* marjoram. [L. *amāra-cus*—Gr. *amārakos*.]

amarant(h), *am'ər-ant(h)*, *n.* a fabled never-fading flower, emblem of immortality: any species of Amarant(h)'us, the love-lies-bleeding genus, with richly coloured spikes, long in withering, giving name to the family Amarant(h)ā'ceae, akin to the goosefoots.—*adjs.* amarant(h)ā'ceous; amarant(h)'ine (-*in*); amarant'ine (*Milt.*), of or like amaranth: fadeless: immortal: purple. [Gr. *amarantos*—*a*-, priv., *marainein*, to wither; the *th* forms from confusion with *anthos*, flower.]

Amaryllis, *am-ə-ril'is*, *n.* the belladonna lily genus, giving name to the narcissus and snowdrop family Amaryllidā'ceae, differing from lilies in the inferior ovary.—*n.* amaryll'id, any member of the family.—*adj.* amaryllidā'ceous. [*Amaryllis*, a girl's name in the Gr. and L. poets, and others.]

amass, *ə-mas'*, *v.t.* and *v.i.* to gather in great quantity: to accumulate.—*adj.* amass'able.— *n.* amass'ment. [Fr. *amasser*—L. *ad*, to, and *massa*, a mass.]

amate, *ə-māt'*, (*Spens.*) *v.t.* to match. [Pfx. a-, intens., and mate.]

amate, *ə-māt'* (*arch.*) *v.t.* to daunt: to dismay. [O.Fr. *amatir*, to subdue; cf. checkmate, mat (2), mate (2).]

amateur, *am'ə-tər*, -*tūr*, -*tûr'*, *n.* an enthusiast, admirer: one who cultivates a study or art for the love of it, and not professionally, often implying that he is superficial, trifling, dilettantish, or inexpert: one who engages in sport purely for pleasure—opp. to *professional*.—Also *adj.*—*adj.* amateur'ish, imperfect and defective, as the work of an amateur rather than a professional hand.—*adv.* amateur'ishly.—*ns.* amateur'ishness; am'ateurism, am'ateurship. [Fr.,—L. *amātor*, -*ōris*, a lover—*amāre*, to love.]

amative, *am'ə-tiv*, *adj.* inclined towards love.—

*n.* am'ativeness, propensity to love or to sexuality. [L. *amāre*, -*ātum*, to love.]

amatol, *am'ə-tol*, *n.* a high explosive composed of ammonium nitrate and trinitro*tol*uene.

amatory, *am'ə-tər-i*, *adj.* relating to or causing love: amorous.—*adj.* amatō'rial, amatō'rian, amatō'-rious.—*adv.* amatō'rially. [L. *amātōrius*.]

amaurosis, *am-ö-rō'sis*, *n.* blindness without outward change in the eye.—*adj.* amaurotic (-*rot'ik*). [Gr. *amaurōsis*—*amauros*, dark.]

amaze, *ə-māz'*, *v.t.* to daze (*obs.*): to bewilder (*obs.*): to stun (*obs.*): to strike with fear (*obs.*): to confound with astonishment or wonder.— *n.* bewilderment (*obs.*): panic (*obs.*): extreme astonishment.—*adv.* amaz'edly.—*ns.* amaz'edness (*rare*), amaze'ment, stupefaction (*obs.*): bewilderment (*obs.*): panic, terror (*obs.*): astonishment mingled with wonder.—*adj.* amaz'ing.—*adv.* amaz'ingly (often hyperbolically). [O.E. *āmasian* (found in the pa.p. *āmasod*).]

Amazon, *am'ə-zon*, -*zən*, formerly *ə-mā'zon*, *n.* in Greek story, one of a nation of women warriors, located in Asia or Scythia: the great river of South America (Port. *Amazonas*, Amazons, perh. based on a misunderstood Tupí-Guaraní word *amassona*, *amaçunu*, tidal bore, connected with records of Amazons living on its banks): an Indian of the Amazons: (also without *cap.*) a female soldier: a warlike, manlike, strong, or vigorous woman: a tropical American green parrot: an amazonant.—Also *adj.*—*adj.* Amazō'nian (also without *cap.*).—*adj.* and *adv.* Ama'zon-like.—*ns.* am'-azon-ant', a European and American ant (genus *Polyergus*) helpless in everything except slave-raiding; am'azon-stone, a green microcline, said to be given by the Brazilian Amazons to the men who visited them. [Gr. *Amazōn*, -*onos*, in folk-etymology referred to *a*-, priv., *māzos*, breast, with the explanation that Amazons cut off the right breast lest it should get in the way of the bowstring.]

ambages, *am-bā'jēz*, *n.pl.* windings: roundabout ways: delays.—Also *n.sing.* ambage (*am'bij*) with *pl.* am'bages.—*adjs.* ambagious (-*bā'jəs*), tortuous: circumlocutory; ambagitory (-*baj'i-tər-i*; *Scott*) [L. *ambāgēs* (pl.)—*ambi*-, about, *agĕre*, to lead.]

amban, *am'ban*, *n.* a Chinese resident official in a dependency. [Manchu, minister.]

Ambarvalia, *amb-är-vā'li-a*, *n.pl.* an ancient Roman festival with processions round the cornfields. [L. *Ambarvālia*—*ambi*-, around, *arvum*, field.]

ambassador, *am-bas'ə-dər*, *n.* a diplomatic minister of the highest order: a messenger or agent:—*fem.* ambass'adress.—*adj.* ambassadorial (-*dō'ri-əl*, -*dö'*).—*ns.* ambass'adorship; am'bassage (-*bəs-ij*), am'bassy, forms of embassage, embassy.— bassador-at-large, an ambassador not accredited to any particular foreign government; ambassador extraordinary, an ambassador sent on a special occasion, as distinguished from the ordinary or resident ambassador. [Fr. *ambassadeur*—L. *ambactus*, a slave, gener. thought to be of Celtic origin.]

ambatch, *am'bach*, *n.* a pith-tree. [Apparently native name.]

amber, *am'bər*, *n.* ambergris (*obs.*): a yellowish fossil resin.—*adj.* made of amber: amber-hued— clear brownish yellow.—*adj.* am'bered, (*obs.*) embedded in amber: flavoured with ambergris.— *ns.* am'ber-fish, a fish (genus *Seriola*) of or near the horse-mackerels; am'berite, an amberlike smokeless powder.—*adjs.* am'bery; am'bery —*n.* am'broid or am'beroid, pressed amber. [Fr. *ambre*—Ar. '*anbar*, ambergris.]

ambergris, *am'bər-grēs*, *n.* an ash-grey stronglyscented substance, found floating or cast up, and in the intestines of the spermaceti whale. [Fr. *ambre gris*, grey amber.]

ambidexter, *am-bi-deks'tər*, *adj.* able to use both

hands alike: on both sides: double-dealing.—*n.* one who, is ambidexter.—*n.* **ambidexterity** (*-ter'i-ti*).—*adj.* **ambidex't(e)rous.** [L. *ambi-*, on both sides, *dexter*, right.]
**ambient,** *am'bi-ənt, adj.* going round: surrounding: investing.—*n.* that which encompasses: the air or sky.—*n.* **ambience,** *am'bi-əns,* environment: surrounding influence: atmosphere: (also **ambiance,** *ä-bë-äs*) use or disposition of accessories in art. [L. *ambiēns, -entis,* pr.p. of *ambire* —pfx. *ambi-*, about, *īre*, to go.]
**ambiguous,** *am-big'ū-əs, adj.* doubtful: undetermined: of intermediate or doubtful nature: indistinct: wavering: admitting of more than one meaning: equivocal.—*n.* **ambigū'ity,** doubtful or double meaning: an equivocal expression.—*adv.* **ambig'uously.**—*n.* **ambig'uousness.** [L. *ambiguus*—*ambigĕre,* to go about, waver—pfx. *ambi-,* both ways, *agĕre,* to drive.]
**ambit,** *am'bit, n.* circuit: scope: compass: precincts: confines. [L. *ambitus,* a going round— pfx. *ambi-,* round, *itus,* going—*īre, itum,* to go.]
**ambition,** *am-bish'ən, n.* aspiration after success or advancement: the object of aspiration.—*adjs.* **ambi'tionless; ambitious** (*am-bish'əs*), full of ambition: strongly desirous (of, to do): aspiring: indicating ambition: pretentious.—*adv.* **ambi'tiously.**—*n.* **ambi'tiousness.** [L. *ambitiō, -ōnis,* canvassing—pfx. *ambi-,* about, and *īre, itum,* to go.]
**ambitty,** *am-bit'i, adj.* devitrified. [Fr. *ambité,* of obscure origin.]
**ambivalence,** *am-biv'ə-ləns,* **ambivalency,** *-i, ns.* co-existence in one person of opposing emotional attitudes towards the same object.—*adj.* **ambiv'-alent.** [L. pfx. *ambi-*, on both sides, *valēns, -entis,* pr.p. of *valēre,* to be strong.]
**ambivert,** *am'bi-vûrt, n.* one neither an extravert nor an introvert. [L. *ambi-*, on both sides, *vertēre,* to turn.]
**amble,** *am'bl, v.i.* to move, as a horse, by lifting together both legs on one side alternately with those on the other side: to move at an easy pace: to go like an ambling horse: to ride an ambling animal.—*n.* an ambling pace.—*n.* **am'bler.**—*n.* and *adj.* **am'bling.** [Fr. *ambler*—L. *ambulāre,* to walk about.]
**amblyopia,** *am-bli-ō'pi-ə, n.* dullness of sight. [Gr. *amblyōpiā*—*amblys,* dull, *ōps,* eye.]
**Amblyopsis,** *am-bli-op'sis, n.* the blindfish of the Mammoth Cave in Kentucky. [Gr. *amblys,* dull, *opsis,* sight.]
**Amblystoma,** *am-blis'to-ma, n.* a genus of tailed amphibians in the gill-less or salamandroid suborder, in the larval stage called axolotl. [Gr. *amblys,* blunt, *stoma,* mouth.]
**ambo,** *am'bō, n.* an early Christian raised reading-desk or pulpit:—*pl.* **am'bos, ambō'nes** (*-nēz*). [L.L. *ambō*—Gr. *ambōn, -ōnos,* crest of a hill, pulpit.]
**Amboyna-wood,** (now usu. **Amboina-**), *amboi'nə-wŏŏd, n.* the finely coloured knotty wood of *Pterocarpus indicus,* a papilionaceous tree.— Amboina pine, a tree (*Agathis alba*), a source of resin. [Island of *Amboina.*]
**ambrosia,** *am-brō'z(h)i-ə, -z(h)yə, n.* the food (later, the drink) of the Greek gods, which conferred everlasting youth and beauty: the anointing oil of the gods: any finely flavoured beverage: something sweet and pleasing: bee-bread: fungi cultivated for food by certain bark-beetles (**ambrosia beetles**) of the Scolytidae: (*cap.*) a genus of Compositae called in America ragweeds. —*adj.* **ambrō'sial,** fragrant: delicious: immortal: heavenly.—*adv.* **ambrōs'ially.**—*adj.* **ambrō'sian.** [Gr. *ambrosiā*—*ambrotos,* immortal—*a-,* priv., and *brotos,* for *mbrotos,* mortal; cf. Sans. *amṛta,* immortal.]
**Ambrosian,** *am-brō'z(h)i-ən,-z(h)yən, adj.* pertaining to St *Ambrose,* 4th-cent. bishop of Milan, to his

liturgy, to the form of plainsong introduced by him, to various religious orders and to the public library at Milan (founded 1602-9 by Cardinal Federigo Borromeo) named in his honour.—*n.* a member of any of these orders.
**ambry, aumbry, almery,** Scot. **awmry, awmrie,** *am', öm'(b)ri, n.* a recess for church vessels: a cupboard: a pantry: a dresser: a safe. [O.Fr. *almerie*—L. *armārium,* a chest, safe—*arma,* arms, tools.]
**ambs-ace, ames-ace,** *āmz'ās, amz'ās, n.* double ace, the lowest possible throw at dice: ill-luck: worthlessness. [O.Fr. *ambes as*—L. *ambōs assēs,* both aces.]
**ambulacrum,** *am-bū-lā'krəm, -la', n.* a radial band in the shell of an echinoderm, bearing rows of pores through which protrude the tube-feet:—*pl.* **ambulā'cra.**—*adj.* **ambulā'cral.** [L. *ambulācrum,* a walk—*ambulāre,* to walk.]
**ambulance,** *am'bū-ləns, n.* a vehicle or (air ambulance) helicopter, etc., for conveying sick or injured: a movable field hospital.—*n.* **am'-bulance-chaser,** a lawyer on the look-out for accidents in order to instigate actions for damages (*U.S.*): a person, firm, offering to pursue a claim on behalf of an accident-victim in return for a percentage of the sum obtained.— *adj.* **am'bulant,** walking: moving from place to place: unfixed (*rare*): allowing or calling for walking.—*n.* a walking case.—*v.i.* **am'bulate,** to walk.—*ns.* **ambula'tion; am'bulātor,** a walker: a wheel for road-measuring.—*adj.* **am'b.·ory** (*-ə-tər-i*), of or for walking: moving from p..e to place, not stationary: mutable.—*n.* a covered walk, as an aisle, cloister, portico, corridor. [L. *ambulāre, -ātum,* to walk about.]
**ambuscade,** *am-bəs-kād', n.* an ambush.—*v.t.* and *v.i.* to ambush.—*n.* **ambuscā'do** (esp. 16th-17th cent.; would-be Sp.), an ambuscade:—*pl.* **ambuscā'do(e)s.** [Fr. *embuscade* or Sp. *emboscada;* see **ambush.**]
**ambush,** *am'bŏŏsh, n.* a lying, or laying, in wait to attack by surprise: a place of lying in wait: a body (or person) lying in wait.—*v.t.* to lay in wait: to waylay.—*v.i.* to lie in wait.—*n.* **am'bushment,** ambush. [O.Fr. *embusche* (Fr. *embûche*)—*em-buscher*—L.L. *imboscāre*—*im,* in, *boscus* (see bush).]
**amearst** (*Spens.*) for **amerced.**
**âme damnée,** *äm da-nā,* (Fr.) lit. damned soul, a tool or agent blindly devoted to one's will; **âme de boue,** *äm də bŏŏ,* a soul of mud, a low-minded person; **âme perdue,** *äm per-dü,* lit. lost soul, a desperate character.
**ameer.** See **amir.**
**Amelanchier,** *am-ə-lang'ki-ər, n.* the shadbush genus of the rose family. [Fr. *amélanchier.*]
**amelcorn,** *am'əl-körn, n.* emmer. [Ger. and Du. *amelkorn;* cf. **amylum, corn.**]
**amelia,** *a-mēl'i-a, -mel',* or *-ya, n.* the condition where one or more limbs are completely absent. [Gr. *a-,* priv., and *melos,* limb.]
**ameliorate,** *ə-mē'lyə-rāt, v.t.* to make better: to improve.—*v.i.* to grow better.—*n.* **amēliorā'tion.**—*adj.* **amē'liorātive.** [Fr. *améliorer*—L. *ad,* to, *melior,* better.]
**amen,** *ä-men', ā-men', interj.* so let it be.—*n.* expression of assent, as by saying 'amen': the last word.—*v.t.* to say amen to: to ratify solemnly: to approve: to conclude. [Heb. *āmēn,* true, truly, retained in Gr. and English translations.]
**amenable,** *ə-mēn'ə-bl, adj.* ready to be led or won over: liable or subject.—*ns.* **amenabil'ity, amen'-ableness.**—*adv.* **amen'ably.** [Fr. *amener,* to lead—*à*—L. *ad,* to, and *mener,* to lead—L.L. *mināre,* to lead, to drive (as cattle)—L. *mināri,* to threaten.]
**amenage,** *am'e-nāj,* (*Spens.*) *v.t.* to tame. [O.Fr. *ame(s)nager*—*à,* to, *mesnage,* household.]

**amenaunce,** *am'e-nöns,* (*Spens.*) *n.* bearing. [O.Fr. *amenance*; see **amenable.**]
**amend,** *ə-mend',* *v.t.* to free from fault or error: to correct: to improve: to alter in detail, with a view to improvement, as a bill before parliament: to rectify: to cure: to mend.—*v.i.* to grow or become better: to reform: to recover.—*adjs.* **amend'able;** **amend'atory,** corrective.—*ns.* **amend'er;** **amend'-ment,** correction: improvement: an alteration proposed on a bill under consideration: a counter-proposal put before a meeting: a counter-motion.—*n.pl.* (in form; usu. treated as *sing.*) **amends',** supply of a loss: compensation: reparation. [Fr. *amender*—L. *ēmendāre*—*ē,* out of, and *mendum,* a fault.]
**amende,** *am-äd',* (Fr.) a fine, penalty.—**amende honorable,** *o-nor-äbl',* orig. an ignominious public confession: now a frank admission of wrong satisfying the honour of the injured.
**amene,** *ə-mēn',* *adj.* (now *rare*) pleasant.—*n.* **amenity** (*-mēn', -men'*), pleasantness, as in situation, climate, manners, disposition: a pleasing feature, object, characteristic: civility. [L. *amoenus,* pleasant.]
**amenorrhoea,** *a-, ā-men-ō-rē'ə, n.* failure of menstruation. [Gr. *a-,* priv., *mēn,* month, *rhoiä,* a flowing.]
**ament,** *ä'mənt, ə-ment', n.* one who is mentally defective by failure to develop: a sufferer from amentia.—*n.* **amentia** (*a-, ā-men'shi-ə*), mental deficiency. [L. *āmēns, -entis—ā,* from, *mēns, mentis,* mind.]
**amentum,** *a-men'təm, n.* a catkin:—*pl.* **amen'ta.**—Also **a'ment.**—*adjs.* **amentā'ceous, amen'tal; amentif'erous,** catkin-bearing. [L., thong.]
**amerce,** *ə-mûrs', v.t.* to fine (esp. at discretion): to deprive: to punish.—*ns.* **amerce'ment, amerce'-iament,** infliction of a fine: a fine.—*adj.* **amerc'-iable.** [A.Fr. *amercier—à merci,* at mercy.]
**American,** *ə-mer'i-kən, adj.* pertaining to America, esp. to the United States.—*n.* a native or citizen of America: the English language as spoken in America.—*v.t.* **Amer'icanise, -ize,** to render American.—*ns.* **Amer'icanism,** a custom, characteristic, word, phrase, or idiom characteristic of Americans: condition of being an American citizen: devotion to American institutions; **Amer'icanist,** a student of American biology, archaeology, and the like.—**American aloe,** Agave; **American blight,** a plant-louse pest of apple-trees; **American bowls,** tenpins, a game like skittles: **American cloth,** cloth with a glazed coating; **American Indian,** a member of the native race of America, thought on discovery to be Indian; **American organ,** an instrument resembling the harmonium, in which air is sucked inwards to the reeds. [From *America,* perh. so called from Richard *Ameryk,* Sheriff of Bristol, who financed John Cabot's voyage; also said to be from Amerigo (L. *Americus*) Vespucci.]
**americium,** *am-ər-ish'i-əm, n.* the chemical element of atomic number 95 (symbol Am), obtained artificially in *America.*
**Amerind,** *am'ər-ind, n.* and *adj. Ameri*can *Ind*ian.
**à merveille,** *a mer-vāy',* (Fr.) wonderfully, perfectly.
**ames-ace.** See **ambs-ace.**
**Ametabola,** *am-et-ab'ə-lə, n.pl.* in some classifications the lowest insects, with little or no metamorphosis.—*n.* **ametab'olism.**—*adjs.* **ametabol'ic** (*-ə-bol'ik*), **ametab'olous.** [Gr. *a-,* priv., and *metabolē,* change.]
**amethyst,** *am'ə-thist, n.* a bluish violet quartz anciently supposed to prevent drunkenness: its colour.—*adj.* of, or coloured like, amethyst.—*adj.* **amethyst'ine** (*-in*).—**oriental amethyst,** a purple corundum. [Gr. *amethystos—a-,* priv., and *methyein,* to be drunken—*methy,* wine; cf. **mead** (1), Sans. *madhu,* sweet.]
**Amharic,** *am-har'ik, n.* an Ethiopic language pre-

vailing in Abyssinia.—Also *adj.* [*Amhara* district.]
**ami,** *a-mē,* (Fr.) a friend:—*fem.* **amie,** *a-mē,* a mistress.—**ami de cour,** *a-mē də kōōr,* a court friend—an untrustworthy friend; **ami du peuple,** *a-mē dü pøpl',* friend of the people (esp. Marat, French revolutionist).
**amiable,** *ām'i-ə-bl, adj.* friendly (*Shak.*): love-inspiring (*Shak.*): lovable: of sweet and friendly disposition.—*ns.* **āmiabil'ity, ām'iableness.**—*adv.* **ām'iably.** [O.Fr. *amiable,* friendly—L. *amicābilis—amicus,* friend; confused in meaning with O.Fr. *amable* (Fr. *aimable*)—L. *amābilis—amāre,* to love.]
**amianthus,** *am-i-anth'əs,* more correctly **amiantus** (*-ant'əs*), *n.* the finest fibrous asbestos, which can be made into cloth readily cleansed by fire. [Gr. *amiantos* (*lithos*), undefiled (stone)—*a-,* priv., and *miainein,* to soil.]
**amicable,** *am'ik-ə-bl, adj.* in friendly spirit.—*ns.* **amicabil'ity, am'icableness.**—*adv.* **am'icably.** [L. *amicābilis—amicus,* a friend—*amāre,* to love.]
**amice,** *am'is, n.* a strip of fine linen, worn formerly on the head, now on the shoulders, by a priest at mass: a cloak, wrap. [O.Fr. *amit*—L. *amictus,* cloak—*amb-,* about, and *jacēre,* to throw.]
**amice,** *am'is, n.* a furred hood with long ends hanging down in front, originally a cap or covering for the head, afterwards a hood, or cape with a hood, later a mere college hood. [O.Fr. *aumuce,* of doubtful origin.]
**amicus curiae.** *a-mī'kus kū'ri-ē, a-mē'kōōs kōō'ri-i,* (L.) a friend of the law-court: a disinterested adviser, not a party to the case: (wrongly) a friend in high quarters.
**amid,** *ə-mid', prep.* in the midst of: among.—*adv.* (*arch.*) in the midst.—*adv.* and *prep.* **amid'most,** in the very middle (*adv.*).—*adv.* **amid'ships,** in, near, towards, the middle of a ship lengthwise (from gen. of ship).—*adv.* and *prep.* **amidst',** amid. [O.E. *on middan* (dat. of adj.), in middle; the *s* is a later adverbial genitive ending, the *t* as in **amongst, betwixt,** etc.]
**amide,** *am'id, n.* a derivative of ammonia in which an acid radical takes the place of one or more of the three hydrogen atoms.—*n.* **amido-group** (*ə-mē'dō*), the group $NH_2$ in such combination. [From **ammonia.**]
**amildar,** *am'il-där, n.* a factor or manager in India: a collector of revenue amongst the Mahrattas. [Hind. *'amaldār*—Ar. *'amal,* work, Pers. *dār,* holder.]
**amine,** *am'in, -ēn, n.* a derivative of ammonia ($NH_2$) in which one or more hydrocarbon radicals take the place of one or more of the three hydrogen atoms.—*ns.* **amino-a'cid** (*a-mē'nō-*), a fatty acid (e.g. **ami'no-acet'ic acid,** glycine) in which the amino-group takes the place of a hydrogen atom of the hydrocarbon radical; **ami'no-group',** the group $NH_2$ in such combination. [From **ammonia.**]
**aminobutene,** *a-mē'nō-bū'tēn, n.* a pain-relieving drug, less addiction-forming than morphine. [amine and butene.]
**a minori** (ad majus), *a min-ör'i* (*ad māj'us*), **ä min-ör'ē** (*ad mi'ūs*), (L.) from the less (to the greater).
**amir, ameer,** *a-mēr', ə-mēr', n.* the title borne by certain Mohammedan princes. [Ar. *amir;* see **admiral, emir.**]
**amis** (*Spens.*). Same as **amice** (1).
**amiss,** *ə-mis', adv.* astray: wrongly: improperly: faultily.—*adj.* out of order: wrong: unsuitable: to be objected to.—*n.* an evil: a misdeed.—**come amiss,** to be unwelcome, untoward; **take amiss,** to take offence at (strictly, by misinterpretation). [Prep. a, and **miss.**]
**amissible,** *ə-mis'i-bl, adj.* liable to be lost.—*n.* **amissibil'ity.** [L. *amittēre, āmissum,* to lose—*ā,* from, *mittēre,* to send.]

**amissing,** *ə-mis'ing,* (*Scot.*) *adj.* wanting: lost. [Prep. **a,** and **missing.**]

**amitosis,** *am-i-tō'sis,* (*biol.*) *n.* cell-division without mitosis.—*adj.* **amitotic** (*-tot'ik*).—*adv.* **amitot'-ically.** [Gr. *a-,* priv., and *mitos,* thread.]

**amity,** *am'i-ti, n.* friendship: goodwill: friendly relations. [Fr. *amitié*—L. *amicus,* a friend.]

**amman.** See **amtman.**

**ammeter,** *am'i-tər, n.* an instrument for measuring electric current. [From **ampere,** and Gr. *metron,* measure.]

**ammiral,** an old form (*Milt.*) of **admiral.**

**Ammon,** *am'on, n.* the ancient Egyptian ram-headed god *Amûn, Amen,* identified by the Greeks with Zeus, famous for his temple and oracle in the Libyan oasis of Siwa: (without *cap.*) the argali (from its gigantic horns).—*n.* **ammonia** (*ə-, ə-mō'ni-ə*), a pungent compound of nitrogen and hydrogen (NH₃) first obtained in gaseous form from *sal-ammoniac*: its solution in water, strictly ammonium hydroxide (*liquid ammonia,* long known as spirits of hartshorn).—*adjs.* **ammō'niac,** of the region of the temple of Ammon (applied only to gum-ammoniac, and to sal-ammoniac, which is said to have been first made in that district from camel-dung): ammoniacal; **ammo-ni'acal,** of ammonia.—*n.* **ammoni'acum** (*am-ə-nī'ə-kəm*), gum-ammoniac (see **gum**).—*adj.* **ammō'niated,** combined, impregnated, with ammonia.—*ns.* **amm'onite,** a fossil cephalopod of many kinds, with coiled chambered shell like Ammon's horn; **ammō'nium,** a univalent radical, NH₄, resembling the alkali metals in chemical behaviour. [Gr. *Ammōn, -ōnos.*]

**ammonal,** *am'ən-al, n.* a high explosive made from *ammon*ium nitrate and *al*uminium.

**ammonia, ammoniacum, ammonite, ammonium.** See under **Ammon.**

**ammophilous,** *am-of'i-ləs, adj.* sand-loving. [Gr. *ammos,* sand, *phileein,* to love.]

**ammunition,** *am-ū-nish'ən, n.* orig. military stores generally: things used for charging fire-arms —missiles, propellants: explosive military devices: anything that can be used in fighting (*lit.* and *fig.*).—*adj.* for ammunition: supplied from army stores.—*v.t.* to supply with ammunition. [Obs. Fr. *amunition,* app. from *l'amunition* for *la munition*; see **munition.**]

**amnesia,** *am-nē'zh(y)ə, n.* the loss of memory.—*n.* **amne'siac,** one who suffers from amnesia.—*adjs.* **amne'si(a)c.** [Gr. *amnēsiā.*]

**amnesty,** *am'nes-ti, n.* a general pardon: an act of oblivion.—*v.t.* to give amnesty to. [Gr. *amnēstiā,* forgetfulness.]

**amnion,** *am'ni-ən, n.* the innermost membrane enveloping the embryo of reptiles, birds, and mammals:—*pl.* **am'nia.**—**amnio-,** in composition; **amnion**: amniotic.—*adj.* **amniot'ic.**—**amniotic fluid,** the fluid within the amnion in which the embryo is suspended. [Gr.]

**amoeba,** *ə-mē'bə, n.* a protozoon of ever-changing shape:—*pl.* **amoebae** (*-bē, -bī*).—*adjs.* **amoe'bic; amoe'biform; amoe'boid.** [Gr. *amoibē,* change.]

**amoebaean,** *ə-mē-bē'ən, adj.* answering alternately, responsive, as often in pastoral poetry. [L. *amoebaeus*—Gr. *amoibaios*—*amoibē,* alternation.]

**à moitié,** *a mwa-tyā,* (Fr.) half, by halves.

**amok,** *ə-mok',* **amuck,** *ə-muk', adj.* and *adv.,* in a frenzy, esp. in phrase **to run amok,** to run forth murderously assailing all who come in the way. [Malay *amoq,* frenzied.]

**Amomum,** *a-mō'məm, n.* a genus of the ginger family including cardamoms and grains of paradise. [Latinised from Gr. *amōmon,* prob. cardamom.]

**à mon avis,** *a mo-n a-vē,* (Fr.) in my opinion.

**among,** *ə-mung',* **amongst,** *ə-mungst', preps.* of the number of: amidst.—*adv.* **among** (*arch.*), meanwhile: all the time: betweenwhiles: here and there. [O.E. *on-gemang,* lit. in mixture, crowd—*gemengan,* to mingle: for *-st* see **against.**]

**amontillado,** *ä-mon-til-(y)ä'dō, n.* a slightly sweet sherry of light colour and body, orig. from *Montilla.* [Sp.]

**amoove** (*Spens.*). Same as **amove** (1).

**amoral,** *a-mor'əl,* also *ä-, adj.* non-moral, outside the domain of morality.—*ns.* **amor'alism,** refusal to recognise the validity of any system of morality; **amor'alist.** [Gr. *a-,* priv., and **moral.**]

**amorce,** *ə-mörs', n.* a percussion cap for a toy pistol. [Fr., priming.]

**amoret,** *am'ər-et, n.* a sweetheart (*obs.*): a love-glance: a love-knot: a love-sonnet or song.—*ns.* **amoret'to,** a lover: a cupid:—*pl.* **amoret'ti** (*-tē*); **amorino** (*-ē'nō*), a cupid:—*pl.* **amori'ni** (*-nē*). [O.Fr. *amorete* and It. *amoretto, amorino,* dims. from L. *amor,* love.]

**amorist,** *am'ər-ist, n.* a lover: a gallant: one who writes of love: a seeker of sexual adventures or experiences.—*n.* **am'orism.** [L. *amor,* love.]

**amornings,** *ə-mörn'ingz,* (*obs.*) *adv.* of a morning. [Prep. **a,** and **morning,** with gen. ending added.]

**amoroso,** *am-or-ō-ō'sō,* (*mus.*) *adj.* tender.—Also *adv.* —*n.* a lover: a gallant:—*fem.* **amoro'sa.** [It.]

**amorous,** *am'ər-əs, adj.* inclined to love: in love: fond: amatory: relating to love.—*n.* **amorosity** (*-os'i-ti; rare*).—*adv.* **am'orously.**—*n.* **am'orous-ness.** [O.Fr. *amorous* (Fr. *amoureux*)—L.L. *amōrōsus*—*amor,* love.]

**amor patriae,** *ä'mör pä'tri-ē, ä'mor pa'tri-ī,* (L.) love of country.

**amorphous,** *ə-mör'fəs, adj.* without definite shape or structure: shapeless: without crystalline structure.—*n.* **amor'phism.** [Gr. *amorphos,* shapeless—*a-,* priv., *morphē,* form.]

**amort,** *ə-mört',* (*obs.* or *arch.*) *adj.* spiritless, dejected. [Fr. *à,* to, *mort,* death; but partly from **alamort** wrongly understood as *all amort.*]

**amortise, -ize,** *ə-mör'tīz, -tiz, v.t.* to alienate in mortmain or convey to a corporation: to wipe out esp. through a sinking-fund.—*n.* **amortisā'-tion, -z-.** [L.L. *a(d)mortizāre*—Fr. *à,* to, *mort,* death.]

**amount,** *ə-mownt', v.i.* to go up (*Spens.*): to come in total: to come in meaning or substance with *to*).—*n.* the whole sum: principal and interest together: quantity: value, import, equivalence. [O.Fr. *amonter,* to ascend—L. *ad,* to, *mōns, montis,* a mountain.]

**amour,** *ə-mōōr', n.* love, friendship (*obs.*): love-making (usu. in *pl.*; *arch.*): a love affair (now usu. discreditable): a loved one.—*n.* **amourette** (*a-mōō-ret'*), a petty amour: an amoretto. [Fr.,—L. *amor, amōris,* love.]

**amour courtois,** *a-mōōr kōōr-twä,* (Fr.) courtly love.

**amour-propre,** *a-mōōr-pro-pr',* (Fr.) self esteem: sometimes in exaggerated form, shown in readiness to take offence at slights.

**amove,** *ə-mōōv', v.t.* to stir up (*obs.*): to affect (*obs.*): to rouse (*Spens.*). [O.Fr. *amover*—L. *admovēre*—*ad,* to, *movēre,* to move.]

**amove,** *ə-mōōv',* (*law*) *v.t.* to remove. [L. *āmovēre* —*ā,* from, *movēre,* to move.]

**amp,** *amp, n.* short for **ampere.**

**ampassy.** See **ampersand.**

**ampelo-, ampeli-,** in composition, of the vine, vine-like.—*n.* **ampelography,** *am-pel-og'rə-fi,* the botany of the vine. [Gr. *ampelos,* vine.]

**ampelopsis,** *am-pi-lop'sis, n.* Virginia creeper. [Gr. *ampelos,* vine, *opsis,* appearance.]

**ampere, ampère,** *am'per, -pēr', ä-per,* (*elect.*) *n.* MKS unit of current, defined as that which, flowing in two parallel conductors, each infinitely thin and long, one metre apart in a vacuum, will produce a force between the conductors of $2 \times 10^{-7}$ newtons per metre length (**international ampere,** a unit formerly defined by means of the rate of deposition of silver from a solution of silver nitrate and slightly less than the practical unit in use; now the same as the unit just defined). —*n.* am′perage, current in amperes. [From A. M. *Ampère*, French physicist (1775-1836).]

**ampersand**, *am′pərs-and*, *n.* the character (&; originally ligatured *E* and *T*, for L. *et*) representing *and.*—Also am′perzand, am′pussy-and, am′-passy (*amp′ə-si*). [*and per se and*—that is, &, by itself, 'and': cf. **a-per-se.**]

**Ampex**, *am′peks*, *n.* a system of magnetic recording of television signals.—*v.t.* to record by Ampex. [Trademark.]

**amphetamine**, *am-fet′ə-mēn*, $C_9H_{13}N$, or its sulphate or phosphate, synthetic drug used to relieve nasal congestion or taken internally to stimulate the central nervous system. [*alpha* methyl *ph*en*e*r*h*yl + *amine.*]

**amphibious**, *am-fib′i-əs*, *adj.* leading two lives: living, or adapted to life, or use, on land and in or on water: of military operations, in which troops are conveyed across the sea or other water in landing barges, assault-craft, etc., and land on enemy-held territory: of double, doubtful, or ambiguous nature.—*n.pl.* **Amphib′ia**, a class of vertebrates typically gill-breathing in the larval state and lung-breathing or skin-breathing as adults—frogs, toads, newts, salamanders, caecilians.—*adj.* **amphib′ian**, amphibious: of the Amphibia.—*n.* a member of the Amphibia: an aeroplane designed to alight on land or water: a vehicle for use on land or water. [Gr. *amphibios* —*amphi*, on both sides, *bios*, life.]

**amphibole**, *am′fi-bōl*, *n.* any mineral of a group differing from the pyroxenes in cleavage angle (about 56° instead of about 87°), silicates of calcium, magnesium, and other metals, including hornblende, actinolite, tremolite, etc.—*n.* **amphib′olite**, a rock composed essentially of amphibole. [Gr. *amphibolos*, ambiguous, on account of the resemblance between hornblende and tourmaline.]

**amphibology**, *am-fi-bol′ə-ji*, *n.* a phrase or sentence ambiguous not in its individual words but in its construction: the use of such ambiguities.—*adjs.* **amphibol′ic**, **amphibological** (-*bō-loj′*), **amphib′-olous** (-*ə-ləs*).—*n.* **amphib′oly**, amphibology. [Gr. *amphibolos*—*amphi*, on both sides, *ballein*, to throw.]

**amphibrach**, *am′fi-brak*, *n.* in prosody, a foot of three syllables, a long between two short, or stressed between two unstressed.—*adj.* **amphibrach′ic**. [Gr. *amphi*, on both sides, *brachys*, short.]

**Amphicar**, *am′fi-kär*, *n.* a car designed for land and water transport. [Gr. *amphi*, on both sides, and car.]

**Amphictyon**, *am-fik′ti-on*, (Gr. *hist.*) *n.* a delegate to an (or the) Amphictyonic council.—*adj.* **Amphictyon′ic.**—*n.* **Amphic′tyony**, a league of neighbouring communities connected with a temple and cult, esp. of Delphi. [Gr. *Amphiktyones*, app. for *amphiktiones*, dwellers around—*amphi*, *ktizein*, to dwell.]

**amphigastrium**, *am-fi-gas′tri-əm*, *n.* a scale-like leaf on the ventral side of some liverworts:—*pl.* **amphigas′tria**. [Gr. *amphi*, about, *gastēr*, belly.]

**amphigory**, *am′fi-gə-ri*, *n.* nonsense-verse. [Fr. *amphigouri*: origin unknown.]

**amphimacer**, *am-fim′ə-sər*, *n.* in prosody, a foot of three syllables, short between two long. [Gr. *amphimakros*—*amphi*, on both sides, *makros*, long.]

**amphimixis**, *am-fi-mik′sis*, *n.* fusion of gametes: sexual reproduction: combination of characters from both parents. [Gr. *amphi*, on both sides, *mixis*, intercourse, mixing.]

**Amphineura**, *am-fi-nū′rə*, *n.pl.* a class of molluscs with two ventral and two lateral nerve-cords, including Chiton. [Gr. *amphi*, on both sides, *neuron*, nerve.]

**Amphioxus**, *am-fi-oks′əs*, *n.* the lancelet, one of the lowest backboned animals. [Gr. *amphi*, at both ends, and *oxys*, sharp.]

**amphipod**, *am′fi-pod*, *n.* one of the **Amphip′oda**, an order of small sessile-eyed crustaceans with swimming feet and jumping feet—sand-hoppers, etc.—*adj.* **amphip′odous**. [Gr. *amphi*, both ways, *pous*, *podos*, a foot.]

**amphisbaena**, *am-fis-bē′nə*, *n.* a fabulous two-headed snake: (*cap.*) a genus of snake-like lizards, chiefly tropical American, whose rounded tails give the appearance of a head at each end.— *adj.* **amphisbae′nic**. [Gr. *amphisbaina*—*amphis*, both ways, *bainein*, to go.]

**amphiscian**, *am-fish′i-ən*, *n.* an inhabitant of the torrid zone, whose shadow is thrown both ways— that is, to the north one part of the year, and to the south the other part.—Also *adj.* [Gr. *amphiskios* —*amphi*, both ways, *skiā*, a shadow.]

**amphistomous**, *am-fis′tə-məs*, *adj.* having a sucker at either end, as some worms. [Gr. *amphi*, on both sides, *stoma*, mouth.]

**amphitheatre**, *am-fi-thē′ə-tər*, *n.* a building with rows of seats one above another, around an open space: a similar configuration of hill slopes: one of the galleries in a theatre.—*adjs.* **amphithe′atral**, **amphitheatrical** (-*at′ri-kəl*).—*adv.* **amphitheat′-rically**. [Gr. *amphitheātron*—*amphi*, *theātron*, theatre.]

**amphitropous**, *am-fit′rə-pəs*, *adj.* (of an ovule) placed T-wise on the funicle. [Gr. *amphi*, on both sides, *tropos*, a turning.]

**Amphitryon**, *am-fit′ri-on*, *n.* in Gr. myth. husband of Alcmene; on Alcmene Zeus, in Amphitryon's semblance, begot Herakles: a hospitable entertainer, esp. of doubtful identity (in allusion to the line in Molière's play, 'Le véritable Amphitryon est l'Amphitryon où l'on dîne'). [Gr. *Amphitryōn.*]

**ampholyte**, *am′fō-līt*, *n.* an *ampho*teric electro*lyte.*

**amphora**, *am′fə-rə*, *n.* a two-handled jar used by the Greeks and Romans for holding liquids:—*pl.* **am′phorae** (-*rē*; -*rī*).—*adj.* **amphor′ic** (-*for′*; *med.*) like the sound produced by speaking into a bottle. [L. *amphora*—Gr. *amphoreus*, *amphiphoreus*— *amphi*, on both sides, and *phoreus*, a bearer.]

**amphoteric**, *am-fō-ter′ik*, *adj.* of both kinds: acting both ways, e.g. as acid and base, electropositive and electronegative. [Gr. *amphoteros*, both.]

**ample**, *am′pl*, *adj.* spacious: wide: large enough: abundant: liberal: copious: full or somewhat bulky in form.—*ns.* **am′pleness**; **amplia′tion**, enlarging: an enlargement.—*ns.* **am′pliātive** (*rare*).—*ns.* **amplificā′tion**, enlargement; **am′-plifier**, one who amplifies: a lens that enlarges the field of vision: a device for giving greater loudness.—*v.t.* am′plify (-*fi*), to make more copious in expression: to add to: to increase loudness of (sound), strength of (current), etc.:—*pr.p.* **am′plifying**; *pa.p.* and *pa.t.* **am′plified.**—*n.* **am′plitude**, largeness: abundance: width: range: extent of vibratory movement (from extreme to extreme, or from mean to extreme): the angular distance from the east point of the horizon at which a heavenly body rises, or from the west point at which it sets.—*adv.* **am′ply** (-*pli*). —**amplitude modulation** (*telecommunications*), modulation in radio transmission by varying the amplitude of the carrier wave—cf. *frequency modulation*. [Fr. *ample*, *amplifier*, *amplitude*— L. *amplus*, *amplificāre*, *amplitūdō.*]

**amplexicaul**, *am-pleks′i-köl*, (*bot.*) *adj.* clasping the stem by a dilated base. [L. *amplexus*, -*ūs*, embrace, *caulis*, stem.]

**ampliation**, **amplification**, etc. See **ample.**

**amplosome**, *am′plə-sōm*, *n.* the short, or stocky, type of human figure. [L. *amplus*, large, Gr. *sōma*, body.]

**ampollosity**, *am-pol-os′i-ti*, ampoule. See **ampulla.**

**ampulla**, *am-pool'ə, n.* a small two-handled flask: a pilgrim's bottle: a vessel for holy oil, as at coronations: cruet for the wine and water used at the altar: a small glass container for a hypodermic dose, etc.: any small membranous vesicle (*biol.*): the dilated end of a semicircular canal in the ear:—*pl.* ampull'ae (*-ē*).—Also am'-poule (or *-pool'*; Fr.), am'pul.—*n.* ampollos'ity (*Browning*), turgidity, bombast. [L. irregular dim. of *amphora*, a flagon; partly directly from L., partly through O.E. *ampulle*, O.Fr. *ampo(u)le*, and It. *ampolla*.]

**ampussy-and.** See ampersand.

**amputate**, *am'pūt-āt, v.t.* to cut off, as a limb—*ns.* **amputā'tion; am'putātor; amputee'.** [L. *amputāre, -ātum—amb-*, around, and *putāre, -ātum*, to lop.]

**amrita**, *am-rē'tä, n.* the drink of the Hindu gods.—*n.* **amritattva**, *am-rē-tät'vä*, immortality. [Sans. *amṛta*, immortal; cf. Gr. *ambrotos*.]

**amtman**, *ämt'män*, **amman**, *am'an, n.* in Germany, Switzerland, the Netherlands, Scandinavia, a district magistrate. [Ger. *amtmann, amman*, Dan. and Norw. *amtmand—amt*, office, administration (from the root of ambassador) and Ger. *mann*, Dan. *mand*, man.]

**amtrack**, *am'trak, n.* an amphibious tracked military motor landing-vehicle. [am for amphibious, and track.]

**amuck**, *ə-muk'.* See amok.

**amulet**, *am'ū-let, -lit, n.* a charm carried about the person: a medicine supposed to have occult operation.—*adj.* amulet'ic. [L. *amulētum.*]

**amuse**, *ə-mūz', v.t.* to put in a muse (*obs.*): to beguile with expectation: to occupy the attention of: to beguile (*arch.*): to occupy pleasantly: to entertain, divert: to excite mirth in.—*adj.* amus'-able.—*adv.* amus'edly.—*ns.* amuse'ment, distraction of attention: beguiling: trifling: a pleasant feeling of the ludicrous: that which amuses: recreation: pastime; amus'er; amus-ette (*am-ū-zet'*), a light field-gun invented by Marshal Saxe.—*adj.* amus'ing, affording amusement: entertaining.—*adv.* amus'ingly.—*adj.* amus'ive, deceptive (*obs.*): recreational (*obs.*): interesting: entertaining: amusing.—*n.* amus'-iveness. [Fr. *amuser—à*, to, *muser*, to stare; see muse, vb.]

**amygdal**, *ə-mig'dəl, n.* (*obs.*) an almond.—*n.* **amyg'dala** (*zool.*), a lobe of the cerebellum: one of the palatal tonsils.—*adj.* amygdalā'ceous, akin to the almond.—*ns.* amyg'dale (*-dāl*) an amygdule; amyg'dalin, a glucoside found in cherry kernels, bitter almonds, etc.—*adjs.* amyg'-daloid, almond-shaped: having amygdules.—*n.* an igneous rock in which almond-shaped steam-cavities have been filled with minerals.—*adj.* amygdaloid'al, having amygdules.—*ns.* amyg'-dule, a mineral-filled steam-cavity in a lava.—**Amyg'dalus**, the almond genus, or section of Prunus. [L. *amygdala*—Gr. *amygdalē*, almond.]

**amyl**, *am'il, n.* an alcohol radical, $C_5H_{11}$.—*ns.* **am'ylase** (*-ās*), any of the enzymes that play a part in hydrolysis of starch and similar substances; **am'ylene**, a hydrocarbon of composition $C_5H_{10}$.—**amyl nitrite**, a fruity-smelling, amber-coloured liquid, inhaled medicinally. [From the first syllable of Gr. *amylon*, starch, fine meal, and *hȳlē*, matter, from having been first got from fusel-oil made from starch.]

**amylum**, *am'il-əm*, (*chem.*) *n.* starch.—*adjs.* amylā'-ceous, am'yloid, amyloid'al. [Gr. *amylon*, the finest flour, starch; lit. unmilled—*a-*, priv., *mylē*, a mill.]

**Amytal** (trademark), amytal sodium. See sodium amytal.

**an**, *an, ən, adj.* one: the indefinite article, used before a vowel sound, and by some (now rarely) before an unstressed syllable beginning with a sounded *h*. [O.E. *ān*; see one.]

**an, an, ən, (arch.) conj.** if: **an', and.** [A form of and.]

**an, an, ən, (obs.) prep.** a form of **on.**

**-ana**, *ä'nä, ä'nä*, also **-iana**, *suff.* things belonging to, or typical of, such as sayings, anecdotes, small objects, etc., e.g. Johnson*iana*, Victor*iana* (gener. used in reference to the time of Queen Victoria rather than to Victoria herself).—**ana**, *n.pl.* or *collective sing.* (with *pl.* ana's, anas) a collection of someone's table-talk or of gossip, literary anecdotes or possessions. [L. neut. pl. ending of adjs. in *-anus*.]

**ana**, *ä-na*, written **āa, ā** (L.L.—Gr.) lit. throughout: (in recipes) in equal quantities.

**anabaptist**, *an-ə-bap'tist, n.* a name given by opponents to one holding that baptism should be of adults only and therefore that those baptised in infancy must be baptised again: (*cap.*) one of a Protestant sect of German origin (1521) rejecting infant baptism and seeking establishment of a Christian communism.—*v.t.* anabaptise', -ize', to baptise anew: to rename.—*n.* anabapt'ism.—*adj.* anabaptist'ic. [Gr. *ana-*, again, and *baptizein*, to dip.]

**Anabas**, *an'a-bas, n.* the genus to which belongs the climbing perch, an East Indian fish that often leaves the water. [Gr. *anabās*, aor. part. of *anabainein*, to climb—*ana*, up, *bainein*, to go.]

**anabasis**, *an-ab'ə-sis, n.* a going up: a military advance up-country, such as that of Cyrus the younger (401 B.C.) related (with the subsequent katabasis or retreat of the 10,000) by Xenophon in his *Anabasis*.—*adj.* anabatic (*-bat'ik*), upward-moving. [Gr.,—*ana*, up, *basis*, going.]

**anabiosis**, *an-ə-bi-ō'sis, n.* (the power of) returning to life after apparent death: a state of suspended animation.—*adj.* anabiot'ic. [Gr. *anabiōsis—ana*, up, back, *bios*, life.]

**Anableps**, *an'ə-bleps, n.* a genus of bony fishes with open air-bladders, and projecting eyes divided in two for vision in air and water. [Gr. *ana*, up, *blepein*, to look.]

**anabolism**, *an-ab'əl-izm, n.* chemical upbuilding of complex substances in living matter—opp. to katabolism.—*adj.* anabolic (*an-ə-bol'ik*). [Gr. *anabolē*, a heaping up—*ana*, up, *bolē*, a throw.]

**anabranch**, *an'ə-bränch*, (*Austr.*) *n.* a stream that leaves a river and re-enters lower. [For anastomosing branch.]

**Anacardium**, *an-ə-kär'di-əm, n.* the cashew-nut genus, giving name to a family **Anacardiā'ceae** akin to the hollies and maples.—*adj.* anacardiā'-ceous. [Gr. *ana*, according to, *kardiā*, heart (from the shape of the fruit).]

**anacatharsis**, *an-ə-ka-thär'sis, n.* vomiting.—*n.* and *adj.* anacathar'tic. [Gr. *anakatharsis*, clearing up —*ana*, up, throughout, *katharsis* (see catharsis).]

**Anacharis**, *an-ak'a-ris, n.* a genus of water-plants including *Anacharis Helodea* or *Elodea canadensis*, a North American weed found in Britain in 1842, soon clogging canals and rivers by vegetative growth. [Gr. *ana*, up, and *charis*, grace.]

**anachronism**, *ə-nak'rə-nizm, n.* an error assigning a thing to an earlier or (less strictly) to a later age than it belongs to: anything out of keeping with chronology.—*adjs.* anachronist'ic, anach'ronous.—*advs.* anachronist'ically, anach'ronously. [Gr. *ana-*, backwards, *chronos*, time.]

**anaclastic**, *an-ə-klas'tik, adj.* refractive. [Gr. *anaklastos*, bent back—*ana-*, back, *klaein*, break.]

**anacoluthia**, *an-ə-ko-lōō'thi-a, -lū', n.* want of syntactical sequence, when the latter part of a sentence does not grammatically fit the earlier.—*n.* anacolu'thon, an instance of anacoluthia: anacoluthia:—*pl.* anacolu'tha. [Gr. *anakolouthiā, anakolouthon—an-*, priv., *akolouthos*, following.]

**anaconda**, *an-ə-kon'də, n.* a gigantic South American water-boa, *Eunectes murinus*. [Perhaps from a Sinhalese name for another snake in Ceylon.]

*fāte, fär; mē, hûr* (her); *mīne, mōte, för; mūte, mōōn, fōŏt; dhen* (then)

**anacoustic zone**, zone of absolute silence in space. [Gr. *an-*, priv.; *acoustic*.]

**Anacreontic**, *an-ak-ri-ont'ik*, *adj*. after the manner of the Greek poet Anacreon (*Anakreōn*; 6th cent. B.C.)—free, convivial, erotic.—*n*. a poem in this vein.—*adv*. **anacreont'ically.**

**anacrusis**, *an-ə-krōō'sis*,(*pros.*)*n*. one or more short syllables introductory to the normal rhythm of a line:—*pl*. **anacru'ses** (*-sēz*).—*adj*. **anacrustic** (*-krus'tik*). [Gr. *anakrousis*, a pushing back, striking up a tune—*ana*, up, back, *krouein*, to strike.]

**anadem**, *an'ə-dem*, *n*. a fillet, chaplet, or wreath. [Gr. *anadēma*—*ana*, up, and *deein*, to bind.]

**anadiplosis**, *an-ə-di-plō'sis*, *n*. rhetorical repetition of an important word (or sometimes phrase). [Gr. *anadiplōsis*—*ana*, back, *diploein*, to double.]

**anadromous**, *an-ad'rə-məs*, *adj*. ascending rivers to spawn. [Gr. *anadromos*, running up—*ana*, up, *dromos*, a run.]

**anadyomene**, *a-na-dī-o'mə-nē*, *adj*. coming up, emerging (esp. of Aphrodite from the sea). [Gr. *anadyomenē*.]

**anaemia**, in U.S. **anemia**, *an-ēm'i-a*, *n*. bloodlessness: lack of red blood corpuscles or of haemoglobin—a condition marked by paleness and languor.—*adj*. **anaem'ic**, suffering from anaemia: sickly, spiritless, washed-out, lacking in body (*fig.*).—**pernicious anaemia**, a severe form of anaemia characterised by abnormalities in the red blood corpuscles, etc. [Gr. *anaimiā*—*an-*, priv., *haima*, blood.]

**anaerobe**, *an'ā*(*ə*)*r-ōb*, *n*. an organism that lives in absence of free oxygen.—Also **anaero'biont.**—*adjs*. **anaerobic** (*-ob'ik*,*-ōb'ik*), **anaerobiotic** (*-ō-bī-ot'ik*), living in the absence of free oxygen: effected by anaerobes, as a biochemical change: involving the activity of anaerobes.—*advs*. **anaerob'ically**, **anaerobiot'ically.**—*n*. **anaerobio'sis**, life in the absence of oxygen. [Gr. *an-*, priv., *āēr*, air, *bios*, life.]

**anaesthesia**, in U.S. **anesthesia**, *an-ēs-thē'zi-a*,*-zya* or *-is-*, **anaesthesis**, *-sis*, *ns*. loss of feeling: insensibility, general or local.—*adj*. **anaesthetic** (*-thet'ik*, *-thēt'ik*), producing or connected with insensibility.—*n*. an anaesthetic agent.—*adv*. **anaesthet'ically.**—*v.t*. **anaes'thetise**, **-ize.**—*ns*. **anaesthetist** (*-ēs'thə-tist*, or *-es'*), one who administers anaesthetics; **anaesthesiol'ogy**, the science of administering anaesthetics; **anaesthesiol'ogist.** [Gr. *anaisthēsiā*, insensibility, *anaisthētos*, insensible—*an-*, priv., *aisthanesthai*, to perceive.]

**anaglyph**, *an'ə-glif*, *n*. an ornament in low relief: a picture composed of two prints, in complementary colours, seen stereoscopically through spectacles of these colours.—*adjs*. **anaglyph'ic**; **anaglyptic** (*-glip'tik*). [Gr. *anaglyphos*, *anaglyptos*, in low relief—*ana*, up, back, *glyphein*, to engrave, carve.]

**anagnorisis**, *an-ag-nō'ri-sis*, *-nö'*, *n*. recognition leading to dénouement. [Gr. *anagnōrisis*.]

**anagoge**, *an-ə-gō'jē*, *n*. mystical interpretation.—Also **an'agogy.**—*adjs*. **anagogic** (*-goj'ik*), pertaining to mystical interpretation: (of the strivings in the unconscious towards morally high ideals; *fig.*).—*adv*. **anagog'ically.** [Gr. *anagōgē*, leading up, elevation—*ana*, up, *agein*, to lead.]

**anagram**, *an'ə-gram*, *n*. a word or phrase formed by the letters of another in different order.—*v.t*. and *v.i*. to **anagrammatise.**—*adjs*. **anagrammat'ic**, **anagrammat'ical.**—*adv*. **anagrammat'ically.**—*v.t*. and *v.i*. **anagramm'atise**, **-ize**, to transpose so as to form an anagram.—*ns*. **anagramm'atism**, the practice of making anagrams; **anagramm'atist**, a maker of anagrams. [Gr. *ana-*, back, *gramma*, letter.]

**anal.** See **anus.**

**analcime**, *an-al'sim*, **analcite**, *an-al'sīt*, *ns*. a cubic zeolite, a hydrated sodium aluminium silicate.

[Gr. *an-*, priv., *alkimos*, *alkis*, strong, because weakly electrified by friction.]

**analects**, *an'ə-lekts*, **analecta**, *-lek'ta*, *ns.pl.* collected literary fragments.—*adj*. **analec'tic.** [Gr. (*pl.*) *analekta*—*ana*, up, *legein*, to gather.]

**analeptic**, *an-ə-lep'tik*, *adj*. restorative: comforting. [Gr. *analēptikos*, restorative—*ana*, up, and the root *lab* of *lambanein*, to take.]

**analgesia**, *an-al-jē'zi-a*, *n*. painlessness: insensibility to pain.—*n*. **analgesic** (*-jē'sik*), an anodyne.—*adj*. producing analgesia. [Gr. *analgēsiā*—*an-*, priv., and *algeein*, to feel pain.]

**analogy**, *an-al'ə-ji*, *n*. an agreement or correspondence in certain respects between things otherwise different: a resemblance of relations: parallelism: relation in general: a likeness: proportion, or the equality of ratios (*math.*): agreement in function, as distinguished from *homology* or agreement in origin (*biol.*): a resemblance by virtue of which a word may be altered on the model of another class of words, as *strove*, *striven*, remodelled upon *drove*, *driven*, *throve*, *thriven*, etc. (*philol.*).—*adjs*. **analogic** (*an-ə-loj'ik*; *rare*); **analog'ical.**—*adv*. **analog'ically.**—*v.t*. **anal'ogise**, **-ize**, to explain or consider by analogy.—*ns*. **anal'ogist**, one who sees, follows, or uses analogies; **anal'ogon** (*-gon*; Gr.), **analogue.**—*adj*. **anal'ogous** (*-gəs*), having analogy: bearing some correspondence or resemblance: similar in certain circumstances or relations (with *to*): positively electrified by heating.—*adv*. **anal'ogously.**—*ns*. **anal'ogousness**; **an'alogue** (*-log*; in U.S. also **analog**) that which is analogous to something else: that which is of like function (distinguished from a *homologue*) (*biol.*).—**analogue computer** (*U.S.* also **analog**), a type of computer in which varying electrical currents or voltages, etc., are used to represent proportionally other quantities (e.g., forces, speeds) in working out problems about these quantities. [Gr. *analogiā*—*ana*, according to, and *logos*, ratio.]

**analphabet(e)**, *an-al'fə-bet*, *-bēt*, *adj*. ignorant of the alphabet.—Also *n*.—*adj*. **analphabet'ic**, totally illiterate: not alphabetic. [Gr. *analphabētos*—*an-*, priv.; see **alphabet.**]

**analysis**, *ən-al'is-is*, *n*. a resolving or separating of a thing into its elements or component parts: ascertainment of those parts: a table or statement of the results of this: the tracing of things to their source, and so discovering the general principles underlying individual phenomena: resolution of a sentence into its syntactic elements (*gram.*): formerly, proof by assuming the result and reasoning back to principles (*math.*): use of algebraical methods: psychoanalysis:—*pl*. **anal'yses** (*-sēz*).—Opp. *synthesis*.—Spellings with *-z-* in following words are chiefly U.S.—*adj*. **analysable**, **-zable** (*an-ə-līz'ə-bl*).—*v.t*. **anal'yse**, **-yze** (*-līz*), to subject to analysis.—*ns*. **analys'er**, **-yzer**, one who analyses: in a polariscope the nicol (or substitute) through which the polarised light passes: a device that analyses; **an'alyst** (*-list*), one skilled in or practising analysis, esp. chemical: a psychoanalyst.—*adj*. **analytic** (*-lit'ik*), pertaining to, performing, or inclined to analysis: resolving into first principles.—*n*. (often *pl*. in form) analytical logic: analytical geometry.—*adj*. **analyt'ical.**—*adv*. **analyt'ically.**—**analysis situs** (*sit'əs*; *math.*), older name for *topology* (*math*. meanings 1 and 2); **analytical chemistry** (also **analysis**), chemistry concerned with determination of the constituents of chemical compounds, or mixtures of compounds; **analytical geometry**, co-ordinate geometry; **analytical languages**, those that use separate words instead of inflexions; **in the last analysis**, when all inessentials are excluded from the problem, or the situation. [Gr. *analysis*—*analȳein*, to unloose, *ana*, up, *lȳein*, to loose.]

Neutral vowels in unaccented syllables: *el'ə-mənt*; for certain sounds in foreign words, see p. viii

**anamnesis,** *an-am-nēs'is,* *n.* the recalling to memory of things past: the recollection of the Platonic pre-existence: a patient's remembrance of the early stages of his illness. [Gr. *anamnēsis* —*ana,* up, back, *mimnēskein,* to remind, recall to memory.]

**anamorphosis,** *an-ə-mör'fə-sis,* or *-fō',* *n.* a deformed figure appearing in proportion when rightly viewed, e.g. in a curved mirror, or in a particular direction.—*adjs.* **anamor'phic, anamor'phous.** [Gr. *anamorphōsis,* a forming anew—*ana,* back, anew, and *morphōsis,* a shaping—*morphē,* shape, form.]

**anan,** *ə-nan',* (*obs.* or *dial.*) *interj.* expressing failure to understand. [anon.]

**ananas,** *ə-nä'nas,* *n.* the pineapple (*Ananas sativus*): the pinguin (*Bromelia Pinguin*), or its fruit.—Also **an'ana.** [From an American Indian language.]

**Ananias,** *an-ə-nī'es,* *n.* a liar. [*Acts of the Apostles,* v. 1-5.]

**ananke,** *a-nangk'ē,* (Gr. *anankē*) necessity.

**anapaest,** in U.S. **anapest,** *an'ə-pēst,* (*pros.*) *n.* a foot of two short (or unstressed) syllables followed by a long (or stressed)—a dactyl reversed.—*adjs.* **anapaes'tic, -al.** [Gr. *anapaistos,* struck back—*ana,* back, *paiein,* to strike.]

**anaphase,** *an'ə-fāz,* *n.* the stage of mitosis at which the daughter-chromosomes move towards the poles of the spindle. [Gr. *ana,* up, back, and phase.]

**anaphora,** *an-af'ə-ra,* *n.* the rhetorical device of beginning successive sentences, lines, etc., with the same word or phrase: use of a word (such as *it, do*) to avoid repetition of a preceding word or group of words: the offering of the Eucharistic elements. [Gr. *anaphorā,* a carrying back, reference—*ana,* back, *pherein,* to bear.]

**anaphrodisiac,** *an-af-rō-diz'i-ak,* *adj.* tending to diminish sexual desire.—*n.* an anaphrodisiac agent. [Gr. *an-,* priv., *aphrodisiakos,* sexual.]

**anaphylaxis,** *an-ə-fil-aks'is,* *n.* an increased susceptibility to injected foreign material, protein or non-protein, brought about by a previous introduction of it.—Also **anaphylax'y.**—*adj.* **anaphyllac'tic.** [Gr. *ana,* back, *phylaxis,* protection.]

**anaplasty,** *an'ə-pläs-ti,* *n.* the reparation of superficial lesions by the use of adjacent healthy tissue, as by transplanting a portion of skin.—*adj.* **anaplas'tic.** [Gr. *ana,* again, *plassein,* to form.]

**anaplerosis,** *an-ə-plē-rō'sis,* *n.* the filling up of a deficiency.—*adj.* **anaplerotic** (*-rot'ik*). [Gr. *anaplērōsis*—*ana,* up; and *plēroein,* to fill.]

**anaptyxis,** *an-əp-tik'sis,* (*phon.*) *n.* development of a vowel between consonants.—*adj.* **anaptyc'tic.** [Gr. *anaptyxis,* gape—*ana,* back, *ptyssein,* to fold.]

**anarak.** See anorak.

**anarchy,** *an'ər-ki,* *n.* complete absence of law or government: a harmonious condition of society in which law is abolished as unnecessary: utter lawlessness: chaos: complete disorder.—*n.* **anarch** (*an'ärk*), an author, promoter, or personification of lawlessness.—*adjs.* **anarchal** (*an-ärk'əl*; *rare*); **anarch'ial** (*rare*); **anarch'ic, anarch'ical.**—*adv.* **anarch'ically.**—*v.t.* **an'ar-chise, -ize** (*an'ər-kīz*), to render anarchic.—*ns.* **an'archism,** the teaching of the anarchists; **an'-archist,** one whose ideal of society is one without government of any kind: one who seeks to advance such a condition by terrorism.—Also *adj.*—*adj.* **anarchist'ic.** [Gr. *anarchiā,* leaderlessness, lawlessness—*an-,* priv., *archē,* government.]

**anarthrous,** *an-är'thrəs,* *adj.* used without the article (of Greek nouns): without distinct joints.—*adv.* **anar'thrously.** [Gr. *an-,* priv., *arthron,* a joint, article.]

**anasarca,** *an-ə-sär'kə,* *n.* diffused dropsy in the skin and subcutaneous tissue. [Gr. phrase *ana sarka,* throughout the flesh.]

**anastasis,** *an-as'tə-sis,* *n.* in Byzantine art, the Harrowing of Hell: convalescence.—*adj.* **anastatic** (*an-ə-stat'ik*), of anastasis: with characters raised in relief. [Gr. *anastasis,* rising or raising up, or again—*ana,* up, again, *stasis,* a setting, standing.]

**anastigmat,** *an-as'tig-mat,* or *-stig',* *n.* an anastigmatic lens.—*adj.* **anastigmat'ic** (*an-ə-*), not astigmatic.—*n.* **anastig'matism.** [Gr. *an-,* priv., and **astigmatic.**]

**anastomosis,** *an-as-tə-mō'sis,* *n.* communication by cross-connections to form a network:—*pl.* **anastomo'ses** (*-sēz*).—*v.i.* **anas'tomose,** to intercommunicate in such a way.—*adj.* **anastomotic** (*-mot'ik*). [Gr. *anastomōsis,* outlet—*ana,* back, *stoma,* mouth.]

**anastrophe,** *an-as'trə-fē,* (*rhet.*) *n.* inversion. [Gr. *anastrophē*—*ana,* back, and *strephein,* to turn.]

**anatase,** *an'ə-tās,* *n.* a mineral consisting of titanium oxide. [Gr. *anatasis,* a stretching, from its long crystals.]

**anathema,** *a-* or *ə-nath'i-mə,* *n.* a solemn ecclesiastical curse or denunciation involving excommunication: a curse, execration: a person or thing cursed ecclesiastically or generally: an object of abhorrence:—*pl.* **anath'emas.**—*adj.* **anathematical** (*-mat'i-kl*).—*n.* **anathematisation, -ization** (*-mə-tī-zā'shən*).—*v.t.* and *v.i.* **anath'-ematise, -ize**—**anathema maranatha** (*mar-ə-na'-tha*; Syriac *māran athā,* the Lord cometh, or Lord come), words happening to occur together in 1 Cor. xvi. 22, wrongly understood as an intensified curse. [Gr. *anathēma,* a thing dedicated or accursed, for *anathēma,* a votive offering.—*ana,* up, and the root of *tithenai,* to place.]

**anatomy,** *ə-nat'ə-mi,* *n.* the art of dissecting an organised body: the science of the structure of the body learned by dissection: a subject for dissection (*obs.*): a skeleton, shrivelled and shrunken body, alive or dead, or mummy (*arch.*): bodily frame or structure: dissection: analysis. —*adjs.* **anatomic** (*an-ə-tom'ik*), **-al.**—*adv.* **anatom'-ically.**—*v.t.* **anat'omise, -ize,** to dissect: to lay open minutely (*fig.*).—*n.* **anat'omist,** one skilled in anatomy. [Gr. *anatomē,* dissection—*ana,* up, *tomē,* a cutting.]

**anatropous,** *a-* or *ə-nat'rə-pəs,* (*bot.*) *adj.* of an ovule, turned back and attached at the side of the funicle, which thus becomes a ridge on the ovule. [Gr. *ana,* back, up, *tropē,* a turning.]

**anatta, anatto.** See annatto.

**a natura rei,** *ä na-tū'ra rē'i,* *na-tōō'rä rā'ē,* (L.) from the nature of the case.

**anax andron,** *a'naks and'rön,* (Gr. *andrōn*) lord of men (esp. Agamemnon).

**anbury,** *an'bər-i,* *n.* a soft bloody wart on horses, etc.: a disease in turnips, cabbages, etc., due to a slime-fungus. [Perh. for *angberry*—O.E. *ange,* narrow, painful, and **berry.**]

**ance, āns.** Northern form of **once.**

**ancestor,** *an'sis-tər,* *n.* one from whom a person is descended: a forefather:—*fem.* **an'cestress.**—*adjs.* **ances'tral** (*-ses'*); **ancestorial** (*-sis-tō'ri-əl,* *-tō'*).—*n.* **an'cestry,** a line of ancestors: lineage. —**an'cestor-wor'ship.** [O.Fr. *ancestre*—L. *antecessor*—*ante,* before, *cēdĕre, cessum,* to go.]

**anchor,** *ang'kər,* *n.* an implement for retaining a ship by chaining it to the bottom, or for holding a balloon to the ground, or the like: anything that gives stability or security (*fig.*).—*v.t.* to fix by an anchor: to fasten.—*v.i.* to cast anchor: to stop, or rest.—*n.* **anch'orage,** the act of anchoring: a place of or for anchoring: a set of anchors (*Shak.*): rest or support to the mind (*fig.*): duty imposed for anchoring.—*adj.* **anch'orless.**—**anchor escapement,** or recoil escapement, a clock escapement in which the pallets push the escape-wheel slightly backwards at the end of each swing, causing a recoil of the pendulum; **anch'or-hold,** the hold of an anchor upon the ground: security (*fig.*); **anch'or-ice',** ground-ice; **anchor (man),** the man at the back of a team in a tug-of-war: the man who runs the last stage of a relay-race: (or **anchorman**) a person on whom the success of an activity depends, esp., on television, the person responsible for smooth running of a dialogue or discussion between or among others; **anch'or-ring,** a solid generated by the revolution of a circle about an axis in its plane but not cutting it and not passing through its centre; **anch'or-stock,** the cross-bar of an anchor, which causes one or other of the flukes to turn to the bottom.—**at anchor,** anchored; **cast anchor,** to let down the anchor; **weigh anchor,** to take up the anchor. [O.E. *ancor*—L. *ancŏra*; cf. Gr. *ankȳra*—*ankos,* a bend; conn. with **angle.**]

**anchor,** *ang'kər* (*Shak.*), **anchoret,** *-et,* **anchorite,** *-it, ns.* a man or woman who has withdrawn from the world, especially for religious reasons: a recluse.—*ns.* **anch'orage,** a recluse's cell; **anch'oress,** **anc'ress,** a female anchorite.—*adjs.* **anchoret'ic, -al.** [Gr. *anachōrētēs*—*ana,* apart, *chōreein,* to withdraw.]

**anchovy,** *an'chō-vi, an-chō'vi, n.* a small Mediterranean fish (*Engraulis encrasicholus*) of the herring family, used for pickling, and making sauce, paste, etc.—**an'chŏvy-pear,** the fruit of a W. Indian lecythidaceous tree (*Grias cauliflora*), often pickled. [Sp. and Port. *anchova*; of doubtful etymology.]

**anchylosis.** The same as **ankylosis.**

**ancien régime,** *ä-syē rā-zhēm,* (Fr.) the old order (esp. before the French Revolution); **ancienne noblesse,** *ä-syen nob-les,* the old nobility: the nobility of the ancien régime.

**ancient,** *ān'shənt, adj.* very old: of former times: of long standing: belonging or relating to times long past, esp. before the downfall of the Western Roman Empire (A.D. 476).—*n.* an aged man: an elder or senior: one who lived in ancient times—usu. in *pl.* and applied esp. to the Greeks and Romans.—*adv.* **an'ciently.**—*ns.* **an'cientness;** **an'cientry,** antiquity: seniority: ancestry: dignity of birth: old people (*Shak.*).—**ancient lights,** the legal right to receive in perpetuity, by certain windows, a reasonable amount of daylight; **Ancient Monument,** a building of historical moment scheduled for preservation, in many cases under the care of a government department; **the Ancient of days** (*B.*), the Almighty. [Fr. *ancien*—L.L. *antiānus,* former, old—L. *ante,* before.]

**ancient,** *ān'shənt,* (*obs.*) *n.* a flag: a standard-bearer: an ensign. [See **ensign.**]

**ancile,** *an-si'lē, an-kē'lā,* (L.) the shield that fell from heaven in the reign of Numa Pompilius, on the safety of which the prosperity of Rome depended.

**ancillary,** *an-sil'ər-i, an'sil-ər-i, adj.* subserving: ministering: auxiliary. [L. *ancilla,* a maid-servant.]

**ancipitous,** *an-sip'i-təs,* (*bot.*) *adj.* two-edged and flattened. [L. *anceps, -cipitis,* two-edged, double—*ambi-,* on both sides, *caput, capitis,* head.]

**ancle,** an obselete spelling of **ankle.**

**ancome,** *an'kəm,* (*obs.* or *dial.*) *n.* a sudden inflammation: a whitlow. [Cf. **oncome, income.**]

**ancon,** *ang'kon, n.* the elbow: a console to support a door cornice: a breed of sheep with very short legs:—*pl.* **ancones** (*-kō'nēz*). [Latinised from Gr. *ankōn,* a bend, elbow.]

**Ancona,** *ang-kō'na, n.* a speckled variety of laying poultry of Mediterranean family. [*Ancona* in Italy.]

**ancora,** *ang-kō'rä, -kō', adv.* encore. [It.]

**and,** *and, ənd, ən, 'n, conj.* indicating addition: also: of another kind: used to introduce a consequence or aim: to introduce a question expressive of surprise, realisation, wonder, incredulity, etc.: sometimes app. meaningless ('When that I was and a little tiny boy'): as a conditional conjunction (from M.E. times only; often in *Shak.*; now *arch.*—also **an, an if**) if: even if, although: as if.—**and all,** not without; **and how** (*coll.*), I should think so indeed; **but and** (*obs.*), and also. [O.E. *and, ond*; cf. Ger. *und,* and L. *ante,* before, Gr. *anti,* against.]

**and,** *and, n.* the sign ampersand: a use of the word 'and': something added.

**and,** *ən, (dial.* and *Shak.) conj.* than. [Perh. O.N. *an, en, enn,* than.]

**Andalusian,** *an-də-lōō'* (or *-lū') z(h)yən, -s(h)yən, n.* a native of *Andalusia* (Sp. *Andalucía*), in Spain: a blue variety of laying poultry, of Mediterranean family.—Also *adj.*—*n.* **andalu'site** (*-sit*), a silicate of aluminium, first found in Andalusia.

**andante,** *an-dan'tā,* (*mus.*) *adv., adj.* and *n.* moving with moderately slow, even expression: a movement or piece composed in andante time.—*adj., adv.* and *n.* **andantino** (*an-dan-tē'nō*), (a movement, etc.) somewhat slower than andante: sometimes intended for somewhat quicker. [It., pr.p. of *andare,* to go.]

**Andean,** *an-dē'ən,* **Andine,** *an'din, adjs.* of, or like, the Andes Mountains.—*ns.* **andesine** (*an'diz-ēn, -in*), a feldspar intermediate between albite and anorthite; **an'desite,** a volcanic rock with plagioclase and some ferromagnesian mineral as phenocrysts in a microlithic ground-mass (both found in the Andes).—*adj.* **andesitic** (*-it'ik*).

**andiron,** *and'i-ərn, n.* an iron bar to support the end of a log in a fire: a fire-dog. [O.Fr. *andier* (Fr. *landier = l'andier*); origin unknown; early confused with **iron.**]

**Andrew,** *an'drōō, n.* one of the twelve Apostles, patron Saint of Scotland.—**St Andrew's cross,** a saltire, or cross of equal shafts crossed diagonally: the saltire of Scotland, white on a blue ground.

**Andrew Ferrara,** *an'drōō fi-rä'rä, n.* a make of sword-blade highly esteemed in Scotland from *c.* 1600.—Also **An'dro,** or **Andrea** (*-drä'ä,* or *an'*), **Ferrara.** [According to some from *Andrea dei Ferrari* of Belluno, to others *Andrew Ferrars* or *Ferrier* of Arbroath, poss. as a native of Ferrara, or—L. *ferrārius,* smith.]

**andro-, andr-,** in composition, man: male.—*adjs.* **androcephalous** (*an-drō-sef'ə-ləs*), man-headed (Gr. *kephalē,* head); **androdioecious** (*-di-ē'shəs*), having hermaphrodite and male flowers on separate plants.—*ns.* **androdioe'cism** (see dioecious); **androecium** (*an-drē'shi-əm,* or *-si-əm*), stamens collectively (Gr. *oikion,* house); **androgen** (*an'drō-jən*), any one of the male sex-hormones: a synthetic compound with similar effect.—*adjs.* **androgen'ic,** pertaining to an androgen; **androgynous** (*an-droj'i-nəs,* or *-drog'*), having the characteristics of both male and female in one individual: hermaphrodite: having an inflorescence of both male and female flowers (*bot.*).—*n.* **androg'yny,** hermaphroditism (Gr. *gynē,* woman).—*adj.* **andromonoecious** (*an-drō-mon-ē'shəs*), having hermaphrodite and male flowers on the same plant.—*ns.* **andromonoe'cism** (see monoecious); **an'drophore** (*-fōr, -för*), a prolongation of the receptacle carrying the stamens (Gr. *phoros,* a bearing). [Gr. *anēr, andros,* man, male.]

**Andromeda,** *an-drom'i-da, n.* a genus of shrubs of the heath family: a northern constellation.—*n.* **andromedotoxin,** *an-drom'i-dō-tok'sin,* a vegetable drug got from Andromeda, used in relief of high blood pressure. [*Andromeda,* in Greek myth, a maiden delivered by Perseus from a sea-monster.]

**andvile** (*Spens.*). Same as **anvil.**

ane, *yin*, *ān* (*Scot.* and *obs.*), *adj.*, *n.* and *pron.* one: an, a. [O.E. *ān.*]

anear, *ə-nēr'*, *adv.* nearly: near.—*prep.* near.— *v.t.* to approach, to come near to. [of, on, and near.]

aneath, *ə-nēth'*, (*Scot. ə-neth'*, *ə-nāth'*), *adv.* and *prep.* (chiefly Scot.) beneath. [Prep. a, and the root of beneath.]

anecdote, *an'ik-dōt*, *n.* a short narrative of an incident of private life.—*n.* an'ecdotage, anecdotes collectively: garrulous old age (with pun on *dotage*); an'ecdotist.—*adjs.* anecdōt'al, anecdotical (-*dot'*). [Gr. *an-*, priv., *ekdotos*, published—*ek*, out, *didonai*, to give.]

anechoic, *an-ək-ō'ik*, *adj.* echoless. [Gr. *an-*, priv., and echoic.]

anelace. See anlace.

anele, *ə-nēl'*, *v.t.* to anoint (*arch.*): to administer extreme unction to. [O.E. *an*, on, *ele*, oil; used in reminiscence of Shakespeare; see unaneled.]

anemia, anemic, etc. Same as anaemia, etc.

anemo-, in composition, wind.—*ns.* anemogram (*ə-nem'ō-gram*), an anemographic record; anem'ograph (-*gräf*), an instrument for measuring and recording the pressure and velocity of the wind.—*adj.* anemographic (-*graf'ik*).—*ns.* anemology (*an-i-mol'ə-ji*), the science of the winds; anemometer (-*mom'i-tər*), a wind-gauge.—*adj.* anemometric (-*mō-met'rik*).—*ns.* anemom'etry; anemone (*ə-nem'ə-ni*), windflower—any member of the genus Anemone of the crowfoot family: a sea-anemone (Gr. *anemōnē*).—*adj.* anemoph'-ilous, wind-pollinated.—*n.* anemoph'ily. [Gr. *anemos*, wind; cf. L. *animus*, *anima.*]

anencephaly, *an-ən-sef'ə-li*, *-kef'*, *n.* congenital absence of all or part of the brain.—Also *angelos*, a messenger.]

anencephal'ia (-*āl'ya*).—*adj.* anencephal'ic. [Gr. *an-*, priv.; see encephalon.]

an-end, *ən-end'*, *adv.* to the end, continuously (*Shak.*): upright (*Shak.*): straight ahead (*naut.*).—most an end (*obs.*), almost always. [Prep. an and end.]

anent, *ə-nent'*, (mainly *Scot.*) *prep.* in a line with: against: towards: in regard to, concerning, about. [O.E. *on efen*, on even.]

anerly, *an'ər-li*, (*arch. Scot.*) *adv.* only. [ane; *r* perh. on analogy of some other word.]

aneroid, *an'ə-roid*, *adj.* dispensing with the use of liquid.—*n.* an aneroid barometer. [Fr. *anéroïde* —Gr. *a-*, priv., *nēros*, wet, *eidos*, form.]

anesthesia, etc. Same as anaesthesia, etc.

anetic, *a-net'ik*, (*med.*) *adj.* soothing. [L. *aneticus* —Gr. *anetikos*, abating sickness.]

aneurin, *an'ū-rin*, *ə-nū'rin*, *n.* vitamin B₁, deficiency of which affects the nervous system.— Also called thiamine. [Gr. *a-*, priv., *neuron*, nerve.]

aneurysm, *an'ūr-izm*, *n.* dilatation of an artery (*path.*): any abnormal enlargement.—*adj.* aneurys'mal.—Also aneurism. [Gr. *aneurysma-ana*, up, *eurys*, wide.]

anew, *ə-nū'*, in U.S. -*nōō'*, *adv.* afresh: again. [of and new.]

anfractuous, *an-frakt'ū-əs*, *adj.* winding, involved, circuitous.—*n.* anfractuosity (-*os'i-ti*). [L. *anfractuōsus*—*ambi-*, about, *frangēre*, to break.]

Angaraland, *ang-gä-rä'land*, (*geol.*) *n.* the primitive nucleus of N.E. Asia. [*Angara* River.]

angary, *ang'gər-i*, *n.* a belligerent's right to seize and use neutral or other property (subject to compensation). [Gr. *angareiā*, forced service— *angaros*, a courier; a Persian word—Assyrian *agarru.*]

angekkok, *ang'gi-kok*, *n.* Eskimo conjurer. [Eskimo.]

angel, *ān'jl*, *n.* a divine messenger: a ministering spirit: an attendant or guardian spirit: a person possessing the qualities attributed to these— gentleness, purity, etc.: a dead person regarded as received into heaven: one supposed to have a

special commission, as the head of the Church in Rev. ii and iii: in the Catholic Apostolic Church, one who corresponds in a limited sense to a bishop: a messenger generally (*poet.*): an old Eng. coin bearing the figure of an angel: a radar echo of unknown origin: a financial backer or adviser (*coll.*): a rich man who is an easy victim for those in search of money (*coll.*). —*adjs.* angelic (*an-jel'ik*), -al.—*adv.* angel'ically. —ān'gel-cake, ān'gel-food, a cake made of flour, sugar, and white of egg; ān'gel-fish, a kind of shark (*Squatina*, or *Rhina*), with large wing-like pectoral fins: a tropical American river-fish (*Pterophyllum*) of the family Cichlidae, much compressed, almost circular in body but cres-cent-shaped owing to the long fin filaments, the whole banded with changing black vertical stripes: applied also to *Pomacanthus* and several other fishes of the Chaetodontidae; ān'gelhood; Angel'ica, a genus of umbelliferous plants with large leaves and double-winged fruit, once highly reputed as a defence against poison and pestilence: (*without cap.*) a garden plant by some included in the genus as *A. Archangelica*, by others called *Archangelica officinalis*: its candied leaf-stalks and midribs; angel'ica-tree', an American Aralia; angelol'atry (*ān-*), angel-worship; āngelol'ogy, doctrine regarding angels; āngeloph'any, the manifestation of an angel to a man; āng'els-on-horse'back, oysters and bacon on toast; ān'gel-water, a perfumed liquid, at first made largely from angelica, then from ambergris, rose-water, orange-flower water, etc. —on the side of the angels, basically in sympathy with traditional virtues and virtuous aims. [Gr. *angelos*, a messenger.]

angelus, *an'ji-ləs*, *n.* a short devotional exercise in honour of the Incarnation, repeated three times daily: the bell rung in Roman Catholic countries at morning, noon, and sunset, to invite the faithful to recite it. [From the introductory words, '*Angelus* domini nuntiavit Mariae'.]

anger, *ang'gər*, *n.* hot displeasure, often involving a desire for retaliation: wrath: inflammation (*now dial.*).—*v.t.* to make angry: to irritate.— *adj.* an'gerless.—*advs.* an'gerly (*arch.*), ang'rily. —*n.* ang'riness.—*adj.* ang'ry, excited with anger: inflamed: of threatening or lowering aspect.—*n.* an angry young man.—angry young man, a young man loud in disgust at what his elders have made of society (from *Look Back in Anger*, play, 1956, by John Osborne, one of a group of writers of the period to whom the term was applied). [O.N. *angr*; cf. agnail, anbury, angina, anguish.]

Angevin, *an'ji-vin*, *adj.* of *Anjou*: relating to the Plantagenet house that reigned in England from 1154 to 1485, descended from Geoffrey V, Count of Anjou.—*n.* a native of Anjou: a member of the house of Anjou—by some reckoned only down to loss of Anjou (1204), by others, till the deposition of Richard II in 1399.

angico, *an'ji-kō*, *n.* a S. American mimosaceous tree (*Piptadenia*): its gum. [Port.—Tupí.]

angina, *an-ji'nə*, better *an'ji-nə*, *n.* any inflammatory affection of the throat, as quinsy, croup, etc.—*adj.* anginal (*an-ji'nl*, *an'ji-nl*).—angina pec'toris, a disease of the heart marked by paroxysms of intense pain, radiating from the breastbone mainly towards the left shoulder and arm. [L. *angina.* See anguish.]

angiocarpous, *an-ji-ō-kär'pəs*, *adj.* having the fruit, or in fungi the hymenium, within a special covering. [Gr. *angeion*, a case, *karpos*, fruit.]

angiogram, *an'ji-ō-gram*, *n.* a photograph made by angiography.—*ns.* angiog'raphy, art or process of making X-ray photographs of blood-vessels by injecting the vessels with a substance opaque to the rays; angioma (*an-ji-ō'ma*), a tumour composed of blood or lymph vessels:—

*pl.* angiō'mata. [Gr. *angeion*, case, vessel; *gramma*, that which is written.]

angiosperm, *an'ji-ō-spûrm, n.* a plant of the Angiosperm'ae, one of the main divisions of flowering plants, in which the seeds are in a closed ovary, not naked as in gymnosperms.— *adjs.* angiosperm'al, angiosperm'ous. [Gr. *angeion*, case, *sperma*, seed.]

angiostomous, *an-ji-os'təm-əs,* angiostomatous, *an-ji-ō-sto'mə-təs, adjs.* narrow-mouthed: with a mouth that is not distensible. [Gr. *angeion*, a vessel, case, confused with L. *angēre*, to compress; Gr. *stōma, stomatos,* mouth.]

angle, *ang'gl, n.* a corner: the point from which lines or surfaces diverge: the inclination of two straight lines, or of two curves measured by that of their tangents, or of two planes measured by that of perpendiculars to their intersection (*geom.*): the spread of a cone, a number of meeting planes or the like, measured by the area on the surface of a sphere subtending it at the centre: an outlying corner or nook: a point of view: frame (*snooker,* etc.).—*v.t.* to put in a corner: to corner: to put in the jaws of a billiard pocket: to move, drive, direct, turn, adjust, present, at an angle: to present (news, etc.) in such a way as to serve a particular end. —*v.i.* to proceed at an angle or by an angular course—*adj.* ang'led, having angles: biased.— *adv.* ang'lewise.—*adj.* ang'ular (*ang'gū-lər*), having an angle or corner: measured by an angle: stiff in manner, the opposite of easy or graceful (*fig.*): bony and lean in figure.—*n.* angūlarity (*-lar'i-ti*).—*adj.* ang'ūlated, formed with angles.—angle iron, an L-shaped iron used in structural work. [Fr.,—L. *angulus*: cog. with Gr. *ankylos*; both from root *ank*, to bend, seen also in anchor, ankle.]

angle, *ang'gl, n.* a fish-hook or fishing-tackle (*obs.*): an act of angling (esp. *fig.*).—*v.i.* to fish with rod and line.—*v.t.* to try to gain by some artifice (with *for*).—*ns.* ang'ler, one who fishes with rod and line, esp. for sport: the devil-fish or fishing-frog, a wide-mouthed voracious fish (*Lophius piscatorius*) that attracts its prey by waving filaments attached to its head: extended to related kinds, some of them remarkable for the dwarf males parasitic on the female; ang'ling.—*n.* ang'le-worm, any worm used as bait by anglers. [O.E. *angul,* hook.]

Angle, *ang'gl, n.* a member or descendant of the German tribe (O.E. *Engle*) from Schleswig that settled in Northumbria, Mercia, and East Anglia.—*adj.* Ang'lian, of the Angles.—*n.* an Angle: the English dialect of the Angles.—*adj.* Ang'lican, of or characteristic of, the Church of England and churches in communion with it: English (esp. *U.S.*).—Also *n.*—*n.* Ang'licanism, the principles of the Church of England: attachment to English institutions, esp. the English Church.—*adj.* anglice (*ang'gli-sē*); L. *ang'gli-kā*), in English.—*v.t.* ang'licise, -ize (*-siz*), to make English.—*v.i.* to assume or conform to English ways.—*ns.* ang'licism (*-sizm*), an English idiom or peculiarity: English principles; ang'licist, ang'list, one who has a scholarly knowledge of the English language, literature, and culture; anglist'ic, the study of these subjects.—*v.t.* ang'lify, to make English.—*pfx.* Anglo- (*ang'-glō-*), English: esp. conjointly English and something else.—*adj.* Ang'lo-Amer'ican, English in origin or birth, American by settlement or citizenship.—Also *n.*—*n.* Anglo-Cath'olic, one who regards himself as a Catholic of Anglican pattern: a High-Churchman.—Also *adj.*—*n.* Anglo-Cathol'icism.—*adj.* Anglo-French', of England and France.—*n.* the form of the French language formerly spoken in England.—*adj.* Anglo-In'dian, of England and India: of English as spoken in India: Eurasian.—*n.* an English-

man long resident in India: a Eurasian.—*n.* Anglo-I'rish, the English language as spoken in Ireland: Irish people of English descent: people of mixed English and Irish descent.—*adj.* of England and Ireland: of the Anglo-Irish people or speech.—*n.* Anglo-Is'raelite, one who believes that the English are descendants of the Jewish 'lost tribes' carried off by the Assyrians 721 B.C. —Also *adj.*—*ns.* anglo-mā'nia, a craze, or indiscriminate admiration, for what is English; anglomā'niac; Anglo-Nor'man, the French dialect of the Normans in England.—Also *adj.* —*n.* ang'lophil (*-fil*), also -phile (*-fīl*), a friend and admirer of England and things English (Gr. *philos,* friend).—Also *adj.*—*n.* ang'lophobe, one who fears or dislikes England and things English (Gr. *phobos,* fear).—Also *adj.*—*n.* anglophō'bia.—*adjs.* anglophō'biac, -phobic (*-fōb', -fob'*); Ang'lophone, of African state, person, speaking English, esp. as opp. to French, in everyday affairs.—*n.* Anglo-Sax'on, Old English: one of the Germanic settlers in England and Scotland, including Angles, Saxons, and Jutes, or of their descendants: a Saxon of England, distinguished from the Old Saxons of the Continent: anybody of English speech.—Also *adj.*—*n.* Anglo-Sax'ondom. [L. *Anglus.*]

anglesite, *ang'gli-sit, n.* orthorhombic lead sulphate, first found in *Anglesey.*

Anglican, etc., Anglo-, etc. See Angle.

Angola, *ang-gō'la, adj.* Angora: pertaining to Angola in Africa.

Angora, *ang-gō'ra, -gö', adj.* of *Ang'ŏra* (Gr. *Ankȳra*; in later times *Angora, Ankara*) a town of ancient Galatia, now capital of Turkey.—*n.* (in all meanings sometimes without *cap.*) an Anatolian goat: its long silky wool (the true mohair): cloth made from it: a silky-haired rabbit or (formerly) cat: yarn or material of Angora rabbit hair.

Angostura, *ang-gos-tū'ra, n.* a town (now Ciudad Bolivar) on the narrows (Sp. *angostura*) of the Orinoco in Venezuela, giving name to an aromatic bitter bark formerly used in medicine (*fam.* Rutaceae, esp. *Cusparia*).—Angostura bitters, trademark for a brand of aromatic bitters first made in Angostura.

angry. See anger.

angst, *ängst,* (Ger.) anxiety.—*adj.* angst'-ridden.

Ångström, angstrom, *ang'* or *ong'strəm, n.* a unit (10⁻¹⁰ metres) used in expressing wavelengths of light, ultraviolet rays, X-rays, molecular and atomic distances.—Formerly, but not now usu., Ång-, angstrom unit. [Anders J. *Ångström* (1814-74), Swedish physicist.]

Anguis, *ang'gwis, n.* generic name not of a snake but of the blindworm.—*n.* ang'uifauna, fauna of snakes.—*adj.* ang'uiform, snake-shaped.—*n.* Anguill'a, the common eel genus.—*adj.* anguill'-iform, eel-like.—*n.* Anguill'ūla, the paste-eel genus of nematode worms.—*adjs.* anguine (*ang'-gwin*) of or like a snake; ang'uiped(e) (*-ped, -pēd*) having feet or legs in the form of snakes. [L. *anguis,* snake; adj. *anguinus*; dim. *anguilla,* eel.]

anguish, *ang'gwish, n.* excessive pain of body or mind: agony.—*v.t.* to afflict with anguish.—*v.i.* to suffer anguish.—*adj.* ang'uished. [O.Fr. *angoisse,* choking—L. *angustia,* tightness, narrowness.]

angular. See under angle.

angusti-, *ang-gus'ti-,* in composition, narrow.— *adjs.* angustifo'liate, narrow-leaved; angustiros'-trate, narrow-beaked. [L. *angustus,* narrow.]

angwantibo, *ang-wän'ti-bō,* a small W. African lemur. [W. African word.]

anharmonic, *an-här-mon'ik, adj.* not harmonic.— anharmonic ratio, cross-ratio (harmonic when= -1). [Gr. *an-,* priv., *harmonikos,* harmonic.]

an-heires (*Shak.*), an obscure word in *Merry*

*Wives* II, i. 227, variously conjectured to be an error for **on** here, for **mynheers**, or for **ameers**.
**anhelation**, *an-hi-lā'shən*, *n.* shortness of breath. [L. *anhēlātiō*, *-ōnis*—*anhēlāre*, to gasp.]
**anhungered.** See **ahungered.**
**anhydride**, *an-hī'drid*, *n.* a compound representing in its composition an acid *minus* water.—*n.* **anhy'drite**, a mineral, anhydrous calcium sulphate.—*adj.* **anhy'drous**, free from water. [Gr. *an-*, priv., *hydōr*, water.]
**aniconic**, *an-ī-kon'ik*, *adj.* symbolising without aiming at resemblance: pertaining to aniconism.—*ns.* **ani'conism** (*-kən-izm*), worship or veneration of an object that represents a god without being an image of him; **ani'conist.** [Gr. *an-*, priv., *eikōn*, image.]
**anicut, annicut,** *an'i-kut*, *n.* a dam. [Tamil *anaikattu.*]
**anigh**, *ə-nī'*, *prep.* and *adv.* nigh. [*a-* as in *anear, afar,* and **nigh**; a modern formation.]
**anight**, *ə-nīt'*, (*Shak.*) *adv.* of nights, at night. [of **and** **night.**]
**anil**, *an'il*, *n.* indigo, plant or dye. [Port. *anil*; Ar. *an-nil*, the indigo plant; Sans. *nīlī*, indigo.]
**anile**, *an'īl*, *ān'īl, adj.* old-womanish: imbecile.— *n.* **anility** (*a-* or *ə-nil'i-ti*), old-womanishness: imbecile dotage. [L. *ănus, -ūs,* an old woman.]
**aniline**, *an'il-ēn, -in,* or *-īn, n.* a product of coal tar extensively used in dyeing and other industrial arts, first obtained from *anil.*—Also *adj.* (as in **aniline** dye).
**anima**, *an'i-ma, n.* the soul, the innermost part of the personality.—**anima mundi**, *mun'dī, mōōn'dē,* the soul of the world. [L.]
**animadvert**, *an-im-ad-vûrt', v.i.* to take cognisance (*law*; usu. with *on, upon*): to take note: to comment critically (**on**): to express censure.— *v.t.* to consider, to observe (*obs.*).—*ns.* **animadver'sion; animadvert'er.** [L. *animus,* the mind, *ad,* to, and *vertĕre,* to turn.]
**animal,** *an'i-məl, n.* an organised being having life, sensation, and voluntary motion—typically distinguished from a plant, which is organised and has life, but apparently not sensation or voluntary motion: often, a lower animal—one below man: a mammal: a brutish or sensual man.— *adj.* of, of the nature of, derived from, or belonging to an animal or animals: brutal, sensual.—*v.t.* **an'imalise, -ize,** to represent or conceive an animal form: to endow with animal life or the properties of animal matter: to convert into animal matter: to brutalise, sensualise. —*ns.* **animalisā'tion, -z-; an'imalism,** exercise or enjoyment of animal life, as distinct from intellectual: the state of being actuated by mere animal appetites: brutishness, sensuality: theory that man is a mere animal being; **an'imalist,** one who practises or believes in animalism: one who paints, carves, or writes stories about, animals; **animality** (*-al'i-ti*), animal nature or life: status of an animal or of a lower animal.—*adv.* **an'imally,** physically.—**animal spirits** (orig. *spirit*), formerly, a supposed principle formed in the brain out of vital spirits and conveyed to all parts of the body through the nerves: nervous force: exuberance of health and life: cheerful buoyancy of temper: the spirit or principle of volition and sensation (*Milt.*); **an'imal-worship; -worshipper.** [L. *animal*— *anima,* air, breath, life, soul.]
**animal bipes,** *an'i-mal bī'pēz, bī'pās,* (L.) a two-footed animal, man; **animal implume,** *im-plōō'mē, -me,* featherless animal; **animal rationale,** *rā-shi-ō-nā'lē, ra-ti-ō-nä'le,* reasoning animal; **animal risibile,** *ri-sī'bi-lē, rē-sī'bi-le,* animal able to laugh.
**animalcule,** *an-im-al'kūl, n.* a small animal: (now) one that cannot be seen by the naked eye:— *pl.* **animal'cules, animal'cula.**—*adj.* **animal'cular.**—*n.* **animal'culist,** one who believes that

the spermatozoon contains all future generations in germ. [L. *animalculum,* dim. of *animal.*]
**animate,** *an'im-āt, v.t.* to give life to: to enliven: to inspirit: to actuate.—*adj.* (*-mit*) living: having animal life.—*adj.* **an'imated,** lively: full of spirit: endowed with life: moving as if alive.—*adv.* **an'imatedly.**—*adj.* **an'imating.**—*adv.* **an'imatingly.**—*ns.* **animā'tion,** act of animating: state of being alive: liveliness: vigour; **an'imator,** primitive attribution of life to natural phenomena and natural objects, but not, as in **animism,** belief that spirits reside in them; **an'imator,** an artist who makes drawings for animated cartoons.—**animated cartoon,** a motion picture produced from drawings, each successive drawing showing a very slight change of position so that a series of them gives the effect of a definite movement. [L. *animāre, -ātum— anima,* air, breath, life.]
**animé, anime,** *an'i-mā, -mē, n.* the resin of the W. Indian locust-tree: extended to other gums and resins. [Said to be Fr. *animé,* living, from the number of insects in it; but perhaps a native name.]
**animism,** *an'im-izm, n.* the attribution of a soul to natural objects and phenomena: G. E. Stahl's theory that the soul is the vital principle.—*n.* **an'imist.**—*adj.* **animis'tic.** [L. *anima,* the soul.]
**animo et fide,** *an'i-mō et fī'dē, fi'dā,* (L.) by courage and faith.
**animosity,** *an-im-os'i-ti, n.* strong dislike: enmity. [L. *animōsitās,* fullness of spirit.]
**animus,** *an'im-əs, n.* intention: actuating spirit: hostility. [L. *animus,* spirit, soul.]
**anion,** *an'i-on, n.* an ion that seeks the anode: an electronegative ion.—*adj.* **anion'ic.** [Gr. *ana,* up, *iŏn,* going, pr.p. neut of *ienai,* to go.]
**anise,** *an'is, n.* an umbelliferous plant (*Pimpinella*) whose aromatic seeds are used in making cordials: in Matt. xxiii. 23 (Gr. *anĕthon*) believed to be dill.—*ns.* **an'iseed,** the seed of anise: anisette; **anisette** (*an-i-zet'*), a cordial or liqueur prepared from anise seed.—**star-anise** (see **star**). [Gr. *anison,* anise.]
**aniso-,** *an-ī'sō-,* or *-so',* in composition, unequal. —*adjs.* **anisocercal** (*-sûr'kl*), with unequal taillobes; **anisodac'tylous** (of birds), with three toes turned forward, one backward; **anisom'erous,** with unequal numbers of parts in the floral whorls; **anisophyll'ous,** with differently formed leaves on different sides of the shoot; **anisotrop'ic,** not isotropic, showing differences of property or of effect in different directions.—*n.* **anisot'ropy.** [Gr. *anisos,* unequal—*an-,* priv., *isos,* equal.]
**anker,** *angk'ər, n.* an old measure for wines and spirits used in Northern Europe, varying considerably—that of Rotterdam 8½ imperial gallons. [Du.]
**ankerite,** *ang'kər-īt, n.* a rhombohedral carbonate of calcium, iron, magnesium, and manganese. [After Professor M. J. *Anker* (1772-1843), Styrian mineralogist.]
**ankh,** *angk, n.* an ansate cross—T-shaped with a loop above the horizontal bar—symbol of life. [Egypt., life.]
**ankle,** or (*arch.*) **ancle,** *angk'l, n.* the joint connecting the foot and leg.—*adj.* **ank'led,** having ankles.—*n.* **ank'let** (*-lit*), an ornamental or supporting ring or chain for the ankle.— **ank'le-boot, ank'le-jack,** a boot reaching above the ankle; **ankle sock,** a sock reaching to and covering the ankle. [O.E. *anclēow*; cf. Ger. *enkel,* and angle.]
**Ankole,** *ang-kō'lē, n.* a breed of large cattle with long horns. [*Ankole,* plateau region in Uganda.]
**ankus,** *ang'kəs, n.* an elephant goad. [Hind.]
**ankylosis, anchylosis,** *ang-ki-lō'sis, n.* fusion of bones or skeletal parts: fixation of a joint by fibrous bands or union of bones.—*v.t.* and *v.i.*

ank'ylose, anch'ylose, to stiffen or fuse, as a joint or bones.—*adj.* ank'ylosed, anch'ylosed. [Gr. *ankylōsis,* stiffening of a joint—*ankyloein,* to crook.]

ankylostomiasis, anchylostomiasis, *ang-ki-lō-sto-mī'ə-sis, n.* hookworm disease or miner's anaemia, caused by a parasitic nematode (*Ankylostomum duodenale* or other). [Gr. *ankylos,* crooked, *stoma,* mouth.]

anlace, anelace, *an'las, -ləs, n.* a short two-edged tapering dagger. [Ety. unknown.]

anlage, *än'lä-gə,* (*biol.*) *n.* the primordium or first rudiment of an organ. [Ger.]

ann, *an,* (*Scot.*) *n.* see annat.

anna, *an'a, n.* an obsolescent coin of India and Pakistan, the sixteenth part of a rupee. (Decimal coinage introduced India, 1957, Pakistan, 1961.) [Hind. *ānā.*]

annabergite, *an'ə-bûrg-īt, n.* an apple-green mineral, hydrous nickel arsenate. [*Annaberg* in Saxony.]

annal, *an'əl, n.* a year's entry in a chronicle: (in *pl.*) records of events under the years in which they happened: historical records generally: year-books.—*v.t.* ann'alise, -ize, to record.—*n.* ann'alist, a writer of annals.—*adj.* annalist'ic. [L. *annālis,* yearly—*annus,* a year.]

annat, *an'ət, n.* annates, *an'āts, n.pl.* the first-fruits, or one year's income of a benefice, paid to the Pope (in England from 1535 to the crown, from 1703 to Queen Anne's bounty; extinguished or made redeemable 1926): annat or ann (*Scots law*) from 1672 to 1925 the half-year's stipend payable after a parish minister's death to his widow or next of kin. [L.L. *annāta*—L. *annus,* a year.]

an(n)atto, a- or *ə-nat'ō,* an(n)atta, -a, arnotto, *är-not'ō, n.* a bright orange colouring matter got from the fruit pulp of a tropical American tree, *Bixa Orellana* (fam. *Bixaceae*). [Supposed to be of Carib origin.]

anneal, *ə-nēl', v.t.* to heat and cool gradually (glass, metals), usu. in order to soften: to heat in order to fix colours on, as glass.—Also *v.i.*—*ns.* anneal'er; anneal'ing. [Pfx. *an-,* and O.E. *ǣlan,* to burn.]

annelid, *an'ə-lid, n.* member of the Annelida (*ə-nel'i-da*), a class comprising the red-blooded worms, having a long body composed of numerous rings. [L. *annellus, ānellus,* dim. of *ānulus,* a ring.]

annex, *ə-neks', v.t.* to add to the end: to join or attach: to take permanent possession of: to purloin, appropriate (*coll.*): to affix: append.—*n.* (*an'eks*) something added: a supplementary building—sometimes (as Fr.) annexe (*a-neks', an'eks*).—*n.* annexā'tion (*an-*).—*n.* and *adj.* annexā'tionist.—*ns.* annexion (*ə-nek'shən*), act of annexing: something annexed (*Shak.*); annex'ment, addition (*Shak.*): the thing annexed; annexure, *a-nek'shər,* something added, esp. an addition to a public document. [L. *annectēre, annexum*—*ad,* to, *nectēre,* to tie.]

annicut. See anicut.

annihilate, *ə-nī'(h)il-āt, v.t.* to reduce to nothing: to put out of existence: to crush or wither by look or word (*fig.*).—*ns.* annihilā'tion, reduction to nothing: the destruction of soul as well as body (*theol.*); annihilā'tionism, the belief that the soul (esp. of the unrepentant wicked) dies with the body.—*adj.* annī'hilātive.—*n.* anni'hilātor. [L. *annihilāre, -ātum*—*ad,* to, *nihil,* nothing.]

anniversary, *an-i-vûrs'ə-ri, adj.* returning, happening or commemorated about the same date every year: pertaining to annual recurrence or celebration.—*n.* the day of the year on which an event happened or is celebrated as having happened in a previous year: the celebration proper to recurrence, esp. a mass or religious

service. [L. *anniversārius*—*annus,* a year, and *vertĕre, versum,* to turn.]

anno, *an'ō,* (L.) in the year; anno Christi, *kris'tī, -tē,* in the year of Christ; anno Domini, *dom'in-ī, -ē,* in the year of our Lord (used as *n.* for 'advancing old age'); anno mundi, *mun'dī, moōn'dē,* in the year of the world (used in reckoning dates from the supposed time of creation); anno regni, *reg'nī, -nē,* in the year of the reign; anno salutis, *sal-ū'tis, -ōō',* in the year of redemption; anno urbis conditae, *ûr'bis kon'dit-ē, ōor'bis kon'dit-ī,* in the year of the founding of the city (i.e. Rome, 753 B.C.).

annotate, *an'ō-tāt, v.t.* to make notes upon.—*v.i.* to append notes.—*ns.* annotā'tion, the making of notes: a note of explanation: comment; an'-notātor. [L. *annotāre*—*ad,* to, *notāre, -ātum,* to mark.]

announce, *ə-nowns', v.t.* to declare: to give public notice of: to make known.—*ns.* announce'ment; announc'er, one who announces: in radio and television, one who reads the news and announces other items in the programme. [O.Fr. *anoncer*—L. *annuntiāre*—*ad,* to, *nuntiāre,* to report.]

annoy, *ə-noi', v.t.* and *v.i.* to trouble: to vex: to tease: to harm, esp. in military sense.—*ns.* annoy' (now poetic), annoy'ance, that which annoys: act of annoying: state of being annoyed.—*adv.* annoy'ingly. [O.Fr. *anoier* (It. *annoiare*); noun *anoi* (mod. *ennui*)—L. L. *inodiāre*—L. phrase, *in odiō,* as in 'est mihi *in odiō*'= it is to me hateful.]

annual, *an'ū-əl, adj.* yearly: coming every year: lasting or living for a year: requiring to be renewed every year: performed in a year.—*n.* a plant that lives for one year only: a publication appearing yearly, esp. an illustrated gift-book: a year-book.—*adv.* ann'ually.—annual rings, rings, as seen in cross-section, in a branch or trunk, representing generally a year's growth of wood. [L.L. *annuālis*—*annus,* a year.]

annuity, *ə-nū'i-ti, n.* a payment (generally of uniform amount) falling due in each year during a given term, such as a period of years or the life of an individual, the capital sum not being returnable.—*n.* annū'itant, one who receives an annuity.—annuity due, one whose first payment is due in advance; certain annuity, one for a fixed term of years, subject to no contingency whatever; complete annuity, one of which a proportion is payable up to the day of death; contingent annuity, one that depends on the continuance of some status, as the life of a person; curtate annuity, one payable only at the end of each year survived; deferred or reversionary annuity, one whose first payment is not to be made until the expiry of a certain number of years. [Fr. *annuité*—L.L. *annuitās, -ātis*—L. *annus,* year.]

annul, *ə-nul', v.t.* to make null: to reduce to nothing: to abolish:—*pr.p.* annull'ing; *pa.t.* and *pa.p.* annulled'.—*n.* annul'ment. [Fr. *annuler*—L.L. *annūllāre*—L. *ad,* to, *nūllus,* none.]

annular, *an'ū-lər, adj.* ring-shaped: cutting in a ring: ring-bearing.—*n.* the ring-finger.—*n.* annularity (*-lar'i-ti*).—*n.pl.* Annūlā'ta (*obs.*), the Annelida.—*n.* ann'ūlate (*obs.*), an annelid.—*adjs.* ann'ūlate, -d, ringed.—*ns.* annūlā'tion, a ring or belt: a circular formation; ann'ūlet, a little ring: a small flat fillet encircling a column, etc. (*archit.*): a little circle borne as a charge (*her.*).—*adj.* ann'ūlose, ringed.—*n.* ann'ūlus (*biol.*), any ring-shaped structure, esp. a ring of cells that brings about dehiscence of a moss sporogonium or a fern capsule:—*pl.* ann'ūli.—annular eclipse, one in which a ring-shaped part of the sun remains visible. [L. *annulāris,* for *ānulāris*—*ānulus,* a ring—dim. of *ānus,* a rounding or ring.]

annunciate, annuntiate, *ə-nun's(h)i-āt, v.t.* to proclaim.—*ns.* annunciā'tion (*-si-*), proclamation: esp. (*cap.*) that of the angel to the Virgin Mary, or its anniversary, 25th March (Annunciā'tion-day, Lady-day); Annunciation-lily, the white lily (*Lilium candidum*), often seen in pictures of the Annunciation.—*adj.* annun'ciative.—*n.* annun'ciator, a device giving audible or visual information, e.g. indicating where a bell or telephone is being rung, now often operated by closed-circuit television: an announcer. [L. *annuntiāre*, -*ātum*—*ad*, to, *nuntiāre*—*nuntius*, a messenger; *c* from mediaeval spelling of Latin; cf. announce.]

annus mirabilis, *an'əs mir-ab'il-is, an'ōōs mēr-ăb'il-is*, (L.) year of wonders—applied to 1666 (year of plague and fire of London), etc.

anoa, *a-nō'a, n.* the sapi-utan, or wild ox of Celebes, like a small buffalo. [Native name.]

anode, *an'ōd, n.* the electrode by which an electric current enters an electrolyte or gas (opp. to cathode): in high vacuum, the electrode to which electrons flow.—*v.t.* anodise, -ize (*an'ō-dīz*), to give a protective or decorative coat to a metal by using it as an anode in electrolysis.—*adjs.* anōd'al (or *an'od-əl*), anodic (*an-od'ik*), of an anode: upwards on the genetic spiral (*bot.*). [Gr. *anodos*, way up—*ana*, up, *hodos*, way.]

anodyne, *an'ō-din, n.* a medicine that allays pain. [Gr. *anōdynos*—*an-*, priv., and *ŏdynē*, pain.]

anoesis, *a-nō-ē'sis, n.* sensation or emotion not accompanied by understanding of it.—*adj.* anoet'ic (-*et*). [Gr. *anoia*, lack of understanding.]

anoint, *ə-noint', v.t.* to smear with ointment or oil: to consecrate with oil: (ironically) to drub.—*n.* anoint'ment.—the Anointed, the Messiah; the Lord's anointed, in royalist theory, king by divine right. [Fr. *enoint*, pa.p. of *enoindre*—L. *inungĕre, inunctum*—*in*, on, *ung(u)ĕre*, to smear.]

anomaly, *ə-nom'ə-li, n.* irregularity: deviation from rule: the angle measured at the sun between a planet in any point of its orbit and the last perihelion (*astron.*).—*adjs.* anomalist'ic, -al, anomalous: departing from established rules: irregular; anom'alous, irregular: deviating from rule: of vision, relatively insensitive to one or more colours.—anomalistic month, year (see month, year); anomalous water, polywater. [Gr. *anōmalos*—*an-*, priv., and *homalos*, even—*homos*, same.]

anomie, *an'ə-mē, n.* in society or in an individual, a condition of hopelessness caused by breakdown of rules of conduct, and loss of belief and sense of purpose.—Also an'omy. [Fr.,—Gr. *anomia*, or -*iē*, lawlessness—*ā-*, priv., *nomos*, law.]

anon, *ə-non', adv.* in one (instant): immediately: soon: at another time: coming (in reply to a call).—*interj.* expressing failure to hear or understand. [O.E. *on*, in, *ān*, one.]

Anona, *ä-nō'na, n.* a tropical genus of dicotyledons, including custard-apple, sweet-sop, and other edible fruits, giving name to the family Anonā'ceae, akin to the magnolias.—*adj.* anonā'ceous. [Latinised from Sp. *anón*, from Taino.]

anonyma, *ə-non'i-mə,* (Latinised Gr.) a showy woman of easy morals.

anonymous, *ə-non'i-məs, adj.* wanting a name: without name of author, real or feigned.—*ns.* anonym (*an'*), a person whose name is not given: a pseudonym; anonym'ity.—*adv.* anon'ymously. [Gr. *anōnymos*—*an-*, priv., and *onyma* = *onoma*, name.]

Anopheles, *an-of'əl-ēz, n.* a genus of germ-carrying mosquitoes.—*adj.* anoph'eline, relating to Anopheles.—*n.* a mosquito of this genus. [Gr. *anōphelēs*, hurtful—*an-*, *ophelos*, help.]

Anoplura, *an-o-plōō'ra, n.pl.* an order or suborder of insects, the bugs. [Gr. *anoplos*, unarmed, *ourā*, tail.]

anorak, anarak, *an'ə-rak, n.* a Greenlander's fur coat: a hooded waterproof outer jacket. [Greenland Eskimo word.]

anorexia, *an-or-ek'si-a,* anorexy, *an'or-ek-si* (or -*ek'*), *n.* want of appetite, esp. (*psych.*) the pathological condition *anorexia nervosa*. [Gr.

an-, priv., *orexis*, longing—*oregein*, to reach out.]

anorthic, *an-ör'thik, adj.* (*crystal.*) triclinic, referable to three unequal oblique axes.—*n.* anor'thite, a plagioclase feldspar, calcium aluminium silicate (from the oblique angles between the prism faces). [Gr. *an-*, priv., *orthos*, right.]

anosmia, *an-oz'mi-ə, n.* loss of sense of smell.

another, *ə-nudh'ər, adj.* and *pron.* a different or distinct (thing or person): one more: a second: one more of the same kind: any other.—*adj.* anoth'erguess (see othergates).—one another, a compound reciprocal pronoun usu. regarded as interchangeable with 'each other', but by some restricted to cases where more than two individuals are involved; one with another, taken all together, taken on an average. [Orig. an other.]

anough (*Milt.*). Same as enough (*sing.*).

anourous. Same as anurous.

anow (*Milt.*). Same as enow, enough (*pl.*).

anoxia, *an-ok'si-a, n.* deficient supply of oxygen to the tissues.—*adj.* anox'ic. [Gr. *an-*, priv., *o*xygen, -*ia*.]

ansate, -d, *an'sāt, -id, adjs.* having a handle.— ansate cross (see ankh). [L. *ansātus*—*ansa*, handle.]

anschauung, *an-show'ōōng,* (*psych.*) *n.* direct perception through the senses. [Ger. *anschauung*, view.]

anschluss, *an'shlōōs,* (Ger.) union, esp. (*cap.*) the political union of Germanv and Austria in 1938.

anserine, *an'sər-in, adj.* of the goose or the goose family: stupid. [L. *anserinus*—*anser*, goose.]

answer, *än'sər, n.* that which is said, written, or done in meeting a charge, combating an argument, objection, or attack: that which is called for by a question or questioning state of mind: the solution of a problem: an acknowledgment: a return in kind: anything given, sent or said in return: an immediate result or outcome in definite relation to the act it follows: a repetition or echo of a sound: restatement of a theme by another voice or instrument (*mus.*).—*v.t.* to speak, write, or act in answer to or against: to say or write as an answer: to give, send, afford, or be an answer to: to behave in due accordance with: to be in proportion to or in balance with: to give a conclusive or satisfactory answer to: to serve the purpose of: to fulfil: to recompense satisfactorily: to be punished for.—*v.i.* to give an answer: to behave in answer: to be responsible: to suffer the consequences: to be in conformity: to serve the purpose: to succeed: to react.—*adj.* an'swerable, able to be answered: accountable: suitable: equivalent: in due proportion.—*n.* an'swerabil'ity.—*adv.* an'swerably.—*n.* an'swerer.—*adj.* an'swerless.—answer back (*coll.*), to answer one who expects silent submission: to answer pertly; answer to (the name of), to show sign of accepting as one's name: to have as one's name (*coll.*); know all the answers, to be in complete command of the situation with no chance of being caught out—statement usu. made with reference to another person who is too self-confident. [O.E. *andswaru* (n.), *andswarian* (vb.)—*and-*, against, *swerian*, to swear.]

ant, *ant, n.* a small hymenopterous insect (of the Formicidae), of proverbial industry, the emmet or pismire: loosely, a termite (*white ant*).—*n.* ant'ing, the introduction by birds of live ants or other stimulants into their plumage, possibly as a pleasurable means of cleaning it and their skin. —ant'-bear, the great ant-eater, the largest species of ant-eaters, found in swampy regions in S. America: the aardvark of S. Africa; ant'-bird, a S. American ant-thrush; ant'-cow, an aphis kept and tended by ants for its honey-dew; ant'-eater, any one of a S. American family of edentates, feeding chiefly on ants: a pangolin: an aardvark: an echidna.—*n.pl.* ant(s)'-eggs, pupae of ants.—ant'-hill, hillock raised as nest by ants or by termites: the earth (*fig.*); ant'-lion, a neuropterous insect (*Myrmeleon*) whose larva traps ants in a funnel-shaped sandhole; ant'-thrush, any bird of the northern S. American family Formicariidae which feed on insects disturbed by travelling ants, or of the long-legged thrushlike Oriental and Australian family *Pittidae*. [O.E. *ǣmete*; cf. emmet.]

an't, *änt*, a contr. of are not, am not, has not, (*ant*) on it, and it = if it.

anta, *an'ta*, *n.* a square pilaster at either side of a doorway or the corner of a flank wall:—*pl.* an'tae (*-tē*). [L.]

antacid, *ant-as'id*, *adj.* counteracting acidity of the stomach.—*n.* a medicine that counteracts acidity. [Gr. *anti*, against, and acid.]

antagonist, *an-tag'ə-nist*, *n.* one who contends or struggles with another: an opponent: a muscle that opposes the action of another: in an organism, something that has an opposite effect: a drug acting against another drug.—Also *adj.*—*n.* antag'onism, opposition: hostility: production of opposing effects, e.g. in a living body: interference with the growth of another organism, as by using up the food supply or producing an antibiotic substance.—*v.t.* antag'onise, -ize, to struggle violently against: to counteract the action of: to arouse opposition in.—*n.* antag'-onisā'tion, -z-.—*adj.* antagonist'ic.—*adv.* antagonis'tically. [Gr. *antagōnistēs—anti*, against, *agōn*, contest. See agony.]

antaphrodisiac, *ant-af-rō-diz'i-ak*, *-rə-*, *adj.* counteracting sexual desire.—*n.* an antaphrodisiac agent. [Gr. *anti*, against, and aphrodisiac.]

antar, *an'tər*, (*Shak.*) *n.* a cave. [Fr. *antre*—L. *antrum*—Gr. *antron.*]

Antarctic, *ant-ärk'tik*, *adj.* opposite the Arctic: of, near, or relating to the south pole.—*n.* the south polar regions.—Antarctic Circle, a parallel of latitude about 23½° from the south pole. [Gr. *antarktikos—anti*, opposite, and *arktikos*; see Arctic.]

Antares, *an-tā'rēz*, or *-tä'*, *n.* a first magnitude red star in the Scorpion. [Gr. *Antarēs*—pfx. *anti-*, like, *Arēs*, Mars.]

antarthritic, *ant-är-thrit'ik*, *adj.* counteracting gout. [Gr. *anti*, against, and arthritic.]

antasthmatic, *ant-as(th)-mat'ik*, *adj.* counteracting asthma. [Gr. *anti*, against, and asthmatic.]

ante-, *ant'i-*, *pfx.* before. [L. *ante*, old form *anti*; conn. with Gr. *anti-*.]

ante, *an'ti*, *n.* a fixed stake put down by a poker player, usu. before the deal: advance payment. (*-v.t.* to stake: to pay. [L., before.]

ante-bellum, *an'ti-bel'əm*, before the war (whichever is in mind). [L. phrase.]

antecedent, *an-ti-sē'dənt*, *adj.* going before in time: prior.—*n.* that which precedes in time: the noun or its equivalent to which a relative pronoun refers (*gram.*): the conditional part of a hypothetical proposition (*logic*): the numerator term of a ratio (*math.*): (in *pl.*) previous principles, conduct, history, etc.—*n.* antecē'dence.—*adv.*— antecē'dently. [L. *antecēdēns*, *-entis*—*ante*, before, *cēdere*, to go.]

antecessor, *an'ti-ses-ər*, or *-ses'*, *n.* a predecessor (*rare*): an ancestor (*obs.*). [L. *antecessor*; cf. preceding word and ancestor.]

antechamber, *an'ti-chām-bər*, *n.* a chamber or room leading to a more important apartment. [Fr. *antichambre*—L. *ante*, before, and *camera*, a vault.]

antechapel, *an'ti-chap-l*, *n.* the outer part of the west end of a college chapel. [L. *ante*, before, and chapel.]

antedate, *an'ti-dāt*, *n.* a date assigned which is earlier than the actual date.—*v.t.* to date before the true time: to assign to an earlier date: to bring about at an earlier date: to be of previous date to:

to accelerate: to anticipate. [L. *ante*, before, and date.]

antediluvian, *an-ti-di-lōō'vi-ən*, *-lū'*, *adj.* existing or happening before Noah's Flood: resembling the state of things before the Flood: very old-fashioned, primitive.—*n.* one who lived before the Flood: one who lives to be very old.—*adj.* antedilu'vial.—*adv.* antedilu'vially. [L. *ante*, before, *dilūvium*, flood.]

antefix, *an'ti-fiks*, *n.* (usually in *pl.*) an ornament concealing the ends of roofing tiles:—*pl.* an'tefixes, antefix'a (L.).—*adj.* antefix'al. [L. *ante*, before, in front, and *figěre*, *fixum*, to fix.]

antelope, *an'ti-lōp*, *n.* a fabulous fierce horned beast (*Spens.*): since the 17th cent., any one of a group of hollow-horned ruminants near akin to goats. [O.Fr. *antelop*—mediaeval L. *antalopus* —Late Gr. *antholops*, of unknown origin.]

antelucan, *an-ti-lū'kən*, *-lōō'*, *adj.* before dawn or daylight (of e.g. worship). [L *antelūcānus— ante*, before, *lūx*, light.]

ante lucem, *an'te lū'səm*, *lōō'kem*, (L.) before light.

antemeridian, *an-ti-mə-rid'i-ən*, *adj.* before midday. [L. *antemeridiānus—ante meridiem*, before noon.]

ante meridiem, *an'te mer-id'i-em*, *mer-ēd'*, (L.) before noon.

antemundane, *an-ti-mun'dān*, *adj.* before the existence of the world. [L. *ante*, before, *mundānus* —*mundus*, world.]

antenatal, *an-ti-nā'tl*, *adj.* before birth.—*n.* antenā'ti (L. *-nā'tē*), those born before a certain time, as opposed to *post-nati*, born after it—of Scotsmen born before 1603, and Americans before the Declaration of Independence (1776).—antenatal clinic, a clinic for the purpose of treating and giving advice to pregnant women. [L. *ante*, before, *nātālis*, natal, *nātus*, born.]

ante-nicene, *an-ti-ni'sēn*, *adj.* before the first council of *Nicaea* in Bithynia, A.D. 325.

antenna, *an-ten'a*, *n.* a feeler or horn in insects, crustaceans, and myriapods: in wireless communication, a structure for sending out or receiving electric waves: an aerial:—*pl.* antenn'ae (*-ē*), antenn'as (radio).—*adjs.* antenn'al, antenn'ary; antenn'iform; antennif'erous.—*n.* antenn'ūle, one of first or smaller pair of antennae in crustaceans. [L. *antemna*, antenna, yard (of a mast).]

antenuptial, *an-ti-nup'shl*, *adj.* before marriage. [L. *ante*, before, and nuptial.]

anteorbital, *an-ti-ör'bit-l*, *adj.* situated in front of the eyes. [L. *ante*, before, and orbit.]

antepast, *an'ti-päst*, (*obs.*) *n.* something to whet the appetite: a foretaste. [L. *ante*, before, and *pāscěre*, *pāstum*, to feed.]

antependium, *an-ti-pend'i-əm*, *n.* a frontlet, or fore-cloth, for an altar: a frontal. [L. *ante*, before, and *penděre*, to hang.]

antepenult, *an-ti-pen-ult'*, *n.* the last syllable but two.—*adj.* antepenult'imate, last but two. [L. *ante*, before, and penult.]

ante-post, *an'ti-pōst*, *adj.* of betting, beginning before the runners' numbers have been posted. [L. *ante*, before, and post.]

anteprandial, *an-ti-prand'i-əl*, *adj.* before dinner. [L. *ante*, before, and *prandium*, dinner.]

anterior, *an-tē'ri-ər*, *adj.* before, in time or place: in front: towards the bract or away from the axis (*bot.*).—*n.* anterior'ity (*-or'i-ti*).—*adv.* antē'-riorly. [L. *antērior* (comp.)—*ante*, before.]

anteroom, *an'ti-rōōm*, *n.* a room leading into another larger room: a waiting-room: an officers' mess sitting-room. [L. *ante*, before, and room.]

anthelion, *an-thē'li-ən*, *-lyən*, *n.* a luminous coloured ring seen on a cloud or fog-bank over against the sun:—*pl.* anthe'lia. [Gr. *ant(h)ēlios*, *-on*,—*anti*, opposite, *hēlios*, the sun.]

anthelix. See antihelix.

anthelminthic, anthelmintic, *an-thel-min'thik*, *-tik*, *adj.* destroying or expelling worms.—*n.* a drug used for that purpose. [Gr. *anti*, against, and *helmins, helminthos*, a worm.]

**anthem,** *an'thəm, n.* an antiphon (*obs.*): a composition for a church choir, commonly with solo passages, usually set to a passage from the Bible: any song of praise or gladness: loosely applied to an officially recognised national hymn or song (*national anthem*).—*v.t.* to praise in an anthem.— *adv.* **an'themwise** (*Bacon*), in the manner of an antiphonal anthem. [O.E. *antefn*—Gr. *antiphōna* (*pl.*) sounding in answer—*anti*, in return, *phōnē*, voice. See **antiphon**.]

**anthemion,** *an-thē'mi-ən, n.* the so-called honeysuckle ornament in ancient art, a conventionalised plant-form more like a palmetto:—*pl.* **anthē'mia.** [Gr. *anthēmion*, dim. of *anthos*, a flower.]

**anther,** *an'thər, n.* that part of a stamen that contains the pollen.—*ns.* **antherid'ium** (*bot.*), the gametangium in which male gametes are produced:—*pl.* **antherid'ia; antherozo'oid, antherozo'id,** a motile male gamete produced in an antheridium (Gr. *zōoeidēs*, like an animal—*zōion*, animal, and *eidos*, shape). [Gr. *anthēra*, a medicine made from flowers, esp. their inner parts—*anthos*, flower.]

**anthesis,** *an-thē'sis, n.* the opening of a flower-bud: the lifetime of a flower from opening to setting of seed. [Gr. *anthēsis*, flowering—*anthos*, flower.]

**Anthesteria,** *an-thes-tē'ri-ə, n.pl.* the Athenian spring festival of Dionysos, held in the month of *Anthestē'rion* (February—March). [Gr. *ta Anthestēria* (Feast of Flowers), *Anthestēriōn* (the month)—*anthos*, flower.]

**antho-,** in composition, flower.—*n.* **anthocarp** (*an'thō-kärp*; Gr. *karpos*, fruit), a fruit resulting from many flowers, as the pineapple: a fruit of which the perianth or the torus forms part.—*adj.* **anthocarp'ous.**—*ns.* **an'thochlore** (*-klōr, -klör*; Gr. *chlōros*, green, yellow), a yellow pigment in flowers; **anthocyan** (*-si'ən*), *-cy'anin* (Gr. *kyanos*, blue), a glucoside plant pigment, violet in neutral, red in acid, blue in alkaline cell-sap.—*adj.* **an'thoid** (Gr. *eidos*, shape), flower-like.—*v.t.* and *v.i.* **anthologise, -ize** (*an-thol'ə-jiz*).—*ns.* **anthol'ogist; anthol'ogy,** a flower-gathering (*lit.*): a choice collection of poems (orig. of Greek epigrams); **anthomā'nia** (Gr. *maniā*, madness), a craze for flowers; **anthomā'niac; Anthonomus** (*an-thon'ə-məs*; Gr. *nomos*, herbage, food), the genus of the cotton-boll weevil.—*adj.* **anthophilous** (*an-thof'i-ləs*), loving, frequenting, or feeding on flowers.— *ns.* **an'thophore** (*-thō-fōr, -för*), an elongation of the receptacle between calyx and corolla; **anthophyllite** (*an-thō-fil'it, -thə-*, sometimes *-thof'*; Mod.L. *anthophyllum*, clove—Gr. *phyllon*, leaf), an orthorhombic amphibole, usually clovebrown; **anthoxan'thin** (Gr. *xanthos*, yellow), a yellow pigment in plants.—*n.pl.* **Anthozō'a** (Gr. *zōia*, animals), the Actinozoa, a class of coelenterates including sea-anemones, corals, etc. [Gr. *anthos*, flower.]

**Anthony,** *an'tən-i*, a 4th-century saint who has a pig and a bell among his symbols and who was believed to have stayed an epidemic (perhaps raphania, but commonly supposed to be erysipelas) in 1089: (also **tantony,** *tan'*, **St Anthony pig, tantony pig),** the smallest pig in a litter: an obsequious follower.—**St Anthony's cross,** a taucross; **St Anthony's fire** (*pop.*), erysipelas; **St Anthony's nut,** earthnut or pignut; **tantony bell,** a small bell.

**anthophilous, etc.** See **antho-**.

**anthrax,** *an'thraks, n.* a carbuncle, malignant boil: malignant pustule, woolsorter's disease, a deadly disease due to a bacillus, most common in sheep and cattle but communicable to men.—*adj.* **anthracic** (*an-thras'ik*).—*ns.* **anthracene** (*an'thrə-sēn*), a product of coal-tar distillation ($C_{14}H_{10}$), a source of dye-stuffs.—**an'thracite** (*an'thrə-sit*), hard lustrous coal that burns nearly without

flame or smoke, consisting almost entirely of carbon.—*adjs.* **anthracitic** (*-thrə-sit'ik*), of, of the nature of, anthracite; **anthracoid** (*an'thrə-koid*), like anthrax.—*n.* **anthracosis** (*-kō'sis*), a diseased state of the lung due to breathing coal-dust. [Gr. *anthrax, -akos*, charcoal, coal, carbuncle (stone or boil).]

**anthropo-, anthropo-,** in composition, man, human, —*adjs.* **anthropic** (*an-throp'ik*), **-al,** human.—*n.* **anthropobiol'ogy,** human biology.—*adj.* **anthropocentric** (*an-thrō-pō-sent'rik*; Gr. *kentron*, centre), centring the universe in man.—*ns.* **anthropogenesis** (*-jen'*); **anthropogeny** (*-poj'ən-i*; Gr. *genos*, race, birth), the study of man's origin; **anthrōpogeog'raphy,** the geography of the races of man; **anthropogony** (*-pog'ə-ni*; Gr. *gonē, gonos,* birth, begetting), the study, or an account, of the origin of man: **anthropography** (*-pog'rə-fi*), study of the geographical distribution of human races. —*adj.* **an'thropoid** (or *-throp'*; Gr. *eidos*, form), manlike: applied esp. to the highest apes— gorilla, chimpanzee, orang-utan, gibbon, but also to the higher Primates generally—man, apes, monkeys, but not lemurs.—*n.* an anthropoid ape. —*adj.* **anthropoid'al.**—*n.* **anthropol'atry** (Gr. *latreiā*, worship), man-worship, the giving of divine honours to a human being.—*adj.* **anthrōpological** (*-loj'*).—*adv.* **anthrōpolog'ically.**—*ns.* **anthropol'ogist; anthropol'ogy,** the science of man in its widest sense.—*adj.* **anthropomet'ric.**— *ns.* **anthropometry** (*-pom'i-tri*; Gr. *metreein*, to measure), measurement of the human body; **anthrō'pomorph** (Gr. *morphē*, shape), a representation, esp. conventionalised, of the human form in art.—*adj.* **anthropomorph'ic.**—*v.t.* **anthropomor'phise,-ize,** to regard as or render anthropomorphic. —*n.* **anthropomorph'ism,** conception or representation of a god as having the form, personality, or attributes of man: ascription of human characteristics to what is not human; **anthropomor'phist; anthropomorph'ite.**—*adj.* **anthropomorphit'ic.**—*ns.* **anthropomorph'itism; anthropomorphō'sis** (or *-mörf'ə-sis*), transformation into human shape.—*adj.* **anthropomorph'ous,** formed like or resembling man; **anthropopathic**(*-path'ik*). —*adv.* **anthropopath'ically.**—*ns.* **anthropopathism** (*-op'ə-thizm*), **anthropop'athy** (Gr. *pathos*, suffering, passion), ascription of human passions and affections (to God, nature, etc.).—*n.pl.* **anthrōpophagi** (*-pof'ə-ji, -gē*; Gr. *phagein*, to eat), man-eaters, cannibals.—*ns.* **anthropophaginian** (*-jin'i-ən*; *Shak.*), a cannibal; **anthropoph'agite** (*-ə-jit*).—*adj.* **anthropoph'agous** (*-ə-gəs*).—*ns.* **anthrōpoph'agy** (*-ə-ji*), cannibalism; **anthropoph'uism** (Gr. *phyē*, nature), the ascription of a human nature to the gods; **Anthropopithē'cus,** the chimpanzee (Gr. *pithekos*, ape); **anthropos'ophist; anthropos'ophy** (Gr. *sophiā*, wisdom), the knowledge of the nature of men: human wisdom: esp. the spiritualistic doctrine of Rudolf Steiner (1861-1925).—*adj.* **anthrōpopsy'chic** (*-si'kik, -psi'kik*).—*adv.* **anthropopsy'chically.**—*ns.* **anthropopsy'chism** (Gr. *psȳchē*, soul), ascription to nature or God of a soul or mind like man's; **anthropot'omy** (Gr. *tomē*, a cut), human anatomy. [Gr. *anthrōpos*, man (in general sense).]

**Anthurium,** *an-thū'ri-əm, n.* a genus of tropical American plants with showy leaves and flowers. [Gr. *anthos*, flower, *oura*, tail.]

**anti-,** *ant'i-*, in U.S. also *an'ti-, pfx.* against, in opposition to, rivalling, simulating.—*n.* and *adj.* (one who is) opposed to anything. [Gr. *anti*, against, instead of, etc.]

**antiaditis,** *an-ti-ə-dī'tis, n.* tonsillitis. [Gr. *antias, -ados*, tonsil.]

**anti-aircraft,** *an'ti-ār'kräft*, in U.S. also *an'ti-, adj.* intended for use against hostile aircraft.

**antiar,** *an'chär, an'ti-är, n.* the upas-tree: its poisonous latex. [Jav. *antjar*.]

antibacchius, *an-ti-bə-ki'əs*, (*pros.*) *n.* a foot of two long (stressed) syllables followed by a short (unstressed). [Gr. *anti*, opposite to; see under bacchanal.]

antibarbarus, *an'ti-bär'bär-us*, (L.L.) a list of words and locutions to be avoided in the classical usage of a language.

antibilious, *an-ti-bil'yəs*, in U.S. also *an-ti-*, *adj.* of use against biliousness.

antibiosis, *an-ti-bi-ō'sis*, in U.S. also *an-ti-*, *n.* antagonistic relation between associated organisms: inhibition of growth by a substance produced by another organism.—*adj.* antibiotic (*-ot'ik*), inimical to life: inhibiting the growth of another organism, used esp. of a substance produced by micro-organisms which, in dilute solution, has the capacity to inhibit the growth of, or to destroy, micro-organisms causing infectious diseases: pertaining to antibiosis.—*n.* an antibiotic substance. [Gr. *anti*, against, *biōsis*, way of life; adj. *biōtikos—bios*, life.]

antibody, *an'ti-bod-i*, *n.* a defensive substance produced in an organism in response to the action of a foreign body such as the toxin of a parasite. [Gr. *anti*, against, and body.]

Antiburgher, *an-ti-bûrg'ər*, *n.* a member of that section of the Scottish Secession Church which parted from the main body (the *Burghers*) in 1747, interpreting the reference in the oath administered to burgesses in Edinburgh, Glasgow and Perth, to 'the true religion presently professed within this realm' to mean the Established Church.—Also *adj.*

antic, *ant'ik*, *adj.* grotesque.—*n.* a fantastic figure or ornament: a grotesque pageant (*Shak.*): a buffoon, clown, mountebank (*arch.*): (usu. in *pl.*) a fantastic action or trick: a caper.—*v.t.* (*Shak.*) to make grotesque.—*v.i.* to cut capers.—Formerly ant'icke, sometimes ant'ique.—*v.i.* anticize (*ant'i-siz*; *Browning*), to play antics.—See also antique. [It. *antico*, ancient—L. *antiquus*; orig. used of the fantastic decorations found in the remains of ancient Rome.]

anticathode, *an-ti-kath'ōd*, in U.S. also *an'ti-*, *n.* the target of an X-ray tube, on which the cathode rays are focused and from which X-rays are emitted.

anticatholic, *an-ti-kath'ə-lik*, *adj.* opposed to the Catholic or the Roman Catholic Church, to Catholics, or to what is catholic.

antichlor, *an'ti-klōr, -klör*, *n.* any substance used in paper-making to free the pulp from the last traces of free chlorine. [Pfx. anti- and chlorine.]

Antichrist, *an'ti-krist*, *n.* an opponent of Christ: the great opposer of Christ and Christianity expected by the early Church, applied by some to the Pope and others.—*adj.* antichristian (*-kris'*), relating to Antichrist: opposed to Christianity.—*n.* antichris'tianism.—*adv.* antichris'tianly. [Gr. *Antichristos—anti-*, against, *Christos*, Christ.]

Antichthon, *an-tik'thon*, *n.* second earth placed by Pythagoreans on the other side of the sun: the southern hemisphere.—*n.pl.* antich'thones (*-thon-ēz*), the antipodeans. [Gr. *anti-*, opposite to, *chthōn*, earth.]

anticipate, *an-tis'ip-āt*, *v.t.* to forestall (person or thing): to preoccupy: to use, spend, deal with in advance or before the due time: to realise beforehand: to foresee or count upon as certain: to expect: to precede: to advance to an earlier time, bring on sooner.—*v.i.* to be before the normal time: to do anything before the appropriate time.—*adj.* and *n.* antic'ipant, anticipating, anticipative.—*n.* anticipa'tion, act of anticipating: assignment to too early a time: introduction of a tone or tones of a chord before the whole chord (*mus.*): intuition: foretaste: previous notion: presentiment: prejudice: imagining beforehand: expectation.—*adjs.* antic'ipative, anti'cipatory.—*advs.* antic'ipatively, antic'ipatorily.—*n.* antic'i-

pātor. [L. *anticipāre, -ātum—ante*, before, *capēre*, to take.]

anticivic, *an-ti-siv'ik*, *adj.* opposed to citizenship, esp. the conception of it engendered by the French Revolution.—*n.* anticiv'ism.

antick, anticke, obsolete forms of antic, antique.

anticlerical, *an-ti-kler'i-kl*, in U.S. also *an'ti-*, *adj.* opposed to the clergy or their power.—*n.* a member of an anticlerical party.—*n.* anticler'icalism.

anticlimax, *an-ti-kli'maks*, *n.* the opposite of climax: a ludicrous drop in impressiveness after a progressive rise.—*adj.* anticlimac'tic.—*adv.* anticlimac'tically.

anticline, *an'ti-klin*, *n.* (*geol.*) an arch-like fold dipping outwards from the fold-axis.—*adj.* anticlin'al, sloping in opposite directions: perpendicular to the surface near the growing-point (*bot.*).—*n.* an anticline.—*n.* anticlinō'rium (*-klin-* or *-klīn-*), a series of folds which as a whole is anticlinal. [Gr. *anti*, against, *klinein*, to lean; *oros*, a mountain.]

anticoagulant, *an-ti-kō-ag'ū-lənt*, in U.S. also *an'ti-*, *n.* a drug that hinders clotting of blood.—Also *adj.*

anticonvulsant, *an-ti-kən-vul'sənt*, in U.S. also *an'ti-*, *n.* a drug used to control epilepsy, etc.—Also *adj.*

anticous, *an-ti'kəs*, (*bot.*) *adj.* on the anterior side, or away from the axis. [L. *anticus*, in front—*ante*, before.]

anticyclone, *an-ti-si'klōn*, *n.* a rotatory outflow of air from an area of high pressure.—*adj.* anticyclonic (*-klon'ik*). [Pfx. anti-, reverse of, cyclone.]

antidote, *an'ti-dōt*, *n.* that which counteracts poison: anything that prevents an evil (with *against*, *for*, *to*) (*fig.*).—*adj.* antido'tal. [Gr. *antidotos—didonai*, to give.]

antient, an obsolete spelling of ancient.

anti-federal, *an'ti-fed'ər-əl*, in U.S. also *an'ti-*, *adj.* opposed to federalism: applied to the U.S. party afterwards called Democratic.—*ns.* anti-fed'eralism; anti-fed'eralist.

antifouling, *an-ti-fowl'ing*, in U.S. also *an'ti-*, *adj.* intended to prevent fouling of ships' bottoms.

antifreeze, *an-ti-frēz'*, *n.* a substance, as ethylene glycol, with low freezing point put into the radiator of an internal-combustion engine to prevent freezing up.

antifriction, *an-ti-frik'shən*, in U.S. also *an'ti-*, *adj.* intended to reduce friction.

anti-Gallican, *an'ti-gal'ik-ən*, *adj.* opposed to what is French, or to Gallicanism.—Also *n.*—*n.* anti-Gall'icanism.

antigen, *an'ti-jen*, *n.* any substance that stimulates the production of an antibody. [Gr. *anti*, against, *gennaein*, to engender.]

antigropelo(e)s, *an-ti-grop'ə-lōz*, *n.pl.* waterproof leggings. [Said to be from Gr. *anti*, against, *hygros*, wet, and *pēlos*, mud.]

antihelix, *an-ti-hē'liks*, in U.S. also *an'ti-*, anthelix, *an'thi-liks*, *an-thē'liks*, *n.* the inner curved ridge of the external ear:—*pls.* antihelices, (*-li-sēz*), anthel'ices. [Gr. *anthēlix—hēlix*, a coil.]

anti-hero, *an'ti-hē'rō*, in U.S. also *an'ti-*, *n.* a principal character who lacks noble qualities and whose experiences are without tragic dignity:—*fem.* anti-heroine (*her'ō-in*).—*adj.* anti-heroic (*hi-rō'ik*).

antihistamine, *an-ti-his'tə-mēn*, *n.* any of a group of drugs that prevents the action of histamines in allergic conditions.

anti-Jacobin, antijacobin, *an'ti-jak'ə-bin*, in U.S. also *an'ti-*, *adj.* opposed to the Jacobins and to the French Revolution or to democratic principles.—*n.* one opposed to the Jacobins: (*cap.*) a weekly paper started in England in 1797 by Canning and others to refute the principles of the French Revolution.—*n.* anti-Jac'obinism.

antiknock, *an-ti-nok'*, in U.S. also *an'ti-*, *n.* a

substance that prevents knock or detonation in internal-combustion engines.

**antilegomena,** *an-ti-leg-om′i-nə, n.pl.* those books of the New Testament not at first universally accepted but ultimately admitted into the Canon —2 Peter, James, Jude, Hebrews, 2 and 3 John, and the Apocalypse:—opp. to *homologoumena.* [Gr., spoken against.]

**antilogarithm,** *an-ti-log′ə-ridhm, -rithm, n.* a number of which a particular number is the logarithm:—*contr.* **an′tilog.**

**antilogy,** *an-til′ə-ji, n.* a contradiction.—*adj.* **antil′- ogous** (*-gəs*), of the contrary kind: negatively electrified by heating. [Gr. *antilogiā,* contra- diction.]

**Antilope,** *an-til′ō-pē, n.* the Indian antelope genus. *adj.* **antil′opine,** of antelopes. [Form of **antelope,** adopted by P. S. Pallas, naturalist.]

**antilymphocyte serum,** *an-ti-lim′fə-sit sē′rəm,* in U.S. also *an′ti-,* serum used to prevent defensive action of lymphocytes, e.g. in cases where they would reject an organ transplanted into the body.

**antimacassar,** *an-ti-mək-as′ər, n.* a covering for chair-backs, etc., to protect them from macassar oil or other grease in the hair, or for ornament.

**antimalarial,** *an-ti-mə-lā′ri-əl,* in U.S. also *an′ti-, adj.* used against malarial.

**antimask, antimasque,** *an′ti-mäsk, n.* a farcical interlude dividing the parts of, or preceding, the more serious mask.

**anti-matter,** *an′ti-mat′ər,* in U.S. also *an′ti-, n.* hypothetical extra-terrestrial matter that would consist of particles similar to those of terrestrial matter but of opposite electrical charge or, in the case of the neutron, reversed magnetic polarity.

**antimetabole,** *an-ti-me-tab′ol-i,* (*rhet.*) *n.* a figure in which the same words or ideas are repeated in inverse order, as Quarles's 'Be wisely worldly, but not worldly wise'. [Gr.]

**antimetathesis,** *an-ti-me-tath′ə-sis, n.* inversion of the members of an antithesis, as in Crabbe's 'A poem is a speaking picture; a picture, a mute poem'. [Gr.]

**antimnemonic,** *an-ti-ni-mon′ik, adj.* tending to weaken the memory.—Also *n.*

**antimonarchical,** *an-ti-mon-ärk′i-kl,* in U.S. also *an′ti-, adj.* opposed to monarchy and monarchical principles.—*n.* **antimon′archist** (*-ər-kist*).

**antimony,** *an′ti-mən-i, n.* a brittle, bluish-white element (at. numb. 51; symbol Sb, for stibium) of metallic appearance: type (*printers′ slang*).— *adj.* **antimonial** (*-mō′ni-əl*), pertaining to, or con- taining, antimony.—*n.* a drug containing anti- mony.—*adjs.* **antimonic** (*-mon′ik*), containing pentavalent antimony; **antimō′nious,** containing trivalent antimony.—*ns.* **an′timonate** (*-mən-*), **antimō′niate,** a salt of any antimonic acid; **an′timonide,** a binary compound with antimony as one of its constituents; **an′timonite,** a salt of antimonious acid: the mineral stibnite (not chemically an antimonite). [L.L. *antimōnium,* of unknown origin, prob. from some Arabic word.]

**anti-national,** *an′ti-nash′ə-nl,* in U.S. also *an′ti-, adj.* hostile to one's nation or to nationalism.

**antinephritic,** *an-ti-ne-frit′ik,* in U.S. also *an′ti-, adj.* acting against diseases of the kidney.

**antineutrino,** *an-ti-nū-trē′nō,* in U.S. also *an′ti-, n.* the antiparticle of the neutrino.

**antineutron,** *an-ti-nū′tron,* in U.S. also *an′ti-, n.* an uncharged particle that combines with the neutron with mutual annihilation and emission of energy.

**antinode,** *an′ti-nōd,* (*physics*) *n.* a point of maximum disturbance midway between nodes.—*adj.* **anti- nōd′al.**

**antinomian,** *an-ti-nō′mi-ən, n.* one who denies the obligatoriness of moral law: one who believes that Christians are emancipated by the gospel from the obligation to keep the moral law, faith

alone being necessary.—Also *adj.—n.* **anti- no′mianism.**—*aajs.* **antinomic** (*-nom′ik*), **-al,** pertaining to, of the nature of, or involving, antinomy.—*n.* **antinomy** (*an-tin′ə-mi*), a contra- diction in a law: a conflict of authority: con- clusions discrepant though apparently logical. [Gr. *anti-,* against, *nomos,* law.]

**anti-novel,** *an′ti-nov′l,* in U.S. also *an′ti-, -nuv′l, n.* a type of novel of the mid-twentieth century which largely discards plot and character and concerns itself with tiny inner dramas on the border of consciousness.

**Antiochian,** *an-ti-ō′ki-ən,* **Antiochene,** *an-ti′ō-kēn,* *adjs.* of the city of *Antioch*: of the eclectic philoso- phy of *Antiochus* of Ascalon: of any of the Seleucid kings of the name.—*n.* **Antio′chianism,** a school of theology in the 4th and 5th centuries in revolt against allegorising of Scripture by the Alexandrian school.

**antiodontalgic,** *an-ti-o-dont-alj′ik,* in U.S. also *an′ti-, adj.* of use against toothache.—Also *n.* [Gr. *anti,* against, *odous, odontos,* tooth, and *algeein,* to suffer pain.]

**antipapal.** See antipope.

**antiparallel,** *an-ti-par′ə-lel,* in U.S. also *an′ti-, adj.* making with a transverse line an internal angle equal to the external angle made by another line. —Also *n.*

**antiparticle,** *an′ti-pär′ti-kl,* in U.S. also *an′ti-, n.* the 'pair' of an elementary particle, particle and antiparticle being mutually destructive.

**antipasto,** *an-ti-päs′tō,* (It.) an hors d'œuvre, a whet. [Cf. antepast.]

**antipathy,** *an-tip′əth-i, n.* opposition in feeling: aversion: repugnance: incompatibility: mutual opposition: an object of antipathy.—*adjs.* **anti- pathet′ic, -al; antipathic** (*an-ti-path′ik*), belong- ing to antipathy: opposite: contrary. — *n.* **antip′athist,** one possessed by an antipathy. [Gr. *anti-,* against, *pathos,* feeling.]

**antiperiodic,** *an-ti-pē-ri-od′ik,* in U.S. also *an′ti-, adj.* destroying the periodicity of diseases.—*n.* a drug with such an effect.

**antiperistaltic,** *an-ti-per-i-stal′tik,* in U.S. also *an′ti-, adj.* contrary to peristaltic motion.

**antiperistasis,** *an-ti-par-ist′ə-sis,* in U.S. also *an′ti-, n.* opposition of circumstances: resistance or reaction. [Gr., surrounding, interchange—*anti,* against, *peristasis,* a circumstance—*peri,* around, *stasis,* a setting, stand.]

**anti-personnel,** *an′ti-pûr-sən-el′,* in U.S. also *an′ti-, adj.* intended to destroy military personnel and other persons.

**antipetalous,** *an-ti-pet′ə-ləs, adj.* opposite a petal.

**antiphlogistic,** *an-ti-floj-ist′ik,* in U.S. also *an′ti-, adj.* acting against heat, or inflammation.—*n.* a medicine to allay inflammation.

**antiphon,** *an′ti-fon, n.* alternate chanting or singing: a species of church music sung by two parties each responding to the other—also **antiph′ony** (*-ən-i*).—*adj.* **antiph′onal.**—*n.* a book of antiphons or of anthems.—Also **antiph′onary** and an- **tiph′oner.**—*adjs.* **antiphonic** (*-fon′*), **-al,** mutually responsive.—*adv.* **antiphon′ically.** [Gr. *anti,* in return, and *phōnē,* voice: a doublet of **anthem.**]

**antiphrasis,** *an-tif′rə-sis,* (*rhet.*) *n.* the use of words in a sense opposite to the literal one.—*adjs.* **anti- phrastic** (*an-ti-fras′tik*), **-al,** involving antiphrasis: ironical.—*adv.* **antiphras′tically.** [Gr., —*anti,* against, *phrasis,* speech.]

**antipodes,** *an-tip′ə-dēz, n.pl.* (also *sing.*) those who live on the other side of the globe, or on opposite sides, standing feet to feet: a point or place diametrically opposite to another on the surface of the earth or of any globular body or sphere: a pair of points or places so related to each other: the exact opposite of a person or a thing—*sing.* (*rare*) **antipode** (*an′ti-pōd*).—*adjs.* **antip′odal, anti- pōdē′an.**—**antipodal cells** (*bot.*), in flowering plants, three cells in the embryo-sac at the end

remote from the micropyle, representing the prothallus. [Gr. *antipŏdēs*, pl. of *antipous*, with feet opposite—*pous, podos*, a foot.]
**antipole**, *an'ti-pōl, n.* the opposite pole: direct opposite.
**antipope**, *an'ti-pōp, n.* a pontiff set up in opposition to one asserted to be canonically chosen, as those who resided at Avignon in the 13th and 14th centuries.—*adj.* antipā'pal, opposed to the pope or the papal system.
**antiproton**, *an-ti-prō'ton,* in U.S. also *an'ti-, n.* a particle comparable to the proton but negatively charged.
**antipruritic**, *an-ti-prōō-rit'ik,* in U.S. also *an'ti-, n.* a substance that reduces itchiness.—Also *adj.*
**antipyretic**, *an-ti-pi-ret'ik,* in U.S. also *an'ti-, adj.* counteracting fever.—*n.* an antipyretic agent. [Gr. *anti-*, against, *pyretos*, fever—*pȳr*, fire.]
**antiquary**, *an'ti-kwər-i, n.* one who studies, collects, or deals in relics of the past, but not usually very ancient things—curiosities rather than objects of serious archaeological interest.—*adj.* (*Shak.*) ancient.—*adj.* antiquarian (*-kwā'ri-ən*), connected with the study of antiquities.—*n.* an antiquary: before metrication a size of drawing-paper, 53 × 31 inches.—*n.* antiquā'rianism. [L. *antiquārius—antiquus*, old.]
**antique**, *an-tēk',* formerly *an'tik* (and sometimes written antick), *adj.* ancient: of a good old age, olden (now generally rhetorical in a good sense): old-fashioned: savouring of bygone times: after the manner of the ancients.—*n.* anything very old: an old relic: a piece of old furniture or other object sought by collectors: a type of thick and bold face with lines of equal thickness.—*v.t.* antiquate (*an'ti-kwāt*), to make antique, old, or obsolete: to put out of use.—*adj.* an'tiquated.—*n.* antiquā'-tion.—*adv.* antique'ly.—*n.* antique'ness.—*ns.* antiquitarian (*an-tik-wi-tā'ri-ən*), one attached to old ways or beliefs; antiq'uity, ancient times, esp. the times of the ancient Greeks and Romans: great age: old age, seniority (*Shak.*): ancient style: the people of old time: a relic of the past: (*pl.*) manners, customs, etc., of ancient times.— the antique, ancient work in art: the style of ancient art.—See also antic. [L. *antiquus*, old, *ancient—ante*, before; influenced by Fr. *antique*.]
**antirachitic**, *an-ti-ra-kit'ik, adj.* tending to prevent or cure rickets.—Also *n.* [Pfx. anti-; for rachitic see rachitis.]
**Antirrhinum**, *an-ti-ri'nəm, n.* the snapdragon genus. [Latinised from Gr. *antirrinon*, snap-dragon—*anti*, like, mimicking, *rhis, rhinos*, nose.]
**antiscian**, *an-tish'i-ən, n.* a dweller on the same meridian on the other side of the equator, whose shadow at noon falls in the opposite direction.—Also *adj.* [Gr. *anti-*, opposite to, *skiā*, shadow.]
**antiscorbutic**, *an-ti-skör-būt'ik, adj.* acting against scurvy.—*n.* a remedy or preventive for scurvy.
**antiscriptural**, *an-ti-skrip'chər-əl, adj.* opposed to the authority of the Bible.
**anti-Semite**, *an'ti-sem'it, -sēm', n.* a hater of Semites, esp. Jews, or of their influence.—*adj.* anti-Semitic (*-sim-it'*).—*n.* anti-Semitism (*-sem', -sēm'*).
**antisepalous**, *an-ti-sep'ə-ləs, adj.* opposite a sepal.
**antisepsis**, *an-ti-sep'sis, n.* destruction, or inhibition of growth, of bacteria.—*adj.* antisep'tic.—*n.* an antiseptic agent.—*n.* antisep'ticism (*-sizm*), antiseptic treatment.—*adv.* antisep'tically.—*v.t.* antisep'ticise, -ize (*-sīz*). [Gr. *anti-*, against, *sēpsis*, putrefaction.]
**antisocial**, *an-ti-sō'shl, adj.* opposed to the good of society, or the principles of society: disinclined to mix in society: without social instincts.—*adv.* antiso'cially.—*ns.* antiso'cialism; antiso'cialist, (formerly) unsociable person: now opponent of socialism; **antisociality** (*-shi-al'i-ti*), unsociableness: opposition to the principles of society.
**antispasmodic**, *an-ti-spaz-mod'ik,* in U.S. also *an'ti-*

*adj.* opposing spasms or convulsions.—*n.* a remedy for spasms.
**antispast**, *an'ti-spast, n.* a foot composed of an iambus and a trochee.—*adj.* antispast'ic. [Gr. *antispastos—antispaein*, to draw back—*spaein*, to draw.]
**antistrophe**, *an-tis'trə-fi, n.* the returning dance in Greek choruses, reversing the movement of the strophe: the stanza answering the strophe in the same metre: repetition in reverse order: retortion of an argument: an inverse relation.—*adj.* antistrophic (*an-ti-strof'ik*).—*adv.* antistroph'ically.—*n.* antis'trophon, an argument retorted on an opponent. [Gr. *antistrophē—strophē*, a turning.]
**antithalian**, *an-ti-thə-li'ən, adj.* opposed to mirth. [Gr. *anti-*, against, *Thaleia*, the comic muse.]
**antitheism**, *an-ti-thē'izm,* in U.S. also *an'ti-, n.* doctrine antagonistic to theism: denial of the existence of a God: opposition to God.—*n.* antithē'ist.—*adj.* antithēist'ic. [Gr. *anti-*, against, *theos*, a god.]
**antithesis**, *an-tith'i-sis, n.* a figure in which thoughts or words are balanced in contrast: a thesis or proposition opposing another: opposition: the direct opposite:—*pl.* antith'eses (*-sēz*)—*n.* an'tithet (*-thet; rare*), an instance of antithesis.—*adjs.* antithet'ic, -al.—*adv.* antithet'ically. [Gr. *antithesis—thesis*, placing.]
**antithrombin**, *an-ti-throm'bin,* in U.S. also *an'ti-, n.* a substance produced by the liver which prevents clotting of the blood in the veins. [Gr. *anti-*, against, *thrombos*, a clot.]
**antitoxin**, *an-ti-tok'sin,* in U.S. also *an'ti-, n.* a substance that neutralises toxin formed in the body.—*adj.* antitox'ic.
**antitrade**, *an'ti-trād,* in U.S. also *an'ti-, n.* a wind that blows in the opposite direction to the trade-wind—that is, in the northern hemisphere from south-west, and in the southern hemisphere from north-west.
**antitragus**, *an-ti-trā'gəs,* in U.S. also *an'ti-, n.* a prominence of the external ear, opposite the tragus.
**antitrinitarian**, *an-ti-trin-i-tā'ri-ən,* in U.S. *an'ti-, adj.* opposed to the doctrine of the Trinity.—Also *n.* antitrinitā'rianism.
**antitype**, *an'ti-tip, n.* that which corresponds to the type: that which is prefigured by the type.—*adjs.* antityp'al, -typic (*-tip'ik*), -al.
**antivaccinationist**, *an-ti-vak-si-nā'shən-ist,* in U.S. also *an'ti-, n.* an opponent of vaccination.—*n.* antivaccinā'tionism.
**antiviral**, *an-ti-vī'rəl,* in U.S. also *an'ti-, adj.* acting against a virus.
**anti-vitamin**, *an'ti-vit'ə-min, -vīt',* in U.S. also *an'ti-, n.* a substance with a chemical structure very similar to a vitamin which prevents that vitamin from having its effect.
**anti-vivisection**, *an'ti-viv-i-sek'shən,* in U.S. also *an'ti-, n.* opposition to vivisection.—*ns.* anti-vivisec'tionism; anti-vivisec'tionist.
**antler**, *ant'lər, n.* a bony outgrowth from the frontal bone of a deer: orig. the lowest branch of a stag's horn, then any branch, then the whole.—*adj.* ant'lered.—*n.* ant'ler-moth, a noctuid moth (*Charaeas graminis*), with antler-like markings on the wings, its larvae very destructive to pastures. [O.Fr. antoillier; assumed derivation from L.L. *ant(e)oculāris* in front of the eyes, is unlikely.]
**antlia**, *ant'li-a, n.* the suctorial proboscis of Lepidoptera (*pl.* ant'liae,-ē): (*cap.*) the Air Pump, a small southern constellation.—*adj.* ant'liate. [L. *antlia*, a pump—Gr. *antliā*, bilge-water.]
**antoninianus**, *an-tō-nin-i-ā'nəs, n.* Roman coin equal to two denarii in value. [From 3rd-cent. emperor *Antoninus*.]
**antonomasia**, *ant-on-o-mā'zi-a, n.* use of an epithet, or the name of an office or attributive, for a person's proper name, e.g. his lordship for an earl; and conversely, e.g. a Napoleon for a great

Neutral vowels in unaccented syllables: el'ə-mənt; for certain sounds in foreign words, see p. viii

conqueror. [Gr. *antonomasiā—onomazein*, to name, *onoma*, a name.]

antonym, *ant'ŏ-nim, n.* a word opposite in meaning to another. [Gr. *onyma = onoma*, a name.]

antre, *an'tar, n.* a cave.—(*Shak.*) an'tar. [Fr.; L. *antrum—*Gr. *antron*, a cave.]

antrorse, *an-trörs', adj.* turned up or forward. [From *anterus*, hypothetical positive of L. *anterior*, front, and L. *versus*, turned.]

antrum, *an'tram, n.* a cavity. [L., cave.]

Antrycide, *an'tri-sid, n.* a drug useful for cure and prevention of trypanosome diseases. [Trademark.]

Anubis, *a-nū'bis, n.* the ancient Egyptian jackal-headed god of the dead. [L.,—Gr. *Anoubis—*Egypt. *Anup.*]

anuria, *an-ū'ri-a, n.* failure in secretion of urine. [Gr. *an-*, priv., *ouron*, urine.]

anurous, *an-ū'ras,* anourous, *an-ōō'ras, adj.* tailless. —*n.pl.* Anu'ra, Anou'ra, the Salientia or tailless amphibians, frogs and toads. [Gr. *an-*, priv., *ourā*, tail.]

anus, *ā'nas, n.* the opening of the alimentary canal by which undigested residues are voided.—*adj.* ā'nal. [L. *ānus, -ī*, a ring.]

anvil, *an'vil, n.* an iron block on which smiths hammer metal into shape: the incus of the ear.— on or upon the anvil, in preparation, under discussion. [O.E. *anfilte, onfilti.*]

anxious, *ang(k)'shas, adj.* uneasy with fear and desire regarding something doubtful: solicitous. —*n.* anxiety (*ang(g)-zī'i-ti*), state of being anxious: a state of chronic apprehension as a symptom of mental disorder.—*adv.* an'xiously.—*n.* an'xiousness.—the age of anxiety, the present time (W. H. Auden, 1947). [L. *anxius—angēre*, to press tightly. See anger, anguish.]

any, *en'i, adj.* and *pron.* one indefinitely: some: whichever, no matter which.—*adv.* at all, to an appreciable extent.—*n.* and *pron.* an'ybody, any single person: a person of any account.—*adv.* an'yhow, in any way whatever: in any case, at least: indifferently, carelessly.—*ns.* and *prons.* an'yone (or any one), anybody at all: anybody whatever; an'ything, a thing indefinitely, as opposed to nothing.—*adv.* any whit, to any extent.—*ns.* anythingā'rian, one with no beliefs in particular; anythingā'rianism.—*advs.* an'ytime, at any time; an'yway, an'yways, in any manner: anyhow: in any case; an'ywhen (*rare*); an'ywhere, in or to any place; an'ywhither (*rare*); an'ywise, in any manner, to any degree.—any day, in any circumstances; any old how, without any special care; at any rate, whatever may happen: at all events; like anything, very much: with great vigour. [O.E. *ǣnig—ān*, one.]

Anzac, *an'zak, n.* an Australasian expeditionary soldier (1914 *et seq.*).—Also *adj.* [Coined from the initials of Australian-New-Zealand Army Corps.]

anziani, *an-sē-än'ē*, (It.) councillors, senators.

Anzus, *an'zas, n.* a political organisation of Australia, New Zealand, and the United States.

Aonian, *ā-ō'ni-an, adj.* pertaining to *Aonia* in Greece, or to the Muses supposed to dwell there. —Aonian fount, the fountain Aganippe, on a slope of Mount Helicon—the Aonian mount.

aorist, *ā'ar-ist, n.* a tense, esp. in Greek, expressing simple past time, with no implications of continuance, repetition, or the like.—*adj.* aorist'ic. [Gr. *aoristos*, indefinite—*a-*, priv., and *horistos*, limited.]

aorta, *ā-ör'ta, n.* the great arterial trunk that carries blood from the heart.—*adjs.* aor'tal, aor'tic.—*n.* aorti'tis, inflammation of the aorta. [Gr. *aortē—aeirein*, to raise up.]

aoudad, *ä'ōō-dad, n.* a North African wild sheep. [Native name in French spelling.]

à outrance, *a ōō-träs*, (Fr.) to the utmost: to the death: to the bitter end.

apace, *a-pās', adv.* at a quick pace: swiftly. [Prep. a, and pace.]

Apache, *a-pa'chi, n.* a Red Indian of a group of tribes in Arizona, New Mexico, etc.: (apache; *a-pash'*) a lawless ruffian or hooligan in Paris or elsewhere. [Perh. Zuñi *āpachu*, enemy.]

apage (Satanas), *ap'a-jē, ap-a-ge (sat'an-as)*, (Gr.) away, avaunt (Satan).

apagoge, *ap-a-gō'jē, n.* reduction to absurdity, indirect proof by showing the falsehood of the opposite.—*adjs.* apagogic (*-goj'ik*), *-al.—adv.* apagog'ically. [Gr. *apagōgē*, leading away, *apagein*, to lead off.]

apaid. See apay.

apanage. See appanage.

apart, *a-pärt', adv.* separately: aside: asunder, parted: separate: out of consideration.—*n.* apart'ness.—to set apart, to separate: to devote. [Fr. *à part—*L. *ad partem*, to the side.]

apartheid, *a-pärt'hāt, -pär'tid, n.* segregation (of races). [Afrikaans.]

apartment, *a-pärt'mant, n.* a separate room in a house occupied by a particular person or party: a suite or set of such rooms (*arch.* and *U.S.*).—now in this sense in the *pl.*: a compartment (*obs.*).— *adj.* apartmental (*-ment'al*). [Fr. *appartement*, a suite of rooms forming a complete dwelling—L. *ad*, to, and *partire, partiri*, to divide—*pars, partis*, part.]

à pas de géant, *a pa da zhā-ä*, (Fr.) with a giant's stride.

apathaton, *a-path'i-tan, n.* (*Shak.*) for epitheton.

apathy, *ap'ath-i, n.* want of feeling, passion, or interest: indifference.—*adjs.* apathet'ic, *-al.— adv.* apathet'ically. [Gr. *apatheia—a-*, priv., *pathos*, feeling.]

apatite, *ap'a-tit, n.* a mineral consisting of calcium phosphate and fluoride (or chloride). [Gr. *apatē*, deceit, from its having been confused with other minerals.]

apay, appay, *a-pā', v.t.* to satisfy (*arch.*): to repay (*obs.*):—*pa.p.* and *pa.t.* ap(p)aid', ap(p)ayd'. [O.Fr. *apayer*—L. *ad*, and *pācāre—pāx*, peace.]

ape, *āp, n.* a monkey: a large monkey without a tail or with a very short one: a mimic: an imitator.—*v.t.* to mimic: to imitate.—*ns.* ape'-dom; ape'hood; ap'ery, conduct of one who apes: any ape-like action: a colony of apes.— *adj.* ap'ish, like an ape: imitative: foppish.—*adv.* ap'ishly.—*ns.* ap'ishness, ap'ism (*Carlyle*).— God's ape, a born fool; lead apes in hell, feigned to be the lot of old maids in after life; make one his ape, to put an ape in one's hood (*obs.*), to make a fool of one. [O.E. *apa*; Ger. *affe.*]

apeak, apeek, *a-pēk', adv.* (*naut.*) vertical. [Prep. a, and peak.]

apepsy, *a-pep'si*, apepsia, *a-pep'si-a, n.* weakness of digestion. [Gr. *apepsiā*, indigestion; *a-*, priv., *peptein*, to digest.]

aperçu, *a-per-sü, n.* a summary exposition: a brief outline: a glimpse: an immediate intuitive insight. [Fr. *aperçu*, survey, sketch—lit. (pa.p. of *apercevoir*) perceived.]

aperient, *a-pē'ri-ant, n.* and *adj.* laxative.—*adj.* aperitive (*a-per'i-tiv*), laxative.—*n.* (usu. as Fr. apéritif, *a-pā-rē-tēf*) a (liquid) appetiser. [L. *aperire, apertum*, to open.]

aperiodic, *ā-pē-ri-od'ik, adj.* not periodic: coming to rest without oscillation.—*n.* aperiodicity (*-a-dis'i-ti*). [Gr. *a-*, priv., and periodic.]

apert. See apert.

a-per-se, *ā-par-sē, n.* the letter a spelling a word by itself (*arch.*): anything unique in excellence (*fig.*). [L. *a per se*, a by itself; cf. ampersand.]

apert (*a-pûrt'*; *arch.*), open, public.—*n.* apert'ness. [O.Fr.,—L. *apertus*, open.]

aperture, *ap'ar-char, n.* an opening: a hole: diameter of the opening through which light passes in an optical instrument. [L. *apertura—aperire*, to open.]

*fāte, fär; mē, hûr* (her); *mīne, mōte, för; mūte, mōōn, fŏŏt; dhen* (then)

apetalous, *ə-pet'əl-əs*, *adj.* (*bot.*) without petals.—*n.* apet'aly. [Gr. *a-*, priv., and *petalon*, a leaf.]

à peu près, *a pø pre*, (Fr.) nearly.

apex, *ā'peks*, *n.* summit, tip, or point: a vertex (*geom.*): the culminating point, climax of anything:—*pl.* ā'pexes, apices (*āp'*, or *ap'i-sēz*). [L. *āpex*, *āpicis*, a tip.]

aphaeresis, *a-fē'ri-sis*, *n.* (*gram.*) the taking away of a sound or syllable at the beginning of a word. [Gr. *aphairesis*, a taking away, *apo*, away, and *haireein*, to take.]

aphagia, *ə-fā'j(i)-a*, *n.* inability to swallow: (of imago of certain insects) inability to feed. [Gr. *a-*, priv., *-phagia—phagein*, to eat.]

Aphaniptera, *af-an-ip'tər-a*, *n.pl.* the flea order (or suborder) of insects.—*adj.* aphanip'terous. [Gr. *aphanēs*, invisible, *pteron*, wing.]

aphasia, *a-fā'z(h)i-a*, *n.* inability to express thought in words, or inability to understand thought as expressed in the spoken or written words of others, by reason of some brain disease.—*n.* and *adj.* aphā'siac.—*adj.* aphasic (*a-fā'zik*, *a-faz'ik*). [Gr. *a-*, priv., *phasis*, speech—*phanai*, to speak.]

aphelion, *a-fē'li-ən*, *n.* a planet's furthest point in its orbit from the sun:—*pl.* aphē'lia.—*adjs.* aphē'-lian, aphē'lic. [Gr. *apo*, from, *hēlios*, sun.]

apheliotropic, *a-fē-li-ō-trop'ik*, *adj.* turning away from the sun.—*n.* apheliot'ropism. [Gr. *apo*, from, *hēlios*, sun, and *tropikos*, belonging to turning.]

apheresis. Same as aphaeresis.

aphesis, *af'i-sis*, *n.* the gradual and unintentional loss of an unaccented vowel at the beginning of a word, as in *squire* from *esquire*—a special form of aphaeresis.—*adj.* aphetic (*ə-fet'ik*).—*v.t.* aph'etise, -ize. [Gr. *aphesis*, letting go—*apo*, from, *hienai*, to send.]

aphis, *af'is*, *āf'is*, aphid, *af'id*, *ns.* a plant-louse or greenfly, a small homopterous insect that sucks plant juices:—*pl.* aph'ides (*-i-dēz*), aph'ids.—*adj.* and *n.* aphid'ian.—*adj.* aphid'ical.—*ns.* aph'icide, aphid'icide (*-sid*), an aphis killer. [Ety. unknown.]

aphonia, *a-fō'ni-a*, aphony, *af'ə-ni*, *n.* loss of voice from hysteria, disease of larynx or vocal cords, etc.—*adjs.* aphonic (*-fon'*), aphonous (*af'ə-nəs*), voiceless. [Gr. *a-*, priv., *phōnē*, voice.]

aphorism, *af'ər-izm*, *n.* concise statement of a principle in any science: brief, pithy saying: adage.—*v.i.* aph'orise, -ize.—*ns.* aph'oriser, -z-; aph'orist.—*adj.* aphoris'tic.—*adv.* aphorist'ically. [Gr. *aphorizein*, to define—*apo*, from, *horos*, a limit.]

aphotic, *a-fō'tik*, *adj.* lightless. [Gr. *a-*, priv., *phōs*, *phōtos*, light.]

aphrodisiac, *af-rō-diz'i-ak*, *-rə-*, *adj.* exciting sexually.—*n.* that which so excites.—*n.* aphrodis'ia, sexual desire, esp. violent.—*adj.* Aphrodis'ian, belonging to Aphrodite. [Gr. *aphrodisiakos*—*Aphroditē*, the goddess of love.]

aphtha, *af'tha*, *n.* the disease thrush: a small whitish ulcer on the surface of a mucous membrane:—*pl.* aph'thae (*-thē*).—*adj.* aph'thous. [Gr. *aphtha*, mostly in pl. *aphthai*.]

aphyllous, *a-fil'əs*, (*bot.*) *adj.* without foliage, leaves. —*n.* aphyll'y. [Gr. *a-*, priv., *phyllon*, a leaf.]

a piacere, ä pē-a-chā'rā, (It.) at pleasure.

apian, *ā'pi-ən*, *adj.* relating to bees.—*adj.* āpiarian (*-ā'ri-ən*), relating to beehives or bee-keeping.— *ns.* ā'piarist, a bee-keeper; ā'piary (*-ər-i*), a place where bees are kept; ā'piculture, bee-keeping; āpicul'turist.—*adj.* āpiv'orous, feeding on bees. [L. *āpis*, a bee, *āpiārium*, a bee-house.]

apical, *ap'*, or *āp'ik-l*, *adj.* of or at the apex.—*adv.* ap'ically.—*n.pl.* ap'ices (see apex).—*adj.* apic-ūlate (*ap-ik'*; *bot.*) with a short sharp point on an otherwise blunt end. [See apex.]

Apician, *ə-pish'(y)ən*, *adj.* relating to *Apicius*, the Roman epicure in the time of Tiberius: luxurious and expensive in diet.

apiece, *ə-pēs'*, *adv.* for each piece, thing, or person: to each individually. [a, piece.]

apiezon oils, *a-pi'zən*, the residue of almost zero vapour pressure left by vacuum distillation of petroleum products. [Gr. *a-*, neg., *piezein*, press.]

aplacental, *ap-lə-sen'tl*, *adj.* without placenta. [Gr. *a-*, priv., and placental.]

aplanatic, *ap-lə-nat'ik*, *adj.* free from spherical aberration.—*ns.* aplanatism (*ə-plan'ə-tizm*); aplan'ogamete, aplan'ospore, a non-motile gamete, spore. [Gr. *a-*, priv., *planaein*, to wander.]

aplasia, *a-plā'z(h)i-a*, *n.* imperfect development of an organ or part.—*adj.* aplastic (*-plas'*). [Gr. *a-*, priv., and Mod. L. *-plasia*—Gr. *plasis*, moulding.]

aplomb, *ə-plom'*, Fr. *a-pl5*, *n.* perpendicularity: self-possession, coolness. [Fr. *aplomb—à plomb*, according to plummet.]

aplustre, *a-plus'tər*, *n.* the stern ornament of an ancient ship. [L. *āplustre*, *āplustre*—Gr. *aphlaston*.]

apnoea, *ap-nē'a*, *n.* a cessation of breathing. [Gr. *apnoia—a-*, priv., *pno(i)ē*, breath.]

Apocalypse, *a-pok'əl-ips*, *n.* the last book of the New Testament, otherwise the Revelation of St John: (without *cap.*), any book purporting to reveal the future or last things: a revelation or disclosure.—*adjs.* apocalypt'ic, pertaining to the Apocalypse: prophetic of disaster or of the end of the world; apocalypt'ical.—*adv.* apocalypt'-ically.—apocalyptic number, the number of the Beast, the mystical number 666, spoken of in the Apocalypse (xiii. 18), supposed to be the sum of the numerical values of the Greek and Hebrew letters of a name, for which many solutions have been offered. [Gr. *apokalypsis*, an uncovering— *apo*, from, *kalyptein*, to cover.]

apocarpous, *ap-ō-kär'pəs*, (*bot.*) *adj.* having the carpels separate. [Gr. *apo*, from, *karpos*, fruit.]

apocatastasis, *ap'ō-ka-tas'tə-sis*, (*theol.*) *n.* the final restitution of all things at the appearance of the Messiah—an idea extended by Origen to the final conversion and salvation of all created beings, the devil and his angels not excepted. [Gr. *apokatastasis—apo-*, again, back, *katastasis*, establishment; cf. catastasis.]

apochromatic, *ap-ō-krō-mat'ik*, *adj.* relatively free from chromatic and spherical aberration.—*ns.* ap'ochromat, an apochromatic lens or instrument; apochro'matism. [Gr. *apo*, from, *chrōma*, *-atos*, colour.]

apocope, *ə-pok'ō-pē*, *n.* the cutting off of the last sound or syllable of a word.—*v.t.* apoc'opate.—*n.* apocopā'tion. [Gr. *apokopē—apo*, off, *koptein*, to cut.]

apocrypha, *ə-pok'rif-a*, *n.pl.* hidden or secret things: applied specially to certain books or parts of books included in the Septuagint and Vulgate translations of the Old Testament but not accepted as canonical by Jews or Protestants, and to later books (Apocrypha of the New Testament) never accepted as canonical or authoritative by any considerable part of the Christian Church:—*sing.* apoc'ryphon.—*adj.* apoc'ryphal, of the Apocrypha: of doubtful authority: spurious: fabulous. [Gr., things hidden—*apo*, from, *kryptein*, to hide.]

Apocynum, *a-pos'i-nəm*, *n.* the dogbane genus, giving name to the periwinkle family Apocynā'-ceae, close akin to the asclepiads.—*adj.* apocynā'-ceous. [Gr. *apokȳnon*, an asclepiad poisonous to dogs—*apo*, off, *kyōn*, *kynos*, a dog.]

apod, *ap'od*, apode, *ap'ōd*, *n.* an animal without feet or ventral fins.—*adjs.* ap'od, ap'odal, ap'ode, ap'odous. [Gr. *a-*, priv., *pous*, *podos*, a foot.]

apodictic, *ap-ō-dik'tik*, apodeictic, *-dik'*, *adj.* necessarily true: demonstrative without demonstration: beyond contradiction.—*adj.* apod(e)ic'-tical.—*adv.* apod(e)ic'tically. [Gr. *apodeiktikos —apodeiknynai* (*apo* and *deiknynai*), to demonstrate.]

apodosis, *ə-pod'ə-sis*, (*gram*.) *n*. in the consequent clause in a conditional sentence:—opp. *protasis*. [Gr. *apodosis*—*apo*, back, *didonai*, to give.]
apodyterium, *ap-ō-di-tēr'i-əm*, *n*. an undressing-room at an ancient bath. [Gr. *apodytērion*—*apodyein*, to undress—*apo*, from, *dyein*, to get into, put on.]
apogamy, *ə-pog'ə-mi*, (*bot*.) *n*. omission of the sexual process in the life-history—the sporophyte developing either from an unfertilised egg-cell or some other cell.—*adj*. apog'amous.—*adv*. apog'amously. [Gr. *apo*, from, *gamos*, marriage.]
apogee, *ap'ō-jē*, *n*. a heavenly body's point of greatest distance from the earth: the sun's greatest meridional altitude (*obs*.): culmination (*fig*.):—opp. *perigee*.—*adjs*. apogaeic (*-jē'ik*), apogē'al, apogē'an; apogeotrop'ic (*biol*.), turning against the direction of gravity.—*adv*. apogeotrop'ically.—*n*. apogeotropism (*-ot'*). [Gr. *apogaion*—*apo*, from, *gaia*, or *gē*, the earth.]
apograph, *ap'ō-gräf*, *n*. an exact copy. [Gr. *apographon*, a copy—*apo*, from, and *graphein*, to write.]
à point, *a pwē*, (Fr.) to a nicety.
apolaustic, *ap-ō-lö'stik*, *adj*. devoted to the search of enjoyment.—*n*. the philosophy of the pleasurable. [Gr. *apolaustikos*—*apolauein*, to enjoy.]
apolitical, *a-pəl-it'ik-əl*, also *ā-*, *adj*. indifferent to political affairs: uninvolved in politics.—*adv*. apolit'ically.—*ns*. apolitical'ity, apolit'icism. [Gr. *a-*, priv., and political.]
Apollo, *ə-pol'o*, *n*. the Greek sun-god, patron of poetry and music, medicine, archery, etc.—*adj*. Apollinarian (*-i-nā'ri-ən*), sacred to Apollo: of Apollinaris, (d. *c*. A.D. 390) Bishop of Laodicea in Syria, or of his doctrine that in Christ the Logos took the place of a soul: of any other Apollinaris.—*n*. a follower of Apollinaris.—*ns*. Apollinā'-rianism; Apollina'ris (water), a mineral water rich in sodium bicarbonate and carbon dioxide, from the Apollinaris spring in the Ahr valley.—*adj*. apoll'ine (*-in*), of Apollo.—*adjs*. Apollōnian (*ap-o-lō'ni-ən*), of Apollo: having the characteristics of Apollo (often opposed to *Dionysian*): of the mathematician Apollonius of Perga (3rd century B.C.), or other Apollonius.—*n*. apollonicon (*-on'i-kən*), a gigantic organ, partly automatic (*mus*.). [Gr. *Apollōn, -ōnos*, L. *Apollō, -inis*.]
Apollyon, *a-pol'yən*, *n*. the destroyer or devil (Rev. ix. 11). [Gr. *apollyōn*, pr.p. of *apollyein*, to destroy utterly—*apo-*, indicating completeness, *ollyein*, or *ollynai*, to destroy.]
apologetic, *ə-pol-ə-jet'ik*, *adj*. (primarily) vindicatory, defensive: (now usu.) regretfully acknowledging fault.—*n*. a defence, vindication.—*adj*. apologet'ical.—*adv*. apologet'ically.—*n*. (*pl*. in form) apologet'ics, the defensive argument or method, esp. the defence of Christianity.—*n*. apologia (*ap-o-lō'ji-a*), a written defence or vindication.—*v.i*. apologise, -ize (*ə-pol'ə-jīz*), to put forward a defence: (now usu.) to express regret for a fault.—*ns*. apol'ogist (*-jist*), a defender by argument; apologue (*ap'ə-log*), a fable: esp. a beast-fable; apology (*ə-pol'ə-ji*), a defence, justification, apologia: an explanation with expression of regret: a regretful acknowledgment of a fault: a poor specimen hardly worthy of its name: an apologue (*obs*.). [Gr. *apologia*, defence, *apologos*, a tale—*apo*, off, *logos*, speaking.]
apomixis, *ap-ō-miks'is*, *n*. omission of sexual fusion in reproduction, as in parthenogenesis, or in apogamy. [Gr. *apo*, from, *mixis*, mingling, intercourse.]
apomorphine, *ap-ō-mör'fēn*, apomorphia, *-fi-a*, *ns*. an alkaloid prepared by dehydrating morphine (morphia)—a rapid and powerful emetic and expectorant. [Gr. *apo*, from, and morphine, morphia.]
aponeurosis, *ap-ō-nū-rō'sis*, *n*. a flat thin tendon.—

adj. aponeurotic (*-rot'ik*). [Gr. *aponeurōsis*—*apo*, off, *neuron*, tendon.]
apoop, *ə-pōōp'*, *adv*. on the poop, astern.
apopemptic, *ap-ō-pemp'tik*, *adj*. valedictory. [Gr. *apopemptikos*—*apo*, away from, *pempein*, to send.]
apophlegmatic, *ap-ō-fleg-mat'ik*, *adj*. promoting the discharge of mucus.—*n*. an apophlegmatic agent. [Gr. *apophlegmatikos*—*apo*, off; see phlegm.]
apophthegm, apothegm, *ap'ō-them*, *n*. a pithy saying, more short, pointed, and practical than the aphorism need be.—*adjs*. apo(ph)thegmat'ic, -al (*-theg-*).—*adv*. apo(ph)thegmat'ically.—*v.i*. apo-(ph)theg'matise, -ize, to speak in apophthegms.—*n*. apo(ph)theg'matist. [Gr. *apophthegma*—*apo*, forth, and *phthengesthai*, to utter.]
apophyge, *a-pof'i-jē*, *n*. the curve where a column merges in its base or capital. [Gr. *apophygē*, escape.]
apophyllite, *a-pof'i-līt*, *ap-ō-fil'īt*, *n*. a mineral, hydrated calcium potassium silicate, that exfoliates on heating. [Gr. *apo*, off, *phyllon*, leaf.]
apophysis, *a-pof'i-sis*, *-zis*, *n*. an outgrowth or protuberance, esp. on a bone, on the end of a pine-cone scale, on a moss stalk below the capsule (*biol*.): a branch from a mass of igneous rock (*geol*.).—*pl*. apoph'yses. [Gr., offshoot—*apo*, off, *phyein*, to grow.]
apoplectic, etc. See apoplexy.
apoplexy, *ap'ō-pleks-i*, *n*. sudden loss of sensation and motion, generally the result of haemorrhage or thrombosis in the brain.—*adjs*. apoplec'tic, -al.—*adv*. apoplec'tically.—*n*. ap'oplex (*arch*.), apoplexy.—*v.t*. (*Shak*.), to affect with apoplexy. [Gr. *apoplēxiā*—*apo-*, expressing completeness, *plēssein*, to strike.]
aporia, *a-pōr'i-a, -pör'*, (Gr.) in rhetoric, a professed doubt of what to say or to choose: a difficulty.
aport, *ə-pört', -pört*, *adv*. on or towards the port side.
à portée, *a por-tā*, (Fr.) within reach or range.
aposematic, *ap-ō-sē-mat'ik*, *adj*. (of animal coloration) warning. [Gr. *apo*, away from, *sēma*, *sēmatos*, sign.]
aposiopesis, *ə-pos-i-ō-pē'sis*, *ap-ō-si-ō-pē'sis*, *n*. a sudden breaking off in the midst of a sentence, e.g. Virgil, *Aeneid*, i. 135, 'Quos ego—' [Gr. *aposiō-pēsis*—*apo*, off, and *siōpē*, silence.]
apositia, *ap-ō-sish'i-a*, *n*. an aversion to food. [Gr. *apo*, away from, *sitos*, bread, food.]
apospory, *ə-pos'po-ri*, (*bot*.) *n*. omission of spore-formation in the life-history—the gametophyte developing vegetatively from the sporophyte.—*adj*. apos'porous. [Gr. *apo*, away from, and spore.]
apostasy, *ə-pos'tə-si*, *n*. abandonment of one's religion, principles, or party: a revolt from ecclesiastical obedience, from a religious profession, or from holy orders: defection.—*n*. apost'ate (*-āt, -it*), one who has apostatised: a renegade.—*adj*.—*adjs*. apostatic (*ap-ō-stat'-ik*), -al.—*v.i*. apostatise, -ize (*ə-pos'tə-tīz*). [Gr. *apostasiā*, a standing away—*apo*, from, *stasis*, a standing.]
a posteriori, *ā pos-tē-ri-ō'rī, -ō'rī, ä pos-ter-i-ō'rē*, *adj*. applied to reasoning from experience, from effect to cause: inductive: empirical: gained from experience:—opp. to *a priori*.—Also *adv*. [L. *ā*, from, *posteriōrī*, abl. of *posterior*, coming after.]
apostil, -ille, *ə-pos'til*, *n*. a marginal note. [Fr. *apostille*. See postil; origin of *a-* doubtful.]
apostle, *ə-pos'l*, *n*. one sent to preach the gospel: esp. one of Christ's twelve: a first introducer of Christianity in a country, e.g. Augustine, the apostle of the English: a principal champion or supporter of a new system, or of a cause: the highest in the fourfold ministry of the Catholic

Apostolic Church: one of the twelve officials form'ng a presiding high council in the Mormon Church.—*ns.* apos'tleship; apost'olate (*ə-post'ə-lāt*), the office of an apostle: leadership in a propaganda.—*adjs.* apostolic (*ap-əs-tol'ik*), -al.— *ns.* apostol'icism (*-i-sizm*), apostolicity (*ə-post-ə-lis'i-ti*), the quality of being apostolic.—Apostles' Creed, the oldest form of Christian creed that exists, early ascribed to the apostles; apostle spoons, silver spoons with handles ending in figures of the apostles, once a common baptismal present; apostolical succession, the derivation of holy orders by unbroken chain of transmission from the apostles through bishops—the theory of the Catholic Church: the assumed succession of a ministry so ordained to apostolic powers and privileges; apostolic fathers, the immediate disciples and fellow-labourers of the apostles, more especially those who have left writings (Barnabas, Clement of Rome, Ignatius, Hermas, Polycarp); apostolic see, the see of Rome; apostolic vicar, the cardinal representing the Pope in extraordinary missions. [Gr. *apostolos*, one sent away, *apo*, away, *stellein*, to send.]

apostrophe, *ə-pos'trə-fi, n.* (in rhet.) a sudden turning away from the ordinary course of a speech to address some person or object present or absent, explained by Quintilian as addressed to a person present, but extended by modern use to the absent or inanimate: the ranging of chloroplasts along the side walls of the cell in intense light (*bot.*).—*adj.* apostrophic (*ap-ō-strof'ik*).—*v.t.* apos'trophise, -ize, to address by apostrophe. [Gr. *apo*, from, and *strophē*, a turning.]

apostrophe, *ə-pos'trə-fi, n.* a mark (') showing (among other uses) the omission of a letter or letters in a word: a sign of the modern Eng. genitive or possessive case—orig. marking the dropping of *e*. [Gr. *apostrophos*, turning away, elision; confused with foregoing.]

apostrophus, *ə-pos'trə-fəs, n.* the symbol Ɔ, used in Roman numerals—IƆ = 500, IƆƆ = 5,000, IƆƆƆ = 500,000.

apothecary, *ə-poth'i-kər-i, n.* a druggist or pharmacist (*arch.*)—still a legal description for licentiates of the Society of Apothecaries: a medical practitioner of an inferior branch, who often kept a shop for drugs (*obs.*).—apothecaries' measure, liquid units of capacity (fluid ounce, etc.) used by pharmacists before 1969; apothecaries' weight, a pre-1969 system based on the troy ounce. [L.L. *apothēcarius*—Gr. *apothēkē*, a storehouse—*apo*, away, and *tithenai*, to place.]

apothecium, *ap-ō-thē's(h)i-əm, n.* an open fructification in Discomycetes and lichens:—*pl.* apothe'-cia.—*adj.* apothe'cial. [Latinised dim. of Gr. *apothēkē*, a storehouse.]

apothegm, etc. See apophthegm.

apothem, *ap'ə-them, n.* the perpendicular from the centre to any of the sides of a regular polygon. [Gr. *apo*, away from, *thema*, that which is placed.]

apotheosis, *ə-po-thi-ō'sis, n.* a deification: glorification:—*pl.* apotheo'ses (*-sēz*).—*v.i.* apoth'eosise, -ize (or *ap-ō-thē'ō-sīz*). [Gr. *apotheōsis—apo-*, expressing completion, *theos*, a god.]

apotropaic, *ə-pot-rō-pā'ik*, or *ap'ō-trō-, adj.* turning aside (or intended to turn aside) evil.—*adj.* apot'ropous (*bot.*), anatropous with ventral raphe. [Gr. *apo*, from, *tropē*, turning.]

apozem, *ap'ō-zem, n.* a decoction. [Gr. *apozema—apo*, off, and *zeein*, to boil.]

appaid. See apay.

appair, *ə-pār'*, an obs. form of impair.

appal, *ə-pöl', v.i.* to wax pale, flat or flavourless (*obs.*): to wax faint (*Spens.*).—*v.t.* to abate (*Spens.*): to horrify, dismay:—*pr.p.* appall'ing; *pa.t.* and *pa.p.* appalled'.—*adj.* appall'ing.—*adv.* appall'ingly. [Perh. from O.Fr. *apalir, apallir*, to wax pale, make pale. See pall and pale.]

appalto, *a-päl'tō*, (It.) a contract or monopoly.

appanage, apanage, *ap'ən-ij, n.* a provision for maintenance, esp. of a king's younger child: dependent territory: a perquisite: an adjunct or attribute.—*adj.* ap(p)'anaged, endowed with an appanage. [Fr. *apanage*—L. *ad*, and *panis*, bread.]

apparat, *ä'pə-rät*, the political machine of the Communist party.—*n.* apparatchik, *ä-pə-räch'ik*, a member of the Soviet bureaucracy. [Russ., apparatus.]

apparatus, *ap-ə-rā'təs, -ra'təs, n.* things prepared or provided, material: set of instruments, tools, natural organs, etc: materials (as various readings) for the critical study of a document (apparatus criticus, *ap-ə-rā'təs krit'i-kəs, ap-a-rā'tōos krit'i-koōs*):—*pl.* appara'tuses or appara'-tus (L. *appārātūs*). [L. *appārātəs, -ūs—ad*, to, *pārāre*, -*ātum*, to prepare.]

apparel, *ə-par'l, v.t.* to equip (*obs.*): to dress, clothe: to adorn:—*pr.p.* appar'elling; *pa.t.* and *pa.p.* appar'elled.—*n.* equipment (*obs.*): rigging (*arch.*): attire, dress: ecclesiastical embroidery (*arch.*).—*n.* appar'elment. [O.Fr. *apareiller*—L. *ad*, to, *pār*, equal.]

apparent, *ə-par'ənt*, or *-pār', adj.* that may be seen: obvious: conspicuous: seeming: obtained by observation without correction, distinguished from *true* or from *mean*.—*n.* (*Shak.*) heir-apparent.—*n.* appar'ency, apparentness: position of being heir-apparent.—*adv.* appar'-ently.—*n.* appar'entness. [L. *appārens, -entis*, pr.p. of *appārēre*; see appear.]

apparition, *ap-ə-rish'ən, n.* an appearing: an appearance: reappearance after occultation: that which appears: a phantom: a ghost.—*adj.* appari'tional. [See appear.]

apparitor, *ə-par'i-tər, n.* an officer in attendance on a court, to execute orders (*obs.*): still, such an officer of an ecclesiastical court: a university beadle: one who appears (*rare*). [L. *appāritor.* See appear.]

appartement, *a-par-t(ə)-mã*, (Fr.) a set of rooms in a house for an individual or a family.

appay, appayd. See apay.

appeach, *ə-pēch', (Shak.) v.t.* to accuse, censure, or impeach.—*n.* appeach'ment. [O.Fr. *empechier*; see impeach.]

appeal, *ə-pēl', v.i.* to call upon, have recourse to (with *to*): to refer (to a witness or superior authority): to make supplication or earnest request (to a person for a thing): to resort for verification or proof (to some principle or person): to make a demand on the feelings that comes home: to demand another judgment by a higher court: to remove to another court.—*v.t.* to remove to a higher court (*arch.* except in U.S.): to accuse (*Spens., Shak.*): to offer up (prayers) (*Spens.*).—*n.* an impeachment (*Shak.*): a challenge (*obs.*): recourse: an act of appealing: a supplication: removal of a cause to a higher tribunal: an evocation of sympathetic feeling.— *adjs.* appeal'able; appeal'ing, making an appeal: imploring: calling forth sympathy.—*adv.* appeal'-ingly.—*n.* appeal'ingness.—appeal to the country, to seek approval by a general election; Court of Appeal, a section of the English High Court of Justice; Court of Criminal Appeal, an English Court created in 1907 for appeal in criminal cases. [O.Fr. *apeler*—L. *appellāre, -ātum*, to address, call by name; also to appeal to, impeach.]

appear, *ə-pēr', v.i.* to become visible: to present oneself formally before an authority or tribunal, hence to act as the representative or counsel for another: to come into view, to come before the public, be published: to be manifest: to seem.— *ns.* appear'ance, the act of appearing, e.g. in court to prosecute or answer a charge: the publication of a book: the effect of appearing conspicuously, show, parade: the condition of

that which appears, form, aspect: outward look or show: a natural phenomenon: an apparition; appear'er.—keep up appearances, to keep up an outward show, often with intent to conceal absence of the inward reality; put in an appearance, to appear in person; to all appearance(s), so far as appears to any one. [O.Fr. *apareir*—L. *appārēre*—ad, to, *pārēre*, *pāritum*, to come forth.]
appease, *ə-pēz'*, *v.t.* to pacify: to propitiate by concessions: to satisfy: to quiet: to allay.—*adj.* appeas'able.—*n.* appease'ment, the action of appeasing: the state of being appeased.—*adv.* appeas'ingly. [O.Fr. *apeser*, to bring to peace—L. *ad*, to, *pāx*, *pācis*, peace.]
appel au peuple, *a-pel ō pœpl'*, (Fr.) a plebiscite.
appellant, *ə-pel'ənt*, *n.* one who appeals: one who impeaches: a challenger to single combat (*obs.*): one who in the Jansenist controversy appealed against the bull Unigenitus (1713) to a pope 'better informed', or to a general council.—*adj.* appell'ate, relating to appeals.—*n.* appellation (*ap-ə-lā'shən*) that by which anything is called: name, esp. one attached to a particular person.—*adj.* appellā'tional.—*n.* appell'ative (*ə-pel'ə-tiv*), a common as distinguished from a proper name: a designation.—*adj.* common (as distinguished from proper): of or pertaining to the giving of names—*adv.* appell'atively. [L. *appellāre*, *-ātum*, to call.]
append, *ə-pend'*, *v.t.* to hang on (to something): to add.—*n.* append'age, something appended: esp. one of the paired jointed structures of arthropods —antennae, jaws, legs.—*adj.* append'ant, attached, annexed, consequent.—*n.* an adjunct, quality. —*ns.* appendec'tomy, more commonly appendicec'tomy (*-dis-*), removal of the vermiform appendix (Gr. *ektomē*, cutting out); appendici'tis, inflammation of the vermiform appendix.—*adj.* appendicular (*ap-en-dik'ū-lər*), of the nature of, or belonging to, an appendix.—*n.* Appendiculā'ria, a genus of Ascidians that retains the larval vertebrate characters which are lost in the more or less degenerate sea-squirts.—*adj.* appendic'ūlate, furnished with appendages.— *n.* appendix (*ə-pen'diks*), something appended or added: a supplement: an addition to a book or document, containing matter explanatory, but not essential to its completeness: a process, prolongation, or projection, esp. the vermiform appendix (*anat.*):—*pl.* append'ixes, append'ices (*-sēz*, *-siz*).—appendix vermiformis, or vermiform appendix, a blind process terminating the caecum. [L. *ad*, to, *pendēre*, to hang.]
apperception, *ap-ər-sep'shən*, *n.* the mind's perception of itself as a conscious agent: an act of voluntary consciousness, accompanied with self-consciousness: the assimilation of a new sense-experience to a mass already in the mind.—*adjs.* appercep'tive; appercipient (*-sip'i-ənt*).—*v.t.* apperceive (*-sēv'*). [L. *ad*, to, and perception, perceive.]
apperil(l), *ə-per'il*, (Shak.) *n.* peril. [L. *ad*, and peril.]
appertain, *ap-ər-tān'*, *v.i.* to belong, as a possession, a right, or attribute.—*n.* appertain'ance, appurtenance.—*adj.* appertain'ing, proper, appropriate (with *to*).—*n.* appertain'ment (Shak.), appurtenance.—*n.* apper'tinent, appertaining. —*n.* (Shak.) appurtenance. [O.Fr. *apartenir*, *apertenir*—L. *ad*, to, *pertinēre*, to belong.]
appetent, *ap'i-tənt*, *adj.* eagerly desirous: craving: longing.—*ns.* app'etence, app'etency. [L. *appetēns*, *-entis*, pr.p. of *appetēre*—ad, to, *petēre*, to seek.]
appetite, *ap'i-tit*, *n.* physical craving accompanied with uneasy sensation (hunger, thirst, sex): natural desire: inclination: desire for food: hunger (with *for*).—*adjs.* app'etible, attractive, desirable.—*v.t.* app'etise, *-ize*, to create or whet appetite in—*ns.* appetise'ment (Scott appeteeze'-

ment); app'etiser, *-z-*, something to whet the appetite.—*adj.* appetis'ing, *-z-*.—*adv.* appetis'-ingly, *-z-*.—*n.* appetition, (*-tish'ən*), direction of desire.—*adj.* app'etitive (or *a-pet'i-tiv*), having or giving an appetite. [O.F. *apetit*—L. *appetitus* —*appetēre*; see foregoing.]
applaud, *ə-plöd'*, *v.t.* to express approbation of by clapping the hands or otherwise: to extol: to commend.—*v.i.* to clap the hands or otherwise express approval.—*n.* applaud'er.—*adj.* applaud'ing.—*adv.* applaud'ingly.—*n.* applause (*-plöz'*), clapping of hands or other sign of approval: general approbation: loud praise: acclamation.—*adj.* applausive (*ə-plös'iv*).—*adv.* applaus'ively. [L. *applaudēre*, *-plausum*—ad, to, *plaudēre*, to clap; cf. explode.]
apple, *ap'l*, *n.* the fruit of the apple-tree: extended to other fruits (as pineapple, custard-apple) or even galls (oak-apple): the fruit of the forbidden tree in the Garden of Eden.—ap'ple-blight, American blight, a woolly plant-louse that infests apple-trees; app'le-blossom; app'le-cart; app'le-jack (*U.S.*), apple brandy, distilled from fermented apple juice; app'le-John (Shak.), a variety of apple considered to be in perfection when shrivelled and withered—also John-app'le; app'le-pie, a pie made with apples; app'le-squire, a prostitute's attendant: a man kept by a woman as concubine; app'le-tree, a tree (*Pyrus Malus*) of the rose family, close akin to the pear-tree; app'le-wife, app'le-woman, a woman who sells apples at a stall.—apple of discord, any cause of envy and contention, from the golden apple inscribed 'for the fairest', thrown among the gods by Eris, goddess of discord, and claimed by Aphrodite, Pallas, and Hera; apple of Sodom or Dead Sea apple, a fruit described by the ancients as fair to look upon but turning when touched to ashes, variously thought to be a gall, or the fruit of an asclepiad *Calotropis procera*: by botanists applied to the poisonous green-pulped fruit of *Solanum sodomaeum*: any fair but disappointing thing; apple of the eye, the pupil of the eye: something especially dear; apple-pie bed, a bed prepared playfully, e.g. with sheets doubled up, so as to be impossible or painful to get into; apple-pie order, perfect order; upset the apple-cart, to throw plans into confusion. [O.E. *æppel*, cf. Ger. *apfel*; O.N. *epli*; Ir. *abhal*; W. *afal*.]
appleringie, *ap-l-ring'i*, (Scot.) *n.* southernwood (*Artemisia abrotanum*). [Anglo-Fr. *averoine*—L. *abrotanum*—Gr. *abrotanon*.]
Appleton layer, *ap'l-tən lā'ər*, an ionised region in the atmosphere, about 150 miles up, that acts as a reflector of radio waves. [From the physicist Sir Edward *Appleton*.]
appliqué, *a-plē'kā, -kä'*, Fr. *ä-plē-kä*, *n.* work applied to, or laid on, another material, either of metal-work or of lace or the like.—Also *adj.* [Pa.p. of Fr. *appliquer*, to apply.]
apply, *ə-pli'*, *v.t.* to lay or put in contact: to administer: to bring to bear: to put to use: to show the reference or relevance of: to assign: to ascribe (*obs.*): to wield or ply: to direct: to devote (to a pursuit): to adapt (*obs.*): to lay on as appliqué: to cover with appliqué.—*v.i.* to suit or agree: to have recourse: to offer oneself as a candidate: to make or lodge a request: to be relevant: to hold good: to give close attention: to betake oneself (*obs.*):—*pr.p.* apply'ing; *pa.t.* and *pa.p.* applied'.—*adj.* appli'able, applicable: compliant (*obs.*).—*ns.* appli'ance, compliance (Shak.): application: apparatus; applicability (*ap-li-kə-bil'i-ti*).—*adj.* app'licable (now also *-plik'* in *adj.* and *adv.*), that may be applied: suitable.— *adv.* app'licably.—*n.* app'licant, one who applies: a petitioner: a candidate for a post.—*adj.* app'licate, put to practical use, applied.—*n.* applica'tion, the act of applying, administering,

or using: a thing applied: formal request, appeal, or petition: diligence: close thought or attention: employment, use of anything in special regard to something else: a bringing to bear: the lesson or moral of a fable: employment of a word with assignment of meaning: a kind of needlework, appliqué: compliance (*obs.*).—*adj.* **app´licâtive**, put into actual use in regard to anything: practical.—*adj.* **app´licatory** (*-kə-tər-i*), having the property of applying.—*adj.* **applied** (*ə-plïd´*), placed with a flat surface against or close to something: turned to use.—**applied mathematics**, mathematics applied to observed facts of nature, or to practical life; **applied science**, science put to use for a purpose, generally utilitarian, other than its own end (opposed to *pure*). [O.Fr. *aplier*, and its source, L. *applicāre*, *-ātum*—*ad*, to, *plicāre*, to fold.]

**appoggiatura**, *äp-pod-jä-tōō´rä*, *n.* a leaning note— a grace-note written in smaller size taking its time at the expense of the following note: a similar note with a stroke through the tail, played very quickly—an acciaccatura. [It.—*appoggiare*, to lean upon; same root as **appui**.]

**appoint**, *ə-point´*, *v.t.* to fix: to settle: to assign, grant: to fix the time of: to engage to meet: to name to an office: to ordain: to prescribe: to destine, devote: to equip (*obs.* except in *pa.p.*): to blame, arraign (*Milt.*).—*adj.* **appoint´ed**, fixed: furnished.—*adj.* **appoint´ive** (*U.S.*), filled by appointment.—*n.* **appoint´ment**, engagement, esp. for a meeting: direction: nomination: an office to which one is or may be nominated: (now usu. in *pl.*) equipment: article of equipment: allowance paid to a public officer (*obs.*). [O.Fr. *apointer—à point*, to (the) point.]

**apport**, *ə-pört´*, *-pört´*, *n.* in psychical research, the (supposed) transport of material objects without material agency: an object brought on the scene at a spiritualistic séance by no visible agency. [Fr.,—L. *apportāre*, to bring.]

**apportion**, *ə-pör´shən*, *-pör´*, *v.t.* to portion out: to divide in just shares: to adjust in due proportion. *n.* **appor´tionment**. [L. *ad*, to, and **portion**.]

**appose**, *ə-poz´*, *v.t.* to apply, e.g. a seal to a document: to place side by side. [Fr. *apposer*—L. *ad*, to, *pausāre*, to cease, rest; confused and blended in meaning with words from *pōnĕre*, *pŏsitum*, to put.]

**appose**, *ə-pōz´*, *v.t.* to confront: to examine, question (*Spens.*).—*ns.* **appos´er**; **apposition** (*ap-ō-zish´ən*), a public examination, a disputation, as on Speech Day at St Paul's School, London. [Variant of **oppose**.]

**apposite**, *ap´ō-zit*, *adj.* apt: to the purpose.—*adv.* **app´ositely**.—*ns.* **app´ositeness**; **apposition** (*-zish´ən*), application: juxtaposition: the position of a word parallel to another in syntactic relation (*gram.*): growth by deposition on the surface (*bot.*).—*adjs.* **apposi´tional** (*ə-poz´*), placed in apposition. [L. *appŏsitus*, pa.p. of *appōnĕre*, to put to—*ad*, to, *pōnĕre*, to put.]

**appraise**, *ə-prāz´*, *v.t.* to set a price on: to value with a view to sale or in U.S. payment of customs duty: to estimate the worth of.—*adj.* **apprais´able**.—*ns.* **apprais´al**, appraisement; **appraise´ment**, a valuation: estimation of quality; **apprais´er**, one who values property: one who estimates quality. [Later form of **apprize**.]

**appreciate**, *ə-prē´shi-āt*, *v.t.* to estimate justly: to be fully sensible of all the good qualities in: to estimate highly: to perceive: to raise in value, to advance the quotation or price of, as opposed to **depreciate**.—*v.i.* to rise in value.—*adj.* **apprē´ciable**, capable of being estimated: perceptible. *—adv.* **apprē´ciably**.—*n.* **apprēciā´tion**, the act of setting a value, especially on a work of literature or art: just—and also favourable—estimation: a sympathetic critical essay: increase in value.— *adj.* **apprē´ciative**, characterised by, implying

appreciation.—*n.* **apprē´ciâtor**, one who appreciates, or estimates justly.—*adj.* **apprē´ciatory** (*-shyə-tər-i*). [L.L. *appretiāre*, *ātum*—*ad*, to, and *pretium*, price.]

**apprehend**, *ap-ri-hend´*, *v.t.* to lay hold of: to arrest: to be conscious of by the senses: to lay hold of by the intellect: to catch the meaning of: to understand: to recognise: to consider: to look forward to, esp. with fear.—*n.* **apprehensibil´ity**.—*adj.* **apprehens´ible**.—*n.* **apprehen´sion**, act of apprehending or seizing: arrest: conscious perception: conception: ability to understand: fear.—*adj.* **apprehens´ive**, pertaining to the laying hold of sensuous and mental impressions: intelligent, clever: having an apprehension or notion: fearful: anticipative of something adverse.—*n.* **apprehens´iveness**. [L. *appraehendēre*—*ad*, to, *praehendēre*, *-hēnsum*, to lay hold of.]

**apprentice**, *ə-prent´is*, *n.* one bound to another to learn a craft: a mere novice.—Also *adj.*—*v.t.* to bind as an apprentice.—*ns.* **apprent´icehood** (*Shak.*), apprenticeship; **apprent´icement**; **apprent´iceship**, the state of an apprentice: a time of training for a trade, or for any activity: hence, (*Hood*) a period of seven years.—**to serve apprenticeship**, to undergo the training of an apprentice. [O.Fr. *aprentis—aprendre*, to learn—L. *appraehendēre*. See **apprehend**.]

**appress**. See **adpress**.

**apprise**, *ə-priz´*, *v.t.* to give notice to: to inform. [Fr. *apprendre*, pa.p. *appris*. See **apprehend**.]

**apprize**, **-ise**, *ə-priz*, *v.t.* to put a selling price on (*Scots law*): to value, appreciate: to have sold for payment of debt (*Scots law*).—*ns.* **appriz´er**, a creditor for whom property is apprized (*Scots law*); **appriz´ing**, the sheriff's sentence directing property to be apprized (*Scott*). [O.Fr. *appriser*, *aprisier—à*, to, and *prisier*, to price, prize. See **appraise**.]

**approach**, *ə-prōch´*, *v.t.* to bring near: to come near in any sense: to come into personal relations or seek communication with: to resemble.—*v.i.* to come near.—*n.* a drawing near: in golf, play on drawing near the putting-green (also **approach-stroke**, **-shot**, etc.): access: an avenue or means of access: approximation: (usually *pl.*) advances towards personal relations: (*pl.*) trenches, etc., by which besiegers strive to reach a fortress, or routes into any area of military importance.—*n.* **approachabil´ity**. *adj.* **approach´able**. [O.Fr. *aprochier*, L.L. *adpropiāre*—L. *ad*, to, *prope*, near.]

**approbation**, *ap-rō-bā´shon*, *n.* a formal sanction: approval: confirmation (*Shak.*): probation (*Shak.*).—*v.t.* **app´robate**, to approve authoritatively (*obs.* except in U.S.): to accept as valid (*Scots law*).—*adj.* **app´robative**, **approbatory** (*ap´rō-bə-tar-i*, or *ə-prō´*)—**approbate and reprobate**, at once to accept and reject the same deed or instrument—forbidden by Scots law; **on approbation** (*coll.* **appro**, *ap´rō*), subject to approbation: without obligation to buy. [L. *approbāre*, *-ātum*; see **approve** (1).]

**approof**, *ə-prōōf´*, *n.* trial, proof: sanction: approval. [O.Fr. *aprover*; see **approve** (1).]

**appropinque**, *ap-rō-pingk´*, **appropinquate**, **-wāt**, (*arch.*) *vs.t.* and *i.* to approach.—*ns.* **appropinquā´tion**, approach; **appropinq´uity**, nearness. [L. *appropinquāre*, to approach—*ad*, to, *propinquus—prope*, near.]

**appropriate**, *ə-prō´pri-āt*, *v.t.* to make to be the private property of any one: to take to oneself as one's own: to filch: to set apart for a purpose, assign: to suit (with *to*).—*adj.* set apart for a purpose: peculiar: suitable.—*adv.* **apprō´priately**.—*ns.* **apprō´priateness**; **apprōpriā´tion**, the act of appropriating: the making over of a benefice to a monastery or other corporation: the assigning of supplies granted by parliament

Neutral vowels in unaccented syllables: *el´ə-mənt*; for certain sounds in foreign words, see p. viii

to particular specified objects: sometimes used loosely for *impropriation*.—*adj.* **apprō′priative.**— *ns.* **apprō′priativeness; apprō′priātor.**—**appro-priation bill,** a bill stating in some detail how the revenue is to be spent. [*L. appropriāre, -ātum— ad,* to, *proprius,* one's own; see **proper.**] **approve,** *ə-prōōv′, v.t.* to show, demonstrate (esp. *refl.*): to confirm: to sanction or ratify: to think well of, to be pleased with: to commend: to test (*Shak.*): to convict (*Shak.*).—*v.i.* to judge favourably, to be pleased (with *of*).—*adj.* **approv′able,** deserving approval.—*ns.* **approv′al, approv′ance** (*rare*), approbation; **approv′er,** one who approves: an accomplice in crime admitted to give evidence against a prisoner (*law*): an informer.—*adv.* **approv′ingly.**—**approved school,** (1933—Scotland 1937—to 1969) a state boarding school for young people who have broken the law or who are pronounced to be in need of care and protection.—**on approval,** on approbation. [O.Fr. *aprover*—L. *approbāre*—*ad,* to, and *probāre,* to test or try—*probus,* good.] **approve,** *ə-prōōv′, (law) v.t.* to turn to one's profit, increase the value of. [O.Fr. *aproer, approuer*— *à,* to (L. *ad*), and *pro, prou,* advantage; see **prowess;** confused with **approve** (1).] **approximate,** *ə-proks′im-it, adj.* close together: nearest or next: approaching correctness (**very approximate,** very nearly exact; but by some used to mean very rough).—*v.t.* (-*āt*) to bring near: to come or be near to.—*v.i.* to come near (to), approach.—*adv.* **approx′imately.**—*n.* **approxima′tion,** an approach: a result in mathematics not rigorously exact, but so near the truth as to be sufficient for a given purpose.—*adj.* **approx′-imative** (-*mā-tiv,* -*mə-tiv*), approaching closely. [L. *approximāre, -ātum*—*ad,* to, *proximus,* nearest, superl. adj.—*prope,* near.] **appui,** *a-pwē, n.* support: the reciprocal action between horse's mouth and rider's hand.— *v.t.* appui, **appuy,** to support: to place beside a *point d'appui:*—*pr.p.* **appuy′ing;** *pa.t.* and *pa.p.* **appuied′, appuyed′.**—**point d'appui** (*pwē da-pwē*), a position of strength or support in a line of defences: a prop: a fulcrum. [Fr.,—O.Fr. *apuyer*—assumed L.L. *appodiāre*—L. *ad,* to, *podium,* support.] **appulse,** *ə-puls′, n.* a striking against something: a coming to conjunction or to the meridian (*astron.;* *obs.*). [L. *appulsus, -ūs*—*appellēre*— *ad,* towards, *pellēre,* to drive.] **appurtenance,** *ə-púr′tən-əns, n.* that which appertains: an appendage or accessory: a right belonging to a property (*law*).—*adj.* and *n.* **appor′tenant.** [A.Fr. *apurtenance*—O.Fr. *aper-tenance*—*apertenir.* See **appertain.**] **apraxia,** *a-praks′i-a, n.* loss of ability to mani-pulate objects, caused by brain lesion. [Gr., inaction.] **après,** *a-pre,* (Fr.) after; **après coup,** *kōō,* too late; **après-goût,** -*gōō,* an after-taste. **après-ski, apres-,** *a-pre-skē,* -*prā-, n.* (evening period of) amusements after skiing.—Also *adj.* [Fr.] **apricate,** *ap′ri-kāt, v.i.* to bask in the sun.—*v.t.* to expose to sunlight.—*n.* **aprica′tion.** [L. *apricāri,* to bask in the sun, *apricus,* open to the sun.] **apricot,** *ā′pri-kot, -kət,* or *a′,* formerly apricock, -*kok, n.* a fruit of the plum genus, roundish, pubescent, orange-coloured, of a rich aromatic flavour: its colour: the tree that bears it. [Port. *albricoque*—Ar. *al-birqūq*—*al,* the, Late Gr. *praikokion*—L. *praecoquum* or *praecox,* early ripe; the form is perh. due to a fancied connec-tion with L. *apricus,* sunny; assimilated to Fr. *abricot;* see **precocious.**] **April,** *ā′pril, -prəl, n.* the fourth month of the year.—*adjs.* **April′ian, A′prilish.**—**A′pril-fish,** an April-fool's errand or hoax (Fr. *poisson* d'Avril); **A′pril-fool,** one sent upon a bootless errand on

the first of April (in Scotland a *gowk*). [L. *Aprilis.*] **a prima vista,** *a prē′ma vēs′ta,* (It.) at first sight. **a priori,** *ā pri-ō′ri, -ō′,* L. *ä prē-ōr′ē,* term applied to reasoning from what is prior, logically or chronologically, e.g. reasoning from cause to effect; from a general principle to its conse-quences; even from observed fact to another fact or principle not observed, or to arguing from pre-existing knowledge, or even cherished prejudices; from the forms of cognition inde-pendent of experience (*Kant*).—*ns.* **apriō′rism, apriority** (-*or′i-ti*); **apriō′rist,** one who believes in Kant's view of a priori cognition. [L. *ā,* from, *priōri* (abl.), preceding.] **apron,** *ā′prən, n.* a cloth or piece of leather or the like worn in front: an English bishop's short cassock: anything resembling an apron in shape or use, as a leg-covering in an open vehicle: a timber behind the stem of a ship: a stage or part of stage in front of the proscenium arch, pro-jecting to greater or less extent into the audi-torium (also a′**pron-stage**): ground-surface at entrance to a hangar, lock, etc.: an extent of e.g. gravel, sand, spread outward from a source (*geol.*).—*v.t.* to cover with, or as with, an apron. —*ns.* a′**pron-man** (*Shak.*), a man who wears an apron, a mechanic; a′**pron-string,** a string by which an apron is tied.—**tied to a woman's apron-strings,** bound as a child to its mother. [M.E. *napron*—O.Fr. *naperon*—*nappe,* cloth, table-cloth—L. *mappa,* a napkin (*an apron from a napron;* cf. **adder**).] **apropos,** *a-prō-pō′, -prə-, adv.* to the purpose: appropriately: in reference to (with *of*): by the way, incidentally.—*adj.* to the purpose. [Fr. *à propos.* See **propose, purpose.**] **à propos de rien,** *a prō-pō də ryē,* (Fr.) apropos of nothing; **à propos de bottes** (*bot*), apropos of boots—*i.e.* without real relevancy: by the way. **apse,** *aps, n.* a semicircular or polygonal recess, esp. at the east end of a church choir—where, in the Roman basilica, stood the praetor's chair: an apsis.—*adj.* ap′sidal, of an apse or apsis.—*ns.* **apsid′iole,** a subsidiary apse; aps′is, in an orbit, the point of greatest or least distance from the central body: an apse:—*pl.* **aps′idēs** (-*z*); or **ïd-ēz**).—*adj.* ap′sidal. [L. *apsis, -idis*—Gr. *hapsis* (*apsis*), -*idos,* a felly, wheel, arch, loop—*haptein,* to fit, connect. See **apt.**] **apsos.** See **Tibetan.** **apt,** *apt, adj.* fitting: fit: suitable: apposite: tending: liable: ready or prone: open to impressions, ready to learn (often with *at*): likely.—*v.t.* to fit (*obs.*).—*adv.* apt′ly.—*n.* apt′-ness.—*n.* **ap′titude,** fitness: tendency: natural ability, readiness to learn (with *for*). [L. *aptus,* fit, suitable.] **apterous,** *ap′tər-əs, adj.* wingless.—*adj.* ap′teral, wingless: without side columns.—*n.* **apterium** (*ap-tē′ri-əm*) a bare patch on a bird's skin:—*pl.* **apte′ria.** [Gr. *a-,* priv., *pteron,* feather, wing, side-wall.] **Apteryx,** *ap′tər-iks, n.* the kiwis, a genus of birds found in New Zealand, wingless and tailless, reddish-brown, about the size of a large hen.— *n.pl.* **Apterygota** (*ap-ter-i-gō′ta*), a class of primitive insects, wingless, without metamor-phosis (bristle-tails, springtails—but see *Col-lembola*). [Gr. *a-,* priv., *pteryx,-ygos,* wing.] **aptote,** *ap′tōt, n.* an indeclinable noun.—*adj.* **aptotic** (-*tot′ik*), uninflected. [Gr. *aptōtos*—*a-,* priv., *ptōsis,* case.] **apyrexia,** *ap-i-reks′i-a, n.* intermission of fever.— *adj.* **apyret′ic.** [Gr. *apyrexiā*—*a-,* priv., *pyres-sein,* to be feverish.] **aqua,** *ak′wə, ə,* (L.) water.—**aqua caelestis** (*sē-les′tis, ki-*), rain water: rectified spirits: cordial (L. *caelestis,* coming from heaven); **aqua fontana** (*fon-tän′a*), spring water (L.

*fontānus, -a, -um,* of a spring); **aqua-fortis, aquafortis,** nitric acid: etching with nitric acid (L. *fortis,* strong); **aquafortist,** an etcher or engraver who uses aqua-fortis; **aqua-mirab´ilis,** a preparation distilled from cloves, nutmeg, ginger, and spirit of wine (L. *mīrābilis,* wonderful); **aqua-regia** (*rē´jya,* L. *rā´gi-a*), a mixture of nitric and hydrochloric acids, which dissolves the royal (L. *rēgius, -a, -um*) metal, gold; **aqua Tofana** (*tō-fän´a*), a secret poison (probably arsenical) made by a 17th-cent. Sicilian woman **Tofana; aqua-vitae** (*vī´tē;* *wē´ti;* of life), alcohol: brandy, whisky, etc. [L. *aqua,* water.] **aqua-,** *ak´wə-, ak´wa-,* in composition, water.—*adj.* **aquabat´ic.**—*ns.* **aquabat´ics,** spectacular feats and evolutions in water; a´**quaboard,** a board for riding on the surface of water; a´**quacade,** an exhibition of swimming, diving, etc., usu. accompanied by music; a´**quadrome,** a centre with facilities for water-skiing competitions; a´**quafer,** aquifer; a´**qualung,** a lightweight, self-contained diving apparatus with compressed-air supply carried on the back; a´**quanaut,** a skin-diver: one who explores and/or lives in the sea at considerable depth; **aquanaut´ics;** a´**quaplane,** a board on which one stands and is towed behind a motor-boat.—*v.i.* to ride on an aquaplane.—a´**quaplaner;** a´**quaplaning; aquifer** (*ak´wi-fer*), **aquafer,** (*geol.*) any formation containing water sufficient to supply wells, etc. [L. *aqua,* water.]
**aquamanile,** *ak´wə-mə-nī´lē, -nē´lä,* **aquamanale,** *-nä´lē, n.* a mediaeval ewer: a basin in which the priest washes his hands during the celebration of mass. [Through L.L.—L. *aquae,* of water, *mānālis,* flowing, or *manus,* hand.]
**aquamarine,** *ak´wə-mə-rēn´, n.* a pale green beryl.—*adj.* bluish-green. [L. *aqua marina,* sea water—*mare,* the sea.]
**aquanaut, aquaplane,** etc. See **aqua-.**
**aquarelle,** *ak´wə-rel´, n.* water-colour painting: a painting in (transparent) water-colours.—*n.* **aquarell´ist.** [Fr.,—It. *acquerella, acquarella*—*acqua*—L. *aqua.*]
**aquarium,** *ə-kwā´ri-əm, n.* a tank or (a building containing) a series of tanks for keeping aquatic animals or plants:—*pl.* **aquā´riums, aquā´ria.**—*adj.* **aquā´rian.**—*n.* one who keeps an aquarium.—*ns.* **aquā´riist, aquā´rist,** an aquarian.—*n.* **Aquā´rius,** the Water-bearer, a sign of the zodiac, and a constellation once coincident with it. [L. *aquārius, -a, -um, adj.*—*aqua,* water.]
**aquatic,** *ə-kwat´ik, -kwot´, adj.* living, growing, practising sports, taking place, in or on water.—*n.* an aquatic plant, animal, or sportsman: (in *pl.*) water sports. [L. *aquāticus*—*aqua,* water.]
**aquatint,** *ak´wə-tint, n.* a mode of etching on copper with resin and nitric acid.—Also **aquatint´a.**—*v.t.* and *v.i.* a´**quatint,** to engrave in aquatint. [It. *acqua tinta,* dyed water—L. *aqua,* water, and *tingĕre, tinctum,* to dye.]
**à quatre,** *a katr´,* (Fr.) of or between four: four together; **à quatre mains,** *mē,* for four hands.
**a quattr' occhi,** *a kwat-ro´kē,* (It.) face to face, tête-à-tête.
**aquavit,** *äk´wə-vēt, ak´, n.* a Scandinavian spirit flavoured with caraway seeds.—Also **ak´vavit.** [Dan., Sw., Norw. *akvavit*—Mediaeval L. *aqua vitae.*]
**aqueduct,** *ak´wi-dukt, n.* an artificial channel or pipe for conveying water, most commonly understood to mean a bridge across a valley: a bridge carrying a canal: a small passage in an animal body. [L. *aqua,* water, *dūcĕre, ductum,* to lead.]
**aqueous,** *ā´kwi-əs, adj.* of water: watery: deposited by water.—**aqueous humour,** the watery fluid between the cornea and the lens in the eye. [L. *aqua,* water.]
**aquifer.** See **aqua-.**
**Aquifoliaceae,** *ak-wi-fō-li-ā´si-ē, n.pl.* the holly

family.—*adj.* **aquifoliā´ceous** (*-shəs*). [L. *aquifolium,* holly—*acus, -ūs,* needle, *folium,* leaf.]
**Aquila,** *ak´wi-la, n.* the golden eagle genus: the Eagle, a constellation north of Sagittarius.—*adj.* **aq´uiline** (*-līn*), of the eagle: hooked like an eagle's beak. [L. *aquila,* eagle.]
**Aquilegia,** *ak-wi-lē´jyə, n.* the columbine genus. [Prob. L. *aquila,* eagle.]
**Aquilon,** *ak´wi-lon,* (Shak.) *n.* the north wind. [L. *aquilō, -ōnis.*]
**a quoi bon?,** *a kwa bõ,* (Fr.) what's the good of it?
**ar, är,** *n.* the eighteenth letter of the alphabet (R, r).
**Arab,** *ar´əb, n.* one of the Semitic people inhabiting Arabia and neighbouring countries: an Arabian horse: a neglected or homeless boy or girl (usually **street** or **city arab**).—*adj.* Arabian, to Arabia or the Arabs.—*n.* a native of Arabia.—*adj.* **Arabian** (*ə-rā´bi-ən, -byən*), of or belonging to Arabia or the Arabs.—*n.* a native of Arabia.—*adj.* **Arabic** (*ar´əb-ik*), relating to Arabia, or to its language.—*n.* the language of the Arabs (see also **gum**).—*ns.* **Ar´abism,** an Arabic idiom; **Ar´abist,** one skilled in the Arabic language or literature; **Araby,** a poetical form of *Arabia.*—**Arabian,** or **Arabic, numerals,** the numerals in ordinary use in arithmetic, transmitted from India to Europe by the Arabs. [L. *Arabs, Arabis*—Gr. *Araps, Arabos.*]
**araba,** *är-ä´bä, n.* a heavy screened wagon used by the Tatars and others.—Also **ar´ba, arõ´ba.** [Ar. and Pers. *'arābah.*]
**arabesque,** *ar-ə-besk´, adj.* after the manner of Arabian designs.—*n.* a fantastic painted or sculptured ornament among the Spanish Moors, consisting of foliage and other forms curiously intertwined: a musical composition with analogous continuity: a posture in ballet dancing in which one leg is stretched out backwards parallel with the ground and the body is bent forward from the hips.—*adj.* **arabesqued´,** ornamented with arabesques. [Fr.,—It. *arabesco; -esco* corresponding to Eng. *-ish.*]
**arabin,** *ar´əb-in, n.* the essential principle of gum-arabic (see **gum**).—**ar´abinose** (or *-ab´*) a sugar got from arabin. [See **Arab.**]
**Arabis,** *ar´ə-bis, n.* the rock-cress genus of Cruciferae. [L.L. *Arabis,* Arabian, perhaps from its dry habitats.]
**arable,** *ar´ə-bl, adj.* fit for ploughing or tillage. [L. *arābilis*—*arāre,* cog. with Gr. *aroein,* to plough, O.E. *erian,* Eng. **ear** (v.t.), Ir. *araim.*]
**Araceae, araceous.** See **Arum.**
**Arachis,** *ar´ə-kis, n.* a Brazilian genus of the pea family, including the monkey-nut, ground-nut, or peanut, which ripens its pods underground. [Gr. *arachos* and *arakis,* names of leguminous plants.]
**Arachnida,** *ə-rak´ni-də, n.pl.* a class of Arthropoda, embracing spiders, scorpions, mites, etc.—*n.* **arach´nid,** any member of the class.—*n.* and *adj.* **arach´nidan.**—*adj.* **arach´noid,** like a cobweb.—*n.* the arachnoid membrane.—*adjs.* **arachnoi´dal; arachnolog´ical.**—*ns.* **arachnol´ogist,** one who studies the Arachnida; **arachnol´ogy.**—**arachnoid membrane,** one of the three coverings of the brain and spinal cord, between the dura-mater and pia-mater, non-vascular, transparent, thin. [Gr. *arachnē,* spider.]
**araeometer, areometer,** *ar-i-om´i-tər, n.* an instrument for determining specific gravity, a hydrometer.—*adjs.* **araeometric, -al** (*-met´*).—*n.* **araeom´etry,** the measuring of specific gravity. [Gr. *araios,* thin, *metron,* measure.]
**araeostyle, areostyle,** *a-rē´ō-stīl, adj.* having columns four diameters or more apart.—*n.* a building or colonnade so built.—*adj.* **araeosystyle, areosystile** (*-sis´tīl*), alternately araeostyle and systyle.—Also *n.* [Gr. *araios,* thin, sparse, *stȳlos,* column.]
**aragonite,** *ar´ə-gə-nīt, ə-rag´ə-nit, n.* an ortho-

rhombic mineral composed of calcium carbonate. [*Aragon*, in Spain.]

**araise, arayse,** *ə-rāz'*, (*Shak.*) *v.t.* to raise from the dead. [Pfx. *a-*, intensive, and **raise**.]

**arak.** Once *obs.*, now more usu., spelling of **arrack.**

**Aralia,** *ə-rā'li-ə, n.* a genus of the ivy family, **Araliā'ceae,** much grown as decorative plants.— *adj.* **araliā'ceous.** [Perh. American Indian origin.]

**Aramaic,** *ar-ə-mā'ik, adj.* relating to Aramaea, or Aram (roughly, modern Syria), or to its language —also **Aramaean** (*-mē'ən*).—*ns.* any of a group of Semitic languages (including that spoken by Christ) once used in this and neighbouring areas in commerce and government.—*n.* **Aramā'ism** an Aramaic idiom. [Gr. *Aramaios*.]

**Aranea,** *a-rā'ni-ə, n.* the garden-spider genus (otherwise *Epeira*):—*ns.pl.* **Arā'neae** (*-ē*), **Araneida** (*ar-ə-nē'i-da*), **-idae** (*-dē*), spiders as a class or order.—*n.* **arā'neid** (*-ni-id*), a spider.—*adj.* **arā'neous,** cobwebby. [L. *arănea,* spider.]

**arapaima,** *ar-ə-pī'mə,* the pirarucu (*Arapaima*, or *Sudis, gigas*; fam. Osteoglossidae), a gigantic South American river-fish, chief food-fish of the Amazon, reaching sometimes 4 cwt. [Tupí origin.]

**arapunga,** *ar-ə-pung'gə, n.* the campanero or South American bell-bird. [Tupí *araponga*.]

**arar,** *är'är, n.* the sandarac tree. [Moroccan name.]

**araroba,** *ä-rä-rō'bə, n.* Goa powder, got from cavities in a papilionaceous Brazilian tree (*Andira*, or *Vataireopsis, araroba*), cultivated in Goa, yielding chrysarobin. [Prob. Tupí.]

**Araucaria,** *a-rö-kā'ri-ə, n.* the monkey-puzzle genus, coniferous trees of S. America and Australasia. [*Arauco,* in S. Chile.]

**à ravir,** *a ra-vēr,* (Fr.) ravishingly.

**arba.** See **araba.**

**arbalest,** *är'bəl-est, n.* a crossbow: a cross-staff.— Also **ar'balist, ar'blast, ar'cubalist.**—*ns.* **ar'balester, ar'balister, ar'blaster,** a crossbowman. [L. *arcuballista*—*arcus,* bow, *ballista* (see **ballista**); partly through O.E. *arblast*—O.Fr. *arbaleste*.]

**arbiter,** *är'bi-tər, n.* a judge: an umpire: one chosen by parties to decide between them: one who has absolute control:—*fem.* **ar'bitress.**— *adj.* **ar'bitrable.**—*n.* **ar'bitrage** (*-trij*), arbitration: traffic in bills of exchange or stocks to profit by different prices in different markets.—*adj.* **ar'bitral** (*Scots law*).—*n.* **arbit'rament** (now less usu. **arbit'rement**), the decision of an arbiter: determination: power of decision.—*v.i.* and *v.t.* **ar'bitrate,** to decide, determine: to refer to arbitration: to judge as arbiter.—*ns.* **arbitrā'tion,** (submission) to the decision of an arbiter; **ar'bitrātor, arbiter:**—*fem.* **ar'bitrātrix.** [L.]

**arbiter elegantiarum,** *ar'bit-er el-e-gan-shi-är'əm, el-e-gan-ti-är'ōōm,* (L.) judge of taste.

**arbitrary,** *är'bi-trər-i, adj.* not bound by rules: despotic, absolute: capricious: arising from accident rather than from rule.—*adv.* **ar'bitrarily.**—*n.* **ar'bitrariness.** [L. *arbitrārius— arbiter*.]

**arbitrium,** *ar-bit'ri-əm, -ōōm,* (L.) power of decision.

**arblast.** See **arbalest.**

**arbor,** *är'bər, n.* (L.) a tree: a shaft or beam: a spindle or axis.—*adjs.* **arborā'ceous,** tree-like: wooded; **arboreal** (*är-bō'ri-əl, -bö'*), of, of the nature of, trees: tree-dwelling; **arbo'reous,** of or belonging to trees: tree-like: in the form of a tree: wooded.—*ns.* **arboresc'ence, arborisā'tion,** *-izā'tion,* tree-like growth.—*adj.* **arboresc'ent,** growing, formed, branched, like a tree: approaching the character of a tree.—*ns.* **ar'boret,** shrubbery (*obs.*): an arboretum (*obs.*): a little tree, shrub (*Milt.*); **arborē'tum** (L. *är-bor-*

**ä'tōōm**), a botanic garden of trees:—*pl.* **arborē'ta.**—*n.* **ar'borist,** one who studies trees.— *adjs.* **ar'borous,** of, or formed by, trees; **arboricul'tural.**—*ns.* **arboriculture,** forestry, the culture of trees, esp. timber-trees; **arboricul'turist.—Arbor Day,** in some countries a day yearly set apart for the general planting of trees; **arbor vitae** (L., tree of life; *vī'tē, wē'ti*), a coniferous genus (*Thuja*) akin to cypress: a tree-like appearance seen when the human cerebellum is cut vertically. [L. *arbor,* tree.]

**arbour,** *är'bər, n.* a grass-plot, garden, herbgarden, or orchard (*obs.*): a grassy seat (*obs.*): hence, a retreat or bower of trees or climbing plants: a shaded walk (*Milt.*).—*adj.* **ar'boured.** [A.F. *herber*—L. *herbārium*—*herba,* grass, herb; meaning changed through confusion with L. *arbor,* tree.]

**Arbutus,** *är-bū'təs, är', n.* the strawberry-tree genus.—*n.* **ar'bute,** the strawberry-tree or other Arbutus. [L. *arbūtus*.]

**arc,** *ärk, n.* a part of the circumference of a circle or other curve: an arch (*Milt.*): a luminous discharge of electricity across a gap between two conductors or terminals.—*v.i.* to form an arc (*elect.*).—*n.* **arc(k)'ing.**—*ns.* **arc-lamp, arc-light,** a lamp whose source of light is an electric arc between carbon electrodes; **arc-welding** (see **weld**). [L. *arcus,* a bow.]

**arcade,** *är-kād', n.* a row of arches, open or closed, on columns or pilasters: a walk arched over: a covered passageway lined with shops.—*adj.* **arcād'ed.**—*n.* **arcād'ing.** [Fr.,—L.L. *arcāta,* arched; see **arch.**]

**Arcadian,** *är-kād'i-ən, adj.* of Arcadia (*poet.* **Arcady,** *är'kə-di*), a district in Greece whose people were primitive in manners and given to music and dancing: pastoral: simple, innocent. —Also *n.*—*n.* **Arcād'ianism.**

**arcanum,** *är-kān'əm, n.* a secret: a mystery: a secret remedy or elixir:—*pl.* **arcan'a.**—*adj.* **arcane'.**—*n.* **arcan'ist** (*-kān'*), one having knowledge of a secret ceramic process. [L., neut. of *arcānus—arca,* a chest.]

**arc de triomphe,** *ärk də trē-ɔ̄f,* (Fr.) triumphal arch.

**arc-en-ciel,** *ärk-ā-syel,* (Fr.) rainbow.

**arch,** *ärch, n.* a structure of wedge-shaped stones or other pieces supporting each other by mutual pressure and able to sustain a superincumbent weight: anything of like form: an archway: the part from heel to toes of the bony structure of the foot, normally having an upward curve: (in *pl.*) with various adjs. (grey, dark, silvery, etc.), collectors' names for moths of different kinds, with markings like arcading.—*v.t.* to cover or furnish with an arch.—*v.t.* and *v.i.* to bend in the form of an arch.—*adj.* **arched,** having the form of an arch: covered with an arch.—*adv.* **arch'wise,** in the manner of an arch.—*ns.* **arch'let,** a little arch; **arch'way,** an arched or vaulted passage.—(**Court of**) **Arches,** the ecclesiastical court of appeal for the province of Canterbury, formerly held at the church of St Mary-le-Bow (or of the Arches, from the arches that support its steeple).—**dropped, fallen, arch,** a flattened foot arch. [O.Fr. *arche*—L. *arcus,* bow (as if *arca*).]

**arch,** *ärch, adj.* chief, principal (*Shak.*): finished, accomplished, pre-eminent, esp in evil (*Bunyan*): cunning: waggish: roguish: shrewd.—*n.* (*Shak.*) chief.—*adv.* **arch'ly.**—*n.* **arch'ness.** [From the prefix *arch-,* in words such as *arch-*rogue, etc.]

**arch-, ärch-** (*ärk-*) in direct borrowings from Greek), *pfx.* first or chief: often an intensive in an odious sense.—*ns.* **arch'-druid,** a chief or presiding druid; **arch'-en'emy,** a chief enemy: Satan—also **arch'-fel'on, arch'-fiend', arch'-foe';** **arch'-flā'men,** a chief flamen or priest; **arch'-**

her'etic, a leader of heresy; arch'-mock' (*Shak.*), the height of mockery; arch'-pi'rate, a chief pirate; arch'-pō'et, a chief poet: a poet-laureate (*obs.*): arch'-prel'ate, a chief prelate; arch'-priest', a chief priest: in early times, a kind of vicar to the bishop—later, a rural dean: a superior appointed by the Pope, to govern the secular priests sent into England from the foreign seminaries during the period 1598-1621; arch'-trait'or, a chief traitor, greatest of traitors, sometimes applied esp. to the devil, or to Judas; arch'-vill'ain, one supremely villainous. [O.E. *arce-, ærce-*, through L. from Gr. *archi—archos*, chief.]

Archaean, är-kē'ən, (*geol.*) *adj.* and *n.* Pre-Cambrian. [Gr. *archaios*, ancient—*archē*, beginning.]

archaeology, ärk-i-ol'ə-ji, *n.* the scientific study of human antiquities.—*adj.* archaeological (-ə-loj'i-kl).—*adv.* archaeolog'ically.—*n.* archaeol'-ogist. [Gr. *archaios*, ancient—*archē*, beginning, *logos*, discourse.]

Archaeopteryx, är-ki-op':ər-iks, *n.* a Jurassic fossil bird, with a long bony tail. [Gr. *archaios*, ancient, *pteryx*, wing.]

Archaeornithes, är-ki-ör-ni'thēz, *n.pl.* the Sauru-rae, or primitive reptile-like birds, the Archaeopteryx and its kin. [Gr. *archaios*, ancient, *ornithēs*, pl. of *ornis*, *ornīs*, bird.]

Archaeus. See Archeus.

archaic, är-kā'ik, *adj.* ancient: savouring of the past: not absolutely obsolete but no longer in general use: old-fashioned.—*adv.* archā'ically. —*n.* archā'icism.—*v.i.* ar'chāise, -ize, to imitate the archaic.—*ns.* ar'châiser, -izer; ar'chāism, inclination to archaise: an archaic word or phrase; ar'châist.—*adj.* archäist'ic, affectedly or imitatively archaic. [Gr. *archaikos—archaios*, ancient—*archē*, beginning.]

archangel, ärch'ān-jl, or -ân', *n.* an angel of the highest order: garden angelica: dead-nettle: a kind of pigeon.—*adj.* archangelic (-an-jel'). [Gr. *archangelos—archos*, chief, *angelos*, messenger.]

archbishop, ärch-bish'əp, or ärch', *n.* a metropolitan bishop who superintends the bishops in his province, and also exercises episcopal authority in his own diocese.—*n.* archbish'opric. [O.E. *ærcebiscop*; see arch-, and bishop.]

arch-chimic, ärch-kim'ik, (*Milt.*) *adj.* supreme in alchemy. [See arch-, chemic.]

archdeacon, ärch-dē'kn, or ärch', *n.* a chief deacon: the ecclesiastical dignitary having the chief supervision of a diocese or part of it, next under the bishop—the 'bishop's eye'.—*ns.* archdeac'onry, the office, jurisdiction, or residence of an archdeacon. [O.E. *ærcediacon*; see arch-, deacon.]

archdiocese, arch-di'ə-sis, -sēs, *n.* an archbishop's diocese. [arch-, chief, and diocese.]

archduke, ärch'dūk, ärch'dūk', (*hist.*) *n.* the title of certain early reigning dukes of importance, and of princes of the imperial house of Austria: —*fem.* archduchess (ärch'duch'is).—*adj.* arch'-dū'cal.—*ns.* arch'duch'y, arch'duke'dom. chief, and duke.]

archegonium, ärk-i-gō'ni-əm, *n.* the flask-shaped female reproductive organ of mosses and ferns, and (in a reduced form) of flowering plants:—*pl.* archego'nia.—*adjs.* archego'nial; archego'niate, having archegonia.—*n.pl.* Archegoniā'tae, a main division of the vegetable kingdom, bryophytes and pteridophytes. [Gr. *archegonos*, founder of a race.]

archenteron, ärk-en'tər-on, *n.* in the embryo, the primitive gut. [Gr. pfx. *arch-*, *enteron*, gut.]

archer, ärch'ər, *n.* one who shoots with a bow and arrows:—*fem.* arch'eress.—*n.* arch'ery, the art or sport of shooting with the bow: a company of archers.—*n.* arch'er-fish, an acanthopterygious fish of India that catches insects by shooting

water at them from its mouth. [O. Fr. *archier*—L. *arcārius—arcus*, a bow.]

archetype, ärk'i-tīp, *n.* the original pattern or model, prototype.—*adj.* archetyp'al. [Gr. *archetŷpon, arche-, archi-*, and *typos*, a model.]

Archeus, Archaeus, or without *cap.*, är-kē'us, *n.* personification by Paracelsus of a supposed spirit dwelling in and controlling all living things and processes. [Mod. L. *archaeus*—Gr. *archaios*, original.]

archgenethliac, ärch'je-neth'li-ak, (*Browning*; in derogatory sense) *n.* greatest of genethliacs or astrologers. [arch-, chief.]

Archibald, är'chi-bəld, Archie, är'chi, (*mil. slang*) *ns.* an anti-aircraft gun. [Arbitrary name.]

Archichlamydeae, är-ki-klə-mid'i-ē, (*bot.*) *n.pl.* one of the main divisions of the Dicotyledons, in which the petals, if present, are in general not united. [Gr. pfx. *archi-* denoting primitiveness, *chlamys, -ydos*, mantle.]

archidiaconal, är-ki-dī-ak'ə-nl, *adj.* of an archdeacon. [Gr. *archidiākonos*; see deacon.]

archiepiscopal, är-ki-i-pis'kə-pl, *adj.* of an archbishop.—*ns.* archiepis'copacy, archiepis'copate, dignity or province of an archbishop.—*archi-*episcopal cross, a patriarchal cross. [Gr. *archiepiskopos*, archbishop.]

archil, är'chil, -kil, *n.* a red or violet dye made from various lichens: a lichen yielding it, esp. species of Roccella.—Also orchel (*ör'chəl*), orchella (-*chel'ə*), or'chil, orchill'a.—*n.* orchill'a-weed, an archil lichen. [O.Fr. *orchel, orseil* (Fr. *orseille*)—It. *orcello*, origin undetermined.]

Archilochian, är-ki-lō'ki-ən, *adj.* of *Archilōchus* (Gr. *Archilōchos*) of Paros (*c.* 714-676 B.C.), Greek lyric poet and lampooner, reputed originator of iambic metre, proverbially bitter.—*n.* an Archilochian verse—dactylic tetrameter catalectic, dactylic trimeter catalectic (*lesser Archilochian*), or dactylic tetrameter combined with trochaic tripody (*greater Archilochian*).

archilowe, är'hhi-lō, (*obs. Scot.*) *n.* a treat in return. [Origin unknown.]

archimage, är'ki-māj, *n.* a chief magician or enchanter. [Gr. *archi-*, chief, *magos*, a magician; older than Spenser's Archimago.]

archimandrite, är-ki-man'drīt, *n.* in the Greek Church, an abbot. [Late Gr. *archimandritēs*—pfx. *archi-*, first, and *mandrā*, an enclosure, a monastery.]

Archimedean, är'ki-mē-dē'ən, or -mē'di-ən, *adj.* pertaining to *Archimedes*, a celebrated Greek mathematician of Syracuse (*c.* 287-212 B.C.).—Archimedean screw, a machine for raising water, etc., in simplest form a tube bent spirally turning on its axis; Archimedean spiral, the curve described by a point moving uniformly along a uniformly revolving radius vector, its polar equation being $r = a\theta$. principle of Archimedes, that a body weighed when immersed wholly or partly in a fluid shows a loss of weight equal to the weight of fluid it displaces.

Archipelago, ärk-i-pel'ə-gō, *n.* the Aegean Sea: (without *cap.*) a sea abounding in islands, hence a group of islands:—*pl.* archipel'ago(e)s.—*adj.* archipelagic (-pi-laj'ik). [An Italian compound *arcipelago* from Gr. *archi-*, chief, *pelagos*, sea, with pfx. restored to Gr. form.]

architect, ärk'i-tekt, *n.* a designer of buildings: a designer of ships (*naval architect*): a maker: a contriver.—*adjs.* architecton'ic, pertaining to architecture: constructive: controlling, directing: pertaining to the arrangement of knowledge.—*n.* (often in *pl.* form) the science of architecture: the systematic arrangement of knowledge.—*adj.* architecton'ical.—*adv.* architecton'ically.—*adj.* architec'tural (-*chər-əl*).—*n.* architec'ture, the art or science of building: structure: in specific sense, one of the fine arts, the art of designing buildings: style of building.

[Gr. *architektōn*, master-builder—*archi-*, chief, and *tektōn*, a builder.]

**architrave**, *ärk'i-trāv*, (*archit.*) *n*. the lowest division of the entablature resting immediately on the abacus of the column: collective name for the various parts, jambs, lintels, etc., that surround a door or window: moulding round an arch.—*adj.* **arch'itraved**. [It. *architrave*—Gr. *archi-*, chief, and L. *trabs*, *trabis*, a beam.]

**archive**, *ärk'īv*, *n*. (in *pl.*) a repository of public records or of records and monuments generally: public records: (rare in *sing.*) a document, monument.—*adj.* **archiv'al** (or *ärk'i-vǝl*).—*n.* **archivist** (*ärk'i-vist*), a keeper of archives or records. [Fr., —L.L. *archi*(*v*)*um*—Gr. *archeion*, magisterial residence—*archē*, government.]

**archivolt**, *är'ki-vōlt*, *n*. the under-curve of an arch: moulding on it. [It. *archivolto*—*arco* (L. *arcus*, an arch) and *volta*, vault.]

**archlute**, *ärch'lōōt*, *-lūt*, *n*. a large double-necked bass lute. [Pfx. **arch-** and **lute**.]

**archology**, *ärk-ol'ǝ-ji*, (*rare*) *n*. doctrine of the origin of things: the science of government. [Gr. *archē*, beginning, rule, *logos*, discourse.]

**archon**, *ärk-on*, *-ǝn*, *n*. one of nine chief magistrates of ancient Athens.—*ns.* **arch'onship**, the office of an archon; **arch'ontate**, the archon's tenure of office.—*adj.* **archontic** (*-ont'ik*). [Gr. *archōn*, *-ontos*, pr.p. of *archein*, to be first, to rule.]

**arco saltando**, *är'kō säl-tän'dō*, *adv.* and *adj.* (played) with rebounding bow.—*n.* a quick staccato. [It., jumping bow.]

**Arctic**, **arctic**, *ärk'tik*, *adj.* relating to the Great Bear, or to the north: extremely cold.—*n.* a waterproof overshoe (*U.S.*): (usu. *cap.* and with **the**) the area lying north of the Arctic Circle or north of the timber line:—*n.pl.* **Arctiidae** (*-ī'i-dē*), the tiger-moth family, whose caterpillars are called woolly-bears.—*adj.* **arc'toid**, bear-like.—**Arctic Circle**, the parallel of latitude 66°33'N, bounding the region of the earth surrounding the north terrestrial pole. [Gr. *arktos*, a bear.]

**Arctogaea**, *ärk-tō-jē'a*, *n*. a zoological region including all lands outside of Notogaea and Neogaea.—*adjs.* **Arctogae'an**, **Arctogae'ic**. [Gr. *arktos*, bear (see preceding), *gaia*, earth.]

**Arctostaphylos**. See **bearberry**.

**Arcturus**, *ärk-tū'rǝs*, *-tōō'*, *n*. the Bear-ward, a yellow star in Boötes, fourth in order of brightness in the entire heavens. [Gr. *Arktouros—arktos*, bear, and *ouros*, guard.]

**arcuate**, *är'kū-āt*, **arcuated**, *-id*, *adjs.* arched.—*n.* **arcua'tion**.—**arcus** (senilis), *är'kǝs* (*sen'il-is*), a bow-shaped or ring-shaped greyish fatty deposit in the cornea (especially in the aged). [L. *arcuātus*, pa.p. of *arcuāre*, to bend like a bow—*arcus*, a bow.]

**arcubalist**, *är'kū-bǝ-list*. See **arbalest**.

**arcus**. See **arcuate**.

**Ardea**, *är'di-a*, *n*. the heron and bittern genus. [L. *ardea*, heron.]

**ardeb**, *är'deb*, *n*. an Egyptian dry measure of 5½ bushels. [Ar. *irdab*.]

**ardent**, *ärd'ǝnt*, *adj.* burning: fiery: fervid: combustible, inflammable (*obs.* exc. in ardent spirits, distilled alcoholic liquors, whisky, brandy, etc.). —*n.* **ard'ency**.—*adv.* **ard'ently**.—*n.* **ard'our**, warmth of passion or feeling: eagerness: enthusiasm (with *for*). [L. *ardēns*, *-entis*, pr.p. of *ardēre*, to burn.]

**ardentia verba**, *ar-den'shi-a*, *ti-a*, *vûr'ba*, *wer'*, (L.) words that burn, glowing language.

**ard-ri(gh)**, **ardri(gh)**, * örd'rē*, or *-rē'*, *n*. a head king. [Ir. *ärd*, noble, *rī*, king.]

**arduous**, *ärd'ū-ǝs*, *adj.* steep, difficult to climb: difficult to accomplish: laborious.—*adv.* **ard'-uously**.—*n.* **ard'uousness**. [L. *arduus*, steep, high.]

**are**, *är*, *n*. the unit of the metric land measure, 100 sq. metres. [Fr.,—L. *ārea*, a site, space, court.]

**are**, *är*, used as plural of the present indicative of the verb *to be*. [Old Northumbrian *aron*, which ousted the usual O.E. *sind*, *sindon*; both from the root *es-*.]

**area**, *ā'ri-a*, *n*. a space or piece of ground: a portion of surface: a region (*lit.* and *fig.*): the floor of a theatre, etc.: a sunken space alongside the basement of a building: superficial extent. —*adj.* **ā'real**.—**ā'rea-sneak'**, a thief who sneaks in by area doors. [L. *ārea*, an open empty place, etc.]

**areach**, *a-rēch'*, (*obs.*) *v.t.* to reach, get at: to seize. —*pa.t.* (*Spens.*) **arraught** (*a-röt'*). [O.E. *ārǣcan*—*ā-*, intens., *rǣcan*, to reach.]

**aread**, **arede**, **arreede**, *a-rēd'*, *v.t.* to declare (*obs.*): to utter (*obs.*): to guess (*arch.*): to interpret, explain (*arch.*): to adjudge (*obs.*): to decide (*obs.*): to counsel (*Milt.* and *Spens.*).—*pa.t.* and *pa.p.* **ared(d)'**. [O.E. *ārǣdan*: see **read**.]

**arear**, **arere**, Spenserian spellings of **arrear** (*adv.*).

**à rebours**, *a rǝ-bōōr*, (Fr.) against the grain.

**Areca**, *ar'i-kǝ*, *ǝ-rē'*, *n*. the betel-nut genus of palms.—*n.* **ar'eca-nut**, betel-nut, the nut of *Areca catechu*, chewed by the Malays with lime in a betel-pepper leaf. [Port.,—Malayalam *adekka*.]

**arefaction**, *ar-i-fak'shǝn*, (*obs.*) *n*. drying.—*v.t.* and *v.i.* **ar'efy**, to dry up, wither. [L. *ārefacēre*, to make dry—*ārēre*, to dry, *facēre*, to make.]

**arena**, *ǝ-rē'nǝ*, *n*. part of the ancient amphitheatre strewed with sand for combats: any place of public contest: any sphere of action.—*adj.* **arenaceous** (*ar-i-nā'shǝs*), sandy: composed of sand or quartz grains: with shell of agglutinated sand-grains: sand-growing.—*ns.* **Arenā'ria**, the sandwort genus, akin to chickweed; **arenā'tion**, remedial application of sand.—*adj.* **arenic'olous**, sand-dwelling.—**arena stage**, a stage which can have audience all round it. (See **theatre-in-the-round**.) [L. *arēna*, sand.]

**areography**, *ar-i-og'rǝ-fi*, *n*. description of the physical features of the planet Mars. [Gr. *Arēs*, Mars, *graphein*, to write.]

**areola**, *a-rē'ō-lǝ*, *n*. a small area: a small space marked off by lines, or a slightly sunken spot (*biol.*): an interstice in a tissue (*physiol.*): any circular spot such as that around the nipple (*physiol.*): part of the iris of the eye bordering on the pupil (*physiol.*):—*pl.* **arē'olae** (*-lē*).—*adjs.* **arē'olar**; **arē'olate**, **arē'olated**, divided into small areas.—*ns.* **arēolā'tion**, division into areolae; **areole** (*ar'i-ōl*), an areola: a spiny or hairy spot on a cactus. [L. *āreola*, dim. of *ārea*.]

**areometer**. See **araeometer**.

**Areopagus**, *ar-i-op'ag-ǝs*, *n*. the Hill of Arēs, on which the supreme court of ancient Athens was held: the court itself: any important tribunal.— *n.* **Areop'agite** (*-git*, *-jit*), a member of the Areopagus.—*adj.* **Areopagitic** (*-git'*, or *-jit'*), pertaining to the Areopagus. [Latinised from Gr. *Areios pagos*, hill of Arēs (identified with Roman Mars).]

**areostyle**, **areosystile**. See **araeostyle**.

**aret**, **arett**, *a-ret'*, *v.t.* to entrust, commit (*Spens.*): to assign, allot (*obs.*): to adjudge, award (*obs.*). [O.Fr. *areter*, *a-*, to, *reter*—L. *reputāre*, to reckon.]

**arête**, *a-ret'*, *n*. a sharp ridge: esp. in French Switzerland, a rocky edge on a mountain. [Fr.,—L. *arista*, an ear of corn, fish-bone, spine.]

**Aretinian**, *ar-i-tin'i-ǝn*, *adj.* pertaining to Guido of Arezzo (d. 1050).—**Aretinian syllables**, the initial syllables of the half-lines of a hymn to John the Baptist, which, falling on successive notes of the diatonic scale, were used (apparently by Guido) as names for the notes:—*Ut* queant laxis *re*sonare fibris *Mi*ra gestorum *fa*muli tuorum, *Sol*ve polluti *la*bii reatum, Sancte Ioannes. Thus C in the bass is *C fa ut*, being the fourth note (fa) of the first hexachord (on G) and the first note (ut) of the second hexachord (on C). See gamut. [L. *Arētinus, Arrētinus*, of Arrētium or Arezzo.]

**arew,** *a-roō', (Spens.) adv.* arow, in a row.

**arfvedsonite,** *är'ved-sən-it, n.* a soda amphibole. [After J. A. *Arfvedson* (1792-1841), Swedish mineralogist.]

**argal,** *är'gl, adv.* Shakespeare's gravedigger's attempt at L. *ergō*, therefore.

**argala,** *är'gə-la, n.* the adjutant stork. [Hind. *hargila.*]

**argali,** *är'gə-li, n.* the great wild sheep (*Ovis ammon*) of Asia. [Mongol.]

**argan,** *är'gan,* a Moroccan timber-tree of the family Sapotaceae: its oil-bearing seed. [N. African pron. of Ar. *arjān.*]

**argand,** *är'gand, n.* a burner admitting air within a cylindrical flame.—Also *adj.* [Invented by Aimé *Argand* (1755-1803).]

**Argathelian,** *är-gə-thē'li-ən, adj.* of the party in Scotland in the 18th century that approved of the political influence of the house of Argyle. [L.L. *Argathelia,* Argyle.]

**argemone,** *är-jem-ō'nē, n.* the prickly poppy. [Gr. *argemōnē*, a kind of poppy.]

**argent,** *ärj'ənt, adj.* and *n.* silver: silvery-white: white (*her.*).—*adjs.* **argentif'erous,** silver-bearing; **ar'gentine** (-*in*), of or like silver: sounding like silver: (*cap.*) of, or belonging to, Argentina or its people.—*n.* white metal coated with silver: spongy tin: a small smelt with silvery sides: **Argentine,** a native or citizen of Argentina (also **Argentino,** -*tē'nō,* Sp. *är-hhen-tē'nō*).—*n.* **ar'-gentite,** silver-glance, native sulphide of silver. [Fr.,—L. *argentum*, silver; the republic is named from the Rio de la Plata (silver river).]

**argent comptant,** *ar-zhã kõ-tã,* (Fr.) ready money.

**Argestes,** *är-jes'tēz, (Milt.) n.* the north-west wind personified. [Gr. *Argestēs*.]

**arghan,** *är'gan, n.* pita fibre, or the plant yielding it. [Origin unknown.]

**argil,** *är'jil, n.* potter's clay: pure clay or alumina.— *adj.* **argillā'ceous,** clayey.—*n.* **ar'gillite,** an indurated clay rock. [L. *argilla*, Gr. *argillos,* white clay—*argēs,* white.]

**Argive,** *är'giv, -jiv, n.* and *adj.* belonging to *Argos*: Greek.

**argle-bargle, argie-bargie.** See under argue.

**Argo,** *är'gō, n.* a large southern constellation consisting of four separate constellations.

**argol,** *är'gol, n.* dried dung used as fuel. [Mongolian.]

**argol,** *är'gol, n.* a hard crust formed on the sides of wine-vessels, from which cream of tartar and tartaric acid are obtainable—generally reddish. [Prob. conn. with Gr. *argos*, white.]

**argon,** *är'gon, n.* a colourless, odourless inert gas (at. numb. 18) discovered in the atmosphere in 1894 by Rayleigh and Ramsay. It constitutes about 1% by volume of the atmosphere from which it is obtained by fractionation of liquid air. It is used in gas-filled electric lamps, radiation counters and fluorescent tubes. [Gr. *ārgon* (neut.) inactive—*a-*, priv., *ergon,* work.]

**Argonaut,** *är'gō-nöt, n.* one of those who sailed in the ship *Argo* in search of the golden fleece: (without *cap.*) the paper nautilus (*Argonauta*).— *adj.* **argonaut'ic.** [Gr. *Argō,* and *nautēs,* a sailor.]

**argosy,** *är'gə-si, n.* a great merchant ship, esp. of Ragusa or Venice. [It. *Ragusa,* Ragusan (ship).]

**argot,** *är-gō, n.* slang, originally that of thieves and vagabonds: cant. [Fr.; of unknown origin.]

**argue,** *ärg'ū, v.t.* to prove or indicate: give reason to believe: to seek to show by reasoning: to discuss with reasoning: to persuade or bring by reasoning (into or out of a course of action): to accuse (*obs.*).—*v.i.* to offer reasons: to contend with reasoning.—*adj.* **arg'ūable,** capable of being maintained: capable of being disputed.—

*adv.* **ar'gūably.**—*n.* **arg'ūer.**—*v.i.* **ar'gūfy** (*coll.*), to bandy arguments: to wrangle.—*v.t.* to beset with wrangling.—*ns.* **ar'gūment,** proof: evidence: a reason or series of reasons offered or possible towards proof or inducement: exchange of such reasons: debate: matter of debate or contention: a summary of subject-matter: hence contents (*Shak.*): a quantity upon which another depends, or under which it is to be sought in a table (*math.*): the angle between a vector and its axis of reference (*math.*); **argūmentā'tion,** reasoning: sequence or exchange of arguments. —*adj.* **argūment'ative,** controversial: addicted to arguing.—*adv.* **argūment'atively.**—*n.* **argūment'-ativeness.**—*v.i.* **ar'gy-bar'gy, ar'gie-bar'gie, ar'gle-bar'gle** (*orig. Scot.*), to argue tediously or vexatiously.—*n.* a bandying of argument. [Fr. *arguer*—L. *argūtāre,* freq. of *argūere,* to show, accuse; *argūmentum,* proof, accusation, summary of contents.]

**argumentum,** *är-gū-men'tum, är-goō-men'toōm,* (L.) argument.—**argumentum ad crumenam,** *ad kroō'mən-əm, -mān-am,* argument addressed to the purse (i.e. to cupidity); — **ad hominem,** *hom'in-em,* an appeal to the known prepossessions or previous admissions of an opponent; — **ad ignorantiam,** *ig-nör-an'shi-əm, ig-nör-an'ti-am,* one founded on the ignorance of an opponent; — **ad invidiam,** *in-vid'i-am, -wid',* an appeal to prejudices; — **ad judicium,** *joō-dish'i-əm, ū-dik'i-oōm,* an appeal to the commonsense of mankind; — **ad rem,** *rem,* argument to the purpose; — **baculinum,** *ba-kūl-in'um, ba-koōl-ēn'oōm,* the argument of the stick—most forcible of arguments; — **per impossibile,** *per im-po-sib'il-ē, -ā,* the proof from the absurdity of a contradictory supposition.—**argumenti causa,** *är-gū-men'ti kō'za, ar-goō-men'tē kow'za,* for the sake of argument.

**Argus,** *är'gəs, n.* in Greek mythology, Io's guardian, whose hundred eyes Hera transferred to the peacock's tail: a vigilant watcher: an East Indian genus of pheasants (**Argus pheasant**): a butterfly with many eye-spots on the wings (as some *Lycaenidae* and *Satyridae*): an ophiuroid with much-divided coiling arms.—*adj.* **Ar'gus-eyed'.** [Gr. *Argos,* lit., bright.]

**argute,** *är-gūt', adj.* shrill: keen: shrewd.—*adv.* **argute'ly.**—*n.* **argute'ness.** [L. *argūtus.*]

**argyria,** *är-jir'i-a, n.* skin-pigmentation caused by taking preparations of silver.—*n.* **ar'gyrodite,** a mineral composed of silver, germanium, and sulphur. [Gr. *argyros,* silver.]

**aria,** *ä'ri-a, (mus.) n.* an air or melody, esp. an accompanied vocal solo in a cantata, oratorio, or opera: a regular strain of melody followed by another in contrast and complement, and then repeated *da capo.* [It., from root of air.]

**Arian,** *ä'ri-ən, adj.* pertaining to, or following, *Arius* of Alexandria (d. 336).—*n.* one who adheres to the doctrines of Arius: a Unitarian.—*v.t.* and *v.i.* **A'rianise, -ize.**—*n.* **A'rianism.**

**Arician,** *a-rish'ən, adj.* of or belonging to *Aricia* in Latium or its Diana cult.

**arid,** *ar'id, adj.* dry: parched: barren: jejune.— *ns.* **arid'ity, ar'idness.**—*adv.* **ar'idly.** [L. *aridus.*]

**Ariel,** *ä'ri-əl, n.* a man's name in the Old Testament: in later demonology, a water-spirit: an angel: a spirit of the air (as Shakespeare's Ariel, a sylph in Pope): (without *cap.*) species of swallow, petrel, and toucan. [Heb. *Ariel,* with meaning influenced by air.]

**ariel,** *ä'ri-əl, n.* a kind of gazelle. [Ar. *aryil.*]

**Aries,** *ä'ri-ēz, n.* the Ram, a constellation giving name to, and formerly coinciding with, a sign of the zodiac.—**first point of Aries,** the intersection of equator and ecliptic passed by the sun in (the northern) spring, now actually in Pisces. [L. *ariēs, -etis,* ram.]

**arietta,** *ar-i-et'ta, (mus.) n.* a little aria or air.—

Also (Fr.) **ariette** (-*et'*). [It. *arietta*, dim. of *aria*.]

**aright**, *ə-rīt'*, *adv.* in a right way: rightly: on or to the right.—a **rights** (*Spens.*), rightly. [Prep. **a**, and **right**.]

**aril**, *är'il*, *n.* a covering or appendage of some seeds, an outgrowth of the funicle: sometimes, a caruncle (*false aril*).—Also **arill'us**:—*pl.* **arill'i**.—*adjs.* **ar'illary**, **ar'illate**, **ar'illated**, having an aril.—*n.* **ar'illode**, a caruncle or false aril, from near the micropyle. [L.L. *arillus*, raisin.]

**Arimaspian**, *ar-i-mas'pi-ən*, *adj.* pertaining to the *Arimaspi*, described by Herodotus as a one-eyed people of the extreme north, warring perpetually with griffins for gold hoards.—Also *n.*—Also **Ar'imasp**, *adj.* and *n.*

**arioso**, *a-ri-ō'sō*, *adj.* and *adv.* in the melodious manner of an aria, or between aria and recitative.—Also *n.* [It. *aria*.]

**ariot**, *ə-rī'ət*, *adv.* in riot, riotously.

**aripple**, *ə-rip'l*, *adv.* in a ripple.

**arise**, *ə-rīz'*, *v.i.* to rise up: to get up: to take rise, originate: to come into being, view, or activity:—*pa.t.* **arose** (*ə-rōz'*); *pa.p.* **arisen** (*ə-riz'n*). [Pfx. *a-*, up, out, and **rise**.]

**arish.** See **arrish**.

**arista**, *ə-ris'ta*, *n.* an awn.—*adj.* **aris'tate** (or *ar'*), awned. [L. *arista*, an awn.]

**Aristarch**, *ar'is-tärk*, *n.* a severe critic. [*Aristarchus*, Alexandrian grammarian (*c.* 160 B.C.).]

**Aristides**, *ar-is-tī'dēz*, (L.,—Gr. *Aristeidēs*) an embodiment of justice, from the Athenian statesman (5th cent. B.C.).

**Aristippus**, *ar-is-tip'əs*, (L.,—Gr. *Aristippos*), an embodiment of self-indulgence, from the founder of the Cyrenaic school of philosophy.

**aristocracy**, *ar-is-tok'rə-si*, *n.* government by, or political power of, a privileged order: a state so governed: a nobility or privileged class: an analogous class in respect of any quality.—*n.* **aristocrat** (*ar'is-tə-krat*, or *ə-ris'*), a member of an aristocracy: one who has the characteristics of or attributed to an aristocracy: a haughty person: one of the, or the, best of its kind.—*adjs.* **aristocrat'ic**, **-al**, belonging to aristocracy: having the character that belongs to, or is thought to befit, aristocracy.—*adv.* **aristocrat'ically**.—*n.* **aristocratism** (-*tok'rə-tizm*), the spirit of, or belief in, aristocracy. [Gr. *aristokratiā*—*aristos*, best, and *kratos*, power.]

**Aristolochia**, *ar-is-tō-lō'ki-ə*, *n.* the birthwort genus, herbs and climbers, specially abundant in tropical South America, giving name to the family **Aristolochiā'ceae**. [Gr. *aristolocheia*—*aristos*, best, *locheiā*, child-birth, from the former repute of birthwort.]

**aristology**, *ar-is-tol'ə-ji*, *n.* the science or art of dining. [Gr. *ariston*, breakfast, luncheon, *logos*, discourse.]

**ariston metron**, *ar-is'ton met'ron*, (Gr.) the middle course is the best: the golden mean.

**Aristophanic**, *ar-is-to-fan'ik*, *adj.* relating to or characteristic of the Greek comic dramatist *Aristophanes*.

**Aristotelian**, *ar-is-to-tē'li-ən*, **Aristotelean**, *ar-is-tot-i-lē'ən*, *adj.* relating to Aristotle (Gr. *Aristotelēs*) or to his philosophy.—*n.* a follower of Aristotle.—*ns.* **Aristotē'lianism**, **Aristot'elism**.—**Aristotle's lantern**, a chewing apparatus in sea-urchins, compared by Aristotle to a ship's lantern.

**arithmetic**, *ə-rith'mə-tik*, *n.* the science of numbers: the art of reckoning by figures: a treatise on reckoning.—*adjs.* **arithmetic** (*ar-ith-met'ik*), **-al**.—*adv.* **arithmet'ically**.—*n.* **arithmetician** (-*mə-tish'n*, or *ar'*), one skilled in arithmetic.—**arithmetical progression**, a series increasing or diminishing by a common difference, as 7, 10, 13, 16, 19, 22; or 12, 10½, 9, 7½, 6. [Gr. *arithmētikē* (*technē*, art), of numbers—*arithmos*, number.]

**arithmometer**, *ar-ith-mom'i-tər*, *n.* a calculating machine. [Gr. *arithmos*, number, *metron*, measure.]

**ark**, *ärk*, *n.* a chest or coffer: in Jewish history, the wooden coffer in which the Tables of the Law were kept: a large floating vessel, as Noah's in the Deluge (Gen. vi-viii): a toy representing Noah's ark.—*v.t.* to put in an ark.—*adj.* and *n.* **ark'ite**.—*n.* **ark'-shell**, a boxlike bivalve shell (*Arca*). [O.E. *arc* (*earc*)—L. *arca*, a chest—*arcēre*, to guard.]

**arkose**, *är-kōs'*, *n.* a sandstone rich in feldspar grains, formed from granite, etc.

**arles**, *ärlz*, also *ärlz*, *n.pl.* earnest, esp, in confirmation of a bargain, or an engagement of a servant.—**arle'-penny**, **arles'-penny**. [Scot. and Northern; M.E. *erles*—app. through O.Fr. from a dim. of L. *arrha*.]

**arm**, *ärm*, *n.* the fore-limb from shoulder to hand, esp. when used for purposes other than locomotion: a tentacle: a narrow projecting part: an inlet: a branch: a rail or support for the arm as on a chair: power (*fig.*).—*v.t.* to take in the arms: to conduct arm-in-arm.—*ns.* **arm'band**, a band of cloth worn round the sleeve; **arm'chair**, a chair with arms.—*adjs.* **arm'chair**, amateur: stay-at-home: doctrinaire; **armed**, having an arm or arms, as *one-armed*.—*ns.* **arm'ful**; **arm'hole**, the hole in a garment through which the arm is put.—*adv.* **arm'-in-arm'**, with arms interlinked.—*adj.* **arm'less**.—*ns.* **arm'let**, a little arm: a ring or band round the arm; **arm'pit**, the hollow under the shoulder.—at arm's length, at a distance (*lit.*, *fig.*), not showing friendliness or familiarity: (of negotiations, etc.) in which each party preserves its independent ability to bargain; in arms, carried as a child: young enough for this; right arm, the main support or assistant; secular arm, the civil authority, opp. to the spiritual or ecclesiastical; with open arms, with hearty welcome. [O.E. *arm* (*earm*); cog. with L. *armus*, the shoulder-joint and with Gr. *harmos*, a joint.]

**arm**, *ärm*, *n.* a weapon: a branch of the fighting forces:—(*in pl.*) weapons of offence and defence: hostilities: fighting: soldiering: heraldic devices.—*v.t.* to furnish with weapons, means of protection, armature, or (*fig.*) equipment: to strengthen with a plate or otherwise.—*v.i.* to take arms.—*ns.* **ar'mament**, a force equipped for war: total means of making war: munitions, esp. for warships: act of arming or equipping for war: defensive equipment; **ar'mature**, armour: any apparatus for defence: a piece of iron set across the poles of a magnet: a moving part in a magnetic circuit to indicate the presence of electric current: that part of a direct-current machine in which, in the case of a generator, the electromotive force is produced, or, in the case of a motor, the torque is produced.—*adj.* **armed**, furnished with arms: provided with means of defence: thorny: with beak, claws, etc., of such and such a tincture (*her.*).—**armed eye**, the aided eye (opp. to naked eye); **arms race**, competition among nations in building up armaments.—**bear arms**, to serve as a soldier: (also give arms) to show armorial bearings; **in arms**, armed: quartered (*her.*); **lay down one's arms**, to surrender, submit; **of all arms**, of every kind of troops; **take (up) arms**, to resort to fighting; **under arms**, armed; **up in arms**, in readiness to resist: protesting hotly. [Fr. *armes*, from L. *arma* (*pl.*); L. *armāmenta*, tackle, equipment; *armātūra*, armour].

**armada**, *är-mä'də*, (sometimes -*mā'*), *n.* a fleet of armed ships, esp. that sent by Philip II of Spain against England in 1588. [Sp., fem. pa.p. of *armar*—L. *armāre*, to arm.]

**armadillo**, *ärm-ə-dil'ō*, *n.* an American edentate armed with bands of bony plates:—*pl.* **arma-**

dill'os. [Sp., dim. of *armado*, armed; see foregoing.]

Armageddon, *är-mə-ged'n*, *n.* the great symbolical battlefield of the Apocalypse, scene of the final struggle between the powers of good and evil: a great war or battle of nations. [*Harmagedōn* or *Armageddōn* given as Heb. name in Rev. xvi. 16; perh. suggested by the famous battlefield of *Megiddo*, in the plain of Esdraelon.]

Armagnac, *är-mä-nyak*, *n.* a dry brandy distilled in S.W. France. [Name of district.]

armament, armature. See under arm (2).

Armenian, *är-mē'nyən*, *adj.* belonging to *Armenia*, in Western Asia, or its people or language, or their branch of the Christian Church.—*n.* a native of Armenia: one of the Armenian people: the language of the Armenians.—*adj.* Armē'noid, of the eastern branch of the Alpine race.—Also *n.*

armes parlantes, *ärm par-lät*, (Fr.) lit. talking arms, arms that indicate the name of the family that bears them, as a press and a tun for Preston.

armet, *är'mit*, *n.* a helmet introduced about 1450 in place of the basinet, consisting of an iron cap, spreading over the back of the neck, having in front the visor, beaver, and gorget. [Fr.]

armgaunt, *ärm'gönt*, (Shak., *Ant. and Cleop.*, I, v. 48), *adj.* perh. with gaunt limbs, or perh. worn with armour, but probably an error.

armiger, *är'mi-jər*, *n.* one entitled to a coat-of-arms: an esquire.—Also armi'gero (Slender's blunder in *Merry Wives*).—*adjs.* armi'geral, armi'gerous. [L., an armour-bearer—*arma*, arms, *gerēre*, to bear.]

armilla, *är-mil'ə*, *n.* bracelet (*archaeol*; also ar'mil): frill on a mushroom stalk (*bot.*).—*adj.* armill'ary (or *är'*).—armillary sphere, a skeleton sphere made up of hoops to show the motions of the heavenly bodies. [L. *armilla*, an armlet, dim. of *armus*, the upper arm, the shoulder.]

Arminian, *är-min'i-ən*, *n.* a follower of *Arminius* (1560-1609), who denied the Calvinistic doctrine of absolute predestination, as well as irresistible grace.—Also *adj.*—*n.* Armin'ianism.

armipotent, *är-mip'ə-tənt*, *adj.* powerful in arms. [L. *arma*, arms, *potēns*, *-entis*, powerful.]

armistice, *är'mi-stis*, *n.* a suspension of hostilities: a truce.—Armistice Day, 11th Nov. 1918, the day fighting ended in the 1st World War, kept since as an anniversary, from 1946 as Remembrance Sunday (*q.v.*). [Fr.,—L.L. armistitium—L. *arma*, arms, *sistēre*, to stop.]

armoire, *är-mwär'*, *n.* an ambry or cupboard. [Fr.]

Armoric, *är-mor'ik*, *adj.* of *Armorica*, or Brittany. —*n.* the Breton language.—*n.*, *adj.* Armor'ican. [L. *Armoricus*—Gallic *are-morici*, dwellers by the sea.]

armour (*U.S.* armor), *är'mər*, *n.* defensive dress: protective covering: armoured vehicles: heraldic insignia.—*adj.* armō'rial, of heraldic arms.—*n.* a book of coats-of-arms.—*ns.* ar'morist, one skilled in heraldry: ar'mory, heraldry: armoury (*U.S.*): drill hall and headquarters of an army unit (*U.S.*): arsenal (*U.S.*); ar'mour-bearer, one carrying another's armour, a squire.—*adj.* ar'mour-clad', clad in armour.—*n.* ar'mour-clad, an armoured ship.—*adj.* ar'moured, protected by armour.—*ns.* ar'moured-car', -crui'ser, -train'; ar'mourer, a maker, repairer, or custodian of arms and armour.—*adj.* ar'mourless.—*n.* ar'mour-plate, a defensive plate for a ship, tank, etc.—*adj.* ar'mour-plat'ed.—*n.* ar'moury, a collection of arms and armour: a place where arms are kept: armour collectively.—armorial bearings, the design in a coat of arms. [O.Fr. *armure*—L. *armātūra*—*arma*, arms.]

armozeen, armozine, *är-mō-zēn'*, *n.* a kind of taffeta or plain silk, usually black, used for clerical gowns. [Fr. *armoisin*.]

army, *ärm'i*, *n.* a large body of men armed for war and under military command: a body of men

banded together in a special cause, whether mimicking military methods as the 'Salvation Army', or not, as the 'Blue Ribbon Army': a host: a great number.—army ant, any of several kinds of stinging ants which move about in vast numbers; army corps (*kōr*, *kör*), a miniature army comprising all arms of the service; army list, a list of all commissioned officers: army worm, the larva of a small fly (*Sciara*) that collects in vast armies: the larva of an American moth (*Leucania*) with the same habit. [Fr. *armée*, pa.p. fem. of *armer*—L. *armāre*, *-ātum* to arm.]

Arnaut, Arnaout, *är-nowt'*, *n.* an Albanian, esp. one in the Turkish army. [Turk.]

arnica, *är'-ni-kə*, *n.* a tincture of the flowers of a composite plant, *Arnica montana*, or mountain tobacco, applied to sprains and bruises. [Origin unknown.]

arolla, *a-rol'a*, *n.* the Swiss stone-pine or Siberian cedar (*Pinus Cembra*). [Fr. *arolle*.]

aroma, *ə-rō'ma*, *n.* a spicy fragrance: flavour or peculiar charm (*fig.*).—*adj.* aromatic (*ar-ō-mat'ik*), fragrant: spicy: in chemistry, belonging to the closed-chain class of organic compounds, or benzene derivatives—opp. to *fatty* or *aliphatic*.— Also *n.*—*v.t.* arō'matise, -ize, to render aromatic: to perfume. [L., from Gr. *arōma*, *-atos*, spice.]

arose. See arise.

around, *ə-rownd'*, *prep.* on all sides of: round: round about: somewhere near.—*adv.* on every side: in a circle: round about, astir.—get around to (*coll.*), to reach the point of (doing something); have been around (*coll.*), to be experienced, sophisticated. [Prep. a, and round.]

arouse, *ə-rowz'*, *v.t.* and *v.i.* to rouse.—*n.* an arousing, alarm.—*ns.* arous'al; arous'er. [Pfx. a-, intensive, and rouse (1).]

arow, *ə-rō'*, *adv.* in a row: one following the other. [Prep. a, and row (1).]

aroynt. Same as aroint.

arpeggio, *är-ped'j(y)ō*, (*mus.*) *n.* a chord of which the notes are performed, not simultaneously, but in rapid (normally upward) succession.—*v.t.* arpegg'iate (*-ji-āt*), to play in this manner. [It. *arpeggiare*, to play the harp—*arpa*, harp.]

arpent, *är'pənt*, *är-pä*, *n.* an old French measure for land still used in Quebec and Louisiana varying from about 50 to 35 ares (1¼ acres to 5/6 of an acre). [Fr.,—L. *arepennis*, said to be a Gallic word.]

arquebus(e), harquebus, (*h*)*är'kwi-bus*, *n.* an old-fashioned handgun.—*ns.* arquebusade (*-sād*) lotion for shot-wounds; arquebusier (*-bus-ēr'*), soldier armed with an arquebus. [Fr. *arquebuse*— Du *haakbus*—*haak*, hook, and *bus*, box, barrel of a gun; Ger. *hakenbüchse*.]

arracacha, *ar-a-käch'a*, *n.* an umbelliferous plant (*Arracacia*) of northern South America, with edible tubers. [Quechua *aracacha*.]

arrack, *ar'ək*, *n.* an ardent spirit used in the East, procured from toddy, or the fermented juice of the coco and other palms, as well as from rice and jaggery sugar. [Ar. *araq*, juice.]

arragonite, another spelling of aragonite.

arrah, *ar'ə*, *interj.* Anglo-Irish expression of emotion, wonder, mild expostulation, etc.

arraign, *ə-rān'*, *v.t.* to call to account: to put upon trial: to accuse publicly.—*ns.* arraign'er; arraign'ment. [O.Fr. *aresnier*—L.L. *arratiōnāre*—L. *ad*, to, *ratiō*, *-ōnis*, reason.]

arrange, *ə-rānj'*, *v.t.* to set in a rank or row: to put in order: to settle: to adapt for other

instruments or voices (*mus.*).—*n.* **arrange'ment**, [O.Fr. *arangier*—à (L. *ad*, to), and *rangier*. *rengier*. See **range**.]
**arrant**, *ar'ənt*, *adj.* downright, unmitigated, out-and-out: notorious: rascally. [A variant of **errant**.]
**arras**, *ar'əs*, *n.* tapestry (made at *Arras* in France): a hanging screen of tapestry for a wall.—*adj.* **arr'ased**, covered with arras.—*n.* **arr'asene**, an embroidery material, of wool and silk.
**arraught**. See **areach**.
**array**, *ə-rā'*, *n.* order: dress: equipage: an imposing, purposeful, or significant, arrangement: an arrangement of terms in rows and columns, (esp. if square) a matrix (*math.*).—*v.t.* to put in order: to arrange: to dress, adorn, or equip.—*n.* **array'ment**, act of arraying: clothing (*obs.*). [A.Fr. *arai*, O.Fr. *arei*, array, equipage—L. *ad*, and the Gmc. root found in Eng. **ready**, Ger. *bereit*.]
**arrear**, *ə-rēr'*, *n.* that which is in the rear or behind: (usu. in *pl.*) that which remains unpaid or undone: (in *sing.* or *pl.*) condition of being behindhand.—*adv.* (*obs.*) aback, backward, behind.—*n.* **arrear'age**, arrear, arrears. [O.Fr. *arere* (Fr. *arrière*)—L. *ad*, to, *retrō*, back, behind.]
**arrect**, *a-rekt'*, *adj.* upright: pricked up: on the alert. [L. *arrēctus*.]
**arrectis auribus**, *ar-ek'tēs ow'ri-bōōs*, (L.) with ears pricked up.
**arreede**. See **aread**.
**arrest**, *ə-rest'*, *v.t.* to bring to a standstill, check: to seize: to catch, fix (as the attention): to apprehend by legal authority: to seize by warrant: to take in security (*Shak.*).—*n.* stoppage: seizure by warrant.—*adj.* **arrest'able**.—*ns.* **arrestation** (*ar-es-tā'shən*), the act of arresting: arrest; **arrestee'**, a person prevented by arrestment from making payment or delivery to another until the arrester's claim upon that other is secured or satisfied; **arrest'er**, one who, or that which, arrests: a lightning-arrester: one who makes an arrestment (also **arrest'or**).—*adj.* **arrest'ive**, tending to arrest.—*n.* **arrest'ment**, a checking: detention of a person arrested till liberated on bail, or by security (*law*): process which prohibits a debtor from handing over to his creditor money or property until a debt due by that creditor to a third party, the arrester, is paid or secured (*Scots law*).—**arrester gear**, shock-absorbing transverse cables on an aircraft-carrier's deck for the arrester hook of an alighting aircraft to catch on; **arrester hook**, a hook put out from an aircraft alighting on an aircraft-carrier, to catch on the arrester gear. [O.Fr. *arester*—L. *ad*, to, and *stāre*, to stand still.]
**arrêt**, *a-ret'*, *ä'-re'*, *ä-rā'*, *n.* decision: judgment of a tribunal. [Fr. See **arrest**.]
**arrhenotoky**, *ar-ən-ot'ə-ki*, *n.* parthenogenetic production of males alone. [Gr. *arrēn*, male, *tokos*, offspring.]
**arriage**, *ar'ij*, *n.* a former feudal service in Scotland, said to have been rendered by the tenant with his beasts of burden, later indefinite. [See **average** and **aver** (2).]
**arride**, *ə-rid'*, (*Lamb*) *v.t.* to please, gratify. [L. *arrīdēre*.]
**arriéré**, *ar-ē-ār-ā*, (Fr.) backward, old-fashioned.
**arrière-ban**, *ar'ē-er-ban'*, *-bä*, *n.* a feudal sovereign's summons to all freemen to take the field: the army thus collected. [O.Fr. *ariereban*—O.H.G. *hari*, army, and *ban*, public proclamation; confused with Fr. *arrière*.]
**rière- garde**, *ar-ē-er-gärd*, (Fr.) rear-guard.
**arrière-pensée**, *ar-ē-er-pä-sā*, (Fr.) a mental reservation: a subsidiary aim.
**arriero**, *ar-i-ā'rō*, *n.* a muleteer. [Sp.].
**arris**, *ar'is*, *n.* a sharp edge on stone or metal at the meeting of two surfaces. [See **arête**.]

**arrish, arish**, *är'ish*, (*dial.*) *n.* a stubble field. [O.E. *ersc* (in compounds).]
**arrive**, *ə-riv'*, *v.i.* to reach shore or port (*obs.*): to reach any place: to attain to any object (with *at*): to achieve success or recognition: to happen.—*v.t.* (*obs.*) to reach.—*ns.* **arriv'al**, the act of arriving: persons or things that arrive; **arriv'ance**, **-ancy** (*Shak.*), company arriving. [O.Fr. *ariver*—L.L. *adripāre*—L. *ad*, to, *ripa*, shore.]
**arrivederci, a rivederci**, *är-ē-vəd-er'chē*, (It.) goodbye until we meet again.
**arriviste**, *a'rē-vēst*, *n.* a person 'on the make': a parvenu: a self-seeker.—*n.* **a'rrivisme**. [Fr.].
**arroba**, *a-rō'ba*, *ä-ro'bä*, *n.* a weight of 25 pounds (11·35 kg) or more, used in Spanish and Portuguese regions. [Sp. and Port.,—Ar. *ar-rub'*, the quarter.]
**arrogate**, *ar'ə-gāt*, *v.t.* to claim as one's own: to claim proudly or unduly: to ascribe, attribute, or assign (to another).—*ns.* **arr'ogance**, **arr'ogancy**, undue assumption of importance.—*adj.* **arr'ogant**, claiming too much: overbearing.—*adv.* **arr'ogantly**.—*n.* **arrogā'tion**, act of arrogating: undue assumption. [L. *arrogāre*—*ad*, to, *rogāre*, -*ātum*, to ask, to claim.]
**arrondissement**, *ä-rō̃-dēs'mä*, *n.* a subdivision of a French department. [Fr.,—*arrondir*, to make round.]
**arrow**, *ar'ō*, *n.* a straight, pointed missile, made to be shot from a bow or blowpipe: any arrow-shaped mark or object: the chief shoot of a plant, esp. the flowering stem of the sugar-cane.—*adj.* **arr'owy**, of or like arrows.—**arr'ow-grass**, a genus of marsh plants (*Triglochin*) whose burst capsule is like an arrow-head; **arr'ow-head**, the head or pointed part of an arrow: an aquatic plant (*Sagittaria sagittifolia*) of the Alismaceae, with arrow-shaped leaves.—*adj.* **arr'ow-headed**, shaped like the head of an arrow.—**arr'ow-poi'son**, poison smeared on arrow-heads; **arr'ow-root**, a West Indian plant, *Maranta arundinacea* or other species: its rhizome, esteemed in S. America as an antidote to arrow-poison: a nutritious starch from the rhizome: extended to other plants and their starch (see **Portland**); **arr'ow-shot**, the range of an arrow. [O.E. *arwe*]; prob. cog. with L. *arcus*, bow.]
**arrow**. See **ary**.
**arroyo**, *ə-roi'ō*, *n.* a rocky ravine: a dry water-course. [Sp.]
**'Arry**, *ar'i*, *n.* a jovial vulgar cockney:—*fem.* **'Arr'iet**.—*adj.* **'Arr'yish**. [Cockney pronunciation of *Harry*, *Harriet*.]
**arse**, *ärs*, (now *vulg.*) *n.* buttocks.—*adv.* and *adj.* **ars'y-vers'y**, backside foremost, contrary. [O.E. *ærs* (ears); Ger. *arsch*, Sw. *ars*; cog. with Gr. *orros* (for *orsos*).]
**arsenal**, *ärs'(i)-nl*, *n.* a dockyard (*hist.*): a magazine or manufactory for naval and military weapons and ammunition: a storehouse (*fig.*). [It. *arzenale*, *arsenale* (Sp., Fr. *arsenal*)—Ar. *dār accinā'ah*, workshop—(*dār*, house), *al*, the *çinā'ah*, art.]
**arsenic**, *ärs'(ə-)nik*, *n.* the chemical element (As) of at. number 33: a poison, the trioxide of the element (As$_2$O$_3$); white arsenic.—*ns.* **ar'senate**, **arseniate** (*-sē'ni-āt*), a salt of arsenic acid.—*adjs.* **arsenic** (*-sen'ik*), **-al**, **arse'nious**, composed of or containing arsenic.—In chemistry **arsen'ic** is applied to compounds in which arsenic is pentavalent, **arse'nious** to those in which it is trivalent.—*ns.* **ar'senide**, a compound of arsenic with a metal; **ar'senite**, a salt of arsenious acid; **arseno-pyri'tēs**, mispickel, a mineral composed of iron, arsenic and sulphur; **arsine**, *är'sēn*, *-sin*, *-sin*, hydride of arsenic (AsH$_3$): a compound in which one or more hydrogen atoms of AsH$_3$ are replaced by an alkyl radical, etc. [Gr. *arsenikon*, yellow orpiment, fancifully associated with Gr.

*arsēn*, male, and the alchemists' notion that metals have sex.]

**arshin, arshine, arsheen,** *är-shēn'*, *n.* an old measure of length, about 28 in. in Russia, about 30 inches (legally a metre) in Turkey. [Turkish.]

**arsis,** *är'sis*, *(Gr. pros.* and *mus.) n. (lit.)* a lift, an up-beat: hence the weak position in a bar or foot: understood by the Romans as the strong position: used in English in both senses: elevation of the voice to higher pitch:—*pl.* (L.) ar'sēs:—opp. to *thesis.* [L.,—Gr. *arsis—airein*, to lift.]

**arsmetrick,** *ärz-met'rik*, *n.* an obs. form of **arithmetic,** founded on the false etymology L. *ars metrica*, art of measuring.

**arson,** *är'sn*, *n.* the crime of feloniously burning houses, haystacks, ships, forests, or similar property.—*ns.* ar'sonist, *(rare)* ar'sonite. [O.Fr. *arson*—L. *arsiō*, *-ōnis—ardēre, arsum*, to burn.]

**arson,** *är'sn*,*(obs.) n.* a saddlebow. [O.Fr. *arçun*—L. *arcus*, a bow.]

**art,** *ärt*, *(arch.* and *poet.)* used as 2nd pers. sing. pres. indic. of the verb *to be.* [O.E. (W.S.) *eart*, (Mercian) *earth*, (Northumbrian) *arth*; from the root *es-* seen in is, **are.**]

**art,** *ärt*, *n.* practical skill, or its application, guided by principles: human skill and agency (opp. to *nature*): application of skill to production of beauty (esp. visible beauty) and works of creative imagination, as in the fine arts: a branch of learning, esp. one of the *liberal* arts (see trivium, **quadrivium**), as in *faculty of arts, master of arts*: skill or knowledge in a particular department: a skilled profession or trade, craft, or branch of activity: magic or occult knowledge or influence: a method of doing a thing: a knack: contrivance: address: cunning: artifice: crafty conduct: a wile.—*adj.* of, for, concerned with, painting, sculpture, etc. (as *art gallery, art historian*): intended to be decorative; produced with studied artistry not arising spontaneously by chance.—*adj.* art'ful, dexterous, clever (*arch.*): cunning: produced by art.—*adv.* art'fully.—*n.* art'fulness.—*adj.* **art'less,** simple: inartistic *(rare)*: guileless, un-affected.—*adv.* art'lessly.—*n.* art'lessness.—*adj.* art'y *(coll.)*, aspiring to be artistic.—**art form,** a set form or arrangement in poetry or music: an accepted medium of artistic expression; **art paper,** paper for illustrations, coated with a composition containing china clay; **arts'man,** a craftsman *(obs.)*: a scholar *(obs.)*; **art'-song,** a song whose words and music are the product of conscious art, the music reflecting every turn of meaning—distinguished from a *folk-song*; **arts student,** a student in the faculty of arts; **art student,** a student of painting, sculpture, etc.—*adj.* **art'y-craft'y,** self-consciously artistic.—**art and part,** originally *(law)* concerned in either by *art* in contriving or by *part* in actual execution; now loosely used in the sense of participating, sharing; **be a fine art,** to be an operation or practice requiring nicety of craftsmanship; **term of art,** a technical word; **the fine arts,** painting, poetry, music, etc.—**art deco** *(dek' ō)*, the style of decorative art characteristic of the 1920s and 1930s.

**art autre,** *är-tō-tr'*, a post World War II movement in painting, including tachisme; **art nouveau** *(nōō-vō)* a decorative form of art (*c.* 1890-1910) in which curvilinear forms are important and fundamentally unrelated images are often combined in a single design. [Fr., different art, new art.]

**artefact, artifact,** *är'ti-fakt*, *n.* (esp. *archaeol.*) a thing made by human workmanship. [L. *arte*, by art (abl. of *ars*), *factum*, made.]

**artel,** *är-tel'*, *n.* a Russian workers' guild. [Russ.]

**Artemisia,** *är-te-miz'i-a*, *n.* a genus of composites including wormwood, southernwood, mugwort, sagebrush, etc. [Gr. *artemisiā*.]

**artery,** *är'tər-i*, *n.* a tube or vessel that conveys blood from the heart: any main channel of communication.—*adj.* **arterial** *(-tē'ri-əl)*.—*v.t,* **artēr'ialise, -ize,** to make arterial.—*ns.* artē'riole. a very small artery; **artēriosc1erō'sis** (Gr. *sklērōsis*, hardening), hardening of the arteries.—*adj.* **arteriosclerotic** *(-ot'ik)*.—*ns.* **artēriot'omy** (Gr. *tomē*, a cut), the cutting or opening of an artery, to let blood; **arteri'tis,** inflammation of an artery. [L. *artēria*—Gr. *artēriā*, windpipe, artery.]

**Artesian,** *är-tē'zyən, -zh(y)ən, adj.* of Artois (L.L. *Artesium*), in the north of France, or a type of well in early use there, in which water rises in a bore-hole by hydrostatic pressure from a basin whose outcrop is at a higher level.

**arthral** *gic.*—*n.* **arthritis,** *är-thri'tis,* inflammation of a joint: gout.—*adj.* **arthritic** *(-thrit'ik)*, of or near a joint: of, of the nature of, arthritis.—*n.* a gouty person. [Gr. *arthron*, a joint, *algos*, pain.]

**arthralgia,** *är-thral'j(i-)a, n.* pain in a joint.—*adj.*

**arthromere,** *är'thrō-mēr*, *n.* a body segment of an articulated animal—a somite. [Gr. *arthron*, a joint, *meros*, part.]

**arthropod,** *är'thrō-pod*, *n.* any member of the **Arthropoda** (*är-throp'od-a*), a great division of the animal kingdom, with segmented bodies and jointed appendages—crustacea, arachnids, perip-atus, millipedes, centipedes, insects, tardigrades, etc.—*adj.* **arthrop'odal.** [Gr. *arthron*, joint, and *pous, podos*, a foot.]

**arthrosis,** *är-thrō'sis*, *n.* connection by a joint: articulation. [Gr. *arthrōsis—arthron*, a joint.]

**arthrospore,** *är'thrō-spōr, -spör, n.* a conidium: (in-appropriately) a veg:tative cell that has passed into a resting state. [Gr. *arthron*, joint, *sporā*, seed.]

**Arthurian,** *är-thū'ri-ən, adj.* relating to King Arthur, a ruler of the Britons, whose court is the centre of many legends, but who himself had perhaps real existence: pertaining to the legends.—*n.* **Arthurian'a,** stories, etc., connected with the court of King Arthur.

**artichoke,** *är'ti-chōk*, *n.* a thistle-like perennial plant (*Cynara Scolymus*) with large scaly heads and edible receptacles.—**Jerusalem artichoke,** a totally different plant, a species of sunflower with edible tubers like potatoes, Jerusalem being a corr. of It. *girasole* (turn-sun), sunflower. [North It. *articiocco* (It. *carciofo*)—Old Sp. *alcarchofa*—Ar. *al-kharshōfa, al-kharshūf*.]

**article,** *är'ti-kl*, *n.* a joint, segment *(obs.)*: a juncture, critical moment, nick of time *(obs.)*: a separate element, member, or part of anything: a particular object or commodity: an item: a single clause or term: a distinct point in an agreement, or *(pl.)* an agreement looked at as so made up, as in *articles of apprenticeship*, etc.: *(pl.)* rules or conditions generally: a section, paragraph, or head: a literary composition in a newspaper, periodical, encyclopaedia, etc., treating of a subject distinctly and independently: the adjective *the* (definite article), a or an (indefinite article) or the equivalent in another language *(gram.).—v.t.* to arrange by agreement, etc. *(obs.)*: to bind by articles of apprenticeship: to set forth as a charge (that): to stipulate *(obs.).—v.i.* to bring specific charges (against): *obs.).—adj.* **ar'ticled,** bound as apprentice.—*adjs.* **artic'ŭlar,** that can be articulated; **artic'ŭlar,** belonging to the joints: at or near a joint.—*n.pl.* **Articulā'ta,** in Cuvier's classification, the arthropods and higher worms.—*adj.* **artic'ŭlate,** jointed: composed of distinct parts: composed of recognisably distinct sounds, as human speech: clear: able to express one's thoughts with ease.—*v.t.* to attach by a joint: to connect by joints: to form distinct sounds, syllables, or words.—*v.i.* to form a joint (with; *lit.* and *fig.*): to come to terms (*Shak.*): to speak distinctly.—*adj.* **artic'ŭlated.**—*adv.* **artic'ŭlately.**—*ns.* **artic'ŭ-**

lateness; articŭlā'tion, jointing: a joint: a segment: distinctness, or distinct utterance: a consonant; artic'ŭlātor, one who articulates or speaks: one who articulates bones and mounts skeletons.—*adj.* artic'ŭlatory.—articulated vehicle, a vehicle made easier to manœuvre by having a detachable cab section, which, when attached, can move at an angle to the rest.— articles of association, regulations for the business of a joint-stock company registered under the Companies Acts; articles of faith, binding statement of points of belief of a Church, etc.; articles or war, code of regulations for the government and discipline of armed services; in the article of death (L. *in articulō mortis*), at the point of death; Lords of the Articles, a standing committee of the Scottish parliament who drafted the measures to be submitted; of great article (*Shak.*), of great importance; Thirtynine Articles, the articles of religious belief finally agreed upon by the bishops and clergy of the Church of England in 1562. [L. *articulus*, a little joint, *articulāre*, *-ātum*, to furnish with joints, to utter distinctly—*artus*, joint.]

artifact. See artefact.

artifice, *är'ti-fis*, *n.* handicraft (*Milt.*): workmanship (*obs.*): skill: contrivance, or trickery: an ingenious expedient: a crafty trick.—*n.* artif'icer, a mechanic: one who creates skilfully: a craftsman: a contriver: (*cap.*) the creator: a trickster (*obs.*).—*adj.* artificial (*-fish'l*, or *är'*), contrived (opp. to *spontaneous*): made by man: synthetic (opp. to *natural*): fictitious, factitious, feigned, made in imitation (opp. to *real*): affected in manners: ingenious (*obs.*): perh. creative, playing the artificer, or perh. merely skilful(*Shak.*): technical(*obs.*).—*v.t.* artific'ialise, -ize, to render artificial.—*n.* artificiality (*-fish-i-al'i-ti*).—*adv.* artific'ially.—*n.* artific'ialness.— artificial kidney, an apparatus used, in cases where the kidney functions badly, to remove by dialysis harmful substances from the blood; artificial porcelain, soft-paste porcelain; artificial respiration, stimulation of respiration manually or mechanically by forcing air in and out of the lungs; artificial silk (see silk); artificial sunlight, light from lamps rich in ultraviolet rays. [L. *artificium—artifex, -ficis*, an artificer—*ars, artis*, and *facēre*, to make.]

artillery, *är-til'ər-i*, *n.* offensive weapons of war, formerly in general, now the heavier kinds— ancient ballistas, catapults, modern cannon, etc.: a branch of the military service using these: missiles (*obs.*): gunnery.—*n.* artill'erist, one skilled in artillery: a gunner.—artill'ery-man, a soldier of the artillery; artill'ery-plant, a tropical American plant (*Pilea*) of the nettle family that ejects its pollen in puffs. [O.Fr. *artillerie*— *artiller*, to arm, of doubtful origin.]

artiodactyl, *är-ti-ō-dak'til*, *adj.* even-toed.—*n.* a member of the Artiodac'tyla or even-toed ungulates, in which the third and fourth digit form a symmetrical pair and the hind-foot bears an even number of digits—cf. Perissodactyla. [Gr. *artios*, even in number, and *daktylos*, finger or toe.]

artisan, *ärt-i-zan'*, or *ärt'*, *n.* a handicraftsman or mechanic. [Fr. *artisan*—It. *artigiano*, ult. from L. *artitus*, skilled—*ars, artis*, art.]

artist, *ärt'ist*, *n.* one who practises or is skilled in an art, now esp. a fine art: one who has the qualities of imagination and taste required in art: a painter or draughtsman: a learned man (*obs.*): one who professes magic, astrology, alchemy, etc., or chemistry (*obs.*): a performer, esp. in music.—*adjs.* artist'ic, -al.—*adv.* artist'ically.—*n.* art'istry, artistic pursuits: artistic workmanship, quality, or ability.—artistic temperament, the emotional and capricious temperament ascribed to artists. [Fr. *artiste*—L. *ars, artis*, art.]

artiste, *är-tēst'*, *n.* a public performer: an adept in a manual art. [Fr.]

Artium Baccalaureus, *är'shi-um* (or *-ti-ōōm*) *bak-a-lö'rē-us* (or *-low'rä-ōōs*), (L.) Bachelor of Arts; Artium Magister (*ma-jis'tər* or *-gis'ter*) or Magister Artium, Master of Arts.

Artocarpus, *är-tō-kär'pəs*, *n.* a genus of the mulberry family including breadfruit and jack. [Gr. *artos*, bread, *karpos*, fruit.]

Arum, *ā'rəm*, *n.* the cuckoo-pint or wakerobin genus: (without *cap.*) any kindred plant.—*n.pl.* Arā'ceae (*a-*), the family of spadicifloral monocotyledons to which it belongs.—*adjs.* araceous (*a-rā'shəs*), aroid (*ā'roid*), of the Araceae: like an arum.—*n.* any plant of the family.—arum lily, Zantedeschia. [L. *arum*—Gr. *aron.*]

arundinaceous, *ə-run-di-nā'shəs*, *adj.* of or like a reed. [L. *arundināceus—arundō, -inis*, a reed.]

arval, *är'vəl*, *adj.* pertaining to ploughed land.— Arval Brethren, in ancient Rome, a college of priests who sacrificed to the field deities. [L. *arvālis—arāre*, to plough.]

Arvicola, *är-vik'ō-la*, *n.* the water-rat genus of voles.—*adj.* arvic'oline. [L. *arvum*, ᴀ field, *colĕre*, to inhabit.]

ary, *ā'ri*, *e'ri*, arrow, *ar'ō*, (*dial.*) *adj.* any. [From *e'er* a, ever a; cf. nary.]

Aryan, *ā'ri-ən* or *ä'*, *adj.* Indo-Germanic, Indo-European: now generally of the Indian, or Indian and Iranian, branch of the Indo-European languages: speaking one of these languages: in Nazi politics, not Jewish.—*n.* the parent Indo-European language: a speaker of an Aryan language.—*v.t.* Ar'yanise, -ize. [Sans. *ārya*, noble.]

Arya Samaj, *är'yä sä-mäj'*, *n.* a reformed Hindu religious body or school, founded by Dayananda Saraswati (1824-83), based on the Vedas, opposing idolatry, caste, child-marriage, and other evils. [Hind. *ārya samāj*, noble association.]

aryballos, *ar-i-bal'os*, *n.* a globular oil-flask with a neck.—*adj.* aryball'oid. [Gr.]

aryl, *ar'il*, *n.* any aromatic univalent hydrocarbon radical. [aromatic, and Gr. *hylē*, matter.]

arytaenoid, arytenoid, *ar-i-tē'noid*, *adj.* pitchershaped.—*n.* a cartilage or a muscle of the larynx. [Gr. *arytainoeidēs—arytaina*, a cup, *eidos*, form.]

as, *az*, *əz*, *adv.* in whatever degree, proportion, manner: to whatever extent: in that degree: to that extent: so far: however: specifically: passing into *conj.* or almost *prep.*, for instance: in the manner, character, part, aspect, of: so far as: whereas.—*conj.* because, since: while, when: as if: that (consequence) (*Milt.*): than (*illiterate* or *dial.*).—*pron.* who, which, that (after such, so, same, or where a statement is treated as antecedent; in *Shak.* after a demons. pron.; otherwise *dial.* or *illiterate*).—as also, likewise; as concerning, as for, as regards, as to, for the matter of; as from, from (a specified time); as how, that (with noun clause) (*illit.* or *dial.*): introducing a question (similarly as why) (*obs.*); as if, as though, as it would be if; as it were, so to speak: in some sort; as many as, all who; as much, the same: just that; as now, as then, just at this, that, time; as well, also: in addition: equally; as yet, up to the moment; so as to, with the purpose or consequence specified; when as, at what time (*arch.*). [O.E. *all-swā* (*eall-swā*), all so, wholly so.]

as, *äs*, *n.* a Norse god, inhabitant of Asgard:—*pl.* aesir (*es'ir*). [O.N. *āss*, a god (pl. *æsir*); cf. O.E. *ōs*, seen in such proper names as Oswald, Osric.]

as, *as*, *n.* a Roman unit of weight, a pound of 12 ounces: a copper coin, originally a pound in weight, ultimately half an ounce:—*pl.* ass'es. [L. *ās, assis*, a unit.]

ås, *ōs*, (*geol.*) *n.* a kame or esker:—*pl.* åsar (*ōs'är*) [Sw.]

asafoetida, *as-ə-fet'i-da*, or *-fēt'*, *n.* an ill-smelling

medicinal gum-resin, got from the root latex of some species of *Ferula*—also asafetida, assafoe-tida, assafetida. [Pers. *azā*, mastic, and L. *fētida* (*fem.*), stinking.]
a salti, *ā säl'tē*, (It.) by fits and starts.
åsar. See ås.
asarabacca, *a-sä-rä-bak'a, n.* hazelwort (*Asarum europaeum*), of the birthwort family, formerly used in medicine. [L. *asarum* (—Gr. *asaron*), *bacca*, a berry.]
asbestos, *az-best'os, n.* a fine fibrous amphibole capable of being woven into incombustible cloth: (commercially) chrysotile, a fibrous serpentine. —*adjs.* asbest'ic, asbest'iform, asbes'tine, asbes'tous, of or like asbestos.—*n.* asbestō'sis, a lung disease caused by inhaling asbestos dust.
asbestos cement, cement containing asbestos fibres, used to make thin slabs for various purposes in building. [Gr., (*lit.*) unquenchable—*a-*, priv., *sbestos*, extinguished.]
asbestos gelōs (Gr.). See Appendices.
ascarid, *as'ka-rid, n.* any nematode worm of the parasitic genus As'caris (family Ascar'idae), infesting the small intestines.—*n.* ascariasis, *as-kə-rī'ə-sis,* infestation with, or disease caused by, ascarids, esp. *Ascaris lumbricoides.* [Gr. *askaris,* pl. *askarides.*]
ascaunt. See askance.
ascend, *ə-send', a-send', v.i.* to go up, mount, rise: to go back in time or ancestry.—*v.t.* to go up, mount, climb: to go up to (*Shak.*).—*ns.* ascend'ance, -ence (both *rare*), ascend'ancy, -ency, dominating influence; ascend'ant, less commonly ascend'ent, (*astrol.*) the part of the ecliptic just risen or about to rise at any instant (a planet in this was supposed to influence a person born at the time): (from the phrase in the ascendant) a position of pre-eminence: an ancestor or relative in the ascending line: one who rises or mounts: a rise, up-slope.—*adj.* rising: just risen above the horizon: predominant.—*n.* ascend'er, one who ascends: a letter that reaches the top of the type-body.—*adjs.* ascend'ible (also -able), scalable; ascend'ing, rising: curving up from a prostrate to an erect position (*bot.*).—*n.* ascension (-*sen'shən*), ascent (a Gallicism when used of a mountain ascent): an ascent to heaven, esp. Christ's.—*adjs.* ascen'sional; ascen'sive, moving or tending upwards.—*n.* ascent', a going up: advancement: a going back in time or ancestry: a way up: an up-slope.—Ascen'sion-day (or Ascension Day), Holy Thursday, ten days before Whitsunday, commemorating Christ's Ascension; Ascen'siontide, Ascension-day to Whitsunday.—right ascension (*astron.*), a co-ordinate of the position of a heavenly body measured (usually in terms of time) eastwards along the celestial equator from the First Point of Aries, the other coordinate being the declination. [L. *ascendĕre, ascēnsum—ad,* to, *scandĕre,* to climb.]
ascertain, *as-ər-tān', v.t.* to apprise (*obs.*): to assure (*obs.*): to make certain, prove (*arch.*): to find out for certain: to insure, prove.—*adj.* ascertain'able.—*n.* ascertain'ment. [O.Fr. *acer-tener—à,* to, *certain,* certain.]
ascesis, *ə-sē'sis, n.* the practice of disciplining oneself: asceticism. [Gr. *askēsis,* exercise, training.]
ascetic, *a-* or *ə-set'ik, n.* one who rigidly denies himself ordinary bodily gratifications for conscience' sake: one who aims to compass holiness through mortification of the flesh: a strict hermit: one who lives a life of austerity.—*adjs.* ascet'ic, -al, rigorous in mortifying the flesh: of asceticism: recluse.—*adv.* ascet'ically.—*n.* ascet'icism (-*sizm*). [Gr. *askētikos—askētēs,* one who is in training—*askeein,* to work, exercise, train.]
asci, pl. of ascus.

ascian, *ash'i-ən, n.* an inhabitant of the torrid zone, shadowless when the sun is right overhead. [Gr. *askios,* shadowless—*a-,* priv., *skiā,* a shadow.]
ascidium, *a-sid'i-əm, n.* a pitcher-shaped leaf or part of a leaf, as the pitcher of the pitcher-plants, the bladder of the bladderwort:—*pl.* ascid'ia.—*n.* ascid'ian, a sea-squirt, or tunicate, a degenerate survivor of the ancestors of the vertebrates, shaped like a double-mouthed flask. [Gr. *askidion,* dim. of *askos,* a leathern bag, wineskin.]
ascites, *a-si'tēz, n.* dropsy of the abdomen.—*adjs.* ascit'ic (-*sit'ik*), ascit'ical. [Gr. *askitēs—askos,* belly.]
ascititious. Same as adscititious.
Asclepius, Asclepios, *as-klē'pi-əs, n.* the Greek god of healing (L. *Aesculapius*).—*n.* ascle'piad, a plant of the genus Asclepias: (*cap.*) a son of Asclepius, a physician: a verse used by the Greek poet *Asclepiades* (*Asklēpiadēs*; 3rd cent. B.C.)—a spondee, two (in the *Greater Asclepiad* three) choriambi, and an iambus ( —́ —/—́ ᴗᴗ—́/—́ ᴗᴗ—́/—ᴗᴗ—/ᴗ—́ ).—*n.pl.* Asclepiadā'ceae, the milkweed and swallow-wort family, close akin to the periwinkle family.—*adj.* asclepiadā'ceous (*bot.*).—*ns.* and *adjs.* Asclepiadē'an, Asclepiad'ic (*pros.*).—*n.* Ascle'pias, a chiefly American genus of the swallow-wort family, milkweed. [Gr. *Asklēpios,* the god, *Asklēpiadēs,* the poet, *asklēpias, -ados,* swallow-wort.]
ascomycete, ascospore. See ascus.
asconce, obs. form of askance (in *Shak.* a sconce).
ascorbic, *ə-skör'bik, adj.* antiscorbutic—only in ascorbic acid, vitamin C (C₆H₈O₆). [Gr. a-, priv., and scorbutic.]
ascribe, *ə-* or *a-skrib', v.t.* to attribute, impute, or assign.—*adj.* ascrib'able.—*n.* ascription (-*skrip'shən*), act, expression, formula of ascribing or imputing, e.g. that ascribing glory to God at the end of a sermon. [L. *ascribĕre—ad,* to, *scribĕre, scriptum,* to write.]
ascus, *as'kəs,* (*bot.*) *n.* an enlarged cell, commonly elongated, in which usually eight spores are formed:—*pl.* asci (*as'i*).—*ns.* comycete (*as'kō-mi-sēt*), any one of the Ascomycetes (-*sē'tēz*), one of the main divisions of the fungi, characterised by formation of asci; as'cospore, a spore formed in an ascus. [Gr. *askos,* bag.]
Asdic, *as'dik, n.* an apparatus for detecting and locating a submarine or other underwater object by means of ultrasonic waves echoed back from the submarine, etc. [Allied (or Anti-) Submarine Detection Investigation Committee.]
aseity, *a-sē'i-ti, n.* self-origination. [L. *ā,* from, *sē* (*abl.*), oneself.]
asepalous, *a-, ā-,* or *ə-sep'ə-ləs, adj.* without sepals. [Gr. *a-,* priv., and sepal.]
aseptate, *a-, ā-,* or *ə-sep'tāt, adj.* not partitioned by septa. [Gr. *a-,* priv., and septum.]
aseptic, *a-, ā-,* or *ə-sep'tik, adj.* not liable to, or preventing, decay or putrefaction: involving or accompanied by measures to exclude micro-organisms.—*n.* an aseptic substance.—*ns.* asep'-ticism (-*sizm*), aseptic treatment; asep'sis, freedom from sepsis or blood-poisoning: rendering or being aseptic: exclusion of micro-organisms. —*v.t.* asep'ticise, -ize (-*ti-siz*), to make aseptic: to treat with aseptics. [Gr. *asēptos—a-,* priv., *sēpein,* to cause to decay.]
asexual, *a-, ā-,* or *ə-seks'ū-əl, adj.* without sex: not involving sexual activity: vegetative.—*n.* asexūality (-*al'i-ti*).—*adv.* asex'ūally. [Gr. a-, priv., and sexual.]
Asgard, *äs'gärd, n.* the heaven of Norse mythology, abode of the twelve gods and twenty-six goddesses, and of heroes slain in battle. [O.N. *Āsgarthr, āss,* a god, *garthr,* an enclosure.]
ash, *ash, n.* a well-known timber tree (*Fraxinus excelsior,* or other species) of the olive family:

its wood, white, tough, and hard: an ashen spear-shaft or spear.—*adj.* **ash′en.—ash′-key,** the winged fruit of the ash; **ash′-plant,** an ash sapling.—**mountain ash,** the rowan-tree; **prickly ash,** the toothache tree (Xanthoxylum); **quaking ash,** the aspen. [O.E. *æsc;* Ger. *esche,* O.N. *askr.*]

**ash,** *ash, n.* (often in *pl.*) the dust or remains of anything burnt: volcanic dust, or a rock composed of it: (*pl.*) remains of human body when burnt: (*pl.*) a dead body (*fig.*).—*adj.* **ash′en,** of the colour of ash.—*n.* **ash′ery,** a place where potash or pearl-ash is made.—*adj.* **ash′y.—ash′-bin,** -bucket, -can, a receptacle for household refuse.—*adj.* **ash′en-grey,** of the colour of wood ashes.—**ash′-heap,** a heap of ashes and household refuse; **ash′-hole,** -pit, a hollow, esp. under a fireplace, to receive ashes; **ash′-leach,** a tub in which alkaline salts are dissolved from wood-ashes; **ash′-pan,** a tray fitted underneath a grate to receive the ashes; **ash′-stand, ash′-tray,** a small tray or saucer for tobacco ash; **Ash Wednesday,** the first day of Lent, from the custom of sprinkling ashes on the head.—*adj.* **ash′y-grey.—the ashes,** a term applied by the *Sporting Times* (in a mock 'In Memoriam' notice) to the loss of prestige in English cricket after the Australians' successful visit in 1882, after which English teams strove to 'bring back the ashes', or mortal remains. [O.E. *asce;* O.N. *aska.*]

**ashake,** *ə-shāk′, adv.* in a shaking state. [Prep. a, and shake.]

**ashamed,** *ə-shāmd′, adj.* affected with shame (with *of* action, person; *for,* meaning on behalf of, person; *to do; that*).—*v.i.* ashame′ (*obs.*), to feel shame.—*v.t.* to put to shame.—*adv.* **ash-amed′ly** (or *-id-li*).—*n.* ashamed′ness (or-*id-nes*).—*adj.* asham′ing. [Pfx. *a-,* intensive, and O.E. *sc(e)amian,* to shame.]

**ashet,** *ash′it,* (now only *Scot.*) *n.* a large meat-plate. [Fr. *assiette.*]

**ashine,** *ə-shīn′, adv.* or predicative *adj.* in a shining state. [Prep. a, and shine.]

**ashiver,** *ə-shiv′ər, adv.* or predicative *adj.* in a shivering or quivering state. [Prep. a, shiver (2).]

**Ashkenazim,** *äsh-kə-näz′im, n.pl.* the Polish and German Jews, as distinguished from the *Sephardim,* the Spanish and Portuguese Jews. [Heb. *Ashkenaz,* a northern people (Gen. x.) by later Jews identified with Germany.]

**ashlar, ashler,** *ash′lər, n.* a squared stone used in building or facing a wall: masonry of such stones.—Also *adj.*—*v.t.* to face with ashlar.—*ns.* **ash′laring, ash′lering,** ashlar masonry or facing: a vertical timber between floor-joist and rafter.—*n.* **ash′lar-work,** ashlar masonry. [O.Fr. *aiseler* —L. *axillāris—axilla,* dim. of *axis,* axle, plank.]

**ashore,** *ə-shōr′,-shör, adv.* on shore. [Prep. a, and shore.]

**ashram(a),** *äsh′rəm(-ə), n.* (*India*) a hermitage, or a place of retreat for a religious group. [Sans. *āśrama.*]

**Ashtaroth, Ashtoreth.** See Astarte.

**Asian,** *ā′sh(i)ən, ā′shyən, -zh-,* **Asiatic,** -*i-at′ik, adjs.* belonging to Asia (esp. Asia Minor): in literature or art, florid.—*n.* a native of Asia.—*adj.* **Asianic** (*-an′ik*), Asian, esp. of a group of non-Indo-Germanic languages of Asia and Europe.—*n.* **Asiat′icism** (*-i-sizm*), imitation of Asiatic or Eastern manners.

**aside,** *ə-sīd′, adv.* on or to one side: privately: apart.—*n.* words spoken in an undertone, so as not to be heard by some person present, words spoken by an actor which the other persons on the stage are supposed not to hear: an indirect effort of any kind.—*adj.* (*U.S.*) private, apart.—*prep.* (now only *Scot.*) beside.—**aside from,** apart from; **to set aside,** to quash (a judgment). [Prep. a, and side.]

**asinico,** *as-i-nē′kō,* (*Shak.*) *n.* a stupid fellow. [Sp. *asnico*—dim. of *asno*—L. *asinus,* ass.]

**asinine,** *as′in-in, adj.* of or like an ass.—*n.* **asininity** (*-in′i-ti*). [L. *asininus—asinus,* ass.]

**ask,** *äsk, v.t.* to beg, request: to make a request of: to inquire: to inquire of: to invite: to proclaim.—*v.i.* to make request or inquiry.—*n.* ask′er.—asking price, price set by the seller of an article before bargaining has begun.—**to ask for it** (*coll.*), to behave in a way likely to bring trouble on oneself. [O.E. *āscian, ācsian;* Ger. *heischen,* O.N. *æskja.*]

**ask,** *ask,* (*dial.*) *n.* a newt.—Also ask′er. [Apparently O.E. *āthexe;* cf. Ger. *eidechse,* lizard.]

**askance,** *ə-skans′,* **askant,** *ə-skant′, adv.* sideways: awry: obliquely.—*v.t.* (*Shak.*) to turn aside.—*prep.* (*Shak.*) **ascaunt′** (folio reading **aslant**), with a slant over.—**to eye, look or view askance,** to look (at) with disdain, disapprobation, envy, or (now usually) suspicion. [Ety. very obscure.]

**askari,** *äs′kä-rē, äs-kä′rē, n.* an East African soldier. [Arab, '*askarī,* soldier.]

**askesis.** See ascesis.

**askew,** *ə-skū′, adv.* obliquely: aside: awry. [App. prep. a, and skew.]

**aslake,** *ə-slāk′, v.t.* to slake (*obs.*): to mitigate (*arch.*): to appease (*obs.*). [O.E. *āslacian;* see slake.]

**aslant,** *ə-slänt′, adv.* (or *adj.*) on the slant.—Also **asklent′** (*Scot.*). [Prep. a, and slant (1).]

**asleep,** *ə-slēp′, adv.* (or *adj.*) in or to a sleeping state: dead: (of limbs) numbed, sometimes with tingling or prickly feeling. [Prep. a, and sleep.]

**aslope,** *ə-slōp′, adv.* or *adj.* on the slope. [O.E. *āslopen,* pa.p. of *āslūpan,* to slip away.]

**asmear,** *ə-smēr′, adj.* smeared over. [Prep. a.]

**Asmodeus,** *as-, az-mə-dē′us,* **Asmoday,** *-dā′, n.* an evil spirit of Semitic mythology. [L.,—Gr. *Asmodaios*—Heb. *Ashmadai.*]

**asmoulder,** *ə-smōl′dər, adv.* in a smouldering state. [Prep. a.]

**asocial,** *a-, ā-sō′shl, adj.* not social: antisocial. [Gr. *a-,* priv., and social.]

**asp,** *asp, äsp, n.* an aspen.

**asp,** *asp, äsp,* **aspic(k),** *asp′ik, n.* a venomous snake of various kinds—*Vipera aspis* of Southern Europe, Cleopatra's asp (prob. the horned viper), the biblical asp (prob. the Egyptian juggler's snake, *Naja Haje*), the cobra da capello. [L.,—Gr. *aspis.*]

**Asparagus,** *əs-par′ə-gəs, n.* a genus of Liliaceae, with leaves reduced to scales, cultivated as ornamental plants, and one species (*A. officinalis*) for its young shoots as a table delicacy.—*ns.* **aspar-ag′inase** (*-aj′*), an enzyme that causes asparagine to hydrolyse to aspartic acid and ammonia; **aspar′agine** (*-jin, -jēn*), an amide found in asparagus and other vegetables.—**aspar′agus-stone,** a pale yellowish green apatite; **aspartic acid,** an amino-acid found in young sugar-cane, etc. [L.,—Gr. *asp(h)aragos.*]

**Aspasia,** *as-pā′zyə, as-pā′zi-a, n.* a gifted Athenian courtesan, mistress of Pericles—any charming and accomplished woman of easy morals.

**aspect,** *as′pekt* (in *Spens., Shak., Milt.,* etc., *as-pekt′*), *n.* a look, a glance: a view: direction of facing: appearance presented: way of viewing: face: the situation of one planet with respect to another, as seen from the earth: in some languages, a verbal form expressing simple action, repetition, beginning, duration, etc. (*gram.*): attitude (*aircraft*).—*v.t.* **aspect′** (*obs.*), to look at or on.—**as′pectable,** visible: worth looking at.—**aspect ratio,** ratio of the width to the height of a reproduced image (*TV*): ratio of the span of an aerofoil to its mean chord. [L. *aspectus.*]

**aspen,** *asp′ən, äsp′, -in* (*Spens.* **aspine**), *n.* the trembling poplar.—*adj.* made of, or like, the aspen:

tremulous: timorous.—*adj.* **as'pen-like.** [O.E. *æspe*; Ger. *espe*.]

**asper,** *as'pər, n.* a small (obsolete) silver Turkish coin. [Gr. *aspron*, rough, later white.]

**asper,** *as'pər, adj. (obs.)* rough, harsh.—*n.* the Greek rough breathing (*spíritus asper*).—*v.t.* **as'perate,** to roughen.—*n.* **asperity** (-*per'*), roughness: harshness: bitter coldness: (in *pl.*) excrescences, rough places.—*adj.* **as'perous,** rough with short hairs. [L. *asper*.]

**asperge,** *as-pûrj', v.t.* to sprinkle.—*n.* an aspergillum for holy water.—*ns.* **aspergation** (-*gā'*); **asper'ger** (-*jər*); **asper'ges,** a short service introductory to the mass, so called from the words *Asperges me, Domine, hyssopo et mundabor* (Ps. li); **aspergill, -um** (*as'pər-jil, -jil'əm*), a holy-water sprinkler; **Aspergillum,** a genus of boring Lamellibranchs in which the shell forms an elongated cone, ending in a disk pierced with numerous small tubular holes; **Aspergill'us,** a genus of minute moulds occurring on decaying substances. [L. *aspergēre—ad,* to, *spargēre,* to sprinkle.]

**asperse,** *as-pûrs', v.t.* to slander or calumniate: to bespatter.—*n.* **asper'sion,** calumny: slander: a shower or spray (*Shak.*).—*adjs.* **aspers'ive,** **aspers'ory,** tending to asperse: defamatory.—*n.* an aspergillum: an aspersorium.—*ns.* **aspersoir** (*äs-per-swär*; Fr.), an aspergillum; **aspersō'-rium** (L.), a holy-water vessel. [L. *aspergēre, aspersum—ad,* to, *spargēre,* to sprinkle.]

**asphalt,** *as'falt,* **asphaltum,** *as-falt'əm, ns.* a black or dark-brown, hard, bituminous substance, found native, and got as a residue in petroleum distillation, etc., anciently used as a cement: a mixture of this with rock chips or other material, used for paving, roofing, etc.—*v.t.* to lay, cover, or impregnate with asphalt.—*adj.* **asphalt'ic.** [Gr. *asphaltos,* from an Eastern word.]

**aspheterism,** *as-fet'ər-izm, n.* denial of the right of private property (*Southey*).—*v.i.* **asphet'erise, -ize.** [Gr. *a-,* priv., and *spheteros,* one's own.]

**asphodel,** *as'fə-del, -fo-, n.* a plant of the lily family—in Greek mythology, the peculiar plant of the dead: applied to other plants, esp. bog asphodel. [Gr. *asphodelos;* cf. **daffodil.**]

**asphyxia,** *as-fik'si-a, n. (lit.)* stoppage of the pulse: suspended animation owing to any cause interfering with respiration.—Also **asphyx'y.**—*n.* and *adj.* **asphyx'iant,** (a chemical substance) producing asphyxia.—*v.t.* **asphyx'iate,** to produce asphyxia in.—*adj.* **asphyx'iāted.**—*ns.* **asphyxiā'-tion,** action of asphyxiating or condition of being asphyxiated; **asphyx'iātor.** [Gr. *asphyxiā—a-,* priv., *sphyxis,* pulse.]

**aspic, aspick.** See **asp.**

**aspic,** *as'pik, n.* a savoury meat-jelly containing fish, game, hard-boiled eggs, etc. [Perh. from *aspic,* asp, because it is 'cold as an aspic' (French proverb).]

**aspic,** *as'pik, n.* the broad-leaved lavender. [Fr., —L. *spica,* spike.]

**Aspidistra,** *as-pid-ist'rə, n.* a genus of plants of the asparagus group of *Liliaceae*—often grown indoors. [Perh. Gr. *aspis,* a shield.]

**Aspidium,** *as-pid'i-əm, n.* the shield-fern genus (by some broken up) of ferns—from the shield-shaped or kidney-shaped indusium.—*adj.* **aspid'ioid.** [Gr. *aspidion,* dim. of *aspis,* shield.]

**aspire,** *əs-* or *as-pir', v.i.* (with *to, after,* or an infinitive) to desire eagerly: to aim at or strive for high things: to tower up.—*n.* **aspir'ant** (or *as'pir-*), one who aspires (with *after, for*): a candidate.—*adj.* ambitious: mounting up (*rare* in both senses).—*v.t.* **aspirate** (*as'pir-āt*), to pronounce with a full breathing, as *h* in *house.*—*n.* (-*it, -ət*) the sound represented by the letter *h*: a consonant sound, a stop followed by an audible breath, as that of *bh* in Sanskrit: sometimes extended to a fricative or spirant: a mark

of aspiration, the rough breathing (') in Greek: a letter representing an aspirate sound.—Also *adj.* —In French '*h* aspirate', no longer sounded, still affects the junction with the preceding word.—*ns.* **aspirā'tion,** eager desire: lofty hopes or aims: breathing (*obs.*): pronunciation of a sound with a full breathing: an aspirated sound (like Gr. *ch, th,* etc.): drawing a gas or liquid in, out, or through; **as'pirātor,** an apparatus for drawing air or other gases through bottles or other vessels: an instrument for removing fluids from cavities of the body (*med.*).—*adjs.* **aspir'atory** (-*ə-tə-ri* or *as'pir-*), relating to breathing; **aspir'ing.**—*adv.* **aspir'ingly.**—*n.* **aspir'ingness.**—to drop one's **aspirates,** to omit to pronounce the sound of *h.* [L. *aspīrāre, -ātum—ad,* to, *spīrāre,* to breathe.]

**aspirin,** *as'pər-in, n.* a drug (acetyl-salicylic acid) used for relieving rheumatic pains, neuralgia, etc.

**Asplenium,** *as-plē'ni-əm, n.* spleenwort, a genus of ferns, mostly tropical, with long or linear sori, with indusium arising from a vein—including wall-rue. [Gr. *asplēnon,* lit. spleenless—*a-,* priv., and *splēn,* spleen: reputed a cure for spleen.]

**asport,** *as-pōrt', -pört', (rare) v.t.* to carry away, esp. wrongfully.—*n.* **asportā'tion.** [L. *asportāre* —*abs,* away, and *portāre,* to carry.]

**aspout,** *ə-spowt', adv.* spoutingly. [Prep. **a.**]

**asprawl,** *ə-spröl', adv.* in a sprawl. [Prep. **a.**]

**aspread,** *ə-spred', adv.* in or into a spreading state. [Prep. **a.**]

**asprout,** *ə-sprowt', adv.* in a sprouting state. [Prep. **a.**]

**asquat,** *ə-skwot', adv.* squattingly. [Prep. **a.**]

**asquint,** *ə-skwint', adv.* and *adj.* towards the corner of the eye: obliquely. [App. prep. **a,** and some such word as Du. *schuinte,* slant.]

**ass,** *as, äs, n.* a small, usually grey, long-eared animal of the horse genus: a dull, stupid fellow (*fig.*).—**asses' bridge,** the *pons asinorum,* or fifth proposition in the first book of Euclid, for some an impassable barrier to further progress. [O.E. *assa*—L. *asinus;* cf. Gr. *onos,* ass.]

**assa**—L. *asinus;* cf. Gr. *onos,* ass.]

**assafetida.** Same as **asafoetida.**

**assagai.** Same as **assegai.**

**assai,** *äs-sä'ē, (mus.) adv.* very. [It.,—L. *ad,* to, *satis,* enough.]

**assai,** *ä-sä'ē, n.* a S. American palm (*Euterpe edulis*): its fruit: a drink made from its fruit. [Tupí.]

**assail,** *ə-sāl', v.t.* to attack.—*adj.* **assail'able.**—*ns.* **assail'ant,** one who attacks; **assail'ment.** [O.Fr. *asaillir*—L. *assilīre—ad,* and upon, and *salīre,* to leap.]

**assart,** *as-art', (hist.) v.t.* to reclaim for agriculture by grubbing.—*n.* a forest clearing: assarted land: grubbing up of trees and bushes. [A.Fr. *assarter*—L.L. *exsartāre*—L. *ex,* out, *sar(r)īre,* to hoe, weed.]

**assassin,** *ə-* or *a-sas'in, n.* a follower of the Old Man of the Mountains, a member of his military and religious order in Persia and Syria (11th-13th cent.), notorious for secret murders: one who, usually for a reward, or for political reasons, kills by surprise or secretly.—*v.t.* **assass'inate,** to murder by surprise or secret assault: to murder (especially a prominent person) violently, often publicly: to maltreat (*Milt.*): to destroy by treacherous means, as a reputation (*fig.*).—*n.* (*obs.*) one who assassinates.—*ns.* **assassinā'tion;** **assass'inator.** [Through Fr. or It. from Ar. *hashshāshin,* hashish-eaters.]

**assault,** *ə-sölt', n.* a sudden attack: a storming, as of a town: in Eng. law, unlawful attempt to apply force to the person of another—when force is actually applied, the act amounts to *battery.*—*v.t.* to make an assault or attack upon.—*adj.* used in attack: preparing, or prepared, for attack.—*n.* **assault'er.**—**assault boat,** a portable boat for landing on beaches or crossing rivers.—

assault at or of arms, a display of attack and defence in fencing. [O.Fr. *asaut*—L. *ad*, upon, *saltus*, a leap, *salire*, to leap. See assail.]

assay, *a*- or *ə-sā', v.t.* to put to the proof: to make trial of: to test: to determine the proportion of a metal, or other component, in: to give as result: to test fatness of (a killed stag) by a trial cut (*obs.*): to taste before presenting (as guarantee against poison) (*obs.*): to put to proof in action: to afflict (*Spens.*): to tempt (*obs.*): to affect (*Spens.*): to experience (*Shak.*): to endeavour (now usu. essay): to assail (*Spens.*, *Shak.*): to challenge (*Shak.*): to accost (*Shak.*).— *v.i.* to adventure, make an attempt: to practise assaying (of ores, etc.)—*n.* (by some *as'ā*) a test, trial: a determination of proportion of metal: a specimen used for the purpose: determination of the fatness of a stag (*obs.*): experiment: experience: endeavour, attempt, tentative effort (usu. essay): assault (*Spens.*, *Shak.*): proof, temper, quality, standard, such as might be found by assaying (*Spens.*, *Shak.*).—*adj.* assay'-able.—*ns.* assay'er, one who assays metals; assay'ing.—assay'-master, an officer who determines the amount of gold or silver in coin or bullion; assay'-piece, a sample chosen for assay: an example of excellence.—cup of assay, a small cup for trial tasting before offering. [O.Fr. *assayer*, n. *assai*. See essay.]

assegai, assagai, (*Afrik.* assegaai) *as'ə-gī*, *n.* a slender spear of hard wood tipped with iron, some for hurling, some for thrusting with—used in South Africa.—*v.t.* to kill or wound with an assegai. [Through Fr. or Port. from Ar. *azzaghāyah*—*az* = *al*, the, *zaghāyah*, a Berber word.]

assemble, *ə-sem'bl, v.t.* to call or bring together: to collect: to put together the parts of.—*v.i.* to meet together.—*ns.* assem'blage, a collection of persons or things: the whole collection of remains found on an archaeological site: (also *a-sä-bläzh*), (putting together) a sculptural or other work of art consisting in whole or in part of selected objects, usu. objects made for another purpose; assem'bla(u)nce, an assembling (*Spens.*): semblance (*Shak.*); assem'bler; assem'bly, the act of assembling: the putting together of parts: a company assembled: a formal ball or meeting for dancing and social intercourse: a reception or at-home: a meeting for religious worship (*arch.*): a deliberative or legislative body, esp. in some legislatures a lower house: a drum-beat, esp. a signal for striking tents (*mil.*).—assembly line, a serial arrangement of workers and apparatus for passing on work from stage to stage in assembling a product; assem'blyman, a member of assembly or lower house; assembly room, a public ballroom.—General Assembly, in Scotland, Ireland and the United States, the highest court of the Presbyterian Church; Legislative Assembly, House of Assembly, the lower or only house of some legislatures; National Assembly (also Constituent Assembly), the first of the revolutionary assemblies in France (1789-91): a body set up in 1920 'to deliberate on all matters concerning the Church of England and to make provision in respect thereof', consisting of houses of Bishops, Clergy, and Laity—also Church Assembly; superseded in 1970 by the General Synod (see synod). [Fr. *assembler*—L.L. *assimulāre*, to bring together—*ad*, to, *similis*, like. See assimilate.]

assemblé, *ä-sä-blä, n.* a ballet dancer's leap with extended leg followed by crossing of legs. [Fr. *assembler*, to bring together.]

assent, *a*- or *ə-sent', v.i.* to express agreement or acquiescence (with *to*).—*n.* an agreeing or acquiescence: compliance.—*adj.* assentaneous (*as-ən-tā'ni-əs*), ready to agree.—*ns.* assentā'tion, obsequious assent, adulation; ass'entātor (*obs.*); assent'er.—*adjs.* assentient (*ə-sen'shənt*), as-

sent'ive.—*adv.* assent'ingly.—*ns.* assent'iveness; assent'or, one who subscribes a candidate's nomination paper in addition to proposer and seconder.—royal assent, the sovereign's formal acquiescence in a measure which has passed the Houses of Parliament. [L. *assentārī*, to flatter, freq. of *assentīrī*, to assent, agree.]

assert, *ə-sûrt', v.t.* to vindicate or defend by arguments or measures (now used only with cause as object, or reflexively): to declare strongly: to lay claim to: to insist upon: to affirm: to bear evidence of (*rare*).—*adj.* assert'able.—*ns.* assert'er, assert'or, a champion: one who makes a positive statement; asser'tion (*-shən*), affirmation: the act of claiming one's rights: averment.—*adj.* assert'ive, asserting or confirming confidently: positive: dogmatic.—*adv.* assert'ively.—*n.* assert'iveness.—*adj.* assert'ory, affirmative.—assert oneself, to defend one's rights or opinions, sometimes with unnecessary zeal: to thrust oneself forward. [L. *asserĕre, assertum*, to lay hands on, claim—*ad*, to, and *serĕre*, to join.]

assess, *ə-ses', v.t.* to fix the amount of, as a tax: to tax or fine: to fix the value or profits of, for taxation (with *at*): to estimate.—*adj.* assess'-able.—*ns.* assess'ment, act of assessing: a valuation for the purpose of taxation: a tax; assess'or, a legal adviser who sits beside a magistrate: one appointed as an associate in office with another: one who assesses taxes, or value of property, income, etc., for taxation: one who shares another's dignity.—*adj.* assessō'rial (*as-*).—*n.* assess'orship. [L. *assidēre, assessum*, to sit by, esp. of judges in a court, from *ad*, to, at, *sedēre*, to sit.]

assets, *as'ets, n.pl.* (*orig. sing.*) the property of a deceased or insolvent person, considered as chargeable for all debts, etc.: the entire property of all sorts belonging to a merchant or to a trading association.—*false sing.* ass'et, an item of property: something advantageous or well worth having (*coll.*). [From the Anglo-Fr. phrase *aver assetz*, to have enough, O.Fr. *asez*, enough—L. *ad*, to, *satis*, enough.]

asseverate, *ə-, ə-sev'ər-āt, v.t.* to declare solemnly —earlier assev'er.—*adj.* assev'erating.—*adv.* assev'eratingly.—*n.* asseverā'tion. [L. *asseverāre*, *-ātum*—*ad*, to, *sevērus*, serious; see severe.]

assez bien, *a-sä byē*, (Fr.) pretty well.

assibilate, *a*- or *ə-sib'i-lāt, v.t.* to sound as a sibilant.—*n.* assibilā'tion. [L. *ad*, to, *sibilāre*, to hiss.]

assiduity, *as-id-ū'i-ti, n.* persistent application or diligence: (*pl.*) constant attentions.—*adj.* assiduous (*ə-sid'ū-əs*), constant or unwearied in application.—*adv.* assid'ūously, unremittingly.— *n.* assid'ūousness. [L. *assiduus*—*ad*, to, at, *sedēre*, to sit.]

assiege, *ə-sēj', (Spens.) v.t.* to besiege. [See siege.]

assiento, *as-ē-en'tō, (hist.) n.* a treaty (esp. that with Britain, 1713) for the supply of African slaves for Spanish American possessions. [Sp. (now *asiento*), seat, seat in a court, treaty.]

assign, *ə-sīn', v.t.* to allot: to designate, appoint: to put forward, adduce: to make over, transfer: to ascribe, refer: to specify: to fix, determine.— *n.* one to whom any property or right is made over: (in *pl.*, *Shak.*) appendages.—*adj.* assign'-able, that may be assigned.—*ns.* assignation (*as-ig-nā'shən*), an appointment to meet, used chiefly of love trysts, and mostly in a bad sense: the making over of any right to another (*Scots law*); assignee (*as-in-ē'*), one to whom any right or property is assigned: a trustee of a sequestrated estate; assignment (*-sīn'*), act of assigning: anything assigned: the writing by which a transfer is made: a task allotted: (*Spens.* altered in 1596 to dessignment) design, enterprise: assignor (*as-i-nör'*), one who makes over (*law*). [Fr. *assigner*—L. *assignāre*, to mark out —*ad*, to, *signum*, a mark or sign.]

**assignat**, *as'ig-nat, a-sēn-yä'*, *n*. one of the notes first issued in 1790 by the French government as bonds on the security of the appropriated church lands. [Fr.]

**assimilate**, *ə-sim'il-āt, v.t*. to make similar or like (with *to*, *with*): to convert into a like substance, as food in the body: to take fully into the mind, experience effects of (e.g. knowledge): to modify (a speech sound), making it more like a neighbouring sound in a word or sentence.—*v.i*. to become like: to be incorporated in.—*adj*. **assim'ilable**.—*n*. **assimilā'tion**.—*adj*. **assim'ilātive**, having the power or tendency to assimilate. [L. *assimilāre*, *-ātum*—*ad*, to, *similis*, like.]

**assist**, *ə-sist'*, *v.t*. to help: to accompany (*Shak*.).—*v.i*. to help: to be present (now a *Gallicism*).—*n*. **assis'tance**, help: relief.—*adj*. **assist'ant**, helping.—*n*. one who assists: a helper.—*adj*. **assis'ted**, for which help (e.g. financial aid, additional power) is supplied. [Fr. *assister*—L. *assistēre*, to stand by—*ad*, to, *sistēre*, to set, take one's stand.]

**assize**, *ə-siz'*, *v.t*. to assess (*obs*.): to set or fix the quantity or price of.—*n*. a statute settling the weight, measure, or price of anything (*hist*.): a trial by jury (*Scot*.): a jury (*Scot*.): judgment, sentence: (in *pl*.) periodical sittings of judges on circuit through the English counties, with a jury (till 1972).—*n*. **assiz'er**, an officer with oversight of weights and measures: a juror (*Scots law*). [O.Fr. *assise*, assembly of judges, set rate —*asseoir*—L. *assidēre*—*ad*, to, *sedēre*, to sit.]

**associate**, *ə-sō'shi-āt*, *v.t*. to join, connect, link: to connect in one's mind: to make a colleague or partner: to accompany (*Shak*.).—*v.i*. to consort, keep company (with *with*): to combine or unite. —*adj*. associated: connected: confederate: joined as colleague or junior colleague.—*n*. one joined or connected with another: a colleague, companion, friend, partner, or ally: a person admitted to a society without full membership.— *n*. **associabil'ity**.—*adj*. **asso'ciable** (*-shi-ə-bl*, or *-shə-bl*), capable of being associated.—*ns*. **asso'- ciateship**; **associā'tion** (*-si-*, or *-shi-*), act of associating: union or combination: a society of persons joined to promote some object: a set of species of plants or animals characteristic of a certain habitat (*biol*.): loose aggregation of molecules (*chem*.): (*football*; also association **football**, *coll*. soccer) the game as formulated by the Football Association (formed 1863), with eleven players a side, opp. to *Rugby*: connection of thoughts, of feelings: (usu. in *pl*.) thought, feeling, memory, more or less permanently connected with e.g. a place, an occurrence, something said.—*adj*. **assō'ciātive**, tending to association: such that (*a*\**b*)\**c* = '*a*\*(*b*\**c*)—where * denotes a binary operation (*math*.).—*n*. **asso- ciativ'ity**.—**association copy**, a copy of a book deriving additional interest from some association, e.g. a copy inscribed as given to or by some person of note.—**association of ideas**, mental linkage that facilitates recollection—by similarity, contiguity, repetition. [L. *associāre*, *-ātum* —*ad*, to, *socius*, a companion.]

**assoil**, *ə-soil'*, (*arch*.) *v.t*. to absolve: to acquit: to discharge: to release: to solve: to dispel: to determine.—*n*. **assoil'ment**.—*v.t*. **assoilzie** (*ə-soil'i, -yi*), to absolve (*Scot*.): to free (defender or accused) of a claim or charge (*Scots law*). [A.Fr. *assoilier*—L. *ab*, from, *solvēre*, to loose.]

**assoil**, *ə-soil'*, *v.t*. to soil, sully, dirty. [L. *ad*, and **soil** (2).]

**assonance**, *as'ən-əns*, *n*. a correspondence in sound: vowel-rhyme, coincidence of vowels without regard to consonants, as in *mate* and *shape*, *feel* and *need*: extended to correspondence of consonants with different vowels: resemblance,

**corresponaence**.—*adjs*. **ass'onant**; **assonantal** (*-ant'əl*).—*v.i*. **ass'onate**, to correspond in vowel sound: to practise assonance. [L. *assonāre*, *-ātum*—*ad*, to, *sonāre*, to sound.]

**assort**, *ə-sört'*, *v.t*. to distribute in classes, classify: to class.—*v.i*. to agree or be in accordance: to suit well: to keep company (*arch*.).—*adj*. **assort'ed**, classified, arranged in sorts: made up of various sorts.—*ns*. **assort'edness**; **assort'ment**, act of assorting: a quantity or number of things assorted: variety. [Fr. *assortir*—L. *ad*, to, *sors*, *sortis*, a lot.]

**assot**, *ə-sot'*, (*obs*.) *v.t*. to befool, to besot.—*p.adj*. **assott'**, or **assott'ed** (*Spens*.), infatuated. [O.Fr. *asoter*—*à*, to, *sot*, fool; see **sot**.]

**assuage**, *ə-swāj'*, *v.t*. to soften, mitigate, or allay.— *v.i*. to abate or subside: to diminish.—*n*. **assuage'ment**.—*n*. and *adj*. **assuag'ing**.—*adj*. **assuā'sive** (*-siv*), soothing: mitigating. [O.Fr. *assouager*—L. *ad*, to, *suāvis*, mild.]

**assubjugate**, *a-sub'joō-gāt*, (*Shak*.) *v.t*. to reduce to subjection. [Pfx. *a-*, intensive, **subjugate**.]

**assuefaction**, *as-wi-fak'shən*, *n*. habituation. [L. *assuēfacĕre*—*assuētus*, accustomed, and *facĕre*, to make.]

**assuetude**, *as'wi-tūd*, *n*. accustomedness: habit. [L. *assuētus*.]

**assume**, *ə-sūm'*, *-soōm'*, *v.t*. to adopt, take in: to take up, to take upon oneself: to take for granted: to arrogate: to pretend to possess.—*v.i*. to make undue claims: to be arrogant.—*adj*. **assum'able**.—*adv*. **assum'ably**.—*adj*. **assumed'**, appropriated, usurped: pretended: taken as the basis of argument.—*adv*. **assum'edly**.—*adj*. **assum'ing**, haughty: arrogant.—*n*. assumption: arrogance: presumption.—*adv*. **assum'ingly**.— *ns*. **assumpsit** (*ə-sump'sit*), an action at law, wherein the plaintiff asserts that the defendant undertook (L. *assūmpsit*) to do a certain act and failed to fulfil his promise; **assumption** (*-sum'*, *-sump'*), an act of assuming: reception: taking upon oneself: arrogance: taking for granted: supposition: that which is taken for granted or supposed: the minor premise in a syllogism (*logic*): a taking up bodily into heaven, especially the **Assumption of the Virgin**, celebrated on the 15th of August (declared a dogma of the Roman Catholic Church on the 1st of November 1950).—*n*. **Assump'tionist**, a member of the Roman Catholic congregation (*Augustinians of the Assumption*) founded at Nîmes in 1843.— Also *adj*.—*adj*. **assump'tive**, of the nature of an assumption: gratuitously assumed: apt, or too apt, to assume.—**deed of assumption** (*Scots law*), a deed executed by trustees under a trust-deed assuming a new trustee or settlement. [L. *assūmĕre*, *assūmptum*—*ad*, to, *sūmĕre*, to take.]

**assure**, *ə-shoōr'*, *v.t*. to make sure or secure: to give confidence: to betroth (*obs*.): to tell positively: to insure.—*adj*. **assur'able**.—*n*. **assur'ance**, confidence: feeling of certainty: subjective certainty of one's salvation (*theol*.): self-confidence: unabashedness: audacity: positive declaration: insurance, now esp. life-insurance: security: the securing of a title to property: a promise: a surety, warrant: a betrothal (*obs*.).—*adj*. **assured'**, secured: pledged: betrothed (*obs*.): certain: confident: beyond doubt: insured: self-confident: over-bold: brazen-faced.—*adv*. **assur'edly**.—*ns*. **assur'edness**; **assur'er**, one who gives assurance: an insurer or underwriter: one who insures his life. [O.Fr. *aseürer* (Fr. *assurer*)—L.L. *adsēcū-rāre*—*ad*, to, *sēcūrus*, safe; see **sure**.]

**assurgent**, *ə-sûr'jənt*, *adj*. rising, ascending: rising in a curve to an erect position (*bot*.): depicted as rising from the sea (*her*.).—*n*. **assur'gency**, the tendency to rise. [L. *ad*, to, *surgĕre*, to rise.]

**asswage**, an old spelling of **assuage**.

**Assyrian**, *a-* or *ə-sir'i-ən*, *adj*. of Assyria.—*n*. an inhabitant or native of Assyria: the Semitic language of ancient Assyria.—*ns*. **Assyriol′ogist**; **Assyriol′ogy**, the science of Assyrian antiquities. [Gr. *Assyrios—Assyriā*.]

**assythment**, *ə-sith′mənt*, (Scots *law*; *obsolescent*) *n*. indemnification by one who has caused a death, etc. [O.Fr. *aset*; see **assets**.]

**astarboard**, *ə-stär′bôrd*, *-bôrd*, *adv*. on or towards the starboard. [Prep. **a**, and **starboard**.]

**astare**, *ə-stär′*, *adv*. in a state of staring. [Prep. **a**, and **stare**.]

**astart**, *ə-stärt′*, (*Spens.*) *v.i*. to start up: to befall. —*adv*. with a start, suddenly. [Pfx. *a-*, up, and **start**.]

**Astarte**, *as-tär′ti*, *n*. the Greek and Roman form of the name of a Semitic goddess whose attributes symbolise the notion of productive power.— Also **Ashtaroth** (*ash′tar-oth*), **Ash′toreth** (*B.*).

**astatic**, *a-stat′ik*, *adj*. having no tendency to stand in a fixed position: without polarity, as a pair of magnetic needles set in opposite directions.—*n*. **astatine** (*as′tə-tēn*), the chemical element of atomic number 85 (symb. At). [Gr. *astatos*, unstable—*a-*, priv., *statos*, verb. adj. of *histanai*, to make to stand.]

**astatki**, *as-tat′kē*, *n*. the residue of petroleum-distillation, used as fuel. [Russ., *pl*. of *ostatok*, residue.]

**asteism**, *as′tē-izm*, *n*. refined irony. [Gr. *asty*, *-eōs*, town.]

**astely**, *a-stē′li*, (*bot.*) *n*. absence of a central cylinder or stele.—*adj*. **astē′lic**. [Gr. *a-*, priv., *stēlē*, column.]

**aster**, *as′tər*, *n*. a star (*obs.*): a starlike figure, as in mitotic cell-division: (*cap.*) a genus of Compositae, with showy radiated heads, white or lilac-blue or purple, flowering in late summer and autumn, hence often called Michaelmas daisies: extended to the kindred China aster (*Callistephus hortensis*) brought from China to France by a missionary in the 18th century.—*ns*. **asteria** (*as-tē′ri-ə*), a precious stone that shows asterism when cut *en cabochon*—star-sapphire, star-ruby; **Astē′rias**, the common crossfish or five-fingers genus of sea-urchins.—*adj*. **astē′riated** (*min.*), showing asterism.—*ns*. **as′terid**, a starfish; **as′-terisk**, a star-shaped mark (*) used as a reference to a note, as a mark of omission, as a mark of a word or root inferred to have existed but not recorded, and for other purposes; **as′terism**, a group of stars: three asterisks placed to direct attention to a passage: in some minerals the property of showing by reflected or transmitted light a star-shaped luminous figure due to inclusions or tubular cavities; **as′teroid**, a minor planet: a starfish.—*adj*. resembling a star, starfish, or aster.—*adj*. **asteroid′al**.—*n.pl*. **Asteroid′ea**, a class of echinoderms, the starfishes. [Gr. *astēr*, star.]

**astern**, *ə-stûrn′*, *adv*. in or towards the stern: behind. [Prep. **a**, and **stern**.]

**astert**, *ə-stûrt′*, *v.i*. Same as **astart**.

**asthenia**, *as-thē′ni-ə*, *-thi-nī′ə*, *n*. debility.—*adj*. **asthenic** (*-then′ik*), of, relating to, asthenia: lacking strength: of a slender type, narrow-chested, with slight muscular development (*anthrop.*).—*n*. a man of asthenic type.—*n*. **asthenosphere** (*-then′ə-sfēr*; *geol.*) a hypothetical sphere lying between the crust and the solid nucleus of the earth, supposed to yield more readily than rock to persistent stresses. [Gr. *astheneia—a-*, priv., *sthenos*, strength.]

**asthma**, *as′mə*, also *asth′*, *ast′*, in U.S. usu. *az′*, *n*. a chronic disorder of the organs of respiration, characterised by difficulty of breathing, wheezing, and a tightness in the chest.—*adjs*. **asthmatic** (*-mat′*), **-al**.—*adv*. **asthmat′ically**. [Gr. *asthma*, *-atos—aazein*, to breathe with open mouth.]

**asthore**, *as-thōr′*, (Ir.) darling.

**Asti**, *as′tē*, *n*. an Italian white wine made round about *Asti* in the Monferrato hills in Piedmont. **astichous**, *as′ti-kəs*, (*bot.*) *adj*. not in rows. [Gr. *a-*, priv., *stichos*, a row.]

**astigmatism**, *ə-stig′mə-tizm*, *n*. a defect in an eye, lens, or mirror, by which rays from one point are not focused at one point.—*adj*. **astigmatic** (*-mat′*). [Gr. *a-*, priv., and *stigma*, *-atos*, a point.]

**astir**, *ə-stûr′*, *adv*. on the move: out of bed: in motion or excitement. [Prep. **a**, and **stir**.]

**astomatous**, *a-stom′ə-təs*, or *-stōm′*, *adj*. mouthless.—Also **astomous** (*as′tə-məs*). [Gr. *a-*, priv., *stoma*, *-atos*, mouth.]

**astonish**, *əs-ton′ish*, *v.t*. to impress with sudden surprise or wonder: to amaze: to daze, to stun (*Shak.*).—Earlier forms **astone** (*ə-stun′*), **astun′**, **astony** (*-ston′i*).—*adjs*. **aston′ied** (*obs.*); **aston′ished**, amazed: dazed, stunned (*obs.*).—*adj*. **aston′ishing**, very wonderful, amazing.—*adv*. **aston′ishingly**.—*n*. **aston′ishment**, amazement: wonder: a cause for astonishment. [Ultimately from L. *ex*, out, *tonāre*, to thunder.]

**astoop**, *ə-stoop′*, *adv*. in a stooping position. [Prep. **a**, and **stoop**.]

**astound**, *əs-townd′*, *v.t*. to amaze, to strike dumb with astonishment.—*adjs*. **astound′** (*arch.*), **astound′ed**, stunned: dazed: amazed; **astound′-ing**.—*adv*. **astound′ingly**.—*n*. **astound′ment**. [From the pa.p. **astoned**; see **astonish**.]

**astraddle**, *ə-strad′l*, *adv*. with legs wide apart. [Prep. **a**, on, and **straddle**.]

**astragal**, *as′trə-gəl*, *n*. a small semicircular moulding round a column or elsewhere (*archit.*): a round moulding near the mouth of a cannon: one of the bars that hold the panes of a window (*archit.*): (in *pl.*) dice.—*n*. **astragalus** (*as-trag′al-əs*), the ankle-bone: (*cap.*) the tragacanth and milk-vetch genus. [Gr. *astragalos*, a vertebra, ankle-bone, moulding, milk-vetch, in *pl*. dice.]

**astrakhan**, *as-trə-kan′*, *n*. lamb-skin with a curled wool from the Middle East; a rough fabric made in imitation of it. [*Astrakhan* on the Caspian Sea.]

**astral**, *as′trəl*, *adj*. belonging to the stars: starry: belonging to a mitotic aster: in theosophy, of a supersensible substance supposed to pervade all space and enter into all bodies.—**astral body**, an astral counterpart of the physical body: a ghost or wraith; **astral spirits**, spirits supposed to animate the heavenly bodies, forming, as it were, their souls. [L. *astrālis—astrum*, a star.]

**astrand**, *ə-strand′*, *adv*. on the strand. [Prep. **a**, on, and **strand**.]

**Astrantia**, *as-tran′shi-ə*, *n*. a genus of umbelliferous plants with showy petal-like bracts. [Gr. *astron*, star.]

**astraphobia**, **astrapophobia**, *as-trə-fō′bi-ə*, *-tra-pə-fō′bi-ə*, *n*. a morbid fear of thunder and lightning. [Gr. *astrapē*, lightning, *phobos*, fear.]

**astray**, *ə-strā′*, *adv*. out of the right way: out of one's reckoning: in a lost state. [Prep. **a**, on, and **stray**.]

**astrex** (**rabbit**). See **Rex**.

**astrict**, *ə-strikt′*, *v.t*. to bind, to compress: to constipate: to restrict.—*n*. **astric′tion** (*-shən*).—*adj*. **astrict′ive**, astringent.—*v.t*. **astringe** (*-strinj′*, *-strinzh′*), to bind: to draw together: to draw tight: to compress: to constipate.—*n*. **astrin′-gency** (*-jən-si*).—*adj*. **astrin′gent** (*ə-strin′jənt*), binding: contracting: drawing together: having power to contract organic tissues: styptic (of e.g. manner) sharp, austere, severe.—*n*. an astringent agent.—*adv*. **astrin′gently**. [L. *astrin-gĕre*, *astrictum—ad*, to, *stringĕre*, to draw tight.]

**astride**, *ə-strid′*, *adv*. in a striding position: with a leg on each side.—*prep*. astride of: on either side of. [Prep. **a**, on, and **stride**.]

**astringency**, etc. See under **astrict**.

**astringer**, a Shakespearian form of **austringer**.

**astro-**, *as′trō-*, *-tro′*, in composition, star.—*ns*. **as′trodome**, a small transparent observation dome on the top of the fuselage of an aeroplane: a sports centre covered by a huge translucent plastic dome, orig. one at Houston, Texas; **astrogeol'ogist**; **astrogeol'ogy**, study of the geology of the moon, etc.; **astroid**, a hypocycloid with four cusps; as'**trolabe** (-*lāb*), an old instrument for taking altitudes (from *lab*-, root of Gr. *lambanein*, to take); **astrol'atry**, star-worship (Gr. *latreiā*, worship); **astrol'oger**.— *adjs.* **astrolog'ic**, -al.—*adv.* **astrolog'ically**.—*ns.* **astrol'ogy**, orig. practical astronomy: now almost confined to the once-supposed art or science of the influence of the stars on human and terrestrial affairs (*judicial astrology*; Gr. *logos*, discourse); **astronaut** (*as'trō-nöt*; Gr. *nautēs*, a sailor), one engaged in space travel; **astronaut'ics**, the science of travel in space; **astron'omer**.—*adjs.* **astronom'ic**, -al, relating to astronomy: prodigiously great, like the distance of the stars—(**astronomical unit**, the earth's mean distance from the sun, about 92.9 million miles, used as a measure of distance within the solar system).—*v.i.* **astron'omise**, -ize, to study astronomy.—*n.* **astron'omy**, the science of the heavenly bodies (Gr. *nomos*, law).—*adj.* **astrophys'ical**.—*ns.* **astrophys'icist**; **astrophys'ics** (*pl.* in form, treated as *sing.*), the science of the chemical and physical condition of the heavenly bodies. [Gr. *astron*, star.]

**astrophel**, **astrofell**, *as'trō-fel*, *n.* an unidentified bitter starlike plant into which Spenser feigns Astrophel and Stella (Sir Philip Sidney and Penelope Devereux) to have been transformed—the seaside aster has been suggested. [Poss. Gr. *astron*, star, *phyllon*, leaf.]

**astrut**, *ə-strut'*, *adv.* protrudingly: distendedly.— *adj.* protruding: distended. [Prep. a, **strut**.]

**astute**, *as-*, *əs-tūt'*, in U.S. *-tōōt*, *adj.* shrewd: sagacious: wily.—Also **astucious** (*-tū'shəs*).— *adv.* **astu'ciously**.—*n.* **astucity** (*-tū'si-ti*).—*adv.* **astute'ly**.—*n.* **astute'ness**. [L. *astūtus—astus* (found in abl. *astū*), craft.]

**astylar**, *a-sti'lər*, *adj.* without columns. [Gr. *a*-, priv., *stylos*, a column.]

**asudden**, *ə-sud'ən*, *adv.* of a sudden. [Prep. a.]

**asunder**, *ə-sun'dər*, *adv.* apart: into parts: separately. [Prep. a.]

**aswarm**, *ə-swörm'*, *adv.* in swarms. [Prep. a, and **swarm** (1).]

**asway**, *ə-swā'*, *adv.* swayingly: in a sway. [Prep. a.]

**aswim**, *ə-swim'*, *adv.* afloat. [Prep. a.]

**aswing**, *ə-swing'*, *adv.* swingingly: in a swing. [Prep. a.]

**aswirl**, *ə-swûrl'*, *adv.* in a swirl. [Prep. a.]

**aswoon**, *ə-swōōn'*, *adv.* in a swoon. [Poss. for *on* or *in swoon*; or orig. a pa.p., M.E. *iswowen*—O.E. *geswōgen*, swooned (not known in other parts of speech).]

**asylum**, *ə-si'ləm*, *n.* a place of refuge for debtors and for those accused of crime: an institution for the care or relief of the unfortunate, as the blind or (*old-fashioned*) mentally ill: any place of refuge or protection:—*pl.* **asy'lums**. [L. *asylum*—Gr. *asylon* (neut.) inviolate—*a*-, priv., *sylon*, *sylē*, right of seizure.]

**asymmetry**, *a-sim'ə-tri*, *n.* want of symmetry.— *adjs.* **asymmetric** (*-et'rik*), -al.—*adv.* **asymmet'rically**. [Gr. *asymmetriā—a*-, priv., *symmetriā*, symmetry.]

**asymptote**, *a'sim-tōt*, (*math.*) *n.* a line that continually approaches a curve but never meets it.— *adjs.* **asymptotic** (*-tot'ik*), -al.—*adv.* **asymptot'ically**. [Gr. *asymptōtos—a*-, priv., *syn*, together, *ptōtos*, apt to fall, *piptein*, to fall.]

**asynartete**, *a-sin'är-tēt*, *adj.* not connected, consisting of two members having different rhythms. —*n.* a verse of such a kind.—Also **asynartetic** (*-tet'ik*). [Gr. *asynartētos—a*-, priv., *syn*, together, *artaein*, to knit.]

**asynchronism**, *a-sing'kro-nizm*, *n.* want of syn-

chronism or correspondence in time.—*adj.* **asyn'chronous**. [Gr. *a*-, priv., *syn*, together, *chronos*, time.]

**asyndeton**, *a-sin'də-ton*, (*rhet.*) *n.* a figure in which the conjunctions are omitted.—*adj.* **asyndet'ic**. [Gr. *asyndeton—a*-, priv., *syndetos*, bound together, *syn*, together, *deein*, to bind.]

**asynergia**, *as-in-ûr'ji-ə*, *n.* lack of coordination in action, as of muscles. [Gr. *a*-, priv., *syn*, together, *ergon*, work.]

**asyntactic**, *as-in-tak'tik*, *adj.* loosely put together, irregular, ungrammatical. [Gr. *asyntaktikos— a*-, priv., *syntaktos*—*syntassein*, to put in order together.]

**asystole**, *a-sis'to-lē*, (*med.*) *n.* inability of the heart to empty itself.—Also **asys'tolism**. [Gr. *a*-, priv., *systolē*, contraction.]

**at**, *at*, *ət*, *prep.* denoting (precise) position in space or time, or some kindred relation, as occupation, aim, activity. [O.E. *æt*; cf. Goth. and O.N. *at*, L. *ad*, Sans. *adhi*.]

**atabal**, *at'ə-bal*, *ä-tä-bäl'*, *n.* a Moorish kettledrum. [Sp.,—Ar. *at-tabl*, the drum.]

**atabeg**, **atabek**, *ät-ä-beg'*, -*bek'*, *n.* a ruler or high official. [Turk. *atabeg—ata*, father, *beg*, prince.]

**atabrin**, **atebrin**, *at'ə-brin*, *n.* mepacrine.

**atacamite**, *a-tak'ə-mit*, *n.* a mineral, a basic chloride of copper. [Atacama, in Chile.]

**atactic**. See **ataxia**.

**ataghan**. Same as **yataghan**.

**Atalanta**, *a-ta-lan'ta*, a fleet-footed Arcadian (or Boeotian) maiden who raced her suitors— defeated by Milanion (or Hippomenes), who dropped golden apples on the course to delay her.

**atalaya**, *ä-tä-lä'yä*, (Sp.,—Ar.) a watch-tower.

**ataman**, *at'a-man*, *n.* a Cossack headman or general—a hetman:—*pl.* **atamans**. [Russ.,— Ger. *hauptmann—haupt*, head, *mann*, man.]

**atap**, **attap**, *at'ap*, *n.* the nipa palm: its leaves used for thatching. [Malay.]

**ataraxia**, *at-ə-rak'si-ə*, **ataraxy**, *at'ə-rak-si*, *n.* calmness, the indifference aimed at by the Stoics. —*adjs.* and *ns.* **atarac'tic**, **atarax'ic**, tranquillising (drug). [Gr. *ataraxiā—a*-, priv., *tarassein*, to disturb.]

**à tâtons**, *a tä-t3*, (Fr.) gropingly.

**atavism**, *at'av-izm*, *n.* appearance of ancestral, but not parental, characteristics: reversion to an ancestral type.—*adj.* **atavist'ic**. [L. *atavus*, a great-great-great-grandfather, an ancestor— *avus*, a grandfather.]

**ataxia**, *a-tak'si-ə*, **ataxy**, *a-tak'si*, *at'aks-i*, *n.* inability to co-ordinate voluntary movements (*med.*; see **locomotor**): lack of order.—*adjs.* **atact'ic**, **atax'ic**, disorder—*a*-, priv., *taxis*, order.]

**Ate**, *ä'tē*, *ä'tē*, *ä'tä*, *n.* the Greek goddess of mischief and of all rash actions and their results. [Gr. *Atē*.]

**ate**, *et*, or *āt*, *pa.t.* of **eat**.

**atebrin**. See **atabrin**.

**ateleiosis**, *a-tel-i-ō'sis*, *n.* dwarfism without disproportion. [Gr. *ateleiōtos*, insufficient—*a*-, priv., *telos*, an end.]

**atelier**, *at'əl-yā*, *n.* a workshop, esp. an artist's studio. [Fr.]

**a tempo**, *ä tem'pō*, (It.) in time, i.e. revert to the previous or original tempo.

**Athanasian**, *ath-ə-nā'sh(y)ən*, -*z(h)yən*, *adj.* relating to Athanasius (*c.* 296-373), or to the creed erroneously attributed to him.

**athanasy**, *ə-than'ə-si*, *n.* deathlessness. [Gr. *athanasiā—a*-, priv., *thanatos*, death.]

**athanor**, *ath'ə-nör*, *n.* an alchemist's self-feeding digesting furnace. [Ar. *at-tannūr—al*, the, *tannūr*, furnace—*nūr*, fire.]

**Atharvaveda**, *ä-tär'vä-vä'dä*, *n.* one of the Vedas. [Sans.—*atharvan*, fire-priest, and *veda*, knowledge.]

atheism 80 atom

atheism, ā′thi-izm, n. disbelief in the existence of a god.—v.i. and v.t. a′theise, -ize, to talk or write as an atheist.—n. a′theist.—adjs. atheist′ic, -al.—adv. atheist′ically.—adj. a′theous (Milt.), atheistic: godless. [Gr. atheos—a-, priv., and theos, god.]
atheling, ath′əl-ing, (hist.) n. a member of a noble family: later, a prince of the blood royal, or the heir-apparent. [O.E. ætheling—æthele, noble; cf. Ger. adel.]
athematic, ath-i-mat′ik, adj. without a thematic vowel.—adv. athemat′ically. [Gr. a-, priv., and thematic.]
Athene, a-thē′nē, Athena, -na, n. Greek goddess of wisdom, born from the head of Zeus, tutelary goddess of Athens, identified by the Romans with Minerva.—n. Athenaeum (ath-ə-nē′əm), a temple of Athene: an ancient institution of learning, or literary university: a name sometimes taken by a literary institution, library, or periodical.—adj. Athenian (a-thē′ni-ən), of Athens.—n. a native or citizen of Athens or Attica.
atheology, ā-thi-ol′ə-ji, n. opposition to theology.—adj. atheological (-ə-loj′i-kl). [Gr. a-, priv., and theology.]
atherine, ath′ər-in, adj. of a genus (Atheri′na) of small fishes of a family (Atherinidae; -in′i-dē), akin to the grey mullets, sometimes sold as smelt.—n. an atherine fish. [Gr. atherinē, atherine.]
athermancy, ath-ûr′mən-si, n. impermeability to radiant heat.—adj. ather′manous. [Gr. a-, priv., thermainein, to heat.]
atheroma, ath′ər-ō-mə, n. a cyst with porridge-like contents: a thickening of the inner coat of arteries.—adj. atherōm′atous.—n. atherosclero′sis (-ō′sis), arteriosclerosis, or a form or stage of it. [Gr. athērōma—athērē or athārē, porridge.]
athetesis, ath-i-tē′sis, n. rejection as spurious.—v.t. ath′etise, -ize, to reject.—n. athetō′sis, involuntary movement of fingers and toes due to a lesion of the brain.—adj. ath′etoid.—n. a spastic who has involuntary movements. [Gr. athetos, without position, set aside, athetēsis, rejection—a-, priv., and the root of tithenai, to set.]
a′thing. See a′.
athirst, ə-thûrst′, adj. thirsty: eager. [O.E. ofthyrst. See thirst.]
athlete, ath′lēt, n. a contender for victory in feats of strength, speed, endurance, or agility: one vigorous in body or mind.—Also athlē′ta (obs.).—adj. athletic (-let′ik), of a long-limbed, large-chested, muscular type of body (anthrop.): relating to athletics: strong, vigorous.—adv. athlet′ically.—n. athlet′icism (-i-sizm), practice of, training in, or devotion to, athletics.—n.pl. athlet′ics, athletic sports: (treated as sing.) the practice of athletic sports.—athlete's foot, a contagious disease of the foot, caused by a fungus. [Gr. athlētēs—athlos, contest.]
at-home. See home.
athrill, ə-thril′, adv. in a thrill. [Prep. a.]
athrob, ə-throb′, adj. and adv. with throbs, throbbing. [Prep. a.]
athwart, ə-thwört′, prep. across.—adv. sidewise: transversely: awry: wrongly: perplexingly. [Prep. a.]
atilt, ə-tilt′, adv. on tilt: as a tilter. [Prep. a, and tilt (2).]
atimy, at′i-mi, n. loss of honour: in ancient Athens, loss of civil rights, public disgrace. [Gr. atimiā—a-, priv., and timē, honour.]
atingle, ə-ting′gl, adj. and adv. in a tingle. [Prep. a, and tingle (1).]
Atkins. See Tommy Atkins.
Atlas, at′ləs, n. the Titan who bore the heavens on his shoulders, and whose figure used to appear on title-pages of atlases: the African mountain range into which he was transformed: (pl.

Atlantes, at-lan′tēz), a figure of a man serving as a column in a building: (without cap.; pl. at′lases), the vertebra supporting the skull: a book of maps, plates, or the like: before metrication a size of drawing-paper.—adjs. Atlantē′-an, of Atlas: gigantic: of Atlantis; Atlan′tic, of Atlas: of the Atlantic Ocean.—n. the Atlantic Ocean, separating Europe and Africa from America.—ns. Atlan′tis, a traditional vanished island in the Atlantic Ocean; Atlantosaurus (-ō-sö′rəs; Gr. sauros, lizard), a gigantic Jurassic dinosaur of Colorado and Wyoming.—Atlantic Charter, an Anglo-American declaration during the Second World War of eight common principles of right in future peace. [Gr. Atlas, Atlantos.]
atlas, at′ləs, n. a silk-satin manufactured in the East. [Ar.]
atman, ät′mən, n. in Hinduism, the divine within the self. [Sans. ātman, self, soul.]
atmology, at-mol′ə-ji, n. the science of the phenomena of aqueous vapour.—n. atmol′ogist. [Gr. atmos, vapour, and logos, discourse.]
atmolysis, at-mol′i-sis, n. a method of separating mixed gases by their different rates of passage through a porous septum.—v.t. at′molyse, -yze, (-liz). [Gr. atmos, vapour, lysis, loosing—lyein, to loose.]
atmometer, at-mom′i-tər, n. an instrument for measuring the rate of evaporation from a moist surface. [Gr. atmos, vapour, metron, measure.]
atmosphere, at′məs-fēr, n. the gaseous envelope that surrounds the earth or any of the heavenly bodies: any gaseous medium: a unit of atmospheric pressure equal to the pressure exerted by a column of mercury 760 millimetres in height at 0°C, practically the same as standard atmosphere (see standard): a feeling of space and distance in a picture: any surrounding influence or pervading feeling (fig.).—adjs. atmospher′ic (-fer′-ik), -al, of or depending on the atmosphere.—adv. atmospher′ically.—n.pl. atmospher′ics, noises interfering with radio reception, due to electric disturbances in the ether.—atmospheric engine, a variety of steam-engine in which the steam is admitted only to the under side of the piston; atmospheric hammer, a hammer driven by compressed air. [Gr. atmos, vapour, sphairā, a sphere.]
atoc. See atok.
atocia, a-tō-shi-ə, n. sterility in a female.—n. atoke (at′ōk), the sexless part in certain polychaete worms.—adjs. atokous (at′ək-əs), at′okal, without offspring. [Gr. atokiā—a-, priv., tokos, birth, offspring.]
atok, atoc, a-tok′, n. a species of skunk. [Peruvian.]
atoll, at′ol, or ə-tol′, n. a coral island consisting of a circular belt of coral enclosing a central lagoon. [Name in Maldive Islands.]
atom, at′əm, n. a particle of matter so small that, so far as the older chemistry goes, it cannot be cut or divided: anything very small.—adjs. atomic (ə-tom′ik), pertaining to atoms: obtained by means of atomic fission, as atomic power: driven by atomic power, as atomic aircraft-carrier, icebreaker, merchantman, submarine, etc.: heated by atomic power, as atomic radiator; atom′ical.—ns. atomicity (at-əm-is′i-ti), state or fact of being composed of atoms: number of atoms in a molecule: valency; atomisā′tion,-z-, the reduction of liquids to the·form of spray.—v.t. at′omise, -ize, to reduce to atoms: to reduce (a liquid or solid) to a fine spray or minute particles: to destroy by bombing.—ns. atomi′ser, an instrument for discharging liquids in a fine spray; at′omism, the doctrine that atoms arranged themselves into the universe: the atomic theory: a theory that mental processes and psychological states can be analysed

fāte, fär; mē, hûr (her); mīne; mōte, för; mūte; mōōn, fōōt; dhen (then)

into simple elements (*psych.*); at′omist, one who believes in atomism.—*adj.* atomis′tic.—*adv.* atomist′ically.—*n.* at′omy, an atom, or mote: a pygmy (*Shak.*).—atom(ic) bomb, a bomb in which the nuclei of uranium or plutonium atoms bombarded by neutrons split with explosive transformation of part of their mass into energy; atomic energy, nuclear energy; atomic clock, a clock in which, to achieve greater accuracy, the oscillations of a quartz crystal (see quartz clock) are regulated by the vibration of certain atoms as a caesium atom; atomic mass unit, 1/12 of the mass of an atom of C-12; atomic number, the number of units of charge of positive electricity on the nucleus of an atom of an element: atomic philosophy, a system of philosophy enunciated by Democritus, which taught that the ultimate constituents of all things are indivisible particles, differing in form and in their relations to each other; atomic pile, a device for the controlled release of nuclear energy, e.g. a lattice of small rods of natural uranium embedded in a mass of pure graphite which serves to slow down neutrons; atomic second, a time interval whose measurement uses the frequency of radiation emitted or absorbed during transition from one energy state to another of a chosen atom; atomic theory, the hypothesis that all atoms of the same element are alike and that a compound is formed by union of atoms of different elements in some simple ratio; atomic time, time whose unit is the atomic second; atomic warfare, warfare using atomic bombs; atomic weight, the inferred weight of an atom of an element relatively to that of oxygen as 16 or, more recently, C-12 = 12; a′tom-smasher (*coll.*), an apparatus for breaking up the atom, any accelerator.—Atomic Energy Authority and Atomic Energy Commission, the respective bodies in Britain and the U.S.A. responsible for the development and control of atomic energy; primaeval atom, a hypothetical dense conglomerate from whose explosion 60 thousand million years ago the universe was (according to one theory) gradually formed. [Gr. *atomos*—*a-*, priv., and *tomos*, verbal adj. of *temnein*, to cut.]

atomy, *at′əm-i*, (*Shak.*) *n.* a skeleton, walking skeleton. [Formerly also *atamy* and *natomy*, for anatomy, mistakingly divided *an atomy.*]

atone (*Spens.* attone), *ə-tōn′*, *adv.* at one, at once, together.—*v.i.* originally to make *at one*, to reconcile; to give satisfaction or make reparation (with *for*): to make up for deficiencies: to agree, be in accordance (*Shak.*).—*v.t.* to appease, to expiate: to harmonise, or reconcile (*arch.*).—*ns.* atone′ment, the act of atoning; reconciliation: expiation: reparations: in Christian theology, the reconciliation of God and man by means of the incarnation and death of Christ; aton′er.—*advs.* aton′ingly; attonce (*ə-tons′*), attones (*ə-tōnz′*; both *Spens.*), at once: together.

atony, *at-ən-i*, *n.* want of tone or energy or of stress: debility: relaxation.—*adj.* atonal (*a-tō′-nl*; *mus.*), not referred to any scale or tonic.—*ns.* atonality (*at-ə-nal′i-ti*); atō′nalism.—*adj.* atonic (*a-ton′ik*), without tone (*pros.*): unaccented (*pros.*): debilitated.—*n.* atonic′ity (*-is′*), debility, weakness. [Gr. *atoniā*—*a-*, priv., *tonos*, tone, strength.]

atop, *ə-top′*, *adv.* on or at the top. [Prep. a, and top.]

à tort et à travers, *a tor ā a tra-ver*, (Fr.) at random; à toute force, *a tōōt fors*, (Fr.) by all means, absolutely; à toute hasard, *a tōō-ta-zär*, (Fr.) at all hazards; à tout prix, *a tōō prē*, (Fr.) at any price; à tout propos, *a tōō prō-pō*, (Fr.) on every occasion.

atrabilious, *at-rə-bil′yəs*, *adj.* of a melancholy temperament: hypochondriac: splenetic, acrimonious. [L. *āter*, *ātra*, black, *bilis*, gall, bile.]

atramental, *at-rə-men′təl*, *adj.* inky, black. [From L. *ātrāmentum*, ink—*āter*, black.]

à travers, *a tra-ver*, (Fr.) across, through.

atremble, *ə-trem′bl*, *adv.* in a tremble. [Prep. a.]

atresia, *ə-trēzh′(i)ə*, *n.* absence of, or closure of, a passage in the body. [Formed from Gr. *trēsis*, perforation.]

atrip, *ə-trip′*, *adv.* (of an anchor when it is just drawn out of the ground), in a perpendicular position: (of a sail) when it is hoisted from the cap, sheeted home and ready for trimming. [Prep. a.]

atrium, *ä′*, *ā′tri-əm* (L. *ät′ri-ōōm*), *n.* the entrance hall or chief apartment of a Roman house: a cavity or entrance (*zool.*):—*pl.* a′tria.—*adj.* a′trial. [L. *ātrium.*]

atrocious, *ə-trō′shəs*, *adj.* extremely cruel or wicked: heinous: very grievous: execrable.—*adv.* atro′ciously.—*ns.* atro′ciousness; atrocity (*ə-tros′i-ti*), atrociousness: an atrocious act. [L. *ātrōx*, *ātrōx*, *-ōcis*, cruel.]

atrophy, *at′rəf-i*, *n.* wasting away: degeneration: diminution of size and functional activity by disuse: emaciation.—*v.t.* and *v.i.* to cause or suffer atrophy: to starve, to waste away.—*adj.* at′rophied. [Gr. *a-*, priv., and *trophē*, nourishment.]

Atropos, *at′rō-pos*, *n.* the Fate that cuts the thread of life.—*ns.* At′ropa, the deadly nightshade genus of the potato family; at′ropin, atropine (*-pēn*, *-pin*, *-pin*), a poisonous alkaloid in deadly nightshade (atropia, *ə-trō′pi-ə*); at′ropism, atropin poisoning. [Gr. *Atropos.*]

atropous, *at′rō-pəs*, (*bot.*) *adj.* of an ovule, orthotropous. [Gr. *a-*, priv., *tropos*, turning.]

Ats, *ats*, *n.pl.* women of the Auxiliary Territorial Service. [From the initial letters; see under *Abbreviations.*]

attach, *ə-tach′*, *v.t.* to bind or fasten: to seize: to gain over: to connect, associate: to join in action, function, or affection: to arrest.—*v.i.* to adhere, to be fastened: to be attributable, incident (*to*): to come into effect (*rare*).—*adj.* attach′able.—*adj.* attached′.—*n.* attach′ment, act or means of fastening: a bond of fidelity or affection: seizure of goods or person by virtue of a legal process. [O.Fr. *atachier*, from *à* (—L. *ad*), and perhaps the root of tack.]

attaché, *ə-tash′ā*, *n.* a junior member of an ambassador's suite.— atta′ché-case, a small rectangular leather hand-bag for documents, etc. [Fr., attached.]

attack, *ə-tak′*, *v.t.* to fall upon violently: to assault: to assail: to begin to affect or act destructively upon.—*v.t.* and *v.i.* (*mus.*) to begin (a phrase or piece).—*n.* an assault or onset: the offensive part in any contest: the beginning of active operations on anything, even dinner: severe criticism or calumny: an access of illness: an executant's approach to a piece, or mode of beginning with respect to crispness, verve, and precision (*mus.*): in lacrosse, certain positions between centre and the opponents' goal.—*adj.* attack′able. [Fr. *attaquer*; a doublet of attach.]

attain, *ə-tān′*, *v.t.* to reach or gain by effort: to arrive at.—*v.i.* to come or arrive.—*adj.* attain′-able, that may be reached.—*ns.* attain′ableness; attain′ment, act of attaining: the thing attained: acquisition: (*pl.*) acquirements in learning. [O.Fr. *ataindre*—L. *attingĕre*—*ad*, to, *tangĕre*, to touch.]

attainder, *ə-tān′dər*, *n.* act of attainting: loss of civil rights through conviction for high treason (*law*).—*v.t.* attaint′, to convict: to deprive of rights by conviction for treason (*law*): to accuse: to disgrace, stain (from a fancied connection with *taint*).—*n.* the act of touching (*arch.*): a hit (in tilting): infection (*Shak.*): attainder: a stain, disgrace.—Older *pa.p.* attaint′ (*Shak.*),

Neutral vowels in unaccented syllables: el′ə-mənt; for certain sounds in foreign words, see p. viii

corrupted, tainted.—*ns.* **attaint'ment, attaint'ure.**
[O.Fr. *ataindre*—see **attain**.]
**attap.** See **atap.**
**attar,** *at'ər, n.* a very fragrant essential oil made in
Bulgaria and elsewhere, chiefly from the damask
rose.—Also **ott'o, ott'ar.** [Pers. *atar.*]
**attask,** *ə-täsk′, v.t.* to take to task (only in the
*pa.p.* **attaskt′,** a doubtful reading in Shak. *King
Lear*). [Pfx. *a-,* intensive, and **task.**]
**attemper,** *ə-tem′pər, v.t.* to mix in due proportion:
to modify or moderate: to adapt.—*adj.* **attem′-
pered.** [L. *attemperāre*—*ad,* to, *temperāre,* to
regulate.]
**attempt,** *ə-temt′, v.t.* to try, endeavour (to do, or
with *n.* of action): to try to obtain (*obs.*): to
tempt, entice (*arch.*): to make an attack upon
(*arch.* or *obs.*).—*v.i.* to make an attempt or trial.
—*n.* an effort: a personal assault: temptation
(*Milt.*): any act that can fairly be described as
one of a series which, if uninterrupted and
successful, would constitute a crime (*law*).—*n.*
**attemptabil′ity.**—*adj.* **attempt′able,** that may be
attempted.—*n.* **attempt′er** (*Milt.*), a tempter.
[O.Fr. *atempter*—L. *attentāre*—*ad,* and *temptāre, tentāre,* to try—*tenděre,* to stretch.]
**attend,** *ə-tend′, v.t.* to wait on: to accompany:
to be present at: to wait for: to give attention
to.—*v.i.* to yield attention: to act as an attendant: to wait, be consequent (with *to, on, upon*).
—*ns.* **attend′ance,** act of attending: attention,
careful regard (*B.*): presence: gathering of
persons attending; **attend′ancy,** attendance, a
retinue (*obs.*): relative position (*obs.*).—*adj.*
**attend′ant,** giving attendance: accompanying.—
*n.* one who attends or accompanies: a servant:
what accompanies or follows: one who owes a
duty or service to another (*law*).—*ns.* **attend′er,**
one who gives heed: a companion; **attend′-
ment** (*rare*), accompaniments: (*Spens.* **atten′de-
ment**), intention.—*adj.* **attent′** (*Spens., Shak.*).
giving attention.—*n.* (*Spens.*) attention.—*n.*
**atten′tion** (*-shən*), act of attending: steady
application of the mind: heed: civility, courtesy:
(in *pl.*) courtship: position of standing rigidly
erect with hands by the sides and heels together.
—*interj.* (*mil.*) a cautionary word calling for an
attitude of readiness to execute a command.—
*adj.* **attent′ive,** full of attention: courteous,
mindful.—*adv.* **attent′ively.**—*n.* **attent′iveness,**
[L. *attenděre, attentum; attentiō, -ōnis.*]
**attenuate,** *ə-ten′ū-āt, v.t.* to make thin or lean: to
break down into finer parts: to reduce in density:
to reduce in strength or value.—*v.i.* to become
thin or fine: to grow less.—*n.* **atten′uant,** anything that attenuates.—*adjs.* **atten′uate, atten′-
uated,** thin: thinned: dilute, rarefied: tapering.
—*n.* **attenuā′tion,** process of making slender:
reduction of intensity, density, force, or (of
bacteria) virulence: in homoeopathy, the reduction of the active principles of medicines to
minute doses: reduction in magnitude, amplitude, or intensity, arising from absorption or
scattering (*nuc., telecommunications*); **atten′-
uator.** [L. *attenuāre, -ātum*—*ad,* to, *tenuis,* thin.]
**attercop,** *at′ər-kop,* (*obs.* or *dial.*) *n.* a spider: an
ill-natured person. [O.E. *attorcoppa*—*attor,*
*ātor,* poison, and perh. *cop,* head, or *copp,* cup.]
**attest,** *ə-test′, v.t.* to testify or bear witness to: to
affirm by signature or oath: to give proof of, to
manifest: to call to witness (*obs.*).—*v.t.* and *v.i.*
to enrol for military service.—*v.i.* to bear witness.
—*n.* (*Shak.*) witness, testimony.—*adjs.* **attest′-
able, attest′ative.**—*n.* **attestā′tion** (*at-*), act of
attesting: administration of an oath.—*adj.*
**attest′ed,** certified free from the tubercle bacillus.
—*ns.* **attest′or, attest′er.** [L. *attestāri*—*ad,* to,
*testis,* a witness.]
**Attic,** *at′ik, adj.* of Attica or Athens: chaste,
refined, classical, in taste, language, etc., like the
Athenians.—*v.t.* **Atticise, -ize** (*at′i-siz*), to make

conformable to the language or idiom of Attica.
—*v.i.* to use the idioms of the Athenians: to side
with the Athenians: to affect Attic or Greek
style or manners.—*n.* **Att′icism** (*-sizm*).—**Attic**
**salt,** wit of a dry, delicate, and refined quality.
[Gr. *Attikos*—*Attikē,* Attica.]
**attic,** *at′ik, n.* in archit., a low story or structure
above the cornice of the main part of an elevation,
usually of the so-called Attic order, i.e. with
square columns or pilasters instead of pillars: a
skylighted room in the roof of a house. [The
structure was supposed to be in the Athenian
manner. See foregoing.]
**attire,** *ə-tīr′, v.t.* to dress, array or adorn: to
prepare.—*n.* dress: any kind of covering.—*ns.*
**attire′ment, attir′ing.** [O.Fr. *atirer,* put in order
—*à tire,* in a row—*à* (L. *ad*), to, and *tire, tiere,*
order, dress. See **tier.**]
**attitude,** *at′i-tūd, n.* posture, or position: a studied
or affected posture: a position on one leg with
the other leg extended behind, modelled on the
position of Giovanni Bologna's flying mercury
(*ballet*): of an aircraft in flight, or on the ground,
the angles made by its axes with the relative
airflow, or with the ground, respectively: the
tilt of a vehicle measured in relation to the surface of the earth as horizontal plane (*space
flight*): any condition of things or relation of
persons viewed as expressing some thought,
feeling, etc.—*adj.* **attitud′inal.**—*n.* **attitudinā′rian,**
one who studies attitudes.—*v.i.* **attitud′inise,
-ize,** to assume affected attitudes.—*n.* **attitudini′-
ser, -izer.**—**attitude angle,** in a cornering motor
vehicle, the slight angle between the track of the
vehicle and the direction in which the tyres are
pointing.—**to strike an attitude,** to assume a
position or figure to indicate a feeling or emotion
not really felt. [Fr. *attitude* or It. *attitudine*—L.
*aptitūdō, -inis*—*aptus,* fit.]
**atto-,** *pfx.* one million million millionth, $10^{-18}$.
**attollent,** *ə-tol′ənt, adj.* lifting up, raising.—*n.* a
muscle that raises. [L. *attollēns, -entis,* pr.p. of
*attollěre,* to lift up—*ad,* to, *tollěre,* to lift.]
**attorn,** *ə-tûrn′,* (*law*) *v.t.* to transfer to another.—
*v.i.* to accept tenancy under a new landlord.—
**attorney** *v.i.* (*pl.* **attor′neys;** O.Fr. pa.p. *atorné*), one
legally authorised to act for another: one legally
qualified to manage cases in a court of law: a
solicitor.—*v.t.* (*Shak.*) to perform by proxy: to
employ as a proxy.—*ns.* **attor′neydom; attor′-
neyism; attor′neyship; attorn′ment,** acknowledgment of a new landlord.—*n.* **Attor′ney-
Gen′eral,** the chief law-officer for England, Eire,
a dominion, colony, etc.: the king's attorney in
the duchies of Lancaster and Cornwall, and the
county palatine of Durham: in the United
States, one of the seven officials who constitute
the president's cabinet, the head of the Department of Justice: also the legal adviser of a State
governor.—**attorney at law,** or **public attorney,** a
professional and duly qualified legal agent;
**attorney in fact,** or **private attorney,** one duly
appointed by power of attorney to act for another
in matters of contract, money payments, and the
like; **letter, warrant,** or **power of attorney,** a
formal instrument by which one person authorises another to perform certain acts for him.
[L.L. *attornāre,* to assign; see **turn.**]
**attract,** *ə-trakt′, v.t.* to draw or cause to approach
otherwise than by material bonds: to allure: to
entice.—*adj.* **attract′able,** that may be attracted.
—*adv.* **attract′ingly.**—*ns.* **attract′ant,** something
that attracts, esp. that effects communication in
insects and animals; **attrac′tion,** act of attracting: an attracting force: that which attracts.—
*adj.* **attract′ive,** having the power of attracting:
alluring.—*adv.* **attract′ively.**—*ns.* **attract′iveness;
attract′or.** [L. *attrahěre, attractum*—*ad,* to,
*trahěre,* to draw.]
**attrahent,** *at′rə-hənt, ə-trā′ənt, adj.* attracting or

drawing.—*n.* that which attracts. [L. *attrahēns, -entis,* pr.p. of *attrahēre.* See **attract.**]

**attrap,** *ə-trap',* (*Spens.*) *v.t.* to adorn with trappings: to dress or array. [L. *ad,* to, **trap** (4).]

**attribute,** *ə-trib'ūt* (*Milt. at'ri-būt*), *v.t.* to ascribe, assign, or consider as belonging.—*n.* (*at'*) that which is attributed: that which is inherent in, or inseparable from, anything: that which can be predicated of anything: a quality or property: an accessory: a conventional symbol: a word added to another to denote an attribute (*gram.*).—*adj.* **attrib'utable.**—*n.* **attribution** (*at-ri-bū'shən*), act of attributing: that which is attributed.—*adj.* **attrib'utive,** expressing an attribute.—*n.* a word added to another to denote an attribute (*gram.*).—*adv.* **attrib'utively.** [L. *attribuēre, -tribūtum—ad,* to, *tribuēre,* to give.]

**attrist,** *ə-trist',* (*obs.*) *v.t.* to sadden. [Fr. *attrister*—L. *ad,* to, *tristis,* sad.]

**attrite,** *ə-trit',* *adj.* worn by rubbing or friction: repentant through fear of punishment, not yet from the love of God (*theol.*).—*n.* **attrition** (*a-* or *ə-trish'ən*), rubbing together: wearing down: a defective or imperfect sorrow for sin (*theol.*): the wearing down of an adversary, resistance, resources, etc (*fig.*). [L. *attritus—atterēre—ad,* to, and *terēre, tritum,* to rub.]

**attuition,** *at-ū-ish'ən, n.* a mental operation intermediate between sensation and perception.—*adjs.* **attui'tional; att'uent,** performing the function of attuition.—*v.t.* **att'uite** (*-it*), to be conscious of by attuition.—*adj.* **attu'itive.**—*adv.* **attu'itively.** [L. *ad,* to, *tuēri,* to attend to.]

**attune,** *ə-tūn',* in U.S. *-tōon, v.t.* to put in tune: to make to accord: to arrange fitly: to make musical.—*n.* **attune'ment.** [L. *ad,* to, and **tune.**]

**atwain,** *ə-twān',* (*arch.*) *adv.* in twain: asunder. [Prep. *a,* and **twain.**]

**atweel,** *ə-twēl',* (*Scot.*) *adv.* or *interj.* well: indeed. [**wat weel,** i.e. wot well.]

**atween,** *ə-twēn',* (*Spens.*) *adv.* betweenwhiles.—*prep.* **between.**—*adv.* and *prep.* **atwixt'** (*Spens.*), **betwixt.**

**atypical,** *a-, ā-tip'i-kl, adj.* not typical. [Gr. *a-,* priv., and **type.**]

**aubade,** *ō-bäd', n.* a musical announcement of dawn: a sunrise song. [Fr.,—*aube,* dawn—Prov. *alba,* dawn.]

**auberge,** *ō-berzh', n.* an inn.—*n.* **aubergiste** (*ō-ber-zhēst'*), an inn-keeper. [Fr., of Gmc. origin. See **harbour.**]

**aubergine,** *ō'ber-jēn, -zhēn, n.* the fruit of the eggplant, the brinjal: its purple colour. [Fr. dim. of *auberge,* a kind of peach—Sp. *albérchigo*—Ar. *al,* the, Sp. *pérsigo*—L. *persicum,* a peach.]

**Aubrietia,** *ō-brē', ō-bri-ē'sh(y)ə, n.* a purpleflowered Mediterranean genus of trailing cruciferous plants, much grown in rock-gardens, etc. [After Claude *Aubriet* (*c.* 1665-1742), naturalist-painter.]

**auburn,** *ō'bûrn, adj.* orig. light yellow: reddish brown. [L.L. *alburnus,* whitish—L. *albus,* white.]

**au contraire,** *ō kɔ̄-trer,* (Fr.) on the contrary.

**au courant,** *ō kōō-rä,* (Fr.) in the stream: well-informed: well up in the facts or situation.

**auction,** *ök'shən, n.* a public sale at which goods are sold to the highest bidder: auction bridge.—*v.t.* to sell by auction.—*adj.* **auc'tionary.**—*n.* **auctioneer',** one who sells or is licensed to sell by auction.—*v.t.* to sell by auction.—**auction bridge,** a development of the game of bridge in which the players bid for the privilege of choosing trump suit or no-trumps.—**Dutch auction,** a kind of auction at which the salesman starts at a high price, and comes down till he meets a bidder. [L. *auctiō, -ōnis,* an increasing —*augēre, auctum,* to increase.]

**auctorial,** *ök-tō'ri-əl, -tō', adj.* of an author or his trade. [L. *auctor, -ōris,* author.]

**Aucuba,** *ō'kū-bə, n.* the Japan laurel genus. [Jap.]

**audacious,** *ö-dā'shəs, adj.* daring: bold: impudent.—*adv.* **audā'ciously.**—*ns.* **audā'ciousness, audacity** (*ö-das'i-ti*). [Fr. *audacieux*—L. *audāx* —*audēre,* to dare.]

**audax et cautus,** *ö'daks et kö'tus, ow'daks et kow'-tōōs,* (L.) bold and cautious.

**au désespoir,** *ō dā-zes-pwär,* (Fr.) in despair.

**audible,** *öd'i-bl, adj.* able to be heard.—*ns.* **audibil'ity, aud'ibleness.**—*adv.* **aud'ibly.**—*n.* **aud'ience,** the act of hearing: a judicial hearing: admittance to a hearing: a ceremonial interview: an assembly of hearers or spectators: a court of government or justice in Spanish America· the territory administered by it.—*adj.* **aud'ient,** listening: paying attention.—*n.* a hearer.—*adj.* **aud'ile,** pertaining to hearing.—*n.* one inclined to think in terms of sound.—**audio-,** in composition, pertaining to sound, esp. broadcast sound: pertaining to, using, or involving, audio-frequencies.—*n.* an acoustic device by which an airman returning to an aircraft-carrier knows when he is at a proper speed for landing.—*ns.* **aud'io-engineer',** one concerned with the transmission and reception of broadcast sound; **audio-frequency** (*ö'di-ō-frē'kwən-si*), a frequency of oscillation which, when the oscillatory power is converted into a sound pressure, is perceptible by the ear; **audio-loca'tion,** echo-location; **audiol'ogist; audiol'ogy,** the science of hearing; **audiom'eter,** instrument for measuring differences in hearing: one for measuring minimum intensities of sounds which, for specified frequencies, are perceivable by the ear.—*adj.* **audiomet'ric.**—*ns.* **audiometrician** (*-mi-trish'ən*); **aud'iophil(e)** (*-fil, -fīl*), an enthusiast for the true reproduction of recorded or broadcast sound; **aud'io-typ'ist,** typist able to type directly material reproduced by a Dictaphone.—*adj.* **audio-vis'ual,** concerned simultaneously with seeing and hearing.—*ns.* **aud'iphone,** an instrument which pressed against the teeth, communicates examination of accounts by an authorised person or persons: a calling to account generally: a statement of account: a periodical settlement of accounts (*obs.*): audience, hearing (*obs.*). —*v.t.* to examine and verify by reference to vouchers, etc.: to attend (a class) without intending to take any examination (*U.S.*).—*ns.* **audi'tion** (*ö-dish'ən*), the sense, or an act, of hearing: a trial performance by an applicant for an acting, etc., position (also *v.t.*): mode of hearing: something heard (*rare*); **aud'itor,** a hearer: one who audits accounts—*fem.* **aud'itress; auditor'ium,** in a theatre, or the like, the space allotted to the hearers: the reception-room of a monastery: hall (*U.S.*); **aud'itorship.** —*adj.* **aud'itory,** relating to the sense of hearing. —*n.* an audience: a place where lectures, etc., are heard.—**audience participation,** drawing audience into a theatrical performance by direct appeals to its members; **audio-visual aids,** material such as pictures, closed-circuit TV, teaching machines, used in the classroom; **audit ale,** an ale of special quality brewed for use on the day of audit. [L. *audīre,* to hear.]

**audita querela,** *ö-dī'tə kwə-rē'lə, ow-dē'tä kwe-rā'lä,* (L.) the suit having been heard—name of a writ giving leave to appeal.

**auf,** *öf, n.* an elf's child, an oaf. [O.N. *ālfr,* elf.]

**au fait,** *ō fe,* (Fr.) well-acquainted with a matter: expert.

**aufgabe,** *owf'gä-bə, n.* (*psych.*) a task set as an experiment, etc. [Ger.]

**aufklärung,** *owf-kle'rōōng,* (Ger.) enlightenment, esp. the 18th-century intellectual movement.

**au fond,** *ō fɔ̄,* (Fr.) at bottom.

**au fromage,** ō fro-mäzh, (Fr.) with cheese.

**auf wiedersehen,** owf vē'dǝr-zā-ǝn, (Ger.) goodbye till we meet again.

**Augean,** ö-, ow-jē'ǝn, adj. filthy: difficult. [From *Augeas*, king of Elis into whose uncleansed oxstalls Herakles turned the river Alpheus.]

**auger,** ö'gǝr, n. a carpenter's boring tool.—ns. **au'ger-bit,** an auger that fits into a carpenter's brace; **au'ger-hole; au'ger-shell,** Terebra; **au'ger-worm,** the goat-moth larva, which bores trees. [From *nauger* (an auger for a nauger)—O.E. *nafugār—nafu,* a nave of a wheel, gār, a piercer. See nave, gore, 2.]

**Auger effect,** ö-zhā, non-radiative transition of an atom from an excited state to one of lower energy with emission of an electron (Auger electron). [Pierre *Auger*, physicist.]

**aught,** öt, n. a whit: ought: anything: a part. [O.E. ā-wiht contr. to āht (whence ought), shortened to aht (whence aught); ā-wiht is from ā, ō, ever, and wiht, creature, whit, wight.]

**augite,** ö-jit -g,it, n. one of the pyroxene group of minerals, closely allied to hornblende, usually greenish, an essential component of many igneous rocks.—adj. augitic (-jit', -git'). [Gr. augē, brightness.]

**augment,** ög-ment', v.t. to increase: to make larger.—v.i. to grow larger.—n. aug'ment (-mǝnt), increase: the prefixed vowel or initial vowel-lengthening in some past tenses of the verb in Sanskrit and Greek: sometimes applied also to such inflectional prefixes as the ge- of the German perfect participle.—adjs. augment'able; augment'ative, having the quality of power of augmenting.—n. a word formed from another to express increase of its meaning (gram.).—ns. augmentā'tion, increase: addition: an additional charge in a coat-of-arms bestowed as a mark of honour (her.): the repetition of a melody in notes of greater length than the original (mus.): in Scots law an increase of stipend obtained by a parish minister by an action raised in the Court of Teinds against the titular and heritors.—adj. augment'ed.—ns. augment'er; augment'or, a nerve that increases the rate of activity of an organ.—augmented interval, one increased by a semitone.—Augmented Roman Alphabet, earlier name for Initial Teaching Alphabet. [L. augēre, increase.]

**au grand sérieux,** ō grä sā-ryø, (Fr.; now très au sérieux, tre-zō), in all seriousness.

**au gratin,** ō gra-tẽ, (Fr.) cooked covered with breadcrumbs or grated cheese, or with both.

**augur,** ö'gǝr, n. among the Romans, one who sought knowledge of secret or future things by observing the flight and the cries of birds: a diviner: a soothsayer: an augury or portent (Shak., app.).—v.t. to foretell from signs.—v.i. to guess or conjecture: to forebode.—adj. au'gural (-ū-rǝl; -yǝr-ǝl).—ns. au'gürer (Shak.), an augur; au'gürship; au'gûry, the art or practice of auguring; an omen. [L.; prob. from avis, bird.]

**august,** ö-gust', adj. venerable: imposing: sublime: majestic.—adv. august'ly.—n. august'ness. [L. augustus—augēre, to increase, honour.]

**august, auguste,** ow-gōōst', n. a circus clown of the maladroit type. [Ger., Augustus.]

**August,** ö'gǝst, n. the eighth month of the year. [After the Roman emperor *Augustus*.]

**Augustan,** ö-gust'ǝn, adj. pertaining to the Emperor Augustus, or to the time in which he reigned (31 B.C.—A.D. 14)—the most brilliant age in Roman literature: hence pertaining to any similar age, as the reign of Anne in English, and that of Louis XIV in French literature: classic: refined.

**Augustine,** ö'gust-in, ö-gust'in, **Augustinian,** -tin'i-ǝn, n. one of any order of monks or nuns whose rule is based on the writings of St.

Augustine: one who holds the opinions of St Augustine, esp. on predestination and irresistible grace (theol.).—adj. Augustin'ian, of or relating to St. Augustine.—n. Augustin'ianism.—Augustinian canons, or Austin canons (see canon); Augustinian or Austin friars, or hermits, the fourth order of mendicant friars, wearing a black habit, but not to be confused with the Black Friars or Dominicans.

**au jour le jour,** ō zhōōr lǝ zhōōr, (Fr.) from day to day, from hand to mouth.

**auk,** ök, n. a short-winged bird of the family Alcidae.—n. auk'let, one of the smaller birds of the family.—great auk, garefowl, extinct c. 1844; little auk, rotche. [O.N. ālka.]

**aula,** ö'la, n. a hall.—adj. aulā'rian, relating to a hall.—n. at Oxford, a member of a hall, as distinguished from a collegian.—adj. au'lic.—Aula Regis, or Curia Regis, (hist.) a feudal assembly of tenants-in-chief: the Privy Council: the Court of King's Bench; Aulic Council (Ger. Reichshofrat), a court or personal council of the Holy Roman Empire, established in 1501 by Maximilian I, and co-ordinate with the Imperial Chamber (Reichskammergericht). [L. aula, Gr. aulē, court, courtyard, hall.]

**auld,** öld, (Scot.) adj. old—adjs. auld'-farr'ant (i.e. old-favouring), old-fashioned: precocious; auld'-warld, old world, ancient.—the Auld Kirk, the Church of Scotland: whisky; auld lang syne, lit. old long since, long ago; Auld Reekie, old smoky, i.e. Edinburgh. [O.E. ald.]

**aumail,** ö-māl', v.t. to enamel: to figure or variegate (Spens.). [See enamel.]

**aumbry,** öm'bri, n. Same as ambry.

**au mieux,** ō myø, (Fr.) on the best of terms.

**aumil,** ö'mil, ä'mil, n. an amildar.

**au naturel,** ō na-tü-rel', (Fr.) in the natural state: cooked plainly.

**aunt,** änt, n. a father's or a mother's sister: an uncle's wife: an old woman (obs.): a gossip (obs.): a procuress (obs.).—dim. aunt'ie, aunt'y.—Aunt Sally, a pastime at fairs, in which sticks or balls are thrown to smash a pipe in the mouth of a wooden figure: a target for abuse (fig.). [O.Fr. ante—L. amita, a father's sister.]

**aunter,** ön'tǝr, n. an old form of adventure. [O.Fr. aventure.]

**au pair,** ō per, (Fr.) adj. orig. by mutual service without payment: used of arrangement whereby girls perform light domestic duties in exchange for board and lodging and pocket-money.—n. an au pair girl.

**au pied de la lettre,** ō pyä dǝ la letr', (Fr.) literally.

**au pis aller,** ō pē-za-lā, (Fr.) at the worst.

**au poids de l'or,** ō pwa dǝ lor, (Fr.) at its weight in gold, very dear.

**au premier,** ō prǝ-myā, (Fr.) on the first (floor).

**aura,** ö'ra, n. a supposed subtle emanation, esp. that essence which is claimed to emanate from all living things and to afford an atmosphere for occult phenomena: air, distinctive character (fig.): peculiar sensations that precede an attack in epilepsy, hysteria, and certain other ailments (path.):—pl. aur'ae (-ē), aur'as.—adj. aur'al, pertaining to the air, or to a subtle vapour or exhalation arising from a body. [L. aura, a breeze.]

**aural,** ö'ral, adj. pertaining to the ear.—adv. aur'ally. [L. auris, ear.]

**aura popularis,** ö'ra po-pū-la'ris, ow-ra po-pōō-lä'ris-), (L.) the breeze of popular favour.

**aurate,** ö'rāt, n. a salt of auric acid.—adjs. au'rated, gold-coloured: compounded with auric acid; aurē'ate, gilded: golden: floridly rhetorical.—ns. aurē'ity, the peculiar properties of gold; Aurē'lia, a common genus of jellyfishes: formerly, a chrysalis, from its golden colour.—adj. aurē'lian, golden: of an aurelia.—Also n. (obs.) a lepidopterist.—ns. aurē'ola, aureole (ö'ri-ōl), a crown, or an increment to the ordinary blessedness of heaven, gained by virgins, martyrs, and doctors (*theol.*): the gold or coloured disk or ring round the head in a picture, symbolising glory: a glorifying halo (*fig.*): a halo or corona around the sun or moon, or the clear space within it (*meteor.*): the coloured rings around the spectre of the Brocken (*meteor.*): (apparently erroneously) a halo surrounding the whole figure (e.g. a *vesica piscis*): any halo-like appearance.—*adj.* au'reoled, encircled with an aureole.—*ns.* aureomycin (*-mi'sin*) an antibiotic used against typhus and other diseases, got from Strepto*myces aureo*faciens; au'reus, a gold coin of the Roman empire.—*adj.* au'ric, pertaining to gold: containing trivalent gold (*chem.*).— auric acid, a hypothetic acid of composition HAuO₂—usually applied to auric hydroxide, Au(OH)₃, or auric oxide, Au₂O₃. [L. *aurum*, gold.]

aurea mediocritas, ö're-a mē-dē-o'kri-tas, ow'rä-a me-di-o'kri-täs, (L.) the golden or happy mean.

au reste, ö rest, (Fr.) as for the rest: besides.

au revoir, ö rə-vwär, (Fr.) goodbye until we meet again.

auricle, ör'i-kl, *n.* the external ear: either of the two upper cavities of the heart into which the blood comes from the veins: an earlike lobe of a leaf, etc.—*adj.* aur'icled, having appendages like ears.—*n.* auric'ula, a species of primula (bear's ear, or dusty-miller): (*cap.*) a genus of gasteropod molluscs.—*adj.* auric'ular, pertaining to the ear: known by hearing, or by report: told privately.—*adv.* auric'üiarly.—*adjs.* auric'ülate, auric'ülated, ear-shaped.—auricular confession, confession to a priest. [L. *auricula*, dim. of *auris*, the ear.]

auriferous, ör-if'ər-əs, *adj.* bearing or yielding gold.—*v.t.* and *v.i.* aur'ify, to turn into gold. [L. *aurifer*—*aurum*, gold, *ferre*, to bear; *facĕre*, to make.]

auriform, ör'i-förm, *adj.* ear-shaped. [L. *auris*, ear, and form.]

Auriga, ö-rī'ga, a northern constellation. [L. *auriga*, charioteer.]

Aurignacian, ö-rig-nä'sh(y)en, *adj.* belonging to an upper Palaeolithic culture that succeeded the Mousterian and preceded the Solutrean. [*Aurignac*, in Haute-Garonne, where objects of this culture have been found.]

aurist, ör'ist, *n.* one skilled in diseases of the ear. [L. *auris*, ear.]

aurochs, ör', owr'oks, *n.* the extinct urus or wild ox: (erroneously), the European bison. [O.H.G. ûr-ohso—ûr (adopted into L. as ūrus, into Gr. as ouros), and ohso, ox.]

Aurora, ö-rö'rə, -rö', *n.* the dawn: the goddess of dawn (without *cap.*) a rich orange colour: a luminous meteoric phenomenon of electrical character seen in and towards the Polar regions, with a tremulous motion, and streamers of light: —*pl.* auro'ras, -rae.—*adjs.* auro'ral, auro'rean, pertaining to the dawn or the aurora: rosy: fresh and beautiful.—*adv.* auro'rally.—aurora borealis (bö-ri-ä'lis, -ä'lis or bö-), or septentrionalis (sep-ten-tri-on-ä'lis), the northern aurora or northern lights; aurora australis (ös-trä'lis), the southern lights, a similar phenomenon in the southern hemisphere. [L. *Aurōra.*]

aurous, ör'əs, *adj.* containing univalent gold. [L. *aurum*, gold.]

aurum potabile, ö'rum po-tab'i-lē, ow'room pö-täb'i-le, (L.) *lit.* potable gold, a former medicine or cordial containing a small quantity of gold.

auscultation, ös-kult-ā'shən, *n.* the art of discovering the condition of the lungs and heart by applying the ear to the stethoscope.—*v.t.* and *v.i.* aus'cultate, to examine by auscultation.—*n.* aus'cultător, one who practises auscultation: an instrument for the purpose: in Germany, formerly one who had passed his first public exa-

mination in law, and who was merely retained, not yet employed or paid by government.—*adj.* auscult'atory. [L. *auscultāre*, to listen.]

au second, ö sə-gõ, (Fr.) on the second (floor).

au secours, ö sə-koor, (Fr.) help!

au sérieux, ö sä-ryø, (Fr.) seriously.

ausgleich, ows'glihh, (Ger.) a settlement: an arrangement: agreement between Austria and Hungary in 1867 (*hist.*).

ausländer, ows'len-dər, (Ger.) a foreigner.

Ausonian, ö-sö'ni-ən, *adj.* Italian. [L. *Ausonia*, a poetical name for Italy.]

auspice, ös'pis, *n.* an omen drawn from observing birds: augury: prognostic: (in *pl.*) patronage. —*v.t.* auspicate (ös'pi-kāt), to foreshow: to initiate or inaugurate with hopes of good luck.— *adj.* auspicious (*-pish'əs*), having good auspices or omens of success: favourable: fortunate: propitious.—*adv.* auspi'ciously.—*n.* auspi'ciousness. [Fr.,—L. *auspicium*—*auspex, auspicis*, a bird-seer, from *avis*, bird, and *specĕre*, to look, to observe.]

Aussie, ös'i, (*slang*.) *n.* and *adj.* Australian.

austenite, ös'tə-nit, *n.* a solid solution of carbon or other substance in one of the forms of iron.— austenit'ic (*-it'*) stainless steels, stainless steels composed chiefly of austenite.

Auster, ös'tər, *n.* the south wind. [L.]

austere, ös-tēr', *adj.* sour and astringent: harsh: severe: stern: grave: severe in self-discipline: severely simple, without luxury.—*adv.* austere'ly. —*ns.* austere'ness, austerity (*-ter'*), quality of being austere: severity of manners or life: harshness: asceticism: severe simplicity of style, dress, or habits.—*adj.* evincing or adopted in austerity. [L. *austērus*—Gr. *austēros—auein*, to dry.]

Austin. See Augustine.

austral, ös'trəl, *adj.* southern.—*adj.* Australasian (*-ā'zhən*), pertaining to Australasia, or the lands that lie south-east of Asia.—*n.* a native or colonist of one of these.—*adj.* Austrā'lian, of or pertaining to Australia.—*n.* an aboriginal native of Australia proper, later also a native or resident white.—*ns.* Australian'ism, an Australian idiom: feeling for Australia; aus'tralite, tektite found in the interior of Australia; Australopithecus (*-pith'ə-kas* or *-pi-thē'kəs*), a genus of extinct primates, represented by skulls, etc., found in southern Africa, belonging to the subfamily Australopithecinae.—*adj.* and *n.* Australopithecine.—*n.* Aus'tralorp, one of an Australian breed of hen.—Australian rules, an Australian mixture of association and rugby football played by eighteen a side with a rugby ball—familiarly rules. [L. *austrālis—Auster*, the south wind.]

Austrian, ös'tri-ən, *adj.* of or pertaining to Austria. —*n.* a native or citizen of Austria.

Austric, ös'trik, *adj.* belonging to a family of languages divided into Austroäsiat'ic (in eastern India and Indo-China, including the Munda or Kolarian, Mon-Khmer and Khasi groups, and the languages of the Semang and Sakai) and Austronē'sian (including the Indonesian, or Malay, Polynesian, Micronesian, and Melanesian groups). [L. *Auster*, south wind, Asiatic, and Gr. *nēsos*, island.]

austringer, ös'strin-jər, *n.* a keeper of goshawks.— Also a'stringer, ostreger (os'tri-jər; *Shak.*). [O.Fr. *ostruchier*.]

Austroasiatic, Austronesian. See Austric.

aut-. See auto-.

autacoid, ö'tə-koid, *n.* an internal secretion that excites or inhibits action in various tissues: a hormone or chalone. [Gr. *autos*, self, *akos*, drug.]

autarchy, öt'är-ki, *n.* absolute power.—*adjs.* autar'chic(al).—*n.* aut'archist. [Gr. *autos*, self, and *archein*, to rule.]

autarky, öt'är-ki, *n.* self-sufficiency.—*adjs.* autar'-

Neutral vowels in unaccented syllables: el'ə-mənt; for certain sounds in foreign words, see p. viii

kic, -al.—n. aut'arkist. [Gr. autarkeiă—autos, self, arkeein, to suffice.]

autecology, ö-tek-ol'əji, n. (study of) the ecology of an individual organism or species.—adjs. autecolog'ic, -al. [aut-, and ecology.]

auteur. ö-tœr, (Fr.) the director/creator of a film.

authentic, -aι, o-thent'ιk, -əι, adjs. genuine: authoritative: true, entitled to acceptance, of established credibility: (of writing) trustworthy, as setting forth real facts: own, proper (Milt.): applied in music to old modes having their sounds within the octave above the final—opp. to plagal: in existentialism, used to describe the way of living of one who takes full cognisance of the meaninglessness of the world yet deliberately follows a consistent course of action.—adv. authent'ically.—v.t. authen'ticate, to make authentic: to prove genuine: to give legal validity to: to certify the authorship of.—ns. authenticā'tion; authen'ticātor; authenticity (ö-thən-tis'i-ti), quality of being authentic: state of being true or in accordance with fact: genuineness. [Gr. authentikos, warranted—autos, self.]

author, öth'ər, n. one who brings anything into being: a beginner of any action or state of things: the original writer of a book, article, etc.: elliptically, an author's writings: one's authority for something (arch.):—Also v.t. —n.fem. auth'oress.—n. auth'orcraft.—adjs. authorial (-thö', -thö'), auth'orish.—v.t. auth'orise, -ize, to give authority to: to sanction: to justify: to establish by authority.—adj. authoris'able.— n. authorisā'tion.—adj. auth'orless, anonymous. —ns. auth'oring; auth'orism, state or quality of being an author; auth'orship.—Authorised Version, the English translation of the Bible completed in 1611. [Through Fr. from L. auctor—augēre, auctum, to increase, to produce.]

authority, öth-or'it-i, n. legal power or right: power derived from office or character or prestige: weight of testimony: permission: a person or body holding power: an expert: a passage ᴏι book referred to in witness of a statement: the original bestower of a name (biol.).—adj. authoritā'rian, setting authority above liberty.—Also n.—n. authoritā'rianism.— adj. author'itātive, having the sanction or weight of authority: dictatorial.—adv. author'itātively.—n. author'itātiveness. [L. auctōritas, -ātis—auctor.]

autism, öt'izm, n. absorption in imaginative activity directed by the thinker's wishes, with loss of contact with reality: an abnormality of childhood development affecting language and social communication.—adj. autis'tic. [Gr. autos, self.]

auto-, aut-, ö-t(ö)-, in composition, self: same: self-caused: automobile: automatic. [Gr. autos, self.]

auto, ö'tö, n. (chiefly U.S.) short for automobile. [Gr. autos, self.]

auto, ä'ōö-tö, (Sp. and Port.) an act: a drama, esp. a short religious one: an auto-da-fé.

autobahn, ow'tö-bän, (Ger.) an arterial double road for motor traffic only.

autobiography, ö-tö-bī-og'rə-fi, n. a person's life written by himself.—n. autobiog'rapher.—adjs. autobiographic (-ö-graf'ik), -al. [Gr. bios, life, graphein, to write.]

autobus, autocar, autocycle, motor-bus, -car, -cycle. [auto-.]

autocade. Same as motorcade.

autocarp, ö'tö-kärp, n. a fruit produced by self-fertilisation. [Gr. autos, self, karpos, fruit.]

autocatalysis, ö-tö-kə-tal'is-is, n. the catalysis of a reaction by a product of that reaction (chem.): reaction or disintegration of a cell or tissue due to the influence of one of its own products (zool.). —v.t. autocatalyse, -yze (-kat'ə-līz).—adj. autocatalytic (-lit'ik). [auto-.]

autocephalous, ö-tö-sef'ə-ləs, adj. having its own head: independent.—n. autoceph'aly, condition of being autocephalous. [Gr. autos, self, kephalē, head.]

autochthon, ö-tok'thon, n. one of the primitive inhabitants of a country: an aboriginal:—pl. autoch'thons, and autoch'thonēs.—adj. autoch'-thonous, (of flora, fauna) indigenous: formed in the region where found (geol.): found in the place of origin: pertaining to ideas unrelated to a person's train of thought which come into the mind (psych.).—ns. autoch'thonism, autoch'-thony, the condition of being autochthonous. [Gr. autochthōn, sprung from the soil—chthōn, chthonos, soil; the Athenians claiming to have actually sprung from the soil.]

autoclave, ö'tö-klāv, n. a strong vessel for carrying out chemical reactions under pressure and at high temperatures, or one in which super-heated steam under pressure is used for sterilising or cooking. [Gr. autos, self, perhaps L. clāvis, key.]

autocrat, ö'tö-krat, n. one who rules by his own power: an absolute sovereign.—n. autocracy (-tok'rə-si), an absolute government by one man: despotism.—adj. autocrat'ic.—adv. autocrat'ically. [Gr. autokratēs—autos, self, kratos, power.]

autocritique, ö-tö-krē-tēk, (Fr.) self-criticism, esp. political.

autocross, ö-tö-kros', n. a motor race round a grass field. [auto-.]

autocue, ö'tö-kū, n. a device showing a speaker the text of what he has arranged to say.

auto-da-fé, ö'tö-da-fä', n. the public declaration of the judgment passed on heretics in Spain and Portugal by the Inquisition: the infliction of the punishment that immediately followed thereupon, esp. the public burning of the victims:—pl. autos-da-fé. [Port. auto da fé (Sp. auto de fe); auto—L. actum, act; da, of the—L. de, of; and fé—L. fidēs, faith.]

autodidact, ö'tö-di-dakt, n. a self-taught person. —adj. autodidact'ic. [Gr. autos, self, didaktos, taught.]

auto-digestion. Same as autolysis.

autodyne, ö'tö-dīn, adj. in radio, of an electrical circuit in which the same elements and valves are used both as oscillator and detector. [auto-, (hetero)dyne.]

autoerotic, ö-tö-e-rot'ik, adj. seeking sensual gratification from one's own person.—ns. auto-er'otism, auto-erot'icism. [Gr. erōtikos, amorous—auto-, and erōtaein, to love.]

autoflare, ö'tö-flär, n. an aircraft automatic landing system operating from an altitude of 50 feet and dependent on a very accurate radio altimeter. [auto-.]

autogamy, ö-tog'ə-mi, n. self-fertilisation.—adjs. autog'amous, autogamic (ö-tö-gam'ik). [Gr. autos, self, gamos, marriage.]

autogenous, ö-toj'ə-nəs, adj. self-generated: independent.—n. autog'eny, spontaneous generation. [Gr. autogenēs—autos, self, genos, offspring.]

autogiro, autogyro, ö-tö-jī'rö, n. a rotating-wing aircraft whose chief support in flight is derived from the reaction of the air upon freely-revolving rotors. [Orig. trademark; invented by Juan de le Cierva: Sp.,—Gr. gyros, circle.]

autograft, ö'tö-gräft, a graft from one part to another of the same body.—Also v.t.

autograph, ö'tö-gräf, n. one's own handwriting: a signature: an original manuscript.—v.t. to write with one's hand.—adj. autographic (-graf'). —adv. autograph'ically.—n. autography (ö-tog'-rə-fi), act of writing with one's own hand: reproduction of the outline of a writing or drawing by facsimile. [Gr. autos, self, graphē, writing.]

autogravure, ö-tö-grav-ūr', or ö', n. a process of photo-engraving akin to autotype. [Gr. autos, self; Fr. gravure, engraving.]

*fāte, fär; mē, hûr (her); mīne, mōte, för; mūte; mōōn, fōot; dhen (then)*

**autoharp,** ö'tō-härp, *n.* a kind of zither, with button-controlled dampers, which produces chords.

**auto-immunisation,** ö'tō-im-ūn-iz-ā'shən, *n.* production by a living body of antibodies which attack constituents of its own tissues, perhaps the cause of certain serious diseases (auto-immune diseases).—*n.* **auto-immun'ity.**

**auto-intoxication,** ö'tō-in-toks-i-kā'shən, *n.* poisoning by substances produced within the body.—*n.* and *adj.* **au'to-intox'icant.**

**autolatry,** ö-tol'ə-tri, *n.* worship of oneself. [Gr. *autos,* self, *latreiā,* worship.]

**autology,** ö-tol'ə-ji, *n.* scientific study of oneself. [Gr. *autos,* self, *logos,* discourse.]

**Autolycus,** ö-tol'i-kəs, *n.* a thief: a plagiarist: a snapper up of unconsidered trifles. [From the character in Shakespeare's *Winter's Tale,* or in Greek mythology.]

**autolysis,** ö-tol'is-is, *n.* the breaking down of dead tissue by the organisms own ferments.—*v.t.* and *v.i.* **aut'olyse, -yze** (-*liz*), to (cause to) undergo autolysis.—*adj.* **autolyt'ic.** [Gr. *autos,* self, *lysis,* loosening.]

**automaton,** ö-tom'ə-tən, *n.* a self-moving machine, or one that moves by concealed machinery: a living being regarded as without consciousness: one who acts by routine, without intelligence:—*pl.* **autom'atons, autom'ata.**—*n.* **aut'omat** (or -*mat*), a restaurant where dishes, hot or cold, are obtained from slot machines: a slot machine of this kind: an automaton.—*v.t.* **automate** (ö'tō-māt), to apply automation to.—*adj.* **automatic** (-tə-mat'ik).—*n.* a device that works automatically, especially an automatic pistol which reloads itself from an internal magazine, or a firearm that goes on firing as long as there is pressure on the trigger.—*adj.* **automat'ical.**—*adv.* **automat'ically.**—*ns.* **automā'tion,** a high degree of mechanisation in manufacture, the handling of material between processes being automatic, and the whole automatically controlled; **autom'atism,** automatic or involuntary action: power of self-moving: power of initiating vital processes from within the cell, organ, or organism, independently of any direct or immediate stimulus from without: the self-acting power of the muscular and nervous systems, by which movement is effected without intelligent determination: action without conscious volition: the doctrine that animals are automata, their motions, etc., being the result of mechanical laws: suspension of control by the conscious mind, so that ideas may be released from the unconscious—a technique of surrealism (*art*); **autom'atist,** one who holds the doctrine of automatism: one who acts automatically.— **automatic pilot,** a device which can be set to steer an aircraft or a ship on a chosen course (also **autopilot); automatic transmission,** power transmission in which gear-changing is automatic; **automatic writing,** writing performed without the volition of the writer. [Gr. *automatos,* self-moving—*autos,* self.]

**automobile,** ö-tō-mō-bēl', or ö', or -mō', *adj.* self-moving.—*n.* a motor-car.—*ns.* **automō'bilism, automō'bilist.** [Gr. *autos,* self; L. *mōbilis,* mobile.]

**automorphism,** ö-tō-mör'fizm, *n.* ascription to others of one's own characteristics.—*adj.* **automor'phic,** marked by automorphism: idiomorphic.—*adv.* **automor'phically.** [Gr. *autos,* self, *morphē,* form.]

**automotive,** ö-tō-mōt'iv, *adj.* self-propelling: pertaining to automobiles: pertaining to the motor-car trade.

**autonomy,** ö-ton'əm-i, *n.* the power or right of self-government, esp. partial self-government: (Kant's *philos.*) the doctrine that the human will carries its guiding principle within itself.—*adjs.* **autonomic,** ö-tō-nom'ik, self-governing: pertaining to the autonomic nervous system: spontaneous (*bot., zool.*); **autonom'ical.**—*ns.* **autonom'ics,** study of self-regulating systems for process control; **auton'omist.**—*adj.* **auton'o-mous.**—**autonomic nervous system,** system of nerve fibres, innervating muscles, glands, etc., whose actions are automatic. [Gr. *autonomos*—*nomos,* law.]

**autonym,** ö'ton-im, or -tən-, a writing published under the author's real name. [Gr. *autos,* self, *onyma (onoma),* name.]

**autophagous,** ö-tof'ə-gəs, *adj.* self-devouring: of a bird, capable of feeding itself from the moment of hatching.—*n.* **autophagy** (-ə-ji), sustenance by self-absorption of the tissues of the body: eating or biting of part of one's own body. [Gr. *phagein,* to eat.]

**autophanous,** ö-tof'ə-nəs, *adj.* self-luminous. [Gr. *phānos,* bright.]

**autophoby,** ö-tof'ob-i, *n.* a shrinking from making any reference to oneself. [Gr. *autos,* self, *phobos,* fear.]

**autophony,** ö-tof'ən-i, *n.* observation of the resonance of one's own voice by speaking with the ear on the patient's chest. [Gr. *phōnē,* sound.]

**autopilot.** See automatic pilot.

**autoplasty,** ö'tō-plas-ti, *n.* grafting of healthy tissue from another part of the same body.—*adj.* **autoplas'tic.** [Gr. *plastos,* formed.]

**autopoint,** ö'tō-point, *n.* a point-to-point over rough country in motor vehicles. [auto-.]

**autopsy,** ö'top-si, or -top', **autop'sia,** *n.* personal inspection: post-mortem examination.—*v.t.* **autopsy.**—*adjs.* **autopt'ic, -al.**—*adv.* **autopt'ically.** [Gr. *autos,* self, *opsis,* sight.]

**autoradiograph,** ö-tō-rā'di-ō-gräf, *n.* in tracer work, the record of a treated specimen on a photographic plate caused by radiations from the radioisotope used.—*n.* **autoradio'graphy** (-og'raf-i), the production of autoradiographs.

**autoschediasm,** ö-tō-sked'i-azm, or -skēd', *n.* anything extemporised.—*v.t.* **autosched'iaze** (-āz).—*adj.* **autoschedias'tic.** [Gr. *autoschedon,* on the spot—*autos,* self, *schedios,* off-hand.]

**autosome,** ö'tō-sōm, *n.* a chromosome other than a sex-chromosome.—*adj.* **autosom'al.** [Gr. *autos,* self, *sōma,* body.]

**autostrada,** ä'ōō-tō-strä-da, (It.) a highway for motor traffic only.

**auto-suggestion,** ö'tō-su-jes'chən, *n.* a mental process similar to suggestion, but originating in a belief in the subject's own mind. [Gr. *autos,* self, and suggestion.]

**autotelic,** ö-tō-tel'ik, *adj.* being an end in itself, or its own justification. [Gr. *autotelēs*—*autos,* self, *telos,* end.]

**autotheism,** ö-tō-thē'izm, *n.* assumption of divine powers: the doctrine of the self-subsistence of God, esp. of the second person in the Trinity.—*n.* **autothe'ist.** [Gr. *autos,* self, *theos,* a god.]

**autotomy,** ö-tot'ə-mi, *n.* reflex separation of part of the body. [Gr. *autos,* self, *tomē,* cut.]

**autotrophic,** ö-tō-trof'ik, *adj.* capable of building up food materials from inorganic matter.—*n.* **au'totroph,** an autotrophic organism. [Gr. *autos,* self, *trophē,* food.]

**autotype,** ö'tō-tip, *n.* a true impress or copy of the original: a process of printing from a photographic negative in a permanent pigment.—*v.t.* to reproduce by such a process.—*n.* **autotypog'-raphy,** a process by which drawings made on gelatine are transferred to a plate from which impressions may be taken. [Gr. *autos,* self, *typos,* a stamp.]

**autovac,** ö'tō-vak, *n.* a vacuum mechanism in a motor-car for raising petrol to a higher tank so that it may flow by gravity to the carburettor. [Gr. *autos,* self, and vacuum.]

**autumn,** ö'təm, *n.* the third season of the year,

when fruits are gathered in, generally (in the northern hemisphere) from August or September to October or November: astronomically, from the autumnal equinox to the winter solstice: a period of harvest or of maturity.—*adj.* **autum'nal** (*ŏ-tum'nl*), pertaining to autumn: blooming in autumn: beyond the prime: withering or withered.—*adv.* **autum'nally.**—**autumn crocus,** a species of *Colchicum*, meadow-saffron. [L. *autumnus.*]

**autunite,** *ŏ'tun-it, n.* a mineral composed of a hydrous phosphate of uranium and calcium. [*Autun* in France, one of its localities.]

**au voleur,** *ō vo-lœr*, (Fr.) stop thief!

**auxanometer,** *ŏks-ən-om'it-ər, n.* an instrument for measuring plant-growth. [Gr. *auxanein*, to grow, *metron*, measure.]

**aux armes,** *ō-zärm*, (Fr.) to arms.

**auxesis,** *ŏk-sē'sis, n.* increase in size: hyperbole: growth of cell, etc.—*adj.* **auxet'ic.**—*n.* something that promotes auxesis. [Gr. *auxēsis*, increase.]

**auxiliar,** *ŏg-zil'yər,* **auxiliary,** *-i, adjs.* helping: subsidiary.—*ns.* **auxil'iar,** an auxiliary; **auxil'iary,** a helper: a verb that helps to form the moods, tenses or voices of other verbs (*gram.*): (esp. in *pl.*) a soldier serving with another nation. [L. *auxiliāris—auxilium*, help—*augēre*, to increase.]

**auxin,** *ŏks'in, n.* any of a number of growth-promoting substances present in minute quantities in plants. [Gr. *auxein*, to increase.]

**auxometer,** *ŏks-om'it-ər*, (*opt.*) *n.* an instrument for measuring magnifying power. [Gr. *auxein*, to increase, *metron*, measure.]

**ava,** *ə-vö'*, (*Scot.*) *adv.* at all. [For of all.]

**ava,** *ä'vä, n.* a species of pepper: an intoxicating drink, also called *kava*, made from its root-stock: any similar drink. [Hawaiian.]

**avadavat.** Same as amadavat.

**avail,** *ə-vāl', v.t.* to be of value or service to: to benefit (used reflexively with *of* in the sense of make use, take advantage): to give (one) the benefit (of), inform (one of) (*U.S.*; *arch.*).—*v.i.* to be of use: to answer the purpose: to draw advantage, be the better (*Shak.*).—*n.* effectual advantage: (in *pl.*) profit, proceeds (*obs.*).—*n.* **availabil'ity,** quality of being available: power of effecting or promoting an end.—*adj.* **avail'able,** that one may avail oneself of: accessible: within reach: obtainable: to be had or drawn upon: valid (*law*): profitable (*obs.*).—*n.* **avail'ableness.**—*adv.* **avail'ably.**—*adjs.* **avail'ful** (*obs.*), of avail: serviceable; **avail'ing.**—*adv.* **avail'ingly.**—**of (no) avail,** (not) producing the desired result. [L. *ad*, to, *valēre*, to be worth, to be strong; app. modelled on vail.]

**avail, availe.** Same as avale.

**aval,** *āv'əl, adj.* pertaining to a grandparent.—[L. *avus*, grandfather.]

**avalanche,** *av'ə-länsh, -länch, -ö-, n.* a hurtling mass of snow, with ice and rock, descending a mountain side: a snow-slip, as from a roof: an overwhelming influx: a shower of particles resulting from the collision of a high-energy particle with matter (*nuc.*).—*v.t.* and *v.i.* to carry or come down as or like an avalanche. [Fr. dial.— *avaler*; see next word.]

**avale, avail, availe,** *v.t.* to lower (*Spens.*): to doff (*obs.*).—*v.i.* (*Spens.*) to come down: to alight. [Fr. *avaler*, to descend—*à* (L. *ad*), to, *val* (L. *vallis*), valley.]

**avant,** *a-vä*, (Fr.) before.—**avant-goût,** *gŏŏ*, a foretaste; **avant-propos,** *prŏ-pō*, preliminary matter: preface.

**avant-courier,** *av-ä-kŏŏr'i-ər, -kŏŏ-ryä, n.* one sent before: (in *pl.*) scouts or advance guard. [Fr. *avant-coureur*, forerunner, scout; *avant-courier*, forerunner.]

**avant-garde,** *av-ä-gärd', n.* those who create or support the newest ideas and techniques in an

art, etc.—Also *adj.*—*ns.* **avant-gard'ism,** avant-garde theory or practice, or support of these; **avant-gard'ist(e),** a member of the avant-garde. [Fr. *avant-garde*, vanguard.]

**avanti,** *a-vän'tē*, (It.) forward!

**avanturine.** See aventurine.

**avarice,** *av'ər-is, n.* eager desire for wealth: covetousness.—*adj.* **avaricious**(*-ish'əs*), extremely covetous: greedy of gain.—*adv.* **avari'ciously.** —*n.* **avari'ciousness.** [Fr.,—L. *avāritia—avārus*, greedy—*avēre*, to pant after.]

**avast,** *ə-väst', (naut.) interj.* hold fast! stop! [Prob. Du. *houd vast*, hold fast.]

**avatar,** *a-və-tär', n.* the descent of a Hindu deity in a visible form: incarnation: supreme glorification of any principle (*fig.*). [Sans. *ava*, away, down, and root *tar-*, to pass over.]

**avaunt,** *ə-vönt', interj.* move on: begone.—*n.* (*Shak.*) dismissal.—*v.i.* to advance (*Spens.*): to depart (*obs.*). [Fr. *avant*, before—L. *ab*, from, *ante*, before.]

**avaunt,** *ə-vönt', (obs.) v.t.* and *v.i.* to boast.—*n.* a boast. [O.Fr. *avanter*—L.L. *vänitāre*, to boast —L. *vānus*, vain.]

**ave,** *ā'vē, ä'vi*, or *ä'vä, interj.* be well and happy: hail.—*n.* an address or prayer to the Virgin Mary, in full, **ave Maria** (*ä'vä mə-rē'ə*), or **ave Mary,** the Hail Mary, or angelic salutation (Luke i. 28). [Imper. of L. *avēre*, to be well. See angelus.]

**ave atque vale,** *ä'vē at'kwi vä'le, ä'vä (-wä) at'kwe vä'lä* (*wä*), (L.) hail and farewell.

**avec plaisir,** *a-vek ple-zēr*, (Fr.) with pleasure.

**Avena,** *a-vē'na, n.* the oat genus of grasses.—*adj.* **avenaceous** (*av-i-nā'shəs*), of the nature of oats. [L. *avēna*, oats.]

**avenge,** *ə-venj', -venzh', v.t.* to vindicate: take vengeance on someone on account of.—*n.* (*obs.*) revenge.—*adjs.* **avenge'ful,** **aveng'ing;**—*ns.* **avenge'ment; avenge'r:**—*fem.* **aveng'eress.** [O.Fr. *avenger*—L. *ad*, to, *vindicāre*, to claim. See vengeance.]

**avenir,** *av-ə-nēr*, (Fr.) future.

**avens,** *av'ənz, n.* any plant of the rosaceous genus *Geum* (water avens, *Geum rivale*; wood avens, herb-bennet): also the related sub-alpine mountain avens (*Dryas octopetala*). [O.Fr. *avence*.]

**aventail, aventaile,** *av'ən-tāl, n.* the flap or movable part of a helmet in front, for admitting air. [O.Fr. *esventail*, air-hole—L. *ex*, out, *ventus*, wind.]

**aventre,** *a-ven'tr*, (*Spens.*) *v.t.* apparently, to thrust, direct. [Origin unknown.]

**aventure,** *ə-ven'chūr*, obsolete form of adventure.

**aventurine,** *a-ven'chū-rin*, **avanturine,** *-van', n.* a brown, spangled kind of Venetian glass: a kind of quartz enclosing spangles of mica or haematite.—*adj.* shimmering or spangled, as kinds of feldspar or sealing-wax. [It. *avventura*, chance— because of the accidental discovery of the glass.]

**avenue,** *av'ən-ū*, in U.S. *-ōō, n.* the principal approach to a country-house, usually bordered by trees: a double row of trees, with or without a road: a wide and handsome street, with or without trees, esp. in America: any passage or entrance into a place: means of access or attainment (*fig.*). [Fr.,—L. *ad*, to, *venire*, to come.]

**aver,** *ə-vûr', v.t.* to declare to be true: to affirm or declare positively: to prove or justify (*law*):— *pr.p.* **averr'ing;** *pa.p.* **averred'.**—*n.* **aver'ment,** positive assertion: a formal offer to prove a plea (*law*): the proof offered (*law*). [Fr. *avérer*—L. *ad*, and *vērus*, true.]

**aver,** *ā'vər, n.* possessions (*obs.*): cattle (*obs.*): a draught animal, esp. an old or worthless cart-horse (*Scot.*). [O.Fr. *aver*, *aver* (Fr. *avoir*), possessions, stock—L. *habēre*, to have.]

**average,** *av'ər-ij, n.* orig. a customs duty or similar charge: any expense other than freight payable by the owner of shipped goods: expense or loss by damage of ship or cargo: equitable distribution of expense or loss: assessment of compensation in the same proportion as amount insured bears to actual worth: arithmetical mean value of any quantities: estimation of such a mean: loosely, ordinary or prevailing value, common run.—*adj.* mean: prevailing, ordinary. —*v.t.* to obtain the average of: to amount to on an average: to do on an average.—*v.t.* and *v.i.* to even out to an average.—**average adjuster,** an assessor employed by an insurance company in marine claims. [Cf. Fr. *avarie*, It. *avaria*, duty on goods; poss. conn. with foregoing.]

**Avernus,** *a-vûr′nəs, a-ver′nōōs, -wer′*, (L.) the infernal regions: any abyss—from Lake Avernus in Campania.

**Averr(h)oism,** *av-er-ō′izm, n.* the doctrine of the Arab philosopher *Averrhoës* (1126-98), that the soul is perishable, the only immortal soul being the world-soul from which individual souls went forth, and to which they return.—*n.* **Averr-(h)ō′ist.**

**averruncate,** *av′ər-ung-kāt, (rare) v.t.* to ward off: (wrongly) to uproot.—*ns.* **averruncā′tion; av′er-runcātor,** an instrument for cutting off branches of trees. [L. *āverruncāre,* to avert, perh. confused with *ēruncāre,* to weed out.]

**averse,** *ə-vûrs′, adj.* disinclined (with *to*; but some prefer *from*): reluctant: turned away or backward.—*adv.* **averse′ly.**—*ns.* **averse′ness;** **aver′sion,** turning aside: dislike: hatred: the object of dislike.—*adj.* **aver′sive,** showing aversion: with purpose, or result, of averting.—*v.t.* **avert′,** turn aside: to prevent: ward off.—*adj.* **avert′ed.**—*adv.* **avert′edly.**—*adj.* **avert′ible,** capable of being averted.—**aversion therapy,** treatment of person suffering from a perversion or a compulsive form of behaviour by associating his or her thoughts about it with something unpleasant such as an electric shock given to him. [L. *āvertĕre, āversus—ab,* from, *vertĕre,* to turn.]
**avert.** See **averse.**

**avertiment,** for **advertisement** (*Milt.*).

**Aves,** *ā′vēz,* L. *ā′vās, -wās, n.pl.* birds as a class of vertebrates.—*adjs.* **ā′vian, avine** (*ā′vin*), of birds.—*ns.* **ā′viarist,** one who keeps an aviary; **ā′viary,** a large cage or the like for keeping birds; **Avicula** (*av-ik′ū-lä;* from the winglike shape), a genus of pearl oysters, giving name to the family **Avicū′lidae** (*-dē*); **Avicūlā′ria,** the bird-catching spider genus, giving name to the family **Avicū-lariidae** (*-lar′i-i-dē*); **ā′viculture,** bird-rearing: bird-fancying; **āvifau′na,** the assemblage of birds found in a region.—*adjs.* **ā′viform,** birdlike in form or structure; **avine, avian.** [L. *avis,* bird, *avicula,* little bird, *aviculārius,* bird-keeper.]

**Avesta,** *ə-ves′tä, n.* the Zoroastrian holy Scriptures.—*adjs.* **Aves′tan, Aves′tic,** of the Avesta or its East Iranian language.—*n.* the language of the Avesta, also called Zend. [Pehlevi *Avistâk,* lore.]

**avian, aviary, Avicula,** etc. See **Aves.**
**aviate,** *ā′vi-āt,* to fly mechanically, navigate the air.—*ns.* **āviā′tion,** mechanical flying; **ā′viātor,** an airman, flying man; **aviatrix** (*ā-vi-ā′triks*), a female pilot; **aviette** (*av-yet′, ā-vi-et′*), an aeroplane driven by man-power.—*adj.* **avion′ic.**—*n.* **āvion′ics,** science concerned with development and use of electronic and electrical devices for aircraft (*aviation electronics*).—**aviation spirit,** a motor fuel with a low initial boiling-point and complying with a certain specification, for use in aeroplanes. [L. *avis,* a bird.]
**avid,** *av′id, adj.* greedy: eagerly desirous.—*n.* **avid′ity.**—*adv.* **av′idly.** [L. *avidus.*]
**aviette.** See **aviate.**
**avion,** *a-vyõ,* (Fr.) aeroplane.—**par avion** (*par av-yõ*), by air: by airmail.
**avionic(s).** See **aviate.**

**avisandum.** See **avizandum.**
**avis au lecteur,** *a-vē ō lek-tœr,* (Fr.) notice to the reader.
**avise, avize, avyze,** *a-vīz′,* obs. forms (*Spens.,* etc.) of **advise.**—*n.* **avise′ment.**—*adj.* **avize′full** (*Spens.*), watchful.—*n.* **avi′so-** a notification: an advice-boat.
**avised.** See **black-a-vised** (under **black**).
**avital,** *ə-vī′tl, av′i-tl, adj.* of a grandfather: ancestral. [L. *avitus—avus,* a grandfather.]
**avitaminosis,** *ā-vit-ə-min-ōs′is, n.* lack of vitamins or a condition due to this. [Gr. *a-,* priv.]
**avizandum,** *av-iz-an′dəm, (Scots law) n.* private consideration of a case by a judge before giving judgment.—Also **avisan′dum.** [Gerund of L.L. *avizāre, avisāre,* to advise.]
**avocado,** *a-vō-kä′dō, n.* the alligator-pear, fruit of a tropical American lauraceous tree. [Sp. *aguacate*—Aztec *ahuacatl.*]
**avocat consultant,** *a-vō-ka kõ-sül-tä,* (Fr.) consulting lawyer, chamber counsel.
**avocation,** *av-ō-kā′shən, n.* properly, a diversion or distraction from one's regular employment: improperly used for **vocation,** business which calls for one's time and attention: diversion of the thoughts from any employment (*arch.*): the calling of a case to a higher court. [L. *āvocātiō, -ōnis,* a calling away—*ab,* from, *vocāre,* to call.]
**avocet, avoset,** *av′ō-set, n.* a wading bird (genus *Recurvirostra*) with webbed feet and long, slender, curved, elastic bill. [Fr. *avocette,* It. *avosetta.*]
**Avogadro's constant, number,** *a-vō-gä′drōz,* the number of specified elementary units (e.g. molecules) in a mole of any substance; **Avogadro's law, rule, hypothesis,** the law that at equal temperature and pressure equal volumes of gases contain the same number of molecules. [A. *Avogadro* (1776-1856), Italian physicist.]
**avoid,** *ə-void′, v.t.* to evade: to shun: to empty (*obs.*): to invalidate (*law*): to leave, to quit (*Shak.*): to dismount from.—*v.i.* to take oneself off.—*adj.* **avoid′able.**—*n.* **avoid′ance,** the act of avoiding or shunning: act of annulling: the shunning of certain relatives among primitive peoples (*anthrop.*). [A.Fr. *avoider,* O.Fr. *es-vuidier*—L. *ex,* out, and root of **void.**]
**avoirdupois,** *av-ər-də-poiz′,* or *av′,* n. a system of weights in which the lb. equals 16 oz.—*adj.* of that system. [O.Fr. *aveir de pes,* to have weight—L. *habēre,* to have, *dē,* from, *pēnsum,* that which is weighed.]
**à volonte,** a *vo-lõ-tā,* (Fr.) at pleasure.
**avoset.** See **avocet.**
**a vostro beneplacito,** a *vos′trō bā-nā-plä′chē-tō,* (It.) at your pleasure, at your will.
**à votre santé,** a *votr′ sä-tā,* (Fr.) to your health.
**avouch,** *ə-vowch′, v.t.* to avow: to acknowledge: to vouch for: to assert positively: to maintain: to guarantee: to own to: to appeal to.—*v.i.* to give assurance.—*n.* (*Shak.*) evidence.—*adj.* **avouch′able.**—*n.* **avouch′ment.** [O.Fr. *avochier*—L. *advocāre,* to call to one's aid. See **vouch,** **advocate.**]
**avoué,** *a-vōō-ā,* (Fr.) attorney, solicitor.
**avow,** *ə-vowr′,* (Spens.) *n.* avowal. [See **avow.**]
**avouterer,** *a-vōōt′ər-ər,* **avoutry, -ri,** old forms of **adulterer, adultery.**
**avow,** *ə-vow′, v.t.* to declare: to acknowledge: to maintain.—*v.i.* (*law*) to justify an act done.—*n.* a solemn promise: a vow.—*adj.* **avow′able.**—*ns.* **avow′ableness; avow′al,** a positive declaration: an acknowledgment: a frank confession.—*adj.* **avowed′.**—*adv.* **avow′edly.**—*n.* **avow′ry,** the act of avowing and justifying in one's own right the distraining of goods (*law*): advocacy considered as personified in a patron saint (*obs.*). [O.Fr. *avouer,* orig. to swear fealty to—L. *ad,* to, and L.L. *võtāre*—L. *võtum,* a vow: with sense affected by L. *advocāre.* See **vow,** **avouch.**]

avoyer, *a-vwa-yā*, (Fr.) formerly the chief magistrate in some Swiss cantons.

a vuestra salud, *a vōō-ās'tra sä-lōōdh'*, (Sp.) to your health.

avulse, *ə-vuls'*, *v.t.* to pluck or tear away.—avul'sion, forcible separation: sudden removal of land by change of a river's course, whereby it remains the property of the original owner (opp. to *alluvion*). [L. *āvellēre, āvulsum.*]

avuncular, *ə-vung'kū-lər*, *adj.* of an uncle. [L. *avunculus*, an uncle.]

avvogadore, *a-vō-ga-dō'rā*, (It.) an official criminal prosecutor in Venice.

await, *ə-wāt'*, *v.t.* to wait or look for: to be in store for: to attend: to lie in wait for, to watch (*obs.*).—*n.* (*Spens.*) ambush, watch. [O.N.Fr. *awaitier—à*, to; see wait.]

awake, *ə-wāk'*, *v.t.* to rouse from sleep: to rouse from inaction.—*v.i.* to cease sleeping: to rouse oneself from sleep or indifference:—*pa.t.* awoke', awaked', *pa.p.* awaked' or awoke', sometimes awōk'en.—*adj.* not asleep: vigilant: aware, cognisant (with *to*).—*v.t.* awak'en, to awake: to rouse into interest or attention: to call to a sense of sin (*theol.*).—*v.i.* to awake: to spring into being.—*adj.* awak'ening, becoming awake: rousing: revivifying, reanimating.—*n.* a becoming awake, aware, active: a throwing off of indifference or ignorance: a rousing.—*n.* and *adj.* awak'ing.—to be awake to, to be fully aware of. [O.E. *āwæcnan* (pa.t. *āwōc*, pa.p. *āwacen*), confused with *āwacian* (pa.t. *āwacode*). See wake, watch.]

awanting, *ə-wont'ing*, (chiefly *Scot.*) *adj.* wanting: missing. [Prep. a, and the gerund of want.]

award, *ə-wörd'*, *v.t.* to adjudge: to determine: to grant.—*n.* judgment: final decision, esp. of arbitrators: that which is awarded: a prize. [O.Fr. *ewarder, eswarder*—L. *ex*, in sense of thoroughly, and the root of ward, guard.]

aware, *ə-wār'*, *adj.* wary: informed, conscious (with *of*).—*n.* aware'ness, state of being aware: consciousness, esp. a dim form. [O.E. *gewær—wær*, cautious. See ware.]

awarn, *a-wörn'*, (*Spens.*) *v.t.* to warn. [Pfx. *a-*, intensive, and warn.]

awash, *ə-wosh'*, *adv.* on a level with the surface of the water: afloat at the mercy of the waves. [Prep. a.]

awatch, *ə-woch'*, *adv.* on the watch. [Prep. a.]

awave, *ə-wāv'*, *adv.* in a wave: in waves. [Prep. a.]

away, *ə-wā'*, *adv.* onward: continuously: without hesitation, stop, or delay: forthwith: out of the place in question: not at home: on the opponents' ground (*sport*): at or to a distance: off: in or into an averted direction: out of existence, life, or consciousness: with effect of removal or elimination: far: about (with *here, there, where*; now *dial.*): with omission of verb = go or (with *with*) take away (usu. *imper.*): to endure (with *with*).—*interj.* begone: get out.—*adv.* aways (*obs.*, *Spens.* awayes'), away.—do away with, to abolish; explain away, to explain so as to make the thing explained seem not to exist; fall away, to dwindle: to waste away: to go on, proceed now without further delay; make away with, to destroy: to murder; once and away (now usu. once in a way), on occasion. [O.E. *aweg, onweg—on*, on, *weg*, way.]

awe, *ö*, *n.* reverential wonder or fear: dread: power to inspire awe (*arch.*).—*v.t.* to strike with or influence by awe or fear.—*adj.* awed (*öd*), awe-stricken: expressive of awe; awe'-inspiring; awe'less, without awe: fearless: regarded without awe (*Shak.*).—*n.* awe'lessness.—*adjs.* awe'some, aw'some, awed: awe-inspiring (*Scot.*): dreadful.—*adv.* awe'somely.—*n.* awe'someness.—*adj.* awe'-stricken, -struck, struck with awe.—*v.t.* awe'strike.—*adj.* aw'ful, inspiring awe: filled with awe: very bad, tiresomely great, etc. (*coll.*).—*adv.* very (*coll.*).—*adv.* aw'fully, in an awe-inspiring or awe-stricken manner: with awe: very (*coll.*).—*n.* aw'fulness. [O.N. *agi*; cf. O.E. *ege*, fear; Gr. *achos*, distress.]

aweary, *ə-wē'ri*, *adj.* weary.—*adj.* awea'ried, weary. [Pfx. a-, intensive, and weary.]

a-weather, *ə-wedh'ər*, (*naut.*) *adv.* towards the weather or windward side—opp. to *alee*. [Prep. a.]

a-week', *ə-wēk'*, *adv.* in the week. [Prep. a.]

aweel, *ə-wēl'*, (*Scot.*) *interj.* well: well then. [ah well.]

a-weigh, *ə-wā'*, *adv.* in the act of being weighed, as an anchor just raised from the bottom. [Prep. a, and weigh.]

aweto, *ä-wā'tō*, *n.* the so-called vegetable caterpillar, the body of a caterpillar filled with a parasitic fungus. [Maori *ahweto*.]

awhape, *ə-(h)wāp'*, (*Spens.*) *v.t.* to confound, amaze. [Cf. Goth. *af-hwapjan*, to choke.]

awheel, *ə-(h)wēl'*, (*obs.* awheels), *adv.* on wheels, esp. on a bicycle. [Prep. a, and wheel.]

a'where. See a'.

awhile, *ə-(h)wīl'*, *adv.* for some time: for a short time. [O.E. *āne hwīle*, a while (dat.): combined as early as 13th century.]

a-wing, *ə-wing'*, *adv.* on the wing. [Prep. a, and wing.]

awkward, *ök'wərd*, *adj.* oblique, inverted, back-handed (*obs.*): clumsy: ungraceful: embarrassed: difficult to deal with: adverse (*Shak.*): embarrassing: froward (*obs.*).—*adj.* awk'ward-ish.—*adv.* awk'wardly.—*n.* awk'wardness, clumsiness: embarrassing or inharmonious quality, or condition. [Prob. O.N. *afug*, turned wrong way, and suff. *-ward*.]

awl, *öl*, *n.* a pointed instrument for boring small holes. [O.E. *æl*; O.N. *alr*, Ger. *ahle*.]

awmous, *ö'məs*, (*Scot.*) *n.* alms. [O.N. *almusa*; cf. O.E. *ælmysse*, alms.]

awn, *ön*, *n.* the beard of barley, or similar bristly process.—*adjs.* awned; awn'less; awn'y.—*n.* awn'er, a machine for removing the awns from grain. [O.N. *ögn* or a lost O.E. cognate; Ger. *ahne*.]

awning, *ön'ing*, *n.* a covering to shelter from the sun or weather.—*v.t.* awn, to shelter with an awning. [Origin unknown; Fr. *auvent*, window-shade, may be connected.]

awoke, *ə-wōk'*, *pa.t.* of awake.

awork, *ə-wûrk'*, *adv.* at work.—*advs.* awrack', in a state of wreck; awrong', wrongly. [Prep. a, on.]

awry, *ə-rī'*, *adj.* twisted to one side: distorted, crooked: wrong: perverse.—*adv.* askew: unevenly: perversely: erroneously.—to look awry, to look askance at anything; to walk awry, to go wrong. [Prep. a, and wry.]

axe, ax, *aks*, *n.* a tool for hewing or chopping, with edge and handle in the same plane: a stone-dressing hammer: ruthless cutting down of expenditure (*fig.*):—*pl.* ax'es (see also axis).—*v.t.* to hew or strike with an axe: to dismiss as superfluous: to cut down, reduce (*fig.*): to dispense with (*fig.*).—axe'-stone, a kind of jade used for making axes.—axe to grind, a private purpose to serve. [O.E. *æx*; cf. Gr. *axinē*.]

axerophthol, *aks-ər-of'thol*, *n.* vitamin A, a pale yellow crystalline substance, defect of which causes xerophthalmia. [Gr. *a-*, priv., and *xerophthalmia*.]

axial, axile. See under axis (1).

axilla, *ak-sil'ə*, *n.* the armpit (*anat.*): axil (*bot.*):—*pl.* axillae (-*ē*).—*n.* ax'il, the angle between leaf and stem.—*adjs.* ax'illar, ax'illary. [L. *āxilla*, the armpit.]

axinite, *aks'in-it*, *n.* a brilliant brown mineral with axe-shaped crystals, containing calcium, aluminium, boron, silicon, etc.—*n.* axin'omancy, divination from the motions of an axe posed upon a stake, or of an agate placed upon a red-hot axe. [Gr. *axinē*, an axe, *manteiā*, divination.]

axiology, aks-i-ol'ə-ji, n. the science of the ultimate nature, reality, and significance of values.—adj. axiological (-ə-loj'i-kl).—n. axiologist (ol'ə-jist). [Gr. axios, worthy, logos, discourse.]

axiom, aks'i-əm, n. a self-evident truth: a universally received principle: a postulate, assumption.—adjs. axiomat'ic, axiomat'ical.—adv. axiomat'ically.—n. axiomat'ics, the study of axioms and axiom systems. [Gr. axiōma, -atos— axioein, to think worth, to take for granted— axios, worthy.]

axioma medium, ak-si-ōm'a mē'di-əm, me'di-ōom, (L.) a generalisation from experience.

axis, aks'is, n. an axle (obs.): a line about which a body rotates, or about which a figure is conceived to revolve: a straight line about which the parts of a figure, body or system are symmetrically or systematically arranged: a fixed line adopted for reference in co-ordinate geometry, curve-plotting, crystallography, etc.: the second vertebra of the neck (zool.): the main stem or root, or a branch in relation to its own branches and appendages (bot.): an alliance of powers, as if forming together an axis of rotation—esp. of Germany and Italy (1936):—pl. axes (aks'ēz).— adj. ax'ial, relating to, or of the nature of, an axis.—adv. ax'ially.—adj. ax'ile (ak'sil, U.S. ak'səl), coinciding with an axis.—ns. ax'oid, a curve generated by the revolution of a point round an advancing axis; ax'on, a process of the nerve cell or neuron which in most cases transmits impulses away from the cell.—adj. axonomet'ric, pertaining to a method of projection in which a drawing of a three-dimensional object has all lines to exact scale and appears distorted.—axis cylinder, the excitable core of a medullated nerve-fibre.—axis of incidence, the line passing through the point of incidence of a ray perpendicularly to the refracting surface; axis of refraction, the continuation of the same line through the refracting medium; axis of the equator, the polar diameter of the earth which is also the axis of rotation. [L. axis; cf. Gr. axōn, Sans. aksa, O.E. eax.]

axis, aks'is, n. a white-spotted deer of India. [L. axis, Pliny's name for an Indian animal.]

axle, aks'l, axle-tree, aks'l-trē, n. the pin or rod in the nave of a wheel on which the wheel turns: a pivot or support of any kind: an axis (arch.).— ax'le-box, the box in which the axle end turns; ax'le-guard, a pedestal or pillow-block. [More prob. O.N. öxull than a dim. from O.E. eax.]

Axminster, aks'min-stər, adj. of a variety of cut-pile carpet. [Axminster in Devon, where it is made.]

axolotl, aks'o-lot-l, n. the larval form of Amblystoma, commonly retaining its larval character in life, though capable of breeding. [Aztec.]

axon, axonometric. See axis (1).

ay, ā, interj. ah: oh: alas: esp. in ay me. [M.E. ey, ei, perh. from Fr. ahi, aï; cf. Sp. ay de mi.]

ay, aye, i, adv. yea: yes: indeed.—n. aye (i), a vote in the affirmative: one who votes in the affirmative. [Perh. a dial. form of aye, ever; perh. a variant of yea.]

ayah, i'ä, n. an Indian or South African waiting-maid or nursemaid. [Hind. āyā; from Port. aia, nurse.]

aye, ay, ā, adv. ever: always: for ever.—for aye, for ever and aye, for ever. to all eternity.—In combination, with sense of ever, as in Shakespeare's aye'-remain'ing, etc. [O.N. ei, ever; O.E. ã; conn. with age, ever.]

aye-aye, i'i, n. an aberrant squirrel-like lemur of Madagascar. [Malagasy aiay.]

ayelp, ə-yelp', adv. in a state of yelping. [Prep. a.]

ayenbite, ä-yen'bit, (obs.) n. remorse, as in the book-title Ayenbite of Inwyt (remorse of conscience). [M.E. ayen, again and bite.]

aygre, ä'gər, (Shak.). Same as eager.

Aylesbury, ālz'bər-i, n. a breed of ducks much valued for the table. [Aylesbury, a market town in Bucks.]

ayont, ə-yont', (Scot.) adv. and prep. beyond. [Pfx. a-, and yond.]

ayrie. Same as aerie.

ayuntamiento, a-yōon-ta-mē-än'tō, (Sp.) municipal council.

ayword, ä'wûrd, (Shak.) n. a byword, proverbial reproach. [Origin obscure; Rowe proposed to read nayword.]

Azalea, a-zā'li-ə, n. a genus close akin to, or subgenus of, Rhododendron, shrubby plants, with five stamens and annual leaves. [Gr. azaleos, dry; reason for name uncertain.]

azeotrope, ə-zē'ə-trōp, n. any liquid mixture which distils over without decomposition in a certain ratio, the boiling-point of the mixture differing from that of any constituent.—adj. azeotrop'ic (-trop'). [Gr. a-, priv., zeein, to boil, tropos, turn.]

Azilian, a-zil'i-ən, adj. belonging to a transition between Palaeolithic and Neolithic. [Mas d'Azil, Ariège, where objects of this culture have been found in a cave.]

azimuth, az'im-əth, n. the arc of the horizon between the meridian of a place and a vertical circle passing through any celestial body.—adj. az'imuthal (or -mūdh', -mūth'), pertaining to the azimuth. [Ar. as-sumūt, as = al, the, sumūt, pl. of samt, direction. See zenith.]

azione (sacra), a-tsi-ō'nä (sak'ra), (mus.) n. a composition, in form like an oratorio, but performed as a drama. [It.]

azo-, az'ō-, in combination, nitrogen.—ns. az'o-com'pound, a compound in which two nitrogen atoms are each attached to (usually) a carbon group, as az'oben'zene, $C_6H_5N : NC_6H_5$; az'o-dye', a dye of such composition. [azote.]

azoic, a-zō'ik, adj. without life: before the existence of animal life: formed when there was no animal life on the globe, as rocks. [Gr. a-, priv., and zōē, life.]

azonal, a-zōn'əl, adj. not arranged in zones or regions. [Gr. a-, priv., zōnē, a belt.]

azonic, a-zon'ik, adj. not limited to a zone, not local. [Gr. a-, priv., zōnē, a belt.]

azote, a-zōt', n. an old name for nitrogen, so called because it does not sustain animal life.— adjs. azot'ic (a-zot'ik), nitric; azō'tous, nitrous. v.t. az'otise, -ize, to combine with nitrogen.—n. Azōtobac'ter, a genus of nitrogen-fixing bacteria. [Gr. a-, priv., zaein, to live.]

azoth, äz'oth, n. the alchemist's name for mercury: Paracelsus's universal remedy. [From Ar. az-zäūg—al, the, zäūg, from Pers. zhiwah, quicksilver.]

Azrael, az'rā-el, n. in Mohammedan mythology, the angel of death.

Aztec, az'tek, n. one of a people dominant in Mexico before the Spanish conquest.—Also adj.

azulejo, a-thōō-lā'hhō, (Sp.) glazed tile.

azure, azh'ər, äzh'ər, or ä'zhūr, adj. of a faint blue: sky-coloured: blue (represented in engraving, etc., by horizontal lines (her.).—n. a delicate blue colour: the sky.—adjs. azure'an, az'urine (-in), azure.—ns. az'urine, a blue-black aniline dye: a fresh-water fish, the blue roach; az'urite, blue basic carbonate of copper, chessy-lite.—adjs. az'urn (Milt.), azure; az'ury, bluish. [O.Fr. azur—L.L. azura—Ar. (al) lazward, Pers. lājward, lapis lazuli, blue colour.]

azygous, az'i-gəs, adj. not yoked or joined with another: unpaired (anat.).—n. azygy (az'i-ji). [Gr. azygos—a-, priv., and zygon, a yoke.]

azymous, az'i-məs, adj. unfermented: unleavened.—ns. az'ym, az'yme, unleavened bread; az'y-mite, a member of any church using unleavened bread in the Eucharist. [Gr. azymos—a-, priv., zymē, leaven.]

# B

**B, b,** *bē, n.* the second letter of our alphabet, called by the Phoenicians *beth,* the house, corresponding to Greek β, beta: in music, the seventh note of the scale of C major (H in German notation, B being used for B flat): the subsidiary series of paper sizes, ranging from B0 (1000 × 1414 mm.) to B10 (31 × 44 mm.): of second class or order, or of a class arbitrarily designated B: see blood-group: as a mediaeval Roman numeral B = 300; B̄ = 3000.—B or B flat, a 19th-cent. euphemism for domestic bedbug; in old music B quadratum, quadrate B, square B, is B natural, B rotundum, round B, is B flat.—the three B's, Bach, Beethoven, Brahms.

**ba',** *bö, n.* Scots form of ball.—*ns.* ba''ing, ba''-spiel (see ball).

**baa,** *bä, n.* the cry of a sheep.—*v.i.* to bleat.—*n.* baa'ing. [Imit.]

**Baal,** *bä'al, n.* a god of the Phoenicians, originally probably a fusion of many local gods: a false god generally:—*pl.* Ba'alim.—*ns.* Ba'alism; Bā'alite. [Heb.]

**baas,** *bäs, n.* (*S. Africa*), master, overseer, sir.—*n.* baaskap, condition in which one section of the population is treated as a master race: the theory used to justify this. [Afrik.—Du.]

**baba,** *bä'bä, n.* a small cake, leavened with yeast, with or without fruit, soaked in a rum syrup.—Also baba au rhum (ō rom). [Fr.—Pol. baba, 'old woman'.]

**babacoote,** *bab'ə-kōōt, n.* a large lemur, the indri or a closely related species. [Malagasy babakoto.]

**babassu,** *bab-ə-sōō', n.* a Brazilian palm (Attalea) or its oil-yielding nut. [Prob. Tupí.]

**Babbitt,** *bab'it, n.* a conventional middle-class business-man (or other person) who esteems success and has no use for art or intellectual pursuits.—*ns.* Babb'itry, Babb'itism. [Eponymous hero of novel (1922) by Sinclair Lewis.]

**babbitt,** *bab'it, v.t.* to fit with Babbitt('s) metal, a soft anti-friction alloy (tin, with copper, antimony, and usu. lead). [Isaac *Babbitt* (1799-1862), the Massachusetts inventor.]

**babble,** *bab'l, v.i.* to speak like a baby: to make a continuous murmuring sound like a brook, etc.: to talk incessantly: to tell secrets: to prate.—*v.t.* to utter confusedly or by rote: to divulge by foolish talk.—*adj.* babb'lative.—*ns.* babb'le, idle senseless talk: prattle: confused murmur, as of a stream; babb'lement; babb'ler, one who babbles: a bird of an ill-defined family somewhat akin to the thrushes (also babbling thrush). —*n.* and *adj.* babb'ling.—*adj.* babb'ly. [Prob. imit., from the repeated syllable *ba*; cf. Du. *babbelen,* Ger. *pappelen,* Fr. *babiller,* perh. influenced by *Babel.*]

**babe,** *bāb, n.* form of baby.

**Babel,** *bā'bl, n.* a foolishly conceived lofty structure: a confused sound of voices: a scene of confusion.—*ns.* bā'beldom, bā'belism.—*adj.* bā'-belish. [Heb. *Bābel,* prob. Assyr. *bāb-ili,* gate of God, associated in Gen. xi. 9, with confusion.]

**Babi, Babee,** *bä'bē, n.* a member of a Persian sect, followers of *Bab*-ed-Din (Mizra Ali Mohammed, 1821-50), who sought to combine the best in all religions.—Also Ba'bist.—*ns.* Ba'bism, Ba'biism, Ba'beeism.

**babingtonite,** *bab'ing-tən-it, n.* a pyroxene, ferrous silicate with admixtures, sometimes worked as an iron ore. [After William *Babington,* mineralogist (1756-1833).]

**babiroussa, -russa,** *bä-bi-rōō'sa, n.* a wild hog found in Celebes, etc., with great up-turned tusks in the male, hence called the horned or deer hog. [Malay *bābi,* hog, and *rūsa,* deer.]

**bablah,** *bab'lə,* babul, *bä'bōōl, n.* a species of acacia (*A. arabica*): the pods of that and other species, used for tanning. [Hind. and Pers. *babūl.*]

**baboo.** See babu.

**baboon,** *bə-bōōn', n.* large monkey of various species, with long face, dog-like tusks, large lips, a tail, and buttock-callosities: a clumsy, brutish person of low intelligence.—*n.* baboon'ery.—*adj.* baboon'ish. [Fr. *babouin,* remoter origin unknown.]

**babouche, babuche, baboosh,** *bə-bōōsh', n.* an Oriental heelless slipper. [Fr.,—Arab. *bābūsh*—Pers. *pā,* foot, *pūsh,* covering.]

**babu, baboo,** *bä'bōō, n.* a title for Hindus in some parts of India corresponding to Mr: an Indian clerk: an Indian with a superficial English education (esp. *hist.*).—Also *adj.*—*ns.* ba'budom, ba'buism. [Hind. *bābū.*]

**babushka,** *bə-bōōsh'kə, n.* triangular headscarf tied under the chin. [Russ. *bábushka,* grandmother.]

**baby,** *bā'bi, ns.* an infant, young child: a doll (*obs.*): the reflection of oneself in the pupil of another's eye (*obs.*): a young animal: a babyish person: a thing small of its kind, as varieties of grand-piano, aeroplane, etc.: a girl (*coll.*): an inexperienced person: one's pet project, invention, machine, etc.: responsibility.—*v.t.* to treat as a baby.—Also *adj.*—*n.* ba'byhood.—*adj.* bā'-byish.—bā'by-farm'er, one who takes in infants to nurse for pay; bā'by-jump'er, a seat suspended by elastic straps, to enable a baby to disport itself; bā'by-ribb'on, a very narrow ribbon. —*v.i.* bab'y-sit, to act as baby-sitter.—bā'by-sitter, one who mounts guard over a baby to relieve the usual attendant; bā'by-sitting, bab'y-snatcher, person marrying another who is much younger; bab'y-talk, speech of babies learning to talk, or a grown-up imitation of it.— to hold the baby, to be left in the lurch with a responsibility. [Prob. imitative. See babble.]

**Babylonian,** *bab-i-lōn'i-ən, adj.* of Babylon: hence huge, gigantic: Romish, popish (*obs.*; from the identification with Rome of the scarlet woman of Rev. xvii.): Babel-like, confused in language.—Also Babylon'ish.—Babylonian or Babylonish captivity, the exile of the Jews deported to Babylon in 597 and in 586 B.C., lasting till *c.* 538: the exile of the popes at Avignon, 1309-77.

**bacca,** *bak'a,* (*bot.*) *n.* a berry.—*adjs.* bacc'ate, having berries: berry-like: pulpy; bacciferous (*bak-sif'ər-əs*), bearing berries; bac'ciform, of the shape of a berry; bacciv'orous, living on berries. [L. *bacca,* a berry.]

**baccalaureate,** *bak-ə-lö'ri-āt, n.* the university degree of bachelor.—*adj.* baccalau'rean. [L.L. *baccalaureus,* altered from *baccalārius.* See bachelor.]

**baccara, baccarat,** *bak'-ə-rä, n.* a French card game played by betters and a banker. [Fr.]

**bacchanal,** *bak'ə-nl, n.* a worshipper, priest or priestess, of Bacchus: a drunken reveller: a dance, song, or revel in honour of Bacchus.—*adj.* relating to drinking or drunken revels.—Also bacchanalian (-*nä'li-ən*):—*ns.pl.* bacchanā'lia,

*fāte, fär; mē, hûr* (her); *mīne; mōte, för; mūte; mōōn, fŏŏt; dhen* (then)

**bacch'anals**, originally feasts in honour of Bacchus: hence, drunken revels.—*n.* **bacchanā'-lianism**.—*n.* and *adj.* **bacchant** (*bak'ant*), a priest or votary of Bacchus: a reveller: a drunkard.— *n.* **bacchante** (*bə-kant'*, *bak'ant*, or after Italian *baccante*, *ba-kant'i*), a priestess of Bacchus: a female bacchanal.—*adjs.* **bacchiac** (*bak-i'ək*), relating to the bacchius; **Bacch'ian**, **Bacchic** (*bak'ik*), relating to Bacchus: jovial: drunken. —*ns.* **bacchi'us** (Gr. and Lat. *pros.*) a foot of two long syllables preceded by one short:—*pl.* **bacchi'i**; **Bacchus**, *ba'kus*, god of wine. [L. *Bacchus*, Gr. *Bakchos*, the wine god.]

**baccy**, **bacco**, *bak'i*, *-ō*, abbreviations of *tobacco*.

**bacharach**, *bak'ər-ak*, *bähh'ə-rähh*, *n.* an excellent wine named from *Bacharach*, on the Rhine.

**bachelor**, *bach'əl-ər*, *n.* a young knight following the banner of another, as too young to display his own (*hist.*): an unmarried man: one who has taken his or her first degree at a university: a young unmated bull-seal or other male animal. —*n.* **bach** (*coll.*), a bachelor.—*v.i.* to live as a bachelor: to do for oneself.—Also *v.t.* with *it*.— *ns.* **bach'elordom**; **bach'elorhood**; **bach'elorism**, habit or condition of a bachelor; **bach'elorship**, the degree of bachelor.—**bach'elor-girl**, a girl with a latch-key (*obs.*); a young unmarried woman who supports herself; **bach'elor's-butt'ons**, a double-flowered yellow or white buttercup: also applied to double feverfew, species of Centaurea, and many other plants; **bachelor's wife**, an ideal woman with none of the shortcomings of married men's wives.—**knight-bachelor** (see knight). [O.Fr. *bacheler*—L.L. *baccalārius*; of doubtful origin.]

**bacillus**, *bə-sil'əs*, *n.* (*cap.*) a genus of Schizomycetes (fam. Bacillaceae), aerobic rod-shaped bacteria: a member of the genus: loosely, any rod-shaped bacterium: popularly any disease-causing bacterium:—*pl.* **bacill'i** (*-i*).—*n.pl.* **Bacillā'ceae**, a family (order Eubacteriales) of endospore-producing bacteria.—*adjs.* **bacill'ar**, **bacill'ary** (or *bas'*), of the shape or nature of a bacillus, rodlike.—*n.* **bacill'icide**, that which destroys bacilli.—*adj.* **bacill'iform**. [L.L. *bacillus*, dim. of *baculus*, a rod.]

**back**, *bak*, *n.* the hinder part of the body in man, and the upper part in beasts, extending from the neck and shoulders to the extremity of the backbone: put for the whole body in speaking of clothes: the hinder part, or the side remote from that presented or that habitually seen or contemplated (opposite to the front): the under side of a leaf or of a violin: part of the upper surface of the tongue opposite the soft palate; the convex side of a book, opposite to the opening of the leaves: the thick edge of a knife or the like: the upright hind part of a chair, bench, etc.: something added to the hinder side: the surface of the sea, or of a river: the keel and keelson of a ship: in football, etc., one of the players behind the forwards—*full back* (who guards the goal), *half* and *three-quarter backs*: in mining, that side of an inclined mineral lode which is nearest the surface of the ground—the *back* of a level is the ground between it and the level above.—*adj.* rearward: remote: reversed: made by raising the back of the tongue (*phon.*): belonging to the past.—*adv.* to or towards the back: to or towards the place from which one came: to a former state or condition: behind: behind in time: in return: again.—*v.t.* to mount or ride: to help or support, as if standing at one's back: to support one's opinion by a wager or bet on: to countersign or endorse: to write or print at the back of as a parliamentary bill, or the like: to furnish with a back: to lie at the back of: to form the back of: to cause to move backward, as a horse: to put or propel backward, or in the opposite direction, by reversing the action, as an engine

or a boat.—*v.i.* to move or go back or backwards: (of the wind) to change counter-clockwise.—*adj.* **backed**, having a back.—*ns.* **back'er**, one who backs or supports another in a contest or venture; one who places a bet, e.g. on a horse; **backing**, support at the back: mounting of a horse: the action of putting or going back: a body of helpers: anything used to form a back or line the back: counter-clockwise change of wind: support for an enterprise: musical accompaniment, esp. of a popular song.—*adj.* and *adv.* **backward**, *bak'wərd*, towards the back: on the back: towards the past: from a better to a worse state: in a direction opposite to the normal.—*adj.* **back'ward**, keeping back: shy, bashful: unwilling: slow in development: late: dull or stupid.—*n.* the past portion of time.—*n.* **backwarda'tion**, percentage paid by a seller of stock for keeping back its delivery till the following account.—*adv.* **back'wardly**.—*n.* **back'-wardness.**—*adv.* **back'wards.**—**back'ache**, a pain in the back; **back'band**, a rope, strap, or chain passing over a cart saddle and holding up the shafts of a vehicle (also **back'-chain**, **back'-rope**); **back'bench'er**, an occupant of a back bench, as in parliament.—*v.t.* **back'bite**, to speak evil of in absence.—*ns.* **back'biter**; **back'biting.**—*adj.* **back'-block**, of the back-blocks.—*n.* **back'-blocker.**—*n.pl.* **back'-blocks** (*Austr.*), the interior parts of a station, far from the river-front.— **back'-board**, a board at the back of a cart, boat, etc.: a board fastened across the back to straighten the body; **back'bond**, a deed attaching a qualification or condition to the terms of a conveyance or other instrument (*Scots law*); **back'-bone**, the spine or vertebral column: a main support or axis: mainstay: firmness.—*adj.* **back'-bone'less.**—*n.* **back'breaker**, a very heavy job.— *adj.* **back'breaking.**—**back'chat**, answering back, retort: impertinence; **back'-cloth**, **back'drop**, the painted cloth at the back of the stage; **back'-country**, districts not yet thickly populated; **back'cross**, a cross between a hybrid and a parent race; **back door**, a door in the back part of a building.—*adj.* **back'-door**, unworthily secret: clandestine.—**back'-draught**, a backward current; **back'-end'**, the rear end: the later part of a season (*dial.*): the late autumn (*dial.*); **back'fall**, an obsolete ornament like an appoggiatura (*mus.*): a fall on the back as in wrestling (often *fig.*): a lever in the coupler of an organ; **back'fire**, ignition of gas in an internal-combustion engine's cylinder at wrong time, or within a bunsen-burner or the like instead of at the outlet. —*v.i.* (*bak-fīr'*) to have a backfire: to go wrong (*coll.*).—**back'-forma'tion**, the making of a word from one that is, in error or jocularity, taken to be a derivative, as the verb *sidle* from the adverb *sidling* treated as if it were a participle; **back'-friend**, a pretended friend (*obs.*): a backer, a friend who stands at one's back.—*adj.* **back'-ganging** (*Scot.*), in arrears.—**back'-garden**, **back'-green**, a garden, green, at the back of a house; **back'ground**, ground at the back: a place of obscurity: the space behind the principal figures of a picture: that against which anything is, or ought to be, seen (*fig.*): upbringing and previous history (*fig.*): environment (*fig.*).—*adj.* in the background (*lit.* or *fig.*).—*adj.* **back'-hair**, the hair at the back of the head; **back'hand**, the hand turned backwards in making a stroke: handwriting with the letters sloping backwards: in the part of the court to the left of a right-handed player, or the right of a left-handed (*tennis*): a stroke made with the hand turned backwards.—*adjs.* **back'hand'**, back-handed; **back'-hand'ed**, with the hand turned backwards (as of a blow): indirect, dubious, sarcastic, insincere.— *ns.* **back'-hand'er**, a blow with the back of the hand: a bribe (*coll.*): an extra glass of wine out of turn, the bottle being passed back; **back'ing-down**, shirking; **back'lash**, the jarring or play of ill-fitting machinery in recoil: reaction or consequence, esp. if violent; **back'-lill**, the left-hand thumb-hole at the back of a bagpipe chanter (*Scott*; sometimes *erron.* **-lilt**); **back'log**, a log at the back of a fire: a reserve or accumulation of business, stock, etc., that will keep one going for some time (*coll.*).—*adj.* **back'most**, farthest to the back.—**back'-numb'er**, a copy or issue of a newspaper or magazine of a bygone date: a person or thing out of date or past the useful stage (*fig.*).—*v.i.* **back'-ped'al**, to press the pedals back, as in slowing a fixed-wheel bicycle: to hold back: to reverse one's course of action: to retreat from an opponent while still facing him (*boxing*).—**back'-ped'alling**; **back'piece**, **back'-plate**, a piece or plate of armour for the back.—*adj.* **back'room** (of persons) doing important work behind the scenes, esp. in secret (*coll.*).—**back'saw**, a saw stiffened by a thickened back.—*v.t.* **back'scratch.**—**back'-scratcher**, a clawed instrument for scratching the back: one who practises back-scratching; **back'-scratching**, doing favours in return for favours, for advantage of both parties: servile flattery; **back'set**, a setting back, reverse: an eddy or countercurrent; **back'sey** (-*sī*; *Scot.*), sirloin; **back'-side**, the back or hinder side or part of anything: the hinder part of an animal: the premises at the rear of a house (*Scot.*); **back'sight**, in surveying, a sight taken backwards: the sight of a rifle nearer the stock; **back'-slang**, slang in which every word is pronounced as if spelt backwards.—*v.i.* **back'slide**, to slide or fall back in faith or morals.—**back'slider**; **back'sliding**; **back'-spaul(d)** (*Scot.*), the back of the shoulder: the hindleg.—*v.t.* and *v.i.* **backspeir'**, **-speer'**, (*Scot.*) to cross-question.—*adj.* and *adv.* **back'stage** (*lit.* and *fig.*), behind the scenes, unobserved by the public.—**back'stairs**, servants' or private stairs of a house.—*adj.* secret or underhand.—**back'stall**, a garrotter's confederate on the lookout behind.—*v.i., pr.p.* (*Spens.*) **backstart'ing**, starting back.—*n.pl.* **back'stays**, ropes or stays extending from the topmast-heads to the sides of a ship, and slanting a little backward: any stay or support at the back.—**back'stitch**, a method of sewing in which, for every new stitch, the needle enters behind, and comes out in front of, the end of the previous one; **back'stroke**, a swimming stroke used when on the back; **back'sword**, a sword with a back or with only one edge: a stick with a basket-handle, singlestick; **backsword'man**.—*v.i.* **back'track**, go back on one's course.—*n.* a return track to starting point: a retracing of steps.—**back'veld** (-*felt*) (*S. Africa*), country remote from towns.—*adj.* remote, rustic, primitive.—*n.* **backvel'der** (-*dər*); **back'wash**, a receding wave: a backward current: a reaction.—*v.t.* to affect with backwash: to clean the oil from (wool) after combing.—**back'water**, water held back by a dam: a pool or belt of water connected with a river but not in the line of its present course or current: water thrown back by the turning of a water-wheel: a place unaffected by the movements of the day (*fig.*): a backward current of water: swell of the sea caused by a passing ship.—*n.pl.* **back'woods**, the forest beyond the cleared country.—**back'woods'man**, a dweller in the backwoods: (*fig.*): a person of uncouth manners (*fig.*): a peer who seldom attends the House of Lords (*fig.*); **back'word**, a withdrawal of a promise, etc.: a retort.—*adj.* **back'-wounding** (*Shak.*), backbiting.—**back'yard'**, a yard behind a house.—**back and fill**, to trim sails so that the wind alternately presses them back and fills them: to vacillate; **back down**, to abandon one's opinion or position; **back of** (*U.S.*), behind; **back out**, to move

out backwards: to evade an obligation or undertaking; **back-seat driver**, one free of responsibility but full of advice: one controlling from a position from which he ought not to control; **back up**, to give support to; **backward and forward**, to and fro; **back water**, to ply the oars or turn the paddle-wheels backward; **bend, fall, lean over backwards**, (*coll.*) to go even to the point of personal discomfort (to be accommodating or to please); **break the back of**, to overburden: to accomplish the hardest part of; **give or make a back**, to take up position for leapfrog; **know backwards**, to have a thorough knowledge of; **on the back of**, close behind: just after (*Scot.*); **put one's back into**, to do with might and main; **ring bells backward**, to begin with the bass bell, in order to give tidings of dismay; **set or put one's back up**, to show or to arouse resentment; **take a back seat**, to sink into obscurity or subordination; **talk through the back of one's neck**, to talk utter nonsense; **to the backbone**, through and through. [O.E. *bæc*; Sw. *bak*, Dan. *bag*.]

**back**, *bak*, *n.* a trough for carrying fuel: a tub.—*n.* **back'et** (*Scot.*), a shallow wooden trough for carrying ashes, coals, etc. [Fr. *bac*, trough, dim. *baquet*, perh. partly through Du. *bak*.]

**backare**, **baccare**, *bak'ār*, or *bak'ā'ri*, (*Shak.*), *interj.* back: stand back. [Perh. for *back there*; or sham Latin.]

**backfisch**, *bäk'fish*, *n.* a young girl, a flapper. [Ger., lit. fish for frying, perhaps in allusion to immaturity.]

**backgammon**, *bak-gam'ən*, or *bak'*, *n.* a game played by two persons on a board with dice and fifteen men or pieces each: a triple game scored by bearing all one's men before the other has brought all to his own table.—*v.t.* to defeat in such a way. [back, because the pieces are sometimes taken up and obliged to go back—that is, re-enter at the table, and M.E. *gamen*, play.]

**backsheesh**, **backshish**. See **baksheesh**.

**backward(s)**, etc. See **back** (1).

**bacon**, *bā'kn*, *n.* swine's flesh (now the back and sides) salted or pickled and dried: a rustic, a chaw-bacon (*Shak.*).—**bring home the bacon** (*coll.*), achieve an object, successfully accomplish a task: provide material support; **save one's bacon**, to come off scatheless with difficulty. [O.Fr. *bacon*, of Gmc. origin; cf. O.H.G. *bahho*, *bacho*; Ger. *bache*.]

**Baconian**, *bā-kō'ni-ən*, *adj.* pertaining to Francis Bacon (1561-1626), or to his inductive philosophy, or to Roger Bacon (d. *c.* 1292) or his teaching, or to the theory that Francis Bacon wrote Shakespeare's plays.—Also *n.*—*n.* **Baco'nianism.**

**bacteria**, *bak-tē'ri-ə*, *n.pl.* the Schizomycetes, a class of microscopic unicellular or filamentous, plants, saprophytic, parasitic or autotrophic, agents in putrefaction, nitrogen fixation, etc., and the cause of many diseases:—*sing.* **bacte'rium**, any member of the class, esp. a rod-shaped schizomycete.—*adjs.* **bactē'rial**, **bactē'rian**, bacteric (-*ter'ik*).—*n.* **bactē'ricide**, a substance that destroys bacteria.—*adj.* **bactērici'dal.**—*ns.* **bacteriochlorophyll** (-*klor'*, -*klōr'ō-fil*), in some bacteria, a substance related to the chlorophyll of green plants; **bactē'rioid, bac'tēroid**, a swollen bacterium living symbiotically in the root-nodules of beans and other plants.—*adj.* **bactēriolog'ical.**—*ns.* **bactēriol'ogist**; **bactēriol'ogy**, the scientific study of bacteria; **bactēriolysin** (or -*ol'i*-), an antibody that destroys bacteria; **bactēriol'ysis**, destruction of bacteria by an antibody (Gr. *lysis*, dissolution).—*adj.* **bactēriol'ic.**—*ns.* **bacteriophage** (*bak-tē'ri-ō-fāj*, -*fäzh*), any of a large number of virus-like agents, present in the atmosphere, soil, water, living things, etc., whose function is to destroy bacteria (Gr. *phagein*, to eat); **bactē̆riŏ'sis**, any bacterial plant-disease; **bactē̆rios'tasis**, inhibition of the growth of bacteria (Gr. *stasis*, standing); **bactē'riostat**, an agent that inhibits their growth.—*adj.* **bactēriostat'ic**.—*v.t.* **bac'-tĕrise, -ize**, to treat with bacteria.—**bacterial leaching**, see **leaching**. [Gr. *baktērion*, dim. of *baktron*, a stick.]

**Bactrian**, *bak'tri-ən*, *adj.* belonging to *Bactria* (Central Asia), esp. applied to a two-humped camel.—*n.* a two-humped camel.

**baculine**, *bak'ū-līn*, *adj.* pertaining to the stick or cane—in flogging. [L. *baculum*.]

**baculite**, *bak'ū-līt*, *n.* a fossil of the genus Bacul**i'tes** (*-i-tēz*), allied to the ammonites, with a straight, tapering shell. [L. *baculum*, a stick.]

**bad**, *bad*, *adj.* ill or evil: wicked: hurtful: incorrect, faulty: poor: unskilful: worthless: unfavourable: unwell: spurious: severe: having serious effects:—*comp.* **worse**; *superl.* **worst**.—*n.* **baddie, baddy** (*slang*), a criminal person or villain, esp. as portrayed in films, television or radio shows.—*adj.* **badd'ish**, somewhat bad: not very good.—*adv.* **bad'ly**, in a faulty or unskilful way: unfavourably: severely: to a marked extent: very much.—*n.* **bad'ness**.—**bad blood**, angry feeling; **bad debt**, a debt that cannot be recovered; **bad lands**, wastes of much eroded soft strata in South Dakota and elsewhere; **bad language**, profane language, swearing; **bad'man'** (*U.S.*), an outlaw; **bad shot**, a wrong guess.—**go bad**, to decay; **go to the bad**, to go to moral ruin; **in bad books**, in disfavour; **to the bad**, in a bad condition: in deficit; **with a bad grace**, ungraciously. [Ety. very obscure. The M.E. *badde* is perh. from O.E. *bæddel*, a hermaphrodite, *bædling*, an effeminate fellow.]

**baddeleyite**, *bad'li-it*, *n.* source of zirconium, consisting of 90% zirconium dioxide; found in beach sands, in Ceylon and Brazil. [Joseph *Baddeley*, who brought specimens to Europe in 19th cent.]

**badderlock**, *bad'ər-lok*, (*Scot.*) *n.* an edible seaweed (*Alaria*) resembling tangle. [Poss. for Balder's locks.]

**bade**, *bad* (*poet. bād*), *pa.t.* of **bid** (both verbs).

**badge**, *baj*, *n.* a distinguishing mark or emblem. [M.E. *bage*. Origin obscure.]

**badger**, *baj'ər*, *n.* a burrowing, nocturnal, hibernating animal of the otter and weasel family: extending to other animals—hyrax, wombat, ratel: a painting, or other, brush made of badger's hair.—*v.t.* to pursue with eagerness, as dogs hunt the badger: to pester or worry.—*adj.* **badg'erly**, like a badger: greyish-haired, elderly.—**badg'er-bait'ing, -drawing**, the sport of setting dogs to draw out‚ a badger from a barrel; **badg'er-dog**, the dachshund, a long-bodied and short-legged dog used in drawing the badger.—*adj.* **badg'er-legged**, having legs of unequal length, as the badger was commonly supposed to have. [Prob. from **badge** and suffix **-ard**, in reference to the white mark borne like a badge on its forehead.]

**badinage**, *bad'in-äzh*, *n.* light playful talk: banter. [Fr. *badinage*—*badin*, playful or bantering.]

**badious**, *bā'di-əs*, (*bot.*) *adj.* chestnut-coloured. [L. *badius*.]

**badmash, budmash**, *bud'mash*, (*India*) *n.* an evil-doer. [Pers.]

**badminton**, *bad'min-tən*, *n.* a cooling summer drink compounded of claret, sugar, and soda-water: a game played with shuttlecocks. [*Badminton* in Gloucester, a seat of the Dukes of Beaufort.]

**bael, bel, bhel**, *bel*, *n.* a thorny Indian rutaceous tree (*Aegle Marmelos*): its edible fruit, the Bengal quince. [Hind.]

**baetyl**, *bē'til*, *n.* a magical or holy meteoric stone. [Gr. *baitỹlos*.]

**baff**, *baf*, *v.t.* to strike the ground with the sole of a golf-club in playing, and so to send the ball up in the air.—*n.* **baffy**, *baf'i*, a club like a brassy, but with a somewhat shorter shaft and a more sloping face.

**baffle**, *baf'l*, *v.t.* to frustrate, confound, impede perplexingly: to cheat, hoodwink, bewilder, bring to nought (*obs.*): to disgrace publicly, as by hanging by the heels (*obs.*).—*n.* confusion, check (*obs.*): a plate or like device for regulating or diverting the flow of liquid, gas, sound-waves, etc. (also **baffle-plate, baff'ler**).—*n.* **baff'ler**, a bewilderer, confounder.—*adj.* **baff'ling**.—*adv.* **baff'lingly**. [Perh. Scottish and connected with *bauchle*, to treat contemptuously; but cf. Fr. *bafouer*, or earlier *beffler*, from O.Fr. *befe*, mockery.]

**baft**, *bäft*, *n.* a coarse fabric, orig. Oriental, later made in and shipped from England. [Pers. *baft*, woven.]

**baft**, *bäft*, (*arch.*) *adv.* and *prep.* behind: abaft, astern (*naut.*). [O.E. *beæftan*—*be*, by, and *æftan*, behind.]

**bag**, *bag*, *n.* a sack, pouch: specially the silken pouch to contain the back-hair of the wig: a bagful: measure of quantity for produce: a game-bag, hence the quantity of fish or game secured, however great: an udder: an unattractive, slovenly or immoral woman (*slang*): (in *pl.*) trousers (*coll.*).—*v.i.* to bulge, swell out: to drop away from the right course (*naut.*).—*v.t.* to cram full: to put into a bag, specially of game: hence to kill (game): to seize, secure or steal:—*pr.p.* **bagg'ing**; *pa.p.* **bagged**.—*n.* **bag'ful**, as much as a bag will hold:—*pl.* **bag'fuls**.—*adj.* **bagged** (*bagd*), in a bag: bulged slackly.—*adv.* **bagg'ily**.—*n.* **bagg'ing**, cloth or material for bags. —*adj.* **bagg'it** (Scots form of **bagged**), bagged: full of spawn, etc.—*n.* a ripe female salmon that has failed to shed her eggs.—*adj.* **bagg'y**, loose like a bag: bulged.—**bag'man**, an old-fashioned name for a commercial traveller; **bag'-wig**, an 18th-cent. wig with back-hair enclosed in an ornamental bag.—**bag and baggage**, originally a military expression, as in the phrase, 'to march out with bag and baggage', i.e. with all belongings saved: now used to mean 'completely' in sentences such as *to clear out bag and baggage*; **bag of bones**, an emaciated living being; **bag of tricks**, the whole outfit; **bags (I)**, (*slang*), I lay claim to; **bags of** (*slang*), plenty of; **in the bag**, secured or as good as secured; **let the cat out of the bag**, to disclose a secret. [M.E. *bagge*, perh. Scand.; not Celtic, as Diez suggests.]

**bagarre**, *ba-gär*, (Fr.) a scuffle, brawl, rumpus.

**bagasse**, *ba-gas'*, *n.* dry refuse in sugar-making.— *n.* **bagassos'is**, industrial disease caused by inhaling bagasse. [Fr.; Sp. *bagazo*, husks of grapes or olives after pressing.]

**bagatelle**, *bag-ə-tel'*, *n.* a trifle: a piece of music in a light style: a game played on a board with nine balls and a cue, the object being to put the balls down into holes at the end. [Fr.,—It. *bagatella*, a conjuror's trick, a trifle.]

**bagel**, *bā'gəl*, (*U.S.*) *n.* a hard leavened roll in the shape of a doughnut. [Yiddish, *beygel*—Ger. *beugel*.]

**baggage**, *bag'ij*, *n.* the tents, provisions, and other necessaries of an army: traveller's luggage: a worthless woman: a saucy woman.—*ns.* **bagg'age-animal**; **bagg'age-car** (*U.S.*), a railway luggage-van; **bagg'age-train**, a train of baggage-animals, wagons, etc. [O.Fr. *bagage*—*baguer*, to bind up, from which we may infer all the meanings, without reference to Fr. *bagasse*, It. *bagascia*, a strumpet.]

**bagnio**, *ban'yō*, *n.* a bathing-house, esp. one with hot baths (*obs.*): an Oriental prison: a brothel. [It. *bagno*—L. *balneum*, a bath.]

**bagpipe**, *bag'pīp*, *n.* a wind-instrument consisting

of a *bag* fitted with *pipes* (often in *pl.*).—*ns.* bag'-piper; bag'piping.

baguette, *bag-et'*, *n.* a small moulding like an astragal (*archit.*): a precious stone cut in the shape of a long rectangle. [Fr., rod, dim.—L. *baculum.*]

baguio, *bä-gē'ō*, *n.* a hurricane. [Philippine Islands Sp.]

bah, *bä, interj.* expressing disgust or contempt. [Fr.]

Bahadur, *bə-hä'dər*, or *-hö'*, (*India*) *n.* a title of respect often added to the names of officers and officials. [Hind. *bahādur*, hero.]

Bahai, Baha'i, *bä-hä'ē*, or *bə-*, *n.* an adherent of a Persian religion, a development of Babism (see Babi).—Also *adj.*—*ns.* Baha'ist; Baha'ism; Baha'ite. [From *Baha*-Ullah and Abdul *Baha*, successors of the Bab.]

baignoire, *ben-wär*, *n.* a theatre box on a level with the stalls. [Fr., bath.]

bail, *bāl*, *n.* one who procures the release of an accused person by becoming security for his appearing in court: the security given: jurisdiction, custody (*Spens.*).—*v.t.* to set a person free by giving security for him: to release on the security of another: to deliver (goods) in trust upon a contract.—*adj.* bail'able.—*ns.* bailee', one to whom goods are bailed; bail'er, one who bails goods; bail'ment, a delivery of goods in trust: the action of bailing a prisoner.—bail'-bond, a bond given by a prisoner and his surety upon being bailed; bail'-dock, bale'-dock, a room at the Old Bailey, London, in which prisoners were formerly kept during the trials; bails'man, one who gives bail for another.—to accept, admit to, allow bail, are all said of the magistrate; the prisoner offers, surrenders to his bail; the one who provides it goes, gives, or stands bail, or bails out a prisoner; give leg bail, to be beholden to one's legs for escape. [O.Fr. *baile*, perh. from *baillier*, to enclose; or L. *baculum*, a stick.]

bail, bayle, *bāl*, *n.* a barrier: a pole separating horses in an open stable: a frame for holding a cow's head during milking (*Australia*).—*v.t.* bail (*Shak.* bale), to confine.—(*Australia*) bail up, to secure in a bail: to stop and disarm in order to rob: to put one's hands up in surrender. [O.Fr. *baile*, perh. from *baillier*, to enclose; or L. *baculum*, a stick.]

bail, *bāl*, *n.* one of the cross pieces on the top of the wicket in cricket.—*ns.* bail'-ball, bail'er, a bowled ball that hits or removes a bail without disturbing the stumps. [Prob. conn. with foregoing.]

bail (also bale), *bāl*, *n.* a bucket or other vessel for ladling out water from a boat.—*v.t.* to clear of water with bails: to ladle (often with *out*).—*n.* bail'er.—to bale (bail) out, to escape from an aeroplane by parachute: to escape from a potentially difficult situation. [Fr. *baille*, bucket, perh. from L.L. *bacula*, dim. of *baca*, a basin.]

bail, *bāl*, *n.* a hoop: a hoop-handle, as in a kettle. [Prob. O.N. *beygla*, hoop, from the Gmc. root *bug-*, to bend.]

bailey, *bāl'i*, *n.* the outer wall of a feudal castle: hence the outer court, or any court within the walls.—the Old Bailey in London was in the ancient bailey between Ludgate and Newgate. [Fr. *baille*, palisade, enclosure, from L.L. *ballium*.]

Bailey bridge, *bā'li brij*, *n.* a prefabricated bridge constructed speedily for emergency use. Designed during World War II by Sir Donald *Bailey*.

bailie, *bāl'i*, *n.* in Scotland, title of magistrate who presides in borough or police court—elected by town council from among the councillors: sheriff's officer (*obs.*; cf. water-bailie): chief magis-

trate of Scottish barony or part of county (*obs.*). —*n.* bail'ieship.—Also baill'ie, baill'ieship. [O.Fr. *bailli*, *baillif*. See bailiff.]

bailiff, *bāl'if*, *n.* formerly any king's officer, e.g. sheriff, mayor, etc., esp. the chief officer of a hundred, surviving in certain cases as a formal title: the first civil officer in Jersey and in Guernsey: a foreign magistrate: a sheriff's officer: an agent or land-steward.—*n.* bail'iwick, the jurisdiction of a bailiff: jurisdiction in general. [O.Fr. *baillif*—L.L. *bājulivus*—*bājulus*, carrier, administrator. See bail (1).]

bailli, *bī-yē*, (Fr.) a magistrate; bailliage, *-äzh*, his jurisdiction.

Baily's beads, *bā'liz bēds*, *n.* bright spots, resembling a string of beads, visible during the last seconds before a total eclipse of the sun. [Detected in 1836 by the astronomer F. *Baily*.]

bain-marie, *ban-ma-rē'*, *bĕ-ma-rē*, *n.* a water-bath (*chem.*): in cooking, a vessel of hot or boiling water into which another vessel is placed to cook slowly or keep hot. [Fr. *bain-marie*, bath of Mary—L. *balneum Mariae*—origin uncertain, perh. from *Mary* or Miriam, sister of Moses, who reputedly wrote a book on alchemy.]

Bairam, *bi'räm*, *bī-räm'*, *n.* the name of two Mohammedan festivals—the *Lesser Bairam* lasting three days, after the feast of Ramadan, and the *Greater*, seventy days later, lasting four days. [Pers.]

bairn, *bārn*, (*Scot.*) *n.* a child.—*adj.* bairn'like, bairn'ly.—*ns.* bairn's'-part, see legitim; bairn'-team, bairn'-time, brood of children. [O.E. *bearn* —*beran*, to bear.]

baisemain, *bāz'mē*, (*obs.*) *n.* mostly in pl., compliment paid by kissing the hand. [Fr. *baiser*, to kiss, *main*, hand.]

bait, *bāt'*, *n.* food put on a hook to allure fish or make them bite: any allurement or temptation: a refreshment, esp. taken on a journey (*arch.*): a stop for that purpose (*arch.*): a rage (*slang*).— *v.t.* to set with food as a lure: to tempt: to give refreshment to, esp. on a journey (*arch.*): to set dogs on (a bear, bull, etc.): to persecute, harass: to exasperate, esp. with malice, tease.— *v.i.* to take, or stop for, refreshment on a journey (*arch.*).—*n.* bait'ing.—bait'fish, fish used as bait: fish that may be caught with bait. [M.E. *beyten*—O.N. *beita*, to cause to bite— *bita*, to bite.]

baize, *bāz*, *n.* a coarse woollen cloth with a long nap, used mainly for coverings, linings, etc.: a table cover.—*v.t.* to cover or line with baize. [Fr. *baies*, pl. (fem.) of *bai*—L. *badius*, bay-coloured.]

bajan, *bā'jən* (*Aberdeen*), bejant, *bē'jənt* (*St Andrews*), *n.* a freshman (so formerly at several continental universities). [Fr. *béjaune*, novice— *bec jaune*, yellow bill, unfledged bird.]

Bajocian, *ba-jō'si-ən*, (*geol.*) *adj.* of a division of the Middle Jurassic. [L. *Bajocassēs*, a people living about Bayeux.]

bajra, bajri, bajree, *bäj'rə*, or *-rä*, *bäj'rē*, (*Hind.*) a kind of Indian millet.

bake, *bāk*, *v.t.* to dry, harden, or cook by the heat of the sun or of fire: to make or cook in an oven: to harden by cold (*Shak.*): to cake (*Shak.*).—*v.i.* to work as a baker: to become firm through heat:—*pa.p.* baked (*bākt*), bāk'en (*arch.*); *pr.p.* bāk'ing.—*n.* (*Scot.*) a kind of biscuit.—*ns.* bak'er, one who bakes bread, etc: an artificial fly used in salmon-fishing; bak'ery, a bakehouse: a baker's shop; bak'ing, the process by which bread is baked: the quantity baked at one time.—bake'board (*Scot.*), a board for kneading dough on; bake'house, a house or place used for baking in; bake'meat (*B.*), pastry, pies; baker's dozen, see dozen; bake'stone, a flat stone or plate of iron on which cakes are baked in the oven; bak'ing-pow'der, a mixture (e.g. tartaric acid and sodium bicarbonate) giving off carbon dioxide, used as a substitute for yeast in baking; **bak'ing-so'da,** sodium bicarbonate. [O.E. *bacan;* cog. with Ger. *backen,* to bake, Gr. *phōgein,* to roast.]

**Bakelite,** *bā'kəl-īt, n.* a synthetic resin made by condensation of cresol or phenol with formaldehyde. [From its inventor, L. H. *Baekeland* (1863-1944); trademark.]

**baksheesh, bakhshish, backsheesh, backshish,** *bak'* or *buk'shēsh, n.* a gift or present of money in the East (India, Turkey, etc.), a gratuity or tip. [Pers. *bakhshish.*]

**Balaam,** *bā'lam,* a prophet who strives to mislead, like Balaam in Numb. xxii-xxiv: unimportant paragraphs kept in readiness to fill up a newspaper.—*n.* Bā'laamite.—*adj.* Bālaamit'ical.— Bā'laam-box, or -bas'ket, a place in which such paragraphs are kept in readiness.

**Balaclava cap, helmet,** *bal-ə-klä'va, n.* a warm woollen head-gear covering ears and back of head, suitable for severe weather. [*Balaklava* in Crimea.]

**baladin, baladine,** *ba-la-dē, -dēn,* (Fr.) a public dancer: a mountebank.

**balalaika,** *ba-lə-lī'ka, n.* a Russian musical instrument, like a guitar, with triangular body and ordinarily three strings. [Russ.]

**balance,** *bal'əns, n.* an instrument for weighing, usually formed of two dishes or scales hanging from a beam supported in the middle: act of weighing two things: equilibrium: harmony among the parts of anything: equality or just proportion of weight or power, as the *balance of power:* the sum required to make the two sides of an account equal, hence the surplus, or the sum due on the account: what is needed to produce equilibrium, a counterpoise: a contrivance that regulates the speed of a clock or watch: remainder.—*v.t.* to weigh in a balance to poise: to set or keep in equilibrium: to counterpoise: to compare: to settle, as an account: to examine and test so as to make the debtor or creditor sides of an account agree (*bookkeeping*).—*v.i.* to have equal weight or power, etc.: to be or come to be in equilibrium: to hesitate or fluctuate.—*adj.* bal'anced, poised so as to preserve equilibrium: well arranged, stable.—*n.* bal'ancer, one who, or that which, balances: a fly's rudimentary hindwing: an acrobat.—bal'ance-sheet, a summary and balance of accounts; bal'ance-wheel, a wheel in a watch or chronometer which regulates the beat or rate. —balance of payments, the difference over a stated period between a nation's total receipts (in all forms) from foreign countries and its total payments to foreign countries; balance of power, a state of equilibrium of forces in which no nation or group of nations has the resources to go to war with another or others with likelihood of success; balance of trade, the difference in value between a country's imports and exports; off balance, unstable, esp. mentally or emotionally; on balance, having taken everything into consideration. [Fr.,—L. *bilanx,* having two scales—*bis,* double, *lanx, lancis,* a dish or scale.]

**Balanus,** *bal'ə-nəs, n.* the acorn-shell genus.—*n.* **Balanogloss'us,** a genus of worm-like animals of the Hemichordata. [Gr. *balanos,* acorn, gland, *glōssa,* tongue.]

**balas,** *bal'as, n.* a rose-red spinel (usu. **balas ruby**). [O.Fr. *balais* (It. *balascio*)—L.L. *balascus*— Pers. *Badakhshān,* a place near Samarkand where they are found.]

**balata,** *bal'ə-ta, n.* the gum of the bullet or bully tree of South America, used as a substitute for rubber and gutta-percha. [Prob. Tupí.]

**balboa,** *bäl-bō'a, n.* the monetary unit of Panama. [Vasco Nuñez de Balboa, c. 1475-1517.]

**Balbriggan,** *bal-brig'ən, n.* a knit cotton fabric like

that made at *Balbriggan,* Ireland: underclothing made of it.

**balbutient,** *bal-bū'sh(y)ənt, adj.* stammering. [L. *balbūtiēns, -entis—balbūtire,* to stutter.]

**balcony,** *balk'ə-ni* (18th cent., *bal-kō'ni*), *n.* a stage or platform projecting from the wall of a building within or without, supported by pillars or consoles, and surrounded with a balustrade or railing: in theatres, usually the gallery immediately above the dress circle (*U.S.* the dress circle itself).—*n.* balconet(te)', a miniature balcony.—*adj.* bal'conied. [It. *balcōne—balco,* of Gmc. origin; O.H.G. *balcho* (Ger. *balken*), Eng. **balk.**]

**bald,** *böld, adj.* without hair, feathers, etc., on the head (or on other parts of the body): bare, unadorned: lacking in literary grace: paltry, trivial (*arch.*): undisguised.—*adjs.* bald'ing, going bald; bald'ish, somewhat bald.—*adv.* bald'ly.—*n.* bald'ness.—bald'-coot, bald'i-coot, the coot, from its pure white wide frontal plate; bald'-eagle, a common but inaccurate name for the American white-headed eagle, used as the national emblem.—*adj.* bald'-faced, having white on the face, as a horse.—*n.* bald'-head, a person bald on the head.—*adj.* bald'-headed, having a bald head.—*adj.* and *adv.* (*slang*) bald'-head'ed, without restraint: out and out.—*n.* bald'pate, one destitute of hair: a kind of wild duck.—*adjs.* bald'pate, -d.—bald as a coot, see coot. [Perh. *balled,* rounded.]

**baldachin, baldaquin,** *böl'da-kin, n.* silk brocade: a canopy over a throne, pulpit, altar, etc.: in R.C. processions, a canopy borne over the priest who carries the host. [It. *baldacchino,* Fr. *baldaquin* a canopy, from It. *Baldacco,* Baghdad, whence was brought the stuff of which they were made.]

**balderdash,** *böl'dar-dash, n.* mixture of liquids (*obs.*): idle senseless talk: anything jumbled together without judgment: obscene language or writing (*dial.*). [Origin unknown.]

**baldmoney,** *böld'mun-i, n.* spignel (*Meum athamanticum*), a subalpine umbelliferous plant: gentian of various kinds. [Ety. unknown.]

**baldric,** also **baldrick,** *böld'rik, n.* a warrior's belt or shoulder sash: (*Spens.* baudricke) the zodiac. [Cf. M.H.G. *Balderich,* girdle.]

**Baldwin,** *böld'win, n.* an American variety of apple. [Personal name.]

**bale,** *bāl, n.* a bundle, or package of goods: the set of dice for any special game (*obs.*).—*v.t.* to make into bales.—*n.* bal'er. [M.E. *bale,* perh. from O.Fr. *bale*—O.H.G. *balla, palla,* ball. See **ball.**]

**bale.** See **bail.**

**bale,** *bāl, n.* evil, injury, mischief (*arch.*): misery, woe (*arch.*).—*adj.* bale'ful, malignant, hurtful: of evil influence: painful (*arch.*): sorrowful (*arch.*): lugubrious.—*adv.* bale'fully.—*n.* bale'-fulness. [O.E. *bealu;* O.H.G. *balo;* O.N. *böl.*]

**balection.** Same as **bolection.**

**baleen,** *bə-, ba-lēn' n.* horny plates growing from the palate of certain whales, the whalebone of commerce.—Also *adj.* [O.Fr. *baleine*—L. *balaena,* whale.]

**bale-fire,** *bāl-fīr, n.* a funeral pyre (*arch.*): a beacon-fire (*Scot.*): a bonfire. [O.E. *bǣl;* cf. O.N. *bál,* bale, Gr. *phalos,* bright, white.]

**Balinese,** *bä-lə-nēz', adj.* pertaining to the island of Bali (east of Java), its people, or their language.—Also *n.*

**balista.** See **ballista.**

**balk, baulk,** *bö(l)k, n.* an unploughed ridge: a place overlooked, an omission (*obs.*): a ridge (*obs.*): part of a billiard table marked off by the balk-line: a forbidden action of the pitcher in baseball: a squared timber: a tie-beam of a house, stretching from wall to wall, esp. when laid so as to form a loft (the balks): the beam of a balance (*obs.*): a rope to connect fishing-nets:

a check, frustration: a disappointment: failure to take a jump or the like.—*v.t.* to ignore, pass over: to shirk: to decline: to avoid: to let slip: to put a balk in the way of: to thwart: to frustrate: to foil: to check: to chop (logic) (*Shak.*).—*v.i.* to pull up or stop short at a difficulty: to jib: to refuse a jump, etc.: to refrain: to desist: to lie out of the way (*Spens.*): to bandy words (*obs.*).—*adj.* balk′d (*Shak.*), prob., heaped in balks.—*n.* balk′er.—*n.* and *adj.* balk′-ing.—*adv.* balk′ingly.—*adj.* balk′y, apt to balk. —*n.* balk′line, a line drawn across a billiard table: a boundary line for the preliminary run in a jumping competition or the like. [O.E. *balca*, ridge; O.H.G. *balcho*, beam.]

**Balkanise, -ize,** also without *cap.*, *böl′kan-iz, v.t.* to reduce to the condition of the *Balkan* countries, where hostile nationalities are or were mixed together.—*n.* **Balk-, balkanisā′tion, -izā′tion.**

**ball,** *böl, n.* anything spherical or nearly so: the orb of sovereignty: a globular body to play with: any rounded protuberant part of the body: a bullet, or solid missile thrown from an engine of war: a throw or delivery of the ball at cricket, etc.: a game played with a ball, esp. (*U.S.*) baseball or football: a spherical clew of yarn, string, etc.: the eyeball: a spherical cake of soap (*obs.*): a bolus for a horse: (in *pl.*) testicles (*vulg.*). —*interj.* (in *pl.*; *vulg.*) nonsense!—*v.t.* to form into a ball: to clog: to entangle.—*v.i.* to gather into a ball: to clog: to cluster, as swarming bees round the queen.—*adj.* **balled,** formed into a ball.—*n.* **ball′ing,** forming into a ball: snowballing: (*Scot.* ba′′ing) a periodical game of football played by the population of a town in the streets (and sometimes the river).—**ball′-bear′ings,** a device for lessening friction by making a revolving part turn on loose steel balls; **ball′cock,** the stopcock of a cistern, turned by a floating ball that rises and falls with the water.—*adj.* **balled′-up** (*vulg.*), utterly confused, mixed-up.—**ball′-flower,** an ornament of Decorated Gothic architecture, resembling a ball within a globular flower; **ball′-game,** any game played with a ball, esp. (*U.S.*) baseball or football; **ball lightning,** a slowly-moving luminous ball occasionally seen during a thunderstorm.—*adjs.* **ball′-point,** of a fountain-pen, having a tiny ball rotating against an inking cartridge as its writing tip; **ball′-proof,** proof against balls discharged from fire-arms.—**ba′′spiel** (*Scots*), **ba′′ing** (see **balling**).—**ball and socket,** a joint formed of a ball partly enclosed in a cup; **no ball,** a delivery adjudged contrary to rule (*cricket*); **keep the ball rolling,** to keep things going; **make a balls of** (*vulg.*), to do badly, to make a mess of; **on the ball,** properly in touch with a situation: on the alert; **the ball at one's feet,** success in one's grasp; **three balls,** the sign of a pawnbroker. [M.E. *bal*—O.N. *böllr*; O.H.G. *ballo, pallo.*]

**ball,** *böl, n.* an assembly for dancing.—*ns.* **ball′-dress; ball′-room.**—Also *adj.*—**have a ball,** to enjoy oneself very much (*coll.*); **open the ball,** to begin operations. [O.Fr. *bal*—*baller,* to dance—L.L. *ballāre,* perh.—Gr. *ballizein,* to dance.]

**ballad,** *bal′ɔd* (*Scot.* **ballant,** *bal′ɔnt,* **ballat,** *-ɔt*), *n.* orig. a song accompanying a dance: a simple narrative poem in short stanzas (usu. of four lines, of eight and six syllables alternately): a popular song, often scurrilous, referring to contemporary persons or events (chiefly *hist.*): formerly, a drawing-room song, usu. sentimental, in several verses sung to the same melody: any slow, sentimental song.—(*obs.*) *v.t.* to make ballads about.—*ns.* **balladeer′,** one who sings ballads; **ball′adist,** a writer or singer of ballads; **ball′admonger,** a dealer in or composer of ballads; **ball′adry,** ballads collectively: ballad-

making.—**ballad concert,** a concert of drawing room ballads; **ballad opera** (*hist.*), opera with spoken dialogue, and songs set to existing popular tunes. [O.Fr. *ballade*—L.L. *ballāre,* to dance; see **ball** (2).]

**ballade,** *ba-läd′, n.* a poem of one or more terns or triplets of stanzas, each of seven, eight, or ten lines, including refrain, followed by an envoy, the whole on three (or four) rhymes: sometimes loosely, any poem in stanzas of equal length: an ill-defined form of instrumental music, often in six-eight or six-four time.—**ballade royal,** rhyme royal (James VI and I's *ballat royal* has an additional line and rhymes *ababbcbc*). [An earlier spelling of **ballad,** with old pronunciation restored.]

**ballan,** *bal′ɔn, n.* a species of wrasse.—Also **ball′-anwrasse′.** [Perh. Irish *ball,* spot.]

**ballant,** *bal′ɔnt,* a Scots form of **ballad.**

**ballast,** *bal′ɔst, n.* heavy material used to weigh down and steady a ship or balloon: broken stone or other material used as the bed of a road or railway: that which renders anything steady: quality giving stability to person's character. —*v.t.* to load with ballast: to make or keep steady: to load (*Shak.*):—*pa.p.* **ball′asted** (*Shak.* **ball′ast**).—*n.* **ball′ast-heav′er.**—**in ballast,** carrying ballast only. [Prob. Old Sw. *barlast*—*bar,* bare, and *last,* load.]

**ballat.** See **ballad, ballade.**

**ballerina,** *bal-ɔ-rē′na, n.* a female ballet-dancer:— *pl.* **balleri′ne** (*-nā*), **balleri′nas.** [It.]

**ballet,** *bal′ā, n.* a theatrical exhibition of dancing and pantomimic action: music for it: the troupe that performs it: a dance (*obs.*): (*bal′ɔt*) a form of madrigal: (*Scot.*; also **ballat**) a ballad. —*ns.* **ball′et-dancer; ball′et-girl; ball′et-master, -mistress,** the director of a ballet; **ballet′omane** (*-et′-ō-mān*), an enthusiast for ballet; **balletomā′nia.** [Fr.; dim. of *bal,* a dance.]

**ballista, balista,** *ba-lis′ta, n.* a Roman military engine in the form of a crossbow for heavy missiles.—*adj.* **ballis′tic,** projectile: relating to projectiles.—*ns.* **ballis′tics** (treated as *sing.*), the science of projectiles; **ballis′tite,** a smokeless powder composed of guncotton and nitroglycerine.—**ballistic missile,** a guided missile that ends in a ballistic descent, guidance being over only part of its course; **ballistic pendulum,** a suspended block for finding the velocity of projectiles. [L.,—Gr. *ballein,* to throw.]

**ballium,** *bal′i-ɔm, n.* the L.L. form of **bailey.**

**ballon d'essai,** *ba-l5 de-sā,* (Fr.) an experimental balloon: a feeler or preliminary sounding of opinion.

**balloon,** *bɔ-lōōn′, n.* an apparatus for travel in the air, or for carrying recording instruments, consisting of a gas-bag and a car: a toy consisting of an inflatable rubber bag: anything inflated, empty (*fig.*): ornamental ball on a pillar, etc. (*archit.*): balloon-shaped drawing enclosing words spoken in a strip cartoon: a game played with a large inflated ball, or the ball itself (*obs.*; also **ballon,** *ba-l5,* *ba-lōn′*).—*v.t.* to inflate: to send high in the air.—*v.i.* to ascend or travel in, or as if in, a balloon: to puff out like a balloon. —*ns.* **ballonet** (*bal-o-net′*), in a balloon or dirigible, a small bag from which air is allowed to escape, and into which air is forced, to compensate for changes of pressure in the gas-bag; **balloon′ing; balloon′ist.**—**balloon barrage,** a system of captive balloons as a protection against hostile aircraft; **balloon tyre,** a large pneumatic tyre of low pressure; **balloon′-vine′,** heartseed, a tropical American climber with bladdery pods.—**when the balloon goes up,** when the trouble starts: when proceedings begin. [It. *ballone,* augmentative of *balla,* ball.]

**ballot,** *bal′ɔt, n.* a little ball or ticket or paper used in voting: a secret vote or method of voting by putting a ball or ticket or paper into an urn or box: in U.S. extended to open voting.—*v.i.* to vote by ballot: to draw lots:—*pr.p.* **ball´oting**; *pa.t.* and *pa.p.* **ball´oted.**—*ns.* **ball´ot-box,** a box to receive ballots; **ball´ot-paper,** a paper on which a ballot vote is recorded. [It. *ballotta,* dim. of *balla,* ball. See **ball.**]

**ballow,** *bal´ō, (Shak.) n.* a cudgel.—Other readings are **bat, battero.** [Perh. a misprint for **baton.**]

**bally,** *bal´i,* (*slang*) *adj.* a euphemism for **bloody,** but almost meaningless.

**ballyhoo,** *bal-i-hōō´,* (*slang*) *n.* noisy propaganda.

**ballyrag,** *bal´i-rag, v.t.* to bullyrag (q.v.).

**balm,** *bäm, n.* an aromatic substance: a fragrant and healing ointment: aromatic fragrance: anything that heals or soothes pain: a tree yielding balm: an aromatic labiate plant of the genus *Melissa:* extended to *Melittis* (*bastard balm*) and other garden herbs.—*v.t.* to embalm (*arch.*): to anoint with fragrant oil (*Shak.*): to soothe (*arch.*).—*n.* **balm´iness.**—*adj.* **balm´y,** fragrant: mild and soothing: bearing balm: see **barmy.**— **balm,** or **balsam, of Gilead,** the resinous exudation of trees of the genus *Commiphora* or *Balsamodendron,* from the belief that it is the substance mentioned in the Bible as found in Gilead: the balsam fir. [O.Fr. *basme*—L. *ba¹samum.* See **balsam.**]

**bal masqué,** *bal mas-kā,* (Fr.) a masked ball.

**balm-cricket,** *bäm-krik´it,* (*Tennyson*) *n.* a cicada. [Ger. *baum,* tree, and **cricket.**]

**balmoral,** *bal-mor´əl, n.* a flat Scottish bonnet: a figured woollen petticoat: a kind of boot lacing in front.—*n.* **balmorality** (*bal-mər-al´i-ti*; *jocular*), the Victorian type of morality. [**Balmoral,** royal residence in Aberdeenshire built in Queen Victoria's reign.]

**balneal,** *bal´ni-əl, adj.* of baths or bathing.—*n.* **bal´neary,** a bath: a bathing-place: a medicinal spring.—*adj.* of or for bathing.—*ns.* **balneā´tion,** bathing; **balneol´ogist; balneol´ogy,** the scientific study of bathing and mineral springs; **balneother´apy,** treatment of disease by baths. [L. *balneum*—Gr. *balaneion,* bath.]

**balneum Mariae,** *bal´ni-əm ma-rī´ē, bal´ne-ōōm ma-rē´ī,* (L.) a bain-marie.

**baloney, boloney,** *ba-, bə-lō´ni,* (*slang*) *n.* deceptive talk: nonsense.

**baloo, balu,** *bä´lōō,* (*India*) *n.* a bear. [Hind. *bhālū.*]

**bal paré,** *bal pa-rā,* (Fr.) a dress ball.

**balsa,** *böl´sa, bäl´sa,* *n.* a raft or float: corkwood, a tropical American tree (*Ochroma Lagopus*) of the silk-cotton family, with very light wood. [Sp., raft.]

**balsam,** *böl´səm, n.* a plant of the genus *Impatiens* (family Balsaminaceae): a liquid resin or resinous oily substance, esp. balm of Gilead: any healing agent (*fig.*).—*v.t.* to heal: (*rare*) embalm. —*adjs.* **balsamic** (*-sam´ik*); **balsamif´erous,** producing balsam.—*n.* **Balsami´na,** a discarded synonym of Impatiens, giving name to the balsam family Balsaminaceae (*-in-ā´si-ē*), close akin to the geraniums.—*adj.* **bal´samy,** fragrant.— **balsam fir,** an American fir (*Abies balsamea*); **balsam of Peru, of Tolu,** see **Peru, Tolu; balsam poplar,** an American species of poplar; **Canada balsam,** a turpentine from the balsam fir. [L. *balsamum*—Gr. *balsamon;* prob. of Semitic origin.]

**Balt,** *bölt, n.* a member of the former land-owning class (of German origin) in the Baltic provinces or states.—*adj.* **Balt´ic,** of the sea separating Scandinavia from Germany and Russia: of the western division of the Baltoslavs.—*n.* **Balt´oslav´.**—*adjs.* **Balt´oslav, -ic, -om´ic,** of a family of Indo-Germanic languages including the Slavonic languages with Lettish, Lithuanian, and (extinct) Old Prussian. [From the *Baltic* Sea—L. *Baltia,* Scandinavia.]

**Baltimore,** *böl´tim-ōr, -ör, n.* a common orange and black North American bird of the hang-nest family, called also *Baltimore oriole, fire-bird,* etc. [From Lord *Baltimore,* whose livery was orange and black.]

**Baluchitherium,** *ba-lōō-chi-thē´ri-əm, n.* a gigantic Tertiary fossil rhinoceros. [*Baluchistan,* where it was found, and Gr. *thērion,* a beast.]

**baluster,** *bal´əs-tər, n.* a small pillar supporting a stair rail or a parapet coping.—*adj.* **bal´ustered.** —*n.* **bal´ustrade,** a row of balusters joined by a rail or coping. [Fr. *balustre*—L.L. *balaustium*—Gr. *balaustion,* pomegranate flower; from its form.]

**balzarine,** *bal´zə-rēn, n.* a light dress material of mixed cotton and worsted. [Fr. *balzorine.*]

**bam,** *bam,* (*coll.*) *n.* a hoax: a false tale.—*v.t.* to cheat or hoax. [See **bamboozle.**]

**bambino,** *bam-bē´nō, n.* a child: a picture or image of the child Jesus. [It.]

**bamboo,** *bam-bōō´, n.* a gigantic tropical and subtropical grass with hollow-jointed woody stem.— **bamboo curtain,** the impenetrable political barrier of Asiatic, esp. Chinese, communism (after **iron curtain**). [Perh. Malay *bambu.*]

**bamboozle,** *bam-bōō´zl, v.t.* to deceive: to confound or mystify.—*n.* **bamboo´zlement.** [Origin unknown: first appears about 1700.]

**ban,** *ban, n.* a proclamation: sentence of banishment: outlawry: anathematisation: a denunciation: a curse: a prohibition: a vague condemnation.—*v.t.* to curse (*arch.*): to chide or rail upon (*dial.*): to anathematise: to proscribe: to forbid or prohibit. [O.E. *gebann,* proclamation, *bannan,* to summon: cf. **banns.**]

**Ban, ban,** (*hist.*) *n.* the governor of a **Ban´at** (**Ban´ate, Bann´at**), or military division of the boundaries of the Hungarian kingdom. [Pers. *bān,* lord.]

**banal,** *bən-al´, bän´əl, ban´əl, adj.* commonplace, trivial, flat.—*n.* **banal´ity,** triviality. [Fr.]

**banana,** *bə-, ba-nä´nə, n.* a gigantic tree-like herbaceous plant (*Musa sapientum*) or its nutritious fruit.—**banana republic,** a small country depending on foreign capital, from the small republics in the tropics depending on exports of fruit and on foreign investment. [Sp. or Port., from the native name in Guinea.]

**banausic,** *ban-ö´sik, adj.* mechanic: befitting or savouring of an artisan: vulgar.—Also **banau´sian.** [Gr. *banausikos*—*banausos,* a handicraftsman.]

**Banbury cake,** *ban´bər-i käk, n.* a kind of mincepie made in *Banbury,* Oxfordshire.

**banc, bank,** *n.* the judges' bench.—**in banc, in banco,** in full court. [Fr.]

**banco,** *bang´kō, n.* standard money in which a bank keeps its accounts, as distinguished from the current money of the place. [It. See **bank.**]

**band,** *band, n.* that by which loose things are held together: a moral bond of restraint or of obligation (*fig.*): a tie or connecting piece: (*pl.*) shackles, bonds, fetters: an agreement or promise given (*arch.*): security given (*arch.*): a pledge (*Spens.*).—*n.* **band´ster,** one who binds the sheaves after the reapers.—**band´-stone,** a stone set transversely in a wall to bind the structure. [M.E. *band, bond*—O.N. *band.* O.E. has *bend.* See **band, below, bind, bond.**]

**band,** *band, n.* a flat strip (of cloth, rubber, metal, etc.) to bind round anything, as a hat-band, waist-band, rubber-band, etc.: a stripe crossing a surface distinguished by its colour or appearance: a flat strip between mouldings, or dividing a wall surface: the neck-band or collar of a shirt, also the collar or ruff worn in the 17th century (termed a *falling-band* when turned down): a belt for driving machinery: (*pl.*) the pair of linen strips hanging down in front from the collar, worn by some Protestant clergymen and by barristers and advocates, formerly by

others: a group or range of frequencies between two specified limits (*radio*): a group of wavelengths (*radio*).—*n.* **band'age,** a strip of cloth for winding round part of the body (esp. *surg.*): a piece of cloth used to blindfold the eyes.—*v.t.* to bind with a bandage.—*adj.* **band'ed,** fastened as with a band: striped with bands.—**band'-box** (or *ban'boks*), a light kind of box for holding (originally bands) caps, millinery, etc.; **band'-brake,** a brake in the form of a flexible band that can be tightened about a wheel or drum; **band'-fish,** a bright red Mediterranean fish (*Cepola*), or other ribbon-shaped fish; **band'-saw,** an endless saw, a toothed steel belt; **band'-string,** an ornamental string for fastening bands or collar; **band'-wheel,** a wheel on which a strap or band runs. [M.E. *bande*—O.Fr. *bande,* of Gmc. origin; cf. O.E. *bindan*; Ger. *binde,* a band; Eng. **band** (1), above, **bind.**]
**band,** *band, n.* a number of persons bound together for any common purpose: a troop of conspirators, confederates, etc.: a body of musicians, esp. performers on wind and percussion instruments, often attached to a regiment: a herd or flock (*U.S.*).—*v.t.* to bind together.—*v.i.* to associate, assemble, confederate.—*ns.* **band'master,** the conductor of a band; **bands'man,** a member of a band of musicians; **band'stand,** a structure for accommodating a band of musicians; **band'-wagon,** the car that carries the band in a circus procession: a party drawing new members by the prestige or possible advantage it seems to offer: a fashionable movement.—**Band of Hope,** an association of young persons pledged to lifelong abstinence from alcoholic drinks—first instituted about 1847; **beat the band,** to be specially good or remarkable; **then the band played,** that was the end of it. [Fr. *bande,* of Gmc. origin, with changed sense; cf. **band** (1 and 2) **bend, bind.**]
**band,** *band, v.t.* (*Spens.*) to ban or banish.
**band,** an obsolete *pa.t.* of **bind.**
**band,** *bant,* (Ger.) a volume of a book or journal:—*pl.* **bände** (*ben'də*).
**bandalore,** *ban'də-lōr, -lör, obs. n.* an 18th-cent. toy resembling a Yo-yo (*q.v.*) which, through the action of a coiled spring, returned to the hand when thrown down. [Origin unknown.]
**bandana, bandanna,** *ban-dan'ə, n.* a silk or cotton coloured handkerchief, with spots or diamond prints, originally from India. [Hind. *bādhnū,* a mode of dyeing.]
**bandar,** *bun'där, n.* a rhesus monkey. [Hind.]
**bandeau,** *ban'dō, ban-dō', n.* a band to bind the hair: a band within a hat: a bandage for the eyes:—*pl.* **bandeaux** (*ban-dōz'*). [Fr.]
**bandelet,** *band'ə-let,* (*archit.*) *n.* a small flat moulding or fillet surrounding a column. [Fr. *bandelette.*]
**bandelier,** *ban-də-lēr', n.* a form of **bandoleer.**
**banderilla,** *ban-, bän-dä-rēl'yä, n.* a dart with a streamer, stuck by bullfighters in the bull's neck.—*n.* **banderillero** (*ban-, bän-dä-rēl-yä'rō*), a bullfighter who uses banderillas.
**banderol, banderole,** *ban'də-rōl,* **bandrol,** *ban'drōl,* **bannerol,** *ban'ə-rōl* (*Spens.* **bannerall,** *-rōl*) *n.* a small banner or streamer, as that borne on the shaft of a lance: a flat band with an inscription, common in Renaissance buildings (*archit.*). [Fr.]
**bandersnatch,** *ban'dər-snach, n.* a monster invented by Lewis Carroll.
**band(h).** Same as **bund** (2).
**bandicoot,** *bun'di-kōōt, n.* the largest species of rat, found in India and Ceylon, called also *Malabar rat* and *pig-rat*: a genus (*Perameles*) of small marsupials. [Telugu *pandikokku,* pig-rat.]
**bandit,** *ban'dit, n.* an outlaw: a brigand: in airman's slang, an enemy plane:—*pl.* **ban'dits,** **banditti** (*ban-dit'ē*); also loosely used as *sing.,*

a body of bandits).—*n.* **ban'ditry.**—**one-armed bandit,** a fruit-machine, so called from the similarity to an arm of the lever pulled to operate it, and the heavy odds against the user. [It. *bandito,* pl. *banditi*—L.L. *bannire, bandire,* to proclaim. See **ban.**]
**bandobast, bundobust,** *bun'dō-bust,* (*Ind.*) *n.* an arrangement, settlement. [Hind: and Pers. *band-o-bast,* tying and binding.]
**bandog,** *ban'dog, n.* a dog tied up as a watch-dog or because of its ferocity. [**band** (1), and **dog.**]
**bandoleer, bandolier,** *ban-dō-lēr', n.* a shoulder belt, esp for ammunition. [O.Fr. *bandouillere*—It. *bandoliera*—*banda,* a band.]
**bandolero,** *ban-dō-lā'rō, n.* a highwayman. [Sp.]
**bandoline,** *ban'dō-lēn, n.* a gummy substance used for stiffening the hair. [Prob. from **band** (1).]
**bandore,** *ban-dōr', -dör, n.* an Elizabethan wirestringed instrument like a cittern, invented by John Rose. [Sp. *bandurria,* Fr. *mandore*; L. *pandura,* Gr. *pandourā,* a three-stringed lute.]
**bandrol,** *band'rōl, n.* Same as **banderol.**
**bandy,** *ban'di, n.* a club bent at the end for striking a ball: a game at ball with such a club: a game played on ice.—**ban'dy-ball,** hockey. [Origin obscure.]
**bandy,** *ban'di, v.t.* to beat to and fro: to toss from one to another (as words *with* any one): to pass from mouth to mouth: to give and take (blows or reproaches): to fight, strive (*Shak.*):—*pr.p.* **ban'dying**; *pa.t.* and *pa.p.* **ban'died.**—*n.* **ban'dying.** [Origin obscure.]
**bandy,** *ban'di, adj.* bent wide apart at the knee: having bandy or crooked legs.—*adj.* **ban'dy-legged'.** [Poss. **bandy** (1).]
**bandy,** *ban'di,* (*Ind.*) *n.* a carriage or (bullock) cart.—**ban'dyman.** [Telugu *bandi.*]
**bane,** *bān, n.* destruction: death: mischief: poison: source or cause of evil.—*v.t.* to harm (*arch.*): to poison (*Shak.*).—*adj.* **bane'ful,** destructive: pernicious: poisonous.—*adv.* **bane'fully.**—*n.* **bane'fulness.**—*n.* **bane'berry,** a black poisonous berry, the fruit of the ranunculaceous plant *Actaea spicata*: the plant itself. [O.E. *bana,* a murderer; O.N. *bani,* death.]
**bang,** *bang, n.* a heavy blow: sudden loud noise: explosion: *fig.* meanings as thrill, burst of activity, sudden success.—*v.t.* to beat: strike violently: slam, as a door: beat or surpass.—*v.i.* to make a loud noise: slam: bounce (*dial.*).—*adv.* with a bang: abruptly.—*n.* **bang'er,** something that bangs: an explosive firework: a sausage (*slang*).—*adj.* **bang'ing,** dealing blows: (*coll.*) overwhelming, very great.—*n.* **bang'ster,** a violent person: a braggart: a victor.—**bang on** (*coll.*), right on the mark; **bang off** (*coll.*), immediately; **bang-'up** (*arch. slang*), in the height of excellence or fashion; **bang up to,** right up to. [O.N. *banga,* to hammer; cf. Ger. *bengel,* a cudgel.]
**bang,** *bang, n.* hair cut square across the brow (often in *pl.*).—*v.t.* to cut square across.—*adj.* **banged,** wearing the hair in such a way.—**bang'-tail,** a tail with the end tuft squared: a beast whose tail hair is banged. [An Americanism, poss. from the phrase *bang-off.*]
**bang.** Same as **bhang.**
**bangle,** *bang'gl, n.* a ring for arm or leg.—*adj.* **ban'gled,** wearing bangles. [Hind. *bangri, bangli.*]
**bangsring.** Same as **banxring.**
**banian, banyan,** *ban'yən, -yan, n.* an Indian fig-tree with vast rooting branches: a Hindu trader, esp. from Gujarat: loosely, out of India, a Hindu: an Indian broker or financier: a loose jacket, gown, or under-garment worn in India.—**banian days** (*obs.*), days on which no meat was served out, hence days of short commons generally, from the abstinence from flesh of the Banian merchants. [Port. *banian,* perh. through Ar. *banyān,* from Hind. *baniyā*—Sans. *vāṇija*—*vaṇij,* a merchant.]

**banish,** *ban'ish, v.t.* to condemn to exile: to drive away: to expel.—*n.* **ban'ishment,** exile. [Fr. *bannir. baniss*—L.L. *bannīre,* to proclaim.]
**banister,** *ban'is-tər, n.* a stair-rail with its supports (often in *pl.*). [baluster.]
**banjo,** *ban'jō, ban-jō', n.* a musical instrument of the guitar kind—played with the fingers or with a plectrum—having a long neck, a body of stretched parchment like a drum, and usually five strings of catgut and wire.—*n.* **ban'joist** (-*ist*). [Negro pronunciation of *bandore.*]
**banjulele,** *ban-jōō-lā'li, n.* a small banjo with gut strings. [banjo and ukelele.]
**bank,** *bangk, n.* a mound or ridge: an acclivity: the margin of a river, lake, etc.: the raised border of a road, railway cutting, etc.: the surface at a pit-mouth: the coal-face in a mine: a shoal or shallow: a bed of shellfish: a mass of cloud or mist: the tilt of an aeroplane.—*v.t.* to enclose with a bank: to deposit or pile up: to cover (a fire) so as to lessen the rate of combustion.—*v.t.* and *v.i.* (of aircraft) to tilt in turning.—*n.* **bank'er** (*Austr.*), a river full to the top of its banks.—*adv.* **bank'-high,** up to the top of the bank.—*n.* **banks'man,** an overseer at a pit-mouth.—**from bank to bank,** from the time the collier begins to descend for his spell of work till he reaches the top again. [M.E. *banke,* prob. Scand.; cog. with **bank** (2, 3), **bench.**]
**bank,** *bangk, n.* a bench in a gallery: a tier or rank of oars: the bench on which judges sat: a range of apparatus or equipment: a working table in various crafts: a pottery: (of birds, esp. swans) a company.—*n.* **bank'er,** a mason's bench.—**bank'er-mark,** a mason's mark on a stone. [O.Fr. *banc,* of Gmc. origin; cog. with **bank** (1 and 3).]
**bank,** *bangk, n.* a bench, office, or institution for the keeping, lending, and exchanging, etc., of money: a money-box for savings: a stock of money, fund, or capital: in games of hazard, the money the proprietor or other, who plays against all, has before him: a pool to draw cards from: any store of material or information, as **blood bank, data bank, eye bank.**—*v.t.* to deposit in a bank.—*v.i.* to have a bank account: to count, rely (on) (*coll.*).—*ns.* **bank'er,** one who keeps a bank: one employed in banking business: a betting card game; **bank'ing,** the business of the banker.—*adj.* pertaining to a bank.—**bank'-â'gent,** formerly in Scotland, the head of a branch-bank (now **bank'-man'ager**); **bank'-bill** (formerly) a bank-note: a bill drawn by one bank upon another; **bank'-book,** a book in which record is kept of money deposited in or withdrawn from a bank; **bank'-cheque',** an order to pay issued upon a bank; **banker's card,** a card issued by a bank guaranteeing the honouring of any cheque up to a specified value; **bank'-hol'iday,** a day on which banks are legally closed, bills falling due on these being payable the following day—in England observed as a general holiday; **bank'-note,** a note issued by a bank, which passes as money, being payable to bearer on demand; **bank'-pap'er,** bank-notes in circulation; **bank'-rate,** until 1972 the rate at which the Bank of England was prepared to discount bills (see **minimum lending rate** in Supplement): **bank'roll,** money resources.—*v.t.* to finance.—**bank'-stock,** a share or shares in the capital stock of a bank.—**clearing bank,** a bank which is a member of the London Clearing-house; **joint-stock bank,** one whose capital is subscribed by a large number of shareholders; **merchant bank,** one whose functions include financing transit of goods and providing financial and commercial advice; **private bank,** one carried on by fewer than ten persons.—**bank of issue,** one that issues its own notes or promises to pay; **break the bank,** in gambling, to win from the

management the sum fixed as the limit it is willing to lose on any one day. [Fr. *banque*—It. *banca;* of Gmc. origin, cog. with two foregoing words.]
**banket,** *bang-ket', (S. Africa) n.* an auriferous pebbly conglomerate. [Du. *banketje,* almond-rock.]
**bankrupt,** *bangk'rupt, n.* one who breaks or fails in business: an insolvent person.—*adj.* insolvent: destitute (with *of*).—*v.t.* to make bankrupt.—*n.* **bank'ruptcy** (-*si*), the state of being or act of becoming bankrupt. [Fr. *banque-route,* It. *banca rotta*—*banca,* bank, and *rotto, -a*—L. *ruptus,* broken.]
**Banksia,** *bangk'si-a, n.* a genus of Australian Proteaceae. [After Sir Joseph *Banks* (1744-1820.]
**banlieue,** *bä-lyø,* (Fr.) a precinct, extramural area, suburb.
**banner,** *ban'ər, n.* strictly, a square flag charged with a coat of arms: a military standard: a flag bearing some device, often carried on two poles, or hanging from a cross-piece, used in processions, etc.: those who serve under a banner, esp. in the Manchu army (*hist.*).—*adj.* **bann'ered,** furnished with banners—**banner cloud,** a stationary lenticular cloud that forms on the lee side of a mountain; **banner headline,** a large-type headline running right across a newspaper page. [O.Fr. *banere*—L.L. *bandum, bannum;* cog. with **band** (1) and **bind.**]
**banneret,** *ban'ər-et, (hist.) n.* a knight of higher grade, orig, one bringing his vassals under his own banner, later, one dubbed on the field of battle (often confused with **baronet**). [O.Fr. *baneret,* lit. bannered.]
**bannerol, bannerall.** See **banderol.**
**bannock,** *ban'ək, n.* a flat home-made cake of oatmeal, barley, or pease-meal, usually baked on a griddle. [O.E. *bannuc.*]
**banns,** *banz, n.pl.* a proclamation of intended marriage.—**to forbid the banns,** to make formal objection to a projected marriage. [**ban.**]
**banquet,** *bangk'wit, n.* a feast: a course of sweetmeats, fruit, and wine, separate, or after a meal—still used in the Scottish phrase, 'a cake and wine banquet'.—*v.t.* to give a feast to.—*v.i.* to fare sumptuously:—*pr.p.* **banq'ueting;** *pa.t.* and *pa.p.* **banq'ueted.**—*ns.* **banq'ueter, banqueteer';** **banq'ueting.**—**banq'ueting-hall, -house.** [Fr.,—*banc,* bench.]
**banquette,** *bang-ket', n.* a raised way inside a parapet: the long seat behind the driver in a French diligence: a built-in wall-sofa used instead of individual seats, e.g. in a restaurant. [Fr.; It. *banchetta,* dim. of *banca,* seat.]
**banshee,** *ban'shē, n.* a female fairy in Ireland and elsewhere who wails and shrieks before a death in the family to which she is attached. [Ir. *bean sidhe,* Old Ir. *ben side,* woman of the fairies.]
**bant.** See **banting.**
**bantam,** *ban'təm, n.* a small variety of the common domestic fowl: a small man, esp. a soldier.—*adj.* of bantam breed: little and combative.—*n.* **ban'tam-weight,** a boxer over 8 st. and not over 8 st. 6 lb. (amateur 7 lb.). [Prob. *Bantam* in Java.]
**banteng, banting,** *ban'teng, -ting, n.* an East Indian wild ox. [Malay.]
**banter,** *ban'tər, v.t.* to assail with good-humoured raillery: to joke or jest at: to impose upon, trick (*arch.*).—*n.* humorous raillery: jesting.—*n.* **bant'erer.**—*n.* and *adj.* **bant'ering.**—*adv.* **bant'eringly.** [Ety. quite unknown.]
**banthine,** *ban'thēn, n.* a synthetic drug used against peptic ulcers.
**banting,** *bant'ing, n.* a system of diet for reducing superfluous fat.—*v.i.* **bant** (back-formation).—*n.* **bant'ingism.** [From W. *Banting* (1797-1878), a London cabinetmaker, who recommended it to the public in 1863.]

**bantling**, *bant'ling*, *n.* a child. [Prob. Ger. *bänkling*, bastard—*bank*, bench.]
**Bantu**, *ban'tōō*, *n.* a name given to a large group of African languages and the peoples speaking them in South and Central Africa: official name for African peoples of South Africa.—Also *adj.* —*n.* Ban'tustan, coined name for semi-independent African area.
**banxring, bangsring**, *bangks'ring*, *n.* a tree-shrew. [Jav. *bangsring*.]
**banyan.** See banian.
**banzai**, *bän'zä-ē*, *interj.* a Japanese battle-cry and salute to the emperor. [Jap., forever.]
**baobab**, *bā'ō-bab*, *n.* a gigantic tropical Western African tree, the monkey-bread tree (*Adansonia digitata*; family Bombacaceae). [Prob. African.]
**bap**, *bap*, (*Scot.*) *n.* a large elliptical breakfast roll. [Ety. uncertain.]
**Baphomet**, *baf'ō-met*, *n.* a mysterious idol the Templars were accused of worshipping.—*adj.* **baphomet'ic.** [For *Mahomet*.]
**baptise, -ize**, *bapt-iz'*, *v.t.* to administer baptism to: to christen, give a name to: to name at launching and break a bottle of wine on the bow of.—*n.* **bapt'ism** (*-izm*), immersion in or sprinkling with water as a religious ceremony.—*adj.* **baptis'mal.**—*adv.* **baptis'mally.**—*ns.* **bapt'ist**, one who baptises: (*cap.*) one of a body who approve only of baptising by immersion, and that only to persons who profess their faith in Christ; **bap'tistery, bap'tistry,** a place for administration of baptism, whether a separate building or part of a church.—**baptismal name,** one given at baptism, a Christian name; **baptismal regeneration,** the doctrine of the remission of sin original and actual, and of the new birth into the life of sanctifying grace, in and through the sacrament of baptism; **clinical baptism,** baptism administered to the sick; **conditional (or hypothetical) baptism,** baptism administered conditionally when it is doubtful whether the person was previously baptised validly or at all; **private baptism,** baptism elsewhere than in church.— **baptism by desire,** the grace held to be given to a believer who ardently desires baptism, but dies before he can receive it; **baptism for the dead,** the vicarious baptism of a living for an unbaptised dead Christian; **baptism of blood,** martyrdom of the unbaptised Christian; **baptism of fire,** the gift of the Holy Spirit: martyrdom by fire regarded as an equivalent to baptism: any trying ordeal, as a first experience of being under fire (*fig.*). [Gr. *baptizein—baptein*, to dip.]
**bapu**, *bä'pōō*, *n.* spiritual father. [Hindi.]
**bar**, *bär*, *n.* a comparatively long and generally massive rod or strip of any solid substance, as metal, soap, wood: a strong rod or long piece used as a lever, door fastening, barrier, part of a gate or grate, etc.: a bolt: a barrier: an obstruction or impediment: that which completely puts an end to an action or claim: a bank or shoal as at the mouth of a river or harbour: a counter across which liquor or food is served: a public-house: a rail or the like marking off a space, as in a house of parliament, or that at which prisoners are arraigned: barristers or advocates collectively: any body pronouncing judgment, often self-appointed: an addition to a medal, a strip of metal below the clasp: a ridge: a stripe, esp. transverse: a horizontal band across a shield (*her.*): a vertical line across the staff marking off a measure (**double bar,** two heavy lines at the end of a section) (*mus.*): the measure itself: (in *pl.*) the game of (prisoner's) base (but see base 1): a counter at which one particular article of food, clothing, etc., is sold, or one particular service is given.—*v.t.* to fasten, secure, shut (out, in), furnish or mark with a bar or bars: to hinder: to obstruct: to exclude the possibility or validity of: to preclude: to divide

into bars:—*pr.p.* **barr'ing;** *pa.t.* and *pa.p.* **barred.**—*prep.* except, but for.—*n.* **barr'ing.**— *prep.* except.—*adj.* **bar'ful** (*Shak.* barrefull), full of obstructions.—**bar'-bell,** a bar weighted at the ends for gymnastic exercises; **bar'fly** (*coll.*), a drinker who spends his time in bars; **bar'-graph,** a diagram representing quantities, such as frequencies, by rectangles: **bar'-iron,** iron in malleable bars; **bar'keeper,** keeper of a refreshment bar or toll-bar; **bar'-magnet,** a permanent magnet in the form of a straight bar; **bar'maid, bar'man,** a woman, man, who serves at a public-house bar; **bar'-par'lour,** a small room adjoining a bar in a public-house; **barr'ing-out',** the shutting out of a schoolmaster from school by the pupils, to enforce demands; **bar'room,** a room in which there is a bar, taproom; **bar'-sin'ister** (see baton); **bar'tender,** a barman; **bar'wood,** a red dye-wood imported in bars from Africa.—**at the bar,** in court: in practice as a barrister or advocate; **called to the bar,** admitted as barrister or advocate; **called within the bar,** made king's (or queen's) counsel. [O.Fr. *barre* —L.L. *barra*.]
**bar**, *bär*, **baur, bawr, bör,** (*Scot.*) *n.* a jest: an amusing incident or story.
**bar**, *bär*, *n.* a fish, the maigre. [Fr.]
**bar**, *bär*, *n.* a unit used in expressing atmospheric pressure (millibar equals a thousand dynes per square centimetre) (*meteor.*). [Gr. *baros*, weight.]
**baracan.** Same as barracan.
**baragouin**, *bä-rä-gwē̃*, *-gwin'*, *n.* any jargon or unintelligible language. [Fr.; from Bret. *bara*, bread, and *gwenn*, white, said to have originated in the Breton soldiers' astonishment at white bread.]
**barathea**, *bar-ə-thē'ə*, *n.* a soft fabric of worsted, or of worsted and silk, etc. [Origin unknown.]
**barathrum**, *ba-rath'room*, (L.—Gr. *barathron*) an abyss: hence, an insatiable extortioner or other person.
**barb**, *bärb*, *n.* the beard-like jag near the point of an arrow, fish-hook, etc.: one of the thread-like structures forming a feather's web: a sting (*fig.*): a wounding or wittily-pointed remark.—*v.t.* to arm with barbs: to shave, trim, mow: to pierce, as with a barb.—*adjs.* **barb'ate,** bearing a hairy tuft; **barb'ated,** barbed: bearded.—*n.* **barbe,** a Waldensian teacher.—*adj.* **barbed,** furnished with a barb or barbs (e.g. **barbed-wire,** used for fences): (by confusion) barded.—*n.* **barb'el,** a freshwater fish of the carp family with beard-like appendages at its mouth: such an appendage.— *adj.* **barb'ellate** (*bot.*), having barbed or bearded bristles.—*ns.* **barb'et,** a tropical bird with bristly beak: a kind of poodle; **barb'ule,** a small barb: a fish's barbel: a process on the barb of a feather. [L. *barba*, a beard.]
**barb**, *bärb*, *n.* a swift kind of horse: a dark-coloured fancy pigeon. [From *Barbary*, whence the breeds came.]
**Barbados, also Barbadoes,** *bär-bā'dōz*, *adj.* of the West Indian island of Barbados.—*n.* and *adj.* **Barbā'dian.**—**Barbados cherry,** the cherry-like fruit of West Indian trees of the genus Malpighia; **Barbados earth,** a diatomaceous marl found in Barbados; **Barbados gooseberry,** the edible fruit of a West Indian climbing cactus, *Pereskia aculeata*; **Barbados leg,** elephantiasis; **Barbados pride,** a West Indian shrub, peacock-flower (*Caesalpinia*, or *Poinciana, pulcherrima*): an Asiatic mimosaceous tree (*Adenanthera pavonina*) naturalised in the West Indies, called red sandalwood.
**barbarous**, *bär'bər-əs*, *adj.* falling short of the standard of correctness, classical purity, and good taste: unscholarly: corrupt or ungrammatical or unidiomatic: uncultured: uncivilised: brutal: harsh.—*n.* **barbār'ian,** orig. one who

was not a Greek, later neither a Greek nor a Roman: a foreigner: one without taste or refinement: a somewhat uncivilised man (but usu. not a savage).—Also *adj.—adj.* **barbar'ic** (*-bar'ik*), foreign: uncivilised: characteristic of barbarians: rude: tastelessly ornate and ostentatious: wild and harsh.—*n.* **barbarisa'tion**, **-ization**, (*-bar-i-zā'shən*).—*v.t.* **bar'barise, -ize,** to make barbarous: to corrupt, as a language.—*ns.* **bar'barism,** savage life: rudeness of manners: a form of speech offensive to scholarly taste; **barbar'ity** (*-bar'i-ti*), savageness: cruelty.—*adv.* **bar'barously.**—*n.* **bar'barousness.** [Gr. *barbaros*, foreign, lit. stammering, from the unfamiliar sound of foreign tongues.]
**Barbary,** *bär'bər-i, n.* the country of the *Berbers*, in North Africa.—*adj.* **barbaresque** (*-esk'*).— **Barbary ape,** the magot; **Barbary sheep,** a North African wild sheep. [Berber.]
**barbastel(le),** *bär-bəs-tel'*, or *bär'*, *n.* a hairy-lipped bat. [Fr. *barbastelle.*]
**barbecue,** *bärb'i-kū, v.t.* to roast whole: to cure on a barbecue.—*n.* a framework for drying and roasting meat: an animal roasted whole: an open floor on which coffee-beans and the like are spread out to dry: a large social entertainment, esp. in the open air, at which food is cooked over a charcoal fire: food so cooked, esp. with a highly seasoned sauce. [Sp. *barbacoa*—Haitian *barbacòa*, a framework of sticks set upon posts.]
**barbel.** See barb (1).
**barber,** *bärb'ər, n.* one who shaves beards and dresses hair.—*v.t.* to shave or cut the hair of.— **barb'er-mon'ger** (*Shak.*), a man decked out by his barber, a fop; **barber's block,** a round block on which wigs are made; **barber's pole,** the barber's sign, a pole striped spirally, generally red and white, having often a brass basin hung at the end; **barb'er-sur'geon,** one who let blood and drew teeth as well as shaved. [O.Fr. *barbour*—L. *barba*, a beard.]
**barberry,** *bär'bər-i, n.* a thorny shrub (*Berberis*) with yellow flowers and red berries, common in hedges. [L.L. *berberis*; the Ar. *barbāris* is borrowed; not connected with berry.]
**barbet.** See barb (1).
**barbette,** *bär-bet', n.* an earthen terrace inside the parapet of a rampart, serving as a platform for heavy guns: an armoured turret in a warship. [Fr.]
**barbican,** *bär'bi-kən, n.* a projecting watch-tower over the gate of a castle or fortified town: esp. the outwork intended to defend the drawbridge. [O.Fr. *barbacane*; origin unknown.]
**barbituric,** *bärb-it-ū'rik,* (*chem.*) *adj.* applied to an acid got from malonic acid and urea, source of important sedatives.—*ns.* **barb'itone** (also **barb'-ital**), veronal, a derivative of barbituric acid; **barbit'urate** (or *-tūr'*), a salt or ester of barbituric acid. [From the lichen Usnea *barbata* and *uric* acid.]
**barbola** (work), *bär-bō'la, n.* ornamentation with small flowers, fruits, etc. made of plastic paste coloured. [Origin obscure.]
**barca,** *bär'ka,* (It.) a boat, barge.
**barcarol(l)e,** *bär'kə-rōl, -rōl', -rol', n.* a gondolier's song: a musical composition of a similar character. [It. *barcarola*, a boat-song—*barca*, a boat.]
**Barclaycard,** *bär'klā-kärd, n.* credit card issued by Barclay's Bank.
**bard,** *bärd, n.* a Celtic poet and singer: a strolling minstrel: a poet.—*n.* **bard'-craft.**—*adj.* **bard'ic.** —*ns.* **bard'ling,** a poetaster; **bardol'atry,** Shakespeare-worship (Gr. *latreiā*, worship); **bard'ship.**—*adj.* **bard'y** (*Scot.*), insolent: impudent. [Gael. and Ir. *bàrd.*]
**bard,** *bärd, n.* piece of bacon or pork fat used to cover meat or game during cooking to prevent

drying-out: (*pl.*) the protective covering of a war-horse or a man-at-arms (*obs.*).—*v.t.* to cover a piece of meat or game with bacon or pork fat: to provide a horse or man with bards (*obs.*). —*adj.* **bard'ed,** caparisoned. [Fr. *barde*—Sp. *albarda*, pack-saddle, perh. from Ar. *al-barda'ah*, —*al,* the, and *barda'ah*, the mule's pack-saddle.]
**bard,** an old spelling of barred; also for barded.
**bare,** *bār, adj.* uncovered: naked: open to view: uncovered, bare-headed: unsheathed: unarmed: disfurnished: napless, threadbare, worn: unprovided or scantily provided: poor: scanty: mere: unadorned: paltry (*Shak.*): laid waste (*Shak.; Milt.*): empty: plain, without luxury (*Spens.*).—*v.t.* to strip or uncover.—*adv.* **bare'ly,** plainly: explicitly: openly: hardly, scarcely: just and no more: not quite.—*n.* **bare'ness.**—*adj.* **bar'ish,** somewhat bare.—*adj.* and *adv.* **bare'back,** without saddle.—*adjs.* **bare'backed,** with bare back: unsaddled; **bare'-breached** (*Scott*), trouserless.—**bare'bone** (*Shak.*), a very lean person.—*adj.* **bare'faced,** with the face uncovered: beardless: avowed (*Shak.*): impudent.—*adv.* **bare'facedly** (*-fāst'li, -fās'id-li*).— **bare'facedness.** — *adv.* **bare'foot.** — *adjs.* **bare'foot, -ed,** having the feet bare: discalced; **bare'headed; bare'legged.** [O.E. *bær*; Ger. *baar, bar*; O.N. *berr.*]
**bare,** *bär,* old *pa.t.* of bear.
**barege, barège,** *bä-rezh', n.* a light, mixed dressstuff.—*n.* **baregine,** *bar'i-jēn,* a gelatinous mass of bacteria and sulphur deposited in thermal waters. [*Barèges* in Hautes-Pyrénées.]
**baresark,** erroneous form of berserk.
**bargain,** *bär'gən, n.* strife (*obs.*): a contract or agreement: a favourable transaction: an advantageous purchase: chaffering (*Shak.*).—*v.i.* to strive (*obs. Scot.*): to make a contract or agreement: to chaffer: to count (*on*), make allowance (*for* a possibility).—*v.t.* to lose by bad bargaining (with *away*).—*n.* **bar'gainer.**—**bar'gain-basement, -counter,** places in a shop where bargains are promised; **bar'gain-hunter,** one who goes shopping in quest of bargains.—**bargain and sale,** in law, a mode of conveyance whereby property may be assigned or transferred for valuable consideration; **into the bargain,** over and above; **sell one a bargain** (*Shak.*), to befool him, esp. to trap him into saying something ridiculous or unseemly; **strike a bargain,** to come to terms. [O.Fr. *bargaine.*]
**barge,** *bärj, n.* a small sailing vessel (*obs.*): a flat-bottomed freight boat, with or without sails, used on rivers and canals: a lighter: the second boat of a man-of-war: a large pleasure or state boat.—*v.i.* to move clumsily: to bump (*into*): to push one's way rudely.—*n.* **barg'ee,** a bargeman.—**barge'man,** manager of a barge; **barge'-master,** proprietor of a barge; **barge'pole,** a pole for propelling a barge.—**barge in,** to intrude: to interfere. [O.Fr. *barge*—L.L. *barga*; cf. bark (2).]
**barge-board,** *bärj'bôrd, -bōrd, n.* a board along the edge of a gable to cover the rafters and keep out rain.—**barge'-coup'le,** gable rafters.—*n.pl.* **barge'-stones,** those making up the sloping edge of a gable. [Perh. L.L. *bargus,* a gallows.]
**barghest, bargest, bargaist,** *bär'gest, -gäst, n.* a dog-like goblin portending death. [Perh. conn. with Ger. *berg-geist,* mountain-spirit.]
**baric.** See barium.
**barilla,** *bar-il'a, n.* an impure sodium carbonate got by burning certain seaside plants. [Sp.]
**barite.** See under baryta.
**baritone,** *bar'i-tōn.* See barytone.
**barium,** *bā'ri-əm, n.* a metallic element (at. numb. 56) present in baryta.—*adj.* **bā'ric.**—*n.* **bā'rite** (*rare*), barytes.—**barium meal,** a mixture of barium sulphate administered to render the alimentary canal opaque to X-rays. [See baryta.]
**bark,** *bärk, n.* the abrupt cry of a dog, wolf, etc.:

Neutral vowels in unaccented syllables: *el'ə-mənt*; for certain sounds in foreign words, see p. viii

report of a gun: cough (*coll.*).—*v.i.* to utter a bark: to clamour: to keep watch: to advertise wares noisily: to cough (*coll.*).—*v.t.* to utter with a bark (*Spens.*): to utter abruptly and peremptorily: to make by barking.—*n.* bark'er, a dog: a barking dog: a tout: a pistol or cannon (*slang*).—barking deer, the muntjac.—bark up the wrong tree, to follow a false scent; his bark is worse than his bite, his angry words are worse than his actual deeds. [O.E. *beorcan.*]

bark, barque, *bärk, n.* formerly, any small sailing ship: a ship of small size, square-sterned, without head-rails: technically, a three-masted vessel whose mizzen-mast is fore-and-aft-rigged (instead of being square-rigged like the fore and main masts): any boat or sailing ship (*poet.*).—*ns.* bark'entine, barqu'entine (-*ən-tēn*), three-masted vessel, with the fore-mast square-rigged, and the main-mast and mizzen-mast fore-and-aft-rigged. [Fr. *barque*—L.L. *barca*; poss. from Gr. *bāris,* a Nile barge.]

bark, *bärk, n.* the rind or covering of the trunk and branches of a tree: that used in tanning or dyeing: that used in medicine (cinchona): an outer covering or skin—*v.t.* to strip or peel bark or skin from: to encrust.—*v.i.* to form a bark.—*v.t.* and *v.i.* bark'en, to dry up into a barky crust. —*adjs.* bark'less; bark'y.—bark'-bed, a hotbed of spent bark; bark'-beet'le, any beetle of the family Scolytidae, tunnellers in and under bark. —*adj.* bark'-bound, compressed by failure to shed the bark. [O.N. *börkr*; Dan. *bark.*]

Barker's mill, *bärk'ərz mil, n.* a device rotated by water, invented by a 17th-cent. Dr *Barker.*

barley, *bär'li, n.* a hardy grass (*Hordeum vulgare* and other species): its grain used for food, and for making malt liquors and spirits.—bar'ley-bree, -broo, -broth, strong ale: whisky; bar'ley-corn (personified as *John Barleycorn*), the grain from which malt is made: a single grain of barley: a measure of length = ⅓ of an inch; barley sugar, sugar candied by melting and cooling (formerly by boiling with a decoction of barley); barley water, a decoction of pearl barley.—pearl barley, the grain stripped of husk and pellicle, and completely rounded by grinding; pot barley, the grain deprived by milling of its outer husk, used in making broth, etc. [O.E. *bærlic,* of barley, from root of bear (3), and suffix -*lic.*]

barley, *bär'li,* (*Scot.*) *interj.* a word used in games in demand of a truce.—*n.* a truce: a breathing-space. [Perh. parley.]

barley-brake, *bär'li-brāk, n.* an old country game, originally played by three couples, of which one, left in a middle 'den called hell, had to catch the others, who could break or separate when about to be overtaken. [Perh. because often played in a *barley*-field; or perh. from the word preceding.]

barm, *bärm, n.* froth of fermenting liquor.—*adjs.* barm'y, frothy: fermenting: mentally unsound (*slang*; also balmy); barm'y-brained. [O.E. *beorma,* Dan. *bärme,* Ger. *bärme.*]

barmbrack, *bärm'brak, n.* a currant-bun. [Ir. *bairigen breac,* speckled cake.]

barm-cloth, *bärm'-kloth,* (*arch.*) *n.* an apron. [O.E. *barm* (W.S. *bearm*) bosom, and cloth.]

Barmecide, *bär'mi-sīd, n.* one who offers an imaginary or pretended banquet or other benefit. —*adjs.* Bar'mecide, Barmeci'dal. [From an imaginary feast given to a beggar in the *Arabian Nights,* by one of the *Barmecide* family.]

bar mitzvah, bar mizvah, *bär mits'və* (sometimes *cap.*), a Jewish religious ceremony at which a boy (usually thirteen years old) is formally recognised as an adult member of the Jewish community having reached the age of religious responsibility: a boy taking part in such a ceremony.

barmkin, *bärm'kin,* (*arch.*) *n.* a battlement, or a turret, on the outer wall of a castle: the wall itself. [Orig. obscure.]

barn, *bärn, n.* a building in which grain, hay, etc., are stored.—*v.t.* to store in a barn.—barn dance, an American dance like a schottische; barn'-door, the door of a barn: in cricket, a player who blocks every ball: humorously, any broad target; barn owl, a species of owl, generally buff-coloured above and white below; barn'-stormer, a strolling player (as type of ranting actor).—*v.i.* barn'storm.—*n.* barn'yard—also *adj.* as in barnyard fowl. [O.E. *bere-ern,* contracted *bern,* from *bere,* barley, *ern,* a house.]

barn, *bärn, n.* unit of effective cross-sectional area of nucleus equal to $10^{-24}$cm$^2$.

Barnaby, *bärn'ə-bi, n.* a form of *Barnabas.*—*n.* Bar'nabite, a member of the Congregation of Regular Clerics of St Paul, founded at Milan in 1530, so called from their church of St Barnabas there.—Barnaby Day, Barnaby Bright or Long Barnaby, St Barnabas' Day, 11th June, in Old Style reckoned the longest day.

barnacle, *bär'nə-kl, n.* a barnacle-goose: a cirri-pede crustacean that adheres to rocks and ship bottoms: a companion not easily shaken off.'—*n.* bar'nacle-goose, ber'nicle-goose, a species of wild goose once believed to develop from a barnacle that grew on a tree. [O.Fr. *bernaque*—L.L. *bernaca.*]

barnacle, *bär'nə-kl, n.* an instrument put on a restless horse's nose to keep him quiet: (in *pl.*) spectacles (*coll.*).—*adj.* barnacled. [O.Fr. *bernac.*]

barney, *bär'ni,* (*coll.*) *n.* humbug: a prize-fight: a quarrel.

barock, another spelling of baroque.

barograph, *bar'ō-gräf, n.* a recording barometer. [Gr. *baros,* weight, *graphein,* to write.]

barometer, *bə-rom'i-tər, n.* an instrument for measuring atmospheric pressure: a weather-glass: an indicator of change (e.g. in public opinion; *fig.*).—*adjs.* barometric (*bar-ō-met'rik*), barometrical (-*met'ri-kl*).—*adv.* baromet'rically. —*n.* barometry (-*rom'*). [Gr. *baros,* weight, *metron,* measure.]

barometz, *bar'ō-mets, n.* the Scythian lamb, at one time supposed to be at once plant and animal, to grow on a stalk, and to eat grass like a lamb, near the Caspian Sea: a fern, *Cibotium* or *Dicksonia Barometz,* of the East Indies and Pacific islands, whose woolly rootstock and leaf bases could easily be shaped into a lamb. [Erroneous form of Russ. *baranets,* club-moss, dim. of *baran,* ram.]

baron, *bar'ən, n.* a title of rank, the lowest in the peerage: a foreign noble of similar grade, as a German freiherr: the owner of a freehold estate, whether titled or not (*Scot. hist.*): a husband (opposed to *feme,* wife; *her.* and *Eng. law*): an industrial magnate (as a *press baron*): formerly a title of the judges of the Court of Exchequer: in feudal times a tenant-in-chief of the crown: later a peer or great lord of the realm generally: till 1832, the name for the parliamentary representatives of the Cinque Ports.—*ns.* bar'onage, the whole body of barons: a list or book of barons; bar'oness, a baron's wife, or a lady holding a baronial title in her own right.—*adj.* baronial (*bə-rō'ni-əl*), pertaining to a baron or barony: applied to a turreted style of architecture favoured by the Scottish land-holding class. —*n.* bar'ony, the territory of a baron: in Ireland, a division of a county: in Scotland, a large freehold estate, or manor, even though not carrying with it a baron's title and rank: the rank of baron.—bar'on-bail'ie (*hist.*), a magistrate appointed by the lord superior in a burgh of barony; bar'on-off'icer (*Scott*), an estate official.—baron of beef, a joint consisting of two

sirloins left uncut at the backbone. [O.Fr.
*barun, -on*—L.L. *barō, -ōnis*, man.]
**baronet,** *bar'ən-et, n.* a lesser baron (*obs.*; confused with *banneret*): a baron's substitute (*obs.*):
now the lowest British hereditary title (of
England, now of Great Britain, since 1611; of
Scotland, or of Nova Scotia, since 1625; of
Ireland, since 1619).—*ns.* **bar'onetage,** the whole
body of baronets: a list or book of baronets;
**bar'onetcy,** the rank or title of baronet; **bar'-
onetess,** a woman who succeeds to a Scottish
baronetcy.—*adj.* **baronet'ical.** [Dim. of baron.]
**baroque, barock,** *bə-rok', -rōk',* **barocco, -rok'ō,**
*n.* originally a jeweller's term applied to a rough
pearl: a bold, vigorous, exuberant style in
architecture, decoration, and art generally, that
arose with the Counter-Reformation and prevailed in Louis XIV's time, degenerating into
tasteless extravagance in ornament: comparable
style in music, or literature.—*adj.* in baroque
style: whimsical: flamboyant: sometimes
rococo. [Fr. *baroque,* from Port. and Sp.; of
architecture, from It.]
**baroscope,** *bar'ō-skōp, n.* an instrument for indicating changes in the density of the air. [Gr.
*baros,* weight, *skopeein,* to look at.]
**barouche,** *ba-* or *bə-rōōsh', n.* a double-seated four-wheeled carriage with a falling top. [Ger. *barutsche*—It. *baroccio*—L. *bis,* twice, *rota,* a
wheel.]
**barque.** Same as bark (2).
**barquentine.** See bark (2).
**barracan, baracan,** *bar'ə-kan,* (*obs.*) *n.* a thick,
strong stuff resembling camlet. [Fr. *barracan*—
Ar. *barrakān,* camlet, Pers. *barak,* a stuff made
of camel's hair.]
**barrace,** *bar'as,* (*obs.*) *n.* the lists in a tournament.
[O.Fr. *barras*—*barre,* bar.]
**barrack,** *bar'ək, n.* a building for soldiers, esp. in
garrison (generally in *pl.*): a huge plain, often
bleak, building, esp. for housing many persons.
—*v.t.* and *v.i.* to lodge in barracks. [Fr. *baraque*
—It. *baracca,* or Sp. *barraca,* tent.]
**barrack,** *bar'ək, v.t.* and *v.i.* to make a hostile
demonstration (against), especially by cheering
ironically, at a cricket-match, etc.—*n.* and *adj.*
**barr'acking.**—*n.* **barr'acker.** [Aboriginal Australian *borak.*]
**barracoon,** *bar-ə-kōōn', n.* a depot for slaves. [Sp.
*barracón,* augmen. of *barraca,* tent.]
**barracouta,** *bar-ə-kōō'tə, n.* a southern food-fish
(*Thyrsites*) of the hairtail family, called snoek in
South Africa and elsewhere: (also **barracoo'ta,
-cuda, -də**) a voracious West Indian fish (*Sphyraena*) akin to the grey mullets. [Sp. *baracuta.*]
**barrage,** *bar'ij,* or (*mil.*) *bar-äzh', bar'äzh, n.* an
artificial bar across a river: the forming of such
a bar; a barrier formed by continuous shower
of projectiles along a fixed or a moving line
(curtain-fire), or by captive balloons, or mines,
or otherwise.—Also *fig.*—*ns.* **barr'age-balloon;
barr'age-fire,** curtain-fire. [Fr. *barrage*—*barre,*
bar.]
**barramunda,** *bar-ə-mun'də, n.* an Australian river-fish of the *Osteoglossidae* (*Scleropages*): the
Australian lung-fish. [Native name.]
**barranca, bar-ang'kə,** (*U.S.*) *n.* a deep gorge.—
Also **barran'co.** [Sp. *barranco.*]
**barrat,** *bar'ət, n.* (*obs.*) deceit, strife or trouble.—
*n.* **barr'ator,** one who vexatiously stirs up law-suits, quarrels, etc.—*adj.* **barr'atrous.**—*adv.* **barr'-
atrously.**—*n.* **barr'atry,** fraudulent practices on
the part of the master or mariners of a ship to
the prejudice of the owners: vexatious litigation:
stirring up of suits and quarrels, forbidden under
penalties to lawyers: traffic in offices of church
or state. [O.Fr. *barat,* deceit; traced by some
to Gr. *prattein,* to do, by others to a Celt. or a
Scand. origin.]
**barrefull** (*Shak.*). See **barful** under **bar** (1).

**barrel,** *bar'əl, n.* a wooden vessel made of curved
staves bound with hoops: its contents or its
capacity (36 imperial gallons of ale and beer;
various weights or quantities of other goods): a
revolving drum: a cylinder: a tube as of a gun:
a button on a braided coat: the trunk of a horse,
etc.: political funds (*U.S.*).—*v.t.* to put in
barrels.—*v.i.* to drive very fast (*U.S.*).—*ns.*
**barr'elage; barr'elful** (*pl.* **barr'elfuls**), as much as
a barrel will hold.—*adj.* **barr'elled,** having a
barrel or barrels: put in barrels.—**barr'el-bulk,**
a measurement of five cubic feet; **barr'el-house,**
a cheap saloon (*adj.* of jazz, crude and rough
in style); **barr'el-or'gan,** a mechanical instrument for playing tunes by means of a revolving
drum set with pins; **barrel vault,** a vault with a
simple hemicylindrical roof (*adj.* **barr'el-vault'ed**).
[Fr. *baril*; perh. conn. with **bar.**]
**barren,** *bar'ən, adj.* incapable of bearing offspring:
not producing fruit, seed, crops, vegetation, etc.:
infertile: unproductive: unfruitful: arid: jejune: dull, stupid (*Shak.*).—*n.pl.* (*cap.*), in
North America, plateaus with small trees but no
timber.—*n.* **barr'enness.**—**barren strawberry,** a
plant (*Potentilla Fragariastrum*) very like the
wild strawberry, but with inedible fruit; **barr'enwort,** a herb (Epimedium) of the barberry family.
[O.Fr. *barain, brahain, brehaing.*]
**barret,** *bar'it, n.* a flat cap: a biretta.—*n.* **barr'et-
cap.** [Fr. *barette*; cf. **beret, biretta.**]
**barricade,** *bar'ik-ād, n.* a temporary fortification
raised to block a street: a barrier.—*v.t.* to block:
to close or enclose with a barricade.—*n.* and *v.t.*
(earlier form) **barricã'do.** [Fr. *barricade* or Sp.
*barricada,* perh.—Fr. *barrique* or Sp. *barrica,*
cask, the first street barricades being of casks
filled with stones, etc.; or from L.L. *barra,* bar.]
**barrico,** *bar-ē'kō, n.* a small cask. [Sp. *barrica.*]
**barrier,** *bar'i-ər, n.* a defensive stockade or palisade: a fence or other structure to bar passage
or prevent access: (in *pl.*) lists: (in *pl.*) a martial
exercise of the 15th and 16th centuries in which
the combatants were on opposite sides of a fence:
a separating or restraining obstacle.—*v.t.* to shut
by means of a barrier.—**barrier cream,** a dressing
for the skin used to prevent dirt from entering
the pores and as a protection against oils and
solvents; **barrier reef,** a coral-reef fringing a
coast with a navigable channel inside.—**Barrier
Act,** an act of the General Assembly of the
Church of Scotland (1697) decreeing that
changes in the law of the Church, even when
approved by the Assembly, should not become
law till approved by a majority of presbyteries.
[O.Fr. *barrière*—L.L. *barrāria*—*barra.*]
**barrister,** *bar'is-tər, n.* one who is qualified to
plead at the bar in a law-court (in Scotland
called *advocate*).—*adj.* **barristerial** (*-tē'ri-əl*).—*n.*
**barr'istership.**—**revising barrister,** a barrister
formerly appointed to revise the voters' lists.
[From L.L. *barra,* bar (i.e. orig. of the Inns of
Court).]
**barrow,** *bar'ō, n.* a small hand or wheeled carriage
used to convey a load.—**barr'ow-boy,** a street-trader with a barrow; **barr'ow-tram,** the shaft
of a barrow. [O.E. *bearwe*—*beran,* to bear.]
**barrow,** *bar'ō, n.* a hill or hillock (*obs.* except in
place names): an ancient grave-mound, tumulus.
[O.E. *beorg*; cf. Ger. *berg.*]
**barrow,** *bar'ō, n.* a long, sleeveless flannel garment
for infants. [Perh. O.E. *beorgan,* to protect.]
**barter,** *bär'tər, v.t.* to give in exchange (with *for,
away*).—*v.i.* to traffic by exchange of commodities.—*n.* trade or traffic by direct exchange of
goods.—*n.* **bar'terer.** [Prob. O.Fr. *barat*; see
**barrat.**]
**Bartholomew,** *bär-thol'ə-mū,* or (*obs.*) **Bartholmew, Bartlemew,** *-t(h)l-mū,* **Bartlemy,** *-tl-mi, adj.*
relating to the Apostle *Bartholomew,* his day
(24th August), or the fair held about that time

Neutral vowels in unaccented syllables: *el'ə-mənt*; for certain sounds in foreign words, see p. viii

at West Smithfield, London (1133-1855): sold at Bartholomew Fair.—*n.* **Barthol'omew-tide,** the time about St Bartholomew's Day.—**Black Bartholomew,** 24th August 1662, on which the Act of Uniformity came into force in England.

**bartisan, bartizan,** *bär'ti-zan, -zan'*, *n.* a parapet or battlement: a projecting gallery on a wall-face: (erroneously) a corbelled corner turret.—*adj.* **bar'tisaned** (*or -zand'*). [Apparently first used by Scott, who found a reading *bertisene,* for **bratticing;** see **brattice.**]

**barton,** *bär'tən*, *n.* a farmyard. [O.E. *bere-tūn,* yard—*bere,* barley, and *tūn,* enclosure.]

**barycentric,** *bar-i-sen'trik, adj.* pertaining to the centre of gravity. [Gr. *barys,* heavy, *kentron,* centre.]

**barye,** *bär'ē.* Same as **microbar.**

**baryon,** *bar'i-on, n.* any one of the heavier class of subatomic particles, which includes protons and neutrons.—Opp. to **lepton.**—**baryon number,** the number of baryons minus the number of antibaryons (antiparticles of baryons) in a system. [Gr. *barys,* heavy.]

**barysphere,** *bar'i-sfēr, n.* the heavy core of the earth within the lithosphere. [Gr. *barys,* heavy, *sphairā,* sphere.]

**baryta,** *bə-rī'tə, n.* barium monoxide.—*n.* **bary'tes** (*-tēz*), heavy-spar, barium sulphate (also **barite,** *bā'rīt*): (loosely) baryta.—*adj.* **barytic** (*ba-rit'ik*), of or containing baryta or barium.—**baryta paper,** paper coated on one side with an emulsion of barium sulphate and gelatine. It is used in moving-pointer recording apparatus and for photographic printing papers. [Gr. *barys,* heavy.]

**barytone,** *bar'i-tōn, n.* a deep-toned male voice between bass and tenor: a singer with such a voice (in these senses now usually **baritone**): (also **baryton**) musical instrument like the viola da gamba with sympathetic strings added: a kind of saxhorn.—*adj.* of the pitch and compass of a baritone or barytone: in Greek, not having an acute accent on the last syllable. [Gr. *barytonos,* deep-sounding, not accented—*barys,* heavy, deep, and *tonos,* a tone.]

**basal.** See under **base.**

**basalt,** *bas'ölt, bas-ölt', n.* an igneous rock composed essentially of plagioclase and pyroxene, and commonly olivine and magnetite or titaniferous iron: esp. a compact rock of this kind.—*adj.* **basalt'ic.** [L. *basaltēs*—Gr. *basanitēs* (*lithos*), touchstone.]

**basan,** *ba'zan, n.* a sheepskin roughly tanned and undressed. [Ar. *bitanah,* lining.]

**basanite,** *bas'ən-it, n.* a black jasper that serves as a touchstone: a variety of basalt containing nepheline, leucite, or analcime. [Gr. *basanos,* touchstone.]

**basbleu,** *bä-blə, n.* a bluestocking. [Fr.]

**bascule,** *bas'kūl, n.* an apparatus of which one end rises as the other sinks.—**bascule bridge,** a bridge that rises when a counterpoise sinks in a pit. [Fr. *bascule,* see-saw.]

**base,** *bās, n.* that on which a thing rests: foot: bottom: foundation: support: the part next the place of attachment: the foot or lower member of a pillar, on which the shaft rests (*archit.*): the side or face on which a geometrical figure is regarded as standing: the lower part of a shield (*her.*): (in *pl.*) a skirt worn by knights on horseback (*Spens.*): a horse's housing (*Milt.*): a number on which a system of numeration or of logarithms is founded: the chief ingredient: an ingredient of a mixture that plays a subsidiary but important part, such e.g. as giving bulk: a starting-point: a base-line a fixed station in games such as baseball: an old game of which prisoner's-base and rounders are forms, and baseball a development (possibly a different word: see **bar**): a place from which operations

are conducted or on which they depend: home or headquarters, of a fleet, with equipment for its safe-keeping, repairs and other needs: in chem. a substance that reacts with an acid to form a salt, or dissolves in water forming hydroxyl ions.—*v.t.* to found or place on a base: —*pr.p.* **bas'ing;** *pa.p.* **based** (*bāst*).—*adj.* **bās'al,** pertaining to or situated at the base: at the lowest level: (loosely) fundamental.—*adj.* **base'less,** without a base or foundation.—*n.* **base'lessness.**—*adj.* **bās'ic,** belonging to or of the nature of a base: containing excess of a base: in geol., poor in silica—opp. to *acid:* (loosely) fundamental.—*adv.* **bas'ically.**—*n.* **basic'ity** (*-is'*). —*adj.* **basilar** (*bas'*), basal.—**basal anaesthesia,** anaesthesia acting as a basis for further and deeper anaesthesia; **basal plane** (*crystallography*), a crystal face or form parallel to the horizontal axes; **base'ball,** the American national game, a development of rounders, played nine-a-side with bat and ball, the players on the batting side making a circuit of four bases: a ball for the game; **base'baller; base line,** an accurately measured line used as a base for triangulation: a line at the end of the court (*lawn tennis*): a line joining bases (*baseball*); **base'man** (*baseball*), a fielder stationed near a base; **base'ment,** an underlying support: lowest story of a building, beneath the principal one, esp. one below ground level; **base'plate,** the foundation plate of a piece of heavy machinery; **base'runner,** a baseball player in course of performing his circuit of bases; **Basic English,** a reduced English vocabulary of 850 words for teaching foreigners or for use as an auxiliary language: (without *cap.*) English using few and simple words; **basic process,** a steel-making process with a furnace lined with material rich in metallic oxides; **basic salt,** a salt having one or more hydroxyl groups in place of an acid radical or radicals; **basic slag,** a by-product of the basic process rich in lime, used as manure. [Fr. *base*—L. *basis*—Gr. *basis*—root of *bainein,* to go.]

**base,** *bās, adj.* low in place, value, estimation, or principle: mean: vile: worthless: debased: counterfeit: servile as opposed to *free* (*law*): humble: lowly (*B.* and *Shak.*): bass (*obs.*).—*adv.* **base'ly.**—*n.* **base'ness.**—*adj.* **base'-born,** lowborn: illegitimate.—**base coin,** spurious coin; **base metal,** any metal other than the precious metals: a metal that alters on exposure to air— opp. to *noble metal.*—*adjs.* **base'-mind'ed,** of a low mind or spirit: mean; **base'-spirited,** meanspirited. [Fr. *bas*—L.L. *bassus,* thick, squat.]

**base,** *bās, v.t.* a form of **abase.**

**baseball.** See **base** (1), and **bar** (1): also **prisoner's-base.**

**basecourt,** *bās'kört, kört, n.* the outer court of a castle or mansion: an inferior court of justice. [Fr. *basse-court* (now *basse-cour*).]

**baselard,** *bas'ə-lärd,* (*obs.*) *n.* a dagger or hanger. [A.Fr.]

**basenji,** *ba-sen'jē, n.* a smallish erect-eared, curlytailed African hunting dog that rarely barks. [Bantu, *pl.* of *mosenji, musengi,* native.]

**bash,** *bash, v.t.* to beat: to smash in.—*n.* a heavy blow: a dint.—*n.* **bash'er** (*slang*), a straw-hat.— **have a bash** (*coll.*), to have a try: to make an attempt (at); **on the bash** (*slang*), on the spree. [Prob. Scand.]

**bashaw,** *ba-shö', n.* a pasha (*arch.*): a haughty man.—*ns.* **bashaw'ism, bashaw'ship.** [Turk. *bāshā;* cf. **pasha.**]

**bashful,** *bash'fŏŏl, adj.* easily confused: modest: shy, wanting confidence.—*v.i.* **bash** (*Spens.*), to be abashed.—*adv.* **bash'fully.**—*n.* **bash'fulness.** —*adj.* **bash'less,** unashamed. [See **abash.**]

**bashi-bazouk,** *bash-ē-bə-zōōk', n.* a Turkish irregular soldier.—*n.* **ba'shi-bazouk'ery.** [Turk. *bashi-bozuq,* wild head.]

**bashlyk**, *bash'lik*, *n.* a hood with long ends worn in Russia, esp. by soldiers. [Russ. *bashluikŭ*, a Caucasian hood.]

**basidium**, *bas-id'i-əm*, *n.* a fungal fructification from which spores (usually four) are abstricted:—*pl.* basidia.—*adj.* basid'ial.—*n.pl.* Basidiomycetes (-*ō-mī-sē'tēz*), one of the main groups of fungi, characterised by the possession of basidia, including the familiar toadstools as well as rusts and smuts.—*n.* basid'iospore, a spore produced by a basidium. [Gr. *basis*, basis, and dim. ending, *-idion.*]

**basifixed**, *bā'si-fikst*, *adj.* attached by the base. [base and fixed.]

**basifugal**, *bās-*, or *bas-if'ū-gl*, *adj.* developing in a direction away from the base. [base, and L. *fugĕre*, to flee.]

**basil**, *baz'il*, *n.* an aromatic labiate plant (*Ocimum*): extended to calamint and other labiates. [O.Fr. *basile*—L. *basilisca*, representing Gr. *basilikon*, lit. royal, perh. with reference to *basiliskos*, basilisk, cobra, as a reputed cure for snakebite.]

**basil.** Same as basan.

**basil.** See bezel.

**Basilian**, *ba-*, *bə-zil'i-ən*, or *-sil'*, *adj.* of St Basil (c. 329-379).—*n.* a monk or nun following his rule.

**basilica**, *bə-sil'i-kə*, *n.* orig. a royal palace: a large oblong hall, with double colonnades and commonly a semicircular apse, used for judicial and commercial purposes: a magnificent church formed out of such a hall, or built after its plan: a Roman Catholic church with honorific privileges.—*adjs.* basil'ical, royal; basil'ican, of a basilica.—*n.* basil'icon, an ointment of various kinds, as of sovereign virtue. [Gr. *basilikos, -ē, -on*, royal—*basileus*, king.]

**basilisk**, *bas'*, *baz'il-isk*, *n.* a fabulous creature, about a foot long, with fiery death-dealing eyes and breath, so named according to Pliny, from its crown-like crest: a harmless crested lizard of tropical America: an ancient brass cannon throwing a shot of about 200 lb. [Gr. *basiliskos*, dim. of *basileus*, a king.]

**basin**, *bā'sn*, (*arch.* bason), *n.* a wide open vessel or dish: a basinful: any hollow place containing water, as a dock: the area drained by a river and its tributaries: a region of synclinal structure (*geol.*).—*n.* ba'sinful, as much as will fill a basin—*pl.* ba'sinfuls.—*adj.* ba'sin-wide (*Spens.* basen wide), wide as a basin.—have a basinful (*coll.*), to have an excess of. [O.Fr. *bacin*—L.L. *bachinus*, perh. from *bacca*, a vessel.]

**basinet**, *bas'i-net*, basnet, *bas'net*, *n.* a light globular headpiece worn alone with a visor, or with the great helm over it. [Dim. of basin.]

**basipetal**, *bās-* or *bas-ip'i-tl*, *adj.* proceeding or developing in the direction of the base. [base, and L. *petĕre*, to seek.]

**basis**, *bās'is*, *n.* the foundation, or that on which a thing rests: a pedestal: the groundwork or first principle: the fundamental ingredient:—*pl.* bas'es (*bās'ēz*). [See base (1).]

**bask**, *bäsk*, *v.i.* to lie in the warmth or sunshine (often *fig.*).—basking shark, a large but harmless shark that shows its great dorsal fin as it basks. [O.N. *bathask*, to bathe.]

**basket**, *bäs'kit*, *n.* a receptacle of plaited twigs, rushes or other flexible materials: a basketful: a net used as goal at basketball: the back part of a stagecoach outside: a basket-hilt.—*ns.* bas'ketful, as much as fills a basket:—*pl.* bas'ketfuls; bas'ketry, basket-making: basketwork.—bas'-ketball, an adaptation of lacrosse in which goals are scored by throwing a ball into a raised net (originally a basket); bas'ket-chair', a wicker chair; bas'ket-hilt', a sword hilt with a protective covering wrought like basketwork; bas'ket-maker; bas'ket-mak'ing; bas'ketwork, any

structure of interlaced twigs or the like. [Origin obscure.]

**basoche**, *ba-sosh*, (Fr.) a mediaeval gild of clerks of the parliament of Paris, performers of mystery plays.

**bason.** See basin.

**Basque**, *bäsk*, *n.* a member of a people (in their own tongue *Euscara, Eskuara*) inhabiting the western Pyrenees, in Spain and France: their agglutinative language: (without *cap.*) a short-skirted jacket, or a continuation of a bodice a little below the waist.—*adjs.* (*cap.*) of the Basques or their language or country; basqued (*bäskt*), furnished with a basque.—*n.* basquine (*-kēn'*), an outer petticoat worn by Basque and Spanish women. [Fr. *Basque*—L. *Vasconēs*, a people of Gascony.]

**bas-relief**, *bas'-ri-lēf'*, or (*Ital.*) basso-rilievo, *bäs'sō- rēl-yä'vō*, popularly -relievo, *bas'ō-ri-lē'vō*, *n.* sculpture in which the figures do not stand far out from the ground on which they are formed. [Fr. and It. See base, low, and relief.]

**bass**, *bäs*, *n.* the low or grave part in music: a bass singer—often in Italian form basso (*bäs'sō*): a bass instrument, esp. (*coll.*) a double-bass.—*adj.* low, deep, grave.—*v.t.* (*rare*) to sound in a deep tone.—bass'-bar, a strip of wood on the belly of a violin, etc., under the bass foot of the bridge, to distribute the vibrations; bass clef, the F clef on the fourth line of the stave; bass drum, the large drum of an orchestra or band; bass fiddle (*coll.*), a double-bass; bass horn, an old wind instrument, a modification of the serpent; bass tuba, the lowest instrument of the saxhorn class—the bombardon; bass viol, a four-stringed instrument, used for playing the bass in concerted music; the viola da gamba: the double-bass (*coll.*). [See base, low.]

**bass**, *bas*, *n.* a container made of bast or the like, used for carrying fish, etc.—bass'wood, limetree or its wood. [See bast.]

**bass, basse**, *bas*, *n.* a European sea-fish of the sea-perch family (*Labrax lupus* or *Morone labrax*): extended to other sea and freshwater fishes. [O.E. *bærs*; cf. Ger. *bars*, the perch.]

**basset**, *bas'it*, *n.* a hound (bass'et-hound) like a badger-dog, but bigger: an old Venetian game at cards, resembling faro, widely popular in the 18th century: outcrop (*geol.*).—*v.i.* to crop out.—basset horn (It. *corno di bassetto*), the richest and softest of all wind instruments, similar to a clarinet in tone and fingering, but with a twice-bent wooden tube. [Fr.,—*bas*, low.]

**bassinet**, *bas'i-net*, *n.* a kind of basket with a hood used as a cradle: a similarly shaped perambulator: a bed in hospital, with necessary equipment, for care of a baby. [Fr. dim. of *bassin*, a basin.]

**basso.** See bass (1).

**bassoon**, *bə-sōōn'*, *-zōōn'*, *n.* (It. *fagotto*) a woodwind instrument filling an important place in the modern orchestra, its compass from B flat below the bass stave to C or F in the treble.—The **double bassoon** (It. *contrafagotto*), sounds an octave lower.—*n.* bassoon'ist. [It. *bassone*, augmentative of *basso*, low, from root of base, bass.]

**basso profondo**, *bä'sō prō-fon'dō*, (It.) a deep bass voice, or singer.

**bast**, *bast*, *n.* phloem: inner bark, esp. of lime: fibre: matting.—Also bass. See bass (2). [O.E. *bæst*; Ger. *bast.*]

**basta**, *bas'tə*, (Shak.) interj. enough. [It. and Sp.]

**bastard**, *bas'tərd*, *n.* a child born of parents not married to each other: a sweet Spanish wine (Shak.): vulgarly, a recalcitrant person or thing, an unpleasant person, an unfortunate person, or almost meaninglessly, a chap.—*adj.* born out of wedlock: not genuine: resembling, but not identical with, the species bearing the name: of abnormal shape or size: false.—*n.* bastardisā'tion, -izā'tion.—*v.t.* bas'tardise, -ize, to pronounce to be or prove to be a bastard: to reduce to a lower state or condition.—*v.i.* to beget bastards (*Shak.*): to degenerate.—*n.* bast′ardism, bastardy.—*adj.* bas′tardly.—*n.* bas′-tardy, the state of being a bastard.—bas′tard-bar, an inaccurate name for the baton-sinister in heraldry; bastard file, file with teeth of a medium degree of coarseness; bastard title, an abbreviated title of a book on an otherwise blank page preceding the full title-page; bastard types, types cast with an extra deep bevel to obviate the use of leads, as longprimer face on pica body; bas′tard-wing, three, four, or five feathers on the first digit (homologue of the thumb) of a bird's wing. [O.F. *bastard* (Fr. *bâtard*), child of the pack-saddle (O.Fr. *bast*).]

bastard, *bas′tard, Afrik.* baster, *bas′tər, (S. Africa) n.* a person of mixed white and coloured parentage, whether legitimately born or not. [Du. *bastaard*, bastard.]

baste, *bäst, v.i.* to beat with a stick.—*n.* bast′ing. [Probl conn. with O.N. *beysta*, Dan. *böste*, to beat.]

baste, *bäst, v.t.* to drop fat or butter over, as in roasting. [Ety. unknown.]

baste, *bäst, v.t.* to tack in sewing. [O.Fr. *bastir*—O.H.G. *bestan*, to sew.]

baster. See bastard (2).

bastide, *bas-tēd,* (Fr.) a French country-house.

bastille, *bas-tēl′, n.* a tower for the defence of a fortress (*hist.*): a movable tower used by besiegers: (*cap.*) an old fortress and state prison in Paris, demolished in the Revolution (July 1789): hence any prison, esp. as a symbol of tyranny.—bastel-house (*bas′tl; Scot.*), a fortified house, usu. with vaulted ground-floor. [Fr.,—O.Fr., *bastir* (Fr. *bâtir*), to build.]

bastinado, bastinade, *bast-in-ād′(ō), v.t.* to beat with a baton or stick, esp. on the soles of the feet (an Eastern punishment):—*pr.p.* bastinād′oing or bastinād′ing; *pa.p.* bastinād′oed or bastinād′ed.—*ns.* bastinade′, bastinād′o. [Sp. *bastonada,* Fr. *bastonnade*—baston, *bâton*; cf. baton, batten.]

bastion, *bast′yən, n.* a kind of tower at the angle of a fortification: a defence (*fig.*).—*adj.* bast′-ioned. [Fr.,—It. *bastione*—*bastire*, to build.]

basto, *bäs′tō, n.* in quadrille, the ace of clubs. [Sp., club.]

Basuto, Basutu, *ba-sōōt′ō* or *′ōō, n.* Bantu people of Lesotho (form. Basutoland): a member thereof: their language (also Sotho).

bat, *bat, n.* a heavy stick: a flattish club for striking the ball in cricket: a club for baseball: in tennis, etc., a racket: a batsman: the clown or harlequin's lath: a piece of brick: speed (*slang*): a drunken spree (*slang*): a blow: a sheet of batting (also batt): a layer of felt used in hat-making (also batt).—*v.t.* and *v.i.* to hit with a bat in cricket, etc.: to hit as with a bat:—*pr.p.* batt′ing; *pa.t.* and *pa.p.* batt′ed.—*ns.* batt′er; batt′ing, the management of a bat in playing games: cotton fibre prepared in sheets, for quilts, etc.—bat′fowling, catching birds at night by showing a light and beating the bushes; bat′man, a man on an aerodrome or aircraft carrier who assists planes to taxi to position using a pair of lightweight bats; bats′man, one who wields the bat at cricket, etc.; bats′manship.—bat around (*slang*), to wander: to go on a bat; to carry (out) one's bat (*cricket*), to be not-out at the end of an innings, esp. when one has gone in first and when all ten wickets have fallen; off one's own bat, by one's own efforts (as a cricketer from his own hits): on one's own initiative; take out one's bat, to be not out at the end of an innings, esp. when one has gone in later than first and when all ten wickets have fallen. [Perh. from O.E. *bat* (a doubtful form), prob. Celt. *bat,* staff.]

bat, *bat, n.* a flying mammal with wings attached mainly to its arms and hands, but extending along its sides to the hind-feet and tail.—bats′-wing, a gas-burner that gives a flame shaped like a bat's wing.—*adj.* batt′y, batlike: bat-infested: crazy (*slang*).—*adj.* bats, (*slang*) batty.—bats in the belfry, crazy notions. [M.E. *bakke,* apparently from Scand.; cf. Dan. *aftenbakke,* evening-bat.]

bat, *bat, v.t.* to flutter, esp. an eyelid.—not to bat an eye(lid), not to sleep a wink: to show no surprise, no emotion. [Cf. bate (3).]

bat, *bat, n.* a spoken language of India or farther east.—sling the bat, to speak such a language. [Hindi, speech, word.]

batable, *bāt′ə-bl, adj.* short for debatable.

batata, *bə-tä′tə, n.* the sweet-potato. [Sp. from Haitian.]

Batavian, *bə-tā′vi-ən, adj.* pertaining to the ancient *Batāvi* in the Low Countries, or to the modern Dutch, or to Batavia (Jakarta).—Also *n.*

batch, *bach, n.* the quantity of bread baked, or of anything made or got ready, at one time: a set: quantity of material for one operation in glass-making, etc., or of concrete prepared at one time.—*adj.* batch′ing.—*v.t.* to collect into, or treat in, batches. [From the root of bake.]

bate, *bāt, v.t.* and *v.i.* to abate: to lessen, diminish: to blunt.—*adj.* bate′less, not to be blunted (*Shak.*): not bated (*obs.*).—*n.* bate′ment, reduction (*obs.*).—bated breath, restrained breathing; batement light, a window whose sill is not horizontal. [Aphetic form of abate (1).]

bate, *bāt, n.* (*Spens.*) strife, contention.—*adj.* bate′-breed′ing (*Shak.*). [Aphetic form of debate.]

bate, *bāt, v.i.* to beat the wings impatiently (*Shak.*): to be impatient (*obs.*). [O.Fr. *batre*—L.L. *batĕre.*]

bate. Same as bait, a rage (*slang*).

bateau, *bä-tō, n.* a light river-boat, esp. on Canadian rivers:—*pl.* bateaux (*-tōz′*). [Fr.]

bateleur, *bat′lər, n.* a short-tailed African eagle. [Fr., mountebank, app. from its characteristic movements.]

bath, *bäth, n.* water for immersing the body: an act of bathing: a receptacle or a house for bathing: a place for undergoing medical treatment by means of bathing: the act of exposing the body to vapour, mud, sunlight, etc.: a liquid or other material (as sand), or a receptacle, in which anything is immersed for heating, washing, or steeping (*chem.*):—*pl.* baths (*bädhz,* also *bäths*).—*v.t.* to give a bath to: to wash (oneself) in a bath.—*v.i.* to take a bath.—*ns.* bath′house; bath′robe (*U.S.*) dressing-gown; bath′room; bath′tub.—Order of the Bath, an English order of knighthood, so named from the bath before installation. [O.E. *bæth;* Ger. *bad.*]

Bath, *bäth,* a famous city in Somerset, with Roman baths.—*n.* Bathō′nian (*geol.*), a division of the Middle Jurassic (also *adj.*).—Bath bun, a rich sweet bun; Bath chair (also without *cap.*), a large wheeled chair for invalids, long in general use in Bath; Bath Oliver, a biscuit invented by Dr W. Oliver of Bath; Bath stone, a building-stone quarried at Bath.

bath, *bäth, n.* the largest Jewish liquid measure, containing about six gallons. [Heb.]

bath-brick, *bäth′-brik, n.* a preparation of siliceous silt, manufactured at Bridgwater in the form of bricks and used in cleaning knives. [Traditionally named after the first maker, one *Bath,* or from its resemblance to *Bathstone.*]

bathe, *bādh, v.t.* to wash as in a bath: to wash or moisten, with any liquid: to moisten, suffuse encompass.—*v.i.* to take a dip or swim: to bask.—*n.* the act of bathing: a swim or dip.—*n.* bäth′er.—bäth′ing-box, -hut′, a small structure for bathers to undress and dress in; bäth′ing-

*fāte, fär, hûr (her); mīne; mōte, för; mūte, mōōn, fōōt; dhen (then)* cost'ume, -dress, -suit, a garb for bathing in; bāth'ing-machine', a small carriage in which a bather may be carried out into water conveniently deep. [O.E. *bathian*.]

**bathmism,** *bath'mizm, n.* a supposed directive force in evolution, or inherent tendency to develop along divergent lines.—*adj.* **bath'mic.** [Gr. *bathmos*, step.]

**batholite,** *bath'ō-līt, n.* a mass of igneous rock that has risen from a great depth.—Also **bath'olith, bath'ylite, bath'ylith.**—*adj.* **batholit(h)ic, bathylit(h)ic** (-*lit'*, -*lith'*). [Gr. *bathos*, depth, *bathys*, deep, *lithos*, a stone.]

**bathometer,** *bath-om'it-ər, n.* a bathymeter. [Gr. *bathos*, depth, *metron*, measure.]

**bathophobia,** *bath'ō-fō-bi-a, n.* morbid fear of falling from a high place. [Gr. *bathos*, depth, *phobos*, fear.]

**bathorse,** *bat'hörs, bät'* (formerly *bä'*), *n.* a packhorse carrying an officer's baggage.—**batman,** *bat'mən* (formerly *bä'mən*), one who has charge of a bathorse: an officer's attendant; **batwoman** (*bat'*). [Fr. *bât*, pack-saddle.]

**bathos,** *bā'thos, n.* a ludicrous descent from the elevated to the mean in writing or speech.—*adj.* **bathetic** (*bə-thet'ik*; irregularly formed on the analogy of *pathos*, *pathetic*). [Gr. *bathos*, depth.]

**bathy-,** *bath'i-, -i', in composition, deep.—n.* **bathyb'ius** (Gr. *bios*, life), a once supposed low form of life on the sea bottom.—*adj.* **bathygraph'ical** (Gr. *graphein*, to write), of maps, indicating depth of water.—*n.* **bathymeter** (-*im'*; Gr. *metron*, measure), a sounding instrument.— *adjs.* **bathymet'ric, -al.**—*n.* **bathym'etry,** the science of sounding seas and lakes.—*adjs.* **bathyorograph'ical** (Gr. *oros*, mountain), representing height and depth—applied to maps that show height of land and depth of water; **bathypelagic** (*-aj'ik*; Gr. *pelagos*, sea) found in the depths of the sea.—*n.* **bath'ysphere** (Gr. *sphaira*, sphere), a submersible observation chamber (**bath'yscaph(e), -scope,** later types). [Gr. *bathys*, deep.]

**batik,** *bat'ik, n.* an East Indian method of producing designs on cloth by covering with wax, for each successive dipping, those parts that are to be protected from the dye. [Malay.]

**bating,** *bāt'ing, prep.* abating, excepting. [bate (1).]

**batiste,** *ba-tēst', n.* a fine fabric of linen, cotton, or wool. [Fr., cambric—*Baptiste*, the original maker; or from its use in wiping the heads of children after baptism.]

**batler,** *bat'lər,* (Shak.) *n.* a beetle for clothes.— Altered by some editors to **bat'let.** [bat (1).]

**batman.** See bat (1) and bathorse.

**batology,** *ba-tol'ə-ji, n.* the study of brambles.— *adj.* **batological** (*-loj'*).—*n.* **batol'ogist.** [Gr. *batos*, bramble.]

**baton,** *bat'(ə)n,* (arch.) **batoon,** *bə-tōōn', n.* a staff or truncheon, esp. of policeman, conductor (e.g. of orchestra), or marshal.—*v.t.* to strike with a baton.—**bat'on-sin'ister,** a heraldic indication of illegitimacy, improperly called *bar-sinister*, a diminutive of a bend-sinister, not extending to the sides of the shield, so as to resemble a marshal's baton laid diagonally over the family arms from sinister to dexter. [Fr. *bâton*.]

**Batrachia,** *bə-trā'ki-a, n.pl.* the Amphibia: the Salientia, tailless amphibia, or frogs and toads.— *adj.* and *n.* **batrā'chian.** [Gr. *batrāchos*, a frog.]

**batsman.** See bat (1).

**batswing.** See bat (2).

**batt.** See bat (1).

**batta,** *bat'a, n.* an allowance in addition to ordinary pay: subsistence money. [Prob. Kanarese *bhatta*, rice.]

**battailous,** *bat'ā-ləs,* (Spens.) *adj.* warlike. [O.Fr. *bataillos*; see **battle** (1).]

**battalia,** *bət-äl'yə* or *-äl', n.* order of battle (arch.):

the main body of an army in array (obs.). [It. *battaglia*; see **battle** (1).]

**battalia pie,** *bət-äl'yə pi, n.* articles like pincushions, embroidered by nuns in convents with scenes from the Bible: titbits in a pie. [Fr. *béatilles*, dim. from L. *beātus*.]

**battalion,** *bə-tal'yən, n.* a body of soldiers consisting of several companies: a body of men drawn up in battle array. [Fr. *batallion*—It. *battaglione*; see **battle** (1).]

**batteilant,** *bat'ā-lant,* (Spens.) *adj.* combatant. [Fr. *bataillant*.]

**battels,** *bat'lz, n.pl.* accounts for provisions received from college kitchens and butteries (*Oxford*): sums charged in college accounts generally.—*v.i.* **batt'el, batt'ill** (Spens.), to have such an account.—*n.* **batt'eler,** one who battels: a student of rank below a commoner (obs.). [Poss. conn. with **battle** (2).]

**batten,** *bat'n, v.i.* to thrive at the expense of (with *on*): to grow fat: to feed abundantly (on; *lit.* and *fig.*).—*v.t.* (obs.) to fatten. [O.N. *batna*, to grow better—*bati*, advantage; cf. Du. *baten*, to avail.]

**batten,** *bat'n, n.* a piece of sawn timber used for flooring, support of laths, etc.: a strip of wood fastened across parallel boards, or used to fasten down hatches aboard ship, etc.: a row of electric lamps or a strip of wood carrying them. —*v.t.* to fasten or furnish with battens.—*n.* **batt'ening,** battens forming a structure. [baton.]

**batter,** *bat'ər, v.t.* to beat with successive blows: to wear with beating or by use: to attack with artillery.—*n.* ingredients beaten along with some liquid into a paste: paste for sticking.— **batt'ering-ram,** a large beam with a metal head like a ram's used for battering down walls.— **battered baby** (or **child**) **syndrome,** collection of symptoms found in a baby or young child, caused by violence on the part of the parent or other adult suffering from social and psychological disturbance; **on the batter** (slang), on the bat, on a spree. [O.Fr. *batre* (Fr. *battre*)—L.L. *battēre* (L. *ba(t)tuĕre*), to beat.]

**batter,** *bat'ər, n.* inward inclination from the perpendicular.—*v.i.* to slope inward. [Origin doubtful.]

**batter, batting.** See bat (1).

**batterie de cuisine,** *bat-(ə-)rē də kwē-zēn,* (Fr.) set of utensils for cooking.

**battery,** *bat'ər-i, n.* the act of battering: a wound (*Shak.*): a number of cannon with their equipment: the place on which cannon are mounted: a unit of artillery or its personnel: a combination of cells, Leyden jars, lenses, or other apparatus: an attack against a person, beating, wounding, or threatening by touching clothes or body (*law*): an arrangement of tiers of cages in which hens are kept, the eggs they lay running down into wire containers outside the cages: apparatus for preparing or serving meals: pitcher and catcher (*baseball*).—**battery of tests** (*psych.*), a set of tests covering various factors relevant to some end purpose, e.g. job selection; **cross batteries,** two batteries commanding the same spot from different directions; **masked battery,** a battery out of the enemy's view.

**battill,** Spenser's spelling of **battle** (2).

**battle,** *bat'l, n.* a contest between opposing armies: a fight or encounter: a battalion (arch.). —*v.i.* to fight: to struggle: to contend (with *against*, dim.).—*v.t.* to dispose in battalions (arch.): to contest.—**batt'le-axe, -ax,** a kind of axe once used in battle: a formidable woman (*coll.*); **batt'le-cruiser,** a large cruiser with battleship qualities; **batt'le-cry,** a war-cry, slogan; **batt'ledress,** a simplified military uniform, close-fitting at the waist, allowing freedom of movement: **battle fatigue,** same as **combat fatigue**; **batt'lefield,** the place on which a battle is or was fought; **batt'le-piece**, a picture or description of a battle; **batt'leplane** (*obs.*), a large fighting aeroplane: **battle royal**, a general mêlée.—*adj.* **batt'le-scarred**, scarred in battle.—**batt'leship**, a warship of the first class.— **half the battle**, anything that brings one well on the way to success. [Fr. *bataille*—L. *battuālia*, fighting.]

**battle**, *bat'l*, *adj.* nourishing (*dial.*): fertile (*dial.*). —*v.t.* and *v.i.* (*obs.*) to feed: to fatten: to make or become fertile. [Perh. conn. with O.N. *bati*, improvement; see **batten**.]

**battle**, *bat'l*, *v.t.* (*obs.*) to furnish with battlements (esp. in *pa.p.*).—*n.* **batt'lement**, a wall or parapet with embrasures.—*adj.* **batt'lemented**. [O.Fr. *batailler*, movable defences.]

**battledore, battledoor**, *bat'l-dōr*, *-dör*, *n.* a wooden bat used for washing, etc.: a light bat for striking a ball or shuttlecock: a hornbook (*obs.*).—**not to know a B from a battledore** (*arch.*), to be thoroughly ignorant. [Perhaps Sp. *batidor*, a beater, a washing beetle.]

**battology**, *bat-ol'ə-ji*, *n.* futile repetition in speech or writing.—*adj.* **battolog'ical**. [Gr. *battologiā*, stuttering, said to be from *Battos*, who consulted the Delphic oracle about his defect of speech (Herodotus iv. 155), and *legein*, to speak.]

**battre la campagne**, *batr' la kā-pan-y'*, (Fr.) to scour the country, to beat the bush.

**batts**. See **bot**.

**battue**, *ba-tōō'*, *ba-tū'*, *bä-tü'*, *n.* a hunt in which animals are driven into some place for the convenience of the shooters: indiscriminate slaughter. [Fr.—*battre*, to beat.]

**battuta**, *bät'tōō'tä*, (It.) beat; **a battuta**, in strict time.

**bauble**, *bō'bl*, *n.* a trifling piece of finery: a child's plaything: a jester's sceptre, a stick surmounted by a head with ass's ears: a piece of childish foolery: a foolish person (*Shak.*).—*adj.* **bau'bling** (*Shak.*), trifling. [O.Fr. *babel*, *baubel*, toy, trinket.]

**bauchle**, *böhh'l*, (*Scot.*) *n.* a loose, down-at-heel, or badly worn, shoe: a worn-out, useless, or clumsy person or thing.—*v.t.* to shamble: to make shapeless: to bungle or spoil. [Origin obscure.]

**baud**, *böd'*, (*teleg.*) *n.* a unit of signalling speed.

**baudekin**, *böd'i-kin*, **bawdkin**, *böd'kin*. Same as **baldachin**.

**baudric, baudrick**, *böd'rik*. Same as **baldric(k)**.

**Baudrons**, *böd'rəns*, *n.* Scottish quasi-proper name for the cat: also for the hare. [Origin obscure.]

**Bauhaus**, *bow'hows*, *n.* a German art school (1919–1933), concerned with functional art of various kinds.

**bauk, baulk**. Same as **balk**.

**bausond**, *bös'ənd*, *adj.* having white spots, esp. on the forehead, or a white stripe down the face.— *adj.* **baus'on-faced**. [O.Fr. *bausant*, black and white spotted.]

**bauxite, beauxite**, *bök'sit*, *-zit*, *bō'zīt*, *n.* a clay compound containing aluminium. [From Les *Baux*, near Arles, and *-ite*.]

**bavardage**, *bäv-är-däzh*, *n.* chattering, prattle. [Fr. *bavard*, garrulous—*bave*, drivel.]

**bavin**, *bav'in*, *n.* a fagot of brushwood.—**bavin wits** (*Shak.*), wits that blaze and die like bavins. [Origin unknown.]

**bawbee**, *bö-bē'*, (*Scot.*) *n.* a halfpenny: originally a silver coin worth three Scots pennies. [Prob. from a Scottish mint-master (1538), Alexander Orrok of Sillebawbee.]

**bawble**. Same as **bauble**.

**bawcock**, *bö'kok*, (*Shak.*) *n.* a fine fellow. [From Fr. *beau*, fine, and *coq*, a cock.]

**bawd**, *böd*, *n.* a procuress (or till about 1700 procurer) of women for lewd purposes.—*ns.* **bawd'iness; bawd'ry**, procuring: unchastity:

**bawdy talk.**—*adj.* **bawd'y**, lewd.—*n.* **bawdy talk.**—*adj.* **bawd'-born** (*Shak.*), born of a bawd.— **bawd'y-house**, a brothel. [Prob. M.E. *bawdstrot*, pander—O.Fr. *baldestrot*, prob.—*bald*, bold, gay, and the root of **strut**.]

**bawd**, *böd*, *n.* (*Shak.* baud) a hare. [Perh. Baudrons.]

**bawl**, *böl*, *v.t.* and *v.i.* to shout or cry out very loudly.—*n.* a loud cry or shout.—*ns.* **bawl'er; bawl'ing**.—**to bawl out** (*coll.*), to reprimand bullyingly. [Perh. L.L. *baulāre*, to bark, but cf. Icel. *baula*, to low like a cow—O.N. *baula*, a cow.]

**bawley**, *bö'li*, (*Essex* and *Kent*) *n.* a small fishing-smack. [Origin obscure.]

**bawn**, *bön*, *n.* a fortification round a house: an enclosure for cattle. [Ir. *bábhun*, enclosure.]

**baxter**, *bak'stər*, (*obs.*) *n.* a baker (of bread, etc.). [bake.]

**bay**, *bā*, *adj.* reddish brown inclining to chestnut. —*n.* a bay horse. [Fr. *bai*—L. *badius*, chestnut-coloured.]

**bay**, *bā*, *n.* an inlet of the sea with a wider opening than a gulf: an inward bend of the shore: a similar recess in a land form, e.g. in a mountain range.—**bay salt**, coarse-grained salt, orig. from sea-water.—**the Bay State**, Massachusetts. [Fr. *baie*—L.L. *baia*, a harbour.]

**bay**, *bā*, *n.* the space between two columns, timbers, walls, etc.: the space under one house gable (*Shak.*): any recess or stall: a passing-place in a military trench: a side-line in a railway station (also **bay'-line**): a compartment (e.g. bomb bay) or section of an aircraft.—**bay window**, any window forming a recess.—*adj.* **bay'-win'dowed**. [O.Fr. *baée*—*baer*, to gape, be open; prob. conn. bay (2).]

**bay**, *bā*, *n.* the laurel tree; extended to other trees and shrubs, species of *Magnolia*, *Myrīca*, etc.: (in *pl.*) an honorary garland or crown of victory, originally of laurel: hence, literary renown.— **bay'berry**, the berry of the bay tree, or of candle-berry: a tree (*Pimenta acris*) akin to all-spice: **bay leaf**, dried leaf of laurel tree (*Laurus nobilis*) used as flavouring agent in cooking; **bay rum**, an aromatic liquid prepared from the leaves of *Pimenta acris*. [O.Fr. *baie*, a berry— L. *băca*.]

**bay**, *bā*, *n.* barking, baying (esp. of a dog in pursuit): the combined cry of hounds in conflict with a hunted animal: the last stand of a hunted animal when it faces the hounds at close quarters.—*v.i.* to bark (esp. of large dogs).—*v.t.* to bark at: to utter by baying: to follow with barking: to bring to bay.—**to bay (at) the moon**, to make a futile gesture; **to keep at bay**, to prevent from coming closer; **to stand, be, at bay**, to face the dogs at close quarters: to face one's pursuers. [Partly O.Fr. *abai*, barking, *bayer*, to bark, partly O.Fr. *bay*, open-mouthed suspense —L.L. *badāre*, to open the mouth.]

**bay**, *bā*, **bez**, *bā*, **bāz**, *n.* (in full **bay'-antler**, **-tine**), the second tine of a deer's horn. [O.Fr. *besantlier*—*bes-*, secondary (—L. *bis*, twice), *antlier*, antler.]

**bay, baye**, *bā*, (*Spens.*) *v.t.* to bathe.

**bayadère**, *bä-yä-der'*, *n.* a Hindu dancing-girl. [Fr.,—Port. *bailadeira*.]

**Bayard**, *bā'är(d)*, Fr. *bä-yär*, *n.* a type of the knight 'without fear and without reproach'. [From the French knight *Bayard* (1476-1524).]

**Bayard**, *bā'ärd*, *-ərd*, *n.* in romance, Rinaldo's horse: (without *cap.*), a bay horse or horse generally: a type of blind recklessness or bold ignorance.

**bayonet**, *bā'ə-nit*, *n.* a stabbing instrument of steel fixed to the muzzle of a fire-arm: military force: a soldier armed with a bayonet.—*v.t.* to stab with a bayonet: to force at the point of the bayonet.—*adj.* **bay'oneted**, armed with a

bayonet. [Fr. baïonnette, perh. from Bayonne, in France; or from O.Fr. bayon, arrow.]
bayou, bi'ōō, (U.S.) n. the marshy offshoot of a lake or river. [Perh. Fr. boyau, gut, or Choctaw bāyuk, little river.]
bayt, a Spenserian spelling of bate (1); also of bait.
bazaar, bazar, bə-zär', n. an Eastern market-place or exchange: a fancy fair in imitation of an Eastern bazaar: sometimes, a big shop. [Pers. bāzār, a market.]
bazooka, bə-zōō'kə, n. a slide wind instrument used for humorous purposes: an anti-tank gun for rocket-driven projectiles: a rocket launcher situated on the wing of an aeroplane.
bdellium, del'i-əm, n. a gum got from Commiphora trees: used to translate, but prob. unconnected with, Heb. b'dōlakh (Gen. ii. 12; meaning unknown). [L.,—Gr. bdellion.]
be, bē, v.i. infin. to live: to exist: to have the state or quality mentioned:—pr.p. bē'ing; pa.p. been (bēn, bin); pr.subj. be; arch. and dial. pr.indic. be (see am, art, is, are); for pa.t. see was, wast, were, wert.—n. be'-all (Shak.), all that is to be (be-all and end-all now often = 'the supreme aim'). [O.E. bēon; Ger. bin (1st pers.); Gael. bi, exist; W. byw, live; Gr. phyein, produce, grow; L. fui, I was, fīō, I become; Sans. bhavati, he is; orig. to grow.]
be-, bi, pfx. used (1) to form verbs with the sense of around, on all sides, in all directions, thoroughly; (2) to form verbs from adjectives and nouns; (3) it was formerly used to make intransitive verbs transitive, as bespeak. [O.E. bi-, weak form of bī.]
beach, bēch, n. the shore of a sea or of a lake, esp. when sandy or pebbly: a marginal terrace formed by waves: the strand.—v.t. to drive or haul up on a beach.—adjs. beached, having a beach: driven on a beach; beachy, pebbly.—beach'comber (-kōm-), a long rolling wave: a loafer about the wharfs in Pacific seaports: a settler on a Pacific island who maintains himself by pearl-fishery, or often by less reputable means; beach'combing; beach'head, an area held on an enemy's shore for purpose of landing; beach'-master, an officer in charge of disembarking troops; beach'-rescue, a person employed to save beach bathers in difficulties. [Orig. a dial. word for shingle.]
beach-la-mar, bēch-lä-mär', n. a South Sea jargon used in the bêche-de-mer trade. [Port. bicho do mar, sea-slug, bêche-de-mer.]
beacon, bē'kn, n. a fire on an eminence used as a sign of danger: a hill on which it could be lighted: an erection with or without a light marking a rock or shoal in navigable waters: a light to guide airmen: a sign marking a street crossing—e.g. a Belisha (bə-lē'shä) beacon, named after the Minister of Transport 1934: a wireless transmitter in which the radiation is concentrated in one or more narrow beams, so as to act as a guide to shipping or aircraft: anything that warns of danger.—v.t. to act as a beacon to: to light up: to mark by beacons.—floating beacon, a lightship. [O.E. bēacn, a beacon, a sign.]
bead, bēd, n. a prayer (obs.): a little ball strung with others in a rosary, for counting prayers: a similar ball or the like pierced for stringing to form a necklace, etc.: a beadlike drop: the front-sight of a gun: a narrow moulding of the semi-circular section, sometimes broken into bead-like parts: the flange of a tire.—v.t. to furnish with beads or beading.—v.i. to form a bead or beads.—adj. bead'ed, having beads or a bead: in beadlike form.—n. bead'ing, bead moulding: work in beads.—adj. bead'y, bead-like, small and bright (as eyes): covered with beads or bubbles.—bead'-house, orig. a chapel:

an almshouse whose inmates were required to pray for the founder's soul.—adj. bead'-proof, of such proof or strength as to carry beads or bubbles after shaking, as alcoholic liquors.—bead'-roll, orig. a list of the dead to be prayed for, hence a list of names, a long series: a rosary; beads'man, bedes'man, one bound or endowed to pray for others: licensed beggar (Scot.):—fem. beads'woman.—draw a bead on (U.S.), to take aim at; tell one's beads, to say one's prayers. [O.E. gebed, prayer; see bid.]
beadle, bēd'l, n. a mace-bearer, esp. (Oxford and Cambridge bedel(l), -del', or bēd') a vice-chancellor's: a petty officer of a church, college, etc.: a parish officer with the power of punishing petty offenders: in Scotland, the church-officer attending on the minister: a messenger or crier of a court (obs.).—ns. bead'ledom, bead'lehood, stupid officiousness; bead'leship, bedel(l)'ship, the office of beadle or bedel. [O.E. bydel—bēodan, to proclaim, to bid; affected by O.Fr. form bedel.]
beadman, bedeman, old forms of beadsman. [See under bead.]
beagle, bē'gl, n. a small hound tracking by scent, formerly much used in hunting hares: sometimes, a harrier: a spy: a bailiff: a small kind of shark.—v.i. to hunt with beagles.—ns. bea'gler; bea'gling, hunting with beagles. [Ety. unknown; poss. O.Fr. beegueulle, clamourer—beer, to gape, guele, throat.]
beak, bēk, n. a bird's bill: a hard or sharp snout: a nose: a pointed process or projection: in the ancient galley a pointed iron fastened to the prow for piercing the enemy's vessel: a magistrate, schoolmaster, or schoolmistress (slang).—adj. beaked (bēkt). [O.Fr. bec—L. beccus (recorded by Suetonius), a cock's bill.]
beaker, bēk'ər, n. a large drinking-bowl or cup, or its contents: a deep glass or other vessel used by chemists.—Beaker Folk, a round-headed, heavy-browed, square-jawed people who appeared in Britain at the dawn of the Bronze Age, makers of round barrows in which bell-shaped beakers are often found. [O.N. bikarr, prob.—L.L. bicārium, or bicārium, app.—Gr. bikos, a drinking bowl.]
beam, bēm, n. a large (obs. except in hornbeam, whitebeam, etc.): a large and straight piece of timber or iron forming one of the main structural members of a building, etc.: a great fault (fig.; Matt. vii. 3): any of the transverse pieces of framing extending across a ship's hull: the greatest width of a ship or boat: breadth: the part of a balance from which the scales hang: the pole of a carriage: the stem, or main part of a deerhorn, an anchor, a plough: a cylinder of wood in a loom: a shaft or ray of light or other radiations: a gleam.—v.t. to send forth: to place on a beam: to transmit by beam system.—v.i. to shine: to smile radiantly.—n. beam'er, a workman or machine that puts yarn on the beam of a loom.—adv. beam'ily, radiantly.—n. beam'iness, radiance: breadth.—n. and adj. beam'ing.—adv. beam'ingly.—adjs. beam'ish, radiant; beam'less, without beams: emitting no rays; beam'y, shining: radiant: massive like a weaver's beam: broad.—beam'-ends, the ends of the transverse beams of a ship; beam'-en'gine, a steam-engine with a beam connecting the piston-rod and the crank of the wheel-shaft; beam sea, one rolling against the ship's side; beam system, a system whereby, with the aid of reflectors, short wireless waves are projected (like a lighthouse beam) in a particular direction, not radiated in all directions; beam trawl, a trawling net kept open by a beam along its upper lip, resting on runners; beam trawling; beam tree, a pleonastic name for the whitebeam.—

abaft, before, **the beam**, behind, before, a line projected from the greatest width of a ship (its beam) at right angles to its course; **fly** or **ride the beam**, to fly an aircraft in the direction down by a radio beam; **lee, weather, beam**, the side away from, or towards, the wind; **off** or **on the beam**, off or on the course shown by a radio beam: off or on the mark (*fig.*); **on her beam-ends**, of a ship, so much inclined to one side that the beams become nearly vertical; **on one's beam-ends**, in acute distress, destitute; **on the beam**, in the direction of a ship's beams, at right angles to her course: see **off the beam**; **on the port, starboard, beam**, applied to any distant point out at sea, at right angles to the keel, and on the left, or right, side. [O.E. *bēam*, tree, stock of a tree, ray of light; Ger. *baum*, tree; perh. akin to Gr. *phȳma*, a growth—*phyein*, to grow.]
**bean**, *bēn*, *n.* the name of several kinds of leguminous plants and their seeds, esp. the common, or broad bean (*Vicia Faba*) and the French kidney, or haricot bean (*Phaseolus vulgaris*): applied also to the seeds of other plants, from their bean-like form, as coffee: a coin (*coll.*): head (*coll.*).—*n.* **bean'o** (*coll.*), a beanfeast, a disturbance, a jollification: bingo.—**bean-bag**, a small cloth bag containing dried beans, used in games; **bean ca'per**, a genus (*Zygophyllum*) of steppe and desert shrubs whose flower-buds are used as capers; **bean'feast**, an annual dinner given by employers to their hands at which beans used to be prominent: a jollification; **bean'-king**, the king of the festivities on Twelfth Night, finder of a bean hidden in the Twelfth Cake; **bean'pole**, a supporting pole up which a bean plant climbs: a tall, very thin person (*coll.*); **beanstalk**, the stem of a bean plant; **bean tree**, a name given to several trees, as Moreton Bay chestnut, coral tree, and Catalpa.—**full of beans**, in high spirits; **give one beans**, to treat one severely; **old bean** (see **old**). [O.E. *bēan*; Ger. *bohne*.]
**bear**, *bār*, *v.t.* to carry: to have: to convey: (*backgammon*) to remove from the board in the final stage of the game: to sustain or support: to thrust or drive: to endure: to admit of: to purport: to be entitled to (*her.*): to afford: to behave or conduct (oneself): to bring forth.—*v.i.* to suffer: to be patient: to have endurance (with *on* or *upon*): to press (with *on* or *upon*): to lie in, or take, a direction: to be capable of sustaining weight: to be productive:—*pr.p.* **bear'ing**; *pa.t.* **bōre** (*arch.* **bare**); *pa.p.* **bōrne** (but born when referring adjectively to something brought forth).—*n.* (*Spens.* **beare**, *bēr*) a burden: also (*Spens.*) a bier (see **bier**).—*adj.* **bear'able**, that may be borne or endured.—*n.* **bear'ableness**.—*adv.* **bear'ably**.—*ns.* **bear'er**, one who or that which bears: the actual holder of a cheque or the like: one who helps to carry a body to the grave: a carrier or messenger: in India a personal, household or hotel servant; **bear'ing**, demeanour: direction: a supporting surface: relation: that which is borne upon an escutcheon: the part of a machine that bears friction, esp. a journal and its support (often in *pl.*: see **ball-bearings**).—Also *adj.*—**bearing cloth**, a mantle or cloth in which a child was carried to the font; **bearing rein**, a fixed rein between the bit and the saddle, by which a horse's head is held up and its neck made to arch.—**bear a hand** (see **hand**); **bear away**, to sail away; **bear down**, to overthrow: (with *upon* or *towards*) to sail with the wind (towards): (with *upon*) to approach (someone or something) rapidly and purposefully; **bear hard** (*Shak.*), have ill-will to; **bear hard, heavily upon** (*lit.* and *fig.*), to press heavily on: to oppress, afflict; **bear in hand**, to make out, maintain (*arch.*): to keep in expectation, to flatter one's hopes (*Shak.*); **bear in mind**, remember (that):

think of, take into consideration; **bear in upon** (usu. in *pass.*) to impress upon, or to make realise, esp. by degrees; **bear out**, to corroborate; **bear up**, to keep up one's spirits; **bear up for** (*a place*), to sail towards; **bear with**, to make allowance for; **bring to bear**, to bring into operation (with *against, upon*); **find, lose one's bearings**, to ascertain, or to become uncertain of one's position or orientation. [O.E. *beran*; Goth. *bairan*, L. *ferre*, Gr. *pherein*, Sans. *bharati*, he carries.]
**bear**, *bār*, *n.* a heavy carnivorous animal with long shaggy hair and hooked claws: any rude, rough or ill-bred fellow: one who sells stocks for delivery at a future date, anticipating a fall in price—opp. to *bull* (the old phrase *a bearskin jobber* suggests an origin in the proverbial phrase, to sell the bearskin before one has caught the bear): the name of two constellations, the Great and Little Bear (Ursa major and minor).—*v.i.* to speculate for a fall.—*adj.* **bear'ish**, like a bear in manners.—*n.* **bear'ishness**.—**bear'-animal'cule**, a tardigrade—one of a group of degenerate arthropods; **bear'-baiting**, the former sport of setting dogs to worry a bear; **bear'-berry**, a trailing plant (*Arctostaphylos*) of the heath family: extended to various plants; **bear'bine**, a bindweed; **bear'-cat**, a panda; **bear garden**, an enclosure for bear-baiting: a turbulent assembly; **bear'-leader**, one who leads about a performing bear: the tutor of a youth on travel; **bear's'-breech**, acanthus; **bear's'-ear**, auricula; **bear's'-foot**, black hellebore; **bear'skin**, the skin of a bear: a shaggy woollen cloth for overcoats: the high fur cap worn by the Guards in England: **bear'ward**, a warden or keeper of bears. [O.E. *bera*; Ger. *bar*; Du. *beer*; apparently from an Indo-Gmc. root *bhero-*, brown.]
**bear, bere**, *bēr*, *n.* barley: in Scotland now the little grown four-rowed (really six-rowed) variety. [O.E. *bere*.]
**bear, beer**, *bēr*. See **bere**.
**beard**, *bērd*, *n.* the hair that grows on the chin and adjacent parts of a grown man's face: the tuft on the lower jaw of a goat, seal, etc.: a fish's barbel: an awn or threadlike spike as on the ears of barley (*bot.*): a tuft of hairs: a barb of a hook, an arrow, etc.: the gills of an oyster, etc.—*v.t.* take by the beard: to oppose to the face.—*adj.* **beard'ed**, having a beard: prickly: awned: barbed.—*adj.* **beard'less**.—**beard'-grass**, a kind of bearded grass (*Polypogon*). [O.E. *beard*; Ger. *bart*, Russ. *boroda*.]
**béarnaise, Béarnaise** (sauce), *bā-ar-nez*, a sauce made from egg yolks, butter, shallots, tarragon, chervil and wine vinegar. [Fr. *béarnaise* (fem. of **béarnais**) of Béarn, region of south-western France.]
**beast**, *bēst*, *n.* an irrational animal, as opposed to man: a four-footed animal: a brutal person: anything beastly (*coll.*): **the Beast**, Antichrist in *Revelation*:—*dim.* **beast'ie**.—*n.* **beast'hood**, state or nature of a beast.—*adv.* **beast'ily** (*Shelley*), bestially.—*n.* **beast'liness**.—*adjs.* **beast'like** (also *adv.*); **beast'ly**, like a beast in actions or behaviour: bestial: foul: sensual: vile, disagreeable (*coll.*).—*adv.* brutishly: abominably (*coll.*).—**beast fable**, a story in which animals play human parts; **beast'ly-head** (*Spens.*), personality or self of a beast.—**mark of the Beast**, a stamp on the forehead or right hand of a worshipper of the Beast of the Book of Revelation, chap. xiii: hence a sign of whatever was considered to be of Antichrist, or (*loosely*) evil or even ill manners; **number of the beast**, the apocalyptic number. [O.Fr. *beste* (Fr. *bête*)—L. *bestia*.]
**beastings.** Same as **beestings**.
**beat**, *bēt*, *v.t.* to strike repeatedly: to break or bruise (*B*): to pound: to batter: to whip up or switch: to flap: to strike (as bushes) in order to

rouse game: to thrash: to defeat, to frustrate: to be too difficult for: to spread flat and thin by beating with a tool (as gold): to mark (time) with a baton, etc.—*v.i.* to give strokes repeatedly: to pulsate: to impinge: to mark time in music: to swindle (with *out of*):—*pr.p.* beat′ing; *pa.t.* beat; *pa.p.* beat′en, now rarely beat.—*n.* a recurrent stroke, its sound, or its moment, as of a watch or the pulse, or a conductor's baton: accent: pulsation, esp. that heard when two notes nearly in tune are sounded together: a round or course, as a policeman's: a place of resort.—*adj.* weary: fatigued: affected with bursitis (as *beat elbow, knee*).—*adj.* beat′en, made smooth or hard by beating or treading: trite: worn by use.—*ns.* beat′er, one that beats or strikes: one who rouses or beats up game: a crushing instrument; beat′ing, the act of striking: thrashing: pulsation or throbbing: rousing of game: exercising the brain.—**beat music**, popular music with a very pronounced rhythm; **beatnik**, *bēt′nik*, one of the **beat generation** (orig. in U.S.), bohemian poets, etc., who, in the 1950s, dissociated themselves from the aims of contemporary society: later used loosely for a young person whose behaviour, dress, etc., were unconventional.—*adj.* beat′-up, dilapidated through excessive use.—**beat about the bush**, to approach a subject in an indirect way; **beat a retreat**, to retreat, originally to beat the drum as a signal for retreat; **beat down**, of a buyer, to try to reduce the price of goods; **beat it** (*slang*), to make off hastily or furtively; **beat off**, to drive back; **beat the air**, to fight to no purpose, or against an imaginary enemy; **beat the bounds**, to trace out boundaries in a perambulation, certain objects in the line of journey being formally struck, and sometimes also boys whipped to make them remember; **beat one's brains**, to puzzle one's brains about something; **beat out**, to flatten or reduce in thickness by beating; **beat up**, to pound or whip into froth, paste, a mixture, etc.: to put up as by beating the bushes: to alarm by a sudden attack: to thrash, to subject to a violent and brutal attack (*slang*): to disturb: to arouse: to go about in quest of anything: to make way against wind or tide. [O.E. *bēatan*, pa.t. *bēot*.]

**beatae memoriae**, *bi-ā′tē me-mō′ri-ē, -mō′, be-ā′ti me-mo′ri-ī*, (L.) of blessed memory.

**beath**, *bēdh*, (*Spens.*) *v.t.* to bathe, heat. [O.E. *bethian*, to foment.]

**beati pacifici**, *bi-ā′ti pa-sif′i-sī, be-ā′tē pa-kif′i-kē*, (L.) blessed are the peacemakers.

**beatify**, *bi-at′i-fī, v.t.* to make blessed or happy: to declare to be in the enjoyment of eternal happiness in heaven.—*adjs.* beatific (*bē-ə-tif′ik*), -al, making supremely happy.—*adv.* beatif′ically. —*n.* beatifica′tion, act of beatifying: in R.C. church, a declaration by the Pope that a person is blessed in heaven, authorising a certain definite form of public reverence payable to him—the first step to canonisation.—**beatific vision**, a glimpse of the glory of heaven. [L. *beātus*, blessed, and *facĕre*, to make.]

**beatitude**, *bi-at′i-tūd, n.* heavenly happiness: happiness of the highest kind: a title given to patriarchs in the Orthodox Churches: (in *pl.*) sayings of Christ in Matt. v, declaring certain classes of person to be blessed. [L. *beātitūdō—beātus*, blessed.]

**beau**, *bō, n.* a man attentive to dress or fashion: a fop or dandy: a lover:—*pl.* beaux (*bōz*):— *fem.* belle.—*adj.* beau′ish.—beau′-idē′al, ideal beauty: (blunderingly) a type or embodiment of the highest excellence; beau-pere (*bū-pēr*); *obs.*; Fr. *père*, father), a term of courtesy for father, used esp. of ecclesiastical persons: (*Spens.*; O.Fr. *per*, equal, peer) a companion. [Fr. *beau, bel*—L. *bellus*, fine, gay.]

**beau**, *bō*, (Fr.) beautiful, handsome, fine; **beau**

garçon, *-gär-sɔ̄*, a handsome man: a dandy; **beau geste**, *zhest*, gracious gesture; **beau jour**, *zhoor*, fine day, good times; **beau monde**, *mɔ̄d*, the gay or fashionable world.

**beaufet, beauffet**, *buf-et′, ns.* obs. forms of buffet, sideboard, cupboard.

**beaufin**, a sophisticated spelling of biffin.

**Beaufort**, *bō′fərt, adj.* devised by Sir Francis *Beaufort* (1774-1857), English admiral and hydrographer.—**Beaufort scale**, a scale of wind velocity, with 0 for calm, 12 for hurricane.

**Beaujolais**, *bō-zho-lā, n.* a red wine of Southeastern France. [From *Beaujolais*, a subdivision of Lyonnais.]

**beaumontag(u)e**, *bō-mon-tāg, -mon′tij, n.* a composition for hiding cracks and holes in wood or iron, of varying composition. [Perh. from Elie de *Beaumont* (1798-1874), French geologist.]

**Beaune**, *bōn, n.* a red wine from *Beaune* in Eastern France.

**beauté du diable**, *bō-tā dü dyäbl′*, (Fr.) an irresistible or overpowering beauty.

**beauty**, *bū′ti, n.* the quality that gives pleasure to the sight, or aesthetic pleasure generally: a particular grace or excellence: a beautiful person (often *ironical*), esp. a woman; also applied collectively: a very fine specimen of its kind: in *pl.*) beautiful passages or extracts.—*v.t.* (*Shak.*) to make beautiful.—*n.* beaut (*slang*), someone or something exceptionally beautiful or remarkable. —*adj.* beau′teous (*-ti-əs*), a bookish word for beautiful.—*adv.* beau′teously.—*ns.* beau′teousness; beautician, *bū-tish′ən*, one engaged in women's hairdressing, facial make-up, manicuring, etc.; beautifica′tion; beau′tifier, one who or that which beautifies or makes beautiful.—*adj.* beau′tiful, fair: with qualities that give delight to the senses, esp. the eye and ear, or which awaken admiration in the mind.—*adv.* beau′tifully.—*v.t.* beau′tify, to make beautiful: to grace: to adorn. —*v.i.* (*rare*) to become beautiful, or more beautiful.—**beauty parlour**, an establishment for the hairdressing, manicuring, face-massaging, etc., of women; **beauty queen**, a girl who is voted the most attractive or best-proportioned in a competition; **beauty sleep**, the sleep before midnight, considered the most refreshing; **beauty spot**, a patch placed on the face to heighten beauty: a birthmark resembling such a patch: a foil: a scene of outstanding beauty. [O.Fr. *biaute* (Fr. *beauté*)—L.L. *bellitās, -ātis*—L. *bellus*.]

**beaux arts**, *bō-zär*, (Fr.) fine arts; **beaux esprits**, *-zes-prē*, see **bel esprit**; **beaux yeux**, *-zyø*, fine eyes: a pretty woman.

**beauxite**. See bauxite.

**beaver**, *bēv′ər, n.* an amphibious rodent (Castor): its valuable fur: a hat of beaver fur or a substitute: a glove of beaver fur: a heavy woollen cloth.— *n.* beav′ery, a place where beavers are kept.— **beaver board**, a building board of wood-fibre; **beaver rat**, the coypu: the musquash: Hydromys; **bea′ver-tree, -wood**, a species of magnolia whose bark beavers eat.—**mountain beaver**, the sewellel. [O.E. *befcr, beofor*; Du. *bever*, Ger. *biber*, Gael. *beaghar*, L. *fiber*.]

**beaver**, *bēv′ər, n.* in mediaeval armour, the covering for the lower part of the face, the visor being that for the upper part—later the movable beaver was confounded with the visor: a beard or bearded man (*slang*).—*adj.* beav′ered. [O.Fr. *bavière*, child's bib—*bave*, slaver.]

**bebeeru**, *bi-bē′rōō, n.* the greenheart tree of Guyana. —*n.* bebee′rine (*-rin, -rēn*), an alkaloid yielded by its bark, a substitute for quinine. [Native name.]

**beblubbered**, *bi-blub′ərd, adj.* disfigured by weeping. [be- (1).]

**bebop**, *bē′bop, n.* a variety of jazz music, from about 1940, which added new harmonies, melodic patterns, and rhythms to accepted jazz characteristics.—Also **bop**.—Also *v.i.* [Imitative of two quavers in the rhythm.]

**bebung**, *bā'boong*, (*mus.*) *n.* a tremolo effect produced on the clavichord by fluctuating the pressure of the finger on the key. [Ger.]

**becall**, *bi-köl'*, *v.t.* to call names. [be- (1).]

**becalm**, *bi-käm'*, *v.t.* to make calm, still, or quiet.—*adj.* **becalmed'**, motionless from want of wind. [be- (1).]

**became**, *bi-kām'*, *pa.t.* of become.

**bécasse**, *bā-käs*, (Fr.) a woodcock: a fool, dupe.

**because**, *bi-koz'*, *bi-köz'*, *adv.* and *conj.* for the reason that: on account (of). [by, cause.]

**beccaccia**, *bāk-kä'chä*, (It.) a woodcock.

**beccafico**, *bek-a-fē'kō*, *n.* a garden warbler or kindred bird, considered a delicacy by the Italians:—*pl.* **beccafi'cos**. [It., from *beccare*, to peck, and *fico*, a fig.]

**béchamel** (sauce), **bechamel**, *bā-sha-mel*, *besh'ə-mel*, *n.* a white sauce with flavouring and/or cream. [Fr.; from name of steward of Louis XIV.]

**bechance**, *bi-chäns'*, *v.i.* (with *dat.*) to happen by chance: to befall.—*adv.* by chance: accidentally. [be- (1), and **chance**, *v.i.*]

**becharm**, *bi-chärm'*, *v.t.* to charm: to enchant. [be- (1).]

**bêche-de-mer**, *besh'-də-mer*, *n.* the trepang or sea-slug, a species of Holothuria, much esteemed in China as a food delicacy: South Sea English, or beach-la-mar. [Fr.,—Port. *bicho do mar*, sea-slug.]

**beck**, *bek*, *n.* a brook. [O.N. *bekkr*; Ger. *bach*.]

**beck**, *bek*, *n.* a sign with the finger or head: a nod: a gesture of salutation (*Scot.*).—*v.i.* to make such a sign.—*v.t.* to call by a nod.—**at one's beck (and call)**, subject to one's will. [A contr. of **beckon**.]

**becke**, *bek*, (*Spens.*) *n.* Same as **beak**.

**becket**, *bek'it*, (*naut.*) *n.* a loop of rope having a knot at one end and an eye at the other: a slung hook, or a wooden bracket used to keep loose tackle or spars in a convenient place. [Perh. Du. *bogt*, *bocht*, a bend of rope.]

**beckon**, *bek'n*, *v.t.* and *v.i.* to nod or make a summoning sign (to). [O.E. *biecnan*—*bēacn*, a sign. See **beacon**.]

**beck-iron**. See **bickern**.

**becloud**, *bi-klowd'*, *v.t.* to obscure by clouds: to dim. [be- (2).]

**become**, *bi-kum'*, *v.i.* to come to be: to arrive, have got (to a place) (*obs.*): to be the fate (followed by *of*).—*v.t.* to suit or befit: to grace: to adorn fittingly: to look well in.—*pa.t.* **became'**; *pa.p.* **become'**.—*adj.* **becom'ingly**.—*n.* **becom'ingness**. [O.E. *becuman*; see **come**.]

**becurl**, *bi-kûrl'*, *v.t.* to curl. [be- (1).]

**bed**, *bed*, *n.* a couch or place to sleep on: a mattress: a bedstead: a garden plot: a layer of oysters, etc.: a place in which anything rests: conjugal union, sexual relationship, the marriage and matrimonial rights and duties, or a marriage as a source of offspring: the channel of a river: sea or lake bottom: a layer or stratum.—*v.t.* to put to bed: to provide, or make, a bed for: to plant in a bed: to lay in layers or on a surface: to embed.—*v.i.* to go to bed: to cohabit:—*pr.p.* **bedd'ing**; *pa.p.* **bedd'ed**.—*ns.* **bedd'er**, a plant suitable for a flower bed; **bedd'ing**, mattress, bed-clothes, etc.: litter for cattle: stratification (false **bedding**, irregular or diagonal bedding due to action of currents).—**bed'bug**, the common bug (*Cimex lectularius*); **bed'chamber**, a bedroom; **bed'-closet**, a closet serving as a bedroom; **bed'clothes**, sheets, blankets, etc., for a bed; **bed'cover**, an upper covering for a bed.—*adj.* **bed'fast**, confined to bed.—**bed'fellow**, a sharer of a bed: a colleague; **bed'-jacket**, light jacket worn when sitting up in bed; **bed'-key**, a tool for tightening a bedstead; **bed'maker**, one who makes the beds and sweeps college rooms at Oxford, etc.;

**bed-of-honour**, the grave of a soldier who has fallen in battle; **bed-of-justice** (Fr. *lit de justice*), the king's throne in the Parlement of Paris: a sitting at which the king was present, chiefly for the registration of his own decrees; **bed'pan**, a chamber utensil for use in sick-bed: a warming-pan; **bed'-plate** (*mech.*), the foundation plate of a machine; **bed'post**, a corner support of a bedstead; **bed'presser** (*Shak.*), a heavy, lazy fellow.—*adjs.* **bed'ridd(en)**, confined to bed by age or sickness: worn out.—**bed'right**, **-rite** (*Shak.*), the privilege or due of the marriage-bed; **bed'rock**, the solid rock underneath superficial formations: fundamental principles (*fig.*): the lowest state.—*adj.* **bottom**, lowest.—**bed'room**, a room with a bed: a sleeping apartment: room in bed, sleeping space; **bed'-sitting-room**, a combined bedroom and sitting-room (abbrevs. **bed'-sit'**, **bed'-sitt'er**); **bed'side**, position by a bed.—Also *adj.* as **bedside book**, one suitable for sleepless nights; *bedside manner*, a doctor's way in the presence of the patient.—**bed'sore**, an ulcer arising from long confinement to bed, esp. over the bony prominences; **bed'spread**, a coverlet put over a bed by day; **bed'-staff**, a staff or stick formerly used for making or fixing a bed, a handy weapon; **bed'-stead**, a frame for supporting a bed; **bed'straw**, any plant of the genus *Galium*, esp. (Our) Lady's Bedstraw (*Galium verum*); **bed'-swerver** (*Shak.*), one who is false to his marriage vow; **bed'-table**, a table for use by a person in bed; **bed'tick**, the case in which stuffing is put for a bed; **bed'time**, the hour for going to bed.—*adv.* **bed'ward(s)**, in the direction of bed: towards bedtime.—**bed'-work** (*Shak.*), work easily performed, as if done in bed.—**bed and board**, food and lodging: full connubial relations; **bed of down, or roses**, any easy or comfortable place; **brought to bed**, confined in childbirth (with *of*); **get out of bed on the wrong side**, to start the day in a bad mood; **keep one's bed**, to remain in bed; **lie in the bed one has made**, to have to accept the consequences of one's own acts; **Lords, Ladies, of the Bed-chamber**, officers in the royal household who wait in turn upon a king or queen; **make a bed**, to put a bed in order. [O.E. *bed(d)*; Ger. *bett*, O.N. *bethr*; prob. akin to L. *fodere*, to dig (as orig. a hole).]

**bed**, *bed*, (*Spens.*). Same as **bid** (order, pray).

**bedabble**, *bi-dab'l*, *v.t.* to dabble or wet. [be- (1).]

**bedad**, *bi-dad'*, *interj.* an Irish minced oath, from **begad** = by God.

**bedaggle**, *bi-dag'l*, *v.t.* to soil by dragging along the wet ground. [be- (1).]

**bedarken**, *bi-därk'n*, *v.t.* to cover with darkness. [be- (1).]

**bedash**, *bi-dash'*, *v.t.* to bespatter, splash. [be- (1).]

**bedaub**, *bi-döb'*, *v.t.* to daub over or smear [be- (1).]

**bedawin**. Same as **bedouin**.

**bedaze**, *bi-dāz'*, **bedazzle**, *bi-daz'l*, *vs.t.* to dazzle or overpower by any strong light.—*pa.ps.* **bedazed'**, **bedazz'led**, stupefied, besotted.—*n.* **bedazz'lement**. [be- (1).]

**bede**. Same as **bead**, a prayer.

**bedeafen**, *bi-def'n*, *v.t.* to make deaf: to stun. [be- (1).]

**bedeck**, *bi-dek'*, *v.t.* to deck or ornament. [be- (1).]

**bedeguar**, *bed'i-gär*, *n.* a soft spongy gall found on the branches of sweet-brier and other roses, called also the sweet-brier sponge. [Fr. *bédeguar*—Pers. and Ar. *bādā-war*, lit. wind-brought.]

**bedel**, **bedell**, old spellings of **beadle**, still used at Oxford and Cambridge.

**bedel**, *bē'dl*, (*Bridges*) *n.* app. for **bevel**, i.e. bevel-wheel.

**bedesman**. Same as **beadsman**.

**bedevil**, *bi-dev'l*, *v.t.* to throw into confusion: to play the devil with: to torment: to treat with

devilish malignity: to possess as a devil.—*pr.p.*
**bedev'illing**; *pa.t.* and *pa.p.* **bedev'illed.**—*n.*
**bedev'ilment.** [be- (2).]
**bedew**, *bi-dū'*, *v.t.* to moisten gently, as with dew.
[be- (2).]
**bedide**, *bi-dīd'*, (*Spens.*). Same as **bedyed.**
**bedight**, *bi-dīt'*, (*arch.* or *poet.*) *v.t.* to equip, array,
furnish: adorn:—*pa.t.* and *pa.p.* **bedight'.** [be-
(1).]
**bedim**, *bi-dim'*, *v.t.* to make dim or dark:—*pr.p.*
**bedimm'ing**; *pa.t.* and *pa.p.* **bedimmed'.**—*n.*
and *adj.* **bedimm'ing.** [be- (2).]
**bedizen**, *bi-dīz'n*, *bi-diz'n*, *v.t.* to dress gaudily.—
*adj.* **bediz'ened.**—*n.* **bediz'enment.** [be- (1).]
**bedlam**, *bed'lam*, *n.* an asylum for lunatics: a mad-
house: a place of uproar: a madman (*obs.*).—
*adj.* fit for a madhouse.—*ns.* **bed'lamism**, anything
characteristic of madness; **bed'lamite**, a madman.
[From the priory St Mary of *Bethlehem*, in
London, afterwards a madhouse (Bethlehem
Royal Hospital).]
**Bedlington (terrier)**, *bed'ling-tən*, *n.* a long-
bodied, lightly-built terrier, swiftest of its kind.
[*Bedlington*, near Morpeth, where it was first
bred.]
**bedouin, beduin, bedawin**, *bed'ŏŏ-in*, *-ēn*, *bed'ä-win*,
*-wēn*, *bed'win*, *n.* a tent-dwelling nomad Arab
(properly *pl.*). [Fr. *bédouin*—Ar. *badāwin*,
dwellers in the desert.]
**bedraggle**, *bi-drag'l*, *v.t.* to soil by dragging in the
wet or dirt.—*adj.* **bedragg'led.** [be- (1).]
**bedral, bederal**, *bed'(ə)rəl*, (*Scot.*) *n.* a beadle,
church-officer, or minister's man: also a grave-
digger. [beadle.]
**bedrench**, *bi-drench'*, *-drensh'*, *v.t.* to drench or wet
thoroughly. [be- (1).]
**bedrop**, *bi-drop'*, *v.t.* to drop upon.—*adj.* **be-
dropped'**, **bedropt'**, sprinkled as with drops:
strewn. [be- (3).]
**beduck**, *bi-duk'*, *v.t.* to duck or plunge under water.
[be- (1).]
**beduin**, a form of **bedouin.**
**bedung**, *bi-dung'*, *v.t.* to manure: to befoul with
dung. [be- (2).]
**bedust**, *bi-dust'*, *v.t.* to cover with dust. [be- (2).]
**bedwarf**, *bi-dwörf'*, *v.t.* to make dwarfish. [be- (2).]
**bedye**, *bi-di'*, *v.t.* to dye or stain:—*pa.t.* and *pa.p.*
**bedyed'** (*Spens.* **bedide'**, **bedyde'**). [be- (1).]
**bee**, *bē*, *n.* a four-winged insect that makes honey:
a gathering of persons to unite their labour for
the benefit of one individual or family, or for some
joint amusement, exercise or competition (as
*quilting bee*, *husking bee*, *spelling bee*; from the
bee's habit of combined labour): a busy person:
(*pl.*) a type of yeast.—**bee'-bread**, the pollen
collected by bees as food for their young; **bee'-
eat'er**, any bird of a brightly-plumaged family
(Meropidae) nearly allied to the kingfishers,
which feed on bees; **bee'-flower**, a flower pollinated
by bees; **bee'-glue**, propolis; **bee'hive**, a case or
box in which bees are kept, of straw-work, wood,
etc. (*adj.* dome-shaped, like an old-fashioned
beehive, as *beehive hairstyle*, *beehive tomb*); **bee'-
house**; **bee'keeper**; **bee'keeping**; **bee'-kite**, the
honey-buzzard; **bee'line**, the most direct road,
like the honey-laden bee's way home; **bee'-
master**, a beekeeper; **bee'-moth**, a moth whose
larvae are very destructive to young bees; **bee'-
or'chis**, an orchid whose flower resembles a bee;
**bee'-skep**, a beehive, properly of straw; **bees'-
wax**, the wax secreted by bees and used by them
in constructing their cells.—*v.t.* to polish with
beeswax.—**bees'wing**, a filmy crust of tartar
formed in port and some other wines after long
keeping.—*adj.* **bees'winged**, so old as to show
beeswing.—**a bee in one's bonnet**, a whimsical or
crazy fancy on some point: an obsession. [O.E.
*bēo*; Ger. *biene*.]
**bee**, *bē*, *n.* the second letter of the alphabet (B, b).
**beech**, *bēch*, *n.* a common forest tree of the genus

*Fagus* with smooth silvery bark: extended to the
kindred genus *Nothofagus* and to many trees not
related.—*adj.* **beech'en.**—**beech'-drops**, cancer-
root, an American orobanchaceous'plant parasitic
on beech roots; **beech'-fern**, a fern of the polypody family (a mistranslation of Phegopteris;
from Gr. *phēgos*, a kind of oak); **beech'-mar'ten**,
the stone-marten; **beech'-mast**, the mast or nuts
of the beech-tree, which yield a valuable oil,
**beech'-oil.** [O.E. *boece*, *bēce*; Ger. *buche*, L.
*fāgus*, Gr. *phēgos* (oak).
**beef**, *bēf*, *n.* the flesh of the ox as food: extended to
that of some other animals, as the horse: muscle:
vigorous muscular force: an ox, esp. one
fattened for the butcher (*arch.*; *pl.* in this sense
**beefs, beeves**, *bēvz*): a complaint: an argument,
quarrel.—*adj.* of beef.—*v.i.* to grumble.—*adj.*
**beef'y**, like beef: fleshy, muscular: stolid.—
*adj.* **beef'-brained**, stupid.—**beef'-brew'is** (*obs.*),
**-broth**, broth made from beef; **beef'cake**, a picture of a muscle-man: brawn as distinct from
brain; **beef'eater**, an ox-bird: a consumer of
beef: a yeoman of the guard: a warder of the
Tower of London (the form *buffetier* supposed
to connect with *buffet* is not known); **beef'-ham'**;
**beef'steak**, a thick slice of beef for broiling or
frying; **beef'tea'**, stimulating rather than nutritious food for invalids, juice of beef strained off,
after simmering in water.—*adj.* **beef'-witt'ed**, dull
or heavy in wits: stupid.—**beef'-wood**, the wood
of Casuarina and other trees.—**beef up** (*coll.*),
to add strength to, to reinforce. [O.Fr. *boef*
(Fr. *bœuf*)—L. *bōs*, *bovis*; cf. Gr. *bous*, Gael. *bò*,
Sans. *go*, O.E. *cū*.]
**beegah.** Same as **bigha.**
**Beelzebub**, *bi-el'zi-bub*, *n.* a form of Baal worshipped by the Philistines at Ekron: the prince
of the evil spirits. [Heb. *ba'al z'būb*, fly-lord.]
**been**, *bēn*, sometimes *bin*, *pa.p.* of be: pres. *infin.*
and *pl. pres. indic.* of be (*arch.*).
**beenah**, *bē'nä*, *n.* a form of marriage (in Ceylon,
etc.) in which the man goes to live with his wife's
relatives and the children belong to her group.
[Ar. *binah*, separate.]
**beer**, *bēr*, *n.* an alcoholic beverage made by fermentation, in which the yeast settles to the
bottom (cf. **ale**), from malted barley flavoured
with hops: the generic name of malt liquor,
including ale and porter.—*adj.* **beer'y**, of, or
affected by beer.—*n.* **beer'iness.**—**beer'-barrel**;
**beer'-bottle**; **beer'-engine**, **beer'-pump**, a machine
for drawing beer up from the casks to the bar;
**beer'-gar'den**, a garden with tables where beer
and other refreshments may be had; **beer'-house**,
a house where beer or malt liquors are sold;
**beer'-money**, money given in lieu of beer and
spirits: a gratuity.—**bitter beer**, pale ale, a
highly hopped beer made from the very finest
selected malt and hops (**mild** or **sweet ale** being
of greater gravity or strength, and comparatively
lightly hopped); **black beer**, a kind of beer made
at Danzig, black and syrupy; **small beer**, weak
beer: hence trifling, unimportant, things, as in
the phrase, *to think no small beer of oneself.*—
**beer and skittles**, idle enjoyment. [O.E. *bēor*;
Ger. and Du. *bier*, O.N. *bjorr*.]
**beer, bear**, *bēr.* See **bere.**
**beesome**, *bē'səm*, (*Shak.*) *adj.* supposed to be for
**bisson.**
**beestings**, *bēst'ingz*, *n.* the first milk drawn from
a cow after calving. [O.E. *bȳsting*, *bēost*; Ger.
and Du. *biest.*]
**beet**, *bēt*, *n.* a plant (genus *Beta*; esp. *Beta vulgaris*)
of the goosefoot family, with a succulent root,
used as food and as a source of sugar.—**beet'-fly**,
a fly whose larvae are injurious to beet and
mangel-wurzel; **beet'root**, the root of the beet
plant; **beet sugar.** [O.E. *bēte*—L. *bēta.*]
**beet, bete**, *bēt*, (*obs.* except *dial.*) *v.t.* to improve:
to mend (esp. a fire): to relieve, assuage.—*n.*

**beet'mister** (*Scott*, **-master**), a help in need. [O.E. *bētan*; cf. *bōt*, **boot** (2).]

**beetle**, *bē'tl*, *n*. any insect of the Coleoptera, an order in which the fore-wings are reduced to hard and horny covers for the hind-wings: a game in which a drawing of a beetle is made up gradually of its component parts, body, head, etc., according to the throw of dice, the object being to produce a completed drawing.—*v.i.* (first found in *Shak.*) to jut: to overhang.—*adj.* (always applied to brows) overhanging, scowling. —*adj.* **beet'ling**, jutting: prominent: overhanging.—*adj.* **beet'le-browed**, with overhanging or prominent brows.—**beet'le-crusher** (*slang*), a big heavy foot or boot: a policeman: an infantryman; **beetle drive**, a progressive game of beetle.— *adj.* **beet'le-eyed**, blind.—**black beetle**, the cockroach, not a beetle.—**beetle off**, to scuttle like a beetle (*coll.*): to fly (*air-force slang*). [M.E. *bityl*—O.E. *bitula, bitela*—*bitan*, to bite; the connection of beetle brows with the insect is not accepted by all.]

**beetle**, *bē'tl*, *n*. a heavy wooden mallet used for driving wedges, crushing or beating down paving-stones, or the like: a wooden pestle-shaped utensil for mashing potatoes, beating linen, etc.— **beet'lehead**, a heavy stupid fellow.—*adj.* **bee'tleheaded**. [O.E. *bietl*—*bēatan*, to beat.]

**beeves**, *bēvz*, *n.pl.* cattle, oxen. [See **beef**.]

**befall**, *bi-föl'*, *v.t.* (or *v.i.* with *dat.*) to fall or happen to: to occur to.—*v.i.* to happen or come to pass: to befit (*Spens.*): to fall in one's way:—*pr.p.* **befall'ing**; *pa.t.* **befell'**; *pa.p.* **befall'en** (*Spens.* **befeld'**). [O.E. *bef(e)allan*; see **fall**.]

**befana, beffana**, *be-fä'nä*, *n*. an Epiphany gift. [It. *La Befana*, a toy-bringing old woman, a personification of Epiphany, Gr. *epiphaneia*.]

**befit**, *bi-fit'*, *v.t.* to be fitting, or suitable to: to beseem.—*v.i.* to be right:—*pr.p.* **befitt'ing**; *pa.p.* **befitt'ed**.—*adj.* **befitt'ing**.—*adv.* **befitt'ingly**. [be- (1).]

**beflower**, *bi-flow'ər*, *v.t.* to cover or besprinkle with flowers. [be- (2).]

**beflum**, *bi-flum'*, (*Scott*) *v.t.* to befool, cajole. [Cf. **flummery**.]

**befoam**, *bi-fōm'*, *v.t.* to bespatter or cover with foam. [be- (2).]

**befog**, *bi-fog'*, *v.t.* to envelop in fog: to obscure. [be- (2).]

**befool**, *bi-fōōl'*, *v.t.* to make a fool of, or deceive: to treat as a fool. [be- (2).]

**before**, *bi-för', -för'*, *prep.* in front of: ahead of: in presence or sight of: under the consideration or cognisance of: previous to: previous to the expiration of: in preference to: superior to.—*adv.* in front: sooner: earlier: in the past: formerly. —*conj.* previous to the time when (sometimes with *that*).—*adj.* (*Shak.*) previous.—*adv.* **before'hand**, before the time: in advance or anticipation: by way of preparation: in advance of one's needs. —*adj.* **before'-men'tioned**.—*adv.* **before'time**, in former time.—**be beforehand with**, to forestall (a person); **before Christ** (abbrev. B.C.), before the date formerly assigned to the birth of Christ (corresponding to the year 753 in Roman reckoning); **beforehand with the world**, comfortably provided for; **before the wind**, in the direction in which the wind is blowing, and hence helped along by it. [O.E. *beforan*. See **fore**.]

**befortune**, *bi-för'tūn*, (*Shak.*) *v.t.* to happen to, to befall. [be- (3).]

**befoul**, *bi-fowl'*, *v.t.* to make foul: to soil. [be- (2).]

**befriend**, *bi-frend'*, *v.t.* to act as a friend to: to favour. [be- (2).]

**befringe**, *bi-frinj'*, *v.t.* to adorn with fringes. [be- (2).]

**befuddle**, *bi-fud'l*, *v.t.* to reduce to a fuddled condition. [be- (1).]

**beg**. Same as **bey**.

**beg**, *beg*, *v.i.* to ask alms or charity, esp. habitually: to sit up on the hind quarters, as a dog for a reward.—*v.t.* to ask earnestly: to beseech: to pray: to take unwarrantedly for granted (esp. to **beg the question**, to fall into the fallacy of *petitio principii*, assuming what is to be proved as part of the would-be proof):—*pr.p.* **begg'ing**; *pa.t.* and *pa.p.* **begged** (*begd*).—*n.* **beggar** (*beg'ər*), one who begs: one who lives by begging (hyperbolically), one who is indigent: a mean fellow: a poor fellow: often used playfully and even affectionately.—*v.t.* to reduce to beggary: to exhaust or impoverish: to go beyond the resources of, as of description (*fig.*).—*ns.* **begg'ardom**, the fraternity of beggars; **begg'arliness**.—*adj.* **begg'arly**, poor: mean: worthless.—*adv.* meanly.—*ns.* **begg'ary**, extreme poverty.—*n.* and *adj.* **begg'ing**.—*adv.* **begg'ingly**.—**begg'ar-man**; **begg'ar-my-neigh'bour**, a game that goes on till one has gained all the others' cards; **begg'ing-lett'er**, a letter soliciting alms or subscriptions.—**beg off**, to obtain another's release through entreaty: to seek remission of some penalty or liability; **beg for a fool** (*obs.*), to sue for the guardianship of, and administration of the estate of, on grounds of mental deficiency; **go a-begging**, to be in want of a purchaser, occupant, etc. [Perh. from **beghard** (q.v.), the verb being a back-formation.]

**begad**, *bi-gad'*, **begar**, *bi-gär'* (*Shak.*), *interjs.* minced oaths for **by God**.

**began**, *bi-gan'*, *pa.t.* of **begin**.

**begar**, *bā'gär*, (*Ind.*) *n.* forced labour. [Hind. *begār*.]

**begem**, *bi-jem'*, *v.t.* to adorn, as with gems. [be- (2).]

**beget**, *bi-get'*, *v.t.* to produce or cause: to generate (commonly of the father): to produce as an effect, to cause:—*pr.p.* **begett'ing**; *pa.t.* **begot'** (*arch.* **begat'**); *pa.p.* **begott'en** (or **begot'**).—*n.* **begett'er**, one who begets: a father: the agent that occasions or originates anything. [O.E. *begitan*, to acquire; see **get**.]

**beghard**, *beg'ärd*, *n.* in Flanders or elsewhere from the 13th century, a man living a monastic life without vows and with power to return to the world. [Flem. *beggaert*; origin doubtful; cf. **béguine**.]

**begift**, *bi-gift'*, *v.t.* to present with gifts. [be- (2).]

**begild**, *bi-gild'*, *v.t.* to gild: to cover or overlay with gold-leaf. [be- (1).]

**begin**, *bi-gin'*, *v.i.* to come into being: to take rise: to perform the first act: to open: to have an opening.—*v.t.* to perform the first act of: to enter on: to start:—*pr.p.* **beginn'ing**; *pa.t.* **began'** (now rarely **begun'**); *pa.p.* **begun'**.—*ns.* **beginne'** (*Spens.*), beginning; **beginn'er**, one who begins: one who is in the early stages of learning or doing anything; **beginn'ing**, origin: a start: an entering upon action: an opening or first part: a rudiment. —*adj.* **beginn'ingless**.—**to begin with**, firstly: at first. [O.E. *beginnan* (less usual than *onginnan*), from pfx. *be-*, and *ginnan*, to begin.]

**begird**, *bi-gûrd'*, *v.t.* to gird or bind with a girdle: to surround or encompass:—*pa.t.* and *pa.p.* **begirt'** (or **begird'ed**). [O.E. *begyrdan*; be- (1), and **gird**.]

**beglerbeg**, *beg'lər-beg*, *n.* formerly, the governor of a Turkish province, in rank next to the grand vizier. [Turk., lit. bey of beys.]

**begloom**, *bi-glōōm'*, *v.t.* to render gloomy. [be- (2).]

**begnaw**, *bi-nö'*, *v.t.* to gnaw or bite, to eat away. [be- (1).]

**bego**, *bi-gō'*, *v.t.* to beset (*obs.* except in compound **woe-begone**). [O.E. *began*, to beset, surround.]

**begone**, *bi-gon'*, *interj.* be gone: be off: get away. [**be gone**.]

**Begonia**, *bi-gō'ni-a*, *n.* a genus (giving name to a family Begoni'ceae) of tropical, especially American, plants cultivated in greenhouses for their pink flowers and their remarkable unequal-sided and often coloured leaves—elephant's ears, angel's wings. [Named from Michel Bégon (1638-1710), patron of botany.]

**begored,** *bi-gōrd', -görd', (Spens.) adj.* besmeared with gore. [be- (2).]

**begorra, begorrah,** *bi-gor'ə, interj.* an Anglo-Irish modification of by God.

**begot,** *bi-got',* **begotten,** *bi-got'n.* See beget.

**begrime,** *bi-grīm', v.t.* to soil with grime. [be- (2).]

**begrudge,** *bi-gruj', v.t.* to grudge: to envy the possession of. [be- (1).]

**beguile,** *bi-gīl', v.t.* to cheat or deceive: to pass with diversion of attention from anything tedious or painful: to wile into some course.—*ns.* beguile'-ment; beguil'er.—*adv.* beguil'ingly. [be- (1) and *obs. v.t.* guile.]

**béguine, beguine,** *bāg'ēn, beg'in, n.* a member of a sisterhood living as nuns but without vows, and with power to return to the world:—*masc.* béguin, beguin (*bāg-ē, beg'in*), a beghard.—*n.* béguin-age (*bāg'ēn-äzh, beg'in-ij*), an establishment for béguines. [Fr. *béguine*; see beghard.]

**beguine,** *bə-gēn', n.* a dance of French West Indian origin or its music, in bolero rhythm. [Fr.]

**begum,** *bā'gəm, bē'gəm, n.* a Moslem princess or lady of rank: a deferential title given to any Moslem lady. [Urdu *begam*; cf. beg, bey.]

**begun,** *bi-gun', pa.p.* (sometimes *pa.t.*) of begin.

**begunk,** *bi-gungk', (Scot.) v.t.* to trick: to befool: to jape: to jilt.—*n.* a trick: a befooling. [Orig. uncertain; *Scot. gunk,* jilt, trick, recorded later.]

**behalf,** *bi-häf', n.* favour or benefit: cause: sake, account: part. [M.E. *behalve*—O.E. *be healfe*, by the side. See half.]

**behappen,** *bi-hap'n, (Spens.) v.t.* to happen to. [be- (1).]

**behave,** *bi-hāv', v.t.* to bear or carry: to wield, manage, conduct (commonly with *self*).—*v.i.* to conduct oneself: conduct oneself well: to act: to function:—*pa.t., pa.p.* behaved'.—*n.* behaviour, in U.S. behavior (*bi-hāv'yər*), conduct: manners or deportment, esp. good manners: general course of life: treatment of others: mode of action: response to stimulus (*physiol.*).—*adj.* behav'ioural, of or relating to behaviour.—*ns.* behav'iourism, a psychological method which substitutes for the subjective element of consciousness, the objective one of observation of conduct in other beings under certain stimuli; behav'iourist, an upholder of behaviourism.—**behavioural science,** a science which studies the behaviour of human beings or other organisms (e.g. psychology, sociology); **behaviour therapy,** treating a neurotic symptom (e.g. a phobia) by desensitising the patient, *i.e.* gradually conditioning him to react normally.—**upon one's best behaviour,** so placed that watchfulness over one's conduct is called for. [be- (1), and have; O.E. had *behabban,* to detain, restrain.]

**behead,** *bi-hed', v.t.* to cut off the head of.—*ns.* behead'al (*rare*); behead'ing. [be- (1), meaning off, away.]

**beheld,** *bi-held', pa.t.* and *pa.p.* of behold.

**behemoth,** *bē'i-moth, bi-hē'moth, n.* an animal described in the book of Job, usually taken to be the hippopotamus: a great beast. [Heb. *b'hēmōth,* pl. of *b'hēmāh,* beast, or a Hebraistic form of the Egyptian *p-ehe-mout,* water-ox.]

**behest,** *bi-hest', n.* promise (*obs.*): command: charge. [O.E. *behǽs,* a promise; see hest.]

**behight,** *bi-hīt',* **behote,** *bi-hōt', (obs.) v.t.* to vow: to promise: to speak to, to ordain, to adjudge, to name (*Spens.*):—*pa.t.* and *pa.p.* behight or **behote.** [O.E. *behātan,* to vow—*be-* and *hātan,* to be called, to call, to command. For the confusion of tenses and voices and for reduplication, see hight.]

**behind,** *bi-hīnd', prep.* at the back of (in place, or as support): in the place or state left by: at the

far side of: after (in time, rank, order): in inferiority to, or less far advanced than.—*adv.* at the back, in the rear: backward: past: in arrears.—*n.* the hinder part: rump.—*adj., adv.* behind'-hand, being behind: tardy: ill-provided: in arrears.—*adj.* behind'-door', surreptitious, clandestine.—**behind one's back,** without one's knowing (when one might feel entitled to know). [O.E. *behindan;* Ger. *hinten;* see hind (3).]

**behold,** *bi-hōld', v.t.* to look upon: to contemplate: to view, see: perhaps, to restrain (*Spens.*).—*v.i.* to look:—*pa.t.* and *pa.p.* beheld'.—*imper.* or *interj.* see: lo: observe.—*adj.* behold'en, bound in gratitude: under an obligation.—*n.* behold'er, one who beholds: an onlooker.—*adj.* behold'ing (*Shak.*), beholden.—*n.* (*Shak.*) sight, contemplation. [O.E. *behaldan* (W.S. *behealdan*), to hold, observe—*be-* and *h(e)aldan,* to hold.]

**behoof,** *bi-hōōf', n.* benefit: convenience. [O.E. *behōf.*]

**behote.** See behight.

**behove, behoove,** *bi-hōōv' (unhistorically bi-hōv'), v.t.* and *v.i.* to be fit, right, or necessary—now only used impersonally with *it.*—*adjs.* behove'ful (*arch.*), behove'ly, (*obs.*) useful: profitable. [O.E. *behōfian,* to be fit, to stand in need of.]

**behowl,** *bi-howl', v.t.* to howl at (Warburton's emendation for 'beholds' in *Midsummer Night's Dream,* V. ii. 2).

**beige,** *bāzh, n.* a woollen fabric of undyed wool.—*adj.* greyish: (*recently*) buff with a slight suffusion of pink. [Fr.]

**bein,** *bēn, (Scot.) adj.* and *adv.* comfortable: well off: well found: good (*arch. slang*).—Also **bien.**—*n.* bein'ness. [M.E. *bene,* of dubious origin; O.N, *beinn,* L. *bene,* and Fr. *bien,* all offer difficulties.]

**being,** *bē'ing, n.* existence: substance: essence: any person or thing existing.—*adj.* existing, present.—*adj.* bē'ingless.—*n.* bē'ingness. [Verbal noun and *pr.p.* of be.]

**beinked,** *bē-ingkt', adj.* smeared with ink. [be- (2).]

**bejade,** *bi-jād', (obs.) v.t.* to tire out. [be- (2).]

**bejant.** See bajan.

**bejewel,** *bi-jeo͞o'it, v.t.* to initiate or seduce into Jesuitism. [be- (2).]

**bejewel,** *bi-jōō'əl, v.t.* to deck with jewels. [be- (2).]

**bekah,** *bē'kä, (B.) n.* a half-shekel. [Heb.]

**bekiss,** *bi-kis', v.t.* to cover with kisses. [be- (1).]

**beknave,** *bi-nāv', v.t.* to call or treat as a knave. [be- (2).]

**beknown,** *bi-nōn', (arch.* or *dial.) adj.* known. [be- (1).]

**bel,** *bel, n.* a measure for comparing intensity of noises, electric currents, etc., the number of bels being the logarithm to the base 10 of the ratio of one to the other. [From Graham Bell (1847-1922), telephone inventor.]

**belabour,** *bi-lā'bər, v.t.* to beat soundly: to assail verbally. [be- (1).]

**bel-accoyle,** *bel-a-koil', (Spens.) n.* favourable or kind reception. [O.Fr. *bel acoil,* fair welcome. See accoil.]

**belace,** *bi-lās', v.t.* to adorn with lace. [be- (2).]

**bel air,** *be-ler,* (Fr.) fine deportment.

**belamoure, bellamoure,** *bel-a-mowr', (Spens.) n.* a beloved one: some kind of flower. [Fr. *bel amour,* fair love.]

**belamy,** *bel'a-mē, (Spens.) n.* a good or intimate friend. [Fr. *bel ami,* fair friend.]

**belate,** *bi-lāt', v.t.* to make late: to retard.—*adj.* belāt'ed, coming too late: out of date: benighted.—*n.* belāt'edness. [be- (2).]

**belaud,** *bi-löd', v.t.* to praise up. [be- (1).]

**belay,** *bi-lā', v.t.* to set, overlay, with ornament: to beset: to besiege: to waylay: to make fast: to secure by a turn about a cleat, belaying pin, point of rock, etc.—*interj.* enough: hold.—*n.* a turn of a rope in belaying: that about which a belay is made.—**belaying pin,** a pin for belaying

Neutral vowels in unaccented syllables: *el'ə-mənt;* for certain sounds in foreign words, see p. viii

ropes about. [O.E. *belecgan*; Ger. *belegen*, Du. *beleggen*. See **lay**.]

**bel canto**, *bel kän'tō*, (It.) a manner of operatic singing that cultivates beauty of tone.

**belch**, *belch, belsh*, *v.t.* and *v.i.* to void (wind) from the stomach by the mouth: to eject violently: to cast up, as of the smoke from a volcano or a cannon.—*n.* eructation. [O.E. *bealcian*; Du. *balken*.]

**belcher**, *bel'chər*, *n.* a dark-blue neckerchief with blue-centred white spots. [From Jim *Belcher*, a famous English boxer.]

**beldam, beldame**, *bel'dəm*, *n.* a grandmother or remoter ancestress (*obs.*): an old woman (formerly a term of address): a hag: a furious woman. [Formed from **dam**, mother, and *bel-*, used like *grand-* —Fr. *bel, belle*, but not a French use.]

**beleaguer**, *bi-lēg'ər*, *v.t.* to lay siege to.—*n.* **beleag'uerment**. [Du. *belegeren*, to besiege—*be-*, and *leger*, camp. See **leaguer**.]

**belee**, *bi-lē'*, (*Shak.*) *v.t.* to place on the lee-side of something. [be- (2).]

**belemnite**, *bel'əm-nīt*, *n.* a fossil pointed like a dart, being the internal shell of a cephalopod, formerly known as *thunderbolt, thunder-stone, elf-bolt*. [Gr. *belemnitēs*—*belemnon*, a dart.]

**bel esprit**, *be-les-prē*, (Fr.) a wit or genius:—*pl.* **beaux esprits**.

**bel étage**, *be-lā-täzh*, (German Fr.) the best storey, the first floor.

**belfry**, *bel'fri*, *n.* the part of a steeple or tower in which bells are hung: a bell-tower, sometimes standing apart: a movable wooden tower, used in the Middle Ages in attacking a fortification. —*adj.* **bel'fried**, having a belfry. [Orig. and properly a watch-tower, from O.Fr. *berfroi*—M.H.G. *berchfrit, bergan*, to protect—*frid, frit*, a tower.]

**belga**, *bel'ga*, *n.* a former currency unit of Belgium used in foreign exchange (from 1926 till the end of World War II), value five paper francs. [L. *Belga*, a Belgian.]

**belgard**, *bel-gärd'*, (*Spens.*) *n.* a fair or kind look. [It. *bel guardo*, lovely look.]

**Belgian**, *bel'jən*, *adj.* of *Belgium*, a country of Europe.—*n.* a native or citizen of Belgium.—*adj.* **Belgic**, of the *Belgae*, who anciently possessed Belgium, or of Belgium.—**Belgian hare**, a harelike breed of domestic rabbit. [L. *Belga, Belgicus*.]

**Belgravian**, *bel-grā'vi-ən*, *adj.* belonging to *Belgravia* (a fashionable part of London), or to fashionable life.

**Belial**, *bēl'yəl*, *n.* the devil: in Milton, one of the fallen angels. Not a proper name in O.T. [Heb. *b'li-ya'al*,—*b'li*, not, *ya'al*, use.]

**belie**, *bi-lī'*, *v.t.* to give the lie to: to speak falsely of: to present in a false character: to counterfeit: to be false to: falsify: to fill with lies (*Shak.*): to fail to fulfil or justify:—*pr.p.* **bely'ing**; *pa.t.* and *pa.p.* **belied'**. [be- (3).]

**believe**, *bi-lēv'*, *v.t.* to regard as true: to accept as true what is said by: to suppose (followed by a noun clause).—*v.i.* to be firmly persuaded: to have faith (with *in, on*): to judge.—*n.* **belief'**, persuasion of the truth of anything: faith: the opinion or doctrine believed: intuition, natural judgment (as used by some philosophers).—*adjs.* belief'less; believ'able.—*n.* believ'er, one who believes: a professor of Christianity, Mohammedanism, or whatever religion is relevant.—*adj.* believ'ing, trustful: having belief.—*adv.* believ'ingly.—I (don't) believe so, I (don't) think so; make believe (see make); the belief (*arch.*), the Apostles' Creed. [M.E. *bileven*—*bi-, be*, and *leven*, superseding O.E. *gelēfan*.]

**belike**, *bi-līk'*, (*arch.*) *adv.* probably: perhaps. [O.E. pfx. *be-*, and **like**.]

**Belisha beacon**. See **beacon**.

**belittle**, *bi-lit'l*, *v.t.* to make small: to cause to appear small, to disparage.—*n.* **belitt'lement**.—*adj.* **belitt'ling**. [be- (2).]

**belive**, *bi-līv'*, (*arch.* and *Scot.*) *adv.* with speed: promptly. [M.E. *bi life*; *bi*, by, *life*, dat. of *lif*, life.]

**bell**, *bel*, *n.* an instrument for giving a ringing sound, typically a hollow vessel of metal with flared mouth struck by a tongue or clapper, but taking many other forms, as a hollow sphere containing a loose ball, a shallow cup, a tube, or a coiled spring struck by a hammer: a corolla shaped like an ordinary bell: the body of a Corinthian or Composite capital, without the surrounding foliage: anything bell-shaped, as in diving-bell, bell-glass, the outward-turned orifice of a wind-instrument, etc.: the sound of a bell: a signal or intimation by bell: a stroke or double stroke of a bell to indicate the number of half-hours of the watch that have elapsed—'two bells', 'three bells', etc., meaning that there are two, three, etc. half-hours past—the watch of four hours is eight bells (*naut.*).—*v.i.* to ring.—*v.t.* to furnish with a bell, esp. in **to bell the cat**, to take the leading part in any hazardous movement, from the ancient fable of the mice who proposed to hang a warning bell round the cat's neck.—**bell'bind** (*dial.*), hedge or field bindweed; **bell-bird**, the campanero: a honey-eater (Manorina) with a tinkling note (*Australia*): also a thickhead (Oreoica) with a clear bell-like call (*Australia*): elsewhere, other birds with bell-like notes.—*adj.* **bell'-bottomed**, widening towards the ankle.—**bell'-boy** (*U.S.*), a hotel attendant; **bell'-buoy**, a buoy carrying a bell, rung by the waves; **bell'cote** (*archit.*), an ornamental structure made to contain one or two bells, and often crowned by a small spire; **bell crank**, a lever having two arms, usu. at right angles, with a common fulcrum at their junction; **bell'-flower**, a campanula; **bell'-founder**, one who casts bells; **bell'-glass**, a bell-shaped glass for sheltering flowers, etc.; **bell'-heather**, heath; **bell'hanger**, one who hangs and repairs bells; **bell'hop**, a bell-boy; **bell'man**, one who rings a bell, esp. on the streets, before making public announcements: a town-crier; **bell'-metal**, the metal of which bells are made—an alloy of copper and tin; **bell'-pull**, a cord or handle used in ringing a bell; **bell'-punch**, a ticket punch containing a signal-bell; **bell'push**, a button used in ringing an electric or spring bell; **bell'-ringer**, one who rings a bell on stated occasions: a performer with musical hand-bells; **bell'-ringing**; **bell'-rope**, the rope by which a bell is rung.—*adj.* **bell'-shaped**.—**bell'-siller** (*sil'ər*; *Scott*), a fee for bell-ringing at a funeral; **bell'-tent**, a bell-shaped tent; **bell'-tower**, a tower built to contain one or more bells, a campanile; **bell'-turret**, a turret containing a chamber for a bell, usually crowned with a spire; **bell'-wether**, the leading sheep of a flock, on whose neck a bell is hung: any loud, turbulent fellow, a ringleader (*fig.*); **bell'wort**, any plant of the *Campanulaceae*: the liliaceous genus *Uvularia* (*U.S.*).—**bear**, or **carry off**, the **bell**, to have or gain the first place; **bell, book, and candle**, a phrase popularly used in reference to a form of excommunication ending, 'Do to (shut) the book, quench the candle, ring the bell'. [O.E. *belle*; cog. with Du. *bel*.]

**bell**, *bel*, *n.* a bubble formed in a liquid. [Ety. dub.; cf. Du. *bel*, a bubble in water, perh. from L. *bulla*, bubble in water.]

**bell**, *bel*, *v.i.* to bellow, roar: to utter loudly.—*n.* the cry of a stag at rutting-time. [O.E. *bellan*; to roar; cf. Ger. *bellen*.]

**belladonna**, *bel'ə-don'ə*, *n.* the deadly nightshade or dwale (*Atropa Belladonna*), all parts of which are narcotic and poisonous from the presence of atropine: the drug prepared from it.—**bella-**

donna lily, a pink-flowered South African Amaryllis. [It. *bella donna*, fair lady; one property of belladonna is to enlarge the pupil of the eye.]

**bellarmine**, *bel'är-mēn*, a greybeard, or large jug with a big belly, decorated with a bearded face, said to represent Cardinal *Bellarmine*, made in mockery by Dutch Protestants.

**Bellatrix**, *bel-ā'triks* (L. *-ä'trēks*), *n.* a second-magnitude star in Orion, one of the corners of the quadrilateral. [L. *bellātrix*, female warrior.]

**belle**, *bel*, *n.* a handsome woman: the chief beauty of a place: a fair lady generally.—*n.* **belle-de-nuit** (*-də-nwē*; Fr.; night beauty), the marvel of Peru. [Fr. *belle* (*fem.*)—L. *bellus*, *-a*, *-um.*]

**belle amie**, *be-la-mē*, (Fr.) a female friend, a mistress; **belle assemblée**, *be-la-sä-blä*, a fashionable gathering; **belle époque, la** (or *caps.*), *bel ā-pok, lä*, 'the fine period', the time of security and gracious living for the well-to-do ended by World War I; **belle laide**, *bel led*, jolie laide; **belle-mère**, *bel-mer*, mother-in-law; **belle passion**, *pa-syɔ̃*, tender passion; **belle peinture**, *pē-tür*, naturalistic painting; **belle vue**, *vü*, fine prospect.

**belles-lettres**, *bel-let'r'*, *n.pl.* polite or elegant literature, including poetry, fiction, criticism, aesthetics, etc.—*n.* **bellet(t)'rist.**—*adjs.* **belletris'tic, -al.** [Fr., lit. fine letters.]

**belleter**, *bel'ə-tər*, *n.* a bell-founder. [For *bell-yetter*—bell, and O.E. *gēotan*, to pour.]

**bellibone**, *bel'i-bōn*, (Spens.) *n.* a beautiful and good woman. [Apparently Fr. *belle* (*et*) *bonne.*]

**bellicose**, *bel'ik-ōs*, *adj.* contentious, war-like.—*adv.* **bell'icosely.**—*n.* **bellicosity** (*-kos'i-ti*). [L. *bellicōsus.*]

**bellied.** See belly.

**belligerent**, *bel-ij'ər-ənt*, *adj.* waging war: recognised legally as waging war: aggressive.—*n.* a party or person waging war: one recognised as so doing.—*ns.* **bellig'erence, bellig'erency.** [L. *belligerāre*, to wage war—*bellum*, war, *gerĕre*, to wage.]

**Bellona**, *bel-ō'na*, *n.* the Roman goddess of war—hence (*fig.*) a woman of great spirit and vigour.

**bellow**, *bel'ō*, *v.i.* to roar like a bull: to make any violent outcry.—*v.t.* to roar out.—*n.* the roar of a bull: any deep sound or cry.—*n.* **bell'ower.** [M.E. *belwen*; O.E. *bylgian*, to roar; cf. bell (3).]

**bellows**, *bel'ōz*, or (old-fashioned) *bel'us*, *n.pl.* (often treated as *sing.*) an instrument for producing a current of air to blow up a fire, or sound an organ, accordion, etc.: a contrivance for expanding a photographic camera or the like: that which fans the fire of hatred, jealousy, etc. (*fig.*): the lungs.—**bell'ows-fish**, the trumpet-fish. [Same as belly; the sing. did not survive the 15th century.]

**bellum internecinum**, *bel'əm, -ōōm, in-tər-nes-in'əm, -ter-nek-ēn'ōōm*, (L.) a war of extermination.

**belly**, *bel'i*, *n.* the part of the body between the breast and the thighs, containing the bowels: the stomach, as the receptacle of the food: the bowels proper: the womb or uterus: the interior of anything: the bulging part of anything, as a bottle, or any concave or hollow surface, as of a sail: the front or under surface, as opposed to the *back*: in a violin or a leaf the upper surface: a sound-board.—*adj.* ventral, abdominal: belonging to the flesh, carnal (*theol.*).—*v.i.* to swell or bulge out (often with *out*):—*pa.t.* and *pa.p.* **bellied** (*bel'lid*).—*adj.* **bell'ied**, with a belly, esp. a big belly, pot-bellied: bulging: puffed out.—*n.* **bell'yful**, a sufficiency: more than enough.—*n.* and *adj.* **bell'ying.**—*n.* **bell'y-ache**', a pain in the belly: a persistent complaint, whine (*slang*).—*v.i.* (*slang*) to complain whining-

ly.—**bell'y-band**, a saddle-girth: a band fastened to the shafts of a vehicle, and passing under the belly of the horse drawing it; **bell'y-dance**, a solo dance with very pronounced movement of abdominal muscles; **bell'y-flop**, a dive in which one lands in the water on one's stomach: a belly-landing.—Also *v.i.*—**bell'y-god**, one who makes a god of his belly, a glutton; **bell'y-landing**, of an aircraft, a landing without using the landing-wheels; **bell'y-laugh**, a deep unrestrained laugh; **bell'y-timber** (*arch*), provisions. [M.E. *bali*, *bely*—O.E. *bælig*, *belig*, *bælg*, *belg*, bag.]

**belomancy**, *bel'ō-man-si*, *n.* divination by means of arrows. [Gr. *belos*, a dart, *manteiā*, divination.]

**belong**, *bi-long'*, *v.i.* to go along (with): to pertain (to): to be the property (of): to be part or appendage (of), or in any way connected (with): to be specially the business (of): to be a native or inhabitant, or member (of)—in all senses usually with *to.*—*n.pl.* **belong'ings**, matters connected with any person: possessions: persons connected, relatives: accessories. [M.E. *bi-, be-longen*, intens. of *longen*. See long (2).]

**Belorussian, Byelorussian**, *byel'ə-rush'ən*, *adj.* White Russian, of a region in European U.S.S.R. to the west of Moscow: of its language or people.—*n.* a native or citizen of White Russia: the language of White Russia, closely related to Russian proper. [Russ. *Belorossiya—beliy*, white.]

**belove**, *bi-luv'*, *v.t.* (*obs.* except in *pa.p.*, **beloved**, *bi-luvd'*), to love.—*adj.* **beloved** (*bi-luv'id*) much loved, very dear—often compounded with *well-, best-*, etc.—*n.* (*bi-luv'id*) one who is much loved.—*adj.* **belov'ing** (*Shak.*), loving. [be- (1).]

**below**, *bi-lō'*, *prep.* beneath in place, rank or quality: underneath: not worthy of.—*adv.* in a lower place: downstairs: on earth, or in hell (*fig.*).—*adj.* and *adv.* **below'stairs.** [be- (2).]

**bel paese**, *bel pä-ā'zē*, *n.* a mild Italian cheese. [Formerly a trademark.]

**bel sangue**, *bel sän'gwä*, (It.) gentle blood.

**belt**, *belt*, *n.* a girdle, zone, or band: a band of leather or other material worn around the waist: a band of flexible material used to transmit motion in machinery: a broad stripe of anything, different in colour or material: that which confines or restrains: a zone of country, a district (*geog.*): a strait: a band for the waist awarded in recognition of a specific (grade of) achievement (see black, Lonsdale).—*v.t.* to surround with a belt, or to invest formally with one, as in conferring knighthood: to encircle: to thrash with a belt.—*v.i.* (*slang*) to hurry.—*adj.* **belt'ed**, wearing a belt, of a knight: marked with a belt.—*n.* **belt'ing**, belts collectively: material for making belts: a beating.—**belt up** (*slang*), to be quiet; hit, etc., below the belt, to hit, etc., an opponent's body lower than the waist (forbidden in some sports): hence (*fig.*) to deliver a mean blow, attack unfairly; hold the belt, to hold the championship in wrestling, boxing, or the like; tighten one's belt, to reduce one's demands or expenditure. [O.E. *belt*—L. *balteus.*]

**Beltane**, *bel'tān*, *n.* an ancient Celtic festival, held in the beginning of May, when bonfires were lighted on the hills: the first day of May (O.S.)—one of the four old quarter-days of Scotland, the others being Lammas, Hallowmas, and Candlemas.—Also *adj.* [Gael. *bealltainn, beilteine*, apparently bright fire. It has nothing to do with Baal.]

**beluga**, *bi-lōō'ga*, *n.* the white whale, one of the dolphin family, closely allied to the narwhal, found in Arctic seas: a great Russian sturgeon—*Acipenser huso.* [Russ. *bæliy*, white.]

**belvedere**, *bel'vi-dēr*, *n.* a pavilion or raised turret or lantern on the top of a house, open for the view, or to admit the breeze: a summer-house on an eminence. [It. *belvedere—bel*, beautiful, *vedere*, to see.]

**bema**, *bē'mə, n.* the tribune or rostrum from which Athenian orators made their speeches: hence the apse or chancel of a basilica. [Gr. *bēma*, a step.]

**bemad**, *bi-mad', v.t.* to madden. [be- (1).]

**bemaul**, *bi-möl', v.t.* to maul thoroughly. [be- (1).]

**bemazed**, *bi-māzd', adj.* stupefied, bewildered. [be- (1).]

**Bembex**, *bem'beks, n.* a genus of sand-wasps, noted for their loud buzz. [Gr. *bembix*, a buzzing insect.]

**bemean**, *bi-mēn', v.t.* to make mean, to lower or debase. [be- (2).]

**bemean**, *bi-mēn',* (*obs.*) *v.i.* to signify. [be- (1).]

**bemedal**, *bi-med'əl, v.t.* to cover with medals. [be- (2).]

**bemete**, *bi-mēt', v.t.* to measure. [Pfx. be- (1).]

**bemire**, *bi-mir', v.t.* to soil with mire.—*adj.* **bemired.** [be- (2).]

**bemoan**, *bi-mōn', v.t.* to lament, bewail: to pity.—*v.i.* to grieve.—*ns.* **bemoan'er; bemoan ing.** [be- (1).]

**bemock**, *bi-mok', v.t.* to mock at, to deride. [be- (1).]

**bemoil**, *bi-moil',* (*Shak.*) *v.t.* to bemire, to bedraggle. [be- (1).]

**bemonster**, *bi-mon'stər, v.t.* to make monstrous: to regard or treat as a monster. [be- (2).]

**bemouth**, *bi-mowdh', v.t.* to mouth about. [be- (1).]

**bemud**, *bi-mud', v.t.* to bespatter with mud: to confuse. [be- (2).]

**bemuddle**, *bi-mud'l, v.t.* to confuse or muddle completely. [be- (1).]

**bemuffle**, *bi-muf'l, v.t.* to wrap or muffle up completely. [be- (1).]

**bemuse**, *bi-mūz', v.t.* to put in confusion: stupefy. [be- (1).]

**ben**, *ben, n.* a mountain peak. [Gael. *beinn*, oblique case of *beann*.]

**ben**, *ben,* (*Scot.*) *prep.* and *adv.* in or toward the inner or better, or (vaguely) another, apartment (of).—*n.* the inner or better apartment of a house, as opposed to the *but* or kitchen through which formerly one had generally to pass first.—**a but and ben,** a two-roomed house; **but and ben,** backwards and forwards in the house (also *fig.*): out and in: at opposite ends of a house or passage; **far ben,** on terms of great intimacy or favour. [M.E. *binne*—O.E. *binnan*, within.]

**ben**, *ben, n.* the winged seed of the horse-radish tree, *Moringa pterygosperma.*—*ns.* **ben'-nut; ben'-oil.** [Ar. *bān*, the ben-tree.]

**bename**, *bi-nām', v.t.* to name, mention: to vow: —*pa.t.* and *pa.p.* **benamed'** (*arch.* **benempt'**). [O.E. *benemnan—nemnan*, to name.]

**bench**, *bench, bensh, n.* a long seat or form with or without a back: a seat in a boat: a work-table or working-place: a judge's seat: the body or assembly of judges: a tribunal: an official seat: a level ledge or set-back in the slope of masonry or earthwork: a level tract between a river and neighbouring hills (*Amer.*): a terrace: in a greenhouse or conservatory, a raised bed or a platform with sides for holding potted plants.— *v.t.* to place on or furnish with benches: to put plants in greenhouse benches: to show (dogs).— *ns.* **bench'er,** a senior member of an inn of court; **bench'ership.—bench'-hole** (*Shak.*), a latrine; **bench'-mark,** a surveyor's mark cut on a rock, etc. indicating a point of reference in levelling (from its horizontal line forming a bench for a levelling instrument); **bench'-warr'ant,** one issued by a judge rather than a justice or magistrate.—**on the bench,** holding the office of a judge or bishop: officiating as judge; **raise to the bench,** to make

a judge or bishop. [O.E. *benc*; cog. with Ger. and Du. *bank*.]

**bend, bend,** *v.t.* to constrain: to subject to tension: to brace: to string: to nerve: to force into (or out of) a curved or angled form: to curve: to bow, turn downwards: to dispose, incline: to aim: to direct: to deflect: to subdue: to fasten (*naut.*): to drink hard at (*Scot.*).—*v.i.* to curve: to stoop: to bow: to give way, yield: to turn: to incline: to drink hard (perh. from the phrase *bend the bicker*, turn up the cup, drink cup-out) (*Scot.*):—*pa.t.* and *pa.p.* **bent;** also **bend'ed.**—*n.* a strengthening band (*Spens.*): a knot by which a line is tied to another, or to itself after passing through a ring, etc.: a band, strip: an ordinary bounded by two parallel lines crossing the shield from dexter chief to sinister base (**bend'-sin'ister** from sinister chief to dexter base), occupying a fifth of the shield, or a third if charged (*her.*): half a butt of leather cut lengthwise: an act of bending: state of being bent: a bent thing: a place of bending: a bow or stoop: a directing of the eye (*Shak.*): a pull of liquor, or a drinking bout (*Scot.*): (in *pl.*) caisson disease: aeroembolism.—*adj.* **bend'ed.**—*n.* **bend'er,** one who or that which, bends: a sixpence (*slang*): a thing very large or fine of its kind (*slang*): a (drunken) spree (*slang*).—*n.* and *adj.* **bend'ing.**—*adv.* **bend'ingly.**—*n.* **bend'let** (*her.*), a half-width bend.—*adv.* **bend'wise** (*her.*), diagonally.—*adj.* **bend'y** (*her.*), divided into bends.—*n.* and *adj.* **bent** (see **bent**).—*n.* **bent'wood,** wood artificially curved for chair-making, etc.—Also *adj.*—**bend over backwards** (see **backwards**); **round the bend,** crazy, mad. [O.E. *bendan*, to constrain, bind, fetter, string (as a bow), *bend*, bond, fetter.]

**bend**, *bend,* (*Spens.*) *n.* Same as **band** (2).

**bene**, *bēn,* (*arch.*; *Wordsworth*) *n.* a prayer: a boon. [O.E. *bēn.*]

**bene**, an old spelling of **been.**

**beneath**, *bi-nēth', adv.* and *prep.* below: in a lower position so as to have overhead, or nearly so, or to be covered: inside, behind, at the back (of): at a lower level relatively to.—*prep.* in a manner unworthy the dignity of, unbecoming to.—*adj.* (*Shak.*) lower. [O.E. *beneothan.*]

**bene decessit**, *be'ne di-se'sit, dā-kā'sit,* (L.L.) he has left well—a leaving certificate given to a schoolboy, curate, etc.

**benedicite**, *ben-i-dis'i-ti, -dis'* (L. *-dēk'i-te*), *interj.* bless you (an old form of greeting).—*n.* a blessing: a grace at table: the canticle beginning *Benedicite omnia opera* (All ye works of the Lord, bless ye) from *The Song of the Three Holy Children.* [L. *benedicite,* plur. imperative of *benedicĕre*, to bless—*bene*, well, *dicĕre*, to say, speak.]

**benedick**, *ben'i-dik,* or (blunderingly) **Benedict**, *-dikt, n.* a name for a newly married man, esp. one who has long held out against marriage— from *Benedick* in Shakespeare's *Much Ado about Nothing.*

**benedict**, *ben'i-dikt,* (*obs.*) *adj.* blessed: benign.— *n.* **benedic'tion** (-*shən*), a blessing: a solemn invocation of the divine blessing on men or things: one pronounced at the end of a religious service: a brief and popular service in the Roman Catholic Church: grace before or after a meal: blessedness.—*adjs.* **benedic'tional; benedict'ive; benedict'ory.**—*n.* **Benedict'us,** the canticle of Zacharias (Luke, i. 68-79), used in the Roman and Anglican services.—*adj.* **benedight** (*-dit'*; *Longfellow*), blessed.—**apostolic benediction,** that at the end of 2 Cor. [L. *benedicĕre, -dictum— bene*, well, *dicĕre*, to say, speak.]

**Benedictine**, *ben-i-dik'tin, tin, adj.* pertaining to St *Benedict* of Nursia (480-543), or his monastic rule.—*n.* a monk or nun of the order founded by him at Monte Cassino: (*-tēn*) a cordial or liqueur resembling Chartreuse, distilled at

Fécamp in Normandy—once distilled by Benedictine monks.

**benefaction,** *ben-i-fak'shan, n.* the act of doing good: a good deed done or benefit conferred: a grant of endowment.—*v.t.* **ben'efact,** to confer a benefit on.—*n.* **ben'efactor** (or *-fak'*), one who confers a benefit: one who aids financially e.g. an institution, a patron:—*fem.* **ben'efactress** (or *-fak'*).—*adj.* **benefac'tory.** [L. *benefactiō, -ōnis*; cf. following words.]

**benefic,** *bi-nef'ik, adj.* kindly: benign: beneficent: favourable (*astrol.*).—*n.* **benefice** (*ben'i-fis*), a church living, esp. with cure of souls: a fief (*hist.*).—*adj.* **ben'eficed,** possessed of a benefice. —*n.* **beneficence** (*bi-nef'i-sans*), active goodness: kindness: charity: a beneficent gift.—*adjs.* **benef'icent; beneficential** (*-sen'shl*).—*adv.* **benef'-icently.**—*adj.* **beneficial** (*ben-i-fish'l*), useful: advantageous: enjoying the usufruct of property (*law*).—*n.* (*Spens.*) app., a letter of presentation to a benefice.—*adv.* **benefic'ially.**—*ns.* **benefic'ialness; benefic'iary,** a holder of a benefice or a fief: one who receives a gift or advantage: one who enjoys or has the prospect of enjoying, any interest or estate held in trust by others. [L. *beneficus,* kindly, beneficent, *beneficium,* a service, benefit—*bene,* well, *facĕre,* to do.] **beneficiate,** *be-ni-fish'i-āt, v.t.* to reduce ores.— *v.i.* to receive profit from working a mine. [Sp. *beneficiar,* to benefit—L. *beneficium,* a service, benefit.]

**benefit,** *ben'i-fit, n.* a kindness: a favour: any advantage, natural or other: a performance whose proceeds go to one of the company or other particular person or object: a right in the form of money or services enjoyed under insurance schemes.—*v.t.* to do good to.—*v.i.* to gain advantage (with *from,* or *by*):—*pr.p.* **ben'efiting;** *pa.t.* and *pa.p.* **ben'efited.**—**benefit of clergy** (see clergy); **benefit of inventory** (*Scots law*), an heir's privilege of securing himself against unlimited liability for his ancestor, by giving up within a year an inventory of his heritage or real estate, to the extent of which alone he was liable; **benefit of the doubt,** favourable judgment when culpability is uncertain; **benefit society,** a friendly society. [M.E. *benfet*—A.Fr. *benfet*—L. *benefactum.*]

**Benelux,** *ben'a-luks, n.* a name for *Be*lgium, the *Ne*therlands and *Lux*embourg.

**bene merentibus,** *be'ne mer-ent'ib-us, -ōōs,* (L.) to the well-deserving.

**benempt.** See **bename.**

**beneplacito,** *be-ne-plä'chē-tō,* (It.) good pleasure: by your leave.

**benet,** *bi-net', v.t.* to catch in a net, to ensnare. [be- (1) or (2).]

**benet,** *ben'it, n.* an exorcist, the third of the four lesser orders in the Roman Catholic church. [O.Fr. *beneit*—L. *benedictus,* blessed.]

**bene vobis,** *be'ne vō'bis, wō'bēs,* (L.) health to you.

**benevolence,** *bi-nev'a-lans, n.* disposition to do good: an act of kindness: generosity: a gift of money, esp. for support of the poor: a kind of forced loan or contribution, levied by kings without legal authority, first so called under Edward IV in 1473 (*Eng. hist.*).—*adj.* **benev'olent,** charitable, generous, well disposed.—*adv.* **benevo'lently.** [O.Fr. *benivolence* and L. *benevolentia.*]

**Bengali,** *ben-gö'lē, adj.* of or belonging to *Bengal. n.* a native of Bengal: the language of Bengal. —*n.* **bengaline** (*beng'ga-lēn*), a light fabric usually of silk and cotton or silk and wool, with a crosswise rib.—**Bengal fire, Bengal light,** a brilliant light, black sulphide of antimony, used as a shipwreck signal, to illuminate country at night, and in fireworks.

**benight,** *bi-nit', v.t.* to involve in darkness: to cloud with disappointment.—*adj.* **benight'ed,** overtaken by night: involved in darkness, intellectual

or moral: ignorant.—*v.t.* **benight'en** (*rare*), to benight.—*ns.* **benight'ening; benight'er; benight'ing** (also *adj.*); **benight'ment.** [Pfx. be- (2) and night.]

**benign,** *bi-nin', adj.* favourable, esp. in astrology, as opposed to *malign:* gracious: kindly: of a mild type, as opposed to *malignant* (*med.*): salubrious.—*n.* **benignancy** (*bi-nig'nan-si*), benignant quality.—*adj.* **benig'nant,** kind: gracious: beneficial.—*adv.* **benig'nantly.**—*n.* **benig'nity,** goodness of disposition: kindness: graciousness: favourable circumstances—of climate, weather, disease, planets.—*adv.* **benign'ly.** [O.Fr. *benigne*—L. *benignus,* prob.—*bene,* well, and root of *genus,* birth, kind.]

**benison,** *ben'i-zn, -sn, n.* a benediction, blessing, esp. blessing of God. [O.Fr. *beneiçun*—L. *benedictiō, -ōnis.*]

**bénitier,** *bā-nē'tyä, n.* a holy-water font, or stoup. [Fr., —L.L. *benedictārium*—L. *benedictus.*]

**benj,** *benj, n.* bhang. [Ar.]

**Benjamin,** *ben'ja-min, n.* a youngest son: a favourite child. [As in Genesis xlii.]

**benjamin,** *ben'ja-min, n.* an old kind of overcoat. [Perh. alluding to Joseph (q.v.); or a tailor's name.]

**benjamin,** *ben'ja-min, n.* gum benzoin (also gum benjamin).—*n.* **ben'jamin-tree,** Styrax: the American spice-bush: a kind of fig-tree. [benzoin.]

**bennet,** *ben'it.* See herb-bennet (at herb).

**bennet,** *ben'it, n.* (*S. England*) *n.* a dry grass stalk. [bent (2).]

**bent,** *bent, pa.t.* and *pa.p.* of **bend.**—*adj.* curved: having a bend: intent, set (upon doing something), determined: obedient, governed (*Spens.*): morally crooked, or criminal: stolen (*slang*).—*n.* curvature: curved part: tendency: trend: inclination: direction: leaning or bias: natural inclination of the mind: the extent to which a bow may be bent: degree of tension: capacity of endurance.—**to the top of one's bent,** to the full measure of one's inclination. [bend.]

**bent,** *bent, n.* any stiff or wiry grass: the old dried stalks of grasses: a genus (*Agrostis*) of grasses, slender and delicate in appearance, some useful as pasture-grasses and for hay: a place covered with bents, a heath: a hillside.—Also **bent'-grass.**—*adj.* **bent'y.**—take (to) the bent (*Scot.*), to take flight. [O.E. *beonet,* found in place-names, as *Beonetlēah,* Bentley.]

**Benthamism,** *ben'tham-izm, n.* the social and political teaching of Jeremy Bentham (1748-1832), whose leading principle is the doctrine of utility, that happiness is identical with pleasure, summed up in Hutcheson's phrase, 'the greatest happiness of the greatest number'.—*n.* **Ben'thamite.**

**benthos,** *ben'thos, n.* the flora and fauna of the sea-bottom—opp. to *plankton* and *nekton.*—*adj.* **ben'thic.** [Gr. *benthos,* depth.]

**benthoscope,** *ben'thō-skōp, n.* a submersible sphere from which to study deep-sea life. [Gr. *benthos,* depth, *skopeein,* to look at.]

**ben trovato,** *ben trō-vä'tō,* (It.) aptly invented; **ben venuto,** *ven-ōōt'ō,* welcome.

**benumb,** *bi-num', v.t.* to make insensible or powerless: to stupefy (now chiefly of *cold*): to deaden the feelings of: to paralyse generally.— *adj.* **benumbed'.**—*ns.* **benumbed'ness, benumb'-ment.** [Pfx. be- (2).]

**Benzedrine,** *ben'zi-drēn, n.* tradename for amphetamine.

**benzene,** *ben'zēn, n.* simplest of the aromatic series of hydrocarbons, discovered by Faraday in 1825, now mostly prepared by destructive distillation of coal-tar, its molecule consisting of a ring or closed chain of six carbon atoms each with a hydrogen atom attached—formerly called **benzine, benzol,** names now used differently

(see below).—*ns.* ben'zal or benzyl'idine, a radical whose oxide is benzal'dehyde or oil of bitter almonds; benz'idine, a base used in preparing azo-dyes; ben'zil, a double benzoyl radical; ben'zine (*ben'zēn*), a mixture of hydrocarbons got by destructive distillation of petroleum, used as a solvent, motor fuel, etc.: improperly, benzene; ben'zoate (*-zō-āt*), a salt of benzoic acid; benzocaine, *ben-zō-kǎ'in*, *ben'zō-kǎn*, a drug used as a local anaesthetic and in the treatment of gastritis (benzine and cocaine). —*adj.* benzo'ic, pertaining to benzoin (see next article), as benzoic acid, an acid, C₆H₅·COOH, found in benzoin and other gums.—*ns.* ben'zol(e), crude benzene, used as a motor-spirit: improperly, benzene; ben'zoline, benzine: impure benzene; benzoyl (*ben'zō-il*), the radical C₆H₅: CO; benzpyrene, *benz-pi'rēn*, a cancer-inducing hydrocarbon (C₂₀H₁₂) found in coal-tar and present in small quantities in smoke, including tobacco smoke (benzene and pyrene); ben'zyl (*-zil*), the radical C₆H₅CH₂. [From benzoin.]
benzoin, ben'zō-in, or -zoin, n. gum benjamin, the aromatic and resinous juice of *Styrax Benzoin*, a tree of Java and Sumatra, used in perfumery, in pastilles, for incense and court-plaster, and friar's balsam.—*adj.* benzo'ic. [In the 16th century, benjoin, most prob. through It. from Ar. *lubān jāwī*, frankincense of Jawa (i.e. Sumatra).]
bepaint, bi-pānt', v.t. to paint over: to colour. [Pfx. be- (1).]
bepat, bi-pat', v.t. to pat frequently, to beat. [Pfx. be- (1).]
bepatched, bi-pacht', adj. mended with patches: wearing patches on the face by way of adornment. [Pfx. be- (1).]
bepearl, bi-pûrl', v.t. to cover over with pearls. [Pfx. be- (1).]
bepelt, bi-pelt', v.t. to pelt vigorously. [Pfx. be- (1).]
bepepper, bi-pep'ər, v.t. to pelt with a rain of shot or blows. [Pfx. be- (1).]
bepester, bi-pest'ər, v.t. to vex or pester greatly. [Pfx. be- (1).]
bepity, bi-pit'i, v.t. to pity greatly. [Pfx. be- (1).]
beplaster, bi-pläs'tər, v.t. to plaster thickly: to daub. [Pfx. be- (1).]
beplumed, bi-plōōmd', adj. adorned with feathers. [Pfx. be- (2).]
bepommel, bi-pum'l, v.t. to pommel soundly. [Pfx. be- (1).]
bepowder, bi-pow'dər, v.t. to powder over. [Pfx. be- (1).]
bepraise, bi-prāz', v.t. to lavish praise on. [Pfx. be- (1).]
beprose, bi-prōz', v.t. to reduce to prose: to discuss in prose and tediously. [Pfx. be- (2).]
bepuff, bi-puf', v.t. to puff out: to praise beyond measure. [Pfx. be- (1).]
bequeath, bi-kwēdh', v.t. to leave by will to another (strictly of personal property): to transmit to posterity, to leave behind: to commit or entrust to any one.—adj. bequeath'able.—ns. bequeath'al; bequeath'ment. [O.E. becwethan— pfx. bi-, be-, and cwethan, to say; see quoth.]
bequest, bi-kwest', n. act of bequeathing: that which is bequeathed, a legacy. [M.E. biqueste— O.E. pfx. bi-, be-, cwethan, to say; see quoth.]
berate, bi-rāt', v.t. to scold or chide vigorously. [Pfx. be- (1).]
beray, bi-rā', (obs.) v.t. to befoul.—Also (erroneously) bewray'. [Pfx. be- (1) and ray (1).]
Berber, bûr'bər, n. a member of one of the Hamitic peoples of Barbary: the language of the Berbers. —Also adj. [Ar. barbar; connection with Gr. barbaros doubtful.]
Berberis, bûr'bər-is, n. the barberry genus, giving name to the family Berberidā'ceae, akin to the buttercup family.—adj. berberidā'ceous.—n. ber'-

berine, an alkaloid got from barberry roots. [Latinised from Ar.; see barberry.]
berceau, ber-sō, (Fr.) a cradle: a covered walk.
berceuse, ber-søz', n. a cradle song: a musical composition in similar rhythm. [Fr.]
bere, another spelling of bear, barley.
bere, beer, bear, bēr, n. a pillow-case (usu. pill'ow-bere). [Origin obscure; cf. Ger. bühre.]
Berean, be-rē'ən, n. one of an extinct Scottish sect of the 18th century.—Also adj. [Beroea, Gr. Beroia, in Macedonia, where the people searched the scriptures daily (Acts, xvii. 11).]
bereave, bi-rēv', v.t. to rob of anything valued: to deprive: to widow, orphan, or deprive by death of some dear relative or friend: to snatch away:—pa.t. and pa.p. bereaved' (usu. by death), bereft' (usu. in general sense); arch. pa.p. bereav'en.—adj. bereaved'.—n. bereave'ment, loss of a relative or friend. [O.E. berēafian, to plunder; see reave.]
beret, ber'i, berret, ber'et, n. a flat, round, woollen cap worn by Basques and others. [Fr. béret.]
berg, bûrg (S.Afr. berhh), a hill or mountain: short for iceberg.—berg'-add'er, a venomous South African viper, living on hill-sides; berg'-ce'dar, a rare conifer (*Widdringtonia juniperoides*) of the Cedarbergen in South Africa; bergfall, (berhh'fäl, bûrg'föl; Ger.), fall of mountain-rock; berghaan (berhh'hän; S.Afr.), the bateleur eagle (Du., mountain cock); bergmehl (berhh'-mäl, or bûrg'), a powdery deposit of diatom frustules (Ger., mountain flour); bergschrund (berhh'shrōōnt), a crevasse formed where a glacier or snowfield starts away from a mountain wall (Ger., mountain cleft). [Ger., Du., Sw. berg, hill; cog. with barrow (O.E. beorg).]
bergamask, bûr'gə-mäsk, n. a native of Bergamo, in Italy: a rustic dance associated with that district.—Also ber'gomask.
bergamot, bûr'gə-mot, n. a kind of citron or orange, whose aromatic rind yields oil of bergamot, used in perfumery: the essence so extracted: a mint of similar smell. [Said to be from *Bergamo* in Italy; or *Bergama* (Pergamum) in Asia Minor; or as next word.]
bergamot, bûr'gə-mot, n. a fine pear. [Fr.,—It.,— Turk. begarmudi, prince of pears.]
bergander, bər-gan'dər, n. the sheldrake. [Perh. equal to burrow-gander.]
Bergsonian, bûrg-sō'ni-ən, adj. pertaining to Henri Bergson (1859-1941) and his philosophy of creative evolution.—n. a follower of Bergson.—n. Berg'sonism (-sən-izm).
bergylt, bûr'gilt, n. a red northern sea-fish of the Scorpaenidae. [Norw. berggylta, rock-pig.]
beribboned, bi-rib'ənd, participial adj. decorated with ribbons. [Pfx. be- (2).]
beriberi, ber'i-ber-i, n. an Eastern disease due to lack of vitamin B. [Sinh. beri, weakness.]
Berkeleian, bärk'lē'ən, bärk'li-ən, in U.S. bûrk-, adj. pertaining to Bishop Berkeley (1685-1753), who maintained that the world we see and touch is not an abstract independent substance, of which conscious mind may be an effect, but is the very world which is presented to our senses, and which depends for its actuality on being perceived.—n. a follower of Berkeley.—n. Berkelei'anism (or bärk').
berkelium, bər-kē'li-əm (earlier bûrk'li-əm), n. an element (Bk; at. number 97), prepared in a cyclotron at *Berkeley*, California.
berlin, bûr'lin, bər-lēn', -lin', n. an old four-wheeled covered carriage, with a seat behind covered with a hood—also ber'line: a closed motor-car with the driver's seat partitioned off. —Berlin blue, Prussian blue; Berlin wool, a fine dyed wool for worsted work, knitting, etc. [From the city of Berlin.]
Bermuda shorts, bər-mū'də, shorts, for men or

women, reaching to just above the knee.—Also **Bermudas.**

**Bernardine,** *bûr'nər-din, -dēn, adj.* Cistercian. [From *Bernard* of Clairvaux, founder of the order.]

**bernicle-goose.** Same as barnacle-goose.

**berob,** *bi-rob', (Spens.) v.t.* to rob or plunder.

**berry,** *ber'i, n.* any small succulent fruit: in bot. a simple fruit with pericarp succulent throughout (thus excluding strawberry, raspberry, blackberry): a coffee-bean: a cereal grain: a lobster's or crayfish's egg: a knob on a swan's bill: (*pl.* **berr'ies**).—*v.i.* to come into berry, to swell: to gather berries.—*adj.* **berr'ied,** bearing berries.— *n.* **berr'ying.** [O.E. *berie.*]

**berry,** *ber'i, n.* a pottage or sop (as in ale-berry, bread-berry). [O.E. *briw* pottage, porridge.]

**bersaglieri,** *ber-säl-yä'rē, n.pl.* the riflemen or sharpshooters of the Italian army, first organised in the Sardinian army in 1836. [It.; pl. of *bersagliere—bersaglio,* a mark.]

**berserk, berserker,** *ber-sûrk'(ər), -zûrk'(ər), n.* a Norse warrior whom the sight of the field of battle would fill with a frenzied and resistless fury.—*adjs., advs.* in a violent frenzy. [O.N. *berserkr,* probably bear-sark.]

**berth,** *bûrth, n.* sea-room: a ship's station at anchor or at a wharf: a room or sleeping-place in a ship, sleeping-carriage, etc.: any allotted or assigned place: a situation or place of employment, usually a comfortable one.—*v.t.* to moor: to furnish with a berth.—to give a wide berth to, to keep well away from generally. [Ety. obscure.]

**bertha,** *bûr'thə, n.* a woman's falling collar (also **berthe**): (with *cap.*; often **Big Bertha**) a big German gun (from Frau *Berta* Krupp of the Krupp steelworks); first used of guns shelling Paris 1918. [Woman's name.]

**Bertholletia,** *bûrth-ō-lē'sh(y)ə, n.* the brazil-nut genus of Lecythidaceae. [Named in honour of the chemist C. L. *Berthollet.*]

**Berthon-boat,** *bûr'thon, n.* a type of collapsible boat. [Edward L. *Berthon* (1813-99), its inventor.]

**bertillonage,** *ber-tē-yon-äzh, n.* a system of criminal identification by measurement, worked out by Alphonse *Bertillon.*

**beryl,** *ber'il, n.* a precious stone of which emerald and aquamarine are varieties, a silicate of beryllium and aluminium crystallising in the hexagonal system, green, colourless, yellow or blue, once esteemed as a magic crystal.—*adj.* pale greenish.—*ns.* **beryll'ium,** a metallic element (Be; atomic number 4), used as a moderator in nuclear reactors, and industrially to harden alloys, etc.; **beryll'ia,** its oxide. [O.Fr. *beryl—* L. *bēryllus—*Gr. *bēryllos.*]

**besaint,** *bi-sānt', v.t.* to make a saint of.—*pa.p.* **besaint'ed,** canonised: haunted with saints. [Pfx. be- (2).]

**bescatter,** *bi-skat'ər, v.t.* to scatter over. [Pfx. be-(1).]

**bescrawl,** *bi-skröl', v.t.* to scrawl or scribble over. [Pfx. be- (1).]

**bescreen,** *bi-skrēn', v.t.* to screen: to overshadow. [Pfx. be- (1).]

**bescribble,** *bi-skrib'l, v.t.* to write in a scribbling hand: to scribble about, over, or upon. [Pfx. be- (1).]

**besee,** *bi-sē' (obs.) v.t.* to look to: to provide for: to treat: to provide, furnish, apparel, adorn:— *pa.p.* **beseen'.**—*adj.* **beseen',** of good appearance, comely: furnished. [O.E. *beséon—be-,* pfx., *séon,* to see.]

**beseech,** *bi-sēch' (Spens.* **beseeke,** *bi-sēk'), v.t.* to entreat, to implore: to ask or pray earnestly: to solicit:—*pa.t.* and *pa.p.* **besought** (*bi-söt'*), also **beseeched'.**—*n. (Shak.)* entreaty.—*n.* **beseech'er.** —*n.* and *adj.* **beseech'ing.**—*adv.* **beseech'ingly.**

**n. beseech'ingness.** [Pfx. be- (1), and M.E. *sechen*; see seek.]

**beseem,** *bi-sēm', v.i.* to seem (*obs.*): to be fitting or becoming.—*v.t.* to be seemly for: to become: to be fit for or worthy of.—*n.* and *adj.* **beseem'-ing.**—*n.* **beseem'ingness.**—*adv.* **beseem'ingly.**— *adj.* **beseem'ly** (*rare*). [Pfx. be- (1).]

**beseen.** See besee.

**beset,** *bi-set', v.t.* to surround or set round with anything (now only in *pa.p.*): to surround with hostile intentions, to besiege: to occupy so as to allow none to go out or in: to assail, perplex, endanger, as by temptations, obstacles, etc.: —*pr.p.* **besett'ing;** *pa.t.* and *pa.p.* **beset'.**—*ns.* **beset'ment; besett'er.**—*adj.* **besett'ing,** constantly assailing: dominant: obsessive. [O.E. *besettan* —*settan,* to set.]

**beshadow,** *bi-shad'ō, v.t.* to cast a shadow over. [Pfx. be- (1).]

**beshame,** *bi-shām', v.t.* to put to shame. [Pfx. be- (1).]

**beshine,** *bi-shīn', v.i.* to light up.—*adj.* **beshone** (*-shon'*). [Pfx. be- (1).]

**beshrew,** *bi-shrōō', v.t.* to invoke evil upon, to curse—now only in imprecations. [Pfx. be- (1) and *obs. v.t.* shrew, to curse.]

**beside,** *bi-sīd', prep.* by the side of, near: over and above, besides (*rare*): outside of: away from: distinct from: apart from, not falling within, as of a question, resolution, etc.—*adv.* near by: besides: apart: to the side.—*adv.* **besides',** in addition: moreover: otherwise, else.—*prep.* over and above: else than: beside (*obs.*): away from, apart from (*obs.*).—**beside oneself,** having lost self-possession: beside the mark, point, question, irrelevant. [O.E. *besídan,* by the side (dat.); the *s* is of the adverbial gen.]

**besiege,** *bi-sēj', v.t.* to lay siege to: to beset with armed forces: to throng round: to importune: to pester.—*ns.* **besiege'ment; besieg'er.**—*n.* and *adj.* **besieg'ing.**—*adv.* **besieg'ingly** (*rare*), urgently. [Pfx. be- (1).]

**besigh,** *bi-sī', v.t.* to sigh over. [Pfx. be- (3).]

**besing,** *bi-sing', v.t.* to celebrate in song.—*adj.* **besung.** [Pfx. be- (3).]

**besit,** *bi-sit', (obs.) v.t.* to besiege: to sit well on, as clothes, to become.—*adj.* **besitt'ing** (*Spens.*), becoming. [O.E. *besittan—sittan,* to sit.]

**beslave,** *bi-slāv', v.t.* to make a slave of: to call slave. [Pfx. be- (2).]

**beslaver,** *bi-slav'ər, v.t.* to slaver or slobber upon: to cover with fulsome flattery. [Pfx. be- (1).]

**beslobber,** *bi-slob'ər, v.t.* to besmear with the spittle running from one's mouth: to cover with drivelling kisses: to flatter fulsomely. [Pfx. be-(1).]

**beslubber,** *bi-slub'ər, v.t.* to bedaub or besmear. [Pfx. be- (1).]

**besmear,** *bi-smēr', v.t.* to smear over: to bedaub: to pollute. [Pfx. be- (1).]

**besmirch,** *bi-smûrch', v.t.* to soil, as with smoke or soot: to sully. [Pfx. be- (1).]

**besmutch,** *bi-smuch', v.t.* to besmirch. [Pfx. be-(1).]

**besmut,** *bi-smut', v.t.* to blacken with soot.—*adj.* **besmutt'ed.** [Pfx. be- (1).]

**besognio,** *bi-zōn'yō, n.* a beggar. [See bezonian.]

**besoin,** *bə-zwē,* (Fr.) need, want, desire.

**beso las manos,** *bā'sō läs mä'nōs,* (Sp.) I kiss yⱺur hands.

**besom,** *bē'zəm, bez'əm, n.* a bunch of twigs for sweeping: (Scot., pron. *biz'əm, buz'əm*) a broom: any cleansing or purifying agent (*fig.*).—*be'som-head,* a blockhead: **be'som-rid'er,** a witch.— **to jump the besom** (see broom). [O.E. *besema*; Ger. *besen,* Du. *bezem.*]

**besom,** *biz'əm, bē'zəm, (Scot.* and *dial.) n.* a term of reproach for a woman, implying generally slatternliness, laziness, impudence, or unscrupulous energy. [Perh. the same word as the preceding; perh. connected with O.E. *bysn, bisn*, example, or O.N. *bȳsn*, wonder.]

**besort,** *bi-sört'*, (*Shak.*) *v.t.* to match, befit, become.—*n.* suitable company. [Pfx. be- (1).]

**besot,** *bi-sot'*, *v.t.* to make sottish, dull, or stupid: to make a sot of: to cause to dote: to infatuate: —*pr.p.* **besott'ing;** *pa.p.* **besott'ed.**—*adj.* **besott'ed,** infatuated.—*adv.* **besott'edly.**—*n.* **besott'edness.** [Pfx. be- (2).]

**besought,** *bi-söt'*, *pa.t.* and *pa.p.* of **beseech.**

**besouled,** *bi-sōld'*, *adj.* endowed with a soul. [Pfx. be- (2).]

**bespangle,** *bi-spang'gl*, *v.t.* to adorn with spangles, or with anything sparkling or shining. [Pfx. be- (1).]

**bespatter,** *bi-spat'ər*, *v.t.* to spatter or sprinkle with dirt or anything moist: to defame. [Pfx. be- (1).]

**bespeak,** *bi-spēk'*, to speak for or engage beforehand, to order or apply for: to stipulate or ask for: to betoken: to bewitch (*obs. dial.*).—*v.i.* (*obs.*) to speak: (*pa.t.* **bespoke**, *arch.* **bespake'**; *pa.p.* **bespōk'en,** also **bespoke').**—*n.* an actor's benefit, so called because his friends and patrons choose the piece to be performed: an application in advance. [Pfx. be- (3).]

**bespeckle,** *bi-spek'l*, *v.t.* to mark with speckles or spots. [Pfx. be- (1).]

**bespectacled,** *bi-spek'tə-kld*, *adj.* having spectacles on. [Pfx. be- (2).]

**bespeed,** *bi-spēd'*, *v.t.* to help on.—*pa.t.* and *pa.p.* **besped'.** [Pfx. be- (1).]

**bespice,** *bi-spis'*, (*Shak.*) *v.t.* to season with spice. [Pfx. be- (2).]

**bespit,** *bi-spit'*, (*arch.*) *v.t.* to spit upon, defile with spittle:—*pa.t.* and *pa.p.* **bespit', bespat'**; *pa.p.* (*Browning*) **bespate'.** [Pfx. be- (1).]

**bespoke,** *bi-spōk'*, **bespoken,** *be-spōk'n*, *pa.p.* of **bespeak,** ordered to be made, as clothes. [Pfx. be- (3).]

**besport,** *bi-spört'*, *-spört'*, *v.t.* to disport. [Pfx. be- (1).]

**bespot,** *bi-spot'*, *v.t.* to cover with spots.—*adj.* **bespott'ed.**—*n.* **bespott'edness.** [Pfx. be- (1).]

**bespout,** *bi-spowt'*, *v.t.* to spout over: to declaim pompously. [Pfx. be- (1).]

**bespread,** *bi-spred'*, *v.t.* to spread over: to cover:—*pr.p.* **bespread'ing;** *pa.t.* and *pa.p.* **bespread'.** [Pfx. be- (3).]

**besprent,** *bi-sprent'*, (*obs.*) *pa.p.* sprinkled over: scattered. [O.E. *besprengan*; see **sprinkle.**]

**besprinkle,** *bi-spring'kl*, *v.t.* to sprinkle over. [Pfx. be- (1).]

**Bessemer,** *bes'əm-ər*, *adj.* pertaining to the steelmaking process invented by Sir Henry *Bessemer.* —**Bessemer iron, pig,** pig-iron suitable for making Bessemer steel.

**best,** *best*, *adj.* (serving as *superl.* of **good**) good in the highest degree: first: highest: most excellent. —*n.* one's utmost endeavour: the highest perfection: the best share, part, success, or lot (as the *best of the bargain*, *the best of three*—tosses, games, etc.).—*adv.* (as *superl.* of **well**) in the highest degree: in the best manner.—*v.t.* (*coll.*) to get the better of.—**best boy, girl** (*coll.*), a favourite associate of the opposite sex; **best man, best maid** (*Scot.*), groomsman and bridesmaid at a wedding; **best part,** greater part; **best'seller,** a book that has had one of the biggest sales of the season: the writer of such a book.—**at best,** on the most favourable supposition; **for the best,** with the best of intentions or outcome; **give one best,** to concede the victory; **have the best of it,** to gain the advantage in a contest; **I had best, I were best** (for earlier *me were best*), it were best for me; **to make the best of one's way,** to go as well as one can; **put one's best foot foremost** (see **foot**); **with the best,** as successfully as anyone. [O.E. *betst, betest*; see **better.**]

**bestain,** *bi-stān'*, *v.t.* to stain all over. [Pfx. be- (1).]

**bestar,** *bi-stär'*, *v.t.* to cover with stars. [Pfx. be- (2).]

**bestead,** *bi-sted'*, *v.t.* to help, relieve: to be of use to, avail.—*v.i.* to profit, be advantageous:— *pa.t.* **bestead'ed;** *pa.p.* **bestead', bested'.** [Pfx. be- (1) and *obs. v.t.* stead.]

**bestead, bested,** *bi-sted'* (*Spens.* **bestad, bestadde,** *bi-stad'*), *adj.* set about (*with*): beset (with *by*, of foes; *with,* of dangers, etc.): situated— usually with *ill, hard,* etc. [Pfx. be- (2) and **stead,** placed.]

**bestial,** *best'i-əl, adj.* like a beast: rude: brutally sensual.—*n.* (*Scot.*) a collective name for cattle.— *v.t.* **best'ialise, -ize,** to make like a beast.—*ns.* **best'-ialism,** irrationality; **bestiality** (*-al'i-ti*), beastliness: disgusting vice. [L. *bestiālis—bestia,* beast.]

**bestiary,** *best'i-ar-i, n.* a book of a class popular in the Middle Ages, describing animals, a mixture of natural and unnatural history allegorised for edification. [L.L. *bestiārium,* a menagerie —*bestia,* a beast.]

**bestick,** *bi-stik'*, *v.t.* to stick over, as with sharp points: to transfix: to stick about, adorn:—*pa.t.* and *pa.p.* **bestuck'.** [Pfx. be- (1).]

**bestill,** *bi-stil'*, *v.t.* to make quiet, to hush. [Pfx. be- (1).]

**bestir,** *bi-stûr'*, *v.t.* to put into lively action: arouse into activity. [Pfx. be- (1).]

**bestorm,** *bi-störm'*, *v.t.* to assail with storms or tumult. [Pfx. be- (1).]

**bestow,** *bi-stō'*, *v.t.* to stow, place, or put by: to give or confer: to accommodate with quarters: to apply (with *on* and *upon*): (*refl., Shak.*) to acquit (oneself).—*ns.* **bestow'al,** act of bestowing: disposal; **bestow'er; bestow'ment.** [Pfx. be- (1).]

**bestraddle,** *bi-strad'l, v.t.* to bestride. [Pfx. be- (3).]

**bestraught,** *bi-ströt'*, (*obs.*) *adj.* distraught: distracted: mad. [Pfx. be- (1); **distraught,** with change of pfx.]

**bestreak,** *bi-strēk'*, *v.t.* to overspread with streaks. [Pfx. be- (1).]

**bestrew,** *bi-strōō'*, *v.t.* to strew loosely with something strewn or scattered over:—*pa.p.* **bestrewed',** **bestrown'** (*-strōn'*), **bestrewn'** (with). [Pfx. be- (1).]

**bestride,** *bi-strīd'*, *v.t.* to stride over: to sit or stand across: to defend, protect, from the sense of standing over a fallen man to defend him:—*pa.t.* **bestrid'**, **bestrode'**; *pa.p.* **bestrid'**, **bestridd'en.**— *adj.* **bestrid'able.** [Pfx. be- (3).]

**bestud,** *bi-stud'*, *v.t.* to adorn as with studs, as the sky with stars. [Pfx. be- (1).]

**bet,** *bet, n.* a wager: something staked to be lost or won on the result of a doubtful issue.—*v.t.* and *v.i.* to lay or stake, as a bet:—*pr.p.* **bett'ing;** *pa.t.* and *pa.p.* **bet** or **bett'ed.**—*ns.* **bett'er,** one who bets—also **bett'or; bett'ing.**—**an even bet,** an equal chance; **you bet** (*slang*), certainly. [Possibly shortened from the noun **abet.**]

**beta,** *bē'tə, n.* the second letter (B, β) of the Greek alphabet: as a numeral β' = 2, ͵β = 2,000: in a constellation, star second in brightness.— *ns.* **be'tacism** (*-sizm*), pronunciation of the sound of b as that of v; **be'tatron** (Gr. *-tron,* agent suffix), see **accelerator** (under **accelerate**).— **beta rays,** streams of beta particles, or electrons, given off by radium and other radio-active substances. [Gr. *bēta*; see B, **beth.**]

**betake,** *bi-tāk'*, *v.t.* to take (oneself) to, to go (with *self*): to apply or have recourse:—*pa.t.* **betook';** *pa.p.* **betāk'en.** [Pfx. be- (1).]

**bête,** *bet,* (Fr.) brute, stupid person; **bête noire,** *nwär,* a black beast: a bugbear; **betise,** *bet-ēz,* stupidity.

**beteem, beteeme,** *bi-tēm'*, (*Spens., Shak.*) *v.t.* to grant, vouchsafe, allow (also with the undermeaning of teem upon). [Perh. from a lost O.E. word answering to Du. *betamen,* to beseem.]

**betel,** *bē'tl, n.* the leaf of the **be'tel-pepp'er** (*Piper* *betle*), which is chewed in the East along with the areca-nut and lime.—*n.* be'tel-nut, the areca-nut. [Through Port. from Malayalam *vettila*.]

**Betelgeuse, Betelgeuze,** *bet'əl-jōōz, n.* a reddish first-magnitude star in Orion's shoulder. [Fr.,—Ar. *bayt-al-jawzā'*, Orion.]

**beth,** *beth, bāth, n.* the second letter of the Hebrew and Phoenician alphabets, resembling a house. [Heb. *bēth*, house; see B, beta.]

**bethankit,** *bi-thangk'it*, (*Scot.*) *interj.* elliptical for *God be thanked.—n.* a grace.

**bethel,** *beth'əl, n.* a Methodist or Baptist church: an old ship fitted as a place of worship for sailors. [Heb. *Bēth-ēl*, house of God.]

**Bethesda,** *be-thez'da*, (Heb.) a healing pool at Jerusalem—often applied to a Nonconformist church.

**bethink,** *bi-thingk', v.t.* to think on or call to mind: to recollect (generally followed by a reflexive pronoun and *of*): to propose to oneself.—*v.i.* to consider:—*pa.t.* and *pa.p.* **bethought** (*bi-thöt'*). [O.E. *bithencan*; cf. Ger. *bedenken*. See think.]

**bethrall,** *bi-thröl'*, (*Spens.*) *v.t.* to enslave [Pfx. be- (2).]

**bethumb,** *bi-thum', v.t.* to mark with the thumbs:—*pa.p.* **bethumbed'**. [Pfx. be- (1).]

**bethump,** *bi-thump', v.t.* to thump or beat soundly. [Pfx. be- (1).]

**bethwack,** *bi-thwak', v.t.* to thrash soundly. [Pfx. be- (1).]

**betide,** *bi-tid', v.t.* to befall, happen to (orig. *dat.* and formerly sometimes followed by *to, unto*): (*erroneous and rare*) to betoken:—*pa.t.* **betid'ed, betid** (*-tid'*); *pa.p.* **betid'** (*Spens.* **betight,** *bi-tit'*). [Pfx. be- (1); see tide (2).]

**betime,** *bi-tim'*, (*Shak.*) *v.i.* to betide. [Pfx. be- (2).]

**betimes,** *bi-timz', adv.* in good time: early: seasonably: speedily. [betime with adverbial gen. -*s*.]

**betitle,** *bi-ti'tl, v.t.* to give a name to. [Pfx. be- (2).]

**betoil,** *bi-toil', v.t.* to weary with toil. [Pfx be- (1).]

**betoken,** *bi-tō'kn, v.t.* to show by a sign: to foreshow: to mean: (*arch.*) to symbolise. [Pfx. be- (1).]

**béton,** *bā'tō, n.* lime concrete: concrete. [Fr.]

**betony,** *bet'ən-i, n.* a common labiate plant (*Stachys* or *Betonica, officinalis*) growing in woods, of great repute in ancient and mediaeval medicine: extended to various labiate and scrophulariaceous plants. [Fr. *bétoine*—L. *betonica, vettonica*.]

**betook,** *bi-tōōk', pa.t.* of **betake.**

**betoss,** *bi-tos', (Shak.) v.t.* to agitate. [Pfx. be- (1).]

**betray,** *bi-trā', v.t.* to give up treacherously: to disclose in breach of trust: to let go basely or weakly: to deceive (the innocent and trustful), to seduce: to discover or show: to show signs of. —*ns.* **betray'al,** act of betraying; **betray'er,** a traitor: the seducer of a trustful girl. [Pfx. be- (1) and O.Fr. *trair* (Fr. *trahir*)—L. *tradēre*, to deliver up.]

**betread,** *bi-tred', v.t.* to tread over or walk upon:—*pa.t.* **betrod'**; *pa.p.* **betrodd'en.** [Pfx. be- (1).]

**betrim,** *bi-trim', v.t.* to trim or set in order, to deck, to dress. [Pfx. be- (1).]

**betroth,** *bi-trōdh',* or *-trōth', v.t.* to contract, or promise, to marry (a woman): to affiance: to pledge oneself to (*obs.*).—*ns.* **betroth'al, betroth'-ment,** an engagement to marry: ceremonious declaration of such an engagement.—*adj.* and *n.* **betrothed'.** [Pfx. be- (2), and troth or truth.]

**better,** *bet'ər, adj.* (serves as *comp.* of **good**) good in a greater degree: preferable: improved: more suitable: larger: kinder: stronger in health: completely recovered, quite well again (*Scot.*).—*adv.* (*comp.* of well) well in a greater degree: more fully or completely: over or more: with greater advantage.—*n.* superior (esp. in *pl.*)—*v.t.* to make better: to surpass.—*v.i.* to grow better.—*adjs.* **bett'ered; bett'ering.**—*ns.* **bett'ering,** amelioration: improvement; **bett'erment,** improvement, esp. in standard of life or value of property.—*adj.*

**bett'ermost, best.**—*n.* **bett'erness.**—**better half,** a jocose term for a wife, once applied seriously to wife or husband, intimate friend, and even the soul as opposed to the body; **be better than one's word,** to do more than one had promised; **better off,** in superior circumstances: more fortunate: richer; **get the better of,** to gain the advantage over, overcome; **had better** (see **have**); **think better of,** to revise one's decision about, esp. to decide not to do so: to have the better opinion of. [O.E. *bet* (adv.), *betera* (adj.): better; Goth. *batiza*, Ger. *besser*; prob. cog. with **boot.**]

**betty,** *bet'i, n.* a man who troubles himself with the women's work in a household: a burglar's jemmy (*old slang*).—**Bett'y Mar'tin** (*obs.*), an expression inviting incredulity (usu. *all my eye and Betty Martin*). [Dim. of *Elizabeth.*]

**Betula,** *bet'ūla, n.* the birch genus, giving name to the family **Betulā'ceae,** which includes hazel and hornbeam. [L. *betūla.*]

**betumbled,** *bi-tum'bld, (Shak.) participial adj.* tumbled or disordered. [Pfx. be- (1).]

**between,** *bi-twēn', prep.* in, to, through, or across the space that separates: intermediate to: on the part of in reciprocal relation: by combined action or influence of: from one to another of: in joint possession of (generally of two).—*adv.* in or to an intermediate place: at intervals.—*n.* an interval (*Shak.*): an intermediate variety of needle.—*ns.* **between'ity** (*playful*), **between'ness,** state of being between.—**between'-decks,** the space between any two decks of a ship (also *adv.*); **between'-maid,** a servant subsidiary to two others (esp. cook and tablemaid)—a tweeny.—*advs.* **between'time, between'whiles,** at intervals.—**between ourselves, between you and me** (*slang* **and the cat,** or **post,** or **bedpost,** etc.), in confidence; **between the devil and the deep sea,** in a desperate dilemma; **go between,** to act as a mediator (*n.* **go'-between**). [O.E. *betwēonum,* and *betwēon*—*be,* by, and *twēgen, twā,* twain, two.]

**betwixt,** *bi-twikst',* and *adv.* between.—**betwixt and between,** in a middling position. [O.E. *betweox*—*twā,* two, and the suffix *-ix, -ish,* with added *-t,* as in *against,* and *amidst.*]

**Beulah,** *bū'la,* (Heb.) a land of rest—a name for Israel in its future condition, in Isa. lxii, 4: a Nonconformist chapel.

**beurré,** *bœ-rā, n.* a soft pear of various kinds. [Fr., buttery.]

**bevatron.** See **accelerator** (under **accelerate**).

**bevel,** *bev'l, n.* a slant or inclination of a surface: an instrument opening like a pair of compasses, and adjustable for measuring angles.—*adj.* having the form of a bevel: slanting.—*v.t.* to form with a bevel or slant:—*pr.p.* **bev'elling;** *pa.t.* and *pa.p.* **bev'elled.**—*adj.* **bev'elled,** cut to an oblique angle, sloped off.—*ns.* **bev'eller, bev'elling, bev'element.**—**bev'el-gear, bev'el-wheels** (*mech.*), wheels working on each other in different planes, the cogs of the wheels being bevelled or at oblique angles to the shafts. [From the older form of Fr. *beveau,* bevel (instrument).]

**bever.** See **beverage.**

**bever,** an obsolete form of **beaver.**

**beverage,** *bev'ər-ij, n.* any liquid for drinking, esp. tea, coffee, milk, etc.: a mixture of cider and water (*obs.*): a drink or drink-money to celebrate an occasion (*dial.*).—*n.* **bever** (*bēv'ər*), a small repast between meals (*dial.*): a time for drinking (*obs.*). [O.Fr. *bevrage* (Fr. *breuvage*), *beivre*—L. *bibēre,* to drink.]

**bevue,** *bā-vü, n.* a blunder. [Fr. *bévue.*]

**bevy,** *bev'i, n.* a company or flock of larks, quails, swans, roes, or ladies. [Origin obscure.]

**bewail,** *bi-wāl', v.t.* to lament: to mourn loudly over (esp. the dead).—*v.i.* to utter lamentations.—*adj.* **bewailed'.**—*n.* and *adj.* **bewail'ing.** [Pfx. be- (1).]

**beware,** *bi-wār', v.i.* (usu. with *of,* or with *that, lest*)

Neutral vowels in unaccented syllables: *el'ə-mənt*; for certain sounds in foreign words, see p. viii

to be on one's guard: to take heed (*obs.*): to take care (of) (*obs.*): to take warning (by) (*obs.*). —*v.t.* to be on one's guard against: to take care of (*obs.*): to take care (with *infin.* or clause) (*arch.*). Used normally only in infinitive and imperative; old writers have *ware*, etc. [be, ware.]

**beweep,** *bi-wēp'*, *v.t.* to weep over, lament: to wet or disfigure by weeping:—*pa.t.* and *pa.p.* **bewept'.** [Pfx. be- (1).]

**beweltered,** *bi-wel'tərd*, (*arch.*) *participial adj.* besmeared by weltering in blood. [Pfx. be- (1).]

**bewet,** *bi-wet'*, *v.t.* to wet or moisten (*Shak.*):— *pa.t.* and *pa.p.* **bewett'ed, bewet'.** [Pfx. be- (1).]

**bewhore,** *bi-hōr'*, *-hör*, (*Shak.*) *v.t.* to call a whore: to make a whore of.—[Pfx. be- (2).]

**bewig,** *bi-wig'*, to cover with a wig.—*adj.* **bewigged'.** [Pfx. be- (2).]

**bewilder,** *bi-wil'dər*, *v.t.* to lead astray (*arch.*): to perplex, confuse.—*adjs.* **bewil'dered,** lost (*arch.*): confused in mind: trackless (*arch.*): confused, mixed up (*arch.*); **bewil'dering.**—*adv.* **bewil'deringly.**—*n.* **bewil'derment.** [Pfx. be- (1) and obs. Eng. *wildern*—O.E. *wilddēoren*, wilderness—*wild*, wild, *dēor*, beast.]

**bewitch,** *bi-wich'*, *v.t.* to affect by witchcraft (mostly malignantly): to fascinate or charm.— *n.* **bewitch'ery.**—*adj.* **bewitch'ing,** charming: enchanting.—*adv.* **bewitch'ingly.**—*n.* **bewitch'- ment.** [Pfx. be- (1).]

**bewray,** *bi-rā'*, (*arch.*) *v.t.* to reveal: to divulge: to show up: to reveal the existence, presence, or whereabouts, of. [M.E. *bewreien*—*be-*, and O.E. *wrēgan*, to accuse.]

**bewray.** See beray.

**bey,** *bā*, *n.* a Turkish governor. [Turk. *bey*.]

**beyond,** *bi-yond'*, *prep.* on the farther side of: farther onward in comparison with: out of reach of: above, superior to: apart from.— *adv.* farther away.—*n.* the unknown: the hereafter.—beyond measure, excessively; beyond one, more than one is able to do: past one's comprehension; beyond seas, abroad; go beyond, to surpass: to circumvent: to over- reach (*B.*, *Shak.*); the back of beyond, a place of extreme remoteness. [O.E. *begeondan*—pfx. *be-*, and *geond*, across, beyond; see yon.]

**bez, bez-antler, -tine.** See bay (6).

**bezant,** *bez'ənt*, or *biz-ant'*, *n.* a gold coin first struck at Byzantium or Constantinople: a small circle or (i.e. yellow), like a gold coin (*her.*).

**bezel,** *bez'l*, *n.* the part of the setting of a precious stone which encloses it: the oblique side or face of a cut gem: the grooved rim in which a watch- glass is set, etc.: a sloped cutting edge (usually *basil*, *baz'l*): an indicator light on a car dashboard. [From an O.Fr. word represented by mod. Fr. *biseau*; ult. origin uncertain.]

**bezique,** *bi-zēk'*, *n.* a game at cards for two, three, or four, played with two to four packs, from which cards below the seven have been removed: the combination of the knave of diamonds and queen of spades. [Fr. *besigue*, of obscure origin.]

**bezoar,** *bē'zōr*, *-zör*, *n.* a stony concretion found in the stomachs of goats, antelopes, llamas, etc., formerly esteemed an antidote to all poisons. —*adj.* **bezoardic** (*bez-ō-ärd'ik*). [Through Sp. *bezoar* and Ar. *bāzahr*—Pers. *pādzahr*, antidote— *zahr*, poison.]

**bezonian,** *bi-zō'nyən*, (*Shak.*) *n.* a beggar. [It. *bisogno*, need.]

**bezzle,** *bez'l*, (*obs.*) *v.i.* to drink hard.—*v.t.* to squander: to despoil: to consume. [O.Fr. *besiler*. See embezzle.]

**bhang,** *bang*, *n.* a narcotic and intoxicant, leaves and shoots of hemp. [Hind. *bhāg*; Pers. *bang*; Sans. *bhanga.*)

**bharal,** *bur'əl*, *n.* the blue sheep of the Himalaya, connecting the true wild sheep with the goats.— Also **burrel, burrell, burhel, burrhel, burhel.** [Hind.]

**Bharat,** *bu'rut*, *n.* Hindi name of the Republic of

India.—*adj.* **Bha'rati.** [*Bharata*, legendary monarch.]

**bhisti, bheesty, bheestie, bhistee,** *bēs'tē*, an Indian water carrier. [Urdu. *bhisti*—Pers. *behisti*— *bihisht*, paradise.]

**bi-, bi,** *pfx.* twice, double. [L. *bis*, twice, *bīnī*, two by two, for *duis*, *duīnī*.]

**biannual,** *bi-an'ū-əl*, *adj.* two-yearly: also half- yearly. [L. *bi-*, twice, *annus*, year.]

**bias,** *bi'əs*, *n.* an obliquity: an oblique line: a bulge or greater weight on one side of a bowl (in the game of bowling), making it turn to one side: a turning to one side: a one-sided inclination of the mind: a prejudice: any special influence that sways the mind.—*adj.* biased: cut slantwise. —*adv.* slantwise.—*v.t.* to cause to turn to one side: to prejudice, or prepossess: to cut obliquely:—*pr.p.* **bi'asing** (by some **bi'assing**); *pa.t.* and *pa.p.* **bi'ased (bi'assed).**—*n.* **bi'asing,** a bias or inclination to one side.—bias binding, a long narrow folded piece of material cut slantwise and used for finishing hems, seams, etc., in sewing; **bi'as-drawing,** (*Shak.*) a turn awry. [Fr. *biais*, slant; of unknown origin.]

**biathlon,** *bi-ath'lon*, *n.* an international competi- tion in ski-ing and shooting. [L. *bi-*, twice, Gr. *athlon*, a contest.]

**biaxial,** *bi-aks'i-əl*, *adj.* having two (optic, etc.) axes.—Also **biax'al.** [L. *bi-*, and axial.]

**bib,** *bib*, *n.* a cloth or plastic shield put under a child's chin: of an apron, overalls, etc., the front part above the waist: the pout, a fish of the cod and haddock genus with a large chin barbel.—*v.t.* and *v.i.* to drink, to tipple.— *adj.* **bibā'cious.**—*ns.* **bibā'tion,** tippling; **bibb'er,** a tippler: chiefly used in composition as (*B.*) wine-bibber; **bib'cock,** a tap with down-turned nozzle.—best bib and tucker, best clothes. [Prob. from L. *bibĕre*, to drink; perh. partly imit.]

**bibble-babble,** *bib'l-bab'l*, (*Shak.*) *n.* idle talk. [Reduplication of babble.]

**Bibby,** *bib'i*, *n.* in a ship, a stateroom on a passage- way. [Name of shipping line.]

**bibelot,** *bēb'lō*, *n.* a knick-knack. [Fr.]

**Bible,** *bi'bl*, *n.* the sacred writings of the Christian Church, consisting of the Old and New Testa- ments: (also bible) a big or authoritative book: the third stomach of a ruminant, with many folds like the leaves of a book.—*adj.* **biblical** (*bib'li-kl*), of or relating to the Bible.—*adv.* **bib'lically.**—*ns.* **bib'licism** (*-sizm*), biblical doctrine, learning, or literature: literal acceptance of the Bible; **bib'licist, bib'list,** one versed in biblical learning: one who makes the Bible the sole rule of faith: one who adheres to its letter. [Fr.,—L.L. *biblia*, fem. sing., earlier neut. pl., from Gr. *biblia*, books, esp. the canonical books (sing. *biblion*, a book, dim. of *biblos*, papyrus, paper).]

**bibli-, bib'li-,** in composition, book.—*n.* **biblio- grapher** (*-og'rə-fər*), one versed in bibliography: the compiler of a bibliography.—*adjs.* **biblio- graphic** (*-ō-graf'ik*), **-al.**—*ns.* **bibliog'raphy,** study, description or knowledge of books, in regard to their outward form, authors, subjects, editions, and history: a descriptive list of books: a book containing such a list; **bibliolater** (*-ol'ə-tər*), **bibliol'atrist,** one given to bibliolatry.—*adj.* **bibliol'atrous.**—*n.* **bibliol'atry** (Gr. *latreiā*, wor- ship), a superstitious reverence for a book, esp. the Bible.—*adj.* **bibliological** (*-ō-loj'i-kl*).—*ns.* **bibliologist** (*-ol'ə-jist*); **bibliol'ogy,** bibliography: book-lore; **bib'liomancy** (*-man-si*; Gr. *manteiā*, divination), divination by opening the Bible or other book at hazard; **bibliomā'nia** (Gr. *maniā*, madness), a mania for collecting or possessing books: love of books; **bibliomā'niac.**—*adjs.* **bibliomaniacal** (*-ma-ni'ə-kl*); **bibliopegic** (*-pej'ik*; Gr. *pēgnynai*, to fix).—*ns.* **bibliopegist** (*-op'i-jist*), a bookbinder: a fancier of bindings; **bibliop'egy,**

the fine art of bookbinding; bibliophagist (-*of'ə-jist*; Gr. *phagein*, to eat), a voracious reader; bib'liophil(e) (-*fil*; Gr. *philos*, friend), a lover or collector of books.—Also *adj.*—*ns.* biblioph'ilism; biblioph'ilist; biblioph'ily; bibliophō'bia (Gr. *phobeein*, to fear), hatred of books; bib'liopole (Gr. *pōlēs*, seller), a bookseller.—*adjs.* bibliopolic (-*pol'ik*), -al.—*ns.* bibliop'olist; bibliop'oly, bookselling; bibliothē'ca (Gr. *bibliothēkē*—*thēkē*, repository), a library; a bibliography: a series of books; biblioth'ecary (*rare*), a librarian. [Gr. *biblion*, book; cf. Bible.]
bibulous, *bib'ū-ləs, adj.* drinking or sucking in: spongy. [L. *bibulus*—*bibēre*, to drink.]
bicameral, *bī-kam'ər-əl, adj.* having two chambers. [L. *bi*, twice, and *camera*, chamber.]
bicarbonate, *bī-kär'bən-āt, n.* an acid salt of carbonic acid. [L. *bi*-, twice, and carbonate.]
bice, *bīs, n.* a pale blue or green paint. [Fr. *bis*.]
bicentenary, *bī-sen-tēn'ər-i*, or -*ten'*, or -*sen'*, *adj.* pertaining to two hundred (years).—*n.* a bicentenial. [L. *bi*-, twice, centēnārius, pertaining to a hundred—*centum*, a hundred.]
bicentennial, *bī-sen-ten'yəl, adj.* pertaining to two hundred years.—*n.* a two hundredth anniversary. [L. *bi*-, twice, *centum*, a hundred, *annus*, a year.]
biceps, *bī'seps, n.* a two-headed muscle: esp. one in front of the upper arm or one on the back of the thigh.—*adj.* bicip'ital, two-headed. [L. *biceps*, two-headed—*bis*, twice, and *caput*, head.]
bichromate, *bī-krō'māt, n.* a dichromate, or salt of dichromic acid. [L. *bi*-, twice, and chromate.]
bicker, *bik'ər, v.i.* to contend in a petty way: to quiver: to glitter: to brawl, as running water: to patter.—*n.* a fight, a quarrel, esp. (*Scot.*) a street or school encounter: a clattering noise: a strife (*Scot.*). [Poss. a freq. conn. with beak.]
bicker, *bik'ər, n.* a bowl, esp. of wood, for holding liquor: a vessel of wooden staves for porridge. [Scot. form of beaker.]
bick-iron, *bik'ī-ərn, n.* a small anvil with one horn: the tapered end of an anvil. [From earlier bickern, a two-horned anvil—Fr. *bigorne*—L. *bicornis*, two-horned.]
biconcave, *bī-kon'kāv, adj.* concave on both sides. [L. *bi*-, twice, and concave.]
biconvex, *bī-kon'veks, adj.* convex on both sides. [L. *bi*-, twice, and convex.]
bicorporate, *bī-kör'pər-āt*, (*her.*) *adj.* double-bodied, as the head of a lion to which two bodies are attached. [L. *bi*-, twice, and corporate.]
bicuspid, *bī-kus'pid, adj.* having two cusps.—*n.* a premolar tooth.—*adj.* bicusp'idate. [L. *bi*-, twice, and cusp.]
bicycle, *bī'si-kl, n.* a vehicle with two wheels, one before the other, driven by pedals or a motor.—*v.i.* to ride a bicycle.—*n.* bi'cyclist. [L. *bi*-, twice, Gr. *kyklos*, a circle, wheel.]
bid, *bid, v.t.* to offer: to propose: to proclaim, as the banns of marriage: to command: to invite (*arch.*): to offer to pay at an auction: to call (in card games).—*v.i.* to make an offer or venture.—*pr.p.* bidd'ing; *pa.t.* bade (*bad*; also, as in the poets, *bād*), bid: *pa.p.* bidd'en, bid.—*n.* an offer of a price: a venturesome attempt or proposal: a call (at cards).—*adj.* bidd'able, tractable.—*ns.* bidd'er; bidd'ing, offer: command: calling.—to bid fair, to seem likely; bid in (of owner or his agent), in an auction, to overbid the highest offer. [O.E. *bēodan*; Goth. *biudan*, Ger. *bieten*, to offer.]
bid, *bid, v.t.* to ask for (*arch.*): to invite: to command: to pray (*obs.*): hence to salute with, say as a greeting:—Tenses are as in the preceding verb, with which it has been confused.—bidd'-ing-pray'er, originally the praying, or saying, of a prayer, then by confusion with the foregoing word taken to mean enjoining or inviting of prayer. [O.E. *biddan*; Goth. *bidjan*; Ger. *bitten*. See bead.]

biddy, *bid'i*, (*dial.*) *n.* a fowl: in *Shak.* applied to Malvolio.—red biddy (see red). [Poss. the woman's name *Biddy* for *Bridget*.]
bide, *bīd, v.i.* (*arch., Scot.*) to wait: to dwell: to remain.—*v.t.* to await (*obs.* except in sense of *bide one's time*): to face unshrinkingly(*poet.*): to endure.—*pa.t.* bid'ed, bode, (*Shak.*) bid, (*Scot.*) bade (*bād*); *pa.p.* bid'ed, (*obs.* and *Scot.*) bidd'en.—*n.* bid'ing (*Shak.*), residence, habitation. [O.E. *bīdan*; but sometimes for abide.]
bident, *bī'dənt, n.* a two-pronged tool: a two-year-old sheep.—*adj.* bidental (*bī-dent'l*), two-pronged: two-toothed.—*n.* a place struck by lightning (possibly consecrated by the Romans by sacrifice of a sheep).—*adjs.* bident'ate, -d, two-toothed. [L. *bi*-, twice, *dēns, dentis*, a tooth.]
bidet, *bē-dā, bi-det', n.* a nag: a bestridable bath and stand. [Fr., pony.]
bield, *bēld*, (chiefly *Scot.*) *n.* shelter: protection.—*adj.* bield'y. [Northern; O.E. *beldo* (W.S. *bieldo*), courage, cf. bold.]
bien, another spelling of bein.
bien, *byē*, (Fr.) well; bien-aimé, *byē -ne-mā*, well-beloved; bien chaussé, *sho-sā*, well-shod; bien élevé, *nā-ləv-ā*, well brought up, well mannered; bien entendu, *-nā-tā-dü*, of course: well designed: well versed: on condition; bien pensant, *pā-sā*, right-thinking: orthodox; bienséance, *-sā-äs*, propriety: (*in pl.*) the proprieties.
biennial, *bī-en'i-əl, -en'yəl, adj.* lasting two years: happening or appearing once in two years.—*n.* a plant that flowers and fructifies only in its second year, then dies.—*adv.* bienn'ially. [L. *biennium*, two years—*bi*-, twice, and *annus*, a year.]
bier, *bēr, n.* a carriage or frame of wood for bearing the dead to the grave.—bier right, (*hist.*) ordeal of appearing before a corpse believed murdered (expected to bleed in presence of murderer). [O.E. *bær*; Ger. *bahre*, L. *feretrum*. From root of verb bear.]
biestings, same as beestings.
bifacial, *bī-fā'shl, adj.* two-faced: having two unlike sides. [L. *bi*-, twice, and facial.]
bifarious, *bī-fā'ri-əs, adj.* double: in two rows. [L. *bifārius*, double.]
biff, *bif*, (*coll.*) *n.* a blow.—*v.t.* to strike hard.
biffin, *bif'in, n.* a variety of apple: such an apple slowly dried and flattened into a cake. [For *beefing*, from its colour of raw beef.]
bifid, *bif'id, bī'fid, adj.* cleft in two. [L. *bifidus*—*bi*-, twice, and *findēre*, to cleave or split.]
bifilar, *bī-fī'lər, adj.* having two threads. [L. *bi*-, twice, *filum*, thread.]
bifocal, *bī-fō'kəl, adj.* composed of parts of different focal lengths.—*n.pl.* bifo'cals, spectacles with bifocal lenses, for far and for near vision. [L. *bi*-, twice, and focal.]
bifold, *bī'fōld, adj.* twofold: of two kinds (*Shak.*). [L. *bi*-, twice, and fold.]
bifoliate, *bī-fō'li-āt, adj.* having two leaves or leaflets.—*adj.* bifo'liolate, having two leaflets. [L. *bi*-, twice, *folium*, leaf.]
biform, *bī'förm, adj.* having two forms. [L. *biformis*—*bi*-, twice, and *förma*, form.]
bifurcate, *bī'fûr-kāt*, or *-fûr', adj.* two-forked; having two prongs or branches.—*v.i.* to divide into two branches.—*ns.* bifurca'tion, a forking or division into two branches.—*adj.* bifurcated. [L. *bifurcus*—*bi*-, *bis*, twice, *furca*, a fork.]
big, *big, adj.* (*compar.* bigg'er; *superl.* bigg'est) large or great: pregnant: grown up: magnanimous: great in air, mien, or spirit: loud: pompous: very important, as in the Big Three, (leaders of) three specified powerful nations or organisations.—Also *adv.* (as in *talk big*).—*adj.* bigg'ish.—*n.* big'ness, bulk, size.—*adj.* big-bell'ied, having a big belly: pregnant (*with*).—big'-bud', a swelling of currant buds owing to a gall-mite; big business, large business enterprises

and organisations, esp. collectively; **Big Brother**, a dictator, as in George Orwell's *Nineteen Eighty-four* (1949); **big end**, in an internal-combustion engine, the larger end of the connecting rod; **big'head** (*coll.*), a swelled-headed person: conceit:—*adj.* **big'headed.**—**big'horn**, the Rocky Mountain goat or sheep; **big house**, (*slang*) prison; **big money**, money in very large sums; **big'-time**, the top level in any pursuit:—*adj.* at the top level: important.—**big'wig**, **big shot** (*coll.*), a leading man, a person of some importance. [M.E. *big*; origin obscure.]

**big**, *big*, (*Scot.*) *v.t.* to build, to pile up.—*n.* **bigg'in**, anything built, a house. [O.N. *byggja*, O.E. *būian*.]

**biga**, *bī'gǝ*, *bē'ga*, (L). a two-horse chariot (in L. earlier in *pl.* form **bigae**, *bī'jē*, *bē'gī*—*bi-*, *jugum*, yoke).

**bigamy**, *big'ǝ-mi*, *n.* the custom, crime, or fact of having two legal, or supposed, wives or husbands at once: a second marriage (*eccl. law*).—*n.* **big'amist**, one who has committed bigamy.—*adj.* **big'amous.**—*adv.* **big'amously.** [L. *bi-*, twice; Gr. *gamos*, marriage.]

**bigener**, *bī'jin-ǝr*, *n.* a hybrid between different genera.—*adj.* **bigeneric** (*-er'ik*). [L. *bǐgěner*, a hybrid.]

**bigg**, *big*, *n.* six-rowed barley: sometimes bear (3). [O.N. *bygg*.]

**biggin**, *big'in*, (*arch.*) *n.* a child's cap or hood: a nightcap: a serjeant-at-law's coif. [Fr. *béguin*, from béguine's cap.]

**bigha**, *bē'ga*, *n.* a land measure in India, ⅓ to ⅝ of an acre. [Hindi.]

**bight**, *bīt*, *n.* a wide bay: a bend or coil. [O.E. *byht*; cf. Dan. and Sw. *bugt*, Du. *bocht*.]

**Bignonia**, *big-nō'ni-a*, *n.* a genus of tropical plants with trumpet-shaped flowers, giving name to the family **Bignoniā'ceae.** [Named after the Abbé *Bignon*, Louis XIV's librarian.]

**bigot**, *big'ǝt*, *n.* one blindly and obstinately devoted to a particular creed or party.—*adj.* **big'oted**, having the qualities of a bigot.—*n.* **big'otry**, blind or excessive zeal, esp. in religious matters. [O.Fr.; origin unknown.]

**bijou**, *bē'zhoō*, *n.* a trinket: a jewel: a little box:—*pl.* **bijoux** (*bē'zhoōz*).—*adj.* small and elegant.—*n.* **bijouterie** (*bē-zhoōt'ǝr-ē*), jewellery, esp. trinkets. [Fr.]

**bijwoner.** Same as bywoner.

**bike**, **byke**, *bik*, (*Scot.*) *n.* a nest of wasps, wild bees, etc.: a swarm of people.—*v.i.* to swarm. [Origin unknown.]

**bike**, *bik*, *n.* and *v.i.* coll. for bicycle.

**bikini**, *bē-kē'nē*, *n.* a much reduced bathing-dress, in two parts, introduced early in the 1950s. [Said to be from *Bikini*, an atoll of the Marshall Islands, scene of atom-bomb experiments.]

**bilabial**, *bi-lā'bi-ǝl*, *adj.* two-lipped: produced by contact or approximation of the two lips, as the sound of b, w (*phon.*).—*n.* a bilabial consonant.—*adj.* **bilā'biate**, two-lipped, as some corollas. [L. *bi-*, twice, and *labium*, a lip.]

**bilander**, *bī'land-ǝr*, *n.* a two-masted hoy, having her mainsail bent to the whole length of her yard, hanging fore and aft, and inclined to the horizontal at an angle of about 45°.—Also **by'-lander**. [Du. *bijlander*.]

**bilateral**, *bi-lat'ǝr-ǝl*, *adj.* having or involving two sides: affecting two parties or participants reciprocally.—*n.* **bilat'eralism**, two-sidedness: equality in value of trade between two countries.—*adv.* **bilat'erally.** [L. *bi-*, twice, *latus*, *-eris*, side.]

**bilberry**, *bil'bǝr-i*, *n.* a whortleberry or blaeberry shrub: its dark blue berry. [Cf. Dan. *böllebær*.]

**bilbo**, *bil'bō*, *n.* a rapier or sword. [From *Bilbao*, in Spain.]

**bilboes**, *bil'bōz*, *n.pl.* a bar with sliding shackles. [Perh. connected with the foregoing.]

**bildungsroman**, *bil'doōngs-rō-män'*, *-doōngz-*, (Ger.) novel concerning the early emotional or spiritual development or education of its hero.

**bile**, *bil*, *n.* a thick bitter fluid secreted by the liver —yellow in man and carnivorous animals, green in vegetable feeders: derangement of its secretion: ill-humour (*fig.*).—*adjs.* **biliary** (*bil'yǝr-i*), belonging to or conveying bile; **bilious** (*bil'yǝs*), pertaining to or affected by bile.—*adv.* **bil'iously.**—*n.* **bil'iousness.**—**bile'-duct**, the duct that conveys the bile to the small intestine. [Fr.,—L. *bilis*.]

**bilge**, *bilj*, *n.* the bulging part of a cask: the broadest part of a ship's bottom: filth such as collects there: piffle (*slang*).—*v.i.* to spring a leak by a fracture in the bilge, as a ship.—*adj.* **bilg'y**, having the appearance and disagreeable smell of bilge-water.—**bilge'-keel**, a ridge along the turn of the bilge of a ship to check rolling; **bilge'-pump**; **bilge'-wat'er**. [Perh. bulge.]

**Bilharzia**, *bil-här'zi-ǝ*, *n.* a genus of trematode worms parasitic in human and other blood with two larval stages, first in water-snails and then in man.—*ns.* **bilhar'zia**, **bilharzi'asis**, **bilharziō'sis**, a disease caused by it, common in tropical countries, esp. Egypt and other parts of Africa (also known as schistosomiasis). [From the helminthologist, Theodor *Bilharz*.]

**bilian**, *bil'i-an*, *n.* a heavy ant-proof lauraceous timber tree of Borneo. [Malay.]

**bilimbi**, *bil-im'bi*, *n.* an East Indian tree of the wood-sorrel family: its acid fruit.—Also **bilim'bing**, **blim'bing**. [Dravidian and Malay.]

**bilingual**, *bi-ling'gwǝl*, *adj.* expressed in two languages: speaking two languages, esp. native or habitual languages.—*ns.* **biling'ualism**; **biling'uist**. [L. *bilinguis*—*bi-*, twice, *lingua*, tongue.]

**bilirubin**, *bil-i-roō'bin*, *n.* a reddish pigment in bile.—*n.* **biliver'din**, a green pigment in bile. [L. *bilis*, bile, *ruber*, red, Fr. *verd*, green.]

**biliteral**, *bi-lit'ǝr-ǝl*, *adj.* of or involving two letters: written in two scripts. [L. *bi-*, twice, *litera*, *littera*, a letter.]

**bilk**, *bilk*, *v.t.* to elude: to cheat.—*n.* **bilk'er**. [Perh. a form of balk; at first a term in cribbage.]

**bill**, *bil*, *n.* a concave battle-axe with a long wooden handle: a kind of hatchet with a long blade and wooden handle in the same line with it, often with a hooked point, used in cutting thorn hedges or in pruning.—**bill'hook**, a bill or hatchet with curved point; **bill'man**, a soldier armed with a bill. [O.E. *bil*; Ger. *bille*.]

**bill**, *bil*, *n.* the beak of a bird, or anything like it: a sharp promontory: the point of an anchor fluke.—*v.i.* to join bills as doves: to caress fondly.—*adj.* **billed**, having a bill.—*n.* and *adj.* **bill'ing.**—**bill'board**, a board used to protect the planking from injury by the bill when the anchor is weighed. [O.E. *bile*, most prob. same word as preceding.]

**bill**, *bil*, *n.* an account of money: a draft of a proposed law: a written engagement to pay a sum of money at a fixed date: a bank-note (*U.S.*): a placard: a slip of paper serving as an advertisement: any written statement of particulars: a written accusation of serious crime (*Eng. criminal law*).—*v.t.* to announce or advertise by bill.—**bill'board**, a board on which placards are posted; **bill'book**, a book used in commerce in which an entry is made of all bills accepted and received; **bill'-broker**, one who deals in bills of exchange and promissory notes; **bill'-chamber**, a department of the Scottish Court of Session dealing with summary business—so called because formerly both summonses and diligence or execution were usually commenced by a writ called a bill; **bill'-discounter**, one who discounts or advances the amount of bills of exchange and notes which have some time to run; **bill'fold**

(*U.S.*), a note-case; **bill´head**, a form used for business accounts, with name and address printed at the top; **bill´poster**, **bill´sticker**, one who sticks or posts up bills or placards.—**bill of adventure**, a writing by a merchant stating that goods shipped by him, and in his name, are the property of another, whose adventure or chance the transaction is; **bill of costs**, an account of a solicitor's charges and disbursements in the conduct of his client's business; **bill of exceptions**, a statement of objections, by way of appeal against the ruling of a judge who is trying a case with a jury in the Court of Session; **bill of exchange**, a document purporting to be an instrument of pecuniary obligation for value received, employed for the purpose of settling a debt in a manner convenient to the parties concerned; **bill of fare**, a list of dishes or articles of food; **bill of health**, an official certificate of the state of health on board ship before sailing; **bill of indictment**, a statement of a charge made against a person; **bill of lading**, a paper signed by the master of a ship, by which he makes himself responsible for the safe delivery of the goods specified therein; **bill of mortality** (*hist.*), an official return of births and deaths—hence **within the bills of mortality**, within the London district for which such returns were made; **bill of rights** (see right); **bill of sale**, in English law, a formal deed assigning personal property; **bill of sight**, an entry of imported goods of which the merchant does not know the quantity or the quality; **bill of store**, a licence from the customs authorities to reimport British goods formerly exported; **bill of victualling**, a list of necessary stores shipped from the bonded warehouse, or for drawback on board vessels proceeding on oversea voyages. [L.L. *billa*—L. *bulla*, a knob, a seal, hence a document bearing a seal, etc.; cf. **bull**.]

**billabong**, *bil´ə-bong*, (*Austr.*) *n.* a cut-off loop of a river, replenished only by floods: an effluent from a river (strictly one that does not rejoin). [Native words *billa*, river, *bung*, dead.]

**billboard**. See bill (2) and (3).

**billet**, *bil´it*, *n.* a little note or paper: a ticket assigning quarters to soldiers or others: quarters requisitioned: a destined resting-place: a post or occupation.—*v.t.* to quarter or lodge, as soldiers.—*pr.p.* **bill´eting**; *pa.t.* and *pa.p.* **bill´eted**. [O.Fr. *billette*, dim. of *bille*; see **bill**.]

**billet**, *bil´it*, *n.* a small log of wood used as fuel: a piece of timber sawn on three sides and rounded on the fourth: a bar of metal: an ornament in Norman architecture in the form of short cylinders with spaces between: a bearing in the form of an upright rectangle (*her.*).—**bill´et-head**, a piece of wood round which a harpoon-line is turned. [Fr. *billette*—*bille*, the young stock of a tree; orig. unknown.]

**billet-doux**, *bil-i-dōō´*, *n.* a love-letter:—*pl.* **billets-doux´** (same pron. as *sing.*). [Fr. *billet*, letter, *doux*, sweet.]

**billiards**, *bil´yərdz*, *n.* a game played with a cue and balls on a table with pockets at the sides and corners.—*adj.* **bill´iard.**—**bill´iard-ball**; **bill´iard-cloth**, a green cloth for covering a billiard table; **bill´iard-marker**, a person who marks the points made by the players; **bill´iard-table**. [Fr. *billard*—*bille*, a stick, hence a cue.]

**billie**. See billy.

**billingsgate**, *bil´ingz-gāt*, *n.* foul and abusive language like that once familiar to the ear at *Billingsgate* (the London fish-market).

**billion**, *bil´yən*, *n.* in Britain, France (since 1948), etc., a million millions (unit and twelve ciphers): in U.S., often now in Britain, one thousand millions (unit and nine ciphers) or milliard.—*n.* **bill´ionair-e.**—*adj.*, *n.* **bill´ionth**. [bi-, **million**.]

**billon**, *bil´ən*, *n.* base metal: esp. an alloy of silver

with copper, tin, or the like. [Fr., from same root as **billet** (2).]

**billow**, *bil´ō*, *n.* a great wave: a wave, the sea (*poet.*).—*v.i.* to roll or swell in great waves: to bulge flowingly.—*adjs.* **bill´owed**, **bill´owing**, **bill´owy**. [App. O.N. *bylgja*; Sw. *bölja*, Dan. *bölge*, wave.]

**billy**, **billie**, *bil´i*, *n.* a brother (*Scot.*): a comrade, a companion-in-arms (*Scot.*): an Australian bushman's (or other's) boiling-pan or tea-pot (also **billy-can**; poss. for *bouilli can*):—*pl.* **bill´ies.**—**bill´y-goat**, a he-goat. [Prob. from *Bill*, a familiar abbrev. of William.]

**billyboy**, *bil´i-boi*, *n.* a bluff-bowed one-masted trading-vessel. [Prob. conn. with **bilander**.]

**billycock**, *bil´i-kok*, *n.* a hard felt hat. [Said to be from William Coke, nephew of Earl (1837) of Leicester.]

**billy-o**, *bil´i-ō*, *n.* in phrase **like billy-o**, vigorously, fiercely. [Origin obscure.]

**bilobar**, *bī-lō´bər*, **bilobed**, *bī´lōbd*, *adjs.* having two lobes.—*adj.* **bilobular**, *bī-lob´ū-lər*, having two lobules. [L. *bi-*, twice, and **lobe**, **lobule**.]

**bilocation**, *bī-lō-kā´shən*, *n.* the power of being in two places at the same time. [Coined from *bi-*, twice, and **location**.]

**bilocular**, *bī-lok´ū-lər*, *adj.* divided into two cells. [L. *bi-*, twice, *loculus*, dim. of *locus*, place.]

**biltong**, *bil´tong*, (*S. Africa*) *n.* sun-dried lean meat. [Du. *bil*, buttock, *tong*, tongue.]

**Bimana**, *bim´ə-na*, *bī-mā´na*, *n.pl.* two-handed animals, an obsolete name for mankind.—*adjs.* **bim´anal**, **bim´anous**. [L. *bi-*, twice, *manus*, hand.]

**bimbashi**, *bim-bä´shē*, *n.* a military officer (in Turkey or Egypt). [Turk. *bin*, thousand, *bash*, head.]

**bimestrial**, *bī-mes´tri-əl*, *adj.* of two months' duration. [L. *bimestris*—*bi-*, and *mēnsis*, a month.]

**bimetallism**, *bī-met´əl-izm*, *n.* a monetary system in which gold and silver are on precisely the same footing as regards mintage and legal tender.—*adj.* **bimetallic** (*bī-mi-tal´ik*).—*n.* and *adj.* **bimet´allist.** [L. *bi-*, twice, and **metal**.]

**bimillenary**, *bī-mil´in-ər-i*, *n.* a period of two thousand years: two thousandth anniversary.—Also *adj.* [L. *bi*, twice, **millenary**.]

**bimillennium**, *bī-mil-en´i-əm*, *n.* Same as **bimillenary**. [L. *bi*, twice, **millennium**.]

**bimonthly**, *bī-munth´li*, *adj.* once in two months: also twice a month. [L. *bi-*, two, and **month**.]

**bin**, *bin*, *n.* a receptacle for corn, wine, dust, etc. [O.E. *binn*, a manger.]

**bin**, *bin*, (*Shak.*) used for be and been.

**binary**, *bī´nər-i*, *adj.* composed of two: twofold.—*n.* binary system, star.—*adj.* **bi´nate**, growing in pairs: double: consisting of two leaflets.—**binary form** (*mus.*), a form of movement founded on two themes; **binary operation**, in math. combining two elements in a collection of elements in such a way as to give another element from the same collection (as addition or multiplication in the ordinary number system); **binary scale**, the scale of notation whose radix or base is 2 (instead of 10); **binary star**, **binary system**; **binary system**, two stars revolving about their centre of gravity (also **binary star**): system using the binary scale of notation: system in which numbers are expressed by using two digits only, viz. 1 and 0. [L. *bīnārius*—*bīnī*, two by two, *bis*, twice.]

**binaural**, *bin-ö´rl*, *adj.* having, employing, or relating to two ears: of reproduction of sound, using two sound channels.—*adv.* **binaur´ally.**—**binaural effect**, the ability to tell the direction from which a sound is coming, arising from the difference in arrival times of the sound at a person's two ears. [L. *bīnī*, two by two, *auris*, ear.]

Neutral vowels in unaccented syllables: *el´ə-mənt*; for certain sounds in foreign words, see p. viii

**bind**, *bind*, *v.t.* to tie or fasten together with a band: to encircle round: to restrain: to fix: to make fast: to sew a border on: to tie up or bandage: to fasten together and put a cover on (a book): to impose an obligation upon: to oblige by oath or promise: to indenture: to hold or cement firmly: to render hard: to constipate. —*v.i.* to become bound:—*pa.t.* and *pa.p.* **bound**, **bownd**.—*n.* a stalk of hop or other twiner: the indurated clay of coal-mines: in music, the tie for indicating that a note is to be held on, not repeated (of the same form as the slur or legato mark): capacity, measure (*Scot.*): a bore (*slang*). —*ns.* **bind'er**, one who binds (books, sheaves, etc.): anything that binds, as a rope, a bandage, a cementing agent, a tie-beam, a header in masonry, a case for binding loose papers: an attachment to a reaping-machine for tying the bundles of grain cut and thrown off: a reaping-machine provided with one; **bind'ery**, a bookbinder's establishment.—*adj.* **bind'ing**, restraining: obligatory.—*n.* the act of one who binds: anything that binds: the covering of a book.— *ns.* **bind'weed**, convolvulus: also (**black bindweed**) a species of *Polygonum.*—**be bound up in**, to be wholly devoted to; **bind over**, to subject to legal obligation; **I dare** or **will be bound, I will be responsible for the statement**. See also **bound** (1) and **bounden**. [O.E. *bindan*; Ger. *binden*, Sans. *badhnōti*, he binds.]

**bine**, *bin*, *n.* the slender stem of a climbing plant: a flexible shoot. [Orig. dial. form of **bind**.]

**binervate**, *bī-nûrv'āt*, *adj.* with two ribs or nerves. [L. *bi-*, twice, and **nerve**.]

**bing**, *bing*, (*dial.*) *n.* a heap or pile (esp. of waste from a coal-mine): a bin. [O.N. *bingr.*]

**bing**, *bing*, (*obs. slang*; *Scott*) *v.i.* to go.

**binge**, *binj*, *binzh*, *v.t.* and *v.i.* to soak (*dial.*): to drink deep.—*n.* (*slang*), a spree.

**bingle**, *bing'gl*, *n.* a hairstyle midway between bob and shingle.—Also *v.t.*

**bingo**, *bing'gō*, *n.* a familiar name for brandy. [Prob. B, for **brandy**, and **stingo**.]

**bingo**, *bing'gō*, *n.* housey-housey. [Orig. uncertain.]

**bink**, *bingk*, (*Scot.*) *n.* a bench, a bank, a shelf: a plate-rack: a wasp's or bee's nest: a small heap of mortar. [Northern form of **bench**.]

**binnacle**, *bin'ə-kl*, (*naut.*) *n.* the box in which a ship's compass is kept. [Formerly *bittacle*— Port. *bitácola*—L. *habitáculum*, a dwelling-place —*habitāre*, to dwell.]

**binocle**, *bin'o-kl*, *-ə-kl*, *n.* a telescope for use with both eyes at once.—*adj.* **binocular** (*bi-*, *bi-nok'ū-lər*), with two eyes: suitable for use with two eyes: stereoscopic.—*n.* a binocular telescope (usually in *pl.*) or microscope.—*adv.* **binoc'ularly**. [L. *bini*, two by two, *oculus*, an eye.]

**binomial**, *bī-nōm'i-əl*, *adj.* (*alg.*) consisting of two terms, as *a+b*.—*n.* a binomial expression.—*adj.* **binominal**, *bī-nom'in-əl*), making use of two names, as the Linnaean nomenclature which names every species by giving first the generic and then the trivial name.—**binomial theorem**, Newton's theorem giving any power of a binomial. [L. *bi-*, twice, and *nōmen*, a name, a term.]

**bint**, *bint*, *n.* a girl, woman (with various shades of meaning). [Arabic.]

**binturong**, *bin'tū-rong*, *n.* an East Indian prehensile-tailed carnivore, akin to the civet. [Malay.]

**bio-**, *bī-ō-*, in composition, life: living organisms: living tissue—as in, e.g. the following.—*n.* **bioastronaut'ics**, science dealing with the effects of travel in space on living organisms.—*adj.* **biobibliograph'ical**, dealing with the life and writings of any one.—*n.* **bi'oblast** (Gr. *blastos*, germ), a hypothetical unit of living matter: a minute granule in protoplasm.—*adj.* **biochem'ical**.—*ns.* **biochem'ist**; **biochem'istry**, the chemistry of living things, physiological chemistry.—*adj.*

**biocid'al** (*-sid'*), killing living material.—*n.* **biocoenosis** (*bī-ō-sē-nō'sis*; Gr. *koinos*, common), an association of organisms ecologically interdependent.—*adjs.* **biocoenotic** (*-not'ik*), ecological; **biodegrād'able**, (of substances) able to be broken down by bacteria.—*n.* **biodegradā'tion**. —*adj.* **biodynam'ic**, dealing with activities of living organisms: (of system of land cultivation) fertilising with organic materials only.—*ns.* **biodynam'ics**; **bioecol'ogy**, the branch of ecology dealing with the interrelationship of plant and animal life; **bioelectric'ity**, electrical phenomena in plants and animals; **bioengineer'ing** (see **biological engineering**, at end of article); **bi'ogen** (*-jen*; Gr. *genos*, race, offspring), a hypothetical unit of protoplasm; **biogen'esis** (Gr. *genesis*, production), the derivation of living things from living things only: biogeny.—*adjs.* **biogenet'ic**, relating to biogens or to biogeny, or to biogenesis; **biogenous** (*-oj'*), parasitic.—*ns.* **biog'eny**, the course of organic evolution or development of the individual or the race; **biogeochem'istry**, the science of plants and animals in relation to chemicals in the soil; **biogeog'rapher**.—*adj.* **biogeograph'ical**.—*ns.* **biogeog'raphy**, the geography of living things: geographical distribution of plants and animals; **bi'ograph** (Gr. *graphein*, to write), a biography: a bioscope; **biog'rapher**, one who writes biography.—*adjs.* **biograph'ic**, **-al**.—*adv.* **biograph'ically**.—*n.* **biog'raphy**, a written account or history of the life of an individual: the art of writing such accounts.—*adj.* **biological** (*-loj'*), of, pertaining to, biology: physiological: produced by physiological means: effected by living organisms.—*adv.* **biolog'ically**.—*ns.* **biol'ogist**; **biol'ogy**, the science of living things: sometimes restricted to ecology; **bioluminesc'ence**, the emission of light by living organisms, as certain insects, marine animals, bacteria, fungi; **biomechan'ics**, the mechanics of movements in living creatures.—*adj.* **biomet'ric** (Gr. *metron*, measure).—*ns.* **biometrician** (*-trish'ən*); **biomet'rics**, **biom'etry**, the statistical or quantitative study of biology; **bi'omorph** (Gr. *morphē*, form), a representation of a living thing in decoration. —*adj.* **biomorph'ic**.—*n.* **bion'ics**, study of methods of working of living creatures and application of the principles observed to design of computers, etc.—*adj.* **bionom'ic**.—*ns.* **bionom'ics** (Gr. *nomos*, law), the study of the relations between the organism and its environment: ecology; **biophor(e)** (*bī'ō-fōr*, *-för*; Gr. *phoros*, carrying), Weismann's hypothetical unit of living matter; **biophys'ics**, a form of biology dealing with biological structures and processes in terms of physics; **bi'oplasm** (Gr. *plasma*, form, *plastos*, moulded), protoplasm; **bi'oplast**, a minute portion of protoplasm; **biopoies's** (*-poi-ēs'is*), creation of living from non-living material as an evolutionary process; **bi'opsy**, a removal of tissue or fluid from a living body for diagnostic examination: such examination; **bi'oscope** (Gr. *skopeein*, to look at), a cinematographic apparatus or theatre; **bi'osphere**, the part of the earth and its atmosphere in which living things are found; **biosyn'thesis**, the production of chemical substances by a living organism.—*adj.* **biosynthet'ic**.—*ns.* **biosystemat'ics**, study of relationships of organisms and of laws of classification; **biō'ta**, flora and fauna of a region.—*adj.* **biotic** (*bī-ot'ik*), pertaining to life.—**biogenetic law**, the law of recapitulation of the history of the race in that of the individual; **biological control**, a method of reducing the numbers of a pest—plant, animal or parasite—by introducing or fostering one of its enemies; **biological engineering**, provision of aids (electronic, electrical, etc.) to functioning of the body, as hearing aids, aids to movement, etc. (also *bioengineering*): engineering required for methods of biosynthesis of animal and plant products, e.g. for fermentation processes (also *bioengineering*): manipulating living cells so as to promote their growth in a desired way; **biological warfare**, methods of fighting involving the use of disease bacteria. [Gr. *bios*, life.]

**biotin**, *bī'ō-tin, n.* one of the members of the vitamin B complex (also known as vitamin H). [Gr. *biotos*, means of living.]

**biotite**, *bī'ō-tīt, n.* a black or dark ferro-magnesian mica. [Named after J. B. *Biot* (1774-1862).]

**biparous**, *bip'ər-əs, adj.* bearing two at a birth: dichasial. [L. *bis*, twice, *parĕre*, to bring forth.]

**bipartite**, *bī-pärt'it, adj.* divided into two parts: having two corresponding parts, as a document: affecting two parties, as an agreement.—*adj.* **bipart'isan** (*-i-zan*), pertaining to, supported by, or consisting of members of, two parties.—*n.* **bipartition** (*-tish'ən*), division into two parts. [L. *bi-*, *bis*, twice, *partitus*, divided—*partire*, *-irī*, to divide.]

**biped**, *bī'ped, n.* an animal with two feet.—*adjs.* **bi'ped**, **bi'pedal**, having two feet. [L. *bipēs*, *-pedis*—*bi-*, twice, *pēs*, *pedis*, foot.]

**bipetalous**, *bī-pet'əl-əs, adj.* having two petals. [L. *bi-*, twice, and **petal**.]

**bipinnaria**, *bī-pin-ā'ri-ə, n.* a starfish larva with two ciliated bands. [L. *bi-*, twice, *pinna*, a feather.]

**bipinnate**, *bī-pin'āt, adj.* pinnate with each pinna itself pinnate. [L. *bi-*, twice, and **pinnate**.]

**biplane**, *bī'plān, n.* an aeroplane or glider with two sets of wings, one above the other. [L. *bi-*, twice, and **plane**.]

**bipod**, *bī'pod, n.* a two-legged stand. [L. *bi-*, twice, Gr. *pous*, *podos*, a foot.]

**bipyramid**, *bī-pir'ə-mid, n.* a form of two pyramids base to base, or with a pyramid at each end.

**biquadratic**, *bī-kwəd-rat'ik, n.* a quantity twice squared, or raised to the fourth power.—**biquadratic equation**, an equation involving the fourth, and no higher, power of the unknown quantity; **biquadratic root**, the square root of the square root. [L. *bi-*, twice, and *quadrātus*, squared.]

**biquintile**, *bī-kwin'til, n.* the aspect of planets when they are twice the fifth part of a great circle (i.e. 144 degrees) from each other. [L. *bi-*, twice, *quintus*, the fifth.]

**birch**, *bûrch, n.* a hardy forest-tree (*Betula*), with smooth white bark and very durable wood: a rod for punishment, consisting of a birch twig or twigs.—*v.t.* to flog.—*adjs.* **birch**, **birch'en**, made of birch.—**birch rod**, a birch for punishment. [O.E. *berc*, *bierce*; O.N. *björk*, Sans. *bhūrja*.]

**bird**, *bûrd, n.* a general name for a feathered animal (orig. applied to the young): a person (*slang*): an object of admiration (*slang*): a girl or woman (*arch.*, *dial.*; later *slang*; orig. confused with **bride** or **burd** (1) or (2)).—*v.i.* to shoot at, seek to catch or snare birds.—*ns.* **bird'ie** (*dim.*), a little bird: the achievement of a hole in golf in one stroke less than par; **bird'ing**, the hunting, shooting, snaring, or catching of birds.—*n.*, *adj.*, *adv.* **bird-alane** (see **burd** (2)).—**bird'bath**, a basin set up for birds to bathe in; **bird'-batting** (*dial.*), bat-fowling; **bird'-bolt** (*Shak.*), a short thick blunted bolt or arrow for killing birds without piercing; **bird'cage**, a cage of wire or wicker for holding birds; **bird'call**, a bird-catcher's instrument for imitating birds' notes; **bird'-catcher**, a professional catcher of birds.—*n.* and *adj.* **bird'-catching** (**bird-catching spider**, see **bird-spider**).— **bird'-cherry**, a small wild cherry tree (*Prunus Padus*): its astringent fruit; **bird'-dog**, one trained to find or retrieve birds for hunters.— *adj.* **bird'-eyed**, quick-sighted.—**bird'-fancier**, one who breeds birds, or keeps them for sale; **bird impact**, **bird strike**; **bird'ing-piece**, a fowling-piece; **bird'-louse**, a louse-like insect of the

Mallophaga, parasitical on birds and mammals (*pl.* **bird'-lice**); **bird'-lime**, a sticky substance for catching birds; **bird'-of-par'adise** (see **paradise**; **bird-of-paradise flower**, Strelitzia); **bird'-pepper**, a species of capsicum; **birdseed**, seed (hemp, etc.) for cage-birds: a thing trifling in amount, chicken feed (*slang*); **bird's'-eye**, a kind of primrose, of speedwell, or of tobacco.—*adj.* such as might be seen by a flying bird: having markings like birds' eyes.—**bird's'-foot**, a papilionaceous genus (*Ornithopus*) with clawlike pods; **bird'-skiing**, water-skiing with winglike device that enables the skier to rise off the water; **bird's'-nest**, the nest in which a bird lays and hatches her eggs: a name given to several plants from their appearance, esp. Monotropa and Neottia (bird's nest orchis); **bird's'-nesting**, **bird'-nesting**, seeking and robbing birds' nests; **bird'-spider**, a large spider (Mygale) that preys on small birds, found in Brazil: extended to others of the Aviculariidae; **bird strike**, collision of a bird with an aircraft resulting in aircraft damage; **bird'-table**, a table, inaccessible to cats, for wild birds to feed on.—*adj.* **bird'-witt'ed**, flighty: incapable of sustained attention.—**a bird in the hand is worth two in the bush**, a certainty is not to be thrown away for a poor chance of something better; **a little bird told me**, I heard in a way I will not reveal; **bird's-eye view**, a general view from above: a general view of a subject; **bird's-foot trefoil**, a papilionaceous genus (Lotus) with clustered pods like birds' feet; **do bird** (*slang*), serve a prison sentence; **for the birds** (*slang*), not to be taken seriously, of little value; **get the bird** (i.e. the goose), in stage slang, to be hissed, hence dismissed; **in bird** (*slang*), in prison; **like a bird**, with alacrity. [O.E. *brid*, the young of a bird, a bird.]

**birefringent**, *bī-rə-frin'jənt, adj.* doubly refracting, like Iceland spar.—*n.* **birefrin'gence**. [L. *bi-*, twice, and **refringent**.]

**bireme**, *bī'rēm, n.* an ancient vessel with two banks of oars. [L. *birēmis—bi-*, twice, and *rēmus*, an oar.]

**biretta**, *bir-et'a, n.* a square cap worn by clergy— by priests, black; bishops, purple; cardinals, red. [It. *berretta*—L.L. *birretum*, cap.]

**birk**, *birk, bûrk, n.* Scots and dial. for **birch**.— *adj.* **birk'en** (*Scot.*), birchen.

**birkie**, *birk'i, (Scot.) n.* a strutting or swaggering fellow: a fellow generally.—*adj.* active. [Perh. conn. with O.N. *berkia*, O.E. *beorcan*, to bark.]

**birl**, *birl, (Scot.) v.t.* and *v.i.* to spin round: to toss (a coin): to spend (esp. on liquor). [Apparently onomatopoeic.]

**birl**, **birle**, *birl, (Scot.) v.t.* and *v.i.* to pour out: to ply with drink: to carouse.—*ns.* **birl'er** (*Cumberland*); **birl'ing**, the act of drawing liquor. [O.E. *byrelian—byrele*, a cup-bearer, *beran*, to bear.]

**birlieman**, *bir'li-mən, (Scott) n.* Same as **byrlawman**.

**birlinn**, *bir'lin, n.* a chief's barge in the Western Isles. [Gael. *birlinn*—O.N. *byrthingr—byrthr*, burden.]

**Birminghamise**, **-ize**, *bûr'ming-əm-iz, v.t.* to make up artificially. [See **Brummagem**.]

**birostrate**, *bī-ros'trāt, adj.* double-beaked. [L. *bi-*, twice, *rōstrātus*, beaked—*rōstrum*, a beak.]

**birr**, *bir, (Scot.) n.* impetuosity: a violent push: stress in pronunciation: any sharp whirring sound. [O.N. *byrr*, a favourite wind.]

**birse**, *birs, (Scot.) n.* bristle.—*adj.* **bir'sy**.—**lick the birse**, to draw a hog's bristle through the mouth —as in admission as a burgess in Selkirk; **set up one's birse**, to rouse the wrath of, from the bristling up of enraged animals. [O.E. *byrst*.]

**birsle**, *birs'l, (Scot.) v.t.* to scorch, to toast. [Origin unknown.]

**birth**, *bûrth, n.* a ship's station at anchor. [Same as **berth**.]

birth, *bûrth*, *n*. the act of bearing or bringing forth: coming into the world: the offspring born: dignity of family: origin.—*n*. birth'dom (*Shak*.), birthright.—birth control, the control of reproduction by contraceptives; birth'day, the day on which one is born, or (usually) its anniversary, or a day officially held instead.—*adj*. relating to the day of one's birth.—birth'day-book, a book for autograph records of friends' birthdays; birthday honours, titles, etc., conferred on the king's (or queen regnant's) official birthday; birth'day-suit, the naked skin; birth'mark, a peculiar mark on one's body at birth: a distinguishing quality (*fig*.); birth'night, the night on which one is born, or the anniversary of that night: the evening of the king's (or queen's) birthday (*obs*.); birth'place, the place of one's birth; birth'-rate, proportion of births to population; birth'right, the right or privilege to which one is entitled by birth: native rights.—*adj*. birth'-strangled (*Shak*.), strangled at birth.—*n*. birth'wort, a plant (*Aristolochia Clematitis*) formerly reputed to help parturition. [Prob. O.N. *byrthr*.]

bis, *bis, adv*. twice: a direction for repetition (*mus*.). [L.]

biscacha. Same as viscacha.

Biscayan, *bis'kā-ən*, or *kā'*, *adj*. and *n*. of or pertaining to *Biscay* in Spain, or its people: Basque generally: a long heavy musket, or its bullet.

biscuit, *bis'kit*, *n*. a small, thin, crisp cake made of unleavened dough: a soft round cake (*U.S.*): pottery that has been fired but not yet glazed: a square mattress (*mil. slang*).—*adj*. pale brown in colour.—*n*. biscuit-root, camass.—to take the biscuit, to surpass all others (*ironically*). [O.Fr. *bescoit* (mod. *biscuit*)—L. *bis*, twice, *coquĕre*, *coctum*, to cook or bake.]

bise, *bēz*, *n*. a cold north or north-east wind prevalent at certain seasons in and near Switzerland. [Fr.]

bisect, *bī-sekt'*, *v.t.* and *v.i.* to divide into two (usu. equal) parts.—*ns*. bisec'tion; bisec'tor, a line that divides an angle, etc., into two equal parts. [L. *bi-*, twice, and *secāre*, *sectum*, to cut.]

biserial, *bī-sē'ri-əl*, *adj*. arranged in two series or rows. [L. *bi-*, twice, and series.]

biserrate, *bī-ser'āt*, doubly serrate. [L. *bi-*, twice, and serrate.]

bisexual, *bī-seks'ū-əl*, *adj*. hermaphrodite: attracted sexually to both sexes. [L. *bi-*, twice, sexual.]

bishop, *bish'əp*, *n*. in the Western and Eastern Churches and in the Anglican communion, a clergyman consecrated for the spiritual direction of a diocese, usu. under an archbishop, and over the priests or presbyters and deacons: a spiritual overseer in the early Christian Church, whether of a local church or of a number of churches: a chessman whose move is in a diagonal line, its upper part carved into the shape of a bishop's mitre (formerly the *archer*): a wholesome hot drink compounded of red wine (claret, Burgundy, etc.) poured warm or cold upon ripe bitter oranges, sugared and spiced to taste: any of several kinds of weaver-bird (bish'op-bird).—*v.t.* to play the bishop, to confirm (*jocularly*): to supply with bishops: to let (milk or the like) burn while cooking.—*ns*. bish'opess, a bishop's wife: a she-bishop (*jocularly*); bish'opric, the office and jurisdiction of a bishop: sometimes a diocese—also bish'opdom.—bishop's cap, a genus (Mitella) of the saxifrage family, with one-sided inflorescences; bishop('s) weed, goutweed or goatweed.—the bishop has put his foot in it, it has burnt while cooking. [O.E. *biscop*—L. *episcopus* —Gr. *episkopos*, an overseer—*epi*, upon, *skopeein*, to view.]

bishop, *bish'əp*, *v.t.* to fill, or otherwise tamper with, the teeth of (to make a horse seem younger). [From a person of the name.]

bisk. See bisque (1).

bismar, *bis'*, *biz'mər*, (*Orkney* and *Shetland*) *n*. a kind of steelyard. [O.N. *bismari*.]

bismillah, *bis-mil'a*, *interj*. in the name of Allah. [Ar.]

bismuth, *bis'* or *biz'məth*, *n*. a brittle reddish-white element, of atomic number 83. [Ger. *bismuth*, *wissmuth* (now *wismut*), origin unknown.]

bisociation, *bi-sō-si-ā'shən*, *-shi-*, *n*. association at the same time of an idea or object with two quite different sets of facts or ideas.—*adj*. bisō'ciative. [L. *bi-*, twice, and association.]

bison, *bī'sn*, *-zn*, *n*. a large wild ox with shaggy hair and a fatty hump—the European bison, almost extinct except in parks, and the American, commonly called buffalo in America. [From L. *bisōn*, *-ontis*, prob. of Gmc. origin; cf. O.H.G. *wisunt*, O.E. *wesend*.]

bisque, bisk, *bisk*, *n*. a rich soup, esp. crayfish soup. [Fr.]

bisque, bisk, *n*. a kind of unglazed white porcelain: pottery that has undergone the first firing before being glazed. [See biscuit.]

bisque, bisk, *n*. a term at tennis, golf, etc., for the handicap whereby a player allows a weaker opponent (at latter's choice of time) to score a point in a set, or deduct a stroke at a hole, to take an extra turn in croquet, etc. [Fr.]

bissextile, *bis-ekst'il*, *adj*. having an intercalary day.—*n*. leap year. [L. *bisextīlis*—bis, twice, *sextus*, sixth, the sixth day before the kalends of March (24th February) being doubled.]

bisson, *bis'ən*, *adj*. (*Shak*. beesome), blind, purblind: (*Shak*. bisson) perh. blinding. [O.E. *bisene*, blind.]

bistable, *bī'stā-bl*, *adj*. (of a valve or transistor circuit) having two stable states.

bistort, *bis'tört*, *n*. adderwort or snakeweed, a plant (*Polygonum Bistorta*) of the dock family with twisted rootstock. [L. *bistorta*—bis, twice, *tortus*, *-a*, *-um*, twisted.]

bistoury, *bis'tər-i*, *n*. a narrow surgical knife for making incisions. [Fr. *bistouri*.]

bistre, bister, *bis'tər*, *n*. a pigment of a warm brown colour made from the soot of wood, esp. beechwood.—*adj*. bis'tred. [Fr. *bistre*; origin unknown.]

bistro, *bē-strō*, *n*. (Fr. *slang*), a small tavern.

bisulcate, *bī-sul'kāt*, *adj*. cleft in two (*zool*.): cloven-footed (*zool*.): with two furrows (*bot*.). [L. *bi-*, twice, *sulcus*, a furrow.]

bisulphate, *bī-sul'fāt*, *n*. an acid sulphate.—*n*. bisulph'ide, a disulphide.

bit, *bit*, *n*. a bite, a morsel: a small piece: a coin: 12½ cents (*U.S.*) (used only in two, four, six bits): the smallest degree: a brief space of time: a small boring tool (see brace): the boring part of a drilling machine: the part of the bridle that the horse holds in his mouth: somewhat (as *a bit of a fool*): in the sense of a bit of, sometimes with the effect of a diminutive (as *a bit of a laddie*, pl. *bits o' laddies*) (*Scot*.): a girl, young woman (*slang*).—*v.t.* to put the bit in the mouth of: to curb or restrain.—*pr.p.* bitt'ing; *pa.p.* bitt'ed.—*ns*. bitt'ie (*Scot*.), a small piece, short distance, or short time; bitt'ock (*Scot*.), a little bit.—*adj*. bitt'y, scrappy, disjointed, made up of odds and ends: not forming an artistic whole.—*n*. bit' (-part), a small part in acting.—bit and sup, something to eat and drink; bit by bit, piecemeal: gradually; do one's bit, do one's due share; take the bit in one's teeth, to throw off control. [From bite.]

bit, *bit*, *n*. the smallest unit of information in computers and communications theory. [Contracted binary dig*it*.]

bitch, *bich*, *n*. the female of the dog, wolf, and fox: (abusively), a woman, very rarely a man: a malicious or arrogant woman.—*v.i.* (*slang*) to complain.—*v.t.* (*slang*) to mess up, spoil (often bitch up).—*adj*. bitch'y.—the bitch goddess,

material success as an object of worship. [O.E. *bicce*; O.N. *bikkja*.]
**bite**, *bit*, *v.t.* and *v.i.* to seize or tear with the teeth: to puncture with the mouth-parts, as an insect: to cut or penetrate: to eat into chemically: to take effect: to grip: to wound by reproach (*arch.*): to deceive, to take in (now only in passive): to accept something offered as bait (also *fig.*): (*pa.t.* bit; *pa.p.* bit or bitt′en).—*n.* a grasp by the teeth: manner in which the teeth come together: a puncture by an insect: the wound or sore caused thereby: a nibble at the bait: something bitten off: a mouthful: biting quality: grip: pungency: corroding action: a playful imposition or befooling (*old slang*).—*n.* bit′er, one who bites: an animal with a habit of biting: a fish apt to take the bait: a cheat (*obs.*, except in the biter bit, the cheater cheated: the wrongdoer paid back).—*n.* bit′ing.—*adj.* which bites: sharp, cold: sarcastic.—*n.* bit′ing-louse, a bird-louse.—**bite** in (*etching*), to eat out the lines of with acid; **bite off** more than one can chew, to over-estimate one's capacities: to undertake that which one cannot achieve; **bite the dust**, to fall, to die; **bite the thumb**, to express defiance by knocking the thumb-nail against the teeth. [O.E. *bitan*; Goth. *beitan*, O.N. *bita*, Ger. *beissen*.]
**bito**, *bē′tō*, *n.* a tree (*Balanites aegyptiaca*; family Zygophyllaceae) of dry tropical Africa and Asia: its oil-yielding fruit.
**bitonal**, *bi′tōn′əl*, *adj.* using two musical keys simultaneously.—*n.* bitonal′ity.
**bitt**, *bit*, (*naut.*) *n.* a post for fastening cables (usu. in *pl.*).—*v.t.* to fasten round the bitts.—*n.* bitt′er, the turn of cable round the bitts, hence perhaps **the bitter end**, the end of the rope that remains aboard, and so the last extremity (but perhaps from **bitter** *adj.*). [Perh. O.N. *biti*, a cross-beam.]
**bittacle**. Same as **binnacle**.
**bitte**, *bit′ə*, (Ger.) please: don't mention it: I beg your pardon.
**bitter**, *bit′ər*, *adj.* having a taste like that of quinine or hops: sharp: painful: acrimonious.—*n.* any substance having a bitter taste, esp. a type of ale.—*adj.* bitt′erish.—*adv.* bitt′erly.—*n.* bitt′erness.—*n.pl.* bitt′ers, a liquid prepared from bitter herbs or roots, and used as a stomachic.—**bitter-apple**, colocynth; **bitter-cress**, Cardamine; **bitter-earth**, magnesia; **bitter-king**, an intensely bitter shrub of the quassia family, growing in the Eastern Archipelago; **bitter-pit**, a disease of apples, etc., characterised by brown spots and depressions; **bitter-root**, an American xerophytic plant of the purslane family; **bitter-spar**, dolomite; **bittersweet**, the woody nightshade (*Solanum Dulcamara*), whose stems when chewed taste first bitter, then sweet: an apple that tastes both sweet and bitter (*Shak.*): a mixture of sweet and bitter (also *fig.*); bitt′erwood, various trees, esp. of the Simarubaceae.—**the bitter end** (see bitt). [O.E. *biter—bitan*, to bite.]
**bitterling**, *bit′ər-ling*, *n.* a small fish (*Rhodeus amarus*).
**bittern**, *bit′ərn*, *n.* a marsh bird of the heron family. [M.E. *bittour*, *botor*—O.Fr. *butor*.]
**bittern**, *bit′ərn*, *n.* an oily liquid remaining in saltworks after crystallisation of the salt. [bitter.]
**bittock**. See bit.
**bittor**, bittour, bittur, *bit′ər*, *n.* (*Spens.*, Dryden) the bittern.
**bitumen**, *bit′ū-mən*, or *bi-tū′*, *n.* name applied to various inflammable mineral substances, as naphtha, petroleum, asphalt.—*v.t.* bitū′minate, to mix with or make into bitumen—also bitū′minise, ize.—*n.* bituminisā′tion, -izā′tion.—*adjs.* bitū′minous, bitūmed′ (or *bit′*; Shak.), impregnated with bitumen.—**bituminous coal**, coal that flames in burning, from richness in volatile hydrocarbons. [L. *bitūmen*, *-inis*.]

**bivalent**, *bi-vā′lənt* or *biv′ə-lənt*, *adj.* having a valency of two (*chem.*): pertaining to one of a pair of homologous chromosomes (also *n.*).—*ns.* **bivalence**, **bivalency**. [L. *bi-*, twice, and valent.]
**bivalve**, *bi′valv*, *n.* an animal having a shell in two valves or parts, like the oyster—esp. a lamellibranch; a seed vessel of like kind.—*adj.* having two valves.—*adj.* bivalv′ular. [L. *bi-*, twice, *valva*, a door-leaf.]
**bivariate**, *bi′vā′ri-āt*, *adj.* of, or involving, two variant qualities.—Also biva′riant.—Also *n.*
**bivious**, *biv′i-əs*, *adj.* leading two, or different, ways.—*n.* biv′ium, in echinoderms the two rays enclosing the madreporite. [L. *bivius—bi-*, twice, *via*, a way.]
**bivouac**, *biv′ōō-ak*, *n.* the resting at night of soldiers (or others) in the open air, instead of under cover in camp.—*v.i.* to pass the night in the open air:—*pr.p.* biv′ouacking; *pa.p.* biv′ouacked.—Also (*slang*) *n.* and *v.* bivv′y. [Fr.,—Ger. *beiwacht*, additional watch.]
**bi-weekly**, *bi-wēk′li*, *adj.* occurring or appearing once in two weeks or twice a week.—Also *adv.*—*n.* a periodical issued twice a week.
**Bixa**, *bik′sa*, *n.* a tropical American genus of plants yielding anatta, giving name to the **Bixā′ceae**, a family of parietal Archichlamydeae. [Sp. *bixa* (*bija*)—Taino *bixa*.]
**biz**, *biz.* Slang for business.
**bizarre**, *bi-zär′*, *adj.* odd: fantastic: extravagant.—*n.* bizarr′erie. [Fr.,—Sp. *bizarro*, gallant, brave, poss.—Basque *bizarra*, beard.]
**bizcacha**. See viscacha.
**bizone**, *bi′zōn*, *n.* a unit formed of two zones, as that comprising the British and U.S. occupation zones in Germany after 1945.
**blab**, *blab*, *v.i.* to talk much: to tell tales.—*v.t.* to let out (a secret):—*pr.p.* blabb′ing; *pa.p.* blabbed.—*n.* one who lets out secrets (*Milt.*): a tattler: tattling.—*ns.* blabb′er, blabber′mouth.—*n.* and *adj.* blabb′ing. [M.E. *blabbe*, cf. O.N. *blabbra*, Ger. *plappern*.]
**blab**, *blab*, *n.* a blister (*obs.*).—*v.t.* to swell.—*adj.* blabb′er, swollen. [bleb.]
**black**, *blak*, *adj.* of the darkest colour: reflecting no light: obscure: dismal: sullen: horrible: dusky: foul, dirty: malignant: dark-haired: wearing dark armour or clothes: illicit: under trade-union ban.—*n.* black colour or absence of colour: a Negro or other dark-skinned person: a black pigment: a smut: smut fungus: black clothes (formerly, still in Scotland, in *pl.*).—*v.t.* to make black: to soil or stain: to draw in black: to put under trade-union ban.—*v.t.* black′en, to make black: to defame.—*v.i.* to become black.—*n.* black′ing, a substance used for blacking leather, etc.—*adj.* black′ish.—*n.* black′ness.—*n.* black′amoor, a black Moor: a Negro.—*adj.* black-and-blue, livid in colour because of bruising.—*adj.* and *n.* black′-and-tan′, (a dog) having black hair on the back, and tan or yellowish-brown elsewhere: (usu. Black′-and-Tan′) (of) an auxiliary policeman in Ireland, about 1920 (from his khaki uniform with black cap and armlet).—*adj.* black′-and-white′, partly black, partly white: drawing or drawn in black on a white ground.—**black art**, magic (perh. a translation of L. *nigromantia*, erroneously used for Gr. *nekromanteiā*, see necromancy).—*adj.* black-a-vised (*blak′-ə-vist*, *-vizd*; perh. Fr. *à vis*, in the face), swarthy.—*v.t.* black′ball, to vote against by putting a black ball into a ballot-box: to ostracise: to vote against, veto.—*n.* black′-balling.—black′band, iron ore containing enough coal to calcine it; **black bass**, a North American freshwater fish (*Micropterus*); black′-bee′tle, a cockroach; **black belt**, a belt showing grade of proficiency in judo: an area with rich dark soil (*U.S.*): a region in which Negroes outnumber whites (*U.S.*); black′berry, the fruit of

the bramble: in some districts, the blackcurrant or the crowberry; **black´bird**, a black species of thrush: a grackle or other bird of the *Icteridae* (*U.S.*): a Negro or Polynesian recruited or kidnapped for labour; **black´birder**, a person or ship engaged in slave-trading: **black´birding**; **black´board**, a board painted black, for writing on.—*adj.* **black´-bod´ing**, of evil omen.—**black body**, one that absorbs all incident radiation, reflecting none; **black book**, an important book bound in black: a book recording the names of persons deserving punishment; **black bottom**, an American dance of late 1920s with sinuous movement of hips; **black box**, a type of seismograph for registering underground explosions: a unit of electronic equipment in package form which can be put into or removed from an aircraft, spacecraft, etc., without dismantling; **black´boy**, the Australian grass-tree; **black bread**, rye-bread.—*adj.* **black´-browed´**, having black eyebrows: sullen.—**black´buck**, the common Indian antelope; **black´-bull´y**, sapodilla; **black´cap**, a warbler with a black crown: an apple roasted until it is black: a black American raspberry; **black cap**, the cap put on by English judges to pronounce sentence of death; **black´-cat´**, the pekan or fisher; **black cattle**, at one time cattle of any colour, orig. Welsh and Scottish cattle; **black chalk**, bluish-black clay-slate, used for drawing, and for making black paint.—*adj.* **black´-coated**, wearing a black coat: of the professional class.—*ns.* **black´cock**, the male of the **black´grouse** or **black´game**, a species of grouse, common in the north of England and in Scotland:—*fem.* **grey´-hen**; **black comedy**, a 'pièce noire' (Jean Anouilh), a play in which, under fantasy and grotesque humour, the hopeless world of reality is clearly seen: also a comedy about dreadful events: a film of either type; **Black Country**, the industrial Midland counties of England; **black´curr´ant**, the small black berry of a garden shrub (*Ribes nigrum*) of the gooseberry genus; **black damp**, air in which the oxygen has been displaced by carbon dioxide; **black death** (also with *caps.*), a deadly epidemic of bubonic plague that swept over Asia and Europe, reaching England in 1348 (from the black spots that appeared on the skin); **black diamond**, carbonado (2): (in *pl.*) coal; **black draught**, a purgative medicine, chiefly senna and Epsom salts; **black drop**, a liquid preparation of opium, vinegar, and sugar; **black earth**, a fertile deposit covering wide regions in S. Russia and in Central India; **black eye**, an eye of which the iris is dark: a discoloration around the eye due to a blow or fall.—*adj.* **black´-faced.**—**black´fellow**, an Australian aboriginal; **black´fish**, a name given to several kinds of fish, e.g. the black ruff, a kind of perch: the ca'ing whale: a salmon after spawning; **black´-fisher**, poacher of fish by night: **black´-fishing**; **black flag**, the flag of a pirate: that hoisted at the execution of a criminal: that waved to call a driver in from a racing circuit; **Black´foot**, a member of a tribe of Algonquin American Indians:—*pl.* **-foot**, or **-feet**:—Also *adj.*—**black´-fox´**, the pekan; **Black Friar** (also without *caps.*), a Dominican, from his black mantle (over a white woollen habit); **black Friday**, Good Friday: an unlucky Friday (*orig. hist.*); **black frost**, frost without rime or snow; **black´game**, blackgrouse, see blackcock: **blackguard** (*blag´ärd*), originally applied to the lowest menials about a court, who took charge of the pots, kettles, etc.: a contemptible scoundrel: a low and scurrilous person.—Also *adj.*—*v.t.* to vituperate.—*v.i.* to play the blackguard.—*n.* **black´guardism.**—*adj. and adv.* **black´guardly.**—**black hand**, a secret society or underground influence, often imaginary; **black´-head**, a bird of various kinds, as the blackheaded

gull: a comedo.—*adj.* **black´headed**, having a black head.—**black´heart**, a dark kind of cherry.—*adj.* **black-heart´ed**, of an evil disposition.—**black hole**, a punishment cell, esp. (*caps.*) that at Calcutta (1756) in which 123 of 146 British prisoners died of suffocation; **black house**, an obsolescent type of house in the Scottish highlands and islands, built of turf; **black humour**, humour which laughs at the tragedy of the human lot and mocks the idea that man can order his world successfully; **black´jack**, a large jug for holding drink. originally made of leather: a pirate flag: zincblende: a short leather-covered club with weighted head: vingt-et-un, or a game like it; **black´lead´**, a black mineral (plumbago, not lead) used in making pencils, blacking grates, etc.; **black´leg**, blackquarter: a turf-swindler: a worker continuing to work during a strike or one taking a striker's place (also **black´-neb**); **black letter**, the Old English (also called Gothic) type (𝔟𝔩𝔞𝔠𝔨=𝔩𝔢𝔱𝔱𝔢𝔯); **black light**, invisible infrared or ultraviolet light; **black´list**, a list of defaulters or persons against whom a warning is necessary; **black´mail**, tribute formerly paid to robbers for protection: hush-money extorted under threat of exposure, often baseless.—*v.t.* to extort money from (a person): to force by threats (into doing something).—*n.* **blackmail´er.**—**black Maria**, a prison van: a shell that emits dense black smoke or a gun discharging it (*mil. slang*); **black market**, surreptitious trade in rationed goods: buying and selling that is against the law or official regulations (e.g. illegal traffic in drugs):—**black´-marketeer´**, one who operates on the black market; **black mass**, a travesty of the mass in diabolism or devil-worship; **black Monday**, Easter Monday: the day of return to school; **Black Monk**, a Benedictine (also without *caps.*); **black´out**, total extinction or concealment of lights: sudden loss of consciousness, or failure of the mind to work.—*adj.* for blacking out with.—**Black Pope**, (*disparagingly*) the head of the Jesuits; **Black Power**, a militant movement to increase Negro influence, esp. in predominantly white countries; **black´pudd´ing**, a blood-pudding (q.v.); **black´-quart´er**, an apoplectic disease of cattle; **black rat**, the smaller of the two British rats (usually brown) now comparatively rare; **Black Rod**, the usher of the chapter of the Garter and of the House of Lords; **black sheep**, a disreputable member of a family or group; **Black´shirt**, a member of a Fascist organisation, esp. in the Nazi SS and in Italy during World War II; **black´smith**, a smith who works in iron; **black snake**, a large agile non-poisonous snake (*Bascanium constrictor*) (*U.S.*): a very venomous snake (*Pseudechis porphyriacus*), nearly allied to the cobra (*Austr.*): a long whip; **black spot**, name given to diseases of various plants, e.g. roses: a small area which has bad conditions or a bad record; **Black Stone**, an Islamic sacred stone in a shrine in Mecca; **black swan**, a swan with black plumage and red beak native to Australia: something rare or non-existent (*fig.*); **black´thorn**, a dark-coloured thorn bearing sloes: a stick made from its stem; **black´top**, layers of bituminous material in specified arrangement used for surfacing roads, etc.: a road so surfaced; **black velvet**, champagne and stout.—*adj.* **black´-vis´aged**, having a black visage or appearance.—**black´-wash**, a lotion of calomel and lime-water: anything that blackens; **Black Watch** (see watch); **blackwater**, a cattle disease (see redwater); **blackwater fever**, a fever in which the urine is dark-coloured; **black widow**, a very venomous American spider, the female with a black body and the habit of eating her mate.—**black in the face**, purple through strangulation, passion, or effort; **black out**, to obliterate with black: to extinguish or cover all lights: to suppress (news or radio communication); **in black and white**, in writing or in print: in art, in no colours but black and white; **in one's black books**, having incurred one's displeasure; **in the black**, solvent, out of debt: making a profit. [O.E. *blæc*, black.]

**blad.** Same as **blaud.**

**bladder,** *blad´ər, n.* a thin distended or distensible bag: any such bag in the animal body, esp. the receptacle for urine.—*adjs.* **bladd´ered, bladd´-ery.**—*ns.* **bladd´er-camp´ion,** a species of Silene with inflated calyx; **bladd´er-cherry,** the winter-cherry or strawberry-tomato; **bladd´er-nut,** a genus (*Staphylea*) of shrubs with inflated capsule; **bladd´er-worm,** the asexual state of a tapeworm or cestode; **bladd´erwort,** a genus (*Utricularia*) of floating plants with bladders that catch small animals; **bladd´er-wrack,** a common brown sea-weed with bladders. [O.E. *blædre—blāwan,* to blow; O.H.G. *blā(h)en, blājen,* to blow; Ger. *blatter—blähen;* cf. L. *flātus,* breath.]

**blade,** *blād, n.* the flat or expanded part of a leaf or petal, esp. a leaf of grass or corn: the cutting part of a knife, sword, etc.: the flat part of an oar: the paddle-like part of a propeller: the free outer part of the tongue: a dashing fellow.—*adj.* **blad´ed.**—**blade´-bone,** the flat bone at the back of the shoulder, the scapula. [O.E. *blæd;* O.N. *blath;* Ger. *blatt.*]

**blae,** *blā, (Scot.) adj.* blackish or dark bluish: livid: bleak.—*n.* (in *pl.*) hardened clay or somewhat carbonaceous shale, often blae in colour.—*n.* **blae´berry,** the whortleberry or bilberry. [O.N. *blār,* livid.]

**blague,** *blāg, n.* humbug: bounce.—*n.* **blagueur** (*blä-gœr*), one given to blague. [Fr.]

**blah,** *blä, (slang) n.* bunkum: pretentious nonsense. Also **blah-blah.**

**blain,** *blān, n.* a boil or blister. [O.E. *blegen.*]

**blain,** *blān, n.* a fish (*Gadus luscus*), the bib or pout.

**blame,** *blām, v.t.* to find fault with: to censure: to impute fault to: to charge with being cause: to bring discredit upon (*Spens.; B.*).—*n.* imputation of a fault: culpability: responsibility for what is amiss: injury (*Spens.*).—*adj.* (*U.S.*) confounded (also *adv.*).—*adj.* **blām´able.**—*n.* **blām´-ableness.**—*adv.* **blām´ably.**—Form. **blame´able, blame´ableness, blame´ably.**—*adjs.* **blamed** (*U.S. slang*), damned, confounded (also *adv.*); **blame´-ful,** meriting blame.—*adv.* **blame´fully.**—*n.* **blame´fulness.**—*adj.* **blame´less,** without blame: guiltless: innocent.—*adv.* **blame´lessly.**—*adj.* **blame´worthy,** worthy of blame: culpable.—**to blame,** blameworthy as being the cause. [Fr. *blâmer,* O.Fr. *blasmer*—Gr. *blasphēmeein,* to speak ill; see **blaspheme.**]

**blanc-de-Chine,** *blä-də-shēn, n.* a white porcelain made at Te-hua under the Ming dynasty. [Fr., white of China.]

**blanch,** *blänch, blänsh, v.t.* to whiten.—*v.i.* to grow white.—*adj.* and *adv.* (see **blench**). [Fr. *blanchir—blanc,* white; see **blank.**]

**blanchisseuse,** *blä-shē-sœz,* (Fr.) a laundress.

**blancmange,** *blə-mäzh´, -mönzh´, n.* a jelly prepared with milk: orig. fowl or other flesh with cream, etc.: shaped milk pudding. [Fr. *blancmanger—blanc,* white, *manger,* food.]

**bland,** *bland, adj.* smooth: gentle: mild: polite, suave: ironical.—*adv.* **bland´ly.**—*n.* **bland´ness.** [L. *blandus.*]

**bland,** *bland, n.* in Orkney and Shetland, buttermilk and water. [O.N. *blanda.*]

**blandish,** *bland´ish, v.t.* to flatter and coax, to cajole.—*n.* **bland´ishment,** act of expressing fondness: flattery: winning expressions or actions. [Fr. *blandir, blandiss-,* from L. *blandiri.*]

**blank,** *blangk, adj.* without writing or marks, as white paper: empty: featureless: expressionless: nonplussed: sheer: unrhymed.—*n.* a paper without writing: a lottery-ticket that brings no prize: an empty space, a void or vacancy: the white mark in the centre of a target (*archery*): a form of document having blank spaces to be filled up (*arch.* except in *U.S.*): a roughly shaped piece to be fashioned into a manufactured article: a dash in place of an omitted word.—*v.t.* to make blank: to make pale: to disconcert (*Milton*): mincingly used for damn, from the once usual form of printing d——.—*adv.* **blank´ly.**—*n.* **blank´ness.**—**blank cartridge,** one without a bullet; **blank cheque,** a signed cheque in which the sum is not filled in: complete freedom to act as one thinks best (*fig.*); **blank door, window,** a recess imitating a doorway or window.—*n.* or *adj.* **blank´ety-blank´, blank´ety, blank´y,** coll. for 'damned' as in verbal sense above.—**blank verse,** unrhymed verse of five feet. [Fr. *blanc,* from root of Ger. *blinken,* to glitter.—O.H.G. *blichen;* cf. Gr. *phlegein,* to shine.]

**blanket,** *blangk´it, n.* originally a white woollen fabric: a covering, generally woollen, for a bed, or used as a garment by American Indians, etc.: a covering generally: fertile material put round a nuclear reactor core to breed new fuel.—*v.t.* to cover, obstruct, or extinguish with, or as with, a blanket (as a ship by taking the wind out of her sails, gun-fire by getting in the way): to toss in a blanket: to bring under a single coverage.—*adj.* applying generally or covering all cases.—*n.* **blank´eting,** cloth for blankets: tossing in a blanket.—**blanket Indian,** Kaffir, one wearing a blanket, not European clothes; **blanket stitch,** a stitch used for the edge of a blanket; **wet blanket,** a damper of spirits: a killjoy.—**on the wrong side of the blanket,** illegitimately. [O.Fr. *blankete,* dim. of *blanc,* white.]

**blanquet,** *blä-ke,* (Fr.) a variety of pear.

**blanquette,** *blä-ket,* (Fr.) a ragout made with a white sauce.

**blare,** *blär, v.i.* to roar: to sound loudly, usu. harshly, as a trumpet.—*n.* roar: noise. [M.E. *blaren.*]

**blarney,** *blär´ni, n.* flattery or cajoling talk.—*v.t.* to cajole.—*n.* **blar´ney-land,** Ireland. [*Blarney* Castle, near Cork, where a stone difficult to reach confers the gift on those who kiss it.]

**blasé,** *blä´zä, adj.* dulled to pleasures: surfeited with enjoyments. [Fr. *pa.p.* of *blaser,* to cloy.]

**blash,** *blash, (Scot.) n.* a dash or splash of liquid or semi-liquid: battering rain: watery stuff.—*adj.* **blash´y.**

**blaspheme,** *blas-fēm´, v.t.* to speak impiously of.—*v.i.* to speak profanely or impiously: to curse and swear.—*n.* **blasphem´er.**—*adj.* **blasphemous** (*blas´fi-məs; Spens., Milt. -fē´*).—*adv.* **blas´-phemously** (*Spens. -fē´*).—*n.* **blas´phemy** (*Spens.* also *-fē´*), impious or profane speaking: contempt or indignity offered to God. [Gr. *blasphēmiā;* see **blame.**]

**blast,** *bläst, n.* a blowing or gust of wind: a forcible stream of air: a sound of a wind instrument: an explosion or detonation: a golf stroke of explosive effect: any scorching, withering or pernicious influence: a blight.—*v.i.* to emit blasts, blow: to use explosives: to swell (*dial.*): to wither (*obs.*): to curse.—*v.t.* to blow up: to rend asunder with an explosive: to blow into: to inflate (*dial.*): to strike with a blast: to blight, wither, scorch: to strike with a curse.—*adj.* **blast´ed,** blighted: cursed, damned.—*n.* **blast´er,** one who blasts: a kind of niblick.—*n.* and *adj.* **blast´ing.**—*n.* **blast´ment** (*Shak.*), blight.—**blast´-furnace,** a smelting furnace into which hot air is blown; **blast´-hole,** a hole in the bottom of a pump through which water enters; **blast´-off,** (the moment of) launching of a rocket-propelled missile or space capsule (*v.t.* and *v.i.* **blast off**); **blast´-pipe,** a pipe in a steam-engine, to convey the waste steam up the chimney.—in, at, **full blast**, in a state of maximum activity. [O.E. *blǣst*; cf. O.N. *blāsa*; Ger. *blasen*.]

**blastema**, *bla-stē'mə*, *n.* primordial material: the primordium of an organ: the protoplasmic part of an ovum, distinguished from the yolk: the axial part of a plant embryo. [Gr. *blastēma*, sprout.]

**blasto-**, *blas'tō-*, in composition, sprout, bud, germ.—*ns.* **blas'tocyst**, the blastula in mammals; **blas'toderm** (Gr. *derma*, skin; *embryology*), the layer or layers of cells arising from the germinal disk, or the portion of a partially segmenting egg which undergoes division; **blastogen'esis** (*-jen'*), transmission of hereditary characters by the germ-plasm: reproduction by budding.—*adj.* **blastogen'ic**, pertaining to the germ-plasm.—*adj.* and *n.* **blast'oid**.—*n.pl.* **Blastoid'ea** (Gr. *eidos*, form), a group of bud-like calcareous fossil echinoderms.—*ns.* **blas'tomere** (Gr. *meros*, part), a cell formed in an early stage of the cleavage of a fertilised ovum; **blas'topore** (Gr. *poros*, a passage), the orifice of a gastrula; **blas'tosphere** (Gr. *sphaira*, a sphere), a blastula; **blas'tūla**, a hollow sphere of cells, one cell thick, formed in the cleavage of a fertilised ovum.—*adj.* **blast'ūlar**.—*n.* **blastulā'tion**. [Gr. *blastos*, a sprout.]

**blat**, *blāt*, *v.i.* to cry like a sheep or calf: to make an ineffectual noise: to talk with little sense.— Also *v.t.* [Imit.]

**blatant**, *blāt'ənt*, (*Spens.* also **blattant**, prob. *blat'ənt*), *adj.* clamorous: calumniously clamorous: egregiously vulgar: (loosely) flagrant.— *adv.* **blat'antly**. [Prob. a coinage of Spenser: for the *blatant beast*, see Faerie Queene, V, xii. 37. onward.]

**blate**, *blāt*, (*Scot.*) *adj.* bashful, timidly awkward. [Perh. O.E. *blā*, pale.]

**blather**, **blatherskite**. See blether.

**blatter**, *blat'ər*, (chiefly *Scot.*) *n.* a clattering rainy blast: a clatter or torrent of words.—*v.i.* to beat with clattering, like rain on a window.—*v.t* to utter volubly. [L. *blaterāre*, to prate, with sense probably modified by sound.]

**blaubok**, *blow'bok*, *Afrik.* **bloubok**, *blō'bok*, *n.* a small South African antelope: also a large extinct species. [Du. *blaauw*, blue, *bok*, goat.]

**blaud**, *blöd*, (*Scot.*) *n.* a fragment: a broken-off slab: a screed or selection of verse.—*v.t.* to strike: to disfigure. [Perh. conn. with O.E. *blāwan*, to blow.]

**Blaue Reiter, Der**, *blow-ə rī'tər*, name given to important art book published by two artists in Munich and transferred (1911) to the group of expressionist painters formed round them. [Ger., the Blue Rider.]

**blawort**, *blā'wərt*, *n.* the harebell: the corn bluebottle.—Also **blewart** (*blōō'ərt*). [Scot. **blae**, and O.E. *wyrt*, herb.]

**blay**, **bley**, *blā*, *n.* the bleak (fish). [O.E. *blǣge*.]

**blaze**, *blāz*, *n.* a rush of light or of flame: an area of brilliant light or colour: a bursting out or active display.—*v.i.* to burn with a strong flame: to throw out a brilliant light: to be furious (*coll.*). —*n.* **blaz'er**, a light sporting jacket, originally bright-coloured.—*n.pl.* **blazes**, the fires of hell, in imprecations like **to blazes**; also **like blazes**, with fury.—**blaze away**, to fire a rapid and repeated stream of bullets: to work very hard (*coll.*); **blaze up**, to burst into flames: to become furious (*coll.*). [O.E. *blǣse*, torch.]

**blaze**, *blāz*, *n.* a white mark on a beast's face: a mark on a tree made by chipping the bark or otherwise.—*v.t.* to mark (a tree or a track) with a blaze.—**blaze the trail**, to show the way as a pioneer. [Perh. Du. *bles* or O.N. *blesi*; or **blaze** (1).]

**blaze**, *blāz*, *v.t.* to proclaim, to spread abroad.— *n.* **blaz'er** (*Spens.*), one who spreads abroad or

proclaims. [Connected with O.N. *blāsa*, to blow; confused with blazon.]

**blazon**, *blā'zn*, *v.t.* to make public: to display: to depict or to explain in heraldic terms (*her.*).— *n.* a coat-of-arms, heraldic bearings (also *fig.*): the science or rules of coats-of-arms.—*ns.* **blaz'oner**, one who blazons: a herald : a slanderer; **blaz'onry**, the art of drawing or of deciphering coats-of-arms: heraldry. [Fr. *blason*, a shield, confused with blaze (3).]

**bleach**, *blēch*, *v.t.* to make pale or white: to whiten, as textile fabrics.—*v.i.* to grow white.— *n.* a process or act of bleaching: a bleaching agent.—*ns.* **bleach'er**, one who or that which bleaches: (in *pl.*) cheap, open-air seats for spectators, e.g. in a baseball ground (*U.S.*): cheap covered seats (*Austr.*); **bleach'ery**, a place for bleaching; **bleach'-field**, a place for bleaching cloth: a bleacher's office or works.—*n.* and *adj.* **bleach'ing**.—**bleaching green**, a green for bleaching clothes on; **bleaching powder**, a compound of calcium, chlorine, and oxygen (CaOCl₂). [O.E. *blǣcan*.]

**bleak**, *blēk*, *adj.* colourless: dull and cheerless: cold, unsheltered.—*adv.* **bleak'ly**.—*n.* **bleak'ness**. —*adj.* **bleak'y**, bleak. [Apparently O.N. *bleikr*, answering to O.E. *blǣc*, *blāc*, pale, shining, black; cf. **bleach**.]

**bleak**, *blēk*, *n.* a small white river-fish. [O.N. *bleikja*, or a lost equivalent O.E. word.]

**blear**, *blēr*, *adj.* dim, watery: blurred as with inflammation.—*v.t.* to dim: to blur: to dim the sight of: to hoodwink.—*adj.* **bleared**.—*n.* **blear'i-ness**.—*adj.* **blear'y**.—*adj.* **blear'-eyed**. [Cf. Ger. *blerr*, soreness of the eyes.]

**bleat**, *blēt*, *v.i.* to cry like a sheep: to complain, grumble: to talk nonsense.—*n.* a sheep's cry or similar quavering sound: a complaint, grumble. —*n.* and *adj.* **bleat'ing**. [O.E. *blǣtan*; imit.; cf. L. *bālāre*, to bleat; Gr. *blēchē*, a bleating.]

**bleb**, *bleb*, *n.* a transparent blister of the cuticle: a bubble, as in water. [Prob. imit.]

**bled**, *bled*, *pa.t.* and *pa.p.* of bleed.

**blee**, *blē*, (*arch.*) *n.* complexion, colour. [O.E. *blēo*.]

**bleed**, *blēd*, *v.i.* to lose blood or sap: to die by slaughter: to issue forth or drop as blood: to have money, etc., extorted from one: to feel great pity (*fig.*).—*v.t.* to draw blood from, esp. surgically: to draw sap from: to extort from: (in bookbinding) to trim so as to encroach on letterpress or illustrations:—*pa.t.* and *pa.p.* bled. —*ns.* **bleed'er**, one who bleeds: an extortioner: one who suffers from haemophilia: a (nasty) person (*slang*); **bleed'ing**, a discharge of blood or sap: letting blood: diffusion or running of colouring matter.—*adj.* full of compassion: emitting sap: terribly weakened by war: bloody (*Shak.*, *coll.*).—**bleeding heart**, a name given to various plants of the genera *Dicentra*, *Colocasia*, etc.: a contemptuous name for a do-gooder.— **bleed like a pig**, to bleed copiously. [O.E. *blēdan*. See bleed.]

**bleep**, *blēp*, *v.i.* to give out a high sound or radio signal.—*n.* bleep'er, a detecting device that bleeps on receiving a certain radio or other signal. [Imit.]

**blemish**, *blem'ish*, *n.* a stain or defect: reproach.— *v.t.* to mark with any deformity: to tarnish: to defame.—*n.* blem'ishment (*Spens.*). [O.Fr. *blesmir*, *blemir*, pr.p. *blemissant*, to stain, of dubious origin.]

**blench**, *blench*, *blensh*, *v.i.* to shrink or start back: to flinch: to start aside, fly off (*Shak.*): to be inconstant (*Shak.*).—*n.* a starting aside (*Shak.*). [O.E. *blencan*.]

**blench**, *blench*, *blensh*, *adj.* or *adv.* on the basis of payment of a nominal yearly duty.—Also **blanch**. [See blank.]

**blend**, *blend*, *v.t.* to mix together, esp. intimately or harmoniously: to pollute, vitiate (*Spens.*).—*v.i.* to be mingled: to harmonise: to shade off:— *pa.t.* and *pa.p.* usu. blend'ed, also, esp. *poet.*, blent.—*n.* a mixture.—*ns.* blend'er; blend'ing. [M.E. *blenden*; cf. O.E. *blandan*, O.N. *blanda*.] blend, *blend*, (*obs.*) *v.t.* to blind: to dazzle: to obscure:—*pa.p.* (y)blent'. [O.E. *blendan*.] blende, *blend, n.* a mineral, zinc sulphide. [Ger. *blende—blenden*, to deceive, from its resemblance to galena.]

Blenheim, *blen'əm, n.* a kind of spaniel named from the Duke of Marlborough's seat.

blennorrhoea, *blen-ō-rē'ə, n.* a discharge of mucus. [Gr. *blennos*, mucus, *rhoiā*, flow.]

blenny, *blen'i, n.* a genus (Blennius) of acanthopterygian fishes, usually slimy. [Gr. *blennos*, mucus.]

blent, *blent, pa.t.* and *pa.p.* of blend (1) and (2).

blepharism, *blef'ər-izm, n.* spasm of the eyelid.— *n.* blephari'tis, inflammation of the eyelid. [Gr. *blepharon*, eyelid.]

blesbok, *bles'bok, n.* a South African antelope with a blazed forehead. [Du. *bles*, blaze, *bok*, goat.]

bless, *bles, v.t.* to consecrate: to make the sign of the cross over: to extol as holy, to pronounce holy or happy: to invoke divine favour upon: to wish happiness to: to make joyous, happy, or prosperous: to glorify:—*pa.p.* blessed (*blest*), or blest.—*adj.* bless'ed, blest, happy: prosperous: in heaven: beatified: (euphemistically) accursed, confounded.—*adv.* bless'edly.—*ns.* bless'edness; bless'ing, a wish or prayer for happiness or success: any means or cause of happiness: a gift or present (*B.*): a form of invoking the favour of God at a meal.—blessed sacrament, the consecrated Host; blessing in disguise, something proving unexpectedly advantageous; single blessedness, the unmarried state. [O.E. *blēdsian*, *blētsian, bletsian*, to bless, prob. from *blōd*, blood.]

bless, *bles*, (*Spens.*) *v.t.* to brandish: to brandish around:—*pa.t.* blest, blist. [Perh. from bless (1) as if to make the sign of the cross; or from bless (3); or poss. conn. with blaze.]

bless, *bles, v.t.* to wound: to beat. [Fr. *blesser*, to wound.]

blest, *blest, pa.p.* of bless.—Also *adj.*

blet, *blet, n.* incipient internal decay in fruit without external sign: a part so affected.— *v.i.* to become soft or sleepy:—*pr.p.* blett'ing; *pa.t.* and *pa.p.* blett'ed. [Fr.]

blether (*Scot.*), *bledh'ər*, blather (*U.S.*, etc.), *bladh'ər, v.i.* to talk garrulous nonsense.—*n.* one who blethers: (often in *pl.*) fluent, garrulous nonsense.—*n.* blethera'tion.—*n.* and *adj.* bleth'ering. —*ns.* bleth'erskate, bleth'eranskate (*Scot.*), blath'erskite (*U.S.*), a loquacious talker of nonsense. [M.E. *blather*—O.N. *blathra*, talk foolishly, *blathr*, nonsense; prob. skate (the fish).]

bleuâtre, *blə-ätr'*, (Fr.) bluish.

blew, *bloo, pa.t.* of blow.

blew, an old spelling (*Spens., Milt.*) of blue.

blewits, *blū'its, n.* a kind of edible mushroom, bluish in part. [Perh. from blue.]

bley, *blā, n.* same as blay.

blight, *blīt, n.* a disease in plants which blasts or withers them: a fungus, insect, or other cause of blight: anything that injures, destroys, depresses, or frustrates: a damp, depression, decay, set-back, check.—*v.t.* to affect with blight: to blast: to frustrate.—*n.* blight'er, a cause of blighting: a term of (usually playful) abuse, scamp, beggar, wretch (*slang*).—*n.* and *adj.* blight'ing.—*adv.* blight'ingly. [17th cent.; origin obscure; poss. conn. with bleach, bleak.]

blighty, *blī'ti, (mil. slang) n.* home: the home country: a wound necessitating return home. [Hind. *bilāyatī*, foreign, European—Ar. *wilāyat* province, country. Cf. vilayet.]

blimbing. Same as bilimbi.

blimey, blimy, *blī'mi, interj.* à Cockney vulgarism for *God blind me.*

blimp, *blimp, n.* a small type of airship for scouting, etc.: an incurably conservative elderly military officer, as Colonel *Blimp* of the cartoonist David Low, or any other person of similar views: soundproof housing for sound-film camera.

blimy. See blimey.

blin, *blin*, (*Spens.*) *v.t.* and *v.i.* to cease from, to cease.—*n.* cessation: stoppage. [O.E. *blinnan*, to cease, pfx. be- (1), and *linnan*, to cease.]

blind, *blind, adj.* without sight: dark: obscure: invisible: concealed: not directed, or affording no possibility of direction, by sight or by foresight: ignorant or undiscerning: unobserving: voluntarily overlooking: without an opening: failing to flower or fruit: in flying, by use of instruments only, without seeing course or receiving directions from wireless: drunk (*coll.*). —*n.* something intended to blind one to the facts: a window-screen: a shade: a stake put up without seeing one's cards (*poker*).—*v.t.* to make blind: to darken, obscure, or deceive: to dazzle: to render matt: to fill in the interstices of.—*n.* blind'age (*mil.*), a temporary wooden screen faced with earth as a protection against splinters of shell and the like.—*adj.* blind'ed, deprived of sight: without intellectual discernment.—*n.* blind'er, one who or that which blinds: a horse's blinker.—*n.* and *adj.* blind'ing.—*adj.* blind'less.—*adv.* blind'ly.—*n.* blind'ness, want of sight: ignorance: folly.—blind'-alley, a cul-de-sac.—*adj.* (of a juvenile employment) leading to no settled occupation in adult life.—blind'-coal, anthracite (as burning without flame): coal partly carbonised by an igneous intrusion; blind date, an appointment with someone one has not seen, as with a dance partner chosen for one: the partner, etc., so chosen.—*adj.* blind'-drunk, so drunk as to be like a blind man.—blind'fish, an eyeless fish (Amblyopsis) of the Kentucky Mammoth Cave.—*adj.* blind'fold (earlier blind-felled, struck blind), having the eyes bandaged so as not to see: thoughtless: performed without seeing: reckless.—Also *adv.*—*v.t.* to cover the eyes of: to mislead.—blind'-gut, the caecum; blind'man's-buff (i.e. buffet), a game in which a blindfold player tries to catch the others; blind road, a grassy track invisible to those that are on it; blind'-side, the side on which a person is blind to danger: weak point; blind spot, the spot on the retina where the optic nerve joins and where there are no visual cells: a point within the normal range of a transmitter at which the field strength is abnormally small (*radio*): a point outside the range of one's vision: a region of understanding in which one's intuition and judgment always fail; blind'-story, a triforium; blind tooling, impression without gilding; blind'worm, a slow-worm, a legless lizard with eyes too small as to be supposed blind. [O.E. blind; O.N. *blindr*.]

blink, *blingk, v.i.* to glance, twinkle, or wink: to see obscurely: to look with the eyes half-closed: to shine unsteadily.—*v.t.* to shut out of sight: to ignore or evade.—*n.* a glimpse, glance, or wink: a gleam, esp. momentary.—*n.* blink'ard, one who blinks or has bad eyes.—*adj.* blinked, affected with blinking.—*n.* blink'er, a leather flap to prevent a horse from seeing sidewise.—*adj.* blink'ing (*slang*), a meaningless substitute for bloody.—*n.* blinks, a mud or water weed (*Montia*) of the purslane family, with minute flowers.—on the blink, (of electrical or electronic device) (going) out of order. [Cf. blench.]

blip, *blip, n.* the image of an object on a radar screen.

bliss, *blis, n.* the highest happiness: the special happiness of heaven.—*adj.* bliss'ful.—*adv.* bliss'-

fully.—*n.* bliss′fulness.—*adj.* bliss′less. [O.E.
*bliths*—*blithe*, blithe.]
blist, *blist*, (*Spens.*) *pa.t.* and *pa.p.* of bless (1 and
2).
blister, *blis′tǝr*, *n.* a thin bubble or bladder on the
skin, often containing watery matter: a similar
spot elsewhere, as on a leaf, metal, paint: the
protective bulging outer hull of a double-hulled
ship, to lessen risk of sinking (*naut.*): a plaster
applied to raise a blister: a transparent bulge
on the upper surface of an aeroplane forming
part of its structure.—*v.t.* to raise a blister or
blisters on: to burn with scathing words (*fig.*):
to ornament with puffs (*Shak.*).—*v.i.* to develop
blisters.—*adjs.* blis′tery; blis′tering, of criticism,
virulent, cruel (*fig.*): painfully intense or
strenuous.—blis′ter-bee′tle, blis′ter-fly, an insect used for blistering, esp. Spanish fly (Cantharis); blis′ter-plas′ter, a plaster made of
Spanish flies used to raise a blister; blis′ter-steel,
blis′tered-steel, steel made from wrought-iron
with blistered surface. [M.E.; most prob. O.Fr.
*blestre*, conn. with O.N. *blāstr, blāsa*, to blow;
Ger. *blase.*]
blite, *blit*, *n.* a name for several plants of the goosefoot family. [Gr. *bliton.*]
blithe, *blidh, adj.* jocund: cheerful: gay: sprightly.
—*adv.* blithe′ly.—*n.* blithe′ness.—*adj.* blithe′-
some, joyous.—*adv.* blithe′somely.—*n.* blithe′-
someness. [O.E. *blithe*, joyful. See bliss.]
blither, *blidh′ǝr*, *v.i.* another form of blather,
blether.—*adj.* blith′ering (used as an expression
of contempt).
blitz, *blits*, *n.* an attack or bombing from the air:
any sudden, overwhelming attack.—*v.t.* to attack
or damage by air-raid. [Ger. *blitzkrieg*, lightning war, the German method in 1939—*blitz*,
lightning, *krieg*, war.]
blive, *bliv*, (*Spens.*) *adv.* Same as belive.
blizzard, *bliz′ǝrd*, *n.* a blinding storm of wind and
snow, a snow-squall.—*adjs.* blizz′ardly, blizz′-
ardous. [A modern coinage, most prob. onomatopoeic, on the analogy of *blow, blast*, etc.]
bloat, *blōt, v.t.* to swell or puff out: to dry partially
by smoke (applied to fish).—*v.i.* to swell or
dilate: to grow turgid.—*n.* hoove (also bloating):
bloatedness: a drunkard.—*adj.* bloat′ed, having
been bloated: swollen (often as a result of
gluttony): (*fig.*) swollen with riches.—*n.*
bloat′er, a herring partially dried in smoke, esp.
at Yarmouth. [Cf. O.N. *blautr*, soft.]
blob, *blob, n.* a drop or globule: anything soft and
round, as a gooseberry: a round spot: zero.—
*v.i.* to make a blob, to form into a blob. [Imit.]
bloc, *blok, n.* a combination of parties, nations, or
other units to achieve a common purpose. [Fr.]
block, *blok, n.* a mass of wood or stone, etc., usu.
flat-sided: a piece of wood or other material used
as a support (as for chopping, beheading), or as a
mould (as for hats), or for printing from (as
wood-engravings, process-blocks), or as a toy
(for building): a pulley with its framework or the
framework alone: a connected group of houses,
seats, sheets of paper, shares, etc.: a section of
territory: a building lot bounded by streets
(*U.S.*): an obstruction: a head: a blockhead: an
impassive person: the place where a batsman
rests his bat (*cricket*): an instance of, or a cause
of, blockage or blocking: an administrative unit
in India.—*adj.* in a block or lump: comprising
a number grouped and dealt with together.—
*v.t.* to enclose or shut up: to restrict: to obstruct:
to make inactive: to shape as on a block, or to
sketch out roughly (often with *in* or *out*): to stop
(a ball) with bat resting upright on the ground.—
*n.* blockade′, cutting a place off by surrounding
it with troops or by ships: obstruction.—*v.t.* to
block up by troops or ships.—*ns.* block′age, set
or instance of obstructing, or state of being
obstructed: resistance to understanding, learn-

ing, etc., set up by existing habits of thought and
action; block′ing, interruption of a train of
thought, esp. by unpleasant thoughts rising in
the mind.—*adjs.* blocked, meanings as *pa.p.* of
verb: subject to restriction in use; block′ish, like
a block: stupid: dull.—blockade′-runner, a
person or ship that passes through a blockading
force; block′-book, a book printed from
engraved blocks, not movable types; block′-
buster, a bomb or explosive charge able to
destroy a number of buildings simultaneously:
a thing or person notably violent and effective
(*fig.*); block′busting.—Also *adj.*—block capital,
a capital letter written in imitation of type;
block′-chain′, an endless chain of blocks and
links; block′-coal, coal that breaks into cuboidal
blocks; block grant, a fixed general grant made
by the central government to a local authority
for all its services, as distinct from a series of
specific grants each a percentage of the amount
spent locally on the various services; block′head,
a wooden head: a dolt; block′house, a small
temporary fort; blocking motion, notice of
intention to bring up a certain matter at a future
date, thus preventing (or blocking) raising of
the subject on a motion for adjournment; block
letter, a block capital: block type; block′-ship, a
warship too old for action, but useful in port
defence: block′-system, a system in which no
train is allowed on to a section of railway so long
as any other is on it; block′-tin, tin in the form of
blocks or ingots; block type, a heavy-letter type,
without serifs. [Fr. *bloc*, probably Gmc.]
bloke, *blōk, n.* a man (*slang*): the commander
(*naut.*). [Origin obscure.]
bloncket, *blongk′et*, (*Spens.*) *adj.* grey. [Fr.
*blanquet, blanchet*, whitish, dim. of *blanc*, white.]
blond (*fem.* blonde), *blond, n.* a person of fair complexion and light-coloured hair—opp. to
*brunet(te).*—*adj.* (of hair) between golden and
light chestnut in colour: of a fair complexion:
fair.—blond beast (or with *caps.*), blond type
of primitive northern European man, admired,
e.g. by Nietzsche, for his physical splendour:
any predatory type of man; blond(e)′-lace,
lace made of silk, originally raw silk. [Fr.]
blood, *blud, n.* the oxygenating fluid (red in the
higher animals) circulating in the body: descent,
good birth: relationship, kindred: (elliptically)
a blood-horse, one of good pedigree: a swaggering dandy about town: the blood-royal (as in
*princes of the blood*): temperament: bloodshed
or murder: the juice of anything, esp. if red: the
supposed seat of passion—hence temper, anger
(as *his blood is up*), etc.: the sensual nature of
man: sensational or melodramatic tale, a penny-
dreadful (*slang*).—*v.t.* to bleed: to smear with
blood: to initiate into blood sports or to war.—
*adj.* blood′ed, having blood: of pure blood,
pedigreed: initiated.—*adj.* blood′ily.—*adj.* blood′-
less, without blood: dead: anaemic: without
bloodshed: without spirit or activity (*Shak.*).
—*n.* blood′lessness.—*adj.* blood′y, of the nature
of blood: stained with blood: murderous,
cruel: (*coll.*) as an *adj.* emphasising anger or the
like, or almost meaningless, and as an *adv.* employed
as an intensive—most prob. from the habits of
the late 17th-century bloods (Etheredge, '*bloody-
drunk*').—*v.t.* to make bloody.—blood agar,
agar-agar for growing bacteria, to which blood
has been added before the jelly set.—*adj.* blood-
and-thunder, sensational, melodramatic.—blood
bank, a supply of blood plasma, or the place
where it is kept; blood′-bath, a bath in warm
blood: a massacre.—*adj.* blood′-bespott′ed,
spotted, sprinkled with blood.—blood′-bird, an
Australian honey-eater with scarlet plumage in
the cock-bird.—*adjs.* blood′-bol′tered, clotted or
matted with blood; blood′-bought (*Shak.*),
bought at the expense of blood or life.—blood′-

broth'er, a brother by blood: among primitive peoples, one who has entered a close and binding friendship with another by ceremonies involving the mixing of blood.—*adj.* blood'-consuming (*Shak.*).—blood count, the number of red or white corpuscles in the blood.—*adj.* blood'-curdling, exciting horror with a physical feeling as if the blood had curdled.—blood donor, one who gives blood for use in transfusion; blood'-dust, haemoconia; blood'-feud, a family feud arising out of an act of bloodshed: a vendetta; blood'-flower, *Haemanthus*: a species of *Asclepias.* —*adj.* blood'-froz'en (*Spens.*), having the blood frozen or chilled.—blood'-group, any one of the four types of human blood (designated O, A, B, AB) which may or may not prove incompatible on transfusion; blood'-guilt'iness, the guilt of shedding blood, as in murder.—*adj.* blood'-guilty.—blood'heat, the temperature of human blood (about 98° Fahr., 37°C); blood'-horse, a horse of the purest and most highly prized blood, origin, or stock.—*adj.* blood'-hot, as hot or warm as blood.—blood'hound, a large, keen-scented (sleuth) hound, noted for its powers of tracing: a detective (*fig.*); blood'letter; blood'-letting, bleeding by opening a vein; blood'lust, desire for bloodshed; blood'-money, money earned by laying or supporting a capital charge against anyone, esp. if the charge be false or made by an accomplice: money paid to a hired assassin: compensation formerly paid to the next of kin of a victim slain; blood orange, a variety of orange with red or red-streaked pulp; blood'-plate, a platelet; blood'-pois'oning, a name popularly, but loosely, used of pyaemia and allied diseases; blood pressure, the pressure of the blood on the walls of the blood-vessels, varying with age and physical condition; blood'-pudding, a pudding made with blood and other materials; blood purge, massacre or execution of large numbers believed by a government or ruler to be disloyal; blood'-rain, rain coloured by red dust from the desert.—*adj.* blood'-red', of the colour of blood.—blood'-rela'tion, one related by common ancestry; blood'root, a plant (*Sanguinaria canadensis*) of the poppy family with red rootstock and sap; blood'-roy'al, royal descent; blood'-sac'rifice (*Shak.*), a sacrifice made with bloodshed; blood'shed, the shedding of blood: slaughter.—*adjs.* blood'shot (of the eye), red or inflamed with blood; blood'-sized, sized or smeared with blood.—blood'-spav'in, a disease of horses consisting of the swelling of a vein on the inside of the hock, from a checking of the blood; blood sports, those involving the killing of animals—fox-hunting and the like.—*adj.* blood'sprent, sprinkled with blood.—blood'stain. —*adj.* blood'stained, stained with blood: guilty of murder.—blood'stock, pedigree horses collectively: young men available as dance partners; blood'stone, a green chalcedony with blood-like spots of red jasper: haematite; blood'stream, the blood flowing through the body: something playing a similarly vital part (*fig.*); blood'sucker, an animal that sucks blood, esp. a leech: an extortioner: one who sponges upon another.— *adj.* blood'sucking, that sucks or draws blood.— blood'-tax, conscription or universal military service, as drawing from the nation, a number of lives or recruits annually; blood test, an examination (chemical, microscopical, bacteriological) of a small specimen of blood usually drawn from a blood-vessel; blood'thirstiness, eager desire to shed blood.—*adj.* blood'thirsty.—blood trans-fusion, transfer of blood taken from the veins of one person to those of another; blood'-vessel, a vein or artery; blood'-wagon (*airmen's slang*), an ambulance; blood'-wite, -wit (*hist.*), a fine for shedding blood: the right to levy it; blood'wood, a name for various trees with red wood or juice,

or their timber, as a lythraceous tree of the East Indies (Lagerstroemia), eucalyptus of different kinds, logwood; blood'-worm, a red aquatic midge larva (*Chironomus*); blood'y-bones' (see rawhead).—*adjs.* blood'y-eyed; blood'y-faced.— bloody flux, dysentery, in which the discharges from the bowels are mixed with blood; blood'y-hand' (see hand); bloody Mary, a cocktail consisting of vodka, tomato juice and seasoning. —*adj.* bloody-mind'ed, liking bloodshed, cruel: in a mood of, or inclined to show, aggressive obstinacy.—bloody-mind'edness; blood'y-sweat, a sweat accompanied by the discharge of blood. —avenger of blood, the next of kin to a murdered man whose duty it was thought to avenge his death; blood and iron (see blut); in blood, in full vigour; in hot or cold blood, under or free from excitement or sudden passion; make one's blood boil, to arouse one's fury. [O.E. *blōd*; O.Fris. *blōd*; Ger. *blut.*]

bloom, *blōōm*, *n.* a blossom or flower (also collectively): the state of being in flower: the prime or highest perfection of anything: the first freshness of beauty of anything: rosy colour: the glow on the cheek: a powdery, waxy, or cloudy surface or appearance: an efflorescence.—*v.i.* to put forth blossoms: to flower: to be in a state of beauty or vigour: to flourish.—*v.t.* to give a bloom to.—*n.* bloom'er, a plant that blooms: a floriated initial letter: an absurd and embarrassing blunder (*slang*).—*adj.* bloom'ing, flowering: flourishing: fresh and youthful: bright: euphemistically for bloody (*slang*).—*adjs.* bloom'less, without bloom; bloom'y, flowery: flourishing: covered with bloom. [O.N. *blōm*; cf. Goth. *blōma*, Ger. *blume.*]

bloom, *blōōm*, *n.* a mass or bar of iron or steel in an intermediate stage of manufacture, esp. one thicker than a *billet.—n.* bloom'ery, a furnace for making iron ore or iron into blooms. [O.E. *blōma.*]

bloomer, *blōōm'ər*, *n.* and *adj.* a dress for women, devised by Mrs *Bloomer* of New York about 1849, consisting of a jacket with close sleeves, a skirt falling a little below the knee, and Turkish trousers: (in *pl.*) bloomer trousers: (in *pl.*) a loose undergarment similar to knickers, but fuller.

Bloomsbury Group, *blōōmz'bər-i*, a group of literary and artistic friends, some living in Bloomsbury, who wrote during and after the First World War; they included Virginia Woolf, Lytton Strachey, and E. M. Forster.—*n.* Blooms'buryite, a member of the Bloomsbury group.

bloosme, *blōōm*, *n.* and *v.i.* Spenser's form of blossom, modified by bloom.

blore, *blōr*, *blör*, *n.* a violent gust of wind. [Prob. related to blare and blow.]

blossom, *blos'əm*, *n.* a flower or bloom, esp. one that precedes edible fruit: the state of being in flower, literally or figuratively.—*v.i.* to put forth blossoms or flowers: to flourish and prosper.— *n.* bloss'oming.—*adj.* bloss'omy, covered with flowers, flowery. [O.E. *blōstm, blōstma*, from the same root as bloom, and L. *flōs.*]

blot, *blot*, *n.* a spot, as of a drop of ink: an obliteration: a stain in reputation: a blemish.— *v.t.* to obliterate: to spot or smudge: to disgrace: to blemish: to dry with blotting-paper:—*pr.p.* blott'ing; *pa.t.* and *pa.p.* blott'ed.—*n.* blott'er, one who blots: a bad author: a sheet, pad, or book of blotting-paper.—*n.* blottesque (*-esk'*), a painting executed with heavy blot-like touches: a daub: a vigorous descriptive sketch (*fig.*).— Also *adj.—n.* blott'ing, spotting as with ink: obliterating: smudging: drying with blotting-paper: blotting-paper.—*adjs.* blott'o (*slang*), helplessly drunk; blott'y, blotted: smudged.— blott'ing-pad, a pad of blotting-paper; blott'ing-paper, unsized paper, used for absorbing ink.—

blot one's copybook, to blemish one's record, esp. by an indiscretion. [Origin obscure.]

blot, *blot*, *n.* a piece liable to be taken at backgammon: exposure of a piece: a weak place in anything. [Cf. Dan. *blot*, Du. *bloot*, naked, exposed.]

blot, *blot*, (*Spens.*) *n.* spawn. [Perh. conn. with blow (3).]

blotch, *bloch*, *n.* an irregular discoloration: a pustule: any plant disease characterised by blotching.—*v.t.* to mark or cover with blotches. —*adj.* blotched.—*n.* blotch′iness.—*n.* and *adj.* blotch′ing.—*adj.* blotch′y. [Prob. formed on blot.]

bloubok. See blaubok.

blouse, *blowz*, *n.* a loose sack-like, belted outer garment, like the smock-frock: a loose-fitting bodice for women, tucked in at the waist.—*v.t.* to arrange in loose folds.—*v.i.* to puff out loosely with air, as a sail. [Fr.]

blouson, *blōō′zon*, *n.* a woman's loose outer garment fastened at the waist by a belt or drawstring.—blouson noir (*blōō-zɔ̄ nwär*), a rebellious young man, usu. one of a group, so called from the black windcheaters worn by many of them. [Fr.]

blow, *blō*, *n.* a stroke or knock: a sudden misfortune or calamity.—at a blow, by a single action, suddenly. [Found from the 15th century; perh. from blow (3) or conn. with Ger. *bläuen*, to beat, beetle.]

blow, *blō*, *v.i.* to bloom or blossom.—*v.t.* (*Milt.*), to put forth, as flowers:—*pr.p.* blow′ing; *pa.t.* blew (*blōō*); *pa.p.* blown (*blōn*).—*n.* blossom, bloom: display of blossom. [O.E. *blōwan*; Ger. *blühen*; cf. bloom, blossom.]

blow, *blō*, *v.i.* to produce a current of air: to move, as air or wind (often *impers.*): to breathe hard: to spout, as whales: to boast: to act as an informer (*slang*): (of insects) to deposit eggs: of an electric fuse, to melt (also *v.t.*).—*v.t.* to drive air upon or into: to drive by a current of air: to sound, as a wind-instrument: to destroy or force by explosive: to spread by report: to inform upon: to fan or kindle: (of insects) to deposit eggs on: to curse: to squander (*slang*):—*pa.t.* blew, *blōō*; *pa.p.* blown, *blōn*, in imprecations blowed, *blōd.*—*n.* a blast: an insect egg.—*n.* blow′er, one who blows: a metal plate on the upper part of a fireplace, to increase the draught: a machine for driving a blast of air: a speaking-tube, telephone, or similar means of sending messages: a communication system, esp. one used by bookmakers and their representatives, or one keeping police headquarters in touch with police cars (*slang*).—*adjs.* blown, out of breath, tired: swelled: stale, worthless; blow′y, windy: gusty.—blow′ball, the downy head of a dandelion in seed; blow′fly, a flesh-fly (*Sarcophaga*): a blue-bottle (*Calliphora*); blow′gun, a blowpipe (weapon); blow′-hole, a whale's nostril: a hole in ice to which seals, etc., come to breathe: a vent for escape of gas, etc.: a bubble in metal: a natural vent from the roof of a cave up to the ground surface, through which air and water are forced by rising tides; blow′lamp, a portable lamp producing heat by a blast; blow′-mould′ing, a process used in fabricating plastic objects, the molten thermoplastic being blown against the sides of the mould; blow′-out, a feast (*slang*): a tyre burst (*coll.*); blow′pipe, a pipe through which air is blown on a flame, to increase its heat, used in *blowpipe analysis*, etc.: a long straight tube from which an arrow, pellet, etc., is blown by the breath: a glass-blower's tube; blow′-valve, a snifting valve.—blow hot and cold, to be favourable and unfavourable by turns, to be irresolute; blow in, to turn up casually; blow off (steam, etc.), to allow to escape, to escape

forcibly; blow one's own trumpet, to sound one's own praises; blow one's top (*coll.*), to explode in anger; blow over, to pass away, as a danger or a scandal; blow up, to come into being: to destroy by explosion: to explode: to finish in disaster: to inflate: to scold: to lose one's temper: to enlarge, as an illustration: to go to pieces (*U.S.*); blow upon, to take the bloom, freshness, or the interest off: to bring into discredit: to inform upon. [O.E. *blāwan*; Ger. *blähen, blasen*; L. *flāre.*]

blowze, *blowz*, *n.* a ruddy, fat-faced wench.—*adjs.* blowzed, blowz′y, fat and ruddy, or flushed with exercise: dishevelled. [Perh. related to blush or blow, or of cant origin.]

blubber, *blub′ər*, *n.* a jellyfish: the fat of whales and other sea animals: excessive fat: a weeping. —*v.i.* to weep effusively (shortened to blub).— *adj.* blubb′ered, of a face, swollen with weeping. [M.E. *blober, bluber*; prob. imit.]

blucher, properly *blühh′ər*, often *blōōk′ər*, or *blōōch′ər*, *n.* a strong leather half-boot or high shoe. [Marshal *Blücher*, the Prussian general at Waterloo.]

blude, *blüd*, *n.* a Scots form of blood.—*adj.* blud′y, blud′ie.

bludge, *bluj*, (*slang*), *n.* a soft job.—*v.i.* to loaf about: to evade work or other responsibility.— *n.* bludg′er.

bludgeon, *bluj′n*, *n.* a short stick with a heavy striking end.—*v.t.* to beat with a bludgeon: to assail heavily. [First in 18th century; origin very obscure.]

blue, *blōō*, *adj.* of the colour of the unclouded sky, or that of wood-smoke, skim-milk, lead: livid : greyish: dismal: depressed: learned, pedantic: indecent or obscene: dressed in blue: symbolised by blue.—*n.* one of the colours of the rainbow: the sky: the sea: a blue pigment: a blue powder or liquid (indigo, Prussian blue, etc.) used in laundries: a member of a party whose colour is blue (as the opponents of the Greens in ancient Constantinople, *hist.* the Presbyterians, and later often the Conservatives): a present or past representative of Oxford or Harrow (dark), Cambridge or Eton (light blue) in sports: a similar representative of any university: the badge awarded to him, or the honour of wearing it: blue clothes: a bluestocking: a butterfly of the family *Lycaenidae*: a former squadron of the British fleet: (in *pl.*) depression, the blue devils: (in *pl.*) slow, sad song orig. American Negro folksong.—*v.t.* to make blue: to treat with blue.—*v.i.* to turn blue. —*ns.* blue′ing, blu′ing, the process of imparting a blue colour, esp. to metal, or of neutralising yellow; blue-rot in wood: laundress's blue (*U.S.*); blue′ness.—*adj.* blue′y (*blōō′i*), inclined towards blue (esp. in compounds, as blu′ey-green′).—*n.* (*Austr.*) a bushman's bundle, often in a blue cloth.—*adj.* blu′ish.—blue baby, a baby with congenital cyanosis; blue′back, the sockeye, chief salmon of the North Pacific; blue′bell, in S. England the wood-hyacinth: (*blōō′bel′*), in Scotland and N. England the harebell; blue′berry, the fruit of *Vaccinium vacillans* and other American species; blue′bird, a small American bird (*Sialia sialis*) akin to the warblers.—*n.* and *adj.* blue′-black, black with a tinge of blue: blue changing in time to black.— Blue Blanket, the banner of the Edinburgh craftsmen; blue blood, aristocratic blood (Sp. *sangre azul*, from the blue veins of descendants of the Visigoths); blue-bonn′et, a round flat blue woollen cap: hence a Scottish peasant, a Scotsman; blue book, a report or other paper printed by parliament (from its blue paper wrapper); blue′bottle, the blue cornflower: a large fly (*Calliphora*) with metallic blue abdomen: a policeman or beadle (*slang*); blue′-buck, the blaubok; **blue′cap**, a salmon of one year, with blue-spotted head: the blue titmouse: a Scotsman (*Shak.*); **blue′-cheese**, blue-veined cheese, e.g. Gorgonzola; **blue′-chip′**, term applied to the most reliable industrial shares; **blue′coat**, a serving-man, almsman, or other wearing a blue coat (*arch.*): a pupil of Christ's Hospital or other *Bluecoat school*, whose garb is a blue coat. —Also *adj.*—**blue devil**, an evil demon: (in *pl.*) the apparitions seen in delirium tremens, hence deep despondency; **Blue Ensign**, a blue flag with the Union Jack in canton, till 1864 flag of the Blue squadron, now flown by the Naval Reserve and certain yachts and merchant vessels; **blue′-eye**, a blue-cheeked Australian honey-eater; **blue′fish**, a large voracious fish (*Pomatomus saltatrix*) of the Serranidae, on the U.S. Atlantic coast; **blue fox**, an arctic fox; **blue funk** (*slang*), great terror; **blue′gown**, one of a former class of licensed beggars in Scotland, a King's Bedesman; **blue′grass**, a slightly glaucous permanent grass (*Poa pratensis*, etc.) of Europe and North America, esp. Kentucky.—*adjs.* **bluegreen**, **blue-grey**, between blue and green or grey (blue-green algae, the *Cyanophyceae*).— **blue ground**, a greyish-blue decomposed agglomerate in which diamonds are got; **blue gum**, species of Eucalyptus, esp. *E. globulus*; **blue hare**, the mountain hare; **blue′jacket**, a seaman in the navy; **blue jay**, an American jay (*Cyanocitta cristata*); **blue John**, ornamental fluorspar; **blue laws**, sumptuary laws; **Blue Mantle**, one of the pursuivants of the English Heralds' College; **blue moon**, a very long but quite indeterminate time; **blue mould**, a fungus that turns bread, cheese, etc., blue; **blue murder**, extreme activity or commotion; **blue′nose**, a straitlaced or puritanical person (*U.S.*): (*cap.*) a nickname for a Nova Scotian; **blue note**, a flattened note, usu. third or seventh, characteristic of the blues.— *v.t.* **blue-pen′cil**, to correct, edit, or censor, as if with a blue pencil.—**Blue Peter**, a blue flag with a white rectangle hoisted when a ship is about to sail: a call for trumps in whist; **blue pill**, a mercurial pill; **blue′print**, a photographic print, white upon blue, on paper sensitised with a ferric salt and potassium ferricyanide from a photographic negative or a drawing on transparent paper—also called cyanotype, ferroprussiate print: a preliminary sketch or plan of work to be done, or a guide or model provided by agreed principles or rules or by conclusions from earlier experiment.—Also *v.t.*—**blue ribbon**, **riband**, the ribbon of the Order of the Garter: any very high distinction or prize: the badge of the teetotal Blue Ribbon Army, founded in America in 1878; **blue′-rot′**, a blue discoloration in coniferous wood, caused by a fungus, *Ceratostomella*; **blue ruin** (*slang*), gin; **blue sheep**, the bharal; **blue-sky laws** (*U.S.*), laws to prevent fraud in the sale of stocks (against capitalising of the blue skies); **blue′stocking**, a learned lady, esp. one inclining to pedantry (said to be from Benjamin Stillingfleet, a member of Mrs Montague's coterie, who preferred worsted to black silk); **blue′stone**, or **blue vitriol**, hydrated copper sulphate; **blue′throat**, or **blue′breast**, a bird akin to the nightingale; **blue tongue**, a viral disease of sheep and cattle transmitted by mosquitoes; **blue water**, open sea; **blue′weed**, viper's bugloss (also **blue thistle**); **blue whale**, Sibbald's rorqual, the biggest living animal; **blue′wing**, an American teal.—**blue-eyed boy**, favourite who can do no wrong, white-headed boy; **burn blue**, to burn with a blue flame, as in the presence of sulphur, terrestrial or infernal; **out of the blue**, from the cloudless sky: hence, entirely unexpectedly; the **Blues**, the Royal Horse Guards; **true blue**, unswervingly faithful, esp. to political party of blue persuasion, orig.

used of Covenanters (see above). [M.E. *blew*— O.Fr. *bleu*, of Gmc. origin; O.N. *blā* gave M.E. *bla*, *blo* and **blae**.]

**blue**, *blōō*, *v.t.* to squander. [Prob. for blow.]

**bluette**, *blü-et*, (Fr.) a spark, flash: a short playful piece of music.

**bluff**, *bluf*, *adj.* steep or upright in front: blustering, surly (*dial.*): rough and hearty in a good-natured way: outspoken: (of the shape of a body) such that, when it moves through air or other fluid, it leaves behind it a large disorderly wake and experiences a large drag.—opp. of *streamlined.*—*n.* a high steep bank.—*adv.* **bluff′ly.**—*n.* **bluff′ness.** [Perh. Du. *blaf* (*obs.*), broad, flat; or M.L.G. *blaff*, even, smooth.]

**bluff**, *bluf*, *v.t.* or *v.i.* to deceive or seek to deceive by concealment of weakness or show of self-confidence or threats (orig. in poker to conceal poor cards).—*n.* a bluffing act or behaviour: a horse's blinker.—*n.* **bluff′er.**—**call one's bluff**, to expose or challenge one's bluff. [Perh. Du. *bluffen*, to brag, boast.]

**bluggy**, *blug′i*, *adj.* jocularly for bloody.

**bluid**, *blüd*, *n.* a Scots form of blood.—*adj.* **bluid′y.**

**blunder**, *blun′dər*, *v.i.* to make a gross mistake: to flounder about.—*v.t.* to utter thoughtlessly: to mismanage, bungle: to achieve, put, render, by blundering.—*n.* a gross mistake.—*n.* **blun′derer.**—*n.* and *adj.* **blun′dering.**—*adv.* **blun′deringly.** [M.E. *blondren*; prob. conn. with bland, to mix.]

**blunderbuss**, *blun′dər-bus*, *n.* a short hand-gun with a wide bore. [Du. *donderbus*—*donder*, thunder, *bus*, a box, gun-barrel, gun; Ger. *donner-büchse*.]

**blunge**, *blunj*, *v.t.* (*pottery*) to mix (clay or the like) with water.—*n.* **blung′er**, machine for doing so: one who blunges. [From blend and plunge.]

**blunk**, *blungk*, (*Scot.*) *v.t.* to spoil: to bungle.—*n.* **blunk′er**, (*Scott*) a bungler, or according to Jamieson, one who prints cloth.

**blunt**, *blunt*, *adj.* having a dull edge or point: rough: outspoken: dull: barren (*Spens.*)—*v.t.* to dull.—*v.i.* to become dull.—*n.* (*slang*) money. —*adj.* **blunt′ish.**—*adv.* **blunt′ly.**—*n.* **blunt′ness.**— *adj.* **blunt′-witted** (*Shak.*), dull, stupid. [Origin unknown.]

**blur**, *blûr*, *n.* an ill-defined spot or smear: a confused impression.—*v.t.* to blot: to render indistinct in outline: to blemish.—*v.i.* to make blurs: —*pr.p.* **blurr′ing**; *pa.t.* and *pa.p.* **blurred.** [Perh. a variety of blear.]

**blurb**, *blûrb*, *n.* a publisher's puff or commendatory description of a book, commonly printed on the jacket. [Attributed to Gelett Burgess, American author.]

**blurt**, *blûrt*, *v.t.* to utter suddenly or unadvisedly (with *out*).—*v.i.* (*Shak.*) to snort or puff in scorn. —*n.* an abrupt outburst.—*adv.* with a blurt.—*n.* and *adj.* **blurt′ing.** [Prob. imit.]

**blush**, *blush*, *n.* a red glow on the skin caused by shame, modesty, etc.: any reddish colour or suffusion.—*adj.* pinkish.—*v.i.* to show shame or confusion by growing red: to grow red.—*ns.* **blush′er**; **blush′et** (*Ben Jonson*), a blushing girl. —*adj.* **blush′ful.**—*n.* and *adj.* **blush′ing.**—*adv.* **blush′ingly.**—*adv.* **blush′less.**—*adv.* **blush′lessly.** —*n.* **blush′-rose′**, a pink variety of rose.—**at the first blush**, at the first glance or sight: off-hand; **put to the blush**, to cause to blush. [Cf. O.E. *blyscan*, to shine.]

**bluster**, *blus′tər*, *v.i.* to blow boisterously: to storm, rage: to bully or swagger.—*v.t.* to utter stormily: to drive by storming.—*n.* a blast or roaring as of the wind: bullying or boasting language: a storm of anger.—*n.* and *adj.* **blus′tering.**—*adv.* **blus′teringly.**—*adjs.* **blus′terous** (*Shak.* **blus′trous**), noisy: boastful; **blus′tery**, stormy: swaggering. [Cf. E. Frisian *blüstern*, to bluster.]

Neutral vowels in unaccented syllables: *el′ə-mənt*; for certain sounds in foreign words, see p. viii

**blut**, *blōōt*, (Ger.) blood; **blut und boden**, *ōōnt bō'dən*, blood and earth, and **blut und ehre**, *ā'rə*, blood and honour (Nazi party slogans); **blut und eisen** or **eisen und blut**, *i'sən*, blood and iron (Bismarck), relentless force.

**blutwurst**, *blōōt'vōōrst*, (Ger.) blood-pudding.

**bo, boh**, *bō, interj.* a word used to drive geese or to frighten children.—**cannot say bo to a goose**, is inarticulate from extreme meekness.

**bo**, *bō*, (*U.S. slang*) *n.* man (as term of address).

**Boa**, *bō'a, n.* a genus, mainly South American, of large snakes that kill their prey by pressure: (without *cap.*) popularly any large constricting snake: long, serpent-like coil of fur, feathers, or the like, worn round the neck by ladies.—**boa constric'tor**, properly the name of one species; popularly any boa, python, or similar snake. [L. *bōa*, a kind of snake.]

**Boanerges**, *bō-ən-ûr'jēz, n.* a noisy preacher or shouting orator (*sing.* and *pl.*). [Sons of thunder—Mark iii. 17.]

**boar**, *bōr, bör, n.* the male swine, or its flesh.— *adj.* **boar'ish**, swinish: brutal.—*ns.* **boar'fish**, a fish (*Capros*) of the horse-mackerel family with hoglike snout; **boar'hound**, a powerful dog used for hunting the wild boar, esp. the great Dane or German mastiff; **boar'-spear**, a spear used in boar-hunting. [O.E. *bār*; Du. *beer*.]

**board** (*Spens.*, etc., **bord, boord, boorde**), *bōrd, börd, n.* a broad and thin strip of timber: a table: supply of food: provision of meals (with or without lodging): a council-table: a council or authorised body: a slab prepared for playing a game (as a chessboard) or other special purpose (as a notice-board, blackboard, knife-board): side (*obs.* except seaboard, and the side of a ship): (in *pl.*) the stage: a kind of thick stiff paper or sheets of paper pasted together, as in pasteboard, Bristol-board, esp. that used in the binding of books: a rectangular piece forming the side of a book-binding: conversation (*Spens.*): coast (*Spens.*).—*v.t.* to cover with boards; to supply with food (and bed) at fixed terms: to enter (a ship or orig. U.S., a train, bus, etc.): to accost, to attack (*Shak.*).—*v.i.* to receive food (and lodging): to border (*Spens.*).—*ns.* **board'er**, one who receives board: one who boards a ship; **board'ing**, the act of covering with boards: a structure or collection of boards: act of boarding a ship.—**board'-foot**, a unit of **board'-measure**, for timber, a piece one inch thick by 12 inches square; **board'ing-house**, a house where boarders are kept; **board'ing-pike**, a pike used in boarding a ship, or in defending it when attacked; **board'-ing-school**, a school in which board and lodging are provided for pupils; **board'-school**, a school under control of a schoolboard; **board'-wa'ges**, payment to a servant in lieu of food.—**above board**, openly; **Board of Trade unit** (*elect.*), a kilowatt-hour (contracted B.T.U.); **board out**, to have board elsewhere than where one lives: to place in a house for board; **go by the board**, to go over the side of a ship: to be discarded or ignored: to meet disaster; **on board**, aboard; **sweep the board**, to take all the cards: to win everything. [O.E. *bord*, board, the side of a ship; O.N. *borth*, connected either with **bear** or with **broad**.]

**boart.** See **bort**.

**boast**, *bōst, v.i.* to talk vaingloriously: to brag (with *of*).—*v.t.* to brag of: to speak proudly or confidently of, esp. justifiably: to possess with pride.—*n.* an expression of pride: a brag: the cause of boasting.—*n.* **boast'er**.—*adj.* **boast'ful**, given to bragging.—*adv.* **boast'fully**.—*ns.* **boast'-fulness, boast'ing**.—*adj.* **boast'less**, without boasting: simple, unostentatious. [M.E. *bōst*; origin unknown; apparently W. *bostio*, Gael. *bòsd*, a bragging, are borrowed from English.]

**boast**, *bōst, v.t.* in stonecutting, to shape roughly.

—**boast'er**, broad steel chisel used for boasting. [Origin unknown.]

**boat**, *bōt, n.* a small open craft usually moved by oars: a ship: a boat-shaped utensil (as sauceboat).—*v.i.* to sail about in a boat.—*v.t.* to put or convey in a boat: to ship (as oars): (with *it*) to go in a boat.—*ns.* **boat'er**, one who boats: a straw hat; **boat'ing**, the art, sport, or practice of sailing in boats.—**boat'bill**, a bird of the heron family (from the shape of its bill); **boat'-builder**, one who constructs boats; **boat'-deck** a ship's top deck, on which the small boats are carried; **boat'-fly**, a water-bug (*Notonecta*), with boat-shaped body, that swims on its back; **boat'-hook**, a hook fixed to a pole used for pulling or pushing off a boat; **boat'house**, a house or shed for a boat; **boat'-load; boat'man**, a man who has charge of a boat: a rower; **boat'race**, a race of rowing-boats: (*cap.*) annual boatrace between Oxford and Cambridge universities; **boat'-racing; boat'-song**, a song sung by a boatman; **boat'tail**, a grackle; **boat'-train**, a train run in connection with a ship.—**have an oar in another's boat**, to meddle with his affairs; **in the same boat**, (of persons) in the same unfavourable circumstances. [O.E. *bāt*; cf. Du. *boot*; Fr. *bateau*.]

**boatswain** (often **bosun, bo's'n, bos'n**), *bō'sn, n.* foreman of a crew (warrant-officer in the navy) who looks after a ship's boats, rigging, flags, etc.: skua (prob. from its aggressiveness): transferred (app.) to the tropic-bird (**boat'swain-bird**).—**boatswain's call, pipe, whistle** (see **whistle**); **boatswain's mate**, boatswain's assistant. [boat, swain.]

**bob**, *bob, v.i.* to move quickly up and down: to curtsey: to ride a bobsled: to fish with a bob.— *v.t.* to move in a short jerking manner: to execute with a bob: to cut (hair) square across: to dock, to bobtail: (*pr.p.* **bobb'ing**; *pa.t.* and *pa.p.* **bobbed**).—*n.* a short jerking motion: a curtsey: a dance (*Scot.*): a slight blow (*obs.*): a jibe (*obs.*): anything that moves with a bob or swing: the weight of a pendulum, plumb-line, or the like: a pendant (*arch.*): a knot of hair: bobbed or docked hair: a bunch or cluster (as of cherries) (*dial.*): a bunch of lobworms, used in catching eels: any small roundish body: the refrain or burden of a song (*arch.*): a short line at or near the end of a stanza: a term in bell-ringing for certain changes—a **bob minor** is rung upon six bells; a **bob major** on eight; a **bob royal** on ten; a **bob maximus** on twelve.— *adj.* **bobb'ish**, in good spirits.—*n.* **bobb'le**, the movement of water in commotion: a woolly ball for trimming dresses.—**bob'cat**, a kind of lynx; **bob'-cherry**, the pastime of catching a swinging cherry with the teeth; **bob'** (-**fly'**), the top drop-fly; **bob'sled, -sleigh**, a short sledge: a sleigh made up of two of these, sometimes with common seat; **bob'tail**, a short or cut tail: an animal with a bobbed tail (also *adj.*): a word applied in contempt to the rabble, as in *rag-tag and bobtail*.—Also *v.t.*—*adj.* **bob'tailed**, with tail cut short.—*ns.* **bob'wheel**, in verse, the bob with the lines following it; **bob'wig**, one with the ends turned up into short curls.—**bob up**, to appear suddenly. [Poss. Gael. *baban, babag*.]

**bob**, *bob*, (*obs.*) *v.t.* to befool: to take by cheating (*Shak.*): to cheat (out of) (*Shak.*). [O.F. *bober*.]

**bob**, *bob*, (slang) *n.* a shilling:—*pl.* **bob**. [Prob. not O.Fr. *bobe* = 1½d.]

**bobak, bobac**, *bō'bak, n.* a species of marmot. [Pol. *bobak*.]

**Bobadil**, *bob'ə-dil, n.* a swaggering boaster, from the soldier in Ben Jonson's *Every Man in his Humour*.

**bobbery**, *bob'ər-i, n.* a noisy row. [Perh. Hind. *bāp re*, O father.]

**bobbin**, *bob'in, n.* a reel or spool for winding yarn,

wire, etc.—**bobb′in-lace′**, lace made on a pillow with bobbins; **bobb′in-net′** or **bobb′inet**, a fine machine-made netted lace. [Fr. *bobine*.]

**bobby**, *bob′i*, (*slang*) *n.* a policeman. [Familiar form of *Robert*, from Sir Robert Peel, Home Secretary at the passing of the Metropolitan Police Act, 1828; cf. peeler.]

**bobby-dazzler**, *bob′i-daz-lər*, *n.* (*Northern*) anything overwhelmingly excellent, striking, or showy, esp. a woman; a young girl who sets out to make an impression.

**bobbysock**, *bob′i-sok*, (*slang*) *n.* an ankle-sock.—*n.* **bobbysox′er**, an adolescent girl, teenager.

**bobolink**, *bob′ō-lingk*, *n.* a North American singing bird. [At first *Bob Lincoln*, from its note.]

**bobsled, bobsleigh.** See bob (1).

**bobstays**, *bob′stāz*, (*naut.*) *n.pl.* ropes or stays used to hold the bowsprit down to the stem or cutwater, and counteract the strain of the foremaststays.

**bob-white**, *bob′(h)wit′*, *n.* an American quail. [Imit.]

**bocage.** See boscage.

**bocca**, *bok′ka*, (*It.*) mouth.

**boche, bosche**, *bosh*, *n.* abusive French slang for a German.

**bock**, *bok*, (*Fr.*, from *Ger.*) a strong German beer—from *Einbocker bier*, *Eimbockbier*—beer from Einbeck (Eimbeck): now often a glass or mug of beer (quarter of a litre).

**bod**, *bod*, (*orig. service slang*) *n.* a person. [Contraction of body (*coll.*).]

**bodach**, *bōd′əhh*, *bod′* (*Gael. bot′*), (*Scot.*) *n.* an old man, a churl: a goblin. [Gael.]

**bode**, *bōd*, *v.t.* to portend: to foreshow: to augur: to have a presentiment of.—*v.i.* to augur.—*n.* (*Scot.*) a bid, offer.—*adj.* **bode′ful**, boding, ominous.—*n.* **bode′ment**, an omen, presentiment. —*adj.* **bod′ing**, presaging.—*n.* an omen or portent. [O.E. *bodian*, to announce—(*ge*)*bod*, a message; allied to bid.]

**bode**, *bōd*. See bide.

**bodega**, *bo-dē′ga*, *n.* a wine-shop. [Sp.]

**bodge**, *boj*, (*dial.*) same as botch (*v.t.* and *v.i.*): (*Shak.*) prob. same as budge.—*n.* (*dial.*) a clumsy patch: a clumsy worker.—Also bodg′er.

**bodger**, *boj′ər*, (*dial.*) *n.* a travelling pedlar who turns beechwood to make chairs, etc. [Origin uncertain.]

**bodgie**, *boj′i*, (*Austr.*) *n.* a delinquent youth, usu. member of a teenage gang. [From bodge, a clumsy worker.]

**Bodhisattva**, *bō-di-sat′wə*, (*Buddhism*) *n.* one who postpones entry into nirvana in order to help others: a future Buddha. [Sans.—*bodhi*, enlightenment, *sattva*, existence.]

**bodhi tree.** See bo tree.

**bodice**, *bod′is*, *n.* a stiffened inner garment (orig. *pl.* of body) (*arch.*): a woman's outer garment covering the waist and bust: the close-fitting waist or body of a woman's gown.

**bodikin**, *bod′i-kin*, *n.* dim. of body, in '*Od's bodikins*, God's little body.

**bodkin**, *bod′kin*, *n.* a small dagger: a small instrument for pricking holes, for dressing the hair, for correcting type, etc.: a large blunt needle.—**to sit, or ride, bodkin**, to be wedged in tight between two others. [Poss. conn. with W. *bidog*, dagger.]

**bodle**, also **boddle**, *bod′l*, *bōd′l*, *n.* a 17th-century Scots copper coin, worth about one-sixth of an English penny, the smallest coin. [Origin unknown.]

**bodrag**, *bod′rag*, (*Spens.*) *n.* a hostile attack, a raid —Also **bord′raging**. [Perh. Ir. *buaidhreadh*, a disturbance.]

**body**, *bod′i*, *n.* the whole frame of a man or lower animal: the main part of an animal, as distinguished from the limbs: the main part of anything: the part of a vehicle which carries the load or passengers: a garment or part of a garment covering the trunk: a bodice: a corpse: matter, as opposed to spirit: substance or substantial quality: fullness, solidity: opacity of a paint or pigment: a mass: a person (*coll.*): a number of persons united by some common tie: size of type:—*pl.* bod′ies.—*v.t.* to give form to: to embody:—*pr.p.* bod′ying; *pa.t.* and *pa.p.* bod′ied.—*adj.* bod′iless, without a body: incorporeal.—*adj.* bod′ily, of the body, esp. as opposed to the mind: actual, real (*Shak.*).—*adv.* in the flesh: as a whole.—bod′y-build′er, a maker of vehicle bodies: an apparatus for exercising muscles: a nutritious food; **body cavity**, the coelom, or cavity in which the viscera of the higher animals lie; **body colour**, degree of consistence, substance, and tingeing power of a paint: water-colour mixed with zinc or other white to give it body; **bod′y-cur′er** (*Shak.*), a doctor; **bod′yguard**, a guard to protect the person, esp. of a sovereign; **body politic,** the collective body of the people in its political capacity; **body servant**, a personal attendant; **bod′y-snatch′er**, one who secretly disinters the bodies of the dead for the purposes of dissection. —**body-line bowling**, in cricket, fast bowling delivered at the batsman's body. [O.E. *bodig*.]

**Boeotian**, *bi-ō′sh(y)ən*, *adj.* of *Boeotia* in Greece, proverbial for the dullness of its inhabitants: hence, stupid, dull.—Also *n.*

**Boer**, *bōōr*, (chiefly *hist.*) *n.* a S. African of Dutch descent, esp. one engaged in farming.—Also *adj.* [Du.; see boor, bower.]

**boffin**, *bof′in*, (*orig. service slang*) *n.* research scientist, esp. one employed by armed forces or government.

**Bofors gun**, *bō′förz*, or *-förs*, *gun*, *n.* a double-barrelled, quick-firing anti-aircraft gun. [From *Bofors*, Sweden, where orig. made.]

**bog**, *bog*, *n.* spongy, usu. peaty, ground: a marsh: a type of vegetation growing on peat deficient in lime: a latrine (*slang*).—*v.t.* to sink.—Also *v.i.* —*n.* bogg′iness.—*adj.* bogg′y.—bog′-as′phodel, a yellow-flowered liliaceous bog-plant (*Narthecium ossifragum*); bog′bean, buckbean; bog′-butt′er, butter-like substance of animal origin found in Irish peat-bogs; bog′land; bog′-Lat′in, Shelta; bog′-moss′, the sphagnum genus; bog′-myrtle′, sweet-gale (*Myrica gale*), a bog plant; bog′oak′, trunks of oak embedded in bogs and preserved from decay—of a deep black colour, often used for making ornaments; bog′-ore, bog′-iron, an iron ore found in boggy land, limonite; bog′-spav′in, distension of the capsule of the hock-joint of the horse; bog′-trotter, one who lives in a boggy country, hence an Irishman.—*n.* and *adj.* bog′trotting.—**bog down**, (*fig.*; with *in*) to make, or to be made, feel helpless through amount of work required or difficulty of task. [Ir. and Gael. *bogach*; *bog*, soft.]

**bogey**, *bō′gi*, *n.* in golf, the score, for a given hole or for the whole course, of an imaginary good player, Colonel *Bogey*, fixed as a standard—the bogey is higher than par or sometimes equivalent to it. [Perh. bogy.]

**bogey.** See bogie, bogy.

**boggard**, *bog′ərd*, **boggart**, *-ərt*, **boggle**, *bog′l*. See bogle.

**boggle**, *bog′l*, *v.i.* to stop or hesitate as if at a bogle: to start with fright: to make difficulties about a thing: to equivocate.—*n.* a scruple, objection: a bungle.—*n.* bogg′ler, one who boggles: a doubter: one who hesitates or swerves (*Shak.*). [bogle.]

**bogie, bogey**, *bō′gi*, *n.* a low heavy truck, a trolley: a railway coach: a pivoted undercarriage, as in a locomotive engine. [Ety. unknown: perh. conn. with bogy.]

**bogle**, *bō′gl*, *n.* a spectre or goblin: a scarecrow (tatt′ie-bo′gle): a bugbear, or source of terror.—

bogg'le, bogg'ard, bogg'art, are North of England forms.—bogle about the bush, stacks, a kind of hide-and-seek. [Scot.; possibly connected with bug (1).]

bogong. See bugong.

bogus, bō'gəs, adj. counterfeit, spurious. [An American cant word, of very doubtful origin—it may possibly be ult. related to bogy.]

bogy, bogey, bō'gi, n. a goblin: a bugbear or special object of dread: the devil: a policeman (slang):—pl. bo'gies, bo'geys.—ns. bog'(e)yism; bo'g(e)y-man'. [Perhaps a form of bogle and boggard.]

bohea, bō-hē', n. the lowest quality of black tea: black tea generally. [From the Wu-i hills in China.]

Bohemian, bō-hē'mi-ən, n. a native or inhabitant of Bohemia: a Czech: a gypsy: a person of loose or irregular habits: an artist or man of letters, or indeed anyone, who sets social conventions aside: the Czech language.—Also adj.—n. Bohē'mianism.—Bohemian ruby, rose quartz; Bohemian topaz, citrine. [Fr. bohémien, a gypsy, from the belief that these wanderers came from Bohemia.]

bohunk, bō'hungk, (slang, esp. U.S.) n. a Slav or Hungarian, esp. an unskilled labourer: his language. [Perh. Bohemian Hungarian.]

boil, boil, v.i. to pass rapidly from liquid into vapour with violent evolution of bubbles: to bubble up as if from the action of heat: to be heated in boiling liquid: to be hot: to be excited or angry.—v.t. to heat to a boiling state: to cook, dress, clean or otherwise treat by boiling.—n. act or condition of boiling: a swirling disturbance made at the surface of the water by a fish coming to the fly.—ns. boil'er, one who boils: that in which anything is boiled: a vessel in which steam is generated: a vessel for heating water for baths, etc.: an electric apparatus for boiling a kettle or the like; boil'ery, a place for boiling, esp. for obtaining salt; boil'ing, the act of causing to boil: the condition of being boiled or at boiling-point: a quantity boiled at once: collection, set (coll.).—adj. at boiling-point: very hot: bubbling: swelling with heat or passion.—boil'ing-point, the temperature at which a liquid, esp. water, boils, esp. at atmospheric pressure; boil'ed shirt, a dress shirt; boiler suit, a workman's overall garment.—boil down, to reduce in bulk by boiling: to extract the substance of: to epitomise; boil over, to bubble over the sides of the containing vessel: to break out into unrestrained indignation. [O.Fr. boillir—L. bullire—bulla, a bubble.]

boil, boil, n. an inflamed swelling. [O.E. býl; Ger. beule.]

boisterous, bois'tər-əs, adj. wild: noisy: turbulent: stormy.—adv. bois'terously.—n. bois'terousness. [M.E. boistous.]

boite de nuit, bwät də nwē, (Fr.) a night-club.

bok, bok, (S. Africa) n. a goat: an antelope—used alike of male and female. [Du. bok, goat.]

boko, bō'kō, n. the nose (slang). [Origin unknown.]

bolas, bō'läs, n. (properly pl.) a South American missile, consisting of two or more balls or stones strung together, swung round the head and hurled so as to entangle an animal. [Sp., balls.]

bold, bōld, adj. daring: actively courageous: forward or impudent: presumptuous: executed with spirit: striking to the sense, standing out clearly, well marked: steep or abrupt: (of e.g. currants) full-flavoured, mature, plump.—v.t. bold'en (obs.), to make bold.—adv. bold'ly, —n. bold'ness.—adj. bold'-faced, impudent: of type, having a heavy face.—bold as brass, utterly unabashed; to make bold, to be so bold as to, to

take the liberty. [O.E. bald; O.H.G. bald, O.N. ballr.]

bold-beating, bōld'-bēt'ing, adj. (Shak.) poss. for bowl-beating, pot-thumping.

bole, bōl, n. the trunk of a tree. [O.N. bolr; Ger. bohle, a plank.]

bole, bōl, n. a friable earthy clay, usually red. [Gr. bōlos, a clod.]

bole, bōl, (Scot.) n. a recess in a wall: an opening to admit light and air. [Origin unknown.]

bolection, balection, bō-, bə-lek'shən, n. a moulding around a panel, projecting beyond the surface of the framing. [Origin unknown.]

bolero, bə-lā'rō, n. Spanish national dance: a tune to which it may be danced: (bo'lə-rō) a jacket-like bodice, coming barely to the waist. [Sp.]

Boletus, bol-ē'təs, n. a genus of fungi, edible and poisonous, with a pore-like surface instead of gills. [L. bōlētus—Gr. bōlitēs, mushroom.]

bolide, bō'lid, n. a large meteor, esp. one that bursts: a fireball. [Fr.,—L. bolis, -idis—Gr. bolis, -idos, a missile.]

bolivar, bol-ē'vär, n. the standard monetary unit of Venezuela. [From Simón Bolívar.]

boliviano, bol-ē-vi-ä'nō, n. a Bolivian dollar (100 centavos).

boll, bōl, n. a swelling: a knob: a round capsule, as in cotton, flax, poppy, etc.—v.i. to swell, to form bolls.—adjs. bolled (bōld), swollen, podded; bollen (bōln; Shak.), swollen.—boll'-weevil, a weevil (Anthonomus grandis) whose larvae infest cotton-bolls; boll'-worm, a moth caterpillar that destroys cotton-bolls, maize, tomatoes, etc.—in U.S. Chloridea obsoleta, in Egypt and India Earias insulana and E. fabia. [A form of bowl—O.E. bolla.]

boll, bōl, n. a measure of capacity for grain, etc., used in Scotland and the north of England—in Scotland usually = 6 imperial bushels; in England varying from 2 to 6 bushels: also a measure of weight, containing, for flour, 140 lb. [Prob. O.N. bolli.]

Bollandist, bol'ən-dist, n. any of the Jesuit writers who continued the Acta Sanctorum by John Bolland (1596-1665).

bollard, bol'ərd, n. a short post on a wharf or ship, etc., round which ropes are secured: one of a line of short posts barring passage of motor vehicles. [Prob. bole.]

bolletrie, bol'ē-trē. Same as bully-tree.

Bologna, bol-ōn'yä, adj. of the town of Bologna in Italy.—adj. and n. Bologn'ese (or -ēz').—Bologna phial, an unannealed bottle that shatters on scratching; Bologna phosphorus, barium sulphide; Bologna sausage; Bologna stone, fibrous barytes. [L. Bonōnia.]

bolometer, bō-lom'i-tər, n. an instrument for measuring radiant energy. [Gr. bolē, stroke, ray (ballein, to throw), metron, a measure.]

boloney. See baloney.

Bolshevik (or bol-), bol'shə-vik, n. a member of the Russian Majority (or Extreme) Socialist party, opp. to Menshevik (hist.): a violent revolutionary Marxian communist: anarchist, agitator, causer of trouble (used loosely as a term of disapprobation).—Also adj.—coll. contracted bol'shie, bol'shy.—v.t. bol'shevise, -ize.—ns. bol'shevism; bol'shevist, a Bolshevik: an extreme revolutionary communist (of any country)—loosely used by opponents.—Also adj. [Russ.—bolshe, greater, from its more thorough-going programme, or from its being in a majority (i.e. at the Russian Social Democratic Congress in 1903), -vik, agent suffix.]

bolster, bol'stər, n. a long round pillow or cushion: a pad: anything resembling it in form or use, esp. any piece of mechanism affording a support against pressure; a form of cold chisel with a broad, splayed-out blade, used in cutting stone slabs, etc.: the jutting-out part of a knife which abuts on the handle.—*v.t.* to support as with a bolster: to hold up.—*adj.* bol'stered, supported: swelled out.—*n.* and *adj.* bol'stering, propping up or supporting. [O.E. *bolster.*]

**bolt,** *bōlt, n.* a bar used to fasten a door, etc.: a stout pin with a head: an arrow, esp. for a crossbow: a thunderbolt: a roll of a definite measure (of cloth, etc.): the uncut edge of a sheet folded for a book: a rush.—*v.t.* to fasten with a bolt: to fetter: to throw or utter precipitately: to expel suddenly: to discharge, as a bolt: to swallow hastily: to break away from, withhold support from (*U.S.*).—*v.i.* to spring, dart: to rush away: to take flight: to run away: to start up: to withhold support from one's party, or its policy or nominee (*U.S.*).—*adv.* like a bolt.—*n.* bolt'er, one who bolts: a horse given to running away.—bolt'-head, the head of a bolt; bolt'hole, a hole to receive a bolt: a secret passage or way of escape: a refuge from danger: a distilling receiver (*arch.*); bolt'-rope, a rope sewed all round the edge of a sail to prevent it from tearing.—a fool's bolt is soon shot, a fool soon gives away the initiative, leaving himself unprotected; bolt from the blue, an unexpected event; bolt upright, upright and straight as an arrow: supine (*obs.*); have shot one's bolt, to be unable to do more than one has done. [O.E. *bolt*; O.H.G. *bolz.*]

**bolt.** See boult.

**bolus,** *bō'ləs, n.* a rounded mass: a large pill. [L. *bōlus*—Gr. *bōlos*, a lump.]

**boma,** *bō'ma, n.* a fenced enclosure. [Swahili.]

**boma,** *bō'ma, n.* a boa or anaconda. [Congo; thence carried by Portuguese to Brazil.]

**bomb,** *bom* (old-fashioned *bum*), *n.* a hollow case containing explosive, incendiary, smoke-producing, poisonous, or other offensive material, deposited, thrown, dropped, or shot from a mortar: a rounded mass of lava thrown out by a volcano.—*v.i.* to throw, discharge, or drop bombs.—*v.t.* to attack, injure, or destroy with bombs.—*n.* bombard (*bom'bärd*), an early cannon, throwing stones, etc.: a large liquorjug, a black-jack (*Shak.*): an old form of bassoon.—*v.t.* bombard', to attack with artillery: to batter or pelt: to subject to a succession of blows or impingements: to assail, as with questions (*fig.*): to subject, as the atom, to a stream of particles at high speed (*phys.*).—*ns.* bombardier (*bom-*, *bum-bər-dēr'*), the lowest non-commissioned officer in the British artillery, formerly a man employed about a bombard; bombardment (*bom-bärd'mənt*); bombar'don (*or bom'*), the bass tuba.—*n.* bomber (*bom'ər*), one who bombs: a bombing aeroplane.—Also *adj.* —bombardier beetle, a name given to beetles (*Brachinus*, etc.) that discharge an acrid volatile fluid with explosive force from the abdomen; bomb'-calorim'eter, an apparatus for determining the calorific value of fuels by ignition in a thickwalled steel vessel; bomb'-dispos'al, the act of removing and detonating previously unexploded bombs.—*adjs.* bomb'-happy', in a state of mind for discharging bombs without compunction; bomb'proof, proof or secure against the force of bombs.—*n.* a bomb-proof structure.—bomb'shell, a bomb: now only *fig.*, a sudden and surprising piece of news; bomb'-site, an area which has been laid waste by air-raid(s); bomb'-vessel, -ketch (*hist.*), a vessel for carrying mortars used in bombarding from the sea.—go like a bomb, to go very well or very quickly. [Fr. *bombe*, prob.—L. *bombus*—Gr. *bombos*, humming sound.]

**bombasine, bombazine,** *bom'bə-zēn,* or *-zēn',* formerly *bum', n.* a twilled or corded fabric of silk and worsted, or of cotton and worsted. [Fr. *bombasin*—L.L. *bombȳcinus*—Gr. *bombȳkinos, bombȳx,* silk-worm.]

**bombast,** *bom'bast, n.* cottonwool: padding: stuffing: inflated or high-sounding language, fustian.—*adj.* (*Shak.*) inflated.—*v.t.* (*-bast'*, also *bom'*) to pad, stuff: to inflate, render grandiose. —*adj.* bombas'tic, high-sounding: inflated.— *adv.* bombas'tically.—*n.* Bom'bax, a genus of tropical, chiefly S. Amer. trees, giving name to the silk-cotton family, Bombacā'ceae.—*adj.* bombacā'ceous. [L.L. *bombax*, cotton—Gr. *bombȳx*, silk.]

**Bombay duck,** *bom'bā duk, n.* a fish, the bummalo.

**bombe,** *bōb,* (Fr.) a dessert, usually ice-cream frozen in a round or melon-shaped mould.

**bombilate, bombinate,** *bom'bil-āt, -bin-āt, v.i.* to hum, buzz, drone, boom.—*ns.* bom'bilation, bom'bination. [L. *bombilāre, bombināre.*]

**Bombyx,** *bom'biks, n.* the silkworm genus, giving name to the family Bombycidae (*-bis'i-dē*).—*n.* bom'bycid, an insect of the family.—Also *adj.* [Gr. *bombȳx.*]

**bon,** *bō,* (Fr.) good; bon accueil, *bo-na-kœy',* good reception, due honour; bon ami (fem. bonne amie), *bo-na-mē,* good friend: lover; bon camarade, *bō ka-ma-rad,* good comrade; bon chrétien, *krā-tyē,* 'good Christian'—a kind of pear, the William; bon diable, *dē-äbl',* goodnatured fellow; bon goût, *gōō,* good taste; bon gré, mal gré, *grā, mal grā,* willing or unwilling, willy-nilly; bonjour, *-zhōōr,* (Fr.) good day: good morning; bon marché, *mar-shā,* bargain: cheapness: cheap: cheaply; bon mot, *mō,* (*pl.* bons mots), a witty saying; bonsoir, *-swär,* (Fr.) good evening; bon ton, *tō,* the height of fashion; bon vivant, *vē-vä,* a jovial companion: one who lives well, esp. one who enjoys fine food (bonne vivante is *not* according to French usage); bon viveur, *vē-vœr* (not used in Fr.), a bon vivant, esp. a man-about-town; bon voyage, *vwa-yäzh,* a good journey to you.

**bona,** *bō'na, bo', (L.) goods; bona mobilia, *mō-bi'-li-a,* movable goods; bona peritura, *per-i-tū'ra, -tōō',* perishable goods; bona vacantia, *va-kan'shi-a, wa-kan'ti-a,* unclaimed goods.**

**bona fide,** *bō'na fid'(ə), bo'nä fi'dä,* (L.) (*abl.*) in good faith—(used as *adj.*) genuine; bona fides, *fi'dēz, fid'äs,* good faith: genuineness.

**bonanza,** *bon-an'za, n.* a rich mass of gold: any mine of wealth or stroke of luck.—*adj.* very prosperous. [Sp., good weather.]

**Bonapartean,** *bō-nə-pärt'i-ən, adj.* of Napoleon Bonaparte or his family.—*n.* Bo'napartism, attachment to his dynasty or policy.—*n.* and *adj.* Bo'napartist.

**bona-roba,** *bō'na-rō'ba, n.* (*Shak.*) a showy wanton, a courtesan. [It. *buona roba,* lit. good stuff (or dress).]

**bonas(s)us,** *bon-as'əs, n.* a bison. [L.,—Gr. *bonasos, bonassos.*]

**bonbon,** *bon'bon, bō-bō, n.* a sweetmeat: a cracker (for pulling).—*n.* bonbonniere (*bō-bon-yer'*), a fancy box for holding sweets. [Fr., redup. of *bon,* good.]

**bonce,** *bons, n.* a large marble for the head. [Origin obscure.]

**bond,** *bond, n.* that which binds, a band: link or connection or union: a writing of obligation to pay a sum or to perform a contract: a debenture: a mortgage (*Scots law*): any constraining or cementing force: in building, the overlapping connection of one stone or brick with another, as in English bond, Flemish bond, etc.: (in *pl.*) imprisonment, captivity: the condition of goods retained in a warehouse, called a bonded warehouse or bonded store, until duties are paid.— *v.t.* to connect, secure, or bind with a bond: to put in a bonded warehouse: to put in a condition of bond: to cause to adhere (e.g. metal to glass or plastic).—*adj.* bond'ed, secured by bond.—*ns.* bond'er, a bondstone or header; bonding.—bonded debt, the debt of a corporation represented by the bonds it has issued, as contrasted with its floating debt; bond'-hold'er, one who holds bonds of a private person or public company; bond paper, a superior kind of paper, originally intended for bonds; bonds'man, a surety; bond'stone, a stone that reaches a considerable distance into or entirely through a wall for the purpose of binding it together; bond'-timber, timber built into a wall as it is carried up for the purpose of binding it together in a longitudinal direction; bond'-washing, an illegal series of deals in bonds designed to avoid payment of tax. [A variant of band—O.E. *bindan*, to bind.]

**bond**, *bond*, *adj.* in a state of servitude.—*ns.* **bond'age**, captivity: slavery; **bond'ager**, a female outworker in the Borders and North of England, whom the *hind* or married cottar was bound to provide for the farm-work.—**bond'maid**, **bond'-woman**, **bonds'woman**, a woman-slave; **bond'man**, **bonds'man**, a man-slave; **bond'man-ship**; **bond'servant**, a slave; **bond'-service**, the condition of a bondservant: slavery; **bond'-slave**, a slave. [O.E. *bonda*, a boor, a householder, from O.N. *bōndi*, *būandi*, a tiller, a husbandman, *būa*, to till, cog. with O.E. *buan*, meaning affected by association with bond (1).]

**bonduc**, *bon'duk*, *n.* the nicker seed. [Ar. *bonduq*, a kind of nut.]

**bone**, *bōn*, *n.* a hard substance forming the skeleton of the higher animals: a separate piece of the skeleton: a piece of whalebone: a bobbin for lace-making: (in *pl.*) the skeleton or anything analogous: (in *pl.*) mortal remains: (in *pl.*) pieces of bone or the like held between the fingers of the hand and rattled together to keep time to music: (in *pl.*) dice.—*v.t.* to take the bones out of, as meat: to furnish with bones: to seize, to steal (*slang*).—*adjs.* **boned**, having bones: having the bones removed; **bone'less**, wanting bones: spineless (*fig.*).—*n.* **bōn'iness**; **boner** (*bōn'ər*) (*U.S. slang*), a howler.—*adj.* **bon'y**, full of, or consisting of, or like bones: thin.—**bone'-ache**, pain in the bones; **bone'-ash**, **bone'-earth**, the remains of bones burned in an open furnace; **bone'-bed**, a deposit of fossil bones; **bone'-brecc'ia**, rock formed of broken fossil bones; **bone'-black**, the carbonaceous remains of bones heated in a close vessel; **bone'-cave'**, a cave containing deposits of fossil bones of animals that lived in it or their prey; **bone china**, china in the making of which calcium phosphate, as in bone ash, is used.—*adj.* **bone'-dry**, as dry as bone: under total prohibition.—**bone'-dust**, ground or pulverised bones, used in agriculture; **bone'head**, a blockhead.—*adj.* **bone'-idle**, utterly idle, idle to the bone.—**bone'-lace'**, lace woven with bobbins, which were often made of bones; **bone'-meal'**, ground bones used as fertiliser and as animal feed; **bone'-mill**, a mill where bones are ground; **bone'-oil'**, a liquid got in dry distillation of bones; **bone'set**, an American species of hemp agrimony; **bone'setter**, one who treats broken bones without being a duly qualified surgeon; **bone'shaker**, a familiar name for earlier forms of bicycle: any crazy vehicle; **bone'-spavin**, a bony excrescence or hard swelling on the inside of the hock of a horse; **bone'-tur'quoise**, blue fossil bone or tooth used as turquoise; **bony fishes**, the Teleostei, an order of fishes including most of the living forms; **bony pike**, the American (and fossil) garfish.—**a bone of contention**, something that causes strife; **a bone to pick**, something to occupy one (*arch.*): a difference to be cleared up (with somebody); **bone up on** (*slang*), to study or collect information about (a subject) for an immediate purpose; **make no bones of, about**, to have no scruples about: to make no fuss, difficulty, about; **near the bone**, mean: on the verge of the indecent; **to the bone**, to the

inmost part: to the minimum. [O.E. *bān*; Ger. *bein*, leg.]

**bonfire**, *bon'fīr*, *n.* a large fire in the open air on occasions of public rejoicing, for consuming garden refuse, etc.—originally a fire in which bones were burnt. [bone, and fire.]

**bongo**, *bong'gō*, *n.* an African bushbuck. [Native name.]

**bongo (drum)**, *bong'gō*, *n.* a small Cuban drum played with the fingers—generally used in pairs.

**bongrace**, *bon'grās*, *n.* a shade from the sun once worn by women on the front of the bonnet: a broad-brimmed hat or bonnet. [Fr. *bonne* (*fem.*) good, *grâce*, grace.]

**bonheur-du-jour**, *bo-nœr-dü-zhōōr*, *n.* a small desk or writing-table popular esp. in 18th-cent. France. [Fr., happiness of the day.]

**bonhom(m)ie**, *bon'-o-mē*, *n.* easy good nature. [Fr.]

**bonie**. See bonny.

**boniface**, *bon'i-fās*, *n.* an inn-keeper—from the hearty *Boniface* of Farquhar's *Beaux' Stratagem*, or the *Bonifazio* of Ariosto's *La Scolastica*.

**boning**, *bōn'ing*, *n.* estimation of straightness by looking along a row of poles, as in **boning-rod** or -telescope.

**bonito**, *bo-nē'tō*, *n.* a tunny of various kinds. [Sp.]

**bonkers**, *bong'kərz*, (*slang*) *adj.* slightly drunk: crazy.

**bonne**, *bon*, *n.* a French maid or nursemaid. [Fr.; fem. of *bon*, good.]

**bonne**, *bon*, fem. of bon, (Fr.).—**bonne chance**, *shãs*, good luck; **bonne compagnie**, *kõ-pa-nyē*, good society; **bonne foi**, *fwa*, good faith; **bonne grace**, *grās*, good grace, gracefulness; in *pl.* favour; **bonne mine**, *mēn*, good appearance; pleasant looks.

**bonne-bouche**, *bon-bōōsh*, *n.* a delicious morsel. [Fr., pleasant taste; *bonne* (fem.), good, *bouche*, mouth.]

**bonnet**, *bon'it*, *n.* a woman's head-covering, tied on by strings: a soft cap: the velvet cap within a coronet: a small work before the salient or flanked angle of the ravelin (*fort.*): an additional part laced to the foot of jibs, or other fore-and-aft sails, to gather more wind (*naut.*): a wire-cowl over a chimney-top: the cover of a motor-car engine, or of various parts of machinery, etc.: the second stomach of a ruminant: a decoy or pretended player or bidder at a gaming-table or an auction, the accomplice of a thimble-rigger or other petty swindler.—*v.t.* to put a bonnet on: to crush his hat over the eyes of.—*adj.* **bonn'eted**.—**bonnet laird** (*Scot.*), a small landowner who wore a bonnet, not the hat of the gentry; **bonn'et-monkey**, an Indian macaque (from the appearance of the head); **bonn'et-piece**, a gold coin of James V of Scotland, on which the king wears a bonnet instead of a crown; **bonn'et-rouge** (Fr.: *bon-ā-rōōzh*), the red cap of liberty of the French Revolution, in the form of a Phrygian cap. [O.Fr.,—L.L. *bonnetum*, orig. the name of a stuff.]

**bon(n)ibell**, *bon-i-bel'*, (*Spens.*) *n.* a good and fair maid. [Fr. *bonne et belle*, good and fair: or for bonny belle.]

**bon(n)ilasse**, *bon'i-läs*, *n.* (*Spens.*) for bonny lass.

**bonny, bonnie**, *bon'i* (*Scot.* also *bō'ni*; Burns **bonie**), *adj.* comely, pretty: plump: healthy-looking: as a general term expressing appreciation, considerable, etc., often ironically: smiling, gay (*obs.*): stout, strong (*Shak.*).—Also *adv.*—*adv.* **bonn'ily**, beautifully: gaily.—*n.* **bonn'iness**, handsomeness: gaiety. [Origin obscure.]

**bonny-clabber**, *bon'i-klab'ər*, *n.* milk naturally clotted on souring. [Ir. *bainne*, milk, *claba*, thick.]

**bonsai**, *bon'sī*, *bōn'*, *n.* a dwarf tree growing in a pot, produced by special methods of cultivation: the art of growing such trees. [Jap.]

# bonspiel

**bonspiel** 147 **boom**

bonspiel, *bon'spēl, n.* a great match, now only a curling match. [App. from some Du. compound of *spel,* play; cf. **ba'spiel.**]

bontebok, *bon'tǝ-bok, n.* a South African antelope. [Du. *bont,* particoloured, *bok,* goat.]

bonus, *bōn'ǝs, n.* a premium beyond the usual interest for a loan: an extra dividend to shareholders: a policy-holder's share of profits: an extra payment to workmen or others: a douceur or bribe.—**bonus issue,** an issue to shareholders in a company of shares for which no payment is made, representing a capitalisation of reserves. [L. *bonus,* good.]

bonxie, *bongks'i, (Shetland) n.* the great skua. [O.N. *bunki,* heap.]

bonze, *bonz, n.* a Buddhist priest. [Jap. *bonzô* or *bonzi,* a priest.]

bonzer, *bon'zǝr, (slang; Austr.) adj.* very good.

boo, booh, *bōō, interj.* expressive of disapprobation or contempt.—*v.t.* and *v.i.* to hoot.—*v.t.* **boo'-hoo',** to weep noisily.

boob, *bōōb, v.t.* to bungle.—*v.i.* to blunder.—*n.* a blunder: a stupid fellow (*U.S.*). [booby.]

boobook, *bōō'bŏŏk, n.* an Australian owl (*Ninox boobook*). [Imit.; from its cuckoo-like cry.]

booby, *bōō'bi, n.* a lubberly lout: a stupid fellow: a boy at the bottom of the class: a sea-bird of the gannet tribe, absurdly easy to catch.—*adjs.* **boo'by, boo'byish,** like a booby: stupid.—*n.* **boo'byism.**—**boo'by-prize,** a prize for the worst score; **boo'by-trap,** a rude form of practical joke, by which something is made to fall upon one entering a door, or the like: a harmless-looking object which on being touched sets off an explosion. [Perh. Sp. *bobo,* a dolt.]

boodle, *bōōd'l, n.* a crowd, pack: stock-in-trade, capital: counterfeit money: money got by political or official corruption: spoil. [Perh. Du. *boedel,* property.]

boodle, *bōōd'l, (slang) n.* a stupid noodle.

boody, *bōōd'i, v.i.* to sulk or mope. [Fr. *bouder,* to pout.]

boogie-woogie, *bōōg'i-wōōg'i, n.* a jazz rhythm in which the piano has an ostinato figure in the bass. [From U.S. slang *boogie,* a Negro performer, and *woogie,* invented to rhyme.]

book, *bŏŏk, n.* a collection of sheets of paper, etc., bound together or made into a roll, either printed, written on, or blank: a large-scale literary composition: a division of a volume or composition: (with **the**) the Bible: a betting-book, or record of bets made with different people: any source of instruction (*fig.*): a libretto: the first six tricks gained by a side in whist: a structure resembling a book: (*pl.*) formal accounts of transactions, as minutes of meetings, records kept of a business.—*v.t.* to write or enter in a book: to engage in advance; of police, to take the name of, for an alleged offence. —*v.i.* to make a reservation in advance.—*adj.* **book'ful,** full of information gathered from books.—*n.* **book'ie** (*coll.*), a bookmaker.—*adj.* **book'ish,** fond of books: acquainted only with books: savouring of books.—*n.* **book'ishness.** —*adj.* **book'less,** without books: unlearned.—*n.* **book'let,** a small book.—*adjs.* **book'sie,** by way of being literary; **book'y,** bookish.—**book'-account',** an account of debt or credit in a book: **book'-binder,** one who binds books; **book'binding,** the cover of a book: the art or practice of binding or putting the boards on books; **book'-canvasser,** one who goes around soliciting orders for a book; **book'case,** a case with shelves for books; **book club,** a society that buys, circulates on loan, or prints books for its members; **book'-debt,** a sum owing to a seller as shown in his business-books.—*adjs.* **booked'-out, booked'-up,** full up: unable to accept further reservations or appointments.—**book'-end,** a prop for the end of a row of books; **book'-hold'er,** one who holds

the book of the play and prompts the actor in the theatre; **book'-hunt'er,** one who hunts for rare books; **book'ing-clerk',** one who sells tickets; **book'ing-hall;** **book'ing-off'ice,** an office where names are booked or tickets sold; **book'keeper;** **book'keep'ing,** the art of keeping accounts in a regular and systematic manner; **book'land** (O.E. *bōcland*), land taken from the *folcland* or common land, and granted by *bōc* or written charter to a private owner; **book'-learn'ing,** learning got from books, as opposed to practical knowledge; **book'lore** (*Scot.* book-, buik-lear, -lār), book-learning: bibliographical lore; **book'louse,** a wingless insect of the Corrodentia, found among books and papers:—*pl.* **book'lice;** **book'mak'er,** one who makes up books from the writings of others, a compiler: one who makes a living by betting at race-courses; **book'making;** **book'man,** a scholar, student; **book'mark, book'marker,** something placed or to be placed in a book to mark one's place; **book'-mate** (*Shak.*), a companion in study: a schoolfellow; **book'-mind'edness,** habitual direction of the mind towards books; **book'-mus'lin,** muslin used in book-binding; **book'-oath** (*Shak.*), an oath made on the Book or Bible; **book'plate,** a label usually pasted inside the cover of a book, bearing the owner's name, crest, coat-of-arms, or peculiar device; **book'-post,** arrangement in the Post Office for the transmission of books; **book'-scor'pion,** a scorpion-like arachnid found in libraries, probably feeding on booklice; **book'-seller,** one who sells books: formerly a publisher; **book'selling; book'shelf,** a shelf for books; **book'shop,** a shop where books are sold; **book'-stall,** a stall or stand, generally in the open air, where books are sold; **book'stand,** a bookstall: a stand or support for holding up a book in reading; **book'-tally, -token,** a paper to be exchanged for books of a stated price, sent as a gift; **book trade,** the trade of dealing in books; **book'worm,** a grub that eats holes in books, esp. a beetle larva (*Anobium*): a hard reader.—**be upon the books,** to have one's name in an official list; **book of words,** directions for use; **bring to book,** to bring to account; **get one's books,** to be dismissed; **in one's good (bad) books,** favourably (unfavourably) regarded by one; **suit one's book,** to be agreeable to or favourable to one; **take a leaf out of another's book,** to profit by his example; **talk like a book,** to talk pedantically, or with precision and readiness; **without book,** from memory: unauthorisedly. [O.E. *bōc,* book, beech; Ger. *buche,* beech, *buch,* book, supposed to be from early Germanic use of beechen boards.]

**Boolean algebra,** *bōō'lē-ǝn al'ji-brǝ,* an algebra closely related to logic in which the symbols used do not represent arithmetical quantities. [Named after George *Boole* (1815-1864).]

boom, *bōōm, n.* a pole by which a sail is stretched: a chain or bar stretched across a harbour: a barrier of floating logs: a long beam: a tree (in combination, as Kaffir-boom, etc.; *S. Africa*).—**boom'-iron,** a ring in which a spar slides; **boom'-slang,** a venomous S. African tree-snake. [Du. *boom,* beam, tree.]

boom, *bōōm, v.t.* to make a hollow sound or roar. —*n.* a hollow roar, as of the sea, the cry of the bittern, etc.—**boom carpet,** area affected by a particular sonic boom. [From a L.G. root found in O.E. *byme,* a trumpet, Du. *bommen,* to drum; late **bomb,** of imit. origin.]

boom, *bōōm, v.i.* to go on with a rush: to become suddenly prosperous: to increase sharply in value.—*v.t.* to push into sudden prominence: to boost by advertising.—*n.* a sudden increase of activity in business, or the like—often specially worked up: sudden rise in price or value.—*n.* and *adj.* **boom'ing.** [Prob. from boom (2).]

Neutral vowels in unaccented syllables: *el'ǝ-mǝnt;* for certain sounds in foreign words, see p. viii

**boomer**, *boom'ər, n.* the sewellel: the chickaree.
**boomerang**, *boom'ə-rang, n.* a bent missile used by the natives of Australia, sometimes so balanced that it returns towards the thrower: an act that recoils upon the agent (*fig.*).— *v.i.* to recoil thus (*fig.*). [Australian.]
**boon**, *boon, n.* a petition: a gift, favour. [O.N. *bōn*, prayer: O.E. *bēn.*]
**boon**, *boon, adj.* gay, merry, or kind. [Fr. *bon*— L. *bonus*, good.]
**boondocks**, *boon'doks*, (*U.S.*) *n.* isolated rough uncivilised country. [Tagálog *bundok*, mountain.]
**boondoggle**, *boon'dog-l*, (*U.S.*) *n.* a Scout's plaited cord of varicoloured leather strips: an article of simple handcraft: work, or operation, of little or no practical value, esp. work officially provided as a palliative for unemployment. [Scout coinage.]
**boong**, *boong, n.* a New Guinea native: an aborigine. [Aborigine word.]
**boor**, *boor, n.* a countryman, a peasant: a Dutch colonist in South Africa: a coarse or awkward person.—*adj.* **boor'ish**, like a boor: awkward or rude.—*adv.* **boor'ishly.**—*n.* **boor'ishness.** [Du. *boer*; perh. partly O.E. *būr, gebūr*, farmer.]
**boord, boorde**, *bōrd, börd*, old spellings of **board** (*Spens.*, etc.).
**boose.** See **booze**.
**boost**, *boost, v.t.* to push up: to raise, as price, morale: to advertise or promote: to supplement voltage of: to increase supply of air to, or pressure of.—Also *n.*—*n.* **boost'er**, a person or thing which boosts: an auxiliary motor in a rocket, usually breaking away after delivery of its impulse: any device to increase effect of another mechanism. [Orig. U.S.; origin unknown.]
**boot**, *boot, n.* a covering for the foot and lower part of the leg, generally made of leather: an instrument of torture for the leg: a box or receptacle in a coach: a compartment in a motor car for luggage, etc.—*v.t.* to put boots on: to kick: to turn out, dismiss.—*adj.* **boot'ed**, having boots on, equipped for riding.—*n.* **bootee'**, a lady's short boot: an infant's woollen boot.— **boot'black**, a shoeblack; **boot'-catcher**, an inn servant who helped to pull off guests' boots; **boot'-closer**, one who closes the upper leathers of boots; **boot'-hook**, an instrument for pulling on long boots; **boot'hose** (*Shak.*), a stocking used instead of a jack-boot:—*pl.* **boot'hose**; **boot'ikin**, the boot for torture: a boot or mitten for the gouty; **boot'-jack**, an instrument for taking off boots; **boot'lace**, a lace for fastening boots; **boot'last, boot'tree**, the last or foot-like mould on which boots or shoes are made or stretched to keep their shape; **boot'leg**, the leg of a high boot.—*v.t.* to smuggle (liquor).— **boot'legger**, one who smuggles alcoholic liquor in a bootleg or elsewhere: an illicit dealer; **boot'legging.**—*adj.* **boot'less**, without boots.— **boot'licker**, a toady (*U.S.* **boot'lick**; also *v.t.*); **boot'licking**; **boot'maker**; **boot'making**; **boots**, an inn servant who cleans boots, runs messages, etc., also used in combination as *lazyboots, slyboots*; **boot'topping**, the part of a ship's hull between the load-line and the water-line when the ship is without cargo: act of coating this: paint, etc., for the purpose.—**boot and saddle** (a corr. of Fr. *boute-selle*, place saddle), the signal for mounting; **like old boots** (*slang*), vigorously; **the boot is on the other leg, foot**, the tables are turned: responsibility is (now) the other way: the reverse is the truth; **die in one's boots**, to die a sudden death, not in bed; **get the boot** (*slang*), to be dismissed; **have one's heart in one's boots**, to have lost courage. [O.Fr. *bote* (mod. *botte*)— L.L. *botta, bota*, of doubtful origin.]
**boot**, *boot, v.t.* to profit or advantage.—*n.* advantage: profit: in old law, any reparation or

compensation paid: booty (*Shak.*).—*adj.* **boot'-less**, without boot or profit: useless.—*adv.* **boot'-lessly.**—*n.* **boot'lessness.**—**to boot**, in addition. [O.E. *bōt*, compensation, amends, whence *bētan*, to amend.]
**Boötes**, *bō-ō'tēz, n.* a northern constellation beside the Great Bear, containing the bright star Arcturus. [Gr. *Boōtēs*, lit. an ox-driver.]
**booth**, *boodh, booth, n.* a hut or temporary erection formed of slight materials: a small shop of simple construction: a covered stall at a fair or market: a polling place. [O.N. *būth*, or a cognate word; cf. Ger. *bude.*]
**booty**, *boot'i, n.* spoil taken in war or by force: plunder, a prize.—**play booty**, to join with others in order to cheat one player: to play a game with intention to lose. [O.N. *bȳti*, share—*bȳta*, to divide.]
**booze, boose,** (*arch.*) **bouse**, *booz, bowz, v.i.* to drink deeply or excessively.—*n.* intoxicating liquor: a drinking bout.—*adj.* **boozed.**—*n.* **booz'er**, one who boozes: a public house (*slang*).—*adjs.* **booz'ing**, drinking: for drinking; **booz'y**, inclined to booze: drunken.—*adv.* **booz'ily.**— See also **bouse**.
**bop.** Short for **bebop**, of which it was a development in the 1950s.
**bo-peep**, *bō-pēp', n.* a simple play among children in which one peeps from behind something and cries 'Bo'.
**bor**, *bö(r), n.* neighbour, an East Anglian form of address to man or woman. [O.E. *būr*, usu. *gebūr*, farmer; cf. **neighbour**.]
**bora**, *bō'rä, bö', n.* a strong north-east wind in the upper Adriatic. [Venetian variant of It. *borea*— L. *boreas*; or Slav.; cf. Serbian *bura*.]
**bora**, *bō'rä, bö', n.* an Australian initiation rite. [Native word.]
**borachio**, *bor-ach'(i-)ō, n.* a Spanish wine-skin: a drunken fellow. [Sp. *borracha, borracho.*]
**borage**, *bur'ij, bor'ij, n.* a blue-flowered bristly plant, *Borago officinalis*, of the family Boraginā'-ceae, tubiflorous dicotyledons with cincinnate inflorescence and four nutlets. [L.L. *borrāgō.*]
**borane.** See **boron**.
**borax**, *bō'raks, bö', n.* a mineral hydrated sodium tetraborate, found on alkaline lake shores.— *adjs.* **bo'ric, boracic** (*bo-ras'ik*), of or relating to borax or boron.—*ns.* **bo'racite** (*-rə-sīt*), a mineral composed of magnesium borate and chloride; **bo'rate**, a salt of boric acid.—**boric** or **boracic** or **orthoborac'ic acid**, an acid (H₃BO₃) obtained by dissolving borax, and also found native in mineral springs in Italy, changing successively by loss of water on heating to metaboric acid, tetraboric or pyroboric acid, and boric anhydride. [Fr. and L.L. *borax*—Ar. *būraq.*]
**borazon.** See **boron**.
**borborygmus**, *bör-bə-rig'məs, n.* sound of flatulence in the intestines.—*adj.* **borboryg'mic.** [Gr. *borborygmos.*]
**bord, borde**, obs. spellings of **board**.
**bordar**, *börd'ər, n.* a villein who held his hut at his lord's pleasure. [L.L. *bordārius*; of Gmc. origin. See **board**.]
**Bordeaux**, *bör-dō', n.* claret, wine of *Bordeaux.*— **Bordeaux mixture**, a mixture of lime and copper sulphate, used to kill fungus and insect parasites on plants.
**bordel**, *bör'dəl*, (*arch.*) *n.* a house for prostitution.—Also **bordello** (*-del'ō*; It.). [O.Fr. *bordel*, a cabin—L.L. *borda.*]
**border**, *börd'ər, n.* the edge or margin of anything: the boundary of a country, etc., esp. (*cap.*)— also *in pl.*) that between England and Scotland: a flower-bed in a garden: a piece of ornamental edging or trimming.—*adj.* of or on the border.— *v.i.* to come near or to be adjacent (with *on, upon, with*).—*v.t.* to furnish with a border: to bound. *adj.* **bord'ered.**—*n.* **bord'erer**, one who dwells

or was born on the border of a country.—*adj.* **bord´erless.**—**bordered pit** (*bot.*), a thin area in the wall between two vessels or tracheides, surrounded by a thickened border; **bord´erland,** a border region.—*adj.* belonging to the undefined margin between two things, e.g. sanity and insanity.—*n.* **bord´erline.**—Also *adj.*, marginal, hardly or doubtfully coming within the definition (esp. of insanity). [O.Fr. *bordure*; from root of **board.**]

**bordereau,** *bor-d(ə)-rō,* (Fr.) a memorandum.

**bordraging,** *börd´rag-ing, n.* See **bodrag.**

**bordure,** *bör´dūr, -jōōr, n.* (*her.*) a border surrounding a shield. [See **border.**]

**bore,** *bör, bör, v.t.* to pierce so as to form a hole: to thrust against (as one racehorse against another): to weary or annoy with tediousness (perh. a different word—not known before mid-18th century).—*n.* a hole made by boring: the size of the cavity of a tube: a person or thing that wearies.—*ns.* **bore´dom,** tedium; **bor´er,** the person or thing that bores: a name common to many animals that pierce wood, rocks, etc.; **bor´ing,** the act of making a hole in anything: a hole made by boring: (in *pl.*) the chips produced by boring.—**bore´hole,** a bore in the earth's crust for investigation or for water, oil, etc. [O.E. *borian,* to bore; cf. Ger. *bohren*; allied to L. *forāre,* to bore, Gr. *pharynx,* the gullet.]

**bore,** *bör, bör, pa.t.* of **bear.**

**bore,** *bör, bör, n.* a tidal flood that rushes with great violence up the estuaries of certain rivers, also called eagre. [O.N. *bāra,* a wave or swell.]

**Boreas,** *bor´, bör´, bör´i-as, n.* the North Wind.—*adj.* **bō´real** (or *bo´, bö´*), of North Wind or North: (*cap.*) of a biogeographical region consisting of the northern and mountainous parts of the Northern hemisphere: (*cap.*) of a postglacial period when the climate of Europe and North America resembled that of the present Boreal region. [L., Gr. *Borěas.*]

**borecole,** *bör´kōl, bör´, n.* kale. [Du. *boerenkool,* lit. peasant's cabbage.]

**boree,** *bö´rē,* (*Austr.*) *n.* any one of several wattle-trees. [Aboriginal.]

**boreen,** *bō-rēn´, n.* a lane: byroad. [Ir. *bóithrin.*]

**borgo,** *bör´gō,* (It.) a borough, a market-town; **borghetto,** *bor-gä´tō,* a big village.

**boric.** Same as **boracic.** [See **borax.**]

**born,** *börn.* (See **bear** (1))—**born again,** having received new spiritual life; **born fool,** mimic, etc., one whose folly, mimic ability, etc., is innate; **born to be,** destined to be; **in one's born days,** in one's whole lifetime; **not born yesterday,** not young in experience.

**borne,** *börn, börn, pa.p.* of **bear,** to carry.

**borné,** *bor´nā, adj.* limited, narrow-minded. [Fr. *pa.p.* of *borner,* to limit.]

**Bornholm disease,** *börn´hōm,* epidemic pleurodynia, a rare infectious disease caused by a virus, named from the Baltic island *Bornholm,* where it was first described.

**bornite,** *börn´it, n.* a copper ore, sulphide of copper and iron. [I. von *Born,* mineralogist (1742-91).]

**boron,** *bö´ron, bö´, n.* a non-metallic element (symbol B), of atomic number 5, present in borax and boric acid, obtained as an amorphous powder or impure in diamond-like crystals.—*ns.* **borane,** *bör´ān, bör´,* any boron hydride, efficient as high-energy fuel; **borazon,** *bör´a-zon, bör´,* ® a man-made substance, compound of boron and nitrogen, hard as diamond; **boride,** *bör´id, bör´,* any of a class of substances made by combining boron chemically with a metal, some of which are extremely hard and heat-resistant. [See **borax.**]

**borough,** *bur´ə, n.* a town with a corporation and special privileges granted by royal charter; a town that sends representatives to parliament.— **bor´ough-English,** a custom in some ancient English boroughs (till 1925), by which estates descended to the youngest son; **bor´oughmonger,** a buyer or seller of the patronage of boroughs; **bor´ough-reeve,** the chief municipal official in some unincorporated English towns prior to 1835; **close** or **pocket borough,** a borough whose representation was in the nomination of some person—common before 1832; **county borough,** a borough (by Acts of 1888, 1926, 1958, respectively above 50,000, 75,000, 100,000, inhabitants) with some of the characters of a county; **rotten borough,** one which still returned members to parliament although the constituency had disappeared—all abolished in 1832.—**The Scottish terms** are grouped under **burgh.** [O.E. *burg, burh,* a city, from *beorgan*; Ger. *bergen,* to protect.]

**borrel, borrell, borel,** *bor´əl,* (*arch.*) *adj.* rustic, clownish. [O.Fr. *burel,* coarse cloth worn by peasantry.]

**borrow,** *bor´ō, n.* a pledge or surety (*arch.*): a borrowing (*Shak.*).—*v.t.* to obtain on loan or trust: to adopt from a foreign source: to derive from another (with *from, of*).—*adj.* **borr´owed,** taken on loan: counterfeit: assumed.—*n.* **borr´ower.**—*n.* and *adj.* **borr´owing.**—**borrowing days,** the last three days of March (O.S.), supposed in Scottish folklore to have been borrowed by March from April, and to be especially stormy.—**to borrow,** for a pledge or surety. [O.E.]

**borgian**—*borg, borh,* a pledge, security.]

**borsch,** *börsh(t), n.* a Russian soup with beetroot, etc. Also **bortsch** (*börch*), etc. [Russ. *borshch.*]

**borstal, borstall,** *bör´stəl, n.* a way up a hill, still used in the district of the Downs: an establishment for the detention of young adult delinquents.—**Borstal system,** a system of detaining 'juvenile adult' delinquents, named from the first reformatory of the kind at Borstal, a suburb of Rochester. [O.E. *beorh,* a hill, and *stigel,* a stile, or *borg,* security, *steall,* place.]

**bort, boart,** *bört, n.* diamond fragments or dust: a coarse diamond or semicrystallic form of carbon. [Fr.]

**borzoi,** *bör´zoi, n.* a dog like a huge greyhound, but with a soft coat about the length of a deerhound's. [Russ., swift.]

**bosbok.** See **bush** (1).

**boscage,** *bosk´ij, n.* thick foliage: woodland. [Fr. *boscage, bocage*—L.L. *boscus,* conn. with Ger. *busch,* Eng. **bush.**]

**bosch,** *bos, bosh.* See **bush.**

**bosche.** See **boche.**

**bosh,** *bosh, n.* nonsense: foolish talk.—Also *interj.* [Turk. *bosh,* worthless, frequent in Morier's novel *Ayesha* (1834).]

**boshta, boshter,** *bosh´ta, tər,* (*Austr. coll.*) *adj.* very good.

**bosk,** *bosk, n.* a thicket: a little wood.—*ns.* **bosk´et,** a thicket: a plantation; **bosk´iness.**—*adj.* **bosk´y,** woody or bushy: shady: somewhat tipsy (*coll.*). [Cf. **bush, boscage.**]

**bosker,** *bos´kər,* (*Austr. coll.*) *adj.* very good.

**bo's´n, bos´n.** See **boatswain.**

**bosom,** *bōōz´əm, n.* the breast of a human being: the part of the dress that covers it: the imagined seat of the passions and feelings: the heart: desire (*Shak.*): embrace, enclosure: any close or secret receptacle.—in composition, confidential: intimate.—*v.t.* to enclose in the bosom.— *adj.* **bos´omed,** having a bosom: enclosed.— **Abraham's bosom,** the abode of the blessed dead. [O.E. *bōsm*; Ger. *busen.*]

**boson,** *bō´son, n.* any of a class of subatomic particles whose behaviour is governed by Bose-Einstein statistics, according to which, under certain conditions, particles of the same kind will accumulate in each low-energy quantum mechanical state. [S. N. *Bose,* physicist.]

**boss,** *bos, n.* a knob or stud: a raised ornament.—

*v.t.* to ornament with bosses.—*adjs.* **bossed**; **boss′y**, having bosses. [O.Fr. *boce* (Fr. *bosse*), from O.H.G. *bōzan*, to beat.]
**boss**, *bos*, *n.* a chief or leader: a master, manager, or foreman: the person who pulls the wires in political intrigues.—*adj.* chief, excellent.—*v.t.* to manage or control: to domineer over.—*adj.* **boss′y**. [New York Dutch *baas*, master.]
**boss**, *bos*, (*Scot.*) *adj.* hollow: empty. [Obscure.]
**boss**, *bos*, *v.i.* (*dial.* and *slang*) to make a mess of.—*adj.* **boss′-eyed**, with one good eye: squint-eyed: out of true. [Origin unknown.]
**bossa nova**, *bos′ə nō′və*, ('new style'), a style of dancing originating in Brazil.
**bostangi**, *bos-tan′ji*, *n.* a Turkish palace guard. [Turk. *bostanji*.]
**boston**, *bost′ən*, *n.* a game of cards, somewhat similar to whist: a kind of waltz.—**Boston terrier**, a breed of dog arising from a cross between a bulldog and a bull-terrier. [From *Boston*, U.S.A.]
**bostryx**, *bos′triks*, (*bot.*) *n.* a cymose inflorescence in which each lateral axis arises on the same side (cyclically) of its parent axis. [Gr., curl.]
**bosun**. See boatswain.
**Boswellian**, *boz-wel′li-ən*, *adj.* after the hero-worshipping, detailedly intimate manner of James Boswell in his biography of Samuel Johnson.—*v.i.* **Boswellise**, **-ize** (*-wəl-īz*), to write like Boswell.—*n.* **Boswell′ism**.
**bot**, *bot*, (*Austr. coll.*) *n.* an irritating interfering person, a pest.
**bot**, **bott**, *bot*, *n.* the maggot of a botfly, parasitic in the intestines of the horse and other animals: (in *pl.*) the diseased condition thereby caused: (*Scot.* batts) colic.—**bot′fly**, a name for various flies of the family Oestridae that lay their eggs on horses, etc.; **bot′hole**, a hole in a hide due to boring by a bot. [Origin unknown.]
**botany**, *bot′ən-i*, *n.* the science of plants: fine wool, orig. from Botany Bay.—*adjs.* **botan′ic**; **botan′ical** (also *n.*, a vegetable drug).—*adv.* **botan′ically**.—*v.i.* **bot′anise**, **-ize**, to seek for and collect plants for study.—*ns.* **bot′anist**, one skilled in botany; **bot′anomancy**, divination by means of plants, esp. the leaves of sage and fig.—**Botany Bay**, early convict settlement near what is now Sydney: convict settlements generally. [Gr. *botanē*, grass, fodder.]
**botargo**, *bot-är′gō*, *n.* a relish made of mullet or tunny roe. [It.,—Ar. *butarkhah*.]
**botch**, *boch*, *n.* a swelling on the skin: a boil, pimple, or sore (*Milt.*): a blemish: a clumsy patch: ill-finished work.—*v.t.* to patch or mend clumsily: to put together unsuitably or unskilfully: to bungle.—*v.i.* to do repairs: to bungle.—*ns.* **botch′er**, a repairer: a bungler; **botch′ery**.—*n.* and *adj.* **botch′ing**.—*adj.* **botch′y**, marked with or full of botches. [Partly O.N.Fr. *boche* (O.Fr. *boce*), ulcer; partly perh. some other root.]
**botfly**. See bot.
**both**, *bōth*, *adj.* and *pron.* the two: the one and the other.—*adv.* or *conj.* as well (sometimes of more than two). [O.N. *bāthar* (superseding O.E. *bēgen*, *bā*); Ger. *beide*; cf. L. *ambō*, Gr. *amphō*, Sans. *ubhau*, orig. *ambha*.]
**bothan**, *bo′han*, *n.* a booth, hut: an illegal drinking den. [Gael.]
**bother**, *bodh′ər*, *v.t.* to perplex or tease: to fluster.—*v.i.* to stir oneself.—*n.* petty trouble, difficulty, or perplexity.—*interj.* expressing irritation.—*n.* **botherā′tion** (*coll.*).—*adj.* **both′ersome**. [First found in 18th-cent. Irish-born writers; poss. Anglo-Irish for pother.]
**bothy, bothie**, *both′i*, *n.* a humble cottage or hut: a one-roomed hut or temporary dwelling: a barely furnished dwelling for farm-servants in the north-east of Scotland.—**bothy ballad**, a folk-song, dealing with country matters, usu. bawdy; **both′yman**. [Cf. booth.]

**botoné, bottony**, *bot′ən-i*, (*her.*) *adj.* having buds or knobs at the extremity, applied to a cross having each arm terminated in three buds, like trefoil. [O.Fr.; see button.]
**bo tree, bodhi tree**, *bō trē, bōd′i, n.* in Ceylon, the pipal (*Ficus religiosa*), holy tree of the Buddhists, under which Buddha found enlightenment, planted close by every temple. [Sinh. *bo*, from Pali *bodhi*, perfect knowledge.]
**botryoid, -al**, *bot′ri-oid, -oid′əl, adjs.* like a bunch of grapes.—*adj.* **bot′ryose**, botryoidal: racemose (*bot.*). [Gr. *botrys*, a bunch of grapes, *eidos*, form.]
**botte**, *bot*, (Fr.) a pass or thrust in fencing.
**bottega**, *bot-tā′gä*, (It.) a wine shop: the studio of an artist and his assistants or apprentices.
**bottine**, *bot-ēn′, n.* a high boot: a half-boot: a lady's boot: a small boot. [Fr., dim. of *botte*, boot.]
**bottle**, *bot′l*, *n.* a bundle (of hay). [O.Fr. *botel*.]
**bottle**, *bot′l*, *n.* a narrow-necked hollow vessel for holding liquids: the contents of such a vessel: liquor or drinking.—*v.t.* to enclose in bottles.—*adj.* **bott′led**, enclosed in bottles: shaped or protuberant like a bottle: kept in restraint: drunk (*slang*).—**bott′le-brush**, a brush for cleaning bottles, with bristles standing out from a central axis: a name given to various plants of like appearance, as horse-tail, mare's-tail, *Banksia*, and *Callistemon*; **bott′le-chart**, a chart showing currents from evidence of bottles thrown into the sea; **bott′le-coaster**, a bottle-slider; **bott′le-fish**, a fish, *Saccopharynx ampullaceus*, that can blow its body out like a bottle; **bott′le-gas**, liquefied butane gas in containers for use in lighting, cooking, heating, etc.; **bott′le-glass**, a coarse green glass used in the making of bottles; **bott′le-gourd**, or *false calabash*, a climbing, musky-scented Indian cucurbitaceous annual, whose fruit is shaped like a bottle, an urn, or a club.—*adj.* and *n.* **bott′le-green**, dark green, like bottle-glass.—*adj.* **bott′le-head**, a bottle-nosed whale; **bott′le-holder**, a boxer's attendant: a backer or supporter generally; **bott′le-imp**, an imp confined in a bottle; **bott′le-neck**, a narrow place in a road where traffic is apt to be congested (often *fig.*); **bott′le-nose**, a large swollen nose: a bottle-nosed toothed whale (Hyperoodon).—*adj.* **bott′le-nosed**.—**bott′le-party**, a more or less improvised drinking party where each brings a bottle.—*adj.* **bott′le-shouldered**, with sloping shoulders like a champagne bottle.—**bott′le-slider**, a tray for passing a decanter round the table; **bott′le-tree**, an Australian sterculiaceous tree with swollen trunk; **bott′le-washer**, one whose business it is to wash out bottles: a factotum generally.—**bottle off**, to draw from the cask and put into bottles; **bottle up**, to enclose as in a bottle: to hold back; **bring up on the bottle**, to rear artificially rather than by the breast; **pass the bottle of smoke**, to acquiesce in some falsehood: to make pretence; **three-bottle man**, one who could drink three bottles of wine without losing his decorum. [O.Fr. *bouteille*, dim. of *botte*, a vessel for liquids—L.L. *butis*, a vessel.]
**bottom**, *bot′əm*, *n.* the lowest part or surface of anything: that on which anything rests or is founded: the sitting part of the body: the bed of the sea, a river, etc.: the part that supports the contents of a vessel: the seat of a chair: the less dignified end: the foot of a page, hill, etc.: low land, as by a river: the lower part of a ship, hence the ship itself: groundwork: fundamental character or ingredient: staying power: financial resources: the portion of a wig hanging down over the shoulder: a ball of thread (Shak.).—*adj.* undermost.—*v.t.* to ground or base: to wind (Shak.).—*v.i.* to find bottom: to found, rest.—*adj.* **bott′omed**.—**bottom drawer**, a supposed receptacle for possessions hoarded by a

young woman against marriage; bott'om-fish, a fish that feeds on the bottom (also collectively); bott'om-glade (*Milt.*), a glade or open space in a bottom or valley; bott'om-grass (*Shak.*), grass growing on low grounds; bott'om-land (*U.S.*), alluvial deposits; bottomless pit, hell; bott'om-sawyer, the sawyer who works at the bottom of the saw-pit.—at bottom, fundamentally; at the bottom of, the real origin of; bet one's bottom dollar, to bet all one has; from the bottom of the heart, with heartfelt sincerity; get to the bottom of, to investigate exhaustively; stand on one's own bottom, to be independent; touch bottom, to reach the lowest point. [O.E. *botm*; Ger. *boden*; conn. with L. *fundus*, bottom, Gael. *bonn*, the sole.]

**bottony.** See botoné.

**botulism,** *bot'ū-lizm*, *n.* sausage-poisoning, or poisoning by tinned or other food infected with *Bacillus botulinus* (or *Clostridium botulinum*). [L. *botulus*, sausage.]

**bouche,** *boōsh*, (Fr.) the staff of cooks in a large house.

**bouché,** *boō-shā*, (Fr.) stoppered: corked while still fermenting.

**bouché,** *boō-shā*, (Fr.) a small patty.

**bouclé,** *boō'klā*, *n.* a yarn having the threads looped to give a bulky effect: a fabric made of such a yarn.—Also *adj.* [Fr., curled, looped.]

**boudoir,** *boōd'wär*, *n.* a lady's private room. [Fr. *bouder*, to pout, to be sulky.]

**bouderie,** *boō-d(ə)-rē*, *n.* (Fr.) pouting, sulking.

**bouffant,** *boō-fä*, (Fr.) puffed out, full, bulging.

**bouffe.** See opera-bouffe.

**Bougainvillaea,** *boōg-ən-vil'i-ə*, or *-vil-ē'ə*, *n.* a Neotropical genus of Nyctaginaceae, frequently trained over trellises, its triplets of flowers almost concealed by rosy or purple bracts.—Also **Bougainvil'ia.** [From the first French circumnavigator of the globe, Louis Antoine de *Bougainville* (1729-1811).]

**bouge.** A Shakespearian form of budge (vb.).

**bouget.** A Spenserian form of budget.

**bough,** *bow*, *n.* a branch of a tree: the gallows.—**bough'pot, bow'pot** (*arch.*), a pot for boughs as an ornament: a flower-pot: a bunch of flowers. [O.E. *bōg, bōh*, an arm, the shoulder; Ger. *bug*, shoulder, the bow of a ship—O.E. *būgan*, to bend.]

**bought, boughten.** See buy.

**bought,** *bowt*, *n.* a bight or bend: a twist or coil (*Spens.*): the bend of a sling. [See bight.]

**bougie,** *boō'zhē*, *n.* a wax candle: an instrument (orig. of waxed linen) for distending contracted mucous canals. [Fr.,—*Bougie* in Algeria.]

**bouillabaisse,** *boō-yä-bes'*, *n.* a Provençal kind of fish chowder, familiar through Thackeray's appreciative ballad. [Fr.]

**bouilli,** *boō-yē*, *n.* boiled or stewed meat.—*n.* **bouillon** (*boō-yɔ̃*), a strong broth. [Fr.; see boil.]

**bouillotte,** *boō-yot*, *n.* a gambling card game resembling poker. [Fr.]

**bouk,** *boōk*, (*Scot.*) *n.* body: bulk. [O.E. *būc*, belly, O.N. *būkr*, coalescing with bulk.]

**boulder,** *bōld'ər*, *n.* a large stone rounded by the action of water: a mass of rock transported by natural agencies from its native bed (*geol.*).—*adj.* containing boulders.—**bould'er-clay,** a stiff stony mass of finely ground rock, usually containing boulders and pebbles, formed as a ground moraine under land-ice. [Origin obscure; Sw. dial. *bullersten*, large stone in a stream, has been compared.]

**boule.** Same as buhl.

**boule,** *boō'lē*, *n.* in ancient Greece, a council or senate. [Gr. *boulē*.]

**boulevard,** *boōl'(ə-)vär*, *n.* a broad road, walk, or promenade bordered with trees, originally applied to those formed upon the demolished forti-

fications of a town: a broad main road.—*n.* **boulevardier** (*boōl-vär-dyā*), a frequenter of boulevards or promenades, chiefly of Paris, a man-about-town. [Fr.,—Ger. *bollwerk*; see bulwark.]

**bouleversement,** *boōl-vers-mä*, *n.* an overturning, overthrow, ruin. [Fr.]

**boult, bolt,** *bōlt*, *v.t.* to sift through coarse cloth: to examine by sifting.—*ns.* **bo(u)lt'er,** a sieve: a machine for separating bran from flour; **bo(u)lt'-ing.**—**bo(u)lting cloth,** a firm silk or nylon fabric with various mesh sizes used for boulting meal or flour, for embroidery, or for photographic enlargements; **bo(u)lt'ing-hutch,** a hutch or large box into which flour falls when it is bolted. [O.Fr. *bulter—buleter*, app. from *bure*—L.L. *burra*, a coarse reddish-brown cloth—Gr. *pyrrhos*, reddish.]

**boun, bowne,** *boōn, bown*, *v.t.* and *v.i.* (used *refl.*) to prepare: to get ready: to dress: to set out.—*adj.* ready. [See bound (4); revived by Scott.]

**bounce,** *bowns*, *v.i.* to jump or spring suddenly: to bound like a ball, to throw oneself about: to burst (into or out of a room, etc.): to boast, to exaggerate: to come back to one, as a cheque that cannot be cashed.—*v.t.* to beat (*obs.*): to cause to rebound: to turn out, eject, dismiss: to reprimand (*slang*): to bring to book.—*n.* a thud: a leap or spring: a boast: dismissal (*U.S.*): a bold lie.—*adv.* and *interj.* expressing sudden movement or the noise of a gun.—*n.* **bounc'er,** one who bounces: something big: a bully: a liar: a chucker-out: a cheque that bounces.—*adjs.* **bounc'ing,** large and heavy: lusty: swaggering; **bounc'y,** given to bouncing, cocky. [Du. *bonzen*, to strike, from *bons*, a blow.]

**bounce,** *bowns*, *n.* the lesser spotted dogfish.

**bound,** *bownd*, *pa.t.* and *pa.p.* of bind.—*n.* **bound'-bail'iff,** a sheriff's officer, so called from his bond given to the sheriff for the discharge of his duty.—**bound to,** obliged to: certain to (perhaps partly from bound (4)). In composition, restricted to or by, as *housebound, stormbound.*

**bound,** *bownd*, *n.* a limit: (in *pl.*) the limit of that which is reasonable or permitted: (in *pl.*) a borderland, land generally within certain understood limits, the district.—*v.t.* to set bounds to: to limit, restrain, or surround.—*adjs.* **bound'ed,** restricted, cramped; **bound'less,** having no limit: vast.—*ns.* **bound'lessness; bound'ary,** limit: border: termination: a hit to the limit of the ground (*cricket*): a score for such a hit.—**boundary layer,** the very thin layer of air on the surface of an aircraft in which the viscosity of the air affects its velocity, causing turbulence to build up and thereby increasing drag (**boundary-layer control,** removal of the boundary layer by a suction system or other means); **bound'ary-rider** (*Austr.*), one who rides around a station and repairs fences. [O.Fr. *bonne*—L.L. *bodina*; cf. Bret. *bonn*, a boundary.]

**bound,** *bownd*, *v.i.* to spring or leap.—*n.* a spring or leap.—*n.* **bound'er,** one who bounds: an obtrusively ill-bred man: one whose moral conduct is objectionable.—*adj.* **bound'ing,** moving forward with a bound: leaping.—**by leaps and bounds,** by startlingly rapid stages. [Fr. *bondir,* to spring, in O.Fr. to resound—L. *bombitāre.*j

**bound,** *bownd*, *adj.* ready, prepared (*obs.*): ready to start (for): on the way to (with *for*, or following an *adv.*, e.g. *homeward bound*). See also bound (1). [O.N. *būinn,* pa.p. of *būa*, to prepare; cf. boun.]

**bounden,** *bownd'n*, *adj.* obligatory. [Archaic pa.p. of bind.]

**bountree,** *boōn'tri.* See bourtree.

**bounty,** *bown'ti*, *n.* liberality in bestowing gifts: the gift bestowed: money offered as an inducement to enter the army, or as a premium to encourage any branch of industry, or (king's, or queen's bounty) to a mother who has three or more children at a birth.—*adjs.* boun'teous, boun'tiful, liberal in giving: generous.—*advs.* boun'teously, boun'tifully.—*ns.* boun'teousness, boun'tifulness; boun'tihood; boun'tyhed (*Spens.*).—Lady Bountiful, a character in Farquhar's *Beaux' Stratagem*: now used for the charitable great lady of a district. [O.Fr. *bontet* (*bonté*), goodness—L. *bonitās*, *-ātis—bonus*, good.]

bouquet, *book'ā*, or *-ā'*, *n.* a bunch of flowers: a nosegay: the perfume exhaled by wine.—*n.* bouquetiere (*boo-k(ə)-tyer*) a flower-girl.—bouquet garni (*boo-kā gär-nē*), a bunch or sachet of herbs used as flavouring, removed before serving (Fr., garnished bouquet.) [Fr. *bouquet*, dim. of *bois*, a wood; cf. It. *bosco*; see boscage, bush.]

bourasque, *boo-rask'*, *n.* a tempest. [Fr. *bourrasque*; It. *borasco*, a storm.]

Bourbon, *boor'bon*, *n.* a reactionary (*U.S.*): a race of roses: (without *cap.*; usu. *bûr'bən*) maize whisky (orig. made in Bourbon County, Kentucky).—*ns.* Bour'bonism; Bour'bonist, an adherent of the Bourbons.—Bourbon biscuit, two chocolate-flavoured pieces of biscuit with chocolate cream between. [From the *Bourbon* family, which long reigned in France and Spain.]

bourd, *boord*, (*obs.*) *n.* a jest, sport.—*n.* bourd'er (*obs.*), a jester. [O.Fr. *bourde*, origin unknown.]

bourdon, *boor'dən*, *n.* the refrain of a song: a drone bass: a bass stop in an organ or harmonium. [See burden.]

bourdon, *boor'dən*, (*obs.*) *n.* a pilgrim's staff: a club. [Fr.,—L.L. *burdō*, *-ōnis*, a mule.]

bourg, *boorg*, *n.* a town, esp. beside a castle: a market-town. [Fr.]

bourgeois, *bûr-jois'*, *n.* a type larger than brevier and smaller than longprimer. [Fr.; perh. from the name of the type-founder.]

bourgeois, *boorzh'wä*, *n.* a citizen: a member of the middle class: a merchant or shopkeeper.—*adj.* middle class: conventional: humdrum: conservative.—*n.* bourgeoisie (*boorzh'wä-zē,-zē'*), the middle class of citizens. [Fr. *bourgeois*, a citizen.]

bourgeon. See burgeon.

Bourignian, *boor-in'yən*, *adj.* of or pertaining to Antoinette *Bourignon* (1616-80), a religious visionary who made religion consist in inward emotion, not in knowledge or practice.

bourkha. Same as burk(h)a.

bourlaw. See byrlaw.

bourn, bourne, *boorn*, *bôrn*, *börn*, *n.* a boundary, a limit, or goal: domain (*Keats*). [Fr. *borne*, a limit.]

bourn, bourne. Same as burn (1).

bourrée, *boor'ā*, *-ā'*, *n.* a brisk dance in duple time, originating in Auvergne or in the Basque provinces: a musical composition in the same rhythm, often introduced in old suites. [Fr.]

bourse, *boors*, *n.* an exchange where merchants meet for business. [Fr. *bourse*. See purse.]

boursier, *boor-syā*, (Fr.) a foundation-scholar: a speculator on 'Change.

bourtree, *boor'tri*, (*Scot.*) *n.* the elder-tree.—Also boun'tree (*boon'tri*).—*n.* bour'tree-gun, a pop-gun made of an elder twig. [Ety. unknown.]

bouse, *booz*, *bowz*, *v.i.* and *n.* arch. form of booze.—*adjs.* bous'ing; bous'y, etc.—*n.* bous'ingken (*obs. thieves' slang*), a low drinking-shop.

bouse, bowse, *bows*, *v.t.* and *v.i.* to haul with tackle. [Orig. unknown.]

boustrophedon, *boo-* or *bow-strof-ē'don*, adj. and adv. (of ancient writing) ploughwise, alternately from right to left and from left to right. [Gr. *boustrophēdon—bous*, ox, *strophē*, a turning.]

bout, *bowt*, *n.* a turn, round: a spell: a trial: a fit. [bought (2).]

boutade, *boo-täd'*, *n.* a sudden outburst: a caprice. [Fr.,—*bouter*, to thrust.]

boutique, *boo-tēk'*, *n.* a shop: a department in a

shop: a tradesman's stock: about 1960, used esp. for a small, expensive, exclusive dress shop for women, but no longer so limited. [Fr.]

bouton, *boo-tŏ*, *n.* an enlargement of the end of a nerve fibre in contact with part of another nerve fibre.—*adj.* boutonné(e) (*-ton-ā*), reticent, buttoned-up.—*n.* boutonnière (*-to-nyer*), flower for the buttonhole, etc. [Fr., button.]

bouts rimés, *boo rē-mā'*, *n.pl.* rhyming words given out by some one as the line-endings of a stanza, for others to fill up the lines. [Fr., rhymed ends.]

bouzouki, *boo-zoo'ki*, *n.* a plucked metal-stringed instrument, used esp. in Greece.

bovate, *bō'vāt*, (*hist.*) *n.* an oxgang. [L.L. *bovāta—bōs*, *bovis*, an ox.]

bovine, *bō'vīn*, *adj.* pertaining to cattle: stupid, dull. [L. *bōs*, *bovis*, an ox or cow.]

bow, *bow*, *v.i.* to bend: to bend the neck or body in saluting, acknowledging a compliment, etc.: to submit.—*v.t.* to bend or incline downwards, to crush down: to usher with a bow: to express by a bow.—*n.* a bending of the neck or body in salutation.—*adj.* bowed (*bowd*), bent forward, esp. in the back.—a bowing acquaintance, a slight acquaintance; bow out, to withdraw from a place, situation, etc.; make one's bow, to retire ceremoniously: to leave the stage; take a bow, to acknowledge applause or recognition. [O.E. *būgan*, to bend; akin to L. *fugēre*, to flee, to yield.]

bow, *bō*, *n.* a piece of elastic wood or other material for shooting arrows, bent by means of a string stretched between its ends: anything of a bent or curved shape, as the rainbow: a yoke (*Shak.*): the instrument by which the strings of a violin, etc., are sounded: a ring of metal forming a handle: a knot with one or two loops: a looped knot of ribbons: a necktie or the like, so tied: a single movement (up or down) or stroke of the bow in playing an instrument.—*v.i.* to handle the bow in playing.—*v.t.* to play with a bow: to distribute between up-bows and down-bows: to mark such distribution.—*adjs.* bow'-backed, with bent back; bow'bent (*Milton*), bent like a bow.—*n.* bow'-boy, a boy archer: Cupid (*Shak.*).—*n.pl.* bow'compasses, a small pair of compasses, often with a bow-shaped spring instead of a hinge.—bow'fin, a North American freshwater fish (*Amia*) of the Holostei; bow'-hand, the hand in which the bow is held—normally in archery, the left, in violin-playing the right; bow'-leg, a bandy leg like a bow.—*adj.* bow'-legged.—bow'-man, an archer; bow'-saw, a saw with a narrow blade stretched like a bowstring in a strong frame; bow'shot, the distance to which an arrow can be shot from a bow; bow'string, the string by which a bow is drawn: a string with which the Turks strangled offenders: a horizontal tie on a bridge or girder.—*v.t.* to strangle with a bowstring (*pa.t.* and *pa.p.* bow'stringed, sometimes bow'strung).—*adj.* of, for, having, a bowstring.—bow'string-hemp, the genus Sansevieria or its fibre; bow'-win'dow, a window projecting in a curve: a pot-belly (*slang*).—*adj.* bow'-win'-dowed.—*n.* bow'yer, a bowman: a maker of bows.—draw the long bow, to make extravagant statements; on the bow hand, wide of the mark; two strings to one's bow, an alternative in reserve. [O.E. *boga*; cog. with Ger. *bogen*.]

bow, *bow*, *n.* the forepart of a ship—often used in *pl.*, the ship being considered to have starboard and port bows, meeting at the stem.—*ns.* bow'er, bow'er-anch'or, an anchor at the bow or forepart of a ship (*best-bower* and *small-bower*); bow'-oar, the oar nearest the bow.—bold, or bluff, bow, a broad bow; lean bow, a narrow one; on the bow, within 45° of the point right ahead. [From a L.G., Du. or Scand. word for shoulder; see bough.]

bowat, bowet, buat, *boo'ət*, (*Scot.*) *n.* a lantern.—

MacFarlane's buat (*Scott*), the moon. [L.L. *boeta*, box.]

**bowdlerise**, **-ize**, *bowd'lər-īz*, *v.t.* to expurgate a book or writing, by removing whatever might raise a blush, esp. to do so unnecessarily.—*ns.* **bowdlerisā'tion** (-iz); **bowd'leriser** (-iz); **bowd'-lerism**. [From Dr T. *Bowdler* (1754-1825), who published an expurgated Shakespeare in ten volumes in 1818.]

**bowel**, *bow'əl*, *n.* an interior part of the body: (in *pl.*) the entrails, intestines: the interior part of anything: the heart, pity, tenderness (the emotions being supposed to be seated in the bowels) (*obs. B.* and *Shak.*).—*v.t.* **bow'el**, to take out the bowels (*pr.p.* **bow'elling**; *pa.p.* and *pa.t.* **bow'-elled**). [O.Fr. *boel*—L. *botellus*, a sausage, an intestine.]

**bower**, *bow'ər*, *n.* a shady enclosure or recess in a garden, an arbour: an inner apartment: a lady's private room, boudoir: a dwelling (*poet.*).—*v.t.* to enclose: to embower (*Shak.*).—*v.i.* (*Spens.*) to lodge.—*adj.* **bow'ery**, having bowers: shady.—**bow'er-bird**, an Australian bird that makes a bower adorned with gay feathers, shells, etc; **bower'woman** (*arch.*), chambermaid. [O.E. *būr*, a chamber; root of *būan*, to dwell.]

**bower**, *bow'ər*, *n.* the name in euchre for the two highest cards, the knave of trumps, and the other knave of the same colour, the *right* and *left* bower respectively. [Ger. *bauer*, peasant.]

**bower**, **bower-anchor**. See bow (3).

**bowery**, *bow'ə-ri* (*U.S.*) *n.* a farm.—**the Bowery**, a street in New York. [Du. *bouwerij*.]

**bowes**. A Miltonic spelling of boughs.

**bowet**. Same as bowat.

**bowget**. A variant of budget.

**bowie knife**, *bō'i*, in U.S. *bōō'i*, *nif*, *n.* a strong, one-edged dagger-knife with a blade about twelve inches long. [From Colonel *Bowie*, its inventor, died 1836.]

**bowl**, *bōl*, *n.* a ball (*obs.*): a heavy wooden ball with a bias: (in *pl.*) a game played by rolling such balls on a green towards a jack: (in *pl.*) sometimes the game of skittles (ninepins) or American bowls (tenpins): (*Scot. bōōl*) a marble: (in *pl.*) the game of marbles.—*v.i.* to play at bowls or ninepins or tenpins: to roll or trundle: to travel swiftly and smoothly in a wheeled vehicle: to pitch the ball to the batsman at the wicket (*cricket*): to be bowler.—*v.t.* to roll or trundle: to deliver by bowling (*cricket*): to put out by hitting the wicket with a bowled ball (also with *out*: *fig.* to overcome).—*ns.* **bowl'er**, one who plays at bowls or bowls in cricket; **bowl'ing**. —**bowl'ing-all'ey**, a long narrow covered place for ninepin- or tenpin-bowling; **bowl'ing-crease** (see crease); **bowl'ing-green**, a smooth grassy plot for bowls.—**to bowl over**, to knock down: to overwhelm. [Fr. *boule*—L. *bulla*.]

**bowl**, *bōl*, *n.* a nearly hemispherical basin for domestic use: a large vessel for brewing punch: a round drinking-cup, rather wide than deep—hence a synonym for conviviality: the round hollow part of anything: the pocket of a pound-net. [O.E. *bolla*.]

**bowlder**, *bōld'ər*, *n.* Same as **boulder**.

**bowler**, *bō'lər*, *n.* a stiff felt hat with a roundish brim.—Also **bow'ler-hat'**.—*v.t.* (*slang*) to discharge, dismiss in civil dress. [Said to be name of a hatter who made it in 1850.]

**bowline**, *bō'lin*, *n.* a rope from the weather side of the square sails (to which it is fastened by *bridles*) to the larboard or starboard bow, to keep the sail close to the wind.—**bowline knot**, a simple but secure knot used in fastening the bowline bridles to the cringles. [M.L.G. *bōline*, M.Du. *boechlijne*.]

**bowpot**. Same as **boughpot**.

**bowr**, *bowr*, (*Spens.*) *n.* muscle. [bow, to bend.]

**bowse**. Same as **bouse**.

**bowser**, *bow'zər*, *n.* (*cap.*; *trademark*) an early form of petrol pump: a light tanker used for refuelling aircraft on an airfield.

**bowsprit**, *bō'sprit*, *n.* a strong spar projecting over the bows of a ship. [M.L.G. *bōgsprēt*, M.Du. *boechspriet*.]

**bowwow**, *bow'wow'*, *n.* a dog's bark: a full-mouthed literary style (*Scott*): a dog (*childish* or *facet.*). [Imit.]

**box**, *boks*, *n.* an evergreen shrub or small tree (*Buxus sempervirens*) with hard smooth yellowish wood, often used to border garden-walks and flower-beds (also **box'-tree**, **box'wood**): its wood (also **box'wood**): extended to various other plants, esp. the *Eucalyptus*.—*adj.* **box'en**, made of or like boxwood. [O.E. *box*—L. *buxus*—Gr. *pyxos*, the box-tree.]

**box**, *boks*, *n.* a case or receptacle for holding anything: the contents of a box: a fund: a (Christmas) present: \a compartment: a ruled off space: a pitcher's standing-place (*baseball*): a small house or lodge, as a *shooting-box*, etc.: in a theatre, a small enclosure with several seats: an old square pew or similar enclosure, as a *sentry-box*, *signal-box*, *bathing-box*, *witness-box*, etc.: the driver's seat on a carriage: the case of a ship's compass: a predicament.—*v.t.* to put into or furnish with boxes: to enclose: to panel, wainscot (*Scot.*): to overturn (a watchman) in his box (*slang*): to mix, as flocks of sheep (*Austr.*).—*n.* **box'ful**, as much as a box will hold: —*pl.* **box'fuls**.—**box'-bed**, a kind of bed long common in Scottish cottages, having its ends, sides and roof of wood, and capable of being closed in front by two sliding panels; **box'car**, (*U.S.*) a box-wagon; **box'-cloth**, a heavy cloth for riding garments; **box'-coat**, a heavy overcoat for coaching: **box'-day**, one of the Court of Session vacation days when papers ordered to be deposited in court must be lodged; **box'-gird'er**, a hollow, square or rectangular, girder.—*v.t.* **box'-haul**, to veer (a ship) by a particular method when circumstances make the usual method impractical.—**Boxing Day**, the day after Christmas, when boxes or presents are given; **box'-iron**, a hollow smoothing-iron heated by a heater put into it; **box junction**, an area at a cross-roads, marked by means of a square criss-crossed by diagonal lines, into which a vehicle must not move unless it can reach the other side before the lights change to red; **box'keeper**, an attendant who opens the doors of boxes at theatres, etc.; **box'-kite**, a kite composed of open-ended boxes; **box'-lobb'y**, the lobby leading to the boxes in a theatre; **box number**, a number to which replies to advertisements may be sent; **box'-office**, in a theatre, etc., the office at which seats may be booked: receipts from a play, etc.: ability to draw an audience: an attraction as judged by the **box-office**.—Also *adj.*—**box'-pleat**, a double fold of cloth turned opposite ways; **box'room**, a room in which boxes are stored; **box'seat**, a driver's seat; **box'-wag'on**, a closed railway wagon; **box'wallah** (see wallah), a pedlar: (*derogatorily*) a young man working in a business house in India.—**box the compass**, to name the 32 points in their order then backwards: hence to make a complete roundabout in any opinion; **in the wrong box**, in a false position, in a scrape; **the box**, the television set. [O.E. *box*—L. *buxem*, acc. of *buxis*—Gr. *pyxis*, a box.]

**box**, *boks*, *n.* a blow on the head or ear with the hand.—*v.t.* to strike with the hand or fist.—*v.i.* to fight with the fists.—*v.t.* and *v.i.* (*Scot.*) to butt.—*ns.* **box'er**, one who boxes or is skilled in boxing: a medium-sized, smooth-haired dog of a breed, with bulldog blood, developed in Germany, and used in war and as a police dog: (*cap.*) a member of a Chinese society hostile to foreigners—name arising from a Chinese phrase applied to them which meant 'righteous harmonious fist'; box'ing, the act or art of fighting with the fists: a combat with the fists; box'ing-glove, a padded glove worn in boxing. [Possibly connected with Gr. *pyx*, with the fist.]

**Box and Cox**, *boks and koks*, two people who never meet, or who alternate in a place, job, etc.—*adj.* and *adv.* alternating. [From play in which two men rent a room by night and day respectively; adapted (1847) by J. M. Morton from French farce, and made into comic opera by F. C. Burnand and A. S. Sullivan (1867).]

**box-calf**, *boks'-käf*, *n.* a chrome-tanned calfskin with rectangular markings made by rolling. [Said to be named after one Joseph *Box*, shoemaker.]

**boy**, *boi*, *n.* a male child: a lad: a young man generally: (Ireland and elsewhere) a man: a camp-follower (*Shak.*): knave (*obs.*): in some countries a native servant or labourer: a slave.—*v.t.* (*Shak.*) to play (a female part) as a boy.—*n.* **boy'hood.**—*adj.* **boy'ish.**—*adv.* **boy'ishly.**—*n.* **boy'ishness.**—**boy bishop**, a mock bishop formerly elected by choirboys or schoolboys, in office from St Nicholas' to Holy Innocents' Day (6th-28th December); **boy'friend**, a girl's favourite boy for the time being; **Boys' Brigade**, an organisation of boys for the promotion of habits of obedience, reverence, discipline, and self-respect; **(Boy) Scout**, a member of the (orig. Boy) Scouts Association, whose aim is to develop alertness and strong character; **boy's love**, southernwood; **boy's play**, trifling. [M.E. *boi*, *boy*; Fris. *boi*; Du. *boef*, Ger. *bube*.]

**boyar**, *bo-yär'*, *boi'är*, *n.* a member of the old Russian aristocracy next in rank to the ruling princes, before the reforms of Peter the Great. [Russ. *boyarin*.]

**boyau**, *bwo'yō*, *bwä'yō*, *boi'ō*, (*fort.*) *n.* a communication trench:—*pl.* bo'yaux. [Fr., bowel.]

**boycott**, *boi'kot*, *v.t.* to shut out from all social and commercial intercourse.—*n.* an act of boycotting, a kind of secular excommunication. [From Captain *Boycott* of County Mayo, who was so treated by his neighbours in Dec. 1880.]

**boyg**, *boig*, *n.* an ogre: an obstacle, problem, difficult to get to grips with. [Norw. *bøig.*]

**Boyle's law.** See law.

**boysenberry**, *boi'sn-ber-i*, *n.* a fruit growing on a bramble, a hybrid of certain raspberries and blackberries. [Rudolph *Boysen*.]

**bozzeto**, *bot-set'tō*, (It.) a small model or sketch of a projected sculpture.

**bra**, *brä*, *n.* short for **brassière**.

**brabble**, *brab'l*, (*arch.*) *v.i.* to babble or clamour: to brawl or wrangle.—*n.* a clamorous contest, a brawl (*Shak.*): a quibble.—*n.* **brabb'lement.** [Du. *brabbelen*, to stammer, to jabber.]

**braccate**, *brak'āt*, *adj.* having feathered legs or feet. [L. *brācātus*, wearing breeches.]

**braccio**, *brät'chō*, *n.* an Italian measure of length, more than half a metre:—*pl.* braccia (*brät'chä*). [It., lit. arm.]

**brace**, *brās*, *n.* armour for the arm (*Shak.*): anything that draws together and holds tightly: an instrument of wood or iron used by carpenters and metal-workers for turning boring tools: a mark (}) connecting words, lines, staves of music, indicating that they are taken together, and also used as a bracket in algebra: a pair or couple (esp. of game shot): (in *pl.*) a combination of straps for supporting the trousers: (in *pl.*) ropes for squaring or traversing horizontally the yards of a ship.—*v.t.* to tighten or strengthen, to give firmness to: to tone up: to embrace, encompass (*Spens.*).—*n.* **brac'er.**—*adj.* **brac'ing**, giving strength or tone. [O.Fr. *brace* (Fr. *bras*), the arm, power—L. *brāchium*, *brācchium*, Gr. *brāchiōn.*]

**bracelet**, *brās'lit*, *n.* an ornament for the wrist: a handcuff (*coll.*). [Fr. dim.,—L. *brāchiāle*—*brāchium*; see brace.]

**brach**, *brach*, *n.* a dog for the chase, a bitch hound.—*n.* **brach'et**, **bratch'et**, a brach: a whelp: a brat. [O.Fr. *brachet*, pl. *brachès*, dim. of *brac*—L.L. *braccō*, of Gmc. origin.]

**brachial**, *brāk'* or *brak'i-əl*, *adj.* of the arm.—*n.* **brachiā'tion**, use of arms as a supplementary means of locomotion.—**brachial artery**, the great arterial trunk supplying the upper extremity between the armpit and the elbow, direct continuation of the axillary artery. [L. *brāchium*; see brace.]

**brachiopod**, *brak'i-ō-pod*, *n.* a member of a class **Brachiopoda** (*-op'o-da*) of shelled animals allied to worms and Polyzoa, having usually two long arm-like processes serving to waft food particles to the mouth. [Gr. *brāchiōn*, an arm, and *pous*, *podos*, a foot.]

**brachistochrone**, *bra-kis'tō-krōn*, *n.* the curve along which a particle acted on by a force (e.g. gravity) will pass in the shortest time from one given point to another. [Gr. *brachistos*, superl. of *brachys*, short, *chronos*, time.]

**brachium civile**, *brā'kē-əm si-vi'lē*, *brā'ki-ōōm kē-wē'le*, (L.) the civil arm; **brachium seculare**, *sek-ū-lā'rē*, *sā-koō-lä're*, the secular arm.

**brachy-**, *brak'i-*, *-i'-*, in composition, short.—*ns.* **brachyax'is** (*crystal.*), brachydiagonal; **brachycephal** (*-sef'l*; Gr. *kephalē*, head), a short-headed person.—*adjs.* **brachycephalic** (*-si-fal'ik*), **brachycephalous** (*-sef'ə-las*), short-headed, having a skull whose breadth is 80 (or 78) per cent. or more of its length.—*n.* **brachyceph'aly**, short-headedness—opp. to *dolichocephaly*.—*adjs.* **brachydac'tyl**, **brachydactyl'ic**, **brachydac'tylous** (Gr. *daktylos*, finger, toe).—*ns.* **brachydac'tyly**, abnormal shortness of fingers and toes; **brachydiag'onal** (*crystal.*), the shorter lateral axis; **brach'ydome**, a dome parallel to the brachydiagonal; **brachyg'raphy**, certain old systems of shorthand; **brachyl'ogy**, condensed expression; **brachypin'akoid**, **brach'yprism**, a pinakoid, prism, parallel to the brachydiagonal.—*adjs.* **brachyp'terous** (Gr. *pteron*, wing), short-winged: short-finned.—*n.pl.* **Brachyura** (*-ū'ra*; Gr. *ourā*, tail), a group of decapod crustaceans having the abdomen reduced and bent forward under the thorax, the crabs.—*adjs.* **brachyu'ral**, **brachyu'rous**. [Gr. *brachys*, short.]

**brack**, *brak*, *n.* a flaw in cloth. [See break (1).]

**bracken**, *brak'ən*, *n.* a fern, esp. *Pteris aquilina*, the commonest British fern, abundant on hillsides, etc. [Ety. obscure.]

**bracket**, *brak'it*, *n.* a projecting support: a small shelf fastened to a wall: a gas-pipe projecting from a wall: in printing, one of the marks used to enclose words or mathematical symbols: one of the side pieces of a gun-carriage, supporting the trunnions: the space intervening between overestimated and underestimated shots at a target in straddling (*artillery*): a bracketed group.—*v.i.* to support by brackets: to enclose by brackets: to group, as in an honour list, implying equality: to straddle (*artillery*). [Fr. *braguette*—Sp. *bragueta*—L. *brāca*, sing. of *brācae*, breeches.]

**brackish**, *brak'ish*, *adj.* saltish, rather salt.—*n.* **brack'ishness.** [Du. *brak*, brackish; prob. the same as *brak*, refuse.]

**bract**, *brakt*, *n.* a leaf (often modified) that bears a flower in its axil.—*adj.* **bract'eal.**—*n.* **bract'-eate** (*archaeology*), a thin-beaten plate of gold or silver.—*adj.* of metal beaten thin: having bracts.—*adj.* **bract'eolate**, having bracteoles.—*n.* **bract'eole**, a small leaf on the axis of a flower.—*adj.* **bract'less.**—*n.* **bract'let**, a bracteole. [L. *bractea*, a thin plate of metal, gold-leaf.]

**brad**, *brad*, *n.* a small nail with a side projection

instead of a head.—*n.* **brad′awl,** a small boring tool. [O.N. *broddr,* spike.]

**Bradshaw,** *brad′shö, n.* a noted railway-guide, 1839-1961, first issued by George Bradshaw.

**brady-,** *brad′i-,* in composition, slow.—*n.* **bradycard′ia** (Gr. *kardiā,* heart), slowness of heartbeat.—*adj.* **bradypept′ic** (Gr. *peptikos,* digesting), slow of digestion.—Also *n.*—*n.* **brad′yseism** (*-sīzm*; Gr. *seismos,* a shake), a slow up and down movement of the earth's crust. [Gr. *bradys,* slow.]

**brae, brā,** (*Scot.*) *n.* the slope bounding a riverside plain: a hill-slope. [O.N. *brā,* eyelid; cf. **brow.**]

**brag,** *brag, v.i.* and *v.t.* to boast or bluster: (*pr.p.* **bragg′ing;** *pa.t.* and *pa.p.* **bragged**).—*n.* a boast or boasting: a thing one boasts of or is proud of: a card game like poker.—*adj.* or *adv.* (*Spens.*) proud, proudly.—*advs.* **bragg′ingly, brag′ly** (*Spens.*). [Origin doubtful.]

**bragadisme.** See under **braggart.**

**Braggadocio,** *brag-ə-dō′shi-ō, -chi-ō, n.* a braggart or boaster: empty boasting. [From *Braggadochio* (prob. *-dok′yō*) in Spenser's *Faerie Queene.*]

**braggart,** *brag′ərt, adj.* boastful.—*n.* a vain boaster. —*n.* **bragg′artism** (*Shak.* **bragadisme**), boastfulness. [Fr. *bragard,* vain, bragging.]

**Brahma,** *brä′mə, n.* a fowl of Chinese breed, modified in Europe and America. [*Brahmaputra,* whence it is said to have been brought.]

**Brahma,** *brä′mə* (*brä-mä′*), *n.* the supreme post-Vedic Hindu deity.—*n.* **Brah′man** (*-mən*), **Brah′min,** one of the highest or priestly caste among the Hindus: (*-min*; derog.) highly cultured person.—*adjs.* **Brahmanic** (*-man′*), **-al, Brahmin′ic, -al, Brah′minee,** appropriated to the Brahmans. —*ns.* **Brah′manism,** or **-min-,** one of the religions of India, worship of Brahma; **Brahmi** (*brä′mē*), an ancient Indian alphabet.—**Brahma Samaj** (*su-mäj′*) or **Brah′mo Somaj′,** a reformed Hindu theistic society or church, founded in 1830; **brahmin** (in U.S. **Brahman**) **bull, cow, zebu,** or **zebu cross.**

**braid, brād,** *v.t.* to jerk, whip out (*obs.*): to plait, intertwine: to arrange in plaits: to thread, wind about through: to trim, bind, or outline with braid.—*v.i.* (*obs.*) to start: to change colour or appearance.—*n.* a sudden movement, start (*obs.*): a plait, especially of hair: a band for the hair: a fabric woven in a narrow band: an interweaving, plaiting: embroidery.—*adj.* **braid′ed,** plaited: entwined: trimmed with braid: tarnished, faded (*obs.*).—*n.* **braid′ing,** plaiting: manufacture of braid: work in braid: embroidery: braids collectively. [O.E. *bregdan,* to move quickly, flash, change colour, plait, weave; O.N. *bregtha.*]

**braid, brād,** (*Shak.*) *v.t.* to upbraid, to reproach. [Prob. from **upbraid;** or **braid** (1).]

**braid, brād,** *adj.* Scots form of **broad.**

**braide, brād,** (*Shak.*) *adj.* dissembling, deceitful. [O.E. *brǣgd,* falsehood—*bregdan,* to weave.]

**Braidism,** *brād′izm,* (*arch.*) *n.* hypnotism. [From Dr James Braid, who practised in *c.* 1842.]

**brail, brāl,** *n.* a piece of leather to bind up a hawk's wing: (in *pl.*) the feathers about a hawk's rump: one of the ropes used to truss up a sail (*naut.*). —*v.t.* to haul in, as a sail, by pulling upon the brails. [O.Fr. *brail*—L. *brācāle,* a waist-belt—*brācae,* breeches.]

**Braille, brāl,** *n.* a kind of type in relief for the blind, having arbitrary signs consisting of varying combinations of six points arranged thus (::), there being sixty-three distinguishable combinations.—also *adj.* [From Louis *Braille,* the inventor (1809-52).]

**brain, brān,** *n.* (often in *pl.*) in vertebrates, that part of the central nervous system that is contained within the skull: in invertebrates, the nervous ganglia near the head end of the body:

the seat of the intellect and of sensation: the intellect (often used in *pl.*): a person of exceptional intelligence (*coll.*).—*v.t.* to dash out the brains of: to conceive of (*Shak.*).—*adjs.* **brain′ed,** having brains; **brain′ish** (*Shak.*), brainsick, hot-headed, furious; **brain′less,** without brains or understanding: silly; **brain′y,** well endowed with brains: intellectual.—*n.* **braini′ness.**—**brain′case,** the cranium; **brain′child,** an original thought or work; **brain coral,** a coral with brain-like convolutions; **brain drain,** continuing loss of citizens of high intelligence and creativity through emigration; **brain fag,** a tired condition of the nerves or brain; **brain fever,** a loose popular term which includes congestion of the brain and its membranes, delirium tremens, and inflammation of the brain substance itself; **brain′pan, brain′case.**—*adj.* **brain′sick,** diseased in the understanding, deranged.—*adv.* **brain′sickl′y** (*Shak.*).—**brain′-sickness; brain′storm,** sudden disturbance of the mind: sudden inspiration; **brains trust,** a committee of experts: a number of reputedly well-informed persons chosen to answer questions of general interest in public and without preparation; **brain′wash, -ing,** subjection of a person to systematic indoctrination or mental pressure with a view to getting him to change his views or to confess to a crime.—*v.t.* **brain′wash.**—**brain′-wave,** sudden bright idea: access of cleverness.— **brain-fever bird,** an Indian cuckoo that sings scales in the night; **on the brain,** as an obsession; **pick someone's brains** (see **pick** (1)). [O.E. *brægen;* Du. *brein,* dial. Ger. *bregen.*]

**braird, brārd, breer, brēr,** *n.* (orig. *Scot.*) the first shoots of corn or other crop.—*v.i.* to appear above ground. [O.E. *brerd,* edge.]

**braise, brāz,** *v.t.* to stew in a closed vessel. [Fr. *braiser.*]

**braise, braize, brāz,** *n.* a sea-bream or porgy. [Perh. conn. with **bream,** or with **bass(e).**]

**brake, brāk,** *adj.* obsolete *pa.t.* of **break.**

**brake, brāk,** *n.* a fern: a bracken. [Perh. **bracken.**]

**brake, brāk,** *n.* a thicket.—*adj.* **brak′y.** [Ety. obscure.]

**brake, brāk,** *n.* an instrument for breaking flax or hemp: a harrow: a contrivance for retarding by friction: a kind of vehicle (see **break** (2)).—*adj.* **brake′less,** without a brake.—**brake′-block,** a block pressed against a wheel as brake; **brake′-shoe,** the rubbing part of a brake; **brakes′-man,** the man whose business it is to manage the brake of a railway train; **brake′-van,** the carriage wherein the brake is worked; **brake′-wheel,** the wheel to which a brake is applied. [From root of **break,** cf. Du. *braak,* a flax-brake.]

**brake, brāk,** *n.* a handle, as of a pump: a lever for working a machine. [Prob. through O.Fr. *brac,* from L. *brāchium,* an arm.]

**brake, brāk,** (*Shak.*) *n.* an obscure word in *Measure for Measure* II, i. 39 (not made clearer by emendation of *ice* to *vice*).

**Bramah-press, brām′ə-pres,** *n.* a hydraulic press invented by Joseph *Bramah* (c. 1748-1814), inventor also of the **Bramah-lock,** etc.

**bramble, bram′bl,** *n.* the blackberry bush, a wild prickly shrub of the raspberry genus (*Rubus*): any rough prickly shrub: a blackberry (*Scot.*).— *adj.* **bram′bly.**—*ns.* **bram′ble-berry; bram′ble-bush,** blackberry bush or thicket; **bram′ble-finch, bram′bling,** a bird nearly allied to the chaffinch. [O.E. *brēmel;* Du. *braam,* Ger. *brombeere.*]

**brame, brām,** (*Spens.*) *n.* sharp passion, longing. [Prob. It. *brama.*]

**bran, bran,** *n.* the refuse of grain: the inner husks of corn sifted from the flour: the coarser part of anything.—*adj.* **brann′y.**—*n.* **bran′fulness.**— **bran′-mash; bran′-pie′, bran′-tub,** a tub of bran from which Christmas presents, etc., are drawn. [O.Fr. *bran*, bran, perh. Celt.]

**brancard**, *brangk'ərd*, *n.* a horse litter. [Fr.]

**branch**, *bränch*, *bränsh*, *n.* a shoot or arm-like limb of a tree: anything like a limb of a tree: any offshoot from a main trunk: a subdivision, a section or department of a subject: any subordinate division of a business, subsidiary shop, office, etc.: a tributary or brook (*U.S.*).—*v.t.* to divide into branches: to adorn with figures of branches, by embroidery or otherwise (*Spens.*, etc.).—*v.i.* to spread out as a branch (with *out*, *off*, *from*), or in branches.—*adj.* **branched**.—*ns.* **branch'er**, a young hawk or other bird when it leaves the nest and begins to take to the branches; **branch'ery**, branches collectively (*lit.* and *fig.*).—*n.* and *adj.* **branch'ing**.—*adj.* **branch'less**, without branches.—*n.* **branch'-let**, a little branch.—*adj.* **branch'y**.—**branch'-officer**, (*navy*; since 1949) any officer holding warrant; **branch'-pi'lot**, one who holds the Trinity House certificate; **branch'-work**, ornamental figured patterns.—**root and branch**, thorough(ly). [Fr. *branche*—L.L. *branca*, a beast's paw.]

**branchia**, *brangk'i-a*, *n.* a gill:—*pl.* **branchiae** (*-ē*).—*adjs.* **branch'ial**; **branch'iate**, having branchiae. [L. *branchia*—Gr. *branchion* (pl. *-a*).]

**Branchiopoda**, *brangk-i-op'o-da*, *n.pl.* a class or subclass of Crustacea with numerous flattened, leaf-shaped, lobed swimming-feet that serve also as breathing organs.—*n.* and *adj.* **branch'iopod**. [Gr. *branchia*, gills, *pous*, *podos*, foot.]

**brand**, *brand*, *n.* a piece of wood burning or partly burned: an instrument for branding: a mark burned into anything with a hot iron: a trademark, made by burning or otherwise, as on casks: a particular class of goods (as if distinguished by a trademark): a sword, from its glitter: a mark of infamy: a general name for the fungoid diseases or blights of grain crops (*bunt*, *mildew*, *rust*, and *smut*).—*v.t.* to burn or mark with a hot iron, or otherwise: to fix a mark of infamy upon.—*adj.* **brand'ed**.—*n.* **brand'er** (*Scot*), a gridiron.—*v.t.* to cook on the gridiron.—*adjs.* **brand'ered**, **brand'ering**.—*ns.* **brandise** (*brand'is*; O.E. *isen*, iron), a trivet; **brand'ling**, a salmon-parr: an earthworm banded in red and yellow, found in dunghills, used by anglers; **brand'reth** (O.N. *brandreith*—*reith*, carriage), a stand of wood for a cask or hayrick: a rail round a well.— **brand'ing-i'ron**; **brand'-i'ron**, a gridiron: an iron to brand with: a trivet or tripod to set a pot or kettle upon: (*Spens.* brondyron, etc.) a sword.— *adj.* **bran(d)'-new**, quite new (as if newly from the fire).—**a brand from the burning**, one snatched out of a pressing danger—from Amos iv. 11. [O.E. *brand*, *brond*, O.N. *brandr*, from root of **burn**.]

**brandish**, *brand'ish*, *v.t.* to wave or flourish as a brand or weapon.—*n.* a waving or flourish. [Fr. *brandir*, *brandiss-* from root of **brand**.]

**brandy**, *brand'i*, *n.* an ardent spirit distilled from wine.—*adj.* **bran'died**, heartened or strengthened with brandy.—**brand'y-ball**, a kind of sweet; **brand'y-bott'le** (*dial.*), candock; **brand'y-paw'nee** (Hind. *pānī*, water), brandy and water; **brand'y-snap**, a thin gingerbread biscuit flavoured with brandy. [Formerly *brand-wine*—Du. *brandewijn*—*branden*, to burn, to distil, and *wijn*, wine; cf. Ger. *branntwein*.]

**brangle**, *brang'gl*, (*arch.*) *v.i.* to wrangle.—*n.* a brawl.—*n.* **brang'ling**, disputing. [Fr. *branler*.]

**brank**, *brangk*, *n.* buckwheat. [Pliny says *brance* (doubtful reading, perh. *brace*) is the Gallic name of a kind of corn.]

**brank**, *brangk*, *v.i.* to prance, toss the head: to strut or swagger.—*adj.* **brank'y** (*Scot.*), showy. [Prob. a variant of **prank**.]

**branks**, *brangks*, *n.pl.*, rarely in *sing.* (*Scot.*) a

**bridle**: a scold's bridle, having a hinged iron framework to enclose the head and a bit or gag. [Ety. very obscure; O.Fr. *bernac* (see **barnacle** (2)); Ger. *pranger*, pillory, Du. *prang*, fetter, have been compared.]

**brankursine**, *brangk'ər-sin*, or *-ûr'*, *n.* acanthus, or bear's-breech. [L.L. *branca ursina*, a bear's paw.]

**bran-new.** See **brand**.

**bran(s)le.** See **brawl** (2).

**brant-goose.** See **brent-goose**.

**brantle**, *brant'l*. See **brawl** (2).

**brasero**, *brä-sā'rō*, *n.* a brazier: a place for burning criminals or heretics. [Sp.,—*brasa*, a live coal.]

**brash**, *brash*, *n.* angular fragments of rock, which occasionally form the basement bed of alluvial deposits: fragments of crushed ice: clippings of hedges or trees.—*adj.* **brash'y**. [Prob. Fr. *brèche*.]

**brash**, *brash*, *n.* an eructation or belching of acid water from the stomach—water-brash: a sudden burst of rain: a slight attack of illness (*Scot.*): an attack or bout (*obs.*).—*v.t.* (*obs.*) to disturb. [Prob. onomatopoeic.]

**brash**, *brash*, *adj.* reckless, impetuous (*U.S.*): forward, bumptious: bold: of wood, brittle (*U.S.*).

**brasier.** Same as **brazier**.

**brass**, *bräs*, *n.* an alloy of copper and zinc: bronze (*obs.*): effrontery (*fig.*): money (*slang*): an article or fixture of brass: a monumental plate of brass, commonly with effigy: (*collectively* and in *pl.*) the brass wind-instruments or their players in an orchestra or band.—*adj.* of brass.—*adv.* **brass'ily**.—*ns.* **brass'iness**; **brass'y**, a brass-soled wooden golf-club (also **brassie**); a bronze-coloured fish, the bib or pout.—*adj.* like brass in appearance, hardness, sound, or otherwise: brazen-faced.—**brass band**, a band of players of (mainly) brass wind instruments: a small military band; **brass'-bounder**, a midshipman: a privileged apprentice on a ship for whom a premium is paid (from his gold braid); **brass farthing**, a whit; **brass'founder**, one who casts objects in brass; **brass'founding**; **brass hat** (*mil. slang*), a staff officer (with gold braid on his hat); **brass tacks**, details of practical business.—**brass**, **brass hats**: those in authority at the top. [O.E. *bræs*.]

**brassard**, *bras'ärd*, *n.* a piece of armour for the arm (also **brassart**, *bras'ərt*, **brass'et**): an armband or armlet: a symbolic band for the arm. [Fr.—*bras*, arm.]

**brasserie**, *bras'(ə-)rē*, *n.* a beer garden or restaurant. [Fr., brewery.]

**Brassica**, *bras'i-ka*, *n.* the turnip and cabbage genus of Cruciferae. [L., cabbage.]

**brassière**, *bras'i-er*, in U.S. sometimes *brə-zēr'*, *n.* a woman's undergarment supporting the breasts. [Fr.]

**brast**, *obs.* and *Northern* for **burst** (*pr.t.*, *pa.t.*, and *pa.p.*).

**brat**, *brat*, *n.* a contemptuous name for a child: an annoying child: any over-garment of coarse cloth (*obs.*): a child's pinafore (*obs.*): an apron (*obs.*).—*n.* **brat'ling**, a little brat.—*adj.* **bratt'ish**. [O.E. *bratt*, prob. Old Ir. *brat*, plaid, Gael. *brat*, apron.]

**bratchet**, *brach'it*, *n.* See **brach**.

**brattice**, *brat'is*, **brattish**, *brat'ish*, **brettice**, *bret'is*, *n.* in mediaeval siege operations, a fixed tower of wood: a covered gallery on a castle wall, commanding the wall-face below (in these senses also **bretesse**, *bri-tes'*, **bretasche**, *bri-tash'*): wooden partition: a wooden lining: a partition to control ventilation in a mine.—*v.t.* to furnish with a brattice.—*ns.* **bratt'icing**, **bratt'ishing**, work in the form of brattices: cresting, or ornamental work along a ridge, cornice or coping (*archit.*).—*n.* **bratt'ice-cloth**, strong tarred cloth

used for mine brattices. [O.Fr. *breteshe*—L.L. *bretachia*; cf. **bartisan**.]
**brattle,** *brat'l, n.* a clattering noise: a quarrel: tumult.—*v.i.* to make a clattering noise.—*n.* and *adj.* **bratt'ling.** [Imit.]
**braunch.** An old spelling of **branch**.
**bravado,** *brav-ä'dō, n.* a display of bravery: a boastful threat: a swaggerer (*obs.*):—*pl.* **brava'do(e)s.**—*v.i.* to display bravado. [Sp. *bravada*; see **brave**.]
**brave,** *brāv, adj.* daring, courageous: noble: making a fine appearance: finely dressed, showy, handsome (*Scot.* braw): a general word for excellent.—*v.t.* to meet boldly: to defy: to face (out).—*n.* a bully (*arch.*): a bravo (*arch.*): a hired assassin (*arch.*): a brave soldier, esp. among the North American Indians: bravado (*arch.*).—*adv.* bravely (*poet.*).—*adv.* **brave'ly.**—*n.* **brav'ery,** bravado (*obs.*): courage: heroism: finery, showy dress. [Fr. *brave*; It. and Sp. *bravo*; origin unknown.]
**bravo,** *brä'vō, n.* a daring villain: a hired assassin: —*pl.* **bravo(e)s.**—*interj.* well done: excellent (also **bra'va** when addressed to a woman, **bravi,** *-vē,* to a number of persons). [Sp. and It.]
**bravura,** *brä-vōō'rä, n.* spirit and dash in execution (*mus.*): a florid air with difficult and rapid passages (*mus.*): brilliant or daring display.— Also *adj.* [It.]
**braw,** *brö, adj.* fine: attired in finery.—*adv.* **braw'ly.**—*predicative adj.*—very well.—*n.pl.* **braws,** fine clothes. [Scots form of **brave**.]
**brawl,** *bröl, n.* a noisy quarrel.—*v.i.* to quarrel noisily: to make a disturbance: to murmur or gurgle.—*n.* **brawl'er.**—*n.* and *adj.* **brawl'ing.** [M.E. *bralle,* of doubtful origin; perh. conn. with Du. *brallen,* Ger. *prahlen,* to boast.]
**brawl,** *bröl, n.* an old French dance or dancetune.—Also **branle, bransle, brantle.** [Fr. *branle*.]
**brawn,** *brön, n.* muscle, esp. of the arm or calf of the leg: thick flesh: muscular strength: a boar: a preparation of meat made from pig's head and ox-feet, cut up, boiled, and pickled.— *adj.* **brawned.**—*n.* **brawn'iness,** quality of being brawny: muscularity.—*adj.* **brawn'y,** fleshy: muscular: strong. [O.Fr. *braon,* flesh (for roasting); cf Gmc. origin, cf. Ger. *braten,* to roast.]
**braxy,** *brak'si,* (*Scot.*) *n.* a bacterial disease of sheep: applied loosely to various diseases of sheep: a sheep so infected: its flesh.—Also *adj.*—**braxy mutton,** the flesh of a braxy sheep or generally of a sheep that has died of disease or accident. [Prob. orig. pl. of *brack,* variant of **break**.]
**bray,** *brā, v.t.* to break, pound, or grind small, as in a mortar.—*n.* **bray'er,** an instrument for grinding or spreading ink in printing. [O.Fr. *breier* (Fr. *broyer*).]
**bray,** *brā, n.* the cry of the ass: any harsh grating sound.—*v.i.* to cry like an ass: to give forth harsh sounds, esp. of the trumpet.—*n.* **bray'er.** [O.Fr. *brai, brait*; *braire*—L.L. *bragĭre,* perh. of Celt. origin.]
**braze,** *brāz, v.t.* to cover with, or make like, brass. —*adj.* **bra'zen,** of or belonging to brass: impudent.—*v.t.* to face (out) with impudence.—*adv.* **brā'zenly.**—*ns.* **brā'zenness, brā'zenry,** effrontery; **bra'zier** (*brāz'yǝr, brāzh'(y)ǝr*), a worker in brass. —**brā'zen-face,** one remarkable for effrontery.— *adj.* **brā'zen-faced.** [brass.]
**braze,** *brāz, v.t.* to join with hard solder.—*adj.* **braze'less,** without soldering.—*n.* **brazier** (*brāz'-yǝr, brāzh'(y)ǝr*), a vessel or tray for hot coals. [O.Fr. *braser,* to burn; perh. influenced by **brass**. Cf. **braise, brasero**.]
**brazier.** See **braze** (1) and (2).
**brazil,** *bra-zil', n.* usually **brazil'-wood,** the hard reddish wood of the East Indian sappan tree or other species of *Caesalpinia,* used in dyeing: also that of *Guaiacum.*—*n.* **Brazil'ian,** a native or

citizen of Brazil, in South America.—*adj.* of Brazil.—*ns.* **Brazilian wax,** carnauba; **Brazil nut,** the edible seed of a large lecythidaceous Brazilian tree (*Bertholletia*). [O.Fr. *bresil* (Sp. *brasil,* It. *brasile*)—L.L. *brasilium,* a red dye-wood brought from the East, itself prob. a corr. of some Oriental word. When a similar wood was discovered in South America the country became known as *terra de brasil,* land of red dye-wood.]
**breach,** *brēch, n.* a break: an act of breaking: an opening, or discontinuity: a breaking of law, contract, covenant, promise, etc.: a quarrel: a broken condition or part of anything: a gap made in a fortification: surf.—*v.t.* to make a breach or opening in.—**breach of promise,** often used simply for breach of promise of marriage; **breach of the peace,** a violation of the public peace by riot or the like. [O.E. *bryce, brice,* related to **break**.]
**bread,** *bred, n.* food made of flour or meal baked: food: livelihood: money (*slang*).—*n.* **bread-and-butt'er,** bread sliced and buttered: livelihood. —*adj.* connected with making a living or with the consumption of bread-and-butter: materialistic, practical: youthfully insipid: descriptive of a letter of thanks for hospitality.—**bread'-basket,** a basket for holding bread: the stomach (*slang*); **bread'berry,** a sop of bread in hot milk; **bread'-chipper** (*Shak.*), one who chips bread, an under-butler; **bread'-corn,** corn of which bread is made; **bread'-crumb,** the inner parts of a loaf: bread crumbled down as for dressing food (also in *pl.*).—*v.t.* to cover with bread-crumbs.—**bread'fruit,** the fruit of a moraceous tree (*Artocarpus incisa*) of the South Sea Islands, which when roasted forms a good substitute for bread; **bread'nut,** the fruit of a tropical American tree (*Brosimum alicastrum*) akin to the bread-fruit tree, used as bread when boiled or roasted; **bread'room,** an apartment in a ship's hold where the bread is kept; **bread'root,** the prairie-turnip, a North American papilionaceous plant (*Psoralea esculenta*) with an edible root: also the yam; **bread study,** any branch of study taken up as a means of gaining a living; **bread'stuff,** bread in any form: any material of which bread is made; **bread tree,** a name for various trees whose seeds or pith yield a substitute for bread, e.g. *Kaffirbread*; **bread'winner,** one who earns a living for a family.—**bread and circuses,** translation of panem et circenses (q.v.); **bread buttered on both sides,** very fortunate circumstances; **know which side one's bread is buttered on,** to know how to act from self-interest; **on the breadline,** at subsistence level, with just enough to make ends meet (from breadline, a queue of poor or derelict people waiting for free food, esp. from government sources); **take the bread out of one's mouth,** to deprive of the means of living. [O.E. *brēad,* prob. from a Gmc. root meaning a fragment; cf. Scots use of **piece**.]
**breaded.** See **brede**.
**breadth,** *bredth, n.* extent from side to side: width: liberality of mind: in art, subordination of details to the harmony of the whole.—*adv.* **breadth'ways, -wise,** in the direction of breadth: broadside on. [O.E. *brǣdu;* Ger. *briete;* see **broad**.]
**break,** *brāk, v.t.* to divide, part, or sever, wholly or partially, by applying a strain: to rupture: to shatter: to crush: to make by breaking: to destroy the continuity or integrity of: to interrupt (a fall, journey, etc.): to bruise or penetrate the surface of: to break a bone in, or separate the bones of: to subject, overcome, or wear out: to tame or habituate to obedience (also with *in*): to crush the spirit of: to cure (of a habit): to violate (as a law, promise, bounds, prison): to set aside (a will): to cut up (an animal's body): to unfurl: to impart (esp. with delicacy): to

make bankrupt: to degrade or cashier: to arpeggiate: to cause to change from a simple vowel to a diphthong.—*v.i.* to separate, come apart, or go to pieces, esp. with suddenness: to give way: to start away: to burst forth: to force a passage: to pass suddenly into a condition or action (as into laughter, revolt, sweat, spots): to become variegated or striped: to open or come into view (as day, hope, a scene): (of news) suddenly to become generally known: to become bankrupt: to crack (as the voice): to collapse: to burst into foam: to sever a connection: to fall out (with a friend): to change direction (as a cricket-ball on pitching): to change from a simple vowel to a diphthong under influence of a neighbouring sound: (*pa.t.* brōke, *arch.* brāke; *pa.p.* brōk′en, less usu. brōke).— *n.* an act of breaking: the state of being broken: an opening: a discontinuity: a pause, interval, or interruption: a consecutive series of successful strokes (*billiards, croquet*): the number of points so scored at billiards: a continuous run of anything: the deviation of a ball on striking the pitch (*cricket*): the dawn (*break of day*): onset (of the monsoon): a social blunder (*U.S.*): a chance (as in *an even break*, a fair or equal chance): a good chance.—*adj.* break′able.— Also *n.*, in *pl.*—*ns.* break′ableness; break′age, act of breaking or its consequences: a broken place; break′er, a person or machine that breaks: a wave broken on rocks or shore.—*n.* and *adj.* break′ing.—break′away, revolt: secession: stampede, stampeding animal (*Austr.*).— *adj.* break′back, crushing.—breakbone fever, dengue; break′down, a stoppage through accident: collapse: disintegration: a vigorous and noisy Negro dance or the like: an analysis; breakdown gang, wreckage clearers after an accident.—*adjs.* break′-jaw, very difficult to pronounce accurately; break′neck, headlong: threatening to break the neck.—break′-prom′ise, break′-vow (both *Shak.*), one who habitually breaks promises or vows; break′through, a forcible passage through a barrier: solving of a problem, esp. scientific, after much effort, opening the way to further developments: any comparable success; break′-up′, dissolution; break′water, a barrier against force of waves; break′-wind, a wind-break.—break a jest, to utter a jest; break a lance with, to enter into a contest with; break away, to go away, escape, abruptly: to sever connection forcibly or abruptly: to be scattered, as clouds after a storm; break bulk, to open the hold and take out a portion of the cargo: to begin to use goods supplied in bulk; break cover, to burst forth from concealment, as a fox; break down, to demolish: crush: collapse: fail completely: analyse; break even, to avoid loss but fail to gain; break forth, to burst out, issue; break ground, to begin working untouched ground: to lead in new work: break in, to make (shoes, etc.) less stiff by use; break in, in upon, or into, to enter violently: to interpose abruptly; break loose, to extricate oneself forcibly: to break through all restraint; break no squares, to make no difference, do no harm, matter little; break off, to detach by breaking: to put an abrupt end to: to leave off abruptly; break one's mind, to communicate one's thoughts to somebody; break out, to appear suddenly: to break through all restraint: to come into sudden activity: to become covered with (with *in*); break sheer (said of a ship riding at anchor), to be forced by wind or tide out of a position clear of the anchor; break the balls (or simply break; *billiards*), to open the game by striking the red ball or giving a miss, or to continue the game thus when a similar position occurs; break the heart, to crush with grief; break the ice (*fig.*), to

get through first difficulties, esp. restraint on first meeting; break through, to force a passage through (a barrier); break up, to break open: to break in pieces: to go to pieces: to put an end to: to disperse: to dig or plough up: to decay in health or faculties; break upon the wheel, to punish by stretching on a wheel and breaking the bones; break wind, to void wind; break with, to cease relations with, esp. to quarrel with: to cease adherence to (tradition, a habit). [O.E. *brecan*; Ger. *brechen*.]

break, brake, *brāk, n.* a long wagonette: a carriage frame all wheels and no body, used in breaking in horses. [break, *v.t.*]

breaker, *brāk′ər, n.* a small water-cask, used on shipboard. [Prob. Sp. *bareca*, barrel.]

breakfast, *brek′fast, n.* a break or breaking of fast: the first meal of the day.—*v.i.* to take breakfast.—*v.t.* to furnish with breakfast.—break′- fast-set, the china or other ware used at breakfast; break′fast-table.

bream, *brēm, n.* a freshwater fish of the carp family, with high-arched back: a fish of the family Sparidae (sea-bream): a fish (Ray's bream, *Brama raii*) akin to the mackerel: extended to other fishes. [O.Fr. *bresme* (Fr. *brême*)—O.H.G. *brahsema* (mod. Ger. *brassen*).]

bream, *brēm, v.t.* to clean, as a ship's bottom, by burning off seaweed, shells, etc. [Prob. conn. with broom, Du. *brem*.]

breare, *brēr, (Spens.) n.* Same as brier.

breast, *brest, n.* the forepart of the human body between the neck and the belly: one of the two mammary glands in women (or rudimentary in men), forming soft protuberances on the chest: the corresponding part of any animal: a swelling slope: conscience, disposition, affections (*fig.*): voice (*obs.*).—*v.t.* to oppose the breast to: to oppose manfully: to mount.—*adj.* breast′ed, having a breast.—*n.* breast′bone, the sternum, the bone running down the middle of the breast, to which the first seven ribs are attached.—*adv.* breast′-deep, deep, as up to the breast.—*n.* breast′-girdle, the pectoral girdle.—*adv.* breast′- high, high as the breast: breast-deep.—breast′- knot, a knot of ribbons worn on the breast; breast′pin, an ornamental pin for the breast; breast′plate, a plate or piece of armour for the breast: an embroidered square of linen with precious stones worn on the breast of the Jewish high-priest (*B.*); breast′plough, a kind of spade for cutting turf, with a cross-bar against which the breast is pressed; breast′rail, the upper rail of a breastwork; breast′stroke, a stroke made in swimming on the breast; breastsummer, bressummer (*bres′ə-mər*), a summer or beam supporting the whole, or a great part, of the front of a building in the manner of a lintel; breast wall, a retaining wall; breast wheel, a water-wheel turned by water delivered upon it at about half its height; breast′work, a hastily constructed earthwork.—make a clean breast, to make a full confession. [O.E. *brēost*; Ger. *brust*, Du. *borst*.]

breath, *breth, n.* the air drawn into and then expelled from the lungs: power of breathing: life: a single act of breathing: breathing without vibrating the vocal cords (*phon.*): a sound so produced: the time occupied by one breathing: a very slight breeze.—*adj.* produced by breath without voice.—*adjs.* breathed (*bretht*), having a breath (esp. in compounds, as long-breathed, see also under breathe); breath′ful (*Spens.*), full of breath or air, also full of scent or odour; breath′less, out of breath: with the breath held or taken away, from excitement, interest, etc.: breezeless: dead.—*adv.* breath′lessly.—*n.* breath′- lessness.—*adj.* breath′y, of a speaking voice, accompanied by much unvocalised breath: of a singer or instrument-player, without proper breath control, causing impure sound.—*adv.* **breath′ily.**—*n.* **breath′iness.**—*n.* **breathalyzer** (in *Britain*, usu. **breathalyser**), *breth′ə-li-zər*, an American machine which indicates amount of alcohol in a person's breath, by means of a chemical reaction whose extent is indicated by a moving pointer: a simpler device also using a chemical reaction.—*adj.* **breath′taking**, astounding.—**above one's breath**, aloud; **below, under, one's breath**, in a low voice; **catch the breath**, to stop breathing for an instant; **out of breath**, having difficulty in breathing; **spend or waste one's breath**, as in profitless talk; **take breath**, to recover freedom of breathing: to stop for breath, rest, or refreshment; **take one's breath away**, to render one breathless through astonishment, delight, etc; **with bated breath**, with breath restrained from reverence or fear. [O.E. *brǣth*; Ger. *brodem*, steam, breath.]

**breathe**, *brēdh*, *v.i.* to draw in or expel breath or air to or from the lungs or other respiratory organs: to respire: to take breath, to rest or pause: to live.—*v.t.* to draw into or expel from the lungs: to infuse: to give out as breath: to utter by breath: to utter softly, whisper: to express: to keep in breath, to exercise: to tire by some brisk exercise.—*adj.* **breathed** (*brēdhd*), pronounced without voice (see also under **breath**).—*ns.* **breath′er**, one who breathes or lives: a spell of exercise: a rest to recover breath; **breath′ing**, the act of breathing: aspiration, secret prayer: respite: one or other of two signs used in Greek to signify presence ('rough breathing') or absence ('smooth breathing') of the aspirate.—*adj.* lifelike.—**breath′ing-space**, **breath′ing-time**, time to breathe or rest: a brief respite; **breath′ing-while**, time sufficient for drawing breath: any very short period.— **breathe again**, to be relieved from an anxiety; **breathe freely**, to be at ease; **breathe upon**, to tarnish the name of. [From **breath**.]

**breccia**, *brech′yä*, *n.* a rock composed of angular fragments.—*adj.* **brecciated** (*brech′i-ā-tid*) reduced to or composed of breccia. [It.]

**brecham**, *brehh′əm*, (*Scot.*) *n.* a horse-collar. [O.E. *beorgan*, to protect, *hama*, covering.]

**bred**, *bred*, *pa.t.* and *pa.p.* of **breed**.

**brede**, *brēd*, *n.* and *v.t.* an archaic form of **braid**. —*pa.t.* and *adj.* (*Spens.*) **bread′ed.**

**bree**, *brē*, *n.* (*Scot.*) the eyebrow. [O.E. *brǣw*, *brēaw*; cf. Ger. (*augen*) *braue*; and **brae**.]

**bree**, *brē*, *n.* the liquor in which anything has been boiled. [O.E. *briw*; cf. **barley** (2), Ger. *brei*.]

**breech**, *brēch*, *n.* (almost always in *pl.*, **breeches**, *brich′iz*; in Amer. also **britches**), a garment worn by men on the lower parts of the body—strictly, as distinguished from trousers, coming just below the knee, but often used generally for trousers: the lower part of the body behind (*arch.*): the hinder part of anything, esp. of a gun (*pl.* in these senses pron. *brēch′iz*).—*v.t.* (*brich, brēch*) to put into breeches: to flog.—*adj.* **breeched.**— *n.* **breeching** (*brich′ing*), a part of a horse's harness attached to the saddle, coming round the breech and hooked to the shafts: a strong rope attached to the breech of a gun to secure it to a ship's side.—*adj.* (*Shak.*), subject to whipping. —*adj.* **breech′less**, trouserless.—**breech birth**, **breech delivery**, one in which the breech comes first; **Breeches Bible**, the Geneva Bible (*q.v.*), with 'breeches' for 'aprons' in Gen. iii. 7; **breech′es-buoy**, a life-saving apparatus enclosing the person like a pair of breeches; **breeches part** (*theat.*), a part in which an actress wears men's clothes; **breech′-loader**, a firearm loaded by introducing the charge at the breech instead of the muzzle.—*adj.* **breech′-loading.**—**wear the breeches** (said of a wife), to be master. [O.E. *brēc*, pl. of *brōc*; cf. Ger. *bruch*, Du. *broek*.]

**breed**, *brēd*, *v.t.* to generate or bring forth: to cause or promote the generation of, or the production of breeds of: to train or bring up: to cause or occasion.—*v.i.* to be with young: to produce offspring: to be produced or brought forth: to be in training (*Scot.*):—*pa.t.* and *pa.p.* **bred.**—*n.* that which is bred, progeny or offspring: a strain, variety or race: a kind.—*ns.* **breed′er**; **breed′ing**, act of producing: education: manners.—**breed′-bate** (*Shak.*), one who foments debate or strife; **breeder reactor**, a nuclear reactor capable of creating more fissile material than it consumes in maintaining the chain reaction.—**breeding in-and-in**, in-breeding, breeding from near kin. [O.E. *brēdan*, to cherish, keep warm; Ger. *brüten*, to hatch.]

**breeks**, *brēks*, *n.pl.* Scots form of **breeches**, trousers.

**breer.** See **braird.**

**breeze**, *brēz*, *n.* a light wind: a disturbance or quarrel: a whispered rumour.—*v.i.* to blow as a breeze: to go briskly (*slang*).—*adjs.* **breeze′less**; **breez′y**, fanned with or subject to breezes: bright, lively, exhilarating.—**to breeze up, to** freshen into a breeze; **get the breeze up, to** get the wind up (see **wind** (1)). [Old Sp. *briz*, north-east wind.]

**breeze, breese, brize**, *brēz*, *n.* a gadfly, botfly, or other dipterous pest of horses and cattle. [O.E. *briosa.*]

**breeze**, *brēz*, *n.* furnace refuse used in making for building **breeze brick**, **breeze blocks**, **breeze** concrete. [Perh. O.Fr. *brese.*]

**bregma**, *breg′ma*, *n.* the part of the skull where the frontal and the two parietal bones join—sometimes divided into the right and left bregmata:— *pl.* **breg′mata.**—*adj.* **bregmat′ic.** [Gr.]

**brehon**, *brē′hon*, *n.* an ancient Irish judge.—**Brehon Law(s)**, the system of jurisprudence in use among the Irish until near the middle of the 17th century. [Ir. *breitheamh*, pl. *breitheamhuin*.]

**breloque**, *brə-lok′*, *n.* an ornament attached to a watch-chain. [Fr.]

**breme, breem**, *brēm*, (*Spens.*) *adj.* fierce, keen. [Perh. related to O.E. *brēman*, to rage.]

**bremsstrahlung**, *brem′shträ-lŏong*, *n.* electromagnetic radiation produced when an electron collides with, or is deflected by, a positively charged nucleus. [Ger. *bremse*, brake, *strahlung*, radiation.]

**bren, brenne, bren,** (*obs.*) *v.t.* and *v.i.* to burn: (*pa.t.* and *pa.p.* **brent**).—*adj.* **brent.** [See **burn** (2).]

**Bren (gun), bren, bren (gun),** *n.* a light machine-gun. [*Brno*, Brünn, in Czechoslovakia, and *Enfield*, in Middlesex.]

**brent, brent,** (*Scot.*) *adj.* lofty: steep: smooth, unwrinkled. [O.E. *brant*, steep; O.N. *brattr.*]

**brent-goose**, *brent′-gōōs*, *n.* a small wild goose, having the head, neck, long wing feathers, and tail black, the belly white, the rest slaty-grey, often confounded with the barnacle goose.— Also **brant′-goose**, or **brent barnacle.** [Prob. *branded*, brindled.]

**brer**, *brûr*, *n.* a Negro pronunciation of **brother.**

**brere**, *brēr*, (*Spens.*) *n.* a form of **brier.**

**bressummer.** Same as **breastsummer.**

**bretasche, bretesse.** See **brattice.**

**brethren**, *bredh′rən*, *pl.* of **brother.**

**Breton**, *bret′ən*, *n.* a native of Brittany (*Bretagne*), France: the Celtic tongue of Brittany, Brezonek: a woman's hat with a rounded crown and turned-up brim.—*adj.* of Brittany: Armoric.

**brettice.** See **brattice.**

**Bretwalda**, *bret-wöl′da*, *n.* a title of certain kings of old English kingdoms, whose superiority over the others was more or less acknowledged. [Prob. Lord of the *Britons*, or of *Britain*.— O.E. *walda*, ruler.]

**breve**, *brēv*, *n.* a pope's letter: the mark (⏑) of a short vowel, opp. to *macron*: an obsolescent note, ‖ ○ ‖, twice as long as the longest now used (the semibreve), but half (or in 'perfect' time one-third) as long as the obsolete long (*mus.*). [L. *brevis*, short.]

**brevet**, *brev'it*, *n.* a military commission entitling an officer to take rank above that for which he receives pay.—*v.t.* to confer such rank on:—*pr.p.* **brev'eting**; *pa.t.* and *pa.p.* **brev'eted** (those who pronounce *bri-vet'* write **brevett'ing, brevett'ed**). [Fr.,—L. *brevis*, short.]

**brevet d'invention**, *brə-ve dē-vā-syɔ̃*, (Fr.) a patent. **breveté**, *brəv-tā*, (Fr.) patented.

**breviary**, *brēv'i-ər-i*, *n.* a book containing the daily service of the R.C. Church. [L. *brĕviārium* —*brevis*, short.]

**breviate**, *brē'vi-āt*, *n.* a short compendium: a lawyer's brief. [L. *brĕviātus—brĕviāre*, to shorten.]

**brevier**, *brə-vēr'*, *n.* a type (8-point) between bourgeois and minion, said (doubtfully) to have been used for breviaries.

**brevi manu**, *brē'vī mān'ū*, *bre'wē man'ōō*, (L.) with a short hand, off-hand.

**brevipennate**, *brev-i-pen'ət*, *adj.* of birds, having short wings. [L. *brevis*, short, *penna*, wing.]

**brevity**, *brev'it-i*, *n.* shortness: conciseness. [L. *brevitās*, *-ātis—brevis*, short.]

**brew**, *brōō*, *v.t.* to prepare by infusion, boiling and fermentation, as beer from malt and other materials, or by infusion, mixing, or boiling, without fermentation, as tea, punch: to contrive or plot. —*v.i.* to perform the operation of brewing ale or beer: to be gathering or forming.—*n.* a brewing: a brewage: a variety of making of a brewed beverage: a variety.—*ns.* **brew'age**, something brewed: mixed liquor; **brew'er**, one who brews; **brew'ery**, a place for brewing; **brew'ing**, the act of making liquor from malt: the quantity brewed at once; **brew'ster** (now mainly *Scot.*; orig. *fem.*), a brewer.—**brew'-house**, a brewery. [O.E. *brēowan*; cf. Ger. *brauen*.]

**brewis**, *brōō'is*, (*arch.* and *dial.*) *n.* broth, esp. beef broth: bread soaked in broth, fat, gravy, or the like. [O.Fr. *broez*, influenced by O.E. *briw*, bree.]

**Brezonek**, *brez'ə-nek*, *n.* See Breton.

**briar.** See brier (1) and (2).

**Briard**, *brē-är(d)*, *n.* a large, heavy, hairy dog of a French breed. [*Brie*, district in N.E. France.]

**Briarean**, *bri-ā'ri-ən*, *adj.* relating to *Briareus* (Gr. *Briārēos*), a hundred-handed giant: hence many-handed. [Gr. *briāros*—strong.]

**bribe**, *brib*, *n.* spoil (*obs.*): something offered to influence the judgment unduly or corrupt the conduct.—*v.t.* to steal (*obs.*): to influence by a bribe: to gain over.—*v.i.* to practise bribery.— *ns.* **brib'er**, one who bribes.—**brib'ery**, the act of giving or taking bribes.—**brib'ery-oath**, an oath taken by an elector that he had not been bribed. [O.Fr. *bribe*, a lump of bread; origin dub.]

**bric-à-brac, bricabrac**, *brik'ə-brak*, *n.* old curiosities, knick-knacks, or other treasured odds and ends. [Fr.]

**brick**, *brik*, *n.* baked or 'burned' clay: a shaped block of burned clay, generally rectangular (the standard dimensions being $9 \times 4\frac{1}{2} \times 3$ inches): a brick-shaped block of other material, often compressed: a child's building block of wood, etc.: a loaf or a bun more or less in the shape of a brick: a spirited good fellow (*slang*).—*v.t.* to build (*in*, *up*, etc.) with brick: to cover with brick or an appearance of brick.—*adj.* **brick'en**, made of brick—*n.* **brick'ing**, brickwork: imitation brickwork.—*adj.* **brick'y**, like or of brick.— **brick'bat**, a piece of brick, esp. as a missile; **brick'-clay**, a clay containing sand and a good deal of iron: any clay, loam, or earth used for brick-making; **brick'-dust**, powdered brick: the colour of powdered red brick; **brick'-earth'**, a clayey silt or loam used for brick-making;

**brick'field**, a place where bricks are made; **brick'fielder** (*Austr.*), a hot dry wind (orig. one bringing dust from the brickfields of Sydney suburbs); **brick'kiln**, a kiln in which bricks are made; **brick'layer**, one who builds with bricks; **brick'laying**; **brick'maker**; **brick'making**; **brick'-nog, -nogging** (see nogging).—*adjs.* **brick'-red**, of the colour of an ordinary red brick; **brick'shaped**, of the shape of a standard brick.— **brick'-tea'**, tea pressed into cakes; **brick'work**, work constructed in brick: bricklaying: a factory for bricks; **brick'yard**, a brickfield.— **drop a brick**, to make an undisguisable and horrifying blunder in speech or action; **like a ton of bricks**, heavily and promptly; **make bricks without straw**, to try to do a piece of work without the materials necessary for it: to make something that will not last; **see through a brick wall**, to be unusually perspicacious. [Fr. *brique*, from the root of break.]

**brickle**, *brik'l*, (*Spens.* and *Scot.*) *adj.* apt to break : weak: troublesome. [Cf. bruckle.]

**brickwall**, *brik'wöl*, a corruption of bricole.

**bricole**, *brik'əl*, or *-ōl*, or *brik-ōl'*, *n.* an ancient engine for throwing stones: the rebound of a ball from the wall of a tennis-court: an indirect stroke: a similar stroke in billiards. [Fr.,—L.L. *briccola*.]

**bridal**, *brid'əl*, *n.* a marriage feast: a wedding.— *adj.* belonging to a bride or a wedding: nuptial. [O.E. *brȳdealo*, lit. bride-ale; see bride and ale (feast).]

**bride**, *brid*, *n.* a woman about to be married or newly married.—*v.i.* and *v.t.* (with *it*; *Shak.*) to act the bride.—**bride'-ale** (*arch.*; see bridal), the ale-drinking at a marriage feast; **bride'-bed**, the marriage bed; **bride'cake**, **bride's'-cake**, a cake distributed at a wedding; **bride'-chamber**, a nuptial apartment: the room in which a wedding is performed; **bride'groom**, a man about to be married or newly married; **bride'maid(en)**, **bride's'-maid**, **brides'maid**, **bride'man**, **bride's'-man**, **brides'man**, young unmarried people who attend the bride and bridegroom at a wedding. [O.E. *brȳd*; O.N. *brūthr*, Ger. *braut*.]

**bridewell**, *brid'wəl*, *n.* a house of correction: a gaol. [From a palace near *St Bride's Well* in London.]

**bridge**, *brij*, *n.* a structure spanning a river, road, etc. giving communication across it: the narrow raised platform whence the captain of a ship gives directions: a thin upright piece of wood supporting the strings in a violin or similar instrument: the bony part of the nose: a support for a billiard cue: a bridge-like structure by which false teeth are borne by natural teeth or roots: in the theatre, a platform that rises above the stage: anything that connects across a gap. —*v.t.* to be or to build a bridge over: to connect the extremities of (a gap) (*fig.*): to make an electrical connection between.—*n.* **bridg'ing**, provision of credit necessary for a business transaction: a method of keeping balance on overhanging rock.—Also *adj.*—*adj.* **bridge'less**. —**bridge'board**, a notch-board; **bridge'head**, a fortification covering the end of a bridge nearest to the enemy's position: a place suitable for such fortification: any advanced position seized in enemy territory; **bridge'-house**, a house at the end of a bridge; **bridge'-of-boats'**, a bridge resting on boats moored abreast across a piece of water. [O.E. *brycg*; Ger. *brücke*, O.N. *bryggja*.]

**bridge**, *brij*, *n.* a modification of whist in which the dealer or his partner chooses the trump-suit, or no-trumps, and the dealer plays his partner's hand as a dummy, with peculiarities in scoring— superseded by *auction bridge* and *contract bridge*.—**bridge'-drive**, a tournament of bridge-playing; **Bridgerama**, an apparatus which shows on large electronically-lit boards the steps of a bridge game in progress in another room; as a card is played, light behind it is switched off. [Earlier known as *bridge whist*, *biritch*; etymology unknown.]

**bridie**, *brī'di*, (*Scot.*) *n.* a meat turnover.

**bridle**, *brīd'l*, *n.* the apparatus on a horse's head by which it is controlled: any curb or restraint: a movement expressing resentment, scorn, or vanity—a throwing back of the head with a forward tilt, like a horse pulled up by the bridle.— *v.t.* to put a bridle on: to manage by a bridle: to check or restrain.—*v.i.* to make the movement described (often with *up*; *at* the thing taken amiss).—*n.* **bri'dler**, one who governs or restrains as by a bridle.—**bri'dle-hand**, the hand that holds the bridle in riding—the left hand; **bri'dle-path, -road,** a path or way for horsemen; **bri'dle-rein,** the strap of a bridle.—**bite on the bridle,** to be impatient, like a restive horse. [O.E. *bridel*; O.H.G. *brittel.*]

**bridoon**, *brid-ōōn'*, *n.* the light snaffle usual in a military bridle in addition to the ordinary bit, controlled by a separate rein. [Fr. *bridon—bride*, a bridle.]

**Brie**, *brē*, *n.* a white, soft cheese made in *Brie*, N.E. France.

**brief**, *brēf*, *n.* a summary of a client's case for the instruction of counsel: a writ: a short statement of any kind: instructions: (in *pl.*) close-fitting legless pants.—*adj.* short: concise.—*v.t.* to issue instructions to.—*n.* **brief'ing**, action, or an instance, of making or giving a brief: instructions.—*adj.* **brief'less.**—*adv.* **brief'ly.**—*n.* **brief'-ness.**—**brief'-bag, -case,** a small case for carrying briefs, or for other papers, etc.—**hold a brief,** to be retained as counsel: to assume the attitude of advocate rather than judge; **in brief,** in few words; **king's briefs,** royal mandates ordering collections to be made in chapels for building churches, etc.; **papal brief,** a papal document issued without some of the solemnities proper to bulls; **take a brief,** to undertake a case; **the brief and the long** (*Shak.*), the short and the long; **to be brief,** to speak in a few words. [Fr. *bref*—L. *brevis*, short.]

**brier, briar,** *brīr*, *brī'ər*, *n.* a prickly shrub: a wild rose bush.—Also (*Spens.*, etc.) **brere** (*brēr*).—*adjs.* **briered, briared,** caught in, covered with, briers; **brier'y,** thorny: abounding in, beset with, briers.—**sweet brier,** eglantine, a wild rose (*Rosa rubiginosa*) with scented leaves. [O.E. (Anglian) *brēr* (W.S. *brǣr*).]

**brier, briar,** *brī'ər*, *n.* the white heath, a shrub grown in Algeria: a tobacco-pipe made of its root.—*ns.* and *adjs.* **bri'er-root, -wood.** [Fr. *bruyère*, heath.]

**brig**, *brig*, *n.* a two-masted, square-rigged vessel: a place of detention on board ship (*U.S. navy*): a prison (*U.S. slang*). [Shortened from *brigantine.*]

**brig**, *brig*, *n.* Scots form of **bridge** (1).

**brigade**, *brig-ād'*, *n.* a body of troops consisting of a group of regiments, battalions, or batteries commanded by a general officer: a band of people more or less organised.—*v.t.* to form into brigades: to organise, esp. oppressively.—*n.* **brigadier,** (*brig-ə-dēr'*), formerly **brigadier'-gen'eral,** a general officer of the lowest grade, who has command of a brigade: (*brē-gä-dyä*), in the French army, a lance-corporal.—**brigade'-mā'jor,** a staff-officer attached to a brigade. [Fr. *brigade*—It. *brigata*—L.L. *briga*, strife.]

**brigand**, *brig'ənd*, *n.* a bandit or freebooter.—*ns.* **brig'andage, brig'andry,** freebooting: plundering: **brigandine, brigantine** (*brig'ən-dēn, -tēn*), a coat-of-mail of steel rings or plates sewed upon linen or leather. [Fr.,—It. *brigante—briga*, strife.]

**brigantine**, *brig'ən-tēn*, *n.* a two-masted vessel,

with the main mast of a schooner and the foremast of a brig. [Fr. *brigantin*—It. *brigantino*, pirate ship.]

**bright**, *brit*, *adj.* shining: full of light: vivid: clear: beautiful (*arch.*): cheerful: vivacious: clever: illustrious.—*adv.* brightly: clearly.—*v.t.* and *v.i.* **bright'en,** to make or grow bright or brighter: to clear up.—*adv.* **bright'ly.**—*n.* **bright'ness.**—*adj.* **bright'some,** bright: brilliant.—**bright and early,** in good time. [O.E. *byrht, beorht*; cog. with Goth. *bairhts*, clear, L. *flagrāre*, to flame.]

**Bright's disease,** *brits diz-ēz'*, *n.* a generic name for diseases of the kidneys with albumen in the urine. [From Dr Richard *Bright* (1789-1858).]

**brigue**, *brēg*, *v.i.* to intrigue.—*n.* strife: intrigue.—*n.* **briguing** (*brēg'ing*), canvassing. [Fr. *brigue.*]

**brill**, *bril*, *n.* a fish akin to the turbot, spotted with white. [Ety. unknown.]

**brilliant**, *bril'yənt*, *adj.* sparkling: glittering: splendid: superlatively bright, having a dazzling hard lustre: of outstanding or conspicuous ability: showily, strikingly, or superficially clever: performing or performed in a hard or showy manner or with great display of technical skill: brilliant-cut.—*n.* a diamond or other gem cut in a many-faceted form resembling two truncated cones base to base: a very small type (about 4-point).—*ns.* **brill'iance, brill'iancy; brill'iantine,** a dressing for making the hair glossy.—*adv.* **brill'iantly.**—*n.* **brill'iantness.** [Fr. *brillant*, pr.p. of *briller*, to shine, which like Ger. *brille*, eyeglass, is from L.L. *beryllus*, a beryl.]

**brim**, *brim*, *n.* the margin or brink of a river or lake: the upper edge of a vessel: the rim of a hat.—*v.t.* to fill to the brim.—*v.i.* to be full to the brim: *pr.p.* **brimm'ing;** *pa.t.* and *pa.p.* **brimmed.**—*adj.* **brim'ful, brim'-full',** full to the brim: brimming with tears.—*n.* **brim'ful(l')ness.**—*adjs.* **brim'less,** without a brim; **brimmed,** brim-full: having a brim (used also in composition).—*n.* **brimm'er,** a bowl full to the brim.—*adv.* and *adj.* **brimm'ing.** [M.E. *brymme.*]

**briming**, *brē'ming, bri'*, (*dial.*) *n.* phosphorescence of the sea. [Origin unknown.]

**brimstone**, *brim'stən*, *n.* sulphur: a virago (*fig.*): (in full, **brimstone butterfly**) a common yellow pierid butterfly (*Gonepteryx rhamni*).—*adj.* **brim'stony.** [Lit. burning stone; from O.E. *brȳne*, a burning—*byrnan*, to burn, and **stone;** cf. Ger. *bernstein.*]

**brinded, brindled,** *brin'did, brin'dld*, **brindle,** *brin'dl*, *adjs.* marked with spots or streaks.—*n.* **brin'dle,** state of being brindled. [See **brand.**]

**brindisi,** *brin'di-zi, brēn-dē'zē*, (It.) a toast: a drinking-song.

**brine**, *brin*, *n.* very salt water: the sea.—*v.t.* to treat with brine.—*adjs.* **brin'ish,** like brine: somewhat salt; **brin'y,** pertaining to brine or to the sea: salt.—**the briny** (*coll.*), the sea.—**brine'-pan, -pit,** a pan or pit in which brine is evaporated to obtain salt: a salt spring: **brine'-shrimp,** a small phyllopod crustacean of salt-lakes and brine-pools. [O.E. *brȳne*, a burning.]

**bring**, *bring*, *v.t.* to fetch: to cause to come: to persuade: to adduce or institute (as an argument, charge, action):—*pa.t.* and *pa.p.* **brought** (*bröt*).—*ns.* **bring'er; bring'ing.—bringings forth** (*Shak.*), the fruits of his own actions; **bringing up,** upbringing, rearing, training.—**bring about,** to bring to pass, effect: to turn round; **bring down,** to humble: to shoot: to overthrow: to lower; **bring down the house,** to call forth a general burst of applause; **bring forth,** to give birth to, produce; **bring forward,** to advance: in book-keeping (used in *pa.p.*) to transfer (a partial sum) to the head of the next column; **bring home,** to prove: to impress; **bring in,** to introduce: to yield: to pronounce (a verdict); **bring off,** to bring away, as by a boat from a ship, to rescue: to achieve: **bring on**, to induce: to cause to advance; **bring out**, to make clear, or prominent: to put before the public, as a book, a play, a singer: to introduce (a young woman) formally into so-called society; **bring over**, to convert; **bring round**, to restore from illness or unconsciousness: to win over; **bring to**, to restore to consciousness: to bring to a standstill (*naut.*); **bring under**, to subdue; **bring up**, to rear or educate: to introduce to notice: to make prominent: to vomit; **bring up the rear**, to come last. [O.E. *bringan*, to carry, to bring; allied perh. to bear.]

**brinjal**, *brin'jöl*, *n.* the egg-plant, or its fruit.— Corrupted **brown jolly**. [Sans. *vātiṅgaṇa*, through Pers., Ar. and Port.]

**brinjarry**, *brin-jär'i*, *n.* a travelling dealer in grain and salt, in Southern India. [Urdu *bānjāra*.]

**brink**, *bringk*, *n.* the edge or border of a steep place or of a river: often *fig.*—**brink'man**, one who practices **brink'manship**, the action or art of going to the very edge of, but not into, war or other disaster in pursuit of a policy. (First used 1956 following statement by J. Foster Dulles that U.S. Diplomacy had three times walked to the brink of war.) [Prob. Dan. *brink*, declivity.]

**brio**, *brē'ō*, *n.* liveliness, vivacity, spirit. [It.]

**brioche**, *brē-osh'*, *n.* a sponge cake or roll. [Fr.]

**briony**. Same as bryony.

**briquette**, *bri-ket'*, *n.* a brick-shaped block made of coal-dust: a small brick-shaped slab. [Fr. *briquette*, dim. of *brique*, brick.]

**brise-soleil**, *brēz-sol-ā'*, (Fr.) a louvred screen to keep sunlight from walls and windows of buildings.

**brisk**, *brisk*, *adj.* spruce (*obs.*): pert (*obs.*): full of life and spirit: lively: promptly active: sharp: effervescing.—*v.t.* and *v.i.* to make or become brisk: to move briskly.—*v.t.* and *v.i.* brisk'en, to make or become brisk.—*adjs.* brisk'ish, brisk'y (*Shak.*).—*adv.* brisk'ly.—*n.* brisk'ness. [First found in Shakespeare's time; poss. Welsh *brysg*, brisk of foot; perh. Fr. *brusque*.]

**brisket**, *bris'kit* (*Scott*, breaskit, *bres'kit*), *n.* the breast: the part of the breast next to the ribs. [Perh. conn. with Fr. *brechet*, *brichet*.]

**brisling**, *bris'ling*, *n.* a Norwegian sprat. [Norw., sprat.]

**brissel-cock**, *bris'l-kok*, (*obs. Scot.*) *n.* a fowl conjectured to be the turkey. [Origin unknown.]

**bristle**, *bris'l*, *n.* a short stiff hair.—*v.i.* to stand erect, as bristles: to be set as with bristles: to have or set bristles erect: to show rage or resistance (*fig.*).—*v.t.* to cover, as with bristles: to make bristly: to erect (as bristles):—*pr.p.* brist'ling; *pa.t.* and *pa.p.* brist'led.—*adj.* brist'led. furnished with bristles.—*n.* brist'liness.—*adj.* brist'ly, set with bristles: rough.—**brist'le-fern'**, a filmy fern (*Trichomanes radicans*) with a bristle on the receptacle; **brist'le-tail**, any insect of the Thysanura; **brist'le-worm**, a chaetopod.—**to set up one's bristles**, to show resistance. [Conn. with O.E. *byrst*; Scot. *birse*; cog. with Ger. *borste*, O.N. *burst*.]

**Bristol**, *bris'tl*, *n.* a city with status of a county on the border between Gloucestershire and Somerset.—**Bris'tol-board'**, a smooth pasteboard; **Bris'tol-brick'**, an earthy material for scouring cutlery, like bath-brick; **Bris'tol-di'amond**, a kind of quartz crystal found near Bristol; **Bris'tol-milk'**, sherry (17th-cent. joke). —**Bristol fashion**, in good order.

**brisure**, *brizh'yər*, *brē-zür'*, *n.* any part of a rampart or parapet which breaks off at an angle from the general direction (*fort.*): a variation of a coat-of-arms showing the relation of a younger to the main line (*her.*). [Fr.—*briser*, to break.]

**brit**, *brit*, *n.* a young herring, sprat, or other fish.

**Britannic**, *brit-an'ik*, *adj.* pertaining to Britannia or Britain (*arch.*, surviving officially in *Britannic*

*majesty*).—**Britannia**, a seated female figure with a trident and helmet, representing Britain or the British Commonwealth.—**Britannia metal**, an alloy, mainly tin with copper, antimony, lead or zinc or a mixture of these, similar to pewter. [L. *Britannia*, *Brittan(n)ia*, Great Britain or the British Islands.]

**britches**. See breech.

**British**, *brit'ish*, *adj.* pertaining to Britain, to its former or present inhabitants or citizens, or to the empire or commonwealth of nations of which it is the nucleus.—*n.* the language of the ancient Britons: Welsh.—*v.t.* and *v.i.* **Brit'icise, -ize**, to make or become British or like the British: to assimilate to the British.—*ns.* **Brit'ishism**, **Brit'icism** (*-sizm*), an expression characteristic of the English spoken in Britain; **Brit'isher** (orig. *U.S.*), a native or citizen of Britain.—**British gum**, dextrin; **British plate**, a kind of German silver; **British Standard Time**, (1968-70) time one hour ahead of Greenwich Mean Time; **British thermal unit** (see heat); international value 1055·06 joules; **British warm** (see warm). [O.E. *Brettisc* —*Bret*, a Briton, Welshman.]

**Briton**, *brit'ən*, *n.* one of the Brythonic inhabitants of Britain before the coming of the English, or one of their present representatives the Welsh: a native or citizen of Great Britain or of any of the associated states: a Breton (rare):—*fem.* (*Spens.*) **Brit'oness**. [L. *Brittō*, *-ōnis*, or *-ōnis*; see Brythonic.]

**brittle**, *brit'l*, *adj.* apt to break: easily broken: frail.—*n.* britt'leness.—**britt'le-star**, an ophiuroid or sand-star. [O.E. *brēotan*, to break.]

**britzka**, **britzska**, **britska**, *brits'kə*, **britschka**, *brich'kə*, *n.* an open four-wheeled carriage with one seat. [Polish *bryczka*.]

**brize**. See breeze (2).

**broach**, *brōch*, *n.* a tapering, pointed instrument, used chiefly for boring or rounding holes: a spit: (also broach-spire) a church spire, now restricted to one without parapets, consisting of a tall octagonal and a low square pyramid interpenetrating each other: a visible corner of the square pyramid in such a spire.—*v.t.* to pierce as a cask, to tap; to open up or begin: to utter.—*n.* broach'er, a broach or spit: one who broaches or utters.—**broach the admiral**, to steal some liquor from a cask in transit or in store; **broach to** (*naut.*), to turn to windward. [Fr. *broche*; cf. brooch.]

**broad**, *bröd*, *adj.* wide: large, free or open: outspoken: coarse, indelicate: liberal minded: widely diffused: giving prominence to main elements, or harmony of the whole, without insisting on detail: slow and full-toned: strongly marked in pronunciation or dialect.—*n.* the broad part: (in East Anglia) a lake-like expansion of a river: a woman (*slang*): sometimes, a prostitute (*slang*).—*advs.* broad, broad'ly.—*v.t.* and *v.i.* broad'en, to make or grow broad or broader.—*adj.* broad'ish.—*n.* broad'ness.— **broad'-arr'ow**, a mark (↑) on government property; **broad'-bean'**, the common bean, (*Vicia Faba*); **broad'-brim**, a hat with a broad brim, such as those once worn by Quakers: a Quaker (*coll.*).—*adj.* broad'cast, scattered or sown over the general surface: dispersed widely: communicated generally, by word of mouth, pamphlets, radio, TV, or any other means: by means of broadcast.—*adv.* in all directions.—*n.* sowing by broadcasting: general dissemination: the sending forth of material by radio or TV for reception by the public.—*v.t.* and *v.i.* to scatter broadcast or freely: to disseminate by any means, esp. by radio or TV transmission:—*pa.t.* and *pa.p.* broad'cast, by some broad'casted.—*ns.* broad'caster; broad'casting.—**Broad Church**, a party within the Church of England favouring a broad and liberal interpretation of dogmatic definitions and creed subscription—name used in 1853 by W. J. Conybeare; **broad'cloth**, a fine woollen fulled black cloth; **broad day(light)**, fully diffused daylight.—*adj.* **broad'-gauge** (see **gauge**).—**broad jump**, (*U.S.*) long jump.—*adjs.* **broad'-leaf**, having broad leaves, not needles; **broad'loom**, (of carpet) woven on a wide loom; **broad'-minded**, liberal: tolerant.—**broad'piece** (or **broad**), a 17th-century 20-shilling coin; **Broad Scots** (also **Scotch**), older, or dialect, Scottish forms of English; **broad'side**, the side of a ship: all the guns on one side of a ship of war: their simultaneous discharge: (also **broad'sheet**) a sheet of paper printed on one side, containing a proclamation, a ballad, or other popular matter. —*adj.* **broad'-spectrum**, wide-spectrum; **broad'- sword**, a cutting sword with a broad blade: a man armed with such a sword; **broad'way**, a broad road, often the name of the chief thorough- fare of a town or district.—*adv.* **broad'ways, -wise**, breadthwise.—**as broad as it is long**, six of one and half-a-dozen of the other. [O.E. *brād*, Goth. *braiths*.]

**Brobdingnagian**, *brob-ding-nag'i-ən, n.* an inhabi- tant of the fabulous region of *Brobdingnag* in *Gulliver's Travels*, where everything was gigantic. —*adj.* **Brbb'dingnag**, immense (often erroneously *Brobdignag.*).

**brocade**, *brōk-ād', n.* a silk stuff on which figures are wrought.—*adj.* **brocād'ed**, woven or worked in the manner of brocade: dressed in brocade. [It. *broccato*, Fr. *brocart*, from It. *broccare*, Fr. *brocher*, to prick, stitch; from root of **broach**.]

**brocage.** See **brokage** (under **broker**).

**brocard**, *brōk'ärd*, or *ərd, n.* an elementary law or principle: a canon: a gibe (Fr.). [Fr. *brocard*, L.L. *brocarda*, from *Brocard* or *Burchard*, Bishop of Worms, who published a book of ecclesiastical rules.]

**brocatel(le)**, *brok-ə-tel', n.* a stiff, silk-and-linen, heavy-figured fabric like brocade. [Fr.—It. *brocatello*, gold tinsel—**broccato**, brocade.]

**broccoli**, *brok'ə-li, n.* a hardy variety of cauli- flower. [It.; pl. of *broccolo*, a sprout, dim. of *brocco*, a skewer, a shoot.]

**broch**, *brohh, n.* an ancient dry-built circular castle with galleries in the thickness of the wall, com- mon in the north of Scotland, very rare in the south: a luminous ring around the moon.—Also **brogh** and **brough**. [Scots,—O.N. *borg*; O.E. *burh*.]

**broch**, *brōch*, obsolete spelling of **broach**, **brooch**.

**brochan**, *brohh'ən*, (*Scot.*) *n.* gruel: sometimes porridge. [Gael.]

**broché**, *brō'shā, adj.* of fabrics, woven with a pattern like brocade.—*n.* such a fabric. [Fr. pa.p. of *brocher*, to stitch.]

**brochure**, *bro'shōōr, shoōr', n.* a pamphlet. [Fr., —*brocher*, to stitch—*broche*, a needle. See **broach**.]

**brock**, *brok, n.* a badger: a dirty, stinking fellow. —*adjs.* **brocked, brock'it** (*Scot.*), variegated, esp. black and white. [O.E. *brocc*—Celt. (as Gael. *broc*).]

**brock**, *brok,* (*Scot.*) *n.* food scraps: pigswill: rubbish. [O.E. (*ge*)*broc*, fragment—*brecan*, to break.]

**brocket**, *brok'it, n.* a stag in its second year, with its first, dagger-shaped, horns. [Fr. *brocard*— *broque*, a spike.]

**brockram**, *brok'rəm,* (*N. England*) *n.* breccia.

**brod**, *brod, n.* a Scots form of **board**: esp. a church collection plate or box.

**brod**, *brod,* (*dial.*) *n.* a goad: a spike: a kind of nail: a prick.—*v.t.* to prod. [O.E. *brord*; O.N. *broddr.*]

**brodekin, brodkin**, *brōd'kin* (*obs.*) *n.* a buskin. [Fr. *brodequin.*]

**broderie anglaise**, *brod-rē ä-glāz*, open-work embroidery. [Fr., English embroidery.]

**brog**, *brog,* (*Scot.*) *n.* an awl.—*v.t.* to prick. [Origin obscure.]

**brogue**, *brōg, n.* a stout shoe (also **brō'gan**): an accent, esp. Irish (perh. a different word). [Ir. *brōg*, dim. *brògan* and Gael. *bròg*, a shoe.]

**broider**, *broid'ər, v.t.* and *v.i.* to embroider.—*ns.* **broid'erer**; **broid'ering**; **broid'ery**. [O.Fr. *brouder, broder*; see **embroider**.]

**broil**, *broil, n.* a noisy quarrel: a confused dis- turbance—(*Scot.*) **brulyie, brulzie** (*brōōl'i*).—*n.* **broil'er**, one who stirs up broils. [Fr. *broullier*, to trouble.]

**broil**, *broil, v.t.* to cook over hot coals: to grill. —*v.i.* to be greatly heated.—*n.* **broil'er**, a very hot day: a quickly-reared young chicken sold ready for broiling. [Ety. dub.]

**brokage.** See **broker**.

**broke**, *brōk, pa.t.* and old *pa.p.* of **break**, surviving as *pa.p.* chiefly in the sense of hard up.—*pa.p.* **brōk'en.**—*adj.* **brok'en**, *adj.* **brok'en**: infirm: humbled or crushed: thrown into disorder: dispersed, routed: altered in direction: shattered in health, spirit, estate or position: bankrupt: outlawed (*obs.*): trained to the saddle or bridle: infringed: variegated: with surface interrupted: incom- plete, fragmentary: interrupted: uncertain: of a language, ill spoken, as by a foreigner.— *adv.* **brok'enly.**—*n.* **brok'enness.**—*adjs.* **brok'en- backed**, having the back dislocated: of a ship, so loosened in her frame as to droop at both ends; **brok'en-down**, disintegrated: decayed: ruined in character or strength; **brok'en-heart'ed**, crushed with grief: greatly depressed in spirit.— **broken home**, the home of children whose parents are divorced or have separated; **broken man**, one under outlawry, esp. in the Highlands and Border country (*hist.*): one whose life is com- pletely shattered; **broken meats**, the leavings of a banquet; **broken music** (*Shak.*), concerted music.—*adj.* **brok'en-wind'ed**, having short breath or disordered respiration, as a horse.— **broke to the wide**, completely penniless.

**broker**, *brōk'ər, n.* one employed to buy and sell for others: a secondhand dealer: a go-between: a pander (*obs.*): a petty or disreputable trafficker (*obs.*).—*v.i.* **broke**, to bargain, negotiate: to act as **broker** (*Shak.*).—*ns.* **brok'erage, brok'age**, the business of a broker: commission for transacting business for others: procuring (*obs.*); **brok'ery** (*obs.*), the business of a broker: broker's wares. [M.E. *brocour*—A.Fr. *brocour*. The original meaning seems to be tapster; cf. **broach**.]

**brolly**, *brol'i,* (*slang*; a clipped form) *n.* um- brella.

**brome-grass**, *brōm'-gräs, n.* a grass (Bromus) strongly resembling oats. [Gr. *bromos*, a kind of oats.]

**Bromelia**, *brə-mēl'ya, n.* a genus of plants giving name to the pineapple family, Bromeliā'ceae, a tropical American family of monocotyledons, mainly epiphytic and xerophytic, with stiff leaves in rosettes.—*adj.* **bromeliā'ceous.**— **bromel'iad**, any plant of the family. [Named in honour of the Swedish botanist Olaus *Bromel* (1639-1705).]

**bromine**, *brō'mēn, -min, -min, n.* a non-metallic chemical element (at. numb. 35), a red liquid giving off an irritating, poisonous brown vapour. —*n.* **brō'mate**, a salt of bromic acid.—*adj.* **brō'- mic.**—*n.* **brō'mide**, a salt of hydrobromic acid: a platitudinous person (from the use of bromides as sedatives): a platitude.—*adj.* **brō'mid'ic**, con- ventionally commonplace.—*ns.* **brōmidrō'sis**, osmidrosis; **brō'moform**, a bromine compound analogous to chloroform.—**bromic acid**, a com- pound of hydrogen, bromine and oxygen, HBrO$_3$; **bromide paper**, in photography, a paper with a sensitive surface containing bromide of silver, used in printing from a negative. [Gr. *bromos*, stink.]

**brommer**, *brom'ər*, (*Afrik.*) *n.* bluebottle fly. [Onomatopoeic.]

**bronco, broncho**, *brong'kō*, (*U.S.*) *n.* a half-tamed horse.—**bronc'o-bust'er**, one who breaks in broncos: a cowboy. [Sp. *bronco*, rough, sturdy.]

**bronchus**, *brong'kəs*, *n.* either of the main forks of the windpipe:—*pl.* **bronch'i** (*-i*).—*n.pl.* **bronch'ia** (erroneously *bronchiae*), the ramifications of the bronchi.—*adj.* **bronch'ial**, pertaining to the bronchi, or the bronchia.—*n.* **bronchiec'tasis** (*-ek'tə-sis*), a chronic viral disease caused by dilated bronchi.—*adj.* **bronchitic** (*-it'ik*), pertaining to bronchitis.—*n.* one suffering from bronchitis.—*n.* **bronchitis** (*-i'tis*), inflammation of the lining of the bronchial tubes.—**bron'cho-**, in composition, relating to the bronchi.—*n.* **bron'cho-dilā'tor**, any drug that causes the air-passages of the bronchi to expand. [Gr. *bronchos*, windpipe; *bronchia*, bronchia.]

**brond.** See **brand**.

**Brontosaurus**, *bron-tō-sör'əs*, *n.* a genus of dinosaurs found fossil in Wyoming and Colorado. [Gr. *brontē*, thunder, *sauros*, lizard.]

**Bronx cheer**, *brongks chēr*, (*U.S.*) a vulgar sound of disapproval. [From the *Bronx* borough of New York City.]

**bronze**, *bronz*, *n.* an alloy of copper and tin used in various ways since prehistoric times: a copper alloy without tin: anything cast in bronze: the colour of bronze: impudence (*obs.*).—*adj.* made of bronze: coloured like bronze.—*v.t.* and *v.i.* to make or become bronze-like: to harden (*fig.*, *obs.*).—*adjs.* **bronzed**, coated with bronze: bronze-coloured, sunburned: hardened (*fig.*, *obs.*); **bronz'en** (*rare*).—*v.t.* **bronz'ify** (*rare*), to make into bronze.—*ns.* **bronz'ing**, the process of giving or assuming the appearance of bronze; **bronz'ite**, an enstatite with bronzy lustre.—*adj.* **bronz'y**, having the appearance of bronze.— **Bronze Age**, a prehistoric condition or stage of culture marked by the use of bronze as the material for tools and weapons—coming between the Stone Age and the Iron Age; **bronzed skin**, Addison's disease; **bronze'-wing, bronze'-pi'geon**, an Australian pigeon of various species with lustrous bronze markings on the wings. [Fr.,— It. *bronzo, bronzino*—perh. from L. (*aes*) *Brundusinum*, (brass) from Brindisi; or perh. from Pers. *birinj, pirinj*, copper.]

**broo**, *brōō, brü*, (*Scot.*) *n.* liquor that comes off from anything or in which anything has been boiled. [Prob. O.Fr. *bro, breu*, broth.]

**broo, brow**, *brōō*, (*Scot.*) *n.* brow in any sense: (perh. a different word) liking (with *of*). [**brow.**]

**brooch**, *brōch*, *n.* an ornamental clasp with a joined pin fitting into a hook.—*v.t.* (*Shak.*) to adorn as with a brooch. [Fr. *broche*, a spit. See **broach.**]

**brood**, *brōōd*, *n.* something bred: offspring, children, or family: a race, kind: parentage, extraction (*arch.*): the number hatched, produced, or cherished at once: condition of breeding or brooding.—*adj.* for breeding (as in *brood*-mare, etc.).—*v.t.* to sit upon or cover in order to breed or hatch: to hatch: to cover, as with wings: to mature or foster with care: to meditate moodily upon.—*v.i.* to sit as a hen on eggs: to hang envelopingly: to think anxiously for some time: to meditate silently (with *on over*).—*ns.* **brood'er**; **broodi'ness.**—*adv.* **brood'-ingly.**—*adj.* **brood'y**, inclined to sit or incubate: apt to brood or to breed.—**brood'-pouch**, a body-cavity in which eggs or embryos are put to develop. [O.E. *brōd*; Du. *broed*; cf. **breed.**]

**brook**, *brōōk*, *n.* a small stream.—*n.* **brook'let**, a little brook.—**brook'weed**, water pimpernel (*Samolus*), a water-plant of the primrose family superficially like a crucifer. [O.E. *brōc*, water breaking forth: Du. *broek*, Ger. *bruch*.]

**brook**, *brōōk*, *v.t.* to enjoy: to bear or endure. [O.E. *brūcan*, to use, enjoy; Ger. *brauchen*, L. *frui, fructus.*]

**brookite**, *brōōk'it*, *n.* a mineral, titanium oxide. [After Henry James *Brooke* (1771-1857), English mineralogist.]

**brooklime**, *brōōk'lim*, *n.* a speedwell that grows in brooks and ditches. [**brook**, and O.E. *hleomoc*, brooklime.]

**brool**, *brōōl*, *n.* a deep murmur. [Ger. *brüll*, a roar.]

**broom**, *brōōm*, *n.* a papilionaceous shrub, *Cytisus scoparius*, or kindred kind: a besom made of its twigs or of anything else: a long-handled domestic sweeping brush.—*v.t.* to sweep with a broom.—*adj.* **broom'y**, abounding in or consisting of broom.—**broom'-corn**, a kind of millet of which brooms are made; **broom'rape** (L. *rapum*, a knob), a genus (*Orobanche*) of plants parasitic on broom and other roots; **broom'staff, broom'stick**, the handle of a broom.—**marry over the broomstick or jump the besom**, to go through an irregular form of marriage in which both jump over a broomstick; **new brooms sweep clean**, people newly appointed to a position work very conscientiously, or try to sweep away abuses. [O.E. *brōm*.]

**broose** (*Scott*, **brouze**), *brōōz, brüz*, (*Scot.*) *n.* a race at a wedding. [Derivation unknown.]

**brose**, *brōz*, *n.* a food made by pouring boiling water or milk on oatmeal or peasemeal, seasoned with salt and butter.—**Athole brose**, a mixture of whisky and honey; **brose and bannock day**, Shrove Tuesday. [Scot.; perh. conn. with **brewis, broo.**]

**broth**, *broth*, *n.* an infusion or decoction of vegetable and animal substances in water, used as soup or as a medium for culture of bacteria.—a **broth of a boy** (*Irish*), the quintessence of a good fellow. [O.E. *broth—brēowan*, to brew. See **brew.**]

**brothel**, *broth'l*, *n.* a house of prostitution. [M.E. *brothel*, worthless person—O.E. *brothen*, ruined, *brēothan*, to go to ruin; influenced in meaning by **bordel.**]

**brother**, *brudh'ər*, *n.* a male in relation to another of either sex born of the same parents or parent (*half-brother*): any one closely united with or resembling another associated in common interests, occupation, etc.: a fellow-member of a religious order, a guild, etc.: a fellow-creature: a fellow-citizen: a co-religionist: a kinsman (*B.*):—*pl.* **broth'ers** and **breth'ren**, the latter esp. used in the sense of fellow-members and in the names of certain bodies, as Christian Brethren, Moravian Brethren, Plymouth Brethren, etc.—*adj.* associated in any relation (also in composition as **brother-man**).—*n.* **broth'erhood**, the state of being a brother: an association of men for any purpose.—*adj.* **broth'erlike.**—*n.* **broth'erliness.**—*adj.* **broth'erly**, like a brother: kind: affectionate.— **broth'er-ger'man**, a full-brother, one having both parents in common, in contradistinction to a *half-brother*; **broth'er-in-law**, the brother of a husband or wife: a sister's husband. [O.E. *brōthor*, pl. *brēther*; cog. with Ger. *bruder*, Gael. *brathair*, L. *frāter*, Sans. *bhrātṛ*; Gr. *phrātēr*, fellow-clansman.]

**brotstudien**, *brōt'shtōō-dē-ən*, (*Ger.*) bread studies, those by which one earns one's living.

**brough.** See **broch** (1).

**brougham**, *brōō'əm, brō'əm*, or **brōōm**, *n.* a one-horse close carriage, named after Lord *Brougham* (1778-1868): an early motor-car with uncovered driver's seat.

**brouhaha**, *brōō-hä'hä, brōō'hä-hä*, *n.* fuss, excitement, clamour, or an instance of this. [Fr.; perh. from Heb.]

**brought**, *brōt*, *pa.t.* and *pa.p.* of **bring**.

**brouze.** See **broose**.

brow, *brow, n.* the eyebrow: the ridge over the eyes: the forehead: the edge of a hill: a gallery in a coal-mine running across the face of the coal: a pit-head: aspect, appearance (*fig.*).—*adj.* brow′less, without eyebrows: without shame.— brow′-antler, -tine, the first tine of a deer's horn.—*v.t.* brow′beat, to bear down with stern looks or speech: to bully.—*adj.* brow′-bound, crowned. [O.E. *brū.*]

brown, *brown, adj.* of a dark or dusky colour, inclining to red or yellow: dark-complexioned: sunburnt: formerly conventionally applied to a sword, perh. burnished, perh. rusty, perh. blood-stained.—*n.* a dark-reddish colour: a copper coin (*slang*).—*v.t.* to give a brown colour to: to roast brown.—*v.i.* to become brown.—*ns.* brown′ie, a drudging domestic goblin (*Scottish folklore*): (*with cap.*) a member of the junior section of the Girl Guides, in brown garb; brown′ing, the process of making or becoming brown: a preparation for the purpose.—*adj.* brown′ish.—*n.* brown′ness.—*adj.* brown′y, of a brownish colour.—brown algae, brown sea-weeds, the Phaeophyceae, one of the main divisions of the algae; brown bear, the common bear of Europe and Asia; brown Bess, the old British flintlock musket—from the brown walnut stock; brown bill, a foot soldier's or watchman's halberd, painted brown; brown bread, any dark coloured bread, esp. that made of unbolted flour; brown coal, lignite; brown George, a hard biscuit: a brown earthen vessel: brown owl, the tawny owl: a woman who has charge of a group of Brownies; brown paper, coarse and strong paper used chiefly for wrapping; brown rat, the larger and commoner of the two British rats (often black); brown rice, rice hulled but not polished; Brown′shirt, a member of Hitler's organisation of storm-troopers: a Nazi; brown spar, a brownish variety of dolomite; brownstone (*U.S.*), a dark brown sandstone, re-garded as the favourite building material of the prosperous classes; brown stout, a kind of porter; brown study, reverie: absent-mindedness; brown sugar, unrefined or partially refined sugar.— browned off (*slang*), fed up: bored: dejected; do brown (*slang*), to do thoroughly, to deceive or take in completely. [O.E. *brūn*; Du. *bruin,* Ger. *braun.*]

Brownian, *brown′i-ən, adj.* pertaining to Robert *Brown* (1773-1858), who drew attention to Brownian movement, an agitation of particles in a colloid solution caused by impact of molecules in the surrounding medium.

Brownist, *brown′ist, n.* one holding the church principles of Robert *Browne* (c. 1550-c. 1633), which may be said to have given birth to the Independents or Congregationalists of England. —*n.* Brown′ism.

brown jolly, *brown jol′i,* a corruption of brinjal.

browse, *browz, v.i.* to feed on rough shoots of plants: to read desultorily.—*v.t.* to browse on.— *n.* a twig: a browsing.—*n.* brows′ing, the shoots and leaves of plants: fodder: the action of the verb browse. [O.Fr. *brouster* (Fr. *brouter*)— *broust,* a sprout.]

browst, *browst, (Scot.) n.* a brewing. [brew.]

brucellosis, *broō-sal-ō′sis, n.* a disease of animals, also called contagious abortion (see abortion), communicable to man as Malta, or undulant, fever. [Sir David *Bruce,* bacteriologist, -*ella,* -*osis.*]

brucine, *broōs′ēn, n.* an alkaloid got from nux vomica, wrongly thought to come from the simarubaceous genus *Brucea,* named after James *Bruce* (1730-94), Scottish African traveller.

brucite, *broōs′it, n.* a mineral, magnesium hy-droxide. [Named after A. *Bruce,* American mineralogist.]

Brücke, Die, *brü′kə, dē,* a group of expressionist

painters formed in Dresden in 1905. [Ger., the Bridge.]

bruckle, *bruk′l, (Scot.) adj.* liable to break, brittle and unstable. [O.E. *brucol—brecan,* to break.]

bruhaha. A spelling of brouhaha.

Bruin, *broō′in, n.* the name of the bear in the beast-epic *Reynard the Fox*; hence in general use. [Du., brown.]

bruise, *broōz, v.t.* to crush by beating or pounding without breaking the surface: to pound: to pulverise by pounding: to mark and discolour part of the surface of, e.g. skin of person, fruit, etc.: to hurt by unkind words.—*v.i.* to box (*obs.*): to ride recklessly (*hunting slang*): to be injured physically or in feelings.—*n.* an injury with discoloration of the human skin made by anything blunt and heavy: a similar injury to fruit or plants.—*n.* bruis′er, one who bruises: a prize-fighter.—*n.* and *adj.* bruis′ing. [O.E. *brȳsan,* to crush, combined with O.Fr. *brisier, bruiser, bruser,* to break.]

bruit, *broōt, n.* noise (*arch.*): something noised abroad: a rumour or report: a murmur heard in auscultation.—*v.t.* to noise abroad: to report: to make famous. [Fr. *bruit*—Fr. *bruire*; cf. L.L. *brugitus*; prob. imit.]

brûlé, *brü-lā,* (Fr.) cooked with brown sugar: compromised.

brulzie, bruilzie, *broōl′(y)i, brül′yi, n.* Scottish and northern form of broil.

Brum, *brum, n.* contraction of Brummagem for Birmingham.

Brumaire, *brü-mer′, n.* the second month in the French revolutionary calendar, about Oct. 22 to Nov. 20. [Fr. *brume,* fog—L. *brūma,* winter.]

brumby, *brum′bi, (Austr.) n.* a wild horse. [Origin unknown.]

brume, *broōm, n.* fog.—*adjs.* brum′al, relating to winter; brum′ous, foggy, wintry. [L. *brūma,* winter, contr. from *brevima,* the shortest day.]

Brummagem, *brum′ə-jəm, n.* a local form of *Birmingham* (the town): a thing made in Birmingham.—*adj.* showy and worthless, sham, counterfeit.

brummer, *broōm′ər, (S. Africa) n.* older form of brommer.

brunch, *brunch, brunsh, n.* a compromise between breakfast and lunch. [Portmanteau word.]

brunette, *broōn-et′, n.* a woman with brown or dark hair and complexion.—Also (esp. *anthrop.*) in *masc.* brunet′. [Fr. dim. of *brun,* brown.]

Brunonian, *broō-nō′ni-ən, adj.* relating to the system of medicine founded by Dr John *Brown* of Edinburgh (c. 1736-88)—all diseases *sthenic* or *asthenic,* depending on excess or deficiency of excitement. [*Brūnō,* -*ōnis,* Latinisation of Brown.]

brunt, *brunt, n.* the shock of an onset or contest: the force of a blow: the chief stress or crisis of anything.—*v.t.* to bear the brunt of.—at the instant brunt, at the outset, at once. [Origin obscure.]

brush, *brush, n.* an instrument set with bristles or the like for cleansing or for applying friction or a coating of some material: a painter's hair pencil: a manner of painting: a painter (*arch.*): a tuft: a bushy tail: a bundle of wires, strips, or the like, making electrical contact between surfaces in relative motion: a brushlike discharge of electricity or any brushlike appearance: an application of a brush: a grazing contact: a skirmish: lopped or broken twigs: an assem-blage of shrubs and small trees: an area covered with thickets: a forest (*Austr.*): the backwoods: a brisk run or race (*U.S.*).—*v.t.* to pass a brush over: to touch or rub as if with a brush: to remove by a sweeping motion (with *off,* or *away*). —*v.i.* to use a brush: to pass with light contact: to make off.—*ns.* brush′er, one who brushes: a small wallaby; brush′ing, the act or process

Neutral vowels in unaccented syllables: *el′ə-mənt*; for certain sounds in foreign words, see p. viii

of brushing.—*adj.* in a lively manner: brisk.—
*adj.* **brush′y,** like a brush: covered with brush.—
**brush kangaroo,** a wallaby; **brush′-off** (*coll.*), a
curt or discourteous setting aside or ignoring:
a rebuff; **brush turkey,** an eastern Australian
mound-bird; **brush′wheel,** a revolving brush:
a friction wheel with bristles on the rubbing
surface; **brush′wood,** loppings and broken
branches: underwood or stunted wood; **brush′-
work,** work done with a brush: a painter's
manner of using the brush.—**brush aside,** to
ignore, dismiss; **brush up,** to brighten: to revive.
[O.Fr. *brosse,* brushwood; prob. connected with
**bristle.**]
**brusque,** brŏŏsk, brusk, *adj.* blunt and abrupt in
manner.—*adv.* **brusque′ly.**—*ns.* **brusque′ness,**
**brusquerie** (brŏŏs′kə-rē). [Fr.]
**Brussels,** brus′əlz, *n.* the capital of Belgium: (in
full **Brussels carpet**), a kind of carpet in which
the worsted threads are arranged in the warp, and
are interwoven into a network of linen, the bulk
of the carpet consisting of wool.—**Brussels lace,**
a fine lace with sprigs applied on a net ground;
**Brussels sprouts,** a variety of the common
cabbage with sprouts like miniature cabbages.
**brust,** brust, (*Spens.*). Same as **burst.**
**brut,** brŏŏt, (Fr.) of wines, raw, unsweetened.
**brute,** brŏŏt, *adj.* belonging to the lower animals:
irrational: stupid: rude: crude.—*n.* one of the
lower animals, esp. the larger mammals: a
brutal man.—*adj.* **brut′al,** like a brute: unfeeling: inhuman: stupidly cruel or sensual.—*v.t.*
**brut′alise, -ize,** to make like a brute, to degrade:
to treat with brutality.—*v.i.* to live like a brute.
—*ns.* **brutalisa′tion, -izā′tion; brutal′ity.**—*adv.*
**brut′ally.**—*n.* **brute′ness,** brutelike state: brutality: stupidity (*Spens.*).—*v.t.* **brut′ify,** to make
brutal, stupid or uncivilised:—*pr.p.* **brut′ifying;**
*pa.p.* **brut′ified.**—*adj.* **brut′ish,** brutal: unwise
(*B.*).—*adv.* **brut′ishly.**—*n.* **brut′ishness.**—**brute
force,** sheer physical strength. [Fr. *brut*—L.
*brūtus,* dull, irrational.]
**brutum fulmen,** brŏŏ′tum (or *-tŏŏm*) ful′ (or
*fŏŏl′*)men, (L.) an ineffectual thunderbolt.
**Brutus,** brŏŏ′təs, *n.* a kind of wig: a way of
wearing the hair brushed back from the forehead,
popular at the time of the French Revolution,
when it was an affectation to admire the old
Romans, as *Brutus.*
**bruxism,** bruks′izm, *n.* habitual grinding of the
teeth. [Gr. *brychein,* to gnash.]
**bryology,** bri-ol′ə-ji, *n.* the study of mosses.—*adj.*
**bryological** (-ə-loj′i-kl).—*n.* **bryol′ogist.** [Gr.
*bryon,* moss, liverwort, and *logos,* discourse.]
**bryony,** bri′ə-ni, *n.* a wild climbing plant (*Bryonia
dioica,* **white bryony**) of the gourd family, common in English hedgerows: **black bryony,** a
climbing plant (*Tamus communis*) of the yam
family, similar to bryony in habit and disposition.
[L. *bryōnia*—Late Gr. *bryōniā.*]
**bryophyte,** bri′ō-fīt, *n.* a member of the **Bryoph′yta**
(*-of′i-ta*), one of the main groups of the vegetable
kingdom, mosses and liverworts. [Gr. *bryon,* a
moss, a liverwort, *phyton,* plant.]
**Bryozoa,** brī-ō-zō′a, *n.pl.* an old name for the
Polyzoa, from their resemblance to mosses. [Gr.
*bryon,* moss, *zōia,* living things.]
**Brython,** brith′on, *n.* a Celt of the group to which
Welsh, Cornish, and Bretons belong—distinguished from Goidel.—*adj.* **Brython′ic.** [Welsh
*Brython,* Briton—introduced in philological use
by Sir John Rhŷs.]
**buat,** Same as **bowat.**
**buaze, bwazi,** bŭ′āz, bwä′zi, *n.* an African fibre-
yielding polygalaceous shrub (*Securidaca*).
[Native name.]
**bub, bub, bubby,** bub′i, (*U.S.*) *n.* boy (in addressing). [Cf. Ger. *bube,* boy.]
**bub, bub,** (*arch.* slang) *n.* strong drink. [Origin
unknown.]

**Bubalis,** bū′bal-is, *n.* the hartebeest genus of
antelopes, not to be confused with Bubalus, the
buffalo.—*adj.* **bub′aline.** [Gr. *boubalis.*]
**bubble, bub′l,** *n.* a bladder of liquid or solidified
liquid blown out with gas: anything empty: an
unsound or fraudulent scheme.—*adj.* unsubstantial: deceptive: fleeting, transient.—*v.i.* to
rise in bubbles: to give off bubbles: to make
sounds as of rising and bursting bubbles: (with
*with*) to show (great joy, rage, etc.): to blubber
(*Scot.*).—*v.t.* to cheat with bubble schemes
(*arch.*).—*adj.* **bubb′ly.**—**bubble-and-squeak,** meat
and cabbage fried together; **bubb′le-car,** a
midget motor-car resembling a bubble in its
rounded line and windowed top; **bubb′le-
chamber,** a device for showing the path of a
charged particle by the string of bubbles left in
its track—a variant of the cloud-chamber;
**bubb′le-gum,** a kind of chewing-gum that can be
blown into large bubbles; **bubb′le-shell,** a
gasteropod (*Bulla*) with thin globose shell;
**bubb′ly-jock** (*Scot.*), a turkey-cock; **bubbly
(water)** (*slang*), champagne.—**bubble over,** to
show uncontrolled anger, mirth, etc. [Cf.
Sw. *bubbla,* Du. *bobbel.*]
**bubinga,** bŏŏ′bing-a, *n.* species of W. African tree,
esp. *Didelotia africana,* its hard wood used in
furniture-making. [Bantu.]
**bubo,** bū′bō, *n.* an inflammatory swelling of the
glands, esp. in the groin or armpit.—*adj.* **bubonic**
(*-bon′*), accompanied by buboes.—*n.* **būb′ukle,**
(*arch.*) a ridiculous word of Fluellen's for a red
pimple, compounded of *bubo* and *carbuncle.*
[L. *bubō*—Gr. *boubōn,* the groin, a bubo.]
**buccal,** buk′əl, *adj.* pertaining to the cheek: pertaining to the mouth, oral. [L. *bucca,* cheek.]
**buccaneer, buccanier,** buk-ən-ēr′, *n.* one of the
piratical adventurers in the West Indies during
the 17th century, who plundered the Spaniards
chiefly.—*v.i.* to act as a buccaneer.—*n.* **buccan-
eer′ing.**—*adj.* **buccaneer′ish.** [Fr. *boucanier*—
*boucan,* a Carib wooden gridiron (used by
French settlers in the West Indies).]
**buccina,** buk′sin-a, a Roman curved trumpet.—*n.*
**buc′cinātor,** a flat cheek muscle used in chewing
and blowing.—*adj.* **buc′cinatory.**—*n.* **buc′cinum,**
the whelk genus of molluscs, with trumpetlike
shell. [L. *būcina,* trumpet, *būcinātor,* trumpeter.]
**bucellas,** bū-, bŏŏ-sel′əs, *n.* a white wine from
*Bucellas* near Lisbon.
**Bucentaur,** bū-sen′tör, *n.* state barge used formerly
in the marriage of Venice with the Adriatic.
[It. *bucentoro, bucintoro;* poss. from Gr. *bous,*
an ox, *kentauros,* a centaur—perh. from the
figurehead.]
**Bucephalus,** bū-sef′ə-ləs, *n.* Alexander the Great's
famous war-horse: a familiar name for a riding-
horse. [Gr. *Boukephalos—bous,* ox, *kephalē,*
head.]
**Buchmanism,** bŏŏhh′mən-izm, *n.* the Oxford Group
movement.—*adj.* and *n.* **Buch′manite** (*-it*). [See
**Oxford.**]
**buchu, bucku,** bŏŏ′hhŏŏ, -chŏŏ, -kŏŏ, (S. *Africa*) *n.*
a rutaceous genus (*Barosma*) with leaves of
medicinal value for wounds, etc. [Zulu.]
**buck,** buk, *n.* the body of a cart.—*ns.* **buck′board,**
a board or rail projecting over cart-wheels:
a plank on four wheels, with a light seat to hold
two persons (*U.S.*): **buck′cart,** a buckboard: a
cart with boards projecting over the wheels;
**buck′-wag′on** (S. *Africa, arch.*), a large canvas-
covered trek wagon. [O.E. *būc,* body.]
**buck,** buk, *n.* the male of the deer, goat, hare, and
rabbit (cf. *doe*): a male fallow-deer: a bok
(*q.v.*): a dashing fellow: a male Negro or
American Indian: a counter (*cards*): a dollar
(*U.S.*): an act of bucking.—*v.i.* (of a horse or
mule) to attempt to throw by rapid jumps into
the air, coming down with the back arched, head
down, and forelegs stiff.—*v.t.* to throw by

bucking: to resist (*U.S.*): to cheer, invigorate, tone up (*slang*).—*ns.* **buckeen´**, a poor Irish gentleman, without means to support his gentility; **buck´er**, an animal that bucks.—*adj.* **buck´ish**, lively, frisky: dandified: goatish.— **buck´-eye**, the American horse-chestnut (genus *Aesculus*); **buck´horn**, **buck´s´-horn**, the material of a buck's horn (**buck´s-horn plantain**, a British plantain with pinnatifid leaves); **buck´hound**, a small kind of staghound used for hunting bucks; **buck´-jumper**, an animal that bucks; **buck´rabb´it**, a male rabbit: a Welsh rabbit with poached egg; **buck´-saw**, a large frame-saw used with a saw-buck; **buck´shot**, a large kind of shot, used in shooting deer; **buck´skin**, a soft leather made of deerskin or sheepskin: a strong twilled woollen cloth, cropped of nap: a horse of buck-skin (greyish-yellow) colour: a backwoods American: (in *pl.*) breeches or suit of buckskin. —*adj.* made of or like the skin of a buck.— **buck´thorn**, a genus (*Rhamnus*) of shrubs whose berry supplies the sap-green used by painters: (see also **sea-buckthorn**); **buck´tooth**, a projecting tooth.—**buck up** (*slang*), to bestir oneself: to cheer up: to improve: to stimulate: to dress up (*dial.*); **pass the buck**, (*slang*) to shift the responsibility to someone else (as one passes a marker to the next dealer in forms of poker). [O.E. *buc*, *bucca*; Du. *bok*, Ger. *bock*, a he-goat.] **buck**, *buk*, *v.t.* to soak or steep in lye, a process in bleaching.—*n.* lye in which clothes are bleached.—*n.* **buck´ing**.—**buck´-basket**, a basket in which clothes are carried to be bucked; **buck´-wash, -ing**. [Ety. obscure: M.E. *bouken*; cog. words are Ger. *bäuchen*, *beuchen*.] **buckaroo**, *buk´ə-rōō*, or *-rōō´*, (*U.S.*) *n.* a cowboy. [Sp. *vaquero*.] **buckbean**, *buk´bēn*, *n.* a marsh plant (*Menyanthes trifoliata*) of the gentian family.—Also **bogbean**. [Flem. *bocks boonen*, goat's beans.] **bucket**, *buk´it*, *n.* a vessel for drawing or holding water, etc.: one of the compartments on the circumference of a water-wheel: one of the scoops of a dredging-machine: a leather socket for holding a whip, carbine or lance: the pitcher in some orchids: a bucketful.—*v.t.* to lift in a bucket: to ride very hard: to push forward m.rcilessly: to swindle (*arch.*).—Also *v.i.*—*ns.* **buck´etful**, as much as a bucket will hold:—*pl.* **buck´etfuls**; **buck´eting**.—**bucket seat**, a round-backed, often forward-tipping, seat for one in a motor-car, aeroplane, etc.; **bucket shop**, the office of an outside broker—a mere agent for bets on the rise or fall of prices of stock, etc.: **buck´et-wheel**, a contrivance for raising water by means of buckets attached to the circumference of a wheel.—**give the buck et, to d'smiss; kick the bucket,** (*slang*) to die. [Prob. conn. with O.E. *būc*, a pitcher: or O.Fr. *buket*, a pail. Not Gael. *bucaid*, a bucket.] **buckie**, *buk´i*, (*Scot.*) *n.* a shellfish such as the whelk: a refractory person. [Prob. related somehow to L. *buccinum*, a shellfish.] **buckle**, *buk´l*, *n.* fastening for a strap or band, consisting of a rim and a tongue: a crisped, curled, or warped condition.—*v.t.* and *v.i.* to connect with a buckle: to prepare for action: to join closely as in fight or marriage: to bend or warp. —*v.i.* to apply oneself zealously (with *to*).—*ns.* **buck´le-beggar**, a hedge-parson; **buck´ler**, a small shield used for parrying. [Fr. *boucle*, the boss or a shield, a ring—L.L. *buccula*, dim. of *bucca*, a cheek.] **buckling**, *buk´ling*, *n.* smoked Baltic herring. **bucko**, *buk´ō*, *n.* a swaggerer, domineering bully (*orig. naut. slang*): young lad, chap (*chiefly Irish*). [buck (2).] **buckra**, *buk´ra*, *n.* a word used by West Indian and American Negroes for a white man—said to mean 'demon' in a dialect of the Calabar coast.

**buckram**, *buk´rəm*, *n.* a coarse open-woven fabric of jute, cotton, or linen made very stiff with size: stiffness in manners and appearance.—*adj.* made of buckram: stiff: precise.—*v.t.* to give the quality of buckram. [O.Fr. *boquerant*.] **buckshish.** Same as **baksheesh.**—*n.* **buckshee**, (*mil. slang*) spoil, a windfall.—*adj.* free, gratuitous. [See **baksheesh, bukshi.**] **bucksom**, a Miltonic spelling of **buxom.** **buckthorn.** See **buck** (2). **bucku.** See **buchu.** **buckwheat**, *buk´(h)wēt*, *n.* a *Polygonum* or *Fagopyrum* used in Europe for feeding horses, cattle and poultry, in America made into cakes for the breakfast table. [Prob. Du. *boekweit*, or Ger. *buchweizen*, beech-wheat, from the shape of the seeds.] **bucolic, -al,** *bū-kol´ik, -əl*, *adjs.* pertaining to tending of cattle: pastoral: rustic, countrified.— *n.* **bucol´ic**, a pastoral poem or poet: a rustic. [L. *būcolicus*—Gr. *boukolikos*—*boukolos*, a herdsman.] **bud**, *bud*, *n.* a rudimentary shoot of a plant: a protuberance that develops asexually into a new individual (*biol.*): a young person (as a term of endearment): a débutante (*U.S.*).—*v.t.* to put forth as buds: to graft by inserting a bud under the bark of another tree.—*v.i.* to put forth buds: to come as a bud: to be in or issue from the bud: (*pr.p.* **budd´ing;** *pa.p.* **budd´ed**).—*n.* and *adj.* **budd´ing.**—*adjs.* **budd´y; bud´less.**—*n.* **bud´-scale,** a leaf specialised as a scale protecting a bud.—**nip in the bud,** to destroy at its very beginning. [M.E. *budde*; perh. related to Du. *bot*, a bud.] **bud**, *bud*, **buddy**, *bud´i*, *n.* brother (*U.S.*): pal, most constant companion. [Childish or Negro for **brother.**] **Buddha**, *boōd´a*, *n.* a title applied to Sakyamuni or G°utama, the founder of the Buddhist religion: a general name for any one of a series of teachers of whom he is one.—*ns.* **Budd´hism,** the religion founded by the Buddha; **Budd´hist,** a believer in Buddhism.—*adjs.* **Budd´hist, Buddhist´ic.**— **Buddhist cross,** the swastika. [Sans. *buddha,* wise, from *bodhati,* he understands.] **buddle**, *bud´l,* *n.* an inclined hutch for washing ore.—*v.t.* to wash with a buddle. [Origin obscure.] **Buddleia**, *bud´li-a, bud-lē´a, n.* a genus of plants of the Loganiaceae, shrubs and trees with opposite leaves and showy clusters of purple or orange flowers. [Named in honour of Adam *Buddle* (d. 1715), botanist.] **buddy.** See **bud** (2). **budge**, *buj, v.i.* and *v.t.* to move or stir.—*n.* **budg´er.** [Fr. *bouger*—L. *bullire,* to bubble.] **budge,** *buj, n.* lambskin fur.—*adj.* pompous: stiff. [Origin obscure.] **budgeree,** *buj´ər-ē, (Austr.) adj.* good. [Native word, *budgeri.*] **budgerigar,** *buj´ər-i-gär, -gär´, n.* a cage and aviary bird, an Australian parrakeet.—*fam.* **budge, buj, budgie, buj´i.** [Australian native *budgeri,* good, *gar,* cockatoo.] **budgerow, budgero,** *bu´jər-ō, (Hind.)* a heavy keelless barge. **budget,** *buj´it, n.* a sack or its contents (*obs.*): a compact collection of things: news: a socket in which the end of a cavalry carbine rests: a financial statement and programme put before parliament by the Chancellor of the Exchequer: a plan of domestic expenditure or the like.—*v.i.* to prepare a budget.—*v.t.* to provide for in a budget: (*pr.p.* **budg´eting;** *pa.t.* and *pa.p.* **budg´eted**). [Fr. *bougette,* dim. of *bouge,* a pouch—L. *bulga.*] **budgie.** See **budgerigar.** **budmash.** See **badmash.** **buenas noches,** *bwān´as nō´ches,* (Sp.) good-night;

buenas tardes, *tar'dhes*, good-afternoon; buenos dias, *bwän'os dē'as*, good-day, good-morning.

**buff**, *buf*, *n.* originally buffalo-hide: now white leather from which the grain surface has been removed, used for army accoutrements: a military coat: the colour of buff, a light yellow: the bare skin: a buff-stick or buff-wheel: (in *pl.*) certain regiments in the British army, from their former buff-coloured facings—e.g. East Kent Regiment, Ross-shire Buffs: a member of a party whose colour is buff: an enthusiast, fan (*coll.*).—Also *adj.*—*v.t.* to polish with a buff.—*n.* buff'er, one who buffs or polishes.—*ns.* buff'-coat, buff'-jer'kin, a strong, military coat: a soldier; buff'-leather'; buff'-stick, buff'-wheel, a stick or wheel covered with buff-leather or the like, and charged with an abrasive for polishing.—in buff, naked. [Fr. *buffle*, a buffalo.]

**buff**, *buf*, *n.* a buffet, blow, or stroke (*obs.*): a dull blow or its sound.—*v.t.* to strike, esp. with a dull sound: to burst out.—*ns.* buff'er, a mechanical apparatus for deadening the force of a concussion, as in railway carriages: a ship's fender: a boatswain's mate: a fellow, esp. a dull or ineffectual fellow (as in *old buffer*): in chemistry, a substance or mixture which opposes change of hydrogen-ion concentration in a solution.—*v.t.* to treat with a buffer.—*adj.* buff'ered.—buffer state, a neutral country lying between two others whose relations are or may become strained. [O.Fr. *buffe*, a blow.]

**buffalo**, *buf'ə-lō*, *n.* a name for certain large animals of the ox kind, esp. the tame, often domesticated Asiatic buffalo, and the entirely wild and fierce Cape buffalo: the American bison (*U.S.*): a bison:—*pl.* buff'aloes.—*v.t.* to bewilder: to overawe.—buff'alo-berry, a North American shrub of the Elaeagnaceae, or its edible fruit; buff'alo-bird, an ox-pecker; buff'alo-grass, a low creeping grass (*Buchloe dactyloides*) growing on the western prairies of the U.S.: any of several other prairie grasses; buff'alo-nut, a North American shrub of the sandalwood family: its oil-yielding nut; buff'alo-robe, a bison-hide rug or cloak. [It. *buffalo*, through L. from Gr. *boubalos.*]

**buffet**, *buf'it*, *n.* a blow with the fist: a slap: a stroke, esp. heavy and repeated, as of the wind, fortune, etc.—*v.t.* to strike with the hand or fist: to struggle against, beat back.—*v.i.* to deal heavy blows.—*n.* buff'eting, a striking with the hand, boxing: contention: repeated blows: irregular oscillation of any part of an aircraft, caused and maintained by an eddying wake from some other part. [O.Fr. *buffet*—*buffe*, a blow, esp. on the cheek.]

**buffet**, *buf'it*, *n.* a sideboard: a low (esp. rectangular) stool (*Scot.*): (usu. *bŏŏf'ā*) a refreshment counter or bar: meal set out on table, etc., from which the diner serves himself.—Also *adj.*—buffet car, a railway coach with light meal or snack service. [Fr. *buffet*; origin unknown.]

**bufflehead**, *buf'l-hed*, *n.* a N. American diving duck resembling the golden-eye: a stupid fellow. [From buffalo and head.]

**buffo**, *bŏŏf'fō*, *adj.* comic.—*n.* the comic actor in an opera:—*pl.* buff'fi (*fē*); *fem.* buf'fa; *pl.* buf'fe (*fä*). [It.]

**buffoon**, *buf-ōŏn'*, *n.* one who sets himself to amuse by jests, grimaces, etc.: a low, vulgar, or indecent jester, one without self-respect.—*n.* buffoon'ery, the practices of a buffoon: low or vulgar jesting. [Fr. *bouffon*—It. *buffone*; *buffare*, to jest.]

**bufo**, *bū'fō*, (*Ben Jonson*) *n.* a black tincture in alchemy. [L. *būfō*, toad.]

**bug**, *bug*, *n.* (*obs.*) an object of terror.—*ns.* bug'aboo, a bogy, or object of terror; bug'bear, an object of terror, dislike, or annoyance.—*n.*

**bug'-word**, (*obs.*) a terrifying or threatening word. [M.E. *bugge*, prob. W. *bwg*, a hobgoblin.]

**bug**, *bug*, *n.* a name applied loosely to certain insects, esp. of the Hemiptera (Heteroptera), and specifically to one (*Cimex lectularius*) that infests houses and beds: any insect or small animal (*U.S.*): a disease-germ: a viral disease (*coll.*): a craze: an enthusiast: a crazy person: an important person (big bug): a snag, a defect: a hidden microphone: a light vehicle stripped of everything inessential: lunar excursion module (see module).—*v.t.* to plant a concealed listening device in: to annoy, irritate (*slang*).—*adj.* bugged.—*n.* and *adj.* bugg'ing.—*ns.* bug'bane, bug'wort, a ranunculaceous plant (*Cimifuga foetida*) akin to baneberry, reputed to drive away insects; bug'house (*U.S.*), an insane asylum.—*adj.* insane.—*n.* bug'-hunter, a collecting entomologist. [Perh. O.E. *budda*, beetle; perh. same as bug (1).]

**bug**, *bug*, (*U.S.*) *v.i.* to start or bulge:—*pr.p.* bugg'ing; *pa.t.* and *pa.p.* bugged.—*adj.* bug'-eyed', with eyes protruding in astonishment, etc.

**bug**, *bug*, (*U.S.*) *v.i.* to leave, as in *n.* bug'-out', desertion: a deserter.—*v.i.* bug out, to desert, esp. in panic. [Perh. from bugger (off).]

**bugger**, *bug'ər*, *n.* orig. a Bulgarian heretic, believed capable of any crime: one guilty of bestiality and unnatural vice: a term of abuse, often quite colourless or even kindly (*vulg. coll.*): a rogue, scamp—applied inoffensively to child or animal (*U.S.*): a difficult or unpleasant task, etc. (*vulg. coll.*).—*v.t.* (*vulg. coll.*) to exhaust: to frustrate, ruin the plans of: to spoil, prevent success in (also with up).—*v.i.* (with off) (*vulg. coll.*) to go away quickly.—*interj.* used to express annoyance (*vulg. coll.*).—*n.* bugg'ery (*law*), bestiality, unnatural vice.—bugger about (*vulg. coll.*), to potter about. [Fr. *bougre*—L. *Bulgarus*, Bulgarian.]

**Buggins' turn**, turn for promotion, etc., in accordance with seniority, by rotation, etc. [Origin unknown.]

**buggy**, *bug'i*, *n.* a light carriage or gig of several kinds—in America, a one-horse, four-wheeled vehicle with one seat; in England, two-wheeled; in India, hooded. [By some conn. with bogie; ety. really quite unknown.]

**bugle**, *bū'gl*, *n.* orig. a buffalo or wild ox: hence (also bū'gle-horn) a horn used as a drinking vessel or hunting-horn: a treble instrument with or without keys, usually made of copper, like the trumpet, but having the bell less expanded and the tube shorter and more conical, used more for signalling than music.—*v.i.* to sound a bugle.—*ns.* bū'gle-band; bū'gle-call; bū'gler, one who sounds the bugle; bū'glet, a small bugle. [O.Fr. *bugle*;—L. *būculus*, dim. of *bōs*, an ox.]

**bugle**, *bū'gl*, *n.* a slender elongated bead, usually black.—*adj.* (*Shak.*) like bugles. [Poss. conn. with L.L. *bugulus*, hair-pad, or with Du. *beugel*, ring.]

**bugle**, *bū'gl*, *n.* a genus (*Ajuga*) of labiate plants without upper-lip. [Fr., It. *bugola*—L.L. *bugula*, *būgillō*.]

**bugloss**, *bū'glos*, *n.* a name for several plants of the borage family, esp. *Lycopsis arvensis*, a common cornfield weed, and viper's bugloss (q.v.). [Fr. *buglosse*—L. *būglōssa*—Gr. *bouglōssos*—*bous*, ox, *glōssa*, tongue.]

**bugong**, *bŏŏ'gong*, *n.* a noctuid moth eaten by Australian aborigines. [Native name.]

**buhl**, *bŏŏl*, *n.* a complicated form of inlay, gold, silver, or brass and pewter, ivory and mother-of-pearl in tortoiseshell, etc., forming panels for furniture decoration: furniture thus decorated.—Also boulle, boule. [From Charles André Boulle (1642-1732), a cabinet-maker in the service of Louis XIV.]

**buhrstone**, *bûr'stōn*, *n.* a variety of quartz, con-

*fāte, fär, hûr (her); mē, hûr (her); mīne, mōte, för; mūte, mōōn, fŏŏt; dhen (then)*

taining many small empty cells, which give it a peculiar roughness of surface particularly adapted for millstones.—Also burr'stone. [Perh. conn. with burr, from its roughness.]
**buik, buke,** *buk, bük, būk, n.* variants of Scots **bouk.**
**build,** *bild, v.t.* to erect, as a house or bridge: to construct, as a railway, etc.: to establish (*fig.*): to base, as hopes (on), to form (combinations) (*cards*).—*v.i.* to depend (with *on, upon*):—*pa.t.* and *pa.p.* **built,** *arch.* **build'ed.**—*n.* form: make. —*ns.* **build'er,** one who builds, or controls the work of building; **build'ing,** the art or process of erecting houses, etc.: a substantial structure for giving shelter, e.g. a house, office-block.— *adj.* **built,** formed or shaped.—**build'ing-block,** a hollow or solid block made of concrete or other material, larger than a brick; **build'ingboard,** an artificial material made in slabs for lining walls; **building society,** a society that advances money to its members towards providing them with dwelling-houses; **build'-up,** a building up, increasing, strengthening: the amount of this: a working up of favourable publicity: preliminaries leading up to a climax in a story, speech, etc.—*adjs.* **built'-in,** formed as part of a main structure, esp. if recessed: present as part of one's genetic inheritance: very firmly fixed; **built'-up,** of an area, covered with buildings.—**build in,** to enclose or fix by building; **build up,** to close up by building, as a door: to cover with buildings: to create, or be created, or to increase, gradually (as a concentration of troops, a reputation, voltage, tension): to put together from parts already made: to edify spiritually. [O.E. *gebyld,* pa.p. of an assumed *byldan,* to build—*bold,* a dwelling.]
**buirdly,** *bûrd'li,* (*Scot.*) *adj.* stalwart, large and well made. [Poss. a variant of burly.]
**buist,** *büst,* (*Scot.*) *n.* a box: a tar-box: an owner's mark on sheep or cattle.—*v.t.* to mark thus. [O.Fr. *boiste* (Fr. *boîte*), box.]
**buke.** See buik.
**bukshi, bukshee,** *buk'shē, n.* a paymaster. See buckshish. [Pers. *bakhshi.*]
**bulb,** *bulb, n.* a subterranean bud with swollen leaf-bases in which reserve materials are stored: a protuberance or swelling: the medulla oblongata: a dilatation or expansion of a glass tube: the glass of an electric light.—*v.i.* to form bulbs: to bulge out or swell.—*adjs.* **bulb'ar, bulbed, bulbif'erous.**—*n.* **bulb'il,** a small bud that may grow into an independent plant.—*adj.* **bulb'ous.**—**bulb of percussion,** a raised cone on a worked flint, marking where a blow was struck. [L. *bulbus*—Gr. *bolbos,* an onion.]
**bulbul,** *bool'bool, n.* properly, a Persian nightingale: in India, extended to a genus (*Pycnonotus*) of birds akin to the babblers: a sweet singer. [Arab.]
**Bulgarian,** *bul-gā'ri-ən, adj.* of Bulgaria or its language.—*n.* a native or citizen of Bulgaria: the Bulgarian language (Slavonic).—*n.* **Bul'gar** (*-gär*), a member of an ancient Finnic or Ugrian tribe that moved from the Volga towards Bulgaria.—*adj.* **Bulgaric** (*-gar'ik*).—*n.* the ancient language of the Bulgars.
**bulge,** *bulj, n.* a protuberance, swelling: a temporary increase.—*v.i.* and *v.t.* to swell out.— *ns.* **bul'ger,** wooden golf-club with a convex face; **bul'giness.**—*adjs.* **bul'ging,** swelling out: overfull; **bul'gy.**—**to get the bulge on one,** (*slang*) to get a decided advantage over a person. [O.Fr. *boulge,* prob. L. *bulga,* a leather knapsack: a Gallic word; cf. bilge.]
**bulimia,** *bū-lim'i-a, n.* morbid voracity (*lit.* and *fig.*).—Earlier forms **būl'imy, buli'mus.** [Gr. *boulimiā*—*bous,* ox, *līmos,* hunger.]
**bulk,** *bulk, n.* a stall or framework built in front of a shop.—*n.* **bulk'er** (*arch.*), a street thief or

strumpet. [Ety. dub.; cf. O.N. *bālkr,* beam, O.E. *bolca,* gangway of a ship.]
**bulk,** *bulk, n.* a heap (now only of tobacco): a cargo: the belly, trunk, or body: a hull or hold: volume or size: great size: the greater part: any huge body or structure: mass.—*v.i.* to be in bulk: to be of weight or importance.—*v.t.* to put or hold in bulk: (often with *out*; also with *up*) to cause to swell, make greater in size.—*n.* **bulk'iness.**—*adj.* **bulk'y,** having bulk: filling much space: unwieldy.—**bulk buying,** largescale purchase of a commodity, esp. on preferential terms and by a single buyer on behalf of a body of consumers: guaranteed purchase by one country of all or most of another's output of a commodity; **bulk carrier,** vessel carrying cargo, such as grain, that is not in the form of separate packages.—**break bulk,** see **break** (1); **load in bulk,** to put cargo in loose; **sell in bulk,** to sell cargo as it is in the hold: to sell in large quantities. [Prob. (hypothetical) O.N. *bulki,* heap or cargo, confused with O.E. *buc,* belly; see bouk.]
**bulkhead,** *bulk'hed, n.* any of the partitions separating one part of a ship's interior from another: a protecting barrier or structure: the roof of a bulk (1): the bulk itself.—**collision bulkhead,** that nearest the bow. [bulk (1) and bulk (2).]
**bull,** *bool, n.* an uncastrated male of the ox kind: a male whale, walrus, elephant, moose, etc.: Taurus (*astron.*): one who seeks to raise the price of stocks, and speculates on a rise (cf. *bear*): a bull's-eye (*musketry*): nonsense (*slang*): spit and polish (*mil. slang*): a policeman (*U.S. slang*). —*adj.* male: massive: favourable to the bulls, rising (*Stock Exchange*).—*v.t.* to try to raise the price of: to copulate with (a cow).—*v.i.* to be in heat, of a cow.—*adj.* **bull'ish,** like a bull: obstinate: inclining towards rising prices (*Stock Exchange*).—*adv.* **bull'ishly.**—*ns.* **bull'ishness; bull'ock,** an ox or castrated bull.—**bull'-bait'**ing, the sport of baiting or exciting bulls with dogs; **bull'bat** (*U.S.*), the night-hawk or goat-sucker; **bull'-beef,** the beef or flesh of bulls, coarse beef: (*Shak.* in *pl.*) **bull'-beeves; bull'-begg'ar** (*dial.*), a hobgoblin, etc.: **bull'-calf,** a male calf: a stupid fellow, a lout; **bull'-dance,** a dance of men only; **bull'dog,** a breed of dogs of great courage, formerly used for baiting bulls: hence a person of obstinate courage: a shortbarrelled revolver of large calibre: a proctor's attendant at Oxford or Cambridge.—*v.t.* to assail like a bulldog: to wrestle with and throw (a steer, etc.) (*U.S.*).—**bull'fight,** a popular spectacle in Spain, Portugal, Southern France, and Latin America, in which a bull is goaded to fury by mounted *picadores* armed with lances, and despatched by a specially skilful *espada* or swordsman; **bull'fight'er; bull'fight'ing; bull'**finch, a plump red-breasted finch: (perh. for *bull-fence*) a kind of high, thick hedge hard to jump; **bull'frog,** a large frog.—*adj.* **bull'-fronted,** having a forehead like a bull.—*n.* **bull'head,** the miller's thumb, a small river fish with large, flat head: extended to various similar fishes, as the pogge (*armed bullhead*).—*adj.* **bull'-head'ed,** impetuous and obstinate.—**bull'-head'edness; bull'-hoof,** a West Indian passion-flower (from the shape of its leaf); **bull'-mastiff,** a cross between the bulldog and the mastiff, the mastiff strain predominating.—*adj.* **bull'-necked,** thicknecked.—**bull'ock's-heart',** the custard-apple; **bull'-pen,** a pen for a bull: a similar enclosure for prisoners (*U.S.*); **bull'-of-the-bog'** (*Scot.*), *†*he bittern; **bull'-pup,** a young bulldog; **bull'-rin,:',** the enclosure for bull-fighting or bull-baiting: a ring for a bull's nose; **bull'-roar'er,** a boy's plaything, made of an oblong slip of wood, whirled at the end of a string to give a loud whirring noise—the native Australian *turndun,*

**bull** 170 **bummalo**

the *rhombos* of the Greek mysteries; **bull's'-eye,** the central boss formed in making a sheet of blown glass: a thick lens, or round piece of glass, as in a lantern: a policeman's lantern: a round opening or window: the centre of a target: a shot that hits it: a big round hard peppermint sweet; **bull'shit,** (*mil. slang*) nonsense; **bull'-terr'ier,** a cross between bulldog and terrier; **bull'-trout,** a variety of sea-trout (*Salmo trutta eriox*): a large trout with a big head: a salmon that has re-entered fresh water after spawning; **bull'whack,** a heavy whip.— *v.t.* to lash with a bull-whack.—**a bull in a china shop,** one who lacks the delicacy that the situation calls for; **bull into,** to plunge hastily into; **take the bull by the horns,** to grapple boldly with a danger or difficulty. [M.E. *bole,* prob. O.N. *bole, boli;* most prob. related to **bellow.**]

**bull,** *bōōl, n.* an edict of the pope with his seal affixed.—*n.* **bull'ary,** a collection of papal bulls. [L. *bulla,* a knob, a leaden seal.]

**bull,** *bōōl, n.* a ludicrous inconsistency in speech often said to be an especial prerogative of Irishmen—'I was a fine child, but they changed me'. [Prob. O.Fr. *boul,* cheat.]

**bull,** *bōōl, n.* drink made by pouring water into a cask that had held liquor. [Origin unknown.]

**bull,** *bōōl, n.* a deck game in which pads are thrown at an inclined board, the **bull'-board.** [Origin unknown.]

**bulla,** *bōōl'a, n.* a round metal ornament worn by ancient Roman children: a seal attached to a document: a blister: anything rounded or globular: (*cap.*) the bubble-shell genus.—*adj.* **bull'ate,** blistered or puckered: bubble-like: knobbed: inflated. [L. *bulla.*]

**bullace,** *bōōl'is, n.* a shrub closely allied to the sloe. [Cf. O.Fr. *beloce.*]

**bulldoze,** *bōōl'dōz, v.t.* to intimidate: to bully: to level and clear by bulldozer.—*n.* **bull'dozer,** one who bulldozes: a pistol or other means of compulsion: a tractor machine for levelling and clearing land. [Origin obscure.]

**buller,** *bōōl'ər, (Scot.) n.* turbulence in water: a bubbling: a bellow.—*v.i.* to seethe: to gurgle: to bellow. [Cf. Dan. *bulder,* Swed. *buller,* rumble, noise, roar; prob. partly from or influenced by O.Fr. *bullir,* Icel. *bulla,* to boil.]

**bullet,** *bōōl'it, n.* a little ball (*obs.*): a projectile, now esp. one (round or conical) discharged from any kind of small-arm: a plumb or sinker in fishing.—*n.* **bull'et-head,** a round head: an obstinate fellow (*U.S.*).—*adjs.* **bull'et-head'ed; bull'et-proof,** proof against bullets. [Fr. *boulette,* dim. of *boule,* a ball—L. *bulla.*]

**bulletin,** *bōōl'i-tin, n.* an official report of public news, or of a patient's progress. [Fr.,—It. *bullettino.*]

**bullet-tree, bulletrie.** Same as **bully-tree.**

**bullion,** *bōōl'yən, n.* gold and silver in the mass and uncoined: occasionally, precious metal, coined and uncoined: a heavy twisted cord fringe, often covered with gold or silver wire.—*n.* **bull'ionist,** one in favour of metallic currency. [Perh. conn. with L.L. *bulliō, -ōnis,* a boiling.]

**bullock.** See **bull** (1).

**bully,** *bōōl'i, n.* a cruel oppressor of the weak: a blustering, noisy, overbearing fellow: a ruffian hired to beat or intimidate anyone (*arch.*): one who lives upon the gains of a prostitute (*obs.*): a term of genial familiarity, esp. to a man (*obs.*).— *adj.* blustering (*arch.*): excellent.—*v.i.* to bluster. —*v.t.* to oppress cruelly: to threaten in a noisy way:—*pr.p.* **bull'ying;** *pa.p.* **bull'ied.**—*interj.* good.—*ns.* **bull'yism; bull'y-rook,** a bully: a comrade. [Perh. Du. *boel,* a lover; cf. Ger. *buhle.*]

**bully,** *bōōl'i, n.* a miner's hammer.

**bully,** *bōōl'i, n.* a scrimmage (*football*): in hockey,

the opening (or reopening) of the game—two opposing players each striking the ground on his own side of the ball and his opponent's stick alternately, three times, and then trying to strike the ball—also **bully-off'.**—*v.t.* and *v.i.* **bull'y** (-**off**).

**bully,** *bōōl'i,* **bully-beef,** *bōōl'i-bēf, ns.* canned or pickled beef. [Prob. Fr. *bouilli,* boiled beef, influenced by **bull.**]

**bullyrag,** *bōōl'i-rag,* **ballyrag,** *bal'i-rag, v.t.* to assail with abusive language or horseplay: to badger. [Origin unknown; perhaps from **rag** (2).]

**bully-tree,** *bōōl'i-trē, n.* a name for several West Indian sapotaceous trees yielding good timber, edible fruits, and balata, esp. *Mimusops Balata.* —Also **bull'et-tree, bull'etrie, boll'etrie.** [Perh. from **bullace;** perh. from **balata.**]

**bulrush,** *bōōl'rush, n.* a name given to two distinct tall marsh or water plants—the reed-mace or cat's-tail, and clubrush, a plant of the sedge family (*Scirpus lacustris*).—*adj.* **bul'rushy.**—**bulrush millet,** pearl millet. [Perh. **bole** (1) or **bull** (1) in sense of great or coarse, and **rush** (2).]

**bulse,** *buls, n.* a bag for or of diamonds, etc. [Port. *bolsa*—L.L. *bursa,* a purse. See **purse.**]

**bulwark,** *bōōl'wərk, n.* a fortification or rampart: a breakwater or sea-wall: the side of a ship projecting above the deck: any means of defence or security.—*v.t.* to defend; to fortify. [Cf. Ger. *bollwerk.*]

**bum,** *bum, n.* the buttocks.—*n.* **bum'bai'liff** (*Shak.*), **bum'-bay'lie),** a bailiff who comes behind to make arrests: a sheriff's officer. [Cf. **bump** in sense of swelling.]

**bum,** *bum, v.i.* to hum or make a murmuring sound, as a bee.—*v.t.* (*Scot.*) to toss, hurl:—(*pr.p.* **bum'ming;** *pa.p.* **bummed.**—*n.* a humming sound.— *ns.* **bum'-bee** (*Scot.*), a bumble bee; **bum'-clock** (*Scot.*), a drone-beetle.—*n.* **bumm'er,** a person or thing that bums.—**head'-bumm'er** (*Scot.*), a manager or person in authority. [Imit.]

**bum,** *bum,* (*U.S. slang*) *n.* a spree: a dissolute fellow: a sponger.—*adj.* worthless: despicable. —*v.i.* to loaf: to sponge: to live dissolutely.—*n.* **bumm'er,** a plundering straggler or camp-follower (during the American Civil War): a dissolute fellow: a loafer: a sponger.

**bumbaze,** *bum-bāz', (Scot.) v.t.* to confound, bamboozle. [Origin obscure.]

**bumble, bummle,** *bum'(b)l, v.i.* to bungle: to utter indistinctly: to bustle about blunderingly. —*n.* confusion: indistinct utterance: a bungler: an idler.—**bum'ble-bee,** a large wild loud-humming bee, a humble bee; **bum'ble-foot,** cellulitis in a fowl's foot, due to pus-forming organisms: club-foot; **bum'ble-puppy,** the old game of nine-holes: unscientific whist: a racket game in which a string is wound round a post by hitting a slung ball or bag. [Freq. of **bum** (2).]

**Bumble,** *bum'bl, n.* a beadle: a self-important minor official.—*n.* **Bum'bledom.** [From Mr *Bumble* in Dickens's *Oliver Twist.*]

**bumbo,** *bum'bō, n.* a mixture of rum or gin, water, sugar, and nutmeg, or similar drink. [Perh. It. *bombo,* a child's word for drink.]

**bum-boat,** *bum'-bōt, n.* orig. a Thames scavenger's boat: a boat bringing vegetables, etc., for sale to ships. [Origin doubtful.]

**bumf, bumf,** *n.* lavatory paper: papers, official papers, documents (*disparagingly*).

**bumkin, bumpkin,** *bum'kin, n.* a short beam of timber projecting from each bow of a ship, for the purpose of extending the lower corner of the foresail to windward: a small outrigger over the stern of a boat, usually serving to extend the mizzen. [From **boom** (1), and dim. termination -*kin.*]

**bummalo, bumalo,** *bum'ə-lō, n.* the Bombay duck, a small Indian fish of a family (*Scopelidae*) akin

*fāte, fär; mē, hûr* (her); *mīne; mōte, för; mūte; mōōn, fōōt; dhen* (then)

to the salmon, dried and eaten as a relish.—Also **bummalō'ti.** [Marathi *bombīl*.]

**bummaree**, *bum-ər-ē'*, *n.* orig. a middleman in Billingsgate fish-market: a porter at Smithfield meat-market. [Ety. unknown.]

**bummer.** See bum (2 and 3).

**bummle.** See bumble.

**bummock**, *bum'ək*, (*Orkney*) *n.* a brewing of ale for a feast. [Ety. unknown.]

**bump**, *bump*, *v.i.* to make a heavy or loud noise: to knock dully: to jolt: to move joltingly: (of a cricket-ball) to bound high on striking the pitch. —*v.t.* to strike with a dull sound: to strike against: in boat-racing, to overtake and impinge upon—the bumper consequently taking the place of the bumped in rank: to spread out in printing so as to fill any desired number of pages.—*n.* a dull heavy blow: a thump: a high rebound of a cricket-ball: a jolt: a lump or swelling: a protuberance on the head confidently associated by phrenologists with qualities or propensities of mind: hence (*coll.*) faculty.—*n.* **bump'er**, anything or person that bumps: a bar on a motorcar to lessen the shock of collision: a railway buffer (*U.S.*): a bumping race: a cup or glass filled to the brim for drinking a toast: anything large or generous in measure: a crowded house at a theatre or concert.—*adj.* full to overflowing.—*v.i.* to drink bumpers.—*ns.* **bump'iness; bumpol'ogy** (*jocose*), phrenology.—*adj.* **bump'y.** —**bumping race**, a boat-race in which the boats seek to bump, not to pass; **bump off** (*slang*), to kill, murder; **bump up** (*coll.*), to raise (prices): to increase size of. [Imit.]

**bump**, *bump*, *n.* the booming cry of the bittern.— *v.i.* to utter that cry. [Imit.]

**bumph.** Same as bumf.

**bumpkin**, *bump'kin*, *n.* an awkward, clumsy rustic: a clown.—*adj.* **bump'kinish.** [Prob. Du. *boomken*, a log.]

**bumpkin.** See bumkin.

**bumptious**, *bump'shəs*, *adj.* offensively self-important.—*adv.* **bump'tiously.**—*n.* **bump'tiousness.** [Prob. formed from bump (1).]

**bun**, *bun*, *n.* a kind of sweet cake: a rounded mass of hair.—**bun-fight** (*slang*), a tea party. [Perh. from O.Fr. *bugne*, a swelling.]

**bun**, *bun*, *n.* a dry stalk: a hare's scut. [Possibly Gael. *bun*, a root, a stump.]

**bun**, *bun*, *n.* a playful name for a rabbit or a squirrel. [Origin unknown.]

**buna**, *bōō'na*, *n.* an artificial rubber made by the polymerisation of butadiene. [Orig. trademark.]

**bunch**, *bunch, bunsh*, *n.* a lump: a lumpish gathering: a number of things aggregated or fastened together: a definite quantity fastened together, as of linen yarn (180,000 yards), etc.: a cluster: a handful of flowers: something in the form of a tuft or knot.—*v.i.* to swell out in a bunch: to cluster.—*v.t.* to make a bunch of: to concentrate. —*adj.* **bunched**, humped, protuberant: lumpy.— *ns.* **bunch'iness; bunch'ing.**—*adj.* **bunch'y**, growing in bunches or like a bunch: bulging.— *adj.* **bunch'-backed** (*Shak.*), hump-backed.—*n.* **bunch'-grass**, a clumped Western American grass of several kinds.—**bunch of fives**, the clenched fist. [Origin unknown.]

**bunco.** See bunko.

**buncombe.** See bunkum.

**bund**, *bōōnt*, (*Ger.*) *n.* a league or confederacy.—*ns.* **bundesrat(h)** (*bōōn'dəs-rät*), federal council in Germany, etc.: upper house of the parliament of the Federal Republic of Germany; **bundestag** (*-tähh*), lower house of the Federal German parliament; **bundeswehr** (*-vär*), the Federal German armed forces.

**bund**, *bund*, *n.* (India, etc.) an embankment or dam: a stoppage of work by employees. [Hind. *band*, from Pers.]

**bundle**, *bun'dl*, *n.* a number of things loosely bound together: a bunch: a loose parcel, esp. one contained in a cloth: a strand of conducting vessels, fibres, etc. (*biol.*): a definite measure or quantity, as two reams of paper, twenty hanks of linen yarn, etc.—*v.t.* to make into bundles: to put hastily or unceremoniously: to hustle.—*v.i.* to pack up one's things for a journey: to go hurriedly or in confusion (with *away, off, out*): to lie in bed together fully clad (an old custom in Wales and New England for sweethearts and others). [Conn. with bind and bond.]

**bundobust.** Same as bandobast.

**bundook**, *bun'dŏŏk*, (*mil. slang*) *n.* a rifle. [Hind. *bandūq*.]

**bung**, *bung*, *n.* the stopper of the hole in a barrel: a large cork.—*v.t.* to stop up or enclose with a bung (also *fig.*).—**bung'-hole**, a hole for a bung; **bung'-vent**, a small hole in a bung to let gases escape, etc. [Ety. dubious.]

**bung**, *bung*, *n.* a large purse (*obs.*; *thieves' cant*): a cutpurse (*Shak.*).—**nip a bung**, to cut a purse. [Cf. O.E. *pung*, purse.]

**bung**, *bung*, (*slang*) *v.t.* to throw or shove carelessly and hurriedly.

**bungalow**, *bung'gə-lō*, *n.* a lightly-built house, properly with a veranda and one story: now loosely, a one-story house.—*adj.* and *n.* **bung'-aloid.**—**dak(-)bungalow, dâk bungalow** (see dâk). [Hindi *banglā*, (house) in the style of Bengal, house.]

**bungle**, *bung'gl*, *n.* anything clumsily done: a gross mismanagement.—*v.i.* to act in a clumsy manner.—*v.t.* to make or mend clumsily: to mismanage grossly: to make a failure of by want of skill.—*n.* **bung'ler.**—*adj.* **bung'ling**, clumsy, awkward: unskilfully or ill done.—Also *n.*—*adv.* **bung'lingly.** [Ety. dub.: prob. onomatopoeic; cf. Sw. dial. *bangla*, to work ineffectually; Hindes Groome suggests Gypsy *bongo*, left, awkward.]

**bunia.** See bunnia.

**bunion**, *bun'yən*, *n.* a lump or inflamed swelling of the first joint of the great toe. [Ety. unknown; poss. It. *bugnone*, a botch.]

**bunk**, *bungk*, *n.* a box or recess in a ship's cabin, a sleeping-berth anywhere.—*v.i.* to occupy a bunk. —*n.* **bunk'er**, a window-seat and chest (*Scot.*): a turf seat (*Scot.*): a large bin or chest, esp. for coals (*Scot.*): slab beside a sink (*Scot.*): compartment for fuel on shipboard: sand-pit or sandy gap in turf, esp. as a hazard in a golf course.—*v.t.* to fuel: to play into a bunker.—*v.i.* to fuel.—*adj.* **bunk'ered**, in a bunker: in difficulties. [Cf. O.N. *bunki*, Scand. *bunke*, heap.]

**bunk**, *bungk*, (*slang*) *n.* flight (esp. in phrase **to do a bunk**).—*v.i.* to flee.

**bunk.** See bunkum.

**bunker**, *bung'kər*, *n.* an underground bombproof shelter. [Ger.]

**bunko**, **bunco**, *bung'kō*, (*U.S.*) *n.* a form of confidence-trick by which a simple fellow is swindled or taken somewhere and robbed.—*v.t.* to rob or swindle in such a way.—*n.* **bunk'o-steer'er**, that one of the swindling confederates who lures the victim.

**bunkum**, *bung'kəm*, *n.* bombastic speechmaking intended for the newspapers rather than to persuade the audience: humbug: claptrap.—Also **bun'combe, bunk.** [From *Buncombe*, a county in North Carolina, whose member is said to have gone on talking in Congress, explaining apologetically that he was 'only talking for Buncombe'.]

**bunnia, bunia**, *bun'i-a*, *n.* a Hindu merchant. [Hind.]

**bunny**, *bun'i*, *n.* a pet name for a rabbit.—*n.* **bunn'y-hug**, a 20th-century American dance— also *v.i.* [Ety. unknown; cf. bun.]

**bunodont**, *bū'nō-dont*, *adj.* having tuberculate

molars—opp. to *lophodont*. [Gr. *bounos*, a rounded hill, *odous, odontos*, a tooth.]

**bunraku,** *bōōn-rä'kōō, n.* a Japanese form of puppet theatre in which the puppets, usu. about 3 ft high, are each manipulated by 3 men who remain visible throughout the performance. [Jap.]

**bunsen,** *bun'sən,* or *bōōn'sən, adj.* invented by the great chemist, R. W. *Bunsen* of Heidelberg.—

**bun'sen-burn'er,** a gas-burner in which a plentiful supply of air is caused to mingle with the gas before ignition, so that a smokeless flame of low luminosity but great heating power is the result.

**bunt,** *bunt, n.* stink-brand, a disease of wheat: the fungus (*Tilletia*) that causes it.—*adj.* **bunt'ed, bunt'y.** [Ety. unknown.]

**bunt,** *bunt, n.* the bagging part of a fishing-net, a sail, etc.—*v.i.* to belly, as a sail.—**bunt'line,** a rope passing from the foot-rope of a square sail to prevent bellying in furling. [Ety. unknown.]

**bunt,** *bunt, v.i.* to push with the horns, butt: to spring, rear: to block a ball with the bat (*baseball*).—Also *v.t.* and *n.*—*n.* a push.—*n.* **bunt'ing,** pushing: a boy's game, played with sticks and a small piece of wood: a strong timber, a stout prop.

**bunter,** *bunt'ər, n.* a rag-picker: a low woman. **Bunter,** *bōōn'tər,* (*geol.*) *n.* the lowest division of the Trias. [Ger., mottled.]

**bunting,** *bunt'ing, n.* a thin worsted stuff for ships' colours: flags, cloth decorations. [Ety. dub.]

**bunting,** *bunt'ing, n.* any finch of a group (*Emberiza,* etc.) nearly allied to the crossbills.

**bunting.** See **bunt.**

**bunya,** *bun'yə,* **bun'ya-bun'ya,** *n.* an Australian monkey-puzzle with large edible seeds. [Native word.]

**bunyip,** *bun'yip, n.* an Australian swamp monster, invisible to whites: an impostor. [Native word.]

**buonamano,** *bwō'na-mä'nō,* or **bonamano,** *bo-na-,* (It.) a tip.

**buona sera,** *bwō'na sā'ra,* (It.) good-evening.

**buon giorno,** *bwōn jor'nō,* (It.) good-day.

**buoy,** *boi,* in U.S. often *bōō'ē* (and in compounds below, *bōō'y-*) *n.* a floating secured mark, serving (by its shape, colour, light, sound, etc.) as a guide or as a warning.—*v.t.* to furnish or mark with buoys or marks: to keep afloat, bear up, or sustain: to raise, lift.—*v.t.* to rise.—*ns.* **buoy'age,** a series of buoys or floating beacons to mark the course for vessels: the providing of buoys; **buoy'ance** (*rare*), **buoy'ancy,** capacity for floating lightly on water or in the air: loss of weight owing to immersion in a fluid: lightness of spirit, cheerfulness (*fig.*).—*adj.* **buoy'ant,** tending to float or to buoy up: light, cheerful, and elastic.—*n.* **buoy'antness.** [Du. *boei,* buoy, fetter, through Romance forms (Norman *boie*), from L.L. *boia,* a collar of leather.]

**Buphaga,** *bū'fä-gə, n.* a small genus of African birds, nearly related to the starlings, feeding on the larvae of gadflies and the like, which they find on the backs of cattle, camels, etc.—Also **beef-eater** and **ox-pecker.** [Gr. *bous,* an ox, *phagein,* to eat.]

**buplever,** *bū-plev'ər, n.* hare's-ear (Bupleurum). [Fr. *buplèvre*—L. *būpleurum*—Gr. *bous,* ox, *pleuron,* rib.]

**Buprestis,** *bū-pres'tis, n.* a genus of beetles, typical of a large family, **Bupres'tidae,** those occurring in warmer countries having lively colour and metallic sheen—some known as golden beetles. [Gr. *houprēstis,* a kind of poisonous beetle—*bous,* ox, *prēthein,* to swell.]

**bur.** See **burr** (1) and (2).

**buran,** *bōō-rän', n.* a violent blizzard blowing from the north-east in Siberia and Central Asia. [Russ.]

**burble,** *bûrb'l, n.* a tangle.—*v.t.* to confuse. [Scot.; prob. conn. with O.Fr. *barbouiller,* to confound.]

**burble,** *bûrb'l, n.* a murmur.—*v.t.* and *v.i.* to murmur: to gurgle: to talk excitedly and rather incoherently (*coll.*).—*n.* **burb'ling,** separation of the flow of air from the upper surface of a moving aerofoil.—**burble point, burbling point,** the angle of attack at which the sharp drop in the ratio of lift to drag (an effect of burbling too near the leading edge) first appears. [Prob. onomatopoeic.]

**burbot,** *bûr'bət, n.* a fresh-water fish, like the ling, with a longish barbel on its lower jaw. [Fr. *bourbotte, barbotte.*—L.L. *borba,* mud, or L. *barba,* a beard.]

**burd,** *bûrd,* (*obs.*) *n.* a maiden: a lady. [O.E. *byrde,* well-born (or perh. *brȳd,* bride), prob. combined or confused with O.N. *byrthr,* O.E. *byrd,* birth, offspring.]

**burd,** *bûrd* (*Scot.*) *n.* a bird: a young bird: a young animal of any kind: offspring, progeny: a term of endearment.—*n.* **burd'ie,** (*dim.*).—**burd'-alane', bird'-alane',** the last remaining of a family.—*adj.* and *adv.* (*Morris* **bird'-alone**) quite alone.

**burdash,** *bûrd'ash, n.* a fringed sash worn by gentlemen in the time of Anne and George I. [Origin unknown.]

**burden,** *bûr'dən* (*arch.* **burthen, -dhən**), *n.* a load: weight: cargo: a ship's carrying capacity (still often **burthen**): that which is grievous, oppressive, or difficult to bear: an obligation: any restriction, limitation, or encumbrance affecting person or property (*Scots law*): a child in the womb (*obs.*): a birth: (in *pl.*) a boat's floorboards.—*v.t.* to load: to oppress: to encumber.—*adjs.* **bur'denous, bur'densome,** heavy: oppressive.—**burden of proof,** the obligation to prove one's contention. [O.E. *byrthen—beran,* to bear.]

**burden,** *bûr'dən,* (*arch.* **burthen, -dhən**), *n.* bourdon or bass: part of a song repeated at the end of every stanza, refrain: the leading idea of anything. [Fr. *bourdon,* a humming tone in music—L.L. *burdō,* a drone bee; confused with **burden** (1).]

**burden,** *bûr'dən, n.* a pilgrim's staff. [See **bourdon** (2).]

**burdock.** See **burr** (1).

**bureau,** *bū'rō, bū-rō', bū-rō', n.* a writing-table combined with chest of drawers: a room or office where such a table is used: a department or office for the transacting of business, such as collecting and supplying information: a government department:—*pl.* **bureaux, bureaus** (*-ōz*). [Fr. *bureau*—O.Fr. *burel,* russet cloth—L. *burrus,* red.]

**bureaucracy,** *bū-rok'rə-si,* or *-rōk', n.* a system of government by officials, responsible only to their departmental chiefs.—*ns.* **bur'eaucrat, bureau'-cratist,** one who practises or favours bureaucracy.—*adv.* **bureaucrat'ically.** [**bureau,** and Gr. *kratos,* power.]

**bureau de change,** *bü-rō də shäzh,* (Fr.) an office where currency can be exchanged.

**burette,** *bū-ret', n.* a graduated glass tube with a tap, for measuring liquids run off: an altar-cruet. [Fr.]

**burg,** *bûrg, bûrg, n.* a fortress or a walled town (*hist.*): a town (*U.S. coll.*; *bûrg*). [West Ger. *burg;* O.E. *burh.*]

**burgage,** *bûr'gij, n.* a tenure in socage for a yearly rent: a tenure in Scotland in royal burghs under nominal service of watching. [L.L. *burgāgium,* from the root of *borough,* **burgh.**]

**burganet, burgonet,** *bûr'gə-net, n.* a light 16th-century helmet with cheek-pieces. [Fr. *bourguignotte,* lit. Burgundian.]

**burgee,** *bûr'jē, n.* a swallow-tailed flag or pennant: a kind of small coal for furnaces. [Origin unknown.]

**burgeon, bourgeon,** *bûr'jən, v.i.* to put forth

sprouts or buds: to grow. [Fr. *bourgeon*, a bud, shoot.]

**burgess**, *bûr'jis*, *n.* a freeman or citizen of a borough: a member of a privileged class in a town: a member of parliament for a borough (*hist.*): a borough magistrate or town councillor (*hist.*). [O.Fr. *burgeis*.]

**burgh**, *bûr'ə*, spelling of **borough**, used for Scottish burghs, otherwise archaic.—*adj.* **burghal** (*bûrg'l*). —*n.* **burgher** (*bûrg'ər*), a freeman or citizen of a borough (burgh): a townsman: a Seceder who felt himself free to take the burgess oath (see **antiburgher** (*Scot. eccles.*): a citizen of one of the South African Boer republics (*hist.*): in Ceylon, a Eurasian, or a person of European race assimilated to the native population.—**parliamentary burgh**, one whose boundaries, as first fixed in 1832 for parliamentary representation, were adopted later for municipal purposes: a burgh which by itself or in combination elects a member of parliament: often applied to one that has ceased to do so; **police burgh**, a burgh constituted by the sheriff for purposes of improvement and police; **royal burgh**, a corporate body deriving its existence, constitution, and rights from a royal charter, actual or presumed to have existed. —**burgh of barony**, a corporation under a feudal superior or baron, who sometimes nominated the magistrates; **burgh of regality**, a burgh of barony enfranchised by crown charter, with regal or exclusive criminal jurisdiction within its territory. [See **borough**.]

**burglar**, *bûrg'lər*, *n.* one who enters a building as a trespasser (before 1969, by night) to commit a felony, e.g. to steal.—*v.i.* to commit burglary.— Also *v.t.*—*adj.* **burglarious** (*-lā'ri-əs*).—*adv.* **burglar'iously.**—*vs.t.* **burg'larise, -ize, burg'le** (a facetious back-formation).—*n.* **burg'lary.** [Ety. dub.]

**burgomaster**, *bûr'gō-mäs-tər*, *n.* the chief magistrate of a Dutch, Flemish or German town. [Du. *burgemeester*; Ger. *bürgermeister*, lit. boroughmaster.]

**burgonet.** See **burganet.**

**burgoo**, *bûr-gōō'*, *bûr'gōō*, *n.* a sailor's dish of boiled oatmeal with salt, butter, and sugar: a stew or thick soup for American picnics. [Derivation unknown.]

**burgrave**, *bûr'grāv*, *n.* the governor or hereditary ruler of a town or castle. [Ger. *burg-graf*.]

**burgundy**, *bûr'gən-di*, *n.* a French wine (generally red), made in *Burgundy*: a similar wine made elsewhere.—**Burgundy mixture**, a fungicide composed of copper sulphate, sodium carbonate, and water; **Burgundy pitch**, a resin prepared by melting and straining the exudation from Norway spruce (now got mainly elsewhere).

**burhel.** Same as **bharal.**

**burial**, *ber'i-əl*, *n.* the act of burying: a tomb (*arch.*).—**bur'ial-ground**, a ground set apart for burials—**bur'ial-place**, a burial-ground: the place where anyone is buried; **burial society**, an insurance society for providing the expenses of burial. [O.E. *byrgels*, a tomb; see **bury**.]

**Buridan's ass**, *bū'ri-danz*, in the sophism doubtfully attributed to the French 14th-century schoolman Jean *Buridan*, an ass dying of starvation through inability to choose between two equidistant and equally desirable sources of food.

**burin**, *būr'in*, *n.* a kind of chisel of tempered steel, used in copper engraving: the distinctive style of an engraver: a palaeolithic flint tool.—*n.* **bur'inist**, an engraver. [Fr.; from root of **bore**.]

**buriti**, *bōō-ri-tē'*, *n.* the miriti palm. [Tupi.]

**burke**, *bûrk*, *v.t.* to murder, esp. by stifling: hence (*fig.*) to put an end to quietly. [From *Burke*, an Edinburgh Irishman (hanged 1829), who committed the crime in order to sell the bodies of his victims for dissection.]

**burk(h)a**, *bōōr'kə*, *n.* a loose garment, with veiled eyeholes, covering the whole body. [Urdu *burga'*—Ar.]

**burl**, *bûrl*, *n.* as mall knot in thread: a knot in wood.—*v.t.* to pick knots, etc., from, in finishing cloth.—*n.* **bur'ler.**—*adj.* **bur'ly.**—**bur'ling-i'ron**; **bur'ling-machine'.**

**burlap**, *bûr'lap*, *n.* a coarse canvas for wrappings, wall-coverings, etc.—usually in *pl.* [Origin unknown.]

**burlesque**, *bûr-lesk'*, *n.* ludicrous imitation: a piece of literature, of acting, or other performance that mocks its original by grotesque exaggeration or by combining the dignified with the low or the familiar: a playful or jocular composition (*mus.*).—*adj.* of the nature of burlesque: practising burlesque.—*v.t.* to mock by burlesque: to make a burlesque of. [It. *burlesco*; prob. from L.L. *burra*, a flock of wool, a trifle.]

**burletta**, *bûr-let'ə*, *n.* a musical farce: comic opera. [It.; dim. of *burla*, a jest.]

**burly**, *bûr'li*, *adj.* big and sturdy.—*n.* **bur'liness.** [M.E. *borlich*; perh. the same as O.H.G. *burlih*, high—*bōr*, a height.]

**Burmese**, *bûr'mēz*, *-mēz'*, *adj.* relating to *Burma* or its people or language.—*n.* a native of Burma: the language of Burma.—Also **Bur'man.**

**burn**, *bûrn*, (now chiefly *Scot.*) *n.* a small stream or brook.—**burn'side**, the ground beside a burn. [O.E. *burna*, brook, spring; cf. Du. and Ger. *born.*]

**burn**, *bûrn*, *v.t.* to consume or injure by fire or great heat: to produce an effect of heat upon (as to bake pottery, calcine lime, scorch food, wither grass): to oxidise: to use (up), e.g. uranium, in a nuclear reactor: to corrode: to make by fire or analogous means.—*v.i.* to be burnt: to be on fire: to give out heat or light: to glow: to feel excess of heat: to be inflamed with passion:— *pa.t.* and *pa.p.* **burnt** or **burned.**—*n.* a hurt or mark due to burning.—*ns.* **burn'er**, one who burns: a fixture or part of a lamp or gas-jet from which a flame comes; **burn'ing**, act of consuming by fire: conflagration: inflammation: a quantity burned at one time: controlled expenditure of rocket propellant for course adjustment purposes.—*adj.* very hot: scorching: ardent: excessive.—Also *adv.*—**burning bush**, emblem of the Church of Scotland and other Presbyterian churches with the motto, 'Nec tamen consumebatur', adopted from Exodus iii. 2, in memory of the unconquerable courage of the Covenanters under the cruel persecutions of the 17th century: applied to various plants, as dittany, whose volatile oil may catch fire in the air, some American species of spindle-tree with bright red fruits, artillery plant, etc.; **burn'ing-glass**, a convex lens concentrating the sun's rays at its focus; **burn'ing-house**, a kiln; **burn'ing-mirr'or**, a concave mirror for producing heat by concentrating the sun's rays; **burning mountain**, a volcano; **burn'ing-point**, the temperature at which a volatile oil in an open vessel will take fire from a match held close to its surface; **burning question**, one keenly discussed; **burnt'-almonds** (*pl.*), almonds in burnt sugar; **burnt'-cork'**, charred cork used for blacking the face.—Also *v.t.*—**burnt'-ear**, a smut in oats, wheat, etc.; **burnt'-off'ering**, something offered and burned upon an altar as sacrifice; **burnt'-sienn'a** (see **sienna**); **burn'-the-wind** (*Scot.*), a blacksmith.— **burn a hole in one's pocket**, said of money when one is eager to spend it; **burn blue** (see **blue**); **burn daylight** (*Shak.*), to waste time; **burn down**, to burn to the ground; **burn in**, to fix and render durable by intense heat, to imprint indelibly; **burn one's boats**, to cut oneself off from all chance of retreat, to stake everything on success; **burn one's fingers**, to suffer from interfering, from embarking in speculations, etc.; **burn out**, to destroy or drive out by burning: to burn till the fire dies down from want of fuel; **burn the candle at both ends (see candle)**; **burn the midnight oil,** to study late into the night; **burn the water,** to spear salmon by torchlight; **burn up,** to consume completely by fire: to be burned completely: to increase in activity of burning: to make short or easy work of; **(money) to burn,** in great abundance. [O.E. the transitive weak verb *bærnan, bærnde, bærned,* has been confused with the intransitive strong verb *beornan, byrnan, barn, bornen;* cf. Ger. *brennen,* to burn.]

**burnet,** *bûr′nit, adj.* dark brown (*obs.*).—*n.* a fine dark woollen cloth of the Middle Ages: the name of two closely related rosaceous plants, the great burnet (*Sanguisorba officinalis* or *Poterium officinale*), a meadow-plant, and common or salad burnet (*P. Sanguisorba*) found on the chalk and sometimes used in salads, cool-tankard, etc., both with close aggregates of brownish-purple flowers.—**burnet moth (or burnet),** a moth of the Zygaenidae, esp. of the genus *Arthrocera,* with red-spotted or red-streaked fore-wings; **burnet (-leaved) rose,** a wild rose (*Rosa spinosissima*) with leaves like burnet, the Scotch rose; **burnet saxifrage,** a plant (*Pimpinella Saxifraga*) neither burnet-coloured nor a saxifrage but a green umbellifer akin to anise, with burnet-like leaves. [O.Fr. *burnete, brunette;* see **brunette.**]

**burnettise, -ize,** *bûr′nit-iz, v.t.* to treat with Burnett's fluid, a solution of zinc chloride, a preservative for timber, etc., against dry-rot and insects, introduced by Sir William *Burnett* (1779-1861).

**burnish,** *bûrn′ish, v.t.* to polish: to make bright by rubbing.—*n.* polish: lustre.—*ns.* **burn′isher,** an instrument employed in burnishing: one who burnishes; **burn′ishing; burn′ishment.** [Fr. *burnir, burniss-,* to burnish—*brun,* brown.]

**burnous,** *bûr-nōōs′,* **burnouse,** *-nōōz′,* n. a mantle with a hood much worn by the Arabs. [Fr.,—Ar. *burnus.*]

**Burnsian,** *bûrnz′i-ən, adj.* pertaining to Robert *Burns* (1759-96), the Scottish poet.—*n.* a student or admirer of Burns.—*n.* **Burns′ite,** a devotee of Burns.

**burnt,** *pa.t.* and *pa.p.* of **burn.**—Also *adj.*

**burp,** *bûrp, v.i.* to belch (*coll.*).—Also *n.*—*v.t.* to rub or pat a baby's back after feeding to cause it to belch.

**burr, bur,** *bûr, n.* the prickly seed-case or head of certain plants, which sticks to clothes or animals: any impediment or inconvenient adherent: any lump, ridge, etc., more or less sharp, an excrescence on a tree, or markings representing it in wood: a knot in thread: a knob at the base of a deer's horn: the rough edge to a line made by an engraving tool, which, when the plate is inked, gives a further quality to the line: waste raw silk: the sweetbread or pancreas: club-moss (*Scot.*): the name for various tools and appliances, as the triangular chisel for clearing the corners of mortises, etc.: the blank driven out of a piece of sheet-metal by a punch: a partly vitrified brick.—*adj.* **burr′y.**—**bur′dock,** a composite plant (*Arctium Lappa*) with hooked involucral bracts and docklike leaves: any species of *Xanthium*; **bur′-mar′igold,** any plant of the composite genus *Bidens,* with barbed pappus: a species of *Xanthium;* **bur′-reed,** a reedlike genus (*Sparganium*) of water-plants with globular flower-heads; **bur′-this′tle,** spear-thistle; **bur′weed,** various bushy plants as burdock, bur-reed, clot-bur (*Xanthium*), etc.—**burr in the throat,** something seeming to stick in the throat, producing a choking sensation. [Cog. with Dan. *borre,* a bur.]

**burr, bur,** *bûr, n.* the rough sound of *r* pronounced in the throat, as by many Northumberland people.—*v.i.* to whisper hoarsely, to murmur.

[Usually associated with burr (1), but perh. from the sound.]

**burramundi,** *bur-ə-mun′di,* a variant of **barramunda.**

**burrel,** *bur′əl, n.* a coarse russet cloth of mediaeval times. [See **bureau.**]

**burrel, burrell.** Same as **bharal.**

**burro,** *bōōr′ō, n.* a donkey. [Sp.]

**burrow,** *bur′ō, n.* a hole in the ground dug esp. by certain animals for shelter or defence: a passage, hole, or gallery dug or eaten through wood, stone, etc.: a refuge.—*v.i.* make holes underground as rabbits: to work one's way through earth, etc.: to dwell in a concealed place.—*v.t.* to make a burrow in: to make by burrowing.—**burr′ow-duck,** the sheldrake or bergander; **burr′owing-owl,** a small long-legged diurnal American owl nesting in burrows. [Prob. a variant of **borough**—O.E. *beorgan,* to protect.]

**burrowstown,** *bur′əs-tōōn,* (*Scot.*) *n.* a town that is a burgh. [burgh.]

**bursa,** *bûr′sa, n.* a pouch or sac, esp. one containing viscid lubricating fluid at points of friction (*zool.*).—*pl.* **bur′sae** (*-sē*).—*adj.* **bur′sal,** relating to a bursa: fiscal.—*n.* **bur′sar,** one who keeps the purse, a treasurer: in Scotland, a student or pupil maintained at a university or school by funds derived from endowment.—*adj.* **bursarial** (*-sā′ri-əl*).—*ns.* **bur′sarship,** the office of a bursar; **bur′sary,** the treasury of a college or monastery: in Scotland, a scholarship; **burse,** a purse: an obsolete form of **bourse.**—*adjs.* **bursic′ūlate,** resembling a small pouch; **bursi′i-form,** pouch-shaped.—*n.* **bursi′tis,** inflammation of a bursa. [L.L. *bursa,* a purse—Gr. *byrsa,* skin or leather.]

**bursch,** *bōōrsh, n.* a German student:—*pl.* **bursch′en.**—*ns.* **bursch′enism; bursch′enschaft** (*-shäft*), a student's association. [Ger. *bursch,* a companion, student.]

**Bursera,** *bûr′sər-a, n.* a tropical American genus of trees yielding elemi and timber, giving name to the family **Burserä′ceae,** akin to the rue family.—*adj.* **burserä′ceous.** [Named after Joachim *Burser* (1593-1689), German botanist.]

**burst,** *bûrst, v.t.* to break into pieces: to break open or cause to give way suddenly or by violence: to make by bursting.—*v.i.* to fly open or in pieces, esp. owing to a force from within: to give way suddenly: to break forth or away: to force a way: to break suddenly into being, or into some condition, activity, or expression of feeling:—*pa.t.* and *pa.p.* **burst,** *arch., dial.,* and *U.S.* **burst′ed, bust′ed;** *pa.p.* **burst′en.**—*n.* an act, occasion, or result of bursting: a sudden outbreak: a hard gallop: a spurt: a drunken bout.—*n.* **burst′er** (see also **buster**).—**burst′-up,** a complete break: disruption: commotion: collapse: failure. [O.E. *berstan;* Ger. *bersten.*]

**burthen,** *bûr′dhən, n.* and *v.t.* See **burden** (1 and 2).

**burton,** *bûr′tn, n.* a tackle of two or three blocks.

**Burton,** *bûr′tn, n.* a town of Staffordshire famous for its beer: a drink.—**gone for a Burton** (*airman's slang*), drowned, dead: absent: missing.

**bury,** *ber′i, bûr′i, v.t.* to hide in the ground: to cover: to consign to the grave, the sea, etc., as a dead body: to hide or blot out of remembrance:—*pr.p.* **bur′ying;** *pa.t., pa.p.* **bur′ied.**—*n.* (*dial.*) a burrow.—**bur′ying-beetle,** a beetle (*Necrophorus* or kindred genus) that buries small animals as food for its larvae; **bur′ying-ground,** ground set apart for burying the dead: a graveyard; **bur′ying-place.**—**bury the hatchet,** to renounce enmity. [O.E. *byrgan,* to bury; Ger. *bergen,* to hide.]

**bus, 'bus,** (*obs.* **buss**), *bus, n.* an omnibus: car, aeroplane, etc. (*slang*):—*pl.* **bus′es.**—**bus′-bar,** an electric conductor connecting with a number of circuits: **bus′boy, bus′girl** (*U.S.*), an assistant waiter or waitress; **bus'-fare**; **bus'man**, the driver or conductor of a bus.—**busman's holiday**, a holiday spent in activities similar to one's work; **miss the bus**, to lose an opportunity. [Short for **omnibus**.]

**busby**, *buz'bi*, *n.* a fur hat with a bag hanging on its right side, worn esp. by hussars. [Prob. Hung.]

**bush**, *boosh*, *n.* a woody plant in size between a tree and an undershrub: a shrub thick with branches: anything of bushy tuft-like shape: forest: wild uncultivated country (even though treeless): country covered with bushes: the wild: a bunch of ivy hung up as a tavern sign: a tavern.—*v.i.* to grow thick or bushy.—*v.t.* to set bushes about: to support with bushes: to cover (seeds) by means of the bush-harrow.— *adj.* **bushed**, lost in the bush: bewildered (*slang*): tired (*slang*).—*n.* **bush'iness**.—*adj.* **bush'y**, full of or like bushes: thick and spreading.—**bush'-ba'by**, a small South African lemur (*Galago maholi*) also called night-ape; **bush'-buck**, a small S. African antelope, or any other of the same genus (Tragelaphus).—Also (Du.) **boschbok** (*bos'-bok*), (Afrik.) **bosbok** (*bos'bok*); **bush'-cat**, the serval; **bush'craft**, practical knowledge of the bush and skill in its ways; **bush'-fruit**, a fruit growing on a bush, as gooseberry, raspberry; **bush'-harr'ow**, a light harrow for covering grass-seeds, formed of a barred frame interwoven with bushes or branches; **bush'man**, a settler, or traveller, in uncleared land: a woodsman: (*cap.*) one of a now almost extinct nomadic, stunted, yellowish-brown, aboriginal race of huntsmen in S. Africa—Cape Du. *Bos(jes)man*.—Also *adj.*— **bush'manship**, bushcraft; **bush'master**, a venomous South American snake (*Lachesis muta*); **bush pilot**, an air-line pilot operating over uninhabited country; **bush'ranger**, in Australia, a lawless person, often an escaped criminal, who takes to the bush and lives by robbery: a woodsman: a rapacious person (*fig.*); **bush'-rope**, a liana; **bush shirt, jacket**, a cotton, etc., garment with four patch pockets and a belt; **bush'-shrike**, any bird of a sub-family of Formicariidae (ant-thrushes); **bush telegraph**, the obscure and rapid transmission of news through a country or population; **bush'-tit**, a small long-tailed titmouse of West America, building a large hanging-nest; **bush'veld, bosch'veld** (*bos'*), veld made up largely of woodland.—*v.i.* **bush'whack**, to range through the bush: to fight in guerilla warfare: to travel through woods, esp. by clearing a way to do so.—*v.t.* to ambush.—**bush'-whacker**, a guerilla fighter: a country lout: a short heavy scythe for cutting bushes: one who clears a way in the bush: a sniper; **bush'-whack'ing**, the habits or practice of bushwhackers: the process of forcing a way for a boat by pulling at the bushes overhanging a stream.—**beat about the bush**, to go round about anything, to evade coming to the point.—[M.E. *busk*, *busch*—O.N. *buskr*, from a Gmc. root found in Ger. *busch*, L.L. *boscus*, Fr. *bois*. Some uses are from the corresponding Du. *bosch*.]

**bush**, *boosh*, *n.* the metal box or lining of any cylinder in which an axle works.—*v.t.* to furnish with a bush.—**bush'-met'al**, hard brass, gunmetal, a composition of copper and tin, used for journals, bearings, etc. [Du. *bus*—L. *buxus*, box-tree.]

**bushel**, *boosh'əl*, *n.* dry measure of 8 gallons, no longer official, for grain, fruit, etc. (*imperial bushel*, 2219·36 cub. in.): container for this quantity. [O.Fr. *boissiel*—root of **box**.]

**bushel**, *boosh'əl* (*U.S.*) *v.t.* and *v.i.* to mend or alter, as men's clothes.—*ns.* **bush'eller**; **bush'elling**.— **bush'el-man, -woman**. [Cf. Ger. *bosseln*.]

**bushido**, *boo'shi-do*, *n.* a Japanese code of chivalry. [Jap.]

**business**, *biz'nis*, *n.* employment: trade, profession, or occupation: a task or errand incumbent or undertaken: matter requiring attention: dealings, commercial activity: a commercial or industrial concern: one's concerns or affairs: a matter or affair: action as distinguished from dialogue (*theat.*): a thing, used quite indefinitely (*coll.*): (*biz'i-nis*, also written **busyness**) state of being busy.—Also *adj.* (*biz'nis*).—**business cycle**, (*U.S.*) trade cycle.—*adj.* **bus'iness-like**, methodical, systematic, practical.—**bus'iness-man'**, one engaged in commercial transactions. —**do the business for**, to settle, make an end of: to ruin; **genteel business** (*theat.*), such parts as require good dressing; **like nobody's business** (*coll.*), keenly, energetically; **make it one's business**, to undertake to accomplish something or see it done; **man of business**, a law agent who conducts one's affairs; **mean business**, to be in earnest; **mind one's own business**, to confine oneself to one's own affairs; **place of business**, the ordinary place for the practice of one's vocation; **send about one's business**, to dismiss promptly. [**busy**.]

**busk**, *busk*, *v.t.* or *v.i.* to prepare: to dress. [O.N. *būa*, to prepare, and *-sk*, contr. of *sik*, the refl. pron. self.]

**busk**, *busk*, *n.* the piece of bone, wood, or steel in the front of a woman's stays: a corset.—*adj.* **busked**. [Fr. *busc*.]

**busk**, *busk*, *v.i.* to cruise along a shore, to beat about (*naut.*): to seek.—*n.* **busk'er**, a wandering musician or actor. [Prob. Sp. *buscar*, to seek.]

**busket**, *busk'ət*, (*Spens.*) *n.* a little bush. [See **bush**.]

**buskin**, *busk'in*, *n.* a high thick-soled boot worn in ancient times by actors in tragedy.—*adj.* **busk'ined**, wearing buskins; tragic. [Ety. uncertain; cf. O.Fr. *brousequin*; Du. *broosken*; Sp. *borceguí*.]

**busky**, *busk'i*, (*Shak.*) *adj.* Same as **bosky**.

**buss**, *bus*, *n.* a rude or playful kiss, a smack.—*v.t.* to kiss, esp. in a rude or playful manner. [Cf. Ger. dial. *buss*, W. and Gael. *bus*, L. *bāsium*.]

**buss**, *bus*, *n.* a small two-masted Dutch vessel, used in the herring and mackerel fisheries. [O.Fr. *busse*, L.L. *bussa*; cf. Ger. *büse*.]

**bussu**, *boos'oo*, *n.* a tropical American palm (*Manicaria*) with gigantic leaves and netted spathe that serves as cloth. [Port. from Tupí *bussú*.]

**bust**, *bust*, *n.* a sculpture representing the head and breast of a person: the upper front part of the human body, esp. a woman's.—*adj.* **bust'ed**, breasted: adorned with busts. [Fr. *buste*; It. and Sp. *busto*.]

**bust**, *bust*, *n.* and *v.* a coll. form of **burst**:—*pa.t.* and *pa.p.* **bust'ed**.—*n.* a drinking bout.—*adj.* ruined, penniless.—*ns.* **bust'er**, something large: a frolic: a roisterer (*coll.*): a horse-breaker (*U.S.*): a stormy south wind (*Austr.*): something that causes a large-scale break-up.—**bust'up**, a burst-up.—**go bust**, to become bankrupt.

**bustard**, *bust'ərd*, *n.* any bird of the genus *Otis*, sometimes made the type of a large family, usually ranked with cranes. [Fr. *bistard*—L. *avis tarda*, slow bird (a misnomer).]

**bustee**, *bus'tē*, *n.* in India, a settlement or a collection of huts. [Hind. *basti*.]

**bustle**, *bus'l*, *v.i.* to busy oneself noisily or fussily. —*n.* hurried activity: stir: tumult.—*n.* **bust'ler**. [M.E. *bustelen*, of doubtful relations.]

**bustle**, *bus'l*, *n.* a contrivance for causing a skirt to hang back from the hips. [Origin doubtful.]

**busy**, *biz'i*, *adj.* fully employed: active: diligent: meddling: fussily active: (of a telephone line) engaged: (of picture or design) unrestful because having too much detail.—*n.* (*slang*) a detective. —*v.t.* to make busy: to occupy:—*pr.p.* **bus'ying**; *pa.t.* and *pa.p.* **bus'ied**.—*adv.* **bus'ily**.—*n.*

# but

—bus'ybody, one who meddles in others' affairs:
mirror(s) at window arranged to show passers-
by; busy Lizzie, a plant of the *Impatiens* genus.
[O.E. *bysig*.]
**but**, *but*, *prep.* without (*obs.*): except: in or toward the outer room of (*Scot.*).—*conj.* on the
other hand: in contrast: nevertheless: unless,
if not: otherwise than (that): except that (merging in *prep.*): that not (developing into a negative *rel. pron.*): than, sooner than (*arch.*).—*adv.*
only: in or to the outer room, outwards (*Scot.*).
—*n.* an objection (as in Mrs Centlivre's 'But me
no buts'): an outer room (*Scot.*).—Also *adj.*—
*v.t.* to put forward as an objection—**but and** (*obs.*),
and also; **but and ben** (see **ben**); **but for, but that**,
were it not for, or that; **but if** (*obs.*), unless:
sometimes equivalent to but alone in various
senses. [O.E. *be-ūtan, būtan*, without—*be*, by
and *ūtan*, out—near, and yet outside.]
**but**, *but*, *n.* Same as **butt**.
**butadiene**, *bū-tə-dī'ēn*, *n.* (L. *dis*, twice) a hydrocarbon, C₄H₆, used in making synthetic rubber.
—*n.* bu'tane, a hydrocarbon of the methane
series, C₄H₁₀. [butyl.]
**butch**, *bōōch*, *n.* a very short haircut for men or
women: an aggressively tough man (*slang*): the
'male' partner in a lesbian relationship (*slang*).
—*adj.* tough, aggressive. [Amer. boy's nickname.]
**butcher**, *bōōch'ər*, *n.* one whose business is to
slaughter cattle for food, or who deals in their
flesh: one who delights in bloody deeds: a
sweet-seller on a railway train (*U.S.*).—*v.t.* to
slaughter for food: to put to a bloody death, to
kill cruelly: to spoil, as a bad actor or the like
(*fig.*).—*ns.* butch'ering, butch'ing (back-formation), the act of killing for food, or cruelly.—
*adv.* butch'erly, butcher-like, cruel, murderous.—
*n.* butch'ery, great or cruel slaughter: a slaughterhouse or shambles.—butch'er-bird, a shrike;
butch'er('s) meat, the flesh of animals slaughtered
by butchers, as distinguished from fish, fowls
and game; butch'er's-broom, an evergreen shrub
(*Ruscus aculeatus*) of the lily family, with
phyllodes, formerly used by butchers for sweeping their blocks. [O.Fr. *bochier, bouchier*, one
who kills he-goats—*boc*, a he-goat; **buck**.]
**Butea**, *būt'i-a*, *n.* the dhak genus of papilionaceous
trees, yielding Bengal kino. [Named after Lord
*Bute*, prime minister and botanist.]
**but-end.** Same as **butt-end.**
**butene**, *bū'tēn*, *n.* butylene.
**butler**, *but'lər*, *n.* a servant who has charge of
liquors, plate, etc.: an officer in a royal household.—*v.i.* to act as butler.—Also butt'le (back-
formation).—*ns.* but'lerage, duty on imported
wine once paid to the king's butler (*obs.*): the
office of butler (*obs.*): a butler's department;
but'lership; but'lery, the butler's pantry. [Norm.
Fr. *butuiller*—L.L. *buticulārius*. See **bottle**.]
**butment.** Same as **abutment.**
**butt**, *but*, *v.t.* to strike with the head, as a goat, etc.
—*v.i.* to strike with the head (*absolutely*, or with
*at, against*): to go or drive head first.—*n.* a
push or blow with the head.—*n.* butt'er, an
animal that butts.—**butt in**, to interfere, thrust
oneself in. [O.Fr. *boter*, to push, strike.]
**butt**, *but*, *n.* a large cask: a wine butt = 126
gallons, a beer and sherry butt = 108 gallons.
[Cf. Fr. *botte*, Sp. *bota*, L.L. *butta*.]
**butt**, *but*, *n.* a mark or mound for archery practice:
a mound behind targets: one who is made an
object of ridicule: a hiding place for grouse-
shooters.—*n.* butt'-shaft (*Shak.*), a shaft for
shooting at butts with. [Fr. *but*, goal.]
**butt**, *but*, *n.* the thick and heavy end: the stump:
a tree-trunk: hinder part of a hide: thick leather:
the fag-end of a cigar or cigarette: remnant:
square end of a plank meeting another.—*v.i.* to
abut: to meet end to end.—butted joint, a joint

formed between the squared ends of the two
jointing pieces, which come together but do not
overlap; butt'-end, butt welding, welding the
seam formed by joining two butt-ends. [Ety.
dub.; prob. connected with butt (3) and abut.]
**butt**, *but*, *n.* a flat-fish of various kinds. [Cf. Sw.
*butta*, turbot, Du. *bot*, flounder; **halibut, turbo**·.]
**butte**, *būt*, *n.* a conspicuous and isolated hill, cliff-
sided, often flat-topped, in the western United
States. [Fr.]
**butter**, *but'ər*, *n.* an oily substance obtained from
cream by churning: extended to various substances resembling or containing it: an old
chemical name for certain oily chlorides (butter
of *antimony*, of *tin*, etc.): flattery.—*v.t.* to spread
over with butter, mortar, or other soft substance:
to flatter: to fail to catch, let slip.—*n.* butt'-
erine (-*ēn*), a margarine made partly from milk.—
*adj.* butter-like: smeared with butter or like
the like.—butt'er-bake (*Scot.*), -bis'cuit, a cake
like a biscuit but softer; butt'er-bean', an
American bean akin to the French-bean; butt'er-
bird, in Jamaica, the bobolink; butt'er-boat, a
table vessel for melted butter; butt'er-box, a box
for butter: an old nickname for a Dutchman;
butt'erbur', butt'erdock', a plant akin to coltsfoot with knobbed masses of flower heads and
great rhubarb-like leaves; butt'er-cloth', -mus'-
lin, a loose-woven cloth suitable for wrapping
butter; butt'er-cool'er, a dish for keeping butter
in water at table; butt'ercup, a crowfoot (*Ranunculus*), esp. of one of those species that have
golden-yellow cup-shaped flowers; butt'er-dish,
-plate, a dish or plate for holding butter at table;
buttered eggs (*arch.*), scrambled eggs; butt'er-
fat', the fat contained in butter, chiefly glycerides
of palmitic and oleic acids.—*adj.* butt'er-fingered,
prone to let things slip.—butt'er-fingers, (*sing.*)
one who lets a ball, etc., he ought to catch slip
through his fingers; butt'er-fish, a name for
various slimy fishes, notably the gunnel; butt'er-
fly, a general name for any of the daylight
Lepidoptera, roughly distinguished from moths
by their clubbed antennae: a gay, flighty person
(*fig.*): butterfly breast-stroke.—*pl.* butt'erflies.—
*adj.* light, flighty, like a butterfly.—butt'erfly-
bow', a bow whose loops and ends are spread like
butterfly's wings; butterfly (breast-)stroke, in
swimming, a faster variation of the breast-stroke
in which the arms are recovered out of the water
and there is a different kick; butt'erfly-fish', a
blenny with an eye-spot on the dorsal fin: any
fish of the family Chaetodontidae; butt'erfly-
flower, one adapted for pollination by butterflies; butt'erfly-orchis, an orchid (of various
kinds) with flowers resembling a butterfly;
butt'erfly-screw', -nut', a screw or nut, turned by
winged finger-grips; butt'erfly-weed', pleurisy-
root; butt'er-knife, a blunt knife for taking
butter from a butter dish; butt'er-milk, the milk
that remains after the butter has been separated
from the cream by churning; butter muslin (see
above); butt'ernut, the oily nut of the North
American white walnut: the tree itself: its light-
coloured close-grained wood: the souari-nut of
Guiana; butt'er-paper, a translucent paper suitable for wrapping butter; butt'er-pat', a pat of
butter: a wooden instrument for working butter
into shape; butt'er-print, a stamp for shaping
butter: a child (old *slang*); butt'er-scotch, a kind
of toffee containing much butter; butt'er-tree, a
name for many trees that yield a buttery substance, notably of the genera *Bassia, Butyrospermum, Caryocar, Pentadesma*; butt'er-wife,
butt'er-wom'an, a woman who makes and sells
butter; butt'erwort, any species of Pinguicula, a
genus of insectivorous bog-plants, (family
*Lentibulariaceae*) with glistening leaves.—
butterflies in the stomach, nervous tremors in the
stomach; butter up, to flatter. [O.E. *butere*;

*fāte, fär; mē, hûr* (her); *mīne; mōte, fŏr; mūte; mōōn, fŏŏt; dhen* (then)

Ger. *butter*; both from L. *bütyrum*—Gr.
*boutyron*, app.—*bous*, ox, *tyros*, cheese.]
**butter.** See butt (1).
**butter-bump**, *but'ər-bump*, *n.* the bittern. [See
bittern, and bump (2).]
**buttery**, *but'əri*, *n.* a domestic storeroom for provisions, esp. liquors.—**butt'ery-bar'**, the ledge for
holding tankards in the buttery; **butt'ery-
hatch'**, a half-door over which provisions are
handed from the buttery. [Fr. *bouteillerie*, lit.
place for bottles; butler, bottle.]
**buttery.** See butter (1).
**buttle.** See butler.
**buttock**, *but'ək*, *n.* the rump or protuberant part
of the body behind: in wrestling, a throw by use
of the buttock.—*v.t.* to throw in this way.—
**butt'ock-mail** (*Scot.*), the fine formerly exacted
by the church in commutation of sitting on the
stool of repentance. [Dim. of butt, end.]
**button**, *but'n*, *n.* a knob or disk, used as a fastening, ornament, or badge: a knob, e.g. that at the
end of a foil, that for winding a watch, that to
which a violin tailpiece is looped: a bud: the
head of an unexpanded mushroom: a pimple:
the knob of an electric bell, etc.: anything of
small value: a person who acts as a decoy; (in
*pl.*) sheep's dung: (*pl.* in form, treated as *sing.*) a
page of livery (also **boy in buttons**).—*v.t.* to fasten
by means of buttons: to close up tightly.—*v.i.*
to admit of fastening with buttons.—*adj.*
**butt'ony**, set with buttons: like a button.—*n.*
**butt'on-bush**, a Nòrth American shrub (*Cephalan-
thus*) of the madder family, having globular
flower-heads.—*adj.* **butt'oned-up** (*slang*), uncommunicative.—**butt'on-hole**, the slit through
which a button is passed: a flower or flowers
therein.—*v.t.* to make button-holes in: to work
with a stitch suitable for defence of edges (*button-
hole-stitch*): to detain in talk (orig. **butt'onhold**).
—**butt'on-hook**, a hook for pulling buttons
through button-holes; **butt'on-wood**, a small
tropical Atlantic coast evergreen tree (*Conocar-
pus erecta*) of the myrobalan family: a plane-
tree (*U.S.*)—also **butt'on-ball**; **button scurvy**,
**yaws**; **butt'on-through**, a woman's dress buttoning in front from top to bottom.—**buttoned up**
(*slang*), successfully fixed up: safe in hand:
ready for action; **in his buttons**, a conjectural
reading in *Merry Wives* where the quarto has
*betmes*, prob. a misprint for *talons*. [Fr. *bouton*,
any small projection, from *bouter*, to push.]
**buttress**, *but'rəs*, *n.* a projecting support built on
to the outside of a wall: any support or prop.—
*v.t.* to prop or support, as by a buttress.—**butt'-
ress-root**, a root, often adventitious, that helps
to keep a plant upright. [App. O.Fr. *bouterez*—
*bouter*, to push, bear against.]
**butty**, *but'i*, (*dial.*) *n.* a chum, comrade, work-
fellow, partner, esp. in a coal-mine: one who
takes a contract for work in a coal-mine:
a barge towed by another.—**butt'y-coll'ier**;
**butt'y-gang.** [App. dim. of dial. *butt*, a companion.]
**butty**, *but'i*, (*dial.*) *n.* a sandwich, snack.
**butyric**, *bū-tir'ik*, *adj.* pertaining to or derived
from butter.—*ns.* **bū'tyl** (*-til*, *U.S.*-*təl*; Gr. *hylē*,
matter), an alcohol radical, $C_4H_9$; **būty'lene**,
(also **bū'tene**), an olefine hydrocarbon ($C_4H_8$) in
three isomers.—*adj.* **būtyrā'ceous**, buttery, containing butter.—*n.* **bū'tyrate**, a salt of butyric
acid.—**butyric acid**, a volatile fatty acid ($C_3H_7$·
COOH), smelling like rancid butter. [See
butter.]
**buvette**, *bü-vet*, (Fr.) a small road-side café
selling drinks and snacks.
**buxom**, *buks'əm*, *adj.* yielding, elastic: gay, lively,
jolly: plump and comely.—*n.* **bux'omness.** [M.E.
*buhsum*, pliable, obedient—O.E. *būgan*, to bow,
yield, suff. *-some*.]
**buy**, *bī*, *v.t.* to purchase for money: to bribe: to

obtain in exchange for something: to accept,
believe (*slang*):—*pr.p.* **buy'ing**; *pa.t.* and *pa.p.*
**bought** (*bôt*), *arch. pa.p.* **bought'en**.—*n.* something
purchased.—*adj.* **buy'able**.—*n.* **buy'er**, one who
buys: one employed to buy goods.—**buyers'
market**, one in which buyers rule the price,
supply exceeding demand.—**a good buy** (*coll.*), a
wise purchase, a bargain; **buy and sell** (*Shak.*),
to traffic in; **buy in**, to collect a stock of by
buying: to buy back for the owner at an auction;
**buy off**, to buy exemption or release for: to get
rid of by paying; **buy out**, to dispossess entirely
by payment: to buy off; **buy over**, to win over
by payment; **buy up**, to purchase the whole stock
of; **I'll buy that**, I don't know, I give it up, tell
me: I'll accept the explanation though it seems
surprising. [O.E. *bycgan*, *bohte*, *boht*; Goth.
*bugjan*.]
**buzz**, *buz*, *v.i.* to make a noise like that of insects'
wings: to murmur: to move quickly (*slang*).—
*v.t.* to utter with a buzzing sound: to whisper or
spread secretly: to transmit by Morse over a
telephone wire by means of a key: to make a
telephone call to: to throw (*slang*): to fly very
low over or very close to: to interfere with in
flight by flying very near to (*aero.*).—*n.* the noise
of bees and flies: a humming sound: a voiced
hiss: a whispered report: a telephone call.—*n.*
**buzz'er**, one who buzzes: a whisperer or tell-
tale (*Shak.*): an apparatus that makes a buzzing
sound, as a hooter, a circular saw, or an electrical
device for signalling, etc.—*n.* and *adj.* **buzz'ing**.—
*adv.* **buzz'ingly**.—*adj.* **buzz'y**.—**buzz bomb**, a
flying bomb; **buzz'-saw** (*U.S.*), a circular saw;
**buzz'-wig**, a great bushy wig. [From the sound.]
**buzz**, *buz*, *v.t.* to drain (a bottle) to the last drop
of wine. [Orig. uncertain.]
**buzzard**, *buz'ərd*, *n.* a large bird of prey of the
genus *Buteo*, despised by falconers: extended to
some others, as the *honey-buzzard*, *turkey-
buzzard*: a blockhead, coward or sluggard. [Fr.
*busard*.]
**buzzard**, *buz'ərd*, *n.* a blundering insect, as a cockchafer or night-flying moth: an ignorant blunderer (often *blind buzzard*).—*n.* **buzz'ard-clock**
(*dial.*), a cockchafer. [buzz.]
**bwana**, *bwä'nä*, *n.* master: sir. [Swahili.]
**by**, *bī*, *prep.* at the side of: near to: along a route
passing through, via: past: in oaths, in the
presence of, or with the witness of: through (denoting the agent, cause, means, etc.): to the
extent of: in quantity measurable in terms of: in
accordance with: in respect of: of time, not
after: multiplied into, or combined with another
dimension of: in succession to: besides (*Scot.*):
in comparison with (*Scot.*).—*conj.* by the time
that (*arch.* and *Scot.*): than (*Scot.*).—*adv.* near:
aside: away: past: in reserve.—*n.* and *adj.* see
bye.—*adv.* **by'-and-by**, at some future time:
before long: successively (*Spens.*).—**by'-blow**, a
side blow: an illegitimate child; **by'-corner**,
an out-of-the-way place; **by'-drinking** (*Shak.*),
drinking between meals; **by'-election**, a parliamentary election for a seat during the sitting of
parliament; **by'-end**, a subsidiary aim; **by'-
form**, a subsidiary form: a form varying from
the usual one; **by'going**, the action of passing by
(esp. in in the by'going, in passing).—*adj.* **by'gone**
(*-gon*).—*n.pl.* **by'gones**, past happenings or
grievances: ornaments, household articles, etc.,
of former times which are not fine enough, or not
old enough, to be valued as antiques (also in
*sing.*).—**by'-lane**, a side lane or passage out of the
common road; **by'line**, a line at the head of a
newspaper or magazine article telling by whom it
is written; **by'-mô'tive**, an unavowed motive;
**by'-name**, a nickname.—*adj.* **by'-ordinar** (*Scot.*),
extraordinary.—**by'pass**, a side track for carrying
traffic, fluids, electricity, etc., round an obstruction, congested place, etc.—*v.t.* to supply with a

Neutral vowels in unaccented syllables: *el'ə-mənt*; for certain sounds in foreign words, see p. viii

bypass: to direct (e.g. fluid) along a bypass: to go round and beyond by a bypass (also *fig.* to ignore, leave out): to evade.—by′-passage, a side passage.—*adj.* by′-past (*Shak.*), past: gone by.—by′path, a secluded or indirect path; by′place, a retired place; by′-play, action subordinate to and apart from the main action of a play; by′-plot, a subsidiary plot; by′-product, a product formed in the process of making something else; by′road, a retired side road; by′room (*Shak.*), a side or private room; by′-speech, a casual speech; by′stander, one who stands by or near one: a looker-on; by′-street, an obscure street; by′-thing, a thing of minor importance; by′-time, leisure time; by′way, a private, secluded, or obscure way; by′word, a common saying, proverb: an object of scorn: a person noted for a specified characteristic; by′work, work for leisure hours.—by and by, presently: in the course of time; by and large (*naut.*), whether close-hauled or before the wind: speaking generally: on the whole; by the by(e), by the way, in passing, incidentally; let bygones be bygones, let the past be ignored. [O.E. *bī, bi, big*; Ger. *bei,* L. *ambi-.* See bye.] by. See bye.

bycoket, *bī′kok-it, n.* a turned-up peaked cap worn by noble persons in the 15th century. [O.Fr. *bicoquet,* prob. *bi-* (L. *bis*), double, *coque,* a shell.]

bye, by, *bī, n.* anything of minor importance, a side issue, a thing not directly aimed at: in games, the state of one who has not drawn an opponent, and passes without contest to the next round: in cock-fighting, a battle not forming part of a main: in golf, the holes remaining after the match is decided, played as a subsidiary game: in cricket, a run made from a ball bowled but not struck or touched by the batsman.—*adj.* subsidiary: apart: indirect. See also by.

Byelorussian. See Belorussian.

byke. Same as bike (1).

bylander. Same as bilander.

bylaw, bye-law, *bī′lö, n.* the law of a local authority or private corporation: a supplementary law or an inferred regulation. [The same as byrlaw, from O.N. *byjar-lög*; Dan. *by-lov,* town-law; from O.N. *būa,* to dwell. See bower.]

bylive (*Spens.*). Same as belive.

bynempt. Obs. pa.t. of bename.

byre, *bir,* (mainly *Scot.*) *n.* a cowhouse.—byre′-

man, byre′woman, a farm-servant with care of cows. [O.E. *bȳre.*]

byrlady, *bər-lā′di,* byrlakin, *bər-lā′kin,* (*arch.*) contractions for By Our Lady, Ladykin.

byrlaw, *bir′lö, n.* a sort of popular jurisprudence long surviving in Scotland in villages and among husbandmen, concerning local matters in dispute.—*n.* byr′law-man (*Scott* bir′lieman), an arbiter, oddsman, or umpire in such matters. [See bylaw.]

byrnie, *bir′ni,* (*hist.*) *n.* a mail-coat: a breastplate. [A Scots form—O.N. *brynja*; O.E. *byrne.*]

byroad, bystander, byway, etc. See by.

Byronic, *bī-ron′ik, adj.* possessing the characteristics of Lord Byron (1788-1824), or of his poetry, overstrained in sentiment or passion, cynical and libertine.—*adv.* Byron′ically.—*n.* By′ronism.

byssus, *bis′əs, n.* a fine yellowish flax: linen made from it (the 'fine linen' of the Bible): the bundle of filaments by which some shellfish attach themselves.—*adjs.* byssā′ceous, composed of a mass of fine threads: delicately filamentous; byss′al, pertaining to a mollusc's byssus; byss′ine, made of fine linen.—*n.* byssinos′is, an allergic lung disease of cotton workers.—*adj.* byss′oid, byssaceous. [L.,—Gr. *byssos,* a fine flaxen substance.]

bytownite, *bī′town-it, n.* a plagioclase intermediate between anorthite and labradorite. [*Bytown,* now Ottawa, where it occurs.]

bywoner, *bi′won-ər, bi′vōn-ər, n.* an authorised squatter on another's farm: a poor white parasite. [Du. *bijwonen,* to be present.]

byzant, *biz′ant,* or *biz-ant′.* Same as bezant.

Byzantine, *biz-an′tin,* or *biz-an′tin,* or *-tin,* or *biz′ən-, adj.* relating to Byzantium (Constantinople, now Istanbul): rigidly hierarchic: intricate, tortuous.—*n.* an inhabitant of Byzantium. —*n.* Byzan′tinism, manifestation of Byzantine characteristics.—Byzantine architecture, the style prevalent in the Eastern Empire down to 1453, marked by the round arch springing from columns or piers, the dome supported upon pendentives, capitals elaborately sculptured, mosaic or other incrustations, etc.; Byzantine Church, the Eastern or Greek Church; Byzantine Empire, the Eastern or Greek Empire from A.D. 395 to 1453; Byzantine historians, the series of Greek chroniclers of the affairs of the Byzantine Empire down to its fall in 1453. [Gr. *Byzantion.*]

*fāte, fär; mē, hûr* (her); *mīne; mōte, för; mūte; mōōn, fōōt; dhen* (then)

# C

**C, c, sē,** *n.* the third letter of our alphabet, a rounded form of the Greek *gamma* (see G), which the Romans used instead of *k*, and in some languages came to have the sound of *s* or one like it: one of the notes of the musical gamut, the sound on which the system is founded—the keynote of the natural scale, C major, having neither flats nor sharps: as a time signature, common time: as a Roman numeral, C = 100: C̄ = 100,000; C3, of poor physique.

**ca', kō, (Scot.)** *v.t.* and *v.i.*, to call: to drive: to propel: to knock (with *down, off, over*, etc.).— *n.* **ca''ing-** or **caa'ing-whale,** a species of dolphin (*Globiocephalus melas*) often taken by ca'ing or driving ashore.—**ca' canny,** to go easy: deliberately to restrict output or effort. [call.]

**caatinga, kä-ting'ga,** *n.* in Brazil, open, comparatively low forest, on white sandy soil derived from granite. [Tupí, white forest.]

**cab, kab,** *n.* a public carriage of various sizes and shapes, with two or four wheels, orig. horsedrawn now usu. motor-driven: a taxi-cab: the driver's shelter on a locomotive, motorlorry, etc.—*ns.* **cabb'y,** familiar dim. of **cab'man,** one who drives a horse cab; **cab'-rank, cab'-stand,** a place where cabs stand for hire; **cab'-runner, cab'-tout,** one whose business it is to call cabs. [Shortened from **cabriolet.**]

**cab, kab,** *n.* a Hebrew dry measure nearly three pints. [Heb. *qab.*]

**caba.** U.S. form of **cabas,** having **cabas** as pl.

**cabal, ka-bal',** *n.* a small party united for some secret design: the plot itself: a name in English history esp. given to five unpopular ministers of Charles II (1672), whose initials happened to make up the word.—*v.i.* to form a party for a secret purpose: to intrigue:—*pr.p.* **caball'ing; pa.t.** and **pa.p. caballed'.**—*n.* **caball'er.** [Fr. *cabale*; from Heb. *qabbalah*; see **cabbala.**]

**caballero, kab-al-yär'ō,** *n.* a Spanish gentleman. [Sp.,—L. *caballārius,* horseman—*caballus,* horse.]

**caballine, kab'ə-lin, adj.** pertaining to, or suited to, a horse. [L. *caballinus—caballus,* a horse.]

**cabala,** etc. See **cabbala.**

**cabana, kə-ban'(y)ə, (U.S.)** *n.* a small tentlike cabin, esp. used as a changing hut on the beach or by a swimming-pool. [Sp. *cabaña.*]

**cabaret, kab'ə-rā,** *n.* a restaurant with variety turns: the kind of entertainment there given. [Fr., tavern; prob. for *cabaneret—cabane,* a hut.]

**cabas, kab'ä,** *n.* a woman's work-basket, reticule, or handbag. See also **caba.** [Fr., flat basket.]

**cabbage, kab'ij,** *n.* a vegetable (*Brassica oleracea*) of the Cruciferae: the edible terminal bud of various palms.—*adj.* **cabb'agy.**—*ns.* **cabb'age-butt'erfly, cabb'age-white',** a large white butterfly (*Pieris*) whose larvae injure the leaves of cabbage and kindred plants; **cabb'age-fly,** a fly (*Anthomyia brassicae*), whose maggots injure cabbage roots; **cabb'age-lett'uce,** a lettuce with cabbage-like head; **cabb'age-moth,** a moth (*Mamestra brassicae*) whose larva feeds on the cabbage; **cabb'age-palm, cabb'age-tree,** *Oreodoxa oleracea* or other palm with an edible cabbage; **cabb'age-rose,** a rose of bunchy cabbage-like form; **cabb'age-worm,** the larva of the cabbage-butterfly or of the cabbage-moth.—**Kerguelen cabbage,** a wind-pollinated plant of the cabbage family growing on Kerguelen Island. [Fr. *caboche,* head; cf. It. *capocchia,* augmentative—*capo,* head—L. *caput.*]

**cabbage, kab'ij,** *v.t.* and *v.i.* to purloin, orig. of tailors who took portions of a customer's cloth as a perquisite.—*n.* cloth so appropriated.

**cabbala, cabala, kab'ə-lə** or **kə-bä'lə,** *n.* a secret traditional lore, theological, metaphysical, and magical, of Jewish rabbis, who read hidden meanings into the Bible.—*ns.* **cab(b)'alism,** the science of the cabbala; **cab(b)'alist,** one versed in the cabbala.—*adjs.* **cab(b)alist'ic, -al,** relating to the cabbala: having a hidden meaning. [Heb. *qabbālāh,* tradition, *qibbēl,* to receive.]

**caber, käb'ər,** *n.* a pole, generally the stem of a young tree, which is poised and tossed or hurled by Highland athletes. [Gael. *cabar.*]

**cabin, kab'in,** *n.* a hut or cottage: a small room, esp. in a ship, for officers or passengers: a compartment for passengers in an aircraft: a railway signal-box.—*v.t.* to shut up in a cabin or in a cramped space: to hamper in action (*fig.*).—*v.i.* to dwell in a cabin.—**cab'in-boy,** a boy who waits on the officers or cabin passengers of a ship; **cabin class,** class between tourist and first class; **cabin crew,** members of aircraft crew who look after passengers; **cabin cruiser,** power-driven boat with full provision for living on board; **cabin passenger,** formerly, one entitled to superior accommodation: a passenger having cabin accommodation; **cabin ship,** a ship carrying only one class of passengers. [Fr. *cabane*—L.L. *capanna.*]

**cabinet, kab'(i-)nit,** *n.* a little cabin or hut (*obs.*): the bed or nest of a beast or bird (*Shak.*): a small room, closet, or private apartment: a case for storing or displaying articles of value: a private room for consultation, esp. a king's: hence (usu. *cap.*) a select inner group of the ministers who govern a country: in U.S., the president's advisory council, consisting of heads of government departments.—**Cabinet Council,** an earlier name for the Cabinet; **cab'inet-edi'tion,** one less in size and price than a library edition, but still elegant in format; **cab'inet-maker,** a maker of cabinets and other fine furniture; **cab'inetmaking,** the occupation or art of the cabinetmaker: the getting together of a new set of cabinet ministers; **cabinet minister,** a member of a cabinet; **cab'inet-pho'tograph,** one of the size larger than a carte-de-visite; **cab'inet-pudd'ing,** a cake-like pudding. [Dim. of **cabin;** cf. Fr. *cabinet.*]

**Cabiri, ka-bi'ri** (L. **kä-bē'rē**), *n.pl.* ancient mystic divinities whose cult spread from Lemnos, Samothrace, and Imbros—also **Cabei'ri.**—*adjs.* **Cabirian, Cabir'ic.** [Latinised from Gr. *Kabeiroi.*]

**cable, kā'bl,** *n.* a strong rope or chain for hauling or tying anything, esp. a ship's anchor: a cable-laid rope: a cable-length: a line of submarine telegraph wires embedded in gutta-percha and encased in coiled strands of iron wire: a bundle of insulated wires laid underground: a cabled message.—Also *v.t.* and *v.i.* to provide with a cable, to tie up: to telegraph by cable.— *n.* **cā'bling,** a bead or moulding like a thick rope: the filling of flutes on a column with a moulding like a cable.—*n.* **cā'blegram,** a telegram sent by cable.—*adj.* **cā'ble-laid,** composed of hawsers with a right-handed twist, twisted together to the left hand; **cā'ble-length, cāble's-length,** a tenth of a naval mile, approximately 200 yards.—*ns.* **cā'ble-mould'ing,** a bead or moulding

Neutral vowels in unaccented syllables: *el'ə-mənt*; for certain sounds in foreign words, see p. viii

carved in imitation of a thick rope; cā'ble-stitch, (a series of stitches producing) a pattern suggestive of cables; cā'ble-tramway, -rail'way, one along which cars or carriages are drawn by an endless cable; cā'bleway, a structure for transport of material in cars suspended from a cable. [Fr.,—L.L. *caplum*, a halter—L. *capēre*, to hold.]

**cabob.** Same as **kabob.**

**caboc,** *ka'bək, n.* a double cream cheese rolled in oatmeal. [Same as **kebbock.**]

**caboceer,** *kab-ō-sēr', n.* a West African headman. [Port. *cabeceira*—*cabo*—L. *caput*, head.]

**caboched, caboshed,** *kə-bosht', (her.) adj.* in full face with no neck showing. [Fr. *caboché*—L. *caput*, head.]

**cabochon,** *ka-bō-shō, n.* a precious stone polished but uncut, or cut *en* (*ā*) **cabochon,** i.e. rounded on top and flat on back, without facets.—Also *adj.* [Fr., *caboche*—L. *caput*, head.]

**caboodle,** *kə-bōō'dl, (slang) n.* crowd, collection. [Origin unknown.]

**caboose,** *kə-bōōs', n.* a ship's kitchen: an open-air cooking stove: car on a goods or construction train for the train crew or workmen (*U.S.*): a hut. [Du. *kombuis*; cf. Ger. *kabuse*.]

**cabotage,** *kab'o-tij, n.* coastal trading: restriction of this within a country's territory. [Fr.]

**cabré,** *kā'brā, adj.* rearing (Fr.): of an aeroplane, flying tail-down. [Fr. *cabrer*, to caper.]

**cabrie,** *kab'rē, n.* a pronghorn.—Also **cab'rit.** [Sp. *cabrito*, kid.]

**cabriole,** *kab'ri-ōl, n.* a capriole.—*adj.* of furniture legs, curved, often like an animal's paw.—*n.* **cabriolet** (*-lā'*), a light carriage with two wheels: (after 1830) a cab: a type of motor-car like a coupé, with folding top: a small armchair of curved design (18th century). [Fr.,—L. *capra*, a goat.]

**cacafogo,** *kak-ə-fō'gō,* **cacafuego,** *-fū'gō* (Sp. *kä-kä-fwā'gō*), (*obs.*) *n.* a spitfire, blusterer. [Sp. *cagar*, to void excrement, Port. *fogo*, Sp. *fuego*, fire.]

**cacao,** *kə-kä'ō, kə-kā'ō, n.* the tropical American tree *Theobroma cacao* (family *Sterculiaceae*) or its seeds from which cocoa and chocolate are made. [Mex. *cacauatl*, cacao tree.]

**cachaemia,** *ka-kē'mi-a, n.* a morbid state of the blood.—*adj.* **cachae'mic.** [Gr. *kakos*, bad, *haima*, blood.]

**cachalot,** *kash'ə-lot, -lō, n.* the sperm-whale. [Fr.]

**cache,** *kash, n.* a hiding-place for treasure, provisions, ammunition, etc.: stores so hidden.—*v.t.* to hide.—*n.* **cache-pot** (*kash'pō, -pot*), an ornamental flower-pot enclosing a common one. [Fr. *cacher*, to hide.]

**cachet,** *kash'ā, n.* a seal: any distinctive stamp (*fig.*), esp. something showing or conferring prestige: a capsule enclosing a medicine.—**lettre de cachet** (*hist.*), a letter under the private seal of the king of France, by which his pleasure was made known to individuals, and the administration of justice often interfered with. [Fr.]

**cachexy, cachexia,** *ka-kek'si, -a, n.* a bad state of body: a depraved habit of mind.—*adjs.* **cachec'tic, -al.** [L.,—Gr. *kachexiā*—*kakos,* bad, *hexis,* condition, from the root of *echein,* to have.]

**cachinnate,** *kak'in-āt, v.i.* to laugh loudly.—*n.* **cachinnā'tion.**—*adj.* **cachinn'atory** (or *kak'*). [L. *cachinnāre,* to laugh loudly.]

**cacholong,** *kach'o-long, n.* a variety of quartz or of opal, generally of a milky colour. [Fr. from Kalmuk.]

**cacholot.** Same as **cachalot.**

**cachou,** *ka-shōō', n.* a pill or lozenge of extract of liquorice, cashew-nut, or the like, used by some smokers in the hope of sweetening the breath. [Fr.]

**cachucha,** *kə-chōō'chə, n.* a lively Spanish dance in 3-4 time, like the bolero. [Sp.]

**cacique,** *ka-sēk', n.* a West Indian chief: a political boss. [Haitian.]

**cack-handed,** *kak'-,* (*slang) adj.* left-handed: clumsy.—Also **kack-handed.**

**cackle,** *kak'l, n.* the sound made by a hen or goose: talk or laughter of similar sound or value.—*v.i.* to make such a sound.—Also *v.t.*—*n.* **cack'ler,** a fowl or person that cackles.—**cut the cackle,** to stop the useless talk. [M.E. *cakelen*; cog. with Du. *kakelen.*]

**cacodaemon, cacodemon,** *kak-ō-dē'mən, n.* an evil spirit: a nightmare (*Shak.*). [Gr. *kakos,* bad, *daimōn,* spirit.]

**cacodoxy,** *kak'ō-dok-si, n.* bad doctrine, wrong opinion, heterodoxy. [Gr. *kakos,* bad, *doxa,* an opinion.]

**cacodyl,** *kak'ō-dil, n.* a colourless stinking liquid, composed of arsenic, carbon, and hydrogen. [Gr. *kakōdēs,* stinking, *hȳlē,* matter.]

**cacoethes,** *kak-ō-ē'thēz, n.* a bad habit or itch. [Gr. *kakoēthēs,* *-ēs,* ill-disposed—*kakos,* bad, *ēthos,* habit.]

**cacoethes loquendi,** *kak-ō-ē'thēz* (or *ka-ko-āth'ās*) *lō-kwen'di* (or *lo-kwen'dē*), (L.) an itch for speaking; **cacoethes scribendi,** *skri-ben'di* (or *skrē-ben'dē*), an itch for scribbling.

**cacogastric,** *kak-ō-gas'trik, adj.* pertaining to a disordered stomach, dyspeptic. [Gr. *kakos,* bad, *gastēr,* the belly.]

**cacogenics,** *kak-ō-jen'iks, n.* the science of race deterioration. [Gr. *kakos,* bad, *genos,* race.]

**cacography,** *kak-og'rə-fi, n.* bad handwriting or spelling.—*adj.* **cacographic** (*-ō-graf'ik*). [Gr. *kakos,* bad, and *graphē,* writing.]

**cacolet,** *kak'ō-lā, n.* a military mule-litter. [Fr., prob. from Basque.]

**cacology,** *ka-kol'ə-ji, n.* faulty vocabulary or pronunciation. [Gr. *kakos,* bad, *logos,* speech.]

**cacomistle, cacomixl,** *ka'kə-mi(k)s-əl, n.* a small carnivore (*Bassariscus*) found in south-west U.S. and Mexico; also **ringtail, ringtailed cat.** [Mex.-Sp.,—Nahuatl *tlaco,* half, *miztli,* cougar.]

**cacoon,** *ka-kōōn', n.* the large seed of a tropical climber (*Entada scandens*) of the mimosa family, used for making scent-bottles, snuff-boxes, etc.: the purgative and emetic seed of a tropical American climber (*Fevillea cordifolia*) of the gourd family. [Origin doubtful.]

**cacophony,** *ka-kof'ə-ni, n.* a disagreeable sound: discord of sounds.—*adjs.* **cacoph'onous, cacophonic** (*-ō-fon'ik*), **-al, cacophonious** (*-fō'ni-əs*), harsh-sounding. [Gr. *kakos,* bad, *phōnē,* sound.]

**cacotrophy,** *ka-kot'rə-fi, n.* bad nourishment. [Gr. *kakos,* bad, *trophē,* nourishment.]

**cactus,** *kak'tus, -təs, n.* a name given to any plant of the American family **Cactā'ceae** (now divided into several genera), fleshy xerophytes whose stems store water and do the work of leaves, which are generally reduced to spines.—*pl.* **cac'ti** or **cac'tuses.**—*adjs.* **cactā'ceous, cac'tiform.** [L.,—Gr. *kaktos,* a prickly plant found in Sicily.]

**cacumen,** *ka-kū'men, n.* a top or point.—*adjs.* **cacū'minal,** pertaining to the top: produced by turning the tip of the tongue up and back (*phon.*); **cacū'minous,** with pointed or pyramidal top. [L. *cacūmen, -inis.*]

**cad,** *kad, n.* an inferior assistant (*obs.*): a hanger-on, tavern-yard loafer, or errand-runner (*obs.*): a bus-conductor (*obs.*): a passenger taken by a conductor for his own profit (*obs.*): a townsman (at Oxford): a low vulgarian: one who lacks the instincts of a gentleman.—*adj.* **cadd'ish.**—*n.* **cadd'ishness.** [Short for **cadet.**]

**cadastral,** *ka-das'trəl, adj.* pertaining to a **cad-as'tre** or public register of the lands of a country for fiscal purposes: applied also to a survey on a large scale. [Fr.,—L.L. *capitastrum,* register for a poll-tax—L. *caput,* the head.]

**cadaverous,** kə-dav′ə-rəs, *adj.* corpselike: sickly-looking: gaunt, haggard —*n.* **cadāv′er** (or *-dav′*; *surg.* and *anat.*), a corpse.—*adj.* **cadăv′-eric.**—*n.* **cadav′erousness.** [L. *cadāver*, a dead body—*cadēre*, to fall (dead).]

**caddie, caddy,** kad′i, *n.* one who attends a golfer at play, carrying the clubs: (18th cent.) a messenger or errand porter in Edinburgh.— *v.i.* to carry clubs.—**caddie car,** or **caddy car,** a device running on two wheels for taking a bag of golf clubs round the course—also **caddie** (or **caddy**) **cart.** [See cadet.]

**caddis,** kad′is, (*Shak.* **caddyss**) *n.* worsted ribbon. [O.Fr. *cadaz, cadas,* tow.]

**caddis, caddice,** kad′is, *n.* the larva of the **cadd′is-fly** (*Phryganea*) or other insect of the Trichoptera, which lives in water in a **cadd′is-case,** a silken sheath covered with fragments of wood, stone, shell, leaves, etc., open at both ends.—Also **cadd′is-worm.** [Origin obscure.]

**caddy,** kad′i, *n.* a small box for holding tea. [Malay *kati,* the weight of a small packet of tea.]

**cade,** kād, *n.* a barrel or cask. [Fr.—L. *cadus,* a cask.]

**cade,** kād, *n.* and *adj.* a lamb or colt brought up by hand, a pet lamb. [Ety. unknown.]

**cadeau,** ka-dō, (Fr.) a gift, present.

**cadence,** kā′dəns, *n.* falling, sinking (*Milton*): the fall of the voice: rise and fall of sound, modulation: rhythm: a succession of chords closing a musical period (see **imperfect, perfect, plagal, cadence**).—*adj.* **cā′denced,** rhythmical.— *n.* **cā′dency,** rhythm: the relative status of younger sons (*her.*).—*adj.* **cā′dent** (*Shak.*), falling. [Fr.—L. *cadēre,* to fall.]

**cadenza** (kä-dent′sa, kə-den′za), an outstanding virtuoso passage or flourish interpolated, sometimes improvised, given by a solo voice or instrument towards the end or at some important stage of a movement. [It. *cadenza*—L. *cadēre,* to fall.]

**cadet,** kə-, ka-det′, *n.* a younger son: a member of the younger branch of a family: one studying or qualifying for a commission in the army, navy, or other service, or (formerly) in the East India Company's service: a boy undergoing training for one of the armed forces: in New Zealand, a newcomer gaining experience.—*n.* **cadet′ship.**— **cadet corps,** an organised body of boys undergoing military training. [Fr. *cadet,* formerly *capdet*—dim. of L. *caput,* the head.]

**cadge,** kaj, *v.t.* and *v.i.* to beg or go about begging: to sponge.—*n.* **cadg′er,** a carrier who collects country produce for disposal: a hawker: a fellow who picks up his living about the streets: a sponger. [Prob. conn. with **catch.**]

**cadge,** kaj, *n.* a padded wooden frame on which a number of hawks may be carried. [Prob. **cage**; perh. **cadge** (1).]

**cadgy,** kaj′i, (*dial.*) *adj.* cheerful and friendly: frolicsome: wanton. [Cf. Dan. *kaad,* wanton, O.N. *kātr,*merry.]

**cadi,** kä′di, kā′di, *n.* a magistrate in Mohammedan countries. [Ar. *qādī,* a judge.]

**Cadmean,** kad-mē′ən, *adj.* relating to Cadmus (Gr. *Kadmos*), who, according to legend, introduced the original Greek alphabet.—**Cadmean victory,** one very costly to both sides (Cadmus sowed the dragon's teeth from which sprang soldiers who fought each other until only five were left).

**cadmium,** kad′mi-əm, *n.* the element of atomic number 48, a white metal, occurring in zinc ores. [Gr. *kadmiā, kadmeiā* (*gē*), Cadmean (earth), calamine.]

**cadrans,** kad′ranz, *n.* an instrument by which a gem is adjusted while being cut. [Fr. *cadran,* a quadrant.]

**cadre,** kad′r′, käd′ri, kad′ər, käd′, *n.* framework, esp. permanent skeleton of a military unit, the commissioned and non-commissioned officers, etc., around whom the rank and file may be

quickly grouped: any nucleus of key persons: (prob. from Fr. through Russ.) a cell of trained Communist leaders: a member of such a cell. [Fr.]

**caduac,** kad′ū-ak, (*obs.*) *n.* a casualty or windfall. [Scot.—L. *cadūcum.*]

**caduceus,** ka-dū′si-us, (*myth.*) *n.* the rod of Hermes, messenger of the gods—a wand surmounted with two wings and entwined by two serpents:—*pl.* cadū′cei.—*adj.* cadū′cean. [L. *cādūceus,* akin to Gr. *kērȳkeion,* a herald's wand —*kēryx, -ykos,* a herald.]

**caducibranchiate,** ka-dū-si-brang′ki-āt, *adj.* losing the gills on attaining maturity. [L. *cadūcus* caducous, *branchiae,* gills.]

**caducous,** ka-dū′kəs, *adj.* falling early, as leaves or flowers: lapsing (*Rom. law*).—*n.* **caducity** (*ka-dū′si-ti*), transitoriness, senility: lapse. [L. *cadūcus*—*cadēre,* to fall.]

**Caecilia,** sē-sil′i-a, *n.* a genus of legless burrowing Amphibia with hidden eyes.—*adj.* **caecil′ian.**— *n.* any member of the class to which Caecilia belongs. [L. *caecus,* blind.]

**caecum,** sē′kəm, in U.S. **cecum,** *n.* a blind sac: a sac or bag having only one opening, connected with the intestine of an animal:—*pl.* cae′ca.— *adj.* cae′cal. [L., neut. of *caecus,* blind.]

**caen-stone,** kā′ən-stōn, *n.* a cream-coloured limestone brought from Caen (*kä*) in France.

**caerulean.** Same as cerulean.

**Caesalpinia,** ses-, sēz-al-pin′i-a, *n.* a genus, including brazil-wood and divi-divi, giving name to a family **Caesalpinia′ceae** of leguminous plants. [Named after Andrea *Cesalpino* (1519-1603), botanist.]

**Caesar,** sē′zər, *n.* an absolute monarch, an autocrat, from the Roman dictator Gaius Julius *Caesar* (100-44 B.C.).—*adj.* **Caesarean, -ian** (*-ā′ri-ən*), relating to Julius Caesar.—*n.* an adherent of Caesar, an imperialist.—*ns.* **Cae′sarism; Cae′sarist; Cae′sarship.**—**caesaropapism** (also *cap.*), (*sē-zə-rō-pā′pizm*), control of the church by a secular ruler or by the state (L.L. *pāpa,* pope).—**Caesarean operation, section,** delivery of a child by cutting through walls of abdomen: in Roman times, enjoined by law if mother died (perh. *Lex Caesarea,* perh. *caedēre,* to cut—Pliny connects with first bearer of cognomen *Caesar*).

**caesium,** sēz′i-əm, in U.S. **cesium,** *n.* the element of atomic number 55, a silver-white, soft, and extensile alkaline metal; used in form of compounds or alloys in photoelectric cells, etc.—*adj.* **caes′ious,** bluish or greyish green. [L. *caesius,* bluish grey.]

**caespitose,** sēs′pi-tōs, *adj.* tufted: turf-like. [L. *caespes, -itis,* turf.]

**caestus.** Variant of cestus (2), or, less often, (1).

**caesura, cesura,** si-zū′ra, (*pros.*) *n.* division of a foot between two words: a pause in a line of verse (generally near the middle).—*adj.* **caes-ū′ral.** [L. *caesūra*—*caedēre, caesum,* to cut off.]

**cafard,** ka-fär′, *n.* depression, the blues. [Fr.]

**café, cafe,** kaf′ā, ka′fi, *n.* a coffee-house, a restaurant: (Fr. **café,** *kaf-ā*) coffee-(house).— **café au lait,** ō le, coffee with hot milk; **café chantant** (*shã-tä*), **café-concert** (*kõ-ser*), café providing musical entertainment; **café filtre,** *fēl-tr′,* strong black filtered coffee; **café noir** (*nwär*), black coffee (i.e. without milk).

**cafeteria,** ka-fi-tē′ri-ə, *n.* a restaurant with a counter for self-service. [Cuban Sp., a tent in which coffee is sold.]

**caff.** Slang term for **café,** coffee-house.

**caffeine,** kaf′ēn, or *kaf-ē′in,* *n.* theine, an alkaloid present in coffee and tea.—*n.* **caff′e(in)ism,** a morbid state caused by caffeine. [Fr. *caféine*; see **coffee.**]

**cafila, caffila,** ka′fēl-a, (Ar.) a caravan.

**Caffre.** See **Kaffir.**

Neutral vowels in unaccented syllables: el′ə-mənt; for certain sounds in foreign words, see p. viii

caftan, *kaf'tən, kaf-tan'*, *n.* a long-sleeved Persian or Turkish garment, reaching to the ankles and often tied with a sash. [Turk. *qaftān.*]

cage, *kāj*, *n.* a box or compartment wholly or partly of open work for captive animals: a prison: a frame with a platform or platforms used in hoisting in a vertical shaft: the framework supporting a peal of bells: a wire guard: any structure resembling a bird's cage: a squirrel's nest (*dial.*).—*v.t.* to imprison in a cage: —*pr.p.* cag'ing; *pa.t.* and *pa.p.* caged.—*adj.* caged, confined.—*n.* cage'ling, a bird that is or has been kept in a cage.—*ns.* cage'bird, a bird of a kind habitually kept in a cage; cage'work, open work like the bars of a cage. [Fr.,—L. *cavea*, a hollow place.]

cagey, cagy, *kāj'i*, (*coll.*) *adj.* artfully shy, wary, chary: not frank, secretive.—*n.* cag'iness, cag'yness. [Perh. conn. with cadgy.]

cagot, *kāg'ō*, *n.* one of an outcast class found scattered in the western Pyrenees, supposed to be the descendants of lepers. [Fr.; origin unknown.]

cahier, *ka-yā*, (Fr.) a writing-book: a memorandum: a report, memorial.

cahoot, *kə-hoot*, *n.* (*U.S.*) company or partnership.—go cahoots, to go shares; in cahoots, in collusion.

cailleach, *kal'yahh*, (*Scot.*) *n.* an old woman.— Also caillach, cailliach. [Gael. *cailleach.*]

caimac, caimacam. Same as kaimakam.

caiman. Same as cayman.

Cain, *kān*, *n.* Adam's son, murderer of Abel (Gen. iv), hence allusively a murderer.—*n.* Cain'ite, a descendant of Cain: a member of a 2nd-century set of Gnostics who revered Cain and Judas.—*adj.* Cain'-col'oured (*Shak.*), of the traditional colour of Cain's beard and hair, red.—raise Cain, to make a determined or angry fuss.

cain, kain, *kān*, *n.* in old Scots law, rent paid in kind, esp. in poultry, etc.: tribute.—*n.* cain'-hen, a hen given up as cain.—pay the cain, to pay the penalty. [Ir. and Gael. *cáin*, rent, tax.]

ca'ing-whale. See ca'.

Cainozoic, *kī-nō-zō'ik*, (geol.) *adj.* and *n.* Tertiary. [Gr. *kainos*, new, *zōē*, life.]

caique, caïque, *kä-ēk'*, *n.* a light skiff used on the Bosporus: the skiff of a galley. [Fr.,—Turk. *kaik*, a boat.]

caird, *kārd*, (*Scot.*) *n.* a tramping tinker, a gypsy, a vagrant. [Gael. and Ir. *ceard.*]

Cairene, *kī'rēn, kī-rēn'*, *adj.* relating to Cairo.—*n.* a native or citizen of Cairo.

cairn, *kārn*, *n.* a heap of stones, esp. one raised over a grave, or as a landmark on a mountaintop or path: a small variety of Scottish terrier (in full cairn terrier) suitable for driving foxes from their earths among cairns.—*n.* cairngorm' (-stone), brown or yellow quartz found among the Cairngorm Mountains. [Gael. *càrn.*]

caisson, *kā'sən, kə-soon'*, *n.* a tumbril or ammunition wagon: a chest of explosive materials: a strong case for keeping out the water while the foundations of a bridge are being built: an apparatus for lifting a vessel out of the water for repairs or inspection: the pontoon or floating gate used to close a dry-dock.—caisson disease, bends, a disease affecting divers, caisson-workers, etc., who are too suddenly subjected to decreased air pressure; it is due to formation of nitrogen bubbles in the body as nitrogen comes rapidly out of solution. [Fr., from *caisse*, a case or chest. (See case.)]

caitiff, *kā'tif*, *n.* a mean despicable fellow.—*adj.* mean, base.—*n.* cai'tive (Spens.), captive, subject. [O.Fr. *caitif* (Fr. *chétif*)—L. *captivus*, a captive—*capēre*, to take.]

cajole, *kə-jōl'*, *v.t.* to coax: to cheat by flattery.— *ns.* cajole'ment, coaxing for the purpose of de-

luding: wheedling, language: flattery; cajol'er; cajol'ery. [Fr. *cajoler*, to chatter; ety. dub.]

cajuput, *kaj'ə-put*, *n.* a pungent, volatile, aromatic oil, distilled from the leaves of an Indo-Malayan and Australian myrtaceous tree *Melaleuca Leucodendron.*—Also caj'eput. [Malay.]

cake, *kāk*, *n.* a piece of dough that is baked: a small loaf of fine bread: any flattened mass baked, as *oatcake* (whence Scotland has been called the 'Land of Cakes'), or formed by pressure or drying, as of soap, clay, snow, blood: a breadlike composition enriched with additions such as sugar, spices, currants, peel, etc.: a separately made mass of such composition: a madcap or fool (*slang*).—*v.t.* and *v.i.* to form into a cake or hard mass.—*n.* and *adj.* cāk'ing,— *adj.* cak'y.—*n.* cake'walk, a prancing movement performed by American Negroes in competition for a *cake*: a dance developed therefrom: music for the dance: something accomplished with supreme ease.—*v.i.* to perform a cakewalk or execute similar movements.—caking coal, a bituminous coal that fuses into a mass in burning.—a piece of cake, a thing easy to do; cakes and ale, vaguely, all the good things of life; eat one's cake and have it, to have the advantage of both alternatives; his cake is dough, his hope has failed; take the cake (*slang*), to carry off the honours, rank first (ironically). [O.N. *kaka*, cog. with Ger. *kuche*(*n*), Du. *koek.*]

Calabar-bean, *kal-ə-bär'-bēn*, or *kal'*, *n.* the seed of the tropical African *Physostigma venenosum* (*Papilionaceae*), used in emulsion in witchcraft ordeal, the accused being acquitted if he can vomit the poison.

calabash, *kal'ə-bash*, *n.* a gourd, or its shell used as a vessel, tobacco-pipe, etc.: the fruit of the calabash tree or its shell similarly used.— calabash nutmeg, the fruit of a tropical anonaceous tree *Monodora myristica*, whose seeds are used as nutmegs; calabash tree, a bignoniaceous tree of tropical America (*Crescentia cujete*) with large melon-like fruit. [Fr. *calebasse*—Sp. *calabaza*—Pers. *kharbuz*, melon.]

caliboose, *kal'ə-boos, -boos'*, (*U.S.*) *n.* a prison. [Sp. *calabozo.*]

Caladium, *kal-ā'di-um*, *n.* an American genus of plants of the arum family, with edible starchy root-stocks. [Latinised from Malay *kélády*, a kindred plant.]

calamanco, *kal-ə-mangk'ō*, *n.* a satin-twilled woollen stuff, checkered or brocaded in the warp. [Du. *kalamink*, Ger. *kalmank*, Fr. *calmande*; origin unknown.]

calamander, *kal-ə-man'dər*, *n.* a hard and valuable cabinet-wood of the ebony genus, brownish with black stripes, brought from India and Ceylon. [Prob. Sinh.]

calamary, *kal'ə-mər-i*, *n.* a squid. [L. *calamārius* —*calamus*—Gr. *kalamos*, pen, from its internal shell.]

calamine, *kal'ə-min, -min*, *n.* a mineral, zinc carbonate (smithsonite): in U.S., hydrous zinc silicate (hemimorphite, or electric calamine). [Fr.—L.L. *calamina*, prob.—L. *cadmia*; see cadmium.]

calamint, *kal'ə-mint*, *n.* a genus (*Calamintha*) of labiate plants allied to mint and thyme. [Fr.— Gr. *kalaminthē*, some related plant.]

calamite, *kal'ə-mīt*, *n.* a general name for a family of fossil plants abundant in the Coal-Measures, gigantic trees related to horse-tails. [L. *calamus*, a reed.]

calamity, *kə-lam'i-ti*, *n.* a great misfortune: affliction.—*adj.* calam'itous, making wretched, disastrous.—*adv.* calam'itously.—*n.* calam'itousness. [Fr. *calamité*—L. *calamitās, -ātis.*]

calamus, *kal'ə-mus*, *n.* the traditional name of the sweet-flag: the reed pen used by the ancients in

writing: a quill (*zool.*): (*cap.*) a genus of palms whose stems make canes or rattans:—*pl.*
cal′ami. [L.—Gr. *kalamos*, reed, cane, pen.]
calando, *kä-län′dō*, (*mus.*) *adj.* and *adv.* gradually slower with diminishing volume of tone. [It., falling off.]
calandria, *kal-an′dri-ə, n.* a sealed vessel used in the core of certain types of nuclear reactor.
Calanus, *ka-lā′nəs, kal′ə-nəs, n.* a genus of copepods, swimming in plankton, important as whale and fish food.
calash, *kə-lash′, n.* a light low-wheeled carriage with a folding top: a hood with hoops formerly worn by ladies over the cap. [Fr. *calèche*; of Slav. origin.]
calavance, *kal′ə-vans, n.* a name for certain varieties of pulse.—Also car′avance. [Sp. *garbanzo*, chick-pea, said to be Basque *garbantzu*.]
calcaneum, *kal-kä′ni-əm, n.* the heel-bone.—*adjs.* calcā′neal, calcā′nean. [L. *calcāneum*, the heel—*calx*, the heel.]
calcar, *kal′kär, n.* a spur or spur-like projection, esp. from the base of a petal (*bot.*): a bird's spur (*zool.*): the prehallux (*zool.*): the hippocampus minor or calcar ā′vis (bird's spur) in the brain (*zool.*).—*adjs.* cal′carate; calcar′iform; cal′carine. [L., a spur—*calx*, the heel.]
calcar, *kal′kär, n.* a fritting furnace, an oven or furnace for calcining the materials of frit before melting: an arch or oven for annealing. [L. *calcāria*, a lime-kiln.]
calcareous, *kal-kā′ri-əs, adj.* chalky: limy. [L. *calcārius*, from *calx*, lime.]
calceamentum, *kal-si-ə-men′tum, n.* a red silk embroidered sandal forming part of the insignia of the Holy Roman Empire. [L. *calceāmentum*, a shoe.]
calced, *kalst, adj.* shod, wearing shoes—opp. to *discalced*—of Carmelites.—*v.t.* cal′ceate, to shoe.—*adjs.* cal′ceate, -d, shod; cal′cēiform, cal′ceolate, slipper-shaped. [L.L. *calceus*, a shoe—*calx*, the heel.]
calcedony. See chalcedony.
Calceolaria, *kal-si-ō-lā′ri-ə, n.* a South American genus of Scrophulariaceae, largely cultivated for the beauty of the slipper-like flowers. [L. *calceolus*, dim. of *calceus*, a shoe.]
calciferol, etc. See calcium.
calcium, *kal′si-əm, n.* the metal, of atomic number 20, present in lime, chalk, gypsum, etc.—*adjs.* cal′cic, containing calcium; cal′cicole, calcic′olous, growing on limestone or limy soils.—*n.* calcif′erol, vitamin D₂ (*calci*ferous and ergosterol).—*adjs.* calcif′erous, containing lime; cal′cific, calcifying or calcified.—*n.* calcificā′tion, the process of calcifying, a changing into lime.—*adjs.* cal′cifuge (-*fūj*), calcif′ugous (-*ū-gəs*), avoiding limestone.—*v.t.* and *v.i.* cal′cify, to make or become limy by secretion, deposition, or substitution.—*adjs.* calcig′erous (-*sij′ə-rəs*), containing lime; cal′cinable.—*n.* calcinā′tion.—*v.t.* cal′cine (or -*sin′*), to reduce to a calx by the action of heat: to subject to prolonged heating, esp. so as to oxidise, or so as to drive off water and carbon dioxide.—*v.i.* to become calx or powder by heat.—*ns.* cal′cite, calcspar (*kalk′spär*), a mineral, calcium carbonate crystallised in the hexagonal system; calc′-sin′ter, calc′-tuff, travertine, a porous deposit from springs charged with calcium carbonate.—Calciferous Sandstone, the lowermost group of Carboniferous rocks in Scotland, answering to part of the English Carboniferous Limestone. [L. *calx, calcis*, lime, limestone.]
calculate, *kal′kū-lāt, v.t.* to count or reckon: to think out, esp. mathematically: to think, purpose, suppose (*U.S.*).—*v.i.* to make a calculation: to estimate.—*adj.* cal′culable.—*p.adjs.* cal′culated, thought out: reckoned: computed: fitted, likely, of such a nature as probably;

cal′culating, given to forethought: deliberately selfish and scheming.—*n.* calculā′tion, the art or process of calculating: estimate: forecast.—*adj.* cal′culātive, relating to calculation.—*n.* cal′culātor, one who calculates: a book, table, or machine for obtaining arithmetical results.—calculated risk, a possibility of failure, the degree of which has been estimated and taken into account before a venture is undertaken; calculating machine, a machine for obtaining arithmetical results without calculation. [L. *calculāre, -ātum*, to reckon by help of little stones—*calculus*, dim. of *calx*, a stone.]
calculus, *kal′kū-lus, n.* a stone-like concretion which forms in certain parts of the body (*pl.* cal′culi): a system of computation used in the higher branches of mathematics (*pl.* cal′culuses).—*adjs.* cal′cular, pertaining to the mathematical calculus; cal′culary, cal′culose, cal′culous, pertaining to or affected with stone or with gravel.—calculus of finite differences is concerned with changes in functions due to finite changes in variables—it does not assume continuity; differential calculus, a method of treating the values of ratios of differentials or the increments of quantities continually varying; integral calculus, the summation of an infinite series of differentials. [L.; see foregoing.]
caldarium, *kal-där′i-um, kal-där′i-ōōm*, (L.) a hot bath.
caldera, *käl-dā′ra, (geol.) n.* a volcanic crater of great size. [Sp., cauldron.]
caldron. Same as cauldron.
Caledonian, *kal-i-dō′ni-ən, adj.* pertaining to ancient Caledonia, to the Highlands of Scotland, or to Scotland generally, or (*geol.*) to a mountain-forming movement with folds and overthrusts trending generally N.E. and S.W. in Silurian and Old Red Sandstone times, well developed in Scotland.—*n.* a Scot. [L. *Cālēdōnia*.]
calefaction, *kal-i-fak′shən, n.* act of heating: state of being heated.—*adj.* calefacient (-*fā′shənt*), warming.—*n.* anything that warms: a blister or superficial stimulant.—*adj.* calefac′tive, communicating heat.—*n.* calefac′tor, a small stove.—*adj.* calefac′tory, warming.—*n.* a room in which monks warmed themselves: a warming-pan, or pome.—*v.t.* and *v.i.* cal′efy, to make or grow warm. [L. *calefacĕre—calēre*, to grow hot; *facĕre, factum*, to make.]
calembour, *kal-ä-bōōr*, (Fr.) a pun.
calendar, *kal′ən-dər, n.* the mode of adjusting the natural divisions of time with respect to each other for the purposes of civil life: an almanac or table of months, days, and seasons, or of special facts, etc.: a list of documents arranged chronologically with summaries of contents: a list of canonised saints, or of prisoners awaiting trial: any list or record.—*v.t.* to place in a list: to analyse and index.—*ns.* cal′endarer, cal′endarist.—calendar-line, the date-line; calendar month, year, see under month, year. [O.Fr. *calandier*—L. *calendārium*, an account-book, *kalendae*, calends.]
calender, *kal′ən-dər, n.* a machine with bowls or rollers for finishing the surface of cloth, paper, etc., by combined moisture, heat, and pressure: a person who calenders (properly a calendrer).—*v.t.* to dress in a calender.—*ns.* cal′endering is done. [Fr. *calandre*—L. *cylindrus*—Gr. *kylindros*, roller.]
calender, *kal′ən-dər, n.* a dervish. [Pers. *qalandar*.]
calends, *kal′əndz, n.pl.* among the Romans, the first day of each month. [L. *kalendae—calāre*, Gr. *kaleein*, to call (because the beginning of the month was proclaimed).]
Calendula, *ka-len′dū-lə, n.* the marigold genus: a preparation of marigold flowers formerly used in plasters, etc., for the healing of wounds. [L.

*kalendae*, calends (but the connection is not obvious).]
**calenture**, *kal'ən-chər*, *n.* a fever or delirium occurring on board ship in hot climates. [Fr.— Sp. *calentura*—L. *calēns*, *-entis*—*calēre*, to be hot.]
**calescence**, *kal-es'əns*, *n.* increase in heat. [L. *calēscĕre*, inchoative of *calēre*, to be hot.]
**calf**, *käf*, *n.* the young of the cow, elephant, whale, and certain other mammals: calfskin leather: a stupid or loutish person: an iceberg in relation to its parent glacier:—*pl.* **calves** (*kävz*).—*v.t.* and *v.i.* **calve** (*käv*), to bring forth a calf: to detach (an iceberg).—*adj.* **calf'-bound**, bound in calf-skin.—**calf'-country**, **-ground**, home of one's youth; **calf'dozer**, a small bulldozer; **calf'-lick**, a cow-lick; **calf'-love**, a boy's or girl's transient amorous attachment; **calf's'-foot**, **calves'-foot**, the foot of the calf, used in making a jelly; **calf'skin**, the skin of the calf, making a good leather for bookbinding and shoes; **calf'-time**, youth.—**divinity calf**, a dark-brown calf book-binding with blind stamping, and without gilding—used on theological books; **golden calf**, the image set up by Aaron during the absence of Moses on Sinai, or one of those erected by Jeroboam at Bethel and Dan; wealth as an object of worship; **half-calf**, a bookbinding in which the back and corners are in calfskin; **mottled calf**, a light-coloured bookbinding, decorated by the sprinkling of acid in drops; **smooth calf**, a binding in plain or undecorated calf leather; **tree calf**, a bright brown calf book-binding, stained by acids with a pattern resem-bling the trunk and branches of a tree. [O.E. (Anglian) *cælf* (W.S. *cealf*); Ger. *kalb*.]
**calf**, *käf*, *n.* the thick fleshy part at the back of the leg below the knee.—*adj.* **calf'less**, with a thin poor calf. [O.N. *kálfi*.]
**caliature-wood**, *kal'i-ə-char-wood*, *n.* red sanders.—Also **caliatour**, **calliature**, etc.
**Caliban**, *kal'i-ban*, *n.* a man of beastly nature, from the monster of that name in Shakespeare's *Tempest.*
**calibre**, **caliber**, *kal'i-bər*, *n.* the size of the bore of a tube: diameter: character, capacity (*fig.*).—*adj.* **cal'ibred**, **cal'ibered**.—*v.t.* **cal'ibrāte**, to determine the calibre of, or the true values answering to the graduations of.—*n.* **calibrā'tion**. [Fr. *calibre*, the bore of a gun; perh. L. *quā librā*, of what weight, or from *L. qālib*, a mould.]
**caliche**, *kä-lē'chä*, *n.* Chile saltpetre. [Sp.]
**calico**, *kal'i-kō*, *n.* a cotton cloth first brought from *Calicut* in India: plain white unprinted cotton cloth, bleached or unbleached: coarse printed cotton cloth:—*pl.* **cal'icos**, **cal'icoes**.—*adj.* made of calico: spotted.—**cal'ico-bush**, **-flower**, **-tree**, kalmia; **cal'ico-print'er**, one em-ployed in printing calico(e)s; **cal'ico-wood**, the snowdrop-tree.
**calid**, *kal'id*, *adj.* warm.—*n.* **calid'ity**. [L. *calidus*, hot.]
**calif.** See caliph.
**californium**, *kal-i-för'ni-əm*, *n.* element 98 (symbol Cf.). [Produced at the University of *California*.]
**caligo**, *kal-i'gō*, *n.* dimness of sight.—*adj.* **caligin-ous** (*kal-ij'i-nəs*), dim, obscure, dark.—*n.* **caligino'ity**. [L. *cālīgō*, *-inis*, fog.]
**caligraphy**, a faulty spelling of calligraphy.
**caliology**, *kal-i-ol'ə-ji*, *n.* the science of birds' nests. [Gr. *kaliā*, *kaliā*, a nest, *logos*, discourse.]
**calipash**, *kal'i-pash*, *n.* the part of a turtle close to the upper shell, a dull greenish fatty gelatinous substance.—*n.* **cal'ipee**, the light-yellowish por-tion from the belly. [Prob. from West Ind. words.]
**calipers.** See callipers.
**caliph**, *kal'if*, or *kā'lif*, *n.* a successor of Moham-med: spiritual leader of Islam.—Also **calif**, **khalif**.—**cal'iphate**, the office, rank, government

or empire of a caliph. [Fr. *calife*—Ar. *khalifah*, a successor.]
**Calippic**, **Callippic**, *ka-lip'ik*, *adj.* pertaining to the Athenian astronomer *Kal(l)ippos* (*c.* 350 B.C.) whose cycle equalled four Metonic cycles less one day, or seventy-six years.
**calisaya**, *kal-i-sā'yə*, *n.* a variety of Peruvian bark.
**calisthenics.** See callisthenics.
**caliver**, *kal'i-vər*, (*Shak.*) *n.* a kind of light musket. [Same as calibre.]
**calix.** See calyx.
**Calixtin**, **Calixtine**, *kal-iks'tin*, *n.* a member of the more moderate party among the Hussites—a Utraquist.—Also *adj.* [From their demanding the cup (L. *calix*) as well as the bread for the laity.]
**Calixtin**, **Calixtine**, *kal-iks'tin*, *n.* a follower of the Syncretist Lutheran divine, George *Calixtus* (1586-1656).
**calk.** Same as caulk.
**calk**, *kök*, *n.* a pointed piece on a horseshoe to prevent slipping—also **calk'in**, **calk'er**, **caulk'er**. —*v.t.* to provide with a calk. [O.E. *calc*, shoe— L. *calx*, a heel.]
**calk**, **calque**, *kök*, *kalk*, *v.t.* to copy by rubbing the back with colouring matter and then tracing with a blunt point. [L. *calcāre*, to tread, *calx*, the heel.]
**call**, *köl*, *v.i.* to cry aloud (often with *out*): to make a short visit (with *upon*, *for*, *at*): to make a telephone call: in poker, to demand a show of hands after repeated raising of stakes.—*v.t.* and *v.i.* in card games, to undertake to score: to declare (trump suit, etc.) in card games.—*v.t.* to name: to summon: to rouse: to appoint or pro-claim: to designate or reckon: to select for a special office, as to the bar: to read out the names in (a roll): to demand the playing of (an exposed card): to apply (offensive name) to (*coll.*).—*n.* a summons or invitation (to the witness-box, the telephone, before the curtain, etc.): a sense of vocation: a demand: a short visit: a signal by trumpet, bell, etc.: a telephone connection or conversation, or a request for one: in card games, a declaration or undertaking, or the right to make it in turn: a cry, esp. of a bird: an instrument mimicking a bird's cry: admission to the rank of barrister: an invitation to the pastorate of a congregation: occasion, cause (*coll.*).—*ns.* **call'er**, one who calls; **call'ing**, vocation; **call'-at-large**, a form of pastoral call sometimes adopted by a presbytery where a congregation is not unanimous, in which the name of the person to be called is not inscribed beforehand, and the names cannot be adhibited by mandate; **call'-bird**, a bird trained to allure others into snares; **call'-box**, a public telephone-box; **call'-boy**, a boy who waits upon the prompter in a theatre, and calls the actors when wanted on the stage; **call'-girl**, a prostitute on call by telephone; **calling card**, a visiting card; **call'ing-crab**, the fiddler-crab, which waves its larger claw when disturbed; **call'-loan**, **call'-mon'ey**, a loan or money payable when asked for; **call'-note**, the note by which a bird or beast calls to its kind; **call'-up**, an act of calling up.—at call, readily available; boatswain's call (see under whistle); call attention to, to point out; call away, to divert the mind; call back, to recall; call cousins, claim kindred; call down, to invoke: to rebuke; call for, to come for and take away with one: to ask loudly for: to demand: to require (called-for, required, necessary; not called for, uncalled-for); call forth, to evoke; call for trumps, to play a card as a signal to a partner to lead a trump; call in, to bring in from outside, as the notes in circula-tion, etc.: to call to one's help (as a doctor, the police); call in question, to challenge, throw doubt on; call off, to summon away: to with-

draw or back out: to cancel or abandon; **call on,** or **upon,** to invoke, appeal to: to make a short visit to; **call out,** to challenge to fight a duel: to summon to service, bring into operation: to instruct (members of a trade union) to come out on strike; **call over,** to read aloud (a list); **call to account** (see **account**); **call to mind,** to recollect, or cause to recollect; **call to order,** to call upon to observe the rules of debate; **call up,** to summon, from beneath, or from another world, to a tribunal, to the colours, to memory; **on call,** at call: ready to answer summons; **within call,** within calling distance. [Found in O.E. (W.S.) as *ceallian;* O.N. *kalla.*]

**call,** *köl, n.* (*Spens.*) a caul or cap.

**Calla,** *kal'ə, n.* a marsh plant of the arum family: erroneously (often **calla lily**) the lily of the Nile (*Zantedeschia*). [Origin doubtful.]

**callant,** *käl'ənt,* (*Scot.*) *n.* a lad. [Du. *kalant.*]

**caller,** *käl'ər, köl'ər,* (*Scot.*) *adj.* fresh: cool. [Prob. the same as **calver.**]

**callet,** *kal'it,* (*Shak.*). *n.* a scold, a woman of bad character, a trull. [Origin obscure.]

**callid,** *kal'id, adj.* shrewd.—*n.* **callid'ity,** shrewdness. [L. *callidus,* expert.]

**calligraphy,** *kə-lig'rə-fi, n.* fine penmanship: characteristic style of writing: artistic script produced with a brush: line or lines in art suggesting this.—*n.* **callig'rapher.**—*adjs.* **calligraph'ic** (*kal-i-graf'ik*), **-al.**—*ns.* **callig'raphist; call'igram(me),** a design using the letters of a word. [Gr. *kallos,* beauty, *graphein,* to write.]

**Calliope,** *kə-li'ə-pi, kal-i'o-pē, n.* the muse of epic poetry: (without *cap.*) a set of steam-whistles played by a keyboard. [Gr. *Kalliópē.*]

**callipers, calipers,** *kal'i-pərz, n.pl.* compasses with legs suitable for measuring the inside or outside diameter of bodies.—Also **calliper-compasses.**—*adj.* **call'iper.**—**calliper** (splint), a splint fitted to the leg, so that the patient may walk without any pressure on the foot. [**calibre.**]

**callippic.** Same as **calippic.**

**callipygous,** *kal-i-pī'gəs, adj.* fair-buttocked.—Also **callipygean, -pij'i-ən.** [Gr. *kallipýgos,* an epithet of Aphrodite—*kallos,* beauty, *pȳgē,* buttock.]

**Callistemon,** *kal-i-stē'mon, n.* an Australian genus of the myrtle family, bottle-brush shrubs. [Gr. *kallos,* beauty, *stēmōn,* a thread (stamen).]

**callisthenics,** *kal-is-then'iks, n.pl.* exercises for cultivating gracefulness and strength.—*adj.* **callisthen'ic.**—Also **calisthenics, -ic.** [Gr. *kallos,* beauty, *sthenos,* strength.]

**Callitriche,** *kal-it'ri-kē, n.* the water-starwort genus, constituting the **Callitricha'ceae,** a family of uncertain affinities, placed by some beside the spurges and boxes, by others with the mare's tails. [Gr. *kallos,* beauty, *thrix, trichos,* hair.]

**callous,** *kal'əs, adj.* hardened: unfeeling, cruel.—*n.* **callos'ity,** a thickening of the skin: callousness.—*adv.* **call'ously.**—*n.* **call'ousness,** lack of feeling, brutality. [L. *callōsus—callus,* hard skin.]

**callow,** *kal'ō, adj.* not covered with feathers: unfledged, unbearded: inexperienced. [O.E. *calu;* Ger. *kahl,* bald.]

**callow,** *kal'ō, adj.* low-lying and liable to be submerged.—*n.* an alluvial flat. [Perh. Irish *calad,* a riverside meadow.]

**Calluna,** *kə-lū'nä, n.* the heather genus. [Gr. *kallȳnein,* to beautify, to sweep—*kalos,* beautiful.]

**callus,** *kal'us, n.* a thickening of the skin: new material by which fractured bones are consolidated (*path.*): soft tissue that forms over a cut surface (*bot.*). [L.]

**calm,** *käm, adj.* still or quiet: (of person, action) serene, tranquil, assured: cool, impudent (*coll*).—*n.* absence of wind—also in *pl.*: repose: serenity of feelings or actions.—*v.t.* and *v.i.* to

make or become calm: to quiet.—*v.t.* to becalm.—*ns.* and *adjs.* (*med.*) **calmant, calmative** (both *kal'* or *kä'*).—*adj.* **calmed** (*kämd*).—*adv.* **calm'ly.**—*n.* **calm'ness.**—*adj.* **calm'y** (*Spens.*), characterised by calm. [Fr. *calme* (It. *calma*), from L.L. *cauma*—Gr. *kauma,* noonday heat—*kaiein,* to burn.]

**calm, calmstane.** See cam (3).

**calmuck.** See **kalmuck.**

**calomel,** *kal'ō-mel, n.* mercurous chloride, used in medicine. [Fr. *calomel,* apparently from Gr. *kalos,* beautiful, *melās,* black, possibly because, itself a colourless crystalline substance, it gives a black product with ammonia, or is got from a black mixture.]

**caloric,** *ka-lor'ik, n.* heat (*arch.*): the once supposed material principle or cause of heat.—*ns.* **calorescence** (*kal-ər-es'əns;* an ill-formed word, meaning the contrary of what it should mean), the transmutation of heat rays into luminous rays; **cal'orie,** the amount of heat needed to raise a gram (*small* or *gram-calorie*), of water (usu. at 15°C) 1° centigrade in temperature (in 1950 it was recommended that this should be superseded as unit by the *joule;* at 15°C, an *international table calorie* (cal$_{IT}$) = 4·1868 joules, a *thermochemical calorie* = 4·1840 joules): the amount of heat needed to raise a kilogram (*great, large, kilogram-calorie*) of water 1° centigrade in temperature (used in expressing the heat- or energy-producing value of foods): the hundredth part of the heat required to raise a gram from 0° to 100°C (*mean calorie;* equal to 4·1897 joules).—*adj.* **calorif'ic,** causing heat: heating.—*ns.* **calorifica'tion; calor'ifier,** an apparatus for heating water in a tank, the source of heat being a coil of heated pipes immersed in the water; **calorim'eter,** an instrument for measuring heat (not temperature) or thermal constants; **calorim'etry; cal'orist,** one who held heat to be a subtle fluid called caloric.—**calorific value,** of a food or fuel, the number of heat units got by complete combustion of unit mass. [L. *calor,* heat.]

**calotte,** *kal-ot', n.* a plain skull-cap or coif worn by R.C. clergy. [Fr.]

**calotype,** *kal'ō-tip, n.* an early kind of photography (invented *c.* 1840 by W. H. Fox Talbot) by means of silver iodide and silver nitrate.—*n.* **cal'otypist.** [Gr. *kalos,* beautiful, *typos,* an image.]

**caloyer,** *kal'o-yər, n.* a Greek monk, esp. of the order of St Basil. [Fr.—It.—Late Gr. *kalogēros.*—Gr. *kalos,* beautiful, *gēras,* old age.]

**calp, kalp, n.** in Ireland, a dark shaly limestone occurring in the middle of the Carboniferous Limestone.

**calpa.** Same as **kalpa.**

**calpac, calpack.** See **kalpak.**

**calque.** See calk (3).

**caltrop,** *kal', köl'trop, n.* an instrument armed with four spikes, so arranged that one always stands upright, used to obstruct an enemy: a sponge spicule of like shape: a name for several plants with fruits so shaped, e.g. (esp. in *pl.*) water chestnut.—Also **cal'trap, cal'throp.** [O.E. *coltetræppe, calcatrippe*—L. *calx,* heel, and the root of trap (1).]

**calumba,** *ka-lum'bə, n.* the root of an East African plant (*Jateorhiza columba,* fam. Menispermaceae) used as a stomachic and tonic. [Perh. from *Colombo* in Ceylon.]

**calumet,** *kal'ū-met, n.* the peace pipe of the North American Indians, a tobacco-pipe smoked in token of peace. [Norman Fr. *calumet,* shepherd's pipe (Fr. *chalumet*)—L. *calamus,* reed.]

**calumny,** *kal'əm-ni, n.* false accusation: slander.—*v.t.* **calumniāte** (*kə-lum'ni-āt*), to accuse falsely: to slander.—*v.i.* to spread evil reports.—*ns.* **calum'niātion; calum'niātor.**—*adjs.* **calum'niātory,**

calum'nious, of the nature of calumny: slanderous.—*adv.* calum'niously. [L. *calumnia*, prob. conn. with *calvī*, to deceive.]

Calvados, *kal'va-dos*, or *-dos'*, *n.* a liqueur made from cider or apple-pulp, esp. in the Calvados department of Normandy.

Calvary, *kal'va-ri*, *n.* the name of the place where Jesus was crucified: a representation of Christ's crucifixion, or a series of scenes connected with it.—Calvary cross, a Latin cross on three steps. [L. *calvāria*, Vulgate rendering of Gr. *krānion*, as that again of Aramaic *gogulthō* or *gogolthā* (Heb. *gulgōleth*—Grecised as *golgotha*), all three words meaning skull.]

calve, calves. See calf.

calver, *kal'var*, *v.t.* to prepare (salmon or other fish) when alive or freshly caught.—*p.adj.* cal'vered. [Cf. caller.]

Calvinism, *kal'vin-izm*, *n.* the doctrines of the great Genevan religious reformer, John *Calvin* (1509-1564), as these are given in his *Institutio*, esp. on particular election, predestination, the incapacity for true faith and repentance of the natural man, efficacious grace, and final perseverance (continuance of the saints in a state of grace until the final state of glory).—*n.* Cal'vinist.—*adjs.* Calvinist'ic, -al.

calvities, *kal-vish'i-ēz*, *n.* baldness. [L. *calvitiēs—calvus*, bald.]

calx, *kalks*, *n.* the substance of a metal or mineral that remains after strong heating:—*pl.* calxes (*kalk'siz*), or calces (*kal'sēz*). [L. *calx, calcis*, lime.]

Calycanthus, etc. See under calyx.

calypso, *ka-lip'sō*, *n.* a West-Indian folk-song, usually dealing with current events, usually made up as the singer goes along.

calyptra, *ka-lip'tra*, *n.* a Greek veil: a hood, covering, esp. that of a moss capsule, or of a root.—*adj.* calyp'trate, capped.—*n.* calyp'trogen, the group of cells giving rise to the root-cap. [Gr. *kalyptrā*, a veil.]

calyx, *kā'liks, kal'iks*, *n.* the outer covering of a flower, its separate leaves termed sepals (*bot.*): applied to various cup-like structures, as the cup of a coral (*zool*; by confusion with L. *calix*, cup):—*pl.* ca'lyces (-*sēz*), or ca'lyxes.—*n.pl.* Calycanthaceae (*kal-ik-an-thā'si-ē*; Gr. *anthos*, flower), the Carolina allspice family of plants, in which there is a transition from sepals to petals.—*ns.* calycanthemy (*kal-ik-an'thi-mi*; Gr. *anthemon*, flower), the condition of having the calyx like a corolla; Calycan'thus, a small North American genus of shrubs, Carolina allspice or strawberry shrub.—*n.pl.* Calyciflorae (*-is-i-flō'rē,-flō*; L. *flōs, flōris*, flower).—*adj.* calyciform (*kal-is'*), having the form of a calyx; calyc'inal, calycine (*kal'i-sin*), pertaining to a calyx.—*n.* cal'ycle, cal'ycule, a whorl of bracts, epicalyx or involucre (*bot.*): a calyx (*zool.*).—*adjs.* cal'ycled, having a calycle; cal'ycoid, calycoi'deous, like a calyx. [Gr. *kalyx*, a covering—*kalyptein*, to cover.]

cam, *kam*, (*mech.*) *n.* an eccentric projection on a revolving shaft, shaped so as to give some desired linear motion to another part.—*ns.* cam'shaft, cam-wheel, a shaft, wheel, bearing a cam or cams. [Du. *kam*, cam, comb; cf. comb, kame.]

cam, *adj.* and *adv.* See kam.

cam, caum, calm, *kām, kōm,* (*Scot.*) *n.* pale blaes: a slate-pencil: pipeclay: limestone (*obs.*).—*v.t.* to whiten with camstone.—*n.* cam'stone, -stane, a white argillaceous stone used for whitening hearthstones and doorsteps.—*adj.* calm'y, clayey. [Origin unknown.]

camaïeu, *kam-a-yø*, *n.* a cameo: a painting in monochrome, or in simple colours not imitating nature: a style of printing pictures producing the effect of pencil-drawing. [Fr.; see cameo.]

Camaldolite, *kam-al'dō-līt*, *n.* a member of a religious order founded by St Romuald at

Camaldoli early in the 11th century.—Also *adj.*—*n.* and *adj.* Camal'dolese.

caman, *kam'an*, *n.* a shinty stick.—*n.* camanachd (*kam-an-ahh'*), shinty. [Gael.]

camaraderie, *kam-a-räd'a-rē*, *n.* good fellowship: the intimacy of comradeship. [Fr.]

camarilla, *kam-a-ril'a*, *n.* a body of secret intriguers, esp. of a court party against legitimate ministers: a small room. [Sp. dim. of *cámara*, a chamber.]

camass, camas, camash, quamash, *kam'as*, -*ash*, *kwom'ash, kwam-ash'*, *n.* a small plant (*Camassia*) of the lily family growing in the north-western United States: its nutritious bulb.—*n.* camassrat, a small gopher rodent that devours the bulbs. [Chinook *kámass*.]

camber, *kam'bar*, *n.* a slight convexity upon an upper surface (as on a road, a beam, the deck of a ship, the wing section of an aeroplane, etc.: a small dock for timber.—*v.t.* and *v.i.* to arch slightly. [Fr. *cambre*—L. *camerāre*, to vault.]

Camberwell beauty, *kam'bar-wal bū'ti, n.* (*Vanessa*, or *Nymphalis, antiopa*) a large and beautiful butterfly, first recorded in England in 1748 at *Camberwell*, then a rural place.

cambist, *kam'bist*, *n.* one skilled in the science of exchange.—*ns.* cam'bism, cam'bistry. [It. *cambista*—L. *cambire*, to exchange.]

cambium, *kam'bi-am*, *n.* a layer or cylinder of meristem by whose differentiation into xylem and phloem new wood and bast are formed.—*adjs.* cam'bial, cam'biform. [L.L.—L. *cambīre*, to change.]

camboge, obsolete form of gamboge.

cambrel, *kam'bral*, *n.* a bent stick or rod for hanging a carcase: an animal's hock. [Perh. conn. with camber, or with gambrel.]

Cambrian, *kam'bri-an, adj.* pertaining to *Cambria* or Wales: Welsh: the geol. system (well represented in Wales) next above the Archaean.—*n.* an inhabitant of Cambria, or Wales: the Cambrian system. [Latinised from W. *Cymry*, Welshmen, *Cymru*, Wales.]

cambric, *kām'brik*, *n.* a fine white linen, originally manufactured at *Kamerijk* (Cambrai) in French Flanders: a cotton imitation.—cambric tea, a beverage made of hot water, milk, sugar and sometimes a small amount of tea.

came, *kām*, *pa.t.* of come.

camel, *kam'al*, *n.* an animal of Asia and Africa with one or two humps on its back, used as a beast of burden and for riding: a watertight structure for raising a vessel in shallow water: a humped type of aeroplane.—*ns.* cam'eleer, one who drives or rides a camel; cam'eline, a material made from camel's hair.—*adj.* of the nature of a camel.—*adjs.* cam'elish, like a camel, obstinate; cam'eloid, of the camel family—also *n.*—*n.* cam'elry.—*adj.* cam'el-backed, humpbacked.—cam'elback, an inferior grade of rubber, made from reclaimed or synthetic rubber, used for retreading tires; cam'el-corps, troops mounted on camels; camel('s) hair, the hair of the camel: the hair of the squirrel's tail used for paint-brushes; camel's thorn, a papilionaceous manna-yielding desert plant (*Alhagi maurorum*) which camels eat greedily. [L. *camēlus*—Gr. *kamēlos*—Phoenician or Heb. *gāmāl*.]

cameleon. See chameleon.

Camellia, *ka-mēl'yā, -mel'*, *n.* a genus of evergreen shrubs close akin to tea, natives of eastern Asia, grown for the singular beauty of their flowers. [Named from Kamel, Latinised *Camellus*, a Moravian Jesuit, who collected plants in the Philippine Islands.]

camelopard, *kam-el'ō-pärd*, or *kam'al-ō-pärd*, *n.* the giraffe.—Also cameleopard (*kam-a-lep'ard*; as by Shelley, by confusion with leopard).—Camelopardalis (*ka-mel-a-pär'da-lis*), a northern constellation. [L. *camēlopardus*—Gr. *kamēlo-*

*pardălis*; from Gr. *kamēlos*, the camel, and *pardălis*, the panther.]

**camelot**, *kam'lot, n.* Same as **camlet.**

**Camembert**, *kam'əm-ber*, Fr. *kam-ā-ber, n.* a soft rich cheese made near *Camembert*, in Normandy.

**cameo**, *kam'i-ō, n.* a gem with figure carved in relief, esp. one in which a differently coloured lower layer serves as ground:—*pl.* **cam'eos.**—**cam'eo-shell'**, a helmet-shell; **cameo ware**, pottery with relief figures against a different colour. [It. *cammeo*—L.L. *cammaeus*, of unknown origin.]

**camera**, *kam'ər-ə, n.* a vaulted room: judge's private chamber: legislative chamber: the papal treasury: the photographer's apparatus, a form of camera obscura in which the outside image is recorded on a light-sensitive plate or film; the apparatus that receives the image of the scene and converts it into electrical impulses for transmission (*TV*):—*pl.* **cam'eras.**—*adjs.* **cam'eral**; **cam'erated**, chambered: vaulted.—*n.* **camerā'tion.**—**camera lucida** (*lū'sid-a*; L., light chamber), a drawing device by which the image of the object is made by reflection to appear as if projected on the paper; **cam'eraman'**, photographer, esp. for press or cinema; **camera obscura** (*ob-skūr'a*; L., dark chamber), dark chamber in which an image of outside objects is thrown upon a screen. [L. *camera*, Gr. *kamarā*, vault.]

**camerlengo**, *kam-ər-leng'gō*, **camerlingo**, *-ling'gō, n.* a papal treasurer. [It.; conn. **chamberlain.**]

**Cameronian**, *kam-ə-rōn'i-ən, n.* a follower of the Covenanter Richard *Cameron*, a member of the Reformed Presbyterian Church, a body that refused to accept the Revolution settlement (mostly united with the Free Church in 1876): a soldier of the Cameronian regiment (26th Foot, later First Battalion of Scottish Rifles; disbandment announced 1968), formed from a body of Cameronians (1689).—Also *adj.*

**camino real**, *kä-mē'nō rā-äl'*, (Sp.) lit. 'royal road': a highway.

**camion**, *kam'i-ən, n.* a heavy lorry, wagon. [Fr.]

**camis**, *kam'is*, **camus**, *kam'əs, n.* (*Spens.*) a loose light robe.—*ns.* **camisâde'**, **camisâ'do** (for Sp. *camisada*), a night attack, probably because shirts were often put on over armour; **cam'isard** (*-sär*, *-zär*), an insurgent Huguenot of the Cevennes, so called from the *camise* or blouse worn by the peasants; **cam'isole**, a sleeved jacket, a woman's loose morning gown or jacket: a loose underbodice with or without sleeves:—*n.pl.* **cam'i-knick'ers**, combined camisole and knickers. [Sp. and Prov. *camisa*, shirt—L. *camisia*.]

**camise**, **camese**, *kam-ēs', n.* the usual Arab shirt. [Ar. *qamiç*, perh. L. *camisia*.]

**camlet**, *kam'lit, n.* a cloth perhaps originally of camel's hair, but now chiefly of wool and goat's hair. [Fr.—L.L. *camelotum*—L. *camēlus*; or perh. Ar. *khamlat*, nap.]

**camomile**, **chamomile**, *kam'ō-mil, n.* a name for several plants akin to chrysanthemum, or their dried flowers, used in medicine, affording a bitter stomachic and tonic—esp. *Anthemis nobilis* (common camomile) and *Matricaria chamomilla* (wild camomile). [Fr. *camomille*—L. *chamomilla*—Gr. *chamaimēlon*, lit. earth-apple, from the apple-like smell of its blossoms—*chamai*, on the ground, *mēlon*, an apple.]

**Camorra**, *kam-or'a, n.* a Neapolitan secret society.—*ns.* **Camorr'ism**; **Camorr'ist.** [It.]

**camouflet**, *kä-mōō-flā, n.* a mine to destroy an underground hostile gallery: an underground cavern filled with gas and smoke formed by a bomb exploding beneath the surface.—*n.* **cam'ouflage** (*-fläzh*), any device (esp. visual) for deceiving an adversary.—*v.t.* and *v.i.* to deceive, to counterfeit, to disguise. [Fr. *camouflet*, a whiff of smoke intentionally blown in the face, an affront, a camouflet.]

**camp**, *kamp, n.* a place on which a tent or tents or the like are pitched: a collection of temporary dwellings, or their inhabitants collectively: temporary quarters of an army, tribe, travellers, holiday-makers, or others: an old fortified site: a permanent military station: a mushroom town, as a mining camp: military service or life (*fig.*): a party or side.—*v.i.* to encamp, or pitch tents: to lodge in a camp (often with *out*, i.e. in the open).—*n.* **camper**, one who camps: a motor vehicle converted for use as temporary living accommodation.—**camp'-bed, -chair, -stool**, a portable folding bed, etc.; **camp'-fe'ver**, typhus, typhoid, or other fever apt to occur in camps; **camp'-fire**, the fire of an encampment: a reunion, lodge, or section, of certain organisations; **camp'-foll'ower**, a non-combatant who follows in the train of an army, as sutler, servant, etc.; **camp'-meet'ing**, a religious gathering in the open air or in a temporary encampment; **camp'-preach'er**, one who preaches at such meetings. [Fr. *camp*, camp.—L. *campus*, a plain.]

**camp**, *kamp*, (*obs.*) *n.* conflict: an old form of the game of football.—*v.i.* to fight, struggle.—*v.i.* **cam'ple**, to wrangle. [O.E. *camp*, battle; cf. Ger. *kampf.*]

**camp**, *kamp, adj.* theatrical, affected, exaggerated: homosexual: characteristic of homosexuals.—*n.* absurd extravagance in manner, deliberate (**high camp**) or without full awareness of the effect.— Also *v.i.*—**camp up**, to make exaggerated, etc.; **camp it up**, to show camp qualities ostentatiously.

**campaign**, *kam-pān', n.* champaign or open country (*arch.*): the time during which an army keeps the field: the operations of that time: an excursion into the country: an organised series of operations in the advocacy of some cause or object.—*v.i.* to serve in a campaign.—*ns.* **campagna** (*käm-pän-yä*; Ital.), once equivalent to champaign, now only a geographical proper name; **campaign'er**, one who has served in several campaigns. [Fr. *campagne*—L. *campania*—*campus*, a field.]

**campana**, *kam-pā'na, n.* a bell-shaped object, as the core of a Corinthian capital: a flower, perhaps the pasque-flower (*Drayton*).—*n.* **campanist** (*kam'pən-ist*), one versed in bells.—*adjs.* **campaniform** (*-pan'*), bell-shaped; **campanolog'ical.**—*ns.* **campanol'ogist**; **campanol'ogy**, the subject or science of bells or bell-ringing; **Campan'ūla**, a genus (giving name to a family **Campanulā'ceae**) commonly known as bell-flowers or bells, the best-known the harebell or Scottish bluebell.— *adjs.* **campanulā'ceous**, **campan'ūlar.**—*n.* **Campanulā'ria**, a common genus of Hydrozoa, with stems simple or branched, the nutritive polyps surrounded by transparent bell-shaped sheaths.—*adj.* **campan'ūlate**, bell-shaped. [It. *campana*, a bell.]

**campanero**, *kam-pa-nē'rō, n.* the South American bell-bird or arapunga, a snow-white chatterer with a note like a church bell. [Sp., bellman.]

**campanile**, *kam-pan-ē'lā, n.* a bell-tower, esp. a tall one detached from the church:—*pl.* **campaniles**, sometimes (It.) **campanili** (*-lē*). [It., from *campana*, a bell.]

**Campbellite**, *kam'bəl-it, n.* a member of the sect known as Disciples of Christ, founded by Alexander *Campbell* (1788-1866).

**campeachy-wood**, *kam-pēch'i-wŏŏd, n.* logwood, first exported from Campeachy (*Campeche*).

**campeador**, *kam-pi-ə-dör', n.* a champion, esp. the Cid. [Sp.]

**campestral**, *kam-pes'trəl, adj.* growing in or pertaining to fields.—Also **campes'trian.** [L. *campester*—*campus*, field.]

**camphire**, *kam'fir, n.* an old name for camphor: henna (*Bible*). [**camphor.**]

**camphor**, *kam'fər, n.* a solid essential oil, got from the camphor laurel (a species of cinnamon-tree) of Formosa, etc., or synthetically manufactured, having a peculiar aromatic taste and smell: any similar compound of the terpene series.—*ns.* camphane (*kam'fān*), a terpene hydrocarbon ($C_{10}H_{18}$), parent substance of the camphor group; camphene (*kam'fēn, -fēn'*), a camphorlike terpene hydrocarbon ($C_{10}H_{16}$); camphine (*kam'fēn, -fīn*), an old name for rectified oil of turpentine.—*adj.* camphorā'ceous, like camphor. —*v.t.* cam'phorate, to impregnate with camphor. —*adj.* camphoric (*-for'ik*), pertaining to camphor. [Fr. *camphre*—L.L. *camphora*—Ar. *kāfūr*.]

campion, *kam'pi-ən, n.* any plant of the genera *Lychnis* (or *Melandryum*) and *Silene*. [Origin unknown.]

Campodea, *kam-pō'di-ə, n.* a genus of bristle-tails. —*adj.* campode'iform, resembling a Campodea, as certain six-legged active insect grubs. [Gr. *kampē*, caterpillar, *eidos*, form.]

campo santo, *kam'pō san'tō*, (It.) a buryingground.

camp-sheathing, -shedding, -sheeting, -shot, *kamp'shē'dhing, -shed'ing, -shēt'ing, -shot, ns.* piles and boarding protecting a river bank or the like. [Origin unknown.]

Camptonite, *kamp'tən-it, n.* an igneous rock composed essentially of plagioclase and hornblende. [*Campton* in New Hampshire.]

campus, *kam'pəs, n.* college grounds (and buildings), or college, or self-contained division of university: a university: the academic world. [L. field.]

Campus Martius, *kam'pəs mär'shəs, kam'pōos mär'ti-ōōs*, (L.) field of Mars, used by the ancient Romans for athletic games, military drill, etc.

campylotropous, *kam-pil-ot'rə-pəs, adj.* of an ovule, curved so as to bring the micropyle near the chalaza. [Gr. *kampylos*, curved, *tropē*, turning.]

camsho, *kam'shō*, camshoch, camsheugh, *kam'-shuhh*, (Scot.) *adj.* crooked. [Cf. cam, and O.E. *sceolh*, awry.]

camstairy, camsteerie, camsteary, *kam-stār'i, -stēr'i*, (chiefly *Scot.*) *adj.* perverse, unruly. [Ety. dub.]

camstone. See cam (3).

camus, *kam'əs, adj.* flat-nosed. [Prob. Fr. *camus*.]

camus. See camis.

cam-wood, *kam'-wōōd, n.* the wood of *Baphia nitida*, a West African papilionaceous tree, at first white, turning red on exposure to air, used as a red dye. [Perh. from African name *kambi*.]

can, kan, *v.t.* (*obs.* in *infin.* except in Scots) to be able: have sufficient power: know (*obs.*): have skill in:—*3rd pers.* can, *2nd sing.* canst; *parts. obs.* except could in Scots; *pa.t.* could.—can is used for *gan* in M.E. and in Spenser. [O.E. *cunnan*, to know (how to do a thing), to be able; *pres. indic. can*; Goth. *kunnan*, Ger. *können*, to be able. See con, ken, know; also cannot, can't, couth.]

can, kan, *n.* a vessel for holding or carrying liquids, generally of tinned iron, with a handle over the top: a chimney-pot: a tin, vessel of tinplate in which meat, fruit, etc., are sealed up: a drinking-mug: a container for various things, as ashes, rubbish (*U.S.*), or film in quantity: a jacket in which a fuel rod is sealed in an atomic reactor: jail (*the can*; *slang*).—*v.t.* to put up for preservation in tins: to store in containers:— *pr.p.* cann'ing, *pa.p.* and *pa.t.* canned.—*p.adj.* canned, packed in tins (or in U.S. jars): drunk (*slang*): (of music) recorded for reproduction by e.g., gramophone.—*ns.* can'ful, as much as a can will hold:—*pl.* can'fuls; cann'er; cann'ery, a place where provisions are tinned.—can it! (*slang*), stop talking about, doing, etc., that!; carry the can (*slang*), to take the blame; can (of motion picture), ready for release: (of

radio, TV, material), recorded and stored for future use. [O. E. *canne*.]

canada, *kän-yä'dä, n.* a narrow cañon. [Sp.]

Canadian, *kə-nä'di-ən, adj.* pertaining to *Canada.* —*n.* a native or citizen of Canada.—Can'ada balsam (see balsam); Canada rice (see Zizania); Canadian waterweed (see Anacharis).

canaigre, *ka-nä'gər, n.* a Texan dock whose root is used in tanning. [Mexican Sp.]

canaille, *kan-äy', kan-i', kən-āl', n.* the mob, the vulgar rabble. [Fr.,—L. *canis*, a dog.]

canakin. See cannikin.

canal, *kə-nal', n.* an artificial watercourse, esp. for navigation: a duct that conveys fluids (*biol.*): a groove.—*adjs.* canalic'ular (*kan-ə-lik'ū-lər*), like or pertaining to a canaliculus; canalic'ulate, -d, channelled, grooved.—*ns.* canalic'ulus (*anat.*), a small furrow or channel:—*pl.* canalic'uli; canalisā'tion (*kan-əl-i-zā'shən*), the construction of canals: formation of an artificial channel: conversion into a canal: direction into a fixed channel (*lit.* and *fig.*).—*v.t.* can'alise, -ize, to make a canal through: to convert into a canal: to direct into a fixed channel (*lit.* and *fig.*).—canal'-boat, a boat for canal traffic; canal'-cell, a cell in the neck of an archegonium; canal'-rays (*phys.*), positive rays, a stream of positively electrified particles through a perforation in the cathode of a vacuum-tube. [L. *canālis*, a waterpipe.]

canape, *ka-na-pä', n.* a piece of bread, sometimes fried or toasted, with caviare, or other dainty, etc. [Fr.]

canard, *ka-när(d'), n.* a false rumour: an early duck-like type of aeroplane. [Fr., lit. duck.]

Canarese. See Kanarese.

canary, *kə-nā'ri, n.* a light sweet wine from the *Canary* Islands: a song-bird (finch) found in the Canary Islands, bright yellow in domestic breeds: a lively dance said to have taken origin in the Canary Islands (often in *pl.*).—*adj.* canarycoloured, bright yellow.—*v.i.* to dance the canary: to prance about.—canā'ry-bird, a canary: a jail-bird (*slang*): a mistress; canā'rycree'per, a yellow-flowered Tropaeolum (popularly but ungrammatically canarien'sis); canā'rygrass, a grass (*Phalaris canariensis*) whose seed (canā'ry-seed) is used to feed canaries; canā'rywood, the timber of two species of *Persea* or *Laurus* of the Canary Islands, Azores and Madeira.

canasta, *kə-nas'ta, n.* a card game of the rummy type, originating in South America. [Sp., basket.]

canaster, *kə-nas'tər, n.* a kind of tobacco, so called from the rush basket in which it was originally brought from Spanish America. [Sp. *canastra*, *canasta*—Gr. *kanastron*.]

cancan, *kan'kan, n.* a stage dance of French origin, orig. considered particularly indecorous. [Fr. *cancan*, chatter, scandal, the cancan; usually referred to L. *quamquam*, the pronunciation of which was long hotly disputed in the French schools; Littré quotes O.Fr. *caquehan*, a noisy assembly.]

cancel, *kan'sl, v.t.* to cross out: to annul or suppress: to abolish or wipe out: to counterbalance or compensate for: to remove as balancing each other, e.g. like quantities from opposite sides of an equation, like factors from numerator and denominator of a fraction:—(*pr.p.* can'celling; *pa.t.* and *pa.p.* can'celled).—*n.* the suppression of a printed leaf or sheet: the part so cancelled, or (usually) the new one substituted.—*n.pl.* cancelli (*kan-sel'i*; L. *kang-kel'ē*), cross-pieces forming a lattice-work or grating, as in the division between the choir and the body of a church: reticulations (*anat.*).—*adjs.* can'cellate, -d, marked latticewise, reticulated.—*n.* cancellā'tion, cancelling: crosswise marking.—*adj.* can'cellous. [L. *cancellāre*,

fāte, fär; mē, hûr (her); mīne; mōte, för; mūte; mōōn, fōōt; dhen (then)

to cross out, *cancellī*, lattice-work, dim. of *cancer*, a lattice.]

**cancelier, canceleer,** *kan-si-lēr'*, (*Scott*) *v.i.* of a hawk, to turn on the wing before stooping.—Also *n.*

**Cancer,** *kan'sər, n.* the genus to which the edible crab belongs: a constellation (the Crab) between Gemini and Leo, and a sign of the zodiac (once coincident with it) whose first point marks the limits of the sun's course northward in summer: **cancer,** loosely any malignant new growth or tumour: properly a carcinoma or disorderly growth of epithelial cells which invade adjacent tissue and spread by the lymphatics and bloodvessels to other parts of the body: any corroding evil (*fig.*).—*v.i.* **can'cerate,** to become cancerous.—*ns.* **cancerā'tion.**—*adj.* **can'cerous,** of, like, affected with, cancer.—*adjs.* **cancriform** (*kang'-kri-förm*), crab-shaped: like cancer; **can'crine** (*kang'krin*), crab-like: palindromic (from the false notion that a crab walked backwards); **cancrizans** (*kang'kri-zanz*; *mus.*), of a canon, having the answer repeating the subject backwards; **cancroid** (*kang'kroid*), crab-like: cancer-like.—Also *n.*—**can'cer-root,** beech-drops. [L., crab.]

**cancionero,** *kän-thyō-nā'rō, n.* a collection of songs. [Sp.]

**cancriform, cancrizans,** etc. See **Cancer.**

**candela,** *kan-del'a, -dē'la, n.* a unit of luminous intensity such that the luminous intensity of a black body radiator at the temperature of solidification of platinum is 60 candelas per sq. cm. [**candle.**]

**candelabrum,** *kan-di-lā'brəm,* or *lä', n.* a branched and ornamented candlestick or lampstand:—*pl.* **candela'bra**—also used as a false *sing.* with *pl.* **candela'bras.** [L. *candēlābrum—candēla,* candle.]

**candelilla,** *kän-dä-lēl'ya, n.* a Mexican wax-yielding spurge. [Sp. dim. of *candela,* candle.]

**candent,** *kan'dant, adj.* glowing: white-hot.—*n.* **candescence,** *kan-des'əns,* a white heat.—*adj.* **candes'cent.** [L. *candēre,* to glow (inceptive *candēscēre*).]

**candid,** *kan'did, adj.* white (*obs.*): shining, clear: frank, ingenuous: free from prejudice: fair, impartial.—*adv.* **can'didly.**—*n.* **can'didness.**—**candid camera,** a type of camera used for taking unposed photographs of people engaged in the normal occupations of their daily life: this style of photography. [L. *candidus,* white.]

**candidate,** *kan'di-dāt, n.* one who offers himself for any office or honour, so called because, at Rome, the applicant used to dress in white.—*ns.* **can'didature, can'didateship, can'didacy** (*-də-si*). [L. *candidātus—candidus,* white.]

**candied.** See **candy.**

**candle,** *kan'dl, n.* a cylinder of wax, tallow, or the like surrounding a wick: a luminary: a candle-shaped object: a jet in a gas-stove: a photometric unit: (or **new candle**) candela: (**international candle**) a former unit of luminous intensity.—*v.t.* to test (as an egg) by holding up before a candle or other light.—**can'dle-berry,** wax-myrtle or bayberry (*Myrica cerifera*) of the spurge family, or its fruit: **can'dle-bomb,** a small glass bomb filled with water, exploding in a candle-flame; **can'dle-coal** (same as **cannel-coal**); **can'dle-dipp'ing,** the method of making candles by dipping instead of moulding; **can'dle-end,** the end-piece of a burnt-out candle; **can'dle-fish,** the eulachon: another West American fish, a cheek-armoured acanthopterygian (*Anoplopoma fimbria*)—the *black candle-fish*; **can'dle-holder,** one who holds a candle to another while working—hence one who abets or connives; **can'dle-light,** the light of a candle: illumination by candles: the time when candles are lighted; **can'dle-lighter,** one whose business is to light the candles:

a spill; **can'dle-nut,** the oil-yielding fruit of a species of *Aleurites* (spurge family) of the Pacific Islands; **can'dle-power,** illuminating power in terms of a standard candle—a name applied to various units of photometry; **can'dle-snuffer,** a snuffer, instrument or person (see **snuff,** 2): also *fig.*; **can'dlestick,** a portable stand for a candle, originally a stick or piece of wood; **can'dle-tree,** a tropical American tree (*Parmentiera cerifera*) of Bignonia family, with candle-like pods; **can'dle-waster,** one who studies late; **can'dlewick,** the wick of a candle: a cotton tufted material used for bedspreads, etc.; **can'dle-wood,** the ·wood of various West Indian and Mexican resinous trees.—**burn the candle at both ends,** to waste or use up in two ways at once; **do a candle,** of a parachute, to fail to inflate; **not fit to hold a candle to,** not to be compared with; **sell by the candle,** to offer for sale as long as a small piece of candle burns, the bid made just before it goes out being successful; **the game is not worth the candle,** the thing is not worth the labour or expense of it. [O.E. *candel*—L. *candēla,* from *candēre,* to glow.]

**Candlemas,** *kan'dl-məs, n.* the R.C. festival for the purification of the Virgin Mary, on 2nd February, when candles are blessed: a quarter-day in Scotland. [**candle, mass.**]

**candock,** *kan'dok, n.* the yellow water-lily. [**can** (2) and **dock** (1).]

**candor.** U.S. spelling of **candour.**

**candour,** in U.S. **candor,** *kan'dər, n.* whiteness (now *rare*): purity (*obs.*): kindness (*obs.*): freedom from prejudice: sincerity: frankness. [Fr. *candeur*—L. *candor,* whiteness, from *candēre,* to shine.]

**candy,** *kan'di, n.* a sweetmeat of sugar boiled and crystallised (also **su'gar-can'dy**): any form of confectionery (*U.S.*): (*U.S. pl.* **candies**).—*v.t.* to preserve or dress with sugar: to crystallise as sugar or the like: to encrust.—*v.i.* to crystallise: to become encrusted.—*adj.* **can'died,** encrusted with candy or sugar: sugared, flattering (*fig.*).—**candy floss,** a fluffy sweetmeat consisting of a ball of spun coloured and flavoured sugar sold on the end of a stick: something insubstantial or ephemeral.—Also *adj.* **candy stripe,** a textile fabric pattern, consisting of narrow coloured stripes on a white background at intervals equal or nearly equal to the width of the stripe. [Fr. *candi,* from Ar. *qandah.* candy.]

**candy,** *kan'di, n.* a South Indian weight, generally containing 20 maunds, about 500 pounds English.—Also **can'die** and **kan'dy.** [Tamil.]

**candytuft,** *kan'di-tuft, n.* a cruciferous plant (*Iberis*), with flowers in tufts or corymbs, the outer petals larger than the inner. [From *Candia* or *Crete,* whence a species was brought, and **tuft.**]

**cane,** *kān, n.* the stem of one of the small palms (as calamus or rattan) or the larger grasses (as bamboo, sugar-cane), or raspberry or the like: a slender rod for beating: a walking-stick.—*v.t.* to beat with a cane: to make or weave with canes, e.g. chairs.—*n.* **can'ing,** a thrashing with a cane.—*adj.* **can'y,** like, made of, or abounding in cane.—*adj.* **cane'-bottomed,** having a seat of interwoven cane strips.—*ns.* **cane'-brake,** a thicket of canes, esp. (in Southern U.S.) of a giant reed; **cane'-chair,** chair made of rattan; **cane'fruit,** fruit borne upon canes, as raspberries, blackberries; **cane'-mill,** a mill for crushing sugar-cane; **cane'-su'gar,** sucrose, esp. that obtained from the sugar-cane; **cane'-trash,** refuse of sugar-cane used for fuel in boiling the juice. [Fr. *canne*—L. *canna*—Gr. *kannē,* a reed.]

**caneh.** See **kaneh.**

**canella,** *kan-el'a, n.* cinnamon (*obs.*): (*cap.*) a genus of low aromatic trees of a small family. **Canellā'ceae** (*-si-ē*), one of which yields white cinnamon or *canella bark*. [L.L., dim. of *canna*, reed.]

**canephor**, *kan'i-fōr, -för*, (*archit.*) *n.* a female (or male) sculptured figure bearing a basket on the head.—Also **canephora, canephore, canephorus** (*ka-nē'for-əs*). [Gr. *kanēphoros*, a basket bearer, as at the Panathenaic festival—*kaneon*, basket, *phoros*, bearing.]

**canescent**, *ka-nes'ənt, adj.* tending to white: hoary.—*n.* **canesc'ence**. [L. *cānēscēns*—*cānēre*—*cānus*, hoary.]

**cangue, cang, kang,** *n.* a Chinese portable pillory borne on the shoulders by petty offenders. [Fr. *cangue*—Port. *cango*, a yoke.]

**canicular**, *ka-nik'ū-lər, adj.* pertaining to the Dogstar (**Canic'ula**) or to the Dog-days: pertaining to a dog (*facetious*).—**canicular year, cycle,** Sothic year, cycle. [L. *caniculāris, canicula*, dim. of *canis*, a dog.]

**canine**, *kan'in, kăn'in, adj.* like or pertaining to the dog.—*n.* any animal of the dog tribe: a canine tooth.—*ns.* **caninity** (*kə-* or *kā-nin'i-ti*); **Ca'nis,** the dog genus, typical of the family **Ca'nidae.**—**canine appetite,** a huge appetite: **canine letter,** R (from its growling sound); **canine tooth,** a sharp-pointed tooth between the incisors and the premolars. [L. *canīnus*—*canis*, a dog.]

**canister**, *kan'is-tər, n.* a box or case, for holding tea, shot, etc.: (for **can'ister-shot**), case-shot.—*vs.t.* **can'ister, can'isterise, -ize,** to put into, pack in, canister(s).—*n.* **canisterisā'tion.** [L. *canistrum*, a wicker-basket; Gr. *kanastron*—*kannē*, a reed.]

**canities**, *ka-nish'i-ēz, n.* whiteness of the hair. [L.]

**canker**, *kang'kər, n.* an eating sore: a gangrene: a fungus disease in trees, esp. one due to Nectria: inflammation in horses' feet: eczema of dogs' ears: an abscess or ulcer in birds: anything that corrupts, consumes, irritates or decays: a canker-worm: a dog-rose (*Shak.*).—*v.t.* to eat into, corrupt, or destroy: to infect or pollute: to make sour and ill-conditioned.—*v.i.* to grow corrupt: to decay.—*adj.* **cank'ered,** corroded (*obs*): polluted (*obs.*): malignant, soured, crabbed.—*adv.* **cank'eredly.**—*n.* **cank'eredness.**—*adj.* **cank'erous,** corroding like a canker.—*n.* **cank'erworm,** a larva that cankers or eats into plants.—*adj.* **cank'ery,** affected with canker: crabbed (*Scot.*). [L. *cancer*, a crab, gangrene.]

**cann.** Same as **con** (3).

**Canna,** *kan'a, n.* the Indian shot (*q.v.*) genus of plants. [L., a reed.]

**canna.** See cannot.

**canna,** *kan'a,* **cannach,** *kan'ahh,* (*Scot.*) *n.* cottongrass. [Gael. *canach*.]

**cannabic,** *kan'əb-ik,* or *-ab', adj.* pertaining to hemp.—*ns.* **cann'abin,** a resin obtained from the hemp plant; **Cann'abis,** the hemp (q.v.) genus: (without *cap.*) narcotic drug variously known as hashish, bhang, marihuana, etc. [Gr. *kannabis*; cf. O.E. *hænep.*]

**cannel,** *kan'l, n.* a bituminous coal that burns with a bright flame, used for making oils and gas.—Also **cann'el-coal, can'dle-coal.** [Prob. form of candle.]

**cannelloni,** *kan-ə-lō'nē, n.* hollow tubelike pieces of paste like macaroni, stuffed with cheese or meat. [It. *cannelloni*, augm. of *cannello*, small tube.]

**cannelure,** *kan'i-lūr, n.* a groove or a fluting: a groove round the cylindrical part of a bullet. [Fr.]

**cannibal,** *kan'i-bl, n.* an eater of the flesh of his own species.—*adj.* relating to or practising cannibalism.—*n.* **cann'ibalism,** the practice of eating one's own kind.—*adj.* **cannibalist'ic.**—*adv.* **cann'ibally** (*Shak.*).—*v.t.* **cann'ibalise, -ize,** to repair (a vehicle, aircraft, etc.) with parts taken from other vehicles, etc.: to take (parts) for such repairs. [Sp. *Canibal, Caribal,* Carib.]

**cannikin,** *kan'i-kin,* a small can.—Also **can'akin, can'ikin.** [Dim. of can.]

**cannon,** *kan'ən, n.* a great gun (*pl.* **cann'ons** or **cann'on**): a cannon bone: a cannon bit: a stroke in billiards in which the cue-ball hits both the red and the opponent's ball (perh. for carom): a similar stroke in certain other games.—*v.i.* to cannonade: to make a cannon at billiards: to strike on the rebound: to collide.—*v.t.* to collide with.—*n.* **cannonade',** an attack with cannon.—*v.t.* to attack or batter with cannon.—*ns.* **cannoneer', cannonier',** one who manages cannon; **cann'onry,** cannonading: artillery.—**cann'onball,** a ball to be shot from a cannon: **can'nonball-tree,** a South American tree (*Couroupita guianensis*) with a large woody fruit; **cannon bit,** a smooth round bit; **cannon bone,** in mammals in which the digits are reduced in number, a bone formed by the fusion of the persisting metacarpals or metatarsals, which supports the limb from 'knee' (wrist) or hock to fetlock: in birds, the tarsometatarsus; **cann'on-fodder,** men regarded merely as material to be consumed in war; **cann'on-game,** a form of billiards in which, the table having no pockets, the game consists in making a series of cannons; **cann'on-met'al,** gun-metal.—*adj.* **cann'on-proof,** proof against cannon-shot.—**cann'on-shot,** a cannonball: the distance to which a cannon will throw a ball. [Fr. *canon*, augmentative—L. *canna,* a reed.]

**cannot,** *kan'ət, v.t.* can not (contracted **can't**, *känt,* Scots **canna,** *kan'ā, kan'a*). [can, not.]

**cannula,** *kan'ū-la, n.* a surgical tube, esp. one enclosing a trocar or perforator, or the breathing-tube inserted in the windpipe after tracheotomy.—*adj.* **cann'ulate.** [Dim. of *canna,* a reed.]

**canny,** *kan'i, adj.* (*Scot.* and *Northern*) knowing: skilful: shrewd: lucky: of good omen: free from taint of the supernatural or dangerous: comfortable: sparing in money matters: gentle: innocent, harmless (sometimes euphemistically): sly or pawky.—Also *adv.*—*adv.* **cann'ily.**—*n.* **cann'iness.**—**ca' canny** (see **ca'**); **no' canny,** preternatural: dangerous. [App. conn. with can.]

**canoe,** *kə-nōō', n.* a boat made of the hollowed trunk of a tree, or of bark or skins: a skiff driven by paddling.—*v.i.* to paddle a canoe.—*ns.* **canoeing; canoe'ist.** [Sp. *canoa*—Haitian *canoa.*]

**cañon, canyon,** *kan'yən, n.* a deep gorge or ravine. [Sp. *cañón,* a hollow, from root of **cannon.**]

**canon,** *kan'ən, n.* a law or rule, esp. in ecclesiastical matters: a general rule or principle: standard or criterion: the books of the Bible accepted as the standard or rule of faith by the Christian Church: the recognised genuine works of any author: a species of musical composition constructed according to a rule, one part following another in imitation: a list of saints canonised: a large kind of type (*print.*).—*adjs.* **canonic** (*kə-non'ik*), **-al,** of the nature of, according to, or included in a canon: regular: ecclesiastical.—*adv.* **canon'ically.**—*n.pl.* **canon'icals,** the official dress of the clergy, regulated by the church canons.—*n.* **canonicity** (*kan-ən-is'i-ti*), the state of belonging to the canon.—*v.t.* **can'onise, -ize** (*Shak. -non'*), to enrol in the canon or list of saints: to recognise as canonical.—*ns.* **canonisā'tion, -z-; can'onist,** one versed in canon law.—*adj.* **canonist'ic.**—**canonical hours,** set hours for prayer: those wherein marriage may take place in an English parish church (formerly 8 a.m. to 12 noon, extended in 1886 to 3, in 1934 to 6 p.m.; **canon law,** a digest of the formal decrees of councils, ecumenical, general, and local, of diocesan and national synods, and of patriarchal decision as to doctrine and discipline.—**canon of the mass,** that part of the mass which begins after the 'Sanctus' with the prayer 'Te igitur', and ends just before the 'Paternoster'.

*fāte, fär; mē, hûr* (her); *mīne; mōte, för; mūte, mōōn, fŏŏt; dhen* (then)

**[O.E.** *canon*—**L.** *canōn*—**Gr.** *kanōn*, a straight rod—*kannē*, a reed.]

**canon,** *kan'ən*, *n.* a member of a body of clergymen serving a cathedral or other church and living under a rule; a clerical dignitary belonging especially to a cathedral, enjoying special emoluments, and obliged to reside there part of the year.—*ns.* **can'oness,** a member of a community of women living under a rule: a woman holding a prebend or canonry, often living in the world; **can'onry,** the benefice of a canon.—**Canon Regular,** a member of an order (Augustinian, Austin, or Black Canons) living under a rule based on St Augustine's teaching, or of an offshoot (Premonstratensians, White Canons), intermediate between monks and secular clergy; **canon residentiary,** a canon obliged to reside at a cathedral and take a share in the duty; **canon secular,** one other than a canon regular; **honorary canon,** one having the titular rank of canon in a cathedral, but without duties or emoluments; **minor canon,** one who conducts cathedral services but is not a member of the chapter. [O.E. *canonic*—L. *canonicus*—*canōn*; see previous article.]

**canoodle,** *ka-nōōd'l*, *(slang)* *v.i.* to fondle amorously. [Origin obscure.]

**canophilist,** *kə-nof'i-list*, *n.* a lover of dogs. [L. *canis*, a dog, Gr. *phileein*, to love.]

**Canopus,** *ka-nō'pus*, *n.* a bright star in the southern constellation *Argo navis*: an Egyptian human-headed vase for holding the entrails taken from an embalmed body.—*adj.* **Cano'pic.** [L.,—Gr. *Kanōpos*, Menelaus's steersman who died at Canopus in Egypt, was stellified as Canopus, and identified with an Egyptian god worshipped in the form of a jar with human head.]

**canopy,** *kan'ə-pi*, *n.* a covering hung over a throne or bed: a covering of state held over the head: any overhanging covering, as the sky: a rooflike projection over a niche, tomb, statue, stall, altar, etc: the transparent cover over the cockpit of an aircraft: the overhead fabric part of a parachute.—*v.t.* to cover with a canopy (*pr.p.* **can'opying;** *pa.t.* and *pa.p.* **can'opied).** [Fr. *canapé*—L. *cōnōpium,* *cōnōpēum*—Gr. *kōnōpion,* a couch with a mosquito curtain—*kōnōps*, a mosquito.]

**canorous,** *kan-ō'rəs*, *-ō'*, *kan'*, *adj.* musical: singing: resonant.—*adv.* **cano'rously.**—*n.* **cano'-rousness.** [L. *canōrus*—*canor,* melody—*canēre,* to sing.]

**canst.** See can (1).

**canstick,** *kan'stik*, *(Shak.)* *n.* a candlestick. [Contr.]

**cant,** *kant*, *v.i.* to speak whiningly: to use language whose meaning has evaporated from continued repetition: to use the language of thieves, etc.: to talk in an affectedly solemn or hypocritical way.—*n.* a hypocritical or affected or perfunctory style of speech or thought: the language peculiar to a sect: odd or peculiar talk of any kind: slang: a common saying: affected use of religious phrases or sentiments.—Also *adj.*—*n.* **cant'er,** one who cants, a beggar: one who makes hypocritical professions.—*adj.* **cant'ing,** whining, pretending to piety: in the form of a rebus, or implying a pun on the bearer's name, allusive (*her.*). [L. *cantāre,* freq. of *canēre,* to sing.]

**cant,** *kant,* *n.* an inclination from the level: a toss or jerk: a sloping or tilted position or face: one of the segments forming a side-piece in the head of a cask: a ship's timber lying obliquely to the line of the keel.—*v.t.* and *v.i.* to turn on the edge or corner: to tilt or toss suddenly.—*n.* **cant'ing,** tilting.—*ns.* **cant'-board,** a sloping board; **cant'ing, tilting; cant'ing-coin,** a piece of wood to prevent rolling of casks; **cant'ing-wheel,** a wheel with bevelled cogs; **cant'-rail,** a timber supporting the roof of a railway carriage.

**[Prob. conn. with Du.** *kant;* Ger. *kante,* corner.]

**cant,** *kant,* *n.* sale by auction.—*v.t.* to sell by auction. [O.Fr. *encant,* auction; der. uncertain; cf. L.L. *incantāre,* to put up to auction.]

**cant,** *kant,* *(Scot.) adj.* brisk: lively. [Cf. L.G. *kant,* and **canty.**]

**can't,** *känt,* a colloquial contraction for **cannot.**

**Cantab,** *kan'tab,* for **Cantabrigian,** *kan-tə-brij'i-ən, adj.* of or pertaining to Cambridge (Latinised *Cantabrigia*).—Also *n.*

**cantabank,** *kan'tə-bangk, n.* a strolling singer. [It. *cantambanco.*]

**cantabile,** *kan-tä'bē-lä, adj.* easy and flowing. [It.]

**cantaloup,** *kan'tə-lōōp, n.* a small, ribbed muskmelon: in U.S. extended to other varieties. [Fr.,—It. *Cantalupo,* near Rome, where it was first grown in Europe.]

**cantankerous,** *kən-tang'kər-əs, adj.* cross-grained: perverse in temper.—*adv.* **cantan'kerously.**—*n.* **cantan'kerousness.** [M.E.*contek,* strife.]

**cantar.** Same as **kantar.**

**cantata,** *kan-tä'ta, n.* originally the name applied to a sort of musical narrative by one person, accompanied by a single instrument; subsequently an air was introduced—the modern concert-aria: now also a choral work, a short oratorio or opera intended for concert performance only.—*n.* **cantatrice** (*kan-ta-trē'chä* or *kan'tə-trēs*), a female singer. [It.,—L. *cantāre,* freq. of *canēre,* to sing.]

**cantate,** *kan-tä'tä, kan-tä'tē,* the 98th Psalm, from its opening words in Latin, 'Cantate Domino'.

**canteen,** *kan-tēn', n.* a vessel used by soldiers, etc., for holding liquids: a box of cooking utensils or of knives, forks and spoons: a barrack-tavern, or refreshment house for soldiers: a restaurant attached to an office, works, or the like: a public house (*S. Africa*).—wet, dry, canteen, one in which alcoholic liquors are, are not, sold. [Fr. *cantine*—It. *cantina,* a cellar; further der. uncertain.]

**canter,** *kan'tər, n.* an easy gallop.—*v.i.* to move at an easy gallop.—*v.t.* to make to canter. [Orig. *Canterbury-gallop,* from the easy pace at which the pilgrims rode to Canterbury.]

**canterbury,** *kan'tər-bər-i, n.* a stand with divisions in it for holding books, music, etc.—**Canterbury bells, bell,** orig. the nettle-leaved bell-flower, or pink bells, in some varieties double: loosely applied to other large-flowered bell-flowers.

**cantharis,** *kan'thər-is, n.* a blister-beetle or Spanish fly (*Lytta*): in *pl.* **cantharides** (*kan-thar'i-dēz*), their dried bodies, used for blistering, etc.—*n.* **can'tharid,** a member of the genus Cantharis, otherwise Lytta.—*adjs.* **canthar'idal, cantharid'-ian, cantharid'ic.**—*n.* **canthar'idine,** the active principle of blistering-flies. [L. *cantharis*—Gr. *kantharis* (a blister-beetle), pl. *kantharides.*]

**cantharus,** *kan'thə-rus, n.* a large two-handled drinking-cup: a laver in the atrium before ancient churches:—*pl.* **can'thari.** [L.,—Gr. *kantharos.*]

**canthus,** *kan'thus, n.* the angle at the junction of the eyelids:—*pl.* **can'thi.** [Gr. *kanthos.*]

**canticle,** *kan'ti-kl, n.* a song: a non-metrical hymn, esp. one used in church service as the *Benedicite:* a canto (*Spens.*): a short canto: (in *pl.*) the Song of Solomon.—*n.* **can'ticum,** a canticle: a part-song in an ancient play. [L. *canticum,* dim. *canticulum.*]

**cantico(y).** See kantikoy.

**cantilena,** *kan-ti-lē'na, n.* a ballad or light song: a vocal or instrumental melody: a cantus firmus or melody for church use: a singing exercise or solfeggio. [L. *cantilēna.*]

**cantilever,** *kan'ti-lēv-ər,* or *-lēv', n.* a large bracket for supporting cornices, balconies, and even stairs.—**cantilever bridge,** one composed of arms projecting from the piers and connected together in the middle of the span. [Perh. **cant**, angle, and **lever**.]

**cantillate**, *kan'ti-lāt, v.t.* and *v.i.* to chant, intone.—*n.* **cantillā'tion**.—*adj.* **can'tillatory.**

**cantion**, *kan'shən*, (*Spens.*) *n.* a song. [L. *cantiō*, *-ōnis*.]

**cantle**, *kan'tl, n.* a corner, edge or slice of anything: the raised hind part of a saddle: the crown of the head or of the causeway (*Scot.*).—*v.t.* to cut a piece from: to divide.—*n.* **cant'let**, a fragment. [**cant**, **edge**.]

**canto**, *kan'tō, n.* a division of a long poem: the part that carries the melody (*mus.*):—*pl.* **cantos**.—Also (*Shak.*) **can'ton**.—**can'to fer'mo**, plainsong, the unornamented melody used in the Western Church from the earliest times, to which later other parts in counterpoint were added. [It.,—L. *cantus—canĕre*, to sing.]

**canton**, *kan'tən, kan-ton', n.* a corner (*obs.*): a division or space (*obs.*): a division of territory, constituting in Switzerland a separate government, in France a subdivision of an arrondissement: a pilastered or quoined corner of a building: an ordinary of a shield, being a square occupying generally the dexter, sometimes the sinister, chief of the field (*her.*).—*v.t.* to divide into cantons: (mil. pron. *kən-tōōn'*) to allot quarters to.—*adjs.* **can'tonal**, pertaining to or divided into cantons; **can'toned**, ornamented at the corners with projecting pilasters (*archit.*): placed in the midst of charges occupying the corners (*her.*).—*n.* **canton'ment** (mil. pron. *kəntōōn'mənt*), the temporary quarters of troops taking part in manoeuvres or active operations: in India, formerly, a permanent military town. [O.Fr. *canton*; It. *cantone*, corner, district—*canto*, a corner: cf. **cant** (2).]

**cantor**, *kan'tör, n.* the leader of the singing in a church, a precentor.—*adjs.* **canto'rial** (*-tö'ri-əl*, *-tö'*); **cantō'ris**, (*gen.* of L. *cantor*) of the cantor, i.e. on the north side of a choir (opposed to *decani*). [L., singer, *canĕre*, to sing.]

**cantred**, *kan'tred*, **cantref**, *kan'trev*, (*hist.*) *n.* a division of the country—a hundred. [W. *cantref—cant*, hundred, and *tref*, town.]

**cantrip**, *kan'trip*, (*Scot.*) *n.* a freak or wilful piece of trickery: a witch's spell. [Ety. unknown.]

**Cantuarian**, *kan-tū-ā'ri-ən, adj.* pertaining to Canterbury as the archiepiscopal see of the primate of the Church of England. [L.L. *Cantuārius*, *Cantuarensis*—O.E. *Cantware* (*pl.*) the people of Kent.]

**cantus**, *kan'təs, n.* a melody, esp. an ecclesiastical style of music:—*pl.* **can'tus**.—**cantus firmus**, **canto fermo**. [L., song—*canĕre*, to sing.]

**canty**, *kan'ti*, (*Scot.*) *adj.* cheerful, lively.—*n.* **can'tiness**. [**cant** (4); cf. L.G. *kantig*.]

**canuck**, *kə-nuk', n.* a Canadian (*U.S.*): a French-Canadian (*Canada*): a small horse.

**canvas**, *kan'vəs, n.* a coarse cloth made of hemp or other material, now esp. cotton, used for sails, tents, etc., and for painting on: the sails of a ship: a piece of stretched canvas, painted or to be painted: material for covering the ends of a racing-boat (whence a canvas-length, win by a canvas).—*v.t.* to cover with canvas.—*ns.* **can'vasback**, a North American duck, very good eating, its back ashy white, crossed by broken, zigzag, dark lines; **can'vas-climb'er** (*Shak.*), a sailor; **can'vas-stretch'er**, a wooden frame on which canvas is stretched for oil-painting; **can'vaswork**, embroidery upon canvas, or upon cloth over which canvas has been laid to guide the stitches.—**under canvas**, having the sails unfurled, under sail: living in tents. [O.Fr. *canevas*—L. *cannabis*—Gr. *kannabis*, hemp.]

**canvass**, *kan'vəs, v.t.* to toss in canvas, or in a blanket (*Shak.*): to toss or turn about: to examine: to discuss: to solicit votes, orders,

contributions, etc., from: (in American elections) to scrutinise.—*v.i.* to solicit votes, etc. (with *for*).—*n.* close examination: a seeking or solicitation: an election scrutiny (*U.S.*).—*n.* **can'vasser**. [**canvas**.]

**cany.** See **cane**.

**canyon.** Same as **cañon**.

**canzone**, *kant-sō'nā, n.* a song or air resembling a madrigal but less strict: an instrumental piece of like character: a series of stanzas in Italian poetry, of various metrical arrangements:—*pl.* **canzoni** (*-nē*).—*ns.* (dim.) **canzonet** (*kan-zō-net'*), **canzonetta** (*kan-tsō-net'ta*; pl. **canzonette**, *-tā*). [It., a song, L. *cantiō*, *-ōnis—canĕre*, to sing.]

**caoutchouc**, *kow'chōōk, n.* india-rubber, gumelastic: the latex of rubber trees. [Fr.,—Carib *cahuchu.*]

**cap**, *kap, n.* a woman's light head-dress: brimless covering for the head: an official or symbolic head-dress or one appropriated to a special class or use, academic, athletic, etc.: membership of a team symbolised by a cap: a caplike covering of any kind: the top of a toadstool: the uppermost or terminal part of anything: a percussion-cap (see **percussion**): a paper disk enclosing a fulminating substance for use with toy pistols, etc.: a lifting of the cap in salutation.—*v.t.* to cover the end or top of: to touch with a cap in conferring a degree: to admit to membership of a team: to outdo or surpass by following with a better.—*v.t.* and *v.i.* to salute by raising the cap (*pr.p.* **capp'ing**, *pa.p.* and *pa.t.* **capped**, *kapt*).—**capping**, a covering: a graduation ceremony.—*ns.* **cap'-case** (*obs.*), a small travelling-case, a chest; **cap'-paper**, a kind of wrapping paper: a size of writing paper.—**black cap** (see **black**); **cap and bells**, the marks of a professional jester; **cap in hand**, submissively: supplicatingly; **cap of liberty**, or *Phrygian cap*, the conical cap given to a Roman slave on enfranchisement, now the symbol of republicanism; **cap of maintenance** (see **maintenance**); **cap verses**, to quote verses in turn, according to rule; **college cap**, a mortarboard or trencher-cap; **set her cap at**, of a woman, to set herself to captivate (a man); **the cap fits**, the allusion is felt to apply; **throw up one's cap**, to make this gesture (*lit.* or *fig.*) in token of immoderate joy. [O.E. *cæppe*—L.L. *cappa*, a cape or cope.]

**cap**, **caup**, *kap, köp*, (*Scot.*) *n.* a wooden drinking-bowl, with two handles. [O.E. *copp*, a cup; or Scand. *koppr*.]

**capa**, *kä'pa, n.* a Spanish cloak: fine Cuban tobacco for the outsides of cigars. [Sp.]

**capable**, *kāp'ə-bl, adj.* comprehensive (*obs.*): having (esp. legal) right, or (with *of*) right to (*obs.*): having practical ability: able (often with *of*): qualified.—*ns.* **capabil'ity**, quality or state of being capable: (usu. in *pl.*) feature capable of being used or developed: ability for the action indicated, because provision and preparation have been made; **cap'ableness**.—**capable of**, able to take in, contain, understand, etc. (*arch.*): able, good, well-made, etc., enough to, or bad, foolish, etc., enough to (fol. by verbal noun or other action noun): susceptible of. [Fr.,—L.L. *capābilis*—L. *capĕre*, to hold, take.]

**capacity**, *kə-pas'i-ti, n.* power of holding, containing, absorbing, or grasping: room: volume: ability: power of mind: character in which one does something: legal competence: maximum possible output or performance: capacitance.—*adj.* attaining the full capacity.—*adj.* **capacious** (*kə-pā'shəs*), including much: roomy: wide: extensive.—*adv.* **capā'ciously**.—*ns.* **capā'ciousness**; **capac'itance**, the property that allows a system or body to store an electric charge: the value of this expressed in farads (q.v.).—*v.t.* **capac'itate**, to make capable:—*n.* **capac'itor**, an electrical device having large capacitance.—**capacity for heat,** power of absorbing heat; **legal capacity,** the power to alter one's rights or duties by the exercise of free will, or responsibility for one's acts; **to capacity,** to the utmost capacity, the fullest extent possible. [Fr. *capacité*—L. *capāx, -ācis,* able to receive—*capēre,* to hold.]

**cap-à-pie,** *kap-ə-pē, adv.* from head to foot, referring to arming, as a knight. [O.Fr. *cap a pie* (mod. *de pied en cap*)—L. *caput,* head, *ad,* to, *pēs,* foot.]

**caparison,** *kə-par'i-sən, n.* the covering of a horse: a rich cloth laid over a warhorse: dress and ornaments generally.—*v.t.* to cover with a cloth, as a horse: to dress very richly.—*adj.* **capar'isoned.** [Fr. *caparaçon*—Sp. *caparazón,* augmentative of *capa,* a cape, cover—L.L. *cappa.*]

**cape,** *kāp, n.* a covering for the shoulders attached as a tippet to a coat or cloak: a sleeveless cloak. [O.F. *cape*—L.L. *cappa.*]

**cape,** *kāp, n.* a head or point of land running into the sea or a lake.—*v.i.* (*naut.*) to keep a course.— **Cape cart,** a two-wheeled vehicle with hood and pole; **Cape Coloured** (*S. Africa*), person of mixed race, mainly in the W. Cape area; **Cape doctor,** a south-east wind at the Cape, so named (as being able to blow away germs) by Anglo-Indians formerly invalided there; **Cape Dutch,** former name for language now (officially and generally) known as *Afrikaans* (*q.v.*): an architectural style of the Cape, characterised by whitewashed, gabled, thatched-roof, single-storey houses; **Cape gooseberry,** the strawberry-tomato (*Physalis peruviana*), a S. American solanaceous plant with bladdery calyx, naturalised in S. Africa: its edible fruit; **Cape nightingale,** a frog; **Cape pigeon,** the pintado petrel; **Cape smoke,** S. African brandy, dop.—**the Cape,** Cape of Good Hope: Cape Province, Capetown, and Cape Peninsula. [Fr. *cap*—L. *caput,* the head.]

**capelin,** *kap'ə-lin, n.* a small fish of the smelt family, abundant off Newfoundland, much used as bait.—Also **cap'lin.** [Fr. *capelan.*]

**capeline,** *kap'ə-lin, n.* a small iron skullcap worn by archers: a light woollen hood for evening wear: a surgical bandage for the head.—Also **cap'elline.** [Fr.,—L.L. *capella*—*capa,* a cap.]

**Capella,** *ka-pel'a, n.* a first-magnitude star in the constellation Auriga. [L., lit. she-goat.]

**capellet,** *kap'ə-lit, n.* a wen-like swelling on a horse's elbow, or on the back part of his hock. [Fr.,—L.L. *capella*—*capa,* a cap.]

**capellmeister.** Same as **kapellmeister.**

**caper,** *kā'pər, n.* the pickled flower-bud of a bush (*Capparis spinosa*) grown in Sicily.—**cā'per-bush;** **cā'per-sauce,** a sauce for boiled mutton, etc., made with capers; **cā'per-spurge,** a kind of spurge whose capsules are sometimes pickled; **cā'per-tea,** a black tea with a knotty curled leaf. [L. *capparis*—Gr. *kapparis.*]

**caper,** *kā'pər, v.i.* to leap or skip like a goat: to dance in a frolicsome manner.—*n.* a leap: a frisk.—*n.* **cā'perer.**—**to cut a caper,** to execute a frisk. [See **capriole.**]

**capercailzie, -llie, -lzie,** *cap-ər-kā'l(y)i, n.* a species of grouse weighing up to 12 pounds. [Gael. *capull coille,* horse of the wood.]

**Capernaite,** *ka-, kə-pûr'ni-it, n.* an inhabitant of *Capernaum* in Galilee: (polemically) a believer in transubstantiation (John vi. 35, 51).—*adj.* **Capernaitic** (*-it'ik*).—*adv.* **Capernait'ically.**

**capernoity, -ie, cappernoity,** *kap-ər-noi'ti* (*Scot.*) *n.* the head, noddle.—*adj.* peevish: crabbed: capricious.—*adj.* **capernoit'ed,** capernoity. [Origin unknown.]

**capillaceous,** *kap-il-lā'shəs, adj.* hairlike.—*ns.* **capillaire** (*-lār'*), orig. an infusion of maidenhair fern (Fr. *capillaire*): a syrup flavoured with orange-flower water; **capillarity** (*-lar'i-ti*), capil-

lary quality: capillary attraction.—*adj.* **capillary** (*kə-pil'ə-ri-* sometimes *kap'*), having to do with hair: hairlike: of very small bore: relating to capillary attraction.—*n.* a fine-bored tube: a minute vessel such as those that connect arteries with veins.—*n.* **capillitium** (*kap-i-lish'i-əm*), a mass of threads.—**capillary attraction,** the force that causes liquids to rise in capillary tubes and wicks, to spread through blotting-paper, etc. [L. *capillus,* hair.]

**capital,** *kap'it-l, adj.* relating to the head: involving the death penalty: placed at the head: main, chief, principal: excellent (*coll.*): relating to capital.—*n.* the chief or most important thing: the chief town or seat of government: a large letter, in the form used at the beginning of a sentence, etc.: the stock (including property and equipment) and/or money used for carrying on a business: possessors of capital collectively, or their political and economic influence and interests: any advantage used as a means of gaining further advantages.—*n.* **capitalisā'tion, -izā'tion.**—*v.t.* **cap'italise, -ize,** to furnish with capital: to convert into capital or money: to turn to account: to print or write with capital letters.—*ns.* **cap'italism,** condition of possessing capital: the economic system which generates capital and gives power to capitalists; **cap'italist,** one who derives income and power from capital.— Also *adj.*—*adj.* **capitalist'ic.**—*adv.* **cap'itally,** chiefly: principally: excellently (*coll.*): by capital punishment.—**capital cross,** a Greek cross with terminations like Tuscan capitals; **capital gains,** profits from the sale of bonds or other assets; **capital goods,** producers' goods; **capital levy,** an exaction by a state, for a specific purpose, of a proportion of the capital (money value—cash, securities, mortgages, houses, machinery, goodwill, etc.) of its members; **capital murder,** a murder involving the death penalty; **capital ship,** a warship of the largest and strongest class; **capital sin,** deadly sin.—**circulating** or **floating capital,** that which constantly changes hands, as wages paid to workmen, raw material used; **fixed capital,** consists of buildings, machines, tools, etc.; **make capital out of,** to turn to advantage; **working capital,** capital needed to carry on a business: liquid capital (see **liquid**): assets after debts have been paid. [O.Fr. *capitel*—L. *capitālis*—*caput,* the head.]

**capital,** *kap'it-l, n.* the head or top part of a column, etc.: a chapter of a book. [L. *capitellum,* dim. of *caput,* head.]

**capitan,** *kāp-i-tän',* or *kap'i-tan,* (*hist.*) *n.* the chief admiral of the Turkish fleet.—*n.* **capitan'o,** a head-man. [Sp. *capitán,* and It. *capitano;* see **captain.**]

**capitate,** *kap'it-āt, adj.* having a head, knob, or capitulum.—*n.* **capitā'tion,** numbering of heads or individuals: a poll-tax.—**capitation grant,** a grant of so much a head. [L. *capitātus,* headed, *capitātiō, -ōnis,* poll-tax—*caput,* head.]

**capitayn,** *kap'it-ān',* (*Spens.*) *n.* captain.

**Capitol,** *kap'it-ol, -əl, n.* the temple of Jupiter at Rome, built on the *Capitoline* hill: the house where Congress or a state legislature meets (*U.S.*).—*adjs.* **capitō'lian, capit'oline.** [L. *Capitōlium*—*caput,* the head.]

**capitular,** *kə-pit'ūl-ər, n.* a statute passed in a chapter or ecclesiastical court: a member of a chapter.—*adj.* relating or belonging to a chapter in a cathedral.—*adv.* **capit'ularly.**—*n.* **capit'ulary,** a collection of ordinances: a heading.—*adj.* of a chapter. [See **chapter.**]

**capitulate,** *kə-pit'ūl-āt, v.i.* to treat: to draw up terms of agreement: to yield or surrender on certain conditions or heads.—*ns.* **capit'ulant,** one who capitulates; **capitulā'tion.**—*adj.* **capit'ulatory.** [L.L. *capitulātus,* pa.p. of *capitulāre,* to arrange under heads—*capitulum,* a chapter.]

**capitulum**, *kə-pit'ū-lum*, *n*. a close head of sessile flowers, as in Compositae (*bot*.): the head of a bone, esp. of a rib (also **capitell'um**) (*anat*.):—*pl*. **capit'ula**, **capitell'a**.—*adjs*. **capit'ulate**; **capit'-ular**. [L., dim. of *caput*, head.]

**caple**, **capul**, *kā'pl*, *n*. a horse. [M.E. *capel*; cf. O.N. *kapall*; Ir. *capall*; L.L. *caballus*, a horse.]

**caplin**. See **capelin**.

**capnomancy**, *kap'nō-man-si*, *n*. divination by smoke. [Gr. *kapnos*, smoke, *manteiā*, divination.]

**capocchia**, *kä-pok'kyə*, (*Shak*. **chipochia**) *n*. a fool. [It.]

**capon**, *kā'pn*, *n*. a castrated cock: (jocularly) a fish, esp. a herring: a letter (*Shak*.).—*v.t.* **cā'-ponise, -ize**. [O.E. *capun*; L. *capō, -ōnis*, Gr. *kapōn*—*koptein*, to cut. See **chop**.]

**caponiere**, *kap-ō-nēr'*, *n*. a covered passage across the ditch of a fortified place.—Also **caponier'**. [Fr. *caponnière*, Sp. *caponera*, capon-coop.]

**caporal**, *kap-or-äl'*, *n*. a kind of shag tobacco. [Fr.]

**capot**, *kə-pot'*, *n*. the winning of all the tricks at the game of piquet, and scoring forty.—*v.t.* to score **capot** against. [Fr.]

**capote**, *kə-pōt'*, *n*. a long kind of cloak or mantle. [Fr. dim. of *cape*, a cloak; see **cape**.]

**capotaine**. See **copataine**.

**Cappagh-brown**, *kap'ä-brown*, *n*. a brown bituminous earth pigment, stained with oxide of manganese and iron from *Cappagh* near Cork. —Also **Capp'ah-brown**.

**Capparis**, *kap'ər-is*, *n*. the caper genus, giving name to the family **Capparidā'ceae**, akin to the crucifers.—*adj*. **capparidā'ceous**. [See **caper**.]

**cappuccino**, *käp-pōōt-chē'nō*, *ka-pōō-*, *n*. black coffee with a little milk, perh. from the colour of a Capuchin's gown. [It., Capuchin.]

**capreolate**, *kap'ri-ō-lāt*, *adj*. tendrilled. [L. *căprēŏlus*, a tendril.]

**capric**, *kap'rik*, **caproic**, *kəp-rō'ik*, **caprylic**, *kəp-ril'ik*, *adjs*. applied to three fatty acids obtained from butter, etc., with goat-like smell.— *ns*. **cap'rate**, **cap'roate**, **cap'rylate**, salts respectively of these. [L. *caper*, a goat.]

**caprice**, *kə-prēs'*, *n*. a change of humour or opinion without reason: a freak: changeableness. —*ns*. **capriccio** (*kä-prē'chō*), a sportive motion: a species of free composition, not subject to rule as to form or figure (*mus*.); **capriccioso** (*-chō'sō*), a direction in music for a free style.—*adj*. **capricious** (*kə-prish'əs*), humorous (*Shak*.): full of caprice: changeable.—*adv*. **capri'ciously**.—*n*. **capri'ciousness**. [Fr. *caprice* and It. *capriccio*; perh. from L. *caper* (m.), *capra* (f.), a goat.]

**Capricorn**, *kap'ri-körn*, *n*. a constellation and a sign of the zodiac represented as a horned goat or monster. See **tropic**. [L. *capricornus*—*caper*, a goat, *cornū*, a horn.]

**caprifig**, *kap'ri-fig*, *n*. a goat-fig, wild fig.—*n*. **caprificā'tion**, a method of promoting the fertilisation and ripening of cultivated figs (which are practically dioecious) by hanging on the trees branches of caprifig (which have male flowers as well as sterile female or gall flowers) so that the gall-wasps emerging from the galls and flying to the cultivated fig to lay their eggs, carry with them some pollen.—*v.t.* **cap'rify**. [L. *capricus*, the wild fig—*caper*, a goat, and *ficus*, a fig.]

**caprine**, *kap'rin*, *adj*. goat-like.

**caprifole**, *kap'ri-fōl* (*Spens*. **caprifoil**, *-foil*), an old name for honeysuckle.—*n.pl*. **Caprifoliā'ceae** (*-si-ē*), the honeysuckle family.—*adj*. **caprifoliā'ceous**. [L. *caper*, goat, *folium*, leaf.]

**capriform**, *kap'ri-förm*, *adj*. goatlike. [L. *caper*, goat, *förma*, form.]

**capriole**, *kap'ri-ōl*, *n*. a caper: a leap without advancing.—*v.i.* to leap: caper. [O.Fr. *capriole*— It. *capriola*—L. *caper* (m.), *capra* (f.), a goat.]

**caps**, *kaps*, (*coll*.) *n.pl*. for **capitals**, capital letters.

**Capsian**, *kap'si-ən*, *adj*. of a Mediterranean culture answering to the Aurignacian. [L. *Capsa*, Gafsa, in Tunisia.]

**Capsicum**, *kap'si-kəm*, *n*. a tropical shrubby genus of the potato family, yielding cayenne pepper.— *n*. **cap'sicin** (*-sin*), an extract from capsicum. [Perh. L. *capsa*, a case.]

**capsid** (bug), *kap'sid*, *n*. any of several small active plant pests. [Gr. *kapsis*, gulping— *kaptein*, to gulp down.]

**capsize**, *kap-siz'*, *v.t.* to upset.—*v.i.* to be upset.— *n*. an overturning.—*adj*. **capsiz'able**. [Origin unknown.]

**capstan**, *kap'stən*, *n*. an upright machine turned by bars or otherwise so as to wind a cable upon it. [Fr. *cabestan*, *capestan*, through L.L. forms from L. *capĕre*, to take, hold.]

**capsule**, *kap'sūl*, *n*. a dry dehiscent fruit of more than one carpel (*bot*.): the spore-bearing part of a moss (*bot*.): a fibrous or membranous covering (*zool*.): a gelatine case for holding a dose of medicine: a small dish: a metallic or other container: a self-contained spacecraft or a part of one, manned or unmanned, recoverable or non-recoverable.—*adjs*. **cap'sular**, **cap'-sulary**; **cap'sulate**. [Fr.,—L. *capsula*, dim. of *capsa*, a case—*capĕre*, to hold.]

**captain**, *kap'tin*, *n*. a head or chief officer: the commander of a troop of horse, a company of infantry, a ship, or a portion of a ship's company: in the navy, an officer ranking with a colonel: in the army, an officer ranking with a naval lieutenant: the overseer of a mine: the leader of a team or club: the head-boy of a school.—*v.t.* to lead.—*ns*. **cap'taincy**, the rank or commission of a captain; **cap'tainship**, **cap'tainry** (*obs*.), rank or condition of a captain: skill in commanding.—**cap'tain-gen'eral**, commander of an army.—**captain of industry**, a great industrial employer. [O.Fr. *capitaine*—L.L. *capitāneus*, chief—L. *caput*, head.]

**caption**, *kap'shən*, *n*. the act of taking: an arrest: the formal title of an indictment or deposition which shows the authority under which it is executed (*Engl. law*): in Scotland, before 1837, a formal warrant to apprehend a debtor or other defaulting obligant, given in the Bill Chamber after letters of horning had been executed: a heading, legend, or accompanying wording of an article, chapter, illustration, or cinematograph picture, etc.—*v.t.* to give a caption (heading, etc.) to.—*adj*. **cap'tious**, ready to catch at faults or take offence: peevish.—*adv*. **cap'tiously**.—*n*. **cap'tiousness**. [L. *captiō, -ōnis capĕre*, to take.]

**captive**, *kap'tiv*, *n*. a prisoner: a person or animal kept in confinement.—*adj*. confined: kept in bondage: restrained by a line (as a balloon): charmed or subdued by anything (*fig*.): pertaining to captivity.—*v.t.* (*kap'tiv*; also in *Spens.*, *Milt. kap-tiv'*) to make captive or to captivate.—*v.t.* **cap'tivate**, to charm: to engage the affections of.—*adj*. **cap'tivating**.—*ns*. **cap'tiva(u)nce** (*Spens*.), captivity; **captiv'ity**; **cap'tor**, one who takes a captive or a prize; **cap'ture**, the act of taking: the thing taken: arrest: transference of a tributary to another river by more active denudation (*geol*.).—*v.t.* to take as a prize: to take by force.—**captive bolt** (pistol), a gunlike device which fires a rod, used in slaughtering animals. [L. *captivus*, *captor*, *captūra*—*capĕre*, *captum*, to take.]

**capuccio**, *kə-pōōt'chō*, (*Spens*.) *n*. a hood. [It.]

**capuche**, *kə-pōōsh'*, *-pōōch'*, *n*. a hood, esp. that worn by the Capuchins.—*n*. **Capuchin** (*kap'ū-chin* or *kap-ōō-shēn'*), a friar of a branch of the Franciscan order so called from the hood he wears: a cloak like a capuchin's: a hooded pigeon: a capuchin monkey.—**capuchin cross**, a cross with each arm terminated by a ball;

capuchin monkey, a South American monkey (*Cebus*) with hair like a cowl. [Fr., cowl— L.L. *cappa*; see cap, cape.]

capul. See caple.

caput, *kap'ut, -ət, n.* a head: a knob:—*pl.* cap'ita. —caput mortuum, the residuum after distillation: worthless residue. [L.]

capybara, *kap-i-bä'ra, n.* the largest living rodent, a native of South America, allied to the guinea-pig. [Port. from Tupí.]

car, *kär, n.* a vehicle moved on wheels, applied to very various forms—a large and splendid vehicle, as a triumphal car, a funeral car, the two-wheeled Irish jaunting-car, a motor-car: a street tramway carriage: in America, applied to all vehicles for railway travelling, as a passenger-car, freight-car, etc.: in Britain, to certain forms of railway carriage, as dining-car, sleeping-car, Pullman-car: a chariot (*poet.*): the part of a balloon or airship that carries passengers and load.—car'man, a man who drives a car or cart: a carter; car'port, a covered parking space, esp. a space under a roof projecting from a building. [O.Fr. *carre*—L.L. *carra*, a Celt. word, seen in Ir. *carr*, Bret. *karr*.]

carabine. See carbine.

carabiniere, *kä-rä-bē-nyä'rä,* (It.) a policeman armed with a rifle.

Carabus, *kar'ə-bəs, n.* a genus of beetles giving name to the ground-beetle family, Carabidae (*kə-rab'i-dē*). [Gr. *kārabos*, a kind of beetle.]

caracal, *kar'ə-kal, n.* the Persian lynx. [Fr., prob.—Turk. *qara-qulaq*, black ear.]

caracara, *kär-rä-kä-rä',* or *kä-rä-kä'rä, n.* a name for several South American vulture-like hawks. [Imit.]

carack. See carrack.

caracol, caracole, *ka'rə-kōl, n.* a half-turn or wheel made by a horseman: a winding stair.— *v.i.* to turn half-round: to prance about. [Fr. *caracole*—It. *caracollo*—Sp. *caracol,* a spiral snail shell.]

caract, *kar'əkt,* (*Shak.*) *n.* mark: sign. [App. Gr. *charaktos,* marked.]

caracul. See karakul.

carafe, *kə-räf', n.* a water-bottle for the table. [Fr. *carafe,* prob. from Ar. *gharafa,* to draw water.]

caramba, *kär-äm'bä,* (Sp.) *interj.* expressing annoyance or surprise.

carambola, *ka-rəm-bō'lə, n.* a small East Indian tree (*Averrhoa Carambola*) of the wood-sorrel family: its acrid pulpy fruit used for tarts, etc. [Port.]

carambole, *ka'rəm-bōl.* See carom.

caramel, *kar'ə-mel, n.* a dark-brown substance produced from sugar by loss of water on heating, used in colouring puddings, whisky, wines, etc.: a tenacious sweetmeat made with sugar, butter, etc.—*adj.* made of or containing caramel: of the colour of caramel.—*vs.t.* and *vs.i.* car'amel, car'amelise, -ize.—Also car'omel. [Fr.,—Sp. *caramelo.*]

caranna, *kar-an'ə,* carauna, *-ön'ə, n.* a resinous substance yielded by various South American burseraceous trees. [Sp. *caraña,* from Tupí.]

Caranx, *kar'angks, n.* the scad genus of fishes, giving name to a family Carangidae (*kar-an'ji-dē*).—*adj.* carangoid (*kar-ang'goid*). [Origin obscure.]

Carapa, *kar'a-pə, n.* a genus of tropical trees of the mahogany family yielding car'ap (or crab')-nuts, -oil, -wood. [*caraipi,* the native Guiana name.]

carapace, *kar'ə-pās, n.* the shell of the crab, tortoise, etc.—*adj.* carapä'cial (*-shl*). [Fr.,— Sp. *carapacho.*]

carat, *kar'ət, n.* a unit of weight (metric carat = 200 milligrams) used for gems: (also *karat*) a unit used in expressing fineness of gold, 24-carat

gold being pure gold: worth, estimate (*obs.*). [Fr.,—Ar. *qīrāt,* perh. from Gr. *keration,* a carob-seed used as a weight.]

carauna. See caranna.

caravan, *kar'ə-van, -van',* a company travelling together for security, esp. in crossing the deserts: a company of people: a fleet with convoy: a covered van: a house on wheels.—*v.i.* to travel in a caravan:—*pr.p.* car'avaning or caravann'ing; *pa.p.* and *pa.t.* car'avaned, caravanned'.—*ns.* caravaneer', the leader of a caravan; caravanserai (*-van'sə-ri*), a kind of unfurnished inn or extensive enclosed court where caravans stop.— Also caravansarai, -sary. [Pers. *kārwān,* caravan. *kär-wänsarāi* (*sarāi,* inn).]

caravel, *kar'ə-vel, n.* a light Mediterranean sailing-ship. [Fr. *caravelle*—It. *caravella;* cf. L.L. *cārabus,* Gr. *kārabos,* a light ship.]

caraway, *kar'ə-wä, n.* an umbelliferous plant (*Carum Carvi*) with aromatic fruits (caraway seeds) used as a tonic and condiment. [Prob. Sp. *alcaravea* (*carvi*) Ar. *karwiyā*—Gr. *karon.*]

carbamide, *kär'bəm-id, kär-bam'id, n.* urea. [carbonyl, amide.]

carbide, *kär'bid, n.* a compound of carbon with another element. [carbon.]

carbine, *kär'bin,* carabin(e), *kar'ə-bin, -bin, n.* a short light musket.—*n.* car(a)bineer', -ier, a soldier armed with a carbine: a light cavalryman: a soldier of the 6th Dragoon Guards (from 1939, 3rd Carabineers). [Fr. *carabine.*]

carbocyclic, *kär-bō-sik'lik, adj.* homocyclic. [carbon, cyclic.]

carbohydrate, *kär-bō-hī'drāt, n.* a compound of carbon, hydrogen, and oxygen, the last two being in the same proportion as in water: extended to kindred compounds. [See carbon, hydrate.]

carbolic, *kär-bol'ik, n.* (in full carbolic acid) phenol. [L. *carbō,* coal, *oleum,* oil.]

carbon, *kär'bən, n.* a non-metallic element (atomic number 6), widely diffused, occurring uncombined as diamond and graphite: a piece of carbon (esp. an electrode or a lamp-filament), or of carbon paper: a carbonado diamond.—Also *adj.*—*adj.* carbonā'ceous, coaly: containing much carbon: like carbon.—*ns.* car'bonate, a salt of carbonic acid.—*v.t.* to combine or impregnate with carbon dioxide: to carbonise. —*n.* carbonā'tion; carbon'alite, an intrusive carbonate rock.—*adjs.* carbonic (*-bon'ik*), pertaining to carbon; carbonif'erous, producing carbon or coal: (*cap.; geol.*) belonging to the carboniferous system.—*n.* carbonisā'tion, -izā'-tion.—*v.t.* carbonise, -ize, to reduce to carbon: to char or coke: to cover with carbon.—*v.i.* to become carbonised.—carbon-14, a radioactive isotope of carbon used, e.g. as a tracer element in biological studies; carbon black, form of finely divided carbon produced by partial combustion of hydrocarbons; carbon copy, a duplicate of writing or typed matter made by interleaving carbon paper, a paper coated with lamp-black: any exact duplicate; carbon dating, estimating the date of death of prehistoric organic material from the amount of carbon-14 still present in it; carbon dioxide, carbonic anhydride, an oxide of carbon ($CO_2$), a colourless, odourless, incombustible gas, present in the atmosphere, popularly called *carbonic acid,* which in solution in water forms carbonic acid ($H_2CO_3$), a weak acid; carbon disulphide ($CS_2$), a solvent for rubber; carbon fibres (see also whiskers), very fine filaments used in bundles, bound together by resins, to reinforce materials; carbon monoxide (CO), a colourless, odourless, very poisonous gas which burns with a blue flame to carbon dioxide; carbon process (*phot.*), printing process using paper coated with gelatine and a pigment and sensitised with potassium bichromate; carbon tetrachloride ($CCl_4$), a solvent, etc; the Carboniferous (System), one of the main divisions of the Palaeozoic rocks, overlying the Devonian or Old Red Sandstone, underlying the Permian, and including the Mountain or Carboniferous Limestone, the Millstone Grit, and the Coal Measures. [Fr. *carbone*—L. *carbō*, -*ōnis*, coal, charcoal.]

carbonado, *kär-bən-ā'dō*, (*obs.*) *n.* a piece of meat cut crossways for broiling on coals.—*v.t.* to cut crossways for broiling: to slash. [Sp. *carbonada*.]

carbonado, *kär-bən-ā'dō*, *n.* a variety of crystalline carbon, black, opaque, harder than diamond, used in drilling, etc., called also *black diamond*, *carbon*. [Port., carbonated.]

Carbonari, *kär-bon-är'ē*, *n.pl.* members of a secret society in Italy at the beginning of the 19th century, founded to help forward a republican government.—*n.* Carbonar'ism. [It., lit. charcoal burners.]

carbonyl, *kär'bə-nil*, (*chem.*) *n.* the radical CO.—*v.t.* carbonylate (*kär-bon'i-lāt*), to introduce the carbonyl group into.—*n.* carbonylā'tion. [carbon, and Gr. *hȳlē*, matter.]

Carborundum, *kär-bər-un'dum*, *n.* a silicon carbide, used as a substitute for corundum. [carbon and corundum; a trademark in some countries.]

carboxyl, *kär-boks'il*, *n.* the radical COOH. [carbon, oxygen, Gr. *hȳlē*, matter.]

carboy, *kär'boi*, *n.* a large glass bottle, with basketwork or other casing, for dangerous chemicals. [Pers. *qarābah*.]

carbuncle, *kär'bung-kl*, *n.* a mythical self-luminous gem: a fiery-red precious stone (almandine or precious garnet): an inflamed ulcer: a pimple on the nose.—*adjs.* car'buncled, set with the gem carbuncle; afflicted with carbuncles: having red inflamed spots; carbun'cular, belonging to or like a carbuncle: red: inflamed. [L. *carbunculus*, dim. of *carbō*, a coal.]

carburet, *kär'bū-ret*, or *ret'*, *n.* a carbide (*obs.*).—*vs.t.* carburet, car'burate, car'burise, -ize, to combine with carbon: to charge with carbon compounds.—*ns.* carburā'tion, carburisā'tion.—*p.adj.* car'buretted (or *ret'*).—*ns.* car'burettor, -er, *U.S.* carburetor, -er, (or *ret'*), an apparatus for charging a gas with carbon compounds, esp. part of an internal-combustion engine in which air is mixed with volatile fuel in the desired proportion; carburetion (-*rāsh'ən*, -*resh'ən*), carburation.—carburetted gas, a mixed illuminant got by passing water-gas over hot hydrocarbons; carburetted hydrogen, marsh-gas, olefiant gas, or other compound of carbon and hydrogen. [Fr. *carbure*—L. *carbō*, coal.]

carcajou, *kär'kə-jōō*, *n.* the glutton or wolverene. [Canadian Fr., prob. from an Indian name.]

carcake, *kär'kāk*, (*Scot.*) *n.* a kind of cake for Shrove Tuesday. [O.E. *caru*, grief, and cake.]

carcanet, *kär'ka-net*, *n.* a collar of jewels: a jewelled head-ornament (*obs.*). [Fr. carband obs. Engl.) *carcan*, an iron collar used for punishment —L.L. *carcannum*, from Gmc.]

carcase, carcass, *kär'kəs*, *n.* a dead body, no longer used of a human corpse: (disrespectfully) a live human body: the framework of anything: a ruin: an incendiary shell: the body of a tyre as distinct from the tread.—*v.t.* to put up the framework of.—carcase meat, carcass meat, raw meat as prepared for the butcher's shop, not tinned. [O.Fr. *carquois* (mod. *carcasse*), a skeleton.]

carcinogen, -ic. See carcinoma.

carcinology, *kär-si-nol'ə-ji*, *n.* the study of crustaceans.—*adj.* carcinolog'ical (-ə-loj'i-kl).—*n.* carcinol'ogist. [Gr. *karkinos*, a crab, *logos*, discourse.]

carcinoma, *kär-si-nō'mə*, *n.* a cancer:—*pl.* carcinō'mata.—*adj.* carcinō'matous.—*ns.* carcin'ogen (-*jen*), a substance that encourages the growth of cancer; carcinogen'esis.—*adj.* carcinogen'ic.—

ns. carcinō'sis, carcinōmatō'sis, spread of cancer in the body. [Gr. *karkinōma*—*karkinos*, crab.]

card, *kärd*, *n.* a small piece of pasteboard: one with figures for playing a game, with a person's name and address, with a greeting, invitation, message, programme, etc. (*playing-card*, *visiting-card*, *Christmas card*, *wedding card*, *race-card*, etc.): a domino: the dial of a mariner's compass: a map: a perforated plate used as a guide in weaving: a personal announcement in a newspaper or elsewhere (*U.S.*): an invitation: a person (*slang*): a wag or eccentric:—(in *pl.*) a game played with cards.—*v.t.* to return on a scoring-card (*golf*).—card'board, a stiff, finely finished pasteboard: card'-case, a case for carrying visiting-cards: card'-castle, an erection of playing cards in storeys: any flimsy or precarious structure; card-catalogue, -index, one with entries on separate cards; card'-sharper, one who cheats at cards; card'-table, a table for playing cards on; card'-vote, a voting system that gives each delegate's vote a value in proportion to the number he represents; cooling card (see cool); knowing card, one who is sharp, wide awake; leading card, a strong point in one's case; sure card, one who is wide awake.—cards in one's hands, everything under one's control; cards on the table, one's resources and moves freely laid open; card up one's sleeve, an advantageous factor or argument kept in reserve; get one's cards, to be dismissed; house of cards, a cardcastle; on the cards, not improbable; play one's cards well, badly, to make, not to make, the best of one's chances; show one's cards, to expose one's secrets or designs; speak by the card, to speak with precision and to the point; throw up (or in) the cards, to give in: to confess defeat. [Fr. *carte*—L. *c(h)arta*—Gr. *chartēs*, paper; cf. carte.]

card, *kärd*, *n.* an instrument for combing wool or flax.—*v.t.* to comb (wool, etc.): to mix, adulterate (*Shak.*).—*n.* card'er. [Fr. *carde*—L. *carduus*, a thistle.]

Cardamine, *kär-dam'i-nē*, *n.* a genus of cress, including the cuckoo-flower or lady's smock. [Gr. *kardaminē*—*kardamon*, cress.]

cardamom, *kär'də-məm*, *n.* the capsules of several tropical plants of the ginger family, which form an aromatic, pungent spice. [L. *cardamōmum*—Gr. *kardamōmon*.]

cardecu, cardecue, *kär'di-kū*, (*obs.*) *n.* an old French silver coin. [Fr. *quart d'écu*, quarter of a crown.]

cardiac, *kär'di-ak*, *adj.* belonging to the heart or to the upper end of the stomach.—*n.* a cordial or heart stimulant: a person with cardiac disease.—*adj.* cardiacal (-*dī'ə-kl*), cardiac.—*ns.* cardialgia (-*di-al'ji-a*; Gr. *algos*, pain), car'dialgy, an uneasy sensation or burning pain at the upper orifice of the stomach, apparently at the heart—hence called heartburn; car'diograph, an instrument for recording movements of the heart; cardio'grapher, one who uses a cardiograph; cardiog'raphy; car'diogram, a tracing obtained from a cardiograph.—*adj.* car'dioid, heart-shaped.—*n.* a heart-shaped curve traced by a point on the circumference of a circle rolling on an equal circle.—*ns.* cardiol'ogy, (-*ol'ə-ji*), the science that deals with the structure, function, and diseases of the heart; cardiol'ogist.—*adj.* cardiovas'cular (-*vas'kū-*), pertaining to, involving, heart and blood-vessels.—*n.* cardit'is, inflammation of the heart. [Gr. *kardiā*, heart, the upper end of the stomach.]

cardigan, *kär'di-gən*, *n.* a knitted woollen jacket, named after Lord *Cardigan* (1797-1868).

cardinal, *kär'di-nl*, *adj.* pertaining to a hinge: on which a thing hinges: of fundamental importance: of a deep scarlet colour, like a cardinal's cassock or hat.—*n.* one of the princes of the church constituting the sacred college at Rome, to whom pertains the right of electing a new pope: a short cloak, formerly worn by ladies: a cardinal-bird.—*ns.* car'dinalate, car'dinalship, the office or dignity of cardinal.—*adv.* car'dinally, fundamentally.—car'dinal-bird, a large American finch, the cock bright red with a crest, a songbird; car'dinal-flower, a scarlet-flowered American lobelia: extended to a blue species (*blue cardinal*); cardinal numbers, numbers expressing how many (1, 2, 3, distinguished from *ordinals*); cardinal points, the four chief points of the compass—north, south, east, and west; cardinal virtues, justice, prudence, temperance, fortitude, upon which the whole of human nature was supposed to hinge. [L. *cardinālis—cardō, cardinis*, a hinge.]

cardio-. See cardiac.

cardoon, *kär-dōōn'*, *n.* a Mediterranean plant close akin to the true artichoke, its leafstalks and ribs eaten like celery. [Obs. Fr. *cardon*—L. *carduus*, a thistle.]

cardophagus, *kär-dof'ə-gəs, n.* a thistle-eater, a donkey. [Latinised from Gr. *kardos*, thistle; *phagos*, eater, glutton.]

carduus, *kär'dū-us*, (Shak.) *n.* a thistle. [L.]

care, *kār, n.* affliction: anxiety: heedfulness: heed: charge, oversight: an object of anxiety or watchfulness.—*v.i.* to be anxious: to be inclined: to be concerned: to mind: to have liking or fondness: to provide, look after, watch over (with *for*).—*adj.* care'ful, full of care: heedful: anxious (*B.*): grievous (*Spens.*): sorrowful (*Spens.*).—*adv.* care'fully.—*n.* care'fulness.—*adj.* care'less, without care: heedless, unconcerned.—*adv.* care'lessly.—*n.* care'lessness.—*adjs.* care'-crazed (*Shak.*), crazed or broken with care and solicitude; care'free, void of anxiety.—*n.* care'-taker, one put in charge of anything, esp. a building.—*adj.* exercising temporary supervision or control.—*adj.* care'worn, worn or vexed with care.—care and maintenance, the keeping of a discontinued plant in sound condition on possibility of its being restarted; care of, to be delivered to the custody of, or at the address of; couldn't care less, do not care in the least; take care, to be careful or cautious; take care of, to look after with care: to make the necessary arrangements regarding (*coll.*). [O.E. *caru*; Goth. *kara*, sorrow; O.N. *kæra*, to lament.]

careen, *kə-rēn', v.t.* and *v.i.* to turn over on the side, esp. for repairing or cleaning.—*n.* a heeling position.—*n.* careen'age, a place where ships are careened: the cost of careening. [L. *carina*, keel.]

carème, *ka-rem,* (Fr.) Lent.

career, *kə-rēr'* (*obs.* cariere; *Spens. kar'*), *n.* a racecourse or lists. a course passed over (*obs.*): a rush: progress through life: (advancement in) profession or occupation.—*adj.* having a career: dedicated to a career.—*v.i.* to gallop: to move or run rapidly.—*ns.* career'ist, one intent on his own advancement; career'ism. [Fr. *carrière*, a racecourse—L.L. *carrāria*, carriage-road—*carrus*, wagon.]

caress, *kə-res', v.t.* to touch endearingly: to fondle.—*n.* an endearing touch.—*n.* and *adj.* caress'ing.—*adv.* caress'ingly. [Fr. *caresser*—It. *carezza*, an endearment—L. *cārus*, dear.]

caret, *kar'ət, n.* a mark, Λ, to show where to insert something omitted. [L., 'there is wanting'.]

Carex, *kā'reks, n.* a genus of sedges. [L. *cārex*.]

carfax, -fox, *kär'faks, -foks, n.* a place where four roads meet—now used mainly of particular examples, as at Oxford. [L. *quadrifurcus*, four-forked.]

carfuffle, curfuffle, *kər-fuf'l*, (orig. *Scot.*) *n.* commotion, agitation.—*v.t.* to disorder.—Other present-day spellings include kefuffle. [Gael. pfx. *car-*, Scot. *fuffle*, to disorder.]

cargo, *kär'gō, n.* the goods carried by a ship or aeroplane:—*pl.* -oes.—cargo cult, a type of religion in certain South Pacific islands based on the belief that ancestors will return bringing products of modern civilisation and thus make the islanders rich and independent: any setting of too high a value on material possessions. [Sp.,—root of car.]

cargoose, *kär'gōōs, n.* the crested grebe:—*pl.* cargeese. [O.N. *kjarr*, copsewood, and goose.]

cariacou, *kar'i-ə-kōō, carjacou, kär'jə-kōō, n.* any deer of the American genus or subgenus *Cariacus*, including the Virginian deer. [Tupí, *cariacu*.]

cariama, *sä-ri-ä'mä, n.* Same as seriema.

Carib, *kar'ib*, one of a race inhabiting parts of Central America and northern South America: their language.—Also *adj.*—*ns.* and *adjs.* Caribbē'an, Caribbee'.—Caribbee bark, the bark of a West Indian rubiaceous genus (*Exostema*) once esteemed a substitute for cinchona. [Cf. cannibal.]

caribe, *kä-rē'bä, n.* the piranha. [Sp., Carib, savage, piranha.]

caribou, *kar-i-bōō', n.* the American reindeer. [Canadian Fr.]

Carica, *kar'i-ka, n.* the papaw genus, giving name to a family Caricā'ceae, akin to the passion-flowers. [L. *Carica (ficus)*, a Carian dried fig.]

caricature, *kar'i-kə-tūr, or -tūr', or -chōōr, or -chōōr', n.* a likeness of anything so exaggerated or distorted as to appear ridiculous.—*v.t.* to turn into ridicule by distorting a likeness: to burlesque.—Formerly caricatū'ra.—*n.* caricatūr'ist. [It. *caricatura—caricare*, to load, from root of car.]

cariere, an obs. form of career.

caries, *kā'ri-ēz, n.* decay, esp. of teeth.—*adj.* cā'rious, decayed. [L. *cariēs*.]

carillon, *kə-ril'yən, kar'il-yən, n.* a set of bells for playing tunes: a mechanism for playing them: a melody played on them.—*n.* carill'onist (or *kar'*). [Fr.,—L.L. *quadriliō, -ōnis*, a quaternary, as formerly rung on four bells.]

carina, *kə-rī'na, n.* a keel or keel-like ridge: the boat-shaped structure formed by the two lower petals in the pea family.—*adj.* carinate (*kar'i-nāt*), keeled. [L. *carina*, a keel.]

carioca, *kar-ē-ō'ka, n.* a Brazilian dance or its tune, a maxixe or variety thereof. [Port.]

cariole, carriole, *kar'i-ōl, n.* a small open carriage: a light cart. [Fr. *carriole*—root of car.]

caritas, *ka'ri-tas* (or *kä'ri-täs*), (L.) (Christian) charity.

cark, *kärk,* (*arch.*) *n.* care, anxiety, or solicitude.—*v.t.* to burden, harass.—*v.i.* to be anxious.—*adj.* cark'ing. [Norm. Fr. *kark(e)*—L.L. *carcāre*—L.L. *carcāre*, to load. See charge.]

carl, *kärl, n.* a husbandman (*obs.*): a churl (*arch.*)—*ns.* carl'-hemp, the female plant of hemp (lit. male-hemp, as stronger than fimble, the true male): car'line (-*lin*) (Scot.), an old woman: a witch.—*adj.* carl'ish (*arch.*), churlish: clownish.—*n.* car'lot (*Shak.*; *As You Like It*), a churl, peasant. [O.N. *karl*, a man, a male: see churl.]

Carley float, *kär'li flōt,* an emergency rubber raft. [From the inventor's name.]

carline, *kär'lin, n.* any plant of a genus (*Carlina*): Carline thistle closely allied to the true thistles. [From a legend that an angel showed the root to Carolus, Karl, or Charlemagne, as a remedy for a plague.]

Carlist, *kär'list, n.* a supporter of the claims of the Spanish pretender Don Carlos de Borbón (1788-1855), second son of Charles IV, and his representatives.—Also *adj.*—*n.* Car'lism.

carlock, *kär'lok, n.* a Russian isinglass. [Russ. *karluk*.]

Carlovingian, *kär-lo-vin'ji-ən, adj.* relating to a dynasty of Frankish kings, so called from *Karl* the Great or Charlemagne (742-814).—Also Carolin'gian.

**Carlylese**, *kär-līl-ēz'*, *n*. the vigorous, irregular phraseology and vocabulary of Thomas *Carlyle* (1795-1881).—*adjs*. **Carlylesque'**, **Carlyl'ean**.— *n*. **Car'lylism** (or *līl'*).

**carmagnole**, *kär-man-yōl'*, *n*. a popular song and dance of the French Revolution: a kind of jacket worn by revolutionists at that time with short skirts, a broad collar and lapels, and several rows of buttons. [Prob. from *Carmagnola* in Piedmont.]

**Carmelite**, *kär'mi-līt*, *n*. a White Friar, or friar of the order of Our Lady of Mount *Carmel*, in Palestine, founded there *c*. 1156, made a mendicant order in 1247—the habit brown, with a white cloak and scapular: a nun of a similar order (from 1452): a variety of pear (*obs*.): (without *cap*.) a fine woollen stuff like beige.

**carminative**, *kär'min-ə-tiv*, or *-min'*, *adj*. expelling flatulence.—*n*. a medicine with that effect. [L. *cärmināre*, to card, comb out—*cärmen*, a card for wool.]

**carmine**, *kär'min*, *-min*, *n*. the red colouring matter of the cochineal insect: its colour.—*adj*. of that colour. [Fr. *carmin* or Sp. *carmin*—Sp. *carmesi*, crimson—Ar. *qirmazī*, crimson. Same root as **crimson**.]

**carnage**, *kär'nij*, *n*. a heap of slain (*obs*.): slaughter. [Fr.,—It. *carnaggio*, carnage—L. *carō*, *carnis*, flesh.]

**carnahuba**. See **carnauba**.

**carnal**, *kär'nl*, *adj*. fleshly: sensual: unspiritual: bodily: sexual: murderous, flesh-eating (*Shak*.). —*v.i*. (*obs*.) to act carnally.—*v.t*. **car'nalise, -ize**, to sensualise.—*ns*. **car'nalism**; **car'nalist**, a sensualist: **carnal'ity** (*-nal'i-ti*), state of being carnal.—*adv*. **car'nally**.—*adj*. **carnass'ial** (Fr. *carnassier*), adapted for flesh-eating.—*n*. a carnivore's scissor-tooth, usually long and large, used for tearing flesh.—*adjs*. **car'neous, carnose'**, fleshy: of or like flesh.—*n*. **car'nifex** (L.), an executioner.—*adj*. **carnificial** (*-fish'l*).—*n*. **carnos'ity**, a fleshy excrescence growing in and obstructing any part of the body.—**carnal knowledge** (*law*), sexual intercourse.—*adj*. **car'nal-mind'ed**, worldly-minded. [L. *carō*, *carnis*, flesh.]

**carnallite**, *kär'nəl-it*, *n*. a milk-white or pinkish hydrous chloride of potassium and magnesium. [Mineralogist Von *Carnall* (1804-74).]

**carnassial**. See **carnal**.

**carnation**, *kär-nā'shən*, *n*. flesh-colour (*obs*.): a colour ranging from light pink to deep crimson: a florists' double-flowering variety of the clove pink.—*adj*. of the colour carnation.—*adj*. **carnā'tioned**, ruddy. [L. *carnātiō*, *-ōnis*, fleshiness.]

**carnauba, carnahuba**, *kär-nä-ōō'ba*, or *-now'*, *n*. a Brazilian palm (*Copernicia*): its yellowish wax—also *Brazilian wax*. [Braz.]

**carnelian**. See **cornelian**.

**carnet**, *kär-nā*, *n*. a customs permit. [Fr.]

**carnival**, *kär'ni-vl*, *n*. a feast observed by Roman Catholics just before the fast of Lent: any season of revelry or indulgence: riotous feasting, merriment, or amusement: a fair-like entertainment. [It. *carnevale*—L.L. *carnelevārium*, apparently from L. *carnem levāre*, to put away flesh.]

**Carnivora**, *kär-niv'ə-ra*, *n.pl*. an order of flesh-eating mammals.—*n*. **car'nivore** (*-vōr*), a carnivorous animal.—*adj*. **carniv'orous**, flesh-eating. —*adv*. **carniv'orously**.—*n*. **carniv'orousness**. [L. *carō*, *carnis*, flesh, *vorāre*, to devour.]

**Carnot cycle**, *kär'nō sī'kl*, an ideal heat engine cycle of maximum thermal efficiency. [Nicolas *Carnot*, French physicist, d. 1832.]

**carnotite**, *kär'nō-tīt*, *n*. a mineral (hydrated vanadate of uranium and potassium) important as a source of radium, later of vanadium, later of

uranium. [Adolphe *Carnot*, French mine inspector, d. 1920.]

**carny, carney**, *kär'ni*, (*dial*.) *v.t*. and *v.i*. to coax, wheedle.—*n*. flattery. [Origin unknown.]

**carob**, *kar'ob*, *-əb*, *n*. the algarroba or locust-tree (*Ceratonia Siliqua*), a caesalpiniaceous Mediterranean tree. [Fr. *carobe*—Ar. *kharrūbah*; cf. **algarroba**.]

**caroche**, *kä-rosh'*, *n*. a carriage, esp. a grand one (*hist*.). [Fr.,—It. *caroccio*, *carro*—L. *carrus*, car.]

**carol**, *kar'əl*, *n*. a ring-dance or the song accompanying it (*arch*.): a song of joy or praise: Christmas song or hymn: an enclosure for a study in a cloister, etc.—*v.i*. to dance or sing a carol: to sing or warble.—*v.t*. to praise or celebrate in song (*pr.p*. **car'olling**; *pa.p*. and *pa.t*. **car'olled**).—*n*. **car'oller**. [O.Fr. *carole*; It. *carola*, orig. a ring-dance; acc. to Diez, a dim. of L. *chorus*, Gr. *choros*.]

**Carolina**, *kar-ə-lī'nə*, *n*. two states (North and South) of the United States.—Also *adj*.— **Carolina allspice** (see **Calycanthus**); **Carolina pink**, an American species of Silene (bladder-campion): pinkroot (see **pink**, 3).

**Carolingian**, *kar-ə-lin'ji-ən*, *adj*. Same as **Carlovingian**.

**Carolus**, *kar'ə-ləs*, *n*. a gold coin of the time of Charles I.—*adj*. **Car'oline**, belonging to the time of Charles (I or II, or Charlemagne, or any other Charles). [L. *Carolus*, Charles.]

**carom**, *kar'əm*, *n*. and *v.i*. an abbreviation for **carambole** (*kar'əm-bōl*), the same as **cannon** in billiards.

**carotene**, *kar'ō-tēn*, *n*. any of a number of reddish-yellow pigments widely distributed in plants, precursors of vitamin A.—*n*. **carotenoid** (*karot'in-oid*), any of a group of pigments similar to carotenes, some of which are precursors of vitamin A.—Also **car'otin**, **carot'inoid**.

**carotid**, *kə-rot'id*, *adj*. relating to the two great arteries of the neck. [Gr. *karōtidēs* (pl.)—*karos*, sleep, the ancients supposing that deep sleep was caused by compression of them.]

**carouse**, *kə-rowz'*, *adv*. (*obs*.) in drinking, all out.— *n*. a drinking-bout: a noisy revel.—*v.i*. to hold a drinking-bout: to drink freely and noisily.—*ns*. **carous'al**, a carouse: a feast: **carous'er**.—*adv*. **carous'ingly**. [O.Fr. *carous*, Fr. *carrousse*—Ger. *gar aus*, quite out, that is, empty the glass.]

**carousel**, in U.S. **carrousel**, *kar-ōō-zel'*, *-ə-sel'*, *n*. a tilting match or tournament, to which were added games, shows, and allegorical representations: a merry-go-round (*U.S.*): a rotating conveyor, e.g. for luggage at an airport or air terminal. [Fr. *carrousel*.]

**carp**, *kärp*, *v.i*. to catch at small faults or errors (with *at*).—*n*. **carp'er**.—*n*. and *adj*. **carp'ing**, cavilling: fault-finding.—*adv*. **carp'ingly**. [Most prob. Scand., O.N. *karpa*, to boast, modified in meaning through likeness to L. *carpĕre*, to pluck, deride.]

**carp**, *kärp*, *n*. a fresh-water fish common in ponds. [O.Fr. *carpe*—L.L. *carpa*; poss. Gmc.]

**carpal**. See **carpus**.

**carpe diem**, *kär'pē dī'em*, *kär'pe dē'em*, (L.) enjoy the present.

**carpel**, *kär'pl*, *n*. a modified leaf forming the whole or part of the gynaeceum of a flower.—*adj*. **car'pellary**.—*n*. **carpogō'nium**, the female organ in red seaweeds, indirectly producing **carp'ospores**.—*adj*. **carpoph'agous**, fruit-eating.—*n*. **carp'ophore**, a prolongation of a flower axis below or between the carpels. [Gr. *karpos*, fruit.]

**carpenter**, *kär'pint-ər*, *n*. a worker in timber as used in building houses, etc.—*v.i*. to do the work of a carpenter.—*n*. **car'pentry**, the trade or work of a carpenter.—*n*. **car'penter-bee'**, a bee that excavates its nest in wood. [O.Fr. *carpentier*

—L.L. *carpentārius—carpentum*, a car, from root of car.]

**carpet**, *kär'pit, n.* the woven or felted covering of floors, stairs, etc.: a tablecloth (*Shak.*): a smooth, or thin, surface or covering: a carpet-moth.—*v.t.* to cover with or as if with a carpet: to have up for reprimand:—*pr.p.* **car'peting;** *pa.p.* and *pa.t.* **car'peted.**—*n.* **car'peting,** material of which carpets are made: carpet, or carpets.—*ns.* **car'pet-bag'**, a travelling-bag made of carpeting; **car'petbagger**, one who comes to a place for political or other ends (as if he carried his whole property qualification for citizenship with him in his carpet-bag); **car'pet-beat'ing**, the removing of dust from carpets by beating; **car'pet-bedd'ing**, a system of horticulture in which plants are arranged in mosaic or geometrical designs; **car'pet-bomb'ing**, systematic bombing of a whole area; **car'pet-knight'**, one dubbed a knight by mere court favour, not on account of his military exploits—hence an effeminate person; **car'petmonger** (*Shak.*), an effeminate person; **car'pet-moth'**, any of the larger moths, with carpet-like markings, of the geometrid family Larentidae; **car'pet-rod**, one of the rods used to keep a stair carpet in its place; **car'pet-slipper**, a slipper made of carpeting; **car'pet-snake**, a variegated python of Australia; **car'pet-sweeper**, an apparatus with a revolving brush and a dust-pan, for sweeping carpets.—**on the carpet**, under discussion (jocular trans. of Fr. *sur le tapis*): up before someone in authority for reprimand; **sweep under the carpet**, to hide irom notice, put out of mind (unpleasant problems or facts). [O.Fr. *carpite*—L.L. *carpeta*, -*pita*, coarse fabric made from rags pulled to pieces—L. *carpěre*, to pluck.]

**carphology**, *kär-fol'ə-ji, n.* floccillation, fitful plucking movements as in delirium. [Gr. *karphos*, straw, *logeiā*, gathering.]

**carpus**, *kär'pəs, n.* the wrist, or corresponding part of the fore-limb.—*adj.* **car'pal**, pertaining to the carpus.—*n.* a bone of the carpus.—*n.* **carpometacar'pus**, in birds, a bone of the wing formed by fusion of some of the carpals with the metacarpals. [Latinised from Gr. *karpos*, wrist.]

**carr**, *kär, n.* (a copse in) boggy ground. [O.N. *kjarr.*]

**carrack**, *kar'ək*, (*hist.*) *n.* a large ship of burden, which was also fitted for fighting.—Also **car'ack**, **carr'act**, **carr'ect**. [O.Fr. *carraque*—L.L. *carraca*; ety. dub.]

**carrag(h)een**, *kar-ə-gēn', n.* a purplish-red North Atlantic seaweed (*Chondrus crispus*) and a related species (*Gigartina mamillosa*), used for making soup and a kind of blancmange, as well as for size—also called *Irish moss.*—*n.* **carrag(h)ee'nin**, a colloid prepared from red algae, used in food processing, pharmaceuticals, etc. [Prob. Ir. *carraigín*, little rock—*carraig*, rock.]

**carrat, carraway.** Same as **carat, caraway.**

**carriage**, *kar'ij, n.* act or cost of carrying: a vehicle for carrying, esp. a luxurious road vehicle, or a railway passenger-car: a wheeled support of a gun: the structures on which an aeroplane lands: a carrying part of a machine: the loop of a sword-belt (*Shak.*): behaviour (*arch.*): bearing: burden (*Shak.*): baggage (*B.*).—*adj.* **carr'iageable**, that may be conveyed in carriages. —**carriage clock**, a small portable clock, usu. with a case; **carriage dog**, a coachdog; **carr'iage-drive**, a road for carriages through parks, etc.—*advs.* **carr'iage-free'**, without charge for transport; **carr'iage-for'ward**, without prepayment of carriage.—**carriage horse**, a horse that draws a carriage.—*adv.* **carriage-paid'**, with prepayment of carriage.—**carriage trade**, trade from the wealthy; **carr'iageway**, a road, or part of a road, used by vehicles.—**carriage and pair**, a turn-out of a carriage and two horses. [See **carry.**]

**carrick bend**, *kar'ik bend', (naut.) n.* a knot for joining two ropes, formed by looping and interlacing the ends together. [Perh. conn. with **carrack**, and the root of **bind.**]

**carrier.** See **carry.**

**carriole.** See **cariole.**

**carrion**, *kar'i-ən, n.* the dead and putrid body or flesh of any animal: anything vile.—*adj.* relating to, or feeding on, putrid flesh.—*ns.* **carr'ion-crow'**, the common crow: the black vulture (*U.S.*): **carr'ion-flower**, a S. African asclepiad (*Stapelia*) with fleshy stem and stinking flowers. [Fr. *charogne*—L.L. *carōnia*—L. *carō, carnis*, flesh.]

**carritch**, *kar'ich*, (*Scot.*) *n.* a catechism. [Fr. *catéchèse*, taken to be a plural.]

**carriwitchet**, *kar-i-wich'it, n.* a quip: a quibble. [Origin unknown.]

**carronade**, *kar-ən-ād', n.* (*hist.*) a short cannon of large bore. [From *Carron*, a town in Stirlingshire with ironworks.]

**carron oil**, *kar'ən oil*, a liniment orig. of linseed-oil and lime-water. [Form. used for burns at *Carron* (see **carronade**) ironworks.]

**carrot**, *kar'ət, n.* a plant of the *Umbelliferae*, having a tapering root of a reddish or yellowish colour: the root itself, which is edible and sweet.—*adj.* **carr'oty**, carrot-coloured, applied to the hair. [Fr. *carotte*—L. *carōta.*]

**carrousel.** U.S. spelling of **carousel.**

**carry**, *kar'i, v.t.* to convey: to bear: to lead or transport: to take by force: to hold in saluting position (*mil.*): to effect: to gain: to behave or demean: (of money) to be sufficient for: to pass, by a majority: to add to another column (*arith.*); (of a newspaper) to publish (e.g. an item of news), or to publish as a regular feature: to do the work of, or perform in sport or entertainment well enough to cover up the deficiencies of (another): —*v.i.* (of a voice, a gun, etc.) to reach, indicating its range (*pr.p.* **carr'ying;** *pa.p.* and *pa.t.* **carr'i⊙**).—*n.* the distance a golf ball goes when struck till it touches the ground: range: an act of carrying: the portage of a boat: land across which a boat has to be carried between one navigable stream or stretch and another: the position of 'carry arms': the sky, cloud-drift (*Scot.*).—*ns.* **carr'ier**, one who carries, esp. for hire: anything that carries: an instrument for carrying: a basket, framework, or the like, for carrying luggage, as on a bicycle: one who transmits disease (without suffering from it) by harbouring germs, virus, etc.: a vehicle for communicating a signal in cases where the medium cannot convey the actual signal (as speech, etc., in radio transmission): a constant frequency in an amplitude-modulation transmission (*telecomm.*): non-active material mixed with, and chemically identical to, a radioactive compound (*nuc.*): a carrier-pigeon.—**carrier bag**, a strong paper or plastic bag for carrying shopping, etc.; **carrier gas**, a gas, e.g. helium, mixed with oxygen for breathing by divers when at great depths; **carr'ier-pig'eon**, a pigeon with homing instinct, used for carrying messages: a pigeon of a fancy breed no longer so used; **carr'ytale** (*Shak.*), a tale-bearer.—**carry all before one**, to bear down all obstacles; **carry away**, to carry off: deprive of self-control by exciting the feelings: to transport; **carry it**, to behave, demean oneself: to gain the advantage, **carry the day** (also **carry it away**): **carry off**, to cause the death of: to gain, to win, as a prize: to cause to pass muster, to make to pass by assurance or dissimulation; **carry on**, manage: continue: proceed: complain or behave unrestrainedly (*ns.* **carry-on, carrying-on**): to flirt (*with*); **carry one's bat** (see **bat**); **carry one's point**, to overrule objections to one's plan or view; **carry out**, to accomplish: to carry out for burial; **carry over**, to bring into the other party: to take to a new page, as an account, etc.: to postpone to next occasion; **carry the day**, to be successful: to win the day; **carry through**, to support through difficulties: to succeed in putting in effect, to accomplish; ca.ry too far, to continue beyond reasonable limits; **carry up**, to continue a building upward: to trace back; **carry weight**, to possess authority: to have force. [O.Fr. *carier*—L.L. *carricāre*, to cart—L. *carrus*, a car.]

**carry-all**, *kar'i-öl*, (*U.S.*) *n.* a light four-wheeled one-horse carriage. [cariole, changed by folk-etymology.]

**carse**, *kärs*, (*Scot.*) *n.* an alluvial river-side plain. [Perh. **carr.**]

**cart**, *kärt*, *n.* a two-wheeled vehicle without springs, used for farm purposes, or for conveying heavy loads: a light two-wheeled vehicle with springs.—*v.t.* to convey in a cart: to carry publicly in a cart as a punishment—formerly done to bawds.—*ns.* **cart'age**, the act or cost of carting; **cart'er**, one who drives a cart.—*ns.* **cart'-horse**, a horse suitable for drawing a cart; **cart'-house**, a shed for keeping carts; **cart'load**, as much as a cart can carry; **cart'-road**, **cart'-way**, a road or way by which carts may pass; **cart's-tail**, the hind part of a cart, formerly a place of punishment; **cart'wheel**, the wheel of a cart: a sideways somersault, or Catherine-wheel; **cart'wright**, a carpenter who makes carts; see also **dogcart, mail-cart, tax-cart,** etc.—**in the cart** (*slang*), in the lurch: in a fix; **put the cart before the horse**, to reverse the natural order of things; **village cart**, an uncovered two-wheeled carriage.for one horse, with a low body and one seat; **Whitechapel cart**, or **chapel cart**, a light two-wheeled spring-cart used in delivering shop goods. [Ety. dub.; O.E. *cræt*, or O.N. *kartr*.]

**carta.** See **charta.**

**carte**, *kärt*, *n.* the fourth position of the wrist in fencing. [Fr. *quarte*—It. (and L.) *quarta*, fourth.]

**carte**, *kärt*, *n.* a bill of fare: a playing-card (*Scot.*): a *carte-de-visite*.—*ns.* **carte'-blanche** (*-bläsh*), a blank paper, duly signed, to be filled up at the recipient's pleasure: freedom of action; **carte-de-visite** (*-də-vē-zēt'*), a small photographic portrait pasted on a card; **carte du jour** (*dü zhoōr*), menu (of the day). [Fr.,—L. *c(h)arta*; see **card.**]

**cartel**, *kär'təl*, *n.* a challenge: an agreement for exchange of prisoners: a card with writing on it: a political condition or bloc: (also *kär-tel'*) a combination of firms for certain purposes, esp. to keep up prices and kill competition.—*v.t.* and *v.i.* **cartelise', -ize'.** [Fr.,—L. *c(h)arta*; see **card.**]

**Cartesian**, *kar-tē'zi-ən*, or *-zhyən*, *adj.* relating to the French philosopher René *Descartes* (1596-1650), or his philosophy, or mathematical methods.—*n.* a follower of Descartes.—**Cartesian co-ordinates**, co-ordinates of a point which have reference to two fixed lines that cross each other in a plane, or to two or three meeting surfaces; **Cartesian devil, diver,** or **bottle-imp,** a scientific toy named after Descartes, a glass container with a floating figure that sinks when the top of the container is pressed.

**carthamine**, *kär'thə-min*, *n.* a dye got from safflower. [L.L. *carthamus*—Ar. *qartum*, saffron.]

**Carthusian**, *kär-thū'zi-ən*, or *-thoō'*, *n.* a monk or (since 1229) a nun of an order founded by St Bruno in 1086, noted for its strictness: a scholar of the Charterhouse School, founded on the site of a Carthusian monastery in London, now in Godalming.—*adj.* of or pertaining to the order or the school. [L. *Cartusiānus—Catorissium*, Chatrousse, a village in Dauphiné, near which

their first monastery, La Grande Chartreuse, was founded.]

**cartilage**, *kär'ti-lij*, *n.* gristle, a firm pearly white substance, often converted later into bone.—*adj.* **cartilaginous** (*-laj'*).—**cartilaginous fishes**, fishes with a cartilaginous skeleton—sharks, rays, chimaeras. [Fr.,—L. *cartilāgō, -inis*; cog. with *crātis*, wickerwork, Gr. *kartallos*, a basket.]

**cartography**, *kär-tog'rə-fi*, *n.* map-making.—*n.* **cartog'rapher**.—*adjs.* **cartographic** (*-tō-graf'ik*), **-al.**—*ns.* car'togram, a map presenting statistical information in diagrammatic form; **cartol'ogy**, the science of maps and charts.—*adj.* **carto-log'ical.** [L. *c(h)arta*—Gr. *chartēs*, a sheet of paper, and Gr. *graphein*, to write.]

**cartomancy**, *kär'tō-mən-si*, *n.* divination by playing-cards. [L.L. *carta*, a card, Gr. *manteiā*, divination.]

**carton**, *kär'tən*, *n.* a thin pasteboard: a box made from it: a small disk within the bull's-eye of the target: a shot that strikes it.—*n.* **car'tonnage**, pasteboard: the outer covering of a mummy.—**carton-pierre** (*kär-tō-pyer*), a kind of papier-maché, imitating stone. [Fr. See **cartoon.**]

**cartoon**, *kär-toōn'*, *n.* a preparatory drawing on strong paper to be reproduced in fresco, tapestry, etc.: any large sketch or design on paper: a comic or satirical drawing commenting on current events or politics: a cinematograph film made by photographing a succession of drawings.—*v.t.* to make a cartoon or working design of: to caricature by a cartoon.—*n.* **cartoon'ist**, one who makes cartoons. [Fr. *carton* or It. *cartone*, augm. of *carta*.]

**cartophily**, *kär-tof'i-li*, *n.* cigarette-card collecting.—*n.* **cartoph'ilist.** [L. *c(h)arta*—Gr. *chartēs*, a sheet of paper, and Gr. *philiā*, a liking.]

**cartouche**, *kär-toōsh'*, *n.* a case for cartridges or formerly for mortar bullets: a scroll-like ornament with rolled ends (*archit.*): an ancient Egyptian oval figure enclosing royal or divine names.—Also **cartouch'.** [Fr.,—It. *cartoccio*—L. *c(h)arta*—Gr. *chartēs*, paper.]

**cartridge**, *kär'trij*, *n.* a case containing the charge for a gun (blank'-car'tridge, with powder only; ball'-car'tridge, with a bullet as well).—**car'-tridge-belt**, a belt having pockets for cartridges; **cartridge-pä'per**, a light-coloured, strong paper, originally manufactured for making cartridges. [A corr. of **cartouche.**]

**cartulary**, *kär'tū-lər-i*, *n.* a register-book of a monastery, etc.: one who kept the records: the place where the register is kept. [L.L. *chartu-lārium*—L. *chartula*, a document—*charta*, paper.]

**carucate**, *kar'ū-kāt*, *n.* as much land as a team of oxen could plough in a season.—*n.* **car'ucage**, a tax on the carucate, first imposed by Richard I in 1198. [L.L. *carrūcāta*, ploughland—*carrūca*, plough, from root of **car.**]

**caruncle**, *ka-, kə-rung'kl*, *n.* a small fleshy excrescence: an outgrowth on a seed near the micropyle.—*adjs.* **carun'cular, carun'culate, carun'culous.** [Fr.—L. *caruncula*.]

**carvacrol**, *kär'və-krol*, *n.* an isomer of and substitute for thymol, obtained from origanum, etc. [Fr. *carvi*, caraway, L. *acer*, sharp, *oleum*, oil.]

**carve**, *kärv*, *v.t.* to cut into forms, devices, etc.: to make or shape by cutting: to cut up (meat) into slices or pieces: to apportion or distribute.—*v.i.* to exercise the art or perform the act of carving: app., to make affected gestures or amorous advances (*Shak.*): *infin.*, *Spens.*, **carv'en**; *pa.p.* **carved, arch.** **carv'en.**—*adj.* **carv'en,** carved.—*ns.* **carv'er**, one who carves: a wood-carver: a sculptor: a carving-knife: a tree used for carving (*Spens.*); **carv'ing,** the act or art of sculpture esp. in wood or ivory: a carved device or figure: the act or art of cutting up meat at table.—**carv'-ing-knife,** a large knife for carving meat.—**carve out,** to hew out: to gain by one's exertions; **cut and carve, to refine. [O.E. *ceorfan*, to cut; Du. *kerven*; Ger. *kerben*, to notch.]

carvel, *kär'vəl*, *n*. older form of caravel.—*adj.* car'vel-built, built without overlap of planks (distinguished from *clinker-built*).

carvy, *kär'vi*, (*Scot.*) *n*. caraway: a caraway seed, esp. one coated with sugar. [Fr. *carvi*; see caraway.]

caryatid, *kar-i-ät'id*, *n*. a female figure used instead of a column to support an entablature:— *pl.* caryat'ids, caryat'ides (*-i-dēz*).—*adjs.* caryat'ic, caryat'idal, caryatidē'an, caryatid'ic. [Gr. *Karyātis*, a priestess of Artemis at *Karyai* (*Caryae*), pl. *Karyātidĕs*.]

Caryocar, *kär'i-ō-kär*, *n*. the butternut genus, giving name to the family Caryocarā'ceae (*-si-ē*). [Gr. *karyon*, nut, *karā*, head.]

caryophyllaceous, *kar-i-ō-fi-lā'shəs*, *adj*. belonging to the pink family (Caryophyllā'ceae; *-si-ē*). [*Caryophyllus*, early botanical name for clovepink—Gr. *karyophyllon*, clove-tree (from similar smell).]

caryopsis, *kar-i-op'sis*, *n*. a dry indehiscent fruit in which the pericarp is united with the testa, characteristic of the grasses. [Gr. *karyon*, a nut, *opsis*, appearance.]

casa, *kä-zä*, (It.) *n*. a house.

Casanova, *kas-ə-nō'və*, *n*. a person conspicuous for his amorous adventures, as was Giovanni Jacopo Casanova de Seingalt (1725-1798).

casbah. Same as kasba(h).

cascabel, *kas'kə-bel*, *n*. the part behind the basering of a cannon. [Sp.]

cascade, *kas-kād'*, *n*. a waterfall: a trimming of lace or other material in a loose wavy fall: connection of apparatus in series.—*v.i.* to fall in cascades. [Fr.,—It. *cascata*—L. *cadĕre*, to fall.]

cascara, *kas-kä'rə*, or (Sp.) *käs'kä-rä*, *n*. (*cascara sagrada*) a Californian buckthorn (*Rhamnus*) bark used as a tonic aperient: (*cascara amarga*), a bitter Honduras bark of the quassia family.— *n*. cascarill'a, the aromatic bitter bark of a West Indian Croton. [Sp. *cáscara*, bark.]

casco, *kas'kō*, *n*. a Philippine lighter. [Sp.]

case, *käs*, *n*. a covering, box, or sheath: a set: a facing for walls: the boards and back of a book: the tray in which a compositor has his types before him.—*v.t.* to enclose in a case: to skin.— *n*. cas'ing, the act of putting on a case, or of skinning: an outside covering of any kind, as of boards, plaster, etc.—case'-bottle, a bottle made to fit into a case with others, a bottle with a covering.—*v.t.* case'-hard'en, to harden on the surface, as by carbonising iron: to make callous or insensitive (*fig.*).—case'-hard'ening; case'-knife, a large knife kept in a sheath: case'-maker, one who makes covers for books; case'-man, a compositor; case'-shot, canister-shot, an artillery projectile for use at close quarters; case'-worm, caddis-worm. [O.N.Fr. *casse* (mod. Fr. *châsse* and *caisse*)—L. *capsa*—*capĕre*, to take.]

case, *käs*, *n*. that which falls or happens, event: state or condition: subject of question or inquiry: an instance of disease: a person under medical treatment: an odd character (*slang*): a legal statement of facts: a law-suit: a plausible contention, something to be said for a position or action: the grammatical relation of a noun, pronoun, or (in some languages) adjective to another word in the sentence, or its variation in form to express that relation—the nominative being imagined as a vertical line, and the oblique cases in various stages of falling or *declension*.— *v.t.* to reconnoitre with a view to burglary.— case'book, a book in which a doctor records the history of his cases: a book recording medical, or legal, etc., cases which are valuable as examples for reference; case history, record of ancestry, environment, personal history, etc., for use in diagnosis and treatment, or for other purpose; case'-law, law as decided in previous cases; case'-work, study of maladjusted individuals or families, their environment and history, often together with supervision and guidance; case'-worker.—in any case, at all events: at any rate; in case, in the event that: lest; in case to, in fit condition for; make out one's case, to give good reasons for one's statements or position; put (the) case, to suppose an instance: to take for example; the case, the fact, the reality. [O.Fr. *cas*—L. *cāsus—cadĕre*, to fall.]

caseation, casein. See caseous.

casemate, *käs'māt*, *n*. any bomb-proof vaulted chamber, even when merely used as quarters for a garrison: orig. a loopholed gallery, from which the garrison of a fort could fire upon an enemy who had obtained possession of the ditch. —*adj.* case'mated. [Fr.; der. uncertain.]

casement, *käs'mənt*, *n*. the case or frame of a window: a window that opens on vertical hinges: a hollow moulding.—*adj.* case'mented, having casements.—case'ment-cloth, a plain cotton fabric, suitable for casement-curtains; case'ment-cur'tain, a curtain hung from a window-sash; case'ment-window. [For encasement (Fr. *enchassement*), or L.L. *casamentum*, house-frame, or directly from case (1).]

caseous, *kā'si-əs*, *adj*. cheeselike.—*ns*. caseätion, becoming cheeselike; casein (*kā'sē-*, *si-in*), principal albuminous constituent of milk, in which it is found as a calcium salt, obtainable by curdling. [L. *cāseus*, cheese.]

casern(e), *kä-zern'*, *n*. a barrack. [Fr.,—Sp. *caserna*.]

cash, *kash*, *n*. coin or money: ready money.—*v.t.* to turn into or exchange for money.—*n*. cashier', one who has charge of the receiving and paying of money.—cash'-account', an account to which nothing is carried but cash (*book-k.*): a form of account with a bank, by which a person is entitled to draw out sums by way of loan—also called cash'-cred'it; cash'-book, a book in which an account is kept of the receipts and disbursements of money; cash dispenser, a machine, usually in or outside a bank which dispenses money on the insertion of a special voucher; cash'-keeper, cashier; cash'-pay'ment, payment in ready money; cash'-rail'way, a mechanical device for interchange of cash between counter and cash-desk in a shop; cash'-reg'ister, a till that automatically and visibly records the amount put in.—cash and carry, sale for cash, with delivery up to the buyer; cash in, to seize an advantage; cash in on, to turn to one's advantage; cash in (one's checks), to exchange counters for money on leaving the gaming-table: to die (*slang*); hard cash (see hard); out of cash, in cash, without, or with, money: out of, or in, pocket. [A doublet of case, a box—O.Fr. *casse*, a box.]

cash, *kash*, *n*. a small Eastern coin. [Port. *caixa*— Sinh. *kāsi*, coin—Tamil *kācu*.]

cashaw, *kə-shö'*, *n*. a kind of pumpkin (*U.S.*): a W. Indian mesquite. [Algonquian.]

cashew, *kə-shōō'*, *kash'ōō*, *n*. a spreading tropical American tree (*Anacardium occidentale*) with kidney-shaped nuts (cash'ew-nuts) whose kernels and fleshy stalks (cash'ew-app'les) are used as food. [Tupí *caju*; cf. acajou.]

cashier, *kash-ēr'*, *v.t.* to dismiss from a post in disgrace: to discard or put away: to annul.—*ns*. cashier'er; cashier'ing, a punishment for army and naval officers, severer than dismissal, in that it disqualifies them from entering the public service in any capacity (abolished 1970); cashier'ment, dismissal. [Du. *casseren* (*kasseren*), to cashier —Fr. *casser*—L. *cassāre—cassus*, void, empty.]

cashier. See cash (1).

cashmere, *kash'mēr*, *n*. (a shawl or fabric made

from) fine soft *Kashmir* goats' hair: any similar product.

casino, *kə-sē'nō, n.* a room for public dancing: a building with public dance halls, gaming tables, etc.: a card-game. [It.: from L. *casa*, a cottage.]

cask, *käsk, n.* a hollow round vessel for holding liquor, made of staves bound with hoops: a measure of capacity: a casque (*obs.*).—*v.t.* to put in a cask. [Fr. *casque*—Sp. *casco*, skull, helmet, cask.]

casket, *käsk'it, n.* a little cask or case: a small case for holding jewels, etc.: a coffin (*U.S.*) [Ety. uncertain; hardly a dim. of cask.]

casque, (*obs.* cask), *käsk, n.* a cover for the head: a helmet. [A doublet of cask.]

Cassandra, *kəs-an'drə, n.* a daughter of Priam, king of Troy, beloved by Apollo, who gave her the gift of prophecy, but not of being believed—hence any one who expresses gloomy views of the political or social future and is not listened to.

cassareep, cassaripe, *kas'ə-rēp, n.* the juice of the bitter cassava, a potent antiseptic, used in sauces, and in the West Indian pepper-pot. [From Tupí.]

cassation, *ka-sā'shən, n.* annulment: in French law, the quashing of a decision of a court—hence court of cassation, the supreme tribunal: an 18th-cent. type of musical composition in several short movements. [L.L. *cassātiō, -ōnis*—*cassāre,* to bring to nought.]

cassava, *kə-sä'və, n.* manioc: tapioca. [From a Taino (language of extinct West Indian tribe) name.]

Cassegrain(ian) telescope, *kas-ə-grān'(i-ən)*, a type of reflecting telescope devised by, and named after, a 17th-cent. Frenchman.

casserole, *kas'ə-rōl, n.* a stew-pan: a vessel in which food is both cooked and served: the outer part of several dressed dishes.—casserole cookery, cooking in the dish in which the food is to be served. [Fr.]

cassette, *kas-et', n.* a small casket: a light-tight container for an X-ray film, or one for film in a miniature camera: a holder with reel of magnetic tape, esp. tape on which there is pre-recorded material. [Fr. dim. of *casse*, case.]

cassia, *kas(h)'yə, n.* a coarser kind of cinnamon (cass'ia-bark'): the tree that yields it: (*cap.*) a genus of shrubs of the Caesalpinia family, yielding senna, and the drug cassia fistula or purging cassia. [L. *casia*—Gr. *kasiā* (also *kassiā*)—Heb. *qetsi'āh.*]

cassimere, *kas'i-mēr, n.* a twilled cloth of the finest wools.—Also kerseymere'. [Corr. of cashmere.]

cassino, *kə-sē'nō, n.* a game at cards. [See casino.]

Cassiopeia, *kas-i-ō-pē'(y)ə, n.* a northern constellation named after the mother of Andromeda.—*n.* cassiope'ium, discarded name for lutetium.

cassis, *kä-sēs, n.* a syrupy black-currant drink or flavouring. [Fr.]

cassiterite, *ka-sit'ə-rīt, n.* a brown native tin dioxide. [Gr. *kassiteros,* tin.]

cassock, *kas'ək, n.* a long robe or outer coat, formerly in common wear, but now worn only by clergy and choristers: a shorter garment, usually of black silk, worn under the Geneva gown by Scottish ministers.—*adj.* cass'ocked. [Fr. *casaque*—It. *casacca.*]

cassolette, *kas'ō-let, n.* a censer: a perfume-box with perforated lid. [Fr.,—Sp. *cazoleta*—*cazo,* a saucepan.]

cassonade, *kas-o-nād', n.* unrefined sugar. [Fr.]

cassone, *kä-sō'nā,* (It.) a large chest, elaborately carved and painted.

cassoulet, *ka-sōō-le,* (Fr.) a stew consisting of beans and various kinds of meat.

cassowary, *kas'ə-wər-i, n.* a genus (*Casuarius*) of

birds, found esp. in New Guinea, nearly related to the emu. [Malay *kasuāri* or *kasavāri.*]

cassumunar, *kas-ōō-mū'nər, n.* an East Indian ginger. [Origin unknown.]

cast, *käst, v.t.* to throw or fling: to throw off, shed, drop: to drop prematurely: to throw down: to throw up: to reckon: to add: to project: to reject, condemn, decide against (*arch.*): to mould or shape: to purpose, devise, consider (*arch.*): to appoint as actor (*for* a part): to assign as his part (*to* an actor): to cut and throw up to dry (peat) (*Scot.*).—*v.i.* to warp (*pa.t.* and *pa.p.* cast).—*n.* act of casting: a throw of anything, as the sounding-lead, a fishing-line: the thing thrown, esp. in angling: the distance thrown: a motion, turn, or squint, as of the eye: a turn or sample performance: a good turn, as a lift or conveyance in a vehicle (*Scot.*): matter ejected by a bird, earthworm, etc.: a throw or turn of fortune, a chance: a mould: form, manner, stamp, or quality: a shade of colour, a degree of guilt, etc.: the assignment of the various parts of a play to the several actors: the company of actors playing rôles: a couple of hawks.—*adj.* moulded: rejected, cast off: defeated at law.—*adj.* cast'ed (*Shak.*), cast off.—*n.* cast'ing, act of casting or moulding: that which is cast: a mould.—cast'away, one shipwrecked in a desolate place: an outcast.—*adj.* worthless, rejected.—cast'ing-net, a species of net for fishing; cast'ing-vote, a chairman's deciding vote in case of equality; cast'ing-weight, the weight that makes the balance cast or turn when exactly poised; cast'-iron, an iron-carbon alloy distinguished from steel by its containing substantial amounts of cementite or graphite, which make it unsuitable for working.—*adj.* hard, rigid: unassailable.—*adj.* cast'-off, laid aside or rejected.—*n.* anything thrown aside.—*n.* cast'-steel, steel that has been cast, not shaped by mechanical working.—cast about, to contrive, to look about, to search for, as game: to turn, to go round (*B.*); cast a horoscope, nativity, to make an astrological calculation; cast anchor, to anchor a ship; cast an eye, a glance, to look; cast a spell upon, to put under an enchantment; cast a vote, to record or make a vote; cast away, to wreck: to waste; cast back, to revert; cast down, to deject or depress in mind: to turn downward; cast loose, to set loose or adrift; cast lots (see lot); cast off, to reject: to loose (hawks, hounds): to unmoor: to eliminate stitches: to estimate amount of printed matter that copy will make; cast on, to make stitches; cast out (*Scot.*), to quarrel; cast up, to throw up: to bring up as a reproach: to turn up, appear, emerge (*Scot.*); cast water (*arch.*), to inspect urine in diagnosis; the last cast, extremities. [O.N. *kasta,* to throw.]

Castalian, *kas-tā'li-ən, adj.* pertaining to *Castalia,* a fountain on Parnassus, sacred to Apollo and the Muses.

Castanea, *kas-tān'i-a, n.* the chestnut genus of the beech family (*Fagaceae*).—*n.* Castanospermum (*kas-tan-ō-sper'məm*), an Australian papilionaceous tree, the Moreton Bay chestnut, so called from the taste of its nuts. [Gr. *kastanon,* chestnut (*sperma,* seed).]

castanets, *kas'tə-nets, -nets', n.pl.* two hollow shells of ivory or hard wood, bound by a band on the thumb, and struck by the finger to produce a clicking sound—much used in Spain as an accompaniment to dances and guitars. [Sp. *castañeta*—L. *castanea,* a chestnut.]

caste, *käst, n.* a social class in India: an exclusive social class: a type of individual in some polymorphic social insects.—caste'-mark, an indication of caste worn on the forehead (also *fig.*).—lose caste, to descend to social rank. [Port. *casta,* breed, race—L. *castus,* pure, unmixed.]

castellan, castellated. See castle.

**caster.** Same as castor (1).
**castigate,** *kas'tig-āt, v.t.* to chastise: to criticise severely: to emend.—*ns.* **castigā'tion; cas'tigā-tor.**—*adj.* **cas'tigatory** (*-ə-tər-i*). [L. *castigāre, -ātum,* from *castus,* pure.]
**Castilian,** *kas-til'yən, adj.* of Castile.—*n.* a native of Castile: the language thereof, standard Spanish.—**Castile soap,** a hard soap made with olive-oil and soda. [Sp. *Castellano.*]
**castle,** *käs'l, n.* a fortified house or fortress: the residence of a prince or nobleman, or a large country mansion generally: a rook in chess: a defensive tower borne on an elephant's back: a large ship, esp. of war.—*v.t.* to enclose or fortify with a castle.—*v.i.* to move the king two squares towards the castle and place the castle on the square the king has passed over.—**castellan,** (*kas'təl-an*), governor or captain of a castle.—*adj.* **cas'tellated** (*kas'tel-āt-id*), having turrets and battlements like a castle.—*adj.* **cas'tled,** furnished with castles.—*n.* **cas'tle-build'ing,** the act of building castles in the air or forming visionary projects; **cas'tle-guard,** the guard for the defence of a castle.—**castles in the air,** or in Spain groundless or visionary projects. [O.E. *castel*—L. *castellum,* dim. of *castrum,* a fortified place.]
**castock,** *kas'tək,* **custock,** *kus', (Scot.) n.* a cabbage stock. [kale, stock.]
**Castor,** *kas'tŏr, -tər, n.* one of the Dioscuri, twin-brother of Pollux, son of Leda, famous for his skill in horse-taming: a bright star in the constellation Gemini (the Twins). [L.,—Gr. *Kastōr.*]
**castor, caster,** *käst'ər, n.* a small solid swivelled wheel on a leg of furniture: a vessel with perforated top for sprinkling.—**castor sugar, caster sugar,** white powdered sugar. [cast.]
**castor,** *käs'tər, n.* the beaver (genus Castor): castoreum: a hat of beaver-fur or substitute.—*ns.* **castoreum** (*-tō'ri-əm,-tŏ'*), the perineal sacs of the beaver, or a brown unctuous strong-smelling substance got from them, once used in medicine and perfumery; **cas'tory** (*Spens.*), a red or pink colour got from castoreum. [L. *castŏr, -ŏris*—Gr. *kastōr, -oros,* beaver.]
**castor-oil,** *käs'tər-oil', n.* a medicinal and lubricating oil obtained from the seeds of a tropical African euphorbiaceous plant, *Ricinus communis.* [Perh. from use as substitute for castor(eum).]
**castral,** *kas'trəl, adj.* belonging to the camp. [L. *castra.*]
**castrametation,** *kas-trə-me-tā'shən, n.* the art of designing a camp. [L. *castra,* a camp, *mētārī, -ātus,* to measure off—*mēta,* a boundary.]
**castrate,** *kas'trāt, v.t.* to deprive of the power of generation: to remove the testicles from, geld, emasculate: to take from or render imperfect.—*adj.* **cas'trated,** gelded: expurgated.—*ns.* **castrā'tion; castrato** (*käs-trä'tō;* Ital.), a male singer castrated in boyhood so as to preserve a soprano or alto voice:—*pl.* **castra'ti** (*-tē*). [L. *castrāre, -ātum.*]
**casual,** *kaz(h)'ū-əl, adj.* accidental: unforeseen: occasional: off-hand: negligent: unceremonious.—*n.* a chance or occasional visitor, labourer, pauper, etc.: a weed not naturalised.—*v.t.* **cas'ualise, -ize,** to turn (regular workers) into casual labourers.—*ns.* **casualisa'tion, -z-;** **cas'ualism,** belief that chance governs all things.—*adv.* **cas'ually.**—*n.* **cas'ualness.**—*n.pl.* **cas'uals,** slip-on flat-heeled shoes: loose-fitting comfortable and informal clothing.—*n.* **cas'ualty,** that which falls out: an accident: a misfortune: loss by wounds, death, desertion, etc. (*mil.*): an incidental charge or payment: a person injured or killed: a thing damaged or done for.—**casual labourer,** a worker without fixed employment; **casualties of superiority,** in the feudal law of Scotland, payments to the superior in certain contingencies (e.g. death)—ultimately redeemed or extinguished by Act of 1914; **casualty department, ward,** a hospital department, ward, in which accidents are treated; **casual ward,** formerly, a workhouse department for casuals. [L. *cāsuālis—cāsus.* See case.]
**Casuarina,** *kas-ū-ə-rī'nə, n.* the she-oak or beef-wood genus of trees, mainly Australian, constituting a family **Casuarinā'ceae,** perhaps akin to birch but superficially like horsetails. [Named from its resemblance to Cassowary plumage.]
**casuist,** *kaz'ū-ist, n.* one who studies and resolves cases of conscience: often, one who argues sophistically in such cases.—*adjs.* **casuist'ic, -al.**—*n.* **cas'uistry,** the science or doctrine of cases of conscience: the reasoning which enables a man to decide in a particular case between apparently conflicting duties—often with a suggestion of sophistry. [Fr. *casuiste*—L. *cāsus;* see case.]
**casus belli,** *kä'sus be'lī, kä'sŏŏs be'lē,* whatever involves or justifies war; **casus conscientiae** (*kon-shi-en'shi-ē, kōn-skē-en'tē-ī*), a case of conscience; **casus foederis** (*fē'də-ris, foi'də-ris*), a case clearly coming within the provisions of a treaty. [L.]
**cat,** *kat, n.* a carnivore of genus *Felis,* esp. the domesticated kind or any of the smaller wild species: a spiteful woman: a movable penthouse to protect besiegers: a double tripod with six legs: a piece of wood tapering at each end, struck with the **cat'-stick** in the game of *tip-cat:* the game itself: short for the **cat-o'-nine-tails,** a whip with nine knotted tails or lashes, once used in the army and navy: a showily dressed man (*slang*): a man, fellow (*slang*): a jazz fan (*slang*): a caterpillar tractor.—*v.t.* to raise the anchor to the cathead: to vomit.—*ns.* **cat'hood,** state of being a cat or having the nature of a cat; **cat'kin,** a crowded spike or tuft of small unisexual flowers with reduced scale-like bracts, as in the willow, hazel, etc.—*adj.* **cat'-like,** noiseless, stealthy.—*ns.* **cat'ling,** a little cat, a kitten: a catgut string (*Shak.*); **catt'ery,** a place where cats are bred or cared for.—*adjs.* **catt'ish, catt'y,** like a cat: spiteful: back-biting.—*ns.* **cat'amount,** the European wild cat: the puma, the lynx, or other beast of the cat family (*U.S.*); **catamoun'-tain,** or **cat o' mountain,** a leopard, panther, or ocelot: a wild mountaineer.—*adj.* ferocious, savage.—*adj.* **cat'-and-dog,** constantly quarrelling.—**cat'bird,** an American bird of the thrush family with a mewing note: an Australian bowerbird; **cat'-bur'glar,** a burglar who performs nimble climbing feats; **cat'call,** a squeaking instrument used in theatres to express disapprobation: a shrill whistle or cry.—*v.i.* to sound a cat-call.—*v.t.* to assail with one.—*adj.* **cat'-eyed,** having eyes like a cat: able to see in the dark.—**cat'fish,** a fish with cat-like features, in Britain usually the wolf-fish, in America a sait or fresh-water fish of the family Siluridae; **cat'-gut,** a kind of cord made from the intestines of sheep and other animals used for violin strings, surgical ligatures, etc.: the violin or other stringed instrument: a coarse corded cloth.—*adj.* **cat'-hammed,** with thin hams like a cat's.—**cat'head,** one of two strong beams projecting from the bow of a ship through which the tackle passes by which the anchor is raised; **cat'-hole,** one of two holes in the after part of a ship through which hawsers may pass for steadying the ship or for heaving astern; **cat'lap,** any thin or despised drink; **cat'mint, cat'nep, cat'nip,** a mint-like labiate plant (*Nepeta Cataria*) of which cats are fond; **cat'nap,** a brief sleep, in a chair, etc.; **cat's'-cradle,** a pastime in which a string looped about the fingers and passed from player to player is transformed from one symmetrical figure to another; **cat's'-ear,** a name given

to two genera of British compositous plants—Hypochoeris, of the ligulate-flowered group, and Antennaria, or mountain-everlasting; **cat's-eye**, a name for various chatoyant minerals, esp. a variety of chrysoberyl, also a fibrous quartz, and a quartz pseudomorph after crocidolite: ⒭ a reflector set in a frame fixed in a road surface; **cat's-foot**, the mountain-everlasting: ground-ivy; **cat'-sil'ver**, a variety of silvery mica; **cat'skin**; **cat's-meat**, horse's flesh, or the like, sold for cats: any rather unappetising food; **cat's'-paw**, a light breeze (*naut.*): a hitch in a rope providing two loops for a hook: one who is made the tool of another—from the fable of the monkey who used the paws of the cat to draw chestnuts out of the fire; **cat's-tail**, a catkin: Timothy grass: the reed-mace or bulrush; **cat'-suit**, a type of one-piece trouser suit; **cat's'-whisk'er** (*radio*), a delicate wire brought in contact with a crystal to rectify the current in some forms of crystal detector and produce audibility.—**cat'-walk**, a narrow footway, as on a bridge.—*adj.* **cat'-witted**, small-minded, conceited, and spiteful.—**bell the cat** (see **bell**); **catted and fished** (of an anchor), raised to the cathead and secured to the ship's side; **care killed the (or a) cat**, even with his proverbial nine lives; **Cheshire cat**, proverbially notable for grinning; **enough to make a cat laugh**, i.e. even the least inclined; **in the catbird seat** (*U.S.*), in an advantageous position; **Kilkenny cats**, proverbial cats who fight till each destroys the other; **like something the cat brought in**, bedraggled, slovenly in dress, etc.; **put the cat among the pigeons**, to stir up trouble; **rain cats and dogs**, to pour down heavily; **room to swing a cat**, a minimum of space; **see which way the cat jumps**, to watch how things are going to turn before committing oneself; **the big cats**, lions, tigers, leopards, etc.; **the cat's pyjamas, the cat's whiskers** (*slang*), the very thing that is wanted: anything very good; **turn (the) cat in (the) pan**, to change sides with dexterity; **whip the cat** (see **whip**). [O.E. *cat*; found also in Celt., Slav., Ar., Finn., etc.]

**cat**, *kat*, *n.* an old name for a coal and timber vessel on the north-east coast of England.—*n.* **cat'boat**, a cat-rigged boat.—*adj. adj.* **cat'-rigged**, having one great fore-and-aft main-sail spread by a gaff at the head and a boom at the foot, for smooth water only. [Obscurely connected with **cat** (1).]

**catabolism.** See **katabolism.**

**catacaustic**, *kat-ə-kös'tik*, (*geom.*) *adj.* belonging to caustic curves formed by reflection. [Gr. *kata*, against and **caustic**.]

**catachresis**, *kat-ə-krē'sis*, (*rhet.*) *n.* misapplication of a word.—*adjs.* **catachrestic** (*-kres'tik*, or *-krēs'tik*), **-al**.—*adv.* **catachres'tically.** [Gr. *katachrēsis*, misuse—*chrēsis*, use.]

**cataclasm**, *kat'ə-klazm*, *n.* a disruption, breaking down.—*adjs.* **cataclas'mic**, pertaining to or of the nature of a cataclasm; **cataclas'tic** (*geol.*), mylonitic, or granular in consequence of crushing. [Gr. *kataklasma*—*kata*, down, *klaein*, to break.]

**cataclysm**, *kat'ə-klizm*, *n.* a flood of water: a debacle: a great revolution.—*adj.* **cataclys'mic.** [Gr. *kataklysmos*—*kata*, downward, *klyzein*, to wash.]

**catacomb**, *kat'ə-kōm*, or *-kōōm*, *n.* a subterranean excavation used as a burial-place, esp. near Rome, where many of the early Christian victims of persecution were buried: any place built with crypt-like recesses for storing books, wine, etc.—*adj.* **catacumbal** (*-kum'bl*). [It. *catacomba*—L.L. *Catacumbas*, perh. in some way—Gr. *kata*, down, and *kymbē*, a cup.]

**catacoustics**, *kat-ə-kōōs'tiks*, or *-kows'*, *n.* the part of acoustics that treats of echoes or sounds reflected. [Gr. *kata*, back, and **acoustics**.]

**catadioptric, -al**, *kat-ə-dī-op'trik*, *-əl*, *adjs.* pertaining to both reflection and refraction. [See **catoptric**, **dioptric**.]

**catadromous**, *kat-ad'rəm-əs*, *adj.* of fishes, descending periodically for spawning to the lower parts of a river or to the sea. [Gr. *kata*, down, *dromos*, a run.]

**catafalque**, *kat'ə-falk*, *n.* a temporary tomb-like structure used in funeral ceremonies: a funeral car.—Also **catafal'co.** [Fr.,—It. *catafalco*.]

**Cataian, Catayan**, *kə-tā'ən*, (*Shak.*) *n.* a Cathayan, Chinese—a vague term of reproach. [*Cathay*, poetical name for China.]

**Catalan**, *kat'ə-lan*, *adj.* of or belonging to Catalonia or its language, a dialect of Provençal.—*n.* a native of Catalonia: the language thereof.

**catalectic**, *kat-ə-lek'tik*, *adj.* incomplete: wanting one syllable in the last foot (*pros.*).—*n.* **catalex'is.** [Gr. *katalēktikos*, incomplete—*katalēgein*, to stop.]

**catalepsy**, *kat'ə-lep-si*, *n.* a state of more or less complete insensibility, with bodily rigidity: cataplexy in animals.—*adj.* and *n.* **catalep'tic.** [Gr. *katalēpsis*, seizure, catalepsy—*kata*, down, *lēpsis*, taking, seizure.]

**catallactic**, *kat-ə-lak'tik*, *adj.* pertaining to exchange.—*adv.* **catallac'tically.**—*n.* **catallac'tics**, political economy. [Gr. *katallaktēs*, a money-changer.]

**catalo.** Same as **cattalo.**

**catalogue**, *kat'ə-log*, in U.S. often **catalog**, *n.* a systematic list of names, books, pictures, etc.—*v.t.* to put in a catalogue: to make a catalogue of.—*n.* **cat'aloguer.**—*v.t.* **cat'aloguise, -ize.**—*n.* **cat'alog** (*U.S.*), a university calendar. [Gr. *katalogos*, from *kata*, in order, *legein*, to reckon.] **catalogue raisonné**, *ka-ta-log re-zon-ā*, (Fr.) a classified descriptive catalogue.

**Catalpa**, *kat-al'pa*, *n.* an American and Japanese genus of low bignoniaceous trees with profuse blossoms and long cigarlike pendent pods. [American Indian (Creek) *kutuhlpa*.]

**catalysis**, *kə-tal'i-sis*, *n.* the chemical influence of a substance not itself permanently changed.—*n.* **cat'alase**, an enzyme that reduces hydrogen peroxide.—*v.t.* **cat'alyse, -yze** (*-līz*), to subject to catalysis.—*ns.* **cataly'ser** (or *-z-*), **cat'alyst** (*-list*), a catalysing agent.—*adjs.* **catalytic** (*-lit'ik*), **-al.** [Gr. *katalysis*—*kata*, down, *lyein*, to loosen.]

**catamaran**, *kat'ə-mə-ran'*, or *kat-am'ə-ran*, *n.* a raft of logs lashed together: a boat with two hulls: an old kind of fire-ship, long superseded: an ill-natured woman. [Tamil, *kattu-maram*, tied wood.]

**catamenia**, *kat-e-mē'ni-ə*, *n. pl.* the menstrual discharge.—*adj.* **catamē'nial.** [Neut. pl. of Gr. *katamēnios*, monthly—*kata*, against, *mēn*, a month.]

**catamite**, *kat'ə-mīt*, *n.* a boy kept for unnatural purposes. [Corruption of **Ganymede**.]

**catamount.** See **cat.**

**catapan**, *kat'ə-pan*, *n.* the governor of Calabria and Apulia for the Byzantine emperor. [Acc. to Littré, from Gr. *katepanō tōn axiōmatōn*, one placed over the dignities.]

**cataphonics**, *kat-ə-fon'iks*, *n.* catacoustics.—*adj.* **cataphon'ic.** [Gr. *kata*, back, *phōnē*, sound.]

**cataphoresis**, *kat-ə-fə-rē'sis*, *n.* electrophoresis: the introduction into the body of medicinal substances by means of an electric current. [Gr. *kata*, down, *phorēsis*, a carrying.]

**cataphract**, *kat'ə-frakt*, *n.* a suit of mail: a soldier in full armour (*Milton*).—*adj.* **cataphrac'tic.** [Gr. *kataphraktēs*, a coat-of-mail—*kata*, inten., and *phrassein*, to enclose, protect.]

**cataphyll**, *kat'ə-fil*, *n.* a rudimentary or simplified leaf.—*adj.* **cataphyll'ary.** [Gr. *kata*, down, *phyllon*, leaf.]

**cataphysical**, *kat-ə-fiz'i-kl*, (*rare*) *adj.* unnatural. [Gr. *kata*, down, against, *physis*, nature.]

**cataplasm**, *kat'ə-plazm*, *n.* a plaster or poultice. [Gr. *kataplasma*.]

**cataplexy**, *kat'ə-plek-si*, *n.* a condition of immobility induced by emotion: in animals the state called shamming death.—*adj.* **cataplec'tic**. [Gr. *kataplēxis*, amazement—*kata*, down, *plēssein*, to strike.]

**catapult**, *kat'ə-pult*, *n.* anciently, an engine of war (properly one resembling the ballista) for throwing stones, arrows, etc.: a small forked stick having an elastic string fixed to the two prongs, used by boys for throwing small stones: any similar device, as for launching aeroplanes.—*v.t.* and *v.i.* to shoot out from, or as if from, a catapult.—*adj.* **catapul'tic**.—*n.* **catapultier'**.—**catapult fruit**, one that shoots out its seeds. [L. *catapulta*—Gr. *katapeltēs*.]

**cataract**, *kat'ə-rakt*, *n.* a portcullis (*obs.*): a water-spout, etc.; a waterfall: a floodgate (*Milton*): an opaque condition of the lens of the eye, painless, unaccompanied by inflammation. [L. *cataracta*—Gr. *kataraktēs*, portcullis, waterfall.]

**catarrh**, *kat-är'*, *n.* a discharge of fluid from the inflammation of a mucous membrane, esp. of the nose, esp. when chronic: a cold in the head.—*adjs.* **catarrh'al, catarrh'ous**. [L. *catarrhus*—Gr. *katarrhous*—*kata*, down, *rheein*, to flow.]

**catarrhine, catarhine**, *kat'ə-rīn*, *adj.* pertaining to that one of the two divisions of Primates, including all the Old World monkeys, having a narrow partition between the nostrils. [Gr. *katarris*, with hanging nose—*kata*, down, *rhis, rhinos*, nose.]

**catasta**, *kat-as'ta*, *n.* a block on which slaves were exposed for sale: a stage or place for torture. [L.]

**catastasis**, *kə-tas'tə-sis*, *n.* the part of a drama in which the action has reached its height. [Gr. *katastasis*, settlement.]

**catastrophe**, *kət-as'trə-fi*, *n.* an overturning: a final event: the climax of the action of the plot in play or novel: an unfortunate conclusion: a sudden calamity: rear (*Shak.*).—*adj.* **catastrophic** (*kat-ə-strof'ik*).—*ns.* **catas'trophism**, the old theory of geological change by vast catastrophes and new creations (opp. to *uniformitarianism*); **catas'trophist**. [Gr. *kata*, down, *strophē*, a turning.]

**catatonia**, *kat-ə-tō'ni-a*, **catatony**, *kat-at'ə-ni*, *ns.* a type of schizophrenia characterised by periodic states of stupor.—*adj.* and *n.* **catatonic** (*-ton'*). [Gr. *kata*, down, *tonos*, stretching, straining—*teinein*, to stretch.]

**catawba**, *ka-tö'ba*, *n.* an American grape (*Vitis Labrusca*): a red wine made from it. [*Catawba* River in Carolina.]

**catbird**; **catcall**. See **cat**.

**catch**, *kach*, *v.t.* to take hold of, esp. of a thing in motion: to gather (the ball) after the batsman has hit it and before it touches the ground (*cricket*): to dismiss (a batsman) thus: to apprehend or understand: to seize after pursuit: to trap or ensnare: to come upon: to be in time for: to strike: to take (a disease) by infection: to take (fire): to take up by sympathy or imitation.—*v.i.* to be contagious: to be entangled or fastened (*infin.* in *Spens.* sometimes **catchen**, *pa.t.* and *pa.p.* **caught**, *köt*, also *obs.* and *dial.* **catched, catcht**; *pa.t.* in *Spens.* also **keight**, *kīt*).—*n.* seizure: an act of catching, esp. the ball at cricket, etc.: a clasp, or anything that seizes or holds: that which is caught or is worth catching: a sudden advantage taken: a concealed difficulty or disadvantage: a round for three or more voices, later seeking comic effect by the interweaving of the words.—*adj.* **catch'-able**, that may be caught.—*ns.* **catch'er**; **catch'-ing**, the action of the verb: a nervous or spasmodic twitching.—*adj.* infectious: captivating:

attractive.—*n.* **catch'ment**, river drainage.—*adj.* **catch'y**, attractive: deceptive: readily caught up, or taking hold of the mind, as a tune, etc.: fitful.—**catch'-as-catch'-can'**, a style of wrestling in which any hold is allowed.—Also *adj.* and *adv.*—**catch'-basin, -pit**, a trap for dirt in a drain; **catch'-drain**, a drain on a hillside to catch the surface-water; **catch'fly**, a name for a species of campion (*Lychnis viscaria*) and several of bladder-campion (*Silene*) with sticky stems; **catchment area**, or **basin**, the area from which a river or reservoir is fed.—Also *fig.*—**catch'penny**, worthless thing made only to sell.—Also *adj.*—**catch'-phrase**, a phrase that becomes popular and is much repeated: a slogan; **catch-the-ten'**, card game in which the aim is to capture the ten of trumps; **catch'weed**, goosegrass or cleavers; **catch'word**, actor's cue: the word at the head of the page in a dictionary or encyclopaedia: the first word of a page given at the bottom of the preceding page: any word or phrase taken up and repeated esp. as the watchword or symbol of a party.—**catch at**, to snatch at; **catch fire**, to become ignited: to become inspired by passion or zeal; **catch hold of**, to seize; **catch it**, to get a scolding or the like; **catch me, him**, etc., an emphatic colloquial phrase implying that there is not the remotest possibility of my or his doing something suggested; **catch on**, to comprehend: to catch the popular fancy; **catch out**, to put out at cricket by catching the ball after it has been hit and before it touches the ground: to detect in error or deceit; **catch sight of**, to get a glimpse of; **catch up**, to overtake; **catch up**, or **away**, to snatch or seize hastily. [From O.Fr. *cachier*—L.L. *captiāre* from *captāre*, inten. of *capĕre*, to take; see **chase**.]

**catchpole, -poll**, *kach'pōl*, *n.* a constable, petty officer of justice. [Through O.Fr. from L.L. *cachepolus, chassipullus*, one who chases fowls. See **chase** and **pullet**.]

**catchup, catsup**. See **ketchup**.

**cat'-cracker**, *n.* (in full, **catalytic cracker**), a plant in which the cracking of petroleum is speeded up by the use of a catalyst.—*n.* **cat'-cracking**.

**cate**, *kāt*, (*arch.*; *Shak.*) *n.* (nearly always in *pl.*) a viand: a dainty, a delicacy. [Aphetic; see **acates**; cf. **cater**.]

**catechise, -ize**, *kat'i-kiz*, *v.t.* to instruct by question and answer: to question as to belief: to examine systematically by questioning.—*adjs.* **catechetic** (*ket'ik*), **-al**, relating to a catechism or oral instruction in the first principles, esp. of Christianity.—*adv.* **catechet'ically**.—*ns.* **catechet'ics**, the art or practice of teaching by question and answer: that part of theology which treats of **catechesis** (*-kē'sis*), or primary oral instruction, as that given to catechumens; **cat'echiser, -z-**; **cat'echising, -z-**; **cat'echism**, any compendious system of teaching drawn up in form of question and answer: a set of questions: an examination by questions; **cat'echist**, one who catechises: a teacher of catechumens: a native teacher in a mission church.—*adjs.* **catechis'tic, -al, catechis'mal**, pertaining to a catechist or catechism. [L. *catēchismus*, formed from Gr. *katēchizein, katēcheein*, to din into the ears—*kata*, back, *echē*, a sound.]

**catechu**, *kat'i-chōō, -shōō*, *n.* a dark extract of Indian plants (acacia, betel-nut, etc.) rich in tannin.—*n.* **cat'echol**, a white crystalline phenol-alcohol derived from catechu. [Cf. Malay, *cachu*.]

**catechumen**, *kat-i-kū'mən*, *n.* one who is being taught the rudiments of Christianity: in the early Christian Church a converted Jew or heathen undergoing instruction preparatory to baptism.—*n.* **catechu'menate**.—*adj.* **catechumen'ical**.—*adv.* **catechumen'ically**.—*ns.* **catechu'menism, catechū'menship**. [Gr. *katēchoumenos*,

being taught, pr.p. pass. of *katēcheein*, to teach;
cf. **catechise**.]
**category,** *kat'i-gər-i, n.* what may be affirmed of a
class: a class or order.—*adjs.* **categorematic**
(*-gor-i-mat'ik*), capable of being used by itself as
a term; **categorial** (*ka-tə-gor'i-əl*), of or pertaining to a category.—*adv.* **categor'ially.**—
*adj.* **categorical** (*-gor'*), positive: absolute:
without exception.—*adv.* **categor'ically,** absolutely: without qualification: expressly.—*n.* **categor'icalness,** the quality of being absolute and
unqualified.—*n.pl.* **cat'egories** (*phil.*), the highest
classes under which objects of philosophy can
be systematically arranged, understood as an
attempt at a comprehensive classification of all
that exists: in Kant's system, the root-notions
of the understanding, the specific forms of the
*a priori* or formal element in rational cognition
(*quantity, quality, relation, modality,* etc.).—*v.t.*
**cat'egorise, -ize,** to place in a category or list:
to class.—*n.* **cat'egorist,** one who categorises.—
**categorical imperative,** in the ethics of Kant, the
absolute unconditional command of the moral
law, irrespective of every ulterior end or aim—
universally authoritative, belonging to the fixed
law of nature. [Gr. *katēgoriā,* assertion, predication, accusation—*katēgoros,* an accuser, *kata,*
down, against, *agorā,* assembly.]
**catelog,** an obs. spelling of **catalogue.**
**catena,** *kə-tē'na, n.* a chain or connected series,
as in **catena patrum,** a chronological series
of extracts from the Fathers on any doctrine of
theology.—*adj.* **catenarian** (*kat-i-nā'ri-ən*), of, of
the nature of, a chain or a catenary.—*n.* **catē'-
nary** (*U.S. kat'*), the curve formed by a flexible
homogeneous cord, hanging freely between two
points of support, and acted on by no other force
than gravity.—*adj.* relating to a chain, like a
chain.—*v.t.* **catenate** (*kat'i-nāt*), to connect as in
or by a chain.—*adj.* linked as in a chain.—*n.*
**catenā'tion.**—**catenary system,** on some electrified railways, an arrangement of wires, supported
above the tracks, from which current is collected.
[L. *catēna,* chain.]
**cater,** *kā'tər, (obs.) n.* an acater: one who provides (sometimes *fig.*).—*v.i.* to provide food,
entertainment, etc. (for).—*ns.* **cā'terer; cā'-
teress; cā'tering.** [See **acater.**]
**cater,** *kā'tər, (dial.), v.t.* and *v.i.* to move diagonally.—Also *adj., adv.—advs., adjs.* **catercor'-
ner(ed),** diagonal(ly). [(M.) Fr. *quatre,* four—L.
*quattuor.*]
**cateran,** *kat'ər-ən, n.* a Highland reiver or freebooter: a robber or brigand generally. [Old
Gael. *ceatharn, ceithern,* a band of soldiers (Ir.
*ceithern,* foot-soldiers; see **kern(e).).**]
**cater-cousin,** *kā'tər-kuz'n, (Shak.) n.* a person
allied by familiarity, affection, sympathy, rather
than kindred. [More prob. conn. with **cater,** to
provide food, than *quarter* or *quarter.*]
**caterpillar,** *kat'ər-pil-ər, n.* a butterfly or moth
grub: extended to other insect larvae: an unproductive consumer (*arch.*): (from **Caterpillar,**
trademark) a tractor or other vehicle running on
endless articulated tracks consisting of flat metal
plates. [Prob. O.Fr. *chatepelose,* hairy cat; see
**cat, pile.**]
**caterwaul,** *kat'ər-wöl, n.* the shriek or cry emitted
by the cat when in heat.—*v.i.* to make such a
noise: to make any discordant sound: to behave
lasciviously: to quarrel like cats.—*n.* **cat'er-
wauling.** [**cat;** the second part prob. imit.]
**cates.** See **cat.**
**catgut.** See **cat.**
**Cathari,** *kath'ər-ī, n.pl.* a mediaeval Manichaean
sect, chiefly in S. France and N. Italy, the Albi-
gensians.—*ns.* **Cath'arism; Cath'arist.** [Gr.
*katharos,* pure.]
**cathartic, -al,** *kath-ärt'ik, -al, adjs.* cleansing,
purifying: having the power of cleansing the

bowels: purgative.—*n.* **cathart'ic,** a purgative
medicine.—*v.t.* **cath'arise, -ize,** to render absolutely clean.—*n.* **cathar'sis,** purification: evacuation of the bowels: purification of the emotions,
as by the drama according to Aristotle: the
purging of the effects of a pent-up emotion and
repressed thoughts, by bringing them to the surface of consciousness (*psych.*). [Gr. *kathartikos,*
fit for cleansing, *katharos,* clean.]
**Cathayan, Cathaian,** *ka-thā'ən, n.* and *adj.*
Chinese. (See **Cataian.**)
**cathead.** See **cat.**
**cathedral,** *kə-thē'drəl, n.* the principal church of a
diocese, containing the bishop's throne.—*adj.*
belonging to a seat of authority or a cathedral.—
*n.* **cathedra** (*-thē'dra, -thed'ra*), a bishop's seat,
the episcopal dignity.—*adj.* **cathedrat'ic,** promulgated *ex cathedra,* authoritative. [L. *cathēdra,*
*cathēdra*—Gr. *kathēdrā,* a seat.]
**Catherine-wheel,** *kath'(ə-)rin-(h)wēl, n.* a rose-
window (*archit.*): a wheel set round with teeth
(*her.*): a rotating firework: a sidewise somersault.—**Catherine pear,** a small and early variety
of pear. [From St *Catherine* of Alexandria (4th
cent.), who miraculously escaped torture on a
wheel.]
**catheter,** *kath'i-tər, n.* a tube for admitting or
removing gases or liquids through channels of
the body, especially for removing urine from the
bladder.—*ns.* **cath'eterism,** use of the catheter;
**cathetom'eter,** an instrument for measuring small
differences of level of different liquids in tubes;
**cath'etus,** a straight line perpendicular to another
straight line or surface. [Gr. *kathetos,* perpendicular, *kathetēr,* a catheter—*kathienai,* to send
down—*kata,* down, *hienai,* to send.]
**cathex'is,** *kə-thek'sis, n.* (*psych.*) a charge of
mental energy attached to any particular idea or
object.—*adj.* **cathec'tic.** [Gr. *kathexis,* holding.]
**cathisma,** *kə-thiz'ma, n.* in Greek use, a section of
the psalter: a troparion or short hymn used as a
response. [Gr.—*kathizein,* to sit down.]
**cathode,** *kath'ōd, n.* the negative terminal of an
electrolytic cell at which positively charged ions
are discharged into the exterior electric circuit:
in valves and tubes, the sources of electrons
(opposed to *anode*).—*adjs.* **cath'odal;** **cathodic.**
—*ns.* **cathod'ograph,** a photograph by X-rays;
**cathodog'rapher; cathodog'raphy.**—**cathode-ray
oscillograph,** the complete equipment for registering transient wave-forms on a photographic
plate within the vacuum of a cathode-ray tube;
**cathode-ray oscilloscope,** the complete equipment
for observing repeated and transient wave-forms
of current or voltage, which present a display
on a phosphor; **cathode rays,** streams of negatively charged particles, electrons, proceeding
from the cathode of a vacuum tube; **cathode-ray
tube,** a device in which a narrow beam of
electrons, which can be deflected by magnetic
and/or electrostatic fields, impinges on a fluorescent screen or photographic surface—used in
television, etc.; **cathodic protection,** protection of
a metal structure underground or under water
against electrolytic corrosion by making it the
cathode in an electrolytic cell. [Gr. *kathodos,*
a going down, *kata,* down, *hodos,* a way.]
**cat-hole.** See **cat.**
**catholic,** *kath'ə-lik, adj.* universal: general, embracing the whole body of Christians: orthodox,
as opposed to *heterodox* and *sectarian:* liberal,
the opposite of exclusive: belonging to the
Christian Church before the great schism between East and West, or to any church claiming
to be in historic continuity with it, esp. after the
schism the Western church, after the Reformation the Church of Rome (Roman Catholic), but
applied also, e.g., to Anglicans: relating to the
Roman Catholics.—*n.* an adherent of the R.C.
Church.—*v.t.* and *v.i.* **cathol'icise, -ize** (*-sīz*), to

*fāte, fär; mē, hûr* (her); *mīne; mōte, för; mūte; mōōn, fŏŏt; dhen* (then)

make or become Catholic.—*ns.* **Cathol'icism,** the tenets of the R.C. Church: (without *cap.*) **catholicity** (*rare*); **catholic'ity** (*-is'i-ti*), universality: liberality or breadth of view: Catholicism (*rare*); **cathol'icon** (*-kon*), a panacea; **cathol'icos,** the Patriarch of Armenia.—**Catholic (and) Apostolic,** Irvingite; **catholic creditor** (*Scots law*), one whose debt is secured over two or more subjects belonging to the debtor—e.g. over two or more heritable estates; **Catholic emancipation,** the relief of the Roman Catholics from certain vexatious penal regulations and restrictions, granted in 1829; **catholic** or **general epistles,** certain epistles in the canon addressed to the Church universal or to a large and indefinite circle of readers; **Catholic King** (*hist.*), the king of Spain; **German Catholics,** a body that broke away from the Roman Catholic Church in Germany in 1844 on the occasion of the exhibition of the Holy Coat at Trier; **Old Catholics,** a body that broke away from the Roman Catholic church in Germany in opposition to the dogma of papal infallibility proclaimed by the Vatican Council in 1870. [Gr. *katholikos,* universal—*kata,* throughout, *holos,* the whole.]

**Catiline,** *kat'i-lin, n.* the type of a daring and reckless conspirator, L. Sergius *Catilina,* whose plot to destroy Rome was foiled by Cicero, 63 B.C.—*adj.* **catilinarian** (*-li-nā'ri-ən*).

**cation, kation,** *kat'ī-ən, n.* an ion that travels towards the cathode: a positively-charged ion. [Gr. *kata,* down, *iŏn,* neut.—*pr.p.* of *ienai,* to go.]

**catkin, catling, catmint.** See **cat.**

**Catonian,** *kə-tō'ni-ən, adj.* resembling or relating to *Cato,* the Roman censor (234-149 B.C.), or Cato Uticensis (95-46 B.C.), both remarkable for gravity of manners—hence grave, severe, unbending.

**catoptric,** *kat-op'trik, adj.* relating to reflection.— *n.pl.* **catop'trics,** the part of optics which treats of reflected light. [Gr. *katoptron,* a mirror—*kata,* back, and the root of *opsomai,* I shall see.]

**cat's-tail.** See **cat.**

**cattabu,** *kat'ə-bū, n.* a cross between common cattle and zebu. [From *catt*le and *zebu.*]

**cattalo,** *kat'ə-lō, n.* a cross between the bison ('buffalo') and the domestic cow. [From *catt*le and *buff*alo.]

**cattle,** *kat'l, n.pl.* beasts of pasture, esp. oxen, bulls, and cows: sometimes also horses, sheep, etc.—**cattle grid,** in U.S. **cattle guard,** a frame of spaced bars covering a trench or depression in a road where it passes through a fence, crossable by motor vehicles or pedestrians but deterring hoofed animals; **catt'le-lift'er,** a stealer of cattle, **catt'le-lift'ing,** **catt'leman,** one who tends cattle, or who rears them on a ranch; **catt'leplague,** plague among cattle, esp. rinderpest or steppe murrain; **cattle show,** an exhibition of cattle or other domestic animals in competition for prizes. [O.Fr. *catel, chatel*—L.L. *captāle,* L. *capitāle*—*caput,* the head.]

**catty,** *kat'i, n.* the Chinese kin or pound, usually a little over 1¼ lb. avoirdupois. [Malay *kati.*]

**Caucasian,** *kö-kā'z(h)i-ən, adj.* pertaining to the *Caucasus* or the country around it.—*n.* and *adj.* as used by Blumenbach (pertaining to) one of the main ethnological divisions of mankind, by some later anthropologists, (pertaining to) the white race: now usu., in some places by law, (pertaining to) a white person.

**cauchemar,** *kōsh-mär,* (Fr.) a nightmare.

**caucus,** *kö'kəs, n.* a meeting of members of a party to nominate candidates or delegates or to decide how to vote on any question, its decision binding on those who attend (*U.S.*): in Britain, (*opprobriously*) any too-influential small group esp. in a constituency.—*v.i.* to hold a caucus: to control by means of a caucus. [Ety. dub.; perh.

John Smith's Algonkin word *Caw-cawaassough,* an adviser; perh. a corr. of '*caulkers'* meetings'.]

**caudal,** *kö'dl, adj.* pertaining to the tail.—*adjs.* **cau'dāte, -d,** tailed.—**caudal anaesthesia,** form of epidural anaesthesia. [L. *cauda,* tail.]

**caudex,** *kö'deks,* (*bot.*) *n.* the stem of a tree, esp. of a palm or tree-fern:—*pl.* **caud'icēs** (*-i-sēz*), **caud'exes.**—*n.* **caudicle,** the stalk of the pollen-masses of certain orchids. [L.]

**caudillo,** *kow-dēl'yō, n.* in Spanish-speaking countries, leader: the head of the state. [Sp.]

**caudle,** *kö'dl, n.* a warm drink, sweetened and spiced, given to the sick, esp. women in childbed. —*v.t.* to give a caudle to: to mix.—**hempen caudle** (*Shak.*), the hangman's noose. [O.Fr. *chaudel*—L. *calidus,* hot.]

**caudron,** *kö'drən, n.* (*Spens.*). Same as **cauldron.**

**caught,** *köt, pa.t.* and *pa.p.* of **catch.**

**cauk, cawk,** *kök, n.* chalk: barytes in platy crystals. [A form of **chalk.**]

**cauker.** See **calk.**

**caul,** *köl, n.* a net or covering for the head: the membrane covering the head of some infants at their birth. [O.Fr. *cale,* a little cap, prob. Celt.; cf. Ir. *calla,* a veil, hood.]

**cauld,** *köld,* (*Scot.*) *n.* a dam in a stream, a weir. [Origin obscure.]

**cauld,** *köld,* (*Scot.*) *adj.* and *n.* cold.—*adj.* **cauldrife** (*köld'rif*), apt to feel chilly: chilling, lifeless, without vigour.

**cauldron, caldron,** *köl'drən, n.* a large kettle for boiling or heating liquids. [O.Fr. *caudron*—L. *caldārium—calidus,* hot—*calēre,* to be hot.]

**cauliflower,** *ko', kö'li-flowr, n.* a variety of cabbage whose young inflorescence is eaten.—**cauliflower ear,** an ear permanently thickened by injury, esp. from boxing. [Earlier *cole-florye, colie-florie*— L.L. *cauliflōra*—L. *caulis,* cabbage; see **cole** and **flower.**]

**caulis,** *kö'lis* (L. *kow'lis*), *n.* the stem of a plant: one of the main stems at the angles of the Corinthian capital (*archit.*):—*pl.* **cau'les** (*-lēz*; *-lās*).—*adj.* **caulesc'ent,** having a stem rising above the ground.—*n.* **cau'licle,** a rudimentary stem.—*adjs.* **caulic'olous,** growing on a stem; **caulic'ūlāte.**—*ns.* **caulic'ūlus,** one of the slender stems springing from the *caules* or main stalks supporting the volutes in the Corinthian capital; **cauliflo'ry,** production of flowers on old stems from dormant buds.—*adjs.* **caul'iform,** having the form of a stem; **cauli'g'enous,** borne upon the stem; **caul'inary, cau'line,** belonging to a stem.— *n.* **cau'lōme,** a plant's stem-structure as a whole. [L. *caulis,* a stalk.]

**caulk, caik,** *kök, v.t.* to render watertight by pressing oakum, etc. into the seams.—*v.i.* (*sailor's slang*), to snooze.—*ns.* **caulk'er,** one who caulks: a dram: a big lie—also **cauk'er;** **caulk'ing.**—**caulk'ing-i'ron,** an instrument like a chisel used for pressing oakum into the seams of ships. [O.Fr. *cauquer,* to press—L. *calcāre,* to tread—*colx,* heel.]

**caulker.** See **calk** (2).

**caum, caumstane.** See **cam** (3).

**cause,** *köz, n.* that which produces an effect: that by or through which anything happens: motive: inducement: a legal action between contending parties: sake, advantage: that side of a question which is taken up by an individual or party: accusation (*Shak.*): matter, affair in general (*Shak.*).—*v.t.* to produce: to make to exist: to bring about: (*Spens.*; *infin.* **caus'en**) to give excuses for.—*conj.* (*dial.*) because (usu. **'cause**) —*adj.* **caus'al,** being the cause, that causes: relating to a cause or causes.—*n.* **causal'ity,** the relation of cause and effect: the working of a cause.—*adv.* **caus'ally.**—*ns.* **causā'tion,** the act of causing: the bringing about of an effect; the relation of cause and effect: **causā'tionism,** the principle of universal causation; **causā'tionist.**—

*adj.* **caus'ative,** causal: of the nature of, or expressing, causation.—*n.* a form of verb expressing causation.—*adv.* **caus'atively.**—*adj.* **cause'less,** without cause: without just cause.—*adv.* **cause'lessly.**—*ns.* **cause'lessness; caus'er.**—**efficient cause,** the means by which a thing took its present form; **final cause,** the end or object for which a thing is done, esp. the design of the universe; **first cause,** the original cause or creator of all; **formal cause,** the essence or idea of a thing; **have** or **show cause,** to have to give reasons for a certain line of action; **hour of cause** (*Scot.*), hour or time of trial; **make common cause** (*with*), to unite for a common object; **material cause,** that out of which a thing is framed; **occasional causes** (*occasionalism*); **secondary causes,** such as are derived from a primary or first cause; **show cause** (*Eng. law*), to argue against the confirmation of a provisional order or judgment. [Fr.,—L. *causa*.]
**cause célèbre,** *kōz sā-lebr'*, (Fr.) a very notable or famous trial.
**causerie,** *kōz'ər-ē, n.* a talk or gossip: a paragraph of chat about literature or art: a short and informal essay on any subject in a newspaper or magazine. [Fr.]
**causeway,** *kōz'wā,* **causey,** *kōz'i, n.* a raised way through a marsh or water: a pathway raised and paved with stone: a paved or cobblestoned road.—*v.t.* to pave.—*p.adjs.* **cause'-wayed, caus'eyed.** [M.E. *causee*—O.Fr. *caucie*—L.L. (*via*) *calciāta,* a trodden way—L. *calx,* heel; **causeway** is for 'causey-way'.]
**caustic,** *kös'tik, adj.* burning: bitter, severe, cutting (*fig.*).—*n.* a substance that exerts a corroding or disintegrating action on the skin and flesh: an envelope of rays of light proceeding from a fixed point and reflected (*catacaustic*) or refracted (*diacaustic*) by a surface or a curve (*math.*).—*adv.* **caus'tically.**—*n.* **causticity** (*-tis'i-ti*), quality of being caustic.—**caustic ammonia,** ammonia as a gas, or in solution; **caustic lime,** quicklime; **caustic potash,** potassium hydroxide; **caustic soda,** sodium hydroxide.—common **caustic, potash:** also **silver nitrate;** **lunar caustic,** silver nitrate in sticks for surgical use. [L. *causticus*—Gr. *kaustikos*—*kaiein,* fut. *kausein,* to burn.]
**cautel,** *kö'tl, n.* craft (*Shak.*): insidious purpose (*Shak.*): caution (*obs.*): wariness (*obs.*): a traditionary caution or written direction about the proper manner of administering the sacraments (*obs.*).—*adj.* **cau'telous,** cautious (*obs.*): insidious (*Shak.*): artful (*Shak.*). [Fr. *cautèle*—L. *cautēla*—*cavēre, cautum,* to guard against.]
**cauterise,** *kö'tər-iz,* **-ize,** *v.t.* burn with a caustic or a hot iron: to sear (*fig.*).—*ns.* **cau'ter, cau'tery,** burning with caustics or a hot iron: burning iron or caustic for burning tissue; **cauterisa'tion, -z-, cau'terism.** [Fr. *cautériser*—L.L. *cautērizāre*—Gr. *kautēr,* a hot iron—*kaiein,* to burn.]
**caution,** *kö'shən, n.* heedfulness: warning: an alarming, amusing, or astonishing person or thing (*coll.*): (also *kā'*) security, surety, bail (*Scots law*).—*v.t.* to warn to take care.—*adj.* **cau'tionary,** containing caution: given as a pledge.—*ns.* **cau'tioner;** one who cautions or advises: (also *kā'*) a surety (*Scots law*); **cautionry** (*Scots law; kā'*), the act of giving security for another.—*adj.* **cau'tious (-shəs),** possessing or using caution: watchful: prudent.—*adv.* **cau'tiously.**—*n.* **cau'tiousness.**—**caution money,** money paid in advance as security for good behaviour. [Fr.,—L. *cautiō, -ōnis*—*cavēre,* to beware.]
**cavalcade,** *kav-əl-kād', kav', n.* a train of persons on horseback: a parade.—*v.i.* to go in a cavalcade. [Fr., through It. and L.L.—L. *caballus,* a horse.]
**cavalier,** *kav-əl-ēr', n.* a knight: a Royalist in the

great Civil War: a swaggering fellow: a gallant or gentleman in attendance upon a lady, as her escort or partner in a dance or the like: in military fortification, a raised work so situated as to command the neighbouring country.—*adj.* like a cavalier: gay: war-like: haughty, supercilious, free-and-easy, off-hand.—*v.i.* to act as cavalier.—*adjs.* **cavalier'ish, cavalier'ly,** like, characteristic of, a cavalier.—*n.* **cavalier'ism.**—*adv.* **cavalier'ly,** off-hand: with supercilious disregard or curtness.—*n.* **cavaliero** (*kav-äl-yā'rō*; Sp. *caballero*). [Fr.,—It. *cavallo*; see **cavalcade.**]
**cavaliere servente,** *kä-vä-lē-er'e ser-ven'te,* (It.) a gallant who waits with fantastic devotion upon a married woman.
**cavally,** *kə-val'i, n.* an American fish of the scad family. [Sp. and Port. *cavalla,* mackerel.]
**cavalry,** *kav'əl-ri, n.* horse-soldiers: a troop of horse or horsemen.—*n.* **cav'alryman.** [Fr. *cavallerie*—It. *cavalleria*—L. *caballārius,* horseman—*caballus,* horse.]
**cavass.** See **kavass.**
**cavatina,** *kav-ät-ē'na, n.* a melody with no second part or da capo: loosely, a short operatic air, of a smooth and melodious character, often part of a grand scena. [It.]
**cave,** *kāv, n.* a hollow place in a rock: a small faction of seceders from a political party (from the Cave of Adullam, 1 Sam. xxii. 1-2).—*v.t.* to hollow out.—*v.i.* to lodge in a cave.—*n.* **cav'ing** (in), falling into a hollow: yielding.—**cave'-bear** (*Ursus spelaeus*), a Pleistocene bear found fossil in caves; **cave'-dweller,** one who lives in a cave, esp. one of the Stone Age of pre-historic times: **cave'-earth',** a fine deposit on cave floors; **cave'man,** a cave-dweller: a modern male of primitive ways (*coll.*).—**cave in,** to slip, to fall into a hollow: to yield to outside pressure, to give way, collapse. [Fr. *cave*—L. *cavus,* hollow.]
**cave,** *kav'i, kāv'i, v.i.* or *interj.* (*schoolboy slang*) beware.—*n.* **caveat** (*kā'vi-at*), a notice or warning: a formal warning, entered in the books of a court or public office, that no step be taken in a particular matter without notice to the person lodging the caveat. [L. *căvē,* imperat. sing., *căvĕat,* 3rd sing. pres. subj., of *căvēre,* to take care.]
**caveat actor,** *kā'vi-at,* (*ka've-at, -we-*) *ak'tör,* (L.) let the doer beware; **caveat emptor** (*emp'tör*), it is the buyer's look-out.
**cave canem,** *kā'vi* (*ka'vä, -wä*) *kā'nəm* (*ka'nem*), (L.) beware of the dog, a frequent inscription on Roman thresholds.
**cavel,** *kāv'l,* (*Scot.*) *n.* a piece of wood, etc., used in casting lots: a lot. [Du. *kavel.*]
**cavendish,** *kav'ən-dish, n.* tobacco moistened and pressed into quadrangular cakes. [Possibly from the name of the original manufacturer.]
**cavendo tutus,** *kā-, ka-ven'dō* (*-wen'*) *tū'təs* (*tōō'tōōs*), (L.) safe through taking care.
**cavern,** *kav'ərn, n.* a deep hollow place in rocks.—*v.t.* to put in a cavern: to hollow out.—*adjs.* **cav'erned,** full of caverns: dwelling in a cavern; **cav'ernous,** hollow: full of caverns.—*adv.* **cav'ernously.**—*adj.* **cav'ern'ŭlous,** full of little cavities. [Fr. *caverne*—L. *caverna*—*cavus,* hollow.]
**cavesson,** *kav'əs-ən, n.* a nose-band for a horse. [Fr. *caveçon*—[It. *cavezzone*—L. *capitia, capitium,* a head-covering.]
**cavetto,** *ka-vet'tō, n.* a hollowed moulding whose curvature is the quarter of a circle, used chiefly in cornices. [It.: dim. of *cavo*—L. *cavus,* hollow.]
**caviare, caviar,** *kav'i-är, kav-i-är',* also *kav-yär',* (*Shak.*) **caviar'ie,** (*obs.*) **cavier** (*kə-vēr'), n.* salted roe of the sturgeon, etc.: something whose flavour is too fine for the vulgar taste (*fig.*). [Prob. the 16th-cent. It. *caviale;* the Turk. *khāvyār* is prob. borrowed.]

**cavicorn**, *kav'i-körn*, *adj.* hollow-horned, as a ruminant.—*n.* one of the Cavicor'nia, or Bovidae. [L. *cavus*, hollow, *cornū*, a horn.]

**cavie**, *kāv'i*, *n.* a hen-coop or cage. [Cf. Du. *kevie*, Ger. *käfig*—L. *cavus*.]

**cavil**, *kav'il*, *v.t.* to make empty, trifling objections: to use false arguments:—*pr.p.* **cav'illing**; *pa.t.* and *pa.p.* **cav'illed**.—*n.* a frivolous objection.— *ns.* **cavillā'tion**, **cav'illing**; **cav'iller**. [O.Fr. *caviller*—L. *cavillāri*, to practise jesting.]

**cavity**, *kav'it-i*, *n.* a hollow: a hollow place: hollowness.—*n.* **cavitā'tion**, the formation of cavities in a structure, or of gas bubbles in a liquid, or of a vacuum, or of a partial vacuum as between a body moving in a fluid and the fluid: a cavity.—*adj.* **cav'itied**.—**cavity wall**, a wall consisting of two layers with a space between. [L. *cavitās*—*cavus*, hollow.]

**cavo-rilievo**, *kä'vō-rē-lyä'vō*, *n.* a kind of relief in which the highest surface is level with the plane of the original stone, which is left round the outlines of the design. [It. *cavo*, hollow, *rilievo*, relief; see **cave** and **relief**.]

**cavort**, *kə-vört'*, *v.i.* to frolic, bound. [Explained as a corr. of **curvet**.]

**cavy**, *kāv'i*, *n.* the guinea-pig genus (*Cavia*) of rodents. [*Cabiai*, native name in French Guiana.]

**caw**, *kö*, *v.i.* to cry as a crow.—*n.* the cry of a crow—also **kaw**.—*n.* **caw'ing**. [From the sound.]

**cawk.** See **cauk, caulk**.

**cawker.** Same as **calker**.

**caxon**, *kak'sən*, *n.* a kind of wig formerly worn. [Origin obscure.]

**Caxton**, *kaks'tən*, *n.* a book printed by William *Caxton* (1422-91), the first English printer: a kind of printing-type in imitation of Caxton's.

**cay**, *kā*, *n.* a low islet, the same as **key**. [Sp. *cayo*.]

**cayenne**, *kā-en'*, *n.* a very pungent red pepper (**cay'enne-pepp'er**), made from several species of Capsicum.—*adj.* **cayenned'**, seasoned with cayenne. [Usually referred to *Cayenne* in French Guiana; but prob. from Tupí.]

**cayman**, *kā'mən*, *n.* an alligator, esp. of South American kinds:—*pl.* **caymans**. [Sp. *caimán*, most prob. Carib.]

**cayuse**, *ki-ūs'*, (*U.S.*) *n.* an Indian pony: a small or poor horse. [Amer. Indian.]

**cazique**, a form of **cacique**.

**Ceanothus**, *sē-ə-nō'thəs*, *n.* an American genus of shrubs of the buckthorn family. [Gr. *keanōthos*, corn-thistle.]

**cease**, *sēs*, *v.t.* and *v.i.* to give over: to stop: to end.—*n.* end: cessation.—*adj.* **cease'less**, without ceasing: incessant.—*adv.* **cease'lessly.**—*n.* **ceas'ing.**—**cease'-fire**, an order to cease firing: an agreed cessation of active hostilities. [Fr. *cesser*—L. *cessāre*, give over—*cēdĕrε*, yield.]

**ceaze**, an obs. spelling of **seize**.

**cebadilla.** See **sabadilla**.

**Cebus**, *sē'bus*, *n.* generic name of the Capuchin monkeys.—*n.pl.* **Cebidae** (*seb'i-dē*) a family including all the New World monkeys except the marmosets. [Gr. *kēbos*, a kind of monkey.]

**Cecidomyia**, *ses-id-o-mī'i-ə*, *n.* a gall-midge, a genus of flies destructive to vegetation. [Gr. *kēkis, -idos*, a gall, *myia*, a fly.]

**cecils**, *ses'*, *sēs'ilz*, *n.pl.* minced meat, breadcrumbs, onions, etc., made into balls and fried. [Ety. dub.]

**cecity**, *sē'si-ti*, *n.* blindness.—*n.* **cecutiency** (*si-kū'shyən-si*), a tendency to blindness. [L. *caecus*, blind.]

**Cecropia**, *si-krō'pi-a*, *n.* a tropical American genus of trees of the mulberry family, some with hollow stems that give food and housing to a protective garrison of ants. [Named after the mythical Attic King *Cecrops* (Gr. *Kekrōps*).]

**cecum.** U.S. spelling of **caecum**.

**cedar**, *sē'dər*, *n.* a large evergreen coniferous tree (*Cedrus*, including *Cedar of Lebanon, Atlantic cedar*, and *deodar*) remarkable for the durability and fragrance of its wood; applied also to many more or less similar trees, as the Barbados cedar, properly a juniper, and the Bastard Barbados cedar, properly a Cedrela.—*adj.* made of cedar.—*adjs.* **cē'dared**, covered with cedars; **cē'darn**, of cedar; **cē'drine**, belonging to the cedar-tree.— **cē'dar-bird**, an American waxwing; **cedar-nut**, the seed of the cembra pine. [L. *cedrus*—Gr. *kedros*.]

**cede**, *sēd*, *v.t.* to yield or give up to another.—*v.i.* to give way. [L. *cēdĕre, cēssum*, to yield, to give up.]

**cedi**, *sed'i*, *n.* (new cedi) unit of Ghana's decimal currency, equal to 100 (new) pesewas:—*pl.* **ced'is.**

**cedilla**, *se-dil'ə*, *n.* a mark placed under the letter c (thus ç), originally a subscript Z, formerly used in Spanish to indicate that it had the sound of (Spanish) Z where that of K would be expected, still used esp. in French and Portuguese to indicate an S- sound as before *a, o, u*. [Sp. (Fr. *cédille*, It. *zediglia*), all dims. from *zēta*, the Greek name of *z*. See **z**.]

**cedrate**, *sē'drāt*, *n.* citron. [Fr. *cédrat*—L. *citrus*.]

**Cedrela**, *sed-rē'la*, *n.* a tropical genus of Meliaceae, allied to mahogany.—*adj.* **cedrelā'ceous.** [Sp.— dim. of *cedro, cedra*, cedar; see **cedar**.]

**cedula**, *sed'ū-lə*, *n.* a S. American promissory-note or mortgage-bond on lands. [Sp.; cf. **schedule**.]

**cee-spring**, **c-spring**, *sē'spring*, *n.* a spring in the shape of a C to support the frame of a carriage.

**ceil**, *sēl*, *v.t.* to overlay the inner roof of: to overlay or line: to provide with a ceiling.—*n.* **ceil'ing**, the inner roof of a room: the limiting height of aircraft: an upper limit.—*adj.* **ceil'inged**, having a ceiling. [Prob. conn. with Fr. *ciel*, It. *cielo*, L.L. *caelum*, a canopy.]

**ceilidh**, *kā'li*, *n.* an informal evening of song and story. [Gael., a visit.]

**ceinture**, *sē-tür*, (Fr.) a girdle, belt.

**celadon**, *sel'ə-don*, *n.* a pale-green colour: a Chinese pottery glaze of the colour. [Fr., perh. after a character in D'Urfé's *Astrée*.]

**celandine**, *sel'an-din*, *n.* swallow-wort (*Chelidonium majus*; greater celandine) a plant of the poppy family, supposed to flower when the swallows came, and to perish when they went: also pilewort (*Ranunculus Ficaria*; lesser celandine). [O.Fr. *celidoine*—Gr. *chelidonion*—*chelidōn*, a swallow.]

**celebrate**, *sel'i-brāt*, *v.t.* to make famous: to distinguish by solemn ceremonies, as a festival or an event: to perform with proper rites and ceremonies, as mass, the eucharist, marriage, etc.: to publish the praises of.—*n.* **cel'ebrant**, one who celebrates: the principal officiant at a rite.—*adj.* **cel'ebrated**, distinguished: famous.— *ns.* **celebrā'tion**, act of celebrating: any solemn ceremony: an extolling; **cel'ebrātor**; **celebrity** (*si-leb'ri-ti*), the condition of being celebrated: fame: notoriety: a person of distinction or fame. [L. *celebrāre, -ātum*—*celeber*, frequented.]

**celerity**, *si-ler'i-ti*, *n.* quickness: rapidity of motion. [Fr. *célérité*—L. *celeritās*—*celer*, quick.]

**celery**, *sel'ər-i*, *n.* an umbelliferous plant (*Apium graveolens*) whose blanched leaf-stalks are eaten cooked or uncooked.—*n.* **celeriac** (*si-ler'i-ak*), a turnip-rooted variety of celery. [Fr. *céleri*—Gr. *selinon*, parsley.]

**celesta**, *si-les'tə*, *n.* a keyboard instrument in which the hammers strike steel plates over wooden resonators. [Fr. *céleste*, heavenly.]

**celeste**, *si-lest'*, *adj.* sky-blue.—*n.* voix céleste, a kind of soft pedal on a piano. [Fr. *céleste*.)

**celestial**, *si-lest'yəl*, *adj.* heavenly: dwelling in heaven: in the visible heavens: Chinese (*coll.*).

—*n.* an inhabitant of heaven: a Chinese.—*adv.* **celest'ially.**—*n.* **celestine** (*sel'is-tēn, -tin, -tin*), a mineral, strontium sulphate, sometimes skyblue.—the **Celestial Empire** (*hist.*), China. [Through French from L. *caelestis—caelum,* heaven.]

**Celestine,** *sel'is-tin,* or *sil-es'tin, n.* a monk of an order founded 1264 by Pietro da Morrone, afterwards Pope *Celestine* V.

**celiac.** Same as **coeliac.**

**celibacy,** *sel'i-bəs-i, n.* unmarried state, esp. under a vow.—*adjs.* **celibatā'rian,** favouring celibacy; **cel'ibate,** living single.—*n.* one who is unmarried, or bound not to marry. [L. *caelebs,* single.]

**cell,** *sel, n.* a small room in a prison, monastery, etc.: a monastery or nunnery dependent on another: a hermit's one-roomed dwelling: a small cavity: a vessel with electrodes and an electrolyte, for electrolysis or for generating an electric current by chemical action: a unit-mass of living matter, whether walled or unwalled, by itself or associated with others in a higher unity: a unit group, esp. of communist propagandists: a part of the atmosphere that behaves as a unit (*meteor.*): the cavity containing pollen in an anther lobe (*bot.*): one chamber in an ovary (*bot.*): one of the spaces into which the wing of an insect is divided (*zool.*): unit of homogenous reactivity in a nuclear reactor core: unit of storage in computing.—*n.* **cell'a,** the naos or inner chamber of a temple.—*adjs.* **celled,** having cells, cellular; **cellif'erous,** having or producing cells; **cell'ūlar,** consisting of, characterised by, or containing cells or compartments: composed of ordinary cells without vessels (as the lower cryptogams): porous: of open texture; **cell'u-lāted.**—*n.* **cell'ule,** a little cell.—*adj.* **cellulif'erous,** having or producing little cells.—*ns.* **cellulī'tis,** spreading infection of subcutaneous tissue with pyogenic bacteria; **cell'uloid,** a thermoplastic, made from nitro-cellulose, camphor, and alcohol, which is elastic and very strong.—*adj.* **cell'ulose,** containing cells.—*n.* a carbohydrate forming the chief component of cell-walls of plants and of wood (cotton down, linen fibre, wood pulp being almost pure cellulose): extended to cellulose acetate, cellulose nitrate, etc., compounds used in making artificial silk, etc.—*adj.* **cellulōs'ic,** containing, or derived from cellulose.—*n.* a compound or substance containing cellulose. [O.Fr. *celle*—L. *cella,* conn. with *celāre,* to cover.]

**cellar,** *sel'ər, n.* any underground room or vault: a room for storing wine, beer, coal, etc.: a stock of wine.—*v.t.* to store in a cellar.—*ns.* **cell'arage,** cellars: charge for storing in cellars; **cell'arer, cell'arist,** one who has charge of the cellar: an officer in a monastery who looks after the provisions; **cell'aret,** a case for holding bottles.— *adj.* **cell'arous** (*Dickens*), belonging to a cellar: excavated: sunken.—**cell'ar-book,** a record of wines kept in a cellar; **cell'ar-flap,** a plate covering an entrance to a cellar; **cell'arman,** one who has the care of a cellar. [O.Fr. *celier*—L. *cellārium—cella.*]

**cellar.** See **saltcellar.**

**cello,** *chel'ō,* for **violoncello:** sometimes written **'cello.**—**cellist, 'cellist,** for **violoncellist.**

**celluloid, cellulose.** See **cell.**

**cellophane,** *sel'ō-fān, n.* a tough, transparent, paperlike wrapping material made from viscose. [Orig. trademark—**cell**(ul)**o**(**se**), and Gr. *phainein,* to show.]

**celsitude,** *sels'i-tūd, n.* loftiness. [L. *celsitūdō—celsus,* lofty.]

**Celsius.** See *cel'si-us.* See **centigrade.**

**celt,** *selt, n.* a prehistoric axe-like instrument. [Founded on *celte,* perh. a misreading for *certe* (surely), in the Vulgate, Job, xix. 24, taken to be from a supposed L. word *celtes,* a chisel.]

**Celt,** *kelt, selt, n.* a Gaul (*hist.*): extended to include members of other Celtic-speaking or recently Celtic-speaking peoples—also **Kelt.**— *adj.* **Celt'ic, Kelt'ic,** pertaining to the Celts: of a branch of the Indo-Germanic family of languages including Breton, Welsh, Cornish, Irish, Gaelic, Manx.—*ns.* **Celt'icism, Kelt'icism,** a Celtic idiom or custom; **Celtomā'nia, Keltomā'nia.**—*adjs.* **P-Celtic** (or **-Keltic**), **Q-Celtic** (or **-Keltic**), pertaining respectively to one of the Celtic languages in which Indo-Germanic *qu* became *p* and to one in which *qu* became *q,* later *k* (written *c*).—*ns.* **P-Celt, -Kelt; Q-Celt, -Kelt.**—**Celtic cross,** a type varying from a cross incised on a flat slate to an elaborate monument carved in the style common to the Celts, Scandinavians, and Northumbrian Angles, sometimes miscalled Runic cross. [L. *Celtae;* Gr. *Keltoi* or *Keltai.*]

**cembalo,** *chem'bä-lō, n.* a musical instrument with strings struck by hammers, a dulcimer: a similar instrument with a keyboard, as a harpsichord or pianoforte.—*n.* **cembalist** (*chem'* or *sem'*). [It.; see **cymbal.**]

**cembra,** *sem'brə, n.* (also **cembra pine),** the Swiss stone-pine. [Ger. dial. *zember*=*zimmer,* timber.]

**cement,** *si-ment',* formerly *sem'ənt, n.* anything that makes two bodies stick together: mortar: a bond of union: the bony substance forming the outer layer of the root of a tooth.—*v.t.* to unite with cement: to join firmly.—*ns.* **cementation** (*sem-ən-tā'shən*), the act of cementing: the process of impregnating the surface of one substance with another by surrounding it with powder and heating, as in steel-making, case-hardening, turning glass into porcelain: precipitation: process of injecting fluid cement mixture for strengthening purposes; **cement'ite,** an iron carbide, $Fe_3C$.—*adjs.* **cement'atory, cementi'-tious,** having the quality of cementing or uniting firmly.—**cement'-copper,** copper obtained by precipitation; **cement gun,** an apparatus for spraying fine concrete or cement mortar; **cement'-stone,** a clayey limestone, suitable for making hydraulic cement; **cement'-water,** water containing copper salts, as in copper mines. [O.Fr. *ciment*—L. *caementum,* chip of stone used to fill up in building a wall, *caedimentum—caedēre,* to cut.]

**cemetery,** *sem'i-tri, n.* a burying-ground. [L.L. *coemētērium*—Gr. *koimētērion,* sleeping-place.]

**cemitare,** Spenser's spelling of **scimitar.**

**cenacle,** *sen'ə-kl, n.* a supper-room, esp. that in which the Last Supper was eaten by Christ and the apostles: a coterie, or its meeting-place. [Fr. *cénacle*—L. *cēnāculum—cēna,* supper.]

**cenesthesis.** Same as **coenaesthesis.**

**cendré,** *sā-drā,* (Fr.) ash-blond.

**cenobite.** Same as **coenobite.**

**cenotaph,** *sen'ō-täf, n.* a sepulchral monument without a burial. [Gr. *kenotaphion—kenos,* empty, and *taphos,* a tomb.]

**Cenozoic,** *sē-nō-zō'ik.* Same as **Cainozoic.**

**cense,** *sens, v.t.* to burn incense before. [*incense.*]

**cense,** *sens,* (*obs.*) *v.t.* to think: to assess.—*n.* a public rate of tax: rank, condition. [L. *cēnsēre,* to estimate.]

**censer,** *sens'ər, n.* a pan in which incense is burned. [O.Fr. *censier, encenser* (mod. *encensoir*)—L.L. *incēnsorium*—L. *incendēre, incēnsum,* to burn.]

**censor,** *sen'sör,* or *-sər, n.* a magistrate who kept account of the property of Roman citizens, imposed taxes, and watched over their morals: an official with analogous functions elsewhere: any of several university officials: an official who examines books, papers, telegrams, letters, films, etc., with powers to delete material, or to forbid publication, delivery, or showing: an unconscious inhibitive mechanism in the mind, that prevents what is painful to conscious aims from emerging into consciousness (*psych.*): one who

*fāte, fär; mē, hûr* (her); *mīne; mōte, för; mūte; mōōn, fōōt; dhen* (then)

censures or blames.—*v.t.* to subject to censorial examination or condemnation.—*adjs.* **censorial** (-ō'ri-əl, -ō'), belonging to a censor, or to the correction of public morals; **censo'rian,** censorial; **censo'rious,** expressing censure: fault-finding.— *adv.* **censo'riously.**—*ns.* **censo'riousness; cen'sorship,** office of censor: time during which he holds office. [L. *cēnsor,* -*ōris.*]
**censor morum,** *sen'sər mōr'əm, kān'sor mō'rōom,* (L.) censor of morals.
**censure,** *sen'shər, n.* an opinion or judgment (formerly general, now unfavourable only): blame: reproof.—*v.t.* to form or give an opinion or judgment (now unfavourable) of: to blame: to condemn as wrong: to sentence (*Shak.*).— *adj.* **cen'surable,** deserving of censure: blamable. —*n.* **cen'surableness.**—*adv.* **cen'surably.** [L. *cēnsūra—cēnsēre,* to estimate.]
**census,** *sen'səs, n.* an official enumeration of inhabitants with statistics relating to them.—*adj.* **cen'sual,** relating to or containing a census. [L. *cēnsus,* -*ūs,* a register.]
**cent,** *sent, n.* a hundredth part, esp. of a dollar: a coin of that value.—*ns.* **cent'age,** rate by the hundred: **cent'al,** a weight of 100 lb.—**per cent,** by the hundred. [L. *centum,* a hundred.]
**centaur,** *sen'tör, n.* a fabulous monster, half man, half horse.—*adj.* **centau'rian.**—*n.* **Centaur'us,** a southern constellation containing Alpha Centauri and Beta Centauri. [Gr. *kentauros.*]
**centaury,** *sen'tö-ri, n.* a name applied to plants of the gentianaceous genera Erythraea and Chlora, and to the composite genus Centaurea (knapweed, etc.). [The *centaur* Chiron is said to have healed a wound with *kentaurion,* one of these plants.]
**centavo,** *sen-tä'vō, n.* a Portuguese and Brazilian money of account, 100 centavos making 1 escudo or cruzeiro. [Port.]
**centavo,** *sen-tä'vō, n.* a Spanish American coin and money of account. [Sp.]
**centenary,** *sen-tēn'ər-i* (also *-ten'* or *sen'*), *n.* a hundred: a century or hundred years: a centennial.—*adj.* pertaining to a hundred.—*ns.* **centenā'rian,** one who is a hundred years old; **centenā'rianism; centenier** (*sen'ten-ēr*), a centurion; a police-officer in Jersey. [L. *centēnārius* —*centēni,* a hundred each—*centum.*]
**centennial,** *sen-ten'yəl, adj.* happening once in a hundred years: having lasted a hundred years.— *n.* a hundredth anniversary. [L. *centum,* a hundred, *annus,* a year.]
**center,** American spelling of **centre.**
**center,** *sen'tər, n.* (*Shak.*) *n.* cincture, waist-belt.
**centering, centreing,** *sen'tər-ing,* (*archit.*) *n.* the framework upon which an arch or vault of stone, brick, or iron is supported during its construction.
**centesimal,** *sen-tes'i-məl, adj.* hundredth: designating a centigrade thermometer.—*adv.* **centes'imally.** [L. *centēsimus—centum.*]
**centesis,** *sen-tē'sis, n.* (*pl.* **-ses, -sēz.**) in surgery, a puncture (usu. used in compound terms). [Gr. *kentēsis—kentein,* to prick.]
**centi-,** *sen-ti-,* in composition 1/100 of the unit named. [L. *centum,* a hundred.]
**centiare,** *sen'ti-är, n.* the hundredth part of an are, 1·196 sq. yards. [L. *centum,* a hundred, *area,* area.]
**centigrade,** *sen'ti-grād, adj.* having a hundred degrees: divided into a hundred degrees, as the centigrade thermometer constructed by Celsius (1701-44), in which freezing-point of water is zero and boiling-point is 100° (to convert degrees Celsius or centigrade to Fahrenheit multiply by $\frac{9}{5}$, and add 32). [L. *centum,* and *gradus,* a step, a degree.]
**centigram(me),** *sen'ti-gram, n.* the hundredth part of a gram(me). [Fr.,—L. *centum,* a hundred, and **gram(me).**]
**centilitre,** *sen'ti-lē-tər, n.* the hundredth part of a

litre, 10 cubic centimetres. [Fr.,—L. *centum,* a hundred, and **litre.**]
**centillion,** *sen-til'yən, n.* the hundredth power of a million—i.e. 1 followed by 600 ciphers: in U.S. the hundredth power of a thousand—i.e. 1 followed by 300 ciphers.—*n.* **centill'ionth.** [L. *centum,* a hundred, and the ending of **million.**]
**centime,** *sä-tēm, n.* a French coin, 1/100 of a franc: other coins 1/100 of their standard. [Fr.,—L. *centesimum,* a hundredth.]
**centimetre, centimeter,** *sen'ti-mē-tər, n.* a lineal measure, the hundredth part of a metre.— **centimetre-gram(me)-second** (contr. C.G.S., CGS) system, a system of scientific measurement with the centimetre, etc., as units of length, mass, time. [Fr.,—L. *centum,* a hundred. and **metre.**]
**centinel(l),** obs. spellings ot **sentinel.**—**centinel** (private), a private soldier.
**centipede,** *sen'ti-pēd, n.* any myriapod of the class Chilopoda, carnivorous flattened animals with many joints, most of which bear one pair of legs. [L. *centum,* a hundred, and *pēs, pedis,* a foot.]
**centner,** *sent'nər, n.* a hundredweight, usually of 50 kg. [Ger.,—L. *centēnārius;* cf. **centenary.**]
**cento,** *sen'tō, n.* a poem manufactured by putting together verses or passages of one author, or of several authors, so as to make a new meaning: a composition formed by joining scraps from other authors: a mere string of commonplace phrases and quotations:—*pl.* usually **cen'tos.**—*adj.* **cen'tonate** (*bot.*), blotched.—*ns.* **cen'toist, cen'tonist.** [L. *centō,* -*ōnis,* Gr. *kentrōn,* patchwork.]
**centonel(l),** Spenserian spellings of **sentinel.**
**centre** (*U.S.* center), *sen'tər, n.* the middle point of anything, esp. a circle or sphere: the middle: a fixed point of reference: the point toward which all things move or are drawn: a nucleus: a resort: the chief leader of an organisation— head-centre: a player in a central position: a centre-forward: the men of moderate political opinions in the French Chamber, sitting right in front of the president: the Ultramontane party in Germany.—*v.t.* to place on or collect to a centre.—*v.i.* to be placed in the middle: to have a centre: to lie or move in relation to a centre:— *pr.p.* **cen'tring, cen'tering;** *pa.t.* and *pa.p.* **cen'tred, cen'tered.**—*adj.* **cen'tral,** belonging to, in, or near, the centre: principal, dominant.— *ns.* **centralisā'tion, -izā'tion, cen'tralism,** the tendency to administer by the sovereign or central government matters which would be otherwise under local management.—*v.t.* **cen'tralise, -ize,** to draw to or concentrate at a centre.—*n.* **centrality** (*-tral'i-ti*), central position. —*adv.* **cen'trally.**—*adjs.* **cen'tric, terete** (*bot.*): relating to, placed in, or containing the centre; **cen'trical.**—*adv.* **cen'trically.**—*ns.* **cen'tricalness, centricity** (*-tris'i-ti*); **cen'tring** (see **centering**); **cen'trum,** the body of a vertebra.—**central conic,** a conic section that has a centre—ellipse or hyperbola; **central fire,** of a cartridge having the fulminate in the centre of the base; **central forces,** forces causing an acceleration towards or from a fixed point, the centre of force; **central heating,** a system of heating a building by water, steam or warm air conducted throughout the building from one point; **cen'tre-bit,** a joiner's tool, turning on a centre, for boring circular holes— one of the chief tools of the burglar; **cen'treboard,** a movable plate, fitted to drop below the keel of a racing yacht; **cen'tre-for'ward,** in association football and hockey, the central player among the forwards; **cen'tre-half (-back),** the central player among the half-backs; **cen'trepiece,** an ornament for the middle of a table, ceiling, etc.; **cen'tre-rail,** a rail between the ordinary rails; **central nervous system** (*zool.*), the main ganglia of the nervous system with their associated nerve cords; **Central Powers,** in and before the war of 1914-18, the German

Neutral vowels in unaccented syllables: *el'ə-mənt;* for certain sounds in foreign words, see p. viii

Empire and Austria-Hungary; **central to**, important for the understanding or working of; **centre of attraction**, the point to which bodies tend by the force of gravity or the like; **centre of buoyancy**, or **displacement**, the centre of gravity of the fluid displaced; **centre of gravity**, the point at which the weight of a body may be supposed to act; **centre of inertia**, or **mass**, the point through which any plane divides a body into two parts of equal mass; **centre of oscillation**, the point in a pendulum such that, if all the matter were concentrated there, the pendulum would have the same period; **centre of percussion**, the point where the direction of a blow meets the plane in which lie the centre of inertia and a possible axis of rotation such that the blow imparts a rotation without pressure on the axis; **centre of pressure**, the point on an immersed surface at which the pressure resultant may be taken to act; **centre of symmetry**, a point in a figure such that any straight line through it meets the figure in two points at equal distances on either side. [Fr.,—L. *centrum*—Gr. *kentron*, a sharp point.]

**centri-**, *sen-tri'*, *sen'tri-*, **centro-**, *sen'tro-*, in composition, centre.—*adj.* **centrifugal** (*sen-trif'ū-gəl*; L. *fugĕre*, to flee from), tending away from a centre: efferent: proceeding in development from the apex towards the base (*bot.*): using, or produced by centrifugal force.—*v.t.* **centrif'-ugalise**, **-ize**, to subject to centrifugal force.—*adv.* **centrif'ugally.**—*n.* **cen'trifuge** (*-fūj*; also **centrifugal machine**), a machine which, by rapid rotation, separates substances of different densities—used in industry, biochemistry, etc.—*v.t.* to subject to such rotation.—*ns.* **centrifugation** (*-fū-gā'shən*), **centrif'ugence** (*-ū-jəns*), centrifugal tendency or force.—**centrifugal force**, the resistance of a revolving body, by virtue of its inertia, to an acceleration towards the centre, equal and opposite to the constraining force.—*adj.* **centrip'etal** (L. *petĕre*, to seek), tending towards a centre: afferent: proceeding from base towards apex.—*n.* **centrip'etalism.**—*adjs.* **centrobaric** (*-bar'ik*; Gr. *baros*, weight), relating to the centre of gravity; **centrocli'nal** (Gr. *klinein*, to lean; *geol.*) dipping towards a centre from all directions.—*ns.* **cen'trode** (Gr. *hodos*, a path), a locus traced out by the successive positions of an instantaneous centre of pure rotation; **cen'troid** (Gr. *eidos*, form), the point where the medians of a triangle intersect; **cen'trosome** (Gr. *sōma*, a body), a small body found in the protoplasm of a cell, forming by division the two poles of the mitotic spindle; **cen'trosphere**, the barysphere. [Gr. *kentron* and L. *centrum* (from Gr.) a sharp point.]

**centry**, *sen'tri*, *n.* centre (*Shak.*): centering (*obs.*).

**centry**, an obs. spelling of **sentry**.

**centum**, *sen'təm*, *ken'tŏom*, a hundred.—**centum languages**, the group of Indo-Germanic languages in which an original palatal consonant appears as a guttural (as in L. *centum*, hundred); cf. **satem languages**; **centumvir** (*sen-tum'vir*; L. *vir*, a man), one of the Roman judges chosen annually for civil suits, orig. 105 in number (three from each of the thirty-five tribes):—*pl.* **centum'-viri.**—*n.* **centum'virate**. [L. *centum*, a hundred.]

**centuple**, *sen'tū-pl*, *adj.* hundredfold.—*v.t.* to multiply or increase a hundred times.—*n.* **centuplica'tion.**—*adj.* **centū'plicate.**—*n.* one of a hundred like things or copies.—*v.t.* to centuple. [L. *centuplus* and *centuplex*—*centum*, *plicāre*, to fold.]

**century**, *sen'tū-ri*, *n.* a set or series of a hundred, as Roman soldiers, runs at cricket, or miles ridden, or consecutive years (esp. reckoned from the conventionally accepted date of Christ's birth).—*adj.* **centūr'ial.**—*ns.* **centuria'tion**, division into hundreds; **centū'riātor**, one of a company of

16th-century Reformed divines of Magdeburg who compiled a church history in 13 vols., each volume covering a century; **centū'rion**, the commander of a century: one who has scored or achieved a hundred in any way.—**century plant** (see agave). [L. *centuria*, a century—*centum*, a hundred.]

**ceorl**, *chä'örl*, *kā'örl*, *n.* before the Norman Conquest an ordinary freeman not of noble birth. [O.E. *ceorl*; see **churl**.]

**cephal-**, *sef'əl-*, *si-fal'-*, *kef'al-*, in composition, head.—*adjs.* **ceph'alate**, having a head; **cephal'ic**, of, belonging to, the head: for curing pains in the head.—*n.* a remedy for head-pains.—*adj.* **ceph'alous**, having a head.—*ns.* **cephalag'ra** (Gr. *agrā*, a catching), gout in the head; **cephalalgia** (Gr. *algos*, pain), headache.—*adj.* **cephalal'gic.**—*ns.* **Cephalas'pis** (Gr. *aspis*, shield), an Upper Silurian and Old Red Sandstone genus of fishes or fishlike animals (ostracoderms) with a head-shield; **cephalic index**, the ratio of the breadth to the length of the skull expressed as a percentage; **cephali'tis**, inflammation of the brain.—*n.pl.* **Cephalochorda** (*-ō-kör'da*; Gr. *chordē*, cord), a lowly class of chordate animals in which the persisting notochord projects beyond the nerve-cord to the end of the snout—the lancelets or amphioxus.—*ns.* **ceph'alopod** (*-pod*; Gr. *pous*, *podos*, foot), a member of the **Cephalopoda** (*-op'od-a*), the highest class of molluscs, usu. large animals, exclusively marine, with the foot modified into arms surrounding the mouth—cuttle-fish, etc.; **cephalothō'rax**, the fused head and thorax in some arthropods; **cephalotomy** (*kef-al-ot'ə-mi*; Gr. *tomē*, a cut), the dissection of the head. [Gr. *kephalē*, head.]

**Cepheus**, *sē'fūs*, *n.* a northern constellation named after Andromeda's father.—*n.* **cepheid** (*sē'fē-id*), any star of the type of the star δ Cephei ('classical' cepheid) or of a similar short-period 'cluster-type', from whose rhythmically varying brightness its distance can be inferred—useful in estimating the dimensions of the Milky Way and the distances of extragalactic bodies. [Gr. *Kēpheus*.]

**ceramic**, **keramic**, *se-* or *ke-ram'ik adj.* pertaining to a ceramic or to ceramics: made of a ceramic.—*ns.* **ceramic**, any product that is first shaped and then hardened by means of heat, or the material from which it is formed—including not only traditional potter's clays but also a large range of new dielectric materials: (*pl.*; treated as *sing.*) the potter's art: articles made of ceramic material; **ceram'ist**, one who makes a scientific study of clays and other ceramic materials, or who puts them to practical use.—**cer'amet**, a cermet; **ceramog'raphy**, description or study of pottery; **cer'met**, a combination of ceramic particles and a *met*al matrix. [Gr. *keramos*, potter's earth.]

**cerargyrite**, *ser-är'jar-it*, *n.* horn-silver—a hornlike mineral, silver chloride. [Gr. *keras*, horn, *argyros*, silver.]

**cerasin**, *ser'ə-sin*, *n.* the insoluble portion of cherry-tree gum. [L. *cerasus*, Gr. *kerasos*, cherry-tree.]

**Cerastes**, *se-ras'tēz*, *n.* the North African horned viper, with a horny process over each eye.—*n.* **Ceras'tium**, the mouse-ear chickweed, with horn-shaped capsules. [Gr. *kerastēs*—*keras*, a horn.]

**cerate**. See **cere**.

**ceratitis**. See **keratitis**.

**Ceratodus**, *ser-at'ō-dəs*, *n.* the barramunda, an Australian lung-fish, now called Neoceratodus, the name Ceratodus being reserved for a fossil genus. [Gr. *keras*, *-atos*, horn, *odous*, tooth.]

**ceratoid**, *ser'ə-toid*, *adj.* horny. [Gr. *keratoeidēs*—*keras*, horn, *eidos*, form.]

**Cerberus**, *sûr'bar-əs*, *(myth.) n.* the monster that guarded the entrance to Hades, a dog with (at

least) three heads.—*adj.* **cerbē′rian.** [L.—Gr. *Kerberos.*]
**cercal.** See **cercus.**
**cercaria,** *sər-kā′ri-ə, n.* a larval stage of many trematodes.—*adj.* **cercā′rian.** [Gr. *kerkos,* a tail.]
**Cercopithecus,** *sûr-kō-pi-thē′kus, n.* an African genus of long-tailed monkeys, including the Diana monkey, vervet, and mona. [Gr. *kerkos,* tail, *pithēkos,* monkey.]
**cercus,** *sûr′kəs,* a tail-like appendage.—*adj.* **cer′cal,** pertaining to a tail. [Gr. *kerkos,* tail.]
**cere,** *sēr, v.t.* to cover with wax.—*n.* the bare waxlike patch at the base of the upper part of a bird's beak.—*adj.* **cērā′ceous,** waxy.—*n.* **cēr′ate,** a paste or stiff ointment containing wax.—*adj.* **cēr′eous,** waxy.—**cere′-cloth, cerement** (*sēr′mənt*), a cloth dipped in melted wax to wrap a dead body in: a winding-sheet or grave-clothes generally. [L. *cēra,* wax.]
**cereal.** See **Ceres.**
**cerebrum,** *ser′i-brəm, n.* the front and larger part of the brain.—*adjs.* **cerebell′ar, cerebell′ous.**—*n.* **cerebell′um,** the hinder and lower part of the brain.—*adj.* **cer′ebral,** pertaining to the brain or the cerebrum: of consonant sounds, produced by inverting the tip of the tongue on the palate (*phon.*).—*ns.* **cer′ebralism,** the theory that all mental operations originate in the brain; **cer′ebralist.**—*v.i.* **cer′ebrate,** to show brain action.—*n.* **cerebrā′tion,** action of the brain, esp. unconscious.—*adjs.* **cer′ebric** (or *sər-eb′rik*), **cerebral; cerebriform** (-*eb′*), brain-shaped.—*adj.* **cerebri′tis,** inflammation of the cerebrum.—*adj.* **cer′ebrospin′al,** relating to the brain and spinal cord together.—*n.* **cerebrotonia** (-*tō′ni-a*), the temperament associated with ectomorphic body type—introversive, hypersensitive (L. *tonus,* tone).—*adj.* **cerebrovas′cular,** relating to the cerebrum and its blood vessels.—**cerebral hemispheres,** the two great divisions of the cerebrum; **cerebrospinal fever, meningitis; cerebrovascular accident,** a paralytic stroke. [L. *cerebrum,* the brain; prob. cog. with Gr. *karā,* the head, *krānion,* the cranium.]
**ceremony,** *ser′i-mə-ni, n.* a rite: a formal act: the outward form, religious or other: any empty form without inwardness: pomp or state.—*adj.* **ceremonial** (-*mō′ni-əl*), relating to ceremony.—*n.* outward form: a system of ceremonies.—*n.* **ceremō′nialism,** adherence to outward form.—*adv.* **ceremō′nially.**—*adj.* **ceremō′nious,** full of ceremony: particular in observing forms: precise.—*adv.* **ceremō′niously.**—*n.* **ceremōniousness.**—**master of ceremonies,** the person who directs the form and order of the ceremonies to be observed on some public occasion: a compère; **stand on ceremony,** to be punctilious about forms. [L. *caerimōnia,* sanctity.]
**Ceres,** *sē′rēz, n.* the Roman name for the Greek Demeter, goddess of tillage and corn: one of the minor planets.—*adj.* **ce′real** (*sē′ri-əl*), relating to edible grain.—*n.* a grain used as food, such as wheat, barley, etc.: a food prepared from such grain, esp. a breakfast food easily got ready.—*n.* **cē′realist,** a specialist in cereals: a feeder on cereals. [L. *Cĕrēs, -eris,* prob. from root of *creāre,* to create.]
**Cereus,** *sē′ri-əs, n.* a large genus of cactuses, including some of the most imposing forms. [L. *cēreus,* waxen, wax-taper (from their stiff form).]
**cerge,** *sûrj, n.* a large wax-candle burned before the altar.—Also **cierge, serge.** [O.Fr.,—L. *cēreus* —*cēra,* wax.]
**Cerinthian,** *sər-in′thi-ən, adj.* pertaining to *Cerinthus,* one of the earliest heretics in the Christian Church, against whose crude Gnosticism the Gospel of John was written, according to Irenaeus.
**ceriph.** Same as **serif.**

**cerise,** *sər-ēz′,* also -*ēs′, n.* and *adj.* light and clear red. [Fr., cherry.]
**cerium,** *sē′ri-əm, n.* the metallic element of atomic number 58.—*ns.* **cē′ria,** its oxide; **cē′rite,** a mineral, its hydrous silicate. [Named from the planet Ceres discovered about the same time.]
**cermet.** See **ceramic.**
**cerne,** *sûrn* (*Shak.*), a short form of **concern.**
**cernuous,** *sûr′nū-əs,* (*bot.*) *adj.* nodding, bowing down, drooping. [L. *cernuus,* inclined forwards.]
**cerograph,** *sē′rō-gräf, n.* a writing on wax: an encaustic painting: engraving by means of a plate spread with wax.—*adjs.* **cerographic** (-*graf′ik*), -al.—*ns.* **cerographist** (-*rog′rə-fist*); **cerog′raphy.** [Gr. *kēros,* wax, *graphein,* to write.]
**ceromancy,** *sē′rō-man-si, n.* divination by dropping melted wax in water. [Gr. *kēros,* wax, *manteiā,* divination.]
**ceroon.** See **seron.**
**ceroplastic,** *sē-rō-plas′tik, adj.* pertaining to wax-modelling.—*n.pl.* **ceroplas′tics,** the art of wax-modelling. [Gr. *kēros,* wax, *plastikos,* plastic— *plassein,* to mould.]
**cerris,** *ser′is, n.* the Turkey oak (*Quercus cerris*).— *adj.* **cerr′ial.** [L. *cerreus.*]
**certain,** *sûr′tn, adj.* sure: not to be doubted: resolved: fixed: determinate: regular: inevitable: some: one.—*adv.* **cer′tainly.**—*ns.* **cer′titude; cer′tainty** (*slang* **cert,** sometimes in phrase **dead cert).—a certain person,** implying some degree of contempt; **a lady of a certain age,** one no longer young; **for certain,** assuredly; **in a certain condition,** euphemism for pregnant; **moral certainty** (see moral). [O.Fr.,—L. *certus* —*cernĕre,* to decide.]
**certes,** *sûr′tiz, adv.* certainly: in sooth.—my **cer′tie, cer′ty** (*Scot.*), assuredly. [Fr.]
**certificate,** *sər-tif′i-kāt, n.* a written declaration, official or formal, of some fact: a statement of qualification(s) or recognised professional status.—*v.t.* to give a certificate to.—*adj.* **cer′tifiable** (-*fī-ə-bl*), capable of being certified (esp. as insane).—*adv.* **cer′tifiably.**—*adj.* **certif′icated,** (of e.g. a teacher) holding a certificate of training and fitness.—*ns.* **certificā′tion; certif′icatory,** a certificate.—Also *adj.*—*n.* **cer′tifier,** one who certifies.—*v.t.* **cer′tify,** to make known as certain: to inform: to declare in writing: to certify as insane:—*pr.p.* **cer′tifying;** *pa.p.* **cer′tified.**— **certified milk,** milk certified as yielded by tuberculin-tested herds, fulfilling required conditions as to bacterial content, etc. [Fr. *certificat* —L. *certificāre, certus,* certain, and *facĕre* to make.]
**certiorari,** *sûr-shi-ō-rā′rī, n.* a writ by which causes are removed from inferior courts into the High Court of Justice. [L.L. *certiōrāri,* to be informed of—*certior,* comp. of *certus,* certain.]
**cerulean, caerulean,** *si-rōō′li-ən, adj.* sky-blue: dark-blue: sea-green.—*adjs.* **caerule** (*sēr′ūl; Spens.*) sky-blue; **ceru′leous.**—*n.* **ceru′lein,** a coal-tar colour, producing fast olive-greens. [L. *caerŭleus,* dark blue or green.]
**cerumen,** *si-rōō′men, n.* ear wax.—*adj.* **ceru′minous.** [L. *cēra,* wax.]
**ceruse,** *sē′rōōs,* or *si-rōōs′, n.* white lead.—*n.* **cērus(s)ite,** native lead carbonate. [Fr.,—L. *cērussa,* conn. with *cēra,* Gr. *kēros,* wax.]
**cervix,** *sûr′viks, n.* the neck of an organ, esp. the uterus.—*adj.* **cervical** (*sûr′vi-kl, sər-vī′kl*). [L. *cervix, cervīcis,* neck.]
**cervine,** *sûr′vīn, adj.* relating to deer: like deer: fawn coloured. [L. *cervīnus—cervus,* a stag.]
**cesarean.** See **caesarean.**
**cesarevitch, -witch, cesarevna.** See **tsar.**
**cesium.** U.S. spelling of **caesium.**
**cespitose.** Same as **caespitose.**
**cess,** *ses,* (*obs.*) *n.* a tax, a local rate.—*v.t.* to impose a tax.—**bad cess to** (in Ireland), ill luck to;

out of all cesse (*Shak.*), excessively, immoderately. [Shortened from *assess*.]

**cessation**, *ses-ā'shən*, *n.* a ceasing or stopping: a rest: a pause. [L. *cessātiō, -ōnis*. See cease.]

**cesse**, *ses*, (*Spens.*) *v.i.* Same as cease.

**cession**, *sesh'ən*, *n.* a yielding up.—*n.* cess'ionary, one to whom an assignment has been legally made.—**cessio** (*ses'i-ō, sesh'i-ō*) bonō'rum (*Scots law*), a debtor's surrender of his estate to his creditors in return for a judicial protection from imprisonment in respect of his debt—after 1880 a summary process in small bankruptcies, finally abolished 1913. [L. *cēssiō, -ōnis*; see cede.]

**cesspool**, *ses'pōōl*, *n.* a pool or pit for collecting filthy water. [Origin obscure.]

**cestode**, *ses'tōd*, *n.* a tapeworm or bladder-worm. —*n.* ces'toid, a cestode: a ribbon-like ctenophoran (Venus's girdle).—Also *adj.*—*n.* and *adj.*

**cestoid'ean.** [Gr. *kestos*, a girdle, a strap, and *eidos*, form.]

**Cestracion**, *ses-trā'si-on*, *n.* an antiquated type of shark represented by the Port Jackson shark. [Perh. Gr. *kestrā*, a kind of fish, or *kestros*, sharp, *akē*, point.]

**cestui**, *set-ē'*, *sest'wē*, *n.* that one—in such phrases as **cestui que trust** (*ki-trust*), a person entitled to the benefit of a trust. [O.Fr., dat. of *cest*, that.]

**cestus**, *ses'təs*, *n.* a girdle, esp. Aphrodite's. [L.,— Gr. *kestos*, girdle.]

**cestus**, *ses'təs*, *n.* an ancient boxing-glove loaded with metal. [L. *caestus*.]

**cesura.** See caesura.

**cesure**, *sē'zūr*, (*Spens.*) *n.* a break: interruption. [caesura.]

**Cetacea**, *si-tā'shi-a, -shya*, *n.pl.* an order of mammals of aquatic habit and fish-like form including the toothed whales, or *Odontoceti* (sperm whales, bottle-noses, dolphins, etc.) and the baleen whales, or *Mystacoceti* (right whale, hump-backs, rorquals).—*n.* and *adj.* cetā'cean.— *adj.* cetā'ceous.—*ns.* cetol'ogy, the study of whales; Ceteosau'rus (Gr. *sauros*, lizard), a large Jurassic dinosaur. [Gr. *kētos*, a sea-monster.]

**cetane**, *sē'tān*, *n.* a paraffin hydrocarbon found in petroleum.—**cetane number**, a measure of the ignition quality of diesel engine fuel; **cetyl**, *sē'til*, *U.S.* *sē'təl* (Gr. *hȳlē*, matter), the univalent radical C₁₆H₃₃.—**cetyl alcohol**, a waxy crystalline solid used in detergents and pharmaceuticals, so called because compounds of it occur in spermaceti. [Gr. *kētos*, a sea-monster.]

**Ceterach**, *set'ər-ak*, *n.* the scale-fern genus. [Mediaeval L. *ceterach*—Ar. *shitarakh*.]

**cetera desunt**, *set'ə-ra dē'sunt, kā'te-ra dā'sōōnt*, (L.) the rest is missing.

**ceteris paribus**, *sē'tər-is par'i-bus, kā'te-rēs pa'ri-bōōs*, (L.) other things being equal.

**cetyl.** See cetane.

**cevadilla.** See sabadilla.

**cevitamic acid**, *sē-vi-tam'ik a'sid*, ascorbic acid. [The letter *c* and *vitamin*.]

**Ceylonese**, *sē-lən-ēz'*, *adj.* of or belonging to Ceylon.—*n.* a native of Ceylon: a Sinhalese.—*ns.* cey'lonite, cey'lanite, a magnesia-iron spinel.

**ch**, *ch*, *pron.* obs. S.W. and conventional dialect for *ich*, I, fused with the verb, as **cham**, I am, **chave**, I have, **chill**, I will. [M.E. *ich*—O.E. *ic.*]

**cha**, *chä*, *n.* tea: rolled tea. [Chin. *ch'a.*]

**chabazite**, *kab'ə-zit*, *n.* a zeolite, a hydrated calcium-aluminium silicate, in pink and glassy white crystals. [From a misreading of Gr. *chalazios*, a kind of stone—*chalaza*, hailstone.]

**Chablis**, *shab'lē*, *n.* a very dry white Burgundy wine made at *Chablis*, department of Yonne, in France.

**chabouk**, *chä'bōōk*, *n.* a horsewhip. [Pers. *chābuk.*]

**chace.** See chase (1).

**cha-cha** (-cha), *chä'-chä'* (-chä'), *n.* a West Indian dance, a later form of the mambo.

**chack**, *chak, chäk*, *n.* (*Scot.*) a snack or slight hasty meal: a snapping or pinching, as by a door or window.—*v.t.* to pinch or nip in such a way. [Imit.]

**chacma**, *chak'ma*, *n.* a large South African baboon. [From Hottentot.]

**chaco.** Same as shako.

**chaconne**, *sha', shə-kon'*, *n.* an old dance, with slow movement: its music, a series of variations on a ground bass, in triple time, appearing in vocal and instrumental music as well as in ballets. [Fr.,—Sp. *chacona*—Basque *chucun*, pretty.]

**chad**, *shad*, *n.* a kind of fish. [See shad.]

**Chaetodon**, *kē'tō-don*, *n.* a tropical genus of fishes with slender teeth, giving name to the family **Chaetodont'idae.** [Gr. *chaitē*, hair, *odous, odontos*, tooth.]

**chaetopod**, *kē'tō-pod*, *n.* a worm (as earthworm, lobworm, sea-mouse) that crawls by the help of bristles. [Gr. *chaitē*, hair, and *pous, podos*, foot.]

**chafe**, *chāf*, *v.t.* to heat, fret, or wear by rubbing: to cause to fret or rage.—*v.i.* to fret or rage (with *against, at*).—*n.* heat caused by rubbing: rage: passion.—*ns.* chaf'er (*obs.*), a chafing-dish, a saucepan; **chaf'ing-dish**, a vessel for heating by hot coals, etc.: a dish for cooking on the table; **chaf'ing-gear**, mats, spun-yarn, battens, etc., put upon the rigging and spars of a ship to prevent their being chafed. [Fr. *chauffer*—L. *calefacēre* —*calēre*, to be hot, and *facēre*, to make.]

**chafer**, *chāf'ər*, *n.* a beetle, esp. of the Scarabaeidae. [O.E. *cefer*; Du. *kever*; Ger. *käfer*.]

**chaff**, *chäf, chaf*, *n.* husks of corn as threshed or winnowed: cut hay and straw: refuse, or worthless matter: light banter, badinage (*slang*; perh. a different word).—*v.t.* (*slang*) to banter.— *n.* and *adj.* chaff'ing.—*adv.* chaff'ingly.—*adjs.* chaff'less; chaff'y.—chaff'-cutt'er, chaff'-en'gine, a machine for cutting up straw or hay. [O.E. *ceaf*; cf. Du. *kaf*.]

**chaffer**, *chaf'ər*, *v.i.* to bargain: to haggle about price: to sell, exchange, or bandy (*Spens.*).—*ns.* chaff'erer, a haggler; chaff'ery, buying and selling: haggling (*Spens.*). [M.E. *chapfare*, a bargain, from O.E. *cēap*, price, *faru*, way.]

**chaffinch**, *chaf'inch, -insh*, *n.* a little song-bird of the finch family. [Said to delight in *chaff*. See finch.]

**chaffron.** See chamfrain.

**chaft**, *chaft, chäft*, (*Scot.* and *Northern English*) *n.* the jaw. [O.N. *kjaptr*; cf. Sw. *kaft*, Dan. *kieft*.]

**chagan**, *kä-gän'*, *n.* an early form of khan.

**chagrin**, *shag'rin, shə-grēn'*, *n.* that which wears or gnaws the mind: vexation: annoyance.—*v.t.* to vex or annoy.—*p.adj.* chagrined'. [Fr. *chagrin*, shagreen, rough skin, ill-humour.]

**chai, chi, chī**, *fem.* of chal.

**chain**, *chān*, *n.* a series of links or rings passing through one another: a number of things connected in series: a linked series: a mountain range: a string of islands: something that binds: a connected course or train of events: a measure of 100 links, or 66 feet (see Gunter): a succession of cigars, or cigarettes smoked without intermission: a number of atoms linked in succession (*chem.*): (*pl.*) fetters, bonds, confinement generally: (in *pl.*) a circular apparatus of metal links fitted to the wheels of a car in icy conditions to prevent skidding.—*v.t.* to fasten: to fetter: to restrain: to embrace (*Shak.*).—*p.adj.* chained, bound or fastened, as with a chain: fitted with a chain.—*adj.* chain'less, without chains: unfettered.—*n.* chain'let, a small chain.—chain'-arm'our, chain-mail; chain'-bolt, a large bolt used to secure the chain-plates to the ship's side; chain'-bridge, a bridge suspended on chains: a suspension-bridge; chain'-cable, a cable composed of iron links; chain'-drive, transmission of power by chain-gear.— *adj.* chain'-driven.—chain'-gang, a gang of convicts chained together; **chain'-gear, -gearing,** gearing consisting of an endless chain and (generally) sprocket-wheels; **chain'-harrow,** a harrow composed of chainwork; **chain'-letter,** a letter soliciting (among other things) the sending of duplicates with or without a limit; **chain'-light'ning,** forked or zigzag lightning: a harsh whisky; **chain locker** (*naut*.), a compartment at the forward end of a ship for storing the anchor chain when the anchor is not being used; **chain'-mail,** armour of connected links, much used in Europe in the 12th and 13th centuries; **chain'-mould'ing,** moulding in the form of a chain; **chain'-pier,** a pier supported by chains like a chain-bridge.—*n.pl.* **chain'-plates,** on shipboard iron plates bolted below the channels to serve as attachments for the dead-eyes, through which the standing rigging or shrouds and backstays are rove and secured.—**chain'-pump,** a pump consisting of an endless chain, usually with disks; **chain reaction,** a process in which each reaction is in turn the stimulus of a similar reaction; **chain reactor, a** nuclear reactor; **chain'-rule,** an arithmetical rule, so called from the terms of the problem being stated as equations, and connected, as if by a chain, so as to obtain by one operation the same result as would be obtained by a number of different operations in simple proportion: the rule for solving problems by compound proportion; **chain'saw,** a power saw with teeth linked in an endless chain; **chain'-shot,** two bullets or half-bullets fastened together by a chain, used formerly to destroy ships' rigging; **chain'-smo'ker,** a non-stop smoker; **chain'-stitch,** a stitch resembling the links of a chain; **chain'-store,** a multiple shop; **chain'work,** work looped or linked like a chain: network. [O.Fr. *chaeine*—L. *catēna*.]

**chair, chār,** *n.* a movable seat for one, with a back to it: a chariot (*hist*.): a vehicle, wheeled or carried, for one person (*hist*.): the seat or office of one in authority, as a judge, a bishop, or the person presiding over any meeting: the chairman: the seat from which a professor delivers his lectures: a professorship: a pulpit (*obs*.): a witness-box (*U.S.*): the instrument or the punishment of electrocution: a support for a railway rail securing it to a sleeper.—*v.t.* to place in a seat of authority: to carry publicly in triumph: to conduct as chairman (a meeting).—*n.* **chair'-bed,** a chair capable of being turned into a bed.—*n.pl.* **chair'days** (*Shak*.; *fig*.) the evening of life.—*ns.* **chair'lift,** a set of seats suspended from cables used to take skiers uphill; **chair'man,** one who takes the chair, or presides at an assembly or meeting: one who carries a sedan or draws a Bath chair; **chair'manship; chair'-or'gan,** a choir-organ (perhaps because it sometimes formed the back of the organist's seat); **chair'woman.** [Fr. *chaire*—L.—Gr. *kathedrā*.]

**chaise, shāz,** *n.* a light open carriage for one or more persons: a travelling carriage (see post-chaise).—*adj.* **chaise'less.**—*n.* **chaise'-cart,** a light vehicle for going about in; **chaise-longue,** (*lõg*) a couch with back at one end and short armrest. [Fr., a form of *chaire*; see chair. **chay** and **shay** are vulgar singulars of imaginary *pl.* **chaise.**]

**chal, chal,** *n.* fellow: person:—*fem.* **chai, chī.** [Romany.]

**chal(l)an, chul'lən,** (*Ind*.) *n.* a way-bill: a pass: the sending up of an accused person before a magistrate: (*technically*) a form used when money due to a government department is paid, not to the department itself, but to the government Treasury.—Also *v.t.* [Hindi *calan*.]

**chalaza, ka-lā'za,** *n.* in a bird's egg, the string that holds the yolk-sac in position (*zool*.): the base of the ovule (*bot*.).—*adj.* **chalazogamic** (*kal-az-ō-*

**gam'ik*).—*n.* **chalazog'amy** (*-og'ə-mi*; *bot*.) entrance of the pollen-tube through the chalaza (opp. to *porogamy*). [Gr. *chalaza*, hail, lump.]

**chalcedony, kal-sed'ə-ni,** or **kal',** *n.* a beautiful mineral composed of silica, usually banded, translucent, of waxy lustre, generally white or bluish-white, apparently amorphous but consisting of crystalline fibres.—*adj.* **chalcedonic** (*-si-don'ik*).—*n.* **chalced'onyx** (or *-on'*; from **onyx**), an agate of alternating white opaque and greyish translucent chalcedony. [Gr. *chalkēdōn,* possibly from *Chalcedon,* in Asia Minor.]

**Chalcidian, kal-sid'i-ən,** *adj.* pertaining to Chalcis in Euboea, or its people.—**Chalcidian alphabet,** the alphabet used by Chalcidian settlers in southern Italy and Sicily, from which the Latin alphabet developed.

**chalcography, kal-kog'rə-fi,** *n.* the art of engraving on copper or brass.—*ns.* **chalcog'rapher, chalcog'raphist.** [Gr. *chalkos,* copper, *graphein,* to write.]

**Chalcolithic, kal-kō-lith'ik.** Same as Aeneolithic. [Gr. *chalkos,* copper, *lithos,* stone.]

**chalcopyrite, kal-kō-pī'rīt,** *n.* copper pyrites. [Gr. *chalkos,* copper, and pyrite.]

**Chaldaic, kal-dā'ik, Chaldee, kal'dē,** *adjs.* relating to *Chaldaea.*—*n.* the language of the Chaldaeans: an ancient inhabitant of Chaldaea: a soothsayer: a member of the Chaldaean church.—*n.* **chal'dāism,** a Chaldaic idiom.—*adj.* **chaldae'an, chalde'an,** Chaldaic.—*n.* a native of Chaldaea.

**chalder, chöl'dər,** *n.* an old Scottish dry measure, containing 16 bolls. [Prob. a form of chaldron.]

**chaldron, chöl'drən,** *n.* an old coal-measure, holding 36 heaped bushels (= 25½ cwt.). [Fr. *chaudron;* see cauldron.]

**chalet, shal'ā,** *n.* a summer hut used by Swiss herdsmen in the Alps: a wooden villa. [Fr.; *châlet* is wrong.]

**chalice, chal'is,** *n.* a cup or bowl: a communion-cup.—*adj.* **chal'iced,** cup-like. [O.Fr. *chalice*—L. *calix, calicis;* cf. Gr. *kylix,* a cup; calyx is a different word.]

**chalk, chök,** *n.* white soft rock, composed of calcium carbonate, chiefly shells of Foraminifera: a substitute for this used for writing, etc.—*v.t.* to write, rub, mark, or manure, with chalk.—*n.* **chalk'iness.**—*adj.* **chalk'y.**—*ns.* **chalk'board,** a blackboard; **chalk'pit,** a pit in which chalk is dug; **chalk'stone,** a stone or piece of chalk: (in *pl.*) the white concretions formed round the joints in chronic gout.—**by a long chalk,** by a considerable distance, referring to the habit of scoring with chalk: **chalking the door,** in Scotland, a form of warning tenants to remove from burghal tenements; **chalk out,** to trace out, as with chalk, to plan; **chalk up,** to make a special note of: to record (a score, etc.): to charge or ascribe (to e.g. a person); **not to know chalk from cheese,** to know nothing about the matter; **the Chalk** (*geol.*), the uppermost part of the Cretaceous system in England. [O.E. *cealc*—L. *calx,* limestone.]

**challenge, chal'inj,** *v.t.* to call on to settle a matter by fighting or by any kind of contest: to claim as one's own: to accuse: to object to: to track (*Spens*.).—*n.* a summons to a contest of any kind, but esp. a duel: a calling of any one or anything in question: exception to a juror: the demand of a sentry: an accusation: a claim: a difficulty which stimulates interest or effort.—*adj.* **chall'engeable,** that may be challenged.—*n.* **chall'enger,** one who challenges to a combat of any kind: a claimant: one who objects, calls in question.—*adj.* **chall'enging.**—*adv.* **chall'engingly.** [O.Fr. *chalenge,* a dispute, claim—L. *calumnia,* a false accusation—*calvī* or *calvĕre,* to deceive.]

**challis, shalli, chal'is, shal'is, shal'i,** *n.* a soft

glossless silk and worsted fabric, later of other materials. [Origin uncertain.]
chalone, kāl', kal'ōn, n. an internal secretion which inhibits action as a hormone excites it.—adj.
chalon'ic. [Gr. chalaein, to relax.]
chalumeau, sha.'-ū-mō', shal-ü-mō', n. an early reed instrument that developed into the clarinet: the lowest register of the clarinet:—pl. chalumeaux (-mōz'). [Fr.,—O.Fr. chalemel—L.L. calamellus, dim. of calamus, a pipe, a reed.]
Chalybean, kal-ib-ē'ən, or ka-lib'i-ən, adj. forged by the Chalybes (Milt.): well tempered.—adj.
chalyb'eate, containing iron.—n. a water or other liquid containing iron.—n. cha'lybite, siderite, a common iron ore, ferrous carbonate. [Gr. chalyps, chalybos, steel, or Chalyps, one of the Chalybēs, a nation in Pontus famous for steel.]
cham, kam, n. an obs. form of khan: an autocrat (fig.).
chamade, sha-mäd', n. a drum or trumpet call for a parley or surrender. [Fr.]
Chamaerops, ka-mē'rops. See palmetto.
chamber, chām'bar, n. a room: the place where an assembly meets: a house of a legislature, esp. the French Chamber of Deputies: an assembly or body of men met for some purpose, as a chamber of commerce: a hall of justice: a compartment: a cavity: the back end of the bore of a gun: a small cannon (Shak.): (in pl.) a suite of rooms in a house occupied separately, esp. by lawyers: a judge's room for hearing cases not taken into court.—v.t. to put in a chamber: to confine.—v.i. to be wanton (arch.).
—adj. cham'bered, confined: having rooms or room, or (of a shell) parts separated by a succession of walls.—ns. cham'berer, a man of intrigue (arch.): a gallant (Shak.); cham'bering (B.), lewd behaviour.—chamber concert, a concert of chamber music; chamber council (Shak.), a private or secret council; chamber-counsel, -counsellor, a counsel who gives his advice privately, but does not plead in court; cham'ber-fellow (arch.), one sharing a chamber.
—n.pl. cham'ber-hangings (Shak.), the hangings or tapestry of a chamber.—cham'ber-lye (Shak.), urine; cham'bermaid, a female servant who has the care of bedrooms in hotels, etc.; formerly, and still in U.S., a housemaid; chamber music, music suitable for a room, rather than a theatre or a large hall, now almost confined to music for strings with or without piano or winds; chamber organ, a small organ suitable for a room; cham'berpot, a bedroom vessel for urine—often merely cham'ber; chamber practice, the business of a chamber-counsel. [Fr. chambre—L. camera—Gr. kamarā, a vault, a room.]
chamberlain, chām'bar-lin, n. an officer appointed by a king or nobleman, or by a corporation, to perform domestic and ceremonial duties or to act as factor or steward.—n. cham'berlainship.—Lord Chamberlain, an officer of high standing in the royal household, having control over all the officers and servants 'above stairs', except those of the bedchamber, over the establishment attached to the Chapel Royal, the physicians, surgeons, and apothecaries of the household; Lord Great Chamberlain, a hereditary officer who has the government of the palace of Westminster and to whom upon solemn occasions the keys of Westminster Hall and of the Court of Requests are delivered. [O.Fr. chambrelenc; O.H.G. chamerling—L. camera, a chamber, and affix -ling or -lenc = Eng. -ling in hireling.]
Chambertin, shā-ber-tē, n. a famous red Burgundy from the vineyard of that name near Dijon.
chambré, shā-brā, (Fr.) of wine, at room temperature.
chameleon, chamaeleon, ka-mēl'yan, n. a small lizard famous for changing its colour: an

inconstant person (fig.).—adjs. chameleonic (-i-on'ik), chamel'eon-like. [L. chamaeleōn—Gr. chamaileōn—chamai (cf. L. humi), on the ground (i.e. dwarf) and leōn, a lion.]
chamelot, cham', or kam'e-lot, (Spens.) n. same as camlet.
chamfer, cham'far, n. a bevel or slope made by paring off the edge of anything originally right-angled: a groove, channel, or furrow.—v.t. to cut or grind off bevel-wise, as a corner: to channel or make furrows upon: to flute, as a column.—adj. cham'fered, bevelled: furrowed, grooved, wrinkled. [Fr. chanfrein—O.Fr. chanfraindre, apparently from chant fraindre—L. cantum frangĕre, to break the edge or side.]
chamfrain, cham'fran, n. a piece of leather or plate of steel to protect the face of a horse in battle.—Also cham'fron, chaf'fron. [Fr. chanfrein; origin unknown.]
chamiso, sha-mē'sō, chamise, sha-mēz', n. a rosaceous shrub (Adenostoma fasciculatum) of California.—n. chamisal', a chamiso thicket. [Sp. chamiza, cane.]
chamlet, cham' or kam'let, n. Same as camlet.
chamois, sham'wä, n. a goat-like antelope inhabiting high mountains in southern and central Europe: (pl. chamois, sham'wä): (sham'i), a soft kind of leather originally made from its skin (in this sense also shammy, or shamoy). [Fr., perh. from Swiss Romanic; cf. Ger. gemse, a chamois.]
chamomile. See camomile.
champ, champ, v.i. to make a snapping noise with the jaws in chewing.—v.t. to bite or chew: to munch: to crush: to mash.—n. a champing. [Cf. jam (2).]
champ, champ, (her.) n. field. [Fr.]
champ, champ, slang abbrev. for champion.
champagne, sham-pān', n. a white sparkling wine, strictly from Champagne in France (sometimes still or coloured red): the amber-like colour of white champagne.
champaign, cham'pān', also sham-pān', adj. level, open.—n. an open level country. [Doublet of campaign, from O.Fr. champaigne—L. campānia, a plain.]
champak, champac, chum'puk, cham'pak, n. an Indian tree (Michelia Champaca) of the magnolia family, of great beauty, with oppressively scented flowers. [Hind.]
champerty, cham'par-ti, n. an illegal bargain whereby the one party is to assist the other in a suit, and is to share in the proceeds.—n. cham'-part, the division of the produce of land, the right of the feudal lord. [Norm. Fr.—L. campi pars, part of the field.]
champignon, cham-, or sham-pin'yan, n. a mush-room or other edible fungus esp. the fairy-ring champignon (Marasmius oreades).
champion, cham'pi-an, n. one who fights in single combat for himself or for another: one who defends a cause: a successful combatant: in sports, one who has excelled all others: a hero.—adj. acting or ranking as champion, first: excellent (coll.).—v.t. to challenge (obs.): to defend: to support.—ns. cham'pioness; cham'pionship, the position of honour gained by being champion: the act of championing. [Fr.,—L.L. campiō, -ōnis—L. campus, a plain, a place for games.]
champlevé, shā-la-vā, n. enamel work done with vitreous powders in channels cut in a metal base.—Also adj. [Fr.]
Champs Élysées, shā-zā-lē-zā, (Fr.) Elysian Fields: also a famous open space and avenue in Paris.
chance, chāns, n. that which falls out or happens fortuitously, or without assignable cause: fortune: an unexpected event: risk: opportunity: possibility of something happening: (sometimes in pl.) probability: (in pl.) misfor-

tunes (*arch.*).—*v.t.* to risk.—*v.i.* to happen.—
*adj.* happening by chance.—*adv.* perchance.—
*adjs.* chance'ful, full of risk or danger (*arch.*):
full of chance(s); chance'less, without an opportunity; chanc'y, lucky, safe (*Scot.*): risky, uncertain.—*n.* chance'-com'er, one who comes by
chance or unexpectedly.—by chance, accidentally; chance one's arm, to take a chance, often
recklessly; chance upon, find by chance; even
chance, equal probability for or against; how
chance? (*Shak.*) how does it happen that?;
stand a good chance, to have a reasonable expectation; take one's chance, to accept what happens: to risk an undertaking; the main chance,
the chief object (esp. an eye to the main chance,
thought for self-enrichment). [O.Fr. *cheance*—
L.L. *cadentia*—L. *cadĕre*, to fall.]

chancel, *chän'sl, n.* the eastern part of a church,
originally separated from the nave by a screen of
latticework, so as to prevent general access
thereto, though not to interrupt either sight or
sound. [O.Fr.,—L. *cancelli*, lattices.]

chancellor, *chän'səl-ər, n.* secretary (*Shak.*): a
chief minister: the president, or a judge, of a
court of chancery or other court: the official
who keeps the registers of an order of knighthood: the titular (or in U.S. active) head of a
university: the foreman of a jury (*Scot.*).—*ns.*
chan'cellorship; chan'cellery, -ory, the position,
department, etc., of a chancellor: the office
attached to an embassy or consulate.—chancellor of a cathedral, an officer who had charge of
the chapter library, custody of the common seal,
superintendence of the choir practices, and headship of the cathedral schools; chancellor of a
diocese, an eclesiastical judge uniting the
functions of vicar-general and official principal,
appointed to assist the bishop in questions of
ecclesiastical law, and hold his courts for him;
Chancellor of the Exchequer, the chief minister of
finance in the British government; Lord Chancellor, Lord High Chancellor, the Speaker of the
House of Lords, presiding judge of the Chancery
Division, keeper of the great seal. [Fr. *chancelier*
—L.L. *cancellārius*, orig. an officer that had
charge of records, and stood near the *cancelli*
(L.), cross-bars surrounding the judgment seat.]

chance-medley, *chäns-med'li, n.* a casualty that is
not pure chance but has a mixture of chance in it:
esp. unintentional homicide in which the killer is
not entirely without blame: action with an element of chance: (wrongly) pure chance. [O.Fr.
*chance medlée*, mingled chance.]

Chancery, *chän'sər-i, n.* formerly the highest
court of justice next to the House of Lords,
presided over by the Lord High Chancellor—
now a division of the High Court of Justice: a
court of record generally: the office of a
chancellor (*obs.*): the political office in an embassy or legation (*Brit. diplomatic*).—Chancery
Office, in Scotland, an office in the General
Register House at Edinburgh, managed by a
director, in which all royal charters of novo-
damus, pateits of dignities, gifts of offices,
remissions, legitimations, presentations, commissions, and other writs appointed to pass the
Great and Quarter Seals are recorded: in
chancery, (of an estate, etc.) in litigation: (of a
boxer's head) held firmly under his adversary's
arm (*slang*): in an awkward predicament (*slang*).
[Fr. *chancellerie*.]

chancre, *shang'kər, n.* the hard swelling that
constitutes the primary lesion in syphilis.—*n.*
chanc'roid, a non-syphilitic ulceration of the
genital organs due to venereally contracted infection.—*adjs.* chanc'roid, chanc'rous. [Fr.; a
form of canker.]

chandelier, *shan-di-lēr', n.* a frame with branches
for holding lights.—*ns.* chandler (*chand'lər*), a
candle-maker: a dealer in candles, oil, soap,

etc,: a dealer generally (as in *corn-chandler, ship-
chandler*); chand'lering.—*adj.* chand'lerly.—*n.*
chand'lery, goods sold by a chandler. [Fr.,—
L.L. *candēlārius*, a candle-maker, *candēlāria*, a
candlestick.—L. *candēla*, a candle.]

Chandler's wobble, *chand'lərz wob'l,* very small
displacement of the earth's axis of rotation which
causes variation in latitude (and also longitude).
[S.C. *Chandler*, astronomer.]

change, *chānj, v.t.* to alter or make different: to
put or give for another: to make to pass from
one state to another: to exchange.—*v.i.* to suffer
change: to change one's clothes or vehicle.—*n.*
the act of changing: alteration or variation of
any kind: exchange (*Shak.*): fickleness (*Shak.*):
a shift: variety: money given for money of a
different kind, or in adjustment of a payment:
small coin: satisfaction (*coll.*): an exchange
(now usu. 'change).—*ns.* changeabil'ity, change'-
ableness, fickleness: power of being changed.—
*adj.* change'able, subject or prone to change:
fickle: inconstant: admitting possibility of
change: showing change of colours, shot
(*Shak.*).—*adv.* change'ably.—*adj.* change'ful,
full of change: changeable.—*adv.* change'fully.
—*n.* change'fulness.—*adj.* change'less, without
change: constant.—*ns.* change'ling, a surreptitious substitute: a child substituted for another,
esp. one supposed to be left by the fairies:
hence, an undersized crabbed child: a half-wit:
one apt to change (*arch.*); chang'er, one who
changes the form of anything: one employed in
changing or discounting money (*obs.*).—*ns.*
change'-house (*Scot.*), a small inn or alehouse;
change'over, transition to a new system or condition; chang'ing-piece (*Shak.*), a fickle person.
—change colour, to blush or turn pale; change
gear (see gear); change of life, the time of life at
which menstruation is about to cease—the menopause; change oneself (now *Scot.*), to change
one's clothes; change one's mind, to form a
different opinion: change one's tune, to change
from joy to sorrow: to change one's manner of
speaking; put the change on, to delude, trick;
ring the changes, to go through all the possible
permutations in ringing a peal of bells: to go
over in every possible order: to pass counterfeit
money: to bemuddle a shopman into giving too
much change; small change, small coin: a petty
thing. [Fr. *changer*—L. *cambire*, to barter.]

chank, *changk,* chank-shell, *changk'-shel, n.* the
shell of several species of Turbinella, gasteropod
molluscs of the East Indian seas, sliced into
bangles for Hindu women. [Hind. *chankh*; cf.
conch.]

channel, *chan'l, n.* the bed of a stream of water: a
strait or narrow sea: a navigable passage: a
passage for conveying a liquid: a groove or
furrow: a gutter: means of passing or conveying: gravel (*Scot.*): (in *pl.*) means of communication: a one-way path for a signal: a path for
information in a computer: a narrow range of
frequencies, part of a frequency band, for the
transmission of radio and television signals without interference from other channels.—*v.t.* to
make a channel: to furrow: to convey (through):
to direct (into a particular course; *lit.* and *fig.*):
—*pr.p.* chann'elling; *pa.t.* and *pa.p.* chann'elled.
—*adj.* chann'elled.—*n.* chann'el-stone, -stane,
(*Scot.*), a curling-stone.—the Channel, the
English Channel. [O.Fr. *chanel, canel*—L.
*canālis*, a canal.]

channel, *chan'l, n.* a flat piece of wood or iron
projecting horizontally from a ship's side to
spread the shrouds and keep them clear of the
bulwarks—*fore, main,* and *mizzen* channels.
[For *chain-wale.*]

chanoyu, *chä'no-ū, n.* a Japanese tea ceremony.
[Jap. lit. *tea of hot water.*]

chanson, *shā'sɔ̃, n.* a song.—*n.* chansonette

(-*son-et'*), a little song, a ditty.—**chansonnier** (-*son'ē-ā*), *n.* collection of songs, esp. old French: cabaret performer of satirical songs.—**chanson de geste** (*də zhest*; see gest, 2), an old French epic poem. [Fr.]

**chant, chaunt,** *chänt, v.t.* to sing: to celebrate in song: to recite in a singing manner: to intone: to sell (a horse) fraudulently.—*n.* song: melody: a kind of church music, in which prose is sung. —*ns.* **chant'er, chaunt'er, chant'or,** a singer: a precentor: in a bagpipe, the pipe with finger-holes, on which the melody is played: one who cries up horses; **chant'ress, chaunt'ress; chant'ry, chaunt'ry,** an endowment, or chapel, for the chanting of masses; **chanty** (see **shanty,** 2). [Fr. *chanter*—L. *cantāre*—*canĕre,* to sing.]

**chantage,** *shă-täzh', n.* blackmail. [Fr.]

**chanterelle,** *shan-,* *shă-tər-el', n.* the highest string of a musical instrument. [Fr.,—L. *cantare,* to sing.]

**chanterelle, chantarelle,** *chan-tər-el', n.* a yellowish edible fungus (*Cantharellus cibarius*). [Fr., dim. from Gr. *kantharos,* cup.]

**chanteuse,** *shan'tōōs* or *-tōōz, shă-tœz, (U.S.) n.* a female night-club singer. [Fr.]

**chanticleer,** *chant'i-klēr, -klēr', n.* a cock. [From the name of the cock in the old beast-epic of *Reynard the Fox*—O.Fr. *chanter,* to sing, *cler,* clear.]

**Chantilly (lace),** *shan'ti-li, shă-tē-yē, (lās), n.* a silk or linen bobbin lace, black or white, of delicate floral or scrolled pattern. [From *Chantilly,* France, where first made.]

**chaos,** *kā'os, n.* the shape of matter before it was reduced to order: disorder: shapeless mass.— *adj.* **chaot'ic,** confused.—*adv.* **chaot'ically.** [Gr.]

**chap, chap,** *v.i.* to crack: to strike, of a clock, etc., or to knock at a door (*Scot.*).—*v.t.* to fissure. —*n.* a crack: an open fissure in the skin, caused by exposure to cold: a knock.—*adj.* **chap'less.**— *adj.* **chapped,** cracked, of a heavy soil in dry weather, or of the skin in cold weather: cut short.—*adj.* **chapp'y.** [M.E. *chappen*; cog. with Du. and Ger. *kappen.*]

**chap, chap,** *n.* a customer (for chapman) (*obs.* or *dial.*): a fellow (*coll.*).—*ns.* **chap'book,** a book or pamphlet of a popular type such as was hawked by chapmen; **chap'man,** one who buys or sells (*arch.*): an itinerant dealer: a pedlar: a purchaser (*obs.*); **chapp'ie,** a familiar dim. of chap. [O.E. *cēap,* trade, *cēapman,* trader; cf. cheap; Ger. *kaufen, kaufmann.*]

**chap, chap,** *n.* a chop or jaw: a cheek.—*adjs.* **chap'fall'en,** (see chopfallen); **chap'less,** without a lower jaw. [Cf. chop (3); Northern Eng. and Scot. *chaft,* O.N. *kjaptr,* jaw.]

**chaparajos,** *shap-ə-rä'ōs, chä-pä-rä'hhos,* **chaparejos,** *n.pl.* cowboy's leather riding leggings (abbrev. **chaps, shaps**). [Mex. Sp.]

**chaparral,** *shap-ə-ral', chäp-ä-räl', n.* dense tangled brushwood.—**chaparral cock,** a ground-cuckoo of the Californian and Mexican chaparral. [Sp.,—*chaparro,* evergreen oak, one of its constituents.]

**chapati, chapatti,** *chəp-ät'i, n.* a thin cake of un-leavened bread. [Hind. *capati.*]

**chapbook.** See chap (2).

**chape,** *chāp, n.* the plate of metal at the point of a scabbard: the catch or hook by which the sheath of a weapon was attached to the belt.— *adj.* **chape'less.** [Fr.,—L.L. *capa,* a cap.]

**chapeau,** *shă-pō, n.* a hat.—**chapeau-bras** (*brä*) a three cornered hat formerly carried under the arm. [Fr.]

**chapel,** *chap'l, n.* a place of worship inferior or subordinate to a regular church, or attached to a house or institution: an oratory in a mausoleum, etc.: a cell of a church containing its own altar: a dissenters' place of worship, as of Noncon-formists in England, Roman Catholics or Episcopalians in Scotland, etc.: a chapel service (*to keep one's chapels,* to make the requisite number of attendances in chapel): a body of musicians, as a choir, an orchestra, or both, whether connected with a chapel or not: a printing office, or an association of workmen therein.—*n.* **chap'elry,** the jurisdiction of a chapel.—**chapel cart** (see cart); **chap'elmaster,** (Ger. *kapellmeister*), a music-director; **chapel royal,** the oratory of a royal palace.—**chapel of ease,** a chapel for worshippers at some distance from the parish church; **lady chapel** (see lady); **proprietary chapel,** one that is private property. [O.Fr. *capele*—L.L. *cappella,* dim. of *cappa,* a cloak or cope; orig. from the cloak of St Martin.]

**chapelle ardente,** *sha-pel ar-dät,* (Fr.) a chapel or chamber in which a corpse lies in state before burial, surrounded by lighted candles.

**chaperon** (now often **chaperone**), *shap'ə-rōn, n.* a kind of hood or cap: one (esp. an older woman) who accompanies a girl for protection, restraint, or appearance' sake.—*v.t.* to attend in such a capacity.—*n.* **chap'eronage.** [Fr., a large hood— *chape,* a hooded cloak—L.L. *cappa*; see cape.]

**chapiter,** *chap'i-tər, n.* the head or capital of a column. [Fr. *chapitre*—L. *capitulum,* dim. of *caput,* the head.]

**chaplain,** *chap'lin, n.* a clergyman attached to an institution, establishment, organisation, or family.—*ns.* **chap'laincy, chap'lainry, chap'lain-ship.** [O.Fr. *chapelain*—L.L. *cappellānus*— *cappella*; see **chapel.**]

**chaplet,** *chap'lit, n.* a garland or wreath for the head: a circlet of gold, etc.: a string of beads used in counting prayers, one-third of a rosary in length: anything in a string: a metal support of a cylindrical pipe.—*adj.* **chap'leted.** [O.Fr. *chapelet—chape,* a head-dress.]

**chapman.** See chap (2).

**chaprassi,** *chu-präs'i, n.* an office messenger: a household attendant: an orderly. [Hind. *chaprāsi,* badge-wearer, messenger—*chaprās,* a badge.]

**chaps.** See chaparajos.

**chapter,** *chap'tər, n.* a main division of a book, or of anything: a subject or category generally: a division of the Acts of Parliament of a session: an assembly of the canons of a cathedral or collegiate church, or the members of a religious or military order (from the custom of reading a chapter of the rule or of the Bible): its members collectively: an organised branch of a society or fraternity: a Roman numeral on a clock or watch face: a chapter (*Spens.*).—*v.t.* to put into chapters: to take to task.—**chap'ter-house.**— **chapter and verse,** the exact reference to the passage of the authority of one's statements; **chapter of accidents** (see accident); **to the end of the chapter,** throughout. [O.Fr. *chapitre*—L. *capitulum,* dim. of *caput,* the head.]

**chaptrel,** *chap'trəl, n.* the capital of a pillar which supports an arch. [Dim. of **chapiter.**]

**char, charr,** *chär, n.* a small fish (*Salvellinus*) of the salmon kind, found in mountain lakes and rivers. [Prob. Celt.; cf. Gael. *ceara,* red, blood-coloured.]

**char,** *chär, v.t.* to reduce to carbon.—*v.t.* and *v.i.* to scorch:—*pr.p.* **charr'ing**; *pa.t.* and *pa.p.* **charred.**—*adj.* **charr'y,** pertaining to charcoal. [Origin obscure.]

**char, chär, chare,** *chär, n.* a turn (*obs.*): an occa-sional piece of work, an odd job: (*pl.*) household work (see chore) a charwoman.—*v.i.* to do odd jobs of work: to do house-cleaning.—*v.t.* (*Scott*) to do, accomplish:—*pr.p.* **charr'ing, chār'ing**; *pa.t.* and *pa.p.* **charred, chāred.**—*n.* **char'woman,** a woman hired to do rough cleaning. [O.E. *cerran, cierran,* to turn; see also **jar** (3), **ajar.**]

char, chär, n. (slang) tea. [Cockney spelling of cha.]

Chara, kā'ra, n. a genus of freshwater plants of a family and class (stoneworts, Charā'ceae, Charoph'yta) more or less akin to the green seaweeds, having stems encrusted with calcareous matter and whorled branches. [L., some plant.]

charabanc, char-à-banc, shar'-ə-bang, -bā, n. a long open vehicle with rows of transverse seats: loosely applied to a tourist coach.—Vulg. contr. cha'ra—pl. char'abancs, char'-à-bancs, or chars-à-bancs. [Fr. char à bancs, carriage with benches.]

Characinidae, kar-ə-sin'i-dē, n.pl. a family of freshwater fishes to which belong the dorado and the piranha.—adj. chara'cinoid. [Gr. charax, a fish of some kind.]

character, kar'ək-tər, (Spens., Shak., etc. -ak') n. a letter, sign, figure, stamp, or distinctive mark: a mark of any kind, a symbol in writing, etc.: writing generally, handwriting: a secret cipher: any essential feature or peculiarity: a quality: nature: personal appearance (obs.): the aggregate of peculiar qualities which constitutes personal or national individuality: esp. moral qualities: the reputation of possessing these: a formal statement of the qualities of a person who has been in one's service or employment: official position, rank, or status, or a person who has filled it: a person noted for eccentricity or well-marked personality: a personality as created in a play or novel (Shak. char'act) or appearing in history: a literary genre, consisting in a description in prose or verse of a human type, or of a place or object on that model, a dominant form of literature in the 17th century under the influence of Theophrastus and the theory of humours: person (slang).—v.t. to engrave, imprint, write: to represent, delineate, or describe (arch.).—n. characterisā'tion (-izā'tion).—v.t. char'acterise, -ize, to describe by peculiar qualities: to be a distinguishing mark or quality of.—ns. char'acterism, a characteristic: a characterisation; characteris'tic, that which marks or constitutes the character: the integral part of a logarithm.—adjs. characteris'tic, -al.—adv. characteris'tically.—adj. char'acterless, without character or distinctive qualities.—ns. char'acterlessness; char'actery (in Shak. -ak'), writing: impression: that which is charactered.—character actor, one who plays character parts; character essay; character literature; character part, a stage or film rôle portraying an unusual or eccentric personality type; character sketch, a short description of the main traits in a person's character.—in character, in harmony with the part assumed, appropriate: in keeping with the person's usual conduct or attitudes: dressed for the part; out of character, not in character, unlike what one would expect from the person concerned. [Fr. caractère—L. charactēr—Gr. charaktēr, from charassein, to cut, engrave.]

charade, shə-räd', in U.S. usu. -rād', n. a species of riddle, the subject of which is a word proposed for solution from an enigmatical description of its component syllables and of the whole: an acted riddle in which the syllables and the whole are uttered or represented in successive scenes. [Fr., perh.—Prov. charrada, chatter, or Sp. charrada, clownishness.]

Charadrius, kar-ad'ri-əs, n. the plover genus, giving name to the family Charad'riidae. [Gr. charadrios, a bird, prob. the thick-knee.]

charas, churrus, chär'əs, chur'əs, n. the resinous exudation of hemp, a narcotic and intoxicant. [Hind.]

charcoal, chär'kōl, n. charred wood, or coal made by charring wood: the carbonaceous residue of substances that have undergone smothered combustion. [char, coal.]

charcuterie, shär-küt-rē, n. a pork-butcher's

shop: a delicatessen, or the meats sold in it. [Fr.]

chard, chärd, n. the edible leafstalk of cardoon, artichoke, or a variety (Swiss chard) of white beet. [L. carduus, thistle.]

chare. See char (3).

charet, char'et, (Spens.) n. same as chariot.

charge, chärj, v.t. to load, to put something into, to fill: to load heavily, burden: to fill completely: to cause to accumulate electricity: to lay a task upon, to enjoin, command: to deliver an official injunction, exhortation, or exposition to: to accuse: to place a bearing upon (with with; her.): to exact or demand from, to ask as the price: to set down as a liability against: to attack at a rush: to advance in accusation (that).—v.i. to make an onset.—n. that which is laid on: cost or price: the load of powder, fuel, etc., for a gun, furnace, etc.: attack or onset: care, custody: the object of care: an accumulation of electricity: command: exhortation: accusation: a device borne on a shield (her.): (pl.) expenses.—adj. charge'able, liable to be charged, imputable: blamable: burdensome (B.).—n. charge'ableness.—adv. charge'ably.—adj. charge'ful (Spens.; Shak.) burdensome, or expensive.—adj. charge'less.—n. char'ger, a flat dish capable of holding a large joint, a platter: a war-horse.—charge account, an account in which goods obtained are entered to be paid for later; charge'-hand, -man, the leader of a gang of workmen; charge'-house (Shak.), a school; charge'-sheet, a police list of accused and the charges against them.—give in charge, to hand over to the police; take charge of, to assume the care of. [Fr. charger—L.L. carricāre, to load—L. carrus, a wagon; see car, cargo.]

chargé-d'affaires, shär'zhā-dä-fer', n. a diplomatic agent of lesser rank, accredited not to the sovereign but to the department for foreign affairs and holding his credentials from the minister: the person in charge for the time. [Fr.]

charily, chariness. See chary.

chariot, char'i-ət, n. a pleasure or state car: a god's car: a car used in ancient warfare or racing: a light four-wheeled carriage with back seats and box.—v.t. to carry in a chariot.—v.i. to ride in a chariot.—n. charioteer', one who drives a chariot.—v.t. and v.i. to drive or to ride in such. [Fr., dim. of char, a car.]

Charis, kar'is (Gr. hhär'is), any one of the three Char'ites (-tēz, Gr. -tes), the Graces (Aglaia, Euphrosyne, Thalia), Greek goddess of whatever imparts graciousness to life.—ns. char'ism, charis'ma, a spiritual power given by God: personal quality or gift that enables an individual to impress and influence many of his fellows: a similar quality felt to reside in an office or position.—adj. charismat'ic, of or pertaining to a charism. [Gr. charis, -itos, grace.]

charity, char'i-ti, n. universal love (N.T.): the disposition to think favourably of others, and to do them good: almsgiving: a charitable foundation, institution, or cause: (pl.) affections.—adj. char'itable, of or relating to, showing, inspired by charity.—n. char'itableness.—adv. char'itably.—char'ity-boy, -girl', a pupil in a char'ity-school', a school for the poor supported by endowments or gifts.—charity begins at home, usually an excuse for not allowing it to get abroad; cold as charity, an ironical phrase. [Fr. charité—L. cāritās, -ātis—cārus, dear.]

charivari, shär-i-vär'i, n. a cacophonous mock serenade, rough music, cats' concert. [Fr.,—L.L. caribaria, a headache.]

chark, chärk, v.t. to burn to charcoal.—n. charcoal, coke. [charcoal.]

charlatan, shär'lə-tən, n. a mere talking pretender: a quack.—adjs. charlatanic (-tan'ik), -al.

Neutral vowels in unaccented syllables: el'ə-mənt; for certain sounds in foreign words, see p. viii

—*ns.* **char'latanism, char'latanry.** [Fr.,—It. *ciarlatano*—*ciarlare*, to chatter; imit.]

**Charles's wain,** *chärlz'iz wān, n.* the seven bright stars in the Plough. [O.E. *Carles wægn*, Carl being Charlemagne.]

**Charleston,** *chärls'tan, n.* a 20th-century dance characterised by spasmodic knee action. [*Charleston* in South Carolina.]

**Charley, Charlie** (also without *cap.*), *chär'li, n.* a night-watchman: the small triangular beard familiar in the portraits of *Charles* I: a small moustache, resembling that worn by *Charlie* Chaplin: a credulous person: an inefficient, forceless person, a fool (often in the phrase *a proper Charlie*): the fox.—**Char'ley-pitch'er** (*slang*), a thimble-rigger. [From the name *Charles*.]

**charlock,** *chär'lok, n.* wild mustard, a common yellow-flowered cornfield weed. [O.E. *cerlic*.]

**charlotte,** *shär'lot, n.* a dish of cooked apple or the like, covered with crumbs of toast: a kind of tart containing fruit.—**charlotte russe** (*rüs*), a custard or cream enclosed in a kind of spongecake. [From the name *Charlotte*.]

**Charol(l)ais,** *shar-ō-lā, n.* a breed of cattle named after an old district of France (Charolais) of which Charolles was the capital.

**charm,** *chärm, n.* a spell: something thought to possess occult power, as an amulet, a metrical form of words, etc.: an amulet, etc.: a trinket: power of fascination: attractiveness: (*pl.*) personal attractions: that which can please irresistibly: a song (*Spens.*).—*v.t.* to influence by a charm: to subdue by secret influence: to enchant: to delight: to allure: to tune or play.—*adj.* **charmed,** bewitched: delighted: protected as by a special charm.—*n.* **charm'er.**—*adj.* **charm'ful,** abounding in charms.—*adj.* **charm'-ing,** highly pleasing: delightful: fascinating.—*adv.* **charm'ingly.**—*adj.* **charm'less,** wanting or destitute of charms.—*adv.* **charm'lessly.** [Fr. *charme*—L. *carmen*, a song.]

**charm.** Same as **chirm.**

**charmeuse,** *shär'mōōz,* Fr. *shär-mœz,* a soft satin material made originally of silk, but now also of synthetic fibres. [Originally a tradename.]

**charneco,** *chär'ni-kō,* (*Shak.*) *n.* a kind of sweet wine. [Prob. from a village near Lisbon.]

**charnel,** *chär'nəl, n.* (*obs.*) a burial place.—*adj.* sepulchral: death-like.—**char'nel-house,** a place where the bones thrown up by grave-diggers are put. [O.Fr. *charnel*—L.L. *carnāle*—L. *carnālis* —*carō, carnis*, flesh.]

**Charon,** *kā'rən, n.* in Greek mythology, the ferryman who rowed the shades of the dead across the river Styx in the lower world: a ferryman. [Gr. *Charōn*.]

**charpie,** *shär'pē,* or *-pē', n.* lint shredded down to form a soft material for dressing wounds. [O.Fr. *charpir*—L. *carpēre*, to pluck.]

**charpoy,** *chär'poi, n.* the common Indian bedstead, sometimes handsomely wrought and painted. [Hind. *chārpāī*—Pers. *chahār-pāī*, four feet.]

**charqui,** *chär'kē, n.* beef cut into long strips and dried in the sun—jerked beef. [Quechua.]

**charr.** Same as **char** (1).

**chart,** *chärt, n.* a marine or hydrographical map, exhibiting part of a sea or other water, with the islands, contiguous coasts, soundings, currents, etc.: an outline-map, curve, or a tabular statement giving information of any kind.—*v.t.* to map.—*adj.* **chart'less.**—**chart'house, chart'-room,** the room in a ship where charts are kept. [O.Fr. *charte*—L. *c(h)arta*, a paper—Gr. *chartēs*.]

**charta, carta,** *kär'ta, n.* a charter.—*adj.* **chartā'-ceous,** papery. [L. *c(h)arta*—Gr. *chartēs*, a sheet of paper.]

**charter,** *chärt'ər, n.* any formal writing in evidence

of a grant, contract, or other transactions, conferring or confirming titles, rights, or privileges, or the like: the formal deed by which a sovereign guarantees the rights and privileges of his subjects: a document creating a borough or other corporation: any instrument by which powers and privileges are conferred by the state on a body of persons for a special object: a patent: grant: allowance: immunity.—*v.t.* to establish by charter: to let or hire, as a ship, on contract.—*adj.* hired, as *charter plane*: made in a hired aeroplane, as *charter flight.*—*n.* **chart'erer.**—*adj.* **chart'ered,** granted or protected by a charter: privileged: licensed: hired by contract.—**chart'er-chest,** a box in which charters are preserved; **chartered accountant,** one qualified under the regulations of the Institute of Accountants; **chartered company,** a trading company acting under a charter from the crown; **chart'er-hand',** court-hand; **chart'er-may'or,** the mayor of a borough at the time of its charter; **char'ter-mem'ber,** an original member of an incorporation. [O.Fr. *chartre*—L. *cartula, c(h)arta*—Gr. *chartēs*, a sheet of paper.]

**Charterhouse,** *chärt'ər-hows, n.* a Carthusian monastery: the famous hospital and school instituted in London in 1611, on the site of a Carthusian monastery.—*ns.* **Chartreuse** (*shär-trœz'*), a Carthusian monastery, esp. the original one, La Grande Chartreuse near Grenoble in France: a famous liqueur, usu. green, or yellow, long manufactured there by the monks from aromatic herbs and brandy: a kind of enamelled pottery: a mould of rice or blancmange enclosing some other food: a pale greenish ish colour; **Chartreux** (*shär-trø*), a Carthusian: the Charterhouse School. [See **Carthusian.**]

**charterparty,** *chärt'ər-pär-ti, n.* the common written form in which the contract of affreightment is expressed—viz. the hiring of the whole or part of a ship for the conveyance of goods. [Fr. *charte partie*, lit. a divided charter, as the practice was to divide it in two and give a half to each person—(L. *c(h)arta partita*; see **charta**).]

**Chartism,** *chärt'izm, n.* a movement in Great Britain for the extension of political power to the working-classes—its programme, the People's Charter (1838), since achieved, except annual parliaments.—Also *adj.* [See **charta.**]

**chartography,** *kär-tog'rə-fi.* See **cartography.**

**chartreuse, chartreux.** See **Charterhouse.**

**chartulary,** *kär'tū-lər-i.* Same as **cartulary.**

**charwoman.** See **char** (3).

**chary,** *chā'ri, adj.* fastidious, shy (*Shak.*): precious (*obs.*): careful (of) (*arch.*): cautious: wary (of doing, saying, giving, etc.).—*adv.* **char'ily.**—*n.* **char'iness.** [O.E. *cearig*—*cearu*, care.]

**Charybdis,** *kə-rib'dis, n.* in the Odyssey a dangerous monster that dwelt under a rock opposite to Scylla, and three times a day swallowed and threw up the waters of the sea, later a current or a whirlpool on the Sicilian side of the Straits of Messina—with Scylla providing a proverbial alternative of evil or disaster.

**chase** (*obs.* **chace**), *chās, v.t.* to pursue: to hunt: seek: to drive away: put to flight.—*v.i.* (*coll.*), to hurry (around).—*n.* pursuit: a hunting: that which is hunted: an unenclosed game preserve: the second impact of an unreturned ball, for which the player scored unless his opponent bettered it (and scored) by a little impact nearer the end wall (*tennis; Shak.*).—*n.* chas'er, a pursuer: a hunter: a horse for steeplechasing: an aeroplane for pursuing hostile aircraft: a woman over-assiduous in pursuit of men: a cooling drink after spirits: a chasse.—**chase'-port,** the porthole at bow or stern (through which a gun is fired during pursuit).—**beasts of**

**chase**, properly the buck, doe, fox, marten, and roe: wild beasts that are hunted generally; go **and chase yourself**, clear out; **wild-goose chase**, a chase hither and thither: any foolish or profitless pursuit of the unattainable. [O.Fr. *chacier*, *chasser*—L. *captāre*, freq. of *capĕre*, to take.]

**chase**, *chās*, *v.t.* to enchase, to decorate by engraving.—*ns.* **chas'er**, one who practises chasing: a tool for chasing; **chas'ing**, the art of engraving on the outside of raised metal work: the art of cutting the threads of screws. [Short for **enchase**.]

**chase**, *chās*, *n.* a case or frame for holding types: a groove. [Fr. *châsse*, a setting—L. *capsa*, a chest. See **case** (1).]

**chasm**, *kazm*, *n.* a yawning or gaping hollow: a gap or opening: a void space.—*adjs.* **chasmed**; **chasm'y**. [Gr. *chasma*, from *chainein*, to gape; cf. **chaos**.]

**chasmogamy**, *kaz-mog'ə-mi*, (*bot.*) *n.* the condition of having open, not cleistogamic, flowers, allowing cross-fertilisation.—*adj.* **chasmogamic** (*-mōgam'ik*). [Gr. *chasma*, a gape, *gameein*, to marry.]

**chasse**, *shas*, *n.* a dram or liqueur taken after coffee.—Also **chasse-café**. [Fr. *chasser*, to chase.]

**chassé**, *shas'ā*, *n.* a gliding step in dancing.—*v.i.* to make such a step.—*v.t.* (*slang*) to dismiss.—**chassé-croisé**, *-krwä-zā*, a dance movement in which partners change places by means of a chassé. [Fr.]

**Chassepot**, *shas'pō*, *n.* a rifle adopted by the French army in 1866. [From the inventor's name.]

**chasseur**, *shas-œr'*, *n.* a hunter or huntsman: one of a select body of French light infantry or cavalry: a liveried attendant. [Fr.,—*chasser*, to hunt; see **chase**.]

**chassis**, *shas'ē*, *-i*, *n.* the frame, wheels, and machinery of a motor-car: an aeroplane's landing-carriage: a casemate gun carriage: a frame, sash (*obs.*):—*pl.* **chassis** (*shas'ēz*). [Fr. *chassis*, frame.]

**chaste**, *chāst*, *adj.* sexually virtuous: modest: refined and pure in taste and style.—*adv.* **chaste'ly**.—*v.t.* **chasten** (*chās'n*), to free from faults by punishing: hence, to punish: to purify or refine: to restrain or moderate.—*p.adj.* **chas'tened**, purified: modest: tempered.—*ns.* **chas'tener**; **chaste'ness**; **chas'tenment**.—*v.t.* **chastise**, *-ize*, (*chas-tiz'*), to refine, purify, correct (*obs.*): to moderate, restrain (*arch.*): to inflict punishment upon for the purpose of correction: to reduce to order or to obedience.—*adj.* **chastis'able**.—*ns.* **chas'tisement** (*chas'tiz-mənt*); **chastity** (*chas'ti-ti*), sexual purity: virginity: refinement of style: moderation.—**chaste tree**, *agnus castus*; **chastity belt**, a defensive device said to have been worn by, e.g. wives of absent crusaders: a device made in modern times according to its supposed design: also *fig.* [O.Fr. *chaste*—L. *castus*, pure.]

**chasuble**, *chaz'* or *chas'ū-bl*, *n.* a sleeveless vestment worn over the alb by the priest while celebrating mass. [Fr.—L.L. *casubula*—L. *casula*, dim. of L. *casa*, a hut.]

**chat**, *chat*, *v.i.* to talk easily or familiarly.—*v.t.* (with *up*) to talk to lightly and informally but with a purpose, e.g. in order to cajole (*pr.p.* **chatt'ing**; *pa.t.* and *pa.p.* **chatt'ed**).—*n.* familiar, easy talk.—*n.* **chatt'iness**.—*adj.* **chatt'y**, given or inclined to chat: of the nature of chat. [From **chatter**.]

**chat**, *chat*, *n.* a genus (*Saxicola*) of small birds in the thrush family, including the stone-chat and the whin-chat. [From the sound of their voice.]

**chat**, *chat*, *n.* (*dial.*) a small potato of poor quality.

**château**, *shä'tō*, *n.* a castle: a great country-seat,

esp. in France: a vineyard estate around a castle, esp. in Bordeaux (common in names of wines associated with such, e.g. Château Lafite, Château Margaux):—*pl.* **chât'eaux** (*-tōz*).—*ns.* **châtelain** (*shat'ə-lē*), a castellan; **chât'elaine** (*-len*), a female castellan: an ornamental bunch of short chains bearing keys, scissors, etc., attached to the waist-belt: a similar thing in miniature attached to the watch-chain.—**châteaux en Espagne** (*shä-tō-zā-nes-päny'*), (Fr.) castles in Spain, castles in the air. [Fr. *château* (O.Fr. *chastel*)—L. *castellum*, dim. of *castrum*, a fort.]

**Chateaubriand** (also without *cap.*), *shä-tō-brē-ä*, a grilled thick fillet steak. [François René, Vicomte de Chateaubriand, 1768-1848, French author and statesman.]

**chaton**, *shä-tō'*, *n.* the head of a finger-ring. [Fr.]

**chatoyant**, *shat-wä-yä*, *shat-oi'ənt*, *adj.* with a changing lustre, like a cat's eye in the dark: iridescent.—*n.* **chatoyance** (*shat-wä-yäs*, *shat-oi'-əns*). [Fr.]

**chatta**, *chät'ä*, *n.* an umbrella. [Hind.]

**chattel**, *chat'l*, *n.* any kind of property which is not freehold, distinguished further into *chattels-real* and *chattels-personal*, the latter being mere personal movables—money, plate, cattle, and the like: the former including leasehold interests.—**goods and chattels**, all corporeal movables. [O.Fr. *chatel*—L.L. *captāle*—L. *capitāle*, etc., property, goods.]

**chatter**, *chat'ər*, *v.i.* to talk idly or rapidly: (of birds) to utter a succession of rapid short notes: to sound as the teeth when one shivers.—*n.* noise like that made by a magpie, or by the striking together of the teeth: idle talk.—*ns.* **chatt'erer**, one that chatters: an idle talker: a name applied to two families of birds, the wax-wings and the cotingas; **chatt'ering**.—**chatt'erbox**, one who talks or chatters incessantly. [From the sound.]

**chatty**. See **chat** (1).

**chatty**, *chat'i*, (*India*) *n.* an earthen water-pot. [Hind.]

**Chaucerian**, *chö-sē'ri-ən*, *adj.* like or pertaining to Chaucer.—*n.* a student or follower of Chaucer. —*n.* **Chau'cerism**, anything characteristic of Chaucer.

**chaudfroid**, *shō-frwä*, *n.* a jellied sauce, or a dish, e.g. of chicken, including it. [Fr., (*lit.*) hot-cold.]

**chaud-mellé**, *shōd-mel'ä*, (Scots law) *n.* a fight arising in the heat of passion: the killing of a man in such a fight. [O.Fr. *chaude-mellee*, hot fight; see **mêlée**.]

**chaufe**, **chauff** (*Spens.*), *chöf*. Forms of **chafe**.

**chauffer**, *chö'fər*, *n.* a metal box for holding fire, a portable furnace or stove. [See **chafer**.]

**chauffeur**, *shō'fər*, *-fər'*, *n.* one employed to drive a motor-car:—fem. **chauffeuse** (*-føz*). [Fr., stoker.]

**chaulmoogra**, **chaulmugra**, *chöl-mōō'grə*, *n.* a name for various Indian trees of the family Flacourtiaceae, yielding **chaulmoogra oil**, used, esp. formerly, in the treatment of leprosy. [Beng.]

**chaunce**, **chaunge**, old forms of **chance**, **change**.

**chaunt(er)**. See **chant(er)**.

**chausses**, *shōs*, or *shō'siz*, *n.pl.* any closely fitting covering for the legs, hose generally: the defence-pieces for the legs in ancient armour.—*n.* **chaussure** (*-ür'*), a general name for boots and shoes. [O.Fr. *chauces*—L. *calcia*, hose.]

**Chautauqua**, *shə-tök'wə*, *n.* a village and lake in U.S. where similar summer educational meetings were instituted in the late 19th cent.: (also without *cap.*) a meeting of this type, with lectures, etc.—*adj.* **Chautauquan** (*shə-tö'kwən*), pertaining to a system of instruction for adults by home reading and study under guidance, evolved from

Neutral vowels in unaccented syllables: *el'ə-mənt*; for certain sounds in foreign words, see p, viii the *Chautauqua* (New York State) Literary and Scientific Circle, organised in 1878.

**chauvinism,** *shō'vin-izm, n.* an absurdly extravagant pride in one's country, with a corresponding contempt for foreign nations: extravagant attachment to any group, place, cause, etc.— *ns.* **chau'vin, chau'vinist.**—*adj.* **chauvinist'ic.** [From Nicolas *Chauvin,* an ardent veteran of Napoleon's, who figures in Cogniard's *La Cocarde tricolore.*]

**chavender,** *chav'ən-dər, n.* the chub. [Cf. **cheven.**]

**chaw,** *chö, (Spens.) n.* a jaw. [See **jaw.**]

**chaw,** *chö, v.t.* to chew (still used of tobacco and in dial.).—*n.* a quantity for chewing.—**chaw'-bā'con,** a country clown, a rustic fellow.—**chawed up** (*U.S. slang*), destroyed: defeated: crushed: reprimanded. [By-form of **chew.**]

**chawdron,** *chö'drən, (Shak.) n.* the entrails of an animal. [O.Fr. *chaudun.*]

**chay,** a vulgar form of **chaise.**

**chay,** *chī, chā, chaya, chi'ə, shaya, shi'ə, n.* an Indian plant (Oldenlandia) of the madder family whose root (**chay-root,** etc.) yields a red dye. [Cf. Tamil *saya.*]

**che,** *chə, (Shak.) pron.* a S.W. dialect form of I. [O.E. *ic;* cf. **ch.**]

**cheap,** *chēp, n. (obs.)* bargain, buyer's advantage.—*adj.* (from the phrase *good cheap*) low in price: charging low prices: of a low price in relation to the value: easily obtained: of small value, or so reckoned: paltry: inferior.—Also *adv.*—*v.t.* **cheap'en,** to ask the price of (*arch.*): to make cheap, to lower the price of: to lower the reputation of: to beat down the price of.—*n.* **cheap'ener.** —*adv.* **cheap'ly.**—*n.* **cheap'ness.**—**cheap Jack,** or **John,** a travelling hawker who professes to give great bargains; **cheap labour,** labour paid at a poor rate; **cheapskate** (*slang*), a miserly or despicable person.—**cheap and nasty,** offensively inferior and of low value; **cheap of** (*Scot.*), having got off lightly with: served right; **dirt cheap,** ridiculously cheap; **feel cheap,** to have a sense of inferiority and humiliation; **on the cheap,** cheap or cheaply. [O.E. *cēap,* price, a bargain, *ceapian.* O.N. *kaupa* Ger. *kaufen,* to buy.]

**cheat,** *chēt, n.* an escheat, a forfeit (*obs.*): a piece of plunder, a stolen thing (*obs.*): a thing in general, esp. the gallows (*thieves' cant*): a fraud: a deception: a card game in which deception is allowed: one who cheats.—*v.t.* to deceive, defraud, impose upon.—*v.i.* to practise deceit.—*ns.* **cheat'er,** one who cheats: an officer who collected the fines to be paid into the Exchequer (*Shak.*): (*pl.*) spectacles (*U.S. slang*): (*pl.*) falsies (*slang*); **cheat'ery** (*coll.*) cheating.—**put a cheat upon,** to deceive; **tame cheater** (*Shak.*), a decoy. [es- **cheat.**]

**chechako.** Same as **cheechako.**

**chéchia,** *shā'shya, n.* a cylindrical skull-cap, worn by Arabs and adopted by French troops in Africa. [Fr.,—Berber *tashashit,* pl. *tishushai* skull-cap.]

**check,** *chek, v.t.* to bring to a stand: to restrain or hinder: to rebuke: to control by comparison: to verify: to punch (as a ticket): to nip, pinch, crush, as by biting or shutting (*Scot.* also **chack**): to deposit or receive in exchange for a check: to send (baggage) on a passenger's ticket (*U.S.*): to place in check at chess: to mark with a pattern of crossing lines.—*v.i.* to forsake the quarry for some other bird (with *at;* falconry): to come to a stop.—*n.* a position in chess when one party obliges the other either to move or guard his king: anything that checks: a sudden stop, repulse, or rebuff: restraint: control: a rebuke (*B., Shak.*): a mark put against items in a list: an order for money (usually written **cheque,** except in U.S.): a means of verification or testing: any counter-register used as security, a counterfoil: a token, given for example to a

person leaving his seat in a theatre with the intention of returning: a restaurant bill: a counter used in games at cards (hence 'to pass in one's checks' = to die): a mechanism that holds a piano hammer after striking: a pattern of cross lines forming small squares, as in a chessboard: any fabric woven with such a pattern.— *adj.* divided into small squares by crossing lines. —*n.* **check'er,** one who hinders, rebukes, or scrutinises: (in *pl.*) draughts.—**check'-ac'tion,** piano action with checks: **check'-clerk.** a clerk who checks accounts, etc.; **check'er-board,** a checked board on which checkers or draughts is played; **check'-key,** a latch-key; **check'list,** a list for verification purposes: a comprehensive list: an inventory; **check'mate,** in chess, a check given to the adversary's king when in a position in which it can neither be protected nor moved out of check, so that the game is finished: a complete check: defeat: overthrow.—*v.t.* in chess, to put in checkmate: to defeat.—**check'-rein,** a coupling rein, a strap hindering a horse from lowering its head; **check'room, check'ing-room,** (*U.S.*) a cloakroom or luggage-room; **check'-string,** a string by which the occupant of a carriage may attract the driver's notice; **check'-tak'er,** one who takes tickets; **check'-till,** a till that records sums received; **check'-up,** a testing scrutiny: one of a series of regular medical examinations; **check'-weigh'er,** one who on the part of the men checks the weight of coal sent up to the pit-mouth.—**check in, out,** record one's arrival or departure from work: to perform the necessary business at a hotel office on arriving, or leaving; **check up,** to investigate: to examine and test (often with *on*).—**hold in check,** restrain, keep back. [O.Fr. *eschec, eschac,* through Ar. from Pers. *shāh* king, *māt*(a), the king is dead.]

**checker.** See **check;** also under **cheque.**

**checker-berry,** *chek'ər-ber-i, n.* the American winter-green (*Gaultheria*).

**checklaton,** s(c)**hecklaton,** *chek-, shek-lat'ən, n.* understood and explained by Spenser as gilded leather used for making embroidered jacks. [**ciclaton,** perh. with association with **latten.**]

**Cheddar,** *ched'ər, n.* a kind of cheese first made at *Cheddar* in Somersetshire.—**Cheddar pink,** a species of pink (*Dianthus caesius*) found on the limestone cliffs at Cheddar.

**cheechako,** *chē-chä'kō, (Canada* and *Alaska) n.* a tenderfoot.—Also **checha'ko, cheechal'ko, checha'quo.** [Chinook jargon, new-come.]

**chee-chee,** *chē'chē, n.* in India, a Eurasian: affected Eurasian English. [Perh. Hind. *chī-chī,* dirt, fie!]

**cheek,** *chēk, n.* the side of the face below the eye, the fleshy lateral wall of the mouth: effrontery, impudence (*coll.*): a side-post of a door, window, etc.: the cheek strap of a horse's bridle: the ring at the end of a bit: anything arranged in lateral pairs.—*v.t.* (*coll.*) to address insolently.— *adj.* **cheek'y** (*coll.*), saucy.—**cheek'-bone,** the bone above the cheek; **cheek'-pouch,** a dilatation of the cheek, forming a bag, as in monkeys, etc.; **cheek'-tooth,** a molar tooth.—**cheek by jowl,** side by side. [O.E. *cēce, cēace,* cheek, jaw; cf. Du. *kaak.*]

**cheep,** *chēp, v.i.* to chirp, as a young bird.—*n.* sound of cheeping.—*n.* **cheep'er,** a young bird, esp. of game. [Imit.]

**cheer,** *chēr, n.* face (*arch.*): disposition, frame of mind (with *good,* etc.): joy: a shout of approval or welcome: kind treatment (*obs.*): entertainment: fare, food.—*v.t.* to comfort: to encourage: to applaud (to inspirit.—*v.i.* to take comfort (*obs.*): to be of good cheer (*obs.*): to shout encouragement or applause.—*n.* **cheer'er.**—*adj.* **cheer'ful,** in, of, promoting, or accompanied by good spirits.—*adv.* cheer'fully.—*n.* cheer'fulness.—*adv.* cheer'ily.—*n.* cheer'iness.—*interj.* cheer'io, cheer'o, cheers, a bright informal goodbye.—*ns.* cheer'ishness (*Milton*), cheerfulness; cheerleader, (*U.S.*) one who directs organised cheering, as at team games.—*adj.* cheer'less, comfortless.—*adj.* cheer'ly, cheerful.—*adv.* in a cheery manner: heartily.—*interj.* cheers! (*coll.*), good health! (used when drinking a toast).—*adj.* cheer'y, cheerful: promoting cheerfulness.—cheer up, (*coll.*) to make, or become, more cheerful. [O.Fr. *chiere*, face.—L.L. *cara*, the face.]

cheese, *chēz, n.* a wholesome article of food, made from the curd of milk coagulated by rennet, separated from the whey, and pressed into a solid mass: a compressed cake of various nature: the receptacle of a thistle-head: the flattened cheese-shaped bowl used in skittles.—*n.* chees'iness.—*adj.* chees'y, having the nature of cheese.—cheese'burger, a hamburger cooked with cheese on top of it; cheese'cake, a cup of pastry containing formerly cheese, now some sort of curd: a pin-up, esp. of a lightly clad woman (*slang*.): female shapely charms (*slang*): a show of leg (*slang*); cheese'cloth, a loose-woven cloth suitable for pressing cheeses; cheese'-cutter, a square-peaked cap; cheese'-hopper, the larva of a small fly, remarkable for its leaping power, found in cheese; cheese'-mite, a very small arachnid that breeds in cheese; cheese'-monger, a dealer in cheese; cheese'-paring, paring, or rind, of cheese (*Shak.*): a very thin man: parsimony.—*adj.* mean and parsimonious.—cheese'-press, a machine in which curds for cheese are pressed; cheese'-renn'et, the plant lady's bed-straw, said to have been used as rennet in curdling milk; cheese'-straw, a long thin biscuit flavoured with cheese; cheese'-taster, a scoop for taking a sample from the inside of a cheese; cheese'-vat, a vat or wooden case in which curds are pressed; cheese'-wring, a cheese-press.—green cheese, cheese not yet dried; make cheeses, to whirl round and then sink down suddenly so as to make the skirt stand out like a cheese. [O.E. *cēse, cȳse,* curdled milk (cf. Ger. *käse,* cheese)—L. *cāseus.*]

cheese, *chēz, n.* the correct thing (*obs. slang*): anything of excellent quality.—big cheese (*slang*), a person of importance. [Prob. Pers. and Hind. *chiz,* thing.]

cheese, *chēz, v.t.* (*slang*) in the phrases cheese it, stop, have done, run off; cheesed off (also cheesed), fed up.

cheetah, *chē'tə, n.* an Eastern animal like the leopard, used in hunting. [Hindi *cītā*—Sans. *citraka, citrakāya,* having a speckled body.]

cheewink. Same as chewink.

chef, *shef, n.* a head-cook (in full chef de cuisine, *də kwē-zēn,* kitchen-head): a reliquary in the shape of a head.—chef d'œuvre (*shā-də-vr'*), a masterpiece:—*pl.* chefs d'œuvre (*shā-*). [Fr. head, chief; see chief.]

cheiro-, *ki'rō-, ki-ro'-,* (see also chiro-) in composition, hand.—*ns.* cheirog'nomy, chirog'nomy (Gr. *gnōmē,* understanding), palmistry; chi'rograph, a written or signed document; ch(e)irog'rapher (*obs.*), an official of the Court of Common Pleas; ch(e)irog'raphist, an expert in handwriting: a palmist (*Pope*); ch(e)irol'ogist; ch(e)irol'ogy, gesture-language: the study of the hand; ch(e)i'-romancy (*-man-si*), fortune-telling by the hand (Gr. *manteiā,* divination).—*adjs.* ch(e)iroman'tic, -al.—*n.* ch(e)iron'omer (Gr. *nomos,* law), a gesticulator.—*adj.* ch(e)ironom'ic.—*n.* ch(e)iron'omy, the art of gesticulation or of pantomime.—*n.pl.* Ch(e)irop'tera (Gr. *pteron,* wing), the order of bats.—*adjs.* ch(e)iropteroph'ilous (Gr. *phileein,* to love), pollinated by bats; ch(e)irop'terous.—*n.* Cheirothe'rium (Gr. *thērion,* beast), a Triassic

labyrinthodont with hand-like footprints. [Gr· *cheir,* hand.]

cheka, *chā'kə, n.* the Russian secret police of 1917-1922.—*n.* chek'ist, a member of the cheka. [Russ. *che ka,* names of the initial letters of the words for extraordinary commission.]

chela, *kē'lə, n.* the prehensile claw of an arthropod.—*adj.* che'late.—*n.* a co-ordination compound (e.g. haemoglobin) in which a central metallic ion is attached to an organic molecule at two or more positions.—*n.* Chē'lifer, the bookscorpion.—*adj.* chelif'erous, having a chela or chelae. [Latinised from Gr. *chēlē.*]

chela, *chā'lə, n.* a novice in Buddhism: a disciple of a religious teacher or leader.—*n.* che'laship. [Hindi *celā,* servant, disciple.]

chelicera, *kē-lis'ə-rə, n.* a biting appendage in Arachnida:—*pl.* chelic'erae (*-rē*). [Gr. *chēlē,* a crab's claw, *keras,* horn.]

Chellean, *shel'i-ən, adj.* belonging to an early Palaeolithic culture, older than Acheulean. [*Chelles,* near Paris, where flints of this stage are found.]

Chelonia, *ki-lō'ni-a, n.* an order of reptiles with horny shell and horny beak, tortoises and turtles.—*adj.* and *n.* chelō'nian. [Gr. *chelōnē,* a tortoise.]

Chelsea, *chel'sē,* district of London noted as an artists' quarter.—Chelsea bun, a rolled bun filled with currants and raisins; Chelsea pensioner, an elderly, often disabled, ex-soldier, connected with the Chelsea Royal Hospital; Chelsea ware, a variety of china made in the 18th cent.

chemin de fer, *shə-mē-də-fer', n.* a variety of baccarat (familiarly chemmy, *shem'i*). [Fr. railway.]

chemic, etc. See under chemistry.

chemise, *shə-mēz', n.* a woman's shirt, a smock or shift.—*n.* chemisette', a kind of bodice worn by women: lace or muslin filling up the open front of a woman's dress. [Fr. *chemise*—L.L. *camisia,* a nightgown, surplice.]

chemistry, *kem'is-tri,* formerly chymistry, *kim'is-tri, n.* the science of the properties of substances elementary and compound, and of the laws of their combination and action one upon another.—*adjs.* chemiat'ric, iatrochemical; chem'ic, alchemical (*obs.*): iatrochemical (*obs.*): chemical.—*n.* an alchemist or a chemist (*obs.*): bleaching powder (*arch.*).—*v.t.* to treat with bleaching powder:—*pr.p.* chem'icking; *pa.t.* and *pa.p.* chem'icked.—*adj.* chem'ical, alchemical (*obs.*): iatrochemical (*obs.*): relating to chemistry: versed in or studying chemistry.—*n.* a substance obtained by chemical means or used in chemical operations.—*adv.* chem'ically.—*ns.* chem'ism, chemical action; chem'ist, an alchemist (*obs.*): one skilled in chemistry: a manufacturer of or dealer in chemicals and drugs: a pharmacist; chem'itype, any chemical process for obtaining impressions from an engraving; chem'itypy, chem'onasty, nastic movement under diffuse chemical stimulus; chemopsychi'atry, treatment of mental illness by drugs.—*adjs.* chemopsychiat'-ric; chemorecep'tive.—*ns.* chemoreceptiv'ity; chemorecep'tion; chem'oreceptor, a sensory nerve-ending, receiving a chemical stimulus; chem'ostat, an apparatus for growth of bacteria, fungi, tissue, etc.—*adj.* chemotac'tic, pertaining to chemotaxis.—*ns.* chemotax'is, movement of a whole organism in a definite direction in response to chemical stimulus; chemotherapeu'tics, chemother'apy, treatment of a disease by means of a chemical compound, having a specific bactericidal or bacteriostatic effect against the microorganism involved; chemot'ropism (*bot.*), orientation by differential growth in response to chemical stimulus.—*adj.* chemotrop'ic.—*n.* chemurgy (*kem'ər-ji*), a branch of applied chemistry concerned with the use of agricultural products, or other organic raw materials, for industry.—*adjs.*

**chemur'gic, -al.**—chemical affinity, the tendency to combine with one another exhibited by many substances, or the force by which the substances constituting a compound are held together; chemical engineering, design, construction, and operation of chemical plant and works, esp. in industrial chemistry; chemical warfare, warfare involving the use of irritating or asphyxiating gases, oil flames, etc.—chemist and druggist, one who has passed the lower, pharmaceutical chemist, one who has passed the higher examinations, qualifying him to practise as a pharmacist. [See alchemy.]

**chenar,** chē-när', *n.* the oriental plane (*Platanus orientalis*). [Pers. *chinār.*]

**chenet,** sha-ne, (Fr.) an andiron.

**chenille,** sha-nēl', *n.* a thick, velvety cord of silk or wool resembling a woolly caterpillar: a velvet-like material used for table-covers, etc. [Fr. *chenille,* caterpillar—L. *canicula,* a hairy little dog, *canis,* a dog.]

**Chenopodium,** ken-ō-pō'di-əm, *n.* the goosefoot genus, giving name to the family **Chenopodiā'-ceae,** akin to the pink family.—*adj.* chenopodiā'-ceous. [Gr. *chēn,* goose, *pous, podos,* foot.]

**cheong-sam,** chong'-sam', *n.* a tight-fitting high-necked dress with slits at the sides. [Chin.]

**cheque,** in U.S. **check,** chek, *n.* a counterfoil (*obs.*): a money order on a banker.—*n.* cheq'uer, a chess-board, also a chess-man (*arch.*): alternation of colours, as on a chess-board (see also checker).—*v.t.* to mark in squares of different colours: to variegate: to interrupt.—*adjs.* cheq'uered, check'ered, variegated, like a chess-board: varying in character: eventful, with alternations of good and bad fortune.—*adv.* cheq'uerwise.—*adj.* cheq'uy, check'y (*her.*), chequered.—cheque'-book, a book of cheque forms; cheq'uer-work, any pattern having alternating squares of different colours—blank cheque, a cheque signed by the drawer without having the amount indicated: concession of power without limit (*fig.*); crossed cheque, an ordinary cheque with two transverse lines drawn across it, which have the effect of making it payable only through a bank account. [See check.]

**cher,** *fem.* **chère,** *sher,* (Fr.) dear.

**cheralite,** cher'a-līt, *n.* a radioactive mineral rich in thorium and uranium. [*Chera,* anc. name of Travancore, where discovered, Gr. *lithos,* a stone.]

**cherchef't,** a Miltonic spelling of kerchiefed.

**cherimoya, cherimoyer,** cher-i-moi'a, -ar, *n.* a Peruvian fruit (*Anona Cherimolia*) resembling the custard-apple. [Quechua.]

**cherish,** cher'ish, *v.t.* to protect and treat with affection: to nurture, nurse: to entertain in the mind.—*n.* cher'ishment. [Fr. *chérir, chérissant*—*cher,* dear—L. *cārus.*]

**chernozem,** chûr'nō-zem, a very fertile soil of sub-humid steppe, consisting of a dark topsoil over a lighter calcareous layer. [Russ., black earth.]

**Cherokee,** cher'a-kē, *n.* (a member of) a tribe of Iroquoian Indians: the language of the Cherokee.

**cheroot,** sha-rōōt', *n.* a cigar not pointed at either end. [Fr. *cheroute,* representing the Tamil name *shuruttu,* a roll.]

**cherry,** cher'i, *n.* a small stone-fruit: the tree (*Cerasus,* a subgenus of *Prunus*) that bears it: extended to many fruits resembling it in some way, as Barbados cherry: in cricket slang, the new ball, taken after so many runs have been scored or balls bowled.—*adj.* like a cherry in colour: ruddy.—cherr'y-bean, cow-pea; cherr'y-bob', in children's games, two cherries joined by the stalks; cherr'y-bounce', cherry brandy: brandy and sugar; cherry brandy, a liqueur made by steeping Morello cherries in brandy;

**cherr'y-coal,** a soft shining coal; cherr'y-lau'rel, a species of cherry with evergreen laurel-like leaves; cherr'y-pepp'er, a West Indian Capsicum; cherr'y-pie, a pie made of cherries: the common heliotrope; cherr'y-pit, a game in which cherry-stones are thrown into a small hole; cherr'y-plum, a plum of flavour approaching a cherry; cherr'y-stone, the hard endocarp of the cherry. [O.E. *ciris*—L. *cerasus*—Gr. *kerasos,* a cherry-tree. It is said to have been introduced from *Kerasous* (*Cerasus*) in Pontus, by Lucullus, but was known in Europe long before his time.]

**cherry,** cher'i, (Spens.) *v.t.* to cheer. [See cherish.]

**chersonese,** kûr'sa-nēz, -nēs, *n.* a peninsula. [Gr. *chersonēsos*—*chersos,* land, dry land, *nēsos,* an island.]

**chert,** chûrt, *n.* a compact flinty chalcedony.—*adj.* chert'y. [Etymology doubtful.]

**cherub,** cher'ab, *n.* a winged creature with human face, represented as associated with Jehovah: a celestial spirit: a chubby-faced person, esp. a child:—*pl.* cher'ubs, cher'ubim (-ə, -ū, -bim), cher'ubims.—*adjs.* cherubic (-ōō'bik), -al, cherubim'ic, angelic.—*adv.* cheru'bically.—*n.* cher'ubin (Shak.), a cherub. [Heb. *k'rub,* pl. *k'rubim.*]

**cherup,** cher'up. Same as chirrup.

**chervil,** chûr'vil, *n.* an umbelliferous plant (*Anthriscus cerefolium*) cultivated as a pot-herb: also other species of Anthriscus (*common, wild,* and *rough chervil*): extended to sweet cicely (*sweet chervil*). [O.E. *cerfille*—L. *caerefolium*—Gr. *chairephyllon.*]

**chesil,** chez'il, *n.* gravel: shingle: bran.—Also chis'el. [O.E. *cisil.*]

**chess,** ches, *n.* a game of skill for two, played with figures or men of different kinds which are moved on a chequered board.—chess'board, the board on which chess is played: a chequered design; chess'man. [O.Fr. *eschès* (Fr. *échecs*). It. *scacchi;* Ger. *schach*)—Pers. *shāh,* a king.]

**chess,** ches, *n.* one of the parallel planks of a pontoon-bridge—generally in *pl.*

**chessel,** ches'l, *n.* a cheese mould. [cheese.]

**chessylite,** ches'i-līt, *n.* basic carbonate of copper, vivid blue in colour, azurite. [*Chessy,* near Lyons, where it occurs.]

**chest,** chest, *n.* a large strong box: the part of the body between the neck and the abdomen, the thorax: a treasury: a chestful.—*adj.* chest'ed, having a chest: placed in a chest.—*n.* chest'ful, enough to fill a chest.—*adj.* chest'y, of the quality of the chest-voice: suggestive of disease of the chest (*coll.*): self-important (*slang*).—chest'-note, in singing or speaking, a deep note; chest'-protec'tor, a covering to keep the chest warm; chest'-register, -tone, -voice, the lowest register of the voice.—chest of drawers, a case in which drawers slide; chest of viols (*arch.*), a set of viols (two trebles, two tenors, two basses); off one's chest (*coll.*), off one's mind. [O.E. *cyst*—L. *cista*—Gr. *kistē;* Scot. *kist.*]

**chesterfield,** chest'ər-fēld, *n.* a long overcoat: a heavily padded sofa. [Lord *Chesterfield.*]

**chestnut** (now rarely chesnut), ches'nut, *n.* a tree of genus Castanea, esp. the *Spanish* or *Sweet Chestnut:* its edible nut, encased (three together) in a prickly husk: its hard timber: the horse-chestnut (*Aesculus hippocastanum*), its fruit or nut: a chestnut horse: in Australia, Castano-spermum: a horny knob of a horse's foreleg: a stale joke (*slang*).—*adj.* of chestnut colour, reddish-brown.—pull the chestnuts out of the fire, to take control and rescue someone from a difficult situation. [O.Fr. *chastaigne*—L. *casta-nea*—perh. from *Castana,* in Thessaly.]

**cheval de bataille,** sha-val da bä-tä-y', (Fr.; *lit.* warhorse) a favourite topic.

**cheval-de-frise,** sha-val'-da-frēz', *n.* a spiky defensive structure used esp. to stop cavalry:—*pl.*

chevaux-de-frise (shə-vō'-). [Fr. cheval, horse, de, of, Frise, Friesland.]

chevalet, shə-va'lä, she', n. the bridge of a stringed instrument (mus.). [Fr. dim. of cheval, a horse.]

cheval-glass, shə-val'gläs, n. a large glass or mirror supported on a frame. [Fr. cheval, horse, stand.]

chevalier, shev-ə-lēr', n. a cavalier: a knight: a gallant. [Fr.,—L.L. caballárius—L. caballus, a horse.]

chevalier d'industrie, shə-va-lyä dē-düs-trē, (Fr.) lit. a knight of industry: an adventurer, one who lives by his wits.

chevelure, shev'(ə-)lür, n. a head of hair: a periwig: the nebulous part of a comet. [Fr.,—L. capillātūra—capillus, hair.]

cheven, chev'ən, n. the chub.—Also chev'in. [Fr. chevin, chevanne.]

cheverel, -il, chev'ər-əl, n. a kid: soft, flexible kidskin leather.—adj. like kid leather, pliable.—ns.

chev(e)ron (shev'; obs.) a kid glove; chevrette (shəv-ret'), a thin kind of goat-skin. [Fr. chevreau, chevrette, a kid—chèvre; L. capra, a she-goat.]

chevesaile, chev'ə-sāl, n. an ornamental collar of a coat. [O.Fr. chevesaile—chevece, the neck.]

cheville, shə-vē', n. the peg of a stringed instrument (mus.): a redundant word or expression used in a verse or sentence for purposes of metre or balance only. [Fr., peg—L. clāvicula, dim. of clāvis, a key.]

Cheviot, chē'vi-ət (or chev'i-ət), n. a hardy breed of short-woolled sheep reared on the Cheviot Hills: a cloth made from their wool.

chevisance, chev'i-zans, n. (obs.) achievement: resource: gain: money dealings: performance (Spens.): an unidentified flower. [Fr.,—chevir, to accomplish; chef, the head, the end.]

chevron, shev'rən, n. a rafter: the representation of two rafters of a house meeting at the top (her.): a V-shaped band on the sleeve, a mark of noncommissioned rank or (in army and R.A.F., inverted) of long service and good conduct: see under cheverel.—adjs. chev'roned; chev'rony. [Fr. chevron, rafter—L. capreolus, dim. of caper, a goat.]

chevrotain, shev'rō-tān, or -tən, n. a mouse-deer, any member of the Tragulidae, an Old World tropical family of small deerlike animals not very near the deer but forming a separate section of artiodactyls. [Fr., dim. of chèvre—L. capra, she-goat.]

chevy, chev'i, chivy, chiv'i, n. a hunting cry: a pursuit: prisoner's base.—v.t. to chase: (often chivvy) to harass.—v.i. to scamper. [Perh. from the Border ballad of battle, Chevy Chase.]

chew, chōō, v.t. to bruise and grind with the teeth: to masticate: to meditate, reflect (fig.).—n. action of chewing: a quid of tobacco.—n. chew'ing-gum, a preparation made from chicle gum, produced by the sapodilla plum tree, sweetened and flavoured.—chew the cud, to masticate a second time food that has already been swallowed and passed into the first stomach: to ruminate in thought (fig.); chew the rag, the fat (slang), to keep on arguing the point. [O.E. cēowan; Ger. kauen; cf. jaw.]

chewet, chōō'it, n. a chough (obs.): a chatterer (Shak.). [Fr. chouette, chough (now owl).]

chewet, chōō'it, (obs.) n. a pie or pudding of miscellaneous chopped meats.

chewink, chə-wingk', n. a large finch of eastern N. America, the red-eyed towhee. [Imit.]

chez, shā, prep. at the home or establishment of. [Fr.]

chi, ki, hhē, n. the twenty-second letter (X, χ) of the Greek alphabet, representing an aspirated k sound: as numeral χ' = 600, ,χ = 600,000: in inscriptions χ = 1,000 (chilioi). [Gr. chei, chī.]

chi, chī. Same as chai.

Chian, ki'ən, adj. pertaining to Chios in the Aegean Sea.

Chianti, kē-an'ti, -än', It. kyän'tē, n. a red (or white) wine of Tuscany. [Chianti Mountains.]

chiao, jow, n. a coin of the People's Republic of China, one-tenth of 1 yuan. [Chin.]

chiaroscuro, kyär-o-skōō'rō, n. management of light and shade in a picture: the effect of light and shade (also fig.).

chiasm, ki'azm, n. (anat.) a decussation or intersection, esp. that of the optic nerves.—also chias'ma.—n. chias'mus (rhet.), contrast by parallelism in reverse order, as Do not live to eat, but eat to live.—adj. chias'tic.—n. chias'tolite, (min.) a variety of andalusite with black cruciform inclusions. [Gr. chiasma, a cross-shaped mark, chiastos, laid crosswise, like the Greek letter X (chi, chei), lithos, a stone.]

chiaus, chows, n. Same as chouse.

chibol, chib'əl. See cibol.

chibouk, chibouque, chi-bōōk', n. a long straight-stemmed Turkish pipe. [Turk. chibūk.]

chic, shēk, n. style, elegance: artistic skill.—adj. having chic: smart and fashionable. [Fr.]

chica, chē'kä, n. an orange-red dye-stuff, got by boiling the leaves of a South American Bignonia. [From a native name.]

Chicago, shi-kä'gō, n. a form of contract bridge played in sets of four deals, not in rubbers.

chicane, shi-kän', v.i. to use shifts and tricks.—v.t. to deceive.—n. a trick or artifice: a bridge hand without trumps, for which a score above the line used to be allowed: a barrier or obstacle in motor-racing, etc.—ns. chicā'ner, one who chicanes: a quibbler; chicā'nery, trickery or artifice, esp. in legal proceedings: quibbling; chicā'ning, quibbling. [Fr. chicane, sharp practice at law, from Late Gr. tzykanion, a game at mall, tzykanizein, to play at mall.—Pers. tchuagan, a crooked mallet.]

chich, chich. Same as chick-pea.

chicha, chēch'a, n. a South American liquor fermented from maize. [Said to be Haitian.]

chichi, chi-chi, shē-shē, chē-chē, adj. pretentious: fussy, precious, affected: stylish, chic, self-consciously fashionable.—n. something that is, or quality of being, chichi: red tape: fuss. [Fr.]

chick, chik, n. the young of fowls, esp. of the hen: a child, as a term of endearment: a girl or young woman (slang).—n. chick'en, the young of birds, esp. of the domestic fowl: the flesh of a fowl, not always very young: a prairie chicken: a youthful person, esp. a girl: a faint-hearted person (coll.).—adj. (coll.) cowardly, frightened.—v.i. (coll.) to show fear: (coll.; with out) to desert, quit, through cowardice.—n. chick'ling, a little chicken.—chick'-a-biddy, chick'-a-didd'le, terms of endearment addressed to children; chicken-feed, poultry food: small change (coll.): something of little value, e.g. information leaked (coll.); chick'en-haz'ard, a game at hazard for low stakes.—adj. chick'en-heart'ed.—chick'en-pox, a contagious febrile disease, chiefly of children, not unlike a mild form of smallpox; chick'-en-run, a run for hens; chick'en-wire, wire-netting; chick'-pea (see chickling); chick'weed, a species of stitchwort, one of the commonest of weeds, much relished by fowls and cage-birds (mouse-ear chickweed, the kindred genus Cerastium); chick'weed-win'tergreen (see wintergreen, under winter). [O.E. cicen; cf. Du. kieken, Ger. küchlein.]

chick, chik, (Ind.) n. a hanging door-screen or sunblind of laced bamboo slips, etc. [Hindi ciq.]

chickadee, chik-ə-dē', n. an American titmouse. [From its note.]

chickaree, chik-ə-rē', n. an American red squirrel. [From its cry.]

chickling, chik'ling, n. a species of pea (also chickling vetch, Lathyrus sativus).—n. chick'-pea,

gram, a plant of the pea family (*Cicer arietinum*):
its edible seed. [Earlier *chich, chichling, chich-pease*—Fr. *chiche*—L. *cicer*, chick-pea.]
chicle, *chik'l, chik'li, n.* the gum of the sapodilla
tree, chewing-gum. [Sp.,—Mex.]
chicory, (also chiccory), *chik'ə-ri, n.* succory, a
blue-flowered composite (*Cichorium intybus*):
its carrot-like root (ground to mix with coffee).
[Fr. *chicorée*—L. *cichorēum*—Gr. *kichorion*.]
chide, *chid, v.t.* to scold, rebuke, reprove by words:
to be noisy about, as the sea.—*v.i.* to make a
snarling, murmuring sound, as a dog or trumpet:
—*pr.p.* chid'ing; *pa.t.* chid, sometimes chid'ed,
chōde (*arch*); *pa.p.* chid, chidden.—*ns.* chid'er
(*Shak.*), a quarrelsome person; chid'ing,
scolding. [O.E. *cidan* (a weak verb).]
chief, *chēf, adj.* head: principal, highest, first:
outstanding, important (with *comp.* chief'er,
*superl.* chief'est): intimate (*Scot.*).—*adv.* chiefly.
—*n.* a head or principal person: a leader: the
principal part or top of anything: the greater
part: an ordinary, consisting of the upper part
of the field cut off by a horizontal line, generally
made to occupy one-third of the area of the
shield.—*ns.* chief'dom, chief'ship, state of being
chief: sovereignty; chief'ery, chief'ry (in *Spens.*
cheverye), an Irish chieftaincy: the dues paid to
a chief or the supreme lord: a chief's lands;
chief'ess, a female chief.—*adj.* chief'less, without
a chief or leader.—*n.* chief'ling.—*adv.* chief'ly, in
the first place: principally: for the most part.—
*ns.* chief'tain, the head of a clan: a leader or
commander:—*fem.* chief'tainess; chief'taincy,
chief'tainry; chief'tainship.—chief'-bar'on, the
President of the Court of Exchequer; chief'-justice (see justice).—in chief (*her.*), borne in the
upper part of the shield: of a tenure, held
directly from the sovereign: at the head, as com-mander-*in-chief*. [Fr. *chef*—L. *caput*, the head.]
chield, *chēld, (Scot.) n.* a lad, a man.—Also chiel.
[Apparently a form of child.]
chiff-chaff, *chif'-chaf, n.* a small warbler. [Imit.]
chiffon, *shif'on, shē'fɔ̃, n.* (in *pl.*) trimmings, or
other adornments: a thin fine clothing fabric of
silk, nylon, etc.—*n.* chiffonier (*shif-ən-ēr'*), an
ornamental cabinet. [Fr., rag, adornment—
*chiffe*, rag.]
chignon, *shē'nyɔ̃, n.* a fold or roll of hair worn on
the back of the head and neck. [Fr., meaning
first the nape of the neck (jointed like a chain)—
*chainon*, link of a chain—*chaine*, a chain.]
chigoe, *chig'ō.* chigre. chigger, *chig'ər, n.* a West
Indian and South American flea (*Sarcopsylla
penetrans*), the gravid female of which buries
itself, esp. beneath the toe-nails: the larva of an
American harvest-mite that burrows in the skin.
—Also jigg'er. [West Indian name.]
chihuahua, *chi-wä'wä, n.* a very small dog (2 lb. or
so) with big eyes and pointed ears. [*Chihuahua*
in Mexico.]
chik. Same as chick (2).
chikara, *chi-kä'ra, n.* a four-horned Indian ante-lope: an Indian gazelle (also chinkara). [Hindi.]
chikara, *chik'ə-ra, n.* an Indian instrument of the
violin class. [Hindi *cikārā*.]
chik(h)or. See chukor.
chilblain, *chil'blān, n.* a painful red swelling, esp.
on hands and feet in cold weather. [chill and
blain (1).]
child, *chīld, n.* a very young person (up to the age
of sixteen for the purpose of some acts of parlia-ment): a female infant (*Shak.*): a son or
daughter: one standing in a relationship of
adoption or origin (to a person, place, etc.):
disciple: youth of gentle birth, esp. in ballads,
etc. (*arch.*; also chalde, chylde): (*pl.*) offspring:
descendants: inhabitants:—*pl.* children (*chil'-drən*; double pl. from older and dial. chil'der).—
*v.t., v.i.(arch.*), bring forth.—*adj.* child'ed (*Shak.*),
possessed of a child.—*n.* child'hood, state of

being a child: the time of being a child.—*adjs.*
child'ing (*Shak.*), fruiting, teeming; child'ish, of
or like a child: silly: trifling.—*adv.* child'ishly.
*ns.* child'ishness, what is natural to a child:
puerility.—*adjs.* child'less, without children;
child'like, like a child: becoming a child: docile:
innocent; child'ly, natural or becoming to a
child.—*n.* child'ness (*Shak.*), nature or character
of a child.—child'bearing, the act of bringing
forth children; child'bed, the state of a woman
brought to bed with child; child'birth, the giving
birth to a child: parturition; child'crowing, a
nervous affection with spasm of the muscles
closing the glottis; child's play, something very
easy to do; child-study, the psychology and
physiology of children; child welfare, health and
well-being of young children as an object of
systematic social work; child'-wife, a very young
wife.—second childhood, the childishness of old
age; with child, pregnant. [O.E. *cild*, pl. *cild*,
later *cildru, -ra*.]
Childermas, *chil'dər-məs, n.* Innocents' Day, a
festival (Dec. 28) to commemorate the slaying of
the children by Herod. [O.E. *cildra*, gen. pl. of
*cild*, child, *mæsse*, mass.]
Chile, *chil'i, adj.* of Chile.—*n.* and adj. Chil'ean
(*obs.* Chil'ian).—Chile(an) pine, the monkey-puzzle; Chile saltpetre, sodium nitrate.
chile, *chil.* Variant form of child.
chili, chile, *chil'i.* Variant forms of chilli.
chili, *shil'ē,* a hot dry wind of North Africa.
[Berber.]
chiliad, *kil'i-ad, n.* the number 1,000: 1,000 of
anything (e.g. years).—*ns.* chil'iagon, a plane
figure with 1,000 angles: chil'iahedron, a solid
figure with 1,000 plane faces; chiliarch (*kil'i-ärk*),
a leader or commander of a thousand men;
chil'iarchy, the position of chiliarch; chil'iasm,
the doctrine that Christ will reign bodily upon
the earth for 1,000 years; chil'iast, one who
holds this opinion: one who believes in a coming
happier time on earth. [Gr. *chilias, -ados*—
*chilioi*, 1,000.]
chill, *chil, n.* coldness: a cold that causes shivering:
anything that damps or disheartens: a foundry
mould.—*adj.* shivering with cold: slightly cold:
opposite of cordial.—*v.i.* to grow cold.—*v.t.* to
make chill or cold: to cool: to preserve by cold:
to injure with cold: to discourage: to cloud or
bloom the surface of (by cold air): to take the chill
off (*dial.*):—*adj.* chilled, made cold: hardened
by chilling, as iron: preserved by cold, as beef.—
*adv.* chill'ily.—*n.* chill'iness.—*n.* and adj. chill'-ing.—*n.* chill'ness.—*adj.* chilly, cold: chilling:
sensitive to cold.—take the chill off, to warm
slightly: to make lukewarm. [O.E. *cele, ciele*,
cold; see cold, cool.]
chilli, *chil'i, n.* the pod of the capsicum, extremely
pungent and stimulant, used in sauces, pickles,
etc., and dried and ground to form Cayenne
pepper. [Nahuatl.]
chillum, *chil'um, n.* the part of a hookah contain-ing the tobacco and charcoal balls: a hookah
itself: the act of smoking it. [Hind. *chilam*.]
Chilognatha, *ki-log'nä-tha, n.pl.* millipedes. [Gr.
*cheilos*, lip, *gnathos*, jaw.]
Chilopoda, *ki-lop'o-da, n.pl.* centipedes. [Gr.
*cheilos*, lip, *pous, podos*, foot.
Chiltern hundreds. See hundred.
chimaera. Older spelling of chimera.
chime, *chim, n.* a set of bells tuned in a scale: the
ringing of such bells in succession (often in *pl.*):
a definite sequence of bell-like notes sounded as
by a clock: the harmonious sound of bells or
other musical instruments: agreement of sound
or of relation: harmony: rhyme: jingle.—*v.i.*
to sound a chime or in chime: to accord or
agree: to jingle: to rhyme: to say words over
mechanically.—*v.t.* to strike, or cause to sound
in chime: to indicate by chiming.—chime in, to

join in, in agreement. [M.E. *chimbe*, prob. O.Fr. *cymbale*—L. *cymbalum*, a cymbal.]

**chime, chimb,** *chim, n.* the rim formed by the ends of the staves of a cask: a hollowed or bevelled channel in the waterway of a ship's deck (*naut.*). [Cog. with Du. *kim*, Ger. *kimme*, edge.]

**chimer,** *chim'ər,* **chimere,** *chi-mēr', n.* a long sleeveless tabard: the upper robe worn by a bishop. [O.Fr. *chamarre*; cf. *cymar*; Sp. *zamarra, chamarra,* sheepskin.]

**chimera, chimaera,** *ki-, ki-mē'rə, n.* (often *cap.*) a fabulous, fire-spouting monster, with a lion's head, a serpent's tail, and a goat's body: any idle or wild fancy: a picture of an animal having its parts made up of various animals: (*cap.*) a genus of cartilaginous fishes, often ranked with the sharks and rays: an organism made up of two genetically distinct tissues.—*adjs.* **chimeric** (*-mer'ik*), **-al,** of the nature of a chimaera: wild: fanciful.—*adv.* **chimĕr'ically.** [L.,—Gr. *chimaira*, a she-goat.]

**chimney,** *chim'ni,* (*dial.* **chimley, chumley,** *chim',* *chum'li*), *n.* a passage for the escape of fumes, smoke, or heated air from a fireplace or furnace: a glass tube surrounding a lamp flame: a volcanic vent: a cleft in a rock-face.—*v.t.* to climb a narrow crevice with back against one wall and feet against the other.—*ns.* **chim'ney-board,** a board blocking up a fireplace; **chim'ney-can,** a **chimney-pot; chim'ney-cor'ner, -nook** (*Scot.* **-nuik**), in old chimneys, the space between the fire and the side-wall of the fireplace: fireside, commonly spoken of as the place for the aged and infirm; **chim'ney-piece,** a shelf over the fireplace; **chim'ney-pot,** a cylindrical pipe of earthenware or other material at the top of a chimney: a top-hat (in full **chim'ney-pot hat**); **chim'ney-shaft,** the stalk of a chimney which rises above the building; **chim'ney-stack,** a group of chimneys carried up together; **chim'ney-stalk,** a very tall chimney; **chim'ney-swallow,** the common swallow: a species of swift (*U.S.*); **chim'-ney-sweep, chim'ney-sweeper,** one who sweeps or cleans chimneys; **chim'ney-top,** the top of a chimney. [Fr. *cheminée*—L. *caminus,* a furnace.]

**chimpanzee,** *chim-pən-zē', n.* one of the African anthropoid apes. [West African.]

**chin,** *chin, n.* the jutting part of the face below the mouth.—*n.* and *v.i.* **chin'wag** (*slang*), talk. [O.E. *cin*; Ger. *kinn*, Gr. *genys* (jaw).]

**china,** *chi'nə, n.* (orig. Chi'na-ware) articles of porcelain brought from China in 16th cent.: Chinese porcelain or, esp., Western imitation or version of it: (*Cockney rhyming slang*) mate (from *china plate*).—*adj.* of china: (*cap.*) of, from, etc., China.—**China aster** (see **aster**); **china clay,** kaolin (*q.v.*), fine white clay used in making porcelain, etc.; **China grass, rami; China ink** (see **ink**); **China jute,** a species of Abutilon; **Chi'naman,** a Chinese (*derog.*): off-break bowled by a left-handed bowler to a right-handed batsman; **chi'naroot,** root-stock of *Smilax china*: China rose, any of several garden roses; **china stone,** partly decomposed granite; **Chi'na-town,** a Chinese quarter in a town.—*n.* **Chinese,** *chi-nēz',* a native or citizen of China (*pl.* **Chinese'** —*arch. coll. sing.* **Chinee'**): the language of China.—Also *adj.* (in names of commodities, sometimes without capital).—**Chinese checkers,** a board game similar to draughts which can be played by 2, 4, or 6 people; **Chinese gooseberry,** subtropical vine (*Actinidia chinensis*) with edible fruit; **Chinese lantern,** a paper lantern; **Chinese lantern plant,** same as winter-cherry; **Chinese paper,** a fine soft brownish paper-like material made from bamboo bark, giving fine impressions of engravings: also the so-called rice paper; **Chinese pavilion** (see **pavilion**); **Chinese white,** a zinc oxide pigment.

**china,** *ki'na, kēn'a.* See **quina**.

**chinampa,** *chin-am'pa, n.* a floating garden. [Sp., —Nahuatl *chinamitl.*]

**chinar.** Same as **chenar.**

**chinch,** *chinch, n.* the bed-bug in America. [Sp. *chinche*—L. *cimex.*]

**chincherinchee, chinkerinchee,** *ching'kə-rin-chē', chin-kə-rin'chē, n.* a white-flowered S. African plant of the star-of-Bethlehem genus.—(*coll.*) **chinks.** [Said to be imitative of the flower-stalks rubbing together in the wind.]

**chinchilla,** *chin-chil'a, n.* a small rodent of South America valued for its soft grey fur: the fur itself: (*cap.*) a breed of rabbits, or of cats, with soft grey fur. [Sp.]

**chin-chin,** *chin'-chin',* (*coll.*) *interj.* hello or good-bye: good health! (as a toast). [Anglo-Chin.— Chin. *ts'ing ts'ing.*]

**chincough,** *chin'kof,* (*dial.*) *n.* whooping-cough. [For **chink-cough;** cf. Scot. *kink-hoast,* Du. *kinkhoest;* see **chink** (3) and **cough.**]

**chindit,** *chin'dit, n.* a member of General Wingate's commando force in Burma during World War II. [Burmese *chinthey,* a griffin, the force's badge.]

**chine,** *chin, n.* the spine or backbone (*arch.*): a piece of the backbone and adjoining parts for cooking: the back (*Spens.*): a ridge crest.—*v.t.* to break the back of. [O.Fr. *eschine,* prob. from O.H.G. *scina,* pin, thorn.]

**chine,** *chin, n.* a ravine. [O.E. *cinu,* a cleft.]

**chine.** Variant form of **chime** (2).

**chiné,** *shē-nā', adj.* mottled, with the pattern printed on the warp. [Fr., dyed in a (supposedly) Chinese way.]

**Chinese.** See **China.**

**chink,** *chingk, n.* a cleft, a narrow opening.—*v.i.* to crack.—*v.t.* to fill up cracks.—*adj.* **chink'y,** full of chinks. [Apparently formed upon M.E. *chine,* a crack—O.E. *cinu,* a cleft.]

**chink,** *chingk, n.* the clink, as of coins: money (in *Shak.* **chinks**) (*slang*).—*v.i.* to give forth a sharp sound.—*v.t.* to clink together. [Imit.]

**chink,** *chingk,* (*Northern* **kink, kingk**), (*dial.*) *n.* a gasp for breath.—*v.i.* to gasp. [Cf. Du. *kinken,* to cough; Ger. *keichen,* to gasp.]

**Chink,** *chingk,* (*slang*) *n.* and *adj.* Chinese. [China.]

**chinkapin, chincapin, chinquapin,** *ching'ka-pin, n.* the dwarf chestnut of the U.S. [Algonquian.]

**chinkara.** See **chikara** (1).

**chinkerinchee, chinks.** See **chincherinchee.**

**chino,** *chē'nō, (U.S.) n.* strong khaki-like twilled cotton: (in *pl.*) trousers made of it. [Amer.— Sp.]

**chinoiserie,** *shē-nwä-z(ə)rē, (Fr.)* Chinese objects, decoration, behaviour, etc.

**Chinook,** *chin-ōōk', a traders' jargon, consisting of words from French, English, Chinook, and other American-Indian tongues: (without *cap.*) a warm dry wind blowing down the eastern side of the Rocky Mts, making winter grazing possible: also a warm moist wind from the Pacific.

**chinovnik,** *chin-ov'nik, n.* a high official in the Russian civil service: a bureaucrat. [Russ., —*chin,* rank.]

**chintz,** *chints, n.* a cotton printed generally in several colours on a white or light ground. —*adj.* **chintz'y,** covered with, or like, chintz: cheap, gaudy. [Orig. *pl.*—Hindi *chīt,* spotted cotton-cloth.]

**Chionodoxa,** *ki-ō-nō-dok'sa, n.* glory of the snow, an early-blooming blue-flowered genus of liliaceous plants. [Gr. *chiōn,* snow, *doxa,* glory.]

**chip,** *chip, v.t.* to strike with small sharp cutting blows: to strike small pieces off the surface of: to remove by chipping: to slice or pare: (of hatching chickens) to crack by pecking: to cut as with an adze: to chaff, tease (*coll.*).—*v.i.* to become chipped: to play a chip-shot (*pr.p.* **chipp'ing;** *pa.t.* and *pa.p.* **chipped**).—*n.* an act of chipping: a piece chipped off, esp. a flattish fragment: a surface flaw: thin slice of fruit, etc.: potato-chip: thin strip of wood, used for making boxes, baskets, etc.: a chip-basket: a counter: a piece of money (*slang*): a piece of dried dung of cow or bison: a key on a musical instrument (*Shak.*).—*adj.* chipp'y, abounding in chips: dry as a chip: seedy from an overdose of liquor.— *ns.* chip'-bas'ket, a fruit basket of interwoven chips; chip'board, reconstructed wood made by consolidation of chips from woodland trimmings, workshop waste, etc., with added resin: a wastepaper cardboard used in box-making; chip'-car'ving, wood carving by removal of splinters; chip'-hat, a hat of palm-leaf strips; chips (*slang*), a ship's carpenter: a regimental pioneer sergeant—usually a carpenter: fried potato-chips (*coll.*): money; chip-shot (*golf*), a short lofted approach.—chip in, to enter the game by putting chips on the table: to interpose: to pay part of the cost of something (*coll.*); chip of the old block, one with the characteristics of his father: chip on one's shoulder, a defiant manner, as if daring anyone to knock it off, readiness to take offence; have had one's chips, to have died: to have had one's chance; when the chips are down, at a critical moment when it is too late to alter the situation. [M.E. *chippen*; M.L.G., M.Du. *kippen*, to hatch by chipping shell.]

chipmunk, chipmuck, *chip'mungk, -muk*, a North American squirrel. [From Indian name.]

chipolata, *chip-ə-lä'tə, n.* a small sausage, used as a garnish, etc. [Fr.,—It. *cipolla*, onion.]

Chippendale, *chip'ən-dāl, adj.* applied to a light style of drawing-room furniture, after the name of a well-known cabinetmaker of the 18th century: also applied to a style of book-plates.

chipper, ·*chip'ər, adj.* brisk and cheerful. [Perh. same word as Northern dial. *kipper*, lively.]

chippy, *chip'i,* (*U.S.*) *n.* a flirtatious or promiscuous woman. [chip, variant of cheep.]

chiquichiqui, *chē-kē-chē'kē, n.* a piassava palm (Leopoldinia). [Tupí.]

chiragra, *ki-rag'ra, n.* gout in the hand.—*adjs.* chirag'ric, -al. [Gr. *cheiragrā—cheir*, hand, *agrā*, a catching.]

chi-rho, *ki-rō', n.* a monogram of XP (*chī, rhō*, ch, r), the first letters of the Greek *Christos* (Christ).

chirimoya. Same as cherimoya.

chirk, *chûrk, v.i.* to chirp or squeak: to grate (*Scot.*). [O.E. *cearcian*, to creak.]

chirl, *chirl,* (*Scot.*) *v.i.* to emit a low sound: to warble.—*n.* a kind of musical warble. [Imit.]

chirm, *chûrm, v.i.* to cry out: to chirp.—*n.* noise, din, hum of voices: a flock of goldfinches (also, charm). [O.E. *cirman*, to cry out; cf. Du. *kermen*.]

chiro-. See cheiro-.

Chironomus, *ki-ron'ō-məs, n.* a large genus of common midges, giving name to the family Chironomidae (*ki-rō-nom'i-dē*).—*n.* chiron'omid, any member of the family. [Gr. *cheironomōn*, gesticulator.]

chiropodist, *ki-rop'ə-dist,* older *ki-,* also *shi-, n.* one who treats minor ailments of the feet, e.g. corns, verrucas.—*n.* chirop'ody. [App. Gr. *cheir*, hand, and *pous, podos,* foot; but *cheiropodēs* means having chapped feet.]

chiropractic, *ki-ra-prak'tik, n.* a method of healing which relies upon the removal of nerve interference by manual adjustment of the spinal column: a chiropractor.—*n.* chiroprac'tor, one who practices chiropractic. [Gr. *cheir*, hand, *praktikos*, concerned with action—*prattein*, to do.]

chirp, *chûrp, n.* the sharp thin sound of certain birds and insects.—*v.i.* to make such a sound: to talk in a cheerful and lively strain.—*v.t.* to urge by chirping.—*n.* chirp'er, a little bird.—*adv.*

chirp'ily.—*adjs.* chirp'ing; chirp'y, lively: merry. [Imit.]

chirr, *chûr, v.i.* to chirp like a cricket or grasshopper. [Imit.]

chirrup, *chir'əp, v.i.* to chirp: to make a sound with the mouth to urge on a horse: to cheer up. —*adj.* chirrup'y, cheerful. [Lengthened form of chirp, associated with cheer up.]

chirt, *chûrt, n.* a squeeze: a squirt.—*v.t.* to squeeze: to squirt. [Conn. with chirr.]

chirurgeon, chirurgery, chirurgical, *kir-ûr'jən, -jər-i, -ji-kl,* old forms of surgeon, surgery, surgical, with pronunciation readjusted to the ultimate Greek etymology.—*adv.* chirur'geonly (*Shak.*), in a manner becoming a surgeon. [Fr. *chirurgien*—Gr. *cheirourgos—cheir,* hand, *ergon,* a work.]

chisel, *chiz'l, n.* a tool with the end bevelled to a cutting edge, esp. the tool of the sculptor.—*v.t.* to cut, carve, etc. with a chisel: to cheat (*slang*) (*pr.p.* chis'elling; *pa.t.* and *pa.p.* chis'elled).— *adj.* chis'elled, cut with a chisel: having sharp outlines, as cut by a chisel (*fig.*).—*ns.* chis'elling; chis'el-tooth, a rodent's chisel-shaped incisor. [O.Fr. *cisel*—L. *caedēre*, to cut.]

chisel, *chiz'l, n.* See chesil.

Chislev. Same as Kislev.

chit, *chit, n.* a short informal letter: an order or pass: testimonial.—Also chitt'y. [Hindi *cițțhī.*]

chit, *chit, n.* a child: a girl (*slightingly*).—*adjs.* chitt'y, chitt'y-faced. [Same as kit (3).]

chit, *chit,* (*dial.*) *n.* a shoot.—*v.i.* to sprout. [Perh. O.E. *cith*, a shoot.]

chital *chē'tal, n.* the axis deer. [Hind.]

chitarrone, *kēt-ə-rō'nā, n.* a large lute-like instrument with a long neck. [It.]

chitchat, *chit'chat, n.* chatting or idle talk: prattle: gossip. [A reduplication of chat.]

chitin, *ki'tin, n.* the substance which forms most of the hard parts of joint-footed animals.—*adj.* chi'tinous. [Fr. *chitine*—Gr. *chitōn*, a tunic.]

chiton, *ki'ton, n.* the ancient Greek tunic: (*cap.*) a genus of marine molluscs with shell of movable plates. [Gr. *chitōn*, a tunic.]

chittagong, *chit'ə-gong, n.* an Indian variety of domestic fowl.—*n.* chitt'agong-wood', a cabinet-maker's wood, usu. that of *Chickrassia tabularis* (mahogany family). [*Chittagong* in Bengal.]

chitter, *chit'ər,* (*Scot.*) *v.i.* to shiver: to chatter.— *n.* chitt'ering. [Cf. chatter.]

chitterling, *chit'ər-ling, n.* the smaller intestines of a pig or other edible animal (usu. *pl.*): a frill (*obs.*).—Also (*dial.*) chid'lings, chitt'lings. [Ety. dub.]

chiv, chiv, shiv, (*slang*) *n.* and *v.t.* knife; also shiv. [From older chive, knife (*thieves' slang*) or perh. Romany *chiv*, blade.]

chivalry, *shiv'əl-ri* (orig. *chiv'-), n.* the usages and qualifications of chevaliers or knights: bravery and courtesy: the system of knighthood in feudal times and its social code.—*adjs.* chivalric (*-al'*), chiv'alrous, pertaining to chivalry: bold: gallant.—*adv.* chiv'alrously.—*n.* chiv'alrousness. [Fr. *chevalerie—cheval*—L.L. *caballus*, a horse.]

chive, *chiv, n.* a herb like the leek and onion, with tufts of leaves (used in soup) and clustered bulbs: a small bulb (*arch.*).—Also cive (*siv*). [Fr. *cive*— L. *cēpa*, an onion.]

chivy, chivvy, *chiv'i, n.* and *v.* See chevy.

Chladni figures. Same as sonorous figures.

chlamys, *klam'is, n.* a short cloak for men: a purple cope:—*pl.* chlam'ydes (*-i-dēz*).—*adjs.* chlam'ydate (*zool.*), having a mantle; chlamyd'-eous (*bot.*), having a perianth.—*n.* chlam'ydo-spore, a thick-walled spore. [Gr. *chlamys,* pl. *chlamydēs.*]

chloasma, *klō-az'ma, n.* a skin disease marked by yellowish-brown patches. [Gr. *chloasma,* greenness, yellowness—*chloē,* verdure.]

chlorine, *klō', klō'rēn, -rin, -rin, n.* a yellowish-green gas (Cl) with a peculiar and suffocating odour, used in bleaching, disinfecting, and poison gas warfare.—*ns.* **chlor'al**, (or *-al'*) a limpid, colourless, oily liquid (CCl₃·CHO), of penetrating odour, formed when anhydrous alcohol is acted on by dry chlorine gas: loosely *chloral hydrate*, a white crystalline substance used as a hypnotic; **chlo'ralism**, the habit, or the morbid effects, of using chloral hydrate; **chloramphenicol**, same as **chloromycetin**; **chlorar'gyrite** (*klō-rär-ji-rit*, *klö-*; Gr. *argyros*, silver) horn silver; **chlo'rate**, a salt of chloric acid; **Chlorella** (*klo-rel'a*), a genus of green freshwater algae (Gr. *chlōros*, pale green).—*adjs.* **chlo'ric**, **chlor'ous**, of or from chlorine.—**chloric acid** (HClO₃), a syrupy liquid, a vigorous oxidising agent.—*n.* **chlo'ride**, a compound of chlorine with another element or radical (*chloride of lime*), not a true chloride.—*v.t.* **chlo'ridise**, **-ize**, to convert into a chloride: to cover with chloride of silver (*phot.*).—Also **chlo'ridate**.—*n.* **chlorim'**-**eter** (same as **chlorometer**).—*adj.* **chlorimet'ric**.—*n.* **chlorim'etry**.—*v.t.* **chlor'inate**, to treat with chlorine (as in sterilisation of water, extraction of gold from ore).—*n.* **chlorinā'tion**.—**chlorine water**, an aqueous solution of chlorine.—*v.t.* **chlo'rinise**, **-ize**, to chlorinate.—*n.* **chlo'rite**, a salt of chlorous acid (*chem.*): a general name for a group of minerals, hydrated silicates of magnesia, iron, and alumina—dark green and rather soft, like mica but not elastic.—**chlo'rite-schist'**, a schistose rock composed of chlorite, usually with quartz, epidote, etc.—*adj.* **chlorit'ic**, pertaining to, of the nature of, or containing, the mineral chlorite.—**chloritic marl**, a marl at the base of the English Chalk stained green with glauconite (not chlorite).—*ns.* **chloritisā'tion**, **-izā'-**, alteration of ferro-magnesian minerals into chlorite or similar material; **chlōrocru'orin**, a green respiratory pigment found in some Polychaeta; **chlo'rodyne**, a patent medicine—anodyne and hypnotic, containing chloroform; **chloroform** (*klor'ō-förm* or *klō'rō-förm*), a limpid, mobile, colourless, volatile liquid (CHCl₃) with a characteristic odour and a strong sweetish taste, used to induce insensibility.—*v.t.* to administer chloroform to. —*ns.* **chlor'oformer**, **-ist**; **chlorom'eter**, apparatus for measuring available chlorine in bleaching-powder, etc.—*adj.* **chloromet'ric**.—*ns.* **chlorom'etry**; **chloromy'cetin** (or-*mi-sēt'in*; orig. trademark), drug used against typhoid, cerebrospinal meningitis, etc.—also **chloramphenicol**.—*n.pl.* **Chlorophyceae** (*-fis'i-ē*; Gr. *phȳkos*, seaweed), the green seaweeds and their kindred, one of the main divisions of the Algae.—*ns.* **chlorophyll**, **-phyl** (*klor'ō-fil*, or *klō'rō-fil*; Gr. *phyllon*, leaf) the ordinary green colouring matter of vegetation; **chlo'roplast** (Gr. *plastos*, moulded), a chlorophyll-bearing plastid; **chlor'oprene**, a colourless fluid derived from acetylene and hydrochloric acid and used in the production of neoprene; **chlo'-roquin(e)**, a drug taken to suppress malaria; **chlorō'sis**, properly *green sickness*, a form of anaemia affecting young women: blanching of the green parts of a plant, esp, for want of iron (*bot.*).—*adj.* **chlorōt'ic**, pertaining to or affected by chlorosis.—**chlorous acid**, a hypothetical acid (HClO₂), known in solution and by its salts.—*n.* **chlorprom'azine hydrochloride**, a drug which induces a feeling of well-being. [Gr. *chlōros*, pale green.]

**chobdar**, *chōb'där*, *n.* in India, an usher. [Pers.]

**chock**, *chok*, *v.t.* to fasten as with a block or wedge.—*n.* a wedge to prevent movement: a log.—*adjs.* **chock-a-block'**, **chock'-full**, **chock'-full**, quite full.—*n.* **chock'stone**, stone(s) jammed in a mountain crack, chimney or crevice.—*adj.* **chock'-tight**, very tight. [See choke.]

**chocolate**, *chok'(ə-)lit*, *n.* a paste made of the ground seeds of *Theobroma cacao* (cocoa), with sugar and flour or similar material: a sweetmeat made of the paste: beverage made by dissolving the paste in hot water or milk.—*adj.* chocolate-coloured, dark reddish-brown: made of or flavoured with chocolate.—*adj.* **choc'olate-box**, pretty-pretty or over sentimental, esp. of a painting. [Sp. *chocolate*; from Nahuatl, *chocólatl*, a mixture containing chocolate.]

**Choctaw**, *chok'tö*, *n.* an American Indian of a tribe formerly chiefly in Mississippi: the tribe, or its language: (sometimes without *cap.*) a skating movement, forward on the edge of one foot, then backward on the opposite edge of the other (cf. **Mohawk**). [Choctaw *Chatha*.]

**chode**, *chōd*, an archaic *pa.t.* of **chide**.

**choice**, *chois*, *n.* act or power of choosing: the thing chosen: alternative: preference: preferable or best part.—*adj.* worthy of being chosen: select: appropriate.—*adjs.* **choice'-drawn** (*Shak.*), selected with care; **choice'ful** (*Spens.*), making many choices, fickle.—*adv.* **choice'ly**, with discrimination or care.—*n.* **choise'ness**, particular value: excellence: nicety.— **for choice**, by preference; **Hobson's choice**, the choice of a thing offered or nothing, from *Hobson*, a Cambridge horsekeeper, who lent out the horse nearest the stable door, or none at all; **make choice of**, to select; **take one's choice**, to take what one wishes. [Fr. *choix—choisir*; cf. **choose**.]

**choir**, *kwir*, *n.* a chorus or band of singers, esp. those belonging to a church: the part of a church appropriated to the singers: the part, the eastern end, often separated from the nave by a rail or screen.—*v.i.* (*Shak.*) to sing in chorus.— **choir'boy**, **choir'man**, a boy, man, who sings in a choir; **choir'-organ**, a department of a large organ, probably originally called chair-organ (renamed as if an organ suitable for accompanying a choir); **choir'-screen**, a screen of latticework, separating the choir from the nave. —*n.pl.* **choir'-stalls**, fixed seats in the choir of a church, generally of carved wood. [Fr. *chœur*—L. *chorus*—Gr. *choros*; see **chorus**.]

**choke**, *chōk*, *v.t.* to stop or interfere with the breathing of (whether by compression, blocking, fumes, emotion, or otherwise): to injure or suppress by obstruction, overshadowing, or deprivation of air, etc.: to constrict: to block: to clog: to obstruct.—*v.i.* to be choked.—*n.* a complete or partial stoppage of breath: the sound of choking: a constriction: a device to prevent the passage of too much gas, electric current, etc., e.g. a *choking-coil*.—*n.* **chok'er**, that which or one who chokes: a large neck-cloth: a very high collar: a large necklace or jewelled collar.—*adj.* **chok'y**, tending to, or inclined to, choke.—**choke'berry**, a small astringent American fruit akin to the apple; **choke'bore**, a gun-bore narrowed at the muzzle: a shot-gun so bored; **choke'cherry**, an astringent American cherry; **choke'damp**, carbon dioxide or other suffocating gas in mines.—*adj.* **choke-full** (see **chock-full**).—**choke'-pear**, an astringent pear: anything that reduces one to silence; **chok'ing-coil**, a coil of thick wire, used to limit the supply of electric light.—**choke back**, **down**, repress as if by a choking action; **choke off**, get rid of; **choke up**, fill completely: block up. [Ety. obscure.]

**choky**, **choky**, *chō'ki*, *n.* a prison: a toll-station: a chokidar.—*n.* **chokidar**, **chowkidar** (*chō'*, *chow'-ki-där*), a watchman. [Hindi *cauki*, *caukidār*.]

**cholaemia**, *ko-lē'mi-ə*, *n.* a morbid accumulation of the constituents of bile in the blood.—*adj.* **cholae'mic**. [Gr. *cholē*, bile, *haima*, blood.]

**cholagogue**, *kol'ə-gog*, *n.* a purgative causing evacuations of bile.—*adj.* **cholagog'ic** (*-goj'ik*, *-goj'ik*). [Gr. *cholē*, bile, *agōgos*, leading.]

**cholecyst**, *kō'li-sist*, *n.* the gall-bladder.—*ns.*

Natural vowels in unaccented syllables: *el'ə-mənt*; for certain sounds in foreign words, see p. viii cholecysti'tis, inflammation of the gall-bladder; cholecystos'tomy (Gr. *stoma*, mouth), cholecystot'omy (Gr. *tomē*, a cut), surgical opening of the gall-bladder; cholecystec'tomy, excision of the gall-bladder. [Gr. *cholē*, bile, *kystis*, a bladder.]

cholelith, *ko'lə-lith, n.* a gall-stone.—*n.* cholelithiasis (*ko-lə-li-thī'ə-sis*), the presence of gall-stones. [Gr. *cholē*, bile, *lithos*, stone.]

choler, *kol'ər, n.* the bile: biliousness (*Shak.*): anger, irascibility.—*adj.* chol'eric, full of choler: passionate. [Gr. *cholerā—cholē*, bile, partly through Fr.]

cholera, *kol'ər-ə, n.* a highly infectious and deadly disease characterised by bilious vomiting and purging.—*adj.* choleraic (*kol-ar-ā'ik*).—British cholera, an acute catarrhal affection of the mucous membrane of the stomach and small intestines; chicken, fowl cholera, a contagious septicaemia of birds; cholera belt, a waist-band of flannel or other material worn as a precaution against disease.—hog cholera, swine fever. [Gr. *cholerā—cholē*, bile.]

cholesterol, *ko-les'tər-ol, n.* an alcohol (C$_{27}$H$_{45}$OH), occurring abundantly in gall-stones, nerves, bloodstream, etc., a white crystalline solid—formerly choles'terin.—*adj.* cholester'ic. [Gr. *cholē*, bile, *stereos*, solid.]

choli, *chō'lē, n.* a short, short-sleeved blouse often worn under a sari. [Hindi *colī*; from Sans. but prob. of Dravidian origin.]

choliamb, *kō'li-amb, n.* a variety of iambic trimeter having a spondee for an iambus as the sixth foot.—*n.* and *adj.* choliam'bic. [Gr. *chōliambos* —*chōlos*, lame, *iambos*, iambus.]

cholic, *kol'ik, kōl'ik, adj.* pertaining to bile, as cholic acid (C$_{24}$H$_{40}$O$_5$) got from bile.—*n.* chol'ine, an alcohol (C$_5$H$_{15}$NO$_2$) discovered in bile. [Gr. *cholē*, bile.]

choltry, *chōl'tri, n.* a caravanserai: a shed used as a place of assembly.—Also choul'try. [From Malayalam.]

chondrus, *kon'drəs, n.* a cartilage: a chondrule: (*cap.*) a genus of cartilaginous red seaweeds to which carrageen belongs:—*pl.* chon'dri.—*adj.* chon'dral.—*ns.* chondre (*kon'dər*), a chondrule; chondrifică'tion, formation of chondrin or development of or change into cartilage.—*v.t.* and *v.i.* chon'drify, to change into cartilage.—*ns.* chon'drin, a firm elastic, translucent, bluish-white gelatinous substance, the ground-substance of cartilage; chon'driosome, a minute body in the cytoplasm of a cell; chon'drite, a meteorite containing chondrules: a fossil resembling *Chondrus*.—*adj.* chondrit'ic.—*ns.* chondrocrăn'ium, a cartilaginous skull, as in embryos, fishes, etc.; chondrogen'esis, chondrification.—*adj.* chon'droid, like cartilage.—*ns.pl.* chondropterygii (*kon-drop-tar-ij'i-i*; Gr. *pteryx, -ygos*, fin), the selachians or elasmobranchs; Chondros'tei (*kon-dros'ti-i*; Gr. *osteon*, bone), an order of fishes including the sturgeon.—*n.* chon'drule, a rounded granule found in meteorites and in deep-sea deposits. [Gr. *chondros*, a grain, grit, cartilage.]

choose, *chōōz, v.t.* to take or pick out in preference to another thing: to select: to will or determine: to think fit.—*v.i.* to make a choice:—*pa.t.* chose, *chōz; pa.p.* chos'en.—*n.* choos'er.—*adj.* choos'(e)y (*coll.*), difficult to please, fastidious.—cannot choose, can have no alternative; choosers of the slain, the Valkyries; not much to choose between, each about equally good or bad; pick and choose, to select with care or at leisure; the chosen people, the Israelites (1 *Chron.* xvi. 13). [O.E. *cēosan*, Du. *kiesen*.]

chop, *chop, v.t.* to cut with a sudden blow: to cut into small pieces: to thrust or clap.—*v.i.* to hack: to come suddenly or accidentally: to thrust: to crack or fissure: to take a direction (running

into chop, 2).—*n.* an act of chopping: chopped food: a piece cut off: a slice of mutton or pork, containing a rib: a crack: a sharp downward blow.—*n.* chopp'er, one who or that which chops: a cleaver: a helicopter (*U.S. slang*).—*n.* and *adj.* chopp'ing.—*adj.* chopp'y, full of chops or cracks: running in irregular waves (also chopp'ing).—chop'-house, a house where mutton-chops and beef-steaks are served: an eating-house; chopp'ing-block, -board, one on which material to be chopped is placed; chopp'ing-knife, a knife for chopping or mincing meat.—chop at, to aim a blow at; chop in, to break in, interrupt; chop up, to cut into small pieces. [A form of chap, 1.]

chop, *chop, v.t.* and *v.i.* to buy and sell, barter, or exchange (*Milton*): to change direction (running into chop, 1).—*n.* an exchange: a change.—chop'-log'ic, chopping of logic: one who chops logic.—chop and change, to buy and sell: to change about: vicissitude; chop logic, to argue contentiously. [Connection with chop, 1 and with chap, 2 is not clear.]

chop, *chop, n.* the chap or jaw:—(in *pl.*) a person with fat cheeks: the mouth or jaws of anything, as a cannon or a vice.—*v.t.* to eat.—*v.i.* to snap. *adj.* chop'fallen, lit. having the chop or lower jaw fallen down: cast-down: dejected. [See chap (3).]

chop, *chop, n.* in China and India, a seal: a brand: a sealed document.—first chop, best quality; no chop, no good. [Hindi *chāp*, seal, impression.]

chop-chop, *chop'-chop', adv.* promptly. [Pidgin English.]

chopin, *chop'in, n.* an old French liquid measure containing nearly an English imperial pint: a Scottish measure containing about an English quart. [O.Fr. *chopine*, Old Du. *schoppe*; Scot. *chappin*, Ger. *schoppen*, a pint.]

chopin, chopine, *chop-ēn', chop'in, n.* a high clog or patten introduced into England from Venice during the reign of Elizabeth I. [Sp. *chapin*.]

chopping, *chop'ing, adj.* stout, strapping, plump. [Perh. chop, 1.; cf. thumping.]

chop-sticks, *chop'-stiks, n.pl.* two small sticks used by the Chinese instead of a fork. [chop-chop, and stick.]

chop-suey, *chop-sōō'i, n.* a miscellaneous Chinese dish, fried in sesame-oil. [Chin., mixed bits.]

choragus, choregus, *ko-rā'gəs, -rē'gəs, n.* in Athens the organiser of a chorus: the leader of a choir. —*adj.* choragic, choregic, (*-raj', -rāj', -rēj'ik*). [Gr. *chorāgos, chorēgos—choros*, chorus, and *agein*, to lead.]

choral, chorale. See chorus.

chord, *kŏrd,* (*mus.*) *n.* the simultaneous union of sounds of a different pitch.—common chord, a note with its third and perfect fifth reckoned upwards. [From accord.]

chord, *kŏrd, n.* a string of a musical instrument: of the emotions (*fig.*): a straight line joining any two points on a curve (*geom.*): a cord (see spinal, vocal): the straight line joining the leading and the trailing edges of an aerofoil section (*aero.*).—*n.pl.* Chordăt'a, the highest phylum of the animal kingdom, including the vertebrates, ascidians, and Hemichordata—animals possessing a notochord.—*n.* chor'date, a member of the Chordata.—Also *adj.*—*n.* chordophone (*kŏr'dō-fōn* (*mus.*)), a stringed instrument.—*adj.* chordophonic (*-fon'ik*). [Gr. *chordē*, a string, intestine.]

chore, *chŏr, chōr, n.* a household task: an unenjoyable task. [Form (orig. U.S.) of char (3).]

chorea, *ko-rē'ə, n.* St Vitus's dance, a nervous disease, causing irregular involuntary movements of the limbs or face. [L.,—Gr. *choreiā*, a dance.]

choree, *kō'rē, kō', n.* a trochee.—Also chorē'us. [Gr. *choreios*.]

choreographer, etc. See chorus.

chorepiscopal, *kō-ri-pis'kə-pl, kō-, adj.* pertaining

to a local or suffragan bishop. [Gr. *chōrā*, place, country.]

**choriamb**, *kor'i-amb*, *n*. a foot of four syllables, the first and last long, the others short.—*adj.* and *n.* **choriam'bic**. [Gr. *choriambos—choreios*, a trochee, *iambos*, iambus.]

**choric**. See chorus.

**chorion**, *kō'ri-on*, *kö'*, *n*. the outer foetal envelope. —*pl.* **cho'ria**.—*adjs.* **cho'rioid**; **cho'roid**.—Also *ns*.—**choroid** (coat) the vascular tunic of the eye, between the retina and the sclerotic. [Gr. *chorion*.]

**chorisis**, *kō'ris-is*, *kö'*, (*bot.*) *n*. multiplication of parts by branching.—*n.pl.* **chōripet'alae**, a series of dicotyledons having the petals separate if present at all.—*ns.* **cho'rizont, -zont'ist**, one who disputes identity of authorship, as of the *Iliad* and *Odyssey*. [Gr. *chōrisis*, separation, *chōrizōn*, *-ontos*, separating.]

**chorography**, *kō-rog'rə-fi*, *kö-*, *n*. geography: topography.—*adjs.* **chorographic** (*-ro-graf'ik*), *-al*; **chorolog'ical**.—*ns.* **chorol'ogist**; **chorol'ogy**, the science of geographical distribution. [Gr. *chōrā*, region, country.]

**choroid**. See chorion.

**chortle**, *chört'l*, *v.i.* to chuckle: to utter a low, deep laugh. [Coined by Lewis Carroll in 1872.]

**chorus**, *kō'rəs*, *kö'*, *n*. a band of singers and dancers: in Greek plays, a number of persons who between the episodes danced, and chanted comment and counsel: a person who performs similar functions by himself: a company of singers: that which is sung by a chorus: the combination of voices in one simultaneous utterance: a refrain, in which the company may join: an obsolete kind of bagpipe.—*v.t.* to sing or say together:—*pr.p.* **cho'rusing**; *pa.t.* and *pa.p.* **cho'rused**.—*adj.* **chor'al**, pertaining to a chorus or a choir.—*n.* (*ko-räl'*; often altered to **chorale'**), a simple harmonised composition with slow rhythm: a psalm or hymn tune: in R.C. usage, any part of the service sung by the whole choir.—*adv.* **chor'ally**, in the manner of a chorus: suitable for a choir.—*adj.* **choric** (*kor'ik, kō'rik*).—*ns.* **chorist** (*kor'ist, kō'rist*), **chŏr'ister, quïr'ister**, a member of a choir; **chorine**, (*kōr'ēn, kör'*) (*slang*) a chorus-girl.—*v.t.* **chor'eograph**, to arrange (a dance, dances, etc.).—*v.i.* to practise choreography.—*ns.* **chor'-eograph**, **choreographer** (*kor-i-og'rə-fər*).—*adj.* **choreograph'ic** (*-graf'ik*). — *ns.* **choreog'raphy**, **choreg'raphy**, the art, or the notation, of dancing, esp. ballet-dancing: the art of arranging dances, esp. ballets: the arrangement of a ba!let; **choreol'ogist**; **choreol'ogy**, study of ballets and their history.—**chor'us-girl**, a woman employed to sing or dance in a chorus on the stage. [L., —Gr. *choros*, dance; see also choir.]

**chose, chosen**. See choose.

**chose**, *shōz*, (*law*) *n*. a thing: a piece of personal property. [Fr.—L. *causa*, thing.]

**chose jugée**, *shōz zhü-zhā*, (Fr.) a settled matter.

**chota-hazri**, *chō'tə haz'ri, häz'*, (*Anglo-Indian*) *n*. early light breakfast. [Hind. *choṭā*, little, *ḥaẓiri*, breakfast.]

**chou**, *shōō*, *n*. cabbage: soft rosette: cream bun: dear, pet:—*pl.* **choux** (*shōō*). [Fr.]

**chough**, *chuf*, *n*. the red-legged crow, or any bird of the genus *Fregilus* or *Pyrrhocorax*: a jackdaw (*obs.*). [Perh. from its cry.]

**chough**. See chuff.

**choultry**. See choltry.

**chouse**, *chows*, *n*. a cheat: one easily cheated (*obs.*): a tool.—*v.t.* to cheat, swindle. [Prob. from Turk. *chaush*, a messenger or envoy.]

**chout**, *chowt*, *n*. one-fourth part of the revenue, extorted by the Mahrattas as blackmail: blackmail, extortion. [Hind. *chauth*, the fourth part.]

**chow-chow**, *chow'chow*, shortened as **chow**, *n*. food: a Chinese mixed condiment: a dog of a Chinese breed.—*adj.* mixed, miscellaneous.—*n*.

**Chow**, a Chinese (*slang*). [Pidgin English, food.]

**chowder**, *chow'dər*, *n*. a dish made of fish with meat and vegetables. [Fr. *chaudière*, a pot.]

**chowkidar**. See choky.

**chow-mein**, *chow'-mēn'*, *-mān'*, *n*. fried noodles: a dish of seasoned shredded meat and vegetables, served with fried noodles. [Chin., fry-dough.]

**chowry**, *chow'ri*, *n*. an instrument used for driving away flies. [Hindi *caūri*.]

**choy-root**. See chay (2).

**chrematist**, *krē'mə-tist*, *n*. a political economist.— *adj.* **chrematist'ic**, pertaining to finance, money-making, or political economy.—*n.* **chrematis'-tics**, the science of wealth. [Gr. *chrēmatistēs*, a money-getter—*chrēma, -atos*, a thing, possession, money.]

**chrestomathy**, *kres-tom'ə-thi*, *n*. a book of selections esp. in a foreign language, usu. for beginners.—*adjs.* **chrestomathic** (*-tō-math'ik*), *-al*. [Gr. *chrēstos*, useful, *mathein*, (aorist) to know.]

**chrism**, *krizm*, *n*. consecrated or holy oil: unction: confirmation: chrisom.—*adj.* **chris'mal**, pertaining to chrism.—*n.* a case for containing chrism: a pyx: a veil used in christening.—*ns.* **chris'matory**, a vessel for holding chrism; **chris'om, christ'om, chris'om-cloth**, a white cloth or robe put on a child newly anointed with chrism after its baptism: the child itself.— **chrisom child** (*Shak.*), a child still wearing the chrisom-cloth: a child that died in its first month, buried in its chrisom-cloth: an innocent child. [O.Fr. *chresme* (Fr. *chrême*)—Gr. *chrisma—chriein*, to anoint.]

**Christ**, *krist*, *n*. the Anointed, a name given to Jesus: a Messiah.—*v.t.* **christen** (*kris'n*), to baptise in the name of Christ: to give a name to. —*ns.* **Chris'tendom**, that part of the world in which Christianity is the received religion: the whole body of Christians; **chris'tening**, the ceremony of baptism; **Christ'hood**, the condition of being the Christ or Messiah; **Christian** (*kris'chən*), a believer in the religion of Christ or one so classified: a follower of Christ: one whose behaviour is considered becoming to a follower of Christ: often a vague term of approbation, a decent, respectable, kindly, charitably minded person: a human being (*coll.*).—*adj.* relating to Christ or his religion: in the spirit of Christ.—*v.t.* **christ'ianise, -ize**, to make Christian: to convert to Christianity.—*ns.* **Christ'ianism**, Christianity (*kris-ti-an'i-ti*), the religion of Christ: the spirit of this religion.—*adjs.* **Christ'ianlike, Christ'ianly**.—*ns.* **Christ'ianness**; **Christ'liness**.—*adjs.* **Christ'less**; **Christ'like**; **Christ'ly**, like Chrïst.—**criss-, Christ-cross-row** (*kris'-kros-rō*), the alphabet, from the use in hornbooks of having a cross at the beginning; **Christian era**, the era counted from the date formerly assigned to the birth of Christ; **Christian name**, the name given at christening: the personal name as distinguished from the surname; **Christian Science**, a religion which includes spiritual or divine healing, founded in 1866 by Mrs Eddy; **Christian Scientist; Christian Socialism**, a mid-nineteenth century movement for applying Christian ethics to social reform: the principles of an Austrian Roman Catholic political party; **Christ's-thorn**, a prickly shrub (*Paliurus spina-christi*) of the buckthorn family common in the Mediterranean region, from which the crown of thorns is fancied to have been made: a kind of jujube tree (*Zizyphus spina-christi*) with the like legend. [O.E. *Crist*—Gr. *Christos—chriein*, to anoint.]

**Christadelphian**, *kris-tə-del'fi-an*, *n*. a member of a small religious body believing in conditional immortality—sometimes called *Thomasites* from Dr John Thomas, of Brooklyn (1805-71). [Gr. *Christos*, Christ, and *adelphos*, brother.]

Neutral vowels in unaccented syllables: *el'ə-mənt*; for certain sounds in foreign words, see p. viii

**christiana.** Variant of **Christiania.**

**Christiania,** *kris-ti-än'i-ə,* **Chris'tie, -ty,** (also without *caps.*), *ns.* a turn with skis parallel executed when descending at speed. [Former name of Oslo.]

**Christmas,** *kris'məs, n.* an annual festival, orig. a mass, in memory of the birth of Christ, held on the 25th of December: the season at which it occurs: evergreens, esp. holly, for Christmas decoration.—Also *adj.*—*adj.* **Christ'mas(s)y,** savouring of Christmas.—**Christ'mas-tide, -time,** the season of Christmas; **Christmas box,** a box containing Christmas presents: a Christmas gift; **Christmas cactus,** S. American cactus with red flowers; **Christmas card,** a card, more or less ornamented sent from friend to friend at Christmas; **Christmas daisy,** the aster; **Christmas eve,** Dec. 24; **Christmas rose,** or **flower** (*Helleborus niger*), flowering in winter; **Christmas tree,** a tree, usu. fir, set up in a room or a public place, and loaded with Christmas gifts and/or gauds: an apparatus fitted to the outlet of an oilwell to control the flow of oil or gas. [Christ and mass.]

**Christolatry,** *kris-tol'ə-tri, n.* worship of Christ. [Gr. *Christos,* Christ, *latreiā,* worship.]

**Christology,** *kris-tol'ə-ji, n.* that branch of theology which treats of the nature and person of Christ.—*adj.* **Christological** (*-to-loj'i-kl*).—*n.* **Christol'ogist.** [Gr. *Christos,* and *logos,* discourse.]

**christom,** *kriz'əm.* Same as **chrisom.**

**christophany,** *kris-tof'ə-ni, n.* an appearance of Christ to men. [Gr. *Christos,* and *phainesthai,* to appear.]

**Christy.** See **Christiania.**

**Christy-minstrel,** *krist'i-min'strəl, n.* one of a troupe of minstrels imitating Negroes. [Instituted by George *Christy,* in New York.]

**chroma,** *krō'ma, n.* quality of colour: a hue.—*n.* **chrō'mate,** a salt of chromic acid.—*adj.* **chrō-mat'ic,** pertaining to, or consisting of, colours: coloured: relating to notes in a melodic progression, which are raised or lowered by accidentals, without changing the key of the passage, and also to chords in which such notes occur (*mus.*).—*ns.* **chromat'icism** (*mus.*), the state of being chromatic: the use of chromatic tones; **chromaticity** (*-tis'*), the colour quality of light depending on hue and saturation (i.e. excluding brightness), one method of defining it being by its purity and dominant wavelength; **chrō-mat'ics** (*pl.* in form), the science of colours; **chrō'matin,** a readily stained substance in the nucleus of a cell; **chrome,** chromium or a chromium compound.—Also *adj.*—*adj.* **chrō'-mic,** pertaining to trivalent chromium.—*ns.* **chrō'minance** (*TV*), difference between any colour and a reference colour (usu. a white of specified chromaticity) of equal luminance; **chro'mium,** a metal (at. numb. 24) remarkable for the beautiful colour of its compounds; **chrō'mō,** chromolithograph; **chrōmatog'raphy,** methods of separating substances in a mixture which depend on selective adsorption, partition between non-mixing solvents, etc., and which present the substances as a **chrōmat'ogram,** such as a series of visible bands in a vertical tube.—*adj.* **chrōmatograph'ic.**—*ns.* **chrōmat'ophore,** a pigment-cell, or a pigment-bearing body in protoplasm or photosynthetic bacteria; **chrō-matop'sia** (Gr. *opsis,* sight), coloured vision; **chrō'matype, chrō'motype,** a photographic process that uses chromium salts: a photograph in colours: a sheet printed in colour; **chromatic scale,** a scale proceeding by semitones; **chrome'-al'um,** potassium chromium sulphate; **chrome'-leath'er,** leather prepared by chrome-tanning; **chrome'-plating,** electroplating with chromium; **chrome'-spinel,** picolite; **chrome'-steel',** an alloy

steel containing chromium; **chrome'-tann'ing,** tanning with salts of chromium; **chrome'-yell'ow,** a pigment of lead chromate; **chromic acid,** an acid of chromium ($H_2CrO_4$), of an orange-red colour, much used in dyeing and bleaching; **chrōmid'ium,** an algal cell in a lichen: a free fragment of chromatin:—*pl.* **chromid'ia;** **chro'mite,** a mineral, a double oxide of chromium and iron; **chrō'mōgram,** a combination of photographs in different colours to give an image in natural colours; **chrō'mōlith'ograph,** or merely **chrōmō,** a lithograph printed in colours; **chrō'mōlithog'raphy; chrō'mōplast** (*bot.*), a chromatophore: **chrō'mōscope,** an apparatus for combining coloured images; **chrō'mōsome,** a rod-like portion of the chromatin of a cell-nucleus, performing an important part in mitotic cell-division, and in the transmission of hereditary characters; **chrō'mōsphere,** a layer of incandescent gas surrounding the sun through which the light of the photosphere passes—also **chrō'matosphere; chrō'mōtypog'raphy,** printing in colours; **chrō'mōxy'lograph** (Gr. *xylon,* wood), a picture printed in colours from wooden blocks; **chrō'-mōxylog'raphy.** [Gr. *chrōma, -atos,* colour.]

**chron-, chrono-,** *kron', -ō-, -ə-, krən-, kron-o',* in composition, time.—*adj.* **chron'ic,** relating to time (*obs.*): lasting a long time: of a disease, deep seated or long continued, as opp. to *acute*: deplorable (*slang*).—*n.* a chronic invalid: a student who repeatedly fails in examinations (*slang*).—*adj.* **chron'ical,** chronic.—*adv.* **chron'-ically.**—*n.* **chron'icle,** a bare record of events in order of time: a history: a story, account; (in *pl., cap.*) the name of two of the O.T. books.—*v.t.* to record as in a chronicle.—*ns.* **chron'icler,** a writer of a chronicle; **chron'ogram** (Gr. *gramma,* letter), an inscription from which a date is got by adding the values of such letters as are Roman numerals; **chron'ograph** (Gr. *graphein,* to write), a chronogram: an instrument for taking exact measurements of time, or for recording graphically the moment or duration of an event; **chronog'rapher,** a chronicler; **chronog'raphy,** chronology; **chronol'oger.**—*adjs.* **chronolog'ic, -al.**—*adv.* **chronolog'ically.**—*ns.* **chronol'ogist; chronol'ogy** (Gr. *logos,* discourse), the science of computing time: a scheme of time: order of time; **chronom'eter** (Gr. *metron,* measure), an instrument for accurate measurement of time.—*adjs.* **chronomet'ric, -al.**—*ns.* **chronom'etry,** the art of measuring time by means of instruments: measurement of time; **chron'oscope** (Gr. *skopeein,* to look), an instrument used for measuring extremely short intervals of time, especially in determining the velocity of projectiles; **chron'otron,** a device which measures very small time intervals by comparing the distance between electric pulses from different sources.—**chronological age,** age in years, etc., opp. e.g. to *mental age.* [Gr. *chronos,* time; adj. *chronikos;* partly through A.Fr. *cronicle* (O.Fr. *cronique*).]

**chronique scandaleuse,** *kro-nēk skä-da-lœz,* (Fr.) a story full of scandalous events or details.

**chrys-,** *kris-,* **chryso-,** *kris'ō-, -ə-, kris-ō',* in composition, gold.—*ns.* **chrys'alid, chrys'alis** (Gr. *chrȳsallis*), orig. a golden-coloured butterfly pupa: a pupa generally: a pupa case:—*pl.* **chrysalides** (*kris-al'i-dēz*), **chrys'alises, chrys'-alids;** **Chrysan'themum** (*kris-* or *kriz-*; Gr. *anthemon,* flower), a genus of composite plants to which belong the corn marigold and ox-eye daisy; **chrysar'ōbin** (see **araroba**), a yellow crystalline mixture got from Goa powder and from rhubarb root: also one of its components, an active purgative.—*adj.* **chryselephan'tine** (Gr. *elephantinos,* made of ivory—*elephas, -antos,* ivory), made of gold and ivory.—*ns.* **chrysober'yl,** a mineral, beryllium aluminate, of various shades

of greenish-yellow or gold colour; chrysocoll'a (Gr. *chrȳsokolla*, gold-solder, perh. applied to this mineral—*kolla*, glue), a silicate of copper, bluish-green; chrysoc'racy (Gr. *krateein*, to rule), the rule of wealth; chrys'olite (Gr. *lithos*, stone), olivine, esp. yellow or green precious olivine; chrys'ophan (Gr. *phainesthai*, to appear), an old name for chrysarobin.—*adj.* chrysophan'ic (chrysophanic acid, an oxidation product of chrysarobin used against skin 'diseases).—*ns.* chrysoph'ilite (Gr. *phileein*, to love), a lover of gold; chrys'oprase (*-prāz*; Gr. *prason*, a leek), a green chalcedony; chrys'otile (Gr. *tilos*, a shred), a fibrous serpentine. [Gr. *chrȳsos*, gold.]
chthonian, *thō'ni-ən, adj.* pertaining to the earth or the underworld and the deities inhabiting it: ghostly.—Also chthonic (*thon'ik*). [Gr. *chthōn, chthōnos*, the ground.]
chub, *chub, n.* a small fat river-fish of the carp family.—*adjs.* chubbed, chubb'y, short and thick, plump; chub'-faced, plump-faced.—*n.* chubb'iness. [Origin unknown.]
Chubb, *chub, n.* a lock invented by *Chubb*, a locksmith in London.—Also chubb'-lock. [Registered trademark.]
chuck, *chuk, n.* the call of a hen: a chicken (dim. chuck'ie): a word of endearment.—*v.i.* to call, as a hen. [A variant of cluck.]
chuck, *chuk, n.* a gentle blow under the chin: a toss or throw, hence dismissal (*coll.*): a pebble or small stone (usu. chuck'ie, chuck'ie-stone, -stane): (in *pl.*) a game with such stones, often called chuck'ies: any game of pitch and toss.—*v.t.* to tap under the chin: to toss : to pitch: to abandon or dismiss.—chuck'er-out, one who expels undesirable people; chuck'-far'thing, a game in which a farthing is chucked into a hole.—chuck it (*coll.*), stop, give over; chuck up (*coll.*), to give up: to give in: to throw up (the sponge). [Fr. *choquer*, to jolt: allied to shock.]
chuck, *chuk, n.* a lump or chunk: an instrument for holding an object so that it can be rotated, as upon the mandrel of a lathe: food (*slang*).—chuck'-wagon, a wagon carrying food, cooking apparatus, etc. [Der. uncertain; cf. It. *cioco*, a block, stump.]
chuck-full. Same as chock-full. [See chock.]
chuckle, *chuk'l, n.* a quiet laugh: the cry of a hen.—*v.t.* to call, as a hen does her chickens.—*v.i.* to laugh in a quiet, suppressed manner, in derision or enjoyment.—*n.* chuck'ling. [Cf. chuck (1).]
chuckle, *chuk'l, adj.* clumsy.—chuck'le-head, a loutish fellow. [Prob. chock, a log.]
chuddar, chuddah, *chud'ä(r), (Ind.) n.* a sheet worn as a shawl or cloak by the women of northern India: a cloth spread on a Mohammedan tomb. [Hindi *caddar*, a square cloth.]
chufa, *chōō'fa, n.* a sedge with edible tubers. [Sp.]
chuff, chough, *chuf, n.* a clown: a surly fellow.—*n.* chuff'iness, boorishness.—*adjs.* chuffed, disgruntled; chuff'y, coarse and surly. [M.E. *chuffe, choffe*, a boor (ety. dub.)]
chuffed, *chuft, (coll.) adj.* very pleased. [Dial. *chuff*, chubby.]
chug, *chug, n.* a rapid explosive noise, as of an internal-combustion engine.—*adj.* chugg'ing.—*v.i.* chug, to make a chugging noise: of a vehicle, to move while making such a noise. [Imit.]
chukker, chukka, *chuk'ər, -a, n.* a period of play in polo. [Hindi *cakkar*, a round.]
chukor, *chu-kōr', chukar, -kär', chik(h)or, chi-kōr', n.* an Indian partridge. [Hindi *cakor*.]
chum, *chum, n.* a chamber-fellow: a friend or associate.—*v.i.* to share a room: to be or become a chum.—*v.t.* to assign as chum (with *on*): to be or become a chum to: to accompany.—*n.* chumm'age, the quartering of two or more persons in one room: a fee demanded from a new chum.—*adj.* chumm'y, sociable.—*n.* a chum: a compact motor-car body for a small company.—

chum up with, to become intimate with. [Perh. a mutilation of chamber-fellow.]
chum, *chum, n.* a dog-salmon or keta.
chummy, *chum'i, (old slang) n.* a chimney sweeper's boy. [chimney.]
chump, *chump, n.* an end lump of wood, mutton, etc.: a thick lump: a blockhead: the head.—off his chump, out of his mind. [Perh. related to chunk.]
chunk, *chungk, n.* a thick piece of anything, as wood, bread, etc.—*adj.* chunk'y, in chunks: short and broad. [Perh. related to chuck.]
Chunnel, *chun'l,* proposed tunnel underneath the English Channel, connecting England and France. [*Channel* tunnel.]
chunter, *chun'tər, (dial.) v.i.* to mutter: to grumble.—Also chunner, etc. [Imit.]
chupati, chupatti. Same as chapati, chapatti.
chuprassy, *chup-räs'i.* Same as chaprassi.
church, *chûrch, n.* a house set apart for public worship, esp. that of a parish, and esp. that of an established or once established form of religion: a church service: the whole body of Christians: the clergy: any particular sect or denomination of Christians: any body professing a common creed, not necessarily Christian.—*adj.* of the church: ecclesiastical.—*v.t.* to perform a service in church with (e.g. a woman after childbirth, a newly-married couple, a new town council.)—*n.* churchian'ity, religion centring in the church rather than in Christ; church'ing; church'ism, adherence to the form of principles of some church, esp. established.—*adjs.* church'less, not belonging to a church: without church approval (Tennyson); church'ly, concerned with the church: ecclesiastical; churchy, obtrusively devoted to the church: savouring of church.—church'-ale, a church festival; Church Army, an organisation of the Church of England, resembling the Salvation Army; church'-bench (*Shak.*), a seat in the porch of a church; church'-court; a court for deciding ecclesiastical causes: a kirk session: a presbytery, synod, or general assembly; church'-goer, one on the way to, or who habitually goes to church; church'-going, the act or habit of going to church; church'man, a clergyman or ecclesiastic: a member or upholder of the established church; church militant, the church on earth in its struggle against evil; church'-mouse, a mouse inhabiting a church, a proverbial type of poverty; church'-off'icer, a church attendant or beadle; church'-parade', military parade for the purpose of church-going: promenade of fashionable church-goers after service; church'-rate, an assessment for the sustentation of the fabric, etc., of the parish church; church'-ser'vice, a religious service in a church: the form followed, a book containing it; church'-text, a thin and tall form of black-letter print; church triumphant, the portion of the church which has overcome and left this world.—*advs.* church'ward, -s.—church'-war'den, an officer who represents the interests of a parish or church: a long clay-pipe; church'way, the public way or road that leads to the church.—Also *adj.* (*Shak.*).—church'woman, a female member or upholder of a church, esp. the Anglican Church; church'yard, a burial-ground round a church. [O.E. *cirice, circe*—Gr. *kȳriakon*, belonging to the Lord—*kȳrios*, lord.]
churinga, *chōō-ring'ga, n.* a stone amulet. [Austr.]
churl, *chûrl, n.* a rustic, labourer: an ill-bred, surly fellow.—*adj.* churl'ish, rude: surly: ungracious.—*adv.* churl'ishly.—*n.* churl'ishness. [O.E. *ceorl*, a countryman; O.N. *karl*, Ger. *kerl*, a man; Scot. *carl*.]
churn, *chûrn, n.* a machine used for the production of butter from cream or from whole milk: a large milk-can suggestive of an upright churn.—*v.t.* to agitate so as to obtain butter: to stir,

agitate, violently: to turn over persistently (ideas in the mind).—*v.i.* to perform the act of churning: to move restlessly and with violence.—*n.* churn'ing, the act of making butter: the quantity of butter made at once.—churn'-drill, a drill worked by hand, not struck with the hammer, a jumper; churn'-milk, buttermilk; churn'-staff, the plunger of an upright churn: the sun-spurge.—churn out, to produce continuously with effort. [O.E. *cyrin*; O.N. *kirna*, a churn, Du. *karnen*, and Ger. *kernen*, to churn.]

churn-owl, *chûrn'-owl, n.* the nightjar. [App. churr and owl.]

churr, *chûr, n.* a low sound made by certain birds and insects.—*v.i.* to make this sound.—*n.* churr'-worm, the fen-cricket. [Prob. imit.]

churrus. See charas.

chuse, *chōōz,* an obs. spelling of choose.

chut, *chut, interj.* an expression of impatience.

chute, shoot, *shōōt, n.* a waterfall, rapid: a passage or sloping trough for sending down goods, water, logs, rubbish, etc.: a narrow passage for controlling cattle. [Fr. *chute,* fall, combined with shoot.]

chute, *shōōt,* abbrev. for parachute.

chutney, *chut'ni, n.* an East Indian condiment, of mangoes, chillies, etc.: an imitation made with home materials, as apples. [Hindi *catnī.*]

chutzpah, *hhōōt'spə, n.* effrontery. [Yiddish.]

chyle, *kil, n.* a white fluid, mainly lymph mixed with fats derived from food in the body.—*n.* chylū'ria (Gr. *ouron,* urine), presence of chyle in the urine. [Gr. *chŷlos,* juice—*cheein,* to pour.]

chyme, *kim, n.* the pulp to which the food is reduced in the stomach.—*n.* chymificā'tion, the act of being formed into chyme.—*v.t.* chym'ify, to form into chyme.—*adj.* chym'ous. [Gr. *chȳmos,* chyme, juice—*cheein,* to pour.]

chymical, chymistry. See chemical, chemistry.

chynd, *chind,* (*Spens.*) *p.adj.* cut into chines.

chypre, *shē'pr', n.* a scent from Cyprus. [Fr., Cyprus.]

ciao, *chä'ō,* Eng. chow, (It.) informal greeting used on meeting or parting.

cibation, *si-bā'shən,* (*obs.*) *n.* the seventh of the twelve processes employed in the search for the philosopher's stone, 'feeding the matter': taking food, feeding. [L. *cibātiō, -ōnis,* feeding.]

cibol, *sib'əl,* chibol, *chib'əl, n.* a variety of onion. [Fr. *ciboule* (Sp. *cebolla*—L.L. *cēpola,* dim. of L. *cēpa,* an onion; see sybo(w)).]

ciborium, *si-bō'ri-əm, bō', n.* a vessel nearly resembling a chalice, usu. with an arched cover, in which the host is deposited: a canopy supported on four pillars over the high altar:—*pl.* cibo'ria. [L., a drinking-cup—Gr. *kibōrion,* the seed-vessel of the Egyptian water-lily.]

cicada, *si-kä'da, -kä'da,* cicala, *-kä'la, n.* a homopterous insect remarkable for its loud chirping sound. [L. *cicāda*; It. *cicala.*]

cicatrice, *sik'ə-tris, n.* a scar over a healed wound: scar in the bark of a tree: mark left where a leaf, etc., has been attached: mark, impression (*Shak.*):—*pl.* cicatri'cēs.—Also cicatrix (*sik-ā'-triks, sik'ə-triks*):—*pl.* cic'atrixes.—*ns.* cicatric'ula, the germinating point in the yolk of an egg; cicatrisā'tion, the process of healing over. —*v.t.* cic'atrise, -ize, to help the formation of a cicatrix on: to scar.—*v.i.* to heal. [L. *cicātrix, -icis,* a scar.]

cicely, *sis'ə-li, n.* a name for several umbelliferous plants allied to chervil, esp. *Myrrhis odorata* (sweet cicely). [L. and Gr. *seseli.*]

Cicero, *sis'ə-rō* (L. *kik-e-rō), n.* a famous Roman orator: cicero, a type-body between pica and English.—*n.* cicerone (*chich-ə-rō'ni,* also *sis-ə-rō'ni*), one who shows strangers the curiosities of a place: a guide:—*pl.* ciceroni (*-nē).—v.i.* to act as cicerone.—*adjs.* Cicero'nian (*sis-*), Ciceronic (*-ron'ik*).—*n.* Cicero'nianism, the character of

Cicero's Latin style. [L. *Cicerō, -ōnis*; It. *Cicerone.*]

cichlid, *sik'lid, n.* any fish of the family Cich'lidae, to which the angel-fish of the Amazon belongs.— *adj.* cich'loid. [Gr. *kichlē,* a kind of wrasse.]

Cichorium, *si-kō'ri-əm, kō', n.* the chicory and endive genus of Compositae.—*adj.* cichorā'ceous. [L. *cichōrium*—Gr. *kichorion.*]

Cicindela, *si-sin-dē'la, n.* a genus of carnivorous beetles, type of the family Cicinde'lidae, the tiger-beetles, active in running down their insect prey. [L. *cicindēla,* glow-worm—*candēla,* a candle.]

cicinnus, *si-sin'əs, n.* a cincinnus. [Latinised from Gr. *kinkinnos,* a ringlet.]

cicisbeo, *chē-chēz-bā'ō, chi-chiz-, n.* a married woman's gallant or *cavaliere servente* in Italy:— *pl.* cicisbe'i (*-ē).—n.* cicisbē'ism. [It.]

ciclaton, ciclatoun, *sik'lə-tən, -tōōn,* (*obs.*) *n.* cloth of gold or other rich stuff: misunderstood by Spenser (see checklaton). [O.Fr. *ciclaton,* from Ar., perh. from the root of scarlet.]

Cicuta, *si-kū'ta, n.* a genus of poisonous umbelliferous plants—*water-hemlock* or *cowbane.* [L. *cicūta,* hemlock.]

Cid, *sid, sēd, n.* a chief, captain, hero—title of the 11th-cent. Castilian champion Rodrigo, or Ruy, Diaz. [Ar. *sayyid,* lord.]

cidaris, *sid'ə-ris, n.* a Persian tiara: (*cap.*) a genus of sea-urchins, mostly fossil. [Gr. *kidaris.*]

cide, *sid, v.t.* a proposed emendation for Shakespeare's side, as if aphetic for decide, adjudge.

cider (sometimes cyder), *si'dər, n.* a drink made from apples.—*ns.* ci'der-and, a mixture of cider and spirits; ci'der-cup, a drink of sweetened cider, with other ingredients; ci'derkin, an inferior cider.—*adj.* ci'dery. [Fr. *cidre*—L. *sicera*—Gr. *sikera,* strong drink—Heb. *shēkār.*]

ci-devant, *sē-də-vä,* (Fr.) before this, former, formerly.

ciel, cieling, variants of ceil, ceiling.

cierge. See cerge.

cigar, *si-gär', n.* a roll of tobacco-leaves with a pointed end for smoking.—*n.* cigarette (*sig-ə-ret'*), finely-cut tobacco rolled in thin paper (contr. cig).—cigarette'-card, a picture card formerly given away with a packet of cigarettes, valued by cartophilists; cigarette'-holder, a mouthpiece for a cigarette; cigarette'-lighter, a mechanical contrivance for lighting cigarettes: cigarette'-paper, paper for making cigarettes; cigar'-tree, a species of Catalpa with long cigar-like pods. [Sp. *cigarro.*]

ci-gît, *sē-zhē,* (Fr.) here lies.

cilice, *sil'is, n.* haircloth: a penitential garment made of haircloth.—*adj.* cilic'ious. [L.,—Gr. *kilikion,* a cloth made of Cilician goat's hair.]

cilium, *sil'i-əm, n.* a hair-like lash borne by a cell: a flagellum:—*pl.* cil'ia.—*adj.* cil'iary.—*n.pl.* Ciliā'ta, a subclass of Infusoria retaining cilia throughout life.—*adjs.* cil'iate, -d, bearing a cilium or cilia: fringed with hairs; cil'iolate, fringed with very short fine hairs.—*n.pl.* Cilioph'ora (Gr. *phoros,* bearing), the Infusoria. [L. *cilium,* eyelash.]

cill, sil, (*building*) *n.* old variant of sill, now usual in the trade.

cimar. Same as cymar.

cimelia, *si-mē'li-ə, n.pl.* treasures. [Gr. *keimēlia.*]

Cimex, *si-meks, n.* the bed-bug genus of Hemiptera, giving name to the family cimicidae (*si-* or *si-mis'i-dē*).

cimier, *sē-myā', n.* the crest of a helmet. [Fr.]

ciminite, *sim'in-īt, n.* a rock intermediate between trachyte and andesite, containing olivine. [Monte Cimini, in Italy.]

Cimmerian, *sim-ē'ri-ən, adj.* relating to the Cimmerii, a tribe fabled to have lived in perpetual darkness.

cimolite, *sim'ō-līt, n.* a species of clay, or hydrous

silicate of aluminium, used as fuller's earth. [Gr. *kimōliā*, prob. from *Kimōlos*, an island of the Cyclades.]

**cinch**, *sinch*, *n.* a saddle-girth (*U.S.*): a secure hold (*coll.*): a certainty (*coll.*): something easy (*coll.*).—*v.i.* to tighten the cinch.—*v.t.* to bind firmly: make sure of (*coll.*). [Sp. *cincha*—L. *cingula*.]

**Cinchona**, *sing-kō′na*, a rubiaceous genus of trees, yielding the bark from which quinine and its congeners are obtained—also called *Peruvian bark.*—*adjs.* **cinchonaceous** (*-kən-ā′shəs*), **cinchonic** (*-kon′ik*).—*n.* **cinch′onine**, an alkaloid obtained from cinchona bark.—*adj.* **cinchonin′ic.**—*n.* **cinchonisā′tion, -z-.**—*v.t.* **cinch′onise, -ize,** to bring under the influence of cinchona or quinine. *n.* **cinch′onism**, a morbid state due to overdoses of cinchona or quinine. [Said to be so named from the Countess of *Chinchón*, who was cured of a fever by it in 1638.]

**cincinnus**, *sin-sin′əs*, (*bot.*) *n.* a uniparous cymose inflorescence in which the plane of each daughter axis is at right angles, alternately to right and left, with that of its parent axis.—*adj.* **cincin′ate.** [L., a curl.]

**cincture**, *singk′chər*, *n.* a girdle or belt: a moulding round a column.—*v.t.* to gird, encompass.—*adjs.* **cinct,** surrounded; **cinc′tured,** having a cincture. [L. *cinctūra*—*cingĕre, cinctum*, to gird.]

**cinder**, *sin′dər*, *n.* the refuse of burned coals: an ember: anything charred by fire: a scoriaceous fragment of lava: a strong stimulant put in tea, soda-water, etc. (*slang*).—**cin′der-cone,** a hill of loose volcanic materials; **Cinderell′a,** a scullery-maid: the despised and neglected one of a set; **Cinderel′la-day,** a dancing-party ending at midnight—from the nursery tale; **cin′der-path, -track,** a path, racing-track, laid with cinders.— *adj.* **cin′dery.** [O.E. *sinder*, slag; cf. Gr. *sinter*; not connected with Fr. *cendre*.]

**cine-, ciné-,** *sin′i-,* in composition, cinematograph, as *ns.* **cin′e-biol′ogy, cin′é-,** the study of biological phenomena by means of cinematographic records; **cin′e-cam′era, cin′é-,** a camera for taking moving photographs; **cinemicrog′raphy,** cinematographic recording of changes under the microscope; **ciné′-project′or; Cinera′ma,** trademark for a method of film projection on a wide curved screen to give a three-dimensional effect; the picture is photographed with three cameras. —**ciné vérité,** cinéma vérité.

**cinéaste, cineast(e),** *sin′ē-ast, n.* one who takes an artistic interest in, or who makes, motion pictures. [Fr.]

**cinema,** *sin′ə-mə, -mä, n.* a cinematograph: a building in which motion pictures are shown: (with *the*) motion pictures collectively, or as an art: material or method judged by its suitability for the cinema.—Also **kin′ema.**—*n.* **cin′emathèque, -theque,** a small, intimate cinema.—*adj.* **cinemat′ic,** pertaining to, suitable for, or savouring of, the cinema.—**cin′emaor′gan,** an organ with showier effects than a church organ; **Cin′emaScope,** proprietary name of one of the methods of film projection on a wide curved screen to give a three-dimensional effect; the picture is photographed with a special type of lens; **cinéma vérité,** realism in films sought by photographing scenes of real life. [cinematograph.]

**cinematograph,** *sin-ə-mat′ə-gräf, n.* apparatus for projecting a series of instantaneous photographs so as to give a moving representation of a scene, with or without reproduction of sound: an exhibition of such photographs.—Also **kinemat′ograph.**—*n.* **cinematog′rapher.**—*adjs.* **cinematograph′ic, cinematograph′ical.**—*ns.* **cinematog′raphist; cinematog′raphy,** the art of making motion pictures. [Fr. *cinématographe*— Gr. *kinēma, -atos*, motion, *graphein*, to write, represent.]

**cineol, -ole,** *sin′i-ol, -ōl, n.* eucalyptol, a camphor-smelling disinfectant liquid ($C_{10}H_{18}O$) got from several essential oils, as eucalyptus, wormwood, cajeput. [From *Artemisia Cina*, a species of wormwood, and L. *oleum*, oil.]

**Cineraria,** *sin-ə-rā′ri-ə, n.* a South African genus of plants, close akin to Senecio, with ashy down on the leaves. [L. *cinerārius*, ashy—*cinis, cineris,* ash.]

**cinerary,** *sin′ə-rə-ri, adj.* pertaining to ashes: for containing ashes of the dead.—*ns.* **cinerā′tion; cinerā′tor; ciné′rea,** grey nerve matter.—*adjs.* **ciné′real,** ashy: cinerary; **ciné′reous, ashy-grey:** ashy; **cineri′tious, ashy-grey:** pertaining to grey nerve matter. [L. *cinereus,* ashy—*cinis, cineris,* ash.]

**Cingalese.** See Sinhalese.

**cingulum,** *sing′gū-ləm, n.* a girdle: a girdle-like structure. [L. *cingĕre*, to gird.]

**cingulum Veneris,** *sing′gū-ləm ve′nə-ris, king′gōō-lōōm ve′ne-ris* (*we′*) (L.) the girdle of Venus.

**cinnabar,** *sin′ə-bär, n.* a mineral, sulphide of mercury, called vermilion when used as a pigment. —*adj.* **vermilion-coloured.**—*adjs.* **cinnabaric** (*-bär′ik*), **cinn′abarine** (*-bə-rēn*).—**cinnabar moth,** a large red moth whose black and yellow caterpillars feed on ragwort. [Gr. *kinnabari,* from Persian.]

**cinnamon,** *sin′ə-mən, n.* the spicy bark of a lauraceous tree of Ceylon: the tree: a light yellowish brown.—Also *adj.*—*adjs.* **cinnamic** (*-am′ik*), **cinnamonic** (*-ə-mon′ik*), obtained from, or consisting of, cinnamon.—**cinn′amon-bear,** a cinnamon-coloured variety of grizzly or American black bear; **cinna′mon-stone,** a yellowish grossular garnet. [Gr. *kinnamōmon,* later *kinnamon* —Heb. *qinnāmōn.*]

**cinquain,** *sing′kän,.n.* a poetic form consisting of five lines of two, four, six, eight and two syllables respectively. [Fr.]

**cinque,** *singk, n.* the number five as on dice.— **cinque-foil,** a common bearing representing a flower with five petals borne full-faced and without a stalk (*her.*): a similar figure formed by cusps in a circular window or the head of a pointed arch (*archit.*): species of the genus *Potentilla* (*bot.*): the five-bladed clover (*bot.*); **cinque′-pace** (*Shak.* also **sinke′-a-pace**), a kind of dance, the pace or movement of which is characterised by five beats.—*adj.* **cinque′-spott′ed** (*Shak.*), having five spots.—**Cinque Ports,** the five ancient ports on the south of England lying opposite to France—Sandwich, Dover, Hythe, Romney, and Hastings (later associated with Winchelsea, Rye, and a number of subordinate ports). [Fr.]

**cinquecento,** *ching′kwe-chen-tō, n.* the 16th century—the art and architecture of the Renaissance period. [It., five hundred, *mil,* one thousand, being understood.]

**cion,** a spelling of scion still used in U.S.

**cipher** (sometimes **cypher**), *si-fər, n.* the character 0 (*arith.*): any of the Arabic numerals: any person or thing of little value: a nonentity: an interweaving of the initials of a name: a secret mode of writing: in an organ, continuous sounding of a note not played.—*v.i.* to work at arithmetic: of an organ, to sound a note continuously when it is not played.—*v.t.* to write in cipher: to calculate: to decipher (*Shak.*).—*n.* **ci′phering**—**ci′pher-key,** a key to a cipher or piece of secret writing. [O.Fr. *cyfre,* Fr. *chiffre* —Ar. *çifr,* zero, empty.]

**cipollino,** *chē-pol-lē′nō, n.* a marble with green bands in which calcite is interfoliated with mica or talc.—Also **cipolin** (*sip′ō-lin*). [It. *cipolla,* an onion.]

**cippus,** *sip′əs, n.* the stocks: a monumental pillar: —*pl.* **cipp′i.** [L. *cippus,* a post.]

**circa,** *sûr′ka, prep.* and *adv.* about, around. [L.]

---

Neutral vowels in unaccented syllables: *el′ə-mənt*; for certain sounds in foreign words, see p. viii

**circadian**, *sûr-kā'di'ən, adj.* pertaining to any biological cycle (e.g. of varying intensity of metabolic or physiological process, or of some feature of behaviour) which is repeated, usu. approx. every 24 hours. [From L. *circa*, about, *di(em)*, day, and suff. *-an*.]

**Circaean**, *sûr-sē'ən, adj.* relating to the beautiful sorceress *Circe*, who transformed the companions of Ulysses into swine by a magic beverage: infatuating and degrading.—Also **Circe'an**.—*n.* **Circae'a**, the enchanter's nightshade genus. [L. *Circē*—Gr. *Kirkē*.]

**circar.** Same as **sircar**.

**Circassian**, *sûr-kas(h)'yən, adj.* belonging to *Circassia*, the country of the *Tcherkesses*, in the western Caucasus.—*n.* a Tcherkess: the language of the Tcherkesses (without *cap.*) a kind of light cashmere (also **circassienne'**).—**Circassian circle,** a progressive dance in reel time.

**circensian,** *sûr-sen'shi-ən, adj.* relating to the Circus Maximus, Rome, where the games were held.—Also **circen'sial** (*obs.*). [L. *circēnsis*—*circus.*]

**circinate,** *sûr'sin-āt, adj.* ring-shaped: rolled inwards (*bot.*). [L. *circināre, -ātum,* make round.]

**circle,** *sûr'kl, n.* a plane figure bounded by one line every point of which is equally distant from a fixed point called the centre: the circumference of the figure so defined: a circular object: a ring: a planet's orbit: a series ending where it began: a figure in magic: a group of things in a circle: a company surrounding or associating with the principal person: those of a certain class or group: an administrative unit.—*v.t.* to move round: to encompass.—*v.i.* to move in a circle: to stand in a circle.—*adj.* **cir'cled,** circular: encircled.—*ns.* **cir'cler; cir'clet,** a little circle: a little circular band or hoop, esp. a metal headband.—*n.* and *adj.* **cir'cling,** moving in a circle.—**cir'cle-rider,** one who rides in circles to round up cattle; **cir'cle-riding.—dress circle** (see **dress**); **great, small, circle,** a circle on the surface of a sphere whose centre is, is not, the centre of the sphere; **reasoning in a circle,** assuming what is to be proved as the basis of the argument; **run round in circles,** to be active without getting anywhere. [O.E. *circul*—L. *circulus,* dim. of *circus*; allied to O.E. *hring,* a ring.]

**circs,** *sûrks, n.pl.* slang abbrev. of **circumstances**.

**circuit,** *sûr'kit, n.* a journey round: a way round: perimeter: a roundabout way: area enclosed: the path, complete or partial, of an electric current: a round made in the exercise of a calling, esp. in England (till 1972) by judges: the judges making the round: a district in which such a round is made, as by Methodist preachers, commercial travellers: a group of theatres, cinemas, etc., under common control, through which an entertainment circulates: the venues visited in turn and regularly by sports competitors, performers, etc.: diadem (*Shak.*).—*v.t.* to go round.—*n.* **circuiteer',** a judge who goes on a circuit.—*adj.* **circuitous** (*-kū'i-təs*), roundabout.—*adv.* **circū'itously.—*ns.* **circū'itousness; cir'cuitry,** detailed plan of a circuit, as in radio or television, or its components; **circū'ity,** motion in a circle: an indirect course.—**cir'cuit-breaker,** a switch or other device for interrupting an electric circuit; **cir'cuit-rider,** a preacher who goes on circuit. [Fr.,—L. *circuitus*—*circuire*—*circum,* round, *ire,* to go.]

**circuitus verborum,** *sûr-kū'it-əs vûr-bō'rəm, -bō', kir-koo̅'it-oo̅s ver-, wer-bō'roo̅m,* (L.) a circumlocution.

**circular,** *sûr'kū-lər, adj.* of or pertaining to a circle: in the form of a circle: round: ending in itself: recurring in a cycle: addressed to a circle of persons.—*n.* an intimation sent to a number of persons.—*v.t.* **cir'cularise, -ize,** to make circular: to send circulars to.—*n.* **circularity**

**(*-lar'i-ti*).—*adv.* **cir'cularly.—circular function** any of the trigonometrical functions with argument in radians; **circular letter,** a letter of which copies are sent to several persons; **circular measure,** the reckoning of angles in radians; **circular note,** a letter of bank-credit for the use of a traveller, being a kind of bill personal to the bearer, who also bears a letter of indication addressed to foreign bankers. [L. *circulāris.*]

**circulate,** *sûr'kū-lāt, v.t.* to make to go round as in a circle: to spread.—*v.i.* to move round: to be spread about: to repeat in definite order (of decimals).—*adj.* **cir'culable,** capable of being circulated.—*n.* and *adj.* **cir'culating.—*ns.* **circulā'-tion,** the act of moving in a circle or in a closed path (as the blood): spreading or moving about: dissemination: the sale of a periodical: the money in use at any time in a country.—*adjs.* **cir'culātive, cir'culatory,** circulating.—*n.* **cir'culātor.—circulating library,** one from which books are circulated among subscribers. [L. *circulāre, -ātum.*]

**circum-,** *sûr'kəm-, sər-kum'-, sûr-kəm-,* in composition, around. [L. *circum.*]

**circumambages,** *sûr-kəm-am-bā'jēz, -am'bi-jiz, n. sing.* and *pl.* roundabout speech.—*adj.* **circum-ambā'gious** (*-jəs*), roundabout in speech. [L. *ambāgēs,* a winding.]

**circumambient,** *sûr-kəm-am'bi-ənt,* going round about, encompassing.—*ns.* **circumam'bience, circumam'biency.** [L. *ambīre,* to go round.]

**circumambulate,** *sûr-kəm-am'bū-lāt, v.i.* to walk round about.—*n.* **circumambulā'tion.** [L. *ambu-lāre, -ātum,* to walk.]

**circumbendibus,** *sûr-kəm-ben'di-bəs, n.* a roundabout way or expression. [Jocular formation from L. *circum,* round, **bend,** and L. abl. pl. ending *-ibus.*]

**circumcentre,** *sûr'kəm-sen-tər, n.* the centre of the circumscribed circle or sphere.

**circumcise,** *sûr'kəm-sīz, v.t.* to cut the foreskin (male) or the clitoris (female): to purify (*fig.*). —*ns.* **cir'cumciser; circumcision** (*-sizh'n*), the act of circumcising: the state of being circumcised: those who are circumcised, esp. the Jews. [L. *circumcidĕre, -cisum*—*caedĕre,* to cut.]

**circumdenudation,** *sûr-kəm-den-ū-dā'shən,* (geol.) *n.* denudation or erosion of surroundings, leaving an isolated elevation.

**circumduct,** *sûr'kəm-dukt, v.t.* to lead around or about, to cause to revolve round an imaginary axis so as to describe a cone.—*v.t.* **circumduce** (*-dūs'*), in Scots law, to declare at an end (of the term for bringing proof).—*n.* **circumduc'tion.**—*adj.* **circumduct'ory.** [L. *circum,* round, *dūcĕre, ductum,* to lead.]

**circumference,** *sər-kum'fər-əns, n.* the boundary-line, esp. of a circle: compass: distance round. —*adj.* **circumferential** (*-en'shl*).—*n.* **circum'-ferentor** (*-en-tər*), an instrument for measuring horizontal angles, consisting of a graduated circle, sights, and a magnetic needle: a graduated wheel for measuring the circumference of wheels. [L. *ferre,* to carry.]

**circumflect,** *sûr'kəm-flekt', v.t.* to bend round: to mark with a circumflex.—*ns.* **cir'cumflex,** an accent (∧) originally denoting a rising and falling of the voice on a vowel or syllable—also *adj.*; **circumflexion** (*-flek'shən*), a bending round. [L. *flectĕre, flexum,* to bend.]

**circumfluence,** *sər-kum'floo-əns, n.* a flowing round: the engulfing of food by surrounding it (as by protozoa, etc.).—*adjs.* **circum'fluent, cir-cumflu'ous.** [L. *fluĕre,* to flow.]

**circumforaneous,** *sûr-kəm-fō-rā'ni-əs, -fō-, adj.* wandering about from market to market, vagrant.—Also **circumfora'nean.** [L. *forum,* the forum, market-place.]

**circumfuse,** *sûr'kəm-fūz', v.t.* to pour around.— *p.adj.* **circumfused'.—*adj.* **circumfus'ile,** molten.

**—n. circumfusion** (*-fū'zhən*). [L. *fundĕre, fūsum,* to pour.]

**circumgyrate,** *sûr-kəm-jī'rāt, v.i.* to whirl round.— **n. circumgyrā'tion.**—*adj.* **circumgy'rātory.** [L. *gȳrāre, -ātum,* to turn.]

**circumincession, -insession,** *sûr-kəm-in-sesh'ən, n.* the reciprocity of existence in one another of the three persons of the Trinity. [L.—*incessus,* pa.p. of *incēdere,* to go, proceed.]

**circumjacent,** *sûr-kəm-jā'sənt, adj.* lying round: bordering on every side.—*n.* **circumjā'cency.** [L. *jacēns, -entis,* lying—*jacēre,* to lie.]

**circumlittoral,** *sûr-kəm-lit'ə-rəl, adj.* adjacent to the shore-line. [L. *littus,* for *lītus, -oris,* shore.]

**circumlocution,** *sûr-kəm-lō-kū'shən, n.* expressing an idea in more words than are necessary: an instance of this: evasive talk.—*v.i.* **circumlocūte',** to use circumlocution.—*n.* **circumlocū'tionist,** one who does this.—*adj.* **circumlocutory** (*-lok'ū-tər-i*). — **Circumlocution Office,** in Dickens's *Little Dorrit,* a very dilatory government department. [L. *loquī, locūtus,* to speak.]

**circummure,** *sûr-kəm-mūr'*, (*Shak.*) *v.t.* to wall around. [L. *mūrus,* a wall.]

**circumnavigate,** *sûr-kəm-nav'i-gāt, v.t.* to sail round.—*adj.* **circumnav'igable.**—*ns.* **circumnavigā'tion; circumnav'igator.**

**circumnutation,** *sûr-kəm-nū-tā'shən, n.* rotation in a nodding position, as in the growing point of a plant.—*v.i.* **circumnū'tate.**—*adj.* **circumnū'tatory.** [L. *nūtāre, -ātum,* to nod.]

**circumpolar,** *sûr-kəm-pō'lər, adj.* situated or ranging round the pole.—**circumpolar stars,** stars so near the pole of the heavens that (for places at the latitude in question) they never set but merely revolve round the pole.

**circumpose,** *sûr-kəm-pōz', v.t.* to place round.— *n.* **circumposi'tion,** the act of placing round.

**circumscissile,** *sûr-kəm-sis'il, adj.* opening by a circular rent. [L. *scissilis,* cleavable.]

**circumscribe,** *sûr-kəm-skrib', v.t.* to draw a line round: to describe a curve or figure touching externally: to enclose within certain limits, to curtail, abridge.—*adj.* **circumscrib'able,** able to be circumscribed.—*ns.* **circumscrib'er,** one who circumscribes; **circumscription** (*-skrip'shən*), limitation: the line that limits: the act of circumscribing: an inscription running round: a defined district.—*adj.* **circumscrip'tive,** marking the external form or outline. [L. *scrībĕre, scriptum,* to write.]

**circumspect,** *sûr'kəm-spekt, adj.* looking round on all sides watchfully: cautious: prudent.—*n.* **cir- cumspec'tion,** watchfulness: caution: examining.—*adj.* **circumspec'tive,** looking around: wary.—*adv.* **cir'cumspectly.**—*n.* **cir'cumspectness.** [L. *specĕre, spicĕre, spectum,* to look.]

**circumstance,** *sûr'kəm-stəns, n.* the logical sur- roundings of an action: an attendant fact: an accident or event: ceremony: detail: (in *pl.*) the state of one's affairs.—*v.t.* to place in particular circumstances.—*adj.* **circumstantial** (*-stan'- shl*), consisting of details: minute.—*n.* **circum- stantiality** (*-stan-shi-al'i-ti*), the quality of being circumstantial: minuteness in details: a detail.—*adv.* **circumstan'tially.**—*n.pl.* **circumstan'tials, incidentals:** details.—*v.t.* **circumstan'tiate** to prove by circumstances: to describe exactly.— **circumstantial evidence,** evidence which is not positive nor direct, but which is gathered in- ferentially from the circumstances in the case; **in good or bad circumstances,** prosperous or un- prosperous; **in, under, the circumstances,** con- ditions being what they are: **not a circumstance to,** (*U.S.*) nothing in comparison to. [L. *stāns, stantis,* standing—*stāre,* to stand.]

**circumvallate,** *sûr-kəm-val'āt, v.t.* to surround with a rampart.—*n.* **circumvallā'tion,** a surroun- ding with a wall or fortification sur- rounding a town or fort: engulfing of food by

surrounding it (as by protozoa) (*zool.*). [L. *vallum,* rampart.]

**circumvent,** *sûr-kəm-vent', v.t.* to go round: to encompass: to surround so as to intercept or capture: to get round, or to outwit.—*n.* **cir- cumven'tion.**—*adj.* **circumvent'ive,** deceiving by artifices. [L. *venīre, ventum,* to come.]

**circumvolve,** *sûr-kəm-volv', v.t.* to roll round.— *v.i.* to revolve.—*n.* **circumvolu'tion** (*-lōō', -lū'*), a turning or rolling round: anything winding or sinuous. [L. *volvĕre, volūtum,* to roll.]

**circus,** *sûr-kəs, n.* a circular building for the exhi- bition of games: a place, building, or tent for the exhibition of feats of horsemanship and other performances: a show of this kind or the com- pany of performers: a group of houses arranged in the form of a circle: an open place at a street junction: a natural amphitheatre: (usu. with *adj.*) a group of people giving a display, esp. in a number of places, as *tennis circus, flying circus:* a noisy entertainment or scene.—*adj.* **cir'cus(s)y.** —*n.* **cirque** (*sûrk;* Fr.), a circus: a ring (*poet.*): a deep round hollow, a natural amphitheatre (*geog.*). [L. *circus*—Gr. *kirkos.*]

**ciré,** *sē-rā, n.* (a fabric with) a highly glazed finish. [Fr. pa.p. of *cirer,* to wax.]

**cire perdue,** *sēr per-dü,* (Fr.) lit. 'lost wax', a method of casting in metal, the mould being formed round a wax model which is then melted away.

**cirl,** *sûrl, n.* a species of bunting (usu. **cirl bunting**). [It. *cirlo.*]

**cirrhopod, Cirrhopoda,** older forms of **cirripede, Cirripedia** (as if from Gr. *kirrhos,* tawny, *pous, podos,* foot); also by confusion, **cirrhipede, Cirrhi- pedia.**

**cirrhosis,** *si-rō'sis, n.* a wasting of the proper tissue of an organ, accompanied by abnormal growth of connective tissue. [Gr. *kirrhos,* tawny— from the colour of the liver so diseased.]

**cirripede,** *sir'i-pēd, n.* one of the Cirripē'dia, a degenerate class of Crustacea, the barnacles and acorn-shells.—Also **cirr'iped** (*-ped*). [L. *cirrus,* con- curl, *pēs, pedis,* foot.]

**cirrus,** *sir'əs, n.* the highest form of clouds, con- sisting of curling fibres: a tendril (*bot.*): any curled filament (*zool.*):—*pl.* **cirr'i.**—*adjs.* **cirr'ate,** **cirr'iform,** like a cirrus; **cirr'igrade,** moving by cirri.—*adjs.* **cirr'ose,** with tendrils; **cirr'ous,** having a cirrus.—*ns.* **cirr'o-cu'mulus,** a cloud of small white flakes or ripples (also *mackerel sky*); **cirr'o-strā'tus,** a high thin sheet of haze-like cloud. [L., a curl, tuft. The common spellings **cirrhus,** etc., are due to confusion with Gr. *kirrhos,* tawny.]

**Cisalpine,** *sis-alp'in, -in, adj.* on this (i.e. the Roman) side of the Alps.—So **Cisatlan'tic; Cisleithan** (*-lī't(h)ən*) on this side of the Leitha (which once in part separated Austria and Hungary): Austrian; **cismon'tane,** on this side of the mountains—opp. to *ultramontane;* **Cispa- dane** (*-pā'dān, sis'pa-dān;* L. *Padus*), on this (Roman) side of the Po; **cispon'tine,** on this side of the bridges, viz. in London, north of the Thames. [L. *cis,* on this side.]

**cisco,** *sis'kō, n.* a variety of Coregonus (*Leuc ichthys*) found in Great Lakes of North America —also *lake herring.* [Fr.-Canadian, *cisco(ette)*— Ojibwa, *pemitewiskawet,* that which has oily flesh.]

**ciselure,** *sēz'lōōr, n.* the art or operation of chasing: the chasing upon a piece of metalwork.—*n.* **cis'eleur** (*-lər*), a chaser. [Fr.]

**cissoid,** *sis'oid, n.* a plane curve consisting of two infinite branches symmetrically placed with ref- erence to the diameter of a circle, so that at one of its extremities they form a cusp, while the tangent to the circle at the other extremity is an asymptote. [Gr. *kissoeidēs,* ivy-like—*kissos,* ivy, *eidos,* form.]

*Neutral vowels in unaccented syllables: el'ə-mənt; for certain sounds in foreign words, see p. viii* cissy, sis'i, (slang) n. an effeminate person.—Also adj. [Partly from the name Cecily, partly from sister; cf. sis.]

cist, sist, n. a tomb consisting of a stone chest covered with stone slabs.—adjs. cist'ed, containing cists: cist'ic, like a cist. [See chest.]

Cistercian, sis-tûr'shən, n. a member of the order of monks established in 1098 in the forest of Cîteaux, (Cistercium), in France—an offshoot of the Benedictines.—Also adj.

cistern, sis'tərn, n. an artificial reservoir or tank for holding water or other liquid: a natural reservoir. [L. cisterna—cista, a chest.]

Cistus, sis'təs, n. the rock-rose genus of shrubby plants, giving name to the family Cistā'ceae, cultivated for the beauty of their flowers. [Gr. kistos, rock-rose.]

cistvaen. See kistvaen.

cit, sit, (arch. slang) n. a term of contempt for a townsman, not a gentleman:—fem. cit'ess (Dryden).—n.pl. cits (U.S. slang), civilian clothes. [citizen.]

citadel, sit'ə-dəl, n. a fortress in or near a city: the place where the guns are kept in a warship. [It. cittadella, dim. of città, a city; see city.]

cite, sit, v.t. to call or summon: to summon to appear in court: to quote: to name: to adduce as proof.—adj. cit'able, that can be cited.—ns. cit'al, summons to appear; citā'tion (sit, sit), official summons to appear: document containing the summons: the act of quoting: the passage or name quoted: mention in dispatches: official recognition of achievement.—adj. cit'atory, having to do with citation: addicted to citation. [L. citāre, -ātum, to call, inten. of ciēre, cire, to make go.]

cithara, sith'ə-ra, n. an ancient Greek musical instrument differing from the lyre in its flat shallow sound-chest.—n. cith'arist, a player on it.—adj. citharist'ic.—ns. cith'er, cith'ern, citt'ern, an early modern metal-stringed musical instrument, played with a plectrum: the Tirolese zither. [L.,—Gr. kitharā; cf. guitar, zither.]

citigrade, sit'i-grād, adj. moving quickly: applied to a tribe of spiders that run down their prey—Lycosidae or wolf-spiders. [L. citus, quick, gradus, a step.]

citizen, sit'i-z(ə)n, n. an inhabitant of a city: a member of a state: a townsman: a freeman: a civilian (U.S.):—fem. cit'izeness.—adj. (Shak.) like a citizen.—v.t. cit'izenise, -ize, to make a citizen of.—ns. cit'izenry, the general body of citizens; cit'izenship, state of being or of having rights and duties of a citizen: conduct in relation to these duties. [M.E. citesein—O.Fr. citeain; see city.]

cito, si', ki'tō, (L.) quickly.

citole, sit'ōl, sit-ōl', n. a mediaeval stringed instrument, prob. an earlier form of cither (see under cithara).

citron, sit'rən, n. the fruit of the citron-tree, resembling a lemon: the tree that bears it (Citrus medica), considered to be the parent of the lemon and lime-fruit.—ns. cit'range (-rənj), a hybrid between citron and orange; cit'rate, a salt of citric acid.—adjs. cit'reous, citrine; cit'ric, derived from the citron (citric acid, the acid to which lemon and lime juice owe their sourness, C₆H₈O₇).—n. cit'rin, the water-soluble vitamin P, found in citrus fruits, etc.—adj. cit'rine (-rin), dark and greenish yellow, like a citron or lemon.—n. citrine colour: a rock-crystal of this colour.—ns. citronell'a, a Ceylon grass (citronella-grass, Cymbopogon nardus) yielding citronella-oil, used in perfumery; citron tree; citron wood, citrus wood, the most costly furniture wood of the ancient Romans (perhaps sandarach); cit'rus, a citron tree: (cap.) a genus of Rutaceae including the citron, lemon, orange, etc; citrus fruits, cit-rons, lemons, limes, oranges, grapefruit.—citric acid cycle, a cycle of chemical changes in living material (e.g. muscle), in course of which citric acid is oxidised, and by which acetic acid or acetyl is converted to carbon dioxide and water, the chemicals released in the process being important to the tissue. [L. citrus, from which comes also Gr. kitron, a citron.]

cittern. Same as cither. [See under cithara.]

city, sit'i, n. a large town: an incorporated town that has or had a cathedral: a town on which the dignity has been conferred by tradition or grant: in various countries a municipality of higher rank, variously defined: the business centre or original area of a large town.—city article, in a newspaper, a financial or commercial article; city company, a London corporation representing any of the mediaeval trade guilds; city editor, the financial editor: editor in charge of local news, etc. (U.S.); city fathers, the magistrates: the town or city council; city man, a man engaged in commercial or financial work in a city; city manager, a man appointed by an elected body to manage the administrative affairs of a city; city mission, a mission for evangelising the poor classes in the large cities; cit'y-slick'er, a sophisticated city-dweller nattily dressed; city state, a sovereign state consisting of a city with a small surrounding territory.—city of God, heavenly city, etc., the ideal of the Church of Christ in glory; city of refuge, by the Jewish law a city where the perpetrator of an accidental homicide might flee for refuge; Eternal City, Rome; Holy City, Jerusalem. [Fr. cité, a city—L. civitās, -ātis, the state—civis, a citizen.]

cive, siv. See chive.

civet, siv'it, n. a perfume obtained from the civet or civet cat, a small cat-like carnivore (Viverra) of Africa, India, etc. [Fr. civette—Ar. zabād.]

civic, siv'ik, adj. pertaining to a city or citizen.—n. civ'ics, the science of citizenship.—civic centre, a place in which the chief public buildings of a town are grouped; civic crown, an oak wreath awarded to a Roman soldier for saving a citizen's life in battle. [L. civicus—civis, citizen.]

civil, siv'il, adj. pertaining to the community: polite (in any degree short of discourtesy): pertaining to ordinary life, not military: lay, secular, temporal, not ecclesiastical: pertaining to the individual citizen: relating to private relations amongst citizens, and such suits as arise out of these, as opposed to criminal (law): naturally good, as opposed to good through regeneration (theol.).—n. civil'ian, a professor or student of civil law (not canon law): one engaged in civil as distinguished from military and naval pursuits. —Also adj.—ns. civ'ilist (arch.), one versed in civil law; civil'ity, civilisation (arch.): good-breeding (obs.): politeness: polite attentions.— adv. civ'illy.—ns. civ'ism, good citizenship: state of being well-affected to French Revolution principles; civv'y (slang), civilian: (in pl. civvies) civilian clothes.—Also adj.—civil day, year, time, the day, year, time, as reckoned for ordinary purposes; civil death, the loss of all civil and legal privileges; civil defence, a civilian service for the wartime protection of the civilian population against the effects of enemy attack by air, etc.; civil disobedience, refusal to obey laws and regulations, pay taxes, etc., used as non-violent means of forcing concessions from government; civil engineer, one who plans and builds railways, docks, etc., as opposed to a military engineer, or to a mechanical engineer, who makes machines, etc.; civil law, as opposed to criminal law, the law laid down by a state regarding the rights of the inhabitants, esp. that founded on Roman law; civil list, formerly a list of charges for civil government purposes: now the expenses of the sovereign's household only;

fāte, fär; mē, hûr (her); mīne; mōte, för; mūte; mōōn, fŏŏt; dhen (then)

(civil list pensions, those granted by royal favour); civil rights (often *cap.*), rights of a citizen to personal freedom, i.e. political, racial, legal, social, etc.—Also *adj.*—civil service, the paid service of the state, in so far as it is not military or naval.—*adj.* civ'il-suit'ed (*Milton*), sombrely clad.—civil war, a war between citizens of the same state; civvy street (*coll.*), civilian life after the Services. [L. *cīvilis—cīvis*, citizen.]

civilise, -ize, siv'il-īz, *v.t.* to reclaim from barbarism: to instruct in arts and refinements.—*adj.* civilis'able.—*n.* civilisā'tion, state of being civilised: culture: cultural condition or complex.—*adj.* civ'ilised, (having) advanced beyond the primitive savage state: refined in interests and tastes: sophisticated, self-controlled and fair-spoken.—*n.* civ'iliser. [See civil.]

civvies. See civil.

cizers, an old spelling (*Shak.*) of scissors.

clabber, klab'ər, (esp. *Ir.*) *n.* mud. [Ir. *clabar*, mud.]

clachan, klä' or kla'hhən (*Scot.*) *n.* a small village. [Gael. *clachan—clach*, stone.]

clack, klak, *v.i.* to make a noise as of a flat thing flapping: to chatter: to cackle.—*n.* a noise of this kind: an instrument making it: sound of voices: the tongue (*coll.*).—*n.* clack'er.—*ns.* clack'-box, the box containing the clack-valve of an engine; clack'dish (*Shak.*), a wooden dish carried by beggars, having a movable cover which they clacked to attract attention; clack'-valve, a valve consisting of a hinged flap or other device that falls back with a clacking noise. [Prob. from the sound.]

clad, klad, *pa.t.* and *pa.p.*, also (*Spens.*) *pres.infin.*, of clothe.—*adj.* clothed, or covered.—*v.t.* to cover one material with another, e.g. one metal with another (as in nuclear reactor), or brick or stonework with a different material (in building). —*n.* cladd'ing.

cladode, klad'ōd, (*bot.*) *n.* a branch with the appearance and functions of a leaf. [Gr. *klados*, a shoot.]

claes, klāz, *n.pl.* Scots for clothes.

clag, klag, (*dial.*) *v.i.* to stick.—*v.t.* to bedaub.—*n.* a sticky mass or clot of dirt, etc.—*adj.* clagg'y, tenacious. [Prob. Scand.; Dan, *klag*, mud; cf. clay.]

claim, klām, *v.t.* to call for: to demand as a right: to maintain or assert.—*n.* a demand for something supposed due: right or ground for demanding: the thing claimed, esp. a piece of land appropriated by a miner or other: (*Spens.* clame) a call, shout.—*adj.* claim'able, that can be claimed.—*ns.* claim'ant, claim'er, one who makes a claim.—claim'-jump'er, one who takes possession of another's mining claim; claiming race, a race in which any horse having taken part in the race may be bought at a previously fixed price by anyone starting a horse at the meeting (cf. selling race); claims assessor, an assessor employed by an insurance company, usu. in motor accident claims.—lay claim to, to assert a right to. [O.Fr. *claimer*—L. *clāmāre*, to call out.]

clairaudience, klār-öd'i-əns, *n.* the alleged power of hearing things not present to the senses.—*n.* and *adj.* clairaud'ient. [Fr. *clair*—L. *clārus*, clear, and audience.]

clair-obscure, clare-obscure, klār-ob-skūr'. Same as chiaroscuro (q.v.). [Fr. *clair*—L. *clārus*, clear, and Fr. *obscur*—L. *obscūrus*, obscure.]

clairschach, klār'shähh, *n.* the old Celtic harp strung with wire. [Gael. and Ir. *clairseach*, a harp.]

clairvoyance, klār-voi'əns, *n.* the alleged power of seeing things not present to the senses.—*n.* and *adj.* clairvoy'ant. [Fr. *clair*—L. *clārus*, clear, and Fr. *voir*—L. *vidēre*, to see.]

clam, klam, *n.* a gripping instrument: a very reticent person (*coll.*): a scallop or scallop-shell (Pecten): in America an edible shellfish of various kinds, esp. the round clam or quahog (*Venus mercenaria*) and the long clam (*Mya arenaria*).—*v.i.* to gather clams (*pr.p.* clamm'-ing; *pa.t.* and *pa.p.* clammed).—*ns.* clam'bake, *n.* a baking of clams on hot stones, with layers of potatoes, fish, Indian corn, etc., popular at picnic parties in U.S.: such a party; clam-chow'der, chowder made with clams; clam'-shell.—clam up (*coll.*), to be silent. [O.E. *clam*, fetter; cf. Ger. *klamm*; Dan. *klamme*.]

clam, klam, *v.t.* to clog (*dial.*): to smear (*dial.*) (*pr.p.* clamm'ing; *pa.t.* and *pa.p.* clammed).—*n.* dampness (*dial.*).—*adv.* clamm'ily.—*n.* clamm'-iness.—*adj.* clamm'y, sticky: moist and adhesive. [O.E. *clǣman*, to anoint: cf. Du., Dan. *klam*, damp.]

clam, klam, *n.* noise produced by ringing two or more bells together.—Also *v.t.* and *v.i.* [Prob. onomatopoeic.]

clamant, klam'ənt, klām'ənt, *adj.* calling aloud or earnestly.—*n.* clam'ancy, urgency. [L. *clāmāre*, to cry out.]

clambe, klām, (*Spens.*) *pa.t.* of climb.

clamber, klam'bər, *v.i.* to climb with difficulty, grasping with hands and feet.—*n.* the act of clambering. [From the root of climb; cf. Ger. *klammern—klemmen*, to squeeze or hold tightly.]

clame (*Spens.*). Same as claim.

clamjamphrie, klam-jam'fri, (*Scot.*) *n.* rubbish: nonsense: rabble.—Also clanjamfray. [Der. uncertain.]

clamour, in U.S. clamor, klam'ər, *n.* a loud continuous outcry: uproar: any loud noise: persistent expression of dissatisfaction.—*v.i.* to cry aloud in demand: to make a loud continuous outcry.—*adj.* clam'orous, noisy, boisterous.—*adv.* clam'orously.—*ns.* clam'orousness; clam'-ourer.—clamour down, into, out of, to force an objective by clamouring. [L. *clāmor, -ōris*.]

clamour, klam'ər, (*Shak.*) *v.t.* to silence, check the ringing of. [Perh. conn. with clam (3).]

clamp, klamp, *n.* a piece of timber, iron, etc., used to fasten things together or to strengthen any framework: any instrument for holding.—*v.t.* to bind with a clamp: to grasp or press firmly: to put (on) authoritatively, impose.—clamp down on, to suppress, or suppress the activities of, firmly. [From a root seen in O.E. *clam*, fetter; Du. *klamp*, a clamp; akin to clip, climb.]

clamp, klamp, *n.* a heavy tread.—*v.i.* to tread heavily. [Prob. from the sound.]

clamp, klamp, *n.* a stack, as of bricks for burning, peats, etc.: a heap: a covered heap of potatoes. —*v.t.* to put in clamps. [Prob. Du. *klamp*, heap.]

clamper, klam'pər, (*Scot.*) *v.t.* to botch up. [Der. unknown; prob. conn. with clamp (1).]

clan, klan, *n.* a tribe or collection of families subject to a single chieftain, commonly bearing the same surname, and supposed to have a common ancestor: a clique, and sect: a collective name for a number of persons or things.—*adj.* clann'ish, closely united and holding aloof from others, like the members of a clan.—*adv.* clann'ishly.—*ns.* clann'ishness; clan'ship, association of families under a chieftain: feeling of loyalty to a clan; clans'man, clans'woman, a member of a clan. [Gael. *clann*, offspring, tribe—L. *planta*, a shoot.]

clandestine, klan-des'tin, *adj.* concealed or hidden: private: sly.—*adv.* clandes'tinely. [L. *clan-destinus—clam*, secretly.]

clang, klang, *v.i.* to produce a loud deep ringing sound.—*v.t.* to cause to clang.—*n.* a ringing sound, like that made by striking large pieces of metal, or that of a trumpet: the sonorous cry of some birds, as cranes or geese.—*n.* clang'er, a singularly ill-timed remark or comment: a stupid mistake.—*n.* and *adj.* clang'ing.—*adj.* clangorous (klang'gər-əs).—*adv.* clang'orously.—

*n.* **clang'our**, in U.S. **clangor**, a clang: loud ringing noise.—*v.i.* to make a clangour. [L. *clangĕre*, to sound; *clangor*, noise of birds or wind instruments.]

**clang.** See **klang.**

**clanjamfray.** See **clamjamphrie.**

**clank**, *klangk*, *n.* a metallic sound, less prolonged than a clang, such as is made by chains hitting together.—*v.i.* or *v.t.* to make or cause to make a clank.—*n.* **clank'ing.**—*adj.* **clank'less**, without clank. [Prob. formed under the influence of **clink** and **clang**.]

**clap**, *klap*, *n.* a sudden blow or stroke (*lit.* or *fig.*): a slap: a pat (*Scot.*): the noise made by the sudden striking together of two things, as the hands: a burst of sound, esp. thunder.—*v.t.* strike together so as to make a noise: to thrust or drive together suddenly: to fasten promptly: to pat (*Scot.*): to applaud with the hands: to bang: to put suddenly (e.g. in prison).—*v.i.* to strike the hands together: to strike or slam with noise: to applaud: to come or go suddenly (*arch.*) (*pr.p.* **clapp'ing**; *pa.t.* and *pa.p.* **clapped**). —*n.* **clapp'er**, one who claps: that which claps, as the tongue of a bell: a contrivance for shaking a mill hopper: an instrument for making a noise, as a rattle, or (in *pl.*) bones for keeping musical time: the tongue (*slang*).—*v.i.* to make a noise like a clapper.—*v.t.* to ring by pulling on a clapper.—*n.* and *adj.* **clapp'ering.**—*n.* **clapp'ing**, noise of striking: applause.—*ns.* **clap'board** (or *klab'ard*), wood for barrel staves, wainscot (*arch.*): a thin board used in covering wooden houses (*U.S.*); **clap'bread**, a kind of hard-baked oatmeal cake; **clap'dish** (same as **clackdish**); **clap'net**, a net made to clap together suddenly by pulling a string; **clapp'erboards**, hinged boards clapped together in front of camera before or after shooting a piece of film to help to synchronise sound and vision; **clapp'erboy**, the person who works the clapperboards.—*v.t.* **clapp'erclaw** (*arch.*), to claw or scratch: to scold. —*n.* **clapp'erclawer.**—**clap'-sill**, a lock-sill, the bottom part of the frame on which lock-gates shut; **clap'trap**, a trick to gain applause (*arch.*): flashy display: empty words.—also *adj.*—*n.* **claptrapp'ery.**—**clap eyes on**, to catch sight of; **clap hands** (*Shak.*), to make an agreement; **clap hold of**, to seize roughly: **clap up** (*Shak.*), to conclude suddenly; **like the clappers** (*coll.*), at top speed. [O.N. *klappa*, to pat; Du. and Ger. *klappen*.]

**clap**, *klap*, *n.* gonorrhoea.—*v.t.* to infect with gonorrhoea. [Cf. Du. *klapoor*.]

**clapper**, *klap'ər*, *n.* (esp. in Devon) a rude bridge of slabs or planks laid across supports (*dial.*): a raised footpath (*dial.*): a rabbit-hole (*obs.*). [L.L. *claperium*, heap of stones, rabbit-hole.]

**claque**, *klak*, *n.* an opera hat: an institution for securing the success of a performance, by preconcerted applause: a body of hired applauders: supporters who are after their own ends.—*n.* **claqueur** (*kla-kûr'*), a member of a claque. [Fr., —*claquer*, to clap.]

**clarabella**, *klar-ə-bel'a*, *n.* an organ-stop of a sweet, fluty tone. [L. *clārus*, clear, *bellus*, beautiful.]

**Clare**, *klär*, *n.* a nun of a Franciscan order founded by St *Clare* (1212).—Also **Poor Clare.**

**clarence**, *klar'əns*, *n.* a four-wheeled carriage, seated inside for two or more persons. [Named after the Duke of *Clarence* (William IV).]

**Clarenceux**, **Clarencieux**, *klar'ən-sū*, (*her.*) *n.* the second king-of-arms in England, so named from the Duke of *Clarence*, son of Edward III.

**clarendon**, *klar'ən-dən*, (*print.*) *n.* a form of type having a heavy face.

**clare-obscure.** See **clair-obscure.**

**claret**, *klar'ət*, *n.* originally applied to wines of a light-red colour, but now used in England for the dark-red wines of Bordeaux: blood (*slang*).—*v.i.* to drink claret.—*ns.* **clar'et-cup**, a drink made up of iced claret, brandy, sugar, etc.; **clar'et-jug**, a fancy jug for holding claret. [Fr. *clairet*—*clair*—L. *clārus*, clear.]

**clarichord**, *klar'i-körd*, *n.* a clavichord. [As if from L. *clārus*, clear; see **clavichord**.]

**clarify**, *klar'i-fī*, *v.t.* to make clear or pure.—*v.i.* to become clear (*pr.p.* **clar'ifying**; *pa.t.* and *pa.p.* **clar'ified**).—*ns.* **clarificā'tion**; **clar'ifier**. [L. *clārus*, clear, and *facĕre*, to make.]

**clarinet**, (*arch.*) **clarionet**, *klar-in-et'*, *klar'*, *n.* wind instrument, usually of wood, in which the sound is produced by a single thin reed, the compass being approximately that of the violin.—*n.* **clarinett'ist**—**the bass clarinet** is pitched an octave lower than the ordinary clarinet. [Fr.,—L. *clārus*, clear.]

**clarion**, *klar'i-ən*, *n.* a kind of trumpet whose note is clear and shrill: the sound of a trumpet, or a sound resembling that of a trumpet. [Fr. *clairon*—*clair*—L. *clārus*, clear.]

**clarionet.** See **clarinet.**

**clarity**, *klar'i-ti*, *n.* clearness. [M.E. *clarte*—L. *clāritās*, -*ātis*.]

**Clarkia**, *klärk'i-a*, *n.* a North American genus of the evening-primrose family, a favourite border plant. [Named in honour of Captain *Clark*, of Lewis and Clark's expedition.]

**clarsach.** Same as **clairschach.**

**clarty**, *klär'ti*, (*Scot.*) *adj.* sticky and dirty. [Der. unknown.]

**clary**, *klā'ri*, *n.* a plant of the sage genus (*Salvia Sclarea*) with pale-blue flowers and large coloured bracts: extended to others of the genus. [L.L. *sclarea*; origin unknown.]

**clash**, *klash*, *n.* a loud noise, such as is caused by the striking together of sheets of metal: opposition: contradiction: chatter, country talk (*Scot.*).—*v.i.* to dash noisily together: to meet in opposition: to act in a contrary direction: to disagree: of events, to coincide disturbingly: to gossip (*Scot.*).—*v.t.* to strike noisily against: to bang, slam (*dial.*).—*n.* **clash'ing**, a striking against: opposition, conflict, disagreement. [Imit; cf., Ger. and Sw. *klatsch*.]

**clasp**, *kläsp*, *n.* a fastening: a supplementary decoration in the form of a bar on the ribbon of a medal: an embrace: a grasp.—*v.t.* to fasten with a clasp: to enclose and hold in the hand or arms: to embrace.—*ns.* **clas'per**, that which clasps: the tendril of a plant: a clasping organ (*zool.*); **clasp'ing.**—**clasp'-knife**, a knife whose blade folds into the handle. [M.E. *clapse*.]

**class**, *kläs*, *n.* a rank or order of persons or things: high rank or social standing: a number of students or scholars who are taught together, or are in the same year of their course: a scientific division or arrangement in biological classification, a division above an order: a grade, as of merit in examination, accommodation in a ship or railway train: a section of a Methodist congregation.—*v.t.* to form into a class or classes: to arrange methodically.—*v.i.* to take rank.—*adj.* (*slang*) of high class.—*adjs.* **class'-able**, **class'ible**, capable of being classed; **classed.** —*n.* **classic** (*klas'ik*), any great writer, composer, or work, esp. in Greek and Latin literature: a student of the ancient classics: a standard work: (in *pl.*) Greek and Latin studies.—*adjs.* **classic**, **-al**, of the highest class or rank, esp. in literature and music: originally and chiefly used of the best Greek and Roman writers: (as opposed to *romantic*) like in style to the authors of Greece and Rome or the old masters in music: chaste, refined, restrained, in keeping with classical art: having literary or historical associations: traditionally accepted, long established: excellent, standard (*slang*): Presbyterian, of a classis (*Milt.*): of clothes, made in simple tailored style that does not soon go out of fashion.—Also *n*.— *n.* **classical'ity.**—*adv.* **class'ically.**—*ns.* **classical-ness**; **class'icism** (*-sizm*), a classical idiom: in literature, music, etc., a principle, character, or tendency such as is seen in Greek classical literature, marked by beauty of form, good taste, restraint, and clarity—opposed to *romanticism*; **class'icist**, one versed in the classics, or devoted to their being used in education: one who is for classicism rather than romanticism.— *adjs.* **class'less**, having no class distinctions: not belonging obviously to any social class; **class'y** (*slang*), of or characteristic of high or upper class. —**class'-book**, a book used in class teaching.— *adj.* **class'-con'scious**, clearly or acutely conscious of membership of a social class.—**class'-fellow**, **class'mate**, a pupil in the same class at school or college; **classic races**, the five chief annual horse-races—the Two Thousand Guineas, One Thousand, Derby, Oaks, and St Leger; **class'-lead'er**, the leader of a class in a Methodist church; **class legislation**, legislation in the interests of a class; **class'man**, one who has gained honours of a certain class at the Oxford examinations—opp. to *passman*; **class'room**, a room in which a class is held; **class'-war'**, hostility or hostilities between different social ranks or classes, esp. between the proletariat and the combined middle and upper classes.—**take a class**, to take honours in an examination, as opposed to the mere pass. [L. *classis*, a division of the Roman people.]

**classes aisées**, *klas e-zā*, (Fr.) the well-off classes.
**classify**, *klas'i-fī*, *v.t.* to arrange in classes: to make secret for security reasons:—*pr.p.* **class'ifying**; *pa.p.* **class'ified**.—*adjs.* **classifi'able**, capable of being classified; **classif'ic**, denoting classes.— *n.* **classifica'tion**, act or system of arranging in classes.—*adjs.* **class'ified**, arranged in classes: of a road, in a class entitled to receive a government grant; **classifica'tory**.—*n.* **class'ifier**.—**classified advertisements**, advertisements in a newspaper or periodical grouped according to the goods or services offered. [L. *classis*, and *facēre*, to make.]
**classis**, *klas'is*, *n.* a group: a presbytery (*obs.*): a bay of a library (*obs.*). [L.]
**clastic**, *klas'tik*, *adj.* composed of fragments, fragmental. [Gr. *klastos—klaein*, to break.]
**clat.** See **claut.**
**clatch**, *klach*, *kläch*, (*Scot.*) *n.* a splashy slapping sound: a slap: anything sloppy and pasty: anything lumbering or clumsy, as an old gig: an ungainly person: a slut: a botched piece of work.— *v.i.* to dabble or work in miry matter.—*v.t.* to daub, plaster: to work up into a pasty mess: to botch. [Cf. Ger. *klatsch*, slap.]
**clathrate**, *klath'rit*, *-rāt*, *adj.* lattice-shaped (*biol.*): of a molecular compound, having one component enclosed in the cavities of the crystals of another component (*chem.*). [L. *clāthrāre*, to furnish with a lattice.]
**clatter**, *klat'ər*, *n.* a repeated rattling noise: a repetition of abrupt, sharp sounds: noisy talk: gossip (*Scot.*, often in *pl.*).—*v.i.* to make rattling sounds: to chatter.—*v.t.* to cause to rattle.—*n.* **clatt'erer**.—*adv.* **clatt'eringly**. [O.E. *clatrung*, clattering (verbal noun).]
**Claude Lorraine glass**, *klōd lor-ān' gläs*, a convex mirror, usu. coloured, employed for viewing landscape. [Named after the painter *Claude Gelée*, known as *le Lorrain* (1600-82).]
**Claudian**, *klö'di-ən*, *adj.* pertaining to the Romans of the name of *Claudius*, esp. the emperors of that gens (Tiberius, Caligula, Claudius, Nero), or to their period (A.D. 14-68).
**claudication**, *klö-di-kā'shən*, *n.* a limp. [L. *claudicātio*, *-ōnis—claudus*, lame.]
**claught**, **claucht**, *klöhht*, (*Scot.*) *v.t.* and *v.i.* to snatch: to clutch.—*n.* a hold: a snatch: a clutch. [From the pa.t. of **cleek**.]

**clause**, *klöz*, *n.* a sentence: part of a sentence with subject and predicate: an article or part of a contract, will, act of parliament, etc.—*adj.* **claus'ular**, pertaining to, or consisting of, a clause or clauses.—**dependent clause**, a part of a sentence which cannot stand in isolation as a sentence in itself—opp. to independent clause. [Fr. *clause*—L. *claudĕre*, to shut.]
**claustral**, *klös'trəl*, *adj.* cloistral, secluded: pertaining to a claustrum.—*ns.* **claustrā'tion**, the act of shutting in a cloister; **claus'trum**, a thin layer of grey matter in the brain hemispheres:—*pl.* **claus'tra**; **claustrophō'bia** (Gr. *phobos*, fear), a morbid dread of confined places.—*adj.* **claustrophobic** (*-fob'ik*). [L. *claustrum*, an enclosed place.]
**ciausula**, *klö'zhə-lə*, *klow'soo-la*, *n.* a short clause ending a period in Latin prose:—*pl.* **clau'sulae**. [L.]
**claut**, *klöt*, *clat*, *klat*, *klät*, (*Scot.*) *n.* a claw: a scratch: a blow: a grasp: a scraping hoe: something scraped together, a lump.—*v.t.* to scratch, claw: to scrape: to hoe. [Perh. conn. with **claw**.]
**clavate**, **-d**, *klā'vāt*, *klav'āt*, *-id*, *adj.* (*biol.*) club-shaped.—*n.* **clavā'tion**, articulation in a socket.— *adjs.* **clav'ūlate**, somewhat club-shaped; **clav'iform**, in the form of a club.—*n.* **clav'iger** (*-i-jər*), a club-bearer.—*adj.* **clavig'erous** (*-ij'ər-əs*), club-bearing (see also under **clavis**). [L. *clāva*, a club.]
**clave**, *klāv*, *pa.t.* of **cleave** (both verbs).
**clave**, *klā'vā*, *n.* one of a pair of small wooden cylinders held in the hands and struck together to mark S. American dance rhythm. [Sp., key to code, etc., clef—L. *clāvis*, key.]
**clavecin**, *klav'ə-sin*, *n.* a harpsichord.—*n.* **clav'e-cinist**. [Fr. *clavecin*—L. *clāvis*, a key.]
**claver**, *klā'vər*, (*Scot.*) *n.* idle talk, gossip.—*v.i.* to talk idly. [Der. uncertain.]
**clavicembalo**, *klav-i-chem'ba-lō*, *n.* a cembalo with keys—a harpsichord. [It.,—L. *clāvis*, key, and **cembalo**.]
**clavichord**, *klav'i-kord*, *-körd*, *n.* an old keyboard stringed instrument in which the tangent which struck the string and produced the sound also determined the vibrating length. [L. *clāvis*, a key, *chorda*, a string.]
**clavicle**, *klav'i-kl*, *n.* collar-bone: merry-thought of birds.—Also **clav'ūla**.—*adj.* **clavic'ūlar**. [Fr. *clavicule*—L. *clāvicula*, dim. of *clāvis*, a key.]
**clavicorn**, *klav'i-korn*, *-körn*, *adj.* having clavate antennae.—*n.* a member of the **Clavicorn'ia**, a group of beetles. [L. *clāva*, a club, *cornū*, a horn.]
**clavicytherium**, *klav-i-si-thēr'i-əm*, *n.* an upright form of spinet. [L. *clāvis*, key, *cytherium—cithara*.]
**clavie**, *klā'vi*, (*Scot.*) *n.* tar barrel burnt for luck at Burghead on Hogmanay (O.S.). [Unknown.]
**clavier**, *klä-vēr'*, *n.* keyboard of a musical instrument: stringed keyboard instrument, esp. clavichord or the pianoforte. [Fr.,—L. *clāvis*, a key.]
**clavis**, *klā'vis* (L. *klä'wis*), *n.* a key, hence a clue or aid for solving problems, interpreting a cipher, etc.:—*pl.* **clā'ves** (*-vēz*; L. *klä'wās*).—*n.* **claviger** (*klav'i-jər*), one who keeps a key, a custodian.— *adj.* **clavig'erous**, keeping keys (see also under **clavate**). [L. *clāvis*, a key.]
**claw**, *klö*, *n.* the hooked nail of a beast or bird: the leg of a crab, insect, etc., or its pointed end or pincer: an instrument shaped like a claw: the narrow basal part of a petal (*bot.*): anything like a claw.—*v.t.* to scratch: to tear: to scrape: to seize: to flatter, fawn on (*fig.*).—*adjs.* **clawed**, having claws; **claw'less**.—**claw'back**, a toady, flatterer; **claw'-hammer**, a hammer with one part of the head divided into two claws, for drawing nails; **claw'-hamm'er-coat**, a facetious name for a dress-coat.—**claw me and I'll claw thee**, favour me and I shall do you good in return. [O.E.

clawu; cog. with Ger. *klaue*; akin to **cleave**, to stick.]

**clay**, *klā, n.* earth in very fine particles, tenacious and impervious (*agri.*): a tenacious ductile earthy material, hydrated aluminium silicates more or less impure (*chem.* and *min.*): earth in general: the human body: (in full **clay-pipe**) a tobacco-pipe of baked clay.—*v.t.* to purify with clay, as sugar.—*adjs.* **clayed**, clay-like; **clay'ey**, made of clay: covered with clay: like clay; **clay'ish**, of the nature of clay.—*adjs.* **clay'-bank** (*U.S.*), brownish yellow; **clay'-brained** (*Shak.*), stupid; **clay'-cold**, cold as clay, lifeless.—**clay'-eat'er**, one addicted to chewing a fatty clay—in Brazil and elsewhere; **clay'-ground**, ground consisting mainly of clay; **clay'-ir'onstone**, a clayey chalybite; **clay'-marl**, a whitish chalky clay; **clay'-mill**, a mill for preparing clay; **clay'-pigeon**, a clay (or usu. other material) disk (or other shape) thrown from a trap and shot at as substitute for a pigeon; **clay'-slate**, hard, fissile argillaceous rock; **clay'-pit**, a pit from which clay is dug.—**feet of clay** (*fig.*), faults and weaknesses of character not at first suspected; **wet one's clay**, to drink. [O.E. *clæg*; cf. Dan. *klæg*, Ger. *klei.*]

**claymore**, *klā-mōr', -mŏr', n.* a large sword formerly used by the Scottish Highlanders: the old Celtic one-handed, two-edged longsword: now applied inaccurately to the basket-hilted sword of the officers of Highland regiments. [Gael. *claidheamhmór*—Gael. and Ir. *claidheamh*, sword, *mór*, great.]

**clean**, *klēn, adj.* clear (*Spens.*): clear-cut: sharply defined: even: neat: free from dirt, stain, or whatever defiles: pure: guiltless: complete: without a catch (*angling*): free of radioactive fall-out: of a design that causes little turbulent wake (*aerodynamics*). — *n.* **clean'ness**. — *adv.* quite: entirely: smoothly: without mishap.—*v.t.* to make clean, or free from dirt.—*n.* **clean'er**, one who or that which cleans.—*n.* and *adj.* **clean'ing**, (the act of) making clean.—*n.* **cleanliness** (*klen'li-nis*), habitual cleanness or purity.—*adj.* **cleanly** (*klen'li*), clean in habits and person: pure: neat.—*adv.* (*klēn'li*) in a clean manner.—*n.* **cleanness** (*klēn'nis*).—**clean hands**, freedom from guilt or corruption.—*adjs.* **clean'-limbed**, with shapely limbs: trim; **clean'-shav'en**, with all facial hair shaved off.—**clean slate**, a fresh start.—*adj.* **clean'-tim'bered** (*Shak.*), well-proportioned.—**clean'-up**, an act of thorough cleaning: the stamping out of an evil.—**clean as a whistle**, completely emptied; **clean out**, to clean the inside of: to take everything, esp. all one's money, away from (one); **clean up**, to make clean: to free from vice, corruption, etc.: to make (large profits); **come clean** (*slang*), to confess, to divulge, everything; **show a clean pair of heels**, to escape by running. [O.E. *clæne*; Ger. *klein*, small.]

**cleanse**, *klenz, v.t.* to make clean or pure.—*adj.* **cleans'able**.—*ns.* **cleans'er**, one who, or that which, cleanses; **cleans'ing**, purification. [O.E. *clænsian.*]

**clear**, *klēr, adj.* pure, bright, undimmed, unclouded, undulled: free from obstruction, difficulty, complication, contents, blame, or accusation: disengaged: plain: distinct: obvious: without blemish, defect, drawback, or diminution: perspicuous: transparent: not coded. —*adv.* in a clear manner: plainly: wholly: quite.—*v.t.* to make clear: to empty: to free from obscurity, obstruction, or guilt: to free, acquit, or vindicate: to leap, or pass by or over: to make as profit: to settle, as a bill: to move on, as wounded from a temporary field hospital (casualty **clear'ing-sta'tion**): to set free for sailing: to decode: to unscramble: to declare free from security, etc., restrictions.—*v.i.* to become

clear: grow free, bright, transparent: sail after satisfying all demands and obtaining permission. —*ns.* **clear'age**, piece of land cleared; **clear'ance**, act of clearing: general removal or emptying: eviction from lands: removal of hindrances: intervening space: play between parts, as of a machine: certificate that a ship has been cleared at the custom-house: declaration of freedom from restrictions; **clear'er**; **clear'ing**, act of making clear: tract of land cleared of wood, etc., for cultivation: method by which bankers change cheques and drafts, and arrange the differences.—*adv.* **clear'ly**, in a clear manner: distinctly.—*n.* **clear'ness**.—*aajs.* **clear'-cut**, sharp in outline: free from obscurity; **clear'-eyed**, clear-sighted, discerning: **clear'-head'ed**, having a clear understanding.—**clear'ing-house**, an office where clearing business is done (**railway clear'ing-house**, an office for adjusting claims of different railways for shares of freights and through tickets); **clear'ing-nut**, the seed of *Strychnos potatorum*, used in the East Indies for clearing muddy water; **clear'-obscure'** (see chiaroscuro).—*adj.* **clear'-sight'ed**, having clearness of sight: discerning.—**clear'-sight'edness**; **clear'-skin** (*Australian*), an unbranded animal; **clear'-starch'er**, a laundress; **clear'-starch'ing**, the act of stiffening linen with clear starch; **clear'-story** (see clerestory); **clear'way**, a stretch of road on which motorists are not allowed to stop; **clear'wing**, a transparent-winged moth.—**clear off**, to get rid of, dispose of: to go away, esp. in order to avoid something (*coll.*); **clear out**, to get rid of: to empty: of a ship, to clear and leave port: to take oneself off; **clear the air**, simplify the situation and relieve tension; **clear the way**, to make the way open; **clear up**, to make or to become clear; **in the clear**, free of suspicion: out of a difficulty: solvent. [Fr. *clair*—L. *clārus*, clear.]

**clearcole**, *klēr'kōl, n.* a priming coat consisting of size or glue with whiting.—Also **clere'cole**, **claircolle** (*klār'*). [Fr. *claire colle*, clear glue.]

**cleat**, *klēt, n.* a wedge: a piece of wood, etc., nailed across anything to keep it in its place or give it an additional strength: a piece attached to parts of a ship for fastening ropes.—*v.t.* to strengthen with a cleat: to fasten to or by a cleat. [From a supposed O.E. *clēat*; cf. Du. *kloot;* Dan. *klode;* Ger. *kloss.*]

**cleave**, *klēv, v.t.* to divide, to split: to separate with violence: to go through: to pierce.—*v.i.* to part asunder: to crack:—*pr.p.* **cleav'ing;** *pa.t.* **clōve**, or **cleft**, *arch.* **clāve;** *pa.p.* **clōv'en** or **cleft**.—*adj.* **cleav'able**, capable of being cleft.— *ns.* **cleav'ableness;** **cleav'age**, a split: a tendency to split, esp. (in rocks and minerals) in certain directions: mitotic cell-division: the hollow between a woman's breasts, esp. as shown by a low-cut dress (*coll.*); **cleav'er**, one who or that which cleaves: a butcher's chopper.—*adj.* **cleav'ing**, splitting.—*n.* a cleft. [O.E. *clēofan*, cog. with Ger. *klieben.*]

**cleave**, *klēv, v.i.* to stick or adhere: to unite:— *pa.t.* **cleaved** or **clave;** *pa.p.* **cleaved.**—*ns.* **cleav'ers**, **clivers** (*kliv'arz*), goose-grass (*Galium Aparine*) which cleaves to fur or clothes by its hooks; **cleav'ing**, the act of adhering.—Also *adj.* [O.E. *clifian;* cog. with Ger. *kleben.*]

**cleché**, *klech'ā, klesh'ā,* (*her.*) *adj.* voided or hollowed throughout, showing only a narrow border. [Fr.]

**cleck**, *klek,* (*Scot.*) *v.t.* to hatch.—*n.* **cleck'ing**, a brood. [O.N. *klekia;* cf. Dan. *klække*, to hatch.]

**cleek**, *klēk, n.* a large hook (*Scot.*): a narrow-faced iron-headed golf-club.—*v.t.* to seize, to hook.—*v.i.* (*Scot.*) to go arm in arm: to link: to marry:—*pa.t.* and *pa.p.* **cleeked**, **cleek'it**, **claught**, pron. *klöhht.* [Northern, perh. related to clutch.]

cleep. See clepe.

clef, *klef, n.* a character placed on the stave by which the absolute pitch of the notes is fixed. [Fr. *clef,* key—L. *clāvis;* Gr. *kleis,* a key.]

cleft, *kleft, pa.t.* and *pa.p.* of cleave (1).—cleft palate. See palate.

cleft, *kleft, n.* an opening made by cleaving or splitting: a crack, fissure, or chink.—Also clift *(B.).* [Cf. Ger. *kluft,* Dan. *klyft,* a hole.]

cleg, *kleg, n.* gadfly, horse-fly. [O.N. *kleggi.*]

cleistogamy, clistogamy, *klis-tog'ə-mi,* (*bot.*) *n.* production of small flowers, often simplified and inconspicuous, which do not open, and in which self-pollination occurs.—*adjs.* cleistogamic (*-tə-gam'ik*), cleistog'amous. [Gr. *kleistos,* closed, *gamos,* marriage.]

cleithral, clithral, *kli'thrəl, adj.* completely roofed over. [Gr. *kleithron,* a bar.]

clem, *klem, v.i.* and *v.t.* to starve. [Dial. Eng. *clam;* Ger. *klemmen,* to pinch.]

Clematis, *klem'ə-tis, n.* a genus of Ranunculaceae, including *Virgin's Bower* or *Traveller's Joy.* [L., —Gr. *klēmatis,* a plant, prob. periwinkle—*klēma,* a twig.]

clement, *klem'ənt, adj.* mild: gentle: kind: merciful.—*ns.* clem'ence (*Spens.*), clem'ency, the quality of being clement: mildness: readiness to forgive.—*adv.* clem'ently. [Fr.,—L. *clēmēns, -entis.*]

clementine, *klem'ən-tēn, n.* a type of orange. Clementine, *klem'ən-tēn, -tin, adj.* relating to any of the popes named *Clement,* esp. Clement I or Clement V.—*n.* a follower of a leader called Clement.

clench, *klench, klensh, v.t.* to close tightly: to grasp: to clinch. [Same as clinch.]

clepe, cleep, *klēp,* (*arch.*) *v.t.* to call: to name:— *pa.p.* yclept (*i-klept'*). [O.E. *clipian,* to call.]

clepsydra, *klep'si-drə, n.* an instrument for measuring time by the trickling of water, a water-clock. [L.,—Gr. *klepsydrā—kleptein,* to steal, *hydōr,* water.]

clerestory, clear-story, *clēr'stō-ri, -stö-, n.* an upper storey or part with its own row of windows—esp. the storey above the triforium in a church. [clear, prob. in sense of lighted, and storey.]

clergy, *klûr'ji, n.* the ministers of the Christian or other religion, as holders of an allotted office, in contradistinction to the laity: learning, education (*arch.*).—*adjs.* cler'gyable, cler'giable, entitled to or admitting of the benefit of clergy: cleric, -al (*kler'ik, -əl*), belonging to the clergy: pertaining to a clerk or scribe.—*ns.* cler'ic, a clergyman; cler'icalism, undue influence of the clergy: sacerdotalism.—*n.pl.* cler'icals, clerical garb.—*ns.* cler'icate, clerical position: clericity (*klər-is'i-ti*), state of being a clergyman; clerisy (*kler'i-si*), the class of learned men, scholars.— black clergy, in Russia, all the regular or monastic, as distinct from the secular or parochial, clergy; cler'gyman, one of the clergy, a regularly ordained minister; cler'gy-woman, a woman who is a minister of religion: a woman belonging to a clergyman's family (*facet.*).—benefit of clergy, originally an exemption of clergymen, in certain cases, from criminal process before a secular judge, but later covering the first offence of all who could read; clergyman's sore throat, chronic pharyngitis. [Fr. *clergé*—L. *clēricus*— Gr. *klērikos,* from *klēros,* a lot, a heritage, then the clergy.]

clerihew, *kler'i-hū, n.* a jingle in two short couplets purporting to quintessentialise the life and character of some notable person. [Started by E. *Clerihew* (Bentley) in his *Biography for Beginners* (1905).]

clerk, *klärk* (*U.S. klûrk*), *n.* a clergyman or priest: a scholar: one who leads the responses in the English Church service: in common use, one employed as a writer, assistant, copyist, accountkeeper, or correspondent in an office: a shopassistant (*U.S.*).—*v.i.* to act as clerk.—*adj.* cler'ical (see under clergy).—*ns.* clerk'dom; clerk'ess, a female clerk.—*adjs.* clerk'ish, like a clerk; clerk'less, ignorant; clerk'-like, scholarly.—*n.* clerk'ling, a young clerk.—*adj.* clerk'ly, scholarly.—*adv.* in a scholar-like or learned manner.—*n.* clerk'ship.—Bible clerk, a scholar who reads the lessons in some college chapels.— clerk of the weather, an imaginary functionary facetiously supposed to direct the weather; clerk of works, one who superintends the erection of a building, etc.; Lord Clerk Register (see register); St Nicholas's clerks (*arch.*), thieves. [O.E. *clerc,* a priest—L.L. *clēricus;* see clergy.]

cleromancy, *kler'o-man-si, n.* divination by lot. [Gr. *klēros,* lot, *manteiā,* divination.]

cleruch, *kler'ōōk, -uk,* (*Greek hist.*) *n.* an allotmentholder in foreign territory retaining his Athenian citizenship.—*n.* cler'uchy, cleruch'ia. [Gr. *klērouchos—klēros,* allotment, *echein,* to have.]

cleuch, cleugh, *klōōhh,* Scottish form of clough.

cleve, *klēv, n.* cliff: hillside. [Now rare. M.E. *cleof,* a variant of cliff.]

cleveite, *klē'vīt, klā'və-it, n.* a pitchblende in octahedral crystals containing helium. [P.T. *Cleve,* Swedish chemist.]

clever, *klev'ər, adj.* able or dexterous: ingenious: skilful: good-natured (*U.S.*).—*ns.* cleveral'ity (*Scot.*); clev'erness.—*adj.* clev'erish, somewhat clever.—*adv.* clev'erly. [Ety. dub.]

clevis, *klev'is, n.* a U-shaped piece of metal through which tackle may pass, fixed at the end of a beam. [Ety. dub.]

clew, clue, *klōō, n.* a ball of thread, or the thread in it: a thread that guides through a labyrinth: anything that points to the solution of a mystery (usu. clue): the corner of a sail.—*v.t.* to coil up into a clew or ball: to tie up to the yards (usu. with *up*): to fix up (*fig.*).—*adj.* clue'less, without trace: trackless: ignorant: stupid.—clew'-garnet (*naut.*), a tackle for clewing up the smaller square sails for furling.—*n.pl.* clew'-lines, ropes on the smaller square sails by which they are clewed up for furling.—not to have a clue, to have no information: to have no idea, no notion, at all. [O.E. *cliwen;* cf. Du. *kluwen;* Ger. *knäuel.*]

cliché, *klē-shā, n.* the impression made by a die in any soft metal: an electrotype or stereotype plate: stereotyped phrase, or literary tag: something hackneyed as idea, plot, situation.— *adj.* cli'ché-ridden, filled with clichés. [Fr.]

click, *klik, n.* a short, sharp ticking sound: anything that makes such a sound, as a small piece of iron falling into a notched wheel: a clucking sound produced by sudden retraction of the tongue from the upper teeth, palate, or elsewhere, characteristic of certain South African native languages, represented by C (dental), Q (palatal), and X (lateral): a latch for a gate.— *v.i.* to make a light, sharp sound: to fit into place opportunely or successfully, esp. to succeed in coming into relations of sociability with a person of the other sex (*slang*).—*ns.* click'er, the compositor who distributes the copy among a companionship of printers, makes up pages, etc.: one who cuts up leather for the uppers and soles of boots; click'ing, the action of the verb.— click'-bee'tle, any beetle of the family Elateridae, characterised by leaping in the air with a click when laid on their backs; click'-clack, a persistent clicking noise. [Dim. of clack.]

cricket, *klik'ət, n.* a latch.—*v.i.* to make a clicking sound. [O.Fr. (and Fr.) *cliquet.*]

client, *kli'ənt, n.* a vassal, dependant, or hangeron: one who employs a lawyer or other professional adviser: a customer.—*n.* cli'entage, the client's whole number of one's clients: the client's

relation to the patron.—*adj.* **cliental** (-*ent'l*).—
*ns.* **clientèle** (*klē-ā-tel*), **clientele** (*klī'ən-tēl*), a
following: the whole connection of a lawyer,
shopkeeper, etc.; **cli'entship**. [L. *cliēns*, -*entis*,
a dependant upon a *patrōnus*.]

**cliff**, *klif*, *n.* a high steep rock: the steep side of a
mountain.—*adjs.* **cliffed**, **cliff'y**, having cliffs:
craggy.—**cliff'hanger**, a tense, exciting adventure
or contest: an ending line that leaves one in
suspense.—*v.i.* **cliff'hang**.—*n.*, *adj.* **cliff'hanging**.
[O.E. *clif*; Du. *clif*; O.N. *klif*.]

**cliff**, *klif*, (*mus.*) *n.* Same as **clef**.

**clift.** See **cleft** (2).

**clift**, *klift*, *n.* same as **cliff** (through the influence
of **cleft**).—*adjs.* **clift'ed**, **clift'y**, broken into
cliffs.

**climacteric**, *klī-mak-ter'ik*, or *klī-mak'tər-ik*, *n.* a
critical period in human life, in which some great
bodily change takes place: a critical time.—*adj.*
pertaining to such a period: critical.—*adj.*
**climacter'ical**.—the grand climacteric, (generally)
the sixty-third year, supposed to be a critical
period for men. [Gr. *klimaktēr*—*klimax*, a
ladder.]

**climate**, *klī'māt*, -*mit*, *n.* the condition of a country
or place with regard to temperature, moisture,
etc.: character of something (*fig.*): region
(*Shak.*).—*v.i.* (*Shak.*) to remain in a certain
place.—*adjs.* **cli'matal**, **climatic** (-*mat'ik*), -**al**.—
*v.t.* **cli'matise**, -**ize** (see **acclimatise**).—*n.* **cli'-
mature** (*Shak.*), region.—*adj.* **climatograph'ical**.
—*n.* **climatog'raphy**, a description of climates.—
*adj.* **climatolog'ical**.—*ns.* **climatol'ogist**; **climatol'ogy**, the science of climates, or an investigation of the causes on which the climate of a place
depends.—**climate of opinion**, the critical atmosphere, complex of opinions prevalent at a particular time or in a particular place. [Fr. *climat*—
L. *clima*—Gr. *klima*, -*atos*, slope—*klinein*, to
slope.]

**climax**, *klī'maks*, *n.* the arranging of discourse in
order of increasing strength (*rhet.*): loosely, the
last term of the rhetorical arrangement: hence, a
culmination: the relatively stable culmination
of a series of plant and animal communities
developing in an area.—*v.i.* to ascend in a climax:
to culminate.—*adjs.* (wrongly formed) **climact'ic**,
-**al**, pertaining to a climax.—*adv.* **climact'ically**.
[Gr. *klimax*, -*akos*, a ladder—from *klīnein*, to
slope.]

**climb**, *klīm*, *v.i.* or *v.t.* to ascend or mount by
clutching with the hands and feet: to ascend
with difficulty: to mount: of plants, to ascend
by clinging to other objects, by means of hooks,
tendrils, twining stems, or otherwise: extended
to similar downward movement (to *climb down*—
also (*fig.*) to abandon an excessive or overweening
demand, position, or attitude):—*pa.t.* and *pa.p.*
**climbed**, (*arch.*) **clomb** (*klōm*).—*n.* an act of
climbing: an ascent.—*adjs.* **climb'able**.—*n.*
**climb'er**, one who or that which climbs: one
who is intent upon his own social advancement:
an old-fashioned name for a bird whose feet are
mainly adapted for climbing: a climbing plant
(*bot.*).—*n.* and *adj.* **climb'ing**.—*n.* **climb'-down**.—
**climb down**, to become more humble: abandon a
firmly stated opinion or resolve. [O.E. *climban*;
cf. Ger. *klimmen*; clamber, cleave (3).]

**clime**, *klīm*, *n.* a country, region, tract. [**climate**.]

**clinamen**, *klin-ā'mən*, *n.* inclination. [L. *clinā-
men*.]

**clinch**, *klinch*, *klinsh*, *v.t.* to fasten or rivet a nail
by bending and beating down the point: to
clench (*obs.*): to drive home (an argument; *fig.*):
to settle or confirm (*fig.*).—*v.i.* to grapple.—*n.*
something set firmly: the fastening of a nail by
beating it back: a holding grapple (*boxing*): a
pun: a punning retort.—*n.* **clinch'er**, one that
clinches: a decisive argument.—*adj.* **clinch'er-
built** (same as **clinker-built**).—**clinch'er-work**,

the disposition of the side planks of a vessel,
when the lower edge of one row overlaps the
row next under it. [Same as **clench**; causal
form of **clink**.]

**cline**, *klin*, (*biol.*) *n.* a gradation of differences of
form, etc., seen, e.g. within one species over a
specified area of the world. [See **clino-**.]

**cling**, *kling*, *v.i.* to stick close by adhesive surface
or by clasp: to adhere in interest or affection: to
remain by an opinion: of wood, to shrink.—*v.t.*
to attach: to shrivel (*pa.t.* and *pa.p.* **clung**).—*n.*
adherence.—*adjs.* **cling**, **cling'stone**, having the
pulp adhering firmly to the stone (of peaches)—
opp. to *freestone*; **cling'y**, sticky. [O.E. *clingan*.]

**clinic**, *klin'ik*, *n.* one confined to bed by sickness
(*arch.*): the instruction of medicine or surgery
at the bedside of hospital patients: a session of
such instruction: a private hospital or nursing-
home: an institution, or a department of one,
or a group of doctors, for treating patients or
for diagnosis or giving advice: any group
meeting for instruction, often remedial, in a
particular field.—Also *adj.*—Also **clinique** (*klin-
ēk'*).—*adj.* **clin'ical**, hospital-like: concerned
with, based on, observation: strictly objective.
—*adv.* **clin'ically**.—*n.* **clinician** (-*ish'ən*).—**clinical
baptism**, baptism administered to persons on
their sick-bed; **clinical convert**, one converted
on his death-bed; **clinical medicine**, or **surgery**,
medicine or surgery as taught by clinics; **clinical
lecture**, one to students at the bedside of the sick;
**clinical thermometer**, one for taking the temperature of patients. [Gr. *klīnikos*—*klīnē*, a bed.]

**clink**, *klingk*, *n.* a ringing sound made by striking
metal, glass, etc.—*v.t.* to cause to make a ringing
sound.—*v.i.* to ring: to go with a clink.—*n.*
**clink'er**, a hard brick (also **klinker**, as Dutch):
a scale or globule of black iron oxide obtained
from red-hot iron under the hammer: incombustible residue of fused ash raked out of furnaces: furnace slag: the cindery crust of some
lava-flows.—**clink'er-block**, a block for building
made from ash from furnaces; **clink'stone**,
phonolite (from its metallic clink when struck).
[A form of **click** and **clank**.]

**clink**, *klingk*, *n.* (*slang*) prison. [Appar. orig. one
in Southwark.]

**clink**, *klingk*, (*Spens.*) *n.* said to mean keyhole, or
latch. [Cf. Du. *klink*, latch.]

**clink**, *klingk*, *v.t.* to clinch: to rivet.—*n.* **clink'er**,
a nail used as a protective stud in footwear,
esp. in climbing boots: anything worthy of
warm admiration in its kind.—*adj.* (*slang*)
**clink'ing**.—*adj.* **clink'er-built**, made of planks
which overlap those below (as distinguished from
carvel-built) and fastened with clinched nails.
[Northern form of **clinch**.]

**clino-**, *klī'nō-*, in composition, oblique.—*ns.*
**cli'noaxis** (*crystal.*), the clinodiagonal; **clino-
diag'onal**, in a monoclinic crystal, that lateral
axis which is not perpendicular to the vertical
axis; **clinometer** (*klin-*, *klin-om'i-tər*), any of
various instruments for measuring slope, elevation, or inclination.—*adj.* **clinomet'ric**.—*ns.*
**clinom'etry**; **clinopin'acoid**, -**pin'akoid**, a form
consisting of two faces parallel to the clinoaxis
and the vertical axis. [Gr. *klinein*, to lean.]

**clinochlore**, *klī'nō-klōr*, -*klör*, *n.* a green mineral, a
distinctly monoclinic variety of *chlorite*.

**clinquant**, *klingk'ant*, *adj.* tinselly (*Shak.*): glittering.—*n.* tinsel: glitter. [Fr.,—Du. *klinken*, to
clink.]

**Clio**, *klī'ō*, *n.* the muse of history. [Gr. *Kleiō*,
proclaimer.]

**Clio**, *klī'ō*, *n.* a genus of shell-less pteropods,
'whales' food'. [Gr. *Kleiō*, a sea-nymph.]

**clip**, *klip*, *v.t.* to cut with shears: to cut off: to
trim or cut off the hair, twigs, ends, edges, etc. of:
to pare down: to reduce or curtail: to shorten
in indistinct utterance: to punch a piece from: to

hit sharply.—*v.i.* to go at a good speed (*pr.p.*
clipp'ing; *pa.p.* clipped, clipt).—*n.* an act of
clipping: the thing removed by clipping: yield
of wool: a smart blow: a high speed: a piece
taken from a film for separate showing.—*adj.*
clipped, clipt.—*ns.* clipp'er, one who clips: a
clipping instrument: a swift mover: a sharp-
built fast sailing-vessel: a showy spirited person
or anything admired (*slang*); clipp'ie (*slang*), a
woman bus or tram conductor; clipp'ing, the act
of clipping, esp. the edges of coins: a small
piece clipped off, shred, paring: a newspaper
cutting.—*adj.* superb: fast-going.—clip'-joint, a
place of entertainment, e.g. a night-club, where
customers are overcharged or cheated.—clip
coin, to pare the edges of coins; clip the wings,
to cut the feathers of a bird's wings to prevent it
from flying: to restrain ambition (*fig.*): to
deprive of the means of rising. [Prob. from O.N.
*klippa*, to cut; Dan. *klippe*.]
clip, *klip, v.t.* to encircle (*arch.*): to encircle: to
hold firmly.—*n.* a device for gripping or clasping,
or holding things together.—*n.* clip'-hook, a
sister-hook. [O.E. *clyppan*, to embrace; Ger.
*kluppe*, pincers.]
clip-clop. See clop.
clipe. See clype.
clique, *klēk, n.* an exclusive group of persons: a
faction: a coterie—used generally in a bad
sense.—*adj.* cliqu'ish, relating to a clique: exclusive.—*ns.* cliqu'ishness; cliqu'ism, tendency
to form cliques. [Fr., orig. in sense of claque;
prob. conn. with click.]
clish-clash, *klish'-klash,* clishmaclaver, *klish'mə-
klāv'ər, n.* gossip. [Scot. See clash, claver.]
clistogamy. See cleistogamy.
clitellum, *kli-, kli-tel'əm, n.* a glandular belt on a
worm, secreting a cocoon:—*pl.* clitell'a.—*adj.*
clitell'ar. [L. *clitellae,* pack-saddle.]
clithral. Same as cleithral.
clitoris, *kli', kli', tə-ris, n.* a homologue of the
penis in the female. [Gr. *kleitoris.*]
clitter, *klit'ər, v.t.* and *v.i.* to make, or cause to
make, a shrill rattling noise.—*n.* clitt'er-clatt'er,
idle talk, chatter. [Related to clatter.]
clivers. Same as cleavers.
cloaca, *klō-ā'kə* (L. -ā'ka), *n.* a sewer: a privy: a
cavity in birds and reptiles, in which the intestinal
and urinary ducts terminate: a sink of moral
filth:—*pl.* cloacae (*klō-ā'sē*; L. -ā-ki).—*adjs.*
cloā'cal, cloā'calin(e), cloacinal (*klō-ə-si'nl*). [L.
*cloāca—cluēre,* to purge.]
cloak, *klōk, n.* a loose outer garment: a covering:
that which conceals: a disguise, pretext.—*v.t.* to
clothe with a cloak: to cover: to conceal.—*ns.*
cloak'-bag (*obs.*), a portmanteau; cloak'room, a
room for keeping coats and hats: a room in a
place of public assembly, e.g. a theatre, in which
outer garments and luggage may be temporarily
deposited: a lavatory.—*adjs.* cloak'-and-dagg'er,
concerned with plot and intrigue; cloak'-and-
sword', concerned with fighting and romance.—
Also (*arch.*) cloke. [O.Fr. *cloke, cloque*—L.L.
*cloca*, a bell, a horseman's bell-shaped cape; see
clock (1).]
cloam, *klōm, n.* and *adj.* earthenware, clay, or
made of such. [O.E. *clām,* mud.]
clobber, *klob'ər, n.* a paste used by shoemakers to
hide the cracks in leather.—*v.t.* to overpaint a
piece of porcelain with enamelled decoration.
[Origin dub.]
clobber, *klob'ər,* (*slang*) *n.* clothing, gear. [Origin
dub.]
clobber, *klob'ər,* (*slang*) *v.t.* to strike very hard:
to defeat overwhelmingly. [Origin unknown.]
clochard, *klo-shär,* (Fr.) *n.* a tramp.
cloche, *klosh, n.* a glass under which plants are
forced: a lady's close-fitting hat. [Fr.; see
clock (1).]
clock, *klok, n.* a machine for measuring time,

strictly one with a bell: a time-measurer in
general: the striking of the hour (*Shak.*).—*v.t.* to
time by a clock or stop-watch: to achieve (a
certain officially attested time for a race).—*v.i.*
to register a time by a recording clock.—*adv.*
clock'wise, in the manner or direction of the
hands of a clock.—clock'-golf, a putting game
on a green marked like a clock dial, in which the
player putts from each hour-figure to a hole near
the centre; clock'maker; clock'work, the works
or machinery of a clock: machinery steady and
regular like that of a clock.—*adj.* automatic.—
against the clock, with effort to overcome shortage of time; clock in, out, on, off, to register
time of coming or going, in, out, on, off; know
what o'clock it is, to be wide awake, to know how
things are; o'clock, for earlier of the clock, as
reckoned or shown by the clock: in a direction
corresponding to that which would be taken by
the hour-hand of a horizontal clock relative to a
person at the centre and facing twelve; put back
the clock, to return to earlier time and its conditions; round the clock, for the whole of the
twenty-four hours. [M.E. *clokke,* prob.
through O.Fr. from L.L. *cloca, clocca,* a bell;
mod. Fr. *cloche,* bell, Du. *klok,* bell, clock, Ger.
*glocke,* bell.]
clock, *klok, n.* an ornament on the side of a
stocking.—*adj.* clocked, ornamented with clocks.
[Ety. dub.]
clock, *klok, klōk,* (Scot. and dial.) *n.* a beetle—*n.*
clock'er, a large beetle. [Origin unknown; cf.
Swed. dial. *klocka,* beetle, earwig.]
clock, *klok,* (Scot.) *v.i.* to cluck: to brood or sit.
—*n.* a brooding hen's cry: a cluck.—*n.* clock'er,
a clocking hen. [O.E. *cloccian*; Du. *klokken.*]
clod, *klod, n.* a thick round mass or lump, that
sticks together, esp. of earth or turf: a concreted
mass: the ground: a bed of fireclay in a coal-
mine: the body of a man, as formed of clay: a
stupid fellow.—*v.t.* to pelt: to throw (*Scot.*).—
*v.i.* to throw clods:—*pr.p.* clodd'ing; *pa.t.* and
*pa.p.* clodd'ed.—*adjs.* clodd'ish; clodd'y, abounding in clods: earthy.—*adv.* clod'ly.—clod'-
hopper, a countryman: a peasant: a dolt.—*adj.*
clod'hopping, boorish.—clod'pate, clod'pole,
clod'poll, a stupid fellow.—*adj.* clod'pated. [A
later form of clot.]
cloff, *klof,* (Scot.) *n.* a cleft. [Cf. O.N. *klof.*]
cloff, *klof, n.* an allowance on buying goods wholesale, of 2 lb. in every 3 cwt., after tare and tret
have been deducted. [Origin obscure.]
clog, *klog, n.* a block of wood: anything hindering
motion: an obstruction: an impediment: a
shoe with a wooden sole.—*v.t.* to fasten a piece
of wood to: to choke up with an accumulation:
to obstruct: to encumber: to sole with wood.—
*adj.* clogged, encumbered.—*ns.* clogg'er, one who
makes clogs; clogg'iness.—*adj.* clogg'y, lumpy,
sticky.—clog'-al'manac, an early form of
almanac having the indicating characters
notched on wood, horn, etc.; clog'dance, a dance
performed with clogs, the clatter keeping time to
the music. [Ety. dub.]
cloison, *klwä-zɔ̃, kloi'zn, n.* a partition, dividing
fillet or band.—*n.* cloisonnage (*klwäz-on-äzh'*),
cloisonné work or process.—*adj.* cloisonné
(*klwäz-on-ā, kloi-zon'ā,* or -ā'), decorated in
enamel, in compartments formed by small fillets
of metal.—*n.* work of this kind. [Fr.]
cloister, *klois'tər, n.* a covered arcade forming part
of a monastic or collegiate establishment: a
place of religious retirement, a monastery or
nunnery: an enclosed place: monastic life.—*v.t.*
to confine in a cloister: to confine within walls.
—*adj.* clois'tered, dwelling in cloisters.—*n.*
clois'terer, one belonging to a cloister.—*adj.*
clois'tral, claustral, pertaining or confined to a
cloister: secluded.—*n.* clois'tress (*Shak.*), a nun.
—clois'ter-garth, the court or yard enclosed by a

Neutral vowels in unaccented syllables: *el'ə-mənt*; for certain sounds in foreign words, see p. viii

cloister. [O.Fr. *cloistre* (O.E. *clauster*)—L. *claustrum*—*claudēre*, *clausum*, to shut.]

cloke. Same as cloak.

clomb, *klōm*, old *pa.t.* and *pa.p.* of climb.

clone, *klōn*, (*biol.*) *n.* the whole stock of individuals derived asexually from one sexually produced. [Gr. *klōn*, shoot.]

clonus, *klō'nəs*, *n.* a spasm of alternate contractions and relaxations of the muscles.—*adj.* clonic (*klon'ik*). [Latinised from Gr. *klŏnos*, tumult.]

cloop, *klōōp*, *n.* the sound of drawing a cork. [Imit.]

cloot, *klōōt*, Scot. *klüt*, *klit*, *n.* a division of a cloven hoof: loosely a hoof.—*ns.* Cloot'ie, Cloots, the devil. [Scot.; ety. dub.]

clop, *klop*, *n.* the sound of a horse's hoof-tread.—*adv.* with a clop.—*v.i.* to make, or go with, such a sound.—Also clip-clop, clop-clop. [Imit.]

cloqué, *klo-kā'*, *n.* an embossed material.—also *adj.* [Fr.]

close, *klōs*, *adj.* shut up: with no opening: confined, unventilated: stifling: narrow: stingy: near, in time or place: intimate: compact: crowded: hidden: reserved: private: secret: (of a vowel) pronounced with slight opening, or with the tongue tense.—*adv.* in a close manner: tightly: nearly: densely: secretly.—*n.* an enclosed place: a small enclosed field: a narrow passage of a street: the precinct of a cathedral. —*adv.* close'ly.—*n.* close'ness.—*adjs.* close'-band'ed, closely united; close'-barred, firmly closed; close'-bod'ied, fitting close to the body; Close Brethren, Exclusive Brethren, branch of the Plymouth Brethren whose members will not associate with (e.g. eat in company with) people outside their group; close call, a narrow escape; close company, firm controlled by five, or fewer, people; close corporation, a corporation which fills up its own vacancies, without outside interference; close'-fist'ed, close'-hand'ed, penurious, covetous; close'-grained, with the particles, fibres, etc., close together, compact; close harmony, harmony in which the notes of chords lie close together; close'-hauled, in trim for sailing as near as possible to the wind.—*adj.* close'-reefed, having all reefs taken in.—close season, time, a time of the year when it is illegal to kill certain game or fish—the breeding season: a prohibited period; close shave, thing, a close call; close'-stool, a chamber utensil enclosed in a box or stool; close tennis, tennis properly so called, distinguished from lawn-tennis.—*adj.* close'-tongued (*Shak.*), cautious in speaking.— close'-up', a photograph or film taken near at hand and thus detailed and big in scale: a close scrutiny.—close to the chest, without revealing one's intentions. [Fr. *clos*, shut—L. *claudēre*, *clausum*, to close, shut up.]

close, *klōz*, *v.t.* to make close: to draw together and unite: to end.—*v.i.* to come together: to grapple: to come to an end.—*n.* the manner or time of closing: a pause or stop: a cadence: the end: junction: encounter (*Shak.*).—*adj.* closed, shut: blocked: not open to traffic: with permanent sides and top: with lid, etc.: exclusive, having few contacts outside itself (e.g. *a closed community*): continuous and finishing where it began.—*ns.* clos'er, one who or that which concludes: any portion of a brick used to close up the bond next to the end brick of a course; clos'ing, enclosing: ending: agreement; clos'-ure, the act of closing: the end: the stopping of a debate by vote of the House.—*v.t.* to apply the closure to.—*adj.* closed'-chain' (*chem.*), having a molecule in which the atoms are linked ringwise, like a chain with the ends united.—closed circuit (*television*), a system in which the showing is for restricted not general viewing; closed shop, an establishment in which only members of a trade union, or of a particular trade union, will be employed: the principle or policy implied in such a regulation: an establishment boycotted by the trade unions: a situation where only specialist personnel have access to a computer (opp. to open shop); closed syllable, one ending in a consonant.—close a bargain, to make an agreement; close down, to come to a standstill or stoppage of work: to give up business; close in upon, to surround and draw near to; close with, to accede to: to grapple with; with closed doors, in private, the public being excluded, as in special cases in court, etc. [Fr. *clore*, *clos*—L. *claudēre*, *clausum*.]

closet, *kloz'it*, *n.* a small private room: a recess off a room: a privy: the private chamber of a sovereign, an apartment for private audience or council, or for private or domestic devotions.— *v.t.* to shut up in or take into a closet: to conceal: —*pr.p.* clos'eting; *pa.t.* and *pa.p.* clos'eted.— clos'et-play, -drama, a play to be read rather than acted; clos'et-strat'egist, a mere theorist in strategy. [O.Fr. *closet*, dim. of *clos*, an enclosure; see close.]

clostridium, *klos-trid'i-əm*, *n.* an ovoid or spindle-shaped bacterium: (*cap.*) a genus of spindle-shaped anaerobic bacteria (fam. Bacillaceae) incl. several species pathogenic to man and animals: —*pl.* clostridia.—*adj.* clostrid'ial. [Gr. *klōstēr*, a spindle.]

clot, *klot*, *n.* a mass of soft or fluid matter concreted, as blood: a fool.—*v.t.* and *v.i.* to form into clots:—*pr.p.* clott'ing; *pa.t.* and *pa.p.* clott'ed.—*v.t.* clott'er, to coagulate.—*ns.* clott'i-ness; clott'ing, coagulation.—*adj.* clott'y.— clot'poll (*Shak.*), a clodpoll, a blockhead; clotted (also clouted) cream, a famous Devonshire dainty, prepared by scalding milk. [O.E. *clott*, a clod of earth; cf. Du. *klos*, block; Dan. *klods*; Ger. *klotz*.]

clote, *klōt*, *n.* the burdock: extended to other plants of burry character.—*n.* clotbur (*klot'bər*), burdock: a species of *Xanthium*.—Also clote'-bur. [O.E. *clāte*.]

cloth, *kloth*, *klŏth*, *n.* woven material from which garments or coverings are made: a piece of this material: clothing: the usual dress of a trade or profession, esp. the clerical: a table-cloth: sails: a theatre curtain:—*pl.* cloths (*kloths*, *klŏdhz*).—*v.t.* clothe (*klōdh*), to cover with a garment: to provide with clothes: to invest as with a garment (*fig.*): to cover:—*pr.p.* clothing (*klōdh'ing*); *pa.t.* and *pa.p.* clothed (*klōdhd*), or clad.—*n.pl.* clothes (*klōdhz*; *coll.* *klōz*), garments or articles of dress: blankets, sheets and cover for a bed.—*ns.* clothier (*klō'dhi-ər*), one who makes or sells cloth or clothes; clothing (*klō'-dhing*), clothes, garments: covering.—clothes'-basket, a large basket for holding and carrying clothes for the wash; clothes'-brush, a brush for clothes; clothes'-horse, clothes'-screen, a frame for hanging clothes on to dry; clothes'-line, a rope or wire for hanging clothes on to dry; clothes'-moth, one of various tineas whose larvae feed on woollens; clothes'-peg, -pin, a forked piece of wood or clamp to secure clothes on a line; clothes'-pole, a pole from which clothes-lines are hung; clothes'-press, a place for holding clothes: apparatus for pressing clothes; clothes'-prop, a movable notched pole for raising or supporting a clothes-line; cloth'-hall, exchange building or market for the cloth trade; cloth-yard, the yard by which cloth was measured, formerly 37 inches.—clothe in words, to express in words; clothe on, or upon, to invest: to cover; cloth of gold, a tissue of threads of gold and silk or wool; cloth of state, a canopy; cloth-yard shaft, an arrow a cloth-yard long; the cloth, the clerical profession: the clergy. [O.E. *clāth*, cloth; Ger. *kleid*, a garment.]

Clotho, *klō'thō*, *n.* in Gr. myth., the Fate that

spins the thread of life: the puff-adder genus. [Gr. *klōthō*.]

**cloture**, *klō'chər*, Fr. *klo-tür, n.* closure: the limitation of a debate in a legislative assembly, usu. by calling for an immediate vote (*U.S.*).—Also *v.t.* [Fr. *clôture*; see **closure**.]

**clou**, *klōō, n.* chief point of interest: dominant idea. [Fr., nail.]

**cloud**, *klowd, n.* a mass of fog, consisting of minute particles of water, often in a frozen state, floating in the atmosphere: anything unsubstantial (*fig.*): a great number or multitude of anything (as cloud of witnesses) (*fig.*): anything that obscures, as a cloud: a dullness: a dark or dull spot: a dark spot on a horse's face (*Shak.*): a great volume of dust or smoke: anything gloomy, overhanging or bodeful.—*v.t.* to overspread with clouds: to darken: to defame: to stain with dark spots or streaks: to dull.—*v.i.* to become clouded or darkened.—*n.* **cloud'age.**—*adj.* **cloud'ed**, hidden by clouds: (*fig.*) darkened, indistinct, dull: variegated with spots.—*adv.* **cloud'ily.**—*ns.* **cloud'iness**; **cloud'ing**, a cloudy appearance.—*adj.* growing dim.—*adj.* **cloud'less**, unclouded, clear.—*adv.* **cloud'lessly.**—*n.* **cloud'let**, a little cloud.—*adj.* **cloud'y**, darkened with, or consisting of, clouds: obscure: gloomy: stained with dark spots: 'shady' (*coll.*).—**cloud'berry**, a low plant related to the bramble, found on elevated moors in Britain, with an orange-red berry of delightful flavour.—*adj.* **cloud'-built**, made of clouds, unsubstantial.—*n.* **cloud'burst**, a sudden flood of rain over a small area.—*adj.* **cloud'-capt** (*Shak.*), capped with or touching the clouds.—**cloud'-castle**, **cloud'land**, **cloud'-cuck'oo-land**, or **-town**, an imaginary situation or land (the last translating Aristophanes's *Nephelokokkȳgiā*); **cloud'-chamber**, an apparatus in which the path of charged particles is made visible by means of water-drops condensed on gas ions.—*adj.* **cloud'-compell'ing**, driving or collecting the clouds, an epithet of Zeus.—**clouded leopard**, an arboreal cat (*Felis nebulosa*) smaller than a leopard.—*—adj.* **cloud'-kiss'ing** (*Shak.*), touching the clouds.—*adj.* **cloud'-topped**, covered with or touching the clouds.—**under a cloud**, in trouble, disgrace, or disfavour. [O.E. *clūd*, a hill (as still in Derbyshire), then a cloud, the root idea being a mass or ball; cf. **clod**, **clot**.]

**clough**, *kluf*, or *klow, n.* a ravine: a valley. [O.E. would be *clōh*; Scot. *cleuch*.]

**clour**, *klōōr,* (*Scot.*) *n.* a knock: a swelling caused by a knock.—*v.t.* to knock: to raise a bump. [Origin doubtful.]

**clout**, *klowt, n.* a piece of cloth, esp. used for mending: a patch: a protective plate or nail: a rag: in archery, the mark or target, usually in long-distance shooting: a shot that hits: a blow or cuff.—*v.t.* to mend with a patch: to protect with a plate or with nails: to cover with a cloth: to cuff.—*adj.* **clout'ed** (*Shak.*), heavy and patched or having nails in the soles, as shoes: covered with a clout.—*adj.* **clout'erly**, clownish.—**clout'-nail**, a large-headed nail: **clout'-shoe**, a shoe with clout-nails: a clown. [O.E. *clūt*; cf. O.N. *klūtr*, a kerchief; Dan. *klud*, rag.]

**clouted**, *klowt'id, adj.* clotted. [See **clot**.]

**clove**, *klōv, pa.t.* of **cleave**.—**clove'-hitch** (see **hitch**); **clove'-hook**, a sister-hook.

**clove**, *klōv, n.* a division of a bulb, as in garlic. [O.E. *clufu*; cf. **cleave**.]

**clove**, *klōv, n.* an old weight (7, 8, or 10 pounds) for wool and cheese. [Fr. *clou*—L. *clāvus*, nail.]

**clove**, *klōv, n.* the flower-bud of the clove-tree (*Eugenia caryophyllata*), a native of the Moluccas, dried as a spice, and yielding an essential oil (*pl.*) a cordial got therefrom.—**clove'-gill'y-flower**, **clove'-pink**, a variety of pink, smelling of

**cloves.** [Fr. *clou*, nail, from its shape—L. *clāvus*, a nail.]

**cloven**, *klōv'n, p.adj.* split: divided.—*adjs.* **clov'en-foot'ed**, **clov'en-hoofed**, having the hoof divided, as the ox or sheep.—**the cloven hoof**, applied to any indication of devilish agency or temptation, from the early representation of the devil with cloven hoofs—prob. from Pan, some of whose characteristics he shares. [*Pa.p.* of **cleave**, to divide.]

**clover**, *klō'vər, n.* a genus (Trifolium) of papilionaceous plants, with heads of small flowers and trifoliate leaves, affording rich pasturage.—*adj.* **clov'ered**, covered with clover.—*adj.* **clov'ery**, abounding in clover.—**clov'er-grass**, clover; **clov'erleaf**, a traffic arrangement in which one road passes over the top of another and the roads connecting the two are in the pattern of a four-leafed clover.—**live in clover**, to live luxuriously or in abundance. [O.E. *clāfre* (usu. *clǣfre*); Du. *klaver*; Dan. *klöver*; Ger. *klee*.]

**clow**, *klow, n.* a Scots form of **clove** (4).—*n.* **clow'-gillieflower**.

**clown**, *klown, n.* a rustic or country-fellow: one with the awkward manners of a countryman: an ill-bred fellow: a fool or buffoon, esp. of the harlequinade or the circus.—*v.i.* to play the clown.—*ns.* **clown'ery**, a clown's performance; **clown'ing**.—*adj.* **clown'ish**, of or like a clown: coarse and awkward: rustic.—*adv.* **clown'ishly**.—*ns.* **clown'ishness**; **clown'ship**. [Perh.—L. Ger., cf. Fris. *klönne*, *klünne*.]

**cloy**, *kloi, v.t.* to prick (a horse in shoeing; *obs.*): to gore: (of a cannon) to spike: to block up: to overcharge with food, to satiate, esp. with sweetness: to disgust, weary.—*v.i.* to cause distaste, become distasteful from excess.—*adjs.* **cloyed**; **cloy'ing**; **cloy'less** (*Shak.*), that cannot cloy.—*n.* **cloy'ment** (*Shak.*), satiety, surfeit.—*adj.* **cloy'some**, satiating. [Apheticised from *accloy*—O.Fr. *encloyer* (Fr. *enclouer*)—L.L. *inclāvāre*, to drive in a nail—*in*, in, *clāvus*, a nail.]

**cloye**, *kloi,* (*Shak.*) *v.t.* app., to claw, stroke with the claw. [Perh. **claw**.]

**club**, *klub, n.* a heavy tapering stick, knobby or massy at one end, used to strike with: a cudgel: a bat used in certain games: an instrument for playing golf, with a wooden, iron, or aluminium head, or a wooden head with brass sole: a bunch: a card of one of the four suits: a combination: a clique, set: an association of persons for social, political, athletic, or other ends: an association of persons who possess a building as a common resort for the members: a clubhouse, or the house occupied by a club.—*v.t.* to beat with a club: to gather into a bunch: to combine: to use as a club: to throw into confusion (*mil.*).—*v.i.* to join together for some common end: to combine together: to share in a common expense.—*adjs.* **club'(b)able**, sociable; **clubbed**, enlarged at the end like a club. —*n.* **clubb'ing**, beating: combination: a thickening, as of finger-ends, or of cabbage-stems attacked by insect larvae.—*adj.* **clubb'ish**, given to clubs.—*ns.* **clubb'ism**, the club system; **clubb'ist**, a clubman.—**club'-face**, the face of a golf-club; **club'-foot**, a deformed foot.—*adj.* **club'-foot'ed.**—*v.t.* **club'-haul** (*naut.*), to tack by dropping the lee anchor and slipping the cable.— **club'-head**, the head of a golf-club.—*adj.* **club'-head'ed**, having a thick head.—**club'house**, a house for the accommodation of a club; **club'-law**, government by violence; **club'-line**, a short line at the end of a paragraph; **club'man**, one who carries a club: a member of a club: a frequenter of clubs, man about town; **club'master**, the manager of, or purveyor for, a club; **club'-moss**, a lycopod; **club'room**, the room in which a club meets; **club'-rush**, any sedge of the genus Scirpus; **club sandwich**, a sandwich of toast, usu.

Neutral vowels in unaccented syllables: *el'ə-mənt*; for certain sounds in foreign words, see ɒ. viii three slices, containing chicken or turkey, bacon or ham, lettuce, tomato, and mayonnaise; **club soda,** soda water; **club'woman.**—*n.pl.* **clubs** (see **clumps**). [O.N. and Sw. *klubba*; same root as **clump.**]

**cluck,** *kluk, n.* the call of a hen to her chickens: any similar sound.—*v.i.* to make such a sound. [Imit.; cf. Du. *klokken,* Ger. *glucken,* Dan. *klukke,* and **clock.**]

**clue,** *klōō.* See **clew.**

**clumber,** *klumb'ər, n.* a kind of spaniel, formerly bred at *Clumber,* in Notts.

**clump,** *klump, n.* a thick, short, shapeless piece of anything: a cluster: a clot: a thick additional sole: a blow.—*v.i.* to walk heavily: to clot: to cluster.—*v.t.* to put in a clump: to beat.—*n.* (*pl.* in form) **clumps,** a parlour game of question and answer—also **clubs.**—*adj.* **clump'y,** abounding in clumps: heavy. [Prob. Scand.; Dan. *klump,* a lump. Cf. Ger. *klump,* and **club.**]

**clumsy,** *klum'zi, adj.* shapeless: ill-made: unwieldy: awkward: ungainly.—*adv.* **clum'sily.**—*n.* **clum'siness.** [M.E. *clumsen,* to be stiff or benumbed.]

**clunch,** *klunch, -sh, n.* a tough clay. [Prob. related to **clump.**]

**clung,** *klung, pa.t.* and *pa.p.* of **cling.**

**Cluniac,** *klōōn'i-ak, n.* a monk or nun of a branch of the Benedictine order originating at *Cluny* in France in A.D. 910.—Also *adj.*

**clunk,** *klungk, n.* the gurgling sound of a liquid or the sound of a cork being drawn from a bottle (*Scot.*): a thump: a dolt (*U.S.*).—*v.i.* to fall with a thumping sound.—*v.t.* (*dial.*), to gurgle while swallowing. [Imit.]

**Clupea,** *klōō'pi-a, n.* the herring genus.—*n.* **clu'peoid,** any fish of the herring family, **Clupē'idae.**—Also *adj.* [L. *clupea,* a kind of river fish.]

**Clusia,** *klōō's(h)i-a, n.* a typical American genus of (mostly) climbing plants, giving an alternative name **Clusiā'ceae** to the Guttiferae. [After the French botanist Charles de Lécluse (L.*Clusius*).]

**cluster,** *klus'tər, n.* a number of things of the same kind growing or joined together: a bunch: a mass: a crowd.—*v.i.* to grow in or gather into clusters.—*v.t.* to collect into clusters: to cover with clusters.—*adjs.* **clus'tered,** grouped; **clus'-tery; clus'tery.**—**clustered column,** a pier which consists of several columns or shafts clustered together; **clus'ter-cup,** an accidium; **clust'er-pine,** the pinaster (*Pinus Pinaster*), a pine with clustered cones. [O.E. *clyster*; L.G. *kluster*; cf. **clot.**]

**clutch,** *kluch, v.t.* to close the hand upon: to hold firmly: to seize or grasp.—*v.i.* to make a snatching movement.—*n.* a claw: a hand (often in *pl.*): a device by which two shafts or rotating members may be connected or disconnected either while at rest or in relative motion: grasp: a snatching movement. [O.E. *clyccan,* to clench.]

**clutch,** *kluch, n.* a brood of chickens: a sitting of eggs.—*v.t.* to hatch. [Cf. **cleck.**]

**clutter,** *klut'ər, n.* a clotted or confused mass: confusion: stir (*dial.*): noise (*dial.*): irregular interference on radar screen from echoes, rain, buildings, etc.—*v.i.* to crowd together: to go about in noisy confusion (*dial.*).—*v.t.* to litter. [From **clot**; influenced in meaning by **cluster** and **clatter.**]

**cly,** *kli,* (*slang*) *v.t.* to seize, steal.—*ns.* **cly'-fāk'er,** a pickpocket; **cly'-fāk'ing,** pocket-picking. [Prob. related to **claw**; referred by some to Du. *kleed,* a garment, *to fake a cly,* to take a garment.]

**Clydesdale,** *klidz'dāl, adj.* originating in *Clydesdale* (of a breed of cart-horses).—*n.* a Clydesdale horse.

**clype, clipe,** *klip,* (*Scot.*) *v.i.* to tell tales:—also *n.* [M.E. *clepien,* to call.]

**clypeus,** *klip'i-əs, n.* the shield-like part of an insect's head.—*adjs.* **clyp'eal,** of the clypeus;

**clyp'eate, clyp'ëiform,** buckler-shaped. [L. *clipeus* (*clypeus*), a round shield.]

**clyster,** *klis'tər, n.* a liquid injected into the intestines.—*n.* **clys'ter-pipe** (*Shak.*), a pipe or syringe for injecting a clyster. [Gr. *klystēr,* a cluster-pipe—*klyzein,* to wash out.]

**Cnicus,** (*k*)*ni'kəs, n.* a genus of thistles. [Gr. *knēkos.*]

**cnida,** (*k*)*ni'da, n.* a nematocyst:—*pl.* **cni'dae** (*-dē*).—*n.pl.* **cnidā'ria,** a division of the Coelenterata characterised by cnidae.—*n.* **cni'doblast,** the mother-cell of a cnida. [Gr. *knidē,* a nettle, a sea-anemone.]

**co-,** *kō-, pfx.* with: together. [L. *co-* for *com,* old form of *cum,* with.]

**co',** *kə,* Scots form of **quoth.**

**co.,** *kō,* an abbreviation for **company.**

**coacervate,** *kō-as'ər-vāt* (or *-ūr'*), *v.t.* to heap: to cause to mass together.—Also *adj.*—*n.* (also **coacervā'tion**) a reversible aggregation of particles of an emulsoid into liquid droplets before flocculation. [L. *coacervāre, -ātum—acervus,* heap.]

**coach,** *kōch, n.* formerly, a private carriage: a large, close, four-wheeled carriage, esp. one for state occasions or one plying for conveyance of passengers: a railway carriage: a bus for tourists and sight-seers: a ship's cabin near the stern: a private tutor: a professional trainer in athletics: a decoy animal.—*v.t.* to carry in a coach (*arch.*): to tutor, instruct, prepare for an examination, boat-race, etc.—*v.i.* to go by coach: to act as tutor: to study with a tutor.—*ns.* **coach'ee, coach'y,** a coachman; **coach'er,** one who coaches: a coach-horse; **coach'ing,** travelling by coach: tutoring: instruction.—*adj.* **coach'y,** pertaining to a coach.—**coach'-box,** the driver's seat on a coach; **coach'builder; coach'-building; coach'dog,** a spotted dog, kept chiefly as an attendant on carriages, a Dalmatian dog; **coach'-hire,** money paid for the use of a hired coach; **coach'-horn,** a post-horn; **coach'-horse,** a horse used for drawing a coach; **coach'-house,** a house to keep a coach in; **coach'man,** the driver of a coach: a servant employed to drive a carriage; **coach'-office,** a coach booking-office; **coach'-road; coach'-stand,** a place where coaches stand for hire; **coach'-way; coach'-wheel; coach'whip,** a coachman's whip: a kind of whip-snake; **coach'whip-bird,** an Australian bird (Psophodes) that utters a sound like the crack of a whip; **coach'work,** the fine work of a motor-car body. [Fr. *coche*—Hung. *kiocs,* from *Kocs,* in Hungary.]

**coact,** *kō-akt', v.i.* to act together.—*n.* **coaction** (*kō-ak'shən*), mutual relations.—*adj.* **coac'tive,** acting together.—*n.* **coactiv'ity.** [Pfx. **co-** and **act.**]

**coact,** *kō-akt', v.t.* to compel.—*n.* **coaction** (*kō-ak'shən*), compulsion.—*adj.* **coac'tive,** compulsory. [L. *cōgēre, coāctum,* to compel.]

**coadjacent,** *kō-a-jās'ənt, adj.* contiguous.—*n.* **coadja'cency.**

**coadjutant,** *kō-aj'ə-tənt, adj.* mutually helping.—*n.* one who helps another.—*ns.* **coadj'utor,** a helper, assistant: an associate:—*fem.* **coadj'utress, coadj'utrix; coadj'utorship.** [L. *adjūtor,* a helper—*ad,* to, *juvāre,* to help.]

**coadunate,** *kō-ad'ū-nāt, v.t.* to unite: to combine.—*n.* **coadūnā'tion.**—*adj.* **coad'ūnātive.** [L. *adūnāre, -ātum,* to unite—*ad,* to, *unus,* one.]

**co-agent,** *kō-ā'jənt, n.* a joint agent.—*n.* **co-ā'gency.**

**coagulate,** *kō-ag'ū-lāt, v.t.* to make to curdle, clot, or set by a chemical reaction.—*v.i.* to curdle, clot, or set irreversibly.—*adj.* **clotted** (*rare*): curdled.—*n.* **coagūlabil'ity.**—*adj.* **coag'ūlable.**—*ns.* **coag'ūlant,** a substance that causes coagulation; **coagūlā'tion.**—*adjs.* **coag'ūlātive; coag'ūlatory.**—*n.* **coag'ūlum,** what is coagulated. [L. *coāgulāre, -ātum—agēre,* to drive.]

**coaita**, kō-ī-tä', the red-faced spider monkey. [Tupí.]

**coal**, kōl, n. charcoal (obs.): a piece of charcoal, esp. glowing: a firm, brittle, generally black combustible carbonaceous rock derived from vegetable matter (the usual sense now): a piece of this rock: a cinder: an ember.—v.i. to take in coal.—v.t. to supply with coal: to char.—n. **coal'ite**, a smokeless fuel got by low-temperature carbonisation of coal.—adj. **coal'y**, of or like coal: covered with coal.—**coal'ball**, a calcareous nodule found in coal; **coal'-bed**, a stratum of coal.—adj. **coal'-black**, black as coal, very black. —**coal'-box**, a box for holding coal: a shell that emits black smoke (mil. slang); **coal'-brass**, iron pyrites found with coal; **coal'-bunker**, a box, recess, or compartment for holding coal; **coal'-cellar**, a cellar or similar place for storing coal; **coal'-cutter**, a machine for undercutting a coal-bed; **coal'-dust**, coal in fine powder; **coal'-face'**, the exposed surface of coal in a mine; **coal'field**, a district containing coal strata; **coal'fish**, a dusky fish of the cod family, with a green back—the saith or sillock; **coal'-flap**, **coal'-plate**, a flap or plate covering the entrance from the pavement to a coal-cellar; **coal'-gas**, the mixture of gases produced by the distillation of coal, used for lighting and heating; **coal'-heaver**, one employed in carrying coal; **coal'-hole**, a small coal-cellar: a hole in the pavement for filling a coal-cellar; **coal'-house**, a covered-in place for keeping coal; **coaling station**, a port at which steamships take in coal; **coal'man**, one who has to do with coals; **coal'master**, the owner or lessee of a coalfield; **Coal Measures** (geol.), the uppermost division of the Carboniferous; **coal'-mine**, -pit, a pit or mine from which coal is dug; **coal'-miner**; **coal'-mouse**, **coal'-tit**, **coal'-tit'mouse** (also cole-), a dark species of tit; **coal'-oil** (U.S.), rock-oil, shale-oil, petroleum; **coal'-own'er**, one who owns a colliery; **coal'-plant**, a fossil plant of the Carboniferous strata; **coal'-porter**, one who carries coal; **coal'-scuttle**, a fireside vessel for holding coal; **coal'-tar**, gas-tar, a thick, black, opaque liquid formed when coal is distilled; **coal'-trimmer**, one who stores or shifts coal on board vessels; **coal'-whipper**, one who unloads coal from vessels to barges.—**blow the coals**, to excite passion, foment strife; **carry coals to Newcastle**, to take a thing where it is already most abundant; **coal-scuttle bonnet**, a bonnet shaped like a coal-scuttle upside down; **haul (or call) over the coals**, to reprimand—from the discipline applied to heretics; **heap coals of fire on the head**, to excite remorse and repentance by returning good for evil (Rom. xii. 20). [O.E. col; cog. with O.N. kol, Ger. kohle.]

**coalesce**, kō-ə-les', v.i. to grow together or unite into one body.—n. **coalesc'ence**, growing into each other: fusion.—adj. **coalesc'ent**.—v.t. and v.i. **co'alise**, **-ize** (kō'ə-līz), to bring or come into coalition.—n. **coalition** (-lish'ən), combination or alliance short of union, esp. of states or political parties.—adj. **coali'tional**.—ns. **coali'tioner**, **coali'tionist**.—**coalition government**, government, by a coalition of parties, sometimes called a national government. [L. coalēscĕre—alēscĕre, to grow up.]

**Coalport**, kōl'pōrt, pört, n. porcelain ware made at Coalport, near Shrewsbury, during the 19th century.

**coamings**, kōm'ingz, (naut.) n.pl. raised work about the edges of the hatches of a ship to keep water out. [Der. unknown.]

**coapt**, kō-apt', v.t. to adjust.—n. **coaptā'tion**. [L. coaptāre—aptāre, to fit.]

**coarb**, kō'ärb, (hist.) n. head of a family in an Irish sept: an ecclesiastical successor.—Also **comarb** (kō'ärb). [Ir. comharba, successor.]

**coarctate**, kō-ärk'tāt, adj. compressed: con-

stricted.—n. **coarctā'tion**. [L. coar(c)tāre, -ātum—ar(c)tāre, to draw together.]

**coarse**, kōrs, körs, adj. common, base, inferior: rough: rude: uncivil: harsh: gross: large in grain, fibre, or mesh, etc.: without refinement: roughly approximate.—adj. **coarse'-grained**, large in grain: coarse in nature (fig.): gross.—adv. **coarse'ly**.—v.t. and v.i. **coars'en**, to make or become coarse.—n. **coarse'ness**.—adj. **coars'ish**, somewhat coarse.—**coarse fish**, freshwater fish other than those of the salmon family:—**coarse fishing**; **coarse metal**, impure cuprous sulphide got in course of smelting. [From phrase 'in course', hence ordinary.]

**coast**, kōst, n. side (obs.): border of land next to the sea: the seashore: limit or border (obs.): region (Milt.): a hill suitable for coasting: an act or spell of coasting; (Spens.) cost, coste (kōst, kost), coast: region: direction: footing, terms: side.—v.i. **coast** (Spens., also cost), to approach (obs.): to sail along or near a coast: to travel downhill on a sledge, on a cycle without pedalling or in a motor-car out of gear: to glide: to succeed or proceed without effort.—v.t. to sail by or near to.—adj. **coast'al**.—ns. **coast'er**, vessel that sails along the coast: foot-rest on bicycle: container for decanter, etc. on table.—adj. **coast'ing**, keeping near the coast: trading between ports in the same country.—n. the act of sailing, or of trading, along the coast: advances towards acquaintance (obs.): sliding downhill.—**coast'guard**, body of men organised to watch along coast for prevention of smuggling, for life-saving, defence, etc.: a member thereof; **coast'guard(s)man**; **coast'line**, the line or boundary of a coast: shoreline; **coast'-wait'er**, a custom-house officer for coasting shipping.—advs. **coast'ward**, **-s**, toward the coast; **coast'wise**, along the coast.—adj. carried on along the coast.—**the coast is clear**, there is no obstacle or danger in the way. [O.Fr. coste (Fr. côte)—L. costa, a rib, side.]

**coat**, kōt, n. an outer garment with sleeves: an overcoat: the hair or wool of a beast: vesture or habit: any covering: a membrane or layer, as of paint, etc.: a coat of arms (see below): a skirt or petticoat (dial.).—v.t. to clothe: to cover with a coat.—ns. **coat'ee**, a short close-fitting coat; **coat'ing**, a covering, layer: cloth for coats.—adj. **coat'less**, without a coat or a coat of arms.—**coat'-arm'our**, coat of arms, or heraldically embroidered garment worn over armour: armorial devices; **coat'-card**, a card bearing the representation of a coated figure, the king, queen, or knave—now, less correctly, called court-card; **coat'-frock**, a dress for use without coat or jacket: a tailored dress with fastening from neckline to hem; also **coat'-dress**; **coat'-hanger**, a curved piece of wood, etc., with a hook, by which a coat may be hung and kept in shape; **coat'rack**, **coat'stand**, a rack or stand with pegs for hanging coats on.—adj. **coat'-style**, of a shirt, buttoning all the way down in front.—**coat of arms**, the family insignia embroidered on the surcoat worn over the hauberk, or coat of mail: the heraldic bearings of a gentleman; **coat of mail**, a piece of armour for the upper part of the body, made of metal scales or rings linked one with another.—**turn one's coat**, to change one's principles, or to turn from one party to another. [O.Fr. cote (Fr. cotte)—L.L. cottus, cotta, a tunic; the further etymology is uncertain.]

**coat**, **coate**, Shakespearian forms of quote.

**coati**, kō-ä'tē or -ti, or kə-wä'tē, n. an American plantigrade carnivorous mammal allied to the raccoons.—Also **coäti-mun'di**, **-mon'di**. [Tupí.]

**coax**, kōks, v.t. to persuade by fondling or flattery: to humour or soothe: to pet.—ns. **coax**, **coax'er**, one who coaxes.—adv. **coax'ingly**. [cokes.]

**coaxial**, kō-ak'si-əl, adj. having the same axis.—

*adv.* **coax'ially.**—coaxial cable, a cable consisting of one or more **coaxial pairs,** each a central conductor within an outer tubular conductor.

**cob, kob,** *n.* a big or notable man (*dial.*): a shortlegged strong horse: a male swan (also **cob'-swan**): a lump (esp. of **coal, ore, clay**): a rounded object: a herring's head (*obs.*): a **cobloaf:** the axis of a head of maize, a corncob: a **cobnut:** an irregularly-shaped Spanish-American dollar (*hist.*).—*adj.* **cobb'y,** iike a cob: stout, brisk, lively, arrogant (*dial.*).—*ns.* **cob'-loaf,** a rounded, round-headed, or misshapen loaf: an expression of contempt (*Shak.*); **cob'-nut,** a large hazelnut: a game played by children with nuts; **cob'-pipe,** a tobacco pipe made from a corncob. [Perh. conn. with **cop** (1).]

**cob, kob,** *n.* a kind of composition of clay and straw for building.—*n.* **cob'-wall.** [Origin unknown.]

**cob, kob,** (*dial.*) *n.* a wicker basket used by sowers. [Origin unknown.]

**cob, kob,** *v.t.* to strike: to thump on the buttocks.

**cobalt, kō'bölt,** *n.* a metallic element, of atomic number 27: a blue pigment prepared from it—also **cō'balt-blue'.**—*adj.* of this deep-blue colour.—**cobalt-60,** a radioactive isotope of cobalt used in the gamma-ray treatment of cancer.—*adjs.* **cobalt'ic; cobaltif'erous.**—*n.* **cō'baltite,** a sulpharsenide of cobalt (also **cobalt glance**).—**cobalt bloom,** erythrite; **cobalt bomb,** a suggested bomb consisting of a hydrogen bomb encased in cobalt—made more dangerous than ever by the cobalt-60 dust released. [Ger. *kobalt,* from *kobold,* a demon, a nickname given by the German miners, because they supposed it to be a mischievous and hurtful metal.]

**cobber, kob'ər,** (*Austr.*; *coll.*) *n.* mate, chum, buddy. [Origin unknown.]

**cobble, kob'l, cobblestone, -stōn,** *ns.* a rounded stone, esp. used in paving.—*v.t.* to pave with cobblestones. [Ety. dub.]

**cobble, kob'l,** *v.t.* to patch up or mend coarsely, as shoes.—*ns.* **cobb'ler,** one who cobbles or mends shoes: an iced drink made up of wine or spirits, sugar, lemon, etc.; **cobb'lery, cobb'ling; cobbler's punch,** a hot drink made of beer, with the addition of spirit, sugar, and spice. [Der. unknown.]

**Cobdenism, kob'dən-izm,** *n.* the policy of Richard *Cobden* (1804-1865), the English 'Apostle of Free Trade'.—*n.* **Cob'denite,** a supporter of Cobdenism, esp. a free-trader.

**co-belligerent, kō-bi-lij'ə-rent,** *adj.* co-operating in warfare.—Also *n.*

**cobia, kō'bi-a,** *n.* the sergeant-fish. [Perh. of West Indian origin.]

**coble, cobble, kōb'l, kob'l,** (*Scot.*) *n.* a small flatbottomed boat. [Cf. W. *ceubal,* a hollow trunk, a boat.]

**Cobol, kō'bōl, -bol,** *n.* a computer programming language, for commercial use, which uses English words. [Common *business oriented language.*]

**cobra, cobra de capello, kō'bra, kob'ra, di ka-pel'ō,** *n.* a poisonous snake, found in India and Africa, which dilates its neck so as to resemble a hood.—*adjs.* **cob'ric; cob'riform,** like or akin to the cobra. [Port., snake of the hood.]

**coburg, kō'bûrg,** *n.* a thin fabric of worsted with cotton or silk, twilled on one side. [*Coburg,* in Germany.]

**cobweb, kob'web,** *n.* a spider's web or net: any snare or device intended to entrap: anything flimsy or easily broken: anything that obscures.—Also *v.t.*—*n.* **cobwebb'ery.**—*adj.* **cob'webby.** [Prob. *attercop-web;* see **attercop, web.**]

**coca, kō'ka,** *n.* a Peruvian shrub (*Erythroxylon coca*) of a family akin to flax, whose leaves furnish an important narcotic and stimulant.—*ns.* **cocaine (ko-kān', kō'kä-in, kō'kä-in),** an alkaloid obtained from coca-leaves, used as a local anaesthetic and as an intoxicant; **cocain-**

**isā'tion, -z-.**—*v.t.* **cōcain'ise, -ize.**—*ns.* **cōcain'ism,** a morbid condition induced by addiction to cocaine; **cocain'ist.** [Sp.—Quechua *coca.*]

**Coca-Cola, kō'ka-kō'la,** *n.* a carbonated soft drink. [Registered trademark.]

**Cocagne, Cocaigne.** Same as **Cockaigne.**

**coccineous, kok-sin'i-əs,** (*obs.*) *adj.* bright red. [L. *coccineus—coccum,* cochineal.]

**cocco, kok'ō, coco, kō'kō,** *n.* the taro or other edible araceous tuber.

**coccolite, kok'ō-līt,** *n.* a variety of pyroxene: a small rounded body found in deep-sea ooze (also **cocc'olith**). [Gr. *kokkos,* a berry, *lithos,* a stone.]

**coccus, kok'əs,** *n.* a one-seeded portion of a dry fruit that breaks up (*bot.*): a spherical bacterium: (*cap.*) a genus of insects in the Hemiptera, type of a family **Coccidea (kok'si-dē):**—*pl.* **cocci (kok'sī).**—*n.* **coccid (kok'sid),** any of the Coccidae.—Also *adj.*—*ns.* **coccidium (kok'sid-i-əm),** a protozoan parasite of the order **Coccidea (kok'sid-ē); coccidiosis (kok-sid-i-ōs'is)** a contagious infection of birds and animals by coccidae; **coccidiostat (kok-sid'i-ō-stat),** an agent which builds up a resistance by the host to coccidae by retarding the latter's life cycle, etc.—*adj.* **cocc'oid.**—*n.* **Cocc'ūlus,** a tropical genus of climbing plants (*Menispermaceae*).—**cocculus indicus,** the dried fruit of *Anamirta Cocculus* (same family), narcotic and poisonous. [L.,—Gr. *kokkos,* a berry.]

**coccyx, kok'siks** (*anat.*) *n.* the terminal triangular bone of the vertebral column:—*pl.* **coccyges (kok-si'jēz).**—*adjs.* **coccygeal (kok-sij'i-əl), coccyg'ian.** [Gr. *kokkyx, -ȳgos,* cuckoo, coccyx (as resembling its bill).]

**coch, kōch,** (*Spens.*) *n.* Same as **coach.**

**Cochin, koch'in, Cochin-China, -chi'na,** *n.* a large feathery-legged domestic hen, originally from Cochin-China.

**cochineal, koch'i-nēl, -nēl',** *n.* a scarlet dye-stuff consisting of the dried bodies of a Coccus insect gathered from a cactus in Mexico, the West Indies, etc.: the insect itself. [Sp. *cochinilla,* dim. of L. *coccinus,* scarlet—*coccum* (Gr. *kokkos*), a berry, as the similar kermes insect was formerly supposed to be the berry or seed of an oak.]

**cochlea, kok'li-a,** *n.* anything spiral-shaped, esp. a snail-shell, a medick-pod, a winding stair: the spiral cavity of the ear (*anat.*).—*adj.* **coch'lear (-li-ər),** pertaining to the cochlea of the ear: spoon-shaped.—*ns.* **coch'lear, cochleār'e** (L.), a spoon.—*n.pl.* **Cochleār'ia,** the scurvy-grass genus.—*adjs.* **cochlear'iform,** spoon-shaped; **coch'leāte, coch'leated,** twisted spirally: spoonlike. [L. *coc(h)lea,* a shell, screw, and *coc(h)-le(ear),* a spoon—Gr. *kochlias,* a snail.]

**cock, kok,** *n.* a male bird, esp. of the domestic fowl (often compounded, as **cock'bird, cock-rob'in, cock-sparr'ow**): the time of cock-crowing (*obs.*): a weathercock: a plucky chap, a term of familiarity: a strutting chief or leader: anything set erect: a tap: part of the lock of a gun, held back by a spring, which, when released by the trigger, produces the discharge: upward turn or upturned part, as of a hat-brim: penis (*low coll.*).—*v.t.* to set erect or upright: to set up the brim of: to draw back, as the cock of a gun: to turn up or to one side: to tilt up knowingly, inquiringly, or scornfully.—*v.i.* to strut: to swagger.—*adj.* **cocked,** set erect: turned up or to one side.—*ns.* **cock'er,** one who follows cock-fighting: a small spaniel employed in pheasant and woodcock shooting; **cock'erel,** a young cock: a young man—also **cock'le,** whence **cock'le-brained,** foolish; **cocks'iness, cox'iness.**—*adj.* **cocks'y, cox'y,** self-important, bumptious; **cock'y,** pert.—**cock-a-dood'le (-doo'),** the crow of a cock.—*v.t.* to crow.—*adj.* **cock-a-hoop',** in exultant spirits.—**cockalō'rum,** a bumptious little person: a boy's jumping game.—*adj.* **cock'-and-**

bull', rambling and incredible.—cock'-broth, the broth made from a boiled cock; cock'chafer, a large greyish brown beetle (*Melolontha vulgaris*), most destructive to vegetation; cock'crow, -ing, early morning, when cocks crow; cocked hat, an old-fashioned three-cornered hat; cocker spaniel, a cocker; cock'eye, a squinting eye: the loop by which a trace is attached to the whippletree.—*adj.* cock'eyed, having a cockeye: off the straight, awry (*coll.*): tipsy (*coll.*).—cock'fight, -ing, a fight or contest between game-cocks: a fight; cockhorse', a child's imaginary or toy horse: a trace-horse for a coach: a spirited animal.—*adj.* prancing, proud.—*adv.* properly a-cockhorse (*i.e.* on cockhorse) on horseback: exultingly.—cockieleek'ie, cockyleek'y, cockaleek'ie (*Scot.*), soup made from a fowl and leeks; cock'laird (*Scot.*), a yeoman; cock'loft, a room just under the roof; cockmatch, a cockfight; cock-of-the-rock', a South American bird of the cotinga family; cock'-pad(d)'le, -paid'le (see paddle 2); cock'pit, a pit or enclosed space where game-cocks fought: a frequent battleground: part of a ship-of-war's lower regions used for the wounded in action: a sheltered depression in the deck of a yacht or small ship: in aircraft, a compartment in the fuselage for pilot or passenger: the driver's seat in a racing car; cock's'-comb, cocks'comb, the comb or crest on a cock's head: a jester's cap: a head (*Shak.*): a crest-like crystalline mineral aggregate (as in *cocks-comb pyrites*): a name for various plants, esp. a monstrous Celosia (fam. Amarantaceae) with fasciated inflorescence like a cock's comb, also yellow-rattle (Rhinanthus), and sainfoin: a cox-comb; cocks'foot, a genus (Dactylis) of grasses with inflorescences like a cock's foot; cock'-shoot (*obs.*), a glade where woodcock were netted as they shot through; cock'shot, a shy at a mark; cock'shut (*Shak.*), twilight, probably referring to the time when poultry are shut up, or when woodcock shoot: cock'shy, a throw at a thing, originally a cock, as for amusement: the object set up, or a showman's outfit for the purpose; cock'spur, spur on the leg of a cock.—*adj.* cock'-sure, quite sure, esp. offensively.—cock'tail, racing horse that is not thoroughbred: one who apes the gentleman: a concoction of spirituous or other liquors, used as an appetiser: a non-alcoholic appetiser consisting e.g. of sea-food with a sauce.—Also *adj.*—cocktail bar, a superior kind of bar, e.g. in a hotel; cocktail dress, one for semi-formal wear.—*adjs.* cock'tailed, having the tail cocked or tilted up; cock-thropp'led, -thrapp'led, of a horse, bending the windpipe on bridling.—cock'-throw'ing, the old sport of throwing sticks at a cock.—*adjs.* cock'-up, turned up: rising above the tops of the other letters, superior (*print.*).—cockyolly (*kok-i-ol'i*), a nursery or pet name for a bird.—cock a snook (see snook); cock of the walk, chief of a set; knock into a cocked hat, to give a profound beating. [O.E. *coc*; O.N. *kokkr.*]

cock, *kok, n.* a small pile of hay, dung, etc.—*adj.* cocked, heaped up in cocks. [Cf. O.N. *kökkr*, a lump.]

cock, *kok*, (*Shak.*) *n.* a cockboat.—*ns.* cock'boat, a ship's small boat: a small frail boat; cock-swain (see coxwain). [Cf. cog (3).]

cock, corr. of god.—cock and pie (see pie (2)).

cock-a-bondy, *kok'ə-bon'di* (coll. *kok'i-bun'di*), *n.* a fly for angling. [Welsh *coch a bon ddu*, red, with black stem.]

cockade, *kok-ād', n.* a rosette worn on the hat as a badge. [Fr. *cocarde*—*coq*, cock.]

Cockaigne, Cockayne, *kok-ān', n.* an imaginary country of luxury and delight. [Ety. dub.; Fr. *cocagne*, acc. to some from L. *coquère*, to cook.]

cockalorum. See cock (1).

cockatoo, *kok-ə-tōō', n.* a large crested parrot of

the Australian region: a small farmer; also cock'y (*Austr.*).—*n.* cockatiel, cockateel (-*tēl'*), a small crested parrot of Australia.—cow cocky (*Austr.*), a dairy farmer. [Malay, *kakatua.*]

cockatrice, *kok'ə-tris, -tris, n.* a fabulous monster like a serpent, often confounded with the basilisk: a cock-like monster with a dragon's tail (*her.*): a prostitute (*obs.*). [O.Fr. *cocatris.*]

cockboat. See cock (3).

cockchafer. See cock (1).

cocker, *kok'ər, v.t.* to pamper: to fondle: to indulge. [Ety. dub.; cf. Du. *kokelen*, O.Fr. *coqueliner*, to dandle.]

Cocker, *kok'ər, n.* a standard of accuracy and orthodoxy. [From Edward *Cocker* (1631-75) author of a popular arithmetic book.]

cocker, cockerel. See cock (1).

cockernony, *kok-ər-non'i*, (*obs. Scot.*) *n.* the gathering of hair in a fillet: a coiffure: a pad of false hair: a starched cap. [Origin obscure.]

cocket, *kok'it, n.* the custom-house seal (*hist.*): a custom-house certificate. [Origin doubtful.]

cock-eye(d), cockhorse. See cock (1).

cockle, *kok'l, n.* a cornfield weed, esp. now the corncockle.—*n.* cock'le-bur, clotbur (*Xanthium*). [O.E. *coccel.*]

cockle, *kok'l, n.* a large bivalve mollusc (*Cardium edule* or other species) with thick, ribbed, heart-shaped, equal-valved shell: its shell: a bivalve shell generally.—*adj.* cock'led, shelled like a cockle.—*ns.* cock'le-hat, a hat bearing a scallop-shell, the badge of a pilgrim; cock'leshell, the shell of a cockle: a frail boat.—cockles of the heart, the heart itself. [Fr. *coquille*—Gr. *konchylion*—*konchē*, a cockle.]

cockle, *kok'l, n.* a pucker.—*v.i.* to pucker.—*v.t.* to cause to pucker. [Perh. Fr. *coquiller*, to blister—*coquille*; see cockle (2).]

cockle, *kok'l, n.* a furnace or stove. [Perh. Du. *kachel.*]

cockle-brained. See cock (1).

cockney, *kok'ni, n.* an egg, esp. a small misshapen egg (*obs.* or *dial.*): a coddled child (*obs.*): a milksop (*Shak.*): one whose experience and knowledge are exclusively townish: (still in *U.S.*) a townsman: (often *cap.*) one born in London, strictly, within hearing of Bow Bells: London dialect.—*adj.* characteristic of a Cockney.—*ns.* cock'neydom, the domain of Cockneys; cock'neyficā'tion.—*v.t.* cock'neyfy, to make Cockney.—*adj.* cock'neyish.—*n.* cock'neyism, a Cockney idiom or characteristic.—the Cockney School, an old nickname for a supposed school of writers belonging to London—Leigh Hunt, Keats and others. [M.E. *coken-ey*, cock's egg. Others would connect with Fr. *coquin*, a rogue—L. *coquus*, a cook.]

cockroach, *kok'rōch, n.* an orthopterous insect, the so-called black beetle. [Sp. *cucaracha*, woodlouse, cockroach.]

cockscomb, cocksfoot, cockshoot, cockshy, cock-tail, etc., See cock (1).

cocky. See cock (1), cockatoo.

coco, *kō'kō, n.* a tropical seaside palm-tree (*Cocos nucifera*), with curving stem (also co'co-palm, co'conut-palm, co'co-tree), producing the coco-nut.—co'co-de-mer (-*də-mer'*; Fr.), the double coconut; co'conut; co'conut, (less correctly) co'coanut, co'kernut, a large edible nut, yielding co'conut-butt'er or co'conut-oil', and co'conut-milk'; co'conut-matt'ing, matting made from the husk of the coconut; co'conut-shy, a cockshy with coconuts as targets or as prizes; double coconut, the large two-lobed nut of the Seychelles palm, Lodoicea Sechellarum. [Port. and Sp. *coco*, a bugbear; applied to the nut from the three marks at the end of it, which form a grotesque face.]

cocoa, *kō'kō, n.* the seed of the cacao or chocolate tree: a powder made from the seeds: a drink made from the powder.—co'coa-beans', the seeds, esp. when dried and fermented; **co'coabutt'er**, **co'coa-fat'**, a fat got from the seeds (different from *coconut* butter); **co'coa-nibs**, cocoa-beans shelled and bruised. [cacao.]

**coconscious**, *kō-kon'shəs*, *adj.* conscious in a subsidiary stream, apart from the main stream.—*n.* **cocon'sciousness**.

**cocoon**, *ko-kōōn'*, *n.* the silken sheath spun by many insect larvae in passing into the pupa stage and by spiders for their eggs: the capsule in which earthworms and leeches lay their eggs: a preservative covering for military and other equipment.—*n.* **cocoon'ery**, a place for keeping silkworms when feeding and spinning cocoons. [Fr. *cocon*, from *coque*, a shell—L. *concha*, a shell.]

**cocoplum**, *kō'kō-plum*, *n.* a West Indian rosaceous tree (*Chrysobalanus icaco*): its edible fruit. [Sp. *icaco*, and **plum**.]

**cocotte**, *ko-kot'*, *n.* a light-o'-love: a loose woman: a small fireproof dish, usu. for an individual portion. [Fr.]

**coco-wood**, **cocoa-wood**, *kō'kō-wŏŏd*, *n.* the wood of a West Indian mimosaceous tree, *Inga vera*: kokra-wood.

**coction**, *kok'shən*, *n.* boiling: cooking.—*adj.* **coc'tile**, baked: hardened by fire, as a brick. [L. *coquĕre*, *coctum*, to boil, cook.]

**cocus-wood**, *kō'kəs-wŏŏd*, *n.* the so-called Jamaica ebony (*Brya ebenus*; Papilionaceae): a tradename for kokra-wood.

**cod**, *kod*, **codfish**, *kod'fish*, *n.* a food fish (*Gadus morrhua*) of northern seas.—*ns.* **cod'-fisher**; **cod'-fish'ery**; **cod'-fishing**; **cod'ling**, small cod. —**cod'-liver oil**, a medicinal oil extracted from the fresh liver of the common cod. [Ety. dub.]

**cod**, *kod*, (*obs.*) *n.* a bag: a pod: the scrotum.— *adjs.* **codd'ed**, enclosed in a cod; **codd'ing** (*Shak.*), lecherous.—**cod'-piece**, a baggy appendage once worn in front of tight hose. [O.E. *codd*, a small bag; cf. next.]

**cod**, *kod*, (*Scot.*) *n.* a pillow or cushion. [O.N. *koddi*, a pillow; cf. foregoing.]

**cod**, *kod*, (*slang*) *n.* a fellow: a codger: a Charterhouse pensioner: a jest: a hoax.—*v.t.* to hoax: to poke fun at. [Ety. dub.]

**coda**, *kō'da*, (*mus.*) *n.* a passage forming the completion of a piece, rounding it off to a satisfactory conclusion. [It.,—L. *cauda*, a tail.]

**coddle**, *kod'l*, *v.t.* to pamper: to fondle: to parboil.—*n.* an effeminate person. [Ety. dub.]

**code**, *kōd*, *n.* a collection or digest of laws: a system of rules and regulations (*specif.* regarding education): established principles or standards (of art, moral conduct, etc.): a volume: a system of signals: a system of words, letters, or symbols which represent sentences or other words, to ensure economy or secrecy in transmission: a cipher.—*v.t.* to codify: to express in code.—*ns.* **codificā'tion** (*kod-*, *kōd-*); **codifier** (*kod'*, *kōd'*), **cōd'ist**, one who codifies.—*v.t.* **codify** (*kod'*, *kōd'*), to put into the form of a code: to digest: to systematise:—*pr.p.* **cod'ifying**; *pa.t.* and *pa.p.* **cod'ified**. [Fr. *code*; see codex.]

**codeine**, *kō'dēn*, *-di-in*, *n.* an alkaloid, obtained from opium, used as an analgesic and sedative. [Gr. *kōdeia*, poppy-head.]

**codex**, *kō'deks*, *n.* a code: a manuscript volume: —*pl.* **codices** (*kōd'i-sēz*). [L. *cōdex* or *caudex*, *-icis*, the trunk of a tree, a set of tablets, a book.]

**codger**, *koj'ər*, *n.* a mean fellow: an old person: a chap. [Prob. a variant of **cadger**.]

**codicil**, *kod'i-sil*, *n.* a supplement to a will.—*adj.* **codicill'ary**. [L. *cōdicillus*, dim. of *cōdex*.]

**codilla**, *kō-dil'ə*, *n.* the coarsest part of hemp or flax. [Dim. of It. *coda*—L. *cauda*, a tail.]

**codille**, *kō-dil'*, *n.* a situation in ombre when the challenger loses. [Fr.]

**codling**, *kod'ling*, **codlin**, *kod'lin*, *n.* an elongated apple.—**cod'lin-moth**, the moth whose larvae

cause 'worm-eaten' apples to fall prematurely. [Ety. dub.]

**codling.** See cod (1).

**codon**, *kō'don*, *n.* a triplet of bases in the DNA of the chromosomes which determines the genetic code. [code.]

**cod's(-)wallop**, **codswallop**, *kodz'wol-əp*, *n.* nonsense put forward as if serious idea or information.

**coeducation**, *kō-ed-ū-kā'shən*, *n.* education of the sexes together.—*n.* **co'ed**, a girl or woman educated at a coeducational institution.—*adjs.* **co'ed**; **coeducā'tional**.

**coefficient**, *kō-if-ish'ənt*, *n.* that which acts together with another thing: a numerical or literal expression for a factor of a quantity in an algebraic term (*math.*): a numerical constant used as a multiplier to a variable quantity, in calculating the magnitude of a physical property (*phys.*).

**coehorn**, **cohorn**, *kō'hörn*, *n.* a small mortar for throwing grenades. [Baron van *Coehoorn* (1641-1704).]

**coelacanth**, *sē'lə-kanth*, *n.* any of a group of cross-opterygian fishes of very great antiquity. [From Gr. *koilos*, hollow, *akantha*, spine.]

**coelanaglyphic**, *sēl-an-ə-glif'ik*, *adj.* in cavorilievo. [Gr. *koilos*, hollow, *ana*, up, *glyphein*, carve.]

**Coelenterata**, *sə-len-tər-ā'tə*, *sē-*, *n.pl.* a phylum of many-celled animals, radially symmetrical, with a single body-cavity, the enteron—Hydrozoa, Scyphozoa, Anthozoa, Ctenophora.—*adj.* and *n.* **coelen'terate**. [Gr. *koilos*, hollow, *enteron*, intestine.]

**coeliac**, **celiac**, *sē'li-ak*, *adj.* relating to the belly. [Gr. *koiliakos—koiliā*, the belly.]

**coelom(e)**, *sē'lōm*, *-lom*, *n.* the body-cavity, or space between the intestines and the body-wall in animals above the Coelenterates.—*n.pl.* **Coelō'mata**, animals possessing a coelom.—*adj.* **coe'lomate**, having a coelom.—*n.* a coelomate animal.—*adjs.* **coelomat'ic**, **coelom'ic**. [Gr. *koilōma*, *-atos*, a cavity.]

**coelostat**, *sē'lō-stat*, *n.* a clock-driven mirror on an axis parallel to the earth's, so as to reflect continuously the same region of the sky. [L. *caelum* (misspelt *coelum*), sky, Gr. *statos*, fixed.]

**coemption**, *kō-emp'shən*, *n.* the buying up of the whole of a commodity: a mode of marriage under the fiction of a mutual sale (*Roman law*). [L. *coemptiō*, *-ōnis*—*emĕre*, to buy.]

**coenaesthesis**, **cenesthesis**, *sē-nēs-thē'sis*, *n.* the general bodily consciousness. [Gr. *koinos*, common, *aisthēsis*, perception.]

**coenenchyma**, *sē-neng'ki-mə*, (*bot.*) *n.* gelatinous material uniting the polyps of an anthozoan colony. [Gr. *koinos*, common, *enchyma*, infusion.]

**coenobite**, **cenobite**, *sēn'o-bit*, *n.* a monk who lives in a community.—*adjs.* **coenobitic** (*-bit'ik*), **-al.**— *ns.* **coen'obitism**; **coenō'bium**, a religious community: a colony of unicellular organisms (*biol.*): —*pl.* **-bia**. [Gr. *koinóbion—koinos*, common, *bios*, life.]

**coenosarc**, *sēn'ō-särk*, *n.* the common tissue uniting the polyps of a coral or the like. [Gr. *koinos*, common, *sarx*, flesh.]

**coenzyme**, *kō-en'zīm*, *n.* the non-protein part of an enzyme system, which is unaffected by heat.

**coequal**, *kō-ē'kwəl*, *adj.* equal with another of the same rank or dignity.—*n.* one of the same rank. —*n.* **coequality** (*-kwol'*).—*adv.* **coē'qually**.

**coerce**, *kō-ûrs'*, *v.t.* to restrain by force: to compel.—*adj.* **coer'cible**.—*adv.* **coer'cibly**.—*ns.* **coer'cion**, restraint: government by force; **coer'cionist**.—*adj.* **coer'cive**, having power to coerce: compelling: tending to, or intended to coerce. —*adv.* **coer'cively**.—*n.* **coer'civeness**. [L. *coercēre* —*arcēre*, to shut in.]

*fāte, fär; mē, hûr* (her); *mīne; mōte, för; mūte; mōōn, fŏŏt; dhen* (then)

**co-essential,** *kō-es-en'shəl, adj.* partaking of the same essence.—*n.* **co-essentiality** (*-shi-al'i-ti*).

**coetaneous,** *kō-i-tā'ni-əs, adj.* of the same age: contemporary. [L. *aetās, aetātis,* age.]

**co-eternal,** *kō-i-tûr'nəl, adj.* alike eternal with another.—*adv.* **co-eter'nally.**—*n.* **co-eter'nity.**

**coeval,** *kō-ē'vəl, adj.* of the same age.—*n.* one of the same age: a contemporary. [L. *coaevus—aevum,* age.]

**co-exist,** *kō-egz-ist', v.i.* to exist at the same time or together.—*n.* **co-exist'ence.**—*adj.* **co-exist'ent.** —peaceful co-existence, a living side by side in mutual toleration.

**co-extend,** *kō-eks-tend', v.i.* to extend equally.—*n.* **co-exten'sion.**—*adj.* **co-exten'sive.**

**coff,** *kof,* (*Scot.*) *v.t.* to buy. [A new present formed from coft, *pa.t.* and *pa.p.* originally of **cope**—M.Du. *copen, cofte,* (*ghe*)*coft* (Mod. Du. *koopen, kocht, gekocht*) to buy.]

**coffee,** *kof'i, n.* a powder made by roasting and grinding the seeds of a tree (*Coffea arabica, robusta,* etc.) of the madder family: a drink made from the powder.—**coff'ee-bean,** the seed of the coffee-tree; **coff'ee-berr'y,** the fruit or the seed of the coffee-tree; **coff'ee-bug,** a coccus destructive to the coffee-tree; **coff'ee-cup,** a cup for coffee; **coff'ee-disease',** a leaf-disease of coffee caused by a rust-fungus, *Hemileia vastatrix*; **coff'ee-house,** a house where coffee and other refreshments are sold; **coff'ee-mill,** a machine for grinding coffee-beans; **coff'ee-pot,** a pot in which coffee is prepared and served; **coff'ee-room,** a room in a hotel where coffee and other refreshments are served: a public room; **coff'ee-stall,** a movable street stall for coffee and other refreshments; **coff'ee-table,** a small, low table.—Also *adj.*—**coff'ee-tree;** white, black coffee, coffee respectively with and without milk. [Turk. *kahveh*—Ar. *qahwah,* orig. meaning wine.]

**coffer,** *kof'ər, n.* a chest for holding money or treasure: a deep panel in a ceiling.—*v.t.* to hoard up.—*adj.* **coff'ered.**—**coff'er-dam,** a water-tight structure allowing under-water foundations to be built dry; **coff'er-fish,** a fish (*Ostracion*) enclosed in a box of bony scales. [O.Fr. *cofre,* a chest—L. *cophinus,* a basket—Gr. *kophinos,* a basket.]

**coffin,** *kof'in, n.* a pie-crust (*obs.*): a chest for a dead body: a thick-walled container, usu. of lead, for transporting radioactive materials.—*v.t.* to place in a coffin.—**coff'in-bone,** a bone enclosed in a horse's hoof; **coff'in-ship,** a dangerously unsound ship.—**drive a nail in one's coffin,** to do something tending to hasten death or ruin. [O.Fr. *cofin*—L. *cophinus*—Gr. *kophinos,* a basket.]

**coffinite,** *kof'in-it, n.* a uranium-yielding ore. [From Reuben Clare *Coffin,* a worker of the ore in Colorado.]

**coffle,** *kof'l, n.* a gang, esp. of slaves. [Ar. *qāfilah,* a caravan.]

**coffret,** *kof'rət, n.* a small coffer: a small presentation box. [Fr., dim. of *coffre,* coffer.]

**cog,** *kog, v.t.* to cheat or deceive: to wheedle: to manipulate (dice) so that they may fall in a given way.—*n.* the act of cheating: deception.—*n.* **cogg'er.** [Thieves' slang.]

**cog,** *kog, n.* a catch or tooth as on a wheel.—*v.t.* to furnish with cogs: to stop (a wheel) by putting a block before it:—*pr.p.* **cogg'ing;** *pa.t.* and *pa.p.* **cogged.**—**cog'-wheel,** a toothed wheel. [M.E. *cogge;* ety. dub.; cf. Sw. *kugge.*]

**cog,** *kog, n.* formerly a large ship of burden or for war: a small boat: a cock-boat. [M.E. *cogge,* perh. from O.Fr. *cogue,* a ship, or O.N. *kuggr,* a merchant ship.]

**cogent,** *kō'jənt, adj.* powerful: convincing.—*ns.* **cō'gence, cō'gency,** convincing power.—*adv.* **cō'gently.** [L. *cōgens, -entis,* pr.p. of *cōgere, co-, agere,* to drive.]

**coggie, cogie,** *kog'i, kōg'i,* (*Scot.*) *n.* a small wooden bowl.—Also cog. [Dim. of cogue.]

**coggle,** *kog'l, v.i.* to be unsteady.—*n.* a cobble-stone.—*adv.* **cogg'ly** (*Scot.*), shaky. [Origin doubtful.]

**cogitate,** *koj'i-tāt, v.i.* to turn a thing over in one's mind: to meditate: to ponder.—*adj.* **cog'itable,** capable of being thought.—*n.* **cogitā'tion,** deep thought: meditation.—*adj.* **cog'itātive,** having the power of thinking: given to cogitating. [L. *cōgitāre, -ātum,* to think deeply, *co-, agitāre,* to put in motion.]

**Cognac,** *kon'yak, n.* a French brandy made near Cognac, in Charente.

**cognate,** *kog'nāt, adj.* of the same family, kind, or nature: derived from the same ancestor, root, or other original: related or allied.—*n.* one related by blood, a kinsman (whether agnate or not) (*Roman law* and *gener.*): often, any kinsman on either side other than an agnate: a relative on one's mother's side (*Scots law*).—*n.* **cognā'tion.** —**cognate object,** a word akin in origin or meaning to a normally intransitive verb, and used as its object. [L. *cognātus—co-,* (*g*)*nāscī,* to be born.]

**cognition,** *kog-nish'ən, n.* a knowledge: apprehension: knowing, in the widest sense, including sensation, perception, etc., distinguished from emotion and conation (*psychol.*).—*adj.* **cognisable, -izable** (*kog'niz-ə-bl;* also *kon'iz-*), that may be known or understood: that may be judicially investigated.—*adv.* **cog'nisably.**—*ns.* **cog'nisance, -zance** (or *kon'iz-*), knowledge or notice, judicial or private: observation: jurisdiction: that by which one is known, a badge.— *adj.* **cog'nisant** (or *kon'iz-*), having cognisance or knowledge of.—*v.t.* **cognise', -ize',** to become conscious of.—*adj.* **cog'nitive,** capable of, or pertaining to, cognition.—*n.* **cognitiv'ity.** [L. *cognitiō, -ōnis—cognōscēre, cognitum—co-,* (*g*)*nōscēre,* to know.]

**cognomen,** *kog-nō'mən, n.* a surname: a nickname: a name: the last of the three names of a Roman, indicating the house or family to which he belonged.—*adj.* **cognominal** (*-nom'*), like-named: relating to a cognomen.—*v.t.* **cognom'-inate,** to name.—*n.* **cognominā'tion.** [L. *cognōmen, -inis—co-,* (*g*)*nōmen,* a name.]

**cognosce,** *kog-nos', (*Scots law*) v.t.* to examine: to give judgment upon: to declare to be an idiot.— *adj.* **cognosc'ible.** [L. *cognōscēre—co-,* inten., (*g*)*nōscēre,* to know.]

**cognoscente,** *kon-nyō-shent'ā, n.* one professing a critical knowledge of works of art, music, literature, etc.: a connoisseur:—*pl.* **cognoscenti** (*-ē*). [It. (mod. *conoscente*)—L. *cognōscēre,* to know.]

**cognovit,** *kog-nō'vit, (law) n.* an acknowledgment by a defendant that the plaintiff's cause is just. [L. *cognōvit actiōnem,* (he) has confessed the action.]

**cogue, cog,** *kōg, kog,* (esp. *Scot.*) *n.* a round wooden vessel, usu. of staves and hoops. [Ety. dub.]

**cohabit,** *kō-hab'it, v.i.* to dwell together as husband and wife, or as if husband and wife.—*ns.* **cohab'-itant,** one dwelling with others; **cohabitā'tion.** [L. *cohabitāre—co-, habitāre,* to dwell.]

**co-heir,** *kō-ār', n.* a joint heir:—*fem.* **co-heir'ess.** —*n.* **coheritor** (*kō-her'it-ər*), a co-heir.

**cohere,** *kō-hēr', v.i.* to stick together: to be consistent.—*ns.* **coher'ence,** a sticking together: consistency; **coher'ency.**—*adj.* **coher'ent,** sticking together: connected: consistent in thought or speech: (of a system of units) such that one unit multiplied or divided by another gives a third unit in the system exactly: (of beam of radiation) showing definite, not random, relationships between points in a cross-section.—*adv.* **coher'ently.**—*n.* **coher'er,** an apparatus for detection

# cohibit

254        cold

of electric waves by reduced resistance of imperfect contact, as if by cohesion.—*adj.* **cohēsible** (*-hēz'*), capable of cohesion.—*n.* **cohē'sion** (*-zhən*), the act of sticking together: a form of attraction by which particles of bodies stick together: concrescence of like parts (*bot.*): logical connection.—*adj.* **cohē'sive**, having the power of cohering: tending to unite into a mass. —*adv.* **cohē'sively.**—*ns.* **cohē'siveness, cohesibil'ity.** [L. *cohaerēre, -haesum—co-, haerēre,* stick.

**cohibit,** *kō-hib'it, v.t.* to restrain.—*n.* **cohibition** (*-ish'ən*).—*adj.* **cohib'itive.** [L. *cohibēre—co-, habēre,* to have, hold.]

**coho, cohoe,** *kō'hō, n.* a Pacific salmon, a species of *Oncorhynchus.*

**cohog.** Same as **quahog.**

**cohort,** *kō'hört, n.* a tenth part of a Roman legion: any band of warriors: (esp formerly) a division of plants between a class and an order: in the classification of higher animals, one of the divisions between subclass and order: a group of individuals: (*popularly*) a companion or follower. [L. *cohors, -tis,* an enclosed place, a multitude enclosed, a company of soldiers.]

**cohortative.** *kō-hör'tə-tiv, adj.* encouraging.—*n.* (*Heb. gram.*) lengthened form of the imperfect. [L. *cohortāri, -ātus—co-,* inten., *hortāri,* exhort.

**cohune,** *kō-hōōn', n.* a Central and South American palm (*Attalea cohune*) yielding **cohune nuts** and **cohune oil.**

**coif,** *koif, n.* a covering for the head, esp. the close-fitting cap of white lawn or silk originally worn by serjeants-at-law: a covering for the head worn by women.—*v.t.* to provide with a coif: to dress (the hair).—*ns.* **coiff'eur** (*kwu-fœr'*), a hairdresser: *fem.* **coiffeuse** (*-œz'*); **coiff'ure** (*kwu-für'*), style of hairdressing: a head-dress.—Also *v.t.* [Fr. *coiffe*—L.L. *cofia,* a cap.]

**coign, coigne, koin.** Same as **coin** (esp. first sense —after *Shak.*), **quoin.**—**coign(e) of vantage,** an advantageous salient corner: hence, a good position generally.

**coil,** *koil, v.t.* to wind in rings: to enclose in twists. —*v.i.* to wind.—*n.* a coiled object: one of the rings into which anything is coiled: a wire wound spirally to conduct electricity. [O.Fr. *coillir* (Fr. *cueillir*)—L. *colligēre—col-,* together, *legēre,* to gather; cf. **cull, collect.**]

**coil,** *koil, n.* tumult: hubbub: noise: fuss.— **mortal coil** (*Hamlet* III. i. 68), the toil and trouble of human life. [Der. unknown.]

**coin,** *koin, n.* a corner-stone, quoin, or coign (*Shak.*): a piece of metal legally stamped and current as money: money.—*v.t.* to convert into money: to stamp: to invent, fabricate: (*Shak.*) to gain money by means of.—*ns.* **coin'age,** the act of coining money: the currency: the pieces of metal coined: the invention, or fabrication, of something new: what is invented; **coin'er,** one who coins money: a maker of counterfeit coins: an inventor; **coin'ing,** minting: invention.— *adj.* **coin-op'erated, coin'-op',** of a machine, operated by inserting a coin in a slot.—**coin money,** to make money rapidly; **pay a man in his own coin,** to give tit for tat: to give as good as one got. [Fr. *coin,* a wedge (see **quoin**), also the die to stamp money—L. *cuneus,* a wedge.]

**coincide,** *kō-in-sid', v.i.* to occupy the same place or time: to agree: to correspond: to be identical. —*ns.* **coincidence** (*kō-in'si-dəns*), fact, event, or condition of coinciding: the occurrence of events simultaneously or consecutively in a striking manner but without any causal connection between them; **coin'cidency.**—*adjs.* **coin'cident, coincidental** (*-dent'l*).—*adv.* **coin'cidently.** [L. *co-, incidēre—in,* in, *cadēre,* to fall.]

**co-inhere,** *kō-in-hēr', v.i.* to inhere together.—*n.* **co-inhēr'ence.**

**co-inheritor,** *kō-in-her'it-ər, n.* a joint heir.—*n.* **co-inher'itance.**

**co-instantaneous,** *kō-in-stən-tā'ni-əs, adj.* exactly simultaneous.—*ns.* **co-instantaneity** (*-tə-nē'i-ti*), **-instantā'neousness.**—*adv.* **co-instantā'neously.**

**co-insurance,** *kō'in-shōō'rəns, n.* insurance jointly with another, esp. when the insurer bears part of the risk.

**Cointreau,** *kwē-trō, kwän' n.* an orange-flavoured liqueur. [Trademark.]

**coir, koir,** *n.* the strong fibre of coconut husk. [From Tamil or Malayalam.]

**coistrel, coistril,** *kois'tril, n.* a groom (*obs.*): a knave (*Shak.*). [See **custrel.**]

**coition,** *kō-ish'ən,* cō'itus, *ns.* sexual intercourse.— **coitus interruptus,** coitus intentionally interrupted by withdrawal before semen is ejaculated. [L. *coitiō, -ōnis—co-,* together, *īre, ītum,* to go.]

**cojoin,** *kō-join', (Shak.) v.t.* Same as **conjoin.**

**coke,** *kōk, n.* a form of fuel obtained by the heating of coal in confined space whereby its more volatile constituents are driven off: residue when any substance (e.g. petrol) is carbonised.—*v.t.* and *v.i.* to make into, or become, coke. [Ety. dub.; not before 17th century.]

**coke,** *kōk, n.* cocaine (*slang*): (properly with *cap.*) Coca-Cola.

**cokernut,** *kō'kər-nut, n.* a faulty form of coconut.

**cokes,** *kōks, (obs.) n.* a simpleton. [Ety. dub.]

**col, kol,** *n.* a depression or pass in a mountain-range (*geog.*): a region between two anticyclones giving a similar figure when represented in contour (*meteor.*). [Fr.,—L. *collum,* a neck.]

**col-.** See **con-.**

**cola, kola,** *kō'lə, n.* a genus of West African trees (*Cola acuminata, C. nitida*) producing nuts used in drugs and for flavouring soft drinks: a soft drink so flavoured. [African name.]

**colander, cullender,** *kul'ən-dər, n.* a perforated vessel used as a strainer in cookery.—*ns.* **colā'tion, col'ature,** straining.—*adj.* **cō'liform,** like a sieve. [L. *cōlāre,* to strain.]

**colatitude,** *kō-lat'i-tūd, n.* the complement of the latitude. [complement, latitude.]

**Colbertine,** *kol'bər-tin, n.* a kind of lace, so called from Jean Baptiste *Colbert* (1619-83), Minister of Finance to Louis XIV, a great patron of the arts.

**colcannon,** *kol-kan'ən, n.* an Irish dish, being a stew of pounded cabbage and potatoes with butter. [*cole,* cabbage; *cannon* unknown.]

**Colchicum,** *kol'ki-kəm, n.* a genus of *Liliaceae* including meadow saffron: its corm and seeds, used for gout and rheumatism and yielding **col'chicine** (*-chi-* or *-ki-sēn*), an alkaloid used to produce polyploidy, etc. [L.,—Gr. *kolchikon,* meadow saffron, neut. of *Kolchikos,* relating to *Kolchis,* the sorceress Medea's country.]

**colcothar,** *kol'kō-thär, n.* a dark-red iron peroxide formed by calcining iron sulphate: a reddish-brown colour. [Ar. *qolqotār.*]

**cold,** *kōld, adj.* giving or feeling a sensation that is felt to be the opposite of hot: chilly: low in temperature: without passion or zeal: spiritless: unfriendly: indifferent: reserved: suggesting cold rather than heat, as blue or grey (*paint.*): without application of heat; used of operations formerly requiring heat, e.g. **cold-casting**, **-forging, -moulding, -welding.**—*n.* a relative want of heat: the feeling or sensation caused by the absence of heat: coldness: a spell of cold weather: a disease caused by cold, a catarrhal inflammation of the mucous membrane of the respiratory organs, usually accompanied by hoarseness and coughing (**cold in the head,** coryza): catarrh: chillness.—*adj.* **cold'ish,** somewhat cold.—*adv.* **cold'ly.**—*n.* **cold'ness.**— *adj.* **cold'-blood'ed,** having body-temperature depending upon environment, as fishes: without feeling: hard-hearted—of persons or actions.— *adv.* **cold'-blood'edly.**—**cold'-blood'edness; cold'-chis'el,** a strong and finely-tempered chisel for cutting cold metal: a tool used with a heavy

*fāte, fär; mē, hûr* (her); *mīne; mōte, för; mūte, mōōn, fŏŏt; dhen* (then) hammer to cut or break stone, concrete, etc.; **cold'-cream'**, a creamy ointment orig. usu. of almond-oil, spermaceti, white wax, and rose-water, used as a cooling dressing for the skin.— *v.t.* (*coll.*) to apply cold-cream to.—*adj.* **cold'-drawn**, drawn through a die without heating: (of vegetable oil) subjected to pressure without heat.—**cold feet**, discouragement: fear; **cold'-frame'**, **cold'house**, a plant frame, greenhouse, without artificial heat; **cold front**, the surface of an advancing mass of cold air where it meets a retreating mass of warmer air; **cold harbour**, a wayside travellers' shelter.—*adj.* **cold'-heart'ed**, wanting feeling: indifferent.—**cold pack**, a wet pack prepared with cold water; **cold pig** (*coll.*), an application of cold water to rouse a sleeper; **cold rubber**, a hard-wearing synthetic rubber made at a temperature of 41°F.—*adj.* **cold'-short**, brittle when cold: of the temper (*fig.*).—*v.t.* **cold'-should'er**, to give the cold shoulder to.—**cold slaw**, cole-slaw; **cold snap**, a sudden spell of cold weather; **cold steel**, cutting or stabbing weapons, opp. to bullets; **cold storage**, storage and preservation of goods in refrigerating chambers: abeyance(*fig.*); **cold turkey**, the plain unvarnished truth: sudden withdrawal of narcotics: narcotics hangover; **cold war** (see **war**); **cold water**, water at its natural temperature in ordinary conditions; **cold wave** (*hairdressing*), an artificial wave produced by a chemical solution; **cold-without'**, brandy with cold water and no sugar.— **catch cold**, to contract a cold; **cold as charity**, a proverbial phrase expressing ironically great coldness or indifference; **give** (**show**) **the cold shoulder**, to show studied indifference: to give a rebuff; **in cold blood**, with deliberate intent, not under the influence of passion; **leave one cold**, to fail to impress; **leave out in the cold**, to neglect, ignore; **throw cold water on**, to discourage. [O.E. (Anglian) *cald* (W.S. *ceald*); Scot. *cauld*, Ger. *kalt*; cf. **cool**, O.N. *kala*, to freeze, L. *gelidus*—*gelū*, frost.]

**cole**, *kōl, n.* a general name for all sorts of cabbage. —**cole'-garth**, a cabbage garden; **cole'-seed**, the seed of rape: rape; **cole'-slaw** (*-slō*) Du. *koolsla*, for *kool salade*, cole salad), cabbage salad; **cole'-wort**, cole—esp. heartless kinds. [O.E. *cawel*; Ger. *kohl*, Scot. **kail**; all from L. *cōlis*, *caulis*, a stem, esp. of cabbage.]

**Coleoptera**, *kol-i-op'tər-ə, n.pl.* an order of insects having the fore-wings hard or horny, serving as wing-cases for the functional wings—the beetles.—*adjs.* **coleop'teral**, **coleop'terous**.—*n.* **coleop'terist**, a student of beetles. [Gr. *koleos*, a sheath, and *pteron*, a wing.]

**coleor(r)hiza**, *kol-i-ō-rī'zə, n.* a protective layer on the radicle of some plants. [Gr. *koleos*, sheath, *rhiza*, root.]

**cole-slaw**. See **cole**.

**coley**, *kō'li, n.* the coalfish.

**colibri**, *kol'ib-rē*. *n.* a humming-bird. [Sp. *colibri*, Fr. *colibri*, said to be the Carib name.]

**colic**. See **colon** (2).

**colin**, *kol'in, n.* the Virginian quail. [Ety. uncertain; perh. Sp.]

**coliseum**. See **colosseum**.

**colitis**. See **colon** (2).

**coll**, *kol,* (*obs.*) *v.t.* to embrace.—*n.* **coll'ing**, embracing. [Fr. *col*—L. *collum*, the neck.]

**collaborate**, *kəl-ab'ər-āt, v.i.* to work in association (sometimes invidiously, with an enemy).—*ns.* **collabora'tion**; **collab'orator**, **collabora'tionist** (in invidious sense). [L. *collabōrāre*, *-ātum*—*labōrāre*, to work.]

**collage'**, *kol-äzh, n.* a picture made from scraps of paper and other odds and ends pasted out: any work put together from assembled fragments. [Fr., pasting.]

**collagen**, *kol'ə-jen, n.* a protein in fibrous connective tissue, readily turned into gelatine. [Gr.

**kolla**, glue, and **gen-**, the root of *gignesthai*, to become.]

**collapse**, *kəl-aps', n.* a falling away or breaking down: any sudden or complete breakdown or prostration.—*v.i.* to cave in: to close or fold up: to break down: to go to ruin: to lose heart.— *adj.* **collaps'able**, **-ible**, capable of collapsing. [L. *collāpsus*—*col-*, together, and *lābi*, *lāpsus*, to slide or fall.]

**collar**, *kol'ər, n.* something worn round the neck by man, horse, dog, etc.: the part of a garment at the neck: a ring: a surrounding band: the junction of root and stem in a plant: a piece of meat rolled up and tied.—*v.t.* to seize by the collar: to put a collar on: to seize (*slang*).—*adj.* **coll'ared**, having, or ornamented with, a collar: rolled up and bound with a string, as a piece of meat having the bones removed: captured.— *n.* **collarette'**, a small collar.—**coll'ar-beam**, a horizontal piece of timber connecting or bracing two opposite rafters, to prevent sagging; **coll'ar-bone**, the clavicle, a bone connecting the shoulder-blade and breast-bone; **coll'ar-stud**, a stud for fastening a collar; **coll'ar-work**, hard work against the horse-collar: drudgery. [O.Fr. *colier*—L. *collāre*—*collum*, the neck.]

**coll'arco**, *ko-lär-kō,* (It.) with the bow.

**collard**, *kol'ərd, n.* cole-wort. [**cole-wort**.]

**collate**, *kol-āt', v.t.* to bring together for comparison: to examine and compare, as books, and esp. old manuscripts: to place in or confer a benefice upon: (to place in order, as sheets of a book for binding and) to examine with respect to completeness and sequence of sheets, etc.:— *adj.* **collā'table**.—*n.* **collā'tion**, act of collating: a bringing together for examination and comparison: presentation to a benefice: a description of a book as collated: a repast between meals, from the habit of reading the *Collationes* of Johannes Cassianus during a slight meal in monasteries.—*adj.* **collā'tive**, having the power of conferring: of livings where the bishop and patron are one and the same person.—*n.* **collā'tor**, one who collates or compares: one who bestows or presents. [L. *collātum*, used as supine of *conferre*—pfx. *col-* and *lātum* (*ferre*, to bring).]

**collateral**, *kol-at'ər-l, adj.* side by side: running parallel or together: corresponding: descended from the same ancestor, but not in direct line.— *n.* a collateral relation: a contemporary: a rival.—*adv.* **collat'erally**.—**collateral security**, an additional and separate security for repayment of money borrowed. [L. *col-*, *latus*, *lateris*, side.]

**colleague**, *kol'ēg, n.* one associated with another in some employment—not a partner in business. —*n.* **coll'eagueship**. [Fr. *collègue*—L. *collēga*— *col-*, *legĕre*, to choose.]

**colleague**, *kol-ēg', (obs.) v.i.* to ally: to conspire:— *pr.p.* **colleaguing** (*kol-ēg'ing*); *pa.p.* **colleagued** (*kol-ēgd'*). [O.Fr. *colliguer*, to join in alliance— L. *colligāre*, to bind together.]

**collect**, *kəl-, kol-ekt', v.t.* to assemble or bring together: to infer: to put (one's thoughts) in order: to receive payment of: to call for and remove.—*v.i.* to run together: to accumulate.— *n.* **collect** (*kol'*), a short prayer, peculiar to the liturgies of the Western Church, consisting of one sentence, conveying one main petition.— *adj.* **collect'able**, **-ible**.—*n.pl.* **collectā'nea**, a collection of passages: a miscellany.—*adj.* **collect'ed**, gathered together: having unscattered wits: cool: firm.—*adv.* **collect'edly**.—*n.* **collect'edness**, self-possession: coolness.—*n.* and *adj.* **collect'ing**.—*n.* **collec'tion**, act of collecting: gathering of contributions, esp. of money: the money collected: an assemblage: a book of selections: inference (*Shak.*): composure: an examination at the end of the terms in certain colleges: range of new fashion clothes shown by a couturier; regular uplifting of mail by a postal official.—*adj.* collect′ive, considered as forming one mass or sum: congregated: common: inferential (*Milt.*): expressing a number or multitude (*gram.*).—*n.* a gathering, assemblage: a unit of organisation in a collectivist system.—*adv.* collect′ively.—*v.t.* collect′-ivise, -ize, to give a collectivist organisation to.—*ns.* collect′ivism, the economic theory that industry should be carried on with a collective capital—a form of socialism: a system embodying this; collect′ivist—Also *adj.*—*ns.* collect′or, one who collects or takes up, as tickets, taxes, etc.: one who sets himself to acquire and set together examples or specimens, as of books, minerals, curiosities: in India, the chief official of a district, collecting revenue and acting as a magistrate; collect′orate, collect′orship.—collect′ing-box, a field-naturalist's box for specimens: a box for receiving money contributions; collective agreement, one reached by collective bargaining; collective bargaining, negotiation on conditions of service between an organised body of workers on one side and an employer or association of employers on the other: collective farm, a state-controlled farm consisting of a number of small-holdings operated on a co-operative basis; collective fruit (*bot.*), a multiple fruit—one derived from several flowers, as fig, mulberry; collective security, general security among nations to be achieved through guarantee of each nation's security by all. [L. *colligĕre*, *collēctum*—*legĕre*, to gather.]

colleen, *kol′ēn*, *kol-ēn′*, *n.* a girl. [Irish *cailín.*]

college, *kol′ij*, *n.* an incorporation, company, or society of persons joined together generally for literary or scientific purposes, and often possessing peculiar or exclusive privileges: a body or society that is a member of a university or is co-extensive with a university: a seminary of learning: a political, political, or religious institution: the edifice appropriated to a college.—*n.* coll′eger, a member of a college: one of the foundationers at Eton College.—*adj.* collegial (*ka-lē′ji-al*), pertaining to a college or university, or to a collegium.—*ns.* collē′gialism, the theory that the church is a self-governing body independent of the state; collegial′ity, sharing by bishops in papal decision-making: colleagueship: adherence to the theory of collegialism; collē′gian, a member or inhabitant of a college: an inmate of a prison (*slang*); collē′gianer, a member of a college, a student.—*adj.* collē′giate, pertaining to or resembling a college: containing a college, as a town: instituted like a college: corporate.—*n.* inmate of a prison, etc.—collegiate church, collegial church, a church having a college or chapter, consisting of a dean or provost and canons, attached to it: in Scotland, a church occupied by two or more pastors of equal rank (also collegiate charge).—College of Arms, Heralds' College, a collegiate body incorporated in 1483, presided over by the Earl Marshal, and including Garter, principal King-of-arms, Clarenceux, and Norroy, besides six heralds and four pursuivants; college of cardinals, the whole body of cardinals, electors of the pope; college of education, a college for training teachers; College of Justice, in Scotland, a great forensic society, composed of judges, advocates, writers to the signet, and solicitors. [Fr. *collège*—L. *collēgium*, from *col-*, and *legĕre*, to gather.]

collegium, *ko-lēj′i-am*, *n.* college of cardinals: an administrative board.—collegium musicum (*ko-lēj′i-am mū′si-kam*, *ko-lāg′i-oom mōō′si-kŏom*), a group of amateur musicians, often connected with a university. [L. *collēgium*; see college.]

col legno, *kol len′yŏ*, *kō lān′yŏ*, (It.) with the wood (of the violin bow).

Collembola, *kol-em′bō-la*, *n.pl.* an order of wingless Apterygota, formerly classified as insects, whose abdomen has six segments or fewer, a forward-pointing springing fork and an adhesive apparatus—the springtails. [Gr. *kolla*, glue, *embolos*, a peg.]

collenchyma, *kol-eng′ki-ma*, (*bot.*) *n.* strengthening tissue of thick-cornered cells.—*adj.* collenchym′-atous. [Gr. *kolla*, glue, *en* in, *chyma*, that which is poured.]

collet, *kol′it*, *n.* a ring or collar: the collar of a plant: the part of a ring which contains the stone. [Fr.,—L. *collum.*]

collide, *ka-līd′*, *v.i.* to dash together: to clash.—*n.* collision (*-lizh′n*), state of being struck together: a violent impact, a crash: conflict: opposition: clashing.—collision course, a course which, if persisted in, will result in a collision (*lit.* and *fig.*); colli′sion-mat, a mat for covering a hole in a ship's side caused by a collision. [L. *collidĕre*, *collisum*—*col-*, *laedĕre*, to strike.]

collie, colly, *kol′i*, *n.* a long-haired, intelligent breed of sheep-dog, originating in Scotland. [Ety. dub.]

collier, *kol′yar*, *n.* a charcoal-burner or dealer in charcoal or coal (*obs.*): a coal-miner: a ship that carries coal: a sailor in such a ship.—*n.* coll′iery, a coal-mine. [coal.]

collieshangie, *kol-i-shang′i*, (*Scot.*) *n.* a noisy wrangling: an uproar: a disturbance. [Origin unknown.]

colligate, *kol′i-gāt*, *v.t.* to bind together.—*n.* colligā′tion, conjunction: bringing together under a general principle or conception.—*adj.* coll′igative (*physical chem.*), depending on concentration, not nature of substance. [L. *colligāre*, *ātum*—*col-*, *ligāre*, to bind.]

collimate, *kol′i-māt*, *v.t.* to make parallel: to adjust accurately parts of (an optical instrument, as a surveying telescope).—*ns.* collimā′tion; coll′imator, a device for obtaining a beam of parallel rays of light or other radiation, or one for obtaining a beam of particles moving in parallel paths: a subsidiary telescope for collimating other instruments. [*collimare*, a wrong reading for L. *collineāre*, to bring into line with—*col-*, together, *linea*, a line.]

collinear, *ko-lin′i-ar*, *adj.* in the same straight line.

Collins, *kol′inz*, *n.* a letter of thanks for hospitality. [From the notable example sent by Mr *Collins* in *Pride and Prejudice.*]

colliquate, *kol′i-kwāt*, (*obs.*) *v.t.* to melt: to fuse.—(*obs.*) *adjs.* colliq′uable, colliq′uant, melting, wasting.—*n.* colliquā′tion, melting: wasting away.—*adj.* colliq′uātive, profuse in flow: wasting.—*n.* colliquesc′ence, readiness to liquefy. [L. *col-*, together, *liquāre*, *-ātum*, to make melt.]

collocate, *kol′ō-kāt*, *v.t.* to place together: to set: to arrange.—*n.* collocā′tion. [L. *collocāre*, *-ātum*, *col-*, *locāre*, to place.]

collocutor, collocutory. See colloquy.

collodion, *kol-ō′di-an*, *n.* a gluey solution of nitrated cotton (or cellulose nitrates) in alcohol and ether, used in surgery and photography. [Gr. *kollōdēs*—*kolla*, glue, *eidos*, form, appearance.]

collogue, *ka-lōg′*, *v.i.* to simulate belief (*obs.*): to conspire (*dial.*): to converse confidentially with.—*v.t.* to coax (*obs.*): to flatter. [Prob. from L. *colloquī*, to speak together.]

colloid, *kol′oid*, *n.* a substance in a state in which, though apparently dissolved, it cannot pass through a membrane: a substance that readily assumes this state: a colloidal system, i.e. the dispersed substance plus the material in which it is dispersed.—*adj.* colloid′al. [Gr. *kolla*, glue, *eidos*, form.]

collop, *kol′ap*, *n.* an egg fried with bacon (*obs.*): a slice of meat, fried or not (*dial.*): a child (*Shak.*).—Collop Monday, the day before Shrove

Tuesday, when collops-and-eggs were eaten.—minced collops (*Scot.*), minced meat. [Origin obscure.]

**colloquy**, *kol'ə-kwi*, *n.* a speaking together: mutual discourse: conversation.—*v.i.* (*rare*), to converse.—*n.* **collocutor** (*kol-ok'ū-tər*).—*adj.* **colloc'ūtory.**—*v.i.* **colloque** (*kol-ōk'*), to hold colloquy.—*adj.* **colloquial** (*kə-lō'kwi-əl*), pertaining to or used in common conversation.—*ns.* **collō'quialism,** a form of expression used in familiar talk; **collō'quialist.**—*adv.* **collō'quially.**—*v.i.* **coll'oquise, -ize,** to converse.—*ns.* **coll'oquist,** a speaker in a colloquy; **collō'quium** (*pl.* -ia, -iums), a conference: a meeting for discussion: a seminar. [L. *colloquium*—*col-*, *loqui*, to speak.]

**collotype,** *kol'ō-tip*, *n.* a form of gelatine process in book illustration and advertising. [Gr. *kolla*, glue, and **type.**]

**colluctation,** *kol-uk-tā'shən*, *n.* strife: opposition. [L. *colluctāri*—*col-*, *luctāri*, to wrestle.]

**collude,** *kol-ūd'*, -*ood'*, *v.i.* to play into each other's hands: to act in concert, esp. in a fraud.—*ns.* **collud'er; collu'sion,** act of colluding: a secret agreement to deceive: deceit: in *Love's Lab. Lost*, Goodman Dull's blunder for **allusion.**—*adj.* **collu'sive,** fraudulently concerted: deceitful.—*adv.* **collu'sively.** [L. *collūdēre*, *collūsum*, from *col-*, and *lūdēre*, to play.]

**colluvies,** *ko-lū'*, *ko-lōō'vi-ēz*, *n.* accumulated filth: a rabble. [L. *colluviēs*, washings—*colluēre*, to wash thoroughly.]

**colly,** *kol'i*, *v.t.* to begrime with coal-dust (*arch.*): to darken (*Shak.*).—*p.adj.* **coll'ied.** [See **coal.**]

**colly.** See **collie.**

**collyrium,** *ko-lir'i-əm*, *n.* eye-wash. [Latinised from Gr. *kollÿrion*, eye-salve, dim. of *kollÿrā*, a roll of bread.]

**collywobbles,** *kol'i-wob-lz*, *n.* (*facet.*) abdominal pain or disorder. [Prob. **colic** and **wabble, wobble.**]

**Colmar,** *kol'mär*, *n.* a kind of fan fashionable in Queen Anne's time. [Perh. *Colmar* in Alsace.]

**Colobus,** *kol'ō-bəs*, *n.* an African genus of monkeys, almost thumbless. [Gr. *kolobos*, maimed.]

**Colocasia,** *kol-ō-kā'zi-ə*, *-si-ə*, (*bot.*) *n.* a genus of plants of the arum family—taro, etc. [Gr. *kolokāsiā*, water-lily root.]

**colocynth,** *kol'ō-sinth*, *n.* a kind of cucumber (*Citrullus colocynthis*): a cathartic drug got from it. [Gr. *kolokynthis.*]

**Cologne-earth,** *ko-lōn'-ûrth*, *n.* a brown earth prepared from lignite, found originally near *Cologne.*—**Cologne water,** or **eau de Cologne** (*ō də ko-lōn'*), a perfumed spirit first made at Cologne in 1709 by Johann Farina.

**colon,** *kō'lən*, *n.* the punctuation mark ( : ) used especially to indicate a distinct member or clause of a sentence. [Gr. *kōlon*, a limb, member.]

**colon,** *kō'lən*, *n.* the large intestine from the caecum to the rectum.—*n.* **colic** (*kol'ik*), a disease attended with severe pain and flatulent distension of the abdomen, without diarrhoea.—*adjs.* **col'ic; col'icky,** like, suffering or causing colic.—*ns.* **coliform (bacillus),** (*kol'i-förm*), any of several bacilli living in the intestines.—Also **colon bacillus; colitis,** *kō-*, *kol'i'tis,* inflammation of the colon; **colos'tomy** (*kə-*), making of an artificial anus by surgical means; **colot'omy,** cutting of or incision into the colon. [Gr. *kōlon*, the large intestine.]

**colon,** *kō-lōn'*, *n.* the monetary unit of El Salvador and Costa Rica. [From Columbus (Sp. *Colón*).]

**colonel,** *kûr'nəl*, *n.* an officer who has command of a regiment or one of equivalent rank—between a lieutenant-colonel and a brigadier (in U.S. brigadier-general): in U.S., also an officer in the marines and one at the air force: in U.S. sometimes, an honorary title given to one not connected with the armed forces.—*ns.* **col'onelcy** (-*si*), the office or rank of colonel; **col'onelling** (or *kor-ō-nel'ing*), playing the colonel; **col'onel-**

ship, colonelcy; quality of being a colonel.—**col'onel-comm'andant,** commander of a brigade; **col'onel-in-chief,** an honorary colonel. [Older Fr. and Sp. *coronel*;—It. *colonello*, the leader of a *colonna*, or column—L. *columna*; spelling assimilated to mod. Fr.]

**colonnade,** *kol-ən-ād'*, *n.* a range of columns placed at regular intervals: a similar row, as of trees.—*adj.* **colonnad'ed.** [Fr.,—L. *columna*.]

**colony,** *kol'ən-i*, *n.* a name vaguely applied to a state's dependencies overseas or abroad (distinguished from a *dominion*): a military settlement planted in subject territory (*Rom. hist.*): a band of emigrants or their new home, connected with the mother city by no political tie (*Gr. hist.*): a body of persons settled in a foreign country, or forming a separate group in any way (as by common occupation), or organised for purposes of support, labour, treatment, etc.: the settlement so formed: the place they inhabit: a number of organisms, esp. of one kind, living together as a community (*biol.*): a coenobium.—*adj.* **colonial** (*kə-lō'ni-əl*), pertaining to or of the nature of a colony.—*n.* an inhabitant, citizen, or member of a colony, a colonist.—*ns.* **colo'-nialism,** a trait of colonial life or speech: the colonial system (see below): policy of obtaining, or maintaining hold over, colonies, esp. with the purpose of exploiting them.—*adj.* and *n.* **colon'ialist.**—*n.* **colonisa'tion,** -z-, act or practice of colonising: state of being colonised.—*v.t.* **col'onise, -ize,** to plant or establish a colony in: to form into a colony: to plant fraudulent voters in (*U.S.*).—*v.t.* to settle.—*n.* **col'onist,** an inhabitant of a colony: a voter set up for election purposes: a weed of cultivated ground (*bot.*).—**colonial animals,** organisms consisting of numerous individuals in bodily union; **colonial experience man** (*Australia*), a jackaroo; **colonial system,** the theory that the settlements abroad should be treated as proprietary domains exploited for the benefit of the mother country. [L. *colōnia*—*colōnus*, a husbandman—*colēre*, to till.]

**colophon,** *kol'ə-fon*, -*fən*, *n.* an inscription at the end of a book or literary composition, often naming the author and scribe or printer, with place and date of execution, etc., as on a modern title-page: a publisher's imprint or device, with name, date, etc. [L. *colophōn*—Gr. *kolophōn*, summit, finishing touch.]

**colophony,** *kol-of'ə-ni*, or *kol'*, *n.* rosin. [Gr. *kolophōniā* (*rhētinē*, gum) from *Kolophōn*, Colophon, in Asia Minor.]

**coloquintida,** *kol-o-kwin'ti-də.* Same as **colocynth.**

**color,** U.S. spelling of **colour.**

**Colorado beetle,** *kol-ər-ä'dō bē'tl*, an American beetle, yellow with black stripes, a potato pest. [State of *Colorado*.]

**coloratura,** *kol-or-ät-ōō'ra*, (*mus.*) *n.* florid vocal passages.—*adj.* **florid.**—**coloratura soprano,** a high and flexible soprano voice, capable of singing coloratura passages: a singer with such a voice. [It., colouring.]

**colossus,** *kəl-os'əs*, *n.* a gigantic statue, esp. that of Apollo at (but not astride of) the entrance of the harbour of Rhodes.—*adj.* **coloss'al,** like a colossus: gigantic.—*ns.* **colossē'um, colisē'um,** a large place of entertainment, from Vespasian's amphitheatre at Rome, which was the largest in the world.—**coloss'us-wise** (*Shak.*), astride. [L.,—Gr. *kolossos.*]

**colostrum,** *ko-los'trəm*, *n.* a mammal's first milk after parturition.—*n.* **colostrā'tion,** a disease of cattle due to colostrum.—*adjs.* **colos'tric, -trous.** [L.]

**colour,** also, esp. in U.S., **color,** *kul'ər*, *n.* a sensation of light induced in the eye by electromagnetic waves of a certain frequency—the colour

Neutral vowels in unaccented syllables: *el'ə-mənt*; for certain sounds in foreign words, see p. viii

being determined by the frequency: a property whereby bodies have different appearances to the eye through surface reflection or absorption of rays: hue, one of the constituents into which white light can be decomposed: appearance of blood in the face: race or race-mixture other than Caucasian: appearance: plausibility: reason, pretext: tint: shade: paint: particle of gold: rhetorical figure: false show: vividness: timbre (*mus.*): variety: (*sing.* or *pl.*) a flag, ensign, or standard: (*pl.*) symbol of membership of a party, club, college, team, etc.—*v.t.* to put colour on: to stain: to paint: to set in a fair light: to exaggerate: to disguise: to misrepresent.—*v.i.* to take on colour: to blush.—*n.* colora′tion (also colouration), colouring: mode of colouring: disposition of colours.—*adj.* colorif′ic (*kol-, kul-*), producing colours.—*n.* colorim′eter (*kol-, kul-*), an instrument for comparison of colours.—*adj.* col′ourable (*kul′*), plausible: feigned.—*adv.* colourably.—*adjs.* col′oured, having colour: having a specious appearance, deceitful (*Spens.*): of the complexion, other than white: of mixed descent—partly Caucasian, partly of darker race: not of Caucasian race; col′ourful, full of colour: vivid.—*ns.* col′ouring, any substance used to give colour: the actual colours of anything, and their arrangement: manner of applying colours: appearance: tone; col′ourist, one who colours or paints: one who excels in colouring.—*adjs.* col′ourless, without colour: transparent: pale: neutral: lacking distinctive character; col′oury, having much colour.—colour bar, social discrimination between whites and other races.—*adj.* col′our-blind, unable to distinguish some colours from others, or to see them at all.—colour blind′ness; colour film, a film for making colour photographs; colour filter, a film or plate transparent for the required colours only or chiefly; colour hearing, the association of colours with sounds heard; colour line, a social and political distinction between white and other races; col′ourman, one who prepares or sells paints; colour music, the art of displaying colours on a screen with effect analogous to music; colour organ, an instrument for doing this; colour party, a guard carrying colours; colour scheme, general conception of combination of colours in a design; colour screen, a colour filter; col′our-sergeant, the sergeant who guards the colours of a regiment.—colour a pipe, to cause a pipe, esp. a meerschaum, to darken by smoking; colour up, blush, flush; come off with flying colours, to do something with éclat; come out in one's true colours, to appear in one's real character; fear no colours, fear no enemy; false colours, a false pretence; give colour, to give plausibility; high colour, ruddiness of complexion; join the colours, to enlist; lose colour, to lose one's good looks: to become pale: to appear less probable (*fig.*); nail one's colours to the mast, to commit oneself to some party or plan of action; off colour, faded: indisposed: past one's best: slightly indecent; pair of colours (see pair); primary colours (see primary); see the colour of a person's money, be sure that a person has money to pay for an article about to be bought. [O.Fr. color—L. color, -ōris; akin to cēlāre, to cover, to conceal.]

colporteur, kol-pōr-tûr′, -pör, or kol′pört-ər, n. a peddler, esp. one selling religious tracts and books.—n. col′portage (or -täzh′), the distribution of books by colporteurs. [Fr. colporteur, from col—L. collum, the neck, and porter—L. portāre, to carry.]

colt, kōlt, n. a young horse: an awkward fellow: an inexperienced youth: a young camel or ass (B.): a rope's end (naut.).—v.i. (Spens.) to frisk like a colt.—v.t. to cheat (Shak.): to give the rope's end, to beat.—adj. colt′ish, like a colt: frisky: wanton.—colts′foot, a composite plant (Tussilago Farfara) with shaggy stalk and large soft leaves; colt's tooth, one of a horse's first set of teeth: love of youthful pleasures (Shak.): wantonness; colt′wood (Spens.), a plant used by Glauce in her incantations (F.Q. III. ii. 49. 8) —said to be coltsfoot, which is not woody. [O.E. colt; Sw. kult, a young boar, a stout boy.]

Colt, kōlt, n. a pistol invented by Samuel Colt (1814-62).

colter. Same as coulter.

Coluber, kol′ū-bər, n. an extensive genus of non-venomous snakes.—ns. colūb′riad (Cowper), the epic of a snake; Colu′bridae, the largest family of snakes—in which some include cobras and other venomous snakes.—adj. colubriform (-ōō′, -ū′), resembling Coluber; col′ūbrine, snakelike: colubriform. [L. coluber, a snake.]

colugo, ko-lōō′gō, n. the so-called flying lemur.

Columba, kəl-um′bə, n. a large genus consisting of the pigeons: Irish apostle (521-597) who founded a monastery at Iona and converted the Northern Picts to Christianity: one of the southern constellations.—adj. Colum′ban. [L. columba, dove.]

Columbian, kəl-um′bi-ən, adj. American: (of type) in size between English and Great Primer—16-point.—n. colum′bate, niobate.—adj. colum′-bic, niobic.—ns. columb′ite, a mineral, niobate and tantalate of iron and manganese; colum′-bium, former name for niobium. [Columbus, discoverer of America.]

columbine, kol′əm-bin, adj. of or like a dove: dove-coloured.—n. any plant of the ranunculaceous genus Aquilegia, with coloured sepals and spurred petals, giving the appearance of a bunch of pigeons: (cap.) in pantomime, the sweetheart of Harlequin.—ns. columbā′rium, a dovecot: a niche for a sepulchral urn: a recess in a wall to receive the end of a rafter; col′umbary, a dovecot. [L. columba, a dove.]

column, kol′əm, n. a long round body, used as support or adornment: any upright body or mass like a column: a body of troops with narrow front: a perpendicular row of figures, etc.: a perpendicular section of a page or of a table: a special section in a newspaper; a bundle of nerve-fibres: the central part of an orchid.—ns. col′ūmel, a small column; colū-mell′a, the central axis of a spiral univalve; the central axis of the spore-case of mosses: in the opening of fruits, what remains in the centre after the carpels have split away.—adjs. columnal (kə-lum′nl), colum′nar, pertaining to columns: like a column: formed in columns.—n. columnar′ity.—adjs. columnated (kol′əm-nāt-id, or kə-lum′); columned (kol′əmd), colum′niated, having columns.—ns. columniation (kə-lum-ni-ā′shən), use or arrangement of columns; columnist (kol′əm-ist, -nist; illit. or facet. kol′ūm-ist), one who conducts a column in a newspaper. [L. columna, akin to celsus, high; Gr. kolōnē, a hill.]

colure, kō-lūr′, kōl′, kol′yər, n. a great circle of the celestial sphere passing through the poles of the equator and either the solstitial or the equinoctial points. [Gr. kolouros—kolos, docked, ourā, tail.]

colza, kol′zə, n. cole-seed, yielding oil. [Du. koolzaad, cabbage-seed.]

coma, kō′mə, n. deep sleep: stupor.—adj. com′-atose, affected with coma: drowsy. [Gr. kōma, -atos.]

coma, kō′ma, n. a tuft (bot.): the head of a tree: the nebulous envelope of the head of a comet (astron.).—adjs. cō′mal, cō′mate, cō′mose, cō′-mous.—Coma Berenices (ber-ə-ni′sēz), Berenice's Hair, a small northern constellation. [Gr. kōmē, hair of head.]

fāte, fär; mē, hûr (her); mīne; mōte, för; mūte; mōōn, fŏŏt; dhen (then)

**comanchero**, kō-man-che'rō, *n.* in 19th cent., one who traded with plains Indians of south-west N. America. [Mex.-Sp.—*Comanche* tribe.]

**comarb.** See **coarb.**

**comart**, kō-märt', (*Shak.*) *n.* an agreement. [Perh. pfx. **co-** and **mart**; or a misprint for *cou'nant*, i.e. *covenant*.]

**comate**, kō'māt', (*Shak.*) *n.* a mate or companion.

**comb, kōm**, *n.* a toothed instrument for separating and cleaning hair, wool, flax, for graining paint, etc.: anything of similar form: the fleshy crest of some birds: the top or crest of a wave, of a roof, or of a hill: an aggregation of cells for honey.—*v.t.* to separate, to arrange, or clean by means of a comb or as if with a comb: to dress with a comb: to search thoroughly: to beat (*Shak.*).—*v.i.* to break with a white foam, as the top of a wave.—*adj.* **combed.**—*n.* **comb'er**, one who or that which combs wool, etc.: a long foaming wave.—*n.pl.* **comb'ings**, hairs combed off.—*adj.* **comb'less.**—*adj.* **comb'y.**—*n.* **comb'-out'**, the process of searching for and removing, e.g. lice, men for military service.—*adv.* **comb'-wise.** [O.E. *camb.*]

**comb, combe.** See **coomb** (1) and (2).

**combat**, kom'bət, kum' (U.S. usu. kum-bat'; not standard in U.K.), *v.i.* to contend or struggle.—*v.t.* to beat against: to contest: to oppose: to debate (*pr.p., pa.t., pa.p.*, **com'bating, com'bated**).—*n.* (kom', kum') a struggle: a fight.—*adjs.* **com'batable**; **com'batant**, disposed to combat: taking part or liable to take part in action—*n.* one who takes part in a combat.—*adj.* **com'bative**, inclined to quarrel.—*n.* **com'bativeness.**—**combat fatigue**, mental disturbance in a fighting soldier, formerly called shell-shock. [Fr. *combattre*, to fight—L. pfx. *com-*, mutual, and *bātuēre*, to strike.]

**comber**, kom'bər, *n.* the gaper (a sea-perch): a species of wrasse.

**combine**, kəm-bīn', *v.t.* to join together: to unite intimately: to bind, restrict (*Shak.*).—*v.i.* to come into close union: to co-operate: to unite and form a new compound (*chem.*).—*n.* (kom'-bīn), a syndicate, a trust, an association of trading companies: a combine harvester: a painting into which articles of everyday use have been fixed.—*adj.* **combinate** (kom'bin-āt), combined: betrothed (*Shak.*).—*n.* **combinā'tion**, the act of combining: union of individual things: a motorcycle with sidecar: persons united for a purpose: in maths., a possible set of a given number of things selected from a given number, irrespective of arrangement within the set (distinguished from a *permutation*): the series of letters or numbers that must be dialled to move the mechanism of a combination lock and so open it.—*n.pl.* **combinā'tions**, an under-garment comprising vest and drawers.—*adjs.* **com'binative**; **combinato'rial**, concerned with arrangement (*math.*); **combin'atory**; **combined'**; **combin'ing.** —*n.* **combo** (kom'bō), a small jazz or dance band: a white man who lives with aborigines and has an aboriginal wife (*Austr.*).—**combination lock**, a lock used on safes, etc., with numbered dials which must be turned in a special order a certain number of times to open it; **combination room**, at Cambridge, a fellows' common room; **combine harvester**, a combined harvesting and threshing machine. [L. *combināre*, to join—*com-*, *bini*, two and two.]

**comble**, kō-bl', (Fr.) acme.

**Combretum**, kom-brē'təm, *n.* a tropical and subtropical genus of trees and shrubs noted for the beauty of their flowers, giving name to the **Combretā'ceae**, a family akin to the myrtles. [L. *combrētum*, an unknown plant.]

**comburgess**, kom-bûr'jis, *n.* a fellow-burgess.

**combust**, kom-bust', *adj.* burnt by the sun (*obs.*): in conjunction with the sun, or apparently very near it, so as to be obscured by its light, said of a planet when it is not more than 8½° from the sun.—*n.* that which is burnt.—*v.t.* to burn up.—*n.* **combustibil'ity.**—*adj.* **combust'ible**, liable to take fire and burn: excitable.—*n.* anything that will take fire and burn.—*ns.* **combust'ibleness**, quality of being combustible; **combust'ion** (-yən), a burning: the action of fire on combustible substances: confusion, turmoil: oxidation or analogous process with evolution of heat.—*adjs.* **combust'ious** (*Shak.*), combustible, inflammable: turbulent; **combust'ive**, disposed to take fire.—**spontaneous combustion**, burning caused by heat generated in the substance itself. [L. *combūrēre*, *combūstum*, to consume—*com-*, intens., *ūrēre*, to burn.]

**come, kum**, *v.i.* to move toward the place that is the point of view (the opposite of *go*): to draw near: to arrive at a certain state or condition: to issue: to happen: to yield (*Shak.*): to become: to turn out: to amount: to reach: to begin to be in some condition: to achieve a sexual orgasm (*slang*; orig. *U.S.*).—*v.t.* (*slang or coll.*) to behave in a certain way (*pr.p.* **com'ing**; *pa.t.* **came**; *pa.p.* **come**).—*interj.* (or *imper.*) expressive of encouragement, protest, or reproof (often in phrases **come come, come now**).—*n.* **com'er** (*Spens.* **comm'er**), one who comes or has come: one who shows promise; **com'ing.**—*interj.* or *pr.p.*, used as a promise of attention.—*adj.* **future**: of future importance: ready to make or meet advances (*arch.*).—*n.* **come'-and-go'**, passage to and fro.—*adj.* **come-at'-able**, accessible. —*ns.* **come'-back**, a return: a revival: a retort; **come'down**, a descent: a humiliating disappointment: a degradation; **come-hith'er**, an invitation to approach: allure.—*adj.* of a look, manner, etc., inviting.—**come'-off**, a conclusion: an evasion of duty; **come'-o'-will**, something that comes of its own accord: an illegitimate child (also **come'-by-chance**); **comeup(p)'ance** (*coll.*), deserved rebuke or punishment.—*n.pl.* **com'ings-in'**, income.—**all comers**, anyone that likes; **as they come**, as they are made, as they are to be had, as they turn up; **come about**, to happen; **come again?** (*slang*), what do you mean?; **come across** (see **across**); **come and go**, to fluctuate: to have freedom of action; **come at**, to reach: to attack; **come back**, to return to popularity, office, etc.: to retort; **come by**, to come near: to pass: to obtain: come in; **come down**, to descend: to be reduced; **come down upon**, to be severe with; **come down with**, to pay down; **come high**, or **low**, to cost much, or little; **come home**, to return to one's house: to touch one's interest or feelings closely (with *to*): to drag or slip through the ground—of an anchor (*naut.*); **come in**, to enter: to reply to a radio signal or call: to give in, to yield, (*fencing*) to get within the opponent's guard (*Shak.*); **come in for**, to receive as, or as if as, one's share: to receive incidentally; **come into**, to fall heir to; **come it over**, to assert one's authority over; **come it strong** (*coll.*), to do or say much, go to great lengths, exaggerate; **come of**, to descend from: become of; **come of age**, to reach full legal age; **come off**, to come away: to turn out: to escape: to pay up (*Shak.*): to desist from: to prove successful; **come on**, to advance: to thrive: to proceed: to begin: often in *imper.* as a challenge or invitation to attack; **come out**, to result: to be published: to become known or evident: to enter society; **come out with**, to utter: to exclaim; **come over**, to surpass (*Shak.*): to befall: to come into the mind of: to over-reach (*slang*): to experience a certain feeling (*coll.*); **come round**, to come by a circuitous path: to happen in due course: to veer: to become favourable: to recover from a faint, etc; **come short**, to fail; **come short of**, to fail to attain;

come to, to obtain: to amount to: to recover consciousness; come to grief, to meet with disaster; come to oneself, return to normal state of mind; come to pass, to happen; come to stay, to become permanent; come true, to be fulfilled; come under, to be included under; come up, to present itself; come upon, to attack: to affect: to hold answerable: to meet; come up with, to overtake; to come, future. [O.E. *cuman*; Ger. *kommen*.]

co-meddle, *kō-med'l*, *v.t.* to mix (*obs.*): to temper (*Shak.*).

comedo, *kom'i-do*, *n.* a blackhead, a small, black-tipped white mass sometimes found in the sebaceous glands. [L. *comedō*, *-ōnis*, glutton—*comedĕre*, to eat up, from its wormlike appearance.]

Comédie Française, La, *ko-mā-dē frä-sez*, *la*, (Fr.) the official name of the Théâtre Français, the French national theatre; Comédie Humaine, La, *ū-men*, (Fr.) the human comedy—Balzac's collection of novels, planned to form a complete picture of contemporary society.

comedy, *kom'i-di*, *n.* a dramatic piece of a pleasant or humorous character: a story with a happy ending: an incident suggesting comic treatment. —*ns.* comedian (*kə-mē'di-ən*), one who acts or writes comedies.—*fem.* (Fr.) comédienne (Eng. *ko-me-*, *mē-*, *di-en'*); comēdiett'a, short comic piece.— comedy of manners, satirical comedy dealing with the manners or fashions of a social class. [Fr. *comédie*—L. *cōmoedia*—Gr. *kōmōidiā*—*kōmos*, revel, or *kōmē*, village, *ōidē*, song.]

comely, *kum'li*, *adj.* pleasing: graceful: handsome.—*adv.* in a comely manner.—*n.* come'-liness, [Conn. O.E. *cymlic*—*cyme*, suitable, *lic*, like.]

comestible, *kom-est'ibl*, *adj.* eatable.—*n.* (usu. in *pl.*) food. [Fr.,—L. *comedĕre*, to eat up.]

comet, *kom'it*, *n.* a heavenly body with a very eccentric orbit, having a definite nucleus, a nebulous light surrounding the nucleus, and commonly a luminous tail turned away from the sun.—*adjs.* com'etary, cometic (*-et'ik*).—*ns.* com'et-finder, a telescope of low power used to search for comets; cometog'raphy; cometol'-ogy. [Gr. *komētēs*, long-haired—*komē*, hair.]

comether, *kəm-edh'ər*, (*dial.*) *n.* wheedling: charm. [come hither, a call to cows, etc.]

comfit, *kum'fit*, *n.* a sweetmeat: a sugar-coated seed or almond.—*n.* com'fiture (*obs.*), conserve. [A doublet of confect; Fr. *confit*, *confiture*.]

comfort, *kum'fərt* (Spens. *kom-fort'*) *v.t.* to strengthen (*obs.*): relieve from pain or distress: soothe, cheer.—*n.* relief: encouragement: ease: quiet enjoyment: freedom from annoyance: whatever gives ease, enjoyment, etc.: a subject of satisfaction.—*adj.* com'fortable, imparting or enjoying comfort.—*n.* (*U.S.*) a bed quilt.—*adv.* com'fortably.—*n.* com'forter, one who administers comfort: the Holy Ghost (*B.*; *A.V.*): a long narrow woollen scarf: a dummy teat: a bed quilt (*U.S.*).—*adj.* com'fortless.—*n.* com'-fortlessness.—*adj.* com'fy (*coll.*), comfortable.— cold comfort, little, if any, comfort; comfort station (*U.S.*), public lavatory. [O.Fr. *conforter*—L. *con-*, inten., and *fortis*, strong.]

comfrey, *kum'fri*, *n.* a rough boraginaceous plant (*Symphytum*). [O.Fr. *confirie*.]

comic, *kom'ik*, *adj.* relating to comedy: raising mirth: droll.—*n.* the quality or element that arouses mirth: an actor of droll parts: an amusing person (*coll.*): a comic paper, strip cartoon (orig. comic, later also serious, even horrific).—*adj.* com'ical, funny.—*ns.* comical'ity, com'icalness.—*adv.* com'ically.—*n.* comique (*kō-mēk'*), a comic actor or singer. [See comedy.]

Cominform, *kom'in-förm*, *n.* the Communist *Inform*ation Bureau (1947-56), which succeeded the Comintern.

Comintern, *kom'in-tûrn*, *n.* the *Com*munist *Intern*ational (1919-43), or Third International (see under international.)

comitadji. Same as komitaji.

comitatus, *kom-i-tā'təs*, *n.* a prince's escort: a county or shire.—*adjs.* com'ital, relating to a count, earl, or county; comita'tive, of a grammatical case, expressing accompaniment.—*n.* a comitative case. [L. *comitātus*, *-ūs*—*comes*, *-itis*, companion, count.]

comitia, *ko-mish'i-a*, *ko-mi'ti-a*, *n.pl.* the assemblies of the Romans for electing magistrates, passing laws, etc; comitia centuriata, *sen-tū-ri-ā'ta*, *ken-toō-ri-ā'ta*, the assembly of Roman people, voting by centuries; comitia curiata, *kū-ri-ā'ta*, *kōō-ri-ā'ta*, that of the patricians, voting by curiae; comitia tributa, *tri-bū'ta*, *tri-bōō'ta*, that of the people, voting by tribes. [L., —*com*, together, *ire*, *itum*, to go.]

comity, *kom'i-ti*, *n.* courteousness: civility.— comity of nations (*comitas gentium*), the international courtesy by which effect is given (within limits) to the laws of one state within the territory of another state: a group of nations adhering to this code of behaviour. [L. *cōmitās*, *-ātis*—*cōmis*, courteous.]

comma, *kom'a*, *n.* a phrase (*rhet.*; *Shak.*): in punctuation, the point (,) that marks the smallest division of a sentence: the smallest interval, break, discontinuity: hence perh. (*Shak.*) a connecting link: a name for various minute intervals, esp. the difference between twelve perfect fifths and seven octaves (*mus.*).—comma bacillus, the micro-organism that causes cholera; comma butterfly, a nymphaline butterfly (Polygonia) with a white comma-shaped mark on the under side of the hind-wing; inverted commas, marks of quotation (". ", '. '). [L.,—Gr. *komma*, a section of a sentence, from *koptein*, to cut off.]

command, *kəm-änd'*, *v.t.* to order: to bid: to exercise supreme authority over: to demand: to cause to act (*Shak.*): to exact (*Shak.*): to have within sight, range, influence, or control.—*v.i.* to have chief authority: to govern.—*n.* an order: authority: control: power to overlook, influence or use: the thing commanded: in a remote-control guidance system, a signal activating a mechanism or setting in motion a sequence of operations by instruments.—*ns.* commandant (*kom-ən-dant'*), an officer who has the command of a place or of a body of troops: commandant'-ship.—*v.t.* commandeer', to compel to military service, or seize for military use (orig. Cape Dutch): to take arbitrarily.—*ns.* command'er, one who commands: an officer in the navy next in rank under a captain: a member of a higher class in an order of knighthood: a district administrator in religious military orders; command'ership; command'ery, the district under a commander, esp. in the religious military orders.—*adj.* command'ing, fitted to impress or control: strategic.—*adv.* command'ingly.—*ns.* command'ment, a command: a precept; command'o, a military party (*S. Africa* from *Port.*): a unit of a special service raiding brigade equivalent to a battalion (*mil.*): one serving in such a unit.— command paper, one laid before Parliament by command of the crown; command performance, a performance by royal command; command'er-in-chief', the officer in supreme command of an army, or of the entire forces of the state.—at command, available for use; commander of the faithful, a title of the caliphs; on commando, on military service in the field; ten commandments, the ten Mosaic laws: the fingernails, esp. a woman's (*Shak.*). [Fr. *commander*—L.L. *commandāre* (L. *commendāre*)—L. *mandāre*, to entrust.]

commeasure, *kəm-ezh'ər*, *v.t.* to equal in measure:

to coincide with.—*n.* commeas'urable (same as commensurable).

commedia dell' arte, *ko-mä'dē-a de-lär'te*, (It.) guild comedy, Italian Renaissance comedy, mainly improvised, performed by a guild of professional actors.

comme il faut, *ko-mël-fō*, (Fr.) as it should be: correct: approved by the fashionable world: genteel.

Commelina, *kom-ə-lī'na, n.* a tropical genus of monocotyledons, giving name to the fam. Commelinaceae (*-li-nā'si-ē*). [After the Dutch botanists Johannes (1629-72) and Caspar (1667-1731) *Commelin.*]

commemorate, *kəm-em'ə-rāt, v.t.* to call to remembrance by a solemn or public act: to celebrate: to preserve the memory of.—*adj.* commem'orable.—*n.* commemorā'tion, preserving the memory of some person or thing, esp. by a solemn ceremony: the specification of individual saints in the prayers for the dead: the great festival of the Oxford academic year, usually taking place on the third Wednesday after Trinity Sunday.—*adjs.* commem'orative, commem'oratory, tending or serving to commemorate.—*n.* commem'orator. [L. *commemorāre, -ātum*, to remember—*com-*, inten., and *memor*, mindful.]

commence, *kəm-ens', v.i.* to begin: to originate: to take rise.—*v.t.* to begin: to originate: to enter upon: to take a university degree (as *commence M.A.*).—*n.* commence'ment, the beginning: at certain universities the act of taking the degrees: the ceremony when these are conferred. [O.Fr. *com(m)encier*—L. *com-*, inten., and *initiāre*, to begin—*in*, into, and *īre*, to go.]

commend, *kəm-end', v.t.* to commit as a charge: to recommend as worthy: to praise: to adorn, set off (*obs.*).—(*Shak.*) *n.* a greeting: praise.—*adj.* commend'able.—*n.* commend'ableness.—*adv.* commend'ably.—*ns.* commend'am (L.L. accus.), an ecclesiastical benefice held, or the tenure or grant of a benefice held, *in commendam*, i.e. theoretically till a pastor was provided for it, but often for life and without duties; commendation (*kom-ən-dā'shən*), the act of commending, esp. of commending the dying or dead to the favour and mercy of God: praise: declaration of esteem; comm'endator, one who holds a benefice *in commendam*: a titular abbot, etc.: the head of a commandery.—*adj.* commend'-atory, commending: containing praise or commendation: presenting to favourable notice or reception: held, or holding, *in commendam.*— commend me to, remember me kindly to: give me by preference. [L. *commendāre*—*com-*, inten., and *mandāre*, to trust.]

commensal, *kə-men'səl, adj.* eating at the same table: living together for mutual benefit (*biol.*): esp. an association of less intimate kind than that called symbiosis.—*n.* a messmate: an organism living in partnership (not parasitism) with another.—*n.* commen'salism.—*adv.* commen'sally. [L. *com-*, together, *mēnsa*, a table.]

commensurable, *kəm-en'sū-rə-bl, adj.* having a common measure: capable of being measured exactly by the same unit: in due proportion.— *ns.* commensurabil'ity, commen'surableness.— *adv.* commen'surably.—*adj.* commen'surate, equal in measure or extent: in due proportion.—*adv.* commen'surately.—*ns.* commen'surateness, commensurā'tion. [L. *com-*, *mēnsūra*, a measure— *mētiri, mēnsus*, to measure.]

comment, *kom'ənt, -ent, n.* a note conveying illustration or explanation: a remark, observation, criticism.—*v.i.* (or *kəm-ent'*) to make critical or explanatory notes: to annotate: to meditate (*Shak.*).—*v.t.* to say in comment: to expound (*Spens.*).—*ns.* comm'entary, a comment: a

remark: a series or book of comments or notes; commentā'tion, annotation; comm'entātor, one who comments; the writer of a commentary: a broadcaster of a running commentary.—*adj.* commentatō'rial, pertaining to the making of commentaries.—*n.* comm'enter, -or (*or -ment'*). [L. *commentārī*, to devise, contrive—*com-* and L. *mēns, mentis*, the mind.]

commerce, *kom'ûrs, n.* interchange of merchandise on a large scale between nations or individuals: extended trade or traffic: intercourse.—*v.i.* commerce (*kəm-ûrs'*), to trade: to have communication with.—*adj.* commer'cial (*-shl*), pertaining to commerce: mercantile.—*n.* a commercial traveller: a commercially-sponsored programme on radio or TV: an advertisement in such a programme.—*n.* commercialese', business jargon. —*v.t.* commer'cialise, -ize, to reduce to a branch of commerce: to subject to the commercial spirit.—*ns.* commer'cialism, the commercial spirit: an expression characteristic of commercial language; commer'cialist; commerciality (*-shi-al'i-ti*).—*adv.* commer'cially.—commercial room, a room in a hotel set apart for commercial travellers; commercial traveller, an accredited travelling representative of a trading house. [Fr., —L. *commercium*—*com-*, mutual, *merx, mercis*, merchandise.]

commère, *kom-er', n.* fem. of compère. [Fr., godmother; cf. cummer.]

commerge, *kə-mûrj', v.i.* to merge together.

commie, *kom'i*, (coll.) *n.*, abbrev. for communist.

comminate, *kom'in-āt, v.t.* to threaten.—*n.* commina'tion, threatening, denunciation: a recital of God's threatenings made on Ash Wednesday and at other times in the English Church.—*adjs.* comm'inative, comm'inatory, threatening punishment. [L. *comminārī, -ātum*—*com-*, inten., and *minārī*, to threaten.]

commingle, *kəm-ing'gl, v.t.* and *v.i.* to mingle or mix together.—*adj.* comming'led.

comminute, *kom'in-ūt, v.t.* to reduce to minute particles: to pulverise.—*n.* comminū'tion.— comminuted fracture (see fracture). [L. *comminuĕre, -ūtum*, to break into pieces—*com-*, inten., *minuĕre*, to make small—root of *minus*, less.]

Commiphora, *kom-if'ər-a, n.* a genus of plants of the family Burseraceae, natives of tropical Asia and Africa, yielding myrrh, bdellium, and other resins. [Gr. *kommi*, gum, *phoreein*, to bear.]

commis, *ko-mē, n.* an agent, deputy: an apprentice waiter, steward or chef. [Fr.]

commiserate, *kəm-iz'ər-āt, v.t.* to feel or express compassion for: to pity: to condole with.—*adj.* commis'erable, requiring commiseration: pitiable.—*n.* commiserā'tion, pity.—*adj.* commis'-erative, feeling or expressing sympathetic sorrow. —*n.* commis'erator. [L. *com-*, with, *miserārī* to deplore—*miser*, wretched.]

commissary, *kom'is-ər-i, n.* one to whom any charge is committed: a deputy: the judge in a commissary court (*Scots law*): a higher officer of police: an officer representing a bishop, and performing his duties in distant parts of the diocese (*eccles.*): an officer who furnishes provisions, etc., to an army: a commissar.—*n.* commissar', a commissary: (*Soviet Union*) a head of a government department (since 1946 called minister).—*adj.* commissā'rial, pertaining to a commissary.—*ns.* commissā'riat, the department charged with the furnishing of provisions, as for an army: the supply of provisions: the office of a commissary or of a commissar: a body of commissars; comm'issaryship.—Commissary Court, a Scottish court with jurisdiction in matters that had belonged to the bishops' courts, abolished in 1836; commissary general, the head of the department for supplying provisions, etc., to an army. [L.L. *commissārius*—*committĕre, commissum*.]

**commission**, *kəm-ish'ən*, *n.* act of committing: the state of being commissioned or committed: that which is committed: an instrument conferring authority, or the authority itself, esp. that of a military, naval, or air officer, or a justice of the peace: a percentage paid to an agent: a body of persons appointed to perform certain duties: an order for a piece of work, esp. of art: (of a warship, etc.) the state of being manned, equipped, and ready for service: (of an office) temporary or permanent delegation to a number of persons who act jointly.—*v.t.* to give a commission to or for: to empower: to appoint: to put in commission.—*v.i.* to be put in commission.—*ns.* **commiss'ion-ag'ent**, **-mer'chant**, one who transacts business for another for a commission; **commissionaire** (*-ār'*), a messenger or doorkeeper in uniform: a member of a corps of old soldiers and sailors employed as doorkeepers, etc.—*adj.* **commiss'ioned.**—*ns.* **commiss'ioner**, one who holds a commission to perform some business: a member of a commission: representative of high authority in a district, etc.; **commiss'ionership.**—**commissioned officer**, one appointed by commission; **High Commission Court**, a court established in 1529 to investigate ecclesiastical cases, abolished as illegal in 1641; **High Commissioner**, the chief representative in a British Commonwealth country of another country that is also a member of the Commonwealth; **Lord High Commissioner**, the representative of the crown at the General Assembly of the Church of Scotland. [See **commit.**]

**commissure**, *kom'is-ūr*, *n.* a joint: a surface of junction: a suture: a bundle of nerve-fibres connecting two nerve-centres.—*adj.* **commissū'ral.** [L. *commissūra*, a joining; see **commit.**]

**commit**, *kə-mit'*, *v.t.* to give in charge or trust: to consign: to become guilty of, perpetrate: to compromise or involve: to pledge (*pr.p.* **committ'ing**; *pa.p.* **committ'ed**).—*adj.* **committ'ed**, having entered into a commitment: (of literature) written from, (of author) writing from, a fixed standpoint or with a fixed purpose, religious, political, or other.—*ns.* **commit'ment**, act of committing: an order for sending to prison: imprisonment: an obligation undertaken: declared attachment to a doctrine or cause; **committ'al**, commitment: a pledge, actual or implied; **committ'ee**, a portion selected from a more numerous body (or the whole body) to which some special business is committed: (*kom-i-tē'*) a person to whom something is committed: one charged with the care of a lunatic or imbecile (*law*); **committ'eeship.**—**committee stage**, the stage in the passage of a bill through parliament, between the second and third readings, when it is discussed in detail in committee.—**Committee of the whole House**, the House of Commons or other legislative body, when it resolves itself into a committee with chairman, etc.; **commit to memory**, to learn by heart; **go into committee**, to resolve itself into a committee; **in committee**, during the deliberations of a committee. [L. *committĕre*—*com-*, with, *mittĕre*, to send.]

**commix**, *kə-miks'*, *v.t.* to mix together.—*v.i.* to mix.—*ns.* **commix'tion** (*-chan*), **commix'ture**, act of mixing together: the state of being mixed: the compound formed by mixing: the rite of putting a piece of the host into the chalice, emblematic of the reunion of body and soul at the resurrection: sexual intercourse (*obs.*).

**commodious**, *kə-mō'dyəs*, *adj.* suitable or convenient (*arch.*): roomy, spacious: serviceable (*Shak.*): comfortable.—*n.* **commode'**, a small sideboard: an ornamental chest of drawers: a night-stool: a large, high head-dress formerly worn by ladies.—*adv.* **commo'diously.**—*ns.*

**commo'diousness**; **commodity** (*-mod'*), convenience (*arch.*): profit, expediency, advantage, privilege (*Shak.*): parcel, portion (*Shak.*): an article of traffic: (in *pl.*) goods, produce. [L. *commodus*—*com-*, together, *modus*, measure.]

**commodore**, *kom'ə-dōr*, *-dör*, *n.* officer intermediate between an admiral and a captain: the senior captain in a fleet of merchantmen: the president of a yacht-club: a commodore's ship. [Perh. from Du. *kommandeur*.]

**common**, *kom'ən*, *adj.* belonging equally to more than one: public: general: usual: frequent: ordinary: easy to be had: of little value: vulgar: of low degree.—*n.* the commonalty (*Shak.*): a tract of open land, used in common by the inhabitants of a town, parish, etc.—*v.i.* to share (*Shak.*): to converse (*Spens*): to board (*arch.*).—*adj.* **comm'onable**, held in common.—*ns.* **comm'onage**, right of pasturing on a common: the right of using anything in common: a common; **commonal'ity**, frequency, widespreadness: (esp. *Scot.*) the common people; **comm'onalty**, the general body of the people: the common people; **comm'oner**, one who is not a noble: a member of the House of Commons: at Oxford, a student who pays for his commons; **comm'oney**, an ordinary playing marble.—*adv.* **comm'only**, in a common manner: meanly, vulgarly: ordinarily: usually: generally: familiarly, intimately (*Spens.*): publicly (*B.*).—*n.* **comm'onness.**—*n.pl.* **comm'ons**, the common people; their representatives—i.e. the lower House of Parliament or **House of Commons**: common land: food at a common table: at Oxford, rations served at a fixed rate from the college buttery: food in general, rations.— **common chord**, a tone with its third (major or minor) and perfect fifth; **Common era**, the Christian era; **common forms**, the ordinary clauses which are of frequent occurrence in identical terms in writs and deeds; **common gender**, the gender of a noun or pronoun having one form for male and female, as L. *bōs*, bull, cow, Eng. *student*; **common law**, in England, the ancient customary law of the land: **common market**, an association of countries as a single economic unit with internal free trade and common external tariffs: **(European) Common Market**, common market formed in 1957 by Treaty of Rome by France, West Germany, Italy, Belgium, the Netherlands and Luxembourg: joined in 1973 by the United Kingdom, Denmark and the Republic of Ireland; **common measure**, a quantity that is a measure of several quantities (*math.*): common time (*mus.*); **common noun**, a name that can be applied to all the members of a class—opp. to *proper* noun.— *adj.* **common-or-garden**, ordinary.—**comm'onplace**, a common topic or subject (*obs.*): a note (*obs.*): a platitude.—*adj.* lacking distinction: hackneyed.—*v.t.* to make notes of: to put in a commonplace book.—*v.i.* to platitudinise.— **commonplace book**, a note or memorandum book; **comm'on-riding**, the Scottish equivalent of beating the bounds; **common room**, in schools, colleges, etc., a room to which the members have common access; **common sense**, an inner consciousness unifying the five outer senses (*obs.*): average understanding: good sense or practical sagacity: the opinion of a community: the universally admitted impressions of mankind. —*adjs.* **comm'onsense'**, **commonsens'ical.**—**common-shore** (see shore (4)); **common school** (*U.S.*), a public elementary school; **common stair**, an interior stair giving access to several independent flats or dwellings; **common time** (*mus.*), four-beat or two-beat rhythm.—**Court of Common Bench**, **Common Pleas**, one of the divisions of the High Court of Justice; **Common Prayer (Book of)**, the liturgy of the Church of England; **in common**, together (*arch.*): shared or possessed equally; make common cause with, to cast in one's lot with: to have the same interest and aims with; philosophy of common sense, that school of philosophy which takes the universally admitted impressions of mankind as corresponding to the facts of things without any further scrutiny; short commons, scant fare; the common, that which is common or usual; the common good, the interest of the community at large: the corporate property of a burgh in Scotland; the common people, the people in general. [Fr. *commun*—L. *commūnis*, prob. from com-, together, and *mūnis*, serving, obliging.]

commonweal, *kom'ən-wēl, n.* the common good, welfare of the community: commonwealth (*arch.*).—*n.* comm'onwealth (*-welth*), the public or whole body of the people: a form of government in which the power rests with the people, esp. that in England after the overthrow of Charles I: a state or dominion, esp. applied to the Australian federation and certain states of America: a group of states united by a strong but elastic link. —*n.* comm'onwealth'sman, comm'onwealthsman (*obs.*), a (good) citizen: an adherent of Cromwell's Commonwealth. [See wealth.]

commorant, *kom'ər-ənt, n.* and *adj.* resident (esp. at a university). [L. *commorāns, -antis*, pr.p. of *commorāri*, to abide.]

commot, *ko'mot*, (*hist.*) *n.* a subdivision of a cantred. [Mediaeval L. *commotum*—W. *cymwd*.]

commotion. See commove.

commove, *kə-mōōv', v.t.* to put in motion: to agitate: to disturb, excite.—*n.* commotion (*-mō'-shən*), a violent motion or moving: excited or tumultuous action, physical or mental: agitation: tumult.—*adj.* commō'tional. [L. *com-*, inten., and *movēre, mōtum*, to move.]

commune, *kom'ūn, n.* a corporation: in France, etc., a small territorial division with some self-government and a mayor: in some communist countries, an agricultural community: a group of people living communally.—*adj.* communal (*kom'ū-nl, kə-mū'*), pertaining to a commune or a community: owned in common, shared.— *ns.* commū'nalisātion, -izā'tion; commū'nalism; commū'nalist.—*adv.* comm'ūnally.—*n.* comm'ūnard (or *-ärd'*), an adherent of the Paris *Commune* in 1871: a communist.—the Commune at Paris in 1871 was a revolt against the national government, the principle of the revolt being that each city or district should be ruled independently by its own commune or local government. [Fr. *commune*. See common.]

commune, *kə-mūn', kom'ūn, v.i.* to converse or talk together: to have intercourse, esp. spiritual: to receive Holy Communion.—*n.* comm'une, converse.—*n.* and *adj.* commūn'ing. [O.Fr. *communer*, to share.]

commune bonum, *ko-mū'nē bō'nəm, ko-mōō'ne bo'nŏom,* (L.) common good.

communibus annis, *ko-mū'ni-bəs an'ēs, ko-mōō'ni-bōōs an'ēs,* (L.) on the annual average.

communicate, *kə-mū'ni-kāt, v.t.* to give a share of, impart: to reveal: to bestow.—*v.i.* to have something in common with another: to have communication: to have means of passage: to have intercourse: to partake of Holy Communion: to succeed in conveying one's meaning to others.—*ns.* commūnicability (*-kə-bil'i-ti*), commū'nicableness.—*adj.* commū'nicable, that may be communicated: affable.—*adv.* commū'nicably.—*ns.* commū'nicant, one who partakes of Holy Communion; commūnicā'tion, act of communicating: that which is communicated: intercourse: correspondence: a means of communicating, a connecting passage or channel: (in *pl.*) means of giving information, as the press, cinema, radio, and television: means of transporting, esp. troops and supplies.—*adj.*

commū'nicātive, inclined to communicate or give information: unreserved.—*adv.* commū'nicātively.—*ns.* commū'nicātiveness; commū'nicātor.—*adj.* commū'nicātory, imparting knowledge.— *n.* communiqué (*kom-ū'ni-kā*), an official announcement. [L. *commūnicāre, -ātum*— *commūnis*, common.]

communi consensu, *ko-mū'nī kon-sen'sū, ko-mōō'nē kon-sen'sōō,* (L.) by common consent.

communion, *kəm-ūn'yən, n.* act of communing: spiritual intercourse: fellowship: common possession: interchange of transactions: union in religious service: the body of people who so unite: (Holy Communion) sacrament commemorating the Last Supper.—Communion of Saints, the spiritual fellowship of all true believers, the blessed dead and the faithful living—in R.C. doctrine held to involve a mutual exchange of examples, prayers, merits and satisfactions. [L. *commūniō, -ōnis*, from *commūnis*, common.]

communism, *kom'ūn-izm, n.* a theory or condition of things according to which private property should be abolished, and all things held in common: Marxian socialism as understood in Russia.—*v.t.* comm'ūnise, -ize, to make common property: to make communist.—*n.* comm'unist, a believer in communism.—*adjs.* comm'ūnist, communist'ic of, or pertaining to, communism: believing in or favouring communism: (communistic) of or favouring communal living and ownership.

community, *kəm-ūn'i-ti, n.* common possession or enjoyment: agreement: communion: commonness (*Shak.*): people having common rights, etc.: the public in general: a body of persons in the same locality: a body of persons leading a common life, or under a socialistic or similar organisation: a monastic body.—*n.* communitā'rian, a member of a community.—community centre, a place where members of a community may meet for social and other activities; community home, school, successor to approved school (see approve); community singing, organised singing by a gathering. [O.Fr. *communité* —L. *commūnitās, -ātis*—*commūnis*, common.]

commute, *kə-mūt', v.t.* to exchange: to exchange for a punishment less severe: to compound for (by a single payment, a simple or more convenient method, etc.): to change (electric current) from alternating to direct or vice versa. —*v.i.* (orig. *U.S.*) to travel regularly, esp. between suburban home and town office.—*n.* commūtabil'ity.—*adj.* commūt'able, that may be commuted or exchanged.—*v.t.* commutate (*kom'*; *elect.*), to commute.—*n.* commūtā'tion, the act of commuting: change or exchange of one thing for another: the change to a lighter penalty, simpler or easier mode of payment, etc. —*adj.* commū'tative (or *kom'*), relating to exchange: interchangeable: such that *x*y = y*x—where * denotes a binary operation (*math.*). —*adv.* commū'tatively.—*ns.* comm'ūtātor, an apparatus for reversing electric currents; commūt'er (orig. *U.S.*), one who commutes.—commutation ticket (*U.S.*), a season ticket. [L. *commūtāre*—com-, with *mūtāre*, to change.]

commutual, *kə-mū'chōō-əl, adj.* mutual, reciprocal.

comose, comous. See coma.

comp, *komp, n.* abbreviated form of compositor.

compact, *kəm-pakt', adj.* closely placed or fitted together: composed or framed: firm: close: brief.—*n.* compact (*kom'*), a compacted body or structure, a combination: a small case containing face-powder for carrying in the handbag (powder compact).—*v.t.* (*-pakt'*) to press closely together: to consolidate: to confirm (*Shak.*).— *adj.* compact'ed.—*adv.* compact'edly.—*n.* compact'edness.—*adv.* compact'ly.—*ns.* compac'tion, act of compacting, or state of being compacted: sediments compacted by pressure from above (*geol.*): an area formed by dumping rock waste, etc., pressing it together by means of heavy machines, and causing or allowing grass to grow over the whole; compact'ness; compac'ture (*Spens.*), close union or knitting together. [L. *compāctus, pa.p.* of *compingĕre—com-, pangĕre,* to fix.]

compact, *kom'pakt, n.* a mutual bargain or agreement: a league, treaty, or union: league, in bad sense (*Shak.*).—*adj.* (*kom-pakt'*) united: leagued: agreed upon, arranged (*Spens.*). [L. *compactum* —*compaciscī,* from *com-,* with, *paciscī,* to bargain.]

compages, *kəm-pā'jēz, n.* structure (also *obs.* compage'):—*pl.* compages.—*n.* compagination (-*paj-i-nā'shən*).—*v.t.* compag'inate, to join, connect. [L. *compāgēs, compāgināre, -ātum, com-* and root of *pangĕre,* to fasten.]

compagnie anonyme, *kõ-pa-nyē a-no-nēm,* (Fr.). Same as société anonyme.

compagnon de voyage, *kõ-pa-ny5 də vwa-yäzh,* (Fr.) travelling companion.

companion, *kəm-pan'yən, n.* one who keeps company or frequently associates with another: a partner (*obs.*): spouse (*obs.*): higher rank of servant, who, though receiving pay, stands rather in the relation of a friend: fellow, rascal (*Shak.*): a member of an order, esp. in a lower grade: one of a pair or set of things.—*v.t.* to accompany.— *adj.* of the nature of a companion: accompanying.—*adjs.* compan'iable (*obs.*), sociable; compan'ionable, fit to be a companion: agreeable.— *n.* compan'ionableness.—*adv.* compan'ionably.— *adjs.* compan'ionate, shared in companionship; compan'ioned, having a companion.—*n.* compan'ionhood.—*adj.* compan'ionless.—*n.* compan'ionship, state of being a companion: company, fellowship: a body of companions.— companionate marriage, a form of marriage proposed in the 1920s with legalised birth-control and divorce by mutual consent; companion star, one appearing to be close to another though not necessarily near it in space, e.g. the fainter component of a double star.—Companion of Literature, C.Litt., an honour (instituted 1961) conferred by the Royal Society of Literature. [Fr. *compagnon,* from L.L. *compānium,* a mess— L. *com-,* with, and *pānis,* bread.]

companion, *kəm-pan'yən,* (*naut.*) *n.* the skylight or window-frame through which light passes to a lower deck or cabin: companion-ladder.— compan'ion-hatch, the covering of an opening in a deck; compan'ion-ladd'er, the ladder or stair leading from the deck to a cabin or to the quarter-deck; compan'ion-way, a staircase from the deck to a cabin. [Cf. Du. *kompanje;* O.F. *compagne;* It. *compagna,* store-room.]

company, *kum'pə-ni, n.* a person or persons associating with one: any assembly of persons, or of beasts and birds: persons associated for trade, etc.: a society: a sub-division of a regiment: the crew of a ship: state of being a companion: presence in association: fellowship: social intercourse.—*v.t.* to accompany.—*v.i.* to associate: to cohabit:—*pr.p.* com'panying, *Spens.* companing; *pa.t.* and *pa.p.* com'panied.— company promoter, one who promotes or superintends the formation of joint-stock companies. —good, or bad, company, having or lacking companionable qualities; keep company, to associate with: to court; know a man by his company, to determine his character by the quality of his friends. [Fr. *compagnie;* same root as companion.]

compare, *kəm-pār', v.t.* to set together so as to ascertain how far things agree or disagree (often with *with*): to liken or represent as similar (with *to*): to give the degrees of comparison of (*gram.*). —*v.i.* to make comparison: to stand in comparison: to vie.—*n.* (*obs.*) compeer: compari-

son.—*adj.* comparable (*kom'pər-ə-bl*).—*n.* com'-parableness.—*adv.* com'parably.—*adj.* comparative (*kəm-par'ə-tiv*), pertaining to or making comparison: estimated by comparing with something else: not positive or absolute: expressing more (*gram.*).—*adv.* com'paratively.— *ns.* compar'ator, any device for comparing accurately, so as e.g. to detect deviations from a standard or to confirm identity; comparison (-*par'i-sən*), the act of comparing: capacity of being compared: a comparative estimate: a simile or figure by which two things are compared: the inflection of an adjective or adverb to express different relative degrees of its quality (*gram.*).—beyond compare, without any rival or like. [L. *comparāre,* to match, from *com-, parāre,* to make or esteem equal—*par, equal.*]

compare, *kəm-pār',* (*Spens.*) *v.t.* to get or provide. [L. *comparāre—com-,* inten., *parāre,* to prepare.]

compartment, *kəm-pärt'mənt, n.* a partitioned off or marked off division of an enclosed space or area: a division of a railway carriage: a division of anything.—*vs.t.* compart', to divide into parts; compartment'alise, -ize, to divide into categories or into units, esp. units with little intercommunication.—*n.* compartmentalisā'tion, -z-. [Fr. *compartiment*—L. *com-,* inten., *partīrī,* to divide —*pars, partis,* a part.]

compass, *kum'pəs, n.* a circuit or circle: space: limit: range of pitch of a voice or instrument: circumference: girth: an instrument consisting of a magnetised needle, used to find directions: (*pl.*) a pair of jointed legs, for describing circles, etc.—*v.t.* to pass or go round: to surround or enclose: to besiege: to grasp, comprehend: to bring about, accomplish, achieve, or obtain: to devise: to contrive or plot: to curve, bend (*Shak.*).—*adj.* com'passable, capable of being compassed.—*n.* com'passing, contrivance, design.—*adj.* com'past (*Spens.*), rounded.— com'pass-card, the circular card of a compass; com'pass-plane, a plane, convex on the under side, for smoothing curved timber; com'pass-plant, any plant (as species of lettuce and *Silphium*) that places its leaves north and south to avoid the midday sun; com'pass-saw, one for cutting in curves; com'pass-sig'nal, a signal denoting a point in the compass; com'pass-tim'ber, curved timber, used for shipbuilding, etc.; com'pass-win'dow, a semicircular bay-window.—box the compass (see box); fetch a compass, to go round in a circuit. [Fr. *compas,* a circle, prob. from L.L. *compassus*—L. *com-,* inten., *passus,* a step.]

compassion, *kəm-pash'ən, n.* fellow-feeling, or sorrow for the sufferings of another: pity.—*v.t.* to pity.—*adjs.* compass'ionable, pitiable; compass'ionate, inclined to pity or mercy: merciful. —*v.t.* to have compassion for: to have pity or mercy upon.—*adv.* compass'ionately.—*n.* compass'ionateness.—compassionate leave, discharge, leave, discharge, in exceptional circumstances for personal reasons. [Fr.,—L.L. *compassiō, -ōnis—com-,* with, *patī, passus,* to suffer.]

compatible, *kəm-pat'i-bl, adj.* consistent: congruous: capable of co-existence: admissible in combination.—*ns.* compatibil'ity, congruity: ability to co-exist: the ability of a system of colour television to transmit a picture signal that can be received in black and white on an ordinary monochrome receiving set; compat'ibleness.—*adv.* compat'ibly. [Fr.,—L. *com-,* with, *patī,* to suffer.]

compatriot, *kəm-pat'ri-ət,* or *-pat', n.* a fellow-countryman.— Also *adj.*—*adj.* compatriotic (-*ot'ik*).—*n.* compa'triotism. [Fr. *compatriote*— L. *compatriōta;* see patriot.]

compear, *kəm-pēr',* (*Scots law*) *v.i.* to appear in court.—*ns.* compear'ance; compear'ant. [Fr.

comparoir—L. *compărēre—com-*, inten., *părēre*, to appear.]

compeer, *kəm-pēr'*, *kom'pēr*, n. an equal: a companion: an associate.—*v.t.* (*-pēr*; *Shak.*) to equal. [L. *compār—com-*, inten., *pār*, equal.]

compel, *kəm-pel'*, *v.t.* to drive or urge on forcibly: to bring with urgency (*Spens.*): to oblige: to force: to obtain by hard labour:—*pr.p.* compell'ing; *pa.t.* and *pa.p.* compelled'.—*adjs.* compell'able; compell'ing, forcing attention. [L. *com-*, inten., *pellĕre*, *pulsum*, to drive.]

compellation, *kom-pə-lā'shan*, n. style of address: an appellation.—*adj.* compellative (*kəm-pel'ə-tiv*).—*n.* compellation. [L. *compellāre*, *-ātum*, to address, freq. of *compellĕre*.]

compen'dium, *kəm-pen'di-əm*; pl. -diums, -dia, compend, *kom'*, ns. a shortening or abridgement: book or treatise containing the substance of a larger one: an epitome: an abstract: a comprehensive, generally compressed, treatise.—*adj.* compen'dious, short: concise: comprehensive. —*adv.* compen'diously.—*n.* compen'diousness. [L. *compendium*, what is weighed together, or saved (opp. to *dispendium*, what is weighed out or spent)—*com-*, together, *pendēre*, to weigh. See compulse.]

compensate, *kom'pən-sāt*, or *kəm-pen'sāt*, *v.t.* to make amends for, or to recompense: to counterbalance.—*v.i.* to make up (for).—*n.* compensā'tion (*kom-*), act of compensating: amends for loss sustained: the neutralisation of opposing forces (*phys.*): payment, remuneration (*U.S.*): process of compensating for sense of failure or inadequacy by concentrating on achievement or superiority, real or fancied, in some other sphere: the defence mechanism involved in this (*psych.*).—*adjs.* compensā'tional, compensative (*kom'*, or *-pen'*), compen'satory, giving compensation.—*n.* com'pensātor, one who or that which compensates.—compensation balance, pendulum, a balance-wheel or pendulum so constructed as to counteract the effect of the expansion and contraction of the metal under variation of temperature. [L. *com-*, inten., and *pēnsāre*, freq. of *pendēre*, to weigh.]

compère, *kō-per*, *kom'per*, n. one who introduces and interlinks items of an entertainment.—*fem.* commère.—*v.t.* to act as compère to. [Fr., godfather, god-mother.]

compesce, *kəm-pes'*, (arch. *Scot.*) *v.t.* to restrain. [L. *compēscĕre*.]

compete, *kəm-pēt'*, *v.i.* to seek or strive for something in opposition to others: to contend for a prize.—*n.* competition (*kom-pi-tish'ən*), the act of competing: rivalry in strife for the same object: a match or trial of ability.—*adj.* competitive (*kəm-pet'i-tiv*), pertaining to or characterised by competition: (of e.g. price) such as to give a chance of successful result in conditions of rivalry.—*n.* compet'itor, one who competes: a rival or opponent: an associate, confederate, fellow (*Shak.*). [L. *competĕre*, to strive together—*com-*, *petĕre*, to seek, strive after.]

competent, *kom'pi-tənt*, adj. suitable: sufficient: fit: efficient: belonging: legally qualified: legitimate.—*ns.* com'petence, com'petency, fitness: efficiency: capacity: sufficiency: enough to live on with comfort: legal power or capacity. —*adv.* com'petently. [L. *competĕre*, to come together, be convenient—*com-*, *petĕre*, to seek.]

compile, *kəm-pil'*, *v.t.* to write or compose by collecting the materials from other books: to draw up or collect: to compose: to heap up, to put or bring together (*Spens.*): to compose (in peace and rest) (*Spens.*): to pile up a score of (cricket slang).—*ns.* compilā'tion (*-pil-* or *-pil-*), the act of compiling: the thing compiled, a literary work made by gathering the material from various authors; compile'ment, a compilation; compil'er, one who compiles: a complex

program(me) which translates a program(me)-language into machine code, thus enabling the computer to function; com'pilātor, one who compiles.—*adj.* compi'latory. [Fr. *compiler*, prob. from L. *compilāre—com-*, together, *pilāre*, to plunder, or *pilāre*, to pound down; influenced by pile.]

compital, *kom'pit-əl*, adj. pertaining to crossroads, or to the intersection of leaf-veins: acutely intersecting. [L. *compita*, cross-roads.]

complacent, *kəm-plā'sent*, adj. showing satisfaction: self-satisfied: pleased: inclined to please.—*ns.* complā'cence, complā'cency, pleasure: satisfaction: complaisance.—*adv.* complā'cently. [L. *complacēre—com-*, inten., *placēre*, to please.]

complain, *kəm-plān'*, *v.i.* (also *refl.*) to express grief, pain, censure: to murmur or express a sense of injury: to accuse: to make a mournful sound: to show that one is ill.—*v.t.* to deplore: to utter as a complaint.—*n.* complaint.—*ns.* complain'ant, one who complains: one who raises a suit, a plaintiff (*law*); complain'er, a murmurer: complainant.—*n.* and adj. complain'-ing.—*adv.* complain'ingly.—*n.* complaint', a complaining: an expression of grief and dissatisfaction: a poem setting forth matter of grief or dissatisfaction: a representation of pains or injuries: a finding fault: the thing complained of: a grievance: a disease: an ailment. [Fr. *complaindre*—L.L. *complangĕre*—L. *com-*, inten., *plangĕre*, bewail.]

complaisant, *kəm-plā'zənt*, *kom'ple-zant*, esp. form. *-zant'*, adj. desirous of pleasing: obliging: facile, ready to condone.—*n.* com'plaisance (or zans', or *-plā'*), care or desire to please, esp. in excess: an obliging civility.—*adv.* complaisantly. [Fr., *complaire*—L. *complacēre*.]

complanate, *kom'plan-āt*, adj. flattened.—*n.* complanā'tion. [L. *complānāre*, *-ātum*, make flat.]

compleat. See complete.

complect, *kəm-plekt'*, *v.t.* to embrace: to interweave.—*adj.* complect'ed, interwoven. [L. *complecti*, to embrace—*com-*, *plectĕre*, to twine.]

complected. See complexion.

complement, *kom'pli-mənt*, n. that which completes or fills up: that by which an angle or arc falls short of a right angle or quadrant: one of the parallelograms not intersected by the diagonal of a given parallelogram when it is divided into four parallelograms by straight lines through a point in the diagonal: that by which a logarithm falls short of 10: that which is added to certain verbs to make a complete predicate: that by which an interval falls short of an octave: one of two colours which together give white: full number or quantity: consummateness, completeness (*Spens.*): fulness (of the moon) (*her.*): politeness (*Spens.*; *Shak.*): all members of a set not included in a given subset (*math.*).—*v.t.* complement (*-ment'* or *kom'pli-mənt*), to be the complement of: to compliment (*arch.*).—*adjs.* complement'al, completing: complimental (*Shak.*); complement'ary, completing: together making up a whole, a right angle, an octave, white.—*n.* complementar'ity, a concept, first adopted in microphysics, which accepts the existence of superficially inconsistent views of an object or phenomenon e.g. which accepts a dual aspect of light (consisting of particles, as shown by certain experiments, and of waves, as shown by others). [L. *complēmentum—com-*, inten., and *plēre*, to fill.]

complete, *kəm-plēt'*, adj. free from deficiency: perfect: finished: entire: fully equipped: consummate:—*arch.* compleat (*-plēt'*).—*v.t.* to finish: to make perfect or entire: to accomplish.—*adjs.* complēt'able; complēt'ed.—*adv.* complete'ly.— *ns.* complete'ness; complē'tion, the act of completing: the state of being complete: fulfilment.

—*adjs.* **complēt′ive**; **complēt′ory**, fulfilling: completing. [L. *complēre*, *-ētum*, to fill up— *com-*, inten., and *plēre*, to fill.]
**complex**, *kom′pleks*, *adj.* composed of more than one, or of many parts: not simple: intricate: difficult.—*n.* a complex whole: a group of (repressed and forgotten) ideas or impressions to which are ascribed abnormal mental conditions and abnormal bodily conditions due to mental causes (*psychology*): loosely applied to the mental condition itself.—*v.t.* **complex′**, to complicate.—*ns.* **complex′edness**, **com′plexness**, **complex′ity**, state of being complex: complication.—*adv.* **com′plexly.**—*n.* **complex′us**, a complicated system: a large muscle of the back, passing from the spine to the head.—**complex number**, the sum of a real and an imaginary number; **complex sentence**, one consisting of a principal clause and one or more subordinate clauses. [L. *complex—com-*, together, and root of *plicāre*, to fold. See **complicate.**]
**complexion**, *kəm-plek′shən*, *n.* disposition: colour: quality: colour or look of the skin, esp. of the face: general appearance, temperament, or texture: bodily constitution (*Shak.*).—*v.t.* to give a colour to.—*adjs.* **complex′ional**, pertaining to the complexion; **complex′ioned** (*U.S.*) **complect′ed**), having a certain complexion, or temperament; **complex′ionless**, colourless: pale. [Fr.,—L. *complexiō*, *-ōnis*, a combination, physical structure of body—*com-*, and *plectĕre*, to plait.]
**compliance**, *kəm-plī′əns*, *n.* a yielding: agreement, complaisance: assent: submission (in bad sense).—*adj.* **compli′able**, disposed to comply.— *n.* **compli′ancy**, compliance.—*adj.* **compli′ant**, yielding: pliant: civil.—*adv.* **compli′antly.** [See **comply.**]
**complicate**, *kom′pli-kāt*, *v.t.* to twist or plait together: to render complex: to entangle.—*adj.* **complex**: involved: folded together.—*n.* **com′-plicacy** (*-kə-si*), the quality or state of being complicated.—*adjs.* **com′plicant**, overlapping; **com′plicated**, intricate, confused.—*n.* **complicā′-tion**, an intricate blending or entanglement.— *adj.* **com′plicātive**, tending to complicate.— **complicated fracture**, a fracture where there is some other injury (e.g. a flesh wound not communicating with the fracture, a dislocation, a rupture of a large blood-vessel).—**complication of diseases**, a number of diseases present at the same time. [L. *com-*, together, and *plicāre*, *-ātum*, to fold.]
**complice**, *kom′plis*, *n.* an associate (*Shak.*): an accomplice (*obs.*).—*n.* **complic′ity**, state or condition of being an accomplice: complexity.
**compliment**, *kom′pli-mənt*, *n.* an expression of regard or praise: delicate flattery: an expression of formal respect or civility: a present.—*v.t.* **compliment′** (*-ment′* or *kom′pli-mənt*), to pay a compliment to: to express respect for: to praise: to flatter: to congratulate: to present in comliment.—*v.i.* to make compliments.—*adjs.* **compliment′al**, expressing or implying compliment; **compliment′ary**, conveying, or expressive of, civility or praise: using compliments: bestowed in compliment, given free.—*n.* **compliment′er**, one who pays compliments.—**compliments of the season**, compliments appropriate to special times, as Christmas and birthdays; **left-handed compliment**, a saying intended to seem a compliment, but in reality the reverse; **pay, or present, one's compliments**, to give one's respects or greeting. [Fr. *compliment*—L. *complimentum*; see **comply.**]
**complin, compline**, *kom′plin*, *n.* the 7th and last service of the day, at 9 p.m., completing the canonical hours. [O.Fr. *complie* (mod. *complies*)—L. *complēta* (*hōra*) (*n.* unexplained.]
**complish**, *kom′plish* (*Spens.*) *v.t.* to accomplish.

**complot**, *kom′plot*, *n.* a conspiracy.—*v.i.* **complot′** (*kəm-*), to plot together: to conspire.—*v.t.* to plan:—*pr.p.* **complott′ing**; *pa.t.* and *pa.p.* **complott′ed.** [Fr.]
**compluvium** *kom-plōō′vi-əm*, *n.* a quadrangular open space in the middle of a Roman house. [L.]
**comply**, *kəm-plī′*, *v.i.* to yield to the wishes of another: to agree or consent to (*with*): to use ceremony (*Shak.*):—*pr.p.* **comply′ing**; *pa.t.* and *pa.p.* **complied′.**—*n.* **compli′er**, one who complies. —*p.adj.* **comply′ing**, compliant. [It. *complire*, to fulfil, to suit, to offer courtesies—L. *complēre*, to fulfil; see **complete.**]
**compo**, *kom′pō*, *n.* a mortar of cement: a mixture of whiting, resin, and glue for ornamenting walls and cornices: a bankrupt's composition. —**compo ration** (*milit.*), a composite 'hard' ration for use in the field when no fresh food is available. [Abbrev. of **composition.**]
**component**, *kəm-pō′nənt*, *adj.* making up: forming one of the elements or parts.—*n.* one of the parts or elements of which anything is made up, or into which it may be resolved.—*n.* **compō′-nency.**—*adj.* **componental** (*kom-pō-nent′l*). [L. *compōnĕre*.]
**compony, componé**, *kom-pō′ni*, (*her.*) *adj.* consisting of a row of squares of alternate tinctures. [Origin doubtful.]
**comport**, *kəm-pōrt′*, *-pört′*, *v.i.* to agree, suit (*with*). —*v.t.* (*refl.*) to bear: to behave.—*n.* manner of acting.—*ns.* **comport′ance** (*Spens.*); **comport′-ment**, behaviour. [L. *comportāre—com-*, with, *portāre*, to carry.]
**compose**, *kəm-pōz′*, *v.t.* to form by putting together or being together: to set in order or at rest: to settle or soothe: to dispose artistically: to set up for printing: to create (esp. in literature and music).—*v.i.* to write (esp.) music: to set type.—*p.adj.* **composed′**, settled: quiet: calm.— *adv.* **compōs′edly.**—*ns.* **compōs′edness**; **com-pōs′er**, a writer or author, esp. of music; **com-posure** (*kəm-pōzh′(y)ər*), calmness: self-posses-sion: tranquillity: composition: temperament, character (*Shak.*).—*n.* **compōs′ing-stick**, a boxlike instrument for holding type before it is placed on the galley. [Fr. *composer*—L. *com-*, with, *pausāre*, to cease, rest; confused and blended in meaning with words from *pōnĕre*, *positum*, to place.]
**composite**, *kom′pəz-it*, formerly *-poz′*, *adj.* made up of distinct parts or elements: blending Ionic and Corinthian (*archit.*): in bot., belonging to the Compositae (*kəm-poz′i-tē*), a great family akin to the bell-flowers but having small flowers crowded together in heads on a common receptacle surrounded by bracts so as to resemble single flowers.—*n.* **com′posite**, a composite thing: a plant of the Compositae.—*ns.* **com′positeness**; **composi′tion**, the act or art of composing: the nature or proportion of the ingredients of anything: a thing composed: a work of art, esp. in music: an exercise in writing prose or verse: disposition of parts: congruity: combination: an artificial mixture, esp. one used as a substitute: mental or moral make-up: a compromise: a percentage accepted by a bankrupt's creditors in lieu of full payment: the compounding of vector quantities, as velocities, forces, into a single resultant: a picture, photograph, formed from several images.—*adjs.* **composi′tional**; **compositive** (*-poz′*).—*ns.* **compos′itor**, one who sets up type; **compost** (*kom′post, -pōst*), com-pōst′ure (*Shak.*), a mixture: a manure consisting of a mixture of decomposed organic substances. —*v.t.* **com′post**, to treat with compost: to convert into compost.—**composite carriage**, a railway carriage with compartments of different class; **composite portrait**, a blend of several portraits: a photograph printed from several negatives representing different persons or the same person

at different times; **com'post-heap**, a pile of plant refuse, soil, and often chemical fertiliser, which decomposes to form compost.—**composition of felony**, compounding of felony; **metal composite**, a metal with steel wires or glass fibres incorporated in it. [L. *compositus, compostus—com-*, together, *pōnĕre*, to place.]

**compos mentis**, *kom'pos men'tis*, (L.) of sound mind, sane.

**compossible**, *kəm-pos'i-bl*, *adj.* possible in coexistence with something else.—*n.* **compossibil'ity.**

**compost.** See **composite.**

**compot, compote**, *kom'pot*, or *kom'pōt*, *n.* fruit preserved in syrup: stewed fruit. [Fr. *compote*; cf. **composite.**]

**compotation**, *kom-pō-tā'shon*, *n.* a carouse together.—*ns.* **compotā'tionship**; **com'potātor**, a bottle-companion.—*adj.* **compot'atory.** [L. *compōtātiō, -ōnis—com-*, together, *pōtāre*, to drink.]

**compound**, *kəm-pownd'*, *v.t.* to make up: to combine: to settle or adjust by agreement: to agree for a consideration not to prosecute (a felony).—*v.i.* to agree, or come to terms: to bargain in the lump.—*adj.* **compound** (*kom'*), mixed or composed of a number of parts: in chem., resolvable into two or more elements, so united that the whole has properties of its own which are not necessarily those of its constituents, as in the case of a mixture: in arith., not simple, dealing with numbers of various denominations of quantity, etc., as in *compound addition*, etc.: or with processes more complex than the simple process, as in *compound proportion.*—*n.* a mass made up of a number of parts: a word made up of two or more words: a compound substance (*chem.*): a compounded drug.—*n.* **compound'er.** —**compound animals** (same as colonial animals); **compound engine**, a condensing engine in which the mechanical action of the steam is begun in one cylinder, and ended in a larger cylinder; **compound fracture** (see **fracture**); **compound householder**, one who pays his rates in his rent, the landlord being immediately chargeable with them; **compound interest**, interest added to the principal at the end of each period (usu. a year) to form a new principal for the next period; **compound leaf**, one divided into leaflets by divisions reaching the mid-rib; **compound quantity** (*alg.*), a quantity consisting of more than one term, as $a+b$; **compound ratio**, the product of ratios; **compound sentence** (*gram.*), one containing more than one principal clause; **compound time** (*mus.*), time in which each bar is made up of two or more simple measures. [O.Fr. *compundre* from L. *compōnĕre—com-*, together, *pōnĕre*, to place.]

**compound**, *kom'pownd*, *n.* an enclosure round a house or factory (in India), or for housing native labourers (S. Africa). [Malay *kampong*, enclosure.]

**comprador(e)**, *kom-prä-dōr'*, *-dōr'*, *n.* an intermediary through whom a foreign firm trades with Chinese dealers. [Port., buyer—L. *com-*, inten., *parāre*, to furnish.]

**comprehend**, *kom-pra-hend'*, *v.t.* to seize or take up with the mind, to understand: to comprise or include.—*ns.* **comprehensibil'ity**, **comprehen'sibleness.**—*adj.* **comprehen'sible**, capable of being understood.—*adv.* **comprehen'sibly.**—*n.* **comprehen'sion**, power of the mind to understand: the intension of a term or the sum of the qualities implied in the term (*logic*): the inclusion of Nonconformists within the Church of England.—*adj.* **comprehen'sive**, having the quality or power of comprehending or containing much: inclusive: compendious.—*adv.* **comprehen'sively.**—*n.* **comprehensiveness.**—**comprehensive school**, one that combines the various types of secondary school in one institution. [L.

*comprehendĕre, -hēnsum—com-, prehendĕre*, to seize.]

**compress**, *kəm-pres'*, *v.t.* to press together: to force into a narrower space: to condense or concentrate: to embrace (*arch.*).—*n.* **compress** (*kom'*; *surg.*), a pad used to apply pressure to any part: a folded cloth applied to the skin.— *adj.* **compressed'**, pressed together: compacted: laterally flattened or narrowed (*biol.*).—*ns.* **compressibil'ity**, **compress'ibleness**, the property of being reduced in volume by pressure: the ratio of the amount of compression per unit volume to the compressing force applied: in aero., a shock-wave phenomenon causing increased drag, which asserts itself when an aircraft in flight approaches the speed of sound, the hypothesis of the air as an incompressible fluid being no longer valid.—*adj.* **compress'ible**, that may be compressed.—*n.* **compression** (*kəm-presh'ən*), act of compressing: state of being compressed: condensation: flattening: deformation by pressure: the stroke that compresses the gases in an internal combustion engine.—*adjs.* **compress'ional**; **compress'ive**, able to compress.— *ns.* **compress'or**, anything that compresses or raises pressure, as a device that compresses air or gas: a muscle that compresses certain parts; **compressure** (*-presh'ər*). —**compression-ignition engine**, an internal-combustion engine in which ignition of the liquid fuel injected into the cylinder is performed by the heat of compression of the air charge. [L. *compressāre, com-*, together, and *pressāre*, to press—*premĕre*, *pressum*, to press.]

**comprint**, *kəm-print'*, *v.t.* to share in printing—of the former privilege shared with the Stationers' Company and the King's Printer by Oxford and Cambridge universities.

**comprise**, *kəm-priz'*, *v.t.* to contain, include: to comprehend: to consist of: to hold together (*Spens.*).—*adj.* **compris'able.**—*n.* **compris'al**, the act, condition, or fact of comprising. [Fr. *compris*, pa.p. of *comprendre*—L. *comprehendĕre*; see **comprehend.**]

**compromise**, *kom'prō-miz*, *n.* arbitration (*Shak.*): a settlement of differences by mutual concession: partial waiving of theories or principles for the sake of settlement: anything of intermediate or mixed kind, neither one thing nor another.—*v.t.* to settle by mutual concession; to involve or bring into question: to expose to risk of injury, suspicion, censure, or scandal.—*v.i.* to make a compromise. [Fr. *compromis*—L. *comprōmittĕre, -missum—com-*, together, *prōmittĕre*, to promise.]

**comprovincial**, *kom-pro-vin'shəl*, (*Spens.*) *adj.* belonging to the same province.

**compt, compter, comptible, kownt, -ər, -ə-bl**, obs. forms of **count**, etc.—*n.* **Comptom'eter** (*komptom'*), a machine that adds, subtracts, multiplies and divides (*trademark*).

**compte rendu**, *kõt rä-dü*, (Fr.) an account rendered: report.

**comptroll, comptroller.** See under **control.**

**compulse**, *kəm-puls'*, *v.t.* (*obs.*) to compel.—*adjs.* **compul'satory**, **compul'sative** (*Shak.*), **compulsory.**—*ns.* **compul'sion**, the act of compelling: force: a strong irrational impulse; **compul'-sionist**, a believer in compulsion; **compul'sitor** (*Scots law*), a means of compelling.—*adj.* **compul'sive**, with power to compel: pertaining to compulsion: (of person) driven by, (of action) caused by, a specific constant and irresistible impulse.—*advs.* **compul'sively**; **compul'sorily.**— *adj.* **compul'sory**, compelled: obligatory: compelling.—**compulsion neurosis**, a disorder in which the patient suffers from compulsions and/or obsessions, depression, etc. [L. *compulsāre*, freq. of *compellere*; see **compel.**]

**compunction**, *kəm-pungk'shən*, *n.* pricking or

uneasiness of conscience (*obs.*): remorse tinged with pity.—*adj.* compunc'tious, of the nature of compunction: feeling compunction.—*adv.* compunc'tiously. [O.Fr.,—L. *compunctiō, -ōnis*—*com-*, intens., and *pungĕre, punctum*, to prick.]

compurgation, *kom-pûr-gā'shən, n.* in Old English and other Germanic law, the clearing of the accused by witnesses joining their oaths to his: evidence in favour of the accused: vindication. —*n.* com'purgator, one who testifies to the innocency or veracity of another.—*adjs.* compurgatō'rial (*kom-*), compur'gatory. [L. *compūrgāre*, to purify wholly—*com-*, intens., *pūrgāre*, to purify: taken as if meaning to clear together; see purge.]

compursion, *kəm-pûr'shən*, (*Sterne*) *n.* a pursing together.

compute, *kəm-pūt', v.t.* to calculate: to number: to estimate.—*adj.* computable (*kom'* or *-pūt'*), calculable.—*ns.* com'putant, com'putātor, com'-putist, a calculator; comput'er, a calculator: a machine or apparatus, mechanical, electric or electronic, for carrying out, esp. complex, calculations, dealing with numerical data or with stored items of other information; also used for controlling manufacturing processes, or coordinating parts of a large organisation; computā'tion, the act of computing: reckoning: estimate: arithmetic.—*adjs.* computā'tional, involving calculation; com'putative (or *-pūt'*), given to computation.—*v.t.* comput'erise, *-ize*, to bring computer(s) into use to control (operation, system of operations): to process (data) by computer.—*n.* computerisā'tion.—computer typesetting, the use of electronic equipment to process an unjustified input of keyed material into an output of justified and hyphenated, etc., lines, the output being either a new tape to be used on a typesetting or filmsetting machine or, in some systems, the final product. [L. *computāre*—*com-*, inten., *putāre*, to reckon.]

com.rade, *kom'rid, kum'rid* (*Shak., Milt.*; *-rād'*), *n.* a close companion: an intimate associate: in some socialist and communist circles used as a term of address, or prefixed to a name.—*n.* com'radeship.—*adj.* and *adv.* com'radely. [Sp. *camarada*, a roomful, a room-mate—L. *camera*, a room—Gr. *kamarā.*]

comsat. Abbrev. for *com*munications *sat*ellite.

Comsomol. Variant of Komsomol.

comstockery, *kum'stok-ə-ri*, or *kom', n.* prudery.— *ns.* com'stocker; com'stockism. [From Anthony Comstock (1844-1915), an American denunciator of the nude in art.]

Comtism, *komt'izm, kōt-ēzm, n.* the philosophical system of Auguste Comte, the founder of Positivism (1798-1857).—*ns.* and *adjs.* Comt'ian; Comt'ist.

Comus, *kō'məs, n.* a god of mirth (*Milt.*): (without *cap.*) a revel. [L.,—Gr. *kōmos*, a revel.]

con, *kon, adv.* and *n.* a contraction of L. *contrā*, against, as in pro and con, for and against.

con (*Spens.* conne, kon), *kon, v.t.* to know (*Spens.*): to learn (*Spens.*): to study carefully, scan, pore over: to commit to memory: to acknowledge (as to *con* thanks'; *obs.*): to teach, show (*obs.*):— *pr.p.* conn'ing; *pa.t.* and *pa.p.* conned, *Spens.*— *n.* cond, *kond.*—*ns.* conn'er; conning. [Another form of can, O.E. *cunnan*, to know; perh. partly *cunnian*, to seek to know, examine. (See conner, 2.)]

con, conn, kun, kon, (*naut.*) *v.t.* to direct the steering of.—Also *v.i.*—*n.* act or station of conning.—*ns.* con'der, conner (*kun'ər, kon'ər*), one who directs steering: a look-out on land, who signals the movements of fish to fishermen; conn'ing.—conning-tow'er, the pilot-house of a warship or submarine. [Older forms cond, condue, etc., apparently—Fr. *conduire*—L. *condūcĕre*; see conduct.]

con, kon, (*dial.*) *n.* a knock. [Fr. *cogner*, to knock.]

con, kon, adj. abbrev. for confidence, as in congame, a swindle, con man, a swindler, esp. one with a persuasive way of talking.—*v.t.* con, to swindle: to trick: to persuade by dishonest means.

conacre, *kon'ā-kər, n.* the custom of letting land in Ireland in small portions for a single crop, for rent in money or labour; a form of this is still found in Eire.—also corn'acre.—*v.t.* to sublet in conacre.—*n.* con'acreism. [corn, acre.]

con amore, kon am-ōr'-e, -ö're, (It.) with love: very earnestly.

conarium, *kō-nā'ri-əm, n.* the pineal gland.—*adj.* conā'rial. [Gr. *kōnarion*, pineal gland, dim. of *kōnos*, cone.]

conation, conative, See conatus.

conatus, *kō-nā'təs, n.* an effort: an impulse: a tendency; nisus;—*pl.* conā'tus.—*n.* conā'tion, the active aspect of mind, including desire and volition.—*adj.* conative (*kon', kōn'ə-tiv*). [L. *cōnātus, -ūs*, effort.]

con brio, kon brē'ō, (It.) with spirit.

concatenate, *kən-kat'ə-nāt, v.t.* to chain or link together: to connect in a series.—*n.* concatenā'-tion, a series of links united: a series of things depending on each other. [L. *con-, catēna*, a chain.]

concause, *kon'köz, n.* a co-operating cause.

concave, *kon'kāv, kon'kāv', adj.* curved inwards (opposed to *convex*).—*n.* a hollow: an arch or vault.—*v.t.* and *v.i.* to make or become hollow.— *adv.* con'cavely.—*n.* concav'ity (*kən-kav'i-ti*), the quality of being concave: a hollow.—*adjs.* concā'vo-con'cave, or doub'le-con'cave, concave on both sides; concā'vo-con'vex, concave on one side, and convex on the other. [L. *concavus*, from *con-*, inten., and *cavus*, hollow. See cave.]

conceal, *kən-sēl', v.t.* to hide completely or carefully: to keep secret: to disguise: to keep from telling.—*adj.* conceal'able.—*n.* conceal'ment, hiding: keeping secret: secrecy: disguise: hiding-place: a mystery (*Shak.*). [O.Fr. *conceler*—L. *concēlāre*, from *con-*, inten., and *cēlāre*, to hide.]

concede, *kən-sēd', v.t.* to yield or give up.—*v.i.* to make concession.—*n.* conced'er. [L. *concēdĕre*, *-cēssum*—*con-*, wholly, and *cēdĕre*, to yield.]

conceit, *kən-sēt', n.* overweening self-esteem: fancy: thought (*obs.*): wit: a witty thought, esp. far-fetched, affected or over-ingenious: idea (*Spens.*): understanding (*Shak.*): estimate. —*v.t.* (*obs.*) to conceive: to think.—*adj.* conceit'ed, clever, witty (*obs.*), fantastical (*dial.*): having a high opinion of oneself: egotistical.— *adv.* conceit'edly.—*n.* conceit'edness.—*adjs.* conceit'ful (*Spens.*) thoughtful; conceit'less (*Shak.*), without conceit, stupid; conceit'y (*dial.*), characterised by conceit.—out of conceit with, displeased with. [From conceive, on the analogy of deceive, deceit.]

conceive, *kən-sēv', v.t.* to receive into or form in the womb: to form in the mind: to imagine or think: to understand: to grasp as a concept: to express.—*v.i.* to become pregnant: to think. —*ns.* conceivabil'ity, conceiv'ableness.—*adj.* conceiv'able.—*adv.* conceiv'ably. [O.Fr. *conceiver*—L. *concipĕre, conceptum*, from *con-*, together, and *capĕre*, to take.]

concent, *kən-sent', (arch.) n.* a harmony or concord of sounds: concert of voices.—*v.t.* (*Spens.*) to fit, adjust duly. [L. *concentus*, pa.p. of *concinĕre* —*con-*, *canĕre*, to sing.]

concentrate, *kon'sən-trāt*, sometimes *kən-sen'-*, *v.t.* to bring towards a common centre: to focus: to direct with exclusive attention upon the matter in hand: to condense, to increase the quantity in unit space.—*v.i.* to draw towards a common centre: to direct one's thoughts or efforts towards one object.—*n.* a product of concentration.—*adj.* con'centrate, concentrated. —*n.* something concentrated, as animal feed.—*n.* concentrā'tion, act of concentrating: condensation: proportion of molecules or ions to unit volume: the keeping of the mind fixed on something.—*adj.* concen'trative, tending to concentrate.—*ns.* concen'trativeness; con'centrator, apparatus for concentrating solutions or for obtaining minerals from ores by physical means.

—concentration camp, a settlement for segregating persons who might be in the way of, or obnoxious to, the authorities. [A lengthened form of concentre.]

concentre, concenter, *kən-sent'ər, v.i.* to tend to or meet in a common centre: to be concentric.
—*v.t.* to bring or direct to a common centre or point—*pr.p.* concent'ring, -cent'ering; *pa.t.* and *pa.p.* concent'red, concent'ered.—*adjs.* concen'tric, -al, having a common centre.—*adv.* concen'trically.—*n.* concentricity (*kon-sən-tris'i-ti*). [Fr. *concentrer*—L. *con-*, *centrum*—Gr. *kentron*, point.]

concept, *kon'sept, n.* a thing conceived, a general notion.—*ns.* conceptacle (*kən-sep'tə-kl; obs.*) a receptacle: a reproductive cavity; concep'tion, the act of conceiving: the fertilisation of an ovum: the formation, or power of forming in the mind, a concept, plan, thought, etc.: a concept: a notion: a mere fancy (*Shak.*): a plan: a thing conceived, esp. in some seaweeds; Concep'tionist, a nun of an order founded in Portugal in 1489 in honour of the Immaculate Conception.—*adjs.* concep'tious (*Shak.*), fruitful; concept'ive, capable of conceiving; concep'tual, pertaining to conception.—*ns.* concep'tualism, the doctrine in philosophy that universals exist in the mind; concep'tualist.—*adj.* conceptualis'-tic. [L. *concipĕre*, *-ceptum*, to conceive.]

concern, *kən-sûrn', v.t.* to relate or belong to: to affect or interest: to involve by interest, occupation or duty: to implicate: to make uneasy: to trouble.—*n.* that which concerns or belongs to one: affair: business: interest: regard: anxiety: a business establishment.—*n.* concern'ancy (*Shak.*, in burlesque), bearing, relevancy.—*adj.* concerned', interested: involved: troubled: under the influence of liquor, drunk (*obs.*).—*adv.* concern'edly.—*n.* concern'edness.—*prep.* concern'ing, regarding: about.—*n.* concern'ment, concern: importance.—as concerns, as regards. [L. *concernĕre*, to distinguish, later to have respect to—*con-*, inten., *cernĕre*, to distinguish.]

concert, *kon'sərt, n.* union or agreement in any undertaking: harmony: musical harmony: a musical entertainment.—*v.t.* concert (*kən-sûrt'*), to frame or devise together: to arrange, adjust. —*n.* concertante (*kon-sər-tan'tē*; It. *kon-cher-tän'te*), a symphonic composition with parts for solo instruments.—*adj.* providing an opportunity for brilliant virtuosity by an instrumentalist.—*adj.* concert'ed (*-sûrt'*), mutually planned: arranged in parts (*mus.*).—*ns.* concertina (*kon-sər-tē'na*), a musical instrument consisting of a pair of bellows, usually hexagonal, the sounds produced by free vibrating reeds of metal, as in the accordion.—*v.i.* to collapse or fold up like a concertina.—*ns.* concertino (*kon-chər-tē'nō*), a short concerto; concerto (*kon-chûr'tō*), a composition for solo instrument(s) and orchestra in sonata form: applied by the older composers to various combinations and forms:—*pl.* concer'tos. —con'cert-goer, a habitual attender of concerts; con'cert-grand, a grand piano suitable for concerts; concert pitch, a standard of pitch that has varied (see international concert pitch, French pitch): also *fig.* [It. *concertare*, sing in concert, perh.—L. *con-*, *certāre*, to strive.]

concession, *kən-sesh'ən, n.* the act of conceding: the thing conceded: a grant.—*adj.* concessible (*-ses'*).—*n.* concessionaire', one who has obtained a concession.—*adj.* concess'ionary.—*n.* concess'ionist.—*adj.* concess'ive, implying concession. [See concede.]

concetto, *kon-chet'tō, n.* an ingenious turn of expression: a conceit:—*pl.* concet'ti, (*-tē*).—*n.* concet'tism, the use of concetti; concet'tist. [It., —L. *conceptum*, conceit.]

conch, *kongk, konch, n.* name for various marine gasteropods, esp. chank and Strombus, and for their shells: a shell used as a trumpet, as by the Tritons: a poor white or other native of the Bahamas or Florida Keys (from their feeding on conchs): a concha.—*n.* conch'a, in archit., the semi-dome of an apse: the apse itself: the outer ear, or its cavity.—*adjs.* conch'ate, conch'iform, shaped like a shell, esp. one valve of a bivalve shell; conchif'erous, having a shell: shelly.—*ns.* conchi'tis, inflammation of the concha: conch'-oid, a plane curve, (*x² + y²*)(*x − a*)² = *l²x²*, locus of point making with fixed straight line constant intercept on ray of pencil through fixed point.—*adjs.* conchoid'al, pertaining to a conchoid: shell-like, applied to a fracture like that seen in glass (*min.*): concholog'ical.—*ns.* conchol'ogist; conchol'ogy, the study of molluscs and their shells. [L. *concha*—Gr. *konchē*, a cockle or mussel; Sans. *śaṅkha*, a shell; conn. with chank, cockle.]

conchy, *kon'shi*, (slang) *n.* a conscientious objector.

concierge, *kɔ̃-si-erzh, n.* a warden: a janitor: a porter or a portress. [Fr.; ety. unknown.]

conciliar, *kən-sil'i-ər, adj.* pertaining to a council. Also concil'iary. [L. *concilium*, council.]

conciliate, *kən-sil'i-āt, v.t.* to gain, or win over: to reconcile.—*v.i.* to make friends.—*adj.* concil'-iable (*obs.*).—*n.* concil'iātion, act of conciliating. —*adj.* concil'iātive.—*n.* concil'iātor.—*adj.* concil'iatory. [L. *conciliāre*, *-ātum*—*concilium*, council.]

concinnity, *kən-sin'i-ti, n.* harmony: congruity: elegance.—*adj.* concinn'ous, elegant: harmonious. [L. *concinnus*, well adjusted.]

concipient, *kən-sip'i-ənt, adj.* conceiving.—*n.* concip'iency. [L. *concipiēns*, *-entis*, pr.p. of *concipĕre*, to conceive.]

concise, *kən-sis', adj.* cut short: brief.—*v.t.* (*Milt.*), to mutilate.—*adv.* concise'ly.—*ns.* concise'ness, the quality of being concise: terseness. —*n.* concision (*-sizh'ən*), mutilation: circumcision (*B.*): conciseness. [L. *concisus*, pa.p. of *concidĕre*—*con-*, inten., *caedĕre*, to cut.]

conclamation, *kon-klə-mā'shən, n.* a shout of many together. [L. *conclāmātiō*, *-ōnis*.]

conclave, *kon'klāv, n.* a private room (*obs.*): the room in which cardinals meet to elect a pope: the body of cardinals: any close assembly.—*n.* con'clavist, an attendant on a cardinal in conclave. [L. *conclāve*—*con-*, with, *clāvis*, a key.]

conclude, *kən-klōōd', v.t.* to enclose (*arch.*): to include (*obs.*): to restrain or debar (*obs.*): to close: to end: to decide: to settle or arrange finally: to infer.—*v.i.* to end: to form a final judgment: to state the object sought (*Scots law*). —*p.adj.* conclud'ed, finished: settled.—*n.* conclud'ing, final, closing.—*n.* conclu'sion (*-zhən*), act of concluding: the end, close, or last part: inference: judgment: an experiment (*obs.*): a problem, a riddle (*Shak.*).—*adjs.* conclusive (*-klōō'siv*), conclu'sory, final: convincing.—*adv.* conclus'ively.—*n.* conclus'iveness.—in conclusion, finally.—to try conclusions, to experiment: to engage in a contest. [L. *conclūdĕre*, *conclūsum* —*con-*, inten., *claudĕre*, to shut.]

concoct, *kən-kokt', v.t.* to digest: to prepare or mature: to make up or put together: to plan, devise: to fabricate.—*ns.* concoct'er, concoct'or; concoc'tion, the action of concocting: ripening:

preparation of a medical prescription, etc.: a made-up story.—*adj.* concoct'ive. [L. *concoquĕre, concoctum*—*con-*, together, and *coquĕre*, to cook, to boil.]

concolor, kon'kul-ər, *adj.* of uniform colour.— Also concol'orate, concol'orous. [L.,—*con-*, together, *color*, colour.]

concomitant, kən-kom'i-tənt, *adj.* accompanying: conjoined.—*n.* he who or thàt which accompanies.—*ns.* concom'itance, concom'itancy, state of being concomitant.—*adv.* concom'itantly. [L. *con-*, inten., *comitāns, -antis*, pr.p. of *comitārī*, to accompany—*comes*, a companion.]

concord, kon'körd, or kong'-, *n.* state of being of the same heart or mind: harmony: agreement: a combination of sounds satisfying to the ear.—*v.i.* concord' (kən-), to agree: to harmonise.—*n.* concord'ance, agreement: an index of the words or passages of a book or author.—*adj.* concord'-ant, harmonious, united.—*adv.* concord'antly.— *n.* concord'at, an agreement, esp. between the pope and a seculaı government.—*adj.* concor'-dial, harmonious. [Fr. *concorde*—L. *concordia* —*concors*, of the same heart, from *con-*, *cor*, *cordis*, the heart.]

concorporate, kən-kör'pər-āt, (arch.) *v.t.* to unite in one body.—*adj.* united in the body.

concours, kõ-kōōr, (Fr.) contest, competition.— **concours d'élégance**, dā-lā-gãs, competition among cars in which marks are allotted for appearance, not speed.

concourse, kon'kōrs, kong', -körs, *n.* assembly of persons or things running or drawn together: concurrence of an officer who has legal right to grant it (*Scots law*): a large hall: an open space, esp. at a road-junction or in a railway station or airport. [Fr. *concours*—L. *concursus*—*con-*, *currĕre*, to run.]

concreate, kon'krē-āt, (arch.) *v.t.* to create with: to create at the same time.

concremation, kon-kri-mā'shən, *n.* complete burning: cremation: burning together: suttee. [L. *concremāre, -ātum*—*con-*, intens., *cremāre*, to burn.]

concrescence, kən-kres'əns, *n.* a coalescence or growing together.—*adj.* concresc'ent. [L. *con-crēscentia*—*con-*, *crēscĕre*, to grow.]

concrete, kon'krēt (or kən-krēt'), *adj.* formed into one mass: the opposite of *abstract*, and denoting a particular thing: (kon') made of concrete.—*n.* (kon') a mass formed by parts growing or sticking together: a mixture of sand, gravel, etc., and cement, used in building.—*v.t.* concrēte', to form into a solid mass: (kon') to cover with concrete.—*v.i.* (krēt') to harden.—*adv.* con-crēte'ly (or kon').—*ns.* concrēte'ness (or kon'); concrētion (-krē'-shən), a mass concreted: a nodule or lump formed within a rock by materials rearranging themselves about a centre (*geol.*): a solid mass formed within an animal or plant body, whether by deposition or by accumulation of foreign matter.—*adj.* concrē'tionary.—*n.* con'cretism, regarding, representing, abstract things as concrete; *n.*, *adj.* con'cretist—*adj.* con-crēt'ive, having power to concrete.—**concrete poetry**, an art form which seeks to introduce a new element into poetry by means of visual effects such as the arrangement of letters on the printed page; **concrete steel**, reinforced concrete. [L. *concrētus*—*con-*, together, and *crēscĕre*, *crētum*, to grow.]

concrew, kon-krōō', (*Spens.*) *v.i.* to grow together. [Fr. *concrû*, pa.p. of *concroître*—L. *concrēscĕre*.]

concubine, kong'kū-bin, *n.* one (esp. a woman) who cohabits without being married.—*n.* concu-binage (kon-kū'bin-āj), state of living together as man and wife without being married.—*adj.* con-cū'binary.—*ns.* concū'bitancy, a custom by which marriage between certain persons is obligatory; concū'bitant, one subject to such an

obligation.—Also *adj.* [Fr.,—L. *concubīna*—*con-*, together, *cubāre*, to lie down.]

concupiscence, kən-kū'pis-əns, *n.* a violent desire: sexual appetite: lust.—*adjs.* concū'piscent; con-cū'piscible. [L. *concupiscentia*—*concupiscĕre*—*con-*, inten., *cupĕre*, to desire.]

concupy, kon(g)'kū-pi, (*Shak.*) *n.* a shortened form of concupiscence (or perh. of concubine).

concur, kən-kûr', *v.i.* to run together: to meet in one point; to coincide: to act together: to agree: to assent:—*pr.p.* concurr'ing; *pa.p.* con-curred'.—*ns.* concurrence (-kur'), meeting of lines in one point: coincidence: joint action: assent: competition (*arch.*); concurr'ency.—*adj.* con-curr'ent, meeting in the same point: running, coming, acting, or existing together: coinciding: accompanying.—*n.* one that concurs: a com-petitor (*arch.*): one who accompanies a sheriff's officer as witness.—*adv.* concurr'ently.—*n.* con-curr'ing, agreeing. [L. *concurrĕre*—*con-*, *cur-rĕre*, to run.]

concuss, kən-kus', *v.t.* to disturb: to shake: to overawei to coerce.—*n.* concussion (-kush'), state of being shaken: a violent shock caused by the sudden contact of two bodies: a violent blow, esp. on the head: the resulting condition: any undue pressure or force exerted upon any-one.—*adj.* concuss'ive, having the power or quality of concussion. [L. *concussus*, pa.p. of *concutĕre*—*con-*, together, *quatĕre*, to shake.]

concyclic, kon-sī'klik, (*geom.*) *adj.* lying on the circumference of the same circle.—*adv.* concy'-clically. [L. *con-*, together, Gr. *kyklos*, wheel.]

cond. See con (2).

condemn, kən-dem', *v.t.* to pronounce guilty: to censure or blame: to sentence: to give up to some fate: to pronounce unfit for use: to reject.—*adj.* condemnable (-dem'na-bl), blamable.—*n.* condemnā'tion (kon-dəm-nā'shən), state of being condemned.—*adj.* condem'natory, expressing or implying condemnation.—*p.adj.* condemned', pronounced to be wrong, guilty, or useless: belonging or relating to one who is sentenced to punishment (e.g. condemned cell): declared dangerous or unfit. [L. *condemnāre*, from *con-*, inten., and *damnāre*, to hurt.]

condense, kən-dens', *v.t.* to reduce to smaller compass: to render more dense or more intense: to reduce to a denser form, as vapour to liquid: to subject to condensation (*chem.*).—*v.i.* to become condensed.—*n.* condensabil'ity.—*adj.* condens'able.—*v.t.* and *v.i.* condens'āte, to con-dense.—*n.* a product of condensation.—*ns.* condensā'tion (kon-), act of condensing: the union of two or more molecules of the same or different compounds with the elimination of water, alcohol, or other simple substances (*chem.*): loosely applied to almost any reaction in which a product of higher molecular weight than the reactant is obtained; condens'er, an apparatus for reducing vapours to a liquid form: a mirror or lens for focusing light: a capacitor; condens'ery, a condensed-milk factory.—con-densation trail (see contrail); condensed milk, milk reduced by evaporation, and sugared; condensed type, printing type of narrow face. [L. *condēnsāre*—*con-*, inten., and *dēnsus*, dense.]

condescend, kon-də-send', *v.i.* to descend willingly from a superior position: to act graciously to inferiors: to deign: to stoop to what is un-worthy: to comply (*obs.*): to agree, consent (*obs.*).—*v.t.* to concede or grant (*obs.*): to specify (*Scot.*).—*n.* condescend'ence, condescen-sion: an articulate statement annexed to a summons, setting forth the allegations in fact upon which an action is founded (*Scots law*).— *adj.* condescend'ing, gracious to inferiors: offensively patronising.—*adv.* condescend'ingly. —*n.* condescen'sion.—condescend upon, to specify: to mention. [L. *con-*, inten., and *dē-*

scendĕre, to descend—dē, down from, scandĕre, to climb.]

condiddle, kən-did'l, (Scott) v.t. to steal. [L. con-, inten., and diddle.]

condign, kən-dīn', adj. well merited (usu. of punishment): worthy, deserving (Spens.).—adv. condign'ly.—n. condign'ness. [L. condignus—con-, inten., dignus, worthy.]

condiment, kon'di-mənt, n. a seasoning.—v.t. to season. [L. condimentum—condire, to preserve, to pickle.]

condisciple, kon-di-sī'pl, n. a fellow-disciple: a schoolfellow: a fellow-student. [L. con-, together, and disciple.]

condition, kən-dish'ən, n. state in which things exist: a good or fit state: a particular manner of being: quality: rank (as a person of condition): prerequisite: temper (obs.): a term of a contract: (in pl.) circumstances: that which must precede the operation of a cause (logic): a provision upon which an obligation depends (law): obligation of passing a future examination to make up a deficiency (U.S.).—v.i. to make terms.—v.t. to agree upon: to restrict, limit: to determine: to put into the required state: to allow to proceed in an education course on condition of passing a future examination (U.S.): to prepare, train (person, animal) for a certain activity or for certain conditions of living: to secure by training (a certain behavioural response to a stimulus).—adj. condi'tional, depending on conditions: expressing condition. —n. conditional'ity.—adv. condi'tionally.—v.t. condi'tionate (obs.), to condition: to qualify.— adj. condi'tioned, having a certain condition, state, or quality: circumstanced: depending: relative—the opposite of absolute: subject to condition.—ns. condi'tioner, a person, substance, or apparatus that brings into good or required condition; condi'tioning.—conditioned reflex, a reflex response to a stimulus which depends upon the former experience of the individual; conditioning house, an establishment in which the true weight, length, and condition of articles of trade and commerce are determined scientifically. [L. condiciō (wrongly conditiō), -ōnis, a compact—condicĕre—con-, together, dicĕre, to say.]

condole, kan-dōl', v.i. to grieve with another: to express sympathy in sorrow: to grieve (Shak.). —adj. condol'atory, expressing condolence.—ns. condole'ment, condol'ence, expression of sympathy with another's sorrow.—adj. condol'ent. [L. con-, with, dolēre, to grieve.]

con dolore, kon do-lō're, -lō're, (It.) with grief.

condom, kon'dom or 'dəm, n. contraceptive rubber sheath. [Perh. from name of inventor in 18th cent.]

condominium, kon-do-min'i-əm, n. joint sovereignty. [L. con-, together, dominium, lordship.]

condone, kən-dōn', v.t. to forgive: to pass over without blame, overlook: to excuse, atone for. —n. condonā'tion (kon-), forgiveness: such forgiveness granted by the injured party as may be urged against divorce for adultery (law). [L. con-, inten., dōnāre, to give. See donation.]

condor, kon'dör, -dər, n. a large South American vulture. [Sp. cóndor—Quechua cuntur.]

condottiere, kon-dot-tyä'rā, n. a leader of a mercenary band of military adventurers:—pl. condottie'ri (-rē). [It.,—condotto, way—L. condūcĕre, to assemble—con-, together, and dūcĕre, to lead.]

conduce, kən-dūs', v.i. to help to bring about, contribute (towards a result): app., to go on, conduct itself, or poss. to assemble (Shak.).—n. conduce'ment (Milt.).—adjs. conduc'ible, conduc'ive, leading or tending: having power to promote: advantageous. [L. con-, together, dūcĕre, to lead.]

conduct, kən-dukt', v.t. to lead or guide: to con-

vey (water, blood, sap, etc.): to direct: to manage: to behave: to carry or transmit (elect.): to beat time for and coordinate (mus.):—n. (kon'dukt), act or method of leading or managing: guidance: escort: guide: management: behaviour.—ns. conduct'ance, a conductor's power of conducting electricity, the reciprocal of the resistance; conductibil'ity.—adj. conduct'ible, capable of conducting heat, etc.: capable of being conducted or transmitted.—n. conduc'tion, act or property of conducting or transmitting: transmission by a conductor, as heat.—adj. conduct'ive, having the quality or power of conducting or transmitting.—ns. conductiv'ity, power of transmitting heat, electricity, stimuli: a substance's specific power of conducting electricity, conductance across a unit cube, reciprocal of the resistivity; conduct'or, the person or thing that conducts: a leader: a manager: a director of an orchestra or choir: one in charge of a bus, etc.: a railway guard (U.S.): that which has the property of transmitting electricity, heat, etc.:—fem. conduct'ress; conduct'orship, the office of conductor. [L. conductus—condūcĕre. See conduce.]

conduit, kon'dit, or kun'-, n. a channel or pipe conveying water or other fluid, or covering electric wires, etc.: a fountain for supplying the public with water. [Fr. conduit—L. conductus—condūcĕre, to lead.]

conduplicate, kan-dūp'li-kāt or -dōōp', adj. folded together lengthwise. [L. conduplicāre, -ātus, to double—con-, and duplex, double.]

condyle, kon'dil, n. a protuberance at the end of a bone serving for articulation with another bone. —adjs. con'dylar, con'dyloid.—n. condylō'ma, an overgrowth of skin about the mucous passages: —pl. condylō'mata.—adj. condylō'matous.— [Gr. kondylos, knuckle.]

cone, kōn, n. an infinite solid figure generated by a straight line passing through a fixed point and intersecting some curve in space: esp. (right circular cone) one generated by revolution of a triangle about one of its sides: a portion of such a figure terminated at the vertex: a surface generated by a line one point of which is fixed and one point of which describes a fixed plane curve: anything shaped like a cone: a form of weather signal: a tapering part of a machine, as a race for ball-bearings: a volcanic hill: a fan of alluvium where a torrent is checked at the foot of a declivity or in a lake: the typical flower (or fruit) or inflorescence of the Coniferae, a more or less conical mass of scale-like sporophylls set closely about an axis: a similar structure in other plants, e.g. horsetails: a sensory body in the retina: an ice-cream cornet. —v.t. to shape like a cone.—v.i. to bear cones.— adjs. conic (kon'ik), -al, having the form of or pertaining to a cone.—n. a conic section: (in pl.) the geometry of the cone and its sections.—adv. con'ically.—adj. cō'niform, in the form of a cone. —adj. cone'-in-cone' (petrology), showing a series of cones, one within another.—cone shell, a Gasteropod mollusc of a family (Conidae) with substantial conical shells; cone wheat, a bearded variety of wheat; conic section, a figure made by the section of a cone by a plane. [Gr. kōnos.]

coney. See cony.

confabulate, kan-fab'ū-lāt, v.i. to chat (coll. confab')—adjs. confab'ūlar; confab'ūlatory.— ns. confabulā'tion (coll. confab', con'fab); confab'ūlātor. [L. cōnfābulārī—con-, fābulārī, to talk.]

confarreation, kən-far-i-ā'shən, n. a Roman patrician mode of marriage, in which a spelt cake was offered up.—adj. confarr'eate. [L. cōnfarreātiō —con-, with, fār, spelt.]

confect, kon'fekt, n. fruit, etc., prepared with sugar: a sweetmeat: a comfit.—v.t. (kən-fekt'), to prepare: to preserve.—*n.* confec'tion, composition, compound: a composition of drugs (*obs.*): a sweetmeat: a ready-made article of dress for women's wear.—*v.t.* to make (into a confection).—*n.* confec'tionary, a confectioner (*B.*): a sweetmeat: a place where confections are made or kept.—*adj.* pertaining to or of the nature of confectionery.—*ns.* confec'tioner, one who makes or sells sweets; confec'tionery, confectioners' work or art: sweetmeats in general. [L. *cōnficĕre*, *cōnfectum*, to make up together—*con-, facĕre*, to make.]

confederate, *kən-fed'ər-āt*, *adj.* leagued together: allied (esp. the seceding American states of the Civil War).—*n.* one united in a league: an ally: an accomplice.—*v.i.* and *v.t.* to league together or join in a league.—*ns.* confed'eracy, a league or mutual engagement: persons or states united by a league: a conspiracy: (*cap.*) (*U.S. hist.*) the league of eleven seceding states in the Civil War; confederā'tion, a league: alliance, esp. of princes, states, etc.—*adj.* confed'erātive, of or belonging to a confederation. [L. *cōnfoederāre*, -*ātum*—*con-, foedus, foedĕris*, a league.]

confer, *kən-fûr'*, *v.t.* to give or bestow: to compare (*obs.*)—in use as abbrev. cf.—*v.i.* to talk or consult together (*pr.p.* conferr'ing; *pa.t.* and *pa.p.* conferred').—*ns.* conferee' (*kon-*), one conferred with; conference (*kon'*), the act of conferring: an appointed meeting for instruction or discussion: (*cap.*) a kind of pear.—*adj.* conferential (*kon-fər-en'shl*).—*n.* confer'ment, bestowal: a thing bestowed.—*adj.* conferr'able.—*n.* conferr'er. [L. *cōnferre*—*con-*, together, *ferre*, to bring.]

conférencier, *kō-fā-rā-syā*, (Fr.) a lecturer.

conferva, *kon-fûr'va*, *n.* a genus of freshwater algae (Heterocontae) forming slimy masses or tufts of unbranched filaments.—*adj.* confer'void, like conferva. [L. *cōnferva*, a kind of water-plant.]

confess, *kən-fes'*, *v.t.* to acknowledge fully (esp. something wrong): to own or admit: to make known, as sins to a priest: to hear a confession from, as a priest: to reveal, betray, or make manifest (*poet.*).—*v.i.* to make confession.—*ns.* confession (*kən-fesh'ən*), acknowledgment of a crime or fault: avowal: the thing confessed: a statement of religious belief: acknowledgment of sin to a priest (*auricular confession*): a religious body of common belief; confess'ional, the seat or enclosed recess where a priest hears confessions: the institution of confession.—*adj.* pertaining to confession.—*ns.* confess'ionalism; confess'ionalist.—*adj.* confess'ionary, of or belonging to confession.—*n.* a confessional.—*ns.* confess'or (or *kon'*), a priest who hears confessions and grants absolution: one who makes avowal, esp. of religious faith: one who endures persecution but not death:—*fem.* confess'oress; confess'orship.—*adjs.* confessed', confest', admitted: avowed: evident.—*advs.* confess'edly, confest'ly.—confession of faith, a formulary embodying the religious beliefs of a church or sect: a creed; confess to, to admit, acknowledge; stand confessed, to be revealed. [Fr. *confesser*—L. *cōnfitēri, cōnfessus*—*con-*, sig. completeness, and *fatēri*, to confess—*fāri*, to speak.]

confetti, *kon-fet'tē, kən-fet'i*, *n.pl.* sweetmeats or comfits: plaster or paper imitations of them flung in carnival: bits of paper flung at brides and bridegrooms. [It. (sing. *confetto*); see comfit, confect.]

confide, *kən-fīd'*, *v.i.* to trust wholly or have faith (with *in*): to impart secrets with trust.—*v.t.* to entrust: to impart with reliance upon secrecy.—*ns.* confidant (*kon-fi-dant'*), one confided in or entrusted with secrets, esp. in love affairs: a bosom friend.—*fem.* confidante'; con'fidence (*kon'fidəns*), firm trust or belief: faith: trust in

secrecy: self-reliance: firmness: boldness: presumption: admission to knowledge of secrets or private affairs: a confidential communication; con'fidency.—*adj.* con'fident, trusting firmly: having full belief: assured: bold.—*n.* a confidential friend.—*adj.* confiden'tial (-*den'shl*), given in confidence: admitted to confidence: private.—*advs.* confiden'tially; con'fidently.—*n.* confid'er, one who confides.—*adj.* confid'ing, trustful.—*adv.* confid'ingly.—*n.* confid'ingness.—confidence trick, a swindler's trick, whereby a person is induced to hand over money as a mark of confidence in the swindler; confident person, in Scots law, a confidential person, partner, agent, etc. [L. *cōnfīdĕre*—*con-*, sig. completeness, and *fīdĕre*, to trust.]

configuration, *kən-fig-ū-rā'shən*, *n.* external figure or shape; outline: relative position or aspect, as of planets: spatial arrangements of atoms in a molecule (*chem.*).—*vs.t.* config'urate, config'ure, to shape. [L. *cōnfigūrāre*, to form.]

confine, *kon'fīn*, *n.* border, boundary, or limit—generally in pl.: (*kən-fīn'*) confinement (*arch.*): a prison (*Shak.*).—*v.t.* confine', to border (*obs.*); to be adjacent to (*obs.*): to limit, enclose: to imprison.—*adjs.* confin'able; confined', limited: imprisoned: narrow; confine'less (*Shak.*), without bound: unlimited.—*ns.* confine'ment, state of being shut up: restraint: imprisonment: accouchement; confin'er, one within the confines (*obs.*): an inhabitant (*Shak.*).—*adj.* confin'ing, bordering: limiting.—be confined, to be limited: to be restrained to bed or indoors by illness. [L. *cōnfīnis*, bordering—*con-*, together, *fīnis*, the end.]

confirm, *kən-fûrm'*, *v.t.* to strengthen: to fix or establish: to. ratify: to verify: to assure: to admit to full communion.—*adj.* confirm'able.—*n.* confirmā'tion, a making firm or sure: convincing proof: the rite by which persons are admitted to full communion in many churches: ratification by a competent court of the appointment of an executor, constituting his right to act (*Scots law*).—*adj.* confirm'ative, tending to confirm.—*n.* con'firmator.—*adjs.* confirm'atory, giving additional strength to: confirming; confirmed', settled: inveterate.—*ns.* confirmee'; one to whom a confirmation is made; confirm'er; confirm'ing; confirm'or. [O.Fr. *confermer*—L. *cōnfirmāre*—*con-*, inten., and *firmāre*—*firmus*, firm.]

confiscate, *kon'fis-kāt*, (*obs.*). *kən-fis'-*, *v.t.* to appropriate to the state, as a penalty: to take possession of by authority.—*adj.* forfeited.—*adjs.* con'fiscable (or -*fis'*), confiscatory (*kon'fis-kā-tər-i* or *kən-fis'kə-tər-i*), of the nature of confiscation.—*ns.* confiscā'tion, the act of confiscating; con'fiscātor, one who confiscates. [L. *cōnfiscāre, -ātum*—*con-*, together, *fiscus*, a basket, purse, treasury.]

confiserie, *kō-fēs-ə-rē*, (Fr.) a confectionery; confiseur, *kō-fēs-œr*, a confectioner.

confit, *kon'fit, n.* (*obs.*). Same as comfit.

confiteor, *kon-fit'i-ör*, *n.* a form of prayer or confession used in the Latin Church. [L. *cōnfiteor*, I confess.]

confiture, *kon'fit-ūr, n.* (*obs.*). Same as comfiture.

confix, *kon-fiks'*, (*Shak.*) *v.t.* to fix firmly. [L. *cōnfīgĕre, -fixum*—*con-*, inten., *fīgĕre*, to fix.]

conflagrate, *kon'flə-grāt, v.t.* and *v.i.* to burn up.—*adj.* conflag'rant (*Milt.*), burning.—*n.* conflagrā'tion, a great burning or fire. [L. *cōnflagrāre*—*con-*, inten., and *flagrāre*, to burn; see flagrant.]

conflate, *kən-flāt'*, *v.t.* to fuse: to combine (two variant readings of a text) into one.—*n.* conflā'tion. [L. *cōnflāre, -ātum*, to blow together—*con-*, and *flāre*, to blow.]

conflict, *kon'flikt*, *n.* violent collision: a struggle or contest: a battle: a mental struggle.—*v.i.*

(*kən-flikt'*), to fight: contend: to be in opposition: to clash.—*adj.* conflict'ing, clashing: contradictory.—*n.* conflic'tion.—*adj.* conflict'ive, tending to conflict. [L. *cōnflīgĕre, -flīctum—con-*, together, and *flīgĕre*, to strike.]
confluence, kon'floo-əns, *n.* a flowing together: meeting-place, as of rivers: a concourse: the act of meeting together.—*adj.* con'fluent, flowing together: running into one: uniting.—*n.* a stream uniting and flowing into with another.—*adv.* confluently.—*n.* con'flux (*-fluks*), a flowing together. [L. *cōnfluĕre*, from *con-*, together, *fluĕre, fluxum*, to flow.]
conform, kən-förm', *v.t.* to make like or of the same form: to adapt.—*v.i.* to be or become of the same form: to comply: to obey.—*adj.* and *adv.* (*Scot.*), in conformity.—*n.* conformabil'ity, state, of being conformable.—*adj.* conform'able, corresponding in form: suitable: compliant: in unbroken continuity of bedding (*geol.*).—*adv.* conform'ably.—*ns.* conformā'tion, particular form, shape, or structure: adaptation; conform'er, conform'ist, one who conforms, esp. to the worship of the Established Church; conform'ity, likeness: compliance: consistency: conformability (*geol.*).—conformal transformation (see transformation); conformation theory, the theory of the structure of molecules, particularly of the arrangement of atoms in very complex molecules.—in conformity with, in accordance with. [L. *cōnförmāre—con-, förmāre—förma*, form.]
confound, kən-fownd', *v.t.* to overthrow, defeat: to mingle so as to make the parts indistinguishable: to confuse, fail to distinguish: to throw into disorder: to defeat in argument: to perplex: to astonish: used in the imperative as a mild curse: (*pa.p.*, *Spens.*, confound').—*adj.* confound'ed, confused: astonished: consummate, egregious (a term of disapprobation; *coll.*).—*advs.* confound'edly (*coll.*), hatefully, shamefully: cursedly; confound'ingly, astonishingly.—confound you, a gentle execration or curse. [O.Fr. *confondre*—L. *cōnfundĕre, -fūsum—con-*, together, *fundĕre*, to pour.]
confraternity, kon-frə-tûr'ni-ti, *n.* a brotherhood: clan: brotherly friendship. [L. *con-, frāter*, brother.]
confrère, kõ-frer', *n.* a colleague: a fellow-member or associate.—confrérie, kõ-frā-rē, a brotherhood. [Fr.,—L. *con-*, together, *frāter*, a brother.]
confront, kən-frunt', *v.t.* to come or be face to face with: to face in opposition: to bring face to face: to compare.—*n.* confrontā'tion (*kon-*), confront'ment, the bringing of people face to face: continued hostile attitude, with hostile acts but without declaration of war.—*adj.* confronté (*kon-frunt'ā*) (*her.*), face to face. [Fr. *confronter*—L. *con-*, together, and *fröns, frontis*, forehead; see front.]
Confucian, kən-fū'shyən, *adj.* of or belonging to Confucius, the Chinese philosopher (551-479 B.C.).—*ns.* Confū'cianism; Confū'cianist.
con fuoco, kon foo-ōk'ō, kon fwō'kō, (It.; *music*) with fire.
confuse, kən-fūz', *v.t.* to pour or mix together so that things cannot be distinguished: to throw into disorder: to perplex: to fail to distinguish.—*v.i.* to be confused.—*adj.* confused', perplexed: disordered.—*adv.* confus'edly, in a confused manner: disorderly.—*ns.* confus'edness, state of being confused: disorder; confū'sion (*-zhən*), the state of being confused: disorder: shame: overthrow: perdition: perplexity: embarrassment: turmoil. [See confound.]
confute, kən-fūt', *v.t.* to prove to be false: to refute: to bring to naught.—*adj.* confūt'able.—*n.* confūtā'tion (*kon-*).—*adj.* confūt'ative, tending to confute.—*n.* confute'ment. [L. *cōnfūtāre.*]
conga, kong'gə, *n.* a Cuban dance in which dancers follow a leader, usu. in single file: music for it. —Also *v.i.* [Amer. Sp., Congo.]
congé, kõ-zhā, congee, kon'ji, *n.* a bow: dismissal leave to depart.—*v.i.* to take leave: to bow.— congé d'élire (*dā-lēr'*; Fr.), permission to elect: the crown's formal permission to a dean and chapter to elect a certain person as bishop. [Fr. *congé*—L. *commeātus*, leave of absence—*com-*, together, *meāre*, to go.]
congeal, kən-jēl', *v.t.* to freeze: to change from fluid to solid by cold: to solidify, as by cold.— *v.i.* to pass from fluid to solid, as by cold: to stiffen: to coagulate.—*adj.* congeal'able.—*ns.* congeal'ableness; congeal'ment, congelation (*kon-ji-lā'shən*), act or process of congealing: anything congealed. [L. *congelāre*, from *con-*, inten., and *gelū*, frost.]
congee. See congé, conjee.
congener, kon'ji-nər, *n.* a person or thing of the same kind or nature: a member of the same genus.—*adj.* akin.—*adjs.* congeneric (*-ner'ik*), -al, of the same genus, origin, or nature; congenerous (*kən-jen'ər-əs*), of the same nature or kind; congenet'ic (*kon-ji-net'ik*), alike in origin. [L. *con-*, with, and *genus, generis*, kind.]
congenial, kən-jē'ni-əl, *adj.* of the same genius, spirit, or tastes: kindred, sympathetic: to one's taste: suitable.—*n.* congēnial'ity (*-al'i-ti*).—*adv.* congē'nially. [L. *con*, with, and *geniālis*, see genial.]
congenital, kən-jen'i-təl, *adj.* begotten or born with one—said of diseases or deformities dating from birth: innate.—*adv.* congen'itally. [L. *congenitus*, from *con-*, together, *gignĕre, genitum*, to beget.]
conger, kong'gər, *n.* a large sea-fish of the eel family—also con'ger-eel. [L.,—Gr. gongros.]
conger, kong'gər, (*hist.*) *n.* a company of co-operating booksellers. [Origin unknown.]
congeries, kon-jer'i-ēz, -jēr', *n.* an aggregation:— *pl.* conger'ies—false *sing.* congery (*kon'jər-i*). [L. *congeriēs—con-*, together, *gerĕre, gestum*, to bring.]
congest, kən-jest', *v.t.* to bring together, or heap up: to accumulate: to cause congestion in.— *adjs.* congest'ed, affected with an unnatural accumulation of blood: overcrowded: packed closely: over-charged: clogged: incapable of supporting its population; congest'ible.—*n.* congest'ion (*-jes'chən*), an accumulation of blood in any part of the body: fullness: an overcrowded condition.—*adj.* congest'ive, indicating or tending to congestion. [L. *congerĕre, congestum—con-*, together, and *gerĕre, gestum*, to bring.]
congiary, kon'ji-ər-i, *n.* a gift to the Roman people or soldiery, originally in corn, oil, etc., later in money. [L. *congiārium—congius*, the Roman gallon.]
conglobe, kən-glōb', *v.t.* or *v.i.* to collect together into a globe or round mass.—*adj.* conglobate (*kon'glō-bāt, kən-glō'bāt*) formed into a globe or ball.—*v.t.* or *v.i.* to form into a globe or ball.—*n.* conglobā'tion.—*v.i.* conglobūlate (*-glob'*), to gather into a globule or small globe. [L. *con-*, together, and *globāre, -ātum—globus*, a ball, globe.]
conglomerate, kən-glom'ər-āt, *adj.* gathered into a clew or mass: bunched: composed of pebbles cemented together (*geol.*).—*v.t.* and *v.i.* to gather into a ball.—*n.* a conglomerate rock (*geol.*): a miscellaneous mass or collection.—*adj.* conglomeratic (*-at'ik; geol.*), of the nature of conglomerate.—*n.* conglomerā'tion, state of being conglomerated: a collection or jumble of things. [L. *conglomerāre, -ātum—con-*, together, and *glomus, glomeris*, a clew, akin to *globus*.]
conglutinate, kən-gloō'tin-āt, *v.t.* to glue together: to heal by uniting.—*v.i.* to unite or grow together.—*adj.* conglu'tinant.—*n.* conglutinā'tion, a

joining by means of some sticky substance: healing.—*adj.* conglu'tinātive, having power to conglutinate.—*n.* conglu'tinator. [L. *conglūtināre*, *-ātum—con-*, together, and *glūten*, glue.]
Congoese, *kong'gō-ēz*, Congolese, *kong'gol-ēz*, *ns.* a native of the Congo.—Also *adjs.*
congou, *kong'gōō*, *n.* a kind of black tea.—Also congo. [Chinese *kung-fu*, labour, referring to that expended in producing it.]
congratulate, *kən-grat'ū-lāt*, *v.t.* to express pleasure in sympathy with: to felicitate: to pronounce or deem happy (esp. *refl.*).—*adjs.* congrat'ūlable; congrat'ūlant, expressing congratulation.—*n.* a congratulator.—*ns.* congratū-lā'tion; congrat'ūlator.—*adj.* congrat'ūlatory. [L. *congrātulārī*, *-ātus—con-*, inten., *grātulārī—grātus*, pleasing.]
congree, *kən-grē'*, (*Shak.*) *v.i.* to agree together: to accord. [L. *con-*, together, and Fr. *gré*, goodwill—L. *grātus*, pleasing.]
congreet, *kən-grēt'*, (*Shak.*) *v.t.* to salute mutually. [L. *con-*, together, and greet.]
congregate, *kong'grə-gāt*, *v.t.* to gather together: to assemble.—*v.i.* to flock together.—*p.adj.* (*Spens.*) congregated.—*p.adj.* congregated, assembled: aggregated.—*n.* congregā'tion, the act of congregating: an assemblage of persons or things: a name given to the children of Israel (*O.T.*): a body of people actually or habitually attending a particular church: the body of Protestant Reformers in Scotland in the time of Mary: a board charged with some department of administration in the Roman Catholic Church: a name given to certain religious orders without solemn vows: an academic assembly—at Cambridge, the senate, at Oxford, the resident masters, doctors, etc., or a smaller degree-conferring body.—*adj.* congregā'tional, pertaining to a congregation: (*cap.*) pertaining to the Independent Church.—*ns.* Congregā'tionalism, a form of church government in which each congregation is independent in the management of its own affairs—also called *Independency*; Congregā'tionalist, an Independent.—Congregation for the Doctrine of the Faith (see Inquisition). [L. *congregāre*, *-ātum—con-*, together, and *grex*, *gregis*, a flock.]
congress, *kong'gres*, *n.* the act of meeting together: intercourse: an assembly of delegates, specialists, ambassadors, etc., for the discussion or settlement of problems: the federal legislature of the United States and of some other American republics.—*v.i.* to meet in congress.—*adj.* congressional (*-gresh'*).—*n.* Con'gressman, a member of Congress, esp. of the House of Representatives.—*fem.* Con'gresswoman. [L. *con-*, together, and *gradi*, *gressus*, to step, to go.]
Congreve, *kong'grēv*, *n.* a rocket for use in war.—Con'greve-match, a kind of friction match. [Both poss. invented by Sir William *Congreve* (1772-1828).]
congrue, *kong-grōō'*, *v.i.* (*Shak.*) to agree.—*ns.* cong'ruence, cong'ruency, quality of being congruent: agreement: suitableness.—*adj.* cong'ruent, agreeing: suitable: congruous: giving the same remainder on division by the same number: capable of coincident superposition (*geom.*).—*n.* congru'ity, agreement, between things: consistency: fitness.—*adj.* cong'ruous, suitable: fit: consistent.—*adv.* cong'ruously.—*n.* cong'ruousness. [L. *congruĕre*, to run together.]
conia. See coniine.
conic, -al. See cone.
conidium, *kon-id'i-əm*, *n.* a spore produced by abstriction, not in a sporangium:—*pl.* conid'ia.—*adj.* conid'ial.—*ns.* conid'iophore (Gr. *phoros*, bearing), a hypha that produces conidia; conid'-iospore, a conidium. [Gr. *konis*, dust.]
conifer, *kon'* or *kōn'i-fər*, *n.* a member of the

Conif'erae, an order of gymnosperms, including yews, pines, firs, etc., which typically bear cones.—*adj.* conif'erous, cone-bearing: of the Coniferae. [L. *cōnus* (Gr. *kōnos*) a cone, *ferre*, to bear.]
coniform. See cone.
coniine, *kō'ni-ēn*, *n.* a liquid, highly poisonous alkaloid ($C_8H_{17}N$) found in hemlock (*Conium*).—Also co'nia, co'nine. [Gr. *kōneion*, hemlock.]
conima, *kon'i-mə*, *n.* the fragrant resin of a tropical American burseraceous tree (*Protium*). [Carib name.]
conirostral, *kōn-i-ros'trəl*, *adj.* having a strong conical beak.—[L. *cōnus* (Gr. *kōnos*), cone, *rōstrālis—rōstrum*, a beak.]
conject, *kən-jekt'*, *v.i.* (*Shak.*) to conjecture.—*n.* conject'ure, a forecast: an opinion formed on slight or defective evidence or none: an opinion without proof: a guess: an idea.—*v.t.* to make conjectures regarding: to infer on slight evidence: to guess.—*adjs.* conject'urable, that may be conjectured; conject'ural, involving conjecture: given to conjecture.—*adv.* conject'urally. [L. *conjicĕre*, *conjectum*, to throw together—*con-*, *jacĕre*, to throw.]
conjee, congee, *kon'jē*, *n.* water in which rice has been boiled.—*v.t.* to starch with conjee. [Tamil *kañji*.]
conjoin, *kən-join'*, *v.t.* to join together: to combine.—*v.i.* to unite.—*adjs.* conjoined', united: in conjunction: conjoint', joined together: united.—*adv.* conjoint'ly. [Fr. *conjoindre*—L. *con-*, *jungĕre*, *junctum*, to join; see join.]
conjugal, *kon'jōō-gəl*, *adj.* pertaining to marriage.—*n.* conjugality (*-gal'i-ti*).—*adv.* con'jugally. [L. *conjugālis—conjux*, a husband or wife—*con-*, together, and *jugum*, a yoke.]
conjugate, *kon'jōō-gāt*, *v.t.* to give the various inflections or parts of (a verb) (*gram.*): to unite (*biochemistry*).—*v.i.* to unite.—*adj.* joined: connected: coupled: occurring in pairs (*bot.*): reciprocally related: of two complex numbers, having their real parts equal and their imaginary parts equal but of opposite sign (*math.*).—*n.* a word agreeing in derivation with another word: anything conjugate with another—joined, or from same root, or reciprocally related.—*n.pl.* Conjuga'tae (*-tē*), class of freshwater algae reproducing by conjugation of like gametes, including desmids, Spirogyra, etc.—*adjs.* con'jugated, conjugate: (of atoms, groups, bonds, or the compounds in which they occur) showing a special type of mutual influence, esp., characterised by an arrangement of alternate single and double bonds between carbon atoms (*chem.*); conjugā'tional, con'jugative, conjugate.—*n.* and *adj.* con'jugating.—*n.* conjugā'tion, the act of joining: union: a connected view or statement of the inflectional forms of a verb (*gram.*): a class of verbs similarly inflected (*gram.*): temporary or permanent union of two cells or individuals preparatory to the development of new individuals esp. the union of isogametes (*biol.*): in *Infusoria*, an exchange of nuclear material.—conjugate diameters, two diameters in a conic section, such that each is parallel to the tangent at the extremity of the other; conjugate foci (see focus); conjugate mirrors, mirrors set so that rays from the focus of one are reflected to that of the other. [L. *conjugāre*, *-ātum—con-*, together, and *jugāre—jugum*, a yoke.]
conjunct, *kən-junkt'*, or *kon'*, *adj.* conjoined: joint.—*n.* conjunc'tion, connection, union: combination: a word that connects sentences, clauses, and words (*gram.*): one of the aspects of the planets, when two bodies have the same celestial longitude or the same right ascension (formerly when they were in the same sign).—*adj.* conjunc'tional, relating to a conjunction.—*adv.* conjunc'tionally.—*n.* conjunctiva (*kon-jungkt-i'-və*),

the modified epidermis of the front of the eye, covering the cornea externally and the inner side of the eyelid.—*adjs.* conjuncti'val, of the conjunctiva; conjunc'tive, closely united: serving to unite: connective: copulative (*gram.*): of the nature of, or introduced by, a conjunction. —*adv.* conjunc'tively.—*ns.* conjunc'tiveness; conjunctivitis (-*iv-i'tis*), inflammation of the conjunctiva.—*adv.* conjunct'ly, conjointly: in union. —*n.* conjunc'ture, combination of circumstances: important occasion, crisis.—conjunctive mood, the subjunctive mood generally, or when used in a principal clause, or in the principal clause of a conditional sentence; conjunct tetrachords (*Greek music*), tetrachords in which the highest note of the lower is the lowest note of the higher. [L. *conjunctiō, -ōnis*—*conjungĕre*; see conjoin.]

conjure, *kun'jər, v.i.* to practise magical arts: to make an invocation: to conspire (*obs.*).—*v.t.* (usu. *kən-jōōr'*) to call on or summon by a sacred name or in a solemn manner: to implore: to implore earnestly: (*kun'jər*) to compel (a spirit) by incantations: to put a spell upon: to call before the imagination: to render, effect, cause to be or become, by magic or jugglery.— *ns.* conjurā'tion, conspiracy: act of summoning by a sacred name or solemnly: enchantment; con'jurātor, a conspirator; conjure'ment, adjuration; con'jurer, -or (*kun', kon'*), one who practises magic: one who produces magical effects by sleight-of-hand, etc.; conju'ror, one bound by oath with others; con'juring, magicworking: the production of effects apparently miraculous by natural means; con'jury, magic. [Fr. *conjurer*—L. *conjūrāre*, to swear together— *con-*, and *jūrāre*, to swear.]

conk, *kongk, n.* the fructification of a fungal parasite on a tree (*U.S.*): timber disease due to the parasite (*U.S.*): the nose (*slang*).—*ns.* conk'er, a strung snail-shell or horse-chestnut used in the game of conkers, in which each seeks to break his opponent's: a horse chestnut; conk'y (*slang*), a large-nosed person.—*adj.* affected by the disease of conk. [conch.]

conk, *kongk,* (*slang*) *v.i.* to get out of order, fail, break down (often with *out*). [Origin unknown.]

con moto, kon mō'tō, (*mus.*) with movement: briskly. [It.]

conn. See con (3).

connascent, *kən- s'ənt, adj.* born or produced at the same time.—*ns.* connasc'ence, connasc'ency. —*n.* connā'tion (*biol.*), union, esp. of like parts. —*adj.* connate (*kon'āt*), inborn: innate: allied: congenital: united in growth.—*adj.* connatural (*kon-ach'ar-əl*), of the same nature with another. —*v.t.* connat'uralise, -ize.—*n.* connatural'ity. *adv.* connat'urally.—*ns.* connat'uralness;—connā'ture.—connate water, water which has been trapped in sediments since their deposition. [L. *con-, nāsci, nātus,* to be born.]

conne. See con (2).

connect, *kən-ekt', v.t.* to tie or fasten together: to establish a relation between: to associate.—*adj.* connect'able, -ible, capable of being connected.— *p.adj.* connect'ed, joined: linked: coherent: related.—*adv.* connect'edly, in a connected manner.—*ns.* connect'er, -or, one who or that which connects; connection, connexion (-*ek'shən*), act of connecting: that which connects: a body or society held together by a bond: coherence: intercourse: context: relation: intimacy: opportunity of change of trains, buses, etc.: a relative.—*adjs.* connect'ive, connex'ive (*obs.*), binding together.—*n.* a word that connects sentences and words.—*adv.* connect'ively.—connecting-rod, in a reciprocating-engine or pump, the rod connecting the piston or cross-head to the crank; connective tissue, an animal tissue including a great variety—e.g. bone, cartilage, ligaments, and enswathing membranes. [L. *con-,* and *nectĕre, nexum,* to tie.]

conner. See con (2) and (3).

conner, *kun'ər, n.* an inspector or tester. [O.E. *cunnere*—*cunnian,* to learn, seek to know.]

conner, cunner, *kun'ər, n.* a kind of wrasse, the goldsinny or corkwing: an allied American fish. [Origin obscure.]

conning-tower. See con (3).

conniption (fit), *kə-nip'shən, n.* a fit of hysterical excitement or rage. [Origin unknown.]

connive, *kən-iv', v.i.* to wink (usu. *fig.*, as at a fault): to take no notice: to have a private understanding: to converge (*biol.*).—*ns.* conniv'ance, -ancy, conniv'ence, -ency.—*adj.* conniv'ent.—*n.* conniv'er. [L. *connivēre, cōnivēre,* to wink.]

connoisseur, *kon'əs-ûr, -əs-ûr', n.* a well-informed judge in the arts, etc.—*n.* connoisseur'ship, the skill of a connoisseur. [Fr. (now *connaisseur*), —*connoitre* (*connaitre*)—L. *cognōscĕre,* to know.]

connote, *kon-ōt', v.t.* to signify secondarily: to imply as inherent attributes: to include.—*v.t.* connotate (*kon'ō-tāt*), to connote.—*n.* connotā'tion, implication of something more than the denotation of an object: the aggregation of attributes connoted by a term.—*adjs.* conn'otã-tive (or -*nōt'*), connō'tive. [L. *con-,* with, *notāre,* to mark.]

connubial, *kən-ū'bi-əl, adj.* pertaining to marriage. —*n.* connubiality (-*al'i-ti*).—*adv.* connū'bially. [L. *con-, nūbĕre,* to marry.]

connumerate, *kən-ū'mə-rāt, v.t.* to count together. —*n.* connumerā'tion.

conoid, *kōn'oid, n.* anything like a cone in form: a solid generated by the revolution of a conic section about its axis.—*adjs.* cōn'oid, cōnoid'al, -ic, -ical. [Gr. *kōnos,* a cone, *eidos,* form.]

conquer, *kong'kər, v.t.* to gain by force or with an effort: to overcome or vanquish.—*v.i.* to be victor.—*adj.* con'querable.—*n.* con'querableness. —*adj.* con'quering.—*adv.* con'queringly.—*ns.* con'queror, one who conquers: a victor:—*fem.* con'queress; conquest (*kong'kwest*), the act of conquering: that which is conquered or acquired by physical or moral force: the act of gaining the affections of another: acquisition otherwise than by inheritance (*Scots law*).—the Conqueror, William I of England (L. *conquestor*); the Conquest, the acquisition of the throne of England by William, Duke of Normandy, in 1066. [O.Fr. *conquerre*—L. *conquirĕre, con-quaerĕre*—*con-,* inten., *quaerĕre,* to seek.]

conquistador, *kong'kēs-ta-dōr', -dōr* or *kwis', n.* a conqueror, applied to the conquerors of Mexico and Peru:—*pl.* -dors, -dores (*dōr'es, dör'es*). [Sp.,—L. *conquirĕre.*]

consanguine, *kon-sang'gwin, adj.* related by blood: of the same family or descent—also consanguin'eous.—*n.* consanguin'ity, relationship by blood: opposed to affinity or relationship by marriage. [L. *cōnsanguineus*—*con-,* with, *sanguis,* or *sanguis,* blood.]

conscience, *kon'shəns, n.* inmost thought, consciousness (*Shak.*): moral sense: scrupulousness, conscientiousness: in genitive case commonly written conscience'.—*interj.* (*Scot.*) an expression of surprise (also my conscience!).— *adjs.* con'scient, aware: conscious; conscien'tious (-*shi-en'shəs*), regulated by a regard to conscience: scrupulous.—*adv.* conscien'tiously.— *n.* conscien'tiousness.—*adj.* con'scionable (-*shən-ə-bl*), governed or regulated by conscience.— *n.* con'scionableness.—*adv.* con'scionably.—conscience clause, a clause in a law to relieve persons of conscientious scruples, esp. against religious instruction; conscience money, money given to relieve the conscience, by discharging a claim previously evaded.—*adjs.* con'-science-proof, unvisited by any compunctions of

Neutral vowels in unaccented syllables: *el'ə-mənt;* for certain sounds in foreign words, see p. viii

with consideration. [L. cōnsiderāre, perh. orig. a term of augury and from con-, and sīdus, sīderis, star; conn. desiderate.]

consign, kən-sin', v.t. to sign or seal: to devote: to transfer: to entrust: to commit: to transmit.— adj. consign'able.—ns. consignation (kon-sig-nā'-shən); consignatory (kən-sig'nə-tər-i), a co-signatory.—adj. consigned', given in trust.—ns. consignee (kon-sin-ē'), one to whom anything is consigned or entrusted; consign'er, consign'or; consign'ment, the act of consigning: the thing consigned: a set of things consigned together. [L. cōnsignāre, to attest.]

consignify, kon-sig'ni-fī, v.t. to mean when taken along with something else.—n. consignificā'tion. —adv. consignif'icative.

consilience, kən-sil'i-əns, n. concurrence: coincidence.—adj. consil'ient, agreeing. [L. con-, together, and salīre, to leap.]

consimilar, kən-sim'i-lər, adj. like each other.—ns. consimilar'ity, consimil'itude, consimil'ity. [L. cōnsimilis.]

consist, kən-sist', v.i. to exist, subsist (obs.): to be composed: to insist (Shak.): to co-exist (obs.): to agree: to hold together (obs.).—ns. consist'-ence, degree of density: substance; consist'-ency, consistence: agreement: self-consistency. —adj. consist'ent, fixed: not fluid: agreeing together, compatible: free from self-contradiction: true to principles.—adv. consist'ently.— adjs. consistō'rial, consistō'rian.—n. con'sistory (or -sist'), properly, a place of assembly: the place where the privy council of the Roman emperor met: the council itself: an assembly or council: a spiritual or ecclesiastical court.—Also adj.—consist in, to inhere in (obs.): to have as essence (obs.): to be composed of; consist of, to be made up of. [L. cōnsistěre—con-, together, sistěre, to set, stand.]

consociate, kon-sō'shi-āt, v.t. and v.i. to associate together.—p.adj. consō'ciated.—n. consociation (-si- or -shi-ā'shən), companionship: association: alliance, esp. of churches: a federal council of Congregational churches: a subdivision of an association dominated by one particular species (bot.).—adj. consocia'tional. [L. cōn-sociāre, -ātum—con-, sociāre, to associate— socius, a companion.]

console, kən-sōl', v.t. to give solace or comfort to: to cheer in distress.—adj. consōl'able.—v.t. consolate (kon-səl-āt; Shak.), to console.—ns. consolā'tion, solace: alleviation of misery: a comforting circumstance.—adj. consolatory (kən-sol'ə-tər-i, or -sōl'), comforting.—n. (Milt.) a message of comfort.—ns. console'ment; con-sol'er:—fem. consolā'trix—consolā'tion-match, -prize, -race, etc., a match, prize, race, etc., for the otherwise unsuccessful. [L. cōnsōlāri—con-, inten., sōlāri, to comfort.]

console, kon'sōl, n. a projection resembling a bracket, frequently in the form of the letter S, used to support cornices, or for placing busts, vases, or figures on: the key-desk of an organ: a large cabinet radio or television set or radiogram: a cabinet for this or similar apparatus: a panel or cabinet with dials, switches, etc., control unit of an electrical, electronic, or mechanical system.—con'sole-ta'ble, a table supported against a wall by consoles or brackets. [Fr. console; prob. conn. with consolidate.]

consolidate, kən-sol'i-dāt, v.t. to make solid: to form into a compact mass: to unite into one: to merge: to rearrange and strengthen (mil.).—v.i. to grow solid or firm: to unite.—adj. made firm or solid: united.—p.adj. consol'idated.—n. con-solidā'tion.—adj. consol'idative, tending to consolidate: having the quality of healing.—n. consol'idator.—consolidated annuities, that part of the British national debt which consists of several stocks consolidated into one fund; con-

solidated fund, a fund made up by uniting the yield of various taxes, etc., from which are paid interest on national debt, grants to royal family, etc.; consolidation acts, acts of parliament which combine into one general statute several special enactments. [L. cōnsolidāre, -ātum—con-, inten., and solidus, solid.]

consols, kon'solz, or kon-solz', n.pl. short for consolidated annuities.

consommé, kɔ-som-ā, n. a soup made from meat by slow boiling: a clear soup. [Fr., pa.p.—L. cōnsummāre, -ātum, to consummate.]

consonant, kon'sən-ənt, adj. consistent: suitable: harmonious.—n. an articulation which can be sounded only with a vowel: a letter of the alphabet representing such a sound.—ns. con'sonance, a state of agreement: agreement or unison of sounds: a combination of musical notes which can sound together without the harshness produced by beats: concord; con'-sonancy, harmony.—adj. con'sonantal (-ant'l).— adv. con'sonantly.—adj. consonous, harmonious. [L. cōnsonāns, -antis, pr.p. of cōnsonāre, to harmonise—con-, sonāre, to sound.]

consort, kon'sört, sərt (Spens., -sört'), n. a partner: a companion: a wife or husband: an accompanying ship: a number of people (obs.): partnership: company: agreement: accord: formerly (by confusion) for concert: a group of instruments played or musicians playing together.—v.t. consort', to accompany: to associate.—v.i. to associate or keep company: to agree.—adj. consort'ed, associated.—ns. consort'er, one who consorts; con'sortism, symbiosis; consortium (kon-sör'ti-əm, -shəm, -shi-əm), fellowship: association: an international banking or financial combination: the association of fungus and alga in a lichen: a lichen thallus:—pl. consor'tia.—in consort, in company: in harmony. [L. cōnsors, -sortis— con-, sors, a lot.]

conspectus, kən-spek'təs, n. a comprehensive view or survey: a synopsis.—n. conspectuity (kon-spek-tū'i-ti; Shak.), sight. [L. cōnspectus— cōnspicěre, to look: see next.]

conspicuous, kən-spik'ū-əs, adj. catching the eye: prominent.—ns. conspicū'ity (kon-), conspic'u-ousness.—adv. conspic'uously. [L. cōnspicuus— cōnspicěre—con-, inten., specěre, to look.]

conspire, kən-spir', v.i. to plot or scheme together: to devise: to act together to one end.—v.t. to plan, devise.—n. conspiracy (-spir'ə-si), the act of conspiring: a banding together for a purpose, often secret, usu. unlawful: a plot: joint action, concurrence.—adj. conspir'ant, conspiring.—ns. conspirā'tion, conspiracy; conspir'ātor, one who conspires:—fem. conspir'atress.—adj. conspī-ratō'rial.—n. conspir'er (Shak.), conspirator.— adv. conspir'ingly. [L. cōnspīrāre—con-, together, spīrāre, to breathe.]

con spirito, kon spir'i-tō, spēr'ē-tō, (It.) with spirit.

conspurcation, kon-spûr-kā'shən, (obs.) n. defilement. [L. cōnspurcāre, -ātum, to defile.]

constable, kun'stə-bl, or kon', n. formerly a state-officer of the highest rank: the warden of a castle: a peace-officer: a policeman.—ns. con'stableship; con'stablewick (arch.), the district of a constable; constabulary (kən-stab'ū-lər-i), an organised body of constables.—adj. of or pertaining to constables, or peace-officers.— Constable of France, chief of the household under the old French kings, then commander-in-chief of the army, judge in questions of chivalry, tournaments, and martial displays; High Constable, one of two constables formerly ordained in every hundred or franchise, to make the view of armour, and to see to the conservation of the peace; Lord High Constable of England, an officer of the crown, formerly a

judge in the court of chivalry; **Lord High Constable of Scotland,** a similar officer (now a mere hereditary title); **outrun the constable,** to go too fast: to get into debt; **petty constable,** a parish constable who was under the High Constable; **special constable,** a person sworn in by the justices to preserve the peace, or to execute warrants on special occasions. [O.Fr. *conestable* (Fr. *connétable*)—L. *comes stabulī,* count or companion of the stable.]
**constant,** *kon'stənt, adj.* fixed: unchangeable: firm: continual: faithful.—*n.* (*math.*) a fixed quantity.—*n.* **con'stancy,** fixedness: unchangeableness: faithfulness: perseverence (*Shak.*): certainty (*Shak.*).—*adv.* **con'stantly.** [L. *cōnstāns, -stantis,* from *cōnstāre,* to stand firm—*con-,* inten., *stāre,* to stand.]
**constantan,** *kon'stən-tən, n.* an alloy of about 40% nickel and 60% copper, having a high resistance to flow of electricity or heat. [constant.]
**Constantia,** *kən-stan'shi-a, n.* a sweet wine produced around *Constantia,* near Cape Town.
**constantia et virtute,** *kon-stan'shi-a (ti-ä) et vûr-tū'tē (vir-tōō'te, wir-),* (L.) by constancy and virtue.
**Constantinian,** *kon-stən-tin'yən, adj.* pertaining to Constantine I (A.D. *c.* 247-337; emperor 306-337).
**Constantinopolitan,** *kon-stan-ti-nō-pol'it-ən, adj.* of or pertaining to *Constantinople.*
**constate,** *kən-stāt', v.t.* to assert (*Gallicism*). [Fr. *constater.*]
**constellate,** *kon'stəl-āt,* or *kən-stel'āt, v.t.* to cluster: to compel or affect by stellar influence. —*v.i.* to cluster together.—*n.* **constellā'tion,** a group of stars: an assemblage of persons distinguished in some way: in astrol., a particular disposition of the planets, supposed to influence the course of human life or character.—*adj.* **constell'atory.** [L. *cōnstellātus,* studded with stars—*con-, stellāre—stella,* a star.]
**conster.** See construe.
**consternate,** *kon'stər-nāt, v.t.* to fill with dismay. —*n.* **consternā'tion,** terror that throws into confusion: dismay. [L. *cōnsternāre, -ātum,* from *con-,* wholly, *sternēre,* to strew.]
**constipate,** *kon'stip-āt, v.t.* to stop up, close (*obs.*): to press together (*obs.*): to make costive, cause an irregular and insufficient action of the bowels of: to deprive of vigour (*fig.*).—*adj.* **con'stipated.** —*n.* **constipā'tion.** [L. *cōnstipāre, -ātum,* to press together—*con-, stīpāre,* to pack.]
**constitute,** *kon'stit-ūt, v.t.* to set up: to establish: to form or make up: to appoint: to give being to.—*n.* **constituency** (*kən-stit'ū-ən-si*), the whole body of voters, or a district, or population, represented by a member of parliament or the like.—*adj.* **constit'uent,** constituting or forming: essential: elemental: component: electing: constitution-making.—*n.* an essential or elemental part: one of those who elect a representative, esp. in parliament: an inhabitant of one's constituency.—*n.* **constitū'tion** (*kon-*), the act of constituting: the natural condition of body or mind: disposition: a system of laws and customs established by the sovereign power of a state for its own guidance: an established form of government: a particular law or usage: in chem., molecular structure, taking into account not only the kinds and numbers of atoms but the way in which they are linked.—*adj.* **constitū'tional,** inherent in the natural frame: natural: agreeable to the constitution or frame of government: essential: legal: reigning subject to fixed laws: supporting the existing constitution.—*n.* a walk for the sake of one's health.—*v.t.* **constitū'tionalise, -ize,** to make constitutional.—*ns.* **constitū'tionalism,** adherence to the principles of the constitution; **constitū'tion(al)ist,** one who

favours or studies a constitution or the constitution; **constitutional'ity.**—*adv.* **constitū'tionally.** —*adj.* **con'stitutive,** that constitutes or establishes: having power to constitute: essential: component. [L. *cōnstituĕre, cōnstitūtum—con-,* inten., *statuĕre,* to make to stand, to place.]
**constrain,** *kən-strān', v.t.* to urge with irresistible power: to bring about by force: to force, compel: to distress: to violate: to confine: to limit: to cause constraint to: to restrict by a condition.—*adj.* **constrain'able.**—*p.adj.* **constrained',** forced, compelled: lacking ease and spontaneity of manner: embarrassed.—*adv.* **constrain'edly.**—*n.* **constraint',** irresistible force: compulsion: confinement: repression of one's feelings: embarrassment: a restricting condition. [O.Fr. *constraindre*—L. *cōnstringĕre—con-, stringĕre,* to press; see following words and **strain.**]
**constrict,** *kən-strikt', v.t.* to press together: to contract: to cramp: to narrow locally.—*p.adj.* **constrict'ed,** narrowed: cramped: narrowed in places (*bot.*).—*n.* **constric'tion,** a pressing together: contraction: tightness: a narrow place.—*adj.* **constrict'ive.**—*n.* **constrict'or,** that which constricts or draws together: a muscle that compresses an organ or structure: a snake that crushes its prey in its folds. [L. *cōnstringĕre, -strictum;* see preceding and following.]
**constringe,** *kən-strinj', v.t.* to draw together: to cause to contract.—*v.i.* to contract.—*n.* **constrin'gency.**—*adj.* **constrin'gent,** having the quality of contracting. [L. *cōnstringĕre;* see preceding.]
**construct,** *kən-strukt', v.t.* to build up: to compile: to put together the parts of: to make: to compose: to put in grammatical relation.—*adj.* **constructed.**—*n.* (*kon'strukt*), a thing constructed, esp. in the mind.—*adjs.* **construct'able, construct'ible,** able to be constructed.—*ns.* **construct'er, construct'or; construc'tion,** the act of constructing: anything piled together: building: a stage structure: manner of forming: the syntactic relations of words in a sentence (*gram.*): interpretation: meaning.—*adj.* **construc'tional,** pertaining to construction: used for structures: making use of structures.—*n.* **construc'tionism,** use of structures: principle of using structures or of following structure.—*adj.* **construc'tive,** capable of, tending towards, or concerned in, constructing: embodying positive advice—opp. to *destructive:* not direct or expressed, but inferred.—*adv.* **construct'ively.** —*ns.* **construct'iveness; construct'ivism,** constructionism: a non-representational style of art, originating in Russia about 1920 and affecting esp. sculpture and architecture, using man-made industrial materials and processes such as twisting, welding: a simplified, non-realistic style in stage sets, using steps, platforms, etc.; **construct'ure.**—**construct state,** in Semitic languages, the state of a noun depending on another noun, where in Indo-Germanic languages the other would be in the genitive case—e.g. House of God—house being in the construct state.— **bear a construction,** to allow of a particular interpretation. [L. *cōnstruĕre, -structum—con-, struĕre,* to build.]
**construe,** *kən-strōō', kon'strōō,* (old form **conster,** *kon'stər*), *v.t.* to exhibit in another language the grammatical structure and literal meaning of: to translate: to explain: to interpret: to construct grammatically: to infer.—*v.i.* to admit of grammatical analysis.—*n.* **con'strue,** an act of construing.—*adj.* **constru'able.**—*ns.* **constru-ability; construer** (*kon',* or *-strōō'*). [L. *cōnstruĕre, cōnstructum,* to pile together.]
**constuprate,** *kon'stū-prāt, v.t.* to ravish.—*n.* **constuprā'tion.** [L. *cōnstuprāre—con-,* intensive, *stuprum,* defilement, disgrace.]

consubsist, *kon-sub·sist'*, *v.i.* to subsist together.
consubstantial, *kon-sub-stan'shl*, *adj.* of the same substance, nature, or essence, esp. of the Trinity. —*ns.* consubstan'tialism, the doctrine of consubstantiation; consubstan'tialist, one who believes in consubstantiation; consubstantiality (*-shi-al'i-ti*).—*adv.* consubstan'tially, with sameness of substance.—*v.t.* and *v.i.* consubstan'tiate (*-shi-āt*), to unite in one common substance or nature.—*adj.* so united.—*ns.* consubstantiā'tion, the Lutheran doctrine of the actual, substantial presence of the body and blood of Christ coexisting in and with the bread and wine used at the Lord's Supper (cf. transubstantiation); consubstantiā'tionist. [L. *con-*, with, and substantial, etc.]
consuetude, *kon'swi-tūd*, *n.* custom: familiarity.—*adj.* consuetū'dinary, customary.—*n.* an unwritten law established by usage, derived by immemorial custom from antiquity: a ritual of customary devotions. [L. *cōnsuētūdō*, *-inis*, custom.]
consul, *kon'səl*, *n.* one of the two chief-magistrates in the Roman republic: one of the three heads of the French republic, 1799-1804: an agent for a foreign government appointed to attend to the interests of its citizens and commerce.—*n.* con'-sulage, duty paid to a consul for protection of goods.—*adj.* con'sular (*-sū-lər*), pertaining to a consul.—*n.* a man of consular rank.—*ns.* con'sulate (*sūl-*, or *səl*), the office, residence, jurisdiction, government, or time of a consul or consuls; con'sulship, the office, or term of office, of a consul. [L. *cōnsul.*]
consult, *kən-sult'*, *v.t.* to ask advice of: to decide or act in favour of: to look up for information or advice: to discuss: to consider: to take measures for the advantage of.—*v.i.* to consider jointly: to take counsel.—*n.* (*kən-sult'*, or *kon'sult*), consultation: council: a meeting for conspiracy or intrigue.—*n.* consultant (*kən-sult'-ənt*), one who seeks advice or information: one who gives professional advice or takes part in consultation.—Also *adj.*—*n.* consultā'tion (*kon'-səl-*,-*sul-*), deliberation, or a meeting for deliberation, esp. of physicians or lawyers.—*adjs.* consult'ative, of or pertaining to consultation, esp. of bodies without vote on the decision; consult'atory, of the nature of consultation.—*ns.* consultee', the person consulted; consult'er, one who consults.—*adjs.* consult'ing, of a physician or lawyer prepared to give advice; consult'ive, consultative.—*n.* consult'or.—*adj.* consult'ory, consultatory.—consult'ing-room, room in which doctor sees patient. [L. *cōnsultāre*, inten. of *cōnsulēre*, to consult.]
consulta, *kon-sōōl'tä*, (It. and Sp.) a meeting of council.
consume, *kən-sūm'*, *-sōōm'*, *v.t.* to destroy by wasting, fire, evaporation, etc.: to use up: to devour: to waste or spend: to exhaust.—*v.i.* to waste away.—*adj.* consum'able.—*adv.* consum'-edly, exceedingly—originally a fantastic variant of *confoundedly*, and prob. influenced in meaning by *consummately*.—*n.* consum'er, one who consumes: as opposed to *producer*, one who uses an article produced.—*n.* and *adj.* consum'ing, wasting or destroying: engrossing.—consumer(s') goods, goods to be used without further manufacturing process to satisfy human needs. [L. *cōnsūmere*, *-sūmptum*, to destroy—*con-*, sig. completeness, *sūmere*, to take.]
consummate, *kon'sum-āt*, or *-səm-*, *v.t.* to raise to the highest point: to perfect or finish: to make (marriage) legally complete by sexual intercourse.—*adj.* (*kən-sum'āt*, *-it*), complete, supreme, perfect of its kind.—*adv.* consumm'ately, perfectly.—*n.* consummā'tion, act of completing: perfection: conclusion of life or of the universe: the subsequent intercourse which makes a

marriage legally valid.—*adj.* consumm'ative.—*n.* con'summātor.—*adj.* consumm'atory. [L. *cōnsummāre*, *-ātum*, to perfect—*con-*, inten., *summa*, highest, perfect, *summa*, a sum.]
consumption, *kən-sum(p)'shən*, *n.* the act or process of consuming or using up: the quantity consumed: wasting of the body: pulmonary tuberculosis.—*n.* consumpt (*kon'sum(p)t*, *kən-sum(p)t'*), quantity consumed.—*adj.* consump'-tive, wasting away; inclined to the disease consumption.—*n.* one affected by consumption.—*adv.* consump'tively.—*ns.* consump'tiveness, consumptiv'ity (*kon-*), a tendency to consumption. [See consume.]
contabescent, *kon-tāb-es'ənt*, *adj.* wasting away, atrophied: failing to produce pollen.—*n.* contabesc'ence. [L. *contābēscēns*, *-entis*—*contābēscere*, to waste away.]
contact, *kon'takt*, *n.* touch: meeting: meeting in a point without intersection (*math.*): close approximation allowing passage of electric current or communication of disease: a place or part where electric current may be allowed to pass: association: means or occasion of communication: a person who has been exposed to contagion: a person through whom one can get in touch (esp. secretly) with an individual or group, esp. with shady person(s).—*v.t.* and *v.i.* (also *kon-takt'*), to bring or to come into contact: to get in touch with, or establish a connection with.—*n.* con'tactor, a device for repeatedly making and breaking an electric current.—*adj.* contact'-ual, pertaining to contact.—contact flight, navigation of an aircraft by ground observation alone; contact lens, a lens, usu. of plastic material, worn in contact with the eyeball, instead of spectacles, to correct defects of vision; con'tact-metamor'phism, alteration of rocks in the neighbourhood of igneous materials; contact man (*coll.*), an intermediary in transactions, esp. shady ones. [L. *contingĕre*, *contactum*, to touch—*con-*, wholly, *tangĕre*, to touch.]
contadino, *kon-tä-dē'nō*, *n.* an Italian peasant:—*pl.* contadini (*-nē*):—*fem.* contadi'na (*-nä*):—*pl.* contadi'ne (*-nä*), contadi'nas. [It.]
contagion, *kən-tā'jən*, *n.* transmission of a disease by direct contact with an infected person or object: a disease or poison so transmitted: the means of transmission: a hurtful influence.—*n.* contā'gionist, one who believes in the contagiousness of a disease.—*adj.* contā'gious, communicable by contact: carrying disease or other contagion: noxious (*obs.*).—*adv.* contā'giously.—*ns.* contā'giousness; contā'gium, contagion: contagious matter. [L. *contāgiō*, *-ōnis*—*con-*, *tangĕre*, to touch.]
contain, *kən-tān'*, *v.t.* to have within, enclose: to comprise, include: to restrain: to keep fixed: to hold back: to keep in check: to retain (*Shak.*).—*adj.* contain'able.—*n.* contain'er, that which contains: that in which goods are enclosed for transport: a vessel for holding gas.—*v.t.* contain'erise, -ize, to put (freight) into standard sealed containers: to use such containers for (e.g. a transport operation).—*ns.* contain'erisā'-tion; contain'ment, the act of containing: act or policy of preventing the spread beyond certain limits of a power or influence regarded as hostile, by means other than war: successful result of this.—container crane, a very large bridge-type quayside crane for handling large containers; container port, terminal port equipped to handle large containers; container ship, ship designed for the most efficient storage of such containers. [O.Fr. (Fr.) *contenir*—L. *continēre*—*con-*, *tenēre*, to hold.]
contaminate, *kən-tam'i-nāt*, *v.t.* to defile by touching or mixing with: to pollute: to corrupt: to infect.—*adj.* contaminated.—*adj.* contam'inable.

—*n*. **contamina'tion**, pollution: the blending into one of several stories, legends or plots: the blending of two or more linguistic forms to produce one new form: the blending into one manuscript of several readings.—*adj*. **contam'inative**. [L. *contāmināre, -ātum—contāmen* (for *contagmen*), pollution; see **contact**.]

**contango**, *kən-tang'gō, n*. a percentage paid by the buyer to the seller of stock for keeping back its delivery to the next settling-day, continuation—opp. to **backwardation**:—*pl*. **contang'os**.—Also *v.t.*—*n*. **contang'o-day** (see **continuation-day**). [Arbitrarily from **continue**.]

**conte**, *kōt, n*. a short story (as a literary genre). [Fr.]

**conté**, *kō-tā, n*. (sometimes *cap*.) hard crayon, usu. black, brown, or red, made of graphite and clay. [N.-J. *Conté*, Fr. chemist.]

**conteck**, *kon'tek*, (*Spens*.) *n*. strife. [O.Fr. *contek*, prob. conn. with *contekier*, to touch.]

**contemn**, *kən-tem', v.t.* to despise:—*pr.p.* **contemning** (*-tem'ing*); *pa.t.* and *pa.p.* **contemned'**, *Spens. pa.p.* **contempt'**.—*n*. **contem'ner** (*-ər, -nər*). [L. *contemnēre, -temptum*, to value little—*con-*, inten., *temnēre*, to slight.]

**contemper**, *kən-temp'ər, v.t.* to blend together, to qualify by mixture: to adapt.—*ns*. **contemperā'tion** (*obs*.), **contem'perature**. [L. *contemperāre*.]

**contemplate**, *kon'tem-plāt*, older *kən-tem'plāt, v.t.* to consider or look at attentively: to meditate on or study: to intend.—*v.i.* to think seriously: to meditate (with *on, upon*).—*adj*. **contemp'lable**.—*ns*. **contem'plant**; **contemplā'tion**, meditation: a meditative condition of mind: attentive viewing or consideration: matter for thought: purpose; **contemp'latist**.—*adj*. and *n*. **con'templātive** (or *kən-tem'plə-*), given to contemplation.—*adv*. **con'templatively** (or *-tem'*).—*ns*. **con'templativeness** (or *-tem'*); **con'templātor**, one who contemplates: a student.—**contemplative life** (*theol*.), life devoted to meditation (opposed to the *active life*). [L. *contemplārī, -ātus*, to mark out carefully a *templum* or place for auguries—*con-*, sig. completeness, and *templum*.]

**contemporaneous**, *kən-tem-pə-rā'nyəs, adj.* living, happening, or being at the same time: in geol., belonging approximately to the same relative place in the succession, not necessarily strictly synchronous.—*n*. and *adj*. **contemporā'nean**, contemporary.—*n*. **contemporaneity** (*-ə-nē'i-ti*).—*adv*. **contemporā'neously**.—*ns*. **contemporā'neousness**; **contem'porariness**.—*adj*. **contem'porary**, belonging to the same time (*with*): of the same age: present day (an inaccurate use), esp. up to date, fashionable: of a style of house decoration and furnishing popular in the 1950s.—*n*. one who lives at the same time: a newspaper or magazine of the same time.—*v.t.* **contem'porise, -ize**, to make contemporary in mind. [L. *con-, tempus, -oris*, time.]

**contempt**, *kən-tempt', n*. scorn: disgrace: in law, disregard of the rule, or an offence against the dignity, of a court (with *of, for*).—*ns*. **contemptibil'ity**, **contempt'ibleness**.—*adj*. **contempt'ible** (*Spens. kon'*), despicable.—*adv*. **contempt'ibly**.—*adj*. **contempt'ūous**, haughty, scornful.—*adv*. **contempt'uously**.—*n*. **contempt'uousness**. [See **contemn**.]

**contend**, *kən-tend', v.i.* to strive: to struggle in emulation or in opposition: to dispute or debate (with *against, for, with, about*): to urge one's course.—*v.t.* to maintain in dispute (with *that*).—*ns*. **contend'ent**, **contend'er**, one who contends.—*n*. and *adj*. **contend'ing**, striving.—*n*. **conten'tion**, a violent straining after any object: strife: debate: a position argued for.—*adj*. **conten'tious**, quarrelsome: given to dispute: in, or relating to, dispute.—*adv*. **conten'tiously**.—*n*. **conten'tiousness**. [L. *contendēre, -tentum—con-, tendēre*, to stretch.]

**contenement**, *kən-ten'i-mənt*, (*obs*.) *n*. property necessary to maintain one's station. [L. *con-*, inten., see **tenement**.]

**content**, *kon'tent, n*. that which is contained: capacity: the substance: (in *pl*.) the things contained: (in *pl*.) the list of chapters, sections, etc., in a book. [See **contain**.]

**content**, *kən-tent', adj.* having the desire limited by present enjoyment: satisfied: quietly happy.—*n*. satisfaction.—*interj*. I am content, agreed!—to formula of assent in the House of Lords.—*v.t.* to make content: to satisfy the mind: to quiet: to please.—*n*. **contentā'tion** (*obs*.).—*adj*. **content'ed**, content.—*adv*. **content'edly**.—*ns*. **content'edness**, **content'ment**.—*adj*. **content'less**, without content: discontented. [Fr.,—L. *contentus*, contained, hence satisfied—*con-*, and *tenēre*, to hold.]

**conterminous**, *kən-tûr'min-əs, adj.* adjacent, meeting along a common boundary: meeting end to end: coincident: co-extensive in range.—*adjs*. **conter'minal**, adjacent: end to end; **conter'minant**, **conter'minate**, adjacent. [L. *conterminus*, neighbouring—*con-*, terminus, a boundary.]

**contesseration**, *kon-tes-ər-ā'shən, n*. (act of) forming friendship or union—in Roman times by dividing a square tablet as token. [From L. *contesserāre—con-*, tessera, square stone, token (*hospitalis*, given by guest to host).]

**contest**, *kən-test', v.t.* to call in question or make the subject of dispute: to strive to gain.—*v.i.* to contend.—*n*. (*kon'*), a struggle for victory: competition: strife: debate.—*adj*. **contest'able**.—*ns*. **contest'ant**, one who contests; **contestā'tion**, the act of contesting: contest, strife: emulation.—*p.adjs*. **contest'ed**; **contest'ing**.—*adv*. **contest'ingly**.—**contested election**, one in which there are more candidates than are to be elected: one whose validity is disputed (*U.S.*). [Fr. *contester*—L. *contestārī*, to call to witness—*con-*, inten., *testārī*, to be a witness—*testis*, a witness.]

**context**, *kon'tekst, n*. the parts of a discourse or treatise which precede and follow a special passage and may fix its true meaning: associated surroundings, setting.—*adj*. **context'ūal**.—*adv*. **context'ūally**.—*n*. **context'ure**, the process or manner of weaving together: structure: fabric. [L. *contextus, contexēre—con-, texēre, textum*, to weave.]

**conticent**, *kon'tis-ənt*, (*Thackeray*) *adj.* silent. [L. *conticēns, -entis—con-*, intens., *tacēre*, to be silent.]

**contignation**, *kon-tig-nā'shən*, (*arch*.) *n*. joining together of timber: framework boarding. [L. *contignātiō, -ōnis—contignāre—con-, tignum*, beam.]

**contiguous**, *kən-tig'ū-əs, adj.* touching, adjoining: near.—*ns*. **contigū'ity**, **contig'uousness**.—*adv*. **contig'uously**. [L. *contiguus—contingēre*, to touch on all sides—*con-*, wholly, *tangēre*, to touch.]

**continent**, *kon'ti-nənt, n*. that which contains (*arch*.): a bank or shore (*arch*.): sum and substance (*arch*.): a great extent of land not broken up by seas: one of the great divisions of the land surface of the globe: the mainland portion of one of these: (usu. *cap*.) the mainland of Europe: solid earth (*obs*.): the main or whole body of anything (*obs*.).—*adj*. restraining within due bounds, or absolutely abstaining from, the indulgence of pleasure, esp. sexual: temperate: virtuous.—*ns*. **con'tinence**, **con'tinency**, self-restraint or abstinence, esp. sexual: chastity.—*adj*. **continental** (*-ent'l*), of, characteristic of, or of the nature of, a continent, esp. the European continent, the colonies of North America at the period of independence, or the main body of the United States.—*n*. a native or inhabitant of a continent: an American soldier of the War of Independence: a currency note of the Conti-

nental Congress.—*ns.* continent′alism, anything peculiar to the usage of a continent, esp. Europe; continent′alist.—*adv.* con′tinently.—continental breakfast, a light breakfast of rolls and coffee; Continental Congress, an assembly of delegates of the revolting American colonies, before the United States constitution was in force; continental drift, hypothetical slow drifting apart of land masses, as e.g. in A. L. Wegener's theory of the formation of world continents from one original land mass; continental shelf, a gently sloping zone, under relatively shallow seas, offshore from a continent or island; Continental System, Napoleon's plan for shutting out England from all commercial connection with Europe. [L. *continēns*, *-entis*—*continēre*, to contain—*con-*, *tenēre*, to hold.]
contingent, *kən-tin′jənt*, *adj.* dependent on something else: liable but not certain to happen: accidental.—*n.* an event liable but not certain to occur: a share, quota, or group, esp. of soldiers. —*ns.* contin′gence, contact: contingency (*obs.*); contin′gency, quality or state of being contingent: contact (*obs.*): close connection: uncertainty: chance: a chance happening or concurrence of events: a possible future event: something dependent on such: an incidental.— *adv.* contin′gently. [L. *contingēns*, *-entis*—*con-*, mutually, *tangēre*, to touch.]
continue, *kən-tin′ū*, *v.t.* to draw out or prolong: to extend: to maintain: to go on with: to resume: to adjourn: to be a prolongation of.— *v.i.* to remain in the same place or state: to last or endure: to persevere.—*adjs.* contin′uable; contin′ual, without interruption: unceasing: persistent.—*adv.* contin′ually.—*n.* contin′uance, duration: uninterrupted succession: stay.—*adj.* contin′uant, continuing: capable of continuing.— *n.* an open consonant.—*adj.* contin′uāte, closely united (*obs.*): unbroken (*Shak.*).—*ns.* continuā′-tion, going on: persistence: constant succession: extension: resumption: a further instalment. —*adj.* contin′uative, continuing.—*n.* contin′uator, one who continues: one who keeps up a series or succession.—*adj.* contin′ued, uninterrupted: unceasing: extended: resumed: in instalments.— *adv.* contin′uedly.—*ns.* contin′uedness; contin′uer, one who continues: one who has the power of persevering; continū′ity, state of being continuous: uninterrupted connection: a complete scenario of a motion-picture: the person who writes it (in full continuity writer); continuo (*kon-tin′ū-ō*; It. *-tēn′wō*), thorough-bass.—*adj.* contin′uous, joined together without interruption. —*adv.* contin′uously.—*ns.* contin′uousness; contin′ūum (L.), that which is continuous: that which must be regarded as continuous and the same and which can be described only relatively: —*pl.* contin′ua.—continuation class, a class for continuing the education of those who have left school; continuā′tion-day, the same as contango-day, that on which contangos are fixed; continuous creation, the notion of creation as going on always, not as a single act at one particular time (*phil.*): the theory that the universe is in a steady state showing no overall change, although new systems are continually being formed to replace those carried away by recession (*astron.*). [L. *continuāre*—*continuus*, joined, connected, from *continēre*, to hold together.]
contline, *kont′lin*, *n.* the space between stowed casks: a spiral interval between the strands of a rope. [Prob. cant, line.]
conto, *kon′tō*, *n.* a Portuguese and Brazilian money of account, 1000 escudos or cruzeiros. [Port., million (reis)—L. *computus*, a sum.]
contorno, *kon-tör′nō*, *n.* contour or outline.—*n.* contor′niate, a coin or medal with a deep groove round the disk.—*adj.* having this. [It. *contorno*, circuit, contour.]

contort, *kən-tört′*, *v.t.* to twist or turn violently: to writhe.—*adj.* contort′ed, twisted: twisted, as some flower-buds when each floral leaf overlaps its neighbour always on the same side round the circle: much and irregularly plicated (*geol.*).—*n.* contor′tion, a violent twisting: deformation.— *adjs.* contor′tional, contor′tionate.—*n.* contor′-tionist, a gymnast who practises contorted postures: one who twists words and phrases.— *adj.* contort′ive. [L. *con-*, inten., and *torquēre*, *tortum*, to twist.]
contour, *kon′tōōr*, *n.* outline: the line that bounds the figure of any object: general character or aspect: artistic quality of outline: a contour line: a point, line, or surface, at, along, or on which some property or characteristic is constant, or its representation in a map or diagram. —*v.t.* to mark with contour lines: to follow the contour lines of.—contour farming, the furrowing and planting of sloping land along the contour lines to counter erosion; contour feathers, those that determine the contours of the body; contour line, a line on the ground whose points are all at the same height above sea-level, or the intersection of the ground surface by a level surface of constant elevation: representation of such a line on a map; contour map, a map in which the configuration of land is shown by contour lines. [Fr. *contour* (It. *contorno*)—It. *contornare*, to surround, outline—L. *con-*, *tornāre*, to turn in a lathe—*tornus* (Gr. *tornos*), a lathe.]
contra, *kon′tra*, *-tra*, *adv.* and *prep.* against.—*n.* an argument against: the other side.—contra-, in composition, against: contrary. [L. *contrā*.]
contraband, *kon-tra-band*, *adj.* excluded by law: prohibited.—*n.* illegal traffic: smuggled or prohibited goods: in the American Civil War, a refugee slave.—*ns.* con′trabandism, trafficking in contraband goods; con′trabandist, a smuggler. —contraband of war, commodities not to be supplied by neutral to belligerent powers. [Sp. *contrabanda*—It. *contrabbando*—L. *contrā*, L.L. *bandum*, ban.]
contrabass, *kon′tra-bās*, *n.* the double bass, playing an octave below the 'cello.—*adj.* applied to other instruments taking a similar part.—Also contra-basso (*-bäs′so*) and coun′terbasse. [It. *contra(b)-basso*—pfx. contra- indicating an octave lower, and *basso*, bass.]
contrabassoon, *kon′tra-bas-ōōn′*, *n.* the double bassoon.
contra bonos mores, *kon′tra bō′nōs* (*bo′*) *mō′rēz* (*′rās*), (L.) against good manners or morals.
contraception, *kon-tra-sep′shan*, *n.* prevention of conception.—*n.* contracep′tive, a means of contraception.—Also *adj.* [conception.]
contract, *kən-trakt′*, *v.t.* to draw together: to lessen: to shorten: to effect by agreement: to come into, become the subject of: to incur, catch (a disease): to bargain for: to betroth.—*v.i.* to shrink: to become less: to become shorter.—*n.* (*kon′trakt*), an agreement on fixed terms: a bond: a betrothal: the writing containing an agreement: a season-ticket: contract bridge: a final bid in contract bridge: an undertaking.—*n.* contractabil′ity.—*adjs.* contract′able (*kən-*), able to be contracted, esp. of a disease or habit; contract′ed, drawn together: shortened: narrow: mean: affianced.—*adv.* contract′edly.—*ns.* contract′edness; contractibil′ity.—*adjs.* contract′-ible, capable of being contracted; contract′ile, tending or having power to contract or to draw in.—*ns.* contractil′ity (*kon-*); contrac′tion (*kən-*), act of contracting: a word shortened in speech or spelling: a symbol for shortening in palaeography, etc.—*adj.* contract′ive, tending to contract.—*n.* contract′or, one of the parties to a bargain or agreement: one who engages to execute work or furnish supplies at a stated rate. —*adj.* contract′ual.—*n.* contract′ure, persistent

muscular contraction: shortening due to spasm or paralysis of muscles, etc.: tapering of a column.—contract bridge, a development of auction bridge, in which tricks beyond the number bid for count only like honours; contract out, to arrange that certain conditions shall not apply. [L. *contractus*—*con*-, together, *trahĕre*, *tractum*, to draw.]

contra-dance. See country-dance.

contradict, *kon-trə-dikt' v.t.* to oppose by words (*obs.*): to deny what is affirmed by: to assert the contrary of: to deny: to be contrary to in character.—*adj.* contradict'able.—*n.* contradic'-tion, act of contradicting: a speaking against: denial: inconsistency.—*adj.* contradic'tious, prone to contradiction.—*adv.* contradic'tiously. —*adj.* contradict'ive, contradicting.—*adv.* contradict'ively.—*n.* contradict'or.—*adv.* contradict'orily.—*n.* contradict'oriness, the quality of being contradictory.—*adj.* contradict'ory, affirming the contrary: inconsistent.—*n.* a word, principle, that contradicts another: either of two propositions such that both cannot be true, or both cannot be false (*log.*).—contradiction in terms, a group of words containing a contradiction. [L. *contrādīcĕre*, *-dictum*.]

contradistinction, *kon-trə-dis-tingk'shən*, *n.* distinction by contrast.—*adj.* contradistinct'ive, distinguishing by opposite qualities.—*v.t.* contradistin'guish, to contrast and mark the difference between.

contrafagotto, *kon-trə-fə-got'tō*, *n.* the contrabassoon. [It. *contra*-, indicating an octave lower, and *fagotto*, bassoon.]

contrahent, *kon'trə-hənt*, *adj.* entering into a contract.—*n.* a contracting party. [L. *contrahēns*, *-entis*—*contrahēre*, to contract.]

contrail, *kon'trāl*, *n.* a trail of condensed vapours left by a high-flying aircraft. [con(densation) and trail.]

contraindicate, *kon'trə-in'di-kāt*, (*med.*) *v.t.* to point to as unsuitable: to forbid.—*ns.* contrain'dicant, con'traindicā'tion.—*adj.* contraindic'-ative.

contrair, *kən-trār'*, an obsolete dial. form of contrary.

contralto, *kən-tral'tō* or *-träl'*, *n.* the lowest musical voice in women: a singer with such a voice: a part for such a voice:—*pl.* contralti (*-tē*), *-tos.*—Also *adj.* [It., *contra*- and alto.]

contra mundum, *kon'tra mun'dum* or *mŏŏn'dŏŏm*, (L.) against the world.

contranatant, *kon-trə-nā'tant*, *adj.* swimming upstream. [L. *contrā*, *natāns*, *-antis*, pr.p. of *natāre*, to swim.]

contraplex, *kon'trə-pleks*, (*teleg.*) *adj.* having messages passing opposite ways at the same time. [L. *contrā*, against, and *-plex*, as in duplex.]

contraposition, *kon-trə-po-zish'ən*, *n.* opposition, contrast: an immediate inference, which consists in denying the original subject of the contradictory of the original predicate (*logic*).—*adj.* and *n.* contrapos'itive.—*n.* contrapposto (*kon-trə-po'stō*; *art*), pose of the human body with hips, shoulders, and head in different planes.

contraprop. Contraction of contrarotating propeller.

contraption, *kən-trap'shən*, *n.* a contrivance. [Perh. *contrivance* a*daption*.]

contrapuntal. See counterpoint.

contrarotating propeller, *kon-trə-rō-tā'ting prə-pel'ər*, *n.* one of a pair of propellers rotating in opposite directions.

contrary, *kon'trə-ri*, *adj.* opposite: contradictory: (usu. *kən-trā'ri*) perverse.—*n.* an extreme opposite: a proposition so related to another that both cannot be true though both may be false (*logic*).—*v.t.* and *v.i.* to oppose: to contradict: to annoy.—*n.* contrariety (*-ri'i-ti*), opposition:

inconsistency.—*adv.* contrarily (*kon'* or *trā'*).—*n.* contrariness (*kon'* or *trā'*).—*adj.* contrarious (*kən-trā'ri-əs*; *arch.*), showing contrariety.—*advs.* contra'riously (*arch.*), contrarily; con'-trariwise (or *trā'*, or *tra'*), in the contrary way: on the other side: on the other hand.—contrary motion (*mus.*), movement of parts in opposite directions—one up, another down.—on the contrary, far otherwise; to the contrary, to the opposite effect. [L. *contrārius*—*contrā*, against.]

contrast, *kən-träst'*, *v.i.* to stand in opposition.—*v.t.* to set in opposition to, in order to show difference.—*n.* contrast (*kon'träst*), opposition or unlikeness in things compared: exhibition of differences.—*adj.* contrast'ive. [Fr. *contraster*—L. *contrā*, opposite to, *stāre*, to stand.]

contrate, *kon'trāt*, *adj.* having cogs parallel to the axis. [L. *contrā*, opposite.]

contra-tenor. Same as counter-tenor.

contraterrene, *kon-trə-ter'ēn*, *adj.* opposite in character to earthy. [L. *contrā*, against, and terrene.]

contrat social, *kō-tra sos'yal*, (Fr.) social contract.

contravallation, *kon-trə-val-ā'shən*, *n.* a fortification built by besiegers about the place invested. [L. *contrā*, *vallāre*, *-atum*, to fortify.]

contravene, *kon-trə-vēn'*, *v.t.* to oppose: to infringe.—*n.* contraven'tion. [L. *contrā*, *venīre*, *ventum*, to come.]

contrayerva, *kon-trə-yûr'va*, *n.* a tropical American plant of the mulberry family, once esteemed as an antidote: a Jamaican birthwort of like reputation. [Sp. (now *contrahierba*)—L. *contrā*, against, *herba*, a herb.]

contrecoup, *kō-tr'-kŏŏ*, (*med.*) *n.*, an injury, esp. to the skull, resulting from a blow on the side exactly opposite to it. [Fr., counterblow.]

contretemps, *kō-tr'-tä*, *n.* something happening inopportunely or at the wrong time, anything embarrassing, a hitch. [Fr. *contre* (L. *contrā*), against, *temps* (L. *tempus*), time.]

contribute, *kən-trib'ūt* (*dial.* *kon'*), *v.t.* to give along with others: to give for a common purpose: to add towards a common result, to a fund, etc.: to write and send for publication with others.—*v.i.* to give or bear a part: to be a contributor.—*adj.* contrib'utable, payable: subject to contribution.—*n.* contribū'tion (*kon*-), the act of contributing: a levy or charge imposed upōn a number of persons: anything furnished to a common stock or done towards a common end: a written composition supplied to a periodical, etc.—*adjs.* contrib'utive, contrib'utory, (contrib'-utary, *obs.*), giving a share: helping.—*n.* contrib'utor. [L. *con-*, *tribĕre*, *-ūtum*, to give.]

contrist, *kən-trist'*, (*obs.*) *v.t.* to sadden.—*n.* contristā'tion. [Fr. *contrister*—L. *contristāre*—*con*-, inten., and *tristis*, sad.]

contrite, *kon'trit*, or *kən-trit'*, *adj.* brokenhearted for sin: penitent.—*adv.* con'tritely.—*ns.* con'-triteness; contrition (*kon-trish'ən*), deep sorrow for sin: remorse. [L. *contrītus*—*conterĕre*—*con*-, wholly, *terĕre*, to bruise.]

contriturate, *kon-trit'ū-rāt*, *v.t.* to pulverise.

contrive, *kən-triv'*, *v.t.* to plan: to invent: to bring about or effect: to manage, arrange: to plot: to conceive, understand (*Spens.*).—*adj.* contriv'able, that may be contrived.—*n.* contriv'ance.—*adj.* contrived, laboured, artificially intricate.—*ns.* contrive'ment, act of contriving: the thing contrived: invention: design: artifice; contriv'er, a schemer, a manager. [O.Fr. *controver*—*con*-, inten., *trover*, to find.]

contrive, *kən-triv'*, (*Shak.*) *v.t.* to spend, as time. [L. *conterĕre*, *contrītum*, perf. *contrīvi*, to wear out.]

control, *kən-trōl'*, *n.* restraint: authority: command: regulation: a check: a means of controlling or testing: a station for doing so: an experiment performed to afford a standard of comparison for other experiments (also **control** experiment): a disembodied spirit or other agency supposed to direct a spiritualistic medium: a lever ('joy-stick') or wheel to move ailerons and elevator, and so control the movements of aircraft (also **control column, lever, stick**): an aerofoil that controls the movements of an aircraft, as rudder, elevator, stabiliser (also **control surface**).—*adj.* pertaining to control.— *v.t.* to check: to restrain: to govern:—*pr.p.* **controll′ing**; *pa.t.* and *pa.p.* **controlled′.**— Formerly **comptroll′, countrol′, controul′.**—*adj.* **controll′able**, capable of, or subject to, control.— *ns.* **controll′er**, one who checks the accounts of others by a counter-roll (also **comptroller**): an official authorised to control some activity or department: one who controls or regulates: an apparatus for regulating—e.g. the speed of an electric car; **controll′ership**; **control′ment**, act or power of controlling: state of being controlled: control.—*ns.* **control room**, a room in which control instruments are placed, e.g. in a broadcasting station; **control tower**, a building at an aerodrome from which take-off and landing instructions are given. [Fr. *contrôle*, from *contre-rôle*, a duplicate register—L. *contrā*, against, *rotulus*, a roll.]

**controvert**, *kon′trə-vûrt*, *v.t.* to oppose: to argue against: to dispute.—*n.* **con′troverse** (*Spens.*), dispute.—*adj.* **controver′sial** (*-shl*), relating to controversy.—*n.* **controver′sialist**, one given to controversy.—*adv.* **controver′sially.**—*n.* **con′-troversy** (also *kən-tro′*), a debate: contention: dispute: a war of opinions, in books, pamphlets, etc.—*adj.* **controvert′ible.**—*adv.* **controvert′ibly.** —*n.* **con′trovertist** (or *vûrt′*). [L. *contrā*, against, and *vertĕre*, to turn.]

**contubernal** (*Chaucer*, **contubernyal**), *kən-tūb′ər-nl*, *adj.* living together (in the same tent): pertaining to companionship. [L. *contubernālis* (*n.*)—*cum*, with, together, *taberna*, hut, tavern.]

**contumacious**, *kon-tū-mā′shəs*, *adj.* opposing lawful authority with contempt: obstinate: stubborn.—*adv.* **contumā′ciously.**—*ns.* **contumā′-ciousness**; **contumacity** (*-mas′i-ti*); **con′tumacy** (*-məs-i*), obstinate disobedience or resistance. [L. *contumāx, -ācis*, insolent, from *con-*, inten., and *tumēre*, to swell, or *temnēre*, to despise.]

**contumely**, *kon′tūm-li* (or *kon′tū-mi-li*), *n.* scornful insolence.—*adj.* **contumē′lious** (*-mē′*), haughtily insolent.—*adv.* **contumē′liously.**—*n.* **contumē′-liousness**. [L. *contumēlia*, prob. from the same source as *contumāx*.]

**contund**, *kən-tund′*, *v.t.* to bruise or pound.—*v.t.* **contūse** (*-tūz′*), to beat or bruise: to crush.—*n.* **contusion** (*-tū′zhən*), act of bruising: state of being bruised: a bruise.—*adj.* **contū′sive**, apt to bruise. [L. *contundĕre, contūsum*—*con-*, inten., *tundĕre*, to bruise.]

**conundrum**, *kən-un′drəm*, *n.* a riddle turning on some odd or fanciful resemblance between things quite unlike: any puzzling question. [Ety. dub.]

**conurbation**, *kən-ûr-bā′shən*, *n.* an aggregation of towns.—*adj.* **conur′ban.**—*n.* **conurbia** (*kən-ûr′bi-ə*) the world of conurbations. [L. *con-*, together, *urbs*, city.]

**convalesce**, *kon-vəl-es′*, *v.i.* to regain health.—*ns.* **convalesc′ence, convalesc′ency**, gradual recovery of health and strength.—*adj.* **convalesc′ent**, gradually recovering health.—*n.* one recovering health. [L. *con-*, inten., *valēscēre*—*valēre*, to be strong.]

**Convallaria**, *kon-və-lā′ri-a*, *n.* the lily-of-the-valley, a genus of Liliaceae. [L. *convallis*, a sheltered valley.]

**convection**, *kən-vek′shən*, *n.* transmission, esp. that of heat or electricity through liquids or gases by means of currents: vertical movement, esp. upwards, of air or atmospheric conditions (*meteor.*).—*adjs.* **convec′tion, convec′tional, con-**

vec′tive.—*n.* **convec′tor**, apparatus for heating by convection. [L. *convectiō, -ōnis*, bringing together—*con-*, and *vehĕre*, to carry.]

**convenable**. See **convenance, convenient.**

**convenance**, *kɔ̄-və-näs, kon′vən-äns, n.* what is suitable or proper: (in *pl.*) the conventional usages or social proprieties.—*adj.* **convenable** (*-äbl′*), conforming to the convenances. [Fr.]

**convene**, *kən-vēn′, v.i.* to come together: to assemble.—*v.t.* to call together.—*adj.* **convēn′-able.**—*n.* **convēn′er**, one who convenes a meeting: the chairman of a committee. [Fr. *convenir*—L. *convenire*—*con-*, together, and *venire*, to come.]

**convenient**, *kən-vēn′yənt, adj.* suitable: handy: commodious.—*adj.* **convenable** (*kon′vən-ə-bl*) (*obs.*), fitting.—*ns.* **convēn′ience, convēn′iency**, suitability: an advantage: any particular domestic accommodation, as a closet, etc.—*adv.* **convēn′iently.—convenience food**, food (partly) prepared before sale so as to be ready, or almost ready, for the table. [L. *convenire*.]

**convent**, *kon′vənt, n.* an association of persons secluded from the world and devoted to a religious life: the house in which they live, a monastery or nunnery.—*adj.* **convent′ual**, belonging to a convent.—*n.* a monk or nun: a member of one of the two divisions of the Franciscans, following a mitigated rule—the other being the *Observants*. [Through Fr. from L. *conventum, convenire*, to come together.]

**convent**, *kən-vent′*, (*Spens., Shak.*) *v.t.* to convene, summon, cite.—(*Shak.*) *v.i.* to be suitable. [L. *convenire, conventum*—*con-*, venire, to come.]

**conventicle**, *kən-vent′i-kl* (earlier *kon′vənt-*), *n.* a secret, illegal, or forbidden religious meeting, applied esp. to those of English dissenters and to the Scottish Presbyterian field-preachings in the persecutions under Charles II and James VII: any private, clandestine, or irregular meeting.— *v.i.* to hold such a meeting.—*n.* **conven′ticler.** [L. *conventiculum*, a secret meeting of monks.]

**convention**, *kən-ven′shən, n.* the act of convening: an assembly, esp. of representatives or delegates for some common object: any extraordinary assembly called upon any special occasion: a parliament not summoned by the sovereign: an assembly for framing or revising a constitution: a meeting of political party delegates for nominating a candidate for the presidency or other purpose (*U.S.*): any temporary treaty: an agreement: established usage: fashion: in card games, a mode of play in accordance with a recognised code of signals, not determined by the principles of the game.—*adj.* **conven′tional**, formed or adopted by convention: bound or influenced by convention: growing out of tacit agreement or custom: customary: not spontaneous: stylised: arbitrary.—*v.t.* **conven′-tionalise, -ize**, to make conventional: to delineate according to a convention rather than nature.—*ns.* **conven′tionalism**, that which is established by tacit agreement, as a mode of speech, etc.; **conven′tionalist**, one who adheres to a convention, or is swayed by conventionalism; **conventional′ity**, state of being conventional: that which is established by use or custom.—*adv.* **conven′tionally.**—*adj.* **conven′-tionary**, acting under contract.—*ns.* **conven′-tioner, conven′tionist.**—**conventional weapons**, weapons that are not nuclear. [L. *conventiō, -ōnis*; see **convene**.]

**converge**, *kən-vûrj′, v.i.* to tend towards or meet in one point or value: to acquire like character independently.—*ns.* **conver′gence, conver′gency.** —*adjs.* **conver′gent**, converging: due to or characterised by convergence; **conver′ging**, meeting in a point: coming nearer together: with gradually approaching tips (*bot.*). [L. *con-*, *vergĕre*, to bend, to incline.]

**conversazione**, *kon-vər-sat-si-ō′ni, n.* a meeting for

conversation, particularly on learned subjects:—*pl.* conversazio'nes, or conversazio'ni (-*nē*). [It.] converse, *kən-vûrs'*, *v.i.* to have intercourse: to talk familiarly: to commune.—*n.* converse (*kon'*), familiar intercourse: conversation: communing.—*adj.* convers'able, disposed to converse: sociable.—*adv.* convers'ably.—*ns.* con'versance, con'versancy, state of being conversant: familiarity.—*adj.* con'versant (also -*vûrs'*), acquainted by study: familiar: concerned or occupied: associating: dwelling (*obs.*).—*n.* conversā'tion, intercourse: talk: familiar discourse: behaviour or deportment (*B.*).—*adj.* conversā'tional.—*ns.* conversā'tionalist, conversā'tionist, one who excels in conversation; conversā'tionism (*rare*), a colloquialism.—*adj.* conver'sative (*obs.*), ready to talk.—conversation piece, a painting of a number of persons, grouped indoors or outside: a play, etc., in which the dialogue is as important as, or more important than, the action: an object that arouses comment by its novelty. [Fr. *converser*—L. *conversārī*, to turn about, go about, associate, dwell—*con-*, intens., and *versāre*, to keep turning—*vertĕre*, to turn.]
convert, *kən-vûrt'*, *v.t.* to turn about (*obs.*): to change or turn from one thing, condition, opinion, party or religion to another: to change from an irreligious to a holy life: to change by a spiritual experience: to change into the converse: to alter into something else (esp. iron into steel, a try into a goal, a merchant ship into a cruiser): to apply to a particular purpose: to exchange for an equivalent, as paper money for specie.—*n.* (*kon'*), one who is converted.—*adj.* con'verse, reversed in order or relation.—*n.* that which is the opposite of another: a proposition in which the subject and predicate have changed places (*log.*): a proposition in which that which is given and that which is to be proved in another proposition are interchanged (*math.*).—*adv.* converse'ly.—*ns.* conver'sion, change from one condition, use, opinion, party, religion or spiritual state to another: appropriation to a special purpose: act of constructing a proposition in accordance with the rules of direct inference, in which the terms of another proposition are interchanged (*logic*); con'vertend, the proposition to be converted; convert'er, one who or that which converts: a vessel in which materials are changed from one condition to another (esp. iron into steel): apparatus for making a change in electric current (also conver'tor); convertibil'ity.—*adj.* convert'ible, that may be converted: of currency, that may be converted into gold (or dollars) at a fixed price: equivalent.—*n.* anything convertible: a car with folding top.—*adv.* convert'ibly.—*n.* con'vertite, a convert: a reformed woman.—convertiplane (*kən-vûr'tə-plān*), an aircraft which takes off vertically like a helicopter but is capable of the great horizontal speed of a conventional aeroplane. [L. *convertĕre*, *conversum*—*con-*, *vertĕre*, to turn.]
convex, *kon'veks*, also *kon-veks'*, *adj.* rising into a round form on the outside, the reverse of concave.—*n.* a convex figure, surface, body, or part: the vault of heaven, etc.—*adj.* convexed', made convex.—*adv.* convex'edly.—*ns.* convex'ity, roundness of form on the outside: a convex part or figure; con'vexness (or *veks'*).—*adv.* con'-vexly (or *veks'*).—*adjs.* convex'o-con'cave, convex on one side, and concave on the other; con-vex'o-con'vex, convex on both sides. [L. *convexus*—*convehĕre*—*con-*, *vehĕre*, to carry.]
convey, *kən-vā'*, *v.t.* to carry: to transmit: to impart: to steal: to communicate, as ideas: to make over in law.—*adj.* convey'able.—*ns.* convey'al; convey'ance, act or means of conveying: trickery: a vehicle of any kind: the act of transferring property (*law*): the writing that transfers

it; convey'ancer, one who prepares deeds for the transference of property; convey'ancing; convey'er, convey'or, a person or thing that conveys in any sense: a mechanism for continuous transport of materials, packages, goods in process of manufacture, etc.—also convey'or-belt. [O.Fr. *conveier*—L. *con-*, *via*, a way.]
convicinity, *kon-vi-sin'i-ti*, *n.* a neighbourhood.
convict, *kən-vikt'*, *v.t.* to prove guilty: to pronounce guilty.—*n.* convict (*kon'*), one convicted or found guilty of crime: one who has been condemned to penal servitude.—*ns.* convic'tion, act of convincing: strong belief: a proving guilty: the condition of being consciously convicted of sin (*theol.*); con'victism, the convict system.—*adj.* convict'ive, able to convince or convict.—carry conviction, to bear irresistibly the stamp or proof of truth. [Root as convince.]
convince, *kən-vins'*, *v.t.* to overcome, get the better of (*Shak.*, *Spens.*): to subdue the mind of by evidence: to satisfy as to truth or error: to convict (*B.*): to refute (*obs.*).—*n.* convince'ment (*obs.*).—*adjs.* convinc'ible; convinc'ing, producing conviction.—*adv.* convinc'ingly. [L. *convincĕre*, *con-*, sig. completeness, and *vincĕre*, *victum*, to conquer.]
convivial, *kən-viv'i-əl*, *adj.* feasting or drinking in company: relating to a feast: social: jovial.—*v.i.* convive (-*vīv'*; *Shak.*), to feast together.—*n.* (*kɔ̄-vēv*, *kon'vīv*), a companion at table.—*ns.* conviv'ialist, a convivial fellow: convivial'ity.—*adv.* conviv'ially. [L. *convivium*, a living together, a feast—*con-*, together, *vivĕre*, to live.]
convoke, *kən-vōk'*, *v.t.* to call together: to assemble —also convocate (*kon'vō-kāt*).—*n.* convocā'tion, act of convoking: a provincial synod of clergy, esp. those of the provinces of Canterbury and York in the Church of England: the great legislative assembly of the university at Oxford and elsewhere.—*adj.* convocā'tional.—*n.* convocā'-tionist. [L. *convocāre*—*con-*, together, and *vocāre*, -*ātum*, to call.]
convolve, *kən-volv'*, *v.t.* to roll together, or one part on another.—*adjs.* convolute (*kon'və-lōōt*, -*lūt*), -d, rolled together, or one part on another: coiled laterally with one margin within, one without (*bot.*): of a flower-bud, contorted (*bot.*): of a gasteropod shell, having the inner whorls concealed or overlapped by the outer (*zool.*).—*n.* convolution (-*lōō'*, -*lū'*), twisting: a fold or sinuosity, esp. of the brain surface. [L. *con-*, together, *volvĕre*, -*ūtum*, to roll.]
Convolvulus, *kən-vol'vu-ləs*, *n.* the bindweed genus of twining or trailing plants, giving name to the family Convolvūlā'ceae, akin to the nightshade family: (without *cap.*) a plant of the genus or of the kindred Calystegia. [L. *convolvĕre*.]
convoy, *kon-voi'*, *v.t.* to accompany for protection.—*n.* (*kon'*), the act of convoying: protection: that which convoys or is conveyed, esp. a ship or ships of war guarding a fleet of merchant-vessels: also the ships so protected: an honourable escort: a supply of stores, etc., under escort: a train of military wagons or the like. [Fr. *convoyer*; see convey.]
convulse, *kən-vuls'*, *v.t.* to agitate violently: to affect by spasms.—*n.* convuls'ant, an agent that causes convulsions.—Also *adj.*—*adj.* convul'-sible, subject to convulsion.—*n.* convul'sion, any involuntary contraction of the voluntary muscles of the body, esp. such seizures in which the body is thrown into violent spasmodic contractions: any violent disturbance.—*adjs.* convul'sional, convul'sionary, pertaining to convulsions.—*ns.* convul'sionary, one who has convulsions, esp. one of a fanatical sect of Jansenists who sprang up in France about 1730; convul'sionist, a religious convulsionary: a believer in the importance of convulsions in geological history (opposed to *uniformitarian*).—*adj.* convuls'ive, attended with

convulsions: spasmodic.—*adv.* convuls'ively.—
*n.* convuls'iveness. [L. *con-*, inten., and *vellĕre*,
*vulsum*, to pluck, to pull.]
cony, coney, kō'ni, or (historically right) kun'i, *n.*
a rabbit: rabbit-skin: a hyrax (*B.*): a term of
endearment for a woman (*obs.*): a dupe (*obs.*).
—co'ny-burr'ow, a rabbit-burrow.—*v.t.* co'ny-
catch (*Shak.*), to cheat.—co'ny-catcher (*obs.*), a
cheat; co'ny-wool, rabbits' fur. [Prob. through
O.Fr. *conil*, from L. *cuniculus*, a rabbit.]
coo, kōō, *v.i.* to make a sound as a dove: to converse fondly.—*v.t.* to murmur softly or ingratiatingly: to effect as by cooing:—*pr.p.* coo'ing;
*pa.t.* and *pa.p.* cooed (kōōd).—*n.* the sound
emitted by doves.—*n.* and *adj.* coo'ing.—*adv.*
coo'ingly. [Imit.]
coo, kōō, (*slang*.) *interj.* expressive of surprise.
cooee, cooey, kōō'ē, *n.* an Australian signal-call.—
*v.i.* to utter the call.—*interj.* a call to attract
attention. [Native word.]
coof, *kof*, *kif*, (*Scot.*) *n.* a lout. [Origin obscure.]
cook, kook, *v.t.* to prepare as food by heat: manipulate for any purpose, or falsify, as accounts,
etc.: concoct: to ruin, tire out (*slang*): spoil (as
a chess-problem, by finding another way out).—
*v.i.* to practise cookery: to undergo cooking.—*n.*
one who undertakes or is skilled in cooking: a
process of heating: an unforeseen alternative
that ruins a chess-problem.—*ns.* cook'er, a stove,
special vessel, or other apparatus for cooking:
a variety suitable for cooking; cook'ery, the art
or practice of cooking.—cook'ery-book, a book
of recipes for cooking dishes (*U.S.* cook'-book);
cook'-gen'eral, cook'-house'maid, a servant
combining the functions of cook and general
servant or housemaid; cook'house, a building
or room for cooking in; cook'ing-app'le, etc.,
apple, etc., specially suitable for cooking; cook'-
ing-range, a stove adapted for cooking several
things at once; cook'maid, a maid who cooks or
assists a cook; cook'out (*U.S.*), a barbecue party;
cook'room, a room in which food is cooked;
cook'shop, an eating-house.—to cook one's goose
(*slang*), to finish off, to kill, to ruin, to spoil one's
plans; what's cooking? (*coll.*), what is afoot?
[O.E. *cōc*, a cook (cf. Ger. *koch*)—L. *coquus*.]
cook, kook, *v.i.* to make the sound of the cuckoo.
cook, kook, kook, (*Scot.*) *v.i.* to appear and disappear by turns: to peep. [Origin obscure.]
cookie, kook'i, *n.* in Scotland, a plain bun: in U.S.
(usu. cook'y), a biscuit: a person (*U.S. slang*).—
*n.* cook'ie-shine (*facet.*), a tea-party. [Du.
*koekje*, a cake.]
cool, kōōl, *adj.* slightly cold: free from excitement:
calm: not zealous, ardent or cordial: indifferent: impudent: colloquially of a large sum
of money, as *a cool thousand*: a slang term of
approval meaning intellectual, not sensual;
excellent and up to date; pleasing, satisfying.—
*v.t.* to make cool: to allay or moderate, as heat,
excitement, passion, etc.—*v.i.* to grow cool: to
lose radioactivity.—*n.* that which is cool: coolness: coolness, self-possession (*U.S. slang*).—*ns.*
cool'ant, a cooling agent: a fluid used to cool the
edge of a cutting tool (*eng.*): a fluid used as the
cooling medium in an engine (*eng.*); cool'er,
anything that cools: a vessel in which something
is cooled: jail (*slang*).—*adj.* cool'ish, somewhat
cool.—*adv.* cool'ly, in a cool manner: indifferently: impudently.—*ns.* cool'ness, moderate
cold: indifference: diminution of friendship:
want of zeal: lack of agitation: self-possession;
coolth (*dial.*), coolness.—*adj.* cool'y (*Spens.*),
cool.—*adj.* cool'head'ed, not easily excited:
capable of acting with composure.—cool'-house,
a greenhouse kept at a cool temperature;
cooling card (*Shak.*), anything that discourages,
or dashes hopes; cool'-tank'ard, a cooling
drink of wine and water, with lemon-juice, spices,
and borage: a local name of borage.—cool off,

become less angry and more amenable to reason:
to grow less passionate; cool one's heels, to be
kept waiting; keep one's cool (*coll.*), to remain
calm, keep one's head; lose one's cool, to become
flustered. [O.E. *cōl*; cf. Ger. *kühl*.]
coolabah, *kool'ə-bä*, *n.* any of several species of
Australian eucalypt. [Native word.]
coolie, cooly, kōōl'i, *n.* an Indian or Chinese
labourer who has emigrated under contract to a
foreign land: a European's name for a hired
native labourer in India and China. [Prob. *Kolī*,
a tribe of W. India; or Tamil, *kūli*, hire.]
coom, kōōm, *n.* soot: coal-dust: dust of various
kinds.—*v.t.* to begrime.—*adj.* coom'y. [App.
Northern form of culm (2).]
coom, kōōm, (*Scot.*) *n.* the wooden centering on
which a bridge is built: anything arched or
vaulted.—*adj.* coom'ceiled, said of a garret with
the inside ceiling sloping from the wall. [Origin
obscure.]
coomb, comb(e), kōōm, *n.* a deep little wooded
valley: a hollow in a hillside. [O.E. *cumb*, a
hollow.]
coomb, comb, kōōm, *n.* a measure of capacity = 4
bushels. [O.E. *cumb*, a measure.]
coon, kōōn, *n.* the raccoon: a sly fellow: a Negro
(*derog.*).—coon'-song, a Negro-song.—a gone coon,
one whose case is hopeless. [U.S.; for raccoon.]
coon-can, kōōn'-kan, *n.* a card game in which one
tries to form sequences. [Sp. *con quién*, with
whom.]
coontie, coonty, kōōn'ti, *n.* an American cycad
yielding a sort of arrowroot. [Seminole *kunti*.]
coop, kōōp, *n.* a wicker basket: a box or cage for
fowls or small animals: a prison: a confined,
narrow space.—*v.t.* to confine in a coop or elsewhere. [Perh. from an unknown O.E. *cūpe*,
collateral with *cȳpe*, cask; cf. L. *cūpa*, cask.]
cooper, kōōp'ər, *n.* one who makes tubs, casks,
etc.: a mixture of stout and porter.—*v.t.* to
repair (tubs, etc.): to prepare, patch up.—*ns.*
coop'erage, the work or workshop of a cooper:
the sum paid for a cooper's work; coop'ering;
coop'ery, the business of a cooper. [Also L.G.,—
L.L. *cūpārius*—*cūpa*, cask; cf. coop.]
cooper, kōp'ər. See coper.
co-op, kō-op', kō'op, (*coll.*) short for co-operative
society or store.
co-operate (also coop- in all words), kō-op'ər-āt,
*v.i.* to work together.—*n.* co-opera'tion, joint
operation: combination in co-operative societies:—*adjs.* co-op'erative (also *n.*); co-op'erant,
working together.—*n.* co-op'erātor, one who
co-operates: a member of a co-operative
society.—co-operating grace (*theol.*), the R.C.,
Arminian, and Socinian doctrine that the human
will co-operates with the divine in the matter of
saving grace; co-operative society, an association
for supplying goods or for carrying on some
branch of industry, the profits going to the
members; co-operative store, the shop of a co-
operative society. [Pfx. co-, together, and
operate.]
co-opt, kō-opt', *v.t.* to elect into any body by the
votes of its members.—*ns.* co-opta'tion, co-
op'tion.—*adj.* co-op'tative. [L. *cooptāre*, *-ātum*
—*co-*, together, *optāre*, to choose.]
co-ordinate (also coor- in all words), kō-ör'di-nāt,
*adj.* of the same order or rank: pertaining to or
involving co-ordination or co-ordinates.—*v.t.*
to place or classify in the same order or rank: to
adjust the relations or movements of: to combine or integrate harmoniously: to harmonise.
—*n.* an element of the same order as another:
each of a system of two or more magnitudes
used to define the position of a point, line, or
surface by reference to a fixed system of lines,
points, etc.: (in *pl.*) outer garments in harmonising colour, material and pattern (cf.
separates).—*n.* co-or'dinance, a joint ordinance.

Neutral vowels in unaccented syllables: *el'ə-mənt*; for certain sounds in foreign words, see p. viii

—*adv.* co-or'dinately.—*ns.* co-or'dinateness; co-ordina'tion.—*adj.* co-or'dinative, co-ordinating: co-ordinated, indicating co-ordination.—co-ordinate geometry, geometry by the use of co-ordinates, analytical geometry; co-ordination compounds (*chem.*), compounds in which the atoms or groups are united by co-ordinate bonds, secondary valences supplementary to the principal valences (e.g. addition compounds), esp. (co-ordination complex compounds) ones in which there is a central atom or ion.

coosen, coosin, obs. spellings of cousin, cozen.

coost, *kūst*, a Scottish form of cast (*pa.t.*).

coot, *kōōt*, *n.* a short-tailed water-fowl, with a characteristic white spot—an extension of the bill—on the forehead; hence called bald, as in phrase, *bald as a coot*: a foolish person (*coll.*). [M.E. *cote*; cf. Du. *koet.*]

coot. See cuit.

cop, *kop*, *n.* a top or head of anything; a conical ball of thread on a spindle.—Also copp'in.—*adj.* copped, rising to a cop or head. [O.E. *cop*, *copp.*]

cop, *kop*, (*slang*) *v.t.* to capture: to catch.—*n.* a policeman: a capture.—*n.* copp'er (*slang*), a policeman. [Perh. Fr. *caper*, to seize—L. *capēre*, *captum*, to take; cf. Du. *kapen*, to steal.]

copacetic, copesettic, *kō-pə-set'ik*, (*U.S. slang*) *adj.* sound: excellent.—*interj.* all clear. [Origin obscure.]

copaiba, copaiva, *kō-pī'bä*, -*vä*, or -*pā'*, *n.* a balsam obtained from S. American caesalpiniaceous trees (*Copaifera*) much used in medicine. [Sp. and Port. from Tupí.]

copal, *kō'pəl*, *n.* a hard resin got from many tropical trees, and also fossil. [Sp.,—Nahuatl *copalli*, resin.]

coparcener, *kō-pär'sən-ər*, *n.* a joint heir to an undivided property.—*n.* and *adj.* copar'cenery, -ary.

copartner, *kō-pärt'nər*, *n.* a joint partner.—*ns.* copart'nership, copart'nery.

copataine, *kop'ə-tān*, (*Shak.*) *adj.* high-crowned like a sugar-loaf. [Ety. obscure.]

copatriot, a form of compatriot.

cope, *kōp*, *n.* a covering: a cap or hood: anything spread overhead: a coping: a semicircular, sleeveless hooded vestment worn over the alb or surplice in processions, at solemn lauds and vespers.—*v.t.* to cover as with a cope.—*n.* cop'ing, the covering course of masonry of a wall.—cope'-stone, cop'ing-stone, a stone that copes or tops a wall; cop'ing-saw, a narrow saw held under tension by a metal frame, for cutting curves. [M.E. *cape*—hypothetical O.E. *cāpe*—L.L. *cāpa*; cf. cap.]

cope, *kōp*, (*dial.*) *v.t.* and *v.i.* to barter or exchange. [Cf. Du. *koopen.*]

cope, *kōp*, *v.i.* (esp. with *with*) to contend: to deal (with) successfully.—*v.t.* to encounter, meet (*Shak.*): to match (*obs.*).—*n.* copes'-mate (*obs.*), a companion (*Shak.*): an accomplice: a partner: an adversary: a paramour. [Fr. *couper*—L. *colaphus* (Gr. *kolaphos*), a buffet.]

cope, *kōp*, (*obs.*) *v.t.* to tie or sew up the mouth of (a ferret). [Origin obscure; cf. uncape, uncope.]

copeck. Same as kopeck.

copepod, *kō'pe-pod*, *n.* a member of the Copep'oda, a class of crustacea, minute animals with oarlike swimming feet. [Gr. *kōpē*, handle, oar, *pous*, *podos*, foot.]

coper, often cooper, *kōp'ər*, *n.* a ship employed in surreptitiously supplying strong drink to deep-sea fishermen.—*v.i.* to supply liquor in such a way. [Du. *kooper*—*koopen*, to trade; cf. Ger. *kaufen*, to buy; O.E. *cēapan.*]

Copernican, *ko-pûr'ni-kən*, *adj.* relating to Copernicus, the famous Prussian astronomer (1473-1543), or to his system, in which the earth revolves about the sun.

copia verborum, *kō'pi-a ver-bō'rəm* (*ver-bō'rōōm, wer-*) (L.) plenty of words, fluency.

copier. See copy.

coping. See cope (1).

co-pilot, copilot, *kō'pī-lət*, *n.* a fellow pilot.

copious, *kō'pi-əs*, *adj.* plentiful: overflowing: abounding: rich in words: not concise.—*adv.* cō'piously.—*n.* cō'piousness. [L. *cōpiōsus*—*cōpia*, plenty—*co-*, inten., and *ops*, *opis*, wealth.]

copita, *ko-pē'tə*, *n.* tulip-shaped sherry glass. [Sp.]

co-polymer, *kō-pol'i-mər*, *n.* a substance polymerised along with another, the result being a chemical compound, not a mixture.—*v.t.* co-pol'ymerise, -ize.—*n.* co-polymerisā'tion.

co-portion, *kō-pōr'shən*, -*pör*, (*Spens.*) *n.* share.

copper, *kop'ər*, *n.* a moderately hard metal (symbol Cu for L. *cuprum*; atomic number 29), of a reddish colour, perhaps the first metal used by man: money, or a coin, made orig. of copper: a copper vessel: a boiler (orig. of copper) for clothes, or soap, etc.—*adj.* made of copper: copper-coloured.—*v.t.* to cover with copper.—*n.* copp'ering, the act of sheathing with copper: a covering of copper.—*adjs.* copp'erish, somewhat like copper; copp'ery, like copper.—Copper Age, a stage in culture in some regions leading up to the Bronze Age, characterised by the use of copper unmixed with tin; copp'er-beech', a variety of the common beech with purplish, copper-coloured leaves.—*adj.* copp'er-bott'omed, having the bottom covered with copper: sound, esp. financially.—Also *v.t.*—*n.* copp'er-cap'tain, one who styles himself captain without grounds. —*adjs.* copp'er-faced, faced with copper, as type; copp'er-fas'tened, fastened with copper bolts.— copp'er-glance', redruthite, cuprous sulphide; copp'erhead, a venomous United States snake akin to the rattle-snake: in U.S. a northern sympathiser with the South in the Civil War; copp'er-nick'el, niccolite, a copper-red mineral, arsenide of nickel; copp'er-nose, a red nose; copp'erplate, a plate of polished copper on which something has been engraved: an impression taken from the plate: faultless handwriting; copp'er-pyri'tes, a yellow double sulphide of copper and iron; copp'erskin, an American Indian; copp'ersmith, work in copper: a smith who works in copper; copp'er-work, a place where copper is wrought or manufactured; copp'er-worm, the ship-worm.—hot coppers, parched tongue and throat after a bout of drinking. [O.E. *copor*—L.L. *cuper*—L. *cuprum*, a form of *cyprium* (*aes*), Cyprian (brass), because found in *Cyprus*.]

copperas, *kop'ər-əs*, *n.* a name formerly applied to copper and other sulphates, now only to ferrous sulphate. [Fr. *couperose* (It. *coparosa*), perh.—L. *cupri rosa*, rose of copper, or *aqua cuprōsa*, copper water.]

coppice, *kop'is*, copse, *kops*, *ns.* a wood of small growth for periodical cutting: a wood of sprouts from cut stumps.—*v.t.* to make into coppice: to cover with coppice.—*adj.* cop'sy.—*n.* copse'-wood. [O.Fr. *copeiz*, wood, newly cut—L.L. *colpare*, to cut—L. *colaphus*—Gr. *kolaphos*, a buffet.]

coppin. See cop (1).

copple, *kop'l*, (*obs.*) *n.* a bird's crest.—*n.* copp'le-crown.—*adj.* copp'le-crowned. [App. from cop.]

copple-stone, an obsolete form of cobble-stone.

copra, *kop'rə*, *n.* the dried kernel of the coconut, yielding coconut oil. [Port., from Malayalam.]

co-presence, copresence, *kō-prez'əns*, *n.* presence together.—*adj.* co'pres'ent.

copro-, in composition, dung.—*n.* coprōlāl'ia (Gr. *lalia*, talk; *phychiatry*), obsessive use of obscene language.—*adj.* coprōlāl'iac.—*n.* coprolite (*kop'rə-lit*; Gr. *lithos*, stone), a piece of fossil dung: loosely applied to phosphatic concretions. —*adj.* coprolitic (-*lit'ik*).—*ns.* coprol'ogy (Gr.

logos, discourse), the unclean in literature and art; coproph'agan (Gr. *phagein*, to eat), a dung-beetle. —*adj.* coprophag'ic.—*n.* coproph'agist (*-jist*), a dung-eater.—*adj.* coproph'agous.—*n.* coprophil'ia (Gr. *philiā*, love), morbid pleasure in dung or filth.—*adj.* coproph'ilous, delighting in dung or filth: growing on or in dung.—*n.* copros'terol, a compound formed from cholesterol in the intestine. [Gr. *kopros*, dung.] copse, copsewood. See coppice.
Copt, *kopt*, *n.* a Christian descendant of the ancient Egyptians.—*adj.* Copt'ic.—*n.* the language of the Copts. [Gr. *Aigyptios*, Egyptian.]
copula, *kop'ū-lə*, *n.* that which joins together: a bond or tie: copulation: the word joining the subject and predicate (*logic*).—*adj.* cop'ular.—*v.t.* and *v.i.* cop'ulāte, to unite in sexual intercourse.—*n.* copulā'tion.—*adj.* cop'ulātive, uniting: indicating combination, not alternative or adversative relation.—*n.* in gram., a conjunction that does this.—*adj.* cop'ulatory. [L. *cōpula—co-*, *apēre*, to join.]
copy, *kop'i*, *n.* abundance, copiousness (*obs.*): an imitation: a transcript: a reproduction: an exemplar: that which is imitated or reproduced: a specimen to be imitated: matter (e.g. a newspaper article) for printing: something newsworthy.—*v.t.* to write, paint, etc. after: to imitate closely: to transcribe: to reproduce or duplicate by copying-press or otherwise.—*v.i.* to make a copy: to follow: to look on a schoolfellow's work and filch the result:—*pr.p.* cop'ying; *pa.t.* and *pa.p.* cop'ied.—*ns.* cop'ier, one who copies: an imitator; cop'yism, servile or plagiaristic copying; copy'ist, one whose business is to copy documents: a mere copier; cop'ybook, a writing or drawing book of models printed for imitation: a letter-book, or collection of copies of documents.—*adj.* conventional, commonplace: (of example, operation, etc.) perfect, or carried out flawlessly.—cop'y-cat (*slang*), term applied in resentful derision to an imitator.—*v.t.* and *v.i.* to imitate.—cop'yhold (*Eng. law*), a species of estate or right of holding land, according to the custom of a manor, by copy of the roll originally made by the steward of the lord's court; cop'yholder, a holder of land by copyhold: an assistant who reads copy aloud to a proof-reader; cop'ying-ink', ink suitable for copying by impression; cop'ying(-ink)-pencil, an ink-pencil; cop'ying-press, a machine for copying manuscript letters by pressure; cop'y-right, the sole right to reproduce a literary, dramatic, musical, or artistic work—also to perform, translate, film, or record such a work (in the United Kingdom, since 1st July 1912, for books the term is the author's lifetime and fifty years after his death).—*adj.* protected by copyright.—*v.t.* to secure the copyright of.—*n.* cop'y-wri'ter, a writer of copy (esp. advertisements) for the press.—a copy of verses, a set of verses, esp. a college exercise. [Fr. *copie*, from L. *cōpia*, plenty; in L.L. a transcript.]
coquelicot, *kok'li-kō*, (*Jane Austen*) *n.* a brilliant red, the colour of the red poppy. [Fr., poppy.]
coquet, coquette, *ko-*, *kō-ket'*, *v.i.* to flirt: to dally.—*v.t.* (*obs.*) to flirt with:—*pr.p.* coquett'ing; *pa.p.* and *pa.t.* coquett'ed.—*ns.* cō'quetry (*-kit-ri*), act of coquetting: attempt to attract admiration, without serious affection: deceit in love: any artful prettiness; coquette', a woman (rarely a man) who seeks admiration from mere vanity: a flirt.—Also *adj.*—*adj.* coquett'ish, practising coquetry: befitting a coquette.—*adv.* coquett'ishly.—*n.* coquett'ishness. [Fr. *coqueter—coquet*, dim. of *coq*, a cock.]
coquilla, *kō-kil'yə*, *n.* the nut of the piassava palm (*Attalea*), whose mottled, dark-brown endosperm is used by button-makers and turners. [Sp.; dim. of *coca*, shell.]

coquimbite, *kō-kim'bīt*, *n.* a yellowish hydrous sulphate of iron found in *Coquimbo*.
coquito, *kō-kē'tō*, *n.* a beautiful Chilean palm, *Jubaea spectabilis*. [Sp.; dim. of *coco*, coco-palm.]
cor, *kör*, *n.* a Hebrew measure, the homer, 10 ephahs or baths (roughly 11 bushels). [Heb. *kōr*, round vessel.]
coracle, *kor'ə-kl*, *n.* a small oval rowing-boat used in Wales, made of skins or tarred or oiled canvas stretched on wickerwork, etc. [Conn. W. *corwg*, anything round; Gael. *curach*, see currach.]
coracoid, *kor'ə-koid*, *adj.* shaped like a crow's beak.—*n.* in anat., a paired ventral bone in the breast-girdle, forming along with the scapula the articulation for the fore-limb: in mammals, except monotremes, reduced to a coracoid process, fused to the scapula. [Gr. *korax, korakos*, a crow, and *eidos*, form.]
co-radicate, coradicate, *kō-rad'i-kāt*, (*philol.*) *adj.* of the same root. [Pfx. co-, together and radicate—see radical.]
coraggio, *kor-ad'jō*, *interj.* courage! [It.]
coral, *kor'əl*, *n.* a hard substance of various colours deposited on the bottom of the sea, skeleton, mostly calcareous, of Anthozoa and of some Hydrozoa: the animal or colony that produces it: a young child's toy of coral or other material for biting: lobster roe, coral red when cooked: (*pl.*) a necklace of coral: a deep orange-pink colour.—*adj.* made of or like coral, esp. red coral.—*adj.* corallā'ceous, like, or having the qualities of, coral.—*n.* Corallian (*-al'*; *geol.*), a Jurassic formation overlying the Oxfordian, including the Coral-Rag and Coralline Oolite.—*adjs.* corallif'erous, containing coral; coralliform (*-al'*), having the form of coral; corallig'enous, producing coral; cor'alline, of, like, or containing coral.—*n.* a common limy seaweed (*Corallina*) of a delicate pinkish or purplish colour: a coral-like substance or animal.—*n.* cor'allite, the cup of a simple coral or of one polyp: a fossil coral.—*adjs.* cor'alloid, coralloid'al, in the form of coral: resembling coral.—*ns.* corallum (*-al'*), the skeleton of a coral colony:—*pl.* corall'a.—cor'alberr'y, an American shrub of the snowberry genus, or its red berry; cor'al-fish, a tropical, spiny-finned fish of many kinds abundant about coral reefs; cor'al - is'land; Coralline Crag (*geol.*), a division of the English Pliocene, shelly sands and clays with fossil polyzoa; Coralline Oolite, a massive limestone underlying the Coral Rag; Cor'al Rag, a coarse limestone rock formed chiefly of coral in the Corallian formation; cor'al-reef', a reef or bank formed by the growth and deposit of coral; cor'al-rock', a limestone composed of coral; cor'al-root', a species of Cardamine with knobbed rootstock: a genus of orchids (*Corallorhiza*) with coral-like rootstock; cor'al-snake, an American genus, Elaps (or Micrurus), of small venomous snakes; cor'al-tree, a tropical genus (Erythrina) of trees and shrubs with red coral-like flowers; cor'al-wort, coral-root, in either sense. [L. *corallum*—Gr. *korallion*.]
coram domino rege, *kō, -kō'ram dom'i-nō rē'jē, rā'ge*, (L.) before our lord the king; coram nobis, *nō'bis, bēs*, before us (*i.e.* the monarch), in our presence; coram populo, *pop'ū-lō, 'ōō-*, in the presence of the public.
coramine, *kor'ə-mīn*. See nikethamide.
coranach. See coronach.
cor anglais, *kör ä-glä'*, an oboe set a fifth lower than the ordinary oboe—also called (It.) corno inglese (*kör'nō ing-glā'sā*). [Fr., English horn, but probably not English.]
coranto, *ko-ran'tō*, *n.* a rapid and lively dance: the music for it, in triple time.—Also courante

**kōōrăt).** [Fr. *courante*, lit. running—L. *currĕre*, to run—(It. *coranta*, from Fr.).]

**corban,** *kör'ban, n.* anything devoted to God in fulfilment of a vow. [Heb. *qorbān*, an offering, sacrifice.]

**corbe,** *körb (Spens.).* See **corbel, courbe.**

**corbeau,** *kör-bō', n.* a blackish green colour. [Fr., raven.]

**corbeil,** *kör'bel, -bā'y', n.* a basket filled with earth, set up as a protection (*fort.*): a carved representation of a basket (*archit.*).—*n.* **corbeille',** a basket of flowers. [Fr. *corbeille*—L. *corbicula*, dim. of *corbis*, a basket.]

**corbel,** *kör'bl, (archit.) n.* a projection from the face of a wall, supporting a weight.—*adj.* **cor'belled.**—*n.* **cor'belling.**—**cor'bel-tā'ble,** a row of corbels and the parapet or cornice they support. [O.Fr. *corbel*—L.L. *corvellus*, dim. of *corvus*, a raven.]

**corbicula,** *kör-bik'ū-lə, n.* the pollen basket of bees, consisting of the dilated posterior tibia with its fringe of long hairs:—*pl.* **corbic'ulae (-lē).**—*adj.* **corbic'ulate.** [L. dim. of *corbis*, a basket.]

**corbie,** *kör'bi, n.* a raven: a crow.—**corbie messenger** (*Scot.*), one who returns too late, or not at all; **cor'bie-steps,** crow-steps. [O.Fr. *corbin*—L. *corvus*, a crow.]

**corcass,** *kör'kas, n.* in Ireland, a salt-marsh, or readily flooded land by a river. [Ir. *corcach*.]

**Corchorus,** *kör'ko-rəs, n.* the jute genus. [Gr. *korchoros*, the name of a plant.]

**cord,** *körd, n.* a small rope or thick string something resembling a cord (as spinal cord, umbilical cord): anything that binds or restrains: a measure of cut wood (128 cubic feet), orig. determined by use of a cord or string: a raised rib on cloth: a string crossing the back of a book in binding.—*v.t.* to supply with a cord: to bind with a cord.—*n.* **cord'age,** a quantity of cords or ropes, as the rigging of a ship, etc.—*adj.* **cord'ed,** fastened with cords: wound about with cords (*her.*): ribbed: piled in cords.—*ns.* **cord'ing,** the act of binding: cordage; **cord'ite,** a cord-like smokeless explosive; **cordot'omy,** cutting in certain parts of the spinal cord to relieve great pain.—**cord'-grass,** a genus (*Spartina*) of grasses of which one species found in muddy salt-marshes is used for making ropes; **cord'-wood,** wood put up in cords. [Fr. *corde*—L. *chorda*; see **chord.**]

**Cordaites,** *kör-dā-ī'tēz, n.* a Palaeozoic genus of fossil plants, typical of the family Cordaitā'ceae, gymnosperms nearer the conifers than the cycads. [Named after A. K. J. *Corda*, botanist (1809-49).]

**cordate,** *kör'dāt, adj.* heart-shaped: having the base indented next the petiole (*bot.*).—*adj.* **cord'iform,** heart-shaped. [L. *cordātus* (in modern sense)—L. *cor, cordis,* the heart.]

**Cordelier,** *kör-də-lēr', n.* a Franciscan friar, from the knotted cord worn as a girdle: (in *pl.*) a club in the French Revolution, meeting in an old Cordelier convent. [O.Fr. *cordele*, dim. of *corde*, a rope.]

**cordial,** *kör'di-əl, adj.* hearty: with warmth of heart: sincere: affectionate: reviving the heart or spirits.—*n.* anything which revives or comforts the heart: a medicine or drink for refreshing the spirits: a beverage containing alcohol or sugar or stimulating drugs.—*v.i.* **cor'dialise, -ize,** to become cordial, to fraternise.—*ns.* **cordiality** (*-al'i-ti*), **cor'dialness.**—*adv.* **cor'dially.** [Fr.,—L. *cor, cordis,* the heart.]

**cordierite,** *kör'di-ər-īt, n.* the mineral iolite or dichroite. [After P. L. A. *Cordier* (1777-1861), French mineralogist.]

**cordillera,** *kör-dil-yä'rä, n.* a chain of mountains, as the Andes and Rocky Mountains. [Sp.,—Old Sp. *cordilla*—L. *chorda*, cord—Gr. *chordē*.]

**cordiner,** *kör'di-nər.* Same as **cordwainer.**

**córdoba,** *kor'dō-bä, n.* the monetary unit of Nicaragua. [Named after Francisco Fernandez de *Córdoba* (d. about 1518).]

**cordon,** *kör'don, -dən, n.* a cord or ribbon bestowed as a badge of honour: a row of stones along the line of a rampart (*fort.*): a line of men set to prevent passage: a single-stemmed fruit-tree.—*v.i.* to enclose with a cordon.—**sanitary cordon,** (now more *usu.*) **cordon sanitaire.** [Fr.]

**cordon bleu,** *kor-dɔ̃ blø,* (Fr.) blue ribbon: a cook of the highest excellence.

**cordon sanitaire,** *kor-dɔ̃ sa-nē-ter,* (Fr.) a sanitary cordon, a line of sentries posted to restrict passage into and out of an area and so keep contagious disease within that area: neutral states keeping hostile states apart: barrier (*lit.* or *fig.*) isolating a state, etc., considered dangerous—sometimes called **sanitary cordon.**

**cordovan,** *kör'do-vən,* **cordwain,** *körd'wän, n.* goatskin leather, originally from *Cordova* (*Córdoba*) in Spain.—*ns.* **cord'wainer, cord'iner,** a worker in cordovan or cordwain: a shoemaker; **cord'-wainery.**

**corduroy,** *kör-də-roi',* or *kör', n.* a ribbed fustian, a cotton stuff made after the fashion of velvet: (in *pl.*) corduroy trousers.—*adj.* of **corduroy.**—**corduroy road,** a track laid transversely with tree-trunks. [Perh. Fr. *corde du roi,* king's cord.]

**Cordyline,** *kör-di-lī'nē, n.* a tropical and subtropical liliaceous genus similar to the dragon-tree. [Gr. *kordylē*, club.]

**core,** *kör, kôr, n.* the innermost part, e.g. of fruit: (also *magnetic core*) a small ferromagnetic ring which, charged or uncharged by electric current, can thus assume two states corresponding to the binary digits 0 and 1; used for computer memory.—*v.t.* to take out the core of.—*adjs.* **cored,** having the core removed: cast by means of a core: having a core; **core'less,** without core: pithless: hollow.—*n.* **cor'er,** an instrument for removing the core. [Poss. L. *cor,* the heart, or Fr. *cor,* horn, corn (on the foot), or *corps,* body.]

**core,** *kör, kôr, n.* company, gang, shift. [corps.]

**Coregonus,** *kor-i-gō'nəs, kör-, n.* whitefish, a genus of herring-like fishes of the salmon family, pollan, vendace, etc.—*adj.* **corego'nine.** [Gr. *korē,* pupil of the eye, *gōniä,* angle.]

**co-relation, co-relative.** See **correlate.**

**co-religionist,** *kō-rə-lij'ən-ist, n.* one of the same religion as another.

**corella,** *kə-rel'ə, n.* an Australian long-billed cockatoo. [Origin uncertain.]

**co-respondent,** *kō-rə-spond'ənt, (law) n.* a man or woman charged with adultery, and proceeded against along with the wife or husband who is the respondent.

**corf,** *körf, n.* a coal-miner's basket, now usu. a tub or trolley: a cage for fish or lobsters:—*pl.* **corves** (*körvz*).—**corf'-house** (*Scot.*), a salmon-curing house. [Du.,—L. *corbis,* basket.]

**corgi,** *kör'gi, n.* a small Welsh dog. [Welsh *corr,* dwarf, *ci,* dog.]

**coriander,** *kor-i-an'ɡər, n.* an umbelliferous plant (*Coriandrum sativum*), whose seeds are used as spice, etc.—**corian'der-seed.** [Fr. *coriandre*—L. *coriandrum*—Gr. *koriannon*.]

**Corinthian,** *kor-inth'i-ən, adj.* of *Corinth* (Gr. *Korinthos*) in Greece: (in architecture) of an ornate style of Greek architecture, with acanthus capitals: overbrilliant in literary style: profligate.—*n.* a profligate: a man of fashion: an amateur sportsman.—*n.* **Cor'inth** (*obs.*), a brothel.—*v.i.* **corinth'ianise, -ize,** to be licentious.—**Corinthian brass, bronze,** an alloy made in Corinth, much valued in ancient times: assurance or effrontery.

**corium,** *kō'ri-um, kö', n.* leather armour (*ant.*): the true skin, under the epidermis (*anat.*).—*adjs.*

**coriăceous, co´rious,** leathery. [L. *corium*—Gr. *chorion,* skin, leather.]

**co-rival, co-rivalry, co-rivalship.** See **corrival.**

**cork, körk,** *n.* the outer bark of the cork-tree, an oak found in S. Europe, N. Africa, etc.: a stopper made of cork: any stopper: a tissue of close-fitting, thick-walled cells, almost air-tight and watertight, forming bark or covering the surfaces of wounds (*bot.*): a piece of cork: a float of cork.—*adj.* made of cork.—*v.t.* to stop with a cork: to stop up.—*n.* **cork´age,** corking or uncorking of bottles: a charge made by hotel-keepers for uncorking of bottles when the liquor has not been supplied from the house.—*adj.* **corked,** stopped as by a cork: tainted as if by the cork, as wine: blackened by burnt cork: drunk (*slang*).—*ns.* **cork´er,** a finisher: a con-clusive argument (*slang*): a person or thing that surpasses; **cork´iness.**—*adjs.* **cork´ing** (*slang*), surpassing; **cork´y,** of, or resembling, cork: withered (*Shak.*).—**cork´-borer,** an instrument for boring holes in corks to receive glass tubes in chemical apparatus; **cork´-cam´bium,** phellogen; **cork´-car´pet, -lino´leum, -mat,** a floor-covering, mat, made of pieces of cork with rubber and linseed oil; **cork´-cutter,** one employed in cutting corks for bottles, etc.: an instrument used for this; **cork´-heel,** a shoe-heel of cork.—*adj.* **cork´-heeled´,** having cork heels; wanton.—**cork´-jack´et,** a jacket made of or lined with cork, to aid in swimming; **cork´-leg,** an artificial leg; **cork´-oak,** a species of oak (*Quercus Suber*) which supplies the cork of commerce in Spain and Portugal; **cork´-screw,** a screw for drawing corks from bottles.—*adj.* like a cork-screw in shape.—*v.i.* to move in a spiral manner.—*v.t.* to pull out with difficulty, as a cork: to obtain information from by force or cunning.—**cork´-sole´,** an inner shoe-sole made of cork; **cork´-tree,** the cork-oak: applied to various trees with corky bark or very light wood; **cork´wing,** the goldsinny; **cork´wood,** very light wood: applied to many trees with light wood, e.g. balsa, alligator apple. [Perh. from Sp. *alcorque,* cork slipper, which may be from L. *quercus,* oak, with the Arabic article *al.* Sp. has also *corche, corcha, corcho,* perh. L. *cortex,* bark, rind.]

**corking-pin, körk´ing-pin,** *n.* a pin of the largest size. [Perh. for **calking-pin.**]

**corkir, korkir, kör´kər,** (*Scot.*) *n.* a lichen used for dyeing (red or purple). [Gael. *corcur*—L. *purpura,* purple.]

**corm, körm,** *n.* a short, bulbous, subterranean stem as in the crocus.—*n.* **corm´ophyte** (*-fīt*), a plant differentiated into leaf, stem, and root.—*adj.* **cormophyt´ic** (*-fīt´*).—*n.* **corm´us,** the differentiated body of a cormophyte: the whole body of a compound animal. [Gr. *kormos,* the lopped trunk of a tree.]

**cormorant, kör´mə-rant,** *n.* a genus (*Phala-crocorax*) of web-footed sea-birds, of great voracity: a glutton. [Fr. *cormoran,* from L. *corvus marinus,* sea crow.]

**corn, körn,** *n.* a grain, hard particle: a ker-nel, small hard seed: collectively seeds of cereal plants, or the plants themselves:—esp. (in England) wheat, (in Scotland and Ireland) oats, (in North America) maize: something old-fashioned or hackneyed.—*adj.* of, for, pertaining to, made from, growing among, feeding upon, corn: granular.—*v.t.* to make granular: to sprinkle with grains of salt: to salt: to give corn to, as a horse (*Scot.*): to intoxicate (*slang*).—*v.i.* to form seed.—*p.adj.* **corned,** granulated: salted (e.g. **corned beef**—also **corn´-beef**); **corn´y,** like corn: produced from corn: tipsy (*slang*): old-fashioned, uninteresting from fre-quent use, dull (*slang*).—**corn´-baby** (see **kirn**); **corn´-ball** (*U.S.*), a sweetened ball of popcorn: a yokel; **corn´-bin,** a bin for corn; **corn´-bor´er,** a

European moth (*Pyrausta nubilalis*) whose larvae have become a maize pest in America; **corn´-brake´,** a maize plantation; **corn´-bran´dy,** spirits made from grain: whisky; **corn´brash** (*geol.*), a clayey limestone of the Oolite, giving good corn soils; **corn´-bread, -cake** (*U.S.*), bread, a cake, made of maize meal; **corn´-chandler,** a retailer of grain; **corn´-chandlery; corn´-cob,** the woody axis of a maize ear: a corn-cob pipe; **corn´cockle,** a tall, beautiful cornfield weed (*Agrostemma* (or *Lychnis*) *Githago*) akin to the campions; **corn´-cracker** (*U.S.*), a poor white: a Kentuckian; **corn´crake,** a rail with character-istic cry, inhabiting cornfields; **corn´-dealer,** -factor, -merchant, one who buys and sells corn; **corn´-dodger** (*U.S.*), a cake, small loaf, or dump-ling of maize; **corn´-exchange´,** a mart for trade in corn.—*adj.* **corn´-fed,** fed on corn: well fed. —**corn´field,** a field in which corn is growing; **corn´-flag,** a gladiolus; **corn´-flour,** finely ground maize, rice, or other grain: a pudding made of it: **corn´flower,** the bluebottle, a beautiful blue-flowered cornfield weed of the Compositae (*Centaurea Cyanus*); **corn´fly,** the gout-fly; **corn´husk** (*U.S.*), a corn-shuck; **corn´husker,** a person or machine that removes cornhusks; **corn´husking; corn´ing-house,** a place where gunpowder is granulated; **corn´-kist** (*Scot.*), a stable grain-chest; **corn´-kister,** a farm-worker's song of his life and work; **corn´land,** ground suitable for growing grain; **corn´-law,** a law regulating trade in grain, esp. (in *pl.*) laws that restricted importation to Britain by a duty, repealed 1846; **corn´loft,** a granary; **corn´-maiden** (see **kirn**); **corn´-mar´igold,** a yellow cornfield chrysanthemum; **corn´-mill,** a flour-mill; **corn´miller; corn´-moth,** a moth of the clothes-moth genus (*Tinea granella*) whose larvae feed on grain; **corn´pipe,** a musical instrument made of a stalk of an oat or other cereal; **corn´-pit** (*U.S.*), part of an exchange where business is done in maize; **corn´-pone** (*U.S.*), maize-bread: a maize loaf; **corn´-popper,** a pan or grating for popping corn; **corn´-rent,** rent paid in corn, not money; **corn´-rig** (*Scot.*), a ridge or strip on which oats are grown; **corn´-sal´ad,** lamb's lettuce, a genus (*Valerianella*) of humble weeds of the valerian family, sometimes used as salads; **corn´-shuck** (*U.S.*), the leaves enclosing a maize ear; **corn´-shucking,** the removal of corn-shucks: an assembly for the purpose; **corn´-snow,** granulated snow; **corn´-spirit,** a vegetation god or spirit concerned in the growth of corn; **corn´stalk,** a stalk of corn: tall thin person, esp. one born in New South Wales; **corn´starch,** maize starch or flour, for puddings; **corn´stone,** a silicious limestone, favourable for corn-growing; **corn´-thrips,** a minute insect of the Thysanura, that sucks the sap of grain; **corn´-van,** an instrument for winnowing corn; **corn´-weevil,** a small weevil (*Calandra granaria*), des-tructive in granaries; **corn´-whisky,** an American whisky made from maize; **corn´worm,** a corn-weevil: a corn-moth larva.—**corn-cob pipe,** a tobacco-pipe with the bowl made of a maize cob; **corn in Egypt,** abundance (Gen. xlii. 2). [O.E. *corn;* Goth. *kaurn;* akin to L. *grānum.*]

**corn, körn,** *n.* a small hard growth chiefly on the toe or foot, resulting from an increase of thickness of cuticle, caused by pressure or friction.—*adj.* **corn´eous,** horny.—*ns.* **corn´icle,** **cornic´ulum,** a little horn: a hornlike process: esp. one of the wax-secreting tubes of a greenfly.—*adj.* **cornic´ulate,** horned: horn-shaped; **cornif´erous,** containing hornstone; **cornif´ic,** producing or forming horn or horns.—*n.* corni-ficā´tion.—*adjs.* **corn´iform,** shaped like a horn; **cornigerous** (*kör-nij´ər-əs*), horned.—*n.* **cor´nū** (L. *kör´nōō*), a horn, hornlike part, or process:—*pl.* **cor´nūa.**—*adj.* **cor´nūal.**—*adj.* **corn´y,** of or pertaining to horns or corns: having corns: horny.—**corn'-cure**, a remedy for corns; **corn'-cutter**, one who cuts corns; **corniferous lime-stone**, a coral limestone with chert nodules in the Devonian of North America; **corn plaster**, a remedial plaster for corns.—**tread on one's corns**, to hurt one's feelings. [L. *cornū*, a horn.]

**cornage**, *körn'ij*, (*hist.*) *n.* a feudal service or rent fixed according to number of horned cattle —horngeld. [O.Fr.,—L. *cornū*, horn.]

**cornea**, *kör'ni-ə*, *n.* the transparent horny membrane that forms the front covering of the eye.—*adj.* **cor'neal.**—**corneal lens**, a contact lens covering the transparent part of the eye only. [L. *cornea* (*tēla*), horny (tissue).]

**cornel**, *kör'nəl*, *n.* the so-called cornelian cherry or cornelian tree, a small tree (*Cornus mas*) of middle and southern Europe: any species of the genus Cor'nus, type of the family **Corna'-ceae** (akin to Umbelliferae), such as dwarf cornel, an alpine herb with four white bracts surrounding its umbel, and dogwood.—**cor'nel-tree, cornē'lian-tree.** [L.L. *cornolium*—L. *cornus*, cornel.]

**cornelian**, *kör-nē'li-ən*, *n.* a fine chalcedony, generally translucent red.—Also **carnē'lian** (*kär-*). [Fr. *cornaline*—L. *cornū*, a horn, or *cornum*, cornelian cherry, from its appearance; confused with *carō, carnis*, flesh.]

**cornemuse**, *kör'ni-mūz*, *n.* a French bagpipe. [Fr.]

**corner**, *kör'nər*, *n.* the point where two lines or several planes meet: an angular projection or recess: a secret or confined place: an embarrassing position, difficulty: a point in a rubber at whist (*obs.*): a free kick given to the opposite side when a player in football kicks the ball over his own goal-line: an operation by which the whole of a stock or commodity is bought up so that the buyers may resell at their own price.—*v.t.* to supply with corners: to put in a corner: to put in a fix or difficulty: to form a corner against: to get control of by forming a corner.—*v.i.* to turn a corner.—*adj.* **cor'nered**, having corners: put in a difficult position.—*adv.* **corn'erwise**, with the corner in front: diagonally.—**corn'er-boy**, a loafer: a street-corner rough: the man at the end of the row in a negro-minstrel performance (also **corner-man**); **cor'ner-stone**, a stone that unites the two walls of a building at a corner: the principal stone, esp. the corner of the foundation of a building: something of very great importance (*fig.*).—*n.pl.* **cor'ner-teeth**, the lateral incisors of a horse.— **cut corners**, to do a piece of work with the minimum of effort; **turn the corner**, to go round the corner: to get past a difficulty or danger; **within the four corners of**, contained in. [O.Fr. *corniere*—L. *cornū*, horn.]

**cornet**, *kör'nit* (*U.S.* also *-net'*), *n.* an old woodwind instrument (usu. **cornett**): an organ stop of various kinds: a treble brass valve instrument, more tapering than the trumpet—also **cornō'pean, cornet-à-piston(s)** (*kor-nā-ä-pēs-t5*): a cornet-player: any funnel-shaped object, as a piece of gold for assaying, a shopkeeper's screwed paper bag, an ice-cream-filled wafer cone, a cream-filled pastry.—*n.* **cor'netist** (*U.S.* **cornett'ist**), a cornet-player. [Fr. *cornet*, dim. of *corne*—L. *cornū*, horn.]

**cornet**, *kör'nit*, *n.* an old form of lady's headdress, with side lappets: a lappet of this: a cavalry standard (*obs.*): till 1871 a cavalry officer —later sub-lieutenant: a standard-bearer at riding the marches.—*n.* **cor'netcy**, commission or rank of cornet. [Fr. *cornette*, ult. from L. *cornū*, horn.]

**cornet.** See coronet.   **cornett.** See cornet (1).

**cornice**, *kör'nis*, *n.* the uppermost member of the entablature, surmounting the frieze (*classical archit.*): a projecting moulding along the top of

a building, window, etc.: a plaster moulding round a ceiling: a support for picture-hooks: an overhanging crest of snow.—*v.t.* to furnish with a cornice.—*adj.* **cor'niced.**—**cor'nice-hook, -pole, -rail**, a hook, pole, rail, for hanging pictures, curtains, etc.; **cor'nice-ring**, a ring or moulding on a cannon next below the muzzle-ring. [Fr.,—It., poss. Gr. *korōnis*, a curved line, cf. L. *corōna*.]

**corniche**, *kor-nēsh*, (Fr.) a coast road built along a cliff-face: in Egypt, a boulevard along a bank of the Nile.

**corniculate**, etc. See corn.

**Cornish**, *kör'nisn*, *adj.* pertaining to Cornwall.—*n.* Celtic language of Cornwall, dead since the later 18th cent.—**Cornish clay**, china-clay; **Cornish pasty**, a pasty (**pasty** (2)) with meat and vegetables.

**corno**, *kör'nō*, *n.* the French horn.—*n.* **corn'ist**, a horn-player.—**corno di basset'to**, the bassethorn: an organ-stop. [It.,—L. *cornū*, a horn.]

**cornopean.** See cornet (1).

**cornu.** See corn (2).

**cornucopia**, *kör-nū-kō'pi-ə*, *n.* the horn of plenty according to one fable, the horn of the goat that suckled Jupiter, placed among the stars as an emblem of plenty: an ornament consisting of a horn overflowing with fruits: an abundant source of supply.—*adj.* **cornucō'pian.** [L. *cornū cōpiae*—*cornū*, horn, *cōpia*, plenty.]

**Cornus.** See cornel.

**cornute**, *kör-nūt'*, *v.t.* (*obs.*) to cuckold.—*adjs.* **cornute'**, **-d**, horned: hornlike: cuckolded (*obs.*). —*n.* **cornūt'o** (or *-nōō'*; It.; *obs.*), a cuckold. [L. *cornūtus*, horned—*cornū*, horn.]

**corny.** See corn (1).

**corocore, corocoro**, *kor'ō-kör, -kör, -ō*, *n.* a Malay form of boat. [Malay *kurakura*.]

**corody.** See corrody.

**corolla**, *kor-ol'ə, -ōl'ə*, *n.* the inner circle or whorl of the floral envelopes.—*adj.* **corollā'ceous.**— *n.pl.* **Corolliflorae** (*-i-flō'rē*; L. *flōs, flōris*, flower), in some classifications the Gamopetalae or Sympetalae.—*adjs.* **corolliflo'ral, corollifloʹrous; coroll'iform; coroll'ine** (or *kor'*). [L. *corolla*, dim. of *corōna*, a crown.]

**corollary**, *kor'ol-ə-ri*, or *kər-ol'ə-ri*, *n.* an easy inference: a consequence or result: a supplement, surplus, or supernumerary. [L. *corollārium*, a garland, money for a garland, a tip— *corolla*.]

**Coromandel**, *ko-rə-man'dəl, -rō-*, *n.* or *adj.* (also **Coromandel wood**) calamander: (also **Coromandel ebony**) a wood of the same genus (*Diospyros*) as calamander: the colour colcothar.—**Coromandel screen**, a Chinese folding lacquered screen; **Coromandel work**, lacquer work in which an incised design is filled with colour or with gold. [*Coromandel* Coast in south-east India.]

**corona**, *ko-rō'nə, kə-*, *n.* the large, flat, projecting member of a cornice crowning the entablature (*archit.*): the trumpet of a daffodil, etc., composed of ligules of the perianth leaves (*bot.*): a coloured ring round the sun or moon, distinguished from halo by having red outermost: convergence point of auroral rays: one of the sun's envelopes, outside the chromosphere, observable during total eclipse (*astron.*): a similar atmospheric envelope of a star (*astron.*): a round pendent chandelier:—*pl.* **corō'nas, corō'nae.**—*n.* **cor'onal** (*-ə-nl*), a circlet, small crown or garland.—*adjs.* **corō'nal, cor'onary** (*-ən-ə-ri*), pertaining to a crown, a corona, or to the top of the head: like a crown: surrounding a part (**coronary arteries**, those that supply the muscle of the heart walls with blood; so **coronary circulation**); **cor'onāte, -d**, crowned: applied to shells with a row of projections round the apex. —*ns.* **corona'tion**, the act of crowning; **corō'-nium**, name given to a hypothetical element in the solar corona assumed to explain spectral lines now known to be due to iron and nickel atoms that have lost a large number of electrons; **coronagraph, coronograph** (*-ōn'a-gräf*), a special telescope used to observe prominences and the corona around the edge of the sun.— **coronary thrombosis,** stoppage of a branch of a coronary artery by a clot of blood. [L. *corōna*, a crown.]

**coronach,** *kor-ə-nähh, -nəhh, n.* a dirge. [Said to be a Gaelic word, but evidence insufficient.]

**coronation** (*Spens.*), for **carnation.**

**coronation.** See **corona.**

**coroner,** *kor'ə-nər, n.* orig. guardian of the pleas of the crown: now an officer whose chief duty is to enquire into the causes of accidental or suspicious deaths. [O.Fr. *corouner*—L. *corōna*, crown.]

**coronet,** *kor'ə-nit, n.* a small crown worn by the nobility: an ornamental head-dress: the part of a horse's pastern just above the coffin—also **cor'net.**—*adj.* **cor'oneted.** [O.Fr. *coronete*, dim. of *corone*, crown—L. *corōna*.]

**coronis,** *ko-rō'nis, n.* in Greek, a sign ( ' ) marking a crasis, as καν̄ = καὶ ἄν. [Gr. *korōnis*, a curved line.]

**coronium.** See **corona.**

**coronoid,** *kor'ə-noid*, or *kor-ō'noid*, (*anat.*) *adj.* like a crow's bill, as the coronoid process of the lower jaw. [Gr. *korōnē*, a crow, and *eidos*, form, shape.]

**corozo,** *kor-ō'sō, n.* a South American short-stemmed palm (*Phytelephas*) whose seed (**corozo nut**) gives vegetable ivory: also the cohune palm, or other. [Sp. from an Indian language.]

**corporal,** *kör'pə-rəl, n.* a non-commissioned officer next under a sergeant: in the navy, a petty officer under a master-at-arms: the leader of a gang of miners, etc.—*n.* **cor'poralship.** [Fr. *caporal*—It. *caporale*—*capo*, the head—L. *caput*, the head.]

**corporal,** *kör'pə-rəl, adj.* belonging or relating to the body: having a body: material: not spiritual.—*n.* the cloth used in Catholic churches for covering the elements of the Eucharist—also **cor'poras** (*obs.*).—*n.* **corporality** (*-al'i-ti*).—*adv.* **cor'porally.**—*adj.* **cor'porate,** legally united into a body so as to act as an individual: belonging to a corporation: united.—*adv.* **cor'porately.**— *ns.* **cor'porateness; corporā'tion,** a body or society authorised by law to act as one individual: a town council: a company (*U.S.*): a belly, esp. a pot-belly (*coll.*).—*adj.* **cor'porātive.** —*n.* **cor'porātor,** a member of a corporation.— *adj.* **corporeal** (*kor-pō'ri-əl, -pō'*), having a body or substance: material.—*v.i.* and *v.t.* **corpō'-realise, -ize.**—*ns.* **corpō'realism,** materialism; **corpō'realist; corpōreality** (*-al'i-ti*).—*adv.* **corpō'-really.**—*ns.* **corporeity** (*-pə-rē'i-ti*); **corporificā'-tion,** act of corporifying.—*v.t.* **corpor'ify,** to embody: solidify.—**aggregate corporation,** a corporation consisting of several persons; **corporal punishment,** punishment inflicted on the body, as flogging, etc; **sole corporation,** a corporation which consists of one person and his successors. [L. *corpus, corpōris*, the body.]

**corposant,** *kör'po-zant, n.* St Elmo's fire, an electrical brush discharge forming a glow about a mast-head, etc. [Port. *corpo santo*—L. *corpus sanctum*, holy body.]

**corps,** *kōr, kör, n.* a division of an army forming a tactical unit: a branch or department of an army: an organised body: a German students' society: a set of people working more or less together:—*pl.* **corps** (*kōrz, körz*). [Fr.,—L. *corpus*, body.]

**corps de ballet,** *kör də ba-le,* (Fr.) the company of ballet dancers at a theatre; **corps d'élite,** *kör dā-lēt,* (Fr.) a small number of people picked out as being the best in any group; **corps diplo-**

**matique,** *dē-plō-ma-tēk,* the whole diplomatic staff at a particular capital.

**corpse,** *körps,* or *körs, n.* a dead human body. —**corpse'-can'dle,** a light seen hovering over a grave—an omen of death; **corpse'-gate,** a lich-gate. [M.E. *corps,* earlier *cors*—O.Fr. *cors* —L. *corpus,* the body.]

**corpus,** *kör'pəs, n.* a body, esp. a dead body: any special structure in the body: a body of literature, law, etc.:—*pl.* **cor'pora** (*-pə-rə*).—*ns.* **cor'pulence, cor'pulency,** fleshiness of body: excessive fatness.—*adj.* **cor'pūlent.**—*adv.* **cor'-pūlently.**—*n.* **cor'puscle** (*-pus-l*); sometimes *-pus'l*), a minute particle—also **corpus'cule.**—*adjs.* **corpus'cular, corpuscūlā'rian.**—*ns.* **corpuscūlā'-rian,** one who holds the corpuscular theory; **corpuscular'ity.**—**corpus Chris'ti** (*-tī, -ti*), the festival in honour of the Eucharist, held on the Thursday after the festival of the Trinity; **corpus delicti** (*di-lik'tī, de-lik'tē; law*), the essential facts of the crime charged, e.g. in a murder trial, that somebody is actually dead and has been murdered; **corpuscular theory of light,** Newton's theory that light consists in the emission of material particles; **Corpus Juris Canonici,** *jōō'ris* (*ū'ris*) *ka-non'i-sī* (*'i-kē*), body of the canon law; **Corpus Juris Civilis,** *si-vī'lis* (*kē-vē', -we'*), the body of the civil law; **corpus vile** (*vī'lē, vē'le, wē'-*), a useless thing (suitable for experiment). [L. *corpus,* the body.]

**corral,** *kə-* or *ko-ral', n.* a pen for cattle: an enclosure to drive hunted animals into: a defensive ring of wagons.—*v.t.* to pen: to form into a corral. [Sp.]

**corrasion** *kə-* or *ko-rā'zhən, n.* wearing away caused by loose solid material, as pebbles in a stream, or wind-borne sand. [L. *corrādĕre,* to scrape together—*con,* together, *rādĕre, rāsum,* to scratch.]

**correct,** *kə-* or *ko-rekt', v.t.* to make right or supposedly right: to remove or mark faults or supposed faults from or in: to do this and evaluate: to set (a person) right: to punish: to counterbalance: to bring into a normal state: to reduce to a standard.—*adj.* right: according to standard: free from faults.—*adjs.* **correct'able, correct'ible.**—*adv.* **correct'ly.**—*n.* **correc'tion,** emendation or would-be emendation: amendment: punishment: reduction: compensation: quantity to be added to bring to a standard or balance an error: bodily chastisement.—*adj.* **correc'tional.**—*ns.* **correc'tioner** (*Shak.*), one who administers correction; **correct'itude,** correctness of conduct or behaviour.—*adj.* **correct'ive,** of the nature of, by way of, correction: tending to correct: correcting.—*n.* that which corrects. —*ns.* **correct'ness; correct'or,** he who, or that which, corrects: a director or governor: a proof-reader.—*adj.* **correct'ory,** corrective.— **corrective training,** reformative imprisonment for persistent offenders of 21 and over for periods from 2 to 4 years.—**under correction,** subject to correction—often used as a formal expression of defence to a superior authority. [L. *corrigĕre, corrēctum*—*cor-,* inten., *regĕre,* to rule.]

**corregidor,** *ko-rehh'-i-dōr, n.* the chief magistrate of a Spanish town. [Sp., corrector.]

**correlate,** *kor'i-lāt, v.i.* to be related to one another.—*v.t.* to bring into relation with each other: to establish relation or correspondence between.—*n.* either of two things so related that one implies the other or is complementary to it: an analogue (*rare*).—*adj.* (*rare*), correlated.—*n.* **correlā'tion,** state or act of correlating: mutual relation, esp. of phenomena regularly occurring together: interdependence, or the degree of it.— *adj.* **correlative** (*-el'ə-tiv*).—*n.* a person or thing correspondingly related to another person or thing.—*adv.* **correl'atively.**—*n.* **correl'ativeness, correlativ'ity.** [L. *cor-,* with, and **relate.**]

correligionist. See co-religionist.

correption, kər-ep'shən, (obs.) n. shortening in pronunciation: reproof. [L. correptiō, -ōnis— cor-, inten., and rapĕre, to seize.]

correspond, kor-i-spond', v.i. to answer, suit, agree (with to, with): to hold intercourse, esp. by letter.—ns. correspond'ence, correspond'ency, suitability: harmony: relation of agreement, part to part, or one to one: friendly intercourse (arch.): communication by letter: a body of letters.—adj. correspond'ent, answering: agreeing: suitable.—n. one with whom intercourse is kept up by letters: one who contributes letters, or is employed to send special reports (e.g. foreign correspondent, war correspondent), to a periodical: a person or firm that regularly does business for another elsewhere.—adv. correspond'ently.—adj. correspond'ing, correspondent: answering: carrying on correspondence by letters.—adv. correspond'ingly.—adj. correspon'sive, corresponding: answering.—correspondence course, school, etc., one conducted by postal correspondence; corresponding member, a member living at a distance who communicates with a society without taking part in its administration.—doctrine of correspondences, the theory of Swedenborg that there is a spiritual antitype corresponding to every natural object and that Scripture contains the key to these correspondences. [L. cor-, with, and respondēre.]

corrida de toros, kō-rē'dhä dä tō'rōs, (Sp.) a bull-fight.

corridor, kor'i-dör, n. a passageway or gallery communicating with separate rooms or dwellings in a building or compartments in a railway train: a strip of territory by which a country has access to a port, etc.: (in pl.) places outside the administrative centre where unofficial news circulates and gossip is carried on (politics).—ns. corr'idor-carr'iage, -train, a carriage, train, in which one can pass along from one compartment to another; corridor work, informal discussion behind the scenes at a meeting.—corridors of power (fig.), higher reaches of government administration. [Fr.,—It. corridore—It. correre, to run—L. currĕre.]

corrie, kor'i, n. a semicircular mountain recess or cirque. [Gael. coire, a cauldron.]

corrigendum, kor-i-jen'dəm or -gen'dōōm, n. that which requires correction:—pl. corrigen'da, esp. corrections to be made in a book. [L., gerundive of corrigĕre, to correct.]

corrigent, kor'i-jənt, adj. and n. corrective.—adj. corr'igible, that may be corrected: open to correction.—n. corrigibil'ity. [L. corrigĕre, to correct; see correct.]

corrival, kor-i'vəl, n. a rival: a competitor: an equal.—adj. contending: emulous.—v.i. to rival. —v.t. to vie.—ns. corri'valry; corri'valship. [L. con-, with, and rival.]

corroborate, kər-ob'ə-rāt, v.t. to confirm: to make more certain.—adj. confirmed: used blunderingly by Ancient Pistol, perh. for corroded or corrupt (Shak.).—adjs. corrob'orable; corrob'o-rant; corrob'orative, tending to confirm.—n. that which corroborates.—ns. corroborā'tion, confirmation; corrob'orator.—adj. corrob'oratory, corroborative. [L. cor-, inten., and rōborāre, -ātum, to make strong; see robust.]

corroboree, kə-rob'ə-rē, n. a dance of Australian aborigines: suiting: a song for such a dance: a festive gathering.—v.i. to hold a corroboree. [Native word.]

corrode, kər-ōd', v.t. to eat away by degrees, esp. chemically: to rust.—v.i. to be eaten away.— adj. corrōd'ent, having the power of corroding.— n. that which corrodes.—n.pl. Corrodentia (-en'-shya), the Psocoptera, or book-lice, etc.—n. corrosibil'ity (-rōz).—adj. corrōs'ible (also cor-

rōd'ible).—n. corrosion (-rō'zhən), act or process of eating or wasting away.—adj. corrōs'ive, having the quality of eating away.—n. that which has the power of corroding.—adv. corrōs'ively.— n. corrōs'iveness.—corrosive sublimate, mercuric chloride. [L. cor-, inten., rōdĕre, rōsum, to gnaw.]

corrody, corody, kor'ō-di, n. an allowance: pension: originally the right of the lord to claim free lodging from the vassal. [O.Fr. conrei, conroi.]

corrugate, kor'ə- or kor'ōō-gāt, v.t. to wrinkle or draw into folds.—ns. corrugā'tion, the act of wrinkling or state of being wrinkled: a wrinkle; corr'ugator (anat.), a wrinkling muscle.—corrugated iron, sheet iron bent by ridged rollers into a wavy form for the sake of strength; corrugated paper, a wrinkled paper used as wrapping material. [L. cor-, inten., rūgāre, -ātum, to wrinkle—rūga, a wrinkle.]

corrupt, kər-upt', v.t. to make putrid: to taint: to debase: to spoil: to destroy the purity of: to pervert: to bribe.—v.i. to rot: to lose purity.— adj. putrid: depraved: defiled: not genuine: much vitiated or debased in transcription: bribed: venal: of the nature of bribery.—ns. corrupt'er; corruptibil'ity, corrupt'ibleness.—adj. corrupt'ible, liable to be corrupted.—adv. corrupt'ibly.—ns. corrup'tion, rottenness: putrid matter: impurity: bribery; corrup'tionist, one who defends or who practises corruption.—adj. corrupt'ive, having the quality of corrupting.— adv. corrupt'ly.—n. corrupt'ness.—corruption of blood, the former inability of an attainted person to inherit or transmit lands, titles or dignities. [L. cor-, inten., and rumpĕre, ruptum, to break.]

corsage, kör-säzh', n. the bodice or waist of a woman's dress: a bouquet to be worn there or elsewhere. [O.Fr.,—cors—L. corpus, the body.]

corsair, kör'sär, n. a privateer (esp. of Barbary): a privateering ship: a pirate. [Fr. corsaire, one who courses or ranges—L. cursus, a running— currĕre.]

corse, körs, n. a poetic form of corpse.

corselet. See corslet.

corset, kör'sit, n. a close-fitting stiff inner bodice: stays: a stiff belt coming down over the hips. —v.t. to furnish with a corset.—pr.p. corseting, pa.t. and pa.p. cor'seted.—corsetier, fem. corsetière (kor-sə-tyä, -tyer), a maker or seller of corsets. [Dim. of O.Fr. cors—L. corpus, the body.]

corsive, kör'siv, (obs.) n. and adj. Same as corrosive.

corslet, corselet, körs'lit, n. a cuirass, a protective body-covering of leather, or steel, etc.: a modified corset, or combined belt and brassière.—adj. cors'leted. [Fr. corselet, dim. of O.Fr. cors—L. corpus, the body.]

corsned, körs'ned, (hist.) n. the ordeal of swallowing a piece of bread or cheese, taken to prove guilt if it stuck in the throat. [O.E. corsnæd— gecor (cf. coren, pa.p. of cēosan, to choose) and snæd, a piece, from snídan, to cut.]

corso, kör-sō, (It.) race, run, course: a race of riderless horses: a procession of carriages: a street where these are held.

cortège, kör-tezh', n. a train of attendants: a procession, a funeral procession. [Fr.,—It. corte, court.]

Cortes, kor'tes, n. the parliament of Spain and of Portugal. [Sp. pl. of corte, a court.]

cortex, kör'teks, n. the bark or skin of a plant between the epidermis and the vascular bundles (bot.): the outer layer of an organ, esp. of the brain (zool.):—pl. cortices (kör'ti-sēz).—adjs. cortical, pertaining to the cortex: external; cor'ticate, -d, furnished with bark.—ns. cor'tico-steroid, cor'ticoid, any of the steroids, e.g. cortisone, extracted from the adrenal cortex; cortico'trophin, adrenocorticotrophin. [L. *cortex*, *corticis*, bark.]

cortile, *kor-tē'lä*, *n.* an enclosed courtyard within a building, generally roofless. [It.]

cortisone, *kör'ti-sōn*, *n.* 'compound E', a steroid isolated from the adrenal cortex, or prepared from ox bile, etc., an anti-inflammatory agent.

corundum, *kə-run'dəm*, *n.* a mineral consisting of alumina, second in hardness only to the diamond —including sapphire, ruby, emery. [Tamil *kurundam*.]

coruscate, *kor'əs-kāt*, *v.i.* to sparkle: to throw off flashes of light.—*adj.* corus'cant, flashing.—*n.* corusca'tion, a glittering: sudden flash of light. [L. *coruscāre*, *-ātum*, to vibrate, glitter.]

corvée, *kör-vā'*, *n.* the obligation to perform gratuitous labour (such as the maintenance of roads) for the sovereign or feudal lord. [Fr.,— L.L. *corrogāta*—L. *corrogāre—cor-*, together, *rogāre*, to ask.]

corves. See corf.

corvet. Same as curvet.

corvette, *kör-vet'*, *n.* formerly a flush-decked vessel, with one tier of guns: now an escort vessel specially designed for protecting convoys against submarine attack. [Fr.,—Sp. *corbeta*— L. *corbita*, a slow-sailing ship, from *corbis*, a basket.]

Corvus, *kör'vəs*, *n.* the crow genus, typical of the family Cor'vidae and subfamily Corvi'nae: a southern constellation: (without *cap.*) a grappling-hook in ancient Roman naval warfare: a hooked ram for destroying walls.—*adj.* cor'vine (*vin*). [L. *corvus*, a raven.]

corybant, *kor'ə-bant*, *n.* a priest of Cybele, whose rites were accompanied with noisy music and wild dances (Eng. *pl.* cor'ybants; L. *pl.* corybant'es).—*adj.* coryban'tic, wildly excited.—*n.* cor'ybantism. [Gr. *korybās*, *korybantos*.]

Corydalis, *kor-id'ə-lis*, *n.* a genus akin to fumitory. —*n.* cor'ydaline, an alkaloid ($C_{22}H_{27}O_4N$) obtained from Corydalis root. [Gr. *korydallis*, crested lark, from a fancied resemblance of the flower.]

Corydon, *kor'i-don*, *n.* generic proper name for a rustic. [L.,—Gr. *Korydōn*, a shepherd's name in Theocritus and Virgil.]

Corylus, *kor'i-ləs*, *n.* the hazel genus. [L.]

corymb, *kor'imb*, (*bot.*) *n.* a flattish-topped raceme.—*adjs.* cor'ymbose (or *-imb'*). [L. *corymbus*—Gr. *korymbos*, a cluster.]

Corypha, *kor'i-fa*, *n.* the talipot genus of gigantic tropical Asian palms. [Gr. *koryphē*, top.]

coryphaeus, *kor-i-fē'əs*, *n.* the chief or leader, esp. the leader of a chorus (*pl.* coryphaei, *-fē'i*).—*n.* coryphee (*kor-ē-fā'*; Fr.), orig. a male dancer (*n.* is *masc.* in Fr.): now, one of group between soloists and corps de ballet (also coryphe). [L., —Gr. *koryphaios—koryphē*, the head.]

coryphene, *kor'i-fēn*, *n.* a fish of the genus *Coryphaena*, called dolphin. [Gr. *koryphaina*.]

coryza, *ko-ri'za*, *n.* a cold in the head: nasal catarrh. [L.,—Gr. *koryza*.]

cos, *kos*, *n.* a long-leaved lettuce. [Introduced from the Aegean island of Cos (Gr. *Kōs*).]

cos. See cosine.

Cosa Nostra, *kō'zä nos'trä*, Mafia organisation, esp. in U.S. [It., 'our thing'.]

coscinomancy, *kos'i-nō-man-si*, *n.* an ancient mode of divination by a sieve and pair of shears. [Gr. *koskinon*, a sieve, *manteiā*, divination.]

cose, *kōz*, *v.i.* to make oneself cosy. [See cosy.]

cosecant, *kō-sek'ənt*, *n.* the secant of the complement of an angle—*abbrev.* cosec (*kō'sek*). —*n.* cosech (*kōsh-ek'*), for hyperbolic cosecant.

coseismal, *kō-siz'məl*, *adj.* experiencing an earthquake shock simultaneously.—Also coseis'mic. [L. *co-*, together, Gr. *seismos*, earthquake.]

co-sentient, *kō-sen'sh(y)ənt*, (*arch.*) *adj.* perceiving together.

cosh, *kosh*, (*Scot.*) *adj.* cosy, snug.

cosh, *kosh*, (*slang*) *n.* a bludgeon, truncheon, leadpipe, piece of flexible tubing filled with metal, or the like, used as a weapon.—Also *v.t.*

cosh. See cosine.

cosher, *kosh'ər*, (*dial.*) *v.t.* to pamper, to coddle.— *v.i.* to chat in a friendly way.

cosher. Same as kosher.

coshery, *kosh'ər-i*, *n.* the ancient right of an Irish chief to quarter himself and his retainers on his tenantry—also cosh'ering.—*v.i.* cosh'er, to live on dependants.—*n.* cosh'erer. [Ir. *coisir*, a feast.]

cosier. See cozier.

co-signatory, *kō-sig'nə-tə-ri*, *adj.* uniting with others in signing.—*n.* one who does so.—*adj.* (*rare*) co-signif'icative, having the same signification.

cosine, *kō'sin*, *n.* the sine of the complement of an angle—*abbrev.* cos (*kos*).—*n.* cosh (*kosh*), for hyperbolic *cosine*.

cosmetic, *koz-met'ik*, *adj.* purporting to improve beauty, esp. that of the complexion: correcting defects of the face, etc., or supplying deficiencies (as *cosmetic surgery*, *hands*).—*n.* a preparation for the purpose.—*adj.* cosmet'ical.—*adv.* cosmet'ically.—*v.t.* cosmet'icise, *-ize* (*-siz*).—*n.* cosmet'icism.—*ns.* cosmē'sis, cosmetic surgery or treatment; cosmetol'ogy, art or profession of applying cosmetics, or of carrying out plastic surgery. [Gr. *kosmētikos—kosmeein*, to adorn —*kosmos*, order.]

Cosmos, *koz'mos*, *n.* an American plant genus of composites akin to the dahlia. [Gr. *kosmos*, ornament.]

cosmos, *koz'mos*, *n.* the world or universe as an orderly or systematic whole—opp. to chaos: order.—*adjs.* cos'mic, relating to the cosmos: universal: orderly; cos'mical, cosmic: happening at sunrise (*astron.*): rising with the sun (*astron.*).—*adv.* cos'mically.—*ns.* cos'mism, notion of the cosmos as a self-existing whole; cos'mist, a secularist; cos'mocrat (*rare*), ruler of the world. —*adjs.* cosmocrat'ic; cosmogon'ic, *-al*, relating to cosmogony.—*ns.* cosmog'onist, one who speculates on the origin of the universe; cosmog'ony (Gr. *kosmogoniā*), a theory or a myth of the origin of the universe, esp. of the stars, nebulae, etc.—Also cosmogeny (*-moj'*); cosmog'rapher.—*adjs.* cosmograph'ic, *-al.*—*n.* cosmog'raphy, a description of the world: the science of the constitution of the universe; cosmol'atry (Gr. *latreiā*, worship) (*rare*), worship of the world.—*adj.* cosmolog'ical.—*ns.* cosmol'ogist; cosmol'ogy, the science of the universe as a whole: a treatise on the structure and parts of the system of creation; cos'monaut (Russian kosmonaut; Gr. *nautēs*, sailor), an astronaut.—*n.* cosmonau'tics.—*adj.* cosmoplas'tic (Gr. *plassein*, to form), moulding the universe: world-forming.—*ns.* cosmopol'icy (*Shelley*); cosmop'olis (Gr. *polis*, city, state), an international city: a world-city; cosmopol'itan, a citizen of the world: one free from local or national prejudices: a cosmopolitan sympathetic towards or tolerant of non-communism in other countries.—*adj.* belonging to all parts of the world: unprejudiced.—*n.* cosmopol'itanism.—*n.* and *adj.* cosmopolite (*koz-mop'ə-līt*).—*adjs.* cosmopol'itic, *-polit'ical.*—*n.* cosmopol'itics, world politics; cosmop'olitism (or *-pol'*); cosmorama (*-rä'ma*; Gr. *horāma*, a spectacle), a view, or a series of views, of different parts of the world, tricked out with mirrors, lenses, etc.— *adj.* cosmoramic (*-ram'*).—*ns.* cos'mosphere, an apparatus for showing the position of the earth at any given time with reference to the fixed stars; cosmothē'ism (Gr. *theos*, god), the belief that identifies God with the cosmos: pantheism. —*adjs.* cosmothet'ic, *-al*, assuming an external world.—cos'motron, see accelerator (under accelerate).—cosmical constant, a number, at present of the order of $10^{78}$, believed to be fundamental to the structure of the universe; cosmic rays, the shortest electro-magnetic waves known, discovered in 1925 by Dr R. A. Millikan, thought to come from interstellar space; cosmological principle, according to the cosmology of general relativity, the principle that, at a given time, the universe would look the same to observers in other nebulae as it looks to us. [Gr. *kosmos*, order, world, universe.]

co-sphered, *kō-sfērd'*, (*arch.*) *adj.* being in the same sphere.

coss, *kos*, *n.* a measure of distance in India, averaging about 1¾ mile. [Hindi *kōs*—Sans. *krōśa*, a call.]

Cossack, *kos'ak*, *n.* one of a people in south-eastern Russia, formerly holding by military tenure and serving as cavalry.—Cossack boots, Russian boots; Cossack post, a small group of mounted troops on outpost duty. [Turk. *quzzāq*, freebooter.]

cosset, *kos'it*, *n.* a hand-reared lamb: a pet.—*v.t.* to fondle: to pamper:—*pr.p.* coss'eting; *pa.t.* and *pa.p.* coss'eted. [Perh. O.E. *cot-sǣta, cotsetla*, cot-dweller.]

cost, *kost*, *v.t.* or *v.i.* to be obtainable at a price of: to involve an expenditure of: to require to be laid out or suffered or lost.—*v.t.* to estimate the cost of production of:—*pa.t.* and *pa.p.* cost.—*n.* what is or would have to be laid out or suffered or lost to obtain anything: (in *pl.*) expenses of a law-suit.—*n.* cost'liness.—*adj.* cost'ly, high-priced: valuable.—cost'-account'ant, one who analyses and classifies elements of cost, as material, labour, etc., or who devises systems of doing this; cost'-account'ing (*v.t.* cost'-account').—*adjs.* cost-effec'tive, giving adequate return for outlay; cost-free, free of charge.—Also *adv.*—*adj.* cost'-plus', used of a work contract where payment is according to actual cost, plus an agreed percentage of that cost as profit.—cost price, the price the merchant pays for goods bought.—at all costs, cost what may, no matter what the cost or consequences may be; cost of living, the total cost of goods ordinarily required in order to live up to one's usual standard; cost of living index, an official number showing the cost of living at a certain date compared with that at another date taken as a standard; prime cost, the price of production, without regard to profit or overhead expenses. [O.Fr. *couster* (Fr. *coûter*)—L. *cōnstāre*, to stand at.]

cost, coste, *kost*, (*Spens.*) *n.* See coast.—*v.t.* and *v.i.* (*Shak., Spens.*) to approach. [coast.]

costa, *kos'ta*, *n.* a rib: a rib-like structure, vein, ridge: the fore-edge of an insect's wing: the nervure next it.—*adj.* cos'tal, of or near the ribs, the costa, or the side of the body.—*n.* the costal nervure.—*adjs.* cos'tāte, -d, ribbed: having the appearance of ribs. [L. *costa*, a rib.]

costard, *kos'tərd*, *n.* a large kind of apple: the human head (contemptuously) (*arch.*).—*ns.* cos'tardmonger, cos'termonger, cos'ter, a seller of apples and other fruit: a seller of fruit and other wares from a barrow: a term of abuse (*Shak.*). [Perh. L. *costa*, a rib.]

costean, *kos-tēn'*, *v.i.* to dig down to bed-rock in prospecting.—*ns.* costean'ing; costean'-pit. [Said to be from Cornish *cothas*, dropped, *stean*, tin.]

costive, *kos'tiv*, *adj.* constipated.—*adv.* cos'tively.—*n.* cos'tiveness. [Fr. *constipé*; see constipate.]

costmary, *kost'mār-i*, *n.* alecost (*Chrysanthemum Balsamita*), a composite of southern Europe, grown in gardens for its fragrant leaves. [L. *costum*—Gr. *kostos*, costus, and *Maria*, the Virgin Mary.]

costrel, *kos'trəl*, (*dial.*) *n.* an eared bottle, to be hung at the waist. [O.Fr. *costerel*.]

costume, *kos'tūm*, in U.S. '*tōōm*, *n.* a manner of dressing: dress, garb: a woman's outer dress as a unit: fancy dress.—*v.t.* (*kos-tūm'*, in U.S. -*tōōm'*), to dress.—*adj.* costumed'.—*ns.* costum'er, costum'ier, one who makes or deals in costumes.—costume jewellery, jewellery worn as an adornment only, without pretence of being genuine gems. [Fr.,—It. *costume*—L. *cōnsuētūdō*, *-inis*, custom.]

Costus, *kos'tas*, *n.* a genus of plants of the ginger family: (without *cap.*) an aromatic root wrongly assigned to it, really that of a composite of Kashmir, *Saussurea hypoleuca*—also cos'tus arabicus, cos'tus-root. [Latinised from Gr. *kostos*.]

cosy, in U.S. cozy, *kō'zi*, (orig. *Scot.*) *adj.* snug: comfortable.—*n.* a covering used for a teapot, to keep the tea warm (also tea'-cosy): a similar covering for a boiled egg.—*adv.* cō'sily. [Ety. unknown.]

cot, *kot*, (*poet.*) *n.* a small dwelling, a cottage.—*adj.* cott'ed, lined with cots.—*ns.* cot'-folk (*Scot.*), cottars; cot'-house (*Scot.*), a house occupied by a cottar; cot'land, land belonging to a cottage; cot'quean (*obs.*), a scolding woman: a man who busies himself with women's affairs (*Shak.*); cot'town (*Scot.*), a group of cot-houses. [O.E. *cot*; cf. O.N. and Du. *kot*.]

cot, cott, *kot*, *n.* a small bed or crib: a swinging bed of canvas (for officers, sick, etc.) (*naut.*): a hospital bed. [Anglo-Ind.,—Hindi *khāṭ*.]

cot (*Spens.* cott), *kot*, *n.* a small boat. [Ir.]

cotangent, *kō-tan'jant*, *n.* the tangent of the complement of an angle—*abbrev.* cot (*kot*).—*n.* cotk (*koth*), for hyperbolic cotangent.

cote, *kōt*, *n.* a cot (1): a place for animals, as dovecote or dove-cot, sheep-cote. [O.E. *cote*; cf. cot (1).]

cote, *kōt*, *v.t.* to pass by (*Shak.*): to outstrip (as one dog another) (*obs.*). [Poss. conn. with coast.]

cote, a Shakespearian form of quote.

coteau, *ko'tō*, (*U.S.*) *n.* a hilly upland area: a valley side.—*pl.* coteaux ('*tō* or '*tōz*). [Canadian Fr.—Fr., a sloping hillside—O.Fr. *costel*, dim. of *coste*, slope.]

cote-hardie, *kōt'-här'di*, *n.* a mediaeval close-fitting tight sleeved body garment. [O.Fr.]

côtelette, *kōt-let*, (Fr.) a cutlet, a chop.

coteline, *kōt-lēn'*, *n.* a kind of muslin, corded or ribbed. [Fr. *côte*, a rib—L. *costa*.]

cotemporaneous, etc. Faulty forms of contemporaneous, etc.

co-tenant, *kō-ten'ənt*, *n.* a joint tenant.—*n.* co-ten'ancy.

coterie, *kō'tə-rē*, *n.* a social, literary, or other exclusive circle. [Fr.; orig. a number of peasants holding land jointly from a lord—L.L. *cota*, a cot.]

coterminous, a faulty form of conterminous.

coth. See cotangent.

cothurnus, *kō-thûr'nəs*, cothurn, *kō'thûrn*, *n.* -*thûrn'*, *n.* the tragedian's buskin (*pl.* cothur'ni). [Latinised from Gr. *kothornos*.]

coticular, *kō-tik'ū-lər*, (*obs.*) *adj.* pertaining to whetstones. [L. *cōticula*, dim. of *cos, cotis*, whetstone.]

co-tidal, *kō-tīd'əl*, *adj.* having high tide at the same time.

cotillion, *ko-til'yən*, cotillon, *ko-tē'yɔ̃*, *n.* a sort of country dance. [Fr., petticoat—*cotte*, a coat—L.L. *cotta*, a tunic; see coat.]

Cotinga, *kō-ting'ga*, *n.* a tropical American genus of bright plumaged passerine birds: (without *cap.*) any bird of its fam., Cotingidae (-*tin'ji-dē*). [Of Tupí origin.]

cotise, cottise, *kot'is*, (*her.*) *n.* one of the diminutives of the bend.—*v.t.* to border with cotises, barrulets, etc. [Fr. *cotice*; origin obscure.]

Cotoneaster, *ko-tō-ni-as'tər*, *n.* a genus of shrubs

or small trees akin to hawthorn. [L. *cotōnea*, quince.]
**Cotswold,** *kots'wōld, n.* a breed of sheep.—**Cots-wold lion** (*jocular*), a sheep. [*Cotswold* Hills.]
**cott.** See cot (2) and (3).
**cotta,** *kot'a, n.* a surplice. [L.L. *cotta*.]
**cottabus,** *kot'ä-bus, n.* an amusement in ancient Greece among young men, consisting in throwing wine into a vessel, success at which betokened fortune in love. [L.,—Gr. *kottabos*.]
**cottage,** *kot'ij, n.* a small dwelling-house: a country residence: a summer residence (*U.S.*): a one-storey house (*Austr.*).—*adj.* **cott'aged,** covered with cottages.—*n.* **cott'ager,** one who dwells in a cottage, esp. of labourers.—**cottage cheese,** soft white loose cheese made from skim-milk curds; **cottage hospital,** a small, simply organised hospital: one housed in a cottage or cottages; **cottage loaf,** a loaf consisting of a smaller lump on the top of a bigger one; **cottage orné** (Fr. *ko-täzh or-nä*), an ornately-designed small country house built in rustic style; **cottage piano,** a small upright piano. [L.L. *cottagium*—O.E. *cot*; see cot (1).]
**cottar, cotter,** *kot'ər, n.* one of a class of mediaeval villeins: a peasant occupying a cot or cottage for which he has to give labour (*Scot.*). [cot (1).]
**cotter,** *kot'ər, n.* a pin or wedge for fastening and tightening.—*n.* **cott'er-pin,** a pin for keeping a cotter in place. [Origin obscure.]
**cottier,** *kot'i-ər, n.* a cottar: an Irish tenant holding land as the highest bidder; **cott'ierism,** the cottier system of land tenure. [Fr. *cotier*; see cot (1).]
**cotton,** *kot'n, n.* a soft substance like fine wool, the long hairs covering the seeds of the cotton-plant: the plant itself, individually or collectively: yarn or cloth made of cotton.—*adj.* made of cotton.—*v.t.* (*arch.*) to provide with cotton.—*v.i.* to agree (the connection of the intransitive meaning is unknown).—*ns.* **cottona'de,** an inferior cotton cloth; **cottono'cracy,** the cotton planting or the cotton manufacturing interests.—*adj.* **cotton'y,** like cotton: soft: downy.—**cott'on-boll,** the pod of the cotton-plant; **cott'on-gin,** a machine for separating the seeds from the fibre of cotton; **cott'on-grass,** a genus (Eriophorum) of sedges with long, silky, or cottony hairs about the ripened ovary; **cott'on-mill,** a factory where cotton is spun or woven; **cott'onmouth,** the venomous water mocassin snake (from the white inside of its mouth); **cott'on-plant,** one of various species of Gossypium (family Malvaceae), yielding cotton; **cott'on-press,** a press for compressing cotton into bales; **cott'onseed,** the seed of the cotton-plant, yielding a valuable oil; **cott'on-spinner,** one who spins cotton, or employs those who do; **cott'ontail,** the ordinary United States rabbit; **cott'on-thistle,** a strong thistle (*Onopordon Acanthium*) covered with a cottony down; **cott'on-tree,** the American cotton-wood: the Indian *Bombax malabaricum*: an Australian Hibiscus; **cott'on-waste,** refuse from cotton mills, used for cleaning machinery, etc.; **cott'on-weed,** cudweed, a cottony seaside composite, *Diotis maritima*; **cott'on-wood,** any one of several American species of poplar; **cott'on-wool',** cotton in its raw or woolly state: loose cotton pressed in a sheet as an absorbent or protective agent, for stuffing, etc.; **cott'on-worm,** the caterpillar of an owlet moth (*Aletia xylina*) destructive to American cotton crops.—**cotton on to** (*slang*), to take to: to understand. [Fr. *coton*—Ar. *qutun*.]
**Cottus,** *kot'əs, n.* a genus of fishes including the bullhead and father-lasher.—*n.* and *adj.* **cott'oid.** [Gr. *kottos,* a fish, perhaps the bullhead.]
**cotyle,** *kot'i-lē, n.* an ancient Greek drinking-cup: a cup-like cavity (*zool.*):—*pl.* **cot'ylae** (*-lē*), and **cot'yles.**—*adjs.* **cotyl'iform** (*bot.*), disk-shaped

with raised rim; **cot'yloid,** cup-shaped. [Gr. *kotylē.*]
**cotyledon,** *kot-i-lē'dən, n.* a seed-leaf (*bot.*): a tuft or patch of villi on the placenta, as in most ruminants (*zool.*): (*cap.*) a genus of S. Afr. plants (from Crassulaceae).—*adjs.* **cotylē'donary; cotylē'donous,** pertaining to or having cotyledons.—*n.pl.* **Cotyloph'ora,** the Pecora, or ruminants other than camels and chevrotains. [Gr. *kotylēdōn*—*kotylē,* a cup.]
**coucal,** *koo'käl, n.* a genus (*Centropus*) of common bush-birds in Africa, India and Australia, the lark-heeled cuckoos. [Imit.]
**couch,** *kowch, v.t.* to lay down: to lower: to cause to lie close: to spread: to level: to arrange in language, to express: to depress or remove (a cataract in the eye).—*v.i.* to lie down for the purpose of sleep, concealment, etc.: to bend or stoop.—*n.* any place for rest or sleep: a bed: a kind of sofa with half back and one raised end: the lair of a wild beast: a layer: that on which something is spread.—*adj.* **couch'ant,** couching or lying down: lying down with head up (*her.*).—*n.* **couch'ing,** embroidery in which the surface is covered with threads and these are secured by stitches forming a pattern.—**couch a spear,** to fix it in its rest at the side of the armour. [Fr. *coucher,* to lay down—L. *collocāre,* to place—*col-,* together, *locus,* a place.]
**couch, couch-grass,** *kowch', koōch' (gräs), ns.* a grass akin to wheat, a troublesome weed owing to its creeping rootstocks. [A variant of quitch.]
**couchee,** *koo'shä, n.* an evening reception. [Fr. *couché,* a reception before going to bed; see couch.]
**couchette,** *koo-shet,* (Fr.) a sleeping berth on a continental train.
**coudé,** *koo-dä, adj.* bent like an elbow: (of reflecting telescope) in which one or more plane mirrors reflect the light down the polar axis. [Fr.]
**Couéism,** *koo'ā-izm, n.* psychotherapy by auto-suggestion.—*n.* **Cou'éist.** [Emile Coué (1857-1926), its expounder.]
**cougar,** *koo'gär, -gər,* **couguar,** *-gwär, n.* a puma. [Fr. *couguar,* adapted from a Guaraní name.]
**cough,** *kof, v.i.* to expel air with a sudden opening of the glottis and a characteristic sound.—*v.t.* to expel by coughing.—*n.* the act or the sound of coughing: an ailment of which coughing is a symptom.—*ns.* **cough'er; cough'ing.—cough'-drop',** a cough-lozenge: a person of spicy character; **cough'-loz'enge,** a medicated lozenge to allay coughing; **cough'-mix'ture.—cough down,** to put to silence by coughing; **cough up** (*slang*), to pay out, hand over, under compulsion. [M.E. *coughen;* cf. Du. *kuchen,* Ger. *keuchen, keichen,* to gasp.]
**could,** *kood, pa.t.* of can. [M.E. *coude, couth*—O.E. *cūthe* for *cunthe,* was able; *l* is inserted from the influence of *would* and *should.*]
**coulée,** *koo-lā', n.* a lava-flow: a ravine (*U.S.* and *Can.*). [Fr. *couler,* to flow.]
**couleur de rose,** *koo-lœr də rōz,* (Fr.) rose coloured: seen or presented in a way that exaggerates attractiveness.
**coulisse,** *koo-lēs', n.* a piece of grooved wood: the slides in which the side-scenes of a theatre run—hence (in *pl.*) the wings. [Fr. *couler,* to glide, to flow—L. *cōlāre,* to strain.]
**couloir,** *kool-wär, n.* a gully. [Fr., passage.]
**coulomb,** *koo-lom', n.* MKSA unit of quantity in measuring current electricity: the quantity furnished by a current of one ampere in one second. [From the French physicist, C. A. de Coulomb (1736-1806).]
**Coulommiers,** *koo-lom-yä, n.* a white, soft cheese, fresh or cured, made near *Coulommiers* in central France.
**coulter, colter,** *kōl'tər (Scot. koo'tər), n.* the iron

Neutral vowels in unaccented syllables: *el'ə-mənt;* for certain sounds in foreign words, see p. viii

cutter in front of a ploughshare. [O.E. *culter*— L. *culter*, knife.]

**coumarin, cumarin,** $k\overline{oo}'m\partial$-rin, *n.* a crystalline compound ($C_9H_6O_2$) obtained from Tonka beans, woodruff, melilot, etc.—*adjs.* **coumaric** (-*mar'*), **coumaril'ic.** [Tupí *cumarú*, Tonka bean.]

**council,** *kown'sl, -sil, n.* an assembly called together for deliberation, advice, administration or legislation: the persons constituting such an assembly: the body directing the affairs of a town, county, parish, etc.: an assembly of ecclesiastics met to regulate doctrine or discipline: a governing body in a university: a committee that arranges the business of a society.—*ns.* **coun'cillor,** (*U.S.*) **coun'cilor,** a member of a council; **coun'cilman** (*London* and *U.S.*), a member of a municipal council.—*adj.* **councilman'ic** (*U.S.*).—**coun'cil-board,** the board or table round which a council meets for deliberation: the council itself; **coun'cil-cham'ber,** the room where a council is held; **council estate,** an area set apart for council houses; **coun'cil-house,** a house in which a council meets: a house erected by a municipal council; **council school,** a school governed by a town or county council; **general council,** one called by an invitation to the church at large, also **oecumenical,** if received by the first seven, 325-787; **legislative council,** a council to assist a governor, with power to make laws.—**Council of Europe,** a consultative body of European states, at first (1949) thought of as the parliament of a future European federation; **council of war,** a conference of officers called to consult with the commander; **in council,** in the council-chamber: in consultation; **Council, House, of States,** upper house of Indian parliament. [Fr. *concile*—L. *concilium*.]

**counsel,** *kown'sl, n.* consultation: deliberation: advice: plan: purpose: a confidential matter: one who gives counsel, a barrister or advocate.—*v.t.* to advise: to warn:—*pr.p.* **coun'selling;** *pa.t.* and *pa.p.* **coun'selled.**—*adj.* **couns'ellable,** that may be counselled.—*n.* **coun'selling** (orig. *U.S.*), (a service consisting of) giving advice on miscellaneous problems to, e.g. citizens, children in a school.—Also *adj.*—*ns.* **coun'sellor,** one who counsels: a barrister; **coun'sellorship.**—**coun'sel-keep'er** (*Shak.*), one who can keep counsel or a secret.—*adj.* **coun'sel-keep'ing** (*Shak.*).—**King's, Queen's Counsel** (K.C., Q.C.), a barrister or advocate appointed by letters-patent: the office is honorary, but gives the right of precedence in all the courts.—**counsel of perfection,** a commendation of something beyond the binding minimum, something not absolutely imperative, but commended as the means of reaching greater 'perfection'; **keep counsel,** to keep a secret. [Fr. *conseil*—L. *consilium,* advice—*consulĕre,* to consult.]

**count,** *kownt, n.* an imperial official (*Rom. hist.*) on the Continent, a noble equal in rank to an earl:—*fem.* **count'ess,** a lady of the same rank: the wife of a count or earl (fem. of *earl*): a size of roofing slate, $20 \times 10$ inches ($508 \times 254$ mm). —*ns.* **count'ship,** a count's dignity or domain (also used as a title); **coun'ty,** a count (*obs.*): a countship (*obs.*): a portion of a country separated for administrative, parliamentary or other purposes, a shire.—*adj.* of a, or the, county: of county family.—**county borough** (see **borough**); **county council,** a council for managing the public affairs of a county; **county councillor; county court,** the highest court of law within a county; **county cricket,** cricket played in matches between clubs representing counties; **county family,** a family of nobility or gentry (**coun'ty-people**), with estates and a seat in the county; **County school,** a school

provided and maintained by a local education authority; **county seat** (*U.S.*), the seat of county government; **county town,** the town in which the public business of the county is transacted; **Count of the Saxon Shore,** in Roman Britain, an official in charge of the S.E. coast (liable to attacks by Saxons). [O.Fr. *conte*—L. *comes, comitis,* a companion, *con-,* with, *īre,* to go.]

**count,** *obs.* **compt,** *kownt, v.t.* to number, sum up: to name the numerals up to: to take into account, reckon as significant or to be recognised: to ascribe: to reckon, esteem, consider. —*v.i.* to number: to be numbered: to be of account: to be recognised in reckoning: to have a certain value: to reckon: to name the numerals in order.—*n.* act of numbering: reckoning: the number counted: a number indicating size of yarn: the counting of the seconds in which a fallen man may rise and resume (also **count-out;** *boxing*): esteem, consideration, account: a particular charge in an indictment.—*adjs.* **count'able** (formerly **compt'-able, -ible**), capable of being counted: to be counted: accountable: sensitive (*Shak.*); **count'ed,** accounted, reckoned.—*n.* **count'er,** he who or that which counts: that which indicates a number: a disk or the like, used in reckoning or as a substitute for a coin in games: a table on which money is counted or goods laid: the name of certain prisons (officially **compter;** *hist.*).— *adj.* **count'less,** that cannot be counted: innumerable.—**count'-down,** a descending count or counted check to a moment of happening regarded as zero, as in the firing of a rocket; **count'er-caster** (*Shak.*), an arithmetician, reckoner; **count'er-jumper, -skipp'er,** contemptuous names for a shopman; **count'ing-house, count'ing-room,** a room in which a merchant keeps his accounts and transacts business; **count'-wheel,** a wheel with notched edge controlling the stroke of a clock in sounding the hours. —**count out,** of a meeting (esp. of the House of Commons), to bring to an end by pointing that a quorum is not present: in children's games, to eliminate players by counting while repeating a rhyme (**counting-out rhyme**): in boxing, etc., to adjudge defeated by counting seconds; **out for the count** (*fig.*), unconscious, or completely exhausted; **under the counter,** hidden from customers' sight (*adj.* **under-the-counter,** reserved for the favoured: secret, furtive). [O.Fr. *cunter* (Fr. *compter*)—L. *computāre.*]

**countenance,** *kown'tэn-эns, n.* the face: the expression of the face: appearance: demeanour shown towards a person: favour: approbation: acquiescence.—*v.t.* to favour or approve: to make a show of (*Spens.*).—*n.* **coun'tenancer.**—**change countenance,** to change expression of the face; **in countenance,** unabashed; **out of countenance,** abashed. [O.Fr. *contenance*—L. *continentia,* restraint, demeanour—*continēre,* to contain.]

**counter,** *kown'tэr, adv.* the opposite way: in opposition.—*adj.* contrary: opposing: opposite.—*n.* that which is counter or opposite: the voice-part set in immediate contrast with the air (*mus.*): an encounter (*Spens.*): a parry in which one foil follows the other in a small circle (*fencing*): the part of a horse's breast between the shoulders and under the neck: the part of a ship's stern from the lower moulding to the water-line (*naut.*).—*v.t.* to encounter: to contradict: to meet or answer by a stroke or move: to strike while reserving or parrying a blow (*boxing*).—**run counter to,** to move in the opposite direction (to): to act, happen, in a way contrary (to instructions, expectations, etc.). [Partly apheitc for **encounter,** partly directly from A.Fr. *countre,* O.Fr. (Fr.) *contre*—L. *contrā,* against.]

**counter.** See **count** (2).

**counter-**, *kown'tər-*, in composition, against.—*v.t.* **counteract'**, to act counter or in opposition to: to hinder or defeat: to neutralise.—*n.* **counterac'tion**.—*adj.* **counteract'ive**, tending to counteract.—*n.* one who or that which counteracts.— *adv.* **counteract'ively**.—*ns.* **coun'ter-ag'ent**, anything which counteracts; **coun'ter-approach'**, a work thrown up outside a besieged place to command or check the approaches of the besieger; **coun'ter-attack**, an attack in reply to an attack; **coun'ter-attrac'tion**, attraction in an opposite direction: a rival show.—*adj.* **coun'ter-attract'-ive**.—*v.t.* **counterbal'ance**, to balance by weight on the opposite side: to act against with equal weight, power, or influence.—*ns.* **coun'ter-balance**, an equal weight, power, or agency working in opposition; **coun'ter-base** (see **contrabass**); **coun'ter-batt'ery** (*mil.*), a battery erected to oppose another; **coun'terblast**, a defiant pronouncement or denunciation; **coun'-terblow**, a return blow; **coun'terbond**, a bond to protect from contingent loss one who has given bond for another.—*v.t.* **coun'ter-brace** (*naut.*), to brace or fasten (the head-yards and after-yards) in opposite ways.—*n.* the lee-brace of the fore-topsail-yard.—*n.* **coun'terbuff**, a stroke that stops motion or causes a recoil: reaction: return blow: rebuff.—*v.t.* to rebuff.—*ns.* **coun'ter-cast** (*Spens.*), a contrary cast, counter-plot, trick; **coun'terchange** (*Shak.*), exchange: re-ciprocation.—*adj.* **coun'terchanged'**, exchanged: having the tinctures reversed or interchanged (*her.*).—*n.* **coun'tercharge**, a charge brought forward in opposition to another charge.—*v.t.* **coun'tercharm**, to destroy or dissolve the effects of (another charm).—*n.* that which destroys the effects of another charm.—*v.t.* **coun'tercheck'**, to check by some obstacle: to rebuke.—*ns.* **coun'tercheck**, a check in opposition to another: a rebuke; **coun'ter-claim** (esp. *law*), a claim brought forward as a partial or complete set-off against another claim.—*adv.* **coun'ter-clock'wise**, in a direction contrary to that of the hands of a clock.—*ns.* **coun'ter-curr'ent**, a current flowing in an opposite direction; **coun'ter-drain**, a drain alongside a canal, etc., to carry off water oozing out.—*v.t.* **coun'terdraw**, to trace on oiled paper or other transparent material.— *ns.* **count'er-esp'ionage**, spying in opposition, espionage directed against the enemy's spy system; **coun'ter-ev'idence**, evidence brought forward in opposition to other evidence.—*adj.* **counter-fleury** (*-flōō'ri, -flū'ri*), *-flo'ry, -flow'ered*, with flowers placed the contrary way.—*ns.* **coun'-terfoil**, the corresponding part of a bank cheque, postal order, ticket, etc., retained by the giver; **coun'ter-force**, an opposing force; **coun'ter-fort**, a buttress or arch supporting a retaining wall; **coun'ter-gauge**, an adjustable scribing gauge for marking the measurements of a mortise on a piece to be tenoned; **coun'ter-glow** (see **gegenschein**); **coun'ter-guard** (*fort.*), an out-work consisting of two lines of rampart running parallel to the faces of the bastion, to guard the bastion from being breached; **coun'ter-in'fluence**, an opposing influence; **counter-intelligence**, activities, as censorship, camouflage, use of codes, etc., aimed at preventing an enemy from obtaining information, or the organisation that carries these out; **coun'ter-irr'itant**, an irritant used to relieve another irritation; **coun'ter-irritā'tion**; **coun'terlight** (*paint.*), a light opposite to any object, disturbing the effect of its light.— *v.i.* **coun'termarch**, to march back or in a direction contrary to a former one.—*n.* a marching back or in a direction different from a former one: an evolution by which a body of men change front, and still retain the same men in the front rank (*mil.*): change of measures.—*ns.* **coun'termark**, an additional mark put on a bale

of goods belonging to several merchants, so that it may not be opened except in the presence of all the owners: a mark put on standard metal by the London Goldsmiths' Company in addition to the artificers: an artificial cavity made in the teeth of horses to disguise their age; **counter-measure**, an action intended to counteract the effect of another action or happening.—*v.t.* **countermine'**, to make a mine in opposition to: to oppose by means of a countermine: to frus-trate by secret working (*fig.*).—*n.* (*kownt'*) a mine or chamber excavated by the besiegers to counteract or destroy the mines made by the besiegers: any means of counteraction (*fig.*).— *ns.* **coun'ter-mō'tion**, an opposite motion; **coun'ter-move**, *-move'ment*, a contrary move, movement; **coun'termure**, a wall-facing: a supplementary wall: a wall raised by besiegers against a wall.—*v.t.* (*-mūr'*) to defend with a countermure.—*ns.* **coun'ter-offen'sive**, counter-attack: attack by the defenders; **coun'ter-o'pening**, an aperture or vent on the opposite side, or in a different place; **coun'ter-pace**, a step in opposition to another, a contrary measure.— *adj.* **coun'ter-paled** (*her.*), divided equally, as an escutcheon, first palewise, then by a line fesswise, with tinctures counterchanged.—*ns.* **coun'ter-parole'**, a word in addition to the password; **coun'terpart**, the part that answers to another part: that which fits into or completes another, having the qualities which another lacks, and an opposite: a duplicate: a double.—*adj.* so **coun'ter-pass'ant** (*her.*), passing each other con-trary ways.—*n.* **coun'terplea**, a replication to a plea or request.—*vs.t.* **counterplead'**, to plead the contrary of; **coun'ter-plot'**, to plot against in order to frustrate another plot.—*n.* a plot or stratagem opposed to another plot.—*v.t.* **coun'terpoise** (*obs.* **coun'terpeise**, *-pēz*), to poise or weigh against or on the opposite side: to act in opposition to with equal effect.—*n.* an equally heavy weight in the other scale.—*ns.* **coun'ter-poison**, a poison used as the antidote of another; **coun'ter-pressure**, opposing pressure.—*adj.* **coun'-ter-produc'tive**, acting against productivity, efficiency, or usefulness.—*ns.* **coun'terproof**, an inverted impression obtained from a newly printed proof of an engraving, by laying it, while the ink is still-wet, upon plain paper, and passing it through the press; **Coun'ter-Refor-mā'tion** (*hist.*), a reform movement within the Roman Catholic Church, following and counter-acting the Reformation; **coun'ter-revolū'tion**, a subsequent revolution counteracting the effect of a previous; **coun'ter-roll**, a copy of the rolls relating to appeals, inquests, etc., serving as a check on another's roll; **coun'ter-round**, a body of officers to inspect the rounds.—*adj.* **coun'ter-sā'lient** (*her.*), salient in opposite directions.—*n.* **coun'terscarp** (*fort.*), the side of the ditch nearest to the besiegers and opposite to the scarp.—*v.t.* **counterseal'** (*Shak.*), to seal along with others.— *ns.* **coun'ter-secur'ity**, security given to one who has become surety for another; **coun'ter-sense**, an interpretation contrary to the real sense; **coun'-tershaft**, an intermediate shaft driven by the main shaft.—*v.t.* **countersign'**, to sign on the opposite side of a writing: to sign in addition to the signature of a superior, to attest the authenticity of a writing.—*n.* (*kownt'*), a military private sign or word, which must be given in order to pass a sentry: a counter-signature.—*ns.* **coun'ter-sig'-nal**, a signal used as an answer to another; **coun'ter-sig'nature**, a name countersigned to a writing.—*v.t.* **coun'tersink**, to bevel the edge of (a hole), as for the head of a screw-nail: to set the head or top of on a level with, or below, the surface of the surrounding material.—*ns.* **coun'ter-stand**, opposition, resistance; **coun'ter-state'ment**, a statement in opposition to another statement; **coun'terstroke** (*Spens.*), a stroke in return; **coun'ter-sub'ject** (*mus.*), part of a figure in which the first voice accompanies the answer of the second; **coun'ter-tall'y**, a tally serving as a check to another; **coun'ter-ten'or**, the highest alto male voice (so called because a contrast to tenor); **coun'ter-time**, the resistance of a horse that interrupts his cadence and the measure of his manège: resistance, opposition; **coun'ter-turn**, a turn in a play different from what was expected.—*v.t.* **countervail'**, to be of avail against: to act against with equal effect: to be of equal value to: to compensate.—*adj.* **counter-vail'able**.—*n.* **coun'ter-view**, an opposing view: a posture in which two persons face each other: opposition: contrast.—*vs.t.* **counter-vote'**, to vote in opposition to; **counter-weigh'**, to weigh against, counterbalance.—*n.* **coun'ter-weight**, weight in an opposite scale.—*v.i.* **coun'ter-wheel**, to wheel in an opposite direction.—*n.* **coun'ter-work**, a work raised in opposition to another.—*v.t.* **counter-work'**, to work in opposition to.—*p.adj.* **coun'ter-wrought**. [A.Fr. *countre*, O.Fr. *contre*—L. *contrā*, against.]

**counterfeit**, *kown'tər-fit*, *-fēt*, *v.t.* to imitate: to copy without authority: to forge.—*n.* something false or copied, or that pretends to be true and original.—*adj.* (*Spens.* **coun'terfect**), pretended: made in imitation: forged: false.—*n.* **coun'ter-feiter**, one who counterfeits.—*adv.* **coun'ter-feitly**, in a counterfeit manner: falsely.—*n.* **coun'terfeisance** (*-fēz'əns*; *Spens.* **counter-fesaunce**), act of counterfeiting: forgery. [O.Fr. *contrefet*, from *contrefaire*, to imitate—L. *contrā*, against, *facĕre*, to do.]

**countermand**, *kown-tər-mänd'*, *v.t.* to give a command in opposition to one already given: to revoke.—*n.* a revocation to a former order.—*adj.* **countermand'able**. [O.Fr. *contremander*—L. *contrā*, against, and *mandāre*, to order.]

**counterpane**, *kown'tər-pān*, *n.* a coverlet for a bed. —Older form (*Shak.*) **coun'terpoint**. [O.Fr. *contrepoint*—*coultepointe*—L. *culcita puncta*, a stitched pillow; see **quilt**.]

**counterpoint**, *kown'tər-point*, *n.* the art of combining melodies (*mus.*): a melody added to another (*mus.*): app. a trick (*Spens.*): an opposite point.—*adj.* **contrapunt'al**.—*n.* **contrapunt'-ist**. [Fr. *contrepoint* and It. *contrappunto*—L. *contrā*, against, *punctum*, a point, from the pricks, points or notes placed against those of the melody; in some senses **counter**- and **point**.]

**country**, *kun'tri*, *n.* a region: a state: a nation: rural districts as distinct from town: land of birth or citizenship: the district hunted by a pack of foxhounds: the rock surrounding a mineral lode (also **coun'try-rock'**).—*adj.* belonging to the country: rural: rustic: rude.—*adj.* **coun'trified**, **coun'tryfied**.—*n.* **coun'tryside**, a district or part of the country.—*adj.* **countrywide'**, all over the country.—**coun'try-box**, a small country-house; **country cousin**, a relative from the country, unaccustomed to town sights or manners; **coun'try-dance**, a dance as practised by country people: a dance in which an indefinite number of couples can take part, arranged in two lines; **coun'try-dan'cing**.—*n.pl.* **coun'try-folk**, fellow-countrymen—**country gentleman**, a landed proprietor who resides on his estate in the country; **coun'try-house**, -**seat**, the residence of a country gentleman; **coun'tryman**, one who lives in the country: a farmer: one belonging to the same country, fellow-countryman; **country party** (*hist.*), the party opposed to the court; **country town**, a small town in a rural district; **coun'trywoman**, a woman who dwells in the country: a woman of the same country.—**go to the country**, to appeal to the community by a general election; **the country** (*cricket slang*), the outfield. [O.Fr. *contrée*—L.L. *contrāta*,

**contrāda**, an extension of L. *contrā*, over against.]
**county**. See **count** (1).
**coup**, *kōō*, *n.* a blow, stroke: a clever and successful stroke in a board or card game: a masterstroke, clever and successful stratagem (*fig.*): act of putting a ball in a pocket without having hit another ball (*billiards*): a coup d'état.—**coup d'essai** (*kōō de-sā*), an experimental work: a first attempt; **coup de foudre** (*də fōō-dr'*), a sudden and astonishing happening: love at first sight; **coup de grâce** (*də gräs*), a finishing blow to put out of pain: a finishing stroke generally; **coup de main** (*də mē*), a sudden overpowering attack; **coup de maître** (*metr'*), a masterstroke; **coup de poing** (*kōō də pwē*), a typical Old Stone Age axe, a roughly pointed piece of stone held in the hand; **coup d'état** (*dā-ta*), a violent or subversive stroke of state policy; **coup de théâtre** (*də tā-atr'*), a sudden and sensational turn as in a play; **coup d'oeil** (*dœy*), a general view at a glance. [Fr.,—L.L. *colpus*—L. *colaphus*—Gr. *kolaphos*, a blow.]

**coup**, *kowp*, (*Scot.*) *v.t.* to exchange or barter.—*n.* **coup'er**, a dealer. [O.N. *kaupa*, to buy.]

**coup**, **cowp**, *kowp*, (*Scot.*) *v.t.* and *v.i.* to overturn: to tip up.—*n.* an upset. [O.Fr. *colp*, blow.]

**coupe**, *kōōp*, (Fr.) a dessert, usu. made with ice-cream, served in a glass bowl: a glass container for serving such a dessert, usu. with a shallow bowl and a short stem.

**coupé**, *kōō-pā*, *n.* the front part of a French stage-coach: a four-wheeled carriage seated for two inside, with a separate seat for the driver: an end compartment of a railway carriage with a seat on one side only: a covered motor-car seated for two.—*adj.* (*her.*), cut evenly off, as the head or limb of an animal.—Also **couped** (*kōōpt*).—*n.* **coupee**, (*kōō-pē'*) in dancing, a salute to a partner, while swinging one foot. [Fr., pa.p. of *couper*, to cut.]

**couple**, *kup'l*, *n.* that which joins two things together: two of a kind joined together, or connected: two: a pair, esp. of married or betrothed persons, dancers, golfers, hunting dogs: a rafter: a pair of equal forces acting on the same body in opposite and parallel directions (*statics*).—*v.t.* to join together.—*v.i.* to pair sexually.—*ns.* **coup'lement**, union: a couple; **coup'ler**, one who or that which couples or unites: an organ mechanism by which stops of one manual can be played from another or from the pedals; **coup'-let**, a pair, couple: a twin: two successive lines of verse that rhyme with each other; **coup'ling**, that which connects: an appliance for transmitting motion in machinery, or for connecting vehicles as in a railway train.—**coup'ling-box**, the box or ring of metal connecting the contiguous ends of two lengths of shafts.—*adj.* **well'-coupled**, of a horse, well formed at the part where the back joins the rump. [O.Fr. *cople*—L. *cōpula*.]

**coupon**, *kōō'pon*, -*pən*, -*pō*, -*pong*, *n.* a billet, check, or other slip of paper cut off from its counterpart: a separate ticket or part of a ticket: a voucher that payments will be made, services performed, goods sold, or the like: a piece cut from an advertisement entitling one to some privilege: a party leader's recommendation of an electoral candidate: a printed betting form on which to enter forecasts of sports results: rate of interest. [Fr. *couper*, to cut off.]

**coupure**, *kōō-pūr'*, *n.* an entrenchment made by the besieged behind a breach: a passage cut to facilitate sallies. [Fr. *couper*, to cut.]

**cour**, **coure**, obsolete forms of **cover**, **cower**.
**courage**, *kur'ij*, *n.* the quality that enables men to meet danger without giving way to fear: bravery: spirit: desire (*obs.*).—*interj.* take courage.—*adjs.* **cour'ageful**; **courageous** (*kə-rā'jəs*), full of courage: brave.—*adv.* **courā'-geously**.—*n.* **courā'geousness**.—**Dutch courage**, a

factitious courage induced by drinking.—**pluck up courage**, to nerve oneself: to gather boldness; **the courage of one's convictions**, courage to act up to, or consistently with, one's opinions. [O.Fr. *corage* (Fr. *courage*), from L. *cor*, the heart.]
**courant**, *kōō-rant'*, (*her.*) *adj*. in a running attitude.
—*ns*. **courante'**, **courant'** (*kōō-ränt'*), an old dance with a kind of gliding step, a coranto: music for it: (*kōō-rant'*) a newspaper (now in titles only). [Fr., pr.p. of *courir*, to run; see **current**.]
**courb**, **curb**, *kōōrb*, *kûrb*, (*Shak.*) *v.i*. to bend, stoop to supplicate.—*adj*. bent (*Spens*. **corbe**). [Fr. *courber*—L. *curvāre*, to bend.]
**courbaril**, *kōōr'bə-ril*, *n*. the West Indian locust-tree: its resin, gum anime. [Fr. from Carib.]
**courbette**, *kōōr-bet'*, French form of **curvet**.
**courd** (*Spens*.), for **covered**.
**courgette**, *kōō'zhet*, *n*. a small marrow. [Fr. *courge*, gourd.]
**courier**, *kōō'ri-ər*, *n*. a runner: a messenger: a state messenger: an official guide who travels with tourists: a frequent title of newspapers. [Fr.,—L. *currēre*, to run.]
**courlan**, *kōōr'lən*, *n*. any bird of the American genus Aramus, akin to the rails. [Fr., from a South American name.]
**course**, *kōrs*, *körs*, *n*. a run (*arch*.): path in which anything moves: the ground over which a race is run, golf is played, or the like: a channel for water: the direction pursued: a voyage: a race: regular progress from point to point: habitual method of procedure: a prescribed series, sequence, process, or treatment, as of lectures, training, pills, etc.: each of the successive divisions of a meal—soup, fish, etc.: conduct: a range of bricks or stones on the same level in building: in lute, etc., one of two or more strings tuned in unison or in octaves: in bell-ringing, the series of positions of a bell in the changing order in which a set of bells is struck: (*naut*.) one of the sails bent to a ship's lower yards (mainsail = *main course*: foresail = *fore course*: cross-jack = *mizzen course*): (in *pl*.) the menses.—*v.t*. to run, chase, or hunt after.—*v.i*. to run: to move with speed, as in a race or hunt.—*ns*. **cours'er**, a runner: a swift horse (*orig*. a charger): one who courses or hunts: a swift running bird (Cursorius); **cours'ing**, hunting with grey-hounds.—**cours'ing-joint**, a joint between two courses of masonry.—**in course**, in regular order: of course (*arch*.); **of course**, by natural consequence: indisputably, often a mere apology for making a statement. [Fr. *cours*—L. *cursus*, from *currēre*, *cursum*, to run.]
**court**, *kōrt*, *kört*, *n*. space enclosed: space surrounded by houses: a piece of ground or floor on which certain games are played: a division marked off by lines on such a place: the palace of a sovereign: the body of persons who form his suite or council: an assembly of courtiers: attention, civility, as 'to pay court': hall of justice (*law*): the judges and officials who preside there: any body of persons assembled to decide causes: a sitting of such a body: a court shoe.—*v.t*. to pay attentions to: to woo: to solicit: to seek.—*ns*. **court'ier**, one who frequents courts or palaces: one who courts or flatters; **court'ier-ism**, the behaviour or practices of a courtier.—*adj*. **and** *adv*. **court'ierlike**.—*adv*. **court'ierly**.—*ns*. **court'ing**, paying addresses, wooing: attendance at court (*Spens*.); **court'let**, a petty court.—*adj*. **court'like**, courtly: polite.—*ns*. **court'liness**; **court'ling**, a hanger-on at court.—*adj*. **court'ly**, having manners like those of, or befitting, a court: politely stately: fair and flattering.—*n*. **court'ship**, courtly behaviour: wooing.—**court'-bar'on**, the assembly of freehold tenants of a manor under a lord; **court'-card** (see **coat-card**); **court'craft**, the courtier's art, intrigue; **court'-**

**cup'board** (*Shak.*), a movable cupboard or side-board on which plate was displayed; **court'-day**, a day on which a judicial court sits; **court'-dress**, the special regulation costume worn on state or ceremonious occasions; **court'-dress'er** (*obs*.), a flatterer; **court'-fool**, a fool or jester, formerly kept at court for amusement; **court'-guide**, a guide to, or directory of, the names and residences of the nobility in a town; **court'-hand**, a modification of the Norman handwriting, as distinguished from the modern or Italian hand-writing, in use in the English law-courts from the 16th century to the reign of George II; **court'-house**, a building where the law-courts are held; **court'-leet**, a court of record held in a manor before the lord or his steward; **court'-mar'tial**, a court held by officers of the army, navy or air force for the trial of offences against service laws (one improvised in time of war round an up-turned drum for summary judgment was a **drumhead court-martial**):—*pl*. **courts'-mar'tial**; **court'-plas'ter**, sticking-plaster made of silk, originally applied as patches on the face by ladies at court; **court'-roll**, the record of a court of justice; **court shoe**, a light high-heeled dress shoe; **court'-sword**, a light sword worn as part of court-dress; **court tennis**, the old game of tennis, distinguished from lawn tennis; **court'-yard**, a court or enclosed ground attached to a house.—**court holy water** (*obs*.), empty compliments: flattery; **out of court**, without claim to be considered. [O.Fr. *cort* (Fr. *cour*)—L.L. *cortis*, a courtyard—L. *cors*, *cohors*, *-tis*, an enclosure; akin to Gr. *chortos*, an enclosed place; L. *hortus*, a garden. See **yard**.]
**Courtelle**, *kōōr-tel'*, *n*. synthetic acrylic woollen fibre. [Trademark.]
**courteous**, *kûrt'yəs*, *kört'yəs*, *adj*. polite, considerate or respectful in manner and action: obliging.—*adv*. **court'eously**.—*ns*. **court'eousness**; **court-esy** (*kûrt'*, or *kört'ə-si*), courteous behaviour: an act of civility or respect: a curtsy: the life interest of the surviving husband in his wife's estate (*law*).—*v.i*. to make a curtsy:—*pr.p*. **court'esy-ing**; *pa.t*. and *pa.p*. **court'esied**.—*n*. **courtesy title**, a title really invalid, but allowed by the usage of society—as to children of peers.—**remember your courtesy** (*obs*.), please put on your hat; **strain courtesy** (see **strain**). [O.Fr. *corteis*, *cortois*; see **court**.]
**courtesan**, **-zan**, *kört'*, *kûrt'i-zan*, or *-zan'*, *n*. a court mistress: a whore. [Fr. *courtisane*—It. *cortigiana*, orig. a woman of the court.]
**couscous**, *kōōs'kōōs*, **couscousou**, *-ōō'*, *n*. granulated wheat flour: a N. African dish of steamed couscous with meat, vegetables, etc. [Fr.,—Ar. *kuskus*—*kaskasa*, to pound; see **cuscus** (2).]
**cousin**, *kuz'n*, *n*. formerly a kinsman generally: now, the son or daughter of an uncle or aunt: a term used by a sovereign in addressing another, or to one of his own nobles: something kindred or related to another.—*ns*. **cous'inhood**, **cous'inship**.—*adj*. **cous'inly**, like, or having the relation of, a cousin.—*n*. **cous'inry**, cousins collectively.—**cous'in-ger'man**, a first cousin: something closely related.—**cross'-cous'in**, the son or daughter of one's father's sister or mother's brother; **first cousins**, children of brothers and sisters, full cousins; **first cousin once removed**, the son or daughter of a cousin-german—sometimes loosely called *second cousin*; **forty-second cousin**, vaguely, a distant relative; **second cousins**, the children of first cousins. [Fr.,—L. *consōbrīnus*—*con-*, sig. connection, and *sobrīnus*, applied to the children of sisters from the root of *soror*, a sister.]
**couter**, *kōō'tər*, (*slang*) *n*. a sovereign. [Said to be from Gypsy *cuta*, a gold piece.]
**couth**, *kōōth*, obsolete *pa.t*. and *pa.p*. of **can**: could: knew: known: did: sometimes used at

Neutral vowels in unaccented syllables: *el'ə-mənt*; for certain sounds in foreign words, see p. viii

present as back formation of **uncouth**, i.e. good-mannered, sophisticated, etc. [O.E. pa.t. *cūthe*, pa.p. *cūth*; see **could**.]

**couthie**, *kōōth'i*, (*Scot.*) *adj.* friendly, kindly: comfortable: snug. [Prob. O.E. *cūth*, known.]

**coutil, coutille**, *kōō-til'*, *n.* a strong cotton fabric used in mattresses, etc. [Fr. *coutil*.]

**couture**, *kōō-tür'*, in U.S. *-tōōr'*, *n.* dressmaking or dress designing.—*n.* **couturier** (*kōō-tür'-yā*, in U.S. *-tōōr-*), *fem.* **couturière** (*-yer'*), a dressmaker or dress designer. [Fr.]

**couvade**, *kōō-väd'*, *n.* a custom among savages in many parts of the world for the father to take to his bed at the birth of a child, and submit to certain restrictions of food, etc. [Erroneously attributed to the Basques; the O.Fr. *couvade*, from *couver*, to hatch, never having had this special meaning.]

**couvert**, *kōō-ver*, (Fr.) cover (at table).

**covalency**, *kō-vā'lən-si*, *n.* the union of two atoms by the sharing of a pair of electrons, one from each atom—cf. **electrovalency**.—*adj.* **covā'lent**. [L. *co-*, together, and **valency**.]

**cove**, *kōv*, *n.* a small inlet of the sea: a bay: a cavern or rocky recess: a curved junction of wall and ceiling (*archit.*).—*v.t.* to overarch.—*adj.* **coved**, formed with an arch.—*n.* **cove'let**, a small cove. [O.E. *cofa*, a room; O.N. *kofi*, Ger. *koben*.]

**cove**, *kōv*, (*slang*) *n.* a fellow, a customer:—*dim.* **cov'ey**. [Origin obscure.]

**covellite**, *kō-vel'it*, *kō'vəl-*, *n.* a blue mineral, cupric sulphide. [*Covelli*, its discoverer.]

**coven**, *kuv'in*, or *-ən*, *n.* a gathering of witches: a gang of thirteen witches. [See **coven**.]

**covenant**, *kuv'ə-nənt*, *n.* a mutual agreement: the writing containing the agreement: an engagement entered into between God and a person or a people—a dispensation, testament.—*v.i.* to enter into an agreement.—*v.t.* to agree to: to stipulate. —*adj.* **cov'enanted**, agreed to by covenant: bound by covenant: holding a position under a covenant or contract.—*ns.* **covenantee'**, the person to whom a covenant is made; **cov'enanter** (usually in Scotland, *kuv-ə-nant'ər*), one who signed or adhered to the *Scottish National Covenant* of 1638 (the *Solemn League and Covenant* of 1643 was in effect an international treaty between Scotland and England for securing civil and religious liberty); **cov'enantor**, that party to a covenant who subjects himself to the penalty of its breach.—**covenant of grace**, redemption, in Christian theology, that by which life is freely offered to sinners on condition of faith in Christ; **covenant of works**, that made with Adam as federal representative of the human race on condition of obedience. [O.Fr.,—L. *con-*, together, and *venire*, to come.]

**covent**, *kov'ənt*, *kuv'ənt*, (*Shak.*) *n.* a variant of **convent**.

**Coventry**, *kov'*, *kuv'ənt-ri*, a town of Warwickshire.—**Coventry blue**, a blue thread once made there.—**send to Coventry**, to exclude from social intercourse.

**cover**, *kuv'ər*, *v.t.* to put or spread something on, over or about: to come or be on, over or about: to hide: to clothe: to protect: to screen: to brood or sit on: to suffice for: to provide for or against: to comprise: to traverse: to take as field of operations: to play a higher card upon: to table upon a coin of equal value in wagering: to set as for a meal: to copulate with—esp. of a stallion: to command with a weapon: to report. —*v.i.* to lay a table for a meal (*obs.*): to put one's hat on.—*n.* that which covers or is intended to cover: a lid: the binding of a book: an envelope: undergrowth, thicket, concealing game, etc.: the table requisites for one person— plate, knife, fork, napkin, etc.: a pretext: a disguise: a confederate: a cover point.—*n.*

**cov'erage**, area or (*fig.*) amount covered or included: the group or section of the community reached by an advertising medium: risks covered by an insurance: amount available to cover liabilities.—*adj.* **cov'ered**, having a cover: sheltered, concealed: roofed over: with a hat on.—*n.* **cov'ering**, anything that covers.—*adj.* **cov'ert**, covered: concealed: secret: concealing (*Spens.*).—*n.* a feather covering the quill-bases of wings and tail: (usu. pron. *kuv'ər*) a cover for game: a shelter.—*adv.* **cov'ertly**, in a covered or concealed manner.—*n.* **cov'erture**, covering, shelter: disguise: secret proceedings (*Spens.*): the condition of a married woman as legally deemed under the protection of her husband (*law*).—**cov'erall** (*U.S.*), a boiler suit; **cover charge**, a charge per person made by a restaurant, in addition to charge for food; **cover crop**, a subsidiary crop grown partly to protect the soil; **covered wagon**, a large wagon with bonnet-shaped canvas hood, esp. that used by pioneers to the American West: symbol of pioneering spirit; **covered way, covert way** (*fort.*), a path outside the ditch of a fort, sunk below the crest of the glacis to afford cover; **cover girl**, a girl pictured on a magazine cover; **covering letter**, letter to explain documents enclosed with it; **cover glass**, a thin glass placed over the object on a microscope slide; **cover point**, in cricket, etc., the player who supports point and stands to his right: the position of such a player; **cov'er slut**, an outer garment worn to hide rags or dirty clothes; **covert coat**, a short light overcoat; **covert coating**, cloth for such.—**cover in**, to fill in: to complete the covering of, esp. of roof of building; **cover into**, to transfer into; **cover shorts**, to buy in such stocks as have been sold short, in order to meet one's engagements, etc.; **cover the buckle**, to execute a certain difficult step in dancing; **cover up**, to cover completely: to conceal, withhold information (*coll.*).—*n.* **cover-up**. [Fr. *couvrir* (It. *coprire*)—L. *co-operire—co-*, and *operire*, to cover.]

**coverlet**, *kuv'ər-lit*, *n.* a bedcover.—Also **cov'erlid**. [Fr. *couvrir*, to cover, *lit* (L. *lectum*), a bed.]

**covet**, *kuv'it*, *v.t.* to desire or wish for eagerly: to wish for wrongfully.—*v.i.* (*Shak.*) to desire (with *for*):—*pr.p.* **cov'eting**; *pa.t.* and *pa.p.* **cov'eted**.— *adjs.* **cov'etable**; **cov'eted**.—*adv.* **cov'etingly**.— *ns.* **cov'etise** (*obs.*), covetousness: ardent desire; **cov'etiveness** (*obs.*), acquisitiveness.—*adj.* **cov'etous**, inordinately desirous: avaricious.—*adv.* **cov'etously**.—*n.* **cov'etousness**. [O.Fr. *coveit(i)er* (Fr. *convoiter*)—L. *cupiditās*, *-ātis—cupĕre*, to desire.]

**covey**, *kuv'i*, *n.* a brood or hatch of partridges: a small flock of game birds: a party, a set. [O.Fr. *covée*—L. *cubāre*, to lie down.]

**covin, covyne**, *kōv'in*, *kuv'in*, *n.* a compact (*arch.*): a conspiracy: a fraud.—*adj.* **covinous** (*kuv'*) (*arch.*), fraudulent.—*n.* **cov'in-tree'**, a tree before a Scottish mansion at which guests were met and parted from. [O.Fr. *covin*.—L.L. *convenium* —*con-*, together, *venire*, to come.]

**coving**, *kō'ving*, *n.* the projection of upper storeys over lower: the vertical sides connecting the jambs with the breast of a fireplace. [See **cove**.]

**cow, kow**, *n.* the female of the bovine animals: the female of certain other animals, as the elk, elephant, whale, etc.: (*vulg.*): an ugly, ungainly, or slovenly woman (*vulg.*): an objectionable or rather despicable person or thing (*Austr. slang*): a trying situation or occurrence (usu. *a fair cow*) (*Austr. slang*):—*pl.* **cows**, older **kine** (*kīn*) and (still in *Scots*) **kye** (*kī*).—*adj.* **cow'ish**, like a cow: cowardly (*Shak.*).—**cow'bane**, the water hemlock (*Cicuta virosa*), often destructive to cattle; **cow'bell**, a bell for a cow's neck; **cow'berry**, the red whortleberry (*Vaccinium vitis-idaea*), **cow'-**

bird, cow black'bird, an American bird (*Molothrus*) of the troupial family, that accompanies cattle, and drops its eggs into other birds' nests; cow'boy, a boy who has the care of cows: a man who has the charge of cattle on a ranch (*U.S.*): a rodeo performer (*U.S.*): a young inexperienced lorry-driver, or anyone who drives an unsafe or overloaded lorry (*slang*):—*fem.* cow'girl; cow'-calf, a female calf; cow'catcher (*U.S.*), an apparatus on the front of a railway engine to throw off obstacles; cow cocky (see cockatoo); cow'-cher'vil, -pars'ley, -weed, wild chervil; cow'feeder, a dairyman; cow'fish, a coffer-fish (with cowlike head): a manati: any small cetacean; cow'grass, perennial red clover: zigzag clover; cow'hand, cow'heel, an oxfoot stewed to a jelly; cow'herd, one who herds cows; cow'hide, the hide of a cow: the hide of a cow made into leather: a coarse whip made of twisted strips of cowhide.—*v.t.* to whip with a cowhide.—cow'house, a building in which cows are stalled, a byre; cow'-leech, a cow-doctor; cow'lick, a tuft of turned-up hair on the forehead; cow'-pars'nip, an umbelliferous plant, hogweed (*Heracleum sphondylium*) used as fodder; cow'-pea, a leguminous plant (*Vigna sinensis*) of Asia, used like French beans; cow'-pil'ot, a West Indian demoiselle fish, said to accompany the cowfish; cow'-plant, an asclepiadaceous plant of Ceylon (*Gymnema lactiferum*) with a milky juice; cow'poke (*U.S.*), a cowboy; cow'pox, a disease that appears in pimples on the teats of the cow, the matter thereof used for vaccination; cow'puncher, a cowboy: a driver of cows; cow'shed, a cowhouse; cow'-tree, a South American tree (*Brosimum galactodendron*) of the mulberry family, that produces a nourishing fluid resembling milk; cow'-wheat, a yellow flowered scrophulariaceous plant (*Melampyrum*), with seeds somewhat like grains of wheat.—till the cows come home, for a long time of unforseeable duration. [O.E. *cū*, pl. *cȳ*; Ger. *kuh*; Sans. *go*, a bull, cow.]

cow, kow, *kow*, (*Scot.*) *n.* a branch, bunch of twigs, besom. [Poss. O.Fr. *coe*—L. *cauda*, tail.]

cow, kow, *v.t.* to subdue the spirit of: to keep under.—*adj.* cowed, abjectly depressed or intimidated. [Perh. from O.N. *kūga*; Dan. *kue*, to subdue.]

cow, kow, (*Dickens*) *n.* a chimney cowl. [A variant of cowl (1).]

cowan, kow'ən, (*Scot.*) *n.* a dry-stone-diker: a mason who never served an apprenticeship: one who tries to enter a Freemason's lodge, or the like, surreptitiously. [Origin doubtful.]

coward, kow'ərd, *n.* a reprehensibly faint-hearted person: one without courage: often applied to one who, whether courageous or not, brutally takes advantage of the weak.—*v.t.* to make cowardly.—*adj.* cowardly; with tail between legs (*her.*).—*ns.* cow'ardice (-*is*), want of courage: timidity; cow'ardliness.—*adj.* cow'ardly, having the character of a coward: befitting a coward: characteristic of a coward.—*adv.* like a coward: with cowardice.—*ns.* cow'ardry (*Spens.* cowardree) cow'ardship (*Shak.*). [O.Fr. *couard* (It. *codardo*)—L. *cauda*, a tail.]

cowdie-gum; -pine; cowrie-pine. See kauri.

cower, kow'ər, *v.i.* to sink down through fear, etc.: to crouch shrinkingly.—*adv.* cow'eringly. [Cf. O.N. *kūra*, Dan. *kure*, to lie quiet.]

cowhage, cowage, cowitch, kow'ij, -ich, *n.* a tropical leguminous climber (Mucuna): the stinging hairs on its pod, used as a vermifuge: its pods. [Hindi *kavăc.*]

cowheard, cowherd, Spenserian spellings of coward.

cowl, kowl, *n.* a cap or hood: a monk's hood: the badge of monkhood: a monk: a cover for a chimney: an engine bonnet: a cowling.—*v.t.* to make a monk of: to cover like a cowl.—*adj.*

cowled, wearing a cowl.—*n.* cowl'ing, the casing of an aeroplane engine. [O.E. *cugele*; O.N. *kofl*; akin to L. *cucullus*, hood.]

cowl, kōl, *kōōl*, kowl, (*dial.* or *arch*:) *n.* a tub or large vessel for liquids.—*n.* cowl'-staff (*Shak.*), a pole on which a basket or vessel is slung. [O.E. *cūfel* or O.Fr. *cuvele*, both—L. *cūpella*, dim. of *cūpa*, a cask.]

cowp, kowp. See coup (2).

cowrie, cowry, kow'ri, *n.* a large genus (Cypraea) of gasteropods used among primitive people as money and magical objects. [Hindi *kauṛi.*]

cowslip, kow'slip, *n.* a species of primrose, with flowers in umbels, common in pastures: in U.S., the marsh-marigold.—*adj.* cow'slip'd, covered with cowslips. [O.E. *cūslyppe*—*cū*, cow, *slyppe*, slime, i.e. cow-dung.]

cox, koks, a shortened form of coxswain.

coxa, koks'a, *n.* the hip: the proximal joint of an arthropod's leg.—*adj.* cox'al.—*n.* coxal'gia (*ji-a*), pain in the hip. [L.]

coxcomb, koks'kōm, *n.* a strip of red cloth notched like a cock's comb, which professional fools used to wear: the head (*Shak.*): a fool: a fop.—*adjs.* coxcombic (-*kōm'*, -*kom'*), -al, coxcom'ical, foppish: vain.—*n.* coxcombical'ity.—*adv.* coxcomb'ically.—*n.* cox'combry, the manner of a coxcomb. [cock's comb.]

coxiness. See cock (1).

coxswain, cockswain, kok'sn, or kok'swān, *n.* one who steers a boat: a petty officer in charge of a boat and crew.—*v.t.* and *v.i.* to act as coxswain (for).—Often contr. cox. [cock, a boat, and swain.]

coxy. See cock (1).

coy, koi, *adj.* bashful: affectedly shy.—*v.t.* to caress (*Shak.*): to disdain (*Shak.*): to affect coyness (with *it*) (*arch.*).—*adj.* coy'ish.—*adv.* coy'ishly.—*n.* coy'ishness.—*adv.* coy'ly.—*n.* coy'ness. [Fr. *coi*—L. *quiētus*, quiet.]

coyote, kō-yō'tä, ki-ōt'ē, ki'ōt, *n.* a prairie-wolf; a small wolf of N. America:—*pl.* coyotes or coyote. [Mex. *coyotl.*]

coypu, koi'pōō, or -pōō', *n.* a large South American aquatic rodent (Myopotamus) yielding nutria fur—now found wild in East Anglia. [Native name.]

coystrel, coystril. Same as coistril.

coz, kuz, *n.* a contraction of cousin.

coze, kōz, *v.i.* to chat.—Also *n.* [Fr. *causer*.]

cozen, kuz'n, *v.t.* to cheat.—*ns.* coz'enage, deceit; coz'ener. [Perh. Fr. *cousiner*, to claim kindred; see cousin.]

cozier, cosier, kō'zi-ər, (*Shak.*) *n.* a cobbler. [O.Fr. *cousere*, tailor—L. *cōnsuĕre*, to sew together.]

cozy. See cosy.

crab, krab, *n.* any of the Brachyura or short-tailed decapod crustaceans: Cancer (sign of the zodiac and constellation): a portable winch: (in *pl.*) the lowest throw at hazard—two aces: a crab-louse.—*v.i.* to drift or fly sideways: to fish for crabs.—*adjs.* and *advs.* crab'like; crab'-wise.—crab'-eat'er, a sergeant-fish: an antarctic seal.—*adj.* crab'-faced, having a peevish countenance.—crab'-louse, a crab-shaped louse infesting the hair of the pubis, etc.—crab's'-eyes, crab'-stones, prayer-beads, the scarlet and black seeds of the Indian liquorice tree (*Abrus precatorius*): a limy concretion in the cray-fish's stomach.—*v.i.* crab'-si'dle, to go sideways like a crab.—crab'-yaws, framboesia tumours on the soles and palms.—catch a crab, to sink the oar too deeply (or not enough) in the water and fall back in consequence. [O.E. *crabba*; Ger. *krebs*.]

crab, krab, *n.* a wild bitter apple: a sour-tempered person.—*ns.* crab'-apple; crab'stick; crab'-tree. [Ety. doubtful.]

crab, krab, *v.t.* (of hawks) to claw: to decry,

criticise: to obstruct, wreck, or frustrate.—*n.*
dejection: fault-finding. [**crab** (1).]
**crabbed,** *krab'id, adj.* ill-natured: harsh: rough
(*arch.*): crooked (*arch.*): undecipherable:
cramped.—*adv.* **crabb'edly.**—*n.* **crabb'edness.**—
*adj.* **crabb'y.** [**crab** (1) intermixed in meaning
with **crab** (2).]
**crab-nut, -oil, -wood.** See **carapa.**
**crack,** *krak, v.t.* and *v.i.* to make or cause to make
a sharp sudden sound: to break into chinks: to
split: to break partially or suddenly: (of
petroleum, etc.) to break into simpler molecules:
to boast (*obs.*).—*v.i.* (*Scot.*) to chat.—*v.t.* to
break open (as safe): to solve the mystery of (a
code).—*n.* a sudden sharp splitting sound: a
chink: a flaw: a blow, a smack: a moment:
break (of day): a friendly chat (*Scot.*): house-
breaking (*slang*): an expert: a pert boy (*Shak.*):
a quip: a try (*slang*).—*adj.* (*coll.*) excellent:
expert.—*adj.* **cracked,** rent: damaged: crazy.—
*n.* **crack'er,** one who or that which cracks: a
boaster, a lie: the pin-tail duck: a thin crisp
biscuit (esp. *U.S.*): a gay favour-filled tubular
package that explodes when the ends are pulled:
a firework tied zigzagwise that bounces at each
explosion; a poor white (*U.S.*): a curl-paper
or curling rag: a rapid pace (*slang*).—*adj.*
**crack'ers,** crazy: unbalanced.—**crack'brain,** a
crazy person.—*adj.* **crack'brained.**—**crack'er-
jack, crack'ajack,** a person or thing of highest
excellence.—Also *adj.*—*adj.* **crack'er-barr'el**
(*U.S.*), of homely philosophy.—**crack'-halt'er,
crack'-hemp, crack'-rope** (*obs.*), one likely or
deserving to be hanged.—*adj.* **crack'jaw,** hard to
pronounce.—**crack'pot,** a crazy person.—Also
*adj.*—**cracks'man,** a burglar; **crack'-tryst** (*obs.*),
one who breaks an engagement.—**crack a
bottle,** open or drink a bottle; **crack a crib**
(*thieves' slang*), to break into a building; **crack a
joke,** to utter a joke with some effect; **crack
credit,** to destroy one's credit; **crack down on,**
to take firm action against; **crack the whip,** to
assert authority suddenly or forcibly; **crack up,**
to praise: to fail suddenly, to go to pieces; **fair
crack of the whip,** a fair opportunity; **get cracking,** to get moving quickly. [O.E. *cracian,* to
crack; cf. Du. *kraken,* Gael. *crac.*]
**crackle,** *krak'l, v.i.* to give out slight but frequent
cracks.—*n.* the giving out of slight cracks: a
kind of china-ware, purposely cracked in the
kiln as an ornament.—*n.* **crack'ling,** the rind of
roast pork: (in *pl.*) skinny part of suet without
tallow.—*adj.* **crack'ly,** brittle.—*n.* **crack'nel,** a
light, brittle biscuit: (in *pl.*) pieces of fat pork
fried crisp. [Freq. of **crack.**]
**Cracovian,** *kra-kō'vi-ən, adj.* pertaining to Cracow.
—*ns.* **cracovienne** (-*en'*), a lively Polish dance:
music for it, in 2-4 time.—Also **krako'wiak;**
**cracowe** (*krak'ow*), a long-toed boot fashionable
under Richard II.
**cradle,** *krā'dl, n.* a bed or crib in which a child is
rocked: infancy (*fig.*): place of origin or
nurture: a framework, esp. one for keeping
bedclothes from pressing on a patient, or one
under a ship for launching: a rocking box for
gold-washing: an engraver's knife used with a
rocking motion.—*v.t.* to lay or rock in a cradle:
to nurture.—*n.* **crā'dling.**—*ns.* **crā'dle-scythe,**
a broad scythe used in a cradle framework for
cutting grain; **crā'dlewalk** (*obs.*), an avenue
arched over with trees. [O.E. *cradol;* ety.
obscure.]
**craft,** *kräft, n.* cunning: artifice (*obs.*): dexterity:
art: skilled trade: occupation: a ship or ships
(of any kind, orig. small): aircraft, spacecraft.—
*v.i.* to exercise one's craft (Shak., *Cor.* IV, vi.
118).—*v.t.* to make or construct, esp. with careful
skill.—*adj.* **craft'y,** having skill: cunning: wily:
(see **arty-crafty**).—*adv.* **craft'ily.**—*n.* **craft'iness.**
—*adj.* **craft'less,** free from craft: unskilled in

any craft.—*ns.* **craft'-broth'er,** a person engaged
in the same trade as another; **craft'-guild,** an
association of men engaged in the same trade.—
*ns.* **crafts'man,** one engaged in a craft; **crafts'-
manship, craft'manship; crafts'master** (*obs.*),
one skilled in a craft. [O.E. *cræft;* Ger. *kraft,*
power.]
**crag,** *krag, n.* a rough steep rock or point: a
shelly deposit mixed with sand, found in the
Pliocene of East Anglia (*geol.*).—*adj.* **cragg'ed,**
craggy.—*ns.* **cragg'edness, cragg'iness.**—*adj.*
**cragg'y,** full of crags or broken rocks: rough:
rugged.—*n.* **crag'-and-tail'** (*geol.*), a hill-form
with steep declivity at one end and a gentle slope
at the other.—*adj.* **crag'fast,** unable to move
from a position on a crag.—*n.* **crags'man,** one
skilled in climbing rocks. [App. conn. with
Gael. *creag, carraig.*]
**crag,** *krag, n.* neck: throat. [Cf. Du. *kraag,* Ger.
*kragen,* the neck.]
**craig,** *krāg, n.* Scots form of **crag** (cliff) and of
**crag** (neck).—**craig'fluke,** the witch (*Pleuronectes cynoglossus*), a flat fish.
**crake,** *krāk,* (*dial.*) *n.* a crow, a raven: a corncrake: a croak: the cry of the corncrake.—*v.i.*
to utter a crake.—**crake'-berry,** crowberry. [Cf.
**corncrake, croak.**]
**crake,** *krāk,* (*Spens.*) *n., v.t.* and *v.i.* boast. [**crack.**]
**cram,** *kram, v.t.* to press close: to stuff: to fill to
superfluity: to overfeed: to feed with a view to
fattening: to make believe false or exaggerated
tales (*slang*): to teach, or get up, hastily for a
certain occasion (as an examination, a lawsuit),
to the extent required for the occasion.—*v.i.* to
eat greedily: to get up by cramming:—*pr.p.*
**cramm'ing;** *pa.t.* and *pa.p.* **crammed.**—*n.* a
crush: a lie (*slang*): information that has been
crammed: the system of cramming.—*adjs.*
**cram'-full; cramm'able; crammed.**—*n.* **cramm'-
er,** a person or machine that crams poultry:
one who crams pupils or a subject: a lie (*slang*).
[O.E. *crammian;* O.N. *kremja,* to squeeze; Dan.
*kramme,* to crumple.]
**crambo,** *kram'bō, n.* a game in which one gives a
word to which another finds a rhyme: rhyme.—
*ns.* **cram'boclink, -jingle,** rhyming. [Prob. from
L. *crambē repetita,* cabbage served up again.]
**crame,** *krām,* (*Scot.*) *n.* a booth for selling goods.
[From Du. or Low Ger.]
**cramoisy, cramesy,** *kram'az-i* (or -*oi-zi*), *adj.* and
*n.* crimson. [See **crimson.**]
**cramp,** *kramp, n.* an involuntary and painful contraction of a voluntary muscle or group of
muscles (in U.S. often in *pl.*): restraint: cramp-
iron: a contrivance with a movable part that
can be screwed tight so as to press things together.
—*adj.* hard to make out (used of handwriting):
cramped: narrow.—*v.t.* to affect with spasms:
to confine: to hamper: to fasten with a cramp-
iron.—*ns.* **cramp'et, cramp'it,** a scabbard-chape:
a cramp-iron: a crampon: an iron foot-board
for curlers; **cramp'on,** a grappling-iron: a
spiked contrivance for climbing mountains or
telegraph poles or walking on ice.—*adj.* **cramp'y,**
affected or diseased with cramp: producing
cramp.—**cramp'-bark** (*U.S.*), the guelder-rose, or
its medicinal bark; **cramp'-bone,** the patella of
the sheep, an old charm for cramp; **cramp'-fish,**
the electric ray or torpedo; **cramp'-iron,** a piece
of metal bent at both ends for binding things
together; **cramp'-ring,** a ring formerly blessed by
the sovereign on Good-Friday against cramp and
falling sickness.—**bather's cramp,** paralysis
attacking a bather; **writer's cramp,** or
*scrivener's palsy,* a common disease affecting
those in the habit of constant writing, the
muscles refusing to obey only when an attempt
to write is made.—**cramp one's style,** to restrict
one's movements or actions. [O.Fr. *crampe;* cf.
Du. *kramp,* Ger. *krampf.*]

**cran**, *kran*, *n.* a measure of capacity for herrings just landed in port—37½ gallons.—**coup the cran** (*Scot.*), to upset, or be upset, as plans. [Prob. from Gael. *crann*, a measure.]

**cranberry**, *kran'bər-i*, *n.* the red acid berry of a small evergreen shrub (*Vaccinium Oxycoccos*; Ericaceae) growing in peaty bogs and marshy grounds: the larger berry of an American species (*V. macrocarpum*): extended loosely to other species of the genus: the shrub itself.—**cran'-berry-tree** (*U.S.*), the guelder-rose. [For *craneberry*; a late word; origin obscure; cf. Ger. *kranbeere* or *kranichbeere*.]

**cranch**, *kranch*, *n.* and *v.t.* Same as **crunch**.

**crane**, *krān*, *n.* any bird of the Gruidae, large wading birds with long legs, neck, and bill: a bent pipe for drawing liquor out of a cask: a machine for raising heavy weights—both named from their likeness to the bird.—*v.t.* to raise with a crane: to stretch as a crane does its neck.—*v.i.* to stretch out the neck: to pull up before a jump.—*n.* **crān'age**, the use of a crane: the price paid for the use of it.—**crane'-fly**, a fly (Tipula) with very long legs.—**the daddy-long-legs.**—*adj.* **crane'-necked.**—**cranes'bill**, **crane's'-bill**, any wild species of Geranium, from the beaked fruit. [O.E. *cran*; Ger. *kranich*, W. *garan*.]

**crane.** Same as **cranium.**

**cranium**, *krā'ni-əm*, *n.* the skull: the bones enclosing the brain:—*pl.* **crā'nia.**—*adj.* **crā'nial.** —*n.pl.* **Crāniā'ta** (*zool.*), the main division of Chordata, having a cranium.—*n.* **crāniog'nomy**, cranial physiognomy.—*adj.* **crāniolog'ical.**—*ns.* **crāniol'ogist**; **crāniol'ogy**, the study of skulls: phrenology; **crāniom'eter**, an instrument for measuring the skull; **crāniom'etry**; **crānios'-copist**, a phrenologist; **crānios'copy**, phrenology; **crāniot'omy** (Gr. *tomē*, a cut; *obstetrics*), the act of breaking down the head of the foetus.—**cranial index**, the breadth of a skull as a percentage of the length. [L.L. *crānium*—Gr. *krānion*, the skull.]

**crank**, *krangk*, *n.* a crook or bend: a conceit in speech: a whim: a faddist: an arm on a shaft for communicating motion to or from the shaft (*mach.*).—*v.i.* to move in a zigzag manner: to turn a crank (often with *up*).—*v.t.* to shape like a crank: to provide with a crank: to move or seek to move by turning a crank.—*adj.* **crooked**: **crabbed**: loose or slack.—*adv.* **crank'ily.**—*n.* **crank'iness.**—*adj.* **crank'y**, crooked: infirm: full of whims: cross.—**crank'case**, a box-like casing for the crankshaft and connecting-rods of some types of reciprocating-engine; **crank'shaft**, the main shaft of an engine or other machine, which carries a crank or cranks for the attachment of connecting rods. [O.E. *cranc*, cf. Ger. *krank*.]

**crank**, *krangk*, *adj.* brisk: merry.—Also *adv.* [Origin unknown.]

**crank**, *krangk*, **crank-sided**, *krangk-sī'did*, (*naut.*) *adj.* liable to be upset.—*n.* **crank'ness**, liability to be upset. [Ety. uncertain.]

**crankle**, *krangk'l*, *n.* a turn, winding, or wrinkle, an angular protuberance.—*v.t.* and *v.i.* to bend: to twist. [Freq. of **crank.**]

**crannog**, *kran'og*, *n.* in Scotland and Ireland a fortified island (partly natural and partly artificial) in a lake: a lake-dwelling. [Gael. *crann*, a tree.]

**cranny**, *kran'i*, *n.* a rent: a chink: a secret place. —*v.i.* to enter crannies.—*adj.* **crann'ied**, having crannies, rents, or fissures. [Fr. *cran*, a notch.]

**cranreuch**, *krän'ruhh*, (*Scot.*) *n.* hoar-frost. [Origin obscure; poss. from Gaelic.]

**crants**, *krants*, (*Shak.*) *n.* the garland carried before the bier of a maiden and hung over her grave. [Ger. *kranz*, a wreath, a garland.]

**crap**, *krap*, *kräp*, *n.* Scots form of **crop.**—*v.t.* to crop: to cram, stuff.—**crappit-head, -heid** (*krap'-*

*it-hēd*, *kräp'*), a haddock's head stuffed with a compound of oatmeal, suet, onions, and pepper.

**crap**, *krap*, *n.* money (*obs. slang*): excrement (*vulg.*): rubbish (*slang*): nonsense (*slang*). —*v.i.* to defecate (*vulg.*). [O.Du. *krappe.*]

**crape**, *krāp*, *n.* a thin silk fabric, tightly twisted, without removing the natural gum—usually dyed black, used for mournings.—*adj.* made of crape.—*v.t.* to clothe with crape: to frizzle (hair). —*adj.* **crap'y.**—**crapehanger, crepehanger** (*coll.*), a pessimist. [O.Fr. *crespe* (Fr. *crêpe*)—L. *crispus*, crisp.]

**craple**, *krap'l*, (*Spens.*) *n.* Same as **grapple.**

**craps**, *kraps*, *n.*, used as if *sing.*, a gambling game in which a player rolls two dice.—**shooting craps**, playing this game. [**crab** (1), lowest throw at hazard.]

**crapulence**, *krap'ū-ləns*, *n.* sickness caused by excessive drinking: intemperance.—*adjs.* **crap'-ulent**, **crap'ulous.**—*n.* **crapulos'ity.** [Fr. *crapule* —L. *crāpula*, intoxication.]

**crare**, **crayer**, *krār*, *n.* a trading vessel. [O.Fr. *craier.*]

**crash**, *krash*, *n.* a noise as of things breaking or being crushed by falling: the shock of two bodies meeting: the failure of a commercial undertaking: a fall or rush to destruction.—*adj.* intended to lessen effects of a crash: planned to meet an emergency quickly: involving suddenness, or speed, great effort.—*v.i.* to fall to pieces with a loud noise: to move with such a noise: to come to grief: (of aircraft) to alight with damage. —*v.t.* to dash in pieces: to drive to a crash: to intrude upon uninvited.—**crash'-dive'**, a sudden dive of a submarine; **crash'-helmet**, a cushioned safety head-dress for racing-motorists, etc.—*v.i.* and *v.t.* **crash'-land**, to land (an aircraft) in such a way as to damage it seriously.—**crash'-landing**; **crash'pad**, padding inside a motor vehicle to protect the occupants in case of accident.—*adj.* **crash'-proof.** [From the sound.]

**crash**, *krash*, *n.* a coarse strong linen. [Perh. from Russ.]

**crasis**, *krā'sis*, *n.* the mixture of different elements in the constitution of the body: temperament: the mingling or contraction of two vowels into one long vowel, or into a diphthong (*gram.*):—*pl.* **crā'sēs** (*-sēz*). [Gr. *krāsis*, mixture.]

**crass**, *kras*, *adj.* gross: thick: dense: stupid.—*ns.* **crassament'um**, the thick part of coagulated blood: the clot; **crass'itude**, coarseness: density: stupidity.—*adv.* **crass'ly.**—*n.* **crass'ness.** —*n.pl.* **Crassūlā'ceae**, a family of succulent plants including stone-crop and house-leek. [L. *crassus.*]

**Crataegus**, *kra-tē'gəs*, *n.* the hawthorn genus. [Latinised from Gr. *krataigos.*]

**cratch**, *krach*, *n.* a crib to hold hay for cattle, a manger.—*n.pl.* **cratches**, a swelling on a horse's pastern, under the fetlock. [Fr. *crèche*, manger; from a Gmc. root, whence also **crib.**]

**crate**, *krāt*, *n.* a wicker-work case for packing crockery in, or for carrying fruit: a packing-case: an open frame-work of spars: a decrepit aeroplane or car.—*v.t.* to pack in a crate. [L. *crātis*, a hurdle.]

**crater**, *krāt'ər*, *n.* a large bowl for mixing wine (*ant.*): the mouth of a volcano: a hole in the ground where a meteor has fallen, or a shell, mine, or bomb exploded: a cavity formed in the carbon of an electric arc.—*n.* **Crāterell'us**, a genus of funnel-shaped fungi.—*adjs.* **crateriform** (*krat-er'i-förm*, or *krā't er-i-förm*), cup-shaped: **crat'erous**—**crater lake**, one formed in the crater of an extinct volcano. [L.,—Gr. *krāter*, a mixing bowl.]

**cratur**, *krā'tər*, (Ir. and Scot.) *n.* creature—**the cratur**, whisky.

**craunch**, *krönch*. A form of **crunch.**

**cravat**, *krə-vat'*, *n.* neckcloth worn chiefly by men.

—*v.t.* to dress in a cravat. [Fr. *cravate*—introduced in 1636 from the *Cravates* or Croatians.] **crave**, *krāv*, *v.t.* to beg earnestly: to beseech: to require: to long for.—*n.* a longing: a claim (*Scots law*).—*ns.* **crav'er**, one who craves: a beggar: **crav'ing**, a longing. [O.E. *crafian*, to crave; O.N. *krefja*.] **craven**, *krāv'n*, *n.* a coward: a spiritless fellow.—*adj.* cowardly: spiritless.—*v.t.* (*Shak.*) to render spiritless.—*adv.* **crav'enly**.—*n.* **crav'enness**.—to cry craven, to surrender. [Origin obscure.] **craw**, *krö*, *n.* the crop, throat, or first stomach of fowls: the stomach of animals generally. [M.E. *crawe*; not found in O.E.; cf. Du. *kraag*, neck.] **crawfish**. See crayfish. **crawl**, *kröl*, *v.i.* to move slowly with the body on or close to the ground: to move on hands and knees: to creep: to move slowly or stealthily: to behave abjectly: to warp: to be covered with crawling things: to swim using the crawl stroke. —*n.* the act of crawling: a slow pace: an alternate overhand swimming stroke.—*n.* **crawl'-er**, one who or that which crawls: an abject person: a sluggish person: a creeping thing: a cab moving slowly in hope of a fare: a caterpillar tractor: a baby's overall.—*n.* **crawl'-ing**.—*adj.* creeping: lousy, verminous.—*adj.* **craw'ly** (*coll.*), with, or like the feeling of, something crawling over one: creepy. [Scand.; O.N. *krafla*, to paw; Dan. *kravle*.] **crawl**, *kröl*, *n.* a pen for keeping fish: a kraal. **Crax**, *kraks*, *n.* the curassow genus of birds. **crayfish**, *krā'fish*, **crawfish**, *krö'fish*, *n.* a large fresh-water decapod crustacean: the Norway lobster: the spiny lobster. [M.E. *crevice*—O.Fr. *crevice* (Fr. *écrevisse*, a crayfish)—O.H.G. *krebiz*, a crab.] **crayon**, *krā'ən*, *n.* a pencil made of chalk or pipeclay, variously coloured, used for drawing: a drawing done with crayons.—*v.t.* to draw with a crayon.—**in crayons**, of a picture, made by crayons. [Fr. *crayon*—*craie*, chalk, from L. *crēta*, chalk.] **craze**, *krāz*, *v.t.* to shatter (*Milt.*): to crack: to cover with fine cracks (as pottery): to weaken: to impair: to derange (the intellect).—*v.i.* to develop fine cracks: to become mad.—*n.* a crack, flaw: a finely cracked condition: insanity: fashion, fad: a small structural defect in plastic. —*adj.* **crazed**.—*adv.* **craz'ily**.—*n.* **craz'iness**.—*adj.* **craz'y**, frail: cracked: insane: demented: fantastically composed of irregular pieces (as a quilt or pavement).—**crazing mill**, a mill for crushing tin-ore. [Scand.; cf. Sw. *krasa*, Dan. *krase*, to crackle; also Fr. *écraser*, to crush.] **creagh**, **creach**, *krehh*, *n.* a foray: booty. [Gael. *creach*.] **creak**, *krēk*, *v.i.* to make a sharp, grating sound, as of a hinge, etc.—*n.* a grating noise, as of an unoiled hinge.—*adv.* **creak'ily**.—*adj.* **creak'y**. [From the sound, like *crake*, and *croak*.] **cream**, *krēm*, *n.* the oily substance that rises on milk, yielding butter when churned: that which rises to the top: the best part of anything: any cream-like substance, as *cold cream* for the skin, etc., or any dish largely made of cream, or like cream, as *chocolate-cream*, *ice-cream*, *whipped-cream*, etc.—*v.t.* to take off the cream from: to treat with cream: to make creamy.—*v.i.* to gather or form as or like cream.—*adj.* of the colour of cream: prepared with cream: of sherry, sweet.—*ns.* **cream'ery**, an establishment where butter and cheese are made from the milk supplied by a number of producers: a shop for milk, butter, etc.; **cream'iness**.—*adj.* **cream'y**, full of or like cream: gathering like cream.—**cream'-cake**, a kind of cake filled with creamy material, etc.; **cream'-cheese'**, cheese made with cream.—*adjs.* **cream'-coloured**, of the colour of cream, light yellow; **cream'-faced**, pale-faced;

**cream'-laid**, of a cream-colour or white with a laid water-mark.—**cream'-nut**, the Brazil nut; **cream'-slice**, a wooden blade for skimming cream from milk.—*adj.* **cream'-wove**, of a cream-colour or white, and wove.—**cream of tartar**, a white crystalline compound made by purifying argol, potassium hydrogen tartrate; **cream of tartar tree**, the baobab: an Australian tree of the same genus. [O.Fr. *cresme*, *creme*—L. *chrisma*—Gr. *chrisma*, unction.] **creance**, *krē'əns*, *n.* the cord which secures the hawk in training. [Fr. *créance*.] **creant**, *krē'ənt*, *adj.* creating: formative. [L. *creāns*, *-antis*, pr.p. of *creāre*; see create.] **crease**, *krēs*, *n.* a mark made by folding or doubling anything: a regulative line, of three kinds —*bowling crease*, from behind or astride of which the bowler must bowl, *popping-crease*, 4 feet in front of it, at which the batsman plays and behind which is his ground, *return-crease*, marking the sideward limits of the bowler (*cricket*).—*v.t.* to make creases in.—*v.i.* to become creased. —*adj.* **creas'y**, full of creases.—*adj.* **crease-resistant**, **-resisting**, of a fabric, not becoming creased in normal wear. [Origin uncertain.] **crease**. See kris. **creasote**. See creosote. **create**, *krē-āt'*, *v.t.* to bring into being or form out of nothing: to bring into being by force of imagination: to make, produce, or form: to design: to invest with a new form, office, or character: to institute: to be the first to act (a part).—*v.i.* (*slang*) to make a fuss.—*adj.* (*Milt.*) created.—*adj.* **creāt'able**.—*n.* **creā'tion** (*krē-ā'-shən*), the act of creating, esp. the universe: that which is created, the world, the universe: a specially designed garment.—*adj.* **creā'tional**.—*ns.* **creā'tionism**, the theory of special creation (opp. to *evolutionism*): the theory that God immediately creates a soul for every human being born (opp. to *traducianism*)—**creā'tionism**; **creā'tionist**.—*adj.* **creā'tive**, having power to create: that creates: showing, pertaining to, imagination, originality.—*adv.* **creā'tively**.—*ns.* **creā'tiveness**; **creativ'ity** (*krē-ə-tiv'*), state or quality of being creative: ability to create; **creā'tor**, one who creates: a maker:—*fem.* **creā'trix**, **creā'tress**; **creā'torship**.—*adjs.* **creat-ural** (*krē'char-əl*), **crea'turely**, pertaining to a creature or thing created.—*ns.* **creature** (*krē'char*), anything that has been created, animate or inanimate, esp. an animated being, an animal, a man: a term of contempt or of endearment: a dependent, instrument, or puppet: (*coll.*—usu. **with** *the*) alcoholic liquor; **crea'tureship**; **creature comforts**, material comforts, food, etc.: liquor, esp. whisky; **the Creator**, the Supreme being, God. [L. *creāre*, *-ātum* to create, *creātūra*, a thing created.] **creatine**, *krē'ə-tin*, *-tēn*, *n.* a constant and characteristic constituent of the striped muscle of vertebrates ($C_4H_9N_3O_2$).—*adj.* **creatic** (*kri-at'ik*), relating to flesh.—*adj.* **crē'atinine**, dehydrated creatine ($C_4H_7N_3O$) found in urine and muscles. [Gr. *kreas*, *kreatos*, flesh.] **crèche**, *kresh*, *n.* a public nursery for children. [Fr. *crèche*, manger.] **credence**, *krē'dəns*, *n.* belief: trust: precautionary tasting of food for a great man's table (*obs.*): a sideboard (*obs.*): the small table beside the altar on which the bread and wine are placed before being consecrated: a shelf over a piscina. —*n.* **credendum** (*kri-den'dəm*), a thing to be believed, an act of faith (*pl.* **creden'da**).—*adjs.* **crē'dent**, credible: credulous: believing; **credential** (*kri-den'shl*), giving a title to belief or credit.—*n.* that which entitles to credit or confidence: (in *pl.*) esp. the letters by which one claims confidence or authority among strangers.—*ns.* **credibil'ity** (*kred-*), **cred'ibleness**,

—*adj.* **cred'ible,** that may be believed: seemingly worthy of belief or of confidence: of a nuclear weapon, in whose use and effectiveness one can believe.—*adv.* **cred'ibly.**—*n.* **cred'it,** belief: esteem: reputation: honour: distinction: good character: acknowledgment: sale on trust: time allowed for payment: the side of an account on which payments received are entered: a sum placed at a person's disposal in a bank up to which he may draw: in American schools and colleges, certified completion of a course of study counting towards a final pass: a credit title.—*v.t.* to believe: to trust: to sell or lend to on trust: to enter on the credit side of an account: to set to the credit of (with *to* or *with*).—*adj.* **cred'itable,** trustworthy: bringing credit or honour.—*n.* **cred'itableness.**—*adv.* **cred'itably.**—*ns.* **cred'itor,** one to whom a debt is due; **crē'dō** (L. *crēdō,* pron. *krā'dō,* I believe), the Creed, or a musical setting of it for church services; **credulity** (*kri-dū'li-ti*), credulousness: disposition to believe on insufficient evidence.— *adj.* **credulous** (*kred'*), easy of belief: apt to believe without sufficient evidence: unsuspecting.—*adv.* **cred'ulously.**—*n.* **cred'ulousness.** **credibility gap,** gap between what is claimed or stated and what seems probable; **credit card,** a card obtainable from a credit card company which, in places where the card is recognised, enables the holder to have purchases, services, etc. debited to an account kept by the company: a similar card issued by other organisations, or by certain banks (to be used with cheque-book); **credit titles,** acknowledgments of the work of participators other than actors, projected on the screen at the showing of a cinematograph film. [L. *crēdĕre, crēditum,* to believe.]
**crédit,** *krā-dē,* (Fr.) credit.—**crédit foncier** (*fɔ̃-syā*), lending of money on security of landed property, repayable by terminable annuity; **crédit mobilier** (*mō-bē-lyā*), lending of money on movable property.
**credit, etc., credulity, etc.** See **credence.**
**cree,** *krē, v.t.* of grain, to soften by boiling or soaking. [Fr. *crever,* to burst.]
**Creed,** *krēd, n.* a form of teleprinter. [From the inventor, Frederick George *Creed* (1871-1957).]
**creed,** *krēd, n.* a summary of articles of religious belief, esp. those called the Apostles', Nicene, and Athanasian: any system of belief.—*adjs.* **creed'al, cred'al.** [O.E. *crēda*—L. *crēdō,* I believe.]
**creek,** *krēk, n.* a small inlet or bay, or the tidal estuary of a river: any turn or winding: in America and Australia, a small river or brook.— *adj.* **creek'y,** full of creeks: winding. [Prob. Scand., O.N. *kriki,* a nook; cf. Du. *kreek,* a bay; Fr. *crique.*]
**Creek,** *krēk, n.* a member of any of the tribes of American Indians who formed the **Creek Confederacy.** [Prob. **creek,** a river.]
**creel,** *krēl, n.* a basket, esp. a fish basket. [Origin obscure.]
**creep,** *krēp, v.i.* to move with the belly on or near the ground: to move or advance slowly or stealthily: to slip or encroach very gradually: to grow along the ground or on supports, as a vine: to fawn or cringe: to have the physical sensation of something creeping over or under the skin: to shudder: to drag with a creeper (*naut.*).—*v.t.* (*Milt.,* etc.) to creep on:—*pa.t.* and *pa.p.* **crept.**— *n.* a crawl: a slow slipping or yielding to stress: crystallisation or rise of a precipitate on the side of a vessel above the surface of a liquid: a narrow passage: (in *pl.*) a horrible shrinking: a silent, boring, or unpleasant person (*slang*).—*ns.* **creep'er,** anything that creeps: a creeping plant, esp. a Virginia creeper: a small bird that runs up trees (Certhia): a kind of grapnel: an endless chain or conveyor.—*adj.* **creep'ered,** covered

with a creeper.—*n.* **creep'ie,** a low stool: a stool of repentence.—*adj.* **creep'ing.**—*adv.* **creep'ingly.** —*adjs* **creep'y, creep'y-crawl'y.**—**creep'-hole,** a hiding hole: a subterfuge.—*adj.* **creep'mouse,** silent and shrinking.—**creeping Jenny,** money-wort, a creeping plant (*Lysimachia Nummu-laria*); **creeping Jesus** (*slang*), a slinking person; **the creeps,** a feeling of horror or revulsion. [O.E. *crēopan;* Du. *kruipen.*]
**creese, crease.** See **kris.**
**creesh,** *krēsh,* (*Scot.*) *v.t.* to grease.—*n.* grease.— *adj.* **creesh'y.** [O.Fr. *craisse*—L. *crassus,* fat.]
**crémaillère,** *krā-mi-yer', n.* a zigzag line of fortification: a rack railway. [Fr., pot-hook.]
**cremaster,** *kri-mas'tər, n.* a muscle of the spermatic cord: the organ of attachment in lepidopterous pupae. [Gr. *kremastēr,* suspender—*kremannynai,* to hang.]
**cremate,** *kri-māt', v.t.* to burn (esp. a dead body). —*ns.* **cremā'tion; cremā'tionist,** one who advocates cremation; **cremāt'or,** one who cremates: a furnace for cremation: an incinerator.—*adj.* **crematorial** (*krem-ə-tō'ri-əl, -tö'*).—*n.* **crematō'-rium,** a place for cremating dead bodies.—*adj.* **crem'atory** (*-ə-tər-i*).—*n.* a crematorium. [L. *cremāre, -ātum,* to burn.]
**crème,** *krem, n.* (for Fr. *crème*) cream—applied to various creamy substances.—**crème de menthe** (*də māt*), a peppermint-flavoured liqueur.
**crème de la crème,** *krem də la krem,* (Fr.) cream of the cream, the very best.
**cremocarp,** *krem'ō-kärp,* (*bot.*) *n.* the characteristic fruit of the Umbelliferae, composed of two one-seeded halves which split apart and dangle from the top of the axis. [Gr. *kremannynai,* to hang, *karpos,* fruit.]
**Cremona,** *krim-ō'nə, n.* a kind of violin made in *Cremona* in Italy.
**cremona, cremorne,** *kri-mō'nə, kri-mör'nə, n.* erroneous forms of **cromorna.**
**cremor,** *krē'mör, n.* thick juice. [L.]
**cremosin, cremsin,** *krem'zin,* (*Spens.*) *adj.* crimson.
**crenate, -d,** *krēn'āt, kren'āt, kren-āt', -id,* (*bot.*) *adj.* having rounded teeth between sharp notches. —*ns.* **crē'na,** a notch or tooth; **crenā'tion;** **cren'ature.**—*adjs.* **cren'ulate, -d,** finely notched or crenate. [From an inferred L. *crēna,* a notch.]
**crenel, kren'l,** (*archit.*) *n.* a notch in a parapet.— *v.t.* to indent with crenels.—*v.t.* **cren'ellate,** *U.S.* **cren'elate,** to embattle.—*adjs.* **cren'ellate, -d,** embattled: indented.—*n.* **crenellā'tion.**—*adj.* **cren'elled.** [O.Fr. *crenel*—inferred L. *crēna,* a notch.]
**creodont,** *krē'ō-dont, n.* any member of a group of primitive fossil carnivores, appearing in Eocene times. [Gr. *kreas,* flesh, *odous, odontos,* tooth.]
**creole,** *krē'ōl, krē-ōl', adj.* and *n.* strictly applied in the former Spanish, French, and Portuguese colonies of America, Africa and the East Indies to natives of pure European blood (in opposition to immigrants born in Europe or to coloured natives): native, but not aboriginal or indigenous: loosely, native, but of mixed blood: applied to the native French or Spanish stock in Louisiana (*U.S.*): a colonial patois (French, Spanish, etc.): a negro born in America—earlier **creō'lian.**—*n.* (*cap.*) (also **creolised language**) a language formerly a pidgin which has developed and become the accepted language of a region. [Fr. *créole*—Sp. *criollo,* dim. of *criado,* nursling—*criar,* lit. to create, hence to bring up, nurse—L. *creāre.*]
**creophagous,** *krē-of'ə-gəs, adj.* flesh-eating. [Gr. *kreas,* flesh, *phagein,* to eat.]
**creosote, creasote,** *krē'ə-sōt, n.* an oily liquid obtained by destructive distillation of wood-tar: a somewhat similar liquid got from coal-tar (**creosote oil,** or **coal-tar creosote**).—*v.t.* to treat with creosote.—**creosote-plant,** an American bush (*Larrea mexicana;* fam. *Zygophyllaceae*)

that smells of creosote and forms dense scrub. [Gr. *kreas*, flesh, *sōtēr*, saviour—*sōzein*, to save.]

crepance, *krē'pəns, n.* a wound on a horse's hind ankle-joint, caused by the shoe of the other hindfoot. [L. *crepāre*, to break.]

crêpe, *krāp, krep, n.* a crape-like fabric: rubber rolled in thin crinkly sheets (crêpe rubber).—*v.t.* to frizz, as hair.—*ns.* crep'oline, a light crapelike dress material; crep'on, a similar fabric made of silk or nylon.—crêpe-de-chine (*da shēn*), a crape-like fabric, originally of silk.—crepe'-hanger (see crape).—*adj.* crêpe'-soled', soled with crêpe rubber.—crêpe paper, thin crinkled paper. [See crape.]

crepitate, *krep'i-tāt, v.i.* to crackle, snap: to rattle: (of beetles) to discharge an offensive fluid.—*adj.* crep'itant, crackling.—*n.* crepitā'tion, the act of crepitating: crackle: a sound detected in the lungs by auscultation in certain diseases.—*adj.* crep'itātive.—*n.* crep'itus. [L. *crepitāre, -ātum,* freq. of *crepāre,* to crack, rattle.]

crept, *krept, pa.t.* and *pa.p.* of creep.

crepuscular, *kri-pus'kū-lər, adj.* of or pertaining to twilight—also crepus'culous.—*ns.* crepuscule, (*krep'əs-kūl,* or *-ūs'*), crepuscle (*krep'əs-l,* or *us'*), twilight. [L. *crepusculum—creper,* dusky, obscure.]

crescendo, *kresh-en'dō,* (*mus.*) *adj.* and *adv.* gradually increasing in loudness.—*n.* increase of loudness: a passage of increasing loudness.— Also *v.i.*—Often cres., cresc., or <. [It., increasing.]

crescent, *kres'ənt, krez', adj.* increasing: shaped like the waxing moon.—*n.* the waxing moon: a figure like the crescent moon: the Turkish (originally Byzantine) standard or emblem: the Turkish power: the Moslem faith: a curved range of buildings (sometimes applied at random): a crescent-shape roll or bun.—*n.* cresc'entade, a religious war for Islam.—*adjs.* cresc'ented, crescentic (-*ent'ik*), formed like a crescent; cresc'ive, increasing. [L. *crēscĕre,* to grow, pr.p. *crēscēns, -entis.*]

cresol, *krēs'ol, n.* a product of distillation of coal-tar resembling phenol—C₇H₈O. [From creosote and alcohol.]

cress, *kres, n.* a name for many pungent-leaved cruciferous plants of Lepidium (garden cress), Rorippa (watercress), Arabis (rock-cress) and other genera: extended to other plants of similar character, as Indian cress (Tropaeolum). —*adj.* cress'y, abounding in cresses. [O.E. *cresse, cerse;* cf. Du. *kers,* Ger. *kresse.*]

cresset, *kres'it, n.* an iron basket, or the like, for combustibles, placed on a beacon, lighthouse, wharf, etc.: a torch generally. [O.Fr. *cresset, crasset* (Fr. *creuset*)—Old Du. *kruysel,* a hanging lamp.]

crest, *krest, n.* the comb or tuft on the head of a cock or other bird: the summit of anything, as a roof-ridge, hill, wave: the mane of a horse, etc.: a ridge along the surface of a bone (*anat.*): a plume of feathers or other ornament on the top of a helmet: an accessory figure originally surmounting the helmet, placed on a wreath, etc., also used separately as a personal cognisance on plate, etc. (*her.*).—*v.t.* to furnish with a crest or serve as a crest for: to surmount.—*adj.* crest'ed, having a crest: having an elevated appendage like a crest (*bot.*).—*adjs.* crest'fallen, dejected: cast-down; crest'less, without a crest: not of high birth. [O.Fr. *creste* (Fr. *crête*)—L. *crista.*]

cretaceous, *kri-tā'shəs, adj.* composed of or like chalk: (*cap.*) belonging to the uppermost system of the Secondary of Mesozoic rocks, including in England the Wealden, the Gault and Greensand, and the Chalk.—Also *n.* [L. *crētāceus—crēta,* chalk.]

Cretan, *krē'tən,* Cretic, *krē'tik, adj.* and *n.*

belonging to *Crete.*—*ns.* cretic, a metrical foot consisting of one short syllable between two long; crē'tism, a lie. [Gr. *krētikos—Krētē,* Crete.]

cretin, *kret'in, krēt'in, n.* one affected with cretinism.—*n.* cret'inism, a state of defective mental development, with bodily deformity or arrested growth, due to failure of secretion of the thyroid gland.—*adjs.* cret'inous, cret'inised, -ized, cret'inoid. [Fr. *crétin—*L. *christiānus,* human creature.]

cretonne, *kret-on',* or *kret'on, n.* a strong printed cotton fabric used for curtains or for covering furniture. [Fr., prob. from *Creton* in Normandy.]

creutzer. Same as kreutzer.

crevasse, *kriv-as', n.* a crack or split, esp. applied to a cleft in a glacier: a breach in a canal or river bank (*U.S.*).—*v.t.* to fissure with crevasses.—*n.* crevice (*krev'is*), a crack or rent: a narrow opening. [O.Fr. *crevace—*L. *crepāre,* to creak, break.]

crève-cœur, *krev-kœr,* (Fr.) heartbreak.

crew, *krōō, n.* a set, gang: a ship's company: oarsmen and steersman manning a racing boat: group in charge of bus, train or aeroplane.—*v.i.* to act as a crew member on a ship, etc. (esp. with *for*).—crew cut, a short, seaman style of hair-cut. [O.Fr. *creue,* increase—*croistre,* to grow.]

crew, *krōō, pa.t.* of crow.

crewe, *krōō,* (*Spens.*) *n.* a pot. [O.Fr. *crue.*]

crewel, *krōō'əl, n.* a fine worsted yarn used for embroidery and tapestry: work in crewels.—*v.t.* to work in crewel.—*ns.* crew'elist, crew'ellery, crewel'work. [Orig. a monosyllable, *crule, crewle;* ety. dub.]

crewels, cruel(l)s, *krōō'əlz,* (*Scot.*) *n.pl.* the king's evil, scrofula. [Fr. *écrouelles.*]

criant, *kri'ənt, krē-ā, adj.* garish, discordantly coloured. [Fr.]

crib, *krib, n.* a manger or fodder-receptacle: a stall for oxen: a bin: a crate: a child's bed: a cabin or hut: a confined place: a house (*thieves'* *slang*): a job (*slang*): a timber framework for a dam, a pier foundation: a mine-shaft lining, etc.: a pilfering, or the thing pilfered: a plagiarism: a key or baldly literal translation, used by schoolboys, etc.: the discarded cards at cribbage, used by the dealer in scoring.—*v.t.* to put in a crib: to confine: to pilfer: to plagiarise:—*pr.p.* cribb'ing; *pa.t.* and *pa.p.* cribbed.—*ns.* cribb'age, a card game in which each player discards a certain number of cards for the *crib,* and scores by holding certain combinations and by bringing the sum of the values of cards played to certain numbers; cribb'age-board, a scoring-board for cribbage, with holes for pegs; crib'-bit'ing, in horses, a vicious habit of biting the manger, etc., and swallowing air; crib'work, work formed of cribs. [O.E. *crib;* Ger. *krippe.*]

cribble, *krib'l, n.* a coarse screen or sieve used for sand, gravel or corn: coarse flour or meal (*obs.*). —*v.t.* to sift or riddle (*obs.*): in engraving, to produce a dotted effect.—*adj.* cribbl'ed.—*n.* cribell'um, an accessory spinning-organ of certain spiders:—*pl.* cribell'a.—*adjs.* cribell'ar; criblé (Fr. *krē-blā*) (*engraving*), punctured like a sieve, dotted: crib'rate (or *krib'*), crib'rose, perforated like a sieve.—*n.* cribrā'tion, sifting.— *adj.* crib'riform, perforated. [L. *cribrum,* dim. *cribellum,* a sieve.]

Cricetus, *kri-sē'təs, n.* the hamster genus. [Mod. L.—Slav. name of hamster.]

crick, *krik, n.* a spasm or cramp of the muscles, esp. of the neck.—*v.t.* to produce a crick in. [Prob. imit.]

cricket, *krik'it, n.* a saltatory, orthopterous insect, allied to grasshoppers and locusts. [O.Fr. *criquet;* cf. Du. *krekel,* Ger. *kreckel.*]

cricket, *krik'it, n.* an outdoor game played with bats, a ball, and wickets, between two sides of

*fāte, fär; mē, hûr* (her); *mīne, mōte, för; mūte; mōōn, fŏŏt; dhen* (then) eleven each: that which is fair and sporting (*coll.*).—*v.i.* to play at cricket.—*n.* crick'eter.—*n.* and *adj.* crick'eting. [Fr. *criquet*; not O.E. *crycc*, a stock.]

cricket, *krik'it* (*dial.*) *n.* a low stool. [Ety. unknown.]

cricoid, *krī'koid*, (*anat.*) *adj.* ring-shaped.—*n.* a cartilage of the larynx. [Gr. *krikoeides*—*krikos*, a ring, and *eidos*, form.]

cri de cœur, *krē də kœr*, (Fr.) a cry from the heart—heartfelt, passionate entreaty, complaint, reproach.

cried, crier, cries. See cry.

crikey, cricky, crickey, *krik'i*, *krik'i*, (slang) *interj.*, a mild oath or expression of surprise. [Euphemism for *Christ*.]

crime, *krīm*, *n.* a violation of law, esp. if serious: an act punishable by law: such acts collectively or in the abstract: an act gravely wrong morally: sin: an accusation (*Spens.*): a cause or motive of wrongdoing (*Spens.*).—*v.t.* (*mil.*) to charge or convict of an infraction of law.—*adjs.* crime'ful, criminal, crime'less, without crime, innocent; criminal (*krim'-*), relating to crime: guilty of crime: violating laws.—*n.* one guilty of crime. —*ns.* crim'inalist, one versed in criminal law; criminal'ity, guiltiness.—*adv.* crim'inally.—*v.t.* crim'inate, to accuse.—*n.* criminā'tion, act of criminating: accusation.—*adjs.* crim'inative, crim'inatory, involving crimination.—*ns.* criminol'ogist; criminol'ogy, that branch of anthropology which treats of crime and criminals.— *adj.* crim'inous, criminal—now chiefly in the phrase 'a criminous clerk'.—*n.* crim'inousness.— crime sheet (*mil.*), a record of offences; criminal conversation, often crim. con., adultery. [Fr.,— L. *crīmen, -inis.*]

crimen falsi, *krī'mən fal'sī, krē'men fal'sē*, (L.) crime of perjury; crimen laesae majestatis, *lē'sē maj-əs-tä'tis, li'si ma-yes-tä'tis*, high treason.

crime passionel, *krēm pa-syo-nel*, (Fr.) a crime due to (sexual) passion.

crimine, crimini, *krim'i-ni*, (arch.) *interj.* an ejaculation of surprise or impatience. [Perh. from *Christ*; see crikey.]

crimp, *krimp*, *adj.* made crisp or brittle.—*v.t.* to press into folds: to curl (hair): to bend into shape: to gash: to seize or decoy.—*n.* a curl or wave: a hindering factor (*coll.*): one who presses or decoys (sailors, etc.).—*n.* crimp'er, one who or that which crimps or corrugates.—*v.t.* crimp'le, to contract or draw together: to plait: to curl.—*adj.* crimp'y, frizzy.—crimp'ing-iron, an iron instrument used for crimping hair or material; crimp'ing-machine', a machine for forming crimps or plaits on ruffles. [O.E. *gecrympan*, to curl; cf. cramp, and Du. *krimpen*, to shrink.]

crimson, *krim'zn*, *n.* a deep red colour, tinged with blue: red in general.—*adj.* deep red.—*v.t.* to dye crimson.—*v.i.* to become crimson: to blush. [M.E. *crimosin*—O.Fr. *cramoisin*; from Ar. *qirmizī*, scarlet—*qirmiz*, kermes, from which it is made.]

crinal, *krī'nal*, *adj.* of or belonging to the hair.— *adjs.* crin'ate, -d, having hair; crinig'erous, hairy; crin'ite, hairy: resembling a tuft of hair (*bot.*); cri'nose, hairy—crinicul'tural, relating to the culture or growth of the hair. [L. *crinis*, the hair.]

crine, *krin*, (*Scot.*) *v.i.* to shrink or shrivel. [Gael. *crion*, dry.]

cringe, *krinj*, *v.i.* to bend or crouch with servility: to submit: to fawn: to flatter with mean servility.—*n.* a servile obeisance.—*ns.* cringe'-ling, crin'ger, one who cringes.—*n.* and *adj.* cring'ing.—*adv.* crin'gingly, in an obsequious manner. [Related to O.E. *crincan, cringan*, to shrink; cf. crank (1).]

cringle, *kring'gl*, *n.* a small piece of rope worked into the bolt-rope of a sail, and containing a metal ring or thimble. [Gmc.; cf. Ger. *kringel.*]

crinite. See crinal, crinoid.

crinkle, *kringk'l*, *v.t.* to twist, wrinkle, crimp.—*v.i.* to wrinkle up, curl.—*n.* a wrinkle.—*adj.* crink'ly, wrinkly.—*n.* and *adj.* crink'um-crank'um, a word applied familiarly to things intricate or crooked. [Related to O.E. *crincan*; see cringe.]

crinoid, *krin'oid, krin'oid*, *n.* a feather-star or sea-lily, an echinoderm of the class Crinoid'ea, with cup-shaped body and branching arms and well developed skeleton, usually attached by a jointed stalk, mouth upwards, well known in fossil forms as encrinites or stone-lilies.—Also *adj.* —*n.* crinite (*krin'* or *krin'it*), an encrinite or fossil crinoid.—*adj.* crinoid'al.—*adj.* and *n.* crinoid'ean. [Gr. *krīnoeidēs*, like a lily—*krīnon*, a lily, *eidos*, form.]

crinoline, *krin'ə-lin, -lēn*, *n.* originally a stiff fabric of horsehair and flax: this or other means to distend women's attire: a hooped petticoat or skirt made to project all round by means of steel-wire: a netting made for ships as a guard against torpedoes.—*n.* crinolette', a small crinoline causing the dress to project behind only.—*adj.* crin'olined. [Fr., *crin*—L. *crinis*, hair, and *lin*— L. *linum*, flax.]

crio-sphinx, *krī'ō-sfingks*, *n.* a ram-headed sphinx. [Gr. *krios*, a ram, *sphinx*, a sphinx.]

cripes, *krips*, (slang) *interj.* expression of surprise or worry. [Euphemism for *Christ*.]

cripple, *krip'l*, *n.* a lame person.—*adj.* lame.—*v.t.* to make lame: to lame: to disable, impair the efficiency of.—*ns.* cripp'ledom; cripp'ling, a prop set up as a support against the side of a building. [O.E. *crypel*; conn. with creep.]

crisis, *krī'sis*, *n.* point or time for deciding anything, the decisive moment or turning-point:— *pl.* crises (*krī'sēz*). [Gr. *krisis*, from *krīnein*, to decide.]

crisp, *krisp*, *adj.* curling closely: having a wavy surface: so dry as to be crumbled easily: brittle: short (of pastry): fresh and bracing: firm, the opposite of limp or flabby.—*v.t.* to curl or twist: to make crisp or wavy: to ripple.—*n.* a piece of food fried or roasted to crispness.—*adjs.* cris'-pâte, -d, having a crisp or wavy appearance.—*ns.* crispâ'tion; crisp'ature, a curling; crisp'er, one who or that which crisps.—*adv.* crisp'ly.—*n.* crisp'ness.—*adj.* crisp'y.—crisp'ing-i'ron, -pin, a curling-iron. [O.E.,—L. *crispus.*]

crispin, *kris'pin*, *n.* a shoemaker, from *Crispin* of Soissons, the patron saint of shoemakers, martyred 25th October 287.

criss-cross, *kris'-kros*, *n.* the cross at the beginning of the alphabet on a hornbook (see criss-cross-row, at Christ): a mark formed by two lines in the form of a cross, as the signature of a person unable to write his name: a network of crossing lines: repeated crossings: cross-purposes: a game of noughts and crosses.—*adj.* and *adv.* crosswise.—*v.t.* and *v.i.* to cross repeatedly. [From christ-cross.]

crista, *kris'ta*, *n.* a crest.—*adjs.* crist'ate, crested; cris'tiform. [L.]

criterion, *krī-tē'ri-ən*, *n.* a means or standard of judging: a test: a rule, standard, or canon:—*pl.* crite'ria. [Gr. *kritērion*—*kritēs*, a judge.]

crith, *krith*, *n.* a unit of mass, that of 1 litre at standard temperature and pressure. [Gr. *krithē*, barleycorn, a small weight.]

crithomancy, *krith'ō-man-si*, *n.* divination by the meal strewed over the victims of sacrifice. [Gr. *krithē*, barley, and *manteiā*, divination.]

critic, *krit'ik*, *n.* one skilled in estimating the quality of literary or artistic work: a professional reviewer: one skilled in textual studies, various readings, and the ascertainment of the original words: a fault-finder.—*adj.* crit'ical, at or relating to a turning-point, transition or crisis: decisive: relating to criticism: rigorously discriminating: captious: of a condition in which a chain reaction is self-sustaining.—*adv.* **crit′ically.**—*ns.* **crit′icalness, critical′ity; crit′icaster,** a petty critic.—*adj.* **criticisable** (-*siz′*).—*v.t.* **crit′icise, -ize,** to pass judgment on: to censure.—*ns.* **crit′icism,** the art of judging, esp. in literature or the fine arts: a critical judgment or observation; **critique** (*kri-tēk′*; Fr.), a critical examination of any production: a review.—**critical angle,** the least angle of incidence at which a ray is totally reflected; **critical path analysis,** working out with the aid of a computer the sequence of operations that must be followed in order to complete a complex piece of work in the minimum time; **critical philosophy,** that of Kant which is based on a critical examination of the faculty of knowledge; **critical temperature,** that temperature above which a gas cannot be liquefied by pressure alone.—**higher or historical criticism,** as distinguished from **textual or verbal criticism,** the inquiry into the composition, date, and authenticity of the books of the Bible, from historical and literary considerations. [Gr. *kritikos*—*krīnein,* to judge.]

**critter, crittur,** *krit′ər, (U.S. dial.* and *coll.) n.* creature: animal.

**croak,** *krōk, v.i.* to utter a low hoarse sound, as a frog or raven: to grumble: to forebode evil: to die (*slang*).—*v.t.* to utter croakingly.—*n.* the sound of a frog or raven.—*n.* **croak′er.**—*adv.* **croak′ily.**—*n.* **croak′ing.**—*adj.* **croak′y.** [Imit.]

**croche,** *krōch, n.* a knob at the top of a deer's horn. [Fr.]

**crochet,** *krō′shā, n.* looping work done with a small hook.—*v.i.* and *v.t.* to work in crochet:—*pr.p.* **crocheting** (*krō′shā-ing*); *pa.t.* and *pa.p.* **crocheted** (*krō′shād*).—**crocheting,** action of crochet: crochetwork. [Fr. *crochet*—*croche, croc,* a hook.]

**crocidolite,** *kro-sid′o-lit, n.* a fibrous mineral consisting mainly of silicate of iron and sodium, called **blue asbestos:** in S. Africa also a golden alteration product or pseudomorph of this mineral, largely quartz. [From Gr. *krokis, -idos,* nap of cloth, and *lithos,* stone.]

**crock,** *krok, n.* a pot or jar: a potsherd.—*n.* **crock′ery,** earthenware: all types of domestic pottery. [O.E. *croc;* Ger. *krug;* perh. of Celt. origin, as in W. *crochan,* a pot, Gael. *crogan,* a pitcher.]

**crock,** *krok,* (*dial.) n.* dirt, smut.—*v.t.* to besmut. [Origin doubtful.]

**crock,** *krok, n.* an old ewe: an old horse: a broken down or decrepit person or thing.—*v.i.* to break down (often with *up*).—*v.t.* to disable. [Cf. Norw. and Sw. *krake,* a poor beast.]

**crocket,** *krok′it,* (*archit.) n.* an ornament on the sloping sides of a pediment, pinnacle, etc., usu. like curled leaves or flowers. [See **croquet.**]

**crocodile,** *krok′ə-dīl, n.* a large reptile of the Nile with bony scutes and horny scales: extended to others of the genus (**Crocodi′lus**) or order (**Crocodil′ia,** or *Loricata,* alligators, gavials, etc.): leather from crocodile skin: a double file of school pupils taking a walk.—*adj.* and *n.* **crocodilian** (*dil′*).—*n.* **crocodil′ite** (*obs.*), captious arguing—from a sophistical problem about a crocodile.—**crocodile bird,** a bird, perh. a plover, said to pick the crocodile's teeth or take leeches from its throat; **crocodile tears,** hypocritical grief—from the old story that crocodiles (which have large lachrymal glands) shed tears over the hard necessity of killing animals for food. [L. *crocodilus*—Gr. *krokodeilos,* a lizard.]

**crocus,** *krō′kəs, n.* a bulbous iridaceous plant with brilliant yellow, purple, or white flowers: in old chemistry, various yellow or red powders (**crocus**

*of Mars,* colcothar).—*adj.* **croceate,** *krō′si-āt* (*obs.*), **croceous** (*krō′shi-əs*), saffron-coloured.—*n.* **crocoite** (*krō′kō-īt*); **crocoisite** (*krō′,* or *kō′*), a bright red mineral, lead chromate. [L. *crocus* —Gr. *krokos;* prob. of Eastern origin; cf. Heb. *karkom,* and Ar. *kurkum,* saffron.]

**crocus,** *krō′kəs,* (*slang) n.* a quack.

**Croesus,** *krē′səs, n.* a very rich man. [*Croesus,* king of Lydia, of fabulous wealth.]

**croft,** *kroft, n.* a small piece of arable land esp. adjoining a dwelling: a small farm.—*ns.* **croft′er; croft′ing.** [O.E. *croft;* perh. cog. with Du. *kroft,* hillock.]

**croissant,** *krwä-sã, n.* a crescent roll. [Fr.]

**croix de guerre,** *krwä də ger,* (Fr.) military decoration for heroism in action.

**cromack.** Same as **crummock, crummack.**

**Cro-Magnon,** *krō-mag′nan, krō-man′yõ, adj.* pertaining to a type of man, long-skulled but short-faced, surviving from Aurignacian times to the present day. [From *Cro-Magnon,* in Dordogne, where the first skulls of this race were found.]

**crome, cromb,** *krōm, krōōm,* (*dial.) n.* a hook or crook.—*v.t.* to draw with a crome. [Cf. Du. *kram.*]

**cromlech,** *krom′lehh, -lek, n.* a stone circle: formerly applied to a dolmen. [W. *cromlech*— *crom,* curved, circular, and *llech,* a stone.]

**cromorna, cromorne,** *krō-mörn′(a), n.* a krummhorn: a krummhorn stop. [Fr. *cromorne*—Ger. *krummhorn.*]

**crone,** *krōn, n.* an old woman, usually in contempt —rarely an old man: an old ewe. [Perh. O.Fr. *carogne,* carrion, hag, directly or through Du.]

**cronet,** *krō′net,* (*obs.) n.* the hair growing over the top of a horse's hoof. [**coronet.**]

**cronk,** *krongk,* (*Austr. slang) adj.* ill: of poor quality: unfavourable. [From **crank** (1).]

**crony,** *krōn′i, n.* an old and intimate companion. [Said to be orig. university slang—Gr. *chronios,* long-continued, perennial.]

**croodle,** *krōōd′l,* (Scot.) *v.i.* to cower down, snuggle. [Origin unknown.]

**croodle,** *krōōd′l, krōōd′l,* (*Scot.) v.i.* to murmur like a dove. [Imit.]

**crook,** *krōōk, n.* a bend, anything bent: a curved tube used to lower the pitch of a wind instrument: the bending of the body in reverence (*obs.*): a staff bent at the end, as a shepherd's or bishop's: an artifice or trick (*obs.*): gibbet (*Spens.*): a professional swindler or thief.—*adj.* (*Austr. slang*), ill: angry: unfair: unscrupulous. —*v.t.* to bend or form into a hook: to turn from the straight line or from what is right (*obs.*).—*v.i.* to bend or be bent.—*adj.* **crook′ed,** bent like a crook: not straight: deviating from rectitude, perverse.—*adv.* **crook′edly.**—*n.* **crook′edness.**—*n.* **crook′back** (*Shak.*), a hunchback.—*adjs.* **crook′backed; crook′-kneed; crook′-shoul′dered.**—**a crook in the lot,** any trial in one's experience; **go crook on** (*Austr. slang*), to upbraid, rebuke. [Prob. O.N. *krōkr;* cf. Dan. *krog.*]

**croon,** *krōōn, v.i.* (Scot. *krün*) to utter a low, monotonous inarticulate sound like a bull: to murmur: to lament murmuringly: to sing or hum in an undertone.—*v.t.* and *v.i.* to sing quietly in an extravagantly sentimental manner. —Also *n.*—*ns.* **croon′er; croon′ing.** [Cf. Du. *kreunen,* to groan.]

**crop,** *krop, n.* the top or end of anything, as a tree or twig (*arch.*): a sprout: a finial (*archit.*): a whip-handle: a hunting whip with loop instead of lash: an end cut off: an act or mode of cutting: mode of cutting or wearing short hair: the total quantity produced, cut, or harvested: the total growth or produce: a cultivated plant, collectively: that which is produced at a time, a growth, supply: a season's yield: an entire hide: the craw, a dilatation of a bird's oesophagus: a similar structure in another animal: an outcrop.—*v.t.* to cut off the top, ends, margins, or loose parts of: to cut short: to mow, reap, or gather: to bite off in eating: to raise crops on: to cut the hair of.—*v.i.* to yield a crop: to come to the surface (with *up* or *out*): hence, to come (up) casually, as in conversation:—*pr.p.* cropp'ing; *pa.t.* and *pa.p.* cropped.—*n.* crop'ful, as much as the crop can hold (*pl.* crop'fuls).— *adj.* crop'full (*Milt.*), satiated.—*ns.* cropp'er, one who or that which crops: a plant that yields a crop: one who raises a crop for a share of it: a kind of pigeon noted for its large crop: a small platen printing machine: a fall: a failure; cropp'ing, act of cutting off: the raising of crops: an outcrop (*geol.*); cropp'y, one of the Irish rebels of 1798 who cut their hair short, like the French Revolutionists.—*adj.* crop'bound, suffering from impaction of the crop.—*ns.* cropdusting, the spraying of crops with fungicides or insecticides from the air; crop-duster, one who does this; crop'-ear, a person, horse, dog, etc., with cropped ears.—*adjs.* crop'-eared, having ears cropped, or hair cropped to show the ears (a Cavalier jibe at a Puritan); crop'sick, sick of a surfeit.—come a cropper, to have a fall, perhaps from phrase *neck and crop.* [O.E. *crop*, the top shoot of a plant, the crop of a bird; Du. *crop*, a bird's crop.]

croquet, *krō'kā, n.* a game in which wooden balls are driven by means of long-handled mallets, through a series of arches.—*v.t.* to drive away by striking another ball in contact. [North Fr. *croquet*, a dial. form of *crochet*, dim. of *croc*, *croche*, a crook.]

croquette, *krō-ket', n.* a ball or round cake, esp. of minced meat or fish, seasoned and fried. [Fr.,—*croquer*, to crunch.]

croquis, *kro-kē*, (Fr.) an outline or rough sketch.

crore, *krōr, krŏr, n.* ten millions, or one hundred lakhs. [Hind. *karoṛ.*]

crosier, crozier, *krō'z(h)yər, n.* the pastoral staff or crook of a bishop or abbot: erroneously, an archbishop's cross.—*adj.* cro'siered. [M.E. *crose* or *croce*—Late L. *crocia*, a crook.]

cross, *kros, n.* a gibbet on which the Romans exposed malefactors, typically consisting of two pieces of timber, one placed transversely to the other: the particular one on which Christ suffered: the symbol of the Christian religion, or of the crusades: the Christian doctrine of atonement: a representation of Christ's cross: any object, figure, or mark formed by two parts or lines transverse to each other, with or without elaboration: a staff surmounted by a cross: a monument not always in the form of a cross, where proclamations are made, etc.: a place in a town or village where such a monument stands or stood: a cross-shaped pendant or medal: the transverse part of an anchor, or the like: a surveyor's cross-staff: a crossing or crossway: anything that crosses or thwarts: adversity or affliction in general: mixing of breeds: a hybrid: something intermediate in character between two other things: unfairness or dishonest practices, esp. in sport where one corruptly allows himself to be beaten: a game or race lost by collusion: the obverse of a coin, formerly often stamped with a cross (*obs.*): hence, a coin (*arch.*).—*adj.* lying across or crosswise: transverse: oblique: adverse: interchanged: peevish: hybrid: dishonest: balancing, neutralising.—*adv.* across (often written 'cross).—*v.t.* to mark with a cross: to make the sign of the cross over: to set something, or draw a line, across: to set in position athwart the mast (*Spens.*): to place crosswise: to cancel by drawing cross lines: to pass from one side to the other of: to extend across: to interbreed: of a cheque, to draw two lines across, with name of a banking company or the words '&

Co.' between (thereby restricting it to payment through a bank): to obstruct: to thwart: to confront (*arch.*): to bestride.—*v.i.* to lie or pass across: to meet and pass: to interbreed:—*pa.t.* and *pa.p.* crossed, sometimes crost.—*adj.* crossed.—*n.* cross'ing, the act of making the sign of the cross: act of going across: a place where a roadway, etc., may be crossed: intersection: esp. transepts and nave: act of thwarting: cross-breeding.—*adjs.* cross'ing, cross'ish. —*n.* cross'let, a small cross.—*adv.* cross'ly.—*n.* cross'ness.—*adv.* cross'wise, in the form of a cross (*arch.*): across.—cross action (*law*), an action brought by the defender against the pursuer; cross aisle (*obs.*), a transept; cross'- and-pile' (or -or-) (*arch.*), heads or tails: a toss-up.—*adjs.* cross'-armed, having the arms crossed; cross'band'ed, having the grain of the veneer run across that of the rail—of a handrail.—cross'band, cross'banding; cross'bar, a transverse bar: a kind of lever.—*adj.* cross'- barred.—crossbar switch, a switch having two sets of paths, one vertical and one horizontal, with an electromagnetically operated means of connecting any path in the one set with any path in the other; crossbar switching, using a crossbar switch system; cross'beam, a large beam stretching across a building and serving to hold its sides together; cross'bearer, one who carries a cross in a procession; cross'-bedd'ing (*geol.*), false bedding; cross'bench, a bench laid crosswise: a bench on which independent members of parliament sometimes sit.—*adj.* independent: impartial.—cross'bencher; cross'- bill, a bill brought by the defendant in a Chancery suit against the plaintiff; cross'bill, a finch of the genus Loxia with mandibles crossing near the points; cross'-birth, a birth in which the child lies transversely in the uterus.—*v.t.* cross'bite (*arch.*), to bite in return: to cheat in return: to outwit: to entrap.—cross'bones, a figure of two thigh-bones laid across each other—forming with the skull a conventional emblem of death or piracy; cross'bow, a weapon for shooting arrows, formed of a bow placed crosswise on a stock; cross'bower, -bow'man, one who uses a crossbow.—*adj.* cross'bred, a breed produced by crossing: the offspring of a cross; cross'breed'ing; cross'-bun (see hot cross bun); cross'-butt'ock, a particular throw over the hip in wrestling.—*v.t.* cross'-check', to test the accuracy of e.g. a statement by consulting various sources of information.—Also *v.i.* and *n.*— cross correspondence (*psychical research*), fitting together of communications separately unintelligible to give an intelligible whole.—*adj.* and *adv.* cross'-coun'try, across the fields rather than by the road.—*ns.* cross'-cross'let, a cross with its ends crossed; cross'cut, a crosswise cutting: a short way across from one point to another.— —*v.t.* (-*kut'*) to cut across.—crosscut saw, a large saw worked by two men, one at each end, for cutting beams crosswise; cross'cutt'ing (*cinema, TV*), cutting and fitting together film sequences so that in the finished picture the action moves from one scene to another and back again, thus increasing dramatic tension; cross'-divi'sion, division into groups or classes that overlap; cross'-examinā'tion.—*v.t.* cross'-exam'ine, to question minutely, or with a view to checking evidence already given: to subject to examination by the other side.—*adj.* cross'-eyed, squinting.—cross'fall, camber on a road; cross'- fertilisā'tion, the fecundation of a plant by pollen from another: fruitful interaction of ideas from e.g. different cultures; crossfire (*mil.*), the crossing of lines of fire from two or more points: (also *fig.*); cross'fish, the common seaurchin *Asterias rubens*; cross'-gar'net, a T-shaped hinge.—*adjs.* cross'-gar'tered (*Shak.*), wearing the garters crossed on the leg; **cross'-grained,** having the grain or fibres crossed or intertwined: perverse: contrary: intractable.—*adv.* across the grain: perversely.—**cross'-grained'ness; cross guard,** the bar, at right angles to the blade, forming the hilt-guard of a sword; **cross'-hatch'ing,** shading by intersecting sets of parallel lines; **cross'-head,** a beam across the head of something, esp. the bar at the end of the piston-rod of a steam-engine; **cross'ing-o'ver** (*biol.*), interchange of parts of two chromosomes when they separate again after synapsis; **cross'-ing-sweeper,** one who sweeps a street crossing; **cross'jack,** a mizzen course; **cross-lat'eral,** a person affected with cross-laterality.—Also *adj.*—**cross-lateral'ity,** a mixture of physical one-sidedness, as the combination of a dominant left eye with a dominant right hand.—*adjs.* **cross'-leaved,** having leaves in four rows, set cross-wise; **cross'-legged,** having the legs crossed.—**cross'light,** a light whose direction makes an angle with that of another light, and which illumines additional parts or regions.—*adj.* **cross'-lighted.**—**cross'over,** a road passing over the top of another; **cross'patch',** an ill-natured person (see patch (2)); **cross'piece,** a piece of material of any kind crossing another: a timber over the windlass, with pins for belaying the running rigging (*naut.*); **cross-ply tyre,** tyre in which the plies of fabric in the carcass are wrapped so as to cross each other diagonally; **cross'-pollina'tion,** transfer of pollen from one flower to the stigma of another; **cross'-pur'pose,** a contrary purpose: (in *pl.*) a game in which answers to questions are transferred to other questions: (in *pl.*) confusion in conversation or action by misunderstanding; **cross-quar'ters,** an ornament of tracery like the four petals of a cruciform flower: a quatrefoil.—*v.t.* **cross'-ques'tion,** to cross-examine.—**cross-ra'tio,** of four points in a range, or rays in a pencil, the quotient of the position ratios of two with respect to the other two; **cross'-ref'erence,** a reference in a book to another title or passage; **cross'-rib,** an arch supporting a vault; **cross'-road,** a road crossing the principal road, a by-path: a road joining main roads: (often *pl.*) a place where roads cross—in *U.S.* often a hamlet: (in *pl.*) a stage at which an important decision has to be made.—*adj.* **cross'roads.**—**cross'-row** (same as **christ-cross-row**); **cross'-ruff',** alternate ruffing by partners, each leading a suit that the other lacks; **cross sea,** a sea that sets at an angle to the direction of the wind; **cross'-sec'tion,** a transverse section: a comprehensive representation: effective target area of a nucleus for a particular reaction under specified conditions, measured in barns (1 barn = $10^{-24}$ sq. cm.); when no reaction can take place, the cross-section is zero.—*v.t.* to make a cross-section of.—**cross'-sill,** a railway sleeper; **cross'-spring'er,** a cross-rib in a groined vault; **cross'-staff,** a surveying instrument consisting of a staff surmounted with a frame carrying two pairs of sights at right angles; **cross'-stitch',** a stitch in the form of a cross; needlework of such stitches; **cross'-stone,** chiastolite: staurolite: harmotome; **cross'-talk',** interference of one telephone conversation with another: backchat; **cross'-tie,** a supporting tie placed transversely: a railway sleeper; **cross'-tin'ing,** a mode of harrowing crosswise; **cross'tree,** a piece of timber or metal placed across the upper end of a ship's mast; **cross'-vault'ing,** vaulting formed by the intersection of simple vaults; **cross'way,** a way that crosses another or links others; **cross'-wind,** a wind blowing across the path of, e.g. an aeroplane; **cross'word (puzzle),** a puzzle in which a square with blank spaces is to be filled with letters which, read across or down, will give

words corresponding to clues given; **cross'wort,** a bedstraw with leaves set crosswise.—**cross as two sticks,** particularly perverse and disagreeable; **cross one's fingers, keep one's fingers crossed,** to place one finger across another to ensure good luck; **cross one's heart,** to emphasise that one is being truthful by making the sign of a cross over one's heart; **cross one's mind,** to flash across one's mind; **cross one's palm,** put a coin in one's hand; **cross one's path,** come in one's way: thwart one; **on the cross,** diagonally: dishonest (*slang*). [O.E. *cros*—O.N. *kross*—L. *crux, crucis.*]

**crossette,** *kro-set'*, *n.* a small projecting part of an impost-stone at the extremity of an arch: a shoulder in an arch-stone fitting into the stone next to it. [Fr.]

**Crossopterygii,** *kros-op-tər-ij'i-ī*, *n.pl.* a subclass of fishes, nearly extinct, whose paired fins have an axis fringed with rays.—*adj.* and *n.* **crossopteryg'ian.** [Gr. *krossoi*, tassels, fringe, *pteryx, -gos,* fin.]

**crotal,** *krō'təl*, *n.* a crotalum: a small spherical bell.—*n.* **Crotalaria** (*krot-*, *krōt-ə-lā'ri-a*), the sunn-hemp genus of Papilionaceae, including the American rattle-boxes (from their inflated pods).—*n.pl.* **Crotalidae** (*-tal'*), the rattlesnake family.—*adjs.* **crotaline** (*krot'ə-lin*), like a rattle-snake.—*ns.* **crot'alism,** poisoning by crotalaria; **crotalum** (*krot'ə-ləm*), a clapper or castanet used in ancient Mysteries; **Crotalus** (*krot'*), the rattle-snake genus. [Gr. *krotalon,* a rattle, castanet.]

**crotal, crottle,** *krot'l*, *n.* a lichen (of various kinds) used for dyeing. [Gael. *crotal.*]

**crotch,** *kroch*, *n.* a fork, as of a tree: the bifurcation of the human body.—*adj.* **crotched.** [Ety. obscure.]

**crotchet,** *kroch'it*, *n.* a hook: a note in music, equal to half a minim, ♩: a crooked or perverse fancy :a whim, or conceit.I—*adjs.* **crotch'eted, crotch'-ety,** having crotchets or peculiarities: whimsical.—*n.* **crotch'eteer,** a crotchety person. [Fr. *crochet,* dim. of *croche,* a hook; see crochet.]

**Croton,** *krō'tən*, *n.* a genus of tropical plants of the spurge family: extended by gardeners, etc., to a tropical hedge-plant of the same family, *Codiaeum variegatum.*—**croton oil,** a powerful purgative got from the seeds of *Croton Tiglium.* [Gr. *krōtōn,* a sheep-tick, which the seed resembles.]

**crouch,** *krowch*, *v.i.* to squat or lie close to the ground, as an animal preparing to spring: to bend low with legs doubled: to cringe: to fawn.—*v.t.* to bend.—*n.* act or position of crouching. [Possibly connected with crook.]

**Crouched-friars, Crutched-friars.** See crutch.

**crouch-ware,** *krowch'-wār, n.* an old salt-glazed stoneware made at Burslem. [Origin unknown.]

**croup,** *krōōp, n.* inflammation of the larynx and trachea in children, associated with a peculiar ringing cough, present especially in diphtheria: a burr.—*v.i.* to croak or speak hoarsely.—*n.* **croup'iness.**—*adjs.* **croup'ous, croup'y.** [From the sound made.]

**croup, croupe,** *krōōp, n.* the rump of a horse: the place behind the saddle.—*n.* **croup'on** (*obs.*), the croup; the human buttocks. [Fr. *croupe,* a protuberance; allied to crop.]

**croupade,** *krōō-pād', n.* a leap in which the horse draws up his hind-legs toward the belly. [Fr.]

**crouper,** *krōōp'ər, n.* obsolete form of crupper.

**croupier,** *krōō'pi-ər,* or *'pi-ā, n.* one who sits at the lower end of the table as assistant chairman at a public dinner: a vice-president: one who officiates at a gaming-table, collecting the stakes and paying the winners. [Fr., one who rides on the croup.]

**crouse,** *krōōs,* (*Scot.*) *adj.* lively, cheerfully confident.—*adv.* boldly, pertly.—*adv.* **crouse'ly.** [M.E. *crūs;* cf. L.G. *krūs,* gay, Ger. *kraus,* Du. *kroes,* crisp, cross.]

croustade, kroōs-täd', n. a case of fried bread or pastry for serving game, etc. [Fr.]

crout, krowt, n. Same as sauerkraut.

croûte, kroōt, n. a thick slice of fried bread for serving entrées.—n. croûton (-tō, -ton'), a small piece of fried bread. [Fr. croûte, crust.]

crow, krō, n. a moderately large black bird, of the genus Corvus—in England C. corone (the so-called carrion crow), in Scotland the rook: extended to other birds: inferior coal: the defiant or triumphant cry of a cock: a child's inarticulate cry of joy: a crow-bar.—v.i. to croak: to utter a crow: to boast, swagger, triumph (often with over):—pa.t. crew (kroō), or crowed; pa.p. crowed, also crown (krōn).— crow'-bar, a large iron bar mostly bent at the end, to be used as a lever; crow'-berry, a small creeping moorland shrub (Empetrum) producing small black berries; crow'-flower (Shak.), perhaps crowfoot; crow'foot, a buttercup, sometimes extended to other plants (pl. in this sense crow-foots): crow's-foot: a number of lines rove through a long wooden block, supporting the backbone of an awning horizontally; crow'-keeper (Shak.), a scarecrow; crow'-quill, a pen made of the quill of a crow, etc., for fine writing or etching; crow's'-bill, crow'-bill (surg.), a kind of forceps for extracting bullets, etc., from wounds; crow's-foot, one of the wrinkles produced by age, spreading out from the corners of the eyes: a caltrop (mil.); crow'-shrike, a piping-crow (see pipe); crow's'-nest (naut.), an elevated shelter for a man on the lookout.—n.pl. crow'-steps, steps on a gable.—crow'-toe (Milt.), probably the same as crowfoot.—as the crow flies, in a straight line; eat crow, eat boiled crow, to be forced to do something very disagreeable, humiliate oneself; have a crow to pluck with, to have something to settle with someone; Royston crow, the hooded crow (Corvus cornix)—said to be common near Royston in Herts. [O.E. crāwe, a crow, crāwan, to crow.]

crowd, krowd, n. a number of persons or things closely pressed together, without order: the rabble: multitude: a set.—v.t. to gather into a lump or crowd: to fill by pressing or driving together: to compress: to thrust, put pressure on.—v.i. to press on: to press together in numbers: to swarm.—adj. crowd'ed.—crowd sail, to carry a press of sail for speed. [O.E. crūdan, to press.]

crowd, krowd, n. (obs.) the crwth.—n. crowd'er (obs.), a fiddler. [See crwth.]

crowdie, krowd'i, (Scot.) n. a mixture of meal and water: brose: a cheese-like preparation of milk. [Der. unknown; perh. in part for crud.]

crown, krown, n. a circular head ornament, esp. as a mark of honour: the diadem or state-cap of royalty: kingship: the sovereign: governing power in a monarchy: honour: the top of anything, as a head, hat, tree, arch: a species of spire or lantern, formed by converging flying buttresses (archit.): a stag's surroyals: the visible part of a tooth: the junction of root and stem: a short footrostock: a clasping metal cap for a bottle: chief ornament: completion or consummation: a coin originally stamped with a crown, esp. a 5s. piece: used to translate various coin names, as krone: the old French écu: a British size of paper before metrication (a U.S. size of paper 15×19 in.), originally water-marked with a crown.—v.t. to cover or invest with a crown: to cap: to invest with royal dignity: to fill with foaming liquor; in draughts, to convert into a king or crowned man by the placing of another draught on the top on reaching the crown-head: to adorn: to dignify: to complete happily: to hit on the head (slang).—adj. crowned.—ns. crown'er (Shak.), a coroner; crown'et, a coronet: (Shak.) that which crowns

or accomplishes; crown'ing.—adj. crown'less.—n. crown'let, a small crown.—crown'-ag'ent, a solicitor in Scotland who prepares criminal prosecutions; crown'-ant'ler, the uppermost tine of an antler; crown'-bark', a kind of cinchona bark; crown'-cap, a lined metal cap for a bottle; crown colony, colony administered directly by the home government; crown courts, the system of courts replacing assize courts and quarter sessions; crown Derby, a late 18th-century porcelain made at Derby, marked with a crown; crowned head, monarch; crown'-gall', bacterial disease of plants, forming tumours; crown'-glass, alkali-lime glass: window-glass formed in circular plates or disks; crown'-graft, insertion of scions between bark and wood; crown'-green, a bowling-green with a crown or arched surface; crown'-head', in draughts, the back row of squares, where a man is crowned; crown'-impe'rial, a plant, a species of fritillary; crown'-jew'el, a jewel pertaining to the crown or sovereign; crown'-land, land belonging to the crown or sovereign; crown'-law'yer, the lawyer who acts for the crown in criminal cases; crown living, a church living in the gift of the crown; crown octavo, an octavo 5×7½ in.; Crown Office, the office for the business of the crown side of the King's Bench: the office in which the great seal is affixed; crown-of-thorns starfish, a starfish that eats living coral; crown'-piece, a five-shilling piece; crown'-post, a king-post; crown prince, the heir apparent to the crown; crown'-saw, saw consisting of a rotating teeth-edged cylinder; crown'-wheel, wheel with teeth set at right angles to its plane; crown witness, a witness for the crown in a criminal prosecution instituted by it; crown'-work (fort.), an outwork composed of a bastion between two curtains, with demi-bastions at the extremes.—crown and anchor, a dicing game; crown of the causeway, middle of the street. [O. Fr. corone—L. corōna; cf. Gr. koronos, curved.]

croze, krōz, n. the groove in the staves of a cask in which the edge of the head is set. [Perh. O.Fr. croz (Fr. creux), groove.]

crozier. See crosier.

cru, krü, (Fr.) a vineyard or group of vineyards.

crucial, cruciate. See crux.

crucian, crusian, kroō'shan, n. the German carp, without barbels. [L.G. karusse (Ger. karausche) —L. coracīnus—Gr. korakinos, a black perch-like fish—korax, raven.]

crucible, kroō'si-bl, n. an earthen pot for melting ores, metals, etc. [L.L. crucibulum.]

crucifer, kroō'si-far, n. a cross-bearer in a procession: a member of the Cruciferae.—n.pl. Crucif'erae, a family of archichlamydeous dicotyledons, with cross-shaped flowers, including cabbage, turnip, cress, wallflower.—adj. crucif'erous, bearing or marked with a cross: with four petals placed crosswise: of the Cruciferae. [L. crux, crucis, a cross, ferre, to bear.]

cruciform, crucigerous. See crux.

crucify, kroō'si-fī, v.t. to expose or put to death on a cross: to fasten to a wheel or the like, as a military field punishment: to subdue completely: to mortify: to torment:—pr.p. cru'cifying: pa.t. and pa.p. cru'cified.—ns. cru'cifier, one who crucifies; cru'cifix, a figure or picture of Christ fixed to the cross; crucifixion (-fik'shan). [O.Fr. crucifier—L. crucifīgĕre, crucifīxum— crux, cross, and figĕre, to fix.]

cruck, kruk, n. in crude building, a curved timber supporting a roof. [Cf. crook.]

crud, krud, kroōd, obs. and dial. form of curd.— v.t. (Spens.) and v.i. crudd'le, curdle.—adj. crudd'y, curdy (Spens.): contemptible (slang).

crude, kroōd, adj. raw, unprepared: not reduced to order or form: unfinished: undigested: immature: unrefined: inartistic.—adv. crude'ly. —ns. crude'ness; crud'ity, rawness: unripeness:

Neutral vowels in unaccented syllables: el'ə-mənt; for certain sounds in foreign words, see p. viii

that which is crude.—*adj.* **crud′y** (*Shak.*), crude, raw. [L. *crūdus*, raw.]

**crue,** a Miltonic spelling of crew (*n.*).

**cruel,** *krōō′əl, adj.* disposed to inflict pain, or pleased at suffering: void of pity, merciless, savage: severe.—*adv.* **cru′elly.**—*ns.* **cru′elness** (*obs.*); **cru′elty.**—*adj.* **cru′el-heart′ed,** delighting in cruelty. [Fr. *cruel*—L. *crūdēlis.*]

**cruels, cruells.** Same as crewels.

**cruet,** *krōō′it, n.* a small jar or phial for sauces and condiments for the table: a vessel for wine, oil, or water for religious ceremonies.—**cru′et-stand,** a stand or frame for holding cruets. [A.Fr., dim. of O.Fr. *cruye,* jar, from root of crock.]

**cruise,** *krōōz, v.i.* to sail to and fro: to fly at a speed economical in fuel, etc.: to wander about seeking something (with *about,* etc.; *coll.*).—*n.* a sailing to and fro: a wandering voyage in search of an enemy or for the protection of vessels or for pleasure or health: a land journey of similar character.—*ns.* **cruis′er,** one who or that which cruises: speedy warship, specially for cruising: a privateer: a cruising yacht.— **cruis′er-weight,** a boxer between middle and heavy, a light-heavyweight. [Du. *kruisen,* to cross.]

**cruisie.** See crusie.

**cruive, cruve,** *krōōv* (*Scot. krŭv, kriv*), *n.* a pen, sty: a hovel: a wattled fish-trap.

**cruller,** *krul′ər,* (*U.S.*) *n.* a friedcake. [Cf. Du. *krullen,* to curl.]

**crumb,** *krum, n.* a small bit or morsel of bread: a small particle of anything: the soft part of bread.—*v.t.* to break into crumbs: to put crumbs in or on: to remove crumbs from.—*v.i.* to crumble.—*adjs.* **crumb′y,** in crumbs: soft; **crum′my,** crumby: plump, or lousy (*slang*).— **crumb′-brush,** a brush for sweeping crumbs off the table: **crumb′-cloth,** a cloth laid under a table to keep crumbs from the carpet: drugget; **crumb′-tray,** a tray for crumbs removed from the table. [O.E. *cruma;* Du. *kruim;* Ger. *krume;* crimp.]

**crumble,** *krum′bl, v.t.* to break into crumbs.—*v.i.* to fall into small pieces: to decay.—*n.* a crumb: that which crumbles easily.—*adj.* **crum′bly.** [Orig. dim. of crumb; Du. *kruimelen;* Ger. *krümeln.*]

**crumen,** *krōō′mən, n.* a deer's tear-pit.—*n.* **cru′-menal** (*Spens.*), a purse. [L. *crumēna,* a purse.]

**crumhorn.** See krummhorn.

**crummock, crummack,** *krum′ək, n.* a crook, stick with curved head. [Gael. *cromag,* hook, crook.]

**crummy.** See crumb, crump.

**crump,** *krump, adj.* crooked: wrinkled: crisp, friable (*Scot.*).—*ns.* **crumm′y,** cow with a crumpled horn: **crump′et,** soft, unsweetened griddle cake: the head (*slang*): a girl (*slang*).— *adj.* **crump′y** (*dial.*), crisp. [O.E. *crump*—crumb, crooked; Ger. *krumm.* Cf. crimp.]

**crumple,** *krump′l, v.t.* to crush into irregular wrinkles: to wrinkle: to cause to collapse.—*v.i.* to wrinkle: to collapse.—*adj.* **crump′led.**—*n.* **crump′ling.** [crump.]

**crunch,** *krunch, v.t.* to crush with harsh noise, with the teeth, under foot, or otherwise: to chew anything hard, and so make a noise.—*v.i.* to make such a noise: to chew with, or as with, such a noise.—*n.* the act or sound of crunching: (with *the*) the real testing moment, trial of strength, etc.—*n.* **crunch′iness.**—*adj.* **crunch′y.**

**crunkle,** *krunk′l, v.i.* to crumple. [Cf. crinkle.]

**cruor,** *krōō′ör, n.* coagulated blood. [L.]

**crupper,** *krup′ər, n.* a strap of leather fastened to the saddle and passing under the horses's tail to keep the saddle in its place: the hind part of a horse. [O.Fr. *cropiere*—*crope,* the croup.]

**crural,** *krōō′rəl, adj.* belonging to or like a leg. [L. *crūrālis,* from, *crūs, crūris,* the leg.]

**crusade,** *krōō-sād′, n.* a military expedition under

the banner of the cross to recover the Holy Land from the Turks: any daring or romantic undertaking: concerted action to further a cause.—*v.i.* to go on a crusade.—*n.* **crusad′er,** one engaged in a crusade. [Fr. *croisade*—Prov. *crozada*—*croz* —L. *crux,* a cross.]

**crusado,** *krōō-sä′dō, n.* a Portuguese coin, so called because marked with a cross. [Port. *cruzado.*]

**cruse,** *krōōz,* also *krōōs, n.* an earthen pot: a small cup or bottle. [Cf. O.N. *krūs;* Ger. *krause.*]

**cruset,** *krōō′sit, n.* a goldsmith's crucible. [Cf. Fr. *creuset,* M.Du. *kruysel,* M.L.G. *krusel.*]

**crush,** *krush, v.t.* to break or bruise: to squeeze together: to beat down or overwhelm: to subdue: to ruin.—*v.i.* to become broken or crumpled under pressure.—*n.* a violent squeezing: a close crowd of persons or things: a drink made from fruit juice; a set of people (*slang*): a narrowing passage for cattle: an infatuation (with *on*), or its object.—*adj.* **crushed.**—*ns.* **crush′er,** one who, or that which, crushes or subdues: a policeman (*slang*).—*adj.* **crush′ing.**—*adv.* **crush′ingly.**— **crush′-barr′ier,** a barrier erected to restrain a crowd; **crushed strawberry,** the pinky colour of strawberries that have been crushed.—also *adj.*— **crush′-hat,** an opera-hat.—**crush′-room,** a room where an audience may promenade during the intervals of the entertainment.—**crush a cup,** to empty a cup: to quaff. [O.Fr. *croissir;* perh. cog. with M.H.G. *krosen,* to crunch.]

**crusie, crusy,** *krōōz′i* (*Scot.*) *n.* an open iron lamp used with a rush wick. [From cruset.]

**crust,** *krust, n.* hard rind or outside coating of anything: outer part of bread: covering of a pie, etc.: solid exterior of the earth: cheek (*slang*).—*v.t.* to cover with a crust or hard case. —*v.i.* to gather into a hard crust.—*adj.* **crust′al,** pertaining to a crust; **crust′ate, crustāt′ed,** covered with a crust.—*n.* **crustā′tion,** an adherent crust.—*adv.* **crust′ily.**—*n.* **crusti′ness.**—*adjs.* **crust′less; crust′y,** of the nature of or having a crust, as port or other wine: having a hard or harsh exterior: hard: snappy: surly. [L. *crusta,* rind.]

**crusta,** *krus′tə, n.* a piece prepared for inlaying: a hard coating: a cocktail served in a glass, its rim encrusted in sugar:—*pl.* **crustae** (-*tē*). [L.]

**Crustacea,** *krus-tā′sh*(*y*)*ə,* -*shi-ə, n.pl.* a large class of arthropod animals, almost all aquatic—crabs, lobsters, shrimps, sand-hoppers, wood-lice, water-fleas, barnacles, etc.—*adj.* and *n.* **crustā′-cean.**—*adj.* **crustā′ceous,** crusty.

**crutch,** *kruch, n.* a staff with a cross-piece at the head to place under the arm of a lame person: any support of like form: a bifurcation, crotch: a small figure inserted to show the number to be carried (*arith.*).—*v.t.* to support: to prop.—*v.i.* to go on crutches.—*adj.* **crutched,** marked by the sign of or wearing a Cross.—*n.pl.* **Crutch′ed-fri′ars,** an order of friars so called from the sign of the cross which they wore—*Crouched-* or *Crossed-friars.* [O.E. *crycc.*]

**crux,** *kruks, n.* a cross: something that occasions difficulty or perplexity (*fig.*): that on which a decision turns: the essential point, as of a problem:—*pl.* **cruxes, cruces** (*krōō′sēz*).—*adjs.* **crucial** (*krōō′shəl*), crosslike: of the nature of a crux: testing or decisive, as if of the nature of a finger-post at a cross-road; **cruciate** (*krōō′shi-āt*), cross-shaped.—*v.t.* to torment.—*adjs.* **cruciform** (*krōō′si-förm*), cross-shaped; **crucigerous** (*krōō′sij′ər-əs*), bearing a cross. [L. *crux, crucis,* a cross.]

**crux criticorum,** *kruks* (*krōōks*) *krit-i-kō′rəm,* -*kö′,* (-*rōōm*), (L.) a puzzle for the critics.

**cruzeiro,** *krōō-zā′rō, n.* the monetary unit of Brazil. [Port. *cruz,* cross.]

**crwth,** *krōōth, n.* the crowd, an old Welsh stringed instrument, four of its six strings played with a bow, two plucked by the thumb. [W. *crwth,* a

hollow protuberance, a fiddle; Gael., Ir. *cruit*.]
**cry**, *krī*, *v.i.* to utter a shrill loud sound, esp. one of pain or grief: to lament: to weep: to bawl.— *v.t.* to utter loudly: to exclaim: to proclaim or make public: to offer for sale by crying: to proclaim the banns of marriage of (*Scot.*):—*3rd pers. sing.* **cries**; *pr.p.* **cry'ing**; *pa.t.* and *pa.p.* **cried** (*krīd*).—*n.* any loud sound, esp. of grief or pain: a call or shout: a fit of weeping: a pack of hounds, hence of people: a particular sound uttered by an animal: the creak of bent tin: bawling: lamentation: prayer: clamour: report or rumour: a general utterance: a watchword, battle-cry, or slogan: a street call of wares for sale or services offered:—*pl.* **cries**.—*ns.* **cri'er**, one who cries, esp. an official maker of proclamations; **cry'ing**, act of calling loudly: weeping. —*adj.* calling loudly: claiming notice: notorious.—**cry'-baby**, one who cries childishly.—**a far cry**, a great distance; **cry against**, to protest against; **cry down**, to decry; **cry for the moon**, to beg, or sigh, for something unattainable; **cry off**, to withdraw from an agreement; **cry on**, to call upon; **cry out** (*obs.*), to be in childbirth; **cry over spilt milk**, to waste time in bemoaning what is irreparable; **cry quits**, to declare a thing even; **cry stinking fish**, decry one's own goods; **cry up**, to praise; **cry you mercy** (*obs.*), I beg your pardon; **great cry and little wool**, much ado about nothing; **hue and cry** (see **hue**); **in full cry**, in full pursuit, used of dogs in hunt; **out of cry** (*obs.*), beyond measure: beyond dispute; **within cry of**, within hearing distance. [Fr. *crier* —L. *quirītāre*, to scream.]
**cryo-**, *krī'ō-*, *krī-o'-*, in composition, frost, ice.—*ns.* **cryoc'onite** (Gr. *konis*, dust), dust found on the surface of polar ice; **cry'ogen** (-*jen*; Gr. root of *gignesthai*, to become), a substance used for obtaining low temperatures, a freezing mixture. —*adj.* **cryogen'ic**, pertaining to the science of cryogenics, or to work done, apparatus used, or substances kept, at low temperatures.—*ns.* **cryogen'ics**, the branch of physics concerned with phenomena at very low temperatures; **cryogeny** (-*oj'ə-ni*), refrigeration: cryogenics; **cry'olite** (Gr. *lithos*, a stone), an ice-stone or Greenland spar, sodium aluminium fluoride, earliest source of aluminium; **cryom'eter** (Gr. *metron*, measure), a thermometer for low temperatures.—*adj.* **cryomet'ric**.—*ns.* **cryoph'orus** (Gr. *pherein*, to bear), an instrument for showing the decrease of temperature in water by evaporation; **cry'ophysics**, low temperature physics; **cry'oscope** (Gr. *skopeein*, to look at), an instrument for determining freezing-points.— *adj.* **cryoscop'ic**.—*ns.* **cryos'copy**, the study of the effect of dissolved substances on the freezing-points of solvents; **cry'ostat**, apparatus for achieving or demonstrating cooling by evaporation: any apparatus for maintaining a low temperature; **cry'osurgery**, surgery using instruments at very low temperatures; **cryother'apy**, medical treatment using extreme cold; **cry'otron**, a tiny form of electronic switch operating in a bath of liquid helium a few degrees above absolute zero. [Gr. *kryos*, frost.]
**crypt**, *kript*, *n.* an underground cell or chapel: a small cavity, a tubular gland (*zool.*).—*adjs.* **cryp'tal**, pertaining to, or of the nature of, a crypt; **cryp'tic**, **-al**, hidden: secret: unseen: mysteriously obscure: protectively concealing (*zool.*). [L. *crypta*—Gr. *kryptē*—*kryptein*, to hide; cf. **grot**.]
**crypto**, *krip'tō*, *n.* a secret member of a party, sect, organisation, etc.
**crypt-**, **crypto-**, *kript-*, *-ō-*, *-o-*, in composition, hidden.—*n.* **cryptaesthesia** (*kript-ēs-thē'zyə*, *-zhə*); Gr. *aisthēsis*, perception), supranormal perception, e.g. clairvoyance.—*adj.* **cryptaesthēt'ic**. —*n.pl.* **cryptadia** (*krip-tā'di-ə*; Gr.), things to

be kept secret.—*ns.* **cryp'to-Christian**; **cryp'to-communist**.—*adj.* **cryptocryst'alline**, with crystalline structure visible only under the microscope. —*n.* **cryp'togam** (Gr. *gamos*, marriage), any member of the **Cryptogamia** (*krip'tō-gā'mi-ə*), the class of flowerless plants, so named by Linnaeus in the expectation that sexual reproduction would one day be discovered in them.— *adjs.* **cryptogā'mian**, **cryptogamic** (-*gam'ik*), **cryptogamous** (-*tog'ə-məs*).—*ns.* **cryptog'amist**; **cryptog'amy**.—*ns.* **cryp'togram**, **cryp'tograph** (Gr. *gramma*, a letter, *graphein*, to write), anything written in cipher.—*ns.* **cryptŏg'rapher**, **-ist**.—*adj.* **cryptograph'ic**.—*n.* **cryptog'raphy**. —*adj.* **cryptolog'ical**.—*ns.* **cryptol'ogist**; **cryptol'-ogy**, secret language: the scientific study of codes. **Cryptomēr'ia** (Gr. *meros*, part), the Japanese cedar; **crypton** (same as **krypton**); **cryp'tonym** (Gr. *onyma*, name), a secret name.—*adj.* **cryptön'ymous**. [Gr. *kryptos*, hidden.]
**crystal**, *kris'tl*, *n.* ice (*obs.*): rock-crystal, a clear quartz, like ice: a body, generally solid, whose atoms are arranged in a definite pattern, outwardly expressed by geometrical form with plane faces: a globe of rock-crystal or the like in which one may see visions: anything bright and clear: a superior glass of various kinds: cut glass: a watch-glass.—*adj.* composed of or like crystal.— *adj.* **crys'talline** (-*in*, *-in*; in the poets also *-tal'*), like crystal or a crystal: composed of crystal, crystals, or parts of crystals: having the structure of a crystal.—*n.* a crystalline substance: aniline (*obs.*): a shining fabric of silk and wool; **crystalli'sable**.—*n.* **crystallisā'tion**.—*v.t.* and *v.i.* **crys'tallise**, **-ize**, to form into crystals: to make or become definite or concrete: of fruit, to coat with sugar crystals.—*ns.* **crys'tallite**, a small, imperfectly formed or incipient crystal: a minute body in glassy igneous rocks; **crystalli'tis**, inflammation of the crystalline lens; **crystallogen'esis**, origination of crystals.—*adj.* **crystal-logenet'ic**.—*n.* **crystallog'rapher**.—*adj.* **crystal-lograph'ic**.—*ns.* **crystallog'raphy**, the science of the structure, forms, and properties of crystals; **crys'talloid**, a substance in a state in which it dissolves to form a true solution which will pass through a membrane: a minute crystalline particle of protein (*bot.*).—*adj.* like a crystal: of the nature of a crystalloid.—*n.* **crys'tallomancy** (Gr. *manteiā*, divination), divination by transparent bodies.—*adj.* **crys'tal-clear**, very, completely clear.—**crys'tal-gazer**; **crys'tal-gazing**, gazing in a crystal or the like to obtain visual images, whether in divination or to objectify hidden contents of the mind; **crystalline heaven**, **sphere**, in ancient astronomy a sphere between the fixed stars and the *primum mobile*, assumed to explain precession of the equinoxes; **crystalline lens**, the transparent refractive body of the eye; **crystal rectifier**, rectifier that depends on differential conduction in semiconductor crystals suitably doped; **crystal set**, a simple wireless receiving apparatus in which a crystal and a cat's-whisker rectify the current. [O.Fr. *cristal*—L. *crystallum* —Gr. *krystallos*, ice—*kryos*, frost.]
**csárdás**, *chär'däsh*, *n.* a Hungarian dance, or its music, in two movements, one slow and the other fast.—Also (wrongly) **czardas**. [Hung.]
**c-spring**. See **cee-spring**.
**ctene**, *tēn*, *n.* a comb-like swimming organ in the Ctenophora.—*adjs.* **cteniform** (*tēn'*, or *ten'*), **cten'oid**, comb-shaped.—*n.pl.* **Ctenoph'ora**, a class of Coelenterates—beautifully delicate, free-swimming marine organisms, moving by means of meridionally placed comb-like plates.— *n.*, *adj.* **ctenoph'oran**.—*n.* **ctenophore**, any member of the Ctenophora. [Gr. *kteis*, *ktenos*, comb.]
**Ctesiphon arch**, *tes'i-fon*, an arch of inverted catenary shape, such as the great ruined arch at Ctesiphon, on the Tigris south-east of Baghdad.

Neutral vowels in unaccented syllables: *el'ə-mənt*; for certain sounds in foreign words, see p. viii

cub, *kub*, *n.* the young of certain animals, as foxes, etc.: a whelp: a young boy or girl (playful or contemptuous, esp. of the ill-conditioned, unmannerly, raw, or conceited): (in full Cub Scout) an embryo Scout: beginner, novice, apprentice, a young or inexperienced reporter.—*v.t.* and *v.i.* to bring forth: to hunt (fox-cubs):—*pr.p.* cubb'ing; *pa.t.* and *pa.p.* cubbed.—*adj.* cubb'ish, like a cub: awkward or ill-mannered.—*ns.* cub'hood; cubb'ing, cub-hunting.—*adj.* cub'less. —*adj.* cub'-drawn (*Shak.*), drawn or sucked by cubs.—cub'-hunting, hunting of young foxes. [Ety. dub.]

cub, *kub*, *n.* a cattle-pen: a chest.—*ns.* cubb'y, cubb'y-hole, a snug enclosed place. [Prob. from L.G.]

Cuban, *kū'bən*, *adj.* pertaining to Cuba or its people.—*n.* a native of Cuba.—Cuban heel, on footwear, a high heel without curves.

cube, *kūb*, *n.* a solid body having six equal square faces, a solid square: the third power of a quantity.—*v.t.* to raise to the third power: to cut into cubes.—*ns.* cub'age, cū'bature, the act of finding the solid or cubic content of a body: the result thus found.—*adjs.* cū'bic, -al, pertaining to a cube: of or involving the third power or degree: solid: isometric (*crystal.*).—*adv.* cū'bically.—*n.* cū'bicalness.—*adj.* cū'biform.—*n.* cū'bism, a modern movement in painting, which seeks to represent several aspects of an object seen from different standpoints arbitrarily grouped in one composition, making use of cubes and other solid geometrical figures.—*n.* and *adj.* cū'bist.—*n.* cū'boid, a rectangular parallelepiped, esp. one whose faces are not all equal.—*adjs.* cū'boid, cū'boid'al, resembling a cube in shape.—cube root, the quantity of which the given quantity is the cube. [Fr.,—L. *cubus*— Gr. *kybos*, a die.]

cubeb, *kū'beb*, *n.* the dried berry of *Piper Cubeba*, a Sumatran climbing pepper shrub—used in medicine. [Fr. *cubèbe*—Ar. *kabābah*.]

cubica, *kū'bi-kə*, *n.* a fine worsted for linings. [Sp. *cubica*.]

cubicle, *kū'bi-kl*, *n.* a bedroom: part of a dormitory or other large room which is partitioned off: a cell or compartment. [L. *cubiculum*—*cubāre*, to lie down.]

cubit, *kū'bit*, *n.* an old measure, the length of the arm from the elbow to the tip of the middle-finger, from 18 to 22 inches—also cū'bitus.—*adj.* cū'bital, of the length of a cubit. [L. *cubitum*, the elbow; cf. L. *cubāre*, to lie down.]

cucking-stool, *kuk'ing-stōōl*, *n.* a stool in which scolds and other culprits were placed, usually before their own door, to be pelted by the mob. [Mentioned in Domesday Book as in use in Chester, and called *cathedra stercoris*. From an obs. word *cuck*, to defecate; cf. O.N. *kūka*.]

cuckold, *kuk'əld*, *n.* a man whose wife has proved unfaithful.—*v.t.* to make cuckold.—*v.t.* cuck'-oldise, -ize, to make a cuckold.—*adj.* cuck'oldly (*Shak.*).—*ns.* cuck'oldom, cuck'oldry, state of a cuckold: act of making a cuckold.—*adj.* cuck'oldy.—cuck'old-mak'er. [O.Fr. *cucuault*—*cucu*, cuckoo.]

cuckoo, *koō'koō*, *n.* a bird (*Cuculus*) that cries *cuckoo*, remarkable for depositing its eggs in the nests of other birds: a silly person.—*adj.* silly.—cuck'oo-bud (*Shak.*), name of a plant; cuck'oo-clock, a clock in which the hours are told by a cuckoo-call; cuck'oo-flower, a species of Cardamine—Lady's-smock: ragged robin; cuck'oo-fly, a gold-wasp—from laying its eggs in wasps' and bees' nests; cuck'oo-pint (-*pint*), the Wake-robin, *Arum maculatum*; cuck'oo-spit, -spitt'le, a froth secreted by frog-hoppers on plants, surrounding the larvae and pupae. [Imit.; cf. Fr. *coucou*, Ger. *kuckuck*, L. *cucūlus*, Gr. *kokkyx*, -*ȳgos*.]

cucullate, -d, *kū'kul-āt*, or -*kul'*, -*id*, *adjs.* hooded: shaped like a hood. [L. *cucullatus*—*cucullus*.]

cucumber, *kū'kəm-bər*, -*kum*-, *n.* a creeping plant (*Cucumis sativus*) of the Cucurbitaceae, with bristly lobed leaves and tendrils: its large oblong fruit, used as a salad and pickle: a cucumber-tree (*U.S.*).—cū'cumber-tree, the bilimbi tree: a magnolia (*U.S.*): also a tulip-tree (*U.S.*).— *adj.* cūcūm'iform. [L. *cucumis*, -*eris*.]

cucurbit, *kū-kûr'bit*, *n.* a chemical vessel used in distillation, originally shaped like a gourd.—*adjs.* cucur'bital, cucurbitā'ceous, pertaining to the Cucurbitā'ceae, a family of sympetalous dicotyledons, including gourd, melon, etc.: gourd-like. [L. *cucurbita*, a gourd.]

cud, *kud*, *n.* food brought back from first stomach of a ruminating animal to be chewed again.— cud'weed, a woolly composite plant of the genus Gnaphalium: extended to kindred plants.— chew the cud (*coll.*), to meditate, to reflect. [O.E. *cwidu*.]

cudbear, *kud'bār*, *n.* a purple dye-stuff, a powder prepared from various lichens. [From Dr Cuthbert Gordon, who made it an article of commerce.]

cuddle, *kud'l*, *v.t.* to hug: to embrace: to fondle. —*v.i.* to lie close and snug together.—*n.* a close embrace. [Origin unknown.]

cuddy, *kud'i*, *n.* a small cabin or cookroom, in the fore-part of a boat or lighter: in large vessels, the officers' cabin under the poop-deck. [Origin uncertain: cf. Fr. *cahute*; Du. *kajuit*; Ger. *kajüte*.]

cuddy, *kud'i*, (*hist.*) *n.* the right of a lord to entertainment from his tenant: rent—(*Spens.*) cuddeehih. [Ir. *cuid oidhche*—*cuid*, a share, *oidche*, night.]

cuddy, cuddie, *kud'i*, (*Scot.*) *n.* a donkey: a stupid person. [Perh. *Cuthbert*.]

cudgel, *kuj'l*, *n.* a heavy staff: a club.—*v.t.* to beat with a cudgel:—*pr.p.* cudg'elling; *pa.t.* and *pa.p.* cudg'elled.—*ns.* cudg'eller; cudg'elling.—cudg'el-play.—*adj.* cudg'el-proof, not to be hurt by beating.—take up the cudgels, to join in defence. [O.E. *cycgel*.]

cue, *kū*, *n.* the seventeenth letter of the alphabet (Q, q).

cue, *kū*, *n.* the last words of an actor's speech serving as a hint to the next speaker: any hint: the part one has to play.—*v.t.* to give a cue to: to insert a cue.—cue someone in (*U.S. slang*), to inform; on cue, just at the right moment. [Acc. to some from Fr. *queue*, tail (see next word); in 17th cent. written Q, and derived from L. *quando*, when, i.e. when the actor was to begin.]

cue, *kū*, *n.* a twist of hair at the back of the head: a rod used in playing billiards.—*v.t.* to form a cue in (hair).—*n.* cue'ist, a billiard-player.—cue ball, the ball struck by the cue. [Fr. *queue*—L. *cauda*, a tail.]

cuerpo, querpo, *kwer'pō*, used formerly in the phrase *in cuerpo*, or *querpo*, without the cloak: in undress: naked. [Sp., body.]

cuesta, *kwes'ta*, *n.* a hill ridge having a steep scarp on one side and a gradual slope on the other, caused by denudation of gently dipping hard rock strata. [Sp.]

cuff, *kuf*, *n.* a stroke with the open hand.—*v.t.* to strike with the open hand: to beat. [Origin obscure; cf. Sw. *kuffa*, to knock.]

cuff, *kuf*, *n.* the end of the sleeve near the wrist: a covering for the wrist: a handcuff: a turned-up fold at the bottom of a trouser leg (*U.S.*).—off the cuff, unofficially and off-hand. [Prob. cog. with coif.]

cuff, *kuf*, *n.* a Scottish form of scuff, scruff.— cuff of the neck. See scruff.

cuffin, *kuf'in*, *n.* a man.—queer cuffin, a justice of the peace: a churl. [Thieves' slang.]

cuffle, *kuf'l*, (*Spens.*) *v.i.* to scuffle.

cuffo, *kuf'ō*, (*U.S. slang*) *adv.* without any admission charge.

Cufic. Same as Kufic.

cui bono?, *ki'*, *kwē'*, *bō'nō*, *kōō'ē bo'nō*, (L.) for whose benefit is it?; who is the gainer?

cuif. Same as coof.

cuirass, *kwi-ras'* (or *kū'*), *n.* a defensive breastplate and backplate fastened together: a breastplate alone.—*v.t.* to furnish with a cuirass.—*n.* cuirassier (*-ēr'*), a horse-soldier armed with cuirass. [Fr. *cuirasse*—*cuir*, leather—L. *corium*, skin, leather.]

cuir-bouilli, *kwēr-bōō'yē*, *n.* leather boiled or soaked in hot water and moulded.—Also cuir-bouilly. [Fr., boiled leather.]

cuisine, *kwē-zēn'*, *n.* a kitchen or cooking department: cookery.—*n.* cuisin'ier (*-yā*), a cook. [Fr.,—L. *coquina*—*coçuēre*, to cook.]

cuisse, *kwis*, cuish, *kwish*, (*Shak.* cush, *kush*) *n.* thigh armour.—*n.* cuisse-madame (*-däm'*), a jargonelle pear. [Fr. *cuisse*—L. *coxa*, hip.]

cuit, cute, coot, *kût, küt, kit*, (*Scot.*) *n.* the ankle.—*n.* cuit'ikin, cut'ikin, coot'ikin, a gaiter. [Cf. Du. *koot*, Flem. *keute*.]

cuiter, *küt'ər*, (*Scot.*) *v.t.* to wheedle: to cocker, pamper.

cuittle, *küt'l*, (*Scot.*) *v.t.* to coax: to cajole: to curry (favour): (perh. by confusion with kittle) to tickle. [Origin obscure.]

culch, cultch, *kulch*, (*S. England*) *n.* rubbish: flooring of an oyster-bed: oyster-spawn. [Origin doubtful.]

Culdee, *kul'dē*, *n.* one of a fraternity of monks living in Scotland from the 8th century in groups of cells. [Old Ir. *cēle de*, servant or companion of God—Latinised by Boece into *Culdei* (pl.) as if *cultōrēs Dei*.]

cul-de-four, *kü(l)-də-fōōr* (Fr. *kü*), *n.* (*archit.*) a sort of low spherical vault, oven-like.—cul-de-lampe (*lăp*), an ornamental design used in filling up blank spaces in a book; cul-de-sac, a street, etc., closed at one end: a blind-alley. [Fr. *cul*, bottom—L. *cūlus*; Fr. *de*, of, *four*, furnace, *lampe*, lamp, *sac*, sack.]

culet, *kū'lit*, *n.* the back of a brilliant-cut diamond: armour protecting the hips. [O.Fr. *culet*, dim. of *cul*; see foregoing.]

Culex, *kū'leks*, *n.* the typical genus of Culic'idae or gnats (*pl.* culices, *kū'li-sēz*).—*adjs.* culiciform (*-lis'*); cu'licine.—*n.* cu'licid. [L. *culex*, *-icis*.]

culinary, *ku'lin-ər-i*, *kū'*, *adj.* pertaining to the kitchen or to cookery: used in the kitchen. [L. *culinārius*—*culīna*, a kitchen.]

cull, *kul*, *v.t.* to gather: to select: to pick out and destroy, as inferior members of a group, e.g. of seals, deer.—*n.* an unsuitable animal eliminated from a flock or herd.—*ns.* cull'er; cull'ing. [Fr. *cueillir*, to gather—L. *colligēre*—*col-*, together, *legēre*, to gather.]

cull. See cully.

cullender. See colander.

cullet, *kul'it*, *n.* waste glass, melted up again with new material. [Fr. *collet*—L. *collum*, neck.]

cullion, *kul'yən*, *n.* a wretch: a rascal.—*adj.* cull'ionly (*Shak.*), mean, base. [Fr. *couillon*, testicle, poltroon (It. *coglione*)—L. *cōleus*, a leather bag—Gr. *koleos*, sheath.]

cullis, *kul'is*, (rare) *n.* a strong broth. [O.F. *coleis* —L. *cōlāre*, to strain.]

cullis, *kul'is*, *n.* a roof gutter or groove. [Fr. *coulisse*.]

cully, *kul'i*, (rare) *n.* a mean dupe: fellow, mate, a man generally.—*v.t.* to deceive meanly:—*pr.p.* cull'ying; *pa.t.* and *pa.p.* cull'ied.—*ns.* cull, a dupe; cull'yism, state of being a cully. [Prob. a contr. of cullion.]

culm, *kulm*, *n.* a grass or sedge stem.—*v.i.* to form a culm.—*adj.* culmif'erous, having a culm. [L. *culmus*, a stalk.]

culm, *kulm*, *n.* coal-dust: anthracite dust: in some

parts of England, anthracite.—*adj.* culmif'erous, producing culm.—Culm, Culm Measures, a Lower Carboniferous formation of Europe and Southwest England, with grits, sandstones, shales, etc. [Origin unknown; cf. coom.]

culmen, *kul'men*, *n.* highest point: the top ridge of a bird's bill. [L.; see next.]

culminate, *kul'min-āt*, *v.i.* to be on, or come to, the meridian, and thus the highest (or lowest) point of altitude (*astron.*): to reach the highest point (with *in*).—*v.t.* to bring to the highest point.— *adj.* cul'minant, at its highest point.—*n.* culminā'-tion, act of culminating: the top: the highest point: transit of a body across the meridian (*astron.*). [L.L. *culmināre*, *-ātum*—*culmen*, or *columen*, *-inis*, a summit.]

culottes, *kōō-lot'*, *n.pl.* a divided skirt.—sans-culotte (see sans). [Fr. *culotte*, breeches.]

culpable, *kul'pə-bl*, *adj.* faulty: criminal.—*ns.* culpabil'ity, cul'pableness, liability to blame.—*adv.* cul'pably.—*adj.* cul'patory, expressive of blame. [L. *culpa*, a fault.]

culpa levis, *kul'pa lē'vis*, (*kōōl'pa le'vis*, *'wis*), (L.) a slight fault.

culprit, *kul'prit*, *n.* one in fault: a criminal: a prisoner accused but not yet tried (*Eng. law*). [From the fusion in legal phraseology of *cul.* (*culpable*, *culpābilis*), and *prit*, *prist* (O.Fr. *prest*), ready.]

cult, *kult*, *n.* a system of religious belief: formal worship: a sect: an unorthodox or false religion: a great, often excessive, admiration for a person or idea: (with *of*) a fad.—Also cult'us.—*adjs.* cult, cult'ic. [L. *cultus*—*colēre*, to worship.]

cultch. Same as culch.

culter, *kul'tər*, *n. obs.* form of coulter.—*adjs.* cul'trate, -d, cul'triform, knife-shaped. [L., knife.]

cultism, *kult'izm*, *n.* Gongorism.—*ns.* cult'ist, cult'orist. [Sp. *culto*, elegant—L. *cultus*.]

cultivate, *kul'ti-vāt*, *v.t.* to till or produce by tillage: to prepare for crops: to devote attention to: to civilise or refine.—*adjs.* cul'tivable, cultivat'able, capable of being cultivated.—*ns.* cultivar (*kul'ti-vär*), a *culti*vated *var*iety of a plant; cultivā'tion, the art or practice of cultivat-ing: civilisation: refinement; cul'tivator, one who cultivates: an agricultural implement—a grubber.—cultivate one's friendship, to seek to gain or foster it. [L.L. *cultivāre*, *-ātum*—L. *colēre*, to till, to worship.]

culture, *kul'chər*, *n.* cultivation: the state of being cultivated: refinement the result of cultivation: a type of civilisation: a crop of experimentally grown bacteria or the like.—*v.t.* to cultivate: to improve.—*adjs.* cul'turable; cul'tural.—*adj.* cul'-tured, cultivated: well educated: refined.—*adj.* cul'tureless.—*n.* cul'turist, a devotee of culture.—culture vulture, derogatory term for one who has an extravagant interest in the arts. [L. *cultūra*—*colēre*.]

cultus. See cult.

culver, *kul'vər*, *n.* a dove, a pigeon: a wood-pigeon.—*n.* cul'ver-key (often in *pl.*), the wild hyacinth: the cowslip: ash-keys.—*adj.* cul'vertailed, dove-tailed. [O.E. *culfre*.]

culverin, *kul'vər-in*, *n.* an early form of cannon of great length, generally an 18-pounder, weighing 50 cwt.—*n.* culverineer'.—*dem'i-cul'verin*, a 9-pounder of 30 cwt. [Fr. *coulevrine*—*couleuvre*, snake—L. *colubrinus*, snake-like—*coluber*, snake.]

Culver's physic, root, *kul'vərz*, the rhizome of speedwell *Veronica virginica*, used medicinally. [From some Dr *Culver*.]

culvert, *kul'vərt*, *n.* an arched channel for carrying water beneath a road, railway, etc. [Perh. from Fr. *couler*, to flow—L. *cōlāre*.]

culvertage, *kul'vərt-tij*, *n.* degradation of a vassal to the position of a serf. [O.Fr. *culvert*, a serf.]

**cum**, *kúm*, *prep.* combined with. [L.]
**cumbent**, *kum'bənt*, *adj.* lying down: reclining.
[L. *cumbēns*, *-entis*, pr.p. of *cumbēre*, to lie down.]
**cumber**, *kum'bər*, *v.t.* to trouble or hinder with
something useless: to get in the way of: to
occupy obstructively.—*n.* encumbrance: cum-
bering.—*adj.* cum'bered, hampered: obstructed.
—*n.* cum'berer.—*adj.* cum'berless, unencumbered.—*n.* cum'berment.—*adj.* cum'bersome,
unwieldy.—*n.* cum'brance, encumbrance.—
*adj.* cum'brous, hindering: obstructing: unwieldy.—*adv.* cum'brously.—*n.* cum'brousness.
—cum'ber-ground, a useless thing, from Luke
xiii. 7. [Apparently O.Fr. *combrer*, to hinder—
L.L. *cumbrus*, a heap—L. *cumulus*, a heap.]
**cum grano salis**, *kum grä'nō sä'lis*, *kōōm grä'nō
sa'lis*, (L.) with a grain of salt.
**cumin, cummin**, *kum'in*, *n.* an umbelliferous
plant (*Cuminum Cyminum*) of the Mediterranean
region, with seeds like caraway, valuable as
carminatives. [O.E. *cymen*—L. *cuminum*—Gr.
*kyminon*, cog. with Heb. *kammon*.]
**cum laude.** See maxima cum laude.
**cummer**, *kum'ər*, **kimmer**, *kim'ər*, (*Scot.*) *n.* a
godmother (*obs.*): a gossip: a woman: a girl.
[Fr. *commère*—L. *con-*, with *māter*, mother.]
**cummerbund**, *kum'ər-bund*, *n.* a waist-belt, a sash.
[Pers. *kamarband*, a loin-band.]
**cum multis aliis**, *kum mul'tis ä'lē-is*, *kōōm mōōl'tēs
a'lē-ēs*, (L.) with many other things.
**cum notis variorum**, *kum nō'tis vä-ri-ō'rəm*, *-ō'*,
*kōōm no'tēs va-ri-ō'rōom*, *wa-*, (L.) with notes of
various (critics).
**cum privilegio**, *kum priv-i-lē'ji-ō*, *kōōm prē-vi-
lä'gi-ō*, *-wi-*, (L.) with privilege.
**cumquat**, same as kumquat.
**cum-savvy**, *kum-sav'i*, (*slang*) *n.* know-how.
**cumshaw**, *kum'shö*, *n.* a gift, a tip. [Pidgin-
English.]
**cumulate**, *kūm'ū-lāt*, *v.t.* and *v.i.* to heap together:
to accumulate.—*adjs.* cum'ulate, -d, heaped up.
—*n.* cumulā'tion, accumulation.—*adj.* cum'ulative, increasing by successive additions.—*adv.*
cum'ulatively.—cumulative vote, a system by
which a voter may distribute a number of votes
at will among the candidates, giving more than
one to a candidate if he chooses. [L. *cumulāre*,
*-ātum*—*cumulus*, a heap.]
**cumulus**, *kū'mū-ləs*, *n.* a heap: a kind of cloud
consisting of rounded heaps with a darker
horizontal base:—*pl.* cū'muli.—*adj.* cū'muli-
form; cū'mulose.—cū'mulo-cirr'us, a delicate
cirrus-like cumulus; cū'mulo-nim'bus, a cumulus
discharging showers. [L. *cumulus*, a heap.]
**cunabula**, *kū-nab'ū-lə*, *n.pl.* a cradle: incunabula.
[L. *cūnābula*.]
**cunctator**, *kungk-tā'tər*, *n.* one who delays or puts
off.—*n.* cuncta'tion, delay.—*adjs.* cuncta'tious,
cunc'tative, cunc'tatory, inclined to delay. [L.
*cunctātor*—*cunctāri*, to delay.]
**cuneal**, *kū'ni-əl*, **cuneate**, *kū'ni-āt*, *adj.* wedge-
shaped.—*adjs.* cuneat'ic, cuneiform; cuneiform
(*kū-nē'i-fŏrm*, *kū'ni-(i-)fŏrm*), wedge-shaped—
specially applied to the old Hittite, Babylonian,
Assyrian and Persian writing, of which the
characters were impressed by the wedge-shaped
facets of a stylus.—*n.* cuneiform writing. [L.
*cuneus*, a wedge.]
**cunette**, *kū-net'*, *n.* a cuvette. [Fr.]
**cunner.** See conner (3).
**cunnilingus**, *kun-i-ling'gəs*, *n.* oral stimulation of
the female genitalia. [L. *cunnus*, vulva, *lingĕre*,
to lick.]
**cunning**, *kun'ing*, *adj.* knowing: skilful: artful:
crafty: dainty or quaintly pleasing (*U.S.*).—*n.*
knowledge: skill: faculty of using stratagem to
accomplish a purpose: craftiness: artifice.—
*adv.* cunn'ingly.—*n.* cunn'ingness, quality of being
cunning: artfulness, slyness. [O.E. *cunnan*, to
know.]

**cunt**, *kunt*, *n.* the female genitalia: a term of
abuse (*vulg.*). [M.E. *cunte*; ety. dub.]
**cup**, *kup*, *n.* a drinking-vessel, usu. nearly hemispherical: an ornamental vessel offered as a
prize: a hollow: a cup-shaped structure: a cupful: half a pint (*U.S.*): the liquid contained in a
cup: a mixed beverage made with wine (as
*claret-cup*): that which we must receive or
undergo: afflictions: blessings.—*v.t.* to form
into a cup: to lodge in a cup: to extract blood
by means of cupping-glasses: to make drunk
(*Shak.*).—*v.i.* to become cup-shaped:—*pr.p.*
cupp'ing; *pa.t.* and *pa.p.* cupped.—*ns.* cup'ful,
as much as fills a cup:—*pl.* cup'fuls; cup'pa (*coll.*),
a cup of tea; cupp'er, a cupbearer: one professionally engaged in cupping; cupp'ing, the
application of cups from which the air has been
exhausted in order to draw blood.—cup'-and-
ball, a ball and socket joint: the game of
catching a tethered ball in a cup on the end of a
stick; cup'-and-ring', a prehistoric marking on
rocks and stones, consisting of a cup surrounded
by rings; cup'bearer, one who attends at a feast
to fill and hand out wine cups; cupboard (*kub'-
ərd*), a place for keeping victuals, dishes, etc.—
*v.t.* to store.—cup'board-love, -faith, love or
faith with a material end; cup'-cor'al, a simple
cup-shaped coral; cup'gall, a cup-shaped gall in
oak-leaves; cup'head, a hemispherical bolt-head
or rivet-head; cup'-li'chen, or -moss, any lichen
with cup-shaped structures; cup'man, a boon
companion; cup'-mark, a cup-shaped hollow
made by prehistoric man on cave walls, standing-
stones, etc.; cupp'ing-glass, a glass used in
cupping; cup'-tie, one of a series of games to
determine the winners of a cup.—cry cupboard,
to cry for food; in his cups, under the influence
of liquor; one's cup of tea (*coll.*), one's preference, taste; there's many a slip 'twixt the cup
and the lip, failure is possible at the last moment.
[O.E. *cuppe*—L. *cūpa*, *cuppa*, a tub.]
**cupel**, *kū'pəl*, *n.* a small vessel used by goldsmiths
in assaying precious metals: the movable hearth
of a reverberatory furnace for refining.—*v.t.* to
assay in a cupel:—*pr.p.* cu'pelling; *pa.t.* and
*pa.p.* cu'pelled.—*n.* cupellā'tion, recovery of
precious metal in assaying. [L. *cūpella*, dim. of
*cūpa*; see cup.]
**Cupid**, *kū'pid*, *n.* the Roman love-god, identified
with Greek Eros: a kind of jam-tart (*U.S.*).—
*adj.* cupid'inous, full of desire, esp. amorous.—
*n.* cupid'ity, covetousness. [L. *Cūpīdo*, *-inis*—
*cupĕre*, to desire.]
**cupola**, *kū'po-lə*, *n.* a spherical vault, or concave
ceiling, on the top of a building: the internal
part of a dome: a dome: a lantern on the top of
a dome: an armoured dome or turret to protect
a gun: a furnace used in iron-foundries.—*v.t.* to
furnish with a cupola.—*adjs.* cū'pola'd (or cū'-
polaed); cū'polar; cū'polated. [It.,—L. *cūpula*,
dim. of *cūpa*, a cask.]
**cuprammonium**, *kū-prə-mō'ni-əm*, *n.* a solution of
cupric hydroxide in ammonia.—cuprammonium
rayon, artificial silk made by dissolving cellulose
in cuprammonium. [L. *cuprum*, copper, and
ammonium.]
**cupreous**, *kū'pri-əs*, *adj.* of, containing, or like
copper.—*adjs.* cū'pric, of or containing bivalent
copper; cūprif'erous, yielding copper.—*n.* cū'-
prite, red copper ore, ruby copper, cuprous
oxide (Cu₂O).—*adj.* cū'prous, of or containing
univalent copper.—*n.* cū'pro-nick'el, an alloy of
copper and nickel. [L. *cupreus*—*cuprum*; see
copper.]
**Cupressus**, *kū-pres'əs*, *n.* the cypress genus. [L.]
**cupule**, *kū'pūl*, *n.* a small cup in a liverwort containing gemmae: a cup-shaped envelope on the
fruit of some trees, e.g. oak, beech, chestnut.—
*adjs.* cū'pūlar, cupulif'erous, cup-like: pertaining
to a cupule.—*n.pl.* Cupulif'erae, in some classifica-

tions a family including beech, oak, chestnut, with or without birch, hazel, and hornbeam.— *adj.* cupulif'erous, of the Cupuliferae: bearing cupules. [L. *cūpula*, dim. of *cūpa*, tub.]

cur, *kûr, n.* a worthless dog, of low breed: a contemptible scoundrel.—*adj.* curr'ish.—*adv.* curr'ishly.—*n.* curr'ishness. [M.E. *curre*; cf. O.N. *kurra*, to grumble.]

curaçoa, curaçao, *kū'rə-sō, kū-ra-sō', kōō-rä-sä-ō, n.* a liqueur flavoured with bitter orange peel. [*Curaçao*, Dutch island in West Indies, where first made.]

curare, curari, *kū-* or *kōō-rä'ri, n.* a paralysing poison extracted from wourali root (*Strychnos toxifera*), etc., by South American Indians for arrows—now a source of valuable drugs.—Also cura'ra.—*n.* cura'rine, a highly poisonous alkaloid therefrom, used, e.g. in surgery, as a muscle relaxant.—*v.t.* cu'rarise, -ize. [Port. from Tupi.]

curassow, *kū'rə-sō, kū-räs'ō, n.* a large turkey-like S. American bird. [From the island of *Curaçao.*]

curat, *kū'rat,* (*Spens.*) *n.* a cuirass. [See cuirass.]

curate, *kūr'it, n.* one who has the cure of souls: a clergyman in the Church of England, assisting a rector or vicar: a small poker (*coll.*): a cake-stand.—*ns.* cur'acy (*-ə-si*), cur'ateship, the office, employment, or benefice of a curate.—curate's egg, anything of which parts are excellent. [L.L. *cūrātus,* L. *cūra,* care.]

curator, *kūr-ā'tər* (in Scots law *kūr'ə-tər*), *n.* one who has the charge of anything: a superintendent, esp. of a museum: one appointed by law as guardian: a member of a board for electing university professors and the like:—*fem.* curā'-trix.—*n.* curā'torship. [L. *cūrātor.*]

curb, *kûrb, n.* a chain or strap attached to the bit for restraining a horse: a hearth fender: a curbstone or kerbstone, pavement edge (often kerb): a curb-market: an edging or margin of various kinds: a check or restraint: a disease of horses, marked by hard swellings on the leg: the swelling itself.—*v.t.* to furnish with or guide by a curb: to restrain or check.—*adjs.* curb'able; curb'less.—curb'-, kerb'-crawling, driving along slowly with the intention of enticing people into one's car; curb'-, kerb'-market, a market in stocks outwith the stock-exchange, originally on the pavement; curb'-, kerb'-merchant, -trader, -vendor, one who sells by the side of the pavement; curb'-roof, a roof whose upper slope is less than its lower; curb'-, kerbside (also *adj.*); curb'stone, kerb'stone, a stone placed edgeways as an edging to a path or pavement; curb'-, kerbstone broker, one outside the stock exchange. —See also courb. [Fr. *courbe*—L. *curvus,* bent.]

curch, *kûrch, n.* a covering for the head, a kerchief. [See kerchief.]

Curculio, *kûr-kū'li-ō, n.* a weevil. [L.]

Curcuma, *kûr-kū'mə, n.* a genus of the ginger family yielding turmeric.—*n.* cur'cumine, the colouring matter of turmeric. [Ar. *kurkum,* saffron.]

curd, *kûrd, n.* milk thickened or coagulated by acid: the cheese part of milk, as distinguished from the whey: any similar substance: in soap-making the granular soap that rises in the lye upon salting: the fatty matter between the flakes of salmon flesh.—*n.* curd'iness.—*v.t.* and *v.i.* curd'le, to turn into curd: to coagulate: to thicken.—*adj.* curd'y, like or full of curd. [Prob. Celt.; Gael. *gruth,* Ir. *cruth.*]

cure, *kūr, n.* care of souls or spiritual charge: care of the sick: act of healing: that which heals: a remedy, or course of remedial treatment: course or method of preserving or arresting decomposition: the total quantity cured: treatment by which a product is finished or made ready for use.—*v.t.* to heal: to preserve as by drying, salting, etc.: to finish by means of chemical change, e.g., to vulcanise (a rubber), or to use heat or chemicals in the last stage of preparing (a thermosetting plastic).—*v.i.* to undergo a process or course of curing.—*adj.* cūr'able.—*ns.* cūr'ableness, cūrabil'ity.—*adjs.* cūr'ative, cūr'atory, tending to cure.—*adj.* cūre'less, that cannot be cured.—*n.* cūr'er.—cūre'-all, a panacea. [O.Fr. *cure*—L. *cūra,* care.]

cure, *kûr,* (*slang*) *n.* odd or queer person. [Ety. dub.]

curé, *kü-rā, n.* a parish priest in France. [Fr.; see curate.]

curettage, *kū-ret'ij, n.* scraping of a body cavity by means of a surgeon's instrument known as a curette'. [Fr. *curer,* to cure.]

curfew, *kûr'fū, n.* in feudal times the ringing of a bell as a signal to put out all fires and lights: the ringing of a bell at a certain hour continued as a traditional custom: a signal for the imposition of restrictions of other kinds, e.g., from being abroad in the streets at night: the time of curfew: the bell itself: a regulation obliging persons to be indoors within certain hours.— cur'few-bell. [O.Fr. *covrefeu; couvrir,* to cover, *feu,* fire—L. *focus.*]

curia, *kū'ri-a, n.* one of the ten divisions of a Roman tribe: a building in which the senate met: a provincial senate: a court, legislative or judicial: the court of the papal see.—*ns.* cū'rialism; cū'rialist.—*adj.* cūrialist'ic.—cu'ria reg'is (see aula). [L. *cūria.*]

curie, *kü-rē, kū'rē, n.* orig., the quantity of radon in radioactive equilibrium with a gram of radium: now, the quantity of a radioactive substance that undergoes $3.70 \times 10^{10}$ radioactive transformations per sec.—*n.* curium (*kū'*), the chemical element of atomic number 96 (symbol Cm).— curiethera'py, treatment of disease by radium. [After Marie and Pierre Curie, discoverers of radium.]

curiet, *kū'ri-et,* (*Spens.*) *n.* a cuirass. [See cuirass.]

curio, *kū'ri-ō, n.* any article of virtu or bric-à-brac, or anything considered rare and curious:—*pl.* cū'rios. [For curiosity.]

curiosa felicitas, *kū-ri-ō'sa fe-lis'i-tas, kōō-ri-ō'sa fä-lē'ki-täs.* [See Appendices.]

curious, *kū'ri-əs, adj.* anxious to learn: inquisitive: showing great care or nicety (*obs.*): solicitous (*Shak.*): skilfully made: singular: rare: (in booksellers' catalogues) indecent: odd.—*n.* curiosity (*-os'i-ti*), state or quality of being curious: inquisitiveness: that which is curious: anything rare or unusual.—*adv.* cū'riously.—*n.* cū'riousness.—curious arts (*B.*), magical practices. [Fr. *curieux*—L. *cūriōsus*—*cūra.*]

curl, *kûrl, v.t.* to twist into ringlets: to coil: to cause to move in a curve: to ripple.—*v.i.* to shrink into ringlets: to move in curves: to writhe: to ripple: to eddy: to play at the game of curling.—*n.* a ringlet of hair, or what is like it: a wave, bending, or twist: an eddy: a plant disease in which leaves curl: a curled condition. —*adjs.* curled; curled'-pate (*Shak.*), having curled hair.—*ns.* curl'er, one who, or that which, curls: a player at the game of curling; curl'icue, a fantastic curl; curl'iness; curl'ing, a game, common in Scotland, consisting in sliding heavy smooth stones along a sheet of ice.—*adj.* curly, having curls: full of curls.—curl'iewurlie (*Scot.*), any fantastic round ornament; curl'ing-i'rons, curl'ing-tongs, an iron instrument used for curling the hair; curl'ing-pond, a pond for curling; curl'ing-stone, a heavy stone with a handle used in curling; curl'-pap'er, a paper twisted into the hair to give it curl; curl'y-greens, kale or borecole.—*adj.* curl'y-head'ed. [M.E. *crull;* Du. *krullen,* Dan. *krolle,* to curl.]

curlew, *kûr'lōō, -lū, n.* a moorland bird (Numenius)

of the woodcock family with long curved bill and long legs, and plaintive whistling cry—the whaup: the thick-knee (stone-curlew). [O.Fr. *corlieu*; prob. from its cry.]

**curmudgeon**, *kər-muj'ən*, *n.* an avaricious, ill-natured churlish fellow: a miser.—*adj.* and *adv.* **curmud'geonly.** [Origin unknown.]

**curmurring**, *kər-mûr'ing*, *n.* a rumbling sound, esp. that made in the bowels by flatulence. [Imit.]

**curn**, *kûrn*, (*Scot.*) *n.* a grain: a particle: a small quantity, a little.—*adj.* **curn'y**, **curn'ey**, granular, coarse-grained. [**corn.**]

**curpel**, *kûr'pl*, *n.* a Scots form of **crupper.**

**curr**, *kûr*, (*Wordsworth*) *v.i.* to make a purring sound. [Imit.]

**currach, -agh**, *kur'ə(hh)*, *n.* a long-shaped boat of similar construction to a coracle. [Ir. *curach*.]

**currant**, *kur'ənt*, *n.* a small black raisin or dried seedless grape (imported from the Levant): extended to several species of Ribes (*black, red, white, flowering currant*), and to various other plants, and their fruits.—*ns.* **curr'ant-bread'**, ordinary bread with some (grape) currants in it; **curr'ant-bun'**, **curr'ant-loaf'**, a dark spiced cake full of currants; **curr'ant-cake'**, a cake with currants in it; **curr'ant-jell'y**, a jelly made from red or black currants; **curr'ant-wine'**.—*adj.* **curr'anty**, full of currants. [**Corinth.**]

**current**, *kur'ənt*, *adj.* running or flowing: passing from person to person: generally or widely received: now 'passing: present: belonging to the period of time now passing.—*n.* a running or flowing: a stream: a portion of water or air moving in a certain direction: a flow of electricity: course.—*n.* **curr'ency**, circulation: that which circulates, as the money of a country: general estimation.—*adv.* **curr'ently.**—*n.* **curr'-entness.**—**currency note**, paper-money, esp. that issued by the Treasury in 1914-28 as legal tender; **current account**, a bank account to meet current expenses; **curr'ent-bedding** (*geol.*), false-bedding.—**pass current**, to be received as genuine. [L. *currēns, -entis*—pr.p. of *currēre*, to run.]

**currente calamo**, *ku-ren'tē* (*kōō-ren'te*) *ka'la-mō*, (L.) with a running pen, off-hand.

**curricle**, *kur'i-kl*, *n.* a two-wheeled open chaise, drawn by two horses abreast. [L. *curriculum*, course, race, racing chariot—*currēre*, to run.]

**curriculum**, *kə-rik'ū-ləm*, *n.* a course, esp. the course of study at a university.—*adj.* **curric'ular**, of relating to a curriculum or to courses of study.—**curriculum vitae**, *kə-rik'ūl-əm vī'tē*, *kōōr-ik'ōō-lōōm vē'ti* (*wē'ti*), (a biographical sketch of) the course of one's life. [L.; see **curricle.**]

**currish, currishly**, etc. See **cur.**

**curry**, *kur'i*, *n.* a meat or other dish prepared with turmeric and mixed spices.—*v.t.* to make a curry of.—*ns.* **curr'y-leaf**, a rutaceous Indian tree (*Murraya koenijii*) whose leaves are an ingredient in curry; **curr'y-pow'der**, ground spices and turmeric. [Tamil *kari*, sauce.]

**curry**, *kur'i*, *v.t.* to dress (leather): to rub down and dress (a horse): to beat: to scratch:—*pr.p.* **curr'ying**; *pa.t.* and *pa.p.* **curr'ied.**—*ns.* **curr'ier**, one who curries or dresses tanned leather; **curr'ying.**—**curr'y-comb**, an iron instrument or comb used for currying or cleaning horses.—**curry favour** (orig. **curry favell**, to curry the chestnut horse), to seek to ingratiate oneself. [O.Fr. *correier* (Fr. *corroyer*), *conrei*, outfit, from L. *con-*, with, and the root seen in **array.**]

**curry, currie**, obsolete forms of **quarry** (2).

**curse**, *kûrs*, *v.t.* to invoke or wish evil upon: to blaspheme: to afflict with: to utter doom or damnation against: to excommunicate.—*v.i.* to utter imprecations: to swear.—*n.* invocation or wishing of evil or harm: evil invoked on another: excommunication sentence: imprecation: any great evil: (with *the*) menstrual period (*coll.*).—

*adj.* **curs'ed**, under a curse: hateful.—*adv.* **curs'edly.**—*ns.* **curs'edness**; **curs'er**; **curs'ing.**—*adj.* **curst**, cursed: ill-tempered (*arch.*).—*n.* **curst'-ness**, state of being curst: peevishness: froward-ness.—**curse of Scotland**, the nine of diamonds (origin unknown). [O.E. *cursian—curs*, a curse; ety. doubtful; not conn. with **cross.**]

**cursitor**, *kûr'si-tər*, *n.* a clerk or officer in the Court of Chancery who made out original writs *de cursu*, i.e. of ordinary course: a vagrant (*obs.*). [L.L. *cursitor.*]

**cursive**, *kûr'siv*, *adj.* written with a running hand, of handwriting: flowing.—*adv.* **cur'sively.** [L.L. *cursivus*—L. *currēre*, to run.]

**cursor**, *kûr'sər*, *n.* a sliding part of an instrument. —*adj.* (*obs.*) **cur'sorary** (*Shak.*; other readings **cur'senary**, **cur'selarie**; prob. intended for **cursi-tory**), cursory.—*n.pl.* **cursores** (*-sō'rēz, -sō'*), in old classifications, running birds, variously limited.—*adj.* **curso'rial**, adapted for running.—*adv.* **cur'sorily** (*-sər-*).—*n.* **cur'soriness.**—*adj.* **cur'sory**, running quickly over: hasty: superficial. [L. *cursor*, pl. *cursōrēs*, a runner—*currēre*, *cursum*, to run.]

**curst.** See **curse.**

**cursus**, *kûr'səs*, (*rare*) *n.* a race-course: a form of daily prayer or service: an academic curriculum. —*adj.* **cur'sal.** [L.]

**curt**, *kûrt*, *adj.* short: concise: discourteously brief or summary.—*adj.* **curt'āte**, shortened or reduced; applied to the distance of a planet from the sun or earth projected on the plane of the ecliptic.—*n.* **curtā'tion**.—*adv.* **curt'ly.**—*n.* **curt'-ness.** [L. *curtus*, shortened.]

**curtail**, *kər-tāl'*, *v.t.* to cut short: to cut off a part of: to abridge.—*ns.* **curtail'ment**; **cur'tail-step**, a round-ended step at the bottom of a flight. [Old spelling *curtal*, O.Fr. *courtault*—L. *curtus*, shortened.]

**curtain**, *kûr'tən*, *n.* hanging drapery at a window, around a bed, etc.: the part of a rampart between two bastions: a curtain wall: a screen of cloth or metal concealing the stage, or restricting the spread of fire (*theat.*): the fall of the curtain, close of a scene or act (*theat.*): a protective barrier in general, as the fire of many guns directed along a certain line to prevent the passage of an enemy (also called **cur'tain-fire**): (in *pl.*) death, the end (*slang*).—*v.t.* to enclose or furnish with curtains.—**curtain call**, a summons from the audience to appear at the end of a scene; **curtain lecture**, a lecture or reproof given in bed by a wife to her husband; **cur'tain-raiser**, a short play preceding the main performance; **curtain speech**, a speech made before a theatre curtain; **curtain wall**, a wall that is not load-bearing, e.g. does not support a roof; **curtain walling**, prefabricated large framed sections of lightweight, usu. predecorated, material used in building.—**bamboo curtain**, (see **bamboo**); **behind the curtain**, away from public view; **draw the curtain**, to draw it aside, so as to show what is behind, or to draw it in front of anything so as to hide it; **iron curtain**, (see **iron**). [O.Fr. *cortine*—L.L. *cortina*; prob. L. *cōrs, cōrtis*, a court.]

**curtal**, *kûr'təl*, (*obs.*) *n.* a horse or other animal with a docked tail: anything docked or cut short.—*adj.* docked or shortened.—*n.* **cur'tal-fri'ar** (*Scott*), a friar with a short frock. [See **curtail.**]

**curtal-ax**, *kûr'təl-aks*, **curtaxe**, *kûrt'aks*, (*Spens.*) *n.* a short, broad sword. [A corr. of the earlier forms *coutelas, coutelas*. See **cutlass.**]

**curtana**, *kûr-tä'na, -tā'na*, *n.* a sword without a point, symbolic of mercy, carried at coronations. [L. *curtus*, short.]

**curtilage**, *kûr'til-ij*, *n.* a court attached to a dwelling-house. [O.Fr. *courtillage*; see **court.**]

**curtsy, curtsey**, *kûrt'si*, *n.* an obeisance, esp. by

women, made by bending the knees.—*v.i.* to make or 'drop' a curtsy. [See **courtesy**.]

**curule**, *kū'rōōl, adj.* like a camp-stool with curved legs, applied to the chair of a higher Roman magistrate. [L. *curūlis—currus*, a chariot.]

**curve**, *kûrv, n.* anything bent: a line that is not straight: a line (including a straight line) answering to an equation: a graph: a curved surface: an arch.—*v.t.* to bend: to form into a curve.—*v.i.* to bend: to move in a curve.—*adjs.* **curvaceous, curvacious** (*kûr-vā'shəs*) (slang), having shapely curves; **cur'vāte, -d**, curved or bent in a regular form.—*n.* **curvā'tion**.—*adj.* **cur'vative** (*-və-tiv*).—*n.* **cur'vature** (*-və-chər*), a curving or bending: the continual bending, or the amount of bending, from a straight line: the reciprocal of the radius at any point.—*adjs.* **curved; curve'some**, curvaceous; **curvicau'date**, having a crooked tail; **curvicos'tate**, having curved ribs; **curvifō'liate**, having curved leaves; **cur'viform**; **curvilin'eal, curvilin'ear**, bounded by curved lines.—*n.* **curvilinear'ity**.—*adjs.* **cur'ving; curviros'tral**, with the bill curved downward; **cur'vital**, of or pertaining to curvature.—*n.* **cur'vity**, the state of being curved.—*adj.* **curv'y**. [L. *curvus*, crooked.]

**curvet**, *kûr'vet, kər-vet', n.* a light leap of a horse in which he raises his forelegs together, next the hind-legs with a spring before the forelegs touch the ground: a leap, frolic.—*v.i.* (*kər-vet', kûr'vet*), to leap in curvets: to frisk:—*pr.p.* **curvett'ing, cur'veting;** *pa.t.* and *pa.p.* **curvett'ed, cur'veted**. [It. *corvetta*, dim. of *corvo*—L. *curvus*.]

**curvilineal, curvilinear.** See **curve**.

**cus-cus**, *kus'-kus*, or *kōōs'-kōōs, n.* a phalanger of the Malay Archipelago. [Native name in the Moluccas.]

**cuscus**, *kus'kus, n.* the grain of the African millet. [Same as **couscous**.]

**cuscus**, *kus'kus, n.* the fragrant fibrous root of an Indian grass (*Andropogon squarrosus*), used for making fans, etc. [Pers. *khas khas*.]

**cusec**, *kū'sek, n.* unit of volumetric rate of flow. [cubic feet per second.]

**cush.** See **cuisse**.

**cushat**, *kush'ət,* (Scot.) *n.* the ringdove or woodpigeon. [O.E. *cūscute*, perh. from its note, and *scēotan*, to shoot.]

**cushion**, *kōōsh'ən, n.* a case filled with some soft, elastic stuff, for resting on: a pillow: a pad: the pillow used in making bone-lace: an engraver's pad: the rubber of an electrical machine: a pad supporting a woman's hair: the cap of a pier (*archit.*): the elastic lining of the inner side of a billiard-table (*coll.* cush): a body of steam remaining in the cylinder of a steam-engine, acting as a buffer to the piston: anything that serves to deaden a blow.—*v.t.* to seat on or furnish with a cushion: to serve as a cushion for or against: to suppress (complaints) by ignoring.—*adj.* **cush'ioned**, furnished with a cushion, padded: having cushion-tires.—*n.* **cush'ionet**, a little cushion.—*adj.* **cush'iony**, like a cushion, soft.—**cush'ion-plant**, a plant of cushion-like form reducing transpiration; **cush'ion-tire, -tyre**, a cycle tire of rubber tubing, with rubber stuffing. [O.Fr. *coissin*—L. *coxinum, coxa,* hip, or perh. L. *culcita,* mattress, cushion.]

**cushy**, *kōōsh'i,* (slang) *adj.* easy and comfortable: not dangerous. [Perh. Hind. *khush*, pleasant, *khushī*, happiness.]

**cusk**, *kusk, n.* the torsk: the burbot.

**cusp**, *kusp, n.* a point: the point or horn of the moon, etc.: a tooth-like meeting of two branches of a curve, with sudden change of direction: a tooth-like ornament common in Gothic tracery (*archit.*): a prominence on a tooth.—*adjs.* **cuspate; cusped; cus'pid; cus'pidal; cus'pidate**,

-d (*biol.*), having a rigid point. [L. *cuspis, -idis,* a point.]

**Cusparia bark**, *kə-spar'i-a*, Angostura bark (q.v.).

**cuspidor(e)**, *kus'pi-dōr* or *-dör,* (*U.S.*) *n.* a spittoon. [Port.,—L. *conspuĕre,* to spit upon.]

**cuss**, *kus,* (slang) *n.* a curse: a fellow.—*adj.* **cuss'ed**, cursed: obstinate.—*ns.* **cuss'edness**, contrariness; **cuss'-word**. [curse; prob. sometimes associated with **customer**.]

**cusser, cuisser, cooser,** *kus'ər, kōōs'ər, küs'ər,* (Scot.) *n.* a stallion. [courser.]

**custard**, *kus'tərd, n.* a composition of milk, eggs, etc., sweetened and flavoured.—*ns.* **cus'tard-apple**, the fruit of a W. Indian tree (*Anona reticulata*) with eatable pulp, like a custard; **cus'tard-coff'in** (Shak.), paste or crust covering a custard: **custard-pie** (comedy), slapstick, esp. of early U.S. films in which comedians threw custard pies at each other. [Earlier *custade,* a corr. of *crustade,* a pie with a crust; see **crust**.]

**custock.** See **castock**.

**custody**, *kus'tə-di, n.* a watching or guarding: care: security: imprisonment.—*adj.* **custō'dial**. —*ns.* **custō'dian, cus'tode, custō'dier, cus'tos**, one who has care, esp. of some public building. [L. *custōdia,* guard, *custōs, -ōdis,* a keeper.]

**custom**, *kus'təm, n.* what one is wont to do: what is usually done by others: usage: frequent repetition of the same act: regular trade or business: any of the distinctive practices and conventions of a people or locality, esp. those of a primitive tribe (applied, *hist.*, to a periodical massacre in parts of West Africa): usages of a manor or of a district: a tax on goods: (in *pl.*) duties on imports and exports: (in *pl.*) the collecting authorities.—*adj.* (*U.S.*) made to order.—*adj.* **cus'tomable** (*arch.*), customary: common: dutiable.—*adv.* **cus'tomarily**.—*n.* **cus'tomariness**.—*adj.* **cus'tomary**, according to use and wont: usual: holding or held by custom: copyhold.—*n.* (also **customary**, *kus'tūm-ər-i*), a body or book of the customs of a manor, etc. or the ritual of a religious community.—*adj.* **cus'tomed**, accustomed: usual.—*n.* **cus'tomer**, one accustomed to frequent a certain place of business: a buyer: a prostitute (Shak.): a person (slang).—*adj.* **cus'tom-built, cus'tom-made**, built (as e.g. a motor-car) or made to a customer's order.—**cus'tom-house**, the place where customs or duties on exports and imports are collected. —*adj.* **cus'tom-shrunk** (Shak.), having fewer customers than formerly.—**customs union**, a territory treated as if one state for purposes of custom duties. [O.Fr. *custume, costume*—L. *cōnsuētūdō, -inis—cōnsuēscēre,* to accustom.]

**custos rotulorum**, *ku'stəs ro-tū-lō'rəm, kōō'stōs ro-tōō-lō'rōōm,* (L.) keeper of the rolls.

**custrel**, *kus'trəl,* (hist.) *n.* an attendant on a knight: a knave. [O.Fr. *coustillier—coustille,* dagger; cf. **coistrel**.]

**cut**, *kut, v.t.* to penetrate with a sharp edge: to make an incision in: to cleave or pass through: to divide: to carve, hew, or make or fashion by cutting: to sever: to reap: to excise: to intersect: to divide (a pack of cards) by lifting the upper portion at random: to expose (a card or suit) in this way: to strike obliquely, imparting spin to: to reduce or lessen: to abridge: (of a book) to trim by guillotine: to wound or hurt: to affect deeply: to shorten: to break off acquaintance with: to pass intentionally without greeting: to renounce, give up: to stay away from: to castrate: to perform or execute (as a caper).—*v.i.* to make an incision: to intersect: to strike obliquely: to be cut: to dash, go quickly: to run away, to be off (slang): to twiddle the feet rapidly in dancing: in motion-picture making, to cease photographing:—*pr.p.* **cutt'ing;** *pa.t.* and *pa.p.* **cut**.—*n.* a cleaving or dividing: an excavation for a road, railway, etc.:

Neutral vowels in unaccented syllables: *el'ə-mənt;* for certain sounds in foreign words, see p. viii

a cross passage: a stroke or blow: in various games, a particular stroke, generally implying obliquity and spin: in cricket, a stroke to the off side with horizontal bat: the spin imparted to the ball: a reduction or diminution: an act of unkindness: the act, or outcome, of cutting a pack of cards: an incision or wound: an excision: a piece cut off: total quantity cut: a varying unit of length for cloth and yarn: an engraved block or the picture from it: manner of cutting, or fashion: a working horse (*Shak.*): a general term of abuse (as in 'call me cut') (*Shak.*): a rake-off (*slang.*).—*ns.* cutt'er, a person or thing that cuts: a cut-throat (*obs.*): a tailor who measures and cuts out the cloth: a small vessel with one mast, a mainsail, a forestay-sail, and a jib set to bowsprit-end: any sloop of narrow beam and deep draught: in quarrying, a joint parallel to the dip of the rocks; cutt'ing, a dividing or lopping off: an incision: piece cut from a newspaper: piece of a plant cut off for propagation: open excavation for road, railway, etc.: editing of film or recording.—cut'away, a coat with the skirt cut away in a curve in front.— Also *adj.*—cut'back, a going back in a plot to earlier happenings: a reduction; cut glass, flint glass shaped by cutting or grinding; cut'-in', out', the act of cutting in or out.—*adj.* cut'-leaved, having leaves deeply cut.—cut'-off, that which cuts off or shortens, a straighter road, a shorter channel cut across a bend of a river: a bend thus cut off: a device for shutting off steam, water, light, electricity, supply of cartridges in a magazine rifle, etc.—*adj.* cut'-price, at a reduced rate.—cut'purse, one who stole by slitting purses worn at the girdle: a pickpocket; cut'-throat, assassin: ruffian: modification of bridge, etc., played by three, each for himself: an open razor.—*adj.* murderous: ruinous.—cut'wa'ter, the forepart of a ship's prow: the angular edge of a bridge-pier; cut'worm, a caterpillar, esp. of the moth genus *Agrotis*, that cuts off young plants near the ground.—a cut above, something distinctly better; cut a dash, or figure, to have a striking appearance; cut and come again, abundant supply, from the notion of cutting a slice, and returning at will for another; cut and cover, a method of forming a tunnel by making an open cutting, arching it over, and covering in; cut and dry, or cut and dried, ready made, fixed beforehand—from the state of herbs in the shop instead of the field; cut and run, to be off quickly; cut back, to prune close to the stem: to revert to a previous scene: to reduce; cut corners, to turn corners by the quickest way, not keeping close to the edge of the road.—Also *fig.*—cut dead, to refuse to recognise; cut down, to take down by cutting the rope on which one has been hanged: to bring down by cutting: to reduce, curtail; cut in, to interpose: to deprive one of a dancing partner: to eavesdrop by telephone: to take one's place in a line of traffic in front of an overtaken vehicle, etc., esp. when meeting others: to come into a game by cutting a card: to give a share; cut it fine, to take risks by calculating too narrowly; cut it out (*coll.*), to make an end of it, leave off; cut it too fat, to overdo a thing; cut off, to sever: to isolate: put to an untimely death: to intercept: to stop: to disinherit; cut off with a shilling, to bequeath only a shilling: to disinherit; cut one's coat according to one's cloth, to adapt oneself to circumstances; cut one's losses, to have done with an unprofitable matter; cut one's stick, to take one's departure; cut out, shape: contrive: debar: supplant: separate from a herd: pass out of a game on cutting a card: pass out of a line of traffic in order to overtake: capture and carry off (a ship) as from a harbour, etc., by getting between her and the shore; cut out for,

fitted naturally; cut short, to abridge: to make short by cutting: to silence by interruption; cut teeth, to have teeth grow through the gums, as an infant; cut up, to cut into pieces: criticise severely: turn out (well or ill) when divided into parts: (in *pass.*) to be deeply afflicted; cut up rough, to take something amiss; draw cuts (*arch.*), to cast lots; short cut, or near cut, a shorter way than the usual one. [Origin unknown.]

**cutaneous.** See cutis.

**cutch,** *kuch, n.* catechu. [Malay *kachu*.]

**cutch, kutch,** *kuch, n.* a set of vellum or tough paper sheets used by gold-beaters. [App.—Fr. *caucher,* cutch—L. *calcāre,* to tread.]

**cutcha,** *kuch'a, adj.* of dried mud: makeshift. [Hindi *kaccā,* raw.]

**cutcherry, cutchery.** Same as kachahri.

**cute,** *kūt, adj.* an aphetic form of acute: daintily or quaintly pleasing.—*n.* cū'tie, cūt'ey, a smart girl.

**Cuthbert,** *kuth'bərt, n.* the apostle of Northumbria (c. 635-687): a derisive name given to one suspected of evading military service, and hence to any shirker.—(St) Cuthbert's beads, perforated joints of encrinites found on Holy Island; (St) Cuthbert's duck, the eiderduck.

**cutikin.** Same as cuitikin.

**cutis,** *kū'tis, n.* the skin: the true skin, as distinguished from the cuticle.—*adj.* cūtān'eous, belonging to the skin.—*n.* cū'ticle, the outermost or thin skin: the dead skin at the edge of finger-and toenails: waxy or corky layer on the epidermis in plants (*bot.*).—*adj.* cūtic'ular.—*ns.* cū'tin, material forming plant cuticle; cūtinisā'tion, -z-.—*v.t.* and *v.i.* cū'tinise, -ize. [L.]

**cutlass,** *kut'las, n.* a short, broad sword, with one cutting edge, used in the navy. [Fr. *coutelas,* augmentative from L. *cultellus,* dim. of culter, a ploughshare, a knife.]

**cutler,** *kut'lər, n.* one who makes or sells knives.—*n.* cut'lery, the business of a cutler: edged or cutting instruments in general: implements for eating food. [Fr. *coutelier*—O.Fr. *coutel*—L. *culter,* knife.]

**cutlet,** *kut'lit, n.* rib and the meat belonging to it or similar piece of mutton, veal, etc.: other food made up in the shape of a cutlet. [Fr. *côtelette,* dim. of *côte,* from L. *costa,* a rib.]

**cuttle,** *kut'l, n.* a cephalopod mollusc (Sepia) remarkable for its power of ejecting a black, inky liquid—also cutt'lefish: extended to other cephalopods.—cutt'le-bone, the internal shell of the cuttlefish, used for making tooth-powder, for polishing the softer metals and for cage-birds to sharpen their beaks on. [O.E. *cudele.*]

**cuttle,** *kut'l, (obs.) n.* a knife: a bully (*Shak.*). [Perh. L. *cultellum,* knife; perh. also for cut-throat, cutpurse, or cuttlefish.]

**cutto, cuttoe,** *kut'ō, n.* a large knife. [Fr. *couteau.*]

**cutty,** *kut'i, (Scot.) adj.* short, curtailed.—*n.* a short clay pipe: a short, dumpy girl: applied to a woman, a term of reprobation, serious or playful: a mischievous or teasing girl or woman.—cutt'y-sark, a short shirt, or its wearer; cutt'y-stool, the stool of repentance in old Scottish church discipline. [cut.]

**cuvée,** *kü-vā, kōō-vā', n.* a vat of blended wine of uniform quality. [Fr.]

**cuvette,** *küv-et, kū-vet', n.* a trench sunk along the middle of a dry ditch or moat, a cunette. [Fr.]

**cwm,** Welsh form of coomb (1).

**cyanogen,** *sī-an'ō-jən, n.* a compound of carbon and nitrogen $(CN)_2$ forming a colourless, poisonous gas with a characteristic odour—an essential ingredient of Prussian blue.—*ns.* cy'an, a greenish blue: printers' blue ink; cyan'amide, the amide of cyanamide, a white crystalline substance ($NCNH_2$): loosely applied to calcium cyanamide ($NCNCa$), a fertiliser; cyanate (*sī'ən-āt*), a salt of cyanic acid.—*adj.* cyan'ic, of or belonging to cyanogen.—*n.* cy'anide, a direct compound of cyanogen with a metal.—*v.t.* to treat with a cyanide.—*ns.* cy'aniding, extraction of gold or silver from ore by means of potassium cyanide; cy'anin, a plant pigment, blue in cornflower, but red in the rose because of its reaction with acids; cy'anine, any of a group of dyes used as sensitisers in photography.—*v.t.* cy'anise, -ize, to turn into cyanide.—*ns.* cy'anite (see kyanite); cyanocobal'amin, vitamin B₁₂, which has a large and complicated molecule, in one form including a cyanide group, in all forms including a cobalt atom; cyanom'eter, an instrument for measuring the blueness of the sky or ocean; cyanō'sis, morbid blueness of the skin. —*adj.* cyanŏt'ic.—*ns.* cyan'otype, blue-print; cyan'ūret (*obs.*), a cyanide.—cyanic acid, an acid composed of cyanogen, oxygen and hydrogen (HCNO). [Gr. *kyanos*, blue.]

Cyanophyceae, sī-ən-ō-fish'i-ē, *n.* the blue-green algae, simply organised unicellular or filamentous thallophytes growing in water and on damp earth, rocks or bark. [See cyanogen.]

cyathus, *sī'a-thəs*, *n.* an ancient Greek filling or measuring cup—about ₁⁄₁₂ of a pint.—*n.* Cyath'ea, a genus of tree-ferns, often with cup-shaped indusium, giving name to the family Cyatheā'-ceae.—*adj.* cy'athiform (or -*ath'*), cup-shaped.— *ns.* cyath'ium, the characteristic inflorescence of the spurges; Cyathophyll'um (Gr. *phyllon*, leaf), a fossil genus of cup-corals. [Gr. *kyathos*.]

Cybele, *sib'i-lē*, *n.* a flora, treatise on the plants of a region. [L. *Cybelē*—Gr. *Kybelē*, the mother goddess.]

cybernetics, *sī-bər-net'iks*, *n.* (*pl.* in form, treated as *sing.*), the comparative study of automatic communication and control in functions of living bodies and in mechanical and electric systems (such as in computers).—*adj.* cybernet'ic. [Gr. *kybernētēs*, a steersman.]

cycad, *sī'kad*, *n.* one of an order of gymnospermous plants, more or less akin to conifers but superficially resembling ferns and palms.—*adj.* cycadā'ceous. [Formed from supposed Gr. *kykas*, a misreading of *koikas*, accus. pl. of *koix*, dum-palm.]

cycl-. See cycl(o)-.

cyclamate, *sik'la-māt*, *sik'*, *n.* any of a number of very sweet substances derived from petrochemicals.

cyclamen, *sik'lə-mən*, *n.* a S. European genus of Primulaceae, with nodding flowers and bent-back petals. [Gr. *kyklaminos*.]

Cyclanthaceae, *sī-klan-thā'si-ē*, *n.pl.* a tropical S. American family of plants akin to the screw-pines, with a spadix sometimes resembling a pile of disks.—*adj.* cyclanthā'ceous. [Gr. *kyklos*, wheel, *anthos*, flower.]

cycle, *sī'kl*, *n.* a period of time in which events happen in a certain order, and which constantly repeats itself: a recurring series of changes: an age: an imaginary cycle or orbit in the heavens: a series of poems, romances, etc., centring in a figure or event (also cy'clus): a group of songs with related subjects: a bicycle or tricycle: complete series of changes in a periodically varying quantity, e.g. an alternating current, during one period: sequence of computer operations which continues until a criterion for stoppage is reached, or the time of this.—*v.t.* to cause to pass through a cycle of operations or events.—*v.i.* to move in cycles: to ride on a cycle.—*n.* cy'cler (*U.S.*), a cyclist.—*adjs.* cy'clic, -al, pertaining to or containing a cycle: recurring in cycles: arranged in a ring or rings.—*ns.* cy'clist, a bicyclist or tricyclist; cy'clograph, an instrument for describing arcs of circles without compasses; cy'cloid, a figure like a circle: a curve made by a point on a radius of a circle

when the circle is rolled along a straight line: a person of cyclothymic temperament, or one suffering from a cyclic type of manic-depressive psychosis.—*adj.* nearly circular: (of fish) having scales with evenly curved border: cyclothymic: characterised by swings of mood (*psych.*).—*adj.* cycloid'al.—*ns.* cycloid'ian, a fish with cycloid scales; cyclom'eter, an instrument for measuring circular arcs: an apparatus attached to the wheel of a cycle for registering the distance traversed; cyclo'sis, circulation.—cycle-car, a small light motor-car; cycle per second (see hertz); cyclic compound, a closed-chain or ring compound in which the ring consists of carbon atoms only (*carbocyclic compound*) or of carbon atoms linked with one or more other atoms (*heterocyclic compound*); cy'clo-cross', a pedal-bicycle race over rough country in the course of which bicycles have to be carried over natural obstacles. [Gr. *kyklos*, circle.]

cyclo, *sī'klō*, *n.* a trishaw (*coll.*). [cycle.]

cycl(o)-, *sīk-l(ō)-*, in composition, cycle: ring: circle: cyclic compound. See cycle, and also entries below. [Gr. *kyklos*, circle.]

cyclone, *sī'klōn*, *n.* a system of winds blowing spirally inwards towards a centre of low barometric pressure: loosely, a wind-storm: a separating apparatus, a kind of centrifuge.—*adj.* cyclŏn'ic. [Gr. *kyklōn*, contr. pr.p. of *kykloein*, whirl round.]

cyclopaedia, cyclopedia, *sī-klō-pē'di-ə*, *n.* a shortened form of encyclopaedia.—*adj.* cyclopae'dic, cyclope'dic.

cyclopean, -pian, etc. See Cyclops.

cyclopropane, *sī-klō-prō'pān*, *n.* a cyclic hydrocarbon C₃H₆, a general anaesthetic. [Gr. *kyklos*, circle, and propane.]

Cyclops, *sī'klops*, *n.* one of a fabled race of giants who lived chiefly in Sicily, with one eye in the middle of the forehead: a one-eyed monster: a genus of minute fresh-water copepods with an eye in front:—*pl.* cyclō'pes (-*pēz*), cy'clopses.— *adjs.* cyclopē'an, cyclō'pian, cyclŏp'ic, relating to or like the Cyclopes: giant-like: vast: pertaining to a prehistoric style of masonry with immense stones of irregular form. [Gr. *kyklōps*, pl. *kyklōpēs*—*kyklos*, a circle, and *ōps*, an eye.]

cyclorama, *sī-klō-rä'mə*, *n.* a circular panorama: a curved background in stage and cinematograph sets, used to give impression of sky distance, and for lighting effects. [Gr. *kyklos*, circle, *horāma*, view.]

cycloserine, *sī-klō-sēr'in*, *n.* an antibiotic used against tuberculosis.

cyclospermous, *sī-klō-spûr'məs*, (*bot.*) *adj.* with embryo bent round the endosperm. [Gr. *kyklos*, circle, *sperma*, seed.]

Cyclostomata, *sī-klō-stō'mə-tə*, *n.pl.* a class of animals with fixed open mouth, including the lampreys.—*n.* cy'clostome, a member of the class. —*adj.* cyclostomous (-*klos'to-məs*). [Gr. *kyklos*, wheel, *stōma*, mouth.]

cyclostyle, *sī'klō-stil*, *n.* an apparatus for multiplying copies of a writing by use of a pen with a small puncturing wheel. [Gr. *kyklos*, circle, and style.]

cyclothymia, *sī-klō-thī'mi-ə*, *n.* a temperament inclined to alternation of high and low spirits.— *adj.* cyclothy'mic. [Gr. *kyklos*, *thymos*, spirit.]

cyclotron. See accelerator (under accelerate).

cyder. Same as cider.

cyesis, *sī-ēs'is*, *n.* pregnancy. [Gk. *kyēsis*.]

cygnet, *sig'nit*, *n.* a young swan. [Dim. from L. *cygnus*, directly or through Fr. *cygne*, which seems to be a reshaping of *cisne*—L.L. *cicinus*, L. *cycnus*—Gr. *kyknos*, a swan.]

cylinder, *sil'in-dər*, *n.* a solid figure of uniform cross-section generated by a straight line remaining parallel to a fixed axis and moving round a closed curve—ordinarily in a circle perpendicular

to the axis (giving a *right circular cylinder*): a roller-shaped object: a cylindrical part, solid or hollow, as a rotating part of a printing press, the tubular chamber in which a piston works (*mech.*).
—*adjs.* cylindrā′ceous, somewhat cylindrical; cylin′dric, -al.—*n.* cylindricity (*-dris′i-ti*).—*adj.* cylin′driform, in the form of a cylinder.—*ns.* cylin′drite, a mineral of cylindrical habit, compound of tin, lead, antimony, and sulphur; cyl′indroid, a body like a cylinder.—Also *adj.*— cyl′inder-head, the closed end of the cylinder of an internal-combustion engine; cyl′inder-block, a casing in which the cylinders of an internal-combustion engine are contained; cyl′inder-seal′ (*ant.*), a stone engraved in intaglio, used in the ancient East for sealing clay tablets by rolling. [Gr. *kylindros*, roller, *kylindein*, to roll.]
cylix, *sil′* or *sil′iks, n.* a shallow two-handled stemmed drinking cup:—*pl.* cyl′ices (*-sēz*).—Also kylix. [Gr. *kўlix, -ikos.*]
cyma, *si′mǝ, n.* an ogee moulding of the cornice (cyma rec′ta, concave in front, convex behind; cyma rever′sa, convex in front, concave behind).
—*ns.* cy′mograph (improperly cy′magraph), an instrument for tracing the outline of mouldings (see also kymograph); cymā′tium, a cyma. [Gr. *kyma*, a billow.]
cymar, *si-mär′, n.* a loose light dress, or loose undergarment, worn by women, mentioned in 17th- and 18th-cent. literature: a chimer. [Fr. simarre.]
cymbal, *sim′bǝl, n.* a hollow brass plate-like musical instrument, beaten together in pairs.—*ns.* cym′balist, a cymbal-player; cym′balo, the dulcimer.—*adj.* cym′biform, boat-shaped. [L. *cymbalum*—Gr. *kymbalon*—*kymbē*, the hollow of a vessel.]
cyme, *sim,* (*bot.*) *n.* a young shoot: any sympodial inflorescence, the main shoot ending in a flower, the subsequent flowers growing on successive lateral branches.—*adjs.* cym′oid, cym′ose, cym′ous. [L. *cȳma, cīma*—Gr. *kȳma*, a sprout.]
cyme, *si′ǝm, n.* (*Shak.*) app. for Sium.
cymophane, *si′mō-fān, n.* cat's eye, a variety of chrysoberyl with wavy opalescence.—*adj.* cymophanous (*-mof′ǝ-nǝs*), opalescent. [Gr. *kȳma*, wave, *phainein*, to show.]
cymotrichous, *si-mot′ri-kǝs,* (*anthrop.*) *adj.* wavy-haired.—*n.* cymot′richy. [Gr. *kȳma*, wave, *thrix*, gen. *trichos*, hair.]
Cymric, *kim′rik, kum′,* or *sim′, adj.* Welsh.—*n.* Cym′ry, the Welsh. [W. *Cymru*, Wales.]
cynanche, *si-nang′kē, n.* disease of the throat, esp. quinsy. [Gr., *kyōn, kynos*, a dog, *anchein*, to throttle.]
cynegetic, *sin-ē-jet′ik, adj.* relating to hunting. [Gr. *kynēgetēs*, huntsman—*kyōn, kynos*, dog, *hēgetēs*, leader.]
cynic, -al, *sin′ik, -ǝl, adjs.* dog-like: surly: snarling: disinclined to recognise goodness or self-lessness.—*ns.* Cyn′ic, one of a sect of philosophers founded by Antisthenes of Athens (born c. 444 B.C.), characterised by an ostentatious contempt for riches, arts, science, and amusements—so called from their morose manners: (without *cap.*) a morose man: a snarler: one who takes a pessimistic view of human motives and actions; cynicism (*-i-sizm*), surliness: contempt for and suspicion of human nature: heartlessness, misanthropy: a cynical remark.—*adv.* cyn′ically.—*n.* cyn′icalness. [Gr. *kynikos*, dog-like—*kyōn, kynos*, a dog.]
Cynips, *sin′ips, sin′ips,* a genus of gall-wasps, giving name to the family Cynip′idae. [Origin doubtful.]
Cynocephalus, *sin-* or *sin′ō-sef-ǝ-lǝs, n.* the so-called flying lemur or Galeopithecus: the dog-faced baboon: a dog-headed man. [Gr. *kyōn*, *kynos*, dog, *kephalē*, head.]
cynosure, *sin′-* or *sin′ō-shōōr, n.* the dog's tail, or

Lesser Bear (*Ursa Minor*), the constellation containing the North Star: the North Star itself: hence anything that strongly attracts attention or admiration.—Cynosur′us, dog's-tail grass. [Gr. *kyōn, kynos*, a dog, *ourā*, a tail.]
Cyperus, *sip-, sip-ē′rus, n.* a tropical genus of the sedge family, Cyperā′ceae, including papyrus.—*adj.* cyperaceous (*ǝ-rā′shǝs*), belonging to, or like, sedge plants. [From Gr. *kypeiros*, sedge.]
cypher. Same as cipher.
cy pres, *sē prā,* in the law of charitable trusts in England, the principle of applying the money to some object *as near as possible* to the one specified, when that is impracticable. [O.Fr., so near.]
cypress, *si′prǝs, -pris, n.* a coniferous tree (Cupressus), whose branches used to be carried at funerals: hence a symbol of death: extended to various other trees, esp. in America to the swamp-growing deciduous conifer *Taxodium distichum.*—*ns.* cy′press-knee, a hollow upgrowth from the root of the swamp-cypress, a breathing organ; cy′press-swamp′. [O.Fr. *ciprès* (Fr. *cyprès*)—L. *cupressus*—Gr. *kyparissos.*]
cypress, *si′prǝs, -pris, n.* a thin transparent black stuff like crape.—*adj.* of cypress.—Also cyprus. [Prob. from the island of *Cyprus.*]
Cyprian, *sip′ri-an, adj.* of the island of Cyprus: lewd, licentious—Cyprus being the place where Aphrodite was worshipped.—*n.* a Cypriot: a lewd woman—*n.* Cyp′riot(e), a native of Cyprus.
—*n.* Cyp′ro-Mino′an, an undeciphered Bronze Age script of Cyprus.—Also *adj.*
cyprid. See Cypris.
Cyprinus, *si-pri′nǝs, n.* the carp genus of fishes, giving name to the fam. Cyprinidae (*si-prin′i-dē*).
—*adjs.* cyprine (*sip′rin*), cyp′rinoid (*-rin-oid*). [L.—Gr. *kyprinos*, a kind of carp.]
Cypriot(e). See Cyprian.
Cypripedium, *sip-ri-pē′di-ǝm, n.* a genus of orchids, lady's slipper. [Gr. *Kypris*, Aphrodite, *podion*, a little foot, modified by L. *pēs*, foot.]
Cypris, *sip′ris, n.* a genus of fresh-water ostracod crustaceans.—*n.* cyp′rid. [Gr. *Kypris*, Aphrodite.]
Cypro-Minoan. See Cyprian.
cyprus. Same as cypress (2).
Cyrenaic, *si-rin-ā′ik, adj.* pertaining to Cyrēnē, or to the hedonism of its philosopher Aristippus.
Cyrillic, *sir-il′ik, adj.* pertaining to the alphabet attributed to St Cyril (9th cent.), distinguished from the other Slavonic alphabet, the Glagolitic.
cyst, *sist, n.* (*biol.*) a bladder or bag-like structure, whether normal or containing morbid matter: a membrane enclosing an organism in a resting stage.—*adjs.* cyst′ic, cyst′iform.—*ns.* Cysticer′cus (Gr. *kerkos*, tail), a bladderworm; cyst′id, cystid′ean, a cystoid; cysti′tis, inflammation of the bladder; cysto′carp (Gr. *karpos*, fruit), the fructification in red seaweeds; cys′tocele (Gr. *kēlē*, tumour), hernia of the bladder; cyst′oid, any echinoderm of the extinct class Cystoid′ea, globular or bladder-like animals enclosed in calcareous plates, stalked or sessile; cyst′olith (Gr. *lithos*, stone), a stalked limy concretion in some plant cells; cyst′oscope (Gr. *skopeein*, to view), an instrument for examining the inside of the bladder; cystos′copy; cystot′omy (Gr. *tomē*, a cut), the operation of cutting into the bladder.—cystic fibrosis (*fi-brō′sis*) a hereditary disease, appearing in infancy or childhood, characterised by too great production of mucus and of fibrous tissue, and presence of cysts, conditions which interfere with digestion, breathing, etc. [L.L. *cystis*—Gr. *kystis*, a bladder.]
cyte, *sit, n.* (*biol.*; *rare*) a cell.—*ns.* cyt′ase, an enzyme that breaks down cellulose; cyt′ochrome, any of a group of substances in living cells, of great importance in cell oxidation; cyt′ode, a protoplasm body without nucleus; cytodiagnos′is, medical diagnosis following the close

examination of the cells of the body tissues or fluids, e.g. the smear test for cervical cancer; **cytogen'esis**, cell formation; **cytogenet'ics**, genetics in relation to cytology.—*adjs.* **cyt'oid**, celllike; **cytolog'ical**.—*ns.* **cytol'ogist; cytol'ogy**, that part of biology that deals with cells; **cytol'ysis** (Gr. *lysis*, loosening), dissolution of cells; **cyt'on**, the body of a nerve-cell; **cyt'oplasm** (Gr. *plasma*, form, body), the protoplasm of a cell apart from that of the nucleus; **cy'tosine**, one of the four bases in deoxyribonucleic acids, in close association with guanine; **cytotox'in**, a substance poisonous to cells.—*adj.* **cytotox'ic**. [Gr. *kȳtos*, vessel, hollow.]

**Cytherean**, *sith-ə-rē'ən*, *adj.* pertaining to Aphrodite. [L. *Cytherēa*—Gr. *Kythereia*, Cytherean

(goddess), Aphrodite, worshipped in the island of *Kythēra*.]

**Cytisus**, *sit'i-səs*, *n.* the broom genus of Papilionaceae.—*n.* **cyt'isine**, a poisonous alkaloid found in laburnum. [Gr. *kytisos*, a kind of medick, laburnum.]

**cyto-**, *si-tō-*, in composition, cell; see **cyte**.

**czar, czarina**, etc. See **tsar**, etc.

**czardas**, a faulty spelling of **csárdás**.

**Czech**, *chek*, *n.* a member of a westerly branch of the Slavs, the Bohemians and Moravians: the language of the Czechs, Bohemian, closely allied to Polish.—Also *adj.* (also **Czech'ic**).—*n.* **Czech'oslovak**, a native or citizen of *Czechoslovakia*: a member of the Slavic people including the Czechs and the Slovaks—also *adj.* [Polish.]

Neutral vowels in unaccented syllables: *el'ə-mənt*; for certain sounds in foreign words, see p. viii

# D

**D, d,** *dē, n.* the fourth letter in our alphabet, as well as in the Phoenician, Hebrew, Greek, and Latin, from which last it was immediately derived—its sound the voiced dental stop: the second note in the natural scale (*mus.*): as a Roman numeral, D = 500.—*ns.* **D-day** (*dē′dā;* D for unnamed *d*ay), the opening day (6th June 1944) of the Allied invasion of Europe in World War II: any critical day of action: decimal day (15th February 1971), day of conversion from £.s.d. to decimal money; **D-mark,** Deutsche mark (see mark (2)); **D′-notice** (D for *d*enial), notice officially sent to newspapers, etc., asking them not to publish certain information.

**′d,** *d,* a shortened form of **had, would.**—′**dst,** hadst, wouldst.

**da, dah,** *dä, n.* a heavy Burmese knife. [Burmese *da.*]

**dab,** *dab, v.t.* to strike gently with something soft or moist: to peck: to smear: to dress (the face of stone) using a steel point:—*pr.p.* **dabb′ing;** *pa.t.* and *pa.p.* **dabbed.**—*n.* a gentle blow: a small lump of anything soft or moist: (usu. in *pl.*) a fingerprint (*slang*): (with *cap.,* in *pl.*) Fingerprint Department of New Scotland Yard: a species (*Limanda limanda*) of fish of the Pleuronectidae: applied to other (esp. to small) flatfish.—*ns.* **dabb′er,** a pad for dabbing ink on blocks or plates; **dab′chick,** the little grebe. [Cf. M. and early Mod. Du. *dabben,* to pinch; Ger. *tappe,* a pat; confused with **daub** and **tap.**]

**dab,** *dab, n.* an expert person.—Also *adj.*—*n.* **dab′ster** (*coll.*).—a **dab hand** at, an expert at. [Origin unknown.]

**dabble,** *dab′l, v.t.* to shake about in liquid: to spatter with moisture.—*v.i.* to play in liquid with hands or feet: to do anything in a trifling or small way.—*n.* the act of dabbling.—*n.* **dabb′ler.** —*n.* and *adj.* **dabb′ling.**—*adv.* **dabb′lingly.** [Freq. of **dab.**]

**da capo,** *dä kä′pō* (*mus.*), an indication in music that the performer must return to the beginning of the piece and conclude at the double bar marked *Fine:* abbrev. **D.C.** [It., from the head or beginning.]

**d′accord,** *da-kör,* (Fr.) agreed: in tune.

**dace,** *dās,* **dare,** *dār,* **dart,** *därt, n.* a small river fish (*Leuciscus vulgaris*) of the carp family and chub genus. [M.E. *darce*—O.Fr. *dars*—L.L. *dardus,* a dart or javelin—of Gmc. origin; from its quickness.]

**dacha,** *dä′chə, n.* a country house in Russia. [Russ., a giving, payment.]

**dachshund,** *däks′hoŏnt, daks′hoŏnd, -hoŏnt, n.* a badger-dog or teckel, of German origin, with long body and very short legs. [Ger. *dachs,* badger, *hund,* dog.]

**dacite,** *dä′sīt, n.* a fine-grained eruptive rock composed of quartz and plagioclase, with mica, etc. [From *Dacia,* a Roman province.]

**dacker,** *dak′ər,* **daker, daiker,** *dä′kər,* (*Scot.*) *v.i.* to lounge, saunter: to potter. [Origin unknown.]

**dacoit, dakoit,** *dä-koit′, n.* one of a gang of robbers in India and Burma.—*ns.* **dacoit′y, dakoit′i, dacoit′age,** robbery by gang-robbers, brigandage. [Hind. *dākait, dakait,* a robber.]

**dactyl,** *dak′til, n.* a digit (*zool.*): a foot of three syllables, one long followed by two short, like the joints of a finger (*classical pros.*):- in English, etc., a foot of three syllables, the first accented.—

*adjs.* **dac′tylar, dactyl′ic.**—*ns.* **dactyliog′raphy, dactyliol′ogy,** the study or lore of finger-rings or engraved gems; **dactyl′iomancy,** divination by means of a finger-ring; **Dac′tylis,** the cock′s-foot grass genus; **dac′tylist,** a writer of dactylic verse; **dactyl′ogram** (or *dak′*), a fingerprint; **dactylog′raphy,** the study of fingerprints: **dactylology; dactylol′ogy,** the art of talking with the fingers, like the deaf and dumb. [Gr. *daktylos,* a finger, *daktylios,* a finger-ring.]

**dad, dad, daddy,** *dad′i,* (*childish* and *coll.*) *ns.* father: used familiarly in addressing any older man.—**dadd′y-long′-legs,** the crane-fly. [History uncertain.]

**dad, daud, dad, död,** (*dial.*) *v.t.* to throw against something: to dash, thump.—*n.* a lump: a blow, thump. [Der. unknown.]

**Dada, Dadaism,** *dä′dä(-izm), n.* a short-lived (from 1916—*c.* 1920) movement in art and literature which sought to abandon all form and throw off all tradition.—*n.* **Da′daist.** [Fr., *dada,* hobby-horse.]

**daddle,** *dad′l,* (*dial.*) *v.i.* to walk in an unsteady manner, as a child or very old person: to totter. [Perh. conn. with **dawdle.**]

**daddle,** *dad′l,* (*dial.*) *n.* the hand. [Uncertain.]

**daddock,** *dad′ək,* (*dial.*) *n.* the heart of a rotten tree. [Perh. conn. with **dodder.**]

**daddy.** See **dad** (1).

**dado,** *dä′dō, n.* the cubic block forming the body of a pedestal (*classical archit.*): a skirting of wood along the lower part of the walls of a room, often merely represented by wall-paper, painting, etc.:—*pl.* **dados, dadoes.** [It.; see **die** (2).]

**daedal, daedale,** *dē′dəl,* **Daedalian,** *dē-dā′li-ən, adjs.* formed with art: displaying artistic or inventive skill: intricate, varied.—Also **de′dal.** [From L. *Daedalus,* Gr. *Daidalos,* the mythical artist who constructed the Cretan labyrinth and made wings for his son Icarus and himself.]

**daemon,** *dē′mən, n.* a spirit holding a middle place between gods and men, as the daemon or good genius of Socrates.—*adj.* **daemonic** (*-mon′ik*), supernatural: of power or intelligence more than human: inspired. [L. *daemōn, -ōnis*—Gr. *daimōn, -ōnos,* a spirit, a genius, and later a devil; see **demon.**]

**daff,** *daf, v.i.* to make sport, to play the fool.—*n.* **daff′ing,** foolery, gaiety. [Origin doubtful.]

**daff,** *daf,* (*Shak.*) *v.t.* to put off: to turn aside, dismiss, put by. [A variant of **doff.**]

**daffodil,** *daf′ə-dil,* often *coll.* **daff′y,** *n.* a yellow-flowered narcissus.—Also (*poet.*) **daffadowndilly,** *daf′ə-down-dil′i,* **daffodill′y.**—*adj.* pale yellow. [M.E. *affodille*—O.Fr. *asphodile*—Gr. *asphodelos,* asphodel; the *d* is unexplained.]

**daffy,** *daf′i, n.* an 'elixir of health' invented by one Thomas *Daffy* (d. 1680).

**daft,** *däft,* (*Scot.* and *N. English*) *adj.* silly: weak-minded: insane: unreasonably merry.—*n.* **daft′ie.**—*adv.* **daft′ly.**—*n.* **daft′ness.**—**daft days** (*Scot.*), days of merriment at New Year (or perhaps Christmas). [M.E. *daffte,* mild, meek. See **deft.**]

**dag,** *dag, n.* a heavy pistol of the 15th and 16th centuries. [Origin uncertain.]

**dag,** *dag, n.* a tag, scallop, or laciniation (*obs.*): a dirt-clotted tuft of wool on a sheep.—*v.t.* to cut into dags: to bedraggle (*obs.*): to cut off a sheep's dags. [Origin uncertain.]

**dagga,** *dag′a, duhh′ə, n.* Indian hemp (called true

*fāte, fär; mē, hûr* (her); *mīne; mōte, för; mūte, moōn, foōt; dhen* (then) dagga): in U.S., marijuana: an African labiate plant *Leonotis leonurus* or other species (Cape or red dagga) smoked as a narcotic, called the love-drug. [Hottentot *dachab*.]

dagger, *dag'ər, n.* a knife or short sword for stabbing at close quarters; a mark of reference † (*print.*); double dagger, diesis ‡.—at daggers drawn, in a state of hostility; look daggers, to look in a hostile manner. [M.E. *dagger*; cf. Fr. *dague*.]

daggle, *dag'l, v.t.* and *v.i.* to wet or grow wet by dragging or sprinkling.—dagg'le-tail, a draggletail. [Freq. of dag.]

dago, *dā'gō, n.* a man of Spanish, Portuguese, or Italian origin:—*pl.* da'goes. [Prob. Sp. *Diego*— L. *Jacōbus*, James.]

dagoba, *dä'gō-bä, n.* in Ceylon, a tope (for Buddhist relics). [Sinh. *dāgaba.*]

Dagon, *dā'gon, -gon, n.* the national god of the Philistines, half-man, half-fish. [Heb. *dāgōn*— *dāg*, fish.]

daguerreotype, *də-ger'ō-tip, n.* a method of photography by mercury vapour development of silver iodide exposed on a copper plate: a photograph so taken: a faithful representation (*obs.*). —*v.t.* to photograph by that process.—*adj.* daguerr'ean.—*n.* daguerre'otypy, the art of daguerreotyping. [Fr., from Louis *Daguerre* (1789-1851).]

dagwood. Same as dogwood. See under dog.

dahabiyah, -iyeh, -ieh, -eeah, *dä-hä-bē'(y)ä, -ə, n.* a Nile sailing boat. [Ar. *dhahabiyah*, golden.]

Dahlia, *däl'ya,* in U.S. *däl'ya, n.* a Mexican genus of garden composites with large brightly-coloured flowers: (without *cap.*) any plant of this genus. [From *Dahl*, an 18th-cent. Swedish botanist.]

daidle, *dā'dl, (Scot.) v.i.* to waddle: to stagger: to idle about: to trifle: to potter.—*adj.* daid'ling, feeble: dawdling. [daddle.]

daiker, *dā'kər, (Scot.) v.i.* to deck out. [Perh. Fr. *décorer*.]

daiker. See dacker.

Dáil (Eireann), *doil (ār'ən), n.* the lower house of the legislature of the Republic of Ireland. [Ir., 'assembly (of Ireland)'.]

daily, *dā'li, adj.* and *adv.* every day.—*n.* a daily paper: a non-resident servant.—daily dozen, (*-duz'n*), physical exercises done regularly, usu. every morning (*coll.*). [day.]

daimen, *dem'ən, däm'ən, (Scot.) adj.* occasional. [Origin obscure.]

daimio, *dī'myō, n.* a Japanese territorial noble under the old feudal system. [Jap.]

daine (*Shak.*). Same as deign.

dainty, *dān'ti, adj.* pleasant to the palate: delicate: tasteful: fastidious: choicely or fastidiously neat: elegant (*Spens.*).—*n.* that which is dainty, a delicacy.—*adj.* (*Spens.*) daint, daynt.—*adv.* dain'tily.—*n.* dain'tiness. [M.E. *daintie*, anything worthy or costly—O.Fr. *daintié*, worthiness—L. *dignitās, -ātis*—*dignus*, worthy.]

daiquiri, *dī'kə-ri, dak'ə-ri, n.* a cocktail containing rum and lime-juice. [Daiquiri, Cuban place name.]

dairy, *dā'ri, n.* a place where milk is kept, and butter and cheese made: a shop where milk and other dairy produce is sold.—*n.* dai'rying.— dairy cattle, cattle reared mainly for the production of milk, as distinct from *beef cattle*, reared primarily for their meat products; dai'ry-farm; dai'rymaid; dai'ryman; dairy products, milk and its derivatives, butter, cheese, etc.; dayr''-house (*Spens.*), a dairy. [M.E. *deye*—O.E. *dæge*, a dairymaid; orig. a kneader of dough; see dough.]

dais, *dās (dā'is* is only a guess from the spelling), *n.* a raised floor at the upper end of the dining-hall where the high table stood: a raised floor, usually with a seat and perhaps a canopy: the canopy over an altar, etc. [O.Fr. *deis*—L.L.

discus, a table—L. *discus*, a quoit—Gr. *diskos*, a disk.]

daisy, *dā'zi, n.* a composite plant (*Bellis perennis*) growing in pastures and meadows: extended to other plants, as the *Ox-eye daisy*, which is a chrysanthemum: a general term of admiration, often ironical.—*adj.* dai'sied, covered with daisies.—dai'sy-chain, a succession of daisies strung one upon another; dai'sy-cutter, a fast-going horse that does not lift its feet high: a cricket-ball skimmed along the ground.—New Zealand daisy bush, a half-hardy shrub of the genus *Olearia*, with daisy-like flowers. [O.E. *dæges ēage*, day's eye.]

dak, *däk, dawk, dōk, n.* in India, the mail-post: hence mail, a letter, a parcel, etc.: method of travelling like that of the mail (orig. by relays of bearers or horses).—dak bungalow, a house for travellers in India; dak runner, a runner or horseman who carries mails. [Hind. *dāk*, a relay of men.]

dakoit. See dacoit.

dal, *däl, n.* the pigeon-pea, a pealike plant (*Cajanus indicus*) cultivated in India and the tropics: pulse: a purée of pulse.—Also dhal, dholl. [Hind. *dal*, to split.]

dalai lama, *dä'li läm'a*, the head of the Tibetan Buddhist hierarchy. [Mongolian, *dalai*, ocean, Tibetan, *lama*, high-priest.]

dale, *dāl, n.* the low ground between hills: the valley through which a river flows.—dales'-man, specifically, a man of the dales of Yorkshire. [O.E. *dæl*, reinforced by O.N. *dalr*; cf. Sw. *dal*; Ger. *tal*.]

dali, *dä'li, n.* a tropical American tree akin to nutmeg yielding staves, etc., and wax seeds. [Native name.]

Dalila. See Delilah.

dalle, *däl, n.* a slab or tile, esp. decorative: in *pl.* a rapid where a river runs in a gorge between steep rocks (*U.S.*). [Fr.]

dallop. See dollop.

dally, *dal'i, v.i.* to lose time by idleness or trifling: to play: to exchange caresses:—*pr.p.* dall'ying; *pa.t.* and *pa.p.* dall'ied.—*ns.* dall'iance, dallying, toying, or trifling: interchange of embraces: delay; dall'ier, a trifler. [O.Fr. *dalier*, to chat.]

dalmahoy, *däl'mə-hoi, -hoi', n.* a bushy bob-wig worn in the 18th cent. [Said to be named from a wearer.]

Dalmatian, *dal-mā'shən, adj.* belonging to Dalmatia.—Dalmatian (dog), the spotted coach-dog, like the pointer in shape.

dalmatic, *dal-mat'ik, n.* a loose-fitting, wide-sleeved ecclesiastical vestment, worn specially by deacons in the R.C. Church, also sometimes by bishops. [L.L. *dalmatica*, a robe worn by persons of rank, on the pattern of a dress worn in *Dalmatia*.]

Dalradian, *dal-rä'di-ən, adj.* applied to a series of Pre-Cambrian rocks well represented in the Scottish Highlands.—Also *n.* [From the ancient kingdom of *Dalriada*.]

dal segno, *däl sān'yō,* an indication in music that the performer must return to the sign (𝄋) abbrev. D.S. [It. *dal segno*, from the sign.]

dalt, dault, dölt, (*Scot.*) *n.* a foster-child. [Gael. *dalta*.]

Daltonism, *döl'tən-izm, n.* colour-blindness: inability to distinguish red from green.—*adj.* Daltō'nian. [From the chemist John *Dalton* (1766-1844), who described his own case.]

Daltonism, *döl'tən-izm, n.* a school method (the Dalton plan) by which each pupil pursues separately in his own way a course suited to himself, mapped out into monthly instalments. [First tried in 1920 at *Dalton*, Massachusetts.]

dam, *dam, n.* an embankment to restrain water: the water thus confined: a mill-stream (*Scot.*).— *v.t.* to keep back by a bank:—*pr.p.* damm'ing;

*pa.t.* and *pa.p.* **dammed.** [Gmc.; Du. *dam,* Ger. *damm,* etc.]
**dam,** *dam, n.* a mother, usu. of beasts, or contemptuous. [A form of **dame.**]
**dam,** *däm, n.* an obsolete Indian copper coin, one fortieth of a rupee. [Hind. *dām.*]
**dam,** *dam, (obs. Scot.) n.* a draughtman.—**dam'-board, dam'brod,** a draughtboard. [Fr. *dame,* lady.]
**damage,** *dam'ij, n.* hurt, injury, loss: the value of what is lost: cost (*coll.*): (*pl.*) the pecuniary reparation due for loss or injury sustained by one person through the fault or negligence of another.—*v.t.* to harm.—*v.i.* to take injury.—*adj.* **dam'-ageable.**—**damage feast** (*fez'ənt*), doing damage (of beasts trespassing); **direct** or **general damages,** damages awarded for the immediate consequences of a hurt as distinct from **indirect** or **special damages** turning on the remoter consequences. [O.Fr. *damage* (Fr. *dommage*)— L. *damnum,* loss.]
**daman,** *dam'an, n.* the Syrian hyrax, the cony of the Bible. [Ar.]
**damar.** Same as **dammar.**
**damascene,** *dam'ə-sēn, dam-ə-sēn', n.* a Damascus or damascened sword: inlay of metal (esp. gold) or other materials on steel, etc.: the structure or surface appearance of Damascus steel: a damson: (with *cap.*) a native or inhabitant of Damascus.—*v.t.* to decorate (esp. steel) by inlaying or encrusting: to ornament with the watered or wavy appearance of Damascus steel, or in imitation of it.—Also **damasceene, damaskeen, -kin, -quin** (*-kēn*).—*n.* **damascen'ing,** inlaying upon steel: production of watered appearance on steel.—**Damascus blade,** a Damascus sword, the surface marked by wavy pattern. [From *Damascus,* famous for its steel and (see **damask**) silk work.]
**damask,** *dam'əsk, n.* figured material, originally of silk, now usually of linen, also of cotton or wool, the figure woven not printed: Damascus steel or its surface appearance: the red colour of the damask rose.—*v.t.* to flower or variegate (cloth): to damascene.—*adj.* red, like a damask rose.—*n.* **dam'assin,** damask with flowered patterns in gold or silver thread.—**damask plum,** the damson; **damask rose,** a bluish-red variety of rose; **dam'ask-steel,** Damascus steel. [From *Damascus* (see **damascene**).]
**damboard, dambrod.** See dam (4).
**dame,** *dām, n.* the mistress of a house, a matron (now usu. jocular or patronising): a mother: a woman (*slang*): the comic vulgar old woman of the pantomime, usually played by a male actor: a noble lady: (title of) a lady of the same rank as a knight: a baronet's or knight's wife (as a formal title prefixed to the lady's first name).—**dame'-school** (*hist.*), a school for young children usually kept by a woman: **dame's'-vi'olet,** a cruciferous plant (*Hesperis matronalis*) formerly cultivated in pots by ladies for its sweet scent at night. [Fr. *dame*—L. *domina,* a lady.]
**dame,** *dam,* (Fr.) *n.* woman, lady.—**dame d'honneur** (*don-œr*), maid of honour; **dames de la halle** (*da la al*), market women.
**dammar,** *dam'ər, n.* a copal used for making varnish, obtained from various conifers. [Malay *damar.*]
**damn,** *dam, v.t.* to censure: to sentence to eternal punishment: to doom: to curse or swear at.—*v.i.* to utter curses.—*n.* an interjection expressing annoyance, disgust or impatience (*coll.*): something of little value (*coll.*): a curse.—*adj.* **damnable** (*dam'nə-bl*), deserving or tending to damnation: hateful: pernicious.—*n.* **dam'-nableness.**—*adv.* **dam'nably.**—*n.* **damnation** (*-nā'shən*), condemnation: the punishment of the impenitent in the future state (*theol.*): eternal punishment.—*adjs.* **dam'natory** (*-nə-tər-i*), con-

signing to damnation; **damned** (*damd*; poet. *dam'nid*), sentenced to everlasting punishment (**the damned,** *äamd,* those so sentenced): hateful, an intensive, meaning merely thorough.—*adv.* very, exceedingly.—*n.* **damnification** (*dam'ni-fi-kā'shən*), infliction of injury or loss.—*v.t.* **dam'nify,** to cause loss to.—*adj.* **damning** (*dam'-ing, -ning*), exposing to condemnation.—**damn all** (*coll.*), nothing at all; **damn with faint praise,** to condemn in effect by expressing too cool approval; **do one's damnedest** (*damd'əst; coll.*), to do one's very best; **not to give a damn** (*coll.*), to be completely unconcerned; **not worth a damn** (*coll.*), of no value. [Fr. *damner*—L. *damnāre,* to condemn—*damnum,* loss.]
**Damoclean,** *dam-ō-klē'ən, adj.* like *Damoclēs,* flatterer of Dionysius of Syracuse, taught the insecurity of happiness by being made to sit through a feast with a sword suspended over his head by a single hair: hence, carrying the threat of imminent calamity.
**damosel, damozel,** *dam'ō-zel, n.* Same as **damsel.**
**damp,** *damp, n.* vapour, mist: moist air: in mines, etc., any gas other than air: lowness of spirits: a gloom: discouragement.—*v.t.* to wet slightly: to discourage: to check: to make dull: to slow down the rate of burning (of a fire): to diminish the amplitude of.—*adj.* moist: foggy.—*v.t.* and *v.i.* **damp'en,** to make or become damp or moist.—*ns.* **damp'er,** one who or that which damps: a depressive influence: a door or shutter for shutting off or regulating a draught: a device for diminishing the amplitude of vibrations or cycles: a mute (*mus.*): a kind of unfermented bread (*Austr.*).—*adj.* **damp'ish.**—*n.* **damp'ishness.**—*adv.* **damp'ly.**—*n.* **damp'ness.**—*adj.* **damp'y** (*poet.*), damp.—**damp'-course,** a layer of moisture-proof material in a masonry wall; **damp'ing-off',** a disease of seedlings caused by Pythium or other fungus in an excess of moisture.—*adj.* **damp'-proof,** impervious to moisture. [M.E. *dampen*; akin to Du. *damp,* Ger. *dampf,* vapour.]
**damsel,** *dam'zl, n.* a young unmarried woman: a girl. [O.Fr. *dameisele* (Fr. *demoiselle*)—L.L. *domicella,* dim. of L. *domina,* lady.]
**damson,** *dam'zn, n.* a rather small oval dark purple plum.—**damson cheese,** damsons pressed into a solid cake. [Shortened from *Damascene*— *Damascus.*]
**Dan,** *dan, n.* a title of honour equivalent to Master or Sir formerly applied esp. to monks, and now by the poets to great poets, etc. [O.Fr. *dan.* (Sp. *don*; Port. *dom*; L. *dominus,* lord.]
**dan,** *dan, (dial.)* a box for carrying coal: a tub.
**dance,** *däns, v.i.* to move with measured steps, esp. to music: to spring.—*v.t.* to make to dance or jump: to perform, execute, as a dance.—*n.* a movement of one or more persons with measured steps: the tune to which dancing is performed: the musical form of a dance-tune: a meeting for dancing.—*ns.* **danc'er, danc'ing.**—**dance'-band;** **dance'-hall,** a public hall providing facilities for dancing to patrons on receipt of an admission fee; **dance'-music,** music specially arranged for accompanying dancing; **dance'-tune; danc'-ing-girl,** a professional dancer; **danc'ing-mas'ter.**—**dance a bear** (*obs.*), to exhibit a performing bear; **dance attendance,** to wait assiduously; **dance of death,** a series of allegorical paintings symbolising the universal power of death, represented as a skeleton; **dance upon nothing,** to be hanged; **lead one a (merry) dance,** to keep one involved unnecessarily in a series of perplexities and vexations; **merry dancers** (*dial.*), the aurora borealis. [O.Fr. *danser,* from Gmc.; O.H.G. *dansôn,* to draw along.]
**dancette,** *dän-set', n.* a zigzag or indented line or figure (*her.*): the chevron or zigzag moulding common in Romanesque architecture.—*adj.* **dan-**

cetté, -ee, -y (*dän'set-i*, or *-set'-*), deeply indented. [O.Fr. *dent*, *dant*, tooth, notch—L. *dēns*, *dentis*.]
dandelion, *dan'di-li-ən*, *n.* a common yellow-flowered composite (*Taraxacum officinale*) with jagged-toothed leaves. [Fr. *dent de lion*, lion-tooth.]
dander, *dan'dər*, daunder, dawner, *dön'(d)ər*, (*Scot.*) *v.i.* to stroll, saunter.—*n.* a stroll, saunter. [Origin unknown.]
dander, *dan'dər*, *n.* a form of dandruff: anger: passion.—raise one's dander, to put him out of temper.
dander, *dan'dər*, (*Scot.*) *n.* furnace cinders. [Origin unknown.]
Dandie Dinmont, *dan'di din'mənt*, *n.* a short-legged rough-coated terrier of Scottish Border breed, of pepper or mustard colour. [From *Dandie Dinmont* in Scott's *Guy Mannering*, whose Peppers and Mustards are represented as the origin of the breed.]
dandiprat, dandyprat, *dan'di-prat*, (*obs.*) *n.* a silver three-halfpenny piece: an insignificant person: a little boy. [Origin unknown.]
dandle, *dan'dl*, *v.t.* to play with: to fondle, toss in the arms or dance lightly on the knee (a baby). [Origin unknown.]
dandruff, dandriff, *dand'rəf*, *n.* a scaly scurf on the skin under the hair. [Origin unknown.]
dandy, *dan'di*, *n.* a foppish, silly fellow: one who pays much attention to dress: a dandy-cock: a dandy-roll.—*adj.* (*coll.*) smart, fine—a word of general commendation.—*adjs.* dandi'acal, dand'i-fied, inclined to be a dandy.—*v.t.* dan'dify, to dress up.—*adv.* dan'dily.—*adj.* dan'dyish.—*n.* dan'dyism.—dan'dy-brush, a hard horse brush of whalebone bristles; dan'dy-cart, a light spring-cart; dan'dy-cock, -hen, a bantam; dan'dy-horse, an early bicycle without pedals, driven by kicking the ground; dan'dy-roll, a wire-gauze cylinder that impresses the ribs and water-mark on paper. [Origin unknown; orig. Scots; poss. one spoiled by overmuch dandling.]
dandy, *dan'di*, *n.* a sloop-like vessel with jigger-mast abaft.—*adj.* dan'dy-rigged.
dandy-fever. See dengue.
Dane, *dän*, *n.* a native or citizen of Denmark: a Northman: a very large dog (great Dane): a Dalmatian dog (lesser Dane).—*adj.* Danish (*dän'ish*), belonging to Denmark.—*n.* the language of the Danes.—Also Dan'isk (*Spens.*). [Dan. *Daner* (pl.); O.E. *Dene*.]
danegeld, *dän'geld*, *n.* a tax imposed in the 10th cent., to buy off the Danes or to defend the country against them. [O.E. *Dene*, Danes, *geld*, payment.]
dane-hole, *dän'hōl*, *n.* Same as dene-hole.
Danelaw, *dän'lö*, *n.* that part of England, N.E. of Watling Street, occupied (9th-11th cent.) by the Danes: (without *cap.*) the Danish law which prevailed there. [O.E. *Dena lagu*, Danes' law.]
dang, *dang*, *v.t.* a minced form of damn.
danger, *dän'jər*, *n.* peril, hazard, or risk: insecurity: power (*obs.*).—*v.t.* (*Shak.*) to endanger.—*adj.* dan'gerous, full of danger: arrogant, stand-offish (*obs.*): unsafe: insecure.—Also *adv.* (*Shak.*).—*adv.* dan'gerously.—*n.* dan'gerousness.—danger line, the boundary between safety and danger; danger money, extra money paid for doing a more than usually perilous job; danger point, the place where safety gives way to danger; dangerous drugs, certain specific drugs, including morphine, cocaine, heroin, etc., to the dispensing of which stringent regulations apply. (Dangerous Drugs Act, the act under which these drugs are scheduled.) [O.Fr. *dangier*, absolute power (of a feudal lord), hence power to hurt.—L.L. *dominium*, feudal authority—L. *dominus*, a lord.]
dangle, *dang'gl*, *v.i.* to hang loosely or with a swinging motion: to follow about.—*v.t.* to make to dangle (often with intent to entice or en-

courage).—*n.* dang'ler, one who dangles about others, esp. about women.—*n.* and *adj.* dang'ling.—dangling participle (*U.S.*), a misrelated participle. [Cf. Dan. *dangle*—O.N. *dingla*.]
Daniel, *dan'yəl*, *n.* a wise judge (in phrases as *a second Daniel*, *a Daniel come to judgment*—both *Merchant of Venice*). [From Daniel in the Apocryphal *Book of Susannah*.]
Danish. See Dane.
Danite, *dan'it*, *n.* one of a secret society amongst the early Mormons. [*Dan*; cf. Gen. xlix. 16, 17].
dank, *dangk*, *adj.* unpleasantly moist, wet.—*n.* (*Milt.*) a wet place.—*adj.* dank'ish.—*n.* dank'ness. [Origin uncertain.]
danke schön, *dang-kə shœn*, (Ger.) many thanks.
dannebrog, *dan'e-brog*, *n.* the Danish national flag: the second of the Danish orders instituted by King Valdemar in 1219. [Dan.]
danse macabre, *däs ma-käbr'*, (Fr.) dance of death (*q.v.*).
danseuse, *dä-sœz'*, *n.* a female dancer: a ballet dancer. [Fr.]
Dansker, *dan'skər*, (*Shak.*) *n.* a Dane.
dant, danton. Earlier forms of daunt, daunton.
Dantean, *dan'ti-ən*, Dantesque, *dan-tesk'*, *adjs.* like the poet *Dante*: sublime: austere.—*ns.* Dan'tist, a Dante scholar; Dantoph'ilist, a lover of Dante.
dap, *dap*, *v.i.* to bounce: to drop bait gently into the water.—*n.* a bait so used: a bounce.—*n.* dapp'er. [Origin obscure.]
Daphne, *daf'ni*, *n.* a genus (fam. Thymelaeaceae) of shrubs, including mezereon and spurge-laurel: (without *cap.*) any plant of this genus. [Gr. *daphnē*, sweet bay.]
dapper, *dap'ər*, *adj.* quick: little and active: neat: spruce.—*n.* dapp'erling, a dapper little fellow. [Du. *dapper*, brave; cf. Ger. *tapfer*, quick, brave.]
dapple, *dap'l*, *adj.* marked with spots.—*v.t.* to variegate with spots.—*adj.* dapp'led.—*adjs.* dapp'le-bay', of bay colour, variegated with dapples; dapp'le-grey'. [Origin unknown.]
dapsone, *dap'sōn*, *n.* a drug widely used in the treatment of leprosy.
darbies, *där'biz*, (*slang*) *n.pl.* handcuffs. [App. from the personal name *Darby*.]
Darby and Joan, *där'bi-ənd-jōn'*, a devoted elderly married couple. [Poss. from characters in an 18th-cent. song.]
Darbyite, *där'bi-it*, *n.* one of the Plymouth Brethren, more particularly of the Exclusive branch of the sect. [From their principal founder, J. N. *Darby* (1800-82).]
dare, *där*, *v.i.* and *v.t.* to be bold enough (to): to venture:—3rd *pers. sing.* dare(s); *pa.t.* durst, commonly in subjunctive sense, dared; *pa.p.* dared.—*v.t.* to challenge: to defy: to face:—3rd *pers.* dares; *pa.t.* and *pa.p.* dared.—*n.* (*Shak.*) boldness: an act of daring or a challenge to perform it.—*adjs.* dare'ful (*Shak.*), full of daring, adventurous: dar'ing, bold: courageous: fearless.—*n.* boldness.—*adv.* dar'ingly.—dare'-devil, a rash, venturesome fellow.—*adj.* unreasonably rash and reckless.—dar'ing-do (see derring-do).—*adj.* dar'ing-hard'y (*Shak.*), fool-hardy.—I dare say, I suppose. [O.E. *durran* (preterite-present vb.), pres.t. *dearr*, pret. *dorste*; Goth. *daursan*; akin to Gr. *tharseein*.]
dare, *där*, (*obs.*) *v.i.* to lurk, crouch, shrink, be dismayed, doze, be fascinated, stare.—*v.t.* (*Spens.*, *Shak.*) to daze: to frighten.—*n.* a contrivance with mirrors used to fascinate larks. [O.E. *darian*, to lurk, be hidden.]
darg, *därg*, (*Scot.*) *n.* a day's work: a task. [Contr. from *dawerk*, *day-wark*, *day-work*.]
darga, *dur'gä*, *n.* (a structure over) a place where a holy person was cremated or buried. [Hind. *dargäh*.]
dargle, *där'gl*, (*Scott*) *n.* a dell. [Prob. from the

Dargle in Co. Wicklow, mistaken by Scott for a common noun.]

dari. See durra.

daric, dar´ik, n. an old gold or silver coin larger than an English sovereign named after Darius I of Persia.

dariole, da´rē-ōl, dar´yöl, n. a shell of pastry, etc., or small round mould: a dish comprising such a shell and its filling. [Fr.]

dark, därk, adj. without light: black, or somewhat blackish: gloomy: difficult to understand: unenlightened: secret: sinister.—n. absence of light: nightfall: a state of ignorance.—adv. (Shak.) in a state of dark.—v.t. dark´en, to make dark or darker: to render ignorant: to sully.—v.i. to grow dark or darker.—adj. dark´ish.—v.i. dark´le, to grow dark (a back-formation from darkling).—adv. and adj. dark´ling, dark: in the dark.—advs. dark´lings (poet.), in the dark; dark´ly.—adj. dark´some, dark: (poet.) gloomy.—ns. dark(e)y, a Negro (coll.; old-fashioned): a dark-lantern (slang); dark´ness.—Dark Ages, the period of intellectual darkness in Europe, from the 5th to the 9th or 12th (or 15th) century; Dark Continent, Africa; dark horse, in racing, a horse whose capabilities are not known: also fig. of a person (usu. implying undisclosed ability): a candidate not brought forward till the last moment; dark´-house (Shak.), a mad-house; dark´-lant´ern, a lantern whose light can be covered; dark´mans (thieves' slang), night; dark´-room, a room free from such light as would affect photographic plates.—darken one's door, (often with negative, often implying unwelcomeness) to appear as a visitor; keep dark, to be silent or secret; keep it dark, to conceal it; prince of darkness, Satan. [O.E. deorc.]

darling, där´ling, n. one dearly beloved (often voc.): a favourite. [O.E. dēorling; see dear.]

Darlingtonia, där-ling-tō´ni-a, n. a Californian pitcher-plant of the Sarracenia family. [Named after William Darlington (1782-1863), American botanist.]

darn, därn, v.t. to mend by interwoven stitches: to embroider or sew with the stitches used in mending holes.—n. a darned place.—ns. darn´er; darn´ing.—darn´ing-need´le. [Etymology unknown.]

darn, därn, a minced form of damn.

darnel, där´nl, n. a species of rye-grass: perh. the tares of the Bible. [Poss. conn. with O.Fr. darne, stupid, from its supposed narcotic properties.]

darraign(e), darrain(e), darrayn, deraign, də-rān´, (obs.) v.t. to vindicate: to justify: to prove: to claim: to challenge: to decide: (Spens., Shak.), to set in battle array, or to do (battle). [O.Fr. derainier, desraisnier, to plead, vindicate.—L.L. dē-, disratiōnāre—L. dē- or dis-, ratiō, reason; cf. arraign.]

darre, där (Spens.). Same as dare (1).—darred (därd), pa.p. of dare (2).

darshan, där´shan, n. a blessing conferred by seeing or touching a great or holy person. [Hindi.]

dart, därt, n. a pointed weapon or toy for throwing with the hand: anything that pierces: a tapering fold sown on the reverse of material in order to shape it: (in pl.) a game in which darts are thrown at a board: in some snails, a calcareous needle supposed to be used as a sexual stimulus: a sudden forward movement: a plan, scheme (Austr.): a cutworm moth (Agrotis) with a dart-like mark on the forewing (in full dart´-moth).—v.t. to hurl suddenly: to send or shoot forth.—v.i. to start or shoot forth rapidly—freq. dar´tle.—n. dart´er, one who or that which darts: a fresh-water diving bird (Plotus) allied to cormorants: an archer-fish: applied also to various small American fishes akin to perch.—adv. dart´ingly.—dart´-board, the target used in the

game of darts; dart´-sac, the gland that secretes the dart in snails.—Old Dart (Austr. slang), Great Britain. [O.Fr. dart; cf. O.E. daroth.]

dart. See dace.

dartre, där´tər, n. herpes.—adj. dar´trous. [Fr.]

Darwinism, där´win-izm, n. the theory of the origin of species propounded by Charles Darwin (1809-82).—adj. and n. Darwin´ian.

darzi, där´zē, dûr´zē, n. a tailor. [Hind. darzī.]

dash, dash, v.t. to throw, thrust, or drive violently: to break by throwing together: to bespatter: to blotch: to frustrate: to confound: to modify by dilution or admixture.—v.i. to rush with violence.—n. a violent striking: a rush: a violent onset: a blow: a splash: a splash of colour: a stroke of the pen or similar mark: a mark (—) at a break in a sentence or elsewhere: a euphemism for damn (sometimes represented by this sign): a staccato mark: an acute accent used in algebra and in lettering of diagrams as a discriminating mark: a long element in the Morse code: verve: ostentation: a slight admixture: a dashboard.—n. dash´er, one who dashes: one who makes a great show (coll.).—adj. dash´ing, spirited: showy: ostentatiously fashionable.—adv. dash´ingly.—dash´board, a board, screen or partition in front of a driver, on a horse-vehicle to keep off splashes of mud, in a motor-car or aeroplane to carry instruments; dash´-pot, a device for damping vibration by a piston moving in a cylinder containing liquid; dash´-wheel, a washing-machine in the form of a partitioned drum.—dash off, to throw off or produce hastily: leave abruptly; dash out, to knock out by striking against something. [M.E. daschen, dassen, to rush, or strike with violence—cf. Dan. daske, to slap.]

dash, dash, n. a gift accompanying a commercial transaction: a gratuity: a bribe. [Port. das, will you (sing.) give?]

das heisst, das hist, (Ger.) that is:—abbrev. d.h.—equivalent to English i.e.

dassie, das´i, (S. Africa) n. the hyrax. [Du. dasje, dim. of das, badger: Afrik. dassie.]

dastard, däs´tərd, n. a cowardly fellow: loosely, one who does a brutal act without giving his victim a chance.—adj. shrinking from danger: cowardly.—adj. and adv. das´tardly.—ns. das´tardness, das´tardliness, das´tardy. [Prob. conn. with dazed.]

dasyphyllous, das-i-fil´əs, adj. having crowded, thick, or woolly leaves. [Gr. dasys, thick, bushy, hairy, phyllon, leaf.]

Dasypus, das´i-poŏs, -pəs, n. a genus of armadillos.—n. das´ypod, any member of the genus.—n.pl. Dasipod´idae, the armadillo family. [Gr. dasypous, a hare—dasys, hairy, pous, podos, foot.]

dasyure, das´i-ūr, n. any marsupial of the flesh-eating genus Dasyu´rus (called native cat) or the fam. Dasyu´ridae (Tasmanian devil, Tasmanian wolf, etc.). [Gr dasys, shaggy, ourā, tail.]

data, dä´ta, (in U.S. and technical Eng. dä´tä), n.pl. (commonly but still erroneously sing.) facts given, from which others may be inferred:—sing. dä´tum, q.v.—n. datamä´tion, shortened term for automatic data processing.—data highway, connecting link between computers at different places rendering all information stored available at each place; data processing (see process). [L. dāta, things given, pa.p. neut. pl. of dāre, to give.]

datary, dä´tə-ri, n. an officer of the papal court charged with registering and dating bulls, etc., and with duties relating to the granting of indults and graces: his office (also datä´ria). [L.L. datārius—L. dāre, to give.]

date, dāt, n. a statement of time, or time and place, of writing, sending, executing, as on a letter, book, document, etc.: the time of an event:

duration, or end, of existence (*arch.*): term of life: death-day, doom (with pun on *debt*; *Spens.*): an appointment or engagement (*coll.*). —*v.t.* to affix a date to: to ascertain the date of: to suggest the date of: to make an appointment with (*coll.*): to go out with (a member of the opposite sex), esp. regularly (*coll.*).—*n.* the person dated (in the last sense of the *v.t.*).—*v.i.* to reckon: to take beginning: to savour of a particular time: hence, to become old-fashioned.—*adjs.* dāt'able; dāt'al; date'less, without date or fixed limit: free from engagements.—*n.* dāt'er.—date'-coding, marking in code on the container a date after which food should not be used; date'-line, the line east and west of which the date differs—the 180th meridian with deviations: a line giving the date, as on a newspaper.—out of date, (see out); up to date, abreast of the times: adapted or corrected to the present time: modern. [O.Fr. *date*—L. *dātum*, given.]

date, dāt, *n.* the fruit of the date-palm.—date'-palm, -tree, a palm (*Phoenix dactylifera*) of N. Africa and S.W. Asia; date'-plum, a fruit of the ebony genus, persimmon; date'-shell, the date-shaped shell of *Lithodomus*, or the animal itself, of the mussel family, a borer in limestone rocks; date'-su'gar. [Fr. *datte*—L. *dactylus*—Gr. *daktylos*, a finger, a date.]

dative, dāt'iv, *adj.* given or appointed: expressing an indirect object (*gram.*).—*n.* the dative case: a word in the dative.—*adj.* datival (*də-tī'vəl*). [L. *dātivus*—*dāre*, to give.]

datolite, dat'ə-līt, *n.* a hydrated silicate of boron and calcium. [Gr. *dateesthai* to divide, *lithos*, stone.]

datum, dā'təm (see data).—dā'tum-line, the horizontal base-line from which heights and depths are measured. [L. *dātum*, given—*dāre*, to give.]

Datura, də-tū'ra, *n.* the thorn-apple genus of the potato family, with strongly narcotic properties. —*n.* datū'rine, atropine, or a mixture of atropine with other alkaloids. [Hind. *dhatūrā*.]

daub, dôb, *v.t.* to smear: to paint coarsely.—*n.* a coarse painting.—*ns.* daub'er, one who daubs: a coarse painter; daub'ery (*Shak.* dawb'ry), a daubing, or crudely artful device, false pretence; daub'ing.—*adj.* daub'y, sticky. [O.Fr. *dauber*, to plaster—L. *dealbāre*, to whitewash—*dē*, down, and *albus*, white.]

daud, dawd, dôd, (*Scot.*) *v.t.* to knock, thump.—*n.* a lump: large piece. [dad (2).]

daughter, dô'tər, *n.* a female in relation to her parent: a female descendant: woman (generally). —*adj.* (*biol.*) derived from another.—*ns.* daugh'terliness; daugh'terling, a little daughter. —*adj.* daugh'terly, like or becoming a daughter. —daugh'ter-in-law, a son's wife: formerly a step-daughter:—*pl.* daugh'ters-in-law. [O.E. *dohtor*; Scot. *dochter*, Ger. *tochter*, Gr. *thygatēr*.]

dault. See dalt.

daunder, dauner. Same as dander.

daunt, dönt, or dänt, *v.t.* to frighten: to discourage: to subdue.—*adj.* daunt'less, not to be daunted.—*adv.* daunt'lessly.—*n.* daunt'lessness. —*v.t.* daun'ton, (*Scot.*), to subdue: to dare. [O.Fr. *danter* (Fr. *dompter*)—L. *domitāre*—*domāre*, tame.]

dauphin, dô'fin, *n.* the eldest son of the king of France (1349-1830).—*n.* dau'phiness, his wife. [O.Fr. *daulphin* (Fr. *dauphin*)—*Delphinus*, family name of the lords of the Viennois—hence dolphins in their crest and name Dauphiné for their province (ceded to the king, 1349).]

daur, dör, a Scots form of dare.

daut, dawt, döt, (*Scot.*) *v.t.* to pet.—*n.* daut'ie, dawt'ie, a pet. [Origin unknown.]

davenport, *dav'n-pört, -pört, n.* a small ornamental writing-desk—also dev'onport: a large sofa. [Prob. from the maker.]

davenport-trick, *dav'n-pört-trik, -pört, n.* an artifice by which a man can free himself from ropes wound round him and tied. [From two impostors who practised it (flor. 1845-65).]

Davis apparatus, *dā'vis ap-ər-ā'təs, n.* a device making possible escape from a crippled submarine. [From the inventor.]

davit, *dav'it, n.* one of a pair of erections on a ship for lowering or hoisting a boat. [App. from the name David.]

Davy, *dā'vi*, Da'vy-lamp, -*lamp, n.* the safety-lamp used in coalmines invented by Sir Humphry Davy (1778-1829).

Davy-Jones, *dā'vi jōnz'*, a sailor's familiar name for the (malignant) spirit of the sea, the devil.—Davy Jones's locker, the sea, as the grave of men drowned at sea. [Origin unknown.]

daw, dö, (*obs.*) *v.i.* to dawn. [O.E. *dagian*—*dæg*, day.]

daw, dö, *n.* a bird of the crow kind, a jackdaw: a simpleton (*arch.*).—*adj.* daw'ish.—daw'cock (*arch.*), a cock jackdaw: a noodle. [M.E. *dawe*.]

dawd. See daud.

dawdle, dô'dl, *v.i.* to waste time by trifling: to act or move slowly.—*n.* daw'dler. [Cf. daddle.]

dawk. See dak.

dawn, dön, *v.i.* to become day: to begin to grow light: to begin to appear.—*n.* daybreak: beginning.—Also dawn'ing.—dawn cypress, redwood, conifer, abundant as a fossil, found living in China in the 1940s and since planted widely; dawn'-man, Eoanthropus (*q.v.*).—dawn on, to begin to become evident to or be understood by. [Appears first as dawning, prob. from O.N.; cf. Sw. and Dan. *dagning*.]

dawner. See dander (1).

dawt, dawtie. See daut.

day, dā, *n.* the time of light, from sunrise to sunset, morning till night: twenty-four hours, from midnight to midnight (formerly by some reckoned from sunrise, or sunset, or—by astronomers—from noon): the time the earth takes to make a revolution on its axis—this being the *sidereal* day (between two transits of the first point of Aries, or approximately of the same star), distinguished from the *apparent solar* day (between two transits of the sun), and the *mean solar* day (between two transits of the mean, or imaginary uniformly moving, sun): the hours devoted to work (*working-day*): a day set apart for a purpose, as for receiving visitors: lifetime: time of existence, vogue, or influence: a time: daylight: space between mullions of a window: ground surface over a mine.—day'-bed (*arch.*), a couch or sofa: day'-blind'ness, a defect of vision in which objects are best seen by a dim light; day'-board'er, a pupil who eats but does not sleep at a boarding school; day'-book, a book for entering the transactions of each day; day'-break, dawn; day'-coal, the upper stratum of coal; day'dream, a dreaming or musing while awake.—Also *v.i.*—day'-fly, a mayfly; day'-là'bour, labour paid by the day; day'-là'bourer, day'-level (*mining*), a level driven from the surface; day'light, the light of day: a clear space: day'light-sav'ing, reduction of loss of daylight, for work or play, by advancing the clock; day'-lil'y, a liliaceous plant (*Hemerocallis*) whose blossoms last only for a day.—*adj.* day'long, during the whole day.—day'mark, an unlighted sea-mark.—*adj.* day'-old, one day old.—day'-peep (*Milt.*), dawn.—*adj.* day'-release', freed from employment during the day so as to attend an educational course.—day'-scholar, a pupil who attends a boarding-school during the school-hours, but boards at home (also day'-boy, day'-girl); day'-school, a school held during the day, as opposed both to a night-school and to a boarding-school; day'-sight, night-blindness; days'man, one who appoints a day to hear a cause: an umpire; day'spring, dawn; day'star, the morning star; day'time, the time of daylight. —*adjs.* day'-to-day', daily, routine; day'-wea'ried (*Shak.*), wearied with the work of the day.—day'-work.—at the end of the day (*fig.*), when all is said and done; call it a day, to announce a decision to leave off; day about, on alternate days; day by day, daily; day in, day out, for an indefinite succession of days; day off, a day's holiday; day out, a servant's free day; days of grace, three days allowed for payment of bills, etc., beyond the day named; in this day and age, at the present time; one of these days, some indefinite time in the near future; see daylight, to arrive at some comprehension, illumination, prospect of a solution; that will be the day (*coll.*), that is very unlikely; the day, the time spoken of or expected: to-day (*Scot.*); the day after the fair, too late; the other day, not long ago; the time of day, the hour of the clock: a greeting; win the day, to gain the victory. [O.E. dæg; Ger. *tag*; not L. *diēs*.]

dayes-man, daynt, dayr'house (all *Spens.*). See day (daysman), dainty, dairy.

day-nettle, dā-net'l, *n.* a dead-nettle: (in Scotland and N. England) the hemp-nettle: a gathering on the finger.—Also dae'-nett'le. [Perh. for dead-nettle; but cf. O.N. (*akr*)*dai*, hemp-nettle.]

day-woman (*Shak.*). Same as dey-woman.

daze, dāz, *v.t.* to stun, to stupefy.—*n.* bewilderment: mica (*arch.*).—*adj.* dazed (dāzd).—*adv.* dazedly (dāz'id-li).—in a daze, stunned. [O.N. dasa-sk (refl.), to be breathless.]

dazzle, daz'l, *v.t.* to daze or overpower with strong light: to confound by brilliancy, beauty, or cleverness.—*v.i.* to be dazzled.—*ns.* dazz'le, dazz'lement, the act of dazzling: that which dazzles; dazz'ler; dazz'ling.—*adv.* dazz'lingly. —dazz'le-paint'ing, fantastic painting for camouflage. [Freq. of daze.]

DDT. See dichlor(o)-.

de-, dē-, di-, *pfx.* (1) meaning down from, away: (2) indicating a reversal of process, or deprivation: (3) used intensively. [L., or Fr.—L.]

deacon, dē'kn, *n.* in Episcopal churches, a member of the order of clergy under priests: in some Presbyterian churches, an officer, man or woman, distinct from the elders, who attends to the secular affairs of the church: in Congregational and some other churches, an officer who advises the pastor, distributes the elements at communion, and dispenses charity: in Scotland, the master of an incorporated company: an adept (*Scot.*): the skin of a very young calf.—*n.* dea'coness, a female servant of the Christian society in the time of the apostles: in a convent, a nun who has the care of the altar: one of an order of women in some Protestant churches whose duties are pastoral, educational, social and evangelical.—*ns.* dea'conhood, dea'conry, dea'conship.—permanent deacon, an officer in the Roman Catholic church, minimally below a priest.—See also diaconate. [L. *diāconus.*—Gr. *diākonos,* a servant.]

deactivate, dē-ak'tiv-āt, *v.t.* to diminish or remove the activity of.—*n.* deactivā'tion. [Pfx. de- (2).]

dead, ded, *adj.* without life: deathlike: at rest, out of play, of a ball: of a golf-ball, within a certain putt: out of use: obsolete: inactive: cold and cheerless: dull: numb: insensitive: as good as dead: inelastic: dull: without vegetation: utter: unerring.—*v.t.* (*obs.*) to deaden, dull: to benumb.—*v.i.* (*obs.*) to lose vitality: to become numb.—*adv.* in a dead manner: absolutely: utterly: directly: exactly (*coll.*).—*n.* one who is dead: the time of greatest stillness, as *the dead* of night.—*v.t.* dead'en, to make dead: to

deprive partly of vigour, sensibility, or sensation: to blunt: to lessen: to make soundproof.—*ns.* dead'ener; dead'ening (also *adj.*); dead'er (*coll.*), a corpse; dead'liness.—*adj.* dead'ly, causing death: fatal: implacable: very great (*coll.*).—*adv.* in a manner resembling death: extremely (*coll.*).—*n.* dead'ness.—*adjs.* dead'-alive', dead'-and-alive', dull, inactive.—dead'-beat, a down-and-out.—*adj.* dead'-beat', quite overcome, exhausted.—dead'-bolt', -lock', one moved by turning key, knob, without intervention of a spring.—*adj.* dead'-born, still-born.—dead'-cart, a cart for collecting the bodies of those dead of a pestilence.—*n.pl.* dead'-clothes, clothes to bury the dead in.—dead'-col'ouring, the first broad outlines of a picture; dead'-deal, a board for measuring and lifting a corpse.—*adjs.* dead'-do'ing (*Spens.*), putting to death, destructive; dead'-drunk', completely drunk.—dead'-end, a pipe, passage, etc., closed at one end: a blind alley (*lit.* and *fig.*); dead'-eye (*naut.*), a round, flattish wooden block with a rope or iron band passing around it, and pierced with three holes for a lanyard; dead'-fall, a trap with a weight that falls when its support is removed; dead'-fin'ish (*Austr.*), a thicket or a thicket-forming shrub of the mimosa family (*Albizzia, Acacia*): a complete standstill or vanquishment; dead'-fire, an appearance of fire taken as a death-omen; dead'-freight, money paid for the empty space in a ship by a person who engages to freight her, but fails to make out a full cargo; dead'-ground (*mil.*), ground that cannot be covered by fire; dead'-hand, mortmain; dead'-head, one who enjoys privileges without paying, as in a theatre, etc.: a sprue; dead'-heat', a heat or race in which two or more competitors are equal; dead'-house, a mortuary; dead language, one no longer spoken; dead'-lett'er, a letter undelivered and unclaimed at the post-office: a law or ordinance made but not enforced; dead'-lev'el, a stretch of land without any rising ground: sameness; dead'-lift, -pull, a lift, pull, made without help, leverage, etc.; hence an effort under discouraging conditions.—*n.pl.* dead'-lights, stormshutters for a cabin window.—dead'line, line in a military prison, on going beyond which a prisoner was liable to be shot: closing date, last possible minute; dead'lock, the case when matters have become so complicated that all is at a complete standstill: (see dead'-bolt'); dead loss, a complete loss: a useless ally (*fig.*); dead'ly-night'shade, belladonna; deadly sin, a mortal sin (see seven); dead'-march', a piece of solemn music played at funeral processions, esp. of soldiers; dead'-meat, the flesh of animals ready for the market.—*n.pl.* dead'-men, empty bottles after a carouse.—dead'-nett'le, any species of *Lamium*, labiate plants superficially like nettles but stingless; dead'-pan, an expressionless face: one having or assuming such.—*adj.* expressionless: emotionless: dead serious or mock serious.—dead'-pay, continued pay dishonestly drawn for men actually dead; dead'-point, a position of a crank in which the force exerted on it does not help to turn it; dead'-reck'oning, an estimation of a ship's place simply by the log-book; dead'-rope, a rope not running in any block; dead'-set, a complete standstill, as of a setting dog: a determined and prolonged onslaught, esp. with a view to captivation; dead'-shot, an unerring marksman; dead's part (*Scots law*), the part of a man's moveable property which he may bequeath by will, and which is not due to wife and children.—*adj.* dead'-stroke, without recoil.—dead'-wall, wall unbroken by windows or other openings; dead'-wa'ter, still water: eddy water closing in behind a ship's stern; dead'-weight, unrelieved weight: heavy and oppressive burden: difference in a ship's displacement loaded and light; **dead'-wind,** calm (in the vortex of a storm): head wind (*obs.*); **dead'-wood,** pieces of timber laid on the upper side of the keel at either end: useless material; **dead'-work,** work, itself unprofitable, but necessary as a preliminary.—**dead as a dodo, door-nail, herring,** absolutely dead; **dead man's handle,** a device, e.g. on an electric train, which allows current to pass only so long as there is pressure on it; **dead man's pedal,** a foot-operated safety device on the same principle, used esp. on diesel trains; **dead-men's bells,** the foxglove; **dead men's fingers,** a very common actinozoan coelenterate (*Alcyonium digitatum*); **dead men's shoes,** succession to one who dies; **Dead Sea apple, fruit,** apple of Sodom; **dead (set) against,** utterly opposed to; **dead spit,** exact image; **dead to the world,** very soundly asleep: unconscious; **put the dead wood on** (*slang*), to gain a great advantage over. [O.E. *dēad*; Goth. *dauths,* Ger. *tot,* from root of **die.**]

**deaf,** *def, adj.* dull of hearing: unable to hear at all: not willing to hear: inattentive: hollow, with no kernel.—*v.t.* **deaf'en,** to make deaf: to stun: to render impervious to sound.—*n.* **deaf'ening,** stuffing put into floors, partition-walls, etc., to prevent sounds from passing through.—*adj.* making deaf (with noise): very loud.—*adv.* **deaf'ly.**—*n.* **deafness.**—**deaf'-aid,** a hearing-aid; **deaf'-mute',** one who is both deaf and dumb; **deaf'-mut'ism.**—**deaf-and-dumb alphabet (language),** digital and manual signs used to express letters (and words and phrases) visually; **turn a deaf ear,** to pretend not to have heard: to ignore. [O.E. *dēaf*; Du. *doof,* Ger. *taub.*]

**deal,** *dēl, n.* a portion: an indefinite quantity: a large quantity: the act of dividing cards: a business transaction (esp. a favourable one): treatment.—*v.t.* to divide, to distribute: to throw about: to deliver.—*v.i.* to transact business: to act: to distribute cards:—*pa.t.* and *pa.p.* dealt (*delt*).—*ns.* **deal'er,** one who deals or whose turn it is to deal, or who has dealt the hand in play: a trader; **deal'ing** (often in *pl.*), manner of acting towards others: intercourse of trade.—**deal with,** to have to do with, to treat of: to take action in regard to. [O.E. *dǣlan—dǣl,* a part; Ger. *teilen—teil,* a part or division; cf. **dole.**]

**deal,** *dēl, n.* a fir or pine board of a standard size: soft wood.—*adj.* of deal.—**deal'fish,** a ribbon-fish (*Trachypterus*). [M.L.G. *dele*; cf. O.E. *thel, thille,* and mod. **thill.**]

**dealbate,** *dē-al'bāt, adj.* whitened.—*n.* **dealbā'tion.** [L. *dealbāre, -ātum,* to whitewash—pfx. *de-,* in sense of over a surface, *albus,* white.]

**deambulatory,** *dē-am'bū-lə-tər-i, n.* a place for walking about in: a passage or aisle round the choir and apse of a church.—[L. *deambulāre, -ātum,* to walk about.]

**dean, dene,** *dēn, n.* a small valley. [O.E. *denu,* a valley; cf. **den.**]

**dean,** *dēn, n.* a dignitary in cathedral and collegiate churches who presides over the canons: the president of a faculty in a college or of the Faculty of Advocates: a resident fellow of a college who has administrative and disciplinary functions: the senior member of a corps or body: the chief chaplain of the Chapel Royal: the chief judge of the Court of Arches: the president of a trade-guild.—*ns.* **dean'ery,** the office of a dean: a group of parishes presided over by a dean: a dean's house; **dean'ship,** the office or dignity of a dean.—**Dean of Arches,** dean of the Court of Arches (see **arch**); **Dean of Faculty,** president of the Faculty of Advocates in Scotland; **Dean of Guild,** a municipal functionary in Scotland who has authority over building and altering of houses; **rural dean,** one who, under the bishop,

has the special care and inspection of the clergy in certain parishes. [O.Fr. *deien* (Fr. *doyen*)—L.L. *decānus* or Gr. *dekānos,* a chief of ten—L. *decem* or Gr. *deka,* ten.]

**deaner,** *dēn'ər, (slang) n.* a shilling. [Prob. L. *denārius.*]

**dear,** *dēr, adj.* high in price: costly: characterised by high prices: scarce: highly valued: beloved: a conventional form of address used in letter-writing: earnest (*Shak.*).—*n.* one who is dear or beloved.—*adv.* at a high price: dearly.—*interj.* indicating surprise, pity, or other emotion.—*n.* and *adj.* **dear'ling** (*Spens.*), darling.—*adj.* **dear'ly.**—*ns.* **dear'ness; dear'y,** one who is dear.—*adj.* **dear'bought.**—**dear(y) me,** an expression of various emotions; **dear knows,** an expression of ignorance. [O.E. *dēore, dȳre*; cog. with Ger. *teuer.*]

**dear, deare, deere,** *dēr, (Spens.; Shak.; Milt.) adj.* grievous.—Also *adv.* [O.E. *dēor.*]

**deare.** See **dere.**

**dearn, dearnful, dearnly.** See **dern,** etc.

**dearth, dürth, n.** dearness, high price: scarcity: want: famine: barrenness. [**dear.**]

**dearticulate,** *dē-är-tik'ū-lāt, v.t.* to disjoint. [Pfx. **de-** (2).]

**deasil,** *dēz'l, des'l, desh'l, dēsh'l, (Scot.) n.* sunwise motion—opp. to *withershins.*—*adv.* sunwise.—also **dea'soil, dei's(h)eal, dea'siul.** [Gael. *deiseil.*]

**deaspirate,** *dē-as'pir-āt, v.t.* to remove the aspirate from.—*n.* **deaspirā'tion.** [Pfx. **de-** (2).]

**death, deth, n.** state of being dead: extinction or cessation of life: manner of dying: mortality: a deadly plague: cause of death·: spiritual lifelessness: the killing of the animal in hunting.—*adjs.* **death'ful,** deadly, destructive: mortal: deathlike; **death'less,** never dying: everlasting.—*n.* **deathless'ness.**—*adj.* **death'like,** deadly: like death.—*n.* **death'liness.**—*adj.* **death'ly,** deadly: deathlike.—*advs.* **death'ward, -s.**—*adj.* **death'y.**—**death'-add'er,** a poisonous Australian snake (*Acanthophis antarcticus*); **death'-ag'ony,** the struggle often preceding death; **death'-bed,** the bed on which one dies: the last illness; **death'-bell,** the passing bell; **death'-blow,** a blow that causes death; **death'-cap, -cup,** a very poisonous toadstool (*Amanita phalloides*) often mistaken for an edible mushroom; **death'-damp,** a cold sweat preceding death.—*adj.* **death'-dealing.**—*n.pl.* **death'-du'ties,** duties paid on inheritance of property.—**death'-fire,** a light supposed to presage death.—*adj.* **death'-marked,** marked for or by death, destined to die.—**death'-mask,** a plaster-cast taken from the face after death.—*adj.* **death'-prac'tised** (*Shak.*), threatened with death by malicious arts.—**death'-rate,** the proportion of deaths to the population; **death'-ratt'le,** a rattling in the throat that so metimes precedes death; **death'-ray,** a pretended ray that could destroy all life; **death'-roll,** a list of the dead; **death's'-head,** the skull of a human skeleton, or a figure of it: a memorial ring bearing such a figure; **deaths'-man** (*Shak.*), an executioner; **death'-song,** a song sung before dying; **death'-stroke,** a death-blow; **death'-throe,** the dying agony; **death'-token** (*Shak.*), a sign or token of impending death, a plague-spot; **death'-trap,** an unsafe structure or place that exposes one to great danger of death; **death'-warrant,** an order from the authorities for the execution of a criminal; **death'-watch,** a watch by a dying person: an insect that produces a ticking noise, esp. a beetle of the genus *Anobium*; **death wish** (*psych.*), wish, conscious or unconscious, for death for oneself or another; **death'-wound,** a wound that causes death.—**at death's door,** very near to death; **death's-head moth,** a hawk-moth with pale markings on the back of the thorax somewhat like a skull; **death on,** to be fatal to, fond of, good at; **do, or**

put, to death, to kill: to cause to be killed; gates, or jaws, of death, the point of death; in at the death, to be up on the animal before the dogs have killed it: often *fig*.; like grim death, tenaciously; to death, to the uttermost: to exhaustion. [O.E. *dēath*; Ger. *tod*; see dead and die.]

deave, *dēv*, (*Scot*.) *v.t.* to deafen: to worry (esp. with noise). [See deaf.]

deaw, deawy, -ie (*Spens*.). See dew, dewy.

deb. Coll. form of débutante.

debacle, débâcle, *di-bak'l*, *dä-bäk'l'*, *n*. a breaking up of ice on a river: a sudden flood of water leaving its path strewed with debris (*geol*.): a complete break-up or collapse: a stampede. [Fr. *débâcle*; *dé*, *des*, and *bâcler*, to bar—L. *baculus*, a stick.]

debar, *di-bär'*, *v.t.* to bar out: to exclude: to hinder:—*pr.p.* debarr'ing; *pa.t.* and *pa.p.* debarred'.—*n.* debar'ment. [Pfx. de- (3).]

debark, *di-bärk'*, *v.t.* or *v.i.* to disembark.—*n.* dēbarkā'tion, dēbarcā'tion. [Fr. *débarquer—des* (—L. *dis-*), away, and Fr. *barque*, a ship.]

debarrass, *di-bar'əs*, *v.t.* to disembarrass, disentangle, free. [Fr. *débarrasser*; *dé-*, *des-* and *barre*, a bar.]

debase, *di-bās'*, *v.t.* to lower: to make mean or of less value: to adulterate.—*adj.* debased', degraded: reversed (*her*.).—*n.* debase'ment, degradation.—*adj.* debas'ing.—*adv.* debas'ingly. [Pfx. de- (1).]

debate, *di-bāt'*, *n*. a contention in words or argument: a (parliamentary) discussion: fight, strife (*obs*.).—*v.t.* to contend for in argument: to argue about: to fight for (*arch*).—*v.i.* to fight, contend (*obs*.): to deliberate: to consider: to join in debate.—*adjs*. debāt'able, also debateable, liable to be disputed: open to argument: contentious; debate'ful (*Spens*.), quarrelsome.—*ns*. debate'ment (*Spens*.; *Shak*.), controversy; debat'er.—*adv.* debāt'ingly.—Debat(e)able Land, a tract of border land between Esk and Sark, formerly claimed by both England and Scotland. [O.Fr. *debatre*—L. *dē*, and *batuēre*, to beat.]

debauch, *di-böch'*, *v.t.* to lead away from duty or allegiance: to corrupt with lewdness: to seduce: to vitiate.—*v.i.* to over-indulge.—*n*. a fit or period of intemperance or debauchery.—*adj.* debauched', corrupt: profligate.—*adv.* debauch'edly.—*ns*. debauch'edness; debauchee (*di-bösh-ē'*), a libertine; debauch'er; debauch'ery, excessive intemperance: habitual lewdness; debauch'ment. [O.Fr. *desbaucher* (Fr. *débaucher*) to corrupt—*des-* (—L. *dis-*), and *baucher*, to hew.]

debby. See début.

debel, *di-bel'*, (*Milt*.) *v.t.* to conquer in war:—*pr.p.* debell'ing; *pa.t.* and *pa.p.* debelled'. [L. *dēbellāre—dē*, down, *bellāre*, to war—*bellum*, war.]

debenture, *di-ben'chər*, *n*. a written acknowledgment of a debt: a security issued by a company for money borrowed on the company's property, having a fixed rate of interest and usually fixed redemption rates: a certificate entitling an exporter of imported goods to a repayment of the duty paid on their importation.—*adj.* debent'ured, entitled to drawback or debenture, as goods. [L. *dēbēre*, there are due, 3rd pers. pl. pass. of *dēbēre*, to owe—the first word of the receipt.]

debilitate, *di-bil'i-tāt*, *v.t.* to make weak: to impair the strength of.—*adj.* debile (*deb'il*, *dēb'il*, *arch*.), weak, feeble.—*ns*. debilitā'tion; debil'ity, weakness and languor: a weak action of the animal functions. [L. *dēbilitāre*, -*ātum*—*dēbilis*, weak—*dē*, from, and *habilis*, able. See ability.]

debit, *deb'it*, *n*. a debt or something due: an entry on the debtor side of an account.—*v.t.* to

charge with debt: to enter on the debtor side of an account.—*n.* deb'itor (*Shak*.), a debtor. [L. *dēbitum*, what is due, from *dēbēre*, to owe.]

debonair, debonnaire, *deb-ə-nār'*, *adj.* of good appearance and manners: elegant: courteous: gay.—*adv.* debonair'ly.—*n.* debonair'ness. [Fr. *de*, of, *bon*, good, and the old word *aire* (*masc*.), manner, origin; mod. Fr. *débonnaire*.]

debosh, *di-bosh'*, an old form of debauch.

debouch, *di-bowch'*, *di-bōōsh'*, *v.i.* to issue, emerge, to march or flow out from a narrow pass or confined place.—*ns*. débouché (*dā-bōō-shā'*), an outlet; debouch'ment, an act or place of debouching; debouchure (*di-bōō-shür'*), the mouth of a river or strait. [Fr. *déboucher—de*, from, *bouche*, mouth—L. *bucca*, cheek.]

Debrett, *di-bret'*, *n*. a peerage edited and published from 1784 until his death by John Field Debrett, still in publication and the type of all exclusive lists.

debrief, *dē-brēf'*, *v.t.* to gather information from a soldier, astronaut, etc., on his return from a mission. [Pfx. de- (2).]

debris, débris, *deb'rē*, *dəb-rē'*, or *dāb'rē*, *n*. wreckage: ruins: rubbish: a mass of rocky fragments. [Fr., from *briser*, akin to bruise.]

debruised, *di-brōōzd'*, (*her*.) *adj.* surmounted or partly covered by one of the ordinaries. [O.Fr. *debruisier—de-*, apart, *bruiser*, to break.]

debt, *det*, *n*. what one owes to another: what one becomes liable to do or suffer: a state of obligation or indebtedness: a duty: a sin (*B*.).—*adj.* debt'ed (*Shak*.), indebted, obliged.—*ns*. debt'ee, a creditor; debt'or, one who owes a debt.—bad debt, a debt of which there is no prospect of payment; debt of honour, a debt not recognised by law, but binding in honour—esp. a gambling or betting debt; debt of nature, death; floating debt, miscellaneous public debt, like exchequer and treasury bills, as opposed to *funded debt*, that which has been converted into perpetual annuities like consols in Britain; National Debt (see nation).—in one's debt, under an obligation (not necessarily pecuniary) to one. [O.Fr. *dette*—L. *dēbitum*, *dēbēre*, to owe.]

debug, *dē-bug'*, *v.t.* to remove concealed listening devices from: to find faults or errors in and remove them from (something mechanical). [L. *dē*, from, and bug.]

debunk, *dē-bungk'*, *v.t.* (*slang*) to clear of bunk or humbug: to remove the whitewash from (a reputation): to show up (e.g. a theory) as false. [Pfx. de- (2).]

début, *dā-bü'*, *n*. a beginning or first attempt: a first appearance before the public, or in society. —*n.* débutant (*dā-bü-tā*, *deb'ū-tant*), one who makes his first appearance:—*fem.* débutante (*-tāt*, *deb'-ū-tant*); U.S. dim. abbrev. deb, debb'y). [Fr. *début*, a first stroke—*débuter—de*, from, *but*, aim, mark.]

Debye (unit), *də-bī'* (*ū'nit*), *n*. a unit of electric dipole moment. [P. J. W. *Debye*, Dutch physicist.]

deca-, *dek-ə-*, prefix signifying ten. [Gr. *deka*.]

decachord, *dek'ə-körd*, *n*. an old ten-stringed musical instrument. [Gr. *dekachordos—deka*, ten, and *chordē*, a string.]

decade, decad, *dek'ād*, *dek-ād'*, *n*. a series of ten years: any group or series of ten.—*adj.* dec'-adal. [Gr. *dekas*, -*ados—deka*, ten.]

decadence, *di-kā'dəns*, or *di-kā'-*, dec'adency (or *di-kā'-*), *n*. state of decay: a decline from a superior state, standard or time: applied to a school in late 19th-century French literature, the symbolists, and their aims.—*adj.* dec'adent (or *di-kā'-*), decaying: lacking in moral and physical vigour: symbolist.—*n.* one who is degenerate: a symbolist. [Fr.,—L.L. *decadentia*, from L. *dē*, down—*cadere*, to fall.]

decagon, *dek'ə-gon*, *n*. a plane figure of ten angles

and sides.—*adj.* decagonal (*-ag'ən-əl*). [Gr. *deka*, and *gōniā*, an angle.]

decagramme, decagram, *dek'ə-gram*, *n.* a weight of ten grammes. [Fr. *décagramme*—Gr. *deka*, ten, and gramme.]

Decagynia, *dek-ə-jin'i-a* (*bot.*) *n.pl.* in the Linnaean system a class of plants with ten pistils.— *adjs.* decagyn'ian, decagynous (*-aj'-*). [Gr. *deka*, ten, *gynē*, a woman.]

decahedron, *dek-ə-hē'drən*, *n.* a solid figure having ten faces.—*adj.* decahē'dral. [Gr. *deka*, and *hedrā*, a seat.]

decal, *dē'kal*, *dek'al*, *n.* a transfer (picture or design). [From Fr. *décalquer*, to trace, copy.]

decalcify, *dē-kal'si-fī*, *v.i.* to deprive of lime.—*n.* decalcificā'tion. [Pfx. de- (2).]

decalescence, *dē-kəl-es'əns*, *n.* the behaviour of iron or steel which in heating from red to white reaches a point where it seems to go back for a little—the opposite of *recalescence*. [L. *dē*, down, *calēscĕre*, to grow hot.]

decalitre, *dek'ə-lēt-ər*, *n.* ten litres, about 2·2 imperial gallons. [Fr. *décalitre*—Gr. *deka*, ten, and *litrā*, a pound.]

decalogue, *dek'ə-log*, *n.* the ten commandments.— *n.* decal'ogist (*di-kal'ə-jist*), an exponent as of the decalogue. [Gr. *deka*, ten, *logos*, a discourse.]

Decameron, *di-kam'ə-ron*, *-rən*, *n.* Boccaccio's book of a hundred tales, supposed to be told in ten days.—*adj.* decameron'ic. [Gr. *deka*, ten, *hēmerā*, a day.]

decamerous, *dik-am'ər-əs*, *adj.* having the parts in tens. [Gr. *deka*, ten, *meros*, part.]

decametre, *dek'ə-mēt-ər*, *n.* ten metres. [Fr. *décamètre*—Gr. *deka*, ten, *metron*, a measure.]

decamp, *di-kamp'*, *v.i.* to make off, esp. secretly: to break camp.—*n.* decamp'ment. [Fr. *décamper*.]

decanal, *dek-ān'əl*, *adj.* pertaining to a dean or deanery: decani.—*adj.* decān'i, dean's, i.e. south (of the side of a choir where the dean sits, opposed to cantoris): used (*mus.*) in antiphonal singing. [L.L. *decānus,-i.*]

Decandria, *de-kan'dri-a*, (*bot.*) *n.pl.* in Linnaean system a class of plants with ten stamens.— *adjs.* decan'drian; decan'drous, with ten stamens. [Gr. *deka*, ten, and *anēr*, *andros*, a man, male.]

decane, *dek'ān*, *n.* a hydrocarbon (C₁₀H₂₂) tenth of the methane series. [Gr. *deka*, ten.]

decani. See decanal.

decant, *di-kant'*, *v.t.* to pour off, leaving sediment: to pour from one vessel into another.—*ns.* decantā'tion (*dē-*); decant'er, an ornamental stoppered bottle for holding decanted liquor. [Fr. *décanter* (It. *decantare*)—L. *dē*, from, *canthus*, beak of a vessel—Gr. *kanthos*, corner of the eye.]

decantate, *dē-kant'āt*, (*obs.*) *v.t.* and *v.i.* to chant or say repeatedly. [L. *dēcantāre*—pfx. *dē-*, *cantāre*, intens. of *canĕre*, to sing.]

decapitate, *di-kap'i-tāt*, *v.t.* to behead.—*n.* decapitā'tion. [L.L. *dēcapitāre*—L. *dē*, from, and *caput*, *capitis*, the head.]

Decapoda, *di-kap'ə-da*, *n.pl.* an order of higher crustaceans with ten feet (including pincers)— crabs, lobsters, shrimps, prawns, etc.: an order of cephalopods with ten arms.—*n.* dec'apod, a member of either of these orders.—Also *adj.*— *adjs.* decap'odal, decap'odan, decap'odous. [Gr. *deka*, ten, and *pous*, *podos*, a foot.]

decarbonise, -ize, *dē-kär'bən-iz*, *v.t.* to remove carbon or carbon dioxide from (also decar'- būrise, -ize; decarbo'nate).—*ns.* decarbonisā'- tion, -z-, decarburisā'tion, -z-. See decoke. [Pfx. de- (2).]

decastere, *dek'ə-stēr*, *n.* ten steres. [Gr. *deka*, ten, and stere.]

decastich, *dek'ə-stik*, *n.* a poem of ten lines. [Gr. *deka*, ten, and *stichos*, a row, a verse.]

decastyle, *dek'ə-stil*, *n.* a portico with ten columns

in front.—Also *adj.* [Gr. *deka*, ten, *stylos*, a column.]

decasyllable, *dek-ə-sil'ə-bl*, *n.* a verse-line, or a word, of ten syllables.—*adj.* decasyllabic (*-ab'ik*). [Gr. *deka*, ten, *syllabē*, a syllable; see syllable.]

decathlon, *dek-ath'lon*, *n.* a two-day contest of ten events held at the modern Olympic Games since 1912. [Gr. *deka*, ten, *athlon*, a contest.]

decaudate, *dē-kö'dāt*, *v.t.* to cut off the tail of. [L. *dē*, from, *cauda*, tail.]

decay, *di-kā'*, *v.i.* to fall away from a state of health or excellence: to waste away: to rot.— *v.t.* to cause to waste away: to impair.—*n.* a falling into a worse or less perfect state: a wearing away: rotting: loss of fortune: ruin, downfall (*obs.*): disintegration of a radioactive substance.—*adj.* decayed', rotten: reduced in circumstances, impoverished. [O.Fr. *decair*—L. *dē*, from, *cadĕre*, to fall.]

Decca, *dek'a*, ® *n.* the Decca Navigator System, consisting of a series of chains of long-wave radio transmitting stations, each chain formed of a master station and three slaves, providing a navigator or pilot with meter readings that have to be interpreted by special charts, or, alternatively, with a direct picture of his track on a Decca Flight Log.

decease, *di-sēs'*, *n.* death.—*v.i.* to die.—*adj.* deceased', dead: lately dead.—*n.* the dead person in question. [O.Fr. *deces* (Fr. *décès*)— L. *dēcessus*, departure, death—*dē*, away, *cēdĕre*, *cēssum*, to go.]

decedent, *di-sē'dənt*, *n.* (*U.S. law*) a deceased person. [L. *dēcēdēns*, *-entis*, pr.p. of *dēcēdĕre*, to depart—*dē*, away, *cēdĕre*, to go.]

deceit, *di-sēt'*, *n.* act of deceiving: anything intended to mislead another: fraud: falseness.— *adj.* deceit'ful, full of deceit: disposed or tending to deceive: insincere.—*adv.* deceit'fully.—*n.* deceit'fulness. [O.Fr. *deceite*—L. *dēcipĕre*, *dē- ceptum*, to deceive.]

deceive, *di-sēv'*, *v.t.* to mislead or cause to err: to cheat: to disappoint.—*adj.* deceiv'able, that may be deceived: exposed to imposture.—*n.* deceiv'- ableness.—*adj.* deceiv'ably.—*n.* deceiv'er. [Fr. *décevoir*—L. *dēcipĕre*, *dēceptum*, to deceive.]

decelerate, *dē-sel'ər-āt*, *v.t.* and *v.i.* to retard.—*ns.* decelerā'tion; decel'erator. [L. *dē*, down, *celer*, swift.]

December, *di-sem'bər*, *n.* formerly the tenth, now the twelfth month of the year.—*adj.* Decem'- berish (*Decem'berly*, wintry, cold.—*n.* Decem'- brist, one of those who took part in the Russian conspiracy of December, 1825. [L. *December*— *decem*, ten.]

decemvir, *di-sem'vər*, *n.* a member of a body of ten men: esp. of those who drew up the Laws of the Twelve Tables at Rome (451-450 B.C.):—*pl.* decem'virs, or decem'viri (*-ri*; L. *dek'em-wi-rē*).— *adj.* decem'viral.—*n.* decem'virāte, a body of ten men in office: the term of office of decemvirs. [L. *decem*, ten, and *vir*, a man.]

decency. See decent.

decennary, *di-sen'ər-i*, *n.* a period of ten years— also decenn'ium.—*adj.* decenn'ial, consisting of, or happening every, ten years. [L. *decem*, ten, and *annus*, a year.]

decennoval, *di-sen'ō-vəl*, (*obs.*) *adj.* pertaining to the number 19. [L. *decemnovalis*—*decem*, ten, *novem*, nine.]

decent, *dē'sənt*, *adj.* becoming: seemly: proper: modest: moderate: fairly good: passable: showing tolerant or kindly moderation (*coll.*).— *n.* dē'cency, becomingness: modesty: considerateness, sense of what may be fitly expected of one (*coll.*).—*adv.* dē'cently. [L. *decēns*, *-entis*, pr.p. of *decēre*, to be becoming.]

decentralise, -ize, *dē-sen'trəl-iz*, *v.t.* to withdraw from the centre: to transform by transferring functions from a central government, organisa-

tion or head to local centres.—*n*. decentralisā'-tion, -z. [Pfx. de- (2).]
deception, *di-sep'shan, n*. act of deceiving: state of being deceived: means of deceiving or misleading: trick: illusion.—*n*. deceptibil'ity.—*adjs*. decept'ible, capable of being deceived; decep'-tious (*Shak*.), deceitful; decep'tive, tending to deceive: misleading.—*adv*. decep'tively.—*n*. decep'tiveness.—*adj*. decep'tory, tending to deceive. [O.Fr.,—L.L. dĕceptiō, -ōnis—dĕcipĕre, to deceive.]
decerebrate, *dē-ser'a-brāt, v.t*. to deprive of cerebrum.—Also decerebrise, -ize.—*n*. decerebrā'tion. [Pfx. de- (2).]
decern, *di-sùrn', (Scots law) v.t*. and *v.i*. to judge: to decree: to pass judgment. [O.Fr. decerner—L. dĕcernĕre—dĕ, and cernĕre, to distinguish.]
decession, *di-sesh'an, (rare) n*. departure. [See decease.]
déchéance, *dā-shā-äs, (Fr.) n*. forfeiture.
dechristianise, -ize, *dē-krist'yan-iz, v.t*. to turn from Christianity. [Pfx. de- (2).]
deci-, *des'i-*, prefix signifying one-tenth. [L. decimus, tenth.]
deciare, *des'i-är, n*. the tenth part of an are. [Fr., —L. deci- (in decimus), and are.]
decibel, *des'i-bel, n*. the tenth part of a bel—unit more commonly used than bel (*q.v.*). [L. deci-, and bel.]
decide, *di-sid', v.t*. to determine: to end: to settle: to resolve.—*v.i*. to make up one's mind.—*adjs*. decid'able, capable of being decided; decid'ed, determined: clear, unmistakable: resolute.—*adv*. decid'edly.—*n*. decid'er, one who, or that which, decides: an action, etc., that proves decisive, as the winning goal in a match (*coll.*). [O.Fr. decider—L. dĕcidĕre—dē, away, caedĕre, to cut.]
deciduous, *di-sid'ū-as, adj*. liable to be shed at a certain period: transitory, not permanent: shedding all the leaves together (opp. to evergreen) (*bot.*): shedding wings (as some insects). —*n*. decid'ua, a membrane of the uterus discharged after parturition.—*adj*. decid'uäte.—*n*. decid'uousness. [L. dĕciduus—dĕcidĕre, dĕ, from, cadĕre, to fall.]
decigram(me), *des'i-gram, n*. the tenth part of a gram(me).
decilitre, *des'i-lē-tar, n*. a tenth part of a litre.
decillion, *di-sil'yan, n*. a million raised to the tenth power: in American notation, a thousand raised to the eleventh power. [L. decem, ten, and million.]
decimal, *des'i-mal, adj*. numbered or proceeding by tens.—*n*. a decimal fraction.—*v.t*. dec'imalise, -ize, to convert to a decimal system, esp. the metric system.—*ns*. decimalisā'tion, -z-; dec'imalism, use or advocacy of a decimal system; dec'imalist.—*adv*. dec'imally.—decimal currency, one in which the basic unit is divided into ten, or a multiple of ten, parts; decimal fraction, a fraction expressed by continuing ordinary decimal notation into negative powers of ten, a point being placed after the unit figure; decimal notation, a system of writing numbers based on ten and powers of ten, our ordinary system; decimal places, the number of figures written after the point (decimal point) which separates the unit and the decimal fraction; decimal system, a system in which each unit is ten times the next below it, esp. the metric system of weights and measures. [L. decima (pars), a tenth (part).]
decimate, *des'i-māt, v.t*. to take the tenth part of: to punish by killing every tenth man: (loosely) to reduce very heavily.—*ns*. decimā'tion, dec'i-mātor. [L. decimāre, -ātum—decimus, tenth—decem, ten.]
décime, *dā-sēm, n*. (*hist*.) a French coin equal to $\frac{1}{10}$ franc. [Fr.,—L. decima (pars), tenth (part).]

decimetre, *des'i-mē-tar, n*. a tenth of a metre.
decinormal, *des-i-nör'mal, (chem.) adj*. of one-tenth of normal concentration. [L. decimus, tenth, and normal.]
decipher, *di-si'far, v.t*. to uncipher: to read or transliterate or interpret from secret, unknown, or difficult writing: to make out: to detect (*Shak*.): to reveal (*Shak*.): to show forth (*obs*.). —*adj*. deci'pherable.—*n*. deci'pherment. [Pfx. de- (2).]
decision, *di-sizh'an, n*. the act or product of deciding: settlement: judgment: the quality of being decided in character.—*adj*. decisive (-*sis'iv*), having the power of deciding: showing decision: final: positive.—*adv*. deci'sively.—*n*. deci'siveness.—*adj*. deci'sory, decisive. [See decide.]
decistere, *des'i-stēr, n*. one-tenth of a stere.
decitizenise, -ize, *dē-sit'i-zan-iz, v.t*. to deprive of citizenship. [Pfx. de- (2).]
decivilise, -ize, *dē-siv'i-liz, v.t*. to reduce from a civilised to a more savage state. [Pfx. de- (2).]
deck, *dek, v.t*. to cover: to clothe: to adorn: to furnish with a deck: to pile up on a platform.— *n*. a covering: a horizontal platform extending from one side of a vessel to the other, thereby joining them together, and forming both a floor and a covering: a floor, platform, or tier as in a bus, bridge, etc.: the ground (*slang*): a pile of things laid flat: a pack of cards: the part of a pack used in a particular game, or the undealt part: the turntable of a record-player: that part of a tape-recorder or computer in which the magnetic tapes are placed, and the mechanism for running them: a set of punched cards. —*adj*. decked (*dekt*), adorned, decorated.— *ns*. deck'er, the person or thing that decks: a vessel, vehicle, or other structure that has a deck or decks (used only in composition, as three-decker): one who adorns; deck'ing, adornment: a platform.—deck'-bridge, a bridge whose upper stringer carries the roadway; deck'-cargo, cargo stowed on the deck of a vessel; deck'-chair, a chair, usually folding and made of canvas, such as passengers sit or lie on deck in; deck'-game, a game played on a ship's deck; deck'-hand, a person employed on deck: an ordinary sailor; deck'-house, a house, room, or box on deck; deck'-load, a deck-cargo; deck'-passage, a passage securing only the right of being on deck, without cabin accommodation; deck'-pass'enger; deck'-quoits, quoits as played on a ship's deck, with rope rings; deck'-tenn'is, lawn-tennis modified for playing on board ship; pedestrian deck, a safeway for pedestrians.—clear the decks, to tidy up, remove encumbrances, esp. in preparation for action (orig. naval action, now often fig.). [Verbal meanings—Du. dekken, to cover; cf. thatch; Ger. decken; L. tegĕre; substantive meanings—M.Du. dec, roof, covering.]
deckle, *dek'l, n*. in paper-making a contrivance for fixing width of sheet: a deckle-edge.—*adj*. deckled (*dek'ld*), deckle edged.—deck'le-edge, the raw or ragged edge of handmade paper or an imitation of it.—*adj*. deck'le-edged, having a rough uncut edge. [Ger. deckel, lid.]
declaim, *di-klām', v.i*. to make a set or rhetorical speech: to harangue: to recite.—*v.t*. to utter, repeat, or recite declamatorily.—*ns*. declaim'ant, declaim'er.—*n*. and *adj*. declaim'ing.—*n*. declamation (*dek-la-mā'shan*), act of declaiming: a set speech in public: display in speaking.—*adv*. declamatorily (*di-klam'a-ta-ri-li*).—*adj*. declam'atory, of the nature of declamation: appealing to the passions: noisy and rhetorical. [L. dē-clāmāre—de-, intens., clāmāre, to cry out.]
declare, *di-klār', v.t*. to make known: to announce: to assert: to make a full statement of, as of goods at a custom-house: to expose and

claim a score for (*bezique*, etc.): to announce one's choice of trump-suit or no trumps (*bridge*).
—*v.i.* to make a statement: to announce one's decision or sympathies: to show cards in order to score: to end an innings voluntarily before ten wickets have fallen (*cricket*).—*adj.* **declār'-able**, capable of being declared, exhibited, or proved.—*ns.* **declār'ant**, one who makes a declaration; **declaration** (*dek-lə-rā'shən*), act of declaring: that which is declared: a written affirmation: a formal announcement (e.g. of war): in the criminal law of Scotland, the statement made by the prisoner before the magistrate: in common law, the pleading in which the plaintiff in an action at law sets forth his case against the defendant.—*adjs.* **declarative** (*di-klar'ə-tiv*), **declār'atory**, explanatory.—*advs.* **declār'atively**, **declār'atorily**.—*n.* **declār'ator**, a form of action in the Court of Session, with the view of having a fact judicially ascertained and declared.—*adj.* **declāred'**, avowed.—*n.* **declār'er**, one who declares.—*adv.* **declā'redly**, avowedly.—**declaratory act**, an act intended to explain an obscure or disputed law.—**declare an interest**, (of member of parliament) formally to make known that he has (financial) connections with an organisation with which parliamentary discussions are concerned; **declare off**, to renounce: to withdraw: (*v.t.*) to cancel; (well) **I declare!** *interj.* expressing surprise. [L. *dēclārāre*, *-ātum*—pfx. *dē-*, wholly, *clārus*, clear (partly through Fr. *déclarer*).]

**declass**, *dē-kläs'*, *v.t.* to remove or degrade from one's class.—*adj.* **déclassé**, *fem.* **déclassée** (*dā-klä-sā*; Fr.) having lost caste or social standing. [Fr. *déclasser*.]

**declassify**, *dē-klas'i-fī*, *v.t.* to take off the security list. [Pfx. de- (2).]

**declension**, *di-klen'shən*, *n.* a falling off: decay: descent: system of cases and case-endings (*gram.*): a class of words similarly declined: a statement in order of the cases of a word. [See decline.]

**decline**, *di-klīn'*, *v.i.* to bend or turn away: to deviate: to refuse: to bend or slope down: to fail or decay: to stoop or condescend: to draw to an end.—*v.t.* to bend down: to turn away from: to refuse: to avoid: to give the various cases of (*gram.*).—*n.* a falling off: deviation: decay: a gradual sinking of the bodily faculties, consumption: a down-slope.—*adjs.* **declin'able**, having inflection for case; **declī'nal**, bending downward; **declinant** (*dek'lin-ənt*; *her.*), having the tail hanging down; **dec'līnate** (*bot.*), curving downwards.—*ns.* **declinā'tion**, act of declining (*U.S.*): a sloping or binding downwards: deviation: angular distance from the celestial equator (*astron.*); **dec'linātor**, an instrument determining declination.—*adj.* **declin'atory**, containing a declination or refusal.—*ns.* **declin'ature**, act of declining or refusing; a plea declining the jurisdiction of a judge (*law*); **declinom'-eter**, an instrument for measuring the declination of the compass.—i.e. the deviation of the magnetic needle from the true north.—**on the decline**, in the process of becoming less, deteriorating. [L. *dēclīnāre*—*dē*, down, away from, *clīnāre*, to bend (partly through Fr. *décliner*).]

**declivity**, *di-kliv'i-ti*, *n.* a place that declines, or slopes downward, opposite of *acclivity*: inclination downwards.—*adjs.* **decliv'itous**, **decli'vous**. [Fr.,—L. *dēclīvitās*, *-ātis*—*dē*, downward, *clīvus*, sloping, akin to *clīnāre*.]

**declutch**, *dē-kluch'*, *v.i.* to release the clutch. [Pfx. de- (2).]

**decoct**, *di-kokt'*, *v.t.* to prepare by boiling: to extract the substance of by boiling: to boil: to devise.—*adjs.* **decoc'tible**, **decoc'tive**.—*ns.* **decoc'tion**, an extract of anything got by boiling; **decoc'ture**, a substance prepared by decoction.

[L. *dēcoquĕre*, *dēcoctum*—*dē*, down, *coquĕre*, to cook.]

**decode**, *dē-kōd'*, *v.t.* to translate from a code. [Pfx. de- (2).]

**decoherer**, *dē-kō-hē'rər*, *n.* a device for bringing a coherer back to its former condition after it has been affected by an electric wave. [Pfx. de- (2).]

**decoke**, earlier **decarb**, *dē-kōk*, *dē'kärb'*, (*coll.*) *v.t.* to decarbonise (an internal combustion engine). [Pfx. de- (2).]

**decollate**, *dē-kol'āt*, *v.t.* to behead.—*adj.* **decoll'ated**, rounded off, as the apex of a shell.—*n.* **decollā'tion**, the act of beheading: a picture of a decapitation, esp. of the head of St John the Baptist on a charger: the festival of the Baptist, 29th Aug. [L. *dēcollāre*—*dē*, from *collum*, the neck.]

**décolleté**, *dā-kol-tā*, *adj.* with neck uncovered: of dress, low cut. [Fr., pa.p. of *décolleter*, to bare the neck and shoulders—*collet*, collar. Cf. **decollate**.]

**decolour**, **decolor**, *dē-kul'ər*, *v.t.* to deprive of colour—also **decol'o(u)rise**, **-ize**.—*n.* **decol'orant**, a substance that bleaches or removes colour.—*v.t.* **decol'orate**, to deprive of colour.—*adj.* without colour.—*ns.* **decolorā'tion**, removal or absence of colour; **decolo(u)risā'tion**, **-z-**. [L. *dēcolōrāre*—*dē*, from, *color*, colour.]

**decomplex**, *dē'kom-pleks*, *adj.* repeatedly compound. [Pfx. de- (3).]

**decompose**, *dē-kom-pōz'*, *v.t.* to separate the component parts of: to resolve into elements.—*v.i.* to decay, rot—*adj.* **decompos'able**. [Fr. *décomposer*—pfx. *dé-* (L. *dis-*, apart), and *composer*; see **compose**.]

**decomposition**, *di-kom-pə-zish'ən*, *n.* act or state of decomposing: decay.—*v.t.* **decompound** (*dē-kom-pownd'*), to decompose.—*adj.* **decompound'able**. [Fr. pfx. *dé-* (L. *dis-*), apart, and **composition**; accidentally associated in meaning with **decompose**.]

**decomposition**, *dē-komp-ə-zish'ən*, *n.* the compounding of things already compound.—*adj.* **decomp'osite**, (or *-oz'-*) doubly or further compounded.—*v.t.* **decompound** (*-kəm-pownd'*), to compound again, or further.—*adj.* (*dē'-*) compounded more than once: having leaflets themselves composed of separate parts (*bot.*). [Pfx. de- (3).]

**decompound**. See decomposition (1) and (2).

**decompress**, *dē-kəm-pres'*, *v.t.* to release from pressure.—*ns.* **decompression** (*-presh'ən*), the act or process of releasing from pressure: the gradual release of air pressure on persons (as divers, construction workers, etc.) on returning to normal atmospheric conditions: any operation to relieve excessive pressure (*surg.*); **decompress'or**.—**decompression chamber**, a chamber in which excessive pressure can be reduced gradually to atmospheric pressure, or in which a person can be subjected gradually to decreased atmospheric pressure; **decompression sickness** (same as caisson disease). [Pfx. de- (2).]

**decongest**, *de-kən-jest'*, *v.t.* to relieve or end the congestion of.—*n.* **decongest'ant** (*med.*), an agent that relieves congestion.—*adj.* **decongest'-ive**. [Pfx. de- (2).]

**deconsecrate**, *dē-kon'si-krāt*, *v.t.* to deprive of the character given by consecration: to secularise.—*n.* **deconsecrā'tion**. [Pfx. de- (2).]

**decontaminate**, *dē-kən-tam'in-āt*, *v.t.* to free from contamination.—*n.* **decontaminā'tion**. [Pfx. de- (2).]

**decontrol**, *dē-kən-trōl'*, *v.t.* to remove (esp. official) control from.—*n.* removal of control. [Pfx. de- (2).]

**décor**, *dā-kōr*, *n.* scenery and stage embellishments: ornament: general decorative effect (colour-scheme, furnishings, etc.) of work of art. [Fr., decoration.]

**decorate**, *dek′ə-rāt*, *v.t.* to ornament, to beautify: to paint, put wallpaper on (a house, etc.): to honour with a badge or medal.—*adj.* **dec′or-ated.**—*n.* **decorā′tion**, ornament: the applied paint and wallpaper in, e.g. a house: badge of an order: (in *pl.*) flags, bunting, paper chains, etc., put out or hung at a time of rejoicing.—*adj.* **dec′orative** (*-rə-tiv*) ornamental.—*ns.* **dec′orativeness; dec′orātor**, one who decorates, esp. houses. —**Decorated style** (*archit.*), a style of Gothic architecture, elaborate and richly decorated, which prevailed till near the end of the 14th century; **Decoration Day** (see **Memorial Day**). [L. *decorāre, -ātum—decus*, what is becoming— *decēre*, to be becoming.]

**decorous**, *de′kə-rəs*, or (*old fashioned*) *-kō′, -kö′*, *adj.* becoming: suitable: proper: decent.—*adv.* **decorously.**—*ns.* **decorousness; deco′rum**, that which is in keeping, congruous: that which is becoming in outward appearance: propriety of conduct: decency. [L. *decōrus*, becoming; L. *decere*, to be becoming.]

**decorticate**, *dē-kör′ti-kāt*, *v.t.* to deprive of the bark, husk, or peel.—*n.* **decorticā′tion.** [L. *dēcorticāre, -ātum—dē*, from, and *cortex*, bark.]

**decoy**, *di-koi′*, *v.t.* to allure: to entrap: to lure into a trap.—*n.* (*dē′koi*) anything intended to lure into a snare (also *fig.*): apparatus of hoops and network for trapping wild-ducks—sometimes *duck-coy*.—**decoy′-duck**, a wild-duck tamed and trained to entice others into a trap: one employed to allure others into a snare (*fig.*; also **decoy**). [Perh. Du. *de*, the, or L. pfx. *dē*, down, and Du. *kool*—L. *cavea*, a cage.]

**decrassify**, *dē-kras′i-fī*, *v.t.* to make less crass. [Pfx. de- (2), and crass.]

**decrease**, *di-krēs′*, *v.i.* to become less.—*v.t.* to make less.—*n.* (*dē′krēs*) a growing less: loss.— *adv.* **decreas′ingly.** [O.Fr. *decrois*, a decrease— L. *dēcrēscere—dē*, from, *crēscēre*, to grow.]

**decree**, *di-krē′*, *n.* an order by one in authority: an edict or law: a judicial decision: a predetermined purpose (*theol.*).—*v.t.* to decide or determine by sentence in law: to appoint.—*v.i.* to make a decree:—*pr.p.* **decree′ing;** *pa.t.* and *pa.p.* **decreed′.**—*adj.* **decree′able**, capable of being decreed.—*n.* **decreet′** (*Scots law*), a court judgment.—*adj.* **decrē′tal** (*Spens. dec′*), pertaining to a decree.—*n.* **decree**, esp. of the pope: book containing decrees: (specif. in *pl.*) the second part of the canon law, the decrees of various popes determining points of ecclesiastical law.—*n.* **decrē′tist**, in mediaeval universities, a student of the decretals, a student of law.—*adjs.* **decrē′tive; decrē′tory**, pertaining to a decree, judicial: having the force of a decree.—**decree nisi** (*nī′sī*; L. *nisi*, unless), a decree that becomes absolute unless cause be shown to the contrary— granted esp. in divorce cases. [O.Fr. *decret* and L. *dēcrētālis*—L. *dēcrētum—dēcernēre*, to decide.]

**decrement**, *dek′ri-mənt*, *n.* the act or state of decreasing: the quantity lost by decrease. [L. *dēcrēmentum.*]

**decrepit**, *di-krep′it*, *adj.* worn out by the infirmities of old age: in the last stage of decay.—*ns.* **decrep′itness; decrep′itude**, state of being decrepit or worn out with age. [L. *dēcrepitus*, noiseless, very old—*dē*, from, *crepitus*, a noise.]

**decrepitate**, *di-krep′i-tāt*, *v.i.* to crackle, as salts when heated.—*v.t.* to roast so as to cause a continual crackling, to calcine.—*n.* **decrepitā′tion.** [L. *dē-*, intens., *crepitāre*, to rattle much, freq. of *crepāre*.]

**decrescent**, *di-kres′ənt*, *adj.* becoming gradually less.—*n.*, *adj.* and *adv.* **decrescendo** (*dā-kre-shen′dō; mus.*; It.), diminuendo. [L. *dē, crēscēre*.]

**decretal.** See **decree.**

**decrew**, *di-krōō′*, (*Spens.*) *v.i.* to decrease. [O.Fr. *decru*, pa.p. of *decroistre*. See **decrease.**]

**decrown**, *dē-krown′*, *v.t.* to discrown. [Pfx. de- (2).]

**decrustation**, *dē-krus-tā′shən*, *n.* removal of a crust. [Pfx. de- (2).]

**decry**, *di-krī′*, *v.t.* to cry down: to condemn: to censure as worthless: to blame:—*pr.p.* **decry′ing;** *pa.t.* and *pa.p.* **decried′.**—*ns.* **decrī′al; decri′er.** [Fr. *dé-, des-* (L. *dis-*), and *crier*, to cry; see **cry.**]

**Dectra**, *dek′tra*, ⓡ *n.* a long-range modification of Decca.

**decubitus.** See under **decumbent.**

**decuman**, *dek′ū-mən*, *adj.* principal, large—of waves, etc.: connected with the principal gate of a Roman camp (near which the 10th cohort of the legion was stationed).—*n.* a great wave, as every tenth wave was supposed to be. [L. *decumānus—decem*, ten.]

**decumbent**, *di-kum′bənt*, *adj.* lying down: reclining on the ground: lying flat with rising tip (*bot.*).—*ns.* **decubitus** (*-kūb′i-təs; med.*), posture in bed; **decum′bence, decum′bency**, the act or posture of lying down.—*adv.* **decum′bently.**—*n.* **decum′biture**, the time when a sick person takes to bed. [L. *dēcumbēns, -entis—dē*, down, and *-cumbēre* (in compounds only), to lie.]

**decuple**, *dek′ū-pl*, *adj.* tenfold.—*n.* a number ten times repeated.—*v.t.* to make tenfold. [Fr. *décuple*—L. *decuplus.*]

**decurion**, *di-kū′ri-ən*, *n.* in a Roman army, an officer over ten soldiers: any overseer of ten: a councillor.—*ns.* **decū′ria, decury** (*dek′ū-ri*), a company of ten (or more); **decū′rionate.** [L.]

**decurrent**, *di-kur′ənt*, *adj.* running or extending downward: continued down the stem (*bot.*).—*n.* **decurr′ency.**—*adv.* **decurr′ently.**—*n.* **decur′sion** (*-kūr′*), a running down: a military manoeuvre or parade.—*adj.* **decur′sive.**—*adv.* **decur′sively.** [L. *dēcurrēns, -entis—dē*, down, *currēre, cursum*, to run.]

**decussate**, *di-kus′āt*, *v.t.* to divide in the form of an X.—*v.i.* to cross in such a form: to cross, as lines, etc.—*adjs.* **decuss′ate, -d**, crossed: arranged in pairs which cross each other, like some leaves. —*adv.* **decuss′ately.**—*n.* **decussā′tion** (*dek-*). [L. *decussāre, -ātum—decussis*, a coin of ten asses (*decem asses*) marked with X, symbol of ten.]

**dedal, dedalian.** See **daedal.**

**dedans**, *də-dā*, *n.* an open gallery at the end of the service side of a tennis-court: spectators at a court-tennis match. [Fr.]

**dedicate**, *ded′i-kāt*, *v.t.* to set apart and consecrate to some sacred purpose: to devote wholly or chiefly: to inscribe to any one: to inaugurate or open (*U.S.*).—*adj.* devoted: dedicated (*Shak.*). —*ns.* **ded′icant**, one who dedicates; **dedicatee** (*ded-i-kā-tē′*), one to whom a thing is dedicated; **dedicā′tion**, the act of dedicating: an address to a patron, prefixed to a book; **ded′icātor.**—*adjs.* **dedicatorial** (*-kə-tō′ri-əl, -tō′*), **ded′icatory** (*-kə-* or *-kā-*). [L. *dēdicāre, -ātum—dē*, down, *dīcāre*, to declare.]

**dedimus**, *ded′i-məs*, *n.* a writ commissioning one not a judge to act as a judge. [From the opening, L. *dedimus* (*potestātem*), we have given (power)—*dāre*, to give.]

**deduce**, *di-dūs′*, *v.t.* to derive: to infer from what precedes or from premises.—*n.* **deduce′ment**, what is deduced.—*adj.* **deduc′ible**, that may be deduced or inferred.—*n.* **deducibil′ity**, the quality of being deducible.—*v.t.* **deduct** (*-dukt′*), to take away: to separate: to subtract: to reduce, weaken (*Spens.*): to deduce (*obs.*).—*adj.* **deduct′-ible.**—*n.* **deduc′tion**, the act of deducing: that which is deduced: the drawing of a particular truth from a general, antecedently known, as distinguished from *induction*, rising from particular truths to a general: the act of deducting: that which is deducted: abatement.—*adj.* **deduct′-ive**, concerned with deduction from premises or accepted principles.—*adv.* **deduct′ively.**—

**deducted spaces** (see **tonnage**). [L. *dēdūcĕre*, *dēductum—dē*, from, *dūcĕre*, to lead.]

**dee**, *dē*, *v.i.* Scottish form of **die**.

**dee**, *dē*, *n.* the fourth letter of the alphabet (D, d): anything shaped like it.—*n.*, *v.t.*, *interj.* a substitute for **damn**.

**deed**, *dēd*, *n.* something done: an act: an exploit: a legal transaction: the written evidence of it.— *adj.* **deed'ful** (*Tenn.*), marked by deeds or exploits. —*adv.* **deed'ily.**—*adjs.* **deed'less** (*Shak.*), not having performed deeds; **deed'y**, industrious, active.—**deed poll**, a deed executed by one party, originally having the edge *polled* or cut even, not indented.—**deed of saying** (*Shak.*), performance of what has been said or promised; **in deed, in reality.** [O.E. *dǣd—dōn*, to do; Ger. *tat*.]

**deed**, *dēd*, a Scottish form of **indeed**; also for **died, dead.**

**dee-jay**, *dē'jā*, or *-jā'*, (*slang*) *n.* a disk-jockey. [Pronunciation of the initials D.J.]

**deem**, *dēm*, *v.t.* or *v.i.* to judge: to think: to believe—*pa.t.* and *pa.p.* **deemed,** *Spens.* **dempt.** —*n.* (*Shak.*) opinion.—*ns.* **deem'ster,** a judge— now only in the Isle of Man; **dempster** (*dem'stər*), a judge (*obs.*): formerly in Scotland an officer who repeated the sentence after the judge (also **doom'ster**). [O.E. *dēman,* to form a judgment— *dōm,* judgment; see **doom.**]

**deen**, *dēn,* (*Spens.*) for **din.**

**deep**, *dēp, adj.* extending or placed far down or far from the outside: far recessed: far involved: engrossed: difficult to understand: secret: wise and penetrating: profoundly versed: cunning: very still: profound: intense: excessive: heartfelt: sunk low: low in pitch: (of a road) encumbered with mud, sand, or ruts: in the out-field, not close to the wickets (*cricket*).— *adv.* in a deep manner.—*n.* that which is deep: the sea: a deep place: the middle, deepest, or most intense part: anything profound or incomprehensible.—*v.t.* **deep'en,** to make deeper in any sense: to increase.—*v.i.* to become deeper.—*n.* **deep'ie** (*coll.*), a three-dimensional cinematograph film.—*adv.* **deep'ly.**—*adj.* **deep'most, deepest.**—*n.* **deep'ness.**—*adjs.* **deep'-browed,** of high intellectual powers; **deep'-draw'ing** (of ships), requiring considerable depth to float in; **deep'-drawn; deep'-dyed,** thorough-going, extreme—in a bad sense; **deep'felt; deep'-fet** (*Shak.*), fetched from a depth.—**deep field,** fielding position deep behind the bowler; **deep'-freeze',** storage of foodstuffs, or other perishable substances, at very low temperature: the container in which the material is stored.—Also *v.t.* —*adj.* **deep'-laid.**—*n.* **deep'-litter,** a method of keeping hens in a henhouse with a peat material on the floor.—*adjs.* **deep'-mouthed,** with deep voice; **deep'-read,** profoundly versed; **deep'-sea,** pertaining to the deeper parts of the sea; **deep'-seat'ed,** not superficial.—**deep'-sink'er** (*Austr.*), a drinking vessel of the largest size; **Deep South,** the region of the S.E. United States that clings to old ways, roughly Georgia, Alabama, Mississippi and Louisiana; **deep therapy,** the treatment of disease by deep X-rays or gamma rays.—*adj.* **deep'-toned',** having a deep tone.— **go (in) off the deep end,** to express strong feelings with abandonment; **in deep water,** in difficulties; **two deep, three deep,** etc., in two, three, etc., **layers or rows.** [O.E. *dēop;* Ger. *tief;* cf. **dip, dive.**]

**deer**, *dēr, n.* any kind of animal (as in *small deer; obs.*): any animal of the Cervidae, a family of even-toed ungulates characterised by the possession of antlers by the males at least— including stag, reindeer, etc.:—*pl.* **deer.**—*n.* **deer'let,** a chevrotain.—**deer'berry,** the huckleberry (*Gaylussacia*): the fruit of Gaultheria: that of *Vaccinium stamineum,* an inedible American whortleberry; **deer'-fence,** a very high

fence that deer cannot jump over; **deer'-forest,** wild tract (not necessarily woodland) reserved for deer; **deer'-hair,** a small species of club-rush; **deer'(-)horn,** a deer's antler or its material: a fresh-water mussel (*U.S.*); **deer'-hound,** a large rough-coated greyhound; **deer'-lick,** a spot of salt ground whither deer come to lick the earth; **deer'-mouse,** the American deer-footed mouse— so called from its agility; **deer'-neck,** a thin ill-shaped neck—of horses; **deer'-park; deer'skin,** skin of the deer, or leather therefrom; **deer'-stalker,** one who stalks deer: a sportsman's helmet-shaped cap; **deer'stalking.** [O.E. *dēor;* Ger. *tier,* Du. *dier;* O.N. *dyr.*]

**deev**, *dēv.* Same as **div.**

**deface**, *di-fās', v.t.* to destroy or mar the face or external appearance of, to disfigure: to obliterate: to put out of countenance (*Spens.*): to defame (*Spens.*).—*n.* **deface'ment,** act of defacing: injury to form or appearance: that which defaces.—*adv.* **defā'cingly.** [O.Fr. *desfacer*—L. *dis-,* away, *faciēs,* face.]

**de facto**, *dē, dā fak'tō,* (L.) actual, if not rightful (e.g. *the de facto ruler*): in fact, actually.

**defaecate.** Same as **defecate.**

**defalcate**, *dē'* or *de'fal-kāt,* or *di-fal'kāt* or (*rare*) *-fōl', v.t.* (*obs.*) to deduct a part of.—*v.i.* to embezzle money held on trust.—*ns.* **defalcā'tion,** a diminution: a defection: a misappropriation of funds entrusted to one: the amount mis-appropriated; **defalcator,** a defaulter. [L.L. *dēfalcāre, -ātum,* to cut away—L. *dē,* from *falcāre,* to cut—*falx, falcis,* a sickle.]

**defame**, *di-fām', v.t.* to take away or destroy the good fame or reputation of: to speak evil of: to charge falsely.—*n.* (*Spens.*) infamy.—*n.* **defamation** (*def-ə-mā'shən*), the act of defaming: calumny: slander.—*adv.* **defamatorily** (*di-fam'ə-tər-i-li*).—*adj.* **defām'atory,** containing defamation: injurious to reputation: calumnious.—*n.* and *adj.* **defā'ming.** [O.Fr. *diffamer*—L. *diffā-māre—dis-,* away, *fāma,* report.]

**defast(e)**, *di-fāst',* Spenserian spellings of **defaced** (*pa.p.*).

**default**, *di-fölt', n.* a fault, failing, or failure: defect: neglect to do what duty or law requires: failure to fulfil a financial obligation: fault or offence (*arch.*).—*v.i.* to fail through neglect of duty: to fail to appear in court when called upon: to fail to fulfil a financial obligation.—*n.* **default'er,** one who fails to appear in court, or to account for money entrusted to his care, or to settle an ordinary debt or debt of honour: a military offender.—**judgment by default,** judgment given against a person because he fails to plead or make an appearance in court; **in default of,** on the absence of: for lack of. [O.Fr. *defaute* (noun) and *default* (3rd sing. of *defaillir*)—L. pfx. *dē-* and *fallĕre;* see **fault.**]

**defeasance**, *di-fēz'əns, n.* undoing (*obs.*): defeat: a rendering null or void (*law*): a condition whose fulfilment renders a deed void.—*adjs.* **defeas'-anced,** liable to be forfeited; **defeas'ible,** that may be annulled.—*ns.* **defeasibil'ity, defeas'ibleness.** —**deed of defeasance** (*Eng. law*), an instrument which defeats the operation of some other deed or estate. [O.Fr. *defesance—desfaire;* see **defeat.**]

**defeat**, *di-fēt', v.t.* to win a victory over: to get the better of: to ruin: to frustrate: to undo (*Shak.*): to disfigure (*Shak.*).—*n.* a frustration of plans: ruin: overthrow, as of an army in battle: loss of a game, race, etc.—*ns.* **defeat'ism,** disposition to accept, welcome, help to bring on, defeat; **defeat'ist.**—Also *adj.*—*n.* **defeat'ure,** undoing (*Spens.*): defeat: disfigurement (*Shak.*): from feature).—*v.t.* to disfigure. [O.Fr. *defait—desfaire,* to undo—L. *dis-,* neg., *facĕre,* to do.]

**defecate**, *def', dēf'i-kāt, v.t.* to clear from dregs or impurities: to purify from extraneous matter.— *v.i.* to void excrement.—*n.* **defecā'tion.** [L.

*dēfaecāre*, *-ātum*, to cleanse—*dē*, from, *faex*, *faecis*, dregs.]

**defect**, *di-fekt'*, *dē'fekt*, *n.* a deficiency: a want: imperfection: blemish: fault.—*v.i.* (*di-fekt'*) to desert one's country, a cause, transferring one's allegiance (to another).—*n.* **defectibil'ity.**—*adj.* **defect'ible,** liable to imperfection: deficient.—*ns.* **defec'tion,** desertion: a failure, a falling away from duty: revolt; **defec'tionist.**—*adj.* **defect'ive,** having defect: wanting in some necessary quality: imperfect: faulty: insufficient: incomplete in inflexions or forms (*gram.*).—*n.* a person deficient in physical or mental powers.—*adv.* **defect'ively.**—*ns.* **defect'iveness; defect'or,** one who deserts his country, etc.—**the defects of one's qualities,** virtues carried to excess, the faults apt to accompany or flow from good qualities. [L. *dēficĕre*, *dēfectum*, to fail—*dē*, down, and *facĕre*, to do.]

**defence,** in U.S. **defense,** *di-fens'*, *n.* a defending: capability or means of resisting an attack: protection: vindication: a defendant's plea (*law*): the defending party in legal proceedings.—*adj.* **defenced'**, fortified.—*adj.* **defence'less.**—*adv.* **defence'lessly.**—*n.* **defence'lessness.**—*v.t.* **defend** (*di-fend'*), to keep off anything hurtful from: to guard or protect: to maintain against attack: to prohibit, forbid (*obs.*): to ward off: to resist, as a claim (*law*): to contest.—*adj.* **defend'able,** that may be defended.—*n.* **defend'ant,** a defender: a person accused or sued (*law*).—*adj.* **defend'ed,** guarded: protected: maintained against attack: forbidden (*Milt.*).—*ns.* **defend'er,** one who defends: the holder of a championship, etc., who seeks to maintain his title: one who accepts a challenge (*obs.*): a person sued or accused (*Scots law*); **defen'sative,** a protection; **defensibil'ity.**—*adj.* **defens'ible,** that may be defended.—*adv.* **defens'ibly.**—*adj.* **defens'ive,** serving to defend: in a state or posture of defence.—*n.* that which defends: posture of defence.—*adv.* **defens'ively.** —**defence mechanism,** an unconscious mental process by which an individual excludes ideas or emotions painful or unacceptable to him (*psych.*); **defender of the faith,** a title borne by the sovereigns of England since Henry VIII, on whom it was conferred in 1521 for his book against Luther; **stand, be, on the defensive,** to be in the attitude of self-defence. [L. *dēfendĕre*, *dēfensum*, to ward off—*dē*, and *fendĕre*, to strike (found in compounds).]

**defenestration,** *dē-fen-is-trā'shǝn*, *n.* a flinging out of a window. [L. *dē*, from, *fenestra*, window.]

**defer,** *di-fûr'*, *v.t.* to put off to another time: to delay:—*pr.p.* **defer'ring;** *pa.t.* and *pa.p.* **deferred'.** —*ns.* **defer'ment; deferr'er,** a procrastinator.— **deferred annuity** (see **annuity**); **deferred pay,** an allowance paid to soldiers on their discharge, or to their relations on their death: a government servant's pension; **deferred payment,** payment by instalments; **deferred shares,** shares not entitling the holder to a full share of profits, and sometimes to none at all, until the expiration of a specified time or the occurrence of some event. [L. *differre*—*dis-*, asunder, *ferre*, to bear, carry; cf. **differ.**]

**defer,** *di-fûr'*, *v.i.* to yield (to the wishes or opinions of another, or to authority).—*v.t.* to submit to or lay before somebody:—*pr.p.* **defer'ring;** *pa.t.* and *pa.p.* **deferred.**—*n.* **deference** (*def'ǝr-ǝns*), a deferring or yielding in judgment or opinion: respectful compliance: submission.—*adj.* **def'erent,** bearing away, carrying off: deferential.—*n.* a deferent duct (as opposed to an *afferent* one) in the body.—*adj.* **deferential** (*-en'shl*), showing deference.—*adv.* **deferen'tially.** [L. *dēferre*—*dē*, down, and *ferre*, to bear.]

**defervescence,** *dē-far-ves'ǝns*, *n.* abatement of heat: coolness: decrease of feverish symptoms. —Also **defervesc'ency.** [L. *dēfervēscĕre*, to

cease boiling—*dē*, down, and *fervēscĕre*, from *fervēre*, to boil.]

**defeudalise,** *-ize*, *dē-fū'dǝl-iz*, *v.t.* to deprive of feudal character. [Pfx. **de-** (2).]

**deffly** (*Spens.*). For **deftly.**

**defiance,** *di-fi'ǝns*, *n.* the act of defying: a challenge to combat: aggressiveness: contempt of opposition.—*adj.* **defi'ant,** full of defiance, insolently bold.—*adv.* **defi'antly.**—*n.* **defi'antness** (*rare*).— —**bid defiance to,** to defy. [defy.]

**defibrinate,** *dē-fi'bri-nāt*, *v.t.* to deprive of fibrin— also **defi'brinise,** *-ize*.—*n.* **defibrinā'tion.** [Pfx. **de-** (2), and **fibrin.**]

**deficient,** *di-fish'ǝnt*, *adj.* wanting (in): less than complete: defective.—*n.* a defective.—*n.* **deficiency** (sometimes **defic'ience**), defect: shortage: the amount which is lacking for completeness.—*adv.* **defic'iently.**—*ns.* **defic'ientness; deficit** (*def'i-sit*, or *-fis'*), deficiency, esp. of revenue, as compared with expenditure: amount of the deficiency.—**deficiency disease,** a disease due to lack of necessary substances (as vitamins) in dietary, such as rickets, scurvy, beri-beri, pellagra. [L. *dēficĕre*; see **defect.**]

**de fide,** *dē fi'dē*, *dā fē'de*, (L.) (of a teaching) in which belief is obligatory.

**defied, defier,** etc. See **defy.**

**defilade.** See **defile** (1).

**defile,** *di-fil'*, *v.i.* to march off in file or line, or file by file.—*n.* (*dē'fil*, *di-fil'*) a long narrow pass or way, in which troops can march only in file, or with a narrow front: a gorge.—*v.t.* **defilade** (*def-i-lād'*), to plan a fortification so as to protect it from enfilading fire.—also *n.*—*n.* **defile'ment,** act of defilading. [Fr. *défiler*—L. *dis-*, and *filum*, a thread.]

**defile,** *di-fil'*, *v.t.* to befoul: to pollute or corrupt: to violate.—*ns.* **defile'ment,** act of defiling: foulness; **defil'er.** [L. *dē*, and O.E. *fȳlan*—*fūl*, foul; confused with O.Fr. *defouler*, to trample, violate.]

**defilement.** See **defile** (1), (2).

**defiliation,** *dē-fil-i-ā'shǝn*, *n.* depriving a parent of his child. [L. *dē*, from, and *filius*, a son.]

**define,** *di-fin'*, *v.t.* to bring to an end (*obs.*): to decide: to fix the bounds or limits of: to determine with precision: to describe accurately: to fix the meaning of.—*adj.* **defin'able.**—*adv.* **defin'-ably.**—*n.* **define'ment** (*Shak.*), description.— *adj.* **definite** (*def'i-nit*), defined: having distinct limits: fixed: exact: clear: sympodial or cymose (*bot.*): referring to a particular person or thing (*gram.*; see also **article**).—*adv.* **def'initely,** in a definite manner: determinately: yes indeed (*coll.*).—*ns.* **def'initeness; defini'tion,** a defining: a description of a thing by its properties: an explanation of the exact meaning of a word, term, or phrase: sharpness of outline. —*adj.* **definitive** (*di-fin'i-tiv*), defining or limiting: positive: final.—*n.* (*gram.*) an adjective used to limit the extent of signification of a noun.— *adv.* **defin'itively.**—*ns.* **defin'itiveness; defin'itude, definitiveness.** [L. *dēfinire*, *-itum*, to set bounds to—*dē*, *finis*, a limit.]

**deflagrate,** *def'lǝ-grāt*, *v.i.*, *v.t.* to burn suddenly, generally with flame and crackling noise.—*ns.* **deflagrabil'ity; deflagrā'tion; def'lagrātor,** apparatus for deflagration.—**def'lagrating-spoon,** a cup with long vertical shank for handling chemicals that deflagrate. [L. *dēflagrāre*—*dē*, down, *flagrāre*, to burn.]

**deflate,** *dē-flāt'*, *v.t.* to reduce from a state of inflation.—*v.i.* to become deflated.—*n.* **deflā'tion,** the act or process of deflating: the state of being deflated: a financial condition in which there is an undue decrease in the amount of money available relative to its buying power—the converse of **inflation** (*econ.*): removal of loose material by the wind.—*adj.* **deflā'tionary.**—*n.* **deflā'tionist,** one who favours deflation of currency.—Also *adj.* [L. *dē*, from, *flāre*, to blow.]

**deflect**, *di-flekt'*, *v.i.* or *v.t.* to turn aside: to swerve or deviate from a right line or proper course.—*adj.* **deflect'ed** (*bot.*), bent abruptly downward.—*ns.* **deflec'tion**, **deflex'ion** (L. *dēflexiō'*), bending: turning: deviation.—*adjs.* **deflec'tional**, **deflex'ional**; **deflec'tive**, causing deflection.—*n.* **deflec'tor**, a device for deflecting a flame, electric arc, etc.—*v.t.* **deflex'** (*zool.*, *bot.*), to bend down.—*adj.* **deflexed'**.—*n.* **deflex'ure**, deviation. [L. *dē*, from, down, and *flectĕre*, *flexum*, to bend, turn.]

**deflorate**, *dē-flō'rāt*, *-flō'*, *adj.* past flowering: of an anther, having shed its pollen.—*v.t.* to **deflower**.—*n.* **deflorā'tion**, the act of deflowering. [L. *dēflōrāre*; see next.]

**deflower**, *di-flowr'*, *v.t.* to deprive of flowers: to deprive of grace and beauty, or of virginity: to ravish.—*n.* **deflower'er**. [O.Fr. *desflorer*—L.L. *dēflōrāre*, to strip flowers off—L. *dē*, from, *flōs*, *flōris*, a flower.]

**defluent**, *def'loō-ənt*, *adj.* running down, decurrent.—*n.* **defluxion** (*di-fluk'shən*; *obs.*), a downflow: a disease supposedly due to a flow of humour: a discharge of fluid in the body. [L. *dēfluĕre*—*dē*, down, *fluĕre*, *fluxum*, to flow.]

**defoliate**, *di-fō'li-āt*, *v.t.* to deprive of leaves.—*adjs.* **defō'liate**, **-d**.—*ns.* **defol'iant**, a chemical preparation used to remove leaves; **defōliā'tion**, the falling off of leaves: the time of shedding leaves; **defō'liātor**. [L.L. *dēfoliāre*, *-ātum*—*dē*, off, *folium*, a leaf.]

**deforce**, *di-fōrs'*, *-fōrs'*, *v.t.* to keep out of possession by force (*law*): to resist (an officer of the law in the execution of his duty) (*Scots law*).—*ns.* **deforce'ment**; **deforc'iant**, one who deforces; **deforciā'tion**, (*obs.*) a legal distress. [A.Fr. *deforcer*—[L. *dis-*); see **force**.]

**deforest**, *dē-for'ist*, *v.t.* to disforest, to deprive of forests.—*n.* **deforestā'tion**. [Pfx. **de-** (2).]

**deform**, *di-förm'*, *v.t.* to alter or injure the form of: to disfigure: to change the shape of without breach of continuity.—*adj.* (*Milt.*, etc.) hideous, unshapely.—*n.* **dēformā'tion**.—*adj.* **deformed'**, misshapen.—*adv.* **deform'edly**.—*ns.* **deformed'ness**; **deform'er**; **deform'ity**, state of being deformed: want of proper form: ugliness: disfigurement: anything that destroys beauty: an ugly feature or characteristic. [L. *dēformis*, ugly—*dē*, from, *fōrma*, beauty.]

**defoul**, *di-fowl'*, *v.t.* to befoul, defile. [O.E. *fūl*, foul, with *de-* from confusion with O.Fr. *defouler*, to trample; cf. **defile**.]

**defraud**, *di-fröd'*, *v.t.* to deprive by fraud: to cheat or deceive.—*ns.* **defraudā'tion**, **defraud'ment**. [L. *dēfraudāre*—*dē*, from, *fraus*, *fraudis*, fraud.]

**defray**, *di-frā'*, *v.t.* to pay: to satisfy, appease (*Spens.*):—*pr.p.* **defray'ing**; *pa.t.* and *pa.p.* **defrayed'**.—*ns.* **defray'al**, **defray'ment**. [O.Fr. *desfrayer*—*des-* = L. *dis-*, and *frais*, expenses.]

**defrost**, *dē'frost'*, *v.t.* to remove frost or ice from: to thaw out.—Also *v.i.*—*n.* **de'frost'er**, a device for defrosting esp. a windscreen. [Pfx. **de-** (2).]

**deft**, *deft*, *adj.* handy, clever.—*adv.* **deft'ly**.—*n.* **deft'ness**. [M.E. *defte*, *dafte*, simple, meek; O.E. *gedæfte*, meek—*dæftan*, *gedæftan*, prepare, make fit; the stem appears in *gedafen*, fit.]

**defunct**, *di-fungkt'*, *adj.* having finished the course of life, dead.—*n.* a dead person.—*n.* **defunc'tion** (*Shak.*), death.—*adj.* **defunc'tive** (*Shak.*), pertaining to the dead. [L. *dēfungī*, *dēfunctus*, to finish—*dē-*, intens., *fungī*, to perform.]

**defuse**, **defuze**, *dē'fūz'*, (*Shak.*) *v.t.* to disorder.—*adj.* **defus'd'**. [For **diffuse**.]

**defuze**, **defuse**, *dē'fūz'*, *v.t.* to remove the fuze from (a bomb or mine). [Pfx. **de-** (2).]

**defy**, *di-fī'*, *v.t.* to challenge (*arch.*): to brave: to flout, or to resist (e.g. convention, order, person):

to discard, dislike (*obs.*):—*pr.p.* **defy'ing**; *pa.t.* and *pa.p.* **defied'**; *3rd pers. pres. ind.* **defies'**.—*n.* (*Dryden*) a defiance.—*n.* **defi'er**. [O.Fr. *defier*—L.L. *diffīdāre*, to renounce faith or allegiance.—L. *dis-*, asunder, and *fīdĕre*, to trust—*fīdēs*, faith.]

**dégagé**, *dā-gä-zhā*, *adj.* unembarrassed, unconstrained, easy. [Pa.p. of Fr. *dégager*, to disentangle.]

**degarnish**. Same as **disgarnish**.

**degauss**, *dē-gows'*, *v.t.* to protect against magnetic mines by equipment for neutralising a ship's magnetic field. [Pfx. **de-**, **gauss**.]

**degender**, *di-jen'dər*, (*Spens.*) *v.i.* to degenerate. [Fr. *dégénerer*, influenced by **gender**, vb.]

**degenerate**, *di-jen'ər-it*, *adj.* having departed from the high qualities of race or kind, become base.—*n.* one who is degenerate.—*v.i.* (*-āt*) to fall from a nobler state: to be or to grow worse.—*v.t.* (*Milton*) to cause to degenerate.—*ns.* **degen'eracy**, **degenerā'tion**, the act or process of becoming degenerate: the state of being degenerate.—*adv.* **degen'erately**.—*n.* **degen'erateness**.—*adj.* **degen'erating**.—*n.* **degenerā'tionist**, one who believes that the tendency of man is not to improve, but to degenerate.—*adj.* **degen'erative**, tending or causing to degenerate.—*adj.* **degen'erous** (*obs.*). [L. *dēgenerāre*, *-ātum*, to depart from its kind—*dē*, from, down, *genus*, *generis*, kind.]

**deglutinate**, *di-gloō'tin-āt*, *v.t.* to separate (things glued together): to remove gluten from. [L. *dēglūtināre*, *-ātum*—*dē*, from, *glūtināre*—*glūten* glue.]

**deglutition**, *dē-gloō-tish'ən*, *n.* the act or power of swallowing.—*adjs.* **deglu'titive**, **deglu'titory**. [L. *dē*, down, and *glūtīre*, to swallow; see **glut**.]

**dégoût**, *dā-goō*, (Fr.) distaste.

**degrade**, *di-grād'*, *v.t.* to lower in grade or rank: to deprive of office or dignity: to lower in character, value, or position, or in complexity: to disgrace: to wear down (*geol.*).—*n.* **degradation** (*deg-rə-dā'shən*), degrading: disgrace: degeneration: abortive structural development: a lowering in dignity.—*adjs.* **degrād'ed**, reduced in rank: base: low: placed on step (*her.*); **degrād'ing**, debasing: disgraceful. [O.Fr. *degrader*—L. *dē*, down, and *gradus*, a step. See **grade**.]

**degras**, *deg'räs*, *n.* a fat got from sheepskins. [Fr. *dégras*—*dégraisser*, to degrease.]

**degrease**, *dē-grēs'*, *v.t.* to deprive of, or cleanse from, grease. [Pfx. **de-** (2).]

**degree**, *di-grē'*, *n.* a grade or step: a gradation on a scale, or that which it measures: a unit of temperature: one of a series of advances or steps: relative position: rank: extent: a mark of distinction conferred by universities, whether earned by examination or granted as a mark of honour: the 360th part of a revolution: 60 geographical miles: nearness of relationship: comparative amount of criminality: one of the three stages (*positive*, *comparative*, *superlative*) in the comparison of an adjective or adverb: the highest sum of exponents in any term (*alg.*): the number of points in which a curve may be met by a straight line.—**by degrees**, by little and little, gradually; **degree of freedom**, one of the independent variables defining the state of a system (e.g. temperature, pressure, concentration): a capability of variation (e.g. a system having two variables one of which is dependent on the other has one degree of freedom); **forbidden degrees**, the degrees of consanguinity within which marriage is not allowed; **Songs of degrees**, or *Songs of ascents*, Psalms cxx-cxxxiv, either because sung by the Jews returning from captivity, or by the Jews coming up annually to attend the feasts at Jerusalem; **third degree**, an American police method of extracting a confession by bullying or torture: any ruthless interrogation; **to a degree**, to a great degree, to an extreme. [Fr. *degré*—L. *dē*, down, *gradus*, a step.]

**dégringoler,** *dā-grē-go-lā,* (Fr.) *v.i.* to descend rapidly or steeply.—*n.* **dégringolade** (-*go-läd*), a sudden descent: a quick deterioration.

**degum,** *dē-gum',* *v.t.* to free from gum. [Pfx. de- (2).]

**degust,** *dē-gust',* *v.t.* to taste, to relish.—*v.i.* to have a relishing taste.—*v.t.* **degust'āte,** to degust. —*n.* **degustā'tion,** the act of tasting.—*adj.* **degust'atory.** [L. *dē*, down, and *gustāre*, to taste.]

**dehisce,** *di-his',* *v.i.* to gape, burst open (*bot.*, etc.). *n.* **dehisc'ence.**—*adj.* **dehisc'ent.** [L. *dēhiscēns,* pr.p. of *dēhiscēre*—*dē*, intens., and *hiscēre*, inceptive of *hiāre*, to gape.]

**dehorn,** *dē-hörn',* *v.t.* to dishorn. [Pfx. de- (2).]

**dehort,** *di-hört',* *v.t.* to dissuade.—*n.* **dehortā'tion** (*dē-*), dissuasion.—*adjs.* **dehor'tative, dehor'tatory,** dissuasive.—*n.* **dehort'er.** [L. *dēhortārī*— *dē*, off, *hortārī*, to exhort.]

**dehumanise, -ize,** *dē-hū'mən-iz,* *v.t.* to deprive of specifically human qualities. [L. *dē*, from, down, and **humanise.**]

**dehumidify,** *dē-hū-mid'i-fī,* *v.t.* to rid of moisture, dry.—*n.* **dehumidificā'tion.** [Pfx. de- (2).]

**dehydrate,** *dē-hī'drāt,* *v.t.* to deprive of water chemically: to remove moisture from, dry: to deprive of strength, interest, etc. (*fig.*).—*v.i.* to lose water.—*n.* **dēhydrā'tion,** loss or withdrawal of moisture: excessive loss of water from the tissues of the body (*med.*). [L. *dē*, from, Gr. *hydōr*, water.]

**de-ice,** *dē'-is',* *v.t.* to dislodge ice from (aircraft surfaces), or to treat them so as to prevent its formation.—*n.* **dē'-ic'er,** any means of doing this, whether a fluid, a paste, or a mechanical or pneumatic device. [Pfx. de- (2).]

**deicide,** *dē'i-sīd,* *n.* the killing or killer of a god. [L. *deus*, a god, and *caedēre*, to kill.]

**deictic,** *dik'tik, adj.* proving directly.—*adv.* **deic'-tically.** [Gr. *deiktikos*—*deiknynai*, to show.]

**deid,** *dēd,* Scots form of **dead, death.**—*n.* **deid'-thraw,** death-throe.

**deify,** *dē'i-fī,* *v.t.* to exalt to the rank of a god: to worship as a deity: to make godlike:—*pr.p.* **dē'ifying;** *pa.t.* and *pa.p.* **dē'ified.**—*adjs.* **dēif'ic, -al,** making god-like or divine.—*n.* **dēificā'tion,** the act of deifying: a deified embodiment. [Fr. *déifier*—L. *deificāre*—*deus*, a god, and *facēre*, to make.]

**deign,** *dān, v.i.* to condescend.—*v.t.* to condescend to give or (*Shak.*) take. [Fr. *daigner*—L. *dignārī*, to think worthy—*dignus*, worthy.]

**dei gratia,** *dē'i grā'shi-ə, dā'ē grä'ti-a,* (L.) by the grace of God.

**deil,** *dēl,* Scots form of **devil.**

**deino-, Deinoceras, Deinornis, deinosaur, Deinotherium.** See **dino-.**

**de integro,** *dē in'ti-grō, dā in-teg'rō,* (L.) *adv.* anew.

**deiparous,** *dē-ip'ə-rəs, adj.* bearing a god—used of the Virgin. [L. *deus*, a god, *parēre*, to bring forth.]

**deipnosophist,** *dīp-nos'ə-fist, n.* one who converses learnedly at dinner, a table-philosopher—from Athenaeus's work, *Deipnosophistai* (end of 2nd century). [Gr. *deipnon*, dinner, *sophos*, wise.]

**deis(h)eal.** Same as **deasil.**

**deist,** *dē'ist, n.* one who believes in the existence of God, but not in a revealed religion.—*n.* **dē'ism.** —*adjs.* **deist'ic, -al.**—*adv.* **deist'ically.** [L. *deus*, a god.]

**deity,** *dē'i-ti, n.* godhood: divinity: godhead: a god or goddess: (*cap.*; with the) the Supreme Being. [Fr. *déité*—L.L. *deitās*—L. *deus*, god; Sans. *deva.*]

**déjà vu,** *dā-zhä vü, n.* in any of the arts, unoriginal material, old stuff; an illusion of having experienced before something that is really being

experienced for the first time, a form of paramnesia (*psych.*). [Fr. already seen.]

**deject,** *di-jekt',* *v.t.* to cast down the countenance or spirits of.—*adj.* (*Shak.*) cast down.—*adj.* **deject'ed,** cast down: dispirited.—*adv.* **deject'edly.** —*ns.* **deject'edness;** **dejec'tion,** lowness of spirits: (in *pl.*) faecal discharge (also **dejec'ta**).— *adj.* **dejec'tory,** promoting evacuations. [L. *dējicĕre, -jectum*—*dē*, down, *jacĕre*, to cast.]

**dejeune,** *di-jōōn',* (*arch.*) *n.* breakfast or luncheon. See **disjune, déjeuner.**

**déjeuner,** *dā-zhə-nā,* (Fr.) *n.* breakfast or lunch.— **petit déjeuner** (*pə-tē*), (little breakfast) coffee and rolls on rising; **déjeuner à la fourchette** (*a la fōōr-shet*), meat (lit. fork) breakfast, early lunch. **de jure,** *dē jōō'rē, dā zhōō're,* (L.) *adj.* and *adv.* by right: rightful.

**Dekabrist,** *dek'ə-brist, n.* Decembrist. [Russ. *Dekabr'*, December.]

**dekko,** *dek'ō,* (*slang*) *n.* look.—*v.i.* to look. [Hind. *dekho*, imp. of *dekhnā*, to see.]

**delaine,** *di-lān', n.* an untwilled light dress material, originally of wool. [Fr. *mousseline de laine*, wool muslin.]

**delaminate,** *di-lam'i-nāt, v.i.* to split into layers.— *n.* **delaminā'tion.** [L. *dēlamināre*—*dē*, *lāmina*, a layer.]

**delapse,** *di-laps', (obs.) v.i.* to sink down.—*n.* **delap'sion.** [L. *dē,* down, *lābī, lapsus,* to slip.]

**délassement,** *dā-las-mä,* (Fr.) *n.* relaxation.

**delate,** *di-lāt',* *v.t.* to pass on: to publish: to charge with a crime.—*ns.* **delā'tion; delā'tor.** [L. *dēlātum,* used as supine of *dēferre,* to bring a report against, to inform—*dē-,* inten., *ferre, lātum,* to bear.]

**delate** (*Shak.*), for **dilate.**

**delay,** *di-lā',* *v.t.* to put off to another time: to defer: to hinder or retard.—*v.i.* to pause, linger, or put off time:—*pr.p.* **delay'ing;** *pa.p.* **delayed.** —*n.* a putting off or deferring: a lingering: hindrance.—*n.* **delay'er.**—*adv.* **delay'ingly.**—**delayed drop** (*aero.*), a live parachute descent in which the parachutist deliberately delays pulling the ripcord; **delayed neutrons,** those neutrons resulting from fission which are emitted with a measurable time delay. [O.Fr. *delaier.*]

**delay,** *di-lā',* (*Spens.*) *v.t.* to temper, dilute, weaken. [Fr. *délayer,* to dilute—L. *dēliquāre,* to clarify or *dis-, ligāre,* to bind.]

**del credere,** *del krād'ər-i, adj.* applied to an agent who becomes surety for the solvency of persons to whom he sells. [It. *del,* of the, *credere,* to believe, trust.]

**dele,** *dē'lē,* *v.t.* delete, efface, a direction in proof-reading to remove a letter or word, indicated by δ or other sign.—*adj.* **deleble, delible** (*del'*), that can be deleted.—*n.pl.* **delen'da,** things to be deleted. [L. *dēlē,* imper. of *dēlēre,* to delete; or for *dēlēātur,* subj. pass.; *dēlenda,* neut. pl. of gerundive.]

**delectable,** *di-lekt'ə-bl,* (*Spens., Shak., del'*), *adj.* delightful: pleasing.—*n.* **delect'ableness.**—*adv.* **delect'ably.**—*n.* **delectā'tion** (*dē-*), delight. [Fr., —L. *dēlectābilis*—*dēlectāre,* to delight.]

**delegate,** *del'i-gāt,* *v.t.* to send as a legate or representative: to entrust or commit.—*n.* one who is delegated: a deputy or representative: a person elected to represent a Territory in Congress, as distinguished from the representatives of the States (*U.S.*).—*adj.* delegated, deputed.—*ns.* **del'-egacy,** act or system of delegating: a delegate's appointment or authority: a body of delegates; **delegā'tion,** a delegating: a deputation: a body of delegates (*U.S.*): a body of delegates that was appointed every ten years by each of the two portions of the Dual Monarchy to negotiate a treaty between the Austrian Empire and the Kingdom of Hungary (*hist.*).—**delegated legislation,** rules and orders with the force of law made by the executive under statutory authority.

[L. *dē*, away, and *lēgāre*, *-ātum*, to send as ambassador.]

delete, *di-lēt'*, *v.t.* to blot out: to erase: to destroy. —*n.* dele'tion.—*adjs.* delē'tive, delē'tory. [L. *dēlēre*, *dēlētum*, to blot out.]

deleterious, *del-i-tē'ri-əs*, *adj.* hurtful or destructive: poisonous.—*adv.* deletē'riously.—*n.* deletē'riousness. [Gr. *dēlētērios*, hurtful—*dēleesthai*, to hurt.]

delf, delft, *delf*, *delft*, *n.* (in full Delft'ware), a kind of earthenware originally made at *Delft*, Holland.

delf, delph, *delf*, *n.* a drain, ditch, excavation: a charge representing a square sod (*her.*):—*pl.* delfs, delphs, delves. [O.E. *delf*; *delfan*, to dig.]

Delian, *dē'li-ən*, *adj.* pertaining to *Dēlos*, in the Aegean Sea, birthplace of Apollo and Artemis.

delibate, *del-i-bāt*, (*obs.*) *v.t.* to sip.—*n.* delibā'tion. [L. *dēlibāre*—*dē*, from, *libāre*, to take, taste.]

deliberate, *di-lib'ər-āt*, *v.t.* to weigh well in one's mind.—*v.i.* to consider the reasons for and against anything: to reflect: to consider: to take counsel: to debate.—*adj.* (*-it*) well considered: not impulsive: intentional: considering carefully: slow in determining: cautious.—*adv.* delib'erately, in a deliberate manner: (loosely) quietly, without fuss or haste.—*ns.* delib'erateness; deliberā'tion, the act of deliberating: mature reflection: calmness: coolness.—*adj.* delib'erative, proceeding or acting by deliberation.—*adv.* delib'eratively. [L. *dēlīberāre*, *-ātum*—*dē*-, inten., and *lībrāre*, to weigh—*libra*, a balance.]

delicate, *del'i-kit*, *adj.* pleasing to the senses, esp. the taste: dainty: nicely discriminating or perceptive: fastidious: of a fine, slight texture or constitution: tender: not robust: pale: requiring nice handling: refined in manners: not immodest: gentle, polite: luxurious.—*n.* a luxurious or fastidious person: a luxury: a delicacy.—*n.* del'icacy (-*kə-si*), state or quality of being delicate: refinement: nicety: tenderness, weakness: luxuriousness: anything delicate or dainty, esp. to eat.—*adv.* del'icately.—*n.* del'icateness.—*n.pl.* delicătess'en (Ger. pl. of Fr. *délicatesse*), prepared foods, esp. meat: a shop selling these. [L. *dēlicātus*, prob. conn. with *dēliciae*, allurements, luxury—*dēlicēre*—*dē*, inten., *lacěre*, to entice.]

delicious, *di-lish'əs*, *adj.* pleasing to the senses, esp. taste: affording exquisite pleasure.—*n.* delice (*di-lēs'*; *Spens. del'is*), delight: a delight: a delicacy.—*adv.* deli'ciously, in a delicious manner: luxuriously (*B.*).—*n.* deli'ciousness.— flower delice (*Spens.*, also *del'is*), see fleur-de-lis. [L. *dēliciōsus*—*dēliciae*, or *dēlicium*, delight.]

delict, *di-likt'*, *n.* a transgression, a misdemeanour. [L. *dēlictum*, an offence; see delinquent.]

deligation, *del-i-gā'shən*, *n.* a binding up, ligature. [L. *dēligāre*, to bind up—*dē*, intens., and *ligāre*, to bind.]

delight, *di-līt'*, *v.t.* to please highly.—*v.i.* to have or take great pleasure: to be greatly pleased.—*n.* a high degree of pleasure: extreme satisfaction: that which gives great pleasure.—*adj.* delight'ed, greatly pleased: delightful (*Shak.*): capable of delight (*Shak.*).—*adjs.* delight'ful, delight'some, full of delight.—*adv.* delight'fully.—*n.* delight'fulness.—*adj.* delight'less, affording no delight. [O.Fr. *deliter*—L. *dēlectāre*, inten. of *dēlicēre*; cf. delicate, delicious; spelling influenced by confusion with light.]

Delilah, *di-lī'lə*, *n.* the Philistine woman who befooled Samson: a courtesan: a temptress: an alluring object.—Also Dali'lah, Dalila (*Milt. dal'i-lə*).

delimit, *di-lim'it*, *v.t.* to fix or mark the limit of.— *n.* delimitā'tion. [L. *dēlimitāre*—*dē*, intens., *limitāre*; see limit.]

delineate, *di-lin'i-āt*, *v.t.* to mark out with lines: to represent by a sketch or picture: to draw: to describe.—*adj.* delin'eable.—*ns.* delineā'tion, the act of delineating: a sketch, representation, or description; delin'eātor. [L. *dēlineāre*, *-ātum*— *dē*, down, and *līnea*, a line.]

delinquent, *di-ling'kwənt*, *adj.* failing in duty.— *n.* one who fails in or leaves his duty: an offender: a person lacking in moral and social sense, without showing impairment of intellect.—*n.* delin'quency, failure in or omission of duty: a fault: a crime.—*adv.* delin'quently. [L. *dēlinquēns*, *-entis*, pr.p. of *dēlinquěre*—*dē*-, inten., and *linquěre*, *lictum*, to leave.]

deliquesce, *del-i-kwes'*, *v.i.* to melt and become liquid by absorbing moisture, as certain salts, etc.—*n.* deliquesc'ence.—*adj.* deliquesc'ent, liquefying in the air: breaking up into branches, as the veins of a leaf (*bot.*). [L. *dēliquēscěre*— *dē*-, inten., *liquēscěre*, to become fluid—*liquěre*, to be fluid.]

deliquium, *di-lik'wi-əm*, *n.* swoon (*obs.*): eclipse (*arch.*): melting away (*Carlyle*). [Really two different words, partly confused: (1) L. *dēliquium*—*dēlinquěre*, to leave, fail; (2) L. *dēliquium*—*dēliquāre*, to melt.]

delirious, *di-lir'i-əs*, *adj.* wandering in mind: lightheaded: insane.—*n.* delirā'tion (*del-*), madness, aberration.—*adj.* delirifacient (*di-lir-i-fā'shənt*), producing delirium.—*n.* that which produces delirium.—*adv.* delir'iously.—*n.* delir'iousness; delir'ium, state of being delirious: strong excitement: wild enthusiasm.—delirium tremens (*trē'menz*), a delirious disorder of the brain produced by over-absorption of alcohol, often marked by convulsive or trembling symptoms. [L. *dēlirus*, crazy—*dēlirāre*, lit. to turn aside— *dē*, from, and *lira*, a furrow; *tremēns*, the pr.p. of *treměre*, to tremble.]

delitescent, *del-i-tes'ənt*, *adj.* latent.—*n.* delitesc'ence. [L. *dēlitēscēns*, *-entis*, pr.p. of *dēlitēscēre*— *dē*, from, and *latēscěre*—*latěre*, to lie hid.]

deliver, *di-liv'ər*, *v.t.* to liberate or set free from restraint or danger: to rescue from evil or fear: to give up: to hand over, distribute: to communicate: to pronounce: to give forth, as a blow, a ball, etc.: to discharge, as water: to disburden, of a child in childbirth.—*adj.* nimble.—*adj.* deliv'erable.—*ns.* deliv'erance, liberation: release: parturition: the utterance of a judgment or authoritative opinion; deliv'erer. —*adv.* deliv'erly.—*n.* deliv'ery, the act of delivering: a giving up: the act or manner of speaking in public, of discharging a shot, or water, of throwing a cricket-ball, etc.: withdrawal of a pattern from a mould: a distribution: a round of distribution: the act of giving birth.— deliv'ery-man, a man who goes round delivering goods; deliv'ery-pipe, *-tube*, one that delivers water, etc., at the place where it is required; deliv'ery-van, a tradesman's van for distributing goods at customers' houses.—deliver the goods (*slang*), to carry out what is required or promised; general delivery, the delivery of letters at a post-office to the persons to whom they are addressed —opp. to house-to-house delivery; gaol, or jail, delivery (see gaol). [Fr. *dēlivrer*—L. *dē*, from, *liberāre*, to set free—*liber*, free.]

dell, del, *n.* a deep hollow or small valley, usually covered with trees: a hole (*Spens.*). [O.E. *dell*; cf. dale.]

dell, del, (*arch. slang*) *n.* a young girl: usu. a trull.

Della-Cruscan, *del-ə-krus'kən*, *del-la-krōōs'kən*, *n.* a member of the old Florentine Accademia *della Crusca* (It., academy of the bran, as sifters of the poetasters crushed by Gifford's *Baviad* and *Maeviad* (1794 and 1796).—Also *adj.*

Della-Robbia, *del-la-rob'bya*, *n.* a term applied to

Neutral vowels in unaccented syllables: *el'ə-mənt*; for certain sounds in foreign words, see p. viii

T.C.D.—12

enamelled terra-cotta, said to have been invented by Luca *della Robbia*.
**delouse,** *dē-lows'*, *v.t.* to free from lice, or (*fig.*) from land-mines, etc. [Pfx. de- (2).]
**delph.** See delf.
**Delphic,** *del'fik*, *adj.* relating to *Delphi*, a town of ancient Greece, or to its famous oracle: oracular.—Also **Del'phian.** [Gr. *Delphikos—Delphoi*.]
**delphin,** *del'fin*, *adj.* pertaining to the *dauphin* (q.v.) of France, or to an edition of the Latin classics prepared for his use, 64 vols., 1674-1730.
**Delphinidae,** *del-fin'i-dē*, *n.pl.* a family of cetaceans, including dolphins, grampuses, etc.—*adj.* **del'phinoid.** [L. *delphīnus*—Gr. *delphīs*, *-īnos*, a dolphin.]
**Delphinium,** *del-fin'i-əm*, *n.* a genus of Ranunculaceae, comprising the larkspurs and stavesacre. [Latinised from Gr. *delphinion*, larkspur, dim. of *delphīs*, dolphin, from the appearance of the flowers.]
**Delphinus,** *del'fin-us*, (*astron.*) *n.* the Dolphin, a northern constellation between Pegasus and Aquila. [L.]
**delta,** *del'tə*, *n.* the fourth letter (Δ δ) of the Greek alphabet, answering to D: an alluvial deposit at the mouth of a stream, Δ-shaped in the case of the Nile: as an ancient Greek numeral Δ' = 4, „Δ = 4000.—*adjs.* **deltā'ic,** belonging to a delta; **del'toid,** of the form of the Greek Δ: triangular.—**del'ta-wing (aeroplane)** a jet aeroplane with triangular wings; **deltoid muscle,** the large triangular muscle of the shoulder. [Gr.,—Heb. *daleth*, a tent-door.]
**deltiology,** *del-ti-ol'ə-ji*, *n.* the study and collection of picture postcards.—*n.* **deltiol'ogist.** [Gr. *deltion*, small writing-tablet.]
**delubrum,** *di-lū'brəm*, *-lōō'*, *n.* a temple, shrine, sanctuary: a church having a font: a font. [L. *dēlūbrum*.]
**deluce.** See fleur-de-lis.
**delude,** *di-lōōd'*, *di-lūd*, *v.t.* to play with (someone) so as to frustrate him or his hopes (*obs.*): to elude (*obs.*): to deceive, cause to accept what is false as true.—*adjs.* **delud'able; delud'ed,** holding or acting under false beliefs.—*n.* **delud'er.** [L. *dēlūdĕre*, to play false—*dē*, down, *lūdĕre*, *lūsum*, to play.]
**deluge,** *del'ūj*, *n.* a great overflow of water: a flood, esp. Noah's: an overwhelming flow (*fig.*). —*v.t.* to inundate: to overwhelm as with water. [Fr. *déluge*—L. *dīluvium—dīluĕre—dis-*, away, *luĕre*, to wash.]
**delundung,** *del'ən-dung*, *n.* the weasel-cat of Java and Malacca, a small carnivore akin to the civet. [Javanese.]
**delusion,** *di-lōō'zhən*, *di-lū'zhən*, *n.* the act of deluding: the state of being deluded: a hallucination: a false belief: error.—*adj.* **delu'-sional,** pertaining to delusions, afflicted with such.—*n.* **delu'sionist.**—*adjs.* **delu'sive** (*-siv*), **delu'sory,** apt or tending to delude: deceptive. *adv.* **delu'sively.**—*n.* **delu'siveness.** [See delude.]
**de luxe,** *də lüks'*, *di lōōks'*, *luks'*, (Fr.) *adj.* sumptuous, luxurious.
**delve,** *delv*, *v.t.* and *v.i.* to dig with a spade: to make deep research (*fig.*): to dip, slope suddenly. —*n.* (*Spens.*) a hollow, hole, depression, a cave. —*n.* **delv'er.** [O.E. *delfan*, to dig; conn. with dale, delf, dell.]
**demagnetise,** *dē-mag'nit-iz*, *v.t.* to deprive of magnetic properties.—*n.* **demagnetisā'tion.** [Pfx. de- (2).]
**demagogue,** *dem'ə-gog*, *n.* a leader of the people: a popular and factious orator.—*adjs.* **demagogic, -al** (*-gog'* or *-goj'*).—*ns.* **demagogism, demagoguism** (*dem'ə-gog-ism*); **dem'agoguery, dem'-agogy** (*-gog-*; *-goj-*). [Gr. *dēmagōgos—dēmos*, people, *agōgos*, leading—*agein*, to lead.]
**demain.** See demesne.

**demaine.** See demean (1).
**demand,** *di-mänd'*, *v.t.* to claim: to ask peremptorily or authoritatively for: to require: to ask (a question; *obs.*).—*n.* the asking for what is due: peremptory asking for something: a claim: desire shown by consumers: inquiry.—*adj.* **demand'able,** that may be demanded.—*ns.* **demand'ant,** one who demands: a plaintiff; **demand'er.—in great demand,** much sought after. [Fr. *demander*—L.L. *dēmandāre*, to demand—L. *dē-*, intens., and *mandāre*, to put into one's charge.]
**demarcation, demarkation,** *dē-märk-ā'shən*, *n.* the act of marking off or setting bounds: separation: a fixed limit: in trade unionism, the strict marking off of the field of one craft from that of another.—*v.t.* **dē'marcate** (or *di-märk'*), to mark off or limit.—Also **demark'.** [Sp. *demarcación—de*, from, *marcar*, to mark. See mark.]
**démarche,** *dā-märsh*, (Fr.) *n.* a step or measure (esp. diplomatic).
**dematerialise,** *dē-mə-tē'ri-əl-iz*, *v.t.* to deprive of material qualities or character.—*v.i.* to become immaterial. [Pfx. de- (2).]
**deme,** *dēm*, *n.* a subdivision of ancient Attica and of modern Greece, a township. [Gr. *dēmos*, people.]
**demean,** *di-mēn'*, *v.t.* to bear, behave, conduct (*refl.*): to treat (*Spens.*): to ill-treat (*Spens.*; *obs. Scot.*).—*n.* (*Spens.* **demaine', demayne',** air, bearing: treatment.—*n.* **demeanour** (*di-mēn'ər*; *Spens.* **demeasnure**), behaviour: bearing towards another. [O.Fr. *demener—de-*, intens., and *mener*, to lead—L. *mināre*, to drive—*mināri*, to threaten.]
**demean,** *di-mēn'*, *v.t.* to lower in status, reputation, or (often *reflex.*) dignity. [Prob. on the analogy of *debase*, pfx. de- (1) and mean.]
**dement,** *di-ment'*, *v.t.* to drive crazy, render insane.—*adj.* insane, demented.—*n.* a demented person.—*v.t.* **dement'āte,** to dement.—*adj.* **dement'ed,** out of one's mind: insane: suffering from dementia.—*n.* **dementia** (*di-men'shi-ə*), (*psychol.*) any form of insanity characterised by the failure or loss of mental powers: the organic deterioration of intelligence, memory, and orientation.—**dementia praecox, precox,** (*prē'koks*), schizophrenia. [L. *dēmēns, dēmentis*, out of one's mind—*dē*, from, and *mēns*, the mind.]
**démenti,** *dā-mä-tē*, *n.* a contradiction, denial. [Fr. *démentir*, to give the lie to.]
**demerara,** *dem-ə-rä'ra*, *n.* brown sugar in large crystals. [*Demerara* (*-rä-*)', in Guyana.]
**demerge,** *dē-mûrj'*, *v.t.* to immerse, plunge. [L. *dē*, down, *mergĕre*, to plunge.]
**demerit,** *dē-*, *di-mer'it*, *n.* desert (*obs.*): ill-desert: fault. [L. *dēmerēri, dēmeritum*, to deserve fully, later understood as to deserve ill—*dē-*, fully, *merēri*, to deserve.]
**demerse,** *di-mûrs'*, (*obs.*) *v.t.* to immerse.—*adjs.* **demer'sal,** subaqueous: found on or near the bottom; **demersed'** (*bot.*), growing under water. —*n.* **demer'sion.** [L. *dē*, down, *mergĕre*, *mersum*, to plunge.]
**demesne,** *di-mān'*, *-mēn'*, **demain,** *di-mān'*, *n.* a manor-house with lands adjacent to it not let out to tenants: any estate in land. [Forms of domain.]
**demi-,** *dem'i*, *pfx.* half, half-sized.—*ns.* **dem'i-bast'ion,** a kind of half-bastion, consisting of one face and one flank; **dem'i-cann'on** (*Shak.*), an old kind of gun which threw a ball of from 30 to 36 lb.; **dem'i-cul'verin,** an old kind of cannon which threw a shot of 9 or 10 lb.—*v.t.* **dem'i-ify,** to treat as a demigod: to go half-way towards deifying.—*ns.* **dem'i-dev'il,** a half-devil; **dem'i-dis'tance** (*fort.*) the distance between the outward polygons and the flank; **dem'i-di'tone** (*mus.*) a minor third; **dem'igod,** a half-god: one

whose nature is partly divine, esp. a hero fabled to be the offspring of a god and a mortal:—*fem.*
**dem′igodd′ess;** **dem′i-gorge** (*fort.*) the part of the polygon remaining after the flank is raised, going from the curtain to the angle of the polygon; **dem′i-lance,** a short, light spear of the 16th century; a soldier armed with such a weapon; **dem′i-lune** (*lōōn; fort.*) a half-moon: an old name for *ravelin;* **demi-monde** (*dem′i-mond, de-mē-mɔ̃d*), a class of women in an equivocal social position, the kept mistresses of society men: the shady section of a profession or group; **demi-mondaine** (-*en′*), a woman member of the demi-monde.—*adj.* **demipique** (*dem′i-pēk*) of an 18th century war-saddle, having a lower peak than usual.—Also *n.*—*ns.* **dem′irep** (for *demi-reputable*), a person, esp. a woman, of dubious reputation; **demirep′dom; demi-semiquaver,** *dem-i-sem′i-kwā-vər,* (*mus.*) *n.* a note equal in time to the half of a semiquaver; **dem′i-volt,** a half-turn of a horse, the forelegs being raised in the air; **dem′i-wolf,** (*Shak.*) a half-wolf, the offspring of a dog and a wolf. [Fr. *demi*—L. *dimidium*—*di-*, apart, *medius,* the middle.]
**demigration,** *dem-i-grā′shən, n.* change of abode. [L. *dēmigrāre, -ātum,* depart—*dē, migrāre.*]
**demijohn,** *dem′i-jon, n.* a glass bottle with a full body and narrow neck, enclosed in wickerwork. [Fr. *dame-jeanne,* Dame Jane, analogous to bellarmine, grey-beard; not from the town *Damaghan.*]
**demi-jour,** *dɔ-mē-zhōōr,* (Fr.) *n.* half-light, twilight, subdued light.
**demipique, demirep.** See demi.
**demise,** *di-miz′, n.* a transferring: death, esp. of a sovereign or a distinguished person: a transfer of the crown or of an estate to a successor.—*v.t.* to send down to a successor: to bequeath by will.—*adj.* **demi′sable.** [O.Fr. *demise,* pa.p. of *desmettre,* to lay down.—L. *dis-,* aside, *mittĕre, missum,* to send.]
**demiss,** *di-mis′,* (*Spens.*) *adj.* humble.—*n.* **demission** (*di-mish′ən*), lowering: degradation: depression: relinquishment: resignation.—*adj.* **demiss′ive** (*obs.*), humble.—*adv.* **demiss′ly.** [L. *dēmittĕre, -missum*—*dē,* down, *mittĕre,* to send.]
**demit,** *di-mit′, v.t.* to send down: to lower. [See demiss.]
**demit,** *di-mit′, v.t.* to dismiss: to relinquish: to resign. [Fr. *démettre*—L. *dīmittĕre*—*dis-,* apart, *mittĕre,* to send.]
**demiurge,** *dem′i-ûrj, n.* the maker of the world: among the Gnostics, the creator of the world and man, subordinate to God the supreme—also **demiur′gus** (*-gɔs*).—*adj.* **demiur′gic** (*-jik*). [Gr. *dēmiourgos*—*dēmos,* the people, and *ergon,* a work.]
**demo.** See demonstrate.
**demobilise, -ize,** *di-mōb′il-īz, v.t.* to take out of mobilisation: to disband: to discharge from the army (*coll.*):—abbrev. **demob′;** *pr.p.* **demobb′ing;** *pa.p.* **demobbed′).**—*n.* **demobilisā′tion, -z-.** [Pfx. de- (2).]
**democracy,** *di-mok′rɔ-si, n.* a form of government in which the supreme power is vested in the people collectively, and is administered by them or by officers appointed by them: the common people: a state of society characterised by recognition of equality of rights and privileges: political, social or legal equality: in the U.S., the Democratic party.—Also **democraty** (-*ok′;* *Milt.*).—*n.* **democrat** (*dem′ō-krat*), one who adheres to or promotes democracy as a principle: a member of the Democratic party in the United States, the party generally inclining to look to the rights of States against centralisation of government, and favouring a low tarriff: a light four-wheeled cart with several seats (*U.S.;* also **democrat wagon**).—*adjs.* **democrat′ic, -al,** relating to democracy: insisting on equal rights and privileges for all.—*adv.* **democrat′ically.**—

*adj.* **democratifi′able,** capable of being made democratic.—*v.t.* **democratise, -ize** (*di-mok′*), to render democratic.—*n.* **democ′ratist,** a democrat. [Fr. *démocratie*—Gr. *dēmokratiā*—*dēmos,* the people, *kratos,* strength.]
**démodé,** *dā-mö-dā,* (Fr.) out of fashion.
**demoded,** *dēmōd′id, adj.* (disparagingly) no longer in fashion. [Pfx. de- (2).]
**Demogorgon,** *dē-mō-gör′gan, n.* a mysterious infernal deity first mentioned about A.D. 450. [Apparently Gr. *daimōn,* deity, *Gorgō,* Gorgon, *gorgos,* terrible.]
**demography,** *dē-mog′rɔ-fi, n.* the study of population.—*n.* **demog′rapher.**—*adj.* **demographic** (*-ō-graf′ik*). [Gr. *dēmos,* the people, *graphein,* to write.]
**demoiselle,** *dɔm-wä-zel′, n.* a young lady (*arch.* or *playful*): a graceful kind of crane (*Anthropoides virgo*): a dragonfly: a fish of the genus *Pomacentrus* or its family (akin to the wrasses): a tiger-shark. [Fr.; see damsel.]
**demolish,** *di-mol′ish, v.t.* to lay in ruins: to destroy, put an end to.—*n.* **demoli′tion** (*dem-ō-*), act of pulling down: ruin. [Fr. *démolir*—L. *dēmōliri,* to throw down—*dē,* down, and *mōliri,* to build—*mōlēs,* a heap.]
**demology,** *dē-mol′ɔ-ji, n.* demography: the theory of the origin and nature of communities. [Gr. *dēmos,* people, *logos,* a discourse.]
**demon,** *dē′mɔn, n.* an evil spirit, a devil: sometimes like daemon, a friendly spirit or good genius: a person of great energy or enthusiasm (*fig.*):—*fem.* **dē′moness.**—*adjs.* **demoniac** (*di-mōn′i-ek*); **demoniacal** (*dē-mɔ-ni′ɔ-kl*), pertaining to or like demons or evil spirits: influenced by demons.—*n.* **demō′niac,** one possessed by a demon or evil spirit.—*adv.* **demoni′acally.**—*n.* **dēmoni′acism** (*-ɔ-sizm*), state of being a demoniac.—*adj.* **demō′nian** (*Milt.*).—*n.* **demō′nianism,** possession by a demon.—*adj.* **demon′ic** (*dē-mon′ik;* see daemonic).—*v.t.* **dē′monise, -ize,** to convert into a demon: to control or possess by a demon.—*ns.* **dē′monism,** a belief in demons; **dē′monist; dēmonoc′racy,** the power of demons; **dēmonol′atry,** the worship of demons; **dēmonol′ater; dēmonol′ogy,** an account of, or the study of, demons and their agency.—*adjs.* **dēmonolog′ic, -al.**—*ns.* **dēmonol′ogist; dēmonomā′nia,** a form of mania in which the subject believes himself possessed by devils; **dē′monry,** demoniacal influence. [L. *daemōn*—Gr. *daimōn,* a spirit, genius; in N.T. and Late Greek, a devil; see daemon.]
**demonetise, -ize,** *dē-mon′i-tiz,* or *-mun′, v.t.* to divest of value as money.—*n.* **demonetisā′tion, -z-.** [Pfx. de- (2).]
**demonstrate,** *dem′an-strāt* (or *di-mon′strāt*), *v.t.* to make manifest: to give proof of: to prove with certainty: to teach, expound, explain, or exhibit by practical means.—*v.i.* to exhibit one's feelings: to act as demonstrator.—*adj.* **demon′strable** (or *dem′an-*), that may be demonstrated.—*ns.* **demon′strableness, -strabil′ity.**—*adv.* **demon′strably** (or *dem′an-*).—*ns.* **demonstrā′tion,** pointing out: proof beyond doubt: expression of the feelings by outward signs: a public expression of feelings, as by a mass-meeting, a procession, etc. (*coll.* abbrev. **demo**): show: a movement to exhibit military intention, or to deceive an enemy: a practical lesson or exhibition.—*adj.* **demon′strative,** pointing out (as a *demonstrative adjective*): making evident: proving with certainty: of the nature of proof: given to the manifestation of one's feelings.—*adv.* **demon′stratively.**—*n.* **demon′strativeness.**—*n.* **dem′onstrātor,** one who proves beyond doubt: a teacher or assistant who helps students with practical work: one who goes about exhibiting the uses and merits of a commodity: one who takes part in a public demonstration.—*adj.*

Neutral vowels in unaccented syllables: *el′ɔ-mɔnt;* for certain sounds in foreign words, see p. viii demon'stratory, demonstrative. [L. *dēmōn-strāre*, *-ātum*—*dē-*, inten., and *mōnstrāre*, to show.]

demoralise, -ize, *dē-mor'əl-īz*, *v.t.* to corrupt in morals: to lower the morale of—that is, to deprive of spirit and confidence: to throw into confusion.—*n.* demoralisā'tion, *-z-*, act of demoralising: corruption or subversion of morals.—*adj.* demoralis'ing. [Pfx. de- (2).]

demos, *dē'mos*, *n.* the people (esp. contemptuously).—*adj.* demot'ic, pertaining to the people: popular: of a simplified kind of writing distinguished from the hieratic, or priestly, and from hieroglyphics (*Egypt. ant.*).—*n.* demot'icist, a student of demotic script. [Gr. *dēmos*.]

Demosthenic, *de-mos-then'ik*, *adj.* of or like *Dēmosthenēs*, the Athenian orator: oratorical: eloquent.

demote, *dē-mōt'*, *v.t.* to reduce in rank.—*n.* demō'tion. [On the analogy of promote; de- (2).]

demount, *dē-mownt'*, *v.t.* to take down from a support, etc.: to take (e.g. a building) to pieces in such a way that it can be reassembled.—*adj.* demount'able. [Pfx. de- (2), mount, to set in position.]

dempster. Same as deemster. [See under deem.]

dempt, *demt* (*Spens.*), *pa.p.* and *pa.t.* of deem.

demulcent, *di-mul'sənt*, *adj.* soothing.—*n.* a medicine that allays irritation. [L. *dēmulcēns*, *-ēntis*—*dē*, down, *mulcēre*, to stroke, to soothe.]

demulsify, *dē-mul'si-fi*, *v.t.* to separate from an emulsion: to make resistant to emulsification. [Pfx. de- (2), emulsify.]

demur, *di-mûr'*, *v.i.* to hesitate from uncertainty or before difficulty: to object.—*v.t.* (*Milt.*) to hesitate about:—*pr.p.* demurr'ing; *pa.t.* and *pa.p.* demurred'.—*n.* a stop: pause, hesitation.—*adj.* demurr'able.—*n.* demurr'age, undue delay or detention of a vessel, railway wagon, etc.: compensation for such detention: a charge made by the Bank of England for exchanging notes or gold for bullion; demurr'er, one who demurs: a plea in law that, even if the opponent's facts are as he says, they yet do not support his case (*law*). [Fr. *demeurer*—L. *dēmorārī*, to loiter, linger—*de-*, inten., and *morārī*, to delay—*mora*, delay.]

demure, *di-mūr'*, *adj.* sober: staid: modest: affectedly modest: making a show of gravity.—*v.i.* (*Shak.*) app., to look demurely.—*adv.* demure'ly.—*n.* demure'ness. [O.Fr. *meur* (Fr. *mûr*)—L. *matūrus*, ripe; pfx. unexplained.]

demy, *di-mi'*, *n.* before metrication a size of printing and writing paper—approximating to A2: in U.S. a writing paper, 21 by 16 in: a holder of certain scholarships in Magdalen College, Oxford, orig. allowed half the commons assigned to a fellow:—*pl.* demies'.—*n.* demy'-ship. [Fr. *demi*—L. *dimidium*, half—*dis-*, apart, *medius*, the middle.]

den, *den*, *n.* the hollow lair of a wild beast: a pit, cave: a haunt of vice or misery: a private retreat for work (*coll.*): a narrow valley, a dean (*dial.*).—*v.i.* to retire to a den. [O.E. *denn*, a cave, lair; akin to *denu*, a valley.]

den, *den*, (*obs.*) *n.* for good-e'en, good-even.

denary, *dēn'ər-i*, *adj.* containing or depending on the number ten: ten.—*n.* the number ten: a group of ten.—*n.* denarius (*di-nā'ri-əs*), the chief Roman silver coin under the Republic, divided into ten asses—about 8d.; translated *penny* in the N.T.—hence the use of d. for penny (before the introduction of decimal coinage). [L. *dēnārius*—*dēnī*, ten by ten—*decem*, ten.]

denationalise, -ize, *dē-nash'ən-əl-īz*, *v.t.* to deprive of national rights or character: return from state to private ownership.—*n.* denationalisā'tion, *-z-*. [Pfx. de- (2).]

denaturalise, -ize, *dē-nach'ər-əl-īz*, *v.t.* to make un-

natural: to deprive of naturalisation.—*n.* dēnaturalisā'tion, *-z-*. [Pfx. de- (2).]

denature, *dē-nā'chər*, *v.t.* to change the nature or properties of, as a protein by heat or other treatment: of alcohol, etc., to render unfit for consumption.—*n.* denā'turant, a substance used to denature another. [Pfx. de- (2).]

denay, *di-nā'*, obs. form of deny, denial.

dendron, *den'dron*, *n.* a branching process of a nerve-cell.—*n.* dendrachate (*den'drə-kāt*; Gr. *achātēs*, agate), arborescent agate.—*adj.* den'-driform, tree-like.—*n.* den'drite (Gr. *dendritēs*, of a tree), a tree-like crystalline aggregate or skeleton crystal: a dendron.—*adjs.* dendrit'ic, *-al*, tree-like, arborescent: marked with branching figures like plants.—*ns.* Dendrō'bium (Gr. *bios*, life), a genus of epiphytic orchids, chiefly of tropical Asia; Dendrocal'amus (Gr. *kalamos*, cane), a genus of bamboos; dendrochronology (*den-drō-kron-ol'ə-ji*), fixing of dates in the past by comparative study of the annual growth rings in ancient trees; den'droglyph (*-glif*; Gr. *glyphē*, carving), an ancient carving on a tree.—*adj.* den'droid, tree-like.—*n.* dendrol'atry (Gr. *latreiā*, worship), the worship of trees.—*adj.* dendrolog'ical.—*ns.* dendrol'ogist; dendrol'ogy, a treatise on trees: the natural history of trees; dendrom'eter, an instrument for measuring trees; Den'drophis (Gr. *ophis*, snake), a genus of tree-snakes, Indian and Australian. [Gr. *dendron*, tree.]

dene, *dēn*, *n.* a small valley. [See dean (1).]

dene, *dēn*, *n.* a sandy tract, a dune. [Ety. doubtful.]

Deneb, *den'eb*, *n.* the brightest star in the constellation Cygnus.—*n.* Deneb'ola, a star at the tail of the constellation Leo. [Ar. *dhanab*, tail, *al-asad*, of the lion.]

denegation, *den-i-gā'shən*, *n.* a denial. [L. *dēnegāre*, *-ātum*, to deny—*dē-*, inten., and *negāre*, to deny.]

dene-hole, *dēn'hōl*, *n.* a prehistoric artificial chamber in the chalk, in Kent, Essex, etc., perhaps a flint-mine or a storehouse. [Perh. from dene (1), or O.E. *Dene*, Danes, from popular association, and hole.]

dengue, *deng'gā*, *n.* an acute tropical epidemic fever, seldom fatal—also *breakbone fever*, *dandy-fever*. [Apparently Swahili, *dinga*.]

denial, *di-ni'əl*, *n.* act of denying: refusal: rejection.—*adj.* deni'able.—*n.* deni'er. [deny.]

denier, *də-nēr'*, *n.* an old small French silver coin (*Shak.*): also later, a copper coin of the value of 1/12 sou—hence a very trifling sum: a unit of silk, rayon, and nylon yarn weight (usu. *den'i-ər*). [Fr.—L. *dēnārius*.]

denigrate, *den'i-grāt*, *v.t.* to blacken (esp. a reputation).—*adj.* blackened.—*n.* denigrā'tion; den'igrātor. [L. *dē-*, inten., *nigrāre*, to blacken, *niger*, black.]

denim, *den'im*, *n.* coloured twilled cotton goods for overalls, etc.: (in *pl.*) a garment made of denim. [Fr. *de*, of, and *Nimes*.]

denitrate, *dē-ni'trāt*, *v.t.* to free from nitric acid or other nitrogen compounds.—*ns.* denitrā'tion; denitrificā'tion, removal of nitrogen or its compounds; deni'trificātor.—*v.t.* deni'trify. [Pfx. de- (2).]

denizen, *den'i-zn*, *n.* an inhabitant (human or animal): one admitted to the rights of a citizen: a wild plant, probably foreign, that keeps its footing: a naturalised foreign word, etc.—Also *adj.*—*v.t.* to make a denizen: to provide with occupants.—*v.i.* to inhabit.—*ns.* denizā'tion, act of making one a citizen; den'izenship. [O.Fr. *deinzein*—*deinz*, *dens* (Fr. *dans*), within—L. *dē intus*, from within.]

dennet, *den'it*, *n.* a light gig. [Prob. a surname.]

denominate, *dē-nom'in-āt*, *v.t.* to give a name to: to call.—*adj.* denom'inable.—*n.* denominā'tion, the act of naming: a name or title: a collection of individuals called by the same name: a sect.—*adj.* denominā′tional, belonging to a denomination or sect.—*n.* denominā′tionalism, a denominational or class spirit or policy: devotion to the interests of a sect.—*adj.* denom′inative, giving or having a title.—*adv.* denom′inatively.— *n.* denom′inātor, he who, or that which, gives a name: the lower number in a vulgar fraction, which names the parts into which the integer is divided (*arith.*).—common denominator, number that is a multiple of each of the denominators of a set of fractions, esp. the least: something that makes comparison, communication, agreement, etc., possible. [L. *dē-*, intens., *nōmināre*, to name—*nōmen*, name.]

denote, di-nōt′, *v.t.* to note or mark off: to indicate by a sign: to signify or mean: to indicate the objects comprehended in a class (*log.*).—*adj.* denō′table.—*v.t.* dē′nōtate, to denote.—*n.* denotā′tion (*log.*), that which a word denotes, in contradistinction to that which it *connotes.*— *adj.* denō′tative (or *dē*′).—*adv.* denō′tatively (or *dē*′).—*n.* denōte′ment (*Shak.*), a sign or indication. [Fr. *dénoter*—L. *dēnotāre, -ātum—dē*, inten., and *notāre.*]

dénouement, dā-nōō-mā, *n.* the unravelling of a plot or story: the issue, event, or outcome. [Fr. *dénouement* or *dénoûment*; *dénouer*, O.Fr. *desnoer*, to untie—L. *dis-, nodāre*, to tie—*nodus*, a knot.]

denounce, di-nowns′, *v.t.* to inform against or accuse publicly: to inveigh against: to proclaim as imminent: to notify formally termination of (treaties, etc.): to announce (*obs.*): to give formal notice of a claim for mining rights covering (*U.S.*; through Sp.).—*ns.* denounce′-ment, denunciation; denounc′er. [Fr. *dénoncer* —L. *dēnuntiāre—dē-*, inten., and *nuntiāre*, to announce.]

de novo, dē nō′vō, dā nō′wō, (L.) anew.

dense, dens, *adj.* thick, close, compact: impenetrably stupid.—*adv.* dense′ly.—*ns.* dense′ness; dens′ity, the quality of being dense: the proportion of a mass to bulk or volume: the quantity of matter per unit of bulk; densim′eter, an instrument for measuring the relative density of the closeness of grain of a substance. [L. *dēnsus*, thick, dense.]

dent, *dent, n.* and *v.t.* Same as dint, dunt. [Confused with next.]

dent, *dent, n.* a notch.—*v.t.* to notch.—*adj.* dent′al, pertaining to or concerned with the teeth or dentistry: produced by the aid of the teeth.— *n.* a sound pronounced by applying the tongue to the teeth or (loosely) the gums.—*ns.* Dent′-ālium, a genus of scaphopod molluscs with shell like an elephant's tusk—tooth-shell or tusk-shell; Dentā′ria, the cruciferous toothwort.— *adj.* dent′ary, belonging to dentition: bearing teeth.—*n.* a bone of the lower jaw of some vertebrates usually bearing teeth.—*adjs.* dent′ate, -d, toothed: notched: set as with teeth.—*ns.* dentā′tion, condition of being dentate: a toothlike projection; dent′el (see dentil); dent′ex, a strongly toothed voracious fish akin to perch, found in the Mediterranean; dent′icle, a small tooth-like structure: a dentil.—*adjs.* dentic′ulāte, -d, notched: having dentils.—*n.* denticulā′tion. —*adj.* dent′iform, having the form of a tooth or of teeth.—*n.* dent′ifrice (L. *fricāre*, to rub), a substance used in rubbing or cleaning the teeth— toothpaste or tooth-powder.—*adj.* dentig′erous (-*ij*′), bearing teeth.—*n.* dent′il, a denticle: one of a series of square blocks or projections as in the bed-moulding of a cornice of columns.— Also dent′el.—*adj.* dentilin′gual (L. *lingua*, tongue), formed between the teeth and the tongue, as *th* in *thin, this.*—*n.* a consonant so formed.—*n.* dent′ine (-*ēn*), the substance of

which teeth are mainly composed.—*adj.* dentiros′tral (L. *rōstrum*, a beak), with notched bill. —*ns.* dent′ist, one qualified to treat diseases and malformations of, and injuries to, teeth; dent′istry, the art or work of a dentist; dent′ition, the cutting or growing of teeth: the conformation, number, and arrangement of the teeth. —*adj.* dent′oid (Gr. *eidos*, form), formed or shaped like a tooth.—*n.* dent′ure, a set of (esp. artificial) teeth.—dental formula, a formula showing the number and distribution of the different kinds of teeth in an animal's jaws. [L. *dēns, dentis*, a tooth; dim. *denticulus.*]

dentelle, *den-tel′*, dā-tel, *n.* lace, lacework: an ornamental pattern or border resembling lace and featuring toothed outlines, used in decorating book covers. [Fr., lit. little tooth—O.Fr. *dentele*, dim. of *dent*, tooth.]

denude, di-nūd′, in U.S. also *-nōōd*, *v.t.* to make nude or naked: to lay bare.—*n.* denudation (*den-ū-dā′shən*), a making nude or bare: the wearing away of rocks whereby the underlying rocks are laid bare (*geol.*). [L. *dēnūdāre—dē-*, inten., *nūdāre, -ātum*, make naked.]

denunciate, *dē′nun′s(h)i-āt*, *v.t.* to denounce.—*n.* denunciā′tion, any formal declaration: act of denouncing: a threat; denun′ciātor, one who denounces.—*adj.* denun′ciatory, containing a denunciation: threatening. [L. *dēnunciāre* or *dēnuntiāre*; see denounce.]

deny, di-nī′, *v.t.* to gainsay or declare not to be true: to reject: to refuse: to refuse to admit: to refuse a visitor access to: to disown:—*pr.p.* deny′ing; *pa.t.* and *pa.p.* denied′.—*adv.* deny′-ingly.—deny oneself, to refuse to allow oneself gratification: to exercise self-denial. [Fr. *dénier* —L. *dēnegāre—dē-*, inten., and *negāre*, to say no.]

Deo, dē′ō, dā′ō, (L.) to, for, with God.—Deo favente, *fə-ven′tē, -wen′tā*, with God's favour; Deo gratias, *grā′shi-as, grä′tē-äs*, thanks to God; Deo Optimo Maximo (abbrev. D.O.M.), *op′ti-mō, mak′si-mō, māk′si-mō*, to God, the best, the greatest (the motto of the Benedictines); Deo volente (abbrev. D.V.), *vo-len′tē, wo-len′tā*, God willing.

deobstruent, *dē-ob′strōō-ənt*, (*med.*) *adj.* removing obstructions.—Also *n.* [L. *dē*, away; see obstruct.]

deoch-an-doruis, *dohh′ən dō′ris, dö′, n.* a stirrup-cup, a parting cup.—Also doch-an-doris, doch-an-dorach (-*ohh*), deuch-an-doris. [Gael. *deoch*, drink, *an*, the, *doruis*, gen. of *dorus*, door.]

deodand, *dē′ō-dand, n.* in old English law, a personal chattel which had been the immediate accidental cause of the death of a human being, forfeited to the crown for pious uses. [L. *deō*, to God, *dandum*, that must be given—*dāre*, to give.]

deodar, *dē′ō-där, n.* a cedar (*Cedrus Deodara*) of the Himalayas, much praised by Indian poets. [Sans. *deva-dāru*, divine tree.]

deodate, *dē′ō-dāt, n.* a gift to God: extended to mean a gift from God. [L. *deō*, to God (ā Deō, by God), *dātum*, given, pa.p. of *dāre*, to give.]

deodorise, -ize, dē-ō′dər-iz, *v.t.* to take the odour or smell from.—*ns.* deō′dorant, deō′doriser, -z-, a substance that destroys or conceals unpleasant smells; deō′dorisā′tion, -z-. [Pfx. de- (2).]

deontology, *dē-on-tol′ə-ji, n.* the science of duty, ethics.—*adj.* deontolog′ical (-*tə-loj′*).—*n.* deon-tol′ogist. [Gr. *deon, -ontos*, neut. pr.p. of *deein*, to be necessary, to behave, *logos*, discourse.]

deoppilate, *dē-op′i-lāt, v.t.* to free from obstruction.—*n.* deoppilā′tion.—*adj.* deopp′ilative. [Pfx. de- (2).]

deoxidate, dē-oks′i-dāt, *v.t.* to take oxygen from, or reduce.—Also deox′idise, -ize.—deoxidā′tion; deoxidi′ser, -z-, a substance that deoxidises.—*v.t.* deoxygenate (*dē-oks′ij-ən-āt*), to deprive of oxygen.—Also deox′ygenise, -ize.—*pfx.* deoxy-, containing less oxygen.—**deoxyribonucleic acids** (*dē-oks-i-rī'bō-nū-klē'ik*), nucleic acids containing deoxyribose (sugar), consisting of complex molecules, present in chromosomes of all plant and animal cells, and carrying in coded form instructions for passing on of hereditary characteristics—abbrev. DNA. [Pfx. de- (2).]

**depaint**, *di-pānt'*, (*Spens.*) *v.t.* to paint: depict. [Fr. *dépeindre*—L. *dēpingĕre*; see **depict**.]

**depart**, *di-pärt'*, *v.i.* to go away: to quit or leave: to die: to separate from one another (*obs.*).—*v.t.* (*obs.*) to separate, divide.—*n.* (*Shak.*; *Spens.*) departure, parting.—*ns.* **depart'er**; **depart'ing**; **depart'ure**, act of departing: a going away from a place: deviation: the distance in nautical miles made good by a ship due east or west: death.—**a new departure**, a change of purpose or method, a new course of procedure; **the departed**, the deceased. [Fr. *départir*—L. *dis-*, apart, and *partire* (*partiri*), to part, to divide.]

**department**, *di-pärt'mənt*, *n.* a part: a special or allotted function, sphere of activity, duty, or competence: a section of an administration, university, office of other organisation: a division of a country, esp. of France.—*adj.* **departmental** (*dē-pärt-ment'l*).—*v.t.* **department'-alise, -ize,** to form into separate departments: to deal with by allotting a specific share to different departments.—*n.* **department'alism,** too strict division of work among departments with little intercommunication.—*adv.* **department'ally.**—**department store** (orig. *U.S.*), a big shop selling a variety of goods in different departments. [Fr. *département*—*départir* (see **depart**).]

**depasture**, *di-päs'chər*, *v.t.* to eat bare: to put to pasture: to afford pasture for.—*v.i.* to graze. [Pfx. de- (2).]

**depauperise, -ize,** *di-pö'pər-iz*, *v.t.* to remove from the state of pauper.—*v.t.* **depau'perate**, to impoverish.—*adj.* impoverished. [Pfx. de- (2).]

**dépêche**, *dā-pesh*, (Fr.) dispatch, message.

**depeinct**, *di-pānt'*, (*Spens.*) *v.t.* to paint. [**depaint**.]

**depend**, *di-pend'*, *v.i.* to hang down: to be sustained by or connected with anything: to be pending: to rely: to rest.—*adj.* **depend'able**, that may be depended on.—*n.* **depend'ant** (also **-ent**), one who depends on another for support or otherwise: a hanger-on.—*adj.* **depend'ent** (also **-ant**), depending, relying, contingent, relative: awaiting settlement.—*ns.* **depend'ence** (rarely **-ance**), state of being dependent: reliance, trust: that on which one depends: a quarrel or duel pending; **depend'ency,** that which depends: connected consistency (*Shak.*): a foreign territory dependent on a country, a kind of subordinate colony without self-government: dependence (rarely; *Shak.* **depend'acie**, submissiveness).—*adj.* **depend'ing,** still undetermined.—*adv.* **depend'ingly.** [Fr. *dépendre*—L. *dēpendēre*—*dē*, from, and *pendēre*, to hang.]

**depersonalise, -ize,** *dē-pûr'sən-əl-iz*, *v.t.* to take away the characteristics of personality of. [Pfx. de- (2).]

**dephlegmate**, *di-fleg'māt*, (old chem.) *v.t.* to free from water: to concentrate, rectify.—*ns.* **dephlegmā'tion** (*dē-*); **dephlegmā'tor.** [Pfx. de- (2).]

**dephlogisticate**, *dē-flo-jis'ti-kāt*, *v.t.* to deprive of phlogiston.—**dephlogisticated air,** Priestley's name for oxygen. [Pfx. de- (2).]

**depict**, *di-pikt'*, *v.t.* .to paint carefully: to make a likeness of: to describe minutely.—*ns.* **depict'er, -or; depic'tion.**—*adj.* **depict'ive.** [L. *dēpingĕre*, *dēpictum*—*dē-*, inten., *pingĕre*, to paint.]

**depicture**, *di-pik'chər*, *v.t.* to picture: to paint: to represent.—*n.* depicting, representation. [Pfx. de- (3), and **picture** vb.]

**depilate**, *dep'i-lāt*, *v.t.* to remove the hair from.—*ns.* **depilā'tion,** removal or loss of hair; depila-

**tory** (*di-pil'ə-tər-i*), an application for removing superfluous hairs.—*adj.* possessing this quality. [L. *dēpilāre, -ātum*—*dē*, out, *pilus*, hair.]

**deplete**, *di-plēt'*, *v.t.* to empty, reduce, exhaust.—*n.* **deplē'tion**, the act of emptying or exhausting: the act of relieving congestion or plethora (*med.*).—*adjs.* **deplē'tive, deplē'tory.** [L. *dēplēre, dēplētum*, to empty, *dē-*, neg., *plēre*, to fill.]

**deplore**, *di-plōr', -plôr', v.t.* to feel or express deep grief for: to disapprove strongly of: to give up as hopeless (*obs.*).—*adj.* **deplor'able**, lamentable: sad: hopelessly bad.—*n.* **deplor'ableness.**—*adv.* **deplor'ably.**—*n.* **deplorā'tion** (*dep-, dēp-*), lamentation.—*adv.* **deplor'ingly.** [L. *dēplōrāre*—*dē-*, inten., *plōrāre*, to weep.]

**deploy**, *di-ploi', v.t.* to unfold: to open out or extend: to spread out and place strategically (any forces).—*v.i.* to open: to extend from column into line, as a body of troops.—*ns.* **deploy', deploy'ment.** [Fr. *déployer*—L. *dis-*, apart, and *plicāre*, to fold.]

**deplume**, *di-plōōm', v.t.* to take the plumes or feathers from.—*n.* **deplumā'tion** (*dē-*). [Pfx. de- (2).]

**depolarise, -ize,** *dē-pō'lər-iz, v.t.* to deprive of polarity.—*n.* **depolarisā'tion, -z-.** [Pfx. de- (2).]

**depone**, *di-pōn', v.t.* to lay down: to deposit: to testify upon oath.—*adj.* **depō'nent** (*gram.*), having a passive form but active signification (as if having laid aside the passive—really middle or reflexive—meaning).—*n.* a deponent verb: one who makes a deposition, esp. under oath, or whose written testimony is used as evidence in a court of justice. [L. *dēpōnēre*; pr.p. *dēpōnēns, -entis*—*dē*, down, *pōnēre*, to place, lay.]

**depopulate**, *dē-, di-pop'ū-lāt, v.t.* to overrun and lay waste (*obs.*): to deprive of population, to dispeople.—*v.i.* to become dispeopled.—*adj.* depopulated.—*ns.* **depopulā'tion**, act of depopulating: havoc: destruction; **depop'ulator.** [L. *dēpopulāri, -ātus*—*dē-*, inten., and *populāri*, to swarm over, to spread over a country, said of hostile people (L. *populus*)—hence to ravage, to destroy; later understood as to deprive of people.]

**deport**, *di-, dē-pōrt', -pôrt', v.t.* to transport, to exile: to expel (e.g. as an undesirable alien).—*n.* **deportā'tion.** [Fr. *déporter*—L. *dēportāre*—*dē-*, away, and *portāre, -ātum*, to carry.]

**deport**, *di-pōrt' -pôrt', v.t.* to behave (*refl.*).—*n.* **deport'ment**, behaviour: bearing: manners. [O.Fr. *deporter*—L. *dē-*, inten., *portāre*, to carry.]

**depose**, *di-pōz', v.t.* to remove from a high station: to degrade: to set down: to remove: to attest: to examine or put upon oath (*Shak.*).—*v.i.* to bear witness: to swear (*Shak.*).—*adj.* **depos'able.**—*n.* **depos'al.** [Fr. *déposer*—L. *dē*, from, *pausāre*, to pause, (late) to place.]

**deposit**, *di-poz'it, v.t.* to put or set down: to place: to lay: to lay up or past: to entrust: to lodge as a pledge: to lay down as a coating, bed, vein or the like:—*n.* that which is deposited or put down: an accumulation by sedimentation, precipitation, sublimation, or other natural means: something entrusted to another's care, esp. money put in a bank: a pledge: a bailment where one entrusts goods to another to be kept without recompense (in Scots law, **depositā'tion**): the state of being deposited.—*ns.* **depos'itary,** a person with whom anything is left for safe keeping: a guardian—sometimes **depos'itory.**—*adj.* **depos'itive.**—*ns.* **depos'itor;** **depos'itory,** a place where anything is deposited—sometimes **depos'itary.**—**depos'it-receipt,** a receipt for money deposited in a bank, etc. [L. *dēpositum*, placed—*dēpōnēre, dē*, down, and *pōnēre*, to place.]

**deposition**, *dēp-ə-zish'ən, n.* act of deposing: act of deponing: declaration, testimony taken authoritatively, to be used as a substitute for the production of the witness in open court: removal: act of depositing: what is deposited, sediment. [**deposit**; blended with root of depose.]

**depot, dépôt,** *dep'ō, di-pō', dā'pō* or *dē'pō, n.* a place of deposit: a storehouse: a military station where stores are kept and recruits trained: the headquarters of a regiment: the portion of a regiment left at home: a railway station (*U.S.*): a place where buses or tram-cars are kept. [Fr. *dépôt*—L. *dēpōnēre, -pŏsitum,* to put down, to place.]

**deprave,** *di-prāv', v.t.* to represent as bad (*obs.*): to make bad or worse: to corrupt.—*n.* **depravation** (*dep-rə-vā'shən*), act of depraving: state of being depraved: depravity.—*adj.* **deprāved',** corrupt.—*adv.* **deprāv'edly.**—*ns.* **deprāv'edness; deprāve'ment,** vitiation.—*adv.* **deprāv'ingly.**—*n.* **depravity** (*di-prav'i-ti*), a vitiated or corrupt state of moral character: extreme wickedness: corruption: the hereditary tendency of man toward sin (*theol.*): original sin (*theol.*). [L. *dēprāvāre* —*dē-,* inten., *prāvus,* bad.]

**deprecate,** *dep'ri-kāt, v.t.* to try to ward off by prayer: to desire earnestly the prevention or removal of: to invoke or beseech with a view to the averting or withholding of evil: to regret deeply: to argue or protest against.—*adj.* **dep'recable,** to be deprecated.—*n.* **depreca'tion,** act of deprecating, earnest prayer, esp. a special petition against some evil, in litanies.—*adv.* **dep'recatingly.**—*adjs.* **dep'recative, dep'recatory.**—*n.* **dep'recātor.** [L. *dēprecāri, -ātus*—*dē,* away, and *precāri,* to pray.]

**depreciate,** *di-prē'shi-āt, v.t.* to lower the worth of: to undervalue: to disparage.—*v.i.* to fall in value.—*n.* **deprecia'tion** (*s(h)i-ā'shən*), the falling of value: disparagement.—*adjs.* **deprē'ciative, deprē'ciatory,** tending to depreciate or lower.—*n.* **deprē'ciātor.** [L. *dēpretiāre, -ātum*—*dē,* down, and *pretium,* price.]

**depredate,** *dep'ri-dāt, v.t.* to plunder or prey upon: to rob: to lay waste: to devour.—*ns.* **depredā'tion,** act of plundering: state of being depredated: **dep'redātor.**—*adj.* **depredatory** (*di-pred'ət-ə-ri*). [L. *dēpraedāri, -ātus*—*dē-,* inten., and *praedāri*—*praeda,* plunder.]

**deprehend,** *dep-ri-hend',* (*obs.*) *v.t.* to catch, seize: to apprehend: to detect. [L. *dēpraehendēre*—*dē-,* aside, and *praehendēre,* to take.]

**depress,** *di-pres', v.t.* to press down: to let down: to lower: to cause to sink: to humble: to make subject: to dispirit or cast a gloom over.—*n.* **depress'ant,** that which lowers activity: a sedative: a chemical that causes a mineral to sink in flotation (*mining*).—Also *adj.*—*adj.* **depressed',** pressed down: lowered: flattened or slightly hollowed: humbled: dejected: dispirited.—*adj.* **depress'ing,** able or tending to depress.—*adv.* **depress'ingly.**—*ns.* **depression** (*di-presh'ən*), a falling in or sinking: a lowering: a region of low barometric pressure: a hollow: abasement: dejection: a reduced condition of trade and prosperity.—*adj.* **depress'ive,** tending to depress.—*n.* **depress'or,** an oppressor: that which lowers activity: a muscle that draws down: a surgical instrument for pressing down.—**depressed area,** a region suffering from depression of trade: a region of specially heavy unemployment. [L. *dēprimēre, -pressum*—*dē,* down, *premēre,* to press.]

**deprive,** *di-priv', v.t.* to dispossess: to keep out of enjoyment: to degrade (esp. a clergyman) from office: to bereave.—*adj.* **depriv'able.**—*ns.* **depriv'al, deprivātion** (*dep'ri-* or *dē'pri-*), act of depriving: state of being deprived: degradation from office: loss: bereavement: suffering from hardship.—*adj.* **depriv'ative.**—*n.* **deprive'ment.** [L.L. *dēprivāre,* to degrade—L. *dē,* from, and *privāre,* to deprive—*privus,* one's own.]

**de profundis,** *dē prə-fun'dis, dä pro-fōōn'dēs,* (L.) *adv.* out of the depths—Psalm cxxx.

**depth,** *depth, n.* deepness: the measure of deepness down or inwards: a deep place: intensity: the innermost or intensest part, as depth of winter: abstruseness: extent of sagacity and penetration. —*adj.* **depth'less,** having no depth: bottomless.— **depth'-bomb, -charge,** a powerful bomb that explodes under water (dropped over or near submarines).—**in depth,** extending far inwards: (of defence) consisting of several successive lines: extensive(ly) and thorough(ly); **out of one's depth,** in water where one cannot touch bottom, or too deep for one's safety: beyond one's understanding; **the depths,** the lowest pitch of humiliation and misery. [Not in O.E.; possibly O.N. *dӯpth*; or formed from **deep,** on analogy of **length,** etc.]

**depurate,** *dep'ū-rāt, di-pū'rāt, v.t.* to purify.— *adj.* and *n.* **dep'ūrant.**—*ns.* **depūrā'tion; dep'- ūrātor.**—*n.* and *adj.* **depurative** (*dep'ū-rā-tiv, di-pūr'ə-tiv*).—*adj.* **depū'ratory.** [L.L. *dēpūrāre, -ātum,* to purify—L. *dē-,* inten., and *pūrāre,* to purify—*pūrus,* pure.]

**depute,** *di-pūt', v.t.* to appoint or send as a substitute or agent: to send with a special commission: to make over (one's authority).—*adj.* (*dep'ūt*) in Scotland, appointed deputy (as in *sheriff-depute*—often simply *the depute*).—*n.* **deputation** (*dep-ū-tā'shən*), act of deputing: the person or persons deputed or appointed to transact business for another: a body of persons sent to state a case: the privilege of shooting game, or a document granting it, formerly given by the lord of a manor, nominally as to a gamekeeper.—*v.t.* **dep'ūtise, -ize,** to appoint as deputy. —*v.i.* to act as deputy.—*n.* **dep'ūty,** one deputed or appointed to act for another, esp. (*London*) for an alderman or (*U.S.*) for a sheriff: a delegate or representative, or substitute: a legislator, member of a chamber of deputies: one who attends to protective arrangements in a coalmine. [L. *dēputāre,* to prune, (later) to select.]

**deracialise, -ize,** *dē'rāsh'əl-īz, yə-liz, v.t.* to divest of racial character. [Pfx. **de-** (2) and **racial.**]

**deracinate,** *dē-ras'i-nāt, v.t.* to root up.—*adj.* **déraciné** (*dā-ras-ē-nä;* Fr.), uprooted. [Fr. *déraciner*—L. *dē,* from, L.L. *rādicina,* dim. of L. *rādix,* a root.]

**deraign.** See **darraigne.**

**derail,** *di-rāl', v.t.* to cause to leave the rails.—*v.i.* to go off the rails.—*ns.* **derail'er; derail'ment.** [Pfx. **de-** (2).]

**dérailleur (gear),** *dā-ra-yœr, n.* a variable bicycle-gear depending on a mechanism by means of which the chain can be transferred from one sprocket wheel to another of different size. [Fr. *dérailler,* to derail.]

**derange,** *di-rānj', v.t.* to put out of place or order: to disorder: to make insane.—*adj.* **deranged'**, disordered: insane.—*n.* **derange'ment,** disorder: insanity: obs. psychiatric term for psychosis. [Fr. *déranger*—*dé-* (L. *dis-*), asunder, *ranger,* rank.]

**derate,** *dē-rāt', v.t.* to relieve (wholly or partially) from local rates.—*n.* and *adj.* **derat'ing.** [Pfx. **de-** (2).]

**deration,** *dē-ra'shən, v.t.* to free from rationing. [Pfx. **de-** (2).]

**deray,** *di-rā',* (*obs.*) *v.t.* to derange.—*v.i.* to go wild.—*n.* tumult, disorder. [O.Fr. *desreer*—*des-,* neg., and *rei, roi,* order; see **array.**]

**Derby,** *där'bi, n.* a kind of porcelain made at *Derby:* a horse-race held annually on Epsom Downs (from *Derby* stakes, instituted by Earl of *Derby,* 1780): (*där'bi*) one run at Churchill Downs, Kentucky: any race attracting much interest, (or) a keen sporting contest, esp. one of local importance: (*dûr'bi*) (*U.S.*), a bowler hat: a strong type of boot.—**Derby dog,** a dog straying on a race-course: an intruder or an interruption (*fig.*); Derbyshire neck, a form of goitre; Derbyshire spar, fluorite.

**der-doing,** *dŭr'dōō'ing,* (*Spens.*) *adj.* doing daring deeds. [See derring-do.]

**dere, deare,** *dēr,* (*obs.*) *v.t.* to injure.—*n.* (*Spens.*) injury. [O.E. *derian.*]

**de règle,** *də regl',* (Fr.) *adj.* and *adv.* according to rule.

**derelict,** *der'i-likt, adj.* forsaken: abandoned, falling in ruins: neglectful of duty (chiefly *U.S.*). *n.* anything (esp. a ship) forsaken or abandoned. —*n.* **derelic'tion,** act of forsaking, unfaithfulness or remissness: state of being abandoned: land gained from the water by a change of water-line. [L. *dērelinquĕre, -lictum—dē-,* inten., *re-,* behind, and *linquĕre,* to leave.]

**dereligionise, -ize,** *dē-ri-lij'ən-iz,* to make irreligious. [Pfx. **de-** (2).]

**deride,** *di-rīd', v.t.* to laugh at: to mock.—*n.* **derid'er.**—*adj.* **derid'ingly.**—*n.* **derision** (*di-rizh'-ən*), act of deriding: mockery: a laughingstock.—*adjs.* **derisive** (*di-rīs'iv,* or *-riz'*), scoffing; **deris'ory,** scoffing: ridiculous.—*adv.* **deris'ively** (or *-riz'*).—*n.* **deris'iveness** (or *-riz'*). [L. *dērīdēre, -risum—dē-,* inten., and *ridēre,* to laugh.]

**de rigueur,** *də rē-gœr,* (Fr.) *adj.* and *adv.* required by strict etiquette, or by fashion, etc.

**derision, derisive,** etc. See deride.

**derive,** *di-rīv', v.t.* to conduct, draw, take, obtain, or receive (from a source or origin): to bring down (upon oneself; *Shak.*): to infer: to trace to an origin.—*v.i.* to descend or issue.—*adj.* **deriv'able.**—*adv.* **deriv'ably.**—*adj.* **derivate** (*der'i-vāt*), derived.—*n.* a derivative.—*n.* **derivā'tion,** act of deriving: a drawing off: the tracing of a word to its root: source: that which is derived: descent or evolution of man or animals.—*adj.* **derivā'tional.**—*n.* **derivā'tionist.**—*adj.* **derivative** (*di-riv'ə-tiv*), derived or taken from something else: not radical or original.—*n.* that which is derived: a word formed from another word.—*adv.* **deriv'atively.** [Fr. *dériver*—L. *dērīvāre—dē,* down, from, *rivus,* a river.]

**derm, dûrm,** *n.* the true skin—also **der'ma, der'-mis.**—*adjs.* **der'mal, dermat'ic, der'mic,** pertaining to the skin: consisting of skin.—*n.pl.* **Dermap'tera,** an order of insects with forewings, when present, in the form of firm elytra—the earwigs; —*ns.* **dermati'tis,** inflammation of the skin; **dermat'ogen** (*bot.*), the layer from which epidermis is formed at the growing-point; **dermatoglyph'ics,** skin patterns, esp. of the skin on the under-surfaces of the hands and feet: the science of the study of skin patterns; **dermatog'raphy,** anatomical description of the skin—also **dermog'raphy.**—*adjs.* **der'matoid,** of the form of skin: skin-like; **dermatolog'ical.**—*ns.* **dermatol'ogist; dermatol'ogy,** the branch of science that treats of the skin; **der'matophyte,** a parasitic fungus of the skin; **Dermop'tera,** an order of mammals, the flying lemurs, sometimes included in Insectivora. [Gr. *derma, -atos,* the skin.]

**dern.** See durn.

**dern, dearn,** *dûrn,* (*arch.* and *dial.*) *adj.* secret: hidden: dreadful (*Shak.*).—*n.* secrecy: hiding. —*adjs.* **dern'ful, dearn'ful,** solitary: mournful.— *advs.* **dern'ly, dearn'ly,** secretly: sorrowfully: grievously. [O.E. *dyrne, derne,* secret.]

**dernier,** *der-nyā,* (Fr.) *adj.* last.—**dernier cri** (*krē*), the last word (lit. cry), the latest fashion; **dernier ressort** (*res-sōr*), a last resort.

**derogate,** *der'ō-gāt, v.i.* to lessen by taking away: to detract. (*Shak.*) degenerate.—*adv.* **der'o-gately** (*Shak.*), in a derogatory manner.—*n.* **derogā'tion,** a taking from: detraction: depreciation.—*adv.* **derogatorily** (*di-rog'ə-tər-i-li*). —*n.* **derog'atoriness.**—*adj.* **derog'atory,** detracting: injurious. [L. *dērogāre, -ātum,* to repeal

part of a law—*dē,* down, from, and *rogāre,* to propose a law.]

**derrick,** *der'ik, n.* an arrangement for hoisting materials, by a boom stayed from a central post: a framework or tower over a borehole or the like.—*v.t.* to luff (the jib of a crane). [From *Derrick,* a 17th-century hangman.]

**derrière,** *der-yer, der'i-er,* (Fr.) *n.* the behind, buttocks.

**derring-do, derring do, doe,** *der'ing-dōō,* (*false* *archaic*) *n.* daring action.—*adj.* **der-do'ing.**—*n.* **derr'ing doo'er.** [Spenser mistook Lydgate's *dorryng do,* i.e. daring (to) do (misprinted *derrynge do*) for a noun.]

**derringer,** *der'in-jər, n.* a short American pistol. [Inventor's name.]

**Derris,** *der'is, n.* a tropical genus of papilionaceous plants whose roots yield an insecticide powder. [Gr. *derris,* a leather coat.]

**der tag,** *dār tähh, täg,* (Ger.) *n.* the day when the struggle begins (orig., in Germany, the day when a career of conquest by Germany was to begin).

**derth,** *dûrth,* (*Spens.*) *n.* Same as **dearth.**

**derv,** *dûrv, n.* diesel engine fuel oil. [From diesel engined road vehicle.]

**dervish,** *dûr'vish, n.* a member of one of numerous Mahommedan fraternities, professing poverty and leading an austere life. [Turkish *dervish*— Pers. *darvish,* a dervish—lit., a poor man.]

**désagrément,** *dāz-ag-rä-mä,* (Fr.) *n.* something disagreeable.

**desalinate,** *dē-sal'in-āt, v.t.* to remove salt from (esp. sea water).—*ns.* **desalinā'tion; desal'inator.** [Pfx. **de-** (2).]

**desalt,** *dē'sōlt', v.t.* to remove salt from.—*n.* **de'salt'ing.** [Pfx. **de-** (2).]

**descant,** *des'kant, n.* an accompaniment above and harmonising with the air: counterpoint (*obs.*): a discourse or disquisition under several heads.—*v.i.* **descant'** (*Shak. des'*), to sing a descant: to discourse at length: to comment. [O.N.Fr. *descant*—L. *dis-,* apart, and *cantus,* a song.]

**descend,** *di-send', v.i.* to climb down: to pass from a higher to a lower place or condition: to pass from general to particulars: to make an invasion: to be derived.—*v.t.* to go down upon, to traverse downwards.—*n.* **descend'ant,** one who descends, as offspring from an ancestor.—*adjs.* **descend'ed,** derived by descent; **descend'ent,** going down: proceeding from an ancestor; **descend'ible** (also **-able**), that may descend or be descended: capable of transmission by inheritance, heritable.— *adj.* **descend'ing.**—*n.* (*Shak.*) **lineage.**—*n.* **descen'sion.**—*adj.* **descen'sional.**—*n.* **descent',** act of descending: transmission by succession: motion or progress downward: slope: a raid or invasion: derivation from an ancestor: a generation, a degree in genealogy: descendants collectively.—**descent from the cross,** a picture representing Christ being taken down from the cross. [Fr. *descendre*—L. *descendĕre* —*dē,* down, *scandĕre,* to climb.]

**describe,** *di-skrīb', v.t.* to trace out or delineate: to give an account of.—*adj.* **describ'able.**—*ns.* **describ'er; description** (*di-skrip'shən*), act of describing: an account of anything in words: (loosely) sort, class, or kind.—*adj.* **descrip'tive,** containing description.—*adv.* **descrip'tively.**—*n.* **descrip'tiveness.** [L. *dēscrībĕre—dē,* down, *scrībĕre, scriptum,* to write.]

**descrive,** *di-skrīv',* (*obs.*) *v.t.* to describe. [O.Fr. *descrivre*—L. *dēscrībĕre.*]

**descry,** *di-skrī', v.t.* to reveal (*Spens.*): to discover by the eye: to espy:—*pr.p.* **descry'ing;** *pa.t.* and *pa.p.* **descried'.**—*n.* discovery: a thing discovered (*Shak.*). [App. two words: O.Fr. *descrire* for *descrivre*—L. *dēscrībĕre,* and O.Fr. *descrier, decryer,* proclaim, announce—*des-, de-,* and *crier,* to cry; cf. **describe, decry.**]

# desecrate

# desperate

desecrate, *des'i-krāt, v.t.* to divert from a sacred purpose: to profane.—*ns.* des'ecrater, -or; desecrā'tion, act of desecrating: profanation. [Coined on the analogy of consecrate—L. *dē*, from. L. *dēsecrāre* meant consecrate.]

desegregate, *dē-seg'ri-gāt, v.t.* to abolish racial segregation in (e.g. a university).—*n.* desegregā'tion. [Pfx. de- (2).]

desensitise, -ize, *dē-sen'sit-īz, v.t.* and *v.i.* to make or become less sensitive. [Pfx. de- (2).]

deserpidine, *di-zûrp'i-din, dēn, n.* a synthetic sedative drug of which the natural base is *Rauwolfia serpentina.*

desert, *di-zûrt', n.* that which is deserved: claim to reward: merit.—*adj.* desert'less, without merit. [O.Fr., pa.p. of *deservir;* see deserve.]

desert, *di-zûrt', v.t.* to leave: to forsake.—*v.i.* to run away: to quit a service, as the army, without permission.—*ns.* desert'er, one who deserts or quits a service without permission; deser'tion, act of deserting: state of being deserted: wilful abandonment of a legal or moral obligation.— desert the diet, (*Scots law*) to give up a charge. [L. *dēserēre, dēsertum—dē-*, neg., and *serēre,* to bind.]

desert, *dez'ərt, adj.* deserted: desolate: uninhabited: uncultivated.—*n.* a desolate or barren tract: a waste: a solitude.—desert pea, an Australian glory-pea (Clianthus) with purple-spotted scarlet flower; desert rat, (from the divisional sign, a jerboa) a soldier of the British 7th Armoured Division with service in North Africa in 1941-42. [O.Fr. *desert—L. dēsertum, dēserēre,* to desert, unbind.]

deserve, *di-zûrv', v.t.* to be entitled to by merit: to merit.—*v.i.* to be worthy of reward.—*adj.* deserved'.—*adv.* deserv'edly.—*adj.* deserv'ing, worthy.—*adv.* deserv'ingly, according to desert: justly. [O.Fr. *deservir—L. dēservīre—dē,* inten., *servīre,* to serve.]

desexualise, -ize, *dē-seks'ū-əl-īz, v.t.* to deprive of sexual character or quality. [Pfx. de- (2).]

déshabillé. Same as dishabille.

desiccate, *des'i-kāt,* formerly *di-sik'āt, v.t.* to dry up: to preserve by drying.—*v.i.* to grow dry.— *adjs.* des'iccant, desiccative (*di-sik'ə-tiv*), drying: having the power of drying.—*ns.* a drying agent. —*ns.* desiccā'tion, the act or process of drying up: state of being dried up; des'iccātor, apparatus for drying. [L. *dēsiccāre, -ātum,* to dry up—*dē-,* inten., *siccus,* dry.]

desiderate, *di-sid'ər-āt, v.t.* to long for or earnestly desire: to want or miss.—*n.* desiderā'tion, the act of desiderating: the thing desiderated.—*adj.* desid erative, implying desire (as in *desiderative verb*).—*ns.* desiderā'tum, something desired or much wanted:—*pl.* desiderā'ta; desiderium (*des-i-dē'ri-əm*), longing: grief for what is lost. [L. *dēsiderāre, -ātum,* to long for; *dēsidērium, dē-,* inten., *siderāre,* to long for, in sense of 'contemplate a star.' A doublet of desire.]

design, *di-zīn', v.t.* to indicate (*Shak.; Spens.*): to draw in: to form a plan of: to contrive: to intend: to set apart or destine.—*n.* a drawing or sketch: a plan in outline: a plan or scheme formed in the mind: plot: intention.—*adj.* design'able.—*v.t.* designate (*dez'ig-nāt*), to mark out so as to make known: to show: to name: to be a name for: to appoint or nominate.— *adj.* nominated to but not yet in possession of an office.—*ns.* designā'tion, a showing or pointing out: name: title: appellation descriptive of occupation, standing, etc.: nomination to office; des'ignātor.—*adv.* designedly (*di-zīn'id-li*), by design: intentionally.—*n.* design'er, one who furnishes designs or patterns: a draughtsman: a plotter.—*adjs.* design'ful, full of design; design'ing, artful: scheming: working secretly for self-interest.—*n.* the art of making designs or patterns.—*adj.* design'less.—*n.* design'ment, the design or sketch of a work: intention, purpose,

enterprise (*Shak.*).—design engineer, a designer in engineering.—argument from design, the argument for the existence of God from evidence of design in creation; by design, intentionally. [Fr. *désigner*—L. *dēsignāre, -ātum—dē-,* off, and *signum,* a mark.]

desilver, *dē-sil'vər, v.t.* to remove silver from— also desil'verise, -ize.—*n.* desilverisā'tion, -z-. [Pfx. de- (2).]

desine (*Spens.*). Same as design.

desinent, *des'in-ənt, adj.* terminal.—*n.* des'inence, ending. [L. *dēsinēns, -entis,* pr.p. of *dēsinēre,* to leave off—*dē,* from, *sinēre,* to allow.]

desipient, *di-sip'i-ənt, adj.* playing the fool: trifling.—*n.* desip'ience. [L. *dēsipiēns, -entis,* pr.p. of *dēsipēre—dē-,* neg., *sapēre,* to be wise.]

desire, *di-zīr', v.t.* to long for: to wish for: to ask: to regret the loss of (*B.*).—*v.i.* to be in a state of desire.—*n.* an earnest longing or wish: a prayer or request: the object desired: lust.— *adj.* desir'able, worthy of desire: to be approved of: pleasing: agreeable.—*n.* a desirable person or thing.—*ns.* desir'ableness, desirabil'ity.—*adv.* desir'ably.—*adj.* desir'eless.—*n.* desir'er.—*adj.* desir'ous, full of desire: wishful: eager: desirable (*obs.*).—*adv.* desir'ously.—*n.* desir'ousness. [Fr. *désirer*—L. *dēsidērāre.*]

desist, *di-zist', -sist', v.i.* to leave off.—*ns.* desist'-ance, -ence. [L. *dēsistēre—dē,* away from, and *sistēre,* to cause to stand.]

desk, *desk, n.* a sloping or flat table for writing or reading, often fitted with drawers, etc.: a shut-up writing-box: a pulpit or lectern: a music-stand: in an orchestra, esp. among strings, (players in) a seating position determined by rank (e.g. the *first desk*).—desk'-work, work done at a desk, as by a clerk or author. [M.E. *deske*—L. *discus*— Gr. *diskos;* see dish, disk.]

desman, *des'mən, n.* a Russian aquatic insectivore with long snout and musk-glands: a kindred Pyrenean species. [Sw. *desman,* musk.]

desmid, *des'mid, n.* one of a group of microscopic algae, unicellular or strung in chains.—*ns.* desmine (*des'mēn, -min*), the mineral stilbite occurring in bundles; Desmōd'ium, the telegraph-plant genus.—*adj.* des'moid, arranged in bundles. [Gr. *desmos,* a chain, *desmē,* a bundle, *eidos,* form.]

désobligeante, *dāz-ob-lēzh-āt, n.* a carriage for one. [Fr., unaccommodating.]

desolate, *des'ō-lāt, v.t.* to make lonely or forlorn: to make joyless: to deprive of inhabitants: to lay waste.—*adj.* (*-lit*) comfortless: dreary: forlorn: lonely: destitute of inhabitants: laid waste.—*adv.* des'olately.—*ns.* des'olateness; de'-solāter, -or; desolā'tion, waste: destruction: a place desolated.—*adj.* des'olatory. [L. *dēsōlāre, -ātum—dē-,* inten., and *sōlāre,* to make alone— *sōlus,* alone.]

désorienté, *dāz-or-ē-ā-tā,* (Fr.) having lost one's bearings, confused.

desorption, *dē-sörp'shən. n.* release from an adsorbed state.—*v.t.* desorb'. [Pfx. de- (2).]

despair, *di-spār', v.i.* to be without hope.—*n.* hopelessness: that which causes despair.—*adj.* despair'ful (*Spens.*).—*adj.* despair'ing, apt to despair: full of despair.—*adv.* despair'ingly. [O.Fr. *desperer*—L. *dēspērāre, -ātum—dē-,* neg., and *spērāre,* to hope.]

despatch. Same as dispatch.

desperado, *des-per-ä'dō, des-pā'dō, n.* a desperate fellow: one reckless of danger: a wild ruffian:— *pl.* despera'do(e)s. [Old Sp. (mod. *desesperado*), —L. *dēspērātus.*]

desperate, *des'pər-it, adj.* in a state of despair: hopeless: beyond hope: despairingly reckless: (loosely) furious: extremely bad.—*adv.* des'perately.—*ns.* desperateness, desperā'tion, state of despair: despairing: disregard of danger: fury. [See despair.]

Neutral vowels in unaccented syllables: *el'ə-mənt;* for certain sounds in foreign words, see p. viii

**despicable**, *des'pik-ə-bl, -pik'*, *adj.* deserving to be despised: contemptible: worthless.—*ns.* **despicabil'ity**, **despicableness.**—*adv.* **despicably.** [See **despise.**]

**despight**, *di-spīt'*, an old spelling of **despite.**

**despise**, *di-spīz'*, *v.t.* to look down upon with contempt.—*adj.* **despis'able.**—*ns.* **despis'al**, contempt; **despis'edness** (*Milt.*); **despis'er.** [O.Fr. *despire* (*despis-*)—L. *dēspicĕre*—*dē*, down, *specĕre*, to look.]

**despite**, *di-spīt'*, *n.* a looking down with contempt: violent malice or hatred.—*prep.* in spite of: notwithstanding.—*adj.* **despite'ful.**—*adv.* **despite'-fully.**—*n.* **despite'fulness.**—*adj.* **despiteous** (*dis-pit'i-əs; Spens.*). [O.Fr. *despit* (mod. *dépit*)—L. *dēspectus*—*dēspicĕre*; see **despise.**]

**despoil**, *di-spoil'*, *v.t.* to plunder completely: to strip: to bereave: to rob.—*ns.* **despoil'er**; **despoil'ment.** [O.Fr. *despoiller* (mod. *dépouiller*; see next).]

**despoliation**, *di-spōl-i-ā'shən*, *n.* despoiling. [L. *dēspoliāre*—*dē-*, inten., and *spolium*, spoil.]

**despond**, *di-spond'*, *v.i.* to be wanting in hope, to be dejected.—*n.* (*Bunyan*) despondency.—*ns.* **despond'ence**, **despond'ency.**—*adj.* **despond'ent.**—*adv.* **despond'ently.**—*n.* and *adj.* **despond'ing.**—*adv.* **despond'ingly.** [L. *dēspondēre*, to promise, to devote, to resign, to despond—*dē*, away, and *spondēre*, to promise.]

**despot**, *des'pot, -pət*, *n.* one invested with absolute power: a tyrant.—*n.* **des'potat(e)**, a territory governed by a despot.—*adjs.* **despot'ic, -al**, pertaining to or like a despot: having absolute power: tyrannical.—*adv.* **despot'ically.**—*ns.* **despot'icalness**; **des'potism**, absolute power: a state governed by a despot; **despotoc'racy**, government by a despot. [O.Fr. *despot*—Gr. *despotēs*, a master.]

**despumate**, *di-spū'māt*, or *des'pū-māt*, *v.i.* to throw off impurities in foam or scum.—*v.t.* to skim.—*n.* **despumā'tion.** [L. *dēspūmāre, -ātum*—*dē-*, off, and *spūma*, foam.]

**desquamate**, *des'kwə-māt*, *v.i.* to scale off.—*n.* **desquamā'tion**, a scaling off: the separation of the cuticle or skin in scales.—*adjs.* **desquamative** (*di-skwam'ə-tiv*), **desquam'atory.** [L. *dēsquāmāre, -ātum*—*dē*, off, and *squā.na*, a scale.]

**desse**, *des*, (*Spens.*) *n.* a desk. [**dais.**]

**dessert**, *diz-ûrt'*, *n.* a final course of fruits, pudding, or other sweet.—**dessert'-serv'ice**, the dishes used for dessert; **dessert'spoon**, a spoon smaller than a tablespoon and larger than a teaspoon; **dessert'spoon'ful.** [O.Fr. *dessert, desservir*, to clear the table—*des-* (L. *dis-*), away, and *servir*, to serve—L. *servire.*]

**dessiatine, dessyatine, desyatin**, *des'yə-tēn*, *n.* a Russian measure of land, 2·7 English acres (about 1·1 hectares). [Russ. *desyatina*, a measure of land, a tenth; *desyati*, ten.]

**destine**, *des'tin*, *v.t.* to ordain or appoint to a certain use or state: to fix: to doom—also **des'tinate** (*obs.*).—*ns.* **destinā'tion**, the purpose or end to which anything is destined or appointed: end: purpose: design: fate: place to which one is going; **des'tiny**, the purpose or end to which any person or thing is appointed: unavoidable fate: necessity. [Fr. *destiner*—L. *dēstināre*—*dē-*, inten., and root of *stāre*, to stand.]

**destitute**, *des'ti-tūt*, *adj.* left alone, forsaken (*obs.*): in utter want: entirely lacking in (with *of*).—*v.t.* (*obs.*) to forsake: to deprive.—*n.* **destitu'tion**, the state of being destitute: deprivation of office: poverty. [L. *dēstituĕre, -ūtum*—*dē-*, away, and *statuĕre*, to place.]

**destrier**, *des'tri-ər, des-trēr'*, (*arch.*) *n.* a warhorse. [Fr.,—L. *dextrārius*, led by the (squire's) right hand.]

**destroy**, *di-stroi'*, *v.t.* to unbuild or pull down: to overturn: to ruin: to put an end to:—*pr.p.*

**destroy'ing**; *pa.t.* and *pa.p.* **destroyed'.**—*n.* **destroy'er**, a person or thing that destroys: a torpedo-boat destroyer. [O.Fr. *destruire* (Fr. *détruire*)—L. *dēstruĕre, dēstructum*—*dē-*, down, and *struĕre*, to build.]

**destruction**, *di-struk'shən*, *n.* act or process of destroying: overthrow: physical or moral ruin: death: a cause of destruction.—*v.t.* **destruct'**, to destroy a rock... or missile in flight.—*adj.* **destruc'tible**, liat le to be destroyed.—*ns.* **destructibil'ity, destruc'tibleness.**—*adj.* **destruc'tional.**—*n.* **destruc'tionist**, one engaged in destruction: one who believes in the final annihilation of the damned.—*adj.* **destruc'tive**, causing or concerned with destruction: mischievous.—*n.* a destroying agent.—*adv.* **destruc'tively.**—*ns.* **destruc'tiveness**; **destruc'tivist**, a representative of destructive principles; **destructiv'ity** (*dē-*); **destruc'tor** (*di-*), a destroyer: a furnace for burning up refuse. [L. *dēstruĕre, -structum*; see **destroy.**]

**desuetude**, *di-sū'i-tūd, des'wi-tūd*, *n.* disuse: discontinuance. [L. *dēsuētūdō*—*dēsuētum, dēsuēscĕre*—*dē*, neg., and *suēscĕre*, to become used.]

**desulphur**, *dē-sul'fər*, *v.t.* to remove sulphur from—also **desul'phūrāte, desul'phūrise, -ize.**—*n.* **desulphūrā'tion.** [Pfx. de- (2).]

**desultory**, *des'əl-tar-i*, *adj.* jumping from one thing to another: without rational or logical connection: rambling: hasty: loose.—*adv.* **des'ultorily.**—*n.* **des'ultoriness.** [L. *dēsultōrius—dēsultor*, a vaulter, *dēsilīre, -sultum*, to leap—*dē*, from, and *salīre*, to jump.]

**desyne** (*Spens.*). Same as **design.**

**detach**, *di-tach'*, *v.t.* to unfasten: to take away or separate: to withdraw: to send off on special service.—*v.i.* to separate.—*adj.* **detach'able.**—*adj.* **detached'**, unconnected: separate: aloof: free from care, passion, ambition, and worldly bonds.—*adv.* **detach'edly.**—*ns.* **detach'edness**; **detach'ment**, state of being detached: that which is detached, as a body of troops. [Fr. *détacher*—O.Fr. pfx. *des-* (L. *dis-*), apart, and root of **attach.**]

**detail**, *di-tāl'*, *v.t.* to relate minutely: to enumerate: to set apart for a particular service.—*v.i.* to give details about anything.—*n.* (*dē'tāl*, also *di-tāl'*) a small part: an item: a particular account: (chiefly *mil.*) a small body set apart for special duty.—*adj.* **detailed**, giving full particulars: exhaustive.—**in detail**, circumstantially, point by point: piecemeal. [Fr. *détailler*—*de-*, inten., and *tailler*, to cut.]

**detain**, *di-tān'*, *v.t.* to hold back: to withhold: to stop: to keep: to keep in custody.—*n.* (*Spens.*) **detention.**—*ns.* **detain'ee**, a person kept in custody; **detain'er**, one who detains: the holding of what belongs to another (*law*): a warrant to a sheriff to keep in custody a person already in confinement; **detain'ment**, detention. [O.Fr. *detenir*—L. *dētinēre*; see **detent.**]

**detect**, *di-tekt'*, *v.t.* to uncover, expose (*obs.*): to accuse (*Shak.*): to discover: discern: to find out (esp. something elusive or secret).—*adjs.* **detect'able, -ible.**—*n.* **detec'tion**, discovery of something hidden or not easily observed: state of being found out.—*adj.* **detect'ive**, employed in or concerned with detection.—*n.* a policeman, usually not in uniform, or other person (*private detective*) who investigates cases of crime or watches behaviour of suspected persons.—*ns.* **detect'ivist**, a writer of detective fiction; **detect'-ōphone**, a secret telephone for eavesdropping; **detec'tor**, one who detects: an apparatus for detecting something, as tampering with a lock, pressure of electric currents, of electric waves.—**detective story**, one in which clues to the detection of a criminal are set forth and unravelled. [L. *dētegĕre, -tēctum*—*dē-*, neg., *tegĕre*, to cover.]

**detent**, *di-tent'*, *n.* that which checks motion: a catch, esp. for regulating the striking of a clock.

**—n. deten'tion**, act of detaining: state of being detained: confinement, or restriction of liberty, esp. of a political prisoner, a military offender, a pupil out of school hours: delay.—**detention centre**, formerly, a place of confinement for young offenders from 14 to 20 years old for periods of up to 6 months. [L. dētinēre, dētentum—dē, from tenēre, to hold.]

**détente**, dä-tät, (Fr.) relaxation of strained relations (esp. between countries).

**détenu**, dā-tə-nü, (Fr.) a prisoner, esp. a political prisoner in India:—fem. **détenue**.

**deter**, di-tûr', v.t. to frighten from: to hinder or prevent:—pr.p. **deterr'ing**; pa.t. and pa.p. **deterred'**.—n. **deter'ment**.—adj. **deterrent** (di-ter'-ənt), serving to deter.—n. anything that deters: specif., a nuclear weapon. [L. dēterrēre—dē, from, terrēre, to frighten.]

**deterge**, di-tûrj', v.t. to wipe off: to cleanse (as a wound).—ns. **deterg'ence, deterg'ency**.—adj. **deterg'ent**, cleansing: purging.—n. that which cleanses: a cleansing agent, as an abrasive, a solvent or mixture of solvents, and certain water-soluble oils, esp. (commonly) a soapless cleanser. [L. dētergēre, dētersum—dē, off, and tergēre, to wipe.]

**deteriorate**, di-tē'ri-ə-rāt, v.t. to make worse.—v.i. to grow worse.—ns. **detēriorā'tion**, the act of making worse: the process of growing worse; **detēriorā'tionist**, a believer in deterioration.—adj. **detē'riorātive**.—ns. **detē'riorism**, the doctrine that the world grows worse; **detēriority** (-or'i-ti; obs.), worseness. [L. dēteriōrāre, -ātum, to make worse—dēterior, worse—dē, down.]

**determine**, dē-tûr'min, v.t. to put terms or bounds to: to limit: to fix or settle: to define: to decide: to resolve: to cause to resolve: to put an end to. —v.i. to come to a decision: to come to an end: to cease to exist (Shak.): to take part in a dispute, esp. in completing the degree of bachelor of arts (obs.).—n. **determinabil'ity**.—adj. **deter'minable**, capable of being determined, decided, or finished. —n. **deter'minableness**.—adv. **deter'minably**.—n. **deter'minacy** (-ə-si).—adj. **deter'minant**, serving to determine.—n. that which serves to determine: the sum of all the products got by taking one from each row and column of a square block of quantities, each product being reckoned positive or negative according as an even or an odd number of transpositions reduces it to the order of the rows (or of the columns)—used for the solution of equations and other purposes (math.): a hypothetical unit in the germ-plasm determining the course of development of a cell: a determining candidate for the B.A. degree (obs.). —adj. **deter'mināte**, determined or limited: fixed: decisive: cymose (bot.).—v.t. (Shak.) to determine.—adv. **deter'minately**.—n. **determinā'tion**, the act of determining: condition of being determined: that which is determined or resolved on: end: direction to a certain end: resolution: fixedness of purpose: decision of character.— adj. **deter'minātive**, that determines, limits, or defines.—n. in hieroglyphics an additional sign attached to a word as a guide to its meaning.— adj. **deter'mined**, ascertained: fixed: firm in purpose: resolute.—adv. **deter'minedly**.—n. **deter'minism**, the doctrine that all things, including the will, are determined by causes—the converse of free-will: necessitarianism.—n. **deter'minist**. —adj. **determinis'tic**. [L. dētermināre, -ātum —dē-, intens., and terminus, a boundary.]

**deterrent**. See **deter**.

**detersion**, di-tûr'shən, n. act of cleansing.—adj. and n. **deter'sive**, detergent. [See **deterge**.]

**detest**, di-test', v.t. to hate intensely.—adj. **detest'able** (Spens. and Shak. dē'), worthy of being detested: extremely hateful: abominable.—n. **detest'ableness**.—adv. **detest'ably**.—n. **detestā'tion** (dē-tes-tā'shən), extreme hatred. [Fr.,—L.

dētestārī—dē-, inten., and testārī, to call to witness, execrate—testis, a witness.]

**dethrone**, di-thrōn', v.t. to remove from a throne. —ns. **dethrone'ment; dethrōn'er; dethrōn'ing**. [Pfx. de- (2).]

**detinue**, det'in-ü, (law) n. wrongful detention of property. [O.Fr. detenue, fem. pa.p. of detenir; see **detain**.]

**detonate**, det'ō-nāt or dēt'ō-nāt, v.t. and v.i. to explode or cause to explode rapidly and loudly: in an internal-combustion engine, to explode by spontaneous combustion with a hammering sound (pinking or knock).—ns. **detonā'tion**, an explosion with report: knock; **det'onātor**, a substance that detonates: a substance or contrivance whose explosion initiates that of another explosive. [L. dētonāre, -ātum—dē, down, and tonāre, to thunder.]

**detort**, di-tört', v.t. to distort: to untwist: to twist the other way.—ns. **detor'sion, detor'tion**. [L. dētorquēre, dētortum; dē, away, also neg., and torquēre, to twist.]

**detour**, dē', dā'tōōr. di-tōōr', n. a winding: a circuitous way.—Also v.t. and v.i. [Fr. dé- (L. dis-). asunder, and tour, turning.]

**detoxicate**, dē-toks'i-kāt, **detoxify**, i-fī, vs.t. to rid of poison or the effects of it.—n. **detoxica'tion**, a substance that detoxicates.—Also adj.—ns. **detoxicā'tion, detoxifica'tion**. [Pfx. de- (2).]

**detract**, di-trakt' v.t. to take away, abate: to defame.—v.i. to take away reputation (with from): to reduce in degree: diminish.—n. **detract'or**:— fem. **detract'ress**.—n. and adj. **detract'ing**.— adv. **detract'ingly**.—n. **detrac'tion**, depreciation: slander.—adjs. **detract'ive, detract'ory**, tending to detract: derogatory. [L. dētrahēre—dē, from, trahēre, tractum, to draw.]

**detrain**, dē-trān', v.t. to set down out of a railway train.—v.i. to alight from a train.—n. **detrain'-ment**. [Pfx. de- (2).]

**détraqué** (fem. **détraquée**), dā-trä-kā, n. a person who is deranged. [Fr., upset, out of order.]

**detriment**, det'ri-mənt, n. diminution: damage: loss.—adj. **detrimental** (-ment'l).—n. a suitor undesirable owing to lack of means or other defect: one whose presence lessens the chances of a good match. [L. dētrimentum—dē, off, and terēre, trītum, to rub.]

**detritus**, di-trī'təs, n. a mass of substance gradually worn off solid bodies: an aggregate of loosened fragments, esp. of rock.—adj. **detri'tal**.—n. **detrition** (di-trish'ən), wearing away. [L. dētrītus, worn—dē, off, and terēre, trītum, to rub.]

**de trop**, də trō, (Fr.) superfluous: in the way.

**detrude**, di-trōōd', v.t. to thrust down.—n. **detru'-sion**. [L. dētrūdēre—dē, down, trūdēre, to thrust.]

**detruncate**, di-trung'kāt, v.t. to cut short: to lop: to mutilate.—n. **detruncā'tion** (dē-). [L. dētruncāre, -ātum—dē, off, truncāre, to lop.]

**detumescence**, dē-tū-mes'əns, n. diminution of swelling—opp. to intumescence. [Pfx. de- (2).]

**deuce**, dūs, n. a card or die with two spots: a situation ('forty all') in which one side must gain two successive points to win the game, or ('five all', 'games all') two successive games to win the set (lawn-tennis).—**deuce'-ace**, a throw of two dice turning up deuce and ace: bad luck. [Fr. deux, two—L. duōs, accus. of duo, two.]

**deuce**, dūs, n. the devil—in exclamatory phrases.— adj. **deuced** (dū'sid); or dūst), devilish: excessive. —adv. confoundedly.—Also **deuc'edly**. [Prob. from the **deuce** (see foregoing), the lowest throw at dice.]

**deus**, dē'əs, dā'ōōs, (L.) god.—**Deus avertat** (a-vûr'tat, ä-wer'tat), God forbid; **Deus det** (det), God grant; **deus ex machina** (usu. eks mak'in-a, sometimes mə-shē'na), a god brought on the stage by a mechanical device: a contrived and inartistic solution of a difficulty in a plot; **Deus vobiscum** (vō-bis'kəm, wō-bēs'kōōm), God be with you; **Deus vult** (*vult*, wōōlt), God wills it (the Crusaders' cry).

**deuter(o)-**, *dū-tər(-ō)-*. in composition, second, secondary.—*ns.* **deuterag′onist**, the second actor in a Gr. drama; **deuterium** (*-tē′ri-əm*), heavy nydrogen, an isotope of hydrogen of double mass.—*adj.* **deuterocanon′ical** (Gr. *kanōn*, rule), pertaining to a second canon of inferior authority —the O.T. Apocrypha and the N.T. Antilegomena.—*ns.* **deuterog′amy** (Gr. *gamos*, marriage), second marriage, esp. of the clergy, after the death of the first wife; **deuterog′amist**, one who allows or practises it; **deu′teron**, the nucleus of heavy hydrogen, of mass 2, carrying unit positive charge; **Deuteronomy** (*-on′ə-mi*, or *dū′*; Gr. *nomos*, law), the fifth book of the Pentateuch, containing a repetition of the decalogue and laws given in Exodus.—*adjs.* **Deuteronom′ic**, **-al**.—*ns.* **Deuteron′omist**, the author of the book of Deuteronomy or part of it; **deuteros′copy** (Gr. *skopiā*, a look-out), a second view or meaning (*obs.*): second sight.—*adj.* **deuteroscop′ic**. [Gr. *deuteros*, *-ā*, *-on*, second.]

**deuton**, *dū′ton*, older form of **deuteron**.

**Deutzia**, *dūt′si-ə*. or *doit′si-ə*, *n.* a genus of saxifragaceous plants with panicles of white flowers, introduced from China and Japan. [After Jan *Deutz*, 18th-cent. Dutch naturalist.]

**Deuxième Bureau**, *də-zyem bü-rō*, (Fr.) the French Department of Military Intelligence.

**deva**, *dā′vä*, (*Hindu myth.*) *n.* a god: a good spirit. [Sans. *deva*, a shining one, a god.]

**devall**, *di-völ′*, *v.i.* to sink, decline (*obs.*): to cease (*Scot.*).—*n.* (*Scot.*) a stop. [Fr. *dévaler*—L. *dē-*, down, *vallis*, a valley.]

**devalue**, *dē-val′ū*, *v.t.* to reduce the value of.—Also *v.i.* (esp. of currency).—*vs.t.* **deval′orise**, **-ize**, **devalu′ate**.—*ns.* **devalōrisā′tion**, **-ization**, **devaluā′tion**. [Pfx. **de-** (2).]

**devanagari**, *dā-və-nä′gə-ri*, *n.* the character in which Sanskrit is usually written and printed: the official script for Hindi: used also for other Indian languages.—Also *cap.* [Sans. *devanāgari*, town-script of the gods; see **nagari**.]

**devastate**, *dev′əs-tāt*, *v.t.* to lay waste, plunder.—*adj.* **dev′astating**, ravaging: (*coll.*) overpoweringly effective.—*adv.* **dev′astatingly**.—*ns.* **devastā′tion**, act of devastating: state of being devastated: havoc: waste of property by an executor; **dēvastā′vit** (L., has wasted), a writ lying against an executor for devastation: the offence of devastation. [L. *dēvastāre*, *-ātum*—*dē-*, inten., *vastāre*, to lay waste.]

**develop** (earlier also **-e**), *di-vel′əp*, *v.t.* to unroll: to lay open by degrees: to free from integuments or that which envelops: to bring out what is latent or potential in: to bring to a more advanced or more highly organised state: to work out the potentialities of: to elaborate: to cause to grow or advance: to evolve: to make more available: to exploit the natural resources of (a region): to build on or prepare for building on (land): to bring into a position useful in attack (*chess*): to disclose: to express in expanded form (*math.*): to unroll into a plane surface: to render visible the image on a negative by the use of chemicals (*phot.*).—*v.i.* to open out: to evolve: to advance through successive stages to a higher, more complex, or more fully grown state:—*pr.p.* **devel′oping**; *pa.t.* and *pa.p.* **devel′oped**.—*adjs.* **devel′opable**; **devel′oped**.—*ns.* **devel′oper**, one who develops: a reagent for developing photographs: an apparatus for developing muscles; **develop′ment**, the act or process of developing: state of being developed: a gradual unfolding or growth: evolution: the expression of a function in the form of a series (*math.*): elaboration of a theme, or that part of a movement in which this occurs (*mus.*): new situations that emerge.—*adj.* **de-**

**velopment′al**, pertaining to development.—*adv.* **development′ally.**—**development area**, a region of heavy unemployment where new industry is given official encouragement. [Fr. *développer*, opposite to *envelopper*, of obscure origin.]

**devest**, *di-vest′*, *v.t.* to undress (*Shak.*): to alienate (*law*): to take off: to strip. [A form of **divest**.]

**deviate**, *dē′vi-āt*, *v.i.* to go from the way: to turn aside from a certain course: to diverge, differ, from a standard, mean value, etc.: to err.—*v.t.* to cause to diverge.—*n.* (*psych.*) one who deviates much from the normal.—*adj.* **dē′viant**, which deviates from the norm.—Also *n.*—*ns.* **dēviā′tion**; **dēviā′tionism**, **dēviā′tionist**, a communist whose doctrine deviates from the strictly orthodox; **dē′viātor.**—**deviation of the compass**, departure of the mariner's compass from the magnetic meridian, owing to the ship's magnetism or other local causes; **standard deviation**, the square root of the variance of a number of observations. [L. *dēviāre*, *-ātum*—*dē*, from, *via*, a way.]

**device**, *di-vīs′*, *n.* that which is devised or designed: contrivance: power of devising: an emblem (*her.*): a motto: a conceit (*obs.*): a masque (*obs.*).—*adj.* **device′ful** (*Spens.*), full of devices. [O.Fr. *devise*; see **devise**.]

**devil**, *dev′l*, *-il*, *n.* an evil spirit: (*cap.*) the supreme spirit of evil: wicked person: reckless, lively person: (usu. pitying) a fellow: an animal, thing, problem, difficult to deal with: one who excels or exceeds in anything: a printer's devil: a drudge (esp. legal or literary): a firework: a grilled or highly seasoned dish: a dust-storm: fighting spirit: a plumber's portable furnace: a machine of various kinds, esp. for tearing: used as a mild oath, an expression of impatience, irritation, etc., or a strong negative.—*v.t.* to season highly and broil.—*v.i.* to perform another man's drudgery:—*pr.p.* **dev′illing**; *pa.t.* and *pa.p.* **dev′-illed.**—*ns.* **dev′ildom**; **dev′iless**; **dev′iling**, **dev′ling**, a young devil: a swift (*dial.*).—*adj.* **dev′-ilish**, fiendish, malignant: very bad.—*adv.* (often *dev′lish*; *coll.*) very, exceedingly.—*adv.* **dev′il-ishly.**—*ns.* **dev′ilism**; **dev′ilkin.**—*adj.* **dev′illed.**—*ns.* **dev′ilment**, frolicsome mischief; **dev′ilry**; **dev′ilship**; **dev′iltry** (*U.S.*).—**dev′il-crab**, the velvet crab; **dev′il-dodger** (*slang*), a preacher, esp. of the ranting kind: one who attends churches of various kinds, to be on the safe side; **dev′il-fish**, the fishing-frog or angler: the giant-ray of the United States: the octopus; **devil-in-a-bush**, a garden flower, love-in-a-mist.—*adj.* **dev′il-may-care**, reckless, audacious.—**dev′il-on-the-neck**, an old instrument of torture; **devil-on-two-sticks**, older name for diabolo; **devil's advocate**, advocatus diaboli, the Promoter of the Faith, an advocate at the papal court whose duty it is to propose objections against a canonisation; **devil's-bit**, a species of scabious (*Scabiosa succisa*) with rootstock as if bitten off; **devil's bones**, dice; **devil's books**, playing-cards; **devil's dozen**, thirteen; **devil's dung**, asafoetida; **devil's dust**, shoddy made by a machine called the devil; **devil's own**, a name given to the 88th Regiment in the Peninsular War, as also to the Inns of Court Volunteers; **devil's tattoo** (see **tattoo** (1)); **dev′il-worship**, the worship of the Devil, or of devils: Satanism: the Yezidi religion; **dev′il-worshipper.**—**between the devil and the deep sea**, in a desperate dilemma; **devil a bit**, **a one**, **a thing**, etc., not at all, not one, etc.; **devil of a mess**, a very bad mess; **devil's coach-horse**, a large dark-coloured beetle (*Ocypus olens*); **devil's snuff-box**, a puff-ball; **devil take the hindmost**, each man for himself; **devil to pay**, serious trouble ahead; **go to the devil**, to become ruined: (*interj.*) go away!; **play the devil**, to make havoc; **printer's devil**, the youngest apprentice in a printing-office: a printer's errand-boy; **talk of the devil**, here comes the person we were

talking of; **the devil and all**, much ado: turmoil.
[O.E. *deofol*, *deoful*—L. *diabolus*—Gr. *diabolos*,
from *diaballein*, to throw across, to slander, from
*dia*, across, and *ballein*, to throw; cf. Ger.
*teufel*, Fr. *diable*, It. *diavolo*, Sp. *diablo*.]
**devious**, *dē'vi-əs*, *adj*. remote: out of the way:
round-about: winding: erring: tortuous of
mind: deceitful.—*adv*. **dē'viously**.—*n*. **dē'viousness**. [L. *dēvius*; see deviate.]
**devise**, *di-vīz'*, *v.t*. to imagine: to compose:
to suppose, guess (*Spens*.): to purpose (*Spens*.):
to meditate (*obs*.): to describe (*obs*.): to depict
(*obs*.): to scheme: to contrive: to bequeath.—
*v.i*. to consider: to talk (*obs*.): to scheme.—*n*.
act of bequeathing: a will: property bequeathed
by will.—*adj*. **devis'able**.—*ns*. **devis'al**; **devisee**
(*dev-i-zē'*), one to whom real estate is bequeathed;
**devi'ser**, one who contrives; **devis'or**, one who
bequeaths. [O.Fr. *deviser*, *devise*—L.L. *dīvisa*, a
division of goods, a mark, a device—L. *dīvidēre*,
*divisum*, to divide.]
**devitalise**, **-ize**, *dē-vī'tə-līz*, *v.t*. to deprive of
vitality or life-giving qualities.—*n*. **devitalisā'tion**,
**-izā'tion**. [Pfx. de- (2).]
**devitrify**, *dē-vit'ri-fī*, *v.t*. to change from glassy to
minutely crystalline.—*n*. **devitrification** (*-fi-kā'*).
[Pfx. de- (2).]
**devocalise**, **-ize**, *dē-vō'kə-līz*, *v.t*. to make voiceless. [Pfx. **de-** (2).]
**devoid**, *di-void'*, *adj*. destitute, free: empty. [O.Fr.
*desvoidier*—*des*- (L. *dis-*, away), *voidier*—L.
*viduāre*—*viduus*, deprived.]
**devoir**, *dev'wär* (historically *dev'ər*), *n*. what is
due, duty: service: an act of civility. [Fr.,—L.
*dēbēre*, to owe.]
**devolution**, *dēv-*, *dev-ə-lōō'shən*, *-lū'*, *n*. a passing
from one person to another: a handing over of
powers: a modified home rule, the delegation
of certain powers to regional governments by a
central government.—*adj*. **devolu'tionary**.—*n*.
**devolu'tionist**. [See devolve.]
**devolve**, *di-volv'*, *v.t*. to roll down: to hand down:
to deliver over.—*v.i*. to roll down: to fall or
pass over in succession.—*n*. **devolve'ment**. [L.
*dēvolvēre*, *-volūtum*—*dē*, down, *volvēre*, to roll.]
**Devonian**, *di-vō'ni-ən*, *adj*. belonging to *Devonshire*: belonging to a system above the Silurian
and below the Carboniferous, and esp. to the
marine type, well seen in Devon—the continental
type being the Old Red Sandstone (*geol*.).—
*n*. a native of Devonshire: the Devonian system.
—**Devonshire cream**, clotted cream.
**devonport**, *dev'n-pōrt*, *-pört*. Same as davenport.
**devote**, *di-vōt'*, *v.t*. to set apart or dedicate by a
vow or solemn act: to dōom: to give up wholly.
—*adj*. (*Shak*.) devoted.—*adj*. **devōt'ed**, given up,
as by a vow: doomed: strongly attached:
zealous.—*adv*. **devōt'edly**.—*ns*. **devōt'edness**;
**devotee** (*dev-o-tē'*, or *dev'*), one wholly or superstitiously devoted, esp. to religion: a votary:
one strongly and consistently interested in something (with *of*); **devōte'ment** (*Shak*.); **devō'tion**,
the act of devoting: state of being devoted:
consecration: giving up of the mind to the
worship of God: piety: prayer: strong affection
or attachment: ardour: faithful service: (in *pl*.)
prayers: religious offerings (*obs*.): alms (*obs*.).
—*adj*. **devō'tional**.—*ns*. **devō'tionalist**, **devō'-
tionist**.—*adv*. **devō'tionally**. [L. *dēvovēre*, *dē-
vōtum*—*dē*, away, and *vovēre*, to vow.]
**devour**, *di-vowr'*, *v.t*. to swallow greedily: to eat
up: to consume or waste with violence or
wantonness: to take in eagerly by the senses or
mind.—*n*. **devour'er**.—*adj*. **devour'ing**.—*adv*. **devour'ingly**.—*n*. **devour'ment**. [O.Fr. *devorer*—L.
*dēvorāre*—*dē*, inten., and *vorāre*, to swallow.]
**devout**, *di-vowt'*, *adj*. given up to religious thoughts
and exercises: pious: solemn: earnest.—*adv*.
**devout'ly**.—*n*. **devout'ness**. [O.Fr. *devot*—L.
*dēvōtus*; see devote.]

**devvel**, **devel**, *dev'l*, (*Scot*.) *n*. a hard blow.—*v.t*.
to hit hard: to stun with a blow. [Ety. dub.]
**dew**, *dū*, *n*. moisture deposited from the air on
cooling, esp. at night, in minute specks upon the
surface of objects: a similar deposit or exudation
of other kinds: early freshness.—*v.t*. to wet with
dew: to moisten.—*n*. **dew'iness**.—*adj*. **dew'y**.—
**dew'-berry**, a kind of bramble or blackberry
(*Rubus caesius*; in America other species)
having a bluish, dew-like bloom on the fruit;
**dew'-bow**, a rainbow-like appearance seen on a
dewy surface; **dew'-claw**, a rudimentary inner
toe, esp. of a dog's hind-foot; **dew'-drop**; **dew'-
fall**, the deposition, or time of deposition, of
dew; **dew'point**, the temperature at which dew
begins to form; **dew'-pond**, a hollow supplied
with water by mist; **dew'-retting**, the process of
rotting away the gummy part of hemp or flax
by exposure on the grass to dew and rain; **dew'-
worm**, the common earth-worm.—**mountain
dew** (*coll*.), whisky. [O.E. *dēaw*; cf. O.N. *dögg*,
Ger. *tau*, dew.]
**dew**, *dū*, *n*. an obsolete spelling of due.—*adj*.
**dew'full** (*Spens*.), due.
**Dewali**. Same as Diwali.
**dewan**, **diwan**, *dē-wän'*, *n*. in India, a financial
minister: a state prime minister: the native
steward of a business house.—*ns*. **dewani**,
**dewanny** (*dē-wä'nē*), the office of dewan. [Pers.
*diwān*; see divan.]
**Dewar-flask**, *dū'ər-fläsk*, *n*. a type of vacuum flask.
[From Sir James *Dewar* (1842-1923), its inventor.]
**dewitt**, *di-wit'*, *v.t*. to lynch—from the fate of Jan
and Cornelius De *Witt* in Holland in 1672.
**dewlap**, *dū'lap*, *n*. the pendulous skin under the
throat of oxen, dogs, etc.: the fleshy wattle of
the turkey.—*adjs*. **dew'lapped**, **dew'lapt**. [Prob.
dew and O.E. *læppa*, a loose hanging piece.]
**dexiotropic**, *deks-i-ō-trop'ik*, *adj*. turning to the
right. [Gr. *dexios*, right, *tropos*, turning.]
**dexter**, *deks'tər*, *adj*. on the right-hand side: right:
of that side of the shield on the right-hand side
of the bearer, the spectator's left (*her*.): so
sometimes in description of a picture, to avoid
ambiguity.—*n*. **dexterity** (*-ter'i-ti*), skill of
manipulation, or generally: adroitness: right-
handedness.—*adjs*. **dex'terous**, **dex'trous**, right-
handed: adroit: subtle.—*adv*. **dex't(e)rously**.—
*n*. **dex't(e)rousness**.—*adv*. **dex'terwise**.—*adj*. **dex'-
tral**, right: turning to the right: of flatfish,
lying right-side-up: of a spiral shell, turning in
the normal manner.—*n*. **dextral'ity**, right-
handedness.—*adv*. **dex'trally**.—*ns*. **dex'tran**, a
carbohydrate formed in sugar solutions by a
bacterium, *Leuconostoc mesenteroides*, a substitute for blood plasma in transfusion; **dex'trin**,
**dex'trine**, British gum, a gummy mixture got
from starch by heating or otherwise.—**dextro-**,
in composition, pertaining to, or towards, the
right.—*n*. **dextrocar'dia** (Gr. *kardiā*, heart), a
condition in which the heart lies in the right side
of the chest, not the left; **dextrocar'diac**, one
who has this condition.—*adjs*. **dextrogyrate**
(*-jī'*), causing to turn to the right hand; **dextro-
ro'tatory**, turning to the right (clockwise), esp.
rotating thus the plane of polarisation of
light.—*ns*. **dextrorotā'tion**; **dex'trose**, glucose.
[L. *dexter*; Gr. *dexios*, Sans. *dakṣiṇa*, on the
right, on the south.]
**dexter**, *deks'tər*, *n*. a small breed of Kerry cattle.
[Prob. breeder's name.]
**dextral**, **dextro-**, etc. See dexter (1).
**dextrorse**, *deks-trors'*, *-trörs'*, or *deks'*, (*biol*.)
*adj*. rising spirally and turning to the left, i.e.
crossing an outside observer's field of view from
left to right upwards (like a screw-nail): formerly
used in the contrary sense (sinistrorse). [L.
*dextrōrsus*, towards the right—*dexter*, *vertēre*,
to turn.]

Neutral vowels in unaccented syllables: *el'ə-mənt*; for certain sounds in foreign words, see p. viii

**dextro tempore**, *deks'trō tem'pər-ē, -por-e*, (L.) at a lucky moment.

**dey**, *dā, n.* a dairy-maid.—Also **dey'-woman.** [See **dairy.**]

**dey**, *dā, n.* the pasha or governor of Algiers before the French conquest. [Turk. *dāi*, orig. a maternal uncle, a familiar title of the chief of the janizaries.]

**dhak**, *däk, n.* an Indian Butea. [Hind. *dhāk*.]

**dhal, dholl.** Same as **dal.**

**dharma**, *dûr'mä, n.* the righteousness that underlies the law. [Sans.]

**dharmsala**, *dürm-sä'lä, n.* a building having a religious or charitable purpose, as a free or cheap lodging for travellers.—Also **dharmshala.** [Hindi *dharmsālā*—Sans. *dharma, śālā*, hall.]

**dharna**, *dûr'nä, n.* calling attention, esp. to injustice, by sitting or standing in a place where one will be noticed, esp. sitting and fasting at the door of an offender. [Hindi.]

**dhobi**, *dō'bi, n.* an Indian washerman. [Hindi *dhobī*.]

**dhole**, *dōl, n.* the Indian wild dog. [Supposed to be from an Indian language.]

**dhooly.** See **doo'lie.**

**dhoti**, *dō'ti*, **dhooti**, *dōō'ti, n.* the Hindu loin-cloth: a cotton fabric used for this. [Hindi *dhotī*.]

**dhow**, better **dow**, *dow, n.* an Arab lateen-sailed vessel of the Indian Ocean. [Origin unknown; cf. Ar. *dāw*, Marathi *dāw*.]

**dhurra.** Same as **durra.**

**dhurrie.** Same as **durrie.**

**di-**, *dī, pfx.* two, twice, double. [Gr. *dis*, twice.]

**dia-**, *dī'a-, -a-, pfx.* through: across: during: composed of. [Gr.]

**diabase**, *dī'ə-bās, n.* (formerly) diorite: an altered dolerite or basalt.—*adj.* **diabā'sic.** [Appar. orig. a faulty derivative of Gr. *di-*, double, *basis*, base; associated with *diabasis*, transition.]

**diabetes**, *dī-ə-bē'tēz, n.* a disease marked by a morbid and excessive discharge of urine—**diabetes insip'idus**, without, **diabetes melli'tus** (L., honied) with, excess of sugar in the blood and urine.—*adjs.* **diabetic** (*-bet'* or *-bet'*), **-al.** [Gr. *diabētēs*, a siphon, *dia*, through, and *bainein*, to go.]

**diablerie, diablery**, *dē-äb'lə-rē, n.* magic: the black art: sorcery: mischief. [Fr. *diable*; see **devil.**]

**diabolic, -al**, *dī-ə-bol'ik, -əl, adjs.* devilish.—*adv.* **diabol'ically.**—*v.t.* **diabolise, -ize** (*-ab'ə-līz*), to render devilish.—*ns.* **diab(ol)ol'ogy**, the doctrine of devils: devil-lore. [Gr. *diabolikos—diabolos*; see **devil.**]

**diabolo**, *di-a'bol-ō*, or *di-, n.* a game in which a two-headed top is spun, tossed, and caught on a string attached to two sticks, held one in each hand. [Gr. *diaballō*, I throw over, toss, or *diabolos*, devil; see article **devil.**]

**diacatholicon**, *dī-ə-kə-thol'i-kon,* (*obs.*) *n.* a purgative electuary: a panacea. [Gr. *dia katholikon*, of universal (ingredients).]

**diacaustic**, *dī-ə-kös'tik, adj.* pertaining to curves formed by the intersections of rays of refracted light.—*n.* a curve so formed. [Pfx. **dia-**, and **caustic** (*math.*).]

**diachylon**, *di-ak'i-lon*, **diachylum**, *-ləm, n.* form. a plaster of plant juices: now lead-plaster. [Gr. *dia chylōn*, through (i.e. composed of) juices or *diachylōn* (*neut.*), juicy.]

**diacid**, *dī-as'id, adj.* having two replaceable hydrogen atoms: capable of replacing two hydrogen atoms of an acid. [Pfx. **di-**.]

**diacodion**, *dī-ə-kō'di-on*, **diacodium**, (*-əm*), *n.* a syrup of poppies. [L.,—Gr. *dia kōdeiōn*, composed of poppy-heads—gen. pl. of *kōdeia*, a poppy-head.]

**diaconate**, *di-ak'ə-nāt, n.* the office of a deacon.—*adj.* **diac'onal**, pertaining to a deacon. [See **deacon.**]

**diaconicon**, *dī-ə-kon'i-kən, n.* a sacristy for sacred vessels, in a Greek church, on the south side of the bema or sanctuary. [Gr. *diākonikon*.]

**diacoustic**, *di-ə-kōōs'tik*, old-fashioned *-kow', adj.* pertaining to the refraction of sound.—*n.* **diacoust'ics**, the branch of physics that deals with refracted sounds. [Pfx. **dia-**, and **acoustic.**]

**diacritic, -al**, *dī-ə-krit'ik, -əl, adjs.* distinguishing —used of marks or points attached to letters. [Gr. *diakritikos—dia*, between, and *kritikos*; see **critic.**]

**diact**, *dī'akt, adj.* two-rayed.—*adjs.* **diactinal** (*-ak'*, or *-tī'*), **diact'ine.** [Pfx. **di-**, and Gr. *aktis aktinos*, ray.]

**diactinic**, *di-a'k-tin'ik, adj.* capable of transmitting actinic rays. [Pfx. **dia-**, and Gr. *aktis, aktinos*, ray.]

**diadelphous**, *di-ə-del'fəs, adj.* of stamens, united by the filaments in two bundles: having stamens so joined.—*n.pl.* **Diadel'phia**, in the Linnaean classification, a class with stamens so joined. [Pfx. **di-**, and Gr. *adelphos*, brother.]

**diadem**, *dī'ə-dem, n.* a crown, head-band, or the like: an arch of a crown.—*adj.* **di'ademed**, wearing a diadem.—**diadem spider**, the common garden spider (from its markings). [O.Fr. *diademe*—L. *diadēma*—Gr. *diadēma—dia*, round and *deein*, to bind.]

**diadochi**, *di-ad'o-kī, n.pl.* the generals who became monarchs of the various kingdoms (Syria, Egypt, etc.) into which the empire of Alexander the Great split after his death (323 B.C.). [Gr. *diadochos*, succeeding, a successor; *diadecheasthai*, to succeed.]

**diadrom**, *dī'ə-drom, n.* a course or passing: a vibration.—*adj.* (of leaf nerves) radiating fanwise. [Gr. *dia*, across, *dromos*, a run.]

**diaeresis, dieresis**, *di-ēr'i-sis, n.* a mark (··) placed over the second of two adjacent vowel-letters to show that each is to be pronounced separately, as *naïf*:—*pl.* **diaer'eses, dier'eses** (*-ēz*). [Gr. *diairesis*, separation—*dia*, apart, *haireein*, to take.]

**diageotropic**, *dī-ə-jē-ō-trop'ik*, (*bot.*) *adj.* taking a position perpendicular to the direction of gravity. —*adv.* **diageotrop'ically.**—*n.* **diageotropism** (*-ot'-*). [Pfx. **dia-**, **geotropic.**]

**diaglyph**, *dī'ə-glif*, or *di-, n.* an intaglio. [Gr. *dia*, through, *glyphein*, to carve.]

**diagnosis**, *di-əg-nō'sis, n.* the identification of a disease by means of its symptoms: a formal determining description:—*pl.* **diagnō'ses** (*-ēz*).—*v.t.* **diagnose** (*-nōz', -nōs'*), to ascertain from symptoms, as a disease.—*adj.* **diagnos'tic**, distinguishing: differentiating.—*n.* that by which anything is known: a symptom.—*n.pl.* **diagnos'tics**, diagnosis as a branch of medicine.—*n.* **diagnostic'ian** (*-nos-tish'-ən*), one skilled in diagnosis. [Gr., *dia*, between, *gnōsis*, knowing.]

**diagometer**, *di-ə-gom'i-tər, n.* a form of electroscope for ascertaining electric conductivity. [Gr. *diagein*, to conduct, *metron*, a measure.]

**diagonal**, *di-ag'ə-nəl, adj.* through the corners, or joining two vertices that are not adjacent, of a polygon: (of a plane) passing through two edges, not adjacent, of a polyhedron: slantwise.—*n.* a straight line or plane so drawn.—*adv.* **diag'onally.** —**diagonal scale**, a scale for laying down small fractions of the unit of measurement, by lengthwise parallel lines intersected by two sets of parallel lines, crosswise and oblique. [L. *diagōnālis*, from Gr. *diagōnios—dia*, through, and *gōniā*, a corner.]

**diagram**, *dī'ə-gram, n.* a figure or plan intended to explain rather than represent actual appearance: an outline figure or scheme: a curve symbolising a set of facts: a record traced by an automatic indicator.—*adj.* **diagrammatic** (*-grə-mat'ik*).—*adv.* **diagrammat'ically.**—*n.* **di'agraph** (*-gräf*), an instrument for copying, enlarging, or projecting

drawings.—*adj.* **diagraphic** (-*graf'ik*). [Gr. *diagramma—dia*, round, *graphein*, to write.]
**diaheliotropic**, *dī-ə-hē-li-ō-trop'ik*, (*bot.*) *adj.* turning transversely to the light.—*n.* **diaheliotropism** (-*ot'rə-pizm*). [Pfx. **dia-, heliotropic.**]
**dial**, *dī'əl*, *n.* an instrument for showing the time of day by the sun's shadow (*sundial*): a timepiece (*obs.*): the face of a watch or clock: graduated plate on which a movable index shows the value of some quantity measured, or can be set to make an adjustment (as in getting a telephone connection): a miner's compass with sights for surveying: a face (*slang*).—*v.t.* to measure or indicate or get into communication with by dial:—*pr.p.* **di'alling**; *pa.t.* and *pa.p.* **di'alled.**—*ns.* **di'alist**, a maker of dials: one skilled in dialling; **di'aller**, one who surveys by dial; **di'alling**, the art of constructing sundials: the science which explains the measuring of time by the sundial: surveying by dial.—**di'alplate**, the plate to which the pillars of a watch are fixed. [L.L. *diālis*, daily—L. *diēs*, a day.]
**dialect**, *dī'ə-lekt*, *n.* a variety or form of a language peculiar to a district or class, esp. but not necessarily other than a literary or standard form: a peculiar manner of speaking.—*adj.* **dialect'al.**—*adv.* **dialect'ally.**—*ns.* **dialect'icism**; **dialectol'ogist**; **dialectol'ogy.** [Through Fr. and L. from Gr. *dialektos*, speech, manner of speech, peculiarity of speech—*dia*, between, *legein*, to speak.]
**dialectic**, -al, *dī-ə-lek'tik*, -əl, *adjs.* pertaining to dialect or to discourse or to dialectics: logical.—*n.* **dialec'tic**, *n.pl.* **dialec'tics**, art of discussing: that branch of logic which teaches the rules and modes of reasoning.—*adv.* **dialec'tically.**—*n.* **dialecti'cian**, one skilled in dialectics, a logician. —**dialectical materialism** (see **materialism**). [Gr. *dialektikos*.]
**diallage**, *dī-al'ə-jē*, (*rhet.*) *n.* a figure of speech by which arguments, after having been considered from various points of view, are all brought to bear upon one point. [Gr. *diallagē*; see next word.]
**diallage**, *dī'əl-āj*, *n.* a mineral nearly allied to augite, brown, grey, or green, with play of colour. —*adjs.* **diallagic** (-*aj'ik*), **diallagoid** (-*al'ə-goid*). [Gr. *diallagē*, change—*dia*, between, *allassein*, to change—*allos*, other.]
**dialogite**, *dī-al'ə-jit*, *n.* a rose-red manganese carbonate. [Gr. *dialogē*, selection, doubt.]
**dialogue**, *dī'ə-log*, *n.* conversation between two or more persons, esp. of a formal or imaginary nature: an exchange of views in the hope of ultimately reaching agreement.—*v.i.* (*Shak.*) to converse.—*v.t.* (*Shak.*) to put into dialogue form.—*adjs.* **dialog'ic** (-*loj'*), **dialogist'ic, -al.**—*v.i.* **dialogise, -ize** (*dī-al'ə-jiz*), to discourse in dialogue.—*n.* **dial'ogist**, a speaker in, or writer of, dialogue. [Fr.,—L. *dialogus*—Gr. *dialogos*, a conversation—*dialegesthai*, to discourse.]
**dialypetalous**, *dī-ə-li-pet'ə-ləs*, *adj.* having the petals separate, polypetalous. [Gr. *dialyein*, to separate—*dia*, asunder, *lyein*, to loose, and *petalon*, a leaf.]
**dialysis**, *dī-al'i-sis*, (*chem.*) *n.* the separation of substances by diffusion through a membranous septum or partition: diaeresis: dissolution: separation:—*pl.* **dial'yses** (-*sēz*).—*adj.* **dialysable**, -z- (*dī-ə-liz'ə-bl*).—*v.t.* **dialyse, -yze** (*dī'ə-liz*), to separate by dialysis.—*n.* **di'alyser**, -z-.—*adj.* **dialytic** (-*lit'ik*). [Gr. *dialysis—dia*, asunder, *lyein*, to loose.]
**diamagnetic**, *dī-ə-mag-net'ik*, *adj.* cross-magnetic —applied to any substance, of which a rod suspended between the poles of a magnet arranges itself across the lines of force (opp. to *paramagnetic*).—*adv.* **diamagnet'ically.**—*n.* **diamag'netism**, the form of magnetic action possessed by diamagnetic bodies: the branch of magnetism

which deals with diamagnetic phenomena. [Pfx. **dia-, magnetic.**]
**diamanté**, *dē-a-mä-tā*, *n.* a decoration, e.g. on a dress, consisting of glittering particles: a fabric so decorated.—Also *adj.* [Fr., *diamant*, diamond.]
**diamantiferous**, *dī-ə-man-tif'ər-əs*, *adj.* yielding diamonds. [Fr. *diamantifère*.]
**diameter**, *dī-am'i-tər*, *n.* the measure through or across: a straight line passing through the centre of a circle or other figure, terminated at both ends by the circumference: in the parabola a straight line parallel to the axis extending from the curve to infinity.—*adjs.* **diam'etral, diametric** (*dī-ə-met'rik*), **-al**, in the direction of a diameter: pertaining to the diameter: as of opposite ends of a diameter (as in *diametrical opposition*).—*advs.* **diam'etrally**, in a diametral manner; **diamet'rically**, along a diameter: as at the ends of a diameter.—**tactical diameter**, the perpendicular distance between a ship's courses before and after turning 180°. [Through Fr. and L. from Gr. *diametros—dia*, through, across, and *metron*, a measure.]
**diamond**, *dī-ə-mənd*, *n.* a highly prized gem stone, and the hardest of all minerals, carbon crystallised in the cubic system: a rhombus: a card of a suit distinguished by pips of that form: a baseball field, or the part between bases (*U.S.*): one of the smallest kinds of English printing type (about 4½-point).—*adj.* resembling diamonds: made of diamonds: marked with diamonds: lozenge-shaped, rhombic.—*adjs.* **di'amonded**, furnished with diamonds; **diamondif'erous**, yielding diamonds.—**di'amond-bee'tle**, a beautiful sparkling S. American weevil; **di'amond-drill**, a borer whose bit is set with bort; **di'amond-dust**, **-pow'der**, the powder made by the friction of diamonds on one another in the course of polishing; **di'amond-field**, a region that yields diamonds; **di'amond-hitch**, a mode of fastening a rope for heavy burdens; **di'amond-ju'bilee**, a sixtieth anniversary (of marriage, **di'amond-wedd'ing**); **di'amond-wheel**, a wheel covered with diamond-dust and oil for polishing diamonds, etc.—**black diamonds**, (*fig.*) coal; **diamond cut diamond**, an encounter between two very sharp persons; **rough diamond**, an uncut diamond: a person possibly of great worth, but of rude exterior and unpolished manners. [M.E. *diamaunt*—O.Fr. *diamant*.—L.L. *diamas*, *-antis* —Gr. *adamas*, *-antos*; see **adamant.**]
**diamyl**, *dī-am'il*, *adj.* having two amyl groups. [Pfx. **di-, amyl.**]
**Diana**, *dī-an'ə*, *n.* Roman goddess of light, the moon-goddess, representative of chastity and hunting—identified with the Greek Artemis: a huntress.—Also **Di'an.**—**Diana monkey**, a large long-tailed W. African monkey (*Cercopithecus diana*) with a white crescent on the forehead; **Diana's tree**, tree of silver (see **tree**).—**Diana of the Ephesians**, a goddess of fertility worshipped at Ephesus. [L. *Diāna*.]
**diandrous**, *dī-an'drəs*, *adj.* having, or allowing, two husbands or male mates (at a time): having two stamens or antheridia.—*n.pl.* **Dian'dria**, in Linnaeus's classification, a class of plants with two stamens.—*n.* **dian'dry**, the practice or condition of being diandrous. [Gr. *dis*, twice, *anēr*, *andros*, a man, male.]
**dianetics**, *dī-ə-net'iks*, *n.* a method of diagnosing and treating psychosomatic ills (held to be caused by pre-natal experiences). [dianoetic.]
**dianodal**, *dī-ə-nō'dl*, (*math.*) *adj.* passing through a node. [Pfx. **dia-, nodal.**]
**dianoetic**, *dī-ə-nō-et'ik*, *adj.* capable of or relating to thought. [Gr. *dianoētikos—dia*, through, *noeein*, to think.]
**Dianthus**, *dī-an'thəs*, *n.* the genus of herbaceous flowers to which carnations and pinks belong.

Neutral vowels in unaccented syllables: *el'ə-mənt*; for certain sounds in foreign words, see p. viii

[Poss. Gr. *Dios anthos*, Zeus's flower; or *dianthēs*, flowering in succession.]

**diapason**, dī-ə-pā′zn, -sn, *n.* a whole octave: a bass part: a harmony: a full volume of various sounds in concord: the whole range or compass of tones: a standard of pitch: a foundation-stop of an organ (*open* or *stopped diapason*) extending through its whole compass.—(*Spens.*) **di′apase.** [Gr. *dia pasōn chordōn symphōniā*, concord through all the notes.]

**diapedesis**, dī-ə-pi-dē′sis, (*physiol*) *n.* the migration of white blood-corpuscles through the walls of the blood-vessels without apparent rupture.—*adj.* **diapedetic** (-det′ik). [Gr. *dia*, through, *pēdēsis*, leaping.]

**diapente**, dī-ə-pen′ti, *n.* the interval of a fifth (*mus.*): a medicine of five ingredients. [Gr. *dia*, through, *pente*, five.]

**diaper**, dī′ə-pər, *n.* linen or cotton cloth with a square or diamond pattern, used chiefly for table linen and towels: esp. in U.S., a baby's napkin: a pattern for ornamentation, woven, not coloured, in textiles: a floral or geometric pattern in low relief in architecture, often repeated over a considerable surface: paving in a chequered pattern.—*v.t.* to variegate with figures, as diaper.—*n.* **di′apering.** [O.Fr. *diaspre*, *diapre*—L.L. *diasprus*—Byzantine Gr. *diaspros*, *dia*, through, *aspros*, white.]

**diaphanous**, dī-af′ə-nəs, *adj.* transparent: translucent: pellucid: clear: light, delicate.—*ns.* **diaphaneity** (dī-ə-fə-nē′i-ti); **diaphanom′eter**, an instrument for measuring the transparency of the air.—*adv.* **diaph′anously.**—*n.* **diaph′anousness.** [Gr. *diaphanēs*—*dia*, through, and *phainein*, to show, shine.]

**diaphone**, dī′ə-fōn, *n.* a siren-like fog-signal: an organ stop made louder by vibrating material: all the variants of a phoneme. [Gr. *dia*, across, *phōnē*, voice.]

**diaphoresis**, dī-ə-for-ē′sis, *n.* sweat, esp. artificially induced.—*adj.* **diaphoretic** (-et′ik), promoting sweating.—*n.* a sudorific. [Gr. *diaphorēsis*, sweating—*dia*, through, *pherein*, to carry.]

**diaphototropic**, dī-ə-fō-tō-trop′ik, *adj.* diaheliotropic.—*n.* **diaphototropy** (-tot′rə-pi). [Pfx. **dia-**, **phototropic.**]

**diaphragm**, dī′ə-fram, -frəm, *n.* a thin partition or dividing membrane: the midriff, a structure separating the chest from the abdomen: a metal plate with a central hole, for cutting off side-rays in optical instruments: a strengthening or stiffening plate (*engineering*).—*adjs.* **diaphragmatic** (-frag-mat′), **diaphrag′mal.**—*n.* **diaphragmati′tis,** inflammation of the diaphragm. [Gr. *diaphragma*, partition, midriff—*dia*, across, *phragma*, a fence.]

**diaphysis**, dī-af′i-sis, *n.* an abnormal elongation of the axis (*bot.*): the shaft of a long bone (*anat.*). [Gr. *diaphysis*, a separation—*dia*, through, *phyesthai*, to grow.]

**diapophysis**, dī-ə-pof′i-sis, *n.* a dorsal transverse process of a vertebra:—*pl.* **diapophysēs** (-sēz).—*adj.* **diapophysial** (dī-ap-ō-fiz′i-əl), apart, *apophysis*, offshoot.]

**diapositive**, dī-ə-poz′i-tiv, *n.* a transparent photographic positive. [Pfx. **dia-**, **positive.**]

**diapyesis**, dī-ə-pī-ē′sis, *n.* suppuration.—*adj.* **diapyetic** (-et′ik), producing suppuration.—*n.* a medicine of this property. [Gr. *diapyēsis*—*dia*, through, *pyon*, pus.]

**diarch**, dī′ärk, (*bot.*) *adj.* having two xylem strands. [Gr. *di-*, twice, *archē*, origin.]

**diarchy**, dī′är-ki, *n.* a form of government in which two persons, states, or bodies are jointly vested with supreme power—less correctly **di′narchy**, **dy′archy.**—*adjs.* **diarch′al**, **diarch′ic.** [Gr. *di-*, twice, *archein*, to rule.]

**diarrhoea**, **diarrhea**, dī-ə-rē′ə, *n.* a persistent purging or looseness of the bowels.—*adjs.* **diar-**

**rhoe′al**, **diarrhoe′ic** (also -rhē′al, etc.). [Gr. *diarroia*—*dia*, through, *rhoiā*, a flow.]

**diarthrosis**, dī-är-thrō′sis, *n.* articulation admitting free movement. [Gr. *diarthrōsis*, jointing—*dia*, through, *arthron*, joint.]

**diary**, dī′ə-ri, *n.* a daily record: a book for making daily records, noting engagements, etc.—*adjs.* **diarial** (dī-ā′ri-əl), **diā′rian.**—*v.t.* or *v.i.* **di′arise**, -ize.—*n.* **di′arist**, one who keeps a diary. [L. *diārium—diēs*, day.]

**diascordium**, dī-ə-skör′di-əm, *n.* a medicine made from water-germander, etc. [Medical L.,—Gr. *dia skordiōn*, composed of *skordiōn* (perhaps water-germander).]

**diaskeuast**, dī-ə-skū′ast, *n.* a reviser: an interpolator. [Gr. *diaskeuazein*, to make ready—*dia*, through, *skeuos*, a tool.]

**Diasone**, dī′ə-sōn, *n.* a proprietary name for a sulphonamide (a derivative of diaminodiphenyl-sulphone) used against leprosy.

**diaspora**, dī-as′por-ə, *n.* dispersion, used collectively for the dispersed Jews after the Babylonian captivity, and also in the apostolic age for the Jews living outside of Palestine.—now, for Jews outside Israel.—Also *adj.* [Gr. *diasporā—dia*, through, *speirein*, to scatter.]

**diaspore**, dī′ə-spōr, -spör, *n.* a mineral, aluminium hydroxide, AlO(OH). [Gr. *diasporā*, scattering, from its decrepitation.]

**diastaltic**, dī-ə-stal′tik, (*Greek mus.*) *adj.* of intervals, extended: of style, bold. [Gr. *diastaltikos*, expanding.]

**diastase**, dī′ə-stās, *n.* an enzyme that converts starch into sugar, produced in germinating seeds and in pancreatic juice.—*adj.* **diastatic** (-stat′ik). [Gr. *diastasis*, division—*dia*, apart, *stasis*, setting.]

**diastasis**, dī-as′tə-sis, (*surg.*) *n.* separation of bones without fracture. [See foregoing.]

**diastema**, dī-ə-stē′mə, *n.* a natural space between two consecutive teeth, or series of teeth:—*pl.* **diastē′mata.**—*adj.* **diastemat′ic.** [Gr. *diastēma*, *-atos*, interval.]

**diastole**, dī-as′to-lē, *n.* dilatation of the heart, auricles, and arteries—opp. to *systole*, or contraction: the lengthening of a short syllable, as before a pause.—*adj.* **diastolic** (dī-ə-stol′ik). [Gr. *diastolē—dia*, asunder, and *stellein*, to place.]

**diastrophism**, dī-as′trō-fizm, (*geol.*) *n.* processes of deformation of the earth's crust.—*adj.* **diastrophic** (dī-ə-strof′ik). [Gr. *diastrophē*, distortion—*dia*, aside, *strophē*, a turning.]

**diastyle**, dī′ə-stil, (*archit.*) *adj.* with columns about three diameters apart.—*n.* a building or colonnade so proportioned. [Gr. *diastȳlos—dia*, apart, *stȳlos*, column.]

**diatessaron**, dī-ə-tes′ə-ron, -rən, *n.* a harmony of the four gospels, especially the earliest, that of Tatian (prob. A.D. 110-180): the interval of a fourth (*mus.*): a medicine of four ingredients. [Gr. *dia tessarōn*, through, or composed of, four.]

**diathermic**, dī-ə-thûr′mik, *adj.* permeable by radiant heat.—Also **diather′mal**, **diather′manous**, **diather′mous.**—*ns.* **diather′macy**, **diather′mancy**, **diathermanē′ity**, permeability by radiant heat; **di′athermy**, heating of internal parts of the body by electric currents. [Gr. *dia*, through, *thermē*, heat.]

**diathesis**, dī-ath′i-sis, *n.* a particular condition or habit of body, esp. one predisposing to certain diseases: a habit of mind.—*adj.* **diathetic** (dī-ə-thet′ik). [Gr. *diathesis—dia*, asunder, *tithenai* to place.]

**diatom**, dī′ə-təm, *n.* one of a class of microscopic unicellular algae with flinty shells in two halves, fitting like box and lid.—*adj.* **diatomā′ceous.**—*n.* **diatomite** (dī-at′əm-it, or dī′ət-), diatomaceous earth or kieselguhr, a powdery siliceous deposit of diatom frustules.—**diatom ooze**, a deep-sea

deposit of diatom frustules. [Gr. *diatomos,* cut through—*dia,* through, *temnein,* to cut.]
**diatomic,** *di-ə-tom'ik, adj.* consisting of two atoms: having two replaceable atoms or groups: bivalent. [Pfx. **di-, atom.**]
**diatonic,** *di-ə-ton'ik, adj.* proceeding by the tones and intervals of the natural scale in music.—*adv.* **diaton'ically.** [Gr. *diatonikos*—*dia,* through, *tonos,* tone.]
**diatribe,** *dī'ə-trīb, n.* a continued discourse or disputation: an invective harangue.—*n.* **di'atribist,** a writer or utterer of such. [Gr. *diatribē,* a spending of time—*dia,* through, *tribein,* to rub, wear away.]
**diatropism,** *di-at'rō-pizm, n.* orientation at right angles to the direction of a stimulus.—*adj.* **diatropic** *(di-ə-trop'ik).* [Gr. *dia,* across, *tropos,* turning.]
**diaxon,** *di-aks'on, adj.* having two axes or two axis-cylinder processes.—*n.* a bipolar nerve-cell. [Gr. *di-,* twice, *axōn,* an axis.]
**diazeuxis,** *di-ə-zūk'sis,* (*Greek mus.*) *n.* the separation of two tetrachords by a whole tone.—*adj.* **diazeuc'tic.** [Gr. *diazeuxis,* disjunction—*dia,* apart, *zeuxis,* yoking.]
**diazo-,** *di-az'ō-,* in combination, applied to compounds containing two nitrogen atoms and a hydrocarbon radical.
**dib,** *dib, v.i.* to dip, as in angling:—*pr.p.* **dibb'ing;** *pa.t.* and *pa.p.* **dibbed.** [Prob. a form of **dab.**]
**dib,** *dib, n.* one of the small bones of a sheep's leg: (*pl.*) a children's game, played by throwing up such small bones or stones (**dib'-stones**) from the palm and catching them on the back of the hand —also **jacks,** in Scots *chuckie-stanes,* or *chucks*: (*pl.*) money (*slang*).
**dibasic,** *di-bā'sik, adj.* capable of reacting with two equivalents of an acid: (of acids) having two replaceable hydrogen atoms. [Pfx. **di-, basic.**]
**dibble,** *dib'l, n.* a pointed tool used for making holes for seeds or plants—also **dibb'er.**—*v.t.* **dibb'le,** to plant with a dibble.—*v.i.* to make holes: to dip, as in angling.—*n.* **dibb'ler.** [Prob. connected with **dab.**]
**dibranchiate,** *di-brang'ki-āt, adj.* having two gills.—*ns.pl.* **Dibran'chia, Dibranchiā'ta,** the two-gilled sub-class of cephalopods. [Gr. *di-,* twice, *branchia,* gills.]
**dibromo-,** *di-brō'mō-,* in composition, having two atoms of bromine, esp. replacing hydrogen.
**dibutyl,** *di-bū'til, adj.* having two butyl groups.—**dibutyl phthalate** (*thal'āt*), the dibutyl ester of phthalic acid, used to keep off insects.
**dicacity,** *di-kas'i-ti, n.* raillery, pert speech.—*adj.* **dicacious** *(di-kā'shəs).* [L. *dicāx,* sarcastic.]
**dicarpellary,** *di-kär'pəl-ər-i,* or *-pel', adj.* of or with two carpels. [Pfx. **di-,**]
**dicast, dikast,** *dik'ast, n.* one of the 6000 Athenians annually chosen to act as judges.—*n.* **dicas'tery,** their court. [Gr. *dikastēs*—*dikē,* justice.]
**dice.** See **die** (2).
**Dicentra,** *di-sen'tra, n.* a genus of the fumitory family including bleeding-heart (*D. spectabilis*) with the two outer petals broadly pouched.— Also **Dielytra** *(di-el'i-tra;* orig. a misprint). [Gr. *di-,* double, *kentron,* a point, spur.]
**dicephalous,** *di-sef'ə-ləs, adj.* two-headed. [Gr. *dikephalos*—*di-,* double, *kephalē,* a head.]
**dich,** *dich,* (*Shak., Timon*) supposed to be for **do it,** may it do.
**dichasium,** *di-kā'zi-əm, n.* a cymose inflorescence in which each axis in turn produces a pair of nearly equal branches (*pl.* **dicha'sia**).—*adj.* **dicha'sial.** [Gr. *dichāsis,* division, halving.]
**dichlamydeous,** *di-klə-mid'i-əs, adj.* having both a calyx and a corolla. [Gr. *di-,* double, *chlamys, -ydos,* mantle.]
**dichlor(o)-,** *di-klōr(-ō)-, -klör-,* in composition,

having two atoms of chlorine, esp. replacing hydrogen.—*n.* **dichlo'rodiphēn'yltrichlo'roeth'ane,** known as DDT, a white powder orig. used to kill lice and thus prevent the spread of typhus; effective also against other insects, but having long-term disadvantages.
**dichogamy,** *dik-* or *dik-og'ə-mi, n.* an arrangement for preventing the self-fertilisation of hermaphrodite flowers, the stamens and stigmas ripening at different times.—*adj.* **dichog'amous.** [Gr. *dicha,* in two, *gamos,* marriage.]
**dichord,** *di'körd, n.* an ancient two-stringed lute. [Gr. *dichordos.*]
**dichotomy,** *dik-* or *dik-ot'ə-mi, n.* a division into two strongly contrasted groups or classes: repeated branching.—*v.t.* and *v.i.* **dichot'omise, -ize.**—*n.* **dichot'omist.**—*adj.* **dichot'omous.**—*adv.* **dichot'omously.** [Gr. *dichotomiā*—*dicha,* in two, *tomē,* a cut—*temnein,* to cut.]
**dichroism,** *di'krō-izm, n.* the property of showing different colours exhibited by doubly refracting crystals when viewed in different directions by transmitted light.—*adjs.* **dichrō'ic, dichröit'ic.**— *ns.* **dichröite,** a strongly dichroic mineral, iolite or cordierite; **di'chrō(o)scope,** an instrument for testing the dichroism of crystals.—*adj.* **dichrō(o)scop'ic.** [Gr. *dichroos,* two-coloured—*di-,* twice, *chroā,* colour.]
**dichromate,** *di-krō'māt,* a salt of **dichro'mic aci** (H₂Cr₂O₇), containing two chromium atoms.— Also **bichromate.** [Pfx. **di-, chromate.**]
**dichromatic,** *di-krō-mat'ik, adj.* having two colours, esp. in different individuals of the same species: able to see two colours and two only, as in red-green colour-blind persons who see only blue and yellow.—*n.* a person of dichromatic vision, a dichromat.—*ns.* **di'chrōmat(e),** a person who can distinguish two colours only; **dichrō'- matism.**—*adj.* **dichrō'mic,** dichroic: dichromatic.—*n.* **dichrō'mism.** [Gr. *di-,* twice, *chrōma,* colour.]
**dichromic.** See (1) **dichromate;** (2) **dichromatic.**
**dicht,** *dihht,* (*Scot.*) *v.t.* to wipe.—*n.* a wipe. [**dight.**]
**dick,** *dik,* (*slang*) *n.* fine words (for **dictionary**): also for **declaration,** as *to take one's dick,* and prob. *up to dick,* excellent (up to declared value).
**Dick** (also without *cap.*), *dik,* (*slang*) *n.* a man: detective.—**clever Dick,** one who thinks himself to be cleverer than he is. [*Dick,* for Richard.]
**dickcissel,** *dik-sis'l, n.* the black-throated bunting, an American migratory bird.
**dickens,** *dik'ənz, n.* the deuce, the devil, as in *what the dickens, play the dickens.* [App. *Dickon,* Richard, as a substitute for **devil.**]
**Dickensian,** *dik-en'zi-ən, adj.* pertaining to Charles Dickens (1812-70), the novelist.—*n.* an admirer or student of Dickens.
**dicker,** *dik'ər,* (*Amer.*) *n.* haggling, bargaining: petty trade by barter, etc.—*v.i.* to haggle. [Prob. the obs. **dicker,** the number ten, esp. of hides or skins.—L. *decuria.*]
**dickey, dicky,** *dik'i, n.* a leathern apron for a gig, etc.: the driver's seat in a carriage: a seat for servants at the back of a carriage: a folding seat at the back of a motor-car: a false shirt-front. [Perh. from *dick,* a dial. Eng. word for a leathern apron; perh. Du. *dek,* a cover.]
**Dickin medal,** *dik'in med'əl, n.* a British award for animal heroism in wartime, instituted in 1943. [Maria Elisabeth *Dickin,* founder of the People's Dispensary for Sick Animals, which makes the awards.]
**Dicksonia,** *dik-sōn'i-ə, n.* a tropical and southern genus of ferns, mainly tree-ferns. [After James *Dickson* (d. 1822), botanist.]
**dicky, dickey,** *dik'i,* (*E. Anglian*) *n.* an ass.—*n.* **dick'y-bird** (*childish*), a small bird. [*Dick,* for Richard.]

Neutral vowels in unaccented syllables: *el'ə-mənt*; for certain sounds in foreign words, see p. viii

**dicky, dickey,** *dik'i,* (*coll.*) *adj.* shaky. [Origin unknown.]

**diclinous,** *dī'kli-nəs,* or *-klī',* *adj.* having the stamens and pistils in separate flowers, whether on the same or on different plants.—*n.* **di'-clinism.** [Gr. *di-,* twice, double, *klīnē,* a bed.]

**dicotyledon,** *dī-kot-i-lē'dən, n.* a plant of the Dicotylē'donēs (*-ēz*) or Dicot'ylae, one of the two great divisions of Angiosperms, having embryos with two cotyledons, leaves commonly net-veined, the parts of the flowers in twos, fives, or multiples of these, and the vascular bundles in the axes usually containing cambium.—*adj.* **di-cotylē'donous.** [Gr. *di-,* twice, and cotyledon.]

**dicrotic,** *dī-krot'ik, adj.* of the pulse, having two beats to one beat of the heart.—Also **di'crotous.**—*n.* **di'crotism.** [Gr. *di-,* twice, double, and *krotos,* beat.]

**Dictaphone,** *dik'tə-fōn, n.* trademark denoting a recording apparatus for dictating letters, etc. [L. *dictāre,* to dictate, Gr. *phōnē,* sound.]

**dicta probantia,** *dik'tə prō-ban'shi-ə, dik'ta prō-ban'ti-a,* (L.) proof texts.

**dictate,** *dik-tāt',* formerly *dik'tat, v.t.* to say or read for another to write: to lay down with authority: to command.—*n.* (*dik'tāt*) an order, rule, direction: impulse.—*n.* dict (*obs.*), a saying.—*v.t.* (*obs.*) to dictate.—*ns.* dictā'tion, act, art, or practice of dictating: speaking or reading of words for a pupil, amanuensis, etc., to write: overbearing command; **dictā'tor,** one invested with absolute authority—originally an extra-ordinary Roman magistrate: one who, or that which, dictates:—*fem.* dictā'tress, dictā'trix.—*adj.* **dictatorial** (*dik-tə-tō'ri-əl*), like a dictator: absolute: overbearing.—*adv.* **dictātō'rially.**—*ns.* **dictā'torship,** dictā'ture.—*adj.* **dic'tātory.** [L. *dictāre, -ātum,* freq. of *dicĕre,* to say.]

**diction,** *dik'shən, n.* a saying or speaking: manner of speaking or expressing: choice of words: style: (*U.S.*) enunciation. [L. *dictiō, -ōnis*—*dicĕre, dictum,* to say.]

**dictionary,** *dik'shən-ə-ri, n.* a book containing the words of a language alphabetically arranged, with their meanings, etymology, etc.: a lexicon: a work containing information on any depart-ment of knowledge, alphabetically arranged. [L.L. *dictiōnārium;* see *diction.*]

**Dictograph,** *dik'tō-gräf, n.* a telephone for trans-mitting speech from room to room, with or without the speaker's knowledge. [Trademark: L. *dictum,* thing said, Gr. *graphein,* to write.]

**dictum,** *dik'təm, n.* something said: a saying: an authoritative saying:—*pl.* dic'ta. [L.]

**dictyogen,** *dik'ti-ō-jen,* (*obs.*) *n.* a monocotyledon with net-veined leaves. [Gr. *diktyon,* a net; *gennaein,* to produce.]

**dicyclic,** *dī-sik'lik, adj.* having two whorls or rings. [Gr. *di-,* twice, double, *kyklos,* wheel.]

**dicynodont,** *dī-sin'o-dont, n.* an extinct tusked reptile, showing affinities with mammals. [Gr. *di-,* twice, *kyōn, kynos,* dog, and *odous, odontos,* tooth.]

**did,** *did,* didst, *didst, pa.t.* of do.

**didactic, -al,** *di-dak'tik, -əl, dī-, adjs.* fitted or intended to teach: instructive: preceptive.—*adv.* didac'tically.—*n.* didac'ticism (*-sizm*).—*n.pl.* **didactics,** the art or science of teaching. [Gr. *didaktikos—didaskein,* to teach; akin to L. *docēre, discēre.*]

**didactyl,** *dī-dak'til, adj.* two-fingered, two-toed, or two-clawed.—Also *n.*—*adj.* didac'tylous. [Gr. *di-,* twice, *daktylos,* finger, toe.]

**didapper,** *dī'dap-ər, n.* the dabchick or little grebe: one who disappears and bobs up again. [dive and dapper, a variant of dipper; cf. O.E. *dūfedoppa,* pelican.]

**didascalic,** *did-as-kal'ik, adj.* didactic. [Gr. *did-askalikos—didaskalos,* teacher.]

**didder,** *did'ər,* (*dial.*) *v.i.* to shake. [See dither.]

**diddle,** *did'l, v.t.* to cajole, swindle.—*n.* **didd'ler.** [Origin uncertain.]

**didelphic,** *dī-del'fik, adj.* having or pertaining to a double womb.—*n.pl.* Didel'phia, the marsupials.—*adjs.* didel'phian, didel'phic, didel'phine, didel'phous.—*n.* Didel'phys (*-fis*), an American genus of opossums.—*n.pl.* Didelphyidae (*-fī'i-dē*), the opossum family. [Gr. *di-,* double, *delphys,* womb.]

**didgeridoo,** *did'jər-i-doō', n.* an Australian abori-ginal musical instrument, consisting of a very long tube.

**dido,** *dī'dō,* (*slang*) *n.* an antic, caper: a frivolous or mischievous act.—act dido, to play the fool; cut up didoes, to behave in an extravagant way. [Origin unknown.]

**didrachma,** *dī-drak'mə,* didrachm, *dī'dram, n.* a double drachma. [Gr. *di-,* double, and drachma.]

**Didunculus,** *di-dung'kū-lus, n.* a remarkable genus of birds—the tooth-billed pigeon of Samoa. [Dim. of *Didus,* zoological name of the dodo, from its similar bill.]

**didymium,** *di-* or *di-dim'i-əm, n.* a supposed ele-ment discovered in 1841, later resolved into neodymium and praseodymium. [Gr. *didymos,* twin, from its constant association with *lantha-num.*]

**didymous,** *did'i-məs, adj.* twin: twinned: growing in pairs: composed of two parts slightly con-nected. [Gr. *didymos,* twin.]

**Didynamia,** *did-i-nā'mi-a, n.pl.* a class of plants in the Linnaean system with two long stamens and two short.—*adjs.* didynā'mian, didyn'amous. [Gr. *di-,* double, *dynamis,* strength.]

**die,** *dī, v.i.* (or *v.t.* with object *death*) to lose life: to perish: to wither: hyperbolically, to lan-guish, suffer, or long: to become insensible: to merge:—*pr.p.* dy'ing; *pa.t.* and *pa.p.* died, did.—*adj.* die'-away', languishing.—die'-hard, an irre-concilable conservative.—die away, to disappear by degrees, become gradually inaudible; die back, to die by degrees from the tip backwards; die down, to subside: to die above ground, leaving only roots or rootstocks; die game, to keep up one's spirit to the last; die hard, to struggle hard against death, to be long in dying; die off, to die quickly or in large numbers; die out, to become extinct, to disappear; die the death (*theat. slang*), to arouse no response from one's audience.—see also dying. [Prob. from a lost O.E. (Anglian) *dēgan;* but commonly referred to a Scand. root seen in O.N. *deyja, döyja;* akin to M.H.G. *touwen,* whence Ger. *tod.* The O.E. word in use was *steorfan.*]

**die,** *dī, n.* a small cube with numbered faces thrown from a box in gaming: a small cubical piece: hazard: a stamp for impressing coin, etc.: applied to various tools for shaping things by stamping or cutting:—*pl.* (gaming, cookery, and the like) dice, (*dīs*); (stamping and shaping) dies (*dīz*).—*v.i.* dice, to play with dice.—*v.t.* cut into dice: to chequer:—*pr.p.* dic'ing; *pa.t.* and *pa.p.* diced, *dīst.*—*adj.* diced (*dīst*), orna-mented with a chequered pattern.—*ns.* dic'er; dic'ing, a chequered pattern: dice-playing.—*adj.* dic'ey (*coll.*), risky: tricky: uncertain in result.—dice'-box, an hour-glass-shaped box from which dice are thrown: dice'-coal, a coal that breaks into cubical blocks; dice'-play; dice'-player; die'-sink'er; die'-sink'ing, the engraving of dies; die'-stock, a contrivance for holding the dies used in screw-cutting; die'-work, ornamentation of a metal surface by im-pressions with a die.—no dice, no answer, or a negative answer: no success; the die is cast, an irrevocable step has been taken: there is no turning back now. [O.Fr. *de,* pl. *dez* (Prov. *dat,* It. *dado*), from L.L. *dadus* = L. *datus,* given or cast.]

**dieb**, *dēb*, *n.* a jackal of northern Africa. [Ar. *dhib*.]

**dièdre**, *dē-ed-r'*, *n.* a rock angle, or re-entrant corner, usu. with a crack in it. [Fr.]

**diegesis**, *di-ē-jē'sis*, (*rhet.*) *n.* in an oration, the narration of the facts. [Gr. *diēgēsis*.]

**dielectric**, *di-i-lek'trik*, *adj.* non-conducting: transmitting electric effects without conducting. —*n.* a substance, solid, liquid or gas, capable of supporting an electric stress, and hence an insulator.—**dielectric heating**, the heating of a non-conducting substance as a result of loss of power in a dielectric. [Gr. *dia*, through, and *electric*.]

**Dielytra**, *di-el'i-tra*, *n.* an erroneous name for *Dicentra* (q.v.). [As if Gr. *di-*, double, and *elytron*, cover.]

**⌣.eresis.** Same as diaeresis.

**dies**, *di'ēz*, *dē'äs*, (L.) day:—*pl.* **dies.**—**dies fasti** *⌣r* **profesti**, *fas'tī*, *fäs'tē*, *pro-fes'tī*, *-tē*, days on which judgment could be pronounced, on which courts could be held in ancient Rome, lawful days; **dies faustus**, *fös'təs*, *fows'tōōs*, lucky day; **dies festi** or **feriae**, *fes'tī*, *-tē*, *fer'i-ē*, *-ī*, days of actual festival; **dies infaustus**, *in-fös'təs*, *in-fows'tōōs*, unlucky day; **dies irae**, *ir'ē*, *ēr'ī*, the day of wrath: the day of judgment (from a Latin hymn); **dies nefasti**, *ni-fas'tī*, *ne-fäs'tē*, days on which a judgment could not be pronounced or assemblies of the people be held, in ancient Rome; **dies non**, *non*, *nōn*, a day on which judges do not sit, or one on which normal business is not transacted.

**diesel**, *dēz'l*, *n.* a diesel engine: a locomotive, train, etc., driven by a diesel engine.—*v.t.* and *v.i.* **dies'elise**, *-ize*, to equip, or be equipped with a diesel engine, locomotive or train.—*n.* **dieselisā'tion**, *-z-*.—*adj.* **dies'el-elec'tric**, using power obtained from a diesel-operated electric generator.—**diesel engine**, a compression-ignition engine in which the oil fuel is introduced into the heated compressed-air charge as a jet of liquid under high pressure.—*adj.* **dies'el-hydraul'ic** (Gr. *hydōr*, water, liquid), using power transmitted by means of one or more mechanisms (torque convertors) filled with oil. [Rudolph *Diesel* (1858-1913), German engineer.]

**diesis**, *di'e-sis*, *n.* the difference between a major and a minor semitone (*mus.*): the double dagger (‡) (*print*):—*pl.* **di'eses** (*-sēz*). [Gr. *diesis*, a quarter-tone.]

**diet**, *di'ət*, *n.* mode of living, now only with especial reference to food: planned or prescribed selection of food: allowance of provisions (*obs.*). —*v.t.* to furnish with food: to prescribe a diet for, put on a diet: to keep fasting.—*v.i.* to feed: to take food according to rule.—*n.* **dietā'rian**, one who observes prescribed rules for diet.—*adj.* **di'etary**, pertaining to diet or the rules of diet.— *n.* course of diet: allowance of food, esp. in large institutions.—*n.* **di'eter** (*Shak.*), one who regulates diet.—*adjs.* **dietet'ic**, *-al*, pertaining to diet.—*adv.* **dietet'ically**.—*ns.* **dietet'ics**, rules for regulating diet; **di'etist**, dietitian, *-cian* (*-ish'ən*), an authority on diet.—**diet-bread**, bread designed for persons on a diet; **di'et-drink**, medicated liquor. [Fr. *diète*—L.L. *diaeta*—Gr. *diaita*, mode of living, diet.]

**diet**, *di'ət*, *n.* a national, federal, or provincial assembly, council, or parliament: a conference: the proceedings under a criminal libel (*Scots law*): a clerical or ecclesiastical function in Scotland, as a *diet of worship*.—*n.* **di'etine**, a minor or local diet.—**desert the diet**, to abandon criminal proceedings under a particular libel—in Scottish usage. [O.Fr. *diete*—L.L. *diēta*—Gr. *diaita*; or acc. to Littré from L. *diēs*, a (set) day, with which usage cf. Ger. *tag*, day, *reichstag*.]

**diethyl**, *di-eth'il*, *adj.* having two ethyl groups.— *n.* **diethylamine** (*-mēn*), a liquid resembling

ethylamine, answering to ammonia, with ethyl replacing two hydrogen atoms. [Pfx. **di-**.]

**Dieu**, *dyø*, (Fr.) God.—**Dieu avec nous**, *a-vek nōō*, God with us; **Dieu et mon droit**, *ä mõ drwä*, God and my right.

**diffarreation**, *di-far-i-ā'shən*, *n.* divorce from a Roman marriage by *confarreation*. [L. *dif-* (= *dis-*), asunder.]

**differ**, *dif'ər*, *v.i.* to be unlike, distinct, or various (used by itself, or followed by *from*): to disagree (with *with*, sometimes *from*): to fall out, dispute (with).—*n.* (*Scot.*) difference.—*ns.* **diff'erence**, (*arch.*) **diff'erency**, dissimilarity: the quality distinguishing one thing from another: a contention or quarrel: the point in dispute: the excess of one quantity or number over another: differentia: a distinguishing mark: a modification to distinguish the arms of a branch from those of the main line (*her.*): discrimination.— *v.t.* to make or perceive a difference between or in.—*adj.* **diff'erent**, distinct: separate: unlike: not the same (with *from*, also *to*, not now *than*): out of the ordinary (*slang*): novel.—*n.* **differentia** (*-en'shi-a*; L.), in logic, that property which distinguishes a species from others:—*pl.* **differen'tiae** (*-ē*).—*adj.* **differen'tial** (*-shəl*), constituting or pertaining to a difference or differentia: discriminating: pertaining to infinitesimal differences (*math.*).—*n.* an infinitesimal difference: a differential gear: a price or wage difference.— *adv.* **differen'tially**.—*v.t.* **differentiate** (*-en'shi-āt*), to make different, cause to develop difference(s): to classify as different: to constitute a difference between: to obtain the differential coefficient of (*math.*).—*v.i.* to become different by specialisation: to distinguish (from, between).—*ns.* **differentiā'tion**, the act of distinguishing: description of a thing by giving its differentia: exact definition: a change by which what was generalised or homogeneous became specialised or heterogeneous: the act or process of differentiating, or determining the ratio of the rates of change of two quantities one of which is a function of the other (*math.*); **differen'tiātor**, one who or that which differentiates.—*adv.* **diff'erently**.—**difference tone, differential tone**, a tone heard when two tones are sounded together, its frequency the difference of their frequencies; **differential calculus** (see calculus); **differential coefficient**, the ratio of the rate of change of a function to that of its independent variable; **differential gear**, a gear permitting relative rotation of two shafts driven by a third; **differential motion**, a mechanical movement in which the velocity of a driven part is equal to the difference of the velocities of two parts connected to it; **differential thermometer**, a thermometer for measuring difference of temperature. [L. *differre—dif-* (for *dis-*), apart, *ferre*, to bear.]

**difficile**, *di-fis'il*, *dif'i-sil* (*arch.* or reintroduced) *adj.* difficult. [O.Fr. and Fr., *difficile*; see **difficult**.]

**difficult**, *dif'i-kəlt*, *adj.* not easy: hard to be done: requiring labour and pains: hard to please: not easily persuaded: unmanageable.—*adv.* **diff'i-cultly** (mainly chem.; e.g. *difficultly soluble*).— *n.* **diff'iculty**, quality or fact of being difficult: laboriousness: obstacle: objection: that which cannot be easily understood or believed: embarrassment of affairs: a quarrel. [The adj. was formed from *difficulty*—Fr. *difficulté*—L. *difficultās*, *-ātis*—*difficilis—dif-* (*dis-*), neg., and *facilis*, easy.]

**diffident**, *dif'i-dənt*, *adj.* distrusting: wanting in self-confidence.—*n.* **diff'idence**.—*adv.* **diff'idently**. [L. *diffīdēns*, *-entis*, pr.p. of *diffīdere*, to distrust —*dif-* (*dis-*), neg., *fīdere*, to trust—*fīdēs*, faith.]

**diffluent**, *dif'lōō-ənt*, *adj.* readily flowing away: fluid: deliquescent. [L. *dis-*, apart, *fluēns*, *-entis*, pr.p. of *fluēre*, to flow.]

**difform**, *di-förm'*, *adj.* unlike: irregular in form.—
*n.* **difform'ity**. [L. *dis-*, apart, *förma*, form.]
**diffract**, *di-frakt'*, *v.t.* to break up: to subject to
diffraction.—*n.* **diffrac'tion**, the spreading of
light or other rays passing through a narrow
opening or by the edge of an onaque body or
reflected by a grating, etc., with interference
phenomena, coloured and other.—*adj.* **diffrac'-
tive**.—*ns.* **diffractom'eter**, an instrument used in
examination of the atomic structure of matter by
means of diffraction of X-rays, electrons, or
neutrons.—**diffrangibil'ity** (*-franj-*).—*adj.* **dif-
frang'ible**, capable of being diffracted. [L.
*diffringĕre*, *diffrāctum—dis-*, asunder, *frangĕre*,
to break.]
**diffuse**, *di-fūz'*, *v.t.* to pour out all round: to send
out in all directions: to scatter: to circulate:
to publish.—*v.i.* to spread.—*adj.* **diffūsed'**, spread
widely: loose.—*adv.* **diffūs'edly**.—*ns.* **diffūs'edness**; **diffūs'er**; **diffūsibil'ity**.—*adj.* **diffūs'ible**.—
*ns.* **diffū'sion**, a spreading or scattering abroad:
extension: distribution: mixture through each
other of gases or liquids in contact.—*adj.*
**diffū'sive** (*-siv*), extending: spreading widely.—
*adv.* **diffū'sively**.—*ns.* **diffū'siveness**; **diffūsiv'ity**.—
**diffused lighting**, lighting that is transmitted or
reflected in all directions and, being evenly distributed, produces no glare; **diffū'sion-tube**, an
instrument for determining the rate of diffusion
for different gases. [L. *diffundĕre*, *diffūsum—
dif-* (*dis-*), asunder, *fundĕre*, to pour out.]
**diffuse**, *di-fūs'*, *adj.* diffused: widely spread:
wordy: not concise.—*adv.* **diffuse'ly**.—*n.* **diffuse'-
ness**. [Root as above.]
**dig**, *dig*, *v.t.* to excavate: to turn up with a spade
or otherwise: to get or put by digging: to poke
or thrust: to taunt: to understand, approve
(*slang*): to take note of (*slang*).—*v.i.* to use a
spade: to seek (for) by digging (*lit.* and *fig.*): to
burrow: to mine: to lodge (*slang*): to study hard
(*U.S. slang*):—*pr.p.* **digg'ing**; *pa.t.* and *pa.p.* **dug**,
(*B.*) **digged**.—*n.* an act or course of digging: an
archaeological excavating expedition: an excavation made by archaeologists: a poke: a
taunt: a hard-working student (*U.S. slang*).—
*adj.* **digg'able**.—*ns.* **digg'er**, a person or animal
that digs: a miner, esp. a gold-miner: an
Australian or New Zealander (*slang*): a machine
for digging.—*n.pl.* **digg'ings**, places where mining
is carried on, esp. for gold: lodgings, rooms
(abbrev. **digs**; *slang*; *orig.* *U.S.*).—**digg'er-
wasp**, a burrowing wasp of various kinds.—**dig
in**, to cover over by digging: to work hard;
**dig oneself in**, to entrench oneself: to establish
oneself in a position; **dig out** (*U.S. slang*), to
decamp; **dig up**, to remove from the ground by
digging: to excavate: to obtain by seeking
(*coll.*): to produce, esp. reluctantly (*coll.*). [Prob.
O.Fr. *diguer*, to dig; of Gmc. origin.]
**digamma**, *dī-gam'ə*, *n.* vau, the obsolete sixth letter
(F, Γ, later ζ) of the Greek alphabet with the
sound of our W: as a numeral ζ' = 6, ,ζ =
6000. See **episemon**. [Gr. *di-*, twice, and
*gamma*, from its form like one capital Γ over
another.]
**digamy**, *dig'ə-mi*, *n.* a second marriage.—*n.*
**dig'amist**.—*adj.* **dig'amous**. [Gr. *di-*, twice,
*gamos*, marriage.]
**digastric**, *dī-gas'trik*, *adj.* double bellied, or fleshy
at each end, as is one of the muscles of the lower
jaw. [Gr. *di-*, double, *gastēr*, the belly.]
**digest**, *di-jest'* (also *di-*), *v.t.* to dissolve in the
stomach: to soften by heat and moisture: to
distribute and arrange: to prepare or classify in
the mind: to think over, to take in gradually,
the meaning and implications of: to endure
without protest (e.g. insult).—*v.i.* to be dissolved
in the stomach: to be softened by heat and moisture.—*adv.* **digest'edly**.—*n.* **digest'er**, one who
digests: a close vessel in which by heat and

pressure strong extracts are made from animal
and vegetable substances.—*n.* **digestibil'ity**.—
*adj.* **digest'ible**, that may be digested.—*n.*
**digestion** (*di-jest'yən*), the dissolving of the food
in the stomach: orderly arrangement: exposing
to slow heat, etc.—*adj.* **digest'ive**, pertaining to
digestion: promoting digestion.—*n.* something
which promotes digestion: (also **digestive
biscuit**) a round, semi-sweet biscuit, the basic
ingredient of which is meal.—*adv.* **digest'ively**.
[L. *digerĕre*, *digestum*, to carry asunder or
dissolve—*di-* (*dis-*), asunder, and *gerĕre*, to bear.]
**digest**, *dī'jest*, *n.* a body of laws collected and
arranged, esp. the Justinian code of civil laws: a
synopsis: an abstract: a periodical abstract of
news or current literature. [L. *digesta*, neut. pl.
of *digestus*, pa.p. of *digerĕre*, to carry apart, to
arrange.]
**dight**, *dit*, (*arch.*) *v.t.* to adorn: to equip.—*adj.*
disposed: adorned. [O.E. *dihtan*, to arrange,
prescribe, from L. *dictāre*, to dictate (whence Ger.
*dichten*, to write poetry); cf. **dicht**.]
**digit**, *dij'it*, *n.* a finger or toe: a finger's breadth or
¾ inch: a figure used in arithmetic to represent a
number: the twelfth part of the diameter of the
sun or moon.—*adj.* **dig'ital**, pertaining to the
fingers, or to arithmetical digits.—*n.* finger: a
key of a piano, etc.—*ns.* **digitalin** (*dij-i-tā'lin*, or
*dij'it-ə-lin*), a glucoside or mixture of glucosides
got from foxglove; **Digita'lis**, the foxglove
genus: dried foxglove leaves used as a drug.—
*adjs.* **dig'itate, -d**, consisting of several finger-
like sections.—*adv.* **dig'itately**.—*n.* **digitā'tion**,
finger-like arrangement: a finger-like division.
—*adj.* **dig'itiform**, formed like fingers; **dig'iti-
grade**, walking on the toes.—*n.* an animal that
walks on its toes.—*v.t.* **digitise, -ize**, to put (data)
into digital form for use in a digital computer.—
*n.* **digitō'rium**, a pianist's dumb keyboard for
finger exercises.—**digital computer**, an electronic
calculating machine using arithmetical digits,
generally binary or decimal notation. [L.
*digitus*, finger, toe.]
**digladiate**, *dī-glad'i-āt*, *v.i.* to fight with swords:
to fence: to wrangle.—*ns.* **digladiā'tion**; **diglad'-
iātor**. [L. *digladiāri*, to contend fiercely—*dis-*,
this way and that, and *gladius*, sword.]
**diglot**, *dī'glot*, *adj.* bilingual. [Gr. *diglōttos—di-*,
double, *glōtta*, tongue.]
**diglyph**, *dī'glif*, (*archit.*) *n.* an ornament consisting
of a double groove. [Gr. *di-*, double, *glyphē*,
carving.]
**dignify**, *dig'ni-fī*, *v.t.* to invest with honour: to
exalt:—*pr.p.* **dig'nifying**; *pa.t.* and *pa.p.* **dig'nified**.—*n.* **dignificā'tion**.—*adj.* **dig'nified**, marked
or consistent with dignity: exalted: noble:
grave: ranking as a dignitary. [L.L. *dignificāre
—dignus*, worthy, *facĕre*, to make.]
**dignity**, *dig'ni-ti*, *n.* the state of being dignified:
elevation of mind or character: grandeur of
mien: elevation in rank, place, etc.: degree of
excellence: preferment: high office: a dignitary.
—*n.* **dig'nitary**, one in a high position or rank,
esp. in the church.—**stand on one's dignity**, to
assume a manner that asserts a claim to deference. [Fr. *dignité*—L. *dignitās*, *-ātis—dignus*,
worthy.]
**digonal**, *dig'ə-nl*, *adj.* of symmetry about an axis,
such that a half-turn (180°) gives the same figure.
[Gr. *di-*, twice, *gōniā*, angle.]
**digoneutic**, *dig-ə-nūt'ik*, *adj.* breeding twice a year.
[Gr. *di-*, twice, *goneus*, a parent.]
**digraph**, *dī'gräf*, *n.* two letters expressing but one
sound, as *ph* in *digraph*. [Gr. *di-*, twice, *graphē*,
a mark, a character—*graphein*, to write.]
**digress**, *di-gres'*, *di-gres'*, *v.i.* to depart from the
main subject: to introduce irrelevant matter.—
*n.* **digression** (*-gresh'ən*), a going from the main
point: a part of a discourse not upon the main
subject.—*adjs.* **digress'ional**, **digress'ive**, of the

nature of a digression: departing from the main subject.—*adv.* digress′ively. [L. *dīgredī, dīgressus —dī-* (*dis-*), aside, *gradī*, to step.]
Digynia, di-jin′i-ə, *n.pl.* in various Linnaean classes of plants, an order with two styles or deeply cleft style.—*adjs.* digyn′ian; digynous (*dij′* or *dij′i-nəs*), digynian: with two styles or two carpels. [Gr. *di-*, twice, and *gynē*, a woman.]
dihedral, di-hē′drəl, *adj.* bounded by two planes, or two plane faces—also diē′dral.—*n.* dihē′dron, the limiting case of a double pyramid when the vertices coincide. [Gr. *di-*, twice, *hedrā*, a seat.]
dihybrid, di-hi′brid, *n.* a cross between parents that differ in two independently heritable characters.—Also *adj.* [Gr. *di-*, double, twice, and hybrid.]
dihydric, di-hi′drik, *adj.* having two hydroxyl groups. [Pfx. di-.]
dijudicate, di-jōō′di-kāt, *v.t.* and *v.i.* to judge: to decide.—*n.* dijudicā′tion. [L. *di-* (*dis-*), asunder, and *jūdicāre*, judge.]
dika, dī′kə, dē′kə, *n.* a West Indian simarubaceous tree, *Irvingia gabonensis*, the so-called wild-mango.—di′ka-bread, a compressed mass of dika and other seeds, smelling like chocolate; di′ka-butter, -oil, a fat expressed from its seeds. [From a W. African name.]
dik-dik, dik′dik, *n.* a name for several very small E. African antelopes, species of *Madoqua*, etc. [Said to be a name in Abyssinia.]
dike, dyke, dik, *n.* a trench, or the earth dug out and thrown up: a ditch: a mound raised to prevent inundation: in Scotland, a wall (dry-stane dike, a wall without mortar; fail-dike, a wall of turf), sometimes even a thorn-hedge: an igneous mass injected into a fissure in rocks, sometimes weathered out into wall-like forms (*geol.*).—*v.t.* to provide with a dike.—*v.i.* to make a dike.—*n.* dik′er, one who makes dikes. [O.E. *dīc*; Du. *dijk*, Ger. *teich*, a pond; see dig, ditch.]
diktat, dik-tät′, *n.* a harsh settlement forced on the defeated or powerless. [Ger., something dictated.]
dilacerate, di-las′ər-āt, *v.t.* to rend or tear asunder. —*n.* dilacerā′tion. [L. *di-*, asunder, and lacerate.]
dilapidate, di-lap′i-dāt, *v.t.* to pull down, stone from stone to waste: to suffer to go to ruin.—*adj.* dilap′idated, in ruins.—*ns.* dilapidā′tion, the state of ruin: (*pl.*) damage done to a building during tenancy: impairing of church property during an incumbency: (*pl.*) money paid at the end of an incumbency by the incumbent or his heirs for the purpose of putting the parsonage, etc., in good repair; dilap′idator. [L. *dilapidāre —dī-*, asunder, *lapis, lapidis*, a stone.]
dilate, di-lāt′, di-lāt′, *v.t.* to spread out in all directions: to enlarge: to set forth at full length (*Shak.*).—*v.i.* to widen: to swell out: to speak at length.—*ns.* dilātabil′ity; dilāt′ancy, property shown by some colloidal systems of thickening or solidifying under pressure or impact; dilatation (-lə-tā′shən), or (irregularly formed) dilā′tion, expansion: a transformation which produces a figure similar to, but not congruent with, the original (*math.*).—*adjs.* dilāt′able, that may be dilated or expanded; dilā′tant.—*adj.* dilāt′ed, expanded and flattened. —*ns.* di′latātor (dilā′tor), an instrument or a muscle that expands; dilāt′er, one who dilates: a dilatator.—*adj.* dilāt′ive. [L. *dilātus* (used as pa.p. of *differre*), from *di-* (*dis-*), apart, and *lātus*, wide.]
dilatory, dil′ə-tə-ri, *adj.* slow: given to procrastination: loitering: tending to delay.—*adv.* dil′atorily.—*n.* dil′atoriness. [L. *dīlātōrius*. See dilate.]
dildo, dil′dō, *n.* an object serving as an erect penis substitute (also dil′doe; *slang*): word used in

refrains of songs (*obs.*): a weak or effeminate man (*obs.*): a cylindrical curl: a W. Indian spiny cactus (*Lemaireocereus hystrix*).—dil′do-glass, a cylindrical glass. [Origin uncertain.]
dilemma, di-, di-lem′ə, *n.* a form of argument in which the maintainer of a certain proposition is committed to accept one of two propositions each of which contradicts his original contention: a position where each of two alternative courses (or of all the feasible courses) is eminently undesirable. The argument was called a 'horned syllogism', and the victim compared to a man certain to be impaled on one or other of the horns of an infuriated bull, hence the horns of a dilemma.—*adj.* dilemmat′ic. [L.,—Gr. *dilēmma —di-*, twice, double, *lēmma*, an assumption— *lambanein*, to take.]
dilettante, dil-et-an′ti, *n.* one who loves the fine arts but in a superficial way and without serious purpose (the *amateur* usually practises them): a dabbler in art, science, or literature:—*pl.* dilettan′ti (-tē).—*adj.* dilettan′tish.—*ns.* dilettan′tism, dilettan′teism. [It., pr.p. of *dilettare—* L. *dēlectāre*, to delight.]
diligent, dil′i-jənt, *adj.* steady and earnest in application: industrious.—*n.* dil′igence, steady application: industry: a warrant to produce witnesses, books, etc., or a process by which persons or goods are attached (*Scots law*): a French or continental stage-coach (also pronounced dē-lē-zhās)—also dill′y.—*adv.* dil′i-gently. [Fr. *diligēns, -entis*, pr.p. of L. *diligĕre*, to choose.]
dill, *dil, n.* an umbelliferous annual akin to parsnip, the fruits or 'seeds' used as condiment and carminative.—dill′-wat′er, a drink prepared from them. [O.E. *dile*; Ger. and Sw. *dill*.]
dilling, dil′ing, *n.* a darling: the youngest child: the weakling of a litter. [Origin doubtful.]
dilly-bag, dil′i-bag, *n.* an Australian native-made rush or bark-bag.—Also dill′i, dill′y. [Native *dilli*.]
dilly-dally, dil′i-dal′i, *v.i.* to loiter, trifle. [Reduplication of dally; cf. shilly-shally.]
dilucidate, di-lū′si-dāt, dil-lōō′, (*obs.*) *v.t.* to elucidate.—*n.* dilucidā′tion. [L. *dīlūcidāre, -ātum*.]
dilute, di-lūt′, di-lōōt′, or di-, *v.t.* to make thinner or more liquid: to diminish the concentration of, by mixing, esp. with water: of labour, to increase the proportion of unskilled to skilled in.—*v.i.* to become mixed.—*adj.* (di- or di-lūt′, -lōōt′, or di′) diminished in concentration by mixing.—*adj.* diluent (dil′ū-ənt), diluting.—*n.* that which dilutes.—*ns.* dilu′tee, an unskilled worker introduced onto a skilled occupation; dilute′ness; dilu′ter, dilu′tor, one who or that which dilutes; dilu′tion. [L. *dīluĕre, dīlūtum—dī-*, away, *luĕre*, to wash.]
diluvium, dil-ū′vi-əm, dil-ōō′, *n.* an inundation or flood: a deposit of sand, gravel, etc., made by extraordinary currents of water (*geol.*; *obs.*).— Also dilu′vion.—*adjs.* dilu′vial, dilu′vian, pertaining to a flood, esp. Noah's: caused by a deluge: composed of diluvium.—*n.* dilu′vialist, one who explains geological phenomena by the flood. [L. *dīluvium*, a deluge—*dīluĕre*, to wash away.]
dim, dim, *adj.* not bright or distinct: obscure: not seeing clearly: mentally dull, stupid (*coll.*). —*v.t.* to make dark: to obscure.—*v.i.* to become dim:—*pr.p.* dimm′ing; *pa.t.* and *pa.p.* dimmed.— *adv.* dim′ly.—*n.* dimm′er, an arrangement for regulating the supply of light.—*adj.* dimm′ish, somewhat dim.—*n.* dim′ness.—dim′wit (*coll.*), a stupid person.—a dim view (*coll.*), an unfavourable view. [O.E. *dimm*; akin to O.N. *dimmr*, dark, and Ger. *dämmerung*, twilight.]
di majorum gentium, di ma-jō′rəm, -jō′, jen′-sh(y)əm, dē ma-yō′rōōm gen′ti-ōōm, (L.) the

divinities of superior rank, i.e. the twelve greater gods of classical mythology.

**dimble**, *dim'bl, n.* a dell, dingle.

**dime**, *dim, n.* the tenth part of an American dollar, 10 cents.—**dime museum,** a cheap show; **dime novel,** a cheap novel, usually sensational. [Fr., orig. *disme,* from L. *decima (pars),* a tenth (part).]

**dimension,** *di-* or *di-men'shən, n.* measure in length, breadth, or thickness (the three dimensions of space): extent: size: the sum of the indices in a term (*alg.*).—*adjs.* **dimen'sional,** concerning dimension: in composition, of so many dimensions; **dimen'sioned; dimen'sionless.**—**dimension work,** masonry in stones of specified size.— **fourth dimension,** an additional dimension attributed to space—in relativity theory, time. [Fr.,— L. *dimēnsiō, -ōnis—dimētiri, dimēnsus—di- (dis-),* apart, *mētiri,* to measure.]

**dimerous,** *dim'ə-rəs, adj.* consisting of two parts: with two members in each whorl (*bot.*): having two-jointed tarsi (*entom.*).—*adj.* **dimeric** (*di-mer'ik*), bilaterally symmetrical: dimerous: having the same empirical formula, but double the molecular weight (*chem.*).—*n.* **dimerism** (*dim'ər-izm*). [Gr. *di-,* double, twice, and *meros,* a part.]

**dimeter,** *dim'i-tər, adj.* containing two measures.— *n.* a verse of two measures. [L.,—Gr. *dimetros— di-,* twice, *metron,* a measure.]

**dimethyl,** *di-meth'il, n.* ethane.—*adj.* containing two methyl radicals in combination.—*ns.* **dimeth'ylamine** (-*ə-mēn'*), a compound answering to ammonia with methyl replacing two hydrogen atoms; **dimethylan'iline,** an oily liquid, aniline heated with methyl alcohol and hydrochloric acid—from which dyes are obtained. [Pfx. **di-, methyl.**]

**dimetric,** *di-met'rik, (crystal.) adj.* tetragonal. [Pfx. **di-,** metric, pertaining to distance.]

**dimidiate,** *di-mid'i-āt, adj.* divided into halves: having a shape that appears as if halved: having only one side developed: split on one side.—*v.t.* (*her.*) to represent the half of.—*n.* **dimidiā'tion.** [L. *dimidiāre, -ātum,* to halve—*dimidius,* half— *dis-,* apart, *medius,* the middle.]

**diminish,** *di-min'ish, v.t.* to make less: to take a part from: to degrade.—*v.i.* to grow or appear less: to subside.—*adj.* **dimin'ishable.**—*adj.* **dimin'ished,** made smaller: humbled: a semitone less than perfect or minor (*mus.*).—*n.* and *adj.* **dimin'ishing.**—*adv.* **dimin'ishingly.**—*n.* **dimin'ishment.**—**diminished responsibility,** limitation in law of criminal responsibility on ground of mental weakness or abnormality, not merely of actual insanity; **diminishing glass,** a lens or combination of lenses that makes objects appear smaller. [Coined from **minish,** in imitation of L. *diminuēre,* to break in pieces—*di- (dis-),* apart, *minuēre,* to make less.]

**diminuendo,** *di-min-ū-en'dō, (mus.) adj.* and *adv.* letting the sound die away, marked thus >. —Also *n.* [It.,—L.L. *diminuendus,* for L. *dēminuendus,* ger. of *dēminuēre, dēminūtum,* to lessen.]

**diminution,** *dim-in-ū'shən, n.* a lessening: degradation.—*adj.* **dimin'utive,** of a diminished size: very small: contracted.—*n. (gram.)* a word formed from another to express a little one of the kind.—*adv.* **dimin'utively.**—*n.* **dimin'utiveness.** [**diminish.**]

**dimissory,** *dim'is-ə-ri, di-, di-mis'ə-ri, adj.* sending away or giving leave to depart to another jurisdiction. [L. *dimissōrius—dimittēre, dimissum— dis-,* apart, *mittēre,* to send.]

**dimity,** *dim'i-ti, n.* a stout white cotton, striped or figured in the loom by weaving with two threads. [Gr. *dimitos—di-,* twice, *mitos,* a thread.]

**dimorphism,** *di-mör'fizm, n.* the occurrence of two forms in the same species (*biol.*): the property of crystallising in two forms (*chem.*).—

*adjs.* **dimor'phic, dimor'phous.** [Gr. *di-,* twice *morphē,* form.]

**dimple,** *dim'pl, n.* a small hollow, esp. on the surface of the body.—*v.i.* to form dimples.—*adj.* **dim'pled.**—*n.* **dim'plement.**—*adj.* **dim'ply.** [Apparently cogn. with Ger. *tumpel,* pool.]

**dimyarian,** *dim-i-* or *di-mi-ā'ri-ən, adj.* having two adductor muscles. [Gr. *di-,* twice, *mȳs, myos,* muscle.]

**din,** *din, n.* a loud continued noise.—*v.t.* to assail (the ears) with noise: to annoy with clamour: to obtrude noisily and persistently:—*pr.p.* **dinn'ing;** *pa.t.* and *pa.p.* **dinned.**—*adj.* **din'ful.** [O.E. *dynn, dyne;* cf. O.N. *dynr, Dan. dön,* noise.]

**dinanderie,** *dē-nä-də-rē, n.* domestic decorative brassware, originally that made at *Dinant* in Belgium: extended to Indian and Levantine brassware. [Fr.]

**Dinantian,** *din-an'shi-ən, (geol.) adj.* Lower Carboniferous. [*Dinant* in Belgium.]

**dinar,** *dē-när', n.* an ancient Arab gold coin of 65 grains' weight: the monetary unit of Algeria, Tunisia, Iraq, and other Arab countries: a Yugoslav franc. [L. *dēnārius.*]

**dinarchy.** See **diarchy.**

**dindle.** See **dinnle.**

**dine,** *din, v.i.* to take dinner.—*v.t.* to furnish with a dinner.—*n. (obs.)* dinner, dinner-time.—*ns.* **din'er,** one who dines: a dining-car; **dinette',** an alcove or other part of a room or kitchen set apart for meals.—**din'er-out,** one who goes much to dinner-parties; **din'ing-car,** a railway carriage in which meals are served; **din'ing-hall; din'ing-room; din'ing-table.**—**dine out,** to dine elsewhere than at home; **dine with Duke Humphrey** (*hist.*), to go without a meal, loiter about Duke Humphrey's Walk in Old St Paul's. [O.Fr. *disner* (Fr. *dîner*) prob.—L. *dis-,* expressing undoing, and *jējūnus,* fasting (cf. **disjune**); according to others—L. *dē-,* inten., and *cēna,* a meal.]

**ding,** *ding, v.t.* to dash: to beat: to thump: to knock: to surpass (*Scot.*).—*v.i.* to beat: to dash:—*pa.t.* **dinged, dang, dung;** *pa.p.* **dinged, dung.**—*n.* **ding'er** (*slang*), anything superlative in its kind.—**ding doun** (*Scot.*), to knock or throw down. [M.E. *dingen, dyngen;* cf. O.N. *dengja,* Sw. *dänga,* to bang.]

**ding,** *ding, v.i.* to ring, keep sounding.—*v.t.* to reiterate to a wearisome degree.—**ding'-dong',** the sound of bells ringing: monotony: sameness: an argument or fight.—*adj.* and *adv.* like a bell ringing: hammer-and-tongs: keenly contested with rapid alternations of success.— *v.t.* and *v.i.* to ring: to nag. [Imit., but partly confounded with preceding.]

**dinges,** *ding'əs, (S. Africa) n.* an indefinite name for any person or thing whose name one cannot or will not remember.—Also **ding'us.** [Du., —Afrik. *ding,* thing; cf. Eng. **thingummy, thingumbob.**]

**dinghy, dingy, dingey,** *ding'gi, n.* a small rowing-boat or ship's tender: an airman's collapsible rubber boat. [Hind. *dingi,* a small boat.]

**dingle,** *ding'gl, n.* a dell. [Origin uncertain.]

**dingle-dangle,** *ding'gl-dang'gl, adv.* with swinging to and fro. [Reduplication of **dangle.**]

**dingo,** *ding'gō, n.* the native dog of Australia:—*pl.* **ding'oes.** [Name in obs. native dialect.]

**dingus.** See **dinges.**

**dingy,** *din'ji, adj.* of a dim or dark colour: dull: soiled.—*n.* **din'giness,** dinginess.—*v.t.* to make dingy. —*n.* **din'giness.** [Origin obscure.]

**dinic,** *din'ik, adj.* relating to vertigo or dizziness.— *n.* a remedy for dizziness. [Gr. *dinos,* whirling.]

**dinitro-,** *di-ni'trō-,* in composition, having two nitro-groups ($NO_2$), esp. replacing hydrogen.—*n.* **dinitroben'zene,** $C_6H_4(NO_2)_2$, answering to benzene, $C_6H_6$.

dink, *dingk*, (*Scot.*) *adj.* neat, trim.—*v.t.* to dress neatly.—*adj.* dink'y (*coll.*), neat: dainty.

dinkum, *ding'kəm*, (*Austr. slang*) *adj.* real, genuine: square, honest.—Also *adv.*—Also dink'y-di(e). [Perh. from E. dial. *dinkum*, a fair share of work.]

dinmont, *din'mənt*, *n.* a Border name for a male sheep between the first and second shearing. [Origin obscure.]

dinner, *din'ər*, *n.* the chief meal of the day: a feast.—*v.i.* to dine.—*v.t.* to provide with dinner.—*adj.* dinn'erless.—dinn'er-dance, a dance following a dinner; dinn'er-gown, a less formal evening dress; dinn'er-hour'; dinn'er-jack'et, a tailless dress-coat; dinn'er-pail', a vessel in which a workman carries his dinner; dinn'er-service, -set, a complete set of plates and dishes for a company at dinner; dinn'er-table; dinn'er-time; dinn'er-wagon, orig. a shelved trolley for a dining-room: a sideboard in two tiers. [O.Fr. *disner*, prop. breakfast; see dine.]

dinnle, *din'l*, (*Scot.*) *v.i.* to tingle.—*n.* a thrill.—Also din'dle. [Prob. imitative.]

dino-, deino-, *dī-nō-*, in composition, huge, terrible.—*ns.* Dinoceras, Deinoceras (*-nos'ə-ras*; Gr. *keras*, horn), a large Eocene fossil stump-footed ungulate of Wyoming, otherwise Uintatherium, named from three pairs of protuberances on the skull; Dinornis (*dī-nör'nis*; Gr. *ornis*, a bird), a genus of moas, including the biggest; dinosaur, deinosaur (*dī'nō-sör*; Gr. *sauros*, a lizard), any extinct (Mesozoic) reptile of the order Dinosaur'ia, in length from two to eighty feet; Dinotherium, Deinotherium (*-thē'ri-əm*; Gr. *thērion*, a beast), a huge extinct (Tertiary) proboscidean, with elephant-like tusks and trunk. [Gr. *deinos*, terrible.]

dinoflagellate, *dī-nō-flaj'ə-lāt*, *n.* a unicellular organism, a plant-like flagellate with two flagella. [Gr. *dinos*, whirl, and flagellate.]

Dinornis, dinosaur, etc. See dino-.

dint, *dint*, *n.* a blow or stroke: the mark of a blow (often dent): force: (as in *by dint of*).—*v.t.* to make a dint in. [O.E. *dynt*, a blow; cf. dunt; O.N. *dyntr*.]

diocese, *dī'ə-sis, -sēs*, *n.* the circuit or extent of a bishop's jurisdiction.—*adj.* diocesan (*dī-os'i-sn, -zn*), pertaining to a diocese.—*n.* a bishop in relation to his diocese: one of the clergy in the diocese. [Through Fr. and L. from Gr. *dioikēsis—dioikeein*, to keep house—*di-*, for *dia-*, sig. completeness, *oikeein*, to keep house—*oikos*, a house.]

diode, *dī'ōd*, *n.* the simplest electron tube with heated cathode and anode: a two-electrode semiconductor device evolved from primitive crystal rectifiers. [Gr. *di-*, twice, *hodos*, way.]

Diodon, *dī'ə-don*, *n.* a genus of globe-fishes with all the teeth in each jaw consolidated. [Gr. *dis-*, twice, double, *odous, odontos*, a tooth.]

dioecious, *dī-ē'shəs*, *adj.* having the sexes separate: having male or female flowers on different plants.—*n.pl.* Dioe'cia, a class in the Linnaean system, dioecious plants.—*n.* dioe'cism (*-sizm*). [Gr. *di-*, twice, *oikos*, a house.]

Diogenic, *dī-ə-jen'ik*, *adj.* pertaining to the Cynic philosopher *Diogenēs* (*c.* 412-323 B.C.): cynical.

Dionaea, *dī-ə-nē'a*, *n.* Venus's fly-trap, an American droseraceous insectivorous plant. [L.,—Gr. *Dīōnaiā*, Aphrodite, from her mother *Diōnē*.]

Dionysia, *dī-ə-niz'i-a*, or *-nis'*, *n.pl.* dramatic and orgiastic festivals in honour of *Dionȳsos* (Bacchus), god of wine.—*adjs.* Dionys'iac, Bacchic; Dionys'ian, relating to *Dionȳsos* or to *Dīonȳsios* (Dionysius—of Syracuse, the Areopagite, Exiguus, or any other of the name).

Diophantine, *dī-ə-fan'tīn*, *adj.* pertaining to the Alexandrian mathematician *Diophantos* (*c.* A.D. 275).—Diophantine analysis, the part of algebra which treats of finding particular rational values for general expressions under a surd form;

Diophantine equations (*maths.*), indeterminate equations for which integral or rational solutions are required.

diopside, *dī-op'sid*, *n.* a strongly birefringent monoclinic calcium-magnesium pyroxene. [Gr. *di-*, double, *opsis*, a view.]

dioptase, *dī-op'tās*, *n.* an emerald-green acid copper silicate. [Gr. *dia*, through, *optazein*, to see; from its internal glitter.]

dioptric, -al, *dī-op'trik, -əl*, *adjs.* pertaining to dioptrics or a diopter: transparent (as a *dioptric bee-hive*).—*ns.* diop'ter, an ancient form of theodolite: the index-arm of a graduated circle: (also diop'tre) a unit of measurement of the power of a lens, the reciprocal of the focal distances in metres, negative for a divergent lens.—*adj.* diop'trate (*entom.*), having the compound eye divided transversely.—*n.* diop'trics, the part of optics that treats of refraction. [Gr. *dioptrā*, a levelling instrument, *dioptron*, a spyglass—*dia*, through, and the root of *opsesthai*, used as fut. of *horaein*, to see.]

diorama, *dī-ə-rä'mə*, *n.* an exhibition of pictures seen through an opening with lighting effects.—*adj.* diorăm'ic. [Gr. *dia*, through, *horāma*, a sight.]

diorism, *dī'ə-rizm*, *n.* distinction, definition.—*adjs.* dioris'tic, -al.—*adv.* dioris'tically. [Gr. *diorizein*, to divide, *dia*, through, *horos*, a boundary.]

diorite, *dī'ə-rit*, *n.* a crystalline granular igneous rock composed of plagioclase and hornblende.—*adj.* diorit'ic. [G *diorizein*, to distinguish—*dia*, through, *horos*, a boundary.]

diorthosis, *dī-ör-thō'sis*, *n.* the reduction of a dislocation (*surg.*): the correction of a deformity: a critical revision of a text.—*adj.* diorthŏt'ic. [Gr. *dia*, through, *orthos*, straight.]

Dioscorea, *dī-os-kōr'i-a, -kōr'i-a*, *n.* the yam genus, of the monocotyledonous family Dioscoreā'ceae.—*adj.* dioscoreā'ceous. [From the 1st century (A.D.) Greek physician *Dioskoridēs*.]

Dioscuri, *dī-os-kū'rī*, *n.pl.* Castor and Pollux, as sons of Zeus. [Gr. *Dios*, gen. of *Zeus*, and *koros* (Ionian *kouros*), a son, a lad.]

diota, *dī-ō'tə*, *n.* a two-handled ancient vase. [Gr. *diōtos*, two-handled—*di-*, twice, *ous, ōtos*, ear.]

Diothelism, Diothelite. See ditheletism.

dioxide, *dī-ok'sid*, *n.* an oxide with two atoms of oxygen in the molecule. [Pfx. di-, oxide.]

dip, *dip*, *v.t.* to immerse for a time: to lower: to lower and raise again (as a flag): to baptise by immersion: to lift by dipping (usu. with *up*): to dye or clean by dipping: to moisten, suffuse (*Milt.*): to involve in money difficulties (*coll.*): to mortgage: to pawn.—*v.i.* to plunge and emerge: to sink: to reach down into something: to enter slightly: to look cursorily: to incline downwards:—*pr.p.* dipp'ing; *pa.t.* and *pa.p.* dipped.—*n.* the act of dipping: a hollow: a sag: that which is taken by dipping: inclination downwards: a sloping: the angle a stratum of rock makes with a horizontal plane (*geol.*): a bath: a short swim: a liquid in which anything is dipped (as sheep, garments, etc.): liquid or creamy mixture into which bread, biscuits, etc., are dipped: a candle made by dipping a wick in tallow: a pickpocket (*slang*).—*n.* dipp'er (q.v.).—dip'-circle or dipp'ing-needle, an instrument for determining magnetic dip: dip'-net, a long-handled net for dipping up fish: dip'-pipe, a pipe with submerged outlet, esp. in gas-works; dip'-sec'tor, an instrument for determining the dip of the visible horizon; dip'-slope' (*geol.*), a slope of ground coinciding with the dip of the rocks; dip'-stick, a rod for measuring depth of liquid in a sump, etc.; dip'-trap, a bend in a pipe containing liquid to cut off gases.—dip of the horizon, the angle of the visible horizon below the level of the eye; dip of the needle, the angle a balanced magnetic needle makes with the horizontal plane. [O.E. *dyppan*, causal of *dȳpan*, to plunge in—*dēop*, deep; cf. Dan. *dyppe*; Ger. *taufen*, to immerse.]

**dipchick, dip′chik.** Same as **dabchick.**

**di penates, dē pə-nā′tēz, dē pe-nä′tās, (L.)** household gods.

**dipetalous, dī-pet′ə-ləs, adj.** having two petals. [Gr. *di-*, twice, and *petalon*, a leaf.]

**diphenyl, dī-fē′nil, n.** a hydrocarbon consisting of two phenyl groups.—*adj.* having two phenyl groups, esp. replacing hydrogen.

**diphone, dī′fōn, n.** a shorthand sign representing a diphthongal sound. [Gr. *di-*, twice, *phōnē*, sound.]

**diphtheria, dif-thē′ri-ə, n.** an infectious throat disease in which the air-passages become covered with a leathery membrane.—*adjs.* **diphtheric** (*-ther′ik*), **diphtheritic** (*-thər-it′ik*).—*n.* **diphtheri′tis,** diphtheria.—*adj.* **diph′theroid.** [Gr. *diphtherā,* leather.]

**diphthong, dif′thong, n.** two vowel-sounds pronounced as one syllable (as in *out,mind*): (loosely) a digraph: the ligature *æ* or *œ*.—*adjs.* **diphthongal** (*-thong′gəl*), **diphthon′gic** (*-gik*).—*adv.* **diphthong′ally.**—*v.t.* **diph′thongise, -ize** (*-giz*). [Gr. *diphthongos*—*di-*, twice, *phthongos*, sound, vowel.]

**diphycercal, dif-i-sûr′kəl, adj.** having the tail symmetrical about the vertebral column, which runs horizontally (of fishes, etc.). [Gr. *diphyēs*, of double nature, twofold, *kerkos*, a tail.]

**diphyletic, di,- dī-fil-et′ik,** (*biol.*) *adj.* of dual origin: descended from two distinct ancestral groups. [Gr. *di-*, double, *phȳletikos*, pertaining to a tribesman—*phȳlē*, a tribe.]

**diphyodont, dif′i-ō-dont, adj.** having two sets of teeth (milk and permanent).—*n.* a mammal with these. [Gr. *diphyēs*, of double nature, *odous, odontos,* a tooth.]

**Diphysite, dif′i-zit, -sit, n.** a believer in the existence of two natures in Christ, a divine and a human—opp. to *Monophysite.*—Also **Dyoph′ysite,** less correctly **Dioph′ysite.**—*n.* **Diph′ysitism** (*-it-izm*). [Gr. *di-*, double, *physis*, nature.]

**dipleidoscope, di-pli′də-skōp, n.** an instrument for ascertaining the moment of meridian passage by observing the coincidence of two images. [Gr. *diploos,* double, *eidos,* appearance, *skopeein,* to view.]

**diplex, dī′pleks, adj.** pertaining to the transmission of two simultaneous messages over one wire in the same direction. [duplex, with substitution of Gr. *di-*, double.]

**dipl(o)-, dip-l(-ō)-,** in composition, double.—*ns.* **Diplod′ocus** (Gr. *dokos*, beam, bar, from its appearance), a genus of gigantic dinosaurs, up to about 80 feet in length, from the Jurassic rocks of the United States; **dip′logen,** (from **hydrogen**), an alternative name for deuterium or heavy hydrogen; **diplogen′esis** (Gr. *genesis*, generation), doubling of parts normally single.—*adj.* **dip′loid** (Gr. *eidos*, form; *biol.*), having the full or unreduced number of chromosomes characteristic of the species, as in body cells: opp. to *haploid.*—*ns.* **diploid′y; dip′lon,** an alternative name for deuteron, the nucleus of heavy hydrogen; **diplō′pia** (Gr. *ōps*, eye), double vision.— *adj.* **diplostē′monous** (Gr. *stēmōn*, a thread; *bot.*), having two whorls of stamens, the outer alternating with the petals, the inner with the outer.—*n.* **Diplozō′on** (Gr. *zōion*, an animal), a flat-worm that lives fused together in pairs parasitically upon the gills of minnows, etc. [Gr. *diploos,* double.]

**diploe, dip′lō-ē,** (*anat.*) *n.* the spongy tissue between the hard inner and outer tables of the skull. [Gr. *diploē,* doubling, fold.]

**diplogen, -genesis, diploid.** See **dipl(o)-.**

**diploma, di-plō′mə, n.** a writing conferring some honour or privilege, as a university degree, etc.— *v.t.* to furnish with a diploma.—*ns.* **diplomacy** (*di-plō′mə-si,* or *-plo′*), the art of negotiation, esp. in relations between states: tact in management of persons concerned in any affair; **diplomat** (*dip′lə-mat*), one employed or skilled in diplomacy; **diplomate** (*dip′lə-māt*), one who holds a diploma.—*v.t.* to confer a diploma on. —*ns.* **diplomatic** (*-mat′ik*), a minister at a foreign court: (in *pl.*) the science of deciphering ancient writings, as charters, etc.—palaeography. —*adjs.* **diplomat′ic, -al,** pertaining to diplomacy: tactful and skilful in negotiation.—*adv.* **diplomat′ically.**—*v.i.* and *v.t.* **diplo′matise, -ize,** to practise, or effect by, diplomacy.—*ns.* **diplo′matist,** a diplomat; **diplomatol′ogy,** the study or science of diplomatics, charters, decrees, etc.— **diplomatic corps,** the whole body of foreign diplomatists resident in any capital. [L.,—Gr. *diplōma,* a letter folded double—*diploos,* double.]

**diplon, diplopia, etc.** See **diplo-.**

**Dipnoi, dip′nō-i, n.pl.** the lung fishes.—*adj.* and *n.* **dip′noan.**—*adj.* **dip′noous,** having both lungs and gills. [Gr. *di-*, double, *pnoē*, breath.]

**dipody, dip′ə-di,** (*pros.*) *n.* a double foot. [Gr. *di-*, double, *pous, podos,* foot.]

**dipolar, di-pō′lər, adj.** having two poles.—*n.* **di′pole,** two equal and opposite electric charges or magnetic poles of opposite sign a small distance apart: a body or system having such: a type of aerial. [Pfx. **di-.**]

**dipper, dip′ər, n.** one that dips: a ladle: a bucket or scoop of a dredge or excavator: a contrivance for directing motor-car headlights upwards or downwards: a dipping bird (*Cinclus*), the waterouzel: dabchick (*U.S.*): (*cap.*) the Plough (*astron.*): a nickname for a Baptist, esp. a Dunker. [**dip.**]

**dippy, dip′i, adj.** crazy: insane. [Origin obscure.]

**diprionidian, di-pri-ə-nid′i-ən, adj.** serrated on both sides (of graptolites). [Gr. *di-*, twice, *priōn*, a saw.]

**diprotodont, dī-prō′tō-dont, n.** any marsupial of the **Diprotodont′ia,** the suborder including kangaroos, wombats, etc., with one pair of incisors in the lower jaw. [Gr. *di-*, twice, *prōtos*, first, *odous, odontos,* tooth.]

**Dipsacus, dip′sa-kəs, n.** the teasel genus, giving name to the **Dipsacā′ceae,** akin to the valerian and madder families. [Gr. *dipsakos*, teasel— *dipsa,* thirst, because the leaf-axils hold water.]

**dipsas, dip′sas, n.** a snake whose bite was believed to cause intense thirst: (with *cap.*) a genus of non-venomous snakes. [Gr. *dipsas*—*dipsa,* thirst.]

**dipsomania, dip-sō-mā′ni-ə, n.** a morbid craving for alcoholic stimulants.—*n.* **dipsomā′niac.** [Gr. *dipsa,* thirst, and *maniā,* madness.]

**Diptera, dip′tar-a, n.pl.** two-winged insects or flies. —*adj.* **dip′teral,** two-winged: with double peristyle.—*ns.* **dip′teran,** a dipterous insect; **dip′terist,** a student of flies; **dip′teros,** a building with double peristyle or colonnade.—*adj.* **dip′terous,** with two wings or winglike expansions. [Gr. *dipteros,* two-winged, *di-*, twice, *pteron,* a wing.]

**dipterocarp, dip′tər-ō-kärp, n.** any tree of the genus **Dipterocar′pus** or its family **Dipterocarpā′ceae** (chiefly Indian), in which some of the sepals enlarge as wings for the fruit.—*adjs.* **dipterocarpā′ceous, dipterocarp′ous.** [Gr. *di-*, double, *pteron,* wing, *karpos,* fruit.]

**diptych, dip′tik, n.** a double-folding writing-tablet: a register of bishops, saints, etc., read aloud during the eucharist: a pair of pictures as folding-tablets. [Gr. *diptychos*—*di-*, and *ptychē,* a tablet, a fold.]

**dirdum, dir′dəm,** (*Scot.*) *n.* uproar: a scolding. [Origin obscure.]

**dire, dīr, adj.** dreadful: calamitous in a high

degree.—*adj.* (*poet.*) **dire'ful.**—*adv.* **dire'fully.**—
*n.* **dire'fulness.** [L. *dīrus.*]
**direct,** *di-rekt', dī'rekt, adj.* straight: straightforward: by the shortest way: forward, not
backward or oblique: at right angles: immediate: without intervening agency or interposed
stages: (of a dye) fixing itself without a mordant:
in the line of descent: outspoken: sincere:
unambiguous: unsophisticated in manner.—*n.*
(*mus.*) an indication of the first note or chord of
next page or line.—*adv.* straight: by the shortest
way: without deviation, intervening agency or
interposed stages.—*v.t.* to keep or lay straight:
to point or aim: to point out the proper course
to: to guide: to order: to address, mark with
the name and residence of a person: to plan and
superintend (the production of a film).—*v.i.* to
act as director: to direct letters, etc.—*n.* **direc'-
tion,** aim at a certain point: the line or course in
which anything moves or on which any point
lies: guidance: command: the body of persons
who guide or manage a matter: the address, or
written name and residence of a person.—*adjs.*
**direc'tional,** relating to direction in space;
**direct'ive,** having power or tendency to direct.—
*n.* a general instruction.—*n.* **directiv'ity.**—*adv.*
**direct'ly,** in a direct manner: without intermediary: immediately (in time and otherwise).
—*conj.* (*coll.*) as soon as.—*ns.* **direct'ness;
direct'or,** one who directs: one who directs the
shooting of a motion picture: a manager or
governor: a member of a board conducting the
affairs of a company: a counsellor: a father
confessor or spiritual guide: part of a machine
or instrument which guides the motion: in
automatic trunk dialling, the apparatus which
obtains a channel through exchange junctions to
the required exchange: a device that continuously calculates the position of a moving target and
supplies firing data:—*fem.* **direct'ress, direct'rix.**
—*ns.* **direct'orate,** the office of director: a body
of directors: (with *cap.*) the French Directory or
Directoire.—*adjs.* **directo'rial** (*-tō', -tō'*); **direct'ory,** containing directions: guiding.—*n.* a
body of directions: a guide: a book with the
names and residences of the inhabitants of a
place: a body of directors: (with *cap.*) the
*Directoire,* or French Republican government of
1795-99.—*ns.* **direc'torship; direct'rix,** a line
serving to describe a conic section, which is the
locus of a point whose distances from focus and
directrix have a constant ratio:—*pl.* **directrices**
(*-trī'sēz*).—**direct action,** coercive methods of
attaining industrial ends as opposed to pacific,
parliamentary, or political action; **direct
current,** an electric current flowing in one direction only; **direct debiting,** an arrangement by
which a creditor can claim payment direct from
the payer's account; **direc'tion-find'er,** a wireless receiver that determines the direction of
arrival of incoming waves; **direct method,** a
method of teaching a foreign language through
speaking it, without translation, and without
formal instruction in grammar; **direct motion**
(*mus.*), progression of parts in the same direction;
**direct object,** word or group of words denoting
that upon which the action of a transitive verb is
directed; **director circle,** the locus of the intersection of a pair of tangents to a conic at right
angles to each other; **direct speech,** speech
reported as spoken, in the very words of the
speaker (L. *ōrātiō rēcta*); **direct tax,** one levied
directly from those on whom its burden falls.
[L. *dīrigĕre, dīrēctum*—*dī-,* apart, *regĕre,* to rule.]
**Directoire,** *dē-rek-twär', n.* the French Directorate
of 1795-99.—*adj.* after the fashion in dress or
furniture then prevailing. [Fr.; see **direct.**]
**dirge,** *dûrj, n.* a funeral song or hymn. [Contrac-
ted from *dirige* (imper. of L. *dīrigĕre,* to direct),
the first word of an antiphon sung in the office

for the dead—the words from the Vulgate,
Psalm v. 8.]
**dirhem,** *dûr-hem', n.* an oriental weight and silver
coin, originally two-thirds of an Attic drachma.
—Also **dirham', derham'.** [Ar., Pers., and
Turk. modifications of the Greek *drachmē,* a
drachma or dram.]
**dirige,** *dir'i-ji, n.* a dirge.
**dirigible,** *dir'i-ji-bl, adj.* that can be directed.—*n.*
a navigable balloon or airship.—*adj.* **dir'igent,**
directing. [See **direct.**]
**dirigism(e),** *dē-rēzh-izm, n.* control by the State in
economic and social spheres. [Fr.,—It. *diri-
gismo.*]
**diriment,** *dir'i-mənt, adj.* nullifying. [L. *dirimēre.*]
**dirk,** *dûrk, n.* a Highland dagger: a side-arm
worn by midshipmen and naval cadets (*hist.*).—
*v.t.* to stab with a dirk. [Ety. unknown.]
**dirk, dirke,** *dûrk, adj., adv.* and *v.t.* (*Spens.*) for
**dark, darkly, darken.**
**dirl,** *dirl,* (*Scot.*) *v.i.* to thrill, vibrate.—*n.* vibration: a tingling as after a blow. [**drill, thrill.**]
**dirndl,** *dûrn'dl, n.* an Alpine peasant woman's
dress with close-fitting bodice and full skirt: an
imitation of this, esp. the skirt. [Ger. dim. of
*dirne,* girl.]
**dirt,** *dûrt, n.* any filthy substance, such as dung
mud, etc.: foreign matter adhering to anything:
loose earth: rubbish: obscenity: spiteful
gossip.—*v.t.* to make dirty.—*adv.* **dirt'ily.**—
*n.* **dirt'iness.**—*adj.* **dirt'y,** foul, filthy: stormy:
obscene: unclean in thought or conversation:
despicable: mean: treacherous.—*v.t.* to soil
with dirt: to sully:—*pr.p.* **dirt'ying;** *pa.t.* and
*pa.p.* **dirt'ied.**—**dirt'-bed,** a quarryman's term for
a layer representing an old soil, esp. in the Purbeck group.—*adj.* **dirt'-cheap,** cheap as dirt, very
cheap.—**dirt'-eating,** a practice of eating clay as
among various primitive peoples: a morbid
impulse to eat dirt; **dirt'-pie,** mud moulded by
children in play; **dirt'-road** (*U.S.*), a soft road,
unpaved and unmacadamised.—*adj.* **dirt'-
rott'en** (*Shak.*), wholly decayed.—**dirt'-track,** a
motor-cycling racing-track, with earthy or
cindery surface; **dirty money,** money earned by
base means: in dock labour, extra pay for unloading offensive cargo; **dirty word,** an obscene
word: a word for something, as a feeling,
principle, or belief, that is regarded with disfavour at the present time; **dirty work,** work
that dirties the hands or clothes: dishonourable
practices, esp. undertaken on behalf of another:
foul play.—**do the dirty on,** to play a low trick on,
cheat; **eat dirt,** submissively to acquiesce in
a humiliation; **throw dirt,** to besmirch a reputation. [M.E. *drit,* prob. O.N. *drit,* excrement; cf.
O.E. *gedrītan,* to defecate.]
**Dis,** *dis, dēs, n.* a name for Pluto, hence, the
infernal world. [L. *Dis,* cog. with *deus, dīvus.*]
**dis-, di-,** *dis-, di-, pfx.* (1) meaning in two, asunder,
apart: (2) meaning 'not' or a reversal: (3)
indicating a removal or deprivation: (4) used
intensively. [L. *dis-, dī-.*]
**disable,** *dis-ā'bl, v.t.* to deprive of power: to
weaken: to cripple, incapacitate: to disqualify:
to depreciate, disparage, undervalue (*Shak.*).—
*ns.* **disā'blement; disābil'ity,** want of power:
want of legal qualification: disqualification.
[Pfx. **dis-** (3).]
**disabuse,** *dis-ə-būz', v.t.* to undeceive or set right.
[Pfx. **dis-** (2).]
**disaccharide,** *dī-sak'ə-rīd, n.* a sugar that hydrolyses into two molecules of simple sugars. [Pfx.
**di-.**]
**disaccommodate,** *dis-ə-kom'ə-dāt, v.t.* to put to
inconvenience.—*n.* **disaccommodā'tion.** [Pfx.
**dis-** (2).]
**disaccord,** *dis-ə-körd',* (*Spens.*) *v.i.* to refuse to
accord: to be at discord.—*adj.* **disaccord'ant.**
[Pfx. **dis-** (2).]

**disaccustom,** *dis-ə-kus'təm, v.t.* to make to be lost through disuse. [Pfx. **dis-** (2).]

**disacknowledge,** *dis-ək-nol'ij, v.t.* to refuse to acknowledge, disown. [Pfx. **dis-** (2).]

**disadorn,** *dis-ə-dörn', v.t.* to deprive of ornaments. [Pfx. **dis-** (3).]

**disadvance,** *dis-əd-väns', v.t.* to cause to retreat: to draw back, cease to put forward (*Spens.*). [Pfx. **dis-** (2).]

**disadvantage,** *dis-əd-vänt'ij, n.* unfavourable circumstance or condition: loss: damage.—*adjs.* **disadvan'tageable** (*obs.*); **disadvantageous** (*dis-ad-vənt-ā'jəs*), attended with disadvantage: unfavourable.—*adv.* **disadvantā'geously.**—*n.* **disadvantā'geousness.** [Pfx. **dis-** (2).]

**disadventurous,** *dis-əd-ven'chə-rəs, adj.* unfortunate.—*ns.* **disadven'ture, disaven'ture** (*Spens.*), a mishap.—*adj.* **disaven'trous** (*Spens.*), unfortunate. [Pfx. **dis-** (2).]

**disaffect,** *dis-ə-fekt', v.t.* to take away the affection of: to make discontented or unfriendly:—*pa.p.* and *adj.* **disaffect'ed,** ill-disposed: tending to break away.—*adv.* **disaffect'edly.**—*ns.* **disaffect'edness; disaffec'tion,** state of being disaffected: want of affection or friendliness: alienation: ill-will.—*adj.* **disaffec'tionate.** [Pfx. **dis-** (3).]

**disaffirm,** *dis-ə-fûrm', v.t.* to contradict: to repudiate.—*ns.* **disaffirm'ance, disaffirmā'tion** (*dis-a-*). [Pfx. **dis-** (2).]

**disafforest,** *dis-ə-for'ist, v.t.* to bring out of the operation of forest laws: to clear of forest, disforest.—*ns.* **disafforestā'tion, disaffor'estment** (see **disforest**). [L. *dis-,* reversal, and L.L. *afforestāre,* to make into a forest. See **forest**.]

**disagree,** *dis-ə-grē', v.i.* to differ or be at variance: to disaccord: to dissent: to quarrel: to prove unsuitable or a source of annoyance, as of food disagreeing with the stomach.—*adj.* **disagree'able,** not amicable: unpleasant: offensive.—*ns.* **disagree'ableness, disagreeabil'ity.**—*n.pl.* **disagree'ables,** annoyances.—*adv.* **disagree'ably.**—*n.* **disagree'ment,** want of agreement: difference: unsuitableness: dispute. [Pfx. **dis-** (2).]

**disallow,** *dis-ə-low', v.t.* to dispraise (*obs.*): not to allow: to refuse to sanction: to deny the authority, validity, or truth of: to reject, to forbid.—*v.i.* (*obs.*) to disapprove.—*adj.* **disallow'able.**—*n.* **disallow'ance.** [Pfx. **dis-** (2).]

**disally,** *dis-ə-li', v.t.* to break the alliance of: to separate, sunder (*Milt.*). [Pfx. **dis-** (2), (1).]

**di salto,** *dē säl'tō,* (It.) *adv.* at a leap.

**disanchor,** *dis-angk'ər, v.t.* to free from the anchor. —*v.i.* to weigh anchor. [Pfx. **dis-** (3).]

**disanimate,** *dis-an'i-māt, v.t.* to deprive of spirit or animation: to deject (*Shak.*). [Pfx. **dis-** (3).]

**disannex,** *dis-ə-neks', v.t.* to disjoin. [Pfx. **dis-** (1).]

**disannul,** *dis-ə-nul', v.t.* to annul completely.—*ns.* **disannull'er; disannul'ment, disannull'ing.** [Pfx. **dis-** (4).]

**disanoint,** *dis-ə-noint', v.t.* to undo the anointing or consecration of. [Pfx. **dis-** (2).]

**disapparel,** *dis-ə-par'əl, v.t.* to disrobe. [Pfx. **dis-** (2).]

**disappear,** *dis-ə-pēr', v.i.* to vanish from sight.—*n.* **disappear'ance,** a ceasing to be in sight: removal from sight, flight, secret withdrawal. [Pfx. **dis-** (3).]

**disappoint,** *dis-ə-point', v.t.* to deprive of what is appointed (*obs.*): to frustrate the hopes or expectations of: to defeat the fulfilment of.—*adjs.* **disappoint'ed,** balked: frustrated: unequipped or ill-equipped (*Shak.*); **disappoint'ing,** causing disappointment.—*n.* **disappoint'ment,** the defeat of one's hopes or expectations: frustration: the vexation accompanying failure. [O.Fr. *desapointer, des-* (L. *dis-*), away, and *apointer,* to appoint. See **appoint**.]

**disapprobation,** *dis-ap-rō-bā'shən, n.* disapproval.

—*adjs.* **disapp'robātive, disapp'robātory.** [Pfx. **dis-** (2).]

**disappropriate,** *dis-ə-prō'pri-āt, v.t.* to take away from the condition of being appropriated.—*adj.* (*-it*) deprived of appropriation. [Pfx. **dis-** (3).]

**disapprove,** *dis-ə-prōōv', v.t.* and *v.i.* to give or have an unfavourable opinion (of): to reject.—*n.* **disapprov'al.**—*adv.* **disapprov'ingly.** [Pfx. **dis-** (2).]

**disarm,** *dis-ärm', v.t.* to deprive of arms: to strip of armour: to render defenceless: to deprive of the power of hurt: to conciliate (*fig.*): to deprive of suspicion or hostility: to reduce to a peace footing.—*v.i.* to disband troops, reduce national armaments.—*n.* **disarm'ament.**—*adj.* **disarm'ing,** charming. [Pfx. **dis-** (3).]

**disarrange,** *dis-ə-rānj', v.t.* to undo the arrangement of: to disorder: to derange.—*n.* **disarrange'ment.** [Pfx. **dis-** (2).]

**disarray,** *dis-ə-rā', v.t.* to break the array of: to throw into disorder: to strip of array or dress.— *n.* want of array or order: undress. [Pfx. **dis-** (2), (3).]

**disarticulate,** *dis-är-tik'ūl-āt, v.t.* to separate the joints of.—*v.i.* to separate at a joint.—*n.* **disarticulā'tion.** [Pfx. **dis-** (1).]

**disassemble,** *dis-ə-sem'bl, v.t.* to take apart.— *n.* **disassem'bly.** [Pfx. **dis-** (1).]

**disassimilate,** *dis-ə-sim'i-lāt, v.t.* to subject to katabolism.—*n.* **dissimilā'tion.**—*adj.* **disassim'**-**ilative.** [Pfx. **dis-** (2).]

**disassociate,** *dis-ə-sō'shi-āt, v.t.* to disconnect (from): to dissociate (from).—*n.* **disassociā'tion.** [Pfx. **dis-** (2).]

**disaster,** *diz-äs'tər, n.* an adverse or unfortunate event: a great and sudden misfortune: calamity. —*adj.* **disas'trous,** calamitous, ruinous: gloomy, foreboding disaster.—*adv.* **disas'trously.** [O.Fr. *desastre, des-* (L. *dis-*), with evil sense, *astre,* a star, destiny—L. *astrum,* Gr. *astron,* star.]

**disattire,** *dis-ə-tir', (Spens.) v.t.* to undress. [Pfx. **dis-** (2).]

**disattune,** *dis-ə-tūn', v.t.* to put out of harmony. [Pfx. **dis-** (2).]

**disauthorise, -ize,** *dis-ö'thər-īz, v.t.* to deprive of authority. [Pfx. **dis-** (3).]

**disavaunce.** See **disadvance.**

**disaventure.** See **disadventure.**

**disavouch,** *dis-ə-vowch', v.t.* to disavow. [Pfx. **dis-** (2).]

**disavow,** *dis-ə-vow', v.t.* to disclaim knowledge of, or connection with: to disown: to deny.—*n.* **disavow'al.** [O.Fr. *desavouer, des-* (L. *dis-*), away, *avouer,* to avow. See **avow**.]

**disband,** *dis-band', v.t.* to disperse, break up, esp. of troops.—*v.i.* to break up.—*n.* **disband'ment.** [O.Fr. *desbander,* to unbind, *des-* (L. *dis-*), reversal, *bander,* to tie.]

**disbar,** *dis-bär', v.t.* to expel from the bar. [Pfx. **dis-** (3).]

**disbark,** *dis-bärk', v.t.* to land from a ship: to disembark. [O.Fr. *desbarquer, des-* (L. *dis-*), reversal, *barque,* bark.]

**disbark,** *dis-bärk', v.t.* to strip of bark, to bark. [Pfx. **dis-** (3).]

**disbelieve,** *dis-bə-lēv', v.t.* to believe to be false: to refuse belief or credit to.—*v.i.* to have no faith (with *in*).—*ns.* **disbelief'; disbeliev'er.** [Pfx. **dis-** (2).]

**disbench,** *dis-bench', -bensh', v.t.* to drive from a bench or seat (*Shak.*): to deprive of the privilege of a bencher (e.g. in the Inns of Court). [Pfx. **dis-** (3).]

**disbodied,** *dis-bod'id, adj.* disembodied. [Pfx. **dis-** (3).]

**disbosom,** *dis-bōōz'əm, v.t.* to make known, reveal. [Pfx. **dis-** (1).]

**disbowel,** *dis-bow'əl, (fig.) v.t.* to disembowel:— *pr.p.* **disbow'elling;** *pa.t.* and *pa.p.* **disbow'elled.** [Pfx. **dis-** (3).]

disbranch, *dis-bränch'*, *-bränsh'*, *v.t.* to remove branches from: to sever. [Pfx. dis- (3).]
disbud, *dis-bud'*, *v.t.* to remove buds from. [Pfx. dis- (3).]
disburden, *dis-bûr'dn*, disburthen, *dis-bûr'dhn*, *v.t.* to rid of a burden: to free: to unload, discharge. [Pfx. dis- (3).]
disburse, *dis-bûrs'*, *v.t.* to pay out.—*ns.* disburs'al, disburse'ment, a paying out: that which is paid. [O.Fr. *desbourser*, *des-* (L. *dis-*), apart, and *bourse*, a purse.]
disc. Same as disk.—*adjs.* disc'al, pertaining to, or of the nature of, a disk; disc'oid, discoid'al, in the form of a disk: of a capitulum, without ray-flowers (*bot.*).—*ns.* discog'raphy, collection, description, etc., of gramophone records: the history or description of musical recording: a list of recordings by one composer or performer; discog'rapher; disc'ophile (*-ō-fil*), one who makes a study of and collects gramophone records. See also disk.
discage, *dis-kāj'*, *v.t.* to free from a cage. [Pfx. dis- (2).]
discalced, *dis-kalst'*, *adj.* without shoes, barefooted, as a branch of the Carmelite order.—*n.* and *adj.* discal'ceate. [L. *discalceātus*—*dis-*, neg., and *calceāre*, *-ātum*, to shoe, *calceus*, a shoe—*calx*, the heel.]
discandy, discandie, *dis-kan'di*, (*Shak.*) *v.i.* to dissolve or melt from a state of being candied.—*n.* discan'dering (*Shak.*), supposed to be for discandying. [Pfx. dis- (2).]
discant, *dis'kant*. Same as descant.
discapacitate, *dis-kə-pas'i-tāt*, *v.t.* to incapacitate. [Pfx. dis- (2).]
discard, *dis-kärd'*, *v.t.* and *v.i.* to throw away, as not needed or not allowed by the game, said of cards: in whist, to throw down a (useless) card of another suit when one cannot follow suit and cannot or will not trump: to cast off: to discharge: to reject.—*n.* (also *dis'*) the act of discarding: the card or cards thrown out of the hand: discharge, dismissal, abandonment: a cast-off, anything discarded.—*n.* discard'ment.—throw into the discard (*U.S.*), to throw on the scrap-heap. [Pfx. dis- (3).]
discase, *dis-kās'*, (*Shak.*) *v.t.* to remove a case or covering from, to undress. [Pfx. dis- (3).]
discept, *di-sept'*, (*Browning*) *v.i.* to dispute, debate.—*n.* disceptā'tion.—*adj.* disceptā'tious.—*n.* disceptā'tor.—*adj.* disceptātō'rial. [L. *disceptāre*, *-ātum*, to contend—*dis-*, *captāre*.]
discern, *di-sûrn'*, *-zûrn'*, *v.t.* to make out: to distinguish by the eye or understanding: to judge (*obs.*, a blunder for decern).—*n.* discern'er.—*adj.* discern'ible.—*adv.* discern'ibly.—*adj.* discern'ing, discriminating, acute.—*n.* discern'ment, power or faculty of discriminating: judgment: acuteness. [L. *discernĕre*—*dis-* thoroughly, and *cernĕre*, to sift, perceive.]
discerp, *di-sûrp'*, *v.t.* to separate.—*n.* discerpibil'ity, capability of being disunited.—*adjs.* discerp'-ible (*obs.*), discerp'tible.—*n.* discerp'tion.—*adj.* discerp'tive. [L. *discerpĕre*, to tear in pieces—*dis-*, apart, *carpĕre*, to pluck.]
discharge, *dis-chärj'*, *v.t.* to free from or relieve of a charge of any kind (burden, explosive, electricity, liability, accusation, etc.): to set free: to acquit: to dismiss: to fire (as a gun): to take the superincumbent weight from: to set down or send forth: to eject: to pour out: to emit or let out: to perform: to pay: to give account for: to distribute (as weight): to forbid (*obs.*).—*v.i.* to unload: to become released from a charged state: to allow escape of contents: to flow away or out.—*n.* the act of discharging: release from a charge of any kind: unloading: liberation: acquittal: dismissal: outflow: rate of flow: emission: release of tension: payment: performance: that which is discharged.—*ns.*

discharg'er, one who discharges: an apparatus for discharging, esp. electricity, e.g. a spark-gap, discharging tongs: apparatus for firing an explosive.—discharge'-tube', a tube in which an electric discharge takes place in a vacuum or in a gas at low pressure; discharging arch, an arch built in a wall to protect a space beneath from the weight above; discharging tongs, metal tongs used for discharging condensers. [O.Fr. *descharger*—*des-*, apart, *charger*; see charge.]
dischurch, *dis-chûrch'*, *v.t.* to deprive of church rank or privileges. [Pfx. dis- (3).]
discide, *di-sid'*, (*Spens.*) *v.t.* to cut asunder, to divide. [L. *dis-*, asunder, and *caedĕre*, to cu·.]
discinct, *di-singkt'*, *adj.* ungirded. [L. *discingĕre*, *-cinctum*, to ungird.]
disciple, *dis-i'pl*, *n.* one who professes to receive instruction from another: one who follows or believes in the doctrine of another: a follower, esp. one of the twelve apostles of Christ.—*v.t.* (*Spens.*) to teach.—*n.* disci'pleship.—Disciples of Christ, a sect that seeks a restoration of New Testament Christianity—by some called Campbellites. [Fr.,—L. *discipulus*, from *discĕre*, to learn: akin to *docĕre*, to teach.]
discipline, *dis'i-plin*, *n.* instruction: a branch of learning, or field of study: training, or mode of life in accordance with rules: subjection to control: order: severe training: mortification: punishment: an instrument of penance or punishment.—*v.t.* to subject to discipline: to train: to educate: to bring under control: to chastise.—*adjs.* disc'iplinable; disc'iplinal (or *-pli'*).—*ns.* disc'iplinant, one who subjects himself to a discipline, esp. one of an order of Spanish flagellants; disciplinā'rian, one who enforces strict discipline; disciplinā'rium, a scourge for penitential flogging.—*adj.* disc'iplinary, of the nature of discipline.—*n.* disc'ipliner, one who disciplines.—First, Second, Book of Discipline, two documents (1560 and 1578) embodying the constitution and order of procedure of the Church of Scotland from the period of the Reformation. [L. *disciplina*, from *discipulus*.]
discission, *di-sish'ən*, *n.* an incision into a tumour or cataract. [L. *discissiō*, *-ōnis*—*discindĕre*, *-scissum*—*di-*, apart, *scindĕre*, to cut.]
disclaim, *dis-klām'*, *v.t.* to renounce all claim to: to refuse to acknowledge or be responsible for: to repudiate: to reject: to cry out against the claim of.—*v.i.* to make a disclaimer: to declaim, cry out (*obs.*).—*ns.* disclaim'er, a denial, disavowal, or renunciation; disclamā'tion (*-kləm-*), a disavowal. [O.Fr. disclaimer—L. *dis-*, apart, *clāmāre*, to cry out.]
disclose, *dis-klōz'*, *v.t.* to unclose: to open: to lay open: to bring to light: to reveal: to hatch (*Shak.*): to transform and give vent to (*Spens.*): —*pa.p.* (*Spens.*) disclo'st.—*n.* a disclosure: emergence from the egg (*Shak.*).—*n.* disclō'sure (*-zhər*), act of disclosing: a bringing to light or revealing: that which is disclosed or revealed. [O.Fr. *desclos*—L. *dis-*, apart, *claudĕre*, *clausum*, to shut.]
discobolus, *dis-kob'ə-ləs*, *n.* a disk-thrower: the name of a famous lost statue ascribed to Myron, of which copies exist. [L.,—Gr. *diskobolos*—*diskos*, a quoit, *ballein*, to throw.]
discographer, -graphy. See disc.
discoid, -al, etc. See disc.
discolour, *dis-kul'ər*, *v.t.* to take away colour from: to change or to spoil the natural colour of: to alter the appearance of: to mark with other colours, to stain: to dirty, disfigure.—*v.i.* to become discoloured.—*n.* discolo(u)rā'tion, act of discolouring: state of being discoloured: stain.—*adj.* discol'oured, stained, etc.: many-coloured (*Spens.*). [O.Fr. *descolorer*—L. *dis-*, apart, and *colōrāre*—*color*, colour.]
discombobulate, -boberate, *dis-kəm-bob'ōō-lāt*,

-ū-lāt, -bob'ər-āt, (U.S. slang) vs.t. to disconcert, upset. [Orig. obscure.]

Discomedusae, dis-kō-me-dū'sē, n.pl. an order of jellyfishes with flattened umbrella.—n. and adj. discomedū'san. [Gr. diskos, disk, and medusa.]

discomfit, dis-kum'fit, v.t. to disconcert, to balk: to defeat or rout:—pr.p. discom'fiting; pa.t. and pa.p. discom'fited.—n. (Milt.) defeat.—n. discom'fiture. [O.Fr. desconfit, pa.p. of desconfire —L. dis-, neg., conficēre, to prepare—con-, inten., facēre, to make.]

discomfort, dis-kum'fərt, n. want of comfort: uneasiness.—v.t. to deprive of comfort: to make uneasy.—adj. discom'fortable, causing discomfort: uncomfortable. [O.Fr. desconforter—des-, priv., conforter, to comfort; see comfort.]

discommend, dis-kəm-end', v.t. to blame: to dispraise.—adj. discommend'able.—ns. discommend'ableness, discommendation (dis-ko-məndā'shən). [Pfx. dis- (2).]

discommission, dis-kə-mish'ən, (Milt.) v.t. to deprive of a commission. [Pfx. dis- (3).]

discommode, dis-kə-mōd', (arch.) v.t. to incommode.—adj. discommō'dious.—adv. discommō'diously.—n. discommōd'ity, inconvenience. [Pfx. dis- (2), obs. vb. commode, to suit.]

discommon, dis-kom'ən, v.t. to deprive of the right of common, or, at Oxford and Cambridge, of dealing with undergraduates. [Pfx. dis- (3), common, n.]

discommunity, dis-kə-mūn'i-ti, n. want of community. [Pfx. dis- (2).]

discompose, dis-kəm-pōz', v.t. to deprive of composure, disturb, agitate: to disarrange, disorder. —n. discompō'sure (-zhər, -zhyər). [Pfx. dis- (2).]

Discomycetes, dis-kō-mi-sē'tēz, n.pl. a group of fungi (Ascomycetes) with open apothecia.—n. dis'comycete.—adj. discomycē'tous. [Gr. diskos, disk, mykētēs, pl. of mykēs, a fungus.]

disconcert, dis-kən-sûrt', v.t. to throw into confusion: to disturb: to frustrate: to defeat: to put out of countenance.—ns. disconcert (dis-kon'sərt), disunion; disconcer'tion, confusion; disconcert'ment. [Obs.Fr. disconcerter, des- (L. dis-), apart, and concerter, to concert.]

disconformable, dis-kən-förm'ə-bl, adj. not conformable.—n. disconform'ity, want of conformity: unconformity (geol.). [Pfx. dis- (2).]

disconnect, dis-kən-ekt', v.t. to separate or disjoin (with from).—adj. disconnect'ed, separated: loosely united, as of a discourse.—adv. disconnect'edly.—ns. disconnec'tion, disconnex'ion. [Pfx. dis- (1).]

disconsent, dis-kən-sent', v.i. to differ, dissent. [Pfx. dis- (2).]

disconsolate, dis-kon'sə-lit, adj. without consolation or comfort.—adv. discon'solately.—ns. discon'solateness, disconsolā'tion. [L. dis-, neg., and consōlāri, consōlātus, to console.]

discontent, dis-kən-tent', adj. not content: dissatisfied.—n. want of contentment: dissatisfaction: a discontented person (Shak.).—v.t. to deprive of content: to stir up to ill-will.—adj. discontent'ed, dissatisfied.—adv. discontent'edly. —n. discontent'edness.—adj. discontent'ful.— adj. discontent'ing, not contenting or satisfying: discontented (Shak.).—n. discontent'ment. [Pfx. dis- (2), (3).]

discontinue, dis-kən-tin'ū, v.t. to cease to continue: to put an end to: to leave off: to stop.—v.i. to cease: to be separated.—ns. discontin'uance, discontinuā'tion, a breaking off or ceasing; discontinu'ity.—adj. discontin'uous, not continuous: broken off: separated: interrupted by intervening spaces.—adv. discontin'uously. [O.Fr. discontinuer—L. dis-, reversal, and continuāre, to continue.]

discophile. See disc.

Discophora, dis-kof'ə-ra, n.pl. the Discomedusae.

—n. and adj. discoph'oran.—adj. discoph'orous. [Gr. diskos, disk, phoros, carrying.]

discord, dis'körd, n. opposite of concord: disagreement, strife: difference or contrariety of qualities: a combination of inharmonious sounds: uproarious noise: a dissonance, esp. unprepared.—v.i. discord', to disagree.—ns. discord'ance, discord'ancy.—adj. discord'ant, without concord or agreement: inconsistent: contradictory: harsh: jarring.—adv. discord'antly.—adj. discord'ful (Spens.).—apple of discord (see apple). [O.Fr. descord—L. discordia—dis-, apart, and cor, cordis, the heart.]

discorporate, dis-kör'pə-rit, adj. disembodied. [Pfx. dis- (2).]

discothèque, -theque, dis'kə-tek, dēs-kō-tek, n. a place where music for dancing is provided by records. [Fr.]

discounsel, dis-kown'səl, (Spens.) v.t. to dissuade. [O.Fr. desconseillier—des-, apart, and conseillier, to counsel.]

discount, dis'kownt, n. a sum taken from the reckoning: a sum returned to the payer of an account: the rate or percentage of the deduction granted: a deduction made for interest in advancing money on a bill: the amount by which the price of a share or stock unit is below the par value.—v.t. discount', to allow as discount: to allow discount on: to pay (rarely to receive) beforehand the present worth of: to put a reduced value on, as in an extravagant statement or fabulous story or an event foreseen: to ignore. —v.i. to practise discounting.—adj. discount'able.—n. discount'er.—dis'count-brok'er, one who cashes notes or bills of exchange at a discount; discount rate, the rate at which a discount is granted: in U.S., bank rate.—at a discount, below par: not sought after: superfluous: depreciated in value. [O.Fr. descompter, des- (L. dis-), away, compter, to count.]

discountenance, dis-kown'tən-əns, v.t. to put out of countenance: to abash: to refuse countenance or support to: to discourage.—n. cold treatment: disapprobation. [O.Fr. descontenancer—des-, reversal, contenance, countenance.]

discourage, dis-kur'ij, v.t. to take away the courage of: dishearten: to oppose by showing disfavour.—n. discour'agement, act of discouraging: that which discourages: dejection.—n. and adj. discour'aging, disheartening, depressing.—adv. discour'agingly. [O.Fr. descourager. See courage.]

discoure, dis-kowr', (Spens.) v.t. to discover.

discourse, dis-körs', -körs', or dis', n. speech or language generally: conversation: the reasoning faculty: a treatise: a speech: a sermon: apparently, process of combat (Spens.).—v.i. to talk or converse: to reason: to treat formally.—v.t. to utter or give forth.—n. discours'er (Shak.).— adj. (obs.) discours'ive. [Fr. discours—L. discursus—dis-, away, and currēre, to run.]

discourteous, dis-kûrt'yəs (or -kört', -kört'), adj. wanting in courtesy: uncivil.—Also (Spens.) discour'teise.—adv. discourt'eously.—ns. discourt'eousness, discourt'esy. [Pfx. dis- (2).]

discover, dis-kuv'ər, v.t. to uncover: to lay open or expose: to exhibit: to reveal: to make known: to find out: to espy.—Also (Spens.) discoure', discure'.—adj. discov'erable.—ns. discov'erer, one who makes a discovery, esp. of something never before known: an informer (obs.): a scout (Shak.); discov'ery, the act of finding out: the thing discovered: gaining knowledge of the unknown: the unravelling of a plot: exploration or reconnaissance (obs. except in voyage of discovery, voyage of exploration). [O.Fr. descouvrir, des- (L. dis-), away, couvrir, to cover; see cover.]

discovert, dis-kuv'ərt, (law) adj. not under the bonds of matrimony, of a spinster or widow.—n.

**discov'erture.** [Lit. uncovered, unprotected; O.Fr. *descovert*; see **discover, cover.**]

**discredit,** *dis-kred'it*, *n.* want of credit: bad credit: ill-repute: disgrace.—*v.t.* to refuse credit to, or belief in: to deprive of credibility: to deprive of credit: to disgrace.—*adj.* **discred'itable,** not creditable: disgraceful.—*adv.* **discred'itably.** [Pfx. **dis-** (2), (3).]

**discreet,** *dis-krēt'*, *adj.* having discernment: wary: circumspect: prudent: discrete, separate, detached (*arch.*).—*adv.* **discreet'ly.**—*n.* **discreet'ness.** [O.Fr. *discret*—L. *discrētus*—*discernēre*, to separate, to perceive; see **discern, discrete.**]

**discrepancy,** *dis-krep'ən-si*, or *dis'*, *n.* disagreement, variance of facts or sentiments.—*n.* **discrep'ance** (or *dis'*).—*adj.* **discrep'ant** (or *dis'*), contrary, disagreeing. [L. *discrepāns, -antis*, different—*dis-*, asunder, and *crepāns*, pr.p. of *crepāre*, to sound.]

**discrete,** *dis'krēt, dis-krēt'*, *adj.* separate: discontinuous: consisting of distinct parts: referring to distinct objects: abstract—opp. to *concrete.*—*adv.* **discrete'ly.**—*n.* **discrete'ness.**—*adj.* **discret'ive,** separating: disjunctive.—*adv.* **discret'ively.** [L. *discrētus*; cf. **discreet.**]

**discretion,** *dis-kresh'ən*, *n.* quality of being discreet: prudence: liberty to act at pleasure.—*adjs.* **discre'tional, discre'tionary,** left to discretion: unrestricted.—*advs.* **discre'tionally, discre'tionarily.**—**age, years, of discretion,** mature years; **at discretion,** according to one's own judgment; **be at one's discretion,** to be completely under one's power or control; **surrender at discretion,** to surrender unconditionally, that is, to another's discretion. [O.Fr. *discrecion*—L. *discrētiō, -ōnis, discernēre, -crētum.*]

**discriminate,** *dis-krim'i-nāt*, *v.t.* to note the difference of or between: to distinguish: to select from others: treat differently because of prejudice (with *against*).—*v.i.* to make or note a difference or distinction: to distinguish.—*adj.* (*-nit*) discriminated: discriminating.—*adj.* **discrim'inant, discriminating.**—*n.* a special function of the roots of an equation, expressible in terms of the coefficients—zero value of the function showing that at least two of the roots are equal.—*adv.* **discrim'inately.**—*adj.* **discrim'inating,** noting distinctions: gifted with judgment and penetration.—*adv.* **discrim'inatingly.**—*n.* **discriminā'tion.**—*adj.* **discrim'inative,** that marks a difference: characteristic: observing distinctions.—*adv.* **discrim'inatively.**—*n.* **discrim'inator.**—*adj.* **discrim'inatory,** discriminative: favouring some, not treating, or falling on, all alike. [L. *discrimināre, -ātum—discrīmen,* that which separates; cf. *discernēre, discern.*]

**discrown,** *dis-krown'*, *v.t.* to deprive of a crown. [Pfx. **dis-** (3).]

**disculpate,** *dis-kul'pāt, v.t.* to free from blame. [Pfx. **dis-** (3).]

**discumber,** *dis-kum'bər, v.t.* to disencumber. [Pfx. **dis-** (2).]

**discure,** *dis-kūr', (Spens.) v.t.* to discover. [Pfx. **dis-** (2).]

**discursive,** *dis-kûr'siv, adj.* running from one thing to another: roving, desultory: proceeding regularly from premises to conclusion: intellectual, rational.—*ns.* **discur'sion,** desultory talk: act of reasoning; **discur'sist,** a disputer.—*adv.* **discur'sively.**—*n.* **discur'siveness.**—*adj.* **discur'sory,** discursive.—*n.* **discur'sus** (L.L.), discourse, reasoned treatment. [See **discourse.**]

**discus,** *dis'kəs, n.* a disk, flat circular image or object: a heavy wooden disk, thickening towards the centre, thrown for distance in athletic contests. [L.,—Gr. *diskos.*]

**discuss,** *dis-kus', v.t.* to examine in detail, or by disputation: to debate: to sift: to consume, as a bottle of wine (*coll.*): to throw off (*Spens.*): to dispel: to settle, decide (*obs.*): to declare,

**make known** (*Shak.*).—*adj.* **discuss'able, -ible.**—*n.* **discussion** (*dis-kush'ən*), debate: dispersion of a tumour (*surg.*).—*adjs.* **discuss'ive, discutient** (*-kū'shi-ənt*), able or tending to discuss or disperse tumours.—*n.* **discū'tient,** a medicine with this property. [L. *discutēre, discussum—dis-*, asunder, *quatēre,* to shake.]

**disdain,** *dis-dān',* or *diz-, v.t.* to think unworthy: to scorn.—*n.* a feeling of contempt, generally tinged with superiority: haughtiness.—*adjs.* **disdained'** (*Shak.*), disdainful; **disdain'ful.**—*adv.* **disdain'fully.**—*n.* **disdain'fulness.** [O.Fr. *desdaigner* with substitution of *des-* (L. *dis-*) for L. *dē* in L. *dēdignārī—dignus,* worthy.]

**disease,** *diz-ēz', n.* uneasiness (in this sense often written **dis-ease** and pron. *dis'ēz'*): a disorder or want of health in mind or body: ailment: cause of pain.—*v.t.* (*Spens.*) to make uneasy.—*adj.* **diseased',** affected with disease.—*n.* **diseas'edness.**—*adj.* **disease'ful.** [O.Fr. *desaise—des-* (L. *dis-*, not), *aise,* ease; see **ease.**]

**disedge,** *dis-ej', (Shak.) v.t.* to deprive of the edge: to blunt: to dull. [Pfx. **dis-** (3).]

**disembark,** *dis-im-bärk', v.t.* to set ashore: to take out of a ship.—*v.i.* to quit a ship: to land.—*ns.* **disembarkā'tion** (*dis-em-, dis-im-*), **disembark'ment.** [O.Fr. *desembarquer—des-* (L. *dis-*, removal), *embarquer.* See **embark.**]

**disembarrass,** *dis-im-bar'əs, v.t.* to free from embarrassment or perplexity.—*n.* **disembarr'assment.** [Pfx. **dis-** (2).]

**disembellish,** *dis-im-bel'ish, v.t.* to deprive of embellishment. [Pfx. **dis-** (2).]

**disembitter,** *dis-im-bit'ər, v.t.* to free from bitterness. [Pfx. **dis-** (2).]

**disembody,** *dis-im-bod'i, v.t.* to take away from or out of the body (esp. of spirits): to discharge from military embodiment.—*adj.* **disembod'ied.**—*n.* **disembod'iment.** [Pfx. **dis-** (3).]

**disembogue,** *dis-im-bōg', v.t.* and *v.i.* to discharge at the mouth, as a stream.—*n.* **disembogue'ment.** [Sp. *desembocar—des-* (L. *dis-*), asunder, *embocar,* to enter the mouth—*en* (L. *in*), into, *boca* (L. *bucca*), cheek, mouth.]

**disembosom,** *dis-im-boōz'əm, v.t.* to separate from the bosom: to disburden. [Pfx. **dis-** (1).]

**disembowel,** *dis-im-bow'əl, v.t.* to take out the bowels of: to tear out the inside of.—*n.* **disembow'elment.** [Pfx. **dis-** (3).]

**disembrangle,** *dis-im-brang'gl, v.t.* to free from dispute. [Pfx. **dis-** (2).]

**disembroil,** *dis-im-broil', v.t.* to free from broil or confusion. [Pfx. **dis-** (2).]

**disemburden,** *dis-im-bûr'dn, v.t.* to disburden. [Pfx. **dis-** (3).]

**disemploy,** *dis-im-ploi', v.t.* remove from employment.—*adj.* **disemployed'.** [Pfx. **dis-** (2).]

**disenable,** *dis-in-ā'bl, v.t.* to make unable: to disable: to deprive of power (*obs.*). [Pfx. **dis-** (2).]

**disenchain,** *dis-in-chān', v.t.* to free from restraint. [Pfx. **dis-** (2).]

**disenchant,** *dis-in-chänt', v.t.* to free from enchantment, to disillusion.—*ns.* **disenchant'er;**—*fem.* **disenchant'ress; disenchant'ment.** [Pfx. **dis-** (2).]

**disenclose,** *dis-in-klōz', v.t.* to free from the condition of being enclosed: to dispark.—Also **disinclose'.** [Pfx. **dis-** (2).]

**disencumber,** *dis-in-kum'bər, v.t.* to free from encumbrance: to disburden.—*n.* **disencum'brance.** [Pfx. **dis-** (2).]

**disendow,** *dis-in-dow', v.t.* to take away the endowments of (esp. of an established church).—*adj.* **disendowed'.**—*n.* **disendow'ment.** [Pfx. **dis-** (3).]

**disenfranchise,** *dis-in-fran'chiz, -shiz, (rare) v.t.* to disfranchise: to deprive of suffrage.—*n.* **disenfran'chisement** (*-chiz-, -shis-*). [Pfx. **dis-** (2).]

**disengage,** *dis-in-gāj', v.t.* to separate or free from being engaged: to separate: to set free: to release.—*v.i.* to come loose.—*adj.* **disengaged',**

at leisure, without engagement.—*ns.* disengag'ed-ness; disengage'ment, a separating, releasing: a mutual withdrawal from a position. [O.Fr. *desengager*—*des*- (L. *dis*-, neg.), *engager*, to engage.]

disennoble, *dis-i-nō'bl*, *v.t.* to deprive of title, or of what ennobles: to degrade. [Pfx. dis- (2).]

disenrol, *dis-in-rōl'*, *v.t.* to remove from a roll. [Pfx. dis- (2).]

disenshroud, *dis-in-shrowd'*, *v.t.* to divest of a shroud, to unveil. [Pfx. dis- (3).]

disenslave, *dis-in-slāv'*, *v.t.* to free from bondage. [Pfx. dis- (2).]

disentail, *dis-in-tāl'*, *v.t.* to break the entail of (an estate): to divest.—*n.* the act of disentailing. [Pfx. dis- (2).]

disentangle, *dis-in-tang'gl*, *v.t.* to free from entanglement or disorder: to unravel: to disengage or set free.—*n.* disentang'lement. [Pfx. dis- (2).]

disenthral, disenthrall, *dis-in-thröl'*, *v.t.* to free from enthralment.—*n.* disenthral'ment. [Pfx. dis- (2).]

disenthrone, *dis-in-thrōn'*, (*Milt.*) *v.t.* to dethrone. [Pfx. dis- (2).]

disentitle, *dis-in-tī'tl*, *v.t.* to deprive of title. [Pfx. dis- (2).]

disentomb, *dis-in-tōōm'*, *v.t.* to take out from a tomb. [Pfx. dis- (2).]

disentrail, disentrayle, *dis-in-trāl*, (*Spens.*) *v.t.* to let forth as if from the entrails. [Pfx. dis- (3).]

disentrain, *dis-in-trān'*, *v.t.* to set down from a train.—*v.i.* to alight from a train.—*n.* disentrain'ment. [Pfx. dis- (3).]

disentrance, *dis-in-träns'*, *v.t.* to awaken from a trance or entrancement: to arouse from a reverie.—*n.* disentrance'ment. [Pfx. dis- (2).]

disentwine, *dis-in-twin'*, *v.t.* to untwine. [Pfx. dis- (2).]

disenvelop, *dis-in-vel'əp*, *v.t.* to free from that in which a thing is enveloped: to unfold. [Pfx. dis- (2).]

disenviron, *dis-in-vī'rən*, *v.t.* to deprive of environment. [Pfx. dis- (3).]

disespouse, *dis-is-powz'*, (*Milt.*) *v.t.* to separate after espousal or betrothal. [Pfx. dis- (1).]

disestablish, *dis-is-tab'lish*, *v.t.* to undo the establishment of: deprive (a church) of established status.—*n.* disestab'lishment. [Pfx. dis- (2).]

disesteem, *dis-is-tēm'*, *n.* want of esteem: disregard.—*v.t.* to disapprove: to dislike.—*n.* disestimā'tion (*-es-tim*-). [Pfx. dis- (2).]

diseuse, *dē-zœz*, masc. diseur, *dē-zœr*, (Fr.) a reciter or entertainer.

disfame, *dis-fām'*, *n.* evil reputation. [Pfx. dis- (2).]

disfavour, *dis-fā'vər*, *n.* want of favour: displeasure: dislike.—*v.t.* to withhold favour from: to disapprove: to oppose.—*n.* disfā'vourer. [Pfx. dis- (2).]

disfeature, *dis-fē'chər*, *v.t.* to deprive of a feature: to deface. [Pfx. dis- (3).]

disfellowship, *dis-fel'ō-ship*, *n.* want of, or exclusion from, fellowship.—*v.t.* to excommunicate. [Pfx. dis- (2).]

disfigure, *dis-fig'ər*, *v.t.* to spoil the figure of: to change to a worse form: to spoil the beauty of: to deform.—*ns.* disfig'urement, disfigurā'tion. [O.Fr. *desfigurer*—L. *dis*-, neg., *figūrāre*, to figure.]

disflesh, *dis-flesh'*, *v.t.* to deprive of flesh, to disembody. [Pfx. dis- (3).]

disforest, *dis-for'ist*, *v.t.* to strip of trees: to disafforest. [Pfx. dis- (3).]

disform, *dis-förm'*, *v.t.* to alter the form of. [Pfx. dis- (2).]

disfranchise, *dis-fran'chiz*, *-shiz*, *v.t.* to deprive of a franchise, or of rights and privileges, esp. that of voting for an M.P.—*n.* disfran'chisement. [Pfx. dis- (2).]

disfrock, *dis-frok'*, *v.t.* to unfrock, deprive of clerical garb or character. [Pfx. dis- (3).]

disfurnish, *dis-für'nish*, (*Shak.*) *v.t.* to strip, render destitute.—*n.* disfur'nishment. [Pfx. dis- (2).]

disgarnish, *dis-gär'nish*, *v.t.* to despoil. [Pfx. dis- (3).]

disgarrison, *dis-gar'i-sn*, *v.t.* to deprive of a garrison. [Pfx. dis- (3).]

disgavel, *dis-gav'l*, *v.t.* to relieve from the tenure of gavelkind. [Pfx. dis- (3).]

disgest, *dis-jest'*, *-jēst'*, disgest'ion (*-yən*), *obs.* or *dial.* forms of digest, -ion.

disglorify, *dis-glō'ri-fī*, *-glö'*, (*Milt.*) *v.t.* to deprive of glory. [Pfx. dis- (3).]

disgodded, *dis-god'id*, *adj.* deprived of divinity. [Pfx. dis- (2).]

disgorge, *dis-görj'*, *v.t.* to discharge from the throat: to vomit: to throw out with violence: to give up: to remove sediment from (champagne) after fermentation in the bottle.—*n.* disgorge'ment. [O.Fr. *desgorger*, *des*, away, *gorge*, throat. See gorge.]

disgospelling, *dis-gos'pəl-ing*, (*Milt.*) *adj.* withholding the gospel, stopping the channel of the gospel. [Pfx. dis- (3).]

disgown, *dis-gown'*, *v.t.* or *v.i.* to strip of a gown: to deprive of or to renounce orders or a degree. [Pfx. dis- (3).]

disgrace, *dis-grās'*, *n.* state of being out of grace or favour, or of being dishonoured: cause of shame: dishonour: disfigurement: ugliness: defect of grace.—*v.t.* to put out of favour: to bring disgrace or shame upon.—*adj.* disgrace'ful, bringing disgrace: causing shame: dishonourable.—*adv.* disgrace'fully.—*ns.* disgrace'fulness; disgra'cer.—*adj.* disgracious (*-grā'shəs*; *Shak.*), ungracious, unpleasing. [Fr. *disgrâce*—L. *dis*-, not, and *grātia*, favour, grace.]

disgrade, *dis-grād'*, *v.t.* to deprive of rank or status.—*n.* disgradā'tion (*-grə-dā'shən*). [O.Fr. *desgrader*, with substitution of *des*- (L. *dis*-), for L. *dē* in L.L. *dēgradāre*—*gradus*, a step.]

disgregation, *dis-gri-gā'shən*, *n.* separation: scattering. [L. *disgregātiō*, *-ōnis*—*dis*-, apart, *grex*, *gregis*, flock.]

disgruntle, *dis-grun'tl*, (*coll.*) *v.t.* to disappoint, disgust.—*adj.* disgrun'tled, out of humour. [Pfx. dis- (4), and gruntle, freq. of grunt.]

disguise, *dis-gīz'*, *v.t.* to change the guise or appearance of: to conceal the identity of by a dress intended to deceive, or by a counterfeit manner and appearance: to intoxicate (usu. *disguised in liquor*; *arch.* and *slang*).—*n.* a dress intended to disguise the wearer: a false appearance: change of behaviour in intoxication.—*adj.* disguised'.—*adv.* disguis'edly.—*n.* disguis'edness.—*adj.* disguise'less.—*ns.* disguise'ment; disguis'er; disguis'ing. [O.Fr. *desguiser*—*des*- (L.*dis*-, reversal), *guise*, manner; see guise.]

disgust, *dis-gust'*, *n.* (formerly, e.g. in Milton, Johnson, Jane Austen) distaste, disfavour, displeasure: (now) loathing: extreme annoyance.—*v.t.* to excite disgust in.—*adv.* disgust'edly.—*adj.* disgust'ful.—*adv.* disgust'fully.—*n.* disgust'fulness.—*adj.* disgust'ing.—*adv.* disgust'ingly.—*n.* disgust'ingness. [O.Fr. *desgouster*—*des*- (L. *dis*-), and *gouster*—L. *gustāre*, to taste.]

dish, *dish*, *n.* a vessel, esp. one that is flat, or shallow, or not circular, or one for food at table: a dishful: the food in a dish: a cup (of tea, coffee, etc.; *arch.*): a particular kind of food: a hollow: concavity of form, as in a wheel, a chair-back: a concave reflector used for directive radiation and reception, esp. for radar or radio telescopes: a good-looking person of the opposite sex (*coll.*).—*v.t.* to put in a dish, for table: to make concave: to outwit, circumvent (*coll.*): to ruin (*coll.*).—*adj.* dished, having a concavity: completely frustrated (*coll.*).—*ns.* dish'ful; dish'ing, putting in a dish: a hollow, concavity.—*adj.* hollow like a dish.—*adj.* **dish'y** (*coll.*), good-looking, attractive.—**dish'-clout, dish'-cloth,** a cloth for drying or wiping dishes; **dish'-cover,** a cover for a dish to keep it hot. —*adj.* **dish'-faced,** having a round, flat face, or (in animals) a concavity in the face.—**dish'-water,** water in which dishes have been washed: a liquid deficient in strength or cleanliness.— **dish out,** to serve out: to share (food) among several people: to give out (*fig.*; *coll.*; usu. *disparagingly*); **dish up,** to serve up, esp. figuratively of old materials cooked up anew. [O.E. *disc*, a plate, a dish, a table—L. *discus*— Gr. *diskos*; cf. disk, desk; Ger. *tisch*, table.]

**dish,** *dish* (*print.*) *v.t.* to distribute (type).

**dishabilitate,** *dis-(h)ə-bil'i-tāt*, *v.t.* to disqualify: to attaint.—*n.* **dishabilitā'tion.** [Pfx. dis- (2).]

**dishabille,** *dis-ə-bēl'*, *n.* a negligent toilet: undress: an undress garment.—Also **déshabillé** (*dā-za-bē-yä*). [Fr. *déshabillé*, pa.p. of *déshabiller*, to undress—*des-* (L. *dis-*), apart, *habiller*, to dress.]

**dishabit,** *dis-hab'it*, (*Shak.*) *v.t.* to drive from a habitation. [O.Fr. *deshabiter*—L. *dis-*, priv., *habitāre*, to inhabit.]

**dishable,** *dis-hā'bl*, an obs. form (*Spens.*) of **disable.**

**dishallow,** *dis-hal'ō*, *v.t.* to desecrate. [Pfx. dis- (2).]

**disharmony,** *dis-här'mə-ni*, *n.* lack of harmony: discord: incongruity.—*adjs.* **disharmonic** (*-mon'*), out of harmony: discordant: incongruous: dysharmonic; **disharmonious** (*-mō'*).—*adv.* **disharmō'niously.**—*v.t.* and *v.i.* **dishar'monise, -ize,** to put out of, or be out of, harmony. [Pfx. dis- (2).]

**dishearten,** *dis-härt'n*, *v.t.* to deprive of heart, courage, or spirits: to discourage: to depress.— *adjs.* **disheart'ened; disheart'ening.** [Pfx. dis- (2).]

**dishelm,** *dis-helm'*, *v.t.* to divest of a helmet. [Pfx. dis- (3).]

**disherit,** *dis-her'it*, (*Spens.*) *v.t.* to disinherit.—*ns.* **disher'ison** (*-zən*); **disher'itor.** [O.Fr. *desheriter* —L. *dis-*, neg., L.L. *hērēditāre*, to inherit—L. *hērēs*, heir.]

**dishevel,** *di-shev'l*, *v.t.* to disorder, as hair: to cause to hang loose: to ruffle.—*v.i.* to spread in disorder:—*pr.p.* **dishev'elling;** *pa.t.* and *pa.p.* **dishev'elled.**—*n.* **dishev'elment.** [O.Fr. *cheveler*—L.L. *discapillāre*, to tear out or disorder the hair—L. *dis-*, in different directions, *capillus*, the hair.]

**dishome,** *dis-hōm'*, *v.t.* to deprive of a home. [Pfx. dis- (3).]

**dishonest,** *dis-on'ist*, *adj.* not honest: wanting integrity: disposed to cheat: insincere: unchaste (*Shak.*).—*adv.* **dishon'estly.**—*n.* **dishon'esty.** [O.Fr. *deshoneste*—*des-* (L. *dis-*), neg., *honeste* (L. *honestus*), honest.]

**dishonour,** *dis-on'ər*, *n.* want of honour: disgrace: shame: reproach.—*v.t.* to deprive of honour: to disgrace: to cause shame to: to seduce: to degrade: to refuse the payment of, as a cheque. —*adjs.* **dishon'orary,** causing dishonour; **dishon'ourable,** not in accordance with a sense of honour: disgraceful.—*n.* **dishon'ourableness.** —*adv.* **dishon'ourably.**—*n.* **dishon'ourer.** [O.Fr. *deshonneur*—*des-* (—L. *dis-*), neg., *honneur* (—L. *honor*), honour.]

**dishorn,** *dis-hörn'*, *v.t.* to deprive of horns. [Pfx. dis- (3).]

**dishorse,** *dis-hörs'*, *v.t.* to unhorse. [Pfx. dis- (3).]

**dishouse,** *dis-howz'*, *v.t.* to deprive of house or housing: to turn out of doors: to clear of houses. [Pfx. dis- (3).]

**dishumour,** *dis-(h)ū'mər*, *n.* ill-humour.—*v.t.* to put out of humour. [Pfx. dis- (2).]

**disillude,** *dis-i-lōōd'*, *-lūd'*, *v.t.* to free from illusion. —*n.* **disillusion** (*dis-i-lōō'zhən, -lū'*), a freeing from illusion: state of being disillusioned.—*v.t.* to

free from illusion, disenchant.—*adjs.* **disillu'sionary; disillu'sioned,** freed from illusion: often, bereft of comfortable beliefs whether they were false or true.—*v.t.* **disillu'sionise, -ize.**—*n.* **disillu'sionment.**—*adj.* **disillu'sive** (*-siv*). [Pfx. dis- (3).]

**disilluminate,** *dis-i-lōō'mi-nāt, -lū'*, *v.t.* to destroy the light of, to darken. [Pfx. dis- (2).]

**disimagine,** *dis-i-maj'in*, *v.t.* to banish from the imagination: imagine not to be. [Pfx. dis- (3), (2).]

**disimmure,** *dis-i-mūr'*, *v.t.* to release from walls. [Pfx. dis- (2).]

**disimpassioned,** *dis-im-pash'ənd*, *adj.* free from the influence of passion, tranquil. [Pfx. dis- (2).]

**disimprison,** *dis-im-priz'n*, *v.t.* to free from prison or restraint.—*n.* **disimpris'onment.** [Pfx. dis- (2).]

**disimprove,** *dis-im-prōōv'*, *v.t.* to render worse.— *v.i.* to grow worse. [Pfx. dis- (2).]

**disincarcerate,** *dis-in-kär'sər-āt*, *v.t.* to free from prison.—*n.* **disincarcerā'tion.** [Pfx. dis- (2).]

**disincentive,** *dis-in-sen'tiv*, *n.* a discouragement to effort.—Also *adj.* [Pfx. dis- (2).]

**disinclination,** *dis-in-kli-nā'shən*, *n.* want of inclination: unwillingness.—*v.t.* **disincline** (*-klīn'*), to turn away inclination from: to excite the dislike or aversion of.—*adj.* **disinclined',** not inclined: averse. [Pfx. dis- (2).]

**disinclose.** Same as **disenclose.**

**disincorporate,** *dis-in-kör'pə-rāt*, *v.t.* to deprive of corporate rights.—*n.* **disincorporā'tion.** [Pfx. dis- (2).]

**disindividualise, -ize,** *dis-in-di-vid'ū-əl-iz*, *v.t.* to deprive of individuality. [Pfx. dis- (2).]

**disinfect,** *dis-in-fekt'*, *v.t.* to free from infection: to purify from infectious germs.—*n.* **disinfect'ant,** anything that destroys the causes of infection.— Also *adj.*—*ns.* **disinfec'tion; disinfect'or.** [Pfx. dis- (2).]

**disinfest,** *dis-in-fest'*, *v.t.* to free from infesting animals.—*n.* **disinfestā'tion.** [Pfx. dis- (2).]

**disinflation,** *dis'in-flā-shən*, *n.* return to the normal condition after inflation.—*adj.* **disinflā'tionary.** [Pfx. dis- (2).]

**disinformation,** *dis-in-fər-mā'shən*, *n.* deliberate leakage of misleading information. [Pfx. dis- (2).]

**disingenuous,** *dis-in-jen'ū-əs*, *adj.* not ingenuous: not frank or open: crafty.—*n.* **disingenu'ity** (*rare*).—*adv.* **disingen'uously.**—*n.* **disingen'uousness.** [Pfx. dis- (2).]

**disinherit,** *dis-in-her'it*, *v.t.* to cut off from hereditary rights: to deprive of an inheritance.—*ns.* **disinher'ison** (*-zən*), act of disinheriting; **disinher'itance.** [Pfx. dis- (3).]

**disinhume,** *dis-in-hūm'*, *v.t.* to take out of the earth, to disinter. [Pfx. dis- (2).]

**disintegrate,** *dis-in'ti-grāt*, *v.t.* and *v.i.* to separate into parts: to break up: to crumble.—*adjs.* **disin'tegrable, disin'tegrative.**—*ns.* **disintegra'tion; disin'tegrātor,** a machine for crushing or pulverising. [Pfx. dis- (1).]

**disinter,** *dis-in-tûr'*, *v.t.* to take out of the earth, from a grave, or from obscurity.—*n.* **disinter'ment.** [Pfx. dis- (2).]

**disinterest,** *dis-in'tər-ist*, *n.* disadvantage: disinterestedness: lack of interest.—*v.t.* to free from interest.—*adj.* **disint'erested,** not influenced by private feelings or considerations: not deriving personal advantage: impartial: unselfish: generous: (revived from obsolescence) uninterested.—*adv.* **disin'terestedly.**—*n.* **disin'terestedness.**—*adj.* **disin'teresting** (*obs.*), uninteresting. [Pfx. dis- (2).]

**disinthral.** Same as **disenthral.**

**disintricate,** *dis-in'tri-kāt*, *v.t.* to free from intricacy. [Pfx. dis- (2).]

**disinure,** *dis-in-ūr'*, (*Milt.*) *v.t.* to render unfamiliar. [Pfx. dis- (2).]

Neutral vowels in unaccented syllables: *el'ə-mənt*; for certain sounds in foreign words, see p. viii

**disinvest**, *dis-in-vest'*, *v.t.* to divest.—*n.* **disinvest'-iture**, the action of disinvesting. [Pfx. **dis-** (2).]

**disinvigorate**, *dis-in-vig'ər-āt*, *v.t.* to weaken. [Pfx. **dis-** (2).]

**disinvolve**, *dis-in-volv'*, *v.t.* to unfold: to disentangle. [Pfx. **dis-** (2).]

**disjaskit**, *dis-jas'kit*, (*Scot.*) *adj.* jaded: worn out. [Prob. dejected.]

**disject**, *dis-jekt'*, *v.t.* to dismember: to scatter.—*n.* **disjec'tion**. [L. *disjicĕre, -jectum*—*dis-*, apart, *jacĕre*, to throw.]

**disjoin**, *dis-join'*, *v.t.* to separate after having been joined.—*v.t.* **disjoint'**, to put out of joint: to separate united parts of: to break the natural order or relations of: to make incoherent.—*adj.* **disjoint'ed**, incoherent, esp. of discourse: badly assorted.—*adv.* **disjoint'edly**.—*n.* **disjoint'edness**. [O.Fr. *desjoindre*—L. *disjungĕre*—*dis-*, apart, *jungĕre*, to join.]

**disjunct**, *dis-jungkt'*, also *dis'*, *adj.* disjoined: deeply constricted (*biol.*): of tetrachords, having the highest note of the lower and the lowest of the upper a tone or semitone apart (*ancient Gr. mus.*).—*n.* **disjunc'tion**, the act of disjoining: disunion: separation.—*adj.* **disjunct'ive**, disjoining: tending to separate: uniting sentences but disjoining the sense, or rather marking an adverse sense (*gram.*).—*n.* a word which disjoins.—*adv.* **disjunct'ively**.—*ns.* **disjunct'or**, a device for breaking an electric circuit: a weak place where separation between conidia occurs (*bot.*); **disjunct'ure**. [O.Fr. *desjoinct, desjoindre*. See above.]

**disjune**, *dis-jōōn'*, (*Scot.*; *arch.*) *n.* breakfast. [O.Fr. *desjun*—L. *dis-*, expressing undoing, *jējūnus*, fasting.]

**disk, disc**, *disk*, *n.* a quoit thrown by ancient Greek athletes: any flat thin circular body or structure: a circular figure, as that presented by the sun, moon, and planets: the enlarged torus of a flower: the inner part of a capitulum in composite plants: a layer of fibrocartilage between vertebrae, the slipping of which causes pressure on spinal nerves and hence pains: a gramophone record.—*v.t.* and *v.i.* to work with a **disk-harrow**.—**disk brake**, one in which the friction is obtained by pads hydraulically forced against a disk on the wheel; **disk'-flower'**, **-flor'et**, one of the tubular inner flowers of a capitulum—opp. to *ray-flower*; **disk'-harr'ow**, **-plough**, a harrow, or plough, in which the soil is cut by inclined disks; **disk'-jockey** (*slang*), one who gives a recital of gramophone records; **disk parking**, a system according to which the motorist himself is responsible for affixing to his car special disk(s) showing his time of arrival and the time when permitted parking ends, there being no charge during the permitted period. See also **disc**. [Gr. *diskos*.]

**disleaf**, *dis-lēf'*, *v.t.* to deprive of leaves.—Also **disleave'**. [Pfx. **dis-** (2).]

**disleal**, *dis-lē'əl*, (*Spens.*) *adj.* disloyal, dishonourable. [See **disloyal**.]

**dislike**, *dis-līk'*, *v.t.* to be displeased with: to disapprove of: to have an aversion to: to displease (*obs.*).—*n.* (*dis-līk'*, sometimes *dis'*) disinclination: aversion: distaste: disapproval.—*adjs.* **dislike'able, dislik'able**; **dislike'ful**.—*v.t.* **dislik'en** (*Shak.*), to make unlike.—*n.* **dislike'ness** (*obs.*), unlikeness. [Pfx. **dis-** (2), and like; the genuine Eng. word is *mislike*.]

**dislimb**, *dis-lim'*, *v.t.* to tear the limbs from: to dismember. [Pfx. **dis-** (1).]

**dislimn**, *dis-lim'*, (*Shak.*) *v.t.* to efface. [Pfx. **dis-** (3).]

**dislink**, *dis-lingk'*, *v.t.* to unlink, to separate. [Pfx. **dis-** (2).]

**disload**, *dis-lōd'*, *v.t.* to unload, to disburden. [Pfx. **dis-** (3).]

**dislocate**, *dis-lō-kāt*, *v.t.* to displace: to put out

of joint.—*adv.* **dis'locately**.—*n.* **disloca'tion**, a dislocated joint: displacement: disorganisation: derangement (of traffic, plans, etc.): a fault (*geol.*). [L.L. *dislocāre, -ātum*—L. *dis*, apart, *locāre*, to place.]

**dislodge**, *dis-loj'*, *v.t.* to drive from a lodgment or place of rest: to drive from a place of hiding or of defence.—*v.i.* to go away.—*n.* **dislodg(e)-ment**. [O.Fr. *desloger*—*des-* (L. *dis-*), apart, *loger*, to lodge.]

**disloign**, *dis-loin'*, (*Spens.*) *v.t.* to put far apart or at a distance, to remove. [O.Fr. *desloignier*—*des-* (L. *dis-*), apart, *loignier*, to remove.]

**disloyal**, *dis-loi'əl*, *adj.* not loyal: unfaithful.—*adv.* **disloy'ally**.—*n.* **disloy'alty**. [O.Fr. *desloyal*—*des-* (L. *dis-*), neg., *loyal, leial*—L. *lēgālis*, legal.]

**dislustre**, *dis-lus'tər*, *v.t.* to deprive of lustre.—*v.i.* to lose lustre. [Pfx. **dis-** (3).]

**dismal**, *diz'məl*, *adj.* gloomy: dreary: sorrowful: depressing.—*n.* unlucky days (*obs.*): a swamp (*U.S.*): a dismal person: (in *pl.*) the dumps: (in *pl.*) mournings (*obs.*).—*adv.* **dis'mally**.—*ns.* **dis'malness, dismality** (*-mal'i-ti*).—**dismal day** (*Spens.*), a day of ill omen; **dismal Jimmy**, confirmed pessimist.—**the dismal science**, political economy. [O.Fr. *dismal*—L. *diēs mali*, evil, unlucky days.]

**disman**, *dis-man'*, *v.t.* to deprive of men (of a country, or ship): to unman: to deprive of human character (of the body by death). [Pfx. **dis-** (3).]

**dismantle**, *dis-man'tl*, *v.t.* to strip: to deprive of furniture, fittings, etc., so as to render useless: to raze the fortifications of: to take to bits, pull down. [O.Fr. *desmanteller*—*des-* (L. *dis-*), away, *manteler*—*mantel*, a mantle.]

**dismask**, *dis-mäsk'*, *v.t.* to strip a mask from: to remove a disguise from: to uncover. [O.Fr. *desmasquer*—*des-* (L. *dis-*), neg., *masquer*, to mask.]

**dismast**, *dis-mäst'*, *v.t.* to deprive of a mast or masts.—*n.* **dismast'ment**. [Pfx. **dis-** (3).]

**dismay**, *dis-*, *diz-mā'*, *v.t.* to appal: to discourage: to distress (*Spens.*).—*v.i.* (*Shak.*) to be daunted.—*n.* loss of strength and courage through fear: discouraging onslaught (*Spens.*).—*n.* **dismay'edness**.—*adj.* **dismay'ful**.—*adv.* **dismay'fully** (*Spens.*). [App. through O.Fr.—L. *dis-*, neg., and O.H.G. *magan* (Ger. *mögen*; O.E. *magan*), to have might or power; see **may**.]

**dismayd**, *dis-mād'*, (*Spens.*) *adj.* apparently, misshapen, deformed, mismade. [Pfx. **dis-** (2).]

**dismayl**, *dis-māl'*, *v.t.* to deprive of mail (armour): to break mail from (*Spens.*). [O.Fr. *desmailler*—*des-* (L. *dis-*), priv., *maille*, mail.]

**disme**, *dim*, (*Shak.*) *n.* a tenth or tithe. [O.Fr.; see **dime**.]

**dismember**, *dis-mem'bər*, *v.t.* to divide member from member: to separate a limb from: to disjoint: to tear to pieces: to carve (certain birds —herons, cranes) for the table (*obs.*).—*adj.* **dismem'bered** (*her.*), without limbs or with limbs detached.—*n.* **dismem'berment**. [O.Fr. *desmembrer*—*des-* (L. *dis-*), apart, *membre*, a member (L. *membrum*).]

**dismiss**, *dis-mis'*, *v.t.* to send away: to dispatch: to discard: to remove from office or employment: to reject, to put out of court, to discharge (*law*): in cricket, to put out (batsman, -men): (*imper.*) as a military command, to fall out.—*ns.* **dismiss'al, dismission** (*-mish'ən*).—*adjs.* **dismiss'ive, dismiss'ory**. [Pfx. **dis-** (3), and L. *mittĕre, missum*, to send; L. *dimissus*.]

**dismoded**, *dis-mōd'id*, *adj.* out of fashion. [Pfx. **dis-** (2), and **mode**.]

**dismount**, *dis-mownt'*, *v.i.* to come down: to come off a horse, bicycle, etc.—*v.t.* to throw or bring down from any elevated place: to unhorse: to remove from a stand, framework, setting,

*fāte, fär; mē, hûr* (her); *mīne; mōte, för; mūte; mōōn, fōōt; dhen* (then)

carriage, or the like. [O.Fr. *desmonter—des-*
(L. *dis-*), neg., *monter*, to mount.]
**dismutation**, *dis-mū-tā'shən*, *n.* in biochemistry,
simultaneous oxidation and reduction. [Pfx.
dis- (2).]
**disnatured**, *dis-nā'chərd*, *adj.* unnatural, devoid
of natural affection.—*v.t.* **disnaturalise, -ize**
(-*nat'*), to make alien or unnatural. [Pfx. dis-
(2).]
**disnest**, *dis-nest'*, *v.t.* to dislodge from a nest: to
clear as of nestlings. [Pfx. dis- (3).]
**disobedient**, *dis-ō-bēd'yənt*, *adj.* neglecting or refusing to obey.—*n.* **disobed'ience.**—*adv.* **disobed'iently.** [Pfx. dis. (2).]
**disobey**, *dis-ō-bā'*, *dis-ə-bā'*, *dis'*, *v.t.* and *v.i.* to
neglect or refuse to obey. [O.Fr. *desobeir—
des-* (L. *dis-*), neg., and *obeir*, to obey.]
**disoblige**, *dis-ō-blīj'*, *-ə-blīj'*, *v.t.* to relieve from
an obligation: to refuse or fail to oblige or grant
a favour to: to offend or injure thereby.—*n.*
**disobligation** (*dis-ob-li-gā'shən*), freedom from
obligation: act of disobliging.—*adj.* **disob'-
ligatory** (-*gə-tə-ri*), releasing from obligation.—
*n.* **disobligement** (-*blīj'*).—*adj.* **disoblig'ing,** not
obliging: not careful to attend to the wishes of
others: unaccommodating: unkind.—*adv.* **disoblig'ingly.**—*n.* **disoblig'ingness.** [Pfx. dis- (2).]
**disorbed**, *dis-örbd'*, (*Shak.*) *adj.* thrown from its
sphere, as a star: deprived of the orb of sovereignty. [Pfx. dis- (3).]
**disorder**, *dis-ör'dər*, *n.* want of order: confusion:
disturbance: breach of the peace: disease.—
*v.t.* to throw out of order: to disarrange: to
disturb: to produce disease in.—*adj.* **disor'-
dered,** confused, deranged.—*n.* **disor'derliness.**
—*adj.* **disor'derly,** out of order: in confusion:
irregular: lawless: defying the restraints of
decency.—*adv.* confusedly: in a lawless manner.
—*n.* a disorderly person.—**disorderly house,** a
brothel: a gaming-house. [O.Fr. *desordre—
des-* (L. *dis-*), neg., *ordre*, order.]
**disordinate**, *dis-ör'di-nit*, *adj.* not in order (*rare*):
disorderly (*rare*): inordinate (*Milt.*).—*adv.* **dis-
or'dinately.** [Pfx. dis- (2).]
**disorganise, -ize**, *dis-ör'gən-iz*, *v.t.* to destroy the
organic structure of: to disorder.—*adj.* **dis-
organic** (-*gan'*).—*n.* **disorganisā'tion.** [Pfx. dis-
(2).]
**disorient**, *dis-ō'ri-ənt*, *-ö'*, *v.t.* to turn from the
east: to confuse as to direction: to throw out
of one's reckoning.—Also **diso'rientate.**—*n.* **dis-
orientā'tion.** [Pfx. dis- (2).]
**disown**, *dis-ōn'* *v.t.* to refuse to own or acknowledge as belonging to oneself: to deny: to
repudiate, cast off.—*n.* **disown'ment.** [Pfx. dis-
(2).]
**dispace**, *dis-pās'*, (*Spens.*) *v.i.* to range about.—
Also *v.t.* (*reflex.*) [Perh. L. *di-*, apart, *spatiāri*, to
walk about; or **dis-** (1), and **pace**.]
**disparage**, *dis-par'ij*, *v.t.* to dishonour by comparison with what is inferior: to match in
marriage with an inferior: to lower in rank or
estimation: to talk slightingly of: to dishearten
(*Spens.*).—*ns.* **dis'parage** (*Spens.*), an unequal
match; **dispar'agement;** **dispar'ager.**—*adv.* **dis-
par'agingly.** [O.Fr. *desparager—des-* (L. *dis-*),
neg., and *parage;* see **parage**.]
**disparate**, *dis'pər-it, -āt, adj.* unequal: incapable
of being compared.—*n.* **dis'parateness.**—*n.pl.*
**dis'parates,** things or characters of different
species. [L. *disparātus—dis-*, not, and *parāre*,
make ready; influenced by *dispar*, unequal.]
**disparity**, *dis-par'i-ti*, *n.* inequality: unlikeness so
great as to render comparison difficult and union
unsuitable. [L. *dispar*, unequal—*dis-*, neg., *par*,
equal.]
**dispark**, *dis-pärk'*, *v.t.* to throw open, deprive of
the character of a park: to remove from a park.
[Pfx. dis- (2, 3).]
**dispart**, *dis-pärt'*, *v.t.* to part asunder: to divide,

to separate.—*v.i.* to separate.—*n.* the difference
between the thickness of metal at the breech
and the mouth of a gun. [Pfx. dis- (1).]
**dispassion**, *dis-pash'ən*, *n.* freedom from passion:
a calm state of mind.—*adj.* **dispass'ionate** (-*it*),
free from passion: unmoved by feelings: cool:
impartial.—*adv.* **dispass'ionately.** [Pfx. dis- (2).]
**dispatch**, **despatch**, *dis-pach'*, *v.t.* to send away
hastily: to send out of the world: to put to
death: to dispose of: to perform speedily.—
*v.i.* (*Shak.*) to make haste.—*n.* a sending away
in haste: dismissal: rapid performance: haste:
taking of life: the sending off of the mails:
that which is dispatched, as a message, esp.
telegraphic: (*pl.*) state-papers (military, diplomatic, etc.).—*n.* **dispatch'er.**—*adj.* **dispatch'ful**
(*Milt.*), swift.—**dispatch'-boat,** a vessel for carrying dispatches; **dispatch'-box,** a box for holding
dispatches or valuable papers; **dispatch'-ri'der,**
a carrier of dispatches, on horse-back or bicycle.
[It. *dispacciare* or Sp. *despachar*—L. *dis-*, apart,
and some L.L. word from the root of *pangěre*,
*pactum*, to fasten; not connected with Fr.
*dépêcher.*]
**dispathy**, a misspelling of **dyspathy**.
**dispauperise, -ize**, *dis-pö'pər-iz*, *v.t.* to free from
pauperism or from paupers.—*v.t.* **dispau'per,**
to declare no longer a pauper. [Pfx. dis- (2).]
**dispeace**, *dis-pēs'*, *n.* lack of peace: dissension.
[Pfx. dis- (2).]
**dispel**, *dis-pel'*, *v.t.* to drive away and scatter: to
make disappear.—*v.i.* to scatter or melt away:
—*pr.p.* **dispell'ing;** *pa.t.* and *pa.p.* **dispelled'.** [L.
*dispellěre—dis-*, away, *pellěre*, to drive.]
**dispence**, *dis-pens'* (*Spens.*). Same as **dispense**.
**dispend**, *dis-pend'*, (*arch.*) *v.t.* to expend, pay out.
[O.Fr. *despendre—*L. *dis-*, out, and *penděre*, to
weigh.]
**dispensary.** See **dispensation**.
**dispensation**, *dis-pən-sā'shən*, *n.* the act of dispensing or dealing out: administration: a dealing of Providence, or of God, or nature: a
method or stage of God's dealing with man
(*Patriarchal, Mosaic, Christian*): licence or permission to neglect a rule: ground of exemption.
—*adj.* **dispens'able,** that may be dispensed, or
dispensed with: pardonable (*arch.*).—*ns.* **dis-
pensabil'ity, dispens'ableness.**—*adv.* **dispens'ably.**
—*n.* **dispens'ary,** a place where medicines are
dispensed (esp. gratis): an out-patient department of a hospital.—*adj.* **dispens'ative,** granting
dispensation.—*adv.* **dispens'atively.**—*n.* **dis'pensātor,** a dispenser: a distributor: an administrator.—*adv.* **dispens'atorily.**—*adj.* **dispens'atory,**
granting dispensation.—*n.* a book containing
medical prescriptions.—*v.t.* **dispense'**, to deal
out: to distribute: to administer: to make up
for distributing or administering.—*v.i.* (*Spens.*)
to make amends: to compound.—*n.* expense:
expenditure: supplies: dispensation (*Milt.*).—
*adj.* **dispensed'.**—*n.* **dispens'er,** one who dispenses, esp. a pharmacist who dispenses medicines: a container, or machine that gives out
in prearranged quantities.—**dispense with,** permit the want of: do without. [Fr. *dispenser*—
L. *dis-*, *pēnsāre*, weigh.]
**dispeople**, *dis-pē'pl*, *v.t.* to empty of inhabitants.
[Pfx. dis- (2).]
**disperse**, *dis-pûrs'*, *v.t.* to scatter in all directions:
to spread: to diffuse: to drive asunder: to
cause to vanish: to put in a colloidal state.—*v.i.*
to separate: to spread abroad: to vanish.—*ns.*
**dispers'al,** dispersion: distribution: the spread
of species to new areas; **dispers'ant,** a substance
causing dispersion.—*adv.* **dispers'edly.**—*ns.* **dispers'edness; dispers'er;** **dispersion** (*dis-pûr'shən*),
a scattering, or state of being scattered: the
removal of inflammation (*med.*): the spreading
out of rays owing to different refrangibility
(*phys.*): the scattering of values of a variable

Neutral vowels in unaccented syllables: *el'ə-mənt*; for certain sounds in foreign words, see p. viii

T.C.D.—13

from the average (*statistics*): the state of a finely divided colloid: a substance in that state: the diaspora.—*adj.* dispers'ive, tending or serving to disperse.—*n.* dispers'oid, a substance in a state of dispersion—also dispersed phase. [L. *dispergĕre, dispersum—dī-*, asunder, apart, *spargĕre*, to scatter.]

dispersonate, *dis-pûr'sən-āt, v.t.* to divest of personality. [Pfx. dis- (2).]

dispirit, *dis-pir'it, v.t.* to dishearten: to discourage.—*adj.* dispir'ited, dejected: feeble, spiritless.—*adv.* dispir'itedly.—*n.* dispir'itedness. —*adj.* dispir'iting, disheartening.—*n.* dispir'itment. [Pfx. dis- (2).]

dispiteous, *dis-pit'i-əs, (obs.) adj.* despiteous: pitiless.—*adv.* dispit'eously.—*n.* dispit'eousness. [See despite; influenced by piteous.]

displace, *dis-plās', v.t.* to put out of place: to disarrange: to remove from a state, office, or dignity: to supplant: to substitute something for.—*adj.* displace'able.—*n.* displace'ment, a putting or being out of place: the difference between the position of a body at a given time and that occupied at first: the quantity of water displaced by a ship afloat or an immersed body. —displaced person, one removed from his country as a prisoner or as a slave labour: a refugee or stateless person. [O.Fr. *desplacer—des-* (L. *dis-*), neg., and *place*, place.]

displant, *dis-plänt', v.t.* to remove from a fixed position: to drive from an abode.—*n.* displantā'tion. [O.Fr. *desplanter*—L. *dis-*, neg., and *plantāre*, to plant.]

display, *dis-plā', v.t.* to unfold or spread out: to exhibit: to set out ostentatiously: to make prominent by large type, wide spacing, etc. (*print*.).—*n.* a displaying or unfolding: exhibition: ostentatious show: the 'picture' on a cathode-ray tube screen making the information visible (*radar* and *navigation*).—*adj.* displayed', unfolded: spread: printed in prominent letters: erect, with wings expanded, as a bird (*her.*).—*n.* display'er. [O.Fr. *despleier—des-* (L. *dis-*), neg., and *plier, ploier*—L. *plicāre*, to fold; double deploy; see ply.]

disple, *dis'pl, (Spens.) v.t.* to discipline, chastise. [Apparently from discipline.]

displease, *dis-plēz', v.t.* to offend: to make angry in a slight degree: to be disagreeable to.—*v.i.* to raise aversion.—*n.* displeasance (*dis-plez'əns, Spens.*), displeasure.—*adj.* displeas'ant (*obs.*).— *adj.* displeased', vexed, annoyed.—*adv.* displeas'edly.—*n.* displeas'edness.—*adj.* displeas'ing, causing displeasure: giving offence.—*adv.* displeas'ingly.—*ns.* displeas'ingness; displeasure (*dis-plezh'ər*), the feeling of one who is offended: anger: cause of irritation.—*v.t.* (*arch.*) to displease, offend. [O.Fr. *desplaisir—des-* (L. *dis-*), reversal, *plaisir*, to please.]

displenish, *dis-plen'ish, v.t.* to deprive of plenishing or furniture, implements, etc.: to sell the plenishing of.—*n.* displen'ishment. [Pfx. dis- (3).]

displode, *dis-plōd', (Milt.) v.t.* to discharge, to explode.—*v.i.* to explode.—*n.* displōsion (*-plō'zhən*). [L. *displōdĕre—dis-*, asunder, *plaudĕre*, to beat.]

displume, *dis-ploōm', v.t.* to deprive of plumes or feathers. [Pfx. dis- (3).]

dispondee, *di-spon'dē, n.* a double spondee.—*adj.* dispondā'ic. [Gr. *dispondeios—di-*, twice, *spondeios*, spondee.]

dispone, *dis-pōn', v.t.* to set in order, dispose (*arch.*): to make over to another (*Scots law*): to convey legally.—*ns.* disponee', the person to whom anything is disponed; dispon'er. [L. *dispōnĕre*, to arrange.]

disponge. See dispunge.

disport, *dis-pōrt', -pört', v.t.* (usually reflex.) and *v.i.*, to divert, amuse: to move in gaiety.—*n.* disport'ment. [O.Fr. (*se*) *desporter*, to carry

(oneself) away from one's work, to amuse (oneself)—*des-* (L. *dis-*), and *porter*—L. *portāre*, to carry; see sport.]

dispose, *dis-pōz', v.t.* to arrange: to distribute: to place: to apply to a particular purpose: to make over by sale, gift, etc.: to bestow: to incline.—*v.i.* to settle things: to ordain what is to be: to make a disposition: (usu. with *of*) to get rid of.—*n.* disposal, management: behaviour, disposition.—*adj.* dispos'able, able to be disposed of: intended to be thrown away or destroyed after use.—*n.* dispos'al, the act of disposing: order: arrangement: management: right of bestowing: availability for one's own use or control.—*adj.* disposed', inclined: of a certain disposition (with *well, ill*, etc.).—*adv.* dispos'edly, in good order: with measured steps.—*n.* dispos'er.—*n.* and *adj.* dispos'ing.—*adv.* disposingly. —*n.* disposure (*-pō'zhər*), disposal, arrangement: disposition.—dispose of, to settle what is to be done with: to make an end of: to have done with to part with: to get rid of: to sell. [Fr. *disposer* —dis- (L. *dis-*), asunder, *poser*, to place—L. *pausāre*, to pause, (late) to place.]

disposition, *dis-pə-zish'ən, n.* arrangement: distribution: plan for disposing one's property, etc.: natural tendency: temper: ministration (*N.T.*): a giving over to another, conveyance or assignment—often *disposition and settlement*, a deed for the disposal of a man's property at his death (*Scots law*).—*adjs.* disposi'tional: disposi'tioned; dispositive (*-poz'i-tiv*).—*adv.* dispos'itively.—*n.* dispos'itor, a planet that disposes or controls another. [Fr.—L., from *dis-*, apart, *pōnĕre, positum*, to place.]

dispossess, *dis-pə-zes', v.t.* to put out of possession. —*adj.* dispossessed', deprived of possessions, property, etc.: deprived of one's home or country: deprived of rights, hopes, expectations, etc.—*n.* dispossess'or. [Pfx. dis- (2).]

dispost, *dis-pōst', v.t.* to displace from a post. [Pfx. dis- (2).]

dispost, *dis-pōst', (Spens.)* for disposed. disposure. See dispose.

dispraise, *dis-prāz', n.* expression of an unfavourable opinion: blame: reproach.—*v.t.* to blame: to censure.—*n.* disprais'er.—*adv.* disprais'ingly. [O.Fr. *despreisier—des-* (L. *dis-*), reversal, *preisier*, to praise.]

dispread, *dis-pred', v.t.* to spread in different ways. —*v.i.* to spread out: to expand.—Spenser has the forms dispred, dispredden (*plur.*), disprad (*pa.p.*). [Pfx. dis- (1).]

disprinced, *dis-prinst', (Tenn.) adj.* deprived of the appearance of a prince. [Pfx. dis- (3).]

disprison, *dis-priz'n, v.t.* to set free. [Pfx. dis- (2).]

disprivacied, *dis-priv'ə-sid, adj.* deprived of privacy. [Pfx. dis- (3).]

disprivilege, *dis-priv'i-lij, v.t.* to deprive of a privilege. [Pfx. dis- (3).]

disprize, *dis-prīz', v.t.* to set a low price upon: to undervalue. [Pfx. dis- (2).]

disprofess, *dis-prə-fes', v.t.* to cease to profess, renounce. [Pfx. dis- (3).]

disprofit, *dis-prof'it, n.* loss, damage. [Pfx. dis- (2).]

disproof, *dis-proōf', n.* a disproving: refutation. [Pfx. dis- (2).]

disproove, *dis-proōv', (Spens.) v.t.* to disprove. of. [Pfx. dis- (2).]

disproperty, *dis-prop'ər-ti, (Shak.) v.t.* to deprive one of possession of. [Pfx. dis- (3).]

disproportion, *dis-prə-pōr'shən, -pör', n.* want of suitable proportion.—*v.t.* to make unsuitable in form or size, etc.—*adj.* dispropor'tionable (*arch.*). —*n.* dispropor'tionableness.—*adv.* dispropor'-tionably.—*adj.* dispropor'tional.—*adv.* dispro-por'tionally.—*n.* dispropor'tionate.—*adv.* dispropor'tionately.—*n.* dispropor'tionateness. [Pfx. dis- (2).]

**dispropriate**, *dis-prō'pri-āt*, *v.t.* to disappropriate. [Pfx. **dis-** (3).]

**disprove**, *dis-prōōv'*, *v.t.* to prove to be false or wrong: to disapprove (*arch.*):—*pa.p.* **disproved'**, **disproven** (*-prōv'*; *prōōv'*).—*n.* **disprov'al**. [O.Fr. *desprover*; see **prove**.]

**disprovide**, *dis-prō-vid'*, *v.t.* to leave or render unprovided. [Pfx. **dis-** (2).]

**dispunge**, *dis-punj'*, (*Shak.*) *v.t.* to sprinkle or discharge as if from a sponge. [Pfx. **dis-** (1).]

**dispurse**, *dis-pûrs'*, (*Shak.*) *v.t.* to disburse. [Pfx. **dis-** (1).]

**dispurvey**, *dis-pər-vā'*, (*arch.*) *v.t.* to deprive of provisions.—*n.* **dispurvey'ance** (*Spens.*). [Pfx. **dis-** (3).]

**dispute**, *dis-pūt'*, *v.t.* to make a subject of argument: to contend for: to oppose by argument: to call in question.—*v.i.* to argue: to debate.— *n.* a contest with words: an argument: a debate: a quarrel.—*adj.* **dis'putable** (also *-pūt'*), that may be disputed: of doubtful certainty.—*n.* **dis'putableness**.—*adv.* **dis'putably**.—*ns.* **dis'putant**, **disput'er**; **disputā'tion**, a contest in argument: an exercise in debate.—*adjs.* **disputā'tious**, **disput'ative**, inclined to dispute, cavil, or controvert. —*adv.* **disputā'tiously**.—*n.* **disputā'tiousness**.— **beyond, or without, dispute**, indubitably, certainly. [O.Fr. *desputer*—L. *disputāre*—*dis-*, apart, and *putāre*, to think.]

**disqualify**, *dis-kwol'i-fī*, *v.t.* to deprive of the qualities or qualifications necessary for any purpose: to make unfit: to disable: to debar: to declare to be disqualified.—*n.* **disqualificā'-tion**, state of being disqualified: anything that disqualifies or incapacitates. [Pfx. **dis-** (3).]

**disquiet**, *dis-kwī'ət*, *adj.* (*arch.*) unquiet, uneasy, restless.—*n.* want of quiet: uneasiness, restlessness: anxiety.—*v.t.* to render unquiet: to make uneasy: to disturb.—Also **disqui'eten**.—*adjs.* **disqui'etful**; **disqui'etive**, **disqui'eting**.—*adv.* **disqui'etly** (*Shak.*).—*ns.* **disqui'etness**, **disqui'etude**. —*adj.* **disqui'etous**. [Pfx. **dis-** (2).]

**disquisition**, *dis-kwi-zish'ən*, *n.* a careful inquiry into any matter by arguments, etc.: an essay.— *adjs.* **disquisi'tional**, **disquisi'tionary**, **disquis'itory**, **disquis'itive**, pertaining to or of the nature of a disquisition. [L. *disquisītiō, -ōnis* —*disquirĕre, dis-*, inten., *quaerĕre, quaesitum*, to seek.]

**disrank**, *dis-rangk'*, *v.t.* to reduce to a lower rank: to throw into confusion. [Pfx. **dis-** (3).]

**disrate**, *dis-rāt'*, (*naut.*) *v.t.* to reduce to a lower rating or rank, as a petty officer. [Pfx. **dis-** (3).]

**disregard**, *dis-ri-gärd'*, *v.t.* to pay no attention to. —*n.* want of attention: neglect: slight.—*adj.* **disregard'ful**.—*adv.* **disregard'fully**. [Pfx. **dis-** (2).]

**disrelish**, *dis-rel'ish*, *v.t.* not to relish: to dislike the taste of: to dislike.—*n.* distaste: dislike: disgust.—*adj.* **disrel'ishing**, offensive. [Pfx. **dis-** (2).]

**disremember**, *dis-ri-mem'bər*, (*dial.*) *v.t.* not to remember, to forget. [Pfx. **dis-** (2).]

**disrepair**, *dis-ri-pār'*, *n.* state of being out of repair. [Pfx. **dis-** (2).]

**disrepute**, *dis-ri-pūt'*, *n.* bad repute: discredit.— Also **disputā'tion** (*dis-rep-*).—*adj.* **disrep'utable**, in bad repute: disgraceful: not respectable: disordered and shabby.—*ns.* **disrep'utableness**, **disreputabil'ity** (*rare*).—*adv.* **disrep'utably**. [Pfx. **dis-** (2).]

**disrespect**, *dis-ri-spekt'*, *n.* want of respect: discourtesy: incivility.—*v.t.* (*arch.*) not to respect.— *adjs.* **disrespect'able** (*rare*), not respectable; **disrespect'ful**, showing disrespect: irreverent: uncivil.—*adv.* **disrespect'fully**.—*n.* **disrespect'fulness**. [Pfx. **dis-** (2).]

**disrobe**, *dis-rōb'*, *v.t.* and *v.i.* to undress: to uncover: to divest of robes. [Pfx. **dis-** (2), (3).]

**disroot**, *dis-rōōt'*, *v.t.* to uproot. [Pfx. **dis-** (3).]

**disrupt**, *dis-rupt'*, *v.t.* and *v.i.* to burst asunder, to break up.—*n.* **disrup'tion**, the act of breaking asunder: the act of bursting and rending: breach: (with *cap.*), in Scottish ecclesiastical history, the separation of the Free Church from the Established Church for the sake of spiritual independence (1843).—*adj.* **disrup'tive**, causing, or accompanied by, disruption. [L. *disruptus, diruptus—dirumpĕre—dis-*, asunder, *rumpĕre*, to break.]

**diss**, *dis*, *n.* an Algerian reedy grass (*Ampelodesma tenax*) used for cordage, etc. [Ar. *dis*.]

**dissatisfactory**, *dis-sat-is-fak'tər-i*, *adj.* causing dissatisfaction.—*ns.* **dissatisfac'tion**, state of being dissatisfied: discontent: uneasiness; **dissatisfac'toriness**. [Pfx. **dis-** (2).]

**dissatisfy**, *dis-sat'is-fī*, *v.t.* to fail to satisfy: to make discontented: to displease.—*adj.* **dissat'-isfied**, discontented: not pleased. [Pfx. **dis-** (2).]

**disseat**, *dis-sēt'*, *v.t.* to unseat. [Pfx. **dis-** (2), (3).]

**dissect**, *di-sekt'*, *v.t.* to cut asunder: to cut into parts for the purpose of minute examination: to divide and examine: to analyse and criticise.— *adj.* **dissect'ed**, deeply cut into narrow segments (*bot.*): cut up by valleys (*geol.*).—*adj.* **dissect'-ible**.—*ns.* **dissect'ing**; **dissec'tion**, the act or the art of cutting in pieces a plant or animal in order to ascertain the structure of its parts: anatomy. —*adj.* **dissect'ive**, tending to dissect.—*n.* **dissect'or**.—**dissected map, picture**, a map or picture on a board cut up, so as to form a puzzle; **dissecting microscope**, a form of microscope that allows dissection of the object under examination; **dissecting room, table**, a room in, table on, which anatomical dissection is practised. [L. *dissecāre, dissectum—dis-*, asunder, *secāre*, to cut.]

**disseise, disseize**, *dis-sēz'*, *v.t.* to deprive of seisen or possession of an estate of freehold: to dispossess wrongfully.—*ns.* **disseis'in**, **disseiz'in**; **disseis'or**, **disseiz'or**. [Pfx. **dis-** (3).]

**dissemble**, *di-sem'bl*, *v.t.* to disguise: to mask: to feign (*obs.*).—*v.i.* to assume a false appearance: to play the hypocrite: to dissimulate.—*ns.* **dissem'blance** (*rare*), want of resemblance: the act of dissembling; **dissem'bler**; **dissem'bling**. —*adj.* deceiving, hypocritical.—*adv.* **dissem'-blingly**. [L. *dissimulāre—dissimilis*, unlike—*dis-*, neg., and *similis*, like; perh. remodelled on *resemble*.]

**dissembly**, *dis-em'bli*, *n.* the breaking up of an assembly: a Dogberryism for assembly (*Shak.*). [Pfx. **dis-** (1).]

**disseminate**, *di-sem'i-nāt*, *v.t.* to sow or scatter abroad: to propagate: to diffuse.—*adj.* **scattered**.—*n.* **disseminā'tion**.—*adj.* **dissem'inative**. —*ns.* **dissem'inātor**; **dissem'inule**, any part or organ of a plant that serves for dissemination.— **disseminated sclerosis**, a chronic progressive disease in which patches of thickening appear throughout the central nervous system, resulting in various forms of paralysis. [L. *dissēmināre, -ātum—dis-*, asunder, *sēmināre*, to sow—*sēmen, sēminis*, seed.]

**dissent**, *di-sent'*, *v.i.* to think differently: to disagree in opinion: to differ (with *from*).—*n.* the act of dissenting: difference of opinion: a protest by a minority: a differing or separation from an established church.—*ns.* **dissen'sion**, disagreement in opinion: discord: strife; **Dissent'er**, one (esp. a Protestant) who is separate from an established church: a nonconformist: (without *cap.*) a dissentient:—*adj.* **dissent'erish**.—*n.* **dissent'erism**.—*adj.* **dissen'tient** (*-shənt*), declaring dissent: disagreeing.—*n.* one who disagrees: one who declares his dissent.—*adj.* **dissent'ing**.—*adv.* **dissent'ingly**.—*adj.* **dissen'tious** (*-shəs*; *Shak.*), disposed to discord, contentious. [L. *dissentīre, dissēnsum—dis-*, apart, *sentīre*, to think.]

**dissepiment**, *di-sep'i-mənt*, *n.* a partition in an

ovary (*bot.*): a partition partly cutting off the bottom of a coral cup (*zool.*).—*adj.* **dissepimental** (-*ment'l*). [L. *dissaepimentum*, a partition —L. *dissaepire—dis-*, apart, *saepire*, to hedge in, to fence.]

**dissertate**, *dis'ər-tāt*, *v.i.* to discourse—(*arch.*) **dissert'.**—*n.* **disserta'tion**, a formal discourse: a treatise.—*adjs.* **disserta'tional**, **diss'ertative.**—*n.* **diss'ertātor.** [L. *dissertāre*, inten. of *disserēre*, to discuss—*dis-*, *serēre*, to put together.]

**disserve**, *dis-sûrv'*, *v.t.* to do an ill turn to: to clear (a table).—*n.* **disserv'ice**, injury: mischief: an ill turn.—*adj.* **disserv'iceable.** [O.Fr. *desservir* —L. *dis-*, neg., *servīre*, to serve.]

**dissever**, *di-sev'ər*, *v.t.* to sever: to part in two: to separate: to disunite.—*ns.* **dissev'erance**, **disseverā'tion**, **dissev'erment**, a dissevering or parting.—*adj.* **dissev'ered**, disunited. [O.Fr. *dessevrer*—L. *dis-*, apart, *sēparāre*, to separate.]

**dissheathe**, *dis-shēdh'*, *v.t.* to unsheathe. [Pfx. **dis-** (2).]

**disshiver**, *dis-shiv'ər*, *v.t.* (*Spens.*) and *v.i.* to shiver in pieces. [Pfx. **dis-** (1).]

**dissident**, *dis'i-dənt*, *adj.* dissenting.—*n.* a dissenter.—*n.* **diss'idence**, disagreement. [L. *dissidēns*, -*entis*, pr.p. of *dissidēre—dis-*, apart, *sedēre*, to sit.]

**dissight**, *di(s)-sīt'*, *n.* an unsightly object. [Pfx. **dis-** (2).]

**dissilient**, *di(s)-sil'yənt*, *adj.* springing asunder: bursting open with force (*bot.*).—*n.* **dissil'ience.** [L. *dissiliēns*, -*entis—dis-*, asunder, *salīre*, to leap.]

**dissimilar**, *di-sim'i-lər*, *adj.* unlike.—*n.* **dissimilarity** (-*ar'*), unlikeness.—*adv.* **dissim'ilarly.**—*v.t.* **dissim'ilate**, to make unlike.—*ns.* **dissimilā'tion**, the act of rendering dissimilar: katabolism; **dissimile** (*di-sim'i-li*), the opposite of a simile, a comparison by contrast; **dissimil'itude.** [Pfx. **dis-** (2).]

**dissimulate**, *di-sim'ū-lāt*, *v.t.* to pretend the contrary of: to conceal or disguise: to dissemble.—*v.i.* to practise dissimulation, play the hypocrite.—*ns.* **dissimulā'tion**, the act of dissembling: a hiding under a false appearance: false pretension: hypocrisy: **dissim'ulātor.** [L. *dissimulāre*, -*ātum*, to dissimulate—*dis-*, neg., *similis*, like.]

**dissipate**, *dis'i-pāt*, *v.t.* to scatter: to squander: to waste: to dispel.—*v.i.* to separate and disappear: to waste away: to be dissolute in conduct: to indulge in trivial amusements.—*adj.* **diss'ipable**, that may be dissipated.—*adj.* **diss'ipated**, dissolute, esp. addicted to drinking.—*n.* **dissipā'tion**, dispersion: state of being dispersed: scattered attention: a course of frivolous amusement or of dissolute life.—*adj.* **diss'ipātive**, tending to dissipate or disperse: connected with the dissipation of energy.—**dissipation of energy**, degradation of energy, or progressive loss of availability of a portion for doing work at each transformation. [L. *dissipāre*, -*ātum—dis-*, asunder, and (archaic) *supāre*, to throw.]

**dissociate**, *di-sō'shi-āt*, *v.t.* and *v.i.* to separate from society or from association of any kind: to separate: to subject to or suffer dissociation.—*adj.* separated.—*n.* **dissōciabil'ity** (-*shə*).—*adjs.* **dissō'ciable**, not sociable: ill associated: incongruous: capable of being dissociated; **dissō'cial**, not social.—*v.t.* **dissō'cialise**, -ize, to make unsocial.—*ns.* **dissociality** (-*sō-shi-al'*); **dissociā'tion** (-*sō-shi-* or -*sō-si-*), act of dissociating: state of being dissociated: separation into simpler constituents, esp. a reversible separation caused by heat, or separation into ions (*chem.*): splitting of personality (*psych.*): splitting off from consciousness of certain ideas and their accompanying emotions: breaking of associations.—*adj.* **dissō'ciative** (*chem.*), tending to

**dissociate.** [L. *dissociāre*, -*ātum—dis-*, asunder, *sociāre*, to associate.]

**dissoluble**, *dis-ol'ū-bl* or *dis'əl-ū-bl*, -*ōō-bl*, *adj.* capable of being dissolved.—*ns.* **dissol'ūbil'ity**, **dissol'ūbleness.**—*adj.* **diss'olute** (-*lōōt* or -*lūt*), loose, esp. in morals, debauched.—*n.* a dissolute person.—*adv.* **diss'olutely.**—*ns.* **diss'oluteness**; **dissolution** (-*lōō'* or -*lū'*), the breaking up of an assembly: loosening: melting: break-up: death: dissoluteness or dissolute behaviour (*arch.*); **dissolu'tionism**; **dissolu'tionist**; **dissolvabil'ity** (*diz-*); **dissolv'ableness.**—*adj.* **dissolv'able**, capable of being dissolved.—*v.t.* **dissolve** (*di-zolv'*), to loose asunder: to undo: to separate or break up: to put an end to (as a parliament): to melt in solution (formerly also in fusion): to disperse: to resolve (as doubts, riddles; *arch.*).—*v.i.* to go into solution: to break up: to waste away: to fade away: to melt.—*n.* **dissolv'ent**, a solvent.—*adj.* having power to melt.—*n.* and *adj.* **dissolv'ing.** [L. *dissolvēre*, *dissolūtum—dis-*, asunder, *solvēre*, -*ūtum*, to loose.]

**dissonant**, *dis'o-nant*, or -*ə-*, *adj.* not agreeing or harmonising in sound: without concord or harmony: disagreeing.—*n.* **diss'onance**, disagreement of sound: want of harmony: discord: disagreement: specif., a combination of musical sounds that calls for resolution or produces beats—also **diss'onancy.** [L. *dissonāns*, -*antis—dis-*, apart, *sonāre*, to sound.]

**dissuade**, *di-swād'*, *v.t.* to give advice against (*obs.*): to seek to divert by advice (*obs.*): to divert by advice.—*ns.* **dissuā'der**; **dissuā'sion** (-*zhən*).—*adj.* **dissuā'sive** (-*siv*), tending to dissuade.—*n.* that which tends to dissuade.—*adv.* **dissuā'sively.**—*n.* and *adj.* **dissuā'sory** (*rare*). [L. *dissuādēre —dis-*, apart, *suādēre*, *suāsum*, to advise.]

**dissunder**, *dis-sun'dər*, *v.t.* to sunder. [Pfx. **dis-** (4).]

**dissyllable**, a faulty spelling of **disyllable.**

**dissymmetry**, *dis-sim'i-tri*, *n.* want of symmetry: enantiomorphy—the symmetry of right and left hand, object and mirror-image.—*adjs.* **dissymmetric**, -**al** (-*et'*). [Pfx. **dis-** (2).]

**distaff**, *dis'täf*, *n.* the stick that holds the bunch of flax, tow, or wool in spinning.—**distaff side**, the female part, line, side, or branch of a family or descent. [O.E. *distæf*, from the root found in L.G. *diesse*, the bunch of flax on the staff; and *stæf*, staff; see **dizen.**]

**distain**, *dis-tān'*, *v.t.* to stain: to sully. [O.Fr. *desteindre*, to take away the colour of—L. *dis-*, neg., and *tingēre*, to colour.]

**distal**, *dis'təl*, (*biol.*) *adj.* far apart, widely spaced: pertaining to or situated at the outer end: farthest from the point of attachment—opp. to *proximal.*—*adv.* **dis'tally.** [Formed from **distant** on the analogy of *central.*]

**distance**, *dis'tans*, *n.* measure of interval between: remoteness: a remote place or region: the remote part of the field of view or the part of a picture representing it: degree of remoteness: opposition: stand-offishness or aloofness of manner: in horse-racing, the space measured back from the winning-post which a horse, in heat-races, must reach before the winner has covered the whole course, in order to run in the final heat.—*v.t.* to place at a distance: to leave at a distance behind.—*adj.* **dis'tanceless**, not allowing a distant view (of hazy weather): having no indications of distance (of pictures).—**keep one at a distance**, to treat with aloofness; **keep one's distance**, to abstain from familiarity with, to keep aloof from. [See **distant.**]

**distant**, *dis'tənt*, *adj.* at a certain distance: at a great distance: remote, in time, place, resemblance, or connection: indistinct: reserved or aloof in manner.—*adv.* **dis'tantly.**—*n.* **dis'tant-signal**, on a railway, a signal farther from the distaste 377 distribute

destination than the home-signal. [Fr.,—L. *distāns, -antis*—*di-*, apart, *stāns, stantis*, pr.p. of *stāre*, to stand.]
**distaste**, *dis-tāst'*, *n.* disrelish: dislike: unpleasant experience (*obs.*): offence (*obs.*).—*v.t.* to dislike (*arch.*): to offend (*obs.*): to spoil the taste of (*Shak.*).—*v.i.* (*Shak.*) to be distasteful.—*adj.* **distaste'ful**, unpleasant to the taste: unpleasant: indicating distaste (*Shak.*): full of distaste.—*adv.* **distaste'fully**.—*n.* **distaste'fulness**.
**distemper**, *dis-temp'ər*, *n.* a mode of painting in size, water-glass, or other watery vehicle giving body to the pigment: paint of this kind—for indoor walls, scenery, etc.—*v.t.* to paint in distemper.—Also **destemp'er**. [L. *dis-*, reversal, *temperāre*, to regulate, mix in proportion; cf. next word.]
**distemper**, *dis-temp'ər*, *n.* a morbid or disorderly state of body or mind: disease, esp. of animals: specifically a disease of the dog and ferret families caused by a filterable virus: ill-humour.—*v.t.* to derange the temper: to disorder or disease.—*adj.* **distemp'erate**, not temperate, immoderate: diseased.—*n.* **distemp'erature** (*arch.*), want of proper temperature: intemperateness, disturbance: uneasiness of mind: indisposition.—*adj.* **distem'pered**, disordered: intemperate, ill-humoured, put out of sorts. [O.Fr. *destemprer*, to derange—L. *dis-*, apart, *temperāre*, to govern, regulate.]
**distend**, *dis-tend'*, *v.t.* to stretch forth or apart: to stretch in three dimensions: to swell.—*v.i.* to swell.—*n.* **distensibil'ity**, capacity for distension.—*adjs.* **disten'sible**, that may be stretched; **disten'sile** (*-sil*), distensible: able to cause distension.—*n.* **disten'sion**, act of distending or stretching: state of being stretched: breadth (*rare*; sometimes **disten'tion**).—*adjs.* **disten'sive**, capable of stretching or of being stretched; **distent'** (*Spens.*), extended: distended, swollen. [L. *distendēre*—*dis-*, asunder, *tendēre, tēnsum* or *tentum*, to stretch.]
**disthene**, *dis'thēn*, *n.* kyanite—so called from its difference in hardness when scratched in different directions. [Gr. *di-*, twice, *sthenos*, strength.]
**disthrone**, *dis-thrōn'*, *v.t.* to dethrone—(*Spens.*) **disthrōn'ize**. [Pfx. dis- (2), (3).]
**distich**, *dis'tik*, *n.* a couple of lines or verses, making complete sense: a couplet:—*pl.* distichs, *-tiks.*—*adj.* having two rows.—*adj.* **dis'tichous**, in or having two rows. [Gr. *distichos*—*di-*, twice, *stichos*, a line.]
**distil**, now rarely **distill**, *dis-til'*, *v.i.* to fall in drops: to flow gently: to use a still.—*v.t.* to let or cause to fall in drops: to convert from liquid into vapour by heat, and then to condense again: to extract by evaporation and condensation:—*pr.p.* **distill'ing**; *pa.t.* and *pa.p.* **distilled'**.—*adj.* **distill'able**.—*n.* **dis'tilland**, that which is to be, or is being, distilled; **dis'tillāte**, the product of distillation; **distillā'tion**, the act of distilling.—*adj.* **distill'atory**, of or for distilling.—*ns.* **distill'er**; **distill'ery**, a place where distilling, esp. of alcoholic spirits, is carried on; **distill'ing**; **distil'ment** (*Shak.*), that which is distilled.—**destructive distillation**, the collection of volatile matters released when a substance is destroyed by heat in a close vessel (as coal in making gas); **fractional distillation**, the separation by distilling of liquids having different boiling-points, the heat being gradually increased and the receiver changed; **vacuum distillation**, distillation under reduced pressure (effecting a lowering of the boiling point). [O.Fr. *distiller*, with substitution of prefix—L. *dēstillāre, -ātum*—*dē*, down, *stillāre*, to drop—*stilla*, a drop.]
**distinct**, *dis-tingkt'*, *adj.* distinguished, differentiated (*Milt.*): separate: different: well-defined: clear: marked, variegated (*Spens., Milt.*).—*n.* **distinction** (*dis-tingk'shən*), separation or divi-

sion: discrimination: a distinguishing mark or character: distinctness (*obs.*): difference: a mark or honorific recognition of excellence: an honour: discriminating favour: noticeable eminence: outstanding merit: impressive and meritorious individuality. — *adj.* **distinc'tive**, marking or expressing difference: characteristic. — *adv.* **distinct'ively**. — *n.* **distinct'iveness**.— *adv.* **distinct'ly**.—*ns.* **distinct'ness**; **distinct'ure** (*-tingk'chər, tyər*), distinctness. [See **distinguish**.]
**distingué**, *dē-stē-gā*, (Fr.) *adj.* distinguished: striking:—*fem.* **distinguée**.
**distinguish**, *dis-ting'gwish*, *v.t.* to mark off, set apart (often with *from*): to recognise by characteristic qualities: to make out: to make distinctions in or concerning (*obs.*): to bring by drawing distinctions: to separate by a mark of honour: to make eminent or known.—*v.i.* to make or show distinctions or differences, to recognise a difference (often with *between*).—*adj.* **disting'uishable**, capable of being distinguished. — *adv.* **disting'uishably**. — *adj.* **disting'uished**, illustrious.—*n.* **disting'uisher**.—*adj.* **disting'uishing**, peculiar.—*n.* **disting'uishment** (*Shak.*), distinction. — **Distinguished Conduct Medal** (**D.C.M.**), **Distinguished Flying Cross** (**D.F.C.**), **Distinguished Service Medal** (**D.S.M.**); also *U.S.*), **Distinguished Service Order** (**D.S.O.**), military decorations awarded for distinguished conduct in action. [L. *distinguēre, distinctum*—*dī-*, asunder, *stinguēre*, orig. to prick, and *-ish*, in imitation of Fr. vbs. in *-ir*.]
**distort**, *dis-tört'*, *v.t.* to twist aside: to put out of shape without breach of continuity: to turn aside from the true meaning: to pervert: to misrepresent.—*adj.* **distort'ed**.—*n.* **distortion** (*-tör'shən*), a twisting awry: deformation without breaking: change of wave-form in course of transmission: crookedness: perversion.—*adj.* **distort'ive**, causing distortion. [L. *dis-*, asunder, *torquēre, tortum*, to twist.]
**distract**, *dis-trakt'*, *v.t.* to draw aside, apart, or in different directions: esp. of the mind or attention: to confuse: to harass: to render crazy.—*adj.* separate (*Shak., dis'-*): distracted (*Milt., -trakt'*).—*adj.* **distract'ed**.—*adv.* **distract'edly**.—*ns.* **distract'edness**; **distrac'tion**, state of being distracted: that which distracts: perplexity: agitation: madness: recreation, relaxation.—*adj.* **distract'ive**, causing perplexity. [L. *distrahēre, -tractum*—*dis-*, apart, *trahēre*, to draw.]
**distrain**, *dis-trān'*, *v.t.* to seize (esp. goods for debt, esp. for non-payment of rent or rates): to pull apart, burst (*Spens.*).—*v.i.* to seize the goods of a debtor.—*adj.* **distrain'able**.—*ns.* **distrain'er**; **distrain'ment**; **distrain'or** (*law*); **distraint'**, seizure of goods. [O.Fr. *destraindre*—L. *dī-*, asunder, *stringēre*, to draw tight.]
**distrait**, *dēs-tre*, (Fr.) absent-minded:—*fem.* **distraite** (*dēs-tret*).
**distraught**, *dis-tröt'*, *adj.* drawn aside (*Spens.*): distracted: mad: perplexed. [**distract**, modified by association with words like **caught**, **taught**.]
**distress**, *dis-tres'*, *n.* extreme pain or suffering: that which causes suffering: calamity: misfortune: acute poverty: exhaustion: peril: difficulty: compulsion (*arch.*): act of distraining goods: in a structure, a sign of weakness arising from stress.—*v.t.* to afflict with pain or suffering: to harass: to grieve: to distrain.—*adj.* **distressed'**.—*adj.* **distress'ful**.—*adv.* **distress'fully**.—*n.* **distress'fulness**.—*adj.* **distress'ing**.—*adv.* **distress'ingly**.—**distressed area**, a region of unusually severe unemployment. [O.Fr. *destresse*—L. *distringēre*; see **strain**.]
**distribute**, *dis-trib'ūt*, or *dis'*, *v.t.* to divide amongst several: to deal out or allot: to classify: to disperse about a space: to spread out: to separate and put back in compartments (*print.*): to use with full extension, including every

Neutral vowels in unaccented syllables: *el'ə-mənt*; for certain sounds in foreign words, see p. viii

individual to which the term is applicable (*log.*).
—*n.* distrib′uend, that which is to be distributed.
—*adjs.* distrib′utable, that may be divided; distrib′utary, distributing.—*n.* a branch of a distributing system: an off-flow from a river that does not return to it.—*ns.* distrib′uter, -or; distribu′tion, the act or process of distributing: dispersal: division: range: allotment: classification: the application of a general term to all the objects denoted by it: the manner in which the products of industry are shared among the people (*econ.*).—*adjs.* distribu′tional; distrib′utive, that distributes, separates, or divides: giving to each his own: such that $a.(x+y+z+\ldots) = a.x+a.y+a.z+\ldots(math.)$.—*n.* a word, like *each* or *every*, that indicates the several individuals of a number taken separately.—*adv.* distrib′utively.—geographical distribution, the department of science that treats of the range and dispersal of animals and plants about the world. [L. *distribuĕre—dis-*, asunder, *tribuĕre*, *tribūtum*, to allot.]

district, dis′trikt, *n.* a portion of territory defined for political, judicial, educational, or other purposes (as a registration district, a militia district, the District of Columbia): a region: a constituency (*U.S.*): a subdivision of a division (*India*).—*v.t.* to divide into districts—district attorney (*U.S.*), a public prosecutor for a district; district council, the council of an urban or rural district; district nurse, a nurse appointed to attend to cases in a district; district visitor, a church worker who visits parishioners in a district. [Fr.,—L.L. *districtus*, jurisdiction—*distringĕre*; see distrain.]

distringas, dis-tring′gas, *n.* an old writ directing a sheriff or other officer to distrain. [Second pers. sing. pres. subj. of L. *distringĕre*; see distrain.]

distrouble, dis-trub′l, (*Spens.*) *v.t.* to trouble greatly, to perplex, to disturb. [L. *dis-*, inten., and trouble.]

distrust, dis-trust′, *n.* want of trust: want of faith or confidence: doubt.—*v.t.* to have no trust in: to disbelieve: to doubt.—*adj.* distrust′ful, full of distrust: apt to distrust: suspicious: to be distrusted (*rare*).—*adv.* distrust′fully.—*n.* distrust′fulness.—*adj.* distrust′less. [Pfx. dis- (2), (3).]

distune, dis-tūn′, *v.t.* to put out of tune. [Pfx. dis- (3).]

disturb, dis-tûrb′, *v.t.* to throw into confusion: to agitate: to disquiet: to interrupt.—*n.* disturbance.—*n.* disturb′ance, agitation: tumult: interruption: perplexity.—*adj.* and *n.* disturb′ant, disturbing.—*adjs.* disturb′ative; disturbed′.—*n.* disturb′er. [O.Fr. *destrouber*—L. *dis-turbāre*, *dis-*, asunder, *turbāre*, to agitate—*turba*, a crowd.]

distyle, dis′til, di′stil, *n.* a portico with two columns. [Gr. *di-*, twice, and *stylos*, column.]

disulphate, di-sul′fāt, *n.* a pyrosulphate: formerly, an acid sulphate.—*n.* disul′phide, a sulphide containing two atoms of sulphur to the molecule —also (*obs.*) disul′phuret.—*adj.* disulphu′ric, pyrosulphuric. [Pfx. di-.]

disunion, dis-ūn′yən, *n.* want of union: breaking up of union or concord: separation.—*n.* disun′ionist, one who favours dissolution of a union.—*v.t.* disunite′, to separate from union: to sever or sunder.—*v.i.* to fall asunder: to part. —*n.* disu′nity, state of disunion. [Pfx. dis- (2), (1).]

disuse, dis-ūs′, or dis′ūs, *n.* the state of being out of use.—*v.t.* (dis-ūz′) to cease to use or practise: to leave out of use.—*n.* disusage (dis-ūz′ij), gradual cessation of use or custom. [Pfx. dis- (2), (3).]

disutility, dis-ū-til′i-ti, *n.* an inconvenience, drawback, disadvantage. [Pfx. dis- (2).]

disvalue, dis-val′ū, (*Shak.*) *v.t.* to disparage. [Pfx. dis- (3).]

disvouch, dis-vowch′, (*Shak.*) *v.t.* to disavow. [Pfx. dis- (3).]

disworship, dis-wûr′ship, (*Milt.*) *n.* dishonour: disgrace. [Pfx. dis- (2).]

disyllable, dis-il′ə-bl, *n.* a word of two syllables.— *adj.* disyllabic (-ab′ik).—*n.* disyllabificā′tion.— *v.t.* disyllab′ify, to make into two syllables.—*n.* disyll′abism, the character of having two syllables. [Through Fr. *dissyllabe*, *dissilabe*, and L. from Gr. *di-*, twice, *syllabē*, a syllable; with *l* as in syllable.]

disyoke, dis-yōk′, (*Tenn.*) *v.t.* to free from the yoke. [Pfx. dis- (3).]

dit, ditt, *dit*, (*arch.*) *n.* a poem: the words of a song. [Apparently formed by Spenser from dite, influenced by ditty.]

dit, *dit*, (now *Scot.*) *v.t.* to stop, block:—*pa.t.* and *pa.p.* ditt′ed, ditt′it; *pa.p.* also dit. [O.E. *dyttan*, to shut.]

dit, *dē*, (Fr.) named: reputed.

dita, *dē′ta*, *n.* an apocynaceous tree (*Alstonia scholaris*) of India and the Philippines, with tonic bark. [Tagálog or Visayan.]

dital, di-təl, *n.* a thumb key for sharpening a lute or guitar string by a semitone. [It. *dito*, finger, with *-al* after pedal, manual.]

ditch, dich, *n.* a trench dug in the ground: any long narrow depression carrying water: the border of a bowling-green: the sea (*slang*).— *v.i.* to make, repair or clean a ditch or ditches. —*v.t.* to dig a ditch in or around: to drain by ditches: to throw, or drive, into a ditch: to abandon, or get rid of (*slang*): to escape from or leave in the lurch (a person; *slang*): to derail (*U.S.*): to bring down into the sea (*slang*).—*n.* ditch′er, a man or machine that makes, cleans or repairs ditches.—ditch′-dog (*Shak.*), a dead dog rotting in a ditch; ditch′-water, stagnant foul water such as is found in ditches, proverbially dull. [O.E. *dīc*, whence also dike.]

dite, *dit*, (*obs.*) *n.* writing: a composition.—*v.t.* to compose, indite: to dictate: to indict. [O.Fr. *dit*, saying, *ditier*, *diter*, to write—L. *dictum*, an utterance, *dictāre*, freq. of *dicĕre*, to say.]

dite, (*Spens.*) *v.t.* Same as dight.

dithecal, di-thē′kl, *adj.* having two thecae.—Also dithē′cous. [Pfx. di-.]

ditheism, di′thē-izm, *n.* the doctrine of the existence of two supreme gods.—*n.* di′theist.—*adjs.* ditheist′ic, -al. [Gr. *di-*, twice, and *theos*, a god.]

Ditheletism, di-thel′et-izm, *n.* the doctrine that Christ on earth had two wills, human and divine —opp. to Monotheletism.—Also Di′thelism, Di-, Dyoth′elism, Dyothel′etism, Dithel′itism.—*n.* Di′-thelēte, a believer in the doctrine.—Also Dio-, Dyoth′elete, -ite.—*adjs.* Dithelēt′ic, -al.—Also Dio-, Dyothelēt′ic, -it′ic, -al. [Gr. *di-*, twice (or dyo, two), *thelētēs*, a willer—*thelein*, to will.]

dither, didh′ər, *v.i.* to tremble, shiver, quake: to waver.—*v.t.* to perturb, confuse.—*n.* a trembling condition: a quaking fit: tremulous excitement: perturbation.—Also didd′er.—all of a dither, nervous, agitated. [Prob. imit.]

dithionate, di-thi′ən-āt, *n.* a salt of dithionic -on′ik) acid, otherwise hyposulphuric acid ($H_2S_2O_6$). [Gr. *di-*, twice, *theion*, sulphur.]

dithyramb, dith′i-ram(b), *n.* an ancient Greek hymn sung in honour of Bacchus: a short poem of a like character.—*adj.* dithyram′bic, of or like a dithyramb: rapturous: wild and boisterous.— *adv.* dithyram′bically.—*n.* dithyram′bist. [Gr. *dithyrambos*.]

ditokous, dit′o-kəs, *adj.* producing two at a birth or in a clutch. [Gr. *di-*, twice, *tokos*, birth.]

ditone, di′tōn, *n.* in ancient Greek music, an interval of two major tones. [Pfx. di-.]

ditriglyph, di-tri′glif, *n.* a space for two triglyphs

*fāte, fär; mē, hûr* (her); *mīne; mōte, för; mūte; mōon, fōot; dhen* (then)

in the entablature between columns.—*adj.* ditriglyph'ic. [Pfx. di-.]
ditrochee, *di-trō'kē*, *n.* a trochaic dipody.—*adj.*
ditroche'an. [Pfx. di-.]
dittander, *di-tan'dər, n.* a pepperwort (*Lepidium
latifolium*), a pungent cruciferous plant: dittany.
[A form of dittany.]
dittany, *dit'ə-ni, n.* an aromatic rutaceous plant
(*Dictamnus albus*), secreting much volatile oil.
[O.Fr. *dïctame*—L. *dictamnus*—Gr. *diktamnos*;
prob. from Mt. *Dïktē* in Crete.]
dittay, *dit'ā,* (*Scots law*) *n.* an indictment, charge.
[O.Fr. *ditté*—L. *dictātum*; cf. ditty, dictate.]
ditto, *dit'ō,* contracted do., *n.* that which has been
said: the same thing.—*adv.* as before, or aforesaid: in like manner.—*v.t.* to duplicate.—*n.pl.*
ditt'os, a suit of clothes of the same colour
throughout. [It. *ditto*—L. *dictum,* said, *pa.p.* of
*dicĕre,* to say.]
dittography, *di-tog'rə-fi, n.* unintentional repetition of letters or words in copying a manuscript. [Gr. *dittos,* double, *graphein,* to write.]
dittology, *di-tol'ə-ji, n.* a double reading or interpretation. [Gr. *dittologiā*—*dittos,* double, *legein,*
to speak.]
ditty, *dit'i, n.* a song: a little poem to be sung.—
*v.t.* to set to music. [O.Fr. *ditie*—L. *dictātum,*
neut. perf. part. (pass.) of *dictāre,* to dictate.]
ditty-bag, *dit'i-bag, n.* a sailor's bag for personal
belongings.—Also ditt'y-box.    [Origin unknown.]
diuretic, *di-ū-ret'ik, adj.* promoting the discharge
of urine.—*n.* a medicine causing this discharge.—
*n.* diurē'sis, discharge of urine, esp. in excess.
[Gr. *diourētikos*—*dia,* through, *ouron,* urine.]
diurnal, *di-ûr'nəl, adj.* daily: relating to or performed in or lasting a day: (of animal) having
one period of rest and one of activity in twenty-
four hours (*biol.*): belonging to the daytime.
—*n.* a service-book containing the day hours,
except matins (a night-office): a diary, journal.
—*n.* diur'nalist, a journalist.—*adv.* diur'nally.
[L. *diurnālis*—*diēs,* a day; see journal.]
diuturnal, *di-ū-tûr'nəl, adj.* lasting long.—*n.* diu-
tur'nity. [L. *diūturnus*—*diū,* long.]
div, *div,* (*Scot.*; in *pres. indic.* only) *v.t.* a form of
do (auxiliary).
div, *dēv* (Pers. *dīv*), *n.* an evil spirit of Persian
mythology.
diva, *dē'vä, n.* a popular female singer: a prima-
donna. [It.,—L. *diva,* fem. of *divus,* divine.]
divagate, *di'və-gāt, v.i.* to wander about: to
digress.—*n.* divagā'tion.    [L. *dīvagārī,* to
wander.]
divalent, *di-vā'lənt* or *div'əl-ənt, n.* a chemical
element or atom capable of uniting with two
atoms of hydrogen or their equivalent.—*adj.*
having two combining equivalents.—Also bivalent. [Gr. *di-,* twice, L. *valēre,* to be worth.]
Divali. Same as Diwali.
divan, *di-van', n.* a collection of poems: a council
of state: a court of justice: poetically, any
council or assembly: a council-chamber with
cushioned seats: an Eastern couch: a couch
of similar type (without back or sides) often
used as couch and bed (**divan-bed**): a smoking-
room: a dewan. [Ar. and Pers. *dīwān,* a long
seat.]
divaricate, *di-var'i-kāt, v.i.* to part into two
branches, to fork: to diverge.—*v.t.* to divide
into two branches.—*adj.* widely divergent,
spreading apart.—*n.* divaricā'tion. [L. *divari-
cāre, -ātum* *dis-,* asunder, *varicāre,* to spread
the legs—*varus,* bent apart.]
dive, *div, v.i.* to dip or plunge into or down
through water or down through the air: to go
headlong into a recess, forest, etc.: to plunge
or go deeply into any matter.—*v.t.* to plunge,
dip.—*n.* a plunge: a swoop: a headlong
descent: a refuge: a resort, generally disreput-

able, often underground (*slang*): a subway.—
*n.* div'er, one who dives or can dive: one who
dives for pearls: one who works from a diving-
bell or in a diving-dress beneath water: a bird
expert at diving, esp. the loon, loosely applied
to auks, grebes, penguins, etc.:   a pickpocket
(*slang*).—*n.* and *adj.* div'ing.—*v.t.* and *v.i.* dive-
bomb, to attack with, or as if with, a dive-
bomber:  to discharge bombs while diving;
dive'-bomber, an aeroplane that discharges a
bomb while in a steep dive; dive'-bombing;
dive-dapp'er (*Shak.*), a didapper, dabchick;
div'ing-bell, a hollow vessel or chamber, originally bell-shaped, open at the bottom and
supplied with air by a tube from above, in which
one may descend into and work under water;
div'ing-board, a board for diving from; div'ing-
dress, a water-tight costume for a diver, with
special provision for receiving air, etc.  [O.E.
*dȳfan, dūfan*—O.N. *dȳfa.*]
divellent, *di-vel'ənt, adj.* drawing asunder.—*v.t.*
divell'icate, to pull in pieces: to pluck apart.
[L. *di,* apart, *vellēre, vellicāre,* to pluck.]
diverge, *di-* or *dī-vûrj', v.i.* to incline or turn apart:
to tend from a common point in different
directions: to vary from the standard.—*ns.*
diverge'ment; diverg'ence, diverg'ency.—*adj.*
diverg'ent.—*adv.* diverg'ently.—*adj.* diverg'ing.
—*adv.* diverg'ingly. [L. *di-,* asunder, *vergĕre,*
to incline.]
divers, *dī'vərz, adj.* sundry: several: more than
one:  same as diverse (*B.*).—*adv.* (*Milt.*) in
different directions.—*adj.* diverse (*di'vərs, di'-,
di'vûrs'*), different: unlike: multiform: various:
distracting (*Spens.*).—*v.i.* (*Spens.*) to turn aside.
—*adv.* di'versely, or diverse'ly.—*adjs.* diversifi'-
able; diver'sified.—*n.* diversificā'tion.—*v.t.* divers'ify, to differentiate (*obs.*): to give variety to:
to make (investments) in securities of different
types so as to lessen risk of loss:  to engage
in production of a variety of (manufactures,
crops).—Also *v.i.*:—*pr.p.* diver'sifying; *pa.t.,
pa.p.* diver'sified.—*ns.* diver'sion, act of diverting
or turning aside: that which diverts: amusement,
recreation: something done to turn the attention of an opponent: a detour round part of
a road which is temporarily closed.—*adj.* diver'sionary, of the nature of a diversion, designed to distract the attention of an opponent.
—*ns.* diver'sionist, a deviationist; diver'sity, state
of being diverse: difference: unlikeness: variety.—*adv.* di'versly, in divers ways.—*v.t.* divert
(*di-vûrt', dī-*) turn aside (also *arch., v.i.*): change
the direction of: turn from business or study:
amuse.—*n.* (*Scot.*) amusing person or thing.—
*adj.* divert'ible.—*ns.* divertibil'ity; divertimen'to
(*It.*) diversion (*obs.*): (the following meanings
all *mus.*) a piece in several movements: a pot-
pourri: a light piece of music: a ballet-interlude
(*pl.* -ti, -tē).—*adj.* divert'ing.—*adv.* divert'ingly.
—*ns.* divertisement (*di-vûrt'iz-mənt*), diversion:
a divertimento; divertissement (Fr.; *dē-ver-
tēs'mä*), a divertimento.—*adj.* divert'ive, tending
to divert.  [Fr.,—L. *divertĕre, diversum*—*di-,*
aside, *vertĕre,* to turn.]
diverticulum, *di-vər-tik'ū-ləm,* (*anat.*) *n.* a blind
tubular branch.—*adjs.* divertic'ular, divertic'-
ulate, -d, [L. *diverticulum,* a byway, retreat.]
Dives, *dī'vēz, n.* the rich man at whose gate
Lazarus lay (Luke xvi. 19): a rich and luxurious
person. [L. *dives,* rich (man), understood as a
proper name.]
divest, *di-* or *dī-vest', v.t.* to strip or deprive of
anything.—*adj.* divest'ible.—*ns.* divest'iture, divest'ment (*rare*). [O.Fr. *desvestir,* with change
of prefix (*dis-* for *dē-*) from L. *dēvestire*—*dē,*
away from, *vestire,* to clothe—*vestis,* a garment.]
divide, *di-vīd', v.t.* to break up, or mark off, into
parts, actually or in imagination: to separate or
distinguish the parts of: to classify: to share: to

allot: to deal out: to ascertain how many times a quantity is contained in (*math.*): to perform with division or floridly (*mus.*): to be a boundary or a subject of difference between: to keep apart: to cause to vote for and against a motion: to sever.—*v.i.* to separate: to fall apart: to branch: to vote for and against a motion: to admit of or be susceptible of division.—*n.* the act of dividing (*coll.*): a watershed (esp. in U.S.).—*adjs.* divid′able (or div′id-), divisible: divided (*Shak.*); divid′ant (*Shak.*), distinguishable, separable.—*adv.* divid′edly.—*n.* divid′er, one who or that which divides: a soup-ladle (*Scot.*): (*pl.*) a kind of compasses for measuring.—*adj.* divid′ing, separating.—*n.* separation.—*adjs.* divid′ual, divisible: separable (*Milt.*): shared in common with others (*Milt.*); divid′uous, divided, special, accidental.—divid′ing-en′gine, an instrument for marking accurate subdivisions or graduating scales. [L. *dividĕre, divisum—dis-,* asunder, root *vid,* to separate.]

dividend, *div′i-dend, n.* that which is to be divided: the share of a sum divided that falls to each individual, by way of interest or otherwise.—dividend stripping, a method of evading tax on dividends by a contrived arrangement between a company liable to tax and another in a position to claim repayment of tax; div′idend-warr′ant, a certificate entitling to payment of dividend.—declare a dividend, to announce the sum per cent. a trading concern is prepared to pay its shareholders. [L. *dividendum,* to be divided, *dividĕre.*]

dividivi, *div′i-div-i, n.* the curved pods of *Caesalpinia coriaria,* imported for tanning and dyeing. [Carib. name.]

divine, *di-vin′, adj.* belonging to or proceeding from a god: holy: excellent in the highest degree: prescient, having forebodings (*Milt.*).—*n.* one skilled in divine things: a minister of the gospel: a theologian.—*v.t.* to foresee or foretell as if divinely inspired: to guess or make out: to prognosticate: to make divine (*Spens.*).—*v.i.* to profess or practice divination: to have forebodings.—*ns.* divinā′tion, the act or practice of divining: seeking to know the future or hidden things by magical means: instinctive prevision: prediction; conjecture; div′inātor, divin′er, one who divines or professes divination: a conjecturer:—*fem.* divin′eress.—*adjs.* divinatō′rial, divin′atory, relating to divination, conjectural.—*adv.* divine′ly.—*n.* divine′ness.—*vs.t.* div′inise, -ize, divin′ify, to treat as divine.—divin′ing-rod, a rod, usually of hazel, used by those professing to discover water or metals under ground. [O.Fr. *devin,* soothsayer, and L. *divinus—divus, deus,* a god.]

diving. See dive.

divinity, *di-vin′i-ti, n.* godhead: the nature or essence of a god: a celestial being: a god: the science of divine things: theology.—divinity hall (*Scot.*), a theological college or department. [O.Fr. *devinite*—L. *divinitās, -tātis;* see divine.]

divisim, *di-vī′zim, dē-wē′sim,* (L.) separately.

division, *di-vizh′ən, n.* act of dividing: state of being divided: that which divides: a partition: a barrier: a portion or section: the taking of a vote: a florid passage or performance in which many short notes may be regarded as taking the place of a long note (*mus.;* *arch.*): a part of a province under a commissioner, divided into districts (*India*): an army unit (usually half an army corps) containing almost all branches of the service: separation: difference in opinion, etc.: disunion: the process of finding how many times one quantity is contained in another (*math.*).—*n.* divisibil′ity (-*viz-*).—*adj.* divis′ible, capable of being divided or separated: capable of being divided without remainder.—*adv.* divis′ibly.—*adjs.* divisional (-*vizh′*), divis′ionary, pertaining to or marking a division or separa-

tion.—*n.* divis′ionism (often *cap.*; *paint.*), pointillism.—*adj.* divisive (-*viz′*), forming division or separation: creating discord.—*ns.* divis′iveness; divis′or (*math.*), the number which divides the dividend.—division of labour, the assigning of different functions to different agents. [L. *divisiō, -ōnis, divisor, -ōris—dividĕre,* to divide.]

divorce, *di-vōrs′, -vörs′, n.* the legal dissolution of marriage: separation (*fig.*).—*v.t.* to dissolve the marriage of: to put away by divorce: to separate.—*v.i.* to obtain a divorce.—*adj.* divorce′able.—*ns.* divorcee′, a divorced person; divorce′ment (*B.*), divorce; divor′cer.—*adj.* divor′cive, having power to divorce. [Fr.,—L. *divortium—divortĕre,* another form of *divertĕre;* see divert.]

divot, *div′ət,* (*Scot.*) *n.* a thin sod, cut for roofing, etc., or accidentally by golfers.—feal and divot (*Scots law*), a right of cutting sods. [Origin unknown.]

divulge, *di-* or *dī-vulj′, v.t.* to spread abroad among the vulgar or the people: to make public: to reveal.—*v.t.* divul′gate (-*gāt*), to publish.—*n.* divulgā′tion. [L. *divulgāre—di-,* abroad, *vulgāre,* to publish, *vulgus,* the common people.]

divulsion, *di-* or *dī-vul′shən, n.* act of pulling or rending asunder or away.—*adj.* divul′sive, tending to pull asunder. [L. *divulsiō, -ōnis—di-, vellĕre, vulsum,* to pull.]

divvy, divi, *div′i,* (*slang*) *n.* a dividend.—*v.t.* and *v.i.* to divide: to go shares.—Also divvy up. [Abbrev. of divide, dividend.]

Diwali, *di-wä′lē, n.* the Hindu festival of lamps held in October or November.—Also Dewali. Divali. [Hindi *divāli.*]

diwan. Same as dewan.

dixi, *dik′sē,* (L.) I have spoken.

dixie, dixy, *diks′i, n.* a military cooking-pail or camp-kettle. [Perh. Hindi *degci*—Pers. *degcha,* dim. of *dig,* large metallic cooking utensil.]

Dixieland, *dik′sē-land, n.* an early style of jazz in New Orleans, played by small combinations of instruments. [*Dixie,* name given to southern states of U.S.]

dizain, *di-zān′, n.* a ten-line stanza or poem. [Fr. *dix,* ten—L. *decem,* ten.]

dizen, *di-zn,* or *diz′n,* (*obs.*) *v.t.* to dress or charge (a distaff) with flax: to dress up, dress gaudily. [From root seen in distaff.]

dizygotic, *di-zi-got′ik, adj.* developed from two zygotes or fertilised eggs.—dizygotic twins, fraternal twins so developed.

dizzard, *diz′ərd, n.* a blockhead. [Perh. M.E. and O.Fr. *disour,* story-teller.]

dizzy, *diz′i, adj.* giddy: confused: causing giddiness: silly (*coll.*): extreme (*coll.*).—*v.t.* to make dizzy: to confuse.—*adv.* dizz′ily.—*n.* dizz′iness.—*adj.* dizz′ying, making dizzy. [O.E. *dysig,* foolish; cf. Dan. *dösig,* drowsy; also doze.]

djellaba, *ja-lä′bə, n.* a cloak with a hood and wide sleeves. [Ar. *jallabah, jallāb.*]

djibbah, *jib′ä.* Same as jibbah.

djinn. See jinn.

DNA, *dē-en-ā, n.* deoxyribo-nucleic acid (*q.v.*).

do, *dōō, v.t.* to put, place (*obs.*): to cause (*obs.*): to put in some condition: to render: to confer: bestow: to perform: to accomplish: to finish: to exhaust: to work at: to perform work upon: to prepare, set in order: to cook: to cheat, or overreach (*slang*): to treat: to make the round of, see the sights of: to spend in prison.—*v.i.* to act, be active: to behave: to fare: to thrive: to suffice: to be good enough to pass:—*2nd sing.* do′est, dost, dust, *3rd* does, duz, also do′eth, doth, *duth; pa.t.* did; *pr.p.* do′ing; *pa.p.* done, dun; in *Spens. infin.* doen, done, donne, *3rd pl.* pa.t. doen.—*Do* serves as a substitute for a verb that has just been used. It is used as an auxiliary verb (where there is no other auxiliary) with an infinitive in negative, interrogative, emphatic, and rhetorically inverted sentences, in some dialects merely periphrastically, and in verse sometimes to gain a syllable or postpone the accent; but these uses are limited with the verbs *have* and *do*.—*n.* activity: what one has to do: fuss (*arch.*): a feast, celebration: a swindle, hoax (*slang*).—*adj.* do'able (*rare*), that can be done.—*n.* do'er, one who does, or habitually does, anything: an agent.—*adj.* do'ing, active (as in *up and doing*).—*n.* (*coll.*) a scolding: thrashing: severe treatment: (in *pl.*) activities, behaviour: (in *pl.*) fancy dishes or adjuncts (*U.S.*): (in *pl.*) what's-its-name (*slang*).—do'all, a factotum; do'-good'er, a slighting name for one who tries to benefit others by social reforms etc., implying that his, her, efforts are unwelcome or ineffectual; do'-good'ery (*slang*); do'-good'ism.—*adj.* do-it-yourself. designed to be built, constructed, etc., by an amateur, rather than one specially trained.—Also *n.*—do'-naught, do'-nought, do'-noth'ing, a lazy or idle person: a fainéant (see donnot); do'-noth'ing-ism; do'-noth'ingness.—be done, to be at an end: to have done, finished (*Scot.*); do away with, to abolish, destroy; do brown, to cook or roast to brownness: to hoax, swindle (*slang*); do by, act towards; do down, put down, subdue (*obs.*): to cheat, get the better of (*slang*); do for, to suit: provide for: ruin: kill (*coll.*): do domestic work for (*coll.*); do in, (*coll.*) to deceive, to get the better of: to exhaust: to ruin, to murder; do one proud (*coll.*), to make one feel flattered: to treat lavishly; do over, to do again: to cover over, as with paint; do to death, to murder: to repeat too often; do up, fasten up: put up, make tidy, arrange, tie up: redecorate: apply cosmetics: dress: fatigue utterly; do well, to be justified: to prosper; do with, to make use of: to meddle with: to get on with; do without, not to be dependent on, to dispense with; have done, desist: stop it: have no more dealings; have to do with, to have any sort of connection with; how do you do? a conventional phrase used on greeting; nothing doing, no; what's to do? what is the matter? [O.E. *dōn*, *dyde*, *gedōn*; Du. *doen*, Ger. *tun*; conn. with Gr. *tithenai*, to put, place.]

do, dō, (*mus.*) *n.* a syllable representing the first note of the scale—Anglicised as doh. [Pers. from G.B. Doni (1593-1647), who is said to have substituted it for the Aretinian syllable *ut* (see gamut).]

doab, dō'äb, *n.* a tongue of land between two rivers (esp. the Ganges and Jumna). [Perh. *dōāb*, two waters.]

doat. Same as dote.

dobbin, *dob'in*, *n.* a workhorse. [An altered dim. of *Robert*.]

dobby, dobbie, *dob'i*, *n.* a dotard: a brownie: an attachment to a loom for weaving small figures. [Perh. from *Robert*.]

dobchick, dob'chik. Same as dabchick.

Doberman(n) pinscher, dōb'ər-man pin'shər, *n.* a breed of terrier—large, smooth-coated, with long forelegs. [*Dobermann*, the first breeder, and Ger. *pinscher*, terrier.]

dobhash, dō'bash, *n.* an interpreter. [Hind. *dōbāshi*, *dūbhāshiya*—dō, dū, two, *bhāshā*, language.]

docent. See privat-dozent.

Docetism, dō-sē'tizm, *n.* a 2nd-century heresy, that Christ's body was only a semblance, or else of ethereal substance.—*ns.* Do'cēte, Docē'tist, a holder of this belief; *n.pl.* Docē'tae (-tē).—*adjs.* Docetic (-set'), -set'), Docetist'ic. [Gr. *dokēsis*, phantom, semblance—*dokeein*, to seem.]

doch-an-doris. See deoch-an-doruis.

dochmius, dok'mi-əs, *n.* a foot of five syllables, typically with first and fourth short, the rest long.—*adjs.* doch'miac, dochmi'acal. [L.—Gr. *dochmios*.]

docile, dō'sil, or dos'il, *adj.* teachable: ready to learn: easily managed.—(*obs.*) do'cible.—*ns.* docibil'ity, doc'ibleness, docil'ity. [Fr.,—L. *docilis*—*docēre*, to teach.]

docimasy, dos'i-mə-si, *n.* scrutiny: application of tests: assaying: examination of drugs.—*adj.* docimastic (-mas'tik).—*n.* docimol'ogy, the art of assaying. [Gr. *dokimasiā*, examination—*dokimazein*, to test—*dechesthai*, to take, approve.]

dock, dok, *n.* a polygonaceous weed (*Rumex*) with large leaves and a long root.—*n.* dock'en (*Scot.*, perh. orig. *pl.*), a dock.—dock'-cress, the nipplewort. [O.E. *docce*.]

dock, dok, *v.t.* to cut short: to curtail: to cut off: to clip: to deprive of pay.—*n.* the part of a tail left after clipping: the rump (*Scot.*). [M.E. *dok*, prob.—O.N. *dokkr*, stumpy tail.]

dock, dok, *n.* an artificial basin for the reception of vessels: the waterway between two wharves or two piers: a wharf or pier: the enclosure in court for the accused: in a railway station, the place of arrival and departure of a train: in the theatre, a space for storing scenery.—*v.t.* to embed in sand or ooze (*Shak.*): to place in a dock: to bring into dock: to equip with docks: to join (space-craft) together in space.—Also *v.i.* —*v.i.* to enter a dock.—*ns.* dock'age, accommodation in docks for ships: dock-dues; dock'er, one who works in the docks; dock'ing; dockisā'tion, -z-.—*v.t.* dock'ise, -ize, to convert into docks.—dock'dues, payments for use of a dock; dock'land, a district about docks; dock'-master, the person superintending a dock; dock'-warrant, a warehouse receipt; dock'yard, a naval establishment with docks, building-slips, stores, etc.—dry dock, a dock from which the water can be pumped, in order to effect repairs to the underside of a ship. [Origin obscure; cf. O.Du. *dokke.*]

docket, dok'it, *n.* a summary of a larger writing: a bill or ticket affixed to anything indicating its contents: a label: a list or register of cases in court, or of legal judgments, or (*U.S.*) business to be transacted: an official permit to buy: a customhouse certificate of payment.—*v.t.* to make a summary of the heads of a writing: to enter in a book: to mark the contents of papers on the back:—*pr.p.* dock'eting; *pa.t.* and *pa.p.* dock'eted.—Also docquet (as if French). [Perh. a dim. of dock, to curtail.]

doctor, dok'tər, *n.* a teacher (*arch.*): a learned father of the church: a cleric especially skilled in theology or ecclesiastical law: one who has received from a university (or the Archbishop of Canterbury) the highest degree in any faculty (originally implying competency to teach): a physician or medical practitioner, whatever be his degree of medicine: in U.S. extended to a dentist or druggist: a mender: in some warm countries, a cool sea-breeze conducive to health: a ship's cook: a name for various contrivances for removing defects or superfluities in manufacture: material used for sophistication: brown sherry: counterfeit coin: (in *pl.*) loaded dice: a fish, the sea-surgeon: an angler's fly.—*v.t.* to treat, as a doctor does: to patch up, repair: to sophisticate, tamper with, falsify: to address as doctor: to confer a doctor's degree upon.—*v.i.* to practice medicine.—*adj.* doc'toral. —*n.* doc'torand, a candidate for the doctorate.— *v.t.* doc'torate, to confer the degree of doctor upon.—*n.* an academic degree of doctor.—*ns.* doc'toress, doc'tress (*facetious*), a female doctor; a doctor's wife.—*adjs.* doctorial (-tō'ri-al, -tō'ri-əl); doc'torly.—*n.* doc'torship.—doc'tor-fish, a sea-surgeon; Doctors' Commons, before the establishment of the Divorce Court and Probate Court in 1857, the college of the doctors of civil law in London, incorporated by royal charter in 1768; doctor's stuff, medicine.—what

Neutral vowels in unaccented syllables: *el'ə-mənt*; for certain sounds in foreign words, see p. viii

the doctor ordered (*slang*), the very thing that's needed. [L., a teacher—*docēre*, to teach.]

**doctrinaire**, *dok-tri-nār'*, *n.* an unpractical theorist, disposed to carry principles to logical but unworkable extremes: in France, in 1815-30, one of a school who desired constitutional government.—*adj.* theoretical.—*n.* and *adj.* **doctrinā'rian**, doctrinaire.—*ns.* **doctrinair'ism**, **doctrinā'rianism**, blind adhesion to one-sided principles. [Fr.,—L.L. *doctrinārius.*]

**doctrine**, *dok'trin*, *n.* teaching (*arch.*): a thing taught: a principle of belief.—*adj.* **doc'trinal** (or *-tri'nal*).—*adv.* **doc'trinally** (or *-tri'*). [L. *doctrina*, *docēre*, to teach.]

**document**, *dok'ū-mənt*, *n.* instruction (*Spens.*): warning (*obs.*): a paper or other material thing affording information, proof, or evidence of anything.—*v.t.* (also *-ment'*), to furnish with documents: to support or prove by documents.—*adjs.* **documental** (*-ment'*), **document'ary**, relating to or found in documents: aiming at presentation of reality.—*n.* a motion-picture presenting an activity or occupation of real life without fictional colouring or professional actors.—*n.* **documentā'tion**, instruction (*arch.*): preparation, setting forth, or use of documentary evidence and authorities: in fiction, realistic reproduction of records, real or supposed. [Fr.,—L. *documentum*—*docēre*, to teach.]

**dod**, *dod*, (*obs.* or *dial.*) *v.t.* to cut the hair of: to poll: to pollard: to clip.—*n.* (*Scot.*) a rounded hill-top, esp. a shoulder of a greater hill.—*adj.* **dodd'ed**, polled: hornless: pollard.—*n.* **dodd'y** (*Scot.*), a hornless cow. [M.E. *dodden.*]

**dod**, *dod*, (*Scot.*) *n.* a slight fit of ill-humour: (in *pl.*; often with *the*) the sulks.—*adj.* **dodd'y**. [Gael. *dod*, peevishness.]

**dod**, *dod*, *n.* a minced form of God, in oaths.

**dodder**, *dod'ər*, *n.* a leafless, twining, pale parasitic plant (*Cuscuta*) of or akin to the convolvulus family. [M.E. *doder*; cf. Ger. *dotter.*]

**dodder**, *dod'ər*, *v.i.* to shake: to tremble: to totter: to potter: to ramble in talk: to be decrepit in mind or body.—*n.* **dodd'erer.**—*adj.* **dodd'ering.**—*adj.* **dodd'ery.** [Perh. conn. with **doddered.**]

**doddered**, **doddard**, *dod'ərd*, *adj.* orig. perh. pollard: decayed with loss of branches. [Cf. **dod** (1).]

**doddypoll**, **doddipoll**, *dod'i-pōl*, (*obs.*) *n.* a blockhead.—Also **dottipoll.** [App. **dote**, and **poll.**]

**dodeca-**, *dō-dek-ə-*, in composition, twelve.—*n.* **dodec'agon** (Gr. *gōniā*, an angle), a plane figure with twelve angles and sides.—*n.pl.* **Dodecagyn'ia** (*jin'i-a*; Gr. *gynē*, a woman, female), in some classes of the Linnaean classification an order of plants with twelve styles.—*adjs.* **dodecagyn'ian**, **dodecag'ynous** (*-aj'i-nəs*).—*n.* **dodecahe'dron** (*-hē'dron*; Gr.; *hedrā*, a seat), a solid figure, having twelve faces (equal pentagons in a *regular* dodecahedron, rhombs in a *rhombic* dodecahedron). — *adj.* **dodecahē'dral.** — *n.pl.* **Dodecan'dria** (Gr. *anēr*, *andros*, a man, male), a Linnaean class of plants, having twelve stamens. —*adjs.* **dodecan'drous**; **dodecaphon'ic** (*mus*; Gr. *phōnē*, voice), twelve-tone.—*ns.* **dodecaph'onist**, a composer or admirer of twelve-tone music; **dodecaph'ony.**—*adj.* **dodecastyle** (*dō'dek-ə-stīl*; *archit.*; Gr. *stȳlos*, a pillar), having twelve columns in front.—*n.* a portico so built.—*n.* **dodecasyll'able** (*pros.*), a line of twelve syllables. —*adj.* **dodecasyllab'ic.** [Gr. *dōdeka*, twelve.]

**dodge**, *doj*, *v.i.* to start aside or shift about: to evade or use mean tricks: to shuffle or quibble. —*v.t.* to evade by a sudden shift of place: to evade: to trick.—*n.* an evasion: a trick: a quibble.—*ns.* **dodg'er**, one who dodges: a screen on a ship's bridge for shelter in rough weather: (*U.S.*) an advertising leaflet, trickery.—*adj.* **dodg'y**, artful, tricky: difficult to

do or carry out: risky.—**dodge the column** (*slang*), evade one's duties. [Origin obscure.]

**Dodgem(s)**, *doj'əm(z)*, *n.* an amusement in which drivers of small electric cars within an enclosure strive to bump others without being bumped. [Trademark.]

**dodkin**, *dod'kin*, *n.* a doit.—Also **doit'kin.** [doit.]
**dodman**, *dod'mən*, (*dial.*) *n.* a snail. [Origin unknown.]
**dodo**, *dō'dō*, *n.* a clumsy flightless bird, about the size of a turkey, a native of Mauritius, extinct about the end of the 17th century:—*pl.* **do'do(e)s.** [Port. *doudo*, silly.]

**Dodonaean**, *dō-dō-nē'ən*, pertaining to *Dodona* in Epirus, or its oracle sacred to Zeus, situated in a grove of oaks.—Also **Dodō'nian.**

**Doe, dō.**—**John Doe** and **Richard Roe**, imaginary plaintiff and opponent in the old legal action for ejectment, proverbial as a legal fiction.

**doe**, *dō*, *n.* the female of the fallow-deer or buck: extended to the female of other deer, of antelope, rabbit, hare, and sometimes other animals.—**doe'-skin**, the skin of a doe: a smooth, closewoven, woollen cloth. [O.E. *dā*; Dan. *daa*, deer.]

**doer, does.** See **do.**

**doff**, *dof*, *v.t.* to take off: to put off: to remove.— *n.* **doff'er**, part of a carding machine that strips the cotton from the cylinder when carded: one who removes full bobbins from a machine. [**do**, off.]

**dog**, *dog*, *n.* a wild or domestic animal of the same genus (Canis) as the wolf: a male of the species: a mean scoundrel: a term of contempt: a fellow (as *a jolly dog*): either of the two constellations, the Greater and the Lesser Dog (Canis Major and Minor): an andiron: a hook for holding logs: a gripping appliance of various kinds: a cock, as of a gun: a dogfish: a prairie dog: heavy ostentation (*slang*): (in *pl.*) greyhound races (*coll.*).—*adj.* (and in composition) of dogs: male (opposed to *bitch*): spurious, base, inferior.—*adv.* (esp. in composition) utterly.—*v.t.* to follow as a dog: to track and watch constantly: to hunt with dogs: to fasten with a dog:— *pr.p.* **dogg'ing**; *pa.t.* and *pa.p.* **dogged.**—*adj.* **dogg'ed**, dog-like: sullen: pertinacious.—*adv.* **dogg'edly.**—*ns.* **dogg'edness** (*slang*) very.—*adv.* **dogg'edly.**—*ns.* **dogg'edness**; **dogg'er**, one who dogs; **dogg'ery**, doggish ways or doings; dogs collectively: rabble: a drinking resort (*U.S.*); **dogg'ess** (*facet.*), a bitch; **dogg'iness**; **dogg'ing**, shooting with dogs: following like a dog.—*adj.* **dogg'ish**, doglike: characteristic of dogs: churlish: brutal.—*adv.* **dogg'ishly.**—*n.* **dogg'ishness.**—*adj.* **dogg'y**, fond of dogs: doglike: dashing, beauish.—*n.* **dog'ship**, the quality or personality of a dog.—**dog'-ape**, a baboon (from the form of its head); **dog('s)'bane**, a plant (*Apocynum*) said to be poisonous to dogs; **dog'-bee**, a drone; **dog'-belt**, a broad belt put round the waist for hauling; **dog'berry**, the fruit of the wild cornel or dogwood: extended to many other plants and their fruits: (with *cap.*) a pompous, muddle-headed fellow (from the character in Shakespeare's *Much Ado About Nothing*); **Dog'berrydom**; **Dog'berryism**, an utterance worthy of Dogberry, verbosely consequential blundering and malapropism; **dog'-bis'cuit**, a biscuit for feeding dogs; **dog'bolt**, orig. a kind of arrow: a contemptible fellow (*obs.*); **dog'cart**, a two-wheeled horse-vehicle with seats back to back, originally used to carry sporting dogs.—*adj.* **dog'-cheap**, extremely cheap.—**dog'-collar**, a collar for a dog: a clerical collar fastened behind: a woman's stiff collar or neck ornament; **dog'-crab**, a very small crab; **dog'-dai'sy**, the common daisy: the ox-eye daisy.—*n.pl.* **dog'days**, the period when the Dogstar rises and sets with the sun (generally reckoned July 3rd to August 11th)—erroneously supposed to be the time when dogs are specially liable to hydrophobia.—dog'-ear, a dog's-ear.— adj. dog'-eared, of pages of a book, turned down like the ears of a dog: hence, shabby, scruffy.— dog'-eat-dog', a ruthless pursuit of one's own interests, savage self-concern.—Also adj.—dog'-end (slang), a cigarette-end.—adj. dog'-faced.— dog'-fan'cier, a breeder or seller of dogs; dog'-fight, a fight between dogs: a confused fight or mêlée; dog'fish, a small shark of various kinds; dog'fox, a male fox; dog'-grass, dog'-wheat, couch-grass or kindred species; dog'-head, hammer of a gunlock; dog'-hip, -hep (dial.), hip or fruit of the dog-rose; dog'hole, a hole fit only for a dog: a wretched dwelling; dog'-house, a dog-kennel: a place of disgrace (fig.); dog-kenn'el; dog'-Lat'in, barbarous Latin; dog'-leech, one who treats diseases of dogs.—adj. dog'-leg(ged), bent like a dog's hind leg: (of stairs) having successive flights running opposite ways without a well-hole: (of a fence) made of poles laid on cross-shaped supports: (also n.; golf) (of) a hole with a bent fairway.—dog'-lett'er, r, from its growling sound; dog'-louse; dog'-pars'ley, fool's parsley; dog'-per'iwinkle, species of Purpura (also dog'-whelk); dog'-rose, species of wild rose, Rosa canina; dog'-salmon, keta and humpback, Pacific species of salmon; dog's'-body (orig. naut. slang), pease-pudding: dish of biscuit, water, and sugar: junior naval (or other) officer: a general drudge; dog('s)'-ear, a fold at the corner of a leaf in a book.— v.t. to fold at the corner.—dog's'-fenn'el, may-weed.—n.pl. dog'shores, pieces of timber used to shore up a vessel before launching.— —adj. dog'-sick', thoroughly sick, sick as a dog.— dog'skin, leather made of or in imitation of dog's skin.—Also adj.—dog'sleep, a light sleep, very easily broken; dog's'-meat, scraps and refuse sold as food for dogs; dog's'-mer'cury, a euphorbiaceous plant Mercurialis perennis; dog's'-nose, gin and beer, or similar mixture; dog's'-tail-grass', a common British pasture grass (Cynosurus); Dog'star, Sirius, in the constella-tion of the Greater Dog, brightest star in the heavens and giving name to the dogdays; dog's'-tongue, hound's-tongue; dog's-tooth, a broken-check pattern used extensively in the weaving of tweeds; dog's'-tooth-grass', a seaside sand-binding grass (Cynodon); dog'-tick.—adjs. dog'-tired, dog'-wea'ry (Shak.), tired as a dog, com-pletely worn out.—dog'tooth, a moulding in later Norman architecture, consisting of a series of ornamental square pyramids: a canine tooth; dog'tooth-spar', calcite crystals like canine teeth; dog'tooth-vi'olet, any plant of the liliaceous genus Erythronium; dog'town, a prairie-dog community; dog'-trick, a low trick; dog'trot, a gentle trot like a dog's; a jogtrot; dog'vane (naut.), a small vane to show direction of wind; dog'-vi'olet, a scentless wild violet, esp. Viola canina; dog'-watch (naut.), on shipboard, a watch 4-6 p.m. or 6-8 p.m., consisting of two hours only, instead of four; dog'-whelk', a gasteropod of the genus Nassa, like a small whelk: a dog-periwinkle; dog'wood, the wild cornel (Cornus sanguinea), a small tree with white flowers and purple berries, the shoots and leaves turning red in autumn: extended to many other shrubs and trees.—dog in the manger, one who will not let others enjoy what he has himself no use for; dog's age (coll.), a long time; dog's breakfast, dinner, anything very untidy; dog's chance, a bare chance; dog's life, a wretched, miserable life; go to the dogs, to be ruined; hot dog, hot sausage sandwich; like a dog's dinner (slang), very smart, dressed up flamboyantly; not to lead the life of a dog, to lead a life so wretched that even a dog would not be content with it; throw, give, or send to the dogs, to throw

away or abandon. [Late O.E. docga—cf. Du. dog, a mastiff; Ger. dogge.]
dog, dog, (obs.) n. used in oaths for God.—interj. doggone(d) (dog-gon(d)'), dog on it (U.S.), ex-pressing vexation.—Also adj.
doge, dōj, or dō'jā, n. the chief magistrate in republican Venice and Genoa.—ns. dogaressa (dō-gä-res'a), a doge's wife; dogate (dō'gāt), doge'ate (dō'jāt), doge'ship. [It. (Venetian dial.) for duce, duke—L. dux, a leader.]
dogger, dog'ər, n. a two-masted Dutch fishing-vessel.—n. dogg'erman. [Du.]
dogger, dog'ər, n. a concretion, esp. of ironstone: a sandy ironstone or ferruginous sandstone: part of the Middle Jurassic. [Origin uncertain; a northern word.]
doggerel, dog'ər-əl, n. irregular measures in bur-lesque poetry, so named in contempt: worthless verses.—adj. irregular in rhythm, mean.—Also dogg'rel. [Origin unknown.]
doggo, dog'ō, (coll.) adj. hidden. [Poss. from dog.]
dogie, dogy, dō'gi, (U.S.) n. a motherless calf. [Origin obscure.]
dogma, dog'mə, n. a settled opinion: a principle or tenet: a doctrine laid down with authority.—adjs. dogmatic (-mat'ik), -al, pertaining to a dogma: asserting a thing as if it were a dogma: asserting positively: overbearing.—adv. dog-n.at'ically.—n. dogmat'ics (theol.), the statement of Christian doctrines, systematic theology.—v.i. dog'matise, -ize (-mə-tīz), to state one's opinion dogmatically or arrogantly.—ns. dog'matiser, -z-; dogmatism', dogmatic or positive assertion of opinion; dog'matist, one who makes positive assertions; dogmatol'ogy, the science of dogma.— adj. dog'matory. [Gr. dogma, -atos, an opinion —dokeein, to think, seem.]
doh. See do (2).
doilt, doilt, (Scot.) adj. crazy, foolish.—Also doiled. [Origin obscure.]
doily, doi'li, n. an old kind of woollen stuff (obs.): a small ornamented napkin, often laid on or under dishes. [From Doily or Doyley, a famous haberdasher.]
doit, doit, n. a small Dutch coin worth about half a farthing: a thing of little or no value. [Du. duit.]
doited, doitit, doit'id, -it, (Scot.) adj. in dotage. [Origin obscure.]
dolabriform, dō-lab'ri-förm, adj. like a hatchet or cleaver. [L. dolābra, a cleaver, fōrma, form.]
dolce, dol'chā, adj. sweet, esp. of music.—n. a soft-toned organ-stop.—adv. dolcemen'te (mus.), softly and sweetly.—dolce far niente (fär nē-en'tā), sweet doing-nothing, pleasant idleness; dolce vita (vē'ta; It., sweet life), a life of wealth, pleasure and self-indulgence. [It.,—L. dulcis.]
doldrums, dol'drəmz, n.pl. those parts of the ocean about the equator where calms and baffling winds prevail (naut.): low spirits. [Prob. conn. with obs. dold, stupid, or dol, dull.]
dole, dōl, n. a share: a dealing out: something given in charity: (usu. contemptuously) state pay to unemployed: a small portion.—v.t. to deal out in small portions. [O.E. dāl; cf. deal.]
dole, dōl, n. pain: grief: heaviness at heart (arch. and poet.).—Also dool, (obs.) doole.—adj. dole'-ful, full of dole or grief: melancholy.—adv. dole'fully.—n. dole'fulness.—adjs. do'lent (obs.), dole'some, dismal.—adv. dole'somely. [O.Fr. doel (Fr. deuil), grief—L. dolēre, to feel pain.]
dole, dōl, n. guile (obs.): criminal intention (Scots law). [L. dolus—Gr. dolos, guile.]
dolerite, dol'ər-it, n. a basic igneous rock like basalt in composition but coarser grained.—adj. dolerit'ic. [Fr. dolérite—Gr. doleros, deceptive.]
dolicho-, dol-i-kō-, in composition, long.—n. dolichocephal (-sef'əl), a long-headed person.— adj. dolichocephal'ic (-sif-al'ik; Gr. kephalē, the

head), long-headed—having a breadth of skull (from side to side) less than 75 (or 78) per cent. of the length (front to back)—opp. to *brachycephalic.*—Also **dolichoceph'alous.**—*ns.* **dolichoceph'aly, dolichoceph'alism;** Dolichos (*dol'i-kos;* Gr., long, also a podded plant), a genus of longpodded leguminous plants allied to the haricot; **Dolichosaurus** (-sö'rəs; Gr. sauros, lizard), the typical genus of **Dolichosau'ria,** a group of Cretaceous fossil reptiles; **Dolichotis** (-kō'tis; Gr. ous, ōtos, the ear), a genus of long-eared S. American rodents—the mara or Patagonian hare. [Gr. *dolichos,* long.]

**dolichurus,** dol-i-kū'rəs, *n.* a dactylic hexameter with a redundant syllable at the end. [Gr. *dolichouros,* long-tailed.]

**dolium,** dō'li-əm, *n.* a Roman earthenware jar for wine, oil, grain, etc.:—*pl.* dō'lia. [L. *dōlium.*]

**doll,** dol, *n.* a puppet: a toy in human form: an insipid woman, esp. one who is over-dressed and silly: a young woman: smallest or pet pig in a litter.—*v.i.* and *v.t.* to dress (often with *up*).—*ns.* **doll'dom; doll'hood; doll'iness.**—*adj.* **doll'ish.**—*ns.* **doll'ishness; doll'y** (girl or bird), dim. of doll, an attractive young girl: formerly, a dolly-mop: a slow, easy catch (*cricket*).—*adj.* **doll'y.**—**doll's'-house; doll'y-mop,** a slut: a prostitute; **doll'y-shop,** a marine store—a low pawn-shop—often having a black doll as sign. [Prob. from *Dolly,* familiar dim. of *Dorothy.*]

**dollar,** dol'ər, *n.* a silver coin (= 100 cents) of U.S.A., Canada, Australia, New Zealand, Mexico, Hong-Kong, etc.: a thaler: five shillings (*slang*).—*adjs.* **doll'ared; doll'arless.**—*ns.* **dollaroc'racy; doll'arship.**—**dollar area,** those countries as a whole whose currencies are linked to the U.S. dollar; **dollar diplomacy,** diplomacy dictated by financial interests: diplomacy that employs financial weapons to increase political power; **dollar gap,** the excess of imports from a dollar country over exports to it, necessitating settlement by dollar exchange or in gold. [Ger. *t(h)aler* (L. *U. daler*), short for *Joachimsthaler,* because first coined at the silver-mines in Joachimsthal (Joachim's dale) in Bohemia.]

**dollop,** dol'əp, *n.* a tuft of grass or weeds: a rank patch in a field: a lump.—Also **dall'op.** [Prob. conn. with Norw. dial. *dolp,* a lump.]

**dolly,** dol'i, *n.* a complimentary offering of flowers, sweetmeats, etc., on a tray. [Anglo-Ind.,—Hindi *dālī.*]

**dolly.** See doll.

**dolly,** dol'i, *n.* a wooden shaft attached to a disk with projecting arms, used for beating and stirring clothes in a washing-tub: somewhat similar apparatus in mining, pile-driving, etc.: a tool for holding the head of a rivet: a trolley, truck, or platform on wheels or roller.—*v.t.* to operate upon, yield, or obtain, with a dolly: to beat with a hammer.—*adj.* **doll'ied.**—*n.* **doll'ier.** —**dolly camera,** a camera moving on a dolly; **doll'y-shop** (see doll); **dolly switch,** an electric light switch pushed up and down vertically; **doll'y-tub,** a tub for washing clothes or ores with a dolly. [Prob. from *Dolly,* the familiar form of *Dorothy.*]

**Dolly Varden,** dol'i var'dən, *n.* a flowered muslin dress for women, with pointed bodice and tucked-up skirt: a large hat, one side bent downwards, abundantly trimmed with flowers: a large American fish of the char genus. [Named from a character in Dickens's *Barnaby Rudge.*]

**dolman,** dol'mən, *n.* a Turkish robe with slight sleeves and open in front: a hussar's jacket, worn like a cloak, with one or both sleeves hanging loose: a woman's mantle. [Turk. *dōlāmān.*]

**dolmen,** dol'mən, *n.* a stone table: a prehistoric sepulchral chamber of erect unhewn stones, supporting a flattish stone. [Fr. *dolmen;* usually

explained as—Bret. *dol, taol,* table, *men,* stone; but *tolmēn* in Cornish meant hole of stone.]

**dolomite,** dol'ə-mit, *n.* a mineral, double carbonate of calcium and magnesium: a rock composed of that mineral, magnesian limestone.—*adj.* **dolomitic** (-mit'ik).—*n.* **dol'omitisation,** -z-.—*v.t.* **dol'omitise,** -ize, to convert into dolomite. [After the French geologist D. Guy de *Dolomieu* (1750-1801).]

**dolour,** dol'ər, dōl'ər, historically dul'ər, *n.* pain: grief: anguish.—*adjs.* **dolorif'erous, dolori'fic,** causing or conveying dolour, pain, or grief.—*adv.* **dolorō'so** (It.; *mus.*), in a soft and pathetic manner.—*adj.* **dol'orous,** full of dolour, pain, or grief: doleful.—*adv.* **dol'orously.**—*n.* **dol'orousness.** [O.Fr.,—L. *dolēre,* to grieve.]

**dolphin,** dol'fin, *n.* an animal of the whale kind, closely resembling the porpoise, about 8 to 10 feet long: the Coryphaena, a fish about 5 feet in length, noted for the brilliancy of its colours when dying: (*cap.*) a northern constellation (see Delphinus).—*n.* **dol'phinet** (*Spens.*), a female dolphin.—**dol'phin-fly,** a black aphis or plantlouse, destructive to bean-plants. [O.Fr. *daulphin*—L. *delphinus*—Gr. *delphis,* -*phinos.*]

**dolt,** dōlt, *n.* a dull or stupid fellow.—*adj.* **dolt'ish,** dull: stupid.—*adv.* **dolt'ishly.**—*n.* **dolt'ishness.** [For dulled or blunted; see dull.]

**Dom,** dom, *n.* the Portuguese form of *Don:* also a title given to certain Catholic dignitaries and members of some monastic orders, esp. the Benedictine. [L. *dominus,* lord.]

**-dom,** -dom, dəm, *suff.* forming nouns, denoting dominion, power, state, act. [O.E. *dōm,* judgment; Ger. -*tum.*]

**domain,** dō-mān', *n.* what one is master of or has dominion over: an estate: territory: ownership of land: the scope or range of any subject or sphere of knowledge: an aggregate to which a variable belongs (*math.*).—*adjs.* **domain'al,** **domā'nial.** [Fr. *domaine*—L. *dominicum*—*dominus,* a master.]

**domal,** dōm'əl, *adj.* relating to a house. [L. *domus,* a house.]

**domatium,** do-mā'sh(y)əm, *n.* a plant structure that harbours mites or other symbiotic organisms:—*pl.* **domātia.** [Latinised form of Gr. *dōmation,* dim. of *dōma,* house.]

**Domdaniel,** dom-dan'yəl, *n.* a hall under the sea inhabited by a sorcerer and his disciples (*Southey*): an infernal cave, den of iniquity generally (*Carlyle*). [Fr.,—Gr. *dōma Daniēl,* house of Daniel; from Chavis and Cazotte's French continuation of the *Arabian Nights.*]

**dome,** dōm, *n.* a structure, usually hemispherical, raised above a large building: a large cupola: a cathedral: a building, esp. a great or stately building (*poet.*): anything approaching the form of a hemispherical vault, esp. a head, the cover of a reverberatory furnace, the steamchamber on a locomotive boiler, a clip-fastener that fits into a hold: a pair of crystal-faces parallel to a lateral axis, meeting in a rooflike edge (*crystal.*).—*v.t.* to furnish with a dome: to form into a dome.—*v.i.* to swell or rise as a dome.—*adjs.* **domed, domical** (dōm', dom'), having a dome; **dom'y.** [L. *domus,* a house; Fr. *dôme,* It. *duoma,* Ger. *dom.*]

**dome** (*Spens.*). Same as doom.—**Domesday-, Doomsday-book** (dōōmz'dā-bōōk), a book compiled by order of William the Conqueror, containing a survey of all the lands in England, their value, owners, etc.—so called from its authority in judgment (O.E. *dōm*) on the matters contained in it.

**domestic,** dō-, də-mes'tik, *adj.* belonging to the house: remaining much at home: private: tame: not foreign.—*n.* a servant in the house:— (in *pl.*) articles of home manufacture, esp. homemade cotton cloths.—*adj.* **domes'tical** (*arch.*).—

*adv.* **domes'tically.**—*v.t.* **domes'ticate,** to make domestic or familiar: to tame.—*adj.* **domes'-ticated,** adapted to or content with home life and activities: tamed.—*ns.* **domestica'tion; domes'ticātor; domesticity** (*dō-, do-mis-tis'*), domestic or domesticated state: home life: (in *pl.*) home conditions and arrangements.— **domestic architecture,** the architecture of mansions, dwelling-houses, cottages, etc.; **domestic economy,** the principles of efficient ordering of a household; **domestic science,** the household arts, as catering, cookery, laundry-work, studied in the light of physiological, chemical, etc., knowledge. [L. *domesticus—domus,* a house.]

**domett,** *dom'ət, -it, n.* a plain cloth with cotton warp and woollen weft. [Perh. a proper name.]

**domicile,** *dom'i-sil, -sil, n.* a dwelling-place, abode: one's legally recognised place of residence.—*v.t.* to establish in a fixed residence.—*adjs.* **dom'iciled; domiciliary** (*-sil'*), pertaining to the domicile. —*v.t.* **domiciliāte** (*-sil'*), to establish in a permanent residence.—*n.* **domiciliā'tion.**—**domiciliary nurse,** a nurse visiting sick persons in their homes; **domiciliary visit,** a visit, under authority, to a private house for the purpose of searching it: a visit made by a doctor to a patient's home. [Fr.,—L. *domicilium—domus,* a house.]

**dominant,** *dom'in-ənt, adj.* prevailing: predominant: overtopping: of an ancestral chracter, appearing in the first generation of cross-bred offspring to the exclusion of the alternative character in the other parent, which may yet be transmitted to later generations (*Mendelism*).— *n.* the fifth above the tonic (*mus.*): a dominant Mendelian character: one of the prevailing species in a plant community.—*ns.* **dom'inance, dom'inancy,** ascendency.—*adv.* **dom'inantly.** [L. *domināns, -antis,* pr.p. of *dominārī,* to be master.]

**dominate,** *dom'in-āt, v.t.* to be lord over: to govern: to prevail over: to tower over: to command a view of: to be the controlling position of.—Also *v.i.*—*n.* the Roman Empire in its later more avowedly absolute form.—*n.* **dominā'tion,** government; absolute authority: tyranny.—*adj.* **dom'inātive,** governing: arbitrary (*rare*).—*n.* **dom'inātor,** a ruler or governor (*Shak.*): a ruling influence. [L. *dominārī, -ātus,* to be master—*dominus,* master—*domāre,* to tame.]

**domineer,** *dom-in-ēr', v.i.* to rule arbitrarily: to command haughtily: to be overbearing.—*adj.* **domineer'ing,** overbearing. [Prob. through Du. from O.Fr. *dominer*—L. *dominārī.*]

**dominical,** *do-min'i-kl, adj.* belonging to the Lord, as the Lord's Prayer, the Lord's Day.—**dominical letter,** one of the first seven letters of the alphabet, used in calendars to mark the Sundays throughout the year. [L.L. *dominicālis*—L. *dominicus—dominus,* lord, master.]

**Dominican,** *do-min'i-kən, adj.* belonging to St. *Dominic* or to the Dominicans.—*n.* a friar or monk of the order of St. Dominic—*Fratres Predicatores,* founded in 1215, or *Black Friars,* from their black mantle.

**dominie,** *dom'i-ni, n.* a schoolmaster, a tutor: a clergyman (*U.S.*). [L. *domine,* voc. of *dominus,* master.]

**dominion,** *dō-, de-min'yən, n.* lordship: sovereignty: a domain or territory with home ruler, owner or government: a completely self-governing colony, not subordinate to but freely associated with the mother-country: control: (in *pl.*) a class of angelic spirits (Col. i, 16).— **Dominion Day,** a Canadian festival on the anniversary of the union of the provinces, 1st July, 1867. [L.L. *dominiō, -ōnis—dominus,* master.]

**domino,** *dom'i-nō, n.* a cape with a hood worn by a master or by a priest: a long cloak of black silk with a hood, used at masked balls, or its wearer:

a mask: one of the oblong pieces with which the game of **dom'inoes** (*-nōz*) is played, usually twenty-eight in number, divided into two compartments, each of which is blank or marked with from one to six spots: a card game played in a similar way: the end. [Apparently Sp. **dominó, dómino,** in some way conn. with L. *dominus,* master.]

**Don, don,** *n.* a Spanish title, corresponding to English Sir, Mr, formerly applied only to noblemen, now to all classes: **don,** a Spanish nobleman, a Spaniard: a fellow of a college, a college authority: a swell, adept (*coll.*):—*fem.* **Doña,** *dōn'ya,* **Don'na** (Italian form); corr. **dona(h),** *dō'nà,* a sweetheart.—*adj.* **donn'ish,** petaining to a don: with the airs of a don.—*ns.* **donn'ism,** self-importance; **don'ship,** rank or dignity of a don.—**Don Juan,** a libertine of Spanish legend, subject of plays, poems, and operas in several European languages: an attractive profligate. [Sp.,—L. *dominus.*]

**don,** *don, v.t.* to do or put on: to assume:—*pr.p.* **donn'ing;** *pa.t.* and *pa.p.* **donned.** [do, on.]

**dona(h).** See under Don.

**Donat, Donet,** *dō'nət, n.* a grammar, a primer. [O.Fr. *donat,* from Aelius *Dōnātus,* author about 358 A.D. of a long-famous Latin grammar.]

**donation,** *dō-nā'shən, n.* act of giving: that which is given, a gift of money or goods: the act by which a person freely transfers his title to anything to another (*law*).—*ns.* **dō'nary,** a thing given to a sacred use; **dō'natary** (*Scots law*), one to whom lands escheated to the crown are made over; **dōn'atory** (or *don'*), a recipient.—*v.t.* **dōnāte'** (a back-formation from **donation**), to give as a gift: to contribute, esp. to charity.—*n.* **dōn'ative** (or *don'*), a gift: a gratuity: a benefice presented by the founder or patron without reference to the bishop.—*adj.* vested or vesting by donation.—*ns.* **dōnā'tor,** one who makes a gift, a donor; **dōn'atory** (or *don'*), a recipient; **dōnee',** the person to whom a gift is made; **dō'nor,** a giver: a benefactor.—**dona nobis,** the last section of the mass, beginning *Dona nobis pacem,* Give us peace. [Fr.,—L. *dōnāre, -ātum —dōnum,* a gift—*dāre,* to give.]

**Donatist,** *dōn', don'ə-tist, n.* a member of an African Christian sect of the 4th and 5th centuries, who protested against any diminution of the extreme reverence paid to martyrs, treated the lapsed severely, and rebaptised converts from the Catholic Church.—*n.* **don'atism.**—*adjs.* **donatis'tic, -al.** [From *Dōnātus,* one of their leaders.]

**done,** *dun, pa.p.* of **do,** often with sense of utterly exhausted: so **done for,** in, out, up: inf. of **do** (*obs.*); see **do.**

**donga,** *dong'gä,* (*S. Africa*) *n.* a gully. [Zulu, bank, side of a gully.]

**donjon,** *dun'jən, n.* a strong central tower in ancient castles, to which the garrison retreated when hard pressed. [A doublet of **dungeon.**]

**donkey,** *dong'ki, n.* an ass: a stupid person:—*pl.* **donkeys.**—**don'key-en'gine,** a small auxiliary engine; **donkey jacket,** a strong jacket, with shoulders of leather or (usu.) a substitute, and patch pockets; **don'key-man,** a man in charge of a donkey-engine; **don'key-pump,** an extra steam-pump; **don'key-work,** drudgery.—**argue, talk, the hind-leg off a donkey,** to do so with invincible pertinacity; **donkey's years,** a long time ( a pun on *ears*). [Still regarded as slang in 1823; perh. a double dim. of *dun,* from its colour; or from *Duncan.*]

**Donna.** See Don.

**donnée,** *do-nā, n.* datum: basic assumption(s), as e.g. a given situation, on which a work of literature is founded: main fact or condition determining the character and timing of an action:—*pl.* **données** (*-ā(z)*). [Fr.]

donnered, donnerd, donnert, don'ərd, -ərt, (Scot.) adj. stupid: dull-witted.

donnerwetter, don'ər-vet-ər, (Ger.) thunderstorm (used as an interjection).

donnot, donnat, don'ət, (Yorkshire) n. a good-for-nothing: an idler. [App. partly do-naught, partly dow-nought.]

Donnybrook, don'i-brŏok, n. a riotous assembly. [From the fair at Donnybrook, Dublin.]

donor. See donation.

donsie, don'si, (Scot.) adj. unlucky, perverse: neat: trim: sickly. [Origin unknown.]

don't, dōnt, for do not.

donut. Same as doughnut.

donzel, don'zəl, (obs.) n. a squire, aspirant to knighthood. [It. donzello—L.L. domnicellus, dim. of L. dominus, lord.]

doo, dōō, n. Scots form of dove.—doocot, dooket (dōōk'ət), a dovecote.

doob, dōōb, n. dog's-tooth grass. [Hind. dūb.]

doodad, dōō'dad, n. a small ornament or trinket: a piece of decoration: a gadget: thingamy.—n. doodah, dōō'dä, a state of agitation, in phrase all of a doodah. [Both coined from do.]

doodle, dōōd'l, (Scot.) v.t. to dandle.

doodle, dōōd'l, (Scot.) v.t. to drone or play, as a bagpipe. [Ger. dudeln.]

doodle, dōōd'l, v.i. scrawl, scribble, meaninglessly.

doodlebug, dōōd'l-bug, n. the larva of an ant-lion or other insect (used in divination in America; U.S.): any instrument, scientific or unscientific, used by prospectors to indicate the presence of minerals: a flying bomb (war slang).

dook, dōōk, (Scot.) n. a plug of wood driven into a wall to hold a nail, etc.: a bung. [Unknown.]

dook, dōōk, (Scot.) v.t. and v.i. to duck: to bathe. —n. an act of plunging, dipping, or bobbing: a bathe: an inclined mine-adit. [duck.]

dook. See duke.

dool, doole. See dole (2), dule.

dool, dōōl, dule, (Scot.) dül, n. a boundary mark: a goal.—hail the dule, to score a goal. [Cf. Du. doel, L. Ger. dole, Fris. dôl, dôle.]

doolie, dōō'li, n. a litter or palanquin. [Hindi dŏli.]

doom, dōōm, n. judgment: condemnation: destiny: ruin: final judgment: a picture of the Last Judgment.—v.t. to pronounce judgment on: to sentence: to condemn: to destine:—pr.p. doom'ing; pa.p. doomed.—adjs. doomed, under sentence: fated; doom'ful (Spens.), dispensing judgment.—adv. dooms (Scot.), very, exceedingly. —ns. dooms'day, the day of doom. the last judgment; dooms'man, one who pronounces doom or sentence, a judge: a pessimist (coll.); doom'ster, a judge: a dempster.—Doomsday-book (see dome (2)).—crack of doom, the last trump. [O.E. dōm, judgment.]

doom-palm. See doum-palm.

door, dōr, dör, n. the usual entrance into a house, room, or passage: a frame for closing up the entrance: a means of approach or access.— doorbell; door'-case, the frame which encloses a door; door'-cheek (Scot.), a side-post of a door; door'-keep'er; door'knob; door'-knocker; door(s)'-man, a porter, doorkeeper; door'mat, a mat for wiping shoes or other purpose at a door: a person whom others trample upon (coll.); door'nail, a stud for a door, proverbially dead; door'-plate, a plate on or at a door with the householder's name on it; door'post, the jamb or side-piece of a door; door'-sill, the threshold of a doorway; door'-stead, a doorway; door'step, a step at a door: a thick slice of bread (coll.); door'stone.—adj. door-to-door, calling at each house in an area for purposes of selling, canvassing, etc.—door'way, an opening where there is or might be a door; door'-yard (U.S.) a yard about the door of a house.—next door (to), in the next house: near, bordering

upon: very nearly (fig.); out of doors (see out); show one the door, to turn out of the house. [O.E. duru (fem.) and dor (neut.); cf. Ger. tür, tor, Gr. thyrā, L. foris, Sans. dvār, a door.]

doorn, dōōrn, (S. Africa) n. thorn.—doorn-boom (dōōrn'bŏŏm), a S. African acacia. [Du. doorn, thorn, boom, tree.]

dop, dop, n. a copper cup in which a gem is fastened for cutting or polishing: Cape brandy made from grape-skins: a drink container (about one third of a bottle): an empty shell (as of a nut): a cartridge-case (usu. doppie.) [Du. dop, shell, husk.]

dop, dop, v.t. and v.i. to dip: to dap.—n. (obs.) a curtsy: a bob.—ns. dopp'er, a didapper: a rod for dapping; dopp'ing, a flock of sheldrake. [O.E. dop- (in compounds); connected with dip.]

dope, dōp, n. a thick liquid, semi-liquid, or pasty material: an absorbent: lubricating grease: aeroplane varnish: a liquid added to improve the efficiency of anything: opium: a drug, esp. one administered to a racehorse or taken by an addict: drug-taking: confidential or fraudulent information in advance: information in general: a wireless news bulletin (U.S.): anything supplied to dull, blind, or blunt the conscience or insight: a fool.—v.t. to give or apply dope to: to drug.—v.i. to take dope.—n. dōp'er, one who applies, administers, deals in, or takes dope.—adj. dōp'y, dope'y, narcotic: stupefied: stupid.—n. dōp'ing, drugging: (electronics) addition of known impurities to a semiconductor, to achieve the desired properties in diodes and transistors.—dope'-fiend, a drug addict. [Du. doop, a dipping, sauce; doopen, to dip.]

doppel-gänger, dop'l-geng'ər, n. a double: a wraith.—Also doppel-gang'er. [Ger., double-goer.]

Dopper, dop'ər, n. a Baptist or Anabaptist: a member of a denomination of the Dutch Reformed Church in S. Africa. [Du. dooper—doopen, to dip.]

doppie. See dop (1).

doppio movimento, dop'pi-ō mō-vē-men'tō, (It.) double speed.

dopplerite, dop'lər-it, n. a black elastic substance (calcium salts of humus acids) found in peat beds. —Doppler's principle, the law of change of wavelength when a source of vibrations is moving towards or from the observer, explaining the fall of pitch of a railway whistle when the engine passes, and enabling astronomers to measure the radial velocity of stars by the displacement of known lines of the spectrum; Doppler effect, this observed change. [From Christian Doppler (1803-53), an Austrian physicist, who announced the principle in 1842.]

dor, dör, (obs.) n. a scoff, mockery, as to give (any one) the dor.—v.t. to mock, put out of countenance. [Prob. O.N. dār, scoff.]

dor, dorr, dör, n. a kind of dung-beetle, also called dor'-beetle and dor'-fly: a cockchafer (in U.S. called dor'-bug): a drone (obs.).—dor'hawk, the nightjar. [O.E. dora, a humble-bee.]

Dora, dō'ra, (coll.) n. the Defence of the Realm Act (1914) which imposed wartime restrictions. [From the initials—Defence Of Realm Act.]

dorado, də-rä'dō, n. the coryphene, so called from its beautiful colour when dying: the so-called golden salmon, a S. American river fish (Salminus) of the Characinidae: (with cap.) a small southern constellation, the Swordfish. [Sp. from dorar, to gild—L. deaurāre, -ātum; see dory, el Dorado.]

Doras, dō'ras, dō', n. a S. American genus of Siluridae, bony-plated river fish with spines, with the habit of walking overland when drought threatens.—n. dō'rad, any member of the genus, or of the group to which it belongs. [Gr. *dory*, spear.]

**Dorcas,** *dör'kəs, n.* in Acts, ix, 36, the Greek translation (*Dorkas*) of *Tabitha* (Aramaic, gazelle), name of a woman famous for good works—hence **Dorcas society,** a ladies' society for making and providing clothes for the poor. [Gr. *dorkas,* gazelle.]

**doree.** See **dory.**

**Dorian,** *dō'ri-ən, dö', adj.* belonging to Doris in Greece or to the Dorians: Doric.—*n.* a native of Doris: a member of one of the main divisions of the ancient Greeks who arrived about 1100 B.C. and made their home in Doris, S.E. Peloponnese, Crete, Rhodes, etc.—**Dorian mode,** a mode of ancient Greek music consisting of two tetrachords with a semitone between the two lowest notes in each, the tetrachords separated by a whole tone (as efga; bcde—but reckoned downwards by the Greeks), traditionally of a stirring, solemn, simple and martial quality: an authentic mode of old church music, extending from d to d with d as its final. [L. *Dōrius*—Gr. *Dōrios*—*Dōris.*]

**Doric,** *dor'ik, adj.* belonging to Doris in Greece, or the Dorians, or their dialect: denoting one of the Greek orders of architecture, distinguished by its simplicity and massive strength.—*n.* a Greek dialect: any dialect imagined to resemble it, esp. Scottish.—*n.* **Doricism** (*dor'i-sizm*), a peculiarity of the Doric dialect.—*v.t.* and *v.i.* **dōr'ise, -ize,** to render or become like the Dorians, in language, manners, etc.—*n.* **Dō'rism,** Doricism: a Dorian characteristic. [L. *Dōricus* —Gr. *Dōrikos*—*Dōris.*]

**Doris,** *dō'ris, dö', n.* a genus of nudibranchiate gasteropods, shell-less molluscs with a plumy tuft of gills on the back, giving name to the family **Dorid'idae.**—*n.* and *adj.* **do'ridoid.** [Gr. *Dōris,* a sea-goddess.]

**Dorking,** *dörk'ing, n.* a square-bodied breed of poultry, variously coloured, and with five claws on each foot—so named from *Dorking* in Surrey.

**dorlach,** *dör'lahh, n.* a bundle, a truss: a sheaf: a valise. [Gael.]

**dormant,** *dör'mənt, adj.* sleeping: with suspended animation or development: torpid: at rest: not used, in abeyance (as a title): in a sleeping posture (*her.*).—*n.* a crossbeam: a joist.—*n.* **dor'mancy.** [O.Fr. *dormant,* pr.p. of *dormir*— L. *dormire,* to sleep.]

**dormer,** *dör'mər, n.* a dormitory or bedroom (*obs.*): a dormer-window.—**dor'mer-win'dow,** a small window with a gable, projecting from a sloping roof (orig. a dormitory window). [O.Fr. *dormeor*—L. *dormitōrium*—*dormire,* to sleep.]

**dormient,** *dör'mi-ənt, adj.* sleeping: dormant. [L. *dormiēns, -entis,* pr.p. of *dormire,* to sleep.]

**dormition,** *dör-mish'ən, n.* falling asleep: death— *n.* and *adj.* **dor'mitive,** soporific. [Fr.,—L. *dormire,* to sleep.]

**dormitory,** *dör'mi-tər-i, n.* a large sleeping-room with many beds, whether in separate cubicles or not: a resting-place: a college hostel (*U.S.*): a suburb where town workers dwell.—**dormitory-car** (*U.S.*), a railway sleeping-carriage. [L. *dormitōrium*—*dormire,* to sleep.]

**dormouse,** *dör'mows, n.* any member of the Myoxidae, a family of rodents akin to mice but somewhat squirrel-like in form and habit: —*pl.* **dor'mice.** [Perh. connected with L. *dōrmire,* to sleep (from their hibernation); prob. mouse.]

**dormy, dormie,** *dör'mi, adj.* in golf, as many holes up or ahead as there are yet to play. [Conjecturally connected with L. *dormire,* to sleep; the player who is *dormy* cannot lose though he go to sleep.]

**dornick,** *dör'nik, n.* a kind of stout figured linen,

originally made at *Doornik,* or Tournai, in Belgium.

**dorp,** *dörp, n.* a village, esp. Dutch. [Du. *dorp;* O.E. *thorp.*]

**dorsal,** *dör'sl, adj.* pertaining or belonging to the back.—*n.* a dorsal fin: a dorsal vertebra: a dossal.—*adv.* **dor'sally.**—*ns.* **dorse** (*obs.*), the back of a book or writing: a dossal: the back; **dor'sel,** a dossal; **dor'ser,** a dosser.—*adjs.* **dorsibranchiate** (*-brangk'),* having gills on the back; **dorsif'erous,** having sori on the back: carrying young on the back; **dor'sifixed** (*bot.*), of an anther, attached by the whole length of the back to the filament; **dor'siflex,** bent towards the back.—*n.* **dorsiflex'ion,** a bending backwards: a bending of the back, a bow.—*adjs.* **dor'sigrade,** walking on the back of the toes; **dorsiven'tral,** possessing two sides distinguishable as upper or ventral and lower or dorsal, as a leaf. —*ns.* **dorsiventral'ity; dors'um,** back.—**dorsal suture,** the seam at the midrib of a carpel.— **send to dorse,** to throw on the back. [L. *dorsum,* the back.]

**dorse,** *dörs, n.* a small cod. [Low Ger. *dorsch.*]

**dort,** *dört, (Scot.) v.i.* to sulk.—*n.pl.* **dorts,** sulks. —*adj.* **dor'ty,** pettish: delicate. [Origin unknown.]

**dorter, dortour,** *dör'tər, (arch.) n.* a dormitory, esp. monastic. [O.Fr. *dortour*—L. *dormitōrium;* see **dormer, dormitory.**]

**dory,** *dō'ri, dö', n.* a golden-yellow fish (*Zeus faber*) of the mackerel family.—Also **John Dory** and **Doree.** [Fr. *dorée,* from *dorer* to, gild—L. *deaurāre,* to gild—*dē-,* in the sense of over, *aurum,* gold.]

**dory,** *dō'ri, dö', (Amer.) n.* a small boat, with flat bottom, sharp bow and stern, especially suited for surf riding. [Origin unknown.]

**dos-à-dos,** *dō-za-dō, adv. (arch.)* back to back.— *n.* a sofa constructed for sitting so: a square-dance figure in which dancers pass each other back to back (*dō-sē-dō';* also **dosi-do**). [Fr.]

**dose,** *dōs,* in Scotland commonly *dōz,* *n.* the quantity of medicine, electric current, X-rays, etc., administered at one time: a portion, esp. a measured portion, of something given or added: anything disagreeable or medicinal to be taken: bout.—*v.t.* to order or give in doses: to give doses to.—*ns.* **dōs'age,** practice, act, or method of dosing: regulation of dose: addition of an ingredient: proper size of dose; **dosim'eter,** an instrument for measuring radiation, a small ionisation chamber with a scale on which can be read the dose which has caused it partially to discharge (also **dose-meter); dos(i)ol'ogy,** science of doses. [Fr.,—Gr. *dōsis,* a giving—*didonai,* to give.]

**doseh,** *dō'se, n.* a religious ceremony at Cairo (abolished 1884), during the festival of the Prophet's birth, when the sheikh of the Sa'di dervishes rode on horseback over the prostrate bodies of his followers. [Ar. *dawsah,* treading.]

**dosi-do.** See **dos-à-dos.**

**doss,** *dos, (slang) n.* a bed, sleeping-place: a sleep.—*v.i.* to sleep: to go to bed.—*n.* **doss'er,** one who lodges in a doss-house, or where he can sleep.—**doss'-house,** a very cheap lodging-house. [Perh. from *doss,* a dial. Eng. name for a hassock; or perh. **dorse** (see under **dorsal**).]

**dossal, dossel,** *dos'əl, n.* a cloth hanging for the back of an altar, sides of a church chancel, etc. [L.L. *dossāle, dorsāle*—L. *dorsum,* back.]

**dosser,** *dos'ər, n.* a rich hanging or tapestry for the walls of a hall or of a chancel: a pannier. [O.Fr. *dossier*—*dos*—L. *dorsum,* back.]

**dossier,** *do-syā, dos'i-ər, n.* a bundle of documents relating to a person or case: a brief. [Fr.,— *dos*—L. *dorsum,* back.]

**dossil,** *dos'il, n.* a plug, spigot: a cloth roll for wiping ink from an engraved plate in printing:

a pledget of lint for dressing a wound (*surg.*).
[O.Fr. *dosil*—L.L. *ducillus*, a spigot.]
**dost**, *dust*, 2nd pers. sing. pres. indic. of **do**.
**dot**, *dot*, *n.* a very small spot: a short element in
the Morse code.—*v.t.* to mark with a dot or dots:
to diversify with objects: to jot: to hit.—*v.i.* to
form dots: to limp:—*pr.p.* **dott′ing**; *pa.t.* and
*pa.p.* **dott′ed**.—*adj.* **dott′ed**, composed of dots:
marked with a dot or dots.—*adj.* **dott′y**, composed of, covered with, dots: unsteady (*coll.*):
feeble (*coll.*): crazed (*coll.*).—**dotted note**, (*mus.*)
one whose length is increased by one half by
a dot placed after it.—**dot and carry**, to set
down the units and carry over the tens to the
next column. [O.E. has *dott*, head of a boil;
Du. *dot*, tuft, knot.
**dot**, *dot*, *n.* a marriage portion.—*adj.* **dotal** (*dō′-
təl*), pertaining to dowry or to dower.—*n.*
**dōtä′tion**, the bestowing of a dowry: an endowment. [Fr.,—L. *dōs, dōtis*.]
**dote, doat**, *dōt*, *v.i.* to be stupid or foolish (*arch.*):
to be weakly affectionate: to show excessive
love (with *upon, on*): of timber, to decay.—*ns.*
**dōt′age**, a doting: childishness of old age:
excessive fondness; **dōt′ant** (*Shak.*), a dotard:
**dōt′ard**, one who dotes: one showing the weakness of old age, or excessive fondness.—*adj.*
**dōt′ed** (*Spens.*), stupid.—*n.* **dōt′er, doat′er**, one
who dotes.—*adj.* and *n.* **dōt′ing, doat′ing**.—*adj.*
**dōt′ish**, silly.—*n.* **dōtt′le** (*Scot.*), a dotard.—
*adjs.* **dōtt′le, -d** (*Scot.*), in dotage; **dōt′y**, decaying (of timber).—**dōt′ing-piece, doat′ing-piece**, one
who is doted on. [Cf. Old Du. *doten*, to be
silly; Fr. *radoter*, to rave, is from the same
root.]
**doth**, *duth*, 3rd pers. sing. pres. indic. of **do**.
**dotterel, dottrel**, *dot′(ə)rəl*, *n.* a kind of plover,
named from its apparent stupidity in allowing
itself to be approached and caught: a stupid
fellow, a dupe. [**dote**.]
**dottle**, *dot′l*, (*Scot.*) *n.* a plug, esp. of tobacco
left at the bottom of a pipe. [**dot**.]
**dottle, dottled**. See **dote**.
**dottle**, *dot′l*, (*Scot.*) *n.* a fool, a silly person.—
*adj.* foolish, crazy.—Also *adj.* **dottled**. [**dote**.]
**douane**, *dōō-än′, dwän*, *n.* a custom-house.—*n.*
**douanier** (*dwä-nyä*), a custom-house officer.
[Fr.,—Ar. *diwānç* cf. divan, diwan.]
**douar, dowar**, *dōō′är*. See **duar**.
**Douay**, *dōō-ā*, among Catholics often *dow′i*, *n.*
the town of *Douai* in France (Nord), historically
famous for its English and other Catholic colleges.—**Douay Bible**, an English Roman Catholic
translation of the Bible, the New Testament in
the Rhemish version, the Old done at Douai in
1609-10.
**double**, *dub′l*, *adj.* twofold: twice as much: of
about twice the weight, size, or quality: two
of a sort together: in pairs: paired: acting
two parts, insincere: folded once: sounding an
octave lower: having stamens in the form of
petals, or having ligulate in place of tubular
florets.—*adv.* to twice the extent: twice over:
two together: deceitfully.—*v.t.* to multiply by
two: to make twofold: to make twice as much
or as many: to be the double of: in acting, to
play by doubling: to be a substitute for or
counterpart of: (in bridge) to double the scoring
value of: to sound in another octave: to line
(*her.*): to fold: to clench: to pass (esp. sail)
round or by.—*v.i.* to increase to twice the
quantity: to turn sharply back on one's course
in running: to act as substitute: in acting, to
play two different parts in the same piece.—*n.*
a quantity twice as much: a score of twice the
amount shown, as in the outer ring of a dart-
board: a combination of two things of the
same kind (as a binary star): in tennis, a game
with two players on each side: in tennis, two
faults in succession: a win, or a defeat, in two

events on the same programme: a combined
bet on two races, stake and winnings from the
first being bet on the second: a Guernsey
copper coin, ⅛th of a penny: a duplicate: an
actor's substitute: a quick pace (short for
**double-quick**): one's wraith or apparition: an
exact counterpart: a turning upon one's course:
a trick: a feast on which the antiphon is said
both before and after the psalms (*eccles.*): a size
of roofing slate, 13 × 6 inches (330 × 152 mm.).—
*ns.* **doub′leness**, the state of being double: duplicity; **doub′ler**, one who or that which doubles;
**doub′ling**, the act of making double: a turning
back in running: a trick: a plait or fold:
mantling (*her.*).—*adj.* shifting, manoeuvring.—
*adv.* **doub′ly**.—*adj.* **doub′le-act′ing**, applying
power in two directions: producing a double
result.—**doub′le-ā′gent**, one secretly acting simultaneously for two opposing powers; **doub′le-
axe′**, a religious symbol of Minoan Crete and
the Aegean, a double-headed axe, associated
with the mother-goddess and her son (*Zeus*).—
*adjs.* **doub′le-banked′**, having two men at each
oar, or having two tiers of oars one above the
other, as in ancient galleys.—**doub′le-bar′**, a
double vertical line marking the end of a movement or piece of music or one of its important
divisions.—*adj.* **doub′le-barr′elled**, having two
barrels: of a surname, hyphened: of a compliment, ambiguous.—**doub′le-bass′**, a stringed instrument—contrabass or *violone*.—*adjs.*
**doub′le-bit′ing**, cutting on either side; **doub′le-
breast′ed**, of a coat, having two breasts, one to
be folded over the other.—*v.t.* **doub′le-charge′**,
to load with double measure.—**doub′le-chin′**,
a chin with a fold of flesh; **doub′le-co′conut**,
the coco-de-mer; **doub′le-cross**, a betrayal of
both sides, as when one who has arranged
to lose a contest sets himself to win.—*v.t.*
to betray by double-cross.—**doub′le-cross′er**;
**doub′le-dagg′er**, a diesis (‡); **doub′le-deal′er**, a
deceitful person; **doub′le-deal′ing**, duplicity.—
*adj.* **doub′le-decked**, having two decks.—**doub′le-
deck′er**, a double-decked ship: a bus, tram-car,
etc., in two stories or tiers; **doub′le-decom-
posi′tion**, a chemical action in which two compounds exchange some of their constituents;
**doub′le-Dutch**, incomprehensible talk.—*adj.*
**doub′le-dyed**, twice-dyed: deeply imbued.—
**doub′le-ea′gle** (*U.S.*), a gold coin worth $20:
heraldic representation of an eagle with two
heads, as in the old arms of Russia and Austria.
—*adj.* **doub′le-edged′**, having two edges: cutting
or working both ways.—**doub′le-end′er**, anything
having two ends alike: a cross-cut sawing machine with two adjustable circular saws for sawing
both ends of timber; **doub′le-en′try** (*book-k.*), a
method by which two entries are made of each
transaction.—*adjs.* **doub′le-eyed**, doubly keen of
sight; **doub′le-faced**, hypocritical, false.—
**doub′le-fā′cedness**; **double figures**, a score or
total of any number from 10 to 99 (inclusive);
**doub′le-first**, a university degree with first-class
honours in two different subjects: one who
takes such a degree; **doub′le-flat′**, a note already
flat flattened again by a semitone: a sign indicating this.—*adjs.* **doub′le-flower′ed**, having
double flowers, as a plant; **doub′le-form′d′**,
having, or combining, two forms; **doub′le-
fount′ed**, having two sources.—*v.t.* **doub′le-
gild**, to gild with double coatings of gold: to
gloze over.—**double-glaz′ing**, a double layer
of glass in a window with an air-space
between the layers to act as insulation.—*adj.*
**doub′le-glazed′**.—**doub′le-Glos′ter**, Gloucestershire cheese of extra richness.—*adj.* **doub′le-
hand′ed**, having two hands: two-handled;
**doub′le-head′ed**, having two heads; **doub′le-
heart′ed**, treacherous.—**double helix**, the DNA
molecule.—*adj.* **doub′le-hung** (of a window) hav-

ing top and bottom sashes each balanced by sash-cord and weights, so as to be capable of vertical movement in its own groove.—**double jeopardy**, second trial for the same offence.—*adjs.* **doub′le-joint′ed**, having joints admitting some degree of movement backward; **doub′le-lived′**, having two lives; **doub′le-locked′**, locked with two locks or bolts: locked by two turns of the key, as in very few locks but many novels; **doub′le-manned′**, furnished with twice the complement of men; **doub′le-meaning′**, ambiguous.—Also *n.*—*adj.* **doub′le-mind′ed**, undetermined, wavering.—**doub′le-mind′edness**.—*adjs.* **doub′le-mouth′d′**, speaking with contradictory voices; **doub′le-nā′tured**, having a twofold nature.—*adj.* and *adv.* **doub′le-quick′**, at a pace approaching a run.—*n.* the double-quick pace.—**double salt**, a salt whose crystals dissolve to give two different salts in solution.—*v.t.* **doub′le-shade′** (*Milt.*), to double the darkness of.— **doub′le-sharp′**, a note already sharp sharpened again by a semitone: a sign indicating this.—*adj.* **doub′le-shott′ed**, of cannon, with double charge.—**doub′le-shuff′le**, a scraping movement made twice with each foot: a dance of such steps: a trick; **doub′le-stopp′ing**, playing on two stopped strings of an instrument at once.—*adj.* **doub′le-sto′rey**, of a building, having two floors, tiers.—**doub′le-stout′**, extra strong stout or porter.—**doub′le-take**, a second look impelled by surprise or admiration: delayed reaction; **doub′le-talk**, talk that sounds to the purpose but amounts to nothing: ambiguous, deceptive talk; **doub′le-think**, the faculty of simultaneously harbouring two conflicting beliefs —coined by George Orwell in his *Nineteen Eighty-Four* (1949).—*adj.* **doub′le-tongued′**, having two tongues or a cleft tongue: self-contradictory: deceitful.—**doub′le-you, -u**, (*dub′l-ū*), the twenty-third letter of the alphabet (W, w).—**double or quits** (see **quit**); **double up**, to fold double: to bend over (as with laughter): to come at the double: to share with another. [O.Fr. *doble*—L. *duplus*, double—*duo*, two, and the root seen in Eng. **fold**, Gr. *haploos*.]

**double entendre**, *dōō-blä-tä-dr′*, *n.* a word or phrase with two meanings, one usually more or less indecent. [Fr. of 17th century, superseded now by (*mot*) *à double entente*.]

**doublet**, *dub′lit*, *n.* a close-fitting garment for the upper part of the body—with *hose*, the typical masculine dress in the 14th-17th c.: a thing that is repeated or duplicated: one of a pair, esp. one of two words orig. the same but varying in spelling and meaning, *e.g. balm, balsam*. [O.Fr., dim. of *double*.]

**doubloon**, *dub-lōōn′*, *n.* an obsolete Spanish gold coin, orig. = 2 pistoles. [Sp. *doblón*, aug. of *doble*, double; see **double**.]

**doubt**, *dowt*, *v.i.* to be undecided in opinion: to be apprehensive (*obs.*).—*v.t.* to hold in doubt: to hesitate or scruple: to incline to believe with fear or hesitation: to distrust: to incline to think (esp. *Scot.*): to suspect (*arch.* also *refl.*): to cause to doubt or fear (*obs.*).—*n.* uncertainty of opinion: suspicion: fear (*obs.*): thing doubtful or questioned (*obs.*): danger (*Spens.*).—*adj.* **doubt′able**.— *adj.* **doubt′ed** (*Spens.*), redoubted: feared: questioned.—*n.* **doubt′er**.—*adj.* **doubt′ful**, full of doubt: undetermined: subject to doubt: not clear: insecure: suspicious: not confident.—*n.* a doubtful person or thing.—*adv.* **doubt′fully**.—*n.* **doubt′fulness**.—*n.* and *adj.* **doubt′ing**.—*adv.* **doubt′ingly**.—*adj.* **doubt′less**, free from doubt or (*Shak.*) fear.—*adv.* without doubt: certainly: no doubt (often a mere concession of possibility).—*adv.* **doubt′lessly**.—**beyond doubt, certain(ly)**; **in doubt**, not certain, undecided; **no doubt** (see **no**). [O.Fr. *douter*—L. *dubitāre*, akin to *dubious*, doubtful, moving in two (*duo*) directions.]

**douc**, *dōōk*, *n.* a variegated monkey in Cochin-China. [Fr., from Cochin name.]

**douce**, *dōōs. adj.* sweet (*obs.*): sober, peaceable, sedate (*Scot.*).—*adv.* **douce′ly**.—*ns.* **douce′ness**; **doucet, dowset** (*dōō′, dow′sit; obs.*), a sweet dish: (in *pl.*) a deer's testicles; **douceur** (*dōō-sûr′*), sweetness of manner (*obs.*): a compliment (*arch.*): a conciliatory present, bribe, or tip. [Fr. *doux, douce*, mild—L. *dulcis*, sweet.]

**douche**, *dōōsh*, *n.* a jet of water directed upon or into the body from a pipe: an apparatus for throwing it.—*v.t.* to turn a douche upon. [Fr.,—It. *doccia*, a water-pipe—L. *dūcĕre*, to lead.]

**doucine**, *dōō-sēn′*, (*archit.*) *n.* a cyma recta. [Fr.]

**dough**, *dō*, *n.* a mass of flour or meal moistened and kneaded, but not baked: money (*slang*).—*n.* **dough′iness**.—*adj.* **dough′y**, like dough: soft: of complexion, pallid, pasty (*coll.*).—*adj.* **dough′-baked**, half-baked, defective in intelligence.—**dough′-boy**, boiled flour dumpling (*U.S.*): an American infantryman (*mil. slang*).—*adjs.* **dough′faced** (*U.S.*), pliable, truckling; **dough′-kneaded** (*Milt.*), soft.—**dough′nut**, sweetened dough fried in fat: an accelerating tube in the form of a toroid (*nucleonics*): a toroidal assembly of enriched fissile material for increasing locally the neutron intensity in a reactor for experimental purposes (*nucleonics*). [O.E. *dāh*; Ger. *teig*, O.N. *deig*, dough; cf. **duff**.]

**doughty**, *dow′ti*, *adj.* able, strong: brave.—*adv.* **dough′tily**.—*n.* **dough′tiness**. [O.E. *dyhtig*, later *dohtig*, valiant—*dugan*, to be strong; Ger. *tüchtig*, able.]

**Douglas fir**, *dug′las fûr*, *n.* a tall western American coniferous timber tree (*Pseudotsuga Douglasii*). [David *Douglas* (1798-1834), who introduced it to Britain.]

**Doukhobor**. See **Dukhobor**.

**doulocracy**. See **dulia**.

**douma**. See **duma**.

**doum-palm**, *dowm′, dōōm′-päm*, *n.* an African palm (*Hyphaene*), with a branched stem, and a fruit with the taste of gingerbread.—Also **doom′-**, **dum′-palm**. [Ar. *daum, dūm*.]

**doup**, *dowp*, (*Scot.*) *n.* the end of an egg-shell: the buttocks.—**can′dle-doup**, a candle-end. [Cf. O.N. *daup*, a hollow.]

**dour**, *dōōr*, (*Scot.*) *adj.* obstinate: sullen: grim.—*n.* **dour′ness**. [Apparently L. *dūrus*, hard.]

**doura**. See **durra**.

**dourine**, *dōō-rēn′, dōō′rēn*, *n.* a contagious disease of horses due to a trypanosome. [Fr. *dourin*.]

**douroucouli, durukuli**, *dōō-rōō-kōō′lē*, *n.* a nightape, any monkey of the S. American genus *Nyctipithecus*. [S. Amer. name.]

**douse, dowse**, *dows, v.t.* to plunge into water.—*v.i.* to fall suddenly into water. [Cf. Sw. *dunsa*, fall heavily; prob. from sound; cf. **souse**.]

**douse, dowse**, *dows, v.t.* to strike: to strike or lower (a sail).—*n.* a heavy blow. [Prob. related to Old Du. *dossen*, to beat.]

**douse, dowse**, *dows, v.t.* to put out, extinguish (esp. in the slang **douse the glim**, put out the light).—*n.* **dous′er**, a shutter for cutting off light in a cinema projector. [Perh. connected with **dout**, or with **douse** (2).]

**dout**, *dowt, v.t.* to put out, extinguish.—*n.* **dout′er**. [**do out**.]

**douzepers**, *dōō′zə-pär, n.pl.* the twelve peers of Charlemagne, or similar group:—*sing.* **douzeper**; **doucepere** (*Spens.*), a champion, grand knight or noble. [O.Fr. *douze pers*, twelve peers.]

**dove**, *duv, n.* a pigeon (esp. in comp., as *ring-dove, turtle-dove*, etc.): a word of endearment: an emblem of innocence, gentleness, also of the Holy Spirit (Matt. iii. 16).—*v.t.* to treat as a dove.—*n.* **dove′let**, a small dove.—*adj.* **dove′-like**, like a dove: innocent.—**dove′-colour**, a greyish, bluish, pinkish colour; **dove′cot, -cote**, a small cot or box in which pigeons breed: a pigeon-house.—*adjs.* **dove'-drawn** (*Shak.*) drawn by doves; **dove'-eyed**, meek-eyed.—**dove'-house**, a dovecot; **dove's'-foot**, a name for some species of cranesbill (*Geranium dissectum, Geranium molle*, etc.); **dove'tail**, a tenon shaped like a dove's spread tail, for fastening boards: a joint of alternate tenons and mortises of that shape.—*v.t.* and *v.i.* to fit by, or as if by, dovetail.—**dove'tailing**.—doves and hawks, the conciliatory and aggressive parties in a political administration, or similarly opposing parties in any conditions where conflict of policy is involved, **flutter the dove-cots**, to disturb commonplace, conventional people, as the eagle would a dovecot (see *Shak., Cor.* V, vi, 115). [O.E. *dūfe*, found only in the compound *dūfe-doppa*, a diving bird; Ger. *taube*.]

**dove**, *dōv*, (*Scot.*) *v.i.* to be half asleep or stupefied. —*v.i.* **do'ver** (*Scot.*), to snooze, doze.—*v.t.* to stun.—*n.* a snooze: a swoon: half-consciousness. [O.E. *dofian*, to be stupid.]

**dove**, *dōv, U.S. pa.t.* of dive.

**dovekie**, *duv'ki, n.* the little auk or rotche: the black guillemot. [Dim. of dove.]

**Dover's powder**, *dō'vərz pow'dər, n.* a sudorific compounded of ipecacuanha root, opium and potassium sulphate. [First prescribed by Dr. Thomas *Dover* (1660–1742).]

**dow.** See dhow.

**dow**, *dow*, (*obs.* and *Scots*) *v.i.* to be good for a purpose: to avail: to be able:—3rd pers. sing. **dow, dows;** *pa.t.* **docht, dought** (*dohht*), **dowed.**—**dow'na** (*neg.*) cannot: cannot be bothered.—*n.* **dow'na-do,** powerlessness. [O.E. *dugan.*]

**dowager**, *dow'ə-jər, n.* a widow with a dower or jointure: a title given to a widow to distinguish her from the wife of her husband's heir: an elderly woman of imposing appearance. [O.Fr. *douagere*—L.L. *dōtārium*, dower—L. *dōtāre*, to endow.]

**dowd**, *dowd*, **dowdy**, *dowd'i, ns.* a woman who wears dull-looking clumsy ill-shaped clothes.— Also *adj.*—*adv.* **dowd'ily.**—*n.* **dowd'iness.**—*adj.* **dowd'yish.**—*n.* **dowd'yism.** [Origin unknown.]

**dowel**, *dow'əl, n.* a pin for fastening things together by fitting into a hole in each.—*v.t.* to fasten by means of dowels.—*ns.* **dow'el-joint; dow'el-pin; dow'el-rod.** [Prob. related to Ger. *döbel*, a plug.]

**dower**, *dow'ər, n.* a jointure: a dowry: an endowment.—*v.t.* to bestow a dowry upon: to endow. —*adj.* **dow'able,** that may be endowed.—*adj.* **dow'erless**—**dow'er-house,** the house set apart for the widow. [O.Fr. *douaire*—L.L. *dōtārium* —L. *dōtāre*, to endow.]

**dowf**, *dowf,* (*Scot.*) *adj.* dull, heavy, spiritless.— *n.* **dowf'ness.** [Prob. O.N. *daufr*, deaf.]

**dowie**, *dow'i,* (*Scot.*) *adj.* dull, low-spirited, sad: dismal. [Prob. O.E. *dol*, dull.]

**dowl, dowle**, *dowl,* (*Shak.*) *n.* a portion of down in a feather: a piece of fluff. [Origin obscure.]

**dowlas**, *dow'ləs, n.* a coarse linen cloth. [From *Daoulas* or *Doulas*, near Brest, in Brittany.]

**down**, *down, n.* soft feathers: a soft covering of fluffy hair.—*adj.* **downed,** filled or covered with down.—*n.* **down'iness.**—*adj.* **down'y,** covered with or made of down: like down: knowing (*slang*). —**down'-bed; down'-quilt.—the downy** (*old slang*), **bed.—The spellings dowlne, dowlney** (*Shak.*) show confusion with dowl. [O.N. *dūnn*; Ger. *daune, dune.*]

**down**, *down, n.* a bank of sand thrown up by the sea (same as **dune**): a treeless upland: (in *pl.*) an undulating upland tract of pasture-land, esp. in S.E. England (**the Downs**) also the roadstead off E. Kent.—*n.* **down'land.** [O.E. *dūn,* a hill—Celt. *dun.*]

**down**, *down, adv.* (passing into *adj.* in predicative use), to a lower position, level or state: away from a centre (capital, great town, university, etc.): southward: to leeward: in a low or lowered position or state: below: on or to the ground: downstairs: under the surface: from earlier to later times: to a further stage in a series: from greater to less (in size, grain, activity, intensity, etc.): to a standstill, exhaustion, or conclusion: to a final state of defeat, subjection, silence, etc.: in a fallen state: in adversity: at a disadvantage: ill: behindhand: in writing or record, in black and white: in flood: on the spot, in cash: in readiness to pounce: in a state of alert awareness and understanding: in watchful opposition or hostility (with *on, upon*).—Also elliptically, passing into an interjection or verb by omission of *go, come, put,* etc., often followed by *with.—adj.* going, reaching, or directed towards a lower position or level: depressed: low.—*prep.* in a descent along, through, or by: to or in a lower position on or in: along in the direction of the current: along.—*n.* a descent: a low place: a reverse of fortune: an act of throwing or putting down: a tendency to be down on one.—*v.t.* to knock, throw or set down: to put down, overthrow: to dispirit.—*advs.* **down'ward, down'wards** (-*wərd(s)*), from higher to lower: from source to outlet: from more ancient to modern: in the lower part.—*adj.* **down'ward.**—*adv.* **down'wardly.**—*n.* **down'wardness,** a sinking tendency: a state of being low.—*adj.* **down'-and-out',** at the end of one's resources.—Also *ns.* **down'-and-out'(er).** —*adj.* **down'-at-heel',** having the back of the shoe trodden down: generally shabby.—**down'-beat,** a downward movement of the conductor's baton: an accented beat; **down'bow** (*mus.*), a movement of bow over strings beginning at the nut end.—*adj.* **down'cast,** dejected.—*n.* a current of air into a mine: a shaft carrying it (**down'-cast-shaft'**): a downward throw: a downthrow. —**down'-come,** a fall, ruin: a heavy pour of rain; **down'-draught,** a current of air downwards; **down'-east'er,** one living *down east* from the speaker, a New Englander, and esp. an inhabitant of Maine; **down'fall,** fall, failure, humiliation, ruin: a falling down, as of rain.—*adjs.* **down'-fallen,** ruined; **down'-going.—down-go'ing** (of *down'*); **down'grade,** a downward slope or course.—*adj.* and *adv.* downhill.—*v.t.* to reduce in status: to belittle, underrate.—*adj.* **down'-gyved** (*Shak.*), hanging down like fetters.— **down'-haul,** a rope by which a jib, etc., is hauled down when set.—*adjs.* **down'-heart'ed,** dejected; **down'hill,** descending, sloping.—Also *n.—adv.* **downhill'.—down'-line,** the line of a railway leading from the capital, or other important centre, to the provinces.—*adj.* **down'looked** (*Dryden*), downcast, gloomy.—**down'-ly'ing** (*dial.*), time of retiring to rest: a woman's lying-in.—*adv.* and *adj.* **down'most,** superlative of *down.*—**down'pour,** a heavy fall of rain, etc.— *adv.* **down'right** (*obs.*), perpendicular: in plain terms: utterly.—*adj.* plain-spoken: brusque: utter, out-and-out (as in *downright madness*).— **down'rightness; down'rush,** a rushing down (as of gas, hot air, etc.); **down'-sett'ing,** a setting down, a snub; **down'-sitt'ing,** sitting down, time of rest (Ps. cxxxix, 2): a sitting, session (*Scot.*): a settlement, establishment (esp. by marriage; *Scot.*).—*advs.* **down'stage',** towards the footlights (also *adj.*); **downstairs',** in, or towards, a lower storey.—*adj.* **down'stair(s).—n.** a position downstairs.—*adv.* **downstream',** with the current.—*adj.* **down'stream,** further down the stream: going with the current.—**down'stroke,** a downward line made by the pen in writing.— *adj.* **down'-the-line,** of a ballet-dancer, inconspicuously placed, unimportant.—**down'-throw,** act of throwing down, state of being thrown down: the amount of vertical displacement of the relatively lowered strata at a fault (*geol.*).— *v.i.* **down'-tools',** to strike.—*adj.* and *adv.* **down'-**

town', in or towards the lower part or (*U.S.*) the business and shopping centre of the town.—down'-train, a railway train proceeding from the chief terminus.—*adj.* down'-trod, -trodden, trampled on: tyrannised over.—down'turn, downward trend, decline.—down east (*U.S.*), in or into Maine and adjoining parts of New England; down in the mouth, in low spirits; down on one's luck, in ill-luck; down south, in the southern states; down to the ground (*coll.*), completely; down town, in or towards the centre of a town; down under, at the antipodes: down with, put down: swallow; go downhill, to deteriorate (in health, prosperity, morality); go down with, be acceptable to: contract (illness); up and down, often merely to and fro. [M.E. *a-down*, *adun*—O.E. *of dūne*, from the hill (dat. case of *dūn*, hill; see foregoing and adown).]

downa. See dow (2).

Downing Street, *down'ing*, the street in London where the Prime Minister's official residence is, as well as the Foreign and Commonwealth Office: the government.

Down's syndrome, *downz*, Mongolism.

dowry, *dow'ri*. *n.* the property which a woman brings to her husband at marriage—sometimes used for dower: sometimes a gift given to or for a wife at marriage: a natural endowment. [See dower.]

dowse, *dows*, *v.t.* and *v.i.* See douse.

dowse, *dowz*, *v.i.* to use the divining-rod.—*n.* dows'er, a water-diviner. [Origin unknown.]

doxographer, *doks-og'rə-fər*, *n.* a compiler of opinions of philosophers.—*ns.* doxog'raphy; doxol'ogy, a hymn or liturgical formula ascribing glory to God. [Gr. *doxa*, opinion, reputation, glory, *graphein*, write, *legein*, speak, *logos*, discourse.]

doxy, *dok'si*, *n.* a mistress (*Shak.*): a woman of loose character. [Origin unknown.]

doxy, *dok'si*, *n.* opinion—'Orthodoxy', said Warburton, 'is my doxy—heterodoxy is another man's doxy'. [Gr. *doxa*, opinion.]

doyen, *doi'ən*, *dwä-yā*, *n.* dean, senior member (of an academy, diplomatic corps, class, profession, etc.):—*fem.* doyenne (*doi-en'*, *dwä-yen*). [Fr.,— L. *decānus*.]

doyley. See doily.

doze, *dōz*, *v.i.* to sleep lightly, or to be half-asleep: to be in a dull or stupefied state.—*v.t.* to spend in drowsiness (with *away*).—*n.* a short light sleep.— *adj.* dōzed, drowsy.—*v.t.* dō'zen (*Scot.*), to stupefy.—*v.i.* to become stupefied.—*ns.* dō'zer: dō'ziness; dō'zing.—*adj.* dō'zy, drowsy: beginning to decay. [Cf. O.N. *dūsa*. Dan. *döse*.]

dozen, *duz'n*, *n.* a set of twelve:—*pl.* dozen, when preceded by a numeral, otherwise dozens.—*adj.* doz'enth—half-a-dozen, six.—baker's, devil's, long, dozen, thirteen; daily dozen (see daily); round dozen, full dozen. [O.Fr. *dozeine*—L. *duodecim* (*duo*, two, and *decem*, ten), and neut. pl. ending -*ēna* (Cf. Sp. *docena*).]

drab, *drab*, *n.* a low, sluttish woman: a whore.— *v.i.* to associate with drabs.—*ns.* drabb'er, one who herds with drabs; drabb'iness.—*adjs.* drabb'- ish, drabb'y, sluttish. [Poss. Gael. *drabag*; Ir. *drabog*, slut; or L.G. *drabbe*, dirt.]

drab, *drab*, *n.* thick, strong, grey cloth: a grey or dull-brown colour, perh. from the muddy colour of undyed wool: uninteresting unvaried dull- ness.—*adj.* of the colour of drab: dull and monotonous.—*n.* drabb'et, a coarse linen fabric used for smock-frocks.—Also drabette'.—*adv.* drab'ly.—*n.* drab'ness. [Perh. Fr. *drap*, cloth— L.L. *drappus*, prob. Gmc.; see drape.]

drabble, *drab'l*, *v.t.* to besmear, bedraggle.—*n.* drabb'ling, a manner of fishing for barbels with a rod and long line passed through a piece of lead.—*n.* drabb'ler, drab'ler, an additional piece of canvas, laced to the bottom of the bonnet of a

sail, to give it greater depth. [L. Ger. *drabbeln*, to wade about.]

Dracaena, *drä-sē'na*, *n.* the dragon-tree genus. [L.L. *dracaena*, a she-dragon—Gr. *drakaina*, fem. of *drakōn*, dragon.]

drachm, *dram*, *n.* a drachma: a dram.

drachma, *drak'ma*, *n.* an ancient Greek weight, and a silver coin of different values: a modern Greek franc:—*pl.* drach'mas, drach'mae (-*mē*) drach'mai (-*mi*). [Gr. *drachmē*—*drassesthai*, to grasp with the hand.]

Draco, *drä'kō*, *n.* the Dragon, a northern constella- tion: a dragon-lizard.—*adj.* draconian (*drak-*, *drak-ō'ni-ən*), draconic (-*on'ik*), of, of the nature of, a dragon.—*ns.* draconites (*drak-ə-ni'tēz*), a precious stone fabled to come from a dragon's brain; dracontiasis (*drak-ən-ti'ə-sis*), Guinea- worm disease; Dracontium (*drə-kon'shi-əm*), a S. American araceous genus once of medical repute; Dracunculus (*drə-kungk'ū-ləs*), the green dragon genus of Araceae; dracunculus, the dragonet: the Guinea-worm. [L. *dracō*, -*ōnis*, and Gr. *drakōn*, -*ontos*, a dragon or snake, dims. L. *dracunculus*, Gr. *drakontion*, prob. from the root of Gr. *derkesthai*, to look.]

Draconian, *drə-* or *drä-kō'ni-ən*, Dracontic (-*kont'ik*), *adjs.* extremely severe, as the laws of Draco (Gr. *Drakōn*), archon at Athens 621 B.C. —*n.* Draconism (*drak'ən-izm*).

drad, *drad*, (*Spens.*) *pa.t.* and *pa.p.* of dread.— *adj.* (*Spens.*) dread.

draff, *dräf*, *n.* dregs: the refuse of malt after brewing.—*adjs.* draff'ish, draff'y, worthless. [Prob. related to Du. *draf*, Ger. *träber*.]

draft, *dräft*, *n.* anything drawn: the selecting of a smaller body of men, animals, things) from a larger: the body so selected (esp. *mil.*): a member of it: conscription (*U.S.*): an order for the payment of money: a demand (upon re- sources, credulity, patience, etc.): a plan: a preliminary sketch: (occasional and *U.S.*) a draught (in various senses).—*v.t.* to draw an outline of: to draw up in preliminary form: to draw off: to detach.—*ns.* draftee', a conscript; draft'er, draught'er, one who drafts: a draught- horse.—draft'-bar, a draw-bar.—draft'-horse, draft'-ox, drafts, drafts'man, drafts'manship (see draught). [draught.]

drag, *drag*, *v.t.* to draw by force: to draw slowly: to pull roughly and violently: to trail: to explore with a drag-net or hook: to apply a drag to.— *v.i.* to hang so as to trail on the ground: to be forcibly drawn along: to move slowly and heavily: to lag: to give the feeling of being unduly slow or tedious:—*pr.p.* dragg'ing; *pa.t.*, *pa.p.* dragged.—*n.* anything dragged: an act of dragging: a dragging effect: the component of the aerodynamic force on an aircraft that lies along the longitudinal axis (*aero.*): a net or hook for dragging along to catch things under water: a heavy harrow: a device for guiding wood to the saw: a car, lorry or wagon (*slang*): a mail-coach: a long open carriage, with trans- verse or side seats: a contrivance for retarding a wheel, esp. an iron shoe that drags on the ground: any obstacle to progress: a tedious, dreary occupation or experience (*slang*): influ- ence, pull (*U.S.*): a trail of scent: an artificial scent dragged on the ground for foxhounds to follow: a short 'draw' on a cigarette (*slang*): a retarded motion of the cue-ball imparted by striking somewhat under the centre (*billiards*): transvestite clothing, now usu. women's dress worn by a man (*slang*): a homosexuals' party (*slang*).—*n.* drag'ster, a car for drag-racing.— drag'-bar, a draw-bar; drag'-chain, a chain used as drag to a wheel: a chain for coupling railway vehicles; drag'hound, a foxhound trained to follow a drag; drag'-hunt; drag'line, an exca- vating machine, crane-like in appearance, moving on articulated tracks (or, **walking drag-line**, on 'legs' having steel plates as 'feet'), and drawing towards itself a bucket suspended from a long jib; **drag'-man**, a fisherman who uses a drag-net; **drag'-net**, a net to be dragged along the bottom of water or the ground; **drag race**, a contest in acceleration, with standing start and quarter-mile course; **drag'-racing**; **drag'-shot**, a shot that imparts drag to a billiard-ball; **drags'man**, the driver of a drag or coach.—**drag one's feet**, to hang back deliberately in doing something. [North.—O.E. *dragan* or O.N. *draga*.]

**dragée**, *drä-zhā, n.* a sweetmeat enclosing a drug, or a nut or fruit, etc.: a chocolate drop: a small silvered ball for decorating a cake. [Fr.]

**draggle**, *drag'l, v.t.* or *v.i.* to make or become wet and dirty, as by dragging along the ground: to trail.—**dragg'le-tail**, a slut.—*adj.* **dragg'le-tailed**. [Freq. of drag, and a doublet of drawl.]

**dragoman**, *drag'ō-mən, n.* an interpreter or guide in Eastern countries:—*pl.* **drag'omans**. [Fr., from Ar. *tarjumān*—*tarjama*, to interpret.]

**dragon**, *drag'ən, n.* a fabulous winged scaly-armoured fire-breathing monster, often a guardian of treasure, ravaging a country when its hoard is rifled: a fierce, intimidating, or watchful person: a paper kite: a dragon-lizard: applied to various plants, esp. Dracunculus (green dragon), and Dracontium; (with *cap.*), a northern constellation (Draco).—*ns.* **drag'oness**, a she-dragon; **drag'onet**, a little dragon: a goby of the genus Callionymus.—*v.t.* **drag'onise**, **-ize**, to turn into a dragon: to watch like a dragon.—*adjs.* **drag'onish**, **drag'onlike**.—*n.* **drag'-onism**, unremitting watchfulness.—*adj.* **dragonné** (*drag-o-nā'*; *her.*), like a dragon in the hinder part.—**drag'on-fish**, a dragonet: a fish of the genus *Pegasus*; **drag'onfly**, a predaceous long-bodied often brilliantly-coloured insect of the *Odonata*; **drag'onhead**, **drag'on's-head**, a labiate garden plant (*Dracocephalum*)—from the shape of the corolla; **dragon lizard**, a small tree-dwelling E. Indian lizard (*Draco*) with parachute of ribs and skin: a S. American lizard (*Thorictis*): a monitor, esp. a species (*Varanus komodoensis*) found in Komodo (in Indonesia), reaching 10 feet in length; **drag'on-root** (*U.S.*), an araceous plant (Arisaema) or its tuberous root, used in medicine; **drag'on's-blood**, a red resinous exudation from the dragon-tree and many other trees, used for colouring varnishes, etc.; **drag'on-stand'ard**, a standard in, or bearing, the form of a dragon; **drag'on-tree'**, a great tree of the Canary Islands (*Dracaena draco*), of the Liliaceae, remarkable for its resin (a variety of dragon's blood), its growth in thickness like a dicotyledon, and the great age it attains. [Fr.,—L. *dracō*, *-ōnis*—Gr. *drakōn*, *-ontos*, perh.—root *drak*, as in *edrakon*, aorist of *derkesthai*, to see clearly.]

**dragonnade**, *drag-ən-ād', n.* the persecution of French Protestants under Louis XIV by means of dragoons: any persecution by military means (usu. in *pl.*). [Fr., from *dragon*, dragoon.]

**dragoon**, *drə-gōōn', n.* an old fire-spitting musket: a mounted infantryman armed with it (*obs.*): a heavy cavalryman, as opp. to hussars and lancers —surviving in the names of certain regiments.—*v.t.* to compel by military bullying: to coerce.—**dragoon'-bird**, the umbrella-bird. [Fr. *dragon*, dragon, dragoon.]

**dragsman**. See drag.

**drail**, *drāl, n.* the iron bow of a plough from which the traces draw: a piece of lead round the shank of the hook in fishing.—*v.i.* to draggle. [Prob. a combination of draggle and trail.]

**drain**, *drān, v.t.* to draw off by degrees: to filter: to draw off water, sewage, or other liquid from: to furnish means of withdrawal of liquid from:

to make dry: to drink dry: to exhaust.—*v.i.* to flow off gradually: to part with liquid by flowing, trickling or dripping: to discharge.—*n.* a water-course: a channel for escape of liquid: a ditch: a sewer: a drink (*slang*): exhausting expenditure.—*adj.* **drain'able**.—*ns.* **drain'age**, act, process, method, or means of draining: mode of discharge of water: the system of drains in a town; **drain'er**, a device on which articles are placed to drain.—**drain'age-basin**, the area of land that drains into one river; **drain'age-tube**, a tube for discharge of pus, etc.; **drain'-pipe**, a pipe to carry away waste water or rainwater: (in *pl.*; *coll.*) very narrow trousers; **drain'-tile**, a contrivance for preventing the escape of foul air from drains, while admitting water to them.—**down the drain** (*slang*), gone for good: wasted. [O.E. *drēahnian*.]

**drake**, *drāk, n.* the male of the duck: a flat stone thrown so as to skip along the surface of water in playing ducks and drakes (also **drake'stone**). [Ety. obscure; cf. prov. Ger. *draak*; O.H.G. *antrahho*, Ger. *enterich*, the first element usually explained as *eend*, *end*, *anut*, duck.]

**drake**, *drāk, n.* a dragon: a fiery meteor: a beaked galley, or viking ship of war; an angler's name for species of Ephemera. [O.E. *draca*, dragon—L. *dracō*.]

**dram**, *dram, n.* a contraction of **drachm**: 1/16th of an ounce. avoirdupois: formerly, with apothecaries, ⅛th of an oz.: a small drink of alcoholic liquor: a tipple.—*v.i.* to drink a dram.—*v.t.* to give a dram to.—**dram'-drink'er; dram'-shop**. [Through Fr. and L., from Gr. *drachmē*. See **drachma**.]

**drama**, *dräm'ə, n.* a story of life and action for representation by actors: a composition intended to be represented on the stage: dramatic literature: theatrical entertainment: a dramatic situation, or series of absorbing events.—*adjs.* **dramat'ic** (*drə-mat'ik*), **-al**, belonging to the drama: appropriate to or in the form of drama: with the force and vividness of the drama.—*adv.* **dramat'ically**.—*ns.* **dramat'icism**; **dramat'ics** (*pl.* treated as *sing.*), the acting, production, study of plays: show of excessive, exaggerated emotion (*coll.*).—*adj.* **dramatis'able** (*dram-*), **-z-**.—*n.* **dramatisa'tion**, **-z-**, the act of dramatising: the dramatised version of a novel or story.—*v.i.* **dram'atise**, **-ize**, to compose in, or turn into, the form of a drama or play: to exaggerate the importance or emotional nature of.—*n. dram'atist*, a writer of plays.—**dram'atis persō'nae** (*-ē*), the characters of a drama or play. [L.,—Gr. *drāma*, *drāmatos*—*drāein*, to do.]

**dramaturgy**, *dram'ə-tûr-ji, n.* the principles of dramatic composition: theatrical art.—*ns.* **dram'aturg** (Ger.), a member of a theatrical company who selects the repertoire and may assist in the arranging and production of the plays, compiling notes for the programme, etc.; **dram'aturge**, **dram'aturgist**, a playwright.—*adj.* **dramatur'gic**. [Through Fr. from Gr. *drāmatourgiā*, *drāmatourgos*, playwright—*drāma*, and *ergon*, a work.]

**drammock**, *dram'ək, n.* meal and water mixed raw. Also **dramm'ach**. [Cf. Gael. *drama(i)g*, a foul mixture.]

**drang nach osten**, *drang nahh ō'stən*, (Ger; *hist.*) eastward thrust—policy of German expansionists.

**drank**, *drangk, pa.t.* of drink.

**drant**, **draunt**, *dränt*, *drönt*, (*dial.*) *v.i.* and *v.t.* to drawl, to drone.—*n.* a droning tone.

**drap**, *drap, n.* and *v.* Scots for drop.—*n.* **drapp'ie**, **drapp'y**, (*Scot.*) a little drop, esp. of spirits.

**drap-de-Berry**, *drä-də-ber-ē*, (*obs.*) *n.* a woollen cloth made in Berry, in France.—Also *adj.* [Fr., Berry cloth.]

**drape**, *drāp, v.t.* to cover as with cloth: to hang

cloth in folds about: (refl.) to assume a casual and graceful pose.—n. (U.S. and theatre), a hanging or curtain.—adj. draped.—n. drăp′er, a dealer in cloth and cloth goods.—adj. drăp′-eried, draped.—n. drăp′ery, cloth goods: hangings: the draper's business: the representation of clothes and hanging folds of cloth (art):— pl. draperies.—v.t. to drape.—ns. drapet (drap′it; Spens.), a cloth covering; drapier (drăp′i-ar; obs.) a draper.—drape suit, a man's suit with very long jacket and narrow trousers. [O.Fr. draper, to weave, drape, drapier, draper—drap, cloth, prob. Gmc.; see drab.]

drastic, dras′tik, adj. forcible, powerful in action: violent: unsparing.—n. a severe purgative.— adv. dras′tically. [Gr. drastikos—drāein, to act, to do.]

drat, drat, v.t. a minced oath used to express vexation. [Aphetic from God rot.]

dratchell, drach′l, (dial.) n. a slut.

draught, dräft, n. drawing or pulling: a pull: attraction: the thing or quantity drawn: readiness for drawing from the cask: the act of drinking: the quantity drunk in one breath: a dose of liquor or medicine: outline of a picture, or a preliminary sketch or plan (usu. draft): that which is taken in a net by drawing: a chosen detachment of men (usu. draft): a current of air: the depth to which a ship sinks in the water: a move in a game (obs.): a thick disk used in the game of draughts: (in pl.) a game played by two persons moving draughtmen alternately on a chequered board: a cesspool or privy (Shak.).— v.t. to sketch out, make a preliminary plan of or attempt at (also draft): occasionally for draft in sense of draw off, set apart from a larger body.—n. draught′iness.—adj. draught′y, full of draughts or currents of air.—draught′-animal, -horse, -ox, etc., one used for drawing heavy loads; draught′board, a chessboard used for playing draughts; draught′-en′gine, the engine over the shaft of a coal-pit.—n.pl. draught′-hooks, large iron hooks fixed on the cheeks of a cannon-carriage.—draught′-house (B.), a sink, privy; draught′man, a piece used for playing draughts; draught′-net, a drag-net; draught′-screen, a screen for warding off a current of air; draughts′man, a piece used in playing draughts; one skilled or employed in drawing: one who draughts or draws up documents (in this sense usually draftsman).—feel the draught (fig.), to be unpleasantly conscious of difficult conditions, esp. economic; on draught, of liquor, sold from the cask. [O.E. draht—dragan, to draw; see drag, draw.]

drave, drāv, old pa.t. of drive.

Dravidian, dra-vid′i-an, adj. belonging to a dark, long-headed, wavy-haired race of the Deccan: belonging to a group of languages in Southern India, including Tamil, Malayalam, Kanarese, Telugu, etc.—Also n. [Sans. Drāviḍa, an ancient province of Southern India.]

draw, drö, v.t. to pull: to drag: to pull along: to bring forcibly towards or after one: to pull into position: to pull back: to pull back the string of: to pull together or awry: to take at random from a number: to entice, attract: to coax into giving information: to stimulate to self-expression (usu. draw out): to inhale: to take out: to unsheathe: to withdraw: to cause to flow out: to evoke or bring out by some artifice: to extract by pulling: to extract the essence of: to eviscerate: to pull through a small hole, as in making wire: to deduce: to lengthen: to extend to the full length: to force to appear (as a badger from its hole): to receive or take from a source or store: to demand by a draft: to get by lot: to trace: to construct in linear form: to make a picture of, by lines drawn: to describe: to put into shape, frame:

to write out (as a cheque): to require as depth of water for floating: to finish without winning or losing: to glance (cricket).—v.i. to pull: to practise drawing: to move: to make one's way, betake oneself: to resort: to approach: to make a draught: to allow a free current: to act as drawer: to draw a card, a sword, lots: to infuse: to end a game without winning or losing: —pa.t. drew, drōō; pa.p. drawn.—n. the act of drawing: assignment by lot, as of prizes, opponents in a game: anything drawn: a drawn or undecided game: an attraction: a drawer (of a chest of drawers; U.S.).—adj. draw′able.—ns. drawee′, the person on whom a bill of exchange is drawn; draw′er, he or that which draws: one who draws beer or fetches liquor in a tavern: (drŏr) a thing drawn out, as the sliding box in a chest of drawers: (in pl.) a close undergarment for the lower part of the body and the legs; draw′ing, the art of representing objects or forms by lines drawn, shading, etc.: a picture in lines: an assigning by lot: act of pulling, etc.—adj. drawn, pulled together: closed: neither won nor lost: unsheathed: eviscerated: strained, tense: etiolated.—draw′-back, a disadvantage: a receiving back some part of the duty on goods on their exportation; draw′-bar, a sliding bar: a bar used in coupling railway vehicles (also drag-, draught-bar); draw′-boy, the boy who pulls the cords of the harness in figure-weaving: a mechanical device for this purpose; draw′bridge, a bridge that can be drawn up or let down at pleasure: bridge played by two persons, with two dummy hands, not exposed; draw′-gear, the apparatus by which railway-cars are coupled; draw′ing-board, a slab on which paper can be pinned for drawing on; draw′ing-frame, a machine in which carded wool, cotton, or the like is drawn out fine; draw′ing-knife, a knife with a handle at each end, used by a cooper for shaving hoops by drawing it towards him; draw′ing-mas′ter; draw′ing-paper; draw′-ing-pen; draw′ing-pencil; draw′ing-pin, a short broad-headed pin for fastening paper to a drawing-board; draw′ing-room, in engineering, a room where plans and patterns are drawn (see also separate article); draw′ing-table, a table which can be extended in length by drawing out sliding leaves; draw′-net (same as drag-net); drawn′-(thread′) work, ornamental work done by pulling out some of the threads of a fabric; draw′-plate, a plate supporting dies for drawing wire or tubing; draw′-sheet, a hospital sheet that can be drawn out from under a patient; draw′-string, a string, cord, etc., in a casing in, or threaded through, material, by which the material may be drawn or gathered up; draw′-tube, a tube sliding within another, as in a form of telescope; draw′-well, a well from which water is drawn up by a bucket and apparatus.— at daggers drawn, openly hostile; draw a bead on (see bead); draw a blank, to get a lottery ticket that wins no prize: to get no result; draw a cover (covert), to send the hounds into a cover to frighten out a fox; draw blank, to do so, but find no fox; draw back, to recoil: to withdraw; draw, hang, and quarter (see hang); draw in, to reduce, contract: to become shorter; draw it fine, to be too precise; draw it mild (coll.), refrain from exaggeration; draw near, to approach; draw off, to cause to flow from a barrel, etc.: to withdraw; draw on, to approach: to pull on; draw on, upon, to make a draught upon: to make a demand upon (one's credulity, patience, resources): to draw one's sword, pistol, against; draw on one's imagination, to make imaginative or lying statements; draw on one's memory, to try to remember: to make use of what one remembers; draw out, to leave the place (of an army, etc.): to lengthen: to entice into talk and self-expression; **draw rein**, to slacken speed, to stop; **draw stumps**, end a game of cricket by removing the wickets; **draw the cloth, board, table** (*arch.*), clear up after a meal; **draw the line**, to fix a limit: **draw the long-bow** (see bow (2)); **draw the teeth of**, to render harmless; **draw to a head**, to mature; **draw up**, to form in regular order: to compose, put into shape: to stop; **in drawing**, correctly drawn; **out of drawing**, inaccurately drawn, or drawn in violation of the principles of drawing; **out of the top drawer**, of top grade, esp. socially. [O.E. *dragan*; cf. **drag**.]

**Drawcansir**, *drö-kan'sər, n.* a blustering bully. [*Drawcansir* (parodying Dryden's *Almanzor*), who 'kills 'em all on both sides' in Buckingham's *Rehearsal* (performed 1671).]

**drawingroom**, *drö'ing-rōōm, n.* a room to which the company withdraws after dinner: a reception of company at court: a private compartment of a 'parlor-car' (*U.S.*).—*adj.* suitable for the drawingroom. [Orig. **withdrawing-room.**]

**drawl**, *dröl, v.i.* to dawdle (*obs.*): to speak in a slow lengthened tone.—*v.t.* to utter in a slow and sleepy manner.—*n.* a slow, lengthened utterance.—*n.* **drawl'er.**—*adv.* **drawl'ingly.**—*n.* **drawl'ingness.** [Connected with **draw.**]

**drawn**, *drön, pa.p.* of draw, and *adj.*

**dray**, *drā, n.* a low strong cart for heavy goods: a timber sledge: that which is dragged or drawn. —*n.* **dray'age.**—**dray'-horse; dray'man; dray'-plough.** [Cf. O.E. *dræge*, drag-net—*dragan*, to draw; see **drag, draw.**]

**dray**. Same as **drey.**

**drazel**, *dräz'l, (dial.) n.* a slut. [Origin unknown.]

**dread**, *dred, n.* great fear: awe: an object of fear or awe: fury (*Spens.*).—*adj.* dreaded: inspiring great fear or awe.—*v.t.* to fear greatly: to reverence: to cause to fear, to affright (*obs.*). —*n.* **dread'er.**—*adj.* **dread'ful**, orig., full of dread: producing great fear or awe: terrible: very bad, unpleasant (*coll.*).—*adv.* **dread'fully.**— *n.* **dread'fulness.**—*adj.* **dread'less.**—*adv.* (*Spens.*) doubtless.—*adv.* **dread'lessly.**—*n.* **dread'lessness.**—*adv.* **dread'ly.**—**dread'nought, dread'-naught**, one who dreads nothing: hence, a thick cloth or garment thereof: a powerful type of battleship or battle-cruiser (dating from 1905-6).—**penny dreadful**, a cheap sensational serial or tale. [M.E. *dreden*—O.E. *ondrædan* to fear; O.N. *ondrēda*, O.H.G. *intratan*, to be afraid.]

**dream**, *drēm, (obs.) n.* joy: mirth: minstrelsy: music: sound.—**dream'hole**, a hole in the wall of a steeple, tower, etc., for admitting light. [O.E. *dréam*, joy, mirth.]

**dream**, *drēm, n.* a train of thoughts and fancies during sleep, a vision: something only imaginary: a distant hope or ideal, probably unattainable.—*v.i.* to fancy things during sleep: to think idly (with *of*): to think (of) as possible, contemplate as imaginably possible.—*v.t.* to see or imagine in, or as in, a dream:—*pa.t.* and *pa.p.* dreamed or dreamt, *dremt.*—*n.* **dream'er; dream'ery**, a place favourable to dreams: dream-like fancies.—*adj.* **dream'ful** (*Tenn.*), dreamy.— *adv.* **dream'ily.**—*n.* **dream'iness.**—*n.* and *adj.* **dream'ing.**—*adv.* **dream'ingly.**—*adj.* **dream'less.** —*adv.* **dream'lessly.**—*n.* **dream'lessness.**—*adj.* **dream'y**, full of dreams: given to dreaming: appropriate to dreams: dream-like: lovely (*coll.*).—**dream'boat** (*slang*), someone wonderful and desirable—usu. of the opposite sex; **dream'-land**, the land of dreams, reverie, or imagination; **dream'while**, the duration of a dream; **dream'-world**, a world of illusions.—**dream up**, to plan in the mind, often unrealistically. [M.E. *dream*, *drēm*; perh. the same word as the foregoing.]

**dreary**, *drēr'i, adj.* gloomy: cheerless.—*adj.* **drear**, dreary.—*n.* (*obs.*; *Spens.* **dreare, drere**)

dreariness: gloom: mishap.—*ns.* **drear'ihead, drear'iment. drear'iness, drear'ing** (all *Spens.*), **drear'ihood.**—*adv.* **drear'ily.**—*adj.* **drear'isome**, desolate, forlorn. [O.E. *drēorig*, mournful, bloody—*drēor*, gore.]

**dredge**, *drej, n.* a bag-net for dragging along the bottom to take oysters, biological specimens, mud, etc.: a machine for deepening a harbour, canal, river, etc., for excavating under water or on land, or for raising alluvial deposits and washing them for minerals, by means of buckets on an endless chain, pumps, grabs, or other devices.—*v.t.* to gather, explore, or deepen with a dredge.—*n.* **dredg'er**, one who dredges: a machine for dredging: a boat, ship, or raft equipped for dredging. [Conn. with **drag, draw.**]

**dredge**, *drej, v.t.* to sprinkle.—*ns.* **dredg'er, dredge'-box, dredg'ing-box**, a vessel with perforated lid for dredging. [O.Fr. *dragie*, sugarplum—Gr. *tragēmata*, dessert.]

**dree**, *drē, (Scot.) v.t.* to endure, bear.—**dree one's weird**, to undergo one's destiny. [O.E. *drēogan*, suffer, accomplish.]

**dregs**, *dregz, n.pl.* impurities in liquor that fall to the bottom, the grounds: dross: the vilest part of anything.—*n.* **dregg'iness.**—*adj.* **dregg'y**, containing dregs: muddy: foul. [O.N. *dreggj.*]

**dreich**, *drēhh*, (*Scot.) adj.* long drawn out: tedious: dreary. [See **dree.**]

**dreikanter**, *drī'kän-tər, n.* a pebble faceted by wind-blown sand, properly having three faces: —*pl.* **drei'kanter(s).** [Ger. *dreikant*, solid angle —*drei*, three, *kante*, edge.]

**drench**, *drench, drensh, v.t.* to fill with drink or liquid: to wet thoroughly: to soak: to physic by force: to drown (*obs.*).—*v.i.* (*obs.*) to drown. —*n.* a draught: dose of physic forced down the throat.—*n.* **drench'er.** [O.E. *drencan*, to cause to drink (*drincan*, to drink), *drenc*, drink, drowning; Ger. *tränken*, to soak. See **drink.**]

**drent**, *drent* (*Spens.*), obsolete *pa.p.* of **drench**, to drown.

**drepanium**, *dri-pā'ni-əm, n.* a cymose inflorescence in which each daughter axis is on the same side of its parent axis, and all in one plane. [Latinised from Gr. *drepanion*, dim. of *drepanon*, a reaping-hook.]

**drere, dreryhead, etc.** Spenserian forms of **drear**, etc.

**Dresden**, (**china, porcelain, ware**), *drez'dən*, fine decorated china made in Saxony (Royal Saxon porcelain factory established at Meissen, 1710).

**dress**, *dres, v.t.* to straighten: to flatten: to smooth: to erect: to set in order: to prepare: to draw (fowl): to manure: to add seasoning to (food): to finish or trim: to treat: to tend: to apply suitable materials to: to clothe: to adorn: to treat with severity: to chide: to thrash.—*v.i.* to come into line: to put on clothes: to put on finer, more elaborate, or more formal clothes: —*pa.t.* and *pa.p.* dressed, sometimes **drest.**—*n.* the covering or ornament of the body: a lady's gown: manner of clothing: ceremonial or formal clothing.—*adj.* pertaining to evening dress. —*ns.* **dress'er**, one who dresses: a medical student who dresses wounds: a tirewoman: a person who assists an actor to dress in a theatre: a tool or machine for dressing: a table on which meat is dressed or prepared for use: a kitchen sideboard: a chest of drawers or dressing-table (*U.S.*); **dress'ing**, dress or clothes: material applied to land, a wound, manufactured goods, etc.: matter used to give stiffness and gloss to cloth: sauce, stuffing, etc., used in preparing a dish for the table, etc.: an ornamental moulding: a thrashing.—*adj.* **dress'y**, fond of dress: showy: indicating care in dressing.—**dress'-cir'cle**, part of a theatre (usually the first gallery) intended for people in evening dress; **dress'-coat**, a fine black coat with narrow or cut-away skirts, worn in full dress.—*n.pl.* **dress′-goods**, cloths for making women's and children's gowns, frocks, etc.—**dress′guard** (*arch.*), an arrangement of strings to protect the rider's dress from contact with a bicycle wheel; **dress′-improver** (*obs.*), a bustle; **dress′ing-case**, a case of toilet requisites; **dress′ing-down**, a severe scolding: a thrashing; **dress′ing-gown**, a loose garment used in dressing, or in deshabille; **dress′ing-jacket, dress′ing-sack**, a jacket worn by women in dressing; **dress′ing-room**; **dress′ing-sta′tion**, a place where wounded are collected and tended by members of a field-ambulance; **dress′ing-tā′ble**; **dress′-length**, enough to make a dress; **dress′maker**, a person who makes dresses for women; **dress′-reform**, a late 19th-cent. movement seeking to make dress more practical; **dress′-rehears′al**, a full rehearsal in costume with everything as for the performance; **dress′-shield**, a device to protect the armpit of a dress against sweat; **dress′-shirt′, dress′-suit′, dress′-tie′**, one for formal evening dress.—**dress down**, to handle with severity: to reprimand: to thrash; **dressed day**, formerly, the second day of a three days' visit; **dress up**, to dress elaborately: to dress for a part: to masquerade: to treat so as to make appear better, more interesting, etc., than it really is; **evening dress, full dress**, the costume prescribed by fashion for evening receptions, dinners, balls, etc. [O.Fr. *dresser*, to prepare—an inferred L.L. *directiāre*, to straighten; see **direct**.]

**dressage**, *dres′äzh, n.* training of a horse in deportment and response to controls. [Fr.]

**drest**, *drest, pa.t.* and *pa.p.* of **dress**.

**drevill**, *drev′il,* (*Spens.*) *n.* a foul person. [Cf. M.Du. *drevel*, scullion.]

**drew**, *droō, pa.t.* of **draw**.

**drey, dray**, *drā, n.* a squirrel's nest. [Ety. dub.]

**drib**, *drib,* (*obs.*) *v.i.* to trickle: to go little by little.—*v.t.* to let trickle: to take a little, filch: to lead gradually: to shoot (an arrow) short or wide.—*n.* a drop: a trickle: a small quantity.—*ns.* **dribb′er; drib′let, dribb′let**, a drop: a trickle: a small quantity.—**dribs and drabs**, small quantities at a time. [Akin to **drip**.]

**dribble**, *drib′l, v.i.* to fall in small drops: to drop quickly: to trickle: to slaver, as a child or an idiot.—*v.t.* to let fall in drops: to give out in small portions: to move the ball forward little by little, tricking opponents (*football, hockey,* etc.): to drib (*archery; Shak.*).—Also *n.*—*n.* **dribb′ler**. [Freq. of **drib**.]

**dried, drier, dries, driest**. See **dry**.

**drift**, *drift, n.* a driving: a drove (*arch.*): a heap of matter driven together, as snow: floating materials driven by water: a driving shower: a streaming movement: the direction in which a thing is driven: a slow current caused by the wind: leeway: passive travel with the current: abandonment to external influences: tendency: a cattle-track, drove-road: a pin or bar driven into a hole: a drift-net: a set of nets: the object aimed at: the meaning of words used: loose superficial deposits, esp. glacial or fluvioglacial (*geol.*): a horizontal or oblique excavation or passage (*mining*): a ford (*S. Africa*; from *Du.*).—*v.t.* to drive: to carry by drift: to cause or allow to drift: to pierce or tunnel.—*v.i.* to be floated along: to be driven into heaps: to leave things to circumstances: to wander around without any definite aim.—*ns.* **drift′age**, that which is drifted: the amount of deviation from a ship's course due to leeway; **drift′er**, one who, or that which drifts: an aimless shiftless person: a fisherman or a fishing-boat that uses a drift-net.—*adjs.* **drift′less**, without drift; **drift′y**, full of or forming drifts.—**drift′-anchor**, an anchor for keeping the ship's head to the wind; **drift′-bolt**, a steel bolt used to drive out

other bolts; **drift′-ice**, floating masses of ice drifting before the wind; **drift′-land**, an old tribute paid for the privilege of driving cattle through a manor; **drift′-mining**, gold-mining by means of drifts in the gravel and detritus of old river-beds; **drift′-net**, a net which is allowed to drift with the tide; **drift′-sail**, a sail immersed in the water, used for lessening the drift of a vessel during a storm; **drift′-way**, a road over which cattle are driven: drift (*min.*); **drift′-weed**, gulf-weed: tangle: seaweed thrown up on the beach; **drift′-wood**, wood drifted by water. [M.E.; O.N. *drift*, snowdrift; root as **drive**.]

**drill**, *dril, v.t.* to bore, pierce: to make with a drill: to exercise (soldiers, pupils, etc.) by repeated practice: to sow in rows.—*n.* an instrument for boring stone, metal, teeth, or other hard substances, actuated by a kind of bow, by a brace, or otherwise: a large boring instrument used in mining: training exercise: a spell of it: a drill-master: a ridge with seed or growing plants on it (turnips, potatoes, etc.): the plants in such a row: the machine for sowing the seed in drill-husbandry: correct procedure or routine (*coll.*).—**drill′-barrow**, a grain-drill driven by hand; **drill′-harrow**, a harrow for working between drills; **drill′-husbandry**, the method of sowing seed in drills or rows; **drill′ing-machine′, drill′ing-lathe, drill′-press**, machines for boring with a drill or drills; **drill′-master**, one who teaches drill, one who trains in anything, esp. in a mechanical manner; **drill′-plough**, a plough for sowing grain in drills; **drill′-sergeant**, a sergeant who drills soldiers. [Prob. borrowed from Du. *drillen*, to bore; *dril, drille*, a borer; cf. **thrill**.]

**drill**, *dril, n.* a W. African baboon, smaller than the mandrill. [Perh. a W. African word.]

**drilling**, *dril′ing, n.* a stout twilled linen or cotton cloth.—Also **drill**. [Ger. *drillich*, ticking—L. *trilix*, three-threaded; *trēs, tria*, three, *licium*, thread.]

**drily**. See under **dry**.

**drink**, *dringk, v.t.* to swallow as a liquid: to smoke (tobacco; *obs.*): to empty, as a glass, bowl, etc.: to absorb: to take in through the senses.—*v.i.* to swallow a liquid: to take intoxicating liquors to excess:—*pr.p.* **drink′ing**; *pa.t.* **drank**, *arch.* **drunk**; *pa.p.* **drunk**.—*n.* an act of drinking: a quantity drunk: something to be drunk: a beverage: intoxicating liquor.—*adj.* **drink′able**.—*ns.* **drink′ableness**; **drink′er**, one who drinks: a tippler.—*interj.* **drink′-hail**, an Early Middle English reply to a pledge in drinking (*waes hail*, be healthy, or lucky, was answered with *drinc hail*, drink healthy or lucky—*hail* being O.N. adj. *heill*, not O.E. *hāl*).—*n.* **drink′-ing**.—Also *adj.* fit to drink: for drinking.—*ns.* **drink′ing-bout**; **drink′ing-foun′tain**; **drink′ing-horn**; **drink′-mon′ey**, a gratuity, ostensibly given to buy liquor for drinking to the health of the giver; **drink′-offering**, an offering of wine, oil, blood, etc., to a god.—**drink himself drunk**, to drink until he is drunk; **drink in**, to absorb (rain, etc.), as dry land does: to take in eagerly (something seen, said, etc.); **drink off**, to quaff wholly and at a gulp; **drink the others under the table**, to continue drinking and remain (comparatively) sober after the others have completely collapsed; **drink to, drink to the health of**, to drink wine, etc., with good wishes for one's health; **drink up**, to exhaust by drinking; **in drink**, intoxicated; **strong drink**, alcoholic liquor; **the drink**, (*slang*) the sea.—See also **drunk**. [O.E. *drincan*; Ger. *trinken*.]

**drip**, *drip, v.i.* to fall in drops: to let fall drops.—*v.t.* to let fall in drops:—*pr.p.* **dripp′ing**; *pa.t.* and *pa.p.* **dripped**—*n.* a falling in drops: that which falls in drops: the edge of a roof: a device for passing a fluid slowly and continuously, esp. into a vein of the body: the material so passed: a forceless person (*slang*): drivel, esp. sentimental (*slang*).—*n.* dripp'ing, that which falls in drops, as fat from meat in roasting. —*adj.* drip'-dry', (of a material or garment) which, when allowed to dry by dripping, requires no, or little, ironing.—Also *v.i., v.t.*—dripp'ing-pan, a pan for receiving the dripping from roasting meat; dripping roast, a source of easy and continuous profit; drip'-stone, a projecting moulding over doorways, etc., serving to throw off the rain; drip'-tip (*bot.*) a prolonged leaf-tip, serving to shed rain.—right of drip, a right in law to let the drip from one's roof fall on another's land. [O.E. *dryppan*—*drēopan.*]

drive, *driv, v.t.* to urge along: to hurry on: to control or guide the movements or operations of: to convey or carry in a carriage: to force in: to push briskly: to furnish motive power to: to urge, as a point of argument: to carry through, as a bargain: to impel: to compel: to send away with force, as a ball, esp. in golf, to play from the tee or with a driver, in cricket to hit strongly down the pitch, in tennis, to return forcibly underarm: to chase: to excavate (e.g. tunnel): to sort out (feathers) in a current of air.—*v.i.* to control an engine, vehicle, draught-animal, etc.: to press forward with violence: to be forced along, as a ship before the wind: to be driven: to go in a carriage: to aim or tend towards a point: to strike with a sword, the fist, etc. (with *at*):—*pr.p.* driv'ing; *pa.t.* drōve, *arch.* drāve, *Spens.* drive (*driv*); *pa.p.* driv'en.—*n.* an excursion in a carriage: a road for driving on, esp. the approach to a house within its own grounds: a driving stroke in games: impulse: impulsive force: power of getting things done: the chasing of game towards the shooters, or the sport so obtained, or the ground over which the game is driven: pushing sales by reducing prices: an organised campaign to attain any end: apparatus for driving.—*n.* driv'er, one who or that which drives, in all senses: a club used in golf to propel the ball from the teeing-ground.—drive'-in, a refreshment halt, store, cinema, etc., where patrons are catered for while still remaining in their motor-cars.—Also *adj.*—drive'way, a carriage drive: a driving road; driv'ing-band, the band or strap that communicates motion from one machine, or part of a machine, to another; driv'ing-box, a box on which a driver sits; driv'ing-gear, apparatus by which power is transmitted from shaft to shaft; driv'ing-shaft, a shaft from a driving-wheel communicating motion to machinery; driving test, a test of ability to drive safely esp. an official and obligatory test; driv'ing-wheel, a main wheel that communicates motion to other wheels: one of the main wheels in a locomotive.—let drive, to aim a blow. [O.E. *drifan*, to drive; Ger. *treiben*, to push.]

drivel, *driv'l, v.i.* to slaver like a child: to be foolish: to speak like an idiot:—*pr.p.* driv'elling; *pa.t.* and *pa.p.* driv'elled.—*n.* slaver: nonsense. —*n.* driv'eller. [M.E. *drevelen, dravelen*; O.E. *dreflian.*]

drizzle, *driz'l, v.i.* to rain in small drops.—*v.t.* (*Shak.*) to shed in small drops.—*n.* a small, light rain.—*adj.* drizz'ly. [Freq. of M.E. *dresen*—O.E. *drēosan*, to fall; Goth. *driusan.*]

droger, drogher, *drō'gǝr, n.* a W. Indian coasting vessel, with long masts and lateen sails. [Du. *droogen*, to dry—orig. a vessel on which fish were dried.]

drogue, *drōg, n.* the drag of boards, attached to the end of a harpoon-line, checking the progress of a running whale: a conical canvas sleeve open at both ends, used as one form of sea-anchor, or to check the way of an aircraft, etc.: a parachute used to reduce speed of a falling object, e.g. one fired from a descending space capsule: a funnel device on the end of the hose of a tanker aircraft: a wind-sock: an air target of similar shape. [Origin obscure.]

droguet, *dro-gā', n.* a ribbed woollen dress fabric, a variety of rep. [Fr.; cf. drugget.]

droich, *drōhh, (Scot.) n.* a dwarf.—*adj.* droich'y, dwarfish. [See dwarf.]

droil, *droil, v.i.* to drudge. [Perh. Du. *druilen*, to loiter.]

droit, *drwä,* (Eng. *droit*), *n.* right, legal claim. —droit administratif (*ad-mēn-ē-stra-tēf'*), in France, administrative law; droit au travail (*ō tra-vä-y'*), right to work; droit des gens (*dā zhä*), international law; droit du seigneur (*dü se-nyœr*), same as *jus primae noctis* (q.v.). [Fr.]

drôle, *drōl, n.* a rogue, a knave.—*adj.* amusing: odd. [Fr.]

droll, *drōl, adj.* odd: amusing: laughable.—*n.* one who excites mirth: a jester.—*v.i.* to practise drollery: to jest.—*ns.* droll'ery, drollness: waggery: a comic show, picture, story: a jest: a puppet-show; droll'ing.—*adjs.* droll'ish, rather droll.—*adv.* drolly (*drōl'li*).—*n.* droll'ness. [Fr. *drôle*, prob. from Du. *drollig*, odd—*trold*, a hobgoblin; cf. Ger. *droll*, a short thick person.]

drome, *drōm, (coll.) n.* an aerodrome.

dromedary, *drum'i-dǝr-i, drom', n.* a thoroughbred camel: a one-humped Arabian camel.—*Spens.* drom'edare. [O.Fr. *dromedaire*—L.L. *dromedārius*—Gr. *dromas, dromados*, running—*dromos*, a course, run.]

dromond, *drom', drum'ǝnd, n.* a swift mediaeval ship of war.—Also drom'on. [O.Fr.,—L.L. *dromō—ōnis*—Byzantine Gr. *dromōn—dromos*, a running, *dramein* (aor.) to run.]

dromophobia, *drom-ō-fō'bi-ǝ, n.* a morbid fear of crossing streets. [Gr. *dromos*, public walk, *phobos*, fear.]

dromos, *drom'os, n.* a Greek race-course: an entrance-passage or avenue, as to a subterranean tomb, etc.:—*pl.* drom'oi.—*adjs.* drom'ic, -al, pertaining to a race-course: basilican. [Gr.]

drone, *drōn, n.* the male of the honey-bee: one who lives on the labour of others, like the drone-bee: a lazy, idle fellow: a deep humming sound: a bass-pipe of a bagpipe: its note: a pedal bass: the burden of a song: a monotonous speaker or speech: an aircraft piloted by remote control.—*v.i.* to emit a monotonous humming sound.—*v.t.* to utter with such a tone.—*adj.* dron'ish, like a drone: lazy, idle.—*adv.* dron'ishly.—*n.* dron'ishness.—*adj.* dron'y. drone'-pipe, a pipe producing a droning sound. [O.E. *drān*, bee, but the quantity of the *a* is doubtful, and relations obscure: perh.—Old Saxon.]

drongo, *drong'gō, n.* any member of the family *Dicruridae*, glossy-black fork-tailed insect-catching birds of the Old World tropics: a nitwit, insignificant twerp (*Austr. slang*).—Also drong'o-shrike.—drong'o-cuck'oo, a cuckoo that resembles a drongo. [From Malagasy.]

drool, *drōōl, v.i.* to slaver: to drivel: to show effusive or lascivious pleasure.—*n.* drivel. [drivel.]

droome, *drōōm,* (*Spens.*) *n.* another form of drum.

droop, *drōōp, v.t.* to hang down: to grow weak or faint: to decline.—*v.t.* to let hang down.—*n.* a drooping position.—*adv.* droop'ingly. [O.N. *drūpa*, to droop; see drop.]

drop, *drop, n.* a small rounded blob of liquid that hangs or falls at one time: a very small quantity of liquid: anything hanging like a drop: a pendant: a round sweetmeat: a curtain dropped between acts (also drop'-cur'tain): (in *pl.*)

a medicine taken in drops: a fall: a vertical descent, difference of level: an unpleasant surprise: a trap in the gallows scaffold, the fall of which allows the criminal to drop: a device for lowering goods into a ship's hold.—*v.i.* to fall in drops: to let drops fall: to fall suddenly, steeply or sheer: to let oneself fall gently: to sink: to lapse: to diminish: to subside into a condition, come gradually to be: to come casually or accidentally: to move slowly with the tide.—*v.t.* to let fall in drops: to let fall: to let go, relinquish, abandon: to omit: to lower: to lay: to give birth to: to spot, bespatter, sprinkle: to utter casually: to write and send (a note) in an offhand manner: to set down, part with: to cause to fall, e.g. by shooting: to hole, etc. (a ball): to score (a goal) with a drop-kick: to set down from a vehicle, a ship: to cease to associate with: to lose (a sum of money, a game as part of a contest): to cause to fall: to bring down by a shot:—*pr.p.* dropp′ing; *pa.t.* and *pa.p.* dropped.—*ns.* drop′let, a little drop; dropp′er, one who or that which drops: a tube or contrivance for making liquid issue in drops: a shoot that grows downward from a bulb and develops a new bulb (*hort.*): a setter or dog that drops to earth on sighting game: an artificial fly attached to the leader (also drop′fly); dropp′ing, that which is dropped: (usu. in *pl.*) dung; dropp′le, a trickle.—*adv.* drop′wise, by drops.—drop′-drill, an apparatus for dropping seed and manure into the soil simultaneously; drop′-forging, the process of shaping metal parts by forging between two dies, one fixed to the hammer and the other to the anvil of a steam or mechanical hammer; drop′-goal (*rugby*), a goal secured by a drop-kick; drop′-hamm′er, drop′-press, a swaging, stamping, or forging machine; drophead coupé, one whose top can be opened; drop′-kick (*rugby football*), a kick made when the ball rebounds from the ground after dropping from the hand; drop′-lett′er (*U.S.*), a letter posted in any place merely for local delivery; drop′-net, a net suspended from a boom, to be suddenly dropped on a passing shoal of fish; dropp′ing-well (*fig.* in Tennyson), a well supplied by water falling in drops from above.—*adj.* drop′-ripe, so ripe as to be ready to drop from the tree.—drop′-scene, a drop-curtain; drop(ped)′-scone, a scone made like a pancake; drop serene (*Milt.*), an old medical name for amaurosis, literally translated from L. *gutta serēna*; drop′-shot (*tennis, etc.*), a ball made to drop close to the net; drop′-stone, a stalactitic calcite; drop′-wort, a species of spiraea (*S. Filipendula*) with bead-like root tubercles.—a drop in the bucket, ocean, a quantity infinitesimal in proportion; at the drop of a hat, immediately: on the smallest provocation; drop a brick (see brick); drop a curtsy, to curtsy; drop astern (*naut.*), to get left more and more behind; drop away, off, to depart, disappear; drop down, to sail, move, or row down a coast, or down a river to the sea; drop in, to come, fall, set, etc. in casually, unintentionally, or one by one; drop off, to fall asleep: to become less, to diminish; drop on (drop down on), to single out for reproof or an unpleasant task; drop out, to disappear from one's place: to withdraw, esp. from an academic course or from conventional life in society (*n.* drop′-out); dropping fire, unremitting irregular discharge of small-arms; get the drop on one (*U.S.*), to be ready to shoot first; hence to have at a disadvantage; let drop, to disclose inadvertently, or seemingly so; (Prince) Rupert's drops, drops of glass that have fallen in a melted state into cold water, and have assumed a tadpole-like shape, the whole falling to dust with a loud report if the point of the tail be nipped off. [O.E. *dropa*, a drop,

dropian, droppian, to drop; Du. *drop*, Ger. *tropfe.*]

dropsy, drop′si, *n.* a morbid accumulation of watery fluid in any part of the body.—*adjs.* drop′sical, drop′sied (*Shak.*), affected with dropsy. [Aphetic for hydropsy.]

Drosera, dros′ə-ra, *n.* the sundew genus of Drosera′ceae, a family of insectivorous plants.—*adj.* droserā′ceous. [Fem. of Gr. *droseros*, dewy —*drosos*, dew.]

droshky, drosh′ki, drosky, dros′ki, *n.* a low four-wheeled open carriage used in Russia: a German four-wheeled cab. [Russ. *drozhki*.]

drosometer, dros-om′i-tər, *n.* an instrument for measuring dew. [Gr. *drosos*, dew, *metron*, measure.]

Drosophila, dros-of′i-la, *n.* a genus of small yellow flies—fruit-flies—which breed in fermenting fruit juices and are utilised in experiments in heredity. [Gr. *drosos*, dew, moisture, *phileein*, to love.]

dross, dros, *n.* the scum of melting metals: waste matter: small or waste coal: refuse: rust: lucre. —*n.* dross′iness.—*adj.* dross′y, like dross: impure: worthless. [O.E. *drōs*.]

drought, drowt, drouth, drowth (Scot. drōōth), *n.* dryness: want of rain or of water: a condition of atmosphere favourable to drying: thirst.— *ns.* drought′iness, drouth′iness.—*adjs.* drought′y, drouth′y, very dry: wanting rain: thirsty. [O.E. *drūgath*, dryness—*drūgian*, to dry.]

drouk, drook, drōōk, (Scot.) *v.t.* to drench.—*n.* drouk′ing, drook′ing.—*adj.* drouk′it, drook′it. [Origin obscure; cf. O.N. *drukna*, to be drowned; Dan. *drukne*.]

drove, drōv, *pa.t.* of drive.—*n.* a number of cattle, or other animals, driven.—*n.* drov′er, one whose occupation is to drive cattle: a fishing boat, drifter (*Spens.*).—drove′-road, an old generally grassy track used or once used by droves of cattle. [O.E. *drāf, drifan*, to drive.]

drow, drow, (Shetland and Orkney) a form of troll (1).

drow, drow, (Scot.) *n.* a drizzling mist: a squall. [Origin obscure.]

drown, drown, *v.i.* to die of suffocation in liquid. —*v.t.* to kill by suffocation in liquid: to submerge: to flood: to extinguish: to make indistinguishable or imperceptible.—*adj.* drownd′ed (*Spens.*; now illiterate): drowned.—*n.* drown′er. —*n.* and *adj.* drown′ing. [M.E. *drounen*; origin obscure; the word used in O.E. was *druncnian*.]

drowse, drowz, *v.i.* to be heavy with sleep.— *v.t.* to make heavy with sleep: to stupefy: to pass in a half-sleeping state.—*n.* a half-sleeping state. —*ns.* drows′ihe(a)d (*Spens.*), drowsiness, sleepiness.—*adv.* drows′ily.—*n.* drows′iness.—*adj.* drows′y, sleepy: heavy: dull: inducing sleep. [Apparently O.E. *drūsian*, to be sluggish; but not known between O.E. times and the 16th century.]

drub, drub, *v.t.* to beat or thrash:—*pr.p.* drubb′-ing; *pa.t.* and *pa.p.* drubbed.—*n.* drubb′ing, a cudgelling. [Ar. *daraba*, to beat, bastinado— *darb*, a beating, has been suggested.]

drucken, druk′ən, (Scot.) *adj.* drunken.—Used also as *pa.p.* of drink.—*n.* druck′enness. [O.N. *drukkinn*, pa.p. of *drekka*, to drink.]

drudge, druj, *v.i.* to do dull, laborious or very mean work.—*n.* one who does heavy monotonous work: a slave: a menial servant: dull task-work.—*ns.* drudg′er; drudg′ery, drudg′ism, the work of a drudge: uninteresting toil: hard or humble labour.—*adv.* drudg′ingly. [Ety. unknown; perh. from root of O.E. *drēogan*, to perform, undergo.]

drug, drug, *n.* any substance used in the composition of medicine: a substance used to stupefy or poison or for self-indulgence: an article that cannot be sold, generally owing to overproduction.—*v.t.* to mix or season with drugs: to administer a drug to: to dose to excess: to poison or stupefy with drugs.—*v.i.* to administer drugs or medicines: to take drugs, esp. narcotics, habitually:—*pr.p.* **drugging**; *pa.t.* and *pa.p.* **drugged.**—*ns.* **drugg′er**, a druggist (*obs.*): one who drugs; **drugg′ist**, one who deals in drugs.—**drug′-add′ict**, **drug′-fiend**, a habitual taker of drugs; **drug′-store**, (*U.S.*) a chemist's shop (usually in America selling a variety of goods, including refreshments). [O.Fr. *drogue*, of uncertain origin.]

**drug**, *drug*, (*Shak.*) *n.* a form of **drudge.**

**drugget**, *drug′it*, *n.* a woven and felted coarse woollen fabric. [O.Fr. *droguet.*]

**Druid**, *drōō′id*, *n.* a priest among the ancient Celts of Britain, Gaul and Germany: a member of a benefit society (founded 1781), its lodges called *groves*: an Eisteddfod official:—*fem.* **Dru′idess.**—*adjs.* **druid′ic**, **-al.**—*n.* **dru′idism**, the doctrines which the Druids taught: the ceremonies they practised.—**druidical circle**, a fanciful 18th-century name for a stone circle (not made by the Druids). [L. pl. *druidae*, from a Celtic stem *druid-*, whence O.Ir. *drai*, Ir. and Gael. *draoi*, magician.]

**drum**, *drum*, *n.* an instrument of percussion, a skin stretched on a frame: anything shaped like a drum: the tympanum of the ear: the upright part of a cupola (*archit.*): a cylinder, esp. a revolving cylinder: a cylindrical barrel: a bundle (*Austr.*): formerly, a large and tumultuous evening party (said to be so called because rival hostesses vied with each other in beating up crowds of guests): a drumfish.—*v.i.* to beat a drum: to beat rhythmically: to solicit orders (*U.S.*).—*v.t.* to expel by beat of drum: to summon: to impress by iteration:—*pr.p.* **drumm′ing**; *pa.t.* and *pa.p.* **drummed.**—*n.* **drumm′er**, one who drums: a commercial traveller: a bush tramp (*Austr.*).—**drum′fish**, any fish of the *Sciaenidae*; **drum′fire**, massed artillery-fire with a rolling sound; **drum′head**, the head or skin of a drum: the top part of a capstan.—*adj.* (*mil.*) improvised in the field (see **court-martial**).—**drum′-mā′jor**, marching leader of a military band; **drum majorette**, a female who twirls a baton at the head of a marching band; **drum′stick**, stick with which the drum is beaten: tibia of a dressed fowl.—**beat the drum**, indulge in publicity. [From a Gmc. root found in Du. *trom*, Ger. *trommel*, a drum; prob. imit.]

**drum**, *drum*, *n.* a ridge (in many place-names).—*n.* **drum′lin** (*geol.*), a ridge formed under the ice-sheet of the Glacial Period (also **drum**). [Ir. and Gael. *druim*, back.]

**drumble**, *drum′bl*, (*Shak.*) *v.i.* to be sluggish.—*n.* **drum′bledor**, a dumbledore.

**drumly**, *drum′li*, (*Scot.*) *adj.* turbid, muddy: gloomy.

**drummock**, *drum′ək.* Same as **drammock.**

**Drummond light**, *drum′ənd līt*, *n.* the limelight or oxy-hydrogen light invented by Captain T. Drummond (1797-1840).

**drunk**, *drungk*, *pa.p.* and old-fashioned *pa.t.* of **drink.**—*adj.* intoxicated (also *fig.*): saturated.—*n.* drunken bout: a drunk person.—*n.* **drunk′ard**, one who frequently drinks to excess: a habitual drinker.—*adj.* **drunk′en**, given to excessive drinking: worthless, besotted: resulting from intoxication: (sometimes) drunk.—*adv.* **drunk′enly.**—*n.* **drunk′enness**, intoxication: habitual intoxication.

**drupe**, *drōōp*, *n.* a fleshy fruit with a stone.—*adj.* **drupā′ceous**, producing or pertaining to drupes or stone-fruits.—*ns.* **drup′el**, **drupe′let**, a little drupe, forming part of a fruit, as in the raspberry. [L. *drūpa*—Gr. *dryppā*, an olive.]

**druse**, *drōōz*, *n.* a rock cavity lined with crystals —by geologists usu. called a drusy cavity.—

**dru′sy**, rough with, composed of, minute crystals: miarolitic. [Ger. *druse*—Czech. *druza*, a piece of crystallised ore.]

**druxy**, *druk-si*, *adj.* of timber, having decayed spots concealed by healthy wood.—Also **drick′-sie.** [Origin unknown.]

**Druz, Druze, Druse**, *drōōz*, *n.* one of a remarkable people inhabiting chiefly a mountainous district in the south of Syria, with a peculiar religion interwoven from the Bible and the Koran.—*adj.* **Drus′ian.** [Perh. from *Darazi*, an early exponent of the religion.]

**dry**, *drī*, *adj.* without water or liquid, contained or adhering: free from, or deficient in, moisture, sap, rain: thirsty: out of water: failing to yield water, or milk, or other liquid: of a fruit, not fleshy: not green: unbuttered: not drawing blood: of wines, etc., free from sweetness and fruity flavour: legally forbidding the liquor trade: enforcing or subjected to prohibition: uninteresting: frigid, precise, formal: of humour, quiet, restrained, and unobtrusive: of manner, distantly unsympathetic:—*comp.* **dri′er**; *superl.* **dri′est.**—*v.t.* to free from or exhaust of water or moisture.—*v.i.* to become dry: to evaporate entirely:—*pr.p.* **dry′ing**; *pa.t.* and *pa.p.* **dried**; *3rd pers. sing. pr.t.* **dries.**—*n.* a prohibitionist.—*n.* **dri′er, dry′er**, one who or that which dries: a machine for extracting moisture from cloth, grain, etc.: a drying agent for oils, paint, etc.—*adv.* **dri′ly, dry′ly**, in a dry manner.—*n.* and *adj.* **dry′ing.**—*adv.* **dry′ish.**—*n.* **dry′ness.**—*n.* **Dry′asdust**, a character in the prefatory manner of some of Scott's novels: a dull, pedantic, learned person.—Also *adj.*—*v.t.* **dry′beat** (*Shak.*), to drub, but without shedding blood.—*n.* **dry′-bi′ble**, a disease of horned cattle in which the third stomach, or bible, is very dry; **dry bob**, at Eton a boy who plays cricket, football, etc.—opp. to the *wet bob*, who rows.—*v.t.* **dry′-clean**, to clean without using water.—**dry′-cell**, an electric cell in which the electrolyte is not a liquid but a paste (as a refill for an electric torch); **dry′-cupping**, application of cups without previous scarification; **dry′-dock**, a dock that can be emptied of water: a graving dock.—*v.t.* to put in dry dock.—*adj.* **dry′-eyed′**, tearless.—**dry farming**, a system of tillage in dry countries, surface soil being kept constantly loose, so as to retain scanty rains and reduce evaporation; **dry′-fist**, a niggard.—*adj.* and *adv.* **dry-fist′ed**, taking payment for gains and owing for losses.—*adj.* **dry′-fly** (of fishing), without sinking the fly in the water.—*adv.* **dry′-foot** (*Shak.*), by scent of the foot alone.—*n.pl.* **dry′-goods**, drapery and the like distinguished from groceries, hardware, etc.—**dry ice** (see **ice**); **dry land**, land as opposed to sea; **dry light**, an undeceptive light: an unprejudiced view; **dry Mass, service**, *Missa sica*, a rite in which there is neither consecration nor communion; **dry measure**, a system of measure by bulk, used for grain, etc. (see **bushel, peck, pint**); **dry′-nurse**, a nurse who does not suckle.—Also *v.t.*—**dry′-plate**, a sensitised photographic plate, with which a picture may be made without the preliminary use of a bath; **dry′-point**, a sharp needle by which fine lines are drawn in copper-plate engraving: a plate or impression produced with it; **dry′-rot**, a decay of timber caused by *Merulius lacrymans* and other fungi which reduce it ultimately to a dry, brittle mass: a concealed decay or degeneration (*fig.*); **dry run**, a practice exercise (military): a rehearsal.—*v.t.* **dry′-salt**, to cure (meat) by salting and drying.—*n.* **dry′salter**, a dealer in gums, dyes, etc.: or (*obs.*) in salted or dry meats, pickles, etc.: **dry′saltery.**—*adj.* and *adv.* **dry′-shod**, without wetting the shoes or feet.—**dry ski**, an adaptation of a ski with which one

can practise skiing on a dry surface; **dry skiing.** —*adj.* **dry′-stone,** built of stone without mortar, as some walls.—**dry steam,** steam unmixed with liquid drops; **dry′-stove,** a kind of hot-house with dry heat; **dry′-wall′er,** one who builds walls without mortar; **dry′-wash′,** the bed of an intermittent stream.—**cut and dried** (see **cut**); **dry up,** to dry thoroughly or completely: to cease to produce liquid (water, milk, etc.): to forget one's lines or part (as an actor, etc.; *coll.*): to stop talking (*slang*); **go dry,** to adopt liquor prohibition; **high and dry** (see **high**). [O.E. *drȳge*; cf. Du. *droog*, Ger. *trocken*.]
**dryad,** *drī′ad, -əd, n.* a wood nymph: a forest-tree:—*pls.* **dry′ads, -adēs.** [Gr. *drȳas, -ados,* from *drȳs,* oak tree.]
**dso, dsobo, dsomo.** See under **zho.**
**dual,** *dū′əl, adj.* two-fold: consisting of two: expressing or representing two things (*gram.*).— *n.* a grammatical form indicating duality: a word in the dual number.—*ns.* **du′ad,** a dyad; **dū′alin,** an explosive mixture of sawdust, salt-petre, and nitroglycerine; **dū′alism** (*philos.*), that view which seeks to explain the world by the assumption of two radically independent and absolute elements—e.g. (1) the doctrine of the entire separation of spirit and matter, thus being opposed both to *idealism* and to *materialism*; (2) the doctrine of two distinct principles of good and evil, or of two divine beings of these characters; **du′alist,** a believer in dualism. —*adj.* **dualis′tic,** consisting of two: relating to dualism.—*ns.* **duality** (*dū-al′i-ti*), doubleness: state of being double: **du′archy,** a faulty form of diarchy.—**dual carriageway,** a road consisting of two separated parts, each for use of traffic in one direction only; **dual control,** joint control or jurisdiction.—*adj.* **du′al-control′,** able to be operated by either or both of two persons.— **dual monarchy,** two (more or less) independent states with one and the same monarch: specifically, Austria-Hungary (before 1918); **dual personality,** a condition in which the same individual shows at different times two very different characters.—*adj.* **du′al-pur′pose,** serving or intended to serve two purposes: (of cattle) bred to produce meat and milk; **dual school,** one for both boys and girls. [L. *duālis—duo,* two.]
**duan,** *dōō′än, -an, n.* a division of a poem, canto. [Gael.]
**duar,** *dōō′är, n.* a circular Arab encampment or tent village.—Also **douar, dowar.** [Ar. *dūār.*]
**dub,** *dub, v.t.* to confer knighthood upon, from the ceremony of striking the shoulders with the flat of a sword: to confer any name or dignity upon: to smooth with an adze: to trim: to cut the comb and wattles from: to rub a softening and waterproof mixture into (leather): to dress (a fly) for fishing:—*pr.p.* **dubb′ing;** *pa.p.* **dubbed.**—*n.* **dubb′ing,** the accolade: (also **dubb′in**) a preparation of grease for softening leather. [O.E. *dubbian,* to dub knight.]
**dub,** *dub,* (*Scot.*) *n.* a pool of foul water: a puddle: (*pl.*) mud. [Cf. L.G. *dobbe.*]
**dub,** *dub, v.t.* to give (a film) a new sound-track, e.g. one in a different language: to add sound effects or music: to transfer (recorded music, etc.) to a new disk or tape: to combine so as to make one record (music, etc., from more than one source, e.g. a live performance and a recording). [Abbrev. of **double.**]
**dubious,** *dū′bi-əs, adj.* doubtful, causing doubt: uncertain: of uncertain event or issue: arousing suspicion or disapproval: hesitating (about).— *n.* **dūbiety** (*bī′i-ti*), doubt.—*adv.* **dū′biously.**— *ns.* **dūbios′ity, dū′biousness.** [L. *dubius.*]
**dubitate,** *dū′bi-tāt, v.i.* to doubt, hesitate.—*adj.* **dū′bitable.**—*ns.* **dū′bitancy, dūbitā′tion.**—*adj.* **dū′bitative.**—*adv.* **dū′bitatively.** [L. *dubitāre, -ātum.*]

**ducal,** *dū′kəl, adj.* pertaining to a duke.—*adv.* **dū′cally.** [Fr.,—L.L. *ducālis—*L. *dux,* leader.]
**ducat,** *duk′ət, n.* a gold coin formerly much used on the Continent, its commonest value being about 9s. 4d., though there were silver ducats in Italy worth 3s. 4d.—*n.* **ducatoon′,** an old silver coin in Venice and elsewhere, worth 5 to 6 shillings. [O.Fr. *ducat—*It. *ducato—*L.L. *ducātus,* a duchy.]
**ducdame,** *dōōk′də-mi, dōōk-dä′mi,* (*Shak. As You Like It*), *interj.* perh. a meaningless refrain: explained as L. **duc ad mē,** bring to me, as Welsh *dewch 'da mi,* come with me, as Romany *dukrā′mē,* I tell fortunes, etc.
**duce,** *dōō′chä, n.* the title assumed by the Italian dictator Mussolini. [It., leader—L. *dux.*]
**duchy,** *duch′i, n.* the territory of a duke, a dukedom.—*ns.* **duch′ess,** the consort or widow of a duke: a woman of the same rank as a duke in her own right: a size of roofing slate, 24 × 12 inches (610 × 305 mm.); **duchesse** (*duch′es, düshes′;* Fr., duchess), a table-cover or centre-piece.—Also **duchesse cover.**—**duchesse lace,** Flemish pillow lace with designs in cord outline; **duchesse set,** a set of covers for a dressing-table; **duch′y court,** the court of a duchy. [O.Fr. *duché* —L.L. *ducātus;* Fr. *duchesse—*L.L. *ducissa.*]
**duck,** *duk, n.* a kind of coarse cloth for small sails, sacking, etc.: (in *pl.*) garments made of duck. [Du. *doek,* linen cloth; Ger. *tuch.*]
**duck,** *duk, v.t.* to dip for a moment in water: to avoid (*coll.*).—*v.i.* to dip or dive: to lower the head suddenly: to cringe, yield.—*n.* a quick plunge, dip: a quick lowering of the head or body, a jerky bow.—*ns.* **duck′er,** one who ducks: a diving-bird; **duck′ing.**—**duck′ing-pond; duck′-ing-stool,** a stool or chair in which offenders were formerly tied and ducked in the water. [M.E. *douken* from an assumed O.E. *dūcan,* to duck, dive; Ger. *tauchen,* Du. *duiken.*]
**duck,** *duk, n.* any bird of the family Anatidae, the prominent marks of which are short webbed feet, with a small hind-toe not reaching the ground, the netted scales in front of the lower leg, and the long bill: the female duck as distinguished from the male *drake:* in cricket (originally *duck's egg*), the zero (O), which records in a scoring-sheet that a player made no runs: a darling, sweetheart (*coll.*): a defaulter, bankrupt.—*ns.* **duck′ing,** duck-hunting; **duck′-ling,** young duck; **ducks, duck′y,** *coll.* endearment.—*adj.* **duck′y.**—**duck′-ant,** a Jamaican termite nesting in trees; **duck′bill,** an aquatic burrowing and egg-laying Australian monotreme (Ornithorhynchus), with broadly webbed feet, and duck-like bill.—*adj.* **duck′-billed,** having a bill like a duck.—**duck′-board,** planking for swampy ground, trenches, etc.; **duck′-hawk,** moor-buzzard or marsh-harrier: (U.S.) peregrine falcon.—*adj.* **duck′-legged,** short-legged.— **duck′mole,** the duckbill; **duck′-pond; duck′s′-foot,** lady's mantle; **duck′-shot,** shot for shooting wild-duck; **duck′s-meat,** duckweed; **duck′-tail,** white Teddy boy of S. Africa; **duck′weed,** any plant of the family Lemnaceae, monocotyledons consisting of a small flat green floating plate, from which a root dangles.—**Bombay duck,** bummalo; **break one's duck** (*cricket*), to make one's first run (see above); **lame duck,** a defaulter: bankrupt: anything disabled; **like a dying duck,** languishing; **make, play, ducks and drakes,** to make flat stones skip on the surface of water: to use recklessly: squander, waste (with *with, of*); **sitting duck,** an easy target, helpless victim; **wild′-duck,** the mallard, esp. the hen-bird. [O.E. *dūce* (or *duce*?), a duck; cf. **duck** (2).]
**duck,** *duk, n.* a kind of amphibious military transport vehicle or landing craft. [From manufacturers' code initials, DUKW.]

Neutral vowels in unaccented syllables: *el′ə-mənt;* for certain sounds in foreign words, see p. viii

**duct**, *dukt*, *n*. a tube conveying fluids in animal bodies or plants: a pipe for an electric cable: an air-passage.—*adj.* **duct'less.**—**ductless glands,** masses of glandular tissue that lack ducts and discharge their products directly into the blood. [L. *ductus*—*dūcĕre*, to lead.]

**ductile**, *duk'til*, *-til*, *adj.* easily led: yielding: capable of being drawn out into threads.—*n.* **ductility** (*-til'*), capacity of being drawn out without breaking. [Fr.,—L. *ductilis*—*dūcĕre*, to lead.]

**dud**, *dud*, (*coll.*) *n.* (in *pl.*) poor or ragged clothes, tatters.—*n.* **dudd'ery**, a shop where old clothes are sold: rags collectively.—*adj.* **dudd'y**, ragged. —**duddy weans** (*wānz*; Burns), ragged children: (with *cap.*) a Scottish literary society. [There is a M.E. *dudde*, birrus, a cloak; cf. O.N. *duthi*, swaddling-clothes.]

**dud**, *dud*, (*slang*) *n.* a bomb or projectile that fails to go off: a dishonoured cheque: a counterfeit: any person or thing useless or ineffective: a failure.—Also *adj.* [Origin unknown.]

**dudder**, *dud'ər*, (*dial.*) *n.* confusion. [Cf. **dither.**]

**dude**, *dūd*, *dood*, (*slang*, orig. *Amer.*) *n.* a fop or dandy: a townsman.—*adj.* **du'dish.**—*n.* **du'dism.** —**dude ranch,** ranch run as a holiday resort or for training in ranching. [Origin unknown.]

**dudeen**, *doo-dēn'*, *-dhēn'*, *n.* a short clay tobacco-pipe. [Ir. *dúidin*, dim. of *dūd*, pipe.]

**dudgeon**, *duj'ən*, *n.* resentment: offended indignation. [Origin unknown.]

**dudgeon**, *duj'ən*, *n.* the haft of a dagger: a small dagger. [Anglo-Fr. *digeon*, knife-handle.]

**due**, *dū*, *adj.* owed: that ought to be paid or done to another: proper: appointed, under engagement, to be ready, arrive, etc.—*adv.* exactly, directly.—*n.* that which is owed: what one has a right to, has earned: fee, toll, charge, or tribute: (in *pl.*) subscription to a club or society.—*adj.* **due'ful, dewfull** (*Spens.*), proper, fit.—**due to,** caused by: (wrongly) owing to, because of; **give the devil his due,** to give a fair hearing or fair-play to one of notorious character; **in due course,** in the ordinary way when the time comes. [O.Fr. *deü*, pa.p. of *devoir*—L. *debēre*, to owe.]

**due**, *dū*, (*Shak.*) *v.t.* to endue.

**duel**, *dū'əl*, *n.* a combat between two persons, pre-arranged and fought under fixed conditions, generally on an affair of honour: single combat to decide a quarrel: any fight or struggle between two parties.—*v.i.* to fight in a duel:—*pr.p.* **dū'elling;** *pa.t.* and *pa.p.* **dū'elled.**—*ns.* **dū'eller; dū'elling; dū'ellist; duello** (*doo-el'lō*; It.), a duel: the laws which regulate duelling.— *adj.* **dū'elsome,** given to duelling. [It. *duello*—L. *duellum*, the original form of *bellum*—*duo*, two.]

**duenna**, *dū-en'a*, *n.* a lady who acts the part of governess in Spain: a lady who watches over or chaperons a younger. [Sp. *dueña*, a form of *doña*, mistress—L. *domina*, fem. of *dominus*, lord.]

**duet**, **duett**, *dū-et'*, **duetto**, *doo-et'tō*, *ns.* a composition in music for two performers: the performance of such: the performers of such: any action involving two parties.—*ns.* **duettino** (*-tē'nō*), a simple duet; **duett'ist** (*dū-*). [It. *duetto*, dim. of *duo*—L. *duo*.]

**duff**, *duf*, *n.* dough: a stiff flour pudding boiled in a bag: decaying vegetable matter, fallen leaves: coal-dust. [A form of **dough.**]

**duff**, *duf*, *v.t.* to make to look new: to alter brands on (stolen cattle): to steal cattle. [Perh. a back-formation from **duffer** (2).]

**duff**, *duf*, *v.t.* to play amiss by hitting the ground behind the ball (*golf*): to bungle. [Back-formation from **duffer** (1).]

**duff**, *duf*, *adj.* no good: broken, not working. [Prob. **duff** (3).]

**duffel**, *duf'l*, *n.* a thick, coarse woollen cloth, with a thick nap—also **duff'le:** sporting or camping kit (*U.S.*).—**duffel coat,** a jacket or coat, usu. hooded, made of duffel. [Du., from *Duffel*, a town near Antwerp.]

**duffer**, *duf'ər*, *n.* an unskilful person: a fogy, useless old fellow: a counterfeit coin: an unproductive mine.—*ns.* **duff'erdom, duff'erism.** [Origin unknown.]

**duffer**, *duf'ər*, *n.* a peddler of sham jewellery, etc.: one who fakes up sham articles or duffs cattle. [Origin unknown: thieves' slang.]

**dug**, *dug*, *n.* a nipple or udder of a cow or other beast. [Cf. Sw. *dægga*, Dan. *dægge*, to suckle.]

**dug**, *dug*, *pa.t.* and *pa.p.* of **dig.**—**dug'out,** a boat made by hollowing out the trunk of a tree: a rough dwelling or shelter dug out of a slope or bank or in a trench: a superannuated person brought back to employment.

**dugong**, *doo'gong*, *n.* a herbivorous marine mammal of the order Sirenia—the supposed original of the mermaid. [Malayan *dúyong*.]

**duiker, duyker,** *di'kər*, *n.* a small S. African antelope: a cormorant (*S. Afr.*). [Du., diver, from plunging into the bush, or into the sea.]

**duke**, *dūk*, *n.* a sovereign prince of a small state: a nobleman of the highest order: a chief (*B.*): (*slang*—*dook*) the fist (also **dook**).—*v.t.* (with *it*) to play the duke.—*ns.* **duke'dom,** the title, rank, or lands of a duke; **duke'ling,** a petty duke; **duk'ery,** a duke's territory or seat; **duke'ship.**— **the Dukeries,** a group of ducal seats in Notts. [O.Fr. *duc*—L. *dux, ducis,* a leader—*dūcĕre*, to lead.]

**Dukhobor, Doukhobor,** *doo'hhō-bör, doo'kō-bör,* *n.* a member of a Russian sect who trust to an inner light, reject the doctrine of the Trinity, and refuse military service, many of them settled in Canada since 1899:—*pl.* **D(o)ukhobors; Dukhobort'sy.** [Russ. *Dukhoborets*—*dukh,* spirit, *borets,* fighter—*boroty'*, to fight.]

**dukkeripen,** *dook-ə-rip'ən,* *n.* fortune-telling. [Romany *drukeriben.*]

**DUKW.** See **duck** (4).

**dulcamara,** *dul-kə-mä'ra,* *n.* the bittersweet. [L. *dulcis,* sweet, *amāra* (fem.) bitter.]

**dulcet,** *duls'it, adj.* sweet: melodious, harmonious. —*n.* **dulciana** (*dul-si-ä'na*), an open diapason organ stop of pleasing tone and small scale; **dulcifica'tion.**—*adj.* **dulcif'luous,** flowing sweetly. —*v.t.* **dul'cify,** to make sweet.—*ns.* **dulcil'oquy,** a soft manner of speaking; **dul'cite, dul'citol;** **dul'cose** (*-kōs*), a saccharine substance derived from various plants—in its crude form, *Madagascar manna;* **Dul'citone** (*trademark*), a keyboard instrument in which graduated tuning-forks are struck by hammers; **dulcitude,** sweetness; **dulcose** (see **dulcite**).—**dulcified spirit,** a compound of alcohol with mineral acid. [L. *dulcis,* sweet.]

**dulcimer,** *dul'si-mər,* *n.* a musical instrument like a flat box, with sounding-board and wires stretched across bridges: a Jewish musical instrument, probably a bagpipe. [Sp. *dulcemele* —L. *dulce melos,* a sweet song—*dulcis,* sweet, Gr. *melos,* a song.]

**Dulcinea,** *dul-sin-ē'a, dul-sin'i-a,* *n.* sweetheart. [From *Dulcinea* del Toboso, the name given by Don Quixote to the mistress of his imagination.]

**dulcite, dulcose.** See **dulcet.**

**dule,** *dül,* (*Scot.*) *n.* woe.—Also *adj.* (*obs.*) **doole.** —*n.* **dule'-tree,** the gallows. [See **dole** (2).]

**dulia, douleia,** *dū-, doo-li'a,* (*R.C. Church*) *n.* the inferior veneration accorded to saints and angels, as opposed to *hyperdulia,* that acorded to the Virgin Mary, and *latria,* that accorded to God alone.—*ns.* **d(o)uloc'racy,** government by slaves; **dulō'sis,** enslavement, practised by certain ants upon other kinds.—*adjs.* **dulōt'ic.** [Gr. *douleiā,* servitude, *doulōsis,* enslavement—*doulos,* a slave.]

**dull,** *dul, adj.* slow of learning, or of understanding:

wanting in keenness of hearing or other sense: insensible: without life or spirit: uninteresting: slow of motion: drowsy: sleepy: sad: downcast: cheerless: lacking brightness or clearness: cloudy: dim: muffled: obtuse: blunt.—*v.t.* to make dull or stupid: to blunt: to damp: to cloud.—*v.i.* to become dull.—*n.* **dull'ard,** a dull and stupid person: a dunce.—*adj.* **dull'ish.**—*ns.* **dull'ness, dul'ness,** the state or quality of being dull.—*adj.* **dull'y,** somewhat dull.—*adv.* **dully** (*dul'li*).—*adjs.* **dull'-brained** (*Shak.*); **dull'-browed; dull'-eyed** (*Shak.*); **dull'-sighted; dull'-witted.** [Related to O.E. *dol.* foolish, and *dwellan,* to err; Du. *dol,* Ger. *toll,* mad.]

**dulocracy,** etc.  See **dulia.**

**dulse, duls,** *n.* an edible red seaweed, esp. *Rhodymenia palmata.* [Gael. *duileasg,* poss.—*duille,* a leaf, *uisge,* water.]

**duly, dū'li,** *adv.* properly: fitly: at the proper time. [See **due.**]

**duma, douma, dōō'ma,** *n.* an elected council, esp. the Russian parliament of 1906-17.—*n.* **dum'aist,** a duma member. [Russ. *duma,* of Gmc. origin; cf. **doom.**]

**dumb, dum,** *adj.* without the power of speech: silent: soundless: stupid (*U.S.* after Ger. or Du.).—*v.t.* (*Shak.*), to render dumb.—*adv.* **dumb'ly,** in silence: mutely.—*ns.* **dumb'ness; dumm'erer** (*old slang*), a dumb person, esp. a rogue who feigns dumbness; **dumm'iness; dumm'y,** one who is dumb: a mere tool, man of straw: a block or lay-figure: a sham or counterfeit article taking the place of a real one: an unprinted model of a book: a rubber teat: an exposed hand of cards: a game in which a hand is exposed: the imaginary player of such a game: a feint of passing (*Rugby football*).—*adj.* silent: sham.—**dumb-bell,** a double-headed weight swung in the hands to develop the muscles: any object or figure of the same shape: a stupid person (*U.S.*); **dumb'-cane,** a tropical American araceous plant (*Dieffenbachia Seguine*) whose acrid juice swells the tongue; **dumb'-pia'no,** a soundless keyboard for piano practice; **dumb'-show,** gesture without words: pantomime; **dumb'-wait'er,** a movable platform used for conveying food, dishes, etc., at meals: a stand with revolving top for holding dessert, etc.: a small lift for food and dishes.—*vs.t.* **dum(b)-found', -er,** to strike dumb: to confuse greatly: to astonish.—**dummy run,** an experimental run: a try-out or testing.—**sell the dummy** (*Rugby football*), to deceive an opponent by a feint of passing the ball: also *fig.*; **strike dumb,** to silence with astonishment. [O.E. *dumb;* Ger. *dumm,* stupid, Du. *dom.*]

**dumbledore,** *dum'bl-dōr, -dör,* (*dial.*) *n.* the bumblebee: the brown cockchafer.

**dumdum,** *dum'dum,* *n.* a soft-nosed expanding bullet, first made at Dum Dum near Calcutta.—**dumdum fever,** kala-azar.

**dumka, dōōm'ka,** (*mus.*) *n.* a lament: a slow movement or piece:—*pl.* **-ky** (*-kē*). [Czech.]

**dummy.**  See **dumb.**

**dumose, dū'mōs,** *adj.* bushy—also **dū'mous.**—*n.* **dumōs'ity.** [L. *dūmus,* a thorn-bush.]

**dump, dump,** *v.t.* to set down heavily or with a thump: to unload: to land and sell at prices below cost of production in the exporting country—or (according to some) in the importing country (*econ.*): to tip (esp. rubbish): to get rid of.—*n.* a thud: a place for the discharge of loads, or for rubbish: a deposit: store (*mil.*): a dirty, dilapidated place. [Cf. Dan. *dumpe,* Norw. *dumpa,* to fall plump.]

**dump, dump,** *n.* dullness or gloominess of mind, ill-humour, low spirits—now only used in the pl.: an obsolete slow dance or dance-tune in 4-4 time: a melancholy strain (*Shak.*): any tune (*obs.*).—*adj.* **dump'ish,** depressed in spirits.—*adv.*

**dump'ishly.**—*n.* **dump'ishness.** [Prob. related to O.Du. *domp,* mist; or Ger. *dumpf,* gloomy.]

**dump, dump,** *n.* a deep hole in a river-bed, a pool. [Prob. Norw. *dump,* pit.]

**dump, dump,** *n.* a short thick person or thing: a marble: a counter: a small coin: (in *pl.*) money (*slang*). [Perh. a back-formation from **dumpy.**]

**dum-palm.**  Same as **doum-palm.**

**dumpling,** *dump'ling,* *n.* a kind of thick pudding or mass of paste: a dumpling-shaped person or animal. [Origin obscure.]

**dumpy, dump'i,** *adj.* short and thick.—*n.* a dumpy person or animal, esp. one of a breed of very short-legged fowls: a short umbrella.—*n.* **dump'iness.**—*v.t.* **dump'le,** to make or cook, as a dumpling: to round into a dumpy shape.—**dump'y-lev'el,** a surveyor's level with rigid connection of the telescope to the vertical spindle. [18th cent.; perh. from **dumpling.**]

**dun, dun,** *adj.* greyish brown: mouse-coloured: dingy: dusky.—*n.* a dun colour: a horse of dun colour.—*v.t.* (*U.S.*) to cure and brown, as cod. —*v.i.* to become dun-coloured.—*n.* **dunn'ing.**—*adj.* **dunn'ish,** somewhat dun.—**dun'-bird,** the pochard, esp. the hen-bird; **dun'-cow,** the shagreen ray; **dun'-div'er,** the merganser; **dun'-fish,** codfish cured by dunning. [O.E. *dun,* prob. not Celt.]

**dun, dun,** *v.t.* to importune for payment:—*pr.p.* **dunn'ing;** *pa.t.* and *pa.p.* **dunned.**—*n.* one who duns: a demand for payment. [Perh. allied to **din.**]

**dun, dun,** *n.* a hill: a fortified mound. [Celt.; in many place-names; adopted in O.E. as *dūn;* see **down.**]

**dunce, duns,** *n.* one slow at learning: a stupid person.—*ns.* **dunce'dom,** the class of dunces; **dun'cery,** stupidity; **Dun'ciad,** Pope's epic of dunces. [*Duns* Scotus (died 1308), the Subtle Doctor, leader of the schoolmen, from him called *Dunses,* who opposed classical studies on the revival of learning—hence any opposer of learning, a blockhead.]

**dunch, dunsh, dunsh,** (*Scot.*) *vs.t.* to jog, nudge, bump: to butt.—Also *n.* [Ety. doubtful.]

**dunder,** *dun'dar,* *n.* lees, dregs of sugar-cane juice. [Sp. *redundar,* to overflow.]

**dunderfunk,** *dun'dar-fungk,* *n.* ship-biscuit, soaked in water, mixed with fat and molasses, and baked in a pan.—Also **dan'dyfunk.**

**dunderhead,** *dun'dar-hed,* *n.* a stupid person—also **dun'derpate.**—*adj.* **dun'derheaded.**—*n.* **dun'derheadism.** [Origin unknown.]

**Dundreary,** *dun-drēr'i,* *adj.* like Lord *Dundreary,* in Tom Taylor's *Our American Cousin*—in Sothern's creation of the part, a lisping and brainless dandy, wearing long side-whiskers.

**dune, dūn,** *n.* a low hill of sand, esp. on the seashore. [Fr.,—O.Du. *duna:* cf. **down.**]

**dung, dung,** *n.* excrement: manure.—*v.t.* to manure with dung.—*v.i.* to void excrement.—*adj.* **dung'y.**—**dung'-bee'tle,** the dor-beetle: a scarabaeoid beetle generally; **dung'-cart; dung'-fork,** a fork used for moving stable manure; **dung'-heap, dung'hill,** a heap of dung: any mean situation; **dung'-hunt'er,** a skua; **dung'mere,** a manure-pit. [O.E. *dung;* cf. Dan. *dynge,* a heap; Ger. *dung.*]

**dungaree,** *dung-ga-rē',* or *dung',* *n.* a coarse Indian calico: (*pl.*) overalls, esp. ones including trousers, made of it. [Hindi *dūgrī.*]

**dungeon,** *dun'jan,* *n.* orig. the principal tower of a castle: a close, dark prison: a cell under ground. —*v.t.* to confine in a dungeon.—*n.* **dun'geoner,** a gaoler. [O.Fr. *donjon*—L.L. *domniō, -ōnis*—L. *dominus,* a lord.]

**duniewassal, dunniewassal, duniwassal,** *dōōn-i-wos'l,* *n.* a Highland gentleman of inferior rank. [Gael. *duine,* man, *uasal,* of gentle birth.]

**dunite, dun'it,** *n.* crystalline rock composed almost

entirely of olivine. [*Dun* Mountain, near Nelson, in New Zealand.]

**dunk,** *dungk, v.t.* and *v.i.* to dip cake, etc., that one is eating in one's coffee or other beverage. [Ger. *tunken,* to dip; cf. **Dunker.**]

**Dunker,** *dungk'ər, n.* a member of a sect of German-American Baptists who practise triple immersion.—Also **tunk'er.** [Ger., dipper.]

**Dunkirk,** *dun-kûrk',* or *dun', n.* a successful military evacuation by sea against odds, as by the British in 1940 at Dunkirk: a complete abandonment of one's position: a rapid or desperate withdrawal.

**dunlin,** *dun'lin, n.* the red-backed sandpiper. [Dim. of **dun.**]

**Dunlop,** *dun-lop', n.* a cheese made of unskimmed milk—from *Dunlop* in Ayrshire.

**dunnage,** *dun'ij, n.* loose wood of any kind laid in the bottom of the hold to keep the cargo out of the bilge-water, or wedged between parts of the cargo to keep them steady: sailor's baggage. [Ety. unknown.]

**dunnock,** *dun'ək, n.* the hedge-sparrow. [Dim. of **dun.**]

**dunny,** *dun'i,* (*dial.*) *adj.* deaf. [Origin obscure.]

**Dunstable,** *dun'stə-bl, n.* a kind of straw-plait, first made at *Dunstable* in Bedfordshire: a straw hat, etc.:—**Dunstable road, highway,** anything plain and direct.

**dunt,** *dunt,* (*Scots.*) *n.* a thump: the wound made thereby.—*v.t.* to thump, beat. [See **dint.**]

**dunt,** *dunt,* (*dial.*) *n.* gid or sturdy in sheep, etc. [Origin obscure.]

**duo,** *dōō'ō, dū'ō, n.* a duet: two persons, etc., associated in some way, e.g. a pair of musicians or variety artists. [It.—L. *duo,* two.]

**duodecennial,** *dū-ō-di-sen'yəl, adj.* occurring every twelve years. [L. *duodecim,* twelve, *annus,* year.]

**duodecimal,** *dū-ō-des'i-ml, adj.* computed by twelves: twelfth: (in *pl.*) a method of calculating the area of a rectangle when the length and breadth are stated in feet and inches.—**duodecimal system,** a system of numbers in which each denomination is twelve times the next, instead of ten times, as in ordinary (decimal) arithmetic: the name given to the division of unity into twelve equal parts. [L. *duodecim,* twelve—*duo,* two, and *decem,* ten.]

**duodecimo,** *dū-ō-des'i-mō, adj.* formed of sheets folded so as to make twelve leaves.—*n.* a book of such sheets—usually written 12mo: an interval of a twelfth (*mus.*). [L. *in duodecimō,* in twelfth (abl. of *duodecimus,* twelfth)—*duo,* two, *decem,* ten.]

**duodenary,** *dū-ō-dē'nə-ri, adj.* relating to twelve, twelvefold. [L. *duodēnārius.*]

**duodenum,** *dū-ō-dē'nəm, n.* the first portion of the small intestine, so called because about twelve fingers'-breadth in length:—*pl.* **duodē'na.**—*adj.* **duodē'nal.**—*ns.* **duodenec'tomy,** excision of the duodenum; **duodeni'tis,** inflammation of the duodenum. [Formed from L. *duodēnī,* twelve each.]

**duologue,** *dū'ō-log, n.* a piece spoken between two. [Irregularly formed from L. *duo* (or Gr. *dyo*) two, Gr. *logos,* discourse.]

**duomo,** *dwō'mō, n.* a cathedral. [It. See **dome.**]

**dup,** *dup,* (*Shak.*) *v.t.* to undo, open. [do up; cf. **don** and **doff.**]

**dupe,** *dūp, n.* one who is cheated.—*v.t.* to deceive: to trick.—*n.* **dūpabil'ity.**—*adj.* **dū'pable.**—*ns.* **dū'per;** **dū'pery,** the art of deceiving others. [Fr. *dupe;* of uncertain origin.]

**duple,** *dū'pl, adj.* double, twofold: having two beats in the bar (*mus.*).—*n.* **dū'plet,** a like throw of two dice: a pair of electrons forming a single bond between two atoms. [L. *duplus;* cf. **double.**]

**duplex,** *dū'pleks, adj.* twofold, double: having some part doubled: communicating in both

directions at the same time.—*n.* **duplicity** (*dū-plis'i-ti*), doubleness, esp. in conduct and intention: insincerity: double-dealing.—**duplex (apartment),** a flat on two floors. [L. *duplex, -icis.*]

**duplicate,** *dū'pli-kit, adj.* double: twofold: like, equivalent or alternative.—*n.* another (esp. subsidiary or spare) thing of the same kind: a copy or transcript: condition of being in two copies. —*v.t.* (*-kāt*) to double: to copy: repeat: to fold. —*ns.* **dūplicand'** (*Scots law*), double feu-duty, due on certain occasions; **dūplicā'tion.**—*adj.* **dū'plicative.**—*ns.* **dū'plicātor,** a copying apparatus; **dū'plicāture,** a doubling: anything doubled: the fold of a membrane; **dūply',** a second reply in Scots law.—*v.t.* to say in duply.—**duplicate bridge,** a form of competition bridge in which each pair or four plays the same set of hands as all other pairs or fours; **duplicate ratio,** ratio of the squares of the quantities.—**in duplicate,** in two copies, or original accompanied by a copy; **duplication of the cube,** the problem eagerly discussed by the early Greek geometers, of constructing a cube equal to twice a given cube, impossible by use of straight line and circle only, but soluble by means of other curves. [L. *duplicāre, -ātum, duo,* two, *plicāre,* to fold.]

**duplicity.** See **duplex.**

**duppy,** *dup'i, n.* a ghost. [West Indian Negro word.]

**dura.** Same as **durra.**

**durable,** *dūr'ə-bl, adj.* able to last or endure: hardy: permanent.—*ns.* **durabil'ity, dur'ableness.**—*adv.* **dur'ably.**—*ns.* **dur'ance,** continuance (*obs.*): durability (*obs.*): a durable cloth (*obs.*): imprisonment; **dur'ant,** a strong cloth in imitation of buff-leather; **durā'tion,** continuance in time: time indefinitely: power of continuance: length of time.—**for the duration** (*coll.*), as long as the war (or the situation under discussion) continues. [L. *dūrāre,* to harden, endure, last.]

**duraluminium,** *dūr-al-ū-min'i-əm, n.* an aluminium alloy.—Also **dural'umin.** [L. *dūrus,* hard, and **aluminium.**]

**dura mater,** *dū'rə mā'tər,* L. *dōō'ra mä'ter, n.* the exterior membrane of the brain and spinal column distinguished from the other two, the arachnoid and the pia mater. [L. *dūra māter,* hard mother, a translation of the Ar. name.]

**duramen,** *dū-rā'mən, n.* heartwood. [L. *dūrāmen,* hardness—*dūrus,* hard.]

**durante bene placito,** *dū-ran'tē ben'ē plas'i-tō, dōō-ran'te ben'e plak'i-tō,* (L.L.) during good pleasure; **durante vita** (*vī'tə, vē', wē'tä*), during life.

**durbar,** *dûr'bär, n.* an audience-chamber: a reception or levee: a court: the body of officials at an Indian court. [Pers. *darbār,* a prince's court, lit. a door of admittance.]

**durchkomponi(e)rt,** *dōōrhh-kom-pon-ērt',* (Ger.; now *-komponiert*) having the music specially adapted to each stanza.

**durchlaucht,** *dōōrhh'lowhht,* (Ger.) Serene Highness.

**durchmusterung,** *dōōrhh-mōōs'tər-ōōng,* (Ger.), examination, scrutiny) a star catalogue.

**durdum.** Same as **dirdum.**

**dure,** *dūr,* (*obs.*) *v.i.* to endure, last or continue.— *adj.* **dure'ful** (*Spens.*), enduring, lasting. [Fr. *durer*—L. *dūrāre*—*dūrus,* hard.]

**duress, duresse,** *dūr-es', dūr'es, n.* constraint: imprisonment: constraint illegally exercised to force a person to perform some act. [O.Fr. *duresse*—L. *dūritia*—*dūrus,* hard.]

**durgan,** *dûr'gən, n.* a dwarf, any undersized creature.—*adj.* **dur'gy.** [Related to **dwarf.**]

**Durham,** *dur'əm, n.* one of a particular breed of shorthorned cattle—from the English county.

**durian,** *dōō'ri-ən,* or *dū', n.* a lofty Indian and Malayan bombacaceous fruit-tree (*Durio Zi-*

*bethinus*), with leaves like a cherry's: its large fruit, with hard rind and pulp of foul smell but fine flavour.—Also du′rion. [Malay *dūri*, thorn.]

**during**, *dū′ring, prep.* throughout the time of: in the course of. [Orig. *pr.p.* of dure.]

**durmast**, *dûr′mäst, n.* a variety of sessile-fruited oak with leaves downy below. (*Quercus petraea* or *sessiliflora*). [Origin unknown: perhaps a blunder for *dun mast*.]

**durn**, *dûrn*, (*dial.*) *n.* a doorpost.—Also **dern**. [Prob. Norse.]

**duro**, *dōō′rō, n.* a Spanish peso:—*pl.* **dūr′os**. [Sp. (*peso*) *duro*, hard (peso).]

**duroy**, *dōō-roi′, n.* an *obs.* form of corduroy.

**durra**, *dōō′rə, n.* Indian millet, a grass (*Sorghum vulgare*) akin to sugar-cane, much cultivated for grain in Asia and Africa, or other species of the genus.—Also **dou′ra, dhu′rra, du′ra,** and **dari** (*dur′i*). [Ar. *dhurah*.]

**durrie**, *dur′i, n.* an Indian cotton carpet fabric with fringes, used for curtains, covers, etc. [Hind. *dari*.]

**durst**, *dûrst, pa.t.* of dare, to venture. [O.E. *dorste*, pa.t. of *durran*, to dare.]

**durum** (wheat), *dū′rəm, n.* a kind of spring wheat (*Triticum durum*), grown esp. in Russia, North Africa and North America, whose flour is used in making spaghetti, etc. [L. *triticum dūrum*, hard wheat.]

**dush**, *dush,* (*Scot.*) *v.t.* to strike heavily against: to throw down.—*n.* a heavy impact.

**dusk**, *dusk, adj.* darkish: of a dark colour.—*n.* twilight: partial darkness: darkness of colour.—*v.t.* and *v.i.* to make or become dusky: to dim.—*v.t.* and *v.i.* **dusk′en,** to make or grow dark.—*adv.* **dusk′ily.**—*n.* **dusk′iness.**—*adj.* **dusk′-ish.**—*adv.* **dusk′ishly.**—*n.* **dusk′ishness.**—*adv.* **dusk′ly.**—*n.* **dusk′ness.**—*adj.* **dusk′y,** partially dark or obscure; dark-coloured: sad: gloomy. [Apparently connected with O.E. *dox*, dark.]

**dust**, *dust, n.* fine particles of solid matter: a cloud of powdery matter: powder: earth: the grave: a mean condition: gold-dust—hence money: turmoil (*slang*): a disturbance, a brawl (also **dust′-up′**).—*v.t.* to free from dust: to sprinkle.—*ns.* **dust′er,** one who dusts: a cloth or brush for removing dust: sprinkler: dust-coat (*U.S.*); **dust′iness.**—*adjs.* **dust′less; dust′y,** covered or sprinkled with dust: like dust: contemptible, bad (in phrase *not so dusty*; slang).—**dust′-ball,** a ball of grain-dust, etc., in a horse's intestine; **dust′-bin,** a receptacle for household rubbish; **dust′-bowl,** a drought area subject to dust-storms, esp. (*caps.*) the region of the U.S. along the western edge of the Great Plains; **dust′-brand,** smut; **dust′-brush,** a light brush for removing dust; **dust′-cart,** a cart for taking away household rubbish; **dust′-coat,** an overall: a light overcoat; **dust′-cover,** the jacket of a book; **dust′-devil, -storm,** a small storm in which a whirling column of dust or sand travels across a dry country; **dust′-hole,** dust-bin; **dust′-jack′et,** the jacket or dust-cover of a book; **dust′man,** one who removes household rubbish; **dust′-pan,** a pan or shovel for removing dust swept from the floor.—*adj.* **dust′proof,** impervious or inaccessible to dust.—**dust′-sheet,** a cloth for protecting furniture from dust; **dust′-shot,** the smallest size of shot.—**dusty answer,** an unsatisfying, unfruitful, or sordid response (*fig.*); **dust′y-foot** (see piepowder); **dust′y-mill′er,** the auricula, from the white dust upon its leaves and flowers.—**bite the dust** (see bite); **dust one's jacket,** to give one a drubbing; **kick up (raise) a dust** (see kick); **throw dust in one's eyes,** to deceive one. [O.E. *dūst*; cf. Ger. *dunst*, vapour.]

**Dutch**, *duch, adj.* pertaining to Holland, its people, or language: German (*obs.*, except *U.S.*): heavy, clumsy, as in *Dutch-built*.—*n.* the language of Holland: German (High and Low

Dutch, Hoch and Nieder or Platt Deutsch, High and Low German; *obs.* and *U.S.*): (*pl.*) the people of Holland: Germans (*obs.* and *U.S.*).—**Dutch′man,** a native or citizen of Holland: an Afrikaner (*S. Afr.; derog.*): a German or Teuton (*U.S.*):—*pl.* **Dutch′men;** *fem.* **Dutch′-woman;** *pl.* **Dutch′women.**—**Dutch auction,** courage, tiles (see auction, courage, tile); **Dutch bargain,** a one-sided bargain; **Dutch carpet,** a mixed material of cotton and wool for floor coverings; **Dutch cheese,** a small round cheese made on the Continent from skim-milk; **Dutch clinker,** a hard yellow brick for paving, etc.; **Dutch clock,** a clock of wood and wire with brass wheels, made in the Black Forest; **Dutch clover,** white clover; **Dutch comfort,** 'Thank God it's no worse'; **Dutch concert,** a concert in which singers sing their various songs simultaneously, or each one sings a verse of any song he likes between bursts of some familiar chorus; **Dutch doll,** a wooden doll with jointed legs; **Dutch drops,** a once popular medicine, composed of oil of turpentine, tincture of guaiacum, etc.; **Dutch gold, leaf, metal,** a copper-zinc alloy, a substitute for gold-leaf; **Dutch hoe,** a hoe with blade attached as in a spade; **Dutch liquid,** ethylene dichloride ($C_2H_4Cl_2$), an anaesthetic discovered by Dutch chemists; **Dutch lunch, supper, treat,** one at which each brings or pays for his own share; **Dutchman's breeches,** Dicentra; **Dutchman's pipe,** a species of Aristolochia; **Dutch oven,** a cooking-pot used by burying in coals: a tin for roasting before an open fire; **Dutch pink** (see pink); **Dutch rush,** a horse-tail (*Equisetum hyemale*) with much silica in its stem, used for polishing; **Dutch wife,** an open frame of rattan or cane used in the East Indies, to rest the limbs upon in bed.—**double Dutch,** any unknown or unintelligible language; **go Dutch** (*coll.*), to pay each for himself; **High Dutch,** see above: formerly, Dutch as spoken in the Netherlands as opp. to S. African Dutch: **double Dutch** (*obs.*); **Pennsylvania Dutch,** mixed German dialect of the descendants of German settlers in Pennsylvania; **talk like a Dutch uncle,** to utter a rebuke. [Ger. *deutsch*, (lit.) belonging to the people—O.H.G. *diutisc*; cf. O.E. *thēod*, Goth. *thiuda*, nation; see **Teutonic**.]

**dutch**, *duch,* (*costermonger's slang*) *n.* a wife. [duchess.]

**duty**, *dū′ti, n.* that which is due: what one is bound by any (esp. moral) obligation to do: one's proper business: service: attendance: supervision of pupils out of school hours: performance of function or service: the work done by a machine under given conditions, or for a specified amount of energy supplied: respect: tax on goods, etc.—*adj.* **dū′teous,** devoted to duty: obedient.—*adv.* **dū′teously.**—*n.* **dū′teousness.**—*adjs.* **dū′tiable,** subject to custom duty; **dū′tied,** subjected to duties and customs; **dū′tiful,** attentive to duty: respectful: expressive of a sense of duty.—*adv.* **dū′tifully.**—*n.* **dū′tifulness.**—*adjs.* **dū′ty-free,** free from tax or duty; **dū′ty-paid,** on which duty has been paid.—**do duty for,** to serve as, to act as substitute for; **on duty,** performing one's duties, or liable to be called upon to do so, during a specified period of time. [Anglo-Fr. *dueté*; see due (1).]

**duumvir**, *dōō-, dū-um′vir, -vər, n.* one of two associated in the same office:—*pl.* **duum′virs, duum′viri, -i:** (L. *dōō-ōōm-wir′ē*).—*adj.* **duum′viral.**—*n.* **duum′virate,** an association of two men in one office: a government by duumvirs. [L. *duumviri,* for *duoviri—duo,* two, and *vir,* a man.]

**duvet**, *dōō′vā,* (Fr. *dü-vā), n.* a quilt stuffed with eider-down or swan's-down. [Fr.]

**dux**, *duks, n.* a leader: the head boy or girl in a school or class. [L., a leader.]

dvornik, *dvor'nēk, dvör'*, *n.* a Russian concierge or porter. [Russ., caretaker—*dvor*, yard, court.]
dwale, *dwāl, n.* deadly nightshade (*bot.*): a stupefying drink: a black colour (*her.*). [O.N. *dvöl, dvali*, delay, sleep.]
dwalm, dwaum, *dwäm, dwöm,* (*Scot.*) *n.* a swoon, a sudden sickness.—*v.i.* to swoon: to fail in health. [O.E. *dwolma*, confusion.]
dwarf, *dwörf, n.* a diminutive man: a small man-like mythological being, esp. a metal-worker: an animal or plant much below the ordinary height: anything very small of its kind: a small star of high density and low luminosity (**white dwarf, red dwarf**, etc. according to colour).—*adj.* dwarfed: dwarfish: very small.—*v.t.* to hinder from growing: to make to appear small.—*v.i.* to become dwarfed.—*adjs.* **dwarfed; dwarf'ish**, like a dwarf: very small: despicable.—*adv.* **dwarf'-ishly.**—*ns.* **dwarf'ishness; dwarf'ism,** condition of being a dwarf.—**dwarfed tree**, bonsai. [O.E. *dweorg;* Du. *dwerg,* O.N. *dverg,* Ger. *zwerg.*]
dwell, *dwel, v.i.* to abide: to reside: to remain: to rest attention (on): to continue long (in; *obs.*).—*v.t.* (*Milt.*) to inhabit: to cause to dwell:—*pr.p.* **dwell'ing;** *pa.t.* and *pa.p.* **dwelt,** or **dwelled.**—*n.* a pause, hesitation.—*ns.* **dwell'er; dwell'ing,** the place where one dwells: a house: habitation: continuance.—**dwell'ing-house,** a house used as a dwelling, in distinction from a place of business or other building; **dwell'ing-place,** a place of residence. [O.E. *dwellan,* to go astray, delay, tarry.]
dwindle, *dwind'l, v.i.* to grow less: to waste away: to grow feeble: to become degenerate.—*v.t.* to lessen.—*n.* decline.—*n.* **dwin'dlement.** [Dim. of dwine.]
dwine, *dwin, v.i.* to pine: to waste away (*Scot.*). [O.E. *dwinan,* to fade: cf. O.N. *dvina,* Dan. *tvine,* to pine away.]
dyad, *di'ad, n.* a pair of units treated as one: a bivalent atom, radical, or element (*chem.*).—*adj.* **dyad'ic.** [Gr. *dyas, -ados—dyo,* two.]
dyarchy, *di'ärk-i, n.* a common but undesirable spelling of diarchy.
dybbuk, *dib'ək,* (*Jewish folklore*) *n.* evil spirit, or soul of dead person, that enters the body of a living person and controls his actions. [Heb. *dibbúq.*]
dye, *di,* (*Spens.*) *n.* Same as die (2).
dye, *di, v.t.* to stain: to give a new colour to:—*pr.p.* **dye'ing;** *pa.t.* and *pa.p.* **dyed.**—*n.* colour: tinge: stain: a colouring liquid.—*adj.* **dyed.**—*ns.* **dye'ing; dye'er,** one whose trade is to dye cloth, etc.; **dyester** (*di'stər; Scot.*), a dyer.—**dye'-house,** a building in which dyeing is done; **dy'er's-green'weed,** or **dy'er's-broom,** a papilionaceous shrub (*Genista tinctoria*), a source of yellow colouring matter; **dy'er's-rock'et, -weld, -yell'owweed,** a plant (*Reseda luteola*) akin to mignonette yielding a yellow dye; **dy'er's-weed,** a name for various plants that yield dyes—woad, weld, dyer's-greenweed, etc.; **dye'stuff,** a material used in dyeing; **dye'-wood,** any wood from which material is obtained for dyeing; **dye'-work(s),** an establishment for dyeing. [O.E. *dēagian,* to dye, from *dēag, dēah,* colour.]
dying, *di'ing, pr.p.* of die.—*adj.* destined for death: mortal: declining: occurring immediately before death, as dying words: pertaining to death.—*n.* death.—*adv.* **dy'ingly.**—*n.* **dy'ing-ness.**—**dying declaration** (*law*), declaration made by a dying person who does not survive through the trial of the accused. [See die (1).]
dyke. Same as dike.
dynamic, -al, *din-am'ik,* or *din-, adj.* relating to force: relating to dynamics: relating to the effects of forces in nature: relating to the activity or things in movement: relating to dynamism: causal: forceful, very energetic.—*n.* a moving force: any driving force instrumental in growth

or change (esp. social): pattern of growth or change.—*adj.* **dynam'ical.**—*adv.* **dynam'ically.**—*ns.* **dynam'ics** (treated as *sing.*), the science of matter and motion, mechanics, sometimes restricted to kinetics; **dyn'amism,** a theory which explains the phenomena of the universe by some immanent energy: operation of force: dynamic quality: quality of restless energy: quality of suggesting forceful movement (*art,* etc.); **dyn'amist.**—*adj.* **dynamis'tic.** [Gr. *dÿnamikos—dÿnamis,* power—*dÿnasthai,* to be able.]
dynamite, *din'ə-mit* (formerly also *din'*), *n.* explosive consisting of absorbent matter, as porous silica, saturated with nitroglycerine.—*v.t.* to blow up with dynamite.—*ns.* **dyn'amitard (-ärd), dyn'amiter,** a user of dynamite, esp. for political purposes. [Gr. *dÿnamis,* power.]
dynamo, *din'ə-mō, n.* the contraction for **dynamo-electric machine,** a machine for generating electric currents by means of the relative movement of conductors and magnets:—*pl.* **dyn'amos.**—*adjs.* **dyn'amo-elec'tric, -al.**—*ns.* **dynamogen'esis, dynamog'eny,** production of increased nervous activity; **dynamograph (-am'),** a recording dynamometer; **dynamom'eter,** an instrument for measuring force, or power.—*adjs.* **dynamomet'ric, -al.**—*n.* **dynamom'etry.**—**human dynamo,** a person of exceptional energy. [Gr. *dÿnamis,* power.]
dynast, *din'ast, -əst,* also *din', n.* a ruler.—*adj.* **dynas'tic,** relating to a dynasty.—*n.* **dyn'asty** (*-əs-ti*), a succession of kings of the same family, or of members of any powerful family or connected group. [Fr. *dynastie,* or L.L. *dynastia*—Gr. *dÿnasteia,* power, dominion—*dÿnasthai,* to be able.]
dyne, *din,* in the C.G.S. unit of force—the force which, acting on a mass of one gramme, produces an acceleration of one centimetre per second per second, equal to $10^{-5}$ of a newton. [Gr. *dÿnamis,* force.]
Dyophysite. Same as Diphysite.
Dyothelete, Dyotheletism, Diothelism. See Ditheletism.
dys-, *dis-, pfx.* ill, bad, abnormal. [Gr.]
dysaesthesia, *dis-əs-thē'si-ə, -zhi-ə, -zhə,* or *-ēs-, n.* impaired sensation, partial insensibility.—*adj.* **dysaesthetic** (*-thet'ik*). [Pfx. **dys-,** and Gr. *aisthēsis,* sensation—*aisthanesthai,* to feel.]
dyschroa, *dis'krō-ə, n.* discoloration of the skin from disease.—Also **dyschroia** (*-kroi'*). [Pfx. **dys-,** and Gr. *chroā, chroiā,* complexion.]
dyscrasia, *dis-krā'si-ə, -zhi-ə, -zhə,* (*path.*) *n.* a disordered condition of the body attributed originally to unsuitable mixing of the body fluids or humours. [Pfx. **dys-,** and Gr. *krāsis,* a mixing.]
dyscrasite, *dis'kras-it, n.* a mineral composed of silver and antimony. [Pfx. **dys-,** and Gr. *krāsis,* mixture.]
dysentery, *dis'ən-tər-i, -tri, n.* a term formerly applied to any condition in which inflammation of the colon was associated with the frequent passage of bloody stools: now confined to *a noebic dysentery,* the result of infection with the *Entamoeba histolytica;* and to *bacillary dysentery,* due to infection with *Bacterium dysenteriae.*—*adj.* **dysenteric** (*-ter'ik*). [Gr. *dysenteria—dys-,* amiss, *enteron,* intestine.]
dysfunction, *dis-fung(k)'shən, n.* impairment or abnormality of the functioning of an organ. [Pfx. **dys-.**]
dysgenic, *dis-jen'ik,* adj. unfavourable to race-improvement.—*n.* **dysgen'ics,** study of race degeneration. [Pfx. **dys-,** and the root of *gennaein,* to beget.]
dysgraphia, *dis-graf'i-ə, n.* inability to write, arising from brain damage or other cause.—*adj.* **dysgraph'ic.** [Pfx. **dys-,** and Gr. *graphein,* to write.]

**dysharmonic,** *dis-här-mon'ik, adj.* unbalanced, wanting in harmony of proportion. [Pfx. **dys-**.]

**dyslexia,** *dis-leks'i-ə, n.* word blindness, great difficulty in learning to read or spell, of which the cause (not lack of intelligence) has not been established.—*adjs.* **dyslec'tic; dyslex'ic.** [Pfx. **dys-,** and Gr. *lexis,* word.]

**dyslogistic,** *dis-lə-jis'tik, adj.* conveying censure, opprobrious.—*adv.* **dyslogis'tically.**—*n.* **dys'-logy,** dispraise. [Pfx. **dys-,** and Gr. *logos,* discourse.]

**dysmelia,** *dis-mēl'i-ə, -mel', -ya, n.* the condition in which one or more limbs are misshapen or incomplete.—*adj.* **dysmel'ic.** [Pfx. **dys-,** and Gr. *melos,* limb.]

**dysmenorrhoea, -rhea,** *dis-men-ō-rē'ə, n.* difficult or painful menstruation.—*adjs.* **dysmenorrh(o)e'al, -ic.** [Pfx. **dys-,** and Gr. *mēn,* month, *rhoiā,* flow.]

**dysodyle, -ile, -il,** *dis'ō-dil, -dil, n.* a yellow or greyish laminated bituminous mineral, often found with lignite, burning vividly, with an odour of asafoetida. [Gr. *dysōdēs,* stinking—*dys-,* ill, *ozein,* to smell, *hȳlē,* matter.]

**dyspathy,** *dis'pə-thi, n.* antipathy, dislike.—*adj.* **dyspathet'ic.** [Pfx. **dys-,** and Gr. *pathos,* feeling.]

**dyspepsia,** *dis-pep'si-ə, n.* indigestion.—Also **dyspep'sy.**—*n.* **dyspep'tic,** a person afflicted with dyspepsia.—*adj.* **dyspep'tic, -al,** afflicted with, pertaining to, or arising from, indigestion: gloomy, bad-tempered (*fig.*).—*adv.* **dyspep'tically.** [Gr. *dyspepsiā—dys-,* ill, *pepsis,* digestion—*peptein,* to digest.]

**dysphagia,** *dis-fā'ji-ə, n.* difficulty in swallowing—also **dys'phagy** (*-fə-ji*).—*adj.* **dysphagic** (*-faj'ik*). [Pfx. **dys-,** and Gr. *phagein* (aorist), to eat.]

**dysphonia,** *dis-fō'ni-ə, n.* difficulty in producing sounds. [Pfx. **dys-,** and Gr. *phōnē,* sound.]

**dysphoria,** *dis-fō'ri-ə, -fō', n.* impatience under affliction: morbid restlessness: uneasiness: want of feeling of wellbeing. [Gr. *dysphōriā,* affliction, pain—*dys-,* ill, and the root of *pherein,* to bear.]

**dyspnoea,** *disp-nē'ə, n.* difficulty of breathing.—*adjs.* **dyspnoe'al, dyspnoe'ic.**—Also **dyspnea,** etc. [Gr. *dyspnoia—dys-,* ill, *pnoē,* breathing.]

**dysprosium,** *dis-prōz'i-əm, n.* a metal of the rare earths, the element of atomic number 66 (symbol Dy). [Gr. *dysprositos,* difficult to reach—*dys-,* ill, difficult, *pros,* to, *ienai,* to go.]

**dystectic,** *dis-tek'tik, adj.* not easily fused. [Gr. *dystēktos—dys-,* ill, *tēkein,* to melt.]

**dysteleology,** *dis-tel-i-ol'ə-ji, n.* the doctrine of purposelessness, or denial of final causes: the study of functionless rudimentary organs in animals and plants.—*adj.* **dysteleological** (*-i-ə-loj'i-kl*).—*n.* **dysteleol'ogist.** [Pfx. **dys-** (in a negative sense).]

**dysthesia,** *dis-thē'si-ə, n.* a morbid habit of body, resulting in general discomfort and impatience. —*adj.* **dysthetic** (*-thet'ik*). [Gr. *dysthesiā—dys-* ill, *thesis,* position.]

**dysthymia,** *dis-thī'mi-ə, n.* morbid anxiety and despondency.—*n.* **dysthym'iac,** one who suffers from dysthymia.—*adj.* **dysthym'ic.** [Pfx. **dys-,** and Gr. *thymiā,* despair.]

**dystrophy,** *dis'trə-fi,* (*biol.*) *n.* imperfect nutrition: any of several disorders in which there is wasting of muscle tissue, etc.—Also **distrō'phia.**—*adj.* **distrophic** (*-tro'fik*).—muscular dystrophy (see **muscle**). [Pfx. **dys-,** and Gr. *trophē,* nourishment.]

**dysuria,** *dis-ū'ri-ə, n.* a difficulty or pain in passing urine—also **dys'ury.**—*adj.* **dysū'ric.** [Gr. *dysouriā—dys-,* ill, *ouron,* urine.]

**Dytiscus,** *di-* or *di-tis'kəs, n.* a genus of carnivorous water-beetles, including a common large British species, *D. marginalis.*—Also **Dyticus** (*dit'*)—*adj.* and *n.* **dytiscid** (*di-* or *di-tis'id*). [Gr. *dytikos,* diving—*dyein,* to dive.]

**dyvour,** *di'vər,* (*Scot.*) *n.* a bankrupt.—*n.* **dyv'-oury,** bankruptcy. [Origin unknown.]

**dzeren,** *dzē'rən, n.* a Central Asian antelope. [Mongolian.]

**dziggetai,** *dzig'ə-tī, n.* a Central Asian wild ass (*Equus hemionus*), rather like a mule. [Mongolian, *tchikhitei.*]

Neutral vowels in unaccented syllables: *el'ə-mənt*; for certain sounds in foreign words, see p. viii

# E

**E, e, ē,** *n.* the fifth letter in our own and cognate alphabets, with various sounds (as in m**e**, g**e**t, England, h**e**r, pr**e**y) and often mute (commonly an indication of a preceding long vowel or diphthong—**cf.** not, not**e**; bit, bit**e**): in music the third note or sound of the natural diatonic scale, the major third above the tonic C: *e* represents the base of the natural system of logarithms, the limit, as *m* approaches infinity, of $\left(1+\dfrac{1}{m}\right)^m$: as a mediaeval Roman numeral E = 250; Ē = 250,000.—**E´-boat** (*enemy boat*), a fast German motor torpedo-boat.

**ea, ē´ə, ē,** (*dial.*) *n.* a river: running water: a drainage canal in the Fens—sometimes **eau,** as if taken from French. [O.E. *ēa;* akin to L. *aqua,* water.]

**each, ēch,** *adj.* and *pron.* every one separately considered.—*adv.* **each´where** (*obs.*), everywhere.—**each other,** a compound reciprocal pronoun, one another, by some restricted in application to two; **each** way, in betting, for a win and for a place. [O.E. *ǣlc—ā,* ever, *gelīc,* alike.]

**eadish,** obsolete form of **eddish.**

**eager, ē´gər,** *adj.* excited by desire: ardent to do or obtain: earnest (*obs.*): keen, severe: (*Shak.* aygre) sour, acid, bitter (*obs.*).—*adv.* **ea´gerly.**—*n.* **ea´gerness.**—**eager beaver,** an enthusiast: a zealous person: one over-eager for work. [O. Fr *aigre*—L. *ācer, ācris,* sharp.]

**eager.** Same as **eagre.**

**eagle, ē´gl,** *n.* a name given to many large birds of prey of the family Falconidae: a military standard carrying the figure of an eagle: a lectern in the form of an eagle: the badge of certain orders, as the Prussian black (1701) and red (1705) **eagle,** the Polish, afterwards Russian, white eagle (1705): a gold coin of the United States, worth ten dollars: a hole at golf played in two strokes less than par.—*n.* **ea´glet,** a young or small eagle.—*adjs.* **ea´gle-eyed, ea´gle-sight´ed,** having a piercing eye: discerning; **ea´gle-flight´ed,** mounting high.—**ea´gle-hawk,** a name applied to several eagles of comparatively small size; **ea´gle-owl,** a genus (Bubo) of large owls; **ea´gle-ray,** a large sting-ray; **ea´gle-stone,** a hard-encrusted nodule of argillaceous oxide of iron.—*adj.* **ea´gle-winged,** having a eagle's wings. [O.Fr. *aigle*—L. *aquila.*]

**eaglewood, ē´gl-wood,** *n.* a genus (Aquilaria) of the daphne family, large spreading trees of Eastern India, whose heartwood contains a resinous substance fragrant in burning. [From the accidental resemblance of its name in some Eastern language to **eagle,** L. *aquila;* cf. **agalloch, agila.**]

**eagre, ā´gər, ē´gər,** *n.* a bore or sudden rise of the tide in a river. [Origin doubtful; hardly from O.E. *ēgor,* flood.]

**ealdorman.** See **alderman** (first meaning and derivation).

**eale,** prob. *ēl,* (*Shak., Hamlet* I, iv, 36) *n.* various conjectures, generally supposed to be for **evil,** but perh. a misprint.

**ean, ēn,** (*Shak.*) *v.t.* and *v.i.* to bring forth.—*n.* **ean´ling,** a young lamb. [O.E. *ēanian.*]

**ear, ēr,** *n.* a spike, as of corn.—*v.i.* to put forth ears.—*adj.* **eared,** of corn, having ears.—**ear´cock´le,** a disease of wheat caused by a thread-worm (*Tylenchus*). [O.E. *ēar;* Ger. *ähre.*]

**ear, ēr,** (*obs.*) *v.t.* to plough or till.—*n.* **ear´ing** (*obs.*), ploughing. [O.E. *erian;* cf. L. *arāre,* Gr. *aroein.*]

**ear, ēr,** *n.* the organ of hearing, or the external part merely: the sense or power of hearing: the faculty of distinguishing sounds esp. of a different pitch: attention: anything projecting or shaped like an ear, as the auricle of a leaf, lug of a vessel, a projecting part for support, attachment, etc.—*adj.* **eared,** having ears, or external ears.—*n.* **ear´ing** (*naut.*), one of a number of small ropes to fasten the upper corner of a sail to the yard.—*adj.* **ear´less,** without ears, or external ears.—**ear´ache,** an ache or pain in the ear; **ear´bob,** an earring; **ear´-bone.**—*adj.* **ear´-bussing** (*Shak.*; another reading **ear´-kissing**), whispered.—**ear´-cap,** a covering to protect the ear from cold or injury; **ear´drop,** an ornamental pendant hanging from the ear; **ear´drum,** the drum or middle cavity of the ear, tympanum; **ear´-hole,** the aperture of the ear; **ear´lap,** the tip of the ear: an ear-cap; **ear´lock,** a curl near the ear worn by Elizabethan dandies; **ear´mark,** an owner's mark on an animal's ear: a distinctive mark.—*v.t.* to put an earmark on: to set aside for a particular purpose.—**ear´muffs,** a pair of ear coverings joined by a band of material across the head; **ear´plug,** a plug of soft ma.erial inserted into the outer ear to exclude unwanted sound, water, etc.: **ear´phone,** a headphone; **ear´pick,** an instrument, for clearing the ear.—*adj.* **ear´-pierc´ing,** shrill, screaming.—**earring** (*ēr´ing*), an ornament hung from the ear; **ear´-shell,** any shell of the family Haliotidae; **ear´-shot,** the distance at which a sound can be heard; **ear´-trum´pet,** a tube to aid in hearing; **ear´wax,** a waxy substance secreted by the glands of the ear; **ear´wig** (O.E. *ēarwicga, ēare,* ear, *wicga,* insect, beetle), any dermapterous insect of the family Forficulidae, once supposed to creep into the ear: a flatterer.—*v.t.* to gain the ear of: to bias: to torment by private importunities.—*adj.* **ear´wiggy.**—**ear´-witness,** a witness that can testify from his own hearing.—**about one's ears,** said of something falling about one (e.g. house), or assailing one all around: also *fig.;* **be all ears,** to give every attention; **give ear,** to attend; **go in at one ear and out at the other,** to make no permanent impression; **have a person's ear,** to be secure of his favourable attention; **have itching ears,** to be desirous of hearing novelties (2 Tim. iv. 3); **have, keep, one's ear to the ground,** to keep oneself well informed about what is going on around one; **lend an ear,** to listen; **make someone's ears burn,** discuss someone in his absence; **over head and ears,** overwhelmed: deeply engrossed or involved; **pin back one's ears,** to listen attentively; **pin back someone's ears,** to subdue someone by beating; **set by the ears,** to set at strife; **tickle the ear of,** to gratify, pander to the taste of, flatter; **turn a deaf ear,** to refuse to listen; **up to one's ears in,** deeply involved in; **walls have ears,** there may be listeners. [O.E. *ēare;* cf. Ger. *ohr,* L. *auris.*]

**eard, eard-hunger.** See **yird.**

**earl, ûrl,** *n.* a British nobleman ranking between a marquis and a viscount:—*fem.* **count´ess.**—*n.* **earl´dom,** the dominion or dignity of an earl.—**Earl Marshal,** an English officer of state, president of the Heralds' College—the Scottish form **Earl Marischal.** [O.E. *eorl,* a warrior,

*fāte, fär; mē, hûr* (her); *mīne; mōte, för; mūte; mōon, fōot; dhen* (then)

hero, a Danish under-king, later a nobleman equivalent to count; cf. O.N. *jarl*.]

**early**, *ûr'li, adv.* near the beginning (of a time, period, series): soon: in good time: before appointed time:—*comp.* **ear'lier**; *sup.* **earliest**.— *adj.* belonging to or happening in the first part of time, period, or series: beforehand: ready, advanced, astir, or on the spot in good time: happening in the remote past or near future.— *v.t.* **ear'lierise, -ize**, to do at a date earlier than that arranged.—*n.* **ear'liness**.—**early bird**, the proverbial catcher of the (early) worm: an early riser; **early closing**, observance of a weekly half-holiday: closing of public houses early in the night; **early door**, an entrance to a theatre or hall open before the ordinary door at a higher price; **Early English**, (*philol.* see **English**) the form of Gothic architecture in which the pointed arch was first employed in Britain—succeeding the *Norman* towards the end of the 12th century, merging into the *Decorated* at the end of the 13th.—*adj.* **ear'ly-Victor'ian**, belonging to or characteristic of the early part of Queen Victoria's reign (reigned 1837-1901).—**early and late**, at all times; **earlier on**, previously; **early on**, before much time has elapsed; **keep early hours**, to rise and go to bed early. [O.E. *ǣrlice* (adv.)—*ǣr*, before.]

**earn**, *ûrn, v.t.* to gain by labour: to deserve: to bring to one.—*n.* **earn'er**.—*n.pl.* **earn'ings**, what one has earned: money saved. [O.E. *earnian*, to earn; cf. O.H.G. *aran*, harvest; Ger. *ernte*.]

**earn**, *ûrn, (dial.) v.t.* and *v.i.* to curdle (of milk).— Also **yearn**. [O.E. *iernan = rinnan*, to run, and *ærnan = rennan*, to cause to run; *gerinnan*, causative *gerennan*, to curdle.]

**earn**, *ûrn, v.i.* (*Spens., Shak.*). See **yearn** (1).

**earnest**, *ûr'nist, adj.* intent: sincere: serious.— *n.* seriousness: reality.—*adv.* **ear'nestly**.—*n.* **ear'nestness**. [O.E. *eornost*, seriousness; Ger. *ernst*.]

**earnest**, *ûr'nist, n.* money given in token of a bargain made (also **ear'nest-money, ear'nest-penny**): a pledge: first-fruits. [Ety. obscure; possibly conn. with **arles**.]

**earst**, obsolete form of **erst**.

**earth**, *ûrth, n.* the third planet in order from the sun: the matter on the surface of the globe: soil, a mixture of disintegrated rock and organic material in which plants are rooted: dry land, as opposed to sea: the world: the inhabitants of the world: dirt: dead matter: the human body: a burrow: an electrical connexion with the earth, usually by a wire soldered to a metal plate sunk in moist earth: an old name for certain oxides of metals (see **alkaline earth, rare earth, metal**).—*v.t.* to bury, inter (*obs.*): to hide or cause to hide in the earth, or in a hole: to connect to earth electrically: to clog, cover, smear, or partially cover with earth (often with *up*).—*v.i.* to burrow: to hide.—*adj.* **earth'en**, made of earth or clay: earthly.—*ns.* **earth'iness**; **earth'liness**; **earth'ling**, a dweller on the earth: a worldly-minded person.—*adj.* **earth'ly**, belonging to the earth: vile: worldly: conceivably possible on earth.—*n.* chance.—*adv.* **earth'ward**, toward the earth.—*adj.* **earth'y**, consisting of, relating to, or resembling earth: inhabiting the earth: gross: unrefined.—**earth'-bag**, a sack of earth used in fortifications; **earth'-bath**, a bath of earth or mud; **earth'-board**, the board of a plough, or other implement, that turns over the earth.—*adjs.* **earth'born**, born from or on the earth; **earth'bound**, bound to earth; **earth'-bred**, bred from earth: mean, grovelling.— **earth'-closet**, a closet in which earth is used for the deodorisation of faecal matters.—*adj.* **earth'-crea'ted**, made of earth.—**earth'enware**, crockery: coarse pottery; **earth'fall**, a landslide.—*adjs.*

**earth'fast**, fixed in the earth; **earth'-fed**, contented with earthly things.—**earth'flax**, asbestos; **earth'-hog**, the aardvark; **earth'-house**, an ancient underground dwelling or storehouse, also called **Picts' house**; **earth'-hunger**, passion for acquiring land; **earthing tires**, aircraft tires that discharge static electricity on grounding.— *adj.* **earth'ly-mind'ed**, having the mind intent on earthly things.—**earth'ly-mind'edness**; **earth'-move'ment**, elevation, subsidence, or folding of the earth's crust; **earth'nut**, the edible root-tuber of *Conopodium flexuosum*, a woodland umbelliferous plant: the plant itself (also *arnut, pignut, earth-chestnut*): the peanut (Arachis); **earth'-pea**, the peanut; **earth'-pillar**, a column of soft material protected from erosion by an overlying stone; **earth'-plate**, a buried plate of metal forming the earth-connexion of a telegraph-wire, lightning-conductor, etc.; **earth'-quake**, a quaking or shaking of the earth: a heaving of the ground.—*adjs.* **earth'quaked**, shaken, destroyed or visited by an earthquake; **earth'quaking**.—**earth'-shine**, the faint light visible on the part of the moon not illuminated by the sun; **earth'-smoke**, fumitory; **earth'-star**, a fungus (Geaster) akin to the puff balls that opens out into a starlike form; **earth'-table**, a course of stone or brick just above the ground; **earth'-tremor**, a slight earthquake; **earth'wax**, ozokerite; **earth'wolf**, the aardwolf; **earth'work**, a fortification of earth: an embankment: work of excavation and embanking; **earth'worm**, the common worm: a mean person, a poor creature. —**green earth** (see **green**).—**go to earth**, seek a hole or hiding place (also *fig.*). [O.E. *eorthe*; cf. Du. *aarde*, Ger. *erde*.]

**ease**, *ēz, n.* freedom from pain or disturbance: rest from work: quiet: freedom from difficulty: naturalness: unconstrained manner.—*v.t.* to free from pain, trouble, or anxiety: to relieve: to relax: to calm: to move gently.—*v.i.* to become less great or severe (often *ease off, up*): to move very gradually: to become less in demand.—*adj.* **ease'ful**, ease-giving: quiet, fit for rest.—*n.* **ease'ment**, relief (*rare*): assistance (*obs.*): support (*obs.*): gratification (*obs.*): legally, the right to use something (esp. land) not one's own or to prevent its owner from making an inconvenient use of it.—*adv.* **eas'ily**. —*n.* **eas'iness**.—*adj.* **eas'y**, at ease: free from pain: tranquil: unconstrained: giving ease: not difficult: yielding: not straitened (in circumstances): not tight: not strict: in plentiful supply: (*of market*) not showing unusually great activity.—Also *adv.*—*interj.* command to lower, to go gently, to stop rowing, etc.—**eas'y-chair**, an arm-chair for ease or rest.—*adjs.* **eas'y-go'ing, -ō'sy**, indolent: placid.—**easy money**, money made without much exertion or difficulty; **easy street** (*coll.*), a situation of comfort or affluence.—**be easy**, to be quite willing to fall in with one arrangement or another; **chapel of ease** (see **chapel**); **ease off**, to slacken gradually: to make or become less intense; **ease oneself**, to defecate; **easy on the eye** (*coll.*), good to look at; **easy money, honours evenly divided (at cards, etc.)**; **ill at ease**, uncomfortable; **stand at ease**, used of soldiers, when freed from attention; **stand easy**, used of a still easier position; **take it easy**, to avoid exertion: to be in no hurry; **take one's ease**, to make oneself comfortable. [O.Fr. *aise*; cog. with It. *agio*; Prov. *ais*, Port. *azo*.]

**easel**, *ēz'l, n.* the frame for supporting a picture during painting. [Du. *ezel*, or Ger. *esel*, an ass.]

**easle, aizle**, *āz'l, (Burns) n.* hot ashes. [O.E. *ysle*.]

**eassel, eassil**, *ēs'l, (Scot.) adv.* eastward: easterly. —*advs.* **eass'elgate, eass'elward**. [east.]

east, *ēst, n.* that part of the heavens where the sun rises at the equinox: one of the four cardinal points of the compass: the east part of a region: the east wind.—*adj.* toward the rising of the sun: blowing from the east.—*v.i.* to move or turn east.—*adjs.* east′er, east′ern, toward the east: connected with the east: dwelling in the east.— *ns.* east′erner, a native or inhabitant of the east, esp. of the United States; east′erling, a native of the east: a trader from the shores of the Baltic.—*adj.* east′erly, situated in the east: coming from the eastward: looking toward the east.—*adv.* on the east: toward the east.—*n.* an east wind.—*adjs.* east′ernmost, east′most, situated furthest east.—Also east′ermost (*obs.*). —*ns.* east′ing, the course gained to the eastward: distance eastward from a given meridian; east′- land, the land in the East.—*adj.* east′ling, -lin (*Scot.*), easterly.—*adv.* east′lings, -lins (*Scot.*), eastward; east′ward, east′wards, toward the east.—*adj.* east′ward.—east-by-north (south), 11¼ degrees north (south) from due east; East End, the eastern part of London or other town, often an area inhabited by people of the poorer classes; East′-end′er; Eastern Church, the Greek Church; East-Indiaman, a vessel used in the East India trade; east-north (south)-east, 22½ degrees north (south) from the east; East Side, the eastern part of New York.—about east (old *U.S. slang*), in proper manner; East Coast fever, African coast fever: a protozoan cattle disease resembling redwater, transmitted by ticks; the East, the countries to the east of western Europe (*Near East*, Turkey, Balkans, etc.: *Middle East*, Turkey, Persia, India, etc.: *Far East*, China, Japan, etc.): the eastern part of the United States, used relatively and vaguely, but commonly that part between the Mississippi and the Ohio. [O.E. *ēast*; Ger. *ost*; akin to Gr. *ēōs*, the dawn.]

Easter, *ēst′ər, n.* a Christian festival commemorating the resurrection of Christ, held on the Sunday after Good Friday.—Easter cactus, a S. American cactus having coral flowers; Easter Day, Easter Sunday; Easter dues, offerings, customary sums paid to the parson by his people at Easter; Easter egg, a stained or artificial egg, given as a present at Easter; East′ertide, East′ertime, either Easter week or the fifty days between Easter and Whitsuntide. [O.E. *ēastre*; Ger. *ostern*. Bede derives the word from *Eostre* (*Eastre*), a goddess whose festival was held at the spring equinox.]

easy. See ease.

eat, *ēt, v.t.* to take into the body by the mouth as food: to consume: to corrode.—*v.i.* to take food: to be eatable, to taste:—*pr.p.* eat′ing; *pa.t.* ate, *et* or *āt; pa.p.* eaten, *ētn,* or, *obs.,* eat, *et.*—*n.* (*arch.* in *sing.,* coll. in *pl.*) food.—*adj.* eat′able, fit to be eaten.—*n.* anything used as food (chiefly in *pl.*).—*ns.* eat′age, grass or fodder for horses, etc.: the right to eat; eat′er, one who, or that which, eats or corrodes: variety suitable for eating uncooked; eat′ery (*slang*), a restaurant.—*n.* and *adj.* eat′ing.—eat′ing-apple etc., one suitable for eating uncooked; eat′ing- house, a restaurant.—eat away, to destroy gradually: to gnaw; eat crow, dirt, humble pie (see crow, dirt, humbles); eat in, used of the action of acid: to eat at home; eat off, to clear (a crop) by setting cattle to eat it; eat one's hat, an undertaking promised on conditions one thinks very improbable; eat one's head off, to cost more for food than one is worth; eat one's heart out, to pine away, brooding over misfortune; eat one's terms, to study for the bar, with allusion to the number of times in a term that a student must dine in the hall of an Inn of Court; eat one's words, to take back what one has said; eat out, to finish eatables: to encroach

upon: to eat in a restaurant; eat the air (Shak.), to be deluded with hopes; eat up, to devour entirely: to consume, absorb: to derive pleasure from (*fig.*); what's eating you? (*coll.*), what is irking you? [O.E. *etan*; cf. Ger. *essen,* O.N. *eta,* L. *edĕre,* Gr. *edein.*]

Eatanswill, *ēt′an-swil, n.* in *Pickwick Papers,* a pocket borough at which an election takes place: any corrupt election or selection.

eatche, *ēch,* (*Scott*) *n.* a Scots form of adze.

eath, eathe, ethe, *ēth, eth,* (*Spens,* etc.) *adj.* easy. —*adv.* easily.—*adv.* eath′ly. [O.E. *ēathe,* easy, easily.]

eau, *ō, n.* the French word for water, used in English in various combinations.—eau des creoles (*dā krā-ol′*), a fine Martinique liqueur, made by distilling the flowers of the mammee-apple with spirit of wine; eau de Cologne (see Cologne); eau de Javelle (see Javel water); eau de vie (*də vē*), brandy.

eau. See ea.

eaves, *ēvz, n.pl.* (orig. *sing.*) the projecting edge of the roof: anything projecting.—eaves′drip, eaves′drop, the water that falls from the eaves of a house: the place where the drops fall.—*v.i.* eaves′drop, to stand under the eaves or near the windows of a house to listen: to listen for secrets.—Also *v.t.*—eaves′dropper, one who thus listens: one who tries to overhear private conversation; eaves′dropping. [O.E. *efes,* the clipped edge of thatch; cf. Ice. *ups.*]

ébauche, *ā-bōsh,* (Fr.) rough draft, sketch.

ebb, *eb, n.* the going back or retiring of the tide: a decline.—*v.i.* to flow back: to sink: to decline.—*adj.* (*obs.* or *dial.; Scott*) shallow.— *adj.* ebb′less.—ebb′-tide, the ebbing tide. [O.E. *ebba.*]

ebenezer, *eb-ən-ēz′ər, n.* a memorial stone set up by Samuel after the victory of Mizpeh (1 Sam. vii. 12): a name sometimes applied to a chapel or meeting-house. [Heb. *eben-hā-'ezer,* stone of help.]

ébéniste, *ā-bā-nēst,* (Fr.) a cabinet-maker.

Ebionite, *ē′bi-ən-it, n.* an early Christian holding the Mosaic law binding and denying the apostolate of Paul and the miraculous birth of Jesus. —*v.t.* e′bionise, -ize.—*adj.* ebionitic (-*it′ik*).—*ns.* e′bionitism, e′bionism. [Heb. *ebyōn,* poor.]

Eblis, *eb′lis,* Iblis, *ib′lis, n.* the chief of the fallen angels in Mohammedan mythology. [Ar. *Iblis.*]

ebon, *eb′ən,* ebony, *eb′ən-i, n.* a kind of wood furnished by various species of Diospyros (family Ebenā′ceae), almost as heavy and hard as stone, usually black, admitting of a fine polish: a tree yielding it: a Negro.—*adj.* made of ebony: black as ebony.—*v.t.* and *v.i.* eb′onise, -ize, to make or become like ebony.—*ns.* eb′onist, a worker in ebony; eb′onite, black vulcanised rubber. [L. (*h*)*ebenus*—Gr. *ebenos;* cf. Heb. *hobnim,* pl. of *hobni, obni*—*eben,* a stone.]

éboulement, *ā-bōōl′mä, n.* the falling in of the wall of a fortification: a landslide or landslip. [Fr.]

ebracteate, *ē-brak′ti-āt,* (*bot.*) *adj.* without bracts. —*adj.* ebract′eolate, without bracteoles. [L. *ē-,* without, from, *bractea,* a thin plate.]

ebriate, ebriated, *ē′bri-āt, -id, adjs.* intoxicated.— *n.* ebriety (*ē-bri′i-ti*), drunkenness.—*adj.* e′briōse, drunk.—*n.* ebrios′ity. [L. *ēbriāre, -ātum,* to make drunk.]

ebrillade, *ā-brē-*(*l*)*yäd, n.* the sudden jerking of a horse's rein when he refuses to turn. [Fr.]

ebullient, *ə-bul′yənt, adj.* boiling up or over: agitated: enthusiastic.—*ns.* ebull′ience, ebull′i- ency, a boiling over; ebull′ioscope, apparatus for determining the boiling-points of liquids.— *adjs.* ebullioscop′ic, -al.—*ns.* ebullios′copy; ebullition (*eb-ə-lish′ən*), act of boiling: agitation: an outbreak. [L. *ēbulliēns, -entis*—*ēbullīre*—*ē,* out, and *bullīre,* to boil.]

eburnean, *eb-ûr'ni-ən, adj.* of or like ivory—also ebur'neous.—*ns.* eburnā'tion (*ēb-* or *eb-*), a morbid change of bone by which it becomes very hard and dense; eburnificā'tion, art of making like ivory. [L. *eburneus*—*ebur*, ivory.]

ecardinate, *ē-kärd'in-āt, adj.* hingeless.—*n.pl.* Ecard'inēs, a class of brachiopods without hinge or arm skeleton. [L. *ē-*, without, *cardō, -inis,* hinge.]

ecarté, *ā-kär'tā, n.* a game in which cards may be discarded for others. [Fr., discarded—L. *ē*, out of, from, Fr. *carte*, a card.]

ecaudate, *ē-kö'dāt, adj.* tailless. [L. *ē-*, without, *cauda*, tail.]

ecblastesis, *ek-blas-tē'sis,* (*bot.*) *n.* proliferation of a floral axis. [Gr. *ekblastēsis*, budding forth —*ek*, out of, *blastos*, a sprout.]

ecbole, *ek'bo-lē, n.* a digression (*rhet.*): the raising or sharpening of a tone (*mus.*).—*adj.* ecbol'ic (*med.*), inducing contractions of the uterus leading to parturition or abortion.—*n.* a drug with this quality. [Gr. *ekbolē*, throwing out—*ek*, out of, *ballein*, to throw.]

eccaleobion, *e-kal-i-ō-bī'on, n.* a kind of incubator. [Gr. *ekkaleō bīon*, I call forth life.]

ecce homo, *ek'sē* (*ek'i*) *hō'mō, ek'e ho'mō,* (*art*) *n.* a picture of Christ crowned with thorns. [L., behold the man (John xix. 5).]

eccentric, *ek-sen'trik, adj.* departing from the centre: not having the same centre as another, said of circles: out of the usual course: not conforming to common rules: odd.—*n.* a circle not having the same centre as another: a contrivance for taking an alternating rectilinear motion from a revolving shaft (*mech.*): an eccentric fellow.— *adj.* eccen'trical.—*adv.* eccen'trically.—*n.* eccentricity (*-sən-tris'*), condition of being eccentric: in a conic section, the constant ratio of the distance of a point on the curve from the focus to its distance from the directrix (usually represented by *e*): singularity of conduct: oddness. [Gr. *ek*, out of, *kentron*, centre.]

ecce signum, *ek'sē sig'nəm, ek'ā sig'nŏŏm,* (L.) behold the sign or the proof.

ecchymosis, *ek-i-mō'sis, n.* discoloration due to extravasation of blood.—*adjs.* ecch'ymosed, ecchymot'ic. [Gr. *ekchymōsis*—*ek*, out of, and *chymos*, juice.]

Eccles cake, *ek'lz kāk, n.* a cake like a Banbury cake. [*Eccles* in Lancashire.]

ecclesia, *i-klē'zi-ə, n.* a popular assembly, esp. of Athens, where the people exercised full sovereignty, and every male citizen above twenty years could vote: applied by the Septuagint commentators to the Jewish commonwealth, and from them to the Christian Church.—*adj.* ecclē'sial.— *ns.* ecclē'siarch (*-ärk*), a ruler of the church; ecclē'siast, the preacher—as the author of Ecclesiastes: an ecclesiastic; Ecclesias'tes, one of the books of the Old Testament, traditionally ascribed to Solomon; ecclesiast'ic, one consecrated to the church, a priest, a clergyman.— *adjs.* ecclesias'tic, -al, relating to the church.— *adv.* ecclesias'tically.—*ns.* ecclesias'ticism (*-sizm*), attachment to ecclesiastical observances, etc.: the churchman's temper or spirit; Ecclesias'-ticus, one of the books of the Apocrypha; ecclesiol'atry (Gr. *latreiā*, worship), excessive reverence for church forms and traditions.— *adj.* ecclesiolog'ical.—*ns.* ecclesiol'ogist; ecclesiol'ogy, the science of church forms and traditions, of building and decorating churches: the science relating to the church. [L.L.,—Gr. *ekklēsia*, an assembly called out of the world, the church—*ek*, out of, and *kaleein*, to call.]

ecco, *ek'kō,* (It.) here is; there: look there.

eccoprotic, *ek-ō-prot'ik, adj.* laxative, mildly cathartic.—*n.* a laxative. [Gr. *ekkoprōtikos*—*ek*, out of, *kopros*, dung.]

eccrinology, *ek-ri-nol'ə-ji, n.* the branch of physi-

ology that relates to the secretions. [Gr. *ek*, out of, *krinein*, to separate, secrete.]

eccrisis, *ek'ri-sis, n.* expulsion of waste or morbid matter.—*n.* eccrit'ic, a medicine having this property. [Gr. *ekkrisis*, secretion—*ek*, out and *krisis*, separation.]

ecdysis, *ek'di-sis, n.* the act of casting off an integument, sloughing.—*n.* ecdysiast (*diz'*; *coll.*) a stripteaser. [Gr. *ekdysis*—*ek*, out of, *dyein*, to put on.]

eche, *ēch,* (*Shak.*) *v.t.* to eke out: to augment. [Other readings, ech, eech, ich; O.E. *ēcan*; akin to L. *augēre*, to increase; see eke.]

echelon, *esh'ə-lon, āsh-lɔ̃, n.* a stepwise arrangement of troops, ships, planes, etc.: a group of persons of one grade in an organisation. [Fr. *échelon*—*échelle*, ladder, stair; see scale.]

Echidna, *ek-id'na, n.* a genus of Australian toothless, spiny, egg-laying, burrowing monotremes. —*n.* echid'nine, snake-poison. [Gr. *echidna,* viper.]

echinus, *e-kī'nas, n.* a sea-urchin: the convex projecting moulding (of eccentric curve in Greek examples) supporting the abacus of the Doric capital (*archit.*).—*adjs.* echinate, -d, *ek'in-āt, -id,* prickly like a hedgehog: bristly.—*ns.* Echi'nocac'tus, a large genus of ribbed, generally very spiny, cactuses; echi'nococc'us, the bladderworm stage (parasitic in cow, sheep, pig, man) of the dog tapeworm; echi'noderm, any one of the Echinoder'ma or Echinoder'mata, a phylum of radially symmetrical marine animals, having the body-wall strengthened by calcareous plates, and moving usually by tube-feet, distensible finger-like protrusions of a part of the coelom known as the water-vascular system—starfishes, sea-urchins, brittle-stars, sea-cucumbers, and sea-lilies.—*adj.* echinoder'matous; echi'noid, like a sea-urchin.—*n.* a sea-urchin.—*n.pl.* Echinoid'ea, the sea-urchins, a class of Echinoderma. —*n.* Echin'ops, a genus of Compositae found in southern Europe, the globe thistle, with flowers in globular clusters. [Gr. *echinos*, a hedgehog.]

echo, *ek'ō, n.* the sending back or reflection of sound or other waves: the repetition of sound by reflection: a reflected sound: a soft-toned organ forming a part of some large organs: a device in verse in which a line ends with a word which recalls the sound of the last word of the preceding line: response: repetition: imitation: an imitator: conventional play to indicate what cards one holds:—*pl.* echoes (*ek'ōz*).—*v.i.* to reflect sound: to be sounded back: to resound: play a card as echo.—*v.t.* send back (sound or other waves): to send back the sound of: to repeat: to imitate: to follow slavishly, -*pr.p.* ech'ōing; *pa.t.* and *pa.p.* ech'oed, -ōd.—*n.* ech'oer.—*adj.* echo'ic, of the nature of an echo: onomatopoeic (*philol.*).—*v.i.* ech'oise, -ize.—*ns.* ech'oism, the formation of imitative words; ech'oist, one who repeats like an echo.—*adj.* ech'oless, giving no echo: unresponsive.—*ns.* ech'ogram, the record produced in echo-sounding; echolalia (*ek-ō-lā'li-a;* Gr. *laliā,* talk), senseless repetition of words heard, occurring in disease of the brain or in insanity; echoprax'ia, echoprax'is (Gr. *praxis,* doing), imitation by an insane person of postures or movements of those near him.—echo location, determining (as a bat does) the position of objects by means of supersonic vibrations echoed from them; ech'o-sounder, the apparatus used in echo-sounding; ech'o-sounding, a method of measuring depth of water, locating shoals of fish, etc., by noting time for return of echo from the bottom, or bottom and shoal, etc.—cheer to the echo, to applaud most heartily. [L.,—Gr. *ēchō,* a sound.]

echt, *ehht,* (Ger.) genuine, authentic.

éclair, *ā-kler',* or *-klār', n.* a cake, long in shape,

with cream filling and chocolate or other icing. [Fr. *éclair*, lightning.]

**éclaircissement**, *ā-kler-sēs'mä*, *n.* the act of clearing up anything: explanation.—**come to an éclaircissement**, to come to an understanding: to explain conduct that seemed equivocal. [Fr. *éclaircir*—L. *ex*, out, *clārus*, clear.]

**eclampsia**, *i-klamp'si-a*, *n.* a condition resembling epilepsy: now confined to acute toxaemia with convulsive fits about the time of childbirth.—Also **eclamp'sy**.—*adj.* **eclamp'tic**. [Gr. *eklampsis*—*eklampein*, to flash forth, to burst forth violently (as a fever)—*ek* out of, *lampein*, to shine.]

**éclat**, *ā-klä*, *n.* a striking effect: showy splendour: distinction: applause. [Fr. *éclat*, from O.Fr. *esclater*, to break, to shine.]

**eclectic**, *ek-lek'tik*, *adj.* selecting or borrowing: choosing the best out of everything: broad, the opposite of exclusive.—*n.* one who selects opinions from different systems, esp. in philosophy.—*adv.* **eclec'tically**.—*n.* **eclec'ticism** (*-sizm*), the practice of an eclectic: the doctrine of the **eclec'tics**, a name applied to certain Greek thinkers in the 2nd and 1st centuries B.C., later to Leibniz and Cousin. [Gr. *eklektikos*—*ek*, from, *legein*, to choose.]

**eclipse**, *i-klips'*, *n.* the total or partial disappearance of a heavenly body by the interposition of another between it and the spectator, or by passing into its shadow: a throwing into the shade: loss of brilliancy: darkness.—*v.t.* to hide wholly or in part: to darken: to throw into the shade, to cut out, surpass.—*n.* **eclip'tic**, the great circle in which the plane containing the centres of the earth and sun cuts the celestial sphere; hence, the apparent path of the sun's annual motion among the fixed stars: a great circle in which that plane cuts the earth's surface at any moment.—*adj.* pertaining to an eclipse or the ecliptic.—**eclipse plumage**, dull plumage apparent in certain usu. brilliant-coloured birds out of the mating season. [O.Fr.—L. *eclipsis*—Gr. *ekleipsis*, failure—*ek*, out of *leipein*, to leave.]

**eclogite**, **eklogite**, *ek'-lə-jit*, *n.* a crystalline rock composed of red garnet and green omphacite or smaragdite. [Gr. *eklogē*, selection (from the unusual minerals that compose it)—*ek*, out of, *legein*, to choose.]

**eclogue**, *ek'log*, *n.* a short pastoral poem like Virgil's *Bucolics*. [L. *ecloga*—Gr. *eklogē*, a selection, esp. of poems—*ek*, out of, *legein*, to choose.]

**eclosion**, *i-klō'zhən*, *n.* emergence, esp. of insect from pupal case or larva from egg.—*v.i.* **eclose'**. [Fr. *éclosion*—L., *ex-*, *claudēre*, to shut.]

**eco-**, *ēk'*, *ek'ō-*, in composition, concerned with habitat and environment in relation to living organisms, as in ecology.—*n.* **ec'osystem**, a unit consisting of a community of organisms and their environment.

**ecology**, *ē-kol'ə-ji*, *ek-ol'*, *ik-*, *n.* study of plants, or of animals, or of peoples and institutions, in relation to environment.—*adjs.* **ecologic** (*-kō-loj'ik*), *-al*.—*adv.* **ecolog'ically**.—*n.* **ecol'ogist**.—Also **oecology**, etc. [Gr. *oikos*, house, *logos*, discourse.]

**economy**, *i-*, *e-*, *ē-kon'ə-mi*, *n.* the management of a household (*arch.*): the administration of the material resources of an individual, community, or country: the state of these resources: a frugal and judicious expenditure of money: thrift: a dispensation, as *the Christian economy*: the efficient use of something, e.g. speech, effort, etc.: an organised system: regular operations, as of nature.—*n.* **economet'rics**, statistical analysis of economic data and their interrelations with the aid of electronic computers.—*adj.* **economet'ric**.—*n.* **econometrician** (*-mə-*

*trish'ən*).—*adjs.* **economic** (*ē-*, *e-kən-om'ik*), pertaining or having reference to economy or to economics: relating to industry or business, e.g. *economic geography*, *history*, etc., from the utilitarian viewpoint: operated at, or capable of yielding, a profit: economical; **econom'ical**, conducive to thrift: frugal: careful: economic.—*adv.* **econom'ically**.—*ns.* **econom'ics**, the science of household management (*obs.*): pecuniary position and management: political economy; **economisā'tion**, *-z-*, act of economising.—*v.i.* **econ'omise**, *-ize*, to manage with economy: to spend money carefully: to save.—*v.t.* to use prudently: to spend with frugality.—*ns.* **economi'ser**, *-i'zer*, one who is economical: a device for saving heat, fuel, etc.; **econ'omist**, one who studies or is an expert on political economy: an economiser. [L. *oeconomia*—Gr. *oikonomiā*—*oikos*, a house, *nomos*, a law.]

**e contra**, *ē* (*ā*) *kon'tra*, (L.L.) contrariwise, conversely.

**e contrario**, *ē kon-trār'i-ō*, *ā kon-trä'ri-ō*, (L.L.) on the contrary.

**e converso**, *ē kon-vûr'sō*, *ā kon-ver'*, (*-wer'*), (L.L.) conversely, by logical conversion.

**écorché**, *ā-kör-shā'*, *n.* a figure in which the muscles are represented stripped of the skin, for the purposes of artistic study. [Pa.p. of Fr. *écorcher*, to flay.]

**écossaise**, *ā-ko-sez'*, *n.* originally a dance or dance-tune of Scottish origin in 3-4 or 2-4 time: later a lively country-dance or its music in 2-4 time.—**douche écossaise**, the alternation of hot and cold douches. [Fr., fem. of *écossais*, Scottish.]

**ecostate**, *ē-kos'tāt*, *adj.* ribless. [L. *ē*, from, *costa*, rib.]

**ecphonesis**, *ek-fō-nē'sis*, *n.* exclamation (*rhet.*): in the Greek Church, the part of the service spoken in an audible tone. [Gr. *ekphōnēsis*—*ek*, out, *phōnē*, voice.]

**ecphractic**, *ek-frak'tik*, (*med. obs.*) *adj.* serving to remove obstructions.—*n.* a drug with such properties. [Gr. *ekphraktikos*—*ek*, from, *phrassein*, to enclose.]

**écritoire**, *ā-krē-twär*, (Fr.) modern form of escritoire.

**ecru**, *e-*, *ā-krōō'*, *-krü'*, *n.* unbleached linen: its colour.—*adj.* like unbleached linen. [Fr. *écru*—L. *ex*, intensive, *crūdus*, raw.]

**ecstasy**, *ek'stə-si*, *n.* a state of temporary mental alienation and altered or diminished consciousness: excessive joy: enthusiasm, or any exalted feeling.—*v.t.* to fill with joy.—*adj.* **ec'stasied**, enraptured.—*v.t.* **ec'stasis**, ecstasy.—*v.t.* **ec'stasise**, *-ize*.—*adj.* **ecstat'ic**, causing ecstasy: amounting to ecstasy: rapturous.—*n.* one given to ecstasy: something spoken in a state of ecstasy.—*adv.* **ecstat'ically**. [Gr. *ekstasis*—*ek*, from, and root of *histanai*, to make to stand.]

**ectasis**, *ek'tə-sis*, *n.* the lengthening of a short syllable: dilatation. [Gr. *ektasis*, stretching.]

**ecthlipsis**, *ek-thlip'sis*, *n.* suppression of a sound, esp. of a syllable ending in *m* in verse before a vowel. [Gr. *ekthlipsis*—*ek*, from, *thlibein*, to rub or squeeze.]

**ecthyma**, *ek-thī'ma*, *n.* a skin eruption in large pustules. [Gr. *ekthȳma*, a pustule.]

**ecto-**, *ek-tō-*, in composition, outside, often opp. to **endo-**, **ento-**. See also **exo-**.—*n.* **ec'toblast** (Gr. *blastos*, a shoot, bud), the outer cell-layer of a gastrula: the epiblast.—*adj.* **ectoblas'tic**:—*n.* **ec'toderm** (Gr. *derma*, skin), the external germinal layer or epiblast of the embryo, or any part of the tissue animal derived from it.—*adjs.* **ectoderm'al**, **ectoderm'ic**.—*n.* **ec'tomorph** (Gr. *morphē*, form), a person of light and delicate build.—*adj.* **ectomorph'ic**.—*ns.* **ec'tomorphy**; **ectopar'asite**, an external parasite; **ec'toplasm** (Gr. *plasma*, mould), the outer layer of cytoplasm of a cell (*biol.*): an emanation of bodily appearance believed by some spiritualists to come from a medium.—*adjs.* **ectoplas'mic, ectoplas'tic.**—*n.* **ec'tosarc** (Gr. *sarx, sarkos,* flesh), ectoplasm.—*adj.* **ectotroph'ic** (Gr. *trophē,* food; *bot.*) of a mycorrhiza, having its hyphae mainly on the outside of the root that it feeds. —*n.* **ectozo'on** (Gr. *zōion,* animal), an animal ectoparasite:—*pl.* **ectozo'a.**—*n.* and *adj.* **ectozo'an.**—*adj.* **ectozo'ic.** [Gr. *ektos,* outside.] **ectogenesis,** *ek-tō-jen'i-sis, n.* development outside the body: variation in response to outside conditions.—*adjs.* **ectogenetic** (*-jɔn-et'ik*), produced by or pertaining to ectogenesis; **ectogen'ic,** of external origin: ectogenous; **ectogenous** (*ek-toj'ɔ-nɔs*), capable of living independently, or outside the body of the host (as some parasites).—*n.* **ectog'eny,** the effect of pollen on the tissues of a plant. [Gr. *ektos,* outside, *genesis,* generation.]

**ectomorph,** etc., **ectoparasite.** See ecto-.

**ectophyte,** *ek'tō-fit, n.* a vegetable ectoparasite. —*adj.* **ectophytic** (*-fit'ik*). [Gr. *ektos,* outside, *phyton,* a plant.]

**ectopia,** *ek-tō'pi-a,* **ectopy,** *ek'to-pi,* (*path.*) *n.* morbid displacement of parts: condition in which the foetus is outside the womb.—*adj.* **ectop'ic.** [Gr. *ek,* from, *topos,* place.]

**ectoplasm,** etc. See ecto-.

**ectosarc ... to ... ectozoic.** See ecto-.

**ectropion, -um,** *ek-trōp'i-on, -ɔm, n.* eversion of the margin of the eyelid, so that the red inner surface is exposed.—*adj.* **ectrop'ic.** [Gr. *ek,* out of, *trepein,* to turn.]

**ectype,** *ek'tip, n.* a reproduction or copy.—*adj.* **ec'typal** (*ek'ti-pɔl*).—*n.* **ectypog'raphy.** [Gr. *ek,* from, and *typos,* a stamp.]

**écu,** *ā-kü,* or *ā-kü', n.* a French silver coin, usually considered as equivalent to the English crown, gold coin weighing about 60 grains, etc. (*hist.*): a common name for the five-franc piece. [Fr.,— L. *scutum,* a shield.]

**écuelle,** *ā-kwel',* or *ā-kü-el', n.* a two-handled soup bowl. [Fr.,—L. *scutella,* drinking-bowl.]

**ecumenic, -al,** *ēk-,* or *ek-ū-men'ik, -ɔl, adj.* general, universal, belonging to the entire Christian Church.—*ns.* **ecumen'icalism, ecumen'icism** (*-is--izm*), **ecumen'ism,** doctrines and practice of the Christian ecumenical movement.—Also **oecumenic,** etc. [L. *oecumenicus*—Gr. *oikoumenikos* —*oikoumenē* (*gē*), inhabited (world).]

**écurie,** *ā-kü-rē,* (Fr.) lit. stable: a team of cars under individual or joint ownership which take part in motor racing.

**eczema,** *ek'si-ma, n.* a skin disease, in which part of the skin is red, with numerous small papules that turn into vesicles.—*adj.* **eczematous** (*-sem',* or *-zem'at-ɔs*). [Gr. *ekzeein*—*ek, zeein,* to boil.]

**edacious,** *i-, ē-, e-dā'shɔs, adj.* given to eating: gluttonous.—*adv.* **edā'ciously.**—*ns.* **edā'ciousness; edacity** (*i-das'i-ti*). [L. *edāx, edācis*— *edēre,* to eat.]

**Edam,** *ē'dam, n.* a kind of Dutch cheese. [After *Edam* near Amsterdam.]

**edaphic,** *i-daf'ik, adj.* pertaining to the soil.— *n.* **edaphology** (*ed-ɔf-ol'ɔ-ji*). [Gr. *edaphos,* ground.]

**Edda,** *ed'a, n.* the name of two Scandinavian books—the *Elder Edda,* a collection of ancient mythological and heroic songs (9th-11th century, or earlier); and the *Younger* or *Prose Edda,* by Snorri Sturluson (*c.* 1230), mythological stories, poetics, and prosody.—*adjs.* **Eddā'ic, Edd'ic.** [O.N. apparently akin to *ōdr,* mad, *ōthr,* spirit, mind, poetry; cf. **wood** (2); Ger. *wut,* fury; L. *vātēs,* poet, seer.]

**eddish,** *ed'ish, n.* pasturage, or the eatable growth of grass after mowing. [Dubiously referred to O.E. *edisc,* a park.]

**eddoes,** *ed'ōz, n.pl.* the tubers of various plants,

especially of taro (*Colocasia*):—*sing.* **edd'o.** [From a W. African word.]

**eddy,** *ed'i, n.* a current running back, contrary to the main stream, thus causing a circular motion: a whirlpool: a whirlwind.—*v.i.* to move round and round:—*pr.p.* **edd'ying;** *pa.t.* and *pa.p.* **edd'ied.** [Cf. O.N. *itha;* prob. conn. with O.E. *ed-,* back.]

**edelweiss,** *ā'dɔl-vis, n.* a small white composite (*Leontopodium alpinum*), with woolly heads, found in damp places on the Alps. [Ger. *edel,* noble, *weiss,* white.]

**edema, edematose, -ous.** See oedema.

**Eden,** *ē'dn, n.* the garden of Adam and Eve: a paradise.—*adj.* **Edenic** (*-den'*). [Heb. *ēden,* delight, pleasure.]

**edentate,** *ē-den'tāt, adj.* without teeth: wanting front teeth.—*n.* a member of the **Edentā'ta,** a New World order of mammals having no front teeth or no teeth at all—sloths, ant-eaters, armadillos, and, formerly, certain Old World edentate animals, as the pangolins.—*adjs.* **eden'tal,** of the edentates; **eden'tulous,** toothless. [L. *ēdentātus,* toothless—*ē,* out of, *dēns, dentis,* a tooth.]

**edge,** *ej, n.* the border of anything: a rim: the brink: the intersection of the faces of a solid figure: a ridge or crest: the cutting edge of an instrument: something that wounds or cuts: keenness: sharpness of mind or appetite: irritability: advantage (*coll.*).—*v.t.* to put an edge on: to place a border on: to border: to egg, urge on (*arch.*): to move gradually: to thrust edgewise: to strike with the edge.—*v.i.* to move sideways: to move gradually.—*adjs.* **edged;** **edge'less,** without an edge: blunt.—*advs.* **edge'ways, edge'wise,** in the direction of the edge: sideways.—*ns.* **edg'iness,** angularity, over-sharpness of outline: state of being on edge; **edg'ing,** any border or fringe round a garment: a border of box, etc., round a flower-bed.—*adj.* **edg'y,** with edges: sharp, hard in outline: irritable, on edge.—**edge coal,** a steeply dipping coalseam; **edge rail,** a rail of such form that the carriage-wheels roll on its edges, being held there by flanges; **edge tool, edged tool,** a tool with a sharp edge.—**edge in a word, get a word in edgeways,** to get a word in with difficulty; **edge out,** to remove or get rid of gradually: to defeat by a small margin (*U.S.*); **have the, an, edge on, against,** to have the, an, advantage over; **inside, outside, edge,** a skating movement on the inner or outer edge of the skate; **on edge,** in a state of expectant irritability: nervous, tense: all agog; **play with edge tools,** to deal carelessly with dangerous matters; **set on edge,** to excite; **set one's teeth on edge,** to cause a strange grating feeling in the teeth: to give a feeling of abhorrent discomfort: formerly, to make eager, stimulate desire. [O.E. *ecg;* cf. Ger. *ecke,* L. *aciēs.*]

**edgebone.** Same as aitchbone.

**edh.** See eth.

**edible,** *ed'i-bl, adj.* fit to be eaten.—*n.* something for food.—*ns.* **edibil'ity, ed'ibleness,** fitness for being eaten. [L. *edibilis*—*edēre,* to eat.]

**edict,** *ē'dikt, n.* something proclaimed by authority: an order issued by a king or lawgiver.—*adj.* **edict'al.**—*adv.* **edict'ally.** [L. *ēdictum*—*ē,* out of, *dicēre, dictum,* to say.]

**edifice,** *ed'i-fis, n.* a building: a large building or house.—*adj.* **edificial** (*-fish'l*), structural. [Fr. *édifice*—L. *aedificium*—*aedificāre;* see **edify.**]

**edify,** *ed'if-i, v.t.* to build (*arch.*): to establish (*obs.*): to furnish with buildings (*Spens.*): to build up the faith of: to strengthen spiritually towards faith and holiness: to improve the mind of:—*pr.p.* **ed'ifying;** *pa.t.* and *pa.p.* **ed'ified.**—*n.* **edifica'tion,** instruction: progress in knowledge or in goodness.—*adj.* **edif'icatory,** tending to edification.—*n.* **ed'ifier,** one who

edifies.—*adj.* ed'ifying, instructive: improving. —*adv.* ed'ifyingly. [L. *aedificāre*—*aedēs*, a temple, house, *facĕre*, to make.]
edile. Same as aedile.
Edinburgh rock, *ed'in-bə-rə rok, n.* a sweetmeat in the form of brittle pastel-coloured sticks. [First manufactured by an Edinburgh confectioner in 1822.]
edit, *ed'it, v.t.* to prepare for publication, broadcasting, etc.: to superintend the publication of: to compile: to garble, cook up: to revise: to censor, bowdlerise: to make up the final version of a motion picture by selection, rearrangement, etc., of material photographed previously.—*ns.* edi'tion, the publication of a book (*obs.*): one of the different forms in which a book is published: the form given to a text by its editor: the number of copies of a book printed at a time, or at different times without alteration: number of identical articles, as e.g. copies of a work of art, issued at one time: reproduction; ed'itor, one who edits books, etc.: one who conducts a newspaper, periodical, etc., or a section of it:— *fem.* ed'itress.—*adj.* edito'rial, of or belonging to an editor.—*n.* an article in a newspaper written by an editor or leader writer.—*adv.* edito'rially. —*n.* ed'itorship. [L. *ēdĕre, ēdĭtum*—*ē*, from, *dăre*, to give.]
edite, bibite, *e'di-tē, bi'bi-tē, e'di-te, bi'bi-te,* (L.), eat, drink.
édition de luxe, *ā-dē-syɔ̄ də lüks,* (Fr.) a splendid and expensive edition of a book.
editio princeps, *i-dish'i-ō prin'seps, ā-dit'i-ō prin'-keps,* (L.) original edition (esp. of a work till then known only in MS).
edriophthalmic, *ed-ri-of-thal'mik, adj.* (of crustacea) with stalkless eyes.—Also edriophthal'-mian, edriophthal'mous. [Gr. *hedrion,* dim. of *hedrā,* seat, *ophthalmos,* eye.]
educate, *ed'ū-kāt, v.t.* to bring up and instruct: to teach: to train.—*adj.* ed'ucable.—*ns.* educabil'ity; educā'tion, bringing up or training, as of a child: instruction: strengthening of the powers of body or mind: culture.—*adj.* educā'tional.—*adv.* educā'tionally.—*ns.*educā'tion(al)ist, one skilled in methods of educating or teaching: one who promotes education.—*adj.* ed'ucātive, of or pertaining to education: tending to teach. —*n.* ed'ucātor. [L. *ēducāre, -ātum,* to rear—*ēdūcĕre*—*ē*, from, *dūcĕre,* to lead.]
educe, *i-* or *ē-dūs', v.t.* to draw out: to extract: to cause to appear, elicit.—*n.* educe'ment.— *adj.* educ'ible.—*ns.* educt (*ē'dukt*), what is educed; eduction (*ē-duk'shən*), the act of educing: exhaust of an engine; educ'tor, he who, or that which, educes. [L. *ēdūcĕre, ēductum*—*ē*, from, and *dūcĕre,* to lead.]
edulcorate, *i-dul'kə-rāt, v.t.* to sweeten (*obs.*): to free from soluble particles by washing.—*adj.* edul'corant.—*n.* edulcorā'tion.—*adj.* edul'corā-tive.—*n.* edul'corātor. [L. *ē-,* intens., *dulcōrāre,* to sweeten—*dulcis,* sweet.]
Edwardian, *ed-wörd'i-ən (U.S.* also *-wärd'), adj.* belonging to or characteristic of the reign of (any) King Edward, esp. Edward VII.—Also *n.*
ee, *ē,* Scottish form of eye:—*pl.* een.
eel, *ēl, n.* any fish of the *Anguillidae, Muraenidae,* or other family of *Apodes,* fishes with long smooth cylindrical or ribbon-shaped bodies, scaleless or nearly, without pelvic fins: extended to various other fishes of similar form, as the sand eel (or launce), electric eel (*Gymnotus*): extended also to some eel-like thread-worms (also eel'worm): a slippery person.—eel'-bas'ket, a basket for catching eels; eel'fare (O.E. *faran,* to travel), a migratory passage of young eels: a brood of young eels: a young eel; eel'grass, eel'wrack, grasswrack (*Zostera*), a grasslike flowering plant of the pondweed family, growing in sea-water; eel'pout (*powt;*

O.E. *ælepūte*), the burbot: the viviparous blenny; eel'-set, a net placed across a river to catch eels; eel'-spear, an instrument with broad prongs for catching eels; eel'worm, a nematode. —salt eel (*obs.*), a rope's end. [O.E. *æl;* Ger., Du. *aal.*]
e'en, *ēn,* a contraction of even.
e'er, *ār,* a contraction of ever.
eerie, eery, *ē'ri, adj.* exciting fear: weird: affected with fear, timorous (*dial.*).—*adv.* ee'rily.—*n.* ee'riness. [Scot.; M.E. *arh, eri*—O.E. *ærg (earg),* timid.]
eeven, eevn, eev'n, eevning, old spellings (*Milt.*) of even (*n., adj., adv.*) and evening.
ef, ef, *n.* the sixth letter of the alphabet (F, f).
effable, *ef'ə-bl, adj.* capable of being expressed. [Fr.,—L. *effāri*—*ex,* out, *fārī,* to speak.]
efface, *i-, e-fās', v.t.* to destroy the surface of: to rub out: to obliterate, wear away.—*adj.* efface'able.—*n.* efface'ment.—to efface oneself, to avoid notice. [Fr. *effacer*—L. *ex,* out, *faciēs,* face.]
effect, *i-fekt', n.* result of an action: impression produced: purport: reality: (in *pl.*) goods, property: (in *pl.*) sound, and also lighting, devices contributing to the illusion of the place and circumstance in which the action is carried on (*theatre, cinema,* etc.).—*v.t.* to produce: to accomplish, bring about.—*n.* effec'ter.—*adjs.* effec'tible, that may be effected; effec'tive, having power to effect: causing something: successful in producing a result or effect: powerful: serviceable: actual: in force.—*n.* a soldier, or a body of soldiers, ready for service.—*adv.* effec'-tively.—*n.* effec'tiveness.—*adj.* effect'less, without effect, useless.—*n.* effect'or (*biol.*), an organ that effects a response to stimulus.—*adj.* effec'-tual, successful in producing the desired effect: decisive (*Shak.*).—*n.* effectual'ity.—*adv.* effec'tu-ally.—*v.t.* effec'tuate, to accomplish.—*n.* effectu-ā'tion.—effectual calling (*theol.*), the invitation to come to Christ received by the elect.—for effect, so as to make a telling impression; general effect, the effect produced, by a picture, etc., as a whole; give effect to, to carry out, perform; in effect, in truth, really: substantially; leave no effects, to die without property to bequeath; take effect, to begin to operate: to come into force. [O.Fr.,—L. *effectus*—*ex,* out, *facĕre,* to make.]
effeir, effere, *e-fēr', (Scot.) n.* affair: appearance, show, array. [affair.]
effeir, effere, *e-fēr', (obs.) v.i.* to appertain: to suit. [O.Fr. *afferir*—L. *ad,* to, *ferrire,* to strike.]
effeminate, *e-, i-fem'in-āt, adj.* womanish: unmanly: weak: soft: voluptuous: feminine (*Shak.*).—*n.* an effeminate person.—*v.t.* to make womanish: to weaken, unman.—Also *v.i.*— Also effem'inise, -ize.—*n.* effem'inacy (*-ə-si*), womanish softness or weakness: indulgence in unmanly pleasures.—*adv.* effem'inately.—*n.* ef-fem'inateness. [L. *effēminăre, -ātum,* to make womanish—*ex,* out, and *fēmina,* a woman.]
effendi, *e-fen'di, n.* a title for civil officials and educated persons generally (abolished in Turkey in 1934). [Turk.; from Gr. *authentēs,* an absolute master.]
efferent, *ef'ə-rant, adj.* conveying outward or away, as (*zool.*) efferent nerve, nerve carrying impulses away from the central nervous system. [L. *ē,* from, *ferēns, -entis,* pr.p. of *ferre,* to carry.]
effervesce, *ef-ər-ves', v.i.* to boil up: to bubble and hiss: to froth up.—*ns.* efferves'cence; effer-vesc'ency.—*adjs.* effervesc'ent, boiling or bubbling from the disengagement of gas; effervesc'-ible. [L. *effervēscĕre*—*ex,* inten., and *fervēre,* to boil.]
effete, *e-fēt', adj.* exhausted: degenerate, decadent: become barren (*obs.*). [L. *effētus,* weak-

ened by having brought forth young—*ex*, out, *fētus*, a bringing forth, young.]

**efficacious**, *ef-i-kā'shəs*, *adj*. able to produce the result intended.—*adv*. **effica'ciously**.—*ns*. **efficā'ciousness**; **efficacity** (*-kas'i-ti*), **eff'icacy** (*-kə-si*), power of producing an effect: effectiveness. [L. *efficāx*, *-ācis*—*efficĕre*; see **efficient**.]

**efficient**, *i-fish'ənt*, *adj*. capable of doing what may be required: effective.—*n*. (*arch*.) the person or thing that effects.—*ns*. **effi'cience** (*arch*.), efficient action or power; **effi'ciency**, power to produce the result intended, adequate fitness: ratio of a machine's output of energy to input.—*adv*. **effi'ciently**. [Fr., L.—*efficiēns*, *-entis*, pr.p. of *efficĕre*—*ex*, out, *facĕre*, to make.]

**effierce**, *e-fērs'*, (*Spens*.) *v.t*. to make fierce.

**effigurate**, *ef-ig'u-rāt*, *adj*. having a definite shape.—*n*. **effigurā'tion**, an axial outgrowth in a flower. [L. *ef-*, *ex-*, intens., and **figurate**.]

**effigy**, *ef'i-ji*, *n*. a likeness or figure of a person: the head or impression on a coin—(*arch*.) *pl*. **effigies** (*ef-ij'i-ēz*): arch. *ef-ij'i-ēz*).—burn in effigy, to burn a figure of a person, as an expression of dislike. [L. *effigiēs*—*effingĕre*—*ex*, inten., *fingĕre*, to form.]

**effleurage**, *ef-lə-räzh*, *n*. a stroking movement in massage.—Also *v.i*. and *v.t*. [Fr., glancing, grazing.]

**effloresce**, *ef-lo-res'*, *v.i*. to blossom forth: to become covered with a powdery crust (*chem*.): to form such a crust.—*n*. **effloresc'ence**, production of flowers: the time of flowering: a redness of the skin: a powdery surface crust: the formation of such a crust: giving up of water of crystallisation to the atmosphere.—*adj*. **effloresc'ent**. [L. *efflōrēscĕre*—*ex*, out, *flōrēscĕre*, to blossom—*flōs*, *flōris*, a flower.]

**effluent**, *ef'loo-ənt*, *adj*. flowing out.—*n*. a stream that flows out of another stream or lake: liquid industrial waste: outflow from sewage during purification.—*n*. **eff'luence**, a flowing out: emanation. [L. *effluēns*, *-entis*, pr.p. of *effluĕre*—*ex*, out, *fluĕre*, to flow.]

**effluvium**, *e-floo'vi-əm*, *n*. minute particles that flow out from bodies: disagreeable vapours rising from decaying matter:—*pl*. **efflu'via**.—*adj*. **efflu'vial**. [L.L.,—L. *effluĕre*.]

**efflux**, *ef'luks*, *n*. act of flowing out: that which flows out.—Also **efflux'ion** (*e-fluk'shən*). [L. *effluĕre*—*ex*, out, *fluĕre*, *fluxum*, to flow.]

**efforce**, *e-fōrs'*, *-fōrs'*, (*obs*.) *v.t*. to compel: to force: to force open: to do violence to: to put forward with force. [Fr., *efforcer*—Late L. *exfortiāre*—*ex*, out, *fortis*, strong.]

**effort**, *ef'ərt*, *n*. a putting forth of strength: attempt: struggle: a piece of work produced by way of attempt: anything done or produced (*coll*.).—*adj*. **eff'ortless**, making no effort, passive: easy, showing no sign of effort. [Fr.,—L. *ex*, out, *fortis*, strong.]

**effray**, **effraide**, obsolete forms of **affray**, **afraid**.

**effrontery**, *i-*, *e-frunt'ər-i*, *n*. shamelessness: impudence: insolence. [Fr. *effronterie*—L. *effrōns*, *effrontis*—*ex*, out, without, *frōns*, *frontis*, forehead.]

**effulge**, *i-*, *e-fulj'*, *v.i*. to shine forth: to beam:—*pr.p*. **efful'ging**; *pa.p*. **efful'ged**.—*n*. **efful'gence**, great lustre or brightness: a flood of light.—*adj*. **efful'gent**, shining forth: extremely bright: splendid.—*adv*. **efful'gently**. [L. *effulgēre*, to shine out, *pr.p*. *effulgēns*, *-entis*,—*ex*, out, *fulgēre*, to shine.]

**effuse**, *e-fūz'*, *v.t*. to pour out: to pour forth (as words): to shed (as blood): to spread: to let loose (*Thomson*).—*v.i*. to flow out.—*n*. (*e-fūs'*; *Shak*.) effusion, shedding.—*adj*. (*e-fūs'*) poured out: loosely spreading (*bot*.): (of shells) with the lips separated by a groove.—*ns*. **effusiometer** (*e-fūz-i-om'i-tər*), an apparatus for comparing molecular weights of gases by observing the

relative time taken to stream out through a small hole; **effusion** (*e-fū'zhən*), pouring or streaming out: emission: shedding (as of blood): an abnormal outpouring of fluid into the tissues or cavities of the body (*med*.): an outpouring, esp. in poetic form: effusiveness.—*adj*. **effusive** (*e-fū'ziv*), poured out abundantly: gushing: poured out at the surface in a state of fusion, volcanic (*geol*.): expressing emotion in a copious and demonstrative manner.—*adv*. **effus'ively**.—*n*. **effus'iveness**. [L. *effundĕre*, *effūsum*—*ex*, out, *fundĕre*, to pour.]

**eft**, *eft*, *n*. a lizard (*obs*.): a newt. [O.E. *efeta*; see **newt**.]

**eft**, *eft*, (*obs*.) *adv*. afterwards: again: forthwith: moreover.—*adv*. **eftsoons** (*eft-soonz'*; *obs*.), soon afterwards, forthwith. [O.E. *æft*, *eft*, after, again; see **aft**.]

**eftest**, *eft'ist*, (*Warwickshire*, *Worcestershire*; *Shak*. Much Ado, IV, ii. 38) *adj. superl*. readiest: most convenient.

**eftsoons**. See **eft** (2).

**egad**, *i-gad'*, *interj*. a minced oath. [Perh. orig. **ah! God!**]

**egal**, *ē'gəl*, (*Shak*.) *adj*. equal.—*adj*. and *n*. **egalitā'rian** (*i-gal-*), equalitarian.—*ns*. **egalita'rianism**; **egality** (*ē-*, *i-gal'*), equality.—*adv*. **ē'gally**. [O.Fr. *egal*—L. *aequālis*—*aequus*, equal.]

**égarement**, *ā-gar-mã*, (Fr.) confusion, bewilderment.

**egence**, *ē'jəns*, **egency** (*-i*, *ns*. need. [L. *ēgēre*, to be in need.]

**eger**, *ē'gər*, *n*. Same as **eagre**.

**Egeria**, *ē-jē'ri-a*, *e-*, *n*. a female adviser. [L. *Ēgēria*, or *Aegēria*, the nymph who instructed Numa Pompilius.]

**egest**, *ə-jest'*, *ē-jest'*, *v.t*. to discharge: to expel from the body in any way.—*n.pl*. **egest'a**, things thrown out: excreta: waste materials removed from the body.—*n*. **egestion** (*e-jest'yən*).—*adj*. **egest'ive**. [L. *ēgerĕre*—*ēgestum*—*ē*, out, *gerĕre*, to carry.]

**egg**, *eg*, *n*. an oval body laid by birds and certain other animals from which the young is hatched: an ovum or female gamete (also **egg'-cell'**): a zygote: anything shaped like a hen's egg: a bomb (*slang*).—*ns*. **egg'er**, one who collects wildfowl's eggs: any moth of the family *Lasio-campidae*, whose cocoons are egg-shaped (also **egg'ar**); **egg'ery**, a place where eggs are laid; **egg'ler**, a dealer in eggs.—*adj*. **egg'y**, abounding in eggs: having just laid or about to lay an egg: savouring of, or marked with, eggs.—**egg'-and-anch'or**, **egg'-and-dart'**, ornaments on mouldings in the form of eggs alternating with anchors or darts; **egg-apparatus** (*bot*.), the egg-cell and two synergidae in the embryo-sac of an angiosperm; **egg'-apple**, the egg-fruit; **egg'-beater** (*slang*), a helicopter; **egg'-binding**, inability to expel an egg; **egg'-bird**, the sooty tern.—*adjs*. **egg'-bound**, in state of being unable to expel eggs; **egg'-box**, used of type of building appearing as if made of numbers of unadorned rectangular sections.—**egg'-capsule**, **-case**, **-purse**, a protective covering in which the eggs of some animals are enclosed; **egg'-cōsy**, a cover for keeping a boiled egg hot; **egg'cup**, a cup for holding a boiled egg at table; **egg'-dance**, a dance performed blindfold among eggs; **egg'-flip**, a drink made of ale, wine, spirits, or milk, with eggs, sugar, spice, etc.; **egg'-fruit**, the fruit of the egg plant; **egg'-glass**, a small sand-glass for regulating the boiling of eggs; **egg'head**, an intellectual; **egg'mass**, intellectuals as a group.—Also *adj*.; **egg'nog**, a drink of eggs and hot beer, spirits, etc.; **egg'-plant**, the aubergine or brinjal, an East Indian annual plant (*Solanum Melongena*) with edible egg-shaped fruit; **egg'-plum**, a yellowish egg-shaped plum; **egg'-powder**, a powder of dried eggs, or a substitute;

egg'-purse, egg-capsule; egg'shell, the calcareous covering of a bird's egg: a smooth gastropod shell: a very thin kind of porcelain.—*adj.* thin and delicate: (of paint, etc.) having a slight gloss.—egg'-slice, a utensil for lifting fried eggs out of a pan; egg-spoon, a small spoon used in eating boiled eggs from the shell; egg'-tim'er, an egg-glass; egg'-tooth, a hard point on the beak by which an unhatched bird or reptile breaks the egg-shell; egg'-whisk, an instrument for beating raw eggs.—a bad egg (*coll.*) a worthless person; egg-and-spoon race, a race in which each competitor lifts and carries an egg in a spoon; good egg! (*coll.*), an exclamation of approval; put all one's eggs into one basket, to risk all on one enterprise; take eggs for money, to be put off with mere promises of payment; teach your grandmother to suck eggs, spoken contemptuously to one who would teach those older and wiser than himself; tread upon eggs, to walk warily, to steer one's way carefully in a delicate situation. [O.N. *egg*; cf. O.E. *æg*, Ger. *ei*, perh. L. *ōvum*, Gr. *ōon*.]

egg, *eg*, *v.t.* (now with *on*) to incite, urge on. [O.N. *eggja*—*egg*, an edge; cog. with O.E. *ecg*; see edge.]

egis. Same as aegis.

eglandular, *ē-glan'dū-lər*, *adj.* having no glands. —*adj.* eglan'dulose.

eglantine, *eg'lən-tin*, *n.* the sweet-brier: perhaps the honeysuckle (*Milt.*). [Fr.,—O.Fr. *aiglent*, as if from a L. *aculentus*, prickly—*acus*, a needle, and suff. *-lentus*.]

eglatere, *eg-lə-tēr'*, (*arch.*) *n.* eglantine.

egma, *eg'mə*, *n.* Costard's attempt at *enigma* (*Shak.*, *Love's Lab.* III, i. 73.]

ego, *e'gō*, *ē'gō*, *n.* the 'I' or self—that which is conscious and thinks.—*adj.* egocen'tric, self-centred: regarding or regarded from the point of view of the ego.—*ns.* egocentri'city; e'gōism, the doctrine that we have proof of nothing but our own existence (*phil.*): the theory of self-interest as the principle of morality (*ethics*): selfishness: egotism; e'gōist, one who holds the doctrine of egoism: one who thinks and speaks too much of himself or of things as they affect himself: an egotist.—*adj.* egōist'ic, -al, pertaining to or manifesting egoism.—*ns.* egō'ity, the essential element of the ego; egomā'nia, morbid egotism; egomā'niac; e'gō-theism (or *-thē'*), the deification of self: identification of oneself with God.—*v.i.* e'gotise, -ize, to talk much of oneself.—*ns.* e'gotism, a frequent use of the pronoun I: thinking or speaking too much of oneself: self-exaltation; e'gotist, one full of egotism.—*adjs.* egotis'tic, -al, showing egotism: self-important: conceited.—*adv.* egotist'ically. [L. *ego*, *egō*, and Gr. *egō*, I.]

egregious, *i-grē'jəs*, *adj.* prominent, distinguished (*arch.*): outrageous: notorious.—*adv.* egrē'giously.—*n.* egrē'giousness. [L. *ēgregius*, chosen out of the flock—*ē*, out of, *grex*, *gregis*, a flock.]

egress, *ē'gres*, *n.* act of going out: departure: the way out: the power or right to depart.—*n.* egression (*i-*, *ē-gresh'ən*), the act of going out: departure. [L. *ēgredī*, *ēgressus*—*ē*, out of, *gradī*, to go.]

egret, *ē'gret*, *n.* a white heron of several species: an aigrette. [See aigrette.]

egurgitate, *ē-gûr'ji-tāt*, (*rare*)' *v.t.* to vomit: to cast forth. [L. *ēgurgitāre*, *-ātum*—*ē*, out of, *gurges*, *-itis*, a whirlpool.]

Egypt, *arch.* Aegypt, *ē'jipt*, *n.* a country of N.E. Africa.—*adj.* Egyptian (*ē-jip'shən*), belonging to Egypt: (of type) antique.—*n.* a native or citizen of Egypt: a gypsy.—*adj.* Egyptolog'ical. —*ns.* Egyptol'ogist; Egyptol'ogy, the science of Egyptian antiquities.—Egyptian darkness, darkness like that of Exod. x. 22.

eh, *ā*, *interj.* expressing inquiry, failure to hear, or slight surprise.—*v.i.* to say 'Eh'.

eident, *i'dənt*, (*Scot.*) *adj.* busy, diligent. [M.E. *ithen*—O.N. *ithinn*, diligent.]

eider, *i'dər*, *n.* the ei'der-duck', a northern sea-duck, sought after for its fine down.—ei'der-down', the soft down of the eider-duck, used for stuffing quilts: a quilt. [Prob. through Sw. from O.N. *æthar*, gen. of *æthr*, an eider-duck.]

eidetic, *i-det'ik*, *adj.* vividly clear: reproducing, or able to reproduce, a vividly clear visual image of what has been previously seen.—*n.* a person with this ability. [Gr. *eidētikos*, belonging to an image—*eidos*, form.]

eidograph, *i'dō-gräf*, *n.* an instrument used for copying drawings. [Gr. *eidos*, form, and *graphein*, to write.]

eidolon, *i-dō'lon*, *n.* an image: a phantom or apparition: a confusing reflection or reflected image:—*pl.* eidō'la. [Gr. See idol.]

eigen-, *i-gən-*, in composition, proper, own.—*ns.* ei'gen-fre'quency, one of the frequencies with which a particular system may vibrate; ei'gen-tone', a tone characteristic of a particular vibrating system; ei'genval'ue, any of the possible values for a parameter of an equation for which the solutions will be compatible with the boundary conditions. [Ger.]

eight, *āt*, *n.* the cardinal number one above seven: a symbol (8, viii, etc.) representing that number: a set of eight things or persons (syllables, leaves, oarsmen, etc.): an eight-oar boat: an eight-cylinder engine or car: a card with eight pips: a shoe or other article of a size denoted by 8: the eighth hour after midday or midnight.—*adj.* of the number eight.—*adj.* and *adv.* eight'fold, in eight divisions: eight times as much.—*adj.* eighth (*ātth*), last of eight: equal to one of eight equal parts.—*n.* an eighth part: an octave (*mus.*).—*adv.* eighthly (*ātth'li*), in the eighth place.—*n.* eight'some, a group of eight: eight together: a Scottish reel for eight dancers. —*adj.* eight'-day, lasting or running for eight days.—eight'foil (*her.*), an eight-leaved flower. —*adj.* eight'foot, eight feet in measure (also *adv.*): (*mus.*) (see foot).—*adjs.* eight'-hour, consisting of eight hours, or eight working hours; eight'-oar, manned by eight oarsmen.—*n.* an eight-oar boat.—eight'pence, the value of eight pennies.—*adj.* eight'penny, costing eightpence.— *n.* and *adj.* eight'score, eight times twenty.— eights'man, one of a crew or team of eight.—*adj.* eight'-square, regularly octagonal.—an eight days, a week; figure of eight, a figure shaped like an 8 made in skating, etc.; one over the eight, one drink too many; piece of eight, an old Spanish coin worth eight reals; the eights, annual bumping boat-races in the summer term between the various Oxford colleges. [O.E. (Anglian) *æhta* (W.S. *eahta*); Ger. *acht*, L. *octō*, Gr. *oktō*.]

eighteen, *ā-tēn'*, *ā'tēn*, *n.* and *adj.* eight and ten.— *adj.* and *n.* eighteen'mo, octodecimo.—*adj.* eigh'teenth (or *-tēnth'*), last of eighteen: equal to one of eighteen equal parts.—*n.* an eighteenth part.—*adv.* eighteenth'ly.—*adj.* eigh'teen-hole, having eighteen golf-holes.—eigh'teen-pence.— eighteen-penny piece, an obsolete English coin.— *adj.* eigh'teen-penn'y. [O.E. (Mercian) *æhtatēne* (W.S. *eahtatīene*).]

eighty, *ā'ti*, *n.* and *adj.* eight times ten:—*pl.* eight'ies, the numbers eighty to eighty-nine: the years so numbered in life or any century.— *adj.* eigh'tieth, last of eighty: equal to one of eighty equal parts.—*n.* an eightieth part. [O.E. *æhtatig* (W.S. *eahtatig*, or *hundeahtatig*).]

eigne, *ān*, *adj.* first born. [Fr. *aîné*.]

eik, *ēk*, Scots form of eke.

eikon. Same as icon.

eild. Same as eld.

**eild**, *ēld*, (*Scot.*) *adj.* not yielding milk. [See **yeld**.]

**eilding**. See **eldin**.

**eine**, *in*, *ēn*, (*obs.*) *n.pl.* eyes. [See **een**, under **ee**.]

**einsteinium**, *in-stin'i-əm*, *n.* the element (symbol Es) of atomic number 99, artificially produced and named after Albert *Einstein* (1879-1955).

**eirack**, *ē'rak*, (*Scot.*) *n.* a young hen. [Gael. *eireag*.]

**eirenicon**, *i-rē'ni-kon*, a proposition or scheme for peace: a peace-making message: the deacon's litany at the beginning of the Greek liturgy—from its opening petitions for peace.—*adj.* **eire'nic** (same as **irenic**). [A partly Latinised spelling of Gr. *eirēnikon*, neut. of *eirēnikos*, peaceful, peaceable—*eirēnē*, peace.]

**eisel(l)**, *ā'səl*, *ī-səl*, (*obs.*) *n.* vinegar. [O.Fr. *aisil*, *aissil*, from L.L. dim. of L. *acētum*, vinegar.]

**eisen und blut**. See **blut und eisen**.

**eisteddfod**, *ās-tedh'vod*. *n.* a congress of Welsh bards and musicians. [W., lit. session—*eistedd*, to sit.]

**either**, *ī'dhər*, *ē'dhər*, *adj.* or *pron.* the one or the other: one of two: each of two.—*conj.* correlative to *or*: or (*B.*). [O.E. *ǣgther*, contraction of *ǣghwæthər—ā*, aye, pfx. *ge-*, and *hwæther*, whether; see also **each**.]

**ejaculate**, *i-jak'ū-lāt*, *v.t.* to eject: to utter with suddenness.—*v.i.* to utter or make an ejaculation: to emit semen.—*n.* **ejaculā'tion**, ejection, emission: a sudden utterance in prayer or otherwise: an unpremeditated emotional prayer or remark: emission of semen.—*adjs.* **ejac'ulative**; **ejac'ulatory**. [L. *ē*, from, and *jaculārī*, *-ātus*—*jacĕre*, to throw.]

**eject**, *ē-jekt'*, *v.t.* to cast out: to dismiss: to turn out: to expel.—*v.i.* to cause oneself to be ejected as from an aircraft or spacecraft.—*n.* **eject** (*ē'jekt*), a mental state other than one's own, a thing thrown out of one's own consciousness, as distinguished from *object*, a thing presented in one's consciousness.—*ns.pl.* **eject'a**, **ejectament'a**, matter thrown out, esp. by volcanoes.—*n.* **ejec'tion**, discharge: expulsion: state of being ejected: vomiting: that which is ejected.—*adj.* **ejec'tive**.—*ns.* **eject'ment**, expulsion: dispossession: an action for the recovery of the possession of land (*law*); **eject'or**, one who ejects or dispossesses another of his land: any mechanical apparatus for ejecting or discharging.—**eject'or-seat**, (*U.S.*) **ejection seat**, seat that can be shot clear with its occupant in an emergency. [L. *ējectāre*, freq. of *ējicĕre*, *ējectum—ē*, from, *jacĕre*, to throw.]

**ejusdem generis**, *ē-jus'dəm jen'ə-ris*, *ā-ūs'dem ge'ne-ris*, (L.) of the same kind.

**eka-**, *ā'ka-*, *ē'ka-*, formerly prefixed to the name of an element to give a provisional name for the hypothetical undiscovered element that should follow in the periodic table. [Sans. *eka*, one.]

**ek dum**, *ek dum*, at once. [Hind. *ek dam*.]

**eke** (*Scot.* eik), *ēk*, *v.t.* to add to: increase: to lengthen: to supplement, make up to the required measure (often with *out*).—*n.* (*Scot.*) an addition, supplement. [O.E. *ēcan* (W.S. *iecan*); cf. **eche**; L. *augēre*; Gr. *auxanein*.]

**eke**, *ēk*, *adv.* in addition: likewise. [O.E. *ēac*; Ger. *auch*, perh. from root of **eke** (1).]

**ekistics**, *ek-is'tiks*, *n.* word coined by a Greek, C. A. Doxiadis, for 'the science of human settlements'.

**ekka**, *ek'a*, *n.* a small one-horse carriage. [Hindi —*ekkā*, one—Sans. *eka*.]

**el**, *el*, *n.* the twelfth letter of the alphabet (L, l): anything of that shape: a wing giving a building the shape of the letter L (*U.S.*).

**el**, *el*, (*U.S. coll.*) *n.* an *el*evated railroad.

**e-la**, *ē'lä'*, *n.* the highest note in old church music, E, the fourth space in the treble, sung to the syllable *la* in the highest hexachord: the highest pitch of anything.—*n.* **e-la-mi**, *ē'lä'mē'*, E, the third space in the bass ('in bass') or the first line in the treble ('in alt'), sung to *la* in the first and fourth hexachords respectively, and *mi* in the second and fifth.

**elaborate**, *i-lab'ər-āt*, *v.t.* to produce by labour: to work out in detail: to build up from raw or comparatively simple materials: to add detail to.—*v.i.* to become elaborate.—*adj.* (*i-lab'-ər-it*) wrought with labour: done with fullness and exactness: highly detailed: complicated.—*adv.* **elab'orately.**—*ns.* **elab'orateness**; **elaborā'tion**, act of elaborating: refinement: the process by which substances are built up in the bodies of animals or plants.—*adj.* **elab'orative**.—*ns.* **elab'-orator**, one who elaborates; **elab'oratory** (*obs.*), a laboratory. [L. *ēlabōrāre*, *-ātum—ē*, from, *labōrāre—labor*, labour.]

**Elaeagnus**, *el-i-ag'nəs*, *n.* the oleaster genus, giving name to the fam. **Elaeagnā'ceae**. [Gr. *elaiagnos*, goat willow.]

**Elaeis**, *el-ē'is*, *n.* the oil-palm genus. [Gr. *elaion*, olive oil.]

**elaeolite**, *el-ē'ō-līt*, *n.* a greasy-looking nepheline. [Gr. *elaion*, olive oil, *lithos*, stone.]

**élan**, *ā-län'*, *ā-lā*, *n.* impetuosity, dash.—**élan vital**, *ā-lä vē-tal*, the creative force responsible for the growth and evolution of an organism (Bergson). [Fr.]

**elance**, *i-läns'*, *v.t.* to throw as a lance. [Fr. *élancer*.]

**eland**, *ē'land*, *n.* a S. African antelope, resembling the elk in having a protuberance on the larynx. [Du.,—Ger. *elend*—Lith. *élnis*, elk.]

**elanet**, *el'ə-net*, *n.* a kite of the genus Elanus. [Gr. *elanos*, a kite.]

**elaphine**, *el'ə-fīn*, *adj.* like or belonging to a red deer. [Gr. *elaphos*, stag.]

**Elaps**, *ē'laps*, *n.* an American genus of snakes, otherwise Micrurus—coral-snake: applied by others to a South African genus, otherwise Homorelaps—garter-snake. [A form of **ellops**.]

**elapse**, *i-laps'*, *v.i.* to slip or glide away: to pass silently, as time.—*n.* passing. [L. *ēlapsus*, *ēlābī—ē*, from, *lābī*, *lāpsus*, to slide.]

**elasmobranch**, *i-laz'mō-brangk*, or *-las'*, *n.* any member of the **Elasmobranch'ii**, a class of fishes including sharks and skates, having a cartilaginous skeleton and plate-like gills. [Gr. *elasmos*, a beaten-metal plate, *branchia*, gills.]

**elastic**, *i-las'tik*, or *-läs'*, *adj.* having a tendency to recover the original form or size: springy: able to recover quickly a former state or condition after a shock (*fig.*): flexible: capable of stretching to include much (*lit.* and *fig.*): made of elastic.—*n.* a string or ribbon with rubber strands.—*n.* **elast'ance**, the reciprocal of the capacity of a condenser, from its electro-mechanical analogy with a spring.—*adv.* **elas'tically.**—*v.t.* **elas'ticate**, to make elastic:—*p.adj.* **elas'-ticated.**—*v.t.* **elas'ticise**, **-ize** (*-ti-sīz*), to make elastic.—*ns.* **elasticity** (*el-* or *ēl-əs-tis'*), power of returning to original form or size: springiness: power to recover from depression; **elas'ticness**, **elas'tin**, a protein, chief constituent of elastic tissue; **elas'tomer**, any rubber-like substance.— **elastic collision** (*nucleonics*), one in which the bombarding particle does not excite or break up the struck nucleus and is simply scattered; **elastic limit**, greatest stress a material can be subjected to without permanent deformation; **elastic tissue**, tissue having fibres with elastic quality, occurring esp. in ligaments and tendons. [Late Gr. *elastikos—elaunein*, to drive.]

**elate**, *i-lāt'*, *adj.* (*rare*) lifted up: puffed up with success: exalted.—*v.t.* to raise or exalt (*obs.*): to make exultant or proud.—*adv.* **elat'edly.**—*ns.* **elat'edness**; **elā'tion**, pride resulting from success: exaltation, high spirits. [L. *ēlātus*, used as pa.p. of *efferre—ē*, from, *lātus*, carried.]

**elater**, *el'ə-tər*, *n.* an elastic filament aiding spore-dispersal in certain fungi, in liverworts and in horse-tails: a skipjack beetle.—*ns.* elatē′rium, a substance contained in the juice of the fruit of the squirting cucumber, yielding the purgative elat′erin; elaterite (*i-lat′ər-īt*), elastic bitumen, a rubber-like mineral resin. [Gr. *elatēr*, driver—*elaunein*, to drive.] elbow, el′bō, *n.* the joint where the arm bows or bends: any sharp turn or bend.—*v.t.* to push with the elbow, to jostle.—el′bow-chair, an armchair; el′bow-grease (humorously), vigorous rubbing: hard work; el′bow-room, room to extend the elbows: space enough for moving or acting: freedom and scope.—at one's elbow, close at hand; bend, crook, or lift the elbow, to drink too much; out at elbow, with coat ragged at the elbows; up to the elbows, completely engrossed. [O.E. *elnboga*; see ell; bow, *n.* and *v.t.*] elchi, eltchi, elchee, *el′chē, chi,* an ambassador. [Turk. *ilchi.*] eld, eld, *n.* age: old age, senility: former times, antiquity. [O.E. *eldo.*] elder, *eld′ər, n.* a shrub or tree (Sambucus) of the Caprifoliaceae, with pinnate leaves, small flowers (the corolla wheel-shaped) and three-seeded fruits.—*ns.* eld′erberry, the acidulous purple-black drupaceous fruit of the elder; eld′er-gun, a popgun made of elder by extracting the pith; eld′erberry wine, a wine made from elderberries; elder-flower water, distilled water made from the flowers. [O.E. *ellærn.*] elder, *eld′ər, adj.* older: having lived a longer time: prior in origin.—*n.* one who is older: an ancestor: one advanced to office on account of age: one of a class of office-bearers in the Presbyterian Church (*presbyter* of the New Testament).—*n.* eld′erliness.—*adj.* eld′erly, somewhat old: bordering on old age.—*n.* eld′ership, state of being older: the office of an elder.—*adj.* eld′est, oldest.—Elder Brethren, the governing members of Trinity House; elder, or eldest, hand, the player on the dealer's left, who leads in card-playing; elders' hours, respectable hours—usually not after 10 p.m.; Elder Statesman, a retired statesman consulted by the government: any administrator of age and experience: (in *pl.*) a reactionary group of retired statesmen who exercised a power behind the throne in Japan. [O.E. *eldra* (W.S. *ieldra, yldra*), comp.; *eldesta* (*ieldesta*), superl. of *ald* (*eald*), old.] eldin, elding, *el′din*(g), (*Scot.*) eilding, *ēl′din,* (*Northern*) *n.* fuel. [O.N. *elding—eldr,* fire.] El Dorado, Eldorado, *el-də-rä′dō,* the golden land (or city) imagined by the Spanish conquerors of America: any place where wealth is easily to be made. [Sp. *el,* the, *dorado,* pa.p. of *dorar,* to gild—'the gilded man', the king of Manoa who smeared himself with gold-dust; afterwards transferred to the city of Manoa itself.] eldritch, *el′(d)rich,* (*Scot.*) *adj.* weird: uncanny. [Perh. connected with elf.] Eleatic, *el-i-at′ik, adj.* belonging to Elea, a Greek city of Lower Italy, or to the school of philosophers connected with it, including Xenophanes, Parmenides, and Zeno.—*n.* one belonging to this school. elecampane, *el-i-kam-pān′, n.* a composite plant (*Inula helenium*) allied to Aster, formerly much cultivated for its medicinal root: a sweetmeat flavoured with an extract from the root. [L. *enula campāna,* field, or Campanian, inula.] elect, *i-lekt′, v.t.* to choose (in preference) to select for any office or purpose: to select by vote.—*adj.* chosen: taken by preference from among others: chosen for an office but not yet in it (almost always after the noun): chosen by God for salvation (*theol.*).—*n.* one chosen or set apart.—*n.* elec′tion (*-shən*), the act of electing

or choosing: the public choice of a person for office, usually by the votes of a constituent body: freewill: the exercise of God's sovereign will in the predetermination of certain persons to salvation (*theol.*): the elected in this way (*B.*).—*v.i.* electioneer′, to labour to secure the election of a candidate.—*n.* electioneer′er.—*n.* and *adj.* electioneer′ing.—*adj.* elect′ive, pertaining to, dependent on, or exerting the power of choice: optional (*U.S.*).—*n.* (*U.S.*) an optional subject of study.—*adv.* elect′ively.—*ns.* electiv′ity (*ē-, e-*); elect′or, one who elects: one who has a vote at an election: in U.S. a member of the so-called electoral college, which elects the President and Vice-President: the title formerly belonging to those princes and archbishops of the German empire who had the right to elect the Emperor: —*fem.* elect′ress, elect′oress.—*adjs.* elect′oral, electō′rial (*ē-, e-*), pertaining to elections or to electors: consisting of electors.—*ns.* elect′orate, the dignity or the territory of an elector: the body of electors; elect′orship.—electoral vote (*U.S.*), the vote of the members of the electoral college, themselves elected by popular vote. [L. *ēligĕre, ēlectum—ē,* from, *legĕre,* to choose.] Electra complex, *i-lek′trə,* (*psych.*) the attachment of a daughter to her father, with hostility to her mother. [Greek story of *Electra,* who helped to avenge her mother's murder of her father.] electric, *i-lek′trik, adj.* pertaining to electricity: charged with or capable of being charged with electricity: producing or produced by, conveying, operated by, or making use of electricity: thrilling (*fig.*): producing a sudden startling effect.—*n.* a non-conductor of electricity, as amber, glass, etc., capable of being electrified by friction.—*adj.* elec′trical.—*adv.* elec′trically.—*ns.* electrician (*el-ik-trish′ən*), one who studies, or is versed in, the science of electricity: one who makes, instals, or repairs electrical apparatus; electricity (*el-ik-tris′i-ti*), the attractive power of amber and other substances when rubbed: an imaginary fluid supposed to explain this and related phenomena: manifestation of a form of energy associated with separation or movement of charged particles, as electrons and protons: the science that deals with this: a feeling of excitement.—*adj.* elec′trifiable.—*n.* electrificā′-tion.—*v.t.* elec′trify, to communicate electricity to: to excite suddenly: to astonish: to adapt to electricity as the motive power:—*pr.p.* elec′-trifying; *pa.t.* and *pa.p.* elec′trified.—*n.* electrisā′tion, -iz-.—*v.t.* elec′trise, -ize, to electrify. electric arc, a luminous space between electrodes when a current passes across; electric battery, a group of cells connected in series or in parallel for generating an electric current by chemical action; electric blanket, a blanket heated by electric current; electric blue, a steely blue colour; electric calamine, the mineral hemimorphite, which becomes positively electrified at one end, negatively at the other, when its temperature rises, and *vice versa* as it cools; electric chair, the seat on which a condemned criminal is put to death by electricity; electric eel, Gymnotus; electric eye, a photo-electric cell: a miniature cathode ray tube; electric fence, a wire fence electrically charged; electric field, a region in which attracting or repelling forces are exerted on any electric charge present; electric fire, heater, radiator, an apparatus using an electric current, for heating a room; electric furnace, an apparatus for getting very high temperatures by means of an electric current; electric guitar, one with an amplifying device built in; electric hare, a dummy animal electrically worked to draw on racing greyhounds; electric motor, any device for converting electrical energy into mechanical energy; electric organ, an organ in which the sound is produced by electrical devices instead of wind (*mus.*): in certain fishes, a structure that generates, stores and discharges electricity (*zool.*); **electric ray**, the fish Torpedo; **electric seal**, dyed rabbit or hare skin; **electric storm**, a violent disturbance in the electric condition of the atmosphere; **electric torch**, a portable electric light. [L. *ēlectrum*—Gr. *ēlektron*, amber, in which electricity was first observed.] **electro-**, *i-lek'trō-*, *el-ik-tro'*, in composition, electric.—*ns.* **elec'tro** (*coll.*), abbrev. of **electroplate** and **electrotype**; **elec'troanal'ysis**, separation by electrolysis; **elec'trobiol'ogist**; **elec'trobio'logy**, the science of the electrical phenomena in living organisms: an old name for hypnotism; **elec'trocar'diogram**, a photographic record of the electrical variations that occur during contraction of the muscle of the heart; **elec'trocar'diograph**, a galvanometer used for making such records; **elec'trocardiog'raphy**, the study of electric currents produced during muscular activity of the heart; **elec'trocement'**, cement made in an electric furnace, by adding lime to molten slag.—*adjs.* **elec'trochem'ic, -al.** —*ns.* **elec'trochem'ist**; **elec'trochem'istry**, the study of the relation between electricity and chemical change; **electro-convulsive therapy**, shock therapy—abbrev. **ECT**; **electrocul'ture**, cultivation of plants under stimulus of electricity.—*v.t.* **elec'trocute**, to inflict a death penalty by means of electricity: to kill by electricity.— *ns.* **electrocū'tion**; **elec'trōde** (Gr. *hodos*, way), a conductor by which a current of electricity enters or leaves an electrolytic cell, gas discharge tube, or thermionic valve; **elec'trodeposi'tion**, deposition of a layer of metal by electrolysis; **elec'trodynam'ics**, the study of electricity in motion, or of the interaction of currents and currents, or currents and magnets; **elec'trodynamom'eter**, an instrument for measuring currents by the attraction or repulsion between current-bearing coils; **elec'troenceph'alogram**, (-*sef'*, -*kef'*) a record made by an **elec'troenceph'alograph**, an instrument recording small electrical impulses produced by the brain; **elec'troencephalog'raphy**; **elec'troextrac'tion**, **elec'trowinn'ing**, recovery of a metal from its salts, by passing an electric current through a solution; **elec'trogild'ing**, electroplating with gold; **elec'trograph**, a recording electrometer; **electrog'raphy**; **electrohydraulic forming**, shaping a piece of metal with a die by means of a shock wave in water set up by discharge of energy between immersed electrodes; **elec'trokinet'ics**, the branch of science that treats of distribution of currents; **electrolier** (-*lēr'*), an electric-light fixture resembling a chandelier; **electrol'ogy**, the science of electricity: electrotherapy; **elec'troluminesc'ence**, luminescence produced by the application of an electric field to a dielectric phosphor.—*v.t.* **elec'trolyse, -yze** (-*liz*), to break up by electric means: to subject to electrolysis. —*ns.* **electrol'ysis** (-*trol'i-sis*; Gr. *lysis*, loosing), decomposition by electric current, with migration of ions shown by changes at the electrodes: term used for the removal of hair by applying an electrically charged needle to the follicle; **elec'trolyte** (-*lit*), a substance that admits of electrolysis.—*adj.* **electrolytic** (-*lit'ik*).—*adv.* **electrolyt'ically.**—**elec'tromag'net**, a piece of soft iron, etc., rendered magnetic by a current of electricity passing through a coil of wire wound round it.—*adj.* **elec'tromagnet'ic.**—**electromagnetic theory**, Clerk Maxwell's theory explaining light in terms of electromagnetic waves; **electromagnetic wave**, a travelling disturbance in space produced by the acceleration of an electric charge, comprising an electric field and a magnetic field at right angles to each other, both moving at the same velocity in a direction normal

to the plane of the two fields; **elec'tromag'-netism**, a branch of science which treats of the relation of electricity to magnetism.—*adj.* **electromechan'ical**, pertaining to any mechanical process or device involving the use of electricity: pertaining to electromechanics.—**electromechan'-ics**, the mechanics of the electric circuit; **elec'-tromer**, a substance showing electromerism. —*adj.* **electromer'ic.**—**electrom'erism**, a form of tautomerism caused by a redistribution of electrons among the atoms of a molecule or group.—*adj.* **electrometallur'gical.**—**electromet'-allurgist**; **electromet'allurgy**, industrial working of metals by means of electricity; **electrŏm'-eter**, an instrument for measuring difference of electric potential.—*adjs.* **electromet'ric, -al.** **electrom'etry**, the science of electrical measurements.—*adjs.* **electromō'tive**, pertaining to the motion of electricity or the laws governing it.— **electromotive force**, difference of potential; **electromō'tor**, an apparatus for applying electricity as a motive power; **elec'tromy'ograph**, instrument for recording voltages produced by muscular contraction; **elec'tromyog'raphy**, the study of electric currents set up in muscles by their working.—*adj.* **electroneg'ative**, carrying a negative charge: tending to form negative ions. —**electrophorē'sis** (Gr. *phoreein*, to bear), migration of suspended particles, as protein macromolecules, under the influence of an electric field.—*adj.* **electrophoret'ic** (-*et'ik*), pertaining to electrophoresis.—**electrŏph'orus**, an instrument for obtaining statical electricity by means of induction; **elec'trophysiol'ogy**, the study of electric phenomena of living organisms. —*v.t.* **elec'troplate**, to plate or cover, esp. with silver, by electrolysis.—*n.* electroplated ware.— **elec'troplating.**—*adjs.* **elec'tropō'lar**, having, as an electrical conductor, one end or surface positive and the other negative; **electropos'itive**, carrying a positive charge: tending to form positive ions. —**elec'troscōpe**, an instrument for detecting the presence of electricity in a body and the nature of it.—*adjs.* **electroscōp'ic**; **electrostat'ic.**—**electrostat'ics**, the branch of science which treats of electricity at rest; **electrotech'nics**, electric technology; **electrothera-peu'tics**, **electrother'apy**, treatment of disease by electricity.—*adjs.* **electrotherm'al**, **electrotherm'-ic**, pertaining to electricity and heat, or heat obtained electrically.—**electrotherm'ics**; **electrotherm'y**; **elec'trotint**, a printing block produced by drawing with varnish on a metal plate, and depositing metal electrically on the parts not covered.—*adj.* **electroton'ic.**—**electrot'onus**, the state of a nerve subjected to a steady discharge of electricity; **elec'trotype**, a printing plate made by electrolytically coating a mould with copper; **elec'trotyp'er**, one who makes electrotypes.— *adj.* **electrotyp'ic.**—**elec'trotȳpist**; **elec'trotȳpy**; **elec'trovalency**, union within a chemical compound achieved by transfer of electrons, the resulting ions being held together by electrostatic attraction—cf. *covalency.*—*adj.* **elec'trovalent.** [Gr. *ēlektro-*, comb. form of *ēlektron*, see electron.]

**electron**, *i-lek'tron*, *n.* a natural alloy of gold and silver used by the ancients (also Latinised as **elec'trum**): a minute particle charged with electricity, or a unit charge having inertia, normally forming part of an atom but capable of isolation as in cathode rays.—*adj.* **electronic** (*el-*, *il-*, *ēl-ik-tron'ik*).—*adv.* **electron'ically.**—*n.pl.* **electron'ics**, the science and technology of the conduction of electricity in a vacuum, a gas, or a semiconductor, and devices based thereon.— **electron camera**, any device that converts an optical image into a corresponding electric current directly by electronic means; **electron gun**, the assembly of electrodes in a cathode ray tube which produce the electron beam; **electronic brain,** any electronic computer; **electronic flash,** an extremely intense and brief flash for high-speed photography produced by passing an electric charge through a gas-filled tube; **electronic music,** music made by arranging sounds previously generated in the laboratory and recorded on tape (cf. musique concrète); **electron microscope,** a microsope that makes use of a beam of electrons instead of light; **electron pair,** a duplet: an electron and a positron; **electron shell,** a group of electrons surrounding a nucleus of an atom and having adjacent energy levels; **electron telescope,** optical instrument with electronic image converter used with a normal telescope; **electron tube,** an electronic device in which the electron conduction is in a vacuum or gas inside a gas-tight enclosure—including a thermionic valve; **electron-volt,** a unit of energy equal to that acquired by an electron when accelerated by a potential of one volt.—**electronic video recording and reproduction,** a process by which material shown on television may be recorded, stored, and later reshown on the television screen; **electron ring accelerator,** an accelerator in which an intense ring of circulating electrons, being accelerated, can carry along and accelerate protons or stripped ions. [Gr. *ēlektron,* amber.]

**electronegative.** See **electric.**

**electronic,** etc. See **electron.**

**electrophoresis** . . . to . . . **electrovalent.** See **electric.**

**electuary,** *i-lek′tū-ər-i, n.* a medicine mixed with honey or the like. [L.L. *ēlectuārium,* perh.—Gr. *ekleikton—ekleichein,* to lick up.]

**eleemosynary,** *el-ē-, el-i-ē-moz′i-nər-i,* or *-mos′, adj.* relating to charity or almsgiving: dependent on charity: of the nature of alms. [Gr. *eleēmosynē,* alms—*eleos,* pity. See **alms.**]

**elegant,** *el′i-gənt, adj.* pleasing to good or fastidious taste: very careful or ornate in dress: graceful in form and movement: refined and luxurious: (of style) polished: (of apparatus or work in science or mathematics) simple and effective: excellent (*slang*).—*ns.* **el′egance, el′egancy,** the state or quality of being elegant: the finest propriety of manners (*arch.*): refinement: an exemplification of elegance.—*adv.* **el′egantly.** [Fr.,—L. *ēlegāns, -antis—ē,* from, and root of *legĕre,* to choose.]

**elegy,** *el′i-ji, n.* a song of mourning: a funeral-song: a poem of serious, pensive, or reflective mood: a poem written in elegiac metre.—*adj.* **elegi′ac,** belonging to elegy: mournful: used in elegies, esp. applied to classical verse in alternate hexameter and pentameter lines.—*n.* elegiac verse.—*adj.* **elegi′acal.**—*ns.* **elegiast** (*-lē′ji-ast; Goldsmith*), **el′egist,** a writer of elegies.—*v.i.* **el′egise, -ize,** to write elegiacally.—*v.t.* to write an elegy on. [L. *elegīa—*Gr. *elegeiā—elegos,* a lament.]

**element,** *el′ə-mənt, n.* a first principle: one of the essential parts of anything: an ingredient: the proper medium, habitat or sphere of any thing or being: any one of the four substances, fire, air, earth, and water, supposed by the ancients to be the foundation of everything: (in *pl.*) the rudiments of learning: (usu. *pl.*) the bread and wine used in the Eucharist: a substance that cannot be resolved by chemical means into simpler substances (*chem.*): a member or unit of a structure: a resistance wire in an electric heater: an electrode: a determining fact or condition in a problem: the sky: a celestial sphere: (in *pl.*) the weather, the powers of nature.—*adj.* **elemental** (*-ment′l*), pertaining to the elements: belonging to or produced by or inhabiting the elements.—*n.* an elemental spirit: a nature spirit: a disembodied spirit.—*n.* **element′alism,**

worship of elemental spirits: the theory which resolves the divinities of antiquity into the elemental powers.—*adv.* **element′ally.**—*adj.* **element′ary,** of a single element: primary: rudimentary: uncompounded: pertaining to the elements: treating of first principles.—**elemental spirits,** beings in mediaeval belief who presided over the four elements, living in and ruling them; **elementary particle,** a particle, esp. electron, proton, neutron, or pion, so-called because supposed indivisible; term is going out of use.—**elements of an orbit,** the data mathematically necessary to determine it; **in one's element,** in the surroundings most natural or pleasing to one. [L. *elementum,* pl. *elementa,* first principles.]

**elemi,** *el′im-i, n.* a fragrant resinous substance obtained from various tropical trees, esp. a species of Canarium. [Perh. Ar.]

**elench,** *i-lengk′,* (*obs.*), **elenchus,** *i-lengk′-əs* (*pl.* **elench′i**), *ns.* refutation: a sophism.—*adj.* **elenc′-tic,** pertaining to argument, cross-examining, refuting. [L.,—Gr. *elenchos—elenchein,* refute.]

**elephant,** *el′i-fənt, n.* a Proboscidean (*Elephas*) of several fossil and two surviving species, the largest living land mammal, having a very thick skin, a trunk, and ivory tusks: a size of paper before metrication.—*n.* **elephanti′asis** (Gr. *elephantiāsis*), a disease chiefly of tropical climates, consisting of an overgrowth of the skin and connective tissue usually of the legs and scrotum.—*adjs.* **elephant′ine,** pertaining to an elephant: like an elephant: very large or ungainly; **elephant′oid,** elephant-like.—**elephant folio,** a folio of the largest size; **elephant grass,** a kind of reed-mace, *Typha elephantum;* **elephant seal,** the largest of the seals, the male measuring about 20 feet in length; **el′ephant's-ears′,** begonia; **el′ephant's-foot,** Hottentot bread, a plant (*Testudinaria elephantipes*) of the yam family, whose root-stock resembles an elephant's foot, eaten by the Hottentots: a tropical composite plant, Elephantopus, from the shape of its radical leaves; **elephant shrew,** any member of the African family Macroscelidae, long-nosed, long-legged Insectivora, agile jumpers over loose sand.—**a white elephant,** anything that gives more trouble than it is worth—a (so-called) white elephant being an honourable but onerous gift of the kings of Siam to a courtier they wished to ruin. [Remodelled after Lat. from M.E. *olifaunt—*O.F. *olifant,* or poss. O.E. *olfend,* camel—L. *elephantus, elephās—*Gr. *elephās, -antos.*]

**Eleusinian,** *el-ū-sin′i-ən, adj.* relating to *Eleusis* in Attica.—**eleusinian mysteries,** the mysteries of Demeter celebrated there.

**eleutherian,** *el-ū-thē′ri-ən, adj.* freedom-giving.—*n.* **eleu′therarch** (*-thər-ärk;* Gr. *archos,* chief; Shelley*), chief of a feigned society of **eleu′theri.**—*adj.* **eleutherodac′tyl** (Gr. *daktylos,* toe; of birds), having the hind-toe free. [Gr. *eleutheros,* free.]

**elevate,** *el′i-vāt, v.t.* to raise to a higher position: to raise in mind and feelings: to exhilarate.—*adjs.* **el′evate, -d,** raised: lofty: exhilarated, esp. by liquor.—*ns.* **eleva′tion,** the act of elevating or raising, or the state of being raised: exaltation: an elevated place: a rising ground: height: a representation of the flat side of a building, drawn with mathematical accuracy, but without any attention to effect (*archit.*): angular height above the horizon: an angle made by a line with the plane of the horizon: a leap with apparent suspension in the air (*ballet*): lifting up (of the Host) in view of the people; **el′evator,** a person or thing that lifts up: a lift or machine for raising grain, etc., to a higher floor: a lift (*U.S.*): a storehouse for grain: a muscle raising a part of the body: movable control surface or surfaces at the tail of an aeroplane by which it is

made to climb or dive.—*adj.* el'evatory, able or tending to raise.—*n.* elevon (*el'ə-vɔn*), a wing flap on delta-wing or tailless aircraft acting both as an *elevator* and as an aileron.—elevated (railroad), a railway borne on pillars or trestles over a roadway, as in some American towns (familiarly el, or L). [L. *ēlevāre, -ātum—ē,* from, *levāre,* to raise—*levis,* light. See light (2).]
**eleven,** *i-lev'n, n.* the cardinal number next above ten: a team of eleven (cricket, association football, etc.): the eleventh hour after noon or midnight.—*adj.* of the number eleven.—*n.* elev'ens, elev'enses (*coll.*), an eleven o'clock snack: morning coffee or the like.—*adj.* elev'-enth, next after the tenth: equal to one of eleven equal parts.—*n.* an eleventh part: an octave and a fourth (*mus.*).—*adv.* eleventh'ly.—e'even and twenty long (*Shak.*), exactly right (the score aimed at in the game of one-and-thirty); **eleventh hour,** the very last moment, referring to Matt. xx. 6, 9.—**eleven-plus** (examination), a school examination taken by pupils about the age of eleven to determine to which type of secondary education (academic, non-academic, or technical) they are to proceed. [O.E. *en(d)-le(o)fan;* cf. Goth. *ainlif;* perh. (ten and) *one left,* from the root of L. *linquĕre,* Gr. *leipein,* to leave.]
**elevon.** See elevate.
**elf,** *elf, n.* in European folklore, a supernatural being, generally of human form but diminutive size, sometimes more malignant than a fairy: a fairy: a dwarf: a tricky, froward, or fairylike being, esp. a child:—*pl.* elves (*elvz*).—*v.t.* (*Shak.*) of the hair, to entangle.—*n.* elf'hood.—*adj.* elf'in, small, with delicate frame: small, mischievous and charming: pertaining to a good-natured elf.—*n.* a little elf: a child.—*adjs.* elf'ish, elv'an, elv'ish, elf-like, mischievous: tricky: distraught: froward.—elf'-arrow, -bolt, an elf-shot: elf'-child, a changeling, or a child supposed to have been left by elves in place of one stolen by them; elf'land, the land of the elves or fairies.—*n.pl.* elf'locks (*Shak.*), locks of hair clotted together, supposedly by elves.—*v.t.* elf'-shoot, to shoot with an elf-arrow, bewitch.— elf'-shot, a prehistoric flint or stone arrow-head, supposed to be used by elves: sickness attributed to it.—*adj.* shot with an elf-arrow: bewitched. [O.E. *ælf;* cf. O.N. *álfr,* Sw. *elf.*]
**Elian,** *ē'li-an, adj.* of, or like the work of, Charles Lamb, who wrote under the name of Elia.—*n.* a devotee or imitator of Lamb.
**eliad.** See œillade.
**elicit,** *i-, ē-, e-lis'it, v.t.* to draw forth: to evoke. *n.* elicitā'tion. [L. *ēlicĕre, ēlicitum.*]
**elide,** *ē-, i-līd', v.t.* to rebut (*arch.*): to cut off, as a syllable: to suppress, abridge.—*n.* elision (*i-lizh'ən*), the suppression of a vowel or syllable: an omission. [L. *ēlīdĕre, ēlīsum—ē,* from, *laedĕre,* to strike.]
**eligible,** *el'i-ji-bl, adj.* fit or worthy to be chosen: legally qualified for election or appointment: desirable.—*n.* (*coll.*) a person or thing eligible.— *n.* eligibil'ity.—*adv.* el'igibly. [Fr.,—L. *ēligĕre;* see elect.]
**eliminate,** *i-, ē-, e-lim'in-āt, v.t.* to thrust out (*arch.*): to remove, cancel, get rid of: to expel waste matter.—*adjs.* elim'inable; elim'inant (*med.*), causing elimination of waste or morbid matter.—*n.* an eliminating agent.—*n.* eliminā'tion. —*adj.* elim'inative.—*n.* elimin'ator, one who or that which eliminates; esp. a device for substituting an electric main for a battery in a wireless receiving set.—*adj.* elim'inatory. [L. *ēlīmināre, -ātum— ē,* from, *limen, -inis,* a threshold.]
**elision.** See elide.
**élite,** *i-, ā-lēt', n.* a chosen or select part: the pick or flower of anything: a size of typewriter type allowing twelve letters to the inch.—Also *adj.*

*n.* **élit'ism,** (belief in) government by an élite: consciousness of belonging to an élite.—*n.* and *adj.* **élit'ist.** [Fr. *élite*—L. *ēlecta* (*pars,* a part, understood); see elect.]
**elixir,** *i-, ē-, e-liks'ər, n.* a liquor once supposed to have the power of indefinitely prolonging life (elixir of life), or of transmuting metals: the quintessence of anything: a substance which invigorates: a panacea: a nostrum: a strong tincture. a compound tincture. [L.L.,—Ar. *al-iksir,* the philosopher's stone, from *al-,* the, *iksir,* prob. from Late Gr. *xērion,* a desiccative powder for wounds—Gr. *xēros,* dry.]
**Elizabethan,** *i-, e-liz-ə-bē'thən, adj.* pertaining to a Queen *Elizabeth* or her reign, esp. to the first Queen Elizabeth (1533-1603) or her reign (1558-1603)—of dress, manners, literature, etc.—*n.* a person, esp. poet or dramatist, of that age.—*n.* **Elizabēth'anism.—Elizabethan architecture,** the mixed style that sprang up on the decline of Gothic, marked by Tudor bow-windows and turrets decorated with classic cornices and pilasters, long galleries, enormous square windows. large apartments, plaster ceilings wrought into compartments, etc.
**elk,** *elk, n.* deer of northern Europe and Asia, identical or close akin with the moose of N. America, the largest of all living deer: the wapiti.—**elkhorn fern,** a genus (Platycerium) of tropical epiphytic ferns, with large leaf like an elk's horn; **elk'hound,** a large strong Norwegian breed of dog with thick coat and curled tail.— **Irish elk,** a giant deer now extinct, known from the remains found in the Pleistocene, esp. of Ireland. [Poss. O.E. *elh* (W.S. *eolh*).]
**ell,** *el, n.* a varying measure of length equally taken from the arm: a cloth measure equal to 1¼ yd (*obs.*).—*n.* ell'wand, a measuring rod.— **give him an inch and he'll take an ell,** a concession will encourage the taking of liberties. [O.E. *eln;* Du. *el,* Ger. *elle,* L. *ulna,* Gr. *ōlenē,* elbow.]
**ell,** *el.* Same as el.
**ellagic,** *e-laj'ik, adj.* pertaining to gall-nuts, applied to an acid, $C_{14}H_6O_8$. [Fr. *galle,* gall, spelt backwards.]
**ellipse,** *i-, e-lips', (geom.) n.* a figure produced by the section of one branch of a right circular cone by a plane passing obliquely and failing to meet the other branch.—*ns.* ellip'sis, a figure of syntax by which a word or words are left out and implied (gram.): mark(s) indicating ellipsis (print.):—*pl.* ellip'sēs; ellip'sograph, an instrument for describing ellipses; ellip'soid (*geom.*), a surface (or the enclosed solid) of which every plane section is an ellipse or a circle.—*adjs.* ellipsoi'dal; ellip'tic, -al, pertaining to an ellipse: oval: pertaining to ellipsis: having a part understood: slightly acute at each end, rather narrow, and broadest in the middle (*bot.*).—*adv.* ellip'tically.—*n.* ellipticity (*el-ip-tis'i-ti*), deviation from the form of a circle or sphere: of the earth, the difference between the equatorial and polar diameters.—**elliptic geometry, space,** Riemannian geometry, space. [L. *ellipsis*—Gr. *elleipsis—elleipein,* to fall short —en, in, *leipein,* to leave.]
**ellops,** *el'ops, (obs.) n.* a kind of snake (*Milt.*): a kind of sturgeon: a sea-serpent (*Goldsmith*). [Gr. *ellops,* also *elops, elaps,* perh. mute, perh. scaly, also an unknown fish, and an unknown snake; cf. Elaps, elops.]
**elm,** *elm, n.* a tree (Ulmus) with serrated leaves unequal at the base, and small flowers in clusters appearing before the leaves.—*adj.* of elm.—*adjs.* elm'en (*obs.*), made of elm; elm'y, abounding with elms. [O.E. *elm;* Ger. *ulme.* L. *ulmus.*]
**elocution,** *el-ə-kū'shən, n.* the art of effective speaking, more esp. of public speaking, regarding solely the utterance or delivery: eloquence

(*obs.*).—*adj.* elocū′tionary.—*n.* elocū′tionist, one versed in or practising elocution: a teacher of elocution: a reciter. [L. *ēlocūtiō*, -*ōnis*, *ēloquī*, -*cūtus*—*ē*, from, *loquī*, to speak.]

**Elodea**, *e-lō′di-a, n.* an American genus of Hydrocharitaceae, to which the Canadian waterweed belongs.—Also called **Helodea**, **Anacharis**, and **Phyllotria**. [Gr. *helōdēs*, marshy, marshdwelling—*helos*, marsh, *eidos*, form.]

**éloge**, *ā-lōzh′*, **elogium** (*obs.*), *ē-lō′ji-əm*, **elogy** (*obs.*), *el′ə-ji, ns.* a funeral oration: a panegyric (*obs.*).—*n.* el′ogist (*obs.*), one who delivers an éloge. [Fr. *éloge*, and its source L. *ēlogium*, a short statement, an inscription on a tomb, perh. confused with eulogy.]

**Elohim**, *e-lō′him, n.* Hebrew name for God.—*n.* **Elō′hist**, the writer or writers of the Elohistic passages of the Old Testament.—*adj.* **Elohist′ic**, relating to Elohim—said of those passages in the Old Testament in which the name Elohim is used instead of Yahweh (Jehovah). [Heb. pl. of *Eloah*—explained by Delitzsch as a plural of intensity.]

**eloin, eloign**, *e-loin′, (arch.) v.t.* to convey to a distance, to separate and remove.—*ns.* **eloin′-ment, eloign′ment.** [O.Fr. *esloignier* (Fr. *éloigner*)—L.L. *ēlongāre.* See elongate.]

**elongate**, *i-, ē′long-gāt*, also -*long′, v.t.* to make longer: to extend.—*v.i.* to grow longer.—*adjs.* **elongate, -d.**—*n.* **elonga′tion**, act of lengthening out: distance (*obs.*): the moon's or a planet's angular distance from the sun. [L.L. *ēlongāre*, -*ātum*—*ē*, from, *longus*, long.]

**elope**, *e-, i-lōp′, v.i.* to escape privately, esp. with a lover (usu. with marital intentions): to run away, bolt.—*ns.* **elope′ment; elop′er.** [Cf. O.Du. *ontlōpen*, Ger. *entlaufen*, to run away.]

**elops**, *el′ops, n.* a genus of fish (fam. *Elopidae*) akin to the tarpon. [See ellops.]

**eloquent**, *el′o-kwənt, adj.* having eloquence: persuasive: strongly expressive.—*n.* **el′oquence**, the power, art, or practice of uttering strong emotion in correct, appropriate, expressive, and fluent language: the art of such language: persuasive speech.—*adv.* **el′oquently.** [L. *ēloquēns, -entis*, pr.p. of *ēloquī.*]

**else**, *els, adj.* (or *adv.*) other (in addition or instead).—*adv.* otherwise: besides: except that mentioned.—*advs.* **elsewhere′**, in or to another place; **elsewhith′er; else′wise**, in a different manner: otherwise. [O.E. *elles*, otherwise, orig. gen. of *el*, other; cf. O.H.G. *alles* or *elles*, L. *alius*, Gr. *allos*, other.]

**elsin**, *el′sin*, **elshin**, *el′shin, (Scot.) n.* an awl. [From O.Du. *elssene* (mod. *els*): cf. awl.]

**elt**, *elt, (dial.) n.* a young sow. [Cf. yelt, gilt (2).]

**eltchi.** Same as elchi.

**eluant, eluate.** See elute.

**elucidate**, *ē-, i-lū′si-dāt*, or *lōō′, v.t.* to make lucid or clear: to throw light upon: to illustrate.—*n.* **elucidā′tion.**—*adjs.* **elu′cidative, elu′cidatory**, making clear: explanatory.—*n.* **elu′cidator.** [L.L. *ēlūcidāre*, -*ātum*—*ē*-, inten., and *lūcidus*, clear.]

**elucubration.** Obs. form of lucubration. [L. *ē*-, inten.]

**elude**, *ē-, i-lūd′* or -*lōōd′, v.t.* to escape by stratagem: to baffle.—*adj.* **elu′dible**—**elu′sion** (-*zhən*), act of eluding: evasion.—*adj.* **elu′sive** (-*ziv*, -*siv*), practising elusion: deceptive.—*adv.* **elu′-sively.**—*n.* **elu′soriness.**—*adj.* **elu′sory**, tending to elude or cheat: evasive: deceitful. [L. *ēlūdēre, ēlūsum*—*ē*, from, *lūdĕre*, to play.]

**Elul**, *e′lal* or *′lōōl, n.* the 12th month of the Jewish civil year, and 6th of the ecclesiastical. [Heb.,—*ālal*, to reap.]

**elution**, *ē-, i-lōō′shən, (chem.) n.* purification or separation by washing.—*ns.* **el′uant**, a liquid used for elution; **el′uate**, liquid obtained by eluting.—*v.t.* **elute′.**—*n.* **elu′tor**, a vessel for

elution. [L. *ēlūtiō, -ōnis*, washing—*ēluĕre*, *ēlūtum*—*ē*, from, *luĕre*, to wash.]

**elutriate**, *ē-, i-lōō′tri-āt, v.t.* to separate by washing into coarser and finer portions.—*ns.* **elutriā′tion, elu′triātor**, apparatus for elutriating. [L. *ēlutriāre*, -*ātum*, to wash out, *ēluĕre*—*ē*, from, *luĕre*, to wash.]

**eluvium**, *i-, ē-lōō′vi-əm*, or -*lū′, n.* an accumulation of rock debris formed on the spot or moved by wind only, as loess.—*adj.* **elu′vial.** [Formed on the analogy of **alluvium, diluvium.** [L. *ē*, from, *luĕre*, to wash.]

**elvan**, *elv′ən, n.* a granular crystalline dyke rock, composed of quartz and orthoclase.—Also **elv′anite.** [Cornish miners' name; prob. Cornish *elven*, spark.]

**elvan, elves, elvish.** See under elf.

**elver**, *el′vər, n.* a young eel. [eelfare; see eel.]

**Elysium**, *ē-, i-, e-liz(h)′i-əm, n.* among the Greeks, the abode of the blessed dead (*myth.*): any delightful place.—*adj.* **Elys′ian.** [L.,—Gr. *elysion* (*pedion*), the Elysian (plain).]

**elytrum**, *el′it-rəm, n.* a beetle's forewing modified to form a case for the hind-wing: a dorsal plate in certain worms.—Also **el′ytron:**—*pl.* **el′ytra.**—*adjs.* **el′ytral; elyt′riform; elytrigerous** (-*trij′ər-əs*). [Latinised from Gr. *elytron*, a sheath.]

**Elzevir**, *el′zi-vēr, -vər, adj.* published by the Elzevirs, a celebrated family of printers at Amsterdam, Leyden, and other places in Holland, whose small neat editions were chiefly published between 1592 and 1681: pertaining to the type used in their 12mo and 16mo editions of the Latin classics.—*n.* a special form of printing types.

**em**, *em, n.* the thirteenth letter of the alphabet (M, m): the unit of measurement (12-point lowercase 'm') used in spacing material and in estimating dimensions of pages (*print.*).

**em-, em-, pfx.** a form of en- used before *b, m* or *p*.

**'em**, *əm, pron.* them: to them. [Orig. the unstressed form of *hem*, dat. and accus. pl. of **he** (O.E. *him, heom*, dat. pl); but now used coll. as if an abbreviation of **them.**]

**emaciate**, *i-mā′shi-āt, -si-, v.t.* to make meagre or lean: to deprive of flesh: to waste.—*v.i.* to become lean: to waste away.—*adjs.* **emā′ciate, -d.**—*n.* **emaciā′tion**, the condition of becoming emaciated or lean: leanness. [L. *ēmaciāre*, -*ātum*—*ē*, inten. *maciāre*, to make lean—*maciēs*, leanness.]

**emanate**, *em′ə-nāt, v.i.* to flow out of or from anything: to proceed from some source: to arise.—*adj.* **em′anant**, flowing out.—*ns.* **emanā′tion**, a flowing out from a source, as the universe considered as issuing from the essence of God: the generation of the Son and the procession of the Spirit, as distinct from the origination of created beings: that which issues or proceeds from some source: a radioactive gas given off by radium, thorium and actinium—radon; **em′anatist.**—*adjs.* **em′anative, em′anatory, emanā′tional.** [L. *ēmānāre*, -*ātum*—*ē*, out from, *mānāre*, to flow.]

**emancipate**, *e-, i-man′si-pāt, v.t.* to set free from restraint or bondage or disability of any kind.—*ns.* **emancipā′tion**, the act of setting free from slavery or disability of any kind: the state of being set free: **emancipā′tionist**, an advocate of the emancipation of slaves; **eman′cipātor; eman′cipist** (*hist.*), a convict who has served his time of punishment in a penal colony. [L. *ēmancipāre, -ātum*—*ē*, away from, *mancipāre*, to transfer property—*manceps, -cipis*, one who gets property, from *manus*, the hand, *capĕre*, to take.]

**emarginate**, *ē-mär′jin-āt, v.t.* to take away the margin of.—*adj.* depressed and notched instead of pointed at the tip, as a leaf (*bot.*): having all the edges of the primitive form crossed by a face (*min.*): having the margin broken by a notch or segment of a circle (*zool*.).—*n*. emargina'tion. [L. *ēmargināre*, *-ātum*—*ē*, out, *margināre*, to provide with a margin—*margō*, a margin.]

emasculate, *i-*, *ē-mas'kū-lāt*, *v.t.* to deprive of the properties of a male: to castrate: to deprive of masculine vigour: to render effeminate.—*adj*. emasculated.—*ns*. emascula'tion; emas'culātor.—*adj*. emas'culatory (*-lə-tər-i*). [L.L. *ēmasculāre*, *-ātum*—*ē*, from, *masculus*, dim. of *mās*, a male.]

embace. See embase.

embail, *im-*, *em-bāl'*, (*obs*.) *v.t.* to encircle: to hoop in: (*pa.p.*, *Spens*., embayld'). [Pfx. em- (en- (1a)).]

embale, *im-*, *em-bāl'*, *v.t.* to make up, as into a bale: to bind up: to enclose. [Fr. *emballer*—*em-* (L. *in*), in, *balle*, a bale.]

emball, *em-böl'*, *v.t.* to ensphere.—*n*. emball'ing (*Shak*.), the receiving of the ball (of sovereignty). [Pfx. em- (en- (1a)).]

embalm, *im-*, *em-bäm'*, *v.t.* to preserve from decay by aromatic drugs, as a dead body: to preserve with fragrance: to preserve unchanged but lifeless: to impregnate with balm, perfume.—*ns*. embalm'er; embalm'ing; embalm'ment. [Fr. *embaumer*, from *em-*, in, and *baume*; see balm.]

embank, *im-*, *em-bangk'*, *v.t.* to enclose or defend with a bank or dike.—*ns*. embank'er; ˌenbank'ment, the act of embanking: a bank or mound made to keep water within certain limits: a mound constructed so as to carry a level road or railway over a low-lying place. [Pfx. em- (en- (1a)).]

embar, *im-*, *em-bär'*, *v.t.* to shut in: to hinder or stop (*arch*.): (*Milt*. imbar') to put under embargo (*arch*.):—*pr.p.* embarr'ing; *pa.t.* and *pa.p.* embarred'.—*n*. embarr'ing.—Also imbar'. [Pfx. em- (en- (1a)).]

embarcation. Same as embarkation.

embargo, *em-bär'gō*, *n*. a temporary order from the Admiralty to prevent the arrival or departure of ships: a stoppage of trade for a short time by authority: a prohibition, ban:—*pl*. embar'goes.—*v.t.* to lay an embargo on: to seize:—*pr.p.* embar'gōing; *pa.t.* and *pa.p.* embar'goed, *-gōd*.—*n*. embarque'ment (*Shak*.) a placing under embargo. [Sp., *embargar*, to impede, to restrain—Sp. pfx. em-, in, L.L. (and Sp.) *barra*, a bar.]

embark, *im-*, *em-bärk'*, *v.t.* to put on board ship: to engage, invest, in any affair.—*v.i.* to go on board ship: to engage in (with *on*, *in*).—*n*. embarka'tion (*em-*), a putting or going on board: that which is embarked: a vessel (*obs*.).—*adjs*. embarked'; embark'ing.—*n*. embark'ment. [Fr. *embarquer*, from *em-*, in, *barque*, bark.]

embarras de (du) choix, *ā-ba-ra də (dü) shwa*, (Fr.) embarrassment in choice, a perplexing number of things to choose from; embarras de(s) richesses, *də (dā) rē-shes*, a perplexing amount of wealth or of abundance of any kind.

embarrass, *im-*, *em-bar'əs*, *v.t.* to encumber: to involve in difficulty, esp. in money matters: to put out of countenance, disconcert: to perplex.—*adj*. embarr'assed, perplexed: constrained: disconcerted.—*n*. embarr'assment, perplexity or confusion: difficulties in money matters: perplexing amount see embarras de choix, etc.). [Fr. *embarrasser*—*em-*, in, *barre*, L.L. *barra*, bar.]

embase, imbase (*Spens*. embace), *im-bās'*, *v.t.* to lower: to bring down: to degrade: to debase: —*pa.p.* and *pa.t.* embased'; (*Spens*.) embaste'.—*adj*. embased'.—*n*. embase'ment. [Pfx. em- (en- (1b)) and base, or Fr. *bas*.]

embassy, *em'bə-si*, *n*. the charge or function of an ambassador: the person or body of persons sent on an undertaking: an ambassador's residence.—*n*. em'bassade (*Shak*.), an embassy.—*adv*. (*Spens*. *-bas'*), on an embassy.—*ns*. ambassador (*-bas'*; *obs*. except *U.S*.), an ambassador;

em'bassage, embassy: the sending or business of an embassy. [See ambassador.]

embathe, imbathe, *im-bādh'*, *v.t.* to bathe: to immerse: to bedew. [Pfx. em- (en- (1c)).]

embattle, *im-bat'l*, *v.t.* to furnish with battlements.—*adj*. embatt'led, furnished with battlements: having the outline like a battlement (*hər*.).—*n*. embatt'lement, battlement. [Pfx. em- (en- (1c)) and O.Fr. *bataillier*, to embattle; see battlement.]

embattle, *im-bat'l*, *v.t.* to range in order of battle: to arm (*Spens*.).—*adj*. embatt'led, arranged for battle. [O.Fr. *embataillier*—*em-*, in, *bataille*, battle.]

embay, *im-bā'*, *v.t.* to enclose in a bay: to land-lock.—*n*. embay'ment, a bay. [Pfx. em- (en- (1a)).]

embay, *em-bā'*, (*Spens*.) *v.t.* to bathe, steep, imbue. [Fr. *em-*, in, and apparently *baigner*; see bagnio.]

embayld. See embail.

embed, imbed, *im-bed'*, to place in a mass of matter (also *fig*.): to lay, as in a bed.—*n*. embed'ment, the act of embedding: state of being embedded. [Pfx. em- (en- (1a)).]

embellish, *im-bel'ish*, *v.t.* to make beautiful with ornaments: to decorate: to make graceful: to illustrate pictorially, as a book.—*n*. embell'isher.—*adv*. embell'ishingly.—*n*. embell'ishment, act of embellishing or adorning: decoration: ornament. [Fr. *embellir*, *embellissant*—*em-*, in, *bel* (*beau*) beautiful.]

ember, *em'bər*, *n*. a piece of live coal or wood: (chiefly in *pl*.) red-hot ashes: smouldering remains of a fire. [O.E. *æmerge*; O.N. *eimyrja*.]

Ember-days, *em'bər-dāz*, *n.pl*. the three Fast-days (Wednesday, Friday, Saturday) in each quarter, following the first Sunday in Lent, Whitsunday, Holy Cross Day (Sept. 14th), and St Lucia's Day (Dec. 13th).—*n*. Em'ber-week, the week in which they occur. [O.E. *ymbryne*, a circuit—*ymb* round (cf. Ger. *um*, L. *ambi-*), and *ryne*, a running, from *rinnan*, to run.]

ember-goose, *em'bər-gōos*, *n*. the great northern diver. [Norw. *emmer*; Ger. *imber*.]

embezzle, *im-bez'l*, *v.t.* to appropriate fraudulently (now only what has been entrusted): to impair (*obs*.).—*ns*. embezz'lement, fraudulent appropriation of property entrusted to one; embezz'ler, [Anglo-Fr. *embesiler*, to make away with, perh. influenced by imbecile (*q.v.*).]

embitter, imbitter, *im-bit'ər*, *v.t.* to make bitter or more bitter: to make more bitterly hostile.—*adj*. embitt'ered, soured: rendered misanthropical, cynical, or disappointed.—*n*. embitt'erer.—*n*. and *adj*. embitt'ering.—*n*. embitt'erment. [Pfx. em- (en- (1b)).]

emblaze, *im-blāz'*, *v.t.* to light up: to set aflame. [Pfx. em- (en- (1b)).]

emblaze, *im-blāz'*, *v.t.* to describe or depict heraldically: to celebrate: to adorn heraldically. [Pfx. em- (en- (1c)).]

emblazon, *im-blā'zn*, *v.t.* in heraldry, to adorn with figures: to depict heraldically: to celebrate.—*ns*. emblā'zoner; emblā'zonment, an emblazoning; emblā'zonry, the art of emblazoning or adorning: devices on shields. [Pfx. em- (en- (1c)).]

emblem, *em'bləm*, *n*. a picture representing to the mind something different from itself: a symbolic device or badge: a type or symbol: an inlaid ornament (*Milton*).—*v.t.* to symbolise.—*ns*. embleme (*em-blē'mə*), an inlaid ornament:—*pl*. emblē'mata.—*adjs*. emblemat'ic, -al, pertaining to or containing emblems: symbolical: representing.—*adv*. emblemat'ically.—*v.t.* emblematise, -ize (*-blem'ə-tiz*), em'blemise, -ize, to represent by an emblem.—*n*. emblem'atist, a writer or inventor of emblems. [L.,—Gr. *emblēma*, *-atos*, a thing inserted—*en*, in, and the root of *ballein*, to throw.]

emblements, *em'bli-mənts*, *n.pl*. crops raised by

the labour of the cultivator, but not tree-fruits or grass. [O.Fr. *emblaer*, to sow with corn—L.L. *imbladāre—in*, in, *bladum*, wheat.]

**emblic**, *em'blik*, *n*. an East Indian tree (*Phyllanthus Emblica*) of the spurge family: its fruit, used for tanning.—Also **emblic myrobalan**. [Ar. *amlaj* —Pers. *amleh*.]

**embloom**, *im-blōōm'*, *v.t.* to cover with bloom. [Pfx. em- (en- (1a)).]

**emblossom**, *im-blos'əm*, *v.t.* to cover with blossom. [Pfx. em- (en- (1a)).]

**embody, imbody**, *im-bod'i*, *v.t.* to form into a body: to make corporeal: to make tangible: to express (in words, in tangible form, etc.): to make part of a body, to incorporate: to organise. —*v.i.* to unite in a body or mass: to become corporeal, carnal, or sensual:—*pr.p.* **embod'y- ing**; *pa.t.* and *pa.p.* **embod'ied**.—*adj.* **embod'ied**. —*n.* **embod'iment**, act of embodying: state of being embodied: that in which something is embodied. [Pfx. em- (en- (1a)).]

**embog**, *im-bog'*, *v.t.* to bog. [Pfx. em- (en- (1c)).]

**embogue**, *im-bōg'*, *v.i.* to disembogue.

**emboil**, *em-*, *im-boil'*, (*obs.*) *v.i.* (*Spens.*) to burn with anger.—*v.t.* to cause to burn with anger: to irritate. [Pfx. em- (en- (1c)).]

**emboîtement**, *ā-bwät-mä*, *n.* encasement.—**em- boîtement theory**, the abandoned theory of old embryologists that the egg contained the germs of all future descendants, box within box. [Fr.]

**embolden**, *im-bōld'n*, *v.t.* to make bold or courage- ous: to give the necessary courage for some action.—*n.* **embold'ener**. [Pfx. em- (en- (1b)).]

**embolism**, *em'bol-izm*, *-bəl-*, *n.* an intercalation of days in the calendar to correct error: an inter- calated prayer for deliverance from evil coming after the Lord's Prayer: the presence of obstruct- ing clots in the blood vessels (*med.*).—*adjs.* **embolic** (*-bol'*), relating to an embolus or to an emboly; **embolis'mal**, **embolis'mic**.—*ns.* **em'- bolus**, a clot obstructing a blood-vessel; **em'boly**, an invagination.—**embolismic year** (see **year**). [Late Gr. *embolismos*, intercalation, Gr. *embolos*, a stopper, *embolē*, insertion, ramming—*em- ballein*, to throw in.]

**embonpoint**, *ä-bõ-pwẽ*, *adj.* stout, plump, full in figure: well-fed.—*n.* stoutness, plumpness, well- fed condition. [Fr.,—*en bon point*, in good form.]

**emborder, imborder**, *im-*, *em-bŏrd'ər*, (*Milt.*) *v.t.* to set as a border: to border. [Pfx. em- (en- (1c)).]

**emboscata**, *em-bos-kä'ta*, *-kä'ta*, *n.* an erroneous form of It. *imboscata*, or Sp. *emboscada*, an ambuscade.

**embosom, imbosom**, *im-bōōz'əm*, *v.t.* to take into the bosom: to receive into the affections: to implant in the bosom or mind: to enclose or surround. [Pfx. em- (en- (1a)).]

**emboss**, *im-bos'*, *v.t.* to cover with bosses: to raise bosses on: to raise in relief: to ornament with raised work.—*adj.* **embossed'**, formed or covered with bosses: raised, standing out in relief: having a protuberance in the centre (*bot.*).—*ns.* **emboss'er**; **emboss'ment**, a prom- inence like a boss: raised work. [Pfx. em- (en- (1a)).]

**emboss, imboss**, *im-bos'*, **imbosk**, *-bosk'*, (*obs.*) *v.i.* to take to the depths of a wood.—*v.t.* to drive to extremity: to make to foam at the mouth: —*pa.p.* **embossed'**, *Milt.* **embost'**. [O.Fr. *em- bosquer*, *em-* (L. *in*, in), *bosc*, a wood; see **ambush**.]

**emboss**, *em-bos'*, (*Spens.*) *v.t.* to clothe: to wrap: to enclose. [Origin obscure.]

**embouchure**, *ä-bōō-shür'*, *n.* the mouth of a river: the mouthpiece of a wind instru.. ent: the disposition of the mouth in playing a wind instrument. [Fr.,—*emboucher*, to put to the mouth, *en*, in, *bouche*, a mouth.]

**embound**, *em-bownd'*, (*Shak.*) *v.t.* to enclose. [Pfx. em- (en- (1a)).]

**embow**, *em-bow'*, *em-bō'*, (*arch.*) *v.t.* to bend: to arch or vault: to ensphere.—*adj.* **embowed'**, bent. [Pfx. em- (en- (1a)).]

**embowel**, *im-bow'əl*, *v.t.* to enclose (*obs.*): to disembowel, to remove the entrails from: to enclose in, or (*Spens.*) thrust into, the bowels (*obs.*):—*pr.p.* **embow'elling**; *pa.t.* and *pa.p.* **em- bow'elled**.—*n.* **embow'elment**. [Pfx. em- (en- (1a)).]

**embower, imbower**, *im-bow'ər*, *v.t.* to place in a bower: to shelter, as with trees.—*v.i.* to take or give shelter.—*n.* **embow'erment**. [Pfx. em- (en- (1a)).]

**embox**, *im-boks'*, *v.t.* to set in a box. [Pfx. em- (en- (1a)).]

**embrace**, *im-brās'*, *v.t.* to take in the arms: to press to the bosom with affection: to take eagerly or willingly: to comprise: to admit, adopt, or receive.—*v.i.* to join in an embrace:— *pr.p.* **embrac'ing**; *pa.t.* and *pa.p.* **embraced'**.—*n.* an embracing: fond pressure in the arms: (in *pl.*) sexual intercourse.—*ns.* **embrace'ment**; **em- brac'er**.—*adjs.* **embrac'ing**, **embrac'ive**.—*adv.* **embrac'ingly**.—*n.* **embrac'ingness**. [O.Fr. *em- bracer* (Fr. *embrasser*)—L. *in*, in, into, *brā*(c)*- chium*, an arm; see **brace**.]

**embrace**, *em-brās'*, (*Spens.*) *v.t.* to brace, to fasten, or bind. [Pfx. em- (en- (1a)).]

**embracer, embraceor, embrasor**, *em-brā'sər*, (*law*) *n.* one who seeks to influence jurors by corrupt means to deliver a partial verdict.—*n.* **em- brac'ery**, the offence of an embracer. [O.Fr. *embraceor*, from *embraser*, to set on fire.]

**embraid**, *em-brād'*, (*Spens.*) *v.t.* to braid. [Pfx. em- (en- (1c)).]

**embranchment**, *im-bränch'mənt,-sh-*, *n.* a branching off, as an arm of a river, a spur of a mountain, etc. [Fr. *embranchement*.]

**embrangle, imbrangle**, *im-brang'gl*, *v.t.* to con- fuse, perplex.—*n.* **embran'glement**. [Pfx. em- (en- (1a)).]

**embrasure**, *em-brās'yər*, (*Shak.*) *n.* embrace. [Pfx. em- (en- (1a)).]

**embrasure**, *im-brā'zhər*, (*archit.*) *n.* an internally splayed recess of a door or window: the slant of such a recess: an opening in a wall for cannon.—Also **embrazure**. [Fr.,—O.Fr. *em- braser*, to slope the sides of a window, *em-* (—L. *in*), *braser*, to skew.]

**embrave**, *em'brāv'*, *v.t.* to make showy, to decor- ate (*Spens.*): to inspire with bravery. [Pfx. em- (en- (1b)).]

**embread**, *em-brēd'*, (*Spens.*) *v.t.* embraid. [Pfx. em- (en- (1c)).]

**embreathe**, *em-brēdh'*, *v.t.* to breathe into: to breathe in. [Pfx. em- (en- (1a)).]

**embrewe** (*Spens.*). See **imbrue**.

**embrocate**, *em'brō-kat*, *v.t.* to moisten and rub, as with a lotion.—*n.* **embroca'tion**, act of em- brocating: the lotion used. [L.L. *embrocāre*, *-ātum*, from Gr. *embrochē*, a lotion—*embrechein*, to soak, embrocate—*en-*, in, into, *brechein*, to wet.]

**embroglio**. See **imbroglio**.

**embroider**, *im-broid'ər*, *v.t.* to ornament with designs in needlework: to add ornament or fictitious detail to.—*ns.* **embroid'erer**; **em- broid'ery**, the art of producing ornamental designs in needlework on textile fabrics, etc.: ornamental needlework: variegation or diver- sity: artificial or elaborate ornamentation: embellishment: exaggeration or invented detail. [M.E. *embrouderie*—O.Fr. *embroder*: confused with or influenced by O.E. *bregdan*, to weave, braid.]

**embroil**, *im-broil'*, *v.t.* to involve in a broil, or in perplexity (with): to entangle: to distract: to throw into confusion.—*n.* **embroil'ment**, a state of perplexity or confusion: disturbance. [Fr. *embrouiller*—pfx. em-, and *brouiller*, to break out.]

**embrown**, imbrown, *im-brown'*, *v.t.* to make brown: to darken, obscure.—*adj.* embrown'ing. [Pfx. em- (en- (1b)).]

embrue. Same as imbrue.

embrute. Same as imbrute.

embryo, *em'bri-ō*, also (*archaic*) embryon, *em'bri-on, n.* a young animal or plant in its earliest stages of development: beginning of anything:—*pl.* em'bryos, em'bryons.—Also *adj.*—*n.* embryogeny (*-oj'i-ni*), the formation and development of the embryo.—*adjs.* embryolog'ic, -al.—*ns.* embryol'ogist; embryol'ogy, the science of the formation and development of the embryo.—*adjs.* em'bryonal, em'bryonate, -d; embry-on'ic, embryot'ic, of or relating to anything in an imperfect state: rudimentary.—*ns.* embryot'omy (Gr. *tomē*, a cut), the division of a foetus to effect removal; embryul'cia (*-ul'shi-ə*; Gr. *holkē*, dragging), forcible extraction of a foetus.—em'bryo-sac, the megaspore of a flowering plant, one of the cells of the nucellus. [L.L.,—Gr. *embrȳon—en*, in, *bryein*, to swell.]

embus, *im-bus'*, *v.t.* to put into a bus (esp. troops).—*v.i.* to mount a bus:—*pr.p.* embuss'ing, *pa.t.* and *pa.p.* embussed'. [Pfx. em- (en- (1a)).]

embusqué, *ä-bü-skä*, (Fr.) in ambush; a slacker, shirker: one who evades military service.

embusy, *em-biz'i*, (*Spens.*) *v.t.* to occupy, make busy. [Pfx. em- (en- (1b)).]

emcee, *em'sē*, *n.* master of ceremonies.—*v.i.* and *v.t.* to act as a master of ceremonies. [From M.C.—abbrev. for *master of ceremonies*.]

eme, *ēm*, (*obs.*) *n.* an uncle. [O.E. *ēam*; Du. *oom*.]

emend, *ē-mend'*, *v.t.* to remove faults or blemishes from (now *rare*): to make alterations in with a view to improving (a text).—*adj.* emend'able, that may be emended.—*n.pl.* emend'als, funds set apart for repairs in the accounts of the Inner Temple.—*v.t.* e'mendate, to correct errors.—*ns.* emendā'tion, removal of an error or fault: correction; e'mendàtor, a corrector of errors in writings: one who corrects or improves.—*adj.* emen'datory, mending or contributing to correction. [L. *ēmendāre*, *-ātum—ē*, from, *mendum*, a fault.]

emerald, *em'ər-əld*, (*Spens.* emeraude), *n.* a very highly esteemed gem-stone, a beautiful velvety green variety of beryl.—em'erald-copp'er, dioptase; Emerald Isle, Ireland, from its greenness; emerald type (*print.*), a small size of type. [O.Fr. *esmeralde*—L. *smaragdus*—Gr. *smaragdos*.]

emerge, *i-*, *ē-mûrj'*, *v.i.* to rise out of anything: to issue or come forth: to reappear after being concealed: to come into view: to crop up.—*ns.* emer'gence, act of emerging: sudden appearance: emergency (*obs.*): in botany, an outgrowth of subepidermic tissue along with epidermic—an appendage more complex in structure than a hair; emer'gency, emergence (*obs.*): an unexpected occurrence, requiring immediate action: pressing necessity: a substitute in reserve.—Also *adj.*—*adj.* emer'gent, emerging: suddenly appearing: arising unexpectedly: urgent: coming into being in the course of evolution.—*adv.* emer'gently.—*adv.* emersed (*ē-mûrst'*; *bot.*), rising above the surface of water (as leaves).—*n.* emer'sion (*-shən*), act of emerging: the reappearance of a heavenly body after eclipse or occultation (*astron.*).—emergency exit, an exit to be used only in an emergency, e.g. fire. [L. *ēmergĕre*, *ēmersum—ē*, out of, *mergĕre*, to plunge.]

emeritus, *i-*, *ē-mer'i-təs*, *adj.* honourably discharged from the performance of public duty, esp. denoting a retired professor.—*n.* one who has been honourably discharged from public duties:—*pl.* emer'iti. [L. *ēmeritus*, having

served one's time—*ēmerērī*, to earn—*ē-*, sig. completeness, and *merērī*, to deserve.]

emerods, *em'ə-rodz*, (*B.*) *n.pl.* now haemorrhoids: representations of them in gold, used as charms.

emery, *em'ər-i*, *n.* a very hard mineral, a variety of corundum, used as powder for polishing, etc.—*v.t.* to rub or coat with emery.—em'ery-bag, a bag of emery-powder for cleaning and sharpening needles; em'ery-board, a small flat strip of wood or card coated with emery-powder, used in manicure; em'ery-cloth, -pā'per, cloth, paper, covered with emery-powder for polishing; em'ery-pow'der, ground emery; em'ery-wheel, a wheel coated with emery for polishing. [O.Fr. *esmeril*, *emeril*—L.L. *smericulum*—Gr. *smēris*, *smȳris*.]

emetic, *i-met'ik*, *adj.* causing vomiting.—*n.* a medicine that causes vomiting.—*n.* emesis (*em'i-sis*), vomiting.—*adj.* emet'ical.—*adv.* emet'ically.—*n.* em'etin, -ine, the alkaloid forming the active principle of ipecacuanha root, violently emetic. [Gr. *emetikos—emeein*, to vomit.]

emeu. See emu.

émeute, *ā-møt'*, sometimes *i-mūt'*, *n.* a popular rising or uproar. [Fr.]

emicate, *em'i-kāt*, *v.i.* to sparkle.—*adj.* em'icant, flashing.—*n.* emicā'tion. [L. *ēmicāre*, *-ātum*.]

emiction, *i-mik'shən*, *n.* the discharging of urine.—*adj.* emic'tory, promoting the flow of urine. [L. *ēmingĕre*, *ēmictum—ē*, from, *mingĕre*, to urinate.]

emigrate, *em'i-grāt*, *v.i.* and *v.t.* to remove from one country (or state) to another as a place of abode.—*adj.* em'igrant, emigrating or having emigrated.—*n.* one who emigrates.—*n.* emigrā'tion.—*adj.* emigrā'tional.—*n.* emigrā'tionist, an advocate or promoter of emigration.—*adj.* em'igrátory.—*n.* émigré (*ā-mē-grā'*; Fr.), a royalist who quitted France during the Revolution. [L. *ēmigrāre*, *ēmigrāre*, *-ātum—ē*, from, *migrāre*, to remove.]

éminence grise, *ā-mē-nãs grēz*, (Fr.) one exercising power in the background, as Cardinal Richelieu's private secretary and *alter ego* Père Joseph, nicknamed *l'Éminence Grise* ('the Grey Eminence').

eminent, *em'i-nənt*, *adj.* rising above others: conspicuous: distinguished: exalted in rank or office.—*ns.* em'inence, a part eminent or rising above the rest: a rising ground: a ridge or knob: height: distinction: a title given in 1631 to cardinals, till then styled Most Illustrious: advantage, upper hand (*Shak.*); em'inency.—*adj.* eminen'tial (*-shəl*: *obs.*).—*adv.* em'inently.—eminent domain, the right by which the supreme authority in a state may compel a proprietor to part with what is his own for the public use. [L. *ēminēns*, *-entis*, pr.p. of *ēminēre—ē*, from, *minēre*, to project.]

emir, *ā-mēr'*, sometimes *ē'mər*, *n.* a title given in the East and in N. Africa to all independent chieftains, and also (perh. improperly) to all the supposed descendants of Mohammed through his daughter Fatima.—*n.* emir'ate, the office, jurisdiction, or state of an emir.—Also ameer, emeer. [Ar. *amir*, ruler.]

emit, *i-*, *ē-mit'*, *v.t.* to send out: to throw or give out: to issue: to utter (a declaration):—*pr.p.* emitt'ing; *pa.t.* and *pa.p.* emitt'ed.—*n.* emissary (*em'is-ər-i*), one sent out on a mission, esp. an underhand or secret mission: a spy: an underground outlet, esp. of a lake.—*adj.* that is sent forth: outgoing.—*adj.* emiss'ile, protrusible.—*n.* emission (*-mish'ən*), the act of emitting: that which is issued at one time: discharge of semen: release of electrons from parent atoms on absorption of energy exceeding the average.—*adj.* emiss'ive, emitting, sending out.—*n.* emissiv'ity (*ē-*), property or power of emitting or radiating.—emission theory, the corpuscular theory. [L. *ēmittĕre*, *ēmissum*—*ē*, out of, *mittĕre*, to send.]

emma, *em'a*, *n.* (formerly) signallers' name for the letter *m*.

Emmanuel, Immanuel, *im-an'ū-əl*, *n.* the symbolical name of the child announced by Isaiah (Isa. vii. 14), and applied to Jesus as the Messiah in Matt. i. 23. [Heb.,—'*im*, with, *ānū*, us, *ēl*, God.]

emmarble, *i-mär'bl*, *v.t.* to turn to marble: to represent in marble: to adorn with marble. [Pfx. em- (en- (1b)).]

emmenagogue, *em-ēn'ə-gog*, or *-en'*, *n.* medicine intended to restore, or to bring on, the menses. —Also *adj.*—*adj.* emmenagogic (*-goj'ik*).—*n.* emmenol'ogy, study of menstruation. [Gr. *emmēna*, menses—*mēn*, a month, *agōgos*, drawing forth.]

Emmental, -thal, Emmentaler, -thaler, *em'ən-täl*, *-ər*, *n.* and *adj.* applied to a Swiss cheese, like Gruyère, made in the Emmental or Emme valley.

emmer, *em'ər*, *n.* a species of wheat, *Triticum dicoccum*. [Ger. dial.]

emmesh. Same as enmesh.

emmet, *em'it*, (*arch.* and *dial.*) *n.* the ant. [O.E. *æmete*.]

emmetropia, *em-e-trō'pi-ə*, *n.* the normal condition of the refractive media of the eye.—*n.* emm'etrope, an emmetropic person.—*adj.* emmetropic (*-trop'ik*). [Gr. *en*, in, *metron*, measure, *ops*, the eye.]

emmew, immew, *i-mū'*, enmew, *in-mū'*, *v.t.* to confine, mew up.—But in *Shak.* app. for enew. [Pfx. em- (en- (1a)).]

emmove, *e-mŏŏv'*, (*Spens.*) *v.t.* to move, to excite.

Emmy, *em'i*, *n.* a television trophy, corresponding to the cinema Oscar, awarded by the American Academy of Television Arts and Sciences.

emollient, *i-mol'yənt*, *adj.* softening: making supple.—*n.* a softening application, as poultices, fomentations, etc. (*med.*).—*n.* emollesc'ence, incipient fusion.—*v.t.* emoll'iate, to soften: to render effeminate.—*n.* emolli'tion, the act of softening or relaxing. [L. *ēmollīre*, *ēmollītum*—*ē*, inten., *mollīre*, to soften—*mollis*, soft.]

emolument, *i-mol'ū-mənt*, *n.* advantage (*obs.*): (often in *pl.*) profit arising from employment, as salary or fees.—*adjs.* emolumen'tal, emolumen'tary. [L. *ēmolimentum*, prob. from *ēmōlĕre*, to grind out—*ē*-, and *mōlĕre*, to grind, rather than from *ēmōlīrī* to work out, *mōlīrī*, to toil.]

emong, emonges, emongest, emongst, old forms of among, amongst.

emotion, *i-mō'shən*, *n.* a moving of the feelings: agitation of mind: one of the three groups of the phenomena of the mind—feeling, distinguished from cognition and will (*phil.*).—*v.i.* emote (*i-mōt'*) to show or express exaggerated emotion.—*adjs.* emō'tionable; emō'tional.—*n.* emō'tionalism, tendency to emotional excitement, the habit of working on the emotions, the indulgence of superficial emotion. —*adv.* emō'tionally.—*adjs.* emō'tionless; emō'tive (*-tiv*), pertaining to the emotions: emotional: tending to arouse emotion.—*v.t.* emove (*i-mŏŏv'*), to affect with emotion. [L. *ēmōtiō*, *-ōnis*— *ēmovēre*, *-mōtum*, to stir up.]

emp-. For words not found under this, see imp-.

empacket, *im-pak'it*, (*Scott*) *v.t.* to pack up. [Pfx. em- (en- (1c)).]

empaestic, *em-pē'stik*, *adj.* pertaining to the art of embossing: stamped, inlaid. [Gr. *empaiein*, to emboss.]

empaire, empare, empayre (*Spens.*). See impair (1).

empale, *em-pāl'*, *v.t.* to impale: to surround with a border (*Spens.*). [impale.]

empanel, *im-pan'əl*, *v.t.* to enter on a panel:— *pr.p.* empan'elling; *pa.t.* and *pa.p.* empan'elled. —*n.* empan'elment.—Also impanel, impannel. [Pfx. em- (en- (1a)).]

empanoply, *im-pan'o-pli*, *v.t.* to invest in full armour. [Pfx. em- (en- (1a)).]

empathy, *em'pə-thi*, *n.* power of entering into another's personality and imaginatively experiencing his experiences: power of entering into the feeling or spirit of something (esp. a work of art) and so appreciating it fully.—*adjs.* empathet'ic, empath'ic.—*v.i.* em'pathise, -ize. [Gr. *en*, in, *pathos*, feeling.]

empatron, *em-pā'trən*, (*Shak.*) *v.t.* to patronise. [Pfx. em- (en- (1c)).]

empennage, *em-pen'ij*, *ā-pen-äzh*, *n.* an aeroplane's tail as a unit, including elevator, rudder, and fin. [Fr., feathering of an arrow—L. *penna*, feather, wing.]

empeople, *im-pē'pl*, (*obs.*) *v.t.* to fill with people: to form into a people or community. [Pfx. em- (en- (1a)).]

emperish, *im-per'ish*, (*Spens.*, etc.) *v.t.* to impair. [Perh. (irregularly)—Fr. *empirer*; cf. impair (1).]

emperor, *em'pər-ər*, *n.* the head of an empire: a high title of sovereignty: before metrication, a paper size (48 × 72 in.):—*fem.* em'press.—*v.t.* em'perise, -ize (*obs.*), to play the emperor.—*ns.* em'perorship; em'pery, empire, power.—emperor moth, except the death's-head, the largest British moth, its expanse of wings being about three inches; emperor penguin, the largest of the penguins. [O.Fr. *emperere*—L. *imperātor*, a commander (fem. *imperātrix*)—*imperāre*, to command.]

empfindung, *emp-fin'dŏong*, (Ger.) sensation, feeling.

emphasis, *em'fə-sis*, *n.* use of language to imply more than is said (*obs.*): forcible or impressive expression: insistent or vigorous way of attributing importance or thrusting upon attention: stress: accent: prominence:—*pl.* em'phases (*-sēz*).—*v.t.* em'phasise, -ize, to make emphatic: to lay stress on.—*adjs.* emphat'ic (*im-*, *em-fat'ik*), -al, expressed or expressing with emphasis: stressed forcibly: impressive: strongly marked. —*adv.* emphat'ically.—*n.* emphat'icalness. [Gr. *emphasis*, image, outward appearance, significance, implied meaning—*en*, in, *phainein*, to show.]

emphlysis, *em'fli-sis*, *n.* a vesicular eruption. [Gr. *en*, in, *phlȳsis*, eruption—*phlȳein*, to bubble, break out.]

emphractic, *em-frak'tik*, *adj.* stopping the pores of the skin.—*n.* a substance with this property. [Gr. *emphraktikos*, obstructive, *en*, in, *phrassein*, to stop.]

emphysema, *em-fis-ē'ma*, (*med.*) *n.* an unnatural distension of a part with air: distension of the lung, with breathing difficulties, etc.—*adj.* emphyse'matous. [Gr. *emphȳsēma*—*emphȳsaein*, to inflate.]

emphyteusis, *em-fit-ū'sis*, *n.* in Roman law, a perpetual right in a piece of land, for which a yearly sum was paid to the proprietor.—*adj.* emphyteu'tic. [Gr.,—*emphyteuein*, to implant.]

empiecement, *em-pēs'mənt*, *n.* an insertion in a garment. [Fr. *empiècement*.]

empierce, emperce, *em-pērs'*, (*Spens.*) *v.t.* to pierce. [Pfx. em- (en- (1c)).]

empight, *em-pit'*, (*Spens.*) *adj.* fixed. [pitch (2).]

empire, *em'pīr*, *n.* (loosely) a widespreading dominion, or group of states, etc., under the same sovereign power—not always an emperor: supreme control or dominion: the government or office of an emperor: the time of its duration: a large industrial organisation embracing many firms: a country whose sovereign owes no allegiance to another (*hist.*).—*adj.* (usu. *cap.*) relating to or in the style of, esp. of dress or furniture, the first French Empire (1804-14).— Empire Day, 24th May (Queen Victoria's birthday); Empire gown, a gown with low neckline and high waist such as was worn

during the first French Empire. [Fr.,—L. *imperium*.]
**empiric**, em-pir′ik, formerly *em′*, *adj.* empirical.—*n.* one who makes trials or experiments: one whose knowledge is got from experience only: a quack.—*adj.* **empir′ical**, resting on trial or experiment: known or knowing only by experience.—*adv.* empir′ically.—*ns.* empir′icism (-sizm), the system which, rejecting all *a priori* knowledge, rests solely on experience and induction (*phil.*): dependence of a physician on his experience alone without a regular medical education: the practice of medicine without a regular education: quackery; **empir′icist** (-sist), one who practises empiricism.—*adj.* **empiricūt′ic** (*Shak.* empirick **qutique**; modelled on therapeutic; *obs.*), empirical.—**empirical formula** (*chem.*), a formula showing in simplest form the ratio of atoms in a molecule, not the absolute number. [Fr.,—L. *empiricus*—Gr. *empeirikos*—*en*, in, *peira*, a trial.]
**emplacement**, im-plās′mənt, *n.* the act of placing: a gun-platform (*mil.*).—*v.t.* **emplace′** (backformation) to put in or provide with an emplacement. [Fr. *emplacement*.]
**emplane**, em-plān′, *v.t.* to put or take on an aeroplane.—*v.i.* to mount an aeroplane. [Pfx. em- (en- (1a)) and plane (2).]
**emplaster**, em-pläs′tər, *n.* and *v.* same as plaster. —*adj.* **emplastic** (-plas′), glutinous: adhesive.—*n.* a medicine that stops the pores.—*ns.* **emplas′tron** (Gr.), **emplas′trum** (L.), a medicated plaster. [Gr. *emplastron*.]
**emplecton**, em-plek′ton, (*arch.*) *n.* ashlar masonry filled up with rubble.—Also (L.) **emplec′tum**. [Gr. *emplekton*—*en*, in, *plekein*, to weave.]
**emplonge** (*Spens.*). See implunge.
**employ**, im-ploi′, *v.t.* to occupy the time or attention of: to use as a means or agent: to give work to.—*n.* employment.—*adj.* employ′able, fit, able, to be employed.—*adj.* **employed′**, having employment, in a job.—*ns.* employ′ee or -é (-ē′), a person employed; **employ′er**; **employ′ment**, act of employing: that which engages or occupies: occupation.—**employment agency**, an agency which finds work for the unemployed and employees for vacant positions; **employment exchange**, a government agency run by the Department of Employment, which finds work for the unemployed, pays out unemployment benefit, etc. (formerly called *Labour Exchange*). [Fr. *employer*—L. *implicāre*, to enfold—*in*, in, and *plicāre*, to fold; cf. imply, implicate.]
**emplume**, im-plōōm′, *v.t.* to furnish with a plume. [Pfx. em- (en- (1a)).]
**empoison**, im-poi′zn, *v.t.* to put poison into: to poison (*obs.*): to embitter, corrupt.—*adj.* **empoi′soned**.—*n.* empoi′sonment. [Pfx. em- (en- (1a)).]
**emporium**, em-pō′ri-əm, -pö′, *n.* a commercial or trading centre or mart: a big shop:—*pl.* empō′ria, **emporiums**. [L.,—Gr. *empŏrion*, a trading station—*empŏros*, a wayfarer, trader, *en*, in, *poros*, a way.]
**empoverish**. Obs. form of impoverish.
**empower**, im-pow′ər, *v.t.* to authorise. [Pfx. em- (en- (1a)).]
**empress**. See emperor.
**empressement**, ã-pres-mã, (Fr.) *n.* demonstrative warmth of manner.—*adj.* **empressé** (-pres-ā), eager, enthusiastic.
**emprise**, em-priz′, (*arch.*) *n.* an enterprise: a hazardous undertaking. [O.Fr. *emprise*—pa.p. fem. of *emprendre*—L. *in*, in, *praehendĕre*, take.]
**emption**, emp′shən, *n.* act of buying, purchase.—*adj.* emp′tional. [L. *emptiō*, -ōnis—*emĕre*, to buy.]
**empty**, emp′ti, *adj.* having nothing within: unoccupied: unfurnished: without effect: unsatisfactory: wanting substance: meaningless: empty-headed: hungry (*coll.*): devoid (of;

*Shak.* with *in*).—*v.t.* to make empty: to deprive of contents: to remove from a receptacle.—*v.i.* to become empty: to discharge:—*pr.p.* emp′tying; *pa.t.* and *pa.p.* emp′tied.—*n.* an empty bottle, box, sack, etc.:—*pl.* emp′ties.—*ns.* emp′-tier; **emp′tiness**, state of being empty: want of substance: unsatisfactoriness: inanity; emp′ty-ing.—*adjs.* **emp′ty-hand′ed**, bringing or taking away nothing or no gift; **emp′ty-head′ed**, frivolous. [O.E. *ǣmetig*—*ǣmetta*, leisure, rest; the *p* is excrescent.]
**emptysis**, emp′ti-sis, *n.* spitting, esp. of blood. [Gr. *emptysis*, spitting—*en*, in, *ptyein*, to spit.]
**empurple**, im-pûr′pl, *v.t.* to dye or tinge purple. [Pfx. em- (en- (1b)).]
**Empusa**, em-pū′za, *n.* a goblin or spectre sent by Hecate (also without *cap.*; also **empuse′**): (*cap.*) a genus of fungi parasitic upon houseflies and other insects. [Gr. *Empousa.*]
**empyema**, em-pi-ē′ma, or -pi-, *n.* a collection of pus in any cavity, esp. the pleura.—*n.* **empyesis** (-ē′sis), pustulous eruption. [Gr. *empyēma*, *empyēsis*—*en*, in, *pyon*, pus.]
**empyreal**, em-pir-ē′al, (*Milt.*, *Pope*, em-pir′i-əl) *adj.* formed of pure fire or light: pertaining to the highest and purest region of heaven: sublime.—*adj.* **empyre′an**, empyreal.—*n.* the highest heaven, where the pure element of fire was supposed to subsist: the heavens. [Gr. *empyros*, fiery—*en*, in, *pŷr*, fire.]
**empyreuma**, em-pir-ū′ma, *n.* the burned smell and acrid taste that come when vegetable or animal substances are burned:—*pl.* empyreu′-mata.—*adjs.* **empyreumat′ic**, -al.—*v.t.* empyreu′-matise, -ize. [Gr. *empŷreuma*, -*atos*, embers—*en*, in, *pŷr*, fire.]
**emu**, **emeu**, ē′mū, *n.* an Australian running bird of the Ratitae, akin to the cassowary, largest of living birds after the ostrich.—**emu wren**, a small Australian bird (Stipiturus), with tail-feathers like emu feathers in structure. [Port. *ema*, an ostrich.]
**emulate**, em′ū-lāt, *v.t.* to strive to equal or excel: to rival successfully: (*loosely*) to imitate.—*adj.* (*Shak.*) ambitious, eager to rival.—*n.* **emulā′tion**, act of emulating or attempting to equal or excel: rivalry: competition: contest: jealous rivalry (*obs.*).—*adj.* **em′ulātive**, inclined to emulation rivalry, or competition.—*n.* em′ulātor:—*fem.* **em′ulātress** (*obs.*).—*v.t.* em′ule (*Southey*), to emulate.—*adj.* **em′ulous**, eager to emulate: desirous of like excellence with another: engaged in competition or rivalry.—*adv.* em′ulously.—*n.* em′ulousness. [L. *aemulāri*, -*ātus*—*aemulus*, emulous.]
**emulge**, i-mulj′, (*arch.*) *v.t.* to milk or drain out.—*n.* emul′gence.—*adj.* emul′gent (*med.*), acting as a drain for. [See emulsion.]
**emulsion**, i-mul′shən, *n.* a colloidal suspension of one liquid in another: a light-sensitive coating on photographic plates: a liquid mixture containing globules of fat (as milk), or of resinous or bituminous material.—*ns.* emulsificā′tion; **emul′sifier**, apparatus for preparing emulsions.—*v.t.* emul′sify.—*n.* emul′sin, an enzyme got from bitter almonds.—*v.t.* emul′sionise, -ize.—*adj.* emul′sive.—*ns.* emul′soid, a colloid easily dispersed, giving a suspension readily formed again after coagulation; **emul′sor**, an emulsifying apparatus.—**emulsifying agent**, substance whose presence in small quantities stabilises an emulsion; **emulsion paint**, a water-thinnable paint made from a pigmented emulsion of a resin in water. [L. *ēmulgēre*, *ēmulsum*, to milk out—*ē*, from, and *mulgēre*, to milk.]
**emunctory**, i-, or ē-mungk′tər-i, *adj.* conveying waste: pertaining to nose-blowing.—*n.* any organ or passage of the body that carries off waste: an excretory duct.—*v.t.* emunge (i-munj′; *obs.*), to clean. [L. *ēmunctōrium*, a pair of

snuffers, a means of cleansing, *ēmungĕre*, *ēmunctum*, to blow the nose, to cleanse.]

**emure,** *i-mūr'*, (*Shak.*) *v.t.* and *n.* a variant of **immure.** [Pfx. em- (en- (1a)).]

**Emys,** *em'is*, *n.* a genus of freshwater and marsh terrapins : (without *cap.*) any member of the genus: *pl.* em'y**dēs.** [Gr. *emys*, *-ydos*.]

**en,** *en*, *n.* the fourteenth letter of the alphabet (N, n): half of an em (*print.*).

**en-,** *en-*, *in-*, *pfx.* (1) in words derived from L. through Fr., (a) used to form verbs with the sense of *in*, *into*, *upon*; (b) used to form verbs with the sense *cause to be*; (c) used intensively or almost meaninglessly; (2) in words derived from Gr. used to form verbs with the sense of *in*.

**enable,** *in-ā'bl*, *v.t.* to make able: to give power, strength, or authority to: to make possible.— **enabling act, bill,** one giving or proposing to give power to act. [Pfx. en- (1b).]

**enact,** *in-akt'*, *v.t.* to perform: to act the part of: to establish by law.—*n.* (*Shak.*) an enactment.— *adjs.* **enact'ing, enact'ive.**—*ns.* **enac'tion** (*-shən*), **enact'ment,** the passing of a bill into law: that which is enacted: a law; **enact'or,** one who practises or performs anything: one who forms decrees or establishes laws; **enac'ture** (*Shak.*), fulfilment. [Pfx. en- (1b), act.]

**enallage,** *en-al'ə-jē*, (*gram.*) *n.* the exchange of one case, mood, tense, etc., for another. [Gr. *enallagē*—*en*, in, and *allassein*, to change.]

**enamel,** *in-am'əl*, *n.* vitrified coating applied to a metal or other surface and fired: any glossy enamel-like surface or coating, esp. that of the teeth: work of art in enamel: a paint giving an enamel-like finish.—*v.t.* to coat with or paint in enamel: form a glossy surface on, like enamel: —*pr.p.* enam'elling; *pa.t.* and *pa.p.* enam'elled.—*ns.* enam'eller, enam'ellist; enam'elling. [O.Fr. *enameler*—*en*, in, *esmail*, enamel; see smelt (2), melt.]

**en ami,** *ä-na-mē*, (Fr.) as a friend.

**enamour,** in U.S. **enamor,** *in-am'ər*, *v.t.* to inflame with love: to charm.—*n.* enamorado (*en-äm-ō-rä'dō*; Sp.) a lover.—*adjs.* enam'oured; enam'-ouring.—enamoured of, in love with. [O.Fr. *enamourer*—pfx. *en-*, *amour*—L. *amor*, *-ōris*, love.]

**enantiomorph,** *en-an'ti-ō-mörf*, *n.* a shape or object (as a crystal, a molecule) exactly similar to another except that right and left are inter-changed, each being a mirror-image of the other. —*adjs.* enantiomorph'ic, enantiomorph'ous.—*ns.* enantiomorph'ism, enantiomorph'y. [Gr. *enan-tios*, opposite, *morphē*, shape.]

**enantiopathy,** *en-an-ti-op'ə-thi*, *n.* allopathy. [Gr. *enantios*, opposite, *pathos*, suffering.]

**enantiosis,** *en-an-ti-ō'sis*, (*rhet.*) *n.* the expression of an idea by negation of its contrary (litotes), or by substitution of the contrary (antiphrasis, irony). [Gr. *enantiōsis*, contradiction.]

**enantiostyly,** *en-an-ti-ō-sti'li*, (*bot.*) *n.* a dimor-phous condition in which the style projects at one side or the other in different flowers.—*adj.* **enantiostÿ'lous.** [Gr. *enantios*, opposite, *stȳlos*, a column.]

**enantiotropy,** *en-an-ti-o'trə-pi*, *n.* the existence in a substance of two crystal forms, one stable above, the other below, a transition temperature.—*adj.* **enantiotro'pic.** [Gr. *enantios*, opposite, *tropos*, turn, habit.]

**enarch.** See inarch.

**enarched,** *en-ärcht'*, (*her.*) *adj.* arched, like an arch. [Pfx. en- (1b).]

**enarm,** *en-ärm'*, *v.t.* to arm (*obs.*): to lard (*obs.*). —*adj.* **enarmed** (*her.*), having horns, hoofs, etc., of a different colour from the body. [Pfx. en- (1b).]

**enarration,** *ē-nə-rā'shən*, (*arch.*) *n.* exposition: detailed narration. [Pfx. en- (1c).]

**en arrière,** *ä-na-ryer*, (Fr.) behind, in the rear.

**enarthrosis,** *en-är-thrō'sis*, (*anat.*) *n.* a ball-and-socket joint.—*adj.* **enarthrō'dial.** [Gr. *enarthrō-sis*—*en*, in, *arthron*, a joint.]

**enate,** *ē'nāt*, *adj.* growing out.—*n.* **ena'tion,** an outgrowth. [L. *ē-*, from, *nātus*, born.]

**en attendant,** *ä-na-tä-dä*, (Fr.) in the meantime, while waiting.

**enaunter,** *en-ön'tər*, *en-än'tər*, (*obs.*; *Spens.*) *conj.* lest by chance. [Contr. from *in a*(*d*)*venture*.]

**en avant,** *ä-na-vä*, (Fr.) forward.

**en badinant,** *ä ba-dē-nä*, (Fr.) roguishly, banter-ingly.

**en beau,** *ä bō*, (Fr.) (of manner of showing person, etc., in a picture), in flattering style, as fair or handsome.

**en bloc,** *ä blok*, (Fr.) as one unit, wholesale.

**en brochette,** *ä bro-shet*, (Fr.) (of food) on a skewer.

**en brosse,** *ä bros*, of hair, cut short and standing up stiffly. [Fr., like a brush.]

**en caballo,** *än kä-bä'lyō*, (Sp.) on horseback.

**encaenia,** *en-sē'ni-a*, *n.* the annual commemora-tion of founders and benefactors at Oxford, held in June. [L.,—Gr. *enkainia* (pl.), a feast of dedication—*en*, in, *kainos*, new.]

**encage, incage,** *in-kāj'*, *v.t.* to shut up in a cage. [Pfx. en- (1a).]

**encalm,** *in-käm'*, (*obs.*) *v.t.* to becalm. [Pfx. en- (1b).]

**encamp,** *in-kamp'*, *v.t.* to form into a camp: to lodge in a camp.—*v.i.* to pitch tents: to make, or stay in, a camp.—*n.* **encamp'ment,** the act of encamping: the place where a camper or company is encamped: a camp. [Pfx. en- (1b).]

**encanthis,** *en-kan'this*, *n.* a small tumour of the inner angle of the eye. [Gr. *enkanthis*—*en*, in, *kanthos*, a canthus.]

**encapsulate,** *in-kap'sūl-āt*, *v.t.* to enclose in a capsule.—*n.* **encapsula'tion.** [Pfx. en- (1a).]

**encarnalise, -ize,** *in-kär'nəl-iz*, *v.t.* to embody: to make carnal. [Pfx. en- (1b).]

**encarpus,** *en-kär'pəs*, *n.* a festoon of fruit orna-menting a frieze. [Gr. *enkarpa* (neut. pl.)—*en*, in, *karpos*, fruit.]

**encase, incase,** *in-kās'*, *v.t.* to enclose in a case: to surround, cover: to line.—*n.* **encase'ment,** the act of encasing: an enclosing substance: a covering: a lining. [Pfx. en- (1a).]

**encash,** *in-kash'*, *v.t.* to convert into cash.— *n.* **encash'ment.** [Pfx. en- (1b).]

**encaustic,** *en-kös'tik*, *adj.* having the colours burned in.—*n.* an ancient method of painting in melted wax.—**encaustic tile,** a decorative glazed and fired tile, having patterns of different coloured clays inlaid in it and burnt with it. [Gr. *enkaustikos*—*enkaiein*, to burn in—*en*, in, *kaiein*, to burn.]

**en cavalier,** *ä ka-va-lyä*, (Fr.) in a cavalier manner.

**encave,** *en-kāv'*, (*Shak.*) *v.t.* to hide. [Fr. *encaver*, to put in a cellar—*en*, in, *cave*, cellar.]

**enceinte,** *ä-sēt*, (*fort.*) *n.* an enclosure, generally the whole area of a fortified place. [Fr.,— *enceindre*, to surround—L. *in*, in, *cingĕre*, *cinctum*, to gird.]

**enceinte,** *ä-sēt*, *adj.* pregnant, with child. [Fr., —L. *incincta*, girt about or ungirt.]

**Encephalartos,** *en-sef-al-är'tos*, *n.* the Kaffir-bread genus of cycads. [Gr. *enkephalos*, within the head, palm-cabbage, *artos*, bread.]

**encephalon,** *en-sef'al-on*, or *-kef'*, *n.* the brain.— *adjs.* **encephalic** (*-al'ik*), belonging to the head or brain; **encephalit'ic,** pertaining to encephalitis. —*ns.* **encephali'tis,** inflammation of the brain; **en-ceph'alocele** (*-əl-ō-sēl*; Gr. *kēlē*, tumour), a pro-trusion of portion of the brain through the skull, where the bones are incomplete in infancy; **enceph'alogram, enceph'alograph,** an X-ray photograph of the brain; **encephalog'raphy,** radiography of the brain, its cavities having been filled with air or dye injected into the space around the spinal cord.—*adj.* enceph'aloid, resembling the matter of the brain.—*n.* encephalot'omy (Gr. *tomē,* a cut), dissection of the brain.—*adj.* enceph'alous, cephalous.—encephalitis lethar'gica (*-ji-kə*), an acute disease marked by profound physical and mental lethargy—popularly called *sleeping-sickness,* better *sleepy-sickness.* [Gr. *enkephalos—en,* in, *kephalē,* head.]

enchafe, *en-chāf'*, (*obs.*) *v.t.* to make warm: to irritate. [Earlier *enchaufe, eschaufe*—O.Fr. *eschauffer—es-* (L. *ex*), *chauffer*; see chafe.]

enchain, *in-chān'*, *v.t.* to put in chains: to hold fast (*fig.*): to link together (*obs.*).—*n.* enchain'ment, act of enchaining: state of being enchained. [Fr. *enchaîner—en,* in, *chaîne,* chain—L. *catēna.*]

enchant, *in-chänt'*, *v.t.* to act on by songs or rhymed formulas of sorcery: to cast a spell upon: to compel by enchantment: to charm: to delight in a high degree.—*adj.* enchant'ed, under the power of enchantment: delighted: possessed by witches or spirits.—*n.* enchant'er, one who enchants: a sorcerer or magician: one who charms or delights:—*fem.* enchant'ress.—*adj.* enchant'ing.—*adv.* enchant'ingly, with the force of enchantment: in a manner to charm or delight.—*n.* enchant'ment, act of enchanting: use of magic arts: enchanted state: that which enchants.—enchanter's nightshade, a plant (*Circaea lutetiana*) of the evening-primrose family, growing in shady places—both names transferred apparently from another plant (perhaps mandrake, or swallow-wort) for no apparent reason. [Fr. *enchanter*—L. *incantāre,* to sing a magic formula over—*in,* on, *cantāre,* to sing.]

encharge, *in-chärj'*, *v.t.* to enjoin (*obs.*): to entrust. [O.Fr. *encharger*; see charge.]

encharm, *in-chärm'*, (*obs.*) *v.t.* to cast a spell on: to charm. [Pfx. en- (1c).]

enchase, *in-chās'*, *v.t.* to fix in a border or setting: to enshrine (*obs.*): to enclose (*obs.*): to enshrine in verse (*obs.*): to insert, let in: to set with jewels: to engrave: to adorn with raised, or embossed work: prob. to fewter (*Spens.*).—*n.* (*Spens.*) enchasing.—*adj.* enchased'. [Fr. *enchâsser—en,* in, *châsse,* shrine, setting—L. *capsa,* a case; see case (1), chase (3); chase (2) is a contraction.]

encheason, *en-chē'zn,* (*Spens.*) *n.* reason, cause, occasion. [O.Fr. *encheson—encheoir,* to fall in; influenced by L. *occāsiō, -ōnis,* occasion.]

encheer, *in-chēr'*, (*arch.*) *v.t.* to cheer, comfort. [Pfx. en- (1c).]

enchiridion, encheiridion, *en*(*g*)*-ki-rid'i-on, n.* book to be carried in the hand for reference: a manual. [Gr. *encheiridion—en,* in, *cheir,* hand.]

enchondroma, *en-kon-drō'ma,* (*path.*) *n.* an abnormal cartilaginous growth. [Gr. *en,* in, *chondros,* cartilage.]

enchorial, *en-kō'ri-əl,* *-kō',* *adj.* belonging to or used in a country (*rare*): used by the people, esp. (in ancient Egypt) demotic.—Also enchoric (*-kor'*). [Gr. *enchōrios—en,* in, *chōrā,* a place, country.]

encincture, *in-singk'chər,* *v.t.* to girdle.—*n.* girdling: an enclosure. [Pfx. en- (1b).]

encipher, *in-si'fər,* *v.t.* to put into cipher. [Pfx. en- (1a).]

encircle, *in-sûrk'l,* *v.t.* to enclose in a circle: to pass round.—*ns.* encirc'ling, encir'clement. [Pfx. en- (1a).]

en clair, *ä kler,* (Fr.) not in cipher.

enclasp, *in-kläsp',* *v.t.* to clasp. [Pfx. en- (1c).]

enclave, *en'klāv,* also *en-klāv',* or *ä-kläv',* *n.* a piece of territory entirely enclosed within foreign territory: an enclosure.—*v.t.* to surround. [Fr.,—L.L. *inclāvāre*—L. *in,* and *clāvis,* a key.]

enclitic, *en-klit'ik,* *adj.* inclined: without accent, as if not a separate word (*gram.*).—*n.* (*gram.*) a

word or particle which always follows another word, so united with it as to seem a part of it.—*n.* enclisis (*eng'klis-is*).—*adv.* enclit'ically. [Gr. *enklitikos—en,* in, *klīnein,* to lean.]

encloister, *in-klois'tər,* (*obs.*) *v.t.* to immure. [Pfx. en- (1c).]

enclose, inclose, *in-klōz',* *v.t.* to close or shut in: to confine: to surround: to put within, esp. of something sent within a letter or within its envelope: to seclude: to fence, esp. used of waste land.—*ns.* enclos'er; enclosure (*-klō'zhər*), the act of enclosing: state of being enclosed: that which is enclosed, esp. in a letter: a space fenced off: that which encloses: a barrier: the framing of a window.—enclosed order, a religious order leading an entirely contemplative life, not going out into the world to work. [Pfx. en- (1a) and close (1).]

enclothe, *in-klōdh',* *v.t.* to clothe. [Pfx. en- (1a).]

encloud, *in-klowd',* *v.t.* to cover with clouds. [Pfx. en- (1a).]

encode, *in-kōd',* *v.t.* to encipher: to record in a form other than plain written or printed text. [Pfx. en- (1a).]

encolour, *in-kul'ər,* *v.t.* to colour, tinge. [Pfx. en- (1b).]

encolpion, *en-kol'pi-on, n.* a reliquary, cross, etc., worn on the breast.—Also (Latinised) encol'pium. [Gr.,—*en,* in, on, *kolpos,* bosom.]

encolure, *en*(*g*)*'kol-ūr',* (*Browning*) *n.* a horse's mane. [Fr., horse's neck.]

encomienda, *än-kō-mē-än'da,* (Sp.) a commandery; encomendero, *än-kō-män-dā'rō,* its commander.

encomium, *en-kō'mi-əm,* also *encō'mion* (*-on*), *n.* high commendation: a eulogy:—*pl.* encō'miums, encō'mia.—*n.* encō'miast, one who utters or writes encomiums: a praiser.—*adjs.* encomias'tic, *-al,* bestowing praise.—*adv.* encomias'tically. [L.,—Gr. *enkōmion,* a song of praise—*en,* in, *kōmos,* festivity.]

encompass, *in-kum'pəs,* *v.t.* to surround or enclose: to go round (*obs.*): to bring about.—*n.* encom'passment. [Pfx. en- (1a).]

encore, *ā-,* *ong-kōr',* *-kör',* *interj.* calling for repetition of a performance, or an additional item.—*n.* a call of encore: an item given in response to such a call.—*v.t.* to call encore to. [Fr., again, still.]

encounter, *in-kown'tər,* *v.t.* to meet face to face, esp. unexpectedly: to meet in a contest: to oppose.—*n.* a meeting unexpectedly: an interview: a fight: manner of meeting or accosting (*Shak.*). [O.Fr. *encontrer*—L. *in,* in, *contrā,* against.]

encourage, *en-kur'ij,* *v.t.* to put courage in: to inspire with spirit or hope: to incite: to patronise: to cherish.—*ns.* encour'agement, act of encouraging: that which encourages; encour'ager.—*n.* and *adj.* encour'aging.—*adv.* encour'agingly. [O.Fr. *encoragier* (Fr. *encourager*)—pfx. en-, *corage,* courage.]

encradle, *en-krā'dl,* (*Spens.*) *v.t.* to lay in a cradle. [Pfx. en- (1a).]

encraty, *en'kra-ti, n.* self-control.—*ns.* En'cratism, the doctrine of the Encratites; En'cratite, one of a heretical sect in the early church who abstained from marriage, and from flesh and wine. [Gr. *enkrateia—en,* in, *kratos,* strength.]

encrease. Obs. form of increase.

encrimson, *en-krim'zn,* *v.t.* to tinge with a crimson colour.—*adj.* encrim'soned. [Pfx. en- (1b).]

encrinite, *en*(*g*)*'kri-nīt,* *n.* a fossil crinoid: a crinoid.—*adjs.* en'crinal, encrin'ic, encrini'tal, encrinitic (*-it'ik*). [Gr. *en,* in, *krinon,* a lily.]

encroach, *in-krōch',* *v.i.* to seize on the rights of others: to intrude beyond boundaries: to extend into territory, sphere, etc., of others.—*n.* encroach'er.—*adv.* encroach'ingly.—*n.* encroach'ment, act of encroaching: that which is taken

by encroaching. [O.Fr. *encrochier*, to seize—
*en*- and *croc*, a hook.]
**en croupe**, *ä krōōp*, (Fr.) on the crupper, on a
pillion.
**encrust, incrust**, *in-krust'*, *v.t.* to cover with a
crust or hard coating: to form a crust on the
surface of.—*v.i.* to form a crust.—*ns.* **encrust'-
ment, encrustā'tion** (*en*-; usu. **incrustā'tion**, *in*-),
act of encrusting: a crust or layer of anything:
an inlaying of marble, mosaic, etc. [L. *in-
crustāre*, *ātum*—*in*, on, *crusta*, crust.]
**en cuerpo**, *än kōō-ār'pō*, (Sp.) in close-fitting
dress; sometimes erroneously for stark naked,
the Spanish for which is **en cueros** (*kōō-ār'ōs*).
**encumber**, *in-kum'bər*, *v.t.* to impede the motion
of: to hamper: to embarrass: to burden: to
load with debts.—*ns.* **encum'berment**, the act of
encumbering: the state of being encumbered;
**encum'brance**, that which encumbers or hinders:
a legal claim on an estate: one dependent on
another, esp. a child; **encum'brancer**. [O.Fr.
*encombrer*, from *en*-, and *combrer*; see **cumber**.]
**encurtain**, *in-kûr'tin*, *v.t.* to curtain, to veil. [Pfx.
**en**- (1a).]
**encyclical**, *en-sik'lik-əl*, or *-sik'*, *adj.* sent round
to many persons or places.—*n.* a letter addressed
by the Pope to all his bishops.—Also **encyc'lic**.
[Gr. *enkyklios*—*en*, in, *kyklos*, a circle.]
**encyclopaedia, encyclopedia**, *en-sī-klō-pē'di-ə*, *n.*
the circle of human knowledge: a work containing information on every department, or on a
particular department, of knowledge, generally
alphabetically arranged: esp. that by Diderot,
D'Alembert, and others.—*adjs.* **encyclopae'dian**,
embracing the whole circle of learning; **encyclopae'dic, -al**, pertaining to an encyclopaedia: all-
comprehensive: full of information.—*ns.* **encyclopae'dism**, comprehensive knowledge: the
rationalistic attitude of the French Encyclopaedists; **encyclopae'dist**, the compiler, or one
who assists in the compilation, of an encyclopaedia: esp. (*Encyclopédiste*) a writer for the
French *Encyclopédie* (1751-65). [False Gr.
*enkyklopaideiā*, a wrong reading for *enkyklios
paideiā*, general education (opposed to professional or special): *enkyklios*, circular, recurring, everyday—*en*, in, *kyklos*, circle; *paideiā*,
education—*pais, paidos*, boy,]
**encyst**, *en-sist'*, *v.t.* or *v.i.* to enclose or become
enclosed in a cyst or vesicle.—*ns.* **encystā'tion**,
**encyst'ment**.—*adj.* **encyst'ed**. [Pfx. **en**- (1a).]
**end**, *end*, *n.* the last point or portion: termination
or close: death: consequence: object aimed
at: a fragment, odd piece: half a unit length
of cloth: a warp thread: a waxed thread ending
in a bristle (*shoemaker's end*), part of a game
played from one end (of the bowling-green,
archery-ground, etc.): an outer district: a
region: a cottage room (*Scot.*)—*v.t.* to bring
to an end: to destroy.—*v.i.* to come to an end:
to cease.—*adj.* **end'ed**, brought to an end:
having ends.—*n.* **end'ing**, termination: conclusion: death: extremity: that which is at the
end: the terminal syllable or portion of a
word (*gram.*).—*adj.* concluding: finishing: completing: dying.—*adj.* **end'less**, without end:
returning upon itself: everlasting: incessant:
objectless.—*adv.* **endlessly.**—*n.* **end'lessness.**—
*adv.* **end'long** (*Scot.* **endlang**), lengthwise (*arch.*):
continuously (*arch.*): straight on (*arch.*): on
end.—*prep.* (*obs.*) along.—*adj.* (*rare*) set on end.
—*adj.* **end'most**, farthest.—*advs.* **end'ways, end'-
wise**, on end: with the end forward.—**end'-all**,
that which ends all; **endless chain**, a chain whose
ends are joined; **endless gearing, screw, worm**,
an arrangement for producing slow motion in
machinery, consisting of a screw whose thread
gears into a wheel with skew teeth; **end man**,
the man at the end of a row of performers, etc.
—*adv.* and *adj.* **end'-on'**, in the direction in

which the end points.—**end organ**, a specialised
sensory or motor structure at a nerve-end; **end'-
paper**, a paper at the beginning or end of a book,
pasted to the binding and leaving an additional
fly-leaf; **end'-product**, the final product of a
series of operations; **end'-reader**, one who peeps
at the end of a novel to see the outcome; **end'-
ship** (*obs.*), a village.—*adj.* **end'-stopped**, having
a pause at the end of each line (of verse).—
**end use**, the final use to which a manufactured
article is put.—**at a loose end, at loose ends**,
with nothing to do; in a state of uncertainty
or confusion as to one's course of action; **at
an end**, terminated: discontinued: exhausted;
**at one's wit's end**, (see **wit** (2)); **at the end of
one's tether**, without further resource; **be the end
of**, to cause the death of (often a coll. exaggeration); **end for end**, with the position of the ends
reversed; **get hold of the wrong end of the stick**,
to misunderstand blunderingly; **in the end**, after
all: at last; **keep one's end up**, to maintain
one's part: to be content to keep one's wicket
standing without trying to score; **loose end**, an
unsettled matter; **make both ends meet**, to live
within one's income (both ends meaning both
ends of the year); **no end** (*coll.*) very much;
**on end**, erect: at a stretch; **the end**, the last
straw: the limit. [O.E. *ende*; cf. Ger. and Dan.
*ende*, Goth. *andeis*; Sans. *anta*.]
**endamage**, *in-dam'ij*, *v.t.* to damage.—*n.* **en-
dam'agement**, damage, injury, loss. [Pfx. **en**-
(1b).]
**endanger**, *in-dān'jər*, *v.t.* to place in danger: to
expose to loss or injury.—*ns.* **endan'gerer**; **endan'germent**, hazard, peril. [Pfx. **en**- (1b).]
**endarch**, *end'ärk*, (*bot.*) *adj.* having the protoxylem on the inner edge. [Gr. *endō*, within,
*archē*, origin.]
**endart**, *in-därt'*, (*Shak.*) *v.t.* to dart in. [Pfx. **en**-
(1a).]
**endear**, *in-dēr'*, *v.t.* to make dear or more dear:
to bind as in gratitude (*Shak.*).—*adjs.* **endeared'**,
beloved; **endear'ing**, making dear: arousing
affection: expressing love (*arch.*).—*adv.* **endear'-
ingly.**—*ns.* **endear'ingness**; **endear'ment**, act of
endearing: state of being endeared: that which
excites or increases affection: a caress or utterance of love. [Pfx. **en**- (1b).]
**endeavour**, *in-dev'ər*, *v.t.* to strive: to attempt:—
*n.* an exertion of power towards some object:
attempt or trial.—*n.* **endeav'ourment** (*Spens.*), endeavour.—**do one's endeavour** (*arch.*), to do one's
utmost. [From such phrases as *to put oneself
in devoir* (Fr. *se mettre en devoir*), to make it
one's duty, do what one can:—Fr. *en*, in,
*devoir*, duty.]
**endecagon**, a faulty form for **hendecagon**.
**endeictic**, *en-dīk'tik*, *adj.* showing, exhibiting,
demonstrating.—*n.* **endeix'is**, an indication. [Gr.
*endeiktikos*.]
**endemic**, *en-dem'ik*, *adj.* prevalent or regularly
found in a people or a district: confined to a
particular area (*biol.*).—*n.* a disease constantly
or generally present in a place.—*adjs.* **endemial**
(*-dē'mi-əl*), **endem'ical**.—*adv.* **endem'ically.**—*ns.*
**endemicity** (*-is'i-ti*), **en'demism**, state of being endemic; **endemiol'ogy** (*-dem*-, or *-dēm*-) knowledge of endemic diseases. [Gr. *endēmios*—*en*,
in, and *dēmos*, a people, a district.]
**endenizen**, *en-den'i-zn*, *v.t.* to naturalise, to make
a denizen. [Pfx. **en**- (1b).]
**endermic, -al**, *en-dûrm'ik*, *-əl*, *adj.* through or
applied directly to the skin—also **endermat'ic.**—
*n.* **en'deron**, the corium, derma, or true skin.
[Gr. *en*, in, *derma*, and *deros*, skin.]
**endew**, *en-dū'*, (*obs.*) *v.t.* (see **endue**): to endow
(*Spens.*).
**endiron**. See **andiron**.
**endite**, obs. form of **indict, indite**.
**endive**, *en'div*, *-div*, *n.* a salad plant (*Cichorium*

*endivia*) of the chicory genus: loosely, chicory. [Fr.,—L. *intubus*.]

**endlong.** See **end**.

**endo-,** *en'dō-, en-do'-*, in composition, inside, often interchanging with **ento-**, and opp. to **ecto-, exo-**.—*n.* **en'doblast** (Gr. *blastos*, a shoot, bud), the inner cell-layer of a gastrula, the hypoblast.—*adjs.* **endocar'diac, endocar'dial,** within the heart.—*ns.* **endocardi'tis,** inflammation of the endocardium, esp. over the valves; **endocar'dium** (Gr. *kardiā*, heart), the lining membrane of the heart; **en'docarp** (Gr. *karpos*, fruit; *bot.*), a differentiated innermost layer of the pericarp, usu. hard, as a plum stone.—*adjs.* **endochylous** (*en-dok'i-ləs*; Gr. *chȳlos*, juice; *bot.*), having internal water-storing cells; **endocri'nal; en'docrine** (Gr. *krinein*, to separate; *physiol.*), secreting internally: applied esp. to certain glands that pour secretions into the blood (also *n.*); **endocrinic** (*-krin'ik*).—*n.* **endocrinol'ogy,** the science of the discharge of ductless glands.—*adj.* **endocritic** (*-krit'ik*), endocrine.—*n.* **en'doderm** (Gr. *derma*, skin), the inner layer of cells in a gastrula: the tissues derived from that layer.—*adjs.* **endoderm'al, endoderm'ic.**—*n.* **endoderm'is,** a close-set sheath, one cell thick, enclosing the central cylinder in plants; **en'dodyne** (same as **autodyne**).—*adjs.* **endogamic** (*-gam'ik*), **endogamous** (*-dog'ə-məs*).—*ns.* **endogamy** (*endog'əm-i*; Gr. *gamos*, marriage), the custom forbidding marriage outside one's own group: inbreeding: pollination between two flowers on the same plant: union of female gametes; **en'dogen** (*-jen*; Gr. *genēs*, born; *obs.*), any plant, including the monocotyledons, regarded as growing from within.—*adjs.* **endogen'ic,** pertaining to the processes of change within the earth; **endogenous** (*en-doj'i-nəs*), increasing by internal growth: formed within.—*ns.* **endog'eny; en'-dolymph,** the fluid within the membranous labyrinth of the ear; **endometri'tis,** inflammation of the endometrium; **endomet'rium** (Gr. *mētra*, womb), the mucous membrane lining the cavity of the uterus; **endomix'is** (Gr. *mixis*, mingling), in Protozoa, a nuclear reorganisation without conjugation; **en'domorph** (Gr. *morphē*, form), a mineral enclosed within another mineral, the latter being termed a perimorph: a person of rounded build.—*adj.* **endomorph'ic.**—*ns.* **endomorph'y; endopar'asite,** an internal parasite.—*adj.* **endophagous** (*en-dof'ə-gəs*).—*n.* **endoph'agy** (*-ə-ji*; Gr. *phagein*, aorist, to eat), cannibalism within the family or tribe: eating away from within.—*adj.* **endophyllous** (*-fil'əs*; Gr. *phyllon*, a leaf; *bot.*), being or formed within a sheathing leaf: living inside a leaf.—*n.* **endophyte** (*en'dō-fīt*; Gr. *phyton*, a plant), a plant living within another, whether parasitically or no.—*adj.* **endophytic** (*-fit'ik*).—*n.* **en'doplasm,** the inner portion of the cytoplasm of a cell.—*adjs.* **endoplas'-mic, endoplas'tic.**—*ns.* **endopleura** (*-plōō'rə*; Gr. *pleurā*, a side; *bot.*), the inner seed coat; **endopodite** (*en-dop'ə-dit*; Gr. *pous, podos*, a foot), the inner branch of a crustacean's leg; **endoradiosonde'**, an electronic device put within the body to send out information about a bodily function such as, e.g. digestion (see **radio**).—*adj.* **endorhizal** (*-rī'zəl*; Gr. *rhiza*, root; *bot.*), having the radicle of the embryo enclosed within a sheath, as in monocotyledons: hence monocotyledonous.—*ns.* **en'dosarc** (Gr. *sarx, sarkos*, flesh), endoplasm; **en'doscope** (Gr. *skopeein*, to look), an instrument for viewing the cavities of internal organs.—*adj.* **endoscopic** (*-skop'ik*).—*n.* **endoscopy** (*en-dos'kə-pi*).—*adj.* **endoskel'etal.**—*ns.* **en'doskeleton** (*en-dos'kə-pi*).—*adj.* **endoskel'etal.**—*ns.* **endoskel'eton,** the internal skeleton or framework of the body; **endosmō'sis,** osmosis inwards, i.e. towards the solution.— Also **en'dosmose** (*-mōs*); **endosmōm'eter,** an instrument for measuring endosmotic action.

—*adjs.* **endosmomet'ric; endosmōt'ic,** pertaining to or of the nature of endosmosis.—*adv.* **endosmot'ically.**—*n.* **en'dosperm** (Gr. *sperma*, seed), in a seed, nutritive tissue formed from the embryo-sac.—*adj.* **endosper'mic.**—*n.* **en'dospore** (Gr. *sporos*, seed), the innermost layer of a spore-wall: a spore formed within a mother-cell.—*adj.* **endos'teal** (Gr. *osteon*, bone), within a bone.—*n.* **endos'teum** (*anat.*), the internal periosteum.—*adjs.* **endotherm'ic** (Gr. *thermē*, heat), accompanied by, characterised by, or formed with absorption of heat; **endotroph'ic** (Gr. *trophē*, food), of a mycorrhiza, occurring mainly within the root of the plant it feeds.— *n.* **endozō'on** (Gr. *zōion*, animal), an entozoon: —*pl.* **endozōa**.—*adj.* **endozō'ic,** entozoic, having seeds dispersed by animals that swallow them (*bot.*). [Gr. *endon*, or *endō*, within.]

**endorse, indorse,** *in-dörs'*, *v.t.* to write on the back of (esp. one's signature, a note of contents, a record of an offence): to assign by writing on the back of: to give one's sanction to: to express approbation of: to lay on the back, to load (*arch.*).—*adj.* **endors'able.**—*ns.* **endorsee'** (*en-*), the person to whom a bill, etc., is assigned by endorsement; **endorse'ment,** act of endorsing: that which is written on the back: sanction; **endors'er.** [See **endoss**; changed under the influence of L.L. *indorsāre—in*, on, *dorsum*, the back.]

**endorse,** *en-dörs'*, (*her.*) *n.* a vertical band or stripe on a shield, one-fourth or one-eighth of the width of a pale.—*adj.* **endorsed'**, (of a pale) with an endorse on each side of it: (of wings) thrown back. [Origin obscure.]

**endoss,** *en-dos'*, (*obs.*) *v.t.* to endorse: to inscribe (*Spens.*). [M.E. *endosse*—O.Fr. *endosser*.]

**endow,** *in-dow'*, *v.t.* to give a dowry or marriage portion to: to settle a permanent provision on: to provide permanent means of support for: to enrich with any gift or faculty: to present.— *ns.* **endow'er; endow'ment,** act of endowing: that which is settled on any person or institution: a quality or faculty bestowed on any-one.—**endowment assurance,** a form of insurance providing for the payment of a certain sum at a certain date or at death if earlier. [Fr. *en* (—L. *in*), *douer*, to endow—L. *dōtāre—dōs, dōtis*, a dowry.]

**endue, indue** (*Spens.*, etc., **endew, indew**), *in-dū'*, *v.t.* to take into the stomach, as a hawk (*obs.*): to digest (*obs.*): to take in, digest mentally (*Spens.*): to bring to (*Shak.*): to put on, as clothes: to invest with: to clothe: to supply. [O.Fr. *enduire*—L. *indūcĕre—in*, into, *dūcĕre*, to lead, with meaning influenced by *indŭĕre*, to put on.]

**endungeon,** *in-dun'jən*, *v.t.* to shut up in a dungeon or the like. [Pfx. **en-** (1a).]

**endure,** *in-dūr'*, *v.t.* to harden (*Spens.*): to remain firm under: to bear without sinking: to tolerate.—*v.i.* to remain firm: to last.—*adj.* **endur'able,** that can be endured or borne: lasting.—*ns.* **endur'ableness.**—*adv.* **endur'ably.**—*ns.* **endur'ance,** state or power of enduring or bearing: a suffering patiently without sinking: patience: continuance: duration (*obs.*): lasting quality: maximum performance under given conditions: captivity (*obs.*); **endur'er.**—*adv.* **endur'ingly.** [O.Fr. *endurer*—L. *indūrāre—in*, *dūrus*, hard.]

**ene,** Same as **en** (even).

**en effet,** *ā-ne-fe*, (Fr.) in effect.

**enema,** *en'i-mə*, *n.* a fluid injected into the rectum: the process of injecting such a fluid:—*pl.* **en'emas, ene'mata.** [Gr. *enēma, -atos—enienai*, to send in—*en*, in, and *hienai*, to send.]

**enemy,** *en'i-mi*, *n.* one who hates or dislikes: a foe: a hostile force.—*adj.* hostile.—**how goes the enemy?** (*slang*), what time is it? **the enemy,** the devil.

the old enemy, the Devil; the last enemy, death. [O.Fr. *enemi* (Fr. *ennemi*)—L. *inimicus*—*in*-, neg., *amicus*, a friend.]
**enemy**, a *dial.* form of **anemone.**
**energumen**, *en-ər-gū'mən, n.* one possessed: a demoniac. [L.L. *energūmenus*—Gr. *energoumenos*—*energeein*—*en*, in, *ergon*, work.]
**energy**, *en'ər-ji, n.* power of doing work: power exerted: vigorous activity: vigour: forcefulness: capacity of a material body or of radiation to do work (*phys.*).—*adjs.* **energet'ic**, **-al**, having or showing energy: active: forcible: effective.—*adv.* **energet'ically.**—*n.pl.* **energet'ics**, the science of the general laws of energy.—*adj.* **ener'gic** (*in-ûr'jik*), exhibiting energy.—*n.* **ener'gid**, a protoplasmic unit: a cell with or without a cell-wall.—*v.t.* **en'ergise**, **-ize**, to give strength or active force to: to stimulate to activity.—*v.i.* to act with force.—**conservation of energy** (see **conservation**). [Gr. *energeia*—*en*, in, *ergon*, work.]
**enervate**, *en'ər-vāt*, still sometimes *i-nûr', v.t.* to deprive of nerve, strength, or courage: to weaken.—*adj.* weakened: spiritless.—*adjs.* **en'ervating**, **ener'vative.**—*n.* **enervā'tion.**—*v.t.* **enerve'** (*obs.*), to enervate. [L. *ēnervāre*, *-ātum*—*ē*, out of, *nervus*, a nerve.]
**enew**, *e-nū', v.t.* in falconry, to drive or (*refl.*) plunge into water. [O.Fr. *enewer*—*en*, in, *eau*, water.]
**enface**, *in-fās', v.t.* to stamp or print on the face of a document, bill, etc.—*n.* **enface'ment.** [Pfx. **en-** (1a).]
**en face**, *ä fas*, (Fr.) in front: opposite: straight in the face: facing forward.
**en famille**, *ä fa-mē-y'*, (Fr.) amongst the family, as at a family gathering, at home, without ceremony.
**enfant**, *ä-fä*, (Fr.), child; **enfant de la maison** (*da la me-zɔ̄*), child of the house, quite at home; **enfant de son siècle** (*da sɔ̄ sye-kl'*), child of his century—one who reflects the spirit of his time; **enfant gâté** (*gä-tä*), spoilt child (fem. **gâtée**); **enfants perdus**, (*ä-fä per-dü*), lit. lost children: forlorn hope, shock troops; **enfant terrible** (*te-rē-bl'*), precocious child whose sayings embarrass his elders; **enfant trouvé** (*trōō-vä*), foundling.
**enfeeble**, *in-fē'bl, v.t.* to make feeble: to weaken.—*n.* **enfee'blement**, weakening: weakness. [Pfx. **en-** (1b).]
**enfelon**, *en-fel'ən*, (Spens.) *v.t.* to make fierce. [Pfx. **en-** (1b).]
**enfeoff**, *in-fef'*, *en-fēf', v.t.* to give a fief to: to invest with a possession in fee: to give up as a fief: to surrender.—*n.* **enfeoff'ment**, act of enfeoffing: the deed which invests with the fee of an estate. [O.Fr. *enfeffer*—*en*-, and *fief*; see **fief, feoff**.]
**enfested**, *en-fest'id*, (Spens.) *adj.* embittered. [Perh. for **infest**, hostile, or **enfestered.**]
**enfestered**, *en-fest'ərd*, *adj.* festered. [Pfx. **en-** (1b).]
**en fête**, *ä fet*, (Fr.) in festivity, keeping holiday.
**enfetter**, *en-fet'ər*, (Shak.) *v.t.* to bind in fetters. [Pfx. **en-** (1c).]
**enfierce**, *en-fērs'*, (Spens.) *v.t.* to make fierce. [Pfx. **en-** (1b).]
**enfilade**, *en-fi-lād', n.* a number of things arranged as if threaded on a string: a series of rooms with the doors in line affording a continuous passage: a vista: a fire that rakes a line or position from end to end (*mil.*): a situation or a body open from end to end.—*v.t.* to rake, or be in position to rake, with shot through the whole length of a line.—Also *adj.* —*adj.* **enfiled** (*en-fīld'*; *her.*), thrust through like a sword. [Fr. *enfiler*—*en* (L. *in*), and *fil*—L. *filum*, a thread. See **file**, a line or wire.]
**enfire**, *en-fīr'*, (Spens.) *v.t.* to set on fire, inflame.
**enfix.** See **infix.**

**enflesh**, *in-flesh', v.t.* to turn into flesh. [Pfx. **en-** (1b).]
**enflower**, *in-flow'ər, v.t.* to cover with flowers. [Pfx. **en-** (1a).]
**enfold**, **infold**, *in-fōld', v.t.* to wrap up: to encompass.—*n.* **enfold'ment**, act of enfolding: that which enfolds. [Pfx. **en-** (1a).]
**enforce**, *in-fōrs', -förs', v.t.* to gain by force: to give force to: to put in force: to give effect to: to urge: to impress: to drive: to compel: to apply force to: to strive (Spens.).—*adj.* **enforce'able.**—*adv.* **enforce'dly**, by violence, not by choice.—*n.* **enforce'ment**, act of enforcing: compulsion: a giving effect to: that which enforces. [O.Fr. *enforcer*—*en* (L. *in*), and *force.*]
**enforest**, *in-for'əst, v.t.* to turn into forest. [Pfx. **en-** (1b).]
**enform** (Spens.). See **inform.**
**enfouldered**, *en-fōl'dərd*, (Spens.) *adj.* charged with or like lightning. [Pfx. **en-** (1c) and O.Fr. *fouldre* (Fr. *foudre*)—L. *fulgur*, lightning.]
**enframe**, *in-frām', v.t.* to put in a frame. [Pfx. **en-** (1a).]
**enfranchise**, **-ize**, *in-fran'chiz*, *-shiz, v.t.* to set free: to give a franchise or political privileges to.—*n.* **enfran'chisement** (*-chiz-*, *-shiz-*), act of enfranchising: liberation: admission to civil or political privileges. [O.Fr. *enfranchir*—*en*, and *franc*, free; see **franchise.**]
**enfree**, *en-frē'*, **enfreedom**, *en-frē'dəm*, (Shak.) *vs.t.* to set free, to give freedom to. [Pfx. **en-** (1b).]
**enfreeze**, *en-frēz', v.t.* to freeze: turn to ice:—*pa.p.* (Spens.) **enfrōs'en.** [Pfx. **en-** (1c).]
**engage**, *in-gāj', v.t.* to pledge (*obs.*): to bind by a gage or pledge: to render liable (*obs.*): to secure for service: to enlist: to win over, attract: to betroth: to bespeak, reserve: to hold or occupy: to enter into contest: to fasten (*archit.*): to interlock: to entangle (*arch.*).—*v.i.* to pledge one's word: to become bound: to take part: to occupy or busy oneself: to enter into conflict.—*adj.* **engaged'**, pledged: promised, esp. in marriage: greatly interested: taken, booked, or bespoke: occupied: partly built or sunk into, or so appearing (*archit.*): geared together, interlocked: of literature or writer, committed.—*ns.* **engage'ment**, act of engaging: state of being engaged: that which engages: betrothal: promise: appointment: employment: a fight or battle; **Engag'er** (*hist.*), an adherent of the *Engagement* of 1647, a secret treaty between Charles I and Scottish Commissioners.—*adj.* **engag'ing**, winning: attractive.—*n.* **engag'ingness.**—*adv.* **engag'ingly.**—**engage'ment-ring**, a ring given in token of betrothal, esp. by the man to the woman.—**engage for**, to answer for. [Fr. *engager*—*en gage*, in pledge; see **gage.**]
**engagé**, *ä-ga-zhä*, (Fr.) committed to a point of view.
**engaol**, *en-jāl'*, (Shak.) *v.t.* to put in gaol. [Pfx. **en-** (1a).]
**en garçon**, *ä gar-sɔ̄*, (Fr.) like a bachelor, in bachelor style.
**en garde**, *ä gärd*, (Fr.) in fencing, a warning to assume a defensive position in readiness for an attack.
**engarland**, *in-gär'lənd, v.t.* to put a garland round. [Pfx. **en-** (1a).]
**engarrison**, *in-gar'i-sn, v.t.* to establish as a garrison. [Pfx. **en-** (1b).]
**engender**, *in-jen'dər, v.t.* to beget: to bear: to breed: to sow the seeds of: to produce.—*v.i.* to be caused or produced.—*ns.* **engen'drure**, **engen'dure**, act of engendering: generation. [Fr. *engendrer*—L. *ingenerāre*—*in*, and *generāre*, to generate.]
**engild**, *en-gild'*, (Shak.) *v.t.* to gild. [Pfx. **en-** (1c).]
**engine**, *en'jin, n.* a mechanical contrivance, esp.

a complex piece of machinery in which power is applied to do work: a locomotive: a military machine: an instrument of torture (*obs.*): anything used to effect a purpose: a device, contrivance, wile (*obs.*): a snare (*obs.*): a person used as a tool (*arch.*): (see also **ingine**) ability, ingenuity, genius, turn of mind (*obs.*).—*v.t.* to equip with an engine or engines: to contrive (*obs.*).—*n.* engineer´, one who designs or makes, or puts to practical use, engines or machinery of any type, including electrical: one who designs or constructs public works, such as roads, railways, sewers, bridges, harbours, canals, etc.: one who constructs or manages military fortifications, etc. (*hist.*), or engines (*obs.*): a soldier of a division of an army called Engineers, concerned with entrenching, road-making, etc.: an officer who manages a ship's engines: an engine-driver (esp. *U.S.*): one who does public work requiring little skill (*U.S.*): one who plots (*obs.*), or who contrives to bring about (with *of*).—*v.i.* to act as engineer.—*v.t.* to arrange, contrive: to manoeuvre, guide.—*ns.* engineer´ing, the art or profession of an engineer; en´giner (*Shak.*), engineer; enginery (*en´jin-ri*), the art of managing engines: engines collectively: machinery.—en´gine-driver, a workman who controls an engine, esp. a railway locomotive; en´gine-fitter, one who fits together the parts of an engine; en´gine-man, one who drives an engine; en´gine-room, the room in a vessel in which the engines are; en´gine-turning, a kind of ornament made by a rose-engine, as on the backs of watches, etc. [O.Fr. *engin*—L. *ingenium*, skill; see **ingenious**.]

**engird**, *in-gûrd´*, *v.t.* to gird round: to encircle: *pa.p.* and *pa.t.* **engirt´**.—*v.t.* **engir´dle**. [Pfx. **en-** (1a).]

**English**, *ing´glish*, *adj.* belonging to England or its inhabitants or language.—*n.* the English people (as *pl.*): a Germanic language spoken in the British Isles, U.S.A., most parts of the British Commonwealth, etc.: 14-point type: side (*billiards*).—*v.t.* to translate into English: to make English: to impart a side to (*billiards*). —*n.* **Eng´lander**, an Englishman.—*adj.* **Eng´lified**, like the English of England in speech or ways: Southroun in speech, esp. affectedly so (*Scot.*).—*ns.* **Eng´lisher**, a translator into English: an Englishman (*Scot.*); **Eng´lishman**, a native or naturalised inhabitant of England; **Eng´lishry**, the fact of being an Englishman: in Ireland, the population of English descent.—**Basic English** (see **base**); **Early English** often means Early Middle English: (*archit.*), see **early**; **little Englander**, an opponent of British imperialism and empire-building; **Old English**, a kind of type—black-letter: the English language down to about 1100 or 1150 A.D. (popularly *Anglo-Saxon*); **Middle English**, from then till about 1500; **Modern English**, from about 1500 onwards.—**presentment of Englishry**, the offering of proof that a person murdered belonged to the English race, to escape the fine levied on the hundred or township for the murder of a Norman; **Young England** (see **young**). [O.E. *Englisc*—*Engle*, Angles.]

**englobe**, *in-glōb´*, *v.t.* to enclose as in a globe: to form into a globe. [Pfx. **en-** (1a,b).]

**engloom**, *in-glōōm´*, *v.t.* to make gloomy. [Pfx. **en-** (1b).]

**englut**, *in-glut´*, *v.t.* to glut, to fill: to swallow. [Pfx. **en-** (1c).]

**engore**, *in-gōr´*, *-gör´*, *v.t.* to gore (*Spens.*): to pierce (*obs.*): to wound (*obs.*): to make gory. [Pfx. **en-** (1c).]

**engorge**, *in-görj´*, *v.t.* to devour (*Spens.*): to glut. —*v.i.* (*Milt.*), to feed voraciously.—*adj.* **en-gorged´**, filled to excess (with blood, etc.).—*n.* **engorge´ment**, the act of swallowing greedily: congestion as with blood (*med.*). [Pfx. **en-** (1c).]

**engouement**, **engoûment**, *ã-gōō-mã*, *n.* excessive fondness: infatuation. [Fr.]

**engouled**, *en-gōōld´*, (*her.*) *adj.* of bends, crosses, etc., having ends that enter the mouths of animals. [Fr. *engoulée*—*en*, in, O.Fr. *goule* (Fr. *gueule*), a beast's mouth.]

**engrace**, *in-grās´*, *v.t.* to put grace into. [Pfx. **en-** (1a).]

**engraff**, obsolete form of **engraft**.

**engraft**, *in-gräft´*, *v.t.* to graft: to insert: to join on (to something already existing): to fix deeply: to cuckold (*obs.*).—*ns.* **engraftã´tion** (*en-*), act of engrafting: **engraft´ment**, engrafting: the thing engrafted: a scion.—Also (*obs.*) **ingraft´**, etc. [Pfx. **en-** (1a).]

**engrail**, *in-grāl´*, *v.t.* to border with little semicircular indents (*her.*): to make rough (*arch.*). —*v.i.* to form an edging or border: to run in indented lines.—*n.* **engrail´ment**, the ring of dots round the edge of a medal: indentation in curved lines (*her.*). [O.Fr. *engresler* (Fr. *engrêler*)—*gresle*, hail.]

**engrain**, **ingrain**, *in-grān´*, *v.t.* to dye of a fast or lasting colour: to dye in the raw state: to infix deeply.—*adj.* **engrained´**, more often **ingrained´** (or *in´*), dyed in grain: deeply coloured or permeated: inveterate (e.g. **engrained** *laziness*): thorough-going (*fig.*).—*n.* **engrain´er**. [Orig. to dye in grain, i.e., with grain; see **grain**.]

**engram**, *en´gram*, **engramma**, *en-gram´a*, *ns.* a permanent impression made by a stimulus or experience: a stimulus impression supposed to be inheritable: a memory trace. [Gr. *en*, in, *gramma*, that which is written.]

**en grande tenue**, *ã grãd t∂-nü*, (Fr.) in full dress.

**en grand seigneur**, *ã grã sen-yær*, (Fr.) like a great lord.

**engrasp**, *in-gräsp´*, (*Spens.*) *v.t.* to grasp. [Pfx. **en-** (1c).]

**engrave**, *in-grāv´*, *v.t.* to cut with a graver on wood, steel, etc.: to cut into: to impress deeply: to form or represent by engraving:—*pa.p.* **engraved´**, **engrāv´en**.—*ns.* **engrāv´er**; **engrāv´ery** (*obs.*), the art of the engraver; **engrāv´ing**, act or art of cutting or incising designs on metal, wood, etc., for the purpose of printing impressions from them—in metal, the lines to be printed are sunk or incised; in wood, the lines to be printed appear in relief, the wood between them being cut away: an impression taken from an engraved plate: a print. [Pfx. **en-** (1a) and **grave**, vb.]

**engrave**, *in-grāv´*, *v.t.* to deposit in the grave. [Pfx. **en-** (1a).]

**engrieve**, *in-grēv´*, (*Spens.*) *v.t.* to grieve. [Pfx. **en-** (1c).]

**engroove**, **ingroove**, *in-grōōv´*, *v.t.* to cut a groove or furrow in: to fit into a groove. [Pfx. **en-** (1a).]

**engross**, *in-grōs´*, *v.t.* to buy up wholesale or completely: to monopolise: to take wholly to oneself: to absorb the whole attention or powers of: to copy in a large hand or in distinct characters: to write in legal form: to name in a list or document (*obs.*): to make thick (*Spens.*): to fatten (*Shak.*).—*n.* **engross´er**.—*adj.* **engross´-ing**, monopolising: absorbing.—*n.* **engross´ment**, buying up wholesale: that which has been engrossed: a fair copy.—**engrossing a deed**, writing it out in full and regular form for signature. [Fr. *en gros*—L. *in*, in, *grossus*, large; see **gross**.]

**enguard**, *en-gärd´*, (*Shak.*) *v.t.* to guard or defend. [Pfx. **en-** (1c).]

**engulf**, **ingulf**, *in-gulf´*, *v.t.* to swallow up wholly, as in a gulf: to cause to be swallowed in a gulf.— Also (*obs.*) **engulph´**, **ingulph´**.—*n.* **engulf´ment**. [Pfx. **en-** (1a).]

**engyscope**, *en´ji-skōp*, (*obs.*) *n.* a microscope, esp. a kind of reflecting microscope.—Erroneously

en'giscope. [Gr. *engys*, near, *skopeein*, to view.]
enhalo, *in-hā'lō*, *v.t.* to surround with a halo. [Pfx. en- (1a).]
enhance, *in-häns'*, *v.t.* to lift (*obs.*): to raise in value or importance: to heighten: to intensify: to add to, increase: to make more important. —*v.i.* to increase: to rise in value.—*n.* enhance'ment.—*adj.* enhanc'ive. [A.Fr. *enhauncer*, prob. from O.Fr. *enhaucer*—L. *in*, and *altus*, high; cf. hance.]
enharmonic, -al, *en-här-mon'ik, -əl, adjs.* pertaining to music constructed on a scale containing intervals less than a semitone: pertaining to that scale of music current among the Greeks in which an interval of 2½ tones was divided into two quarter tones and a major third: distinguishing between those tones that are identified in equal temperament.—*adv.* enharmon'ically.
—enharmon'ic modulation, for instruments of equal temperament, change of notation without change of tone. [Gr. *enharmonikos*—*en*, in, *harmoniā*, harmony.]
enhearse. See inhearse.
enhearten, *in-härt'n*, *v.t.* to encourage: to cheer. [Pfx. en- (1b).]
enhunger, *en-hung'gər*, *v.t.* to make hungry. [Pfx. en- (1b).]
enhydros, *en-hī'dros*, *n.* a chalcedony nodule with water or other liquid in a cavity.—*n.* enhy'drite, a mineral with fluid inclusions.—*adjs.* enhydrit'ic, enhy'drous. [Gr. *enydros*, containing water—*en*, in, *hydōr*, water.]
enhypostasia, *en-hi-pō-stā'zi-a*, *n.* substantial or personal existence: personality not existing independently but by union with another, as the human nature of Christ was said to be dependent on his divine nature.—*adj.* enhypostatic (-*stat'ik*). —*v.t.* enhypostatise, -ize (-*pos'tə-tiz*). [Gr. *en*, in, and *hypostasis*; see hypostasis.]
eniac, *en'i-ak*, *n.* an American pioneer electronic computer, in full *electronic numerical integrator and calculator.*
enigma, *in-ig'ma*, *n.* a statement with a hidden meaning to be guessed: anything very obscure: a mysterious person or situation: a riddle.—*adjs.* enigmat'ic, -al (*en-*), relating to, containing, or resembling an enigma: obscure: puzzling.—*adv.* enigmat'ically.—*v.t.* enig'matise, -ize, to express enigmatically or symbolically.—*ns.* enig'matist, one who concocts or deals in riddles: one who expresses himself riddlingly; enigmatog'raphy, the composition of enigmas. [L. *aenigma*—Gr. *ainigma*—*ainissesthai*, to speak darkly—*ainos*, a fable.]
enisle, inisle, *in-il'*, *v.t.* to put on, or make into, an island: to isolate. [Pfx. en- (1a, b).]
enjambment, enjambement, *in-jam(b)'mənt, ā-zhäb-mä, n.* in verse, the continuation of the sense without a pause beyond the end of the line. —*v.t.* and *v.i.* enjamb (*in-jam'*). [Fr. *enjambement*—*enjamber*, to stride, encroach—*en*, in, *jambe*, leg.]
enjoin, *in-join'*, *v.t.* to lay upon, as an order: to order or direct with authority or urgency: (*law* and *U.S.*) to forbid, to prohibit by *injunction.*— *ns.* enjoin'er, enjoin'ment. [Fr. *enjoindre*—L. *injungēre*—*in*, and *jungēre*, to join.]
enjoy, *in-joi'*, *v.t.* to joy or delight in: to feel or perceive with pleasure: to possess or use with satisfaction or delight: to have the use of: to have sexual intercourse with.—*adj.* enjoy'able, capable of being enjoyed: giving pleasure, delightful.—*n.* enjoy'ableness.—*adv.* enjoy'ably. —*ns.* enjoy'er; enjoy'ment, state or condition of enjoying: satisfactory possession or use of anything: pleasure: happiness.—enjoy oneself, to feel pleasure, have a pleasant time. [O.Fr. *enjoier*, to give joy to—*en* (L. *in*), *joie*, joy; or O.Fr. *enjoir*, to enjoy—*en*, and *joir*—L. *gaudēre*, to rejoice.]

enkernel, *in-kûr'nəl*, *v.t.* to enclose in a kernel. [Pfx. en- (1a).]
enkindle, *in-kin'dl*, *v.t.* to kindle or set on fire: to inflame: to rouse.—*adj.* enkin'dled. [Pfx. en- (1c).]
enlace, *in-lās'*, *v.t.* to encircle: to embrace: to entwine: to entangle: to cover with a network or with lace: to interlace.—*n.* enlace'ment.— Also inlace'. [Pfx. en- (1c).]
en l'air, *ā ler*, (Fr.) in the air, being discussed or expected: without reality.
enlard, *in-lärd'*, (*Shak.*) *v.t.* to grease, to baste. [Pfx. en- (1a).]
enlarge, *in-lärj'* (*Spens.* enlarg'en), *v.t.* to make wider: to increase in size or quantity: to expand: to amplify: to reproduce on a larger scale (esp. of a photograph): to set free.—*v.i.* to grow large or larger: to be diffuse in speaking or writing: to expatiate.—*adj.* enlarged'.—*adv.* enlar'gedly.—*ns.* enlar'gedness; enlarge'ment, act of enlarging: state of being enlarged: increase: extension: diffuseness of speech or writing: a photograph reproduced on a larger scale: a setting at large: release. [O.Fr. *enlarger*—*en* (L. *in*), *large*, large.]
enlevement, *in-lēv'mənt, n.* (esp. *Scots law*) abduction of a woman or child.—Also (as Fr.) enlèvement (*ā-lev-mä*).—enlevé, *ā-lə-vā*, carried away, kidnapped.
enlight, *in-līt'*, (*arch.*) *v.t.* to shed light on: to light up, kindle.—*v.t.* enlight'en, to lighten or shed light on (*arch.*): to give light to (*arch.*): to make clear to the mind (*obs.*): to impart knowledge or information to: to elevate by knowledge or religion: to free from prejudice and superstition.—*n.* enlight'enment, act of enlightening: state of being enlightened: (usu. *cap.*) the spirit of the French philosophers of the 18th century. [O.E. *inlīhtan*—*in*, in, *lihtan*, to light; or independently formed later.]
enlink, *in-lingk'*, *v.t.* to connect closely. [Pfx. en- (1c).]
enlist, *in-list'*, *v.t.* to enrol: to engage as a soldier, etc.: to employ in advancing an object.—*v.i.* to engage in public service, esp. as a soldier: to enter heartily into a cause.—*n.* enlist'ment, act of enlisting: state of being enlisted. [Pfx. en- (1a).]
enliven, *in-līv'n*, *v.t.* to put life into: to excite or make active: to make sprightly or cheerful: to animate.—*ns.* enliv'ener; enliv'enment. [Pfx. en- (1b).]
enlock, *in-lok'*, *v.t.* to lock up, enclose. [Pfx. en- (1a).]
enlumine, *en-lōō'min*, (*Spens.*) *v.t.* Same as illumine.
en masse, *ā mas*, (Fr.) in a body, all together.
enmesh, *in-mesh'*, emmesh, immesh, *em-(m)esh'*, *im-(m)esh'*, *vs.t.* to catch in a mesh or net, to entangle. [Pfx. en- (1a).]
en militaire, *ā mē-lē-ter*, (Fr.) as a military man.
enmity, *en'mi-ti*, *n.* the quality of being an enemy: unfriendliness: ill-will: hostility. [O.Fr. *enemistié*—L. *inimicus*; see enemy.]
enmossed, *in-most'*, *adj.* covered with moss. [Pfx. en- (1a).]
enmove, *en-mōōv'*, (*Spens.*) *v.t.* Same as emmove.
ennea-, *en'i-a-*, in composition, nine.—*n.* ennead (*en'i-ad*; Gr. *enneas, -ados*), the number nine: a set of nine things.—*adj.* ennead'ic.—*n.* enn'eagon (*-ə-gon*; Gr. *gōniā*, angle), a polygon with nine angles.—*adj.* enneagonal (*-ag'ən-əl*).—*n.* enneahē'dron, a solid figure with nine faces.—*adj.* enneahē'dral.—*n.pl.* Ennean'dria (Gr. *anēr, andros*, man, male), the ninth Linnaean class of plants, with nine stamens.—*adjs.* ennean'drian; ennean'drous; enn'eastyle (Gr. *stýlos*, column), having nine columns. [Gr. *ennea*, nine.]
ennoble, *i-nō'bl*, *v.t.* to make noble: to elevate, distinguish: to raise to nobility.—*n.* ennō'ble-

ment, the act of making noble: that which en-nobles. [Fr. *ennoblir*—Fr. *en* (L. *in*), and *noble*.]

ennui, *ā-nwē*, *on'wē*, *on-wē'*, *n.* a feeling of weariness or languor: boredom: the occasion of ennui.—*v.t.* to weary: to bore.—*adj.* ennuyé (*-yā*), bored. [Fr., distress—O.Fr. *anoi*—L. *in odiō*, as in *odiō habeō*, I hold in hatred, i.e. I am tired of; see annoy.]

enodal, *ē-nō'dl*, *adj.* without nodes.

enomoty, *e-nom'o-ti*, *n.* a band of sworn soldiers, esp. the smallest Spartan subdivision. [Gr. *enōmotiā*—*en*, in *omnynai*, to swear.]

enormous, *i-nör'məs*, *adj.* abounding, exceeding the normal, esp. in a bad sense (*arch.*): immense: huge: outrageous (*arch.*): atrocious (*arch.*): —(*obs.*) enorm'.—*n.* enor'mity, a great crime: great wickedness: outrage: iniquity: abnormality (*obs.*): hugeness.—*adv.* enor'mously.—*n.* enor'mousness. [L. *ēnormis*—*ē*, out of, *norma*, rule.]

enosis, *en'ō-sis*, *en-ō'sis*, *n.* union, the aim and rallying-cry of the Greek Cypriot movement for union with Greece. [Gr. (anc. and mod.) *henosis*—*heis*, *henos*, one.]

enough, *i-nuf'*, *adj.* as much as need be: sufficient: giving content: satisfying want.—*adv.* sufficiently.—*n.* sufficience: as much as satisfies desire or want. [O.E. *genōh* (nom., neut. accus., and adv., for earlier *genōg*); Goth. *ganōhs*; Ger. *genug*; O.N. *gnōgr*.]

enounce, *i-* or *ē-nowns'*, *v.t.* to enunciate: to proclaim: to utter or articulate. [Fr. *énoncer*—L. *ēnuntiāre*.]

enow, *i-now'*, (*arch.*) *adj.* and *adv.* enough: formerly used as plural of enough. [O.E. *genōg* (*genōh*), with *g* preserved in inflective forms: cf. enough.]

enow, *ē-nōō'*, *adv.* (*Scot.* and *dial.*) a moment ago, or presently. [Prob. even now.]

en pantoufles, *ā pā-tōō-fl'*, (Fr.) lit. in slippers: unconstrained, at one's ease.

en papillote, *ā pa-pē-yot*, (Fr.) (of food) cooked and served in an envelope of oiled paper or foil.

en passant, *ā pa-sā*, (Fr.) in passing: by the way: applied in chess to the taking of a pawn that has just moved two squares as if it had moved only one.

en pension, *ā pā-syɔ̄*, (Fr.) at a fixed rate for board and lodging.

en plein air, *ā ple-ner*, (Fr.) in the open air.

en plein jour, *ā plē zhōōr*, (Fr.) in broad daylight.

en prince, *ā prēs*, (Fr.) in princely style.

en principe, *ā prē-sēp*, (Fr.) in principle.

enprint, *en'print*, *n.* an enlarged photographic print, e.g. 5 × 3½ in.

en prise, *ā prēz*, (Fr.) (of a pawn in chess) exposed to capture.

en pure perte, *ā pür pert*, (Fr.) to mere loss, to no purpose.

en queue, *ā kø*, (Fr.) like a tail, in a string or line.

enquire, *en-kwīr'*, (Spens.) *v.t.* to implant. [Pfx. en- (1a).]

enrace, *en-rās'*, (Spens.) *v.t.* to implant. [Pfx. en- (1a).]

enrage, *in-rāj'*, *v.t.* to make angry.—*adj.* enraged', angered: furious.—*n.* enrage'ment, act of enraging, state of being enraged: rapture (Spens.). [O.Fr. *enrager*—*en* (L. *in*), and *rage*, rage.]

enranckle, *in-rang'kl*, (Spens.) *v.t.* to enrage. [Pfx. en- (1b).]

enrange, *en-rānj'*, enraunge, *en-rönj'*, (Spens.) *v.t.* to arrange: to rove over. [Pfx. en- (1c).]

enrank, *en-rangk'*, (Shak.) *v.t.* to place in order. [Pfx. en- (1a).]

en rapport, *ā ra-por*, (Fr.) in direct relation: in close touch or sympathy.

enrapture, *in-rap'chər*, *v.t.* to put in rapture or ecstasy: to transport with pleasure or delight.— *adjs.* enrap'tured, enrapt', in ecstasy. [Pfx. en- (1a).]

enravish, *en-rav'ish*, *v.t.* to enrapture. [Pfx. en- (1c).]

enregiment, *in-rej'(i-)mənt*, *v.t.* to form into a regiment. [Pfx. en- (1b).]

enregister, *in-rej'is-tər*, *v.t.* to register: to enrol: to record: to put on record as ratified. [Pfx. en- (1c).]

en règle, *ā re-gl'*, (Fr.) in due order: according to rule.

en retraite, *ā rə-tret*, (Fr.) in retirement, on half-pay.

en revanche, *ā rə-vāsh*, (Fr.) in return or requital.

enrich, *in-rich'*, *v.t.* to make rich: to fertilise: to adorn: to enhance: to increase the proportion of some valuable substance in: to increase the proportion of a particular isotope in a mixture of the isotopes of an element.—*n.* enrich'ment, act of enriching: that which enriches: ornamentation. [Pfx. en- (1b).]

enridged, *en-rij'id*, (Shak.) *adj.* formed into ridges. [Pfx. en- (1b).]

enring, *in-ring'*, *v.t.* to encircle: to put a ring on. [Pfx. en- (1a).]

enriven, *en-riv'n*, (Spens.) *adj.* torn. [Pfx. en- (1c).]

enrobe, *in-rōb'*, *v.t.* to dress, clothe, or invest. [Pfx. en- (1c).]

enrol, enroll, *in-rōl'*, *v.t.* to insert in a roll, list or register: to enter in a list as pupil, member, etc.: to enlist: to record: to put in writing: to form into a roll (Spens.): to enwrap (Spens.).—*v.i.* to enrol oneself:—*pr.p.* enroll'ing; *pa.t.* and *pa.p.* enrolled'.—*ns.* enroll'er; enrol'ment, act of enrolling: that in which anything is enrolled: a register. [O.Fr. *enroller* (Fr. *enrôler*)—*en*, and *rolle*, roll.]

enroot, *in-rōōt'*, *v.t.* to fix by the root: to implant firmly: to entangle, as root by root (Shak.). [Pfx. en- (1c).]

enrough, *in-ruf'*, (*arch.*) *v.t.* to make rough. [Pfx. en- (1b).]

enround, *en-rownd'*, (Shak.) *v.t.* to surround. [Pfx. en- (1a).]

en route, *ā rōōt*, (Fr.) on the road: let us go: march.

ens, *enz*, *n.* an entity, as opp. to an attribute:—*pl.* entia, *en'shi-a*.—ens per accidens, *enz pər ak'si-dənz*, *per a-ki-dāns'*, that which exists only as an accident of a substance or ens par se (*sē*, *sā*); ens rationis, *rā-shi-ō'nis*, *ra-ti-ō'*, an entity of reason, existing purely in the mind—opp. to ens reale, *rē-ā'-lē*, *re-ā'le*, which exists actually or potentially outside of the mind. [L.L. *ēns*, pr.p. from L. *esse*, to be.]

ensample, *en-säm'pl*, (*arch.*) *n.* example.—*v.t.* to give an example of. [O.Fr. *essample*; see example.]

ensanguine, *in-sang'gwin*, *v.t.* to stain or cover with blood.—*adj.* ensan'guined, bloody. [Fr. pfx. *en-*, in, L. *sanguis*, *-inis*, blood.]

ensate, *en'sāt*, *adj.* sword-shaped. [L. *ēnsis*, sword.]

enschedule, *en-shed'ūl*, (Shak.) *v.t.* to insert in a schedule. [Pfx. en- (1a).]

ensconce, *in-skons'*, *v.t.* to cover or protect as with a sconce or earthwork (*obs.*): to hide safely: to settle comfortably. [Pfx. en- (1a).]

enseal, *en-sēl'*, (*arch.*) *v.t.* to put one's seal to: seal up. [Pfx. en- (1c).]

enseam, *en-sēm'*, *v.t.* to mark as with a seam. [Pfx. en- (1c), and seam (2).]

enseam, *en-sēm'*, *v.t.* to grease (*obs.*): to defile (Shak.): to free from superfluous fat (*obs.*). [Pfx. en- (1c), and seam (1).]

enseam, *en-sēm'*, (*obs.*) *v.t.* to contain: to introduce to company. [Der. obscure; cf. M.E. *in* seam, *en-sēm*; same, O.E. *ætsomne*, *tosomne*, together, O.N. *semja*, to put together.]

ensear, *en-sēr'*, (Shak.) *v.t.* to dry up. [Pfx. en- (1b), and sear (2).]

ensemble, *ä-sä-bl'*, *n.* all parts of a thing taken together: union of performers in a concerted number (*mus.*): the group of musicians so combining: the combined effect of the performance: a costume consisting of several (matching) garments: a group of supporting dancers, corps de ballet.—Also *adj.*—tout ensemble (*tōō-tä-*), general appearance or effect. [Fr. *ensemble*, together—L. *in*, in, *simul*, at the same time.]

ensepulchre, *en-sep'əl-kər*, *v.t.* to put in a sepulchre. [Pfx. en- (1a).]

ensew (*Spens.*). Same as ensue.

ensheathe, ensheath, insheathe, *en-shēdh'*, *v.t.* to enclose as a sheath. [Pfx. en- (1a).]

enshell. Same as inshell.—*adj.* enshield' (*Shak.*), prob. enshelled or inshelled.

enshelter, *en-shel'tər*, (*Shak.*) *v.t.* to put in shelter. [Pfx. en- (1a).]

enshield, *en-shēld'*, *v.t.* to shield or protect. [Pfx. en- (1c).]

enshrine, *en-shrin'*, *v.t.* to enclose in or as in a shrine. [Pfx. en- (1a).]

enshroud, *en-shrowd'*, *v.t.* to cover up: to cover with a shroud. [Pfx. en- (1a).]

ensiform, *en'si-förm*, *adj.* sword-shaped. [L. *ēnsis*, a sword, *förma*, form.]

ensign, *en'sin*, *-sin*, *n.* badge, sign, or mark: sign or flag, distinguishing a nation or a regiment (see also under blue, red, white): one who carries the colours: until 1871, the officer of lowest commissioned rank in the British infantry: officer of lowest commissioned rank (*U.S. navy*).—*v.t.* (*-sin'*) mark with a badge or sign, in heraldry, with one placed above.—*ns.* en'signcy, en'signship, rank or commission of an ensign in the army. [O.Fr. *enseigne*—L. *insignia*, pl. of *insigne*, a distinctive mark—*in*, and *signum*, a mark.]

ensilage, *en'sil-ij*, *n.* the storing of green fodder in pits or silos.—*v.t.* ensile (*en-sil'*, or *en'sil*), en'silage, to store by ensilage. [Fr.,—Sp. *en*, in, and *silo*—L. *sirus*—Gr. *siros*, *siros*, *seiros*, pit for corn.]

ensky, *en-ski'*, (*Shak.*) *v.t.* to place in the sky. [Pfx. en- (1a).]

enslave, *in-slāv'*, *v.t.* to reduce to slavery: to subject to a dominating influence.—*adj.* enslaved'.—*ns.* enslave'ment, act of enslaving: state of being enslaved: slavery: bondage; enslav'er. [Pfx. en- (1b).]

ensnare, *in-snār'*, *v.t.* to catch in a snare: to entrap: to entangle. [Pfx. en- (1a).]

ensnarl, *en-snärl'*, (*Spens.*) *v.t.* to entangle. [Pfx. en- (1a).]

ensorcell, *in-sör'səl*, *-sör'*, *v.t.* to bewitch. [O.Fr. *ensorceler*—*en*, and *sorcier*, a sorceror.]

ensoul, insoul, *in-sōl'*, *v.t.* to join with the soul; to animate as a soul. [Pfx. en- (1b).]

en spectacle, *ä spek-ta-kl'*, (Fr.) as a spectacle.

ensphere, insphere, *in-sfēr'*, *v.t.* to enclose or place in a sphere: to give a spherical form to:—*pa.p.* (*Milt.*) insphear'd. [Pfx. en- (1a).]

enstamp, *in-stamp'*, *v.t.* to mark as with a stamp. [Pfx. en- (1c).]

enstatite, *en'stat-it*, *n.* a rock-forming mineral, an orthorhombic pyroxene, magnesium silicate. [Gr. *enstatēs*, adversary, from its refractory character.]

ensteep, *en-stēp'*, (*Shak.*) *v.t.* to steep: to lay under water. [Pfx. en- (1c).]

enstyle, *in-stil'*, (*arch.*) *v.t.* to style, call. [Pfx. en- (1c).]

ensue, *in-sū'*, *v.i.* to follow, to come after: to result (with *from*).—*v.t.* (*B.*, *arch.*) to follow after:—*pr.p.* ensü'ing; *pa.t.* and *pa.p.* ensüed'. [O.Fr. *ensuir* (Fr. *ensuivre*)—L. *in*, after, L.L. *sequēre*—L. *sequi*, to follow.]

en suite, *ä swēt*, (Fr.) in succession or connected series: forming a unit, or a set (not in Fr.).

ensure, *in-shōōr'*, *v.t.* to make sure: to make safe:

to betroth (*obs.*): to insure (*obs.*). [See insure.]

enswathe, inswathe, *in-swädh'*, *v.t.* to wrap.—*n.* enswathe'ment. [Pfx. en- (1c).]

ensweep, *in-swēp'*, (*arch.*) *v.t.* to sweep over. [Pfx. en- (1c).]

entablature, *en-tab'lə-chər*, *n.* in classic architecture that part which surmounts the columns and rests upon the capitals: an engine framework upon columns. [It. *intavolatura*—*in*, in, *tavola*—L. *tabula*, a table.]

entail, entayle, *en-tāl'*, (*obs.*) *v.t.* and *v.i.* to carve.—*n.* cut, fashion. [O.Fr. *entailler*—L.L. *intaleāre*—*in*, into, *taleāre*, to cut.]

entail, *in-tāl'*, *v.t.* to settle on a series of heirs, so that the immediate possessor may not dispose of the estate: to bring on as an inevitable consequence.—*n.* the settlement of an entailed estate: an estate entailed: the transmission, or the rule of descent, of an estate.—*ns.* entail'er; entail'-ment, act of entailing: state of being entailed. [Pfx. en- (1a), and tail (2).]

entame, *en-tām'*, (*Shak.*) *v.t.* to tame. [Pfx. en- (1c).]

entangle, *in-tang'gl*, *v.t.* to twist into a tangle, or so as not to be easily separated: to involve in complications or in an embarrassing or a compromising situation: to perplex: to ensnare.—*n.* entang'lement, a confused state: perplexity: a tangled obstacle: a tangle: condition of being entangled: an entangling connection. [Pfx. en- (1c).]

entasis, *en'tə-sis*, (*archit.*) *n.* the swelling outline of the shaft of a column or the like. [Gr. *entāsis*—*en*, in, *tasis*, a stretch.]

entelechy, *en-tel'ə-ki*, (*phil.*) *n.* actuality: distinctness of realised existence: a vital principle supposed by vitalists to direct processes in an organism towards realisation of a certain end. [Gr. *entelecheia*—*en*, in, *telos*, perfection, end, *echein*, to have.]

entellus, *en-tel'əs*, *n.* the hanuman monkey of India. [App. from *Entellus* the old Sicilian in *Aeneid*, book V, from its old-mannish look.]

entender, intender, *in-tend'ər*, (*obs.*) *v.t.* to make tender: to weaken. [Pfx. en- (1b).]

entente, *ä-tät'*, *n.* an understanding: a friendly agreement or relationship between states—as the entente cordiale (*kör-dē-äl'*) between Britain and France (1904). [Fr.]

enter, *en'tər*, *v.i.* to go or come in: to penetrate: to come upon the stage: to take possession: to become a member: to put down one's name (as competitor, candidate, etc.): to become a party or participator.—*v.t.* to come or go into: to penetrate: to join or engage in: to begin: to put into: to enrol or record: to admit: to inscribe or cause to be inscribed: to register (as a vessel leaving a port, a horse for a race, a pupil for a school, etc.): to insert a record of: to initiate: to become a member of: to take possession of: to obtain right of preemption to by recording one's name in a land office, etc. (*U.S.*).—*n.* (*Shak.*) ingoing.—*adj.* en'terable.—*n.* en'terer.—*n.* and *adj.* en'tering.—enter a protest, to write it in the books: thence simply, to protest: enter into, to become a party to: to be interested in: to participate actively or heartily in: to understand sympathetically: to take up the discussion of: to be part of: enter on, upon, to begin: to engage in. [Fr. *entrer*—L. *intrāre*, to go into, related to *inter*, between.]

enter-. Form of inter-, orig. through Fr. *entre*, between, etc.

enterchaunge, *en-tər-chönj'*, an obs. form of interchange.

enterdeale, (*Spens.*). See interdeal.

enter(o)-, *en'tər(-ō)-*, in composition, intestine.—*adjs.* en'teral, pertaining to, within, or by way of, the intestine; en'terate, having an alimentary canal.—*n.* enterec'tomy (Gr. *ektomē*, a cutting

out), surgical removal of part of the bowel.—
*adj.* **enteric** (*en-ter'ik*), pertaining to the intestines:
possessing an alimentary canal.—*n.* **enteric
fever** (**enteric fever,** typhoid fever, an infectious
disease due to a bacillus, characterised by fever,
rose-red rash, enlargement of the spleen and
ulceration of the intestines).—*ns.* **enteri'tis,** inflammation of the intestines, esp. the small intestine; **en'terocele** (*-sēl*; Gr. *kēlē*, tumour), a hernia
containing intestine; **enterocentesis** (*-sen-tē'sis*;
Gr. *kentēsis*, pricking), operative puncturing of
the intestine; **en'terolith** (Gr. *lithos*, stone), a
concretion of organic matter with lime, bismuth
or magnesium salts formed in the intestine;
**Enteromor'pha** (Gr. *morphē*, form), a genus of
green seaweeds of tubular form; **en'teron,** in
coelenterates the body-cavity: in higher
animals the gut or alimentary canal:—*pl.*
**en'tera.**—**en'teropneust,** any animal of the
**Enteropneus'ta** (gut-breathers; Gr. *pneein*, to
breathe), the Hemichordata, or a division of
them including Balanaglossus; **enteroptos'is,**
downward displacement of the intestines; **en-
teros'tomy** (Gr. *stoma*, mouth), surgical formation of an opening in the intestine; **enterot'omy,**
incision of the intestinal wall. [Gr. *enteron*, gut.]
**enterprise,** *en'tər-priz, n.* an undertaking: a bold
or dangerous undertaking: readiness, initiative,
and daring in undertaking: a business concern.
—*v.t.* to undertake.—*n.* **en'terpriser,** an adventurer (*arch.*): an entrepreneur.—*adj.* **en'ter-
prising,** forward in undertaking: adventurous:
full of initiative.—*adj.* **en'terprisingly.** [O.Fr.
*entreprise,* pa.p. of *entreprendre*—*entre,* between
(L. *inter*), and *prendre*—L. *praehendēre,* to seize.]
**entertain,** *en-tər-tān', v.t.* to maintain, keep up
(*obs.*): to take on (as servant, etc.) (*obs.*): to
treat (*obs.*): to receive (*obs.*): to provide
lodging or refreshment for: to treat hospitably:
to hold the attention or thoughts of: to hold the
attention of pleasurably: to amuse: to receive
and take into consideration: to keep or hold in
the mind: to meet or experience (*Spens.*).—*n.*
(*Spens.*; *Shak.*) entertainment.—*n.* **entertain'er,**
one who gives or offers entertainment in any
sense: one who gives amusing performances
professionally.—*adj.* **enter'taining,** affording entertainment: amusing.—Also *n.*—*adv.* **entertain'ingly.**—*n.* **entertain'ment,** act of entertaining:
reception of and provision for guests: hospitality
at table: that which entertains: the provisions
of the table (*arch.*): a banquet (*arch.*): amusement: a performance or show intended to give
pleasure. [Fr. *entretenir*—L. *inter,* among,
*tenēre,* to hold.]
**entertake,** *en-tər-tāk',* (*Spens.*) *v.t.* to receive.
**entertissued.** See intertissued.
**entêté,** *ã-te-tā,* (Fr.) infatuated: opinionative:—
*fem.* **entêtée.**
**enthalpy,** *en-thal'pi, en'thəl-pi, n.* the heat content
of a substance per unit mass, defined as $h = u + pv$
(*u* =internal energy, *p* =pressure, and *v* =
volume). [Gr. *enthalpein,* to warm in.]
**enthrall, enthral,** *in-thröl', v.t.* to bring into thral-
dom or bondage: to hold in thrall: to hold
spellbound:—*pr.p.* **enthrall'ing;** *pa.t.* and *pa.p.*
**enthralled'.**—*ns.* **enthral'dom,** condition of
being enthralled; **enthral'ment,** act of enthrall-
ing: slavery.—Also (*obs.*) **inthrall', inthral'.**
[Pfx. en- (1a).]
**enthrone,** *in-thrōn', v.t.* to place on a throne: to
exalt to the seat of royalty: to install as bishop:
to exalt.—*ns.* **enthrōne'ment, enthrōnisā'tion,** the
act of enthroning or of being enthroned.—*v.t.*
**enthrō'nise, -ize** (or *en'*), to enthrone, as a
bishop: to exalt. [Pfx. en- (1a).]
**enthusiasm,** *in-, en-thū'zi-azm,* or *-thōo', n.* possession by a god, inspiration, or religious
exaltation (*obs.*): religious extravagance (*obs.*):
intense interest: passionate zeal.—*v.t.* and *v.i.*

**enthuse'** (back-formation), to make, be, become,
or appear enthusiastic.—*n.* **enthu'siast,** one filled
with enthusiasm.—*adjs.* **enthusias'tic, -al,** filled
with enthusiasm: zealous: ardent.—*adv.* **enthusias'tically.** [Gr. *enthousiasmos,* a god-
inspired zeal—*enthousiazein,* to be inspired by
a god—*en,* in, *theos,* a god.]
**enthymeme,** *en'thi-mēm, n.* an argument of
probability only (*rhet.*): a syllogism in which
one premise is suppressed (*logic*).—*adj.* **enthy-
memat'ical.** [Gr. *enthymēma,* a consideration—
*enthýmeesthai,* to consider—*en,* in, *thýmos,* the
mind.]
**entia.** See ens.
**entice,** *in-tis', v.t.* to induce by exciting hope or
desire: to tempt: to lead astray.—*adj.* **entice'-
able.**—*ns.* **entice'ment,** act of enticing: that
which entices or tempts: allurement; **entic'er.**—
*n.* and *adj.* **entic'ing.**—*adv.* **entic'ingly.** [O.Fr.
*enticier,* provoke; prob. related to L. *titiō,* a
brand.]
**entire,** *in-tir', adj.* whole: complete: unmingled:
intact: unimpaired: untired (*Spens.*): not
castrated (esp. of a horse): with untoothed and
unlobed margin (*biol.*): inner, inward (*Spens.*):
genuine (*arch.*).—*adv.* within (*arch.*): sincerely
(*arch.*).—*n.* the whole: completeness: a stallion:
porter or stout as delivered from the brewery.—
*adv.* **entire'ly.**—*ns.* **entire'ness, entire'ty,** completeness: the whole.—**in its entirety,** in its
completeness. [O.Fr. *entier*—L. *integer,* whole,
from *in-,* not, and root of *tangēre,* to touch; in
some senses showing confusion with **interior.**]
**entitle,** *en-ti'tl, v.t.* to give a title to: to style: to
give a right or claim to. [O.Fr. *entiteler*—L.L.
*intitulāre*—in, in, *titulus,* title.]
**entity,** *en'ti-ti, n.* being, existence: something
with objective reality: an abstraction or arche-
typal conception. [L.L. *entitās, -ātis—ēns*; see
ens.]
**ento-,** *en'tō-, en-to',* **ent-, ent-,** in composition,
inside, often interchanging with **endo-** and
opp. to **ecto-, exo-.**—*ns.* **en'toblast** (Gr. *blastos,*
shoot, bud), endoderm: a cell nucleolus;
**en'toderm,** endoderm.—*adj.* **entophytal** (*-fi'tl*).—
*n.* **entophyte** (*-fit;* Gr. *phyton,* plant), an endophyte.—*adjs.* **entophytic** (*-fit'ik*), **entophytous**
(*en-tof'i-təs* or *en-tō-fi'tas*); **entop'ic,** developed,
etc., in the usual place; **entoplas'tral.**—*n.* **entoplas'tron,** the unpaired plate behind the epi-
plastra in a turtle's plastron.—*adj.* **entopt'ic** (Gr.
*ōps, ōpos,* eye), within the eyeball: pertaining to
the visibility to the eye of objects within itself.—
*n.* (*pl.* treated as *sing.*) **entop'tics,** the study of
such appearances.—*adj.* **ento'tic** (Gr. *ous, ōtos,*
ear), of the interior of the ear.—*n.* **entozō'on**
(Gr. *zōion,* an animal), an animal living parasitically within the body of its host:—*pl.*
**entozō'a.**—*adjs.* **entozō'al; entozō'ic.** [Gr. *entos,*
within.]
**entoil,** *in-toil', v.t.* to entangle or ensnare.—*n.*
**entoil'ment.** [Pfx. en- (1a).]
**entomb,** *in-tōōm', v.t.* to place in a tomb: to bury.
—*n.* **entomb'ment,** burial. [O.Fr. *entoumber—en,*
in, *tombe,* a tomb.]
**entomic,** *en-tom'ik, adj.* pertaining to insects.—
*adj.* **entomolog'ical.**—*adv.* **entomolog'ically.**—
*v.t.* **entomol'ogise, -ize.**—*ns.* **entomol'ogist,** one
learned in entomology.—*n.* **entomol'ogy,** the
science of insects.—*adjs.* **entomoph'agous** (Gr.
*phagein,* to eat—aorist), insectivorous; **entomoph'ilous** (Gr. *phileein,* to love), specially
adapted for pollination by insects.—*n.* **entomoph'ily,** pollination by insects: adaptation to
pollination by insects. [Gr. *entoma,* insects—
*entomos,* cut up—*en,* in, *tomē,* a cut.]
**Entomostraca,** *en-tō-mos'trə-ka, n.pl.* a general
name for the lower orders of Crustacea—
*Phyllopods, Ostracods, Copepods,* and *Cirripedes.*—*n.* and *adj.* **entomos'tracan.**—*adj.*

Neutral vowels in unaccented syllables: *el'ə-mənt;* for certain sounds in foreign words see p. viii

**entomos'tracous.** [Gr. *entomos*, cut up—*en*, in, *tomē*, a cut, *ostrakon*, a shell.]

**entourage,** *ä-tōō-räzh'*, *n.* surroundings: followers, attendants. [Fr.,—*entourer*, to surround —*en*, in, *tour*, a circuit.]

**en tout cas,** *ä tōō kä*, a parasol that can be used as an umbrella: ⑧ a hard tennis court that can be used in all weathers. [Fr., in any case.]

**entr'acte,** *ä-trakt'*, *n.* the interval between acts in a play: a piece of music or other performance between acts. [Fr.,—*entre*, between, *acte*, act.]

**entrail,** *en-trāl'*, (*Spens.*) *v.t.* to interlace, entwine. —*n.* twisting, entanglement. [O.Fr. *entreillier—en*, and *treille*, trelliswork.]

**entrails,** *en'trālz*, (*Spens.* entralles, *en'trölz*), *n.pl.* the internal parts of an animal's body, the bowels: the inside of anything: the seat of the emotions (*obs.*):—*sing.* (*rare*) **entrail** (*Spens.* entrall, *en-tröl'*). [O.Fr. *entraille*—L.L. *intrālia—inter*, within.]

**entrain,** *in-trān'*, *v.t.* to put into a railway train, esp. used by troops.—*v.i.* to get into a train: to take a train.—*n.* entrain'ment. [Pfx. en- (1a).]

**entrain,** *in-trān'*, *v.t.* to draw after (*arch.*): to transport one substance, e.g. small liquid particles, in another, e.g. a vapour: to suspend bubbles or particles in a moving fluid.—*n.* entrain'ment. [Fr. *entrainer*.]

**entrain,** *ä-trē*, (Fr.) liveliness, spirit; **entrainement,** *ä-tren-mä*, enthusiasm.

**en train,** *ä trē*, (Fr.) in progress.

**entrammel,** *in-tram'l*, *v.t.* to trammel, fetter. [Pfx. en- (1c).]

**entrance,** *en'trəns*, *n.* act of entering: coming upon the stage: power or right to enter: a place of entering: a door: the beginning (*arch.*).—*n.* **en'trant,** one who, or that which, enters.— **entrance fee,** the money paid on entering a society, club, etc. [Fr. *entrer*—L. *intrāre*, to enter.]

**entrance,** *in-*, *en-träns'*, *v.t.* to put into a trance: to fill with rapturous delight.—*n.* entrance'ment, state of trance or of excessive joy.—*adj.* en**tranc'ing,** charming, transporting. [Pfx. en- (1a).]

**entrap,** *in-trap'*, *v.t.* to catch, as in a trap: to ensnare: to entangle.—*ns.* entrap'ment, act of entrapping: the state of being entrapped; en**trapp'er.** [O.Fr. *entraper—en*, in, *trappe*, a trap.]

**en travesti,** *ä tra-ves-tē*, (Fr.) of female dancer, actress, in male dress.

**entreasure,** *in-trezh'ər*, (*arch.*) *v.t.* to lay up, as in a treasury. [Pfx. en- (1a).]

**entreat,** *in-trēt'*, *v.t.* to ask earnestly: to beseech: to beg for: to induce (*obs.*): to treat, deal with, behave towards (*obs.*): to occupy oneself with (*Spens.*): to pass, spend (time; *Shak.*).—*v.i.* to beseech, ask.—*adjs.* entreat'able (*obs.*); entreat**full** (*Spens.*); entreat'ing.—*adv.* entreating'ly.— *adj.* entreat'ive (*obs.*).—*ns.* entreat'ment, act of entreating: treatment (*obs.*): perhaps discourse, verbal intercourse, or favours as objects of entreaty (*Shak.*); **entreat'y,** act of entreating: earnest prayer.—Also (*Spens.*) intreat', etc. [O.Fr. *entraiter—en*, and *traiter*, to treat.]

**entrechat,** *ä-tr'-shä*, (*ballet*) *n.* a leap during which a dancer beats his heels together. [Fr.,—It. *intrecciata*, plaited, complicated (caper).]

**entrecôte,** *ä-tr'-kōt*, (Fr.) a steak cut from between two ribs.

**entrée,** *ä'*, *on'trä*, *n.* entry, freedom of access, admittance: a dish served at dinner between the chief courses or as a substitute: an introduction or prelude (*mus.*): the act of entering, a formal entrance, or music for it.—**entrée dish,** a dish, usually silver, with a cover, suitable for an entrée. [Fr.]

**entremets,** *ä'trə-mä*, *-me*, *n.* any dainty served at table between the chief courses—formerly **entremes, entremesse.** [O.Fr. *entremes—entre*, between, *mes* (Fr. *mets*), dish.]

**entrench, intrench,** *in-trench'*, *-trensh'*, *v.t.* to dig a trench around: to fortify with a ditch and parapet: to establish in a strong position: to cut into, wound (*Spens.*).—*v.i.* to encroach.—*n.* **entrench'ment,** a defensive earthwork of trenches and parapets: any protection: an encroachment (*obs.*).—**entrenched provisions,** in the constitution of South Africa, provisions specially safeguarded by being made subject to amendment or repeal only by exceptional procedure. [Pfx. en- (1c).]

**entre nous,** *ä-tr' nōō*, (Fr.) between ourselves.

**entrepot,** *ä-trə-pō*, *n.* a storehouse: a bonded warehouse: a seaport through which exports and imports pass. [Fr.]

**entrepreneur,** *ä-trə-prə-nœr'*, *n.* one who undertakes an enterprise: a contractor or employer: an organiser of musical or other entertainments: —*fem.* **entrepreneuse** (*-nœz'*).—*adj.* entrepre**neur'ial** (*-nœr'i-əl*, *-nū'*, *-nōō'*).—**entrepreneur'ship.** [Fr.]

**entresol,** *en'tər-sol*, or *ä-tr'-sol*, *n.* a low storey between two main storeys of a building, generally between the ground floor and the first floor. [Fr.,—*entre*, between, *sol*, the ground.]

**entrez,** *ä-trä*, (Fr.) come in.

**entrold,** another reading **introld,** *in-tröld'*, (*Spens.*) apparently a past participle, meaning unknown —enrolled, in the sense of encircled, has been conjectured.

**entropion, -um,** *en-trō'pi-on*, *-əm*, *n.* inversion of the edge of the eyelid. [Gr. *en*, in, *tropē*, turning.]

**entropy,** *en'trə-pi*, (*phys.*) *n.* a measure of unavailable energy, energy still existing but lost for purpose of doing work: a measure of heat content, regarded as increased in a reversible change by the ratio of heat taken in to absolute temperature. [Gr. *en*, in, *tropē*, turning, intended to represent 'transformation content'.]

**entrust, intrust,** *in-trust'*, *v.t.* to give in trust: to commit as a trust: to charge trustingly.—*n.* **entrust'ment.** [Pfx. en- (1c).]

**entry,** *en'tri*, *n.* act of entering in any sense: coming upon the stage: coming in of an instrument or performer: entrance: a narrow lane between houses (*dial.*): a lobby or vestibule: a hostel (*obs.*): act of committing to writing in a record: the thing so written: a list of competitors: a young hound, or hounds collectively, old enough to begin training: taking possession (*law*).—**entry fee,** entrance fee.—**card of entry** (*bridge*, etc.), a card to bring in one's hand with; **port of entry** (see port (4)). [Fr. *entrée—entrer*— L. *intrāre*, to go into.]

**entwine,** *in-twin'*, *v.t.* to interlace: to weave. [Pfx. en- (1c).]

**entwist,** *in-twist'*, *v.t.* to twist round. [Pfx. en- (1c).]

**enucleate,** *in-ū'kli-āt*, *v.t.* to deprive of a kernel or nucleus: to explain: to extract, e.g. tumour, swelling, etc. (*surg.*).—*adj.* without a nucleus.— *n.* enuclea'tion. [L. *ēnucleāre—ē*, from, *nucleus*, a kernel.]

**enumerate,** *i-nū'mər-āt*, *v.t.* to count the number of: to name over.—*n.* enūmerā'tion, act of numbering: a detailed account: a summing-up (*rhet.*).—*adj.* enū'merative.—*n.* enū'merātor, one who enumerates. [L. *ē*, from, *numerāre*, *-ātum*, to number.]

**enunciate,** *i-nun's*(*h*)*i-āt*, *v.t.* to state formally: to pronounce distinctly: to utter.—*adj.* enun'ciable (*-shi-* or *-si-*), capable of being enunciated.—*n.* **enunciation** (*i-nun-si-ā'shən*), act of enunciating: manner of uttering or pronouncing: a distinct statement or declaration: the words in which a proposition is expressed.—*adjs.* enun'ciative (*-si-ā-*, *-syā-*, *-sh*(*y*)*ā-*, or *-shə-*), enun'ciatory, containing enunciation or utterance: declarative.—*n.* enun'ciātor, one who enunciates. [L.

**ēnuntiāre, -ātum—ē,** from, *nuntiāre,* to tell—*nuntius,* a messenger.]

**enure.** See inure.

**enuresis,** *en-ū-rē'sis, n.* incontinence of urine.—*adj.* and *n.* **enūret'ic.** [Gr. *en,* in, *ourēsis,* urination.]

**envassal,** *en-vas'əl, (obs.) v.t.* to reduce to vassalage. [Pfx. en- (1c).]

**envault,** *en-völt', (obs.) v.t.* to enclose in a vault. [Pfx. en- (1a).]

**enveigle.** See inveigle.

**envelop,** *in-vel'əp, v.t.* to cover by wrapping: to surround entirely: to hide.—*n.* **envelope** *(en'vəl-ōp),* that which envelops, wraps, or covers: a cover for a letter (in this sense sometimes but quite unnecessarily pronounced *on', ä'* in imitation of French): one of the coverings of a flower—calyx or corolla *(bot.):* the gas-bag of a balloon or airship: the locus of ultimate intersections of a series of curves *(math.):* the outer containing vessel of a discharge tube *(electronics):* the curve connecting the peaks of successive cycles of a modulated carrier wave *(telecomm.).* —*adj.* **envel'oped** *(her.),* entwined, as with serpents, laurels, etc.—*n.* **envel'opment,** a wrapping or covering on all sides. [O.Fr. *enveloper;* origin obscure.]

**envenom,** *in-ven'əm, v.t.* to put venom into: to poison: to taint with bitterness or malice. [O.Fr. *envenimer—en,* and *venim,* venom.]

**en ventre sa mère,** *ä vä-tr' sa mer, (law,* Fr.) in his mother's womb.

**en vérité,** *ä vä-rē-tā,* (Fr.) in truth.

**envermeil,** *en-vûr'mil, (Milt.) v.t.* to dye red, to give a red colour to. [O.Fr. *envermeiller—en,* in, *vermeil,* red, vermilion.]

**en ville,** *ä vēl,* (Fr.) in town: not at home.

**environ,** *in-vī'rən, v.t.* to surround: to encircle. —*n.* **envi'ronment,** a surrounding: conditions influencing development or growth.—*adj.* **environment'al.**—*n.pl.* **environs** *(in-vī'rənz,* or *en'vi-),* the places that environ: the outskirts of a city: neighbourhood. [Fr. *environner—environ,* around—*virer,* to turn round; cf. veer.]

**envisage,** *in-viz'ij, v.t.* to face *(arch.):* to consider: to present to view or to mental view: to visualise.—*n.* **envis'agement.** [Fr. *envisager—en,* and *visage,* the face.]

**envision,** *in-vizh'ən, v.t.* to see as in a vision: to visualise: to envisage. [Pfx. en- (1c).]

**envoy,** *en'voi, n.* a messenger, esp. one sent to transact business with a foreign government: a diplomatic minister of the second order.—*n.* **en'voyship.** [Fr. *envoyé—*pa.p. of *envoyer,* to send.]

**envoy, envoi,** *en'voi, n.* the concluding part of a poem or a book: the author's final words, esp. now the short stanza concluding a poem written in certain archaic metrical forms. [O.Fr. *envoye* —*envoiier,* to send—*en voie,* on the way—L. *in,* on, *via,* a way.]

**envy,** *en'vi, n.* ill-will, hostility *(obs.):* a feeling of chagrin at the good looks, qualities, fortune, etc., of another: an object or person contemplated with grudging or emulous feeling.—*v.t.* (formerly *in-vī'),* to feel vexation at *(obs.):* to feel envy towards, or an account of: to grudge *(obs.):* to desire with emulation or rivalry:— *pr.p.* **en'vying;** *pa.t.* and *pa.p.* **en'vied.**—*adj.* **en'viable,** that is to be envied.—*n.* **en'viableness.** —*adv.* **en'viably.**—*n.* **en'vier,** one who envies.— *adj.* **en'vious,** feeling envy: directed by envy: enviable *(Spens.).*—*adv.* **en'viously.**—*ns.* **en'viousness;** **en'vying** *(B.),* jealousy, ill-will. [Fr. *envie* —L. *invidia—invidēre,* to look askance at, to envy —*in,* on, *vidēre,* to look.]

**enwall, inwall,** *in-wöl', v.t.* to enclose within a wall. [Pfx. en- (1a).]

**enwallow,** *en-wol'ō, (Spens.) v.t.* to roll about wallowingly. [Pfx. en- (1c).]

**enwheel,** *en-(h)wēl', (Shak.) v.t.* to encircle. [Pfx. en- (1a).]

**enwind, inwind,** *in-wind', v.t.* to wind about, to enwrap. [Pfx. en- (1a).]

**enwomb,** *en-wōōm', v.t.* to make pregnant *(Spens.):* to conceive or have in the womb *(Shak.):* to contain. [Pfx. en- (1a).]

**enwrap, inwrap,** *in-rap', v.t.* to cover by wrapping: to enfold: to engross.—*n.* **enwrap'ment.**—*adj.* and *n.* **enwrapp'ing.** [Pfx. en- (1a).]

**enwreathe, inwreathe,** *in-rēdh', v.t.* to wreathe: to envelop: to encircle, as with a wreath. [Pfx. en- (1a).]

**enzone,** *in-zōn', v.t.* to engirdle: to enclose as with a zone. [Pfx. en- (1a).]

**enzootic,** *en-zō-ot'ik, adj.* of animal diseases, prevalent in a particular district or at a particular season.—*n.* a disease of this character. [Gr. *en,* in, *zōion,* animal, in imitation of *endemic.*]

**enzyme,** *en'-zim, n.* any one of a large class of protein substances produced by living cells which, usu. in the presence of other substances, e.g. of coenzymes, act as catalysts.—*adj.* **enzymat'ic.**—*ns.* **enzymol'ogist; enzymol'ogy,** scientific study of enzymes. [Gr. *en,* in, *zȳmē,* leaven.]

**E O,** *ē'-ō', n.* a mid-18th-century gambling game, depending on a ball falling into a slot marked E or O.

**eoan,** *ē-ō'ən, adj.* of or pertaining to dawn. [L., —Gr. *ēōs,* dawn.]

**Eoanthropus,** *ē-ō-an-thrō'pəs, n.* a once-supposed very early form of a man represented by parts of a skull found at Piltdown, Sussex (1912); in 1953 a hoax was exposed and the mandible shown to be an ape's. [Gr. *ēōs,* dawn, *anthrōpos,* man.]

**Eocene,** *ē'ō-sēn, (geol.) adj.* belonging to the oldest division of the Tertiary formation.—*n.* the Eocene system, period, or strata. [Gr. *ēōs,* dawn, *kainos,* new—from the very small proportion of living species of molluscs among its fossils.]

**Eohippus,** *ē'ō-hip-əs, n.* the oldest known horselike animal, an Eocene fossil. [Gr. *ēōs,* dawn, *hippos,* horse.]

**EOKA,** *ā-ō'ka, n.* a secret Greek Cypriot combatant organisation contending for the union of Cyprus with Greece. [Gr. Ethnikē Organōsis Kypriōn Agōnistōn, National Organisation. of Cypriot Combatants.]

**Eolian, Eolic, eolipile, eon.** See Aeolian, Aeolic, etc.

**éolienne,** *ā-ol-yen', n.* dress material of fine silk and wool. [Fr.]

**eolith,** *ē'ō-lith, n.* a very early roughly-broken stone implement, or one naturally formed but assumed to have been used by man.—*adj.* **eolith'ic.** [Gr. *ēōs,* dawn, *lithos,* stone.]

**eonism,** *ē'ə-nizm,* (*psychiatry) n.* adoption by a male of female dress and manner. [Chevalier d'*Éon,* French diplomat (d. 1810), who chose female dress as a disguise.]

**eo nomine,** *ē'ō nom'i-nē, e'ō no'mi-ne,* (L.) by that name, on that claim.

**eorl.** See earl (derivation).

**eosin,** *ē'ō-sin, n.* a red dyestuff, $C_{20}H_8Br_4O_5.$—*adj.* **eosin'ophil,** readily staining with eosin. [Gr. *ēōs,* dawn.]

**eothen,** *ē-ō'then,* (arch.) *adv.* from the east—the name given by Kinglake to his book of travel in the East (1844). [Gr. *ēōthen,* lit. from morn, at earliest dawn.]

**Eozoon,** *ē-ō-zō'on, n.* a once supposed fossil organism in the Archaean system of Canada, which would have been the oldest known living thing, or the banded arrangement of calcite and serpentine at that time supposed to be its remains.—*adj.* **Eozō'ic.** [Gr. *ēōs,* dawn, and *zōion,* an animal.]

Neutral vowels in unaccented syllables: *el'ə-mənt;* for certain sounds in foreign words, see p. viii

**Epacris**, *ep-ak'ris, ep'ə-kris, n.* a chiefly Australian genus of heath-like plants, giving name to the fam. **Epacridā'ceae**, close akin to the heaths.— *n.* **epac'rid** (or *ep'*), any member of the genus, or of the family. [Gr. *epi*, upon, *akris*, a summit.]
**epact**, *ē'pakt, n.* the moon's age at the beginning of the year: the excess of the calendar month or solar year over the lunar. [Fr. *épacte*—Gr. *epaktos*, brought on—*epi*, on, *agein*, to bring.]
**epaenetic**, *ep-ə-net'ik*, **epainetic**, *ep-ī-net'ik, (arch.) adj.* eulogistic. [Gr. *epainetikos*—*epainein*, to praise.]
**epagoge**, *ep-ə-gō'gē, -jē, (log.) n.* induction.—*adj.* **epagōg'ic.** [Gr. *epagōgē*—*epi*, on, *agōgē*, leading.]
**epanadiplosis**, *ep-a-nə-di-plō'sis, (rhet.) n.* a figure by which a sentence begins and ends with the same word, as in Phil. iv. 4 (Authorised Version). [Gr.]
**epanalepsis**, *ep-a-nə-lep'sis, (rhet.) n.* repetition or resumption, as in 1 Cor. xi. 18 and 20 (esp. Authorised Version). [Gr.]
**epanaphora**, *ep-ə-naf'o-ra.* Same as **anaphora**.
**epanodos**, *ep-an'o-dos, (rhet.) n.* recapitulation of the chief points in a discourse. [Gr. *epanodos*.]
**epanorthosis**, *ep-an-ör-thō'sis, (rhet.) n.* the retracting of a statement in order to correct or intensify it, as *For Britain's guid! for her destruction!* [Gr. *epanorthōsis*.]
**eparch**, *ep'ärk, n.* the governor of a modern Greek province: a metropolitan.—*ns.* **ep'archate, ep'-archy**, the province, territory or diocese of an eparch. [Gr. *eparchos*—*epi*, upon, *archē*, dominion.]
**épatant**, *ā-pa-tä,* (Fr.) wonderful, marvellous.
**epaule**, *e-pöl', n.* the shoulder of a bastion.—*n.* **epaule'ment**, a side-work of a battery or earth-work to protect it from a flanking fire: a particular placing of a dancer's shoulders, one forward, one back (*ballet*). [Fr. *épaule*, shoulder —L. *spatula*.]
**epaulet, epaulette**, *ep'əl-et, n.* a shoulder-piece: a badge of a military or naval officer (now disused in the British army): an ornament on the shoulder of a lady's dress. [Fr. *épaulette*—*épaule*, the shoulder.]
**epaxial**, *ep-aks'i-əl, adj.* above the axis. [Gr. *epi*, on, over, and **axis**.]
**epedaphic**, *ep-ə-daf'ik, adj.* pertaining to atmospheric conditions. [Gr. *epi*, above, *edaphos*, ground.]
**épée**, *ā-pā', n.* a sharp-pointed, narrow-bladed sword, without a cutting edge, used for duelling, and, with a button on the point, for fencing practice. [Fr.]
**Epeira**, *ep-ir'a, n.* a genus of spiders, the type of the **Epeir'idae** including the common garden spider.—*n.* **epeir'id**, a member of the family. [Perh. Gr. *epi*, on, *eirein*, to string.]
**epeirogenesis**, *ev-ī-rō-jen'i-sis, (geol.) n.* continent-building.—Also **epeirogeny** (*-roj'i-ni*).—*adjs.* **epeirogen'ic, epeirogenetic** (*-jin-et'ik*). [Gr. *ēpeiros*, mainland, *genesis*, formation.]
**epencephalon**, *ep-en-sef'ə-lon,* or *-kef', n.* the cerebellum.—*adj.* **epencephalic** (*-si-fal'ik,* or *-ki-*). [Gr. *epi*, on, *enkephalon*, brain.]
**epenthesis**, *e-pen'thə-sis, n.* the insertion of a sound within a word.—*adj.* **epenthetic** (*-thet'ik*). [Gr.]
**epeolatry**, *ep-i-ol'ə-tri, n.* worship of words. [Gr. *epos*, word, *latreiā*, worship.]
**éperdu**, (*fem.* **éperdue**) *ā-per-dü,* (Fr.) distracted; **éperdument amoureux** (*fem.* amoureuse), *ā-per-dü-mä a-mōō-rø* (*-ræz*), desperately in love.
**epergne**, *i-púrn', n.* a branched ornamental centre-piece for the table. [Fr. *épargne* (saving), as used in phrases *taille* or *gravure d'épargne*, metal or etching with parts left in relief.]
**epexegesis**, *ep-eks-i-jē'sis, n.* the addition of words to make the sense more clear.—*adjs.* **epexeget'ic**

(*-jet'ik*), *-al.*—*adv.* **epexeget'ically.** [Gr. *epexē-gēsis*—*epi*, in addition, *exēgeesthai*, to explain.]
**epha, ephah**, *ē'fa, n.* a Hebrew measure for dry goods. [Heb.; prob. of Egyptian origin.]
**ephebe**, *ef-ēb', **ephē'bus**, -os, n.* in ancient Greece, a young citizen from 18 to 20 years of age:—*pl.* **ephē'bi.**—*adj.* **ephēb'ic**, pertaining to an ephebe: pertaining to the adult period in the life-history of an individual (*biol.*). [L. *ephēbus*—Gr. *ephēbos*—*epi*, upon, *hēbē*; early manhood.]
**Ephedra**, *ef'ed-ra, ef-ēd'ra, ef-ed'ra, n.* sea-grape, a genus of jointed, all but leafless desert plants of the Gnetaceae.—*n.* **eph'edrine** (or *ef-ed'rin*), an alkaloid got from Ephedra, used in treating hay fever, etc. [Gr. *ephedrā*, horsetail.]
**Ephemera**, *ef-em'ər-a,* or *-ēm', n.* a genus of insects whose adult life is very short, mayfly: (*without cap.*) that which lasts a short time.—*adj.* **ephem'eral**, existing only for a day: short-lived: fleeting.—*n.* anything very short lived.—*ns.* **ephemeral'ity; ephem'erid**, an insect of the mayfly family, **Ephemer'idae** (*-mer'i-dē*); order Plectoptera or Ephemerop'tera).—*adj.* **ephemerid'ian.**—*ns.* **ephem'eris**, an account of daily transactions (*arch.*): a journal (*arch.*): an astronomical almanac tabulating the daily positions of the sun, moon, planets and certain stars, etc.:—*pl.* **ephemerides** (*ef-e-mer'i-dēz*); **ephem'erist**, one who studies the daily motions of the planets; **ephem'eron**, an insect that lives but by day.—*adj.* **ephem'erous.**—**ephemeris time**, time measured by orbital movement of earth, moon and planets, differing from mean solar time in that it allows for irregularities due to variations in rate of rotation of the earth; an ephemeris second has the same value as had the mean universal second for the 19th cent. [Gr. *ephēmeros*, living a day—*epi*, for, *hēmerā*, a day.]
**Ephesian**, *ef-ē'zi-ən, -ē'zhən, adj.* of or pertaining to Ephesus.—*n.* an inhabitant of Ephesus: a jolly companion (*Shak.*).
**ephialtes**, *ef-i-al'tēz, (arch.) n.* an incubus: a nightmare. [Gr. *ephialtēs*.]
**ephod**, *ef'od, n.* a kind of linen surplice worn by the Jewish priests: a surplice, generally. [Heb. *ēphōd*—*āphad*, to put on.]
**ephor**, *ef'ör, ef'ər, n.* a class of magistrates whose office apparently originated at Sparta, being peculiar to the Doric states.—*n.* **eph'oralty.** [Gr. *epi*, upon, and root of *horaein*, to see.]
**epiblast**, *ep'i-blȧst, n.* the outer germinal layer of an embryo.—*adj.* **epiblast'ic.** [Gr. *epi*, upon, *blastos*, a germ, shoot.]
**epic**, *ep'ik, adj.* applied to a long narrative poem that relates heroic events in an elevated style: characteristic of an epic poem: impressive: large-scale.—*n.* an epic poem: epic poetry as a genre: a story comparable to that of an. epic poem, esp. a long adventure novel or film: an epic poet (*obs.*).—*adj.* **ep'ical.**—*adv.* **ep'ically.** —*ns.* **ep'icism** (*-sizm*), **ep'icist.**—**epic dialect,** Homer's Greek; **epic theatre,** the theatre of epic drama, episodic drama with alienation (q.v.), narrative passages, etc. [Gr. *epikos*—*epos*, a word.]
**epicalyx**, *ep-i-kāl'iks,* or *-kal', n.* an apparent accessory calyx outside of the true calyx, composed of bracts or of fused stipules of sepals. [Gr.]
**epicanthus**, *epi-kan'thəs, n.* a fold of skin over the inner canthus of the eye, characteristic of the Mongolian race.—*adj.* **epican'thic.** [Gr. *epi*, on, and **canthus**.]
**epicarp**, *ep'i-kärp, (bot.) n.* the outermost layer of the pericarp or fruit. [Gr. *epi*, upon, *karpos*, fruit.]
**epicede**, *ep'i-sēd,* **epicedium**, *ep-i-sē'di-əm,* or *-dī', n.* a funeral ode.—*adjs.* **epicē'dial, epicē'-dian**, elegiac. [L. *epicēdium*—Gr. *epikēdeion*—*epi*, upon, *kēdos*, care.]
**epicene**, *ep'i-sēn, adj.* common to both sexes:

having characteristics of both sexes, or neither: effeminate: of common gender (*gram.*): sometimes restricted to those words that have one grammatical gender though used for both sexes. —Also *n.* [Gr. *epi*, upon, *koinos*, common.] **epicentre,** *ep'i-sen-tər, n.* that point on the earth's surface directly over the point of origin of an earthquake.—*adj.* **epicen'tral.** [Gr. *epi*, upon, over, *kentron*, a point.]
**epicheirema,** *ep-i-ki-rē'ma, n.* a syllogism confirmed in its major or minor premise, or both, by an incidental proposition. [Gr. *epicheirēma*, attempt, an attempted proof short of demonstrating.—*epi*, upon, *cheir*, hand.]
**epicier,** *ā-pē-syā,* (Fr.) a grocer.
**epiclesis,** *ep-i-klē'sis, n.* in the Eastern church, an invocation of the Holy Spirit at the consecration of the elements (bread and wine). [Gr. *epiklēsis*, invocation—*epikalein*, to summon.]
**epicotyl,** *ep-i-kot'il, n.* the stem of an embryo plant or seedling between the cotyledons and the next leaf. [Gr. *epi*, over, and *cotyledon.*]
**epicure,** *ep'i-kūr, n.* an Epicurean (*obs.*): one given to sensual enjoyment (*obs.*): a person of refined and fastidious taste, esp. in food, wine, etc.—*adj.* **Epicurē'an,** pertaining to Epicurus (341-270 B.C.), the Greek philosopher, who taught an atomic materialism in physics and hedonism in ethics, misrepresented by opponents as brutish sensuality: (without *cap.*) given to luxury, esp. refined luxury.—*n.* **Epicurē'an,** a follower of Epicurus: (without *cap.*) a hedonist, an epicure.—*n.* **Epicurē'anism,** the doctrines of Epicurus: attachment to these doctrines: epicurism.—*v.i.* **ep'icurise, -ize** (*arch.*), to play the epicure: to profess the philosophy of Epicurus. —*n.* **ep'icurism,** pursuit of pleasure: fastidiousness in luxury: (also *ep-i-kūr'izm, arch.*) Epicureanism. [L. *Epicūrus*—Gr. *Epikouros.*]
**epicycle,** *ep'i-sī-kl, n.* a circle whose centre is carried round the circumference of a greater circle.—*adj.* **epicy'clic.**—*n.* **epicy'cloid,** a curve described by a point on the circumference of a circle rolling on the outside of the circumference of another circle.—*adj.* **epicycloi'dal.** [Gr. *epi*, upon, *kyklos*, a circle.]
**epideictic, -al,** *ep-i-dīk'tik, -əl, adjs.* done for show or display. [Gr. *epi*, upon, *deiknynai*, to show.]
**epidemic,** *ep-i-dem'ik, adj.* affecting a community at a certain time: prevalent.—*n.* a disease that attacks great numbers in one place, at one time, and itself travels from place to place: a widespread outbreak.—*adj.* **epidem'ical**—*adv.* **epidem'ically.**—*ns.* **epidemiol'ogy** (-*dēm*-), science of epidemics: **epidem'iologist.** [Gr. *epidēmos*, general—*epi*, among, *dēmos*, the people.]
**epidermis,** *ep-i-dûr'mis, n.* scarf-skin or cuticle, forming an external covering of a protective nature for the true skin or corium (*zool.*): an outer sheath of close-set cells, usually one deep (*bot.*).—*adjs.* **epider'mal, epider'mic, epiderm'oid.** [Gr. *epidermis*—*epi*, upon, *derma*, the skin.]
**epidiascope,** *ep-i-dī'ə-skōp, n.* a lantern for projecting images of objects whether opaque or transparent. [Gr. *epi*, upon, *dia*, through, *skopeein*, to look at.]
**epidiorite,** *ep-i-dī'ə-rit, n.* a dioritic or gabbroitic rock more or less metamorphosed, the pyroxene being changed to amphibole. [Gr. *epi*, after, and *diorite.*]
**epidote,** *ep'i-dōt, n.* a greenish mineral, silicate of calcium, aluminium, and iron.—*n.* **epidosite** (*ep-id'ə-sit*), a rock composed of epidote and quartz.—*adj.* **epidotic** (-*dot'*).—*n.* **epidotisā'tion, -ization.** [Gr. *epididonai*, to give in addition, superadd, from the great length of the base of the crystal.]
**epidural,** *ep-i-dūr'əl, adj.* situated on, or administered outside, the dura mater.—**epidural anaes-**

thesia, loss of painful sensation in the lower part of the body produced by injecting an anaesthetic into the lowest portion of the spinal canal. [Gr. *epi*, upon.]
**epifocal,** *ep-i-fō'kl, adj.* epicentral.
**epigaeal, epigeal,** *ep-i-jē'əl,* **epigaeous, epigeous** (-*əs*), **epigaean, epigean** (-*ən*), *adjs.* growing or living close to the ground: with cotyledons above ground. [Gr. *epigaios, epigeios*—*epi*, on *gaia, gē,* earth.]
**epigamic,** *ep-i-gam'ik, adj.* attractive to the opposite sex. [Gr. *epigamos,* marriageable—*epi*, upon, *gamos,* marriage.]
**epigastrium,** *ep-i-gas'tri-əm, n.* the part of the abdomen extending from the sternum towards the navel—the pit of the stomach—*adj.* **epigas'tric.** [Gr. *epi*, upon, *gastēr*, the stomach.]
**epigeal, etc.** See **epigaeal.**
**epigene,** *ep'i-jēn, (geol.) adj.* acting or taking place at the earth's surface. [Fr. *épigène*—Gr. *epigenēs,* born after.]
**epigenesis,** *ep-i-jen'i-sis, n.* the theory, now universally accepted, that the development of an embryo consists of the gradual production and organisation of parts, as opposed to the theory of preformation, which supposed that the future animal or plant was already present complete, although in miniature, in the germ.— *ns.* **epigen'esist, epigenet'icist.**—*adj.* **epigenet'ic,** pertaining to epigenesis: (of minerals) formed subsequently to the enclosing rock.—*n.* **epigenet'ics,** science which studies the causes at work in development. [Gr. *epi*, upon, after, *genesis,* formation.]
**epiglottis,** *ep-i-glot'is, n.* a cartilaginous flap over the glottis.—*adj.* **epiglott'ic.** [Gr. *epiglōttis*—*epi*, over, *glōttis,* glottis.]
**epigon,** *ep'i-gon,* **epigone,** *ep'i-gōn, n.* one of a later generation:—*pl.* **ep'igons, ep'igones** (-*gōnz*), **epig'oni,** sons (esp. of the Seven against Thebes), or successors (esp. of Alexander): undistinguished descendants of the great. [Gr. *epi*, after, *gonē,* birth.]
**epigram,** *ep'i-gram, n.* any concise and pointed or sarcastic saying: a short poem expressing an ingenious thought with point, usually satirical.— *adjs.* **epigrammat'ic** (-*grəm-at'ik*), **-al,** relating to or dealing in epigrams: like an epigram: concise and pointed.—*adv.* **epigrammat'ically.** —*v.t.* **epigramm'atise, -ize,** to make an epigram on.—*n.* **epigramm'atist,** one who writes epigrams. [Through Fr. and L., from Gr. *epigramma*—*epi*, upon, *gramma,* a writing—*graphein,* to write.]
**epigraph,** *ep'i-gräf, n.* an inscription, esp. on a building: a citation or motto at the beginning of a book or its part.—*v.t.* to provide with an epigraph.—*ns.* **epigrapher** (*ep-ig'rə-fər*), **epig'raphist.**—*adj.* **epigraphic** (-*graf'ik*).—*n.* **epig'raphy.** [Gr. *epigraphē*—*epi*, upon, *graphein,* to write.]
**epigynous,** *e-pij'i-nəs,* (*bot.*) *adj.* growing upon the top of the ovary: having calyx, corolla, and stamens inserted on the top of an inferior ovary. —*n.* **epig'yny.** [Gr. *epi*, upon, *gynē,* woman, female.]
**epilate,** *ep'i-lāt, v.t.* to remove (hair) by any means.—*ns.* **epilā'tion; ep'ilator.** [Fr. *épiler*— L. *ex,* from, *pilus,* hair.]
**epilepsy,** *ep'i-lep-si, n.* a chronic functional disease of the nervous system, manifested by recurring attacks of sudden insensibility or impairment of consciousness, commonly accompanied by peculiar convulsive seizures.—*n.* **epilep'tic,** an epileptic patient.—*adjs.* **epilep'tic, -al.** [Gr. *epilēpsia*—*epi*, upon, and root of *lambanein,* to seize.]
**Epilobium,** *ep-i-lōb'i-əm, n.* a willow-herb. [Gr. *epi*, upon, *lobos,* a pod, from the position of the petals.]
**epilogue,** *ep'i-log, n.* the concluding section of a

book, etc.: a short poem or speech at the end of a play: the speaker thereof: the conclusion of a radio or TV programme.—*adjs*. **epilogic** (*-loj'ik*), **epilogistic** (*-jis'*).—*v.i*. **epilogise, -ize** (*ep-il'ə-jiz*), or *ep'*), **epiloguise, -ize** (*-giz*), to speak or write an epilogue. [Fr.,—L. *epilogus*—Gr. *epilogos*, conclusion—*epi*, upon, *legein*, to speak.]

**epimeletic**, *ep-i-mel-et'ik*, (*animal behaviour*) *adj*. of a type of social behaviour covering the care of the young by the parents, or other individuals of the same species, e.g. worker bees.

**epinasty**, *ep'i-nas-ti*, (*bot*.) *n*. down-curving of an organ, caused by a more active growth on its upper side—opposed to *hyponasty*.—*adj*. **epinas'tic**.—*adv*. **epinas'tically**. [Gr. *epi*, upon, *nastos*, pressed close.]

**epinephrine**, *ep-i-nef'rin, -rēn, n*. adrenaline. [Gr. *epi*, upon, *nephros*, kidney.]

**epinikion**, *ep-i-nik'i-ən*, **epinicion**, *ep-i-nis*(*h*)*'i-ən, n*. a song of victory: an ode in honour of a victor or winner.—*adj*. **epinik'ian, epinic'ian**. [Gr. *epinikion*—*epi*, on, after, *nikē*, victory.]

**epinosic**, *ep-i-nos'ik, adj*. unhealthy: unwholesome. [Gr. *epi-*, and *nosos*, disease.]

**epipetalous**, *ep-i-pet'ə-ləs*, (*bot*.) *adj*. inserted or growing on a petal or petals.

**Epiphany**, *e-pif'ə-ni, n*. a church festival celebrated on 6th Jan., in commemoration of the manifestation of Christ to the wise men of the East: the manifestation of a god. [Gr. *epiphaneia*, appearance—*epi*, to, *phainein*, to show.]

**epiphenomenon**, *ep-i-fin-om'ən-ən, n*. an accompanying phenomenon outside the chain of causation: something appearing after, a secondary symptom of a disease (*path*.):—*pl*. **epiphenom'ena**.—*n*. **epiphenom'enalism**, interpretation of mind as an epiphenomenon upon the physical.—*n*. and *adj*. **epiphenom'enalist**. [Gr. *epi*, after, *phainomenon*, neut. pr.p. pass. of *phainein*, to show.]

**epiphonema**, *ep-i-fō-nē'mə*, (*rhet*.) *n*. an exclamation: a phrase or reflection added as a finishing touch. [Gr. *epiphōnēma*.]

**epiphragm**, *ep'i-fram, n*. the disk with which certain molluscs close the aperture of their shell. [Gr. *epiphragma*, covering—*epiphrassein*, to obstruct.]

**epiphyllous**, *ep-i-fil'əs*, (*bot*.) *adj*. growing upon a leaf, esp. on its upper surface. [Gr. *epi*, upon, *phyllon*, a leaf.]

**epiphysis**, *ep-if'i-sis, n*. any portion of a bone having its own centre of ossification: the pineal gland (*epiphysis cerebri*): an ossicle of Aristotle's lantern in a sea-urchin: an upgrowth around the hilum of a seed:—*pl*. **epiph'ysēs**. [Gr., excrescence.]

**epiphyte**, *ep'i-fīt, n*. a plant growing on another plant, without being parasitic: a vegetable parasite on the surface of an animal (*path*.).—*adjs*. **epiphyt'al, epiphytic** (*-fit'ik*), **-al**.—*n*. **ep'iphytism** (or *fīt'*), the condition of being epiphytic: a similar relation among animals. [Gr. *epi*, upon, *phyton*, a plant.]

**epiplastron**, *ep-i-pläs'tron, n*. the anterior lateral one of the (nine) pieces forming the plastron of a turtle:—*pl*. **epiplas'tra**.—*adj*. **epiplas'tral**.

**epiploon**, *e-pip'lō-on, n*. the great omentum.—*adj*. **epiplō'ic**. [Gr. *epiploon*—*epipleein*, to float on.]

**epipolism**, *e-pip'o-lizm, n*. fluorescence.—*adj*. **epipol'ic**. [Gr. *epipolē*, surface.]

**epirrhema**, *ep-i-rē'mə, n*. in Greek comedy the address of the Coryphaeus to the audience after the parabasis.—*adj*. **epirrhēmat'ic**. [Gr.—*epi*, on, after, *rhēma*, word.]

**episcopacy**, *e-pis'kə-pəs-i, n*. church government by bishops: the office of a bishop: a bishop's period of office: the bishops, as a class.—*adj*. **epis'copal**, governed by bishops: belonging to or vested in bishops.—*adj*. **episcopā'lian**, belonging to bishops, or government by bishops, or to an

episcopal church.—*n*. one who belongs to an episcopal (especially Anglican) church.—*n*. **episcopā'lianism**, episcopalian government and doctrine.—*adv*. **epis'copally**.—*ns*. **epis'copant** (*Milt*.), a holder of a bishopric; **epis'copate**, a bishopric: the office of a bishop: a bishop's period of office: the order of bishops.—*v.i*. (*Milt*.) to act as a bishop.—*v.t*. **epis'copise, -ize**, to make a bishop of: to make episcopalian.— *v.i*. to play the bishop (also *v.t*. with *it*).—*n*. **epis'copy** (*Milt*.), survey, superintendence. [Gr. *episkopos*, an overseer.]

**episcope**, *ep'i-skōp, n*. a lantern for projecting images of opaque objects. [Gr. *epi*, on, over, *skopeein*, to look.]

**episemon**, *ep-i-sē'mon, n*. a badge or characteristic device: one of three obsolete Greek letters used as numerals—ϛ or Ϲ, vau or digamma (6); Ϙ, koppa (90); and ϡ, san, sampi (900).—*adj*. **episēmat'ic** (*zool*.), serving for recognition. [Gr. *episēmon*, a badge—*epi*, on, *sēma*, a sign.]

**episepalous**, *ep-i-sep'əl-əs, adj*. growing or inserted upon a sepal or sepals.

**episiotomy**, *ep-iz-i-ot'ə-mi, n*. an incision made in the perinaeum to facilitate delivery of a foetus. [Gr. *epision*, pubic region, and -tomy.]

**episode**, *ep'-i-sod, n*. a story introduced into a narrative or poem to give variety: an interesting incident: a passage affording relief from the principal subject (*mus*.): an incident or period detachable from a novel, play, etc.: a part of a radio or television serial which is broadcast at one time.—*adjs*. **ep'isōdal, episō'dial, episodic** (*-sod'*), **episōd'ical**, pertaining to or contained in an episode: brought in as a digression: abounding in episodes.—*adv*. **episōd'ically**, by way of episode: incidentally. [Gr. *epeisodion* —*epi*, upon, *eisodos*, a coming in.]

**epispastic**, *ep-i-spas'tik, adj*. blistering.—*n*. a blistering agent. [Gr. *epispastikos*—*epi*, upon, *spaein*, to draw.]

**episperm**, *ep'i-spûrm, n*. the outer seed-coat. [Gr. *epi*, upon, and *sperma*, seed.]

**epispore**, *ep'i-spōr, -spōr, n*. the outermost layer of a spore-wall.

**epistaxis**, *ep-i-stak'sis, n*. bleeding from the nose. [Gr. *epistazein*, to shed in drops.]

**epistemology**, *ep-is-tə-mol'ə-ji, n*. the theory of knowledge.—*adj*. **epistemological** (*-ə-loj'*).—*n*. **epistemol'ogist**. [Gr. *epistēmē*, knowledge, *logos*, discourse.]

**episternum**, *ep-i-stûr'nəm, n*. the interclavicle: the epiplastron: the presternum of mammals.— *adj*. **epister'nal**.

**epistilbite**, *ep-i-stil'bīt, n*. a zeolite close akin to stilbite. [Gr. *epi*, on, after, in addition to, and stilbite.]

**epistle**, *i-pis'l, n*. a writing sent to one, a letter: esp. a letter to an individual or church from an apostle, as the Epistles of Paul: the extract from one of the apostolical epistles read as part of the communion service: a verse composition in letter form.—*v.t*. (*Milt*.) to preface.—*ns*. **epistler** (*pis'* or *pist'*), **epistoler** (*i-pist'ə-lər*), a letter-writer: one who reads the liturgical epistle in the communion service; **epistolā'rian**, a letter-writer.—*adjs*. **epistolā'rian, epis'tolary, epis'tolatory**, **epistolic** (*ep-is-tol'ik*), **-al**, pertaining to or consisting of epistles or letters: suitable to an epistle: contained in letters.—*n*. **epis'tolet**, a short letter.—*v.i*. **epis'tolise, -ize**, to write a letter.—*ns*. **epis'tolist**, a writer of letters; **epistolog'raphy**, letter-writing.—**epistle side** of a church, the south side, opp. to *gospel side*. [O.Fr.,—L. *epistola*—Gr. *epistolē*—*epi*, on the occasion of, *stellein*, to send.]

**epistrophe**, *e-pis'trə-fē, n*. ending of successive clauses with the same word, as in 2 Cor. xi. 22 (A.V.) (*rhet*.): a refrain in music. [Gr. *epistrophē*, a return—*epi*, upon, *strephein*, to turn.]

epistyle, *ep'i-stil*, *n*. architrave. [Gr. *epi*, upon, *stȳios*, a pillar.]

epitaph, *ep'i-täf*, *n*. a tombstone inscription: a composition in the form of a tombstone inscription.—*v.t.* to compose an epitaph upon.—*ns*. epitapher (*ep'i-täf-ər*), ep'itaphist, a composer of epitaphs.—*adjs*. epitaph'ian, epitaph'ic. [Gr. *epitaphion*—*epi*, upon, *taphos*, a tomb.]

epitasis, *e-pit'ə-sis*, *n*. the main action of a Greek drama leading to the catastrophe—opp. to *protasis*.

epithalamium, epithalamion, *ep-i-thə-lā'mi-əm*, *-on*, *n*. a song or poem in celebration of a marriage:—*pl*. epithalā'mia.—*adj*. epithalām'ic. [L. *epithalamium*, Gr. *epithalamion*—*epi*, upon, *thalamos*, a bride-chamber.]

epithelium, *ep-i-thē'li-əm*, *n*. the cell-tissue that invests the outer surface of the body and the mucous membranes connected with it, and also the closed cavities of the body.—*adj*. epithē'lial.—*n*. epithēliō'ma, carcinoma of the skin.—*adj*. epithēliō'matous. [Mod.L.,—Gr. *epi*, upon, *thēlē*, nipple.]

epithem, *ep'i-them*, *n*. a soft external application (*med*.): a group of cells exuding water in some leaves (*bot*.).—Also epithema (*ep-i-thē'mə*, *ep-ith'i-mə*):—*pl*. epithems, epithe'mata. [Gr. *epithema*, epithēma, *-atos*—*epi*, on, *tithenai*, to place.]

epithermal, *ep-i-thûr'məl*, *adj*. having energy just above the energy of thermal agitation.

epithesis, *ep-ith'i-sis*, *n*. paragoge. [Gr., setting on.]

epithet, *ep'i-thet*, *n*. an adjective expressing some real quality of the thing to which it is applied: a descriptive term: term, expression (*Shak*.).—*v.t.* to term.—*adj*. epithet'ic, pertaining to an epithet: abounding with epithets.—*n*. epith'eton (*Shak*. apath'aton), epithet. [Gr. *epitheton*, neut. of *epithetos*, added—*epi*, on, *tithenai*, to place.]

epithymetic, *ep-i-thim-et'ik*, *adj*. pertaining to desire. [Gr. *epi*, upon, *thȳmos*, the soul.]

epitome, *i-pit'ə-mē*, *n*. an abridgment or short summary of anything, as of a book: an embodiment in little.—*adjs*. epitomic (*ep-i-tom'ik*) *-al*.—*v.t.* epit'omise, *-ize*, to make an epitome of: to shorten: to condense.—*ns*. epit'omiser, *-z-*, epit'omist, one who abridges.—in epitome, on a small scale. [Gr. *epi*, *tomē*, a cut.]

epitonic, *ep-i-ton'ik*, *adj*. overstrained. [Gr. *epitonos*—*epi*, upon, *teinein*, to stretch.]

epitrachelion, *ep-i-tra-kē'li-ən*, *n*. an Orthodox priest's or bishop's stole. [Gr., on the neck—*epi*, upon, *trachēlos*, neck.]

epitrite, *ep'i-trit*, (*pros*.) *n*. a foot made up of three long syllables and one short. [Gr. *epitritos*—*epi*, in addition to, *tritos*, third.]

epitrochoid, *ep-i-trō'koid*, *n*. a curve like an epicycloid, but generated by any point on a radius. [Gr. *epi*, on, *trochos*, wheel.]

epizeuxis, *ep-i-zūk'sis*, (*rhet*.) *n*. the immediate repetition of a word for emphasis. [Gr., joining on.]

epizoon, *ep-i-zō'on*, *n*. an animal that lives on the surface of another animal, whether parasitically or commensally:—*pl*. epizō'a.—*adj*. and *n*. epizō'an.—*adjs*. epizō'ic, dwelling upon an animal: having seeds dispersed by animals; epizootic (*ep-i-zō-ot'ik*), pertaining to epizoa: containing fossil remains, as subsequent to the appearance of life (*geol*.; *obs*.): affecting animals as an epidemic does mankind.—*n*. an epizootic disease: (*pl*.) the science or study of epidemic animal diseases. [Gr. *epi*, upon, *zōion*, an animal.]

epoch, *ēp'ok*, *ēp'ohh*, *ep'ok*, *n*. a point of time fixed or made remarkable by some great event from which dates are reckoned: the particular time, used as a point of reference, at which the data had the values in question (*astron*.): a planet's heliocentric longitude at the epoch (*astron*.): a precise date: a time from which a new state of things dates: an age, geological, historical, or other.—Also (*arch*.) ep'ocha.—*adjs*. epochal (*ep'ok-l*).—ep'och-mäking, important enough to be considered as beginning a new age; ep'och-marking. [Gr. *epochē*—*epechein*, to stop, take up a position—*epi*, upon, *echein*, to hold.]

epode, *ep'ōd*, *n*. a kind of lyric poem invented by Archilochus, in which a longer verse is followed by a shorter one: the last part of a lyric ode, sung after the strophe and antistrophe.—*adj*. epodic (*-od'ik*). [Gr. *epōidos*—*epi*, on, *ōidē*, an ode.]

eponychium, *ep-o-nik'i-əm*, *n*. a narrow band of cuticle over the base of a nail. [Gr. *epi*, on, *onyx*, *onychos*, nail.]

eponym, *ep'o-nim*, *n*. one who gives his name to something: a hero invented to account for the name of a place or people: a character who gives a play, etc., its title: a distinguishing title.—*adj*. epon'ymous. [Gr. *epōnymos*, eponymous—*epi*, to, *onyma*, *onoma*, a name.]

epopee, *ep'o-pē*, epopoeia, *ep-o-pē'ya*, *n*. epic poetry: an epic poem. [Gr. *epopoiiā*—*epos*, a word, an epic poem. *poieein*, to make.]

epopt, *ep'opt*, *n*. one initiated into the Eleusinian mysteries. [Gr. *epoptēs*—*epi*, upon, and root *op-*, to see.]

epos, *ep'os*, *n*. the elementary stage of epic poetry: an epic poem: a series of events such as are treated in epic poetry. [Gr. *epos*, a word.]

epoxy, *e-pok'si*, *adj*. containing oxygen bound to two other atoms, often carbon, which are already attached in some way.—epoxy (or epoxide) resins, synthetic polymers used as structural plastics, surface coatings, adhesives and for encapsulating and embedding electronic components.

épris, (*fem*. éprise), *ā-prē*, (*-prēz*), (Fr.) captivated, smitten.

éprouvette, *ā-prōō-vet'*, *n*. an apparatus for testing the strength of gunpowder. [Fr. *éprouver*, to try.]

epsilon, *ep-si'lən*, *n*. fifth letter (E, ε) of the Greek alphabet, short e: as a numeral ε' = 5, ,ε = 5000. [Gr. *e psilon*, bare or mere e.]

epsomite, *ep'səm-it*, *n*. a mineral, hydrated magnesium sulphate ($MgSO_4 \cdot 7H_2O$).—Ep'som salt(s)', a purgative medicine of like composition, originally got from the springs at Epsom, in Surrey—used also in dyeing, etc.

épuisé, (*fem*. épuisée), *ā-pwē-zā*, (Fr.) worn out.

epulation, *ep-ū-lā'shən*, *n*. feasting. [L. *epulāri*, *-ātus*, to feast.]

epulis, *e-pū'lis*, *n*. a tumour of the gums, either benign or malignant, and growing from the periosteum of the jaw. [Gr. *epi*, upon, *oulon*, gum.]

epulotic, *ep-ū-lot'ik*, *adj*. cicatrising.—*n*. a cicatrising medicament. [Gr. *epoulōtikos*—*epi*, upon, *oulē*, a scar.]

epurate, *ep'ū-rāt*, *v.t.* to purify.—*n*. epurā'tion. [Fr. *épurer*.]

epyllion, *e-pil'i-ən*, *n*. a poem with some resemblance to an epic but shorter. [Gr.; dim. of *epos*, word.]

Epyornis. Spelling of Aepyornis.

equable, *ek'wə-bl*, *adj*. even, uniform: smooth: without great variations or extremes: of even temper.—*ns*. equabil'ity, e'quableness.—*adv*. e'quably. [L. *aequābilis*—*aequāre*—*aequus*, equal.]

equal, *ē'kwəl*, *adj*. identical in quantity: of the same value: adequate: in just proportion: fit: adequate: uniform: equitable: evenly balanced: just: equally developed on each side (*bot*.).—*n*. one of the same age, rank, etc.: equality (*Spens*.)—*v.t.* to be, or to make, equal to: to

reach the same level as (*bot.*):—*pr.p.* e´qualling; *pa.t.* and *pa.p.* e´qualled.—*n.* equalisā´tion, the act of making equal: state of being equalised. —*v.t.* e´qualise, -ize, to make equal or uniform: to equal (*obs.*).—*v.i.* to become equal: to make one's score equal to one's opponent's.—*n.* equali´ser, a person or thing that equalises: a score that makes both sides alike.—*adj.* equalitār´ian (*-kwol-*), of or pertaining to the equality of mankind.—*n.* one who believes in or favours political and social equality of mankind.—*ns.* equalita´rianism; equality (*ē-kwol´i-ti*), the condition of being equal: sameness: evenness.— *adv.* equally (*ē´kwə-li*).—*n.* e´qualness, equality: equability.—*v.t.* equâte´, to reduce to an average or to a common standard of comparison: to state as equal: to regard as equal.—*n.* equā´tion, the act of making equal: a statement of the equality of two quantities: reduction to a common standard: correction to compensate for an error, irregularity, or discrepancy: the quantity added for this purpose: a formula expressing a chemical action and the proportions of the substances involved.—equal temperament (see temperament).—equal to the occasion, fit or able for an emergency; equation of time, mean solar time minus apparent solar time, or the right ascension of the true sun minus that of the mean sun; personal equation, a correction to be applied to the reading of an instrument on account of the observer's tendency to read too high, too low, etc.: any tendency to error or prejudice due to personal characteristics for which allowance must be made. [L. *aequālis*, equal, *aequāre*, *-ātum*, to make equal—*aequus*, equal.]
equanimity, *e-kwə-nim´i-ti*, *ē-*, *n.* evenness of mind or temper.—*adj.* equanimous (*i-kwan´i-məs*).— *adv.* equan´imously. [L. *aequanimitās*—*aequus*, equal, *animus*, the mind.]
equation. See equal.
equator, *i-kwā´tər*, *n.* an imaginary great circle passing round the middle of the globe and equidistant from N. and S. poles (*obs.*): the corresponding great circle of another body: the imaginary great circle in which the plane of the earth's equator intersects the celestial sphere (so called because day and night are equal when the sun reaches it): the middle belt or line of any globular or nearly globular body that has some sort of polarity.—*adj.* equatorial (*ek-wə-tō´ri-əl*, *-tö´*, or *ēk-*), of, pertaining to, of the nature of, or in the neighbourhood of an equator.—*n.* a telescope mounted on an axis, capable of moving parallel to the equator and so following a star in any part of its diurnal course.—*adv.* equato´rially, so as to have motion or direction parallel to the equator. [See equal.]
equerry, *ek´wə-ri*, *ik-wer´i*, *n.* princely stables (*obs.*): an officer thereof: an official in attendance upon a prince or personage. [Fr. *écurie*— L.L. *scūria*, a stable.]
equestrian, *i-kwes´tri-ən*, *adj.* pertaining to horsemanship, or to the Roman order of *equitēs* or knights: on horseback.—*n.* a horseman: a performer on horseback:—*fem.* (sham Fr.) equestrienne´.—*n.* eques´trianism, horsemanship. [L. *equester*, *equestris*—*eques* a horseman— *equus*, a horse.]
equi-, *ē-kwi-*, a prefix meaning equal, from L. *aequus*.—*adj.* equian´gular, having equal angles (equiangular spiral, a curve whose radius vector makes a constant angle with the tangent —the *logarithmic spiral*).—*n.* equiangular´ity. *n.* and *v.t.* equibal´ance, equipoise.—*adj.* equidiff´erent, having equal differences.—*n.* equidis´tance.—*adj.* equidis´tant, equally distant.— *adv.* equidis´tantly.—*adj.* equilat´eral (L. *latus*, *-eris*, side), having all sides equal.—*n.* equi-

mul´tiple, a number multiplied by the same number as another.—*adjs.* equipo´tent, of equal power; equipoten´tial, of equal power, capability, potential, or potentiality.—*adj.* equiprob´able, equal in degree of probability.—*n.* equiprobabil´ity.—*adj.* e´quivalve, having valves alike in size and form.
Equidae, *ek´wi-dē*, *n.pl.* a family of ungulate mammals consisting of the genus Eq´uus (horse, ass, zebra) and various fossil forms. [L. *equus*, horse.]
equidifferent . . . to . . . equilateral. See equi-.
equilibrium, *ēk-*, *ek-wi-lib´ri-əm*, *n.* balance: state of even balance: a state in which opposing forces or tendencies neutralise each other.—*v.t.* and *v.i.* equilibrate (*ēk-wi-lib´rāt*, or *-lib´rāt*, or *-kwil´*), to balance: to counterpoise.—*ns.* equilibrā´tion; equil´ibrator (*or -lib´*), a balancing or stability device, esp. an aeroplane fin; equil´ibrist (or *-lib´*, or *-lib´*), one who does balancing tricks; equilib´rity. [L. *aequilibrium*—*aequus*, equal, *libra*, balance.]
equimultiple. See equi-.
equine, *e´*, *ē´kwin*, equinal, *e-*, *ē-kwin´əl*, *adj.* pertaining to, or of the nature of, a horse.—*ns.* equinia (*i-*, *ē-kwin´i-ə*), glanders; equin´ity, equine nature. [L. *equinus*—*equus*, a horse.]
equinox, *ek´*, *ēk´wi-noks*, *n.* the time when the sun crosses the equator, making the night equal in length to the day, about 21st March and 23rd Sept.—*adj.* equinoc´tial, pertaining to the equinoxes, the time of the equinoxes, or to the regions about the equator.—*n.* the celestial equator or *equinoctial line*.—*adv.* equinoc´tially, in the direction of the equinox.—equinoctial gales, high gales popularly supposed to prevail about the times of the equinoxes—the belief is unsupported by observation. [L. *aequus*, equal, *nox*, *noctis*, night.]
equip, *i-kwip´*, *v.t.* to fit out: to furnish with everything needed:—*pr.p.* equipp´ing; *pa.t.* and *pa.p.* equipped´.—*n.* equipage (*ek´wi-pāj*), that with which one is equipped (*arch.*): apparatus required for any operation, e.g. making tea (*arch.*): a carriage and attendants: retinue.— *v.t.* (*obs.*) to equip.—*n.* equip´ment, the act of equipping: the state of being equipped: things used in equipping or furnishing: outfit. [Fr. *équiper*, prob. O.N. *skipa*, to set in order, *skip*, a ship; partly influenced by confusion with L. *equus*, horse.]
équipe, *ā-kēp*, (Fr.) in motor-racing and other sport, a team.
equipoise, *ek´wi-poiz*, *n.* a state of balance: a counterpoise.—*v.t.* to balance: to counterpoise. [L. *aequus*, equal, and poise.]
equipollent, *ē-*, *e-kwi-pol´ənt*, *adj.* having equal power or force: equivalent.—*n.* an equivalent. —*ns.* equipoll´ence, equipoll´ency. [L. *aequus*, equal, *pollēns*, *pollentis*, pr.p. of *pollēre*, to be strong, able.]
equiponderate, *ē-*, *e-kwi-pon´dər-āt*, *v.i.* to be equal in weight: to balance: equal in weight.—*n.* equipon´derance.—*adj.* equipon´derant. [L. *aequus*, equal, *pondus*, *ponderis*, weight.]
equipotent . . . to . . . equiprobability. See equi-.
Equisetum, *ek-wi-sē´təm*, *n.* the only surviving genus of the family Equisetā´ceae, constituting the Equiseti´nae or Equisetā´les, a class of pteridophytes, stiff herbaceous plants with almost leafless articulated and whorled stems and branches—also *horse-tail*.—*adjs.* equisetā´ceous; equisēt´ic; equisēt´iform. [L. *equus*, a horse, *sēta*, a bristle.]
equitation, *ek-wi-tā´shən*, *n.* the art of riding on horseback.—*adjs.* eq´uitant, riding: straddling, overlapping: of leaves, folded lengthwise over succeeding leaves. [L. *equitāre*, to ride— *equus*, a horse.]

**equity**, *ek-wi-ti, n.* right as founded on the laws of nature: moral justice, of which laws are the imperfect expression: the spirit of justice which enables us to interpret laws rightly: fairness: an equitable right: the value of property in excess of any charges upon it (*U.S.*): (in *pl.*) ordinary shares: (with *cap.*) British actors' trade-union.—*adj.* **eq'uitable,** possessing or showing or in accordance with equity: held or exercised in equity.—*n.* **eq'uitableness.**—*adv.* **eq'uitably.** [O.Fr. *equité*—L. *aequitās, -ātis*—*aequus,* equal.]

**equivalent,** *i-kwiv'ə-lənt, adj.* equal in value, power, meaning, etc.: interchangeable: of like combining value (*chem.*).—*n.* a thing equivalent: an equivalent weight (*chem.*).—*ns.* **equiv'alence, equiv'alency.** — *adv.* **equiv'alently.** — **equivalent weight** (*chem.*), that weight which displaces or combines with or otherwise represents a standard unit—atomic weight, or atomic weight divided by valence. [Fr.,—L. *aequus,* equal, *valēns, valentis,* pr.p. of *valēre,* to be worth.]

**equivalve.** See **equi-.**

**equivocal,** *i-kwiv'ə-kl, adj.* capable of meaning two or more things: of doubtful meaning: capable of a double explanation: suspicious: questionable.—*adv.* **equiv'ocally.**—*n.* **equiv'ocalness.**—*v.i.* **equiv'ocāte,** to use equivocal or doubtful words in order to mislead.—*ns.* **equivocā'tion; equiv'ocātor.**—*adj.* **equiv'ocatory,** containing or characterised by equivocation.—*ns.* **equivoke, equivoque** (*ek'wi-vōk*), an equivocal expression: equivocation: a quibble: a pun. [L. *aequus,* equal, and *vōx, vōcis,* the voice, a word.]

**er,** *ûr, interj.* expressing hesitation.

**-er,** *-ər, suff.* marks the agent (person or thing) designating persons according to occupation (e.g. writer), or place of abode (e.g. Londoner) (O.E. *-ere*). Some similar words, e.g. grocer, officer, are from Fr. *-ier* (L. *-arius*).

**era,** *ē'ra, n.* a series of years reckoned from a particular point, or that point itself: an important date: an age: a main division of geological time. [L.L. *aera,* a number, orig. counters, pieces of copper used in counting, pl. of *aes,* copper.]

**eradiate,** *i-, ē-rā'di-āt, v.t.* and *v.i.* to shoot out like a ray of light.—*n.* **eradiā'tion.** [L. *ē-,* from, *radius,* a ray.]

**eradicate,** *i-rad'i-kāt, v.t.* to pull up by the roots: to root out: to extirpate.—*adj.* **erad'icable.**—*adj.* **erad'icāted,** rooted up: of a tree, or part of a tree, torn up by the roots (*her.*).—*n.* **eradicā'tion,** the act of eradicating: state of being eradicated.—*adj.* **erad'icātive,** serving to eradicate or drive thoroughly away.—*n.* **erad'icātor.** [L. *ērādicāre, -ātum,* to root out—*ē,* from, *rādix, -icis,* a root.]

**erase,** *i-rāz', v.t.* to rub or scrape out: to efface: to destroy.—*adj.* **erā'sable.**—*adj.* **erased',** rubbed out: effaced: torn off, so as to leave jagged edges (*her.*).—*ns.* **erā'ser,** one who, or that which, erases, as ink-eraser; **erā'sion** (-*zhən*), **erase'ment, era'sure** (-*zhər*), the act of erasing: a rubbing out: scraping away: the place where something written has been rubbed out. [L. *ērādēre—ē,* from, *rādēre, rāsum,* to scrape.]

**Erastian,** *e-ras'ti-ən, -tyən, n.* a follower of Thomas *Erastus* (1524-83), a Swiss physician, who denied the church the right to inflict excommunication and disciplinary penalties: one who would subordinate the church jurisdiction to the state—a position not held by Erastus at all.—*adj.* relating to the Erastians or their doctrines.—*n.* **Eras'tianism,** control of church by state.

**Erato,** *er'ə-tō, n.* the Muse of amatory lyric poetry. [Gr. *Eratō.*]

**erbium,** *ûr'bi-əm, n.* a rare metal (Er; at. numb.

68), found in gadolinite, at **Ytt**erby, near Stockholm.

**erdgeist,** *ārt-gist,* (Ger.) earth-spirit.

**ere,** *ār, adv., prep.* and *conj.* before.—*advs.* **ere-long', ere long,** before long: soon; **erenow',** ere now, before this time; **erewhile',** formerly: some time before. [O.E. *ǣr;* cf. Du. *eer.*]

**ere.** Same as **ear** (2).

**Erebus,** *er'i-bəs, (myth.) n.* the dark and gloomy cavern between earth and Hades: the lower world, hell. [L.,—Gr. *Erebos.*]

**erect,** *i-rekt', adj.* upright: directed upward: right end up, not inverted: not decumbent (*bot.*): turgid and raised (*zool.*).—*v.t.* to set upright: to set up: to set at right angles: to raise: to build: to exalt: to establish.—*adj.* **erect'ed.**—*ns.* **erect'er, erect'or,** one who, or that which, erects or raises: a muscle which assists in erecting a part or an organ: an attachment to a compound microscope for making the image erect instead of inverted.—*adj.* **erect'ile** (-*il*), that may be erected.—*ns.* **erectility** (*e-, ē-rek-til'i-ti*); **erec'tion,** act of erecting: state of being erected: exaltation: anything erected: a building of any kind.—*adj.* **erect'ive,** tending to erect.—*adv.* **erect'ly.**—*n.* **erect'ness.** [L. *ērigēre, ērēctum,* to set upright—*ē,* from, *regēre,* to direct.]

**eremacausis,** *er-i-ma-kö'sis,* (*chem.*) *n.* very slow oxidation. [Gr. *ērema,* quietly, slowly, *kausis,* burning—*kaiein,* to burn.]

**eremic,** *e-rē'mik, adj.* belonging to deserts. [Gr. *erēmikos—erēmiā,* desert, solitude.]

**eremite,** *er'i-mit, n.* a recluse who lives apart, esp. from religious motives: a hermit.—*adjs.* **eremi'tal, eremitic** (-*mit'ik*), **-al.**—*n.* **er'emitism.** [L.L. *erēmita—*Gr. *erēmitēs—erēmos,* desert.]

**e re nata,** *ē rē nā'ta, ā rā nä'ta,* (L.L.) from the circumstances arisen, according to the exigencies of the case.

**erepsin,** *e-rep'sin, n.* an enzyme of the fresh intestine, acting upon casein, gelatine, etc. [L. *ēripēre, ēreptum—ē,* from, *rapēre,* to snatch.]

**erethism,** *er'e-thizm, n.* excitement or stimulation of an organ: abnormal irritability.—*adjs.* **erethis'mic, erethis'tic, erethit'ic.** [Gr. *erethismos.*]

**Erewhon,** *er'e-(h)won, n.* the imaginary country of Samuel Butler's satirical Utopian romances *Erewhon* (1872) and *Erewhon Revisited* (1901).—*n.* and *adj.* **Erewhō'nian.** [Formed from *nowhere* spelt backwards.]

**erf,** *ûrf,* (S. Afr.) *n.* a garden plot or small piece of ground:—*pl.* **er'ven.** [Du.; cf. O.E. *erfe,* inheritance.]

**erg,** *ûrg, n.* the unit of work in the centimetre-gramme-second system—that is, the quantity of work done when the point of operation of a force of one dyne is allowed to move one centimetre in the direction of the force.—*ns.* **er'gograph,** an instrument for measuring and recording muscular work; **er'gometer,** an instrument for measuring work done; **ergonom'ics,** study of man in relation to his working environment: adaptation of machines and general conditions to fit the individual so that he may work at maximum efficiency; **ergon'omist; ergopho'bia,** morbid dislike of work.—**erg'-nine', erg'-ten',** etc., an erg multiplied by ten to the power nine, ten, etc. [Gr. *ergon,* work.]

**ergates,** *ûr'gə-tēz,* **ergate,** *ûr'gāt, ns.* a worker ant, an undeveloped female.—*ns.* **ergatan'dromorph** (Gr. *andromorphos,* of male form), an ant combining characters of males and workers; **ergatan'er** (*ûr-gə-tā'nər, -tä'nər;* Gr. *anēr,* man), a worker-like wingless male ant; **ergatoc'racy** (Gr. *kratos,* power), rule by the workers; **ergatogyne** (-*ji'nē;* Gr. *gynē,* woman), a worker-like wingless female ant.—*adj.* **er'gatoid,** worker-

like, wingless but sexually perfect.—*n.* er'gatomorph, an ergatoid ant.—*adj.* ergatomorph'ic. [Gr. *ergatēs*, workman—*ergon*, work.]
ergo, *ûr'gō*, (*logic*) *adv.* therefore, used to introduce the conclusion of a syllogism.—*v.i.* er'gotise, -ize, to wrangle. [L. *ergō*, therefore.]
ergodic, *ər-god'ik*, *adj.* pertaining to the probability that in a system any state will occur again.—*n.* ergodic'ity (-*dis'*). [Gr. *ergon*, work, *hodos*, way.]
ergogram, ergonomics, etc. See erg.
ergon, *ûr'gən*, er'gon, (Gr.) work, business.
ergot, *ûr'got*, *n.* a disease of grasses (esp. rye) and sedges due to *Claviceps purpurea*: a seed so diseased.—*n.* ergos'terol, an unsaturated sterol got from ergot.—*v.t.* er'gotise, -ize, to affect with ergot or with ergotism.—*n.* er'gotism, poisoning caused by eating bread made of rye diseased with ergot. [Fr.]
eric, er'ik, *n.* the blood-fine paid by a murderer to his victim's family in old Irish law.—Also er'iach, er'ick. [Ir. *eiric*.]
Erica, er'i-kə, *n.* the heath genus.—*adjs.* ericaceous (er-i-kā'shəs), belonging to plants of the genus Erica, or its family Erica'ceae: heathlike; er'icoid, with heatherlike leaves. [L.,—Gr. *ereikē*, heath.]
Erigeron, e-rij'ə-ron, *n.* the flea-bane genus of composites. [Gr. *ērigerōn*, groundsel—*ēri*, early, *gerōn*, old.]
eringo. Same as eryngo.
erinite, er'i-nīt, *n.* a basic arsenate of copper found in Cornwall and Ireland. [*Erin*, Ireland.]
Erinys, e-ri'nis, *n.* a Fury:—*pl.* Erinyes (e-rin'i-ēz). [Gr. *Erinȳs*, pl. *Erinȳēs*.]
erio-, er-i-ō-, -o-, in composition, wool, fibre.—*ns.* Eriocaulon (-ō-kö'lon; Gr. *kaulos*, stalk), the pipewort genus, giving name to the Eriocaul-(on)ā'ceae, a family of monocotyledons, akin to the Bromelias; Eriōden'dron (Gr. *dendron*, tree), the silk-cotton genus of trees; eriometer (-om'ət-ər; Gr. *metron*, measure), an optical instrument for measuring small diameters, of fibres, etc.; Eriophorum (-of'ər-əm; Gr. *phoros*, carrying), the cotton-grass or cotton-sedge genus.—*adj.* eriophorous (-of'ər-əs), very cottony. [Gr. *erion*, wool.]
eristic, -al, er-is'tik, -al, *adj.* of or pertaining to controversy or disputatious reasoning. [Gr. *eristikos*—*eris*, strife.]
erk, ûrk, (airmen's slang) *n.* an aircraftsman. [From *airk*, for aircraftsman.]
erl-king, ûrl'-king, *n.* for German *erlkönig*, which was a mistranslation (alder-king) of the Danish *ellerkonge* (for *elverkonge*, king of the elves).
ermelin, ûr'mə-lin, *n.* arch. for ermine.
ermine, ûr'min, *n.* the stoat: a white fur, the stoat's winter coat in northern lands, used for the robes of judges and magistrates with the black tail-tip (or an imitation) attached.—*adj.* er'mined, adorned with ermine. [O.Fr. *ermine* (Fr. *hermine*), perh. from L. (*mūs*) *Armēnius*, lit. (mouse) of Armenia, whence it was brought to Rome; but acc. to some from O.H.G. *harmin* (Ger. *hermelin*), ermine-fur.]
ern, an old spelling (*Milt.*) of earn.
erne, ûrn, *n.* the eagle. [O.E. *earn*; cf. O.N. *örn*, Du. *arend*.]
erne, ûrn (Spens.). Same as earn (3), yearn.
Ernie, ûr'ni, *n.* the electronic machine which picks, by methods that allow full scope for chance, numbers to be used as winning numbers on premium bonds. [Abbreviation of electronic random number indicator equipment.]
erode, i-, e-rōd', *v.t.* to eat away, wear away: to form by wearing away.—*adjs.* erō'ded, erose (-rōs'), irregularly notched as if bitten.—*adj.* and *n.* erō'dent, caustic.—*n.* erosion (-rō'zhən), eating away, wearing down: the denuding action of weathering, water, ice, wind, etc. (*geol.*).—*adj.*

erosive (-rō'ziv). [L. *ē*, from, *rōděre*, *rōsum*, to gnaw.]
Erodium, e-rō'di-əm, *n.* the stork's-bill genus of the geranium family. [Gr. *erōdios*, a heron.]
erogenic, erogenous. See Eros.
Eros, *ēr'os* (though the initial E is short in Gr.), er'os, er'ōs, *n.* the Greek love-god, identified by the Romans with Cupid: a minor planet discovered in 1898, notable for its near approach to the earth.—*adj.* erotic (e-rot'ik), -al, pertaining to sexual love; amatory: amorous.—*n.* an amatory poem or composition.—*n.pl.* erot'ica, erotic literature.—*ns.* erot'icism (-*sizm*), amorous temperament or habit: erotism; er'otism, sexual desire: the manifestations of sex in its widest application.—*adj.* erotogenic (er-ət-ō-jen'ik), erotogenous (*oj'*), less correctly erogen'ic, erog'enous, productive of erotic desire or gratification.—*ns.* erōtomā'nia, morbid sexual passion; erōtomā'niac. [Gr. *Erōs*, -*ōtos*.]
erostrate, ē-ros'trāt, (*bot.*) *adj.* beakless. [L. *ē*, from, *rōstrum*, a beak.]
erotema, er-ō-tē'ma, eroteme, er'ō-tēm, erotesis, er-ō-tē'sis, *ns.* a rhetorical question.—*adj.* erotetic (-*tet'ik*), interrogatory. [Gr. *erōtēma*, *erōtēsis*—*erōtaein*, to question.]
erotic, erotism, etc. See Eros.
err, ûr, *v.i.* to wander (*arch.*): to wander from the right way (*arch.*): to go astray (*arch.*): to miss the mark: to be inaccurate: to make a mistake: to sin:—*pr.p.* erring (ûr'ing or er'ing); *pa.t.* and *pa.p.* erred (ûrd).—*adjs.* err'able (er'; *obs.*), capable of erring; errant (er'ənt), wandering: roving: quixotic: thorough (*obs.*; cf. arrant): erring.—*n.* a knight-errant.—*adv.* err'antly.—*n.* err'antry, an errant or wandering state: a rambling about like a knight-errant.—*adj.* erra'tic, wandering: having no certain course: not stationary: irregular, capricious, irregular or unpredictable in behaviour.—*n.* a wanderer: an erratic block or boulder.—*adj.* errat'ical.—*adv.* errat'ically.—*n.* errat'tum, an error in writing or printing, esp. one noted in a list in a book (*pl.* errā'ta).—*adj.* err'ing, wandering (*arch.*): straying from the truth or right conduct.—*n.* wandering (*arch.*): straying (*arch.*): making mistakes.—*adv.* err'ingly.—*adj.* erroneous (i-rō'ni-əs), erring: full of error: wrong: mistaken: wandering, straying (*arch.*).—*adv.* errō'neously.—*ns.* errō'neousness; error (er'ər), wandering, winding course (*arch.*): deviation from the right way (*arch.*): mistaken opinion: difference between a quantity obtained by observation and the true value: a blunder or mistake: wrong-doing; err'orist.—erratic block, a mass of rock transported by ice and deposited at a distance. [L. *errāre*, to stray; cog. with Ger. *irren*, and *irre*, astray.]
errand, er'ənd, *n.* a verbal message (*arch.*): a mission (*arch.*): a commission to say or do something usually involving a short journey: (in *pl.*) marketing (*dial.*).—err'and-boy, -girl.—a fool's errand, a sleeveless errand, a futile journey; make an errand, to invent a reason for going; once (yince, ance) errand (*Scot.*), for the express purpose and nothing else; run errands, to be sent to convey messages or perform small pieces of business. [O.E. *ǣrende*; O.N. *eyrindi*; prob. conn. with Goth. *āirus*, O.N. *ārr*, a messenger.]
errhine, er'in, *adj.* and *n.* sternutatory. [Gr. *errinon*—*en*, in, *rhis*, *rhinos*, the nose.]
ers, ûrs, *n.* the bitter vetch. [Fr.,—L. *ervum*.]
ersatz, ər-zats', er', *n.* a substitute: a supplementary reserve from which waste can be made good (*mil.*).—*adj.* substitute: fake. [Ger.]
Erse, ers, ûrs, *n.* the name given by Lowland Scots to the language of the people of the West Highlands, as being of Irish origin: now sometimes used for Irish Gaelic, as opposed to Scottish Gaelic. [Variant of Irish.]

**erst**, *ûrst*, *adv*. at first: formerly.—*adv.* **erst'-while**, **erstwhile'**, formerly.—*adj.* former. [O.E. *ǣrest*, superl. of *ǣr*. See **ere**.]

**erubescent**, *er-ōō-bes'ənt*, *adj*. growing red: blushing.—*ns*. **erubesc'ence**, **erubesc'ency**; **erubesc'ite**, the mineral bornite. [L. *ērubēscĕre*, to grow red; see **rubescent**, **ruby**.]

**eruciform**, *e-rōō'si-förm*, *adj*. like a caterpillar. [L. *ērūca*, caterpillar, *fōrma*, form.]

**eruct**, *i-rukt'*, **eructate**, *-āt*, *vs.t.* to belch out, as wind from the stomach.—*n.* **eructā'tion** (*ē-*). [L. *ēructāre*, *-ātum—ē*, from, *ructāre*, to belch forth.]

**erudite**, *er'ōō-dīt*, *-ū-*, *adj*. learned.—*n.* a learned person.—*adv.* **er'uditely.**—*n.* **erudī'tion**, state of being learned: knowledge gained by study: learning, esp. in literature. [L. *ērudītus*, *ērudīre*, *ērudītum*, to free from rudeness—*ē*, from, *rudis*, rude.]

**erupt**, *i-rupt'*, *v.i.* to break out or through, as a volcano.—*n.* **erup'tion**, a breaking or bursting forth: that which bursts forth: a breaking out of spots on the skin: the action of a volcano.—*adjs.* **erup'tional**; **erupt'ive**, breaking forth: attended by or producing eruption: produced by eruption.—*n.* **erupt'iveness.** [L. *ērumpĕre*, *ēruptum—ē*, from, *rumpĕre*, to break.]

**eryngo**, *e-ring'gō*, *n.* the candied root of sea-holly: the plant itself (Eryngium), a superficially thistle-like umbellifer. [Gr. *ēryngos.*]

**Erysimum**, *er-is'i-məm*, *n.* the treacle-mustard genus of Cruciferae. [Latinised from Gr. *ērўsĭmŏn*, hedge-mustard.]

**erysipelas**, *er-i-sip'i-ləs*, *n.* an inflammatory disease, generally in the face, marked by a bright redness of the skin.—*adj.* **erysipelatous** (*-el'ə-təs*). [Gr.; prob.—root of *erythros*, red, *pella*, skin.]

**erythema**, *er-i-thē'mə*, *n.* redness of the skin.—*adjs.* **erythemat'ic**, **erythem'atous**. [Gr. *erythēma*—*erythainein*, to redden—*erythros*, red.]

**erythr(o)-**, *er-ith-r(ō)-*, in composition, red.—*ns.* **Erythri'na**, the kaffir-boom genus of Papilionaceae, tropical and subtropical trees with brilliant red flowers; **eryth'rism**, red colouring, esp. exceptional or abnormal; **eryth'rite**, a reddish hydrous arsenate of cobalt.—*adj.* **erythrit'ic.**—*ns.* **eryth'rocyte** (Gr. *kytos*, case), a red blood corpuscle; **erythromycin** (*-mī'sin*; Gr. *mўkēs*, fungus), an antibiotic similar to penicillin; **erythropoiesis** (*-poi-ēs'is*; Gr. *poiēsis*, making), formation of red blood cells. [Gr. *erythros*, red.]

**erziehungsroman**, *er-tsē'ōŏngs-rō-män'* (Ger.). Same as **bildungsroman**.

**es**, *es*, *n.* the nineteenth letter of the alphabet (S, s); anything of that shape.—Also **ess**.

**escalade**, *es-kə-lād'*, *n.* the scaling of the walls of a fortress by means of ladders.—Also **escalā'dō** (for Sp. *escalada*).—*v.t.* to scale: to mount and enter by means of ladders.—*v.i.* **es'calate**, to increase rapidly in scale or intensity.—Also *v.t.—n.* **escalā'tion.**—*n.* **es'calātor**, a moving staircase.—**escalator clause**, a clause in an agreement allowing for adjustment up or down according to change in circumstances, as in cost of material in a work contract or in cost of living in a wage agreement. [Fr.,—Sp. *escalada—escala*, a ladder—L. *scāla*.]

**escalier**, *es-ka-lyā*, (Fr.) staircase; **escalier dérobé** (*dā-ro-bā*), private staircase.

**Escallonia**, *es-kal-ōn'i-ə*, a South American genus of shrubs of the Saxifrage family. [*Escallon*, the discoverer.]

**escallop**, *is-kal'əp*, *n.* a variant of **scallop**.—*adj.* **escall'oped** (*her.*), covered with scallop-shells.

**escalop**. A variant of **escallop** or **scallop** except in heraldry.

**escamotage**, *es-ka-mo-täzh*, (Fr.) juggling.

**escape**, *is-kāp'*, *v.t.* to free oneself from: to pass out of danger from: to evade, elude.—*v.i.* to come off or come through in safety: to emerge into or gain freedom: to flee: to slip out: to issue: to leak.—*n.* act of escaping: a means of escaping: flight: flight from reality: an outlet: a leakage: an accidental or inadvertent emission: an outburst: a sally: a prank (*obs.*): a venial offence (*obs.*): a transgression (*obs.*): a person or thing that has escaped, esp. a garden plant maintaining itself wild.—*adj.* of literature, providing escape from reality: of a clause in an agreement, defining the conditions under which a party is relieved of obligation.—*adj.* **escap'able.**—*ns.* **escapade** (*es-ka-pād'*), an escape (*arch.*): a mischievous adventure; **escapado** (*-ä'dō*), an escaped evil-doer: an escapade (Sp. *escapada*); **escapee'**, one who has escaped, e.g. from prison.—*adj.* **escape'less.**—*n.* **escape'ment**, an escape: part of a timepiece connecting the wheelwork with the pendulum or balance, and allowing a tooth to escape at each vibration: the clearance in a pianoforte between the string and the hammer after it has struck the string, while the key is held down; **escap'ism**; **escāp'ist**, one who seeks escape, esp. from reality.—Also *adj.*—*ns.* **escapol'ogist**; **escapol'ogy**, the study of methods of escape from any sort of constraint or confinement and the putting into practice of these methods: (*loosely*) escapism.—**escape mechanism** (*psych.*), a mental process by which one evades the unpleasant; **escape valve**, a valve to let steam, etc., escape when wanted; **escape wheel**, the wheel that the pallets act upon in a clock. [O.Fr. *escaper* (Fr. *échapper*)—L.L. *ex cappā*, (lit) out of one's cape or cloak.]

**escargot**, *es-kar-gō*, (Fr.) a snail.

**escarmouche**, *e-skär'mōōsh*, (*obs.*) *n.* a skirmish. [Fr.]

**escarole**, *es-ka-rōl*, *-röl*, *n.* a broad-leaved, non-curly endive. [Fr.]

**escarp**, *is-kärp'*, *v.t.* to make into a scarp or sudden slope.—*n.* a scarp or steep slope: the side of the ditch next the rampart (*fort.*).—*n.* **escarp'ment**, the precipitous side of a hill or rock: escarp. [Fr. *escarper*, to cut down steep, from root of **scarp**.]

**eschalot**. See **shallot**.

**eschar**, *es'kär*, *n.* a slough or portion of dead or disorganised tissue, esp. an artificial slough produced by caustics.—*adj.* **escharot'ic**, tending to form an eschar: caustic.—*n.* a caustic substance. [L.,—Gr. *escharā*, a hearth, mark of a burn.]

**eschatology**, *es-kə-tol'ə-ji*, (*theol.*) *n.* the doctrine of the last or final things, as death, judgment, the state after death.—*adjs.* **eschatolog'ic**, **-al.**—*n.* **eschatol'ogist**. [Gr. *eschatos*, last, *logos*, a discourse.]

**escheat**, *is-chēt'*, *n.* property that falls to the feudal lord or to the state for want of an heir, or by forfeiture: plunder, gain (*obs.*; *Spens.* **excheat'**).—*v.t.* to confiscate.—*v.i.* to fall to the lord of the manor or the state.—*adj.* **escheat'able.**—*ns.* **escheat'age**, **escheat'ment**; **escheat'or**, an official who watched over escheats. [O.Fr. *eschete—escheoir* (Fr. *échoir*)—L. *ex*, from, *cadĕre*, to fall.]

**eschew**, *is-chōō'*, *v.t.* to shun: to flee from (*obs.*): to abstain from. [O.Fr. *eschever*; cog. with Ger. *scheuen*, to shun.]

**Eschscholtzia**, *e-sholt'si-ə*, *n.* a genus of Papaveraceae, including the Californian poppy, a showy garden annual. [J. F. von *Eschscholtz*, a member of the expedition that discovered the plant in 1821.]

**esclandre**, *es-klä-dr'*, *n.* notoriety: any unpleasantness. [Fr.,—L. *scandalum*.]

**escolar**, *es-kō-lär'*, *n.* an Atlantic and Southern fish of spectacled appearance. [Sp., scholar.]

**escopette**, *es-kō-pet'*, (*U.S.*) *n.* a carbine. [Sp. *escopeta*.]

**escort**, *es'kört*, *n.* a person or persons, ship or ships, etc., accompanying another or others for protection, guidance, or merely courtesy: an armed guard: a man who accompanies a woman on an evening out: a member of an aircraft, etc., crew whose duty is to look after children travelling alone: attendance.—Also used as *adj.*—*v.t.* **escort'**, to attend as escort.—*n.* **escort'age.**—**escort carrier**, a small aircraft-carrier used for escorting naval convoys or in support of military landings. [Fr. *escorte*—It. *scorta*—*scorgere*, to guide—L. *ex*, out, *corrigĕre*, to set right.]

**escot**, *es-kot'*, (*Shak.*) *v.t.* to pay for, to maintain. [O.Fr. *escoter*, *escot*, a tax; of Gmc. origin; cf. **scot** (1), **shot** (2).]

**escribano**, *ā-skrē-bä-nō*, (Sp.) a notary.

**escribe**, *ē-skrīb'*, *v.t.* to describe (e.g. a triangle) so as to touch one side externally, the others (produced) internally. [L. *ē*, out, *scrībĕre*, write.]

**escritoire**, *es-krē-twär'*, *n.* a writing-desk.—*adj.* **escritō'rial.** [Fr. *escritoire*—L.L. *scriptōrium*—L. *scrībĕre*, *scriptum*, to write.]

**escroc**, *es-krō*, (Fr.) a swindler.

**escroll, escrol**, *es-krōl'*, *n.* an escrow: a scroll (*her.*).—*n.* **escrow** (*es-krō'*), a deed in the hands of a third party, to take effect when a condition is fulfilled. [A.Fr. *escroele*, *escroe*; see **scroll, scrow.**]

**escuage**, *es'kū-ij*, *n.* scutage. [A.Fr.; see **scutage.**]

**escudo**, *es-kōō'dō*, *n.* a coin or currency unit of various kinds, in Portugal one milreis. [Port. and Sp., shield.]

**Esculapian.** See **Aesculapian.**

**esculent**, *es'kū-lənt*, *adj.* eatable: fit to be used for food by man.—*n.* something that is eatable. [L. *esculentus*, eatable—*esca*, food—*edĕre*, to eat.]

**escutcheon**, *es-kuch'ən*, *n.* a shield on which a coat of arms is represented: a family shield: the part of a vessel's stern bearing her name: a shield-shaped object or ornament, etc., as a shield over a keyhole.—*adj.* **escutch'eoned**, having an escutcheon.—**a blot on the escutcheon**, a stain on one's good name; **escutcheon of pretence**, an escutcheon placed with the arms of an heiress in the centre of her husband's coat. [O.Fr. *escuchon*—L. *scūtum*, a shield.]

**esemplastic**, *es-əm-plas'tik*, *adj.* unifying.—*n.* **esem'plasy** (*es-em'plə-si*), the unifying power of imagination. [Gr. *es*, into, *hen* (neut.), one, *plastikos*, moulding.]

**esile**. Same as **eisel(l).**

**esker**, *esk'ər*, (*geol.*) *n.* a kame, or ridge of gravel and sand laid down by a subglacial stream or one which issues from a retreating glacier. [Ir. *eiscir*, a ridge.]

**Eskimo**, *es'ki-mō*, *n.* and *adj.* one of a people inhabiting arctic America with its islands, Greenland, and the nearest Asiatic coast: their language:—*pl.* **Es'kimo, -s.**—**Eskimo dog**, one of a breed of powerful dogs, with a double coat of hair, widely distributed in the Arctic regions, and indispensable for drawing sledges; **Eskimo roll** (*canoeing*), a complete roll-over under water. [Prob. from an Indian word meaning eaters of raw flesh.]

**esloin, esloyne**, *es-loin'*. See **eloin.**

**esne**, *ez'ni*, (*hist.*) *n.* a domestic slave in O.E. times. [O.E.]

**esnecy**, *es'na-si*, (*obs.*) *n.* the eldest daughter's right of first choice in dividing an inheritance. [O.Fr. *aisneece* (Fr. *aînesse*).]

**esophagus.** U.S. spelling of **oesophagus.**

**esoteric**, *es-ō-ter'ik*, *adj.* inner: secret: mysterious: taught to a select few—opp. to *exoteric* (*phil.*).—*n.pl.* **esoter'ica**, esoteric objects, etc.—*adv.* **esoter'ically.**—*ns.* **esoter'icism** (*-i-sizm*), **esoterism** (*es-ot'ər-izm*), the holding of esoteric opinions; **es'otery**, secret doctrine.—

**esoteric Buddhism** (see **theosophy**). [Gr. *esōterikos*—*esōterō*, comp. of *esō*, *eisō*, within.]

**espada**, *es-pä'dha*, (Sp.) a sword: a matador.

**espadrille**, *es-pə-dril'*, *n.* a rope-soled shoe. [Fr.,—Prov. *espardillo*—*espart*, esparto.]

**espagnolette**, *es-pan-yō-let'*, *n.* the fastening of a French window. [Fr., dim. of *espagnol*, Spanish.]

**espalier**, *es-pal'yər*, *n.* a lattice-work of wood to train trees on: a fruit-tree trained on stakes: a row of trees so trained (*obs.*).—*v.t.* to train as an espalier. [Fr.,—It. *spalliera*, a support for the shoulders—*spalla*, a shoulder; cf. **epaulet.**]

**esparto**, *es-pär'tō*, *n.* a strong grass (*Stipa tenacissima*, and others) grown in Spain, N. Africa, etc., and used for making paper, baskets, cordage, etc. [Sp.,—L. *spartum*—Gr. *sparton*, a kind of rope.]

**especial**, *is-pesh'l*, *adj.* special: particular: principal: distinguished.—*adv.* **espec'ially.**—in **especial**, in particular. [O.Fr.,—L. *speciālis*—*speciēs*, species.]

**esperance**, *es'pər-əns*, (*Shak.*) *n.* hope. [Fr. *espérance*—L. *spērāre*. to hope.]

**Esperanto**, *es-pər-an'tō*, *n.* an international language devised by Dr Zamenhof, published 1887.—Also *adj.*—*n.* **Esperan'tist**, a speaker of Esperanto. [Inventor's pseudonym, the hoping one.]

**espial.** See **espy.**

**espiègle**, *es-pē-eg'l'*, *adj.* roguish, frolicsome: arch.—*n.* **espièg'lerie**, roguishness: frolicsomeness. [Fr.,—Ger. *Eulenspiegel*; see **owl.**]

**espionage**, *es-pyon-äzh'*, *es'pi-ə-nij*, *es-pī'ə-nij*, *n.* spying: use of spies. [Fr. *espionner*—*espion*, spy.]

**esplanade**, *es-plə-nād'*, *n.* a level space between a citadel and the first houses of the town: any level space for walking or driving in. [Fr.,—Sp. *esplanada*—L. *explānāre*—*ex*, out, *plānus*, flat.]

**espouse**, *is-powz'*, *v.t.* to give or take in marriage or betrothal: to take upon oneself or embrace, as a cause.—*ns.* **espous'al**, the act of espousing or betrothing: the taking upon oneself as a cause: (*pl.*) a contract or mutual promise of marriage: a wedding: a formal betrothal; **espous'er.** [O.Fr. *espouser* (Fr. *épouser*)—L. *spōnsāre*, to betroth—*spondēre*, *spōnsum*, to vow.]

**espresso**, *es-pres'ō*, *n.* a form of coffee-making machine giving high extraction under pressure: coffee so made.—Also *adj.*, esp. of a type of coffee bar. [It., pressed.]

**esprit**, *es-prē*, *n.* wit, liveliness.—**esprit de corps** (*es-prē də kor*), regard for the honour of the body to which one belongs: loyalty of a member to the whole; **esprit de l'escalier** (*də-les-kal-yā*), thinking of an apt or witty retort after the opportunity of making it is past; **esprit fort** (*for*), a free-thinker. [Fr. *esprit*, spirit, *de*, of, *corps*, body, *escalier*, staircase, *fort*, strong.]

**esprit follet**, *es-prē fo-le*, (Fr.) mischievous goblin.

**espy**, *es-pī'*, *v.t.* to watch: to see at a distance: to catch sight of: to observe: to discover unexpectedly:—*pr.p.* **espy'ing**; *pa.t.* and *pa.p.* **espied**; *3rd pers. sing.* **espies'.**—*n.* **espi'al**, the act of espying: observation. [O.Fr. *espier* (Fr. *épier*)—*scūtum*, a shield.]

**Esquimau**, *es'ki-mō* (*pl.* **Esquimaux**, *es'ki-mōz*), a French spelling of **Eskimo.**

**esquire**, *es-kwīr'*, sometimes *es'-*, *n.* orig. a squire or shield-bearer: an attendant on a knight (*arch.*): a landed proprietor: a title of dignity next below a knight: a gentleman acting as escort: a general title of respect in addressing letters. [O.Fr. *esquier* (Fr. *écuyer*)—L. *scūtārius*—*scūtum*, a shield.]

**esquisse**, *es-kēs*, (Fr.) sketch, outline.

**ess**, *es*, see **es.**—**collar of esses**, a chain of links (also written SS) in the form of the letter S, worn by various dignitaries.

**essay**, *es'ā*, *n.* an attempt: a tentative effort: a first draft (*arch.*): a trial (*arch.*): an experiment

fāte, fär; mē, hûr (her); mīne; mōte, för; mūte; mōōn, fōōt; dhen (then)

(*arch.*): a written composition less elaborate than a treatise.—*v.t.* **essay'**, to try: to attempt: to make experiment of (*arch.*):—*pr.p.* **essay'ing;** *pa.t.* and *pa.p.* **essayed'.**—*ns.* **essay'er; ess'ayist,** one who essays: a writer of essays; **essayette'**, a little essay.—*adjs.* **ess'ayish; essayis'tic.** [O.Fr. *essai*—L. *exagium*, weighing—*exagēre*, to try, examine.]

**esse,** *es'i, n.* actual existence: essence.—**in esse,** in existence, opposed to *in posse*, in potentiality. [L. *esse*, to be.]

**essence,** *es'əns, n.* the inner distinctive nature of anything: the qualities which make any object what it is: a being: an alcoholic solution of a volatile or essential oil: a perfume of such composition: the extracted virtues of any drug: a liquid having the properties of the substance from which it is got.—*adj.* **essential** (*is-, es-en'shl*), relating to, constituting, or containing the essence: necessary to the existence of a thing: indispensable or important in the highest degree: highly rectified: pure: of e.g. disease, having no known cause.—*n.* something necessary: a leading principle.—*n.* **essentiality** (*is-en-shi-al'i-ti*), the quality of being essential; an essential quality or element.—*adv.* **essen'tially.** — *n.* **essen'tialness.** — **essential minerals,** those whose presence is considered necessary to entitle a rock to the name it bears—opp. to *accessory* minerals; **essential oils,** oils forming the odorous principles of plants, also called *ethereal oils, volatile oils;* **essential organs** (*bot.*), stamens and carpels.—**of the essence,** of the utmost importance. [Fr.,—L. *essentia*—*essēns, -entis,* assumed pr.p. of *esse*, to be.]

**Essene,** *es-ēn', es'ēn, n.* one of a small religious fraternity among the ancient Jews leading retired ascetic lives and holding property in common.—*n.* **Ess'enism.** [Gr. *essēnos;* origin doubtful.]

**essive,** *es'iv,* (*gram.*) *adj.* denoting a state of being. —*n.* the essive case. [Finn. *essivi*—L. *esse,* to be.]

**essoin, essoyne,** *es-oin',* n. excuse for not appearing in court (*law*): excuse (*Spens.*).—*n.* **essoin'er.** [O.Fr. *essoine* (Fr. *exoine*), *es*—L. *ex,* out of, *soin,* care.]

**essonite,** *es'ən-it,* **hessonite,** *hes'ən-it, n.* cinnamon-stone. [Gr. *hēssōn,* inferior (i.e. in hardness, to hyacinth which it resembles).]

**establish,** *is-, es-tab'lish, v.t.* to settle or fix: to set up: to place in fixed position, possession, or power: to make good: to confirm (*arch.*): to prove: to ordain: to found: to set up in business: to institute by law as the recognised state church, and to recognise officially.—*adj.* **estab'lished,** fixed: ratified: instituted by law and backed by the state.—*ns.* **estab'lisher; estab'lishment,** act of establishing: fixed state: that which is established: a permanent civil or military force: permanent staff: one's residence, household, and style of living: a business: a settlement: the church established by law: (*cap.*) *derog.*) the class in a community, or in a field of activity, who hold power, usu. because they are linked socially, and who are usu. considered to have conservative opinions and conventional values.—*adj.* **establishmentār'ian,** maintaining the principle of church establishment.—Also *n.* [O.Fr. *establir,* pr.p. *establissant*—L. *stabilire*—*stabilis,* firm—*stāre,* to stand.]

**estacade,** *es-tə-kād', n.* a dike of piles in a morass, river, etc., against an enemy. [Fr.,—Sp. *estacada.*]

**estafette,** *es-tə-fet', n.* a military courier or express. [Fr.,—It. *staffetta*—*staffa,* stirrup; cf. O.H.G. *stapho,* a step.]

**estaminet,** *es-tam'ē-nā,* a small café. [Fr.]

**estancia,** *es-tän'sya, n.* a Spanish-American cattle-estate.—*n.* **estanciero** (*-syē'rō*), a farmer. [Sp., station—L. *stāre,* to stand.]

**estate,** *is-, es-tāt', n.* state (*arch.*): rank: worldly condition: total possessions: property, esp. landed: a landed property, esp. of some size: an order or class of men in the body politic: a chair or canopy of state, or a dais (*obs.*).—*v.t.* to give an estate to (*arch.*): to bestow upon (*arch.*). —**estate agent,** manager of landed property: intermediary in the sale of landed property; **estate car,** a car of large enough interior for both passengers and goods; **estates'man** (*N. of England*), statesman.—**man's estate,** the state of manhood; **the estates of the realm** are three—Lords Spiritual, Lords Temporal, and Commons: often misused for the legislature—king, lords, and commons.—The ancient parliament of Scotland consisted of the king and the **three estates**—viz.: (1) archbishops, bishops, abbots, and mitred priors; (2) the barons and the commissioners of shires and stewartries; (3) the commissioners from the royal burghs;—in France, the nobles, clergy, and **third estate** (*tiers état*) remained separate down to 1780; the **fourth estate** (*coll.*), the press; **real estate** (see **real** (1)). [O.Fr. *estat* (Fr. *état*)—L. *status,* a state.]

**esteem,** *is-, es-tēm', v.t.* to set a high estimate or value on: to regard with respect or friendship: to consider or think.—*n.* high estimation or value: favourable regard: estimation of worth. —*adj.* **esteemed',** respected: in commercial correspondence, a colourless complimentary word. —*adj.* **es'timable,** that can be estimated or valued: worth of esteem: deserving our good opinion.—*adv.* **es'timably.**—*v.t.* **es'timate,** to judge of the worth of: to ascertain how much is present of: to calculate.—*n.* reputation (*Shak.*): a valuing in the mind: judgment or opinion of the worth or size of anything: a rough calculation: a preliminary statement of the probable cost of a proposed undertaking: estimation.—*n.* **estimā'tion,** act of estimating: a reckoning of value: esteem, honour: importance (*arch.*): conjecture.—*adj.* **es'timātive.**—*n.* **es'timātor.**—**hold in estimation,** to esteem highly.—**the estimates,** accounts laid before parliament, etc., showing the probable expenditure for the year. [Fr. *estimer*—L. *aestimāre.*]

**ester,** *es'tər, n.* a compound formed by the condensation of an alcohol and an acid, with elimination of water.—*n.* **esterifica'tion** (*-ter-*).—*v.t.* **ester'ify** (or *es'*). [Invented by Leopold Gmelin (1788-1853).]

**esthesia, esthesiogen,** etc. U.S. spelling of **aesthesia,** etc.

**Est(h)onian,** *es-t(h)ō'ni-ən, adj.* pertaining to *Est(h)onia,* a Baltic republic, till 1918 a province of Russia, admitted in 1940 as a republic of the U.S.S.R.—*n.* a native or citizen thereof: its language.—*n.* **Esth,** an Esthonian of the original Finnish stock.

**estimate, estimation.** See **esteem.**

**estival,** etc. U.S. spelling of **aestival,** etc.

**estoc,** *es-tok', n.* a short sword. [Fr.]

**estoile,** *es-twäl',* (*her.*) *n.* a star with wavy points. [O.Fr. *estoile* (Fr. *étoile*), a star.]

**Estonian.** See **Est(h)onian.**

**estop,** *es-top', v.t.* to stop or bar (*arch.*): to hinder, preclude (*law*):—*pr.p.* **estopp'ing;** *pa.t.* and *pa.p.* **estopped'.**—*n.* **estopp'age,** the state of being estopped; **estopp'el,** a conclusive admission, which cannot be denied by the party whom it affects. [O.Fr. *estoper*—*estoupe*—L. *stuppa,* flax; see **stop, stuff.**]

**estover,** *es-tō'vər, n.* a right to necessaries allowed by law, as wood to a tenant for necessary repairs, etc.—common of estovers, the right of taking necessary wood from another's estate for household use and the making of implements of industry. [O.Fr. *estover,* to be necessary, necessaries.]

estrade, *es-träd'*, *n.* a low platform. [Fr.,—Sp. *estrado.*]

estramazone. Same as stramazon.

estrange, *is-tränj'*, *v.t.* to cut off, remove: to alienate, esp. from friendship: to divert from original use or possessor.—*adj.* estranged', alienated: disaffected.—*ns.* estrang'edness; estrange'ment; estrang'er. [O.Fr. *estranger* (Fr. *étranger*)—L. *extrāneāre*—*extrāneus*; see strange.]

estrang(h)elo, *es-trang'gə-lō*, *n.* a cursive form of the old Syriac alphabet.—Also *adj.* [Syriac, perh. —Gr. *strongylos*, round.]

estrapade, *es-tra-pād'*, *n.* a horse's attempt to throw its rider. [Fr.]

estray, *e-strā'*, *n.* a beast found within a manor or lordship, wandering from its owner.—*v.i.* to stray. [See astray.]

estreat, *es-trēt'*, (*law*) *n.* a true extract, copy, or note of some original writing or record, esp. of fines and amercements to be levied by bailiffs or other officers.—*v.t.* to extract from the records of a court, as a forfeited recognisance: to levy, exact. [O.Fr. *estraite*—L. *extrahēre*—*ex*, from, *trahēre* to draw; see extract.]

estrepe, *es'trēp*, (*law*) *v.t.* to commit waste (as a tenant) on lands, e.g. cutting down trees, etc.— *n.* estrepe'ment. [M.Fr. *estreper*—L. *exstirpāre*, to root out.]

estrich, *es'trich*, estridge, *es'trij*, (*obs.*) *n.* the ostrich.

estro, *es'trō*, (It.) enthusiasm, height of poetic inspiration.

estrogen, estrum, etc. U.S. spellings of oestrogen, oestrum, etc.

estuary, *es'tū-ər-i*, *n.* the wide lower tidal part of a river.—*adjs.* estūarial (*-ā'ri-əl*), estūā'rian, es'tūarine (*-ə-rin*). [L. *aestuārium*—*aestus*, burning, boiling, commotion, tide.]

esurient, *es-ū'ri-ənt*, *adj.* hungry: rapacious.—*n.* esū'rience, esū'riency, greedy hunger: needy rapacity. [L. *ēsuriēns*, *-entis*, pr.p. of *ēsurīre*, to be hungry—desiderative of *edere*, to eat.]

eta, *ē'ta*, *ā'ta*, *n.* the seventh letter of the Greek alphabet, long e (H, η): as a numeral η' = 8, ,η = 8000.—*n.* etacism (*ā'ta-sizm*), pronunciation of eta as close e (in this dictionary represented as ā)—opposed to *itacism*. [Gr. *ēta*.]

etaerio, *et-ē'ri-ō*, (*bot.*) *n.* an aggregated fruit, a group of achenes or drupels. [Gr. *hetaireiā*, association.]

étage, *ā-täzh*, (Fr.) floor, storey; bel étage (*q.v.*) is not a French usage.

étagère, *ā-ta-zher*, (Fr.) an ornamental stand of shelves for bric-à-brac, etc.

étalage, *ā-ta-läzh*, (Fr.) display, esp. of goods in a shop window.

et alia (alii), *et ā'li-ə, a'li-a* (*ā'li-ī, a'li-ē*), (L.) and other things (people); abbrev. et al.

etalon, *āt'əl-on*, *n.* an interferometer consisting of an air film enclosed between half-silvered plane-parallel glass or quartz plates. [Fr.,—M.Fr. *estalon*, standard of weights and measures— O.Fr. *estal*, place.]

étape, *ā-tap*, (Fr.) a storehouse: a halting-place: a day's march: rations: forage.

état, *ā-ta*, (Fr.) state, rank; état-major, *ma-zhor*, the staff of an army, regiment, etc.

États-Généraux, *ā-ta zhā-nā-rō*, (Fr.) the States-General.

et cetera, et *set'ər-a* usually written etc. or &c., a Latin phrase meaning and the rest: and so on.— *n.* something in addition, which can easily be understood.

etch, *ech*, *v.t.* and *v.i.* to design on metal, glass, etc. by eating out the lines with an acid: to eat away, corrode.—*ns.* etch'er, one who etches; etch'ing, the act or art of etching or engraving: the impression from an etched plate.—etching ground, the coating of wax or varnish on a plate prepared

for etching; etching needle, a fine-pointed steel instrument used in etching. [Ger. *ätzen*, to corrode by acid; from same root as Ger. *essen*. See eat.]

eten, ettin, *et'ən*, (*arch.*) *n.* a giant. [O.E. *eten*, *eoten*; O.N. *jötunn*.]

etepimeletic, *et-ep-i-mel-et'ik*, (*animal behaviour*) *adj.* of a type of social behaviour shown by young animals to elicit epimeletic behaviour.

eternal, *i-*, *ē-túr'nl*, *adj.* without beginning or end of existence: everlasting: ceaseless: unchangeable.—(*arch.*) eterne'.—*v.t.* eter'nalise, -ize, eter'nise, -ize (or *ē'tər-niz*), to make eternal: to immortalise with fame.—*n.* eter'nalist, one who thinks that matter has existed from eternity.— *adv.* eter'nally.—*n.* eter'nity, eternal duration: the state or time after death.—eternity ring, a ring set all round with stones, emblematic of everlasting continuity.—The Eternal, an appellation of God; the Eternal City, Rome; the eternities, the eternal reality or truth. [Fr. *éternel*—L. *aeternus*—*aevum*, an age.]

etesian, *e-tē'zh(y)ən*, *-zyən*, *adj.* periodical: blowing at stated seasons, as certain winds, esp. the north-west winds of summer in the Aegean. [L. *etēsius*—Gr. *etēsios*, annual—*etos*, a year.]

eth, *edh*, *edh*, *n.* a letter (Ð ð), a barred D, used in Old English, without distinction for thorn, for voiced or voiceless th, in Icelandic and by phoneticians set apart for the voiced sound, thorn standing for the voiceless.

ethal, *ē'thal.* Same as cetyl alcohol.

ethane, *eth'ān*, *n.* a hydrocarbon ($H_3C \cdot CH_3$) of the methane series.—*n.* eth'anol, ethyl alcohol. —*n.pl.* ethanol'amines, derivatives of ethanol used in detergents and cosmetics. [ether.]

ethe. See eath.

ethene. See under ethyl.

Etheostoma, *e-thi-os'to-ma*, *n.* a genus of small American freshwater fishes akin to perch.—*adj.* etheos'tomine. [Gr. *ētheein*, to sift, *stoma*, mouth.]

ether, *ē'thər*, *n.* the clear, upper air: a medium, not matter, assumed in 19th cent. to fill all space and transmit electromagnetic waves—(in these senses also aether): a colourless transparent, volatile liquid ($C_2H_5 \cdot O \cdot C_2H_5$) of great mobility and high refractive power, fragrant odour and a fiery, passing to a cooling, taste (specifically ethyl ether or diethyl ether): extended to the class of compounds in which two alkyl groups are united with an oxygen atom.—*adj.* ethē'real, ethē'rial, consisting of ether: heavenly: airy: spirit-like.—*n.* ethērealisā'tion.—*v.t.* ethē'realise, -ize, to convert into ether, or the fluid ether: to render spirit-like.—*n.* ethēreal'ity.—*adj.* ethē're-ally.—*adjs.* ethē'reous (*Milt.*), etheric (*ē-ther'ik*), -al, ethereal.—*n.* etherificā'tion (*-ther-*).—*ns.* ethē'rion, a very light gas once supposed to exist in air; ethērisā'tion, *-z-*.—*v.t.* ethē'rise, -ize, to convert into ether: to stupefy with ether.— *n.* ethērism, the condition induced by using ether: addiction to the taking of ether; e'thērist, one who takes or who administers ether; etherōmā'nia, addiction to the ether habit; etheromā'niac.—ethereal oils, essential oils. [L. *aethēr*—Gr. *aithēr*, the heavens—*aithein*, to light up.]

ethercap. See ettercap.

ethic, *eth'ik*, (now *rare*) *adj.* ethical.—*n.* (more commonly eth'ics) the science of morals, that branch of philosophy which is concerned with human character and conduct: a system of morals, rules of behaviour: a treatise on morals. —*adj.* eth'ical, relating to morals, the science of ethics, professional standards of conduct: denoting a proprietary pharmaceutical not advertised to the general public.—*adj.* eth'ically. —*v.t.* eth'icise, -ize (*-siz*), to make ethical: to treat as ethical.—*ns.* eth'icism, tendency to moralise or ethicise; **eth'icist**, one versed in ethics: one who detaches ethics from religion.—**ethical**, (still often) **ethic**, dative, dative implying an indirect interest in the matter, used to give a livelier tone to the sentence (e.g. *He could swear me as fluently as any bargee*); **ethical** genitive, genitive implying interest (e.g. *talking as usual about his Roman heating system*; see **your**); **situation ethics**, ethics based on the proposition that no conduct is good or bad in itself and that one must determine what is right or wrong in each situation as it arises. [Gr. *ēthikos—ēthos*, custom, character.]

**Ethiopian**, *ē-thi-ō'pi-ən*, *adj.* pertaining to Ethiopia or its natives: pertaining to the countries south of Egypt inhabited by Negro races: Negro.—*n.* a native of Ethiopia: a Negro.—*n.* (*arch.*) **E'thiop** (-*op.*).—*adj.* **Ethiöp'ic**, belonging to Ethiopia, to the Ethiopian church, or to a group of Semitic languages including Ge'ez, Amharic, Tigre.—*n.* the Ge'ez language.—*n.* **e'thiöps**, in old chemistry, a name given to various, dull, dingy, or black compounds.—Also **Aethiopian**, etc.—**Ethiopian region**, a biological region consisting of Africa and Arabia south of the Tropic of Cancer. [Gr. *Aithiops—aithein*, to burn, *ops*, *ōps*, face.]

**ethmoid**, *eth'moid*, *adj.* like a sieve.—*adj.* **ethmoid'al**.—**ethmoid bone**, one of the bones forming the anterior part of the brain-case. [Gr. *ēthmos*, a sieve, and *eidos*, form.]

**ethnic, -al**, *eth'nik*, *-əl*, *adjs.* concerning nations or races: pertaining to gentiles or the heathen.—*ns.* **eth'nic** (*obs.*), a gentile, a heathen; **eth'narch** (-*närk*; Gr. *archos*, leader) a ruler or governor of a people; **eth'narchy**; **eth'nicism** (-*sizm*) (*obs.*), heathenism: gentile religion.—*adj.* **ethnocen'tric**.—*n.* **ethnocen'trism**, belief in superiority of one's own cultural group or society and corresponding dislike or misunderstanding of other such groups; **ethnog'rapher**.—*adj.* **ethnograph'ic**.—*n.* **ethnog'raphy**, the scientific description of the races of the earth.—*adj.* **ethnolog'ical**.—*adv.* **ethnolog'ically**.—*ns.* **ethnol'ogist**; **ethnol'ogy**, the science that treats of the varieties of the human race: cultural anthropology; **ethnomusicol'ogist**, one who makes a study of the music and/or musical instruments of primitive peoples in relation to their cultures; **ethnomusicol'ogy**. [Gr. *ethnos*, a nation.]

**et hoc** (or **id**) **genus omne**, *et hok* (*id*) *jē'nəs om'nē*, *gen'ōōs om'ne*, (L.) and all that sort of thing.

**ethos**, *ē'thos*, *n.* habitual character and disposition of individual, group, race, etc.: moral significance.—*adjs.* **etholog'ic, -al**.—*ns.* **ethol'ogist**; **ethol'ogy**, the science of character: bionomics: scientific study of the function and evolution of animal behaviour patterns. [Gr. *ēthos*, custom, character.]

**ethyl**, *eth'il*, *ēth'il*, *n.* the base (C₂H₅) of common alcohol, ether, etc.: (*cap.* in U.S. trademark) an anti-knock compound containing lead tetraethyl Pb(C₂H₅)₄: petrol using the compound.—*ns.* **eth'ylamine** (-*ə-min*), a substance (NH₂C₂H₅) resembling ammonia with one atom of hydrogen replaced by ethyl.—*n.* **eth'ylene** (also **eth'ene**), olefiant gas, heavy carburetted hydrogen (C₂H₄). —**ethyl alcohol**, ordinary alcohol. [ether, and Gr. *hȳlē*, matter.]

**ethyne**, *eth'in*, *n.* acetylene.

**etiolate**, *ē'ti-o-lāt*, *v.t.* to cause to grow pale with long whitish internodes and small yellow leaves for want of light, to blanch (*bot.*): to make pale.—*v.i.* to become pale.—*ns.* **etiolā'tion**; **e'tiolin**, a yellow pigment found in etiolated plants. [Fr. *étioler*, to become pale, to grow into stubble, *éteule*, stubble—L. *stipula*, a stalk, straw.]

**etiology**. U.S. spelling of **aetiology**.

**etiquette**, *et'i-ket*, or -*ket'*, *n.* forms of ceremony or decorum: ceremony: the conventional laws of courtesy observed between members of the same profession, players, etc. [Fr. *étiquette*; see **ticket**.]

**etna**, *et'na*, *n.* a vessel for heating liquids in a saucer of burning alcohol.—*adjs.* **Aetnē'an**, **Etnē'an**, of, pertaining to, resembling, or characteristic of, the volcano Etna. [L. *Aetna*—Gr. *Aitnē*.]

**étoile**, *ā-twal*, (Fr.) star: a star-shaped object.

**Eton**, *ē'tn*, *n.* a town opposite Windsor with an old public school: (in *pl.*) an Eton suit.—*n.* **Etonian** (*ē-tōn'i-an*), one educated at *Eton* College.— Also *adj.*—**Eton collar**, a boy's broad starched turned-down collar: a like-shaped collar to a woman's jumper, etc.; **Eton crop**, a fashion of cutting ladies' hair short and sleeking it; **Eton jacket**, a boy's black dress-coat, untailed; **Eton suit**, an Eton jacket with waistcoat and trousers in keeping.

**étourdi**, *fem.* **étourdie**, *ā-tōōr-dē*, (Fr.) thoughtless, foolish, light-minded; **étourderie** (*ā-tōōr-drē*), heedlessness, stupid blundering.

**étranger** (*fem.* **étrangère**), *ā-trä-zhā*, (-*zher*), (Fr.) strange: a foreigner.

**étrenne** (usu. in *pl.* **étrennes**), *ā-tren*, (Fr.) New Year's gift.

**étrier**, *ā-trē-yā*, *n.* a small rope ladder of 1-4 rungs used as a climbing aid by mountaineers. [Fr., stirrup.]

**Etruria**, *i-trōō'ri-a*, *n.* an ancient state of Italy north of the Tiber: part of Hanley, Stoke-on-Trent, where Josiah Wedgwood made *Etruria* ware.—*n.* and *adj.* **Etru'rian**.—*adj.* **Etruscan** (*i-trus'kən*), Etrurian.—*n.* an Etruscan: the language of the Etruscans, of undetermined affinities.—*ns.* **Etruscol'ogist**; **Etruscol'ogy**. [L. *Etrūria, Etrūscus*.]

**et sequens**, *et sē'kwənz*, *se-kwäns'*, (L.) and that which follows; **et sequentes**, *si-kwen'tēz*, *se-kwen'täs* (*neut.* **et sequentia**, *si-kwen'shi-ə*, *se-kwen'ti-a*), and those that follow.

**et sic de ceteris**, *et sik dē set'ə-ris*, *et sēk dā kā'te-rēs*, (L.L.) and so about the rest.

**et sic de similibus**, *et sik dē si-mil'i-bas*, *et sēk dā si-mil'i-bōōs*, (L.L.) and so of the like.

**ettercap**, *et'ər-kap*, **ethercap**, *edh'ər-kap*, *n.* Scots forms of **attercop**.

**ettle**, *et'l*, (*Scot.*) *v.t.* to purpose, intend: to aim: to aspire.—*n.* purpose, intent. [O.N. *ætla*, to think.]

**étude**, *ā-tüd'*, (*mus.*) *n.* a composition intended either to train or to test the player's technical skill. [Fr., study.]

**etui, etwee**, *ā-twē'*, *et-wē'*, *n.* a small case for holding small articles. [Fr. *étui*, a case, sheath.]

**etymon**, *et'i-mon*, *n.* the true origin of a word: an original root: the genuine or literal sense of a word (*rare*).—*adjs.* **etym'ic**; **etymolog'ical**.—*adv.* **etymolog'ically**.—*ns.* **etymolog'icon, -cum**, an etymological dictionary.—*v.i.* **etymol'ogise**, (-*ize*, to inquire into or discuss etymology.—*v.t.* to trace or propound an etymology for.—*ns.* **etymol'ogist**; **etymol'ogy**, the science or investigation of the derivation and original signification of words: an etymon. [Neut. of Gr. *etymos*, true.]

**etypic, -al**, *ē-tip'ik*, *-əl*, *adj.* unconformable to type. [L. *ē*, from Gr. *typos*, type.]

**Eubacteriales**, *ū-bak-tē-ri-ā'lēz*, *n.pl.* an order of Schizomycetes, nonfilamentous, unbranched bacteria.—*n.* **eubactē'rium**, a member of the Eubacteriales: any typical bacterium:—*pl.* **eubactē'ria**. [Gr. *eu*, well, and **bacteria**.]

**eucaine, eucain**, *ū-kā'in*, *-kā'in*, *-kän*, *n.* a safer substitute for cocaine as a local anaesthetic. [Gr. *eu*, well, and **cocaine**.]

**Eucalyptus**, *ū-kə-lip'təs*, *n.* a large characteristically Australian genus of the myrtle family, forest trees, some gigantic, and mallee shrubs, with leathery often glaucous leaves turned edgewise

Neutral vowels in unaccented syllables: *el'ə-mənt*; for certain sounds in foreign words, see p. viii

to the sun and flower-buds opening lid-wise, yielding timber, oils, and gum: eucalyptus oil:— *pl.* eucalyp′tuses, eucalyp′ti.—*ns.* eu′calypt, a eucalyptus; eucalyp′tol, eucalyp′tole, cineol, a constituent of the various oils got from eucalyptus leaves. [Latinised from Gr. *eu*, well, *kalyptos*, covered.]

Eucharist, ū′kə-rist, *n.* the sacrament of the Lord's Supper: the elements of the sacrament.—*adjs.* Eucharist′ic, -al. [Gr. *eucharistiā*, thanksgiving —*eu*, well, and *charizesthai*, to show favour— *charis*, grace, thanks.]

euchlorine, ū-klō′rin, -klör′, *n.* a very explosive green-coloured gas, a mixture of chlorine with chlorine peroxide.—*adj.* euchlō′ric. [Gr. *eu*, well, *chlōros*, green.]

euchologion, ū-ko-lō′ji-on, *n.* a formulary of prayers, primarily that of the Greek Church.— Also euchology (-kol′ə-ji). [Gr. *euchologion*— *euchē*, a prayer, *logos*—*legein*, to speak.]

euchre, ū′kər, *n.* an American card game for two, three, or four persons, with the 32, 28, or 24 highest cards of the pack—if a player fails to make three tricks he is *euchred*, and his adversary scores against him.—*v.t.* to score over, as above: to outwit. [Ety. unknown.]

euclase, ū′klās, *n.* a hydrated beryllium aluminium silicate occurring in pale-green transparent crystals. [Fr.,—Gr. *eu*, well, *klasis*, breaking.]

Euclidean, ū-klid′i-ən, ū-kli-dē′ən, *adj.* pertaining to Euclid, a geometrician of Alexandria *c.* 300 B.C., or to space according to his assumptions.— Euclidean geometry, a geometry based on the postulates of Euclid.

eucrite, ū′krit, *n.* a gabbroitic rock composed of lime-feldspar, pyroxenes, and olivine.—*adj.* eucritic (-krit′ik). [Gr. *eu*, well, *kritos*, distinguished.]

eucyclic, ū-si′klik, (*bot.*) *adj.* having the same number of floral leaves in each whorl. [Gr. *eu*, well, *kyklos*, wheel.]

eudaemonism, eudemonism, ū-dē′mən-izm, *n.* a system of ethics that makes happiness the test of rectitude—whether *egoistic*, as Hobbes's, or *altruistic*, as Mill's.—*ns.* eudae′monist, eudē′- monist. [Gr. *eudaimoniā*, happiness—*eu*, well, *daimōn*, a spirit.]

eudialyte, ū-di′ə-lit, *n.* a silicate of zirconium, sodium, calcium and iron, occurring in Greenland, easily dissolved by acids. [Gr. *eu*, well, *dialyein*, to dissolve.]

eudiometer, ū-di-om′i-tər, *n.* an apparatus for gas analysis, a graduated tube holding the gas over mercury, usually with wires for sparking—early used for testing the air at different times. [Gr. *eudios*, clear, fine (as weather), *metron*, measure.]

euge, ū′jē, *interj.* well! well done! [Gr. *euge*.]

Eugenia, ū-jē′ni-a, *n.* the clove genus of the myrtle family.—eugenol (ū′jin-ol), the chief constituent of oil of cloves (C₁₀H₁₂O₂)—also eugenic (-jen′) acid. [Named after Prince *Eugene*.]

eugenic, ū-jen′ik, *adj.* pertaining to race improvement by judicious mating and helping the better stock to prevail.—*adv.* eugen′ically.—*n.* (treated as *sing.*) eugen′ics, the science of race improvement.—*ns.* eu′genism (-jin-), eu′genist. [Gr. *eugenēs*, of good stock.]

eugh, eughen, ewghen, *obs.* spellings (*Spens.*, *Shak.*) of yew, yewen.

Euglena, ū-glē′na, *n.* a genus of aquatic unicellular organisms of the order Euglenoidi′na or (*bot.*) Euglenā′les, with a single flagellum and reddish eyespots. [Gr. *eu*, well, *glēnē*, eyeball.]

Eugubine, ū′gū-bin, -bin, *adj.* pertaining to the ancient town of *Eugubium* or *Iguvium* (mod. *Gubbio*), or to its famous seven tablets of bronze, the chief monument of the ancient Umbrian tongue.

euharmonic, ū-här-mon′ik, *adj.* in just intonation. [Gr. *eu*, well, *harmoniā*, harmony.]

Euhemerism, ū-hē′mə-rizm, *n.* the system which explains mythology as growing out of real history, its deities as merely magnified men.— *v.t.* and *v.i.* euhē′merise, -ize.—*n.* and *adj.* euhē′merist.—*adj.* euhemeris′tic.—*adv.* euhemer- is′tically. [From *Euhēmerus*, Gr. *Euēmeros*, a 4th-cent. (B.C.) Sicilian philosopher.]

euk, ewk, ūk. See yuke.

eulachon, ū′lə-kən, *n.* the North Pacific candlefish, so oily that it is dried for use as a candle.— Also oulakan, oulakan, -chon, ulicon, -chon, -kon. [Chinook jargon, *ulākân*.]

eulogium, ū-lō′ji-əm, eulogy, ū′lə-ji, *n.* praise: a speech or writing in praise.—*v.t.* eu′logise, -ize, to extol.—*n.* eu′logist, one who extols another.— *adj.* eulogist′ic, full of praise.—*adv.* eulogist′ic- ally. [Late L. *eulogium*—Gr. *eulogion* (classical *eulogiā*)—*eu*, well, *logos*, a speaking.]

eumelanin, ū-mel′ə-nin, *n.* any melanin pigment of darker type. [*eu*-, good, most typical—Gr. *eu*, well.]

Eumenides, ū-men′i-dēz, *n.pl.* euphemistic name for the Erinyes or Furies. [Gr. *Eumenidēs*, gracious ones—*eu*, well, *menos*, disposition.]

eumerism, ū′mər-izm, (*biol.*) *n.* aggregation of similar parts. [Gr. *eu*, well, *meros*, part.]

Eumycetes, ū-mi-sē′tēz, *n.pl.* the higher fungi, Ascomycetes and Basidiomycetes. [Gr. *eu*, well, and mycetes.]

eunuch, ū′nək, *n.* a castrated man, esp. one in charge of a harem, or a high-voiced singer.—*ns.* eu′nuchism, condition of being a eunuch; eu′nuchoidism, condition in which there is some deficiency of sexual development and in which certain female sex characteristics, e.g. high voice, are often present.—*n.* and *adj.* eu′nuchoid. [Gr. *eunouchos*—*eunē*, bed, *echein*, to have (charge of).]

euoi. See evoe.

Euonymus, ū-on′-i-məs, *n.* the spindle tree and burning bush genus of Celastraceae.—*n.* euon′y- min, an extract of bark of burning bush. [Gr. *euōnymos*, (spindle tree).]

eupatrid, ū-pat′rid, *n.* a member of the aristocracy in ancient Greek states. [Gr. *eupatridēs*—*eu*, well—*patēr*, father.]

eupepsy, ū-pep′si, eupepsia, -ə, *n.* good digestion— opp. to *dyspepsia*.—*adj.* eupep′tic, pertaining to good digestion: cheerful (*fig.*).—*n.* eupepticity (-tis′i-ti). [Gr. *eupepsiā*, digestibility—*eu*, well, *pepsis*, digestion—*peptein*, to digest.]

euphemism, ū′fim-izm, *n.* a figure of rhetoric by which an unpleasant or offensive thing is designated by a milder term.—*v.t.* eu′phemise, -ize, to express by a euphemism.—*v.i.* to use euphemistic terms.—*adj.* euphemist′ic.—*adv.* euphe- mist′ically. [Gr. *euphēmismos*—*euphēmizein*, to speak words of good omen—*eu*, well, *phanai*, to speak.]

euphony, ū′fə-ni, *n.* an agreeable sound: a pleasing, easy pronunciation—also (*obs.*) euphonia (-fō′).—*n.* eu′phon, a form of glass harmonica invented by Chladni in 1790.—*adjs.* euphonic (-fon′), -al, euphō′nious, agreeable in sound.— *adv.* euphō′niously.—*v.t.* eu′phonise, -ize, to make euphonious.—*n.* euphō′nium, the bass saxhorn: the euphon. [Gr. *euphōniā*—*eu*, well, *phōnē*, sound.]

Euphorbia, ū-för′bi-ə, *n.* the spurge genus of plants, giving name to the Euphorbiā′ceae, an isolated family of archichlamydeous dicotyledons.—*adj.* euphorbiā′ceous.—*n.* euphor′- bium, a gum resin got from some spurges. [*Euphorbos*, Greek physician to Juba, king of Mauritania.]

euphoria, ū-fō′ri-ə, *fō′*, euphory, ū′fə-ri, *ns.* a feeling of well-being.—*adj.* euphoric (-*for′*). [Gr. *euphōriā*.]

euphrasy, ū′frə-si, -zi, (*bot.*) *n.* eyebright (*Eu- phrasia*) once thought good for disorders of the

fāte, fär; mē, hûr (her); mīne; mōte, för; mūte; mōōn, fōōt; dhen (then)

eyes. [Gr. *euphrăsiă*, delight—*euphrainein*, to cheer—*eu*, well, *phrēn*, the mind.]

Euphrosyne, *ū-froz'i-nē*, or *-fros'*, *n.* one of the three Charites or Graces. [Gr. *Euphrosynē*—*euphrōn*, cheerful.]

Euphuism, *ū'fū-izm*, *n.* the affected and bombastic literary style brought into vogue by John Lyly's romance *Euphues* (1579-80): a high-flown expression in this style.—*v.i.* eu'phuise *-ize*.—*n.* eu'phuist.—*adj.* euphuist'ic.—*adv.* euphuist'ically. [Gr. *euphyēs*, graceful, goodly.]

Eur(o)-, *ū'r(ō)-*, in composition, European (and).—*adj.* Eura'frican, pertaining to Europe and Africa, or Europe and North Africa, jointly: of a human race common to Europe and North Africa, the Mediterranean race: of mixed European and African parentage or descent.—*n.* a person of Eurafrican race in either sense.—*adj.* Euras'ian, of mixed European and Asiatic parentage or descent: of, or pertaining to, Europe and Asia (*Eurasia*) taken as one continent.—*n.* a Eurasian half-caste.—*ns.* Eurat'om, the European Atomic Energy Community (1958), an association for joint peaceful development of nuclear energy; Eu'ro-Amer'ican; Eu'rocrat, an official concerned with the administration of any organisation within the European Economic Community; Eu'ro-doll'ars, U.S. dollars deposited in European banks to facilitate financing of trade; Eu'romarket, Eu'romart, the European Common Market; Eu'rovision, the European television network.

Euraquilo, *ū-rak'wi-lō*, *n.* See Euroclydon.

eureka, rarely heureka, (*h*)*ū-rē'ka*, *interj.* announcing a discovery.—*n.* a brilliant discovery. [Gr. *heurēka*, I have found, perf. tense of *heuriskein*, to find, the cry of Archimedes when he thought of a method of detecting the adulteration of the gold for Hiero's crown.]

eurhythmy, eurythmy, *ū-rith'mi*, or *ridh'*, *n.* rhythmical movement or order: harmony of proportion.—*adj.* eurhyth'mic.—*n.pl.* eurhyth'mics, the art or system of rhythmic movement expounded by E. Jaques-Dalcroze (1865-1950). [Gr. *eurythmiă*—*eu*, well, *rhythmos*, rhythm.]

euripus, *ū-rī'pəs*, *n.* an arm of the sea with strong currents, spec. that between Euboea and Boeotia: a ditch round the arena in a Roman amphitheatre. [L.,—Gr. *euripos*.]

Euro-. See Eur-.

euro, *ū'rō*, *n.* a wallaroo. [Native name.]

Euroclydon, *ū-rok'li-don*, *n.* the tempestuous wind by which St Paul's ship was wrecked (Acts xxvii. 14). [Gr. *Euroklydōn*, as if—*Euros*, east wind, *klydōn*, a wave; supposed to be a wrong reading for Eurakylōn, L. *Euraquilō*—*Eurus* (Gr. *Euros*) and *Aquilō*, north wind.]

European, *ū-rō-pē'ən*, *adj.* belonging to Europe.—*n.* a native of Europe: a member of the white race of man characteristic of Europe.—*v.t.* europe'anise, *-ize*, to assimilate to European character or ways.—European plan (*U.S.*), in hotels, the system of charging for lodgings and service without including meals. [Gr. *Eurōpē*.]

europium, *ū-rō'pi-əm*, *n.* a metal of the rare earths (Eu; at. numb. 63), discovered spectroscopically by Demarçay in 1896. [Europe.]

Eurus, *ū'rəs*, *n.* the south-east wind. [L.,—Gr. *Euros*.]

Eurypharynx, *ū-ri-far'ingks*, *n.* the pelican-fish. [Gr. *eurys*, wide, *pharynx*, pharynx.]

Eurypterus, *ū-rip'tər-əs*, *n.* a genus of Eurypterida.—*n.* euryp'terid, any member of the Eurypterida.—*n.pl.* Eurypter'ida (*-ter'i-də*), a Palaeozoic fossil order of Arachnida, scorpion-like aquatic animals, sometimes over six feet long, with the last (sixth) pair of appendages expanded.—*adj.* euryp'teroid, like or of the Eurypterida.—*n.* a eurypterid. [Gr. *eurys*, wide, *pteron*, wing.]

eurythmy. Usu. American spelling of eurhythmy.

Eusebian, *ū-sē'bi-ən*, *adj.* pertaining to Eusebius of Caesarea, father of ecclesiastical history (died 340), or to the Arian Eusebius of Nicomedia (died 342).

Euskarian, *ūs-kā'ri-ən*, *adj.* Basque. [Basque *Euskara*, the Basque language.]

eusporangiate, *ū-spor-an'ji-āt*, (*bot.*) *adj.* of a group of ferns, having each sporangium derived from a group of cells—opp. to *leptosporangiate*. [Gr. *eu*, well, and sporangium.]

Eustachian, *ū-stā'ki-ən*, *adj.* pertaining to the Italian physician Bartolommeo *Eustachio* (died 1574).—Eustachian tube, the tube leading from the middle ear to the pharynx; Eustachian valve, the rudimentary valve at the entrance of the inferior vena cava in the heart.

eustacy, eustasy, *ū'sta-si*, *n.* changes in world shore-line level, prob. caused by rise or fall of the sea-level and not by subsidence or elevation of the land.—*adj.* eustat'ic. [Gr. *eu*, well, *stasis*, standing; *statikos*, causing to stand.]

eustyle, *ū'stil*, *adj.* with columns spaced at about two diameters and a quarter.—*n.* a colonnade or building so proportioned. [Gr. *eustylos*, well intercolumniated—*eu*, well, *stylos*, column.]

eutaxy, *ū'tak-si*, *n.* good order.—*n.* eutax'ite, a volcanic rock with banded structure.—*adj.* eutaxit'ic, having such a structure. [Gr. *eu*, well, *taxis*, arrangement.]

eutectic, eutectoid. See eutexia.

Euterpe, *ū-tûr'pē*, *n.* the Muse of music and lyric poetry: a genus of palms.—*adj.* Euter'pean, pertaining to Euterpe, or to music. [Gr. *Euterpē*—*eu*, well, *terpein*, to delight.]

eutexia, *ū-tek'si-ə*, *n.* the property of being easily melted.—*n.* eutec'tic, a mixture in such proportions that the melting-point (or freezing-point) is a minimum, the constituents melting (or freezing) simultaneously.—*adj.* of maximum fusibility: pertaining to a eutectic.—*n.* eutec'toid, an alloy similar to a eutectic but involving formation of two or three constituents from another solid constituent.—Also *adj.* [Gr. *eutēktos*, easily melted—*eu*, well, *tēkein*, to melt.]

euthanasia, *ū-thən-ā'zi-ə*, *n.* an easy mode of death: the act or practice of putting painlessly to death, esp. in cases of incurable suffering.—Also euthanasy (*-than'ə-si*). [Gr. *euthanasiă*—*eu*, well, *thanatos*, death.]

euthenics, *ū-then'iks*, *n.* (treated as *sing.*) the science concerned with the improvement of living conditions. [Gr. *euthēneein*, to flourish.]

Eutheria, *ū-thē'ri-ə*, *n.pl.* the placental mammals.—*n.*, *adj.* eutherian. [Gr. *eu*, well, *thēr*, a beast.]

Euthyneura, *ū-thi-nū'rə*, *n.pl.* a subclass of gasteropods in which the visceral nerve-loop is not twisted. [Gr. *euthys*, straight, *neuron*, nerve.]

eutrophy, *ū'trə-fi*, *n.* healthy nutrition: (of lake) the state of being eutrophic.—*adj.* eutrophic (*ū-trof'ik*), pertaining to healthy nutrition: (of lake) over-rich in nutrients either naturally or as a result of artificial pollutants, and hence having a too-abundant growth of water-plants and animals.—*n.* eutrophica'tion. [Gr. *eutrophiă*.]

eutropy, *ū'trə-pi*, *n.* regular variation of the crystalline form of a series of compounds with the atomic number of the element.—*adjs.* eutropic (*-trop'ik*), according to eutropy: turning sun-wise (*bot.*); eu'tropous. [Gr. *eu*, well, *tropos*, a turn.]

Eutychian, *ū-tik'i-ən*, *adj.* of or pertaining to the doctrine of *Eutyches*, a 5th-cent. archimandrite of Constantinople, who held that Christ's human nature was merged in the divine.—*n.* a follower of Eutyches.

euxenite, *ūks'ə-nīt*, *n.* a mineral, niobate and titanate of yttrium, erbium, cerium, and uranium. [Gr. *euxenos*, hospitable, as containing many rare elements.]

Neutral vowels in unaccented syllables: *el'ə-mənt*; for certain sounds in foreign words, see p. viii

**evacuate**, *i-, ē-vak'ū-āt, v.t.* to throw out the contents of: to discharge: to withdraw: to remove, as from a place of danger: to clear out troops, inhabitants, etc., from: to nullify (*law*). —*adj.* and *n.* **evac'uant**, purgative.—*n.* **evacuā'-tion**, act of evacuating: withdrawal: that which is discharged.—*adj.* **evac'uātive**.—*ns.* **evac'uātor**; **evac'ūee**, a person removed in an evacuation. [L. *ē*, from, *vacuāre, -ātum,* to empty—*vacuus,* empty.]

**evade**, *i-, ē-vād', v.i.* to escape, slip away (*rare*).— *v.t.* to escape or avoid artfully: to shirk: to baffle, elude. [L. *ēvādēre—ē,* from, *vādēre,* to go.]

**evagation**, *ē-,* or *e-vag-ā'shən, n.* wandering: a digression. [L. *ēvagāri—ē,* from, *vagāri,* wander.]

**evaginate**, *i-, ē-vaj'i-nāt, v.t.* to turn outside in: to evert: to remove from a sheath.—*adj.* without a sheath.—*n.* **evaginā'tion**. [L. *ēvāgin-āre, -ātum,* to unsheathe—*ē,* from, *vāgina,* a sheath.]

**evaluate**, *i-, ē-val'ū-āt, v.t.* to determine the value of.—*n.* **evaluā'tion**.—*adj.* **eval'uative**, tending, serving, to evaluate. [Fr. *évaluer.*]

**evanescent**, *ev-ən-es'ənt, adj.* fleeting; vanishing. —*v.i.* **evanesce'**, to fade away.—*n.* **evanesc'ence**. —*adv.* **evanesc'ently**. [L. *ēvānēscēns, -entis—ē, vānēscēre,* to vanish—*vānus,* empty.]

**evangel**, *i-van'jəl, n.* good news (*poet.*): gospel: a doctrine set up as a saving principle, esp. in morals or politics.—*ns.* **evangeliar** (*ev-ən-jel'*), **evangeliā'rion**, **evangeliā'rium**, **evangel'iary**, a book of passages from the Gospels to be used at mass or in other services.—*adjs.* **evangelic** (*ev-* or *ēv-ən-jel'ik*), **-al**, of or pertaining to the Gospel: relating to the four Gospels: according to the doctrine of the Gospel: maintaining the teaching of the Gospel: Protestant: of the school that insists especially on the total depravity of unregenerate human nature, the justification of the sinner by faith alone, the free offer of the Gospel to all, and the plenary inspiration and exclusive authority of the Bible. —*n.* **evangel'ical**, one who belongs to the evangelical school.—*n.* **evangel'icalism**.—*adv.* **evangel'ically**.—*ns.* **evangel'icalness**; **evangel'icism** (*-sizm*), evangelical principles; **evangelisā'tion**, **-z-** (*i-van-jəl-*), act of proclaiming the Gospel: Christianisation.—*v.t.* **evan'gelise, -ize,** to make acquainted with the Gospel: to Christianise. —*v.i.* to preach the Gospel from place to place. —*ns.* **evan'gelism**, evangelising, evangelicalism; **evan'gelist**, one who evangelises: an author of a Gospel, especially one of the canonical Gospels: an assistant of the apostles: one who is authorised to preach but who is without a fixed charge: an itinerant preacher: a lay missionary in the Catholic Apostolic Church, a minister of the third grade; **evangelis'tary**, a book of the Gospels, or of passages from them to be read at divine service: a table of such passages —also **evangelistā'rion**.—*adj.* **evangelis'tic**, tending or intended to evangelise.—*n.* **evan'gely** (*obs.*), the Gospel.—**Evangelical Union** (for Morisonian). [L. *evangelicus*—Gr. *euangelikos—eu,* well, *angellein,* to bring news.]

**evanish**, *i-van'ish, v.i.* to vanish: to die away. —*ns.* **evan'ishment, evanition** (*ev-ə-nish'ən*). [O.Fr. *evanir, evaniss-*—L. *ex,* from, *vānus,* empty; cf. evanesce.]

**evaporate**, *i-vap'ər-āt, v.i.* to fly off in vapour: to pass into an invisible state: to depart, vanish. —*v.t.* to convert into vapour: to dry by evaporation: of a metal, to sublimate in order to deposit as a film.—*adj.* **evap'orable**, able to be evaporated or converted into vapour.—*n.* **evaporā'tion**, act of evaporating or passing off in steam or gas: the process by which a substance changes into the state of vapour.—*adj.* **evap'orātive**.—*ns.* **evap'orātor**; **evaporim'eter**, an instrument for

measuring rate of evaporation; **evap'orograph**, a device giving direct or photographic images of objects in darkness by focusing infra-red radiations from them on to an oil-film, which evaporates in proportion to the amount of radiation, leaving an image. [L. *ē*, from, *vapōrāre, -ātum—vapor,* vapour.]

**evasion**, *i-vā'zhən, n.* act of evading or eluding: an attempt to escape the force of an argument or accusation: an excuse.—*adj.* **evasible** (*i-vā'zi-bl*), capable of being evaded; **evā'sive** (*-siv*), that evades or seeks to evade: elusive: not straightforward: shuffling.—*adv.* **evā'sively**.—*n.* **evā'-siveness**.—**take evasive action,** to move or act in such a way as to avoid an object or consequence. [L. *ēvādēre, ēvāsum;* see evade.]

**eve**. See even (2).

**evection**, *i-, ē-vek'shən, (astron.) n.* a lunar inequality, combined effect of the irregularity of the motion of the perigee and alternate increase and decrease of the eccentricity of the moon's orbit. [L. *ēvectiō, -ōnis—ē,* from, *vehēre, vectum,* to carry.]

**even**, *ēv'n, ēvn, adj.* flat: level: smooth: uniform: in a straight line or plane: straightforward (*Shak.*): balanced: equal: on an equality: exact: divisible by 2 without a remainder: denoted by such a number.—*v.t.* to make even or smooth: to put on an equality: to liken: to equal: to act up to (*Shak.*).—*v.i.* to become even.—*adv.* exactly: nearly: indeed: so much as: still: extreme as the case may be, nevertheless.—*adv.* **ev'enly**.—*ns.* **ev'enness**; **ev'ens**, even money.—*adv.* quits.—**ev'en-Chris'tian** (*obs.*), fellow-Christian; **even date,** the same date.— *adj.* **ev'en-down,** straight-down (of rain): downright, honest.—*adv.* thoroughly.—*adjs.* **ev'en-hand'ed,** impartial: just; **ev'en-mind'ed,** having an even or calm mind: equable.—**even money,** an equal sum each on each side.—**even-even nuclei,** nuclei in which there are an even number of protons and of neutrons; **even-odd nuclei,** nuclei in which there are an even number of protons and an odd number of neutrons; **be even with,** be revenged on: be quits with; **even now** (*arch.*), a very little while ago; **even on** (*Scot.*), without intermission; **even up on,** to require, come square with. [O.E. *efen;* Du. *even,* Ger. *eben.*]

**even**, *ēv'n, n.* evening (*poet.*): eve (*obs.* or *dial.*)— also **e'en** (*ēn*).—*ns.* **eve** (*ēv*), evening (*poet.*): the night, or the whole day, before a festival: the time just preceding an event; **evening** (*ēv'ning*) the close of the daytime: the decline or end of life: an evening party, gathering or entertainment.—*adv.* **eve'nings** (*U.S.*), in the evening.— **eve'jar** (*dial.*), the nightjar; **ev'enfall,** early evening, twilight; **eve'ning-dress,** the dress conventionally appropriated to social functions in the evening; **eve'ning-prim'rose,** a N. American plant (Oenothera) with pale yellow flowers that open in the evening; **eve'ning-star,** a planet, usu. Venus or Mercury, seen in the west setting soon after the sun; **ev'ensong,** evening prayer, the Anglican form appointed to be said or sung at evening: the time proper for such; **ev'en-tide,** the time of evening, evening. [O.E. *æfen, æfnung.*]

**event**, *i-vent', n.* that which happens: result: any incident or occurrence: contingency: an item in a programme of sports: fortune or fate (*obs.*). —*adjs.* **event'ful,** full of events: momentous; **event'ūal,** happening as a consequence: final.— *v.i.* **event'ūalise, -ize,** to come to pass: to come into being.—*n.* **eventūal'ity,** a contingency: propensity to take notice of events, changes, or facts (*phrenology*).—*adv.* **event'ūally,** finally: at length.—*v.i.* **event'ūate,** to turn out. [L. *ēventus —ēvenīre,* to come out, happen—*ē,* from, *venīre,* to come.]

*fāte, fär; mē, hûr* (her); *mīne; mōte, för; mūte; mōōn, fōōt; dhen* (then)

**eventration,** *ē-ven-trä´shən, n.* act of opening the belly: protrusion of an organ from the abdomen. [Fr. *éventration*—L. *ē*, from, *venter*, belly.]

**ever,** *ev´ər, adv.* always: eternally: at all times: continually: at any time: on record (as *the biggest ever*, the biggest that ever was or happened): in any degree: at all: in the world. —As a suffix, giving complete generality to relative adverbs and pronouns.—*adj.* ev´ergreen, in leaf throughout the year: always fresh and green: unfading.—*n.* a tree or shrub that is green throughout the year.—*adj.* everlast´ing, endless: perpetual: unceasing: eternal: wearisomely long-continued.—*n.* eternity: a flower (of *Helichrysum, Antennaria,* or other genus) that may be kept for years without much change of appearance: a very durable cloth.—*adv.* everlast´ingly.—*n.* everlast´ingness.—*adj.* ev´er-liv´ing (*Shak.*), immortal: deathless.—*adv.* evermore´ (or *ev´*), for all time to come (also for evermore): ever: unceasingly.—ever and anon, from time to time; ever so, to any extent: to a very great extent; for ever, to all eternity. [O.E. *ǣfre.*]

**everglade,** *ev´ər-glād, n.* a large shallow lake or marsh: (chiefly in *pl.*) such a marsh in southern Florida, enclosing thousands of islets covered with dense thickets. [Perh. ever, and glade.]

**evert,** *ē-,* or *i-vûrt´, v.t.* to turn inside out: to turn outwards.—*n.* ever´sion. [L. *ēvertĕre—ē*, from, *vertĕre, versum,* to turn.]

**every,** *ev´ri, adj.* each of a number: all taken separately.—*prons.* ev´erybody, ev´eryone, every person.—*adj.* ev´eryday, of or belonging to every day, daily: common, usual: pertaining to weekdays, not Sunday.—Also *n.*—*ns.* ev´erydayness; Ev´eryman, the hero of an old morality play, representing mankind, everybody, anybody. —*pron.* ev´erything, all things taken singly: all. —*advs.* ev´eryway, in every way or respect; ev´erywhen, ev´erywhence, ev´erywhither (*all rare*); ev´erywhere, in every place.—every bit, whit, the whole: quite.—every here and there, all over dispersedly; every man Jack, every mother's son, every one without exception; every now and then, or again, at intervals; every other, every second or alternate; every so often, at intervals; every which way (*U.S.*), every way: in disorder. [O.E. *ǣfre,* ever, and *ǣlc,* each.]

**evet,** *ev´it, n.* Same as eft (1).

**evict,** *i-, ē-vikt´, v.t.* to dispossess by law: to expel. —*ns.* evic´tion, the act of evicting from house or lands: the dispossession of one person by another having a better title of property in land; evic´tor. [L. *ēvictus,* pa.p. of *ēvincĕre,* to overcome.]

**evident,** *ev´i-dənt, adj.* that can be seen: clear to the mind: obvious.—*n.* that which serves as evidence.—*n.* ev´idence, that which makes evident: means of proving an unknown or disputed fact: support for a belief: indication: information in a law case: testimony: a witness or witnesses collectively.—*v.t.* to render evident: to attest, prove: to indicate.—*adjs.* evidential (-*den´shəl*), eviden´tiary, furnishing evidence: tending to prove.—*advs.* eviden´tially; ev´idently, visibly (*N.T.*): obviously: manifestly.—in evidence, received by the court as competent evidence: plainly visible, conspicuous—a hackwriter's phrase adopted from the Fr. *en évidence*; turn King's (Queen's) evidence, to give evidence against an accomplice in a crime. [L. *ēvidēns, -entis—ē,* from, *vidēre,* to see.]

**evil,** *ē´v(i)l, adj.* wicked: bad: mischievous: disagreeable: unfortunate.—*adv.* in an evil manner: badly.—*n.* that which produces unhappiness or calamity: harm: wickedness: depravity: sin.—*adv.* evilly (*ē´vil-i*), in an evil manner: not well.—*n.* e´vilness, state of being evil: wickedness.—e´vil-doer, one who does evil; evil eye, a supposed power to cause harm by a

look.—*adj.* e´vil-fā´voured, having a repulsive appearance: ugly.—e´vil-fā´vouredness (*B.*), ugliness: deformity.—*adj.* e´vil-mind´ed, inclined to evil: malicious: wicked.—e´vil-speak´ing, the speaking of evil: slander.—*adj.* e´vil-starred´ (*Tenn.*), born under the influence of an unpropitious star, unfortunate.—e´vil-work´er, one who works or does evil.—the evil one, the devil; speak evil of, to slander. [O.E. *yfel*; Du. *euvel*; Ger. *übel*; cf. ill.]

**evince,** *i-vins´, v.t.* to overcome, overpower (*arch.*): to prove beyond doubt: to show clearly: to make evident: to give indication of.—*n.* evince´-ment.—*adj.* evinc´ible.—*adv.* evinc´ibly.—*adj.* evinc´ive, tending to evince, prove, or demonstrate. [L. *ēvincĕre,* to vanquish—*ē-,* inten., *vincĕre,* to overcome.]

**Evipan,** *ev´i-pan, n.* proprietary name of a drug, hexobarbitone sodium, used intravenously and intramuscularly as a basic anaesthetic.

**evirate,** *ē´-* or *e´vir-āt, v.t.* to castrate: to render weak or unmanly. [L. *ēvirāre—ē,* from, *vir,* a man.]

**eviscerate,** *ē-* or *i-vis´ər-āt, v.t.* to tear out the viscera or bowels of: to gut.—*n.* eviscerā´tion. [L. *ē,* from, *viscera,* the bowels.]

**evite,** *i-vīt´, v.i.* to avoid.—*adj.* evitable (*ev´it-ə-bl*). —*v.t.* ev´itate (*Shak.*), to avoid.—*n.* evitā´tion, the act of shunning [L. *ēvitāre, -ātum—ē,* from, *vitāre,* to shun.]

**eviternal,** *ēv-i-tûr´nl, adj.* eternal.—*adv.* eviter´nally.—*n.* eviter´nity. [L. *aeviternus*; see eternal.]

**evocation, etc. See evoke.**

**evoe, evhoe, euoi,** *ē-vē, ē-vō´i, ū-oi´, interj.* expressing Bacchic frenzy. [L. *eu(h)oe*—Gr. *euoi, eu hoi.*]

**evoke,** *i-vōk´, v.t.* to call out: to draw out or bring forth: to call up or awaken in the mind.—*v.t.* evocate (*ev´ō-kāt*), to evoke: to call up from the dead.—*n.* evocā´tion.—*adjs.* evocative (*i-vok´ə-tiv*), evoc´atory.—*n.* evoc´ativeness. [L. *ēvocāre—ē,* from, and vocāre, to call.]

**évolué,** *ā-vol-wā, n.* a member of a primitive group of people who has been educated to the standards of a more advanced civilisation. [Fr., developed.]

**evolution,** *ēv-, ev-ə-loo´shən, n.* the act of unrolling or unfolding: gradual working out or development: a series of things unfolded: the doctrine according to which higher forms of life have gradually arisen out of lower: the extraction of roots (*math.*): (usu. *pl.*) orderly movements as of a body of troops, flock of birds, etc.—*n.* ev´olute (*math.*), an original curve from which another curve (the *involute*) is described by the end of a thread gradually unwound from the former.—*adj.* rolled back.—*adjs.* evolu´tional, evolu´tionary, of or pertaining to evolution.—*ns.* evolu´tionism, the doctrine of evolution; evolu´tionist, one skilled in evolutions or military movements: one who believes in evolution as a principle in science.—*adj.* ev´olutive. [L. *ēvolū-tiō, -ōnis,—ēvolvĕre*; see evolve.]

**evolve,** *i-,* or *ē-volv´, v.t.* to unroll: to disclose: to develop: to unravel.—*v.i.* to disclose itself: to result.—*adj.* evolv´able, that can be drawn out.—*n.* evolve´ment.—*adj.* evolv´ent. [L. *ēvolvĕre—ē,* from, *volvĕre, volūtum,* to roll.]

**evulgate,** *ē-,* or *ē-vul´gāt, v.t.* to divulge: to publish. [L. *ēvulgāre, -ātum—ē,* out, *vulgus,* the people.]

**evulse,** *i-, ē-vuls´, v.t.* to pluck out.—*n.* evul´sion. [L. *ēvellĕre, ēvulsum—ē,* from, *vellĕre, vulsum,* to pluck.]

**ewe,** *ū, n.* a female sheep.—ewe´-cheese, cheese made from the milk of ewes; ewe´-lamb, a female lamb: a poor man's one possession—used in reference to 2 Sam. xii; ewe´-milk; ewe´-neck, of horses, a thin hollow neck.—*adj.*

**ewe'-necked.** [O.E. *ēowu*; cf. L. *ovis*, Gr. *oïs*, Sans. *avi*, a sheep.]

**ewer,** *ū'ər, n.* a large water jug with a wide spout. [Through Fr. from L. *aquārium* (neut. of *aquārius*, of water)—*aqua*, water.]

**ewest,** *ū'ist*, (*Scot.*) *adj.* or *adv.* near. [App. from O.E. *on nēaweste*, in the neighbourhood, wrongly divided as *on ewest.*]

**ewftes,** *ūfts*, (*Spens.*) *n.pl.* efts. [See **eft** (1).]

**ewghen,** an old spelling of **yewen.**

**ewhow,** *ā'(h)wow'*, (*Scot.*) *interj.* an exclamation of deploration.

**ewigkeit,** *ā'vihh-kit, n.* eternity. [Ger.]

**ewt.** See **newt.**

**ex-,** *eks-*, as a living *pfx.* former but surviving, as **ex-emperor.**—*prep.* without, as **ex dividend.**— *n.* ex, one who is no longer what he was (*pl.* **ex's, ex'es**).

**ex,** *eks, n.* the twenty-fourth letter of the alphabet (X, x).

**ex,** *eks*, (L.) from, out of.—**ex abundantia** (*a-bən-dan'shi-ə, a-bōōn-dan'ti-ä*), out of abundance; **ex abundanti cautela** (*-dan'ti kö-tē'lə, -dan'tē kow-tā'lä*), from excessive caution; **ex accidenti** (*ak-si-den'ti, a-ki-den'tē*; L.L.), accidentally, as opposed to essentially.

**exacerbate,** *iks-*, or *igz-as'ər-bāt, v.t.* to embitter: to provoke: to render more violent or severe, as a disease.—*ns.* **exacerbā'tion, exacerbesc'ence,** increase of irritation or violence, esp. the increase of a fever or disease: embitterment. [L. *exacer-bāre, -ātum—ex*, and *acerbāre*, from *acerbus*, bitter.]

**exact,** *igz-akt', v.t.* to force out: to compel payment of: to demand and obtain: to extort: to require as indispensable.—*v.i.* to practise extortion.—*adj.* precise: rigorous: accurate: absolutely correct: finished: consummate: strict. —*adj.* **exact'ing,** compelling full payment: unreasonable in making demands: demanding much.—*ns.* **exac'tion,** act of exacting or demanding strictly: an oppressive demand: that which is exacted, as excessive work or tribute; **exact'i-tude,** exactness: correctness.—*adv.* **exact'ly.**— *ns.* **exact'ment; exact'ness,** quality of being exact: accuracy; **exact'or, -er,** one who exacts: an extortioner: one who claims rights, often too strictly:—*fem.* **exact'ress.**—**exact sciences,** the mathematical sciences, whose results are precise or quantitative. [L. *exigĕre, exāctum*, to demand, to weigh strictly—*ex*, from, *agĕre*, to drive.]

**ex aequo,** *eks ē-kwō, ī-*, (L.L.) equally, equitably.

**exaggerate,** *igz-aj'ər-āt, v.t.* to magnify unduly: to overstate: to represent too strongly: to intensify.—*n.* **exaggerā'tion,** extravagant representation: a statement in excess of the truth.— *adjs.* **exagg'erative, exagg'eratory,** containing exaggeration or tending to exaggerate.—*n.* **exagg'erator.** [L. *exaggerāre, -ātum—ex-, agger-āre*, to heap up—*agger*, a heap.]

**exalbuminous,** *eks-al-bū'min-əs*, (*bot.*) *adj.* without albumen.

**exalt,** *igz-ölt', v.t.* to set aloft: to elate or fill with the joy of success: to extol: to refine or subtilise (*old chem.*).—*n.* **exaltā'tion** (*egz-ol-*), elevation in rank or dignity: high estate: elation: a planet's position of greatest influence (*astrol.*): a flight of larks (*arch.*).—*adj.* **exalt'ed,** elevated: lofty: dignified.—*n.* **exalt'edness.** [L. *exaltāre —ex-, altus*, high.]

**examine,** *igz-am'in, v.t.* to test: to inquire into: to question: to look closely into: to inspect.—*n.* **exā'men,** examination.—*adj.* **exam'inable.**—*ns.* **exam'inant,** an examiner: one who is being examined; **exam'inate,** one who is examined; **examinā'tion,** careful search or inquiry: close inspection: trial: a test of capacity and knowledge, familiarly contracted to **exam'; examinee',** one under examination; **exam'iner, exam'inā-tor,** one who examines.—*adj.* **exam'ining.** [Fr.

**examiner**—L. *exāmināre—exāmen*, the tongue of a balance.]

**example,** *igz-äm'pl, n.* a specimen: an illustration: a copy of a book: a person or thing to be imitated or not to be imitated: a pattern: a warning: an instance.—*v.t.* (*rare*) to exemplify: to instance.—*n.* **exam'plar** (*arch.*), an exemplar. [O.Fr.,—L. *exemplum—eximĕre*, to take out— *ex*, out of, *emĕre, emptum*, to take.]

**exanimate,** *egz-, igz-an'i-māt, adj.* lifeless: spiritless: depressed.—*n.* **exanimā'tion.** [L. *exani-mātus—ex*, from, *anima*, breath.]

**ex animo,** *eks an'i-mō*, (L.) from the mind, earnestly.

**exanthem,** *eks-an'thəm*, **exanthema,** *eks-an-thē'mə, ns.* a skin eruption, esp. accompanied by fever; a disease so characterised:—*pl.* **exanthems, exan-thē'mata.**—*adjs.* **exanthēmat'ic, exanthēm'atous.** [Gr. *exanthēma, -atos—ex-*, out, *anthæein*, to blossom.]

**exarate,** *eks'ər-āt, adj.* containing grooves or furrows: said of pupae in which the wings and legs are free.—*n.* **exara'tion** (*rare*), the act of writing: composition. [L. *exarātus—exarāre*, to plough up, to trace letters on a tablet.]

**exarch,** *eks'ärk, n.* a Byzantine provincial governor, esp. of Italy: a metropolitan (*Gr. Ch.*): a bishop of rank between a patriarch and a metropolitan (*Gr. Ch.*): the head of the Bulgarian church: an ecclesiastical inspector: a legate.—*ns.* **exarch'ate** (or *eks'*), the office, jurisdiction or province of an exarch; **exarch'ist** (or *eks'*), a supporter of the Bulgarian exarch. [Gr. *exarchos*, leader.]

**exarch,** *eks'ärk*, (*bot.*) *n.* having the protoxylem on the outer edge. [Gr. *ex-*, out, *archē*, beginning, origin.]

**exasperate,** *igz-äs'pər-āt, v.t.* to make rough, harsh (*obs.*): to make more grievous or painful: to make very angry: to irritate in a high degree.— *adj.* irritated: rough with hard points (*bot.*). —*adjs.* **exas'perating, exas'perative.**—*ns.* **exas-perā'tion; exas'perātor.** [L. *ex-* inten., *asperāre*, to make rough—*asper*, rough.]

**ex auctoritate mihi commissa,** *eks ök-to-ri-tā'tē mi'hi kə-mis'ə, owk-tō-ri-tä'te mi'hi ko-mi'sa*, (L.) by the authority entrusted to me.

**Excalibur,** *eks-kal'ib-ər, n.* the name of King Arthur's sword. [O.Fr. *Escalibor* for *Caliburn*; cf. *Caladbolg*, a famous sword in Irish legend.]

**excambion,** *eks-kam'bi-on*, (*Scots law*) *n.* exchange of lands—also **excam'bium.**—*v.t.* **excamb',** to exchange. [L.L. *excambiāre*; cf. **cambist, cambium, exchange.**]

**ex cathedra,** *eks kə-thē'drə*, or *eks-kath'ə-dra*, (L.L.) from the chair of office, esp. the Pope's throne in the Consistory, or a professor's chair: hence authoritatively, judicially.

**excavate,** *eks'kə-vāt, v.t.* to hollow or scoop out: to dig out: to lay bare by digging.—*ns.* **excavā'-tion,** act of excavating: a hollow or cavity made by excavating; **ex'cavātor,** one who excavates: a machine used for excavating. [L. *excavāre— ex-*, out, *cavus*, hollow.]

**exceed,** *ik-sēd', v.t.* to go beyond the limit or measure of: to surpass or excel.—*v.i.* to go beyond a given or proper limit (*arch.*): to be intemperate (*arch.*): to be outstanding.—*adj.* **exceed'ing,** surpassing: excessive: projecting beyond a neighbouring member (*bot.*).—Also *adv.* (*arch.*) exceedingly.—*adv.* **exceed'ingly,** very much: greatly. [L. *ex-*, beyond, *cēdĕre, cessum*, to go.]

**excel,** *ik-sel', v.t.* to be superior to: to surpass: to exceed (*Milt.*).—*v.i.* to have good qualities in a high degree: to perform very meritorious actions: to be superior:—*pr.p.* **excell'ing;** *pa.t.* and *pa.p.* **excelled'.**—*ns.* **excellence** (*eks'ə-ləns*), **exc'ellency,** great merit: any excellent quality: worth: greatness: a title of honour given to persons high in rank or office.—*adj.* **exc'ellent,** surpassing others in some good quality: of great virtue, worth, etc.: good in a high degree. —*adv.* **exc'ellently.**—*interj.* **excel'sior** (L. *comp. adj.*, taller, loftier), higher still (after Longfellow). —*n.* a trade name for wood shavings for packing (*U.S.*). [L. *excellĕre*—*ex-*, out, up, *celsus*, high.]

**excellence, el̃-se-läs,** (Fr.) excellence.—**par excellence,** eminently, by way of ideal.

**excentric.** Same as **eccentric.**

**except, ik-sept',** *v.t.* to take out, or leave out: to exclude.—*v.i.* to object (usually with *to* or *against*).—*prep.* leaving out: excluding: but. —*conj.* (*arch.*) unless.—*adj.* and *n.* **except'ant.** —*prep.* **except'ing,** with the exception of, except. —*n.* **excep'tion,** the act of excepting: that which is excepted: exclusion: objection: offence.— *adj.* **excep'tionable,** objectionable.—*adv.* **excep'- tionably.**—*adj.* **excep'tional,** unusual (esp. in a good sense).—*adv.* **excep'tionally.**—*adjs.* **excep'- tious** (*arch.*), disposed to take exception; **excep'tive,** including, making, or being an exception; **except'less** (*Shak.*), making no exception, usual.—*n.* **excep'tor.**—**the exception proves the rule,** the making of an exception proves that the rule holds in cases not excepted. [L. *excipĕre, exceptum*—*ex*, from, *capĕre*, to take.]

**exceptis excipiendis, ik-sep'tis ik-sip-i-en'dis, eks- kep'tēs eks-ki-pi-en'dēs,** (L.L.) excepting what is to be excepted: with proper exceptions.

**excerpt, ek'sûrpt,** or **ek-sûrpt',** *n.* a passage selected from a book, opera, etc., an extract.— *v.t.* **excerpt',** to select: to extract.—*ns.* **excerpt'- ing,** **excerp'tion;** **excerp'tor.** [L. *excerptum,* pa.p. of *excerpĕre*—*ex*, from, *carpĕre*, to pick.]

**excerpta, ik-sûrp'tə, eks-kerp'ta,** (L.; *pl.* of **ex- cerptum, 'təm, 'tōom**), extracts, selections.

**excess, ik-ses',** *n.* a going beyond what is usual or proper: intemperance: that which exceeds: the degree or amount by which one thing exceeds another: usury (*Shak.*).—*adj.* in excess.—*adj.* **excess'ive,** beyond what is usual or right: immoderate: extreme.—*adv.* **excessively.**—*adv.* **excess'ively.**—*n.* **excess'iveness.**—**excess fare,** payment for distance travelled beyond, or in a class superior to, that allowed by the ticket; **excess luggage,** luggage above the weight allowed free.—**excess profits tax,** a tax on profits in excess of those for a specified base period or over a rate adopted as a reasonable return on capital; **carry to excess,** to do too much. [L. *excessus*—*excēdĕre, excēssum,* to go beyond.]

**exchange, iks-chānj',** *v.t.* to give or give up in return for something else: to receive in return for something else (*obs.*): to give and take mutually: to barter: to change (*obs.*).—*v.i.* to pass by exchange of office with another.—*n.* the giving and taking of one thing for another: barter: the thing exchanged: process by which accounts between distant parties are settled by bills instead of money: money-changing business: exchanging currency of one country for that of another: the difference between the value of money in different places: a stock exchange: the building where merchants, etc., meet for business: a central office where telephone lines are connected: a bar-room (*U.S. slang*): (see **employment exchange**).—*n.* **ex- changeabil'ity.**—*adj.* **exchange'able,** that may be exchanged.—*n.* **exchan'ger,** one who ex- changes or practises exchange: a money- changer, a banker (*B.*).—**exchange control,** the official control of a country's foreign exchange settlements so as to conserve its holding of foreign currency. [O.Fr. *eschangier* (Fr. *échanger*)—L.L. *excambiāre*—L. *ex*, from, L.L. *cambiāre*, to barter.]

**excheat, eks-chēt',** (*Spens.*) *n.* Same as **escheat.**

**exchequer, iks-chek'ər,** *n.* a department of state

having charge of revenue, so named from the chequered cloth which covered the table, and on which the accounts were reckoned: the Court of Exchequer: a national treasury: one's funds, finances, purse.—*v.t.* to proceed against in the Court of Exchequer.—**exchequer bill,** a bill issued at the Exchequer, as security for money advanced to the government.—**Chan- cellor of the Exchequer** (see **chancellor**); **Court of Exchequer,** in England originally a revenue court developed out of the judicial branch of the Exchequer, acquired a general common-law jurisdiction by a legal fiction, became a division of the High Court of Justice in 1875, and is now merged in the King's (Queen's) Bench Division: in Scotland a revenue court, abolished in 1886, its jurisdiction transferred to the Court of Session. [See **chequer, check, chess.**]

**excide, ek-sīd',** *v.t.* to cut off. [L. *excīdĕre*—*ex,* from, *caedĕre,* to cut.]

**excipient, ek-sip'i-ənt,** *n.* a substance mixed with a medicine to give it consistence, or used as a vehicle for its administration. [L. *excipiēns, -entis,* pr.p. of *excipere,* to take out, receive— *ex,* from, *capēre,* to take.]

**excise, ek-sīz',** *n.* a tax on certain home com- modities, and on licences for certain trades: the department in the civil administration con- cerned with this tax.—Also *adj.*—*v.t.* to subject to excise duty.—*adj.* **excis'able,** liable to excise duty.—**excise law** (*U.S.*), a liquor law, licensing law; **excise'man,** an officer charged with col- lecting the excise. [M.Du. *excijs*—O.Fr. *acceis,* tax—L.L. *accensāre,* to tax—*ad,* to, and *cēnsus,* a tax.]

**excise, ek-sīz',** *v.t.* to cut out or out.—*n.* **excision** (ek-sizh'ən), a cutting out or off of any kind: extirpation. [L. *excīdĕre,* to cut out—*ex,* from, *caedĕre,* to cut.]

**excite, ik-sīt',** *v.t.* to call into activity: to stir up: to rouse: to energise: to produce electric or magnetic activity in: to sensitise: to stir emotionally: to raise (a nucleus, atom, mole- cule, etc.) to an excited state.—*n.* **excitabil'ity.** —*adj.* **excit'able,** capable of being excited: responsive to stimulus: easily excited.—*ns.* **excit'ableness; excitancy** (*eк'si-tan-si*), excitant property; **excitant** (*ek'si-* or *ek-sī'*), that which excites or rouses the vital activity of the body: a stimulant: the electrolyte in an electric cell. —*adj.* **exciting:** stimulating.—*n.* **excitā'tion** state of excitement.—*adjs.* **excit'ative, excit'- atory,** tending to excite.—*adj.* **excit'ed,** agitated: roused emotionally: in a state of great activity: having energy higher than that of the ground, or normal, state.—*ns.* **excite'ment,** agitation: that which excites; **excit'er,** one who or that which excites: an auxiliary machine supplying current for another machine: a sparking apparatus for producing electric waves.—*adj.* **excit'ing,** tending to excite: stirring, thrilling. —*ns.* **excit'on,** a bound hole-electron pair; **ex- ci'tor,** exciter: an afferent nerve stimulating a part. [Fr. *exciter*—L. *excitāre, -ātum*—*exciēre* —*ex-*, out, *ciēre,* to set in motion.]

**exclaim, iks-klām',** *v.t.* and *v.i.* to cry out: to utter or speak vehemently.—*n.* an exclamation, outcry.—*n.* **exclamation** (eks-klə-mā'shən), vehe- ment utterance: outcry: an uttered expression of surprise and the like: the mark expressing this (!): an interjection.—*adjs.* **exclamative** (*eks- klam'ə-tiv*), **exclam'atory,** containing or express- ing exclamation. [Fr. *exclamer*—L. *exclāmāre, -ātum*—*ex-*, out, *clāmāre,* to shout.]

**exclaustration, eks-klôs-trā'shən,** *n.* the return of a religious to the outside world on release from his or her vows. [L. *ex,* out, *claustrum,* an en- closed place.]

**exclave, eks'klāv,** *n.* a part of a country, province

etc., disjoined from the main part, being enclosed in foreign territory. [See enclave.]
**exclosure**, *eks-klō'zhər, n.* an area shut off from intrusion. [L. *ex-*, from, and close (1).]
**exclude**, *iks-klōōd', v.t.* to shut out: to thrust out: to hinder from entrance: to emit: to hinder from participation: to except: to hatch.—*adj.* **exclud'ed** (*bot.*), exserted.—*ns.* **exclu'sion** (*-zhən*), a shutting or putting out: ejection: exception; **exclu'sionism**; **exclu'sionist**, one who excludes, or would exclude, another from a privilege.—*adj.* **exclu'sive** (*-siv*), able or tending to exclude: incompatible: debarring from participation: of the nature of monopoly: socially inaccessible or aloof: sole: not to be had elsewhere or from another: select, fashionable: without taking into account: not included.—*n.* one of a number who exclude others from their society: an exclusive product.—*adv.* **exclu'sively.**—*ns.* **exclu'siveness**; **exclu'sivism.**—*adj.* **exclu'-sory**, exclusive.—**exclusion principle**, fundamental law of quantum mechanics that no two particles of a group called fermions can exist in identical quantum states; **Exclusive Brethren** (see Close Brethren); **exclusive dealing**, the act of abstaining deliberately from any business or other transactions with persons of opposite political or other convictions to one's own— a euphemism for *boycotting.*—**law of excluded middle** (*log.*), that everything is either A or not-A. [L. *exclūdĕre*, *-clūsum*—*ex-*, out, *claudĕre*, to shut.]
**excogitate**, *eks-koj'i-tāt, v.t.* to discover by thinking: to think out earnestly or laboriously.—*n.* **excogitā'tion**, laborious thinking: invention: contrivance. [L. *excōgitāre*, *-ātum*—*ex-*, out, *cōgitāre*, to think.]
**excommunicate**, *eks-kəm-ūn'i-kāt, v.t.* to put out of or expel from the communion of the church: to deprive of church privileges.—*adjs.* **excommun'icable**; **excommun'icate**, excommunicated. —Also *n.*—*ns.* **excommunicā'tion**, act of expelling from the communion of a church; **excommun'ion** (*Milt.*).—*adj.* **excommun'icatory**, of or pertaining to excommunication. [From L.L. *excommūnicāre*—L. *ex*, *commūnis*, common.]
**ex concessis** (or **concesso**), *eks kən-se'sis* (*kən-se'sō*), *kon-kä'sēs* (*kon-kä'sō*), (L.L.) from what has been conceded.
**ex consequenti**, *eks kon-si-kwen'tī*, *-se-kwen'tē*, (L.L.) by way of consequence.
**ex converso**. Same as **e converso**.
**excoriate**, *eks-kō'ri-āt*, *-kö'ri-*, *v.t.* to strip the skin from: to criticise severely (*fig.*).—*n.* **excoriā'tion**, the act of excoriating: the state of being excoriated. [L. *excoriāre*, *-ātum*—*ex*, from, *corium*, the skin.]
**excorticate**, *eks-kör'ti-kāt*, *v.t.* to strip the bark off.—*n.* **excorticā'tion**. [L. *ex*, from, *cortex*, *-icis*, bark.]
**excrement**, *eks'kri-mənt, n.* dregs: useless matter discharged from the animal system: dung.—*adjs.* **excremental** (*-ment'l*), **excrementitial** (*-tish'l*), **excrementi'tious**, pertaining to or containing excrement. [L. *excrēmentum*—*excernĕre* ex-, out, *cernĕre*, to sift.]
**excrement**, *eks'kri-mənt*, (Shak.), *n.* an outgrowth, a moustache.—*adj.* **excremental** (*-ment'l*). [L. *excrēmentum*—*ex-*, out, *crēscĕre*, to grow.]
**excrementa**, *eks-kri-men'tə*, *-kre-men'ta* (L; *pl.* of excrementum, *'təm*, *'tōōm*), refuse matter.
**excrescence**, *iks-kres'əns*, *n.* an outgrowth or projection, esp. abnormal, grotesque, or offensive: a wart or tumour: a superfluous part: an outbreak.—*n.* **excresc'ency**, state of being excrescent: excrescence.—*adjs.* **excresc'ent**, growing out: superfluous; **excrescential** (*eks-kri-sen'shl*). [L. *excrēscĕre*—*ex-*, out, *crēscĕre*, to grow.]
**excrete**, *eks-krēt', v.t.* to separate and discharge: to eject.—*n.pl.* **excrē'ta**, matters discharged from

the animal body.—*n.* **excrē'tion**, the excreting of matter from an organism: that which is excreted.—*adjs.* **excrē'tive**, able to excrete: concerned with excretion; **excrē'tory** (or *eks'kri-tər-i*), having the quality of excreting.—*n.* a duct that helps to receive and excrete matter. [L. *ex*, from, *cernĕre*, *crētum*, to separate.]
**excruciate**, *iks-krōō'shi-āt*, *v.t.* to torture: to rack: to inflict severe pain: to irritate greatly. —*adj.* **excru'ciāting**, extremely painful: racking: torturing: agonising: intensely irritating.—*adv.* **excru'ciatingly.**—*n.* **excruciā'tion**, torture: vexation. [L. *ex-*, out, *cruciāre*, *-ātum*, to crucify— *crux*, *crucis*, a cross.]
**excubant**, *eks'kū-bant*, *adj.* on guard. [L. *excubāns*, *-antis*, pr.p. of *excubāre*, to sleep out, lie on guard—*ex*, *cubāre*, to lie.]
**excudit**, *eks-kū'dit*, *-kōō'*, (L.) (he) struck, hammered, forged, printed (this).
**exculpate**, *eks'kul-pāt*, also *-kul', v.t.* to clear from the charge of a fault or crime: to absolve: to vindicate.—*n.* **exculpā'tion**.—*adj.* **excul'patory**, tending to free from the charge of fault or crime. [L. *ex*, from, *culpa*, a fault.]
**ex curia**, *eks kū'ri-a*, *kōō'ri-ä*, (L.) out of court.
**excurrent**, *eks-kur'ənt*, *adj.* having the main stem reaching to the top: having the midrib reaching beyond the lamina: flowing outwards: carrying an outgoing current. [L. *ex*, from, *currēns*, *-entis*, pr.p. of *currēre*, to run.]
**excursion**, *iks-kûr'shən*, *n.* a going forth: a raid: a sally: a deviation: an escapade: a pleasure trip: a company or collection of people on a pleasure outing: a wandering from the main subject: a digression.—Also *v.i.*—*vs.i.* **excurse'**, to digress; **excur'sionise**, *-ize*, to go on an excursion.—*n.* **excur'sionist**, one who goes on a pleasure trip.—*adj.* **excur'sive**, rambling: deviating.—*adv.* **excur'sively.**—*ns.* **excur'siveness**; **excur'sus** (*pl.* **excur'suses**), a dissertation on some particular matter appended to a book or chapter. —**excursion train**, a special train, usually with reduced fares, for persons making an excursion. [L. *ex-*, out, *currēre*, *cursum*, to run.]
**excuse**, *iks-kūz', v.t.* to free from blame or guilt: to exonerate: to pass over, overlook: to pardon or condone (in small matters): to free from an obligation: to release, dispense with: to allow to absent oneself: to seek to extenuate or justify: to make an apology or ask pardon for.—*v.i.* to make excuse.—*n.* (*iks-kūs'*) a plea offered in extenuation: indulgence.—*adj.* **excūsable** (*iks-kūz'ə-bl*).—*n.* **excūs'ableness.**—*adv.* **excūs'ably.**—*n.* **excūs'al.**—*adjs.* **excūs'atory**, making or containing excuse: apologetic; **excusive** (*eks-kūs'iv*).—**excuse me**, an expression used as an apology for any slight or apparent impropriety, or for controverting a statement that has been made. [L. *excūsāre*—*ex*, from, *causa*, a cause, accusation.]
**ex debito justitiae**, *eks deb'i-tō jəs-tish'i-ē*, *dā'bi-tō ūs-ti'ti-ī*, (L.L.) from what is due to justice.
**ex delicto**, *eks di-lik'tō*, *dā-lik'tō*, (L.L.) owing to a crime.
**ex dono**, *eks dō'nō*, (L.) by gift, as a present from.
**exeat**, *eks'i-at, n.* formal leave of absence, esp. for a student to be out of college for more than one night. [L., let him go out: 3rd pers. sing. pres. subj. of *exire*.]
**execrate**, *eks'i-krāt, v.t.* to curse: to denounce evil against: to denounce: to detest.—*adj.* **ex'ecrable**, deserving execration: detestable: accursed.—*adv.* **ex'ecrably.**—*n.* **execrā'tion**, act of execrating: a curse pronounced: that which is execrated.—*adjs.* **ex'ecrātive**, of or belonging to execration.—*adv.* **ex'ecrātively.**—*adj.* **ex'ecrātory.** [L. *exsecrārī*, *-ātus*, to curse—*ex*, from, *sacer*, sacred.]
**execute**, *eks'i-kūt, v.t.* to perform: to give effect

to: to carry into effect: to put to use, bring into action: to put to death by law.—*adj.* **execūtable** (*eks'i-kūt-ə-bl, ek-sek'ūt-ə-bl*), that can be executed.—*ns.* **exec'ūtancy** (*eg-zek'*), technique in music; **exec'ūtant** (*eg-zek'*), one who executes or performs: a technically accomplished performer of music; **execūter** (*eks'*); **execū'tion,** act of or skill in executing or performing: accomplishment: completion: carrying into effect the sentence of a court of law: the warrant for so doing: the infliction of capital punishment; **execū'tioner,** one who executes, esp. one who inflicts capital punishment.—*adj.* **executive** (*eg-zek'ū-tiv*), designed or fitted to execute or perform: concerned with performance, administration, or management: active: qualifying for or pertaining to the execution of the law: administrative.—*n.* the power or authority in government that carries the laws into effect: the persons who administer the government or an organisation: a person in an executive position in government or business: the head of an executive, as president, governor, mayor, etc. (*U.S.*; also **chief executive**).—*adv.* **exec'ūtively.**—*n.* **exec'ūtor** (*eg-zek'*), one who executes or performs: a person appointed to see a will carried into effect:—*fem.* **exec'ūtrix** (*pl.* -trixes, or **execūtri'cēs**); also **exec'utress.**—*adj.* **execūtō'rial.**—*n.* **exec'ūtorship.**—*adj.* **exec'- ūtory,** executing official duties: designed to be carried into effect.—*n.* **exec'ūtry,** executorship: moveable estate and effects (*Scots law*).—**executive session** (*U.S.*), a meeting of the Senate for executive business, usu. held in private: hence, any meeting in private. [L. *exsequī, exsecūtus* —*ex,* out, *sequī,* to follow.]

**exedra,** *eks'i-drə, eks-ed'rə, n.* a portico, hall, or vestibule: a seated room: a raised platform with steps, in the open air: an apse, recess, niche—also **exhedra:**—*pl.* **ex'(h)edrae.** [Gr. *exedrā*—*ex-,* out, *hedrā,* seat.]

**exeem, exeme,** *eks-ēm',* (*obs. Scot.*) *v.t.* to release, exempt. [L. *eximēre*—*ex,* from, *emēre,* to take.]

**exegesis,** *eks-i-jē'sis, n.* interpretation, esp. Biblical.—*ns.* **ex'egēte, exegēt'ist,** one who interprets or expounds.—*adjs.* **exegetic** (*-jet'ik*), **-al,** pertaining to exegesis: explanatory.—*adv.* **exegēt'i-cally.**—*n.pl.* **exegēt'ics,** the science of exegesis. [Gr. *exēgēsis*—*exēgeesthai,* to explain—*ex-,* out, *hēgeesthai,* to guide.]

**exempla,** *ig-zem'plə, eks-em'pla* (L.; *pl.* of **exem-plum,** *ig-zem'pləm, eks-em'plōōm*) examples.

**exemplar,** *egz-em'plər, -plär, n.* a person or thing to be imitated: the ideal model of an artist: a type: an example: a copy of a book.—*adv.* **exem'plarily.**—*ns.* **exem'plariness; exemplarity** (*-plar'*), exemplariness: exemplary conduct.— *adj.* **exem'plary,** worthy of imitation or notice: serving as model, specimen, illustration, or warning. [L. *exemplar*—*exemplum,* example.]

**exemple,** *eg-zäpl',* (Fr.) example, model.—**par exemple,** for example.

**exemplify,** *igz-em'pli-fī, v.t.* to illustrate by example: to make an attested copy of: to prove by an attested copy:—*pr.p.* **exem'plifying;** *pa.t.* and *pa.p.* **exem'plified.**—*adj.* **exem'plifiable.**—*n.* **exemplificā'tion,** act of exemplifying: that which exemplifies: an attested copy or transcript. [L. *exemplum,* example, *facĕre,* to make.]

**exempli gratia,** *ig-zem'pli grä'shi-ə, eks-em'plē grä'ti-ä* (L.) by way of example, for instance— cften abbreviated, e.g.

**exempt,** *igz-emt', v.t.* to set apart (*Milt.*): to free, or grant immunity (with *from*).—*adj.* taken out: not liable.—*n.* one who is exempt: an officer who commanded in absence of his superiors, exempted on this account from ordinary duties (*hist.*).—*n.* **exemp'tion,** act of exempting: state of being exempt: freedom from any service, duty, burden, etc.: immunity.

[Fr.,—L. *eximēre, exemptum*—*ex,* from, *emēre,* to buy.]

**exenterate,** *eks-en'tər-āt, v.t.* to disembowel.— *adj.* (*-it*) disembowelled.—*n.* **exenterā'tion.** [L. *exenterāre*—Gr. *exenterizein*—*ex,* from, and *enteron,* intestine.]

**exequatur,** *eks-i-kwä'tər, n.* an official recognition of a consul or commercial agent given by the government of the country in which he is to be. [L. *exequātur,* let him execute—the opening word.]

**exequy,** *eks'i-kwi* (usu. in *pl.* **exequies, -kwiz**), *n.* a funeral procession: funeral rites.—*adj.* **exequial** (*eks-ē'kwi-əl*). [L. *exequiae—ex,* from, *sequī,* to follow.]

**exercise,** *eks'ər-sīz, n.* a putting in practice: exertion of the body for health or amusement or acquisition of skill: a similar exertion of the mind: a task designed or prescribed for these purposes: a written school task: a study in music: a set of problems, passages for translation, etc., in a text-book: an academical disputation: accomplishment (*Shak.*): (in *pl.*) military drill or manoeuvres: a ceremony or formal proceeding (*U.S.*): an act of worship or devotion: a discourse, the discussion of a passage of Scripture, giving the coherence of text and context, etc. (the *addition* giving the doctrinal propositions, etc.): a meeting of a presbytery for this purpose; hence formerly the presbytery itself.—*v.t.* to train by use: to improve by practice: to give exercise to: to trouble: to put in practice: to use: to wield. —*v.i.* to take exercise: to drill.—*adj.* **ex'ercis-able.**—**ex'ercise-book,** a book for writing school exercises in. [O.Fr. *exercice*—L. *exer-citium*—L. *exercēre, -citum,* pfx. *ex-,* and *arcēre,* to shut up, restrain.]

**exercitation,** *egz-ûr-sit-ā'shən, n.* putting into practice: employment: exercise: a discourse. [L. *exercitātiō, -ōnis—exercēre,* to exercise.]

**exergue,** *eks', or eks-ûrg', n.* part on the reverse of a coin, below the main device, often filled up by the date, etc.—*adj.* **exer'gual.** [Fr.,—Gr. *ex,* out of, *ergon,* work.]

**exert,** *igz-ûrt', v.t.* to put forth (*obs.*); to bring into active operation: to do or perform (*obs.*). —*n.* **exer'tion,** a bringing into active operation: striving: activity.—*adj.* **exert'ive,** having the power or tendency to exert: using exertion. [L. *exserēre, exsertum—ex,* from, *serēre,* to put together.]

**exes,** *eks'əz, n.pl.* a slang abbreviation for **expenses.**

**exeunt,** *eks'i-unt, -ōont,* (L.) go out (*pl.*), leave the stage; **exeunt omnes,** *om'nēz, -nās,* all go out. See **exit.**

**exfoliate,** *eks-fō'li-āt, v.t.* to shed in flakes: to remove in flakes.—*v.i.* to come off in flakes: to separate into layers.—*n.* **exfoliā'tion.**—*adj.* **exfō'-liative,** exfoliative cytology, study for diagnostic purposes of cells shed from internal body surfaces. [L. *exfoliāre, -ātum,* to strip of leaves— *ex,* from, *folium,* a leaf.]

**ex gratia,** *eks grā'shi-ə, grä'ti-ä,* (L.) as an act of grace.

**exhale,** *eks-hāl, egz-āl', v.t.* to breathe forth: to emit or send out as vapour, smell, etc.: to cause or allow to evaporate: to emit through a membrane.—*v.i.* to breathe out: to rise or come off as a vapour, smell, emanation: to evaporate: to ooze out.—*adjs.* **exhāl'able; ex-hāl'ant,** exhaling: emitting vapour or liquid.— *n.* an organ or vessel that emits vapour or liquid.—*n.* **exhalation** (*eks-, egz-ə-lā'shən*), act or process of exhaling: evaporation: that which is exhaled, vapour, effluvium, emanation: a mist: a meteoric phenomenon, a meteor (*arch.*). [L. *exhālāre—ex,* from, *hālāre, -ātum,* to breathe.]

exhale, eks-hāl', (Shak.) v.t. to hale or draw out. [Pfx. ex-, and hale.]

exhaust, igz-öst', v.t. to draw off: to draw out the whole of: to use the whole strength of: to use up: to empty: to wear or tire out: to treat of or develop completely.—n. an outward current, or means of producing it: the exit of used working fluid from the cylinder of an engine: the period of discharge of the fluid: the fluid so escaping (exhaust'-gas, -steam).—adj. exhaust'ed, drawn out: emptied: consumed: tired out.—n. exhaust'er, he who or that which exhausts.—adj. exhaust'ible, that may be exhausted.—n. exhaustion (-öst'yən), act of exhausting or consuming: state of being exhausted: extreme fatigue.—adjs. exhaust'ive, tending to exhaust: investigating all parts or possibilities; exhaust'less, that cannot be exhausted.— exhaust'-pipe', valve', the pipe, valve, through which exhaust gases pass out. [L. exhaurīre, exhaustum—ex, from, haurīre, to draw.]

exheredate, eks-her'i-dāt, (rare) v.t. to disinherit. —n. exheredā'tion. [L. exhērēdāre—ex, out, hērēs, -ēdis, heir.]

exhibit, igz-ib'it, v.t. to hold forth or present to view: to present formally or publicly: to show: to give as a remedy (med.; arch.).—n. a document or object produced in court to be used as evidence (law): something exhibited: an article at an exhibition.—ns. exhib'iter; exhibition (eks-i-bish'ən), presentation to view: display: showing off: a public show, esp. of works of art, manufactures, etc.: that which is exhibited: a public performance at the end of a school year: a grant or gift: an allowance towards support, esp. to scholars in a university: administration of a remedy (arch.); exhibi'- tioner, one who enjoys an exhibition at a university; exhibi'tionism, extravagant behaviour aimed at drawing attention to self: perversion involving public exposure of one's sexual organs (psychiatry); exhibi'tionist.—adj. exhibitionist'ic.—adv. -ist'ically.—adj. exhib'itive (igz-), serving for exhibition: representative.— n. exhibitor (igz-ib'i-tər).—adj. exhib'itory, exhibiting.—make an exhibition of oneself, to behave foolishly, exciting ridicule. [L. exhibēre, -itum—ex-, out, habēre, -itum, to have.]

exhilarate, igz-il'ə-rāt, v.t. to make hilarious or merry: to raise the spirits of: to enliven: to cheer.—adj. exhil'arant, exhilarating: exciting joy, mirth, or pleasure.—n. an exhilarating medicine.—adj. exhil'arāting, cheering: gladdening.—adv. exhil'arātingly.—n. exhilarā'tion, state of being exhilarated: joyousness.—adjs. exhil'arātive, exhil'aratory. [L. exhilarāre, -ātum —ex-, inten., hilaris, cheerful.]

exhort, ig-zört', v.t. to urge strongly and earnestly: to counsel.—n. exhortā'tion (eks- or egz-), act of exhorting: language intended to exhort: counsel: a religious discourse.—adjs. exhort'a- tive, exhort'atory (igz-), tending to exhort or advise.—n. exhort'er, one who exhorts: in some churches a layman appointed to give religious exhortation. [L. exhortāri, -ātus—ex- inten., hortāri, to urge.]

exhume, eks-hūm', ig-zūm', v.t. to take out of the ground or place of burial: to disinter: to bring to light.—Also exhumate (eks'hūm-āt).—ns. ex- humā'tion (eks-); exhum'er. [L. ex, out of, humus, the ground.]

ex hypothesi, eks hī-poth'ə-si, (L.L.) from the hypothesis.

exies, ek'sāz, (Scot.) n.pl. a fit, as of hysterics, ague. [access.]

exigent, eks'i-jənt, adj. pressing: urgent: exacting: demanding immediate attention or action. —n. extremity (obs.): the last strait, the end of all (Shak.): a needed amount (Browning).—adj. exigeant (egz-ē-zhā, Fr.), exacting (fem. exi-

geante, -zhät).—ns. ex'igence, ex'igency (or -ij'), pressing necessity: emergency: distress. [L. exigēns, -entis—pr.p. of exigēre—pfx. ex-, agēre, to drive.]

exigible, eks'i-jib-l, adj. liable to be exacted. [See exact.]

exiguous, egz-, eks-ig'ū-əs, adj. scanty: slender. —ns. exigū'ity (eks-); exig'ūousness. [L. exiguus—exigēre, to weigh strictly; see exact.]

exile, eks', or egz'il, n. enforced or regretted absence from one's country or home: banishment (in these senses formerly egz-il'): one who is in exile: a banished person.—v.t. (formerly egz-il') to expel from one's country, to banish.—n. ex'ilement, banishment.—adj. exilic (egz-il-ik, or eks-), pertaining to exile, esp. that of the Jews in Babylon. [O.Fr. exil —L. exsilium, banishment—ex, out of, and root of salīre, to leap; affected by L. exsul, an exile.]

exility, egz-, eks-il'i-ti, (obs.) n. slenderness, smallness: refinement. [L. exilitās, -ātis—exilis, slender.]

eximious, eg-zim'i-əs, (arch.) adj. excellent, distinguished. [L. eximius—eximēre—ex, from, emēre, to take.]

ex improviso, eks im-prə-vī'zō, im-prō-vē'sō, -wē', (L.) unexpectedly.

exine, eks'in, -in. See extine. [L. ex, out of.]

exist, igz-ist', v.i. to have an actual being.—n. exist'ence, state of existing or being: livelihood: life: anything that exists: being.—adjs. exist'ent, having being: at present existing; existential (eks-is-ten'shal).—ns. existen'tialism, a term covering a number of related doctrines denying objective universal values and holding that a man must create values for himself through action and by living each moment to the full; existen'tialist. [L. existēre, exsistēre, to stand forth—ex-, out, sistēre, to stand.]

exit, ek'sit, eg'zit, n. departure of a player from the stage: any departure: a passage out: a way of departure: death:—pl. ex'its.—v.i. to make an exit: to die:—pa.p. and pa.t. ex'ited. [Partly from the L. stage direction exit, goes out (in pl. exeunt, go out)—exīre, to go out—ex-, out, and īre, itum, to go; partly—L. exitus, a way out.]

ex-libris, eks-lī'bris, lī', n. a bookplate.—ns. ex- li'brism; ex-li'brist, a collector or student of bookplates. [L. ex libris, from the books (of so-and-so).]

ex mero motu, eks mē'rō mō'tū, me'rō mō'tōō, (L.) from his own impulse: of his, its, own accord.

ex natura rei, eks na-tū'rə rē'i, na-tōō'ra re'ē, (L.L.) from the nature of the case; ex natura rerum, rē'rəm, rā'rōōm, from the nature of things.

exo-, eks'ō-, eks-ō', in composition, outside, often opp. to endo-, ento-. See also ecto-.—ns. ex'o- carp (Gr. karpos, fruit), the epicarp of a fruit; exoder'mis (Gr. dermis, skin), the outer cortex layer of a root.—adj. exoderm'al.—n. exog'amy (Gr. gamos, marriage), the practice of marrying only outside of one's own group: union of gametes not closely related (biol.).—adjs. exo- gam'ic, exog'amous.—n. ex'ogen (Gr. gen-, root of gignesthai, to be produced; obs.), a dicotyledon—so called because its stem thickens by layers growing on the outside of the wood.— adj. exog'enous, growing by successive additions to the outside.—n. exoph'agy (Gr. phagein, to eat), the custom among cannibals of eating only the flesh of persons not of their own kin. —adj. exoph'agous.—n. exop'odite (Gr. pous, podos, foot), the outer branch of a crustacean limb.—adj. exopod'itic.—n. exoskel'eton, a hard supporting or protective structure secreted externally by the ectoderm.—adj. exoskel'etal.

—*n.* ex'osphere (Gr. *sphaira*, sphere), the boundary of the earth's atmosphere and interplanetary space.—*adjs.* exospher'ic, -al.—*n.* ex'ospore (Gr. *sporos*, a seed), the outer layer of a spore wall: a spore formed by abstriction, not within a mother-cell.—*adjs.* exospor'al, exospor'ous; exother'mal, exother'mic (Gr. *thermē*, heat; *chem.*), involving evolution of heat.—*n.* exothermi'city. [Gr. *exō*, outside.] exode, *ek'sōd, n.* the concluding part of a Greek drama: a farce or afterpiece. [Gr. *exŏdion.*] exodus, *eks'ə-dəs, n.* a going out, esp. that of the Israelites from Egypt: (*cap.*) the second book of the Old Testament.—*adj.* exodic (-*od'*). —*n.* ex'odist, one who goes out: an emigrant. [L.,—Gr. *exodos*—*ex*-, out, *hodos*, a way.] ex officio, *eks o-fish'i-ō, -fik', (L.)* by virtue of his office. exomis, *eks-ō'mis, n.* a one-sleeved or (in Rome) sleeveless garment—(*Browning*) exo'mion. [Gr. *exōmis*—*ex*-, out, *ōmos*, shoulder.] exon, *eks'on, n.* an officer of the Yeomen of the Guard. [App. intended to express the pronunciation of Fr. *exempt*; see exempt.] exonerate, *igz-on'ər-āt, v.t.* to free from the burden of blame or obligation: to acquit.—*n.* exonerā'tion, act of exonerating.—*adj.* exon'-erative, freeing from a burden or obligation. [L. *exonerāre, -ātum*,—*ex* from, *onus, oneris*, burden.] ex opere operato, ex opere operantis. See opus. exophthalmia, -mos, -mus, *eks-of-thal'mi-a, -məs, ns.* a protrusion of the eyeballs.—*adj.* exoph-thal'mic. [Gr. *ex*, out, *ophthalmos*, eye.] exorable, *eks'ər-ə-bl, adj.* capable of being moved by entreaty.—*n.* exorā'tion (*obs.*), entreaty. [L. *exōrāre*—pfx. *ex*- in the sense of thoroughly, *ōrāre*, to entreat.] exorbitant, *igz-ör'bi-tənt, adj.* going beyond the usual limits: excessive.—*ns.* exor'bitance, exor'-bitancy, great excess.—*adv.* exor'bitantly.—*v.i.* exor'bitate (*obs.*), to stray. [L. *exorbitāns, -antis*, pr.p. of *exorbitāre*—*ex*, out of, *orbita*, a track—*orbis*, a circle.] exorcise, -ize, *eks'ör-sīz, v.t.* to adjure by some holy name: to call forth or drive away, as a spirit: to deliver from the influence of an evil spirit.—*ns.* ex'orcism (-*sizm*), act of exorcising or expelling evil spirits by certain ceremonies: a formula for exorcising: ex'orcist, one who exorcises or pretends to expel evil spirits by adjuration (also exorcis'er, -z-): the third of the minor orders (*R.C. Church*). [L.L. from Gr. *exorkizein*—*ex*-, out, *horkos*, an oath.] exordium, *egz-ör'di-əm, n.* the introductory part of a discourse or composition:—*pl.* exor'diums, -ia.—*adj.* exor'dial, pertaining to the exordium: introductory. [L.—*exordiri*—*ex*, out of, *ordiri*, to begin.] exosmosis, *eks-os-mō'sis, n.* osmosis outwards, i.e. away from the solution—also ex'osmose (-*mōs*).—*adj.* exosmotic (-*mot'ik*). [Gr. *ex*-, out, and osmosis.] exostosis, *eks-os-tō'sis, (anat.) n.* morbid enlargement of a bone. [Gr. *exostōsis*—*ex*-, out, *osteon*, a bone.] exoteric, *eks-ō-ter'ik, adj.* external: fit to be communicated to the public or multitude—opp. to esoteric.—*adj.* exoter'ical.—*adv.* exoter'ically. —*n.* exoter'icism (-*sizm*). [Gr. *exōterikos*—*exōterō*, comp. of *exō*, outside.] exotic, *igz-ot'ik, adj.* introduced from a foreign country: alien: foreign-looking: outlandish: romantically strange, or rich and showy, or glamorous: pertaining to strip-tease.—*n.* anything of foreign origin: something not native to a country, as a plant, a word, a custom.—Also *n.* —*n.* exot'icism (-*sizm*). [Gr. *exōtikos*—*exō*, outside.] expand, *iks-pand', v.t.* to spread out: to lay open:

to enlarge in bulk or surface: to develop, or bring out in fuller detail: to express at length, as in terms of a series, or without contractions.— *v.i.* to become opened: to increase in volume: to enlarge: to spread: to become communicative (*fig.*).—*ns.* expanse (-*pans'*), a wide extent: a stretch: amount of spread or stretch: the firmament; expansibil'ity.—*adj.* expans'ible, capable of being expanded.—*adv.* expans'ibly.— *adj.* expans'ile (-*il*), capable of expansion.—*n.* expan'sion, act of expanding: state of being expanded: enlargement: that which is expanded: amount of expanding: territorial extension: immensity: extension.—*adjs.* expan'sional; expan'sionary, tending to expansion.—*ns.* expan'sionism; expan'sionist, one who favours territorial or currency expansion.— Also *adj.*—*adj.* expans'ive, widely extended: diffusive: causing expansion: worked by expansion: effusive: talkative, communicative: marked by excessive feeling of well-being and delusions of self-importance (*psychiatry*).—*adv.* expans'ively.—*ns.* expans'iveness; expansiv'ity (*eks*-).—expanded metal, steel, etc., stretched to form a mesh, used for reinforcing concrete, etc.; expanded plastic, foam plastic; expanding universe (*astron.*), the theory that as part of continuous creation the whole universe is constantly expanding. [L. *expandēre*—*ex*-, out, *pandēre, pānsum*, to spread.] ex parte, *eks pär'tē, pär'te, adj.* on one side only: partial: prejudiced. [L. *ex*, from, *parte*, abl. of *pars, partis*, party, side.] expatiate, *eks-pā'shi-āt, v.t.* to walk about: to range at large (usu. *fig.*): to enlarge in discourse, argument, or writing.—*n.* expatiā'tion.—*adjs.* expā'tiative, expā'tiatory, expansive.—*n.* expā'-tiātor. [L. *exspatiāri, -ātus*—*ex*, out of, *spatiārī*, to roam—*spatium*, space.] expatriate, *eks-pā'tri-āt, v.t.* to send out of one's country: banish, exile.—Also *n.* and *adj.*—*n.* expatriā'tion, act of expatriating: exile, voluntary or compulsory. [L.L. *expatriāre, -ātum*—*ex*, out of, *patria*, fatherland.] expect, *iks-pekt', v.t.* to await (*obs.*): to look forward to as likely to come or happen, or as due: to suppose.—*v.i.* (*obs.*) to wait.—*n.* (*Shak.*) expectation.—*ns.* expect'ance, expect'ancy, act or state of expecting: that which is expected: hope.—*adj.* expect'ant, looking or waiting for something: in expectation: not yet but expecting to be: pregnant.—*n.* one who expects: one who is looking or waiting for some benefit or office.—*adv.* expect'antly.—*ns.* expectā'tion (*eks*-), act or state of expecting: prospect of future good: that which is or may fairly be expected: degree of probability: the value of something expected: (in *pl.*) prospect of fortune or profit by a will.—*adj.* expect'ative, giving rise to expectation: reversionary.—*n.* an expectancy: an anticipatory grant of a benefice not yet vacant. —*adj.* expect'ed.—*adv.* expect'edly.—*n.* expect'er. —*n.* and *adj.* expect'ing.—*adv.* expect'ingly, in a state of expectation.—Expectation Week, the period betweeen Ascension Day and Whit Sunday—commemorating the Apostles' expectation of the Comforter.—be expecting (*coll.*), to be pregnant. [L. *expectāre, -ātum*—*ex*, out, *spectāre*, to look, freq. of *specēre*, to see.] expectorate, *eks-pek'tə-rāt, v.t.* to expel from the breast or lungs by coughing, etc.: to spit forth. —*v.i.* to discharge or eject phlegm from the throat: to spit.—*adj.* expec'torant, tending to promote expectoration.—*n.* a medicine that promotes expectoration.—*n.* expectorā'tion, act of expectorating: that which is expectorated: spittle.—*adj.* expec'torātive, having the quality of promoting expectoration. [L. *expectorāre*, *-ātum*—*ex*, from, *pectus, pectoris*, breast.] expedient, *iks-pē'di-ənt, adj.* suitable: advisable:

expeditious (*Shak.*).—*n.* that which serves to promote: means suitable to an end: contrivance, shift.—*ns.* expē'dience, haste, despatch (*Shak.*): enterprise (*Shak.*): expediency; expē'diency, fitness: desirableness: conduciveness to the need of the moment: that which is opportune: self-interest.—*adj.* expēdien'tial (*-en'shl*).—*adv.* expē'diently.  [L. *expediēns, -entis,* pr.p. of *expedīre*; see expedite.]
expeditate, *eks-ped'it-āt, v.t.* to deprive of three claws or of the ball of the foot.—*n.* expeditā'tion. [L.L. *expeditāre, -ātum—ex,* from, *pēs, pedis,* foot.]
expedite, *eks'pi-dīt, v.t.* to free from impediments: to hasten: to send forth: to despatch.—*adj.* (*obs.*), free from impediment: unencumbered: quick: prompt.—*adv.* ex'peditely.—*n.* expedition (*-di'shən*), speed: promptness: an organised journey to attain some object, as hunting, warfare, exploration, etc.: the party undertaking such a journey.—*adjs.* expedi'tionary, belonging to an expedition: of the nature of an expedition; expedi'tious, characterised by expedition or rapidity: speedy: prompt.—*adv.* expedi'tiously. *n.* expedi'tiousness.—*adj.* exped'itive.  [L. *expedīre, -itum—ex,* from, *pēs, pedis,* a foot.]
expel, *iks-pel', v.t.* to drive out: to eject: to discharge in disgrace (from school, etc.): to banish: to keep off (*Shak.*):—*pr.p.* expell'ing; *pa.t.* and *pa.p.* expelled'.—*adj.* and *n.* expell'ant, -ent.  [L. *expellēre, expulsum—ex, pellēre,* to drive.]
expend, *iks-pend', v.t.* to lay out: to employ or consume in any way: to spend.—*adj.* expend'-able, that may be expended, esp. that may be sacrificed to achieve some end.—Also *n.*—*ns.* expend'iture, act of expending or laying out: that which is expended: the process of using up: money spent; expense (*-pens'*), expenditure: outlay: cost: (in *pl.*) money out of pocket, or an allowance therefor: (in *pl.*: *Scots law*) costs in a lawsuit.—*adj.* expens'ive, causing or requiring much expense: costly: lavish.—*adv.* expens'ively.—*n.* expens'iveness.—expense(s) account, statement of outlay incurred in carrying out a business commission (often with the implication that the account may be made to cover a great deal).—be at the expense of, to pay the cost of.  [L. *expendēre—ex-,* out, *pendēre, pēnsum,* to weigh.]
experience, *iks-pē'ri-əns, n.* test, trial, experiment (*obs.*): practical acquaintance with any matter gained by trial: long and varied observation, personal or general: wisdom derived from the changes and trials of life: the passing through any event or course of events by which one is affected: an event so passed through: anything received by the mind, as sensation, perception, or knowledge.—*v.t.* to have practical acquaintance with: to prove or know by use: to have experience of: to suffer, undergo.—*adj.* expē'-rienced, taught by experience: having much experience: skilful: wise.—*adjs.* expē'rienceless, having little or no experience; expērien'tial (*-en'shl*), pertaining to or derived from experience.—*ns.* expērien'tialism, the doctrine that all knowledge comes from experience; expērien'tialist.—experience meeting, one for the relating of religious experiences.  [Fr. *expérience* and L. *experientia,* from *experīrī—ex-,* inten., and old verb *perīrī,* to try.]
experiment, *iks-per'i-mənt, n.* experience (*obs.*): a trial: something done to test a theory, or to discover something unknown.—*v.i.* (also *-ment'*) to make experiment or trial: to search by trial.— *v.t.* (*obs.*) to make trial of.—*adj.* experiment'al, experienced, having experience (*obs.*): pertaining to experiment: based on or proceeding by experiment: tentative.—*v.i.* experiment'alise, -ize.—*ns.* experiment'alism, reliance on experi-

ment;  experiment'alist;  exper'imenter (or -*ment'*), exper'imentist, one who makes experiments.—*adv.* experiment'ally.—*n.* experimentā'-tion.—*adjs.* experiment'ative; exper'imented, experienced (*obs.*): practised.  [L. *experi-mentum,* from *experīrī,* to try thoroughly; see experience.]
experimentum crucis, *iks-per-i-men'təm krōō'sis, eks-pe-ri-men'tōōm krōō'kis* (L.) a crucial test.
expert, *eks-pûrt', adj.* taught by practice: having a familiar knowledge: having a facility of performance: skilful, adroit.—*v.t.* (*Spens.*) to experience.—*ns.* ex'pert, one who is skilled in any art or science: a specialist: a scientific or professional witness; expertise (*-ēz'*; Fr.), expert knowledge: expertness: expert appraisal, valuation.—*adv.* expert'ly.—*n.* expert'ness. [Fr., —L. *expertus—experīrī,* to try thoroughly; see experience.]
expiate, *eks'pi-āt, v.t.* to make complete atonement for: to make satisfaction or reparation for.—*adj.* (*Shak.*) expired, at an end.—*adj.* ex'-piable, capable of being expiated, atoned for, or done away.—*ns.* expiā'tion, act of expiating: the means by which atonement is made: atonement; ex'piātor.—*adj.* ex'piatory (*-ə-,* or *-ā-tər-i*).  [L. *expiāre, -ātum—ex-,* inten., *piāre,* to appease, atone for.]
expire, *iks-, eks-pīr', v.t.* to breathe out: to emit: to bring to an end (*Spens.*).—*v.i.* to breathe out: to die: to come to an end: to lapse: to become invalid by lapse of time: to fulfil a term (*Spens.*).—*adj.* expī'rable, that may expire or come to an end.—*ns.* expī'rant, one expiring; expirā'tion (*eks-pi-* or *-pī-*), the act of breathing out: death (*obs.*): end: that which is expired.—*adj.* expī'ratory, pertaining to expiration, or the emission of the breath.—*adjs.* expired', dead: extinct: lapsed: obsolete; expī'ring, dying: pertaining to or uttered at the time of dying.—*n.* expī'ry, the end or termination, esp. by lapse of time: expiration.  [Fr. *expirer—*L. *ex,* from; *spīrāre, -ātum,* to breathe.]
exspicate, *eks-pis'kāt,* (*Scot.*) *v.t.* to find out by skilful means or by strict examination.—*n.* exspiscā'tion.—*adj.* expis'cātory.  [L. *expiscārī, expiscātus—ex,* from, *piscārī,* to fish—*piscis,* a fish.]
explain, *iks-plān', v.t.* to make plain or intelligible: to unfold and illustrate the meaning of: to expound: to account for.—*v.i.* to give an explanation.—*adj.* explain'able.—*ns.* explain'er; explana'tion (*eks-plə-nā'shən*), act of explaining or clearing from obscurity: that which explains or clears up: the meaning or sense given to anything: a mutual clearing up of matters.—*adv.* explan'atorily (*iks-plan'ə-tər-i-li*).—*adj.* explan'a-tory, serving to explain or clear up: containing explanations.—explain away, to modify the force of by explanation, generally in a bad sense. [L. *explānāre—ex-,* out, *plānāre,* to level—*plānus,* flat, plain.]
explantation, *eks-plän-tā'shən, n.* the culture in an artificial medium of a part or organ removed from a living individual.—*n.* and *v.t.* explant'.  [L. *explantāre—ex-,* out, *plantāre,* to plant.]
expletive, *eks-, iks-plē'tiv,* or *eks'pli-tiv, adj.* filling out: added merely to fill up.—*n.* a word inserted to fill up a sentence or line of verse: a meaningless word serving a grammatical purpose only: anything present merely to fill a gap: a meaningless oath.—*adj.* exple'tory (also *eks'*), serving to fill up: expletive: supplementary.  [L. *explētīvus—ex,* out, *plēre,* to fill.]
explicate, *eks'pli-kāt, v.t.* to unfold, develop: to lay open or explain the meaning of.—*adj.* explic'-able (older *eks'*), capable of being explicated or explained.—*n.* explicā'tion, act of explicating or explaining: explanation.—*adjs.* explic'ative, explic'atory (older *eks'*), serving to explicate or

explain. [L. *explicāre, explicātum* or *explicitum* —*ex*, out, *plicāre*, to fold.]

explicit, *iks-plis'it, adj.* not implied merely, but distinctly stated: plain in language: outspoken: clear: unreserved.—*adv.* explic'itly.—*n.* explic'-itness. [See explicate.]

explicit, *eks'pli-sit, n.* a conclusion. [From the mediaeval custom of writing *explicit* at the end of a book or section: originally apparently for L. *explicitum est*, is completed: later taken to be 3rd sing. pres. indic., and supplied with a plural *expliciunt*; see explicate.]

explode, *iks-plōd', v.t.* to cry down, hoot off, as an actor (*arch.*): to bring into disrepute, and reject: to cause to blow up.—*v.i.* to burst with a loud report: to burst out, break forth suddenly.—*adj.* explō'ded, blown up: rejected because proved false (of a theory, etc.).—*ns.* explō'der; explō'sion (*-zhən*), act of exploding: a sudden violent burst with a loud report: an outburst: breaking out of feelings, etc.: a great and rapid increase or expansion as *population explosion*: release of breath after stoppage in articulating a stop consonant in certain positions.—*adj.* explō'sive (*-siv, -ziv*), liable to or causing explosion: worked, set in place, etc., by an explosion: bursting out with violence and noise.—*n.* something that will explode: a stop consonant pronounced with explosion.—*adv.* explō'sively.—*n.* explō'siveness.—explosion shot, a golf stroke to send a ball forcibly out of a bunker; explosion welding, welding metals with very different melting points by means of pressure produced by an explosion; explosive bolt, a bolt that can be blown out of position because it contains a small explosive charge; explosive rivet, a rivet fixed in inaccessible places by detonation of a small charge in its end. [L. *explōdĕre, explōsum—ex*, from, *plaudĕre*, to clap the hands.]

exploit, *eks'ploit, n.* a deed or achievement, esp. an heroic one: a feat.—*v.t.* (*iks-ploit'*) to work, make available: to turn to use: to make gain out of or at the expense of.—*adj.* exploit'able.—*ns.* exploit'age, exploitā'tion (*eks-*), the act of successfully applying industry to any object, as the working of mines, etc.: the act of using for selfish purposes; exploit'er. [O.Fr. *exploit*—L. *explicitum*, unfolded; see explicate.]

explore, *iks-plōr'*, or *-plör', v.t.* and *v.i.* to search or travel through for the purpose of discovery: to examine thoroughly.—*n.* explorā'tion (*eks-*), act of searching thoroughly: travel for the sake of discovery.—*adjs.* explor'ative, explor'atory, serving to explore or investigate: searching out.—*n.* explor'er.—*adj.* explor'ing. [Fr.,—L. *explōrāre, -ātum*, to search out.]

explosion. See explode.

exponent, *eks-pō'nənt, adj.* setting forth: expounding.—*n.* an expounder: an interpreter of an art by performance: an example, illustration, type: a symbol showing what power a quantity is raised to, an index (*math.*).—*adj.* exponential (*eks-pō-nen'shl*), pertaining to or involving exponents.—*n.* an exponential function.—*adv.* exponen'tially.—exponential curve, a curve expressed by an exponential equation; exponential equation, one in which the variable occurs in the exponent of one or more terms; exponential function, a quantity with a variable exponent, esp. $e^x$, where $e$ is the base of natural logarithms; exponential series, a series in which exponential quantities are developed; exponential theorem gives a value of any number in terms of its natural logarithm, and from it can at once be derived a series determining the logarithm. [L. *expōnēns, -entis*, setting forth—*ex-*, out, *pōnĕre*, to place.]

exponible, *eks-pō'ni-bl, adj.* able to be, or requiring to be, explained. [L. *expōnĕre*; see exponent.]

export, *eks-pōrt', -pört', v.t.* to carry or send out of a country, as goods in commerce.—*n.* ex'port, act of exporting: that which is exported: a commodity which is or may be sent from one country to another in traffic.—*adj.* export'able.—*ns.* exportā'tion; export'er.—invisible exports, such items in a national trade balance as money spent by tourists from abroad, etc.; opp. to visible exports, goods sold abroad by traders. [L. *exportāre, -ātum—ex-*, out of, *portāre*, to carry.]

expose, *iks-pōz', v.t.* to lay forth to view: to deprive of cover, protection, or shelter: to make bare: to abandon (an infant): to submit (to an influence, as light, weather): to put up (for sale): to explain (*arch.*): to disclose: to show up.—*n.* (*U.S.*) exposé.—*ns.* expōs'al, exposure: exposition; exposé (*eks-pō-zā*; Fr.), an exposing: a shameful showing up: a formal statement or exposition.—*adj.* exposed, unprotected: shelterless.—*ns.* expos'edness, the state of being exposed; expos'er; exposure (*-pō'zhər, -zhyər*), act of laying open or bare: subjection to an influence: act of allowing access of light (*phot.*): duration of such access: act of showing up an evil: state of being laid bare: openness to danger: shelterless state: position with regard to the sun, influence of climate, etc. [Fr. *exposer*—L. *ex-*, out, and *pausāre*, to rest, confused with *expōnĕre*, to expose; see exponent, exposition, and cf. pose, compose, repose, etc.]

exposition, *eks-pō-zish'ən, n.* act of exposing: a setting out to public view: the abandonment of a child: a public exhibition: act of expounding: explanation: commentary: an expository discourse: enunciation of themes in a composition: that part of a sonata, fugue, etc., in which themes are presented.—*adj.* expositive (*-poz'*), serving to expose or explain: explanatory: exegetical.—*n.* expos'itor, one who, or that which, expounds: an interpreter—*fem.* expos'itress.—*adj.* expos'itory, serving to explain: explanatory.—*n.* exposture (*-pos'chər*; Shak.), exposure. [L. *expositiō, -ōnis, expositor, -ōris—expōnĕre, expositum*, to expose, set forth; see exponent.]

ex post facto, *eks pōst fak'tō*, (L.) (*lit.* from what is done or enacted after): retrospective: retrospectively.

expostulate, *iks-post'ū-lāt, v.i.* to remonstrate: to discuss (Shak.): to claim (Milt.).—*n.* expostulā'tion.—*adjs.* expost'ūlātive (or *-ə-tiv*), expost'-ūlatory (*-ā-* or *-ə-tər-i*), containing expostulation.—*n.* expost'ūlator. [L. *expostulāre, -ātum —ex*, inten., *postulāre*, to demand.]

expound, *iks-pownd', v.t.* to expose, or lay open the meaning of: to explain: to interpret: to explain in a certain way.—*n.* expound'er. [O.Fr. *espondre*—L. *expōnĕre—ex-*, out, *pōnĕre*, to place.]

express, *iks-pres', v.t.* to press or force out: to emit: to represent or make known by a likeness, words, signs, symbols, etc.: to put into words: to symbolise: to state explicitly: to reveal: to designate: to despatch.—*adj.* clearly brought out: exactly representing: directly stated: explicit: clear: intended or sent for a particular purpose: expeditious.—*adv.* with haste: specially: by express train or messenger: by express.—*n.* a messenger or conveyance sent on a special errand: a special message: a regular and quick conveyance: a system for the speedy transmission of messages or goods: an express train: an express messenger.—*n.* express'age, the system of carrying by express: the charge for doing so.—*adj.* express'ible.—*ns.* expression (*-presh'ən*), act of forcing out by pressure: act, or mode, or power, of representing or giving utterance: representation or revelation by language, art, the features, etc.: the manner in which anything is expressed: a word, phrase: a symbol: intonation: due indication of feeling in performance of music.—*adj.* express'ional, of, or pertaining to, expression.—*ns.* express'ionism, in literature and painting a revolt against impressionism, turning away from the outer life to the inner; express'ionist.—*adjs.* express'-ionless; express'ive, serving to express or indicate: full of expression: vividly representing: emphatic: significant.—*adv.* express'ively. —*n.* express'iveness.—*adv.* express'ly, explicitly: for the express purpose: definitely.—*ns.* express'man; express'ness; expressure (*ekspresh'ər*), pressing out: expression (*Shak.*): representation (*Shak.*).—express agency, company, one that undertakes speedy transmission of goods; express delivery, immediate delivery by special messenger: delivery by express agency; express fee, a fee for express delivery; express stop, a stop in a harmonium by which the performer can regulate the air to produce expression; express letter, packet, parcel, one sent by special messenger; express messenger, a special messenger; express rifle, a rifle for big game at short range, with heavy charge of powder and light bullet; express train, a railway-train at high speed and with few stops; express'way, a road for fast motor traffic, with dual-carriageway and no crossings on the same level.—to express oneself, to give expression to one's thoughts. [L. *exprimĕre, expressum—ex*, from, *premĕre, pressum*, to press; partly through Fr. *exprès*, etc.]

expressis verbis, eks-pre'sis vûr'bis, eks-pre'sēs wer'bēs, (L.) in express terms.

exprobrate, eks'prō-brāt, (*arch.*) *v.t.* to reproach with: to upbraid.—*n.* exprobrā'tion.—*adjs.* expro'brative; expro'bratory. [L. *exprobrāre*, *-ātum*—pfx. *ex-*, indicating source, *probrum*, disgrace.]

ex professo, eks prə-fe'sō, pro-, (L.) avowedly.

expromission, eks-pro-mish'ən, *n.* the intervention of a new debtor, substituted for the former one, who is consequently discharged by the creditor. —*n.* expromissor (*-mis'ər*). [L. *exprōmittĕre*, *-missum*, to promise to pay—*ex-*, intens., *prōmittĕre*, to promise.]

expropriate, iks-prō'pri-āt, *v.t.* to dispossess.—*n.* expropriā'tion. [L. *expropriāre*, *-ātum—ex*, from, *proprium*, property.]

ex propriis, eks prō'pri-is, prō'prē-ēs (*pro'*), (L.) from one's own resources.

ex proprio motu, eks prō'pri-ō mō'tū, pro'pri-ō, mō'tōō, (L.L.) of his own accord.

expugn, iks-pūn', *v.t.* to take by storm: to storm: to overcome.—*adj.* expugnable (*-pug'* or *-pū'-nəbl*), capable of being taken or vanquished.—*n.* expugnā'tion (*-pug-*). [L. *expugnāre*.]

expulse, iks-puls', (*obs.*) *v.t.* to expel forcibly, eject.—*n.* expul'sion, the act of expelling: banishment.—*adj.* expul'sive, able or serving to expel. [L. *expulsāre*, freq. of *expellĕre.* See expel.]

expunge, iks-punj', expunct, iks-pungt', *vs.t.* to wipe out: to efface: to mark for deletion.—*n.* expunc'tion (*-pungk'shən*). [L. *expungĕre*, *-punctum* to mark for deletion by a row of dots—*ex-*, out, *pungĕre*, to prick.]

expurgate, eks'pûr-gāt, also *-pûr'*, *v.t.* to purge out or render pure: to purify from anything supposed to be offensive, noxious, or erroneous. —*ns.* expurgā'tion, act of expurgating or purifying: the removal of anything hurtful or evil: bowdlerising: exculpation; expurgator (*eks'-pûr-gā-tər*, or *eks-pûr'gə-tər*), one who expurgates or purifies.—*adjs.* expurgato'rial (*-gə-tō'ri-əl*, *-tö'*), expur'gatory, pertaining to expurgation: tending to expurgate or purify.—*v.t.* expurge (*pûrj'*), to purify, expurgate. [L. *expurgāre*, *-ātum—ex*, out, *purgāre*, to purge.]

exquisite, eks'kwiz-it, also *-kwiz'*, *adj.* far-fetched

(*Shak.*): abstruse (*obs.*): delicious: of consummate excellence: compelling the highest admiration: of delicate perception or close discrimination: not easily satisfied: fastidious: exceeding, extreme, as pain or pleasure.—*n.* one exquisitely nice or fastidious in dress: a fop.— *adv.* ex'quisitely.—*n.* ex'quisiteness. [L. *exquisitus—ex*, out, *quaerĕre*, to seek.]

ex quocunque capite, eks kwō-kun'kwi, *-kōōn'kwe*, *kap'it-ē, -e*, (L.) from whatever source.

ex re nata, (L.). Same as e re nata.

exsanguinous, iks-sang'gwin-əs, *adj.* without blood: anaemic—also exsang'uine, *-d*, exsanguin'eous.—*n.* exsanguin'ity. [L. *ex-*, without, *sanguis, -inis*, blood.]

exscind, ik-sind', *v.t.* to cut off. [L. *ex*, from, *scindĕre*, to cut.]

exsect, ik-sekt', *v.t.* to cut out.—*n.* exsec'tion. [L. *ex*, from, *secāre, sectum*, to cut.]

exsert, ik-sûrt', *v.t.* to protrude.—*adj.* exsert'ed, projecting.—*adj.* exser'tile (*-til, U.S. -til*).—*n.* exser'tion. [L. *exserĕre, -sertum.* See exert.]

ex-service, eks-sûr'vis, *adj.* formerly in one of the fighting services.—*n.* ex-ser'viceman.

exsiccate, ek'si-kāt, *v.t.* to dry up.—*adj.* exsicc'ant. —*n.* exsiccā'tion.—*adj.*exsicc'ative (or *-āt'*).— *n.* ex'siccātor, a drying agent or apparatus. [L. *exsiccare—ex-, siccus*, dry.]

exstipulate, iks-tip'ū-lāt, (*bot.*) *adj.* without stipules.

exsuccous, ik-suk'əs, *adj.* sapless. [L. *exsuccus— ex-, succus*, juice.]

exsufflicate, ik-suf'li-kāt, *adj.* puffed out (*Shak.*). —*v.t.* exsuff'late, to blow away: to exorcise by blowing away.—*n.* exsufflā'tion, expiration: forced expiration: exorcism by blowing. [L. *ex-*, out, and *sufflāre*, to blow out—*sub*, under, *flāre*, to blow.]

ex tacito, eks ta'si-tō, ta'ki-tō, (L.) silently.

extant, iks-tant', eks'tənt, *adj.* standing out, or above the rest (*arch.*): still standing or existing. [L. *extāns, -antis—ex-*, out, *stāre*, to stand.]

exstasy, extatic. Same as ecstasy, ecstatic.

extempore, iks-tem'pə-ri, *adv.* on the spur of the moment: without preparation: suddenly.—*adj.* sudden: rising at the moment: without help of manuscript: composed and delivered or performed impromptu.—*n.* an impromptu.—*adj.* extem'poral.—*n.* extemporaneity (*-ə-nē'i-ti*).— *adj.* extemporā'neous.—*adv.* extemporā'neously. —*n.* extemporā'neousness.—*adv.* extem'porarily. —*n.* extem'porariness.—*adj.* extem'porary, done on the spur of the moment: hastily prepared: speaking extempore: done without preparation: off-hand.—*n.* extemporisā'tion, *-z-*.—*v.t.* extemporise, -ize, to speak, or compose and play, extempore or without previous preparation: to discourse without notes: to speak off-hand. [L. *ex*, out of, and *tempore*, abl. of *tempus*, time.]

extend, iks-tend', *v.t.* to stretch out: to prolong in any direction: to enlarge: to expand: to widen: to unfold: to straighten out: to hold out: to offer, accord: to exert to the full: to seize (*law, Shak.*): to value, assess.—*v.i.* to stretch, reach: to be continued in length or breadth.—*adjs.* extend'able; extend'ant (*her.*), displayed; extend'ed, occupying space: having extension: stretched out: extensive.—*adv.* extend'edly.—*n.* extend'er, one who or that which extends: a university extension lecture: substance added to paint to give body.—*adjs.* extend'ible; extense (*-tens'; obs.*), extensive.— *n.* extensibil'ity.—*adjs.* extens'ible, extensile (*eks-ten'sil, -sil*), that may be extended.—*n.* extension (*iks-, eks-ten'shən*), an act of extending: condition of being extended: an added piece: a wing or annex of a house (*U.S.*): the property of occupying space: extent of the application of a term or the number of objects included under it—opp. *intension* (*logic*): word or words added to subject, predicate, or object (*gram*.): an additional telephone using the same line as the main one: (university extension, the enlargement of the aim of a university, in providing instruction for those unable to become regular students).—*adj.* exten'sional.—*adv.* exten'sionally.—*ns.* extensional'ity; exten'sionist, an advocate of extension: a university extension lecturer or student; exten'sity, massiveness or spatial quality in sensation from which perception of extension is derived.—*adj.* extens'ive, large: wide-spread: comprehensive: (*eks*-) pertaining to extension: seeking or deriving a comparatively small crop cheaply from a wide area—opp. to *intensive*—*adv.* extens'ively.—*ns.* extens'iveness; extensom'eter (*eks*-), an instrument for measuring small strains in metal; exten'sor, a muscle that extends or straightens any part of the body; extent', the space or degree to which a thing is extended: bulk: compass: scope: degree or amount (as *to some extent*): a stretch or extended space: a valuation of property: a writ directing the sheriff to seize the property of a debtor, for the recovery of debts of record due to the Crown (*law*): seizure (*Shak.*): attack (*Shak.*): an act of extending (justice, courtesy, etc.) (*Shak.*).—*adj.* stretched out.—extended play, of a gramophone record, giving longer reproduction because of a closer groove and the use of a larger part of its surface area. [L. *extendĕre*, *extentum*, or *extēnsum*—*ex*-, out, *tendĕre*, to stretch.]

extenuate, *iks-ten'ū-āt*, *v.t.* to lessen: to underrate: to weaken the force of: to palliate.—*n.* and *adj.* exten'ūāting, palliating.—*adv.* exten'ūātingly.—*n.* extenuā'tion, act of representing anything as less wrong or criminal than it seems: palliation: mitigation.—*adjs.* exten'ūātive, exten'ūātory, tending to extenuate: palliative.—*n.* exten'ūātor. [L. *extenuāre*, *-ātum*—*ex*-, inten., *tenuis*, thin.]

exterior, *eks-tē'ri-ər*, *adj.* outer: outward, external: on or from the outside: foreign.—*n.* the outside, outer surface: outward form or deportment: appearance: a representation of an outdoor scene: an outer part (esp. in *pl.*).—*v.t.* extēr'iorise, -ize, to externalise: to bring an internal part temporarily outside the body (*surg.*).—*n.* extērior'ity (*-or'i-ti*).—*adv.* extē'riorly, outwardly. [L. *exterior*, comp. of *exter*, *exterus*, outward—*ex*, from.]

exterminate, *iks-tûr'mi-nāt*, *v.t.* to drive out (*obs.*): to destroy utterly: to put an end to: to root out.—*adj.* exter'minable, that can be exterminated: illimitable (*Shelley*).—*n.* exterminā'tion, complete destruction or extirpation.—*adjs.* exter'minātive, exter'minatory, serving or tending to exterminate.—*n.* exter'minātor.—*v.t.* exter'mine (*Shak.*), to exterminate. [L. *extermināre*, *-ātum*, to drive beyond the boundary—*ex*, out of, *terminus*, boundary.]

external, *iks-tûr'nəl*, *adj.* exterior: lying outside: outward: belonging to the world of outward things: that may be seen: not innate or intrinsic: accidental: foreign.—*n.* exterior: (in *pl.*) the outward parts: (in *pl.*) outward or non-essential forms and ceremonies: (in *pl.*) outward circumstances or appearances.—*adj.* extern', externe', external, outward.—*n.* a non-resident, as a day-scholar, an out-patient, non-resident physician or surgeon.—*n.* externalisā'tion.—*v.t.* exter'nalise, -ize, to give form or apparent reality to: to give external expression to: to extravert (one's personality): to ascribe to causes outside oneself: to regard as consisting of externals only.—*ns.* exter'nalism, undue regard to mere externals or non-essential outward forms, esp. of religion: externality (*-nal'i-ti*), external character: superficiality: undue regard to externals.—*adv.* exter'nally.—*n.* externat (*-nä*)

Fr.), a day-school.—external examiner, an examiner from another seat of learning who has had no part in teaching the examinees; external student, one examined by a university in which he has not studied. [L. *externus*, outward—*exter*, outside.]

exterritorial, *eks-ter-i-tō'ri-əl*, *-tö'*. Same as extraterritorial.

extinct, *iks-tingkt'*, *adj.* put out: extinguished: no longer existing: dead.—*adj.* extinct'ed (*Shak.*), extinguished.—*n.* extinc'tion, extinguishing, quenching or wiping out: destruction: suppression: the cutting off of polarised light at certain angles when a section of doubly refracting mineral is rotated between crossed nicols.—*adj.* extinct'ive, tending to extinguish.—*n.* extinct'ure (*Shak.*), extinction. [L. *ex(s)tinctum*; see extinguish.]

extine, *eks'tin*, *-tēn*, *-tin*, (*bot.*) *n.* the outer membrane of a pollen-grain or spore.—Also ex'ine. [From the root of L. *exter*, *extimus*, outer, outmost.]

extinguish, *iks-ting'gwish*, *v.t.* to quench, put out: to render extinct: to put an end to: to destroy, annihilate: to obscure by superior splendour.—*v.i.* to die out.—*adj.* exting'uishable.—*ns.* exting'uisher, one who, or that which, extinguishes: a small hollow conical instrument for putting out a candle, etc.: a device for putting out fire: a conical structure resembling a candle extinguisher; exting'uishment, the act of extinguishing: putting an end to a right by consolidation or union (*law*). [L. *ex(s)tinguĕre*, *ex(s)tinctum*—*ex*-, out, *stinguĕre*, to quench.]

extirpate, *eks'tər-pāt*, *v.t.* to root out: to destroy totally: to exterminate—(*Spens.*, *Shak.*, etc.) extirp (*eks-tûrp'*).—*adj.* extirp'able (*eks-tûrp'ə-bl*).—*ns.* extirpā'tion, extermination: total destruction; ex'tirpātor, one who extirpates: an implement for weeding.—*adj.* extirp'atory (*eks-tûrp'ə-tər-i*). [L. *exstirpāre*, *-ātum*—*ex*, out, and *stirps*, a stock, root.]

extol, *iks-tōl'*, *-tol'*, *v.t.* to lift up (*Spens.*): to praise highly:—*pr.p.* extoll'ing; *pa.t.* and *pa.p.* extolled'; *Spens.* extold'.—*n.* extol'ment, the act of extolling: the state of being extolled. [L. *extollĕre*—*ex*-, up, *tollĕre*, to lift or raise.]

extort, *iks-tört'*, *v.t.* to wring out: to gain or draw out by compulsion or violence.—*adj.* extorted: wrongfully obtained.—*adj.* extors'ive, serving or tending to extort.—*adv.* extors'ively.—*n.* extor'tion (*-tör'shən*), illegal or oppressive exaction: that which is extorted.—*adjs.* extor'tionary, pertaining to or implying extortion; extor'tionate, oppressive.—*n.* extor'tioner, one who practises extortion.—*adj.* extort'ive. [L. *extorquēre*, *extortum*—*ex*-, out, *torquēre*, to twist.]

extra, *eks'trə*, *adj.* beyond or more than the usual or the necessary: extraordinary: additional.—*adv.* unusually.—*n.* what is extra or additional, as an item above and beyond the ordinary school curriculum, something over and above the usual course or charge in a bill, etc.: a special edition of a newspaper containing later news: a run scored at cricket from a bye, leg-bye, wide, or no-ball (not hit): a film actor temporarily engaged for a minor part, as to be one of a crowd.—*adjs.* ex'tra-condensed' (*print.*), extremely narrow in proportion to the height; extracurric'ular, of a subject or activity, outside and additional to, the regular academic course.—*v.t.* ex'tra-ill'ustrate (or *-lus'*), to grangerise.—*ns.* ex'tra-illustrā'tion.—*adjs.* extra-sen'sory, outside the ordinary senses, as in clairvoyant and telepathic perception; ext'ra-spec'ial, much out of the way.—*n.* a special late edition of an evening newspaper called for by some news of great importance.—extra time, additional time allowed at the end of a match because of time

Neutral vowels in unaccented syllables: *el'ə-mənt*; for certain sounds in foreign words, see p. viii

lost through injury, or for other reason. [Prob. contracted from extraordinary.]

**extra,** *eks'tra, eks'trä,* (L.) outside.—**extra modum** *(mō'dam, mo'dōōm),* beyond measure, extravagant; **extra muros** *(mū'rōs, mōō'rōs),* beyond the walls.

**extra-,** *eks'-tra-, -tra-, pfx.* outside.—*adjs.* **ex'-tra-ax'illary,** not in the axil of a leaf; **ex'tracellular,** outside the cell-walls; **extradō'tal,** not forming part of the dowry; **ex'traflo'ral,** not in a flower; **extraforā'neous,** out-door; **ex'tragalac'tic,** outside the Milky Way; **extrajudi'cial,** not made in court, beyond the usual course of legal proceeding.—*adv.* **ex'trajudi'cially.**—*adjs.* **ex'tralim'ital,** not found within a given faunal area: lying outside a prescribed area—also **extralim'itary;** **extra-marital,** (of relations, etc.) outside marriage, though properly confined to marriage; **ex'tramet'rical,** in excess of the recognised number of syllables in the line; **ex'tramun'dane,** beyond the material world; **ex'tramū'ral,** without or beyond the walls: connected with a university but not under its direct control; **ex'tra-parō'chial,** beyond the limits of a parish; **ex'tra-phys'ical,** not subject to physical laws; **ex'tra-profess'ional,** not belonging to a particular profession: outside the usual limits of professional duty or practice; **extr'a-provin'cial,** outside the limits of a particular province; **ex'tra-reg'ular,** unlimited by rules; **ex'tra-sō'lar,** beyond the solar system; **extra-terres'trial,** outside, or from outside, the earth; **ex'traterrito'rial,** outside a territory or territorial jurisdiction—also **exterritor'ial.**—*n.* **extraterritorial'ity,** the privilege of being outside the jurisdiction of the country one is in.—Also **exterritorial'ity.**—*adjs.* **ex'tra-trop'ical,** outside the tropics; **ex'tra-ū'terine,** outside the uterus; **extravas'cular,** outside the vascular system or a vessel: not vascular. [L. *extrā,* outside.]

**extract,** *iks-, eks-trakt', v.t.* to draw out by force or otherwise: to choose out or select: to find out: to derive: to extort: to take a copy of *(Scots law):* to copy passages from: to withdraw by chemical or physical means from containing or combined matter: to exhaust or treat by extraction.—*adj. (obs.* except *Scots law)* extracted: derived.—*n.* **extract** *(eks'),* anything drawn from a substance by heat, distillation, solvents, etc., as an essence: a passage taken from a book or writing: wool from rags from which cotton has been chemically removed.—*adjs.* **extract'able** (also **extract'ible**).—*ns.* **extrac'tant** *(chem.),* a solvent used for extraction; **extrac'tion,** act of extracting: derivation from a stock or family: birth: lineage: that which is extracted.—*adj.* **extract'ive,** tending or serving to extract: of the nature of an extract.—*n.* an extract (**extractive matter,** the soluble portions of any drug).—*n.* **extract'or,** he who, or that which, extracts.—**extract the root of a quantity,** to find its root by a mathematical process. [L. *extrahĕre, extractum—ex,* from, *trahĕre,* to draw.]

**extradition,** *eks-tra-dish'an, n.* a delivering up of accused persons by one government to another. —*adj.* **extradi'table** *(-dīt'a-bl).*—*v.t.* **ex'tradite,** to hand over for trial or punishment to a foreign government. [L. *ex,* from, *trāditiō, -ōnis—trādĕre, trāditum,* to deliver up.]

**extrados,** *eks-trā'dos, n.* the convex surface of an arch: the external curve of the voussoirs. [Fr., —L. *extrā,* outside, Fr. *dos,* back.]

**extrait,** *eks-tre,* (Fr.) extract.

**extraneous,** *eks-trān'yas, adj.* external: foreign: not belonging to or dependent on a thing: not essential.—*n.* **extraneity** *(-tra-nē'i-ti).*—*adv.* **extrān'eously.** [L. *extrāneus,* external, *extrā,* outside.]

**extraordinary,** *eks-trörd'(i-)nar-i,* or *eks-tra-örd',* or *iks-trörd', adj.* beyond ordinary: not usual or

regular: remarkable, wonderful: special or supernumerary, as 'physician extraordinary' in a royal household, and 'extraordinary professor' in a German university, both being inferior to the ordinary official.—*n.pl.* **extraord'inaries,** things that exceed the usual order, kind, or method.—*adv.* **extraord'inarily.**—*n.* **extraord'inariness.**—**extraordinary ray,** in double refraction, the ray that does not obey the ordinary law of refraction. [L. *extraordinārius—extrā,* outside, *ordō, -inis,* order.]

**extrapolate,** *iks-trap'ō-lāt, -a-lāt, eks', v.t.* to estimate from observed tendencies the value of (any variable) outside the limits between which values are known: to infer, conjecture from what is known: to project into a new area of experience or activity.—Also *v.i.*—*n.* **extrapolā'tion.** [L. *extrā* and **interpolate.**]

**extraught,** *iks-tröt', (Shak.) pa.p.* of **extract.**

**extravagant,** *iks-trav'a-gant, adj.* wandering beyond bounds: irregular: unrestrained: excessive: profuse in expenses: wasteful.—*ns.* **extrav'agance,** excess: lavish expenditure: digression *(Milt.);* **extrav'agancy,** vagrancy *(Shak.):* extravagance.—*adv.* **extrav'agantly.**—*v.i.* **extrav'agate,** to wander: to exceed proper bounds. [L. *extrā,* beyond, *vagāns, -antis,* pr.p. of *vagārī,* to wander.]

**extravaganza,** *iks-trav-a-gan'za, n.* an extravagant or eccentric musical, dramatic, or literary production: extravagant conduct or speech. [It. *(e)stravaganza.]*

**extravasate,** *iks-trav'a-sāt, v.t.* to let, or force (blood) out of the proper vessels: to pour out (lava).—*adj.* **extravasated.**—*n.* **extravasā'tion,** act of extravasating: the escape of any of the fluids of the living body from their proper vessels. [L. *extrā,* out of, *vās,* a vessel.]

**extravert, extrovert,** *eks-tra-* or *-trō-vûrt', v.t.* to turn outward or outside in: to make manifest.— *n. (eks')* a person interested mainly in the world external to himself—opp. to **introvert.**—*n.* **extraver'sion, extrover'sion.** [L. *extrā,* outside, *vertĕre,* to turn: the *extro-* forms by analogy with **introvert.**]

**extreat,** *eks-trēt', (Spens.) n.* extraction. [estreat.]

**extreme,** *iks-trēm' (arch. eks'), adj.* outermost: most remote: last: highest in degree: greatest: most violent: of opinions, etc., not moderate, going to great lengths: stringent:—*superl., Shak.,* etc., **extrēm'est;** *comp., rare,* **extrēm'er.**— *n.* the utmost point or verge: end: utmost or the highest limit or degree: (in *pl., obs.)* great necessity.—*adv.* **extrēme'ly.**—*ns.* **extrē'mism;** **extrē'mist,** one ready to go to extremes: a holder of extreme opinions: an advocate of extreme action; **extremity** *(-trem'i-ti),* the utmost limit: the highest degree: greatest necessity or distress: extreme condition: an end: hand or foot.—**extreme unction** (see **unction**).—**extremely high frequency** (see **frequency**); **go to extremes,** to go too far: to use extreme measures; **in the extreme,** in the last, highest degree: extremely; **the last extremity,** the utmost pitch of misfortune: death. [O.Fr. *extreme—*L. *extrēmus,* superl. of *exter, exterus,* on the outside.]

**extricate,** *eks'tri-kāt, v.t.* to free from entanglements or perplexities: to disentangle: to set free.—*adj.* **ex'tricable.**—*n.* **extricā'tion,** disentanglement: act of setting free. [L. *extricāre, -ātum—ex,* from, *tricae,* hindrances.]

**extrinsic,** *iks-trin'sik, adj.* external: not contained in or belonging to a body: foreign: not essential: of a muscle, running from the trunk to limb or girdle—opp. to *intrinsic.—adj.* **extrin'sical.**—*n.* **extrinsical'ity.**—*adv.* **extrin'sically.** [Fr. *extrinsèque—*L. *extrinsecus—exter,* outside, suff. *-in, secus,* beside.]

**extrorse,** *iks-trörs', adj.* turned outward: (of an anther) opening towards the outside of the flower. [Fr.,—L. *extrorsus*—*extrā*, outside, *versus*, turned.]

**extrovert, extroversion.** Same as **extravert**, etc.

**extrude**, iks-tr $\overline{oo}$ d', *v.t.* to force or urge out: to expel: to protrude.—*v.i.* to protrude.—*n.* **extrusion** (*-tr* $\overline{oo}$ *'zhən*), act of extruding, thrusting, or throwing out: expulsion: the operation of producing rods, tubes, etc., by forcing suitable material through a die by means of a ram (*metallurgy*).—*adjs.* **extrusive** (*tr* $\overline{oo}$ *'-siv*), extru'sory (*-sər-i*). [L. *extrūděre*, *extrūsum*—*ex-*, out, *trūděre*, to thrust.]

**exuberant**, eg-, ig-z *ū'bər-ant*, z $\overline{oo}$ *'*, *adj.* luxuriant: overflowing: abounding: in high spirits: lavish.—*ns.* **exu'berance**, **exu'berancy**, quality of being exuberant: luxuriance, an overflowing quantity: redundancy: outburst.—*adv.* **exu'-berantly**.—*v.i.* **exu'berate**, to be exuberant. [L. *exūberāns*, *-antis*, pr.p. of *exūberāre*—*ex-*, inten., *über*, rich.]

**exude**, igz-, iks-ūd', *v.t.* to discharge by sweating: to discharge through pores or incisions.—*v.i.* to flow out of a body through the pores: to ooze out.—*ns.* **exudate** (*eks'*), exuded matter; **exudā'-tion** (*eks-*), act of exuding or discharging through pores: that which is exuded. [L. *exūdāre*—*ex*, from, *sūdāre*, to sweat.]

**exul**, ek'sul, (*Spens.*) *n.* an exile. [L. *ex*(*s*)*ul*.]

**exulcerate**, igz-ul'sər-āt, *v.t.* to exasperate, afflict as with an ulcer.—*n.* **exulcerā'tion**, ulceration: exasperation. [L. *exulcerāre*, *-ātum*—*ex-*, intens., *ulcerāre*, to ulcerate.]

**exult**, igz-ult', *v.i.* to rejoice exceedingly: to triumph.—*ns.* **exult'ance**, **exult'ancy**, exultation: triumph.—*adj.* **exult'ant**, exulting: triumphant. —*n.* **exultā'tion** (*egz-*), triumphant delight: transport.—*adv.* **exult'ingly**. [L. *ex*(*s*)*ultāre*, *-ātum*, from *ex*(*s*)*ilire*—*ex-*, out or up, *salire*, to leap.]

**ex utraque parte**, eks ū-trä'kwi pär'tē, $\overline{oo}$-trä'kwe pär'te (L.) on either side.

**exuviae**, igz-, iks-ū'vi-ē, *n.pl.* cast-off skins, shells, or other coverings of animals: fossil remains of animals (*geol.*).—*adj.* exū'vial.—*v.i.* exū'viate, to shed, cast off, for a new covering or condition.—*n.* exuviā'tion, the act of exuviating. [L., *exuěre*, to draw off.]

**ex voto**, eks v $\overline{o}$ 'tō, w $\overline{o}$', (L.) according to one's prayer, by reason of a vow: votive: a votive offering.

**eyalet**, ä-yä'let, *n.* a division of Turkey—a *vilayet*. [Turk.,—Ar. *iyālah*.]

**eyas**, i'əs, *n.* an unfledged hawk.—*adj.* (*Spens.*) unfledged.—ey'as-mus'ket, an unfledged male hawk: a child (*Shak.*). [*An eyas* for *a nyas*—Fr. *niais*—L. *nidus*, nest.]

**eye**, i, (*obs.*) *n.* a brood, esp. of pheasants. [*An eye* for *a nye*—O.Fr. *ni*—L. *nidus*, nest.]

**eye**, i, *n.* the organ of sight or vision: more narrowly the globe or movable part of it: the power of seeing: sight: a tinge, suffusion (*Shak.*): regard: aim: keenness of perception: anything resembling an eye, as an eye-spot: a central spot: the hole of a needle: the aperture for inserting the bias in a bowl: a round aperture: a mine entrance: a spring of water: a wire loop or ring for a hòok: a round hole or window: the seed-bud of a potato: a spot on an egg: a spectacle lens: the central calm area of a cyclone: (*pl.*) the foremost part of a ship's bows, the hawse-holes:—*pl.* eyes; *arch.* eyne, in; *Scot.* een, ēn.—*v.t.* to look on: to observe narrowly.—*v.i.* (*Shak.*) to appear:—*pr.p.* ey'ing or eye'ing; *pa.t.* and *pa.p.* eyed, *id.*—*adj.* eyed, having eyes: spotted as if with eyes.—*n.* eye'ful, as much as the eye can take in: something worth looking at, a fascinating sight (*slang*).—*adj.* sightly (*dial.*): careful, having an eye (*dial.*). —*adj.* eye'less, without eyes or sight: deprived of eyes: blind.—eye'-ball, the ball or globe of

the eye; eye bank (see bank, 3); eye'-bath, a cup that can be held in the orbit to bathe the eye; eye'-beam, a glance of the eye; eye'bright, a little plant of the genus Euphrasia (fam. Scrophulariaceae), formerly used as a remedy for eye diseases; eye'brow, the hairy arch above the eye. —*v.t.* to provide with artificial eyebrows.—*adjs.* eye'browless, without eyebrows; eye'-catching, striking.—eye'-drop (*Shak.*), a tear; eye'-flap, a blinker on a horse's bridle; eye'-glance, a quick look; eye'glass, a glass to assist the sight, esp. one held on the bridge of the nose by a spring: an eye-piece: the lens of the eye (*Shak.*); eye'-hole, an eyelet; eye'lash, the row, or one, of the hairs that edge the eyelid; eye'lid, the lid or cover of the eye: the portion of movable skin by means of which the eye is opened or closed; eye'-opener, something that opens the eyes literally or figuratively, a startling enlightenment: a drink, esp. in the morning; eye'-piece, the lens or combination of lenses at the eye end of an optical instrument; eye'-pit, the socket of the eye; eye'-rhyme, a would-be rhyme between words that are spelt as if they rhymed but do not; eye'-salve, salve or ointment for the eyes; eye'-servant, one who does his duty only when under the eye of his master; eye'-service, service so performed: formal worship; eye'-shadow, a coloured cosmetic for the eyelids; eye'-shot, the reach or range of sight of the eye: a glance; eye'sight, power of seeing: view: observation; eye'sore, anything that is offensive to look at; eye'-splice, a kind of eye or loop formed by splicing the end of a rope into itself; eye'-spot, a spot like an eye: a rudimentary organ of vision. —*adj.* eye'-spott'ed (*Spens.*), marked with spots like eyes.—eye'-string, the muscle that raises the eyelid; eye'-tooth, a canine tooth, esp. in the upper jaw, below the eye; eye'-wash, a lotion for the eye: humbug: deception; eye'-water, water flowing from the eye: a lotion for the eyes; eye'-wink (*Shak.*), a rapid lowering and raising of the eyelid: a glance: the time of a wink; eye'-wit'ness, one who sees a thing done. —all my eye (*slang*), humbug; be all eyes, to give all attention; be a sheet in the wind's eye, to be intoxicated (*coll.*); clap, lay, set, eyes on, to see; cry one's eyes out, to weep copiously; cut one's eyeteeth, to cease to be a child: to be shrewd; eyeball to eyeball (of discussion, confrontation, diplomacy) at close quarters, dealing with matters very frankly and firmly; electric eye (see electric); eye for eye, lex talionis (Ex. xxi. 24); eye of day, the sun; eyes down, the start of a bingo-game, or of any non-physical contest; give an eye to, to attend to; glad, green eye (see glad, green); have an eye to, to contemplate: to have regard to: to incline towards; in eye, in sight; in one's mind's eye, in imagination; in the eyes of, in the estimation, opinion, of; in the wind's eye, against the wind; keep one's (or an) eye on, to observe closely: to watch; keep one's eye skinned, to be keenly watchful; make a person open his eyes, to cause him astonishment; make eyes at, to look at in an amorous way, to ogle; mind your eye (*slang*), take care; my eye! a mild asseveration; naked eye (see naked); one in the eye, a rebuff; open a person's eyes, to make him see: to show him something of which he is ignorant; pipe, or put a finger in, the eye, to weep; put a person's eye out, blind him: supplant him in favour; see eye to eye, from Is. lii. 8, but used in the sense of to think alike; see with half an eye, to see without difficulty; throw sheep's eyes at, to ogle; turn a blind eye on, feign not to see, wink at; under the eye of, under the observation of; up to the eyes, deeply involved. [O.E. *ēage*; cf. Goth. *augo*, Ger. *auge*, Du. *oog*, O.N. *auga*.]

**eyelet**, i'lit, *n.* a small eye or hole to receive a lace

or cord, as in garments, sails, etc.: a small hole
for seeing through (also eye'let-hole): a little
eye.—*v.t.* to make eyelets in. [O.Fr. *oillet*—L.
*oculus*, influenced by eye.]
**eyeliad, eyliad,** *i'li-ad, n.* old variants of oeillade.
**Eyeti, Eyetie, Eytie,** *i'ti, (slang) n.* an Italian.
**eyne,** *īn, (arch.) n.pl.* eyes. [O.E. *ēagan*.]

**eyot,** *āt.* Same as ait.
**eyra,** *i'ra, n.* a South American wild cat.
[Guarani.]
**eyre,** *ār, n.* a journey or circuit: a court of itinerant justices. [O.Fr. *eire*, journey, from L. *iter*,
a way, a journey—*ire, itum*, to go.]
**eyry, eyrie.** See aerie.

*fāte, fär; mē, hûr* (her); *mīne; mōte, för; mūte; mōōn, fŏōt; dhen* (then)

# F

**F, f,** *ef, n.* the sixth letter in the English and Latin alphabets, derived from the Greek digamma—its sound a labiodental fricative formed by bringing the lower lip into contact with the upper teeth: the fourth note of the natural diatonic scale of C (*mus.*): as a mediaeval Roman numeral F = 40; F̄ = 40,000: F is used as a contraction for Fahrenheit; $F_1$, $F_2$ (Mendelism) first and second filial generations: ff in mediaeval script was used instead of a capital F.—**F'-clef,** a clef marking F, the fourth line in the bass, the bass-clef; **f'-hole,** either of a pair of holes in the belly of a violin, etc., shaped like an italic *f.*—**the three F's,** free sale, fixity of tenure, fair rent.

**fa, fä,** *n.* the fourth note in the sol-fa notation—also anglicised in spelling as **fah.** [See **Aretinian.**]

**fa', fō, fa'ard, faurd, färd, förd,** Scots for **fall,** favoured.

**fab,** *fab,* (*slang*) *adj.* excellent, marvellous. [Abbrev. for **fabulous.**]

**fabaceous,** *fə-bāsh'əs, adj.* bean-like. [L. *faba,* a bean.]

**Fabergé,** *fa-ber-zhā, fab-ər-jā', n.* delicate gold and enamel ware made in Russia in the 19th and early 20th centuries. [Peter Carl *Fabergé* (1846-1920).]

**Fabian,** *fā'bi-ən, adj.* delaying, avoiding battle, cautious, practising the policy of delay: favouring the gradual introduction and spread of Socialism.—*n.* a member or supporter of the *Fabian Society* (founded 1884) for this purpose.—*n.* **Fā'bianism.** [From Q. *Fabius* Maximus, surnamed Cunctator (delayer), from the masterly tactics with which he wore out the strength of Hannibal, whom he dared not meet in battle.]

**fable,** *fā'bl, n.* a narrative in which things irrational, and sometimes inanimate, are, for the purpose of moral instruction, feigned to act and speak with human interests and passions: any tale in literary form, not necessarily probable in its incidents, intended to instruct or amuse: the plot or series of events in an epic or dramatic poem: a fiction or myth: a ridiculous story, an old wives' tale: a falsehood: subject of common talk.—*v.i.* to tell fictitious tales: to tell falsehoods (*obs.*).—*v.t.* to feign: to invent: to relate as if true.—*adj.* **fā'bled,** mythical: renowned in story: feigned.—*n.* and *adj.* **fā'bling.**—*n.* **fā'bler,** a writer or narrator of fictions.—*adj.* **fabular** (*fab'ū-lər*).—*v.i.* **fab'ulise, -ize,** to write fables, or to speak in fables.—*ns.* **fab'ulist,** one who invents fables; **fabulos'ity.**—*adj.* **fab'ulous,** feigned, false: related in fable: celebrated in story: immense, amazing: excellent (*coll.*).—*adv.* **fab'ulously.**—*n.* **fab'ulousness.** [Fr. *fable* and L. *fābula*—*fārī,* to speak.]

**fabliau,** *fab'li-ō, n.* a metrical tale after the type of those, usually satirical in quality, produced in France in the 12th and 13th centuries:—*pl.* **fabliaux** (*fab'li-ōz*). [Fr.,—dim. of *fable.*]

**fabric,** *fab'rik, n.* the act of constructing: texture: anything framed by art and labour: a building: manufactured cloth: any system of connected parts: framework (also *fig.*).—*v.t.* (*Milt.*) to construct.—*n.* **fab'ricant,** a manufacturer.—*v.t.* **fab'ricate,** to put together by art and labour: to manufacture: to produce: to devise falsely.—*n.* **fabrica'tion,** construction: manufacture: that which is fabricated or invented: a story: a falsehood.—*adj.* **fab'ricātive.**—*n.* **fab'ricātor.** [L. *fābrica,* fabric—*fāber,* a worker in hard materials: partly through Fr. *fabrique.*]

**faburden,** *fa'bər-dən,* (*arch.*) *n.* harmony in thirds and sixths: an early kind of counterpoint: an undersong: a refrain. [Fr. *faux-bourdon*—*faux,* false, *bourdon,* bourdon.]

**façade,** *fa-säd', n.* the exterior front or face of a building: the appearance presented to the world, esp. if showy and with little behind it (*fig.*). [Fr.,—*face,* after It. *facciata,* the front of a building—*faccia,* the face.]

**face,** *fās, n.* the front part of the head, including forehead, eyes, nose, mouth, cheeks, and chin: the outside form or appearance: front or surface of anything: a flat surface of a solid geometrical figure, crystal, etc.: the striking surface of a golf-club, etc.: the edge of a cutting-tool, etc.: the front or upper surface, or that usually presented: the exposed surface in a cliff, mine, or quarry: a principal cleavage-plane: the dial of a watch, etc.: the printed surface of a playing card: a style of letter (*print.*): special appearance or expression of the countenance: aspect, look, configuration: command of facial expression and bearing: boldness, effrontery: a grimace: presence: anger or favour (*B.*).—*v.t.* to meet in the face or in front: to stand opposite to or looking towards: to confront: to stand up to: to brave: to resist: to put an additional face or surface on: to cover in front: to trim.—*v.i.* to direct or turn the face: to take or have a direction: to show a face, esp. bold or false (*obs.*).—*adjs.* **faced,** having a face: having the outer surface dressed: with the front covered with another material; **face'less,** without a face: (of person(s) concerned in some action) with identity concealed.—*n.* **fac'er,** one who faces something: one who puts on a false show (*obs.*): a bold-faced person (*obs.*): a severe blow on the face (*slang*): an affront (*coll.*): anything that staggers one (*coll.*).—*adj.* **facial,** *fā'shl,* of or relating to the face: for the face.—*n.* a beauty treatment to the face (*coll.*).—*adv.* **fa'cially.**—*n.* **fac'ing,** a covering in front for ornament or protection.—**face'-ache,** neuralgia in the nerves of the face; **face'-card,** a playing-card bearing a face (king, queen or knave); **face'-cloth,** a cloth laid over the face of a corpse or living person: a cloth used in washing the face; **face'-guard,** a kind of mask to guard or protect the face; **face'-lift,** renovating process, esp. one applied to the outside of a building (also *fig.*): **face-lifting; face'-lifting,** an operation aiming at smoothing and firming the face; **face'-powder,** a cosmetic powder for the face; **face'-saving,** saving one's face.—Also *adj.*—**face value,** the value, as stated on the face of a coin, etc.: nominal worth; **facial angle,** in craniometry, the angle formed by lines drawn from the middle of the forehead to the upper jaw above the incisor teeth and from the opening of the ear to the opening of the nose.—**face down,** to abash by stern looks; **face out,** to carry off by bold looks; **face the music** (*slang*), to accept the unpleasant consequences at their worst: to brave a trying situation, hostile reception, etc.; **face to face,** opposite: in actual presence; **face up to,** to face, stand up to: to recognise (fact, facts) and prepare to endure or act bravely; **fly in the face of,** to set oneself directly against; **have two faces,** to be two-faced (see **two**); **in the face of,** in defiance of, despite; **lose face,** lose prestige; **loss of face,** humiliation, loss of dignity; **on the**

face of it, on its own showing: palpably plain: at first glance; pull a long face, to look dismal; put a good face on, to assume a bold or contented bearing as regards; right face! left face! right about face!, words of command, on which the soldiers turn to the side specified; run one's face (*U.S. slang*), to obtain things on credit by sheer impudence; save one's face, to avoid humiliation or appearance of climbing down; set one's face against, to oppose strenuously; show (one's) face, to appear; to one's face, in one's presence, openly. [Fr. *face*—L. *faciēs*, form, face; perh. from *facēre*, to make.]

facet, *fas'it, n.* a small surface, as of a crystal: an aspect or view.—*v.t.* to cut a facet upon, or cover with facets.—*adj.* fac'eted, having or formed into facets. [Fr. *facette*, dim. of *face*, face.]

facetious, *fə-sē'shəs, adj.* witty, humorous, jocose: waggish: would-be-funny: pertaining to facetiae.—Also facete (-*sēt*'; *arch.*).—*n.pl.* face'tiae (*shi-ē*), witty or humorous sayings or writings: . a bookseller's term for improper books—of all degrees of indecency.—*adv.* facē'tiously.—*n.* facē'tiousness. [L. *facētia*—*facētus*, merry, witty.]

facia. Same as fascia.

facies, *fā'shi-ēz, n.* general aspect. [L. *faciēs*, face.]

facile, *fas'il,* or -*il, adj.* affable (*obs.*): easily persuaded: yielding: in Scots law, mentally weak, short of idiocy but so as to be easily persuaded to actions prejudicial to oneself: easy of accomplishment: easy: working with ease: fluent (usu. depreciatory).—*adv.* fac'ilely.—*n.* fac'ileness.—*v.t.* facilitāte (*fə-sil'*), to make easy or easier.—*ns.* facilitā'tion; facil'ity, ease in performance or action: fluency: easiness to be persuaded: pliancy: affability (*obs.*): a condition of being facile (*Scots law*): (esp. in *pl.* facil'ities) means or opportunities that render anything readily possible: anything specially arranged or constructed to provide recreation, a service, etc. [Fr.,—L. *facilis*, easy—*facēre*, to do.]

facile princeps, *fas'i-le prin'seps, fa'ki-le prin'keps,* (L.) obviously pre-eminent, an easy first.

facinorous, *fa-, fə-sin'ə-rəs, adj.* atrociously wicked.—Also facinē'rious (Shak.).—*n.* facin'orousness. [L. *facinorōsus*—*facinus*, a crime—*facēre*, to do.]

façon de parler, *fa-sõ da par-lā,* (Fr.) way of speaking, a mere form of words.

façonné, *fa-so-nā, fas-ə-nā', fas'-, n.* fabric with self-coloured pattern of small figures woven into it: the pattern on such a fabric.—Also adj. [Fr., pa.p. of *façonner,* to work, fashion.]

facsimile, *fak-sim'i-li, n.* an exact copy, as of handwriting, a coin, etc.: accurate reproduction: facsimile telegraph, esp. in later more sophisticated forms:—*pl.* facsim'iles.—*adj.* exactly corresponding.—*v.t.* to make a facsimile of, to reproduce.—*n.* facsim'ilist—facsimile telegraph, the transmission of a still picture over a telegraph circuit and its reproduction. [L. *fac*, imper. of *facēre,* to make, *simile,* neut. of *similis,* like.]

fact, *fakt, n.* a deed, act, or anything done (*arch.*): anything that comes to pass: a truth: truth: reality, or a real state of things, as distinguished from a mere statement or belief: an assertion of fact: a crime committed (*obs.* except in after, before the fact).—*adj.* fact'ual, pertaining to facts: actual.—*ns.* factual'ity; fact'ualness; fact'um, a thing done, a deed.—*adj.* fact'-finding, appointed to ascertain, directed towards ascertaining, all the facts of a situation.—as a matter of fact, in reality; facts of life, the details of reproduction, esp. human reproduction: the realities of a situation; in fact, in point of fact, indeed; the fact of the matter, the plain truth about the subject in question. [L. *factum,* neut. pa.p. of *facēre,* to do.]

faction, *fak'shən, n.* a company of persons associated or acting together, mostly used in a bad

sense: a contentious party in a state or society: dissension.—*adj.* fac'tional.—*ns.* fac'tionalism; fac'tionalist; fac'tionary, a member of a faction; fac'tionist.—*adj.* fac'tious, turbulent: given to faction: proceeding from party spirit: seditious. —*adv.* fac'tiously.—*n.* fac'tiousness. [L. *factiō, -ōnis*—*facēre,* to do.]

factitious, *fak-tish'əs, adj.* artificial: made: produced by artificial conditions.—*adv.* facti'tiously. —*n.* facti'tiousness.—*adjs.* fac'titive, causative; fac'tive (*obs.*), making. [L. *facticius, factitivus*—*facēre,* to make.]

factor, *fak'tər, n.* a doer or transactor of business for another: one who buys and sells goods for others, on commission: an agent managing heritable estates for another (*Scot.*): in math. one of two or more quantities, which, when multiplied together, result in the given quantity —e.g. 6 and 4 are factors of 24: an element in the composition of anything, or in bringing about a certain result: in heredity, a gene.—*n.* fac'torage, the fees or commission of a factor.— *adj.* factō'rial, of or pertaining to a factor.—*n.* the product of all whole numbers from a given number down to one.—*v.t.* fac'torise, -ize, to resolve into factors: to warn not to pay or give up goods (*U.S.*): to attach (effects of a debtor in the hands of another—e.g. of his heir).—*ns.* fac'torship; fac'tory, a manufactory: a trading settlement in another country.—factory farm, one carrying out factory farming, farming by methods of feeding and housing animals in which everything is subordinated to achieving maximum production, rapid growth, and qualities in demand on the market; fac'tory-ship, a whaling-ship on which whales are processed.— judicial factor, a person appointed by the Court to manage the estate of a person under some incapacity. [L. *facēre,* to do.]

factotum, *fak-tō'təm, n.* a person employed to do all kinds of work for another:—*pl.* facto'tums. [L.L.,—L. *fac,* imper. of *facēre,* to do, *tōtum,* all.]

facture, *fak'chər, n.* the act or the result of making, workmanship. [L. *factūra*—*facēre,* to make.]

facula, *fak'ū-la, n.* a spot brighter than the rest of the surface, sometimes seen on the sun's disk: —*pl.* fac'ulae, -lē. [L. *facula,* dim. of *fax,* torch.]

faculty, *fak'əl-ti, n.* facility or power to act: any particular ability or aptitude: an original power of the mind: any physical capability or function: personal quality or endowment: right, authority, or privilege to act: licence: a department of learning at a university, or the professors constituting it: the members of a profession: executive ability.—*adj.* fac'ultātive, optional: incidental: of or pertaining to a faculty: conferring privilege, permission or authority: able to live under different conditions (*zool.*).—*adv.* fac'ultatively.—Court of Faculties, a court established by Henry VIII, whereby authority is given to the Archbishop of Canterbury to grant dispensations and faculties. [Fr. *faculté*—L. *facultās, -ātis*—*facilis,* easy.]

facundity, *fa-kun'di-ti, n.* eloquence. [L. *fācunditās, -ātis.*]

fad, *fad, n.* a weak or transient hobby, crotchet, or craze: any unimportant belief or practice intemperately urged.—*n.* fadd'iness.—*adj.* fadd'-ish.—*ns.* fadd'ishness, fadd'ism; fadd'ist, one who is a slave to some fad.—*adj.* fadd'y. [Ety. unknown.]

faddle, *fad'l,* (*dial.*) *v.i.* to trifle.—*n.* nonsense, trifling—usually in fiddle-faddle.

fade, *fād, v.i.* to lose strength, freshness, loudness, brightness, or colour gradually: to grow pale, dull, or faint: to die away: to disappear.—*v.t.* to cause to fade: to cause to change gradually in distinctness (as *fade out, fade in*).—*n.* a fading.— *adj.* (*arch.*) faded, weak.—*adv.* fa'dedly.—*adj.* fade'less, unfading: not liable to fade.—*adv.*

**fade'lessly.**—*n.* and *adj.* **fåd'ing.**—*adj.* **fâ'dy,** wearing away.—**fade'-away',** a gradual disappearance; **fade'-out',** a graded fading out; **fade'-in',** in cinematography, gradual appearance and growth in distinctness. [O.Fr. *fader*—*fade*— L. *vapidum,* acc. to Gaston Paris.]

**fade,** *fad,* (Fr.) insipid, colourless; **fadaise,** *fa-dez,* a silly saying: twaddle; **fadeur** (*fa-dær*), dullness.

**fadge,** *faj,* (arch.) *v.i.* to agree, hit it off: to succeed, turn out. [Ety. dub.; not conn. with O.E. *fēgan,* to join.]

**fading,** *fā'ding, n.* an old dance, probably Irish: the burden of a song (*with a fading;* Shak.). [Origin unknown.]

**fado,** *fä'doō, n.* a type of Portuguese folk song or dance. [Port., fate—L. *fātum.*]

**faeces,** *fē'sēz, n.pl.* sediment after infusion or distillation: dregs: excrement.—*adj.* **faecal** (*fē'kl*). [L., pl. of *faex, faecis,* dregs, grounds.]

**faerie, faery,** *fā'(ə)ri,* (arch.) *n.* the world of fairies, fairyland: a fairy.—Also *adj.* [A variant of **fairy.**]

**faex populi,** *fēks pop'ū-lī, fiks po'poō-lē,* (L.) dregs of the people, the mob.

**fag,** *fag, v.i.* to become weary or tired out: to work hard: to be a fag.—*v.t.* to weary: to use as a fag: —*pr.p.* **fagg'ing;** *pa.t.* and *pa.p.* **fagged.**—*n.* a schoolboy forced to do menial offices for another: a tiresome piece of work: drudgery: orig. an inferior cigarette (for fag-end; *slang*): hence any cigarette (*slang*).—*n.* **fagg'ery,** drudgery: fagging.—*n.* and *adj.* **fagg'ing.**—**fag'-end',** the end of a web of cloth that hangs loose: the untwisted end of a rope: the refuse or meaner part of a thing: the stump of a cigar or cigarette (*slang*).— **to fag out,** to field, as a fag, in cricket. [Ety. dub.; perh. a corr. of **flag,** to droop, which see.]

**faggot, fagot,** *fag'ət, n.* a bundle of sticks for fuel, fascines, etc.: a stick: anything like a faggot: a bundle of pieces of iron or steel cut off into suitable lengths for welding: a soldier numbered on the muster-roll, but not really existing (*hist.*): a voter who has obtained his vote expressly for party purposes, on a spurious or sham qualification (*hist.*): a roll of internal organs, etc., of a pig mixed with bread and savoury herbs: derogatory term for an old woman: a male homosexual (*slang*).—*adj.* got up for a purpose, as in *faggot vote.*—*v.t.* to tie together.—*ns.* **fagg'oting, fag'oting,** a kind of embroidery in which some of the cross-threads are drawn together in the middle.—**to burn one's faggot,** to recant a heresy. [Fr. *fagot,* a bundle of sticks.]

**fagotto,** *fəg-ot'ō, n.* a bassoon.—*n.* **fagott'ist,** one who plays on the bassoon. [It.]

**Fagus,** *fā'gəs, n.* the beech genus of trees, giving name to the fam. **Fagā'ceae.**—*adj.* **fagā'ceous.** [L. *fāgus,* beech; cf. Gr. *phēgos,* oak, O.E. *bōc,* beech.]

**fah.** See **fa.**

**fahlband,** *fäl'bänt, n.* in crystalline rocks, a pale band rich in metals; **fahl'erz** (*-erts*), tetrahedrite: also tennantite; **fahl'ore** (*-ōr, -ör*), tetrahedrite or tennantite. [Ger. *fahl,* dun-coloured, *band,* band, *erz,* ore, and Eng. **ore.**]

**Fahrenheit,** *fa', fä'rən-hit, adj.,* of a thermometer or thermometer scale, having the freezing-point of water marked at 32, and the boiling-point at 212 degrees (to convert °F into °C, subtract 32, and take 5/9 of remainder). [Named from the inventor, Gabriel D. *Fahrenheit* (1686-1736).]

**faible,** *feb'l, n.* a foible (of which it is a variant): the part of a foil blade between the middle and the point—the weak part. [Fr., weak.]

**faience,** *fä-yäs, n.* glazed coloured earthenware. [Fr.; prob. from *Faenza* in Italy.]

**faik,** *fāk,* (Scot.) *v.i.* and *v.t.* to abate: to excuse.

**fail,** *fāl,* (Scot.) *n.* a turf, sod.—**fail'-dike,** a turfwall. [Perh. Gael. *fàl,* a sod.]

**fail,** *fāl, v.i.* to fall short or be wanting (with *in*):

to fall away: to decay: to die: to prove deficient under trial, examination, pressure, etc.: to miss achievement: to be disappointed or baffled: to become insolvent or bankrupt.—*v.t.* to be wanting to: not to be sufficient for: to leave undone, omit: to disappoint or desert: to deceive (*Spens.*): to declare deficient after examination.—*n.* failure (*Shak.*).—*adj.* **failed,** that has failed: decayed, worn out: bankrupt.— *n.* **fail'ing,** a fault, weakness: a foible: failure.— *adj.* that fails.—*prep.* in default of.—*n.* **fail'ure,** a falling short, or cessation: omission: decay: bankruptcy: an unsuccessful person.—*adj.* **fail'-safe,** pertaining to a mechanism incorporated in a system to ensure that there will be no accident if the system does not operate properly. —**fail of,** to come short of accomplishing (a purpose); **without fail,** for certain. [O.Fr. *faillir* —L. *fallĕre,* to deceive; cf. Du. *feilen,* Ger. *fehlen,* O.N. *feila.*]

**faille,** *fāl, fil, fä-y', n.* a soft, closely-woven silk or rayon fabric with transverse ribs. [Fr.]

**fain,** *fān,* (arch. and *poet.*) *adj.* glad or joyful: eager (with *to*): content for want of better: compelled: wont (*Spens.*).—*v.t.* (*Spens.*) to delight in: to desire.—*adv.* gladly.—*adv.* **fain'ly,** gladly.—*n.* **fain'ness,** eagerness. [O.E. *fægen,* joyful: cf. O.N. *feginn,* glad.]

**fain, faine,** *fān,* (*Spens.*) *v.t.* Same as **feign.**

**fainéant,** *fen'ā-ä, adj.* and *n.* do-nothing, applied esp. to the later Merovingian kings of France, mere puppets, whose mayors of the palace governed the country.—*ns.* **fai'néance** (*-ãs*), **fai'neancy** (*-ən-si*), **fainéantise** (*-tēz'*). [Fr., as if—*faire,* to do, *néant,* nothing; really—O.Fr. *faignant,* pr.p. of *faindre,* to skulk.]

**faint,** *fānt, adj.* wanting in strength (*arch.*): dim: lacking distinctness: not bright or forcible: weak in spirit (*arch.*): lacking courage (*arch.*): done in a feeble way: inclined to faint: sickly-smelling, oppressive (*arch.*).—*v.i.* to become feeble or weak (*arch.*): to lose strength, colour, etc. (*arch.*): to swoon: to fade or decay (*arch.*): to vanish (*arch.*): to lose courage or spirit (*arch.*). —*v.t.* (rare) to render faint.—*n.* a swoon.—*adj.* **faint'ed** (*Milt.*), exhausted.—*n.* and *adj.* **faint'ing.** —*adj.* **faint'ish,** slightly faint.—*n.* **faint'ishness.** —*adv.* **faint'ly.**—*n.* **faint'ness,** want of strength: feebleness of colour, light, etc.: dejection.— *n.pl.* **faints,** impure spirit that comes over at the beginning and end of distillation (also **feints**).— *adj.* **faint'y,** faintish.—*adjs.* **faint'-heart** (also *n.*), **faint'-heart'ed,** spiritless: timorous.—*adv.* **faint'-heart'edly.**—*n.* **faint'-heart'edness.** [O.Fr. *feint, feigned*—L. *fingĕre,* to feign.]

**fair,** *fār, adj.* bright: clear: clean: free from blemish: pure: pleasing to the eye: beautiful: of a light hue: free from rain, fine, dry: unobstructed: open: smoothly curving: prosperous: impartial: just: equitable: good, pleasing: plausible: civil: specious: reasonable: likely: favourable: pretty good: passable: out-and-out, veritable (*dial.*): a general expression of commendation or courtesy (as *fair sir; arch.*).—*n.* that which is fair; a woman (*arch.*): beauty (*Shak.*).—*v.t.* to make fair.—*v.i.* to clear up, as the weather from rain.—*adv.* in a fair manner (in all senses): full, square, directly (e.g. *hit fair in the centre*): quite (*dial.*). —*n.* **fair'ing,** adjustment or testing of curves in ship-building: means of reducing head-resistance in an aeroplane.—*adj.* **fair'ish,** somewhat fair: pretty well: pretty drunk (*dial.*).—*adv.* **fair'ly:** faithfully (*arch.*): neatly (*arch.*): justly: reasonably: plainly: gently (*obs.*): fully, quite: tolerably.—*n.* **fair'ness.**—*adjs.* **fair'-and-square',** honest—also *adv.;* **fair'-hand'ed** (*Shak.*), auspicious.—**fair copy,** a clean copy after correction; **fair'-deal'ing,** *adj.* **fair'-faced,** with a light complexion: beautiful: specious.—**fair field,** just

Neutral vowels in unaccented syllables: *el'ə-mənt;* for certain sounds in foreign words, see p. viii

conditions; **fair game,** an object for justifiable attack or ridicule.—*adj.* **fair'-haired, fair'-headed,** having light-coloured hair.—**Fair Isle,** type of design used in knitwear named from a Shetland island; **fair'-lead(er),** a ring, (set of) hole(s), etc., or more elaborate device, for guiding rope, etc., so as to reduce friction.—*adj.* **fair'-minded,** judging fairly.—**fair play,** honest dealing: justice.—*adjs.* **fair'-seem'ing,** appearing fair; **fair'-spok'en,** bland and civil in language and address.—**fair trade,** euphemism for smuggling: a mild form of the protective system, in which the basis of economic policy is supposed to be recipiocity or free-trade only with such nations as grant similar privileges—also used adverbially; **fair'way,** the navigable channel or usual course of vessels in a river, etc.: in golf, the smooth turf between tee and putting-green, distinguished from the uncut rough and from hazards.—*adj.* **fair'-weath'er,** suitable only for, or found only in, fair weather or (esp. of friends or supporters) favourable circumstances.—**bid fair** (see **bid**); **fair (be)fall** (*arch.*), good luck to; **fair enough!,** expressing acceptance, though not necessarily full agreement; **in a fair way** to (use way); **keep fair with,** to keep on amicable terms with; **speak fair** (see **speak**); **stand fair with,** to be in the good graces of; **the fair, the fair sex,** the female sex. [O.E. *fæger*.]

**fair,** *fār, n.* a great periodical market for one kind of merchandise, or for the general sales and purchases of a district, with or without amusements: often reduced to a collection of shows, swing-boats, etc.: charity bazaar: trade show.—*n.* **fair'ing,** a present given at or from a fair: any complimentary gift.—**fair'-day; fair'-ground.**—**a day after the fair, behind the fair,** too late; **get one's fairing** (*Scot.*), to get one's deserts. [O.Fr. *feire*—L. *fēria,* holiday.]

**fairy,** *fār'i, n.* an imaginary being, generally of diminutive and graceful human form, capable of kindly or unkindly acts towards man: fairy-folk: fairyland: enchantress: creature of overpowering charm: male homosexual.—*adj.* like a fairy, fanciful, whimsical, delicate.—*adv.* **fair'ily.**—*ns.* **fair'ydom; fair'yhood; fair'yism.**—*adj. and adv.* **fair'ylike,** like fairies or like something in fairyland: very delicate and charming.—**fair'y-beads,** joints of the stems of fossil crinoids; **fair'y-butt'er,** a name applied in northern England to certain gelatinous fungi; **fai'rycy'cle,** a child's bicycle; **fair'y-god'mother,** a benefactress such as Cinderella had; **fair'yland,** the country of the fairies: **fairy light,** tiny coloured light used as decoration; **fair'y-mon'ey,** money given by fairies, which changes into withered leaves, slate, stones, etc.: money that comes unsought; **fair'y-ring',** a ring of darker-coloured grass due to outward spread of a fungus (as the fairy-ring champignon, *Marasmius oreades*), attributed to the dancing of fairies; **fair'y-stone',** a fossil sea-urchin: a concretion; **fairy tale,** a story about fairies or other supernatural beings: a folk-tale: a romantic tale: an incredible tale: euphemistically, a lie: a marvel.—*adj.* (**fair'y-tale**) beautiful, fortunate, etc., as in a fairy tale. [O.Fr. *faerie,* enchantment—*fae* (mod. *fée*); see **faerie, fay** (1).]

**fait accompli,** *fe-ta-kɔ̄-plē,* (Fr.) an accomplished fact, a thing already done.

**faites vos jeux,** *fet võ zhø,* (Fr.) place your stakes! (e.g. in roulette).

**faith,** *fāth, n.* trust or confidence: belief in the statement of another: belief in the truth of revealed religion: confidence and trust in God: the living reception of religious belief: that which is believed: any system of religious belief, esp. the religion one considers true: fidelity to promises: honesty: word or honour pledged: faithfulness.—*interj.* by my faith: indeed.—*v.t.*

(*fādh; Shak.*) to believe.—*adj.* **faith'ful,** full of faith, believing: firm in adherence to promises, duty, friendship, love, etc.: loyal: constant: conformable to truth: worthy of belief: true: exact.—*adv.* **faith'fully,** with confidence: with fidelity: with sincerity: with scrupulous exactitude: solemnly (*coll.*): a meaningless word used in concluding a letter.—*n.* **faith'fulness.**—*adj.* **faith'less,** without faith or belief: not believing, esp. in God or Christianity: not adhering to promises, duty, etc.: inconstant: adulterous: untrustworthy: delusive.—*adv.* **faith'lessly.**—*ns.* **faith'lessness; faith'worthiness,** trustworthiness.—*adj.* **faith'worthy,** worthy of faith or belief.—**faith'-heal'er; faith'-heal'ing,** or **-cure,** a system of belief based on James v. 15, that sickness may be cured without medical advice or appliances, if the prayer of Christians be accompanied in the sufferer by true faith: cure by suggestion.—**bad faith,** treachery; **Father of the faithful,** Abraham: the caliph; **in good faith,** with sincerity; **the Faithful,** believers, esp. Mohammedans. [M.E. *feith, feyth*—O.Fr. *feid*—L. *fīdēs*—*fīdĕre,* to trust.]

**faitor,** *fā'tər,* (*obs.*) *n.* an imposter.—Often **fai'tour.** [O.Fr. *faitor*—L. *factor, -ōris,* doer.]

**faix,** *fāks,* (*dial.*) *interj.* faith. [Prob. short for **faykins;** see **fay** (2).]

**fake,** *fāk, v.t.* to fold, coil.—*n.* a coil or rope, etc. [Origin obscure.]

**fake,** *fāk, v.t.* to rob or attack: to filch: to doctor, cook, or counterfeit.—*n.* a swindle, dodge, sham: a faked article—also **fake'ment.**—*adj.* false, counterfeit.—*n.* **fak'er.** [Prob. the earlier *feak, feague,* Ger. *fegen,* to furbish up.]

**fakes, faikes,** *fāks, n.pl.* thin-bedded shaly or micaceous sandstone or sandy shale.

**fakir,** *fä-kēr',* or *fā'kər, n.* religious (esp. Mohammedan) mendicant, ascetic, or wonderworker in India, etc.—*n.* **fakir'ism** (or *fā'*). [Ar. *faqīr,* a poor man.]

**fa-la,** *fā-lä, n.* an old kind of madrigal.—**fa la** (**la,** etc.), syllables used as a refrain.

**Falange,** Sp. *fä-läng'hhä,* also *fə-lanj', fā', n.* a Spanish fascist group.—*ns.* **Falangism** (*fə-lan'-jizm*), also **fa-; Falan'gist,** also **fa-.** [Sp.,—Gr. *phalanx,* phalanx.]

**falbala,** *fal'ba-lə, n.* a trimming or flounce: a furbelow. [Ety. dub.; cf. **furbelow.**]

**falcade,** *fal'kād', n.* the motion of a horse when he throws himself on his haunches in a very quick curvet. [Fr.,—L. *falcāta* (fem.) bent.]

**falcate, -d,** *fal'kāt, -id, adj.* bent like a sickle.—*ns.* **falcā'tion; fal'cūla,** a falcate claw.—*adjs.* **falciform** (*fal'si-förm*), sickle-shaped; **fal'cūlate.** [L. *falx, falcis,* a sickle.]

**falchion,** *föl'shən, -chən, n.* a short, broad sword, bent somewhat like a sickle. [O.Fr. *fauchon,* through L.L., from L. *falx,* a sickle.]

**falciform.** See **falcate.**

**falcon,** *föl'kən, fö'kən, n.* a bird of prey of a kind trained to the pursuit of game: by falconers confined to the female: any of the long-winged birds of prey of the genus Falco or its kindred: a kind of cannon.—*ns.* **fal'coner,** one who sports with, or who breeds and trains, falcons or hawks for taking wild-fowl; **fal'conet,** a small field-gun in use till the 16th century.—*adj.* **fal'conine.**—*n.* **fal'conry,** the art or practice of training, or hunting with, falcons.—*adj.* **fal'con-eyed,** keen-eyed.—**fal'con-gen'til, -gen'tle,** the female of the peregrine falcon. [O.Fr. *faucon*—L.L. *falcō, -ōnis.*]

**faldage,** *föld'ij, fald'ij, (hist.) n.* the right of the lord of a manor of folding his tenant's sheep in his own fields for the sake of the manure: a fee paid in commutation therefor. [Law L. *faldāgium*—O.E. *fald,* fold.]

**falderal,** *fal'dər-al', n.* a meaningless refrain in songs: any kind of flimsy trifle—also **fol'derol**

(*fol'dər-ol'*) and **fal de rol.**—**falderal it,** to sing unmeaning sounds.
**faldetta,** *fäl-det'a, n.* a Maltese woman's combined hood and cape. [It.]
**faldstool,** *föld'stool, n.* a folding or camp stool: a coronation stool: a bishop's armless seat: a small desk in churches in England, at which the litany is to be sung or said.—*n.* **fald'istory** (*obs.*), a bishop's seat within the chancel. [L.L. *faldistolium, faldistorium*—O.H.G. *faldstuol—faldan* (Ger. *falten*), to fold, *stuol* (Ger. *stuhl*), stool.]
**Falernian,** *fa-lûr'ni-ən, adj.* pertaining to a district (*Falernus ager*) in Campania, famous of old for its wine.
**fall,** *föl, v.i.* to descend, esp. to descend freely and involuntarily by force of gravity: to drop: to drop prostrate: to throw oneself down: to be dropped in birth: to collapse: to become lower literally or figuratively (in position, degree, intensity, value, pitch, etc.): to die away: to subside: to abate: to ebb: to decline: to sink: (of the face) to relax into an expression of dismay: to flow downwards: to slope or incline down: to hang, dangle, or trail down: to be cast or shed: to drop dead or as if dead, esp. in fight: to be overthrown: to come to ruin: to lose power, station, virtue or repute: to be degraded: to be taken or captured: to become a victim: to yield to temptation: to pass into any state or action, to become, to begin to be (as *fall asleep, fall in love, fall a-weeping*): to rush: to become involved: to betake oneself: to come to be: to befall: to come about: to come by chance or as if by chance: to come in due course: to occur: to chance, light: to issue: to come forth: to appertain: to be apportioned, assigned: to come as one's share, lot, duty, etc.: to take position or arrangement: to find place: to be disposed: to impinge: to lapse: to terminate: to revert.—*v.t.* to cause to fall (*arch.* or *U.S.*): to let fall (*arch.*): to get (as what befalls one) (*obs.*; *Burns*):—*pr.p.* **fall'ing**; *pa.t.* **fell**; *pa.p.* **fallen,** *fö'lən.*—*n.* the act, manner, occasion, or time of falling or of felling: descent by gravity, a dropping down: that which falls: as much as comes down at one time: onset: overthrow: descent from a better to a worse position: slope or declivity: descent of water: a cascade: length of drop, amount of descent: decrease in value: a sinking of the voice: a cadence: the time when the leaves fall, autumn (chiefly *U.S.*): a bout of wrestling: the passing of a city or stronghold to the enemy: a lapse into sin, esp. that of Adam and Eve—'the Fall (of Man)': a falling band, a hanging fringe, flap, or ornament: lot (*arch.*): a lowering or hoisting rope.—*adj.* **fall'en,** having fallen: killed, esp. in battle: overthrown: seduced: in a degraded state, ruined.—*n.* **fall'ing.**—**fallen star,** a gelatinous mass of a blue-green alga (Nostoc, etc.) once popularly thought of meteoric origin; **fall-in',** noun corresponding to verb **fall in**; **falling band,** a seventeenth-century collar of fine material turned down on the shoulders; **fall'ing-off',** decline; **falling sickness,** epilepsy; **falling star,** a meteor; **falling stone,** a portion of an exploded meteor; **fall'-out,** noun corresponding to verb **fall out**: by-product, side benefit (*coll.*): a deposit of radioactive dust from a nuclear explosion or plant; **fall'-trap,** a trap that operates by a fall.—**fall across** (*arch.*), to meet by chance; **fall among,** to find oneself in the midst of; **fall away,** to decline gradually: to languish: to grow lean: to revolt or apostatise; **fall back,** to retreat, give way; **fall back, fall edge** (*obs.*), no matter what may happen; **fall back upon,** to have recourse to as an expedient or resource in reserve; **fall behind,** to lag: to be outstripped: to get in arrears; **fall down on** (*coll.*), to fail in;

**fall flat,** to fail of effect; **fall for** (*coll.*), to become enamoured of: to be taken in by; **fall foul of** (see foul); **fall in,** to (cause to) take places in ranks (*mil.*): to become hollowed: to revert; **fall in with,** to concur or agree with: to comply with: to meet by chance; **fall off,** to become detached and drop: to deteriorate: to die away, to perish: to revolt or apostatise: to draw back; **fall on,** to begin eagerly: to make an attack: to meet (*arch.*); **fall on one's feet,** to come well out of a difficulty: to gain any unexpected good fortune; **fall out,** to quarrel: to happen or befall: to (cause to) quit ranks (*mil.*); **fall over,** to go over to the enemy (*Shak.*): to go to sleep (*Scot.*); **fall over backwards** (see backwards under back); **fall over oneself** (*coll.*), to put oneself about (to do something); **fall short,** to turn out to be short or insufficient: to become used up: to fail to attain or reach what is aimed at (with *of*); **fall through,** to fail, come to nothing; **fall to,** to begin hastily and eagerly: to apply oneself to: to begin to eat; **fall upon,** to attack: to rush against: to devolve upon: to chance upon; **try a fall,** to take a bout at wrestling. [O.E. *fallan* (W.S. *feallan*); Ger. *fallen*; prob. conn. with L. *fallĕre,* to deceive.]
**fall,** *föl, n.* a trap.—*n.* **fall'-guy,** a dupe, easy victim: a scapegoat. [O.E. *fealle*—*feallan,* to fall.]
**fall,** *föl, n.* the cry given when a whale is sighted, or harpooned: the chase of a whale.—**loose fall,** the losing of a whale. [Perh. from the north-eastern Scottish pronunciation of **whale.**]
**fallacy,** *fal'ə-si, n.* something fallacious: deceptive appearance: an apparently genuine but really illogical argument: deception, deceitfulness (*obs.*): a wrong but prevalent notion.—*adj.* **fallacious** (*fə-lā'shəs*), of the nature of fallacy: deceptive: misleading: not well founded: causing disappointment: delusive.—*adv.* **fallā'ciously.**—*n.* **fallā'ciousness.** [L. *fallācia*—*fallāx, -ācis,* deceptive—*fallĕre,* to deceive.]
**fallal,** *fal-al', n.* a streamer of ribbon: any trifling ornament.—*adj.* (*obs.*), foppish, trifling.—*n.* **fallal'ery.**—*adv.* **fallal'ishly.**
**fallible,** *fal'i-bl, adj.* liable to error or mistake.—*n.* **fallibil'ity,** liability to err.—*adv.* **fall'ibly.** [L.L. *fallibilis*—*fallĕre,* to deceive.]
**Fallopian,** *fə-lō'pi-ən, adj.* relating to the Italian anatomist Gabriele *Fallopio* (1523-62).—**Fallopian tubes,** two tubes or ducts through which the ova pass from the ovary to the uterus, perhaps discovered by him.
**fallow,** *fal'ō, adj.* left untilled or unsown for a time.—*n.* land that has lain a year or more untilled or unsown after having been ploughed.—*v.t.* to plough without seeding.—*n.* **fall'owness.**—**fall'ow-chat, fall'ow-finch,** the wheatear.—**green fallow,** fallow where land is cleaned by a green crop, as turnips. [O.E. *fealgian,* to fallow; *fealh,* fallow land.]
**fallow,** *fal'ō, adj.* brownish-yellow.—**fallow deer,** a yellowish-brownish deer smaller than the red deer, with broad flat antlers. [O.E. *falu (fealu)*; cf. Ger. *fahl,* O.N. *fölr.*]
**false,** *föls, adj.* wrong: erroneous: deceptive or deceiving: untruthful: unfaithful: untrue: not genuine or real, counterfeit: improperly so called: artificial, as opposed to natural, of teeth, etc.: incorrect, not according to rule: out of tune.—*adv.* incorrectly: untruly: dishonestly: faithlessly.—*n.* (*obs.*), falsehood: untruth.—*v.t.* (*obs.*), to deceive, be false to: to feign: to falsify.—*n.* **false'hood,** state or quality of being false: want of truth: deceitfulness (*obs.*): false appearance (*obs.*): an untrue statement: the act of lying: a lie.—*adv.* **false'ly.**—*ns.* **false'ness; fals'er,** a falsifier, counterfeiter (*obs.*): a deceiver, a liar, (*Spens.*); **fal'sie(s),** pad(s) of rubber or other material inserted into a brassière to enlarge or improve the shape of

the breasts.—*adj.* **fals'ish**, somewhat false.—*ns.* **fals'ism**, a self-evident falsity; **fals'ity**, quality of being false: a false assertion.—**false acacia**, Robinia; **false alarm**, a warning without danger.—*adj.* **false-bedd'ed.**—**false bedding** (*geol.*), irregular lamination running obliquely to the general stratification, due to deposition in banks by varying currents; **false bottom**, a partition cutting off a space between it and the true bottom; **false card**, the card played to deceive.—*v.i.* **false-card'.**—**false conception**, a uterine growth consisting of some degenerate mass instead of a foetus; **false dawn**, deceptive appearance simulating dawn; **false face**, a mask.—*adj.* **false'-faced** (*Shak.*), hypocritical.—**false gallop** (*arch.*), a canter.—*adj.* **false'-heart'ed**, treacherous, deceitful.—**false imprisonment**, illegal detention by force or influence; **false leg**, a proleg; **false pregnancy**, pseudocyesis (see under **pseud-**); **false quantity**, pronunciation or use of a long vowel as short or short as long; **false relation** (*mus.*), occurrence in different parts together or in succession of a tone and a chromatic derivative; **false rib**, one that does not reach the breastbone; **false shame**, shame for that which is not shameful.—**play one false**, to act falsely or treacherously to a person; **put in a false position**, to bring any one into a position in which he must be misunderstood. [O.Fr. *fals* (mod. *faux*)—L. *falsus*, pa.p. of *fallĕre*, to deceive.]

**falsetto**, *föl-set'ō*, *n.* usu. in a man, forced voice of range or register above the natural: one who uses such a voice: false or strained sentiment.—*adj.* and *adv.* in falsetto. [It. *falsetto*, dim. of *falso*, false.]

**falsi crimen**, *fal-si kri'mən, fal'sē krē'men*, (L.L.) the crime of falsification, esp. forgery.

**falsidical**, *föl-sid'i-kəl*, (*rare*) *adj.* conveying a meaning that is false. [L. *falsus*, and *dicĕre*, to say.]

**falsify**, *föls'i-fī*, *v.t.* to forge or counterfeit: to tamper with: to misrepresent: to prove or declare to be false: to be false to (*obs.*): to feign (*obs.*).—*v.i.* (*obs.*) to lie:—*pr.p.* **fals'ifying**; *pa.t.* and *pa.p.* **fals'ified.**—*adj.* **fals'ifiable.**—*ns.* **falsifiabil'ity**; **falsificā'tion**; **fals'ifier**. [Fr. *falsifier*—L.L. *falsificāre*—L. *falsus*, false, *facĕre*, to make.]

**Falstaffian**, *föl-stäf'i-ən*, or *-staf'*, *adj.* like or pertaining to Shakespeare's *Falstaff*—corpulent, jovial, humorous, dissolute, and irrepressibly impudent.

**faltboat, foldboat**, *fölt'bōt*, or *folt'*, *föld'bōt*, *n.* a small collapsible boat of rubberised sailcloth. [Ger. *faltboot*, folding boat.]

**falter**, *föl'tər*, *v.i.* to stumble: to go unsteadily: to hesitate in speech as if taken aback: to flinch: to waver: to flag: to fail.—*v.t.* to utter falteringly.—*n.* unsteadiness.—*n.* and *adj.* **fal'tering**.—*adv.* **fal'teringly**. [Prob. a freq. of M.E. *falden* to fold; conn. with *fault* (in which the *l* is late) is not possible.]

**falx**, *falks*, *n.* a sickle-shaped part or process, as of the dura mater:—*pl.* **falces** (*fal'sēz*). [L., a sickle.]

**fame**, *fām*, *n.* public report or rumour (*arch.*): renown or celebrity, chiefly in a good sense.—*v.t.* to report: to make famous.—*adjs.* **famed**, renowned; **fame'less**, without renown.—**fama clamo'sa** (*Scot.*), any notorious rumour ascribing immoral conduct to a minister or officebearer in a church; **house of ill fame**, a brothel. [Fr.,—L. *fāma*, report, rumour, fame, from *fāri*, to speak; cf. Gr. *phēmē*, from *phanai*, to say.]

**familiar**, *fə-mil'yər*, *adj.* well acquainted or intimate: in the manner of an intimate: free: unceremonious: having a thorough knowledge: well known or understood: private, domestic:

common, everyday.—*n.* one well or long acquainted: a spirit or demon supposed to attend a person at call: a member of a pope's or bishop's household: the officer of the Inquisition who arrested the suspected.—*v.t.* **famil'iarise, -ize**, to make thoroughly acquainted with: to make easy by practice or study.—*n.* **familiarity** (*-i-ar'i-ti*), intimate acquaintanceship: freedom from constraint: any unusual or unwarrantable freedom in act or speech toward another, act of licence—usu. in *pl.*—*adv.* **famil'iarly**. [O.Fr. *familier*—L. *familiāris*, from *familia*, a family.]

**famille jaune, noire**, *fam-ē zhōn, nwär*, Chinese porcelain in which the background of the design is respectively yellow, black; **famille rose, verte**, *rōz, vert*, Chinese porcelain with design in which pink, green, is prominent. [Fr., family, yellow, black, pink, green.]

**family**, *fam'i-li*, *n.* the household, or all those who live in one house (as parents, children, servants): parents and their children: the children alone: the descendants of one common progenitor: race: honourable or noble descent: a group of animals, plants, languages, etc., more comprehensive than a genus: a collection of curves in the equations of which different values are given to the parameter(s) (*math.*).—*adjs.* **famil'ial** (*fəm-*), characteristic of a family; **famil'iar** (see above).—*ns.* **familism** (*fam'*), the family feeling: (*cap.*) the principles of the Familists; **Fam'ilist**, one of the 16th-cent. mystical sect known as the Family of Love, which based religion upon love independently of faith.—**family baker, butcher**, etc., small retailer who supplies families, not merely institutions; **family Bible**, a large Bible for family worship, with a page for recording family events; **family circle**, the members of the family taken collectively: one of the galleries in a theatre; **family coach**, a large carriage able to carry a whole family: a parlour game; **family man**, a man with a family: a domesticated man; **family name**, surname; **family planning**, regulating size and spacing of family, e.g. by using contraceptives; **family tree**, a diagram showing the branching of a family.—**in a family way**, in a familiar informal manner; **in the family way**, pregnant; **official family** (*U.S.*), the cabinet. [L. *familia—famulus*, a servant.]

**famine**, *fam'in*, *n.* extreme general scarcity of food: scarcity of anything: hunger: starvation. [Fr.,—L. *famēs*, hunger.]

**famish**, *fam'ish*, *v.t.* to starve.—*v.i.* (*arch.*) to die of or suffer extreme hunger or thirst.—*n.* fam'ishment, starvation.—**be famished, famishing**, to feel very hungry. [Obs. *fame*, to starve—L. *famēs*, hunger.]

**famous**, *fā'məs*, *adj.* renowned: noted: excellent (*coll.*).—*v.t.* (*arch.*) to make famous.—*adv.* **fā'mously**.—*n.* **fā'mousness**. [O.Fr.,—L. *fāmōsus—fāma*, fame.]

**famulus**, *fam'ū-ləs*, *n.* a private secretary or factotum: an attendant, esp. on a magician or scholar. [L., a servant.]

**fan**, *fan*, *n.* a basket formerly used for winnowing corn by throwing it in the wind: any instrument for winnowing: a broad, flat instrument esp. used by women to cool themselves—typically in or spreading into the shape of a sector of a circle: any fan-shaped structure, as a deposit of alluvium: anything spreading in a fan shape, e.g. a bird's wing or tail: a small sail to keep a windmill to the wind: a whale's tail-fluke: a propeller screw or propeller blade: a rotating ventilating or blowing apparatus.—*v.t.* to winnow: to move by a fan or the like: to direct a current of air upon: to cool or to kindle with, or as with, a fan.—*v.i.* to move like a fan: to spread out like a fan:—*pr.p.* **fann'ing**; *pa.t.* and *pa.p.* **fanned.**—*n.* **fann'er**, a fanning apparatus for winnowing, ventilation, etc.—**fan dance**, solo dance in nude (or nearly so) in which the performer attempts concealment (or nearly so) by tantalising manipulation of a fan or fans or bunch of ostrich plumes; **fan'-jet'**, (a plane with) an engine in which air is taken in through a fan and some of it, bypassing compressors, combustion chamber and turbines, mixes with the jet formed by the rest; **fan'light**, a window resembling in form an open fan; **fan palm**, any palm with palmate leaves, esp. palmetto.—*adj.* **fan'-shaped**, forming a sector of a circle.—**fan'tail**, tail shaped like a fan: a variety of domestic pigeon with tail feathers spread out like a fan: various other classes of fantailed birds such as the Australian genus *Rhipidura*: an artificially bred goldfish with double anal and caudal fins; **fan tracery, fan vaulting** (*archit.*), tracery rising from a capital or a corbel, and diverging like the folds of a fan over the surface of a vault; **fan wheel**, a wheel with fans on its rim for producing a current of air.—**fan out**, to fan, spread as a fan from a centre. [O.E. *fann*, from L. *vannus*, a basket for winnowing; cf. Fr. *van*.]

**fan,** *fan, n.* a devotee or enthusiastic follower of some sport or hobby, or public favourite.—*n.* **fan'dom.**—**fan club**, group united by devotion to a celebrity; **fan mail**, letters from devotees to a celebrity. [From **fanatic**.]

**fanal,** *fā'nəl, (arch.) n.* a lighthouse, a beacon. [Fr.,—Gr. *phanos*, a lantern, *phainein*, to show.]

**Fanariot.** See Phanariot.

**fanatic,** *fə-nat'ik* (by some *fan'ə-tik*), *adj.* extravagantly or unreasonably zealous, esp. in religion: excessively enthusiastic.—*n.* a person frantically or excessively enthusiastic, esp. on religious subjects.—*adj.* **fanat'ical,** fanatic: extravagant (*Shak.*).—*adv.* **fanat'ically.**—*v.t.* **fanat'icise, -ize** (*-i-siz*), to make fanatical.—*v.i.* to act as a fanatic.—*n.* **fanat'icism** (*-sizm*), wild and excessive religious or other enthusiasm. [L. *fānāticus*, belonging to a temple, inspired by a god, *fānum*, a temple.]

**fan-cricket.** Same as fen-cricket (under fen).

**fancy,** *fan'si, n.* that faculty of the mind by which it recalls, represents, or makes to appear past images or impressions—imagination, esp. of a lower, passive, or more trivial kind: an image or representation thus formed in the mind: an unreasonable lightly-formed or capricious opinion: a whim: a fantasia: capricious inclination or liking: taste: love (*Shak.*).—*adj.* pleasing to, or guided by, or originating in fancy or caprice: fantastic: capriciously departing from the ordinary, the simple, or the plain: ornate: parti-coloured (of flowers).—*v.t.* to picture in the mind: to imagine: to be inclined to believe: to have a liking for: to be pleased with: to breed or cultivate, with a view to development of conventionally accepted points:—*pr.p.* **fan'cying;** *pa.t.* and *pa.p.* **fan'cied.**—*interj.* exclamation of surprise.—*adj.* **fan'cied,** formed or conceived by the fancy: imagined: favoured.—*n.* **fan'cier,** one who fancies: one who has a liking for anything and is supposed to be a judge of it: a breeder for points.—*adj.* **fan'ciful,** guided or created by fancy: imaginative: whimsical: wild: unreal.—*adv.* **fan'cifully.**—*n.* **fan'cifulness.**—*adj.* **fan'ciless,** destitute of fancy.—**fancy bread,** bread other than plain bread; **fancy dress,** dress arranged according to the wearer's fancy, to represent some character; **fancy dress ball, fancy ball,** a ball at which fancy dress is worn; **fancy fair,** a special sale of fancy articles for some charitable purpose.—*adj.* **fan'cy-free',** free from the power of love.—*n.pl.* **fancy goods,** fabrics of variegated rather than simple pattern, applied generally to articles of show and ornament.— **fancy man,** a woman's lover (*derog.*): a pimp; **fancy monger** (*Shak.*), one who concerns himself

with love.—*adj.* **fan'cy-sick** (*Shak.*), love-sick.— **fancy stitch,** a more intricate and decorative stitch than *plain stitch*; **fancy woman,** mistress: prostitute; **fan'cywork,** ornamental needlework. —**fancy oneself,** to be conceited; **the fancy,** sporting characters generally, esp. pugilists: pugilism. [Contracted from **fantasy**.]

**fand,** *fand (Scot.), pa.t.* of find.

**fand,** *fand, fond, fond, (obs.) v.i.* to try, attempt: to proceed:—*pa.t.* and *pa.p.* **fanded, fonded,** or (*Spens.*) **fond.** [O.E. *fandian.*]

**fandangle,** *fan-dang'gl, n.* elaborate ornament: nonsense. [Perh. from **fandango.**]

**fandango,** *fan-dang'gō, n.* an old Spanish dance for two or its music in 3-4 time, with castanets: a gathering for dancing, a ball (*U.S.*). [Sp.]

**fane,** *fān, (obs.) n.* a flag: a weathercock. [O.E. *fana,* flag; cf. Ger. *fahne;* cf. **vane** and L. *pannus,* a cloth.]

**fane,** *fān, n.* a temple. [L. *fānum.*]

**fanfare,** *fan'fār, n.* a flourish of trumpets or bugles: an elaborate style of bookbinding.— *ns.* **fanfarade** (*fan-fər-ād'*), a fanfare; **fan'faron,** one who uses bravado: a blusterer, braggart; **fanfarō'na** (*Scott;* Sp. *fanfarrona,* trumpery), a gold chain; **fanfaronade,** vain boasting: bluster: ostentation.—*v.i.* to bluster. [Fr., perh. from the sound.]

**fang,** *fang, n.* the tooth of a wolf, dog, etc.: a claw or talon (*obs.*): the venom-tooth of a serpent: the embedded part of a tooth, etc.: a tang: a prong: a grip, catch (*Shak.*): grip or power of suction in a pump (*Scot.*).—*v.t. (obs.; Shak.* **phang**) to seize upon, catch: to prime a pump.—*adjs.* **fanged,** having fangs or anything resembling them; **fang'less.** [O.E. *fang,* from the same root as *fōn,* to seize.)

**fangle,** *fang'gl, n. (Milt.; Bunyan)* fancy.—*v.t. (Milt.)* to fabricate, trick out.—*adj.* **fang'led** (*Shak.*), foppish. [Mistaken back-formation from **newfangle(d).**]

**fango,** *fang'gō, n.* a clay or mud from thermal springs in Italy, esp. at Battaglio, used in treatment of gout, rheumatism, etc. [It., mud—Gmc.]

**fanion,** *fan'yən, n.* a small flag, esp. for surveying.—*n.* **fan'on,** a cloth for handling holy vessels or offertory bread: a maniple: a short cape worn by the Pope when celebrating High Mass. [O.Fr. *fanion, fanon*—L.L. *fanō, -ōnis,* banner, napkin—O.H.G. *fano;* cf. **fane, vane.**]

**fank,** *fangk, (Scot.) n.* a coil: a noose: a tangle. —*v.t.* **fank'le,** to entangle.—*n.* a tangle, muddle. [Conn. with **fang.**]

**fank,** *fangk, (Scot.) n.* a sheepfold. [Gael. *fang.*]

**fannel, fannell,** *fan'əl, n.* a maniple. [L.L. *fanonellus, fanula,* dims. of *fanō;* see **fanion.**]

**fanny,** *fan'i, (slang) n.* buttocks.

**Fanny Adams,** *fan'i ad'əmz, (slang)* tinned mutton.—**sweet Fanny Adams, sweet FA** (*slang,* in Services a euphemism), nothing at all. [From a girl murdered and cut up c. 1812.]

**fanon.** See fanion.

**fan-tan,** *fan'-tan, n.* a Chinese gambling game. [Chin.]

**fantasia,** *fan-tā'zi-ə, -tä', 'zhə,* or *-tə-zē'ə, n.* a musical or literary composition not governed by the ordinary rules of form. [It.,—Gr. *phantasiā;* see **fantasy.**]

**fantasy, phantasy,** *fan'tə-si, -zi, n.* fancy: imagination: mental image: love (*obs.*): caprice: fantasia: a story, film, etc., not based on realistic characters or setting: preoccupation with thoughts associated with unobtainable desires. —*v.t. (arch.)* to fancy, conceive mentally.— *adj.* **fan'tasied,** filled with fancies.—*v.t.* and *v.i.* **fan'tasise, -ize.**—*n.* **fan'tasm** (same as **phantasm**).—*adj.* **fantasque** (*-task'*), fantastic.—*n.* **fantasy.**—*ns.* **fan'tast,** a person of fantastic ideas; **fantas'tic** (*obs.*), one who is fantastical:

a dandy, a fop.—*adjs.* fantas′tic, -al, fanciful: not real: capricious: whimsical: wild: foppish (*obs.*): incredible: excellent (*slang*).—*adv.* fantas′tically.—*n.* fantas′ticalness.—*v.t.* and *v.i.* fantas′ticate.—*ns.* fantas′ticism (-*sizm*); fantas′-tico (*Shak.*; It.), a fantastic; fan′tastry. [O.Fr. *fantasie*—through L. from Gr. *phantasiā*—*phantazein*, to make visible; cf. fancy, fantasia.]

Fanti, Fantee, *fan′tē, n.* a Ghanaian people: their language.—to go Fanti (*Kipling, G. K. Chesterton*), to adopt the ways of the natives.

fantoccini, *fan-to-chē′nē, n.pl.* marionettes: marionette show. [It., pl. of *fantoccino*, dim. of *fantoccio*, a puppet—*fante*, a boy—L. *infāns*, -*antis.*]

fantod, *fan′tod*, fantad, -tăd, (*slang*) *n.* a fidgety fussy person, esp. a ship's officer: (usu. in *pl.*) fidgets.—*n.* fantigue, fanteeg (*fan-tēg′*), anxiety, unpleasant excitement.

fantom. Same as phantom.

fap, *fap*, (*Shak.*) *adj.* fuddled, drunk.

faquir, *fäk-ēr′, n.* Same as fakir.

far, *fär, adj.* remote: more distant of two (in *Shak.* as *comp.*): advanced (*obs.*)—*adv.* to, at, or over a great distance or advanced stage: remotely: in a great degree: very much: long (*obs.*): (of an animal) off, right-hand (i.e. the side remote from one leading it).—*v.t.* (*dial.*) to remove to a distance.—*adv.* far′most, most distant or remote.—*n.* far′ness, the state of being far: remoteness, distance.—*adj.* far away, distant: abstracted, absent-minded.—*n.* the distant. —faraway′ness; far cry, a long distance; Far East, Eastern Asia (China, Japan, etc.).—*adjs.* far′-fetched (*obs.* far′fet), fetched or brought from a remote place (*arch.*): forced, unnatural; far′-flung, thrown far and wide: extensive.—*adv.* far′-forth (*Spens.*), far.—Far North, the Arctic regions.—*adj.* and *adv.* far′-off, in the distance.—*adjs.* far-out, of jazz or its addicts, more up to date than 'cool': intellectual: satisfying; far′-reach′ing, having wide validity, scope, or influence; far′-see′ing, prescient; far′-sighted, seeing far: having defective eyesight for near objects: prescient; far′-sought, sought for at a distance.—Far South, the Antarctic regions.—*adj.* far′-spent, far advanced.—Far West, the Great Plains, Rocky Mountains and Pacific side of North America.—by far, in a very great degree; far and away, by a great deal; far and near, far and wide, everywhere, all about; far between, at wide intervals: rare; far be it, God forbid; far from it, on the contrary; I'll see you far (or farther) first, I will not do it by any means; in so far as, to the extent that.—See also farther. [O.E. *feor(r)*; Du. *ver*; O.N. *fiarre*.]

farad, *far′ad, n.* a unit of electrical capacitance, the capacitance of a capacitor between the plates of which appears a difference of potential of one volt when it is charged by one coulomb of electricity.—*n.* far′aday, a unit used in electrolysis, equal to 96,500 coulombs.—*adj.* faradic (-*ad′ik*), pertaining to Faraday, esp. in connection with induced currents.—*n.* faradisā′tion, -z-.—*v.t.* far′adise, -ize (*med.*), to stimulate by induced currents.—*ns.* far′adism, treatment by induced currents; microfar′ad, the millionth part of a farad. [From Michael Faraday (1791-1867).]

farand, farrand, farrant, *far′ənd, fär′, -ənt,* (*Scot.*) *adj.* having a certain appearance or manner, esp. in such compound forms as *auld-farand*—old-fashioned, quaint, precocious, sagacious; *fair-farand*, goodly, specious. [M.E. *farand*, comely. Origin obscure; prob. pr.p. of fare.]

farandine, farrandine, *far′ən-dēn*, ferrandine, *fer′, (obs.) n.* a cloth or a dress of silk with wool or hair. [Fr. *ferrandine*.]

farandole, *far-ən-dōl′, n.* a Provençal dance per-

formed in a long string: music for it, in 6-8 time. [Prov. *farandoula.*]

farborough, *fär′bər-ə, n.* Goodman Dull's pronunciation of thirdborough (*Love's Lab. Lost* I, i. 182).—Another reading, tharborough.

farce, *färs, v.t.* to cram: to stuff, fill with stuffing: to swell out (*Shak.*).—*ns.* stuffing, force-meat: comedy of extravagant humour, buffoonery, and improbability: ridiculous or empty show: a hollow formality.—*n.* farceur (*fär-sœr′*; Fr.), a joker, buffoon: one who writes or acts in farces: —*fem.* farceuse (-*sœz′*).—*adj.* far′cical.—*n.* farcical′ity, farcical quality.—*adv.* far′cically.—*v.t.* far′cify, to turn into a farce.—*n.* farc′ing, stuffing.—*adj.* farci (*fär-sē*; Fr.), stuffed. [Fr. *farce*, stuffing, from L. *farcire*, to stuff; the connecting links of meaning seem to be interpolation, theatrical gag, buffoonery; cf. farse.]

farcy, *fär′si, n.* chronic glanders.—(*obs.*) far′cin. —*adj.* far′cied.—far′cy-bud, a swollen lymphatic gland, as in farcy. [Fr. *farcin*—L.L. *farciminum.*]

fard, *färd, n.* white paint for the face.—*v.t.* to paint with fard: to gloss over: to trick out. [Fr., of Gmc. origin.]

fardage, *fär′dij*, (*naut. obs.*) *n.* dunnage. [Fr.]

fardel, *fär′dl*, (*obs.*) *n.* a fourth part. [O.E. *fēortha dǣl*, fourth deal.]

fardel, *fär′dl, n.* a pack: anything cumbersome or irksome: the manyplies or omasum.—far′-del-bag, the omasum.—*adj.* far′del-bound, constipated, esp. of cattle and sheep, by the retention of food in the omasum. [O.Fr. *fardel* (Fr. *fardeau*), dim of *farde*, a burden, possibly—Ar. *fardah*, a package.]

farden, farding, *fär′dən* (*obs.* or *dial.*). Same as farthing.

fare, *fär, v.i.* to travel: to get on or succeed: to happen well or ill to: to be in any particular state, to be, to go on: to be fed.—*n.* (*orig. Spens.*) a course or passage: the price of passage: a passenger (or passengers): food or provisions for the table.—*interj.* farewell′, may you fare well!, a parting wish for safety or success: goodbye.—*n.* well-wishing at parting: the act of departure.—*adj.* (*fär′wel*) parting: valedictory: final. [O.E. *faran*: Ger. *fahren.*]

farina, *fə-rī′nə, fə-rē′nə, n.* ground corn: meal: starch: pollen: a mealy powder.—*adjs.* farinaceous (*far-i-nā′shas*), mealy: consisting of cereals; far′inose (-*i-nōs*), yielding farina. [L. *farina*—*fär*, corn.]

farl(e), *färl*, (*Scot.*) *n.* the quarter of a round cake of flour or oatmeal: a cake. [fardel (1).]

farm, *färm, n.* a fixed payment (*obs.*): a lease (*Spens.*): a fixed payment in composition of taxes, etc.: the letting out of revenue to one who collects it in exchange for a fixed sum: a tract of land (originally one leased or rented) used for cultivation and pasturage, along with a house and other necessary buildings: farmhouse: farmstead: piece of land or water used for breeding animals (as *fox*-, *oyster-farm*): place for treatment and disposal (*sewage-farm*): place where e.g. children are handed over to be taken care of.—*v.t.* to grant or receive the revenues of for a fixed sum: to rent to or from another: to cultivate: use as farm: to arrange for maintenance of at fixed price.—*v.i.* to practise business of farmer.—*ns.* farm′er, one who farms land: the tenant of a farm: one who receives taxes, etc., for fixed payment:—*fem.* far′meress.—*ns.* farm′ery, buildings of a farm; farm′ing, business of cultivating land.—farmer general, one of those who, in France before the Revolution, leased the public revenues; farmer's lung, a lung disease caused by the spores of actinomycetes which develop in hay baled while it is still damp; farm′house, farmer's house attached to farm; farm′-hand, -labourer,

one who works on a farm.—*n.pl.* **farm'-offices**, outbuildings on a farm.—**farm'-place, farm'-stead, farm steading,** farmhouse with buildings belonging to it—*Scot.* **farm'-toun** (*-tōōn*); **farm'-yard**, yard or enclosure surrounded by farm buildings.—**farm out**, to board out for fixed payment: to give, e.g. work for which one has made oneself responsible, to others to carry out. [L.L. *firma*, a fixed payment—L. *firmus*, firm.]
**farmost.** See **far.**
**faro**, *fär'ō, n.* a game of chance played by betting on the order of appearance of certain cards. [Perh. from *Pharaoh*; reason unknown.]
**farouche**, *fə-rōōsh', fa-*, shy, ill at ease: sullen and unsociable: socially inexperienced and lacking polish. [Fr., wild, shy, savage.]
**farrago**, *fə-rä'gō, fä-rä'gō, n.* a confused mass of objects or persons (*obs.*): a disordered mixture. —*adj.* **farraginous** (*fə-rāj'in-əs, -raj'*), miscellaneous, jumbled. [L. *farrāgō, -inis*, mixed fodder—*fär*, grain.]
**farrand, farrant.** See **farand.**
**farrandine.** See **farandine.**
**farrier**, *far'i-ər, n.* one who shoes horses: one who cures horses' diseases: one in charge of cavalry horses.—*n.* **farr'iery**, the farrier's art: veterinary surgery. [O.Fr. *ferrier*—L. *ferrum*, iron.]
**farrow**, *far'ō, n.* a litter of pigs.—*v.i.* or *v.t.* to bring forth (pigs). [O.E. *fearh*, a pig; Ger. (dim.) *ferkel*; L. *porcus.*]
**farrow**, *far'ō, adj.* not with calf for the time being. [Ety. dub.; with *farrow cow* cf. Flem. *verwekoe, varwekoe.*]
**farruca**, *fa-rōō'ka*, (Sp.) a Spanish gypsy dance with abrupt variations of tempo and mood.
**farse**, *färs, n.* an explanation of the Latin epistle in the vernacular.—*v.t.* to extend by interpolation. [**farce.**]
**fart**, *färt,* (*vulg.*) *v.i.* to break wind from the anus.—Also *n.* [O.E. (assumed) *feortan*; cf. Gr. *perdesthai.*]
**farthel**, *fär'dhəl*, (*Scot.*) *n.* Same as **farl.**
**farther**, *fär'dhər,* **far'thermore, far'thermost, far'thest.** Same as **further**, etc., and sometimes preferred where the notion of distance is more prominent. [A variant (M.E. *ferther*) of **further** that came to be thought a comp. of **far.**]
**farthing**, *fär'dhing, n.* a fourth part (*obs.*): the fourth of a pre-1971 penny (from Jan. 1961, not legal tender): anything very small: the Gr. *assarion* (L. *as*) and also *kodrantēs* (L. *quadrāns*), fourth of an *as* (B.).—*adj.* **far'thingless.**—*n.* **far'thingsworth**, as much as a farthing will buy. —**far'thingland,** a varying area of land. [O.E. *fēorthing*, a fourth part—*fēortha*, fourth, and suff. *-ing.*]
**farthingale**, *fär'dhing-gäl, n.* a kind of crinoline of whalebone for distending women's dress. [O.Fr. *verdugale*—Sp. *verdugado*, hooped, *verdugo*, rod.]
**fasces**, *fas'ēz, n.pl.* the bundle of rods, with or without an axe, borne before an ancient Roman magistrate of high grade. [L. *fascēs*, pl. of *fascis*, bundle.]
**fasching**, *fa'shing*, (Ger.) (Shrovetide) carnival.
**fascia**, *fas(h)'i-ə, n.* a band, fillet (*obs.*): a broad flat band, as in an architrave, or over a shopfront (*archit.*): a board in like position, commonly bearing the shopkeeper's name: (also **fascia-board**) the instrument-board of a motorcar: any bandlike structure, esp. of connective tissue ensheathing a muscle (*zool.*).—*adjs.* **fasc'ial, fasc'iated.**—*n.* **fasciā'tion** (*bot.*), union of a number of parts side by side in a flat plate; **fasciola** (*fə-si'ō-lə*), **fasciole** (*fas'i-ōl*), a band of colour. [L. *fascia*, band, bandage.]
**fascicle**, *fas'i-kl, n.* a bundle or bunch, esp. a bunched tuft of branches, roots, fibres, etc.: a part of a book issued in parts.—Also **fasc'icule**,

**fascic'ulus:**—*pl.* **fascic'uli.**—*adjs.* **fasc'icled, fascic'ular, fascic'ulate, -d.** [L. *fasciculus*, dim. of *fascis*, bundle.]
**fascinate**, *fas'i-nāt, v.t.* to bewitch, enchant, cast the evil eye upon (*obs.*): to control by the eye like a snake: to entangle the attention of: to charm: to captivate.—*adj.* **fasc'inating**, charming, delightful: binding the attention.—*n.* **fascinā'tion**, the act of charming: power to harm, control, allure, or render helpless by looks or spells: state of being fascinated: **fasc'inātor**, one who fascinates: a woman's light, soft head-covering. [L. *fascināre, -ātum*; perh. allied to Gr. *baskainein*, to bewitch.]
**fascine**, *fas-ēn', n.* a brushwood faggot, used to fill ditches, protect a shore, etc. [Fr.,—L. *fascina—fascis*, a bundle.]
**fascio**, *fä'shō, n.* an organised political group or club:—*pl.* **fasci** (*fä'shē*)—*ns.* **Fascist**, *fas(h)'ist*, **Fascista**, *fä-shēs'tə*, a member of a political party in Italy (and elsewhere in imitation) representing a nationalist reaction against socialism and communism, that came into power by violent means in 1922 and fell in 1943 (*pl.* **Fasc'ists, Fascisti**, *fä-shēs'tē*)—**fascist**, without *cap.* when expressing attitude not official party membership.—Also *adj.*—*n.* **Fasc'ism** (also **fascism), Fascis'mo**, the policy of forceful methods of the Fascisti. [Ital. *fascio*, bundle, group, with a hint of *fasces* (q.v.).]
**fash**, *fash,* (Scot.) *v.t.* to trouble, annoy.—*v.i.* to be vexed: to take trouble or pains: to annoy. —*n.* pains, trouble: annoyance.—*n.* **fash'ery.** —*adj.* **fash'ious** (*fash-əs*), troublesome, vexatious. —*n.* **fash'iousness**—never fash your thumb, take no trouble in the matter. [O.Fr. *fascher* (Fr. *fâcher*)—L. *fastidium*, disgust.]
**fashion**, *fash'n, n.* the make or cut of a thing: form or pattern: vogue: prevailing mode or shape of dress or that imposed by those whose lead is accepted: a prevailing custom: manner: genteel society: appearance.—*v.t.* to make: to mould according to a pattern: to suit or adapt. —*adj.* **fash'ionable**, according to prevailing fashion: prevailing in or use at any period: observant of the fashion in dress or living: moving in high society: patronised by people of fashion.—*n.* a person of fashion.—*n.* **fash'ionableness.**—*adv.* **fash'ionably.**—*ns.* **fash'ionist.—fashion house**, an establishment in which fashionable clothes are designed, made and sold.—*adjs.* **fash'ionmongering, fash'ionmonging** (Shak.), behaving like a fop.—**fash'ionplate**, a pictorial representation of the latest style of dress: a very smartly dressed person (*fig.*).—**after** or **in a fashion**, in a way: to a certain extent; **in the fashion**, in accordance with the prevailing style of dress, etc. [O.Fr. *fachon*—L. *factiō, -ōnis—facēre*, to make.]
**fashions**, *fash'ənz*, (Shak.) *n.pl.* for **farcins, farcy.**
**fast**, *fäst, adj.* firm: fixed: steadfast: fortified: (of sleep) sound: (of colours) not liable to fade or run.—*adv.* firmly, unflinchingly: soundly or sound (asleep): close: near.—*adv.* **fast'ly** (Shak.), firmly.—*n.* **fast'ness**, fixedness: a stronghold, fortress, castle.—**fast-and-loose'**, a cheating game practised at fairs, the dupe being invited to put a stick in the loop of a coiled belt so that it cannot be pulled away—called also **prick-the-garter.**—*adj.* **fast'-hand'ed**, closefisted.—**fast by**, close to, close by; **play fast and loose** (from the cheating game), to be unreliable, shifty: to behave without sense of moral obligation. [O.E. *fæst*; Ger. *fest.*]
**fast**, *fäst, adj.* quick: rapid: before time (as a clock): promoting fast play: seeking excitement: rash: dissipated.—*adv.* swiftly: in rapid succession: extravagantly.—*adj.* **fast'ish**, somewhat fast.—*n.* **fast'ness.**—**fast worker**, one who gains his ends quickly and easily, esp. by

unscrupulous means.—**pull a fast one**, to gain an advantage by trickery. [A special use of **fast** (1), derived from Scand. sense of urgent.]
**fast**, *fäst*, *v.i.* to keep from food: to go hungry: to abstain from food in whole or part, as a religious duty.—*n.* abstinence from food: special abstinence enjoined by the church: the day or time of fasting.—*ns.* **fast′er**, one who fasts; **fast′ing**, religious abstinence.—**fast′-day**, a day of religious fasting: a day for humiliation and prayer, esp. before communion; **Fast′ens**, short for **Fastens-eve** (*Scot.* **Fasten-e′en** and **Fastern′s-e′en**), **Fastens Tuesday**, Shrove Tuesday (O.E. *fæstenes*, gen. of *fæsten*, fast). [O.E. *fæstan*, to fast; Ger. *fasten*.]
**fast**, *fäst* (*Spens.*) a spelling of **faced.**
**fasten**, *fäs′n*, *v.t.* to make fast or firm: to fix securely: to attach.—*v.i.* to admit of being fastened: to remain stationary: to fix: to lay hold: to make assault.—*ns.* **fastener** (*fäs′nər*), a clip, catch, or other means of fastening; **fas′tening** (*fäs′ning*), that which fastens.—**fasten on**, to direct (one's eyes) on: to seize on, e.g. a fact: to fix the blame, responsibility for, on (a person; *slang*). [fast (1).]
**fasti**, *fas′tī*, L. *fäs′tē*, *n.pl.* those days among the ancient Romans on which it was lawful to transact legal or public business—opp. to *nefasti*: an enumeration of the days of the year, a calendar: annals. [L.]
**fastidious**, *fas-tid′i-əs*, *adj.* affecting superior taste: over-nice: difficult to please: exacting in taste: nicely critical.—*adv.* **fastid′iously.**—*n.* **fastid′iousness.** [L. *fastidiōsus*—*fastidium*, loathing.]
**fastigiate**, *fas-tij′i-āt*, *adj.* pointed, sloping to a point or edge: with branches more or less erect and parallel (*bot.*): conical.—*adj.* **fastig′iated.** —*n.* **fastig′ium**, the apex of a building: gable-end: pediment. [L. *fastigium*, a gable-end, roof.]
**fastuous**, *fas′tū-əs*, *adj.* haughty: ostentatious. [L. *fastuōsus*—*fastus*, arrogance.]
**fat**, *fat*, *adj.* plump, fleshy: well-filled out: thick, full-bodied (as of printing types): corpulent: obese: having much, or of the nature of, adipose tissue or the substance it contains: oily: fruitful or profitable: rich in some important constituent: gross: fulsome:—*comp.* **fatt′er**; *superl.* **fatt′est.**—*n.* a substance found in adipose tissue: solid animal or vegetable oil: any member of a group of naturally occurring substances consisting of the glycerides of higher fatty acids, e.g. palmitic acid, stearic acid, oleic acid (*chem.*): the richest part of anything: a piece of work offering more than usual profit for effort: a passage that enables an actor or musician to show what he can do: inclination to corpulency: a fat animal: money (*slang*).—*v.t.* to make fat.—*v.i.* to grow fat:—*pr.p.* **fatt′ing**; *pa.t.* and *pa.p.* **fatt′ed.**—*n.* **fat′ling**, a young animal fattened for slaughter.—*adj.* **small and fat.**—*adv.* **fat′ly**, grossly: lumberingly. —*n.* **fat′ness**, quality or state of being fat: fullness of flesh: richness: fertility: that which makes fertile.—*adj.* **fatt′ed** (**fatted calf**, the not always approved fare for the returned prodigal —Luke xv. 23, etc.).—*v.t.* **fatt′en**, make fat or fleshy: make fertile.—*v.i.* grow fat.—*ns.* **fatt′-ener**; **fatt′ening**; **fatt′iness.**—*adjs.* **fatt′ish**, somewhat fat; **fatt′y**, containing fat: having qualities of fat.—*n.* a fat person.—*adjs.* **fat′-brained** (*Shak.*), stupid; **fat′-face, -d**, having a fat or broad face.—**fat′-head**, a dullard.—*adj.* **fat′-head′ed.**—**fat′-hen**, any one of various thick-leaved plants, esp. of the goosefoot family.— *adj.* **fat′-kidney′d** (*Shak.*).—**fat′-lute**, a mixture of pipe-clay and linseed-oil, for filling joints, etc.— *adj.* **fat′-tailed**, having much fat in the tail, as certain Asiatic and African sheep.—**fat stock**,

livestock fattened for market; **fatty acids**, acids which with glycerine form fats; **fatty degeneration**, morbid deposition of fat; **fatty heart**, etc., fatty degeneration of the heart, etc.—*adj.* **fat′-witted**, dull, stupid.—**a fat lot** (*slang*), not much; **the fat is in the fire**, a critical act has precipitated the trouble. [O.E. *fætt*, fatted.]
**fat**, *fat*, *n.* a vessel for holding liquids: a vat: a dry measure of nine bushels. [See vat.]
**fatal**, **fatalism**, etc. See fate.
**fata Morgana**, *fä′tä mör-gä′nä*, a striking kind of mirage seen most often in the Strait of Messina. [Supposed to be caused by the fairy (It. *fata*) *Morgana* of Arthurian romance.]
**fate**, *fāt*, *n.* inevitable destiny or necessity: appointed lot: destined term of life: ill-fortune: doom: final issue: (in *pl.*) the three goddesses of fate, Clotho, Lachesis, and Atropos, who determine the birth, life, and death of men— the fatal sisters.—*adj.* **fāt′al**, belonging to or appointed by fate: announcing fate: causing ruin or death: mortal: calamitous.—*ns.* **fāt′alism**, the doctrine that all events are subject to fate, and happen by unavoidable necessity: acceptance of this doctrine: lack of effort in the face of threatened difficulty or disaster; **fāt′alist**, one who believes in fatalism.—*adj.* **fātalist′ic**, belonging to or partaking of fatalism. —*n.* **fatality** (*fə-tal′i-ti*), the state of being fatal or unavoidable: the decree of fate: fixed tendency to disaster or death: mortality: a fatal occurrence.—*adv.* **fāt′ally.**—*adjs.* **fāt′ed**, doomed: destined: invested with the power of destiny (*Shak.*): enchanted (*Dryden*); **fate′ful**, charged with fate.—*adv.* **fate′fully.**—*n.* **fate′fulness.** [L. *fātum*, a prediction--*fātus*, spoken—*fārī*, to speak.]
**father**, *fä′dhər*, a male parent: an ancestor or forefather: a fatherly protector: a contriver or originator: a title of respect applied to a venerable man, to confessors, monks, priests, etc.: a member of certain fraternities: (usu. in *pl.*) a member of a ruling body, as *conscript fathers*, *city fathers*: the oldest member, or member of longest standing, of a profession or body: one of a group of ecclesiastical writers of the early centuries, usually ending with Ambrose, Jerome, and Augustine: the first person of the Trinity. —*v.t.* to adopt: to ascribe to one as his offspring or production.—*n.* **fa′therhood**, state or fact of being a father: fatherly authority (*arch.*). —*adj.* **fa′therless**, destitute of a living father: without a known author.—*ns.* **fa′therlessness**; **fa′therliness.**—*adj.* **fa′therly**, like a father: paternal.—*n.* **fa′thership.**—**fa′ther-figure**, a senior person of experience and authority looked on as a trusted leader; **fa′ther-in-law**, the father of one's husband or wife: step-father (*arch.*):—*pl.* **fathers-in-law**; **fa′therland**, native land, esp. Germany (Vaterland); **fa′ther-lash′er**, a name applied to two bull-heads found on the British coasts.—**be gathered to one's fathers** (*B.*), to die and be buried; **Holy Father**, the Pope. [O.E. *fæder*; Ger. *vater*, L. *pater*, Gr. *patēr*.]
**fathom**, *fadh′əm*, *n.* originally, the reach of the outstretched arms: now, a nautical measure, six feet: penetration of mind: a timber measure, 216 cubic feet:—*pl.* **fathom, fathoms.**—*v.t.* to measure or encompass with outstretched arms (*arch.*): to try the depth of: to comprehend or get to the bottom of.—*adjs.* **fath′omable**; **fath′omless.**—*n.* **fathom′eter**, a sonic depth-finder.—**fath′om-line**, sailor's line and lead for taking soundings. [O.E. *fæthm*; Du. *vadem*, Ger. *faden*.]
**fatidical**, *fā-, fə-tid′i-kl*, *adj.* having power to foretell future events: prophetical.—*adv.* **fatid′ically.** [L. *fātidicus*—*fātum*, fate, *dīcere*, to tell.]
**fatigue**, *fə-tēg′*, *n.* weariness from labour of body or of mind: toil: lessened power of response

to stimulus, resulting from activity: failure under repeated stress as in metal: fatigue-duty (sometimes allotted as a punishment).—*v.t.* to reduce to weariness: to exhaust the strength or power of recovery of:—*pr.p.* **fatigu'ing**; *pa.t.* and *pa.p.* **fatigued'.**—*adj.* **fatig(u)able** (*fat'ig-ə-bl*), capable of being fatigued: easily fatigued.—*n.* **fat'ig(u)-ableness.**—*adj.* **fatigate** (*fat'i-gāt*; *Shak.*), fatigued.—*v.t.* (*obs.*) to fatigue.—*adv.* **fatigu'ingly.** —**fatigue'-dress**, working dress; **fatigue'-dū'ty**, the part of a soldier's work distinct from the use of arms; **fatigue'-party.** [Fr. *fatigue*—L. *fatigāre*, to weary.]

**Fatimid,** *fat'i-mid, n.* a descendant of Mohammed's daughter, *Fatima*, and his cousin, Ali, esp. one of a dynasty ruling parts of northern Africa from 909 to 1171.—*Also adj.*

**fatiscent,** *fā-, fə-tis'ənt, adj.* gaping with cracks. —*n.* **fatis'cence.** [L. *fatiscēns, -entis,* pr.p. of *fatiscĕre,* to gape.]

**fattrels,** *fat'rəlz, fät', (Scot.) n.pl.* ends of ribbon. [O.Fr. *fatraille,* trumpery.]

**fatuous,** *fat'ū-əs, adj.* silly: imbecile.—*adj.* **fatū'-itous.**—*ns.* **fatū'ity, fat'ūousness,** unconscious stupidity: imbecility.—**fatuous fire,** ignis fatuus, Will-o'-the-wisp. [L. *fatuus.*]

**faubourg,** *fō-bōōr, n.* a suburb just beyond the walls or a district recently included within a city. [Fr.]

**fauces,** *fö'sēz, n.pl.* the upper part of the throat, from the root of the tongue to the entrance of the gullet: the throat of a flower.—*adjs.* **fau'cal** (*-kl*), of, produced, in the fauces, as certain Semitic guttural sounds; **faucial** (*fö'shl*), of the fauces. [L. *faucēs.*]

**faucet,** *fö'sit, n.* a pipe inserted in a barrel to draw liquid: a tap (*U.S.*). [Fr. *fausset.*]

**faugh,** *fö, interj.* expressing disgust.

**faulchion, faulkins,** obsolete forms of falchion.

**fault,** *fölt,* formerly *föt, n.* a failing: error: blemish: imperfection: a slight offence: a dislocation of strata or veins (*geol.*): a stroke in which the player fails to serve the ball into the proper place (*tennis*): culpability for that which has happened amiss.—*v.i.* to fall short (*obs.*): to be faulty: to commit a fault.—*v.t.* to find fault with: to find flaw(s) in (e.g. *cannot fault the performance*): to ʿause a fault in (*geol.*). —*adj.* **fault'ful** (*Shak.*), full ʌf faults or crimes.— *adv.* **fault'ily.**—*n.* **fault'iness.**—*adj.* **fault'less,** without fault or defect.—*adv.* **fault'lessly.**—*n.* **fault'lessness.**—*adj.* **fault'y,** imperfect, defective: guilty of a fault: blamable.—**fault'-finder; fault'-finding; find'-fault** (see **find**).—**at fault** (of dogs) unable to find the scent: at a loss; **in fault,** to blame; **find fault,** to carp, be critical: (with *with*), to censure for some defect; **to a fault,** excessively. [O.Fr. *faute, falte*—L. *fallĕre,* to deceive.]

**fauna,** *fö'na, n.* the assemblage of animals of a region or period: a list or account thereof:— *pl.* **faun'as, faun'ae.**—*n.* **faun,** a Roman rural deity, protector of shepherds.—*adj.* **faun'al.**—*n.* **faun'ist,** one who studies faunas.—*adj.* **faunist'ic.** [L. *Fauna, Faunus,* tutelary deities of shepherds —*favēre, fautum,* to favour.]

**faute de mieux,** *fōt də myø, (*Fr.) for want of better.

**fauteuil,** *fō-tœ-y', also *fō'til, n.* an armchair, esp. a president's chair: the seat of one of the forty members of the French Academy: a theatre-stall. [Fr.]

**fautor,** *fö'tər, n.* a favourer: patron: abettor. [L. *fautor—favēre,* to favour.]

**Fauve, Fauvist,** *fōv, -ist, ns.* one of a group of painters at the beginning of the 20th century, including Matisse, who viewed a painting as essentially a two-dimensional decoration in colour, not necessarily imitative of nature.—*n.* **Fauv'ism.** [Fr. *fauve,* wild beast.]

**fauvette,** *fō-vet', n.* a warbler. [Fr.]

**fauxbourdon,** *fō-bōōr-dɔ.* Same as **faburden.**
**faux pas,** *fō pä,* (Fr.) a false step: a mistake.
**faveolate,** *fə-vē'ō-lāt, adj.* honeycombed. [L. *favus,* honeycomb.]
**favism,** *fā'vizm, n.* acute hepatitis caused by eating broad beans, occurring in people with an inherited abnormality of the red blood cells. [L. *fava,* broad bean, and *-ism.*]
**Favonian,** *fə-vō'ni-ən, adj.* pertaining to the west wind, favourable. [L. *Favōnius,* the west wind.]
**favour, or** (esp. *U.S.*) **favor,** *fā'vər, n.* countenance: good-will: a kind deed: an act of grace or lenity: indulgence: partiality: advantage: a concession of amorous indulgence: a knot of ribbons worn at a wedding, election, etc.: a thing given or worn as a token of favour: appearance, face (*arch.*): a letter or written communication (*commercial jargon*): an attraction or grace (*Shak.*): an object of favour (*Milt.*).— *v.t.* to regard with good-will: to be on the side of: to treat indulgently: to give support to: to afford advantage to: to resemble (*coll.*): to choose to wear, etc.—*adj.* **fā'vourable,** friendly: propitious: conducive: advantageous: satisfactory, promising.—*n.* **fā'vourableness.**—*adv.* **fā'vourably.**—*adj.* **fā'voured,** enjoying favour or preference: wearing favours: having a certain appearance, featured—as in *ill-favoured, well-favoured.*—*ns.* **fā'vouredness; fā'vourer; fā'vour-ite** (*-it*), a person or thing regarded with marked preference: one unduly loved and indulged, esp. by a king: one expected to win: a kind of curl of the hair, affected by ladies of the 18th century. —*adj.* esteemed, preferred.—*n.* **fā'vouritism,** inclination to partiality: preference shown to favourites.—*adj.* **fā'vourless,** without favour: not favouring (*Spens.*).—**curry favour** (see **curry**); **favours to come,** favours still expected; **in favour of, for:** on the side of: for the advantage of; **in (or out of) favour,** (not) approved of. [O.Fr.,—L. *favor—favēre,* to favour, befriend.]
**favus,** *fāv'əs, n.* a fungal skin disease, chiefly of the scalp, giving a honeycombed appearance.— *adjs.* **favose.** (*fə-vōs', fā'vōs*), honeycombed; **fā'vous,** like a honeycomb: relating to favus. [L. *favus,* a honeycomb.]
**faw,** *fö, n.* a gypsy. [From the surname *Faa.*]
**fawn,** *fön, n.* a young deer, esp. a fallow deer: its colour, light yellowish brown.—*adj.* resembling a fawn in colour.—*v.t.* and *v.i.* to bring forth (a fawn). [O.Fr. *faon,* through L.L. from L. *fētus,* offspring.]
**fawn,** *fön, v.i.* to cringe, to flatter in a servile way (with *upon*).—*n.* (*rare*) a servile cringe or bow: mean flattery.—*n.* **fawn'er,** one who flatters to gain favour.—*n.* and *adj.* **fawn'ing.**—*adv.* **fawn'ingly.**—*n.* **fawn'ingness** [A variant of **fain,** to rejoice—O.E. *fægen,* glad.]
**fay,** *fā, n.* a fairy. [O.Fr. *fae*—L.L. *fāta;* see **fate.**]
**fay,** *fā,* (*Shak.*) *n.* faith. [O.Fr. *fei.*]
**fay.** Same as **fey.**
**fay,** *fā, v.t., v.i.* to fit, unite closely.—**fay'ing-face,** prepared surface of contact. [O.E. *fēgan;* Ger. *fügen.*]
**fay, fey,** *fā, (dial.) v.t.* to clean out, as a ditch. [O.N. *fægja,* to cleanse.]
**fayalite,** *fā'ə-lit, fā-yäl'it,* iron-olivine, a silicate of iron found in slag and occurring naturally. [*Fayal,* in the Azores, whence it was first, probably in ballast.]
**fayence,** See **faience.**
**faze,** *fāz.* See **feeze.**
**feague,** *fēg,* (*obs.*) *v.t.* to whip: to perplex. [Cf. Du. *vegen,* Ger. *fegen.*]
**feal,** *fēl,* (*obs.*) *adj.* loyal, faithful. [O.Fr. *feal*—L. *fidēlis.*]
**feal,** *fēl, (dial.) v.t.* to conceal. [O.N. *fela.*]
**feal,** *fēl.* Same as **fail** (1).
**fealty,** *fē'əl-ti,* or *fēl'ti, n.* the vassal's obligation

Neutral vowels in unaccented syllables: *el'ə-mənt;* for certain sounds in foreign words, see p. viii

of fidelity to his feudal lord (*hist.*): loyalty.
[O.Fr. *fealte*—L. *fidēlitās, -tātis,—fidēlis*, faithful
—*fīdĕre*, to trust.]
**fear,** *fēr, n.* a painful emotion excited by danger:
apprehension of danger or pain: alarm: solicitude: an object of alarm: that which causes
alarm: reverence (*B.*): piety towards God: risk.
—*v.t.* to regard with fear: to expect with alarm:
to be regretfully inclined to think: to be anxious
or in fear about (*obs.*): to stand in awe of (*B.*):
to venerate (*B.*): to terrify (*obs.*): to make
afraid (*obs.*).—*v.i.* to be afraid: to be in doubt.
—*adjs.* **feared** (*fērd; arch.* and *Scot.*), afraid;
**fear'ful,** timorous: exciting intense fear: terrible: loosely, very great, very bad.—*adv.* **fear'-**
**fully.**—*n.* **fear'fulness.**—*adj.* **fear'less,** without
fear: daring: brave.—*adv.* **fear'lessly.**—*n.*
**fear'lessness.**—*adj.* **fear'some,** causing fear,
frightful.—*adv.* **fear'somely.**—**fear'nought,** dreadnought cloth.—**for fear,** in case, lest; **no fear**
(*interj.*; *slang*), definitely not. [O.E. *fǣr*, fear,
*fǣran*, to terrify.]
**fear(e).** Same as **fere.**
**feasible,** *fē'zi-bl, adj.* practicable, possible:
(loosely) probable, likely.—*ns.* **feas'ibleness,**
**feasibil'ity.**—*adv.* **feas'ibly.** [Fr. *faisable*, that
can be done—*faire, faisant*—L. *facĕre*, to do.]
**feast,** *fēst, n.* a day of unusual solemnity or joy:
a festival in commemoration of some event—
*movable,* of varying date, as Easter; *immovable,*
at a fixed date, as Christmas: a rich and abundant repast: rich enjoyment: festivity.—*v.i.* to
hold a feast: to eat sumptuously: to receive
intense delight.—*v.t.* to entertain sumptuously:
to delight.—*n.* **feast'er.**—*adj.* **feast'ful,** festive,
joyful, luxurious.—*n.* **feast'ing.**—**feast'-day;**
**feast'-rite,** a rite or custom observed at feasts.—
*adj.* **feast'-won** (*Shak.*), won or bribed by feasting.
—**Feast of Fools, Feast of Asses,** mediaeval
festivals held between Christmas and Epiphany,
in which a mock bishop was enthroned in
church, a burlesque mass was said, and an ass
driven round in triumph; **Feast of Lots,** purim.
[O.Fr. *feste* (Fr. *fête*)—L. *fēstum*, a holiday,
*fēstus,* solemn, festal.]
**feat,** *fēt, n.* act, deed (*obs.*): a deed manifesting
extraordinary strength, skill, or courage, an
exploit, achievement: art, skill (*Spens.*).—*v.t.*
(*Shak.*) perh., to fashion, to make feat or neat.—
*adj.* (*Shak.*) neat, deft.—*adv.* (*Shak.*) **feat'ly,**
neatly: dexterously. [Fr. *fait*—L. *factum*—
*facĕre,* to do: cf. **fact.**]
**feateous, -ly.** See **featous.**
**feather,** *fedh'ər, n.* one of the growths that form
the covering of a bird: a featherlike appearance,
ornament or flaw: the feathered end of an
arrow: plumage: condition: birds collectively:
anything light or trifling: a projecting longitudinal rib or strip: a wedge: a formation of hair:
the act of feathering an oar: a foamy wave or
wave-crest.—*v.t.* to furnish or adorn with a
feather or feathers: to move edgewise (as an oar,
to lessen air-resistance), or to make a propeller-
blade, etc., rotate in such a way as to lessen
resistance.—*v.i.* to take the appearance of a
feather: to quiver the tail.—*adj.* **feath'ered,**
covered or fitted with feathers, or anything
featherlike: like the flight of a feathered animal,
swift: smoothed as with feathers.—*ns.* **feath'eri-**
**ness; feath'ering,** plumage: the addition of a
feather or feathers: a featherlike appearance:
an arrangement of small arcs separated by cusps,
within an arch (*archit.*).—*adj.* **feath'ery,** pertaining to, resembling, or covered with feathers or
appearance of feathers.—**feath'er-bed,** a mattress
filled with feathers.—*v.t.* to pamper.—**feath'er-**
**board'ing** (same as **weather-boarding**); **feath'er-**
**bonn'et,** a Highland soldier's feather-covered
head-dress; **feath'er-brain, feath'er-head,**
**feath'er-pate,** a frivolous person; **feath'er-**

dust'er, a brush of feathers, used for dusting;
**feath'er-edge,** an edge of a board or plank
thinner than the other edge; **feath'er-grass,** a
perennial grass (*Stipa*) with feathery awns;
**feath'er-palm',** any palm with pinnate leaves;
**feath'er-star,** a crinoid; **feath'er-stitch,** one of a
series of stitches making a zigzag line; **feath'er-**
weight, lightest weight that may be carried by a
racing-horse: boxer (over 8 st. 6 lb., amateur
7 lb., and not over 9 st.), wrestler, etc., below
a lightweight: anyone of small moment.—**a**
**feather in one's cap,** a striking distinction; **birds**
of a feather, persons of like character; **feather**
one's nest, to accumulate wealth for oneself
while serving others in a position of trust; **in**
full or high feather, greatly elated or in high
spirits; **make the feathers fly,** to throw into
confusion by a sudden attack; **show the white**
feather, to show signs of cowardice—a white
feather in a gamecock's tail being considered as a
sign of degeneracy. [O.E. *fether*; Ger. *feder*;
L. *penna,* Gr. *pteron.*]
**featous,** *fēt'əs,* **feat'eous,** *-i-əs,* **feat'uous,** *-ū-əs,*
(*arch.*) *adjs.* shapely: well-made: handsome:
dexterous: neat.—*adv.* **feat'eously** (*Spens.*),
dexterously, neatly. [O.Fr. *fetis*—L. *facticius*—
*facĕre,* to make; cf. **factitious.**]
**feature,** *fē'chər, n.* form, outward appearance:
beauty (*obs.*): shape, phantom (*arch.*): cast of
face: an element or prominent trait of anything:
a characteristic: a part of the body, esp. of the
face: (*pl.*) the face: a non-news article in
a newspaper: anything offered as a special
attraction or distinctive characteristic.—Also
*adj.*—*v.t.* to have features resembling (*coll.*): to
be a feature of: to make a feature of: to present
prominently.—*adjs.* **feat'ured,** with features well
marked; **feat'ureless,** destitute of distinct
features; **feat'urely** (*arch.*), handsome.—**feature**
film, a long cinematograph film forming the
basis of a programme; **feature programme,** a
radio or TV programme that reconstructs
dramatically the life of a prominent person, or
an important event, or gives a dramatic picture
of an employment or activity. [O.Fr. *faiture*—
L. *factura*—*facĕre,* to make.]
**febrile,** *fēb', feb'ril,* or *-ril, adj.* of or like fever:
feverish.—*ns.* **febricity** (*fi-bris'i-ti*), feverishness;
**febricula** (*fi-brik'ū-lə*), **febricule** (*feb'*), a slight
short fever.—*adjs.* **febrifacient** (*fē-bri-fā'shənt*);
L. *faciēns, -entis,* making), producing fever;
**febrif'ic** (*fi-*), febrifacient: feverish; **febrifugal**
(*fi-brif'ū-gl, feb-ri-fū'gl;* L. *fugāre,* to drive off).
—*ns.* **febrifuge** (*feb'* or *fēb'ri-fūj*), that which
drives off fever; **febril'ity.** [L. *febris,* fever.]
**Febronianism,** *feb-rō'ni-ən-izm, n.* a system of
doctrine antagonistic to the claims of the Pope
and asserting the independence of national
churches, propounded in 1763 by Johann
Nikolaus von Hontheim under the pseudonym
Justinus *Febronius.*
**February,** *feb'roo-ər-i, n.* the second month of the
year. [L. *Februārius* (*mēnsis*), the month of
expiation, *februa,* the feast of expiation.]
**feces, fecal.** Same as **faeces, faecal.**
**fecht,** *fehht,* **fechter,** *-ər,* Scots forms of **fight,**
**fighter.**
**fecial.** See **fetial.**
**fecit,** *fē'sit, fā'kit,* (L.) (he) made or executed
(this).
**feck,** *fek,* (*Scot.*) *n.* purport (*obs.*): substance
(*obs.*): efficacy: quantity, number: the bulk.—
*adj.* **feck'less,** spiritless: helpless: futile.—*adv.*
**feck'ly,** mostly: nearly. [Aphetic for **effect.**]
**fecula,** *fek'ū-lə, n.* starch got as a sediment:
sediment, dregs.—*ns.* **fec'ulence, fec'ulency.**—
*adj.* **fec'ulent,** containing or consisting of faeces
or sediment: foul: turbid. [L. *faecula,* dim. of
*faex,* dregs.]
**fecund,** *fek'und, fēk'und, -ənd, adj.* fruitful

fertile: prolific.—*v.t.* fec'undāte, to make fruitful: to impregnate.—*ns.* fecundā'tion; fecundity
(*fi-kund'i-ti*), fruitfulness: prolificness.  [L.
*fēcundus*, fruitful.]
fed, *fed*, *pa.t.* and *pa.p.* of feed (1).
fedarie, foedaire, *fē'dər-i*, federarie, -ary, *fed'ər-
ər-i*, *ns.* Shakespearian words for a confederate,
accomplice.  [L. *foedus*, *-eris*, treaty; moulded
on feudary.]
fedayee, *fə-dä'yē*, *n.* Arab commando, esp. one
involved in the conflict against Israel:—*pl.*
feda'yeen.  [Ar. *fidā'i*.]
fedelini, *fed-e-lē'nē*, *n.* vermicelli.  [It.]
federal, *fed'ər-əl*, *adj.* pertaining to or consisting
of a treaty or covenant: confederated, founded
upon mutual agreement: of a union or government in which several states, while independent
in home affairs, combine for national or general
purposes, as in the United States (in the American Civil War, *Federal* was the name applied to the
states of the North which defended the Union
against the *Confederate* separatists of the South).
—*n.* a supporter of federation: a Unionist
soldier in the American Civil War.—*n.* fed'eracy.
—*v.t.* fed'eralise, -ize.—*ns.* fed'eralism, the
principles or cause maintained by federalists;
fed'eralist, a supporter of a federal constitution
or union; fed'erary (*Shak.*; see fedarie).—*v.t.*
and *v.i.* fed'erate, to join in league or federation.—*adj.* united by league: confederated.—*n.*
federā'tion, the act of uniting in league: a
federal union.—*adj.* fed'erātive, united in league.
—federal (or covenant) theology, that first
worked out by Cocceius (1603-69), based on the
idea of two covenants between God and man—
of Works and of Grace (see covenant).—Federal
Bureau of Investigation, in the U.S., a bureau or
subdivision of the Department of Justice that
investigates crimes, such as smuggling and
espionage, that are the concern of the federal
government.  [L. *foedus*, *foederis*, a treaty,
akin to *fidēre*, to trust.]
federarie, federary. See fedarie.
fedora, *fi-dō'*, *dö'rə*, *n.* a felt hat dented lengthwise,
orig. with curled brim.  [*Fédora*, a play by
Sardou.]
fee, *fē*, *n.* cattle, livestock (*obs.*): property (*obs.*):
money (*obs.*): price paid for services, as to a
lawyer or physician: recompense, wages: the
sum exacted for any special privilege: a grant of
land for feudal service (*hist.*): feudal tenure:
service (*obs.*): fee simple: inheritance (*obs.*):
possession (*obs.*): ownership (*obs.*).—*v.t.* to pay
a fee to: to hire (*Scot.*):—*pr.p.* fee'ing; *pa.t.*
and *pa.p.* feed or fee'd.—fee'-farm (*Shak.*),
tenure by fee simple at a fixed rent without
services; fee'-grief (*Shak.*), a private grief;
fee'ing-mar'ket (*Scot.*), a fair or market at which
farm-servants are hired for the year or half-year
following; fee simple, unconditional inheritance; fee tail, an entailed estate, which may
descend only to a certain class of heirs.—base fee,
qualified fee, a freehold estate of inheritance to
which a qualification is annexed; conditional
fee, a fee granted on condition, or limited to
particular heirs: the estate of a mortgagee of
land, possession of which is conditional on payment; great fee, the holding of a tenant of the
Crown.  [Partly O.E. *feoh*, cattle, property;
Ger. *vieh*, O.N. *fē*; allied to L. *pecus*, cattle,
*pecūnia*, money; partly A.Fr. *fee*, probably
ultimately Gmc. and of the same origin.]
fée, *fā*, (Fr.) a fairy: féerie, *fā-rē*, fairyland: an
extravaganza (*theat.*).
feeble, *fē'bl*, *adj.* very weak: forceless: vacillating: faint.—*v.t.* (*Spens.*) to make feeble.—*ns.*
fee'bleness; fe'blesse (*Spens.*).—*adv.* fee'bly.—
*adj.* fee'ble-mind'ed, weak-minded to the extent
of being unable to compete with others or to
manage one's affairs with ordinary prudence:

irresolute.  [O.Fr. *foible*, for *floible*—L. *flēbilis*,
lamentable, from *flēre*, to weep.]
feed, *fēd*, *v.t.* to give, furnish, or administer food
to: to nourish: to furnish with necessary material: to foster: to give as food or as material to
be used progressively: to furnish (an actor) with
cues or opportunities of achieving an effect: in
football, to pass the ball to.—*v.i.* to take food:
to nourish oneself by eating:—*pr.p.* feed'ing;
*pa.t.* and *pa.p.* fed.—*n.* an allowance of provender, esp. to cattle: fodder: feeding: pasture: a
plentiful meal: material supplied progressively
for any operation: the means, channel, motion
or rate of such supply: rate of progress of a tool:
a theatrical feeder.—*n.* feeder, one who feeds:
an actor who feeds another: that which supplies
(water, electricity, ore, paper, etc.): a tributary:
a feeding-bottle: a bib: one who fattens cattle:
a shepherd (*obs.*): a dependant, a servant.—
*adj.* secondary, subsidiary, tributary.—*n.* feed'-
ing, act of eating: that which is eaten: pasture:
the placing of the sheets of paper in position for a
printing or ruling machine.—feed'-back, return of
part of the output of a system to the input as a
means towards improved quality or self-correc-
tion of error; used also in speaking of biological,
etc., self-adjusting systems; feed'-head, a cistern
that supplies water to a boiler; feed'-heat'er,
an apparatus for heating water for a boiler;
feed'ing-bott'le, a bottle for supplying liquid food
to an infant; feed'lot, a unit in which cattle are
kept indoors and made to put on weight rapidly
by means of processed and blended feed supplied
to them automatically; feed'-pipe, a pipe for
supplying liquid, as water to a boiler or cistern;
feed'-pump, a force-pump for supplying a boiler
with water; feed'-water, water supplied to a
boiler, etc.—fed to the (back) teeth (*slang*), fed
up; fed up (*slang*), sated: jaded: nauseated;
off one's feed, without appetite, disinclined to
eat.  [O.E. *fēdan*, to feed.]
feed, *fēd*, *pa.t.* and *pa.p.* of fee.
fee-faw-fum, *fē'-fō'-fum'*, *n.* a nursery word for
anything frightful.  [From *Jack the Giant-
killer.*]
feel, *fēl*, *v.t.* to perceive by the touch: to try by
touch: to be conscious of: to be keenly sensible
of: to have an inward persuasion of: to
experience.—*v.i.* to know by the touch: to have
the emotions excited: to produce a certain
sensation when touched, as to feel hard or hot:
—*pr.p.* feel'ing; *pa.t.* and *pa.p.* felt.—*n.* the
sensation of touch.—*ns.* feel'er, a remark
cautiously dropped, or any indirect stratagem,
to sound the opinions of others: a tentacle: a
jointed organ in the head of insects, etc., possessed of a delicate sense—an *antenna*; feel'ing, the
sense of touch: perception of objects by touch:
consciousness of pleasure or pain: tenderness:
emotion: sensibility, susceptibility, sentimentality: opinion as resulting from emotion: the
affections or passions (*pl.*).—*adj.* expressive of
great sensibility or tenderness: easily or strongly
affected by emotion: sympathetic: compassionate: pitying: deeply felt.—*adj.* feel'ingless.—
*adv.* feel'ingly.—bad feeling, animosity: ill-
feeling; feel after (*B.*), to search for; good
feeling, kindly feeling: amicable relations.
[O.E. *fēlan*, to feel; Ger. *fühlen*; prob. akin to
L. *palpāri*, to stroke.]
feer. Same as fere.
feer, *fēr*, *v.i.* to draw the first furrow in ploughing,
to mark out the rigs.  [Perh. O.E. *fȳrian*, to
make a furrow—*furh*, furrow.]
feet, *fēt*, *pl.* of foot.—*adj.* feet'less, footless; see
foot.
feeze, pheeze, pheeze, phese, *fēz*, *v.t.* to drive,
drive off (*obs.*): to settle the business of (*Shak.*):
to beat (*obs.*): to worry, perturb, discompose.—
Also (*U.S.*) faze, phase (*fāz*).—*n.* a rush (*dial.*):

a rub (obs.): perturbation. [O.E. fēsian, to drive away.]

fegary, fi-gā'ri, n. a variant of vagary.

fegs, fegz, interj. in faith, truly. [See fay (2), faith, and faix.]

fehmgericht. Same as vehmgericht.

feign (Spens. fain, faine, fayne), fān, v.t. to fashion (obs.): to invent: to imagine falsely (obs.): to assume fictitiously: to imagine (arch.): to make a show or pretence of, to counterfeit, simulate: to dissemble (Spens.).— adj. feigned, pretended: simulating: imagined (arch.): fictitious.—adv. feign'edly.—ns. feign'edness; feign'ing. [Fr. feindre, pr.p. feignant, to feign—L. fingĕre, fictum, to form.]

feint, fānt, n. a false appearance: a pretence: a mock-assault: a deceptive movement in fencing, boxing, etc.—v.i. to make a feint. [Fr. feinte, see above.]

feint, fānt, adj. a printers' or stationers' spelling of faint.—n.pl. feints (same as faints).

feis, pl. feiseanna, fesh, fesh'ə-nə, n. an ancient Irish assembly for the proclamation of laws and the holding of artistic, intellectual and sports competitions: an Irish festival on the ancient model, including sports events, folk music and dancing. [Ir., festival, assembly.]

feldgrau, felt'grow, n. and adj. field-grey, the colour of German military uniforms. [Ger. feld, field, grau, grey.]

feldsher, fel(d)'shər, n. (in Russia and parts of Eastern Europe), a partly trained person who practises medicine: one who assists a doctor, esp. on the battlefield. [Russ. fel'dsher—Ger. feldscher, army surgeon.]

feldspar, fel(d)'spär, felspar, fel'spär, n. any member of the most important group of rock-forming minerals, anhydrous silicates of aluminium along with potassium (as orthoclase, microcline), sodium, calcium, or both (the plagioclases), or sodium and barium (hyalophane)—also (obs.) feld'spath.—adj. fel(d)spathic (-spath'ik).—n. fel(d)'spathoid, any mineral of a group chemically akin to feldspar, including nepheline, leucite, sodalite, etc. [Swed. feldtspat, a name given in 1740 by D. Tilas—Sw. feldt or fält, field, spat, spar, apparently because of the abundance of feldspar in tilled fields of S.W. Finland; confused with Ger. fels, rock.]

Félibre, fā-lē'br', n. a member of the Félibrige (-brēzh'), a Provençal literary brotherhood, founded in 1854 by Joseph Roumanille (1818-91) and six others. [Prov., perh. doctors of the law.]

feliciter, fi-lis'i-tər, fā-lē'ki-ter, (L.) happily: successfully.

felicity, fi-lis'i-ti, n. happiness: delight: a blessing: a happy event: a happiness of expression. —v.t. felic'itate, to express joy or pleasure to: to congratulate.—n. felicitā'tion, the act of congratulating.—adj. felic'itous, happy: prosperous: delightful: appropriate.—adv. felic'itously. [O.Fr. felicité—L. fēlicitās, -ātis, from fēlix, -icis, happy.]

feline, fē'lin, adj. pertaining to the cat or the cat kind: like a cat.—n. any animal of the cat tribe. —ns. felinity (fi-lin'i-ti); Fē'lis, the cat genus, typical of the family Fē'lidae and sub-family Fēli'nae. [L. fēlinus—fēlēs, a cat.]

fell, fel, n. a hill: an upland tract of waste, pasture, or moorland. [O.N. fjall; Dan. fjeld.]

fell, fel, pa.t. of fall.

fell, fel, v.t. to cause to fall: to knock down: to bring to the ground: to cut down: to prostrate (as by illness; dial.): to stitch down with an overturned edge.—n. a quantity felled at a time: a falling of lambs: a felled hem.—adj. fell'able. —n. fell'er. [O.E. fælla(n), fella(n) (W.S. fiellan), causative of fallan (feallan), to fall.]

fell, fel, n. a skin: a membrane: covering of rough hair.—fell'monger, one who prepares skins

for the tanner. [O.E. fell; cf. Ger. fell, L. pellis, Gr. pella.]

fell, fel, (Spens.) n. gall, bitterness. [L. fel.]

fell, fel, adj. cruel: fierce: dire: ruthless: deadly: keen: doughty: pungent (Scot.): great, mighty (Scot.).—adv. in a fell manner: very (Scot.): very much (Scot.).—n. fell'ness.—adv. felly (fel'-li).—adj. fell-lurk'ing (Shak.), lurking with treacherous purpose. [O.Fr. fel, cruel—L.L. fellō, -ōnis; see felon.]

fellah, fel'ə, n. a peasant, esp. in Egypt:—pl. fell'ahs, fellahin, -hēn'. [Ar. fellāh, tiller.]

fellatio, fe-lā'shi-ō, n. oral stimulation of the male genitalia. [L.—fellātus, pa. p. of fellāre, to suck.]

felloe. See felly.

fellow, fel'ō, n. an associate: a companion and equal: one of a pair, a mate: a counterpart: the like: a member of a university who enjoys a fellowship: a member of a scientific or other society: a man generally: a worthless or contemptible person.—adj. fell'owly (Shak.), companionable.—n. fell'owship, the state of being a fellow or partner: friendly intercourse: communion: an association: an endowment in a college for the support of graduates called Fellows: the position and income of a fellow: reckoning of proportional division of profit and loss among partners.—fell'ow-cit'izen, one belonging to the same city; fell'ow-comm'oner, at Cambridge and elsewhere, one of a privileged class of undergraduates, dining at the Fellows' table; fell'ow-coun'tryman, a man of the same country; fell'ow-crea'ture, one of the same creation, a creature like oneself; fell'ow-feel'ing, feeling of common interest: sympathy; fell'ow-heir, a joint-heir; fell'ow-man', one who shares humanity with oneself; fell'ow-mem'ber, a member of the same body; fell'ow-serv'ant, one who has the same master; fell'ow-towns'man, a dweller in the same town; fell'ow-trav'eller, one who travels in the same railway carriage, bus, etc., or along the same route: derogatory term for one who, though not a party member, is in the same political road, a sympathiser (trans. of Russ. word).—good fellowship, companionableness; right hand of fellowship, the right hand given esp. by one minister or elder to another at an ordination in some churches. [M.E. felawe— O.N. fēlagi, a partner in goods, from fē (O.E. feoh; Ger. vieh), cattle, property, and root lag-, a laying together, a law. Cf. fee, law, lay.]

felly, fel'i, felloe, fel'i, fel'ō, n. a curved piece in the circumference of a wheel: the circular rim of the wheel. [O.E. felg; Ger. felge.]

felo de se, fē'lō dē sē, fe'lō də sē, (Anglo-L.) a suicide, lit. felon of himself.

felon, fel'ən, n. one guilty of felony: a wicked person (obs.).—adj. (arch.) wicked or cruel: fell: fierce: mighty.—adj. felonious (fi-lō'ni-əs), wicked (arch.): depraved (arch.): pertaining to felony.—adv. felō'niously.—n. felō'niousness, the quality of being felonious.—adj. fel'onous (Spens.), fell.—ns. fel'onry, a body of felons; fel'ony, orig. a crime punished by total forfeiture of lands, etc.: a grave crime, formerly classed legally as one more serious than a misdemeanour. [O.Fr.,—L.L. fellō, -ōnis, a traitor.]

felon, fel'ən, n. an inflamed sore. [Perh. felon (1).]

felsite, fel'sit, n. a fine-grained intimate mixture of quartz and orthoclase: a devitrified acid igneous rock, characterised by felsitic structure.—adj. felsitic (-sit'ik), consisting of a fine patchy mosaic of quartz and feldspar. [feldspar.]

felspar. See feldspar.

felstone, fel'stōn, n. felsite—an old-fashioned name. [Ger. felsstein, partly anglicised.]

felt, felt, pa.t. and pa.p. of feel.

felt, felt, n. a fabric formed without weaving, using the natural tendency of the fibres of wool and certain kinds of hair to interlace and cling together.—*v.t.* to make into felt: to cover with felt.—*v.i.* to become felted or matted.—*v.t.* felt′er, to mat like felt.—*n.* felt′ing, the art or process of making felt or of matting fibres together: the felt itself. [O.E. *felt*; cf. Du. *vilt*, Ger. *filz*.]

**felucca**, *fe-luk′ə, n.* a small merchant-vessel used in the Mediterranean, with two masts, lateen sails, and often a rudder at each end. [It. *feluca*; cf. Ar. *falūkah*.]

**felwort**, *fel′wûrt. n.* a gentian. [O.E. *feldwyrt*—*feld*, field, *wyrt*, wort.]

**female**, *fē′māl, n.* a woman or girl (sometimes used derogatorily): any animal or plant of the same sex as a woman.—*adj.* of the sex that produces young or eggs, fructifications or seeds: for, belonging to, characteristic of, or fancifully attributed to that sex: womanish (*Shak.*): of the sex characterised by relatively large gametes (*biol.*): of parts of mechanism, hollow and adapted to receive a counterpart (*mach.*).—Also (*Milt.*) fe′māl.—*ns.* fe′māleness, femality (-*mal′i-ti*).—female screw, a cylindrical hole with a thread or groove cut on the inward surface. [Fr. *femelle*—L. *fēmella*, a girl, dim. of *fēmina*, woman; the second syllable influenced by association with male.]

**feme**, *fem, fēm, (law) n.* a woman.—feme covert (*kuv′ərt*), a married woman; feme sole, a spinster, widow, or married woman legally in the position of an unmarried. [O.Fr. *feme*.]

**femerall**, *fem′ər-əl, n.* an outlet for smoke in a roof. [O.Fr. *fumeraille*—L. *fūmus*, smoke.]

**femetary.** See fumitory.

**feminal**, *fem′in-əl, adj.* female: feminine.—*ns.* feminal′ity (-*al′i-ti*), feminē′ity, feminil′ity, fem′inineness, feminin′ity, femin′ity, femaleness: the quality of being female, feminine, womanly or womanish.—*adj.* fem′inine (-*in*), female: characteristic of, peculiar or appropriate to, woman or the female sex: womanish: of that gender to which words denoting females, and in some languages various associated classes of words, belong (*gram.*).—*n.* the female sex or nature: a word of feminine gender.—*adv.* fem′ininely.—*n.* fem′ininism, an idiom or expression characteristic of woman: addiction to feminine ways.—*v.t.* and *v.i.* fem′inise, -ize, to make or become feminine.—*ns.* fem′inism, advocacy of women's rights, of the movement for the advancement and emancipation of women; fem′inist, an advocate or favourer of feminism: a student of women.—feminine caesura, one which does not immediately follow the ictus; feminine ending, (Fr. *pros.*) ending of a line in mute *e* (the French feminine suffix): ending in one unstressed syllable; feminine rhyme, a rhyme on a feminine ending. [L. *fēmina*, woman, dim. *fēminina*.]

**femiter**, *fem′i-tər, fenitar, fen′.* See fumitory.

**femme**, *fam,* (Fr.) woman, wife; femme de chambre, *də shä-br′,* lady's-maid: chambermaid; femme du monde, *dü mōd,* woman of the world: society woman; femme fatale, *fa-tal,* an irresistibly attractive woman who brings difficulties or disaster on men: a siren; femme incomprise, *ē-kō-prēz,* a woman misunderstood or unappreciated; femme savante, *sa-vāt,* a learned woman, a blue-stocking. See also feme.

**femto-**, *fem′tō-, pfx.* a thousand million millionth (10⁻¹⁵).

**femur**, *fē′mər, n.* the thigh-bone: the third segment of an insect's leg:—*pl.* fē′murs, fēm′ora, *fem′ər-ə.*—*adj.* femoral (*fem′*), belonging to the thigh.—femoral artery, the main artery of the thigh. [L. *fēmur, -ōris,* thigh.]

**fen**, *fen, n.* low marshy land often, or partially, covered with water: a morass or bog.—*adjs.* fenn′ish; fenn′y.—fen′-berry, the cranberry;

fen′-crick′et, the mole cricket; fen′-fire, the Will-o'-the-wisp; fen′land; fen′man, a dweller in fen country.—*adj.* fen′-sucked (*Shak.*), drawn out of bogs. [O.E. *fenn*; O.N. *fen.*]

**fen**, *fen, v.t.* an exclamation in boys' games, used to bar a right or privilege. [Cf. fend.]

**fen**, *fen, n.* a Chinese coin, 0·1 yuan. [Chin.]

**fence**, *fens, n.* a barrier, esp. of wood or of wood and wire for enclosing, bounding or protecting land: the art of fencing: defence: a receiver of stolen goods, also a receiving-house (*thieves' slang*).—*v.t.* to enclose with a fence: to fortify: to shield: to keep off.—*v.i.* to guard: to practise fencing: to be a receiver or purchaser of stolen goods: to answer or dispute evasively: to leap fences.—*adjs.* fenced, enclosed with a fence; fence′less, without fence or enclosure, open.—*n.* fenc′er, one who practises fencing with a sword.—*adj.* fenc′ible, capable of being fenced or defended.—*n.* (*hist.*) a militiaman or volunteer enlisted at a crisis.—*adj.* fenc′ing, defending or guarding.—*n.* the act of erecting a fence: material for fences: fences collectively: the leaping of fences: receiving stolen goods (*thieves' slang*): the act or art of attack and defence with a sword or the like.—fence′-lizard, a small American lizard (*Sceloporus*); fence month, close season; fenc′ing-master, one who teaches fencing.—fence the tables, in the ancient usage of Scotland, to debar the unworthy from partaking in communion; sit on the fence, to avoid committing oneself: to remain neutral; sunk fence, a ditch or water-course. [Aphetic from defence.]

**fend**, *fend, v.t.* to ward off: to shut out: to defend.—*v.i.* to offer resistance: to provide.—*n.* self-support, the shift one makes for oneself.—*adj.* fend′y (*Scot.*), resourceful: thrifty. [Aphetic for defend.]

**fend**, *fend,* (*Milt.*). Same as fiend.

**fender**, *fend′ər, n.* a guard before a hearth to confine the ashes: a protection for a ship's side against piers, etc., consisting of a bundle of rope, etc.: any structure serving as a guard against contact or impact.—fend′er-stool, a long stool placed beside a fireside fender. [fend.]

**fenestella**, *fen-is-tel′ə, n.* a small window or window-like opening; a niche containing the piscina: (*cap.*) a Palaeozoic genus of lace-like Polyzoa. [L., dim. of *fenestra*, a window.]

**fenestra**, *fi-nes′trə, n.* a window or other wall-opening: a perforation: a translucent spot.—*n.* fenes′tral, a window with some translucent material instead of glass.—*adj.* of or like a window: perforated: with translucent spots.—*adj.* fenestrate (*fen′is-trit, fi-nes′trit, -trāt*), -d, having windows or appearance of windows: pierced: perforated: having translucent spots. *n.* fenestrā′tion, the arrangement of windows in a building: fact of being fenestrate: perforation: the operation of making an artificial fenestra when the fenestra ovalis has been clogged by growth of bone.—fenestra ovalis, rotunda, the oval and round windows, two membrane-covered openings between the middle and inner ear. [L.]

**Fenian**, *fē′nyən, n.* a member of an association of Irishmen founded in New York in 1857 for the overthrow of the English government in Ireland. —*adj.* belonging to the legendary *fiann,* or to the modern Fenians.—*n.* Fē′nianism. [Old Ir. *Féne,* one of the names of the ancient population of Ireland, confused in modern times with *fiann,* militia of Finn and other ancient Irish kings.]

**fenks**, *fengks,* finks, *fingks, n.* the refuse of whale-blubber. [Origin unknown.]

**fennec**, *fen′ək, n.* a little African fox with large ears. [Ar. *fenek.*]

**fennel**, *fen′əl, n.* a genus (*Foeniculum*) of yellow-flowered umbelliferous plants, allied to dill, but distinguished by the cylindrical, strongly-ribbed fruit.—fenn'el-flower, Nigella.—giant fennel, an umbelliferous plant, *Ferula communis*. [O.E. *finul*—L. *fēniculum, fēnuc(u)lum*, fennel—*fēnum*, hay.]

fent, *fent, n.* a slit, crack: a remnant or odd, short, or damaged piece of cloth (*N. Eng.*).— fent'-merchant. [O.Fr. *fente*—L. *findēre*, to cleave.]

fenugreek, *fen'ū-grēk, n.* a plant (*Trigonella foenum-graecum*), allied to melilot. [L. *fēnum graecum*, Greek hay.]

feod, feodal, feodary. Same as feud, feudal, feudary.

feoff, *fef, n.* a fief.—*v.t.* to grant possession of a fief or property in land.—*ns.* feoffee', the person invested with the fief; feoff'er, feoff'or, he who grants the fief; feoff'ment, the gift of a fief. [O.Fr. *feoffer* or *fiefer*—O.Fr. *fief*. See fee.]

feracious, *fi-rā'shəs, adj.* fruitful.—*n.* feracity (*fi-ras'i-ti; rare*). [L. *ferāx, -ācis*—*ferre*, to bear.]

ferae naturae, *fē'rē nə-tū'rē, fe-ri na-tōō'ri,* (L.) (of animals) wild, undomesticated.

feral, *fē'rəl, adj.* wild: untamed: uncultivated: run wild: brutish.—*adjs.* fer'alised, -ized, run wild from domestication; ferine (*-rin, -rin*), pertaining to or like a wild beast: wild: brutish.— *n.* ferity (*fer'i-ti*), wildness: uncultivated state: savagery. [L. *fera*, a wild beast.]

feral, *fē'rəl, adj.* deadly: funereal. [L. *ferālis*.]

fer-de-lance, *fer'də-läs, n.* the lance-headed or yellow viper of tropical America. [Fr., lance-head (*lit.* iron).]

fere, feare, feer, fiere, pheere, *fēr,* (*arch.*) *n.* a companion: a mate: a spouse: an equal.—*n.* fere, or (*adv.*) yfere', together, in company. [O.E. *gefēra*, companion, *gefēre*, company.]

fere, *fēr,* (*Scot.*) *adj.* able, sound. [O.E. *fēre*.]

feretory, *fer'i-tər-i, n.* a shrine for relics carried in processions. [L. *feretrum*—Gr. *pheretron*, bier, litter—*pherein*, to bear.]

ferial, *fē'ri-əl, adj.* pertaining to holidays: belonging to any day of the week which is neither a fast nor a festival. [L. *fēria*, a holiday.]

Feringhi, Feringhee, *fer-ing'gē, n.* a Hindu name for a European.—Also Farin'gee. [Frank.]

ferly, *fūr'li, adj.* fearful: sudden: singular.—*n.* (*Scot.; fär'li*) a wonder.—*v.i.* to wonder. [O.E. *fǣrlic*, sudden; cf. Ger. *gefährlich*, dangerous.]

ferm, *fūrm, n.* a farm: lodging (*Spens.*). [Variant of farm.]

fermata, *fūr-mä'tä, (mus.) n.* a pause. [It.]

ferment, *fūr'mənt, n.* a substance that excites fermentation: internal motion amongst the parts of a fluid: agitation: tumult.—*v.t.* ferment (*-ment'*), to excite fermentation in: to work up, excite.—*v.i.* to rise and swell by the action of fermentation: to work, used of wine, etc.: to be in excited action: to work in the mind, as emotions.—*n.* fermentabil'ity.—*adj.* ferment'- able, capable of fermentation.—*n.* fermentā'tion, the act or process of fermenting: a slow decomposition process of organic substances induced by micro-organisms, or by complex nitrogenous organic substances (*enzymes*) of vegetable or animal origin, usually accompanied by evolution of heat and gas, e.g. alcoholic fermentation of sugar and starch, and lactic fermentation: restless action of the mind or feelings.—*adj.* ferment'ative, causing or consisting in fermentation.—*n.* ferment'ativeness.— *adjs.* ferment'ed; fermentesc'ible, capable of being fermented; fermentitious (*-ish'əs*); ferment'ive. [Fr.,—L. *fermentum*, for *fervimentum* —*fervēre*, to boil.]

fermi, *fūr'mi, n.* a unit equal to 10⁻⁵ angstrom or 10⁻¹³ cm.—*ns.* fer'mion, one of a group of subatomic particles having half integral spin and obeying the exclusion principle; fer'mium, the element (symbol Fm) of atomic number 100. [Italian physicist Enrico *Fermi* (1901-54).]

fern, *fūrn, n.* one of the class of higher or vascular cryptogamous plants, Filices.—*n.* fern'ery, a place for rearing ferns.—*adj.* fern'y.—fern'-ally' (or *-al'*), a pteridophyte other than a fern; fern'- owl, the night-jar: the short-eared owl; fern'- seed, the spores of ferns, once held to confer invisibility; fern'shaw, a thicket of ferns; fern'tic(k)le (*obs.* or *dial.*), also ferni-, fairni-, ferny-, fairny- (*Scot.*), a freckle.—*adj.* fern'- tic(k)led. [O.E. *fearn;* Ger. *farn.*]

ferocious, *fə-rō'shəs, adj.* savage, fierce: cruel.— *adv.* ferō'ciously.—*ns.* ferō'ciousness; ferocity (*-ros'i-ti*), savage cruelty of disposition: untamed fierceness. [L. *ferōx, ferōcis*, wild—*ferus*, wild.]

ferrandine. See farandine.

ferrate, *fer'āt, n.* a salt of ferric acid.—*adjs.* ferr'eous, pertaining to, containing, or like iron; ferr'ic, of iron; of trivalent iron (ferr'ic acid, a hypothetical acid H₂FeO₄) (*chem.*); ferrif'erous, bearing or yielding iron.—*n.* ferr'ite, a form of pure iron: any of a number of new magnetic materials (generally mixtures of iron oxide with one or more other metals) which are also electric insulators.—*adjs.* ferrit'ic, consisting mainly of ferrite; ferr'ous, of bivalent iron: loosely, containing iron.—ferricy'anide, a salt of hydroferricyanic acid; ferricyan'ogen, the trivalent radical, Fe(CN)₆, of the ferricyanides; ferr'o-all'oy (or *-oi'*), an alloy of iron and some other metal; ferr'o-chro'mium, ferr'o-mang'anese, ferr'o-molyb'denum, ferr'o-nick'el, an alloy of iron with much chromium, etc. (as the case may be); ferr'o-con'crete, reinforced concrete; ferrocy'anide, a salt of hydroferrocyanic acid; ferrocyan'ogen, the quadrivalent radical, Fe(CN)₆, of the ferrocyanides.—*adjs.* ferromagnē'sian, containing iron and magnesium; ferromagnet'ic, strongly magnetic: formerly, paramagnetic.—ferr'o-print, a photograph made by means of iron salts; ferropruss'iate, ferrocyanide.—*adj.* ferrosoferr'ic, combining ferrous and ferric.—ferr'otype, an old form of photograph upon a film on an iron plate. [L. *ferrum*, iron.]

ferret, *fer'it, n.* narrow silk or cotton ribbon.— Also *adj.* [It. *fioretto*, dim.—L. *flōs, flōris*, flower.]

ferret, *fer'it, n.* a half-tamed albino variety of the polecat, employed in unearthing rabbits.—*v.t.* to drive out of a hiding-place: to search out persistently.—*v.t., v.i.* to hunt with a ferret:— *pr.p.* ferr'eting; *pa.p.* ferr'eted.—*n.* ferr'eter, one who ferrets.—*adj.* ferr'ety. [O.Fr. *furet*, a ferret, dim.—L.L. *fūrō, -ōnis*, ferret, robber—L. *fūr*, a thief.]

Ferris wheel, *fe'ris (h)wēl*, (orig. *U.S.*) an amusement device, a large upright wheel having seats suspended on the circumference which remain horizontal while the wheel rotates. [G. W. G. *Ferris*, American engineer.]

ferro-alloy, etc. See ferrate.

ferron(n)ière, *fer-on-yer', n.* a jewel held on the forehead by a chain, as in Leonardo da Vinci's 'La Belle Ferronnière'. [Fr. *ferronnière*, fem. of *ferronnier*, ironmonger.]

ferruginous, *fe-, fə-rōō'jin-əs, adj.* of the colour of iron-rust: impregnated with iron.—Also ferrugin'eous (*fer-*).—*n.* ferru'go (*-gō*), rust disease of plants. [L. *ferrūgō, -inis*, iron-rust—*ferrum*.]

ferrule, *fer'ōōl, -əl, n.* a metal bard, ring or cap on a stick, etc.—Also ferr'el (*Scot.* virl). [O.Fr. *virole*—L. *viriola*, a bracelet.]

ferry, *fer'i, v.t.* to carry or convey over a water, etc., in a boat, ship or aircraft: to deliver (an aircraft coming from a factory) under its own power.—*v.i.* to cross by ferry:—*pr.p.* ferr'ying; *pa.t.* and *pa.p.* ferr'ied.—*n.* a place or route of carriage over water: the right of conveying passengers: a ferry-boat.—*n.* ferr′iage, provision for ferrying: the fare paid for it.—ferr′y-boat; ferr′y-house, a ferryman's house: a place of shelter or refreshment at a ferry; ferr′yman. [O.E. *ferian*, to convey, *faran*, to go; Ger. *fähre*, a ferry—*fahren*, to go, to carry.]

fertile, *fūr′til*, *U.S. -təl*, able to bear or produce abundantly: rich in resources: inventive: fertilising: capable of breeding, hatching, or germinating.—*adv.* fer′tilely.—*n.* fertilisa′tion, -z-, (-*ti-li-zā′shən*), the act or process of fertilising.— *v.t.* fer′tilise, -ize, to make fertile or fruitful: to enrich: to impregnate: to pollinate.—*ns.* fer′-tiliser, -z-, one who, or that which, fertilises; fertility (-*til′i-ti*), fruitfulness: richness: abundance.—Fertile Crescent, a crescent-shaped region stretching from Armenia to Arabia, formerly fertile but now mainly desert, considered to be the cradle of civilisation; fertile material, an isotope (as uranium-238) that can be readily transformed into fissionable material; fertility drug, a drug given to apparently infertile women to induce ovulation. [Fr.,—L. *fertilis*— *ferre*, to bear.]

ferule, *fer′ōōl*, *n.* a cane or rod used for punishment.—*n.* fer′ula, a ferule: a staff of command: (*cap.*) the giant fennel genus.—*adj.* ferulā′ceous, like a cane, reed, or Ferula. [L. *ferula*, a giant fennel—*ferire*, to strike.]

fervent, *fūr′vənt*, *adj.* hot: ardent: zealous: warm in feeling.—*n.* fer′vency, heat: eagerness: emotional warmth.—*adv.* fer′vently.—*adjs.* fervescent (-*ves′ənt*), growing hot; fer′vid, very hot: having burning desire or emotion: glowing: zealous.—*n.* fervid′ity.—*adv.* fer′vidly.—*ns.* fer′-vidness; Fervidor′, Thermidor; fer′vour, heat: heat of emotion: zeal.—*adj.* fer′vorous. [L. *fervēre*, to boil, *fervēscĕre*, *fervidus.*]

Fescennine, *fes′ə-nīn*, -nin, *adj.* scurrilous.— Fescennine verses, rude extempore verses, generally in Saturnian measure, in which the parties rallied and ridiculed one another. [The Etruscan town of *Fescennium.*]

fescue, *fes′kū*, *n.* a genus (Festuca) of grasses, very nearly allied to brome-grass, and including many pasture and fodder grasses: a pointer used in teaching. [O.Fr. *festu*—L. *festūca*, a straw.]

fesse, fess, (*her.*) *n.* one of the ordinaries—a horizontal band over the middle of an escutcheon, usually one-third of the whole.—*adv.* fesse(e)′-wise.—fesse′-point, the centre of an escutcheon. [Fr. *fasce*—L. *fascia*, a band.]

-fest, -*fest*, *n.* in composition, a party or gathering, esp. for a particular activity, e.g. songfest. [Ger. *fest*, festival.]

festa, *fes′ta*, (It.) holiday: festival: saint's day.

festal, *fes′tl*, *adj.* pertaining to a feast or holiday: joyous: gay.—*n.* a festivity.—*adv.* fes′tally.—*n.* festil′ogy, festol′ogy, a treatise on ecclesiastical festivals. [See feast.]

fester, *fes′tər*, *v.i.* to become corrupt or malignant: to suppurate.—*v.t.* to cause to fester or rankle.— *n.* a wound discharging corrupt matter. [O.Fr. *festre*—L. *fistula*, an ulcer.]

festinate, *fes′ti-nāt*, *v.t.* to accelerate.—*adj.* (*Shak.*) hurried, hasty.—*adv.* fes′tinately (*Shak.*). —*n.* festinā′tion. [L. *festināre*, -*ātum*, to hurry.]

festive, *fes′tiv*, *adj.* festal: mirthful.—*n.* fes′tival, a joyful or honorific celebration: a feast: a season of performances of music, plays, or the like.—*adv.* fes′tively.—*n.* festiv′ity, social mirth: joyfulness: gaiety.—*adj.* fes′tivous (or -*ti′*), festive. [L. *fēstivus*—*fēstus.*]

festoon, *fes-tōōn′*, *n.* a garland suspended between two points: an ornament like a garland (*archit.*). —*v.t.* to adorn, hang, or connect with festoons.— *v.i.* to hang in festoons.—*n.* festoon′ery, festoons collectively.—festoon′-blind, a window-blind consisting of cloth gathered into rows of festoons

running across its width. [Fr. *feston*, app. conn. with L. *fēstum.* a festival.]

festschrift, *fest′shrift*, *n.* a festival publication, commonly a collection of learned papers or the like, presented by their authors and published in honour of some person. [Ger., festival writing.]

fet, fett, *fet*, *v.t.* obsolete form of fetch.

fetal. See foetus.

fetch, *fech*, *v.t.* to bring: to go and get: to obtain as its price: to cause to come: to call forth: to recall from a swoon: to draw (as blood, breath): to achieve the gaining over of, to take: to derive: to strike: to perform, make, take, utter (as a leap, a sigh, a circuit): to achieve: to reach or attain.—*v.i.* to make one's way: to arrive: to be effective.—*n.* the act of bringing: space carried over: a stratagem.—*adj.* fetch′ing, fascinating.—fetch a compass, circuit, to go round in a wide curve; fetch and carry, to perform humble services for another; fetch a pump, to pour water in so as to make it draw; fetch off, to bring out of danger or difficulty: to make away with (*Shak.*): to fleece (*Shak.*); fetch out, to draw forth, develop; fetch up, to recover: to come to a stop: to bring up, rear (*U.S.*). [O.E. *feccan*, app. an altered form of *fetian*, to fetch; cf. Ger. *fassen*, to seize.]

fetch, *fech*, *n.* the apparition, double, or wraith of a living person.—fetch′-can′dle, a nocturnal light, supposed to portend a death. [Ety. unknown.]

fête, *fet*, *fāt*, *n.* a festival: a holiday: the festival of the saint whose name one bears.—*v.t.* to entertain at a feast: to honour with festivities.— fête champêtre (*shā-pe-tr′*), a rural festival, garden party; Fête-Dieu (*dyø*), Corpus Christi; fête galante (*ga-lāt*), a painting depicting the amusements of elegantly attired groups in a pastoral setting, associated mainly with the French painter Jean Antoine Watteau (1684-1721). [Fr.]

fetial, *fē′shəl*, *adj.* pertaining to the Roman *fētiālēs*, a priestly college of heralds: heraldic, ambassadorial.—Also fē′cial.

feticide. See foetus.

fetid, *fē′tid*, or *fet′id*, *adj.* stinking: having a strong offensive smell.—*ns.* fē′tidness, fē′tor.—Less justifiable spellings are foetid, foetor. -[L. *fētidus*, *fētor*—*fētēre*, to stink.]

fetish, fetich, fetiche, *fe′tish*, *fē′tish*, *n.* an object believed to procure for its owner the services of a spirit lodged within it: something regarded with irrational reverence.—*ns.* fet′ishism, fet′ichism, the worship of a fetish: a belief in charms: pathological attachment of sexual interest to an inanimate object; fet′ishist, fet′ichist.—*adjs.* fetishist′ic, fetichis′tic. [Fr. *fétiche*—Port. *feitiço*, magic: a name given by the Portuguese to the gods of W. Africa—Port. *feitiço*, artificial —L. *facticius*—*facĕre*, to make.]

fetlock, *fet′lok*, *n.* a tuft of hair that grows above a horse's hoof: the part where this hair grows.— *adj.* fet′locked, having a fetlock: tied by the fetlock. [History obscure; long felt as a compound of foot and lock (of hair); cf. Ger. *fissloch.*]

fetter, *fet′ər*, *n.* (usu. in *pl.*) a chain or shackle for the feet: (usu. in *pl.*) anything that restrains.— *v.t.* to put fetters on: to restrain.—*adj.* fett′erless. —fett′erlock (*her.*), a shackle for a horse, as a charge. [O.E. *feter*; conn. with *fōt*, foot.]

fettle, *fet′l*, *v.t.* to make ready, set in order, arrange: to tidy up (*dial.*): to line (a furnace).— *v.i.* to potter fussily about.—*n.* condition, trim, form: lining for a furnace.—*ns.* fett′ler; fett′ling. [Prob. O.E. *fetel*, a belt.]

fetus. See foetus.

fetwa, *fet′wä*, *n.* a Moslem legal decision. [Ar.]

feu, *fū*, (Scot.) *n.* a tenure where the vassal, in place of military services, makes a return in grain or in money: a right to the use of land, houses, etc., in perpetuity, for a stipulated annual payment (feu'-dū'ty): a piece of land held in feu.—*v.t.* to vest in one who undertakes to pay the feu-duty.—*n.* feu'ar, one who holds real estate in consideration of payment of feu-duty.—*adj.* feud'al, pertaining to a feu. [O.Fr. *feu*; see fee.]

feu (*pl.* feux) d'artifice, *fø dar-tē-fēs*, (Fr.) fireworks; feu de joie, *də zhwä*, a bonfire; (in English, *not* in French) a firing of guns in token of joy.

feud, *fūd, n.* a war waged by private individuals, families, or clans against one another on their own account: a bloody strife: a persistent state of private enmity.—Also *v.i.*—*n., adj.* feud'ing.—right of feud, the right to protect oneself and one's kinsmen, and punish injuries. [O.Fr. *faide, feide*—L.L. *faida*—O.H.G. *fēhida*; vowel change unexplained; see foe.]

feud, feod, *fūd, n.* a fief or land held on condition of service.—*adj.* feud'al, pertaining to feuds or fiefs: belonging to feudalism.—*n.* feudalisā'tion, -z-.—*v.t.* feud'alise, -ize.—*ns.* feud'alism, the feudal system or its principles: a class-conscious social or political system resembling the mediaeval feudal system; feud'-alist; feudal'ity, the state of being feudal: the feudal system.—*adv.* feud'ally.—*adjs.* feud'ary, feud'atory, holding lands or power by a feudal tenure.—Also *ns.*—*n.* feud'ist, a writer on feuds: one versed in the laws of feudal tenure.—feudal system, the system by which vassals held lands from lords-superior on condition of military service. [L.L. *feudum*; see fee.]

feudal. See feu (1) and feud (2).

feuilleton, *fœy-tɔ̃, n.* in French and other newspapers, a part ruled off the bottom of a page for a serial story, critical article, etc.: a contribution of such a kind.—*ns.* feu'illetonism (-tən-izm); feu'illetonist. [Fr. dim. of *feuillet* a leaf—L. *folium.*]

feutre. Same as fewter.

fever, *fē'vər, n.* disease (esp. infectious) marked by great bodily heat and quickening of pulse: extreme excitement of the passions, agitation: a painful degree of anxiety.—*v.t.* to put into a fever.—*v.i.* to become fevered.—*adjs.* fē'vered, affected with fever: excited; fē'verish, slightly fevered: indicating fever: restlessly excited: morbidly eager.—*adv.* fē'verishly.—*n.* fē'verishness.—*adj.* fē'verous, feverish: marked by sudden changes: apt to cause fever.—fē'verfew (O.E. *fēferfūge*), a composite perennial *Matricaria* (or *Chrysanthemum*) *Parthenium*, closely allied to camomile, so called from its supposed power as a febrifuge; fē'ver-heat, the heat of fever: an excessive degree of excitement; fever therapy, cure by inducement of fever. [O.E. *fēfor*—L. *febris.*]

few, *fū, adj.* small in number: not many.—*n.* few'ness, smallness of number: few words, brevity (*Shak.*).—a few, a small number (of)—used as a noun, or virtually a compound adjective; also facetiously as an *adv.*, a little; a good few, quite a few (*coll.*), a considerable number; in few, in a few words, briefly; some few, an inconsiderable number; the few, the minority. [O.E. *fēa*, pl. *fēawe*; cf. L. *paucus*, small.]

fewmet. Same as fumet.

fewter, feutre, *fū'tər, n.* (*obs.*) a spear-rest.—*v.t.* (*Spens.*) to set in rest. [O.Fr. *feutre*, felt, a felt-lined socket.]

fewtrils, *fū'trilz,* (*dial.*) *n.pl.* little things, trifles. [See fattrels.]

fey, fay, fie, *fā, adj.* doomed, fated soon to die, under the shadow of a sudden or violent death—imagined to be marked by extravagantly high spirits (chiefly *Scot.*): foreseeing the future, esp.

calamity (chiefly *Scot.*): eccentric, slighty mad: supernatural: fairy-like: elfin. [M.E. *fay, fey*—O.E. *fǣge*, doomed; cf. Du. *veeg*, about to die.]

fez, *fez, n.* a red brimless truncated conical cap of wool or felt, with black tassel, worn in Egypt, formerly in Turkey—the *tarboosh:—pl.* fezz'es, fez'es.—*adj.* fezzed (*fezd*). [From *Fez* in Morocco.]

fiacre, *fē-ak'r', n.* a hackney-coach: a cab. [Fr., from the Hôtel de St *Fiacre* in Paris, where first used.]

fiancé, fem. fiancée, *fē-ā'sā, n.* one betrothed.—*n.pl.* fiançailles (*fē-ā-sī-y'*), betrothal. [Fr.]

fianchetto, *fyäng-ket'to,* (*chess*) *n.* the early movement of a knight's pawn to develop a bishop on a long diagonal.

Fianna Fáil, *fē'an-ä foil,* the Irish republican party. [Ir., militia of Fál (a stone monument at Tara, hence Ireland); cf. Fenian.]

fiars, *fē'ərz,* (*Scot.*) *n.pl.* the prices of grain legally struck or fixed for the year at the Fiars Court, so as to regulate the payment of stipend, rent, and prices not expressly agreed upon—usu. fiars prices. [O.Fr. *feor, fuer*, fixed price, standard—L. *forum*, market.]

fiasco, *fē-as'kō, n.* a flask, bottle: a failure in a musical performance: a complete failure of any kind. [It. *fiasco*, bottle, perh. from L. *vasculum*, a little vessel, *vas*, a vessel.]

fiat, *fī'at,* L. *fē'ät, n.* a formal or solemn command: a short order or warrant of a judge for making out or allowing processes, letters-patent, etc.—(*Spens.* fiaunt').—*v.t.* to sanction. [L. *fiat* (*fiant*), let it (them) be done, 3rd pers. sing. (plur.) pres. subj. of *fiĕrī*, serving as passive of *facĕre*, to do.]

fib, *fib, n.* something said falsely: a not very serious lie.—*v.i.* to tell a fib or lie: to speak falsely:—*pr.p.* fibb'ing; *pa.p.* fibbed.—*ns.* fibb'er, one who fibs; fibb'ery (*rare*), the habit of fibbing; fib'ster, a fibber. [Perh. fable.]

fib, *fib, v.t.* to punch: to pummel:—*pa.t.* and *pa.p.* fibbed; *pr.p.* fibb'ing. [Ety. unknown.]

fiber. See fibre.

Fibonacci numbers, sequence, series, *fē-bō-nä'chē,* a series of numbers in which each term is the sum of the preceding two terms. [Leonardo (*Fibonacci*) of Pisa (1170-1230).]

fibre, fiber, *fī'bər, n.* any fine thread-like object, of animal, vegetable, or mineral origin, natural or synthetic: a structure or material composed of fibres: texture: stamina.—*adjs.* fi'bred, having fibre; fi'breless, without fibre, strength, or nerve; fi'briform, fibre-like.—*ns.* fi'bril, a small fibre: a root-hair: a minute thread-like structure such as the longitudinal contractile elements of a muscle-fibre; fibrill'a, a fibril filament (*pl.* fibrill'ae, -ē).—*adjs.* fi'brillar, fi'brillary, fi'bril-late, -d, pertaining to, of the nature of, or having fibrils or fibrous structure.—*v.i.* fi'brillate, to undergo fibrillation.—*n.* fibrillā'tion, formation of fibrils: a mass of fibrils: a twitching of muscle fibres: uncoordinated contraction of muscle-fibres in the heart (*med.*).—*adjs.* fi'brillose, having, or covered with small fibres or the appearance of small fibres; fi'brillous, pertaining to or having small fibres.—*ns.* fi'brin, an insoluble protein precipitated as a network of fibres when blood coagulates; fibrin'ogen (-jən), a protein that forms fibrin; fibrinol'ysin, an enzyme in the blood which causes breakdown of fibrin in blood clots: a drug having the same effect.—*adj.* fi'brinous, of or like fibrin.—*n.* fibrocar'tilage, cartilage with embedded fibres.—*adj.* fi'broid, of a fibrous character.—*n.* a fibrous tumour.—*ns.* fibroin (*fī'brō-in*), the chief chemical constituent of silk; fi'broline (-lēn), a yarn of flax, hemp, and jute waste, used with linen or cotton for backs of carpets, etc.; fi'brolite, the mineral sillimanite, a fibrous aluminium silicate; **fibrō′ma**, a tumour composed of fibrous tissue:—*pl.* **fibrō′mata**.—*v.i.* **fibrose** (*fi-brōs′*), to form fibrous tissue.—*adj.* **fibrose** (*fi′brōs*), fibrous.—*ns.* **fibrō′sis**, a morbid growth of fibrous tissue; **fibrosi′tis**, inflammation (esp. rheumatic) of fibrous tissue.—*adjs.* **fibrŏt′ic**, pertaining to fibrosis; **fi′brous**, composed of or like fibres; **fibrova̧s′cūlar**, composed of fibres and conducting elements.—**fi′breboard**, a building-board made from compressed fibrous materials; **fi′breglass**, a synthetic fibre made of extremely fine filaments of molten glass, used in textile manufacture, in heat and sound insulation, and in reinforced plastics; **fibre optics**, technique using fibre optic(s) bundles (as *adj.* usu. **fibre optic**); **fibre optic(s) bundle**, bundle of extremely thin flexible glass fibres suitably coated, used in optical instruments to transmit maximum light, and images of maximum clarity, and designed, because of their flexibility, for seeing into otherwise inaccessible places. [Fr.,—L. *fibra*, thread, fibre.]

**fibula**, *fib′ū-lə, n.* a brooch: the outer of the two bones from the knee to the ankle.—*adj.* **fib′ūlar.** [L. *fibula*, brooch.]

**fichu**, *fi′shōō, fē-shü, n.* a three-cornered cape worn over the shoulders, the ends crossed upon the bosom: a triangular piece of muslin, etc., for the neck. [Fr.]

**fickle**, *fik′l, adj.* inconstant: changeable.—*v.t.* (*Scot.*) to perplex, puzzle.—*n.* **fick′leness.** [O.E. *ficol; gefic,* fraud.]

**fico**, *fē′kō, (Shak.) n.* a fig, as a type of insignificance, a whit: a motion of contempt by placing the thumb between two fingers. [It., fig.]

**fictile**, *fik′til, -til, adj.* used or fashioned by the potter: plastic. [L. *fictilis—fingĕre,* to form or fashion.]

**fiction**, *fik′shən, n.* a feigned or false story: a falsehood: romance: the novel, story-telling as a branch of literature: a supposition of law that a thing is true, which is either certainly not true, or at least is as probably false as true.—*adj.* **fic′tional.**—*v.t.* **fic′tionalise, -ize,** to give a fictional character to (a narrative dealing with real facts).—*adj.* **fic′tionalised, -z-.**—*n.* **fic′tionist,** a writer of fiction.—*adj.* **fictitious** (-*tish′əs*), of the nature of fiction: imaginary: not real: feigned.—*adv.* **ficti′tiously.**—*adj.* **fic′tive,** fictitious, imaginative.—*n.* **fic′tor** (*obs.*), one who makes images of clay, etc. [Fr.,—L. *fictiō, -ōnis—fictus,* pa.p. of *fingĕre* to form, fashion.]

**fid,** *fid, n.* a conical pin of hard wood, used by sailors to open the strands of rope in splicing: a square bar, with a shoulder, used to support the weight of the topmast or top-gallant mast. [Origin unknown.]

**fiddious,** *fid′i-əs, (Shak.) v.t.* app., to treat as Coriolanus treated *Aufidius.*

**fiddle,** *fid′l, n.* the violin: extended to like instruments, as *bass fiddle*: a violin-player: a device to keep dishes from sliding off a table at sea: a swindle, esp. petty (*slang*).—*v.t.* and *v.i.* to play on a fiddle.—*v.t.* swindle: falsify.—*v.i.* to be busy over trifles, to trifle.—*n.* **fidd′ler,** one who fiddles: a small crab of the genus *Uca* or Gelasimus, also **fiddler crab** (from the attitude of its enlarged claw).—*adj.* **fidd′ling,** trifling, busy about trifles.—**fiddle block** (*naut.*), a block having two sheaves of different diameters one above the other; **fidd′le-bow,** a bow strung with horsehair, with which the strings of the fiddle are set vibrating.—*interj.* **fiddle-de-dee′,** nonsense!—*v.i.* **fidd′le-fadd′le,** to trifle, to dally.—*n.* trifling talk or behaviour.—*adj.* fussy, trifling. —*interj.* nonsense! **fidd′le-fadd′ler.**—*adj.* **fidd′le-fadd′ling.**—**fidd′lehead,** an ornament at a ship's bow, over the cutwater, consisting of a scroll turning aft or inward; **fiddler's green,** a

sailor's heaven; **fiddler's money,** small coins, as sixpences; **fidd′lestick,** a violin bow: derisively, a mere nothing or anything.—*interj.* **fidd′lestick(s),** nonsense!—**fidd′le-string,** a string for a fiddle; **fidd′lewood,** a tropical American tree (Citharexylum; fam. Verbenaceae) yielding valuable hard wood.—**a face like a fiddle,** a long or dismal face; **as fit as a fiddle,** in the best of condition; **play first,** or **second fiddle,** to act as a first-violin or a second-violin player in an orchestra: to take a leading, or a subordinate, part in anything; **Scotch fiddle,** the itch (from the motion of the fingers against the palm). [O.E. *fithele;* Ger. *fiedel;* see **viol.**]

**fiddley,** *fid′li, n.* iron framework round a hatchway opening. [Origin obscure.]

**fide et amore,** *fi′dē et a-mō′rē, fi′dā et a-mō′re,* (L.) by faith and love; **fide et fiducia,** *fi-dū′shi-a, fi-dōō′ki-ä,* by faith and confidence; **fide et fortitudine,** *for-ti-tū′di-nē, for-ti-tōō′di-ne,* by faith and fortitude; **fidei defensor,** *fi′dē-ī di-fen′-sör, fi-dā′ē dā-fen′sör,* defender of the faith; **fide non armis,** *non är′mis, ar′mēs,* by faith, not arms; **fides et justitia,** *fi′dēz et jus-tish′i-a, fi′däz et üs-ti′ti-a,* fidelity and justice; **fides Punica,** *pū-ni-kə, pōō′ni-ka,* Punic faith: treachery.

**fidelity,** *fi-del′i-ti, n.* faithfulness: faithfulness to a husband or wife: honesty: firm adherence: exactitude in reproduction. [L. *fidēlitās, -ātis—fidēlis,* faithful—*fidĕre,* to trust.]

**fidget,** *fij′it, v.i.* to be unable to rest: to move about uneasily:—*pr.p.* **fidg′eting;** *pa.t.* and *pa.p.* **fidg′eted.**—*n.* one who fidgets: irregular motion: restlessness: (in *pl.*) general nervous restlessness with a desire of changing position.—*v.i.* **fidge** (*dial.*), to move about restlessly: to be eager.—*n.* **fidg′etiness.**—*adj.* **fidg′ety,** restless: uneasy. [Perh. related to **fike.**]

**fidibus,** *fid′i-bəs, n.* a paper spill for lighting a pipe, etc. [Ger.]

**Fido,** *fi′dō, n.* a method of dispersing airfield fog by burning petrol. [*F*og *I*nvestigation *D*ispersal *O*peration.]

**fi donc!,** *fē dö, (Fr.)* for shame!

**fiducial,** *fi-dū′sh(y)əl, adj.* serving as a basis of reckoning: showing confidence or reliance: of the nature of trust.—*adv.* **fidū′cially.**—*adj.* **fidū′ciary,** of the nature of a trust: depending upon public confidence: held in trust.—*n.* one who holds anything in trust: one who depends for salvation on faith without works, an antinomian (*obs. theol.*). [L. *fidūcia,* confidence—*fidĕre,* to trust.]

**fidus et audax,** *fi′dəs et ö′daks, fi′dōōs et ow′däks,* (L.) faithful and bold.

**fie,** *fī, interj.* denoting disapprobation or disgust real or feigned.—**fie upon,** an expression of disapprobation of the thing named. [Cf. Fr. *fi;* L. *fi;* O.N. *fy, fei;* Ger. *pfui.*]

**fief,** *fēf, n.* land held in fee or on condition of military service. [Fr.,—L.L. *feudum;* see **fee, feoff.**]

**field,** *fēld, n.* country or open country in general: a piece of ground enclosed for tillage or pasture or sport: the range of any series of actions or energies: speciality: area of knowledge, interest, etc.: region of space in which forces are at work (*phys.*): the locality of a battle: the battle itself: a wide expanse: area visible to an observer at one time (e.g. in a microscope): one of the two interlaced sets of scanning lines making up the picture (*TV*): a region yielding a mineral: the surface of a shield (*her.*): those taking part in a hunt: the entries collectively against which a contestant has to compete: all parties not individually excepted (as *to bet on the field* in a horse-race): disposition of fielders: a system or collection of elements upon which binary operations of addition, subtraction, multiplication, and division can be performed except that division by 0 is excluded (*math.*).— *v.t.* at cricket and baseball, to catch or stop and return to the fixed place: to put into the field for play, or for military action.—*v.i.* to stand in position for catching or stopping the ball in cricket. **field′ed** (*Shak.*), encamped.—*ns.* **field′er,** one who fields; **field′ing,** the acting in the field at cricket as distinguished from batting.—*advs.* **field′ward, -wards,** toward the fields.— **field ambulance,** medical unit on field of battle; **field allowance,** a small extra payment to officers on active service; **field artillery,** mobile ordnance for active operations in the field; **field battery,** a battery of field artillery; **field bed,** a camp or trestle bedstead: a bed in the open air; **field book,** a book used in surveying fields, etc.; **field′boots,** knee-length boots; **field botany, field geology,** etc., botany, geology, etc., pursued in the open air; **field club,** a club of field naturalists.—*n.pl.* **field colours,** small flags used for marking the position for companies and regiments, also any regimental headquarters' flags.—**field′-cor′net,** the magistrate of a township (*S. African hist.*): rank equivalent to lieutenant, *assistant field-cornet* equal to second-lieutenant (*S. African mil.*); **field day,** a day when troops are drawn out for instruction in field exercises: any day of unusual activity or success; **field′-dew** (*Shak.*); **field event,** an athletic event other than a race; **field′fare** (ety. doubtful), a species of thrush, having a reddish-yellow throat and breast spotted with black; **field glass(es),** a binocular telescope for use in the field or open air; **field gray, field grey,** a grey (*feldgrau*) adopted for uniforms in the German army in 1st World War: a German soldier so clad; **field gun,** a light cannon mounted on a carriage; **field hand,** an outdoor farm labourer; **field hospital,** a temporary hospital near the scene of battle; **field ice,** ice formed in the polar seas in large surfaces, distinguished from icebergs; **field kitchen,** portable cooking equipment for troops, or the place where it is set up; **field lark,** an American bird (*Sturnella*) of the Icteridae, not a lark; **field marshal,** an army officer of highest rank; **field meeting,** a conventicle; **field′mouse,** a name for various species of mouse and vole that live in the fields; **field naturalist,** one who studies natural history out of doors; **field night,** a night marked by some important gathering, discussion, etc.—*n.pl.* **field notes,** data noted in the field, to be worked up later.—**field officer,** a military officer above the rank of captain, and below that of general; **field′piece,** a cannon or piece of artillery used in the field of battle; **field preacher,** an open-air preacher; **field preaching.**—*adj.* **field′-sequen′tial** (*TV*), relating to the association of individual primary colours with successive fields.—**fields′man,** a fielder.—*n.pl.* **field sports,** sports of the field, as hunting, racing, etc.—**field′stone** (chiefly *U.S.*), stone used for building as taken from a field; **field train,** a department of the Royal Artillery responsible for the safety and supply of ammunition during war; **field trial,** a test in practice, as distinct from one under laboratory conditions; **field′work,** farm work in fields: work (scientific surveying, etc.) in the field, opposed to laboratory, office, etc.: (often in *pl.*) a temporary fortification thrown up by troops in the field, either for protection or to cover an attack upon a stronghold; **field′worker,** a practical research worker.—**field-emission microscope,** a microscope in which a very strong electric field is applied to a metal point and movement of atoms at the point is seen on a fluorescent screen; **field of view, vision,** what is visible at one moment; **keep the field,** to keep the campaign open: to maintain one's ground; **take the field,**

to begin warlike operations. [O.E. *feld*; cf. Du. *veld,* the open country, Ger. *feld.*]

**fiend,** *fēnd, n.* a devil: one actuated by the most intense wickedness or hate: an addict: a devotee.—*adj.* **fiend′ish,** like a fiend: devilishly cruel.—*n.* **fiend′ishness.**—*adj.* **fiend′-like,** like a fiend: fiendish. [O.E. *fēond,* enemy, orig. pr.p. of *fēon,* to hate; Ger. *feind,* Du. *vijand.*]

**fierce,** *fērs, adj.* savage: ferocious: violent.—*adv.* **fierce′ly.**—*n.* **fierce′ness.** [O.Fr. *fers* (Fr. *fier*)—L. *ferus,* wild, savage.]

**fieri facias,** *fī′ə-ri fā′shi-as, fi′e-rē fak′i-äs,* (L.L.) cause to be done—the name of a writ commanding the sheriff to distrain the defendant's goods.

**fiery,** *fīr′i, adj.* like or consisting of fire: ardent: impetuous: irritable: of ground in games, dry, hard, fast.—*adv.* **fier′ily.**—*n.* **fier′iness.**—**fiery cross,** a charred cross dipped in blood, formerly carried round in the Scottish Highlands as a call to arms. [**fire.**]

**fiesta,** *fē-es′tə, n.* saint's day: holiday: festivity. [Sp.]

**fife,** *fīf, n.* a smaller variety of the flute.—*v.i.* to play on the fife.—*n.* **fif′er,** a fife-player.—**fife′-ma′jor** (*obs.*), the chief fifer in a regiment; **fife rail,** the rail round the mainmast, where a fifer sat at heaving of the anchor. [Ger. *pfeife,* pipe, or Fr. *fifre,* fifer, both—L. *pipāre,* to cheep.]

**Fifish,** *fīf′ish, adj.* cranky: queer: like a **Fif′er,** an inhabitant of *Fife,* Scotland.

**fifteen,** *fif′tēn,* or *fif-tēn′, adj. and n.* five and ten: a set, group, or team of fifteen (as formerly the Court of Session).—*n.* **fifteen′er,** a verse of fifteen syllables.—*adj.* **fifteenth′** (or *fif′*), last of fifteen: equal to one of fifteen equal parts.—*n.* a fifteenth part: a double octave (*mus.*): an organ stop sounding two octaves above the diapason.—**the Fifteen,** the Jacobite rebellion of 1715. [O.E. *fīftēne;* see **five, ten.**]

**fifth,** *fifth, adj.* last of five: equal to one of five equal parts.—*n.* one of five equal parts: an interval of four (conventionally called five) diatonic degrees (*mus.*): a tone at that interval from another: a combination of two tones separated by that interval.—*adv.* **fifth′ly,** in the fifth place.—**Fifth Amendment,** an amendment to the U.S. constitution which allows a person on trial not to testify against himself and forbids a second trial if a person has been acquitted in a first; **fifth column,** sympathisers among the enemy, awaiting their time (expression used by a Spanish insurgent general when four columns were advancing upon Madrid); **fifth columnist** (*kol′əm-ist*); **Fifth′-mon′archism; Fifth′-mon′-archist.**—**Fifth-monarchy men,** an extreme sect at the time of the Puritan revolution, who looked for a new reign of Christ on earth in succession to Daniel's four great monarchies of Antichrist. [O.E. *fifta,* assimilated to other ordinals in *-th.*]

**fifty,** *fif′ti, adj. and n.* five tens or five times ten: *pl.* **fif′ties,** the numbers fifty to fifty-nine: the years so numbered (of a life or century).—*adj.* **fif′tieth,** last of fifty: equal to one of fifty equal parts.—*n.* a fiftieth part.—*adj.* **fif′tyish,** apparently about fifty years old.—*n.* and *adj. and adv.* **fif′ty-fif′ty,** half-and-half: fifty per cent. of each of two things: share and share alike. [O.E. *fiftig—fīf,* five, and *-tig,* the suff. *-ty.*]

**fig,** *fig, n.* the fig-tree (*Ficus,* of the mulberry family), or its fruit, growing in warm climates: a thing of little or no consequence: piles (*obs.*).—*v.t.* (*Shak.*) to insult by putting the thumb between the fingers.—**fig′-leaf,** the leaf of the fig-tree: a representation of such a leaf for veiling the private parts of a statue or picture: any scanty clothing (from Gen. iii. 7): any prudish evasion: a makeshift: something intended to conceal the reality of actions or motives, esp. political or international; **fig′-pecker,** beccafico; **fig′-tree,** the tree which fig 487 file

produces figs; **fig′wort**, any species of Scrophularia: pilewort. [Fr. *figue*—L. *fīcus*, a fig, fig-tree.]

**fig**, *fig*, (*coll.*) *n.* figure: dress: form.—*v.t.* to dress, get up (with *out*): (of a horse) to display in an artificially lively condition (with *out* or *up*): —*pr.p.* **figg′ing**; *pa.t.*and *pa.p.* **figged.**—*n.* **figg′ery**, dressy ornament. [Perh. figure.]

**fight**, *fit*, *v.i.* to strive: to contend in war or in single combat.—*v.t.* to engage in conflict with: to contend against: to maintain or contend for by combat, action at law, or otherwise: to manipulate in fight: to achieve by struggle: to cause to fight:—*pr.p.* **fight′ing**; *pa.t.* and *pa.p.* **fought**(*föt*).—*n.* a struggle: a combat: a strong disagreement: a battle or engagement: fighting spirit: inclination to fight: a screen to cover the men in a naval fight (*Shak.*).—*n.* **fight′er**, one who fights: a boxer: an aircraft engaged in war. —*adj.* **fight′ing**, engaged in, eager for, or fit for war or strife.—*n.* the act of fighting or contending.—**fighting chance**, a chance of success given supreme effort; **fighting cock**, a gamecock: a pugnacious fellow; **fighting fish** (*Betta pugnax*), a small freshwater fish of Thailand, kept for its extraordinary readiness for fighting, bets being laid on the issue.—*adj.* **fight′ing-fit**, in good condition.—**fight it out**, to struggle on until the end; **fight shy of**, to avoid from mistrust; **fight to the finish**, to the ropes, to the last ditch, to fight until completely exhausted; **live like fighting cocks**, to get the best of meat and drink. [O.E. *fehtan* (W.S. *feohtan*); Ger. *fechten*.]

**figment**, *fig′mant*, *n.* a fabrication or invention. [L. *figmentum*—*fingĕre*, to form.]

**figo**, *fē′gō*, (*Shak.*) *n.* a fico. [O.Sp.]

**figuline**, *fig′ū-lin, -lin*, *adj.* of earthenware: fictile. —*n.* an earthen vessel. [L. *figulinus*—*figulus*, potter.]

**figure**, *fig′ar*, (*U.S.*) *-yar*, (old-fashioned) *fig′ūr*, *n.* the form of anything in outline: appearance: a shape: a geometrical form: a diagram: a horoscope (*Shak.*): a design: an illustration: bodily shape: a human form or representation of it: a personality, personage, character: an impressive, noticeable, important, ludicrous, or grotesque person: a character denoting a number: amount: value or price: a deviation from the ordinary mode of expression (*rhet.*): the form of a syllogism with respect to the position of the middle term (*logic*): a group of notes felt as a unit (*mus.*): a series of steps or movements in a dance or in skating: a type or emblem.—*v.t.* to form or shape (*obs.*): to make an image of: to represent: to mark with figures or designs: to imagine: to reckon, to work out (often with *out*): to symbolise (*arch.*): to foreshow (*obs.*): to note by figures.—*v.i.* to make figures: to appear as a figure, make an appearance or show: to follow as a logical consequence, be expected (*coll.*).—*n.* **figūrabil′ity**, the quality of being figurable.—*adjs.* **fig′ūrable**; **fig′ūral**, represented by figure.—*n.* **fig′ūrant, figūrante** (*fig′ū-rant*; It. *fēg-ōō-rän′tä*) a ballet dancer, one of those who form a background for the solo dancers.—*adj.* **fig′ūrate**, of a certain determinate form: florid (*mus.*).—*n.* **figūrā′tion**, act of giving figure or form: representation by or in figures or shapes, esp. significant, typical or emblematic, figures: a figure of this kind: ornamentation with a design: florid treatment (*mus.*).—*adj.* **fig′ūrative**, representing by, containing, or abounding in figures of speech (*rhet.*): metaphorical: representing a figure: emblematic, symbolic.—*adv.* **fig′ūratively.**—*n.* **fig′ūrativeness.**—*adj.* **fig′ured** (*-ard*), having a figure: marked or adorned with figures: delineated in a figure: in the form of figures.—*ns.* **fig′ūrine** (*-ēn, -ēn′*), a small carved or moulded figure; **fig′urist**, one who uses or interprets by figures.—

**figurate numbers**, a series of numbers such that if each be subtracted from the next, and the series so formed be treated in the same way, by a continuation of the process equal differences will ultimately be obtained; **fig′ure-cast′er** (*obs.*), an astrologer; **fig′ure-cast′ing**, the art of preparing casts of animal or other forms; **fig′ure-dance**, a dance consisting of elaborate figures; **figured bass**, a bass with numerals added to indicate chords; **fig′urehead**, the figure or bust under the bowsprit of a ship: a nominal head; **fig′ureweav′ing**, the weaving of figured fancy fabrics.—**cut a figure**, to make a conspicuous appearance; **figure on**, to count upon: to plan (*U.S.*). [Fr.,—L. *figūra*—*fingĕre*, to form.]

**fike**, *fīk*, (*Scot.*) *v.i.* to fidget restlessly.—*n.* restlessness: any vexatious requirement or detail in work; a pernickety, exacting person.—*n.* **fik′ery**, fuss.—*adjs.* **fik′ish, fik′y**. [Prob. O.N. *fīkja*.]

**filabeg**. See **filibeg**.

**filacer**, *fil′a-sar*, *n.* formerly an officer who filed writs.—Also **fil′azer**. [O.Fr. *filacier*—*filace*, a file for papers—apparently L. *filum*, a thread.]

**filagree**. Same as **filigree**.

**filament**, *fil′a-mant*, *n.* a slender or threadlike object: a fibre: the stalk of a stamen (*bot.*): a chain of cells: a thread of high resistance in an incandescent lamp or thermionic valve (*elec.*).— *adjs.* **filamentary** (*-ment′a-ri*), like a filament; **filament′ous**, threadlike. [L. *filum*, a thread.]

**filander**, *fil-and′ar*, threadlike intestinal worm in hawks: (in *pl.*) the disease it causes. [O.Fr. *filandre*—L. *filum*, thread.]

**Filaria**, *fi-lā′ri-a*, *n.* a genus of nematode worms of the fam. *Filarioidea* introduced into the blood by mosquitoes.—*adj.* **filā′rial.**—*n.* **filariasis** (*-la-ri′a-sis*), a disease due to the presence of filaria in the blood. [L. *filum*, thread.]

**filasse**, *fil-as′*, *n.* vegetable fibre ready for manufacture. [Fr.,—L. *filum*, thread.]

**filature**, *fil′a-char*, *n.* the reeling of silk, or the place where it is done.—*n.* **fil′atory**, a machine for forming or spinning threads. [Fr.,—L. *filum*, a thread.]

**filazer**. Same as **filacer**.

**filbert**, *fil′bart*, *n.* the nut of the cultivated hazel —(*obs.*) **fil′berd**. [Prob. from St *Philibert*, whose day fell in the nutting season, Aug. 22 (O.S.).]

**filch**, *filch*, *v.t.* to steal: to pilfer.—*n.* **filch′er**, a thief.—*n.* and *adj.* **filch′ing.**—*adv.* **filch′ingly**. [Ety. unknown.]

**file**, *fil*, *n.* a thread or wire on which papers are strung (*obs.*): a line or wire on which papers are strung: any contrivance for keeping papers in order: a collection of papers arranged for reference: a roll or list (*Shak.*): a line of soldiers, chessboard squares, etc., ranged one behind another: a small body of soldiers.—*v.t.* to put upon a file: to arrange in an orderly way: to put on record: to bring before a court: to deposit, lodge.—*v.i.* to march in file.—*adjs.* **filaceous** (*fil-ā′shas*), composed of threads; **filar** (*fī′lar*), having threads or wires; **filiform** (*fil′*), threadlike; **filipen′dulous** (*fil-*), hanging by or strung on a thread.—*n.* **fil′oplume** (*fil′*), a slender hairlike feather.—*adj.* **filose** (*fī′lōs*), threadlike: having a threadlike end.—**file copy**, a copy filed for reference: an editor's copy of a book in which errors, possible changes, etc., are noted; **file′-lead′er.—file off**, to wheel off at right angles to their first direction; **file with** (*arch.*), to rank with, to be equal to; **single file, Indian file**, one behind another. [L. *filum*, a thread.]

**file**, *fil*, *n.* an instrument with sharp-edged furrows for smoothing or rasping metals, etc.: a small metal or emery-paper instrument for smoothing fingernails: a shrewd, cunning person, a deep fellow: a pickpocket (*obs.*).—*v.t.* to cut or smooth with, or as with, a file: to polish, improve, esp. of a literary style.—*adj.* **filed**, polished, smooth.—*ns.* **fil′er**, one who files;

**fil′ing,** a particle rubbed off with a file.—**file′-cutter,** a maker of files; **file′-fish,** a fish of Balistes or kindred genus, the skin granulated like a file. [O.E. *fȳl* (W.S. *fēol*); Ger. *feile*; Du. *vijl*.]

**file,** *fīl,* (*Shak.*; *Scot.*) *v.t.* to defile, pollute. [O.E. *gefylan*; cf. **foul.**]

**filemot,** *fil′i-mot, adj.* of a dead-leaf colour—*n.* the colour itself.—Also **philamot, philomot.** [Fr. *feuillemorte,* dead leaf.]

**filet,** *fē-le* (Fr.) undercut of beef, tenderloin: a kind of lace consisting of embroidery on a square-mesh net.

**filet mignon,** *fē-le mē-nyõ,* (Fr.) a small cut of beef from the thick end of an undercut.

**filial,** *fil′i-əl, adj.* pertaining to or becoming a son or daughter: bearing the relation of a child.—*adv.* **fil′ially.** [Fr.,—L.L. *filiālis*—L. *filius,* a son.]

**filiate, filiation.** Same as **affiliate, affiliation.**

**filibeg, filabeg, fillibeg, phil(l)abeg, phil(l)ibeg,** *fil′i-beg, n.* the kilt, the dress or petticoat reaching nearly to the knees, worn by the Highlanders of Scotland. [Gael. *feileadhbeag—feileadh,* plait, fold, *beag,* little.]

**filibuster,** *fil′i-bus-tər, n.* a piratical adventurer, buccaneer: ᴘ military adventurer, one who makes unauthorised war: one who obstructs legislation by speeches, motions, etc.: obstruction in a legislative body.—*v.i.* to act as a filibuster.—*ns.* **filibus′terer; filibus′tering; filibus′terism.**—*adj.* **filibus′terous.** [Sp. *filibustero,* through Fr. *flibustier, fribustier,* from Du. *vrijbuiter* (cf. Eng. **freebooter** (under **free**), Ger. *freibeuter*), from *vrij,* free, *buit,* booty.]

**Filices,** *fil′i-sēz, n.pl.* the ferns: esp. the true (homosporous leptosporangiate) ferns.—*ns.pl.* **Filicales** (*-kā′lēz*), **Filicineae** (*-sin′i-ē*), the ferns, leptosporangiate and eusporangiate, with or without water-ferns.—*adj.* **filicin′ean.** [L. *filix,* -*icis,* fern.]

**filigree,** *fil′i-grē, n.* a kind of ornamental metallic lacework of gold and silver, twisted into convoluted forms, united and partly consolidated by soldering: a delicate structure resembling this (also **fil′agree;** earlier forms, **fil′igrain, fil′igrane**).—*adj.* **fil′igreed,** ornamented with filigree. [Fr. *filigrane*—It. *filigrana*—L. *filum,* thread, *grānum,* a grain.]

**filioque,** *fil-i-ō′kwi, n.* the clause inserted into the Nicene Creed at Toledo in 589, which asserts that the Holy Ghost proceeds from the Son, as well as from the Father—not accepted by the Eastern Church. [L., and from the son.]

**Filipino,** *fil-i-pē′nō, n.* a native of the *Philippine* Islands:—*fem.* **Filipi′na.** [Sp.]

**filius nullius,** *fil′i-əs nul′i-əs, fē′li-ōōs nōō′li-ōōs,* (L.) son of nobody, a bastard; **filius populi,** *po′pū-lī, po′pōō-lē,* son of the people; **filius terrae,** *te′rē, te′rī,* son of the soil; one of mean birth.

**fill,** *fil, v.t.* to make full: to put into until all the space is occupied: to supply abundantly: to satisfy: to glut: to perform the duties of: to supply (a vacant office): to adulterate (of soap, cotton fabrics, etc.): to fulfil, carry out (esp. *U.S.*): to make up (a prescription) (*U.S.*).—*v.i.* to become full: to become satiated.—*n.* as much as fills or satisfies: a full supply: the fullest extent: a single charge of anything.—*ns.* **fill′er,** he who, or that which, fills: a vessel for conveying a liquid into a bottle: a substance added to various materials to impart desired qualities; **fill′ing,** anything used to fill up, stop a hole, to complete, etc., as the woof, in weaving.—**filling station,** a roadside installation where petrol and oil are sold to motorists.—**fill in,** to occupy (time): to add what is necessary to complete, e.g. a form: to act as a temporary substitute (for; *coll.*); **fill one in** (*coll.*), to give one detailed

information about a situation; **fill the bill,** to be adequate; **fill up,** to fill, or be filled, by addition of more; **fill up with,** to stuff with (*lit.* and *fig.*). [O.E. *fyllan—full,* full.]

**fill, fil,** *fil,* (*Shak.*) *n.* a thill or shaft.—**fill′-horse,** *p(h)il′-horse* (*Shak.*), a thill-horse. [See **thill** (1).]

**fille,** *fē-y′,* (Fr.) girl: daughter; **fille de chambre** (*də shä-br′*), a chambermaid; **fille de joie** (*zhwä*), a prostitute; **fille d'honneur** (*do-nœr*), a maid of honour.

**fillet,** *fil′ət, n.* a narrow piece of wood, metal, etc.: a band for the hair: meat or fish boned and rolled: a piece of meat without bone, esp. the fleshy part of the thigh or the undercut of the sirloin: a thick boneless slice of fish: a small space or band used along with mouldings (*archit.*).—*v.t.* to bind or adorn with a fillet: to make into fillets: to bone:—*pr.p.* **fill′eting;** *pa.t.* and *pa.p.* **fill′eted.**—**fillet weld,** a weld at the junction of two parts at right angles to each other, a fillet of welding material being laid down in the angle created by the intersection of the surfaces of the parts. [Fr. *filet,* dim. of *fil,* from L. *filum,* a thread.]

**fillibeg.** See **filibeg.**

**fillip,** *fil′ip, v.t.* to strike with the fingernail released from the ball of the thumb with a sudden jerk: to incite, stimulate:—*pr.p.* **fill′iping;** *pa.t.* and *pa.p.* **fill′iped.**—*n.* a jerk of the finger from the thumb: a stimulus. [A form of **flip.**]

**fillipeen.** U.S. form of **philop(o)ena.**

**fillister,** *fil′is-tər, n.* a kind of rabbeting plane. [Origin unknown.]

**filly,** *fil′i, n.* a young mare: a lively, wanton girl. [Dim. of **foal;** prob. from O.N.]

**film,** *film, n.* a thin skin or membrane: a thin layer or coating: a pellicle: a very slender thread: a mistiness: a coating of a sensitive substance for taking a photograph: a sheet or ribbon of celluloid or the like prepared with such a coating for ordinary photographs or for instantaneous photographs for projection by cinematograph: a motion picture, or connected series of motion pictures setting forth a story, etc.: (in *pl.*) the cinema.—*v.t.* to cover with a film: to make a motion picture of: to adapt and enact for the cinema.—*v.i.* to become covered with a film.—*adj.* **film′able,** suitable for making a film of.—*ns.* **film′dom, film′land,** the cinematic industry.—*adj.* **film′ic,** pertaining to the cinema.—*adv.* **filmi′ness.**—*adjs.* **film′ish,** savouring of the cinema; **film′y,** composed of or like a film: covered with a film: gauzy: clouded.—**film colour** (*psychol.*), a vague textureless area of colour, as the sky or that seen with closed eyes, as opposed to colour seen on the surface of an object; **film fan,** a devotee of the cinema; **film′goer,** a devotee of the cinema; **film′star,** a favourite cinema performer; **filmy ferns,** a family of ferns with very thin leaves, the Hymenophyllaceae.—**sheet film,** film in same sizes as photographic plates and superseding plates. [O.E. *filmen,* conn. with *fell,* skin.]

**filose.** See **file** (1).

**filoselle,** *fil-ō-sel′, n.* coarse floss silk. [It. *filosello*—L.L. *folexellus,* cocoon); infl. by It. *filo,* thread.]

**fils, fēs,** (Fr.) son: (following a name) junior.

**filter,** *fil′tər, n.* an apparatus for purifying a fluid of solid matter by pouring it through porous material: a device for wholly or partly eliminating undesirable frequencies from light or electric currents: at a road junction an auxiliary traffic light in the form of a green arrow which allows one lane of traffic to move while the main stream is held up.—*v.t.* to pass through a filter: to separate by a filter (esp. with *out*).—*v.i.* to pass through a filter: to percolate: to pass gradually and dispersedly through obstacles: to join gradually a stream of traffic: a lane of traffic, to move in the direction specified by the filter: to become known gradually (*fig.*).—*adj.* **fil′terable, fil′trable**, able to pass through a filter (see below): capable of being filtered.—*n.* **filt(e)rability.**—*v.t.* and *v.i.* **fil′trate**, to filter or percolate.—*n.* a filtered liquid.—*n.* **filtrā′tion**, act or process of filtering.—**fil′ter-bed**, a bed of sand, gravel, clinker, etc., used for filtering water or sewage; **fil′ter-paper**, porous paper for use in filtering; **fil′ter-passer, filterable virus**, terms used formerly for virus in sense of submicroscopic disease agent; **filter-tip**, a cigarette with a filter at the mouth end. [O.Fr. *filtre*—L.L. *filtrum*, felt.]

**filth**, *filth*, *n.* foul matter: anything that defiles, physically or morally: obscenity.—*adv.* **filth′ily.** —*n.* **filth′iness.**—*adj.* **filth′y**, foul: unclean: impure. [O.E. *fȳlth*—*fūl*, foul.]

**filtre** (Fr.). See café **filtre.**

**fimble**, *fim′bl*, *n.* the male plant of hemp, weaker and shorter in fibre than **carl-hemp**. [Du. *femel*, female.]

**fimbria**, *fim′bri-ə*, *n.* a fringing filament.—*adj.* **fim′briate**, fringed: having a narrow border (*her.*).—*v.t.* **fim′briate**, to fringe: to hem.— *adj.* **fim′briated.**—*n.* **fimbria′tion.** [L. *fimbriae*, fibres, fringe.]

**fimicolous**, *fim-ik′ə-ləs*, *adj.* growing on dung. [L. *fimus*, dung, *colēre*, to inhabit.]

**fin**, *fin*, *n.* an organ by which an aquatic animal steers, balances, or swims: a fixed vertical surface on the tail of an aeroplane: a portion of a mechanism like a fish's fin in shape or purpose: a thin projecting edge or plate: hand, arm (*slang*).—*n.* **finn′er**, finback.—*adjs.* **fin′less; finned**, having fins; **finn′y**, finned.—**fin′back**, **fin′-whale**, a rorqual.—*adj.* **fin′-foot′ed**, web-footed: with fringed toes.—**fin′-ray′**, a horny rod supporting a fin.—*adj.* **fin′-toed′**, having lobate or fringed toes. [O.E. *finn*; L. *pinna*, a feather, a fin.]

**fin**, *fin*, (*U.S. slang*), *n.* a five-dollar bill. [Yiddish *finf*, five.]

**finable.** See **fine.**

**finagle**, *fi-nā′gəl*, *v.t.* to wangle: to obtain by guile or swindling: to cheat (a person; usu. with *out of*).—Also *v.i.* [Eng. dial. *fainaigue*, cheat, shirk.]

**final**, *fī′nl*, *adj.* last: decisive, conclusive: respecting the end or motive: of a judgment ready for execution.—*n.* last of a series (as the letters of a word, games in a contest, examinations in a curriculum, etc.): in the old church modes, the keynote or tonic, the lowest note in the authentic modes, a fourth above it in the plagal.—*v.t.* **fi′nalise, -ize**, to put the finishing touches to: to put an end to completely.—*ns.* **fi′nalism**, teleology, interpretation in terms of purpose: belief that an end has been reached; **fi′nalist**, teleologist: one who reaches the final stage in a competition: one who believes that finality has been reached; **finality** (-*al′i-ti*), state of being final: completeness or conclusiveness: the principle of final cause: that which is final.—*adv.* **finally.** —**final cause** (see **cause**). [Fr.,—L. *finālis*—*finis*, an end.]

**finale**, *fi-nä′lä, -li*, *n.* the end: the last movement in a musical composition: the concluding number of an opera or the like. [It. *finale*, final —L. *finālis*.]

**finance**, *fi-, fi-nans′*, *n.* money affairs or revenue, esp. of a ruler or state: public money: the art of managing or administering the public money: (in *pl.*) money resources.—*v.t.* to manage financially: to furnish with money.—*v.i.* to engage in money business.—*adj.* **finan′cial** (-*shəl*), pertaining to finance.—*n.* **finan′cialist**, a financier.—*adv.* **finan′cially.**—*n.* **finan′cier** (-*si-ər*; *U.S. fin-an-sēr′*), one skilled in finance; one who administers the public revenue.—*v.i.* and *v.t.*

(-*sēr′*) to finance: to swindle. [Fr.,—O.Fr. *finer*, to settle—L. *finis*, an end.]

**finback.** See **fin.**

**finch**, *finch*, -*sh*, *n.* a name applied to many passerine birds, esp. to those of the genus Fringilla or family Fringillidae—**bullfinch**, **chaffinch**, **goldfinch**, etc.—*adj.* **finched**, **finch-backed.**—*adj.* **finch′-backed**, striped or spotted on the back. [O.E. *finc*; Ger. *fink*.]

**find**, *find*, *v.t.* to come upon or meet with: to discover or arrive at: to come to perceive: to experience: to supply: to determine after judicial inquiry: to succeed in getting.—*v.i.* to come upon game:—*pr.p.* **find′ing**; *pa.t.* and *pa.p.* **found.**—*n.* an act of finding: something found, esp. of value or interest.—*ns.* **find′er**, one who finds: a small telescope attached to a larger one, or a lens attached to a camera, to facilitate the directing of it upon the object required; **find′ing**, act of one who finds: that which is found: a judicial verdict: (*pl.*) the appliances which some workmen have to supply, esp. of shoemakers—everything save leather: accessories (*U.S.*).—**find′-fault** (*Shak.*), one who finds fault with another.—**finders keepers** (*coll.*), those who find something are entitled to keep it; **find one in**, to supply one with; **find one's account in**, to find satisfactory profit or advantage in; **find one's feet**, to become able to stand, able to cope readily with new conditions; **find oneself**, to feel, as regards health, happiness, etc.: to come to terms with oneself: to discover one's true vocation and interests; **find out**, to discover, to detect. [O.E. *findan*; Ger. *finden*.]

**fin de siècle**, *fẽ də sye-kl′*, (Fr.) the end of the (19th) century, or of an era: characteristic of the ideas, etc., of that time: decadent.

**findon-haddock.** See **finnan.**

**fine**, *fin*, *adj.* excellent: beautiful: fair: not coarse or heavy: consisting of small particles: subtle: thin, slender: sharp: keen: exquisite: nice: delicate: sensitive: over-refined: over-elaborate: pretentious: showy: splendid: striking or remarkable: excellent (often ironically): egregious: pure: refined: containing so many parts of pure metal out of twenty-four (as 22 carats, or ounces, fine, 22/24 gold or silver), or out of a thousand.—*v.t.* to make fine: to refine: to purify: to change by imperceptible degrees.— *adj.* and *adv.* at a more acute angle with the line of flight of the ball (as, *fine leg*).—*adv.* well, well enough (*coll.*): narrowly: with little to spare.—*adj.* **fine′ish** (also **fin′ish**), somewhat fine.—*adv.* **fine′ly.**—*ns.* **fine′ness**, state, fact, or degree of being fine: state of subdivision: of gold or silver, number of parts in a thousand; **fin′er**, refiner; **fin′ery**, splendour: showy adornments: a place where anything is fined or refined: a furnace for making iron malleable.— *n.pl.* **fines**, material (ore, coal, etc.) in a fine state of division separated out by screening; **fin′ing**, process of refining or purifying: a clarifying agent (often in *pl.*).—**fine arts** (see under **art**).— *v.t.* **fine′-draw**, to draw or sew up so finely that no rent is seen: to draw out finely or too finely. —*adj.* **fine′-drawn.**—**fine gentleman, lady**, an idle person, usu. ostentatiously fashionable, sometimes refined; **fine metal**, comparatively pure cuprous sulphide got from *coarse metal*.—*adjs.* **fine′-spoken**, using fine phrases; **fine′-spun**, finely spun out: over-subtle.—**fine writing**, literary matter or style pretentiously ornate; **fin′ing-pot**, a vessel used in refining. [Fr. *fin*, prob. a back-formation from L. *finītus*, finished. *pa.p.* of *finire*, to finish—*finis*, an end.]

**fine**, *fin*, *n.* (*obs.* except in phrase *in fine*) end, conclusion: a final settlement: a fee paid on some particular occasion: a fictitious suit as a means of conveying property or barring an entail: a composition by money payment: a

**fine** 490 **fire**

money penalty.—*v.t.* to bring to an end (*Shak.*): to impose a fine on: to punish by fine: to pledge or pawn (*Shak.*).—*adjs.* fin'able, liable to a fine; fine'less (*Shak.*), endless.—foot of fine (see foot). [L. *finis*, an end.]

fine, *fēn, n.* ordinary French brandy.—fine Champagne, *shā-pany'*, brandy distilled from wine made from grapes grown in the Champagne area of France. [Fr.]

fineer, *fi-nēr'*, an old form of veneer (*n.* and *v.t.*).

fineer, *fi-nēr'* (*obs.*), *v.i.* to get goods on credit by fraudulent artifice. [Prob. Du.; cf. finance.]

Fine Gael, *fē'ne gāl*, (*lit.* United Ireland) the moderate party led orig. by W. T. Cosgrave.

finem respice, *fī'nəm rəs-pi'sē, fē'nem re'spi-ke*, (L.) consider the end.

fines herbes, *fēn-zerb*, (Fr.) (*cook.*) a mixture of herbs used as a garnish or, chopped, as a seasoning.

finesse, *fi-nes', n.* subtlety of contrivance: artifice: an endeavour by a player holding a higher card to take the trick with a lower, risking loss.—*v.t.* and *v.i.* to play in finesse.—*v.i.* to use artifice.—*ns.* finess'er; finess'ing. [Fr.]

fingan, *fin-gän', n.* a small coffee-cup without a handle—used with a zarf.—Also finjan (-jän'). [Egyptian *fingān*, Ar. *finjān*.]

finger, *fing'gər, n.* one of the five terminal parts of the hand, or of the four other than the thumb: anything shaped like a finger: part of a glove that covers a finger: a finger-breadth: touch: agency (esp. of God): share, interest: (in *pl.*) grip, control.—*v.t.* to handle or perform with the fingers: to pilfer: to toy or meddle with: to make or indicate choice of fingers in performing (*mus.*).—*v.t.* to use the fingers.—*adj.* fing'ered, having fingers, or anything like fingers, or indication of fingering.—*n.* fing'ering, act or manner of touching with the fingers: the choice of fingers as in playing a musical instrument: the indication thereof.—*adj.* fing'erless.—*n.* fing'erling, a very diminutive being: the parr.—fing'eral'phabet, a deaf and dumb alphabet; fing'er-and-toe', a disease of turnips in which the tap-root branches: another turnip disease, anbury; fing'erboard, the part of a violin, etc., against which the strings are stopped by the fingers; fing'erbowl, -glass, a bowl for water to cleanse the fingers at table; fing'er('s)-breadth, the breadth of a finger, a digit, ¾ of an inch; fing'er('s)-end'; fing'er-grass, grass of genus Digitaria, with fingerlike spikes; fing'erguard, the quillons of a sword-handle; fin'gerhold, a grasp by the fingers: something by which the fingers can hold (also *fig.*); fin'gerhole, a hole in a wind instrument closed by the finger to modify the pitch; fing'ermark, a mark, esp. a soil, made by the finger; fing'ernail; fing'erplate, a plate to protect a door from dirty fingers; fing'er-point'er, reprover; fing'erpost, a post with a finger pointing the way; fing'erprint, an impression of the ridges of the finger-tip.—*v.t.* to take the fingerprints of.—fin'gerprinting; fing'erstall, a covering for protecting the finger; fing'ertip.—a finger in the pie, a share in the doing of anything (often said of vexatious meddling); cross one's fingers (see cross); have at one's finger(s')-ends, -tips, to be master of a subject; have one's fingers all thumbs, to be awkward in handling; not to lift a finger, to take no action; point the finger at, to call attention to in reproof; put a finger on, to touch; put one's finger on, to indicate, comprehend and express, or recall, precisely. [O.E. *finger.*]

fingering, *fing'gər-ing, n.* a thick woollen yarn for stockings. [Perh. Fr. *fin grain*, fine grain.]

finial, *fin'i-əl, n.* the bunch of foliage, etc., on the top of a pinnacle, gable, spire, etc. [L. *finis*, end.]

finical, *fin'i-kl, adj.* affectedly or excessively pre-

cise in trifles: nice: foppish.—*n.* finicality (-*kal'i-ti*), state of being finical: something finical.—*adv.* fin'ically.—*ns.* fin'icalness, fin'icking, fussiness and fastidiousness.—*adjs.* fin'icking, fin'icky, fin'ikin, particular about trifles. [Prob. conn. with fine (1).]

fining. See fine (1).

finis, *fī'nis, n.* the end: conclusion. [L. *finis*.]

finish, *fin'ish, v.t.* to end: to complete the making of: to perfect: to give the last touches to: to complete the education of, esp. for life in society: to complete the course of a race: to put an end to, to destroy.—Also *v.i.*—*n.* that which finishes or completes: the end of a race, hunt, etc.: last touch, elaboration, polish: last coat of plaster or paint.—*adj.* fin'ished, brought to an end or to completion: complete: consummate: perfect.—*n.* fin'isher, one who finishes: one who completes or perfects, esp. in crafts.—*n., adj.* fin'ishing.—finishing post, the post marking the end of a race. [Fr. *finir*, *finissant*—L. *finire*, to end.]

finite, *fī'nīt, adj.* having an end or limit: subject to limitations or conditions—opp. to *infinite.*—*adv.* fi'nitely.—*ns.* fi'niteness, finitude (*fin'i-tūd*).—finite verb, a verb limited by person, number, tense, mood, opp. to infinitive, gerund, participle. [L. *finītus*, pa.p. of *finīre*, to limit.]

finjan. See fingan.

fink, *fingk, (slang) n.* a strike-breaker: an informer: loosely, an unpleasant person.—Also *v.i.* [Origin uncertain.]

finks, *fingks.* Same as fenks.

fin mot de l'affaire, *fē mō də la-fer*, (Fr.) the bottom of the matter, the explanation.

Finn, *fin, n.* a member of a people dwelling in Finland and adjacent regions: more generally, a member of the group of peoples to which the Finns proper belong.—*n.* Fin'lander, a native or citizen of Finland.—*adjs.* Finn'ic, pertaining to the Finns or the Finno-Ugrians; Finn'ish, pertaining to the Finns, or to Finland, or its language.—*n.* the Finno-Ugrian language of Finland.—*adjs.* Finno-Ugrian, Finno-Ugric (*fin'ō-ū'gri-ən, -ōō'gri-ən, -grik*), belonging to the north-western group of Ural-Altaic languages and peoples—Finnish, Estonian, Lapp, Cheremiss, Mordvin, Zyrian, Votyak, etc.—also U'gro-Finn'ic. [O.E. *finnas*, Finns.]

finnan, *fin'ən, obs.* findram, *fin'rəm, n.* a kind of smoked haddock, probably named from Findon, Kincardineshire, not from the Findhorn river.— Also finn'an-, fin'don-hadd'ock.

finnesko, finnsko, finsko, *fin'(e-)skō, n.pl.* reindeer-skin boots with the hair on. [Norw. *finnsko*—*Finn*, Lapp, *sko*, shoe.]

finnock, finnack, finnac, *fin'ək, n.* a young sea-trout. [Gael. *fionnag—fionn*, white.]

fino, *fē'nō, n.* a dry sherry.

fiord, fjord, *fyör(d), fyör(d), n.* a long, narrow, rock-bound inlet. [Norw. *fjord*.]

fiorin, *fī'ə-rin, n.* a variety of creeping bent-grass (*Agrostis alba*, var. *stolonifera*). [Ir. *fiorthán*.]

fioritura, *fyor-i-tōō'rə, n.* a florid embellishment:—*pl.* fioriture, -rā. [It., flowering—L. *flōs*, *flōris*.]

fippence, *fip'əns*, a shortened form of fivepence.

fipple, *fip'l, n.* the under-lip (*dial.*): an arrangement of a block, and a sharp edge against which it directs the wind, in the recorder, etc.—fipp'le-flute', a flute with a fipple, a recorder or flageolet. [Cf. O.N. *flipi*, a horse's lip.]

fir, *fûr, n.* the name of several conifers, esp. of the genera Abies and Picea, resinous trees, valuable for their timber.—*adj.* firr'y, abounding in firs: of fir.—fir'-cone; fir'-tree; fir'-wood. [O.E. *fyrh*; cf. Ger. *föhre*.]

fire, *fīr, n.* a once-supposed substance reckoned one of the four elements: the heat and light of

*fāte, fär; mē, hûr* (her); *mīne, mōte, för; mūte; mōon, fōot; dhen* (then) burning: a mass of burning matter, as of fuel in a grate: flame or incandescence: a conflagration: firing: fuel: a heating apparatus: heat or light due to other causes than burning: lightning (*poet.*): volcanic or plutonic heat: great heat: the heat of fever or inflammation: glowing appearance: a sparkle of light: discharge of fire-arms (also *fig.*): enthusiasm: ardour: passion: spirited vigour or animation. —*v.t.* to ignite: to cause to explode: to expose to heat: to bake: to cauterise: to fuel: to affect as if by fire: to discharge: to drive out: to dismiss (from employment, etc.): to inflame: to animate: to rouse to passion of any kind. —*v.i.* to take fire: to shoot with firearms: to become inflamed: to break out in anger.—*adjs.* fired, affected, or having the appearance of having been affected, with fire: baked: ignited: kindled: discharged; fire′less.—*ns.* fir′er, one who fires, in any sense; fir′ing, ignition: discharge of guns, etc.: simultaneous ringing of a peal of bells: fuelling: firewood: fuel: cautery: injury by overheating: subjection to heat.—fire′-alarm′, apparatus for giving warning of fire: a warning of fire; fire′-arm, a weapon discharged by explosion (usu. in *pl.*); fire′-arrow, a dart or arrow carrying a combustible; fire′-back, a red-backed Sumatran pheasant: the back wall of a fireplace: an ornamental plate of iron so placed; fire′ball, a bolide: ball-lightning: an incendiary or illuminating projectile; fire′-balloon′, a balloon carrying fire and raised by the heating and rarefaction of air: a balloon discharging fireworks in the air; fire′-bar, a bar of a fire-grate: a heating element in an electric radiator; fire′-bas′ket, a portable firegrate; fire′-bird, the Baltimore oriole, or other bird of orange and red plumage; fire′-blast, a blight of hops, due to a mite, giving a scorched appearance; fire-blight, a bacterial disease of fruit-trees, giving a scorched appearance; fire′-bote, a tenant's right to cut wood for fuel; fire′box, a chamber for the fire in a steam-engine, etc.; fire′brand, a burning piece of wood: one who foments strife; fire′brat, a small insect found in bakehouses; fire′-break, a strip of land cleared to stop the spread of a fire; fire′brick, a brick refractory to fire, used for furnace-linings, etc.; fire′-brigade′, a body of firemen; fire′-buck′et, a water bucket for putting out fires; fire′bug, an incendiary; fire′-clay, a clay poor in lime and iron, suitable for making refractory pottery and firebricks; fire′-control′, a system of controlling the whole gun-fire of a ship from one centre; fire′-cracker, a device for making a noise, a cylinder of paper or cardboard containing an explosive and a fuse; fire′crest, the gold crest, or fire′-crested wren, a bird close akin to the gold crest, a kinglet; fire′damp, a combustible gas given off by coal, etc., chiefly methane; fire′dog, an andiron; fire′-drake, a fire-breathing dragon: a luminous phenomenon: a kind of firework; fire′-drill, a primitive instrument for getting fire by twirling a stick: practice in putting out or escaping from fire; fire′-eat′er, a juggler who seems to eat fire: a seeker of quarrels; fire′-edge (*dial.*), a cutting edge hardened by fire: crispness in a newly baked cake: first eagerness; fire′-engine, an engine or pump for extinguishing fires; fire′-escape′, a fixed or movable way of escape from a burning building; fire′-extinguisher, a contrivance for ejecting chemicals to put out fires.—*adj.* fire′-eyed (*Shak.*), having fiery eyes.—fire′-fighter, a fireman; fire′-fighting; fire′-flag (*Coleridge*), fire′-flaught (*Swinburne*), a flash of fire, lightning, etc.; fire′float, a boat or raft used in harbours for extinguishing fires; fire′fly, an insect, generally a beetle, that emits light by night; fire′-grate, a grating to hold a fire; fire′guard, a

protective wire-frame or railing in front of a fireplace; fire′-hook, a hook formerly used to tear down burning buildings; fire′-hose, hose for extinguishing fires; fire′house, a house with a fireplace, a dwelling house; fire′-insu′rance, insurance against loss by fire; fire′-irons, fireside implements—poker, tongs, shovel—not necessarily of iron; fire′light, the light of a domestic fire; fire′lighter, a readily inflammable material or other means of lighting a fire; fire′-lock, a gun discharged by a lock with flint and steel; fire′man, one whose function is to assist in putting out fires and rescuing those in danger: a stoker: a train driver's assistant (stoker on steam engine): one who attends to conditions of safety in a mine: one who explodes charges; fire′mark, a metal plate formerly placed by insurance companies to mark an insured building; fire′-mar′shal (*U.S.*), fire′-mas′ter, head of a fire brigade.—*adj.* fire′-new, new from the fire: brand-new.—fire′-office, a fire insurance office; fire′-o′pal, a flame-coloured variety of opal; fire′pan, a metal vessel for holding fire; fire′-place, the place in a house appropriated to the fire, as the opening of a chimney into a room; fire′-plough (*U.S.* -plow; *archaeol.*), a stick rubbed in a wooden groove to make fire; fire′-plug, a hydrant for use against fires; fire′-pol′icy, a written instrument of insurance against fire; fire′pot, an earthen pot full of combustibles, used as a missile; fire′-power (*mil.*), the weight of missiles that can be fired with effect in a given time.—*adj.* fire′proof, proof against fire: incombustible (see curtain).—*v.t.* to render fire-proof.—fire′proofing; fire′-raiser, an incendiary; fire′-raising, arson.—*adjs.* fire′-resist′ing, immune to effects of fire up to a required degree; fire′-risk; fire′-robed (*Shak.*), robed in fire.—fire′screen, a screen for intercepting the heat of a fire; fire′ship, a ship carrying combustibles sent among the enemy's ships; fire′-shovel; fire′side, the side of the fireplace: the hearth: home.—*adj.* domestic: familiar.—fire′-step, fir′ing-step, a ledge on which soldiers stand to fire over a parapet: a banquette; fire′-stick, a primitive implement for getting fire by friction; fire′stone, a rock, esp. a sandstone, that stands much heat without injury; fire′-tube, a tube through which fire passes; fire′-walk, -ing, the ceremony of walking barefoot over hot stones, ashes, etc.; fire′-walker; fire′-war′den (*U.S.*), an official charged with prevention and extinction of fires; fire′-watch′er, one who watches against fire; fire′-watch′ing; fire′-wa′ter, ardent spirits; fire′weed, the rose-bay willow-herb, which springs up after forest, etc., fires; fire′-wood, wood for fuel; fire′work, a combustible or explosive composition used in warfare, or a projectile carrying it (*obs.*): a contrivance for producing sparks, jets, flares, or glowing pictorial designs in fire for amusement: (now only *pl.*) a display of these: (*pl.*) a florid technical display in music, talk, etc.; fire′worm, a glow-worm: a firefly; fire′-wor′ship, worship of fire: loosely, homage to fire (as among Parsees) as a symbol of deity but not itself a god; fire′-wor′shipper; fir′ing line, area or troops within range of the enemy for practical purposes; fir′ing par′ty, a detachment told off to fire over a grave or shoot a condemned prisoner; fir′ing pin, a pin that strikes the detonator and explodes the cartridge in a rifle; fir′ing point, the temperature at which an inflammable oil takes fire spontaneously; firing squad, firing party, a detachment told off to shoot a condemned prisoner.—catch or take fire, to become ignited: to become aroused about something; fire and brimstone, hell—an exclamation of wrath or extreme irritation; fire and sword, military devastation; fire away, (*interj.*; *coll.*), go ahead: begin;

**fire off**, to discharge: to ask, utter in rapid succession; **fire out** (*Shak.*), to expel; **fire up**, to start a fire: to fly into a passion; **hang fire** (see **hang**); **on fire**, in a state of fiery combustion; **play with fire**, to expose oneself to unnecessary risk: to treat lightly a situation which could prove dangerous; **St Anthony's**, **St Elmo's fire** (see **Saint**); **set on fire**, **set fire to**, to ignite; **under fire**, exposed to the enemy's fire: exposed to criticism. [O.E. *fȳr*; Ger. *feuer*; Gr. *pȳr*.]

**firk**, *fûrk*, *v.t.* to drive: to rouse: to whip or beat (*Shak.*). [O.E. *fercian*, to conduct.]

**firkin**, *fûr'kin*, *n.* a measure equal to the fourth part of a barrel (*brewing*): 9 gallons (*brewing*): 56 lb. of butter. [With dim. suf. *-kin*, from Old Du. *vierde*, fourth.]

**firlot**, *fûr'lət*, *n.* an old Scottish dry measure, the fourth part of a boll. [Earlier *ferthelot*; cf. O.N. *fiŏrthe hlotr*, fourth lot.]

**firm**, *fûrm*, *adj.* fixed: compact: strong: not easily moved or disturbed: unshaken: resolute: decided.—Also *adv.*—*v.t.* to make firm.—*v.i.* to become firm.—*adj.* **firm'less**, wavering.—*adv.* **firm'ly.**—*n.* **firm'ness.** [O.Fr. *ferme*—L. *firmus.*]

**firm**, *fûrm*, *n.* the title under which a company transacts business: a business house or partnership. [It. *firma*, from L. *firmus*; see **farm**.]

**firmament**, *fûr'mə-mənt*, *n.* the solid sphere in which the stars' were thought to be fixed: the sky.—*adj.* **firmament'al** (*-ment'l*). [L. *firmāmentum*—*firmus*, firm.]

**firman**, *fûr'man*, or *fer-män'*, *n.* a decree. [Pers. *fermän*.]

**firn**, *firn*, or *fûrn*, *n.* snow on high glaciers while still granular. [Ger. *firn*, of last year; cf. obs. Eng. *fern*, former.]

**firring.** Same as **furring.**

**first**, *fûrst*, *adj.* foremost: before all others: most eminent: chief: referring to the speaker or writer (*gram.*).—*n.* one who or that which is first or of the first class: a place in the first class: first gear.—*adv.* before anything else.— *n.* **first'ling**, the first produce or offspring, esp. of animals.—*adv.* **first'ly**, in the first place.— **first'-aid'**, treatment of a wounded or sick person before the doctor's arrival.—*adjs.* **first'-begott'en**, begotten first: eldest; **first'-born**, born first.—*n.* the first in the order of birth: the eldest child.—*adj.* **first'-class'**, of the first class, rank, or quality.—**first'-day**, Sunday; **first'-floor'** (*adj.* **first'-floor**; see **floor**); **first'-foot'** (*Scot.*), the first person to enter a house after the beginning of the new year.—*v.t.* to visit as first-foot.—*v.i.* to go around making visits as first-foot.—**first'-foot'er**; **first'-fruit(s)'**, the fruits first gathered in a season: first products or effects of anything: payment such as annates to a superior; **first gear** (see **gear**). —*adj.* **first'-hand**, obtained directly, without an intermediary.—*adv.* **first-hand'.—first name**, Christian name, or name that comes first in full name; **first'-night'**, the first night of a performance; **first-night'er**, one who habitually goes to the theatre on first-nights; **first'-offend'er**, one convicted for the first time.— *adj.* **first'-rate'**, of highest rate or excellence: pre-eminent in quality, size, or estimation.— *n.* a warship so rated.—*adv.* **first-rate'**, excellently.—*adj.* **first'-time**, immediate.—**first water**, the first or highest quality, purest lustre—of diamonds and pearls.—**first-class mail**, mail sent at a higher rate to obtain quicker delivery.—**not to know the first thing about**, to know nothing about; **(the) first thing**, before doing anything else. [O.E. *fyrst*, superl.; cf. *fore*, before.]

**firth**, *fûrth*, *n.* an arm of the sea, esp. a river-mouth.—Also **frith.** [O.N. *fiŏrthr*; Norw. *fjord*.]

**firth.** See **frith** (3).

**fisc, fisk**, *fisk*, *n.* the state treasury: the public revenue: one's purse.—*adj.* **fisc'al**, pertaining to the public treasury or revenue.—*n.* a treasurer (*obs.*): a public prosecutor, chief law officer of the crown under the Holy Roman Empire (*hist.*): in Scot. an officer who prosecutes in criminal cases in local and inferior courts—in full, *procurator-fiscal.*—**the fiscal question**, free trade or protection. [L. *fiscus*, a basket, a purse.]

**fisgig.** See **fizgig.**

**fish**, *fish*, *n.* a vertebrate that lives in water and breathes through gills: loosely, any exclusively aquatic animal: fish flesh: person:—*pl.* **fish**, or **fish'es.**—*v.i.* to catch or try to catch or obtain fish, or anything that may be likened to a fish (as seals, sponges, coral, compliments, information, husbands; often with *for*): to serve the purpose of fishing.—*v.t.* to catch and bring out of water: to bring up or out from a deep or hidden place, obscurity or the like: to elicit (with *out*): to practise the fisher's craft in: to ransack: to hoist the flukes of.—*adj.* **fish'able.** —*ns.* **fish'er**, one who fishes for sport or gain: the pekan or wood-shock (an inappropriate name); **fish'ery**, the business of catching fish: a place for catching fish: right of fishing.—*adj.* **fish'ful**, abounding in fish.—*v.t.* **fish'ify** (*Shak.*), to turn to fish.—*n.* **fish'iness.**—*adj.* **fish'ing**, used in fishing.—*n.* the art or practice of catching fish.—*adj.* **fish'y**, consisting of fish: like a fish abounding in fish: dubious, as a story: equivocal, unsafe.—**fish'ball**, **-cake**, a ball of chopped fish and mashed potatoes, fried.—*adj.* **fish'-bell'ied**, swelled out downward like the belly of a fish.—**fish'-bone**; **fish'-carv'er**, **fish'-slice**, **fish'-trowel**, a large flat implement for carving fish at table; **fish'-creel**, an angler's basket: a fishwife's basket: **fish'-day**, a day on which fish is eaten instead of meat.—**fish'(-dive')** (*slang*), a ballerina's leap on to a partner's outstretched arms; **fish'erman**, a fisher; **fisherman's luck**, getting wet and catching no fish; **fisherman's ring**, a signet ring, with the device of St Peter fishing, used in signing papal briefs; **fish'eye** (*slang*), an unfriendly, suspicious stare; **fish'eye lens** (*phot.*), an ultra-wide-angle lens covering up to 180°; **fish'-fag**, a woman who sells fish; **fish'-farming**, rearing fish in ponds or tanks; **fish'-garth**, an enclosure on a river for the preserving or taking of fish—also **fish'-weir**; **fish'-glue**, glue made from the sounds of fish; **fish'-god**, a deity in form wholly or partly like a fish, like the Philistine Dagon; **fish'-guano**, fishmanure.—*n.pl.* **fish'-guts.**—**fish'-gutter**; **fish'-gutting**, fish-hatch'ery, a station for artificial rearing of fish; **fish'-hawk**, osprey; **fish'-hook**, a barbed hook for catching fish; **fish'ing-frog**, the angler-fish; **fish'ing-rod**, a long slender rod to which a line is fastened for angling; **fish'ing-tack'le**, tackle—nets, lines, etc.—used in fishing; **fish'-kett'le**, a long oval dish for boiling fish; **fish'-ladd'er**, **fish'-way**, an arrangement of steps and shelters for enabling a fish to ascend a fall, etc.; **fish'-louse**, a copepod or other crustacean parasitic on fishes; **fish'-manure**, fish used as a fertiliser; **fish'-meal**, dried fish ground to meal: (*Shak.*) a meal of fish: abstemious diet; **fish'monger**, a dealer in fish.—*adj.* **fish'-net**, woven as a fine net.—**fish'-oil**, oil got from fishes and other marine animals; **fish'-packing**, the process of canning fish; **fish'-pond**, a pond in which fish are kept—formerly also **fish'-stew**; **fish'-sales'man**, one who receives consignments of fish for sale by auction to retail dealers; **fish'-sauce**, sauce proper to be eaten with fish; **fish'-scrap**, fish or fish-skins from which oil or glue has been extracted; **fish'skin**, the skin of a fish: ichthyosis; **fish'-spear**, a spear or dart for striking fish; **fish'-stew**, fish-pond; **fish'-strainer**, a metal colander for taking fish from a boiler.— *adj.* **fish'-tail**, shaped like the tail of a fish.—

*v.i.* to swing the tail of an aircraft from side to side to reduce speed while gliding downward; fish'-torpē'do, a self-propelling torpedo; fish'-way, fish-ladder; *obs.* fish'-weir, fish-garth; fish'wife, fish'-woman, a woman who carries fish about for sale; fish'yback (*U.S.*), transportation of freight containers and trailers by ship or barge.—a fish out of water, a person in an unaccustomed, unsuitable situation which makes him ill at ease; drink like a fish, to drink to excess; fish in troubled waters, to take advantage of disturbed times to further one's own interests; have other fish to fry, to have something else to do or attend to; make fish of one and flesh (or fowl) of another, to make invidious distinctions; neither fish nor flesh (nor good red herring), or neither fish, flesh, nor fowl, neither one thing nor another; odd fish or queer fish, a person of odd habits, or of a nature with which one is not in sympathy; pretty kettle of fish (see kettle). [O.E. *fisc*; Ger. *fisch*; O.N. *fiskr*; L. *piscis*; Gael. *iasg*.]

fish, *fish, n.* a piece of wood placed alongside another to strengthen it (*naut.*): a counter for games.—*v.t.* to strengthen with a fish or fish-plate.—fish'-joint, a joining by fish-plates; fish'-plate, an iron plate used in pairs to join railway rails. [Prob. Fr. *fiche*, peg, mark.]

fishgig. See fizgig.

fisk, *fisk, (obs.) v.i.* to frisk, to gad. [Prob. a freq. of O.E. *fỹsan*, to hurry, or of *fỹsian*, to feeze.]

fisnomie, *fiz'no-mi, n.* Shak. for physiognomy.

fissile, *fis'il, -il, adj.* readily split.—*ns.* fissility (*-il'*), cleavableness; fission (*fish'ən*), a cleaving: reproduction by dividing: the splitting of the nucleus of an atom into two roughly equal parts accompanied by great release of energy.—*adjs.* fiss'ionable, capable of nuclear fission; fiss'ive.—*n.* fissure (*fish'ər*), act of cleaving: a narrow opening—chasm, cleft, groove: a sulcus, esp. one of the furrows on the surface of the brain, as the longitudinal fissure separating the hemispheres.—*adj.* fiss'ured, cleft, divided.—*adjs.* fissicos'tate (L. *costa*, rib), with divided ribs; fissiling'ual (L. *lingua*, tongue), with cloven tongue.—*ns.* fissip'arism (L. *parēre*, bring forth), fissipar'ity.—*adj.* fissip'arous, reproducing by fission.—*adv.* fissip'arously.—*adj.* fiss'ipēd, fiss'ipēde (L. *pēs, pedis*, foot), with digits separate.—*n.* an animal with digits separate.—*adjs.* fissiros'tral (L. *rōstrum*, beak), with deep-cleft or gaping beak.—fission bomb, a bomb deriving its energy from atomic fission; fission fungus, a bacterium; fission spectrum, the wide range of elements and isotopes formed in fission. [L. *findēre, fissum*, to cleave.]

fissle, *fis'l, (Scot.) v.i.* to rustle. [Imitative.]

fissure, fissured. See fissile.

fist, *fist, n.* the closed or clenched hand: handwriting (*coll.*).—*v.t.* to strike or grip with the fist.—*n.* fistiana (*-ä'nə, -ā'nə*; *facet.*), anecdotes about boxing and boxers.—*adjs.* fist'ic, -al (*facet.*), pugilistic.—*n.* fist'ful, a handful.—*adj.* fist'y.—fisti'cuff, a blow with the fist: (*pl.*) boxing: (*pl.*) a fight with fists; fist'-law, the law of brute force. [O.E. *fŷst*; Ger. *faust.*]

fistula, *fist'ū-lə, n.* a narrow passage or duct: an artificially-made opening (*med.*): a long narrow pipe-like ulcer (*path.*): a tube through which the wine of the eucharist was once sucked from the chalice—also *calamus.*—*adjs.* fist'ūlar, fist'ūlose, fist'ūlous. [L. *fistula*, a pipe.]

fit, *fit, adj.* suitable: in suitable condition: of suitable ability: convenient: befitting: well trained and ready: in good condition.—*n.* success in fitting: adjustment and correspondence in shape and size: a thing (esp. a garment) that fits.—*v.t.* to make suitable or able: to alter or make so as to be in adjustment: to adjust: to

piece together: to be suitable or becoming for: to be of such size and shape as to adjust closely to: to be in agreement or correspondence with: to furnish, supply: to drive by fits (*Shak.*).—*v.i.* to be suitable or becoming: to go into place with accurate adjustment to space: to be of such size and shape as to be able to do so:—*pr.p.* fitt'ing; *pa.t.* and *pa.p.* fitt'ed.—*adv.* fit'ly (*comp.* fit'lier; *superl.* fit'liest).—*ns.* fit'ment, due (*Shak.*): something fitted to an end (*Shak.*): an article of furniture or equipment: a fitting; fit'ness; fitt'er, he who, or that which fits or makes fit: one who fits on clothes: one who assembles the parts of a machine, etc.—*adj.* fitt'ing, fit: appropriate.—*n.* anything used in fitting up, esp. in *pl.*, equipment accessories: a fixture: the work of a fitter.—*adv.* fitt'ingly.—fit'-out, outfit; fitt'ing-out, a supply of things fit and necessary; fitt'ing-shop, a shop in which pieces of machinery are fitted together; fit'-up, (*theat.*) temporary, improvised stage and properties.—fit on, to try on: to try on a garment upon; fit out, to furnish, equip; fit up, to provide with fittings. [Origin obscure.]

fit, *fit, n.* a crisis (*obs.*): the approach of death (*Spens.*): a painful experience (*Spens.*): an attack of illness, esp. epilepsy: a convulsion or paroxysm: an access, temporary attack, or outburst of anything, as laughter: a sudden effort or motion: a mood or passing humour.—*v.t.* (*Shak.*), to wrench, cause to start, as by a fit.—*adj.* fit'ful, marked by sudden impulses: capriciously intermittent: spasmodic.—*adv.* fit'fully.—*n.* fit'fulness.—fit of the face, a grimace; fits and starts, spasmodic and irregular bursts of activity; throw a fit (see under throw). [O.E. *fitt*, a struggle.]

fit, *fit, (arch.) n.* a song: a division of a poem, a canto: a strain.—Also fitt, fitte, fytte. [O.E. *fitt*, a song.]

fitch, *fich, n.* vetch: in Isa. xxviii. 25, black cummin (*Nigella sativa*): in Ezek. iv. 9, spelt. [vetch.]

fitch, *fich, n.* a polecat: polecat fur: a paintbrush of polecat-hair: a small hog's-hair brush.—*ns.* fitch'et, fitchew (*fich'ōō*), the polecat or its fur. [M.Du. *visse* and O.Fr. *fissel, fissau*, from the root of Du. *visse*, nasty.]

fitché, fitchée, *fich'ā*, (*her.*) *adj.* cut to a point.—Also fitch'y. [Fr. *fiché*, pa.p. of *ficher*, to fix.]

fitz, *fits, pfx.* son of: used in England, esp. of the illegitimate sons of kings and princes, as *Fitzclarence*, etc. [A.Fr. *fiz* (Fr. *fils*)—L. *filius.*]

five, *fiv, adj.* and *n.* four and one.—*n.* a group of five: a score of five points, strokes, etc.: a card with five pips: an article of the size so numbered: the fifth hour after midnight or midday.—*adj.* and *adv.* five'fold, in five divisions: five times as much: folded in five thicknesses.—*n.* fiver (*coll.*), a five-pound note.—Five Articles, Five Points, statements of the distinctive doctrines of the Arminians and Calvinists respectively—the former promulgated in 1610, the latter sustained by the Synod of Dort in 1619 (see Calvinism); five'-a-side, a form of association football played by five men on each side, instead of eleven.—Also *adj.*—*adj.* five'-bar, having five bars.—five-day week, a week, five days of which are working days; five'finger(s), a name for various plants (cinquefoil, oxlip, etc.): a starfish.—*adj.* five'-finger, for five fingers, as a piano exercise.—Five Nations, a confederacy of five northern Iroquoian Indian tribes.—*adj.* five'-parted, in five parts: divided into five nearly to the base.—five'pence.—*adj.* five'penny.—*n.* five'pins, a game with five 'pins', resembling ninepins and tenpins.—*adj.* five'pin, as in fivepin bowling alley.—*adj.* five'-square (*B.*), regularly pentagonal.—bunch of fives, the

fist. [O.E. *fíf*; Ger. *fünf*; Goth. *fimf*; W. *pump*;
L. *quinque*; Gr. *pente, pempe*; Sans. *pañca*.]
**fives**, *fīvz*, (*Shak*.) *n*. Same as vives.
**fives**, *fīvz*, *n.pl*. a ball game played with the
(gloved) hand (or a bat) in a walled court.
[Origin obscure.]
**fix**, *fiks*, *v.t*. to make firm or fast: to establish:
to drive in: to settle: to make or keep permanent, solid, rigid, steady, or motionless: to
fasten or attach: to put to rights, mend: to
arrange, attend to (a matter; sometimes by
means of trickery): to prepare: to prevent from
causing further trouble (*slang*): to get even with
(*slang*): to chastise (*slang*).—*v.i.* to settle or
remain permanently: to become firm, stable or
permanent.—*n*. a difficulty (*coll.*): a dilemma
(*coll.*): the position of an aircraft as calculated
from instrument readings: a shot of heroin or
other drug (*slang*).—*adj*. fix′able, capable of
being fixed.—*v.t*. fix′āte, to fix, make stable:
to direct (the eyes) upon an object: to arrest the
emotional development of (*psych.*).—*ns*. fixā′-
tion, act of fixing, or state of being fixed: steadiness, firmness: state in which a body does not
evaporate: conversion of atmospheric nitrogen
into a combined form: emotional arrest of
personality, instinctive forces maintaining their
earlier channels of gratification: loosely, an
abnormal attachment, or an obsession; fix′ā-
tive, a fixing agent; fix′ature, a gummy preparation for fixing the hair.—*adj*. fixed, settled: not
apt to evaporate: steadily directed: fast, lasting,
permanent: substantively for fixed stars (*Par.
Lost* III, 481).—*adv*. fix′edly.—*ns*. fix′edness;
fix′er; fix′ing, act or process of making fixed:
arrangement: (in *pl.*) adjuncts, trimmings:
equipment; fix′ity, fixedness.—*adj*. fix′ive.—*ns*.
fix′ture, fixing: a movable that has become
fastened to land or to a house: a fixed article
of furniture: a thing or person permanently
established in a place: a fixed or appointed
time or event, as a horse-race; fix′ure (*Shak.*),
stability, position, firmness.—fixed air, the name
given by Dr Joseph Black in 1756 to what in
1784 was named by Lavoisier carbonic acid;
fixed capital (see capital); fixed odds, a betting
method whereby a stated amount per unit
stake is offered for a certain result or combination of results; fixed oils, those which, on the
application of heat, do not volatilise without
decomposition; fixed stars, stars which appear
always to occupy the same position in the
heavens—opp. to *planets*.—fix on, to single out,
decide for; fix up, to arrange or make arrangements for: to settle: to put to rights, attend to.
[L. *fĭgĕre, fĭxus*, to fix, prob. through L.L.
*fixāre*.]
**fizgig, fisgig**, *fiz′gig*, *n*. a giddy girl: a firework of
damp powder: a gimcrack: a crotchet: a
harpoon (also fish′gig). [gig.]
**fizz, fiz**, *fiz*, *v.i*. to make a hissing or sputtering
sound:—*pr.p.* fizz′ing; *pa.t.* and *pa.p.* fizzed.—
*n*. a sputtering sound: a frothy drink, esp.
champagne.—*n*. fizz′er, that which fizzes: anything excellent (*coll.*): a very fast ball.—*n.* and
*adj*. fizz′ing.—*v.i*. fizz′le, to hiss or sputter: to
go out with a sputtering sound (often with *out*):
to come to nothing, be a fiasco: to fail.—*n*. an
abortive effort.—*adj*. fizz′y. [Formed from the
sound.]
**fizzen.** See foison.
**fjord.** Same as fiord.
**flabbergast**, *flab′ər-gäst*, (*coll.*) *v.t*. to stun, confound. [Prob. conn. with flabby and gast, to
astonish.]
**flabby**, *flab′i*, *adj*. soft, yielding: hanging loose.—
*n*. flabb′iness. [flap.]
**flabellum**, *flə-bel′əm*, *n*. a fan, anciently used to
drive away flies from the chalice during the
celebration of the eucharist: a fan-like structure

(*biol.*).—*adj*. flabell′ate, fan-shaped.—*n*. flabella-
tion (*flab-ə-lā′shən*), the action of fanning.—*adj*.
flabell′iform. [L., a fan.]
**flaccid**, *flak′sid*, *adj*. limp: flabby: lax: easily
yielding to pressure: soft and weak: clammy.
—*adv*. flac′cidly.—*ns*. flac′cidness, flaccid′ity.
[L. *flaccidus—flaccus*, flabby.]
**flacker**, *flak′ər*, (*dial.*) *v.i*. to flap, flutter. [Cf.
O.E. *flacor*, fluttering.]
**flacket**, *flak′it*, *n*. a flask, bottle. [O.Fr. *flasquet*.]
**flacon**, *flak-з′*, *n*. a scent-bottle, etc. [Fr.]
**flaff**, *flaf*, (*Scot.*) *v.i*. to flap: to pant.—*n*. a
flutter of the wings: a puff.—*v.i*. flaff′er, to
flutter. [Imit.]
**flag**, *flag*, *v.i*. to droop: to flap feebly: to grow
languid or spiritless:—*pr.p.* flagg′ing; *pa.t.* and
*pa.p.* flagged.—*n*. flagg′iness.—*adj*. flagg′y, limp,
drooping: flabby. [Perh. O.Fr. *flac*—L. *flaccus*;
prob. influenced by imit. forms as flap.]
**flag**, *flag*, *n*. an iris: reed-grass (*B.*).—*n*. flagg′i-
ness.—*adj*. flagg′y, abounding in flags.—flag′-
basket, a reed basket for tools; flag′-worm, a
worm or grub bred among flags or reeds. [Ety.
obscure; cf. Du. *flag*.]
**flag**, *flag*, *n*. a piece usually of bunting with a
design, used as an emblem for military or
naval purposes, signalling, decoration, display,
propaganda, etc.: a conspicuous sign to mark
a position, e.g. of a golf-hole, or convey information, as that a taxi is disengaged: flagship: a
bushy tail.—*v.t*. to decorate with flags: to inform by flag-signals.—*adj*. flagg′y, like a banner:
spreading.—flag′-cap′tain, the captain of a flagship; flag′-day, a day on which collectors levy
contributions to a fund in exchange for small
flags as badges to secure immunity for the rest
of the day: in U.S. the 14th of June, anniversary
of the adoption of the Stars and Stripes; flag′-
lieutenant′, an officer in a flagship, corresponding to an aide-de-camp in the army; flag′-
off′icer, a naval officer privileged to carry a
flag denoting his rank—admiral, vice-admiral,
rear-admiral, or commodore; flagship, the ship
carrying an admiral and flying his flag; flag′-
pole, flag′staff, flag′stick, pole, etc., for displaying a flag; flag′-wagging, signalling by flag:
aggressive patriotism or imperialism (also flag′-
waving).—flag down, to signal (e.g. a car) to
stop; flag of convenience, a foreign flag under
which a shipping company registers its tonnage
to avoid taxation or other burdens at home;
flag of distress, a flag displayed as a signal of
distress—usually upside down or at half-mast;
flag of truce, a white flag displayed during war
when some pacific communication is desired;
black, red, white, yellow flag (see black, red,
white, yellow): dip the flag, to lower the flag
and then hoist it—a token of respect; show
the flag, to put in an appearance, or otherwise
ensure that one, or the nation, firm, etc., one represents, is not overlooked; strike, or lower the
flag, to pull it down as a token of relinquishment of command, respect, submission, or
surrender. [Origin unknown; cf. Dan. *flag*;
Du. *vlag*, Ger. *flagge*.]
**flag**, *flag*, *n*. a stone that separates in slabs: a
flat paving stone.—*v.t*. to pave with flagstones.
—*n*. flagg′ing, flagstones: a pavement thereof.
—*adj*. flagg′y.—flag′stone. [O.N. *flaga*, a slab.]
**flagellum**, *flə-jel′əm*, *n*. a scourge: a long runner
(*bot.*): a long cilium or whip-like appendage
(*biol.*):—*pl.* flagell′a.—*n.pl.* Flagellata (*flaj-ə-
lā′tə*), unicellular organisms with flagella.—*v.t*.
flag′ellate, to scourge.—*adj*. having a flagellum
or flagella.—*adjs*. flag′ellated; flag′ellant, scourg-
ing.—*n*. one who scourges, esp. himself in
religious discipline.—*ns*. flag′ellantism; flagellā′-
tion, flag′ellātor.—*adjs*. flag′ellatory; flagellif′-
erous; flagell′iform. [L. *flagellum*, dim. of
*flagrum*, a whip.]

flageolet, *flaj-ō-let'*, *flaj'*, *n.* a small fipple flute. [Fr., dim. of O.Fr. *flageol*, *flajol*, a pipe; not L. *flauta*, flute.]

flageolet, *flaj-ō-let'*, *n.* a variety of kidney bean. [Corr. of Fr. *fageolet*; L. *faseolus*.]

flagitate, *flaj'i-tāt*, *v.t.* to entreat, importune.—*n.* flagitā'tion. [L. *flagitāre*, *-ātum*.]

flagitious, *flə-jish'əs*, *adj.* grossly wicked: guilty of enormous crimes.—*adv.* flagi'tiously.—*n.* flagi'tiousness. [L. *flāgitiōsus—flāgitium*, a disgraceful act—*flagrāre*, to burn.]

flagon, *flag'ən*, *n.* a large, esp. wide, bottle: a liquor-jug. [Fr. *flacon—flascon*—L.L. *flascō*, *-ōnis*; see flask.]

flagrant, *flā'grənt*, *adj.* burning or raging (*arch.*): notorious: outrageous, conspicuous.—*ns.* flā'grance, flā'grancy.—*adv.* flā'grantly. [L. *flagrāns*, *-antis*, pr.p. of *flagrāre*, to burn.]

flagrante bello, *flə-gran'tē be'lō*, *fla-gran'te*, (L.) while war is raging; flagrante delicto, *di-lik'tō*, *dä-lik'tō*, in the very act (lit. 'while the crime is blazing').

flail, *flāl*, *n.* an implement for threshing corn, consisting of a wooden bar (the *swingle*) hinged or tied to a handle: a mediaeval weapon with spiked iron swingle.—*v.t.* to strike with, or as if with, a flail.—Also *v.i.* [O.E. *fligel*, influenced by O.Fr. *flaiel*, prob. from L. *flagellum*, a scourge.]

flair, *flār*, *n.* intuitive discernment: faculty for nosing out: popularly and loosely, a natural aptitude. [Fr., scent.]

flak, *flak*, (*mil. slang*) *n.* anti-aircraft protection, missiles, or fragments. [Initials of Ger. *flieger-* (or *flug-*)*abwehrkanone*, anti-aircraft cannon.]

flake, *flāk*, *n.* a small flat scale or layer: a very small loose mass, as of snow: a spark or detached flame: a flash (*Spens.*).—*v.t.* to form into flakes.—*v.i.* to come off in flakes.—*n.* flak'iness.—*adj.* flak'y.—flake'-white, the purest white-lead for painting, made in the form of scales or plates.—flake out, to collapse from weariness or illness. [Perh. conn. with O.N. *flōke*, flock of wool; O.H.G. *floccho*.]

flake, *flāk*, *n.* a movable hurdle for fencing: a stage hung over a ship's side for caulking, etc. (*naut.*): a frame or rack. [Cf. O.N. *flake*; Du. *vlaak*.]

flam, *flam*, *n.* a whim (*arch.*): an idle fancy (*arch.*): a falsehood.—*v.t.* to deceive. [Perh. flim-flam or flamfew.]

flam, flamm. Same as flawn.

flambé, *fläm'bā*, *flä-bā*, *adj.* of a Chinese ceramic glaze, dense and iridescent with streaky colour effect (usu. red and blue) produced by irregular application or uneven firing: decorated with such a glaze: (also flambéed, *fläm-bād*) in cookery, prepared or served with a dressing of flaming liquor, usu. brandy. [Fr., pa.p. of *flamber*, to flame, singe.]

flambeau, *flam'bō*, *n.* a flaming torch:—*pl.* flam'-beaux, *-bōz*. [Fr.,—O.Fr. *flambe*—L. *flamma*.]

flamboyant, *flam-boi'ənt*, *adj.* late French Gothic (15th-16th cent.) with flame-like tracery (*archit.*): of wavy form: gorgeously coloured: (of person, style, action, etc.) ostentatious, colourful.—*n.* (also flamboy'ante) a tropical tree of the Caesalpinia family (*Poinciana regia*) with flame-coloured flowers.—*ns.* flamboy'ance, flamboy'-ancy.—*adv.* flamboy'antly.—flamboy'ant(e)-tree. [Fr., pr.p. of *flamboyer*, to blaze.]

flame, *flām*, *n.* a gaseous matter undergoing combustion: the gleam or blaze of a fire: rage: ardour of temper: vigour of thought: warmth of affection: love or its object.—*v.i.* to burn as flame: to break out in passion.—*v.t.* to set aflame.—*adj.* flamed (*Spens.*), inflamed.—*adj.* flame'less.—*n.* flame'let, a small flame.—*adj.* flam'ing, brilliantly red: gaudy: violent: furious: flagrant.—*adv.* flam'ingly.—*n.* flammabil'ity.—*adjs.* flamm'able, inflammable.

flammif'erous, producing flame; flam'y, pertaining to, or like, flame.—*adj.* flame'-coloured (*Shak.*), of the colour of flame, bright reddish-yellow.—flame'-leaf, Poinciana; flame'-thrower, an apparatus for throwing jets of flame in warfare. [O.Fr. *flambe*—L. *flamma*.]

flamen, *flā'mən*, *n.* in ancient Rome a priest of one particular god.—*adj.* flamin'ical. [L. *flāmen*, *-inis*.]

flamenco, *flä-meng'kō*, *n.* a type of gypsy song or dance from Andalusia. [Sp., 'Flemish', flamingo, gypsy.]

flamfew, *flam'fū*, *n.* a fantastic trifle. [Fr. *fanfelue*.]

Flamingant, *flä-mē-gä*, *n.* one who favours the Flemish language or Flemish nationalism. [Fr.]

flamingo, *flə-ming'gō*, *n.* a tropical or subtropical bird of a pink or bright-red colour, with long legs and neck:—*pl.* flaming'o(e)s. [Sp. *flamengo* (now *flamenco*).]

flammability, flammable. See flame.

flammenwerfer, *fläm'ən-ver-fer*, (Ger.) a flame-thrower.

flammiferous. See flame.

flammule, *flam'ūl*, *n.* a little flame, as in a picture of a Japanese god.—*adj.* flamm'ūlāted, ruddy.—*n.* flammūlā'tion, flamelike marking. [L. *flammula*, dim. of *flamma*, flame.]

flan, *flan*, *n.* a flat open tart. [See flawn.]

flanch, *flanch*, *-sh*, *n.* a flange: an ordinary formed on each side of a shield by the segment of a circle (*her.*).—*adj.* flanched, charged with a pair of flanches. [Prob. related to flank.]

flanch, *flanch*, *-sh*, *v.i.* to widen, esp. outwards or upwards: to flare. [Ety. obscure.]

flanconade, *flang-kə-nād'*, (*fencing*) *n.* a thrust in the flank or side. [Fr., from *flanc*, the side.]

flâneur, *flä-nœr'*, *n.* one who saunters about, a stroller.—*n.* flânerie (*flän-rē*), idling. [Fr. *flâner*, to lounge.]

flange, *flanj*, *n.* a projecting or raised edge of flank, as of a wheel or of a rail.—*v.i.* to widen out.—*v.t.* to put a flange on.—*adj.* flanged. [Perh. conn. with flank.]

flank, *flangk*, *n.* the side of an animal from the ribs to the thigh: the side or wing of anything, esp. of an army or fleet: a body of soldiers on the right or left extremity.—*v.t.* to be on, pass round, attack, threaten, or protect the flank of.—*n.* flank'er, a fortification that commands the flank of an assailing force.—*v.t.* (*obs.*), to defend by flankers: to attack sideways. [Fr. *flanc*.]

flannel, *flan'əl*, *n.* a soft woollen cloth of loose texture for an undergarment, etc.: the garment itself: a piece of flannel or other material used to wash or rub something: flattery, soft-soap: (*pl.*) trousers worn as sportswear or casual wear.—*v.t.* to wrap in or rub with flannel: to flatter, to soft-soap.—*n.* flannelette', a cotton imitation of flannel.—*adjs.* flann'elled; flann'elly.—*n.* flann'en (*obs.* or *dial.*), flannel.—flann'elgraph, a board covered with flannel or felt, and letters, pictures, etc., backed with material which will stick when pressed against the board. [Poss. O.Fr. *flaine*, blanket, or Welsh *gwlanen—gwlan*, wool.]

flap, *flap*, *n.* the blow or motion of a broad loose object: anything broad and flexible hanging loose, as material covering an opening: skin or flesh detached from the underlying part for covering and growing over the end of an amputated limb: a fluster, a panic (*coll.*): any surface attached to the wing of an aircraft which can be adjusted in flight to alter the lift as a whole.—*v.t.* to beat or move with a flap: to fluster.—*v.i.* to move as wings: to hang like a flap: to get into a panic or fluster:—*pr.p.* flapp'ing; *pa.t.* and *pa.p.* flapped.—*ns.* flapp'er, one who or that which flaps: a flipper; young wild duck or partridge: a girl nearing womanhood (*slang*): a

flighty young girl (*slang*); **flapp′erhood.**—*adjs.*
**flapp′erish; flapp′ing,** moving with or like a flap:
not subject to Jockey Club or National Hunt
Committee regulations (*racing*): not registered
under the National Greyhound Racing Club
(*greyhound racing*).—**flap′doodle,** the food of
fools: gross flattery, etc.: nonsense; **flap′-
dragon,** a game in which small edibles, as raisins,
are snatched from burning brandy, and swallowed.—*adj.* **flap′-eared** (*Shak.*).—**flap′jack,** a
kind of broad, flat pancake (*Shak.*): an apple-
puff (*dial.*): a biscuit made with rolled oats and
syrup: a flat face-powder compact.—*adj.* **flap′-
mouthed.** [Prob. imit.]
**flare,** *flār, v.i.* to spread: to wave: to widen out
bell-wise: to burn with a glaring, unsteady
light: glitter, flash: blaze up, lit. or in anger
(with *up*): display glaringly.—*n.* a widening out,
as in the bell of a horn, a bowl, a skirt: an
unsteady glare: an unshaded flame: a sudden
blaze: a torch: a signalling light.—*adj.* **flār′ing.**
—*adv.* **flā′ringly.**—*adj.* **flā′ry.**—**flare′-up; flare′-
path,** a path lit up to enable an aircraft to land
or take off when natural visibility is insufficient.
[Poss. conn. with Norw. *flara,* to blaze.]
**flaser,** *flā′zər, n.* irregular streaky lenticular
structure developed in metamorphic rocks.
[Ger., streak.]
**flash,** *flash, n.* a momentary gleam of light: a
sudden burst, as of merriment: a moment, an
instant: a sudden rush of water: a board for
deepening or directing a stream of water: a
bright garter or ribbon worn with knickerbockers or kilt, a small portion showing below
the knee: a distinctive mark on a uniform:
thieves′ slang: a brief news dispatch by telegraph: in a film, a scene shown momentarily by
way of explanation or comment, especially
(**flash-back**) a scene of the past: vulgar ostentation (*coll.*): a thin piece of metal at the sides of a
forging, or a similar extrusion in other materials:
excess material forced out of a mould.—*adj.*
showy: vulgar: pertaining to the criminal class
and its speech: fashionable (*arch.*).—*v.i.* to
break forth, as a sudden light (*lit.* and *fig.*): to
give forth flashes of light: to sparkle brilliantly:
to blaze out: to break out into intellectual
brilliancy: to burst out into violence: to move
like a flash.—*v.t.* to cause to flash: to expand, as
blown glass, into a disk: to send by some
startling or sudden means.—*n.* flash′er, one who
flashes: a device for turning off and on lights
in an advertising display.—*adv.* flash′ily.—*ns.*
**flashi′ness; flash′ing,** the act of blazing: a
sudden burst, as of water: (a method of producing) irregular colouring of bricks (by
periodically stopping air supply in burning them,
or other means): a strip put over a junction
to make it watertight.—*adj.* emitting flashes:
sparkling.—*adj.* flash′y, dazzling for a moment:
showy but empty: vapid (*Milt.*): gaudy:
tawdry.—**flash′-board,** one of a set of boards set
up at the sides of a water-channel to deepen it;
**flash′-bulb,** an oxygen-filled electric bulb in
which aluminium or other foil or filament may
be fired to provide a brilliant flash; **flash′-gun,**
device holding and firing a flash-bulb; **flash′-
house,** a brothel; **flash′light,** a light that flashes
periodically: a sudden light used to take
photographs: an electric torch; **flash′-point,**
the temperature at which a liquid gives off
enough inflammable vapour to flash when a light
is applied to it: a point in the development of a
tense situation when violent action takes place.—
**flash in the pan** (see **pan**); **news′-flash,** brief
preliminary dispatch about news just becoming
known. [Prob. imit.; cf. Sw. dial. *flasa,* to
blaze.]
**flask,** *flåsk, n.* a narrow-necked vessel for holding
liquids: a bottle: a pocket-bottle: a horn or

metal vessel for carrying powder.—*n.* **flask′et,** a
vessel in which viands are served: a basket
(*Spens.*). [O.E. *flasce*; Ger. *flasche*; prob. from
L.L. *flascō*—L. *vasculum,* a flask.]
**flat,** *flat, adj.* smooth: level: wanting points of
prominence or interest: monotonous: uniform:
vapid, no longer brisk or sparkling: defeated:
failing of effect: dejected: downright, out-and-
out, sheer: (of feet) having little or no arch:
relatively low (*mus.*): below the right pitch
(*mus.*): having flats in the key-signature (*mus.*):
voiced (*phon.*).—*n.* a level part: a plain: a tract
covered by shallow water: something broad: a
story or floor of a house, esp. one, or part of one,
used as a separate residence: the floor of a
particular compartment (*naut.*): a flat piece of
scenery slid or lowered on to the stage: an
insipid passage: a simpleton: a character (♭)
that lowers a note a semitone (*mus.*): a note so
lowered (*mus.*): black key on a piano: a
punctured tyre.—*adv.* in or to a flat position:
evenly: too low in pitch: without qualification:
exactly (used in giving time taken for e.g. a race).
—*n.* flat′let, a small flat of two or three rooms.
—*advs.* flat′ling, flat′lings, flat′long (*Spens.,
Shak.*), with the flat side: flat side on: not
edgewise: prostrate; flat′ly.—*n.* flat′ness.—*adj.*
flatt′ed, made flat: divided into flats.—*v.t.*
flatt′en, to make flat: to knock to the ground: to
knock out: to amaze.—*v.i.* to become flat.—*n.*
flatt′ing, painting leaving a non-glossy finish.—
*adj.* flatt′ish, somewhat flat.—*adj.* or *adv.*
flat′ways, flat′wise, with or on the flat side.—
**flat′boat,** large flat-bottomed boat for floating
goods downstream; **flat′-cap,** low-crowned cap
worn by London citizens in 16th and 17th
centuries: London citizen or apprentice; **flat′-
fish,** marine fish that habitually lies on one side,
with unsymmetrical flat body—flounder, turbot,
etc.; **flat′-foot,** condition in which arch of instep
is flattened: policeman (*slang*).—*adj.* **flat′-
footed,** having flat feet: resolute (*U.S.*): ponderous: unimaginative: uninspired.—**flat′-
footedness.**—*adj.* **flat′head,** having an artificially
flattened head, as some American Indians.—
Also *n.*—(as *U.S. slang*) simpleton.—**flat′iron,**
an iron for smoothing cloth; **flat′-race,** a race
over open or clear ground; **flat rate,** a fixed
uniform rate; **flat spin,** rotation about a
horizontal axis: confused excitement; **flat tyre**
(*U.S.*), a dull and spiritless person; **flat′-worm,** a
tapeworm or other member of the Platyhelminthes.—**flatten out,** to bring an aeroplane into
a horizontal position; **flat out,** at full speed:
using every effort; **that′s flat,** I tell you plainly;
**the flat,** the horse flat-racing season. [O.N.
*flatr,* flat.]
**flatter,** *flat′ər, v.t.* to treat with insincere praise
and servile attentions: to please with false
hopes or undue praise: to overpraise: to represent over-favourably: to coax: to please with
belief: to gratify.—*n.* flatt′erer.—*adj.* flatt′ering.
—*adv.* flatt′eringly.—*n.* flatt′ery, exaggerated or
insincere praise. [Conn. with O.Fr. *flater* (Fr.
*flatter*); Gmc.; cf. O.N. *flathra*.]
**flatus,** *flā′təs, n.* a puff of wind: a blast: a breath:
gas generated in the stomach or intestines.—*ns.*
flatulence (*flat′ū-ləns*), flat′ulency, distension of
stomach or bowels by gases formed during
digestion: windiness: emptiness of utterance.—
*adj.* flat′ulent.—*adv.* flat′ulently.—*adj.* flat′ious.
[L. *flātus, -ūs,* a blowing—*flāre,* to blow.]
**flaught,** *flöt,* (*Scot. flöhht*), *n.* a flight, a flapping.—
*n.* flaugh′ter, a fluttering motion.—*v.i.* to flutter,
flicker. [Related to **flight**.]
**flaught,** *flöt* (*Scot. flöhht*), *n.* a flake: a hide: a
gust: a flash: a spark: a turf.—*v.t.* to pare,
skin, card.—*v.i.* flaugh′ter, to cut turfs, etc.—*n.* a
paring of turf. [Cf. **flake** (1), **flaw** (1), **flay**.]
**flaune.** See **flawn**.

**flaunt**, *flönt*, *v.i.* to wave in the wind: to move ostentatiously: to carry a gaudy or saucy appearance.—*v.t.* to display ostentatiously.—*n.* (*Shak.*) anything displayed for show.—*n.* **flaunt′er**—*adjs.* **flaunt′ing**, **flaunt′y**.—*adv.* **flaunt′ingly**. [Prob. Scand.]

**flautist**, *flöt′ist*, *n.* a flute player. [It. *flautista.*]

**flavescent**, *fla-*, *flā-ves′ənt*, *adj.* yellowish or turning yellow. [L. *flāvēscēns*, *-entis*, pr.p. of *flāvēscĕre*, to become yellow—*flāvus*, yellow.]

**Flavian**, *flāv′i-ən*, *adj.* of or pertaining to *Flavius* Vespasian and his sons Titus and Domitian, the Flavian emperors of Rome (A.D. 69-96).

**flavin**, *flā′vin*, **flavine**, *flā′vēn*, *n.* a yellow dye made from quercitron bark. [L. *flāvus*, yellow.]

**flavour**, *flā′vər*, *n.* that quality of anything which affects the smell or taste: a smack or relish: characteristic quality or atmosphere (*fig*).—*v.t* to impart flavour to.—*adj.* **flā′vourous.**—*n.* **flā′vouring**, any substance used to give a flavour.—*adjs.* **flā′vourless**; **flā′voursome.** [O.Fr. *flaur*; prob. influenced by savour.]

**flaw**, *flö*, *n.* a gust of wind: a sudden rush: an outburst of passion: uproar. [Cf. Du. *vlaag*, Sw. *flaga.*]

**flaw**, *flö*, *n.* a flake, fragment, splinter (*Shak.*): a break, a crack: a defect.—*v.t.* to crack or break.—*adjs.* **flawed**, **flaw′less**; **flaw′y**. [O.N. *flaga*, a slab.]

**flawn**, **flaune**, *flön*, **flam**, **flamm**, *flam*, (*arch.*) *n.* a custard: a pancake. [O.Fr. *flaon*—L.L. *flado̅*, *-o̅nis*,—O.H.G. *flado.*]

**flax**, *flaks*, *n.* the fibres of the plant *Linum*, which are woven into linen cloth: the plant itself.—*adjs.* **flax′en**, made of or resembling flax: light yellow; **flax′y**, like flax: of a light colour.—**flax′-bush**, **flax′-lil′y**, a New Zealand plant (Phormium) of the lily family, yielding a valuable fibre, **New Zealand flax**; **flax′-comb**, a toothed instrument or heckle for cleaning the fibres of flax; **flax′-dresser**, one who prepares flax for the spinner by the successive processes of rippling, retting, grassing, breaking, and scutching; **flax′-mill**, a mill for working flax into linen; **flax′-seed**, linseed; **flax′-wench**, a female who spins flax.—**purging flax**, a small wild species of flax (*Linum catharticum*). [O.E. *flæx* (W.S. *fleax*); Ger. *flachs.*]

**flay**, *flā*, *v.t.* to strip off the skin from: to flog: to subject to savage criticism:—*pr.p.* **flay′ing**; *pa.t.* and *pa.p.* **flayed.**—*n.* **flay′er.**—**flay′-flint**, a skinflint. [O.E. *flēan*; O.N. *flā*, to skin.]

**flay.** See **fley.**

**flea**, *flē*, *n.* any of an order of wingless, very agile, blood-sucking insects.—*adj.* **flea′some.**—**flea′-bane**, a name for various composite plants (Erigeron, Pulicaria, etc.), whose strong smell is said to drive away fleas; **flea′-bite**, the bite of a flea: a small mark caused by the bite: a trifle (*fig.*).—*adj.* **flea′-bitten**, bitten by fleas: mean (*fig.*): having small reddish spots on a lighter ground, esp. of horses.—**flea′-circus**, a show of performing fleas; **flea′-pit**, a public building, e.g. a cinema, supposedly infested with vermin.—**a flea in one's ear**, a stinging rebuff. [O.E. *flēah*; cf. Ger. *floh*, Du. *vloo.*]

**fleam**, *flēm*, *n.* an instrument for bleeding cattle. [O.Fr. *flieme* (Fr. *flamme*)—Gr. *phlebotomon*, a lancet—*phleps*, *phlebos*, a vein, and *tomē*, a cut.]

**flèche**, *flesh*, *n.* a spire: a slender spire rising from the intersection of the nave and transepts in some large churches: a parapet with two faces forming a salient angle at the foot of a glacis (*fort.*): a point on a backgammon board. [Fr., arrow.]

**fleck**, *flek*, *n.* a spot or speckle: a little bit of a thing.—*vs.t.* **fleck**, **fleck′er**, to spot: to streak.—*adjs.* **flecked**, spotted, dappled; **fleck′less**, without spot. [O.N. *flekkr*, a spot; Ger. *fleck*, Du. *vlek.*]

**flecti non frangi**, *flek′ti non fran′ji*, *flek′tē non fran′gē*, (L.) to be bent, not broken.

**flection**, a bad spelling of **flexion.**

**fled**, *fled*, *pa.t.* and *pa.p.* of **flee.**

**fledge**, *flej*, *v.t.* to furnish with feathers or wings.—*v.i.* to acquire feathers for flying.—*adj.* (*Milt.*) **fledged.**—*adj.* **fledged.**—*n.* **fledg′ling** (*rarely* **fledge′ling**), a bird just fledged: a very immature or inexperienced person.—*adj.* **fledg′y** (*Keats*), feathery. [M.E. *fligge*, *flegge*—an assumed O.E. (Kentish) *flecge*; cf. O.E. *unflycge*, unfledged; see **fly.**]

**flee**, *flē*, *v.i.* to run away, as from danger: to disappear.—*v.t.* to keep at a distance from:—*pr.p.* **flee′ing**; *pa.t.* and *pa.p.* **fled.**—*n.* **flē′er.** [O.E. *flēon*; Ger. *fliehen*; not akin to *fly*, but influenced by it, the *f* representing an earlier *th.*]

**fleece**, *flēs*, *n.* a sheep's coat of wool: the wool shorn from a sheep at one time: anything like a fleece.—*v.t.* to shear: to plunder: to cover, as with wool.—*adjs.* **fleeced**, having a fleece; **fleece′less.**—*n.* **fleec′er**, one who strips or plunders.—*adj.* **fleec′y**, woolly: like a fleece.—**fleece′-wool**, that got at clippings after the first. [O.E. *flēos*; Du. *vlies*, Ger. *fliess*, now *vlies.*]

**fleech**, *flēch*, (*Scot.*) *v.t.* and *v.i.* to flatter, coax, beg.—*ns.* **fleech′ing**, **fleech′ment.** [Origin obscure.]

**fleer**, *flēr*, *v.i.* to make wry faces in contempt: to leer.—*v.t.* to mock.—*n.* mockery.—*n.* **fleer′er.**—*n.* and *adj.* **fleer′ing.**—*adv.* **fleer′ingly.** [Cf. Norw. *flira*, Sw. *flissa*, to titter.]

**fleet**, *flēt*, *n.* a number of ships (birds, aircraft, motor-cars, etc.) in company or otherwise associated: a navy: a division of a navy under an admiral. [O.E. *flēot*, a ship—*flēotan* to float; conn. with Du. *vloot*, Ger. *flotte.*]

**fleet**, *flēt*, *adj.* swift: nimble: transient.—*adjs.* **fleet′-foot** (*Shak.*), fleet or swift of foot; **fleet′ly.**—*n.* **fleet′ness.** [Prob. O.N. *fliōtr*, swift; but ult. cog. with succeeding word.]

**fleet**, *flēt*, *v.i.* to float (*obs.*): to flow (*Spens.*): to flit, pass swiftly.—*v.t.* (*Shak.*) to make to pass quickly.—*adj.* (*dial.*) shallow.—*adj.* **fleet′ing**, passing quickly: temporary.—*adv.* **fleet′ingly.** [O.E. *flēotan*, to float.]

**fleet**, *flēt*, *n.* a shallow creek, bay, brook or drain, as in North *fleet*, *Fleet*-ditch, etc.—**Fleet Prison**, or **the Fleet**, a London gaol down to 1842, near the Fleet, long a place of confinement for debtors—clandestine marriages were solemnised here down to 1754 by **Fleet parsons**, broken-down clergymen confined for debt; **Fleet Street**, journalism or its ways and traditions, from the street near the Fleet with many newspaper offices. [O.E. *flēot*, an inlet.]

**fleg**, *fleg*, (*Scot.*) *n.* a fright.—*v.t.* to frighten. [O.E. *flecgan*, to put to flight.]

**fleme**, *flēm*, (*Scot.*) *v.t.* to put to flight:—*pa.t.* and *pa.p.* **flem′it.** [O.E. *flieman.*]

**Flemish**, *flem′ish*, *adj.* of or belonging to the *Flemings* or people of Flanders, or their language.—*n.* **Flem′ing**, a native of Flanders.—**Flemish bond**, a bricklayer's bond of alternate headers and stretchers in every course; **Flemish school**, a school of painting formed by the brothers Van Eyck, reaching its height in Rubens, Vandyck, and Teniers; **Flemish stitch**, a stitch used in making certain kinds of point-lace. [Du. *Vlaamsch.*]

**flench**, *flench*, **flense**, *flens*, **flinch**, *flinch*, *v.t.* to cut up the blubber of, as a whale: to flay. [Dan. *flense.*]

**flesh**, *flesh*, *n.* muscular tissue: all the living substance of the body of similar composition to muscle: the soft substance that covers the bones of animals: animal food: the bodies of beasts and (sometimes) birds; not fish: the body, not the soul: animals, or animal nature: human bodily nature: mankind: kindred: bodily appetites: the soft substance of fruit, esp. the part fit to be eaten.—*v.t.* to reward with flesh: to train to an appetite for flesh, as dogs for hunting: to inure: to glut: to use upon flesh, as a sword: to use for the first time: to gratify with fleshly indulgence: to put flesh upon: to scrape flesh from.—*adj.* **fleshed** (*flesht*), having flesh: fat.—*ns.* **flesh′er**, an instrument for scraping hides: a butcher (esp. *Scot.*); **flesh′-hood** (*Mrs Browning*), the state of being in the flesh; **flesh′iness**.—*n.pl.* **flesh′ings**, flesh-coloured tights.—*adj.* **flesh′less**, without flesh: lean.—*ns.* **flesh′liness**; **flesh′ling**, a sensualist.—*adj.* **flesh′ly**, corporeal: carnal: not spiritual.—Also *adv.*—*n.* **flesh′ment** (*Shak.*), act of fleshing or initiating, excitement arising from success.—*adj.* **flesh′y**, fat: pulpy: plump.—**flesh′-broth**, broth made by boiling flesh; **flesh′-brush**, a brush used for rubbing the skin to excite circulation; **flesh′-colour**, the normal colour of the skin of a European; **flesh′-eater**; **flesh′-fly**, a fly (esp. *Sarcophaga*) whose larvae feed on flesh; **flesh′-hook**, a hook for drawing flesh from a pot; **flesh′-market**; **flesh′-meat**, flesh of animals used for food; **flesh′-monger**, one who deals in flesh: a whoremonger (*Shak.*): a procurer, a pimp, a slave-dealer; **flesh′-pot**, a pot or vessel in which flesh is cooked: abundance of flesh, high living (*fig.*); **flesh′-pottery**, sumptuous living; **flesh′-tint**, a tint or colour that represents the human body; **flesh′worm**, a worm or maggot that feeds on flesh; **flesh′-wound**, a wound not reaching beyond the flesh.—**an arm of flesh**, human strength or help; **flesh and blood**, human nature: one's own kindred; **in flesh**, in good condition: fat; **in the flesh**, in bodily life, alive: incarnate; **make one's flesh creep**, to arouse a feeling of horror in one; **one flesh**, united in marriage; **proud-flesh** (see **proud**). [O.E. *flǣsc*; cog. forms in all Gmc. languages; Ger. *fleisch*, etc.]

**fletch**, *flech*, *v.t.* to feather.—*n.* **fletch′er**, one who makes arrows. [Fr. *flèche*, an arrow, O.Fr. *flecher*, a fletcher.]

**fletton**, *fle′tən*, *n.* a type of brick made near *Fletton* in Huntingdonshire, of a mottled yellow and pink colour, with sharp arrises.

**fleur-de-lis**, **-lys**, *flœr-də-lē′*, *-lēs′*, *n.* the iris: an ornament and heraldic bearing of disputed origin (an iris, three lilies, etc.), borne by the kings of France:—*pl.* **fleurs-de-lis**, **fleurs-de-lys**, (*flœr-*).—Also **flower(-)delice**, **flower-de-luce**, **flower(-)deluce**.—*ns.* **fleuret** (*-et′*), an ornament like a small flower: a fencing foil; **fleuron** (*flœ-rõ*), a flowerlike ornament, in architecture, printing, etc.—*adj.* **fleury** (*flōō′ri*), having fleurs-de-lis—also **flo′ry**. [Fr.; *lis*, being O.Fr. *liz*—L. *lilium*, lily.]

**flew**, *flōō*, *pa.t.* of **fly**; coll. used for **fled** (*pa.t.*). See also **flue**.

**flew**, *flōō*, *n.* a dog's pendulous chop (usu. in *pl.*). —*adj.* **flewed** (*Shak.*). [Ety. unknown.]

**flex**, *fleks*, *v.t.* and *v.i.* to bend.—*n.* a bending: a flexible cord or line, esp. of insulated wire.—*n.* **flexibil′ity**.—*adj.* **flex′ible**, easily bent: pliant: docile.—*n.* **flex′ibleness**.—*adv.* **flex′ibly**.—*adj.* **flex′ile** (*-il*, *-əl*), flexible.—*ns.* **flexion** (*flek′shən*), a bend: a fold: the action of a flexor muscle: inflexion (*gram.*); **flex′or**, a muscle that bends a joint, as opposed to *extensor*.—*adjs.* **flex′ūose**, **flex′ūous**, full of windings and turnings: undulating; **flexural** (*flek′shər-el*).—*n.* **flex′ure**, a bend or turning: the curving of a line or surface (*math.*): the bending of loaded beams: obsequious bowing (*Shak.*). [L. *flectĕre*, *flexum*, to bend.]

**fley**, *flay*, *flā*, *v.t.* (*Scot.*) to cause to flee: to frighten.—*v.i.* to be frightened. [M.E. *flayen*—O.E. *flēgan* (as in compound *āflēgan*, *āfliegan*, to put to flight); cf. O.N. *fleyja*, Goth. *flaugjan*.]

**flibbertigibbet**, *flib′ər-ti-jib′it*, *n.* a flighty person: an imp. [Most prob. jargon.]

**flic**, *flēk*, (Fr.) (*slang*) a policeman.

**flichter**, *flihh′tər*, (*Scot.*) *n.* a flutter.—*v.t.* and *v.i.* to flutter, quiver.

**flick**, *flik*, *v.t.* to strike lightly, as with a lash or a finger-nail.—*n.* a stroke of this kind.—**flick′-knife**, a knife the blade of which springs out on pressure of a button in the handle. [Echoic.]

**flick**, *flik*, (*slang*) *n.* a cinematograph film: (*pl.*) a cinematograph performance. [flicker.]

**flicker**, *flik′ər*, *v.i.* to flutter and move the wings, as a bird: to burn unsteadily, as a flame.—*n.* an act of flickering, a flickering movement or light. —*adv.* **flick′eringly**.—**flick′ertail** (*U.S.*), a ground-squirrel. [O.E. *flicorian*; imit.]

**flicker**, *flik′ər*, *n.* an American woodpecker. [Echoic.]

**flier**, **flies**. See under **fly**.

**flight**, *flīt*, *n.* a passing through the air: a soaring: distance flown: a sally or digression, e.g. of imagination, fancy: a series of steps: a flock of birds flying together: the birds produced in the same season: a volley: a long-distance arrow (*Shak.*): the power of flying: the art or the act of flying with wings or in an aeroplane or other machine: a unit of the Air Force answering to a platoon in the army: a regular air journey, numbered and at a fixed time.—*v.t.* to cause (birds) to fly up: to shoot (wild-fowl) in flight: to put a feather in (an arrow): to impart a deceptive trajectory to (a cricket ball). —*v.i.* of birds, to rise or migrate in a flock.—*adj.* **flight′ed** (*Milt.*), flying.—*adv.* **flight′ily**.—*n.* **flight′iness**.—*adjs.* **flight′less**, without power of flying; **flight′y**, swift (*Shak.*): fanciful: changeable: giddy-minded.—**flight′-deck**, the deck of an aircraft-carrier where the planes take off or land; **flight′-feather**, a quill of a bird's wing; **flight′-lieuten′ant**, an Air Force officer of rank answering to naval lieutenant or army captain; **flight′-recorder**, a device which records on tape or wire information about the functioning of an aircraft and its systems.—**in the first**, **top**, **flight**, in the highest class. [O.E. *flyht—flēogan*, to fly.]

**flight**, *flīt*, *n.* an act of fleeing.—**take** (**to**) **flight**, to flee: to disappear quickly (*fig.*). [Assumed O.E. *flyht*; cf. *flēon*, to flee.]

**flim-flam**, *flim′-flam*, *n.* a trick. [Cf. **flam**.]

**flimp**, *flimp*, (*slang*) *v.t.* to rob while a confederate hustles. [Cf. West Flem., *flimpe*, knock, rob.]

**flimsy**, *flim′zi*, *adj.* thin: without solidity, strength, or reason: weak.—*n.* transfer-paper: a bank-note (*slang*): reporters' copy written on thin paper.—*adv.* **flim′sily**, in a flimsy manner.—*n.* **flim′siness**. [First in 18th century; prob. suggested by **film**.]

**flinch**, *flinch*, *-sh*, *v.i.* to shrink back: to fail.—*n.* **flinch′er**.—*n.* and *adj.* **flinch′ing**.—*adv.* **flinch′ingly**. [Prob. conn. with M.E. *fleechen*, O.Fr. *flechir*, L. *flectĕre*, to bend.]

**flinch**. Same as **flench**.

**flinder**, *flin′dər*, *n.* a splinter or small fragment—usually in *pl.* [Norw. *flindra*, a splinter.]

**Flindersia**, *flin-dûr′si-ə*, *n.* an Australian genus of valuable trees of the *Rutaceae*. [From the explorer, Matthew *Flinders*, 1774-1814.]

**fling**, *fling*, *v.t.* to throw, cast, toss: to dart: to send forth: to send suddenly: to cause to fall.—*v.i.* to throw the body about: to kick out: to dash or rush, throw oneself impetuously: to throw missiles:—*pr.p.* **fling′ing**; *pa.t.* and *pa.p.* **flung**.—*n.* a cast or throw: a try: a passing attack: a jibe: a taunt: complete freedom, full enjoyment of pleasure: a lively Scottish country-dance.—**fling out**, break out in impetuous plain-speaking; **full fling**, at the utmost speed, reck-lessly. [Cf. O.N. *flengja*; Sw. *flänga*.]

**flint**, *flint*, *n.* a hard mineral, a variety of quartz, from which fire is readily struck with steel: a concretion of silica: a piece of flint, esp. one used for striking fire, or one manufactured into an implement before (or after) the use of metals: anything proverbially hard: a tailor or other who refuses low wages (*obs. slang*).—*adj.* made of flint: hard.—*v.t.* flint′ify, to turn to flint.—*adv.* flint′ily.—*n.* flint′iness.—*adj.* flint′y, consisting of, abounding in, or like flint: hard: cruel.—flint′-glass, a very fine and pure lead glass, originally made of calcined flints.—*adjs.* flint′-heart, -ed (*Shak.*), having a hard heart.—flint′-knapp′er, one who flakes or chips flints; flint′-knapp′ing; flint′lock, a gunlock or gun with a flint. [O.E. *flint*; Dan. *flint*; Gr. *plinthos*, a brick.]

flip, *flip*, *v.t.* and *v.i.* to fillip: to flick: to flap.—*n.* a fillip: a flick: a hot drink of beer and spirits sweetened, or similar concoction: a trip in an aeroplane, a pleasure-flight (*coll.*).—*adj.* flippant: pert, over-smart.—*n.* flipp′er, a limb adapted for swimming: a hand (*coll.*): a rubber foot-covering imitating an animal's flipper, worn by swimmers.—*adj.* and *adv.* flipping, nasty, unpleasant: often used intensively or meaninglessly.—flip′-dog, an iron for heating flip.—*adv.* flip′-flap′, flip′-flop′, with repeated flapping.—*n.* a coster's dance: a form of somersault: a cracker: the sound of regular footfall: a flighty woman: a revolving apparatus for public amusement.—flip′flop, orig., and still in U.S., a bistable pair of valves or transistors, two stable states being switched by pulses: in Britain, a similar circuit with one stable state temporarily achieved by pulse; flip′-side, the side of a gramophone record carrying the song, etc., of lesser importance, the reverse of the side on whose merits the record is expected to sell.—*adj.* flipp′-erty-flopp′erty, loose, dangling. [Cf. fillip, flap.]

flippant, *flip′ənt*, *adj.* pert and frivolous of speech: showing disrespectful levity: nimble (*obs.*): playful (*obs.*).—*ns.* flipp′ancy, flipp′antness, pert fluency of speech: pertness: levity.—*adv.* flipp′-antly. [Cf. flip, and O.N. *fleipa*, to prattle.]

flirt, *flûrt*, *v.t.* to jerk: to move about quickly like a fan, to flick, rap.—*v.i.* to trifle with love: to play at courtship: to move briskly about.—*n.* a pert, giddy girl: one who coquets for amusement, usually a woman.—*n.* flirtā′tion, the act of flirting.—*adj.* flirtā′tious (*coll.*), given to flirting.—*n.* flirt′ing.—*adv.* flirt′ingly.—*adj.* flirt′-ish, betokening a flirt.—flirt′-gill (*jil*; *Shak.*), a pert or wanton woman. [Origin obscure; perhaps conn. with Fr. *fleureter*, to talk sweet nothings.]

flisk, *flisk*, (*Scot.*) *v.i.* to skip or caper about: to be restive.—*n.* a whim.—*adj.* flisk′y. [Onomatopoeic.]

flit, *flit*, *v.i.* to move about lightly: to fly silently or quickly: to be unsteady or easily moved: to change one's abode (*Scot.*).—*v.t.* to remove, transfer:—*pr.p.* flitt′ing; *pa.t.* and *pa.p.* flitt′ed, *Spens.* flitt.—*n.* flitt′ing. [O.N. *flytja*; Sw. *flytta*.]

flit, flitt, *flit*, (*obs.*) *adj.* fleet: fleeting: light. [fleet.]

flitch, *flich*, *n.* the side of a hog salted and cured. [O.E. *flicce*; O.N. *flikki*.]

flite. Same as flyte.

flitter, *flit′ər*, *v.i.* to flutter.—flitt′er-mouse, a bat. [flit.]

flitter, *flit′ər*, *n.* fragments, tatters.

flittern, *flit′ərn*, (*dial.*) *n.* a young oak.

flivver, *fliv′ər*, (*slang*) *n.* a failure: a small cheap motor-car or aeroplane: a small destroyer.

flix, *fliks*, *n.* fur, beaver-down.

flix-weed, *fliks′wēd*, *n.* a species of hedge-mustard.

float, *flōt*, *v.i.* to be supported on or suspended in a fluid: to be buoyed up: to move lightly, supported by a fluid: to seem to move in such a way: to be free from the usual attachment: to drift about aimlessly: to flow (*Milt.*): to be flooded (*Spens.*, *Pope*): in weaving, to pass threads without interweaving with them: to use a float.—*v.t.* to cause to float: to cover with liquid: to convey on floats: to levitate: to separate by flotation: to smooth: to pare off (as turf): to launch (e.g. scheme): to circulate (e.g. rumour): to offer for sale (stocks, etc.) to raise capital: to negotiate (a loan).—*n.* state of floating (*Keats*, etc.): a wave (*lit.* and *fig.*; *obs.*): a contrivance for floating or for keeping something afloat, as a raft, the cork or quill of a fishing-line, the ball of a ball-cock, etc.: a tool for smoothing: a plasterer's trowel: a low cart for carrying cattle, etc.: a footlight or the footlights collectively: money in hand for a purpose such as to give change to customers, to provide for expenses.—*adj.* float′able.—*n.* float′age, buoyancy: that which floats: the part above the water-line; float′ant, an agent that causes something to float; floatā′tion (see flotation); float′er, one who or that which floats: a person who is a vagrant, or who drifts from job to job or allegiance to allegiance: a blunder (*slang*).—*adj.* float′ing, that floats, in any sense: not fixed: fluctuating: circulating.—*n.* action of the verb: the spreading of plaster on the surface of walls.—*adv.* float′ingly.—*adj.* float′y.—float′-board, a board of an undershot water-wheel or a paddle-wheel; float glass, glass hardened floating on the surface of a liquid; float grass, floating grass, floating meadow-grass (*Glyceria fluitans*); floating battery, a vessel or hulk heavily armed, used in the defence of harbours or in attacks on marine fortresses; floating bridge, a bridge supported on pontoons; floating capital, goods, money, etc.: capital not permanently invested; floating crane, a large crane carried on a pontoon, used in docks; floating debt, unfunded debt, short-term government loan; floating dock, a floating structure that can be sunk by admitting water to its air chambers, and raised again carrying a vessel to be repaired; floating island, a floating aggregation of driftwood, or a mass of vegetation buoyed up from the bottom by marsh gas, or the like; floating kidney, an abnormally mobile kidney; floating light, a light-ship; floating vote, the votes of electors who are not permanently attached to any one political party; float plane, a seaplane; float′-stone, a porous sponge-like variety of silica, so light as to float for a while on water: a bricklayer's smoothing tool. [O.E. *flotian*, to float; O.N. *flota*.]

floccus, *flok′əs*, *n.* a tuft of woolly hair: a tuft, esp. at the end of a tail: the covering of unfledged birds:—*pl.* flocci, *flok′si*.—*n.* floccillā′-tion (*flok-si-*), fitful plucking at the bed-clothes by a delirious patient; floc′cinau′cini′hilipil′ifi-cā′tion (*facet.*), setting little or no value (from the Latin genitives *flocci*, *nauci*, at a trifle, *nihili*, at nothing, *pili*, at a hair, and *facēre*, to make.)—*adjs.* flocc′ose (or *-ōs′*), woolly; flocc′ular; flocc′ulate, (or *-ōs′*), woolly; flocc′ūlate.—*v.t.* and *v.i.* flocc′ūlate, to aggregate in tufts, flakes or cloudy masses.—*ns.* flocculā′-tion; flocc′ule, a flocculus; flocc′ulence, flocculated condition.—*adj.* flocc′ulent, woolly: flaky: flocculated.—*n.* flocc′ulus, a small flock, tuft, or flake: a small outgrowth of the cerebellum: a tuft or dark patch on the sun's surface, usu. near sunspots, caused by calcium or hydrogen vapour:—*pl.* flocculi (*flok′ū-li*). [L. *floccus*, a lock, a trifle; dim. *flocculus*.]

flock, *flok*, *n.* a company of animals, as sheep, birds, etc.: a company generally: a congregation.—*v.i.* to gather or go in flocks or in crowds.—flock′-mas′ter, an owner or overseer of a flock. [O.E. *flocc*, a flock, a company; O.N. *flokkr*.]

flock, *flok*, *n.* a lock of wool: a tuft: cloth refuse,

waste wool (also in *pl.*): a woolly-looking precipitate (also *pl.*).—**flock'-bed**, a bed stuffed with wool; **flock'-pa'per**, a wall-paper dusted over with flock. [O.Fr. *floc*—L. *floccus*, a lock of wool.]

**floe**, *flō*, *n.* a field of floating ice. [Prob. Norw. *flo*, layer—O.N. *flō*.]

**flog**, *flog*, *v.t.* to beat or strike: lash: chastise with blows: sell, sometimes illicitly (*slang*):—*pr.p.* **flogg'ing**; *pa.t.* and *pa.p.* **flogged**.—*n.* **flogg'ing**. [Late; prob. an abbrev. of **flagellate**.]

**flong**, *flong*, *n.* papier-mâché for stereotyping. [Fr. *flan*.]

**flood**, *flud*, *n.* a great flow of water: an inundation: a deluge: a condition of abnormally great flow in a river: a river or other water (*poet.*): the rise of the tide: any great inflow or outflow, as of light, tears, visitors: a floodlight (*coll.*).—*v.t.* to overflow: to inundate: to supply in excessive quantity.—*v.i.* to overflow: to bleed profusely, as after parturition.—*adj.* **flood'ed**.—*n.* **flood'ing**. —**flood'gate**, a gate for allowing or stopping the flow of water, a sluice or lock-gate; **flood lamp**, a floodlight; **flood'light**, lighting of a large area or surface by illumination from lamps situated at some distance (also **floodlighting**): a floodlight lamp.—Also *v.t.*:—*pa.p.* **flood'lighted, flood'lit**.— **floodlight projector**, housing and support for a floodlight lamp with a reflector for directing the light into a suitable beam; **flood'mark**, the mark or line to which the tide or a flood has risen; **floodtide**, the rising tide; **flood'wa'ter**, the mark or line to which the tide or a flood has risen; **flood'way**, an artificial passage for floodwater.— **the Flood**, Noah's deluge. [O.E. *flōd*; Du. *vloed*, Ger. *flut*; cf. **flow** (2).]

**floor**, *flōr*, *flōr*, *n.* the lower supporting surface of a room, etc.: a platform: rooms in a building on the same level: a bottom surface: that on which anything rests or any operation is performed: a levelled area: the ground (*coll. S. Africa*): the part of a legislative assembly where members sit and speak: the part of an exchange on which dealers operate: a lower limit of prices, etc.: a quantity of grain spread out to germinate.—*v.t.* to furnish with a floor: to throw or place on the floor: to vanquish, stump (*coll.*).—*adj.* **floored**.—*ns.* **floor'er**, a knock-down blow: a decisive retort, etc.: an examination question one cannot answer; **floor'ing**, material for floors: a platform.—**floor'cloth**, a covering for floors, esp. of linoleum or the like: a cloth for washing floors; **floor'head**, the upper end of a floor timber; **flooring saw**, saw curved towards the toe with extra teeth on the back above the toe, used for cutting floorboards, etc.; **floor show**, a performance on the floor of a ballroom, dining-room, etc., not on a platform; **floor timber**, a timber placed immediately across a ship's keel, on which her bottom is framed; **floor'walker**, supervisor of section of large store, who attends to customers' complaints, etc.—**first floor**, the floor in a house above the ground floor, the second storey: usu. the ground floor (*U.S.*).— Also *adj.*—**hold the floor**, to dominate a meeting by much speaking: to speak boringly much; **take the floor**, to rise to address a meeting, or to take part in a dance. [O.E. *flōr*; Du. *vloer*; a flat surface, Ger. *flur*, flat land; W. *llawr*.]

**floosie**, *flōō'zi*, *n.* an attractive young woman esp. of loose morals: a prostitute, esp. a slovenly one.—Also **floosy, -zy, -zie**. [Origin uncertain.]

**flop**, *flop*, *n.* a limp, heavy, flapping movement, fall, or sound: a collapse: a fiasco: a failure.— *adv.* with a flop.—*v.t.* and *v.i.* to move with a flop: to drop plump: to change over in nature or politics (*U.S.*).—*v.i.* to collapse: to fail dismally.—*adv.* **flopp'ily**.—*n.* **flopp'iness**.—*adj.* **flopp'y**.—**flop'house** (*U.S.*), a cheap hotel: a doss-house. [A form of **flap**.]

**flora**, *flō'ra*, *flō'*, *n.* the assemblage of vegetable species of a region, or age: a list or descriptive enumeration of these.—*adj.* **flo'ral** pertaining to the goddess Flora, to floras, or to flowers.—*adv.* **flo'rally**.—*ns.* **Floréal** (Fr.; *flō-rā-äl'*), the 8th month of the French revolutionary calendar, about 20th April—20th May; **florescence** (*flores'ans*), a bursting into flower: time of flowering (*bot.*).—*adj.* **floresc'ent**, bursting into flowers.— *n.* **floret** (*flor'it*), a small flower: a single flower in a close-packed inflorescence.—*adjs.* **flo'riated**, **flo'reated**, decorated with floral ornament.—*adj.* **floricul'tural** (*flōr*, *flōr-*).—*ns.* **flor'iculture**, the culture of flowers or plants; **floricul'turist**.— *adj.* **flōr'id**, abounding in flowers (*obs.*): flowery: bright in colour: flushed with red: characterised by flowers of rhetoric, melodic figures, or other ornament: overadorned: richly ornamental; **flōrid'ity**.—*adv.* **flōr'idly**.—*n.* **flōr'idness**.—*adjs.* **flōrif'erous**, bearing or producing flowers; **flo'riform**, flower-shaped.—*ns.* **flōr'igen** (*-i-jən*; Gr. *gennaein*, to produce), a postulated flower-forming hormone; **florilegium** (*-lē'ji-əm*; L. *legēre*, to gather), an anthology or collection of choice extracts:—*pl.* **florilē'gia**; **flōr'ist**, a cultivator or seller of flowers: (*flō'*, *flō'rist*) a student of flowers or of floras.—*adj.* **flōrist'ic**.— *ns.* **flōrist'ics**, the study of floras; **flōr'istry**, the art of cultivating or selling flowers.—*adj.* **flo'ry**, showy, conceited (*Scott*).—**floral diagram**, a figure showing the arrangement of the parts of a flower in ground-plan. [L. *Flōra*, goddess of flowers; *flōs*, *flōris*, a flower.]

**floreat**, *flō'rē-at*, *flō'rā-at*, (L.) let (it) flourish.

**Florentine**, *flor'ən-tin*, *adj.* pertaining to *Florence* in Tuscany.—*n.* a native or inhabitant thereof: a durable silk textile fabric—also **flor'ence**: a pie with no crust beneath the meat.—**Florence flask**, a long-necked round flask; **Florentine iris** (see **orris** (1)). [L. *Flōrentinus*—*Flōrentia*.]

**florid, florist**, etc. See **flora**.

**Florideae**, *flor-id'i-ē*, (*bot.*) *n.pl.* a large subclass of the Rhodophyceae or red seaweeds.—*n.* and *adj.* **florid'ean**.—*adj.* **florid'eous**. [L. *flōridus*, florid.]

**florin**, *flor'in*, *n.* orig. a Florentine gold coin with a lily stamped on one side, first struck in the 13th century: an English silver or cupro-nickel coin worth one-tenth of a pound first minted in 1849 (a **double florin** was coined in 1887): in Holland, the gulden. [Fr., from It. *fiorino*—*fiore*, a lily—L. *flōs*, *flōris*.]

**floruit**, *flō'rū-it*, *flō'roō-*, *n.* period during which a person flourished or guiding date indicating when he or she was alive. [L., 3rd pers. sing. perf. indic. of *flōrēre*, to flourish.]

**floscule**, *flos'kūl*, *n.* a floret.—*adjs.* **flos'cular**, **flos'culous**. [L. *flōsculus*, dim. of *flōs*, a flower.]

**floss**, *flos*, *n.* the rough outside of the silkworm's cocoon, and other waste of silk manufacture: fine silk in spun strands not twisted together, used in embroidery and tooth-cleaning: any loose downy or silky plant substance: fluff— also **flosh**.—*adj.* **flossy**, made of, like, or pertaining to floss: stylish, overdressed (*slang*).— **floss silk, flox silk**. [Prob. O.Fr. *flosche*, down: or from some Gmc. word cog. with **fleece**; cf. O.N. *flos*, nap.]

**flota**, *flō'ta*, *n.* a commercial fleet: formerly the fleet which annually conveyed the produce of America to Spain. [Sp.]

**flote**, *flōt*, *n.* (*obs.*) a wave.—*n.* **flōt'age** (see **floatage**).—*adj.* **flo'tant** (*her.*), floating in air or in water.—*n.* **flotā'tion**, the act of floating: the science of floating bodies: act of starting a business, esp. a limited liability company: a method of separating ore from gangue by forming a froth, the ore particles clinging to the bubbles.—**plane**, or **line**, **of flotation**, the plane or line in which the horizontal surface of a fluid cuts a body floating in it. [See **float**.]

**flotilla**, *flo-til'ə*, *n.* a fleet of small ships. [Sp., dim. of *flota*, a fleet.]

**flotsam**, *flot'səm*, *n.* goods lost by shipwreck and found floating on the sea (see jetsam). [Anglo-Fr. *floteson* (Fr. *flottaison*)—O.Fr. *floter*, to float.]

**flounce**, *flowns*, *v.i.* to move abruptly or impatiently.—*n.* an impatient fling, flop, or movement.—*adv.* with a flounce. [Prob. cog. with Norw. *flunsa*, to hurry, Sw. dial. *flunsa*, to plunge.]

**flounce**, *flowns*, *n.* a hanging strip sewed to the skirt of a dress by its upper edge.—*v.t.* to furnish with flounces.—*n.* **floun'cing**, material for flounces. [See **frounce**.]

**flounder**, *flown'dər*, *v.i.* to struggle with violent and awkward motion: to stumble helplessly in thinking or speaking.—*n.* an act of floundering. [Prob. an onomatopoeic blending of the sound and sense of earlier words like **founder**, **blunder**.]

**flounder**, *flown'dər*, *n.* a name given to a number of species of flatfish of the family Pleuronectidae —in Europe *Platichthys flesus*, in America certain species of Pseudopleuronectes, Limanda, etc. [Anglo-Fr. *floundre*, O.Fr. *flondre*, most prob. of Scand. origin; cf. O.N. *flythra*; Sw. *flundra*.]

**flour**, *flow(ə)r*, *n.* the finely-ground meal of wheat or other grain: the fine soft powder of any substance.—*v.t.* to reduce into or sprinkle with flour.—*v.i.* to break up into fine globules of mercury in the amalgamation process.—*adj.* **flour'y**, covered with flour: like flour.—**flour bolt**, a machine for bolting flour; **flour mill**, a mill for making flour. [Same word as **flower**.]

**flourish**, *flur'ish*, *v.i.* to bloom (*obs.* and *Scot.*): to grow luxuriantly: to thrive: to be in full vigour: to be prosperous: to use copious and flowery language: to move in fantastic figures: to display ostentatiously: to play or sing ostentatious passages, or ostentatiously (*mus.*): to play a fanfare: to make ornamental strokes with the pen: to show off.—*v.t.* to adorn with flourishes or ornaments: to make fair (*Shak.*): to brandish in show or triumph or exuberance of spirits.—*n.* decoration (*obs.*): showy splendour: a figure made by a bold stroke of the pen: the waving of a weapon or other thing: a parade of words: a showy, fantastic, or highly ornamental passage of music: a mass of blossom of a fruit-tree (*dial.*). —*adjs.* **flour'ished**, decorated with flourishes; **flour'ishing**, thriving: prosperous: making a show.—*adv.* **flour'ishingly**.—*adj.* **flour'ishy**, abounding in flourishes.—**flourishing thread**, thread used in fancywork.—**flourish of trumpets**, a fanfare heralding great persons; any ostentatious introduction. [O.Fr. *florir*, *floriss-* —L. *flōs*, *flōris*, flower.]

**flouse**, *flows*, (*dial.*) *v.t.* and *v.i.* to splash.—Also **floush** (*flowsh*). [Cf. **flush** (1).]

**flout**, *flowt*, *v.t.* to jeer at: to mock: to treat with contempt.—*v.i.* to jeer.—*n.* a jeer.—*adv.* **flout'ingly**.—**flout'ingstock** (*Shak.*), an object for flouting. [Prob. a specialised use of *floute*, M.E. form of **flute**, to play on the flute; so with Du. *fluiten*.]

**flow**, *flō*, *v.i.* to run, as water: to move or change form like a fluid: to rise or come in, as the tide: to move in a stream: to glide smoothly: to abound, run over: to run in smooth lines: to stream or hang loose and waving: to melt (*obs.*). —*v.t.* to cover with water:—*pa.t.* and *pa.p.* **flowed**; *pa.p.*, *Shak.*, *Milt.*, **flown**, *flōn*.—*n.* a stream or current: movement of, or like that of, a fluid: that which flows or has flowed: mode of flowing: the setting in of the tide: copious fluency.—*n.* **flow'age**, act of flowing: state of being flooded.—*adj.* **flow'ing**, moving, as a fluid: fluent: smooth and continuous: falling in folds or in waves.—*adv.* **flow'ingly**.—*n.* **flow'ing-ness.**—**flow chart**, a flow sheet: a chart pictorially representing the nature and sequence of operations to be carried out in a computer programme; **flow'meter**, a device for measuring, or giving an output signal proportional to, the rate of flow of a fluid in a pipe; **flow sheet**, a chart showing the successive stages of an industrial process. [O.E. *flōwan*.]

**flow**, *flō*, *flow*, (*Scot.*) *n.* a morass: a flat, moist tract of land: a quicksand: a moorland pool: a sea basin or sound. [Cf. Icel. *flōi*, a marshy moor; Norw. dial. *floe*, pool in a swamp; O.N. *flōa*, to flood.]

**flower**, *flow(ə)r*, *n.* a growth comprising the reproductive organs of seed plants: the blossom of a plant: the flowering state: a flowering plant, esp. one valued for its blossoms: the prime of life: the best of anything: the person or thing most distinguished: the embodiment of perfection: a figure of speech: ornament of style: (in *pl.*) menstrual discharge (*obs.*): (in *pl.*) a sublimate (as **flowers of sulphur**): (in *pl.*) applied to some fungous growths, as **flowers of tan**, a slime-fungus on tan-bark.—*v.t.* to adorn with figures of flowers.—*v.i.* to blossom: to flourish.—*n.* **flower'age**, flowers collectively: flowering state.—*adj.* **flowered**, decorated with figures of flowers: fleury.—*ns.* **flower'er**, a plant that flowers: embroiderer of floral figures; **flower'et**, a little flower: a floret; **flower'iness.** —*n.* and *adj.* **flowering.**—*adjs.* **flower'less; flower'y**, full of, or adorned with, flowers: highly embellished, florid.—**flower'-bed**, a garden bed for flowers; **flower'-bell**, a blossom shaped like a bell; **flower'-bud**, a bud with the unopened flower; **flower'-clock**, a collection of flowers so arranged that the time of day is indicated by their times of opening and closing; **flower-de-luce** (*-di-lōōs'*), **-delice** (*-di-lēs'*, *-lis'*, *-del'is*), old names for the iris, or for the **fleur-de-lis**; **flower'-garden**; **flower'-girl**, a girl or woman who sells flowers in the street; **flower'-head**, a close inflorescence in which all the florets are sessile on the receptacle; **flowering rush**, a monocotyledonous plant (Butomus), with large linear three-edged leaves and an umbel of rose-coloured flowers; **Flower People**, colourfully dressed adherents of a cult arising in the mid nineteen sixties which rejected materialism and advocated universal love; **flower'pot**, a pot in which a plant is grown; **flower'-serv'ice**, a church service where offerings of flowers are made; **flower'-show**, an exhibition of flowers; **flower'-stalk**, the stem that supports the flower.—*adj.* **flower'y-kir'tled** (*Milt.*).—**flower of Jove**, a campion with heads of purple or scarlet flowers, and leaves silky-white with hairs; **the flowery land**, China. [O.Fr. *flour* (Fr. *fleur*)—L. *flōs*, *flōris*, a flower.]

**flown**, *flōn*, *pa.p.* of **fly**; old *pa.p.* of **flow**.

**flox silk**. Same as **floss silk**.

**flu**, *floo*, *n.* shortened form of **influenza**.

**fluate**, *flōō'āt*, (*obs.*) *n.* a fluoride.

**flub**, *flub*, (*U.S. slang*) *v.t.* to botch, fail at.—*v.i.* to perform badly: to blunder.—*n.* a blunder, [Ety. unknown.]

**fluctuate**, *fluk'tū-āt*, *v.i.* to move like a wave: to go up and down or to and fro: to vary this way and that.—*v.t.* to throw into fluctuation.—*adjs.* **fluc'tuant; fluc'tuating.**—*n.* **fluctuā'tion**, rise and fall: motion to and fro: wavelike motion: alternate variation. [L. *fluctuāre*, *-ātum*—*fluctus*, a wave—*fluĕre*, to flow.]

**flue**, *flōō*, *n.* a pipe for conveying hot air, smoke, flame, etc.: a small chimney: a flue pipe (*mus.*): the opening by which the air escapes from the foot of a flue pipe.—**flue pipe**, a pipe, esp. in an organ, in which the sound is produced by air impinging on an edge; **flue'work**, in an organ, the flue pipes collectively. [Origin doubtful.]

**flue**, *floo̅*, *n.* light fluff, such as collects in unswept places: soft down or fur.—*adj.* **flu'ey.** [Origin doubtful.]

**flue**, **flew**, *floo̅*, (*dial.*) *adj.* shallow, flat: flared: splayed. [Origin uncertain.]

**fluellin**, *floo̅-el'in*, *n.* a name given to various speedwells (esp. *Veronica serpyllifolia* and *V. officinalis*) and toadflaxes (esp. *Linaria Elatine* and *L. spuria*). [W. *llysian Llewelyn*, Llewelyn's herbs.]

**fluent**, *floo̅'ənt*, *adj.* ready in the use of words: voluble: marked by copiousness: smooth, easy, graceful.—*n.* (*math.*), the variable quantity in fluxions.—*ns.* **flu'ence** (*Milt.*), **flu'ency**, **flu'entness.**—*adv.* **flu'ently.** [L. *fluēns, fluentis*, pr.p. of *fluēre*, to flow.]

**fluff**, *fluf*, *n.* a soft down from cotton, etc.: anything downy: faulty acting: a duffed stroke at golf, etc.: a girl (*coll.*).—*v.t.* to make fluffy.— *v.t.* and *v.i.* to bungle.—*n.* **fluff'iness.**—*adj.* **fluff'y.** [Perh. conn. with **flue**, light down.]

**flügel**, **flugel**, *flü'hhəl, floo̅'gl*, (Ger.) *n.* a grand piano.—*ns.* **flügelhorn**, **flugelhorn**, a hunting-horn, a kind of keyed bugle; **flugelman** (*floo̅'gl-man*; see **fugleman**). [Ger., wing.]

**fluid**, *floo̅'id*, *adj.* that flows: unsolidified: likely to, tending to change: easily changed.—*n.* a substance whose particles can move about with freedom—a liquid or gas.—*adjs.* **flu'idal**; **fluid'ic.**—*n.* **fluid'ics**, the science and technology of using a flow of liquid or gas for certain operations in place of a flow of electrons.— *vs.t.* **fluid'ify**; **flu'idise, -ize**, to make fluid: to cause (fine particles) to move as a fluid, e.g. by suspending them in a current of air or gas: to fill with a specified fluid.—*ns.* **fluidisā'tion**, **-izā'tion**; **fluid'ity**, **flu'idness.**—**fluid drive**, a system of transmitting power smoothly through the medium of the change in momentum of a fluid, usu. oil. [L. *fluidus*, fluid—*fluēre*, to flow.]

**fluke**, *floo̅k*, *n.* a flounder: a trematode worm, esp. that which causes liver-rot in sheep, so called because like a miniature flounder (also **fluke'-worm**): a variety of kidney potato. [O.E. *flōc*, a plaice; cf. O.N. *flōke*.]

**fluke**, *floo̅k*, *n.* the barb of an anchor: a barb: a lobe of a whale's tail.—*adj.* **fluk'y.** [Prob. a transferred use of the foregoing.]

**fluke**, *floo̅k*, *n.* an accidental success.—*adj.* **fluk'(e)y.** [Origin unknown.]

**flume**, *floo̅m*, *n.* an artificial channel for water to be applied to some industrial purpose: a ravine occupied by a torrent (*U.S.*).—**be**, or **go**, **up the flume**, to come to grief, to be done for. [O.Fr. *flum*—L. *flūmen*, a river—*fluēre*, to flow.]

**flummery**, *flum'ər-i*, *n.* an acid jelly made from the husks of oats, the Scots sowens: blanc-mange: anything insipid: empty compliment, humbug. [W. *llymru—llymrig*, harsh, raw—*llym*, sharp, severe.]

**flummox**, *flum'əks*, (*coll.*) *v.t.* to perplex. [Ety. unknown.]

**flump**, *flump*, (*coll.*) *v.t.* to throw down heavily.— *v.i.* to move with a flop or dump.—*n.* the dull sound so produced. [Imit.]

**flung**, *flung*, *pa.t.* and *pa.p.* of **fling**.

**flunk**, *flungk*, (*slang*) *v.i.* to fail in an examination (sometimes with *out*).—Also *v.t.* and *n.* [Perh. combined flinch, funk (1).]

**flunkey**, *flung'ki*, *n.* a livery servant: a footman: a mean cringer.—*n.* **flun'keydom.**—*adj.* **flun'-keyish.**—*n.* **flun'keyism.** [Perh. orig. *flanker*, one who runs alongside.]

**Fluon**, *floo̅'on*, *n.* trademark for polytetrafluoro-ethylene.

**fluor**, *floo̅'ər, -or*, *n.* fluorite.—*v.i.* **fluoresce** (*-ər-es'*).—*ns.* **fluorescein** (*es'ē-in*), a fluorescent dyestuff, $C_{20}H_{12}O_5$; **fluoresc'ence**, the property of some substances (e.g. fluor) of emitting, when exposed to radiation, rays of greater wavelength

than those received.—*adjs.* **fluoresc'ent**; **fluoric** (*-or'ik*).—*vs.t.* **flu'oridate, -idise, -ize**, to add a fluoride to (a water or milk supply).—*ns.* **fluoridā'tion**; **flu'oride**, a compound of fluorine with another element or radical.—*v.t.* **flu'orinate**, to introduce fluorine into a chemical compound. —*ns.* **fluorinā'tion**; **flu'orine** (*-ēn*), an element (F), a pale greenish-yellow gas; **fluorite** (*floo̅'ər-it*), a mineral, calcium fluoride, commonly purple, also green, colourless, etc., crystallising in cubes and octahedra, found abundantly in Derbyshire. Its coloured varieties may fluoresce strongly in ultraviolet light; **flu'orocarbon**, any of a series of compounds of fluorine and carbon (corresponding to the hydrocarbons) highly resistant to heat and chemical action; **flu'oroscope**, an instrument for X-ray examination by means of a fluorescent screen; **fluoros'copy**; **fluorō'sis**, chronic poisoning by fluorine; **flu'orotype** (*obs.*), photography by means of fluorides; **fluorspar**, fluorite.—**fluorescent lighting**, brighter lighting obtained for the same consumption of electricity, by using fluorescent material to convert ultra-violet radiation in the electric lamp into visible light. [L. *fluor*, flow, from its use as a flux.]

**Fluothane**, *floo̅'ō-thān*. See **halothane**.

**flurry**, *flur'i*, *n.* a sudden blast or gust: agitation: bustle: the death-agony of the whale: a fluttering assemblage of things, as snowflakes.— *v.t.* to agitate, to confuse:—*pr.p.* **flurr'ying**; *pa.t., pa.p.* **flurr'ied.**—*v.t.* **flurr** (*flŭr*), scatter.— *v.i.* to fly up. [Prob. onomatopoeic, suggested by **flaw, hurry**, etc.]

**flush**, *flush*, *n.* a sudden flow: a flow of blood to the skin, causing redness: a suffusion of colour, esp. red: a sudden growth: a renewal of growth: a rush of feeling: a puddle (*obs.*): a watery place about a spring, etc. (*obs.*): bloom, freshness, vigour: abundance.—*v.i.* to glow: to become red in the face: to flow swiftly, suddenly, or copiously.—*v.t.* to cleanse by a copious flow of water: to clear by a blast of air: to cause to glow: to elate, excite the spirits of.—*adj.* overflowing: abounding: well supplied, as with money: in full bloom (*Shak.*): flushed.— *adj.* **flushed**, suffused with ruddy colour: excited. —*ns.* **flush'er**, one who flushes sewers; **flush'ing**; **flush'ness.**—*adj.* **flush'y**, reddish.—**flush'-box**, a tank for flushing a water-closet. [Prob. next word influenced by **flash, blush**.]

**flush**, *flush*, *v.i.* to start up like an alarmed bird.— *v.t.* to rouse and cause to start off.—*n.* the act of starting: a bird, or a flock of birds so started (*Spens.*). [Prob. onomatopoeic; suggested by **fly, flutter, rush**.]

**flush**, *flush*, *v.t.* to make even: to fill up to the level of a surface (often with *up*).—*adj.* having the surface in one plane with the adjacent surface: of a deck, having the same level throughout the ship's length.—Also *adv.* [Prob. related to **flush** (1).]

**flush**, *flush*, *n.* in card-playing, a hand in which all the cards or a specified number are of the same suit.—*adj.* in poker, consisting of cards all of the same suit.—**straight flush**, in poker, a sequence of five cards of the same suit (**royal flush**, if headed by ace). [Prob. Fr. *flux*—L. *fluxus*, flow; influenced by **flush** (1).]

**fluster**, *flus'tər*, *n.* hurrying: flurry: heat (*obs.*): confused agitation.—*v.t.* to make hot and flurried: to fuddle with drink: to confuse.— *v.i.* to bustle: to be agitated or fuddled.—*n.* **flus'terment.**—*adj.* **flus'tery**, confused.—*v.t.* **flus'trate**, to fluster.—*n.* **flustrā'tion.** [O.N. *flaustr*, hurry.]

**Flustra**, *flus'trə*, *n.* one of the commonest genera of marine Polyzoa. [Ety. unknown.]

**flute**, *floo̅t*, *n.* a musical pipe with finger-holes and keys sounded by blowing: in organ-building, a stop with stopped wooden pipes, having a flute-like tone: a longitudinal groove, as on a pillar: a tall and narrow wine-glass: a shuttle in tapestry-weaving, etc.—*v.i.* to play the flute: to make fluty sounds.—*v.t.* to play or sing in soft flute-like tones: to form flutes or grooves in.— *adj.* flut′ed, ornamented with flutes, channels, or grooves.—*ns.* flut′er; flutina (-*tē*′), a kind of accordion; flut′ing, flute-playing or similar sounds: longitudinal furrowing; flut′ist.—*adj.* flut′y, in tone like a flute.—flûte-à-bec (*flüt-à-bek*; Fr.), a fipple flute; flute′-bird, a piping crow; flute′mouth, a fish (*Fistularia*) akin to the sticklebacks. [O.Fr. *fleûte*; ety. dubious.]

flutter, *flut′ər*, *v.i.* to move about nervously, aimlessly, or with bustle: of a bird, to flap wings: of a flag, etc., to flap in the air: to vibrate, e.g. of a pulse, to beat irregularly: to be in agitation or in uncertainty: to be frivolous (*obs.*): to toss a coin (*arch.*).—*v.t.* to throw into disorder: to move in quick motions.—*n.* quick, irregular motion: agitation: confusion: a gambling transaction (*coll.*): a small speculation (*coll.*). [O.E. *flotorian*, to float about, from the root of *flēotan*, to float.]

fluvial, *flōō′vi-əl*, *adj.* of or belonging to rivers.— *n.* flu′vialist, one stressing rivers in explanation of phenomena.—*adjs.* fluviat′ic, flu′viatile (-*til*, -*til*), belonging to or formed by rivers.—*adj.* fluvioglā′cial, pertaining to glacial rivers. [L. *fluviālis* —*fluvius*, a river, *fluĕre*, to flow.]

flux, *fluks*, *n.* act of flowing: a flow of matter: a state of flow or continuous change: a discharge generally from a mucous membrane: matter discharged: excrement: an easily fused substance, esp. one added to another to make it more fusible: the rate of flow of mass, volume, or energy (*phys.*).—*v.t.* to melt.—*v.i.* to flow: to fuse.—*n.* fluxion (*fluk′shən*), a flowing or discharge: excessive flow of blood or fluid to any organ (*med.*): a difference or variation: the rate of change of a continuously varying quantity (*math.*): (in *pl.*) the name given after Newton to that branch of mathematics which with a different notation is known after Leibniz as the differential and integral calculus.—*adjs.* flux′ional, flux′ionary (*arch.*), variable: inconstant.—*n.* flux′ionist, one skilled in fluxions. —*adj.* flux′ive (*Shak.*), flowing with tears. [O.Fr., —L. *fluxus*—*fluĕre*, to flow.]

fly, *flī*, *v.i.* to move through the air, esp. on wings or in aircraft: to move swiftly: to pass quickly: to flee: to burst quickly or suddenly: to flutter. —*v.t.* to avoid, flee from: to cause to fly, as a kite: to conduct or transport by air: to cross or pass by flying:—*pr.p.* fly′ing; *pa.t.* flew, *flōō*; *pa.p.* flown, *flōn*; 3rd *sing. pres. ind.* flies.—*n.* any insect of the *Diptera*: often so widely used, esp. in composition—e.g. butterfly, dragonfly, mayfly—as to be virtually equivalent to insect: a fish-hook dressed in imitation of a fly: (collectively) an insect pest: a familiar spirit (*arch.*): an attendant parasite (*obs.*): a flight: a flap, esp. a tent-door: a flap of material covering, e.g. a trouser opening: the trouser fastener, e.g. zip: the free end of a flag, or the like: a fast stagecoach: a light vehicle on hire, at first drawn by a man, later by a horse: a flywheel: (in *pl.*) the large space above the proscenium in a theatre, from which the scenes, etc., are controlled: —*pl.* flies.—*adj.* (*slang*) wideawake, knowing.— *ns.* flier, flyer (*flī′ər*), one who flies or flees: airman: an object, e.g. train, moving at top speed: a financial speculation (*slang*): part of a machine with rapid motion: a rectangular step in stairs.—*adj.* fly′able, (of weather) in which it is safe to fly.—*n.* fly′ing.—*adj.* that flies or can fly: moving, or passing, very rapidly: organised for speedy action: (of a visit) very brief.—fly agaric, a poisonous mushroom-like fungus that has been used for killing flies;

fly ash, a fine ash from the pulverised fuel burned in power stations, used in brick-making and as a partial substitute for cement in concrete.—*adj.* fly′away, streaming: flighty.—fly′bane, poison for flies: a name for various plants so used; fly′belt, a belt of country infested by tsetse fly.— *adj.* fly′-bitten, marked as by the bite of flies.— fly′blow, the egg of a fly.—*adj.* fly′-blown, tainted with flies′ eggs or maggots (also *fig.*).— fly′boat, a long, narrow, swift boat used on canals; fly′book, a case like a book for holding fishing-flies; fly′-by, a flight, usu. low-altitude, past a place for observation; fly′-by-night, one who gads about at night: an absconding debtor: an irresponsible person.—*adj.* irresponsible, esp. in business matters: unreliable: transitory.— fly′catcher, name for various birds that catch flies on the wing; fly′-fisher, one who uses artificial flies as lure; fly′-fishing; fly′flap, device for driving away flies; fly′-flapp′er; fly′-half (*rugby*), a stand-off half; flying bedstead, a testing framework resembling a bedstead in shape, that can be raised vertically from the ground by a ϳet engine; flying boat, a seaplane with boat body; flying bomb, a bomb in the form of a jet-propelled aeroplane; flying bridge, a ferry-boat moving under the combined forces of the stream and the resistance of a long cable: a pontoon bridge: the highest bridge of a ship; flying buttress, an arch-formed prop; flying camp, flying column, a body of troops for rapid motion from one place to another.—*n.pl.* flying colours, flags unfurled: triumphant success.—Flying Corps, the precursor (1912-18) of the Royal Air Force; flying doctor, a doctor, esp. orig. in the remote parts of Australia, who can be called by radio, etc., and who flies to visit patients; Flying Dutchman, a black spectral Dutch ship, or its captain, condemned to sweep the seas around the Cape of Storms for ever; flying fish, a fish that can leap from the water and sustain itself in the air for a short time by its long pectoral fins, as if flying; flying fox, a large frugivorous bat; flying lemur, an animal (*Cynocephalus* or *Galeopithecus*) of the Eastern Archipelago, whose fore and hind limbs are connected by a fold of skin—included in the Insectivora or made a separate order Dermoptera; flying lizard, a dragon lizard; flying machine, a power-driven aircraft; flying officer, an officer in the Air Force of rank answering to sub-lieutenant in the navy and lieutenant in the army (formerly called observer); flying party, a small body of soldiers, equipped for rapid movements, used to harass an enemy; flying phalanger, a general name for animals akin to the phalangers with a parachute of skin between fore and hind legs; flying saucer, a disk-like flying object reported to have been seen by sundry persons; flying shore, a horizontal baulk or shore; flying shot, a shot at something in motion; flying squad, a rapidly moving body of police or the like; flying squid, a squid with broad lateral fins by which it can spring high out of the water; flying squirrel, a name for several kinds of squirrels with a parachute of skin between the fore and hind legs: also applied to a flying phalanger; flying start, in a race, a start given after the competitors are in motion (also *fig.*); flying wing, an arrow-head-shaped aircraft designed to minimise drag at very high speeds; fly′-kick, a kick made while running; fly′leaf, a blank leaf at the beginning or end of a book; fly line, a line for angling with an artificial fly; fly′maker, one who ties artificial flies for angling; fly-man, one who works the ropes in theatre flies: one who drives a fly; fly orchis, an orchid (*Ophrys muscifera* or *insectifera*) with a flylike flower; fly′over, a processional flight of aircraft: a road or railway-line carried over the top of

# flype 504 foil

another one at an intersection; **fly'paper**, a sticky or poisonous paper for destroying flies; **fly past**, a ceremonial flight analogous to a march past; **fly powder**, a powder used for killing flies; **fly rail**, a flap that turns out to support the leaf of a table; **fly rod**, a light flexible rod used in fly-fishing, usually in three pieces—butt, second-joint, and tip.—*adj.* **fly'-slow** (*Shak.*; doubtful reading and sense), slow-flying.—**fly'-trap**, a trap to catch flies: a plant that traps flies, esp. the American dog-bane, and Venus's flytrap (*bot.*); **fly'-under**, a road or railway-line carried under another one at an intersection; **fly'weight**, a boxer of eight stone or less; **fly'wheel**, a large wheel with a heavy rim applied to machinery to equalise the effect of the driving effort.—**a fly in the ointment**, some slight flaw which corrupts a thing of value (Eccles. x. 1): a minor disadvantage in otherwise favourable circumstances; **fly a kite** (see kite-flying); **fly at, upon,** to attack suddenly; **fly in the face of,** to insult: to oppose, defy; **fly off the handle** (*slang*), to lose one's temper; **fly open,** to open suddenly or violently; **fly out,** to break out in a rage; **let fly,** to attack: to throw or send off; **make the feathers fly** (see feather); **no flies on,** no want of alertness in. [O.E. *flēogan*, to fly, pa.t. *flēah*; *flēoge*, fly, insect; Ger. *fliegen, fliege.*]

**flype,** *flip, v.t.* to strip back: to turn partly outside in. [Prob. Scand.; cf. Dan. *flip,* a flap.]

**Flysch,** *flish, n.* a great Alpine mass of Cretaceous and Lower Tertiary sandstone with shales. [Swiss Ger.]

**flyte, flite,** *flit,* (*Scot.*) *v.i.* to scold, to brawl.—*ns.* **flyte, flyt'ing,** a scolding-match, esp. as a poetical exhibition. [O.E. *flitan,* to strive; Ger. *befleissen.*]

**foal,** *fōl, n.* the young of the horse family.—*v.i.* and *v.t.* to bring forth (a foal).—**foal'foot,** coltsfoot. [O.E. *fola;* Ger. *fohlen,* Gr. *pōlos;* L. *pullus.*]

**foam,** *fōm, n.* bubbles on surface of liquor: a suspension of gas in a liquid: sea (*poet.*).—*v.i.* to gather or produce foam: to come in foam.—*v.t.* to pour out in foam: to fill or cover with foam. —*n.* and *adj.* **foam'ing.**—*adv.* **foam'ingly.**—*adjs.* **foam'less; foam'y,** frothy.—**foam glass,** glass in a form full of tiny air-cells through admixture of carbon under heat, used in insulation, filling lifebelts, etc.; **foam, or foamed, plastics,** very light plastics, soft and flexible like sponges, or rigid, with excellent heat-insulation properties; **foam rubber,** rubber in the form of a foam-like substance, used chiefly in upholstery. [O.E. *fām;* Ger. *feim,* prob. akin to L. *spūma.*]

**fob,** *fob, n.* (*arch.*) a trick.—*v.t.* (*arch.* except with *off*) to cheat: to give as genuine: to put off: to foist, palm. [Cf. Ger. *foppen,* to jeer.]

**fob,** *fob, n.* a small watch pocket in the waistband of trousers: a chain with seals, etc., hanging from the fob.—*v.t.* to pocket. [Perh. conn. with L. Ger. *fobke,* little pocket, H.Ger. dial. *fuppe,* pocket.]

**fo'c'sle,** *fōk'sl,* contr. form of **forecastle.**

**focus,** *fō'kəs, n.* in geom., a fixed point such that the distances of a point on a conic section from it and from the directrix have a constant ratio: in optics, a point in which rays converge after reflection or refraction, or from which (*virtual focus*) they seem to diverge: any central point: the point or region of greatest activity: the point of origin (as of an earthquake): the position, or condition, of sharp definition of an image:—*pl.* **foci,** *fō'sī,* or **fo'cuses.**—*v.t.* to bring to a focus: to adjust to focus: to adjust so as to get a sharp image of: to concentrate:—*pr.p.* **fo'cusing;** *pa.t.* and *pa.p.* **fo'cused;** some double the *s.*—*adj.* **fō'cal,** of or belonging to a focus.—*v.t.* **fō'calise, -ize,** to focus.—*n.* **focimeter** (*fō-sim'i-tar*), apparatus to help in focusing.—**focusing cloth,**

a cloth thrown over a photographic camera and the operator's head and shoulders to exclude extraneous light in focusing.—**conjugate foci,** two points such that each is focus for rays proceeding from the other; **focal-plane shutter,** camera shutter in the form of a blind with a slot, which is pulled rapidly across, and as close as is practicable to, the film or plate, speed being varied by adjusting the width of the slot; **in focus,** placed or adjusted so as to secure distinct vision, or a sharp, definite image; **principal focus,** the focus for rays parallel to the axis. [L. *fŏcus,* a hearth.]

**fodder,** *fod'ər, n.* food supplied to cattle: food (*slang*).—*v.t.* to supply with fodder.—*ns.* **fodd'erer; fodd'ering.** [O.E. *fōdor;* Ger. *futter;* cf. **food, feed.**]

**foe,** *fō, n.* an enemy:—*pl.* **foes;** *Spens.* **fone, foen,** *fōn.*—**foe'man,** an enemy in war (*pl.* **foe'men**). [M.E. *foo*—O.E. *fāh, fā* (adj.) and *gefā* (noun).]

**foedarie.** See **fedarie.**

**foederatus,** *fed-ə-rā'təs, foi-de-rā'tōōs* (*pl.* **foederati,** *-rā'tī, -rā'tē;* L.) a (conquered) ally of Rome: an auxiliary soldier fighting for the Romans.

**foetid, foetor.** See **fetid, fetor.**

**foetus,** the usual but etymologically unsatisfactory form of **fetus,** *fē'təs, n.* the young animal in the egg or in the womb, after its parts are distinctly formed.—*adj.* **foe'tal, fē'tal.**—*n.* **foe'ticide, fē'ticide,** destruction of a foetus.—*adj.* **foetici'dal, fē-.** [L. *fētus,* offspring.]

**fog,** *fog, n.* a thick mist: watery vapour condensed about dust particles in drops: cloudy obscurity: confusion, bewilderment.—*v.t.* to shroud in fog: to obscure: to confuse.—*v.i.* to become coated, clouded, blurred, confused.—*adj.* **fogged** (*fogd*), clouded, obscured: bewildered.—*ns.* **fogg'er, fog'man,** one who sets railway fog-signals.— *adv.* **fogg'ily.**—*n.* **fogg'iness.**—*adjs.* **fogg'y,** misty: damp: fogged: clouded in mind: stupid; **fog'-less,** without fog, clear.—**fog'-bank,** a dense mass of fog like a bank of land; **fog'-bell,** a bell rung by waves or wind to warn sailors in fog.— *adj.* **fog'bound,** impeded by fog.—**fog'-bow,** a whitish arch like a rainbow, seen in fogs; **fog'-dog,** a whitish spot seen near the horizon in fog; **fog'horn,** a horn used as a warning signal by or to ships in foggy weather: a siren: a big bellowing voice; **fog'-signal,** a detonating cap or other audible warning used in fog; **fog'-smoke,** fog.— **not to have the foggiest,** not to have the least idea. [Origin obscure; perh. conn. with next word; perh. with Dan. *fog,* as in *snee-fog,* thick falling snow.]

**fog, fog, foggage,** *fog'ij, n.* grass that grows after the hay is cut: moss (*Scot.*).—*v.i.* to become covered with fog.—*adj.* **fogg'y.** [Origin unknown; W. *ffwg,* dry grass, is borrowed from English.]

**fogash,** *fog'osh,* the pike-perch. [Hung. *fogas.*]

**fogle,** *fō'gəl,* (*slang*) *n.* a silk handkerchief. [Origin obscure.]

**fogy, fogey,** *fō'gi, n.* a dull old fellow: one with antiquated notions.—*adj.* **fō'gram,** antiquated. —*n.* a fogy.—*ns.* **fō'gramite; fogram'ity; fō'gydom.**—*adj.* **fō'gyish.**—*n.* **fō'gyism.** [Prob. from **foggy,** moss-grown.]

**foh, pho, phoh,** *fō, interj.* expressing disgust or contempt.

**föhn, foehn,** *fœn, n.* a hot dry wind blowing down a mountain valley. [Ger.,—Romansch *favugn*— Lat. *Favōnius,* the west wind.]

**foible,** *foi'bl, n.* a weakness: a penchant: a failing: a faible. [O.Fr. *foible,* weak; cf. **faible, feeble.**]

**foie gras,** *fwä grä,* (Fr.) fat liver (of goose) made into *pâté de foie gras* (or *foies gras*) (*pä-tä də*).

**foil,** *foil, v.t.* to defeat: to baffle: to frustrate: to beat down or trample with the feet (*obs.*): in hunting, to destroy a trail by crossing.—*n.* a check, repulse, frustration (*obs.*): an incomplete

*fāte, fär; mē, hûr* (her); *mīne; mōte, fōr; mūte; mōōn, fŏŏt; dhen* (then) fall in wrestling: a blunt fencing sword with a button on the point.—**put on the foil**, to overcome, bring to naught. [O.Fr. *fuler*, to stamp or crush— L. *fullō*, a fuller of cloth.]

**foil**, *foil*, *n*, a leaf or thin plate of metal, as tinfoil: a mercury coating on a mirror: metalcoated paper: a thin leaf of metal put under a precious stone to show it to advantage: anything that serves to set off something else: a small arc in tracery.—*adj.* **foiled**.—*n.* **foil'ing**. [O.Fr. *foil* (Fr. *feuille*)—L. *folium*, a leaf.]

**foin**, *foin*, *v.i.* to thrust with a sword or spear.— *n.* a thrust with a sword or spear.—*adv.* **foin'ingly**. [O.Fr. *foine*—L. *fuscina*, a trident.]

**foison**, *foi'zn*, *n.* plenty (*arch.*): plentiful yield (*arch.*): strength, vitality, essential virtue (*Scot*; also **fushion**, *foōzh'ən*, *fizh'ən*, *fizz'*en).—*adj.* **foi'sonless**, weak, feeble (*Scot*; also **fush'ionless**, **fizz'enless**). [O.Fr.,—L. *fūsiō*, *-ōnis*—*fundĕre*, *fūsum*, to pour forth.]

**foist**, *foist*, *v.t.* to bring in by stealth: to insert wrongfully: to pass off (*in* or *into* the thing affected, *upon* the person).—*n.* **foist'er**. [Prob. Du. dial. *vuisten*, to take in hand; *vuist*, fist.]

**fold**, *fōld*, *n.* a doubling of anything upon itself: a crease: the concavity of anything folded: a part laid over on another.—*v.t.* to lay in folds, double over: to enclose in a fold or folds, to wrap up: to embrace.—*v.i.* to become folded: to be capable of folding: to yield (*obs.*).—*suff.* **-fold** (with numerals), times, as in **ten'-fold**.—*n.* **fold'er**, the person or thing that folds: a flat knife-like instrument used in folding paper: a folding case for loose papers: a folded circular. —*adj.* **fold'ing**, that folds, or that can be folded. —*ns.* **fold'ing**, a fold or plait: the bending of strata, usu. as the result of compression (*geol.*).— **folded mountains**, mountains produced by folding processes; **fold'ing-door**, a door consisting of two parts hung on opposite jambs; **fold'ingmachine**, a mechanism that automatically folds printed sheets.—**fold in**, to mix in carefully and gradually (*cook.*); **fold up**, to cease to function. [O.E. *faldan* (W.S. *fealdan*), to fold; Ger. *falten*.]

**fold**, *fōld*, *n.* an enclosure for protecting domestic animals, esp. sheep; a flock of sheep: a church (*fig.*): the Christian Church (*fig.*).—*v.t.* to confine in a fold.—*n.* **fold'ing**. [O.E. *falod*, *fald*, a fold, stall.]

**folic acid**, *fō'lik* (*fo'lik*) *as'id*, an acid in the vitamin B complex, found in leaves, liver, etc., or a similar acid which cures some of the symptoms of pernicious anaemia (see **pterin**). [See **folium**.]

**folie**, *fo-lē*, (Fr.) madness, insanity: folly.

**folio**, *fō'li-ō*, *n.* a leaf (two pages) of a book: a sheet of paper once folded: a book of such sheets: the size of such a book: one of several sizes of paper adapted for folding once into well-proportioned leaves: a page in an accountbook, or two opposite pages numbered as one (*book-k.*): a certain number of words taken as a basis for computing the length of a document (*law*): page number in a book (*print.*): a wrapper for loose papers.—*adj.* consisting of paper only once folded: of the size of a folio.— *v.t.* to number the leaves or the pages of: to mark off the end of every folio of, in law copying. —**in folio**, in sheets folded once: in the form of a folio. [L. *in foliō*, on leaf (so-and-so), used in references; L. *folium*, a leaf, a sheet of paper.]

**folium**, *fō'li-əm*, *n.* a leaf, lamina, or lamella:— *pl.* **fō'lia**.—*adj.* **fōliāceous** (*-ā'shəs*), leaflike: like a foliage leaf: leaf-bearing: laminated.—*n.* **fō'liage**, leaves collectively: a mass of leaves: plant forms in art.—*adjs.* **fō'liaged**, having foliage: worked like foliage; **fō'liar**, pertaining to leaves: resembling leaves.—*v.t.* **fō'liate**, orig., to beat into a leaf: to cover with leaf-metal: to number the leaves (not pages) of.—*adj.* **fō'liated**,

beaten into a thin leaf: decorated with leaf ornaments or foils: consisting of layers or laminae.—*ns.* **fō'liāticn**, the leafing, esp. of plants: the act of beating a metal into a thin plate, or of spreading foil over a piece of glass to form a mirror: the numbering of leaves in a book: the alternation of more or less parallel layers or folia of different mineralogical nature, of which the crystalline schists are composed (*geol.*): decoration with cusps, lobes, or foliated tracery (*archit.*); **fō'liature**, foliation; **fō'liole**, a leaflet of a compound leaf (*bot.*): a small leaflike structure.—*adjs.* **fō'liolate**, **fō'liolose**, composed of or pertaining to leaflets; **fō'liose**, leafy: leaflike.—**foliage leaf**, an ordinary leaf, not a petal, bract, etc.; **foliage plant**, one grown for the beauty of its foliage. [L. *folium*, a leaf; cf. **blade**; Gr. *phyllon*.]

**folk**, *fōk*, *n.* people, collectively or distributively: a nation or people: the people, commons (*arch.*): those of one's own family, relations (*coll.*): now generally used as a pl. (either **folk** or **folks**).—*adj.* handed down by tradition of the people (found also in **folk-art**, **folk-craft**, **folkmedicine**, **folk-music**, etc.).—*adj.* **folk'sy** (*U.S.*), everyday: friendly: sociable.—*n.* **folk'siness**.— **folk'-dance**, a dance handed down by tradition of the people; **Folketing** (Dan. *fōl'ke-ting*), the lower house of the Danish parliament or Rigsdag; **folk'-etymol'ogy**, popular unscientific attempts at etymology.—*adj.* **folk'-free**, having the rights of a freeman.—**folk'land** (O.E. *folcland*), in old English times, probably land held by folk-right, opposed to *bōcland* (bookland); **folk'lore**, the study of ancient observances and customs, the notions, beliefs, traditions, superstitions, and prejudices of the common people—the science of the survival of archaic belief and custom in modern ages (a name suggested by W. J. Thoms in 1846); **folk'lōrist**, one who studies folklore; **folk-memory**, a memory of an event that survives in a community through many generations: power of remembering as attributed to a community; **folk'moot**, an assembly of the people among the Old English; **folk'-right**, the common law or right of the people; **folk'rock**, a form of popular music which adapts folk melodies to the rhythm of rock-and-roll; **folk'-song**, any song or ballad originating among the people and traditionally handed down by them; **folk'-speech**, the dialect of the common people of a country, in which ancient idioms are embedded; **folk'-tale**, a popular story handed down by oral tradition from a more or less remote antiquity; **folk'-tune**, a tune handed down among the people; **folk'way**, a traditional way of thinking, feeling, or acting, followed unreflectingly by a social group; **folk'-weave**, a loosely woven fabric. [O.E. *folc*; O.N. *folk*; Ger. *volk*.]

**follicle**, *fol'i-kl*, *n.* a fruit formed from a single carpel containing several seeds, splitting along the ventral suture only (*bot.*): any small saclike structure, as the pit surrounding a hair-root (*zool.*).—*adjs.* **follic'ūlated**, **follic'ūlar**, **follic'ū-lose**, **follic'ūlous**. [L. *folliculus*, dim. of *follis*, a wind-bag.]

**follow**, *fol'ō*, *v.t.* to go after or behind: to keep along the line of: to come after, succeed: to pursue: to attend: to imitate: to obey: to adopt, as an opinion: to keep the eye or mind fixed on: to grasp or understand the whole course or sequence of: to result from, as an effect from a cause: to strive to obtain (*B.*).— *v.i.* to come after: to result: to be the logical conclusion.—*n.* a stroke that causes the ball to follow the one it has struck (*billiards*); commonly **follow-through'**): a second helping.—*ns.* **foll'-ower**, one who comes after: a copier: a disciple: a retainer, an attendant: a servant-girl's sweetheart: a part of a machine driven by another part; **foll'owing**, body of supporters.—*adj.* coming next after: to be next mentioned.— *prep.* after.—**foll'ow-board**, in moulding, the board on which the pattern is laid; **follow-my-lead'er**, a game in which all have to mimic whatever the leader does; **follow-on'**, **-through'**, an act of following on or through.—**follow home**, to follow to point aimed at, heart of the matter; **follow on**, to continue endeavours (*B.*): in cricket, to take a second innings immediately after one's first, as compulsory result of being short in number of runs: to follow immediately (*coll.*): to start where another left off (*coll.*); **follow out**, to carry out (e.g. instructions): to follow to the end or conclusion; **follow suit**, in card-playing, to play a card of the same suit as the one which was led: to do what another has done; **follow through**, to complete the swing of a stroke after hitting the ball; **follow up**, to pursue an advantage closely: to pursue a question that has been started. [O.E. *folgian*, *fylgan*; Ger. *folgen*.]

**folly**, *fol'i*, *n.* silliness or weakness of mind: a foolish thing: sin (*obs.*): a monument of folly, as a great useless structure, or one left unfinished, having been begun without a reckoning of the cost.—*v.i.* (*arch.*), to act with folly. [O.Fr. *folie* —*fol*, foolish.]

**Fomalhaut**, *fō'məl-howt*, *-höt*, *n.* a first-magnitude star in the constellation of the Southern Fish. [Ar. *fam-al-hūt*, the whale's mouth.]

**foment**, *fō-ment'*, *v.t.* to apply a warm lotion to: to cherish with heat (*obs.*): to foster (usu. evil). —*ns.* **fomentā'tion**, the application of a warm lotion (extended sometimes to a dry or cold application): the lotion so applied: instigation; **fomen'ter**. [L. *fōmentum* for *fovimentum*— *fovēre*, to warm.]

**fomes**, *fō'mēz*, *n.* a substance capable of carrying infection:—*pl.* **fomites**, *fō'mi-tēz*. [L. *fōmes*, *-itis*, touchwood.]

**fon**, *fon*, (*obs.*) *n.* a fool.—*v.i.* to be foolish, play the fool.—*v.t.* to befool: to toy with.—*adv.* **fon'ly**, foolishly. [See **fond**.]

**fonctionnaire**, *fōk-syo-ner*, (Fr.) official: civil servant.

**fond**, *fond*, *adj.* foolishly tender and loving: credulous, foolishly hopeful: weakly indulgent: prizing highly (with *of*): very affectionate: kindly disposed: foolish.—*v.i.* to dote.—*v.t.* **fond'le**, to handle with fondness: to caress.—*ns.* **fond'ler**; **fond'ling**, a pet: a fool (*obs.*).—*adv.* **fond'ly**.—*n.* **fond'ness**. [Pa.p. of **fon**—M.E. *fonnen*, to act foolishly, *fon*, a fool.]

**fond** (*Spens.*), *pa.t.* of **fand** (2) and *pa.t.* and *pa.p* of **find**.

**fond**, *fõ*, (Fr.) basis, foundation, background.

**fonda**, *fon'dä*, (Sp.) a tavern.

**fondant**, *fon'dant*, *n.* a soft sweetmeat that melts in the mouth. [Fr.,—*fondre*, to melt—L. *fundēre*.]

**fonds**, *fõ*, (Fr.) landed property: capital: money: fund (*lit.* and *fig.*)

**fondue**, *fon'dōō*, *fõ-dü*, *n.* a sauce made from cheese and wine, etc., and which is eaten by dipping pieces of bread, etc., in the mixture: a soufflé with bread or biscuit crumbs. [Fr.,— fem. pa.p. of *fondre*, to melt.]

**fone**, *fōn*, *n.* See **foe**.

**fons et origo**, *fons et o-ri'gō*, *-rē'*, (L.) the source and origin.

**font**, *font*, *n.* a vessel for baptismal water: a fount, fountain (*poet.*).—*adj.* **font'al**, pertaining to a font or origin.—*n.* **font'let**, a little font.— **font'-stone**, a baptismal font of stone. [O.E. *font*—L. *fōns*, *fontis*, a fountain.]

**font**, *font*. See **fount** (1).

**fontanelle**, **fontanel**, *fon-tə-nel'*, *n.* a gap between the bones of the skull of a young animal: an opening for discharge. [Fr. dim.,—L. *fōns*, *fontis*, fountain.]

**fontange**, *fõ-tãzh'*, *n.* a tall head-dress worn in the 17th and 18th centuries. [Fr., from *Fontanges*, the territorial title of one of Louis XIV's mistresses.]

**Fontarabian**, *fon-tə-rä'bi-ən*, *adj.* pertaining to *Fontarabia* or Fuenterrabia at the west end of the Pyrenees (confused by Milton with Roncesvalles).

**fonticulus**, *fon-tik'ū-las*, *n.* the depression just over the top of the breast-bone. [L. *fonticulus* dim. of *fōns*, fountain.]

**Fontinalis**, *fon-tin-ä'lis*, *n.* a genus of aquatic mosses allied to *Hypnum*. [L. *fontinālis*, of a spring—*fōns*.]

**food**, *fōōd*, *n.* what one feeds on: that which, being digested, nourishes the body: whatever sustains or promotes growth (also *fig.*): substances elaborated by the plant from raw materials taken in (*bot.*).—*adjs.* **food'ful**, able to supply food abundantly; **food'less**, without food.—**food'-card**, a card entitling its holder to obtain his quota of rationed food-stuffs; **food chain**, a series of organisms connected by the fact that each forms food for the next higher organism in the series; **food'-controll'er**, an official who controls the storing, sale, and distribution of food in time of emergency; **food poisoning**, gastrointestinal disorder caused by the ingestion of foods naturally toxic to the system or of foods made toxic by contamination with bacteria or chemicals; **food'-stuff**, a substance used as food; **food values**, the relative nourishing power of foods. [O.E. *fōda*; Goth. *fōdeins*, Sw. *föda*.]

**food**, *fōōd*, Spens. for **feud** (1).

**fool**, *fōōl*, *n.* one wanting in wisdom, judgment or sense: a person of weak mind: a jester: a tool or victim, as of untoward circumstances, a dupe: a vague term of endearment (*obs.*): nothing in comparison: one with a weakness for (with *for*). —*v.t.* to deceive: to make to appear foolish: to get by fooling.—*v.i.* to play the fool: to trifle. —*adj.* (*Scot.* and *U.S.*) foolish.—*ns.* **fool'ery**, an act of folly: habitual folly: fooling; **fool'ing**, playing the fool: acting the jester: vein of jesting: trifling.—*adj.* **fool'ish**, weak in intellect: wanting discretion: unwise: ridiculous: marked with folly: paltry.—*adv.* **fool'ishly**.—*n.* **fool'ishness**.—*adjs.* **fool'begged** (*Shak.*), perh., foolish enough to be begged for a fool (in allusion to the custom of seeking the administration of a lunatic's estate for one's own advantage); **fool'-born** (*Shak.*), born of a fool or of folly; **fool'-y**, happy or lucky without contrivance or judgment.—**fool'hard'iness** (*Spens.* **foolhardise**, **-ize**; *-iz'* or *härd'*).—*adjs.* **foolhard'y**, foolishly bold: rash or incautious; **fool'ish-witt'y** (*Shak.*), wise in folly and foolish in wisdom; **fool'proof**, not liable to sustain or inflict injury by wrong usage: infallible.—**fool's cap**, a jester's head-dress, usu. having a cockscomb hood with bells; **fool's err'and**, a silly or fruitless enterprise: search for that which cannot be found; **fool's gold**, iron pyrites; **fool's mate** (*chess*), the simplest of the mates (in four moves); **fool's paradise**, a state of happiness based on fictitious hopes or expectations; **fool's pars'ley**, a poisonous umbelliferous plant (*Aethusa Cynapium*) that a great enough fool might take for parsley.—**All Fool's Day** (*see* **April**); **fool around**, to waste time: to trifle: to trifle with someone's affections; **fool away**, to squander to no purpose or profit; **fool with**, to meddle with officiously: **make a fool of**, to bring a person into ridicule: to disappoint; **nobody's fool**, a sensible person; **play the fool**, to behave as a fool: to sport. [O.Fr. *fol* (Fr. *fou*)—L. *follis*, a wind-bag.]

**fool**, *fōōl*, *n.* a crushed fruit or the like scalded or stewed, mixed with cream and sugar, as *gooseberry fool*. [Prob. a use of preceding suggested by *trifle*.]

**foolscap**, *fōōlz'kap*, *n.* before metrication, a long folio writing- or printing-paper, generally 17 × 13½ in., originally bearing the watermark of a *fool's cap* and bells.

**foot**, *fōōt*, *n.* the part of its body on which an animal stands or walks: a muscular development of the ventral surface in molluscs: the absorbent and attaching organ of a young sporophyte (*bot.*): the part on which a thing stands: the base: the lower or less dignified end: a measure = 12 in., orig., the length of a man's foot: the corresponding square or cubic unit (sq. ft. 144 sq. inches; cu. ft. 1728 cu. inches): footsoldiers: a division of a line of poetry:—*pl.* **feet**; also, as a measure, **foot**; in some compounds and in sense of dregs, or footlights, **foots.**—*v.t.* and *v.i.* to dance: to walk: to sum up.—*v.t.* to kick: to pay: to add a foot to: to grasp with the foot:—*pr.p.* **foot′ing**; *pa.t.* and *pa.p.* **foot′ed.**—*n.* **foot′age**, measurement or payment by the foot: length of organ pipe giving the lowest note.—*adj.* **foot′ed**, provided with a foot or feet: having gained a foothold (*Shak.*).—*ns.* **foot′er** (*slang*), football; **foot′ing**, place for the foot to rest on: standing: terms: installation: an installation fee or treat: foundation: lower part: position: settlement: track: tread: dance: plain cotton lace.—**foot′ball**, a a large ball for kicking about in sport: a game played with this ball; **foot′baller**, **foot′ballist**, a football player; **foot′bar**, the bar controlled by the pilot's feet, for operating the rudder in aircraft; **foot′-bath**, act of bathing the feet: a vessel for this purpose; **foot′board**, a support for the foot in a carriage or elsewhere: the footplate of a locomotive engine; **foot′boy**, an attendant in livery; **foot′breadth**, the breadth of a foot; **foot′bridge**, a bridge for foot-passengers; **foot′cloth**, a sumpter-cloth reaching to the feet of the horse; **foot′fall**, the sound of setting the foot down; **foot′fault** (*lawn tennis*), an overstepping of the line in serving.—Also *v.t.* and *v.i.* —**foot′gear**, shoes and stockings.—*n.pl.* **foot′-guards**, guards that serve on foot.—**foot′hill**, a minor elevation below a higher mountain or range (usually in *pl.*); **foot′hold**, a place to fix the foot in: a grip: a firm starting position; **foot′-jaw**, a maxilliped; **foot′-land′-raker** (*Shak.*), a footpad; **foot′-licker**, a fawning, slavish flatterer; **foot′light**, one of a row of lights along the front of the stage.—*adj.* **foot′-loose**, free, unhampered.—**foot′man**, one who goes on foot: servant or attendant in livery: foot-soldier: servant running before a coach or rider (*pl.* **foot′men**); **foot′mark** (see **foot′print**); **foot′muff**, muff for keeping the feet warm; **foot′note**, a note of reference or comment at the foot of a page; **foot′pace**, a walking pace: a dais; **foot′pad**, a highwayman on foot; **foot′page**, a boy attendant; **foot′-pass′enger**, one who goes on foot; **foot′path**, a way for foot-passengers only: a side pavement; **foot′plate**, platform for footplatemen, train driver and assistant (on steam locomotive, stoker); **foot′post**, a post or messenger that travels on foot; **foot′-pound**, the energy needed to raise a mass of one pound through the height of one foot; **foot′-pump**, a pump held or operated by the foot; **foot′-race**, a race on foot; **foot′-racing**, **foot′rest**, a support for the foot; **foot′-rope**, a rope stretching along under a ship's yard for the men to stand on when furling the sails: the rope to which the lower edge of a sail is attached; **foot′rot**, ulceration of the coronary band, or other affection of the feet in sheep; **foot′rule**, a rule or measure a foot in length or measured off in feet.—*v.i.* **foot′slog**, to march, tramp.—**foot′slogger**; **foot′slogging**;

**foot′-soldier**, a soldier serving on foot.—*adj.* **foot′sore**, having sore or tender feet, as by much walking.—**foot′stalk** (*bot.*), the stalk or petiole of a leaf; **foot′-stall**, a side-saddle stirrup; **foot′step**, a tread: a footfall: a footprint: a raised step for ascending or descending: (in *pl., fig.*) course, example; **foot′stool**, a stool for placing one's feet on when sitting.—*adj.* **foot′stooled.**—**foot′-warm′er**, a contrivance for keeping the feet warm; **foot′way**, a path for passengers on foot: a mine shaft with ladders; **foot′wear**, a collective term for boots and shoes; **foot′work**, use or management of the feet, as in games.—*adj.* **foot′worn**, worn by many feet: **footsore.**—**at the feet of**, in submission, homage, supplication, or devotion to, under the spell of; **cover the feet** (*B.*), to defecate.—*adj.* **eight′-foot** (*mus.*), having the pitch of an open organ-pipe eight feet long, or having that pitch for the lowest note.—**foot-and-mouth disease**, a contagious disease of cloven-footed animals, characterised by vesicular eruption, esp. in the mouth and in the clefts of the feet; **foot it**, to walk: to dance; **foot of fine**, the bottom part (preserved in the records) of a tripartite indenture in case of a fine of land; **foot the bill**, to pay up; **have one foot in the grave**, to be not far from death; **have one's feet on the ground**, to act habitually with practical good sense; **on foot**, walking or running: in activity or being; **put one's best foot forward**, to make one's best effort; **put one's foot down**, to take a firm decision, usu. against something; **put one's foot in it**, to spoil anything by some indiscretion; **set foot in** (on), to enter; **set on foot**, to originate; **the ball is at his feet**, he has nothing to do but seize his opportunity; **the footlights**, the theatre as a profession; **the wrong foot**, disadvantageous position or circumstances; as **catch on the wrong foot**, to catch unprepared, **get off on the wrong foot**, to make a bad beginning. [O.E. *fōt*, pl. *fēt*; Ger. *fuss*, L. *pēs*, *pedis*, Gr. *pous*, *podos*, Sans. *pad*.]

**footle**, *fōōt'l*, *v.i.* to trifle, to show foolish incompetence, to bungle.—*n.* silly nonsense.—*n.* and *adj.* **foot′ling.** [Origin obscure.]

**footy**, *fōōt'i*, (*dial.*) *adj.* mean. [Origin obscure.]

**foozle**, *fōōz'l*, (*coll.*) *n.* a tedious fellow: a bungled stroke at golf, etc.—*v.i.* to fool away one's time.—*v.i.* and *v.t.* to bungle.—*n.* fooz′ler.—*n.* and *adj.* fooz′ling. [Cf. Ger. dial. *fuseln*, to work badly, to potter.]

**fop**, *fop*, *n.* an affected dandy.—*ns.* fop′ling, a vain affected person; fopp′ery, vanity in dress or manners: affectation: folly.—*adj.* fopp′ish, vain and showy in dress: affectedly refined in manners.—*adv.* fopp′ishly.—*n.* fopp′ishness. [Cf. Ger. *foppen*, to hoax.]

**for**, *för*, *fər*, *prep.* in the place of: in favour of: on account of: in the direction of: with respect to: in respect of: by reason of: appropriate or adapted to, or in reference to: beneficial to: in quest of: notwithstanding, in spite of: in recompense for: during: in the character of: to the extent of.—*conj.* because.—**as for**, as far as concerns; **for all** (that), notwithstanding; **for that** (*obs.*), because; **for to** (*arch.*; *dial.*), in order to: to; **for why** (*obs.*), why: because; **nothing for it but**, nothing else to be done in the case; **to be (in) for it**, to have something unpleasant impending; **what is he for a man?** (*obs.*), what kind of man is he? [O.E. *for.*]

**for-**, *för-*, *fər-*, *pfx.* (1) in words derived from O.E., used to form verbs with the senses: (a) away, off; (b) against; (c) thoroughly, utterly: intensive; (d) exhaustion; (e) destruction. (2) used in words derived from O.E. to form adjs. with superlative force. (3) a contraction of *fore-*. (4) in words derived from L. *foris*, outside, *forās*, forth, out. No longer a living prefix.

**forage**, *for'ij*, *n.* fodder, or food for horses and cattle: provisions: the act of foraging.—*v.i.* to go about and forcibly carry off food for horses and cattle: to rummage about for what one wants.—*v.t.* to plunder.—*n.* for'ager.—for'age-cap, the undress cap worn by infantry soldiers. [Fr. *fourrage*, O.Fr. *feurre*, fodder, of Gmc. origin; cf. fodder.]

**foramen**, *fō-rā'mən*, *fō-*, *n.* a small opening:—*pl.* foramina, *-ram'i-nə*.—*adjs.* foram'inated, foram'-inous, pierced with small holes: porous.—*n.* foraminifer (*for-ə-min'i-fər*; L. *ferre*, to bear), any member of the Foraminif'era (*-am-*, or *-ām-*), an order of rhizopods with a shell usu. perforated by pores (*foramina*).—*adjs.* foraminif'eral, foraminif'erous.—forāmen magnum, the great hole in the occipital bone through which the spinal column joins the medulla oblongata. [L. *forāmen*—*forāre*, to pierce.]

**forane**, *for-ān'*, *adj.* a form of foreign, outlying, rural, as in vicar forane (q.v.).

**forasmuch**, *för-*, *fər-əz-much'*, *conj.* because, since (with *as*).

**foray**, *for'ā*, *n.* a raid.—*v.t.* and *v.i.* to raid: to forage.—*n.* for'ayer. [Ety. obscure, but ult. identical with forage (q.v.).]

**forbad(e)**. See forbid.

**forbear**, *för-*, *fər-bār'*, *v.i.* to keep oneself in check: to abstain.—*v.t.* to abstain from: to avoid voluntarily: to spare, to withhold: to give up (*obs.*):—*pa.t.* forbore'; *pa.p.* forborne'.—*n.* forbear'ance, exercise of patience: command of temper: clemency.—*adjs.* forbear'ant, forbear'ing, long-suffering: patient.—*adv.* forbear'-ingly. [O.E. *forberan*, pa.t. *forbær*, pa.p. *forboren*; see pfx. for- (1a), and bear.]

**forbear**, *för'bār*. Same as forebear.

**forbid**, *fər-*, *för-bid'*, *v.t.* to prohibit: to command not to:—*pa.t.* forbade, *-bad'*, by some *-bād'*, or forbad'; *pa.p.* forbidd'en.—*ns.* forbidd'al, forbidd'ance, prohibition: command or edict against a thing.—*adj.* forbidd'en, prohibited: unlawful.—*adv.* forbidd'enly (*Shak.*), in a forbidden or unlawful manner.—*n.* forbidd'ing.—*adj.* uninviting: sinister: unprepossessing: threatening or formidable in look.—*adv.* forbidd'ingly.—*ns.* forbidd'ingness; forbode (*för-bōd*; arch.), prohibition.—forbidden degrees (see degree); forbidden fruit, that forbidden to Adam (Gen. ii. 17): anything tempting and prohibited: (or *Adam's apple*) a name fancifully given to the fruit of various species of Citrus, esp. to one having tooth-marks on its rind.—over God's forbode, God forbid. [O.E. *forbēodan*, pa.t. *forbēad*, pa.p. *forboden*; see pfx. for- (1a), and bid; cf. Ger. *verbieten*.]

**forby**, (*Spens.* foreby), *fər-bi'*, *adv.* and *prep.* near (*obs.*): past (*obs.*): by (*obs.*): besides (*Scot.*). [for, *adv*, by.]

**forçat**, *för'sä*, *n.* in France, a convict condemned to hard labour. [Fr.]

**force**, *förs*, *förs*, *n.* strength, power, energy: efficacy: validity: influence: vehemence: violence: coercion: group of men assembled for collective action (as *police force*), (*pl.*) navy, army, air force: an armament: any cause which changes the direction or speed of the motion of a portion of matter.—*v.t.* to draw or push by main strength: to thrust: to compel: to constrain: to overcome the resistance of by force: to do violence to: to achieve or bring about by force: to ravish: to take by violence: to strain: to cause to grow or ripen rapidly (*hort.*): to work up to a high pitch: to induce to play in a particular way (*cards*): to cause the playing of (*cards*): to strengthen (*Shak.*): to attribute importance to (*obs.*).—*v.i.* to strive (*obs.*): to make way by force: to care (*obs.*).—*adj.* forced, accomplished by great effort, as a forced march: strained, excessive, unnatural:

artificially produced. — *adv.* forc'edly. — *n.* forc'edness, the state of being forced: constraint: unnatural or undue distortion.—*adj.* force'ful, full of force or might: energetic: driven or acting with power.—*adv.* force'fully.—*adj.* force'less, weak.—*ns.* forc'er, the person or thing that forces, esp. the piston of a force-pump.—*adj.* Forc'es, of or pertaining to the armed forces, army, navy, or air force.—*adj.* forc'ible, having force: done by force.—*n.* forc'ibleness.—*adv.* forc'ibly.—*v.i.* force'-land, to make a forced landing.—forced landing (*aero.*), a landing at a place where no landing was orig. planned, necessary because of some mishap; force'-pump, forc'ing-pump, a pump that delivers liquid under pressure greater than its suction pressure: a pump for cleaning out pipes by blowing air through; forcible detainer, and entry, detaining property or forcing an entry into it by violence or intimidation; forcible feeble, a weak man with show of valour (in allusion to Francis Feeble in II. Hen. IV, III, ii. 180); forc'ing-house, a hothouse for forcing plants; forc'ing-pit, a frame sunk in the ground over a hotbed for forcing plants.—force and fear (*Scot.*), that amount of constraint or compulsion which is enough to annul an engagement or obligation entered into under its influence; force the pace, to bring and keep the speed up to a high pitch by emulation. [Fr.,—L.L. *fortia*—L. *fortis*, strong.]

**force**, *förs*, *förs*, foss, *fos*, *n.* a waterfall. [O.N. *fors*.]

**force**, *förs*, *förs*, (*cook.*) *v.t.* to stuff, as a fowl.—force'meat, meat chopped fine and highly seasoned, used as a stuffing or alone. [For farce.]

**force majeure**, *fors mä-zhœr*, (Fr.) superior power.

**forceps**, *för'seps*, *n.* a pincer-like instrument or organ for holding, lifting, or removing:—*pl.* for'ceps, also for'cepses, for'cipēs, *-si-pēz*.—*adj.* for'cipated, formed and opening like a forceps.—*n.* forcipā'tion, torture by pinching with forceps. [L.,—*formus*, hot, *capěre*, to hold.]

**ford**, *förd*, *förd*, *n.* a place where water may be crossed by wading.—*v.t.* to wade across.—*adj.* ford'able. [O.E. *ford-faran*, to go; cf. Ger. *furt-fahren*, Gr. *poros*, L. *portus*, and fare, ferry, far.]

**fordo**, *för-*, *fər-dōō'*, (*arch.*) *v.t.* to destroy: to ruin: to overcome: to exhaust:—*pr.p.* fordo'ing; *pa.t.* fordid'; *pa.p.* fordone, *-dun'*.—*adj.* fordone', exhausted.—from fordonne (*Spens.*), from being fordone. [O.E. *fordōn*; Ger. *vertun*, to consume.]

**fore**, *för*, *för*, *adj.* in front: former, previous.—*adv.* at or towards the front: previously. *n.* the front: the foremast.—*interj.* (*golf*) a warning cry to anybody in the way of the ball.—*adj.* foremost (*för'mōst*, *för'*; double superl. —O.E. *forma*, first, superl. of *fore*, and superl. suffix *-st*), first in place: most advanced: first in rank and dignity.—*adj.* and *adv.* fore'-and-aft', lengthwise of a ship: without square sails. —fore-and-aft'er, a vessel of fore-and-aft rig: a hat peaked before and behind; fore'bitt, one of the bitts at the foremast; fore'bitter, a ballad sung at the forebitts.—at the fore, displayed on the foremast (of a flag); fore-and-aft sail, any sail not set on yards and lying fore-and-aft when untrimmed; to the fore, at hand: in being, alive (*Scot.*): (loosely) prominent. [O.E. *fore*, radically the same as for, prep.]

**fore-**, *för-*, *för-*, *pfx.* before: beforehand: in front.—*vs.t.* fore-admon'ish, to admonish beforehand; fore-advise', to advise beforehand.—*n.* fore'arm, the part of the arm between the elbow and the wrist.—*v.t.* forearm', to arm or prepare beforehand.—*n.* forebear, forbear (*för'bār*, *för'*;

*Scot.*), an ancestor (from be and suff. -er).—*v.t.* **forebode'**, to prognosticate: to have a premonition of (esp. of evil).—*ns.* **forebode'ment**, feeling of coming evil; **forebod'er**; **forebod'ing**, a boding or perception beforehand; apprehension of coming evil.—*adv.* **forebod'ingly.**—*ns.* **fore'-body**, the part in front of the mainmast; **fore'-brace**, a rope attached to the fore yard-arm, for changing the position of the foresail; **fore'-brain**, the front part of the brain.—*prep.* **foreby'**, (*Spens.*; same as forby).—*ns.* **fore'cabin**, a cabin in a ship's forepart; **fore'-caddy**, a caddy posted where he may see where the balls go; **fore'car**, a small car carrying a passenger in front of a motor-cycle; **fore'carriage**, the front part of a carriage, with arrangement for independent movement of the fore-wheels.—*v.t.* **forecast'**, to contrive or reckon beforehand: to foresee: to predict.—*v.i.* to form schemes beforehand:—*pa.t.* and *pa.p.* **forecast'**, sometimes **forecast'ed.** —*ns.* **fore'cast**, a previous contrivance: foresight: a prediction; **forecast'er**; **forecastle**, **fo'c'sle** (*fōk'sl*, sometimes *fōr'käs-l*, *fōr*), a short raised deck at the fore-end of a vessel: the forepart of the ship under the maindeck, the quarters of the crew.—*adjs.* **forechos'en**, chosen beforehand; **fore-ci'ted**, quoted before or above. —*ns.* **fore'course**, a foresail; **fore'court**, a court in front of a building: an outer court.—*v.t.* **foredate'**, to date before the true time.—*ns.* **fore'day** (*Scot.*), forenoon; **fore'deck**, the forepart of a deck or ship.—*v.t.* **foredoom'**, to doom beforehand.—*ns.* **fore'edge**, the outer edge of a book, furthest from the back—placed outward in a mediaeval library; **fore'-end**, the early or fore part of anything: **fore'father**, an ancestor.— *v.t.* **forefeel'**, to feel beforehand.—*adv.* **forefeel'ingly.**—*adj.* **forefelt'.**—*ns.* **fore'finger**, the finger next the thumb; **fore'foot**, one of the anterior feet of a quadruped: the foremost end of the keel, whereon rests the stem (*naut.*):— *pl.* **forefeet**; **fore'front**, the front or foremost part; **foregath'er** (see forgather); **fore'gleam**, a glimpse into the future.—*v.t.* and *v.i.* **forego'**, to go before, precede: chiefly in its *pr.p.* **forego'ing** (or *fōr'*, *fōr'*) and *pa.p.* **foregone'** (or *fōr'*, *fōr'*); *pa.t.* **forewent'** (*rare*); formerly also *pa.p.*—*ns.* **foregō'er** (or *fōr'*, *fōr'*); **foregoing.**—*adj.* **fore'gone** (**foregone conclusion**, a conclusion come to before examination of the evidence: an obvious or inevitable conclusion or result).—*ns.* **fore'gone'ness**; **fore'ground**, the part of a picture or field of view nearest the observer's eye, as opp. to the *background* (also *fig.*); **fore'-hammer**, a sledge-hammer; **fore'hand**, the front position or its occupant: the upper hand, advantage, preference: the part of a horse that is in front of its rider: the part of the court to the right of a right-handed player or to the left of a left-handed player (*tennis*): a stroke played forehand (*tennis*).—*adj.* done beforehand: anticipating, of anticipation (*Shak.*): with the palm in front— opp. to *backhand*: (of an arrow; *Shak.*) for shooting point-blank.—*adv.* with hand in forehand position.—*adj.* **fore'handed**, forehand, as of payment for goods before delivery, or for services before rendered: seasonable: well off (*U.S.*): shapely in the foreparts.—*ns.* **forehead** (*for'id*, -*ed*, *fōr'hed*), the forepart of the head above the eyes, the brow: confidence, audacity; **fore'-horse**, the foremost horse of a team.—*v.t.* **forejudge'**, to judge before hearing the facts and proof.—*ns.* **forejudg'ment**; **fore'king** (*Tenn.*), a preceding king.—*v.t.* **foreknow** (*fōr-*, *fōr-*), to know beforehand: to foresee.—*adj.* **foreknow'ing.**—*adv.* **foreknow'ingly.**—*n.* **foreknowl'edge** (-*nol'ij*).—*adj.* **foreknown'.**—*n.* **fore'land**, a point of land running forward into the sea, a headland: a front region.—*vs.t.* **forelay'**, to contrive antecedently: to lay wait for in ambush:

to hinder; **forelay'**, *pa.t.* of forelie.—*n.* **fore'leg**, a front leg.—*vs.t.* **forelend'**, **forlend'**, to grant or resign beforehand:—*pa.p.* and *pa.t.*, *Spens.*, **forelent'**, **forlent'**: forelie', to lie before:—*pa.t. Spens.*, **forelay'**; **forelift'** (*Spens.*), to raise in front.—*ns.* **fore'lock**, the lock of hair on the forehead (**take time by the forelock**, to seize an opportunity betimes); **fore'man**, the first or chief man, one appointed to preside over, or act as spokesman for, others: an overseer:—*pl.* **fore'men**; **fore'mast**, the mast that is forward, or next the bow of a ship; **fore'mastman**, any sailor below the rank of petty officer.—*v.t.* **foremean'**, to intend beforehand.—*adjs.* **fore'-men'tioned**, mentioned before in a writing or discourse; **foremost** (*fōr'mōst*, *fōr'*, -*məst*; double superl.—O.E. *forma*, first, superl. of *fore*, and superl. suffix -*st*), first in place: most advanced: first in rank or dignity.—*n.* **fore'-name**, the first or Christian name.—*adj.* **fore'-named**, mentioned before.—*ns.* **fore'night** (*Scot.*), the early part of the night before bedtime, the evening; **forenoon** (*fōr-nōōn'*, *fōr-*, *fōr'nōōn*, *fōr'*; chiefly *Scot.* and *Ir.*), the part of the day before midday, as opposed to early morning.— *adj.* (*fōr'*, *fōr'*), pertaining to this time.—*n.* **fore'-no'tice**, notice of anything in advance of the time.—*v.t.* **fore'-ordain'**, to arrange beforehand: to predestinate.—*ns.* **fore'-ordinā'tion**; **fore'part**, the front: the early part.—*adj.* **fore'past**, bygone.—*ns.* **fore'pay'ment**, payment beforehand; **fore'peak**, the contracted part of a ship's hold, close to the bow.—*vs.t.* **foreplan'**, to plan beforehand; **forepoint'**, to foreshadow.—*adj.* **fore-quo'ted**, quoted or cited before.—*v.t.* **foreran'**, *pa.t.* of forerun.—*n.* **fore'-rank**, the front rank.—*v.i.* **forereach'** (*naut.*), to glide ahead, esp. when going in stays (with *on*).—*v.t.* to sail beyond.—*v.t.* **foreread'**, to foretell:—*pa.t.* **foreread** (-*red'*).—*n.* **fore'reading.**—*adj.* **fore-reci'ted** (*Shak.*), recited or named before.—*v.t.* **forerun'**, to run or come before: to precede.—*n.* **fore'runner**, a runner or messenger sent before: a precursor: a prognostic.—*adj.* **fore'said**, already mentioned (see also foresay).—*n.* **fore-sail** (*fōr'sl*, *fōr'*, -*sāl*) the chief and lowest square sail on the foremast: a triangular sail on the forestay.—*v.t.* **foresay'**, to predict or foretell: to ordain (*Shak.*) (see also forsay).—*v.t.* and *v.i.* **foresee'**, to see or know beforehand:—*pa.t.* **foresaw'**; *pa.p.* **foreseen'.**—*adj.* **foresee'ing.**— *adv.* **foresee'ingly.**—*v.t.* **foreshad'ow**, to shadow or typify beforehand: to give, or have, some indication of in advance.—*ns.* **foreshad'owing**; **fore'ship**, the forepart of a ship; **fore'-shore**, the space between high and low water marks.—*v.t.* **foreshort'en**, to draw or cause to appear as if shortened, by perspective.—*n.* **fore-short'ening.**—*v.t.* **foreshow**, **foreshew** (*fōr-shō'*, *fōr-*), to show or represent beforehand: to foretell:—*pa.t.* **foreshowed**, **foreshewed**, -*shōd'*; *pa.p.* **foreshown**, **foreshewn**, -*shōn'*, also *Spens.* **foreshewed'.**—*ns.* **fore'side**, the front side: outward appearance (*Spens.*); **fore'sight**, act or power of foreseeing: wise forethought, prudence: the sight on the muzzle of a gun: a forward reading of a levelling staff.—*adjs.* **fore'sighted**; **fore'sightful**; **fore'sightless.**—*v.t.* **foresig'nify**, to betoken beforehand: to foreshow: to typify.—*ns.* **fore'skin**, the skin that covers the glans penis, the prepuce; **fore'skirt** (*Shak.*), the loose part of a coat before.—*v.i.* and *v.t.* **foreslack'** (see forslack).—*vs.t.* **forespeak'**, to predict: to engage beforehand (*Scot.*) (see also forspeak); **forespend'**, to spend beforehand:— *pa.p.* **forespent'**; (see also forspend.—*ns.* **fore-spurr'er** (*Shak.*), one who rides before; **fore'-stair** (*Scot.*), an outside stair in front of a house. —*v.t.* **forestall** (*fōr-stōl'*, *fōr-*; O.E. *foresteall*, ambush, lit. a place taken beforehand—*steall*, stand, station), to buy up before reaching the market, so as to sell again at higher prices: to anticipate: to hinder by anticipating: to bar.— *ns.* forestall′er; forestall′ing; forestal′ment; fore′stay, a rope reaching from the foremast-head to the bowsprit end to support the mast.—*v.t.* foretaste′, to taste before possession: to anticipate: to taste before another.—*n.* fore′taste, a taste beforehand: anticipation.—*vs.t.* foreteach′, to teach beforehand:—*pa.t.* and *pa.p.* foretaught′; foretell′, to tell before: to prophesy.—*v.i.* to utter prophecy:—*pa.t.* and *pa.p.* foretold′.—*n.* foretell′er.—*v.t.* forethink′, to anticipate in the mind: to have prescience of:—*pa.t.* and *pa.p.* forethought′.—*ns.* forethink′er; fore′thought, thought or care for the future: anticipation: thinking beforehand.—*adj.* fore′thought′ful.—*n.* fore′token, a token or sign beforehand.—*v.t.* foretō′ken, to signify beforehand.—*n.* and *adj.* foretō′kening.—*ns.* fore′tooth, a tooth in the forepart of the mouth:—*pl.* fore′teeth; fore′top, the platform at the head of the foremast (*naut.*): the forepart of the crown of the head (*obs.*): a lock (usu. upright) over the forehead: an appendage to a shoe (*obs.*); foretop′mast, the mast erected at the head of the foremast, at the top of which is the fore′top-gall′ant-mast. — *adj.* forevouched′ (*Shak.*), affirmed or told before.—*n.* fore′ward, advance-guard: the front (*Shak.*).—*v.t.* forewarn′, to warn beforehand: to give previous notice (see also forwarn).—*n.* forewarn′ing.—*vs.t.* foreweigh′, to estimate beforehand; forewent′, *pa.t.* (*Spens., pa.p.*) of forego (see also forgo).—*ns.* fore′-wheel, one of the pair of front wheels of a wheeled vehicle; fore′wind, a favourable wind; fore′woman, a woman overseer, a headwoman, a spokeswoman for a group (e.g. for a jury):—*pl.* fore′women; fore′word, a preface.′ [O.E. *fore*; Ger. *vor*.]

foreclose, *fōr-klōz′, fōr-, v.t.* to preclude: to prevent: to stop: to bar the right of redeeming. —*n.* foreclosure (-*klō′zhər*), a foreclosing: the process by which a mortgagor, failing to repay the money lent on the security of an estate, is compelled to forfeit his right to redeem the estate (*law*). [O.Fr. *forclos*, pa.p. of *forclore*, to exclude—L. *foris*, outside, and *claudēre*, *clausum*, to shut.]

fore-damned, *fōr-dam′ned,* (*obs.*) *adj.* utterly damned (or poss. damned beforehand). [Pfx. for- (1c), (or poss. fore-).]

forego, better forgo.

forehent. See forhent.

foreign, *for′in, adj.* belonging to another country: from abroad: alien: extraneous: not belonging: unconnected: not appropriate.—*ns.* for′eigner, a native of another country; for′eignness, the quality of being foreign: want of relation to something: remoteness.—*adj.* foreign-built, built in a foreign country.—foreign legion, an army unit consisting of aliens: (*caps.*) a former French army unit, consisting of soldiers of all nationalities, serving outside France; Foreign Office, government department dealing with foreign affairs. [O.Fr. *forain*—L.L. *forāneus*—L. *forās*, out of doors.]

forel, *for′əl, n.* a kind of parchment for covering books. [O.Fr. *forrel*, dim. of *forre, fuerre*, sheath.]

forensic, *fə-ren′sik, adj.* belonging to courts of law, held by the Romans in the forum: used in law pleading: appropriate to, or adapted to, argument: loosely, of or pertaining to sciences or scientists connected with legal investigations.—forensic medicine, medical jurisprudence, the application of medical knowledge to the elucidation of doubtful questions in a court of justice. [L. *forēnsis*—*forum*, market-place, forum.]

forensis strepitum, *for-en′sis strep′it-əm, -ōōm,* (L.) the clamour of the forum.

forest, *for′ist, n.* a large uncultivated tract of land covered with trees and underwood: woody ground and rude pasture: a preserve for big game: a royal preserve for hunting, governed by a special code called the forest law.—*adj.* pertaining to a forest: silvan: rustic.—*v.t.* to cover with trees.—*n.* for′estage, an ancient service paid by foresters to the king: the right of foresters.—*adj.* for′estal.—*n.* foresta′tion, afforestation.—*adj.* for′ested.—*n.* for′ester, one who has charge of a forest: one who has care of growing trees: a member of the Ancient Order of Foresters or similar friendly society: an inhabitant of a forest.—*adj.* for′estine.—*n.* for′estry, the art of planting, tending, and managing forests; forest country: an extent of trees.—*adjs.* for′est-born (*Shak.*), born in a forest; for′est-bred.—for′est-fly, a dipterous insect (*Hippobosca equina*) that annoys horses; Forest Marble, a Middle Jurassic fissile limestone of which typical beds are found in Wychwood Forest, Oxfordshire; for′est-oak, Australian beefwood (*Casuarina*); for′est-tree, a tree, esp. a timber-tree, that grows in forests. [O.Fr. *forest* (Fr. *forêt*)—L.L. *forestis* (*silva*), the outside wood, as opposed to the *parcus* (park) or walled-in wood—L. *foris*, out of doors.]

forever, *fər-ev′ər, adv.* for ever, for all time to come: eternally: everlastingly.—*adv.* forev′ermore′, for ever hereafter.

forfair, *fər-fār′, v.i.* to perish, decay (*obs.*).—*adj.* (*Scot.*) forfairn′, worn out: exhausted. [O.E. *forfaran.*]

forfeit, *fōr′fit, n.* that to which a right is lost: a penalty for a crime, or breach of some condition: a fine: something deposited and redeemable by a sportive fine or penalty, esp. in *pl.*, a game of this kind.—*adj.* forfeited.—*v.t.* to lose the right to by some fault or crime: to confiscate (*arch.*): to penalise by forfeiture: loosely, to give up voluntarily.—*adj.* for′feitable.—*ns.* for′feiter (*Shak.*), one who incurs punishment by forfeiting his bond; forfeiture, act of forfeiting: state of being forfeited: the thing forfeited.—Also (*obs.*) for fault, etc., by association with fault. [O.Fr. *forfait*—L.L. *forisfactum*—L. *foris*, outside, *facēre*, to make.]

forfend, *fər-fend′,* (*arch.*) *v.t.* to ward off, avert. [Pfx. for- (1a), and fend (1).]

forfex, *fōr′feks, n.* a pair of scissors, or pincers: the pincers of an earwig, etc.—*n.* Forfic′ula, the common genus of earwigs.—*adj.* forfic′ulate, like scissors. [L. *forfex, -icis*, shears, pincers.]

forfoughten, *fər-fō′tən,* (*Scot.* forfoughen, *fər-fohh′ən*, forfeuchen, *-fühh′*), (*dial.*) *adj.* exhausted. [Pfx. for- (1c).]

forgat. See forget.

forgather, foregather, *fər-gadh′ər, v.i.* to meet, esp. by chance: to fraternise. [Pfx. for- (1c).]

forgave. See forgive.

forge, *fōrj, fōrj, n.* the workshop of a workman in iron, etc.: a furnace, esp. one in which iron is heated: a smithy: a place where anything is shaped or made.—*v.t.* to form by heating and hammering, by heating and pressure, or by pressure alone: to make falsely: to fabricate: to counterfeit for purposes of fraud: to form by great pressure, electricity, or explosion.—*v.i.* to commit forgery.—*ns.* forg′er, one who forges; forg′ery, fraudulently making or altering anything, esp. a writing: that which is forged or counterfeited: deceit (*obs.*).—*adj.* forg′etive (*Shak.*), creative.—*n.* forg′ing, a piece of metal shaped by hammering: act of one who forges.—forge′man. [O.Fr. *forge*—L. *fabrica*—*faber*, a workman.]

forge, *fōrj, fōrj, v.i.* to move steadily on (usu. with ahead). [Origin obscure.]

forge, *fōrj, förj*, *v.i.* in a horse, to click the hind shoe against the fore. [Origin obscure.]

forget, *fər-get'*, *v.t.* to lose or put away from the memory: to fail to remember or think of: to leave behind accidentally: to neglect:— *pr.p.* forgett'ing; *pa.t.* forgot' *(arch.* forgat'); *pa.p.* forgot'en *(arch.* forgot').—*adj.* forget'ful, apt to forget: inattentive.—*adv.* forget'fully.— *n.* forget'fulness.—*adj.* forgett'able.—*ns.* forgett'er; forgett'ery, a capacity for forgetting, a bad memory.—*n.* and *adj.* forgett'ing.—*adv.* forgett'ingly.—*adj.* forgott'en.—*n.* forgott'en-ness.—forget'-me-not, any plant of the genus Myosotis, regarded as an emblem of loving remembrance.—forget oneself, to lose one's self-control or dignity, to descend to words and deeds unworthy of oneself. [O.E. *forgetan (forgietan)*—pfx. *for-*, away, *getan (gietan)*, to get.]

forgive, *fər-giv'*, *v.t.* to pardon: to overlook: to remit a debt or offence *(Shak.)*: to give up *(Spens.)*.—*v.i.* to be merciful or forgiving:— *pa.t.* forgave', *pa.p.* forgiv'en.—*adj.* forgiv'able, capable of being forgiven.—*n.* forgive'ness, pardon: remission: disposition to pardon.— *adj.* forgiv'ing, ready to pardon: merciful: compassionate. [O.E. *forgiefan*—pfx. *for-*, away, *giefan*, to give; cf. Ger. *vergeben*.]

forgo, forego, *fōr-, för-, fər-gō'*, *v.t.* to leave: to give up: to relinquish: to do without: to forbear the use or advantage of: to forfeit *(arch.)*.—*v.i.* to go or pass away.—*pr.p.* for(e)-go'ing; *pa.p.* for(e)gone'; *pa.t.*—for(e)went. See also forego. [O.E. *forgān*, to pass by, abstain from —pfx. *for-*, away, *gān*, to go.]

forgot, forgotten. See forget.

forhaile, *for-hāl'*, *(Spens.)* *v.t.* to distract. [Pfx. for- (1a).]

forhent, forehent, *för-hent'*, *v.t.* to overtake: to seize:—*pa.p.*, *Spens.*, forhent'. [Pfx. for- (1c).]

forhow, *för-how'*, *v.t.* to despise *(obs.)*: (also forhoo(ie), *fər-hōō(ē))*, to desert or abandon *(Scot.)*. [O.E. *forhogian*, pfx. *for-*, away, *hogian*, to care.]

forinsec, *fər-in'sek*, *adj.* (of feudal service) due to the lord's superior.—*adj.* forin'secal *(obs.)*, foreign: alien: extrinsic. [L. *forinsecus*, from without—*foris*, out of doors, *secus*, following.]

forint, *for'int*, *n.* the monetary unit of Hungary since 1946.

forisfamiliate, *för-, for-is-fə-mil'i-āt*, *(law)* *v.t.* to emancipate from paternal authority: to put in possession of land which is accepted as the whole portion of the father's property, said of a father. —*v.i.* to renounce one's title to a further share, said of a son.—*n.* forisfamiliā'tion. [L.L. *forisfamiliāre, -ātum*—L. *foris* out of doors, *familia*, a family.]

forjeskit, *fər-jes'kit*, forjaskit, *-jas'*, *(Scot.)* *adj.* tired out. [Pfx. for- (1c); cf. disjaskit.]

fork, *förk*, *n.* a pronged instrument: anything that divides into prongs or branches: a branch or prong: the space or angle between branches, esp. on a tree or between the legs: a confluent, tributary, or branch of a river: one of the branches into which a road divides: a bifurcation: a place of bifurcation: a barbed arrow-head: part of a bicycle to which a wheel is attached: the appearance of a flash of lightning: the bottom of a sump in a mine.—*v.i.* to branch: to follow a branch road.—*v.t.* to form as a fork: to move with a fork: to stab with a fork: to menace simultaneously *(chess)*: to pump dry.— *adj.* forked, shaped like a fork.—*adv.* fork'edly. —*ns.* fork'edness; fork'er; fork'iness.—*adj.* fork'y.—fork'-chuck, forked lathe-centre in wood-turning; fork'head, an arrowhead *(Spens.)*: the forked end of a rod; fork'it-tail, fork'y-tail *(dial.)*, an earwig; fork lunch(eon), supper, etc., a buffet-type meal eaten with a fork; fork'tail, a name for various fishes and birds, as the kite.—

fork-lift truck, a power-driven truck with an arrangement of steel prongs which can lift, raise up high, and carry heavy packages and stack them where required (often used with a pallet); fork out, over *(slang)*, to hand or pay over. [O.E. *forca*—L. *furca*.]

forlana, *för-lä'na*, furlana, *fōōr-, n.* a Venetian dance in 6-8 time. [It. *Furlana*, Friulian.]

forlend. See forelend.

forlorn, *fər-lörn'*, *adj.* quite lost: forsaken: neglected: wretched.—*n.* *(Shak.)* a forsaken person: a forlorn hope.—orig. *pa.p.* of the *obs.* forlese *(for-lēz')*, *v.t.* to lose: to forsake *(pa.t.* and *pa.p., Spens.* forlore, *-lōr'*, *-lör')*.—*adv.* forlorn'ly.—*n.* forlorn'ness. [O.E. *forloren*, pa.p. of *forlēosan*, to lose—pfx. *for-*, away, and *lēosan*, to lose; Ger. *verloren*, pa.p. of *verlieren*, to lose.]

forlorn-hope, *fər-lörn'-hōp'*, *n.* a body of soldiers selected for some service of uncommon danger: a desperate enterprise of last resort: a vain or faint hope (from association with hope = expectation). [Du. *verloren hoop*, lost troop.]

form, *förm*, *n.* shape: a mould: something that holds, shapes, e.g. a piece of formwork: species: pattern: mode of being: mode of arrangement: order: regularity: system, as of government: beauty *(obs.)*: style and arrangement: structural unity in music, literature, etc.: a prescribed set of words or course of action: ceremony: behaviour: condition of fitness or efficiency: a schedule to be filled in with details: a specimen document for imitation: the inherent nature of an object *(phil.)*: that which the mind itself contributes as the condition of knowing: that in which the essence of a thing consists: a complete set of crystal faces similar with respect to the symmetry of the crystal *(crystal.)*: type from which an impression is to be taken arranged and secured in a chase—*U.K.* usu. forme *(print.)*: wooden or metal temporary structure used in building, as a mould for setting concrete: a long seat, a bench: a school class: bed of a hare, shaped by the animal's body: criminal record *(slang)*: condition of fitness of e.g. horse, athlete: *(coll.;* with *the)* the correct procedure in an operation; also the situation, position. —*v.t.* to give form or shape to: to bring into being: to make: to contrive: to conceive in the mind: to go to make up: to constitute: to establish.—*v.i.* to assume a form.—*adj.* form'al, according to form or established mode: relating to form: ceremonious, punctilious, methodical: having the form only: sane *(Shak.)*: having the power of making a thing what it is: essential: proper.—*v.t.* and *v.i.* form'alise, -ize. —*ns.* form'alism, excessive observance of form or conventional usage, esp. in religion: stiffness of manner; form'alist, one having exaggerated regard to rules or established usages; formal'ity, the precise observance of forms or ceremonies: a matter of form: a ceremonious observance: established order: sacrifice of substance to form. —*adv.* form'ally.—*n.* form'ant, a component of a speech sound determining its quality: a determinative.—*v.i.* formate', to join, or fly, in formation (of aircraft): to form *(obs.)*: to state precisely, formulate *(obs.)*.—*n.* formā'tion, a making or producing: structure: arrangement of e.g. troops, aircraft, players: a stratigraphical group of strata *(geol.)*: a plant community *(bot.)*. —*adj.* form'ative, giving form, determining, moulding: capable of development: growing: serving to form, not radical *(gram.)*.—*n.* *(gram.)* a derivative.—*adj.* formed.—*ns.* form'er, form'-ing.—*adj.* form'less.—*adv.* form'lessly.—*n.* form'-lessness.—formal logic (see logic); form class *(linguistics)*, a class of forms (words and phrases) that will fit into the same position in a construction; form critic; form criticism, biblical criticism that classifies parts of scripture according to literary form and relates literary forms to historical background; **form'work**, shuttering to contain concrete.—**good, or bad form**, according to good or recognised social usage, or the opposite. [L. *fŏrma*, shape.]

**-form**, *fŏrm*, *suff.* having the form of, having a form. [L. *fŏrma*, form.]

**formaldehyde, formalin.** See under **formic.**

**formaliter**, *fŏr-mal'i-tər*, *-ter*, (L.L.), formerly, in respect of the formal element.

**format**, *fŏr'mat*, *fŏr'mä*, *n.* of books, etc., the size, form, shape in which they are issued. [Fr.]

**forme** (*print.*). See **form.**

**former**, *fŏrm'ər*, *adj.* (*comp.* of *fore*) before in time: past: first mentioned (of two): beforehand, first (of two) (*Shak.*).—*adv.* **form'erly**, in former times: heretofore. [Formed late on analogy of M.E. *formest*, foremost, by adding comp. suff. *-er* to base of O.E. *forma*, first, itself superlative.]

**formic**, *fŏr'mik*, *adj.* pertaining to ants.—*ns.* **formal'dehyde**, a formic aldehyde, formalin; **for'malin, for'mol** (*-mol*, *-mōl*), a formic aldehyde used as an antiseptic, germicide, or preservative; **for'mate**, a salt of formic acid.—Also **for'miate.** —*adj.* **for'micant**, crawling like an ant: very small and unequal, of a pulse.—*ns.* **formicā'rium**, **for'micary**, an ant-hill, ants' nest, or colony. —*adj.* **for'micate**, resembling an ant.—*n.* **formicā'tion**, a sensation like that of ants creeping on the skin.—**formic acid**, a fatty acid H·CO·OH, found in ants and nettles. [L. *formica*, an ant.]

**formidable**, *fŏr'mid-ə-bl*, by some *-mid'*, *adj.* causing fear: inspiring awe: redoubtable.— *ns.* **formidabil'ity; for'midableness.**—*adv.* **for'- midably.** [Fr.,—L. *formidābilis*—*formidō*, fear.]

**formol.** See under **formic.**

**formula**, *fŏrm'ū-lə*, *n.* a prescribed form: a formal statement of doctrines: recipe: a milk mixture used as baby food: a statement of joint aims or principles worked out for practical purposes by diplomats of divergent interests: technical specification governing cars entered for certain motor-racing events: a general expression for solving problems (*math.*): a set of symbols expressing the composition of a body (*chem.*): a list of ingredients of a patent medicine:—*pl.* **formulae** (*fŏrm'ū-lē*), **form'ūlas.**—*adjs.* **form'ūlar, formūlaris'tic.**—*v.t.* **form'ūlarise, -ize.**—*ns.* **form- ūlarisā'tion, -z-, formūlā'tion; form'ūlary**, a formula: a book of formulae or precedents.— *adj.* prescribed: ritual.—*vs.t.* **form'ūlate, form'- ūlise, -ize,** to reduce to or express in a formula: to state or express in a clear or definite form. [L. *fŏrmula*, dim. of *fŏrma.*]

**fornent**, *fər-nent'*, (*Scot.*) *adv.* and *prep.* right opposite to.—Also **foreanent', fornenst'.** [**fore, anent.**]

**fornicate**, *fŏr'ni-kāt*, *adj.* arched: arching over (*bot.*).—*n.* **fornicā'tion.** [L. *fornicātus*—*fornix*, a vault, arch.]

**fornicate**, *fŏr'ni-kāt*, *v.i.* to commit fornication.— *ns.* **fornicā'tion**, voluntary sexual intercourse of the unmarried, sometimes extended to cases where only one of the pair concerned is unmarried: adultery (*B.*), or idolatry (*fig.*); **for'nicător; for'nicātress.** [L. *fornicāri*, *-ātus*— *fornix*, a vault, brothel.]

**fornix**, *fŏr'niks*, *n.* something resembling an arch: an arched formation of the brain. [L.]

**forpine**, *fŏr-pīn'*, *v.i.* (*Spens.*) to waste away. [Pfx. **for-** (1c).]

**forpit, forpet**, *fŏr-pət*, (*Scot.*) *n.* a fourth part (now of a peck). [**fourth part.**]

**forrad**, *fŏr'əd*, (*dial.*), **forrit**, *fŏr'ət*, *fŏr'it*, (*Scot.*) *adv.* forms of **forward**—*comp.* **forr'ader.**

**forray**, *fo-rā'*, *n.* and *v.t.* Spenser's form of **foray.**

**forren** (*Milt.*). Same as **foreign.**

**forsake**, *fər-sāk'*, *fŏr-*, *v.t.* to desert: to abandon: —*pr.p.* **forsak'ing;** *pa.t.* **forsook';** *pa.p.* **forsāk'en.**—*adj.* **forsāk'en.**—*adv.* **forsāk'enly.**—*ns.* **forsāk'enness; forsāk'ing,** abandonment. [O.E. *forsacan*—*for-*, away, *sacan*, to strive.]

**forsay, foresay**, *fŏr-sā'*, *v.t.* to forbid (*obs.*): to renounce (*Spens.*): to banish (*Spens.*). [O.E. *forsecgan*—*for-*, against, *secgan*, to say.]

**forset-seller.** See **fosset-seller.**

**forslack, foreslack**, *fŏr-slak'*, *v.i.* (*obs.*) to be or become slack or neglectful.—*v.t.* (*Spens.*) to injure by slackness. [Pfx. **for-** (1c).]

**forslow, forsloe, foreslow**, *fŏr-slō'*, *v.t.* (*Spens.*) to delay.—*v.i.* (*Shak.*) to delay. [O.E. *forslāwian* —*for*, intensive, *slāwian*, to be slow.]

**forsooth**, *fər-sōōth'*, *fŏr-*, *adv.* in truth: certainly (now only ironically). [**for sooth.**]

**forspeak, forespeak**, *fər-spēk'*, *fŏr-*, *v.t.* to forbid (*obs.*): to speak against (*Shak.*): to bewitch (*Scot.*). [Pfx. **for-** (1b).]

**forspend, forespend**, *fər-spend'*, *v.t.* to wear out physically: to exhaust (resources):—*pa.t.* and *pa.p.* **forspent'.** [Pfx. **for-** (1c).]

**forswatt**, *fŏr-swŏt'*, (*Spens.*) *adj.* covered with sweat. [Pfx. **for-** (1c) and *swat*, old pa.p. of *sweat.*]

**forswear**, *fər-swār'*, *fŏr-*, *v.t.* to deny or renounce upon oath.—*v.i.* to swear falsely:—*pa.t.* **forswore';** *pa.p.* **forsworn'.**—*adj.* **forsworn'**, perjured, having forsworn oneself.—*n.* **forsworn'- ness.**—**forswear oneself**, to swear falsely. [Pfx. **for-** (1b).]

**forswink**, *fər-swingk'*, *fŏr-*, *v.t.* to exhaust by labour.—*adj.* **forswunk'** (*Spens.* **forswonck'**), overworked. [Pfx. **for-** (1b), O.E. *swincan*, to labour.]

**Forsythia**, *fŏr-sī'thi-ə*, *-si'thi-a*, *n.* a genus of oleaceous shrubs with flowers like jasmine. [After William Forsyth (1737-1804), botanist.]

**fort**, *fŏrt*, *fŏrt*, *n.* a small fortress: (in N. America) an outlying trading-station.—*v.t.* to fortify.— **hold the fort**, to take temporary charge. [Fr.,— L. *fortis*, strong.]

**fortalice**, *fŏrt'ə-lis*, *n.* a fortress: a small outwork of a fortification. [L.L. *fortalitia*—L. *fortis*.]

**forte**, *fŏrt*, by some *fŏrt'i* (incorrectly) *n.* that in which one excels: the upper half of a sword or foil blade—the strong part. [Fr. *fort*, strong.]

**forte**, *fŏr'ti*, (*mus.*) *adj.* and *adv.* loud:—*superl.* **fortis'simo**, *double superl.* **fortissis'simo**, as loud as possible.—*n.* a loud passage in music.—*n.* **fortepia'no**, 18th-century name for early type of piano.—*adj.* and *adv.* loud with immediate relapse into softness. [It.]

**forth**, *fŏrth*, *fŏrth*, *adv.* forward: onward: out: into the open: in continuation: abroad.— *prep.* (*Shak.*) out of, forth from.—*n.* **forthcom'ing**, just coming forth: about to appear: approaching: at hand, ready to be produced: (of a person) friendly, communicative.—*ns.* **forth'- going**, a going forth; **forth'-putting**, action of putting forth: undue forwardness (*U.S.*).—*adj.* (*U.S.*) forward.—*adv.* **forth'right** (or *-rīt'*), straightforward: at once.—*n.* (*Shak.*) a straight path.—*adj.* straightforward: downright.—*adv.* **forthwith** (*-with'*, *-widh'*, or *-fŏrth'*), immediately. —and so forth, and so on. [O.E. *forth*—*fore*, before; Du. *voort*, Ger. *fort*.]

**forthink**, *fər-thingk'*, *v.t.* (*Spens.*) to be sorry for, regret: to rethink.—*v.i.* (*dial.*) to change one's mind. [From O.E. *forthencan*—*thencan*, to think, and O.E. *for-*, *thyncan*, to seem.]

**forthy**, *fŏr-dhī'*, (*Spens.*) *adv.* therefore: for that. [O.E. *forthȳ*—*for*, and *thȳ*, instrumental case of *thæt*, that.]

**forties, fortieth.** See **forty.**

**fortify**, *fŏr'ti-fī*, *v.t.* to strengthen with forts, etc., against attack: to invigorate: to confirm: to strengthen (esp. certain wines) by adding alcohol: to enrich (a food) by adding e.g. vitamins: —*pr.p.* **for'tifying;** *pa.t.* and *pa.p.* **for'tified.**— *adj.* **for'tifiable.**—*ns.* **fortifica'tion,** the art of strengthening a military position by means of defensive works: the work so constructed: that which fortifies; **for'tifier.** [Fr. *fortifier*—L.L. *fortificāre*—*fortis,* strong, *facĕre,* to make.]

**fortilage,** *för'ti-lāj, för',* (*Spens.*) *n.* a variant of **fortalice.**

**fortissimo.** See **forte.**

**fortiter et recte,** *för'ti-tər et rek'tē, for'ti-ter et rek'te,* (L.) bravely and uprightly.

**fortitude,** *för'ti-tūd,* in *U.S.* -*tōōd, n.* courage in endurance: strength (*obs.*).—*adj.* **fortitū'dinous.** [L. *fortitūdō,* -*inis*—*fortis,* strong.]

**fortlet,** *fört'lət, fört', n.* a little fort.

**fortnight,** *fört'nit, n.* two weeks or fourteen days.— *adj.* and *adv.* **fort'nightly,** once a fortnight. [O.E. *fēowertȳne niht,* fourteen nights.]

**Fortran,** *för'tran, n.* a problem-orientated computer language widely used in scientific work. [*Formula translation.*]

**fortress,** *för'trəs, n.* a fortified place: a defence.— *v.t.* (*Shak.*) to guard. [O.Fr. *forteresse,* another form of *fortelesce* (see **fortalice**).]

**fortuitous,** *för-tū'i-təs,* in *U.S.* -*təs, adj.* happening by chance: fortunate.—*ns.* **fortū'itism,** belief in evolution by fortuitous variation; **fortū'itist.**— *adv.* **fortū'itously.**—*ns.* **fort'ūitousness, fortū'ity.** [L. *fortuitus.*]

**fortune,** *för'chən, n.* whatever comes by lot or chance: luck: the arbitrary ordering of events: the lot that falls to one in life: success: a great accumulation of wealth: an heiress (*obs.*).—*v.i.* (*obs.*) to befall.—*v.t.* (*obs.*) to determine the fortune of.—*adj.* **for'tunate,** happening by good fortune: lucky: auspicious: felicitous.—*adv.* **for'tunately.**—*n.* **for'tunateness.**—*adjs.* **for'tuned,** supplied by fortune; **for'tuneless,** without a fortune: luckless.—*v.t.* (*Spens.*) **for'tunize,** to make fortunate or happy.—**for'tune-book,** a book for use in fortune-telling; **for'tune-hunter,** one who hunts for a wealthy marriage.—*v.i.* **for'tune-tell** (back-formation).—**for'tune-teller,** one who professes to foretell one's fortune; **for'tune-telling.** [Fr.,—L. *fortūna.*]

**forty,** *för'ti, adj.* and *n.* four times ten.—*n.* (*cap.* with *the*) the French Academy:—*pl.* **for'ties,** esp. the fortieth to forty-ninth years (of life, a century): (*cap.* with *the*) sea area lying between NE Scotland and SW Norway, with a minimum depth of 40 fathoms.—*adj.* **for'tieth,** the last of forty: equal to one of forty equal parts.—*n.* one of forty equal parts.—*adj.* **for'tyish,** apparently about forty years old.—**forty-five,** a microgrooved disk record played at a speed of 45 revolutions per minute: (*cap.* with *the*) the Jacobite rebellion of 1745; **forty-nin'er,** a gold-seeker in the 1849 rush in California; **forty winks,** a short nap, esp. after dinner.—**roaring forties,** the tract of stormy west winds south of 40°S latitude (occasionally also in the Atlantic north of 40°N). [O.E. *fēowertig*—*fēower,* four, -*tig,* ten (as suffix).]

**forum,** *fō'rəm, fö', n.* a market-place, esp. that in Rome where public business was transacted and justice dispensed: the courts of law as opposed to Parliament: a meeting to discuss topics of public concern. [L. *forum,* akin to *forās,* out of doors.]

**forwander,** *fər-won'dər, v.i.* to wander till wearied (*arch.*): to stray far (*Spens.*).—*adj.* **forwan'dered,** strayed. [Pfx. **for-** (1d).]

**forward,** *för'wərd, adj.* near or at the forepart: in advance: well advanced: ready: too ready: presumptuous: officious: earnest (*arch.*): early ripe.—*v.t.* to help on: to send on.—*advs.* **for'ward, for'wards,** towards what is in front or onward: progressively.—*adv.* **forward** (*for'əd*)

towards, in, the front part of a ship.—*ns.* **for'ward,** in football, etc., a player in the front line; **for'warder;** **for'warding,** the act of sending forward merchandise, etc.—*adv.* **for'wardly.**—*n.* **for'wardness.**—*adj.* **for'ward-looking,** having regard to the future: progressive. [O.E. *foreweard* (W.S. *foreweard*)—*fore,* and -*ward* (-*weard*) sig. direction; the *s* of *forwards* is a gen. ending (cf. Ger. *vorwärts*).]

**forwarn, forewarn,** *fər-, för-wörn', v.t.* to forbid. —See also **forewarn.** [Pfx. **for-** (1b), against, and **warn.**]

**forwaste,** *för-wāst', (Spens.) v.t.* to waste utterly. [Pfx. **for-** (1c).]

**forweary,** *fər-, för-wē'ri, (Spens.) v.t.* to weary out. [Pfx. **for-** (1c).]

**forwent,** *fər-, för-went'.* See **forgo.**

**forwhy,** *för-(h)wī', (arch.) conj.* because. [**for,** and **why.**]

**forworn,** *fər-wörn', -wörn', (Spens.) adj.* much worn. [Pfx. **for-** (1c).]

**forzando, forzato.** See **sforzando.**

**foss, fosse,** *fos, n.* a ditch, moat, trench, or canal.— *adj.* **fossed.**—*ns.* **fossette',** a small fossa; **Foss(e)' Way,** the Roman road that runs between Exeter and Lincoln: (without *cap.*) any of the British Roman roads having a fosse on either side. [Fr. *fosse*—L. *fossa*—*fodēre, fossum,* to dig.]

**fossa,** *fos'ə,* (anat.) *n.* a pit or depression.—*ns.* **foss'ula,** a small depression or groove.—*adj.* **foss'ūlate.** [L., a ditch.]

**fossa,** *fos'a,* **foussa,** *fōōs'a, n.* a Madagascan animal more or less akin to the civets. [Malagasy.]

**fosset-seller,** *fos'it-sel'ər,* (*Shak.*) *n.* apparently one who sells faucets.—Another reading **for'set-seller.** [*fosset, forset,* obs. forms of **faucet.**]

**fossick,** *fos'ik,* (*Austr.*) *v.i.* to undermine another's diggings, or work over waste-heaps for gold: to search about for any kind of profit: to prospect. —*v.t.* to dig out.—*ns.* **foss'icker** a mining gleaner who works over old diggings, and scratches about in the beds of creeks; **foss'icking.** [Perh. conn. with Eng. dial. *fossick,* a troublesome person.]

**fossil,** *fos'l,* or -*il, n.* a rock or mineral substance dug from the earth (*obs.*): a relic or trace of a former living thing preserved in the rocks (*geol.*): an antiquated, out-of-date, or unchanging person or thing (*fig.*).—*adj.* dug out of the earth: in the condition of a fossil: antiquated.—*adj.* **fossilif'erous,** bearing or containing fossils.—*n.* **fossilisā'tion.**—*v.t.* **foss'ilise,** -**ize,** to convert into a fossil (also *fig.*).—*v.i.* to become fossil: to look for fossils (*coll.*).—**fossil fuel,** coal, oil, etc., produced in the earth by process of fossilisation. [Fr. *fossile*—L. *fossilis*—*fodēre,* to dig.]

**fossor,** *fos'or, n.* a grave-digger.—*adj.* **fossorial** (-*ō'ri-əl,* -*ō'*; *zool.*) adapted for digging. [L. *fossor*—*fodēre,* to dig.]

**foster,** *fos'tər, v.t.* to bring up or nurse, esp. a child not one's own: to put a child into the care of one not its parent: to encourage: to promote: to cherish.—*ns.* **fos'terage,** the act or custom of fostering or nursing: the condition or relation of foster-child: the care of a foster-child: the act of encouraging or cultivating; **fosterer; fostress;** **fosterling,** a foster-child.—**fos'ter-brother,** a male child nursed or brought up with a child or children of different parents; **fos'ter-child,** a child nursed or brought up by one who is not its parent; **fos'ter-daughter; fos'ter-father,** one who brings up a child in place of its father; **fos'ter-mother,** one who brings up a child not her own: an apparatus for rearing chickens; **fos'ter-nurse; fos'ter-parent; fos'ter-sister; fos'ter-son.** [O.E. *fōstrian,* to nourish, *fōster,* food.]

**fother,** *fodh'ər, v.t.* to cover (a sail, etc.) with yarn and oakum, as stopping for a leak. [Perh. Du. *voederen* (mod. *voeren*), or L.G. *fodern*, to line.]

**fother,** *fodh'ər, n.* a load, quantity (*dial.*): a cart-load (*dial.*): a definite weight—of lead, 19½ cwt. [O.E. *fōther*; Ger. *fuder*.]

**fother,** *fodh'ər,* dial. variant of **fodder.**

**fothergilla,** *fo-dhər-gil'ə, n.* a genus of North American deciduous shrubs of the witch hazel family (*Hamamelis*); also called witch alder. [Dr John *Fothergill,* 18th-century British physician and botanist.]

**fou,** *foo,* (*Scot.*) *adj.* full: drunk.

**fou,** *foo,* (*obs. Scot.*) *n.* a bushel. [Perh. **full.**]

**fouat, fouet,** *foo'ət,* (*Scot.*) *n.* the house-leek.

**foud,** *fowd, n.* a bailiff or magistrate in Orkney and Shetland.—*n.* **foud'rie,** his jurisdiction. [O.N. *fōgeti*; Ger. *vogt*; from L. *vocātus*—*vocāre,* to call.]

**foudroyant,** *foo-droi'ənt, -drwä'yä, adj.* thundering: dazzling: sudden and overwhelming. [Fr., pr.p. of *foudroyer*—*foudre,* lightning.]

**fouetté,** *fwe'tā,* (Fr.) *n.* ballet-step in which the foot makes a whip-like movement.

**fougade,** *foo-gäd',* **fougasse,** *foo-gäs',* (*mil.*) *ns.* a small land mine charged with powder or shells, and loaded with stones. [Fr.]

**fought,** *föt, pa.t.* and *pa.p.,* **foughten,** *föt'n,* old *pa.p.,* of **fight.**

**foughty,** *fow'ti, foo'ti,* (*dial.*) *adj.* musty: mouldy: tainted. [O.E. *fūht,* moist.]

**foul,** *fowl, adj.* filthy: dirty: disfigured: untidy: loathsome: obscene: impure: shameful: gross: in bad condition: stormy: unfavourable: unfair: of little worth: choked up: entangled: full of errors (*print.*): ugly (*Shak.*): bad (*coll.*). —*v.t.* to make foul: to collide with, come in accidental contact with: obstruct.—*v.i.* to collide. —*n.* act of fouling: any breach of the rules in games or contests.—*adv.* in a foul manner: unfairly.—*adv.* **foul'ly.**—*n.* **foul'ness.**—**foul'-brood,** a bacterial disease of bee larvae; **foul'-fish,** fish during the spawning season; **foul'mart** (see **foumart**).—*adjs.* **foul'-mouthed, foul'-spok'en,** addicted to the use of foul or profane language. —**foul'-mouth'edness; foul'-play',** unfair action in any game or contest: dishonest dealing generally: violence or murder.—**claim a foul,** to assert that a rule has been broken, and claim the penalty; **fall foul of,** to come against: to clash with: to assail; **foul (be)fall** (*obs.*), bad luck to; **make foul water** (*naut.*), to come into such shallow water that the keel raises the mud. [O.E. *fūl*; Ger. *faul,* Goth. *fūls.*]

**foulard,** *foo-lärd', -lär', n.* a soft untwilled silk fabric: a silk handkerchief. [Fr.]

**foulder,** *fowl'dər,* (*Spens.*) *v.i.* to thunder. [O.Fr. *fouldre*—L. *fulgur,* lightning.]

**foulé,** *foo'lā,* (Fr.) *n.* fulled cloth, esp. a light woollen smooth-surfaced dress material.

**foumart,** *foo'märt, -mərt, n.* a polecat. [M.E. *fulmard*—O.E. *fūl,* foul, *mearth,* a marten.]

**found,** *pa.t.* and *pa.p.* of **find.**—*n.* **found'ling,** a little child found deserted.—**found money,** money gain got for nothing; **found object,** a natural or man-made object displayed as a work of art, either exactly as found or touched up ('composed').

**found,** *fownd, v.t.* to lay the bottom or foundation of: to establish on a basis: to originate: to endow.—*v.i.* rely (with *on*).—*ns.* **founda'tion,** act of founding: the base of a building: the groundwork or basis: a permanent fund for a benevolent purpose or for some special object: a cosmetic preparation used as a base for facial make-up: a priming substance applied to a canvas or board as a base for oil-painting; **founda'tioner,** one supported from the funds or foundation of an institution; **found'er,** one who founds, establishes or originates: an endower.— *fem.* **found'ress:**—foundation: garment, a woman's

undergarment for supporting or controlling the figure; **founda'tion-mus'lin, -net,** gummed fabrics used for stiffening dresses and bonnets; **founda'-tion-stone,** one of the stones forming the foundation of a building, esp. a stone laid with public ceremony; **founda'tion-stop,** any organ stop whose sounds are those belonging to the keys, or differing by whole octaves only: a fundamental flue stop; **found'er-member,** one of those members of a society who were instrumental in its foundation; **founders' shares,** same as **deferred shares.** [Fr. *fonder*—L. *fundāre, -ātum,* to found—*fundus,* the bottom.]

**found,** *fownd, v.t.* to merit: to make by melting and allowing to harden in a mould (esp. metals): to cast.—*ns.* **found'er; found'ing; found'ry,** the art of founding or casting: a place where founding is carried on: articles produced by founding. [Fr. *fondre*—L. *fundĕre, fūsum,* to pour.]

**founder,** *fownd'ər, v.i.* (of a building) to subside: to collapse in ruins (also *fig.*): to go to the bottom: (of a ship) to fill with water and sink: to stumble: to go lame: to stick in mud.—*v.t.* to cause to founder.—*n.* a collapse: laminitis.— *adj.* **found'erous,** causing to founder. [O.Fr. *fondrer,* to fall in, *fond,* bottom—L. *fundus,* bottom.]

**fount,** *fownt,* (*print.*) *n.* a complete assortment of types of one sort, with all that is necessary for printing in that kind of letter.—Also (esp. in U.S.) **font.** [Fr. *fonte*—*fondre*—L. *fundĕre,* to cast.]

**fount,** *fownt, n.* a spring of water: a source.—*adj.* **fount'ful** (*poet.*), full of springs. [L. *fōns, fontis.*]

**fountain,** *fownt'in, n.* a spring of water, a jet: a structure for supplying drinking water or other liquid: an ornamental structure with jets, spouts, and basins of water: a reservoir from which oil, ink, etc., flows, as in a lamp, a pen: the source.—*adj.* **fount'ainless.**—**fount'ain-head,** the head or source: the beginning; **fount'ain-pen,** a pen with a reservoir for ink. [Fr. *fontaine*—L.L. *fontāna*—L. *fōns, fontis,* a spring.]

**four,** *for, för, n.* the cardinal number next above three: a symbol representing that number: a set of four things or persons (leaves, oarsmen, etc.): a four-oar boat: a four-cylinder engine or car: a shoe or other article of a size denoted by 4: a card with four pips: a score of four points, tricks, strokes, etc.: the fourth hour after midday or midnight: (in *pl.; dial.*) a snack taken at 4 o'clock (also **fours'es**): (in *pl.*) the four extremities (in the phrase *on all fours*).— *adj.* of the number four.—*adj.* and *adv.* **four'fold,** in four divisions: folded in four thicknesses: four times as much.—*ns.* **four'foldness; four'some,** a group of four: anything in which four act together, esp. a game of golf (two against two, partners playing the same ball) or a reel—also *adj.*—**four'-ale,** ale sold at fourpence a quart (*obs.*): cheap ale.—*adj.* **four'-ball** (*golf*), played two against two with four balls, best ball counting.—**four'-by-two',** a rifle pull-through: an army biscuit.—*n. sing.* **four'-eyes,** the fish *Anableps*: a person wearing spectacles (*slang*).— *adj.* **four'-figure,** running into four figures: to four places of decimals.—**four-flush,** four cards of the same suit in a five-card poker hand.—*v.i.* to bluff with a four-flush: to bluff.—*adj.* **bluffing:** not genuine.—**four'-flush'er.**—*adjs.* **four'-foot,** measuring four feet (four-foot way in railways, space of 4 ft 8½ in. (1·435 m.) between rails): having the pitch of an open organ pipe four feet long, or having that pitch for its lowest note; **four'-foot'ed,** having four feet; **four'-hand'ed,** having four hands: played by four players (*cards*); **four'-horse,** drawn by four horses.—**four'-hours** (Scot. *fowr-ōorz*), a refreshment about four o'clock.—*adj.* **four'-inched**

(*Shak.*), four inches wide.—**four'-in-hand,** a coach drawn by four horses, two by two, driven by one person: the team drawing it: a necktie tied with a flat slip-knot, with dangling ends.— Also *adj.* and *adv.—adjs.* **four'-leaved, four'-leafed, four'-leaf; four'-legged'.—four'-oar,** a boat rowed with four oars; **four'-o-clock,** brightly coloured flowering plant *Mirabilis jalapa,* also known as the marvel of Peru: similar red-flowered plant *M. Laevis* found in California: the friar-bird.—*adjs.* **four'-part, four-part'ed,** in four parts: divided into four nearly to the base. —**four'pence,** the value of four pennies; **four'-penny,** an old silver coin worth fourpence.—*adj.* sold or offered for fourpence.—**four'-post'er,** large bed with four curtain posts; **four'-pound'er,** a gun that throws a four-pound shot: a four-pound loaf.—*adjs.* **four'score,** eighty; **four'-scorth** (*obs.*), eightieth.—**four'-seat'er,** a vehicle seated for four.—*adjs.* **four'square'** (also *adv.*), square: presenting a firm bold front; **four'-wheel,** acting on or by means of four wheels; **four'-wheeled.—four'-wheel'er,** a cab or other vehicle with four wheels.—**four-letter word,** any of a number of vulgar short words, esp. of four letters, referring to sex or excrement, formerly taboo; **four-stroke cycle,** in an internal-combustion engine, a recurring series of four strokes of the piston—an out-stroke drawing the mixed gases into the cylinder, an in-stroke compressing them, an out-stroke impelled by their explosion and working the engine, and an in-stroke driving out the burnt gas; **on all fours,** on four feet or hands and feet, hands and knees: analogous, strictly comparable; **The Four Freedoms,** the four essential human freedoms as proclaimed by President Franklin D. Roosevelt in 1941— freedom of speech, freedom of worship, freedom from want, freedom from fear; **the four hundred** (*U.S.*), the exclusive social set; **the four seas** (see sea). [O.E. *fēower;* Ger. *vier.*]

**fourchette,** *fōōr-shet',* *n.* anything forked: a forked piece between glove fingers, uniting the front and back parts: a combination of the card next above and that next below the one just played: the furcula, or wishbone, of a bird: an animal's web foot: part of the external female genitals. [Fr., dim. of *fourche*—L. *furca,* fork.]

**Fourcroya,** *fōōr-kroi'ə.* Same as **Furcraea.**

**fourgon,** *fōōr-gɔ̃, n.* a baggage-wagon. [Fr.]

**Fourierism,** *fōō'ri-ər-izm, n.* the socialistic system of F. M. Charles *Fourier* (1772-1837), in which society is reorganised into small cooperative communities, or *phalanges,* allowing free development to human talent and emotions.

**fou rire,** *fōō rēr,* (Fr.) wild laughter, helpless giggling.

**fourteen,** *fōr-,* *för-tēn',* or *fōr', för'tēn, n.* and *adj.* four and ten.—*n.* **fourteen'er,** a verse line of fourteen syllables.—*adj.* **four'teenth** (or *-tēnth'*), last of fourteen: equal to one of fourteen equal parts.—*n.* a fourteenth part.—*adv.* **fourteenth'ly.** [O.E. *fēowertēne* (*-tiene*); see four and ten.]

**fourth,** *fōrth, förth, adj.* last of four: equal to one of four equal parts.—*n.* one of four equal parts: an interval of three (conventionally called four) diatonic degrees: a tone at that interval from another: a combination of two tones separated by that interval.—*adv.* **fourth'ly.—fourth dimension,** of time, as opposed to the three spatial dimensions: that which is beyond ordinary experience.—*adj.* **fourth'-dimen'sional.—fourth estate,** a group of people other than the lords, commons and clergy, who influence a country's politics: the press; **fourth wall,** idea of the naturalistic theatre, that the open front of the stage-set represents as solid a wall as the other three sides.—*adj.* **fourth'-rate,** of the fourth order: inferior. [O.E. *fēowertha, fēortha.*]

**fouter, foutre,** *fōō'tər,* **footra** (*Shak.*), **foutra** (*Shak.*), *-trə, n.* a fig (as a type of worthlessness): a worthless despicable fellow (*Scot.*). [O.E. *foutre*—L. *futuĕre,* to copulate with.]

**fouth, fowth,** *fōōth,* (*Scot.*) *n.* abundance. [full, suff. *-th.*]

**fovea,** *fō'vi-ə,* (*anat.*) *n.* a depression or pit:—*pl.* **foveae,** (*-ē.*)—*adjs.* **fo'veal; fo'veate,** pitted.—*n.* **fovē'ola,** a small depression—also **fo'veole.** [L. *fovea.*]

**fowl,** *fowl, n.* a bird: a bird of the barn-door or poultry kind, a cock or hen: the flesh of fowl:— *pl.* **fowls, fowl.**—*v.i.* to kill or try to kill wildfowl. —*ns.* **fowl'er,** one who takes wildfowl; **fowl'ing.** —**fowl'ing-net,** a net for catching birds; **fowl'ing-piece,** a light gun for small-shot, used in fowling; **fowl'-pest,** an acute contagious virus disease of birds (**fowl-plague**): another similar disease. [O.E. *fugol;* Ger. *vogel.*]

**fox,** *foks, n.* an animal akin to the dog having upright ears and a long bushy tail:—*fem.* **vix'en:** extended to other animals, as black-fox (pekan), flying-fox: anyone notorious for cunning: a kind of sword (*obs.*).—*v.t.* (*coll.*) to baffle, deceive, cheat.—*v.i.* (*coll.*) to act cunningly, to cheat.—*v.i.* and *v.t.* (of paper) to discolour, showing brownish marks.—*adj.* **foxed,** of books, discoloured: drunk: baffled.—*ns.* **fox'iness,** craftiness: decay: a harsh, sour taste: spotted state as in books; **fox'ing,** act of one who foxes; **fox'ship** (*Shak.*), the character of a fox, craftiness.—*adj.* **fox'y,** of foxes: fox-like: cunning: reddish brown.—**fox'-bat,** a flying-fox, a fruit-bat; **fox'berry,** the bearberry: the cowberry; **fox'-brush,** the tail of a fox; **fox'-earth,** a fox's burrow.—**fox'-ē'vil,** alopecia; **fox'glove,** a plant (Digitalis) with flowers like glove-fingers; **fox'-grape,** an American grape (*Vitis labrusca;* also *V. rotundifolia*); **fox'hole,** a fox's earth; a small entrenchment (*mil.*); **fox'hound,** a hound used for chasing foxes; **fox'-hunt; fox'-hunt'er; fox'-hunting,** the chase of a fox by hounds; **fox'-shark,** a large long-tailed shark, the thresher; **fox'-tail,** a fox's brush: a genus (Alopecurus) of grasses, with head like a fox's tail; **fox'-terr'ier,** a kind of terrier trained to unearth foxes; **fox'-trap; fox'-trot,** a horse's pace with short steps, as in changing from trotting to walking: a shuffling dance to syncopated music.—**fox and geese,** a game played with pieces on a board, where the object is for certain pieces called the geese to surround or corner one called the fox or prevent him from passing. [O.E. *fox;* Ger. *fuchs.*]

**foy,** *foi,* (*Spens.*) *n.* allegiance. [Fr. *foi,* faith.]

**foy,** *foi,* (*dial.*) *n.* a parting entertainment or gift. [Du. *fooi.*]

**foyer,** *foi'ā, foi'ər* (Fr. *fwä-yā*), *n.* in theatres, a public room opening on the lobby. [Fr.,—L. *focus,* hearth.]

**foyle, foyne,** Spenserian spellings of **foil, foin.**

**fozy,** *fōz'i,* (*Scot.*) *adj.* spongy: wanting in freshness: fat: dull-witted.—*n.* **foz'iness,** softness, want of spirit. [Cf. Du. *voos,* spongy.]

**fra,** *frä,* (It.) brother, friar.

**frab,** *frab,* (*dial.*) *v.t.* to worry.—*adj.* **frabb'it,** peevish.

**frabjous,** *frab'jəs, adj.* perh. joyous: surpassing. [Invented by Lewis Carroll.]

**fracas,** *frak'ä, frä-kä', n.* uproar: a noisy quarrel: —*pl.* **fracas,** *-käz.* [Fr.,—It. *fracasso—fracassare,* to make an uproar.]

**frack,** *frak, fräk,* (*Scot.*) *adj.* prompt: eager: lusty. [O.E. *fræc, frec.*]

**fract,** *frakt, v.t.* to break, to violate (*Shak.*).—*adj.* **fract'ed,** broken: violated: having a part displaced, as if broken (*her.*).—*n.* **frac'tion** (*-shən*), a fragment or small piece: any part of a unit (*arith.*; see **decimal** and **vulgar, proper** and **improper**): a breach of amity (*Shak.*): a portion separated by fractionation: the breaking of the bread in the Eucharist.—*adj.* **frac'tional**, belonging to a fraction or fractions: of the nature of a fraction.—*v.t.* **fractionalise, -ize,** to break up into parts.—*ns.* **frac'tionalist,** a breaker up of political unity; **frac'tionalism,** state of consisting of discrete units: action of forming a fraction within the Communist party.—*adj.* **frac'tionary,** fractional: fragmentary.—*v.t.* **frac'tionate,** to break up into smaller units: to separate the components of by distillation or otherwise.—*ns.* **fractiona'tion; frac'tionator,** plant for carrying out fractional distillation.—*v.t.* **frac'tionise, -ize,** to break up into fractions.—*n.* **frac'tionlet,** a small fraction.—*adj.* **frac'tious,** ready to quarrel: cross.—*adv.* **frac'tiously.**—*ns.* **frac'tiousness; frac'ture** (-*char*), breaking: the breach or part broken: the surface of breaking, other than cleavage: the breaking of a bone.—*v.t.* and *v.i.* to break through: to crack.—**fractional distillation,** a distillation process for the separation of the various constituents of liquid mixtures by means of their different boiling points.—**compound fracture,** breaking of a bone, communicating with a co-existing skin wound; **comminuted fracture,** a fracture in which the bone is splintered; **greenstick fracture,** a fracture where the bone is partly broken, partly bent, occurring in limbs of children; **impacted fracture,** a fracture in which the ends of bone are driven into each other; **simple fracture,** a fracture of bone without wound in the skin. [L. *frangĕre, frāctum,* to break (partly through Fr.).]

**frae.** See **fro.**
**fraenum.** Same as **frenum.**
**Fragaria,** *frə-gā'ri-ə, n.* the strawberry genus. [L. *frăgum,* the strawberry.]
**fragile,** *fraj'īl,* in U.S. *-əl, adj.* easily broken: frail: delicate.—*n.* **fragility** (*frə-jil'*), the state of being fragile. [Fr.,—L. *fragilis—frangĕre, frāctum.*]
**fragment,** *frag'mənt, n.* a piece broken off: an unfinished portion.—*adj.* **fragmental** (-*ment'*; also *frag'mən-təl*), composed of fragments of older rocks: in fragments.—*adv.* **frag'mentarily.**—*n.* **frag'mentariness.**—*adjs.* **frag'mentary, fragment'ed,** consisting of fragments: broken: in fragments: existing or operating in separate parts, not forming a harmonious unity.—*n.* **fragmenta'tion,** division into fragments: cell division without mitosis (*biol.*). [L. *fragmentum* —*frangĕre, frāctum,* to break.]
**fragor,** *frā'gör, n.* a crash. [L. *frăgor.*]
**fragrant,** *frā'grənt, adj.* sweet-scented.—*ns.* **fra'grance, fra'grancy,** pleasantness of smell: sweet or pleasant influence (*fig.*).—*adv.* **fra'grantly.**—*n.* **fra'grantness.** [L. *frāgrāns, -antis,* pr.p. of *frāgrāre,* to smell.]
**fraicheur,** *fre-shœr',* (Fr.) freshness, coolness.
**frail,** *frāl, adj.* very easily shattered: feeble and infirm (*esp. Scot.*): decrepit: morally weak: (euphemistically) unchaste: tender (*Spens.*).—*n.* (*slang*) a woman.—*adj.* **frail'ish,** somewhat frail.—*adv.* **frail'ly.**—*ns.* **frail'ness, frail'ty** (*Spens.* **fra'iltee**), weakness: infirmity. [O.Fr. *fraile*—L. *fragilis,* fragile.]
**frail,** *frāl, n.* a rush: a rush-basket. [O.Fr. *frayel.*]
**fraim.** See **fremd.**
**fraise,** *frāz, n.* a horizontal or nearly horizontal palisade (*fort.*): a tool for enlarging a drillhole: a 16th-cent. ruff.—*v.t.* to fence with a fraise. [Fr.]
**fraise,** *frāz,* (*dial.*) *n.* commotion.
**fraise,** *frāz.* See **froise.**
**fraktur,** *fräk-tōōr',* n. a German black-letter typeface. [Ger.,—L. *frāctūra,* breaking.]
**framboesia,** *fram-bē'zi-ə, n.* yaws. [Fr. *framboise,* raspberry.]
**frame,** *frām, v.t.* to form: to shape: to put together: to plan, adjust, or adapt: to contrive or devise: to concoct: to bring about: to

articulate: to direct (one's steps): to set about: to enclose in a frame or border: to make victim of a frame-up.—*v.i.* to make one's way: to resort: to pretend (*dial.*): to make a move: to give promise of progress or success: to contrive (*B.*).—*n.* the body: a putting together of parts: structure: a case made to enclose, border or support anything: the skeleton of anything: the rigid part of a bicycle: a structure on which embroidery is worked: a stocking-making machine: a loom (*obs.*): a structure on which bees build a honeycomb: in gardening, a structure for cultivation or sheltering of plants: state (of mind), mood: act of devising (*Shak.*): unit picture in cinema film: formerly British term for field (*TV*): the total *TV* picture: triangular support in which balls are grouped for the break (*snooker,* etc.): balls so grouped (*snooker,* etc.): in jargon of certain games, a definite part of a game, a game, or a definite number of games.—*ns.* **fram'er,** one who forms or constructs: one who makes frames for pictures, etc.; one who devises: one who formulates (e.g. law); **fram'ing,** the act of constructing: a frame or setting.—**frame'-breaker,** one who broke stocking-frames on their introduction; **frame'-house,** a house consisting of a skeleton of timber, with boards or shingles laid on; **frame'-maker,** a maker of picture-frames; **frame'-saw,** a thin saw stretched in a frame; **frame'-up,** a trumped-up affair, esp. a false criminal charge against an innocent person: a staged or preconcerted event; **frame'work,** the work that forms the frame: the skeleton or outline of anything.—**frame of reference,** a set of axes with reference to which the position of a point, etc., is described (*lit.*): the structure of standards, arising from the individual's experience, and continually developing, to which he refers, in all cases from the simplest to the most complicated, when judging or evaluating (*fig.*). [O.E. *framian,* to be helpful, *fram,* forward.]
**frampold,** *fram'pōld, -pəld,* (*obs.*) *adj.* peevish, cross-grained: fiery.—Also **fram'pal** (*Scott*).—*n.* **fram'pler** (*Scott*), a brawler. [Ety. obscure.]
**franc,** *frangk, n.* a coin forming since 1795 the unit of the French monetary system (**new, or heavy,** **franc** introduced 1960—'new' dropped 1963): unit also in Belgium, Switzerland, etc. [O.Fr. *franc,* from the legend *Francorum rex* on the first coins.]
**franchise,** *fran'chīz, -shiz, n.* liberty: a privilege or exemption by prescription or grant: the right of voting, esp. for an M.P.: voting qualification: a commercial concession by which a retailer is granted by a company the exclusive right of retailing its goods in a specified area (*U.S.*): a percentage below which the underwriter incurs no responsibility (*insurance*).—*v.t.* (*obs.*) to enfranchise.—*ns.* **fran'chisement** (-*chiz-, -shiz-*; *obs.*), liberation; **fran'chiser,** a voter: a firm which grants a commercial concession (*U.S.*). [O.Fr.,—*franc,* free.]
**franchise,** *frä-shēz,* (Fr.) candour, frankness.
**Franciscan,** *fran-sis'kən, adj.* belonging to the order of mendicant friars in the R.C. Church, founded by St *Francis* of Assisi (1182-1226).—*n.* a monk of this order. [L. *Franciscus,* Francis.]
**francium,** *fran'si-əm, n.* the chemical element of atomic number 87, symbol Fr, discovered by a Frenchwoman, Mlle Perey. [France.]
**franco,** *fräng'kō,* (It.) post-free, franked.
**Franco-,** *frangk'ō-,* in composition, French: French and, as Franco-German, Franco-Russian, etc.—**Francomania, -phil(e), -phobe** (same as **Gallomania,** etc.; see under **Gallic**).—*adj.* **Franc'ophone,** French-speaking (used of Africans for whom French is a second mother-tongue).
**francolin,** *frang'kō-lin, n.* a genus (*Francolinus*) of partridges. [Fr.]

franc-tireur, *frä tē-rœr*, (Fr.) sniper: guerrillero.
frangible, *fran'ji-bl*, *adj.* easily broken.—*n.*
frangibil'ity. [L. *frangĕre*, to break; see fraction.]
frangipani, *fran-ji-pä'nē*, *n.* the red jasmine or other species of *Plumeria*, tropical American apocynaceous shrubs with scented flowers: a perfume from or in imitation of red jasmine: (also frangipane, *fran'ji-pän*), a pastry-cake filled with cream, almonds, and sugar. [From the name *Frangipani*.]
Franglais, *frä-gle*, *n.* French with many English words and forms. [Fr. *Francais* and *Anglais*.]
franion, *fran'yən*, *n.* a paramour (*obs.*): boon-companion (*obs.*): loose woman (*Spens.*). [Ety. dub.]
Frank, *frangk*, *n.* a German of a confederation in Franconia of which a branch conquered Gaul in the 5th century, and founded France: in the East, Western European.—*adj.* Frank'ish. [See frank (1).]
frank, *frangk*, *adj.* free, open: liberal (*obs.*): open or candid in expression: unrestrained (*obs.*): unmistakable, true (*med.*; as *frank pus*, *asthma*).—*v.t.* to sign so as to ensure free carriage: to send thus signed: to mark by means of a franking-machine to show that postage has been paid.—*n.* the signature of a person who had the right to frank a letter: a franked cover.—*adv.* frankl'y.—*n.* frank'ness.—frank'-fee, tenure in fee-simple; frank'-pledge, a mutual suretyship by which the members of a tithing were made responsible for one another; frank'-ten'ement, freehold. [O.Fr. *franc*—L.L. *francus*; O.H.G. *Franko*, Frank, hence a free man.]
frank, *frangk*, (*Shak.*) *n.* a pig-sty.—*v.t.* to shut up in a sty: to cram, to fatten. [O.Fr. *franc*.]
frankalmoign, *frangk'al-moin*, (*Eng. law*) *n.* a form of land-tenure in which no obligations were enforced except religious ones, as praying, etc. [O.Fr. *franc*, free, *almoigne*, alms.]
Frankenia, *frang-kē'ni-ə*, *n.* the sea-heath genus, constituting a family Frankeniä'ceae, akin to the tamarisk family. [Named after John *Frankenius* (1590-1661), Swedish physician and botanist.]
Frankenstein, *frangk'ən-stin*, *n.* the hero of Mrs. Shelley's romance so named, who by his skill forms an animate creature like a man, only to his own torment: hence, by confusion, any creation that brings disaster to its author.
Frankfurter, *frangk'fûr-tər*, *-fŏŏr-tər*, (Ger.) a small smoked sausage.
frankincense, *frangk'in-sens*, *n.* olibanum, a sweet-smelling resin from Arabia, used as incense: spruce resin.—herb frankincense, laser. [O.Fr. *franc encens*, pure incense.]
franklin, *frangk'lin*, (*hist.*) *n.* an English free-holder, free from feudal servitude to a subject-superior. [L.L. *francus*; see frank.]
franklinite, *frangk'lin-it*, *n.* a zinc-manganese spinel, mined at *Franklin Forge*, New Jersey.
frantic, *fran'tik*, *adj.* mad, furious: wild.—*advs.* fran'tically, fran'ticly (*Shak.*).—*n.* fran'ticness, the state of being frantic.—*adj.* fran'tic-mad, raving mad. [O.Fr. *frenetique*—L. *phreneticus*—Gr. *phrenētikos*, mad—*phrēn*, the mind; see frenetic, frenzy.]
franzy, *fran'zi*, (*dial.*) *adj.* cross: peevish. [Variant of frenzy.]
frap, *frap*, *v.t.* to strike (now *dial.*): to secure by many turns of a lashing (*naut.*). [Fr. *frapper*, to strike.]
frappant, *fra-pä*, (Fr.) striking, affecting.
frappé, fem. frappée, *fra-pä*, (Fr.) iced, artificially cooled.
frass, *fras*, *n.* excrement or other refuse of boring larvae. [Ger.,—*fressen*, to eat; cf. fret.]
fratch, *frach*, (*dial.*) *n.* a quarrel or brawl.—*adjs.* fratch'ety, fratch'y; fratch'ing. [Perh. imit.]
frate, pl. frati, *frä'tä*, *-tē*, (It.) a friar, a mendicant Franciscan.

frater, *frä'tər*, *n.* a refectory: sometimes applied in error to a monastic common-room or to a chapter-house (by confusion with next word).—Also frä'ter-house, frä'try. [O.Fr. *fraitur* for *refreitor*—L.L. *refectōrium*.]
frater, *frä'tər*, *n.* a friar: a comrade.—*n.* Fratercula (*fra-tûr'kū-lə*), the puffin genus.—*adj.* frater'nal (*frə-tûr'nl*), belonging to a brother or brethren: brotherly.—*adv.* frater'nally.—*n.* fraterni'sä'tion (*frat-*), the associating as brethren.—*v.i.* frat'ernise, -ize, to associate as brothers: to seek brotherly fellowship: to come into friendly association.—*ns.* frat'erniser; frater'nity, the state of being brethren: a brotherhood: a society formed on a principle of brotherhood: an American college association: any set of people with something in common; fratry (*frāt'ri*), frāt'ery, a fraternity: a convent of friars (see also foregoing article).—fraternal twins, dizygotic twins. [L. *frāter*, a brother; cf. brother, Gr. *phrātēr*, a clansman, Sans. *bhrātṛ*.]
fratricide, *frat'ri-sid*, or *frāt'*, *n.* one who kills his brother: the murder of a brother.—*adj.* fratrici'dal. [Fr.,—L. *frāter*, *frātris*, *caedēre*, to kill.]
frau, Frau, *frow*, *n.* a woman: a wife: Mrs.—*n.* fräulein, Fräulein (*froi'lin*), an unmarried woman: often applied to a German governess: Miss. [Ger.]
fraud, *fröd*, *n.* deceit: imposture: a snare (*Milt.*): a deceptive trick: a cheat, swindler (*coll.*): a fraudulent production.—*adj.* fraud'ful, deceptive.—*adv.* fraud'fully.—*ns.* fraud'ster, swindler; fraud'ulence, fraud'ulency.—*adj.* fraud'ulent, using fraud.—*adv.* fraud'ulently.—fraudulent bankruptcy, a bankruptcy in which the insolvent is accessory, by concealment or otherwise, to the diminution of the funds divisible among his creditors. [O.Fr. *fraude*—L. *fraus*, fraud.]
frauendienst, *frow'ən-dēnst*, (Ger.) courtly love.
fraught, *fröt*, *n.* a load, cargo: the freight of a ship.—*v.t.* to fill, store.—*v.i.* to form the freight of a vessel (*Shak.*).—*adj.* freighted, laden: filled (*with*): anxious, distressed.—*n.* fraught'age, fraut'age (*Shak.*), loading, cargo. [Prob. Old Du. *vracht*. Cf. freight.]
Fraunhofer's lines, *frown'hō-fərz*. See line (2).
fraus pia, *frös pī'ə*, frows pē'a, (L.) a pious fraud.
Fraxinus, *frak'si-nəs*, *n.* the ash genus.—Fraxinell'a, dittany (from its ashlike leaves). [L.]
fray, *frā*, *n.* an affray: a brawl.—*v.t.* to frighten. [Aphetic from affray.]
fray, *frā*, *v.t.* to wear off by rubbing: to ravel out the end or edge of: to cause a strain on (e.g. nerves, temper, etc.).—*v.i.* to become frayed: to rub off the velvet from the new antlers.—*n.* fray'ing, the action of the verb: frayed off material. [Fr. *frayer*—L. *fricāre*, to rub.]
frazil, *fraz'il*, *frā'zil*, *n.* ground-ice: ice in small spikes and plates in rapid streams. [Canadian Fr. *frasil*; prob. Fr. *fraisil*, cinders.]
frazzle, *fraz'l*, *v.t.* to fray, wear out.—*n.* state of being worn out: a shred. [Origin unknown.]
freak, *frēk*, *n.* caprice: sport: an abnormal production of nature, a monstrosity: an eccentric.—*adj.* capricious: unusual.—*ns.* freak'iness, freak'ishness.—*adjs.* freak'ish, freak'ful, freak'y, apt to change the mind suddenly: unusual, odd.—*adv.* freak'ishly.—freak'out (*slang*), a (drug-induced) hallucinatory or (loosely) exciting experience or occurrence (*v.i.* freak (out)). [A late word; cf. O.E. *frīcian*, to dance.]
freak, *frēk*, *v.t.* to fleck, spot or streak (*Milt.*): to variegate (*Milt.*).—*n.* a streak of colour. [Perh. the same as the foregoing.]
freckle, *frek'l*, *v.t.* to spot: to colour with spots.—*n.* a yellowish or brownish-yellow spot on the skin, esp. of fair-haired persons: any small spot.—*n.* freck'ling, a little spot.—*adjs.* freck'ly, freck'led, full of freckles. [O.N. *freknur* (pl.), Dan. *fregne*.]

Neutral vowels in unaccented syllables: *el'ə-mənt*; for certain sounds in foreign words, see p. viii

**fredaine,** *frə-den,* (Fr.) escapade, prank.
**free,** *frē, adj.* not bound: at liberty: not under arbitrary government: not strict, or bound by rules: not literal: unimpeded: unconstrained: readily cut, separated or wrought: ready (esp. in phrase *free to confess*): guiltless: frank: lavish: uncombined: unattached: exempt (with *from*): having a franchise (with *of*): without payment: bold: indecent:—*compar.* **freer,** *frē″ər;* *superl.* **freest,** *frē′ist.*—*adv.* freely: without payment: without obstruction.—*v.t.* to set at liberty: to deliver from what confines: to rid (with *from, of*):—*pr.p.* **free′ing;** *pa.t.* and *pa.p.* **freed.**—*n.* **free′dom,** liberty: frankness: outspokenness: unhampered boldness: separation: privileges connected with a city (often granted as an honour merely): improper familiarity: licence. *adv.* **free′ly.**—*ns.* **free′ness;** **freer** *(frē′ər),* liberator.—**free′-ag′ency,** state or power of acting freely, or without necessity or constraint upon the will; **free′-ag′ent;** **free′-and-eas′y,** an informal public-house club.—*adj.* Informal in manners, without ceremonious restraint.—*adj.* **free′-arm,** with unsupported arm.—**free association,** a technique in psychoanalysis based either on the first association called forth by each of a series of words or on a train of thought suggested by a single word; **free atom, radical,** short-lived atom, radical, assumed to exist during certain chemical reactions; **free′-bench,** a widow's right to dower out of her husband's lands; **free′-board,** the distance between water-line and deck: a strip of land outside a fence, or a right thereto; **free′booter (Du.** *vrijbuiter),* one who roves about freely in search of booty; **free′bootery.**—*adj., n.* **free′booting.**—**free′booty.** —*adj.* **free′born,** born free.—**Free Church,** that branch of the Presbyterians in Scotland which left the Established Church in the Disruption of 1843: the small minority thereof who refused to combine with the United Presbyterians in the **United Free Church** (see under **presbyter**): in England, a Nonconformist church generally; **free′-cit′y,** a city constituting a state in itself; **free companion,** a member of a **free company,** or mediaeval band of mercenaries ready for any service; **free′-cost,** freedom from charges; **free′-diver, -diving,** skin-diver, -diving; **freed′man,** a man who has been a slave and has been freed:— *pl.* **freed′men;** *fem.* **freed′woman;** *pl.* **freed′-women; free enterprise,** the conduct of business without interference from the state; **free′-fall,** the motion of an unpropelled body in a gravitational field, as that of a spacecraft in orbit: the part of a parachute jump before the parachute opens; **free fight,** a confused or promiscuous fight; **free′-fish′er,** one who has a right to take fish in certain waters; **free′-food′er,** an opponent of taxes on food.—*adj.* **free′-foot′ed** *(Shak.),* not restrained in movement.—**free′-for-all′,** a contest open to anybody: a free fight.—Also *adj.*— *adj.* **free′-hand,** executed by the unguided hand. —**free hand,** complete freedom of action.—*adjs.* **free′-hand′ed,** open-handed: liberal; **free′-heart′ed,** open-hearted: liberal.—**free′-heart′edness; free′hold,** a property held free of duty except to the king; **free′holder,** one who possesses a freehold; **free house,** a public-house that is not tied to a particular supplier; **free kick,** a kick allowed without interference; **free′-lā′bour,** voluntary, not slave, labour; **free′-lance,** one of the mercenary knights and men-at-arms who after the Crusades wandered about Europe: an unattached journalist, politician. etc.: anyone who works for himself, without an employer; **free list,** the list of persons admitted without payment to a theatre, etc., or of those to whom a book, etc., is sent; **free′-liv′er,** one who freely indulges his appetite for eating and drinking: a glutton; **free′loader** *(U.S.),* a

sponger; **free′-love,** the claim to freedom in sexual relations, unshackled by marriage or obligation to aliment; **free′man,** a man who is free or enjoys liberty: one who holds a particular franchise or privilege:—*pl.* **free′men;** *fem.* **free′woman;** *pl.* **free′women; free′mā′son,** in the Middle Ages, a stone-mason of a superior grade: a member of a secret fraternity, united in lodges for social enjoyment and mutual assistance.— *adj.* **freemason′ic.**—**freemā′sonry,** the institutions, practices, etc. of freemasons: instinctive understanding and sympathy.—*adj.* **free′-mind′-ed,** with a mind free or unperplexed: without a load of care.—**free′-port,** a port where no duties are levied on articles of commerce; **free radical,** a free atom.—*adjs.* **free′-range′,** (of poultry) allowed some freedom to move about: (of eggs) laid by free-range hens; **free′-reed** *(mus.),* having a reed that does not touch the side of the aperture.—**free′-rid′er** *(coll.),* one who enjoys benefits obtained for workers by a trade union without being a member of that trade union; **free′-school,** a school where no tuition fees are exacted.—*v.i.* **free′-select** *(Austr.),* to take up crown-land under the Land Laws.—**free′-selec′tion,** the process of doing so: the land so taken; **free′-selec′tor** (also **selec′tion, selec′tor); free′-shot** (Ger. *freischütz),* a legendary hunter and marksman who gets a number of bullets *(freikugeln)* from the devil, six of which always hit the mark, while the seventh remains at the devil's disposal.—*adj.* **free′-soil,** in favour of free territory, opposed to slavery.—**free-soil′er.**—*adj.* **free′-spōk′en,** accustomed to speak without reserve.—**free′-spōk′enness; Free States,** in America, before the Civil War of 1861-65, those of the United States in which slavery did not exist, as opposed to *Slave States;* **free′stone,** any easily wrought building stone without tendency to split in layers.—*adj.* having a stone from which the pulp easily separates, as a peach—opp. to *clingstone.*—*adj.* **free′-swimming′,** swimming about, not attached. —**free′thinker,** one who rejects authority in religion: a rationalist; **free′-thinking; free′-thought.**—*adj.* **free′-tongued,** free-spoken.—**free′-trade,** free or unrestricted trade: free interchange of commodities without protective duties; **free′-trad′er,** one who practises or advocates this: a smuggler: a smuggling vessel; **free verse,** verse defying usual metrical laws in length of lines, etc.: rhythmic prose arranged as irregular verses; **free′-vers′er,** a writer of free verse, a verslibrist; **free vote,** a vote left to individual choice, free from party discipline; **freeway** *(U.S.),* a toll-free road for high-speed traffic; **free′-wheel,** the mechanism of a bicycle by which the hind-wheel may be temporarily disconnected and set free from the driving-gear.— *v.i.* to cycle with wheel so disconnected: (of motor vehicle or its driver) to coast: to move, act, live, without restraint or concern *(fig.).—* **free′-wheel′ing;** **free′-will′,** freedom of the will from restraint: liberty of choice: power of self-determination.—*adj.* **free′-will,** spontaneous.— **Free World,** the collective name used of themselves by non-communist countries.—**for free** *(coll.),* given without desire for payment or other return; **free on board (f.o.b.),** delivered on a vessel or other conveyance without charge; **make free with,** to be familiar with, to take liberties with: to help oneself liberally to; **make so free as to,** to venture to. [O.E. *frēo;* Ger. *frei;* O.N. *frī.*]
**freemartin,** *frē″mär-tin, n.* a calf (twin with a bull) with internal male organs and external and rudimentary internal female: a similar animal of another species. [Ety. unknown; perh. conn. with Ir. *mart,* a heifer.]
**Freesia,** *frē″zi-ə,* a South African genus of the iris

family, scented greenhouse plants. [E. M. *Fries* (1794-1878), Swedish botanist.]

**freeze**, *frēz*, *v.i.* to become ice: to become solid by fall of temperature: to be at a temperature at which water would freeze: to be very cold: to become motionless, stiff, attached, or stopped by, or as if by, cold.—*v.t.* to cause to freeze: to fix: to stabilise: to prevent the use of or dealings in:—*pr.p.* **freez'ing**; *pa.t.* **frōze**, (*Milt.*) **freez'd**; *pa.p.* **frōz'en**; *obs.* **frōze, frōre, frōrn.**— *n.* a frost: a stoppage.—*adj.* **freez'able.**—*ns.* **freez'er**, a freezing apparatus: anything that freezes: a special compartment in a refrigerator designed to freeze fresh foods; **freez'ing.**— **freeze'-dry'ing**, evaporation to dryness in a vacuum for preservation or storage of a substance, e.g. an antibiotic; **freeze'-up**, in U.S. and Canada, the period when ice forms on lakes, etc., at onset of winter; **freez'ing-down**, lowering of the body temperature; **freez'ing-mixture**, a mixture, as of pounded ice and salt, producing cold enough to freeze a liquid by the rapid absorption of heat; **freez'ing-point**, the temperature at which a liquid solidifies—that of water being 32° Fahrenheit, 0° Celsius (centigrade).— **freeze down**, to lower the body temperature in preparation for heart and other operations; **freeze out** (*coll.*), to oblige to leave: to exclude. [O.E. *frēosan*, pa.p. *froren*; Du. *vreizen*, Ger. *frieren.*]

**freight**, *frāt*, *n.* the lading or cargo, esp. of a ship: the charge for transporting goods by water or land.—*v.t.* to load (esp. a ship): to hire, let out. —*adj.* (*obs.*) freighted: fraught.—*ns.* **freight'age**, money paid for freight; **freight'er**, one who freights a vessel: a cargo-carrying boat, etc.; a transporting agent (*U.S.*): a goods wagon (*U.S.*).—**freight'-car** (*U.S.*), a luggage van: a goods van or wagon; **freight'liner**, a train having specially designed containers and rolling stock and used for rapid transport of goods.— Also *adj.*—**freight'shed**, a goods shed or warehouse; **freight'-train**, a goods train. [Prob. Old Du. *vrecht*, a form of *vracht.*]

**freit, freet**, *frēt*, (*Scot.*) *n.* an omen.—*adj.* **freit'y, freet'y**, superstitious. [O.N. *frētt*, news.]

**fremd**, *fremd*, *frāmd*, **fremit**, *frem'it*, *frām'it*, **fraim**, *frām*, (*Scot.*) *adj.* foreign: strange: not akin: estranged, cold, unfriendly.—*n.* a stranger: strange folk, other than kindred.—*Spens.* **frenne** (*fren*). [O.E. *fremde*; cf. Ger. *fremd.*]

**fremescent**, *frəm-es'ənt*, (*rare*) *adj.* growling, muttering.—*n.* **fremesc'ence.** [L. *fremĕre*, to growl.]

**fremitus**, *frem'i-təs*, *n.* a palpable vibration, as of the walls of the chest. [L., a murmur.]

**French**, *french*, *-sh*, *adj.* belonging to *France* or its people: originating in France (in names of commodities now sometimes spelt without *cap.*). —*n.* the people or language of France.—*n.* **Frenchificā'tion.**—*v.t.* **French'ify**, to make French or Frenchlike: to infect with the manner of the French.—*n.* **French'iness.**—*adj.* **French'y**, with an exaggerated French manner.—*n.* contemptuous name for a Frenchman.—**French bean**, the common kidney-bean (*Phaseolus vulgaris*) eaten, pods and all, as a table vegetable; **French berry**, the berry of species of buckthorn, used in dyeing yellow; **French chalk**, soapstone; **French fry**, fried a potato-chip; **French heel**, a way of turning the heel in knitting: a high curved heel for ladies' shoes; **French horn**, the orchestral horn; **French letter** (*slang*), a condom; **French loaf**, bread with crusty top baked in long narrow shape with tapered ends; **French'man**:—*pl.* **French'men**; *fem.* **French'woman**:—*pl.* **French'-women**; **French pitch** (*mus.*), a standard pitch established by the French government in 1859, and later widely adopted—435 cycles per second at 15°C for A (see **international concert pitch**);

**French plum**, a prune, a dried plum; **French polish**, a varnish for furniture, consisting chiefly of shellac dissolved in spirit.—*v.t.* to treat with French polish.—**French polisher; French polishing; French pox** (*obs.*), syphilis; **French roof**, a modified mansard roof—really American; **French sash, window**, a doorlike window; **French seam**, seam stitched on right side then on wrong side to cover raw edges; **French toast**, bread dipped in egg (and milk) and fried.—**Free** (from 1942 **Fighting**) **French**, continuers under General de Gaulle of resistance to Germany in World War II after the French capitulation of 1940; **take French leave**, to depart without notice or permission, to disappear suspiciously. [O.E. *Frencisc*—L. *Francus*—O.H.G. *Franko.*]

**frenetic, phrenetic**, *fri-net'ik*, formerly *fren'*, *adj.* delirious: frantic: frenzied: mad: distracted. —*n.* a madman.—*adj.* **frenet'ical, phrenet'ical.**— *adv.* **frenet'ically, phrenet'ically.** [O.Fr. *frénétique*—L. *phreneticus*—late Gr. *phrenētikos*—Gr. *phrenitis*, delirium—*phrēn*, heart, mind. See **phrenesiac.**]

**frenne**, *fren*, (*Spens.*). See **fremd**.

**frenum, fraenum**, *frē'nəm*, *n.* a ligament restraining the motion of a part. [L. *frēnum*, a bridle.]

**frenzy**, *fren'zi*, *n.* a violent excitement: a paroxysm of madness.—*v.t.* to drive to frenzy.— *adjs.* **fren'zical, fren'zied.** [O.Fr. *frenesie*—L. and late Gr. *phrenēsis*—Gr. *phrenitis*; see **frenetic.**]

**Freon**, *frē'on*, *n.* any of a family of chemicals containing fluorine used as refrigerants, etc.; Freon-12, dichlorodifluoromethane ($CF_2Cl_2$), is widely used in household refrigerators. [Trademark.]

**frequent**, *frē'kwənt*, *adj.* coming or occurring often: crowded: addicted (*Shak.*).—*v.t.* (*fri-kwent'*), to visit often: to associate with: to resort to: to crowd.—*ns.* **frē'quence**, a crowd, an assembly (*Milt.*): frequency; **frē'quency**, **resort** (*obs.*): commonness of recurrence: number of vibrations, cycles, or other recurrences in unit time (in ascending order, high, very high, ultra-high, extremely high, super high frequency); **frêquentā'tion**, the act of visiting often.—*adj.* **frequentative** (*fri-kwent'ə-tiv;gram.*), denoting the frequent repetition of an action.— *n.* (*gram.*) a verb expressing this repetition.—*n.* **frequent'er.**—*adv.* **frē'quently.**—*n.* **frē'quentness.** —**frequency modulation**, modulation in radio transmission by varying the frequency of the carrier wave, giving greater fidelity than amplitude modulation and almost freedom from atmospherics. [L. *frequēns, frequentis*; conn. with *farcire*, to stuff.]

**frescade**, *fres-kād'*, *n.* a cool walk. [Fr.,—It. *frescata.*]

**fresco**, *fres'kō*, *n.* a mode of painting upon walls covered with damp freshly-laid plaster (*true fresco*), or partly-dried plaster (*dry fresco* or *fresco secco*): a picture so painted:—*pl.* **fres'coes, fres'cos.**—*v.t.* to paint in fresco.—*adj.* **fres'coed** (*-kōd*).—*ns.* **frescoer** (*fres'kō-ər*); **fres'coing; fres'coist.** [It. *fresco*, fresh.]

**fresh**, *fresh*, *adj.* in a state of activity and health: in new condition: not stale, faded or soiled: new, recently added: raw, inexperienced: in youthful bloom: cool, invigorating: brisk: amorously over-free (*slang*): without salt: not preserved by pickling, drying, salting, etc.: not frosty (*Scot.*): cheeky, pert.—*adv.* freshly: afresh: newly.—*n.* time of freshness: a small stream of fresh water (*Shak.*): a warm, open weather (*Scot.*).—*v.t.* to freshen.—*v.t.* **fresh'en**, to make fresh: to take the saltness from.—*v.i.* to grow fresh: to make oneself fresh by washing, etc. (often with *up*).—*ns.* **fresh'ner; fresh'er**, a student in his or her first year, a freshman;

**fresh'erdom; fresh'et**, a stream of fresh water: a flood.—*adj.* **fresh'ish.**—*adv.* **fresh'ly**, with freshness: newly: anew.—*n.* **fresh'ness.**—*adj.* **fresh'-blown**, newly blown, as a flower.—*ns.* **fresh'man**, a newcomer: a student in his first year; **fresh'-manship.**—*adjs.* **fresh'-new** (*Shak.*), quite new; **fresh'-run**, newly come up from the sea, as a salmon; **fresh'water**, of or pertaining to water not salt: accustomed to sail only on fresh water. —**freshwater college** (*U.S.*), a small college. [O.E. *fersc*; cf. Ger. *frisch*.]

**fret**, *fret*, *v.t.* to eat into: to corrode: to wear away by rubbing: to rub, chafe: to ripple, disturb: to vex, to irritate.—*v.i.* to wear away: to vex oneself: to worry: to chafe: of a liquid, to work, ferment (*dial.*):—*pr.p.* **frett'ing;** *pa.t.* and *pa.p.* **frett'ed.**—*n.* agitation of the surface of a liquid: irritation: worry: a worn or eroded spot: sea fret.—*adj.* **fret'ful**, peevish. —*adv.* **fret'fully.**—*n.* **fret'fulness.**—*adj.* **frett'ing**, vexing.—*n.* peevishness. [O.E. *fretan*, to gnaw— pfx. *for-*, inten., and *etan*, to eat; Ger. *fressen*.]

**fret**, *fret*, *v.t.* to ornament with interlaced work: to variegate:—*pr.p.* **frett'ing;** *pa.t.* and *pa.p.* **frett'ed.**—*n.* ornamental network: an ornament consisting of small fillets meeting usually at right angles—a key pattern (*archit.*): bendlets, dexter and sinister, interlaced with a mascle (*her.*).— *adjs.* **frett'ed, frett'y**, ornamented with frets.— **fret'saw**, a ,saw with a narrow blade and fine teeth, used for fretwork, scrollwork, etc.; **fret'-work**, ornamental work consisting of a combination of frets: perforated woodwork. [O.Fr. *freter*, to adorn with interlaced work, *frete*, trelliswork; prob. influenced by or confused with O.E. *frætwa*, ornament.]

**fret**, *fret*, *n.* wooden or metal ridges on the fingerboards of a guitar or other instrument to help stop the strings correctly.—*v.t.* to furnish with frets. [Prob. same as the above.]

**Freudian**, *froid'i-ən*, *adj.* pertaining to Sigmund Freud (1856-1939), his theory of the libido, or his method of psychoanalysis.—*n.* a follower of Freud.

**friable**, *fri'ə-bl*, *adj.* apt to crumble: easily reduced to powder.—*ns.* **fri'ableness, friabil'ity.** [Fr.,— L. *friābilis*—*friāre, friātum*, to crumble.]

**friand**, *frē-ā*, fem. **friande**, *frē-âd*, (Fr.) dainty, delicate: an epicure.

**friar**, *fri'ər*, *n.* a member of one of the mendicant monastic orders in the R.C. Church—the Franciscans (*Friars Minor* or *Grey Friars*), Dominicans (*Friars Preachers*, or *Black Friars*), Carmelites (*White Friars*), Augustinians (*Austin Friars*), and others: a pale patch on a printed page.—*adj.* **fri'arly**, like a friar.—*n.* **fri'ary**, a convent of friars.—**fri'arbird**, an Australian honey-eater with featherless head.—**friar's balsam**, a tincture of benzoin, storax, tolu and aloes; **friar's cap.** wolf's-bane; **friar's cowl**, wake-robin; **friar's lantern**, the Will-o'-the-wisp. [O.Fr. *frere*—L. *frāter*, a brother.]

**fribble**, *frib'l*, *v.i.* to trifle.—*n.* a trifler.—*n.* **fribb'ler.**—*adjs.* **fribb'ling, fribb'lish**, trifling. [Onomatopoeic; prob. influenced by frivol.]

**fricandeau**, *frik-ən-dō'*, or *frik'*, *n.* a thick slice of veal, etc., larded:—*pl.* **fricandeaux** (*-dōz*). [Fr.]

**fricassee**, *frik-ə-sē'*, *n.* a dish of fowl, rabbit, etc. cut into pieces served in sauce.—*v.t.* to dress as a fricassee:—*pr.p.* **fricassee'ing;** *pa.t.* and *pa.p.* **fricasseed'.** [Fr. *fricassée*; origin unknown.]

**friction**, *frik'shən*, *n.* rubbing: a force acting in the tangent plane of two bodies, when one slides or rolls upon another, in direction opposite to that of the movement (*statics*): disagreement, jarring.—*adj.* **fric'ative**, produced by friction.—*n.* a consonant produced by the breath being forced through a narrow opening.—*adjs.* **fric'tional; fric'tionless.**—**friction welding**, welding in which the necessary heat is produced by

means of friction, e.g. by rotating one part and forcing the parts together. [L. *fricāre, frictum*, to rub.]

**Friday**, *fri'di*, *n.* the sixth day of the week.—**Black Friday**, Good Friday, from the black vestments of the clergy and altar in the Western Church: any Friday marked by a great calamity; **Good Friday**, the Friday before Easter, kept in commemoration of the Crucifixion; **Holy Friday**, Friday in an Ember-week—also **Golden Friday**, sometimes put for Good Friday itself; **Man, Girl, Friday** (see man, girl). [O.E. *Frigedæg*, day of (the goddess) Frig.]

**fridge**, *frij*, (*coll.*) *n.* short for refrigerator.

**fridge**, *frij*, (*Sterne*) *v.t.* rub, fray. [Prob. imit.]

**fried.** See fry.

**friend**, *frend*, *n.* one loving or attached to another: an intimate acquaintance: a favourer, wellwisher: one of a society so named; a relative (*Scot.*).—*v.t.* (*arch.*) to befriend.—*adj.* **friend'ed** (*arch.*), supplied with friends.—*n.* **friend'ing** (*Shak.*), friendliness.—*adj.* **friend'less**, without friends: destitute.—*n.* **friend'lessness.**—*adv.* **friend'lily.**—*n.* **friend'liness.**—*adj.* **friend'ly**, like a friend: having the disposition of a friend: favourable: amicable: of a football match, etc., played for amusement rather than competitively: pertaining to the Friends or Quakers.—*n.* **friend'ship**, attachment from mutual esteem: friendly assistance.—**friendly lead** (*arch.*), an entertainment for the benefit of one in need; **friendly society**, benefit society, an association for relief in sickness, old age, widowhood, by provident insurance.—**be friends with**, to be on good terms with, well disposed towards; **have a friend at court**, to have a friend in a position where his influence is likely to prove useful; **Society of Friends**, the designation proper of a sect of Christians better known as Quakers. [O.E. *frēond* (orig. a pr.p.; cf. *frēon*, to love); Ger. *freund*.]

**frier**, *fri'ər*, (*Milt.*) *n.* a friar.

**frier, fries.** See fry.

**Friesian.** See Frisian.

**frieze**, *frēz*, *n.* a rough, heavy woollen cloth.—*adj.* **friezed**, napped. [Fr. *frise*.]

**frieze**, *frēz*, (*archit.*) *n.* the part of the entablature between the architrave and cornice, often ornamented with figures: a decorated band along the top of a room wall.—*v.t.* to put a frieze on. [O.Fr. *frise*; It. *fregio*; perh. L. *Phrygium* (*opus*), Phrygian (work).]

**frig**, *frig*, (*vulg.*) *v.i.* and *v.t.* to masturbate: loosely, to have sexual intercourse with: (often with *about*) to potter about.—*n.* masturbation. —*n.* **frigg'ing**, masturbation: pottering about.— *adj.* and *adv.* as an intensive, to a great extent, very: often used as a colourless descriptive. [Late M.E. *friggen*—L. *fricāre*, to rub.]

**frig**, *frij*, (*coll.*) *n.* short for refrigerator.

**frigate**, *frig'it*, *n.* formerly a vessel in the class next to ships of the line: now denoting an escort vessel.—*n.* **frigatoon'**, a small Venetian vessel with square stern and two masts.—**frigate bird**, a large tropical sea-bird (*Fregata*) with very long wings. [O.Fr. *fregate*—It. *fregata*; ety. dub.]

**frigger**, *frig'ər*, *n.* a glass ornament.

**fright**, *frit*, *n.* sudden fear: terror: a figure of grotesque or ridiculous appearance (*coll.*).—*vs.t.* **fright** (now *rare*, except as Scot. **fricht, frikht**), **fright'en**, to make afraid: to alarm: to drive by fear.—*adjs.* **fright'ened; fright'ening.**—*adv.* **fright'eningly.**—*adj.* **fright'ful**, terrible: horrible: unpleasant (*coll.*): great (*coll.*).—*adv.* **fright'fully**, dreadfully: very (*coll.*).—*n.* **fright'fulness**, the quality of being frightful: terrorism.—*adj.* **fright'some**, frightful: feeling fright. [O.E. *fyrhto*; cf. Ger. *furcht*, fear.]

**frigid**, *frij'id*, *adj.* frozen or stiffened with cold: cold: chillingly stiff: without spirit or feeling:

unanimated: leaving the imagination untouched: of a woman, sexually irresponsive.— *n.* **frigid'ity**, coldness: coldness of affection: want of animation: sexual irresponsiveness.— *adv.* **frig'idly**.—*n.* **frig'idness**.—**frigid zones**, the parts of the earth's surface within the polar circles. [L. *frigidus*—*frigēre*, to be cold—*frigus*, cold.]

**frigidarium**, *frij-i-dār'i-əm*, *frig-i-där'i-ōōm*, (L.) *n.* the cooling room of Roman public baths, often with a swimming bath.

**frigorific**, *frig-ər-if'ik*, *adj.* causing cold: freezing. —*n.* **frigorif'ico** (Sp.), a slaughtering and meat-freezing establishment. [L. *frigus*, *-oris*, cold, *facĕre*, to make.]

**frigot**, *frig'ət*, (*Spens.*) *n.* Same as **frigate**.

**frijol, frijole**, *frē'hhōl*, *n.* the kidney-bean, or any species of Phaseolus:—*pl.* **frijoles** (*-les*). [Sp. *frijol, fréjol*.]

**frill**, *fril*, *v.i.* (*arch.*) to ruffle, as a hawk its feathers, when shivering.—*v.t.* to furnish with a frill.—*n.* a ruffle: a ruffled or crimped edging: superfluous ornament: (in *pl.*) affected airs.—*ns.* **frill'ies**, light and pretty women's underwear; **frill'ing**.—*adj.* **frill'y**.—**frilled liz'ard**, a large Australian lizard (Chlamydosaurus) with an erectile frill about its neck. [Origin unknown.]

**Frimaire**, *frē-mār'*, *n.* the third month of the French revolutionary calendar, about Nov. 21-Dec. 20. [Fr. *frimas*, hoar-frost.]

**fringe**, *frinj*, *n.* a border of loose threads: hair falling over the brow: a border: anything bordering on or additional to an activity.—*v.t.* to adorn with fringe: to border.—*adjs.* **fringed**; **fringe'less**; **fring'y**, ornamented with fringes.— **fringe benefit**, something in addition to wages or salary that forms part of the regular remuneration from one's employment; **fringe tree**, a large American shrub (*Chionanthus virginica*) of the olive family, whose very numerous snow-white flowers have long narrow corolla-segments. [O.Fr. *frenge*—L. *fimbria*, threads, akin to *fibra*, a fibre.]

**fringillaceous**, *frin-ji-lā'shəs*, *adj.* pertaining to the finches or Fringill'idae.—*adjs.* **fringill'iform**, **fringill'ine**. [L. *fringilla*, a finch.]

**fripon**, *frē-pɔ̃*, (Fr.) knave, scamp.—**friponnerie** (*frē-pon-ə-rē*), knavery.

**frippery**, *frip'ər-i*, *n.* cast-off clothes (*obs.*): an old-clothes shop, or the old-clothes trade (*obs.*): tawdry finery: foppish triviality: useless trifles. —*adj.* useless: trifling.—*n.* **fripp'er, fripp'erer** (*arch.*), an old-clothes dealer. [O.Fr. *freperie*— *frepe*, a rag.]

**fris**, *frish*, **friska**, *frish'kö*, *ns.* the quick movement of a csárdás. [Hung.]

**frisette**, *frē-zet*, (Fr.) fringe of curls on the forehead; **friseur**, *frē-zœr*, a hairdresser; **frisure**, *frē-zür*, a mode of curling.

**Frisian**, *friz'i-ən*, *n.* a native of *Friesland*: the Low German language of Friesland.—*adj.* of Friesland, its people, or their language.—*adj.* **Friesian** (*frēz'*), Frisian, esp. of a heavy breed of dairy-cattle.—*n.* a Frisian: a Friesian bull or cow.—*adjs.* **Friesic, Fries'ish**.

**frisk**, *frisk*, *v.i.* to gambol: to leap playfully.—*v.t.* to search (a person or pockets) (*slang*): to search for radioactive radiation by contamination meter.—*n.* a frolicsome movement.—*n.* **frisk'er**.—*adj.* **frisk'ful**, brisk, lively.—*adv.* **frisk'ily**.—*n.* **frisk'iness**.—*n.* and *adj.* **frisk'ing**.— *adv.* **frisk'ingly**.—*adj.* **frisk'y**, lively: jumping with gaiety: frolicsome. [O.Fr. *frisque*.]

**frisket**, *frisk'it*, (*print.*) *n.* the light frame between the tympan and the forme, to hold in place the sheet to be printed. [Fr. *frisquette*.]

**frisson**, *frē-sɔ̃*, *n.* shiver: shudder: thrill. [Fr.]

**frist**, *frist*, (*obs.*) *n.* delay, respite.—*v.t.* to postpone: to grant time, as for payment. [O.E. *first*, time, respite.]

**frit**, *frit*, *n.* the mixed materials for making glass, pottery glazes, etc.—*v.t.* to fuse partially:—*pr.p.* **fritt'ing**; *pa.t.* and *pa.p.* **fritt'ed**.—**frit porcelain**, an artificial soft-paste English porcelain (from its vitreous nature). [Fr. *fritte*—It. *fritta*—L. *frigĕre, frictum*, to roast.]

**frit**, *frit*, *n.* a small fly destructive to wheat. [Ety. unknown.]

**frith**, *frith*. See **firth** (1).

**frith**, *frith*, (*obs.* or *hist.*) *n.* peace: sanctuary.— **frith'borh** (*-borhh*), a surety for keeping the peace, frankpledge; **frith'gild**, a union of neighbours pledged to one another for the preservation of peace; **frith'soken** (O.E. *frith-sōcn*) sanctuary, asylum; **frith'stool** (O.E. *frithstōl*) a chair of sanctuary, placed near the altar in a church—as at Hexham and Beverley. [O.E. *frith*, peace; Ger. *friede*.]

**frith, firth**, *frith, fürth*, *n.* wooded country: brushwood: underwood. [O.E. *(ge)fyrhthe*.]

**fritillary**, *frit'il-ər-i*, or *-il'*, *n.* a genus (Fritillaria) of the lily family, the best-known species with chequered purple flowers: a name for several butterflies of similar pattern. [L. *fritillus*, a dice-box.]

**fritter**, *frit'ər*, *n.* a piece of fruit, etc., fried in batter. [O.Fr. *friture*—L. *frigĕre, frictum*, to fry.]

**fritter**, *frit'ər*, *n.* a fragment.—*v.t.* to break into fragments: to squander piecemeal.—*n.* **fritt'erer**, one who wastes time. [Perh. O.Fr. *freture*—L. *fractūra*—*frangĕre, frāctum*, to break.]

**fritto misto**, *frē'tō mēs'tō*, (It.) mixed dish of fried food.

**friture**, *frē-tür*, (Fr.) a dish of fried food: a fritter.

**frivolous**, *friv'ə-ləs*, *adj.* trifling: silly.—*v.t.* and *v.i.* **friv'ol** (back-formation), to trifle.—*n.* **frivolity** (*-ol'*), trifling habit or nature: levity.— *adv.* **friv'olously**.—*n.* **friv'olousness**. [L. *frīvolus*.]

**frize**. Obs. form of **freeze, frieze**.

**frizz, friz**, *friz*, *v.t.* to curl tightly.—*n.* a curl: frizzed hair.—*adjs.* **frizzed**, having the hair crisped into frizzes; **frizz'y**. [O.Fr. *friser*, to curl; perh. conn. with **frieze** (1).]

**frizzle**, *friz'l*, *v.t.* to form in small short curls.— *v.i.* to go into curls.—*n.* a curl: frizzled hair.— *adj.* **frizz'ly**. [Related to **frizz** and **frieze** (1).]

**frizzle**, *friz'l*, *v.t.* and *v.i.* to fry: to scorch. [Perhaps onomatopoeic adaptation of **fry**, from sputtering noise.]

**fro**, *frō*, *prep.* (*obs.* except in Scots form **frae**, *frā*) from.—*adv.* away, only used in **to and fro** (see **to**). [O.N. *frā*.]

**frock**, *frok*, *n.* a monk's wide-sleeved garment: a frock-coat: a smock-frock: a sailor's jersey: a woman's or child's dress: an undress regimental coat: a wearer of a frock (*obs.*).—*v.t.* to furnish with a frock: to invest with priestly office.—*adj.* **frocked**, clothed in a frock.—*n.* **frock'ing**, cloth suitable for frocks, coarse jean.—*adj.* **frock'less**. —**frock'-coat**, a double-breasted full-skirted coat for men. [O.Fr. *froc*, a monk's frock—L.L. *frocus*—L. *floccus*, a flock of wool; or from L.L. *hrocus*—O.H.G. *hroch* (Ger. *rock*), a coat.]

**Froebelian**, *frœ-bēl'i-ən*, *adj.* pertaining to Friedrich *Froebel*, German educationist (1782-1852), or to his system of kindergarten schools.—*n.* **Froe'belism**.

**frog**, *frog*, *n.* a tailless web-footed amphibian, esp. one of the genus Rana, more agile than a toad: a swelling in the throat: (*cap.*) contemptuous name for a Frenchman: on a railway, a structure in the rails allowing passage across or to another track: a depression made in the face(s) of a brick: in a violin the block by which the hair is attached to the heel of a bow.—*n.* **frogg'ery**, frogs collectively: place where frogs abound or are kept.—*adj.* **frogg'y**, froglike: having or abounding in frogs.—*ns.* **frog'let**, frog'ling, a little frog.—frog'bit, a small aquatic plant (*Hydrocharis Morsus-ranae*), allied to the water-soldier, but with floating leaves; frog'-eater, one who eats frogs: a Frenchman; frog'fish, name for various fishes, esp. the angler; frog'-hopper, a froth-fly; frog'man, underwater swimmer fitted with webbed froglike feet; frog'-march, method of carrying a refractory or drunken prisoner face downwards between four men, each holding a limb.—*v.t.* to carry in such a way.—frog'mouth, any bird of the mopoke family or subfamily (Australian and S. Asian) akin to or included in the goatsuckers; frog's'-mouth, antirrhinum, snapdragon; frog'-spit, cuckoo-spit.—frog in the throat, hoarseness. [O.E. *frogga*; also *frox*; cog. with O.N. *froskr*; Ger. *frosch*.]

frog, *frog*, *n.* a V-shaped band of horn on the underside of a horse's hoof. [Perh. same as frog (1). Gr. *batrachos* means frog in both senses—also influenced by It. *forchetta*, dim. of fork.]

frog, *frog*, *n.* an ornamental fastening or tasselled or braided button: an attachment to a belt for carrying a weapon.—*adj.* frogged, having ornamental stripes or workings of braid or lace, mostly on the breast of a coat. [Perh. Port. *froco*—L. *floccus*, a flock, lock.]

froise, *froiz*, fraise, *frāz*, *n.* a thick pancake, often with slices of bacon. [Origin unknown.]

frolic, *frol'ik*, adj. (*arch.*), merry: pranky.—*n.* gaiety: a prank: a gambol: a merrymaking.—*v.i.* to play wild pranks or merry tricks: to gambol:—*pr.p.* frol'icking; *pa.t.* and *pa.p.* frol'icked.—*adj.* frol'icsome, gay: sportive.—*adv.* frol'icsomely.—*n.* frol'icsomeness. [Du. *vrolijk*, merry; cf. Ger. *fröhlich*, joyful, gay.]

from, *from*, *frəm*, *prep.* out of: away, to or at a greater distance relatively to: springing out of: beginning at: apart relatively to: by reason of. [O.E. *fram*, *from*; akin to Goth. *fram*, O.N. *frā*.]

frond, *frond*, *n.* a leaf, esp. of a palm or fern: a leaflike thallus, or a leaflike organ of obscure morphological nature.—*n.* frond'age, fronds collectively.—*adjs.* frond'ed, having fronds; frond'ent, leafy.—*n.* frondesc'ence, development of leaves.—*adjs.* frondesc'ent, leaflike: leafy: springing into leaf; frondif'erous, bearing or producing fronds; frond'ose, leaflike: leafy. [L. *frōns, frondis*, a leaf.]

Fronde, *frönd, frȝd*, *n.* the opposition to Mazarin and the court in France during Louis XIV's minority.—*n.* frondeur (*frön-dûr', frȝ-dœr*), a member of the Fronde: an irreconcilable, dissident. [Fr., sling—L. *funda*, sling.]

front, *frunt*, *n.* the forehead (*poet.*): the face, appearance: the forepart of anything: the side presented to view: the face of a building, esp. the principal face: the part facing the sea or other water: a seaside promenade: the foremost line: the scene of hostilities: a combined face presented against opponents: a set of false curls for the forehead: the breast of a man's shirt, a dickey: the middle part of the tongue: the auditorium of a theatre: the bounding surface between two masses of air of different density and temperature: the apparent or nominal leader behind whom the really powerful man works anonymously, also front man: something acting as a cover or disguise for secret or disreputable activities: boldness: impudence.—*adj.* of, relating to, in, the front: articulated with the front of the tongue.—*v.t.* to stand in front of or opposite: to face towards: to meet, or to oppose, face to face: to add a front to: to serve as a front to: to change into or towards a front sound.—*v.i.* to be foremost (*Shak.*): to face: to act as a front for someone else or as a cover for something secret

or illicit.—*n.* front'age, the front part of a building: extent of front: ground in front.—*adj.* front'al (*frunt'l*, also *front'l*), of or belonging to the front, or the forehead.—*n.* the façade of a building: something worn on the forehead or face: a pediment over a door or window (*obs.*): a hanging of silk, satin, etc., embroidered for an altar—now usually covering only the top, the *superfrontal*—formerly covering the whole of the front, corresponding to the *antependium*.—*adjs.* front'ed, formed with a front: changed into or towards a front sound; front'less, lacking a front: void of shame or modesty (*arch.*).—*adv.* front'lessly.—*n.* front'let, a band worn on the forehead.—*advs.* front'ward(s), towards the front; front'ways, -wise, with face or front forward.—*adj.* front'-bench, sitting on a front bench, as a minister, or an opposition member of like standing.—*ns.* front'-bench'er; front door.—*adj.* front'-page, suitable for the front page of a newspaper: important.—*v.t.* to print a story on the front page of a newspaper.—*adj.* front'-rank, of foremost importance.—front'-ranker; front'-runner, in a race, one who runs best while leading the field or one who sets the pace for the rest of the runners: one who leads in any kind of competition.—come to the front, to become noticeable: to attain an important position; in front (of), before; front of the house, in a theatre, the collective activities such as box-office and programme selling carried on in direct contact with the public. [L. *frōns, frontis*, the forehead.]

frontier, *frunt'* or *front'ēr*, -*yər*, or -*ēr'*, *n.* the border of a country: the border of settled country, esp. in U.S. the advancing limit of the West pioneered in the 19th cent.: an outwork (*Shak.*): (in *pl.*) the extreme limit of knowledge and attainment in a particular discipline or line of inquiry.—*adj.* belonging to a frontier: bordering.—*v.t.* (*Spens.*) to border.—front'iersman (or -*tērz'*), a dweller on a frontier. [O.Fr. *frontier*—L. *frōns, frontis*.]

frontispiece, *frunt'is-pēs* (or *front'*), *n.* the principal face of a building (*archit.*): a figure or engraving at the front of a book.—*v.t.* to put as a frontispiece: to furnish with one. [Fr. *frontispice*—L.L. *frontispicium*—*frōns, frontis*, forehead, and *specēre, spicēre*, to see; not connected with piece.]

fronton, *frun'tən*, (*archit.*) *n.* a pediment.—Also frontoon (-*tōōn'*). [Fr.,—It. *frontone.*]

frore, *frōr, frör*, froren, frorne, frorn, *frōr'ən*, *frörn*, adj. frozen, frosty.—*adj.* frō'ry (*Spens.*), frozen. [O.E. *froren*, pa.p. of *frēosan*, to freeze.]

frost, *frost*, *n.* a state of freezing: temperature at or below the freezing-point of water: frozen dew, or hoar-frost: a disappointment, a failure (*slang*): coldness of manner or relations.—*v.t.* to affect with frost: to cover with hoar-frost: to make like hoar-frost: to sharpen (the points of a horse's shoe) that it may not slip on ice.—*v.i.* to assume a frostlike appearance.—*adj.* frost'ed, covered by frost: having a frost-like appearance (as a cake or Christmas card by sprinkling, glass by roughening): injured by frost.—*adv.* frost'ily.—*ns.* frost'iness; frost'ing, coating with hoar-frost: material or treatment to give appearance of hoar-frost.—*adjs.* frost'less, free from frost; frost'y, producing, attended with, covered with, frost: chill: frost-like.—frost'bite, injury, sometimes ending in mortification, in a part of the body by exposure to cold.—*v.t.* to affect with frost.—adjs. frost'bitten, bitten or affected by frost (also *fig.*); frost'bound, bound or confined by frost.—frost'-nail, a projecting nail in a horse-shoe serving as an ice-calk.—*v.t.* to furnish with frost-nails.—frost'-smoke, vapour frozen in the atmosphere, and having a smokelike appearance; frost'work, tracery wrought by frost, as on windows: work resembling frost tracery, etc. [O.E. *frost, forst—frēosan*; cf. Ger. *frost*.]

**froth**, *froth*, *n*. foam: chatter (*fig*.): something frivolous or trivial.—*v.t.* to cause froth on.—*v.i.* to throw up froth.—*n.* **froth'ery**, mere froth.—*adv.* **froth'ily**.—*n.* **froth'iness**.—*adjs.* **froth'less**; **froth'y**, full of or like froth or foam: empty: unsubstantial.—**froth'-blower** (*slang*), a beer-drinker; **froth flotation** (see **flotation** at **flote**); **froth'-fly**, **froth'-hopp'er**, a frog-hopper, any insect of the family Cercopidae, whose larvae live surrounded by froth (cuckoo-spit) on plants.—*adj.* **froth-fo'my** (*Spens.*), foaming. [O.N. *frotha*: Dan. *fraade*.]

**frottage**, *fro-täzh*, *n*. rubbing: use of rubbing(s) to obtain texture effect(s) in a work of art: a work of art made by this means: a type of sexual perversion in which orgasm is obtained by rubbing against someone (*psych.*).—*n.* **frotteur**, one who practises frottage (*psych.*). [Fr.]

**frou-frou**, *frōō-frōō*, *n*. the rustling of silk: elaborate trimmings, as frills, etc.: fussy decoration. [Fr.]

**froughy**. Same as **frowy**.

**frounce**, *frowns*, (*obs.*) *v.t.* to plait: to curl: to wrinkle up.—*v.i.* to wrinkle: to frown.—*n.* a wrinkle, a plait or curl: affected ornament. [O.Fr. *froncier*; see **flounce** (2).]

**frounce**, *frowns*, (*obs.*) *n*. a disease of the mouth in hawks. [Origin unknown.]

**frow**, *frow*, *n*. a Dutchwoman. [Du. *vrouw*.]

**froward**, *frō'ərd*, (*arch.*) *adj*. turned away: self-willed: perverse: unreasonable—opp. to *toward*.—*adv.* (*Spens.*), in an averse direction.—*prep.* (also **fro'wards**) in a direction away from.—*adv.* **fro'wardly**.—*n.* **fro'wardness**. [fro, and suffix. -*ward*.]

**frown**, *frown*, *v.i.* to wrinkle the brow as in anger: to look angry, gloomy, threatening: to show disapprobation.—*v.t.* to express, send, or force by a frown.—*n.* a wrinkling or contraction of the brow in displeasure, etc.: a stern look.—*adj.* **frown'ing**, gloomy: disapproving: threatening.—*adv.* **frown'ingly**. [From O.Fr. *froignier* (Fr. *refrogner*), to knit the brow; origin unknown.]

**frowst**, *frowst*, *v.i.* to luxuriate in hot stuffiness and stupefaction.—*n.* hot stuffy fustiness: a spell of frowsting.—*ns.* **frowst'er**; **frowst'iness**. *adj.* **frowst'y**, fusty: close-smelling: ill-smelling. [Origin unknown.]

**frowy**, **froughy**, (*Spens.* **frowie**), *frō'i*, *frow'i*, *adj*. musty, rancid (*Spens.*): of timber, soft and brittle (*dial.*). [Prob. O.E. *thrōh*, rancidity.]

**frowzy**, **frowsy**, *frow'zi*, (*dial.*) *adj*. fusty: stuffy, offensive: unkempt. [Origin unknown.]

**frozen**, *frōz'n*, *pa.p.* of **freeze**.—*adj*. preserved by keeping at a low temperature: very cold: stiff and unfriendly.—**frozen shoulder**, shoulder joint which has become stiff owing to enforced immobilisation, or to injury to the joint or its surrounding tissue.

**Fructidor**, *frük-tē-dör*, *n*. the twelfth month in the French revolutionary calendar, about Aug. 18–Sept. 16. [Fr.,—L. *frūctus*, fruit; Gr. *dōron*, a gift.]

**fructed**, *fruk'tid*, *adj.* (*her.*) bearing fruit.—*adj.* **fructif'erous**, bearing fruit.—*n.* **fructifica'tion**, fruit-production: a structure that contains spores or seeds (*bot.*).—*v.t.* **fruc'tify**, to make fruitful: to fertilise.—*v.i.* to bear fruit.—*adj.* **fructiv'orous** (L. *vorāre*, to devour), frugivorous. —*ns.* **fruc'tose**, fruit sugar or laevulose; **fruc'-tuary**, one enjoying the fruits of anything.—*v.i.* **fruc'tuate**, to come to fruit: to fructify.—*n.* **fructuā'tion**, coming to fruit, bearing fruit.—*adj.* **fruc'tuous**, fruitful. [L. *frūctus*, fruit.]

**frugal**, *frōō'gl*, *adj.* economical in the use of means: sparing: spare: thrifty.—*ns.* **fru'galist**, one who is frugal; **frugality** (-*gal'*), economy:

thrift.—*adv.* **fru'gally**. [L. *frūgālis—frūx, frūgis*, fruit.]

**frugiferous**, *frōō-jif'ə-rəs, adj.* (L. *ferre*, to bear) fruit-bearing.—*adj.* **frugiv'orous** (L. *vorāre*, to eat), feeding on fruits or seeds. [L. *frūx, frūgis*, fruit.]

**fruit** (*obs.* **fruict**), *frōōt, n.* the produce of the earth, which supplies the wants of men and animals: an edible part of a plant, generally sweet, acid, and juicy, esp. a part that contains the seed, but sometimes extended to include other parts (e.g. the leaf-stalk in rhubarb): in bot., a fructification, esp. the structure that develops from the ovary and its contents after fertilisation, sometimes including also structures formed from other parts of the flower or axis: the offspring of animals: (often in *pl.*) product, effect, advantage: a male homosexual (*U.S. slang*).—*v.i.* to produce fruit.—*ns.* **fruit'age**, fruit collectively: fruits; **fruitā'rian**, one who lives on fruit.—Also *adj.*—*ns.* **fruit'erer**, one who deals in fruit—also (now *dial.*) **fruit'er**:—*fem.* **fruit'eress**; **fruit'ery**, a place for storing fruit: fruitage.— *adj.* **fruit'ful**, productive.—*adv.* **fruit'fully**.—*ns.* **fruit'fulness**; **fruit'ing**, process of bearing fruit.— *adj.* **fruit'less**, barren: without profit: useless: in vain.—*adv.* **fruit'lessly**.—*n.* **fruit'lessness**.— *adj.* **fruit'y**, like, or tasting like, fruit: rich: crazy (*U.S. slang*): male homosexual (*U.S. slang*).—**fruit'-bat**, any bat of the suborder Megacheiroptera, large fruit-eating bats of the Old World; **fruit'-bud**, a bud that produces fruit; **fruit'-cake**, a cake containing raisins, etc.; **fruit'-fly**, an insect of genus Drosophila; **fruit'-knife**, a knife with a blade of silver, etc., for cutting fruit; **fruit'-machine**, a coin-operated gaming machine in which chance must bring models of different fruits together in a certain combination to give a win; **fruit salad, cocktail**, a mixture of pieces of fruit, fresh or preserved; **fruit'-tree**, a tree yielding edible fruit.—**bush fruits**, small fruits growing on woody bushes; **first-fruits** (see **first, annat**); **small fruits**, strawberries, currants, etc. [O.Fr. *fruit, fruict*—L. *frūctus—fruī, frūctus*, to enjoy.]

**fruition**, *frōō-ish'ən, n.* enjoyment: use or possession, esp. accompanied with pleasure: now often used for fruiting, for bearing of, coming into, fruit.—*adj.* **fru'itive**. [O.Fr. *fruition*—L. *fruī*, to enjoy.]

**frumentation**, *frōō-mən-tā'shən, n.* a largess of grain bestowed on the starving or turbulent people in ancient Rome.—*adjs.* **frumentā'ceous**, made of or resembling wheat or other grain; **frumentā'rious**, pertaining to corn. [L. *frūmentātiō, -ōnis—frūmentāri*, to provide with corn—*frūmentum*, corn.]

**frumenty**, *frōō'mən-ti, n.* hulled wheat boiled in milk.—Also **fur'menty**, **fur'mety**, **fur'mity** (*für'*). [O.Fr. *frumentee—frument*—L. *frūmentum*.]

**frump**, *frump, n.* a dowdy woman: a flout or snub (*obs.*).—*v.t.* (*obs.*) to snub.—*adjs.* **frump'ish**, **frump'y**, ill-dressed, dowdy.

**frumple**, *frum'pl*, (*dial.*) *v.t.* to wrinkle.

**frush**, *frush*, *v.t.* (*Shak.*) to break or bruise.—*adj.* (*Scot.*) brittle.—*n.* (*Scot.*) a crash: splinters. [O.Fr. *froissier*, to bruise—L. *frustum*, fragment.]

**frush**, *frush, n.* (*dial.*) the frog of a horse's foot: a disease in that part of a horse's foot. [Origin uncertain; cf. O.E. *forsc*, frog (animal); see **frog** (2).]

**frust**, *frust, n.* (*Sterne*) a fragment.—*ns.* **frust'ule**, the siliceous two-valved shell of a diatom, with its contents; **frust'um**, a slice of a solid body: the part of a cone or pyramid between the base and a parallel plane, or between two planes:—*pl.* **frust'a**. [L. *frustum*, a bit.]

**frustrate**, *frus-trāt', frus'trāt, v.t.* to make vain or of no effect: to bring to naught: to balk: to thwart.—*adj.* (*frus'*) vain, ineffectual: balked.—

rte

j. frustrated, thwarted: having a sense of discouragement and dissatisfaction.—n. frustra'tion.
—frustrated export, an article orig. intended for export which for some reason has to be offered for sale on the home market. [L. frustrāri.]
frutex, frōō'teks, n. a shrub:—pl. fru'tices, -ti-sēz. —adj. fru'ticose, shrubby. [L. frutex, -icis, shrub.]
frutify, frōō'ti-fī, (Shak.) v.t. Launcelot Gobbo's blunder for notify or specify.
fry, frī, v.t. to cook in oil or fat in a pan: to burn or scorch (often fig.): to torture with heat (obs.). —v.i. to undergo frying: to foam (Spens.):— pr.p. fry'ing; pa.t. and pa.p. fried; 3rd pers. pres. indic. fries.—n. a dish of anything fried.—n. fri'er (fry'er), one who fries (esp. fish): a vessel for frying: a fish suitable for frying.—n. and adj. fry'ing.—fried'cake (U.S.), a cake fried in deep fat: a doughnut; fry'ing-pan, a flat pan for frying with; fry'-up (coll.), mixed fried foods. —fry in one's fat, suffer the consequences of one's behaviour; out of the frying-pan into the fire, out of one evil into a greater. [Fr. frire—L. frigĕre; cf. Gr. phrȳgein.]
fry, frī, n. young, collectively: a swarm of young, esp. of fishes just spawned: a number of small things.—small fry, small things collectively, persons or things of little importance. [O.N. friō, seed; Dan. and Sw. fro.]
fub, fub, v.t. (arch.) to put off: to fob.—n. fubb'ery (obs.), a deception.—fub off, (Shak.) to put off or evade by a trick or a lie. [See fob.]
fubby, fub'i, fubsy, fub'zi, (dial.) adj. chubby: squat. [Ety. dub.]
fuchsia, fū'shə, n. any plant of a S. American genus (Fuchsia) of the evening primrose family, with long pendulous flowers.—n. fuchsine (fōōks'-ēn), the dyestuff magenta, a green solid, purplish red in solution (from its colour). [Named after Leonard Fuchs, a German botanist, 1501-66.]
fuchsite, fōōks'īt, n. a brilliant green chromium mica. [J. N. von Fuchs (1774-1856), German mineralogist.]
fuck, fuk, (old word, long taboo; all words, meanings, still vulg.) v.i. to have sexual intercourse (with): (with about) to play around: (with off) to go away.—Also v.t. (of males).—n. an act of sexual intercourse.—p. adj. fuck'ed, exhausted. —n. fuck'ing, sexual intercourse.—adj. expressing scorn or disapprobation: as an intensive, to a great extent: often used as meaningless qualification.—adv. very. [Ety. dub.; perh. Ger. ficken, to strike, to copulate with.]
fucus, fū'kəs, n. (obs.) paint for the face, cosmetic (pl. fūci, -sī, fūcuses): (cap.) the bladder-wrack genus of seaweeds.—adj. fū'coid, like, pertaining to, or containing bladder-wrack, or seaweed, or seaweed-like markings.—n. a marking like a fossil seaweed.—adjs. fūcoid'al; fū'cused, painted. [L. fūcus, orchil, rouge; Gr. phȳkos.]
fud, fud, (Scot.) n. a rabbit's or hare's tail: the buttocks.
fuddle, fud'l, v.t. to stupefy, as with drink: to confuse.—v.i. to drink to excess or habitually:— pr.p. fudd'ling; pa.t. and pa.p. fudd'led.—n. intoxicating drink (obs.): intoxication: drinking bout: confusion.—n. fudd'ler, a drunkard.—n. and adj. fudd'ling, tippling.—fudd'le-cap (obs.), a hard drinker. [Origin obscure.]
fuddy-duddy, n. an old fogy, stick-in-the-mud: a carper.—adj. old-fogyish: old-fashioned: stuffy: prim: censorious. [Origin unknown.]
fudge, fuj, n. stuff: nonsense: humbug: a soft sweetmeat.—interj. bosh. [Origin obscure.]
fudge, fuj, n. an inserted patch in a newspaper, or space reserved for it.—v.i. to fadge (arch.): to cheat: to fail: to dodge.—v.t. to patch up: to fake: to distort: to dodge. [Variant of fadge.]
fuel, fū'əl, n. material for a fire: something that

maintains or intensifies emotion, etc. (fig.): food, as maintaining bodily processes: fissile material for a nuclear reactor.—v.t. to furnish with fuel.—v.i. to take or get fuel:—pr.p. fū'elling; pa.t. and pa.p. fū'elled.—n. fū'eller.— fu'el-cell', a cell generating electricity for an external circuit as part of a chemical reaction between an electrolyte and a combustible gas or vapour supplied from outside the cell (the reaction taking place at more or less ordinary temperatures). [O.Fr. fowaille—L.L. focāle— L. focus, a fireplace.]
fuero, fwā'rō, n. a code or body of law or privileges, esp. in the Basque provinces, a constitution. [Sp.,—L. forum.]
fuff, fuf, (Scot.) n. a puff: the spitting of a cat: a burst of anger.—v.t. and v.i. to puff: to spit as a cat.—adj. fuff'y, light and soft. [Imit.]
fug, fug, n. a very hot close state of atmosphere: one who fugs: dusty fluff.—v.i. to sit or revel in a fug.—v.t. to cause a fug.—adj. fugg'y. [Origin unknown.]
fugacious, fū-gā'shəs, adj. apt to flee away: fleeting: readily shed.—ns. fugā'ciousness, fugacity (-gas').  [L. fugāx, -ācis, from, fugĕre, to flee.]
fugato. See fugue.
fugitive, fū'ji-tiv, adj. apt to flee away: fleeing: fleeting: evanescent: occasional, written for some passing occasion.—n. one who flees or has fled: one hard to be caught: an exile.—ns. fū'gie (Scot.), a cock that will not fight: a runaway; fūgitā'tion (Scots law), absconding from justice: sentence of outlawry.—adv. fū'gitively. —n. fū'gitiveness.—fū'gie-warr'ant (Scot.), a warrant to apprehend a debtor supposed to be about to abscond, prob. from the phrase in meditatione fugae. [L. fugitivus—fugĕre, to flee.]
fugleman, fū'gl-mən, n. a soldier who stands before a company at drill as an example: a ringleader, mouthpiece of others.—v.i. fū'gle (Carlyle), to act like a fugleman. [Ger. flügelmann, the leader of a file—flügel, a wing, mann, man.]
fugue, fūg, n. in mus. a form of composition in which the subject is given out by one part and immediately taken up by a second (in answer), during which the first part supplies an accompaniment or counter-subject, and so on: a form of amnesia which is a flight from reality.— adj. fū'gal.—adv. fū'gally.—adj. and adv. fugato (fōō-gä'tō; It.) in the manner of a fugue without being strictly a fugue.—Also n.—n. fughetta (fōō-get'ta), a short fugue.—n. fuguist (fūg'ist), one who writes or plays fugues. [Fr.,—It. fuga —L. fuga, flight.]
Führer, fü'rər, n. the title taken by Hitler as dictator of Nazi Germany. [Ger., leader, guide.]
fulcrum, ful'krəm, fōōl', n. the prop or fixed point on which a lever moves (mech.): a support: a means to an end (fig.):—pl. ful'crums, ful'cra. —adj. ful'crate, supported with fulcrums. [L. fulcrum, a prop—fulcīre, to prop.]
fulfil, fōōl-fil', v.t. to fill full (arch.): to complete: to accomplish: to carry into effect: to bring to consummation: to develop and realise the potential of:—pr.p. fulfil'ling; pa.t. and pa.p. fulfilled'.—ns. fulfil'er; fulfil'ing, fulfil'ment, full performance: completion: accomplishment. [O.E. fullfyllan—full, full, fyllan, to fill.]
fulgent, ful'jənt,adj. shining: bright.—n. ful'gency. —adv. ful'gently.—adj. ful'gid, flashing.—ns. ful'gor, ful'gour (-gör, -gər), splendour.—adj. ful'gorous, flashing.  [L. fulgēns, -entis, pr.p. of fulgēre, to shine, fulgidus, shining, fulgor, brightness.]
fulgurate, ful'gū-rāt, v.i. to flash as lightning.— adjs. ful'gūral, pertaining to lightning; ful'gūrant, flashing like lightning.—ns. fulgūrā'tion, flashing: in assaying, the sudden and final brightening of the fused globule; ful'gūrite, a tube of vitrified sand formed by lightning.—adj.

fāte, fär; mē, hûr (her); mīne; mōte, för; mūte, mōōn, fŏŏt; dhen (then)

**ful´gŭrous**, resembling lightning. [L. *fulgur*, lightning.]

**fulham**, *fool´əm*, *n.* a die loaded at the corner.—Also **full´am**, **full´an**. [Prob. the place-name *Fulham*.]

**fuliginous**, *fū-lij´i-nəs*, *adj.* sooty: dusky.—*n.* **fūlinos´ity**.—*adv.* **fūlig´inously**. [L., *fūligō*, *-inis*, soot.]

**full**, *fool*, *adj.* holding all that can be contained: having no empty space: replete: abundantly supplied or furnished: abounding: copious: filling: containing the whole matter: complete: perfect: strong: clear: intense: swelled or rounded: protuberant: having excess of material: at the height of development or end of course: having thoughts completely engrossed: drunk (*coll.*):—*compar.* **full´er**; *superl.* **full´est**.—*n.* completest extent, as of the moon: highest degree: the whole: time of full moon.—*v.t.* to make with gathers or puckers.—*v.i.* to become full.—*adv.* quite: thoroughly, veritably: directly. —*adj.* **full´ish**, inclined to fullness.—*n.* **full´ness**, **ful´ness**, the state of being full: moment of fulfilment: plenty, wealth (*Shak.*).—*adv.* **full´y**, completely: entirely: quite.—*adjs.* **full´-a´corned** (*Shak.*), full-fed with acorns; **full´-aged**, having reached majority.—**full back** (see **back**); **full blast**, full operation (*adv.* with maximum energy and fluency); **full´-blood**, an individual of pure blood.—*adjs.* **full´-blood´ed**, having a full supply of blood: vigorous: thoroughbred, of unmixed descent: related through both parents; **full´-blown**, fully expanded, as a flower: beyond the first freshness of youth: fully qualified or admitted: puffed out to fullness; **full´-bod´ied**, with much body or substance.—**full´-bottom**, a full-bottomed wig.—*adjs.* **full´-bott´omed**, having a full or large bottom, as a wig; **full´-bound**, with the boards covered as well as the back.—**full brother, sister**, son, daughter, of the same parents. —*adj.* **full´-charged**, fully loaded (*lit.* and *fig.*).—*adv.* **full´ cir´cle**, round in a complete revolution. —**full´-cock´**, the position of a gun cock drawn fully back, or of a tap fully open.—*adv.* in that position.—*adj.* **full´-cocked´**.—**full cousin**, son or daughter of an uncle or aunt, first cousin.—*adj.* **full-dress**, in the dress worn on occasions of state or ceremony (**full-dress debate**, a set debate of some importance in which the leaders take part).—*adjs.* **full´-eyed**, with large prominent eyes; **full´-face**, **full´-faced**, having a full or broad face: (of type) bold-faced: showing the face in direct front view; **full´-fash´ioned**, or **fully-fashioned**, of garments, esp. stockings, conforming to the body contour; **full´-fed**, fed to plumpness or satiety; **full´-fledged´**, completely fledged: having attained full membership; **full´-fraught** (*Shak.*), fully charged, equipped, endowed, all-round; **full´-grown**, grown to full size.—**full hand, full house**.—*adjs.* **full´-hand´ed**, bearing something valuable, as a gift; **full´-heart´ed**, full of heart or courage: fraught with emotion; **full´-hot** (*Shak.*), heated to the utmost.—**full house**, a performance at which every seat is taken (*theat.*): three cards of a kind and a pair (*poker*; also **full hand**).—*adj.* **full´-length´**, extending the whole length.—*n.* a portrait showing the whole length.—*adv.* stretched to the full extent.—*adj.* **full´-manned** (*Shak.*), having a full crew.—**full moon**, the moon with its whole disk illuminated, when opposite the sun: the time when the moon is full.—*adjs.* **full´-mouthed**, having a full set of teeth: having food in plenty: loud: sonorous; **full´-orbed**, having the orb or disk fully illuminated, as the full-moon: round.—**full organ**, the organ, or great organ, with all or most of the stops in use.—*adjs.* **full´-out**, at full power: total; **full´-page**, occupying a whole page.—*advs.* **full´-pelt**, **full´-speed**, **full´-split**, **full´-tilt´**, with highest speed and impetus.—**full pitch**, in cricket a ball which does not or would not pitch before passing or hitting the batsman's wicket—also **full toss**.—*adv.* **full´-sail´**.—*adjs.* **full´-sailed**, having all sails set: having sails filled with wind: advancing with speed and momentum; **full´-scale**, of the same size as the original: involving full power or maximum effort.—**full score**, a complete musical score with a staff for every part; **full stop**, a point marking the end of a sentence: an end, a halt.—*adjs.* **full´-summed**, complete in all its parts; **full´-throat´ed**, **full´-voiced**, singing with the whole power of the voice; **full´-time**, occupied during or extending over the whole working day, week, etc.—**full´-tim´er**.—*adjs.* **full´-winged** (*Shak.*), having wide, strong wings; **full´y-fashioned**, full-fashioned.—**at the full**, at the height, as of one's good fortune, etc.; **full and by**, closehauled to the wind; **full of years**, old, aged: at a good old age; **full up**, full to the limit; sated, wearied (*slang*); **in full**, without reduction; **in full cry**, in chase together, giving tongue; **in full rig**, with maximum number of masts and sails; **in full swing**, at the height of activity; **in the fullness of time**, at the due or destined time; **to the full**, in full measure, completely. [O.E. *full*; Goth. *fulls*, O.N. *fullr*, Ger. *voll*.]

**full**, *fool*, *v.t.* to scour and beat, as a means of finishing or cleansing woollens: to scour and thicken in a mill.—*ns.* **full´age**, the charge for fulling cloth; **full´er**, one who fulls cloth.—**fuller's earth**, an earthy hydrous aluminium silicate, capable of absorbing grease: a division of the English Jurassic; **fuller's-herb**, soapwort; **full´ing-mill**, a mill in which woollen cloth is fulled. [O.Fr. *fuler* (see foil 1) and O.E. *fullere*, fuller, both—L. *fullō*, a cloth-fuller.]

**fulmar**, *fool´mär*, *-mər*, *n.* a gull-like bird of the petrel family. [Perh. O.N. *fūll*, foul, *mär*, gull.]

**fulminate**, *ful´min-āt*, *v.i.* to thunder or make a loud noise: to detonate: to issue decrees with violence, or threats: to inveigh: to flash.—*v.t.* to cause to explode: to send forth, as a denunciation: to denounce.—*n.* a salt of fulminic acid (often dangerously detonating).—*adj.* **ful´minant**, fulminating: developing suddenly (*path.*).—*n.* a thunderbolt: an explosive.—*adj.* **ful´mināting**, detonating.—*n.* **fulminā´tion**, act of thundering, denouncing, or detonating: a denunciation.—*adj.* **ful´minatory**.—*v.t.* and *v.i.* **fulmine** (*ful´min*; *Spens.*, *Milt.*), to fulminate.—*adjs.* **fulmin´eous**, **ful´minous**, pertaining to thunder and lightning. —**fulminating gold**, a green powder made from auric oxide and ammonium hydroxide; **fulminating mercury**, mercuric fulminate; **fulminating silver**, a black solid made from silver oxide and ammonium hydroxide; **fulmin´ic acid**, an acid isomeric with cyanic acid. [L. *fulmināre*, *-ātum*—*fulmen*, *-inis*, lightning—*fulgēre*, to shine.]

**fulsome**, *fool´səm*, *adj.* copious (*obs.*): cloying or causing surfeit: nauseous: offensive: gross: rank: disgustingly fawning.—*adv.* **ful´somely**.—*n.* **ful´someness**. [full and affix *-some*.]

**fulvous**, *ful´vəs*, *adj.* dull yellow: tawny.—*adj.* **ful´vid**. [L. *fulvus*, tawny.]

**fum.** See fung.

**fumado**, *fū-mä´dō*, *n.* a smoked fish, esp. a pilchard. [Sp., smoked—L. *fūmāre*, to smoke.]

**Fumaria**, *fū-mä´ri-ə*, *n.* the fumitory genus, giving name to the **Fumariā´ceae**, a family akin to the poppies.—**fumaric** (*fū-mar´ik*) **acid**, an acid isomeric with maleic acid, found in Fumaria and other plants. [L. *fūmus*; see fumitory.]

**fumarole**, *fūm´ə-rōl*, *n.* a hole emitting gases in a volcano or volcanic region. [Fr. *fumerolle* or It. *fumaruola*—L. *fūmus*, smoke.]

**fumble**, *fum´bl*, *v.i.* to grope about awkwardly: to make bungling or unsuccessful attempts: to

# fume 526 funk

mumble.—*v.t.* to handle, manage, or effect awkwardly or bunglingly: to huddle (*arch.*): to mumble.—*n.* fum'bler.—*adv.* fum'blingly. [Cf. Du. *fommelen,* to fumble; Dan. *famle*; O.N. *fālma,* to grope about.]

**fume,** *fūm, n.* smoke or vapour, often odorous (often in *pl.*): any volatile matter: heat of mind, rage, fretful excitement: a passionate person (*arch.*): anything unsubstantial, vain conceit.— *v.i.* to smoke: to throw off vapour: to come off or pass in fumes: to be in a rage.—*v.t.* to treat with fumes: to give off: to offer incense to.—*ns.* **fūm'age,** hearth-money; **fūm'atory,** a place for smoking or fumigation; **fūmos'ity** (*arch.*), a fuming condition: an exhalation: breath stinking of food or drink.—*adjs.* **fūm'ous, fūm'y.**— **fume'-cham'ber, -cup'board,** a case for laboratory operations that give off fumes; **fumed oak,** oak darkened by ammonia fumes. [L. *fūmus,* smoke.]

**fumet, fewmet,** *fū'mit,* (*arch.,* usu. in *pl.*) *n.* the dung of deer, hares, etc. [Appar. Anglo-Fr.,— L. *fimāre,* to dung.]

**fumet, fumette,** *fū-met', n.* the scent of game when high. [Fr. *fumet.*]

**fumigate,** *fūm'i-gāt, v.t.* to expose to fumes, esp. for purposes of disinfecting, or destroying pests: to perfume (*arch.*).—*ns.* **fūm'igant,** a source of fumes, esp. a substance used for fumigation; **fūmigā'tion, fūm'igātor,** a fumigating apparatus. —*adj.* **fūm'igatory.** [L. *fūmigāre, -ātum.*]

**fumitory,** *fūm'i-tər-i, n.* a plant of the genus Fumaria.—Also (*Shak.*) **fem'iter** or **fen'itar,** **fem'etary.** [O.Fr. *fume-terre,* lit. earth-smoke— L. *fūmus,* smoke, *terra,* earth; so called because its rapid growth was thought to resemble the dispersal of smoke.]

**fun,** *fun, n.* a hoax, trick (*obs.*): merriment: sport: a source of merriment or amusement.—*v.t.* (*obs.*) to trick.—*v.i.* to make sport:—*pr.p.* **funn'ing.**—*adj.* providing amusement.—**fun'fair,** a fair with side-shows and other amusements.— **all the fun of the fair,** all the amusements of the occasion; **be great fun,** to be very amusing; **in fun,** in joke, not seriously; **like fun** (*coll.*), rapidly: not at all; **make fun of, poke fun at,** to ridicule. [Prob. a form of obs. *fon,* to befool.]

**funambulist,** *fū-nam'bū-list, n.* a rope-walker or rope-dancer.—*v.i.* **fūnam'būlate.**—*ns.* **fūnambū-lā'tion; fūnam'būlātor.**—*adj.* **fūnam'būlatory.** [L. *fūnambulus,* a rope walker—*fūnis,* rope, *ambulāre,* to walk.]

**function,** *fung(k)'shən, n.* the doing of a thing: performance (*obs.*): activity (*obs.*): activity appropriate to any person or thing: duty peculiar to any office: faculty, exercise of faculty: the peculiar office of anything: a profession (*obs.*): a solemn service: a ceremony: a social gathering: in math., a variable so connected with another that for any value of the one there is a corresponding value for the other: a correspondence between two sets of variables such that each member of one set can be related to one particular member of the other set: the technical term in physiology for the vital activity of organ, tissue, or cell: the part played by a linguistic form in a construction.—*v.i.* to perform a function: act: operate: work.—*adj.* **func'tional,** pertaining to or performed by functions: of disease, characterised by impairment of function, not of organs: designed with special regard to purpose and practical use: serving a function.—*ns.* **func'tionalism,** the theory or practice of adapting method, form, materials, etc., primarily with regard to the purpose in hand; **func'tionalist.**—*adv.* **func'tion-ally.**—*n.* **func'tionary,** one who discharges any duty: one who holds an office.—*v.i.* **func'tionate,** to perform a function.—*adj.* **func'tionless,** having no function. [O.Fr.,—L. *functiō, -ōnis—fungi, functus,* to perform.]

**functus officio,** *fungk'təs of-ish'i-ō, fo͞ongk'to͞os of-ik'i-ō,* (L.) having fulfilled an office, out of office: no longer having official power to act: (of a power) that can no longer be exercised.

**fund,** *fund, n.* a sum of money on which some enterprise is founded or expense supported: a supply or source of money: a store laid up: supply: (*pl.*) permanent government debts paying interest: money (*pl.; slang*).—*v.t.* to form into a stock charged with interest: to place in a fund.—*adj.* **fund'able,** capable of being converted into a fund or into bonds.—*adjs.* **fund'ed,** invested in public funds: existing in the form of bonds; **fund'less,** destitute of supplies or money. —**fund'-holder,** one who has money in the public funds. [L. *fundus,* the bottom.]

**fundamental,** *fun-də-men'təl, adj.* basal: serving as foundation: essential: primary: important. —*n.* that which serves as a groundwork: an essential: the root of a chord or of a system of harmonics (*mus.*).—*ns.* **fund'ament** (-*mənt*), the lower part or seat of the body; **fundamen'talism,** belief in the literal truth of the Bible, against evolution, etc.; **fundamen'talist,** one who professes this belief; **fundamental'ity.**—*adv.* **fundamen'tally.**—**fundamental particle** (same as elementary particle); **fundamental units** (see absolute units). [L. *fundāmentum,* foundation, *fundāre,* to found.]

**fundamentum relationis,** *fun-də-men'təm ri-lā-shi-ōn'is, fo͞on-dä-men'to͞om re-lä-ti-ōn'is,* (L.L.) ground of relation, principle of, or the nature of, the connection.

**fundus,** *fun'dəs, n.* the bottom of anything: the rounded bottom of a hollow organ (*anat.*). [L.]

**funèbre,** *fü-ne-br',* (Fr.) mournful.

**funeral,** *fū'nər-əl, n.* disposal of the dead, with any ceremonies or observances connected therewith: a procession to the place of burial or cremation, etc.: death (*Spens., Shak.*): tomb (*Spens.*).— *adj.* pertaining to the disposal of the dead.—*adjs.* **fūnē'bral, fūnē'brial,** funereal; **fū'nerary,'** pertaining to or suiting a funeral; **fūnē'real,** pertaining to a funeral: dismal: mournful.— **funeral director,** an undertaker; **funeral home, funeral parlour,** a room that can be hired for funeral ceremonies.—**your, my** (etc.) **funeral,** your, my (etc.) affair, or look-out. [L.L. *fūnerālis* and L. *fūnerārius, fūnebris, fūnēreus—*L. *fūnus, fūnĕris,* a funeral procession.]

**funest,** *fū-nest', adj.* deadly: lamentable. [Fr.,— L. *fūnestus,* destructive.]

**fung,** *fung, fum, n.* a fabulous Chinese bird, sometimes called phoenix. [Chin. *fung, fêng.*]

**fungibles,** *fun'ji-blz,* (*law*) *n.pl.* movable effects which perish by being used, and which are estimated by weight, number, and measure. [L.L. *fungibilis—*L. *fungī,* to perform; see function.]

**fungus,** *fung'gəs, n.* a plant of one of the lowest groups, thallophytes without chlorophyll, including mushrooms, toadstools, mould, etc.: proud-flesh formed on wounds:—*pl.* **fungi,** *fun'jī, -gī,* **funguses.**—*adjs.* **fung'al,** pertaining to fungus; **fungicid'al,** fungi-destroying: pertaining to a fungicide.—*n.* **fungicide** (*fun'ji-sīd*), a means of killing fungi.—*adjs.* **fungiform** (*fun'ji-förm*), mushroom-shaped; **fung'oid** (-*goid*), **-al,** fungus-like: of the nature of a fungus.—*n.* **fungos'ity,** quality of being fungous.—*adj.* **fung'ous,** of or like fungus: soft: spongy: growing suddenly: ephemeral. [L. *fungus,* a mushroom; cf. Gr. *sphongos, spongos,* a sponge.]

**funicle,** *fū'ni-kl, n.* a small cord or ligature: a fibre: the stalk of an ovule (*bot.*).—*adjs.* **fūnic'ū-lar;** **fūnic'ūlate.**—*n.* **fūnic'ūlus,** the umbilical cord: a funicle.—**funicular railway,** a cable-railway. [L. *fūniculus,* dim. of *fūnis,* a rope.]

**funk,** *fungk,* (*coll.*) *n.* a state of fear: panic: shrinking or shrinking from loss of courage: one

*fāte, fär; mē, hûr* (her); *mīne; mōte, för; mūte; mōon, fŏŏt; dhen* (then) who funks.—*v.i.* to flinch: to draw back or hold back in fear.—*v.t.* to balk at or shirk from fear.— *n.* funk′iness.—*adj.* funk′y.—funk′hole (*mil. slang*), a place of refuge, dug-out: a coward's place of retreat. [Poss. Flem. *fonck.*]

funk, *fungk, n.* touchwood: a spark. [Cf. Du. *vonk.*]

funk, *fungk, v.t.* to stifle with smoke.—*v.i.* to smoke and/or cause a strong unpleasant smell. —Also *n.* [Ety. dub.]

Funkia, *fungk′i-ə, n.* an E. Asiatic genus allied to the day lilies. [From the German botanist, H. C. *Funck,* 1771-1839.]

funnel, *fun′l, n.* a vessel, usually a cone ending in a tube, for pouring fluids into bottles, etc.: a passage for the escape of smoke, etc.—*adj.* funn′elled, with a funnel: funnel-shaped.— funn′el-net, a net shaped like a funnel. [Prob. through Fr. or Port. from L. *infundibulum— fundēre,* to pour.]

funnel, *fun′l,* (*dial.*) *n.* the offspring of a stallion and a she-ass. [Origin unknown.]

funny, *fun′i, adj.* full of fun: droll: mirth-provoking: queer, odd (*coll.*).—*n.pl.* funn′ies (*U.S.*), the comic section of a newspaper.—*adv.* funn′ily. —*n.* funn′iness.—funny bone (a punning translation of L. *humerus*), the bone at the elbow with the comparatively unprotected ulnar nerve which, when struck, shoots a tingling sensation down the forearm to the fingers; funny peculiar, or funny ha-ha, funny meaning 'queer, odd'; or funny, meaning 'amusing'. [fun.]

funny, *fun′i, n.* a light clinker-built pleasure-boat, with a pair of sculls. [Perh. from the foregoing.]

Funtumia, *fun-tū′mi-ə, n.* an African genus of apocynaceous trees, yielding Lagos rubber. [From a Ghanaian name.]

fur, *fûr, n.* the thick, soft fine hair of certain animals: the skin with this hair attached: a garment of fur: furred animals (opposed to *feather*): a patched or tufted tincture (*her.*): a coating on the tongue: a crust in boilers, etc.: a strengthening piece nailed to a rafter.—*v.t.* to clothe, cover, coat, trim or line with fur: to coat. —*v.i.* to become coated:—*pr.p.* furr′ing; *pa.t.* and *pa.p.* furred.—*adj.* furred.—*ns.* furr′ier, a dealer or worker in furs; furr′iery, furs in general: trade in furs; furr′ing, fur trimmings: a coating on the tongue: (also firr′ing) strips of wood fastened to joists, etc.: a lining to a wall to carry lath, provide an air-space, etc.—*adj.* furr′y, consisting of, like, covered with, or dressed in fur.—fur′-seal, a sea-bear, an eared seal with close fur under its long hairs. [O.Fr. *forrer* (Fr. *fourrer*), to line, encase—*forre, fuerre,* sheath.]

furacious, *fū-rā′shəs, adj.* thievish.—*ns.* fūrā′-ciousness, fūrac′ity (*-ras′i-ti*). [L. *fūrax, -ācis— fūr,* thief.]

furbelow, *fûr′bi-lō, n.* a plaited border or flounce: a superfluous ornament.—*v.t.* to flounce. [Fr., It., and Sp. *falbala*; of unknown origin.]

furbish, *fûr′bish, v.t.* to purify or polish: to rub up until bright: to renovate.—*n.* fur′bisher. [O.Fr. *fourbir, fourbiss-,* from O.H.G. *furban,* to purify.]

furcate, furcated, *fûr′kāt, -id, adjs.* forked.—*adj.* fur′cal.—*n.* furcā′tion.—*adj.* furcif′erous (*-sif′*), bearing a forked appendage: rascally (*facet.*): in allusion to the *furca* or yoke of criminals).— *n.* fur′cūla, the united clavicles of a bird—the merry-thought.—*adj.* fur′cūlar, furcate: shaped like a fork. [L. *furca,* fork.]

Furcraea, *fûr-krē′ə,* Fourcroya, *fōōr-kroi′ə, n.* a tropical American genus of plants akin to Agave, yielding Mauritius hemp. [After A. F. de *Fourcroy* (1755-1800), French chemist.]

furder, *fûr′dər,* an obs. form (*Milt.*) of further.

fureur, *fû-rœr,* (Fr.) extravagant admiration.

furfur, *fûr′fûr, -fər* (*Browning,* furfair), *n.* dandruff,

scurf.—*adj.* furfuraceous (*fûr-fū-rā′shəs*), branny: scaly: scurfy.—*ns.* furfural (*fûr′fū-ral, -fə-ral*), in full furfural′dehyde; also called fûr′al, fur′-fūrol(e), fûr′ol(e), a liquid ($C_4H_3O \cdot CHO$) got by heating bran with dilute sulphuric acid; fur′furan (also called fûr′an), a colourless liquid ($C_4H_4O$) got from wood-tar.—*adj.* fur′furous (*fûr′fū-rəs, -fə-rəs*), furfuraceous. [L. *furfur,* bran.]

furibund, *fū′ri-bund, adj.* raging. [L. *furibundus— furia,* rage.]

furious. See fury.

furioso, *fōō-ri-ō′sō, n.* a furious person, madman. —*adj.* and *adv.* (*mus.*) with fury. [It.; cf. furious.]

furl, *fûrl, v.t.* to roll up. [Perh. fardel.]

furlana, *fōōr-lä′nə.* Same as forlana.

furlong, *fûr′long, n.* 40 poles, one-eighth of a mile. [O.E. *furlang—furh,* furrow, *lang,* long.]

furlough, *fûr′lō, n.* leave of absence.—*v.t.* to grant furlough to. [Du. *verlof*; cf. Ger. *verlaub.*]

furmenty, furmety, furmity. See frumenty.

furnace, *fûr′nis, n.* an enclosed structure in which great heat is produced: a time or place of grievous affliction or torment.—*v.t.* to exhale like a furnace: to subject to the heat of a furnace. [O.Fr. *fornais—*L. *fornāx, -ācis—fornus,* an oven.]

furniment, *fûr′ni-ment,* (*Spens.*) *n.* furnishing.

furnish, *fûr′nish, v.t.* to fit up or supply completely, or with what is necessary: to supply, provide: to equip.—*adj.* fur′nished, equipped: stocked with furniture.—*n.* fur′nisher.—*n.pl.* fur′nishings, fittings of any kind, esp. articles of furniture, etc., within a house: any incidental part (*Shak.*).—*n.* fur′nishment. [O.Fr. *furnir, furniss-*; of Gmc. origin; cf. O.H.G. *frummen,* to further.]

furniture, *fûr′ni-chər, n.* movables, either for use or ornament, with which a house is equipped: equipment (*Shak.*): the trappings of a horse: decorations (*Shak.*): the necessary appliances in some arts: accessories: metal fittings for doors and windows: the pieces of wood or metal put round pages of type to make margins and fasten the matter in the chase (*print.*). [Fr. *fourniture.*]

furor, *fū′rör, n.* fury: excitement, enthusiasm.— furor loquendi (*fū′rör lok-wen′dī, fōō′ror lok-wen′dē*) a rage for speaking; furor poeticus (*pō-et′ik-əs, po-āt-ik-ōōs*) poetic frenzy; furor scribendi (*:kri-ben′dī, skrē-ben′dē*) a rage for writing. [L.]

furore, *fū′rör, -rör, fōō-rör′ā, n.* a craze: wild enthusiasm: wild excitement. [It.]

furrow, *fur′ō, n.* the trench made by a plough: a groove: a wrinkle.—*v.t.* to form furrows in: to groove: to wrinkle.—*adj.* furr′owy.—furr′ow-weed (*Shak.*), a weed of ploughed land. [O.E. *furh*; cf. Ger. *furche,* L. *porca,* ridge.]

furth, *fûrth,* (*Scot.*) *adv.* forth: outside of.—furth of, outside: beyond the bounds of. [Variant of forth.]

further, *fûr′dher, adv.* at or to a greater distance or degree: in addition.—*adj.* more distant: additional.—*adv.* fur′thermore, in addition to what has been said, moreover, besides.—*adj.* fur′thermost, most remote.—*adv.* fur′thest, at or to the greatest distance.—*adj.* most distant.— further education, post-school education other than university education.—see one further, to see one hanged, or the like. [O.E. *furthor* (adv.), *furthra* (adj.)—*fore* or *forth* with comp. suffix *-ther.*]

further, *fûr′dhər, v.t.* to help forward, promote.— *ns.* fur′therance, a helping forward; fur′therer, a promoter, advancer.—*adj.* fur′thersome, helpful: advantageous: rash. [O.E. *fyrthran.*]

furtive, *fûr′tiv, adj.* stealthy: secret.—*adv.* fur′-tively. [L. *fûrtivus—fûr,* a thief.]

furuncle, *fū′rung-kl, n.* a boil.—*adj.* furun′cular, furun′culous. [L. *fūrunculus,* lit. a little thief.]

**fury**, *fū'ri*, *n.* rage: violent passion: madness: (*cap.*; *myth.*) one of the three goddesses of vengeance, the Erinyes, or euphemistically Eumenides—Tisiphone, Alecto, and Megaera (in *Milt.* a Fate): hence a passionate, violent woman.—*adj.* **furious** (*fū'ri-əs*), full of fury: violent.—*n.* **fūrios'ity**, madness.—*adv.* **fū'riously**.—*n.* **fū'riousness**. [Fr. *furie*—L. *furia*—*furēre*, to be angry.]

**furze**, *fûrz*, *n.* whin or gorse.—*adj.* **furz'y**, overgrown with furze. [O.E. *fyrs*.]

**fusain**, *fū-zān'*, *n.* an important constituent of coal, resembling charcoal and consisting of plant remains from which the volatiles have been eliminated (also *fū'zān*): artists' fine charcoal. [Fr., the spindle-tree, or charcoal made from it.]

**fusarole**, **fusarol**, *fū'sə-rōl*, or *-zə-*, (*archit.*) *n.* an astragal moulding. [Fr. *fusarolle*—It. *fusaruolo*, spindle-whorl—L. *fūsus*, spindle.]

**fuscous**, *fus'kəs*, *adj.* brown: dingy.—Also (*Lamb*) **fusc**. [L. *fuscus*.]

**fuse**, *fūz*, *v.t.* to melt: to liquefy by heat: to join by, or as if by, melting together: to cause to fail by melting of a fuse (*elect.*):—*v.i.* to be melted: to be reduced to a liquid: to melt together: blend, unite: of electric appliance, to fail by melting of a fuse.—*n.* a bit of fusible metal, with its mounting, inserted as a safe-guard in an electric circuit.—*n.* **fūsibil'ity**, the degree of ease with which a substance can be fused.—*adjs.* **fū'sible**, able to be fused or easily fused; **fū'sil** (*fū'zil*; *Milt.*), cast: fusible: molten.—Also **fūsile** (*fū'zil*, *-sil*, *-zil*).—*ns.* **fū'sion** (*-zhən*), melting: the state of fluidity from heat: a close union of things, as if melted together: coalition (*U.S.*); **fū'sionism**, a policy that favours union or coalition; **fū'sionist**.—

**fuse box**, a box containing the switches and fuses for the leads of an electrical system; **fusible metal**, an alloy of bismuth, lead, and tin (sometimes with mercury or cadmium) that melts at temperatures of 60° to 180°C; **fū'sing-point**, melting-point; **fusion bomb**, one deriving its energy from fusion of atomic nuclei, as the hydrogen bomb. [L. *fundēre*, *fūsum*, to melt.]

**fuse**, *fūz*, *n.* a train of combustible material in waterproof covering, used with a detonator to initiate an explosion. [It. *fuso*—L. *fūsus*, a spindle.]

**fusee**, **fuzee**, *fū-zē'*, *n.* the spindle in a watch or clock on which the chain is wound: a match with long, oval head for outdoor use: a fuse for firing explosives. [O.Fr. *fusée*, a spindleful—L. *fūsus*, a spindle.]

**fusee**. Same as **fusil** (2).

**fuselage**, *fū'zil-ij*, or *fū-zə-läzh'*, *n.* the body of an aeroplane. [Fr. *fuseler*, to shape like a spindle—L. *fūsus*, spindle.]

**fusel-oil**, *fū'zl-oil*, *n.* a nauseous oil in spirits distilled from potatoes, grain, etc. [Ger. *fusel*, bad spirits.]

**fushion**, **fusion**. See **foison**.

**fusiform**, *fū'zi-förm*, *adj.* spindle-shaped. [L. *fūsus*, spindle, *förma*, shape.]

**fusil**, *fū'zil*, (*her.*) *n.* an elongated rhomboidal figure. [O.Fr. *fusel*—L. *fūsus*, a spindle.]

**fusil**, *fū'zil*, *n.* a flint-lock musket.—*ns.* **fusilier'**, **fusileer'**, formerly a soldier armed with fusil, now simply a historical title borne by a few regiments; **fusillade** (*-äd'*), simultaneous or continuous discharge of firearms: anything assaulting one in similar way (*lit.*, *fig.*).—*n.* **fusilla'tion**, death by shooting. [O.Fr. *fuisil*, a flint-musket, same as It. *focile*—L.L. *focile*, steel (to strike fire with), dim. of L. *focus*, a fireplace.]

**fusil**, **fusile**, **fusion**. See under **fuse** (1).

**fuss**, *fus*, *n.* a bustle: flurry: commotion, esp. over trifles: petty ostentatious activity or attentions.—*v.i.* to be in a fuss, agitate about trifles.—*v.t.* to agitate, flurry.—*n.* **fuss'er**.—*adv.* **fuss'ily**.—*n.*

**fuss'iness**.—*adj.* **fuss'y**, given to making a fuss: finicky: requiring careful attention: over-trimmed.—**fuss'-pot**, one who fusses. [Origin obscure.]

**fuss-ball**. See **fuzz**.

**fust**, *fust*, *n.* a mouldy or musty smell: the shaft of a column.—*v.i.* to mould: to smell mouldy: to taste of the cask.—*ns.* **fustilâ'rian**, **fustil(l)ir'ian** (*Shak.*), a term of abuse; **fust'ilugs** (*obs.*), a gross overgrown person, esp. a woman; **fust'iness**.—*adj.* **fust'y**, smelling of the cask: musty: stale: stuffy: wanting in freshness. [O.Fr. *fust* (Fr. *fût*), cask—L. *fūstis*, cudgel.]

**fustanella**, *fus-tə-nel'ə*, *n.* a white kilt worn by Greek men. [Mod. Gr. *phoustanella*, dim. of *phoustani*, Albanian *fustan*—It. *fustagno*, fustian.]

**fustet**, *fus'tət*, *n.* Venetian sumach (*Rhus cotinus*), or its wood, source of the dye called young fustic. [Fr.,—Prov. *fustet*—Ar. *fustuq*; see **fustic**.]

**fustian**, *fus'chən*, *n.* a kind of coarse, twilled cotton fabric including moleskin, velveteen, corduroy, etc.: a pompous and unnatural style of writing or speaking: bombast: a liquor made of white wine with yolk of eggs, lemon, spices, etc.—*adj.* made of fustian: bombastic.—*v.i.* **fust'ianise**, **-ize** (*Holmes*), to write bombastically.—*n.* **fust'ianist**, one who writes bombast. [O.Fr. *fustaigne* (Fr. *futaine*)—It. *fustagno*—L.L. *fustāneum*, prob. from *El-Fustāt* (Old Cairo) where it may have been made.]

**fustic**, *fus'tik*, *n.* formerly, fustet (now called **young fustic**): now, the wood of a tropical American tree (*Chlorophora tinctoria*), yielding a yellow dye.—Also **fus'toc**. [Fr. *fustoc*—Sp. *fustoc*—Ar. *fustuq*—Gr. *pistakē*, pistachio.]

**fustigate**, *fus'ti-gāt*, *v.t.* to cudgel.—*n.* **fustigā'tion**. [L. *fūstigāre*, *-ātum*—*fūstis*, a stick.]

**Fusus**, *fū'səs*, *n.* a genus of gasteropods, allied to whelks—the spindle-shells. [L. *fūsus*, spindle.]

**futchel**, *fuch'əl*, *n.* a piece of timber lengthwise of a carriage, supporting the splinter-bar and the pole.

**futhork**, **futhorc**, **futhark**, *fōō'thörk*, *-thärk*, *n.* the Runic alphabet. [From the first six letters, *f, u, p (th), o or a, r, k*.]

**futile**, *fū'til*, *U.S. -təl*, *adj.* ineffectual: trifling: tattling (*obs.*).—*adv.* **fu'tilely**.—*ns.* **futilitā'rian**, one who gives himself to profitless pursuits: one who believes all to be futile; **futil'ity**, uselessness. [L. *fūtilis*, leaky, futile—*fundēre*, to pour.]

**futtock**, *fut'ək*, *n.* one of the crooked timbers of a wooden ship.—**futt'ock-plate**, an iron plate with dead-eyes, for the topmast or topgallant rigging.—*n.pl.* **futt'ock-shrouds**, short pieces of rope or chain securing the futtock-plates to a band round a lower mast. [Perh. for **foot-hook**.]

**future**, *fū'chər*, *adj.* about to be: that is to come: expressive of time to come (*gram.*).—*n.* time to come: life, fate or condition in time to come: the future tense (*gram.*): (in *pl.*) goods bought and sold to be delivered at a future time.—*adj.* **fut'urism** (*art*), a movement claiming to anticipate or point the way for the future, esp. a 20th-century revolt against tradition; **fut'urist**, one whose chief interests are in what is to come: a believer in futurism.—*adj.* **futurist'ic**.—*ns.* **futurition**, future existence: accomplishment: futurity; **futurity** (*fū-tū'ri-ti*), time to come: an event, or state of being, yet to come.—*adj.* **futurolog'ical**.—*ns.* **futurol'ogist**; **futurol'ogy**, the science and study of sociological and technological developments, values, and trends, with a view to planning for the future.—*adj.* **fu'ture-per'fect** (*gram.*), expressive of action viewed as past in reference to an assumed future time.—*n.* the future-perfect tense: a verb in that tense. [Fr. *futur*—L. *futūrus*, used as fut.p. of *esse*, to be.]

fuze, *fūz, n.* a device used to cause a bomb, shell, mine, rocket, etc., to detonate. [fuse (2).]

fuzz, *fuz, n.* light fine particles or fibres, as dust: fluff: blurr: police (*slang*).—*v.i.* disintegrate in fuzz.—*adv.* fuzz'ily.—*n.* fuzz'iness.—*adj.* fuzz'y, covered with fuzz: fluffy: blurred.—fuzz'-ball, fuss'-ball, a puff-ball. [Origin doubtful.]

fuzzle, *fuz'l, (dial.) v.t.* to fuddle.

fy, *fī, interj.* Same as fie.

fyke. Same as fike.

fyke, *fīk, (U.S.) n.* a bag-net. [Du. *fuik.*]

fyle (*Spens.*). See file.

fylfot, filfot, *fil'fot, n.* a swastika, esp. one turned counter-clockwise. [Prob. from misunderstanding of a manuscript, *fylfot* = fill-foot, really meaning a device for filling the foot of a painted window.]

fyrd, *fûrd, fërd, n.* the militia of Old English times. [O.E. *fyrd*, army.]

fytte. See fit (3).

Neutral vowels in unaccented syllables: *el'ə-mənt*; for certain sounds in foreign words, see p. viii

# G

**G, g, jē, n.** the seventh letter of our alphabet, and of the Roman; originally a form of C, inserted in the place of the disused Z, its ordinary sound (as in Latin) a voiced guttural stop, but in some words in English the same as J: the fifth note of the diatonic scale of C major—also *sol* (*mus.*): the scale or key having that note for its tonic (*mus.*): a symbol (*g*) for acceleration due to gravity (see **gravity**): a symbol (*G*) for the constant of gravitation (see **gravity**): as a mediaeval Roman numeral G = 400, Ḡ = 400,000: symbol for general intelligence.— **G-agents,** highly effective poisonous gases for poss. military use; **G´-clef,** a clef on the second line of the treble stave, marking G, the treble clef; **G´-man** (*U.S.*), an agent of the Federal Bureau of Investigation (for Government-man); **G-string** (same as **gee-string**); **g´-suit,** a close-fitting suit with cells that inflate to prevent flow of blood away from the head, worn by airman as defence against blackout due to high acceleration and resultant great increase in weight (*g* for acceleration of gravity).

**gab, gab,** (*coll.*) *v.i.* to chatter, prate.—*n.* idle or fluent talk: mouth.—*n.* **gabb´er,** a chatterer.— *adj.* **gabb´y,** garrulous.—**gift of the gab,** a talent (or propensity) for talking. [Origin doubtful; possibly variant of **gob.**]

**gab, gab,** (*obs.*) *n.* mockery: a jest: a vaunt.—*v.i.* to brag. [O.Fr. *gabber,* to mock.]

**gab, gab, n.** a Scots form of **gob.**

**gabbart, gab´ərt,** (esp. *Scots.*) *n.* a barge.—Also **gabb´ard.** [Fr. *gabare*—Prov. and It. *gabarra.*]

**gabble, gab´l,** *v.i.* to talk inarticulately: to chatter: to cackle like geese.—*ns.* **gabb´le,** gabbling; **gabb´ler; gabb´ling, gabb´lement.** [Perh. freq. of **gab** (1), perh. M.Du. *gabbelen*—imit.]

**gabbro, gab´rō, n.** a coarsely crystalline igneous rock composed of labradorite or similar plagioclase and pyroxene, often with olivine and magnetite.—*adjs.* **gabbr´oic, gabbroitic** (*-it´ik*); **gabb´roid,** resembling gabbro. [It.]

**gabelle, gab-el´, n.** a tax, esp. formerly in France, on salt.—*n.* **gabell´er,** a collector of gabelle. [Fr. *gabelle*—L.L. *gabella, gablum*; of Gmc. origin.]

**gaberdine, gabardine, gab´ər-dēn, n.** a loose cloak, esp. a Jew's (*hist.*): a closely woven twill fabric, esp. of cotton and wool: a coat of this material. [O.Fr. *gauvardine*; perh. M.H.G. *wallevart,* pilgrimage, whence also Sp. *gabardina,* etc.]

**gaberlunzie, gab-ər-lün´i, -yi,** later-*lun´zi,* (*Scot.*), *n.* a beggar's pouch: a strolling beggar, orig. a bluegown.

**gabion, gā´bi-ən, n.** a bottomless basket of earth, used in fortification and engineering (*fort.*): a small curiosity (*Scott*).—*ns.* (*fort.*) **gā´bionade,** a work formed of gabions; **gā´bionage,** gabions collectively.—*adj.* **gā´bioned,** furnished with gabions. [Fr.,—It. *gabbione,* a large cage— *gabbia*—L. *cavea,* a cage.]

**gable, gā´bl,** (*archit.*) *n.* the triangular part of an exterior wall of a building between the top of the side-walls and the slopes on the roof—(*Scot.*) **gā´vel.**—*adj.* **gā´bled.**—*n.* **gā´blet** (*dim.*), a small gable over a niche, buttress, tabernacle, etc.— **gā´ble-end,** the end-wall of a building on the side where there is a gable; **gā´ble-win´dow,** a window in a gable-end: a window with its upper part shaped like a gable. [The northern form *gavel* is prob. O.N. *gafl;* Sw. *gafvel,* Dan.

*gavl;* the southern form *gable* is prob. through O.Fr. *gable,* from O.N. *gafl.*]

**gabnash, gab´nash,** (*Scot.*) *n.* prattle: chatter: a pert prattler. [Cf. **nashgab.**]

**gaby, gā´bi,** (*dial.*), *n.* a simpleton. [Origin unknown.]

**gad, gad, n.** a metal spike or pointed bar (*obs.*): a miner's wedge or chisel: a spear (*obs.*; also **gade, gaid, gād**): a stylus (*Shak.*): a rod or stick (*obs.*): a goad (*dial.*): the bar across a Scottish condemned cell, on which the iron ring ran which fastened the shackles (*hist.*).—*n.* **gad´ling** (*obs.*), one of the spikes on the knuckles of a gauntlet.—**upon the gad** (*Shak.*), upon the spur of the moment. [O.N. *gaddr,* a spike; confused with O.E. *gād;* see **goad.**]

**gad, gad, interj.** a minced form of **God.**—*interj.* (*arch.*) **gad-zooks´,** an obs. minced oath (app. for *God's hooks*; see **gadso.**

**gad, gad, v.i.** to rush here and there in a wayward uncontrolled manner (*obs.*): to wander about, often restlessly, idly or in pursuit of pleasure (often with *about*): to straggle:—*pr.p.* **gadd´ing;** *pa.t.* and *pa.p.* **gadd´ed.**—*n.* **gadd´er,** one who wanders about.—*n.* **gadd´er.**—**gad´about,** one who wanders restlessly from place to place. [Prob. back-formation from **gadling;** or from **gadfly.**]

**gadfly, gad´fli, n.** blood-sucking fly (Tabanus) that distresses cattle: sometimes applied to a botfly: a mischievous gadabout. [**gad** (1) or O.E. *gād* (see **goad**) and **fly.**]

**gadge, gaj,** (*Browning*) *n.* an instrument of torture.

**gadget, gaj´it, n.** any small ingenious device: a what-d'ye-call-it.—*n.* **gad´getry,** gadgets: making of gadgets. [Origin obscure.]

**Gadhel, gad´əl, n.** a Gael, a Celt of the branch to which the Irish, the Scottish Highlanders, and the Manx belong (orig. not including Scottish).—*adj.* **Gadhelic** (*-el´ik, -ēl´ik,* or *gad´*).—See also **Gael, Goidel.** [Ir. *Gaedheal* (pl. *Gaedhil*).]

**gadi, gäd´ē, gud´ē, n.** an Indian throne. [Marathi *gādi,* Bengali *gadi.*]

**gadling, gad´ling,** (*obs.*) *n.* a vagabond. [O.E. *gædeling,* orig. companion.]

**gadling.** See **gad** (1).

**gadoid.** See under **Gadus.**

**gadolinite, gad´ə-lin-it, n.** a silicate of yttrium, beryllium, and iron.—*n.* **gadolin´ium,** a metal of the rare earths (Gd; at. numb. 64). [From the Finnish chemist *Gadolin* (1760-1852).]

**gadroon, ga-drōōn´, n.** a boss-like ornament, used in series in plate, etc., to form a cable or bead.— *adj.* **gadrooned´.**—*n.* **gadroon´ing.** [Fr. *godron.*]

**gadsman, gadz´man,** (*Scot.*) *n.* one who drives horses at the plough. [**gad** (1), or O.E. *gād* (see **goad**), and **man.**]

**gadso, gad´sō,** (*arch.*) *interj.* expressing surprise. [It. *cazzo,* the penis, assimilated to **gad** (2).]

**Gadus, gā´dəs, n.** the cod genus, typical of the family Gadidae (*gad´i-dē*).—*ns.* **gade, gād´oid,** a fish of the family.—*adj.* **gad´oid,** codlike. [Latinised from Gr. *gados,* the hake or similar fish.]

**gadwall, gad´wöl, n.** a northern freshwater duck.

**gae, gā,** a Scots form of **go:**—*pr.p.* **gaun;** *pa.t.* and *pa.p.* **gane.**

**Gaekwar, gik´wär, n.** the title given to the ruler of the former Indian state of Baroda.—Also **Gaikwar, Guicowar.** [Marathi *gāekwār,* cowherd.]

**Gael, gāl, n.** one whose language is Gadhelic, esp.

*fāte, fär; mē, hûr* (her); *mīne, mōte, för; mūte, mōōn, fōōt; dhen* (then) a Scottish Highlander.—*adj.* Gaelic (*gāl'ik*, *gal'ik*), pertaining to the Gaels.—*n.* Gadhelic, the language of Ireland and (now *esp.*) that of the Scottish Highlands.—*v.t.* gael'icise, -ize, (-*sīz*).—*n.* gael'icism (-*sizm*).—See also Goidel. [Scottish Gael. *Gaidheal.*]

Gaeltacht, *gāl'tähht, n.* the Irish-speaking districts of Ireland. [Ir. *gaedhealtacht.*]

gaff, *gaf, n.* a hook used esp. for landing large fish: the spar to which the head of a fore-and-aft sail is bent (*naut.*).—*v.t.* to hook or bind by means of a gaff.—gaff'-top-sail, a small sail, the head of which is extended on a small gaff which hoists on the top-mast, and the foot on the lower gaff. [Fr. *gaffe.*]

gaff, *gaf,* (*slang*) *n.* a low theatre: a fair. [Origin obscure.]

gaff, gaffe, *gaf, n.* a blunder. [Fr. *gaffe.*]

gaff, *gaf,* (*slang*) *v.i.* to gamble.—*ns.* gaff'er; gaff'ing. [Origin obscure.]

gaff, *gaf,* (*slang*) *n.* humbug, nonsense.—to blow the gaff, to disclose a secret, to blab. [Prob. connected with gab (2) or gaff (3); cf. O.E. *gegaf-sprēc,* scurrility.]

gaffer, *gaf'ər, n.* originally a word of respect applied to an old man, now familiar (*fem.* gammer): the foreman of a squad of workmen. [grandfather, or godfather.]

gag, gag, *v.t.* to stop the mouth of forcibly: to silence: to choke up.—*v.i.* to choke: to retch:—*pr.p.* gagg'ing; *pa.t.* and *pa.p.* gagged.—*n.* something put into the mouth or over it to enforce silence (also *fig.*), or to distend jaws during an operation: the closure applied in a debate: a nauseous mouthful, boiled fat beef (*Lamb*).—*n.* gagg'er, one who gags. [Prob. imitative of sound made in choking.]

gag, gag, (*slang*) *v.t.* to deceive.—*v.i.* to practise imposture.—*n.* a made-up story, lie. [Possibly gag (1).]

gag, gag (*coll.*), *n.* an actor's interpolation into his part: a joke: a hoax.—*v.i.* to introduce a gag: to joke.—*v.t.* to introduce a gag into. [Possibly gag (1).]

gaga, *gä'gä,* (*slang*) *adj.* fatuous: in senile dotage. [Fr.]

gage, *gāj, n.* a pledge: something thrown down as a challenge, as a glove.—*v.t.* to bind by pledge or security: offer as a guarantee: to stake, wager. [O.Fr. *guage;* ∩mc.; see wage, wed.]

gage. See gauge.

gage, *gāj.* Same as greengage.

gaggle, *gag'l, n.* a flock of geese, or of women.—*v.i.* to cackle.—*n.* gagg'ling, cackling.—*adj.* garrulous. [Prob. imit.]

gag-tooth, *gag'-tōōth, n.* a projecting tooth.—*adj.* gag'-toothed.

gahnite, *gän'it, n.* a zinc spinel. [J. G. *Gahn* 1745-1818), Swedish chemist.]

Gaidhealtachd, *gä'yal-tähht, n.* the Gaelic-speaking districts of Scotland. [Gael.]

gaiety, gaily. See gay.

Gaikwar. See Gaekwar.

gaillard. Form of galliard.

gain, *gān, v.t.* to obtain to one's advantage: to earn: to win: to be successful in: to increase (speed, weight): to draw to one's own party: to reach.—*v.i.* to profit: to become or appear better, to progress: (of clock, etc.) to go fast by so much in a given time.—*n.* that which is gained: profit: an instance of gaining, a win: ratio of actual power delivered to that which would be delivered if an amplifier were not used (*telecomm.*): ratio of output and input voltages (*telecomm.*): (or gain-control) volume control in amplifier, receiving set (*telecomm.*).—*adj.* gain'able.—*n.* gain'er.—*adj.* gain'ful, lucrative: profitable: engaged in for pay, paid.—*adv.* gain'fully.—*n.* gain'fulness.—*n.pl.* gain'ings.—*adj.* gain'less.—*n.* gain'lessness.—gain ground

(see ground); gain on, upon, to overtake by degrees: to increase one's advantage against: to encroach on. [O.Fr. *gain, gaain, gaigner, gaaignier,* from Gmc., as in O.H.G. *weidenen,* to graze, to seek forage, *weida,* pasture.]

gain, *gān* (*dial.*) *adj.* near, straight: convenient. [O.N. *gegn.*]

gaingiving, *gān'giv-ing,* (*Shak.*) *n.* misgiving.

gainly, *gān'li,* (*dial.*) *adj.* shapely: comely: graceful. [gain (2).]

gainsay, *gān-sā', gān'sā, v.t.* to contradict: to deny: to dispute:—*pr.p.* gainsay'ing, or *gān';* *pa.t.* and *pa.p.* gainsaid, *gān-sād', -sed';* 3rd *pers. sing. pres. indic.* gainsays, -*sāz.*—*n.* gain'say (or -*sā'*), denial.—*ns.* gainsay'er (*B.*), an opposer; gainsay'ing. [O.E. *gegn,* against, and say.]

gainst, 'gainst, genst, a poetic abbreviation of against.

gainstrive, *gān-strīv',* (*obs.*) *v.t.* to strive against.—*v.i.* to resist.

gair, *gār,* (*Scot.*) *n.* gore (of cloth or land). [See gore (2).]

gairfowl. Same as garefowl.

gait, *gāt, n.* way of walking: a horse's pace.—*adj.* gait'ed, having a particular gait. [gate (2).]

gait, *gāt,* (*dial.*) *n.* a sheaf of corn set on end.

gait(t) (*Scott*), spelling of get, a child, gyte (2).

gaiter, *gāt'ər, n.* a covering for the ankle, fitting down upon the shoe. [Fr. *guêtre.*]

gajo. See gorgio.

gal, *gal,* dial. for girl.

gala, *gä'lə, gā', n.* festivity.—ga'la-dress, gay costume for a gala-day. [Fr. *gala,* show—It. *gala,* finery.]

galactic, *gə-lak'tik, adj.* pertaining to or obtained from milk: pertaining to a galaxy or galaxies (see Galaxy).—*ns.* galac'tagogue (-*tə-gog;* Gr. *agōgos,* bringing), a medicine that promotes secretion of milk; galactom'eter (Gr. *metron,* measure), an instrument for finding the specific gravity of milk.—*adjs.* galactoph'orous (Gr. *phoros,* bringing), milk-carrying; galactopoiet'ic (Gr. *poiētikos,* productive), milk-producing.—*ns.* galactorrhoea (-*rē'ə;* Gr. *rhoiā,* a flow), a too abundant flow of milk; galac'tose, a sugar, ($C_6H_{12}O_6$), got by hydrolysis from lactose; galactosae'mia (-*sēm'i-ə*), the presence of galactose in the blood. [Gr. *gala, galaktos,* milk.]

galage, *gəl-āj',* an obs. form of galosh.

Galago, *gä-lā'gō, n.* a genus of large-eared, long-tailed nocturnal African lemurs.

galah, *gə-lä', n.* an Australian cockatoo with pink underparts: a fool, a boaster. [Native name.]

Galam butter, *gä-läm',* shea butter. [*Galam,* a district on the Senegal.]

galangal. See galingale.

galant, *gə-länt', adj.* of a musical style, current in the 18th cent., characterised by lightness, elegance and technical accomplishment. [Fr.]

galantine, *gal'ən-tēn, -tin, n.* a dish of poultry, veal, etc., served cold in jelly. [Fr.; see gelatine.]

galanty show, *gəl-an'ti shō,* a shadow pantomime. [Prob. It. *galanti,* pl. of *galante;* see gallant.]

galapago, *gə-lap'ə-gō, n.* a tortoise. [Sp.]

galatea, *gal-ə-tē'ə, n.* a cotton fabric usu. with coloured stripe. [19th cent. H.M.S. *Galatea.*]

Galaxy, *gal'ək-si, n.* the Milky Way, the luminous band of stars stretching across the heavens: (without *cap.*) any similar system or 'universe': a splendid assemblage. [Through Fr. and L., from Gr. *galaxias—gala, -aktos,* milk.]

galbanum, *gal'bə-nəm, n.* a gum-resin got from Eastern species of Ferula. [L.,—Gr. *chalbanē,* prob. an Eastern word.]

galdragon, *gal'drə-gən,* (*Scott*) *n.* an obs. Shetland word for a sorceress, witch. [O.N. *galdra-kona*—*galdr,* crowing, incantation, witchcraft, *kuna,* woman.]

gale, *gāl, n.* a strong wind between a stiff breeze

Neutral vowels in unaccented syllables: *el'ə-mənt;* for certain sounds in foreign words, see p. viii

and a hurricane: in old poetic diction, a gentle wind: a wafted smell: an outburst. [Origin obscure.]

**gale**, *gāl, n.* (usu. **sweet'-gale**) bog-myrtle. [Prob. O.E. *gagel*; cf. Ger. *gagel*.]

**gale**, *gāl, n.* a periodic payment of rent: a mining licence. [Perh. **gavel**.]

**galea**, *gal'i-ə, gāl'i-ə, (biol.) n.* a helmet-shaped structure.—*adjs.* **gal'eate, -d.** [L. *galea*, a skin helmet.]

**galena**, *gə-lē'nə, n.* lead-glance, native sulphide of lead.—Also **galē'nite.**—*adj.* **galē'noid.** [L. *galēna*, lead-ore.]

**Galenic**, *gə-len'ik, adj.* pertaining to *Galen (Galēnos)*, the 2nd-cent. Greek physician, or to his methods and theories.—*adj.* **Galen'ical.**—*n.* a remedy such as Galen prescribed, a vegetable simple.—*ns.* **Galenism** (*gā'lən-izm*); **Gā'lenist.**

**Galeopithecus**, *gā-li-ō-pi-thē'kəs, -pith', n.* the so-called flying-lemur.—*adjs.* **galeopithē'cine** (*-sin*), **galeopithē'coid.** [Gr. *galeē*, weasel, marten, *pithēkos*, ape.]

**Galilean**, *gal-i-lē'ən, adj.* of or pertaining to *Galileo*, the great Italian mathematician (1564-1642).

**Galilean**, *gal-i-lē'ən, adj.* of or pertaining to *Galilee* (L. *Galilaea*, Gr. *Galilaiā*), one of the Roman divisions of Palestine.—*n.* a native of Galilee: a Christian.

**galilee**, *gal'i-lē, (archit.) n.* a porch or chapel at the west end of some churches, in which penitents were placed, and where ecclesiastics met women who had business with them.— **galilee porch,** a galilee in direct communication with the exterior. [Perh. suggested by Mark xvi. 7, or Matt. iv. 15.]

**galimatias**, *gal-i-mā'shi-əs, mat'i-äs, n.* nonsense: any confused mixture of unlike things. [Fr.]

**galingale**, *gal'ing-gāl, n.* the aromatic rootstock of certain E. Indian plants of the ginger family (*Alpinia* and *Kaempferia*), formerly much used like ginger: the rootstock of a sedge (*Cyperus longus*), of ancient medicinal repute: also the whole plant.—Also **gal'angal, gal'engale, galang'a.** [O.Fr. *galingal*—Ar. *khalanjān*—Chin. *ko-liang-kiang—Ko,* a district near Canton, *liang,* mild, and *kiang,* ginger.]

**galiongee**, *gal-yən-jē', n.* a Turkish sailor. [Turk. *qālyūnjī,* deriv. of *qālyūn*—It. *galeone*, galleon.]

**galipot**, *gal'i-pot, n.* the turpentine that exudes from the cluster-pine. [Fr.]

**gall**, *göl, n.* bile, the greenish-yellow fluid secreted from the liver: bitterness: malignity: assurance, presumption.—*adj.* **gall'-less,** without gall: mild: free from rancour.—**gall'-bladder,** a reservoir for the bile; **gall'-duct,** a tube for conveying bile or gall; **gall'-stone,** a concretion in the gall-bladder or biliary ducts. [O.E. *galla, gealla,* gall; cf. Ger. *galle,* Gr. *cholē,* L. *fel.*]

**gall**, *göl, n.* an abnormal growth on a plant owing to attack by a parasite (fungus, insect, etc.).—*n.* **gallate** (*gal'āt*), a salt of gallic acid.—**gall'-fly** (*göl'-*), **gall'-wasp,** an insect of the hymenopterous family Cynipidae that causes galls by depositing its eggs in plants; **gallic acid** (*gal'ik*), a crystalline substance obtained from gall-nuts, etc.—used in making ink; **gall'-midge,** a Cecidomyia or kindred gall-making midge; **gall'-nut,** a nutlike gall produced on an oak by a gall-wasp, used esp. formerly for making ink. [Fr. *galle*—L. *galla,* oak-apple.]

**gall**, *göl, n.* a painful swelling, esp. in a horse: a sore due to chafing: a state or cause of irritation: a chafed place: a bare place (*arch.*): a flaw (*arch.*): a fault or a dyke (*mining*).—*v.t.* to fret or hurt by rubbing (*arch.*): to irritate.—*v.i.* to become chafed: to scoff (*Shak.*).—*adj.* **gall'ing,** irritating. —*adv.* **gall'ingly.** [O.E. *galla, gealla,* a sore place.]

**gallant**, *gal'ənt, adj.* brave: noble: gay, splendid, magnificent (*rare*): attentive (esp. formally or obsequiously) to ladies: amorous (sometimes *gə-lant'* in the last two senses).—*n.* a gay, dashing person: a man (*arch.*; woman *obs.*) of fashion: a lover (also *gə-lant'* in this sense).—*adv.* **gall'antly.**—*ns.* **gall'antness; gall'antry,** bravery: intrepidity: attention or devotion to ladies, often in a bad sense, amorous intrigue: gallants collectively (*Shak.*).—**the honourable and gallant member,** a mode of referring in parliament to a member who is an officer in the fighting services. [Fr. *galant*—O.Fr. *gale,* a merrymaking; prob. Gmc.; cf. **gala.**]

**galleass**, *gal'i-as, (Shak.) n.* a vessel of the same construction as a galley, but larger and heavier. —Also **gall'iass.** [O.Fr. *galeace*—It. *galeazza*, augmentative from *galea,* galley.]

**galleon**, *gal'i-ən, n.* a large vessel with lofty stem and stern, mostly used formerly by Spaniards for carrying treasure. [Sp. *galeón;* cf. **galley.**]

**gallery**, *gal'ə-ri, n.* a covered walk: a long balcony: a long passage: an upper floor of seats, esp. in a theatre, the highest: the occupants of the gallery: a body of spectators: a room for the exhibition of works of art: an underground passage, drift, or level.—*v.t.* to tunnel.—*adj.* **gall'eried,** furnished with, or arranged like, a gallery.—*n.* **gall'eryite,** one who frequents the gallery in the theatre.—**play to the gallery,** to play for the applause of the least cultured. [O.Fr. *galerie* (It. *galleria*).]

**galley**, *gal'i, n.* a long, low-built ship with one deck, propelled by oars and sails: a Greek or Roman warship: a large open rowing-boat: the cooking place on board ship: a flat oblong tray for type that has been set up (*print.*): an galley-proof (*print.*).—**gall'ey-foist** (*obs.*), a state barge; **gall'ey-proof,** an impression taken from type on a galley, a slip-proof; **gall'ey-slave,** one condemned to work as a slave at the oar of a galley: a drudge; **gall'ey-worm,** a myriapod. [O.Fr. *galie, galee*—L.L. *galea.*]

**galley-west**, *gal-i-west', (U.S. slang) adv.* into confusion or unconsciousness.

**galliambic**, *gal-i-am'bik, adj.* in or of a metre $(\cup\cup—\cup—\cup—|\cup\cup—\cup\cup\cup—)$ said to have been used by the Phrygian priests of Cybele, best known from the *Attis* of Catullus.—*n.pl.* **galliam'-bics,** galliambic verses. [Gr. *galliambikos*— *Gallos,* a priest of Cybele, *iambos,* an iamb.]

**galliard**, *gal'yərd, adj.* (*arch.*) brisk, lively.—*n.* a spirited dance for two, in triple time, common in the 16th and 17th centuries: a gay fellow (*arch.*).—*n.* **gall'iardise** (*arch., -ēz, -iz*), gaiety: a merry trick. [O.Fr. *gaillard.*]

**gallic.** See **gall** (2).

**Gallic**, *gal'ik, adj.* and *n.* Gaulish.—*adj.* **Gall'ican,** of or pertaining to France: esp. pertaining to the Roman Catholic Church in France, regarded as national and more or less independent.—*n.* one holding Gallican doctrines.—*n.* **Gall'icanism,** the spirit of nationalism within the French Church— as opposed to *Ultramontanism,* or the absolute subjection of everything to the personal authority of the pope.—*adv.* **Gallice** (*gal'i-sē;* L. *gal'i-kā*), in French.—*v.t.* and *v.i.* **Gall'icise, -ize,** to assimilate or conform to French habits, etc.— *ns.* **Gall'icism,** the use in another language of an expression or idiom peculiar to French; **Gallomā'nia,** a mania for French ways; **Gall'ophil(e),** one who is friendly to France; **Gall'ophobe,** one who dislikes or fears France; what is French; **Gallopho'bia.** [L. *Gallus,* a Gaul; *Gallicus,* Gaulish.]

**galligaskins**, *gal-i-gas'kinz, n.pl.* wide hose or breeches worn in 16th and 17th centuries: leggings. [O.Fr. *garguesque*—It. *grechesco,* Greekish—L. *graecus,* Greek.]

**gallimaufry**, *gal-i-mö'fri, (Shak.) n.* any inconsistent or absurd medley: a miscellaneous gathering. [Fr. *galimafrée*, a ragout, hash.]

**gallinaceous**, *gal-in-ā′shəs*, *adj.* akin to the domestic fowl. [L. *gallina*, a hen—*gallus*, a cock.]

**gallinazo**, *gal-i-nä′zō*, *n.* a turkey-buzzard or other vulture. [Sp.,—*gallina*—L. *gallina*, hen.]

**gallinule**, *gal′i-nūl*, *n.* a water-hen. [L. *gallinula*, a chicken—*gallina*, a hen.]

**Gallio**, *gal′i-ō*, *n.* one who keeps himself free from trouble and responsibility. [From *Gallio*, Acts xviii. 12-17.]

**galliot, galiot**, *gal′i-ət*, *n.* a small galley: an old Dutch cargo-boat. [Fr. *galiote*—L.L. *galea*, galley.]

**gallipot**, *gal′i-pot*, *n.* a small glazed pot, esp. for medicine. [Prob. a pot brought in galleys.]

**gallise, -ize**, *gal′īz*, *v.t.* in wine-making, to bring to standard proportions by adding water and sugar to inferior must.—Also **gall′isise, -ize**. [Ger. *gallisieren*, from the name of the inventor, Dr L. *Gall*.]

**gallium**, *gal′i-əm*, *n.* a metallic element (symbol Ga; atomic number 31). In the form of gallium arsenide it is an important semiconductor. [L. *gallus*, a cock, from the discoverer's name, Lecoq de Boisbaudran, or *Gallia*, Gaul, France, his country.]

**gallivant**, *gal-i-vant′*, *v.i.* to spend time frivolously, esp. in flirting: to gad about. [Perh. **gallant**.]

**gallivat**, *gal′i-vat*, *n.* a large two-masted Malay boat. [Port. *galeota*; see **galliot**.]

**galliwasp**, *gal′i-wosp*, *n.* a W. Indian lizard.

**galloglass, gallowglass**, *gal′ō-glas*, *n.* a soldier or armed retainer of a chief in ancient Ireland and other Celtic countries. [Ir. *gallōglāch*—Ir. *gall*, foreign, *ōglāch*, soldier.]

**gallon**, *gal′ən*, *n.* a unit of capacity equal to 277·4 cubic inches, in U.S. 231 cubic inches. [O.N.Fr. *galun, galon* (O.Fr. *jalon*).]

**galloon**, *gə-lōōn′*, *n.* a kind of lace: a narrow tape-like trimming or binding material, sometimes made with gold or silver thread.—*adj.* **gallooned′**, adorned with galloon. [Fr. *galon, galonner*; prob. cog. with **gallant**.]

**galloon**, *gə-lōōn′*, *n.* a variant of galleon.

**gallop**, *gal′əp*, *v.i.* to go at a gallop: to ride a galloping animal: to move very fast.—*v.t.* to cause to gallop.—*n.* the fastest pace of a horse, etc., at each stride of which all four feet are off the ground: a ride at a gallop: also *fig.*: a track for galloping.—*n.* **gall′oper**, one who, or that which, gallops.—*adj.* **gall′oping**, proceeding at a gallop: advancing rapidly, as *galloping consumption* (*fig.*).—**Canterbury gallop**, a moderate gallop of a horse (see **canter**). [O.Fr. *galoper, galop*; prob. Gmc.; cf. **wallop**.]

**gallopade**, *gal-əp-ād′*, *n.* a quick kind of dance: the music appropriate to it: a sidewise gallop.—*v.i.* to move briskly: to perform a gallopade. [Fr.]

**Gallovidian**, *gal-ō-vid′i-ən*, *adj.* belonging to Galloway.—*n.* a native thereof. [*Gallovidia*, Latinised from Welsh *Gallwyddel*.]

**gallow**, *ga′lō*, (*Shak.*) *v.t.* to frighten. [O.E. *āgælwan*, to frighten, to astonish.]

**Galloway**, *gal′ō-wā*, *n.* a small strong horse, 13-15 hands high: a breed of large black hornless cattle, orig. from *Galloway* in Scotland.

**gallows**, *gal′ōz*, or (old-fashioned) *gal′əs*, *n.* orig. *pl.* treated as *sing.*, wooden frame for hanging criminals: one who deserves the gallows (*Shak.*): the look of one destined to hang (*Shak.*): any contrivance with posts and crossbeam for suspending things: a rest for the tympan of a hand printing-press: the main frame of a beam-engine: one of a pair of trouser braces:—*pl.* (really double *pl.*) **gal(l)′owses** (used by *Shak.*, in first sense above): used *Scot.* and *dial.*, with various spellings—**gall′uses**, etc.—for trouser braces).—*adj.* deserving the gallows: villainous (*dial.*):

**mischievous** (*dial.*): in some dialects, a mere intensive.—*adv.* (*dial.*) damnably, confoundedly.—*n.* **gall′owsness** (*slang*), recklessness.—**gall′owsbird**, one who deserves hanging or has been hanged; **gall′ows-foot**.—*adj.* **gall′ows-free**, free from the danger of hanging.—**gall′ows-lee**, the place of hanging; **gall′ows-maker**.—*adj.* **gall′ows-ripe′**, ready for the gallows.—**gall′ows-tree′**, a gallows.—**cheat the gallows**, to deserve but escape hanging. [M.E. *galwes* (pl.)—O.E. *galga*; Ger. *galgen*.]

**Gallup poll**, *gal′əp*, a method of gauging public opinion by questioning suitably distributed sample individuals, devised by George Horace *Gallup* (b. 1901).

**gallus**. An old spelling of **gallows**.

**gally**, *gal′i*, (*dial.*) *v.i.* to scare, daze.—**gall′y-bagg′er, -begg′ar, -crow** (also **galli-**), a scarecrow. [See **gallow**.]

**galoot**, *gə-lōōt′*, (*slang*) *n.* a soldier: a marine: a clumsy fellow.

**galop**, *gal′əp, gə-lop′*, *n.* a lively dance or dance-tune in duple time.—*v.i.* to dance a galop. [Fr.; cf. **gallop**.]

**galopin**, *gal′ə-pin*, *n.* an errand boy (*Scott*): a kitchen boy (*obs.*). [Fr.]

**galore**, *gə-lōr′, -lōr′, adv.* in abundance. [Ir. *go*, an adverbialising participle, *leōr*, sufficient.]

**galosh, golosh, galoche**, *gə-losh′*, *n.* a rustic shoe, sandal, or clog (*obs.*): a piece running round a shoe or boot above the sole: an overshoe.—*v.t.* to furnish with a galosh. [Fr. *galoche*—prob. L.L. *gallicula*, small Gaulish shoe.]

**galravage, -itch**. See **gilravage**.

**galumph**, *gə-lumf′*, *v.i.* to march along boundingly and exultingly. [A coinage of Lewis Carroll.]

**galut(h)**, *gä-lōōt′, gō′ləs*, *n.* (often *cap.*) forced exile of Jews, esp. (diaspora) from Palestine. [Heb. *gālūth*, exile.]

**galvanism**, *gal′van-izm*, *n.* current electricity (*obs.*): medical treatment by electric currents.—*adj.* **galvanic** (*-van′*), of, producing, produced by, galvanism (*obs.*): also *fig.*—*n.* **galvanisā′tion**, *-z-.*—*v.t.* **gal′vanise, -ize**, to subject to action of an electric current: to stimulate to spasmodic action by, or as if by, an electric shock: to confer a false vitality upon: to coat with metal by an electric current: to coat with zinc without using a current.—*ns.* **gal′vaniser, -z-**; **gal′vanist**; **gal′vanom′eter**, an instrument for measuring electric currents; **galvanom′etry**.—*adj.* **galvanoplas′tic** (*obs.*).—*ns.* **galvanoplas′ty** (*obs.*), electrodeposition; **galvan′oscope**, an instrument for detecting electric currents.—**galvanic battery, cell** (*obs.*), an electric battery, cell; **galvanic belt** (*obs.*), a belt supposed to benefit the wearer by producing an electric current; **galvanised iron**, iron coated with zinc. [From Luigi *Galvani*, of Bologna, the discoverer (1737-98).]

**Galwegian**, *gal-wē′ji-ən*, *adj.* belonging to Galloway.—*n.* a native thereof.—Also **Gallowe′gian**. [On the analogy of *Norwegian*.]

**gam**, *gam*, *n.* a school of whales: social intercourse or visit at sea (*U.S.*).—*v.i.* to associate in a gam.—*v.t.* (*U.S.*), to call on, exchange courtesies with. [Ety. dub.]

**gam**, *gam*, (*Scot.*) *n.* a tooth or tusk: the mouth. *gam.* See **gamb**.

**gama-grass**, *gä′ma-gräs*, *n.* a tall N. American forage grass (*Tripsacum dactyloides*). [Perh. Sp. *grama*.]

**gamash**, *gəm-ash′*, *n.* a kind of legging.—Also **gramash** (*Scott*), **gramoche** (*Scott*). [Fr. (now *dial.*) *gamache*, Prov. *garamacha*, apparently from *Ghadames*, famous for leather.]

**gamb, gamb**, *n.* (*her.*) a beast's whole foreleg.—*n.* **gam**, (*slang*) a human leg. [L.L. *gamba*, a leg.]

**gamba**, *gam′ba*, *n.* short for *viola da gamba*: an organ-stop of string-like quality.—*n.* **gam′bist**, a gamba-player.

Neutral vowels in unaccented syllables: *el′ə-mənt*; for certain sounds in foreign words, see p. viii

T.C.D.—18

gambado, *gam-bā'dō*, *n.* a leather covering or boot attached to a saddle. [It. *gamba*, leg.]

gambado, *gam-bā'dō*, *n.* a bound or spring of a horse: a fantastic movement, a caper. [Sp. *gambada*; cf. gambol.]

gambeson, *gam'bi-sən*, *n.* an ancient leather or quilted cloth coat worn under the habergeon. [O.Fr.,—O.H.G. *wamba*, belly.]

gambet, *gam'bit*, *n.* the redshank.

gambetta, *gam'bit*, *n.* the redshank. [It. *gambetta*, ruffe, *gambetta fosca*, spotted redshank.]

gambier, gambir, *gam'bēr*, *n.* an astringent substance prepared from the leaves of *Uncaria gambir*, a rubiaceous climbing shrub of the East Indies, used in tanning and dyeing. [Malay.]

gambit, *gam'bit*, *n.* the offer of a sacrifice for the sake of an advantage in timing or position in the opening stages of a game (gam'bit-pawn', -piece', one so offered; *chess*): an initial move in anything, esp. one with an element of trickery (*fig.*). [Sp. *gambito*—It. *gambetto*, a tripping up—*gamba*, leg.]

gamble, *gam'bl*, *v.i.* to play for money, esp. for high stakes: to engage in wild financial speculations: to take great risks for the sake of possible advantage.—*v.t.* to squander or lose by staking: to take a chance (with *on*).—*n.* a transaction depending on chance.—*n.* gam'bler, one who gambles, esp. one who makes it his business.— gam'bling-house, -hell, a house kept for the accommodation of people who play at games of hazard for money. [Freq. of game.]

gamboge, *gam-bōōzh'*, *-bōj'*, *-bōōj'*, *n.* a yellow gum-resin, chiefly got from *Garcinia morella*, used as a pigment and in medicine.—*adjs.* gambogian (*-bōj'*, *-bōōj'*), gambogic (*-bōj'*). [From *Cambodia*, whence it was brought about 1600.]

gambol, *gam'bl*, *v.i.* to leap: to frisk in sport:— *pr.p.* gam'bolling; *pa.t.* and *pa.p.* gam'bolled.—*n.* a frisk: a frolic. [Formerly *gambold*—O.Fr. *gambade*—It. *gambata*, a kick—L.L. *gamba*, leg.]

gambrel, *gam'brəl*, *n.* the hock of a horse: a crooked stick for hanging a carcass, etc.— gambrel roof, a mansard roof. [O.Fr. *gamberel*; cf. Fr. *gambier*, a hooked stick; connection with cambrel, obscure.]

gambroon, *gam-brōōn'*, *n.* a twilled cloth of worsted and cotton, or linen. [Prob. *Gambrun*, in Persia.]

game, *gām*, *n.* sport of any kind: (in *pl.*) athletic sports: a contest for recreation: a competitive amusement according to a system of rules: the state of a game: manner of playing a game: form in playing: the requisite number of points to be gained to win a game: jest, sport, trick: any object of pursuit: scheme or method of seeking an end, or the policy that would be most likely to attain it: fighting spirit (*arch.*): gallantry (*Shak.*): prostitution (*slang*): thieving (*slang*): the spoil of the chase: wild animals hunted by sportsmen: the flesh of such animals: a flock of swans (formerly of other animals) kept for pleasure.—*adj.* of or belonging to animals hunted as game: having the spirit of a fighting cock (*coll.*): plucky, courageous (*coll.*): having the necessary spirit and willingness for some act (*coll.*).—*v.i.* to gamble.—*adv.* gam'ely. —*n.* game'ness.—*adj.* game'some, playful.—*ns.* game'someness; game'ster, a gambler: a lewd person (*Shak.*): a maker of sport (*Shak.*); gam'ing, gambling.—*adj.* gam'y, having the flavour of game, esp. that kept till tainted: spirited, plucky (*coll.*).—game'-bag, a bag for holding a sportsman's game; game'-bird, a bird hunted for sport; game'-chick'en, game'-cock, a cock of a breed trained to fight; game'-dealer; game fish, a fish that affords sport to anglers—opp. to *coarse fish*; game'keeper, one who has the care of game; game laws, laws relating to the protection of game; game

licence, a licence to kill, or to sell, game; game preserve, a tract of land stocked with game preserved for sport or with protected wild animals; game preserver, one who preserves game on his land; games'manship (*facet.*— *Stephen Potter*), the art of winning games by talk or conduct aimed at putting one's opponent off; game tenant, one who rents the privilege of shooting or fishing over a particular area; gam'ing-house, a gambling-house; gam'ing-tā'ble, a table used for gambling.—big game, the larger animals hunted; die game, to keep up courage to the last; give the game away, to disclose a secret; have a game with, make game of, to make sport of, to ridicule; play a waiting game (see wait); play the game, to act in a fair, sportsmanlike, straightforward manner; red game, grouse; round game, a game, as at cards, in which the number of players is not fixed; the game is not worth the candle (see candle); the game is up, the game is started: the scheme has failed. [O.E. *gamen*, play; O.N. *gaman*, Dan. *gammen*.]

game, *gām*, *adj.* lame. [Origin obscure.]

gamelan, *gam'ə-lan*, *n.* an instrument resembling a xylophone: an orchestra of S.E. Asia consisting of percussion (chiefly), wind, and stringed instruments. [Javanese.]

gamete, *gam'ēt*, *gamēt'*, *n.* a sexual reproductive cell—an egg-cell or sperm-cell.—*adjs.* gam'etal (or *-ēt'*), gametic (*et'* or *-ēt'*).—*ns.* gametangium (*gam-it-an'ji-əm*), a cell or organ in which gametes are formed:—*pl.* gametan'gia; gametogen'esis, the formation of gametes; gamē'tophyte (or *gam'*; Gr. *phyton*, plant), in alternation of generations, a plant of the sexual generation, producing gametes. [Gr. *gametēs*, husband, *gametē*, wife—*gameein*, to marry.]

gamic, *gam'ik*, *adj.* sexual: sexually produced. [Gr. *gamikos*—*gamos*, marriage.]

gamin, *gam'in*, *ga-mē*, *n.* a street Arab, a precocious and mischievous imp of the pavement: —*fem.* gamine, *-mēn*, a girl of a pert, boyish, impish appearance and disposition.—Also *adj.*, boyish or impish.—*n.* gaminerie (*gam'in-ri*, *gam-ēn-(ə-)rē*). [Fr.]

gamma, *gam'ə*, *n.* the third letter of the Greek alphabet (Γ, γ = G, g): as a numeral γ' = 3, ,γ = 3000.—*ns.* gammad'ion, gamma'tion (*-ti-on*), a figure composed of capital gammas, esp. a swastika.—gamma rays, a penetrating radiation given off by radium and other radioactive substances. [Gr.]

gammer, *gam'ər*, *n.* an old woman (*masc.* gaffer). [grandmother, or godmother.]

gammerstang, *gam'ər-stang*, (*dial.*) *n.* a tall, awkward person, esp. a woman: a wanton girl. [Perh. gammer and stang.]

Gammexane, *gam-eks'ān*, *n.* trademark for a powerful insecticide. [γ-hexachlorocyclohexane.]

gammock, *gam'ək*, (*dial.*) *n.* a frolic, fun.—*v.i.* to frolic, to lark.

gammon, *gam'ən*, *n.* backgammon (*arch.*): a double game at backgammon, won by bearing all one's men before one's opponent bears any: patter, chatter, esp. that of a thief's confederate to divert attention (*slang*): nonsense, humbug.— *v.t.* to defeat by a gammon at backgammon: to hoax, impose upon.—*v.i.* to talk gammon: to feign.—*ns.* gamm'oner; gamm'oning. [Prob. O.E. *gamen*, a game.]

gammon, *gam'ən*, *n.* the ham of a hog, esp. when cured, now usually with the adjacent parts of the side. [O.N.Fr. *gambon*, *gambe*, leg.]

gammon, *gam'ən*, (*naut.*) *n.* the lashing of the bowsprit.—*v.t.* to lash (the bowsprit).

gammy, *gam'i*, (*dial.*) *adj.* lame: maimed. [Cf. game (2).]

gamo-, *gam'ō-*, *gam-o'-*, in composition, united, uniting.—*n.* gamogen'esis, sexual reproduction.

—*adjs.* gamopet′alous, with petals united; gamophyll′ous, with perianth leaves united; gamosep′alous, with sepals united; gamotrop′ic.—*n.* gamot′ropism, tendency of gametes to attract each other. [Gr. *gamos*, marriage.]

gamp, *gamp*, (*coll.*) *n.* a large, untidy umbrella: an umbrella.—*adj.* gamp′ish, bulging. [From Mrs Sarah *Gamp*, in Dickens's *Martin Chuzzlewit*.]

gamut, *gam′ət*, *n.* the note G on the first line of the bass stave (*hist. mus.*): Guido of Arezzo's scale of six overlapping hexachords, reaching from that note up to E in the fourth space of the treble (*hist. mus.*): any recognised scale or range of notes: the whole compass of a voice or instrument: the full extent of anything. [From *gamma*, the Greek letter G, adopted when it was required to name a note added below the A with which the old scale began, and *ut*, the Aretinian (q.v.) syllable.]

gan, *gan*, *pa.t.* of gin (5).

ganch, gaunch, *gänsh*, -*ch*, *gönsh*, -*ch*, *v.t.* to impale: to lacerate.—*n.* impaling apparatus: a wound from a boar's tusk. [O.Fr. *gancher*—It. *gancio*, a hook.]

gander, *gan′dər*, *n.* the male of the goose: a simpleton: a man living apart from his wife (*U.S. arch.*).—*n.* gan′derism.—gan′der-moon, -month, the month of a wife's lying-in (*U.S. dial.*); gan′der-mooner, a husband during his gander-moon (*U.S. dial.*).—take a gander at (*slang*), to take a look at. [O.E. *ganra, gandra*; Du. and L.G. *gander*.]

gane, *gän*, *pa.p.* of gae.

Ganesa, *gon-ä′sha*, *n.* the elephant-headed Hindu god of foresight.

gang, *gang*, *n.* a band of roughs or criminals: a number of persons or animals (esp. elk) associating together: a number of labourers working together: a set of boys who habitually play together: a set of tools, etc., used together.—*v.t.* and *v.i.* to associate in a gang or gangs.—*v.t.* to adjust in co-ordination.—*ns.* ganger (*gang′ər*); gang′ing; gang′ster, a member of a gang of roughs or criminals; gang′sterism.—gang mill, a sawmill with gang saws; gang saw, a saw fitted in a frame with others; gangs′man, the foreman of a gang; gang punch (*computers*), to punch (the same information) in a number of cards, or (a number of cards) with the same information; gang up on, to make a concerted attack on; gang up with, to join in the (doubtful activities) of. [O.E. *gang* (Dan. *gang*, Ger. *gang*)—*gangan*, to go.]

gang, *gang*, *v.i.* and *v.t.* (*Scot.*) to go:—*pr.p.* gang′-ing (*rare*); *pa.p.* and *pa.t.* not in use.—*n.* (*Scot.*) the range of pasture allowed to cattle.—*ns.* gang′er, a walker (*Scot.*): a fast horse (*dial.*); gang′rel (*Scot.*), vagrant: a child beginning to walk.—Also *adj.*—gang′board (*naut.*), a gangway, plank, or platform for walking on; gang′-bye (*Scot.*), the go-by; Gang Days (*obs. Scot.*), Rogation Days; gang′plank, a long, narrow, portable platform providing access to and from a ship.—*adj.* gang′-there-out (*arch. Scot.*), vagrant.—gang′way (O.E. *gangweg*), a passage into, out of, or through any place, esp. a ship: a way between rows of seats, esp. the cross-passage about halfway down the House of Commons (ministers and ex-ministers with their immediate followers sitting *above the gangway*).—*interj.* make way: make room to pass. [O.E. *gangan*, to go.]

gangling, *gang′gling*, *adj.* loosely-built, lanky.—Also gangly, *gang′gli*. [Orig. Scot. and Eng. dialect; O.Fr. *gangan*, to go.]

ganglion, *gang′gli-ən*, *n.* a tumour in a tendon sheath: a nerve-centre:—*pl.* gang′lia, gang′-lions.—*adjs.* gang′liar, ganglionic (-*on′ik*), pertaining to a ganglion; gang′liate, -d, provided with ganglion or ganglia; gang′liform. [Gr.]

gangrel. See gang (2).

gangrene, *gang′grēn*, *n.* death of part of the body: the first stage in mortification.—*v.t.* to mortify: to cause gangrene in.—*v.i.* to become gangrenous. —*adj.* gangrenous (*gang′grin-əs*), mortified. [Gr. *gangraina*, gangrene.]

gangue, gang, *gang*, *n.* rock in which ores are embedded. [Fr.,—Ger. *gang*, a vein.]

gangway. See gang (2).

ganister, gannister, *gan′is-tər*, *n.* a hard, close-grained siliceous stone, found in the Lower Coal Measures of N. England. [Origin unknown.]

ganja, *gän′ja*, *n.* an intoxicating preparation, the female flowering tops of Indian hemp. [Hind. *gãjã*.]

gannet, *gan′ət*, *n.* a large white sea-bird of the family Sulidae, with black-tipped wings: a greedy person (*coll.*).—Also solan(d). [O.E. *ganot*, a sea-fowl; Du. *gent*.]

ganoid, *gan′oid*, *adj.* (of fish scales) having a glistening outer layer over bone: (of fishes) belonging to an order Ganoid′ei (-*i-ī*) in some classifications, variously defined, having commonly such scales, including many fossil forms. —*n.* a ganoid fish.—*n.* ganoin (*gan′ō-in*), a calcareous substance, forming an enamel-like layer on ganoid scales. [Gr. *ganos*, brightness, *eidos*, appearance.]

gant, gaunt, *gänt, gönt*, (*Scot.*) *v.i.* to yawn.—*n.* a yawn. [Prob. freq. of O.E. *gānian*, to yawn.]

gantlet. Same as gauntlet (1 and 2).

gantline, *gant′lin*, (*naut.*) *n.* a rope used in a single-block hoist. [Variation of girt or girth and line.]

gantlope, *gant′lōp*. See gauntlet (2).

gantry, *gan′tri*, *n.* a stand for barrels: a platform or bridge for a travelling-crane, railway signals, etc.—Also (in first sense) gauntry (*gön′tri*), gaun′tree.—gantry crane, a crane in bridge form with vertical members running on parallel tracks. [Perh. O.Fr. *gantier*—L. *cantērius*, a trellis—Gr. *kanthēlios*, a pack-ass.]

Ganymede, *gan′i-mēd*, *n.* a cupbearer, potboy, from *Ganymēdēs*, the beautiful youth who succeeded Hebe as cupbearer to Zeus: a catamite (*arch.*).

gaol, etc. See jail, etc.

gap, *gap*, *n.* an opening or breach: a cleft: a passage: a notch or pass in a mountain-ridge: a breach of continuity.—*v.t.* to notch: to make a gap in.—*adjs.* gapp′y, full of gaps; gap′-toothed, with teeth set wide apart. [O.N. *gap.*]

gape, *gāp*, *v.i.* to open the mouth wide: to yawn: to stare with open mouth: to be wide open: to bawl (*Shak.*).—*n.* act of gaping: the extent to which the mouth can be opened: the angle of the mouth: a wide opening, parting, fissure, chasm, or failure to meet: in a fish-hook, the width between the point and the shank: (in *pl.*) a yawning fit: (in *pl.*) a disease of poultry of which gaping is a symptom, caused by a thread-worm, Syngamus, or gape′worm, in the windpipe and bronchial tubes.—*n.* gäp′er, one who gapes: a mollusc (Mya) with shell gaping at each end: a sea-perch (Serranus): an easy catch (*cricket*).— *n.* and *adj.* gāp′ing.—*adv.* gāp′ingly.—gape′seed (*dial.*), an imaginary commodity that the gaping starer is supposed to be seeking or sowing: hence, the act of staring open-mouthed, or the object stared at. [O.N. *gapa*, to open the mouth; Ger. *gaffen*, to stare.]

gapó, *gä-pō′*, *n.* riverside forest periodically flooded. [Port. (*i*)*gapó*—Tupí *igapó, ygapó*.]

gar. See garfish.

gar, *gär*, (chiefly *Scot.*) *v.t.* to cause, to compel:—*pa.t.* and *pa.p.* garred, gart (*Scot.*).—Also (*Spens.*) gar.

garre. [Norse *ger(v)a*; cf. yare.]

garage, *gar′äzh, gə-räzh′, gar′ij*, *n.* a building where motor-vehicles are housed or tended.— *v.t.* to put into or keep in a garage. [Fr.,—*garer*, to secure; cf. ware (3).]

**garam masala**, *gar'əm mas-al'a*, a spice mixture used in making curry.

**Garamond**, *gar'ə-mənd*, *n.* a form of type-face like that designed by Claude *Garamond* (d. 1561).

**Garand rifle**, *gar'ənd* or *gə-rand' ri'fl*, a semi-automatic, gas-operated, clip-fed, .30 calibre, U.S. army rifle; also called **M1**. [After U.S. inventor J. C. *Garand*, b. 1888.]

**garb**, *gärb*, *n.* external appearance (*obs.*): fashion of dress: dress: semblance, appearance (*fig.*).— *v.t.* to clothe, array. [It. *garbo*, grace; of Gmc. origin; cf. **gear**.]

**garb, garbe**, *gärb*, (*her.*) *n.* a sheaf. [O.Fr. *garbe*; of Gmc. origin.]

**garbage**, *gär'bij*, *n.* refuse, as animal offal: any worthless matter: household food and other refuse.—**gar'-bageman** (*U.S.*), a dustman; **garbage can** (*U.S.*), a bin for food-waste, etc. [Of doubtful origin.]

**garble**, *gär'bl*, *v.t.* to cleanse, sift (*arch.*): to select what may serve one's own purpose from, esp. in a bad sense (*arch.*): to misrepresent or falsify by suppression and selection: to mangle, mutilate. —*ns.* **gar'bler**; **gar'bling**. [It. *garbellare*—Ar. *ghirbál*, a sieve, perh.—L.L. *cribellum*, dim. of *cribrum*, a sieve.]

**garboard**, *gär'börd, -börd*, *n.* first range of planks or plates laid on a ship's bottom next to the keel.—Also **garboard strake**. [Du. *gaarboord*.]

**garboil**, *gar'boil*, (*Shak.*) *n.* disorder, uproar [O.Fr. *garbouil*—It. *garbuglio*, conn. with L. *bullire*, to boil.]

**Garcinia**, *gär-sin'i-ə*, *n.* a tropical genus of Gutti-ferae, trees yielding gamboge, kokum butter, and mangosteen. [After the French botanist Laurent *Garcin*.]

**garçon**, *gär-sɔ̃*, *n.* boy: male servant, esp. a waiter in a restaurant. [Fr.]

**gardant** (*her.*). Same as **guardant** (see under **guard**).

**garden**, *gär'dn*, *n.* a piece of ground on which flowers, etc., are cultivated: a pleasant spot: a fertile region: (in *pl.*) used in street-names.— *adj.* of, used in, grown in, a garden or gardens.— *v.i.* to cultivate or work in a garden.—*ns.* **gar'dener**, one who gardens, or is skilled in gardening: one employed to tend a garden; **gar'dening**, the laying out and cultivation of gardens.—**garden city, suburb, village**, a model town, suburb, village, laid out with broad roads, trees, and much garden ground between the houses; **gardener's garters**, variegated garden ribbon-grass; **gar'den-glass**, a bell-glass for covering plants; **gar'den-house**, a summer-house (*Shak.*): a house in a garden: a house kept for sensual indulgence (*obs.*); **garden party**, a social gathering held in the garden of a house; **garden patch; garden path; garden stuff, garden produce** for the table.—**hanging garden**, a garden formed in terraces rising one above another; **lead one up the garden (path)**, to draw one on insensibly, to mislead one; **market garden**, a garden in which vegetables, fruits, etc., are raised for sale; **market gardener**; **philosophers of the garden**, followers of Epicurus, who taught in a garden. [O.Fr. *gardin* (Fr. *jardin*); from Gmc.; cf. **yard** (2), **garth**.]

**Gardenia**, *gär-dē'ni-ə*, *n.* a genus of the madder family, Old World tropical and sub-tropical trees and shrubs, with beautiful and fragrant flowers. [Named from the American botanist Dr Alex. *Garden* (c. 1730-91).]

**garderobe**, *gärd'rōb*, (*hist.*) *n.* a wardrobe or its contents: an armoury: a private room: a privy. [Fr.; cf. **wardrobe**.]

**gardyloo**, *gär'di-lōō*, *interj.* the old warning cry in Edinburgh before throwing slops out of the window into the street.—*n.* the slops so thrown, or the act of throwing. [Recorded in this form by Smollett; supposed to be would-be Fr. *gare*

**de l'eau** for *gare l'eau*, beware of the water; Sterne has *garde d'eau* (*Sent. Journey*), for Paris.]

**gare**, *gär*, (*Scot.*) *adj.* greedy, miserly. [O.N. *gerr*; cf. **yare**.]

**garefowl**, *gär'fowl*, *n.* the great auk. [O.N. *geirfugl*.]

**garfish**, *gär'fish*, *n.* a pike-like fish (Belone) with long slender beaked head: the bony pike, an American ganoid river-fish (Lepidosteus): an Australian half-beak.—Also **gar, gar'pike**. [O.E. *gār*, spear.]

**garganey**, *gär'gə-ni*, *n.* a bird akin to the teal, the summer teal. [It. *garganello*.]

**Gargantuan**, *gär-gan'tū-ən*, *adj.* like or worthy of Rabelais's hero *Gargantua*, a giant of vast appetite: enormous, prodigious (without *cap.*). —*ns.* **Gargan'tuism**; **Gargan'tuist**.

**gargarism**, *gär'gə-rizm*, (*obs.*) *n.* a gargle.—*v.t.* and *v.i.* **gar'garise, -ize**.

**garget**, *gär'git*, *n.* inflammation of the throat or udder in cows, swine, etc.: pokeweed (*U.S.*).

**gargle**, *gär'gl*, *v.t.* and *v.i.* to wash (the throat) preventing the liquid from going down by expelling air against it.—*n.* a liquid for washing the throat. [O.Fr. *gargouiller*—*gargouille*, the throat.]

**gargoyle**, *gär'goil*, *n.* a projecting spout, usually grotesquely carved, from a roof-gutter.—Also **gur'goyle**. [O.Fr. *gargouille*—L.L. *gurguliō*, throat.]

**garial**. See **gavial**.

**garibaldi**, *gar-i-böl'di, -bal'di*, *n.* a woman's loose blouse, an imitation of the red shirts worn by followers of the Italian patriot *Garibaldi* (1807-1882).—**Garibaldi biscuit**, a biscuit with a layer of currants.

**garish**, *gär'ish*, *adj.* showy: gaudy: glaring.—*adv.* **gar'ishly**.—*n.* **gar'ishness**. [Formerly also **gaurish, gawrish**, perh.—obs. **guare**, to stare, perh. a freq. of obs. **gaw**, to stare; cf. O.N. *gā*, to heed.]

**garish**. See **guarish**.

**garjan**. Same as **gurjun**.

**garland**, *gär'lənd*, *n.* a crown (*obs.*): a wreath of flowers or leaves: a book of selections in prose or poetry: ornament, glory (*Spens.*; *Shak.*).— *v.t.* to deck with a garland.—*n.* **gar'landage** (*Tenn.*), a decoration of garlands.—*adj.* **gar'-landless**.—*n.* **gar'landry**, garlands collectively. [O.Fr. *garlande*.]

**garlic**, *gär'lik*, *n.* a bulbous liliaceous plant (*Allium sativum*) having a pungent taste and very strong smell: extended to others of the genus, as **wild garlic** (ramsons).—*adj.* **gar'licky**, like garlic. —**garlic mustard**, a tall cruciferous hedge plant (*Sisymbrium alliaria*) with garlicky smell. [O.E. *gārlēac*—*gār*, a spear, *lēac*, a leek.]

**garment**, *gär'mənt*, *n.* any article of clothing.—*v.t.* to clothe as with a garment.—*adjs.* **gar'mented**; **gar'mentless**.—*n.* **gar'menture**, clothing. [O.Fr. *garniment*—**garnir**, to furnish.]

**garner**, *gär'nər*, *n.* a granary: a store of anything. —*v.t.* to store.—*v.i.* (*Tenn.*) to accumulate. [O.Fr. *gernier* (Fr. *grenier*)—L. *grānārium* (usu. in pl.), a granary.]

**garnet**, *gär'nit*, *n.* a mineral, in some varieties a precious stone, generally red, crystallising in dodecahedra and icositetrahedra, an ortho-silicate of a bivalent and a tetravalent metal.—*adj.* **garnetif'erous**.—**gar'net-paper**, abrasive paper similar to glass-paper; **gar'net-rock**, a rock composed of garnet with hornblende and mag-netite. [O.Fr. *grenat*—L.L. *grānātum*, pome-granate; or L.L. *grānum*, grain, cochineal, red dye.]

**garnet**, *gär'nit*, *n.* a hoisting tackle. [Origin obscure.]

**garnet**, *gär'nit*, *n.* a T-shaped hinge. [Possibly O.Fr. *carne*—L. *cardō, -inis*, hinge.]

**garnierite**, *gär'ni-ər-it*, *n.* a green hydrated nickel magnesium silicate. [Jules *Garnier*, who discovered it in New Caledonia.]

**garnish**, *gär'nish*, *v.t.* to adorn: to furnish: to add herbs, etc., to a dish for flavour or decoration: to garnishee.—*n.* a gift of money, esp. that formerly paid to fellow-prisoners on entering prison or sometimes by workmen on starting a new job: something placed round a principal dish at table, whether for embellishment or relish: decoration, embellishment.—*adj.* **garni** (*gär-nē*), garnished.—*n.* **gar'nishee**, a person warned not to pay money owed to another, because the latter is indebted to the garnisher who gives the warning.—*v.t.* to attach in this way: to serve with a garnishment.—*ns.* **garnishee'ment**; **gar'-nisher**, one who garnishes; **gar'nishing**; **gar'-nishment**, that which garnishes or embellishes: ornament: a garnisheement; **gar'nishry**, adornment; **gar'niture**, that which garnishes or embellishes: trimming: apparel: ornamentation, esp. set of ornaments, e.g. vases: set of armour. [O.Fr. *garniss-*, stem of *garnir*, to furnish (old form *warnir*), from a Gmc. root seen in O.E. *warnian*, Ger. *warnen*; cf. **warn.**]

**garotte.** See **garrotte.**

**garpike.** See **garfish.**

**garran.** Same as **garron.**

**garret**, *gar'it*, *n.* a turret or watch-tower (*obs.*): a room just under the roof of a house.—*adj.* **garr'eted**, provided with garrets: lodged in a garret.—*ns.* **garreteer'** (*arch.*), one who lives in a garret, esp. a poor author.—**garr'et-master**, a cabinet-maker, locksmith, etc., working on his own account for the dealers. [O.Fr. *garite*, a place of safety, *guarir*, *warir*, to preserve (Fr. *guérir*), from the Gmc. root seen in **ware.**]

**garrison**, *gar'i-sn*, *n.* a supply of soldiers for guarding a fortress: a fortified place.—*v.t.* to furnish with troops: to defend by fortresses manned with troops.—**garrison town**, a town in which a garrison is stationed. [O.Fr. *garison—garir*, *guerir*, to furnish; Gmc.; see foregoing article.]

**garron, garran**, *gar'ən*, *n.* a small horse. [Ir. *gearran.*]

**garrot**, *gar'ət*, *n.* a name for various ducks. [Fr.]

**garrot**, *gar'ət*, (*surg.*) *n.* a tourniquet. [Fr.]

**garrotte, garotte**, (*U.S.* **garrote**), *gä-rot'*, *gə-rot'*, *n.* a Spanish mode of putting criminals to death: apparatus for the purpose—originally a string round the throat tightened by twisting a stick, later a brass collar tightened by a screw, whose point enters the spinal marrow.—*v.t.* to execute by the garrotte: suddenly to render insensible by semi-strangulation in order to rob:—*pr.p.* **garrott'ing**, **garott'ing**; *pa.t.* and *pa.p.* **garrott'ed**, **garott'ed**.—*ns.* **gar(r)ott'er**; **gar(r)ott'ing**. [Sp. *garrote*; cf. Fr. *garrot*, a stick.]

**garrulous**, *gar'ōō-ləs*, *-ə-*, *-ū-*, *adj.* talkative: loquacious.—*n.* **garrulity** (*-ōō'li-ti*, or *-ū'*), loquacity.—*adv.* **garr'ulously**.—*n.* **garr'ulousness**. [L. *garrulus—garrire*, to chatter.]

**garter**, *gär'tər*, *n.* a band used to support a stocking: (the badge of) the highest order of knighthood in Great Britain.—*v.t.* to put a garter on: to support, bind, decorate, or surround with a garter.—**gar'ter-snake'**, in N. America, any snake of the genus Eutaenia, nonvenomous, longitudinally striped: in S. Africa applied to two venomous snakes, with black and red rings (see **Elaps**); **gar'ter-stitch'**, a plain stitch in knitting: ribbed knitting made by using plain stitches only.—**Garter King-of-Arms**, the chief herald of the Order of the Garter. [O.Fr. *gartier* (Fr. *jarretière*)—O.Fr. *garet* (Fr. *jarret*), ham of the leg, prob. Celt, as Bret. *gar*, shank of the leg.]

**garth**, *gärth*, *n.* an enclosure or yard: a garden: a weir in a river for catching fish. [O.N. *garthr*, a court; cf. **yard, garden.**]

**garuda**, *gur'ōō-dä*, *n.* a Hindu demigod, part man, part bird. [Sans.]

**garvie**, *gär'vi*, (*Scot.*) *n.* a sprat.—Also **gar'vock**. [Gael. *garbhag* is perh. from Scots.]

**gas**, *gas*, *n.* a substance in a condition in which it has no definite boundaries or fixed volume, but will fill any space: often restricted to such a substance above its critical temperature: a substance or mixture which is in this state in ordinary terrestrial conditions: esp. coal-gas, or other gas for lighting or heating, or one used for attack in warfare: gaslight: laughing gas (see **laughing**): empty, boastful, frothy, garrulous, or pert talk (*coll.*): short for gasoline (petrol) (*U.S.*):—*pl.* **gas'es**.—*v.t.* to supply, attack, poison, light, inflate, or treat with gas: to impose on by talking gas (*U.S.*).—*v.i.* to emit gas: to talk gas:—*pr.p.* **gass'ing**; *pa.t.* and *pa.p.* **gassed**.—*ns.* **gasalier'**, **gaselier'**, a hanging frame with branches for gas-jets (formed on false analogy after *chandelier*); **gasē'ity**.—*adj.* **gaseous** (*gäz'*, *gās'*, *gas'*, *gaz'i-əs*), in a state of gas: of gas.—*ns.* **gas'eousness**; **gasificā'tion**, conversion into gas.—*v.t.* **gas'ify**, to convert into gas.—*ns.* **gas'ogene** (see **gazogene**); **gas'olene, -oline** (*-ə-lēn*), a low-boiling petroleum distillate: the ordinary name for petrol (*U.S.*); **gasom'eter**, a storage tank for gas.—*adjs.* **gasomet'ric, -al**, pertaining to the measurement of gases.—*ns.* **gasom'etry**; **gass'ing**, poisoning by gas: idle talking.—*adj.* **gass'y**, full of gas: abounding in or emitting gas: gaseous: given to vain and boastful talk (*slang*).—**gas'-bag**, a bag for holding gas, esp. in a balloon or airship: a talkative person; **gas'-bott'le**, a steel cylinder for holding compressed gas; **gas'-bracket**, a gas pipe projecting from the wall of a room for lighting purposes; **gas'-buoy**, a floating buoy carrying a supply of gas to light a lamp fixed on it; **gas'-burn'er**, the perforated part of a gas-fitting where the gas issues and is burned; **gas'-car'bon**, a hard dense carbon deposited in coal-gas retorts; **gas chamber, oven**, an enclosed place designed for killing by means of gas; **gas chromatography**, a widely used form of chromatography in which a gas is passed down the column which contains the mixture to be separated and a solvent; **gas'-coal**, any coal suitable for making gas: cannel coal; **gas'-coke'**, coke made in gas retorts; **gas'-condens'er**, an apparatus for freeing coal-gas from tar; **gas'-cook'er**, a gas cooking-stove; **gas'-en'gine**, an engine worked by the explosion of gas; **gas'-escape'**, a leakage of gas; **gas'-field**, a region in which natural gas occurs.—*adj.* **gas'-filled**, filled with gas.—**gas'-fire**, a heating-stove in which gas is burned.—*adj.* **gas'-fired'**, fuelled, or heated, by gases.—**gas'-fitter**, one who fits up the pipes etc. for gas appliances.—*n.pl.* **gas'-fittings**, gas pipes, etc., for lighting and heating by gas.—**gas'-fur'nace**, a furnace of which the fuel is gas; **gas'-globe**, a glass used to enclose and shade a gaslight; **gas'-heat'er**, any heating apparatus in which gas is used; **gas'-hel'met**, a gas-mask in the form of a helmet completely covering the head; **gas'-holder**, a large vessel for storing gas: a gasometer; **gas'-jar**, a jar for collecting and holding a gas in chemical experiments; **gas'-jet**, a jet of gas: a gas-flame: a burner; **gas'-lamp**, a lamp that burns gas; **gas'light**, light produced by combustion of gas: a gas jet, burner, or lamp.—*adj.* of, concerned with, for use by, gaslight.—**gas'-lime**, lime that has been used in purifying gas; **gas'-liquor**, a solution of ammonia and ammonium salts got in gas-making.—*adj.* **gas'-lit**, lighted by gas.—**gas'-main**, a principle gaspipe from the gas-works; **gas'man**, a man employed in gas-making or in the reading of gas-meters; **gas'-man'tle**, a gauze covering, chemically prepared, enclosing a gas-jet, and becoming incandescent when heated; gas'-mask, a respiratory device (covering nose, mouth, and eyes) as a protection against poisonous gases; gas'-mē'ter, an instrument for measuring gas consumed; gas'-mo'tor, a gas-engine; gas'-pipe, a pipe for conveying gas; gas'-plant, dittany (see burning-bush); gas'-po'ker, a gas-jet that can be inserted among fuel to kindle a fire; gas'-retort, a closed heated chamber in which gas is made; gas'-ring, a hollow ring with perforations serving as gas-jets; gas'-shell', a shell that gives off a poisonous gas or vapour on bursting; gas'-stove, an apparatus in which coal-gas is used for heating or cooking; gas'-tank, a reservoir for coal-gas; gas'-tap; gas'-tar, coal-tar.—adj. gas'-tight, impervious to gas.—gas'-trap, a trap in a drain to prevent escape of foul gas; gas'-turbine, a machine consisting of a combustion chamber, to which air is supplied by a compressor and in which the air is heated at constant pressure, and a turbine driven by the hot expanding gases; gas'-water, water through which coal-gas has been passed in scrubbing: gas-, or ammoniacal, liquor; gas'-well, a boring from which natural gas issues; gas'-works, a factory where gas is made.—gas and gaiters, nonsense; gas-discharge tube, any tube in which an electric discharge takes place through a gas; natural gas (see natural); step on the gas (i.e. gasoline), to press the accelerator pedal of a motor-car: 'to speed up. [A word invented by J. B. van Helmont (1577-1644); suggested by Gr. chaos.]

Gascon, gas'kən, n. a native of Gascony: a boaster.—adj. of Gascony.—n. Gasconade', boasting talk.—v.i. to boast extravagantly.—ns. Gasconād'er; Gas'conism, boastfulness. [Fr.]

gash, gash, v.t. to cut deeply into.—n. a deep, open cut. [Formerly garse—O.Fr. garser, to scarify—L.L. garsa, scarification, possibly—Gr. charassein, to scratch.]

gash, gash, (Scot.) adj. talkative.—v.i. to tattle.

gash, gash, (chiefly Scot.) adj. ghastly, hideous.— Also gash'ful, gash'ly.—n. gash'liness.—adv. gash'ly. [Perh. ghastful, ghastly.]

gash, gash, (naut. slang) adj. spare, extra.

gasket, gas'kit, n. a canvas band used to bind the sails to the yards when furled (naut.): a strip of tow, etc., for packing a piston, etc.: a layer of packing material, esp. a flat sheet of asbestos compound, sometimes between thin copper sheets, used for making gas-tight joints between engine cylinders and heads, etc.—Also gas'kin. [Cf. Fr. garcette, It. gaschetta; ety. dub.]

gaskins, gas'kinz, (Shak.) n. Same as galligaskins.

gasolene, gasoline. See under gas.

gasp, gäsp, v.i. to gape for breath: to catch the breath: to desire eagerly.—v.t. to breathe: to utter with gasps.—n. the act of gasping.—ns. gasp'er, one who gasps: a cheap cigarette (slang); gasp'iness.—n. and adj. gasp'ing.—adv. gasp'ingly.—adj. gasp'y.—the last gasp, the point of death. [O.N. geispa, to yawn; cf. geip, idle talk.]

gaspereau, gas'pə-rō, (Canada) n. the alewife (fish). [Fr. gasparot, a kind of herring.]

gast, gäst, v.t. (Shak.) to make aghast, to frighten or terrify.—adj. gastfull (Spens.; see ghastful).— n. gast'ness(e), (obs.; Shak.) dread. [O.E. gæstan; cf. aghast.]

gastero-, gastro-, gastr-, in composition, belly.— n.pl. Gasteromycetes (gas'tar-ō-mī-sē'tēz; Gr. mykētēs, pl. of mykēs, mushroom), an order of fungi—Basidiomycetes with fructification closed till the spores ripen—puffballs, stinkhorns, etc.—n. gas'teropod, gas'tropod (Gr. pous, podos, foot), any member of the Gast(e)rop'oda, a class of asymmetrical molluscs in which the foot is broad and flat, the mantle undivided, the shell in one piece, usually conical—limpets, whelks,

snails, slugs, etc.—adj. gast(e)rop'odous.—ns. gastraea (gas-trē'ə), Haeckel's hypothetical ancestor of the Metazoa, like a gastrula; gastraeum (gas-trē'əm), the under surface of the body, esp. in birds; gastralgia (gas-tral'ji-ə; Gr. algos, pain), pain in the stomach.—adj. gastral'gic.—n. gastrectomy (gas-trek'tə-mi; Gr. ek, out, tomē, cutting), surgical removal of the stomach, or part of it.—adj. gas'tric, belonging to the stomach.—ns. gastri'tis, inflammation of the stomach; gastrocnemius (gas-trok-nē'mi-əs; Gr. knēmē, leg), the muscle that bulges the calf of the leg:—pl. -mii.—adj. gastroenter'ic, gastrointestinal.—ns. gastroenteri'tis, inflammation of the lining of the stomach and intestines; gastroenterol'ogist; gastroenterol'ogy (med.), the study of the stomach and intestines.—adj. gastrointest'inal (or -īn'), of, relating to, consisting of, the stomach and intestines.—n. gastrol'oger.—adj. gastrolog'ical.—ns. gastrol'ogy, cookery, good eating; gastromancy (gas'trō-man-si; Gr. manteiā, sooth-saying), divination by sounds from the belly, i.e. ventriloquism: divination by large-bellied glasses; gastronome (gas'trə-nōm; Gr. nomos, law), gastronomer (-tron'ə-mər), an epicure.—adjs. gastronomic (-nom'ik), -al.—ns. gastron'omist; gastron'omy, the art or science of good eating; gas'trosoph (Gr. sophos, wise), one skilled in matters of eating; gastros'opher; gastros'ophy; gastros'tomy (Gr. stoma, mouth), the making of an opening to introduce food into the stomach; gastrot'omy (Gr. tomē, a cut), the operation of cutting open the stomach or abdomen; gastrula (gas'troō-lə), an embryo at the stage in which it forms a two-layered cup by the invagination of its wall; gastrulā'tion, formation of a gastrula.—gastric fever, typhoid; gastric juice, the acid liquid secreted by the stomach for digestion. [Gr. gastēr, belly.]

gat, gat, (slang) n. a gun, revolver. [gatling.]

gat, gat (B.) pa.t. of get.

gat, gat, n. an opening between sandbanks: a strait. [Perh. O.N.]

gate, gāt, n. a passage into a city, enclosure, or any large opening: a narrow opening or defile: a frame for closing an entrance: an entrance, passage, or channel: the people who pay to see a game: the total amount of money paid for entrance—(also gate'-money): electronic circuit which passes impressed signals when permitted by another independent source of similar signals: the location of a film in a projector, printer or camera when it is being acted on or scanned: an H-shaped series of slots for controlling the movement of a gear-lever in a gear-box.—v.t. to supply with a gate: to punish (students or school-children) by imposing a curfew on or by confining to school precincts for a time.— adjs. gāt'ed, having a gate or gates (often in composition, as hun'dred-gated): punished by gating; gate'less.—n. gāt'ing.—v.i. gate'-crash, to enter without paying or invitation: also fig.— gate'-crasher; gate'-fine, the fine imposed upon the gated for disobedience; gate'-house (archit.), a building over or at a gate; gate'-keeper, gate'-man, one who watches over the opening and shutting of a gate.—adj. gate'-legged, of a table, having a hinged and framed leg that can swing in to let down a leaf.—gate'-post, a post from which a gate is hung or against which it shuts; gate'-tower, a tower beside or over a gate; gate'-vein, the great abdominal vein; gate'way, the way through a gate: a structure at a gate: any entrance.—break gates, at Oxford and Cambridge, to enter college after the prescribed hour; gate of justice, a gate as of a city, temple, etc., where a sovereign or judge sat to dispense justice; ivory gate, gate of horn (or in Spenser silver), in Greek legend and poetical imagery, the gates through which false and true dreams respectively come; **stand in the gate** (*B.*), to occupy a position of defence. [O.E. *geat*, a way; Du. *gat*, O.N. *gat*.]

**gate**, *gāt*, (*Scot.* and *north. dial.*) *n.* a way, path, street (often in street-names, as *Cowgate*, *Kirkgate*): manner of doing. See also **gait**. [O.N. *gata*; Dan. *gade*, Ger. *gasse*.]

**gate**, *gāt*, (*Spens.*) *n.* a Northern form of goat.

**gâteau**, *gät-ō*, *n.* a fancy cake.—**veal gâteau**, minced veal made up like a pudding, and boiled in a shape or mould. [Fr.]

**gather**, *gadh'ər*, *v.t.* to collect: to assemble: to amass: to cull: to pick up: to draw together: in sewing, to draw into puckers by passing a thread through: to learn by inference: to have increase in (e.g. speed).—*v.i.* to assemble or muster: to increase: to suppurate: to make way (*naut.*): to arrange signatures of a book in correct sequence for binding.—*n.* a plait or fold in cloth, made by drawing threads through: (*pl.*) that part of the dress which is gathered or drawn in.—*ns.* **gath'erer**, one who collects, amasses, assembles, or culls: a workman who collects molten glass on the end of a rod preparatory to blowing; **gath'ering**, the action of one who gathers: a crowd or assembly: a narrowing: a number of leaves of paper folded one within another: the assembling of the sheets of a book: a suppurating swelling.—**gath'ering-coal, -peat**, a coal, peat, put into a fire, to keep it alive till morning; **gath'ering-cry**, a summons to assemble for war; **gath'ering-ground**, catchment area.—**gather breath**, to recover wind; **gather ground**, to gain ground; **gather oneself together**, to collect all one's powers, like one about to leap; **gather to a head**, to ripen: to come into a state of preparation for action or effect; **gather way**, to get headway by sail or steam so as to answer the helm. [O.E. *gaderian, gæderian*; (*tō*)*gædere*, together; *geador*, together, *gæd*, fellowship.]

**gatling-gun**, *gat'ling-gun*, *n.* a machine-gun invented by R. J. *Gatling* about 1861.

**gau**, *gow*, *n.* a district.—*n.* **gauleiter** (*gow'lī-tər*) chief official of a district under the Nazi régime: an overbearing wielder of petty authority. [Ger. *gau*, district, *leiter*, leader.]

**gauche**, *gōsh*, *adj.* clumsy: tactless.—*n.* **gaucherie** (*gōsh'ə-rē, -rē'*), clumsiness: social awkwardness. [Fr., left.]

**gaucho**, *gow'chō*, *n.* a cowboy of the pampas, usually of mixed Spanish and Indian descent. [Sp.]

**gaucie, gaucy, gawcy, gawsy**, *gö'si*, (*Scot.*) *adj.* portly, jolly. [Origin unknown.]

**gaud**, *göd*, *n.* a large ornamental bead on a rosary (*obs.*): a prank (*obs.*): an ornament: a piece of finery: showy ceremony: festivity (*obs.*).—*v.i.* (*obs.*) make merry.—*v.t.* to adorn with gauds (*obs.*): to paint, as the cheeks (*Shak.*).—*ns.* **gaudeā'mus** (in Scotland *gow-di-ā'mōōs*; L., let us be glad: opening word of a students' song), a rejoicing, students merrymaking; **gaud'ery**, finery.—*adv.* **gaud'ily**.—*ns.* **gaud'iness**; **gaud'y**, an English college, or other, festival.—*adj.* showy: gay: vulgarly bright.—**gaud'y-day, gaud'y-night**. [In part app.—O.Fr. *gaudir*—L. *gaudēre*, to be glad, *gaudium*, joy; in part directly from L.]

**gaudeamus igitur**, *gö-di-ām'əs ij'-i-tər, gow-de-äm'ōōs ig'i-tōōr*, (L.) let us therefore rejoice.

**gaudium certaminis**, *gö'di-əm sûr-tam'in-is, gow'di-ōōm ker-täm'in-is*, (L.) joy of combat.

**gaudy-green**, *gö'di-grēn*, (*obs.*) *n.* and *adj.* yellowish green. [O.Fr. *gaude*, weld, dyer's-rocket.]

**gauge** (also **gage**), *gāj*, *n.* a measuring apparatus: a standard of measure: a means of limitation or adjustment to a standard: a measurement, as the diameter of a wire, calibre of a tube, width of a row of slates: distance between a pair of wheels or rails: a means of estimate: relative position of a ship (in this sense usu. **gage**; see **lee**, **weather**).—*v.t.* to measure: to estimate: to adjust to a standard.—*v.i.* to measure the contents of casks.—*adj.* **gauge'able**, capable of being gauged.—*ns.* **gaug'er**, one who gauges: an excise man; **gaug'ing**, the measuring of casks holding excisable liquors.—**gauge'-glass**, a tube to show height of water; **gaug'ing-rod**, an instrument for measuring the contents of casks.—*adjs.* **broad'-**, **narr'ow-gauge**, in railroad construction greater or less than standard gauge. in Britain 56½ inches (1·435 metres). [O.Fr. *gauge* (Fr. *jauge*).]

**Gaul**, *göl*, *n.* a name of ancient France: an inhabitant of Gaul.—*adj.* **Gaul'ish**.—*n.* the Celtic (Brythonic) language of the Gauls. [Fr. *Gaule*—L. *Gallia, Gallus*; perh. conn. with O.E. *wealh*, foreign.]

**Gaullist**, *göl'ist*, *n.* a follower of the French soldier and statesman General Charles A. J. M. de *Gaulle* (President of the Fifth Republic 1958-69).—*n.* **Gaull'ism**, principles and policies of Gaullists.

**Gault**, *gölt*, *n.* a series of beds of clay and marl between the Upper and the Lower Greensand; **gault**. brick earth: a brick of gault clay.—*n.* **gault'er**, one who digs gault. [Origin obscure.]

**Gaultheria**, *göl-thē'ri-ə*, *n.* a genus of evergreen aromatic plants of the heath family, including the American wintergreen and salal. [From the Swedish-Canadian botanist Hugues *Gaulthier*.]

**gaum**, *göm*, *v.t.* to smear: to daub: to clog: to handle clumsily (*obs.*).—*n.* a smear: a daub: a shiny lustre as on new varnish: stickiness: a sticky mass.—*adj.* **gaum'y**, dauby. [Ety. dub. perh. variant of **gum** (2).]

**gaum**, *göm*, (*dial.*) *n.* notice, heed, regard, attention: understanding.—*v.t.* to pay attention to, to heed: to understand.—*adj.* **gaum'less**, clumsy: stupid, witless. [O.N. *gaumr*, heed, attention.]

**gaun**, *gön*, Scots for **going** and **go**.

**gaunt**, *gönt*, *adj.* thin: of a pinched appearance: grim.—*adv.* **gaunt'ly**.—*n.* **gaunt'ness**. [Origin obscure.]

**gauntlet**, *gönt'lit*, *n.* the iron glove of armour, formerly thrown down in challenge and taken up in acceptance: a long glove covering the wrist: an extension of a glove covering the wrist.—*adj.* **gaunt'leted**, wearing a gauntlet or gauntlets.—**gaunt'let-guard**, a guard of a sword or dagger, protecting the hand very thoroughly.—**throw down, take up, the gauntlet**, to give, to accept a challenge. [Fr. *gantelet*, dim. of *gant*, glove, of Gmc. origin; cf. Sw. *vante*, a mitten, glove, O.N. *vöttr*, a glove, Dan. *vante*.]

**gauntlet**, *gönt'lit*, **gantlope**, *gant'lōp*, *n.* the military punishment of having to run through a lane of soldiers who strike as one passes.—**run the gauntlet**, to undergo the punishment of the gauntlet: to be exposed to unpleasant remarks or treatment. [Sw. *gatlopp*—*gata*, lane (cf. **gate**, (2)), *lopp*, course (cf. **leap**); confused with **gauntlet** (1).]

**gauntry**. See **gantry**.

**gaup, gawp**, *göp*, (*coll.*) *v.i.* to gape in astonishment.—*ns.* **gaup'us, gawp'us**, a silly person. [From obs. *galp*; cog. with **yelp**.]

**gaur**, *gowr*, *n.* a species of ox inhabiting some of the mountain jungles of India. [Hindustani.]

**gauss**, *gows*, *n.* C.G.S. unit of magnetic flux density (formerly used for other magnetic units).—*adj.* **Gauss'ian**, of or due to Johann Karl Friedrich *Gauss* (1777-1855), German mathematician and physicist.

**gauze**, *göz*, *n.* a thin, transparent fabric: material slight and open like gauze.—*n.* **gauz'iness**.—*adj.* **gauz'y**.—**gauze'-tree**, the lace-bark.—*adj.* **gauze'-**

winged, having gauzy wings. [Fr. *gaze*, dubiously referred to *Gaza* in Palestine.]

**gavage**, *gä-väzh'*, *n.* feeding by stomach-tube: cramming of poultry. [Fr. *gaver*—*gave*, bird's crop.]

**gave**, *gāv*, *pa.t.* of give.

**gavel**, *gā'vl*, a dial. form of gable.

**gavel**, *gav'l*, (*hist.*) *n.* tribute or rent.—**gav'elkind**, a tenure long prevailing in Kent by which lands descended from the father to all sons (or, failing sons, to all daughters) in equal portions, and not by primogeniture; **gav'elman**, a tenant holding land in gavelkind. [O.E. *gafol*, tribute; conn. with *giefan*, to give.]

**gavel**, *gav'l*, *n.* a mallet: a chairman's hammer. **gavelock**, *gav'ə-lək*, *n.* a javelin: a crow-bar. [O.E. *gafeluc*.]

**gavial**, *gā'vi-əl*, **garial**, **gharial**, *gûr'i-əl*, *n.* an Indian crocodile (Gavialis) with very long slender muzzle. [Hindi *ghaṛiyāl*, crocodile.]

**gavotte**, *gä-vot'*, *n.* a dance, somewhat like a country-dance, originally a dance of the Gavots, people of the French Upper Alps: the music for such a dance in common time, often occurring in suites.

**gawd**, *göd*, (*Shak.*) *n.* Same as gaud.

**gawk**, *gök*, *n.* an awkward or ungainly person, esp. from tallness, shyness, or simplicity: one who stares and gapes.—*v.i.* to stare and gape.—*ns.* gawk'ihood; gawk'iness.—*adj.* gawk'y, awkward: ungainly.—*n.* a tall awkward person: a gawk. [Ety. obscure: prob. not Fr. *gauche*, left.]

**gawp**. See gaup.

**gawsy**. Same as gaucie.

**gay**, *gā*, *adj.* lively: bright: sportive, merry: dissipated: of loose life: showy: spotted (*dial.*): homosexual (*slang*): considerable (*Scot.*; usu. *gey*, *gī*): often by hendiadys instead of an adv., as *gey and easy*, easy enough: unduly familiar (*U.S.*):—*compar.* gay'er; *superl.* gay'est.—*adv.* (*Scot.*; *gey*) rather, fairly, considerably.—*n.* gai'ety.—*adv.* gai'ly.—*n.* gay'ness.—*adj.* gay'-some, gladsome.—**gay deceiver**, a libertine: a foam-padded brassière (*slang*); **gay science**, a rendering of *gai saber*, the Provençal name for the art of poetry. [O.Fr. *gai*—perh. O.H.G. *wâhi*, pretty.]

**gayal**, **gyal**, *gi'al*, *n.* an Indian domesticated ox, akin to the gaur, with curved horns. [Hindi.]

**Gay-Lussac's law**. See law (1).

**gay-you**, *gi'ū*, *gā'ū*, *n.* a narrow flat-bottomed Anamese boat with outrigger and masts. [Anamese *ghe hâu*.]

**gaze**, *gāz*, *v.i.* to look fixedly.—*n.* a fixed look: the object gazed at—(*Spens.*) gaze'ment.—*adj.* gaze'-ful (*Spens.*), looking intently.—*n.* gaz'er.—*adj.* gaz'y, affording a wide prospect: given to gazing.—**gaze'-hound**, a hound that pursues by sight; **gaz'ing-stock**, one exposed to public view, generally unpleasantly.—**at gaze**, in the attitude of gazing. [Prob. cog. with obs. *gaw*, to stare; cf. O.N. *gā*, to heed; Sw. dial. *gasa*, to stare.]

**gazebo**, *gə-zē'bō*, *n.* a belvedere. [Ety. dub.]

**gazelle**, **gazel**, *gə-zel'*, *n.* a small antelope (*Gazella Dorcas*) of N. Africa and S.W. Asia, with large eyes, or kindred species. [Fr.,—Ar. *ghazāl*, a wild-goat.]

**gazette**, *gə-zet'*, *n.* a newspaper: (*cap.*) an official newspaper containing lists of government appointments, legal notices, despatches, etc.—*v.t.* to publish or mention in a gazette:—*pr.p.* gazett'ing; *pa.t.* and *pa.p.* gazett'ed.—*n.* gazetteer' (*gaz*-), a geographical dictionary: orig, a writer for a gazette, official journalist.—*v.t.* to describe in gazetteers.—*adj.* gazetteer'ish.—**gazetted officer**, one of a higher grade who is listed in an official gazette.—**appear, have one's name in the Gazette**, to be mentioned in one of the official newspapers, esp. of bankrupts. [Fr.,

—It. *gazzetta*, a small coin; or from It. *gazzetta*, dim. of *gazza*, magpie.]

**gazogene**, *gaz'ə-jēn*, **gasogene**, *gas'*, *n.* an apparatus for making aerated waters. [Fr. *gazogène*—*gaz*, gas, Gr. suff. *-genēs*—root of *gennaein*, to generate.]

**gazon**, **gazoon**, *gə-zōōn'*, *n.* a sod in fortification: used erroneously by Hogg for a compact body of men. [Fr., turf.]

**geal**, *jēl*, *v.t.* and *v.i.* to congeal. [Fr. *geler*.]

**gealous**, **gealousy**, Spenser's spellings of jealous, jealousy.

**gean**, *gēn*, *n.* the European wild cherry. [O.Fr. *guigne*.]

**geanticline**, *jē-an'ti-klīn*, *n.* an anticline on a great scale.—*adj.* geanticli'nal. [Gr. *gē*, earth, and anticline.]

**gear**, *gēr*, *n.* equipment: accoutrements: tackle: clothes: armour: harness: apparatus: a set of tools or a mechanism for some particular purpose: household stuff: possessions: stuff: matter: affair, business, doings (often contemptuous): any moving part or system of parts for transmitting motion, e.g. levers, gear-wheels: connection by means of such parts: the actual gear ratio in use, or the gear-wheels involved in transmitting that ratio, in an automobile gearbox, e.g. first gear (low gear), fourth gear (high gear): working connection: working order: the diameter in inches of a wheel whose circumference equals the distance a bicycle would go for one turn of the pedals.—*v.t.* to harness: to put in gear, as machinery: to connect in gear: to make to work in accordance with requirements of (a project or a larger organisation; *fig.*; with *to*).—*v.i.* to be in gear.—*adj.* (*slang*) unusually good, or (later) very up to date.—*adj.* geared.—*n.* gear'ing, harness: working implements: means of transmission of motion, esp. a train of toothed wheels and pinions.—*adj.* gear'-less.—**gear'-box**, the box containing the apparatus for changing gear; **gear'-case**, a protective case for the gearing of a bicycle, etc.; **gear'-lever**, **-shift**, **-stick**, a device for selecting or engaging and disengaging gears; **gear'-ratio**, the ratio of the driving to the driven members of a gear mechanism; **gear'-wheel**, a wheel with teeth or cogs which impart or transmit motion by acting on a similar wheel or a chain.—*adjs.* **high'-gear**, **low'-gear**, geared to give a high or a low number of revolutions of the driven part relatively to the driving part—also *ns.*—**gear down, up**, to make the speed of the driven part lower, higher, than that of the driving part; **multiplying gearing**, a combination of cog-wheels for imparting motion from wheels of larger to wheels of smaller diameter, by which the rate of revolution is increased; **straight gear**, the name given when the planes of motion are parallel—opposed to **bevelled gear** (see bevel): **three-speed gear, two-speed gear, variable gear**, a contrivance for changing gear at will. See also synchromesh. [M.E. *gere*, prob. O.N. *gervi*; cf. O.E. *gearwe*, O.H.G. *garawi*; yare, gar (vb.).]

**geare**, Spens. for gear, jeer.

**geason**, *gē'zn*, (*obs.*) *adj.* rare (*Spens.*): out of the way: wonderful. [O.E. *gǣne*, *gēsne*, wanting, barren.]

**geat**, *jēt*, *n.* the hole in a mould through which the metal is poured in casting. [jet.]

**gebur**, *gə-bōōr'*, *yə-bōōr'*, (*hist.*) *n.* a tenant-farmer. [O.E. *gebūr*.]

**geck**, *gek*, (*Scot.*) *n.* a dupe: object of scorn: a derisive gesture: scorn.—*v.t.* to mock.—*v.i.* to scoff: to toss the head: to show disdain. [Prob. L.G. *geck*; Du. *gek*, Ger. *geck*.]

**gecko**, *gek'ō*, *n.* any lizard of the genus Gecko or the subclass Gecko'nēs, mostly thick-bodied, dull-coloured animals with adhesive toes and vertebrae concave at both ends. [Malay gēkoq; imit. of its cry.]

ged, ged, (dial.) n. the pike or luce. [O.N. gedda.]

gee, jē, n. the seventh letter of the alphabet (G, g).

gee, gē, (dial.) n. a fit of perversity.

gee, jē, v.i. of horses, to move to the right or to move on.—n. gee'-gee, a child's word for a horse.—v.i. gee up, gee hup, to proceed faster, chiefly used as a command to horses.

gee, jē, (dial.) v.i. to go, to suit, to get on well.

gee, jē, n. a radio-navigation system in which three ground stations A (master), B and C (slave), give for AB and AC two sets of intersecting hyperbolas which, charted, give an equipped aircraft its geographical position over a few hundred miles' range from A. [Ground electronics engineering.]

gee, jē, (U.S.) interj. expressing surprise, sarcasm, enthusiasm, etc.: sometimes used only for emphasis—gee whiz, interj. expressing surprise, admiration, etc. [Perh. Jesus.]

geebung, jē'bung, n. an Australian proteaceous tree (Persoonia) or its fruit. [Native name.]

geese, pl. of goose.

gee-string, jē'string, n. a string or strip worn round the waist and between the legs.—Also G-string. [Origin obscure.]

Geëz, gē-ez', gē'ez, Giz, gēz, n. the ancient language of Ethiopia, a Semitic tongue closely related to Arabic.

geezer, gēz'ər, (slang) n. a queer elderly person: a man. [guiser.]

gefuffle, gə-fuf'l. Form of carfuffle.

gegenschein, gā'gən-shin, n. a glow of zodiacal light seen opposite the sun. [Ger.]

Gehenna, gi-hen'ə, n. the valley of Hinnom, near Jerusalem, in which the Israelites sacrificed their children to Moloch, and to which, at a later time, the refuse of the city was conveyed to be slowly burned: hence hell (N.T.): a place of torment. [Heb. Ge-hinnōm, valley of Hinnom.]

Geiger (-Müller) counter, gī'gər (mül'ər) kown'tər, an instrument for detecting radioactivity by means of the ionising effect of the charged particles and counting the particles mechanically. [Geiger and Müller, German physicists.]

geisha, gā'sha, n. a Japanese girl trained to provide entertainment (as conversation, performance of dances, etc.) for men. [Jap.]

geist, gist, n. spirit, any inspiring or dominating principle. [Ger.]

geit. Same as get, a child, gyte (2).

geitonogamy, gī-tən-og'ə-mi, n. pollination from another flower on the same plant.—adj. geitonog'amous. [Gr. geitōn, neighbour, gamos, marriage.]

gel, jel, n. a jelly-like apparently solid colloidal solution.—v.i. to form a gel:—pr.p. gell'ing; pa.t. and pa.p. gelled.—n. gelā'tion (see separate article). [gelatine.]

gelastic, jel-as'tik, adj. pertaining to or provoking laughter. [Gr. gelastikos—gelaein, to laugh.]

gelatine, gelatin, jel'ə-tēn, -tin, n. colourless, odourless, and tasteless glue, prepared from albuminous substances, e.g. bones and hides, used for food-stuffs, photographic films, glues, etc.—vs.t. gelatinate (ji-lat'i-nāt), gelat'inise, -ize, to make into gelatine or jelly.—vs.i. to be converted into gelatine or jelly.—ns. gelatinā'tion, gelatinisā'tion, -z-.—adj. gelat'inous, resembling or formed into jelly.—blasting gelatine, a violently explosive rubbery substance composed of nitroglycerine and nitrocotton. [Fr.,—It. gelatina, gelata, jelly—L. gelāre, to freeze.]

gelation, jel-ā'shən, n. solidification by cooling: formation of a gel from a sol. [Partly L. gelātiō, -ōnis—gelāre, to freeze; partly gel.]

geld, geld, (hist.) n. a tax.—v.t. to tax. [O.E. geld, gyld, payment; O.N. giald, money: cf. yield.]

geld, geld, v.t. to emasculate, castrate: to spay:

to deprive of anything essential, to enfeeble, to deprive: to expurgate:—pa.t. and pa.p. gelt, geld'ed.—ns. geld'er; geld'ing, act of castrating: a castrated animal, esp. a horse. [O.N. gelda; Dan. gilde.]

gelder(s)-rose. Same as guelder-rose.

gelid, jel'id, adj. icy cold: cold.—adv. gel'idly.—ns. gel'idness, gelid'ity. [L. gelidus—gelū, frost.]

gelignite, jel'ig-nit, n. a powerful explosive used in mining, made from nitroglycerine, nitrocotton, potassium nitrate, and wood-pulp. [gelatine and L. ignis, fire.]

gelliflowre (Spens.). Same as gillyflower.

gelly, jel'i, (Spens.) adj. jellied.

gelosy (Spens.). Same as jealousy.

Gelsemium, jel-sē'mi-əm, n. the so-called yellow or Carolina jasmine, an American climbing-plant of the Loganiaceae.—ns. gel'semine (-səm-ēn) and gelseminine (-sem'), two alkaloids yielded by its rhizome and rootlets. [It. gelsomino, jasmine.]

gelt, gelt, pa.t. and pa.p. of geld.

gelt, gelt, (Spens.) n. a madman. [Ir. geilt.]

gelt, gelt, (slang) n. money: profit. [Ger. and Du. geld.]

gelt, gelt, an obsolete erroneous form of geld (1): (Spens.) apparently for gilt.

gem, jem, n. any precious stone, esp. when cut: anything extremely admirable or flawless: a size of type smaller than diamond: a bud (obs.).—v.t. (obs.) to bud: to adorn with gems: to bespangle:—pr.p. gemm'ing; pa.t. and pa.p. gemmed.—adj. gemm-ous (-i-əs), pertaining to gems: like a gem.—ns. gemm'ery, gems generally; gemmol'ogist, one with special knowledge of gems; gemmol'ogy, science of gems.—adj. gemm'y, full of gems: brilliant.—gem'-cutting, the art of cutting and polishing precious stones; gem'-engraving, the art of engraving figures on gems; gem'stone. [O.E. gim; O.H.G. gimma—L. gemma, a bud; later remodelled on L. or reintroduced.]

Gemara, gə-mä'rə, n. the second part of the Talmud, consisting of commentary and complement to the first part, the Mishna. [Aramaic, completion.]

gematria, gə-mä'tri-ə, n. a cabbalistic method of interpreting the Hebrew Scriptures by interchanging words whose letters have the same numerical value when added. [Rabbinical Heb. gēmatriyā—Gr. geōmetriā, geometry.]

gemel, jem'əl, n. a twin (obs.): a gimmal: a hinge (obs.): a pair of bars placed close together (her.).—gem'el-ring (see gimmal). [O.Fr. gemel (Fr. jumeau)—L. gemellus, dim. of geminus, twin.]

geminate, jem'in-āt, v.t. to double.—adj. (bot.) in pairs.—n. geminā'tion, a doubling.—n.pl. Gemini (jem'in-ī), the twins, a constellation containing the two bright stars Castor and Pollux: the third sign of the zodiac.—n. Gem'inid, a meteor of a swarm whose radiant is in the constellation Gemini.—adj. gem'inous (bot.), double, in pairs.—n.pl. gem'iny (Shak.), a pair, esp. of eyes.—interj. expressing surprise—spelt also gemini, gemony, jiminy. [L. geminus, twin.]

gemma, jem'ə, n. a plant bud, esp. a leaf-bud (rare): a small multicellular body produced vegetatively, capable of separating and becoming a new individual (bot.): a bud or protuberance from the body that becomes a new individual (zool.):—pl. gemm'ae (-ē).—adjs. gemmā'ceous, bud-like: relating to gemmae; gemm'ate, having or reproducing by buds or gemmae.—v.t. to deck with gems.—v.i. to reproduce by gemmae.—n. gemmā'tion, budding or gemma-formation.—adj. gemm'ative, pertaining to gemmation; gemmif'erous, bearing gemmae; gemmip'arous, reproducing by gemmae.—ns. gemmūlā'tion, formation of gemmules; gemm'ule, Darwin's hypothetical particle produced by each part of

the body, as a vehicle of heredity: a plumule (*obs.*): an internal bud in sponges.—gemm′a-cup, a liverwort cupule. [L. *gemma*, a bud.]
gemman, *jem′ən*, *n.* a corr. of gentleman:—*pl.* gemmen (*jem′ən*). [gentleman.]
gemmologist, -ology. See gem.
gemmy. See jemmy (2).
gemot, *gə-mōt′*, *yə-mōt′*, (*hist.*) *n.* a meeting or assembly. [O.E. *gemōt*; cf. moot.]
gemsbok, hhemz′bok (S. Afr.), *gemz′bok*, *n.* (*Oryx gazella*) S. African antelope, about size of stag, with long straight horns. [Du., male chamois—Ger. *gemsbock*.]
gemütlich, *gə-müt′lehh*, (Ger.) *adj.* amiable: comfortable.—*n.* gemütlichkeit (*-kīt*), kindness: comfort.
gen, jen, (*slang*) *n.* general information: the lowdown or inside information.—gen up, to learn.
gena, *jē′nə*, *n.* the cheek or side of the head.—*adj.* gē′nal. [L. *gēna*.]
genappe, *jə-nap′*, *n.* a smooth worsted yarn used with silk in fringes, braid, etc. [*Genappe* in Belgium.]
gendarme, *zhä-därm′*, *n.* originally man-at-arms, horseman in full armour: since the French Revolution one of a corps of French military police: a similar policeman elsewhere: a rockpillar on a mountain:—*pl.* gen′darmes′, occasionally gens′darmes′.—*n.* gendarm′erie (*-ə-rē*), an armed police force. [Fr. *gendarme*, sing. from pl. *gens d'armes*, men-at-arms—*gens*, people, *de*, of, *armes*, arms.]
gender, *jen′dər*, *n.* kind (*obs.*): a distinction of words roughly answering to sex (*gram.*): loosely or jocularly, sex. [Fr. *genre*—L. *genus*, kind.]
gender, *jen′dər*, (*arch.*) *v.t.* to beget: to generate.—*v.i.* to copulate. [Fr. *gendrer*—L. *generāre*.]
gene, *jēn*, (*biol.*) *n.* one of the units of DNA, arranged in linear fashion on the chromosomes, responsible for passing on specific characteristics fro.n parents to offspring.—*adj.* gēn′ic, of or relating to a gene.—*ns.* gēn′ome, the full set of chromosomes of an individual: the total number of genes in such a set; gēn′otype, genetic or factorial constitution of an individual: group of individuals all of which possess the same genetic constitution.—*adj.* genotypic (*-tip′ik*). [Gr. *genos*, a race.]
gene, Fr. gêne, *zhen*, *n.* embarrassment.
genealogy, *jē-ni-al′ə-ji*, or *jen′i-*, *n.* history of the descent of families: the pedigree of a particular person or family.—*adj.* genealogical (*-ə-loj′i-kl*).—*adv.* genealog′ically.—*v.i.* geneal′ogise, -ize, to investigate or treat of genealogy.—*n.* geneal′ogist, one who studies or traces genealogies or descents.—genealogical tree, a table of descent in the form of a tree with branches. [Gr. *geneālogiā—geneā*, race, *logos*, discourse.]
genera, *pl.* of genus.
general, *jen′ə-rəl*, *adj.* relating to a genus or whole class: including various species: not special: not restricted or specialised: relating to the whole or to all or most: universal: nearly universal: common: prevalent: widespread: public: vague: (after an official title, etc.) chief, of highest rank, at the head of a department (as director-general, postmaster-general): socially accessible and familiar with all (*obs.*).—*adv.* (*Shak.*) generally.—*n.* the total: the most part, majority: an officer who is head over a whole department: a general officer: the chief commander of an army in service: one skilled in leadership, tactics, management: in the R.C. Church the head of a religious order, responsible only to the Pope: the head of the Salvation Army: a general servant: the public, the vulgar (*Shak.*).—*v.t.* to act as general of.—*n.* generâl′e (L. *gen-er-ä′le*), general principles, esp. in *pl.* generâl′ia.—*adj.* gen′eralisable, -z-.—*n.* generalisâ′tion, -z-.—*v.t.* gen′eralise, -ize, to

make general: to include under a general term: to reduce to a general form: to comprehend as a particular case within a wider concept, proposition, definition, etc.: to represent or endow with the common characters of a group without the special characters of any one member: to bring to general use or knowledge: to infer inductively.—*v.i.* to make general statements: to form general concepts: to depict general character: to reason inductively.—*ns.* generaliss′imo (It. *superl.*), supreme commander of a great or combined force; generalist, one whose knowledge and skills are not restricted to one particular field: opp. of *specialist*; general′ity.—*adv.* gen′erally, in a general or collective manner or sense: in most cases: upon the whole.—*n.* gen′eralship, the position of a military commander: the art of manipulating armies: tactical management and leadership.—General Assembly (see assemble); general election, an election of all the members of a body at once; general epistles (see catholic); general line, the party line; general officer, an officer above rank of colonel; general post, formerly, dispatch of mail to all parts, opp. to local *twopenny* or *penny post*: the first morning delivery of letters: a general change of positions, etc. (from a parlour game); general practitioner, a physician who devotes himself to general practice rather than to special diseases; general principle, a principle to which there are no exceptions within its range of application.—*adj.* general-purpose, generally useful, not restricted to a particular function.—general servant, one whose duties embrace domestic work of every kind; General Synod (see synod).—General Certificate of Education, in secondary education in England and Wales, a certificate obtainable at ordinary, advanced, and scholarship levels for proficiency in one or more subjects; general post office, formerly, an office receiving letters for the general post: the head post office of a town or district; in general, as a generalisation: mostly, as a general rule. [O.Fr.—L. *generālis—genus*.]
generate, *jen′ər-āt*, *v.t.* to produce: to bring into life or being: to evolve: to originate: to trace out (*geom.*).—*adj.* gen′erable, that may be generated or produced.—*ns.* gen′erant, a begetter, producer, parent: a line, point, or figure that traces out another figure by its motion (*geom.*); generâ′tion, production or originating: a single stage in natural descent: the people of the same age or period: descendants removed by the same number of steps from a common ancestor: the ordinary time interval between the births of successive generations—usu. reckoned at 30 or 33 years: offspring, progeny, race: (in *pl.*) genealogy, history (*B.*); generâ′tionism, traducianism.—*adj.* gen′erative, having the power of, or concerned with, generating or producing.—*n.* gen′erâtor, begetter or producer: apparatus for producing gases, etc.: apparatus for turning mechanical into electrical energy: a fundamental tone (*mus.*):—*fem.* gen′erātrix, a mother: a generator: a generant (*geom.*).—generating station, a plant where electricity is generated; generation gap, a lack of communication and understanding between one generation and the next.—alternation of generations (see alternate); motion generative (*Shak.*), a male puppet: or perh. one who is a mere puppet so far as engendering is concerned; spontaneous generation, the origination of living from non-living matter. [L. *generāre*, *-ātum—genus*, a kind.]
generic, -al, generically. See genus.
generous, *jen′ə-rəs*, *adj.* of a noble nature: courageous (*obs.*): liberal: bountiful: invigorating in its nature, as wine: nobly born (*obs.*): ample.—*adv.* gen′erously.—*ns.* gen′erousness, generos′ity, nobleness or liberality of nature: nobility

of birth (*arch.*). [L. *generōsus*, of noble birth—*genus*, birth.]

genesis, *jen'i-sis*, *n.* generation, creation, or production: (*cap.*) the first book of the Bible:—*pl.* (L.) gen'esēs.—*adjs.* Genesiac (*ji-nē'si-ak*), -al, Genesit'ic, pertaining to Genesis. [Gr.]

genet. See jennet.

genet, genette, *jen'it, ji-net'*, *n.* a carnivorous animal (Genetta) allied to the civet: its fur, or an imitation. [Fr. *genette*—Sp. *gineta*—Ar. *jarnait*.]

genethliac, *ji-neth'li-ak, adj.* relating to a birthday or to the casting of nativities.—*n.* a caster of nativities: a genethliacon.—*adj.* genethliacal (*jen-ith-li'a-kl*).—*adv.* genethli'acally.—*n.* genethli'acon, a birthday ode.—*adjs.* genethlialog'ic, -al.—*n.* genethlial'ogy (Gr. *genethliālogiā*), the art of casting nativities. [Gr. *genethlē*, birth.]

genetic, -al, *ji-net'ik, al, adjs.* pertaining to origin.—*adv.* genet'ically.—*ns.* genet'icist (-*i-sist*), a student of genetics; genetics (treated as *sing.*), the branch of biology dealing with heredity and variation: inherited characteristics of an organism: origin: development.—genetic code, the system by which genes pass on instructions that ensure transmission of hereditary characters; genetic engineering, a biological science whose ultimate aim is to control heredity defects by the modification or elimination of certain genes; genetic spiral, line through insertions of successive leaves on a stem. [genesis.]

genetrix. See genitor.

genette. See genet (2).

geneva, *ji-nē'va, n.* a spirit distilled from grain and flavoured with juniper berries, made chiefly in the Netherlands. Also called *Hollands*; see gin.—*n.* genevrette (*jen-av-ret'*), a wine made from wild fruits flavoured with juniper-berries. [O.Du. *genever*, O.Fr. *genevre*—L. *jūniperus*, juniper; confused with town of *Geneva*.]

Genevan, *ji-nē'van, adj.* pertaining to *Geneva.*—*n.* an inhabitant of Geneva: an adherent of Genevan or Calvinistic theology.—*adj.* and *n.* Genevese (*jen'i-vēz*).—*n.* Genē'vanism, Calvinism.—Geneva Bible, a version of the Bible, long popular, produced by English exiles at Geneva in 1560; Geneva Convention, an international agreement of 1865 providing for the neutrality of hospitals, and the security of sanitary officers, naval and military chaplains; Geneva cross, a red cross on a white ground displayed for protection in war of persons serving in hospitals, etc.; Geneva gown, the dark, long preaching gown of the early Geneva reformers, and still the common form of pulpit-gown among Presbyterians; Genevan theology, so called from Calvin's residence in Geneva and the establishment of his doctrines there.

genevrette. See geneva.

genial, *jē'ni-al, adj.* pertaining to marriage and generation (*arch.*): favouring growth: cheering: kindly: sympathetic: healthful.—*v.t.* gē'nialise, -ize, to impart geniality to.—*ns.* gēniality (-*al'i-ti*), gē'nialness.—*adv.* gē'nially. [L. *geniālis* (-*genius*, the tutelary spirit.]

genial, *ja-ni'al, adj.* of or pertaining to the chin. [Gr. *geneion*, chin—*genys*, under jaw.]

genic. See gene (1).

geniculate, -d, *ja-nik'ū-lāt, -id, adjs.* bent like a knee: jointed: knotted.—*v.t.* genic'ulate, to form joints in.—*n.* genicula'tion. [L. *geniculātus*—*geniculum*, a little knee—*genū*, the knee.]

genie, *jē'ni, n.* a jinnee (see jinn). [Fr. *génie*—L. *genius*, adopted because of its similarity to the Arabic word.]

genipap, *jen'i-pap, n.* a large West Indian tree (*Genipa americana*; Rubiaceae): its excellent fruit. [From Tupí.]

Genista, *ja-nis'ta, n.* a genus of shrubby, papilionaceous plants, with simple leaves and yellow flowers—green-weed and petty whin. [L. *genista*, broom.]

genital, *jen'i-tal, adj.* belonging to generation or the act of producing.—*n.pl.* gen'itals (also genitā'lia), the organs of generation, esp. external.—*adj.* genito-ūr'inary, pertaining to genital and urinary organs or functions. [L. *genitālis*—*gignēre, genitum,* to beget.]

genitive, *jen'i-tiv, adj.* pertaining to generation (*obs.*): of or belonging to case expressing origin, possession, or similar relation (*gram.*).—*n.* (*gram.*) the genitive case: a word in the genitive case.—*adj.* geniti'val.—*advs.* geniti'vally, gen'itively. [L. *genitivus* (-*gignēre, genitum,* to beget) for Gr. *genikē* (*ptōsis*), properly, generic (case)—*genos*, a class.]

genitor, *jen'i-tar, n.* a father: a parent: a progenitor:—*fem.* gen'etrix, gen'itrix.—*n.* gen'-iture, engendering: birth. [L.]

genius, *jēn'yas*, or *jē'ni-as, n.* the special inborn faculty of any individual: special taste or natural disposition: consummate intellectual, creative, or other power, more exalted than talent: one so endowed: a good or evil spirit, supposed to preside over every person, place, and thing, and esp. to preside over a man's destiny from his birth: a person who exerts a power, influence (whether good or bad) over another: prevailing spirit or tendency: type or generic exemplification:—*pl.* ge'niuses; in sense of spirit, genii (*jē'ni-ī*). [L. *genius*—*gignēre, genitum,* to beget.]

genius loci, *jē'ni-as lō'sī, gen'i-ōōs lo'kē,* (L.) the spirit of the place.

genizah, *ga-nēz'a, n.* a room adjoining a synagogue for the safe-keeping of old or damaged books, documents or valuables. [Heb.]

gennet. See jennet.

genoa, Genoa, *jen'ō-a, ja-nō'a,* (*naut.*) *n.* a large jib which overlaps the mainsail.—Genoa cake, a rich cake containing fruit, with almonds on the top. [Genoa in Italy.]

genocide, *jen'ō-sīd, n.* deliberate extermination of a race or other group: one who exterminates, or approves extermination of, a race, etc.—*adj.* genocid'al. [Gr. *genos*, race, and L. *caedēre,* to kill.]

Genoese, *jen'ō-ēz,* or *-ēz', n.* Genovese, -*vēz,* adjs. relating to Genoa.—*ns.* an inhabitant, citizen, or native of Genoa:—*pl.* Genoese, Genovese. [L. *Genua,* It. *Genova,* Genoa.]

genotype. See gene.

genouillère, *zha-nōō-yer, n.* the knee-piece in armour. [Fr.]

genre, *zhä-r', n.* kind: a literary species: a style of painting scenes from familiar or rustic life.—Also *adj.* [Fr.,—L. *genus.*]

Genro, *gen-rō', n.* the Japanese Elder Statesmen. [Jap.]

gens, *jenz* (L. *gāns*), *n.* in ancient Rome, a clan including several families descended from a common ancestor: a tribe:—*pl.* gen'tēs.—*adj.* gea'-tile (q.v.).—gens togata, the toga-wearing nation, i.e. the Romans. [L. *gēns, gentis.*]

gens, *zhā,* (Fr.) people; gens de bien, *da byē,* honest, respectable people; gens de condition, *da kō-dēs-yō,* people of rank; gens d'église, *dā-glēz,* churchmen; gens de lettres, *da letr',* men of letters; gens de loi, *da lwa,* lawyers; gens de guerre, *da ger,* military men; gens de peu, *da po,* people of humble condition; gens du monde, *dü mōd,* people of fashion.

gent, *jent,* (Spens.) *adj.* noble: gentle. [O.Fr.,—L. *genitus,* born.]

gent, *jent, n.* (vulg. or facetious) abbrev. of gentleman: one who apes the gentleman:—*pl.* gents.—*n.* gents', men's public lavatory.

genteel, *jan-tēl', adj.* well-bred: graceful in manners or in form: fashionable: now used mainly with mocking reference to a standard of obsolete

snobbery or false refinement.—*adj.* genteel'ish.—
*n.* genteel'ism, a would-be refined substitute for
the right word or phrase.—*adv.* genteel'ly.—*n.*
genteel'ness. [Fr. *gentil*—L. *gentilis*; see gentle.]
gentian, *jen'shan*, any plant of the genus Gentiana,
herbs, usually blue-flowered, abounding chiefly
in alpine regions, typical of the family Gentianā'-
ceae (sympetalous dicotyledons with corolla
twisted in bud and unilocular ovary): the root
and rhizome of the yellow gentian used as a tonic
and stomachic.—*n.* gentianell'a, a name for
several species of gentian, esp. *Gentiana acaulis*,
with deep-blue flowers.—gentian violet, a
mixture of three dyes, methyl rosaniline, methyl
violet, and crystal violet, which is antiseptic and
bactericidal. [L. *gentiāna*, acc. to Pliny from
*Gentius*, king of Illyria, who introduced it in
medicine (2nd cent. B.C.).]
Gentile, gentile, *jen'til*, *n.* anyone not a Jew (*B.*), or
not a Christian (now *rare*), or not a Mormon
(*U.S.*).—*adjs.* gentile, of or belonging to a *gens*
or clan: belonging to the Gentiles: denoting a
race or country (*gram.*); gentilic (*-til'ik*), tribal;
gen'tilish, heathenish.—*n.* gen'tilism (*-til-*, or
*-til-*), paganism.—*adjs.* gentilitial (*jen-ti-lish'l*),
gentili'tian, gentili'tious, pertaining to a gens.
[L. *gentilis*—*gēns*, a nation, clan.]
gentilhomme, *zhä-tē-yom*, (Fr.) a nobleman: a
gentleman.
gentle, *jen'tl*, *adj.* well-born (*arch.*): mild and
refined in manners: mild in disposition or action:
amiable: soothing: moderate: gradual.—*v.t.* to
ennoble (*arch.*): make gentle: handle gently.—
*n.* one well born (*arch.*): a trained falcon: hence
a peregrine falcon (*masc.* ter'cel-gen'tle; *fem.*
fal'con-gen'tle): a soft maggot used as a bait
in angling.—*n.* gentilesse (*-til-es'*), quality of
being gentle, courtesy.—*v.t.* gen'tilise, -ize, to
raise to the class of gentleman.—*n.* gentil'ity,
good birth or extraction: good breeding:
politeness of manners: genteel people: marks of
gentility.—*ns.* gen'tlehood, position or character
attaching to gentle birth; gen'tleness; gen'tle-
nesse (*obs.*), same as gentilesse.—gentle craft,
shoemaking: angling.—*n.pl.* gen'tlefolk, people
of good family.—*adj.* gen'tle-heart'ed, having a
gentle or kind disposition.—gen'tleman, a man
of good birth or high social standing: one who
without a title bears a coat of arms (*hist.*):
more generally every man above the rank of
yeoman, including the nobility (*hist.*): a man
of refined manners: a well-to-do man of no
occupation: a man of good feeling and instincts,
courteous and honourable: a polite term used
for man in general: a body-servant (*Shak.*):—*pl.*
gen'tlemen—also a word of address:—*fem.*
gen'tlewoman, a personal attendant on a lady of
rank (*hist.*): a woman of quality, or of good
breeding, a lady (*old-fashioned*):—*pl.* gen'tle-
women.—Gen'tleman-at-arms, a member of the
royal bodyguard, instituted in 1509, and now
composed of military officers of service and distinction only; gen'tleman-cadet', a student in a
military college; gen'tleman-comm'oner, (*formerly*) at Oxford and Cambridge, undergraduate
with special privileges; gentleman farmer, a landowner who lives on his estate superintending
the cultivation of his own soil: a farmer who
deputes the work of his farm to a farm manager
and other staff; gen'tlemanhood, gen'tlemanship,
the condition or character of a gentleman.—
*adjs.* gen'tlemanlike, like or characteristic of a
gentleman; gen'tlemanly, befitting a gentleman:
well-bred, refined, generous.—gen'tlemanliness;
gentleman's (*-men's*) agreement, an agreement
resting on honour, not on formal contract;
gentleman's gentleman, a valet; gentleman usher
(*pl.* gentlemen ushers), a gentleman who serves as
an usher at court, or as an attendant on a person
of rank; gentle reader, courteous reader, an old-

fashioned phrase common in the prefaces of
books.—*adj.* gen'tlewomanly, like a refined and
well-bred woman.—*n.* gen'tlewomanliness.—
Gentleman of the Chapel Royal, a lay singer who
assists the priests in the choral service of the
royal chapel. [O.Fr. (Fr.) *gentil*—L. *gentilis*,
belonging to the same *gens* or clan, later, well-
bred; see genteel.]
Gentoo, *jen-tōō'*, *n.* Telugu, a Telugu-speaker,
a pagan of India, a Hindu (*hist.*): (without *cap.*)
a Falkland Island penguin.—Also *adj.* [Port.
*gentio*, a Gentile.]
gentry, *jen'tri*, *n.* the class of people next below the
rank of nobility: people of a particular, esp. an
inferior, stamp (*coll.*): rank by birth: the rank of
gentleman: good manners and courtesy (*Shak.*).
—*n.* gen'trice (*-tris*), gentle birth: good breeding.
[O.Fr. *genterise*, *gentelise*, formed from adj.
*gentil*, gentle.]
genty, *jen'ti*, (*Scot.*) *adj.* neat, dainty: graceful.
genuflect, *jen'ū-flekt*, *v.i.* to bend the knee in
worship or respect.—*n.* genūflex'ion (also genū-
flec'tion). [L. *genū*, the knee, *flectēre*, *flexum*, to
bend.]
genuine, *jen'ū-in*, *adj.* natural: native: not
spurious: real: pure: sincere.—*adv.* gen'uinely.
—*n.* gen'uineness. [L. *genuīnus—gignĕre*, to
beget.]
genus, *jē'nəs*, *n.* a taxonomic group of lower rank
than a family, consisting of closely related species,
in extreme cases of one species only (*biol.*): a
class of objects comprehending several subordinate species (*log.*):—*pl.* genera (*jen'ə-ra*).—
*adjs.* generic, -al (*ji-ner'ik*, *-al*), general, applicable to any member of a group or class.—*adv.*
gener'ically.—generic name (*biol.*), the name of
the genus, placed first in naming the species,
thus *Equus caballus* (horse), *Equus asinus* (ass),
*Equus zebra*, etc., are species of the genus Equus,
and Equus is the generic name. [L. *gĕnus*,
*generis*, birth; cog. with Gr. *genos*.]
geo, gio, *gyō*, (*Orkney*, *Shetland*) *n.* a gully, creek.
[O.N. *gjá*.]
geo-, *jē'ō-*, in composition, of the earth. [Gr.
*gē*, the earth.]
geocarpy, *jē-ō-kär'pi*, *n.* production, or ripening,
of fruit underground.—*adj.* geocarp'ic. [Gr. *gē*,
earth, *karpos*, fruit.]
geocentric, *jē-ō-sen'trik*, *adj.* having the earth for
centre: as viewed or reckoned from the centre
of the earth (*astron.*): taking life on earth as the
basis for evaluation.—Also geocen'trical.—*adv.*
geocen'trically.—*n.* geocen'tricism (*-sizm*), belief
that the earth is the centre of the universe. [Gr.
*gē*, the earth, *kentron*, point, centre.]
geochemistry, *jē-ō-kem'is-tri*, *n.* the chemistry of
the crust of the earth.—*adj.* geochem'ical.—*adv.*
geochem'ically.—*n.* geochem'ist. [geo-.]
geochronology, *jē-ō-kron-ol'ə-ji*, *n.* the science of
measuring geological time.—*adj.* geochrono-
log'ical.—*n.* geochronol'ogist. [geo-.]
geode, *jē'ōd*, *n.* a rock cavity lined with crystals
that have grown inwards (*geol.*): a rounded
hollow nodule of ironstone (*mining*).—*adj.*
geōd'ic. [Fr. *géode*—Gr. *geōdēs*, earthy—*gē*,
earth, *eidos*, form.]
geodesy, *jē-od'i-si*, *n.* earth measurement on a large
scale: surveying with allowance for the earth's
curvature.—*adjs.* geodesic (*jē-ō-des'ik*, *-dēs'ik*),
-al, geodet'ic, -al, pertaining to or determined by
geodesy.—*n.* geod'esist, one skilled in geodesy.—
geodesic dome, a light strong dome made by
combining a grid of triangular or other straight-
line elements with a section of a sphere; geodesic
or geodetic (line), the shortest line on a surface
between two points on it; geodetic surveying,
geodesy, surveying large areas with allowance
for the earth's curvature. [Gr. *geōdaisiā—gē*,
the earth, *daisis*, division.]
geodynamics, *jē-ō-dī-nam'iks*, *n.* the study of the

dynamic processes and forces within the earth.—*adjs.* geodynam'ic(al). [geo-.]

geognosy, *jē-og'nə-si*, *n.* knowledge of the general structure, condition, and materials of the earth.—Also (*rare*) geognosis (*jē-əg-nō'sis*).—*n.* gē'ognost.—*adjs.* gēognostic (*-nos'tik*), -al.—*adv.* gēognost'ically. [Fr. *géognosie*—Gr. *gē*, the earth, *gnōsis*, knowledge.]

geogony, *jē-og'ə-ni*, *n.* the science or theory of the formation of the earth.—Also geogeny (*-oj'*).—*adj.* geogonic (*jē-ō-gon'ik*). [Gr. *gē*, the earth, *gonē*, generation.]

geography, *jē-og'rə-fi*, *n.* the science of the surface of the earth and its inhabitants: a book containing a description of the earth.—*n.* geog'rapher.—*adjs.* geographic (*jē-ō-graf'ik*), -al.—*adv.* geograph'ically.—geographical distribution (see distribution); geographical mile (see mile).—physical, political geography (see physic, politic). [Gr. *geōgraphiā*—*gē*, earth, *graphein*, to write.]

geoid, *jē'oid*, *n.* the figure of the earth's mean sea-level surface assumed to be continued across the land, approximately an oblate ellipsoid of revolution.—*adj.* geoid'al. [Gr. *geōdēs, geoeidēs*, earth-like—*gē*, earth, *eidos*, form.]

geolatry, *jē-ol'ə-tri*, *n.* earth-worship. [Gr. *gē*, earth, *latreiā*, worship.]

geology, *jē-ol'ə-ji*, *n.* the science relating to the history and development of the earth's crust, with its successive floras and faunas.—*ns.* geologian (*jē-ə-lō'ji-ən*), geol'ogist.—*adjs.* geologic (*-loj'ik*), -al.—*adv.* geolog'ically.—*v.i.* geol'ogise, -ize, to work at geology in the field.—*v.t.* to investigate the geology of.—geological time, time before written history, divided into epochs each of which saw the formation of one of the great rock systems.—dynamical geology, the study of the work of natural agents in shaping the earth's crust—wind, frost, rivers, volcanic action, etc.; structural geology, the study of the arrangement and structure of rock masses. [Fr. *géologie*—Gr. *gē*, earth, *logos*, a discourse.]

geomagnetism, *jē-ō-mag'nət-izm*, *n.* terrestrial magnetism: the study of this.—*adj.* geomagnet'ic. [geo-.]

geomancy, *jē'ō-man-si*, *n.* divination by figures of or on earth.—*n.* gē'omancer.—*adj.* gēoman'tic. [Gr. *gē*, earth, *manteiā*, divination.]

geomedicine, *jē-ō-med'sin*, *n.* study of diseases as influenced by geographical environment.—*adj.* geomed'ical. [geo-.]

geometry, *jē-om'i-tri*, *n.* that part of mathematics which treats the properties of points, lines, surfaces, and solids, either under classical Euclidean assumptions, or (in the case of elliptic, hyperbolic, etc., *geometry*) involving postulates not all of which are identical with Euclid's: any study of a mathematical system in which figures undergo transformations, concerned with discussion of those properties of the figures which remain constant: textbook of geometry.—*ns.* geom'eter, a geometrician: a geometrid; geometrician (*-me-trish'ən*), one skilled in geometry.—*adjs.* geometric (*-met'*), -al, relating to or according to geometry: consisting of or using simple figures such as geometry deals with.—*adv.* geomet'rically.—*n.* geom'etrid, any moth of the family or superfamily Geomet'ridae, whose caterpillars are loopers.—*v.t.* and *v.i.* geom'etrise, -ize, to work geometrically.—*n.* geom'etrist.—geometrical progression, a series of quantities each of which has the same ratio to its predecessor; geometric mean (see mean (2)). [Gr. *geōmetriā*—*gē*, earth, *metron*, a measure.]

geomorphology, *jē-ō-mör-fol'ə-ji*, *n.* morphology of land forms including those under the sea.—*adj.* geomorpholog'ical.—*n.* geomorphol'ogist. [geo-.]

Geomys, *jē'ō-mis*, *n.* the typical genus of Geomyidae (*-mi'i-dē*), the pouched rats.—*adj.* geomy'oid. [Gr. *gē*, earth, *mȳs*, mouse.]

geophagy, *jē-of'ə-ji*, *n.* earth-eating.—Also geoph'agism.—*n.* geoph'agist.—*adj.* geoph'agous (*-gəs*). [Gr. *gē*, earth, *phagein*, to eat.]

geophilous, *jē-of'il-əs*, *adj.* living in or on the ground: geocarpic: having a short stem with leaves at ground-level.—*adj.* geophil'ic. [Gr. *gē*, earth, *phileein*, to love.]

geophysics, *gē-ō-fiz'iks*, *n.* the physics of the earth.—*adj.* geophys'ical.—*n.* geophys'icist (*-i-sist*). [geo-.]

geophyte, *jē'ō-fīt*, *n.* a plant that survives the winter by subterranean buds.—*adj.* geophytic (*-fit'ik*). [Gr. *gē*, earth, *phyton*, plant.]

geopolitics, *jē-ō-pol'it-iks*, *n.* a science concerned with problems of states, such as frontiers, as affected by their geographical environment: the special combination of geographical and political considerations in a particular state: a Nazi doctrine justifying expansion by necessity for lebensraum, etc. [Ger. *geopolitik*; see geo-.] geoponic, -al, *jē-ō-pon'ik*, *-əl*, *adjs.* agricultural.—*n.* geopon'ics (treated as *sing.*), the science of agriculture. [Gr. *geōponikos*—*gē*, earth, *ponos*, labour.]

geordie, *jör'di*, *n.* a guinea, from the figure of St *George*: a safety-lamp for miners invented by *George* Stephenson: a coal-pitman: a collierboat: (usu. *cap.*) a native of Tyneside.—*adj.* pertaining to Tyneside.

George, *jörj*, *n.* a jewelled figure of St *George* slaying the dragon, worn by Knights of the Garter: the automatic pilot of an aircraft.—George Cross, an award for outstanding courage or heroism given in cases where a purely military honour is not applicable—instituted during World War II; George Medal, an award for gallantry given to civilians and members of the armed forces.—St George's cross, the Greek cross of England, red on a white ground.

georgette, *jör-jet'*, *n.* a thin silk stuff. [Named after a milliner.]

Georgian, *jörj'i-ən*, *adj.* relating to or contemporary with any of the various *Georges*, kings of Great Britain: relating to or following Henry *George*, Lloyd *George*, or other of the name: belonging to *Georgia* (*Gurjestan, Gruzia*) in the Caucasus, its people, language, etc.: of or pertaining to the American State of *Georgia*.—Also *n.*—Georgian planet, Uranus, named after George III by its discoverer, Sir William Herschel.

georgic, *jörj'ik*, *adj.* relating to agriculture or rustic affairs.—*n.* a poem on husbandry. [L. *geōrgicus*—Gr. *geōrgikos*—*geōrgos*, agriculture—*gē*, earth, *ergon*, work.]

geosphere, *jē'ō-sfēr*, *n.* the solid part of the earth, distinguished from *atmosphere* and *hydrosphere*. [Gr. *gē*, earth, *sphaira*, sphere.]

geostatic, *jē-ō-stat'ik*, *adj.* capable of sustaining the pressure of earth from all sides.—*n.* geostat'ics (treated as *sing.*), the statics of rigid bodies. [Gr. *gē*, the earth, *statikos*, causing to stand.]

geostationary, *jē-ō-stā'shən-ə-ri*, *adj.* of a communications satellite, orbiting round the earth at a speed such that it appears to be stationary in the sky. [geo-.]

geostrophic, *jē-ō-strof'ik*, *adj.* of a virtual force used to account for the change in direction of the wind relative to the surface of the earth arising from the earth's rotation: of a wind whose direction and force are partly determined by the earth's rotation. [geo-.]

geosyncline, *jē-ō-sin'klin*, *n.* a syncline on a great scale.—*adj.* geosyncli'nal. [geo-.]

geotaxis, *jē-ō-taks'is*, *n.* response of an organism to the stimulus of gravity.—*adjs.* geotact'ic, -al, [Gr. *gē*, earth, *taxis*, arrangement.]

Neutral vowels in unaccented syllables: *el'ə-mənt*; for certain sounds in foreign words, see p. viii

**geotectonic**, *jē-ō-tek-ton'ik, adj.* relating to the structure of rock masses.—*n.* **geotecton'ics** (treated as *sing.*), structural geology. [Gr. *gē*, earth, *tektōn*, a builder.]

**geothermic**, *jē-ō-thûr'mik,* **geothermal**, *-əl, adjs.* pertaining to the internal heat of the earth.—*n.* **geothermom'eter**, an instrument for measuring subterranean temperatures. [Gr. *gē*, earth, *thermē*, heat.]

**geotropism**, *jē-ot'rop-izm, (bot.) n.* geotaxis (positive downwards, negative upwards).—*adj.* **geotrop'ic.**—*adv.* **geotrop'ically.** [Gr. *gē*, earth, *tropos*, a turning.]

**gerah**, *gē'ra, (B.) n.* the smallest Hebrew weight and coin, 1/20 of a shekel. [Heb. *gērāh*.]

**geraniol.** See geranium.

**geranium**, *ji-rān'yəm, n.* a plant of a genus (Geranium) with seed-vessels like a crane's bill, typical of the family Geraniaceae (*-i-ā'si-ē*): loosely, a pelargonium.—*n.* **geran'iol**, an alcohol (C₁₀H₁₈O) forming a constituent of many of the esters used in perfumery. [L.,—Gr. *geranion—geranos*, a crane.]

**gerbe**, *jûrb, n.* a wheat-sheaf (*her.*): a fountain or firework resembling a wheat-sheaf. [Fr. *gerbe*; cf. garb (2).]

**Gerbera**, *gûr'bə-rə, jûr', n.* a genus of composite plants of S. Africa, etc. [T. *Gerber*, German naturalist.]

**gerbil**, *jûr'bil, n.* a small desert-dwelling rodent which can be kept as a pet.—Also (esp. formerly) **gerbille.** [Fr. *gerbille.*]

**gere** (*Spens.*). Same as gear.

**gerent**, *jē'rənt, n.* controller, ruler. [L. *gerēns, -entis,* pr.p. of *gerēre,* to manage.]

**gerfalcon, gyrfalcon, jerfalcon,** *jûr'fö(l)-kn, n.* a large northern falcon. [O.Fr. *gerfaucon*—L.L. *gyrofalcō,* most prob. O.H.G. *gir,* a vulture (Ger. *geier*); see falcon.]

**geriatrics**, *jer-i-at'riks, n.* medical care of the old. —*adj.* **geriat'ric.**—*ns.* **geriatrician** (*-ə-trish'ən*), **geriatrist** (*-at'rist*); **geriatry** (*jer-i'ə-tri*), care of the old, old people's welfare. [Gr. *gēras,* old age, *iātros,* physician.]

**gerle** (*Spens.*). Same as girl.

**germ**, *jûrm, n.* a rudimentary form of a living thing, whether plant or animal: a plant ovary (*obs.*): a shoot: that from which anything springs, the origin or beginning: a first principle: that from which a disease springs: a micro-organism, esp. a malign one.—*v.i.* to put forth buds, sprout.—*ns.* **ger'men, ger'min** (*Shak.* **ger'main, ger'maine**), a rudiment: a shoot: the ovary in a flower (*obs.*); **germ'icide**, that which kills germs.—*adjs.* **germ'inal**, pertaining to a germ or rudiment: in germ, or (*fig.*) earliest stage of development: seminal (*fig.*); **germ'inant**, sprouting: budding: capable of developing.—*v.i.* **germ'inate**, to begin to grow (esp. of a seed or spore).—*v.t.* to cause to sprout.—*n.* **germinā'tion.**—*adj.* **germ'inative.**—**germ'-cell**, a sperm or ovum, a gamete or cell from which it springs; **germ'-lay'er**, a primary layer in an embryo—ectoderm, mesoderm, or endoderm; **germ'-plasm**, that part of the nuclear protoplasmic material which, according to early theories of inheritance, is the vehicle of heredity, and maintains its continuity from generation to generation; **germ warfare**, warfare in which bacteria are used as weapons. [Partly through Fr. *germe,* from L. *germen, -inis,* a sprout, bud, germ, *germināre, -ātum,* to sprout.]

**german**, *jûr'mən, adj.* of the first degree: full (see brother, cousin): closely allied.—*n.* a full brother or sister: a near relative.—*adj.* **germane** (*-mān'*), nearly related: relevant, appropriate. [O.Fr. *germain*—L. *germānus.*]

**German**, *jûr'mən, n.* a native or citizen of Germany, or one of the same linguistic or ethnological stock:—*pl.* **Ger'mans:** the German language, esp. High German.—*adj.* of or from Germany, one of the Germans: German-speaking.—*adjs.* **Germanesque'**, marked by German characteristics; **Germanic** (*-man'ik*), of Germany: of the linguistic family to which German, English, Norwegian, etc., belong—Teutonic.—*n.* an extinct Indo-Germanic tongue which differentiated into East Germanic (Gothic and other extinct languages), North Germanic or Scandinavian (Norwegian, Danish, Swedish, Icelandic), and West Germanic (English, Frisian, Dutch, Low German, High German).—*adv.* **German'ically.**—*v.t.* **Ger'manise, -ize,** to make German.—*v.i.* to become German: to adopt German ways.—*n.* **Germanisā'tion, -z-.**—*adj.* **Ger'manish,** somewhat German.—*ns.* **Ger'manism**, a German idiom: German ideas and ways; **Ger'manist**, one learned in German philology or other matters relating to Germany.—*adj.* **Germanis'tic,** pertaining to the study of German.—*ns.* **German'ophil,** a lover of the Germans and things German, now usu. **German'ophile; German'ophobe,** one who fears or hates the Germans and things German.—**Ger'man-band',** street-musicians, orig. from Germany; **German flute,** the ordinary modern flute; **German measles,** rubella; **German silver,** an alloy of copper, nickel, and zinc, white like silver, and first made in Germany; **German sixth,** a chord with major third, perfect fifth, and augmented sixth.—**German shepherd (police) dog** (see Alsatian).—**High German,** the speech, originally of High or Southern Germany, the literary language throughout Germany; **Low German,** Platt-Deutsch, the language of Low or Northern Germany: formerly applied to all the West Germanic dialects except High German. [L. *Germānus,* German.]

**germander**, *jər-man'dər, n.* a labiate herb (Teucrium) with aromatic, bitter, and stomachic properties.—**germander speedwell,** a bright blue-flowered veronica (*V. Chamaedrys*). [L.L. *germandra*—Late Gr. *chamandrya*—Gr. *chamaidrys —chamai,* on the ground, *drȳs,* oak.]

**Germanice**, *jûr-man'i-sē,* **ger-man'ik-e,** (L.) in German.

**germanium**, *jər-mā'ni-əm, n.* a metallic element (Ge; atomic number 32), much used in diodes, transistors and rectifiers for its properties as a semiconductor. [Discovered in 1885 by Clemens Winkler (1838-1904), a *German.*]

**Germinal**, *zher-mē-nal', n.* the seventh month of the French revolutionary calendar, about 21st March to 19th April. [See germ.]

**germinal, germinate.** See germ.

**gerne**, *gûrn, (Spens.) v.i.* to grin or gape. [grin.]

**gerontocracy**, *ger-* or *jer-on-tok'rə-si, n.* government by old men.—*adj.* **geront'ic** (*biol.*), pertaining to the senescent period in the life-history of an individual.—*ns.* **gerontol'ogy,** scientific study of the processes of growing old; **geron'tophil(e)** (*-fil, -fīl*), one who experiences gerontophilia (*-fil'i-ə*), sexual feeling towards old people; **gerontotherapeut'ics,** the science of medical treatment of the diseases of old age. [Gr. *gerōn, -ontos,* an old man, *kratos,* power.]

**geropiga**, *jer-ō-pē'gə, n.* a mixture of grape-juice, brandy, etc., used to doctor port-wine. [Port.]

**Gerry.** See Jerry.

**gerrymander**, *jer'i-man-dər,* also *ger', v.t.* to rearrange (voting districts) in the interests of a particular party or candidate: to manipulate (facts, arguments, etc.) so as to reach undue conclusions.—*n.* an arrangement of the above nature. [Formed from the name of Governor Elbridge *Gerry* (1744-1814) and sala*mander,* from the likeness to that animal of the gerry-mandered map of Massachusetts in 1811.]

**gerund**, *jer'ənd, n.* a part of a Latin verb with the value of a verbal noun, as *amandum,* loving: in English, a noun with the ending *-ing* formed from a verb and having some of the qualities of a verb, as the possibility of governing an object, etc.; often preceded by a possessive (e.g. *My leaving it was unwise*).—*adjs.* **gerundial** (*ji-rund'i-əl*), **gerundival** (*jer-ən-dī'vl*), **gerundive** (*ji-rund'iv*). —*n.* **gerund'ive,** a Latin verbal adjective expressing necessity, as *amandus, -a, -um,* deserving or requiring to be loved.—**ger'und-grind'er,** a pedantic teacher. [L. *gerundium*—*gerēre,* to bear.]

**gesellschaft,** *gə-zel'shäft,* (Ger.) a commercial company.

**Gesneria,** *jes-nē'ri-ə, n.* a tropical American genus typical of the **Gesneriä'ceae,** a family close akin to the Scrophulariaceae. [Named after Konrad von *Gesner* (1516-65), Swiss botanist and scholar.]

**gessamine** (*Milt.*). Same as **jasmine.**

**gesse** (*Spens.*). Same as **guess.**

**gesso,** *jes'ō, n.* plaster of Paris: a plaster surface prepared as a ground for painting. [It.,—L. *gypsum*; see **gypsum.**]

**gest,** *jest,* (*Shak.*) *n.* time fixed for a stay in a place. [O.Fr. *giste,* a stopping-place.]

**gest, geste,** *jest, n.* an exploit: a tale of adventure, a romance. [O.Fr. *geste*—L. *gesta,* things done —*gerēre, gestum,* to bear, behave; cf. jest.]

**gest, geste,** *jest, n.* bearing: gesture.—*adj.* **gest'ic.** [Fr. *geste*—L. *gestus*—*gerēre, gestum,* to bear, behave.]

**gestalt,** *gə-shtält', n.* form, shape, pattern: organised whole or unit—**gestalt psychology,** revolt from the atomistic outlook of the orthodox school, starts with the organised whole as something more than the sum of the parts into which it can be logically analysed. [German.]

**gestant.** See **gestation.**

**gestapo,** *gə-stä'pō, n.* the Nazi secret police in Germany. [From Ger. *geheime staats* polizei, secret state police.]

**gestate,** *jes-tāt', v.t.* to carry in the womb during the period from conception to birth: to conceive and develop slowly in the mind.—*v.i.* to be in the process of gestation.—*adj.* **ges'tant,** laden (also *fig.*).—*n.* **gestation,** *jes-tā'shən,* being carried in a vehicle, a boat, etc. (*arch.*): the act of gestating (*biol.* and *fig.*).—*adjs.* **gestatō'rial, ges'tatory,** pertaining to carrying (*arch.*), or to carriage in the womb. [L. *gestāre, -ātum,* to carry—*gerēre,* to bear.]

**gesticulate,** *jes-tik'ū-lāt, v.i.* to make vigorous gestures.—*ns.* **gesticulā'tion; gestic'ulātor.**—*adj.* **gestic'ulatory.** [L. *gesticulārī, -ātus*—*gesticulus,* dim. of *gestus,* gesture—*gerēre,* to carry, behave.]

**gesture,** *jes'chər, n.* a posture, or movement of the body (*obs.*): an action expressive of sentiment or passion or intended to show inclination or disposition: the use of such movements: an action dictated by courtesy or diplomacy, or by a desire to impress: behaviour (*Shak.*).—*adj.* **ges'tural.** [L.L. *gestūra*—L. *gestus,* from L. *gerēre,* to carry, behave.]

**gesundheit,** *gə-zōōnt'hīt,* (Ger.) your health.

**get,** *get, v.t.* to obtain: to acquire: to procure: to receive: to attain: to come to have: to catch: to grasp or take the meaning of: to learn: to commit to memory: to hit: to descry: to make out: to succeed in coming into touch or communication with (e.g. a wireless station): to worst, have the better of, gain a decisive advantage over: to baffle: to irritate: to grip emotionally, take, captivate, hit the taste of exactly: to induce: to cause to be, go, or become: to betake: to beget.—*v.i.* to arrive, to bring or put oneself (in any place, position, or state): to become: to become richer: to clear out:—*pr.p.* **gett'ing;** *pa.t.* **got,** *obs.* **gat;** *pa.p.* **got,** *arch., Scot.,* and *U.S.* **gott'en.**—*n.* that which is got (*obs.*): output (*obs.*): offspring: (spelt also **gait(t), geit,** etc., **gyte**—see **gyte** (2)) a child, brat (*Scot.* contemptuously): begetting (*obs.*).—*n.* **gett'er,** one who,

or that which evacuates: a material used, when evaporated by high-frequency induction currents, for evacuation of gas left in vacuum valves after sealing during manufacture.—*v.t.* to evacuate (a valve) using a getter.—*v.i.* to use a getter.—*ns.* **gett'ering,** evacuation using a getter; **gett'ing,** a gaining: anything gained: procreation.—*adj.* **get-at'-able,** easily accessible.—**get'away,** an escape: a start: breaking cover; **get'-together,** a social gathering: an informal conference; **get'-up,** (style of) equipment, outfit, make-up.—**get across** (*coll.*), communicate successfully; **get ahead, along,** to make progress, advance; **get at,** to reach, attain: to poke fun at (*slang*): to mean: to attack verbally: to influence by underhand or unlawful means; **get away with it,** pull it off: carry a thing through successfully or with impunity; **get by,** to succeed in passing: to elude notice and come off with impunity, manage satisfactorily, be sufficiently good (*coll.*); **get down,** to alight; **get down to,** set to work on, tackle seriously; **get off,** to escape: to learn: to gain the affection of someone of the opposite sex (with *with*; *coll.*); **get on,** to proceed, advance: to prosper: to agree, consort harmoniously: to fare; **get out,** to produce: to extricate oneself: to take oneself off; **get over,** to surmount: to recover from: to make an impression on an audience; **get round,** to circumvent: to persuade, talk over; **get round to,** to bring oneself to do (something); **get there** (*slang*), to achieve one's object, succeed; **get through,** to finish: to reach a destination: to receive approval, or to obtain it for (something): to be put in telephonic communication: to communicate with, reach the comprehension of (with *to*); **get together,** to meet for social intercourse or discussion; **get up,** to arise: to ascend: to arrange: to prepare: to learn up for an occasion: to commit to memory; **to have got** (*coll.*), to have; **to have got to,** to be obliged to. [O.N. *geta*; cog. with O.E. *-gietan* (in compounds).]

**Geum,** *jē'əm, n.* the avens genus of the rose family. [L.]

**gewgaw,** *gū'gö, n.* a toy: a bauble.—*adj.* showy without value. [Origin unknown.]

**gey** (*Scot.*). See **gay.**—*adv.* **geyan** (*gī'ən*), gey and.

**geyser,** *gā', gē'* or *gi'zər, n.* a spring that spouts hot water into the air: (usu. *gē'*) apparatus for heating water as it is drawn.—*n.* gey'serite, sinter. [*Geysir,* a geyser in Iceland—Ice. *geysa,* O.N. *göysa,* to gush.]

**Ghanaian,** *gä-nä'yən, -nä', adj.* of or pertaining to Ghana.—*n.* a native or citizen of Ghana.

**gharial.** Same as **gavial, garial.**

**gnarri, gharry,** *ga'ri, n.* in India, a wheeled vehicle, generally for hire. [Hind. *gārī,* a cart.]

**ghast, gast,** *v.t.* (*Shak.*) to strike aghast: to affright.—*adj.* **ghast'ful** (*Spens.* gastfull), dreary, dismal.—*adj.* **ghast'fully,** frightfully.—*n.* **ghast'liness.**—*adj.* **ghast'ly,** death-like: hideous: deplorable (*coll.*).—Also *adv.*—*n.* **ghastness** (*Shak.* **gastness,** *q.v.*). [O.E. *gǣstan*; cf. gast.]

**ghat, ghaut,** *göt, n.* in India, a mountain-pass: a landing-stair: a place of cremation (*burning ghat*). [Hindi *ghāt,* descent.]

**ghazal,** *gaz'al, n.* a Persian and Arabic verse-form, of not more than 18 couplets, the first two lines and the even-numbered lines thereafter rhyming together, mainly amatory and bacchanalian.—Also **gazal, ghazel.** [Ar. *ghazal.*]

**ghazi,** *gä'zē, n.* a veteran Mohammedan warrior: a slayer of infidels: a high Turkish title. [Ar. *ghāzi,* fighting.]

**Gheber, Ghebre.** Same as **Gueber.**

**ghee, gni,** *gē, g'hē, n.* clarified butter, esp. buffalo butter. [Hind. *ghī.*]

**gherkin,** *gûr'kin, n.* a small cucumber used for

pickling. [From an earlier form of Du. *aug-urk*(*je*), a gherkin; app. from Slavonic.]

**ghesse** (*Spens.*). Same as guess:—*pa.t.* and *pa.p.*

**ghest, ghessed.**

**ghetto,** *get'ō, n.* Jews' quarter in Italian or other city, to which they used to be confined: a quarter esp. poor, inhabited by any racial group. [It., perh. *borghetto*, borough.]

**ghi.** See ghee.

**Ghibeline,** *gib'ə-lēn, -lin, -lin, n.* one of a party in Mediaeval Italy, orig. supporters of Hohenstaufen emperors against Guelfs and pope. [It. *Ghibellino,* app.—*Waiblingen,* a Hohenstaufen town.]

**ghillie.** Same as gillie.

**ghost,** *gōst, n.* a spirit: the soul of a man: a spirit appearing after death: a dead body (*Shak.*): one who does another's work for him, as writing speeches or the like (*slang*): a faint or false appearance: a semblance: a duplicated image due to additional reception of a delayed similar signal which has covered a longer path (*TV*).—*v.t.* to haunt as a ghost.—*v.i.* (*slang*) to play the ghost for another.—*adj.* ghost'-like.—*n.* ghost'liness.—*adjs.* ghost'ly, spiritual: religious: pertaining to apparitions: ghost-like: faint; ghost'y.—ghost'-moth, a moth (*Hepialus humuli*), the male of ghostly white appearance, the caterpillar destructive to hop-gardens; ghost'-story, a story in which ghosts figure; ghost town, one which once flourished owing to some natural resource in the vicinity but which is now deserted since the natural resource has been exhausted; ghost'-word, a word that has originated in the blunder of a scribe or printer; ghost'-writer.—give up the ghost (*B.*), to die; Holy Ghost, the Holy Spirit, the third person in the Christian Trinity; not to have a ghost (of a chance), not to have the least chance of success. [O.E. *gāst*; Ger. *geist*; the *h* from Caxton (Flemish *gheest*).]

**ghoul,** *gōōl,* now often *gowl, n.* an Eastern demon that preys on the dead: a gruesome fiend: a person of gruesome or revolting habits or tastes. —*adj.* ghoul'ish. [Ar. *ghūl.*]

**ghubar.** Same as gobar.

**ghyll,** *gil.* See gill (4).

**giambeux** (*Spens.*) for jambeaux.

**giant,** *jī'ant, n.* a huge mythical being of more or less human form: a person of abnormally great stature: anything much above the usual size of its kind: a person of much greater powers than his fellows:—*fem.* gi'antess.—*adj.* gigantic.—*ns.* gi'anthood, gi'antism, the quality or character of a giant: the occurrence of giants: gigantism; gi'antry, giants collectively: giant stories or mythology; gi'antship.—*adj.* gi'antly, giantlike. —gi'ant-pow'der, a kind of dynamite.—*adj.* gi'ant-rude, (*Shak.*) enormously rude or uncivil. —giant's-kett'le, a great pot-hole believed to have been formed by subglacial water; giant'(s)-stride, a gymnastic apparatus enabling one to take great strides around a pole. [O.Fr. *geant* (Fr. *géant*)—L. *gigās*—Gr. *gigās, gigantos.*]

**giaour,** *jowr, n.* infidel, a term applied by the Turks to all who are not of their own religion. [Through Turk.—Pers. *gaur*; see guebre.]

**gib,** *jib, gib, n.* wedge-shaped piece of metal holding another in place, etc.—*v.t.* to fasten with a gib. [Origin obscure.]

**gib,** *gib, n.* a tom-cat, esp. one castrated: a term of reproach.—Also gib'-cat (*Shak.*). [From the name *Gilbert.*]

**gibber,** *jib'ər, v.i.* to utter senseless or inarticulate sounds. [Imit.]

**Gibberella,** *jib-ər-el'ə, n.* a genus of fungi found esp. on grasses—e.g. wheat scab.—*n.* gibberell'in, any of several plant-growth regulators produced by a gibberella.—gibberell'ic acid, an acid having similar effects.

**gibberish,** *gib'ər-ish,* or *jib', n.* rapid, gabbling talk: unmeaning words.—*adj.* unmeaning. [Imit.]

**gibbet,** *jib'it, n.* a gallows, esp. one on which criminals were suspended after execution: the projecting beam of a crane.—*v.t.* to expose on, or as on, a gibbet. [O.Fr. *gibet,* a stick; origin unknown.]

**gibble-gabble,** *gib'l-gab'l, n.* senseless chatter. [gabble.]

**gibbon,** *gib'ən, n.* an E. Indian anthropoid ape (of several species) with very long arms. [Origin unknown.]

**gibbous,** *gib'əs, adj.* hump-backed: humped: unequally convex on two sides, as the moon between half and full.—Also gibb'ose.—*ns.* gibbos'ity, gibb'ousness.—*adv.* gibb'ously. [L. *gibbōsus—gibbus,* a hump.]

**gibe, jibe,** *jīb, v.i.* to scoff: to flout.—*v.t.* to scoff at: to taunt.—*n.* a flout: a taunt.—*n.* gib'er.—*adv.* gib'ingly. [Origin obscure.]

**gibel,** *gib'əl, n.* the Prussian carp, without barbules.

**Gibeonite,** *gib'i-ən-it, n.* a slave's slave—from Josh. ix.

**giblets,** *jib'lits, n.pl.* the internal eatable parts of a fowl, etc.: entrails.—*adj.* gib'let, made of giblets. [O.Fr. *gibelet*; origin uncertain.]

**Gibraltarian,** *jib-röl-tā'ri-ən, n.* and *adj.* (an inhabitant) of Gibraltar.

**gibus,** *ji'bəs, n.* an opera-hat. [Fr.]

**gid,** *gid, n.* sturdy, a disease of sheep. [giddy.]

**giddy,** *gid'i, adj.* unsteady, dizzy: causing giddiness: whirling: light-headed: flighty.—Also *v.i.* and *v.t.*—*adv.* gidd'ily.—*n.* gidd'iness.—*adjs.* gidd'y-head'ed, thoughtless, wanting reflection; gidd'y-paced (*Shak.*), moving irregularly. —play the giddy goat, to act the fool. [O.E. *gidig, gydig,* insane, possessed by a god.]

**gie,** *gē, vb.* a Scots form of give:—*pa.t.* gied, gēd, gae, gā; *pa.p.* gien, gēn.

**gier-eagle,** *jēr'ē'gl,* (*B.*) *n.* a vulture. [Du. *gier.*]

**gif,** *gif, conj.* an obsolete form (except in Scots) of if.

**giff-gaff,** *gif'-gaf',* (*Scot.*) *n.* give and take. [give.]

**gift,** *gift, n.* a thing given: a bribe (*arch.*): a quality bestowed by nature: the act of giving: something easily obtained, understood, etc.—*v.t.* to endow, esp. with any power or faculty: to present.—*adj.* gift'ed, highly endowed by nature.—gift'-book, a book suitable or intended for presentation; gift horse, a horse given as a present; gift token (see token).—look a gift horse in the mouth, to criticise a gift (orig. to look at a gift horse's teeth to tell its age). [See give.]

**gig,** *gig, n.* a whip-top (*obs.*): a flighty girl (*obs.*): a light, two-wheeled carriage: a long, light boat: a machine for raising the nap on cloth (in full, gig mill): sport, fun (*dial.*).—*v.t.* and *v.i.* gigg'it (*arch. U.S.*), to convey or move rapidly.—*n.pl.* gig'-lamps, (*slang*) spectacles.—gig'man, one who drives or keeps a gig: a narrow middle-class philistine (*Carlyle*).—*n.* gigman'ity. [M.E. *gigge,* a whirling thing (cf. whirligig); origin obscure.]

**gig,** *gig,* (*slang*) *n.* an engagement, esp. of a band, for one performance only. [Ety. unknown.]

**giga-,** *ji-gə, pfx.* meaning ten to the ninth power ($10^9$).—giga-electron-volt, a unit equal to a thousand million electron-volts.

**gigantic,** *ji-gan'tik, adj.* of, like or characteristic of a giant: huge.—Also gigantē'an.—*adj.* gigantesque', befitting or suggestive of a giant.—*adv.* gigan'tically.—*ns.* gigan'ticide, the act of killing a giant; gigant'ism, hugeness, of a business concern, etc.: excessive overgrowth, usually owing to overactivity of the pituitary gland; gigantol'ogy, giant-lore; gigantom'achy (-*ki;* Gr. *maché,* fight), a war of giants, esp. against the gods. [L. *gigās, gigantis,* Gr. *gigās, -antos,* a giant.]

**giggle,** *gig'l, v.i.* to laugh with short catches of the breath, or in a silly manner.—*n.* a laugh of

this kind: something unimportant (*slang*).—*ns.*
gigg′ler; gigg′ling.—*adjs.* gigg′lesome, gigg′ly.
[Echoic.]
giglet, giglot, *gig′lit, -lət, n.* a giddy girl: a wanton
(*arch.*).—*adj.* (*Shak.*) inconstant. [Perh. conn.
with gig; later associated with giggle.]
gigolo, *jig′ō-lō, n.* a professional male dancing
partner: a young man living at the expense of
an older woman. [Fr.]
gigot, *jig′ət, n.* a leg of mutton, etc.: a leg-of-
mutton sleeve. [Fr.]
gigue, *zhēg,* (*mus.*) *n.* a lively dance-form in triple
time, common in old suites.—Also (It.) giga
(*jē′ga*). [Fr.; cf. jig.]
gila, *hhē′la* (in full gila monster), *n.* either of the
two *Heloderma* species, the only venomous
lizards known. [*Gila* River, Arizona.]
gilbert, *gil′bərt, n.* the C.G.S. unit of magnetomotive force. [From the English physician and
physicist William Gilbert (1540-1603).]
Gilbertian, *gil′bûrt′i-ən, adj.* whimsically or para-
doxically humorous. [Sir W. S. *Gilbert* (1836-
1911), librettist, playwright, poet, etc.]
Gilbertine, *gil′bûrt-in, -in, n.* a member of the order
of canons and nuns founded (*c.* 1148) by St
*Gilbert* of Sempringham.—Also *adj.*
gilcup. See giltcup.
gild, *gild, v.t.* to cover or overlay with gold or with
any goldlike substance: to smear with blood
(*obs.*); to flush (*obs.*): to furnish with gold:
to gloss over, give a specious appearance to: to
adorn with lustre:—*pr.p.* gild′ing; *pa.t.* and
*pa.p.* gild′ed or gilt.—*ns.* gild′er, one who coats
articles with gold; gild′ing, act or trade of a
gilder: gold or imitation thereof laid on a
surface.—Gilded Chamber, the House of Lords;
gilded spurs, an emblem of knighthood; gilded
youth, rich young people of fashion.—gild the
lily, to embellish to an unnecessary extent;
gild the pill, to make a disagreeable thing seem
less so. [O.E. *gyldan—gold;* see gold.]
gild. See guild.
gilder. See guilder.
gilden, gylden, *gil′dən,* orig. *adj.* golden, adopted
later (as *Spens.*) as a *pa.p.* of gild. [O.E. *gylden.*]
gilet, *zhē-lā, n.* a waistcoat: in a woman's dress,
a front part shaped like a waistcoat: in ballet
dress, a bodice shaped like a waistcoat. [Fr.]
gill, *gil, n.* an organ for breathing in water: the
flesh under the jaw: the wattle below the bill of
a fowl: one of the radiating plates under a
mushroom or toadstool cap: a projecting rib of
a heating surface.—*v.t.* to gut (fish): to catch
(fish) by the gills in a net.—gill cover, a fold of
skin, usu. with bony plates, protecting the
gills. [Cf. Dan. *giælle;* Sw. *gäl.*]
gill, *jil, n.* a small measure, having various
values; in recent times = ¼ pint.—*n.* gill′-
house (*obs.*), a dram-shop. [O.Fr. *gelle.*]
gill, *jil, n.* a girl, also jill (*obs.*): a female ferret,
also jill: ground ivy (*dial.*): beer with an
infusion of ground ivy, also gill ale, gill beer
(*obs.*).—*n.* gillet (*Scot.*), a skittish, flighty, or
loose young woman, also jillet.—gill′flirt (*arch.*),
a wanton girl, also jill′flirt. [*Gillian* or *Juliana*
(from *Julius*), a woman's name.]
gill, ghyll, *gil, n.* a small ravine, a wooded glen:
a brook. [O.N. *gil.*]
gillaroo, *gil-ə-rōō′, n.* an Irish trout with thickened
muscular stomach. [Ir. *giolla ruadh,* red lad.]
gillie, *gil′i, n.* a Highland chief's attendant (*hist.*):
an attendant on or guide of hunting and fishing
sportsmen.—*v.i.* to act as gillie.—gillie-wet′foot
(*obs.*), -white-foot (*obs.*), a barefoot Highland
lad, esp. a messenger or chief's attendant.
[Gael. *gille,* a lad, Ir. *giolla.*]
gillravage, -itch. See gilravage.
gillyflower, *jil′i-flowr* (*Shak.* gillyvor, *-vər*), *n.* a
flower that smells like cloves, esp. clove-gilly-
flower, stock-gillyflower (see clove (4), stock (1)).

[O.Fr. *girofle*—Gr. *karyophyllon,* the clove-tree
—*karyon,* a nut, *phyllon,* a leaf.]
gilpy, gilpey, *gil′pi,* (*Scot.*) *n.* a boisterous girl
or (formerly) boy.
gilravage, gillravage, galravage, -itch, *gəl-rav′ij,*
*-ich,* or *rāv′,* (*Scot.*) *n.* a noisy frolic: riotous
merrymaking.—*v.i.* to behave riotously.—*n.*
gilrav′ager.
gilt, *gilt, pa.t.* and *pa.p.* of gild.—*adj.* gilded: gold-
coloured.—*n.* gilding: money (*Shak.*).—gilt′cup,
gil′cup, a butter-cup.—*adj.* gilt′-edged, having
the edges gilt: of the highest quality (gilt-edged
securities, those stocks whose interest is considered perfectly safe).—*ns.* gilt′edged, gilts.—
gilt′-head, a name for several fishes, esp. a sparoid
fish with a half-moon-shaped gold spot between
the eyes; gilt′-tail, a yellow-tipped worm
(*Dendrobaena subrubicunda*) of old dung-hills.
gilt, *gilt,* (*dial.*) *n.* a young sow (in various conditions locally). [O.N. *gyltr;* cf. O.E. *gilte.*]
gimbal, *jim′bl, n.* a gimmal (*obs.*): (in *pl.*) a contrivance for keeping a hanging object level (*sing.*
in composition, as gimbal ring). [See gemel.]
gimcrack, jimcrack, *jim′krak, n.* a trumpery
knick-knack: a paltry, ill-made flimsy article:
a trivial mechanism.—*adj.* trumpery.—*n.* gim-
crack′ery. [Origin obscure.]
gimlet, *gim′lit, n.* a small tool for boring holes by
turning it by hand: half a glass of whisky, gin,
or vodka, and lime-juice.—*v.t.* to pierce as with
a gimlet: to turn like a gimlet.—*adj.* gim′let-
eyed′, very sharp-sighted. [O.Fr. *gumbelet,*
from Gmc.; cf. wimble (1).]
gimmal, *jim′l, n.* a ring (also gimmal ring) that
can be divided into two (or three) rings: a joint
or part in a piece of mechanism (also gimm′er;
*Shak.* gimm′or).—*adj.* gimm′alled (*Shak.* jymold),
jointed, hinged. [See gemel.]
gimme, *gi′mi,* (*slang*) contracted form of *give me.*
gimmer, *gim′ər,* (*Scot.*) *n.* a young ewe: (contemptuously) a woman. (O.N. *gymbr;* cf. Sw.
*gimmer,* Dan. *gimmer.*]
gimmick, *gim′ik, n.* secret device for performing
a trick: a device (often peculiar to the person
adopting it) to catch attention, publicity: an
ingenious mechanical device.—*n.* gimm′ickry,
gimmicks in quantity: use of gimmick(s).—*adj.*
gimm′icky, pertaining to a gimmick: loosely,
of little worth, importance. [Origin unknown.]
gimp, *gimp, n.* a yarn with a hard core: a trimming thereof: a fishing-line bound with wire:
a coarse thread in lace-making.—*v.t.* to make or
furnish with gimp.—Also guimp, gymp, gymp. [Fr.
*guimpe,* app. from O.H.G. *wimpal;* cf. wimple;
perhaps confused with Fr. *guipure;* see
guipure.]
gimp, *jimp,* (*rare*) *v.t.* to scallop, notch: to
corrugate.
gin, *jin, n.* geneva: a spirit distilled from grain or
malt and flavoured with juniper berries or
other aromatic substances, made chiefly in
Britain and the U.S.—gin′-fizz, a drink of gin,
lemon-juice, effervescing water, etc.; gin′-
palace, (*derog.*) a showily pretentious public
house; gin′shop; gin′-sling, a cold gin and
water, sweetened and flavoured.—gin and it,
gin and Italian vermouth.—Contr. from
geneva.]
gin, *jin, n.* a scheme, artifice, contrivance (*Spens.*):
a snare or trap: a machine, esp. one for
hoisting: a cotton-gin: an instrument of
torture (*Spens.*).—*v.t.* to trap or snare: to clear
of seeds by a cotton-gin:—*pr.p.* ginn′ing; *pa.t.*
and *pa.p.* ginned.—*ns.* ginn′er, one who gins
cotton; ginn′ery, gin′house, a place where
cotton is ginned.—gin trap, a powerful spring
trap fitted with teeth. [engine.]
gin, *jin, n.* Australian aborigine woman. [Native
word.]
gin, *jin, n.* a type of rummy in which a player

whose unmatched cards count ten or less may stop the game.—Also **gin rummy.** [Origin uncertain.]

**gin,** *gin,* (*arch.*) *v.t.* and *v.i.* to begin:—*pa.t.* **gan,** used poetically in the sense of *did.* [Aphetic from O.E. *beginnan* or *onginnan,* to begin.]

**gin,** *gin,* (*Scot.*) *prep.* by (the time of). [M.E. *gain,* app.—O.N. *gegn,* against.]

**gin,** *gin,* (*Scot.*) *conj.* if. [Perh. pa.p. of give as a substitute for gif; perh. from gin, prep.]

**ging,** *ging,* (*obs.*) *n.* a gang or company. See **gang** (1).

**gingal, gingall.** See **jingal.**

**gingelly.** See **gingili.**

**ginger,** *jin'jər, n.* the root-stock of *Zingiber officinale,* or other species of the genus (family Zingiberaceae) with a hot taste, used as a condiment or stomachic: ginger beer: stimulation: mettle.—*adj.* (*coll.*) sandy, reddish.—*v.t.* to put ginger into: to make spirited.—*adj.* **gin'gerous,** like ginger.—**gingeràde',** ginger ale, an aerated drink flavoured with ginger; **ginger beer,** an effervescent drink made with fermenting ginger; **ginger cordial,** a cordial made of ginger, lemon-peel, raisins, water, and sometimes spirits; **ginger group,** a group within e.g. a political party seeking to inspire the rest with its own enthusiasm and activity; **ginger nut,** a small thick gingersnap; **ginger pop,** weak ginger beer (*coll.*); **gin'gersnap,** a gingerbread biscuit; **ginger wine,** liquor made by the fermentation of sugar and water, and flavoured with various spices, chiefly ginger; **ginger beer plant,** a symbiotic association of a yeast and a bacterium, by which ginger beer can be prepared, also called *Californian bees.* [M.E. *gingivere*—O.Fr. *gengibre*—L.L. *gingiber*—L. *zingiber*—Gr. *zingiberis*—Sans. *śṛnga,* horn, *vera,* body; Malayalam *inchiver.*]

**gingerbread,** *jin'jər-bred, n.* a cake flavoured with treacle and usually ginger.—*adj.* of ornamental work, cheap and tawdry.—**take the gilt off the gingerbread,** to destroy the glamour. [O.Fr. *gingimbrat*—L.L. *gingiber;* see ginger; confused with bread.]

**gingerly,** *jin'jər-li, adv.* with soft steps: with extreme wariness and delicate gentleness.—Also *adj.* [Possibly O.Fr. *gensor,* compar. of gent; see gent (1).]

**gingham,** *ging'əm, n.* a kind of cotton cloth, woven from coloured yarns into stripes or checks: an umbrella (*coll.*). [Fr. *guingan,* orig. from Malay *ginggang,* striped.]

**gingili, gingelly, jinjili,** *jin'ji-li, n.* a species of sesame: an oil got from its seeds. [Hind. *jinjalī,* prob.—Ar. *juljulān.*]

**gingival,** *jin-ji'vl, adj.* pertaining to the gums.—*ns.* **gingivec'tomy,** the cutting back of inflamed or excess gum; **gingivi'tis,** inflammation of the gums. [L. *gingiva,* gum.]

**gingle.** Same as **jingle.**

**ginglymus,** *jing'gli-məs* (or *ging'-*), *n.* a joint that permits movement in one plane only:—*pl.* **ging'lymi.**—*adj.* **ging'limoid.** [Latinised from Gr. *ginglymos.*]

**gink, gink,** (*slang*) *n.* fellow. [Origin unknown.]

**ginkgo,** *gingk'go, n.* the maidenhair tree, holy in Japan, perhaps still wild in China, forming by itself an order (Ginkgoā'les) of Gymnosperms.—Also **ging'ko.** [Jap. *gingko*—Chin. *yin,* silver, *hing,* apricot.]

**ginseng,** *jin'seng, n.* a species of *Panax* or *Aralia;* its root, a Chinese panacea. [Chin. *jên-shên,* perh. image of man.]

**gio.** See **geo** (gully, creek).

**Giorgi system,** *jör'jē sis'tim,* metre-kilogram(me)-second system. [After Giovanni *Giorgi,* Italian physicist, d. 1950.]

**gip,** *jip, n.* Same as **gyp.**

**gipsen,** *jip'sən,* (*Spens.*) *n.* an obs. form of gypsy.

**gipsy.** See **gypsy.**

**giraffe,** *ji-räf', n.* the camelopard, an African ruminant with remarkably long neck and forelegs.—*adj.* **giraff'ine.** [Ar. *zarāfah.*]

**girandole,** *jir'an-dōl, n.* a branched chandelier or similar structure: a pendant, etc., with small jewels attached around it: a rotating firework. [Fr.,—It. *girandola—girare*—L. *gỹrāre,* to turn round—*gỹrus*—Gr. *gỹros,* a circle.]

**girasol, girasole,** *jir'ə-sol, -sōl, n.* a fire-opal or other stone that seems to send a firelike glow from within in certain lights: the plant heliotrope (*obs.*): the sunflower (*obs.*). [It.,—*girare* (see girandole), and *sole*—L. *sōl,* the sun.]

**gird,** *gûrd, v.i.* to gibe, jeer (with *at*).—*v.t.* (*obs.*) to taunt.—*n.* (*arch.*) a taunt, dig, gibe. [Origin obscure; not from O.E. *gyrd, gierd,* rod.]

**gird,** *gird,* (*Scot.*) *n.* a hoop.—Also **girr** (*gir*). [A form of girth.]

**gird,** *gûrd, v.t.* to bind round: to make fast by a belt or girdle: to encompass: to surround: to clothe, furnish:—*pa.t.* and *pa.p* **gird'ed** and **girt.** —*ns.* **gird'er,** a great beam, simple or built up, of wood, iron, or steel, to take a lateral stress, e.g. to support a floor, wall, roadway of a bridge; a strip of strengthening tissue (*bot.*); **gird'ing,** that which girds.—**girder bridge,** a bridge whose load is sustained by girders resting on supports. —**gird oneself,** to tuck up loose garments under the girdle: to brace the mind for any trial or effort. [O.E. *gyrdan;* cf. Ger. *gürten.*]

**girdle,** *gûrd'l, n.* a waist-belt: a cord worn about the waist by a monk, etc.: anything that encloses like a belt: a woman's lightweight, close-fitting undergarment, a form of corset: a bony arch to which a limb is attached: a worm's clitellum: a ring-shaped cut around a tree: the rim of a brilliant-cut gem.—*v.t.* to bind, as with a girdle: to enclose: to cut a ring round.—*adj.* **gird'led.** —*n.* **gird'ler,** one who girdles: a maker of girdles. —**girdle'stead** (*arch.*), the waist. [O.E. *gyrdel—gyrdan.* to gird.]

**girdle,** *gird'l.* See **griddle.**

**girkin,** *gûr'kin, n.* Same as **gherkin.**

**girl,** *gûrl, n.* a female child: a young unmarried woman: a woman irrespective of age: a sweetheart (*coll.*): a maid servant.—*n.* **girl'hood,** the state or time of being a girl.—*adjs.* **girl'ie, girl'ish,** of or like a girl.—*adv.* **girl'ishly.**—*n.* **girl'ishness.**—**Girl Friday,** a young woman who acts as secretary or personal assistant in a business office; **girl'friend,** sweetheart, or girl who is often one's companion: (**girl friend**) a girl's young female friend; **Girl Guide,** a member of an organisation for girls, analogous to the (Boy) Scouts' Association; **Girl Scout,** a member of a similar American organisation.—**old girl,** a female former pupil: a kindly disrespectful mode of address or reference to a female of any age or species. [Origin obscure.]

**girlond,** obsolete form of garland.—In Spens. *Faerie Queene,* IV, x. 51, 9, *girlonds* may be a misprint for *girlands* (or *guerdons*).

**girn, girn,** (*Scot.; Spens.*) *v.i.* to grin, snarl: to complain peevishly.—*n.* an act or manner of girning.—*adj.* **girn'ie,** ill-tempered. [grin.]

**girnel,** *gir'nl,* (*Scot.*) *n.* a granary (*obs.*): a meal chest. [Variant of garner.]

**Giro,** *ji'rō, n.* a banking system by which money can be transferred direct from the account of one holder to that of another person (or to those of others). [Ger., transfer—Gr. *gyros,* ring.]

**giron.** See **gyron.**

**Girondist,** *ji-rond'ist, n.* a member of the moderate republican party during the French Revolution, so-called because its earliest leaders were deputies for the *Gironde* department.—Also **Giron'din.**

**girr.** See **gird** (2).

girt, *gûrt, pa.p.* of gird in all senses: of a ship, moored so taut by her cables to two oppositely placed anchors as to be prevented from swinging to the wind or tide.—*v.t.* to gird: to girth.—*v.i.* to girth.

girth. See grith.

girth, *gûrth, n.* belly-band of a saddle: circumferential measure of thickness.—*v.t.* to put a girth on: to measure the girth of.—*v.i.* to measure in girth.—Also girt.—girthline or girtline, a gantline. [O.N. *gjörth.*]

gist, *jist, n.* the main point or pith of a matter. [O.Fr. *gist* (Fr. *git*)—O.Fr. *gesir* (Fr. *gésir*), to lie—L. *jacēre.*]

gitano, *jē-tän'ō, hhē-,* (Sp.) male gypsy:—*fem.* gitan'a.

gite, *zhēt,* (*arch.*) *n.* a resting-place. [Fr. *gîte*—O.Fr. *giste;* see gest (1).]

gittern, *git'arn. n.* a kind of guitar, a cithern.—*v.i.* to play on the gittern. [O.Fr. *guiterne,* conn. Gr. *kithará;* see cithern, guitar, zither.]

giust, *just,* (*Spens., Scott*) *n., v.i.* Same as joust.

giusto, *jōōs'tō,* (*mus.*) *adj.* suitable: regular: strict. [It.,—L. *jūstus,* just.]

give, *giv, v.t.* to bestow: to impart: to yield: to grant: to donate: to permit: to afford: to furnish: to pay or render, as thanks: to pronounce, as a decision: to show, as a result: to apply, as oneself: to allow or admit.—*v.i.* to yield to pressure: to begin to melt: to grow soft: to open, or give an opening or view, to lead (with *upon, on, into,* a gallicism):—*pr.p.* giv'ing; *pa.t.* gāve; *pa.p.* given, *giv'n.*—*n.* yielding: elasticity.—*adj.* giv'en, bestowed: specified: addicted, disposed: granted: admitted.—*ns.* giv'enness; giv'er, one who or that which gives or bestows; giv'ing, the act of bestowing: the thing given.—*adj.* that gives.—giveaway, a betrayal, revelation, esp. if unintentional: something given free with the aim of increasing sales; given name, the name bestowed upon the individual, not that of the family—the first or Christian name, distinguished from the *surname.*—give and take, reciprocity in concession: mutually compensatory variations: fair exchange of repartee; give away, to give for nothing: to betray: to bestow ceremonially (as a bride); give-away programme, a theatrical or other programme in which some members of the audience seek to gain prizes by performing certain tasks in a given time; give birth to, to bring forth: to originate; give chase, to pursue; give ear, to listen; give forth, to emit: to publish: to expatiate (*coll.*); give ground, place, to give way, yield; give in to (*obs.* give into), to yield to; give it to one (*coll.*), to scold or beat anybody severely; give line, head, rein, etc., to give more liberty or scope—the metaphors from angling and driving; give me, I would choose if I had the choice; give oneself away, to betray one's secret unawares; give out, to report: to emit: to run short: to relinquish (*Shak.*); give over, to cease; give the lie to, to charge openly with falsehood; give tongue, to bark: to utter, expound; give up, to abandon: to surrender: to desist from; give way, to fall back, to yield, to withdraw: to break, snap, collapse, under strain: to begin rowing—usually as a command to a crew: to allow traffic in a direction crossing one's path to proceed first. [O.E. *gefan* (W.S. *giefan*), the back *g* prob. owing to Scand. influence; O.N. *gefa,* Sw. *g'fva,* Dan. *give,* Goth. *giban,* Ger. *geben.*]

give. Same as gyve.

Giz. Same as Geëz.

gizz, *jiz, jiz,* (*Scot.*) *n.* a wig. [Origin unknown.]

gizzard, *giz'ard, n.* a muscular stomach, esp. the second stomach of a bird.—to stick in one's gizzard, to be more than one can accept or tolerate. [M.E. *giser*—O.Fr. *guiser,* supposed

to be—L. *gigeria* (pl.), cooked entrails of poultry.]

gizzen, *giz'n,* (*Scot.*) *v.i.* to shrink from dryness so as to leak: to wither.—*adj.* leaky: shrivelled. [O.N. *gisna.*]

gju. See gue.

glabella, *glə-bel'ə, n.* part of the forehead between the eyebrows and just above their level.—*adj.* glabell'ar. [L. *glaber,* bald, smooth.]

glabrous, *glā'brəs, adj.* hairless. [L. *glāber.*]

glacé, *glā'sā, adj.* frozen, or with ice: iced with sugar: glossy, lustrous, esp. of a thin silk material or kid leather. [Fr.]

glacial, *glās'yəl, glā'si-əl,* or *'shəl, adj.* icy: frozen: readily or ordinarily solidified (as glacial acetic acid, practically pure acetic acid): pertaining to ice or its action.—*ns.* glā'cialist, glaciol'ogist, one who studies the geological action of ice.—*v.t.* glaciate (*glās', glāsh'*), to polish by ice action: to subject to the action of land-ice: to freeze. *n.* glaciā'tion.—*adj.* glaciolog'ical.—*n.* glaciol'ogy, the study of the geological nature, distribution, and action of ice.—Glacial Period, the Ice Age, or any ice age. [L. *glaciālis,* icy, *glaciāre, -ātum,* to freeze—*glaciēs,* ice.]

glacier, *glas'yər* or *i-ər, glās'yər* or *glā'shər, n.* a mass of ice, fed by snow on a mountain, slowly creeping downhill to where it melts or breaks up into icebergs. [Fr.,—*glace,* ice—L. *glaciēs,* ice.]

glacis, *glās-ē, glas'is, glās'is, n.* a gentle slope, esp. in fortification:—*pl.* glacis (*glās-ē, glas'iz, glās'iz*), glacises. [Fr., orig. a slippery place—L. *glaciēs,* ice.]

glad, *glad, adj.* pleased: cheerful: bright: giving pleasure.—*v.t.* (*arch.*) to make glad:—*pr.p.* gladd'ing; *pa.t.* and *pa.p.* gladd'ed.—*v.t.* gladd'en, to make glad: to cheer.—*adj.* glad'ful (*Spens.*).—*n.* glad'fulness.—*adv.* glad'ly.—*n.* glad'ness.—*adj.* glad'some: glad: joyous: gay.—*adv.* glad'somely.—*n.* glad'someness.—glad eye (*slang*), an ogle; glad hand (*U.S.*), the hand of welcome; glad'-hand'er (*U.S.*), one out to make up to all and sundry; glad rags (*coll.*), best clothes, dress clothes.—glad of, glad to have: glad because of; the glad and sorry (*facet.*), the hire-purchase system. [O.E. *glæd;* Ger. *glati,* smooth, O.N. *glathr,* bright, Dan. *glad.*]

gladdon, *glad'ən,* (*dial.*) *n.* an iris. [Origin obscure.]

glade, *glād, n.* an open space in a wood.—*adj.* glā'dy, having glades. [Origin obscure; poss. conn. with glad.]

gladius, *glad'i-əs, glād', n.* a sword (*rare*): a cuttlefish pen.—*adj.* gladiate (*glad', glād'*), sword-shaped.—*n.* gladiator (*glad'i-ā-tər*), in ancient Rome, a professional combatant with men or beasts in the arena.—*adjs.* gladiatorial(*-ə-tō'ri-əl*), gladiato'rian (*obs.*), gladi'atory (*obs.*).—*ns.* glad'iatorship (*obs.*); gladiole, gladiolus (*glad-i-ō'ləs,* rarely *glə-dī'o-ləs*), any plant of a genus (Gladiolus) of the Iris family, with sword-shaped leaves: the middle part of the sternum:—*pl.* gladioli, gladioluses. [L. *glādius,* sword, dim. *glādīŏlus;* *glādiātor,* a gladiator.]

Gladstone, *glad'stən,* statesman and four times prime minister (W. E.; 1809-1898).—*adj.* Gladstonian (*-stō'ni-ən*), pertaining to Gladstone.—*n.* a follower of Gladstone.—Gladstone bag, a travelling bag or small portmanteau, opening out flat, named in his honour; Gladstone sherry, cheap sherry (with ref. to reduction in duty, 1860).

Glagolitic, *glag-ō-lit'ik, adj.* of or pertaining to Glagol, an ancient Slavonic alphabet, apparently derived from the cursive Greek of the 9th century. [Old Slav. *glagolu,* a word.]

glaik, *glāk, n.* (*obs. Scot.;* usu. in *pl.*), a flash: dazzling: mocking deception: a trick: a puzzle-game.—*adj.* (*Scot.*) glaik'it, giddy: foolish.—*n.* (*Scot.*) glaik'itness, levity.—fling the glaiks in folk's een (*obs. Scot.*), to throw dust in people's eyes, dazzle. [Origin obscure.]

**glair**, *glār*, *n.* the clear part of an egg used as varnish: any viscous, transparent substance.—*v.t.* to varnish with white of eggs.—*adjs.* **glair′y, glair′eous** (*arch.*), **glār′eous** (*arch.*).—*n.* **glair′in**, organic matter in mineral waters. [Fr. *glaire*, perh.—L.L. *clāra* (*ōvi*), white (of egg)—L. *clārus*, clear.]

**glaive**, *glāv*, (*obs.*) *n.* a sword: a spear: a long-shafted weapon like a halberd, its edge on the outer curve. [O.Fr. *glaive*.]

**glamour**, in U.S. **glamor**, *glam′ər*, *n.* the supposed influence of a charm on the eyes, making them see things as fairer than they are: fascination: enchantment: witchery (*arch.*): groomed beauty and studied charm.—*v.t.* to enchant, bewitch, cast a spell over.—*adjs.* **glam** (*slang*), **glamorous; glam′orous**, full of glamour: bewitching, alluring.—*n.* **glamorisā′tion**, **-z-**.—*v.t.* **glamor′ise, -ize**, to make glamorous: to romanticise.—**glamour boy, girl** (*coll.*), a man or woman considered to be very glamorous (often *derog.*). [gramary.]

**glance**, *gläns*, *v.i.* to fly (off) obliquely on striking: to make a passing allusion, esp. unfavourable (with *at*): to dart a reflected ray: to flash: to snatch a momentary view.—*v.t.* (*arch.*), to cause to glance: to direct glancingly: to deflect: to glance at.—*n.* an oblique impact or movement: a stroke by which the ball is allowed to glance off an upright bat to fine leg (*cricket*): a passing allusion, esp. satirical: a sudden shoot of reflected light: a darting of the eye: a momentary look.—*n.* and *adj.* **glanc′ing.**—*adv.* **glanc′ingly.** [Origin obscure.]

**glance**, *gläns*, *n.* a black or grey mineral with metallic lustre, usually a sulphide, selenide, or telluride, e.g. redruthite or copper-glance, galena or lead-glance, argentite or silver-glance.— **glance′-coal**, anthracite. [Ger. *glanz*, glance, lustre.]

**gland**, *gland*, *n.* a secreting structure in plant or animal.—*adjs.* **glandif′erous**, bearing acorns or nuts; **gland′iform**, resembling a gland: acorn-shaped; **gland′ūlar**, **gland′ūlous**, containing, consisting of, or pertaining to glands.—*n.* **gland′ūle**, a small gland.—*adj.* **glandūlif′erous.**—*n.* **glans** (*glanz*), an acorn or similar fruit: a glandular structure (**glans clitoris, penis**, the extremity of the clitoris, penis).—**glandular fever**, infectious mononucleosis, a disease characterised by slight fever, enlargement of glands, and increase in the white cells of the blood. [L. *glāns*, *glandis*, an acorn.]

**glanders**, *gland′ərz*, *n.* a malignant, contagious, and fatal disease of the horse and ass (and man), showing itself, esp. on the mucuous membrane of the nose, upon the lungs, and on the lymphatic system.—*adj.* **gland′ered**, affected with glanders. [O.Fr. *glandre*, a gland.]

**glandular**, etc., **glans**. See **gland**.

**glare**, *glār*, *n.* an oppressive or unrelieved dazzling light (also *fig.*): overpowering lustre (*arch.*): cheap or showy brilliance: a glassy or icy surface (*U.S.*): a fierce stare.—*adj.* (*U.S.*) glassy (of ice).—*v.i.* to emit a hard, fierce, dazzling light: to be obtrusively noticeable, to shine dazzlingly: to stare fiercely.—*v.t.* to send forth or express with a glare.—*adj.* **glar′ing**, bright and dazzling: flagrant.—*adv.* **glar′ingly.**—*n.* **glar′ingness.**— *adj.* **glar′y**, glaring: shining harshly. [M.E. *glāren*, to shine; cf. glass, O.E. *glær*, amber, L.Ger. *glaren*, to glow.]

**glareous**, *glā′ri-əs*, *adj.* gravelly: growing on gravel.—*adj.* **glā′real**, growing on dry exposed ground. See also **glair**. [L. *glārea*, gravel.]

**glass**, *gläs*, *n.* a hard, amorphous, brittle substance, a bad conductor of electricity, usually transparent, made by fusing together one or more of the oxides of silicon, boron, or phosphorus with certain basic oxides (e.g. sodium, magnesium, calcium, potassium), and cooling the product rapidly to prevent crystallisation: an article made of or with glass, esp. a drinking-vessel, a mirror, a lens, the cover of a watch-face, a weather-glass, a telescope, etc.: the quantity of liquid a glass holds: any fused substance like glass, with a vitreous fracture: a rock, or portion of rock, without crystalline structure: (*pl.*) spectacles.—*adj.* made of glass.—*v.t.* to glaze: to polish highly: to put in, under, or behind glass: to furnish with glass: to reflect in glass.—*adj.* **glass′en** (*arch.*), of or like glass.— *n.* **glassful**, as much as a glass will hold:—*pl.* **glass′fulls.**—*adv.* **glass′ily.**—*ns.* **glassine** (*en′*), a transparent paper; **glassiness.**—*adj.* **glass′y**, like glass: of eyes, expressionless.—**glass′-blower; glass′-blowing**, the process of making glassware by inflating a viscid mass: **glass chin** or **glass jaw**, a chin or jaw exceptionally vulnerable to punches, used chiefly of boxers; **glass′-cloth**, a cloth for drying glasses: a material woven from glass threads: a polishing cloth covered with powdered glass; **glass′-coach** (*obs.*), a coach (esp. one for hire) having glazed windows; **glass′-crab**, the transparent larva of the spiny lobster; **glass′-cutter**, a tool for cutting sheets of glass: one who does cut-glass work; **glass′-cutting**, the act or process of cutting, shaping, and ornamenting the surface of glass; **glass eye**, an artificial eye made of glass: (*pl.*) spectacles (*obs.*): a form of blindness in horses.—*adj.* **glass-faced** (*Shak.*), reflecting the sentiments of another, as in a mirror.—**glass fibre**, glass melted and then drawn out into extremely fine fibres, which are later to be spun, woven, etc.; **glass-gall**, a scum formed on fused glass.— *adj.* **glass′-gaz′ing** (*Shak.*), addicted to looking in a mirror; **glass′-grinding**, the ornamenting of glass by rubbing with sand, emery, etc.; **glass′-house**, a glass factory: a house made of glass or largely of glass, esp. a greenhouse: military detention barracks (from one with a glass roof at Aldershot; *slang*).—*adj.* **glass′-like.**—**glass jaw** (see glass chin); **glass′man**, a maker or seller of glass: a beggar hawking glass as a pretext (*arch.*); **glass′-painting**, the art of producing pictures on glass by means of staining it chemically; **glass′-paper**, paper coated with finely pounded glass, used like sand-paper; **glass′-rope**, a silicious sponge (Hyalonema) with a long anchoring tuft; **glass′-snake**, a legless lizard (Ophisaurus) with brittle tail; **glass′-soap**, manganese dioxide or other substance used by glass-makers to remove colouring from glass; **glass′ware**, articles made of glass; **glass wool**, glass spun into woolly fibres; **glass′work**, a glass factory: furnishings or articles made of glass; **glass′wort**, a name for plants of the genera Salicornia and Salsola yielding soda, once used in making glass.—*adj.* **glass′yheaded** (*Tenn.*), shiny-pated.—**live in a glass house**, to be open to attack or retort; **musical glasses** (see **harmonica**); **water**, or **soluble, glass**, sodium or potassium silicate. [O.E. *glæs*.]

**Glassite**, *gläs′īt*, *n.* a Sandemanian, or follower of John *Glas* (1695–1773), deposed in 1730 from the ministry of the Church of Scotland for maintaining that a congregation with its eldership is, in its discipline, subject to no jurisdiction but that of Jesus Christ.

**Glaswegian**, *glas-, gläs-, wēj′(y)ən*, *n.* a native or citizen of *Glasgow.*—Also *adj.* [Modelled on Norwegian.]

**glauberite**, *glö′bər-it*, *n.* a greyish-white mineral, sodium calcium sulphate found chiefly in rock-salt, named after the German chemist Johann Rudolf *Glauber* (1604–68).—**Glauber('s) salt**

(glow'bər, glö'bər), hydrated sodium sulphate, discovered by him.

**glaucoma**, glö-kō'ma, n. an insidious disease of the eye, marked by increased tension within the eyeball and growing dimness of vision.—adj. **glaucomatous** (-kōm'ə-təs, -kom'). [Gr. glaukōma, cataract; see glaucous.]

**glauconite**, glök'ə-nīt, n. a mineral now forming in the sea, a hydrated potassium iron and aluminium silicate, which gives a green colour to some of the beds of the Greensand.—adj. **glauconitic** (-nit'ik).—n. **glauconitisā'tion**, -**ization**, conversion into glauconite. [Gr. glaukos, bluish-green.]

**glaucous**, glö'kəs, adj. sea-green: greyish-blue: covered with a fine greenish or bluish bloom (bot.).—n. **glaucescence** (-ses'əns).—adj. **glaucesc'ent**, somewhat glaucous. [L. glaucus—Gr. glaukos, bluish-green or grey (orig. gleaming).]

**Glaucus**, glö'kəs, n. a genus of translucent blue nudibranch gasteropods of warm seas. [Gr. glaukos, bluish-green.]

**glaum**, glöm, (Scot.) v.i. to clutch (with at).

**glaur**, glör, (Scot.) n. mire.—adj. **glaur'y**. [Origin unknown.]

**Glaux**, glöks, n. the generic name of sea-milkwort or black saltwort, a fleshy seaside plant of the primrose family, with pink sepals and no petals, once used in soda-making. [Gr. glaux, wartcress.]

**glaze**, glāz, v.t. to furnish or set with glass: to cover with a thin surface of glass or something glassy: to give a glassy surface to.—n. the glassy coating put upon pottery: a thin coat of transparent colour: any shining exterior.—v.i. to become glassy.—adj. **glāz'en** (arch.), glassy: glazed.—ns. **glāz'er**, a workman who glazes pottery, paper, etc.: **glā'zier** (-zyər), one who sets glass in window-frames, etc.; **glāz'ing**, the act or art of setting glass: the art of covering with a vitreous substance: semi-transparent colours put thinly over others to modify the effect (paint.). [M.E. glasen—glas, glass; see glass.]

**gleam**, glēm, v.i. to glow or shine, usu. not very brightly.—v.t. to flash.—n. a faint or moderate glow: a small stream of light: a beam: brightness: often used fig. as a gleam of hope, a gleam of understanding.—n. **gleam'ing**.—adj. **gleam'y**, casting gleams or rays of light. [O.E. glǽm, gleam, brightness; see glimmer.]

**glean**, glēn, v.t. to gather in handfuls after the reapers: to collect (what is thinly scattered, neglected, or overlooked): to learn by laboriously scraping together pieces of information.—v.i. to gather the corn left by a reaper or anything that has been left by others: to gather facts bit by bit.—n. that which is gleaned: the act of gleaning.—ns. **glean'er**; **glean'ing**. [O.Fr. glener (Fr. glaner), through L.L. glenāre; origin unknown.]

**glebe**, glēb, n. the soil (arch.): a clod (arch.): a field (arch.): the land attached to a parish church.—adjs. **gleb'ous**, **gleb'y**, (arch.) cloddy, turfy.—**glebe'-house**, a manse. [L. glēba, a clod.]

**glede**, glēd, gled, gled, (B.) n. the common kite. [O.E. glida, from glīdan, to glide.]

**gledge**, glej, (Scot.) v.i. to squint: to cast an eye around: to look cunningly.—n. a knowing look: a side-glance: a glimpse. [Cf. gley.]

**glee**, glē, n. joy: mirth and gaiety: impish enjoyment: a song or catch in parts, strictly one without an accompaniment (mus.): app. glitter (proverbially coupled with gold; Spens).—adjs. **glee'ful**, **glee'some**, merry.—**glee'maiden**, a female minstrel; **glee'man**, a minstrel. [O.E. glēo, glīw, mirth; O.N. glȳ.]

**glee.** Same as gley.

**gleed**, glēd, (dial.) n. a hot coal or burning ember. [O.E. glēd; cf. Du. gloed, Ger. glut, Sw. glöd.]

**gleek**, glēk, (obs.) n. (Shak.) a jest or gibe, a trick.—v.i. to gibe at (Shak.): to jest.—v.t. to play a trick upon. [Cf. glaik.]

**gleek**, glēk, (hist.) n. a game at cards for three, each having twelve, and eight being left for the stock. [O.Fr. glic, ghelicque, possibly—M.Du. ghelic, alike.]

**gleet**, glēt, n. a viscous, transparent discharge from a mucous surface.—v.t. to discharge gleet. —adj. **gleet'y**. [O.Fr. glette, glecte, a flux.]

**gleg**, gleg, (Scot.) adj. clever: apt: alert: keen. [O.N. gleggr, clever; cf. O.E. glēaw, wise, Ger. glau, clear.]

**gleichschaltung**, glīhh'shäl-tōong, n. elimination of all opposition, enforcement of strict conformity, in politics, culture, etc. [Ger., co-ordination— gleich, like, schalten, to govern.]

**glen**, glen, n. a narrow valley with a stream, often with trees: a depression, usu. of some extent, between hills. [Gael. gleann; cf. W. glyn.]

**glendoveer**, glen-dō-vēr', (Southey) n. a heavenly spirit. [Fr. grandouver.]

**glengarry**, glen-gar'i, n. a Highlander's cap of thick-milled woollen, generally rising to a point in front, with ribbons hanging down behind. [Glengarry in Inverness-shire.]

**Glenlivet**, glen-liv'it, n. proprietary name for a noted whisky [Glenlivet, a valley in Banffshire.]

**glenoid**, -al, glē'noid, -əl, adjs. socket-shaped: slightly cupped.—Also n. [Gr. glēnoeidēs— glēnē, a socket.]

**glent**, glent, v.t., v.i., and n. an earlier form of glint.

**gley**, glī, glē, (Scot.) v.i. to squint.—adj. **gleyed**, squint-eyed.—Also glee, gleed. [Origin obscure; cf. gledge.]

**glia**, glī'ə, glē'ə, n. neuroglia.—adj. **glial**.—n. **gli'adin**, prolamine, a protein in gluten. [Gr. glīā, glue.]

**glib**, glib, adj. smooth (arch.): slippery (arch.): easy: facile: fluent and plausible.—adv. (arch.) **glibly**.—v.t. (arch.) to make glib.—adj. **glibb'ery** (obs.), slippery.—adv. **glib'ly**.—n. **glib'ness**. [Cf. Du. glibberig, slippery.]

**glib**, glib. (Spens.) n. a bush of hair over the eyes. [Ir.]

**glib**, glib, (Shak.) v.t. to castrate. [Cf. lib.]

**glidder**, glid'ər, (dial.) adj. slippery.—Also glid (Scot.), **glidd'ery**. [O.E. glidder.]

**glide**, glīd, v.i. to slide smoothly and easily: to flow gently: to pass smoothly or stealthily: to travel through the air without expenditure of power: to travel by glider: to play a glide stroke.—n. act of gliding: a transitional sound produced in passing from one position to another (phon.): a glance stroke (cricket): a smooth and sliding dance-step: an inclined plane or slide: stretch of shallow gliding water.— ns. **glid'er**, one who or that which, glides: an aircraft like an aeroplane without engine (a powered glider has a small engine): a hydroplane; **glid'ing**, the action of the verb in any sense: the sport of flying in a glider.—adv. **glid'ingly**.— **glide slope**, **path**, the slope along which aircraft are assumed to come in for landing, marked out, e.g. by a radio beam. [O.E. glīdan, to slip; Ger. gleiten.]

**gliff**, glif, (Scot.) n. a fright: a scare: a glimpse or other transient experience: a moment.—Also **glift**.—n. **gliff'ing**, a moment. [Ety. dub.]

**glike**, glik, (Shak.) n. Same as gleek.

**glim**, glim, n. a glimpse (Scot.): a scrap (Scot.): a light (slang): an eye (slang). [Cf. gleam, glimmer; and Ger., a spark.]

**glimmer**, glim'ər, v.i. to burn or appear faintly. —ns. a faint light: feeble rays of light: an inkling, faint perception; **glimm'ering**, a glimmer: an inkling.—adv. **glimm'eringly**.—adj. **glimm'ery**. —**glimm'er-gowk** (Tenn.), an owl. [M.E. glemern, freq. from root of gleam.]

Neutral vowels in unaccented syllables: el'ə-mənt; for certain sounds in foreign words, see p. viii

glimmer, *glim'ər, n.* mica. [Ger.]
glimpse, *glimps, n.* a short gleam: a passing appearance: a momentary view.—*v.i.* to glimmer: to appear by glimpses.—*v.t.* to get a glimpse of. [M.E. *glymsen,* to glimpse.]
glint, *glint, v.i.* to flash with a glittering light.—*v.t.* to reflect.—*n.* a gleam. [Earlier *glent*; prob. Scand.]
Glires, *glī'rēz, n.pl.* a division of mammals including the typical rodents (e.g. the genus *Glis,* Old World dormice), etc. [L. *glis, glīris,* dormouse.]
glisk, *glisk,* (*Scot.*) *n.* a glimpse. [Perh. from the same root as O.E. *glisian,* to shine.]
glissade, *glēs-äd', v.i.* to slide or glide down.—*n.* act of sliding down a slope: a gliding movement in dancing. [Fr.]
glissando, *glēs-än'dō, n.* effect produced by sliding finger along keyboard or strings: similar effect on trombone, etc.—Also *adj.* and *adv.* [It., sliding.]
glisten, *glis'n, v.i.* to shine, as light reflected from a wet or oily surface.—*n.* gleam. [M.E. *glistnen*—O.E. *glisnian,* to shine; cf. Du. *glinsteren.*]
glister, *glis'tər,* (*arch.*) *v.i.* to sparkle, glitter.—*adj.* glis'tering. [M.E. *glistren*; cf. glisten, and Du. *glisteren.*]
glit, *glit, n.* sticky, slimy or greasy material: gleet. [gleet.]
glitch, *glich, n.* an instance of imperfect functioning in a spacecraft, as, e.g. a minute change in voltage on a line.
glitter, *glit'ər, v.i.* to sparkle with light: to be splendid: to be showy.—*n.* sparkle: showiness.—*adj.* glitt'erand (*Spens.*), glittering.—*n.* and *adj.* glitt'ering.—*adv.* glitt'eringly. [M.E. *gliteren*; cf. O.N. *glitra,* Ger. *glitzern.*]
gloaming, *glōm'ing, n.* twilight, dusk. [Apparently from a short-vowelled derivative of O.E *glōmung—glōm,* twilight.]
gloat, *glōt, v.i.* to gaze exultingly, esp. with a wicked or malicious joy.—*n.* an act of gloating. [Perh. O.N. *glotta,* to grin.]
globe, *glōb, n.* a ball: a round body, a sphere: the earth: a sphere representing the earth (terrestrial globe), or one representing the heavens (celestial globe): an orb, emblem of sovereignty: a lamp glass: a nearly spherical glass vessel: a group (*obs.*).—*v.t., v.i.* to form into a globe.—*adj.* glōb'al, spherical: world-wide: affecting, or taking into consideration, the whole world or all peoples.—*adv.* glōb'ally.—*adjs.* glōb'ate, -d, globe-shaped; glōbed, globe-shaped: having a globe; glōb'oid, glōbose' (*Milt.*; or glōb'), globate.—*ns.* a globosity.—*n.* glōbos'ity, (something having) the quality of being globate.—*adjs.* glōb'ous; globular (*glob'ū-lər*), spherical.—*n.* globularity (*glob-ū-lar'i-ti*).—*adv.* glōb'ularly.—*ns.* glōb'ūle, a little globe or round particle: a drop: a small pill: glōb'ūlet; glōb'ūlin, any one of a class of proteins soluble in dilute salt solutions but not in pure water; glōb'ūlite, a minute spheroidal crystallite occurring esp. in glassy rocks.—*adjs.* glōbūlous; glōb'y (*Milt.*), round.—globe'-fish, any fish of the families Diodontidae and Tetrodontidae, capable of blowing itself up into a globe; globe'-flower, a ranunculaceous plant (Trollius) with a globe of large showy sepals enclosing the small inconspicuous petals; globe'-thistle (see Echinops); globe'-trotter, one who goes sight-seeing about the world; globe'-trotting. [L. *globus.*]
Globigerina, *glob-i-jə-rī'nə, n.* a genus of foraminifers with calcareous shell of globose chambers in a spiral.—globigerina ooze, a deep-sea deposit of globigerina shells. [L. *globus,* globe, *gerēre,* to carry.]
glockenspiel, *glok'ən-shpēl, n.* an orchestral instrumental consisting of a set of bells or bars

struck by hammers, with or (more usually) without a keyboard. [Ger. *glocke,* bell, *spiel,* play.]
glode, *glōd,* (*Spens.*) *pa.t.* of glide.
gloire, *glwär,* (Fr.) glory.
glomerate, *glom'ər-āt, v.t.* (*rare*) to gather into a ball.—*adj.* balled: clustered in heads.—*n.* glomerā'tion.—*adj.* glomerular (*glom-er'ū-lər*).—*n.* glomerule (*glom'ər-ōōl*), a little ball of spores: a cluster of short-stalked flowers. [L. *glomerāre,* -*ātum—glomus, glomeris,* a clew of yarn.]
gloom, *glōōm, n.* partial darkness: cloudiness: a dark place: heaviness of mind: hopelessness: sullenness: a scowl, sullen look (*Scot.*).—*v.i.* to be or look sullen or dejected: to be or become cloudy, dark, or obscure: to scowl: to dusk.—*v.t.* to fill with gloom.—*adj.* gloom'ful.—*adv.* gloom'ily.—*n.* gloom'iness.—*adj.* gloom'ing (*Spens.*), shining obscurely.—*n.* twilight: gloaming: scowling.—*adj.* gloom'y, dim or obscure: dimly lighted: depressed in spirits: dismal. [M.E. *gloumbe*; see glum.]
gloria, *glō', glō'ri-ə, n.* an aureole: a halo. [L.]
gloria, *glō'ri-a, glō'ri-ə,* (L.) glory; gloria in excelsis, *in ek-, ik-sel'sis, eks-chel'sis, eks-kel'sēs,* glory (to God) on high; gloria Patri, *pat'ri, 'ri, pät'rē,* glory (be) to the Father.
glorify, *glō', glō'ri-fī, v.t.* to make glorious: to cast glory upon: to honour: to exalt to glory or happiness: to ascribe honour to: to ascribe great charm, beauty, etc., to, usually to a markedly exaggerated extent: to worship:—*pr.p.* glo'rifying; *pa.t.* and *pa.p.* glo'rified.—*n.* glorificā'tion, an act of glorifying: a doxology: riotous festivity (*coll.*). [L. *glōria,* glory, *facĕre,* to make.]
glory, *glō', glō'ri, n.* renown: exalted or triumphant honour: the occasion of praise: an object of supreme pride: splendour, beauty: resplendent brightness: summit of attainment, prosperity or gratification: in religious symbolism, a combination of the nimbus and the aureola, but often erroneously used for the nimbus: a burst of sunlight: a ring or glow of light about the moon, the Brocken spectre, or other object or phenomenon: boastful or self-gratulatory spirit (*obs.*): the presence of God: the manifestation of God to the blessed in heaven: a representation of the heavens opened: heaven.—*v.i.* to boast (*obs.*): to exult proudly: to rejoice.—*v.t.* (*obs.*) to glorify:—*pr.p.* glo'rying; *pa.t.* and *pa.p.* glo'ried.—*interj.* expressing surprise.—*ns.* glo'riole, a halo or glory; Gloriō'sa, a tropical genus of leaf-climbers of the lily family.—*adj.* glo'rious, noble: splendid: conferring renown: elated, tipsy (*coll.*): boastful (*obs.*).—*adv.* glo'riously.—*n.* glo'riousness.—*n.* glo'ry-pea', the papilionaceous genus Clianthus, consisting of Sturt's desert-pea (in Australia) and the parrot-bill (in New Zealand).—glory be, a devout ascription of Glory to God: hence, an ejaculation of exultation: an interj. expressing surprise; glory of the snow, the plant Chionodoxa; Old Glory, the Stars and Stripes. [O.Fr. *glorie* and L. *glōria.*]
glory-hole, *glō', glō'ri-hōl, n.* a glass-maker's supplementary furnace: a hole for viewing the inside of a furnace: a nook or receptacle for miscellaneous odds and ends: a steward's room on a ship: a hiding-place: an excavation. [Perh. M.E. *glory,* to defile, or glaury, or glory, and hole.]
gloss, *glos, n.* brightness or lustre, as from a polished surface: external show.—*v.t.* to give a superficial lustre to: to render plausible: to palliate.—*adv.* gloss'ily.—*n.* gloss'iness.—*adj.* gloss'y, smooth and shining: highly polished.—*n.* (*coll.*), a glossy magazine.—glossy magazine, a woman's magazine of the lusher type, usually printed on glossy paper, and abounding in

illustrations and advertisements. [Cf. O.N. *glossi*, blaze, *glōa*, to glow; see **glass**.]
**gloss**, *glos, n.* a marginal or interlinear explanation, e.g. of an obscure or unusual word: an explanation: a sophistical explanation: a collection of explanations of words.—*v.t.* to give a gloss on: to explain away.—*v.i.* to comment or make explanatory remarks.—*adj.* **glossä′rial**, relating to a glossary: containing explanation.—*ns.* **gloss′arist** (*-ə-rist*), a writer of a gloss or of a glossary; **gloss′ary**, a collection of glosses: a partial dictionary for a special purpose; **glossä′- tor**, **gloss′er**, a writer of glosses or comments, a commentator; **Gloss′ic**, a phonetic alphabet devised by A. J. Ellis (1814-90); **Glossi′na**, the tsetse fly genus; **glossi′tis**, inflammation of the tongue; **glossodynia** (*-din′i-ə*; Gr. *odynē*, pain), pain in the tongue; **glossog′rapher.**—*adj.* **glossograph′ical.**—*ns.* **glossog′raphy**, the writing of glosses or comments; **glossolā′lia** (Gr. *laleein*, to talk), the 'gift of tongues', abnormal utterance under religious emotion.—*adj.* **glosso-log′ical.**—*ns.* **glossol′ogist; glossol′ogy** (*obs.*), comparative philology (also **glottol′ogy**): terminology. [Gɪ. *glōssa*, *glotta*, tongue, a word requiring explanation.]
**glottis**, *glot′is, n.* the opening of the larynx or entrance to the windpipe.—*adjs.* **glott′al**, of the glottis; **glott′ic**, pertaining to the glottis or to the tongue: linguistic.—**glottal stop**, a consonant sound produced by opening or shutting the glottis, recognised in Hebrew and Arabic, and often substituted for *t* by careless speakers of English, esp. in Scotland. [Gr. *glōttis—glōtta*, the tongue.]
**glottology.** See **glossology** under **gloss** (2).
**glout**, *glowt*, (*arch.*) *v.i.* to be sulky.—*n.* a sulky look, the sulks. [Perh. a variant of **gloat**.]
**glove**, *gluv, n.* a covering for the hand, with a sheath for each finger: a boxing-glove.—*v.t.* to cover with, or as with, a glove.—*adj.* **gloved.**—*n.* **glov′er**, one who makes or sells gloves.—**glove′- fight**, a boxing-match in which the hands are gloved; **glove′-money** (*hist.*), a gratuity given to servants, officers of a court, etc.; **glove′-shield** (*hist.*), a shield worn by a knight on the left-hand gauntlet to parry blows; **glove′-stretcher**, a scissors-shaped instrument for stretching the fingers of gloves. [O.E. *glōf*, perh. conn. with **loof**.]
**glow**, *glō, v.i.* to shine with an intense heat: to burn without flame: to emit a steady light: to flush: to tingle with bodily warmth or with emotion: to be ardent.—*n.* a shining with heat: a luminous appearance: a feeling of warmth: brightness of colour: warmth of feeling.—*adj.* **glow′ing.**—*adv.* **glow′ingly.**—**glow′lamp**, an incandescent lamp, usually electric; **glow′-worm**, a beetle, esp. *Lampyris noctiluca*, whose larvae and wingless females are luminous. [O.E. *glōwan*, to glow; Ger. *glühen*, O.N. *glōa*, to glow.]
**glower**, *glow′ər*, *glowr*, *v.i.* to stare frowningly: to scowl.—*n.* a fierce or threatening stare. [Origin obscure.]
**Gloxinia**, *glok-sin′i-ə, n.* a tropical American genus of Gesneriaceae, with bright bell-shaped flowers: generally applied to the allied Sinningia. [*Gloxin*, a German botanist.]
**gloze**, *glōz, v.i.* (*arch.*) to flatter: to comment.— *v.t.* to make glosses on, explain (*arch.*): to palliate by specious explanation: to flatter (*arch.*): to deceive with smooth words (*arch.*).— *n.* (*arch.*) an explanation: a false show.— *n.* **glō′zing**, flattery, deceit. [O.Fr. *glose*—L. *glōssa*—Gr. *glōssa*; see **gloss** (2).]
**glucinum**, *gloo-si′nəm*, also **glucinium**, *gloo-sin′i- əm, ns.* beryllium.—*n.* **gluci′na**, beryllia. [Gr. *glykys*, sweet, from the taste of its salts.]
**glucose**, *gloo′kōs, n.* grape-sugar or dextrose.— *ns.* **glu′coside**, a vegetable product which, on

treatment with acids or alkalis, yields glucose or kindred substance; **glucosū′ria**, glycosuria. [Gr. *glykys*, sweet.]
**glue**, *gloo, n.* an impure gelatine got by boiling animal refuse, used as an adhesive.—*v.t.* to join with, or as with, glue or other adhesive:—*pr.p.* **glu′ing**; *pa.t.* and *pa.p.* **glued.**—*n.* **glu′er**, one who cements with glue.—*adj.* **glu′ey**, containing glue: sticky: viscous.—*n.* **glu′eyness.**—*adj.* **glu′ish** (*obs.*), having the nature of glue.—**glue′- pot**, a vessel for melting or holding glue: a sticky place.—**marine glue**, not a glue, but a composition of rubber, shellac, and oil, that resists sea-water. [Fr. *glu*—L.L. *glus, glūtis.*]
**glum**, *glum, adj.* sullen: gloomy.—*adv.* **glum′ly.**— *n.* **glum′ness.**—*adj.* **glump′ish** (*arch.*), glum.—*n.pl.* **glumps** (*arch.*), the sulks.—*adj.* **glump′y** (*arch.*), sulky. [M.E. *glombe, glomɛ,* to frown.]
**glume**, *gloōm, n.* an outer sterile bract which, alone or with others, encloses the spikelet in grasses and sedges.—*adj.* **glumā′ceous**, like a glume, thin, brownish and papery.—*n.* **glumell′a**, a palea.—*adj.* **glumif′erous**, having glumes.— *n.pl.* **Glumiflō′rae**, an order of monocotyledons consisting of grasses and sedges. [L. *glūma*, husk —*glūbĕre*, to peel.]
**glut**, *glut, v.t.* to gorge: to feed to satiety: to saturate:—*pr.p.* **glutt′ing**; *pa.t.* and *pa.p.* **glutt′ed.**—*n.* a glutting: a surfeit: an over-supply. [L. *gluttire*, to swallow.]
**glutaeus**, **gluteus**, *gloo-tē′əs, n.* one of the natal or buttock muscles.—*adj.* **glutae′al**, **glutē′al.** [Gr. *gloutos*, the rump.]
**gluten**, *gloo′tən, n.* the nitrogenous part of the flour of wheat and other grains, insoluble in water.—*adj.* **glu′tinous**, gluey: tenacious: sticky. —*adv.* **glu′tinously.**—**glutam′ic acid**, an important amino-acid, HOOC · CH₂ · CH₂ · CH(NH₂) · COOH. [L. *glūten, -inis,* glue; cf. **glue.**]
**glutton**, *glut′n, n.* one who eats to excess: a northern carnivore (Gulo) of the weasel family, reputed a great eater: one greedy for, a devourer, e.g. of books (*jig.*).—*v.i.* **glutt′onise, -ize,** to eat tɔ excess.—*adjs.* **glutt′onous**, **glutt′onish**, given to, or consisting in, gluttony.—*adv.* **glutt′onously.** —*n.* **glutt′ony**, excess in eating. [Fr. *glouton*—L. *glūtō, -ōnis—glūtire, glutire,* to devour.]
**glycerine**, **glycerin**, *glis′ə-rēn, -in,* **glycerol**, *-ol, ns.* a trihydric alcohol, a colourless, viscid, neutral inodorous fluid, of a sweet taste, soluble in water and alcohol.—*ns.* ˌ**lyc′eride**, an ester of glycerol; **gly′ceryl**, a radical of which glycerine is the hydroxide. [Gr. *glykeros*, sweet—*glykys.*]
**glycin**, **glycine**, *glis′in, gli′sin, -sēn, -sēn′, n.* amino-acetic acid or glycocoll, CH₂(NH₂) · COOH, a sweetish colourless crystalline solid first prepared from glue. [Gr. *glykys*, sweet.]
**glycocoll**, *glik′ō-kol,* or *glik′, n.* glycin. [Gr. *glykys*, sweet, *kolla*, glue.]
**glycogen**, *glik′ō-jan,* or *glik′, n.* animal starch, a starch found in the liver, yielding glycose on hydrolysis. [Gr. *glykys*, sweet, and the root of *gennaein*, to produce.]
**glycol**, *glik′ol, glik′ol, n.* the type of a class of compounds with two hydroxyl groups on adjacent carbon atoms, and so intermediate between alcohol and glycerine. [From *glyc*erine and *alcoh*ol.]
**glyconic**, *gli-kon′ik,* (*Greek pros.*) *adj.* consisting of four feet—one a dactyl, the others trochees.— *n.* a glyconic verse. [The poet *Glycon* (Gr. *Glykōn*).]
**glycose**, *gli′kōs, n.* glucose.—*n.* **glycosū′ria** (Gr. *ouron*, urine), the presence of sugar in the urine. [Gr. *glykys*, sweet.]
**glyph**, *glif, n.* (*archit.*) an ornamental channel or fluting, usually vertical: a sculptured mark.— *adjs.* **glyph′ic**, carved; **glyphograph′ic.**—*ns.* **glyph′ograph**, a plate formed by glyphography; **glyphog′raphy**, a process of taking a raised copy

of an engraved plate by electrotype. [Gr. *glyphē—glyphein*, to carve.]

**glyptal resins**, *glip'tǝl rez'inz*, almost colourless, tacky, adhesive resins made by heating glycerol or other polyhydric alcohol with a polybasic acid, used as bonding materials for mica, and (modified) in the paint and varnish trades.

**glyptic**, *glip'tik*, *adj*. pertaining to carving, esp. gem-carving.—*n*. **glyp'tics** (treated as *sing*.), the art of gem-engraving.—*adj*. **glyptograph'ic.**—*ns*. **glyptog'raphy**, the art of engraving on precious stones; **glyptothē'ca** (Gr. *thēkē*, receptacle), a place for keeping sculpture. [Gr. *glyptos*, carved.]

**Glyptodon**, *glip'tō-don*, *n*. a gigantic S. American Post-Tertiary fossil member of the Edentata with fluted teeth. [Gr. *glyptos*, carved, *odous, odontos*, tooth.]

**gmelinite**, (g)*mel'in-it*, (*min*.) *n*. a sodium aluminium zeolite. [After C. G. *Gmelin* (1792-1860), German chemist.]

**gnamma hole**, *nam'ǝ hōl*, (*Austr*.) *n*. a rock hollow in a desert area, perh. containing water. [Aboriginal.]

**Gnaphalium**, *na-fā'li-ǝm*, *n*. the cudweed genus of composites. [Latinised from Gr. *gnaphallion*, cottonweed.]

**gnar**, *när*, *v.i.* to snarl or growl.—Also **gnarr, knar, gnarl.** [Onomatopoeic; cf. O.E. *gnyrran*, to grind the teeth, creak, Ger. *knurren*, Dan. *knurre*, to growl.]

**gnarl, knarl**, *närl*, *n*. a lump or knot in a tree.— *adjs*. **gnarled, gnarl'y**, knotty: contorted: rugged, weatherbeaten. [After Shakespeare's *gnarled* for **knurled**.]

**gnash**, *nash*, *v.t.* and *v.i.* to strike (the teeth) together in rage or pain: to bite with a snap or clash of the teeth.—*n*. a snap of the teeth.—*adv*. **gnash'ingly.** [M.E. *gnasten*; prob. from O.N., ultimately onomatopoeic.]

**gnat**, *nat*, *n*. any small fly of the family Culicidae, of which the females are commonly bloodsuckers: a mosquito: extended to other small insects.—*n*. **gnat'ling**, a little gnat: an insignificant person. [O.E. *gnæt*.]

**gnathic**, *nath'ik*, *adj*. of the jaws.—*n*. **gnath'ite**, in arthropods, an appendage used as a jaw.—*n.pl*. **Gnathobdell'ida** (Gr. *bdella*, leech), an order of leeches with (usu.) jaws but no proboscis. [Gr. *gnathos*, jaw.]

**gnathonic, -al**, *na-thon'ik*, *-ǝl*, *adjs*. flattering. [From *Gnathō*, a character in Terence's *Eunuchus* —Gr. *gnathos*, jaw.]

**gnaw**, *nö*, *v.t.* and *v.i.* to bite with a scraping or mumbling movement: to wear away: to bite in agony or rage: to distress persistently (*fig*.):— *pa.t.* **gnawed**; *pa.p.* **gnawed, gnawn.**—*n*. **gnaw'er**, one who gnaws: a rodent. [O.E. *gnagan*; cf. nag (2); Du. *knagen*, Mod. Ice. *naga*.]

**gneiss**, *nis*, *n*. coarse-grained foliated metamorphic rock, usually composed of quartz, feldspar, and mica.—*adjs*. **gneiss'ic, gneissit'ic**, of the nature of gneiss; **gneiss'oid**, like gneiss; **gneiss'ose**, having the structure of gneiss. [Ger. *gneis*.]

**Gnetum**, *nē'tam*, *n*. a tropical genus of trees and shrubs constituting with Ephedra and Welwitschia the family **Gnetā'ceae** and order **Gnetā'lēs**, gymnosperms differing from conifers in having a perianth, vessels in secondary wood, and no resin canals. [Said to be from *gnemon*, a name used in the island of Ternate.]

**gnocchi**, *no'kē*, *nö'kē*, *nyök'kē*, *n*. a dish of small dumplings made from flour, semolina, or potatoes, sometimes with the addition of cheese, and served with a sauce.

**gnome**, *nōm*, *nō'mē*, *n*. a pithy and sententious saying, generally in verse, embodying some moral sentiment or precept:—*pl*. **gnomes** (*nōmz, nō'mēz*), **gnomae** (*nō'mē*).—*adj*. **gnōm'ic.**— **gnomic aorist** (*gram*.), a past tense of the Greek

verb, used in proverbs, etc., for what once happened and is generally true. [Gr. *gnōmē*, an opinion, maxim.]

**gnome**, *nōm*, *n*. a sprite guarding the inner parts of the earth and its treasures: a dwarf or goblin. —*adj*. **gnōm'ish.**—the gnomes of Europe, Zürich, etc., the big bankers. [Paracelsus's Latin *gnomus*.]

**gnomon**, *nō'mon*, *n*. the pin of a dial, whose shadow points to the hour: an upright rod for taking the sun's altitude by its shadow: an index or indicator: jocularly, the nose (*obs*.): that which remains of a parallelogram when a similar parallelogram within one of its angles is taken away (*geom*.): a geometrical figure which, added to or subtracted from another, gives a figure similar to the original one.—*adjs*. **gnomonic, -al** (*-mon'*), pertaining to a gnomon or to the art of gnomonics.—*adv*. **gnomon'ically.**—*ns*. **gnomon'ics** (treated as *sing*.), the art of measuring time by the sundial; **gnomonol'ogy**, a treatise on gnomonics. [Gr. *gnōmōn*, a gnomon, a carpenter's square—*gnōnai* (aorist), to know.]

**gnostic**, *nos'tik*, *adj*. having knowledge: knowing, shrewd: (with *cap*.) pertaining to Gnosticism.— *n*. (with *cap*.) an adherent of Gnosticism.—*ns*. **gnō'sis**, knowledge: mystical knowledge; **Gnos'ticism**, the eclectic doctrines of the Gnostics, whose philosophy, esp. in early Christian times, taught the redemption of the spirit from matter by spiritual knowledge, and believed creation to be a process of emanation from the original essence or Godhead. [Gr. *gnōstikos*, good at knowing—*gignōskein*, to know.]

**gnothi seauton**, *gnō'thi se-ow-ton'*, (Gr.) know thyself—inscribed on temple of Apollo at Delphi.

**gnotobiology**, *nō-tō-bī-ol'ǝ-ji*, *n*. study of life under germ-free conditions.—*adj*. **gnotobiolog'ical.**— *ns*. **gnotobiō'sis**, condition of being germ-free, or germ-free and then inoculated with known micro-organisms; **gnotobiote** (*-bī'ōt*), a gnotobiotic animal.—*adj*. **gnotobiot'ic**, in the condition of gnotobiosis.—*n*. **gnotobiot'ics**, study of gnotobiotic animals. [Gr. *gnōtos*, known, *bios*, life, *logos*, discourse.]

**gnu**, *noō, nū*, *n*. a large African antelope (*Connochaetes* or *Catoblepas*), superficially like a horse or buffalo. [From Hottentot.]

**go**, *gō*, *v.i.* to pass from one place to another: to be in motion: (of a path, etc.) to lead or give access (to): to proceed: to run (in words or notes): (of verse) to flow smoothly: to walk (*obs*.): to depart: to work, to be in operation: to sound (as a bell, gun): to take a direction: to extend: (as *pr.p.* + *infin*.) to be about (to do): to intend: (of a rumour, etc.) to be current: to be valid, hold true: to be reckoned, to be regarded (as): to be known (*by* or *under* a name): to be on the whole or ordinarily: to tend, serve as a means: to be or continue in a particular state (as in fear, in rags): to elapse: to be sold: to be spent, consumed: to move, act, in a way shown or specified: to be assigned or awarded (to): to harmonise (as colours): to die: (with *by*, (*up*)*on*) to be directed by, to act according to: (with *on*) to become chargeable to (an account, etc.): (with *to*) to subject oneself (to expense, trouble, etc.): to be pregnant (usu. with *with*): to become, or become as if: to happen in a particular way: to turn out: to fare: to contribute (to, towards, a whole, purpose or result): to be spoken of as: to be able to pass: to give way.—*v.t.* to pass through or over (*obs*. except with cognate obj., or *road*, etc.): to stake, bet: to call, bid, declare:—*pr.p.* **gō'ing**; *pa.p.* **gone** (*gon*) (see separate articles); *pa.t.* **went** (supplied from **wend**).—*n*. a going: affair, matter (*coll*.): (with *the*) current fashion (*coll*.): success (*coll*.): energy, activity (*coll*.): a bargain, deal (*coll.*): a spell, turn, bout (*coll.*): a portion supplied at one time (*coll.*); an attempt (*coll.*): failure to play (*cribbage*): a score for an opponent's failure to play (*cribbage*).—*adj.* ready: in perfect condition.—*interj.* (called to start race, etc.) begin!—*ns.* gō′er; gō′ing (see separate article).—*adj.* go′-ahead, dashing, energetic: enterprisingly progressive.—go′-ahead, permission to proceed.—*adj.* go′-as-you-please, not limited by rules: informal.—go′-between, an intermediary; go′-by′, escape by artifice: evasion: any intentional disregard: in coursing, the act of passing by or ahead in motion; go′-cart, a wheeled apparatus for teaching children to walk: a form of child's carriage; go′-gett′er, (*coll.*), forceful aggressive person who sets about getting what he wants; go′-kart, a low racing vehicle consisting of a frame with wheels, engine, and steering gear (now usu. kart); go′-off (*coll.*), start.—*adj.* go-to-meeting (see under Sunday).—all systems go, everything in the spacecraft operating as it should: everything in readiness; all the go (*coll.*), very fashionable; a pretty go (*coll.*, *iron.*), an awkward turn of events; from the word go, from the very beginning; go about, to pass from place to place: to busy oneself with: to seek, endeavour to (with *pr.p.*): (of rumour, etc.) to circulate: (of a ship) to change course; go about one's business, to attend to one's own affairs: to be off; go abroad, to go to a foreign country or out of doors: (of rumour, etc.) to circulate; go against, to turn out unfavourably for: to be repugnant to: to be in conflict with; go ahead, to proceed at once; go along with, to agree with, support; go along with you! (*coll.*), none of that!; go aside, to err (*arch.*): to withdraw, retire; go at, to attack vigorously; go back on, to betray, fail to keep (promise, etc.); go bail, to give security for; go down, to sink, decline: to be swallowed, believed, or accepted (esp. with pleasure): to fail to fulfil one's contract (*bridge*): to leave a university; go down the drain (*coll.*), to be wasted: to become valueless; go down with (*coll.*), to contract (an illness); go Dutch (see Dutch); go far, to go a long way (*lit.* and *fig.*): achieve success; go for, to assail: to set out to secure: to go to get or fetch: be attracted by; go for nothing, to have no value; go halves, to share equally between two; go hang (*slang*), to be forgotten, neglected: to be no longer of concern; go hard with, to prove difficult or unfortunate for; go in, to enter: (of church, school, scholars, etc.), to assemble regularly (*coll.*): (of sun, moon) to become concealed behind cloud: to take the batting (*cricket*); go in and out, to come and go freely; go in for, to make a practice of: to take up as a career or special interest: to take part in (a competition, etc.); go into, to enter: to examine thoroughly, investigate: to adopt as a profession, etc.; go in unto (*B.*), to have sexual intercourse with; go in with, to enter into partnership with: to join, combine with; go it, to act in a striking or dashing manner—often in *imper.* by way of encouragement; go native, to assimilate oneself to an alien culture or to the way of life of a foreign country (usu. less advanced than one's own); go off, to leave: to die (*Shak.*): to explode: to deteriorate: to proceed to an expected conclusion: to cease to operate; go on, to continue, to proceed: an exclamation expressing disbelief (*coll.*): to behave, conduct oneself (*coll.*): to talk at length (*coll.*): to take the bowling, begin to bowl (*cricket*): to be capable of being fitted on to: to appear on stage: to fare: to begin to function; go one better, in some card games, to take a bet and increase the stake (also go better): to excel: to cap a performance; go one's way, to depart; go

out, to become extinguished: to become unfashionable: to mingle in society; go over, to pass in review: to recall: to revise; go over to, to transfer allegiance to; go places, to travel widely: to go far in personal advancement; go round, to be enough for all; go slow, (of workers) deliberately to restrict output or effort in order to obtain concessions from employers.—*adj.* and *n.* go′-slow′; go slow with, to be sparing with; go steady, to court; go the whole hog (see hog); go through, to perform to the end, often perfunctorily: to examine in order: to undergo; go through fire and water, to undertake any trouble or risks (from the usage in ancient ordeals); go through with, to carry out; go to (*arch.*), come now (a kind of interjection, like the L. *agedum*, the Gr. *age nyn*); go to pieces (see piece); go to the wall (see wall); go under, to become submerged, overwhelmed, or ruined: to die (*arch.*); go up, to ascend: to be erected: to increase (as e.g. price): to enter a university; go with, to accompany: to agree with: accord with: to court; go without, suffer the want of; go without saying, to be self-evident (a Gallicism; Fr. *cela va sans dire*); great go, at Cambridge University, a degree examination, contrasted with little go, a preliminary examination; I could go (*coll.*), I should enjoy (usu. food or drink); let go (see let); no go, not possible: futile: in vain; on the go, very active; that goes for, that applies to. [O.E. *gān*, to go; cf. Ger. *gehen*, Du. *gaan*.]

go, gō, *n.* a Japanese game for two, played with black and white stones (or counters) on a board, the object being to capture opponent's stones and be in control of the larger part of the board. [Jap.]

Goa, gō′ə, *n.* Union Territory in west of India.—Goa bean, a papilionaceous plant (*Psophocarpus*) of tropical Asia and Africa, grown for its beans and root: its bean; Goa butter, kokum butter; Goa powder, araroba.

goad, gōd, *n.* a sharp-pointed stick, often tipped with iron, for driving oxen: a stimulus.—*v.t.* to drive with a goad: to urge forward: to incite.—*ns.* goads′man, goad′ster, one who uses a goad. [O.E. *gād.*]

goaf, gōf, (*dial.*) *n.* a rick in a barn. [O.N. *gōlf*, floor.]

goaf, gōf, (*mining*) *n.* the space left by the extraction of a coal-seam, into which waste is packed. [Origin obscure.]

goal (Milt. gole), gōl, *n.* a limit, boundary (*obs.*): a competition, race (*obs.*): the finishing point of a race: the winning-post or a similar marker: sometimes used for the starting-post (*obs.*): a pillar marking the turning-point in a Roman chariot race: the target in archery (*obs.*): the structure or station into which the ball is driven in some games: the sending of the ball between the goalposts or over the crossbar: a score for doing so: an end or aim.—goal′keeper, a player charged with defence of the goal (*coll.* goal′ie); goal′-kick (*soccer*), a free kick awarded to a defending player when an opponent has sent the ball over the goal-line but not between the posts; goal′-line, the boundary marking each end of the field, on which the goals are situated; goal′post, one of the upright posts at the goal. [Origin obscure.]

goanna, gō-an′ə, (*Austr.*) *n.* any large monitor lizard. [iguana.]

goary. Milton's spelling of gory.

goat, gōt, *n.* a ruminant (*Capra*) allied to the sheep: a lecher: a foolish person: (in *pl.*) the wicked (*B.*): (with *cap.*) the zodiacal sign or the constellation Capricorn.—*adj.* goat′ish, resembling a goat, esp. in smell: lustful: foolish.—*ns.* goat′ishness; goat′ling, a young goat in its second year.—*adj.* goat′y.—goat′-ant′elope, a goatlike antelope, or animal intermediate between goat and antelope, as the chamois, the goral; **goat'-fig**, the wild fig; **goat'fish**, red mullet; **goat'-god**, Pan; **goat'herd**, one who tends goats; **goat'-moth**, a large moth whose larva, feeding on willow-wood, etc., exudes a goatlike smell; **goat'-sall'ow, -will'ow**, the great sallow (*Salix caprea*); **goat's'-beard**, a composite plant of the genus *Tragopogon*, John-go-to-bed-at-noon: a herbaceous perennial of the genus *Aruncus sylvester*; **goat's'-hair**, cirrus clouds; **goat's'-rue**, a papilionaceous border and fodder plant, *Galega officinalis*; **goat'skin**, the skin of the goat: leather, or a wine-skin, made from it; **goat'sucker**, the nightjar, a bird akin to the swift falsely thought to suck goats; **goat's'-thorn**, an Astragalus shrub; **goat'weed**, goutweed.—**get one's goat**, to enrage one: play (or act) the (giddy) goat (see **giddy**). [O.E. *gāt*; Ger. *geiss*, Du. *geit*.]

**goatee**, *gō-tē'*, *n.* a tuft on the chin, resembling a goat's beard.—*adj.* **goateed'**. [goat and *-ee*, suff. of uncertain meaning.]

**gob**, *gob*, *n.* the mouth (*slang*): a mouthful, lump (*dial.*): a space left in a mine by extraction of coal: waste packed into it. [O.Fr. *gobe*, mouthful, lump; cf. Gael. *gob*, mouth; perh. partly from **goaf** (2).]

**gob**, *gob*, (*U.S. slang*) *n.* a sailor in U.S. Navy. [Origin obscure.]

**gobang**, *gō-bang'*, *n.* a game played on a board of 256 squares, with fifty counters, the object being to get five in a row. [Jap. *goban*.]

**gobar numeral**, *gō'bär nū'mər-əl*, any of a set of numerals forming the stage between ancient Hindu numerals and present-day Arabic numerals. [Ar. *ghubār*, sanded board.]

**gobbelines**, *gob'ə-lēnz*, *n.pl.* Same as **goblins**.

**gobbet**, *gob'it*, *n.* a mouthful: a lump to be swallowed: a clot: a lump, esp. of flesh hacked or vomited: an extract, esp. for translation or comment. [O.Fr. *gobet*, dim. of *gobe*; see **gob**.]

**gobble**, *gob'l*, *v.t.* to swallow in lumps: to swallow hastily: to play with a gobble (*golf*).—*v.i.* to eat greedily: to make a noise in the throat, as a turkey-cock.—*n.* (*golf*), a rapid straight putt so strongly played that if the ball had not gone into the hole, it would have gone a good way past.—*n.* **gobb'ler**, a turkey-cock. [O.Fr. *gober*, to devour.]

**gobbledegook**, **gobbledygook**, *gob-əl-di-gook'*, (*U.S. slang*) *n.* official jargon. [Imit. of pomposity.]

**Gobelin, Gobelins**, *gōb'ə-lin, -linz, gob'(ə)-, goblē*, *n.* a rich French tapestry.—Also *adj.* [From the *Gobelins*, a famous family of French dyers settled in Paris as early as the 15th century.]

**gobe-mouches**, *gob-mōōsh*, (Fr.) a fly-catcher (bird): an insectivorous plant: a credulous person.

**goblet**, *gob'lit*, *n.* a large drinking-cup, properly one without a handle: a kind of saucepan (*Scot.*). [O.Fr. *gobelet*, dim. of *gobel*, of doubtful origin.]

**goblin**, *gob'lin*, *n.* a frightful sprite: a bogy or bogle. [O.Fr. *gobelin*—L.L. *gobelinus*, perh. —*cobālus*—Gr. *kobālos*, a mischievous spirit.]

**gobony**, *gob-ō'ni*. Same as **compony**.

**goburra**, *gō-bûr'a*. Same as **kookaburra**.

**goby**, *gō'bi*, *n.* any fish of the genus Gobius or the family Gobi'idae, small fishes with ventral fins forming a sucker. [L. *gōbius*—Gr. *kōbios*, a fish of the gudgeon kind.]

**go-cart**. See under **go** (1).

**god**, *god*, *n.* a superhuman being, an object of worship: (with *cap.*) the Supreme Being of monotheist religions, the Creator: an idol: an object of excessive devotion: a man of outstandingly fine physique: (usu. in *pl.*) an occupant of the gallery (*theat.*): (*pl.*) the gallery (*theat.*):—

*fem.* **godd'ess**.—*v.t.* (*Spens., Shak.*), to deify:—*pa.t.* **godd'ed**.—*ns.* **godd'ess-ship**, state or quality of a goddess; **god'head** (M.E. -*hēd*, -*hēde*, variant of -*hōd*), state of being a god: divine nature: (*cap.* with *the*) God; **god'hood** (O.E. -*hād*, M.E. -*hōd*), position or state of being divine: a deity (*obs.*).—*adj.* **god'less**, without a god: living without God.—*adv.* **god'lessly.**—*n.* **god'lessness.**—*adj.* **god'like**, like a god: divine.—*adv.* (*arch.*) **god'lily.**—*ns.* **god'liness; god'ling** (*Dryden*), a little god.—*adj.* **god'ly**, like God in character: pious: according to God's laws.—Also *adv.* (*arch.*).—*n.* **god'ship**, the rank or character of a god: a divinity.—*adj.* and *adv.* **god'ward**, towards God.—*adv.* **god'wards.**—*interj.* **God'-a-mercy!** (*arch.*), †hank God: many thanks to.—*n.* (*obs.*) an expression of thanks.—*adj.* **god-aw'ful** (*coll.*), very bad: unpleasant, distasteful.—**god'child**, a person to whom one is a godparent.—*adjs.* (*coll.*), **godd'am(n)**, **god'dam-ned**, damned, accursed, hateful: utter, complete.—Also *adv.*—**god'daughter**, a female godchild; **god father**, a male godparent: a sponsor (*fig.*): one who pays the bill (*slang*).—*adjs.* **God'-fearing**, reverencing God; **god'-forgotten**, **god'-forsaken** (or with *cap.*), remote, miserable, behind the times; **God'-gift'ed**; **God'-given.**—**god'mother**, a female godparent; **god'parent**, one who, at baptism, guarantees a child's religious education; **God's acre**, a burial-ground (imitated from Ger. *Gottesacker*); **god'send**, a very welcome piece of good fortune; **god'-smith** (*Dryden*), a maker of idols; **god'son**, a male godchild; **god'speed**, a wish for good fortune, expressed at parting; **God's truth**, an absolute truth—an emphatic asseveration.—**for God's sake**, an expression of urgent entreaty: *interj.* expressing, e.g. annoyance, disgust; **God knows**, God is my, his, etc., witness that: (*flippantly*) it is beyond human understanding; **God's (own) country**, a particularly well-favoured (esp. scenically beautiful) region: one's homeland or native region (esp. *U.S.*); **God willing**, if circumstances permit; **household gods**, among the Romans, the special gods presiding over the family: anything bound up with home interests. [O.E. *god*; Ger. *gott*, Goth. *guth*, Du. *god*; all from a Gmc. root *guth-*, God, and quite distinct from *good*.]

**god day**, *god dā*, (*Spens.*) for good-day.

**god-den**, *god-en'*, a dial. variant of good-even.

**godet**, *gō-dā'*, -*det'*, *n.* a triangular piece of cloth inserted in a skirt, e.g. to make a flare. [Fr.]

**Godetia**, *gō-dē'sh(y)ə, gə-*, *n.* an American genus closely akin to the evening primrose. [C. H. *Godet*, Swiss botanist.]

**godown**, *gō-down'*, *n.* a warehouse, or a storeroom, in the East. [Malay *gudang*.]

**go-down**, *gō'down*, *n.* a cutting in the bank of a stream allowing animals to get to the water. [go, down.]

**godroon**, *gō-drōōn'*, *gə-*. Same as **gadroon**.

**godso**. Same as **gadso**.

**godwit**, *god'wit*, *n.* a bird (*Limosa*) of the plover family, with long slightly up-curved bill and long slender legs, with a great part of the tibia bare. [Origin obscure.]

**goe**, *gō*, (*Spens.*). Same as **go**, **gone**.

**goe**, a variant of **geo** (gully, creek).

**goel**, *gō'el, -āl*, *n.* the avenger of blood among the Hebrews, the nearest relative, whose duty it was to hunt down the murderer. [Heb.]

**goety**, *gō'ə-ti*, *n.* black magic.—*adj.* **goetic** (*-et'*). [Gr. *goēteiā*, witchcraft.]

**gofer, gopher, gaufer, gaufre**, *gō'* or *gō'fər*, *n.* a wafer with pattern in crossed lines. [Fr. *gaufre*, honeycomb.]

**goff**, *gof*, *n.* an arch. variant of **golf**.

**goffer**, *göf'ər, gof'*, *gōf'*, *v.t.* to plait, crimp.—*n.* **goff'ering**, plaits or ruffles, or the process of making them: indented tooling on the edge of a book. [O.Fr. *gauffrer*—*goffre*, a wafer.]

**gog**, *gog, n.* obs. for God (in oaths).

**Gog and Magog**, *gog' ənd mā'gog*, the nations represented in the Apocalypse as the forces of Satan at Armageddon (*Rev.* xx. 8): the last two survivors of a mythical race of giants inhabiting ancient Britain.

**go-getter.** See go (1).

**goggle**, *gog'l, v.i.* to strain or roll the eyes: (of the eyes) to protrude.—*v.t.* to turn about (the eyes).—*adj.* (of the eyes) rolling: staring: prominent.—*n.* a stare or affected rolling of the eyes: (*pl.*) spectacles with projecting eye-tubes: (*pl.*) protective spectacles: (*pl.*) spectacles, esp. with round lenses (*coll.*): the eyes (*coll.*).—*adj.* **gogg'led**, wearing goggles.—*ns.* **gogg'ler**, a person with goggle eyes (*coll.*): an eye (*slang*): an assiduous television-viewer (*coll.*); **gogg'ling.** —Also *adj.*—*adj.* **gogg'ly.**—**gogg'le-box** (*coll.*), a television-set.—*adj.* **gogg'le-eyed**, having bulging, staring, or rolling, eyes.—Also *adv.* [*Poss.* related to Ir. and Gael, *gog*, to nod.]

**goglet**, *gog'lit, n.* a water-cooler. [Port. *gorgoleta.*]

**go-go, gogo.** See à gogo.

**Goidel**, *goi'dəl, n.* a Gael in the general sense (Gadhel, *q.v.*, now has the same meaning).—*adj.* **Goidelic** (*-del'*), Gadhelic. [O.Ir. *Góidel.*]

**going**, *gō'ing, n.* the act of moving: departure: course of life (*B.*): condition of the ground for, e.g., walking, racing: progress: gait (*obs.*).—*adj.* (for earlier a-go'ing) in motion or activity: about, to be had: in existence.—**going concern**, a business in actual activity (esp. successfully); **going forth** (*B.*), an outlet, exit; **goings-on**, behaviour, activities, now esp. if open to censure; **goings-out** (*obs.*), expenditure.—**going-away dress**, etc., that worn by a bride when leaving on the honeymoon. [go.]

**going**, *gō'ing, pr.p.* of go, in any sense: about (to).—**going (on for)**, approaching (an age or time); **going strong**, in full activity, flourishing.

**goitre**, in U.S. also **goiter**, *goi'tər, n.* morbid enlargement of the thyroid gland, producing a swelling in front of the throat.—*adjs.* **goi'tred**; **goi'trous.** [Fr. *goitre*—L. *guttur*, the throat.]

**go-kart.** See under go (1).

**Golconda**, *gol-kon'də, n.* a rich source of wealth. [Ruined city near Hyderabad, India, once famous for diamond-cutting.]

**gold**, *gōld, n.* a heavy yellow element (Au; atomic number 79), one of the precious metals, used for coin, etc.: articles made of it: money in the form of gold coins: a standard of money value which varies with the price of the metal: riches: anything very precious: the centre of an archery target: yellow, the colour of gold.—*adj.* made of or like gold.—*adj.* **gold'en**, of gold: of the colour of gold: bright, shining like gold: most valuable: happy: most favourable: of outstanding excellence.—*v.t.* (*rare*), to gild, make golden.—*v.i.* (*rare*), to become golden in colour. —*adv.* **gold'enly.**—*adjs.* **gold'ish**, somewhat golden; **gold'less**; **gold'y**, somewhat like gold. —**gold'-beater**, one whose trade is to beat gold into gold-leaf; **gold'-beating**; **gold'-bee'tle** (*U.S.*), a beetle of the family *Chrysomelidae* or the *Cassididae*; **gold'-brick'**, a block of gold or (orig. *U.S. slang*) of pretended gold, hence a sham or swindle; **gold'-bug** (*U.S.*), a gold beetle: a plutocrat: one who favours a gold standard; **gold'-cloth'**, cloth of gold; **gold'crest**, a golden-crested bird of the genus *Regulus* (also **golden-crested wren**); **gold'-digger**, one who digs for gold, esp. a placer-miner: a woman who treats a man chiefly as a source of material gain; **gold'-digging**; **gold'-dust**, gold in fine particles, as found in some rivers; **golden age**, an imagi-

nary past time of innocence and happiness: any time of highest achievement; **gold'enberry**, the Cape gooseberry; **golden bough**, the bough plucked by Aeneas before visiting the underworld; **golden bowler**, dismissal from the Army followed by a job in Whitehall; **golden boy**, a young man of outstanding talents likely to win renown in his career; **golden bull** (L. *bulla aurea*), an edict issued by the Emperor Charles IV in 1356, mainly for the purpose of settling the law of imperial elections; **golden calf** (see calf). —*adj.* **gold'en crest'ed.**—**gold-end'-man** (*obs.*), a dealer in gold'-ends' (*arch.*), broken remnants of gold; **golden eagle**, the common eagle, from a slight golden gleam about the head and neck; **gold'en-eye**, a northern sea-duck (*Clangula*): the lace-wing fly; **golden fleece**, in Greek mythology, the fleece of the ram Chrysomallus, the recovery of which was the object of the famous expedition of the Argonauts—it gave its name to a celebrated order of knighthood in Austria and Spain, founded in 1429: **golden goose**, the fabled layer of golden eggs, killed by its over-greedy owner; **golden handshake**, a large sum given to an employee or member forced to leave a firm, etc.; **golden horde**, the Kipchaks, a Turkic people, whose empire was founded in central and southern Russia by Batu in the 13th century; **Golden Legend** (L. *Legenda Aurea*), a celebrated mediaeval collection of saints' lives, by Jacobus de Voragine (1230-98); **golden mean**, the middle way between extremes: moderation; **golden mole**, a bronze-coloured S. African insectivore (*Chrysochloris*) superficially like a mole; **golden number**, a number marking the position of a year in the Metonic Cycle of nineteen years; **golden opportunity**, a very favourable one; **golden pheasant**, a golden-crested Chinese pheasant; **golden plover**, a plover with yellow-speckled feathers; **golden rectangle**, one in which the ratio of width to length is the same as that of length to the sum of width and length; **gold'enrod**, any plant of the composite genus *Solidago*, with rodlike stems and yellow heads crowded along the branches; **golden rose**, a rose of wrought gold, blessed by the Pope on the 4th Sunday in Lent; **golden rule**, the precept that one should do as one would be done by: a rule of the first importance, a guiding principle; **golden salmon**, the S. American dorado; **golden saxifrage**, a greenish-yellow plant (*Chrysoplenium*) of the saxifrage family; **golden scoop**, a system (judged to be illegal) according to which winners in bingo games in separate clubs can qualify for prizes offered by a large group of clubs acting together; **gold'en-seal**, a N. American ranunculaceous plant, *Hydrastis canadensis*: its yellow rhizome, used in medicine; **golden section**, division of a line so that one segment is to the other as that to the whole; **golden thistle, tulip**, top award respectively in film-making, advertising; **golden wedding** (see wedding); **gold'eye**, a N. American freshwater fish (*Hyodon*); **gold'-fe'ver**, a mania for seeking gold; **gold'field**, a gold-producing region; **gold'finch**, a beautiful finch, black, red, yellow and white, fond of eating thistle seeds; **gold'finny**, same as **gold'-sinny**; **gold'fish**, a Chinese and Japanese freshwater fish closely allied to the carp, golden or (*silverfish*) pale in its domesticated state, brownish when wild; **gold'-foil'**, gold beaten into thin sheets, but not as thin as gold-leaf: **gold'ilocks**, a golden-haired person: a species of buttercup, *Ranunculus auricomus*; **gold ink**, a writing fluid in which gold or an imitation is in suspension; **gold'-lace'**, lace made from gold-thread.—*adj.* **gold'-laced.**—**gold'-leaf**, gold beaten extremely thin; **gold'-mine**, a mine producing gold: a source of great profit; **gold'-miner**;

gold'-of-pleas'ure, a cruciferous plant of the genus *Camelina*; gold paint, bronze powders mixed with transparent varnish or amyl acetate; gold'-plate', vessels and utensils of gold collectively: metal esp. silver, plated with gold; gold'-rush, a rush to a new goldfield; gold'-sinny, a kind of wrasse, the corkwing; gold'-size, an adhesive, of various kinds, used to attach gold-leaf to a surface; gold'smith, a worker in gold and silver; gold'smithry, -ery; gold'spink (*Scot.*, also gowd'spink), the goldfinch; gold standard, a monetary standard or system according to which the unit of currency has a precise value in gold; gold'stick, a colonel of Life Guards who carries a gilded wand before the sovereign; gold'-thread', gold-wire used in weaving: silk wound with gilded wire: a European ranunculaceous plant (*Coptis*) with yellow roots; gold'-washer, one who obtains gold from sand and gravel by washing: a cradle or other implement for washing gold; gold-wasp, any wasp of a family (*Chrysididae*) with brilliant metallic colouring and telescopic abdomen, whose larvae feed on those of wasps and bees—cuckoo-fly or ruby-tail, ruby-wasp; gold'-wire', wire made of or covered with gold.— as good as gold, behaving in an exemplary manner (usu. of children); gold'-beater's skin, the outer coat of the caecum of the ox, used to separate the leaves of gold during beating; goldfish bowl, a glass aquarium for goldfish: a situation entirely lacking in privacy; on, off, the gold standard, using or not using, gold as standard. [O.E. *gold*, O.N. *gull*, Ger. *gold*, Goth. *gulth*.]

gold, *gōld*, *n.* the marigold (*obs.*): the corn-marigold (*dial.*).—Also (*Scot.*) gool, gule (*gōōl*), (*Spens.*) goold (*gōōld*). [O.E. *golde*, apparently related to gold (1), gollan, gowan; cf. marigold.]

golem, *gō'lem*, -*ləm*, in Jewish folklore, a human image brought to life: a robot: a dolt. [Yiddish *goylem*—Heb. *gōlem*, a shapeless thing, an embryo.]

golf, *golf* (sometimes *gof*, or (*Scot.*) *gowf*), *n.* a game played with a club or set of clubs over a prepared stretch of land, the aim being to propel a small ball into a series of holes.—*v.i.* to play golf.—*ns.* golf'er, golf'ing.—golf'-bag, a bag for carrying golf-clubs; golf'-ball, a small ball used in golf; golf'-club, a club used in golf: a golfing society; golf'-course, golf'-links, the ground on which golf is played. [Origin uncertain; Du. *kolf*, a club, has been suggested.]

Golgi bodies, *gol'jē*, easily stained bodies around the centrosome in animal cells, studied by Camillo *Golgi* (1843-1926).

Golgotha, *gol'ga-tha*, *n.* a burial-ground: a charnel-house: a place littered with bones. [See under Calvary.]

goliard, *gō'li-ärd*, or -*lyərd*, *n.* a disreputable vagrant mediaeval cleric given to revelry, buffoonery, and satirical Latin versifying, follower of an imaginary Bishop Golias.—*adj.* goliardic (-*ärd'ik*).—*ns.* go'liardy, goliard'ery.—*v.i.* go'lias (*Tenn.*), to play Golias. [O.Fr., glutton—L. *gūla*, gluttony.]

Goliath, *gō-li'əth*, *gə-*, *n.* a giant.—*v.i.* goli'athise, -ize, to play Goliath, exaggerate extravagantly. —goli'ath-bee'tle, a tropical beetle (*Goliathus*) reaching four inches in length. [From *Goliath*, the Philistine giant in 1 Sam. xvii.]

gollan, golland, *gol'ən(d)*, gowland *gow'lənd*, *n.* a northern name for various yellow flowers (marigold, corn-marigold, globeflower, etc.). [Perh. conn. with gold (2): see gowan.]

gollar, *gol'ər*, (*Scot.*) *n.* a loud inarticulate gurgling sound: a thick or guttural bawl.—Also *v.i.* [Imitative.]

golliwog. Same as gollywog.

gollop, *gol'əp*, *v.t.* and *v.i.* to gulp greedily or hastily. [Perh. gulp.]

golly, *gol'i*, *interj.* expressing surprise. [Negro modification of God.]

gollywog, golliwog, *gol'i-wog*, *n.* a fantastical doll with black face, staring eyes, and bristling hair: a person who has fuzzy hair or is in some way grotesque. [*Golliwogg*, a doll in certain U.S. children's books, the first of which was published in 1895.]

goloe-shoes. A spelling of galoshes.

golomynka, *go-lo-ming'kə*, *n.* a very oily fish found in Lake Baikal, resembling the gobies. [Russ.]

golosh. Same as galosh.

golp, golpe, *golp*, (*her.*) *n.* a roundel purpure. [Perh.—Sp. *golpe*, bruise.]

goluptious, *gol-up'shəs*, goloptious, -*op'*, (*jocular*) *adj.* delicious: voluptuous.

gombeen, *gom'bēn'*, (*Ir.*) *n.* usury.—*n.* gombeen'-man, a grasping usurer. [Ir. *gaimbín*.]

gombo, gombro. Same as gumbo.

gomeril, gomeral, *gom'ər-l*, (*Scot.*) *n.* a simpleton: a dunderhead. [Origin obscure.]

gomphosis, *gom-fō'sis*, *n.* an immovable articulation, as of the teeth in the jaw. [Gr. *gomphōsis*—*gomphos*, a bolt.]

gomuti, *gō-mōō'ti*, *n.* a palm, *Arenga saccharifera*: the black fibre it yields.—Also gomu'to. [Malay *gumuti*.]

gonad, *gon'ad*, (*biol.*) *n.* an organ that produces sex-cells.—*adjs.* gonadial (-*ād'i-əl*), gonadic (-*ad'*); gonadotrop(h)'ic, stimulating the gonads.—*n.* gonadotrop(h)'in, a substance that does this, used as a drug to promote fertility. [Gr. *gonē*, generation.]

gondelay. See gondola.

gondola, *gon'də-lə*, *n.* a long, narrow boat used chiefly on the canals of Venice: a lighter (*U.S.*): a flat railway wagon (*U.S.*): the car of an airship: the car of a balloon: a car resembling this suspended from an earth-supported structure.— (*Spens.*) gon'delay.—*n.* gondolier (-*lēr'*), one who rows a gondola. [It.; origin obscure.]

Gondwanaland, *gond-wä'nä-land*, *n.* an ancient continent held to have connected India with S. Africa, S. America, Antarctica and Australia from Carboniferous times to Jurassic. [*Gondwana* district in India, i.e. forest of the Gonds.]

gone, *gon*, *pa.p.* of go, in an advanced stage: lost, passed beyond help: departed: dead: weak, faint, feeling a sinking sensation: wide of the mark, of an arrow: enamoured of (with *on*; *slang*): in an exalted state (*slang*).—*ns.* gone'ness, a sinking sensation; gon'er (*slang*), one dead or ruined beyond recovery: a thing beyond hope of recovery.—gone under, ruined beyond recovery.

gonfalon, *gon'fə-lon*, *n.* an ensign or standard with streamers.—*ns.* gonfalonier (-*ēr'*), one who bears a gonfalon: the chief magistrate in some Italian republics; gon'fanon, a gonfalon: a pennon. [It. *gonfalone* and O.Fr. *gonfanon*—O.H.G. *gund-fano*—*gund*, battle, *fano* (Ger. *fahne*), a flag; cf. O.E. *gūthfana*.]

gong, *gong*, *n.* a metal disk, usu. rimmed, that sounds when struck or rubbed with a drumstick: an instrument of call, esp. to meals: a steel spiral for striking in a clock: a flat bell sounded by a hammer: medal (*slang*).—*v.t.* to call upon to stop by sounding a gong.—*n.* gong'ster, one who gongs.—gong'-stick. [Malay.]

Gongorism, *gong'gor-izm*, *n.* a florid, inverted, and pedantic style of writing, introduced by the Spanish poet Luis de *Góngora* y Argote (1561-1627), some of whose distinctive features reappeared in Euphuism.

goniatite, *gō'ni-ə-tit*, *n.* a fossil cephalopod of a group with comparatively simple angular septa.—*n.* and *adj.* goniati'toid. [Gr. *gōniā*, an angle.]

gonidium, *gon-id'i-əm*, *n.* an algal cell in a lichen:

—*pl.* **gonid′ia.**—*adj.* **gonid′ial.** [Gr. *gonē*, generation, seed.]

**gonimoblast,** *gon′i-mō-bläst, n.* in the red seaweeds, a spore-bearing filament that springs from the fertilised carpogonium. [Gr. *gonimos*, productive, *blastos*, a shoot.]

**goniometer,** *gōn-, gon-i-om′i-tər, n.* an instrument for measuring angles, esp. between crystal-faces: a direction-finding apparatus.—*adjs.* **goniometric** (-ə-*met′rik*), **-al.**—*n.* **goniom′etry.** [Gr. *gōniā*, an angle, *metron*, measure.]

**gonococcus,** *gon-ō-kok′əs, n.* the bacterium that causes gonorrhoea.—*adj.* **gonococc′al.** [Gr. *kokkos*, a berry.]

**gonophore,** *gon′ə-fōr, -för, n.* a prolongation of the axis bearing stamens or carpels (*bot.*): a reproductive zooid of a hydrozoan, answering to a medusa but remaining fixed (*zool.*). [Gr. *gonos*, seed, *phoreein*, to bear.]

**gonorrhoea,** *gon-ō-rē′ə, n.* a contagious infection of the mucous membrane of the genital tract.—*adj.* **gonorrhoe′al.**—U.S. **gonorrhea, gonorrheal.** [Gr. *gonorroiă*—*gonos*, seed, *rheein*, to flow, from a mistaken notion of its nature.]

**goo,** *gōō,* (*slang*) *n.* a sticky substance: sentimentality.—*adj.* **goo′ey.** [Origin unknown.]

**good,** *gōōd, adj.* having suitable or desirable qualities: promoting health, welfare, or happiness: virtuous: pious: kind: benevolent: well-behaved: not troublesome: of repute: doughty: worthy: commendable: suitable: adequate: thorough: competent: sufficient: valid: sound: serviceable: beneficial: genuine: pleasing: favourable: ample, moderately estimated: considerable, as in *a good deal, a good mind*: to be counted on:—*comp.* **bett′er;** *superl.* **best.**—*n.* the end of ethics: that which is good: prosperity: welfare: advantage, temporal or spiritual: benefit: avail: virtue: possessions (*arch.*): (in *pl.*) movable property, chattels, merchandise, freight.—*interj.* well: right: be it so.—*adv.* well.—*n.* **good′iness,** weak, priggish, or canting goodness.—*adj.* **good′ish,** pretty good, of fair quality or quantity.—*n.* **good′liness.**—*adv.* **good′ly** (*Spens.*), graciously: excellently, kindly.—*adj.* comely: good-looking: fine: excellent: ample:—*comp.* **good′lier;** *superl.* **good′liest.**—*ns.* **good′lyhead, good′lihead** (*Spens.*), goodness; **good′ness,** virtue: excellence: benevolence: substituted for God in certain expressions and as *interj.*—*n.* **good′y,** good-wife: good-woman (probably formed from *good-wife*): a sweetmeat.—*adj.* **good′y, good′y-good′y,** mawkishly good: weakly benevolent or pious.—**good′-breed′ing,** polite manners formed by a good bringing-up; **good-broth′er, -fath′er, -moth′er, -sis′ter, -son′** (*Scot.*; also **gude-**), a brother-in-law, father-in-law, etc.—*n.* or *interj.* **good-bye′,** for *God be with you:* farewell, a form of address at parting.—*adjs.* **good′-cheap′** (*arch.*), cheap (lit. good-bargain); **good′-condi′tioned,** in a good state.—**good-dame′** (**gude-dame′,** *güd-, gid-*; *obs. Scot.*), a grandmother.—*ns.* or *interjs.* **good-day′,** a common salutation at meeting or parting; **good-den′** (from *good-e′en*), **good-e′en′, good-ēv′en, good-eve′ning,** a salutation on meeting or parting in the evening.—*adj.* **good′-faced** (*Shak.*), having a handsome face.—**good′-fell′ow,** a jolly or boon companion: a reveller; **good′-fell′owship,** merry or pleasant company: conviviality; **good folk, good people.**—*adj.* **good′-for-nothing,** worthless, useless.—*n.* an idle or worthless person.—**Good Friday** (see under **Friday**); **good-hū′mour,** cheerful, tolerant mood or disposition.—*adj.* **good-hū′moured.**—*adv.* **good-hū′mouredly.**—**good′-King-Hen′ry,** a goosefoot formerly grown as a pot-herb.—*interj.* **good-lack′,** an expression of surprise or pity (prob. a variation of *good Lord*, under the influence of **alack**).—*adj.* **good′-look′ing,** handsome.—**good′-look′er**

(*coll.*); **good′man** (*arch.*), a yeoman: formerly prefixed to name of a man of yeoman's rank: (*gōōd-man′,* chiefly *Scot.*; also **gude-**) a householder or husband (*fem.* **goodwife′**) or euphemistically the devil; **goodman's croft,** a patch once left untilled in Scotland to avert the malice of the devil from the crop.—*ns.* and *interjs.* **good-morn′ing** or (*arch.*) **good-morr′ow,** a salutation at meeting or parting early in the day.—**good-nā′ture,** natural goodness and mildness of disposition.—*adj.* **good′-nā′tured.**—*adv.* **good′-nā′turedly.**—*n.* and *interj.* **good-night′,** a common salutation on parting at night or well on in the day.—*interj.* **good′-now,** an exclamation of wonder, surprise, or entreaty.—**good offices,** mediation; **good people, good folk,** the fairies (euphemistically); **good sailor,** a person not liable to seasickness; **goods′-en′gine,** an engine used for drawing goods-trains; **good′-sense′,** sound judgment; **goodsire′** (**gudesire′,** *güd-, gid-*; **gutcher,** *gut′shər*; *obs. Scot.*), a grandfather.—*n.* and *interj.* **good′-speed′,** a contraction of *I wish you good speed* (i.e. success).—**goods′-train,** a train of goods wagons.—*adj.* **good′-tem′pered,** possessing a good temper.—**Good Templar,** a member of a temperance society, modelled on the Freemasons; **goodwife′** (or *gōōd′*), the *fem.* of **goodman; good′will′,** benevolence: well-wishing: the established custom or popularity of any business or trade: often appearing as one of its assets, with a marketable money value.—*adjs.* **good′-will;** (*Scot.*) **good-will′y,** well-wishing: expressive of good-will.—**as good as,** the same as, no less than: virtually; **be as good as one's word,** to fulfil one's promise; **for good (and all),** permanently: irrevocably; **good and** (*coll.*), very; **goodies and baddies,** characters in a drama regarded respectively as definitely good and definitely bad; **good for anything,** ready for any kind of work; **good for you,** *interj.* expressing approval; **good neighbour policy,** a U.S. policy from 1931 for co-operation in all fields between all the countries of North, South, and Central America; **goods and chattels** (see **chattel**); **in one's good books,** in favour; **make good,** to fulfil, perform: to compensate: to come to success, esp. unexpectedly: to do well, redeeming a false start: to repair: to justify; **no good,** useless: unavailing: worthless; **not, hardly,** etc., **good enough,** not sufficiently good: mean, unfair, very different from what was expected or promised; **stand good,** to be lastingly good: to remain; **the goods** (*slang*), the real thing: that which is required, promised, etc.; **think good,** to be disposed, to be willing; **to the good,** for the best: on the credit or advantage side. [O.E. *gōd;* Du. *goed,* Ger. *gut,* O.N. *gōthr,* Goth. *gōths.*]

**goodyear, -s,** *gōōd′yēr(z),* (*Shak.*) *n.* the devil, the plague, or the like—a meaningless imprecation. [Of obscure origin. Perh. orig. 'as I hope for a *good year*'.]

**goof,** *gōōf, n.* a stupid or awkward person.—*v.i.* to make a blunder.—*adj.* **goof′y.**—**goof′ball** (*slang*), a barbiturate pill used as an exhilarant. [Perh. Fr. *goffe*.]

**googly,** *gōōg′li,* (*cricket*) *n.* an off-breaking ball with an apparent leg-break action on the part of the bowler, or conversely.—Also *adj.*—*v.i.* **goog′le,** to behave or bowl in such a manner. [Ety. dub.]

**googol,** *gōō′gol, n.* 1 followed by a hundred zeros, $10^{100}$ [Coined by E. Kasner, mathematician.]

**gook,** *gōōk,* (*slang*) *n.* one of Asiatic race, esp. a Japanese or Korean soldier.

**gool, goold.** See gold (2).

**goon,** *gōōn, n.* hired thug (*U.S. slang*): stupid person.

**gooney(-bird),** *gōō′nē, n.* an albatross. [Prob. dial., simpleton—obs. *gony*.]

goop, gōōp, n. a fool: a fatuous person.—adj.
goop'y. [Cf. goof.]

goor, Goorkha, gooroo. Alternative spellings of
gur, Gurkha, guru.

goosander, gōōs-an'dǝr, n. a large duck of the
merganser genus. [Perh. goose, and O.N. önd,
pl. ander, duck.]

goose, gōōs, n. any one of a group of birds of the
duck family, intermediate between ducks and
swans: a domesticated member of the group,
descended mainly from the grey-lag: the female
of such a bird:—masc. gander: a tailor's smoothing-iron, from the likeness of the handle to the
neck of a goose: a stupid, silly person: a game of
chance once common in England, in which the
players moved counters on a board, with right to
a double move on reaching a picture of a goose:
—pl. geese, gēs, or, of tailor's goose, goos'es.—
v.t. (slang) to hiss off the stage.—ns. goos'ery,
a place for keeping geese: stupidity; goos'ey, a
goose: a blockhead.—adj. like a goose: affected
with gooseflesh; goose'-cap, a silly person;
goose'-club, a combination for saving to buy
geese for Christmas, or to raffle for a goose;
goose'-egg, the egg of a goose: a zero score
(U.S.); goose'-fish (U.S.), the angler-fish;
goose'-flesh, a puckered condition of the skin,
like that of a plucked goose: the bristling
feeling in the skin due to erection of hairs through
cold, horror, etc.; goose'-flower, the pelican-
flower, a gigantic Aristolochia; goose'foot, any
plant of a genus (Chenopodium) of the beet
family, from the shape of the leaf:—pl. goose'-
foots; goose'-girl, a girl who herds geese; goose'-
herd, one who herds geese; goose'-grass,
cleavers: silverweed; goose'-neck, a hook,
bracket, pipe, etc., bent like a goose's neck;
goose-pimples, goose-flesh; goose'-quill, one of
the quills or large wing-feathers of a goose, esp.
one used as a pen; goose'-skin, goose-flesh, horripilation; goose'-step (mil.), a method of marching
(resembling a goose's walk) with knees stiff and
soles brought flat on the ground; goose'-wing,
one of the clews or lower corners of a ship's
mainsail or foresail when the middle part is
furled or tied up to the yard.—adj. goose'-
winged, having only one clew set: in fore-and-
aft rigged vessels, having the mainsail on one side
and the foresail on the other, so as to sail wing-
and-wing. [O.E. gōs (pl. gēs); O.N. gās, Ger.
gans, L. anser (for hanser), Gr. chēn.]

gooseberry, gōōz'bǝ-ri, n. the fruit of the goose'-
berry-bush (Ribes grossularia), a prickly shrub of
the saxifrage family: a fermented effervescing
drink (also goose'berry-wine) made from goose-
berries: an imitation champagne: an unwanted
third person.—goose'berry-cat'erpillar, a creamy
looper with orange spots and black dots, feeding
on gooseberry leaves, the larva of the goose'-
berry-moth' or magpie moth (Abraxas grossu-
lariata), a yellow-bodied moth with black-
spotted white wings; goose'berry-fool' (see fool
(2)); goose'berry-stone', grossular; goose'gog
(coll. and dial.), a gooseberry.—Cape gooseberry,
or gooseberry tomato (see cape); Chinese gooseberry, a sub-tropical vine, Actinidia chinensis,
with brown, hairy, edible fruit; Coromandel
gooseberry, carambola (q.v.). [Perh. goose and
berry; or goose may be from M.H.G. krus
(Gr. kraus, crisp, curled); cf. O.Fr. groisele,
grosele, gooseberry, Scot. grossart.]

gopak, gō'pak, n. a folk-dance from the Ukraine.
[From Russ.]

gopher, gō'fǝr, n. a name in America applied to
various burrowing animals—the pouched rat,
the ground squirrel, the land tortoise of the
Southern States, and a burrowing snake.—v.i. to
burrow: to mine in a small way. [Perh. Fr.
gaufre, honeycomb.]

gopher, gō'fǝr, n. a kind of wood, generally
supposed to be cypress (B.): yellow-wood
(Cladastris) (U.S.). [Heb.]

gopura, gō'pōō-rǝ, n. in Southern India, a pyramidal tower over the gateway of a temple. [Sans.
gopura.]

goral, gō'rǝl, gö', n. a Himalayan goat-antelope.

goramy, gourami, gurami, gō', gö', gōō'rǝ-mi, or
-rä'mi, n. a large freshwater food-fish (Osphro-
menus olfax) of the Eastern Archipelago. [Malay
gurāmi.]

gor-belly, gör'-bel-i, n. a big belly: a big-bellied
person.—adj. (Shak.) gor'-bellied. [Perh. O.E.
gor, filth, and belly.]

gorblimy, gö-bli'mi, (Cockney) interj. for God
blind me.

gorcock, gör'kok, n. the red grouse cock. [Origin
obscure.]

gorcrow, gör'krō, n. the carrion-crow. [O.E. gor,
filth, and crow.]

Gordian, görd'yan, adj. pertaining to Gordium the
capital, or Gordius the king, of ancient Phrygia,
or to the intricate knot he tied: intricate: difficult.—v.t. (Keats) to tie up, knot.—n. Gordius,
a genus of hairworms.—cut the Gordian knot,
to overcome a difficulty by violent measures as
Alexander cut the knot with his sword.

gore, gör, gör, n. filth (obs.): clotted blood: blood.
—adv. gor'ily.—adj. gor'y, like gore: covered
with gore: bloody.—gore'-blood (Spens.); gory
dew, a dark-red slimy film sometimes seen on
damp walls, etc., a simple form of vegetable
life, Porphyridium cruentum. [O.E. gor, filth,
dung; O.N. gor, cud, slime.]

gore, gör, gör, n. a triangular piece of land: a
triangular piece let into a garment to widen it:
a skirt (obs.): a sector of a curved surface.—v.t.
to shape like or furnish with gores: to pierce
with anything pointed, as a spear or horns.—n.
gor'ing, an angular, tapering, or obliquely-cut
piece.—adj. forming a gore. [O.E. gāra, a
pointed triangular piece of land, and gār, a spear.]

gorge, görj, n. the throat: a ravine: the entrance
to an outwork (fort.): a hawk's crop: the maw:
the contents of the stomach: a gluttonous feed:
a fish-catching device, to be swallowed by the
fish.—v.t. to swallow greedily: to glut.—v.i. to
feed gluttonously.—adj. gorged, having a gorge
or throat: glutted: having a crown or coronet
about the neck (her.).—n. gorg'et, a piece of
armour for the throat: a metal badge formerly
worn on the breast by army officers: a wimple:
a neck ornament.—have one's gorge rise, to be
filled with loathing; heave the gorge, to retch.
[O.Fr.]

gorgeous, gör'jǝs, adj. showy: splendid: magnificent: loosely, pleasant, good, etc.—adv. gor'-
geously.—n. gor'geousness. [O.Fr. gorgias,
gaudy.]

gorgio, gör'jō, gör'ji-ō, n. one who is not a gipsy.
—Also gajo, gö'jō. [Romany.]

Gorgon, gör'gǝn, n. one of three fabled female
monsters (Stheno, Euryale, and Medusa), of
horrible and petrifying aspect, winged, with
hissing serpents for hair: anybody, esp. a woman,
very ugly or formidable.—adjs. gor'gon, gorgō'nian.—n. gorgoneion (-ī'on), a mask of the
gorgon.—v.t. gor'gonise, -ize, to turn to stone.
[Gr. Gorgō, pl. -önēs—gorgos, grim.]

Gorgonia, gör-gō'ni-ǝ, n. a genus of sea-fans or
horny corals.—adj. gorgo'nian.—n. a horny
coral. [L. gorgōnia, coral—Gorgō, Gorgon (from
hardening in the air).]

Gorgonzola, gör-gǝn-zō'lǝ, n. a blue cheese of
cow's milk. [From Gorgonzola, a small Italian
town near Milan.]

gorilla, gor-il'ǝ, n. a great African ape, the largest
anthropoid: a thug (slang).—adj. gorill'ine.
[Gr. Gorillai (pl.), reported by Hanno the
Carthaginian as a tribe of hairy women;
supposed to be an African word.]

# gorm

563

## gout

gorm, a variant of gaum ((1) and (2)).

gormand, *gör'mand, n.* older form of gourmand.—*v.i.* gor'mandise, -ize, to eat hastily or voraciously.—*n.* gourmandise: gluttony: gormandising.—*ns.* gor'mandiser; gor'mandising; gor'mandism, gluttony. [See gourmand.]

gorse, *görs, n.* furze or whin, a prickly papilionaceous shrub (Ulex).—Also gosse (*Shak.*).—*adj.* gors'y. [O.E. gorst.]

gorsedd, *gor'sedh, n.* a meeting of bards and druids. [W.]

gosh, *gosh,* (*coll.*) *interj.* for God.

goshawk, *gos'hök, n.* a short-winged hawk, once used for hunting wild-geese and other fowl, not having a toothed bill like the falcons proper. [O.E. *göshafoc—gös,* goose, *hafoc,* hawk.]

Goshen, *gö'shan, n.* a happy place of light and plenty. [From the abode of the Israelites during the plague of darkness in Egypt, Exod. x. 23.]

goslarite, *gos'lər-it, n.* a mineral, hydrated zinc sulphate, found at *Goslar* in Harz Mts.

gosling, *goz'ling, n.* a young goose.—*n.* gos'let, an Eastern dwarf goose (Nettapus). [O.E. *gös,* goose, double dim. *-l-ing.*]

gospel, *gos'pəl, n.* the teaching of Christ: a narrative of the life of Christ, esp. one of those included in the New Testament, Matthew, Mark, Luke, and John: the principles set forth therein: the stated portion of these read at service: any strongly advocated principle or system: absolute truth (*coll.*).—*v.t.* (*Shak.*) to instruct in the gospel.—*v.t.* gos'pel(l)ise, -ize, to evangelise: to square with the gospel.—*n.* gos'peller, a preacher: an evangelist: a Wycliffite, Protestant, or Puritan (often in derision): one who reads the gospel in church.—gospel side, the north side or gospeller's side of the altar. [O.E. *godspel(l),* a translation of L. *evangelium—göd,* good (with shortened vowel being understood as *God,* God) and *spel(l),* story.]

gospodar. See hospodar.

gossamer, *gos'ə-mər, n.* very fine spider-threads that float in the air or form webs on bushes in fine weather: any very thin material.—*adj.* light, flimsy.—*adj.* goss'amery, like gossamer: flimsy. [M.E. *gossomer;* perh. goose-summer, a St Martin's summer, when geese are in season and gossamer abounds; cf. Ger. *sommerfäden,* summer-threads, also *mädchensommer,* maiden-summer.]

gossan, gozzan, *gos', goz'ən, n.* decomposed rock, largely quartz impregnated with iron compounds, at the outcrop of a vein esp. of metallic sulphides. [Cornish miner's term; origin unknown.]

gosse, *gos,* (*Shak.*) *n.* a form of gorse.

gossip, *gos'ip, n.* a sponsor at baptism (in relation to child, parent, or other sponsor) (*arch.*): a woman friend who comes at a birth (*arch.*): a familiar friend (*arch.; Spens.* goss'ib): one who goes about telling and hearing news, or idle, malicious, and scandalous tales: idle talk: tittle-tattle: scandalous rumours: easy familiar writing.—*v.i.* to run about telling idle or malicious tales: to talk much: to chat.—*v.t.* (*Shak.*) to stand godfather to.—*n.* and *adj.* goss'iping.—*n.* goss'ipry.—*adj.* goss'ipy. [O.E. *godsibb,* godfather, one who is sib in God, spiritually related.]

gossoon, gorsoon, *go-, gör-söön', n.* a boy or boy-servant. [Anglo-Ir.,—Fr. *garçon,* boy.]

Gossypium, *go-sip'i-əm, n.* a tropical genus of the mallow family, yielding cotton.—*adj.* goss'ypine, cottony.—*n.* goss'ypol, a poisonous principle in cotton-seed. [L. *gossypion.*]

got, gotten. See under get.

Goth, *goth, n.* one of an ancient Germanic nation, originally settled on the southern coasts of the Baltic, migrating to Dacia in the 3rd century, and later founding kingdoms in Italy, southern France, and Spain: a rude or uncivilised person, a barbarian.—*adj.* Goth'ic, of the Goths or their language: barbarous: romantic: denoting style of architecture with high-pointed arches, clustered columns, etc. (applied in reproach at time of the Renaissance): black-letter (*print.*): a square-cut type without serifs (*U.S.*): orig. applied to 18th-cent. tales, novels, of mystery with gloomy sinister backgrounds, now denoting psychological horror-tales.—*n.* language of the Goths, an East Germanic tongue: Gothic architecture.—*v.t.* goth'icise, -ize (-*siz*), to make Gothic.—*n.* Goth'icism (-*sizm*), a Gothic idiom or style of building: rudeness of manners. [The native names *Gutans* (sing. *Guta*) and *Gutōs* (sing. *Guts*), and *Gutthiuda,* people of the Goths; Latinised as *Gothi, Gotthi;* Gr. *Gothoi, Gotthoi;* O.E. *Gotan* (sing. *Gota*).]

Gothamite, *göt', got'əm-it,* Gothamist, -ist, *ns.* a simpleton: a wiseacre: (*goth', göth'*) a New Yorker (*U.S.*). [From *Gotham,* a village in Nottinghamshire, with which name are connected many of the simpleton stories of immemorial antiquity.]

gothite, *gæt'it, n.* a mineral, hydrated ferric oxide. [Named in honour of the poet *Goethe.*]

gouache, *goo-äsh, goo', (chiefly U.S.) gwäsh, n.* watercolour painting with opaque colours, mixed with water, honey, and gum, presenting a matt surface: work painted according to this method. [Fr.]

Gouda, *gow'də, n.* a kind of cheese from *Gouda* in the Netherlands.

gouge, gowj, also *gooj, n.* a chisel with a hollow blade for cutting grooves or holes.—*v.t.* to scoop out, as with a gouge: to force out, as the eye with the thumb. [O.Fr.,—L.L. *gubia,* a kind of chisel.]

gouge, *gooj, (Scott) n.* a wench. [O.Fr.]

goujeers, an editor's would-be-improvement upon goodyear (q.v.), from a spurious Fr. *goujère,* the French disease.

gouk. See gowk.

goulash, *goo'lash, n.* a stew of beef, vegetables, esp. onions, and paprika: a re-deal of cards that have been arranged in suits and order of value, so many (as e.g. 5) cards at a time (*bridge*). [Hung. *gulyás* (*hús*), herdsman (meat).]

Goura, *gow'rə, n.* a New Guinea genus of beautifully crested, ground-loving pigeons. [From a native name.]

gourami. See gourami.

gourd, *goord, görd, görd, n.* a large hard-rinded fleshy fruit characteristic of the cucumber family: rind of one used as a bottle, cup, etc.: a gourd-bearing plant.—gourd'-worm, a fluke-worm resembling a gourd-seed, esp. the liver-fluke. [O.Fr. *gourde,* contr. from *cougourde*—L. *cucurbita,* a gourd.]

gourde, *goord, n.* the monetary unit of Haiti, consisting of 100 centimes. [Fr. fem. of *gourd*—L. *gurdus,* dull, stupid.]

gourds, *gördz, goordz, gördz, n.pl.* a kind of false dice. [Cf. O.Fr. *gourd,* swindle.]

gourdy, *goord'i, görd', goord', adj.* swollen in the legs (of a horse).—*n.* gourd'iness. [O.Fr. *gourdi,* swollen.]

gourmand, *goor'mənd, -mä, n.* one who eats greedily: a glutton: a lover of good fare.—*adj.* voracious: gluttonous.—*n.* gourmandise (*goor'-mən-diz, goor-mä-dēz*), skill, or indulgence, in good eating: voracious greed (*Spens.*). [Fr.; cf. gormand.]

gourmet, *goor-mä, -me, n.* an epicure, originally one with a delicate taste in wines. [Fr., a wine-merchant's assistant.]

goustrous, *gows'trəs, (Scot.) adj.* boisterous, rude.

gousty, *gows'ti, (Scot.) adj.* dreary: desolate: empty.

gout, *gowt, n.* a drop, spot (*arch.*): a disease in which excess of uric acid in the blood is deposited as urates in the joints, etc., with swelling esp.

Neutral vowels in unaccented syllables: el'ə-mənt; for certain sounds in foreign words, see p. viii

of the great toe: a kindred disease of poultry: a swelling of the stalk in wheat and other grasses.—*n.* gout'iness.—*adj.* gout'y, relating to gout: diseased with or subject to gout.—gout'fly, a fly (Chlorops) whose larvae cause gout by boring in wheat, etc.; gout'weed, -wort, bishopweed or goatweed (*Aegopodium podagraria*), an' umbelliferous weed, long supposed to be good for gout. [O.Fr. *goutte*—L. *gutta*, a drop, the disease supposed to be caused by a defluxion of humours.]

gout, *gōō, n.* taste: relish. [Fr. *goût*—L. *gustus*, taste.]

goutte, *gōōt,* (Fr.) drop (of liquid); goutte à goutte, drop by drop.

gouvernante, *gōō-ver-nät, n.* a female ruler (*obs.*): a housekeeper: a duenna: a governess. [Fr.]

govern, *guv'ərn, v.t.* to direct: to control: to rule with authority: to determine: to determine the case of (*gram.*): to require as the case of a noun or pronoun.—*v.i.* to exercise authority: to administer the laws.—*adj.* gov'ernable.—*ns.* gov'ernall (*Spens.*), government; gov'ernance, government: control: direction: behaviour (*obs.*); gov'ernante (*obs.*), a gouvernante; gov'erness, a female governor (*arch.*; *fig. Milt.*): a lady who has charge of the instruction of the young at home or in school (nursery governess, one having charge of young children only, tending as well as teaching them).—*v.i.* to act as governess.—*v.t.* to be governess to.—*adjs.* gov'ernessy, like a governess, esp. prim; gov'erning, having control.—*n.* government (*guv'ər(n)-mənt*), a ruling or managing: control: system of governing: the body of persons authorised to administer the laws, or to govern a state: tenure of office of one who governs: an administrative division (*arch.*): territory (*arch.*): the power of one word in determining the case of another (*gram.*): conduct (*Shak.*).—*adj.* of or pursued by government.—*adj.* governmental (*-ment'l*), pertaining to government.—*ns.* gov'ernor, a real or titular ruler, esp. of a state, province, colony: the head of an institution or a member of its ruling body: the commander of a fortress: a tutor (*arch.*): (usu. *guv'nər*) a father, chief, or master, applied more generally in kindly, usually ironically respectful, address (*slang*): a regulator, or contrivance for maintaining uniform velocity with a varying resistance (*mach.*): a pilot (*B.*); gov'ernorship.—governess car, cart, a light low two-wheeled vehicle with face-to-face seats at the side; governmental atonement (see Grotian); gov'ernor-gen'eral, orig. the supreme governor of a country, etc., with deputy governors under him: the representative of the British crown in Commonwealth countries which recognise the monarchy as head of state:—*pl.* gov'ernors-gen'eral; gov'ernor-gen'eralship. [O.Fr. *governer*—L. *gubernāre*—Gr. *kybernaein*, to steer.]

gowan, gow'ən, (*Scot.*) *n.* the wild daisy: the ox-eye daisy (also horse'-gow'an).—*adj.* gow'any.—*n.* luck'en-gow'an, the globe-flower. [Apparently a form of gollan(d).]

gowd, gowdspink. Scots form of gold, goldspink.

gowf, *gowf,* (*Scot.*) *v.t.* to strike, cuff.—*v.i.* to golf.—*n.* golf.—*n.* gowf'er, golfer.—gowf'-ba', golf-ball. [See golf.]

gowk, gowk, *gowk,* (*Scot.*) *n.* a cuckoo: a fool: an April fool. [O.N. *gaukr*; O.E. *gēac.*]

gowl, *gowl,* (*Scot.*) *v.i.* to cry or howl. [O.N. *gaula.*]

gowland. See gollan.

gown, *gown, n.* a loose flowing outer garment: a woman's dress: an academic, clerical, or official robe.—*v.t.* and *v.i.* to dress in a gown.—*v.t.* to invest or furnish with a gown.—*adj.* gowned.—gown'boy, a school foundationer, wearing a gown; gown'man, gowns'man, one who wears a gown, as a divine or lawyer, and esp. a member

of an English university: a civilian (*arch.*). [O.Fr. *goune*—L.L. *gunna*; origin unknown.]

gowpen, *gowp'ən,* (*Scot.*) *n.* the hollow of the two hands held together: a double handful.—*n.* gow'-penful. [O.N. *gaupn.*]

goy, *goi, n.* a non-Jew, Gentile:—*pl.* goy'im.—*adj.* goy'ish. [Heb., nation.]

Graafian, *grä'fi-ən, adj.* pertaining to the Dutch anatomist Regnier de *Graaf* (1641-73) who discovered the Graafian follicles, in which the ova are contained in the ovary of higher vertebrates.

graal. See grail (3).

grab, grab, *n.* an Eastern coasting vessel. [Ar. *ghurāb.*]

grab, grab, *v.t.* to seize or grasp suddenly: to lay hands on.—*v.i.* to clutch:—*pr.p.* grabb'ing; *pa.t.* and *pa.p.* grabbed.—*n.* a sudden grasp or clutch: unscrupulous seizure: a double scoop hinged like a pair of jaws: a simple card-game depending upon prompt claiming.—*n.* grabb'er, one who grabs: an avaricious person.—grab'-bag, a bag or other receptacle for miscellaneous articles: one from which gifts are drawn (*U.S.*).—Also *fig.*—grabbing crane, an excavator consisting of a crane and a large grab, so hinged as to scoop in to the earth as it is lifted. [Cf. Sw. *grabba,* to grasp.]

grabble, grab'l, *v.t.* and *v.i.* to grope. [Freq. of grab.]

graben, *grä'ben, n.* same as a rift valley. [Ger. ditch.]

Grace, grās, *n.* an automatic telephone system whereby all calls, trunk as well as local, can be dialled directly by subscribers. [group routing and charging equipment.]

grace, grās, *n.* easy elegance in form or manner: what adorns and commends to favour: a grace note (*mus.*): favour: kindness: pardon (*arch.*): the undeserved mercy of God: divine influence: eternal life or salvation: a short prayer before or after a meal: an act or decree of the governing body of an English university: a ceremonious title in addressing a duke, an archbishop, or formerly a king: (in *pl.*) favour, friendship (with *good*): (*cap.* in *pl.*) the three sister goddesses in whom beauty was deified (the Greek Charites), Euphrosyne, Aglaia, Thalia (*myth.*).—*v.t.* to mark with favour: to adorn.—*adjs.* graced (*Shak.*), favoured, endowed with grace or graces, virtuous, chaste; grace'ful, elegant and easy: marked by propriety or fitness, becoming: having or conferring grace, in any sense.—*adv.* grace'fully.—*n.* grace'fulness.—*adj.* grace'less, wanting grace or excellence: without mercy or favour (*obs.*): depraved (*arch.*): indecorous.—*adv.* grace'lessly.—*n.* grace'lessness.—*ns.* graciosity (*grä-shi-os'i-ti*), graciousness; gracioso (*grä-shi-ō'sō*; Sp. *grä-thyō'sō*), a favourite (*obs.*): a clown in Spanish comedy.—*adj.* gracious (*grä'shəs*), abounding in grace or kindness: proceeding from divine favour (*obs.*): acceptable: affable: becoming in demeanour: favourable (*arch.*).—*n.* used as substitute for God.—*adv.* gra'ciously.—*n.* gra'ciousness.—*adj.* grace-and-favour, (of a residence) belonging to the British sovereign and granted rent-free to a person of importance.—grace cup, a cup or health drunk at the end of a feast; grace note (*mus.*), a note introduced as an embellishment, not being essential to the harmony or melody; gracious living, (living in) conditions of ease, plenty, and good taste.—days of grace, (three) days allowed for the payment of a note or bill of exchange after it falls due; fall from grace, to backslide, to lapse from the state of grace and salvation or from favour; good gracious, an exclamation of surprise; saving grace (*Christian theology*), divine grace so bestowed as to lead to salvation: a compensating virtue or quality; take heart of grace, to pluck up courage (orig. of 'of grace' uncertain); with good (bad) grace, in amiable (ungracious) fashion; year of grace, year of Christian era, A.D. [Fr. *grâce*—L. *grātia*, favour—*grātus*, agreeable.]

grâce à Dieu, *gräs a dyø*, (Fr.) thanks to God.

gracile, *gras'il*, *adj.* slender: gracefully slight in form.—*-n.* gracil'ity. [L. *gracilis*, slender.]

gracious, gracioso, etc. See grace.

grackle, grakle, *grak'l*, *n.* a myna (hill myna) or kindred bird: an American 'blackbird' of the family Icteridae. [L. *grāculus*, jackdaw.]

gradate, etc. See grade.

graddan, *grad'ɔn*, (*Scot.*) *n.* parched grain.—*v.t.* to parch in the husk. [Gael. *gradan*.]

grade, *grād*, *n.* a degree or step in quality, rank, or dignity: a stage of advancement: rank: a yearly stage in education (*U.S.*): a pupil's mark of proficiency (*U.S.*): (in *pl.*, *the grades*) the elementary school (*U.S.*): position in a scale: a class, or position in a class, according to value: position in an ablaut series (*philol.*): one-hundredth part of a right angle (*math.*): gradient or slope: an inclined or level stretch of road or railway (*U.S.*): a class of animals produced by crossing a breed with one purer.—*v.t.* to arrange according to grade: to assign a grade to: to adjust the gradients of.—*v.i.* to shade off.—*adj.* of improved stock.—*v.t.* and *v.i.* gradate (*grɑ-dāt'*), to shade off imperceptibly.—*adv.* grādā'tim (L. *grä-dä'tim*), step by step.—*n.* grādā'tion, a degree or step: a rising step by step: progress from one degree or state to another: position attained: state of being arranged in ranks: a diatonic succession of chords (*mus.*): a gradual shading off: ablaut (*philol.*).—*adjs.* grādā'tional; grādā'tioned, formed by gradations or stages; gradatory (*grad'ɔt-ɔ-ri*), proceeding step by step: adapted for walking; gradient (*grā'di-ɔnt,-dyɔnt*), rising or falling by degrees: walking.—*n.* the degree of slope as compared with the horizontal: rate of change in any quantity with distance, e.g. in barometer readings: an incline.—*ns.* grād'-ienter, a surveyor's instrument for determining grades; gradin, gradine (*grā'din*, *grɔ-dēn'*), a rising tier of seats, as in an amphitheatre: a raised step or ledge behind an altar; gradino (*grä-dē'nō* It.), a decoration for an altar gradin; gradiometer (*grā-di-om'ɔ-tɔr*), a magnetometer for measuring the gradient of a magnetic field, etc.—*adj.* gradual (*grad'ū-ɔl*), advancing by grades or degrees: gentle and slow (of a slope). —*n.* in the R.C. Church, the portion of the mass between the epistle and the gospel, formerly always sung from the steps of the altar: the book containing such anthems—also grail.— *ns.* grad'ūalism, the principle or policy of proceeding by degrees; gradual'ist; gradual'ity. *adv.* grad'ūally.—*n.* grad'ūand, one about to receive a university degree.—*v.t.* gradū'ate, to divide into regular intervals: to mark with degrees: to proportion: to confer a degree upon (*U.S.*): to admit to a university degree (*arch.*).—*v.i.* to pass by grades: to receive a university degree.—*n.* one who has obtained a university degree: one who has completed a course in any educational institution (*U.S.*).— *adj.* grad'ūated, marked with degrees, as a thermometer.—*ns.* grad'ūateship; gradūā'tion; grad'ūātor, an instrument for dividing lines at regular intervals; grā'dus, a dictionary of Greek or Latin prosody—for *Gradus ad Parnassum*, a step, or stairs, to Parnassus.—grade crossing (*U.S.*), a level crossing; grade separation (*U.S.*), a crossing at which one road, etc., is an underpass or an overpass.—at grade (*U.S.*), on the same level; make the grade, orig. to succeed in climbing a steep hill: to overcome obstacles: to succeed: to be up to standard. [L. *gradus*, a step—*gradī*, to step.]

gradely, *grād'li*, (*dial.*) *adj.* decent: proper: fit:

fine.—*adv.* properly: readily: very.—Also graith'ly. [See graith.]

Gradgrind, *grad'grind*, *n.* one who regulates all human things by rule and compass and the mechanical application of statistics, allowing nothing for sentiment, emotion, and individuality. [From Thomas *Gradgrind* in Dickens's *Hard Times*.]

gradient, etc., graduand, etc. See grade.

Graecise, -ize, *grē'sīz*, *v.t.* to make Greek: to hellenise.—*v.i.* to become Greek: to conform to Greek ways or idioms: to use the Greek language.—*n.* Grae'cism, a Greek idiom: the Greek spirit: a following of the Greeks.—*adj.* Graeco-Ro'man (*grē'kō-*), of or pertaining to both Greece and Rome, esp. the art of Greece under Roman domination: applied to a mode of wrestling imagined to be that of the Greeks and Romans.—Also Grecise, -ize, etc. [L. *Graecus*— Gr. *Graikos*, Greek; *graikizein*, to speak Greek.]

graf, *gräf*, *n.* a count, earl:—*fem.* gräfin (*gref-in*). [Ger.]

graff, *gräf*, (*Scot.*) *n.* a variant of grave (1).

graff, *gräf*, *n.* and *vb.* an older form of graft (1).

graffito, *gräf-fē'tō*, *n.* a mural scribbling or drawing, as by schoolboys and idlers at Pompeii, Rome, and other ancient cities (*ant.*): (in *pl.*) scribblings or drawings, often indecent, found on public buildings, in lavatories, etc.: sgraffito: —*pl.* graffiti (*-fē'tē*). [It.,—Gr. *graphein*, to write.]

graft, *gräft*, *n.* a small piece of a plant or animal inserted in another individual or another part so as to come into organic union: the act of inserting a part in this way: the place of junction of stock and scion: the double plant composed of stock and scion: a sucker, branch, plant (*obs.*). —*v.t.* to insert a graft in: to insert as a graft: to cuckoldise (*obs.*).—*v.i.* to insert grafts.— *ns.* graft'er; graft'ing.—graft hybrid, a hybrid form produced, as some have believed, by grafting: a patchwork compound of two species propagated from the junction of tissues in a graft, each part retaining the specific character proper to the cells from which it arose. [From older graff—O.Fr. *graffe* (Fr. *greffe*)—L. *graphium*—Gr. *graphion*, *grapheion*, a style, pencil—*graphein*, to write.]

graft, *gräft*, *n.* a ditch, excavation (*dial.*): a spade's depth: a ditching spade: hard work (*slang*): a criminal's special branch of practice (*slang*): illicit profit by corrupt means, esp. in public life (*slang*): corruption in official life (*slang*).— *v.i.* to dig (*dial.*): to work hard (*slang*): to engage in graft or corrupt practices (*slang*).—*n.* graft'er. [Cf. O.N. *gröftr*, digging: the slang uses of corruption in public life, etc., may belong to graft (1).]

grail, *grāl*, *n.* gravel.—Also (*Spens.*) graile, grayle. [Perh. gravel; or O.Fr. *graile* (Fr. *grêle*), hail— L. *gracilis*, slender.]

grail. See gradual (under grade).

grail, *grāl*, *n.* in mediaeval legend, the platter (sometimes supposed to be a cup) used by Christ at the Last Supper, in which Joseph of Arimathaea caught his blood, said to have been brought by Joseph to Glastonbury, and the object of quests by King Arthur's Knights.— Also graal, grayle. [O.Fr. *graal* or *grael*, a flat dish—L.L. *gradālis*, a flat dish, ultimately from Gr. *krātēr*, a bowl.]

grain, *grān*, *n.* a single small hard seed: corn, in general: a hard particle: a very small quantity: the smallest British weight (the average weight of a seed of corn) = $\frac{1}{7000}$ of a pound avoirdupois: (in *pl.*) refuse malt after brewing or distilling: the arrangement, size and direction of the particles, fibres, or plates of stone, wood, etc.: texture: a granular surface: dried bodies of kermes or of cochineal insects, once thought to be seeds: the

Neutral vowels in unaccented syllables: *el'ɔ-mɔnt*; for certain sounds in foreign words, see p. viii red dye made from these: any fast dye—to *dye in grain* is to dye deeply, also to dye in the wool: dye in general: innate quality or character.—*v.t.* to form into grains, cause to granulate: to paint in imitation of grain: to dye in grain: in tanning, to take the hair off.—*n.* **grain'age,** duties on grain.—*adj.* **grained,** granulated: subjected to graining: having a grain: rough: furrowed.—*ns.* **grain'er,** one who grains: a paint-brush for graining; **grain'ing,** specif., painting to imitate the grain of wood: a process in tanning in which the grain of the leather is raised.—*adj.* **grain'y,** having grains or kernels.— **against the grain,** against the nbre of the wood— hence against the natural temper or inclination; **grains of Paradise,** the aromatic and pungent seeds of an African Amomum; **in grain,** in substance, in essence; **with a grain of salt,** with reservation, as of a story that cannot be admitted (L. *cum grānō salis*). [Fr. *grain*, collective *graine*—L. *grānum*, seed and *grāna*, orig. pl.; akin to **corn** (1).]

**grain,** *grān, n.* a branch, prong, fork (*dial.*): (in pl., used as *sing.*) a kind of harpoon. [O.N. *grein.*]

**graine,** *grān, n.* silkworm eggs. [Fr.]

**graining,** *grān'ing, n.* (in Lancashire) dace—once thought a different species. [Origin unknown.]

**graining.** See **grain** (1).

**graip,** *grāp,* (*Scot.*) *n.* a three- or four-pronged fork used for lifting dung or digging potatoes. [A form of **grope**; cf. Sw. *grep*, Dan. *greb.*]

**graith,** *grāth,* (*Scot.*) *n.* apparatus: equipment.— *v.t.* to make ready, to dress. [O.N. *greithr,* ready; cf. O.E. *geræde,* ready.]

**grakle.** See **grackle.**

**Grallae,** *gral'ē,* **Grallatores,** *-ə-tō'rēz, -tö', ns. pl.* in old classifications, an order of wading birds.— *adj.* **grallatō'rial.** [L. *grallātor,* a stilt-walker— *grallae,* stilts—*gradus,* a step.]

**gralloch,** *gral'əhh, n.* a deer's entrails.—*v.t.* to disembowel (deer). [Gael. *grealach.*]

**gram,** *gram,* **grame,** *grān;,* (*obs.*) *n.* anger: grief, trouble. [O.E. *grama,* anger.]

**gram,** *gram, n.* chick-pea: pulse generally. [Port. *grāo* (sometimes *gram*)—L. *grānum,* a grain.]

**gram, gramme,** *gram, n.* a unit of mass in the metric system—formerly that of a cubic centimetre of water at 4°C, now a thousandth part of the International Prototype Kilogram (see **kilogram**).—**gram'-at'om, gram'-mol'ecule,** the quantity of an element, a compound, whose mass in grams is equal to its atomic weight, molecular weight (a now discarded concept); **gram'-equiv'alent,** the quantity of a substance whose mass in grams is equal to its equivalent weight. [Fr. *gramme*—L. *gramma*—Gr. *gramma,* a letter, a small weight.]

**-gram, -gram,** in composition, something written or drawn to form a record. [Gr. *gramma,* letter.]

**grama,** *grä'mə, n.* an American pasture grass (*Bouteloua*) with one-sided spikes. [Sp.,—L. *grāmen,* grass.]

**gramary, gramarye,** *gram'ə-ri, n.* magic: enchantment. [M.E. *gramery,* skill in grammar, hence magic; see **grammar, glamour.**]

**gramash.** See **gamash.**

**grame.** See **gram** (1).

**gramercy,** *grə-mûr'si,* (*arch.*) *interj.* great thanks. —*n.* thanks. [O.Fr. *grant merci,* great thanks.]

**gramicidin,** *gram-i-sī'din, n.* an antibiotic obtained from certain bacteria, used against Grampositive bacteria.—*adjs.* **Gram-neg'ative** (*gram'-*) (also gram-), losing a stain of methyl violet and iodine on treatment with alcohol; **Grampos'itive** (also gram-), retaining the stain. [H. J. C. *Gram,* deviser of the method, L. *caedēre,* to kill.]

**Gramineae,** *grə-, gra-, grā-min'i-ē, n.pl.* the grass family.—*adjs.* **graminā'ceous** (*grā-, gra-*), **gramin'-**

eous; **graminiv'orous** (*gra-*), grass-eating. [L *gramen, grāminis,* grass.]

**grammalogue,** *gram'ə-log, n.* a word represented by a single sign: a sign for a word in shorthand. [Gr. *gramma,* a letter, *logos,* a word.]

**grammar,** *gram'ər, n.* the science of language, from the points of view of pronunciation, inflexion, syntax, and historic development: the art of the right use of language by grammatical rules: a book that teaches these subjects: any elementary work.—*n.* **gramma'rian,** one versed in grammar, a teacher of or writer on grammar.—*adjs.* **grammat'ic, -al,** belonging to, or according to the rules of, grammar.—*adv.* **grammat'ically.**— *n.* **grammat'icaster** (*arch.*), a piddling grammarian.—*v.t.* **grammat'icise, -ize** (*-sīz*), to make grammatical.—*v.i.* to act the grammarian.—*ns.* **grammat'icism** (*rare*), a point of grammar; **gramm'atist,** a strict grammarian.—**grammar school,** orig. a school in which grammar, esp. Latin grammar, was taught: now a higher school in which academic subjects predominate. [Gr. *gramma, -atos,* a letter; partly through O.Fr. *gramaire.*]

**gramme.** See **gram** (3).

**gramoche,** *gra-mosh'.* See **gamash.**

**gramophone,** *gram'ə-fōn, n.* an instrument for reproducing sounds by means of a needle moving along the grooves of a revolving disk— invented by E. Berliner (trademark in U.S.).— *adj.* **gramophonic** (*-fon'ik*).—*adj.* **gramophon'- ically.**—*ns.* **gramophonist** (*gram-of'ə-nist, gram'ə-fōn-ist*); **gramoph'ony.** [Ill-formed from Gr. *gramma,* letter, record, *phōnē,* sound.]

**grampus,** *gram pəs, n.* a popular name for many whales, esp. the killer: technically, Risso's dolphin (*Grampus griseus*): one who puffs. [16th century *graundepose,* earlier *grapays*—O.Fr. *graspeis*—L. *crassus,* fat, *piscis,* fish, confused with Fr. *grand,* big.]

**gran,** *gran,* (It.) great; **gran turismo,** *tōō-rēs'mō,* (a motor car) designed for touring in luxury and at high speed (term sometimes used loosely).

**granadilla,** *gran-ə-dil'ə,* **grenadilla,** *gren', n.* an edible passion-flower fruit.—**granadilla tree,** the cocus-wood tree. [Sp.]

**granary,** *gran'ə-ri, n.* a storehouse for grain or threshed corn: a rich grain-growing region. [L. *grānārium*—*grānum.*]

**grand,** *grand, adj.* pre-eminent: supreme: chief: main: exalted: magnificent: dignified: sublime: imposing: would-be-imposing: on a great scale: in complete form: in full proportions: very good (*coll.*): (in composition) of the second degree of parentage or descent, as **grandchild, granddaughter, grandfather, grandmother, grandson,** etc.—*n.* a grand piano: a thousand dollars (*U.S. slang*).—*ns.* **grandee',** from the 13th century a noble of the most highly privileged class in the kingdom of Castile, the members of the royal family being included: a man of high rank or station; **grandeur** (*grand'- yər*), vastness: splendour of appearance: loftiness of thought or deportment; **grandil'oquence.** —*adj.* **grandil'oquent** (L. *loquēns, -entis,* speaking), speaking, or expressed bombastically— (*arch.*) **grandil'oquous.**—*adv.* **grandil'oquently.**— *adj.* **gran'diose,** grand or imposing: bombastic. —*adv.* **gran'diosely.**—*n.* **grandios'ity.**—*adv.* **grand'ly.**—*ns.* **grand'ness.**—**grand(d)ad,** old man: a grandfather; **gran'dam** (*arch.*), **grann'am** (*arch.*), an old dame or woman: a grandmother; **grand'-aunt,** a great aunt; **grand'child,** a son's or daughter's child; **grand'daughter,** a son's or daughter's daughter.—**grand'- du'cal.**—**grand duke,** a title of sovereignty over a grand duchy, first created by the Pope in 1569 for the rulers of Florence and Tuscany, assumed by certain German and Russian imperial princes (*fem.* **grand duchess**); **grand'father,** a father's or mother's father.—*adj.* grand'fatherly, like a grandfatner, kindly.—grandfather('s) clock, an old-fashioned clock (long case clock) standing on the ground—larger than a grandmother('s) clock; grand juror, member of a grand jury, a special jury in the U.S. and until 1933 in Britain which decides whether there is sufficient evidence to put an accused person on trial; grand'mamma, grand'ma, a grandmother; grand march, processional opening of a ball; Grand Master, the head of a religious order of knighthood (Hospitallers, Templars, and Teutonic Knights), or of the Freemasons, etc.; grand'mother, a father's or mother's mother.—*adj.* grand'motherly, like a grandmother, over-anxious, fussy.—Grand National, a steeplechase held annually at Aintree in Liverpool; grand'-neph'ew, a great-nephew; grand'-niece, a great-niece; grand'-papa, grand'pa, a grandfather; grand'parent, a grandfather or grandmother; grand piano, a large harp-shaped piano, with horizontal strings; grand'son, a son's or daughter's son; grand'sire, a grandfather (*arch.*): any ancestor (*arch.*): a method of ringing changes on bells; grand slam, the winning of every trick at bridge: in sports such as tennis, golf, etc., the winning of all major championships in a season; grand'stand, an elevated erection on a racecourse, etc., affording a good view; grandstand finish, a close and rousing finish to a sporting contest: a supreme effort to win at the close of a sporting contest; grand style, a style adapted to lofty or sublime subjects; grand total, the sum of all subordinate sums; Grand Tour (see tour); grand touring (same as gran turismo); grand'-un'cle, a great uncle. [Fr. *grand*—L. *grandis*, great.]

grand, grä, (Fr.) great; grand amateur (*da-ma-tœr*), a collector of beautiful objects on a large scale; grand atelier (*dat-əl-yä*), a top-ranking fashion house; grand coup (*kōō*), a successful stroke: in bridge or whist the trumping of a trick that could have been trumped by the winner's partner; grand cru (*krü*), of a wine, from a famous vineyard or group of vineyards; Grand Guignol (see Guignol); grand luxe (*lüks*), great luxury; grand mal (*mal*), a violently convulsive form of epilepsy, see *petit mal*; grand merci (*mer-sē*), many thanks; grand monde (*mɔd*), high society; grand prix (*prē*), chief prize: (*cap.*) any of several international motor races (orig. *Grand Prix de Paris*, a famous horse race): —*pl.* grands prix; grand seigneur (*sen-yœr*), a dignified aristocratic gentleman or noble (now usu. *ironic*); (le) Grand Siècle (*syekl'*), the great century, i.e., the Classical age of French literature during the reign of Louis XIV.

grande, gräd, (Fr.) *fem.* of grand; grande amoureuse (*a-mōō-rœz*), a woman greatly involved in love affairs; (la) Grande Armée (*ar-mä*), the great army, i.e. that led by Napoleon to invade Russia in 1812; grande cocotte (*ko-kot*), a high-class prostitute, usu. one kept by a rich lover; grande dame (*däm*), a great and aristocratic lady, or a socially important and very dignified one (now, as *grand seigneur*, often *ironic*); grande école (*ā-kol*), a French technical college with military connections; grande entrée (*ä-trä*), admission to Court, etc., on occasions of state; grande marque (*märk*), of motor cars, etc., a famous make; grande passion (*pas-yɔ̃*), a serious love affair or intense attachment; grande tenue (*tə-nü*), full dress, esp. military, etc.; grande toilette (*twa-let*), full dress, esp. women's evening dress; grande vedette (*və-det*), a leading film or theatre star.

Grandisonian, gran-di-sō'ni-ən, *adj.* like the novelist Richardson's hero, Sir Charles *Grandison*, beneficent, polite, and chivalrous.

granfer, gran'fər, (*dial.*) *n.* contr. of grandfather.

grange, gränj, *n.* a granary (*Milt.*): a farmhouse

with its stables and other buildings: a country house (*obs.*): an abiding place (*Spens.*): a lodge of the order of Patrons of Husbandry (*U.S.*).—*n.* gran'ger, the keeper of a grange: a member of a grange. [O.Fr. *grange*, barn—L.L. *gränea*—L. *gränum*, grain.]

Grangerism, grän'jer-izm, *n.* the practice of cutting plates and title-pages out of many books to illustrate one book.—*v.t.* gran'gerise, -ize, to practise Grangerism on. [From James *Granger* (1716-76), whose *Biographical History of England* (1769) gave an impetus to this.]

granite, gran'it, *n.* a coarse-grained igneous crystalline rock, composed of quartz, feldspar, and mica.—*adj.* of granite: hard like granite.—*adj.* granit'ic, pertaining to, consisting of, or like granite.—*n.* granitifica'tion.—*adj.* granit'iform.—*n.* gran'itite, muscovite granite; granitisä'tion, -z-.—*v.t.* gran'itise, -ize.—*adj.* gran'itoid, of the form of or resembling granite.—*n.* granodi'-orite, a rock resembling diorite but containing quartz.—*adj.* granolith'ic (Gr. *lithos*, stone), composed of cement and granite chips.—Also *n.*—*n.* gran'ophyre (-*fir*; with -*phyre* after *porphyry*), a quartz-porphyry with graphic intergrowth of quartz and orthoclase for groundmass.—*adj.* granophyric (*fir'ik*, -*fir'ik*). [It. *granito*, granite, lit. grained—L. *gränum*, grain.]

granivorous, gran-iv'ər-əs, *adj.* grain-eating: feeding on seeds. [L. *gränum*, grain, *vorāre*, to devour.]

granny, -ie, gran'i, *n.* a grandmother: an old woman: an old-womanish person: a revolving cap on a chimney-pot.—granny knot, a knot like a reef knot, but unsymmetrical, apt to slip or jam. [grannam (under grand).]

grant, gränt, *v.t.* to bestow: to admit as true: to concede.—*v.i.* (*Shak.*) to consent.—*n.* a bestowing: something bestowed, an allowance: a gift: conveyance of property by deed (*Eng. law*).—*adj.* grant'able.—*ns.* grantee' (*law*), the person to whom a grant, gift, or conveyance is made; grant'er, grant'or (*law*), the person by whom a grant or conveyance is made.—grant-in-aid, an official money grant for a particular purpose.—take for granted, to presuppose, assume, esp. tacitly or unconsciously. [O.Fr. *graanter*, *craanter*, *creanter*, to promise—L. *crēdēre*, to believe.]

Granth, grunt, *n.* the holy book of the Sikhs. [Hind.]

granule, gran'ül, *n.* a little grain: a fine particle.—*adjs.* gran'ular, gran'ulary (*arch.*), gran'ulose, consisting of or like grains or granules.—*adv.* gran'ularly.—*v.t.* gran'ulate, to form or break into grains or small masses: to make rough on the surface.—*v.i.* to be formed into grains.—*adj.* granular: having the surface covered with small elevations.—*n.* granulä'tion, act of forming into grains, esp. of metals by pouring them through a sieve into water while hot: (in *pl.*) the materials of new texture as first formed in a wound or on an ulcerated surface.—*adjs.* granül'erous; gran'üliform.—*n.* gran'ülite, a schistose but sometimes massive aggregate of quartz and feldspar with garnets: a granular-textured metamorphic rock.—*adj.* gran'ülit'ic, of the texture of granulite.—*n.* granüliti-sä'tion, -izätion, reduction of the components of a rock to crystalline grains by regional metamorphism. [L. *gränulum*, dim. of *gränum*, grain.]

grape, gräp, *v.i.* a Scottish form of grope.

grape, gräp, *n.* the fruit of the grapevine: a mangy tumour on the legs of horses: grapeshot.—*adj.* grape'less, without the flavour of the grape, said of wine.—*n.* grap'ery, a place where grapes are grown.—*adj.* grap'y, made of or like grapes.—grape'fruit, a fine variety of the shaddock, the pomelmoose, with sometimes a slightly grapelike taste; grape hyacinth, (Muscari) a near ally to the hyacinths, with

**graph** 568 **grate**

clusters of small grapelike flowers; **grape´-louse** (see **phylloxera**); **grape´seed**, the seed of the vine; **grape´seed-oil**, an oil expressed from it; **grape´shot**, shot that scatters; **grape´stone**, the pip of the grape; **grape sugar**, glucose or dextrose; **grape´tree**, a tropical American tree (*Coccoloba uvifera*) of the dock family, or its edible fruit; **grape´vine**, *Vitis vinifera* or other species of *Vitis*: the bush telegraph: rumour (from its far-stretching branches).—**sour grapes**, things decried because they cannot be attained (from Aesop's fable of the fox and the grapes). See also **Ephedra**. [O.Fr. *grape*, *grappe*, a cluster of grapes—*grape*, a hook; orig. Gmc.]

**graph**, *gräf*, *n.* a symbolic diagram: a curve representing the variation of a quantity: -**graph**, is used as a terminal in many compounds to denote an agent that writes, records, etc., as *telegraph*, *seismograph*, or the thing written, as in *autograph*, etc.— *n.* **grapheme** (*graf´ēm*), a letter of an alphabet: all the letters or combinations of letters together that may be used to express one phoneme.—*adj.* **graphēm´ic.**—*n.* **graphēm´ics**, study of systems of representing speech sounds in writing.—*adjs.* **graphic** (*graf´ik*), **-al**, pertaining to writing, describing, delineating, or diagrammatic representation: picturesquely described or describing: vivid.—*n.* (**graph´ic**) a painting, print, or illustration or diagram.—*adv.* **graph´ically.**—*ns.* **graph´icness; graph´ics**, graphic means of presenting, or means of reproducing, informational material: the art or science of mathematical drawing, and of calculating stresses, etc., by geometrical methods; **Graph´is**, a genus of lichens, with fructifications like writing; **graph´ite**, a mineral, commonly called blacklead or plumbago, though composed of carbon.—*adjs.* **graphit´ic, graph´itoid.**—*v.t.* **graph´itise, -ize**, to convert wholly or partly into graphite.—*ns.* **graph´ium**, stylus; **graphol´ogy**, the art of estimating character, etc., from handwriting.—**graphic arts**, painting, drawing, engraving, as opposed to music, sculpture, etc.; **graphic formula**, a chemical formula in which the symbols for single atoms are joined by lines representing valency bonds; **graphic granite**, a granite with markings like Hebrew characters, owing to intergrowth of quartz and feldspar. [Gr. *graphē*, a writing—*graphein*, to write.]

**grapnel**, *grap´nəl*, *n.* a small anchor with several claws or arms: a grappling-iron: a hooking or grasping instrument. [Dim. of O.Fr. *grapin*—*grape*, a hook; of Gmc. origin.]

**grappa**, *grä´pä*, *n.* a brandy orig. Italian made from residue from a wine-press. [It., grape stalk.]

**grapple**, *grap´l*, *n.* an instrument for hooking or holding: a grasp, grip, hold, or clutch: a state of being held or clutched.—*v.t.* to seize: to lay fast hold of.—*v.i.* to contend in close fight (also *fig.*).—Also (*Spens.*) **graple.**—*n.* **grapplement** (*Spens.*), a close fight.—**grapp´le-plant´**, a S. African plant (*Harpagophytum procumbens*) of the sesame family, with strongly hooked fruits; **grapp´ling-i´ron**, an instrument for grappling: a large grapnel for seizing hostile ships in naval engagements. [Cf. O.Fr. *grappil*—*grape*, a hook.]

**graptolite**, *grap´tə-līt*, *n.* one of a group of fossil Hydrozoa with one or two rows of hydrothecae on a simple or branched polypary—characteristic Silurian fossils like writing upon shales.—*adj.* **graptolit´ic**. [Gr. *graptos*, written, *graphein*, to write, *lithos*, stone.]

**grasp**, *gräsp*, *v.t.* to seize and hold: to take eagerly: to comprehend.—*v.i.* to endeavour to seize (with *at*, *after*): to seize or accept eagerly (with *at*).—*n.* grip: power of seizing: mental power of apprehension.—*adj.* **grasp´able.**—*n.* **grasp´er.**—*adj.* **grasp´ing**, seizing: avaricious.—*adv.* **grasp´ingly.**—*n.* **grasp´ingness.**—*adj.* **grasp´less**, feeble, relaxed. [M.E. *graspen*, *grapsen*, from the root of *grāpian*, to grope.]

**grass**, *gräs*, *n.* common herbage: any plant of the monocotyledonous family Gramineae, the most important to man in the vegetable kingdom, with long, narrow leaves and tubular stems, including wheat and other cereals, reeds (but not sedges), bamboo, sugar-cane: pasture grasses: pasturage: time of grass, spring or summer: the surface of a mine: an informer (*slang*): temporary or casual work in a printing office: marijuana (*slang*).—*v.t.* to cover with grass: to feed with grass: to bring to the grass or ground: to inform on (*slang*).—*v.i.* to inform (*slang*): to do temporary or casual work (*print.*).—*ns.* **grass´er** (*print.*), an extra or temporary worker; **grass´iness**; **grassing**, bleaching by exposure on grass. —*adj.* **grass´y**, covered with or resembling grass, green.—**grass´cloth**, a name for various coarse cloths (rarely made of grass), esp. ramie; **grass´cloth plant**, ramie; **grass´-cutter**, a mowing machine: in India, one who provides provender for baggage cattle (perh. really Hindustani *ghăskatā*).—*adjs.* **grass´-green**, green with grass: green as grass; **grass´-grown**, grown over with grass.—**grass´hopper**, a name for various saltatorial, orthopterous insects akin to locusts and crickets, that lurk among grass and chirp by rubbing their wing-covers; **grass´land**, permanent pasture; **grass´-moth**, a small light-coloured moth that frequents grass, a veneer-moth; **grass´-of-Parnass´us** (see **Parnassus**); **grass´-oil**, a name for several volatile oils derived from widely different plants, some of them grasses; **grass´-plot**, a plot of grassy ground; **grass´-roots** (orig. *U.S.*), the rural areas of a country: the dwellers there, regarded as representing the true character of a people: foundation, basis, origin, primary aim or meaning.—Also *adj.*— **grass´-snake**, the harmless common ringed snake; **grass´-tree**, an Australian plant (*Xanthorrhoea*) of the lily family, with shrubby stems, tufts of long wiry foliage at the summit, and a tall flower-stalk, with a dense cylindrical spike of small flowers; **grass´-wid´ow**, a wife temporarily separated from or deserted by her husband; **grass´-wrack**, eel-grass.—**go to grass**, to be turned out to pasture, esp. of a horse too old to work: to go into retirement, to rusticate: to fall violently (of a pugilist); **hear the grass grow**, to have exceptionally acute hearing: to be exceptionally alert; **let the grass grow under one's feet**, to loiter, linger, and so lose opportunity. [O.E. *gærs*, *græs*; O.N., Ger., Du., and Goth. *gras*; prob. allied to **green** and **grow**.]

**grass**, *gräs*, *n.* for **sparr´ow-grass**, a corruption of **asparagus**.

**grassum**, *gräs´əm*, (Scots law) *n.* a lump sum paid by persons who take a lease of landed property —in England, 'premium' and 'fine'. [O.E. *gærsum*, treasure, rich gift, etc.]

**graste**, *gräst*, (*Spens.*) pa.p. of **grace**.

**grate**, *grāt*, *n.* a framework of bars with interstices, esp. one for holding a fire or for looking through: a door, etc.: a cage: a grid.—*adj.* **grāt´ed**, having a grating.—*ns.* **graticulā´tion** (*gra-* or *grə-tik-ū-lā´shən*), the division of a design into squares for convenience in making an enlarged or diminished copy; **graticule** (*grat´i-kūl*), a ruled grating for identification of points in a map, the field of a telescope, etc.; **grāt´ing**, the bars of a grate: a perforated cover for a drain or the like: a partition or frame of bars: a surface ruled closely with fine lines to give a diffraction spectrum. [L.L. *grāta*, a grate—L. *crātis*, a hurdle; see **crate**.]

**grate**, *grāt*, *v.t.* to rub hard or wear away with anything rough: to irritate or jar on, or fret into anger or sorrow (*arch.*): to grind (the teeth): to emit or utter jarringly.—*v.i.* to make

*fāte, fär; mē, hûr* (her); *mīne; mōte, för; mūte; mōon, fŏŏt; dhen* (then) a harsh sound: to jar, rasp (on, against): to fret, irritate (usually with *on*, *upon*).—*n.* grat′er, an instrument with a rough surface for rubbing down to small particles.—*adj.* grat′ing, rubbing harshly: harsh: irritating.—*adv.* grat′ingly. [O.Fr. *grater*, through L.L., from O.H.G. *chrazzōn* (Ger. *kratzen*), to scratch, akin to Sw. *kratta*.]

grateful, *grāt′f(ōō)l*, *adj.* causing pleasure: acceptable: thankful: having a due sense of benefits: expressing gratitude.—*adv.* grate′fully.—*ns.* grate′fulness; gratificā′tion (*grat-*), a pleasing or indulging: that which gratifies: delight, feeling of satisfaction: a recompense, tip, or bribe (*arch.*); grat′ifier.—*v.t.* grat′ify, to do what is agreeable to: to please: to satisfy: to indulge:—*pr.p.* grat′ifying; *pa.t.* and *pa.p.* grat′ified.—*adj.* grat′ifying—*adv.* grat′ifyingly. [O.Fr. *grat*—L. *grātus*, pleasing, thankful.]

graticule. See grate (1).

gratillity, *grə-til′i-ti*, (*Shak.*) *n.* a small gratuity.

gratis, *grā′*, *grä′tis*, *adv.* for nothing: without payment or recompense.—gratis dictum (*dik′-təm,-tōōm*), mere assertion. [L. *grātis*, contr. of *grātiis*, abl. pl. of *grātia*, favour—*grātus.*]

gratitude, *grat′i-tūd*, *n.* warm and friendly feeling towards a benefactor: thankfulness. [Fr.,—L.L. *grātitūdō*—L. *grātus.*]

grattoir, *grät-wär*, (*archaeol.*) *n.* a scraper. [Fr.]

gratuity, *grə-tū′i-ti*, *n.* a present: an acknowledgment of service, usu. pecuniary: a tip: a bounty: a payment to a soldier, etc., on discharge.—*adj.* gratu′itous, done or given for nothing: voluntary: benefiting one party only (*law*): without reason, ground, or proof: uncalled for.—*adv.* gratu′itously. [Fr. *gratuité*—L.L. *grātuitās*, *-ātis*—L. *grātus.*]

gratulate, *grat′ū-lāt*, (*arch.*) *v.t.* to congratulate: to welcome: to express joy at.—*adj.* (*Shak.*) gratifying.—*adj.* grat′ulant, congratulatory.—*n.* gratulā′tion, congratulation.—*adj.* grat′ulatory, congratulatory.

gravamen, *grəv-ā′men*, *n.* grievance: the substantial or chief ground of complaint or accusation: a statement of abuses, grievances, etc. in the Church sent by the Lower to the Upper House of Convocation:—*pl.* gravā′mina. [L. *gravāmen*—*gravis*, heavy.]

grave, *grāv*, *v.t.* to dig (*obs.*): to engrave on hard substance: to fix deeply (e.g. on the mind): to bury (*obs.*).—*v.i.* to engrave:—*pa.p.* graved or grav′en.—*n.* a pit dug out, esp. one to bury the dead in: any place of burial: the abode of the dead (*B.*): death, destruction (*fig.*): a deadly place.—*adj.* grave′less (*Shak.*).—*ns.* grav′er, an engraver: a burin; grav′ing.—*n.pl.* grave′-clothes, the clothes in which the dead are buried. —grave′-digger; grave′-maker (*Shak.*), a grave-digger; grave′stone, a stone placed as a memorial at a grave; grave′yard, a burial-ground.—with one foot in the grave, on the brink of death. [O.E. *grafan*, to dig, *græf*, a cave, grave, trench; Du. *graven*, Ger. *graben.*]

grave, *grāv*, *v.t.* to clean (by burning, etc.) and pay with tar (a wooden ship's bottom).—grav′ing-dock, a dry-dock for cleaning and repair of ships. [Perh. Fr. *grave*, *grève*, beach.]

grave, *grāv*, *adj.* of importance: serious: not gay or showy: sedate: solemn: weighty: calling for anxiety: low in pitch.—*n.* (also *grāv*), grave accent.—*adv.* grave′ly.—*n.* grave′ness.—grave accent (*U.K. grāv*), a mark (`) originally indicating a pitch falling somewhat, or failing to rise, now used for various purposes. [Fr.,—L. *gravis.*]

grave, *grāv*, *n.* a count, prefect, a person holding office (now only in compounds, as *landgrave*, *margrave*, *burgrave*). [Du. *graaf*, Ger. *graf.*]

gravel, *grav′l*, *n.* an assemblage of small rounded stones: small collections of gravelly matter in

the kidneys or bladder.—*v.t.* to cover with gravel: to run aground on gravel (*obs.*): to puzzle, perplex: to irritate (*coll.*):—*pr.p.* grav′elling; *pa.t.* and *pa.p.* grav′elled.—*adj.* grav′elly.—*adjs.* grav′el-blind′ (*Shak.* high′-grav′el-blind′), after Shakespeare, punningly, in a state somewhere between sand-blind and stone-blind.—grav′el-pit, a pit from which gravel is dug.—*adj.* grav′el-voiced, *adj.* harsh-voiced.—grav′el-walk′, a footpath covered with gravel. [O.Fr. *gravele* (Fr. *gravier*); prob. Celt., as in Bret. *grouan*, sand, W. *gro*, pebbles.]

graven, *grāv′n*, *pa.p.* of grave, to carve, engrave.—graven image, an idol: a solemn person.

graveolent, *grəv-ē′ō-lənt*, or *grav′i-*, rank-smelling. [L. *graveolēns*, *-entis*—*gravis*, heavy, *olēns*, pr.p. of *olēre*, to smell.]

Graves, *gräv*, *n.* a white, or red, table wine from the Graves district in the Gironde department of France.

graves. Same as greaves.

gravid, *grav′id*, *adj.* pregnant.—*n.* gravid′ity. [L. *gravidus*—*gravis*, heavy.]

gravimeter, *grə-vim′i-tər*, *n.* a kind of hydrometer. —*adjs.* gravimetric (*grav-i-met′rik*), *-al*, pertaining to measurement by weight.—*n.* gravim′etry. [L. *gravis*, heavy, Gr. *metron*, measure.]

gravity, *grav′i-ti*, *n.* weightiness: gravitational attraction or acceleration: graveness: lowness of pitch.—*v.i.* gravitāte, to be acted on by gravity: to tend towards the earth or other body: to be attracted, or move, by force of gravitation: to sink or settle down: to be strongly attracted or move (towards; *fig.*).—*n.* gravitā′tion, act of gravitating: the force of attraction between bodies, this being directly proportional to the product of the masses and inversely to the square of the distances (the Newtonian *constant of gravitation* (symbol *G*) is $6·67 \times 10^{-11}$ MKS units).—*adjs.* gravitā′tional; grav′itātive.—*n.* grav′iton, a hypothetical quantum of gravitational field energy.—acceleration due to gravity (symbol *g*), the acceleration of a body falling freely under the action of gravity in a vacuum, about 32·174 feet or 9·8 metres per second per second; specific gravity (see specific). [L. *gravitās*, *-ātis*—*gravis*, heavy.]

gravure, *grə-vūr′*, *n.* any process of making an intaglio printing plate, including photogravure: the plate, or an impression from it. [Fr., engraving.]

gravy, *grāv′i*, *n.* the juices from meat while cooking: money, profit, or pleasure, unexpected or in excess of what one might expect (*coll.*).—graft (*slang*).—grav′y-boat, a vessel for gravy; grav′y-soup, soup like gravy, made from fresh meat; gravy train, a position in which one can have excessive profits or advantages in contrast to other people. [Perh. *gravé*, a copyist's mistake for O.F. *grané*—*grain*, a cookery ingredient.]

gray. Same as grey.—*n.* gray′ling, a silvery-grey fish (Thymallus) of the salmon family, with a smaller mouth and teeth, and larger scales: a grey butterfly of the Satyridae.—grey′fly (*Milt.*), an unknown insect.

grayle. See grail (1) and (3).

graywacke. Same as greywacke.

graze, *grāz*, *v.t.* to eat or feed on (growing grass or pasture): to feed or supply with grass.—*v.i.* to eat grass: to supply grass.—*ns.* graz′er, an animal that grazes; graz′ier, one who pastures cattle and rears them for the market; graz′ing, the act of feeding on grass: the feeding or raising of cattle. [O.E. *grasian*—*græs*, grass.]

graze, *grāz*, *v.t.* to pass lightly along the surface of.—*n.* a passing touch or scratch. [Ety. dub.; perhaps only a special use of graze above; perh. from *rase* (Fr. *raser*), the *g* due to the analogy of grate.]

grease, *grēs*, *n.* a soft thick animal fat: oily

matter of any kind: condition of fatness: an inflammation in the heels of a horse, marked by swelling, etc.—*v.t.* (in U.K. usu. pron. *grēz*) to smear with grease: to lubricate: to bribe (*slang*): to facilitate.—*n.* greaser (*grēz'ər*, or *grēs'ər*), one who greases: a ship's engineer: a Mexican or a Sp. American (*U.S.*; *not polite*).— *adv.* greas'ily.—*n.* greas'iness.—*adj.* greas'y (in U.K. usu. *grēz'i*), of or like grease or oil: smeared with grease: having a slippery coating: fatty: oily: obscene.—grease'-gun, a lubricating pump; grease'-heels, grease in horses; grease'-mon'key (*U.S.*), a mechanic; grease paint, a tallowy composition used by actors in making up.—*adj.* grease'-proof, resistant or impermeable to grease.—grease'wood, a name for various oily American shrubs of the goosefoot family.—grease one's palm (see palm); grease the wheels (*fig.*), to make things go smoothly; hart of grease, a fat hart. [O.Fr. *gresse*, fatness, *gras*, fat—L. *crassus*.]

great, *grāt*, *adj.* big: large: of a high degree of magnitude of any kind: capital (of letters; *arch.*): elevated in power, rank, station, etc.: pre-eminent in genius: highly gifted: chief: sublime: weighty: outstanding: pregnant, teeming (*arch.*): swelling with emotion: much addicted or given to, or excelling in the thing in question: favourite: habitual: in high favour or intimacy: in a high degree: on a large scale: excellent (*coll.*; often ironic): in composition indicating one degree more remote in the direct line of descent (as great'-grand'father, great'-grand'son, and similarly great'-great'-grand-father, and so indefinitely).—*n.* bulk, mass (*obs.*): whole (*obs.*): wholesale (*obs.*): one who has achieved renown: used collectively for those who have achieved renown.—*adv.* (*coll.*) very well.—*v.t.* great'en, to make great or greater.—*v.i.* to become great.—*adj.* great'er, comp. of great: (with geographical names) in an extended sense (as *Greater London*).—*adv.* great'ly.—*n.pl.* Greats, the final honour School of Literae Humaniores (*Classical Greats*) or of Modern Philosophy (*Modern Greats*) at Oxford.— great'-aunt, a grandparent's sister.—*adjs.* great'-bellied (*Shak.*), pregnant.—great circle (see circle); great'coat, an overcoat; Great Dane, a large close-haired dog; great'-grand'child, the child of a grandchild; great'-grand'father, -grand'mother, the father (mother) of a grandparent.—*adj.* great'-hearted, having a great or noble heart: high-spirited: magnanimous.— great'-nephew, -niece, a brother's or sister's grandson, granddaughter; great primer (see primer); great schism, great Eastern schism, Western schism—see schism; great Scot(t), exclamation of surprise; Great Sea, the Mediterranean; great'-uncle, a grandparent's brother; Great War, term applied esp. to war of 1914-18.— the great unwashed, a contemptuous term for the populace. [O.E. *great*; Du. *groot*, Ger. *gross*.]

greave, *grēv*, (*Spens.*) *n.* a thicket. [O.E. *grǣfa*, *grǣfe*; cf. grove.]

greave. Same as grieve (1) and (2).

greave, *grēv*, *n.* armour for the leg below the knee. [O.Fr. *greve*, shin, greave.]

greaves, *grēvz*, graves, *grāvz*, *n.pl.* dregs of melted tallow. [L.G. *greven*; cf. Ger. *griebe*, greaves; O.E. *grēofa*, pot.]

grebe, *grēb*, *n.* a short-winged almost tailless freshwater diving bird (Podiceps). [Fr. *grèbe*.]

grece. See gree (2).

Grecian, *grēsh'(y)ən*, *adj.* Greek.—*n.* a Greek: one well versed in the Greek language and literature: a hellenising Jew (*B.*): a senior boy of Christ's Hospital: an Irish labourer newly in England (*old slang*).—Grecian bend, a mode of walking with a slight bend forward, at one time affected by a few women who fondly

thought to imitate the pose of a figure such as the Venus of Milo; Grecian nose, a straight nose which forms a continuous line with the forehead. [L. *Graecia*, Greece—Gr. *Graikos*, Greek.]

grecise, -ize, grecism, greco-roman. See graecise, -ize, etc.

grecque, *grek*, *n.* a Greek fret. [Fr. (*fem.*), Greek.]

gree, *grē*, *n.* (*Spens.*) good-will, favour.—*v.i.* (*Shak.*, *Scot.*) to agree. [O.Fr. *gré*—L. *grātus*, pleasing; the vb. may be from O.Fr. *gréer* or aphetic from agree.]

gree, *grē*, *n.* degree, rank (*obs.*): a step (*obs.*): superiority (*dial.*): victory (*dial.*): prize (*dial.*). —*n.* grece (*grēs*, *obs.* or *dial.*; from the Fr. plur.), a flight of steps: a step: a degree—also spelt grees, greese, greece, greese, grice, griece, grise, grize (grees'ing, gress'ing, and even grē'cian, are obs. forms).—*adj.* grieced (*her.*), having steps. [O.Fr. *gré*—L. *gradus*; see grade.]

greedy, *grēd'i*, *adj.* having a voracious appetite: inordinately desirous of increasing one's own share: covetous: eagerly desirous.—*n.* greed, an eager desire or longing: covetousness.—*adv.* greed'ily.—*n.* greed'iness. [O.E. *grǣdig*; Du. *gretig*.]

greegree. See grigri.

Greek, *grēk*, *adj.* of Greece, its people, or its language.—*n.* a native or citizen of Greece, of a Greek state, or of a colony elsewhere of a Greek state: the language of Greece: a member of the Greek Church: a hellenising Jew (*B.*): a cunning rogue, a merry fellow (*arch.*): an Irishman (*old slang*): any language of which one is ignorant, jargon, anything unintelligible.—*n.* Greek'dom, the Greek world: a Greek community.—*adjs.* Greek'ish; Greek'less, without knowledge of Greek.—*n.* Greek'ling, a contemptible Greek.—Greek architecture, that developed in ancient Greece (Corinthian, Doric, Ionic); Greek Church, the church that follows the ancient rite of the East and accepts the first seven councils, rejecting papal supremacy—(*Greek*) *Orthodox* or *Eastern* Church; Greek cross, an upright cross with arms of equal length; Greek fire, a composition that took fire when wetted, used in war, long a secret of the Byzantine Greeks; Greek gift, a treacherous gift (from Virgil's *Aeneid*, ii. 49); Greek nose (see Grecian nose).—the Greek calends, never, the Greeks having no calends. [O.E. *Grēcas*, *Crēcas*, Greeks, or L. *Graecus*—Gr. *Graikos*, Greek.]

green, *grēn*, *adj.* of the colour usual in leaves, between blue and yellow in the spectrum: growing: vigorous: hale: new: young: unripe: fresh: undried: raw: incompletely prepared: immature: unseasoned: inexperienced: jealous: easily imposed on.—*n.* the colour of green things: a grassy plot, esp. that common to a village or town, or for bowling, or bleaching, drying of clothes: a golf-course: the prepared ground (*putting-green*) round a golf-hole: a green pigment: (*pl.*) fresh leaves: (*pl.*) green vegetables for food, esp. of the cabbage kind: (*pl., cap.*) a political party at Constantinople, under Justinian, opposed to the Blues.—*v.t.* and *v.i.* to make or become green.—*ns.* green'ery, green plants or boughs: verdure; green'ing, a becoming or making green: a kind of apple green when ripe.—*adj.* green'ish.—*ns.* green'ishness; green'let, any bird of the American family Vireonidae.—*adv.* green'ly, immaturely, unskilfully.—*ns.* green'ness; greenth, greenness, verdure.—*adj.* green'y.—green algae or seaweeds, the Chlorophyceae; green'back, an American note (often printed in green on the back), first issued in 1862; green'-bag, a lawyer's bag: a lawyer (*old slang*); green belt, a strip of open land surrounding a town; green'-bone, a garfish: a viviparous blenny; green'bottle, a metallic green fly (*Lucilia*); green'cloth, a gaming-table: a department of the royal household chiefly concerned with the commissariat—from the green cloth on the table round which its officials sat; green crop, a crop of green vegetables, as grasses, turnips, etc.; green dragon, a European aroid (Dracunculus): dragon-root (*U.S.*); green'-drake', a mayfly; green earth, any green earthy mineral used as a pigment usu. a silicate of iron.—*adjs.* green'ery-yall'ery, in or favouring greens and yellows, hence decadently aesthetic; green'-eyed, having green eyes: jealous (the green-eyed monster, jealousy).—green'finch, green linnet, a finch of a green colour, with some grey and brown; green fingers (or thumb), a knack of making plants grow well; green flash or ray, a flash of green light sometimes seen at the moment of sunrise or sunset; green'fly, a plant-louse or aphis; green goose, a young goose: a simpleton; green gown (*arch.*), a roll on the grass (sometimes but not always understood to imply loss of virginity); green'grocer, a dealer in fresh vegetables; green'hand, an inferior sailor; green'-heart, bebeeru (*Nectandra rodiei*), a S. American tree of the laurel family with very hard wood; green'horn, a raw, inexperienced youth; green'-house, a glasshouse for plants, esp. one with little or no artificial heating: the cockpit of an aircraft—from the transparent sides (*airman's slang*); Green, or Emerald, Isle, Ireland; green'-keeper, one who has the care of a golf-course or bowling-green; green light, permission to go ahead; green manuring, growing one crop to fertilise its successor; green'room, the retiring-room of actors in a theatre, which originally had the walls coloured green; green'-sand, a sandstone containing much glauconite: (*cap.*) two divisions (Lower and Upper) of the Cretaceous system, separated by the Gault; green'shank, a large sandpiper with long, somewhat greenish legs; green sickness, chlorosis; green snake, a harmless colubrine snake common in southern U.S.; greenstick fracture (see fract); green'stone, nephrite: a vague name for any compost basic or intermediate igneous rock; green'stuff, green vegetables, esp. of the cabbage kind; green'sward, sward or turf green with grass; green tea (see tea); green turtle, a tropical and sub-tropical sea turtle (*Chelonia mydas*) with a greenish shell (see turtle); green vit'riol, ferrous sulphate; green'weed, a name given to certain half-shrubby species of Genista; green'wood, a leafy wood or forest.—Also *adj.*—Green Cross Code, a code of road-safety rules for children issued in 1971; green in my eye, mark of credulity. [O.E. *grēne*; Ger. *grün*, Du. *groen*, green; O.N. *grænn*.]

green, grein, grēn, (*Scot.*) *v.i.* to long, yearn. [Cf. O.N. *girna*.]

greengage, grēn'gāj', *n.* a green and very sweet variety of plum. [Said to be named from Sir W. *Gage* of Hengrave Hall, near Bury, before 1725.]

greenockite, grēn'ək-it, *n.* a rare mineral, cadmium sulphide, discovered by Lord *Greenock* (1783-1859).

Greenwich time, grin'ij, mean solar time for the meridian of *Greenwich*.

grees(e), greesing. See gree (2).

greet, grēt, *v.t.* to accost with salutation or kind wishes: send kind wishes to: congratulate (*obs.*): offer congratulations on (*Spens.*): meet, receive: become evident to.—*v.i.* (*obs.*) to meet and salute:—*pr.p.* greet'ing; *pa.p.* greet'ed.—*n.* greet'ing, expression of kindness or joy: salutation. [O.E. *grētan*, to greet, to meet; Du. *groeten*, Ger. *grüssen*, to salute.]

greet, grēt, (*Scot.*; *Spens.* greete) *v.i.* to weep (*pa.t.*, *Scot.*, grat; *pa.p.*, *Scot.*, grutt'en).—*n.*

weeping: a spell of weeping.—greeting meeting, the last meeting of a town-council before an election. [O.E. (Anglian) grētan; Goth. grētan.]

greffier, gref'yā, *n.* a registrar: a notary. [Fr.]

gregale, grā-gä'lā, *n.* a north-east wind in the Mediterranean. [It.,—L. *graecus*, Greek.]

gregarious, gri-gā'ri-əs, *adj.* associating in flocks and herds: growing together but not matted (*bot.*): fond of the company of others (*fig.*).—*adj.* gregā'rian, of the common rank.—*ns.* gregā'rianism, gregariousness; Gregarina (greg-ə-ri'nä), a genus of Protozoa, typical of the Gregarinida (-rin'), a group of parasites; greg'arine (-rin, -rin), a member of the Gregarinida.—*adv.* gregā'riously.—*n.* gregā'riousness. [L. *gregārius*—*grex*, *gregis*, a flock.]

gregatim, gri-gā'tim, gre-gä'tim, (L.) in flocks.

grego, grā'gō, grē'gō, *n.* a Levantine hooded jacket or cloak: an overcoat. [Port. *grego* or other deriv. of L. *graecus*, Greek.]

Gregorian, gri-gō'ri-ən, -gö', *adj.* belonging to or established by *Gregory*—as the Gregorian chant or tones, introduced by Pope Gregory I (6th cent.), the calendar, reformed by Gregory XIII (1582), the reflecting telescope of James Gregory (1638-75), a wig attributed to a barber Gregory.—*n.* follower of any Gregory: member of an 18th-century English brotherhood.—*n.* gregory (greg'ər-i; *coll.*), Gregory's mixture or powder, a laxative powder of rhubarb, magnesia and ginger, compounded by Dr James *Gregory* (1753-1821), great-grandson of aforementioned James.

greisen, gri'zən, *n.* a rock composed of quartz and mica, often with topaz, formed from granite by fluorine exhalations.—*n.* greisenisā'tion, -z-.—*v.t.* greis'enise, -ize. [Ger.]

greisly (*Spens.*, *Milt.*). Same as grisly.

gremial, grē'mi-əl, *adj.* pertaining to the lap or bosom: intimate: resident: in full membership.—*n.* a full or resident member: a cloth laid on a bishop's knees to keep his vestments clean from oil at ordinations. [L. *gremium*, the lap.]

gremlin, grem'lin, *n.* orig. a goblin accused of vexing airmen, causing mechanical trouble to aircraft: an imaginary mischievous agency.

gren, gren, (*Spens.*) *v.i.* Same as grin.

grenade, gri-nād', *n.* a small bomb thrown by the hand or shot from a rifle: a glass projectile containing chemicals for putting out fires, testing drains, dispensing poison-gas or tear-gas, etc.—*ns.* grenadier (gren-ə-dēr'), orig. a soldier who threw grenades: then, a member of the first company of every battalion of foot: now used as the title (Grenadier Guards) of part of the Guards Division of infantry; grenadine (-dēn'), a pomegranate (or other) syrup: slices of veal or poultry fillets. [Fr.,—Sp. *granada*, pomegranate—L. *grānātus*, full of seeds (*grāna*).]

grenadilla, gren-ə-dil'ə. Same as granadilla.

grenadine. See under grenade.

grenadine, gren'ə-dēn, *n.* a thin silk or mixed fabric. [Fr., perh. *Granada*.]

grenzgänger, grents'gengər, (Ger.) one who crosses a national or political border, esp. from the communist countries to the West:—*pl.* grenz-gänger.

grese. See gree (2).

Gresham's law. See law (1).

gressorial, gres-ō', ö'ri-əl, (*zool.*) *adj.* adapted for walking. [L. *gressus*, pa.p. of *gradi*, to walk.]

greve, a variant of greave.

grew, grōō, pa.t. of grow; variant of grue, see gruesome.

grew, grōō, grewhound, grōō'hownd, (*dial.*) *ns.* a greyhound. [By confusion with obs. *Grew*, Greek.]

grex venalium, greks ven-āl'iəm, wen-āl'i-ōōm, (L.) the herd of hirelings.

**grey, gray,** *grā, adj.* of a mixture of black and white with little or no hue: dull: dismal: grey-haired, old, mature.—*n.* a grey colour: a grey or greyish animal, esp. a horse: a badger (*obs.*): a middle-aged or old person (*slang*).—*v.t.* to make grey or dull.—*v.i.* to become grey or dull.—*adj.* **grey′ish,** somewhat grey.—*adv.* **grey′ly.**—*n.* **grey′ness.**—**grey′beard,** one whose beard is grey: an old man: a stoneware jar for liquor, a bellarmine; **grey′-coat,** one who wears a grey coat, esp. a pupil in certain schools: a Confederate soldier.—Also *adj.* **grey′-coat′ed.**— **grey eminence** (see eminence grise).—*adj.* **grey′-eyed.**—**grey-fish,** a dogfish: a young coalfish; **Grey Friar** (also without *caps.*), a Franciscan; **grey′-goose, grey′lag,** the common wild goose (perh. from its lateness in migrating).—*adjs.* **grey′-haired, grey′-headed.**—**grey′hen,** the female of the blackcock; **grey mare** (see mare); **grey matter,** the ashen grey active part of the brain and spinal cord; **grey owl,** the tawny owl; **grey parrot,** a red-tailed grey African parrot; **grey squirrel,** a N. American squirrel naturalised in Britain; **grey-weth′er,** a block of sandstone or quartzite, a relic of denudation, looking at a distance like a grazing sheep; **grey wolf,** the N. American timber wolf.—**grey-goose quill, shaft, wing,** an arrow; **the Greys, the Scots Greys** (see Scots). [O.E. *græg*; cf. Ger. *grau*.]

**greyhound,** *grā′hownd, n.* a tall and slender dog with great speed and keen sight. [O.E. *grighund* (cf. O.N. *greyhundr*—grey, bitch), *hund,* dog.]

**greywacke,** *grā-wak′i, n.* an indurated sedimentary rock composed of grains (round or angular) and splinters of quartz, feldspar, slate, etc., in a hard matrix.—**greywack′e-slate′,** a fine-grained fissile greywacke. [Ger. *grauwacke,* partly translated, partly adopted.]

**gribble,** *grib′l, n.* a small marine isopod (genus *Limnoria*) that bores into timber under water. [Perh.—*grub.*]

**grice,** *grīs,* (*dial.*) *n.* a little pig:—*pl.* **grices, grice.** [O.N. *griss.*]

**grice.** See gree (2).

**grid.** See gridiron.

**griddle,** *grid′l, n.* a flat iron plate for baking cakes. —Also (*Scot.*) **gird′le.**—**griddle car,** a coach on a train where simple cooked meals can be obtained. [Anglo-Fr. *gridil,* from a dim. of L. *crātis,* a hurdle.]

**gride,** *grid, v.t.* and *v.i.* to pierce: to cut, esp. with a grating sound: to graze: to grate.—*n.* a harsh grating sound. [gird.]

**gridelin,** *grid′ə-lin, n.* and *adj.* violet-grey. [Fr. *gris de lin,* grey of flax.]

**gridiron,** *grid′i-ərn, n.* a frame of iron bars for broiling over a fire: a frame to support a ship during repairs: a network: a football field (*U.S.*).—*v.t.* to cover with parallel bars or lines. —*n.* **grid** (back formation), a grating: a gridiron: a framework: a network: a network of power transmission lines: a perforated screen or spiral of wire between the filament and the plate of a thermionic valve: a grated luggage-carrier on a motor-car: a network of lines for finding places on a map, or for other purpose: framework above a theatre stage from which scenery and lights may be suspended. [M.E. *gredire,* a *griddle*; from the same source as **griddle,** but the term. *-ire* became confused with M.E. *ire,* iron.]

**griece.** See gree (2).

**grief,** *grēf, n.* sorrow: distress: great mourning: affliction: bodily pain (*Shak.*): cause of sorrow. —*adjs.* **grief′ful,** full of grief; **grief′less; grief′-shot,** pierced with grief (*Shak.*); **grief′-stricken,** crushed with sorrow.—**come to grief,** meet with reverse, disaster, mishap. [O.Fr.,—L. *gravis, heavy.*]

**griesie, griesy, griesly,** Spenserian forms of grisy (see under gris, grise), grisly.

**grieve,** *grēv, v.t.* to cause grief or pain of mind to: to make sorrowful: to vex: to inflict bodily pain on or do bodily harm to (*obs.*): to show grief for (*poet.*).—*v.i.* to feel grief: to mourn.—*ns.* **griev′ance,** cause or source of grief: ground of complaint: condition felt to be oppressive or wrongful: distress: burden: hardship: injury (*obs.*): grief; **griev′er.**—*adv.* **griev′ingly.**—*adj.* **griev′ous,** causing grief: burdensome: painful: severe: hurtful.—*adv.* **griev′ously.**—*n.* **griev′ousness.** [O.Fr. *grever*—L. *gravāre—gravis,* heavy.]

**grieve,** *grēv, n.* a farm overseer (*Scot.*): a governor or sheriff (*hist.*). [O.Northumbrian *græfa* (W.S. *gerēfa*); cf. reeve.]

**griff, griffe,** *grif, n.* a claw: a clawlike architectural ornament: a mulatto, or person of mixed Negro and mulatto or Negro and American Indian blood: a steep narrow valley (*dial.*). [Fr. *griffe.*]

**griffin, griffon, gryphon,** *grif′in, -ən, n.* an imaginary animal with lion's body and eagle's beak and wings: a newcomer in the East, a novice: a pony never before entered for a race: a watchful guardian, esp. over a young woman, a duenna (*obs.*): a tip, a signal or warning.—*adj.* **griff′inish.** —*n.* **griff′inism.**—**griffon vulture,** a European vulture, *Gyps fulvus.* [Fr. *griffon*—L. *grȳphus*— Gr. *gryps,* a bird, probably the *lämmergeier,* a griffin—*grȳpos,* hook-nosed.]

**griffon,** *grif′ən, n.* a dog like a coarse-haired terrier.—**Brussels griffon,** a toy dog with a rather snub nose. [Prob. from griffin.]

**grig,** *grig, n.* a cricket: a grasshopper: a small lively eel, the sand-eel: a small, lively person.— *v.t.* to tease, irritate.—*v.i.* to fish for grigs (eels). —**merry as a grig,** very merry and lively. [Origin obscure.]

**gri(-)gri.** See gris(-)gris.

**grike, grik,** *n.* a fissure in limestone rock formed or widened by the dissolvent effect of rain: a deep valley, ravine.—Also **gryke.** [O.N. *kriki,* a crack.]

**grill,** *gril, v.t.* to broil on a gridiron or scallop-shell: to torment: to cross-examine harassingly. —*v.i.* to undergo grilling.—*n.* a grating: a gridiron: a grill-room: a grilled dish: an act of grilling.—*ns.* **grillade′,** anything grilled; **grill′-age,** a foundation of crossbeams on marshy grounds.—*adj.* **grilled,** embossed with small rectangular indentations as those on certain late 19th-century postage stamps of the United States and Peru.—*n.* **grill′ing.**—**grill′-room,** part of a restaurant where beefsteaks, etc., are served grilled to order. [Fr. *griller*—*gril,* a gridiron, from a dim. of L. *crātis,* a grate.]

**grille,** *gril, n.* a lattice, or grating, or screen, or openwork of metal, generally used to enclose or protect a window, shrine, etc.: a grating in a convent or jail door, etc. [Fr.; see grill.]

**grilse,** *grils, n.* a young salmon on its first return from salt water. [Origin unknown.]

**grim,** *grim, adj.* forbidding: ferocious: ghastly: sullen: repellent: stern: unyielding: unpleasant.—*adv.* **grim′ly.**—*n.* **grim′ness.**—*adj.* **grim′looked** (*Shak.*), having a grim or dismal aspect. [O.E. *grim(m)*; Ger. *grimmig*—*grimm,* fury, Du. *grimmig,* O.N. *grimmr.*]

**grimace,** *gri-mās′, n.* a distortion of the face, in jest, etc.: a smirk.—*v.i.* to make grimaces. [Fr.]

**grimalkin,** *gri-mal′kin, -möl′kin, n.* an old cat: a cat generally. [grey and **Malkin,** a dim. of *Maud.*]

**grime,** *grim, n.* sooty or coaly dirt: ingrained dirt. —*v.t.* to soil deeply.—*adv.* **grim′ily.**—*n.* **grim′iness.**—*adj.* **grim′y.** [Cf. Flem. *grijm.*]

**Grimm's law.** See law.

**grimoire,** *grē-mwär′, n.* a magician's book for calling up spirits. [Fr.; cf. **gramary.**]

**grin,** *grin, v.i.* to set the teeth together and withdraw the lips in pain, derision, etc: to give a

broad smile.—*v.t.* to set (the teeth) in a grin (*obs.*): to express by grinning:—*pr.p.* **grin'ing**; *pa.t.* and *pa.p.* **grinned.**—*n.* an act of grinning. [O.E. *grennian*; O.N. *grenja*, Ger. *greinen*, Du. *grijnen*, to grumble, Scot. **girn**; allied to **groan.**]
**grin,** *grin*, (*dial.*) *n.* a snare or trap.—Also *v.t.* [O.E. *grin*.]
**grind,** *grind* (*Spens.*). Same as **grinned.**
**grind,** *grind*, *v.t.* to reduce to powder by friction or crushing: to wear down, sharpen, smooth or roughen by friction: to rub together: to force (in, into; *lit.* and *fig.*): to produce by great effort, or by working a crank (with *out*): to oppress or harass: to work by a crank.—*v.i.* to be moved or rubbed together: to jar or grate: to drudge at any tedious task: to read hard:—*pr.p.* **grind'ing;** *pa.t.* and *pa.p.* **ground, grownd.**—*n.* the act, sound, or jar of grinding: drudgery: laborious study for a special examination, etc.: a student who gives all his time to study.—*ns.* **grind'er,** one who, or that which, grinds: a tooth that grinds food: a coach or crammer of students for examination: a hard-working student; **grind'ery,** a place where knives, etc., are ground: shoemakers' materials; **grind'ing,** act or process of the verb to grind: reducing to powder.—*adj.* for grinding: wearing down: very severe: extortionate: (of sound) harsh: giving a harsh sound.—*adj.* (*arch.*) **ground'en,** sharpened. —**grind'stone,** a circular revolving stone for grinding or sharpening tools; **ground glass,** glass obscured by grinding, sandblast, or etching.— **grind the face(s) of,** to oppress as by taxation; **keep one's nose to the grindstone,** to subject one to severe continuous toil or punishment; **take a grinder** (*Dickens*), to put the left thumb to the nose and to work a visionary coffee-mill round it with the right hand—a gesture of derision. [O.E. *grindan*.]
**gringo,** *gring'gō*, *n.* in Spanish-speaking America, one whose language is not Spanish. [Sp., gibberish, prob.—*Griego*, Greek.]
**grip,** *grip*, *n.* a small ditch, gutter, or trench, a drain.—*v.t.* to trench.—Also **gripe** (*grip*). [O.E. *grype*, cf. L.G. *gruppe*, *grüppe*.]
**grip,** *grip*, *n.* a grasp or firm hold, esp. with the hand or mind: strength of grasp: the handle or part by which anything is grasped: a mode of grasping: a particular mode of grasping hands for mutual recognition: a gripsack, travelling bag (orig. *U.S.*): holding or clutching device: power: pinch of distress: mastery: power of holding the mind or commanding the emotions: **gripe:** grippe.—*v.t.* to take or maintain fast hold of: to hold fast the attention or interest of: to command the emotions of.—Also *v.i.*:—*pr.p.* **gripp'ing;** *pa.t.* and *pa.p.* **gripped** (*gript*).—*n.* **gripp'er,** one who, that which, grips: a clutch: a claw.—*adj.* **gripp'le** (*Spens.* **grip'le**), griping, grasping: greedy.—*n.* a grip.—*adj.* **gripp'y,** (*Scot.*) inclining to avarice: having grip.— **grip'sack** (*U.S.*), a bag for travel.—**come to grips (with),** to tackle at close quarters, or (*fig.*) seriously and energetically. [O.E. *gripe*, grasp, *gripa*, handful.]
**gripe,** *grip*, *v.t.* to grasp: to seize and hold fast: to squeeze: to afflict: to oppress: to give pain to the bowels of.—*v.i.* to clutch: to keep on complaining (*coll.*).—*n.* fast hold: grasp: forcible retention: a usurer (*slang*): a grumble (*coll.*): lashing for a boat on deck: pain: (esp. in *pl.*) severe spasmodic pain in the intestines.—*n.* **grip'er.**—*adj.* **grip'ing,** avaricious: of a pain, seizing acutely.—*adv.* **grip'ingly.** [O.E. *gripan* (*grāp, gripen*); O.N. *grīpa,* Ger. *greifen,* Du. *grijpen.*]
**gripe,** *gripe*, *n.* a griffin: vulture.—**gripe's egg,** a cup like a large egg. [Gr. *gryps*.]
**gripe,** *grip.* Same as **grip** (1).
**grippe,** *grēp, n.* influenza. [Fr.,—*gripper*, to seize.]

**Griqua,** *grēk'wä*, *n.* one of a people of Griqualand, South Africa: one of a mixed Hottentot and European race (Hottentot prevailing).
**gris, grise,** *gris, adj.* (*obs.*) grey.—*n.* (*arch.*) a grey fur.—*adjs.* **griseous** (*griz', gris'i-əs*), grey: blue-grey or pearl-grey; **grisy** (*Spens.* **griesie, gryesy;** all *gri'zi*), grey (*obs.*). [Fr.]
**gris.** See **gree** (2).
**grisaille,** *grē-zāl', -zä'ē, n.* a style of painting on walls or ceilings, in greyish tints in imitation of bas-reliefs: a similar style of painting on pottery, enamel, glass: a work in this style.—Also *adj.* [Fr.,—*gris,* grey.]
**gris-amber,** *griz'-am'bər,* (*obs.*) *n.* ambergris.—*adj.* **gris-amb'er-steam'd'** (*Milt.*), flavoured by steam from melted ambergris.
**grise,** *griz,* (*obs.*) *v.i.* to shudder at: to affright.— *v.i.* to shudder.—*adj.* **gri'sy** (*Spens.* **griesy, grysie**), grim: horrible: grisly. [From the verb of which O.E. *āgrīsan* is a compound; cf. **agrise.**]
**grise.** See **gree** (2).
**Griselda,** *griz-el'də, n.* a woman of excessive meekness and patience, from the heroine of an old tale retold by Boccaccio, Petrarch, and Chaucer.
**griseofulvin,** *griz-i-o-fōōl'vin,* (*med.*) *n.* oral antibiotic used as treatment for fungus infections.
**grisette,** *griz-zet', n.* a gay young working-class Frenchwoman. [Fr. *grisette,* a grey gown, which used to be worn by that class—*gris,* grey.]
**grisgris, grigri, greegree** (also **gris-gris,** etc.), **grēgrē,** *n.* African charm, amulet, or spell. [Fr.; prob. of African origin.]
**griskin,** *gris'kin,* (*dial.*) *n.* lean from a loin of pork. [grice.]
**grisled,** *griz'ld.* Same as **grizzled.**
**grisly,** *griz'li, adj.* frightful, ghastly (*Spens., Milt.* **greisly;** *Spens.* **griesly, grisely, gryesly**). —Also *adv.* (*rare*).—*n.* **gris'liness.** [O.E. *grislic*; cf. **grise.**]
**grison,** *griz'ən, griz'ən, -on, n.* a large grey S. American weasel: a grey S. American monkey. [Fr.,—*gris,* grey.]
**grist,** *grist, n.* corn for grinding, or ground: corn for grinding, or ground, at one time: malt for one brewing: supply, portion, quantity (*U.S.*): a measure of the thickness of rope or yarn: profit (*fig.*).—**grist'-mill,** a mill for grinding grain.—**bring grist to the mill,** to be a source of profit. [O.E. *grist*; cf. **grind.**]
**gristle,** *gris'l, n.* cartilage.—*n.* **grist'liness.**—*adj.* **grist'ly.** [O.E. *gristle.*]
**grisy.** See **grise.**
**grit,** *grit, n.* gravel (*obs.*): small hard particles of sand, stone, etc.: small woody bodies in a pear: a coarse sandstone, often with angular grains: texture of stone: firmness of character, spirit.— *n.* **gritt'iness.**—*adj.* **gritt'y,** having or containing hard particles: of the nature of grit: grating: determined, plucky.—*v.t.* and *v.i.* to grind: to grate: to spread with grit.—**grit blasting,** a process used in preparation for metal spraying which cleans the surface and gives it the roughness required to retain the sprayed metal particles; **grit'stone.** [O.E. *grēot;* Ger. *griess,* gravel.]
**grit,** *grit,* a Scottish form of **great.**
**grith,** *grith, n.* sanctuary, asylum; **grith'-stool,** a seat in which a fugitive was in sanctuary. [O.E. *grith.*]
**grits,** *grits, n.pl.* coarsely ground grain, esp. oats. [O.E. *grytta;* cf. **groats.**]
**grivet,** *griv'it, n.* a north-east African guenon monkey. [Fr.; origin unknown.]
**grize.** See **gree** (2).
**grizzle,** *griz'l, n.* a grey colour.—*adjs.* **grizz'led,** grey, or mixed with grey; **grizz'ly,** of a grey colour.—*n.* the grizzly bear (*Ursus horribilis*) of the Rocky Mountains. [M.E. *grisel*—Fr. *gris,* grey.]
**grizzle,** *griz'l, v.i.* to grumble: to whimper: to

fret.—*n.* a bout of grizzling.—*n.* grizz′ler. [Origin unknown.]

groan, *grōn*, *v.i.* to utter a deep rumbling or voiced sound as in distress or disapprobation: to be afflicted (*fig.*).—*n.* a deep moan: a grinding rumble.—*adj.* groan′ful (*arch.*; *Spens.* grone′full).—*n.* and *adj.* groan′ing.—groaning board, a table weighed down with very generous supplies of food. [O.E. *grānian.*]

groat, *grōt* (formerly *grōt*), *n.* an English silver coin, worth fourpence—after 1662 coined only as Maundy money—the silver fourpenny-piece, coined 1836–56, was not officially called a groat: a very small sum, proverbially.—*n.* groats′worth. [O.L.G. *grote*, or Du. *groot*, lit, great, i.e. thick.]

groats, *grōts*, *n.pl.* the grain of oats deprived of the husks. [O.E. *grotan* (pl.).]

Grobian, *grō′bi-ən*, *n.* a boorish rude sloven.—*n.* Gro′bianism. [Ger. *Grobianus*, a character in German satire of the 15th and 16th centuries—*grob*, coarse.]

grocer, *grōs′ər*, *n.* a dealer in staple foods, general household supplies.—*ns.* groc′ery, the trade or business of a grocer: articles sold by grocers (generally used in *pl.*): a grocer's shop or liquor shop (*U.S.*); grocetē′ria, a self-service grocery store. [Earlier *grosser*, a wholesale dealer; O.Fr. *grossier*—L.L. *grossārius*—*grossus*; cf. gross.]

grog, *grog*, *n.* a mixture of spirits and water: bricks or waste from a clayworks broken down and added to clay to be used for brick manufacture.—*v.i.* to drink grog.—*v.t.* to extract the spirit from the wood of empty spirit-casks by soaking with hot water.—*ns.* grogg′ery (*U.S.*), a low public-house; grogg′iness, state of being groggy.—*adj.* grogg′y, affected by grog, partially intoxicated (*arch.*): dazed, unsteady from illness or exhaustion: weak and staggering from blows (*boxing*): applied to a horse that bears wholly on his heels in trotting.—grog′-blossom, a redness of the nose due to drinking; grog′-shop, a dram-shop. [From Old *Grog*, the nickname (apparently from his *grogram* cloak) of Admiral Vernon, who in 1740 ordered that rum (until 1970 officially issued to sailors) should be mixed with water.]

grogram, *grog′rəm*, *n.* a kind of coarse cloth of silk and mohair. [O.Fr. *gros grain*, coarse grain.]

groin, *groin*, *n.* the fold between the belly and the thigh: the line of intersection of two vaults, also a rib along the intersection (*archit.*).—*v.t.* to form into groins, to build in groins.—*adj.* groined.—*n.* groin′ing.—groin′-cen′tring, the centring of timber during construction. [Early forms *grind*, *grine*, perh.—O.E. *grynde*, abyss.]

groin. Spelling of groyne (*q.v.*) usu. in U.S.A.

groin, *groin*, (*obs.*) *v.i.* to grunt, to growl: to grumble. [O.Fr. *grogner*—L. *grunnire*, to grunt.]

Grolier, *grō′lyā*, *n.* a book or a binding from the library of the French bibliophile Jean *Grolier* (1479–1565).—*adj.* Grolieresque (*grō-lyər-esk′*), after the style of Grolier's bindings, with geometrical or arabesque figures and leaf-sprays in gold lines.

groma, *grōm′ə*, *n.* surveying instrument used by the Romans, in which plumblines suspended from the arms of a horizontal cruciform frame were used to construct right angles. [L. *grōma*, a surveyor's pole, measuring rod.]

gromet, grommet. Same as grummet (1).

gromwell, *grom′wəl*, *n.* any plant of the genus Lithospermum: the oyster-plant (*Mertensia*)—both of the borage family. [O.Fr. *gromil.*]

grone, obs. form of groan.

groof. See under grovelling.

grooly, *grōōl′i*, (*slang*) *adj.* gruesome. [*gruesome* and *grisly.*]

groom, *grōōm*, *grōōm*, *n.* a boy, young man, esp. a servant (*obs.*): one who has the charge of horses: a title of several household officers (groom of the stole, grooms-in-waiting): a bridegroom.—*v.t.* to tend, esp. a horse: to smarten: to prepare for political office, stardom, or success in any sphere.—grooms′man, the attendant on a bridegroom. [Origin obscure; cf. Du. *grom*, fry, offspring, O.Fr. *gromet*, boy (see gourmet, grummet (2)); encroaching on O.E. *guma* (as in bridegroom), a man.]

groove, *grōōv*, *n.* a furrow, or long hollow, such as is cut with a tool: the track cut into the surface of a gramophone record along which the needle of the gramophone moves: a set routine: an exalted mood, one's highest form (*jazz slang*).—*adj.* groov′y (also in the groove; *jazz slang*), in top form, oi in perfect condition: up to date in style: a general term of approval: following a set routine.—*v.t.* to grave or cut a groove or furrow in. [Prob. Du. *groef*, *groeve*, a furrow; cog. with Ger. *grube*, a pit, O.N. *grōf*, Eng. grave.]

grope, *grōp*, *v.i.* to search, feel about, as if blind or in the dark.—*v.t.* to search by feeling (one's way).—*adv.* grop′ingly. [O.E. *grāpian*; allied to grab, gripe.]

groper. Same as grouper.

grosbeak, *grōs′bēk*, *n.* the hawfinch, or other finch of the same subfamily, with thick, heavy, seed-crushing bill: extended to various more or less related birds, as the cardinal and the rose-breasted grosbeak. [Fr. *grosbec*—*gros*, thick, *bec*, beak.]

groschen, *grō′shən*, *n.* an Austrian coin, a 100th part of a schilling: a small silver coin current in the north of Germany from the 13th to the late 19th century, varying in value between 1/24 and 1/36 of a thaler: a ten-pfennig piece. [Ger.]

groser, *grō′zər*, grosert, grossart, *-zərt*, groset, *-zit*, (*Scot.*) *n.* a gooseberry. [Fr. *groseille.*]

grosgrain, *grō′grān*, *n.* a heavy corded silk used especially for ribbons and hat bands. [Fr.]

gros point, *grō point*, *n.* a large cross-stitch: embroidery composed of this stitch. [Fr.]

gross, *grōs*, *adj.* coarse: rough: dense: palpable: flagrant, glaring: extreme: shameful: whole: coarse in mind: stupid: sensual: obscene: total, including everything: of a horse, naturally large-girthed, as opposed to overweight (*racing*).—*n.* the main bulk: the whole taken together: twelve dozen:—*pl.* gross.—*v.t.* to make a total profit.—*adv.* gross′ly.—*n.* gross′ness.—great gross, a dozen gross; in gross, in bulk, wholesale. [Fr. *gros*—L. *grossus*, thick.]

grossièreté, gros-yer-tā, (Fr.) grossness, rudeness, coarseness.

grossular, *grōs′ū-lər*, grossularite, *-it*, *ns.* gooseberry-stone, a lime alumina garnet, often green. [Fr. *groseille*, gooseberry, Latinised as *grossulāria.*]

grot, grot, (*poet.*) *n.* a grotto.

grotesque, *grō-tesk′*, *adj.* extravagantly formed: fantastic.—*n.* extravagant ornament, containing animals, plants, etc., in fantastic or incongruous forms (*art*): a bizarre figure or object.—*adv.* grotesque′ly.—*ns.* grotesque′ness; grotesqu′ery. [Fr. *grotesque*—It. *grottesca*—*grotta*, a grotto.]

Grotian, *grō′shi-ən*, *adj.* of or pertaining to Hugo Grotius, or Huig van Groot (1583–1645), founder of the science of international law.—Grotian theory, the theory that man is essentially a social being, and that the principles of justice are of perpetual obligation and in harmony with his nature.—Grotian, or governmental, (theory of the) Atonement, the theory that Christ paid the penalty of human sin in order that God might for His sake forgive sinners while preserving the law that punishment should follow sin.

grotto, *grot′ō*, *n.* a cave: an imitation cave, usu.

fantastic:—*pl.* grott'oes, grott'os.—grott'o-work.
[It. *grotta* (Fr. *grotte*)—L. *crypta*—Gr. *kryptē*, a
crypt, vault.]
**grotty,** *grot'i, (slang) adj.* ugly, in bad condition,
or useless. [grotesque.]
**grouch,** *growch, v.i.* to grumble.—*n.* a grumbling:
sulks: a grumbler.—*adv.* grouch'ily.—*n.* grouch'-
iness.—*adj.* grouch'y. [See grutch, grudge.]
**grouf.** See under grovelling.
**ground, grounden.** See grind.
**ground,** *grownd, n.* bottom, esp. sea-bottom
(*arch.*): the solid land underlying an area of
water (*naut.*): the solid surface of the earth: a
portion of the earth's surface: land: soil: the
floor, etc.: earth (*elect.*): position: field or
place of action: that on which something is
raised (*lit.* or *fig.*): foundation: sufficient reason:
the surface on which the work is represented
(*art*): a first coat of paint: surrounding rock
(*mining*): the space behind the popping-crease
with which the batsman must be in touch by bat
or person if he is not to be stumped or run out
(*cricket*): (*pl.*) an area of land attached to or
surrounding a building: (*pl.*) dregs or sediment:
(*pl.*) basis of justification.—*v.t.* to fix on a
foundation or principle: to put or rest on the
ground: to cause to run aground: to instruct
in first principles: to cover with a layer of
plaster, etc., as a basis for painting: to coat with
a composition, as a surface to be etched: to put
to earth (*elect.*): to keep on the ground, prevent from flying: to attach to the ground-staff
(*aero.*).—*v.i.* to come to the ground: to strike
the bottom and remain fixed.—*n.* ground'age, a
charge on a ship in port.—*adj.* ground'ed.—*adv.*
ground'edly, on good grounds.—*ns.* ground'er, a
ball that keeps low; ground'ing, foundation:
sound general knowledge of a subject: the
background of embroidery, etc.: act or process
of preparing or laying a ground: act of laying
or of running aground.—*adj.* ground'less, without ground, foundation, or reason.—*adv.*
ground'lessly.—*ns.* ground'lessness; ground'ling,
a fish that keeps near the bottom of the water,
esp. the spinous loach: formerly a spectator in
the pit of a theatre—hence one of the common
herd.—*adj.* (*Lamb*) base.—ground'-ang'ling, fishing without a float, with a weight placed a few
inches from the hook—bottom-fishing; ground
annual, (*Scots law*) an annual payment forming a
burden on land; ground'-ash, a sapling of ash:
a stick made of an ash sapling; ground'bait,
bait dropped to the bottom to bring fish to the
neighbourhood; ground'-bass, a bass part
constantly repeated with varying melody and
harmony (*mus.*); ground'-beetle, any beetle of
the Carabidae, a family akin to the tiger-beetles;
ground'-cherry, any of the European dwarf
cherries: any of several plants of the genus
Physalis, also called husk-tomato, Cape gooseberry, etc.: the fruit of these plants; ground'-
control, control, by information radioed from a
ground installation, of aircraft observed by
radar; ground cover, low plants and shrubs
growing among the trees in a forest: various
low herbaceous plants used to cover an area
instead of grass; ground crew (see ground staff);
ground'-cuckoo, a name for several ground-
running birds akin to the cuckoo, as the chaparral
cock, the coucal; ground'-dove, -pigeon, various
small American pigeons of terrestrial habits;
ground'-feed'er, a fish that feeds at the bottom;
ground floor, storey, the floor on or near a level
with the ground; ground game, hares, rabbits,
etc., as distinguished from winged game;
ground'-hog, the woodchuck: the aardvark;
ground'-hold (*Spens.* and *naut.*), ground-tackle;
ground ice, the ice formed at the bottom;
ground'-ivy, a British labiate creeping-plant
(Nepeta) whose leaves when the edges curl

become ivy-like; gr(o)und mail (*Scot.*), payment
for right of burial; ground'mass, the fine-
grained part of an igneous rock, glassy or
minutely crystalline, in which the larger crystals
are embedded; ground moraine, a mass of
mud, sand, and stones dragged along under
a glacier or ice-sheet; ground'-nut, the peanut
or monkey-nut (Arachis): the earth-nut;
ground'-oak, a sapling of oak: various species
of *Teucrium*; ground'-off'icer, one who has
charge of the grounds of an estate; ground'-
plan, plan of the horizontal section of the lowest
or ground storey of a building: first plan, general
outline; ground'plot, the plot of ground on
which a building stands: method of calculating
the position of an aircraft by relating the ground
speed and time on course to the starting position;
ground'-rent, rent paid to a landlord for the use
of the ground for a specified term, usually in
England ninety-nine years; ground'-robin, the
chewink, or towhee; ground'sel, ground'sell,
ground'sill, the lowest timber of a structure;
ground'sheet, a waterproof sheet spread on the
ground by campers, etc.; ground'-sloth, a heavy
extinct ground-going sloth; grounds'man,
ground'man, a man charged with the care of a
cricket-ground or a sports-field: an aerodrome
mechanic; ground'speed, (*aero.*) speed of an
aircraft relative to the ground; ground'-squirr'el,
the chipmunk or hackee; ground staff, ground
crew, aircraft mechanics, etc., whose work is on
the ground: paid staff of players (*cricket*);
ground'-state, state of nuclear system, atoms,
etc., when at their lowest (or normal) energy;
ground swell, a broad, deep undulation of the
ocean caused by a distant gale or earthquake:
a movement, as of public, or political opinion
or feeling, which is evident although the cause,
or leader is not known; ground tackle, tackle
for securing a vessel at anchor; ground'-water,
water naturally in the subsoil; ground'work,
that which forms the ground or foundation of
anything: the basis: the essential part: the
first principle; ground'-ze'ro, the point on the
ground directly under the explosion of a nuclear
weapon in the air.—break ground, to take the
first step in any project; down to the ground (see
down); fall to the ground, to come to nothing;
gain ground, to advance: to become more
widely influential: to spread; give ground, to
fall back, retreat (*lit.* and *fig.*); hold, or stand,
one's ground, to stand firm; let in on the ground
floor, admit on the same terms as the original
promoters; lose ground, to fall back: to decline
in influence, etc.; off the ground, started, under
way; on one's own ground, in circumstances
with which one is familiar; run to ground, hunt
out, track down; shift one's ground, change one's
standpoint in a situation or argument; to
ground, into hiding. [O.E. *grund*; cog. with
Ger. *grund*, O.N. *grunnr.*]
**groundsel,** *grown(d)'sl, n.* a very common yellow-
flowered composite weed of waste ground
(*Senecio vulgaris*). [O.E. *gundeswilge*, appar.—
*gund*, pus, *swelgan*, to swallow, from its use in
poultices, influenced by *grund*, ground.]
**group,** *grōōp, n.* a number of persons or things
together: a number of individual things related
in some definite way differentiating them from
others: a clique, school, section of a party: a
scientific classification: a combination of figures
forming a harmonious whole (*art*): a system of elements having a binary operation
that is associative, an identity element for the
operation, and an inverse for every element
(*math.*): a division in the Scout organisation.
—*v.t.* to form into a group or groups.—*v.i.*
to fall into harmonious combination.—*ns.*
group'er, a member of the Oxford group;
group'ing, the act of disposing and arranging

figures in a group (*art*); group'ist, an adherent of a group.—Also *adj.*—group'-captain, an air-force officer answering to a colonel or naval captain; group dynamics, the interaction of human behaviour within a small social group; group insurance, insurance issued on a number of people under a single policy; group marriage, a hypothetical primitive relation by which every man of a group is husband to every woman of a group; group therapy, therapy in which a small group of people with the same psychological or physical problems discuss their difficulties under the chairmanship of, e.g., a doctor.—pop group (see pop). [Fr. *groupe*—It. *groppo*, a bunch, knot—Gmc.; cf. Ger. *kropf*, protuberance.]

grouper, *groōp'ər*, (*Amer.*), groper, *grōp'ər* (*Austr.*), *ns.* names given to many fishes, esp. various kinds resembling bass. [Port. *garoupa*.]

grouse, *grows*, *n.* the heathcock or moorfowl (*Lagopus scoticus*; the red grouse), a plump bird with a short curved bill, short legs, and feathered feet, found on Scottish moors and hills and in certain other parts of Britain: extended to other birds of the family Tetraonidae, incl. the black grouse or blackcock, the willow-grouse and various birds of North America:—*pl.* grouse.—grouse'-disease', a nematode infection of grouse. [Origin unknown.]

grouse, *grows*, *v.i.* to grumble.—*n.* a grumble.—*n.* grous'er. [Cf. grutch.]

grout, *growt*, *n.* coarse meal: the sediment of liquor: lees: a thin coarse mortar: a fine plaster for finishing ceilings.—*v.t.* to fill and finish with grout.—*n.* grout'ing, filling up or finishing with grout: the material so used.—*adj.* grout'y, thick, muddy: sulky. [O.E. *grūt*, coarse meal: or perh. in part Fr. *grouter*, to grout.]

grout, *growt*, *v.i.* to root or grub with the snout. [Perh. conn. with O.E. *grēot*, grit.]

grove, *grōv*, *n.* a wood of small size, generally of a pleasant or ornamental character: an avenue of trees: often used (quite fancifully) in street-names: an erroneous translation of *Asherah*, the wooden image of the goddess Ashtoreth, also of Heb. *eshel*, tamarisk, in Gen. xxi. 33 (*B.*): a lodge of a benefit society called Druids. [O.E. *grāf*, possibly tamarisk.]

grovelling, *gruv'*, *grov'(ə)-ling*, *adv.* and *adj.* prone: face-down: later felt to be the pr.p. or verbal noun of the new *v.i.* grov'el, to crawl on the earth, esp. in abject fear, etc.: to be base or abject—*pa.t.* and *pa.p.* grov'elled.—*n.* grov'eller. —*n.* groof, grouf (*groōf*; *Scot.*), the front of the body. [M.E. *groveling*, *grofling*, prone—O.N. *grūfa*, and suff. -*ling*.]

grow, *grō*, *v.i.* to have life: to have a habitat: to become enlarged by a natural process: to advance towards maturity: to increase in size: to develop: to become greater in any way: to extend: to pass from one state to another: to become.—*v.t.* to cause or allow to grow: to produce: to cultivate: (in *pass.*) to cover with growth:—*pa.t.* grew, *groō*; *pa.p.* grown, *grōn.— n.* grow'er.—*n.* and *adj.* grow'ing.—*n.* growth, a growing: gradual increase: progress: development: that which has grown: a morbid formation: increase in value (growth-orientated, providing increased capital rather than high interest).—*n.pl.* grow'ing-pains', neuralgic pains in young persons (also *fig.*).—grow'ing-point (*bot.*), the meristem at the apex of an axis, where active cell-division occurs and differentiation of tissues begins; grown'-up, an adult.— Also *adj.*—grow on, upon, to gain a greater hold on: to gain in the estimation of; grow out of, to issue from, result from: to pass beyond in development: to become too big for; grow to, to advance to, come to: of milk, to stick to the

pan and develop a bad taste in heating (so prob. Shak. *Merch. of Ven.*, II, ii.); grow together, to become united by growth; grow up, to advance in growth, become full-grown, mature, or adult: to spring up. [O.E. *grōwan*; O.N. *grōa*.]

growl, *growl*, *v.i.* to utter a deep rough murmuring sound like a dog: to grumble surlily.—*v.t.* to utter or express by growling.—*n.* a murmuring, snarling sound, as of an angry dog: a surly grumble.—*ns.* growl'er, one who growls: a N. American river fish, the large-mouthed black-bass, so named from the sound it emits: a small iceberg: a four-wheeled horse-drawn cab (*slang*): a jug or pitcher used for carrying beer (*Amer.*); growl'ery, a retreat for times of ill-humour; growl'ing.—*adv.* growl'ingly.—*adj.* growl'y. [Cf. Du. *grollen*, to grumble: allied to Gr. *gryllizein*, to grunt.]

groyne, *groin*, *n.* breakwater, of wood or other material, to check erosion and sand-drifting. [Prob. O.Fr. *groign*, snout—L. *grunnīre*, to grunt, but perh. the same as groin (1).]

grub, *grub*, *v.i.* to dig in the dirt: to be occupied meanly: to eat (*slang*).—*v.t.* to dig or root out of the ground (generally followed by *up* or *out*): to supply with victuals (*slang*):—*pr.p.* grubb'ing; *pa.t.* and *pa.p.* grubbed.—*n.* an insect larva, esp. one thick and soft: food (*slang*): a ball bowled along the ground (*cricket*).—*n.* grubb'er, he who, or that which, grubs: an implement for grubbing or stirring the soil: a grub (*cricket*).—*adj.* grubb'y, dirty: infested with grubs.—grub'-stake (*U.S.*), outfit, provisions, etc., given to a prospector for a share in finds.—*v.t.* to provide with such.—Grub Street, a former name of Milton Street, Moorfields, London, once inhabited by booksellers' hacks and shabby writers generally: applied adjectivally to any mean literary production. [M.E. *grobe*; origin uncertain.]

grubble, *grub'l*, a variant of grabble.

grudge, *gruj*, *v.t.* to murmur at (*obs.*): to look upon with envy: to give or allow unwillingly (something to a person): to be loth (to do).—*v.t.* to murmur, to show discontent (*obs.*).—*n.* secret enmity or envy: an old cause of quarrel.—*adj.* grudge'ful (*Spens.*).—*n.* and *adj.* grudg'ing.—*adv.*, grudg'ingly.—grudge a thought (*Shak.*), to thank with ill-will. [grutch.]

gruel, *groō'al*, *n.* a thin food made by boiling oatmeal in water: punishment, severe treatment (*coll.*).—*v.t.* to subject to severe or exhausting experience.—*n.* and *adj.* gru'elling. [O.Fr. *gruel* (Fr. *gruau*), groats—L.L. *grūtellum*, dim. of *grūtum*, meal, of Gmc. origin; cf. O.E. *grūt*.]

gruesome, *groō'səm*, *adj.* horrible: grisly: macabre.—*n.* grue, grew (*Scot.*), a creeping of the flesh: a shiver: a shudder: a pellicle of ice.— *v.i.* grue, grew (*Scot.*), to shudder: to feel the flesh creep: to creep (as the flesh): to curdle (as the blood).—*n.* grue'someness. [Cf. Du. *gruwzaam*, Ger. *grausam*.]

gruff, *gruf*, *adj.* rough, or abrupt in manner or sound.—*adj.* gruff'ish.—*adv.* gruff'ly.—*n.* gruff'-ness. [Du. *grof*; cog. with Sw. *grof*, Ger. *grob*, coarse.]

gru-gru, groo-groo, *groō'groō*, *n.* a name for several tropical American palms akin to the coconut palm, yielding oil-nuts: an edible weevil grub (also gru-gru worm) found in their pith.

grum, *grum*, *adj.* morose: surly: deep in the throat, as a sound.—*adv.* grum'ly.—*n.* grum'ness. [Cf. Dan. *grum*.]

grumble, *grum'bl*, *v.i.* to murmur with discontent: to express discontent: to mutter, mumble, murmur: to growl: to rumble.—*n.* the act of grumbling: an instance of grumbling: a cause of grumbling.—*ns.* grum'bler; Grumbletō'nian,

one of the country party as opposed to the court party, after 1689.—*n.* and *adj.* grum'bling.—*adv.* grum'blingly.—*adj.* grum'bly, inclined to grumble. [Cf. Du. *grommelen*, freq. of *grommen*, to mutter; Ger. *grummeln*.]
grume, groõm, *n.* a thick fluid: a clot.—*adjs.* grum'ous, grum'ose, composed of grains. [O.Fr. *grume*, a bunch—L. *grūmus*, a little heap.]
grummet, grommet, gromet, *grum'it, n.* a ring of rope: a hole edged with rope: a washer of hemp and red-lead putty: a metal ring lining an eyelet: an eyelet: a washer to protect electrical wire passing through a hole.—grumm'ethole. [Perh. 15th-cent. Fr. *gromette*, curb of a bridle.]
grummet, *grum'it, n.* a cabin-boy. [O.Fr. *gromet*; see gourmet.]
grumose, -ous. See grume.
grumph, *grumf,* (*Scot.*) *n.* a grunt.—*v.i.* to grunt. —*n.* grumph'ie (*Scot.*), a swine. [Imit.]
grumpy, *grum'pi, adj.* surly.—*adv.* grum'pily.—*n.* grump'iness. [Obs. *grump,* snub, sulkiness.]
Grundyism, *grun'di-izm, n.* conventional prudery, from the question 'But what will Mrs *Grundy* say?' in Thomas Morton's play, *Speed the Plough* (1798).
grunt, *grunt, v.i.* to make a sound like a pig.— *v.t.* to utter with a grunt.—*n.* a sound made by a pig: a similar sound: a fish (Haemulon, etc.) of a family akin to the snappers, that grunts when taken from the sea.—*n.* grunt'er, one who grunts: a pig: a grunting fish of various kinds.—*n.* and *adj.* grunt'ing.—*adv.* grunt'ingly.—*v.i.* grunt'le, to grunt, keep grunting.—*n.* a grunt: a snout. [O.E. *grunnettan,* freq. of *grunian.*]
gruppetto, *groõ-pet'õ,* (*mus.*) *n.* a turn. [It. a small group.]
grutch, *gruch,* (*Spens.*) *v.t.* or *v.i.* to grudge.—*n.* a grudge. [O.Fr. *groucher, grocher, gruchier,* to grumble.]
Gruyère, *grü'* or *groõ'yer,* or *-yer', n.* a wholemilk cheese, made at *Gruyère* (Switzerland) and elsewhere.
gryde; gryfon, gryphon; grype; grysely; grysie. See gride, griffin, gripe, grisly, grisy.
grypt, *gript,* (*Spens.*) prob. for griped or gripped, in the sense of bitten, pierced.
grysbok, *hhrãs'bok* (S.Afr.), *gris'bok, n.* a small S. African antelope, ruddy chestnut with white hairs. [Du., greybuck—*grys,* grey, and *bok,* a buck.]
G-string. Same as gee-string.
gu. See gue.
guacharo, *gwä'chä-rõ, n.* the oil-bird, a S. American nocturnal frugivorous bird (*Steatornis*) allied to the goatsuckers. [Sp. *guácharo.*]
guaco, *gwä'kõ, n.* a tropical American name for plants reputed antidotes against snakebite, esp. species of Mikania (climbing composites), and of Aristolochia: the medicinal substance got from them. [Amer. Sp.]
Guaiacum, *gwi'ə-kəm, n.* a tropical American genus of trees of the bean-caper family, yielding lignum-vitae: their greenish resin, used in medicine. [Sp. *guayaco,* from a Haitian word.]
guan, *gwän, n.* a large noisy American arboreal game-bird.
guana, *gwä'nä, n.* any large lizard. [For iguana.]
guanaco, *gwä-nä'kõ, n.* a wild llama.—Also huana'co (*wä-*). [Quechua *huanaco.*]
guanazolo, *gwä-nä-zõ'lõ, n.* a synthetic substance (amino-hydroxy triazolo pyrimidine) closely resembling guanine, used experimentally in controlling cancer by the starving of tumours.
guanin(e). See guano.
guano, *gwä'nõ, n.* the dung of sea-fowl, used as manure.—*adj.* guanif'erous.—*n.* gua'nin(e), a yellowish-white, amorphous substance, found in guano, liver, pancreas, and other organs of animals, and germ cells of plants—a constituent

of nucleic acids. [Sp. *guano, huano*—Peruv. *huanu,* dung.]
guar, *gwär, n.* a legume grown for forage and for its seeds which yield guar gum.
guaraná, *gwä-rä-nä', n.* a Brazilian liana (*Paullinia cupana*; Sapindaceae): a paste of its seeds (guaraná bread): a drink or drug made therefrom. [Tupi.]
Guarani, *gwä-rä-në', n.* an Indian of a group of tribes of southern Brazil and Paraguay (*pl.* Guarani): their language, derived from Tupí: guarani (*pl.* guaranies), the monetary unit of Paraguay.—Also *adj.*
guarantee, *gar-ən-të', n.* a person who makes a contract to see performed what another has undertaken: such a contract: surety or warrant: one responsible for the performance of some action, the truth of some statement, etc.—*v.t.* to undertake as surety for another: to secure: to engage, undertake:—*pr.p.* guarantee'ing; *pa.t.* and *pa.p.* guaranteed'.—*ns.* guar'antor (or *-tor'*), one who makes a guaranty; guar'anty, a securing, guaranteeing: a written undertaking to be responsible: a person who guarantees: a security.—*v.t.* to guarantee.—guarantee association, company, society, a joint-stock company on the insurance principle, which becomes security for the integrity of employees, e.g. cashiers. [Anglo-Fr. *garantie*—*garant,* warrant and prob. Sp. *garante*; see warrant.]
guard, *gärd, v.t.* to ward, watch, or take care of: to protect from danger or attack: to escort: to protect the edge of, as by an ornamental border: to furnish with guards: to trim (*lit., fig.*; Shak.). —*v.i.* to watch: to be wary.—*n.* ward, keeping: protection: watch: that which guards from danger: a man or body of men stationed to watch, protect, or keep in custody: one in charge of stage-coach or railway train: state of caution: posture of defence: the position in which a batsman grounds his bat in facing the bowling (*cricket*): a trimming, or a stripe (*obs.*): part of a sword hilt: a watch-chain: a cricketer's pad: in a book, a strip for attachment of a plate, map, or additional leaf: (*pl.*) household troops (Foot, Horse, and Life Guards).—*adj.* guard'able (Shak.), wardship.— *adj.* guard'ant, gardant (*her.*), having the face turned towards the beholder.—*n.* (Shak.) protector.—*adj.* guard'ed, wary: cautious: uttered with caution: trimmed, or striped (*obs.*).—*adv.* guard'edly.—*ns.* guard'edness; guard'ian, one who guards or takes care: one who has the care of the person, property, and rights of another (e.g. a minor; *law*): a member of a board (in England till 1930) administering the poor laws.— *adj.* protecting.—*n.* guard'ianship.—*adj.* guard'less, without a guard: defenceless.—guard'-book, a blank book with guards; guard'-cell (*bot.*), one of the lips of a stoma; guard'-house, guard'-room, a house or room for the accommodation of a guard of soldiers, where defaulters are confined; guardian angel, an angel supposed to watch over a particular person: a person specially devoted to the interests of another; guard'-ring, a keeper, or finger-ring that serves to keep another from slipping off; guard'-ship, a ship of war that superintends marine affairs in a harbour and protects it: guardianship (*Swift*); guards'man, a soldier of the guards.—mount guard, to go on guard; on, or off, one's guard, on (or not on) the alert for possible danger: wary about what one says or does (or the reverse); run the guard, to get past a guard or sentinel without detection. [O.Fr. *garder*—O.H.G. *warten*; O.E. *weardian,* mod. Eng. ward.]
guarish, garish, *gär'ish,* (*Spens.*) *v.t.* to heal. [O.Fr. *guarir* (Fr. *guérir*), to heal.]
guava, *gwä'və, n.* a small tropical American myrtaceous tree (Psidium): its yellow, pear-shaped

Neutral vowels in unaccented syllables: el'ə-mənt; for certain sounds in foreign words, see p. viii

fruit; often made into jelly. [Sp. *guayaba*, guava fruit; of S. Amer. origin.]

**guayule**, *gwä-ū'lā*, *n.* a Mexican composite plant (*Parthenium argentatum*): the rubber yielded by it. [Sp.; of Nahuatl origin.]

**gubernator**, *gū'bər-nā-tər*, *n.* a governor.—*n.* **gubernā'tion**, control, rule.—*adj.* **gubernatorial** (*-nə-tō'ri-əl, -tö'*). [L. *gubernātor*, a steersman.]

**guddle**, *gud'l*, (*Scot.*) *v.t.* and *v.i.* to fish with the hands by groping under the stones or banks of a stream.

**gude, guid,** *güd, gid,* Scottish form of good.— **gudesire** (see under **good**).

**gudgeon**, *guj'ən*, *n.* an easily caught small carp-like freshwater fish (*Gobio*): a person easily cheated.—*adj.* foolish.—*v.t.* to impose on, cheat. [O.Fr. *goujon*—L. *gōbiō, -ōnis*, a kind of fish— Gr. *kōbios*; see **goby**.]

**gudgeon**, *guj'ən*, *n.* the bearing of a shaft, esp. when made of a separate piece: a metallic journal-piece let into the end of a wooden shaft: a pin. [O.Fr. *goujon*, the pin of a pulley.]

**gue, gu, gju,** *gōō, gū, n.* a rude kind of violin used in Shetland. [O.N. *gigja.*]

**Guebre, Gueber,** *gä'bər, gē'bər, n.* a Zoroastrian. [Fr. *guèbre*—Pers. *gabr*; see **giaour.**]

**guelder-rose,** *gel'dər-rōz, n.* the snowball-tree, a Viburnum with large white balls of flowers. [From *Geldern* or from *Gelderland.*]

**Guelf, Guelph,** *gwelf, n.* one of a papal and popular party in mediaeval Italy, opposed to the Ghibel-lines and the emperors.—*adj.* **Guelf'ic,** pertaining to the Guelf family or party. [*Guelfo,* Italian form of the German family name *Welf,* said to have been the war-cry of Henry the Lion at the battle of Weinsberg (1140) against the Emperor Conrad III.]

**guenon,** *gen'ən, gə-nõ, n.* any species of the genus Cercopithecus, long-tailed African monkeys. [Fr.]

**guerdon,** *gûr'dən, n.* a reward or recompense.— *v.t.* to reward. [O.Fr. *guerdon, gueredon* (It. *guidardone*)—L.L. *widerdonum*—O.H.G. *widarlōn* (O.E. *witherlēan*)—*widar,* against, and *lōn,* reward; or more probably the latter part of the word is from L. *dōnum,* a gift.]

**guereza,** *ger'ə-zə, n.* a large, long-haired, black-and-white African monkey, with a bushy tail: any species of the same genus (*Colobus*). [App. of Somali origin.]

**guernsey,** *gûrn'zi, n.* a close-fitting knitted upper garment, worn by sailors: (*cap.*) one of a breed of dairy cattle from *Guernsey,* in the Channel Islands: (*cap.*) Channel Island patois derived from Norman-French.—**Guernsey lily,** a Nerine (*q.v.*).

**guerra al cuchillo,** *gā'rä äl kōō-chē'lyō,* (Sp.) war to the knife.

**guerre à mort,** *ger a mor,* (Fr.) war to the death; **guerre à outrance,** *ōō-träs,* war to the uttermost, to the bitter end.

**guerrilla, guerilla,** *gər-il'ə, n.* harassing an army by small bands: petty warfare: loosely, one who takes part in such warfare (properly **guerrillero,** *-yə'ro*).—Also *adj.*—**guerrilla strike,** a sudden and brief industrial strike. [Sp. *guerrilla,* dim. of *guerra,* war—O.H.G. *werra*; cf. **war**; Fr. *guerre.*]

**guess,** *ges, v.t.* to think, believe, suppose (*arch.* and *U.S.*): to judge upon inadequate knowledge or none at all: to conjecture: to hit on or solve by conjecture.—*v.i.* to make a conjecture or con-jectures.—*n.* judgment or opinion without sufficient evidence or grounds: a random surmise: a riddle, conundrum (*Scot.*).—*adj.* **guess'able.**—*n.* **guess'er.**—*n.* and *adj.* **guess'-ing.**—*adv.* **guess'ingly.**—*n.* **guess'timate,** (*slang*) estimate based on very little knowledge.—**guess'-work,** process or result of guessing.—**anybody's guess,** purely a matter of individual conjecture.

[M.E. *gessen*; cog. with Du. *gissen*; Dan. *gisse,* mod. Icel. *giska,* for *gitska—geta,* to get, think; see **get, forget.**]

**guess.** See **othergates.**

**guest,** *gest, n.* a visitor received and entertained gratuitously or for payment: an animal inhabit-ing or breeding in another's nest.—*adj.* and *n.* (an artist, conductor, etc.) not a regular member of a company, etc., or not regularly appearing on a programme, but taking part on a special occasion.—*v.i.* **guest'en** (*Scott*), to stay as a guest.—*adv.* **guest'wise,** in the manner or capacity of a guest.—**guest'-chamber** (*B.*), **guest'-room,** a room for the accommodation of a guest; **guest'-house,** a hospice: a boarding-house; **guest'-night,** a night when non-members of a society are entertained. [O.E. (Anglian) *gest* (W.S. *giest*), perh. influenced by O.N.; allied to Du. and Ger. *gast,* L. *hostis,* stranger, enemy.]

**Gueux,** *gə, n.pl.* the name assumed by the con-federation (1565) of nobles and others to resist the introduction of the Inquisition into the Low Countries by Philip II of Spain. [Fr., beggars.]

**guff,** *guf,* (*slang*) *n.* nonsense, humbug. [Perh. imit.]

**guffaw,** *guf-ö', v.i.* to laugh loudly.—*n.* a loud laugh. [From the sound.]

**guggle,** *gug'l, v.i.* to gurgle.—*n.* a gurgle. [Cf. **gurgle.**]

**guichet,** *gē'shä, n.* a small opening in a wall, door, etc.: a ticket-office window. [Fr.; cf. **wicket.**]

**Guicowar.** See **Gaekwar.**

**guid.** See **gude.**

**guide,** *gid, v.t.* to lead, conduct, or direct: to regulate: to influence.—*n.* he who, or that which, guides: one who conducts travellers, tourists, mountaineers, etc.: one who directs another in his course of life: a soldier or other employed to obtain information for an army: a Girl Guide (see **girl**): a guide-book: anything serving to direct, show the way, determine direction of motion or course of conduct.—*adj.* **guid'able.**— *ns.* **guid'age,** guidance; **guid'ance,** direction: leadership; **guid'er,** one who guides: a device for guiding: a captain or lieutenant in the Girl Guides.—*adj.* **guide'less.**—*n.* **guide'ship.**—*n.* and *adj.* **guid'ing.**—*n.* **guid'on,** a pennant carried by a cavalry company or mounted battery: the officer bearing it.—**guide'-book,** a book of information for tourists; **guided missile,** a jet- or rocket-propelled projectile carrying a warhead and electronically directed to its target for the whole or part of the way by remote control; **guide dog,** a dog trained to lead blind persons; **guide'line,** a line drawn, or a rope, etc., fixed, to act as a guide: an indication of course that should be followed, or of what future policy will be (*fig.*); **guide'-post,** a post to guide the traveller; **guide'-rail,** an additional rail to keep rolling-stock on the rails at a bend; **guide'-rope,** a rope for guiding the movement of· a thing hoisted or hauled. [O.Fr. *guider*; prob. from a Gmc. root, as in O.E. *witan,* to know, *wîs,* wise, Ger. *weisen,* to show, conn. with **wit, wise.**]

**Guignol,** *gē-nyol, n.* the chief puppet in French puppet shows.—**Grand** (*grä*) **Guignol,** a small theatre in Paris that specialised in short plays of horror: horror plays of this type. [Name originated in Lyons in 18th century; said to be that of a local 'character'.]

**guild,** *gild, gild, n.* an association for mutual aid: a corporation: a mediaeval association pro-viding for masses for the dead, maintenance of common interests, mutual support and protec-tion (*hist.*): meeting-place of a guild (*obs.*; *Spens. gyeld*): a group of plants distinguished by their way of life (e.g. saprophytes, or para-sites).—*n.* **guild'ry** (*Scot.*), the corporation of a royal burgh: membership thereof.—**guild'-brother,** a fellow-member of a guild; **guild'hall,**

the hall of a guild: a town-hall; **Guild Socialism**, a form of socialism that would make trade unions or guilds the authority for industrial matters. [O.E. *gield*, influenced by O.N. *gildi*.]

**guilder, gilder,** *gild′ər, n.* an old Dutch and German gold coin: a modern Dutch gulden: a coin vaguely (*Shak.*). [Du. *gulden*.]

**guile, gil,** *n.* wile, jugglery: cunning: deceit.—*v.t.* (*Spens.*) to beguile.—*adjs.* **guiled,** armed with deceit: treacherous; **guile′ful,** crafty: deceitful.—*adv.* **guile′fully.**—*n.* **guile′fulness.**—*adj.* **guile′less,** without deceit: artless.—*adv.* **guile′lessly.**—*ns.* **guile′lessness; guil′er, guyler** (*Spens.*), a deceiver. [O.Fr. *guile*, deceit, perh. Gmc.; cf. **wile.**]

**guillemot,** *gil′i-mot, n.* a diving bird (Uria) of the auk family. [Fr., dim. of *Guillaume*, William, perh. suggested by Bret. *gwelan*, gull.]

**guilloche,** *gi-lōsh′, n.* an ornament formed of interlacing curved bands enclosing circles.—*v.t.* to decorate with intersecting curved lines. [Fr., a guilloching tool; said to be named from one *Guillot*.]

**guillotine,** *gil′ə-tēn, -tēn′, gē′yə-, n.* an instrument for beheading by descent of a heavy oblique blade—adopted during the French Revolution, and named after Joseph Ignace *Guillotin* (1738–1814), a physician, who first proposed its adoption: a machine for cutting paper, straw, etc.: a surgical instrument for cutting the tonsils: a specially drastic rule or closure for shortening discussion.—*v.t.* to behead, crop, or cut short by guillotine.

**guilt, gilt,** *n.* the state of having done wrong: sin, sinfulness: the state of having broken a law: liability to a penalty.—*adv.* **guilt′ily.**—*n.* **guilt′iness.**—*adj.* **guilt′less,** free from crime: innocent.—*adv.* **guilt′lessly.**—*n.* **guilt′lessness.**—*adj.* **guilt′y,** justly chargeable: wicked: involving, indicating, burdened with, or pertaining to guilt.—*adv.* **guilt′y-like** (*Shak.*), guilty.—**guilty of, to** (*Shak.*), having committed (evil or injudicious act): to blame for (a happening; *arch*): (sometimes in *B.*) deserving (of; *obs.*). [Orig. a payment or fine for an offence; O.E. *gylt*.]

**guilt** (*Spens.*). Same as **gilt** (gilded).

**guimp.** See **gimp.**

**guinea,** *gin′i, n.* an obsolete English gold coin first made of gold brought from *Guinea*, in Africa: its value, finally 21s.—*adj.* priced at a guinea.—**guin′ea-corn,** durra (*Sorghum vulgare*): pearl millet (*Pennisetum typhoideum*), a cereal; **guin′ea-fowl,** an African bird (Numida) of the pheasant family, dark-grey with white spots; **guin′ea-grass,** a tall African grass of the millet genus (Panicum); **guin′ea-hen,** a guinea-fowl: formerly, a turkey: a courtesan (*Shak.*); **guin′ea-pig,** a small S. American rodent, the cavy: a fainéant company director (*slang*): a person used as the subject of an experiment—as the cavy commonly is in the laboratory; **guin′ea-worm,** a very slender threadlike parasitic nematode worm (Filaria) common in tropical Africa.

**guipure,** *gē-pōōr′, n.* a kind of lace having no ground or mesh, the pattern sections fixed by interlacing threads: a species of gimp. [Fr. *guipure*—O.Fr. *guiper*, prob. Gmc.; cf. Goth. *weipan*, to weave.]

**guise,** *gīz, n.* manner, behaviour: custom: external appearance: dress.—*v.t.* to dress.—*v.i.* to act as a guiser.—*ns.* **guis′er, guis′ard** (both chiefly *Scot.*), a person in disguise: a Christmas (or now usu. Hallowe'en) mummer. [O.Fr. *guise*; cf. O.H.G. *wīsa* (Ger. *weise*), a way, guise, O.E. *wise*, way, *wis*, wise.]

**guitar,** *gi-tär′, n.* a fretted musical instrument, now six-stringed—like the lute, but flat-backed.—*n.* **guitar′ist.** [Fr. *guitare*—L. *cithara*—Gr. *kitharā*; see **cithara.**]

**Gujarati,** *gōōj-ə-rä′tē, n.* an Indic language spoken

in the region and state of *Gujarat* in north-western India.—Also **Gujar** (or -er-)**athi.** [Hind.—Sans. *Gurjara*, Gujarat.]

**gula,** *gū′lə, n.* the upper part of the throat: in some insects a plate on the under side of the head.—*adj.* **gū′lar.** [L. *gula*, throat.]

**gulch,** *gulch, gulsh, n.* (*U.S.*) a ravine or narrow rocky valley, a gully.—*v.t.* (*dial.*) to swallow greedily. [Origin doubtful.]

**gulden,** *gōōl′dən, n.* a gold or silver coin in Germany in the Middle Ages: the old unit of account in Austria (before 1892): a Dutch coin, the guilder or florin. [Ger., lit. golden.]

**gule** (*Scot.*). See **gold** (2).

**gules,** *gūlz,* (*her.*) *n.* a red colour, marked in engraved figures by perpendicular lines.—*adj.* **gū′ly** (*obs.*). [O.Fr. *gueules*, perh.—L. *gula*, the throat.]

**gut** (*arch.* **gulph**), **gulf,** *n.* an indentation in the coast: a deep place: an abyss: a whirlpool: anything insatiable: in Oxford and Cambridge examinations, the place of those candidates for honours who are allowed a pass without honours.—*v.t.* to engulf.—*v.i.* to flow like a gulf.—*adj.* **gulf′y,** full of gulfs or whirlpools.—**gulf′weed,** a large olive-brown seaweed (*Sargassum*) that floats unattached in great 'meadows' at the branching of the Gulf Stream and elsewhere in tropical oceans. [O.Fr. *golfe*—Late Gr. *kolphos*—Gr. *kolpos*, the bosom.]

**gull,** *gul, n.* a sea-mew, a sea-bird of the family Laridae, esp. of the genus Larus. [Prob. W. *gwylan.*]

**gull,** *gul,* (*Shak.*) *n.* an unfledged bird. [Perh. O.N. *gulr*, yellow.]

**gull,** *gul, n.* a dupe: an easily duped person: a hoax (*obs.*).—*v.t.* to beguile, hoax.—*ns.* **gull′er; gull′ery** (*arch.*), deception; **gullibil′ity.**—*adjs.* **gull′ible,** easily deceived (also **gull′able**); **gull′ish.**—**gull′-catcher** (*Shak.*), a cheat. [Perh. from **gull** (1 or 2).]

**Gullah,** *gu′lə, gōō′, n.* one of a group of Negroes in islands and coastal districts of south-east United States: their language, a creolised English.

**gullet,** *gul′it, n.* the passage in the neck by which food is taken into the stomach: the throat: a narrow trench, passage, water channel, or ravine. [O.Fr. *goulet*, dim. of *goule* (Fr. *gueule*)—L. *gula*, the throat.]

**gully, gulley,** *gul′i,* (*Scot.*) *n.* a big knife.

**gully, gulley,** *gul′i, n.* a channel worn by running water, as on a mountain-side: a ravine: a ditch: a grooved rail, as for a tramway: the position between point and slips (*cricket*).—*pl.* **gull′ies, gull′eys.**—*v.t.* to wear a gully or channel in.—*adj.* **gull′ied.**—**gull′y-hole,** a passage by which a gutter discharges into a drain; **gull′y-hunt′er,** one who picks up things from gutters. [Prob. **gullet.**]

**gulosity,** *gū-los′i-ti, n.* gluttony. [L. *gulōsus,* gluttonous—*gulō,* glutton—*gula,* throat.]

**gulp, gulp,** *v.t.* to swallow spasmodically or in large draughts.—*v.i.* to make a swallowing movement.—*n.* a spasmodic or copious swallow: a movement as if of swallowing: a quantity swallowed at once: capacity for gulping. [Cf. Du. *gulpen, gulp.*]

**gulph.** See **gulf.**

**gum,** *gum, n.* the firm fleshy tissue that surrounds the bases of the teeth: insolence (*old slang*).—*adj.* **gumm′y,** toothless.—*n.* **gum′boil,** a small abscess on the gum. [O.E. *gōma,* palate; O.N. *gōmr,* Ger. *gaumen,* palate.]

**gum,** *gum, n.* a substance that collects in or exudes from certain plants, and hardens on the surface, dissolves or swells in water, but does not dissolve in alcohol or ether: a plant gum or similar substance used as an adhesive, a stiffener, or for other purpose: any gumlike or sticky substance:

chewing-gum: a hard gelatinous kind of sweet: a gum tree: gummosis: a rubber overshoe (*U.S.*): a beehive, orig. one made from a hollow gum tree (*U.S.*): a humbug (*arch. U.S.*).—*v.t.* to smear, coat, treat, or unite with gum: to humbug (*arch. U.S.*).—*v.i.* to become gummy: to exude gum:—*pr.p.* gumm'ing; *pa.t.* and *pa.p.* gummed.—*n.* gumm'a, a syphilitic tumour:—*pl.* gumm'ata.—*adjs.* gumm'atous; gummif'erous, producing gum.—*ns.* gumm'iness; gumm'ing, act of fastening with gum: application of gum in solution to a lithographic stone: gummosis: becoming gummy; gumm'ite, a hydrated oxide of uranium and lead; gummo'sis, pathological conversion of cell walls into gum; gummos'ity, gumminess.—*adjs.* gumm'ous, gumm'y, consisting of or resembling gum: producing or covered with gum.—gum ammoniac, ammoniacum, a gum resin, inspissated juice of a Persian umbelliferous plant (Dorema), used in medicine and manufactures: that of an African species of Ferula; gum arabic, a gum obtained from various acacias; gum benjamin (see benjamin); gumboot, a rubber boot; gum dragon, tragacanth, tragacanth; gum elastic, rubber; gum juniper, sandarac; gum resin, a resin mixed with gum; gum'shoe (*U.S.*), a rubber overshoe: a shoe with rubber sole: a detective or policeman (*slang*).—Also *v.i.* (*slang*), to snoop, pry.—gum tree, a tree that exudes gum, or gum resin, kino, etc., esp. a Eucalyptus tree, or an American tree of the cornel family (Nyssa). —gum up the works (*coll.*), to make (e.g. a machine, a scheme) unworkable; up a gum tree, in straits (from the opossum's refuge). [O.Fr. *gomme*—L. *gummi*—Gr. *kommi*; prob.—Egyptian *kemai*.]

gum, *gum, n.* material that gathers in the corner of the eye.—gum rash, red-gum. [Perh. O.E. *gund,* matter, pus.]

gum, *gum, n.* used in oaths for God.

gumbo, *gum'bō, n.* the okra or its mucilaginous pods: a soup of which okra is an ingredient: a dish of okra pods seasoned: in central U.S. a fine soil which becomes sticky or soapy when wet: a Negro patois in Louisiana, etc. [Angolan Negro (*ki)ngombo.*]

gump, *gump,* (*Scot.*) *v.t.* and *v.i.* to guddle.

gump, *gump,* (*dial.*) *n.* a foolish person.

gumphion, *gum'fi-ən,* (*obs. Scot.*) *n.* a funeral banner. [gonfanon.]

gumple-foisted, *gum'pl-foist'id,* (*Scott*) *adj.* sulky. [*gumps,* sulks (gump, 2); the second element appears in other words as—*faced, -feist,* etc.]

gumption, *gum(p)'shən, n.* sense: shrewdness: commonsense: art of preparing colours.—*adj.* gump'tious. [Poss. conn. with O.N. *gaumr,* heed.]

gun, *gun, n.* a tubular weapon from which projectiles are discharged, usually by explosion: a cannon, rifle, revolver, etc.: a device for spraying, squirting, or otherwise propelling material: a signal by gun: one who carries a gun, a member of a shooting-party: a professional killer (*U.S. slang*): the throttle of an aircraft: the accelerator of a car.—*v.t.* to shoot: to shoot at: to provide with guns: to open the throttle of, to increase speed (also give the gun).—*v.i.* to shoot: to go shooting.—*ns.* gunn'age, the number of guns carried by a ship of war; gunn'er, one who works a gun: a private in the Artillery: a branch officer in charge of naval ordnance (*naut.*); gunn'ery, the art of managing guns, or the science of artillery; gunn'ing.—gun barrel, the tube of a gun; gun'boat, a small vessel of light draught, fitted to carry one or more guns; gunboat diplomacy, show or threat of (orig. naval) force in international negotiation; gun carriage, a carriage on which a cannon is mounted; gun'cotton, an explosive prepared by saturating cotton with nitric and sulphuric acids;

gun deck, a deck in old warships carrying guns below the main deck (earlier below spar deck); gun dog, dog trained to work with a shooting-party; gun'fight, fight involving two or more people with guns, esp. in old American West.— Also *v.i.*—gun'fighter; gun'fire, the firing of guns: the hour at which the morning or evening gun is fired: an early cup of tea; gun'flint, a piece of flint fitted to the hammer of a flintlock musket; gun'layer, one who sets the sights of a ship's gun; gun'maker; gun'man, a man who carries a gun, esp. an armed criminal; gun'metal, an alloy of copper and tin in the proportion of about 9 to 1, once used in making cannon: an imitation thereof: the colour of the alloy; gun moll (*slang*), a woman who associates with criminals: a gunman's moll; gun'port, a porthole or similar opening for a gun; gun'powder, an explosive mixture of saltpetre, sulphur, and charcoal; gun'room, a room where guns are kept: on board ship, orig. the gunner's apartment, now a mess-room for junior officers; gun'runner; gun'running, smuggling guns into a country; gun'shot, the shot fired from a gun: the distance to which shot can be thrown from a gun.—*adj.* caused by the shot of a gun.—*adj.* gun'-shy, frightened by guns.—gun'slinger (*coll.*), a gunfighter; gun'smith, a smith or workman who makes or repairs guns or small arms; gun'stick, a ramrod; gun'stock, the piece on which the barrel of a gun is fixed; gun'stone (*Shak.*), a stone shot.—as sure as a gun, quite sure, certainly; beat the gun, jump the gun (see jump); blow great guns, to blow tempestuously—of wind; great gun, a cannon (*obs.*): a person of great importance (*coll.*; also big gun); gun for, to seek, try to obtain: to seek to ruin; kiss the gunner's daughter, to be tied to a gun for a flogging; son of a gun, a soldier's bastard (*obs.*): a rogue, rascal (*slang*): used as an affectionate greeting: also *interj.* (*U.S.*); stand, stick, to one's guns, maintain one's position staunchly. [M.E. *gonne,* poss. from the woman's name *Gunhild.*]

gunite, *gun'it, n.* a finely-graded cement concrete (a mixture of cement and sand) sprayed into position under air pressure by a cement gun. [Orig. trademark.]

gunk, *gungk,* (*coll.*) *n.* unpleasant dirty sticky material, or semi-solid usu. valueless residue from a chemical process.

gunnel, *gun'l, n.* See gunwale.

gunnel, *gun'l,* the butter-fish (Centronotus), a small long coast fish of the blenny family. [Origin unknown.]

Gunnera, *gun'ər-a, n.* a gigantic-leaved herb of the mare's-tail family. [After J. E. *Gunner* (1718-73), Norwegian botanist.]

gunny, *gun'i, n.* a strong coarse jute fabric. [Hindi *gani, goṇi,* sacking—Sans. *goṇi,* a sack.]

gunsel, *gun'səl,* (*U.S. slang*) *n.* a stupid or inexperienced youth: a catamite: a gunman. [Yiddish *genzel,* gosling—M.H.G. *gensel,* dim. of *gans,* goose; *gunman* meaning influenced by gun.]

gunter, *gun'tər, n.* a Gunter's scale: a rig with topmast sliding on rings (from its resemblance to a sliding variety of Gunter's scale).—Gunter's chain, a surveyor's chain of 100 links, 66 feet long (10 chains = 1 furlong; 10 sq. chains = 1 acre); Gunter's scale, a scale graduated in several lines for numbers, logarithmic sines, etc., so arranged that trigonometrical problems can be roughly solved by use of a pair of compasses, or in another form by sliding. [From the inventor, Edmund *Gunter* (1581-1626), astronomer.]

gunwale, gunnel, *gun'l, n.* the *wale* or upper edge of a ship's side next to the bulwarks, so called because the upper *guns* were pointed from it.

gunyah, *gun'ya,* (*Austr.*) *n.* an Australian aboriginals' hut: a roughly-made shelter in the bush. [Aboriginal.]

Günz, *günts*, *n.* the first (Pliocene) stage of glaciation in the Alps.—*adjs.* Günz, Günz'ian. [From a Bavarian tributary of the Danube.]

gup, *gup*, (*obs.*) *interj.* expressing remonstrance or derision. [Prob. go up.]

gup, *gup*, (*slang*) *n.* gossip: prattle. [Urdu *gap*.]

guppy, *gup'i*, *n.* a small West Indian fish (*Lebistes*) that multiplies very rapidly and feeds on mosquito larvae; also called *millions*. [From R. J. L. *Guppy*, who sent it to the British Museum.]

gur, goor, *gûr*, *gōōr*, *n.* an unrefined sweet cane sugar. [Hindi, coarse sugar—Sans., *guḍa*.]

gurami. Same as goramy.

gurdwara, *gûr'dwär-a*, *n.* a Sikh place of worship. [Panjabi *gurduārā*—Sans. *guru*, teacher, *dvāra*, door.]

gurge, *gûrj*, (*Milt.*) *n.* a whirlpool. [L. *gurges*.]

gurgitation, *gûr-ji-tā'shən*, *n.* surging. [L. *gurges*, *-itis*, whirlpool.]

gurgle, *gûr'gl*, *v.i.* to flow in an irregular noisy current: to make a bubbling sound.—*n.* the sound of gurgling. [Cf. It. *gorgogliare*.]

gurgoyle. See gargoyle.

gurjun, *gûr'jun*, *n.* an East Indian dipterocarp yielding timber and a balsamic liquid used against leprosy. [Hind. *garjan*.]

Gurkha, Goorkha, *gōōr'kə*, *gûr'kə*, *n.* one of the dominant people of Nepal, a broad-chested fighting race claiming Hindu origin, but Mongolised.

gurl, *gûrl*, (*Scot.*) *n.* a growl.—*v.i.* to growl.—*adj.* gur'ly, grim: lowering: rough: surly. [Cf. growl.]

gurlet, *gûr'lit*, *n.* a pickaxe with a head pointed at one end, bladed at the other.

Gurmukhi, *gōōr'mə-kē*, *n.* the script in which the sacred texts of the Sikhs are written, which is used also for modern secular writing and printing. [Punjabi *Gurmukhī*, lit. from the mouth of the *guru* or teacher.]

gurnard, *gûr'nərd*, gurnet, *-nit*, *n.* a fish (Trigla; of many species) with large angular head and three finger-like walking rays in front of the pectoral fin. [O.Fr. *gornard*, related to Fr. *grogner*, to grunt—L. *grunnire*, to grunt; from the sound they emit when taken.]

gurrah, *gur'ə*, *n.* a coarse Indian muslin. [Hind. *gârhā*, thick.]

gurry, *gur'i*, *n.* whale offal: fish offal.

guru, gooroo, *gōō'rōō*, *n.* a spiritual teacher: a venerable person. [Hind. *gurū*—Sans. *guru*, venerable.]

gush, *gush*, *v.i.* to flow out with violence or copiously: to be effusive, or highly sentimental. —*n.* that which flows out: a violent issue of a fluid.—*n.* gush'er, one who gushes: an oil-well that does not have to be pumped.—*adj.* gush'ing. —*adv.* gush'ingly.—*adj.* gush'y, effusively sentimental. [M.E. *gosshe*, *gusche*; the connection, if any, with O.N. *gusa*, *gjōsa*, Du. *gudsen*, is not clear.]

gusla, *gōōs'lə*, gusle, *-le*, gusli, *-lē*, *n.* a one-stringed Balkan musical instrument: a Russian instrument with several strings.—*n.* guslar', a performer on it. [Bulg. *gusla*, Serb. *gusle*, Russ. *gusli*.]

gusset, *gus'it*, *n.* the piece of chainmail covering a joint in armour, as at the armpit: an angular piece inserted in a garment to strengthen or enlarge some part of it or to give freedom of movement.—*v.t.* to make with a gusset: to insert a gusset into. [O.Fr. *gousset*—*gousse*, a pod, husk.]

gust, *gust*, *n.* a sudden blast of wind: a violent burst of passion.—*v.i.* to blow in gusts.—*adjs.* gust'ful, gust'y, stormy: irritable.—*n.* gust'iness. [O.N. *gustr*, blast.]

gust, *gust*, *n.* sense of pleasure of tasting (*arch.*): relish (*arch.*): gratification (*arch.*): taste, experience (*obs.*): flavour (*arch.*).—*adj.* and *n.* gust'able (*arch.*).—*n.* gustā'tion, the act of tasting: the sense of taste.—*adjs.* gust'ātive, gust'ātory, of or pertaining to the sense of taste; gust'ful (*arch.*), savoury: enjoyable.—*n.* gust'o (It.), taste: zest.—*adj.* gust'y (*Scot.*), savoury: appetisingly flavoured. [L. *gustus*, taste; cf. Gr. *geuein*, to make to taste.]

gut, *gut*, *n.* the alimentary canal: sheep's or other intestines or silkworm's glands prepared for violin-strings, etc.: a narrow passage: a strait: a channel: a lane: (in *pl.*) the viscera: (in *pl.*) the inner or essential parts: (in *pl.*) stamina, toughness of character, tenacity, staying power, endurance, forcefulness (*coll.*).—*v.t.* to take out the guts of: to remove the contents of: to reduce to a shell (by burning, dismantling, plundering, etc.): to extract what is essential from:—*pr.p.* gutt'ing; *pa.t.* and *pa.p.* gutt'ed.—*n.* guts'iness (*Scot.*), greediness.—*adj.* guts'y, gluttonous (*Scot.*): having pluck or nerve (*slang*): lusty, passionate (*slang*).—*n.* gutt'er.—*v.t.* and *v.i.* gutt'le, to eat greedily.—gut'-scrap'er (*facet.*), a fiddler. [O.E. *guttas* (pl.); cf. *geotan*, to pour; dial. Eng. *gut*, Ger. *gosse*, a drain.]

gutta, *gut'ə*, *n.* a drop: a small drop-like ornament on the under side of a mutule or a regula of the Doric entablature: a small vacuole: a small round colour-spot (*zool.*):—*pl.* gutt'ae (-*ē*).— *adjs.* gutt'ate, -d, containing drops: spotted.— *n.* guttā'tion, exudation of drops of liquid from an uninjured part of a plant (whence *v.i.* gutt'ate).—*n.pl.* Guttif'erae, a family of archichlamydeous dicotyledons with abundant oil-glands and passages, and entire exstipulate opposite leaves, including mangosteen, mammeeapple, and according to some St John's wort.— *adj.* guttif'erous, exuding drops: of the Guttiferae.—gutta serena, amaurosis. [L. *gutta*, drop.]

gutta, *gut'ə*, *n.* the coagulated latex of sapotaceous and other trees, esp. gutta-percha: a hydrocarbon (empirically $C_{10}H_{16}$) found in gutta-percha: a solid gutta-percha golf-ball, used in the 19th century—(*coll.*) gutt'y.—gutta-percha (-*pûr'chə*), a substance like rubber, but harder and not extensible, got chiefly from the latex of Malaysian trees of the Sapotaceae (Palaquium, Payena, etc.).—Also *adj.* [Malay *getah*, gum, *percha*, a tree producing it.]

gutter, *gut'ər*, *n.* a channel for conveying away water, esp. at the roadside or at the eaves of a roof: a furrow, groove: a grooved piece, used to separate pages of type in a form (*print.*): (in *pl.*) loosely, the inner margins between two pages (*print.*): slum-life, social degradation (*fig.*): (in *pl.*) mud, dirt (*Scot.*).—*v.t.* to cut or form into small hollows.—*v.i.* to become hollowed: to trickle: to run down in drops, as a candle: (of flame) to be blown downwards, or threaten to go out.—gutt'erblood (*Scot.*), a lowborn person; gutt'er-man, -mer'chant, a pavement-side seller of cheap trifles; gutter press journalism, sensational journalism; gutt'ersnipe, a street urchin: a neglected child from a slum area. [O.Fr. *goutiere*—*goute*—L. *gutta*, a drop.]

guttiferous, Guttiferae. See under gutta (1).

guttural, *gut'ər-əl*, *adj.* pertaining to the throat: formed in the throat: throaty in sound.—*n.* a sound pronounced in the throat or (loosely) by the back part of the tongue (*phon.*): a letter representing such a sound.—*v.t.* gutt'uralise, -ize, to sound guttural: to make guttural.— *adv.* gutt'urally. [L. *guttur*, the throat.]

guy, *gi*, *n.* a rope, rod, etc., used to steady anything, or hold it in position.—*v.t.* to keep in position by a guy.—guy'-rope. [O.Fr. *guis*, *guie*; Sp. *guia*, a guide.]

guy, *gī, n.* an effigy of *Guy* Fawkes, dressed up grotesquely on the anniversary of the Gunpowder Plot (5th Nov.): an odd figure: a fellow (*coll.*): a joke, lark (*slang*): flight, decamping (*slang*).—*v.t.* to turn to ridicule.—*v.i.* to decamp.

guyle, guyse (*Spens.*), forms of guile, guise.

guyot, *gē-ō, n.* a flat-topped submarine mountain. [A. H. *Guyot*, Swiss-born Amer. geologist.]

guzzle, *guz'l, v.t.* and *v.i.* to swallow (esp. liquor, in Scotland food) greedily.—*n.* a bout of guzzling.—*n.* guzz'ler. [Perh. conn. with Fr. *gosier*, throat.]

gwyniad, gwiniad, *gwin'i-ad, n.* a whitefish (*Coregonus pennanti*), found in Bala Lake. [W. *gwyniad—gwyn*, white.]

gybe, *jib, v.i.* (of a sail) to swing over from one side to the other: to alter course in this way.—*v.t.* to cause to gybe.—*n.* a gybing. [Origin obscure; see jib.]

gyeld, a Spenserian form of guild(hall).

gylden. See gilden.

gym, *jim, n.* and *adj.* a familiar abbreviation of gymnasium, gymnastic, gymnastics.—gym shoe, a plimsoll; gym slip, tunic, a belted pinafore dress worn by schoolgirls.

gymkhana, *jim-kä'nə, n.* a public place for athletic games, etc.: a meeting for such sports: now esp., a meeting for equestrian sports. [Hindi *gend-khāna* (ball-house), racket-court, remodelled on *gym*nastics.]

gymmal. Same as gimmal.

gymnasium, *jim-nā'zi-əm, n.* a place, hall, building, or school for gymnastics: orig. a public place or building where the Greek youths exercised themselves, with running and wrestling grounds, baths, and halls for conversation: (usu. *gimnä'zi-ōōm*) a (German) secondary school:—*pl.* gymna'siums, -ia, for continental schools gymnasien (*gim-nä'zi-ən*).—*adj.* gymnä'sial.—*ns.* gymnäs'iarch (-*ärk*; Gr. *archos*, chief), head of a gymnasium; gymnäs'iast, a pupil in a gymnasium: a gymnast.—*adj.* gymnä'sic.—*ns.* gym'nast (*-nast*), one skilled in gymnastics; gymnas'tic, a system of training by exercise: (in *pl.* used as *sing.*) exercises devised to strengthen the body: (in *pl.*) feats or tricks of agility.—*adjs.* gymnas'tic, -al, pertaining to athletic exercises: athletic, vigorous.—*adv.* gymnas'tically. [Latinised from Gr. *gymnasion—gymnos*, naked.]

gymnic, *jim'nik,* (*Milt.*) *adj.* gymnastic. [Gr. *gymnikos—gymnos*, naked.]

gymn(o)-, *gim'n(ō)-, jim'n(ō)-, gimn(o)'-, jimn(o)'-*, in composition, esp. of biol. terms, naked.—*adj.* gymnorhi'nal (Gr. *rhis, rhinos*, nose), with unfeathered nostrils.—*ns.* gym'nosoph, gymnos'ophist (Gr. *sophos*, wise), an ancient Hindu philosopher who wore little or no clothing, and lived solitarily in mystical contemplation; gymnos'ophy; gym'nosperm (Gr. *sperma*, seed), any of the lower or primitive group of seedplants whose seeds are not enclosed in an ovary.—*adj.* gymnosper'mous. [Gr. *gymnos*, naked.]*

gymp. Same as gimp (1) and (2).

gynaeceum, *gin-, jin-, jin-ē-sē'əm, n.* women's quarters in a house: the female organs of a flower (*bot.*). [Gr. *gynaikeion*, women's quarters.]

gynaeco-, in U.S. gyneco-, *gin-, jin-, jin-ē'kō-,* or *-i-ko'-, gyno-, gin'-, jin'-,* or *jin'ō,* or *-o'-,* in composition, woman, female.—*n.* gyn(aec)o'cracy (Gr. *kratos*, power), government by women or a woman.—*adjs.* gyn(aec)ocrat'ic; gynaecolog'ical.—*ns.* gynaecol'ogist; gynaecol'ogy, branch of medicine treating of women's diseases; gynaecomas'tia, gynaecomas'ty, abnormal enlargement of the male breast; gyn'aecomast (Gr. *anēr, andros*, man, male), hermaphroditism.—*adj.* gynan'drous, hermaphroditic: with stamen concrescent with the carpels, as in orchids.—*n.* gynan'dromorph (Gr.

morphē, form), an animal combining male and female secondary characters.—*adjs.* gynandromorph'ic, gynandromorph'ous.—*ns.* gynandromorph'ism, gynan'dromorphy.—*adj.* gynodioe'cious, having hermaphrodite and female flowers on different plants.—*ns.* gynodioe'cism; gyn(o)ecium (*jin-, jin-ē'si-əm; bot.*), U.S. spellings of gynaeceum.—*adj.* gynomonoe'cious, having hermaphrodite and female flowers on the same plant.—*ns.* gynomonoe'cism; gyn'ophore (Gr. *phoros*, carrying), an elongation of the receptacle of a flower carrying carpels only; gynostē'mium (Gr. *stēma*, stamen), a united gynaeceum and androecium, as the column of an orchid. [Gr. *gynē*, -*aikos*, woman.]

gynn(e)y, Shakespearian spellings of guinea(-hen).

gyp, *jip, n.* a college servant at Cambridge and Durham. [Perh. gypsy; or perh. obs. *gippo,* a short jacket, a varlet—obs. Fr. *jupeau.*]

gyp, *jip,* (*slang*) *n.* a swindle: a cheat.—*v.t.* to swindle:—*pr.p.* gypp'ing; *pa.t.* and *pa.p.* gypped.

gyp, *jip,* (*slang*) *n.* pain, torture.—give one gyp, to cause one pain, hurt one. [gee up.]

Gypsophila, *jip-sof'i-lə, n.* a hardy perennial akin to the pinks, but of more chickweed-like aspect. [Gr. *gypsos*, chalk, *phileein*, to love.]

gypsum, *jip'səm, gip'sam, n.* a soft mineral, hydrated calcium sulphate, source of plaster of Paris and other plasters.—*adjs.* gyp'seous; gypsif'erous, producing or containing gypsum.—gypsum block, a building block (usu. hollow) made of a gypsum plaster; (gypsum) plasterboard, a building board consisting of a core of gypsum or anhydrous gypsum plaster between two sheets of paper. [L.,—Gr. *gypsos*, chalk.]

gypsy, gipsy, *jip'si, n.* a Romany, a member of a wandering people of Indian origin: a cunning rogue: a dark-skinned person.—*adj.* of the gypsies: out-of-door: unconventional.—*v.i.* to live like a gypsy, camp out, or picnic.—*ns.* gyp'sydom, gyp'syism.—gypsy moth, a kind of tussock-moth; gyp'sywort, a labiate plant (Lycopus) with which gypsies were reputed to stain their skin. [Egyptian, because once thought to have come from Egypt.]

gyre, *jir, n.* a ring, circle: a circular or spiral turn or movement.—*v.t.* and *v.i.* (in Lewis Carroll pronounced *gīr*) to spin round, gyrate.—*adj.* gyr'al, gyr'ant.—*adv.* gyr'ally.—*v.i.* gyrate', to revolve, spin, whirl.—*adj.* gyr'ate, curved round in a coil.—*n.* gyrā'tion, a whirling motion: a whirl: a whorl.—*adjs.* gyrā'tional; gyr'atory, revolving: spinning round: of traffic, revolving in one-way lines; gyroid'al, spiral: rotatory; gyr'ose, having a folded surface: marked with wavy lines or ridges; gyr'ous.—*n.* gyr'us, a convoluted ridge between two grooves: a convolution of the brain.—*ns.* gyr'ōcar, a monorail car balanced by a gyroscope; gyrōcom'pass, a compass which indicates direction by the freely moving axis of a rapidly spinning wheel—owing to the earth's rotation, the axis assuming and maintaining a north and south direction; gyr'odyne, a rotorcraft in which the rotor(s) are power-driven for take-off, landing, etc., but unpowered for cruising flight.—*adj.* gyromagnet'ic, pertaining to magnetic properties of rotating electric charges.—*ns.* gyromagnet'ism; gyr'omancy (Gr. *manteiā*, divination), divination by walking in a circle and falling from giddiness; gyr'oplane, gyrocop'ter, a rotorcraft with unpowered rotor(s) on a vertical axis, e.g. an *autogiro*; gyr'oscope, an apparatus in which a heavy flywheel or top rotates at high speed, the turning movement resisting change of direction of axis, used as a toy, an educational device, a compass, etc.—*adj.* gyroscōp'ic.—*ns.* gyrostab'iliser, a gyroscopic device for countering the roll of a ship, etc.; gyr'ostat, a gyroscope fixed in a rigid case.—*adj.* **gyrostat'ic.**—*n.* **gyro'-vague** (L. *gyrovagus:*—*pl. gyrovagi*), a wandering monk of the Middle Ages.—**gyromagnetic compass,** a compass used in aircraft in which, in order to eliminate errors caused by changes of course and speed (greater in an aircraft than in a ship), a gyroscope is combined with a magnet system. [L. *gӯrus*—Gr. *gӯros*, a circle, ring.]

**gyre-carlin,** *gīr-kär'lin,* (*Scot.*) *n.* a witch. [O.N. *gӯgr,* a witch, ogress, and carline.]

**gyrfalcon.** See **gerfalcon.**

**gyron, giron,** *jī'ron,* (*her.*) *n.* two lines drawn from the edge of the escutcheon and meeting at right angles in the fesse-point.—*adj.* **gyronn'y.** [Fr. *giron*, older *geron*; O.H.G. *gēro*; cf. **gore** (2).]

**gyte,** *git,* (*Scot.*) *adj.* crazy, mad.

**gyte,** *git,* (*Scot.*) *n.* a child (*obs.*): a first-year boy at Edinburgh High School or Academy.—Also **gait, geit.** [get, offspring.]

**gytrash,** *gi'trash,* (*dial.*) *n.* a ghost.

**gyve,** *jiv,* earlier *gīv,* *v.t.* to fetter.—*n.* a shackle: a fetter. [M.E. *gives, gyves.*]

Neutral vowels in unaccented syllables: *el'ə-mənt*; for certain sounds in foreign words, see p. viii

# H

**H, h,** *āch,* sometimes spelt out **aitch,** *n.* the eighth letter in our alphabet, representing in Old English a guttural sound, gradually softened down to a spirant, and now often silent: in German notation = B natural (*mus.*): in mediaeval Roman notation = 200, H̄ = 200,000.—**H′-bomb** (**H** for *hydrogen*), hydrogen bomb.

**ha, hä,** *interj.* denoting surprise, joy, or grief, and, when repeated, laughter: often an involuntary expression of hesitation. [Spontaneous utterance.]

**ha′, hā, hə,** a shortened form of **have.**

**ha′, hö,** *n.* Scots form of **hall.**

**haaf, häf,** (*Orkney* and *Shetland*) *n.* a deep-sea fishing-ground.—**haaf′-fish′ing.** [O.N. *haf,* sea.]

**haanepoot.** See **hanepoot.**

**haar, här,** (*East Coast*) *n.* a raw sea-mist. [O.N *härr,* hoary; cf. **hoar.**]

**habanera,** (*h*)ä-bä-nā′ra, *n.* a Cuban Negro dance or dance-tune in 2-4 time. [*Habana* or Havana, in Cuba.]

**habeas-corpus,** hā′bi-as-kör′pəs, *n.* a writ to a jailer to produce a prisoner in person, and to state the reasons of detention. [L., lit. have the body (*ad subjiciendum,* to be brought up before the judge).]

**haberdasher,** hab′ər-dash-ər, *n.* a seller of smallwares, as ribbons, tape, etc.: a men's outfitter (*U.S.*).—*n.* **hab′erdashery,** a haberdasher's goods, business, or shop. [O.Fr. *hapertas;* origin unknown.]

**haberdine,** hab′ər-dēn, -dīn, -din, *n.* dried salt cod. [Old Du. *abberdaen,* also *labberdaen;* prob. from Le Labourd, or *Lapurdum,* Bayonne.]

**habergeon,** hab′ər-jən (*Milt.* hab-ûr′ji-on), *n.* a sleeveless mail-coat, orig. lighter than a hauberk. [O.Fr. *haubergeon,* dim. of *hauberc.*]

**habiliment,** hə-bil′i-mənt, *n.* attire (esp. in *pl.*).—*adjs.* **hab′ilable** (*Carlyle*), capable of being clothed: **habil′atory,** of clothes or dressing. [Fr. *habiller,* to dress—L. *habilis,* fit, ready—*habēre.*]

**habilitate,** hə-bil′i-tāt, *v.t.* to qualify: to equip or finance (as a mine): to attire.—*v.i.* to qualify, esp. as a German university lecturer (Ger. *habilitieren*).—*ns.* **habilitā′tion; habil′itātor.** [L.L. *habilitāre,* to enable—L. *habilis,* able.]

**habit,** hab′it, *n.* ordinary course of behaviour: tendency to perform certain actions: custom: accustomedness: familiarity: bodily constitution: characteristic mode of development: outward appearance: dress, esp. official or customary: a garment, esp. a riding-habit.—*v.t.* to dress: to inhabit (*arch.*).—*adj.* **hab′itable,** that may be dwelt in.—*ns.* **habitabil′ity, hab′itableness.**—*adv.* **hab′itably.**—*ns.* **hab′itant,** an inhabitant: (ab-ē-tä; Fr.) a native of Canada or Louisiana of French descent (*pl.* in this sense sometimes **habitans**); **habitā′tion,** act of inhabiting: a dwelling or residence: a lodge of a society; **hab′itaunce** (*Spens.*), dwelling-place.—*adj.* **habit′ual,** customary: usual: confirmed by habit.—*n.* one who has a habit: a habitual drunkard, drug-taker, frequenter, etc.—*adv.* **habit′ually.**—*v.t.* **habit′ūāte,** to accustom: to settle (in), or to frequent (*arch.*).—*ns.* **habitūā′tion,** act of accustoming: process of becoming accustomed: acquired tolerance for a drug, which thereby loses in effect: development of psychological, without physical, dependence on a drug; **hab′itūde,** constitution: characteristic condition: habit: relation (*obs.*): familiar acquaintance (*obs.*); **habitué** (*hab-it′ū-ā, a-bĕ-tü-ā*), a habitual frequenter.—**hab′it-cloth,** a light broadcloth.—*adj.* **hab′it-forming,** of a drug, such as a taker will find it difficult or impossible to give up using.—**hab′it-maker,** a maker of riding-habits.—**habit and repute** (*Scots law*), public knowledge that affords strong and generally conclusive evidence of fact. [L. *habitus,* state, dress—*habitāre,* to dwell.]

**habitat,** hab′i-tat, *n.* the normal abode or locality of an animal or plant (*biol.*): the physical environment of any community: the place where a person or thing can usually be found: a capsule on the sea bed, in which men can live for a prolonged period and from which they can explore their surroundings, the capsule being at the same pressure as the water around it. [L., (it) dwells.]

**hable, hā′bl,** (*Spens.*) *adj.* Same as **able.**

**haboob, hä-bōōb′,** *n.* a sand-storm. [Ar. *habūb.*]

**hachis, (h)ä-shē,** *n.* hash. [Fr.]

**hachure,** hash′ūr, ä-shür, *n.* a hill-shading line on a map. [Fr.]

**hacienda,** as-i-en′də, (*Sp. Amer.*) *n.* an estate or ranch: establishment: factory. [Sp.,—L. *facienda,* things to be done.]

**hack,** hak, *v.t.* to cut with rough blows: to chop or mangle: to notch: to roughen with a hammer: to kick the shins of.—*v.i.* to slash, chop: cough.—*n.* act of hacking: gash: a notch: chap in the skin: a kick on the shin.—*n.* **hack′ing.**—*adj.* short and interrupted, as a broken, troublesome cough.—**hack′-log,** a chopping-block; **hack′-saw,** a saw for metals. [Assumed O.E. *haccian,* found in composition *tō-haccian;* cf. Du. *hakken,* Ger. *hacken.*]

**hack,** hak, *n.* a horse (or formerly, still in U.S., a vehicle) kept for hire, esp. a poor one: an ordinary riding-horse: any person overworked on hire: a literary drudge: anything hackneyed (*obs.*).—*adj.* hired: mercenary: hackneyed.—*v.t.* to make a hack of: to use as a hack: to hackney.—*v.i.* to work as a hack: to journey on horseback.—**hack′ing-jacket, -coat,** a waisted jacket with slits in the skirt and flapped pockets on a slant; **hack′-work,** literary drudgery for publishers. [**hackney.**]

**hack,** hak, *n.* a grating or rack, as for feeding cattle: a bank for drying bricks. [O.E. *hæcc,* hæc, grating, hatch; cf. **hatch** (1) and **heck.**]

**hack,** hak, (*Shak.*) *v.i.* meaning unknown—poss. to take to the highway (or the street), or to have spurs hacked off.

**hackamore,** hak′ə-mōr, -mör, *n.* a bridle consisting of a single length of rope with a loop to serve instead of a bridle. [Sp. *jáquima.*]

**hackberry,** hak′ber-i, *n.* the hagberry: an American tree (Celtis) allied to the elm. [See also **hagberry.**]

**hackbolt,** hak′bōlt, *n.* the greater shearwater.—Also **hag′bolt, hag′den, hag′don, hag′down.** [Origin obscure.]

**hackbut, hak′but, hagbut, hag′,** *n.* an arquebus.—*n.* **hackbuteer′.** [O.Fr. *haquebute,* from O.Du. *hakebus;* see **arquebus.**]

**hackee, hak′ē,** *n.* the chipmunk. [Imit.]

**hackery,** hak′ər-i, *n.* an Indian bullock-cart. [Perh. Bengali *hăkărī,* shouting.]

**hackle, hak′l,** *n.* a comb for flax or hemp: a cock's neck feather: (in *pl.*) the hair of a dog's neck: (in *pl.*) hair, whiskers: an angler's fly made of a cock's hackle, or its frayed-out part.— *v.t.* to dress with a hackle.—*n.* hack′ler.—*adj.* hack′ly, rough and broken, as if hacked or chopped: jagged and rough (*min.*).—make one's hackles rise, to make one angry. [Cf. hatchel, heckle; Du. *hekel*; Ger. *hechel*; perh. partly from O.E. *hacele, hæcele*, cloak, vestment.]

hacklet, *hak′lit*, haglet, *hag′, n.* prob. the shearwater: the kittiwake. [Origin unknown.]

hackmatack, *hak′mə-tak, n.* an American larch. [Indian word.]

hackney, *hak′ni, n.* a horse for general use, esp. for hire: a horse with a high-stepping action, bred to draw light carriages: a person hired for drudgery (*obs.*).—*v.t.* to carry in a hackney-coach: to use overmuch: to make commonplace.—*adjs.* hack′ney, let out for hire; hack′-neyed, devoted to common use: trite: dulled by overmuch use.—hack′ney-carr′iage, -coach, a vehicle let out for hire; hack′ney-coach′man; hack′neyman, one who keeps hackney horses. [O.Fr. *haquenée*, an ambling nag: further history unknown.]

hac lege, *hak lē′jē, lā′ge*, (L.) with this law, under this condition.

hacqueton. Same as acton.

had, *had, pa.t.* and *pa.p.* of have.

had, *häd, höd, hud*, a Scots form of hold:—*pa.p.* hadden (*häd′n, hud′n*).

haddock, *had′ək, n.* a sea-fish of the cod family—(*Scot.*) hadd′ie. [M.E. *haddok*; ety. unknown.]

hade, *hād*, (*min.*) *n.* the angle between the plane of a fault, etc., and a vertical plane.—*v.i.* to incline from the vertical. [Origin obscure.]

Hades, *hā′dēz, n.* the underworld: the abode of the dead: hell. [Gr. *Aidēs, Haidēs*, the god of the underworld: the abode of the dead.]

hadith, *had′ith, hä-dēth′, n.* the body of traditions about Mohammed, supplementary to the Koran. [Ar. *hadīth*.]

had-I-wist, *had-ī-wist′*, (*obs.*) *n.* vain regret: remorse. [had I wist.]

hadj, hajj, *häj, n.* a Mohammedan pilgrimage to Mecca.—*n.* hadj′i, hajj′i (-*ē, -i*), one who has performed a hadj: a Christian who has visited Jerusalem. [Ar. *hajj*, pilgrimage.]

hadrome, *had′rōm*, (*bot.*) *n.* xylem. [Gr. *hadros*, thick.]

hadron, *häd′ron, n.* one of a class of subatomic particles, including baryons and mesons.

Hadrosaurus, *had-rō-sö′rəs, n.* a great Cretaceous dinosaur. [Gr. *hadros*, thick, *sauros*, a lizard.]

hae, *hā*, a form of have, esp. Scots.

haecceity, *hek-sē′i-ti, hēk-, n.* Duns Scotus's word for that element of existence on which individuality depends, hereness-and-nowness. [Lit. thisness, L. *haec*.]

haem-, *hēm-, hem-*, haemat-, haemo-, (in U.S. hem-, hemat-, hemo-), in composition, blood.— *n.* haem (also hem, heme), the pigment combined with the protein (globin) in haemoglobin.—*adj.* haemal, hemal (*hē′məl*), of the blood or blood-vessels: ventral—opp. to neural.—*ns.* Haeman′thus (Gr. *anthos*, flower), blood-flower, a S. African amaryllid; haematem′esis (Gr. *emesis*, vomiting), vomiting of blood from the stomach. —*adj.* haemat′ic, pertaining to blood.—*ns.* hae′matin, a brown substance containing ferric iron obtainable from oxyhaemoglobin or from dried blood; hae′matite, a valuable iron ore, Fe₂O₃, often blood-red, with red streak; hae′matoblast (Gr. *blastos*, a germ), a blood platelet.—*adj.* hae′matoid, bloodlike.—*ns.* hae′-matocele (Gr. *kēlē*, a tumour), a cavity containing blood; haematogen′esis, blood formation; haematol′ogist; haematol′ogy, the study of blood; haematol′ysis, haemolysis; haematō′ma, a swelling composed of blood effused into connective tissue; haematō′sis, the formation of

blood: conversion of venous into arterial blood; haematox′ylin, a dye got from logwood; Haematox′ylon (Gr. *xylon*, wood), the logwood genus; haematū′ria (Gr. *ouron*, urine), presence of blood in the urine; hae′min, the chloride of haematin; haemoco′nia (Gr. *kŏniā*, dust), blood-dust, small colourless granules in the blood; haemocy′anin (Gr. *kuanos*, blue), a blue respiratory pigment with functions similar to haemoglobin, in the blood of Crustacea and Mollusca; haemoglo′bin (L. *globus*, a ball), the red oxygen-carrying pigment in the red blood-corpuscles; haemol′ysis (Gr. *lysis*, dissolution), breaking up of red blood-corpuscles.—*adj.* haemolyt′ic, pertaining to haemolysis.—*ns.* hae′mony (prob. Gr. *haimōnios*, blood-red), a plant with sovereign properties against magic, etc., in Milton's *Comus*; haemophil′ia (Gr. *phileein*, to like), a constitutional tendency to excessive bleeding when any blood-vessel is even slightly injured; haemophil′iac, one who suffers from haemophilia; haemop′tysis (Gr. *ptysis*, a spitting), spitting of blood from the lungs; haemorrhage (*hem′ər-ij*; Gr. *haimorragiā*— *rhēgnynai*, to burst), a discharge of blood from the blood-vessels.—*adj.* haemorrhagic (-*raj′*).— *n.* haemorrhoid (*hem′ər-oid*; Gr. *haimorrois, -idos*—*rheein*, to flow), dilatation of a vein about the anus—usu. in *pl.* piles.—*adj.* haemorrhoid′al. —*n.* hae′mostat, an instrument for stopping bleeding.—*n.* and *adj.* haemostat′ic (Gr. *statikos*, causing to stand), styptic. [Gr. *haima, -atos*, blood.]

haet, ha′it, *hāt*, (*Scot.*) *n.* a whit. [From the phrase *deil ha′ it*, devil have it.]

haff, *haf*, (Ger.) a lagoon separated from the sea by a long sandbar.

haffet, haffit, *haf′, häf′it*, (*Scot.*) *n.* the side of the head: the temple: locks of hair on the temple. [half-head; cf. O.E. *healf-hēafod*, the sinciput.]

hafflin, *häf′lin* (*Scot.*). Same as halfling (see under half).

hafnium, *haf′ni-əm, n.* an element (Hf; at. numb. 72) discovered in 1922 by Profs. Coster and Hevesy of Copenhagen. [L. *Hafnia*, Copenhagen.]

haft, *häft, n.* a handle: a winged leaf-stalk.—*v.t.* to set in a haft: to establish firmly. [O.E. *hæft*; Ger. *heft*.]

hag, *hag, n.* an ugly old woman, originally a witch: one of the round-mouths, allied to the lamprey (also hag′fish).—*adjs.* hagg′ed, haglike: haggard; hagg′ish.—*adv.* hagg′ishly.—*adj.* hag′-ridd′en, ridden by witches, as a horse: troubled by nightmare: obsessed: troubled.—*v.t.* hag′-ride.—hag′-seed, a witch's offspring; hag′-ta′per, the great mullein; hag′-weed, the common broom-plant—a broomstick being a witch's supposed mode of transport. [Perh. O.E. *hægtesse*, a witch; cf. Ger. *hexe*.]

hag, hag, (*Scot.*) *v.t.* and *v.i.* to hack, hew. [O.N. *höggva*.]

hag, hagg, *hag*, (*Scot.*) *n.* any broken ground in a moss or bog: a place from which peat has been dug: a pool or hole in a bog: a relatively high and firm place in a bog: the rough overhanging edge of a peat-hole or stream-bank: brushwood to be cut down. [O.N. *högg*, a gash, ravine, a cutting of trees.]

hagberry, *hag′ber-i*, hackberry, *hak′, n.* the bird-cherry: the American hackberry. [Cf. O.N. *heggr*.]

hagbolt, hagden, hagdon, hagdown, *hag′dən*. See hackbolt.

hagbut. See hackbut.

hagg. See hag (3).

Haggada, *hä-gä′da, n.* a free Rabbinical homiletical commentary on the whole Old Testament, forming, with the Halachah, the Midrash: the Passover ritual.—Also Hagga′dah, Aga′dah.—

*adjs.* **Haggad'ic, Haggadist'ic.**—*n.* **Hagga'dist.** [Heb.]

**haggard,** *hag'ərd, n.* an untamed hawk, or one caught when adult, esp. a female.—*adj.* untamed: intractable: lean: hollow-eyed.—*adv.* **hagg'ardly.** [O.Fr. *hagard*.]

**haggis,** *hag'is, n.* a Scottish dish made of the heart, lungs, and liver of a sheep, calf, etc., chopped up with suet, onions, oatmeal, etc., seasoned and boiled in a sheep's stomach-bag. [Ety. unknown.]

**haggle,** *hag'l, v.t.* to cut unskilfully: to mangle.— *v.i.* to bargain contentiously or wranglingly: to stick at trifles: to cavil.—*n.* **hagg'ler.** [Freq. of **hag,** at least in part.]

**hagi-,** *hag'i-* (sometimes *haj'i-*), in composition, holy: saint.—*ns.* **hag'iarchy,** rule or order of saints or holy persons; **hagioc'racy** (Gr. *kratos,* power), government by holy ones.—*n.pl.* **Hagiog'rapha,** those books which with the Law and the Prophets make up the Old Testament.— *ns.* **hagiog'rapher,** a writer of the Hagiographa: a sacred writer: a writer of saints' lives.—*adjs.* **hagiograph'ic, -al.**—*ns.* **hagiog'raphist; hagiog'- raphy; hagiol'ater,** a worshipper of saints; **hagiol'atry** (Gr. *latreiā,* worship).—*adjs.* **hagiolog'ic, -al.**—*ns.* **hagiol'ogist,** a writer of, or one versed in, saints' legends; **hagiol'ogy; hag'ioscope,** a squint in a church, giving a view of the high altar.—*adj.* **hagioscop'ic.** [Gr. *hagios,* holy.]

**haglet.** Same as **hacklet.**

**hah, hah,** *interj.* Same as **ha.**

**ha-ha,** *hä-hä, interj.* in representation of a laugh. —*n.* the sound of laughter.—*v.i.* to laugh. [Imit.]

**ha-ha,** *hä'hä,* **haw-haw,** *hö'hö, n.* a sunk fence. [Fr. *haha*.]

**haick.** See **haik.**

**haiduk, heyduck,** *hi'dōōk, n.* a brigand: a guer- rilla warrior: a liveried servant. [Hung. *hajduk,* pl. of *hajdú*.]

**haik, haick, haique, hyke,** *hīk, n.* an oblong cloth worn by Arabs on head and body. [Ar. *hayk*.]

**haikai,** *hī'kī, n.* an informal type of prose or verse, developed in Japan in the 17th cent. [Jap.]

**Haikh,** *hīhh, n.* and *adj.* Armenian. [Armenian.]

**haiku,** *hī'kōō, n.* a Japanese poem in three lines of 5, 7, 5 syllables.—Also **hokk'u,** *hō'kōō* (orig. the first verse of a linked verse series). [From Jap.]

**hail,** *hāl, n.* health (*obs.*): a call from a distance: a greeting: earshot.—*adj.* (*obs.*) sound, hale.— *v.t.* to greet: to address, accost: to call to from a distance: to summon to stop or come.—*interj.* of greeting or salutation.—*adj.* **hail'-fellow (-well- met'),** readily friendly and familiar.—Also *n.* and *adv.*—**hail from,** to come from. [O.N. *heill,* health, sound; cf. **hale, heal.**]

**hail,** *hāl, n.* frozen rain or grains of ice falling from the clouds: a shower of hail or the like.— *v.i.* and *v.t.* to shower hail: to shower vigorously or abundantly.—*adj.* **hail'y.**—**hail'shot,** small shot that scatters like hail; **hail'stone,** a ball of hail; **hail'-storm.** [O.E. *hægl* (*hagol*); Ger. *hagel*.]

**hail,** *hāl,* (*Scot.*) *n.* in ball-games, a goal: a score. —*v.t.* to score (a goal): to put into the goal. [App. from **hail** (1), from the shout with which the player claimed a goal.]

**hain,** *hān,* (*Scot.*) *v.t.* to save, preserve: to spare. —*adj.* **hained.**—*n.* **hain'ing,** an enclosure. [O.N. *hegna,* to enclose, protect; cf. Sw. *hägna;* Dan. *hegne*.]

**hainch,** *hänsh, hänch,* Scots form of **haunch.**

**haique.** See **haik.**

**hair,** *hār, n.* a filament growing from the skin of an animal: an outgrowth of the epidermis of a plant: a fibre: a mass or aggregate of hairs, esp. that covering the human head: anything very small and fine: a hair's-breadth: type or character (*obs.*): a locking spring or other safety

contrivance in a firearm.—*v.t.* to free from hair: to furnish with hair.—*n.* **hair'iness.**—*adjs.* **hair'less; hair'y,** of or like hair: covered with hair.—**hair'-ball,** a concretion of hair in the stomach; **hair'bell** (same as **harebell**); **hair('s)'- breadth,** the breadth of a hair: a minute distance. —*adj.* extremely close or narrow.—**hair'-brush,** a brush for the hair; **hair'cloth,** cloth made wholly or partly of hair; **hair'cut,** a cutting of the hair; **hair'-do** (*coll.*), act or style of hairdressing; **hair'dresser,** one whose occupation is the cutting and dressing of hair: a barber; **hair'dressing,** a dressing of the hair; **hair'-eel,** a hair-worm; **hair'-grass,** a genus (Aira) of coarse grasses (perh. only a modification of the generic name); **hair'line,** a line made of hair: a very fine line in writing, type, etc.: a finely striped cloth: the edge of the hair on the forehead.—*adj.* (of e.g. a crack) very thin: also *fig.*—**hair'-net,** a net for confining a woman's hair; **hair'-oil,** a scented oil for dressing the hair; **hair'-pen'cil,** a fine paint-brush; **hair'-piece,** a length of false hair, or a wig covering only part of the head; **hair'pin,** a bent wire or the like used for fastening up the hair.—*adj.* narrowly U-shaped, as a bend on a road.—**hair'-powd'er,** powdered starch formerly dusted on the hair or wig; **hair'-rais'er,** a tale of terror.—*adj.* **hair'-rais'ing.**—**hair-restor'er,** a preparation claiming to make hair grow on bald places; **hair'-seal,** a sea-lion, or eared seal with coarse hair only; **hair'-shirt,** a penitent's gar- ment of haircloth: an intimate or secret afflic- tion (*fig.*); **hair'-space,** the thinnest metal space used by compositors; **hair'-splitt'er,** a maker of over-fine distinctions; **hair'-splitt'ing; hair'- spring,** a slender spring regulating a watch balance; **hair'streak,** a butterfly (Thecla, etc.) with fine white band under the wing; **hair'- stroke,** a hairline in penmanship; **hair'-tail,** a fish of the family Trichiuridae, with whiplike tail; **hair'-trigg'er,** a trigger that releases the hair of a gun; **hair'-wave,** a wavelike appearance artificially given to hair; **hair'-waver** **hair'- waving;** **hair'-work,** work done or something made with hair, esp. human; **hair'-worm,** a worm, like a horse-hair, which when young lives in the bodies of insects.—**against the hair** (*arch.*), against the grain: contrary to inclination; **a hair of the dog that bit him,** a smaller dose of that which caused the trouble: a morning glass after a night's debauch—a homoeopathic dose; **by the short hairs,** in a powerless position, at one's mercy; **get in one's hair,** to become a source of irritation; **keep one's hair on** (*coll.*), to keep cool; **let one's hair down,** to forget reserve and speak or behave freely; **lose one's hair,** to grow angry; **make one's hair curl,** to shock one extremely; **make one's hair stand on end,** to cause one great astonishment or fright; **not to turn a hair,** (of a horse) to show no sweat: not to be ruffled or disturbed; **put up the hair,** to dress the hair up on the head instead of wearing it hanging—once the mark of passage from girl- hood to womanhood; **split hairs,** to make super- fine distinctions; **tear one's hair,** to display frenzied grief or (*coll.*) great irritation; **to a hair, to the turn of a hair,** exactly, with perfect nicety. [O.E. *hǣr,* Ger., Du., and Dan. *haar,* etc.: vowel perh. influenced by Fr. *haire,* a hair-shirt.]

**hairst,** *härst,* a Scottish form of **harvest.**— **hairst-rig',** a harvest-field, or a section of it, formerly cut in competition.

**haith,** *hāth,* (*Scot.*) *interj.* by my faith. [faith.]

**hajj, hajji.** See **hadj, hadji.**

**haka,** *hä'kä, n.* a Maori ceremonial war-dance: a similar dance performed by New Zealanders, e.g. before a rugby game.

**hakam,** *häk'äm, n.* a sage: a rabbinical commen- tator, esp. one during the first two cents. A.D. [Heb. *hākhām,* wise.]

hake, *hāk, n.* a gadoid fish resembling the cod. [Prob. Scand.; cf. Norw. *hake-fisk*, lit. hookfish.]

hakenkreuz, *hä'kən-kroits, n.* the swastika. [Ger., hook-cross.]

hakim, *hä-kēm', n.* a physician. [Ar. *hakim.*]

hakim, *hä'kim, n.* a judge, governor, or official in Pakistan. [Ar. *hakim.*]

Halachah, Halakah, Halacha, *hä-lä'hhä, -kä, n.* the legal element in the Midrash.—*adj.* Halach'ic. [Heb.,—*hālak*, to walk.]

halal, *häl-äl', v.t.* to slaughter according to Mohammedan law.—*n.* an animal that may lawfully be eaten as so slaughtered. [Ar. *halāl*, lawful.]

halation, *hə-, ha-lā'shən, n.* blurring in a photograph by reflection and dispersion of light: a bright area around a bright spot on a fluorescent screen. [halo.]

halberd, *hal'bərd, n.* an axe-like weapon with a hook or pick on its back, and a long shaft, used in the 15th and 16th centuries, in the 18th century denoting the rank of sergeant.—Also hal'bert.—*n.* halberdier (*-dēr'*), one armed with a halberd. [O.Fr. *halebard*—M.H.G. *helmbarde* (Ger. *hellebarde*)—*halm*, handle, or *helm*, helmet; O.H.G. *barta* (Ger. *barte*), axe.]

halbstarker, *halp'shtärk'ər,* (Ger.) a juvenile delinquent.

halcyon, *hal'si-ən, n.* the kingfisher, once believed to make a floating nest on the sea, which remained calm during hatching.—*adj.* calm: peaceful: happy.—halcyon days, a time of peace and happiness. [L. *halcyōn*—Gr. *alkyōn*, fancifully changed to *halkyōn* as if from *hals*, sea, *kyōn*, conceiving.]

hale, *hāl, adj.* healthy: robust: sound of body: whole (*Scot.*; also *n.*, with definite article).—*n.* hayle (*Spens.*), welfare.—*n.* hale'ness. [Northern from O.E. *hāl*; see whole; cf. hail (1), heal.]

hale, *hāl, v.t.* to drag. [O.Fr. *haler*; Germanic in origin.]

half, *häf, n.* one of two equal parts: a half-year, term: a half-back: a halved hole in golf:—*pl.* halves, *hävz.*—*adj.* having or consisting of one of two equal parts: being in part: incomplete, as measures.—*adv.* to the extent of one-half: in part: imperfectly.—*adj.* half'en (*Spens.*), half.—*adv.* half'endeale (*Spens.*), half.—*ns.* half'lin, half'ling (*Scot.*), half-grown person, between boy and man: half a silver penny.—*adj.* halfgrown.—*adv.* half'lin(g)s (*Scot.*), half: partially.—*adj.* half-grown.—half'-and-half, a mixture of two things in equal proportions, esp. beer or porter and ale.—*adj.* and *adv.* in the proportion of one to one, or approximately: in part one thing, in part another.—half'-ape, a lemur; half'-back, in football, a player or position directly behind the forwards—in Rugby (*scrum half* and *stand-off* half), a link between forwards and three-quarters.—*adj.* half'-baked, underdone: incomplete: crude: immature: halfwitted.—*v.t.* half'-baptise', -ize', to baptise privately and hastily.—half'-beak, a fish (Hyporhynchus, etc.) with spear-like under jaw; half'bind'ing, a bookbinding with only backs and corners of leather or the like; half'-blood, relation between those who have only one parent in common: a half-breed.—*adj.* half'-blood'ed.—half'-blue', at Oxford and Cambridge, a substitute for a full blue, or the colours awarded him; half'-board (*naut.*), a manoeuvre by which a sailing-ship gains distance to windward by luffing up into the wind; half'-boot, a boot reaching halfway to the knee.—*adjs.* half'-bound, bound in half-binding; half'-bred, poorly bred or trained: mongrel.—half'-breed, one of mixed breed (esp. a mixture of white and coloured races); half'-brother, half'-sister, a brother or sister by one parent only; half'-cap

(*Shak.*), a cap only partly taken off, a slight salute; half'-caste, a half-breed, esp. a Eurasian.—*adj.* half'-checked (*Shak.*), with reins attached halfway up the side-piece of the bit, giving little leverage.—half'-cheek (*Shak.*), a face in profile; half'-close (*mus.*), an imperfect cadence; half'-cock', the position of the cock of a gun drawn back halfway and retained by the first notch: a stroke made by playing neither forward nor back (*cricket*).—*adv.* in that position.—*adj.* half'-cocked'.—half'-crown', a coin worth half-a-crown', or two shillings and sixpence, from 1970 no longer legal tender: a sum of money equivalent to this; half'-doll'ar, an American coin worth 50 cents.—Also *adjs.*—*adj.* half'-done, partly done: partly cooked.—half'-door, the lower part of a divided door.—*n.* and *adj.* half'-doz'en, six.—*adj.* halfe'-hors'y (*Spens.*), of the Centaurs, partly of the nature of horses.—half'-face, profile.—*adjs.* half'-faced (*Shak.*), showing only part of the face: thin-faced; half'-hard'y, able to grow in the open air except in winter; half'-heart'ed, lacking in zeal.—*adv.* half'-heart'edly.—half'-heart'edness; half'-hitch, a simple knot tied around an object; half'-hol'iday, half of a working day for recreation; half'-kir'tle, a kind of jacket worn by women in 16th and 17th cent.; half'-landing, small landing at the bend of a staircase; half'-length, portrait showing the upper part of the body.—*adj.* of half the whole or ordinary length.—half'-life, the period of time in which activity of a radioactive substance falls to half its original value; half'-light, dim light: twilight; half'-loaf', a loaf of half the standard weight; half'-mast, the position of a flag partly lowered, in respect for the dead or in signal of distress.—Also *adv.* and *v.t.*—half'-meas'ure, any means inadequate for the end proposed; half'-moon, the moon at the quarters when half the disk is illuminated: anything semicircular; half'-mourn'ing, mourning attire less than deep or full mourning: the condition of having one black eye (*slang*); half'-nel'son, a hold in wrestling, one arm under arm, hand on back of the neck: a disabling restraint (*fig.*); half'-note (*mus.*), a minim; half'-one' (*golf*), a handicap of one stroke every second hole; half'-pay', reduced pay, as of an officer not on active service.—*adj.* half'-pay, on half-pay.—halfpenny (*hāp'ni*), a coin worth half a penny: its value: anything very small (*Shak.*): —*pl.* halfpence, *hā'pəns*, also half-pennies, *hāp'niz*).—*adj.* valued at a halfpenny.—halfpennyworth (*hāp'ni-wûrth*—also hap'orth, *hāp'ərth*), as much as is sold for a halfpenny or is worth a halfpenny: half'-pike, a short-shafted pike: a spontoon; half'-pint (*slang*), a very small person; half'-plate (see plate); half'-pound, half a pound.—*adj.* weighing half a pound.—half'-pound'er, a fish or other thing weighing half a pound: a gun that throws a half-pound shot; half'-price, a charge reduced to half.—*adj.* and *adv.* at half the usual price.—half'-round', a semicircle.—*adj.* (*Milt.*) semicircular.—half'-roy'al, a kind of millboard.—*adj.* and *adv.* half'-seas-o'ver, halfway across the sea: half-drunk.—half'-shell, one shell or valve of a bivalve; half'-shift', a position of the hand in violin-playing giving notes a semitone above the open-string position; half'-sove'reign, a gold coin worth half-a-sove'reign, or ten shillings.—*adj.* half'-starved, very inadequately fed.—half'-sword, fighting within half a sword's length: close fight.—half'-term, about the middle of a term.—half'-text, handwriting half the size of text.—Also *adj.*—half'-tide, the stage midway between flood and ebb.—*adj.* uncovered at half-tide.—*adj.* half'-tim'bered, built of a timber frame, with spaces filled in.—half'-time', half of full or whole time: the middle of the whole time: a short break halfway through a game (*sport*): in industry, half the time usually worked.—*adj.* half′time, at or for half-time.—half′-tim′er, one who works half the full time; half′-tint, intermediate tone, between light and dark; half′-ti′tle, a short title preceding the title page or before a section of a book.—*adj.* half′-tone, representing light and shade photographically by dots of different sizes.—*n.* (*mus.*) a semitone.—half′-track, a motor vehicle with wheels in front and caterpillar tracks behind.—Also *adj.*—half′-truth, a belief containing an element of truth: a statement conveying only part of the truth; half′-voll′ey (see volley).—*adv.* halfway′ (sometimes *häf′wä*), midway: at half the distance: imperfectly.—*adj.* half′way, equidistant from two points.—half′-wit, a would-be wit (*obs.*): an idiot.—*adj.* half′-witt′ed, mentally defective.—half′-year, half of a year, six months.—*adj.* half′year′ly, occurring or appearing every half-year.—*adv.* twice a year.—*n.* a half-yearly publication.—at half-cock, only partially prepared; by half, by a long way; cry halves, to claim half; go halves, to share equally; not half (*slang*), not moderately: not even half: not at all: very much, exceedingly. [O.E. (Anglian) *half* (W.S. *healf*), side, half; cf. Ger. *halb*; Dan. *halv*.]

halfa, alfa, (*h*)*al′fə*, *n.* N. African esparto-grass. [Ar. *halfā*.]

halfpace, *häf′pās*, *n.* a landing or broad step: a raised part of a floor. [O.Fr. *halt* (Fr. *haut*), high, *pas*, step.]

halibut, *hal′i-bət*, *n.* a large flatfish, more elongated than flounder or turbot.—Also hol′ibut. [App. holy butt, as much eaten on holy days; see holy, butt (5); cf. Du. *heilbot*, Ger. *heilbutt*.]

halicore, *hal-ik′o-rē*, *n.* the dugong. [Gr. *hals*, sea, *korē*, girl.]

halide, *hal′id*, *n.* a compound of a halogen with a metal or radical—a chloride, bromide, etc. [Gr. *hals*, salt.]

halidom, *hal′i-dəm*, (*arch.*) *n.* holiness: a holy place or thing—esp. in an oath. [O.E. *hāligdōm* —*hālig*, holy.]

halieutic, *hal-i-ū′tik*, *adj.* pertaining to fishing.—*n.* halieu′tics, the art of fishing: a treatise thereon. [Gr. *halieutikos*—*halieus*, fisher—*hals*, sea.]

halimot(e), *hal′i-mōt*, *n.* an erroneous form of hall-moot (as if a holy or church court).

Haliotis, *hal-i-ō′tis*, *n.* earshell or ormer, a genus of gasteropods with ear-shaped shell with perforations, belonging to the family Haliōt′idae. [Gr. *hals*, sea, *ous*, *ōtos*, ear.]

halite, *hal′it*, *n.* rock-salt. [Gr. *hals*, salt.]

halitus, *hal′i-təs*, *n.* a vapour.—*n.* halitō′sis, foul breath.—*adj.* hal′itous, vaporous. [L.]

hall, *höl*, *n.* the main room in a great house: a building containing such a room: a manor-house: the main building of a college: in some cases the college itself: an unendowed college: a licensed residence for students: a college dining-room: hence, the dinner itself: a place for special professional education, or the conferring of diplomas, licences, etc.: the head-quarters of a guild, society, etc.: a servants' dining-room and sitting-room (*servants' hall*): a building or large chamber for meetings, concerts, exhibitions, etc.: a large room entered immediately by the front door of a house: a passage or lobby at the entrance of a house: a clear space (*arch.*).—hall′-bed′room (*U.S.*), a bedroom over an entrance-hall; hall′-door, front-door; hall′mark, the authorised stamp impressed on gold or silver articles at Goldsmiths' Hall or other place of assaying, indicating date, maker, fineness of metal, etc.: any mark of authenticity or good quality.—*v.t.* to stamp with such a mark.—hall′-moot, the court of the lord of a manor: the court of a guild; hall′stand, a tall piece of furniture on which hats,

coats and umbrellas can be left; hall′way (*U.S.*), an entrance hall.—a hall, a hall (*arch.*), a cry at a masque for room for the dance, etc.; bachelor's hall, a place free from the restraining presence of a wife; Liberty Hall, a place where everyone may do as he pleases; the halls, music-halls. [O.E. hall (*heall*); Du. *hal*, O.N. *höll*, etc.]

hallal. Same as halal.

hallali, *hal′ə-lē*, *n.* a bugle-call.

hallaloo, *hal-ə-lōō′*, (*Fielding*) *n.* halloo.

hallan, *häl′ən*, (*Scot.*) *n.* a partition or screen between the door and fireplace in a cottage.—hallan-shäk′er (or -shäk′ər), a sturdy beggar. [Perh. hall.]

hälleflinta, *hel′ə-flin-ta*, *n.* a very compact rock composed of minute particles of quartz and feldspar. [Sw., hornstone.]

hallelujah, halleluiah, *hal-ə-lōō′yə*, *n.* and *interj.* the exclamation 'Praise Jehovah': a song of praise to God: a musical composition based on the word.—Also alleluia. [Heb. *hallelū*, praise ye, and *Jáh*, Jehovah.]

halliard. See halyard.

halling, *hal′ing*, *höl′ing*, *n.* a Norwegian country dance in 2-4 time, or its tune. [Perh. *Hallingdal*, N.W. of Oslo.]

hallion, hallian, hallyon, *hal′yən*, *n.* a lout: a lazy rascal. [Origin unknown.]

hallo, halloa, *hə-lō′*, *hu-lō′*, *interj.* expressing surprise, discovery, becoming aware: used also in greeting, accosting, calling attention.—*n.* a call of hallo.—*v.i.* to call hallo.—Also hello, hullo. [Imit.]

halloo, *hə-lōō′*, *n.* a cry to urge on a chase or to call attention.—*v.i.* to cry dogs on: to raise an outcry.—*v.t.* to encourage with halloos: to hunt with halloos.—don't halloo till you're out of the wood, keep quiet till you are sure you are safe. [Imit.]

hallow, *hal′ō*, *v.t.* to make holy: to consecrate (*arch*): to reverence.—*n.* (*obs.*) a saint.—*ns.* Hallowe′en′, (esp. *Scot.*) the eve of, or the evening before, All Hallows; Hall′owmas, the feast of All Hallows or All Saints, 1st November. [O.E. *hālgian*, to hallow, *hālga*, a saint—*hālig*, holy.]

halloysite, *hal-oiz′it*, *n.* a clayey mineral, a hydrated aluminium silicate. [Omalius d'*Halloy* (1783-1875), Belgian geologist.]

Hallstatt, *häl′shtät*, *adj.* of the transition from the Bronze to the Iron Age. [From finds at *Hallstatt* in upper Austria.]

hallucinate, *həl-ōō′sin-āt*, *həl-ū′*, *v.t.* to affect with hallucination.—*v.i.* to experience hallucination.—*n.* hallucinā′tion, a perception without objective reality: loosely, delusion.—*adjs.* hallu′-cinative, hallu′cinatory.—*n.* hallu′cinogen, a drug producing hallucinatory sensations.—*adj.* hallu-cinogen′ic, causing hallucinations.—*n.* hallucino′sis, a mental disorder characterised by the repeated occurrence of hallucinations. [L. *hallūcinārī* (better *ālūcinārī*), *-ātus*, to wander in the mind.]

hallux, *hal′uks*, *n.* the innermost digit of the hind-limb: the great toe: a bird's hind-toe:—*pl.* halluces (*-ū′sēz*). [Wrong form of L. (*h*)*allex*, *-icis*.]

halm, *häm*. Same as haulm.

halma, *hal′ma*, *n.* in the Greek pentathlon, a long jump with weights in the hands (*hist.*): a game played on a board of 256 squares, in which the men move by jumps. [Gr., a jump.]

halo, *hā′lō*, *n.* a ring of light or colour, esp. one round the sun or moon caused by refraction by ice-crystals, or one round the head of a holy person: an ideal or sentimental glory or glamour attaching to anything:—*pl.* hā′loes, hā′los.—*v.t.* to surround with a halo (*lit.* and *fig.*):—*pa.p.* ha′loed, ha′lo'd. [Gr. *halōs*, a threshing-floor, disk, halo.]

**halogen,** etc. See haloid.

**haloid,** *hal'oid, n.* a halide.—*adj.* having the composition of a halide.—*n.* **halogen** (*hal'ə-jen*), of certain elements in the seventh group of the periodic table, fluorine, chlorine, bromine, iodine, and astatine (the first four defined in the 19th cent. as forming salts by direct union with metals; astatine discovered in 1940).—*v.t.* **halogenate** (*-oj'*), to combine with a halogen.—*adjs.* **halog'enous; hal'ophile** (*-fil, -fīl*; Gr. *phileein*, to like), **haloph'ilous,** tolerant of salt: capable of living in salt water.—*ns.* **haloph'ily,** adaptation to life in the presence of much salt; **halophyte** (*hal'ō-fīt*; Gr. *phyton,* a plant), a plant adapted to life in soil or water containing much salt.—*adj.* **halophytic** (*-fit'*).—*n.* **hal'ōthane,** a general, inhalation anaesthetic known proprietarily as Fluothane. [Gr. *hals,* salt.]

**Haloragis,** *hal-ə-rā'jis, n.* sea-berry, an Australasian genus of plants giving name to the family **Haloragidā'ceae,** a reduced offshoot of the evening primrose family, including mare's-tail and water milfoil. [Gr. *hals,* sea, *rhāx, rhāgos,* a berry.]

**halothane.** See haloid.

**halse,** *höls, Scot.* and *Northern* **hause, hawse,** *hös,* (*obs.* or *dial.) n.* the neck: the throat: a pass, defile, or connecting ridge.—*v.t.* to embrace:— *pa.t.* **halsed** (*Spens.*), **haulst.**—**hause'-bane** (*Scot.*), collar-bone; **hause'-lock** (*Scot.*), the wool of a sheep's neck. [O.E. *hals* (*heals*), neck; Ger. *hals.*]

**halse,** *häls, hös,* (*obs.) v.t.* to salute, greet. [O.E. *halsian.*]

**halser,** *höz'ər, n.* See hawser.

**halt,** *hölt, v.i.* to come to a standstill: to make a temporary stop.—*v.t.* to cause to stop.—*n.* a standstill: a stopping-place: a railway station not fully equipped. [Ger. *halt,* stoppage.]

**halt,** *hölt, v.i.* to be lame, to limp (*arch.*): to walk unsteadily: to vacillate: to proceed lamely or imperfectly, to be at fault, as in logic, rhythm, etc.—*adj.* (*arch.*) lame, crippled, limping.—*n.* a limp (*arch.*): foot-rot (*dial.*): an impediment in speech (*Scot.*).—*n.* and *adj.* **halt'ing.**—*adv.* **halt'ingly.** [O.E. *halt* (*healt*); Dan. *halt.*]

**halter,** *hölt'ər, n.* a rope for holding and leading an animal, or for hanging criminals: a woman's backless bodice held in place by straps round the neck and across the back.—*v.t.* to put a halter on. —**halter neck,** a dress neckline fashioned on the style of a halter. [O.E. *hælftre;* Ger. *halfter.*]

**halteres,** *hal-tēr'ēz, n.pl.* the rudimentary hindwings of flies. [Gr. *haltērēs,* dumb-bells held by jumpers—*hallesthai,* to jump.]

**halva(h), halavah,** *häl'va, n.* a sweetmeat, orig. Turkish, containing sesame seeds, honey, etc. [Yiddish *halva;* ult. from Ar.]

**halve,** *häv, v.t.* to divide in half: in golf, to draw: in carpentry, to join by cutting away half the thickness of each.—*n.* **halv'er,** one who halves: a half-share.—*interj.* **halv'ers,** used in claiming half a find. [**half.**]

**halyard, halliard,** *hal'yərd, n.* a rope or purchase for hoisting or lowering a sail, yard, or flag. [For *halier*—hale, by association with **yard.**]

**ham,** *ham, n.* the back of the thigh or hock: the thigh of an animal, esp. of a hog salted and dried.—*adjs.* **hamm'y; ham'-fist'ed, ham'-hand'ed,** clumsy. [O.E. *hamm;* cf. dial. Ger. *hamme.*]

**ham,** *ham,* (*coll.) n.* actor who rants and overacts: overacting: part that lends itself to this: inexpert boxer: an amateur, esp. an amateur radio operator.—Also *adj.*—*v.i.* to overact. [Prob. **hamfatter.**]

**hamadryad,** *ham-ə-drī'ad, n.* a wood-nymph who died with the tree in which she dwelt: a large poisonous Indian snake, *Naja hamadryas:* a large baboon of Abyssinia:—*pl.* **hamadry'ads,**

**hamadry'ades** (*-ēz*). [Gr. *hamadryas—hama,* together, *drȳs,* (oak) tree.]

**Hamamelis,** *ham-ə-mē'lis, n.* the American witch-hazel genus, giving name to a family, **Hamamelidā'ceae,** akin to the planes. [Gr. *hamamēlis, medlar—hama,* together with, *mēlon,* an apple.]

**hamarthritis,** *ham-är-thrī'tis, n.* gout in all the joints. [Gr. *hama,* together, *arthrītis,* gout.]

**hamartia,** *ha-mär'tē-a, n.* in a literary work, the flaw or defect in the character of the hero which leads to his downfall (orig. and esp. in ancient Greek tragedy; see Aristotle's *Poetics*).—*n.* **hamartiol'ogy,** that section of theology which treats of sin. [Gr. *hamartiā,* failure, error of judgment, sin.]

**hamate,** *hā'māt, adj.* hooked. [L. *hāmātus—hāmus,* hook.]

**hamble,** *ham'bl, v.t.* to mutilate, make useless for hunting (by cutting the balls of a dog's feet).— *v.i.* to limp, to stumble (*dial.*). [O.E. *hamelian.*]

**Hamburg, Hamburgh,** *ham'bûrg, 'b(ə)-rə, n.* a black variety of grape (often *black Hamburg*): a small blue-legged domestic fowl.—*n.* **ham'-burg(h)er,** Hamburg steak, finely chopped meat: this shaped into a round flat cake, fried, and put into a bread roll: a large sausage. [*Hamburg* in Germany.]

**hame,** *hām, n.* one of the two curved bars of a draught-horse's collar. [Cf. Du. *haam,* L.G. *ham.*]

**hame,** *hām,* Scots form of **home.**—*adv.* **hame'-with,** homewards.

**hamesucken,** *hām'suk-n,* (*Scots law) n.* the assaulting of a man in his own house. [O.E. *hāmsōcn—hām,* home, *sōcn,* seeking, attack; cf. Ger. *heimsuchung.*]

**hamfatter,** *ham'fat-ər, n.* a third-rate minstrel, variety artist, actor.—*v.t.* and *v.i.* to act badly or ineffectively. [Perh. from an old Negro minstrel song, The *Hamfat* Man.]

**Hamiltonian,** *ham-il-tō'ni-ən, adj.* pertaining to James *Hamilton* (1769-1829), or his method of teaching languages without grammar, to the philosopher Sir William *Hamilton* (1788-1856), to Sir William Rowan *Hamilton* (1805-65), Irish mathematician, or other of the name.

**Hamite,** *ham'it, n.* a descendant or supposed descendant of *Ham,* son of Noah: a member of a dark-brown long-headed race of N.E. Africa (Galla, Hadendoa, etc.), sometimes understood more widely to cover much of N. Africa: a speaker of any language of a N. African family distantly related to Semitic (ancient Egyptian, Berber, etc.).—*adj.* **Hamitic** (*-it'ik*).

**hamlet,** *ham'lit, n.* a cluster of houses in the country: a small village. [O.Fr. *hamelet,* dim. of *hamel* (Fr. *hameau*), from Gmc.; cf. **home.**]

**hammal, hamal,** *hum-äl', n.* an Eastern porter. [Ar. *hammāl.*]

**hammam,** *hum-äm', hum'um, ham'am, n.* an Oriental bathing establishment, a Turkish bath. —Also **humm'aum, humm'um.** [Ar. *hammām.*]

**hammer,** *ham'ər, n.* a tool for beating metal, breaking rock, driving nails, or the like: a striking-piece in the mechanism of a clock, piano, etc.: the apparatus that causes explosion of the charge in a firearm: the mallet with which an auctioneer announces that an article is sold: a small bone of the ear, the malleus: a trouncer. —*v.t.* to beat, drive, shape, or fashion with or as with a hammer: to contrive by intellectual labour, to excogitate (with *out*): to trounce or criticise severely: to teach by frequent and energetic reiteration (with *in* or *into*): to declare a defaulter on the Stock Exchange: to beat down the price of (a stock), to depress (a market).—*v.i.* to use a hammer: to make a noise as of a hammer: to persevere pertinaciously (with *away*).— *n.* and *adj.* **hamm'ering.**—*adj.* **hamm'erless.**— **hamm'er-beam,** a horizontal piece of timber in place of a tie-beam at or near the feet of a pair of rafters; **hamm′er-brace**, a curved brace supporting a hammer-beam; **hamm′erhead**, a shark with hammer-shaped head (also **hamm′er-fish, hamm′er-head′ed shark**): the umbrette (also **hamm′erkop**, Du.).—*adj.* **hamm′er-head′ed**, with a head shaped like a hammer: dull in intellect, stupid.—**hamm′erlock**, a hold in wrestling in which opponent's arm is twisted upwards behind his back; **hamm′erman**, one who wields a hammer, as a blacksmith, goldsmith, etc.; **hamm′er-pond**, an artificial pond at a water-mill; **hamm′er-toe**, a condition in which a toe is permanently bent upwards at the base and doubled down upon itself.—**bring to the hammer**, to sell, or cause to sell, by auction; **(come) under the hammer**, (come up for sale) by auction; **hammer and sickle**, crossed hammer and sickle emblem of the Soviet Union, or of Communism; **hammer and tongs**, with great noise and violence; **hammer home**, to impress (a fact) strongly and effectively on someone. [O.E. *hamor*; Ger. *hammer*, O.N. *hamarr*.]

**hammercloth**, *ham′ər-kloth*, *n.* a cloth covering a coach-box. [Origin unknown.]

**hammerklavier**, *ham-ər-kla-vēr′*, (Ger.) pianoforte.

**hammock**, *ham′ək*, *n.* a cloth or netting hung by the ends, for use as a bed or couch. [Sp. *hamaca*, from Carib.]

**hamose**, *hā′mōs*, *adj.* hooked—also **hā′mous.**—*adjs.* **hamular** (*ham′ū-lər*), like a small hook; **hăm′ūlate**, tipped with a small hook.—*n.* **hăm′ūlus**, a small hook or hook-like process. [L. *hāmus*, hook.]

**hamper**, *ham′pər*, *v.t.* to impede: to distort: to curtail.—*n.* a shackle: that which impedes: essential but somewhat cumbrous equipment on a vessel (*naut.*). [First, about 1350, in Northern writers; cf. O.N. and Mod. Icel. *hemja*, to restrain, Ger. *hemmen*.]

**hamper**, *ham′pər*, *n.* a large basket.—*v.t.* to give a hamper to, to bribe.—*ns.* **han′ap**, an ornate mediaeval drinking goblet, often having a cover; **han′aper**, a case for a hanap: a receptacle for treasure, paper, etc.: a former department of Chancery. [O.Fr. *hanapier—hanap*, drinking-cup; cf. O.H.G. *hnapf*; O.E. *hnæpp*, a bowl.]

**hampster.** See hamster.

**hamshackle**, *ham′shak-l*, *v.t.* to shackle by tying head to foreleg: to fetter, restrain. [shackle; otherwise obscure.]

**hamster, hampster**, *ham′stər*, *n.* a rodent (Cricetus) with cheek-pouches reaching almost to the shoulders. [Ger.]

**hamstring**, *ham′string*, *n.* the great tendon at the back of the knee or hock of the hindleg.—*v.t.* to lame by cutting the hamstring: to make powerless:—*pa.t.* and *pa.p.* **ham′stringed, ham′strung.** [ham, string.]

**han**, *han*, an old *pl.* (*Spens.*) of have.

**hanap, hanaper.** See hamper (2).

**hance**, *häns, hans, n.* a curved rise from a lower to a higher part (*naut.*): the arc of smaller radius at the springing of an elliptical or many-centred arch (*archit.*).—Also **haunch.** [O.Fr. *hauce, haulce*, rise: cf. enhance.]

**hanch**, *hänsh*, (*Scot.*) *v.i.* and *v.t.* to snap (at) with the jaws. [Older Fr. *hancher*.]

**hand**, *hand*, *n.* in man the extremity of the arm below the wrist: any corresponding member in the higher vertebrates: the forefoot of a quadruped: the extremity of the hind-limb when it is prehensile: a pointer or index: a measure of four inches: a division of a bunch of bananas: side, direction, quarter: a worker, esp. in a factory or a ship: a performer: a doer, author, or producer: instrumentality: influence: share in performance: power or manner of performing: style: skill: handiwork: touch: stroke:

control: (often *pl.*) keeping, custody: possession: assistance: style of handwriting: signmanual: pledge: consent to or promise of marriage, or fulfilment of such promise: feel, handle (of a textile): the set of cards held by a player at one deal: the play of a single deal of cards: loosely, a game of cards: a turn, round, or innings in a game: a round of applause: (in *pl.*) skill in handling a horse's reins.—*v.t.* to lay hands on, set hand to, manipulate, handle (*obs.*): to join hands with (*rare*): to pass with the hand: to lead, escort, or help, esp. in entering a carriage: to transfer or deliver (often with *over*).—**hand-**, in composition, by hand, or direct bodily operation (as **hand′-knitt′ed, hand′made, hand′-painted, hand′-set, hand′-sewn, hand′-weed′ed**): operated by hand (as **hand′-or′gan**): held in the hand (as **hand′-bask′et**).—*suffs.* **-handed**, (as left-handed); **-handedness.**—*adj.* **hand′ed**, having hands: with hands joined (*Milt.*).—*ns.* **hand′er**, one who hands: a blow on the hand; **hand′ful**, enough to fill the hand: a small number or quantity: a charge that taxes one's powers:—*pl.* **hand′fuls.**—*adv.* **hand′ily.**—*n.* **hand′iness.**—*adjs.* **hand′less**, without hands: awkward; **hand′y**, dexterous: ready to the hand: convenient: near.—**hand′bag**, a bag for small articles, carried in the hand by women: a light travelling-bag; **hand′-ball**, a game between goals in which the ball is struck with the palm of the hand: **(hand′ball)** a game similar to fives in which a ball is struck with the gloved hand against a wall or walls (usu. four); **hand′-barrow**, wheelless barrow, carried by handles: handcart; **hand′bell**, small bell with a handle, rung by hand, **hand′bill**, a light pruning-hook: a bill or loose sheet bearing an announcement; **hand′book**, a manual: a bookmaker's book of bets (*U.S.*); **hand(s)′breadth**, the breadth of a hand; **hand′car** (*U.S.*), a workman's vehicle driven by hand on a railway; **hand′-cart**, a light cart drawn by hand; **hand′clap**, a clap of the hands; **hand′craft**, handicraft; **hand′cuff**, (esp. in *pl.*) a shackle locked upon the wrist.—*v.t.* to put handcuffs on.—**hand′fast** (*arch.*), a firm grip: custody: a handle (*dial.*): a contract, esp. a betrothal.—*adj.* (*arch.*) bound: espoused: tight-gripping.—*v.t.* (*arch.*) to betroth: to join by handfasting.—**hand′fasting** (*arch.*), betrothal: probationary marriage: private marriage; **hand′-feeding**, feeding of animals or machinery by hand; **hand′-gall′op**, an easy gallop, restrained by the bridle-hand; **hand′-glass**, a glass or glazed frame to protect plants: a mirror or a lens with a handle; **hand′-grenade′**, a grenade to be thrown by hand; **hand′grip**, a grasp with the hand: something for the hand to grasp: (in *pl.*) close struggle; **hand′-gun**, a gun which can be held and fired in one hand; **hand′hold**, a hold by the hand: a place or part that can be held by the hand; **hand′-horn**, an early form of horn without valves.—*n.pl.* **hand′icuffs**, fisticuffs.—**hand′-in** (badminton, etc.), the player who is serving; **hand′-line**, a fishing-line without a rod; **hand′-list**, a list without detail, for handy reference, **hand′-loom**, a hand-worked weaving loom.—*adj.* **hand′made.—hand′maid, hand′maiden**, a female servant.—*adj.* **hand′-me-down′**, ready-made, usually cheap: second-hand.—*n.* a cheap ready-made or second-hand garment.—**hand′-mill**, a quern: a coffee-mill, pepper-mill, etc., worked by hand; **hand′-off**, act or manner of pushing off an opponent in Rugby football; **hand′out**, a portion handed out, esp. to the needy: an issue: a prepared statement issued to the press; **hand′out**, a player whose side is receiving the service: the situation when the first player on the serving side loses his service; **hand′-pa′per**, paper with a hand for watermark.—*v.t.* **hand′-pick**, to pick by hand: to select carefully for a particular purpose.

*ns.* hand'play, dealing of blows; hand'-post, a finger-post; hand'-press, a printing or other press worked by hand; hand'-prom'ise (*Irish*), formerly a solemn form of betrothal; hand'rail, a rail to hold by, as on stairs.—*adv.* hand'-runn'ing (*dial.*), consecutively.—hand'saw, a saw worked by hand, specif. with a handle at one end: perh. heronshaw (*Shak.*); hand'-screen, a screen against fire or sun, held in the hand; hand'-screw, a clamp: a jack for raising weights; hand'shake, hand'shaking, a shaking of hands; hand'spike, a bar used as a lever; hand'spring, a cartwheel or somersault with hands on the ground; hand'staff, a staff-like handle, as of a flail: a staff as a weapon: a javelin:—*pl.* hand'-staves, hand'staffs; hand'stand, act of balancing one's body on the palms of one's hands with one's trunk and legs in the air; hands'turn, a single or least act of work; hand'work, work done by hand.—*adjs.* hand'worked, hand'-wrought, done by hand.—hand'writing, writing, script: style of writing; hand'yman, a man for odd jobs: a blue-jacket.—at any hand, in any hand (*Shak.*), at any rate, in any case; at first hand, directly from the source; at hand, conveniently near: within easy reach: near in time: at the beginning (*Shak.*); at the hand of, by the act of; bear a hand, to take part, lend aid; bloody or red hand, the arms of Ulster, a sinister hand erect couped at the wrist gules, borne by baronets in a canton or inescutcheon; by hand, by use of the hands, or tools worked by the hand, not by machinery or other indirect means; by the strong hand, by force; change hands, to pass to other ownership or keeping; come to hand, to arrive: to be received; come to one's hand, to be found easy: to come to close quarters; for one's own hand, to one's own account; get one's hand in, to get control of the play so as to turn one's cards to good use: to get into the way or knack; good hands, a trustworthy source: good keeping: care of those who may be trusted to treat one well; hand and foot, orig. with respect to hands and feet: with assiduous attention; hand and (or in) glove, on very intimate terms: in close co-operation; hand down or on, transmit in succession or by tradition; hand in hand, with hands mutually clasped: in close association: conjointly.—*adj.* hand-in-hand; hand it to one (*slang*), admit his superiority, esp. as shown by his success in a difficult matter; hand of God, unforeseen and unavoidable accident, as lightning, tempest; hand over hand, by passing the hands alternately one before or above another, as in climbing a rope or swimming with a certain stroke: progressively: with steady and rapid gain (also hand over fist); hand over head, headlong; hands down, with utter ease (as in winning a race); hands off, keep off: do not touch or strike; hands up, hold the hands above the head in surrender; hand to hand, at close quarters.—*adj.* hand-to-hand; hand to mouth, with provision for immediate needs only.—*adj.* hand-to-mouth; handwriting on the wall (see write); in hand, as present payment: in preparation: under control: of a ball that has to be played from balk (*billiards*); keep one's hand in (see keep); lay hands on, to seize: to obtain or find: to subject physically to rough treatment: to bless or to ordain by touching with the hand(s)—also to lay on hands; laying on of hands, the touch of a bishop or presbyters in ordination; lend a hand, to give assistance; off one's hands, no longer under one's responsible charge; old hand, see old; on all hands, on all sides, by everybody; on hand, ready, available: in one's possession; on one's hands, under one's care or responsibility: remaining as a burden or encumbrance; out of hand, at once, immediately, without premeditation: out of control; poor hand, an unskilful

one; set or put one's hand to, to engage in, undertake: to sign; show of hands, a vote by holding up hands; show one's hand, to expose one's purpose; sit on one's hands, to take no action; slow handclap, slow rhythmic clapping showing disapproval; stand one's hand (*slang*), to pay for a drink for another; take in hand, to undertake: to take charge of in order to educate, etc.; take off one's hands, to relieve one of; throw in one's hand, give up a venture or plan; tie one's hands, render powerless; to one's hand, in readiness; try one's hand at, to attempt: test one's prowess at; under one's hand, with one's proper signature attached; upper hand, mastery; wash one's hands (of), to disclaim responsibility (Matt. xxvii, 24). [O.E. *hand*; in all Gmc. tongues, perh. rel. to Goth. *hinthan*, to seize.]

handicap, *hand'i-kap*, *v.t.* to impose special disadvantages or impediments upon, in order to offset advantages and make a better contest: to place at a disadvantage (*fig.*).—*n.* any contest so adjusted, or the condition imposed: amount added to or subtracted from one's score in stroke competitions (*golf*): a disadvantage (*fig.*).—*adj.* hand'icapped, suffering from some disability or disadvantage.—*n.* hand'icapper, one who handicaps. [App. *hand i' cap*, from the drawing from a cap in an old lottery game.]

handicraft, *hand'i-kräft*, *n.* a manual craft or trade. —*n.* hand'icraftsman, a man skilled in a manual art:—*fem.* hand'icraftswoman. [O.E. *handcræft* —*hand*, *cræft*, craft, assimilated to handiwork.]

handiwork, handywork, *hand'i-wûrk*, *n.* work done by the hands, performance generally: work of skill or wisdom: creation: doing. [O.E. *hand-gewerc*—*hand* and *gewerc* (*geweorc*), work.]

handjar, hanjar, *han'jär*, *n.* a Persian dagger. [Pers. and Ar. *khanjar*.]

handkerchief, *hang'kər-chif*, *-chêf*, *n.* a cloth or paper for wiping the nose, etc.: a neckerchief:—*pl.* hand'kerchiefs, sometimes hand'kerchieves.— Also (*Shak.*, etc.; now *illit.*) hand'kercher.— throw the handkerchief, to summon to pursuit, call upon to take one's turn—as in children's games and royal harems. [hand, kerchief.]

handle, *hand'l*, *v.t.* to hold, move about, feel freely, with the hand: to make familiar by frequent touching: to manage: to discuss: to deal with, treat: to cope with: pass through one's hands: to trade or do business in.—*n.* a part by which a thing is held: anything affording an advantage or pretext to an opponent: feel, as of a textile: one's name (*slang*).—*adj.* hand'led, having a handle.—*ns.* hand'ler, one who handles: a pugilist's trainer or second: one who holds, controls, incites, or shows off an animal at a show, fight, etc.: one who trains and uses a dog which works for the police or an armed service; hand'ling.—hand'lebar, the steering-bar of a cycle, or one half of it; hand'lebar mou\u0074ache, a wide, thick moustache with curved ends thought to resemble handlebars.—a handle to one's name, a title; fly off the handle (see fly). [O.E. *handle*, *handlian*—*hand*.]

hand of glory, *hand əv glō'ri*, *glō'*, *n.* a charm made originally of mandrake root, afterwards of a murderer's hand from the gallows. [A translation of Fr. *main de gloire*—O.Fr. *mandegloire*, mandrake—*mandragore*.]

handsel, hansel, *han(d)'səl*, *n.* an inaugural gift, e.g. a present on Handsel Monday, a coin put in the pocket of a new coat, or the like: an inauguration or beginning, as the first money taken, earnest-money, a first instalment, the first use of anything: app. payment, penalty (*Spens.*).—*v.t.* to give a handsel to: to inaugurate: to make a beginning on: to cut off, kill (Chatterton, from a blundering reading of a dictionary explanation, 'to cut off a first slice'):—

*pr.p.* han(d)'selling; *pa.p.* and *pa.t.* han(d)-selled.—Handsel Monday (*Scot.*), the first Monday after New Year's Day, when handsels were given. [O.E. *handselen*, hand-gift, giving; or O.N. *handsal*.]

handsome, *han'səm, adj.* convenient, handy (*obs.*): suitable, becoming, gracious (*arch.*): good-looking: well-proportioned: dignified: liberal or noble: generous: ample.—*adv.* hand'somely.—*n.* hand'someness. [hand and suff. -some; cf. Du. *handzaam*.]

handy. See hand.

handy-dandy, *hand'i-dand'i, n.* a children's game of guessing which hand a thing is in.—*interj.* (*Shak.*) the formula used in the game. [hand.]

handywork. See handiwork.

hanepoot, *hän'ə-pōōt,* (S.Afr.) *n.* a kind of grape. Also haanepoot, honeypot. [Du. *haane-poot—haan,* cock, *poot,* foot.]

hang, hang, *v.t.* to support from above against gravity: to suspend: to decorate with pictures, tapestry, etc., as a wall: to put to death by suspending by the neck: to suspend (meat and game) until mature: to cause to be brought to justice: to fix, to fit: to fasten, to stick: to exhibit (works of art): to prevent (a jury) from coming to a decision:—(in the *imper.* and *pass.*) a euphemism for damn.—*v.i.* to be suspended, so as to allow of free lateral motion: to be put to death by hanging: to be brought to justice: to weigh down, to oppress (with *on* and *over*): to cling (with *on*): to drape well: to be exhibited: to be undecided: to be in suspense: to hover: to impend: to linger: to hold back: to depend (with *on*): to have things hanging: to remain in close attention (with *on*):—*pa.t.* and *pa.p.* hanged (by the neck), or hung (in all senses).—*n.* hang, action or mode of hanging: principle of connection, plan: knack of using: meaning: a declivity: a slackening of motion: a hanging mass: euphemistically, a damn.—*n.* hangabil'ity.—*adj.* hang'able, liable to be hanged: punishable by hanging.—*n.* hang'er, one who hangs: that on which anything is hung: a wood on a hillside: a short sword.—*adj.* hang'ing, suspending: suspended: drooping: downcast: deserving or involving death by hanging.—*n.* death by the halter: (esp. in *pl.*) that which is hung, as drapery.—hang'bird, a Baltimore oriole (from its pensile nest); hang'dog, a low fellow.—*adj.* with a sneaking, cowed look.—hang'er-on', one who hangs on or sticks to a person or place: an importunate acquaintance: a dependent; hang'fire, delay in explosion; hanging buttress, a buttress supported by a corbel or the like; hanging committee, a committee which chooses the works of art to be shown in an exhibition; hanging garden (see garden); hanging matter, a crime leading to capital punishment: a serious matter (*coll.*); hanging valley, a tributary valley not graded to the main valley, a product of large-scale glaciation; hang'man, a public executioner.—*adj.* rascally.—hang'nest, a hangbird; hang'out, haunt; hang'over, a survival: after-effects, esp. of drinking; hang-up (*slang*), a problem about which one is obsessed; hung'-beef, beef cured and dried; hung jury, a jury that fails to agree.—*adj.* hung'over, suffering from a hangover.—hang about, to loiter; hang back, to show reluctance; hang by a thread, to depend upon very precarious conditions (from the sword of Damocles); hang, draw, and quarter, to hang, cut down while still alive, disembowel and cut in pieces for exposure at different places; draw, hang, and quarter, to drag on a hurdle or otherwise to the place of execution, then hang and quarter; hang fire, to be long in exploding or discharging: to be slow in taking effect: to hesitate; hang in the balance, to be in doubt or

suspense; hang off, to let go: to hold off; hang on, to wait; hang on one's lips or words, to give close, admiring attention to; hang one's head, to look ashamed or sheepish; hang out, to display, as a sign: to lodge or reside (*slang*); hang out for, to insist on; hang over, to project over or lean out from; hang together, to keep united: to be consistent: to connect; hang up, to suspend: to delay: to replace a telephone receiver, break off communication; hang up one's hat, to take up one's abode; hung up, obsessed. [O.E. *hangian,* pa.t. *hangode,* pa.p. *hangod* (intrans.) and *hōn,* pa.t. *heng,* pa.p. *hangen* (trans.), and O.N. *hanga* and *hengja;* cf. Du. and Ger. *hangen.*]

hangar, *hang'ər, hang'gär, n.* a shed for carriages, aircraft, etc. [Fr.]

hangnail, *hang'nāl.* See agnail.

hanjar. See handjar.

hank, *hangk, n.* a coil or skein of a specified length, varying with the type of yarn: a loop: a restraining hold (*dial.*).—*v.t.* to catch, as on a loop.—*v.i.* to catch, be entangled. [O.N. *hanki,* a hasp.]

hanker, *hangk'ər, v.i.* to linger about (*dial.*): to yearn (with *after, for*).—*n.* a yearning.—*n.* hank'ering. [Perh. conn. with hang; cf. Du. *hunkeren.*]

hankie, hanky, *hangk'i, n.* a coll. dim. of handkerchief.

hanky-panky, *hangk'i-pangk'i, n.* jugglery, underhand trickery. [Arbitrary.]

Hanoverian, *han-ə-vē'ri-ən, adj.* pertaining to Hanover (Ger. *Hannover*): of the dynasty that came thence to the British throne in 1714.—*n.* a native of Hanover: a supporter of the house of Hanover, *opp.* to a Jacobite.

Hansard, *han'särd, n.* the printed reports of debates in parliament, from Luke *Hansard* (1752-1828), whose descendants continued to print them down to 1889.—*v.t.* han'sardise, -ize, to confront with one's former recorded opinions.

Hanse, *hans, n.* a league, esp. one of German commercial cities.—*adjs.* Hanse, Hanseatic (*han-si-at'ik*). [O.H.G. *hansa,* a band of men (Ger. *hanse*).]

hansel. See handsel.

hansom, *han'səm, n.* a light two-wheeled cab with driver's seat raised behind.—Also han'som-cab. [From the inventor, Joseph A. *Hansom* (1803-82).]

ha'n't, *hänt,* a coll. contr. for have not or has not.

hantle, *han'tl, hän'tl,* (*Scot.*) *n.* a good many: a good deal. [Poss. hand and tale, number.]

hanuman, *han-ōō-män', n.* a long-tailed sacred monkey of India—the entellus monkey. [*Hanumān,* Hindu monkey god.]

haoma, *how'ma, n.* a drink prepared from the haoma vine, used in Zoroastrian ritual: (*cap.*) a deity, personification of haoma. [Avestan; see soma (1).]

hap, *hap, n.* chance: fortune: accident.—*v.i.* to chance, happen:—*pr.p.* happ'ing; *pa.t.* and *pa.p.* happed.—*n.* and *adj.* hap'haz'ard, random: chance.—*adv.* at random.—*n.* haphaz'ardness.—*adj.* hap'less, unlucky: unhappy.—*adv.* hap'lessly.—*n.* hap'lessness.—*adv.* hap'ly, may be: perhaps: it may be. [O.N. *happ,* good luck.]

hap, *hap,* (*Scot.* and *E. Angl.*) *v.t.* to cover up: to wrap up.—*n.* a wrap. [Origin unknown.]

hapax legomenon, *hap'aks leg-om'en-on,* (Gr.) lit. said once: a word or phrase that is found once only.

ha'pence, *hā'pəns,* for halfpence.

ha'penny, *hāp'ni,* for halfpenny.

haplo-, in composition, single.—*ns.* haplography (*hap-log'rə-fi*), the inadvertent writing once of what should have been written twice; haplol'ogy, omission in utterance of a sound resembling a neighbouring sound (as *idolatry* for *idololatry*).—*adj.* hap'loid (*biol.*), having the reduced number of chromosomes characteristic of the species, as in germ-cells (opp. to *diploid*).—*n.* haploid'y.—*adj.* haplostē'monous (Gr. *stēmōn*, thread; *bot.*), with one whorl of stamens. [Gr. *haploos*, single, simple.]

**hap'orth,** *hā'pərth*, for halfpennyworth.

**happen,** *hap'ən*, *v.i.* to fall out: to come to pass: to take place: to chance.—*adv.* (*N. Engl.*) perhaps.—*ns.* **happ'ening,** event: a performance consisting of discrete events, in which elements from everyday life are put together in a nonrealistic way, usu. demanding audience participation (*theatre*): one such event in the theatre or in other activities including those of everyday life; **happ'enstance,** chance: a chance circumstance.—**if anything should happen,** in case of death; **happen into, on, upon,** to meet or come across by chance. [hap.]

**happy,** *hap'i*, *adj.* lucky: fortunate: expressing, or characterised by, content, wellbeing, pleasure, or good: apt: felicitous: mildly intoxicated (*slang*): in combination, delighted by the possession of or use of, as *power-happy, bomb-happy*—usu. implying irresponsibility—or dazed as result of.—*v.t.* (*Shak.*) to make happy.—*adv.* **happ'ily,** in a happy manner: in happiness: by chance: perhaps.—*n.* **happ'iness.**—*adj.* **happ'y-go-luck'y,** easy-going: taking things as they come.—*adv.* in any way one pleases.—**happy dispatch,** a euphemism for hara-kiri; **happy event,** a euphemism for a birth; **happy hunting-ground,** (also in *pl.*) the Paradise of the Red Indian: any place that one frequents, esp. to make acquisitions or to profit in any way; **happy medium,** a prudent or sensible middle course. [hap.]

**hapteron,** *hap'tər-on*, *n.* a holdfast or attachment organ of a plant thallus.—*adj.* **haptotrop'ic,** curving in response to touch, as a tendril.—*n.* **haptot'ropism.** [Gr. *haptein*, to fasten, *tropos*, turning.]

**haptic,** *hap'tik*, *adj.* pertaining to the sense of touch.—*n.* **hap'tics,** science of studying data obtained by means of touch. [Gr. *haptein*, to fasten.]

**haqueton,** *hak'tən.* Same as **acton.**

**hara-kiri,** *ha'*, *hä'rä-kē'rē*, *n.* ceremonious Japanese suicide by ripping the belly. [Japanese *hara*, belly, *kiri*, cut.]

**haram.** See **harem.**

**harangue,** *hə-rang'*, *n.* a loud speech addressed to a multitude: a pompous or wordy address.—*v.i.* to deliver a harangue.—*v.t.* to address by a harangue:—*pr.p.* haranguing (-*rang'ing*); *pa.t.* and *pa.p.* harangued (-*rangd'*).—*n.* harangu'er. [O.Fr. *arenge, harangue*—O.H.G. *hring* (Ger. *ring*), ring (of auditors).]

**harass,** *har'əs*, *v.t.* to distress, wear out: to annoy, pester.—*adj.* har'assed.—*adv.* har'assedly.—*n.* har'asser.—*n.* and *adj.* har'assing.—*adv.* har'assingly.—*n.* har'assment. [O.Fr. *harasser*; prob. from *harer*, to incite a dog.]

**harbinger,** *här'bin-jər*, *n.* a host (*obs.*): one sent before to provide lodging (*obs.*): a forerunner, pioneer.—*v.t.* to precede as harbinger. [M.E. *herbergeour*; see **harbour.**]

**harbour** (in U.S. harbor), *här'bər*, *n.* a refuge or shelter: a shelter, natural or artificial, for ships: a haven.—*v.t.* to lodge, shelter, entertain, or give asylum to: to trace to its lair.—*v.i.* to take shelter.—*ns.* har'bourage, place of shelter: entertainment; har'bourer.—*adj.* har'bourless.—har'bour-bar', a sandbank at a harbour's mouth.—*n.pl.* har'bour-dues, charges for the use of a harbour.—har'bour-light, a guiding light into a harbour; har'bour-master, an officer who has charge of a harbour.—**harbour of refuge,** a harbour constructed to give shelter to ships: protection in distress. [M.E. *herberwe*—O.E. *herebeorg*—*here*, army, *beorg*, protection; cf. Ger. *herberge*, O.N. *herbergi*.]

**hard,** *härd*, *adj.* not easily penetrated or broken: unyielding to pressure: firm, solid: difficult to scratch (*min.*): difficult: strenuous: laborious: vigorous: bodily fit: coarse and scanty: stingy, niggardly: difficult to bear: difficult to please: unfeeling: insensitive: severe: rigorous: stiff: constrained: intractable: obdurate: (of coal) anthracitic: (of water) difficult to lather owing to calcium or magnesium salt in solution: harsh: brilliant and glaring: over-sharply defined: lacking in finer shades: (of drink) (very) alcoholic: (of drug) habit-forming: (of news) definite, substantiated: (of letters) representing a guttural, not a sibilant, sound: voiceless (*obs.* *phon.*): (of radiation) penetrating.—*n.* hardship: hard state: hard ground: a firm beach or foreshore: hard labour.—*adv.* with urgency, vigour, etc.: earnestly, forcibly: uneasily: in excess: severely: to the full extent (as **hard aport**): with difficulty: harshly: close, near, as in **hard by.**—*v.t.* **hard'en,** to make hard or harder or hardy: to make firm: to strengthen: to confirm in wickedness: to make insensitive.—*v.i.* to become hard or harder, *lit.* or *fig.*—*adj.* **hard'ened,** made hard: unfeeling: obdurate.—*n.* **hard'ener.**—*adj.* **hard'ish,** somewhat hard.—*adv.* **hard'ly,** with difficulty: scarcely, not quite: severely, harshly.—*ns.* **hard'ness,** quality of being hard: power of, and resistance to, scratching (*min.*); **hard'ship,** a thing, or conditions, hard to bear: privation: an instance of hard treatment (*obs.*).—*adv.* **hard'-a-lee',** close to the lee-side, etc.—*adj.* **hard'-and-fast',** rigidly laid down and adhered to.—**hard-and-fast'ness; hard'bake,** almond toffee; **hard'beam,** the hornbeam.—*adjs.* **hard'-billed,** having a hard bill or beak; **hard'-bitt'en,** given to hard biting, tough in fight; **hard'-boiled,** boiled until solid: callous or cynical: practical.—**hard'board,** a compressed fibreboard; **hard case,** a person difficult to deal with or reform; **hard cash,** specie: ready money; **hard'core,** rubble, etc., used under foundations of road; **hard core,** something very resistant to change, as, e.g. the most loyal or the most die-hard members of a group.—*adjs.* **hard'-core,** pertaining to a hard core: blatant; **hard'-cured,** thoroughly cured, as fish, by drying in the sun.—**hard currency,** metallic money: a term without precise meaning applied to the currency of any country with which one has an adverse balance of payments.—*adj.* **hard'-drawn,** of wire, etc., drawn when cold to give the required thickness.—**hard drinker,** one who drinks persistently and excessively.—*adj.* **hard'-earned,** earned with toil or difficulty.—**hard'face,** a soullessly relentless person; **hard facts,** undeniable, stubborn facts.—*adjs.* **hard'-fav'oured, hard'-feat'ured,** of hard, coarse, or forbidding features.—**hard'-fav'ouredness; hard'-feat'uredness; hard'-fern,** the northern fern (Lomaria or Blechnum).—*adjs.* **hard'-fist'ed,** having hard or strong fists or hands: close-fisted: niggardly; **hard'-fought,** sorely contested; **hard'-got, hard'-gotten,** obtained with difficulty; **hard'-grained,** having a close firm grain: forbidding.—**hard'grass,** cock's-foot or other coarse grass; **hard'-hack,** an American Spiraea.—*adj.* **hard'-hand'ed,** having hard hands: rough: severe.—**hard'head,** knapweed: a fish of various kinds (gurnard, menhaden, fatherlasher).—*adjs.* **hard'-head'ed,** shrewd; **hard'-heart'ed,** unfeeling: cruel.—*adv.* **hard'-heart'edly.**—*n.* **hard'-heart'edness.**—*adjs.* **hard'-hit,** seriously hurt as by a loss of money: deeply smitten with love; **hard'line,** of an attitude or policy (**hard line**), definite and unyielding: having an attitude or policy.—**hard'liner; hard lines,** a hard lot: bad luck; **hard'-metal,** sintered tungsten carbide, used for the tip of high-speed cutting tools; **hard money,** coin.—*adj.* **hard'-mouthed,** with mouth

insensible to the bit: not easily managed.—
**hard pad,** once considered to be a neurotropic
virus disease of dogs, now recognised as a
symptom of distemper; **hard'-pan,** a hard layer
often underlying the superficial soil: the lowest
level.—*adjs.* **hard'-paste,** (of porcelain) made of
china-clay and altered granite; **hard'-pressed,**
**hard'-pushed,** in difficulties; **hard'-rid'ing,**
strenuously riding; **hard'-ruled** (*Shak.*), ruled
with difficulty; **hard'-run,** greatly pressed;
**hard'-set,** beset by difficulty: rigid.—**hard sell,**
aggressive and insistent method of advertising
or selling.—*adj.* **hard'shell,** having a hard shell:
rigidly orthodox: uncompromising. — **hard
swearing,** persistent and reckless swearing (by a
witness): (often) perjury; **hard'tack,** ship-
biscuit.—*adjs.* **hard'-up,'** short of money, or of
anything else; **hard'-vis'aged,** of a hard, coarse,
or forbidding visage.—**hard'ware,** goods made of
the baser metals, such as iron or copper: mechanical equipment, including war equipment:
(computer) equipment used in processing information; **hard'wareman.**—*adj.* **hard'-won,** won
with toil and difficulty.—**hard words,** words that
give difficulty to a half-educated reader: harsh
words: angry words; **hard'wood,** timber of
deciduous trees, whose comparatively slow
growth produces compact hard wood.—*adj.*
**hard'work'ing.**—**die hard,** to die only after a
desperate struggle for life: to survive obstinately:
to die impenitent (*obs.*); **go hard but,** will not
easily fail that; **go hard with,** turn out ill for;
**hard as nails,** very hard: callous: tough;
**hard of hearing,** pretty deaf; **hard put to it,** in
great straits or difficulty; **hold hard,** stop;
**Mohs's scale of hardness,** a series of minerals
each of which will scratch the one before it:
(1) talc, (2) gypsum, (3) calcite, (4) fluorite,
(5) apatite, (6) orthoclase, (7) quartz, (8) topaz,
(9) corundum, (10) diamond. [O.E. *hard*
(*heard*); Du. *hard,* Ger. *hart,* Goth. *hardus*;
allied to Gr. *kratys,* strong.]
**hard,** *härd,* (*Spens.* and *Scot.*) for **heard.**
**hardoke,** *här'dok,* (*Shak., King Lear,* folio) *n.*
perhaps burdock.—The quartos have **hor'dock.**
[Prob. O.E. *hār,* hoary, and **dock.**]
**hards,** *härdz,* **hurds,** *hûrdz, n.pl.* coarse or refuse
flax or hemp: tarred rags used as torches
(*Scott*).—*n.* **hard'en, herd'en, hurd'en,** a coarse
fabric made from hards. [O.E. *heordan.*]
**hardy,** *härd'i, adj.* daring, brave, resolute: confident: impudent: able to bear cold, exposure,
or fatigue.—*ns.* **hard'ihead** (*arch.*), **hard'ihood,**
boldness: audacity: robustness (*rare*).—*adv.*
**hard'ily.**—*ns.* **hard'iment** (*arch.*), hardihood: a
deed of hardihood; **hard'iness.**—**hardy annual,**
an annual plant which can survive frosts: a story
or topic of conversation which comes up
regularly. [O.Fr. *hardi*—O.H.G. *hartjan,* to
make hard.]
**hare,** *här, n.* a common very timid and very swift
rodent, in appearance like, but larger than, a
rabbit.—*v.i.* (*slang*) to run like a hare, hasten.—
*adj.* **har'ish,** somewhat like a hare.—**hare'-and-
hounds',** a paper-chase; **hare'bell,** the Scottish
bluebell (*Campanula rotundifolia*).—*adjs.* **hare'-
brained,** giddy: heedless: headlong; **hare'-foot,**
swift of foot.—**hare'-lip,** a fissured upper lip like
that of a hare.—*adj.* **hare'-lipped.**—**hare's-ear,**
an umbelliferous plant (Bupleurum, various
species) with yellow flowers; **hare's'-foot**
(tre'foil), a clover with long soft fluffy heads.—
**first catch your hare,** make sure you have a thing
first before you think what to do with it—from
a direction in Mrs Glasse's cookery-book,
where catch was a misprint for case, skin; **hold
(run) with the hare and run (hunt) with the hounds,**
to play a double game, to be with both sides at
once. [O.E. *hara;* Du. *haas,* Dan. *hare,* Ger.
*hase.*]

**l.areld,** *har'ld, n.* a long-tailed northern sea-duck.
[Mod. Icel. *havella—hav,* sea.]
**harem,** *hā'rem, hä-rēm', n.* women's quarters in a
Mohammedan house: a set of wives and concubines.—Also **haram', harim** (*-ēm'*).—**harem skirt,**
an early 20th-century divided skirt in imitation
of Turkish trousers. [Ar. *harim, haram,* anything forbidden—*harama,* to forbid.]
**haricot,** *har'i-kō, -kot, n.* a kind of ragout or stew
of mutton and beans or other vegetables: the
kidney-bean or French bean (plant or seed). [Fr.
*haricot.*]
**harigal(d)s,** *har'i-glz,* (*Scot.*) *n.pl.* viscera.
**Harijan,** *ha'rē-jan, n.* one of the caste of untouchables, the name proposed by Gandhi. [Sans.
*Hari,* a name of Vishnu, and *jana,* person.]
**hari-kari,** *här'ē-kär'ē,* an incorrect form of hara-
kiri.
**harim.** See **harem.**
**hariolate,** *har'i-ō-lāt, v.i.* to divine.—*n.* **hariolā'-
tion.** [L. *hariolāri, -ātus.*]
**hark,** *härk, v.i.* to listen: to listen (to; also with
*at*): to go (away, forward, etc.): to go in quest,
or to follow (with *after*).—*v.t.* to listen to (*arch.*).
—*n.* a whisper (*Scot.*).—**hark'-back,** a going
back again (*lit.* and *fig.*).—**hark away, back,
forward,** cries to urge hounds and hunters;
**hark back,** to revert. [See **hearken.**]
**harken,** *här'kən, v.i.* Same as **hearken.**
**harl,** *härl,* **herl,** *hûrl, n.* a fibre of flax, etc.: a barb
of a feather, esp. one used in making an artificial
fly. [M.E. *herle*—L.G.]
**harl,** *härl,* (*Scot.*) *v.t.* to drag along the ground:
to roughcast.—*v.i.* to drag oneself: to troll for
fish.—*n.* act of dragging: a small quantity, a
scraping of anything: a haul: roughcast.—*n.*
**har'ling.**
**Harleian,** *här-lē'ən, här'li-ən, adj.* pertaining to
Robert *Harley,* Earl of Oxford (1661-1724), and
his son Edward, or the library collected by them.
—**Harley Street,** in London, a favourite abode
of physicians and surgeons, hence symbolically.
**harlequin,** *här'lə-kwin, n.* a pantomime character,
in tight spangled dress, with visor and magic
wand: a buffoon: a breed of small spotted dogs.
—*v.i.* to play the harlequin.—*n.* **harlequināde',**
part of a pantomime in which the harlequin
plays a chief part.—**harlequin duck,** a variegated
northern sea-duck. [Fr. *harlequin, arlequin* (It.
*arlecchino*), prob. the same as O.Fr. *Hellequin,* a
devil in mediaeval legend, perh. of Gmc. origin.]
**harlot,** *här'lət, n.* a general term of opprobrium
applied to man or woman (*obs.*): a whore: a
prostitute.—*adj.* lewd: base.—*n.* **har'lotry,** prostitution: unchastity: meretriciousness: a harlot
(*obs.*).—*adj.* (*obs.*) base, foul. [O.Fr. *herlot,*
*arlot,* a base fellow; origin unknown.]
**harm,** *härm, n.* injury: moral wrong.—*v.t.* to
injure.—*adj.* **harm'ful,** hurtful.—*adv.* **harm'-
fully.**—*n.* **harm'fulness.**—*adj.* **harm'less,** not injurious, innocent: unharmed.—*adv.* **harm'lessly.**
—*n.* **harm'lessness.**—**harm-do'ing.** [O.E. *herm*
(*hearm*); Ger. *harm.*]
**harmala,** *här'mä-lə, n.* the so-called African or
Syrian rue (*Peganum harmala*) of the bean-caper
family.—Also **har'mel.**—*ns.* **har'malin(e), har'-
min(e),** alkaloids derived from its seeds. [Gr.,
from Semitic; cf. Ar. *harmil.*]
**harman,** *här'man,* (*old thieves' slang*) *n.* a constable
(in *pl.*) the stocks.—**har'man-beck,** a constable.
[Origin obscure; see **beak.**]
**harmattan,** *här-mä-tan', här-mat'ən, n.* a dry
dusty N.E. wind from the desert in W. Africa.
[Fanti *haramata.*]
**harmonic,** *här-mon'ik, adj.* in harmony: in harmonious proportion: pertaining to harmony:
musical: concordant: in accordance with the
physical relations of sounds in harmony or
bodies emitting such sounds (*math.*).—*n.* a
component whose frequency is an integral

*fāte, fär, mē, hûr* (her); *mīne; mōte, för; mūte; mōōn, fŏŏt; dhen* (then) multiple of the fundamental frequency: an overtone: a flutelike sound produced on a violin, etc., by lightly touching a string at a node and bowing: one of the components of what the ear hears as a single sound (in *pl.* form treated as *sing.*) musical acoustics.—*n.* harmon'ica, the musical glasses, Benjamin Franklin's instrument, revolving bell-glasses touched on the rim by a wet finger: an instrument composed of a sound-box and hanging strips of glass or metal, struck by a hammer: a mouth-organ.—*adj.* harmon'ical. —*adv.* harmon'ically.—*ns.* harmon'ichord, a keyboard instrument of violin tone, in which the strings are rubbed by rosined wheels; harmon'icon, a harmonica: an orchestrion: a pyrophone (*chemical harmonicon*).—*adj.* harmonious (*-mō'ni-əs*), in, having, or producing harmony: in agreement: justly proportioned: concordant: congruous.—*adv.* harmōn'iously.— *ns.* harmōn'iousness; harmoniphon(e) (*-mon'i-fon, -fōn*), a keyboard wind instrument with reeds; harmonisation, *-z-* (*här-mən-i-zā'shən,* or *-i-*).—*v.i.* har'monise, *-ize,* to be in harmony: to agree: to be compatible.—*v.t.* to bring into harmony: to reconcile: to provide parts to (*mus.*).—*ns.* harmonis'er, *-z-*; har'monist, one skilled in harmony (in theory or composition): a reconciler: one who seeks to reconcile apparent inconsistencies: (*cap.*) member of a Second Adventist celibate sect (also Har'monite) founded by George Rapp (d. 1847), from its settlement at *Harmony,* Pennsylvania; harmōn'ium, a reed-organ, esp. one in which the air is forced (not drawn) through the reeds; harmōn'iumist; harmonogram (*-mon'*), a curve drawn by a harmonograph; harmon'-ograph, an instrument for tracing curves representing vibrations; harmonom'eter, an instrument for measuring the harmonic relations of sounds; harmony (*här'mən-i*), a fitting together of parts so as to form a connected whole: agreement in relation: in art, a normal and satisfying state of completeness and order in the relations of things to each other: a simultaneous and successive combination of accordant sounds (*mus.*): the whole chordal structure of a piece, as distinguished from its melody or its rhythm (*mus.*): concord: music in general: a collation of parallel passages to demonstrate agreement—e.g. of Gospels.—harmonic conjugates, two points dividing a line internally and externally in the same ratio; harmonic division, division by such conjugates; harmonic mean, the middle term of three in harmonic progression; harmonic minor, a minor scale with minor sixth and major seventh, ascending and descending; harmonic motion, the motion along a diameter of a circle of the foot of a perpendicular from a point moving uniformly round the circumference; harmonic pencil (*math.*), a pencil of four rays that divides a transversal harmonically; harmonic progression, a series of numbers whose reciprocals are in arithmetical progression, such numbers being proportional to the lengths of strings that sound harmonics; harmonic proportion, the relation of successive numbers in harmonic progression; harmonic range, a set of four points in a straight line such that two of them divide the line between the other two internally and externally in the same ratio; harmonic receiver, a receiver for electric waves, in harmony with the impulses producing them; harmonic triad (*mus.*), the common chord.— harmony of the spheres (see sphere); pre-established harmony, the divinely established relation, according to Leibniz, between body and mind— the movements of monads and the succession of ideas being in constant agreement like two clocks. [Gr. *harmoniā—harmos,* a joint fitting.] harmony. See harmonic.

harmost, *här'most, n.* a Spartan governor of a sub-

ject city or province.—*n.* har'mosty, the office of harmost. [Gr. *harmostēs.*]

harmotome, *här'mo-tōm, n.* a zeolite, hydrated silicate of aluminium and barium. [Gr. *harmos,* joint, *tomē,* a cut.]

harn, *härn, n.* a coarse linen fabric. [See harden, under hards.]

harness, *här'nis, n.* tackle: gear: equipment, esp. now of a draught animal: armour for man or horse (*arch.*): an arrangement of straps, etc., for attaching a piece of equipment to the body, as a parachute harness, a baby's leading-strings, a seat belt, etc.—*v.t.* to equip with armour: to put harness on: to attach by harness.—har'ness-cask (*naut.*), a cask for salt meat for daily use; harnessed antelope, any antelope of the striped genus Tragelapas; har'ness-mak'er; harness racing, trotting or pacing races between specially bred horses harnessed to sulkies; har'ness-room. —in harness, occupied in the routine of one's daily work, not on holiday or retired. [O.Fr. *harneis,* armour.]

harns, *härnz,* (*Scot.*) *n.pl.* brains.—harn'-pan, brain-pan. [O.E. *hærn,* prob.—O.N. *hjarne*; cf. Ger. *hirn*; Gr. *krānion.*]

haro. See harrow (2).

harp, *härp, n.* a musical instrument played by plucking strings stretched from a curved neck to an inclined sound-board.—*v.i.* to play on the harp: to dwell tediously.—*v.t.* to render on or to the harp: to lead, call, or bring by playing the harp: to give voice to (*arch.*): to guess at (*obs.*). —*ns.* harp'er, harp'ist, a player on the harp.— *n.pl.* harp'ings (*naut.*), the foreparts of the wales at the bow.—harp'-seal, the Greenland seal, a grey animal with dark bands curved like an old harp; harp'-shell, a genus (Harpa) of gasteropods with ribs suggesting harp-strings.—harp on (one string), to dwell constantly on one topic [O.E. *hearpe*; Ger. *harfe.*]

harpoon, *här-pōōn', n.* a barbed dart, esp. for killing whales.—*v.t.* to strike with a harpoon.— *ns.* harpoon'er, harpooneer'.—harpoon-gun'. [Fr. *harpon,* a clamp—L. *harpa—*Gr. *harpē,* sickle.]

harpsichord, *härp'si-körd, n.* a keyboard instrument in which the strings are twitched by quills or leather points. [O.Fr. *harpechorde*; see harp, chord.]

harpy, *här'pi, n.* a rapacious and filthy monster, part woman, part bird (*myth.*): a large South American eagle (also har'py-ea'gle): a rapacious woman. [Gr. *harpyia,* lit. snatcher, in Homer a personification of the storm-wind—*harpazein,* to seize.]

harquebus, harquebuse, harquebuss, *här'kwi-bus, n.* Same as arquebus.

harridan, *har'i-dən, n.* a vixenish old woman. [Prob. O.Fr. *haridelle,* a lean horse, a jade.]

harrier, *har'i-ər, n.* a medium-sized keen-scented dog for hunting hares: a cross-country runner. [hare, or harry.]

harrier. See harry.

Harrovian, *har-ō'vi-ən, adj.* pertaining to *Harrow.* —*n.* one educated at Harrow school.

harrow, *har'ō, n.* a spiked frame or other contrivance for smoothing and pulverising land and covering seeds.—*v.t.* to draw a harrow over: to tear or harass.—*adj.* harr'owing, acutely distressing.—*adv.* harr'owingly.—harrowing, or harrying, of hell, Christ's delivery of the souls of patriarchs and prophets. [M.E. *harwe.*]

harrow, haro, *har'ō, har-ō', interj.* alas (*arch.*): out upon it (*arch.*): in the Channel Islands a cry announcing a claim to legal redress. [O.Fr. *haro, harou*; not an appeal to *Rou* or Rollo.]

harrumph, *hə-rumf', v.i.* to make a noise as of clearing the throat, usu. implying pomposity: to disapprove. [Imit.]

harry, *har'i, v.t.* to plunder: to ravage: to destroy: to harass:—*pr.p.* harr'ying; *pa.t.* and *pa.p.* harr'ied.—*n.* harr'ier, one who, or that which, harries: a kind of hawk (Circus) that harries small animals.—harrying of hell (see harrow, 1). [O.E. *hergian*—here, army; Ger. *heer.*]

harsh, *härsh, adj.* rough: jarring on the senses or feelings: rigorous.—*v.t.* harsh'en.—*adv.* harsh'ly.—*n.* harsh'ness. [M.E. *harsk,* a Northern word; cf. Sw. *härsk* and Dan. *harsk,* rancid, Ger. *harsch,* hard.]

harslet. See haslet.

hart, *härt, n.* a male deer (esp. red deer) esp. over five years old, when the crown or surroyal antler begins to appear:—*fem.* hind.—harts'horn, the antler of the red deer: a solution of ammonia in water, orig. a decoction of the shavings of a hart's horn (*spirit of hartshorn*); hart's'-tongue, a fern (*Scolopendrium vulgare*) with strap-shaped leaves. [O.E. *heort.*]

hart, (*Spens.*) for heart.

hartal, *här'tal, hŭr'täl, (India) n.* a stoppage of work in protest or boycott. [Hindi *hartāl.*]

hartebeest, *här'tə-bēst (Afrik.* hartbees, *härt'bēs), n.* a large South African antelope.—bastard hartebeest, the sassaby. [S.Afr.Du., hart-beast.]

hartely, harten, hartlesse, (*Spens.*) for heartly, hearten, heartless.

harum-scarum, *hä'rəm-skä'rəm, adj.* flighty: rash.—*n.* a giddy, rash person. [Prob. from obs. hare, to harass, and scare.]

haruspex, *ha-rus'peks, n.* one (among the Etruscans) who foretold events from inspection of entrails of animals:—*pl.* harus'pices (*-pi-sēz*).—*ns.* haruspication (*-kā'shən*), harus'picy (*-si*).—*adjs.* harus'pical, harus'picate.—*v.i.* harus'picate. [L., perh. from an Etruscan word and L. *specēre,* to view.]

harvest, *här'vist, n.* autumn (*obs.* and *dial.*): the time of gathering in crops: crops gathered in: fruits: product of any labour or act.—*v.t.* to reap and gather in.—*v.i.* to gather a crop.—*n.* har'vester, a reaper: a reaping-machine: any member of the Opiliones, a class of Arachnida with very long legs (also har'vestman, harvest spider).—har'vest-bug, -louse, -mite, -tick, a minute larval form of a mite (Trombidium) abundant in late summer, a very troublesome biter; har'vest-feast; har'vest-festival, a church service of thanksgiving for the harvest; har'vest-field; har'vest-fly, in U.S., a cicada of various kinds; har'vest-goose, a goose eaten at a harvest-home feast; har'vest-home, a celebration of the bringing home of the harvest; harvest lady, harvest lord, the head reapers at the harvest; har'vestman, a harvester; harvest moon, the full moon nearest the autumnal equinox, rising nearly at the same hour for several days; harvest mouse, a very small mouse that nests in the stalks of corn; harvest queen, the corn-maiden: the harvest lady; harvest spider, a harvester. [O.E. *hærfest;* Ger. *herbst,* Du. *herfst.*]

has, *haz.* See have.—has'-been, a person or thing whose day is over:—*pl.* has'-beens.

hash, *hash, v.t.* to hack: to mince: to chop small.—*n.* that which is hashed: a mixed dish of meat and vegetables in small pieces: a mixture and preparation of old matter: a mess: a stupid fellow (*Scot.*).—*adj.* hash'y.—settle one's hash (*slang*), to silence or subdue one. [Fr. *hacher*—*hache,* hatchet.]

hashish, hasheesh, *hash'ish, -ēsh, n.* leaves, shoots, or resin of hemp, smoked, or swallowed, as an intoxicant. [Ar. *hashish.*]

hask, *hask, (Spens.) n.* a fish-basket. [Cf. hassock.]

haslet, *häz'lit,* also häs', häs', harslet, *härs', n.* edible entrails, esp. of a hog. [O.Fr. *hastelet,* roast meat—*haste,* spit—L. *hasta,* a spear.]

hasp, *häsp, n.* a clasp: a slotted part that receives a staple, as for a padlock: a fourth part of a

spindle (*dial.*): a skein of yarn (*dial.*).—*v.t.* to fasten with a hasp. [O.E. *hæpse;* Dan. and Ger. *haspe.*]

hassar, *has'ər, n.* a South American nest-building land-walking catfish (in the American sense). [Amer. Indian origin.]

hassock, *has'ək, n.* a tuft or tussock of grass, rushes, etc.: a stuffed stool: in Kent a soft calcareous sandstone.—*adj.* hass'ocky. [O.E. *hassuc.*]

hast, *hast.* See have.

hasta, *äs'tä,* (Sp.) until.—hasta la vista (*lä vē'stä*), until we meet again.—hasta luego (*lōō-ā'gō*), see you later, hasta mañana (*män-yän'ä*), see you tomorrow—all three common terms of farewell.

hastate, -d, *hast'āt, -id, adjs.* spear-shaped: with basal lobes turned outward (*bot.*). [L. *hastātus*—*hasta,* spear.]

haste, *hāst, n.* urgency calling for speed: hurry: inconsiderate speed.—*vs.t.* haste, hasten (*hās'n*), to put to speed: to hurry on: to drive forward.—*vs.i.* to move with speed: to hurry.—*n.* hastener (*hās'n-ər*).—*adv.* hastily (*hāst'i-li*).—*ns.* hast'iness, hurry: rashness: irritability; hast'-ings (*dial.*), early fruit or vegetables, esp. peas.—*adj.* hast'y, speedy: quick: rash: eager: irritable.—hasty pudding, flour, milk, or oatmeal and water porridge.—*adj.* hast'y-witt'ed (*obs.*), rash.—make haste, to hasten. [O.Fr. *haste* (Fr. *hâte*), from Gmc.; cf. O.E. *hǣst,* Du. *haast,* Ger. *hast.*]

hat, *hat, n.* a covering for the head, often with crown and brim: dignity of cardinal, from former red hat: a salutation by lifting the hat (*Scot.* or *obs.*).—*v.t.* to provide with or cover with a hat: to lift one's hat to (*arch.*).—*v.i.* (*Austr.*) to work alone:—*pa.t.* and *pa.p.* hatt'ed.—*n.* hat'ful, as much as will fill a hat:—*pl.* hatfuls.—*adj.* hat'less.—*n.* hat'lessness.—*adj.* hatt'ed, provided or covered with a hat.—*ns.* hatt'er, a maker or seller of hats: a miner or other who works by himself, one whose 'hat covers his family' (*Austr.*); hatt'ing; hatt'ock (*arch. Scot.*), a little hat.—hat'band, a ribbon round a hat; hat'box; hat'brush; hat'guard, a string for keeping a hat from being blown away; hat'peg, a peg for hanging a hat on; hat'pin, a long pin for fastening a hat to the hair; hat'-plant, the sola plant, used for making topees; hat'rack, a set of hatpegs; hat'stand, a piece of furniture with hatpegs; hat trick, a conjurer's trick with a hat: the taking of three wickets by consecutive balls (deserving a new hat) in cricket, or corresponding feat (as three goals) in other games.—a bad hat (*slang*), a rascal; hang up one's hat (see hang); hats off to, all honour to; horse and hattock! to horse! (signal of witches or fairies); mad as a hatter (see mad); my hat! an exclamation of surprise; pass, send, round the hat, to take up a collection, solicit contributions; take off one's hat to, to acknowledge in admiration (*fig.*): to praise; talk through one's hat, to talk wildly or at random; under one's hat, in confidence. [O.E. *hæt;* Dan. *hat.*]

hatch, *hach, n.* a half-door: a small gate (*dial.*): the covering of a hatchway: a hatchway.—*v.t.* to close as with a hatch.—hatch boat, a kind of half-decked fishing-boat; hatch'way, an opening in a deck, floor, wall, or roof.—under hatches, below deck, esp. in confinement: in servitude or depressed state: dead. [O.E. *hæcc, hæc,* grating, half-gate, hatch; cf. hack (3), heck (1); Du. *hek,* gate.]

hatch, *hach, v.t.* to bring out from the egg: to breed: to originate, develop or concoct.—*v.i.* to bring young from the egg: to come from the egg: to develop into young.—*n.* act of hatching: brood hatched.—*ns.* hatch'er; hatch'ery, a place for artificial hatching, esp. of fish eggs.—count one's chickens before they are hatched, to depend too securely on some uncertain future event; **hatches, matches, and dispatches** (*coll.*), newspaper announcements of births, marriages, and deaths. [Early M.E. *hacchen*, from an assumed O.E. *hæccean*.]

**hatch**, *hach*, *v.t.* to mark with fine lines, incisions, or inlaid or applied strips.—*n.* **hatch'ing**, shading in fine lines. [O.Fr. *hacher*, to chop.]

**hatchel**, *hach'əl*, *n.* and *vb.* Same as **hackle**.

**hatchet**, *hach'it*, *n.* a small axe for one hand.—*adj.* **hatch'ety**, like a hatchet.—*adj.* **hatch'et-faced**, having a narrow face with profile like a hatchet. —**hatchet man**, a gunman: a militant journalist: one who does shady jobs for a politician or political party.—**bury the hatchet**, to end war, from a habit of North American Indians. [Fr. *hachette—nacher*, to chop.]

**hatchettite**, *hach'it-it*, *n.* mountain tallow, a natural waxy hydrocarbon. [After Charles *Hatchett* (d. 1847), English chemist.]

**hatchment**, *hach'mənt*, *n.* the arms of a deceased person within a black lozenge-shaped frame, formerly placed on the front of his house. [achievement.]

**hate**, *hāt*, *v.t.* to dislike intensely.—*n.* extreme dislike: hatred: object of hatred.—*adjs.* **hāt'-able, hate'able**, deserving to be hated; **hate'ful**, exciting hate: odious: detestable: feeling or manifesting hate.—*adv.* **hate'fully.**—*n.* **hate'fulness.**—*adj.* **hate'less.**—*ns.* **hate'lessness**; **hāt'er**; **hate'rent** (*Scot.*), hatred.—*adj.* **hate'worthy.**—*n.* **hāt'red**, extreme dislike: enmity: malignity. [O.E. *hete*, hate, *hatian*, to hate; Ger. *hasz*.]

**hate**. Same as **haet**.

**hath**. See **have**.

**hatter**. See **hat**.

**hatter**, *hat'ər*, *v.t.* to trouble, annoy (*arch.*): to batter (*dial.*).

**Hatteria**, *hat-ē'ri-ə*, *n.* Sphenodon. [Origin unknown.]

**hatti-sherif**, *ha'ti-she-rēf'*, (*hist.*) *n.* a decree signed by the Sultan of Turkey. [Pers. *khatt-i-sharif*, noble writing, from Ar.]

**hattock**. See **hat**.

**hauberk**, *hö'bərk*, *n.* a long coat of chain-mail sometimes ending in short trousers: originally armour for the neck. [O.Fr. *hauberc*—O.H.G. *halsberg—hals*, neck, *bergan*, to protect.]

**haud**, *höd*, *n.* and *vb.* a Scottish form of **hold**:— *pa.p.* **hudd'en.**

**haugh**, *höhh*, (*Scot.*) *n.* a riverside meadow or flat. [O.E. *halh* (W.S. *healh*), corner.]

**haughty**, *hö'ti*, *adj.* proud: arrogant: contemptuous: bold (*arch.*): high (*Spens.*).—*adjs.* **haught, hault, haut** (*höt*; *Shak.*, *Spens.*, *Milt.*), haughty: exalted.—*adv.* **haught'ily.**—*n.* **haught'-iness**. [O.Fr. *halt, haut*, high—L. *altus*, high.]

**haul**, *höl*, *v.t.* to drag: to pull with violence or effort: to transport (*U.S.*).—*v.i.* to tug, to try to draw something: to alter a ship's course: to change direction.—*n.* act of pulling, or of pulling in: contents of hauled-in net: a take, gain, loot: a hauled load: distance hauled.—*ns.* **haul'age**, act of hauling: transport, esp. heavy road transport: charge for hauling; **haul'er, haulier** (*höl'yər*; this form is used esp. for a man who conveys coal from the workings to the foot of the shaft, or for one who engages in road haulage business).— **haul over the coals** (see **coal**); **haul round** or **off**, to turn a ship's course away from an object; **haul up**, to come or bring to rest after hauling: to call to account. [A variant of **hale**.]

**hauld**, *höld*, *n.* a Scottish form of **hold**, as in the *dial.* phrase *out of house and hauld*, homeless.

**haulm, halm**, *höm, häm*, *n.* straw, esp. of gathered plants: a strawy stem: a culm: straw or stems of plants collectively. [O.E. *halm* (*healm*).]

**haulst**. See **halse**.

**hault**. See **haughty**.

**haunch**, *hönch, hönsh*, also (old-fashioned) **hanch**,

**hänsh**, *n.* the expansion of the body at and near the pelvis: the hip with buttock: the leg and loin of venison, etc.: the side or flank of an arch between the crown and the springing: the rear (*Shak.*): a jerked underhand throw (*dial.*).—*v.t.* to throw with an underhand movement (*dial.*).— **haunch bone**, the innominate bone. [O.Fr. *hanche*, prob. of Gmc. origin; cf. O.H.G. *anchâ*, leg.]

**haunt**, *hönt*, *v.t.* to frequent: to associate much with: to intrude upon continually: to inhabit or visit (as a ghost): to cling, or keep recurring, to the memory of.—*v.i.* to be much about, to visit frequently (with *about*, etc.).—*n.* place much resorted to: resort, habit of frequenting (*Shak.*): a ghost (*U.S. dial.*).—*adj.* **haunt'ed**, frequented, infested, esp. by ghosts or apparitions: obsessed: worried.—*n.* **haunt'er.**—*n.* and *adj.* **haunt'ing.**— *adv.* **haunt'ingly**. [O.Fr. *hanter*.]

**haurient, hauriant**, *hö'ri-ənt*, (*her.*) *adj.* rising as if to breathe. [L. *hauriēns, -entis*, pr.p. of *haurire*, to draw up, drink.]

**hause**. See **halse** (1).

**hausfrau**, *hows'frow*, *n.* a housewife, esp. a woman exclusively interested in domestic matters. [Ger.]

**haussmannise, -ize**, *hows'mən-iz*, *v.t.* to open out, generally rebuild, as Baron *Haussmann*, as prefect of the Seine (1853-70), did Paris.—*n.* **haussmannisä'tion, -z-**.

**haustellum**, *hös-tel'əm*, *n.* a sucking proboscis or its sucking end, as in flies:—*pl.* **haustell'a.**—*adj.* **haus'tellate**, having a haustellum.—*n.* **haustō'-rium**, the part by which a parasitic plant fixes itself and derives nourishment from its host:—*pl.* **haustō'ria**. [L. *haurire, haustum*, draw up, drink.]

**haut**. See **haughty**.

**haut**, *ō*, (Fr.) high; **haut monde** (*mɔ̃d*), high society; **haut pas** (*pä*), a dais; **haut relief** (*rə-lyef*), high relief; **haut ton** (*tɔ̃*), high fashion.—**de haut en bas** (*də ō tä bä*), downwards, or from top to bottom (*lit.*): with an air of superiority, contemptuously.

**hautboy**, *(h)ō'boi*, *n.* arch. name for **oboe**: a large kind of strawberry. [Fr. *hautbois—haut*, high, *bois*, wood.]

**haute**, *ōt*, (Fr.) fem. of **haut**; **haute bourgeoisie** (*bōōr-zhwä-zē*), the richer, more influential part of the middle class; **haute couture** (*kōō-tür*), fashionable, expensive dress designing and dressmaking; **haute cuisine** (*kwē-zēn*), cookery of a very high standard; **haute école** (*ā-kol*), horsemanship of the most difficult kind; **haute époque** (*ā-pok*), in relation to architecture, furniture, etc., the period during which Louis XIV, XV and XVI reigned in France; **haute politique** (*po-lē-tēk*), the higher reaches of politics; **haute vulgarisation** (*vül-gar-ēz-as-yɔ̃*), popularisation of scholarly subjects.

**hauteur**, *ō'tər, ō-tœr*, *n.* haughtiness: arrogance. [Fr.]

**haüyne**, *hö'in, hä'win*, *n.* a blue mineral, in composition like nosean, with calcium. [After the French mineralogist René J. *Haüy* (1743-1822).]

**Havana**, *hə-van'ə*, *n.* a fine quality of cigar, made in *Havana* or Cuba generally.

**have**, *hav*, *v.t.* to hold: to keep: to possess: to own: to hold in control: to bear: to be in a special relation to (analogous to, if short of, ownership; e.g. *to have a son, an assistant, no government*): to be characterised by: to be in enjoyment of: to experience: to know: to entertain in the mind: to grasp the meaning or point of: to have received as information: to put, assert, and express: to suffer, endure, tolerate: to hold or esteem: to cause or allow to be: to convey, take, cause to go: to accept, take: to get: to obtain: to give birth to: to be obliged: to get the better of, hold at a disadvantage or in one's power in a dilemma: to take in, deceive: as an auxiliary verb, used with the *pa.p.* in

Neutral vowels in unaccented syllables: *el'ə-mənt*; for certain sounds in foreign words, see p. viii

forming the perfect tenses:—*2nd pers. sing.* hast; *3rd has, arch.* hath; *pl.* have; *pres. subj.* have; *pa.t.* and *pa.p.* had, *2nd pers. pa.t.* hadst; *pa.subj.* had; *pr.p.* hav'ing.—*n.* one who has possessions:—*pl.* haves.—*ns.* hav'er, one who has or possesses, a holder: the person in whose custody a document is (*Scots law*); hav'ing, act of possessing: possession, estate: (esp. in *pl. hăv'ingz*) behaviour, good manners (*Scot.*).—*adj.* greedy.—have-at'-him (*Shak.*), a thrust; have'-not, one who lacks possessions:—*pl.* have'-nots; have-on', a deception, a hoax: a piece of humbug or chaff.—had as good (*arch.*), might as well; had as lief (*arch.*), would as willingly; had better, best, would do best to; had like (see like (1)); have at, (let me) attack: here goes; had rather, would prefer; have done, have to do with (see do); have in (*coll.*), to entertain in one's home; have it, to prevail: to exceed in any way: to get punishment, unpleasant consequences; have it in for (someone), to have a grudge against (someone); have it out, to discuss or express explicitly and exhaustively; have on, to wear: to take in, hoax, chaff; have up, to call to account before a court of justice, etc.; have what it takes, to have the necessary qualities or capabilities to do something; have with you (*arch.*), I am ready to go with you; he's had it (*slang*), he is ruined: he has missed his opportunities: it's all up with him: he's been killed. [O.E. *habban*, pa.t. *hæfde*, pa.p. *gehæfd*; Ger. *haben*, Dan. *have*.]

havelock, hav'lǝk, *n.* a white cover for a military cap, with a flap over the neck. [From Gen. Henry *Havelock*, 1795-1857 ]

haven, hā'vn, *n.* an inlet affording shelter to ships. a harbour: any place of retreat or asylum.—*v.t.* to shelter.—*adj.* hā'vened. [O.E. *hæfen*; Du. *haven*, Ger. *hafen*.]

haveour. See haviour.

haver, hăv'ǝr, (*Scot.*) *v.i.* to talk nonsense, or foolishly.—*n.* (usu. in *pl.*) foolish talk: nonsense. —*ns.* hav'erel, a foolish person; haver'ings, havers.

haver, hav'ǝr, *n.* oats (*Northern*): the wild oat (grass; *Northern*).—*n.* hav'ersack, a bag worn over one shoulder for carrying provisions, etc., (orig. horse's oats) on a journey. [O.N. (pl.) *hafrar*; cf. Ger. *hafer, haber*, oats.]

haversine, hav'ǝr-sīn, *n.* half the *versine*.

havildar, hav'il-där, *n.* an Indian sergeant. [Pers. *hawāl-dār*.]

haviour, haveour, hāv'yǝr, *n.* possession (*obs.*): behaviour (*Spens.*). [Partly O.Fr. *aveir*, possession, partly behaviour.]

havoc, hav'ǝk, *n.* general destruction: devastation. —*v.t.* to lay waste:—*pr.p.* hav'ocking; *pa.t.* and *pa.p.* hav'ocked.—*interj.* an ancient war-cry, signal for plunder. [A.Fr. *havok*—O.Fr. *havot*, plunder; prob. Gmc.]

haw, hö, *n.* a hedge (*hist.*): an enclosure (*hist.*): a messuage (*hist.*): the fruit of the hawthorn.— haw'buck, a bumpkin; haw'finch, the common grosbeak; haw'thorn, a small tree of the rose family, much used for hedges. [O.E. *haga*, a yard or enclosure, a haw; Du. *haag*, a hedge, Ger. *hag*, a hedge, O.N. *hagi*, a field.]

haw, hö, *v.i.* to speak with hesitation or drawl, natural or affected.—*adj.* haw'-haw', affectedly superior in enunciation.—*n.* a hesitation or affectation of superiority in speech: loud vulgar laughter.—*v.i.* to guffaw, to laugh boisterously. [Imit.]

haw, hö, *n.* the nictitating membrane: a disease of the nictitating membrane. [Origin unknown.]

Hawaiian, ha-wī'(y)ǝn, *adj.* pertaining to Hawaii, to its citizens, or to its language.—Also *n.*

haw-haw. See ha-ha (1), haw (2).

hawk, hök, *n.* any bird of the falcon family other than the eagles, esp. of the sparrow-hawk (Accipiter) or the goshawk genus (Astur): a predatory

or a keen-sighted person: a hawk-moth.—*v.t.* and *v.i.* to hunt with trained hawks: to hunt on the wing.—*ns.* hawk'er; hawk'ing, falconry.—*adj.* practising falconry: hawklike, keen (*Shak.*). —*adj.* hawk'ish.—*adj.* hawk'-beaked, -billed, with a beak, or nose, like a hawk's bill.—hawk'bell, a small bell attached to a hawk's leg; hawk'bit, a plant (Leontodon) close akin to the dandelion. —*adj.* hawk'-eyed, sharp-sighted.—hawk'-moth, any member of the Sphinx family, heavy moths with hovering flight.—*adj.* hawk'-nosed, hook-beaked.—hawks'beard, a plant (Crepis) very like hawkweed; hawks'bill, a hawk-beaked turtle; hawk'weed, a genus (Hieracium) of yellow-headed ligulate-flowered composites.— doves and hawks (see dove); know a hawk from a handsaw (prob. for *heronshaw*), to be able to judge between things pretty well. [O.E. *hafoc*; Du. *havik*, Ger. *habicht*, O.N. *haukr*.]

hawk, hök, *v.t.* to force up from the throat.—*v.i.* to clear the throat noisily.—*n.* the act of doing so. [Prob. imit.]

hawk. See hawker.

hawk, hök, *n.* a plasterer's slab with handle below. [Origin unknown.]

hawked, hökt, (*Scot.* hawk'it), *adj.* streaked: white-faced.—*ns.* hawk'ey, hawk'ie, a cow with white-striped face.

hawker, hök'ǝr, *n.* one who goes about offering goods for sale: now confined to one who uses a beast of burden or vehicle (distinguished from a pedlar, who carries his wares bodily).—*v.t.* hawk, to convey about for sale: to cry for sale. [Cf. L.G. and Ger. *höker*, Du. *heuker*.]

hawkey. See hockey (2).

hawm, höm, (*dial.*) *v.i.* to lounge about. [Origin unknown.]

hawse, höz, *n.* part of a vessel's bow in which the hawseholes are cut.—hawse'hole, a hole for a ship's cable; hawse'pipe, a tubular casting, fitted to a ship's bows, through which the anchor chain or cable passes. [O.N. *hāls*, neck.]

hawse. See halse (1).

hawser, hö'zǝr, *n.* a small cable, a large rope used in warping: a hawser-laid rope.—*adj.* haw'ser-laid, composed of strands with a left-handed twist twisted together to the right hand. [O.Fr. *haucier, haulser*, to raise.—L.L. *altiāre*—L. *altus*, high.]

hawthorn. See haw (1).

hay, hā, *n.* grass, etc., cut down and dried for fodder or destined for that purpose.—*v.t.* and *v.i.* to make hay.—*ns.* hay'ing, the making or harvesting of hay; hay'sel (O.E. *sæl*, season; *dial.*), the hay season.—hay'band, a rope of twisted hay; hay'box, an airtight box of hay used to continue the cooking of dishes already begun; hay'cock, a conical pile of hay in the field; hay fever, irritation by pollen of the nose, throat, etc., with sneezing and headache—also hay asthma; hay'field, a field where hay is made; hay'fork, a long-handled fork used in turning and lifting hay; hay knife, a broad knife with a handle set crosswise at one end, used for cutting hay from a stack; hay'loft, a loft in which hay is kept; hay'maker, one who makes hay: a wild swinging blow (*slang*): (in *pl.*) a kind of country-dance; hay'making; hay'mow, a rick of hay: a mass of hay stored in a barn; hay'rick, a hay-stack; hay'seed, grass seed dropped from hay: a rustic (*coll.*); hay'stack; hay'wire, wire for binding hay.—*adj.* (*slang*), tangled: crazy: all amiss.—Also *adv.*—hit the hay (*slang*), go to bed; make hay, to toss and turn cut grass: to throw things into confusion (with *of*); make hay while the sun shines, to seize an opportunity while it lasts. [O.E. *hieg, hig, hēg*; Ger. *heu*, Du. *hooi*; O.N. *hey*.]

hay, hā, (*arch.*) *n.* a hedge, fence.—hay'-bote; hedge-bote; hayward, one who had charge of fences and enclosures and prevented cattle from breaking through: one who herded the common cattle of a town. [O.E. *hege*—*haga*, a hedge.]

**hay,** *hā,* (*obs.*) *interj.* used on hitting in fencing.— *n.* (*Shak.*) a hit or home-thrust. [It. *hai,* thou hast (it)—*avere*—L. *habēre,* to have.]

**hay.** See hey (2).

**hayle** (*Spens.*). See hale (1).

**hazard,** *haz'ərd, n.* an old dicing game: chance: accident: risk: the thing risked: the pocketing of the object ball (*winning* hazard), of the player's own ball after contact (*losing* hazard; *billiards*): the side of the court into which the ball is served (*court tennis*): any difficulty on golf links—bunker, long grass, road, water, whins, etc.—*v.t.* to expose to chance: to risk: to venture: to venture to say or utter.—*adj.* **haz'ardable.**—*n.* **haz'ardize** (*Spens.*), hazard.— *adj.* **haz'ardous,** dangerous: perilous: uncertain. —*adv.* **haz'ardously.**—*ns.* **haz'ardousness; haz'- ardry** (*Spens.*), playing at games of hazard or chance: rashness. [O.Fr. *hasard;* prob. through the Sp. from Arab. *al zār,* the die; according to William of Tyre from *Hasart,* a castle in Syria, where the game was invented during the Crusades.]

**haze,** *hāz, n.* vapour or mist, often shining and obscuring vision: mistiness: lack of definition or precision.—*v.t.* to make hazy.—*v.i.* to form a haze.—*adv.* **haz'ily.**—*n.* **haz'iness.**—*adj.* **haz'y,** thick with haze: ill-defined: not clear: confused (of the mind). [App. not O.E. *hasu, haswe,* grey.]

**haze,** *hāz, v.t.* to vex with needless or excessive tasks, rough treatment, practical jokes: to rag: to bully.—*ns.* **haz'er; haz'ing.** [O.Fr. *haser,* to annoy.]

**hazel,** *hā'zl, n.* a tree (Corylus) of the birch family.—*adj.* of hazel: light-brown, like a hazelnut.—*adj.* **hā'zelly.**—**hazel grouse, hen,** the ruffed grouse; **hā'zelnut,** the edible nut of the hazel-tree. [O.E. *hæsel;* Ger. *hasel,* O.N. *hasl,* L. *corulus, corylus.*]

**he,** *hē* (or when unemphatic *hi, ē, i*), *nom.* (irregularly or ungrammatically *accus.* or *dat.*) *masc. pron. of 3rd pers.* the male (or thing spoken of as if male) named before, indicated, or understood:— *pl.* **they.**—*n.* a male:—*pl.* **hes.**—*adj.* male (esp. in composition).—**he'-man,** a man of exaggerated or extreme virility, or what some women take to be virility. [O.E. *hē, he.*]

**head,** *hed, n.* the uppermost or foremost part of an animal's body: the brain: the understanding: self-possession: a chief or leader: a headmaster, principal: the place of honour or command: the front or top of anything: a rounded or enlarged end or top: a capitulum: a mass of leaves, flowers, hair, etc.: a head-dress or dressing for the head (*arch.*): a headache (*coll.*): the peg-box and scroll of a violin, etc.: the membrane of a drum: the essential part of an apparatus: in a bicycle, the tube in which the front-fork is socketed: an individual animal or person as one of a group: a title, heading: a topic or chief point of a discourse: a source: energy of a fluid owing to height, velocity, and pressure: strength (*arch.*): insurrectionary force (*arch.*): highest point of anything: culmination: a cape: a froth on liquor poured out: point of suppuration: headway: a head's length or height: a mine tunnel: (in *pl.*) the obverse of a coin: one who takes hallucinogenic drugs (*slang*).—*adj.* of, pertaining to, the head: for the head: chief, principal: at, or coming from, the front.—*v.t.* to remove the head or top from: to behead (*obs.*): to supply with a head, top, or heading: to be the head, or at the head, of: to get ahead of and turn: to go round the head of: to face: to meet in the face: to cause to face or front: to strike with the head.—

*v.i.* to form a head: to face, front: to shape one's course, make (for).—*adj.* h**ea**d'ed, having a head: come to a head (*Shak.*).—*ns.* **head'er,** one who or a machine which removes heads from or supplies heads for casks, etc.: a dive head foremost: a brick or stone at right angles to the wall surface: the act of heading a ball.—*adv.* **head'ily.**—*ns.* **head'iness; head'ing,** the action of the verb head in any sense: a part forming a head: a small passage to be enlarged into a tunnel: words placed at the head of a chapter, paragraph, etc.—*adj.* **head'less.**—*adv.* **head'long,** with the head foremost or first: without thought, rashly: precipitately.—*adj.* **rash: precipitate: precipitous.**—*adj.* **head'most,** most advanced or forward.—*n.* **head'ship,** the position or office of head or chief.—*adj.* **head'y,** affecting the brain: intoxicating: inflamed: rash: violent.—**head'- ache,** a pain in the head: a source of worry (*coll.*).—*adj.* **head'achy.**—**head'band,** a band or fillet for the head: a band round the top of trousers, etc.: the band at each end of a book: a thin slip of iron on the tympan of a printing-press; **head'-boom,** a jib-boom or a flying jib-boom; **head'borough** (*hist.*), the head of a frank-pledge, tithing, or decennary: a petty constable; **head boy,** the senior boy in a school; **head'chair,** a high-backed chair with headrest; **head'cheese** (*U.S.*), brawn; **head'cloth,** a kerchief worn instead of a hat; **head'-dress,** a covering for the head: a mode of dressing the hair (*arch.*): **head'fast,** a mooring rope at the bows of a ship; **head'frame,** the structure over a mine-shaft supporting the winding machinery; **head'gear,** gear, covering, or ornament of the head: apparatus at the head of a mine-shaft; **head'-hugger,** a woman's close-fitting headgear of kerchief type; **head'hunt'er; head'hunt'ing,** the practice of collecting human heads; **head'- land,** a point of land running out into the sea: a cape: the border of a field where the plough turns, ploughed separately afterwards; **head'- light, head'lamp,** a light on the front of a vehicle; **head'line,** line at the top of a page containing title, folio, etc.: title in a newspaper, caption: a news item given very briefly (*radio, TV*): (in *pl.*) the sails and ropes next the yards. —*v.t.* to give as a headline, mention in a headline: to publicise.—*v.i.* to be a headliner.—**head- lin'er,** one whose name is made most prominent in a bill or programme.—*adj.* **head'-lugged** (*Shak.*), dragged by the head.—**head'man,** a chief, a leader; **head'mark,** a peculiar characteristic; **headmas'ter,** the principal master of a school; **headmis'tress; head money,** a poll tax: prize money by head of prisoners: a reward for a proscribed outlaw's head; **head'note,** a note placed at the head of a chapter or page, esp. a condensed statement of points of law involved introductory to the report of a legal decision: a tone produced in the head register (*mus.*).—*adj.* and *adv.* **head'-on',** head to head: with head pointing directly forward: directly opposed.— **head'phone,** (usu. in *pl.*) a telephone receiver worn in pairs on a headband, esp. for wireless listening: a hairdressing of similar form; **head'- piece,** a helmet: a hat: head, skull (*arch.*); *Spens.* **headpeace:** a brain: a man of intelligence: a top part: a decorative engraving at the beginning of a book, chapter, etc. (*print.*).—*n.pl.* **headquar'ters,** the quarters or residence of a commander-in-chief or general: a central or chief office, etc.—**head'race,** the race leading to a water-wheel; **head'rail,** one of the rails at a ship's head; **head'reach,** the distance made to windward in tacking.—*v.i.* to shoot ahead, in tacking.—**head register** (*mus.*), high register: of the voice in which nose and head cavities vibrate sympathetically: (in male voice) falsetto; **head rent,** rent payable to the freeholder;

head'rest, a support for the head; head rhyme, alliteration; head'rig (Scot.), a headland in a ploughed field; head'ring, a palm-leaf hair ornament worn by S. African native men after marriage; head'room, uninterrupted space below a ceiling, bridge, etc.: space overhead; head'rope, a rope for tying or leading an animal; head sea, a sea running directly against a ship's course; head'shake, a significant shake of the head; head'shrinker, a headhunter who shrinks the heads of his victims: a psychiatrist (coll.); heads'man, an executioner who cuts off heads; head'square, a square cloth worn as a covering for the head; head'stall, the part of a bridle round the head: a choir-stall with back to screen (obs.); head'-sta'tion, the dwelling-house, etc., on an Australian sheep or cattle station; head'stick (print.), formerly a straight piece of furniture placed at the head of a form, between the chase and the type; head'stock (mach.), a device for supporting the end or head of a member or part; head'stone, the principal stone of a building: cornerstone: gravestone; head'-stream, a headwater: a high tributary: the stream forming the highest or remotest source.— adj. head'strong, obstinately self-willed.—head'-tire (obs.), a head-dress; head voice, tones in the head register; head waiter, a person placed over the waiters of a restaurant or hotel; head-wat'er, the highest part of a stream, before receiving affluents; head'way, motion ahead, esp. of a ship: progress; head wind, a directly opposing wind; head'word, a word serving as a heading: a word under which others are grouped, as in a dictionary; head'work, mental work; head'work'er.—above, over, one's head, beyond one's comprehension; come to a head, to reach a climax; eat one's head off (see eat); give a horse his head, to let him go as he chooses (now also fig.); go by the head (naut.), to sink head foremost; go to one's head, to disturb one's sobriety or good sense; have a head on one's shoulders, to have ability and balance; have one's head screwed on the right way, to behave sensibly; head and shoulders, very much, as if taller by a head and shoulders: violently (arch.); head first, foremost, with the head first; head off, to get ahead of so as to turn back: to deflect from path or intention; heads or tails, an invitation to guess how a coin will fall; head over heels, headlong, as in a somersault; hit the headlines, to get prominent notice in the press; keep, lose, one's head, to keep, lose, one's self-possession; lay, put, heads together, to confer and co-operate; off, out of, one's head, crazy: out of one's own head, spontaneously: of one's own invention; over head and ears, deeply submerged or engrossed; show one's head, to allow oneself to be seen; take it into one's head, to conceive the notion; turn one's head (see turn). [O.E. hēafod; cf. Du. hoofd, Ger. haupt.]
-head. See -hood.

heal, hēl, v.t. to make whole and healthy: to cure: to restore to soundness: to remedy, amend.— v.i. to grow sound.—n. (arch. and Scot.) health: soundness: welfare.—adj. heal'able.—n. heal'er. —n. and adj. heal'ing.—adv. heal'ingly.—adj. heal'some (Scot.), wholesome. [O.E. hǣlan (vb.), hǣlu (n.).—hāl, whole; cf. Ger. heil, Du. heel; O.N. heill; hail (1), hale (1), whole.]
heal. See hele.
heald, hēld, n. the same as heddle.—Also an old form of heel (2).
health, helth, n. sound bodily or mental condition: soundness: condition of wholesomeness: well-being: state with respect to soundness: a toast.—adj. health'ful, enjoying, indicating, or conducing to health.—adv. health'fully.—n. health'fulness.—adv. health'ily.—n. health'iness. —adj. health'less.—n. health'lessness.—adjs.

health'some, healthy, wholesome; health'y, in good health: morally or spiritually wholesome: conducive to or indicative of good health.— health centre, centre for clinical and administrative health welfare work; health resort, a place noted for its health-giving conditions, esp. climatic. [O.E. hǣlth—hāl, whole.]
heame, hēm, (Spens.) adv. for home.
heap, hēp, n. a mass of things resting one above another: a mound: a company (Shak.): a great number, a great deal (often in pl.), a collection: an old dilapidated motor car: a ruin (B.).—v.t. to throw in a heap: to amass: to load with a heap or heaps: to pile high, or above the rim or brim.—adj. heap'y, full of heaps.—heap'stead, the buildings and works around a mine-shaft.— knock, strike all of a heap, to confound utterly. [O.E. hēap; cf. O.N. hōpr, Ger. haufe, Du. hoop.]
hear, hēr, v.t. to perceive by the ear: to accede to: to listen to: to listen to in trial of ability to repeat: to try judicially: to be informed: to be a hearer of: to be called (Milt., a Latinism).—v.i. to have or exercise the sense of hearing: to listen: to have news of or from: to be spoken of (Spens., a Graecism):—pa.t. and pa.p. heard (hûrd).—adj. heard (hûrd).—ns. hear'er; hear'ing, power or act of perceiving sound: opportunity to be heard: audience: audition: judicial investigation and listening to evidence and arguments, esp. without a jury: earshot: news: a scolding (dial.).—hear'ing-aid, any device, electrical or other, for enabling the deaf to hear or to hear better; hear'say, common talk: report: rumour.—adj. of the nature of, or based on, report given by others.—hear, hear!, an exclamation of approval from the hearers of a speech; hear tell of, to hear some one speak of; will not hear of, will not allow, tolerate. [O.E. (Anglian) hēran (W. S. hieran, hȳran); Du. hooren, O.N. heyra, Ger. hören, Goth. hausjan.]
heard, heare, hēr, hearie, (Spens.) forms of herd, hair, hairy.
hearken, härk'n, v.i. to hear attentively: to listen. —v.t. to listen to, pay attention to, heed (poet.): to seek by enquiry (obs.).—n. heark'ener. [O.E. hercnian (heorcnian); cf. hark, hear; Ger. horchen.]
hearse, (Spens.) herse, hûrs, n. orig. a canopy or frame over a bier, designed to hold candles: a funeral service (Spens.): a bier (obs.): a car for carrying the dead.—v.t. to put on or in a hearse. —adjs. hearse'-like, hears'y.—hearse'-cloth, a pall. [O.Fr. herse (It. erpice)—L. hirpex, -icis, a harrow.]
heart, härt, n. the organ that circulates the blood: the stomach (obs.): the innermost part: the core: the chief or vital part: the breast, bosom: the (imagined) seat of the affections, understanding, and thought, as opposed to the head, the seat of reason: courage: inmost feelings: vigour, spirit: cordiality: compassion: a term of endearment or encouragement: a heart-shaped figure or object: a playing-card with heart-shaped pips: the centre of a cabbage, lettuce, etc.: a diseased state of the heart.—v.t. to hearten (arch.); to fill up a centre space with rubble (building).—v.i. to form a compact head or inner mass, as a lettuce.—adj. heart'ed, having a heart, esp. of a specified kind (hard-hearted, etc.): seated or fixed in the heart, laid up in the heart.—v.t. heart'en, to encourage, stimulate: to add strength to.—v.i. to take courage.—n. heart'ikin, a little heart (in an obs. minced oath). —adv. heart'ily.—n. heart'iness.—adj. heart'less, without heart, courage, or feeling: callous.— adv. heart'lessly.—ns. heart'lessness; heart'let, a little heart, a nucleus; heart'ling (Shak.), little heart, used in a minced oath (ods heartlings, God's heart).—adv. heart'ly (Spens. harte'ly heartily.—adjs. heart'some, exhilarating: merry;

**heart'y**, full of heart: heartfelt: sincere: cordial: robust: lusty: enthusiastic: unrestrained: in, or indicating, good spirits, appetite, or condition: sound: in good heart.—*n.* a hearty fellow, esp. a sailor: a student who goes in for sports, distinguished from an *aesthete*.—**heart'ache**, sorrow: anguish; **heart'-beat**, a pulsation of the heart: a throb; **heart'-block**, a condition in which the ventricle does not keep time with the auricle; **heart('s)'-blood**, blood of the heart: life, essence; **heart'-bond**, in masonry, a bond in which two headers meet in the middle of a wall and one header overlaps them; **heart'-break**, a crushing sorrow or grief.—*v.t.* (*Burns*) to break the heart of.—**heartbrea'ker**, a flirt: a curl, lovelock.—*adjs.* **heart'brea'king**; **heart'-broken**.—**heart'burn**, a burning, acrid feeling in throat or breast; **heart'burning**, discontent: secret grudging; **heart cam**, a heart-shaped cam in a stop-watch, etc.; **heart cockle**, **heart shell**, a mollusc (Isocardia) or its shell, like a cockle coiled at the bosses.—*adj.* **heart'-dear** (*Shak.*), dear to the heart, sincerely beloved.—**heart disease'**, any morbid condition of the heart.—*adj.* **heart'-eas'ing**, giving peace to the mind.—**heart'-failure**, stoppage or inadequate functioning of the heart: shock producing faintness.—*adjs.* **heart'felt**, felt deeply: sincere; **heart'-free**, having the affections disengaged.—**heart'-grief**, deep-seated affliction; **heart'-heav'iness**, depression of spirits; **heart'land**, an area of a country that is centrally situated and/or vitally important; **heart'-quake**, trembling, fear.—*adj.* **heart'-rend'ing**, agonising.—**heart'-rot**, decay in the hearts of trees, caused by various fungi; **heart'-search'ing**, examination of one's feelings; **heart's(-)ease**, the pansy; **heart'seed**, or **heart'pea**, balloon-vine, from the heart-shaped scar left by the seed; **heart'-ser'vice**, sincere devotion, as opp. to *eye-service*.—*adjs.* **heart'-shaped**, shaped like the conventional representation of the human heart; **heart'-sick**, despondent.—**heart'-sick'ness**.—*adj.* **heart'-sore**, sore at heart: caused by soreness of heart (*Shak.*).—*n.* grief: cause of grief (*Spens.*).—**heart'-spoon** (*dial.*), the depression in the breastbone: the breastbone: the pit of the stomach.—*adj.* **heart'-stirr'ing**, rousing: exhilarating.—*v.t.* **heart'-strike** (*arch.*), to strike to the heart: to dismay: to drive into the heart:—*pa.p.* **heart'-stricken**, **heart'-struck** (*obs.* -strook).—**heart'-string**, orig. a nerve or tendon imagined to brace and sustain the heart: (in *pl.*) affections; **heart'-throb** (*slang*), a sentimental emotion for one of the opposite sex: the person causing it.—*adj.* **heart'-to-heart'**, candid, intimate, and unreserved.—Also *n.*—**heart'-ur'chin**, a sea-urchin of the Spatangoidea, typically heart-shaped.—*adjs.* **heart'warming**, emotionally moving: gratifying, pleasing; **heart'-whole**, whole at heart: sincere: with affections disengaged: undismayed: out-and-out.—**heart'wood**, the duramen or hard inner wood of a tree.—*adj.* **hart'ie-hale** (*Spens.*), good for the heart, healthy.—**after one's own heart**, exactly to one's own liking; **at heart**, in real character: substantially; **break one's heart**, to die of, or be broken down by, grief or disappointment: to cause deep grief to anyone: **by heart**, by rote: in the memory; **cross one's heart**, emphasise the truth of a statement; **eat one's heart** (see eat); **find in one's heart**, to be able to bring oneself; **from the bottom of one's heart**, most sincerely; **have a change of heart**, alter one's former opinion or viewpoint; **have at heart**, to cherish as a matter of deep interest; **have one's heart in one's boots**, to feel a sinking of the heart; **have one's heart in one's mouth**, to be in trepidation; **have one's heart in the right place**, to be basically decent, generous; **heart and hand**, **heart and soul**, with complete heartiness,

with complete devotion to a cause; **heart of heart(s)**, the inmost feelings or convictions: deepest affections; **heart of oak**, heartwood of the oak-tree: a brave, resolute heart; **in good heart**, in sound or fertile condition: in good spirits or courage; **lay**, **take**, **to heart**, to store up in the mind for future guidance: to be deeply moved by something; **set the heart at rest**, to render easy in mind; **set the heart upon**, to come to desire earnestly; **speak to the heart** (*B.*), to comfort, encourage; **take heart**, to be encouraged; **take heart of grace** (see grace); **take to heart**, to come to feel in earnest; **wear one's heart on one's sleeve**, to show the feelings openly; **with all one's heart**, most willingly. [O.E. *heorte*; cf. Du. *hart*, Ger. *herz*; L. *cor*, *cordis*; Gr. *kardiā*.]

**hearth**, *härth*, *n.* the part of the floor on which the fire is made: the fireside: the house itself: the home circle: the lowest part of a blast-furnace: a brazier, chafing-dish, or fire-box.—**hearth'-brush**, a brush for sweeping the hearth; **hearth'-mon'ey**, **-penn'y**, **-tax**, a tax on hearths; **hearth'-rug**, a rug laid over the hearth-stone; **hearth'-stone**, a stone forming a hearth: a soft stone used for whitening hearths, doorsteps, etc. [O.E. *heorth*; Du. *haard*, Ger. *herd*.]

**heast**, **heaste**, *hēst* (*Spens.*) *n.* Same as **hest**.

**heat**, *hēt*, *n.* that which excites the sensation of warmth: sensation of warmth, esp. in a high degree: degree of hotness: exposure to intense heat: a high temperature: the hottest time: redness of the skin: vehemence, passion: sexual excitement, or its period, esp. in the female, corresponding to *rut* in the male: a single course in a race: a division of a contest from which the winner goes on to a final test: animation: pressure intended to coerce (*coll.*): period of intensive search, esp. by the police for a criminal after a crime has taken place (*coll.*).—*v.t.* to make hot: to agitate: perh., to run over, as in a race (*Shak.*).—*v.i.* to become hot.—*adj.* **heat'ed**.—*n.* **heat'er**, one who, or that which, heats: apparatus for heating a room or building: means of heating a flat iron, etc.—*n.* and *adj.* **heat'ing**.—**heat'-ap'oplexy**, sunstroke; **heat barrier**, difficulties caused by a thin envelope of hot air which develops round aircraft at high speeds and occasions structural and other problems; **heat en'gine**, an engine that transforms heat into mechanical work; **heat'er-shield**, a triangular shield, like the heater of a flat-iron; **heat exchanger**, device for transferring heat from one fluid to another; **heat pump**, a device (on the refrigerator principle) for drawing heat from water, air, or the earth, and giving it out to warm, e.g. a room; **heat sink**, something into which unwanted heat can be shot; **heat'spot**, an area of skin with nerve-ends sensitive to heat: a spot or blotch on the skin caused by heat: a freckle; **heat'stroke**, exhaustion, illness, or prostration due to exposure to heat: sunstroke; **heat unit**, amount of heat required to raise a pound of water 1 degree F in temperature (*British thermal unit*; mean value, the 180th part of heat required to raise temperature from 32°F to 212°F, being equal to 1055·06 joules); **heat wave**, heated state of atmosphere passing from one locality to another: a hot spell.—**latent heat**, the heat required to change solid to liquid, or liquid to gas, without change of temperature; **mechanical equivalent of heat**, the energy required to produce one heat unit; **specific heat** (see specific); **turn on the heat** (*slang*), to use brutal treatment, mental or physical, esp. in order to coerce. [O.E. *hātu*, heat; *hāt*, hot; Ger. *hitze*.]

**heath**, *hēth*, *n.* barren open country, esp. covered with ericaceous and other low shrubs: any shrub of genus Erica, sometimes extended to Calluna (heather) and others of the family

Ericaceae: a butterfly of the Satyridae.—*adj.*
**heath'y,** abounding with heath.—**heath bell,**
heather bell: harebell; **heath'bird, heath'-fowl,**
the black grouse; **heath'cock,** the male black
grouse; **heath'-hen,** the grey-hen or female black
grouse: an extinct American bird akin to the
prairie-chicken; **heath'-poult,** the black grouse,
esp. the female or young. [O.E. *hǣth*; Ger.
*heide,* Goth, *haithi,* a waste.]

**heathen,** *hē'dhn, n.* one who belongs to a people of
some lower form of religion, esp. polytheistic, or
of no religion: any person neither Christian nor
Jewish (*arch.*): a pagan: one who is ignorant or
unmindful of religion: an uncivilised person
(*coll.*):—*pl.* **heath'en** (collectively), **heath'ens**
(individually). — *adj.* pagan: irreligious — *ns.*
**hea'thendom, heath'enesse** (*arch.*), heathenism:
the condition of a heathen: those regions of the
world where heathenism prevails.—*v.t.* **hea'then-**
**ise, -ize,** to make heathen or heathenish.—*adj.*
**hea'thenish,** relating to the heathen: rude:
uncivilised: cruel. — *adv.* **hea'thenishly.** — *ns.*
**hea'thenishness; hea'thenism,** the religious
system of the heathens: paganism: barbarism;
**hea'thenry,** heathenism: heathendom. [O.E.
*hǣthen*; Du. *heiden.*]

**heather,** *hedh'ər, n.* ling, a common low shrub
(*Calluna vulgaris*) of the heath family: sometimes extended to the heaths (Erica): an assemblage of heather plants.—*adj.* of the colour of
(red) heather: composed of or from heather.—
*adj.* **heath'ery.**—**heather ale,** a famous liquor
traditionally brewed in Scotland from the bells
of heather a lost art; **heather bell,** the flower
of the cross-leaved heath (*Erica tetralix*) or of
the common heath (*Erica cinerea*); **heath'er-**
**mix'ture,** a woollen fabric speckled in colours
like heather.—**set the heather on fire,** to create a
disturbance or a sensation; **take to the heather,**
to become an outlaw. [Older Scots *hadder*;
origin unknown; prob. influenced by heath.]

**heather-bleat, heather-bleater,** *hedh'ər-blēt', -ər,*
(*Scot.*) *ns.* a snipe. — Also **heather-bluiter,**
**-blutter** (*-blüt', -blut'*). [O.E. *hǣfer-blǣte* —
*hǣfer,* goat, *blǣtan,* to bleat, from its cry; influenced by heather; cf. also Scots *bluiter,*
bittern.]

**Heath(-)Robinson,** *hēth'-rob'in-sən,* used adjectivally to describe an over-ingenious mechanical
contrivance (usually destined not to work).
[Heath Robinson (1872-1944), an artist who
drew such contraptions.]

**heaume,** *hōm,* (*arch.*) *n.* a massive helmet. [Fr.]

**heave,** *hēv, v.t.* to lift up, esp. with great effort: to
throw: to haul: to swell or puff out: to force
from the breast (as a sigh): in mining, to displace (as a vein).—*v.i.* to be raised: to rise like
waves: to retch: to strive or strain to lift or
move something: to move into a certain position, orig. of a ship, now also *fig.*:—*pa.t.* and
*pa.p.* **heaved,** (*naut.*) **hōve;** *pa.p.* in sense of
swollen, **hōv'en.**—*n.* an effort upward: a throw:
a swelling: an effort to vomit: a sigh (*Shak.*):
horizontal displacement (*mining*): in space flight,
motion perpendicular to the surge (q.v.): (in *pl.*)
broken wind in horses.—*ns.* **heav'er; heav'ing.**—
**heave'-off'ering, heave'-shoul'der** (*B.*), an offering, an animal's shoulder, elevated in sacrifice.—
**heave ho!** a sailors' call to exertion, as in heaving
the anchor; **heave in sight,** to come into view;
**heave the lead,** take a sounding with a lead, to
determine the depth of water (*naut.*); **heave the**
**log,** to cast the log into the water in order to
ascertain the ship's speed; **heave to,** to bring a
vessel to a standstill, to make her lie to. [O.E.
*hebban,* pa.t. *hōf,* pa.p. *hafen*; Ger. *heben.*]

**heaven,** *hev'n, hevn, n.* the vault of sky overhanging
the earth (commonly in *pl.*): the upper regions
of the air: a very great and indefinite height:
any one of the concentric revolving spheres

imagined by the old astronomers: (often *cap.*)
the dwelling-place of God or the gods, and the
blessed: (often *cap.*) the Deity as inhabiting
heaven: supreme happiness.—*interj.* (in *pl.*)
expressing surprise, disbelief, dismay, etc.—*n.*
**heavenliness** (*hevn'*).—*adj.* **heavenly** (*hevn'*), of or
inhabiting heaven: of or from God or the angels
or saints: celestial: pure: supremely blessed:
excellent (*coll.*).—*adv.* divinely, exceedingly
(*arch.*): by the influence of heaven (*Milt.*).—*adj.*
**heaven'ward.**—*advs.* **heaven'ward, heaven'wards.**
—*adjs.* **heav'en-born,** descended from heaven;
**heav'en-bred** (*Shak.*), bred or produced in
heaven; **heav'en-direct'ed,** pointing to the sky:
divinely guided; **heaven-fallen** (*hevn-föln'*;
*Milt.*), fallen from heaven; **heaven-gift'ed,**
bestowed by heaven; **heav'en-kiss'ing** (*Shak.*), as
it were, touching the sky.—**heavenly bodies,** the
sun, moon, planets, comets, stars, etc.; **heavenly**
**host,** a multitude of angels.—*adj.* **heaven'ly-**
**mind'ed,** with mind set upon heavenly things:
pure. — **heaven'ly-mind'edness.** — *adj.* **heaven'-**
**sent,** sent by heaven: very timely.—**heaven of**
**heavens** (*B.*), the highest heavens, abode of God;
**in the seventh heaven,** in a state of the most
exalted happiness—from the Cabbalists, who
divided the heavens into seven in an ascending
scale of happiness up to the abode of God;
**move heaven and earth,** to do everything possible;
**tree of heaven,** ailanto. [O.E. *heofon.*]

**Heaviside layer.** See Kennelly-Heaviside layer.

**heavy,** *hev'i, adj.* weighty: ponderous: laden:
abounding: of high specific gravity: not easy to
bear: grievous: oppressive: grave: dull,
lacking brightness and interest: wanting in
sprightliness: pedantic: pompous: laborious:
sad: in low spirits: drowsy: with great momentum: deep-toned: massive: thick: not easily
digested: doughy: impeding the feet in walking: heavy-armed (*mil.*): strong, as liquor: dark
with clouds: gloomy: pertaining to grave or
serious roles (*theat.*):—*compar.* **heav'ier;** *superl.*
**heav'iest.**—*adv.* heavily.—*n.* the villain on stage
or screen.—*adv.* **heav'ily.**—*n.* **heav'iness.**—*adjs.*
**heav'ier-than-air',** of greater specific gravity than
air, not sustained by a gasbag; **heav'y-armed,**
bearing heavy armour or arms.—**heavy chemi-**
**cals,** those produced on a large scale for use in
industry (e.g. sulphuric acid and sodium carbonate).—*adjs.* **heavy duty,** made to withstand
very hard wear or use; **heav'y-hand'ed,** clumsy,
awkward: oppressive; **heav'y-head'ed,** having a
heavy or large head: dull: stupid: drowsy;
**heav'y-heart'ed,** weighed down with grief.—
**heavy hydrogen,** deuterium: also tritium;
**heavy industry** (see industry).—*adj.* **heav'y-**
**lād'en,** with a heavy burden.—**heavy metal,** a
metal of high specific gravity, usu. above 5:
guns or shot of large size: great influence or
power: a person to be reckoned with; **heavy**
**spar,** barytes; **heavy water,** water in which
deuterium takes the place of ordinary hydrogen;
**heav'yweight,** person or thing well above the
average weight: one in the heaviest class (*sport*):
in boxing, light-heavyweight, over 11 st. 6 lb.
and not over 12 st. 7 lb., amateur 11 st. 11 lb. and
12 st. 10 lb.; **heavyweight,** any weight above
these; **heavy wet** (*slang*), a drink of strong ale
or ale and porter mixed.—**heavy marching**
**order,** the condition of troops fully equipped for
field service; **the heavies,** the heavy cavalry (*mil.*):
those who play heavy parts (*theat.*). [O.E. *hefig*
—*hebban,* to heave; O.H.G. *hebig.*]

**hebdomad,** *heb'dō-mad, n.* a set of seven: a week:
in some Gnostic systems, a group of superhuman beings.—*adj.* **hebdomadal** (*-dom'ə-dl*),
weekly.—*adv.* **hebdom'adally.**—*n.* **hebdom'adar,**
**-er,** in Scottish Universities, a senior member
appointed weekly for the supervision of student
discipline.—*adj.* **hebdom'adary,** weekly.—*n.* a

member of a chapter or convent taking weekly turn to officiate.—**hebdomadal council**, an administrative board of Oxford university, meeting weekly. [Gr. *hebdomas, -ados*, a set of seven, a week—*hepta*, seven.]

**Hebe**, *hē'bē, n.* a daughter of Zeus and Hera, cup-bearer of Olympus, a personification of youth.—*n.* **hebephrenia** (*hē-bi-frē'ni-ə*), a form of insanity beginning in late childhood, arresting intellectual development, and ending in complete dementia.—*adjs.* and *ns.* **hebephrē'niac**, **hebephrenic** (*-fren'ik*). [Gr. *hēbē*, youth, puberty (*Hēbē*, the goddess), *phrēn*, mind.]

**heben**, *heb'n, (Spens.) n., adj.* Obs. form of ebony.

**hebenon**, *heb'ə-non*, **hebona**, *-nə*, *(Shak.) n.* something with a poisonous juice. [Perh. ebony or henbane, or Ger. *eibenbaum*, yew-tree.]

**hebetate**, *heb'i-tāt, v.t.* to dull or blunt.—*v.i.* to become dull.—*adj.* dull: blunt: soft-pointed.—*adj.* heb'etant, making dull.—*ns.* **hebetā'tion**, **heb'etude**; **hebetūdinos'ity**.—*adj.* **hebetū'dinous**. [L. *hebetāre, -ātum—hebes, -etis*, blunt.]

**hebona.** See hebenon.

**Hebrew**, *hē'brōō, n.* a Jew:—*fem.* **Hē'brewess** (*B.*): the Semitic language of the Hebrews: unintelligible speech (*coll.*).—*adj.* of the Hebrews or their language.—*adjs.* **Hebraic** (*hē-brā'ik*), **-al**, relating to the Hebrews or to their language.—*adv.* **Hebrā'ically**, after the manner of the Hebrew language: from right to left.—*n.* **Hebrā'icism.**—*v.t.* **Hē'brāise**, **-īze**, to make Hebrew.—*v.i.* to use a Hebrew idiom: to conform or incline to Hebrew ways or ideals.—*ns.* **Hē'brāiser**, **-z-**; **Hē'brāism**, a Hebrew idiom; **Hē'brāist**, one skilled in Hebrew.—*adjs.* **Hebrāist'ic**, **-al**, of or like Hebrew.—*adv.* **Hebrāist'ically**.—*n.* **Hē'brewism.** [O.Fr. *Ebreu* and L. *Hēbraeus*—Gr. *Hēbraios*—Aram. *'ebrai* (Heb. *'ibri*), lit. one from the other side (of the Euphrates).]

**Hebridean**, *heb-ri-dē'ən*, **Hebridian**, *-rid'i-ən, adj.* of the Hebrides (*heb'ri-dēz*).—*n.* a native of the Hebrides.—*adj.* **He'brid.** [Due to a misprint of L. *Hebūdēs*—Gr. *Heboudai*.]

**Hecate**, *hek'ə-tē, Shak.* **Hecat(e)**, *hek'ət, n.* a mysterious goddess, in Hesiod having power over earth, heaven, and sea—afterwards identified with Artemis, Persephone, and other goddesses: in Shakespeare, etc., the chief or goddess of witches. [Gr. *Hekatē*.]

**hecatomb**, *hek'ə-tom, -tōm* (sometimes *-tōōm*), *n.* a great public sacrifice: any large number of victims. [Gr. *hekatombē—hekaton*, a hundred, *bous*, an ox.]

**hech**, *hehh, (Scot.) interj.* an exclamation of surprise, weariness, etc.

**hecht**, *hehht*, Scottish form of the verb hight.

**heck**, *hek, (dial.) n.* the lower part of a door: an inner door: a grating, esp. in rivers or streams: a rack for animal fodder: a piece of spinning machinery, for guiding the yarn to the reels.—**heck and manger**, rack and manger. [O.E. *hec* (*hæc*), grating, hatch; cf. hack (3), hatch (1); Du. *hek*, gate.]

**heck**, *hek, n.* and *interj.* euphemistic for hell.

**heckle**, *hek'l, v.i.* to comb out, of flax or hemp fibres: orig. *Scot.*, to ply with embarrassing questions (as at an election).—*n.* a hackle.—*n.* **heck'ler**. [Cf. hackle, hatchel.]

**hecogenin**, *hek'ō-jen-in, hek-oj'ən-in, n.* a synthetic form of cortisone, prepared chiefly from sisal. [*Hec(htia texensis)*, the plant from which first isolated and suffs. *-gen* and *-in*.]

**hectare.** See under hecto-.

**hectic**, *hek'tik, adj.* pertaining to the constitution or habit of body: affected with hectic fever: feverish, agitated, rushed (*coll.*): flushed (*Shelley*).—*n.* a hectic fever: a consumptive: a flush.—*adj.* **hec'tical.**—**hectic fever**, fever occurring in connection with certain wasting diseases

of long duration. [Gr. *hektikos*, habitual—*hexis*, habit.]

**hecto-**, *hek'tō*, **hect-**, in composition (esp. in the metric system) 100 times.—*ns.* **hectare** (*hek'tär*), 100 ares or 10,000 sq. metres; **hec'togram(me)**, 100 grammes; **hec'tograph**, a gelatine pad for printing copies.—*v.t.* to reproduce in this way.—*adj.* **hectograph'ic.**—*ns.* **hec'tolitre**, 100 litres; **hec'tometre**, 100 metres; **hec'tostere**, 100 cubic metres or steres. [Fr. contraction of Gr. *hekaton*, a hundred.]

**hector**, *hek'tər, n.* a bully, a blusterer.—*v.t.* to treat insolently: to annoy.—*v.i.* to play the bully: to bluster.—*ns.* **hec'torer**; **hec'torism**.—*adv.* **hec'torly**.—*n.* **hec'torship**. [Gr. *Hektōr*, the Trojan hero.]

**heddle**, *hed'l, n.* a series of vertical cords or wires, each having in the middle a loop (**hedd'le-eye**) to receive a warp-thread, and passing round and between parallel bars.—*v.t.* to draw through **heddle-eyes**.—Also **heald**. [An assumed O.E. *hefedl*, earlier form of hefeld.]

**Hedera**, *hed'ər-ə, n.* the ivy genus of the Aralia family.—*adjs.* **hed'eral**; **hed'erated**, ivy-crowned. [L.]

**hedge**, *hej, n.* a close row of bushes or small trees serving as a fence: a barrier (*fig.*): an act of hedging.—*v.t.* to enclose with a hedge: to obstruct: to surround: to guard: to protect oneself from loss on, by compensatory transactions, e.g. bets on the other side.—*v.i.* to make hedges: to shuffle, as in argument: to be shifty.—*adj.* living in or frequenting hedges: wayside: used by, or only fit for, vagrants: low: debased.—*ns.* **hedg'er**, one who hedges or dresses hedges; **hedg'ing**, the work of a hedger.—*adj.* **hedg'y.**—**hedge'-accen'tor**, the hedge-sparrow: **hedge'bill**, **hedg'ing-bill**, a bill for dressing hedges.—*adj.* **hedge'-born**, born under a hedge, low-born.—**hedge'-bote**, a tenant's right to cut wood for repairing hedges or fences; **hedge'-creep'er**, a sneaking rogue; **hedge'hog**, a small prickly-backed insectivorous animal that lives in hedges and bushes, and has a snout like a hog: a prickly fruit, or prickly-fruited plant (*whose manners keep others at a distance*: an offensive person: a small, strongly fortified, defensive position.—*v.i.* **hedge'-hop** (*airman's slang*), to fly low as if hopping over hedges.—**hedge'-hyss'op**, a plant (Gratiola) of the figwort family; **hedge'-mar'riage**, a clandestine marriage; **hedge'-mus'tard**, a tall stiff cruciferous roadside weed (*Sisymbrium officinale*) with small yellow flowers, or kindred species; **hedge'-pars'ley**, an umbelliferous roadside weed (Torilis or Caucalis) with leaves somewhat like parsley; **hedge'-par'son**, **hedge'-priest**, a disreputable, vagrant, or illiterate parson or priest; **hedge'pig**, a hedgehog; **hedge'row**, a line of hedge, often with trees; **hedge'-school**, an open-air school, common in Ireland in 17th and 18th centuries during the ban on Catholic education: a mean school; **hedge'-schoolmaster**; **hedge'-sparr'ow**, **hedge'-war'bler**, a warbler, superficially like a sparrow, that frequents hedges; **hedge'-wri'ter**, a Grub Street author. [O.E. *hecg*; Du. *hegge*, Ger. *hecke*.]

**hedonism**, *hē'dən-izm, n.* in ethics, the doctrine that pleasure is the highest good.—*adjs.* **hēdonic** (*-don'*), **hēdonist'ic**.—*n.* (treated as *sing.*) **hēdon'ics**, that part of ethics or of psychology that treats of pleasure.—*n.* **hē'donist.** [Gr. *hēdonē*, pleasure.]

**hedyphane**, *hed'i-fān, n.* a white variety of green lead ore, arsenate, phosphate, and chloride of lead and calcium with barium. [Gr. *hēdys*, sweet, pleasant, and the root of *phainein*, to show.]

**heebie** (**heeby**)-**jeebies**, the (*slang*), a fit of nerves: irritation or depression: the creeps.

**heed**, *hēd, v.t.* to observe: to look after: to

attend to.—*v.i.* to mind, care.—*n.* notice: caution: attention.—*adj.* heed'ful, attentive: cautious.—*adv.* heed'fully.—*ns.* heed'fulness; heed'iness.—*adj.* heed'less.—*adv.* heed'lessly.—*n.* heed'lessness.—*adj.* heed'y (*Spens.*), heedful, careful. [O.E. *hēdan*; Du. *hoeden*, Ger. *hüten.*]

heehaw, *hē'hö*, *v.i.* to bray.—*n.* a bray. [Imit.]

heel, *hēl*, *n.* hind part of the foot below the ankle: the whole foot (esp. of beasts): the covering or support of the heel: a spur: the hinder part of anything, as a violin bow: a heel-like bend, as on a golf-club: a knob: the top, bottom, or end of a loaf or a cheese: a cad (*slang*).—*v.t.* to execute or perform with the heel: to strike with the heel: to furnish with a heel: to arm with a spur, as a fighting cock: to seize by the heels: to tie by the heels: to follow at the heels of: to supply with a weapon, money, etc.—*v.i.* to follow well (of a dog): to move one's heels to a dance rhythm: to kick the ball backwards out of the scrum with the heel (*Rugby football*).—*adj.* heeled, provided with a heel, shod: comfortably supplied with money, etc.—*ns.* heel'er, one who heels, in any sense: one who follows at heel, as an unscrupulously faithful follower of a party boss; heel'ing, a heel-piece (*Spens.*): the act of making or attaching a heel.—heel'-ball, a black waxy composition for blacking the edges of heels and soles of shoes and boots, and for taking rubbings; heel'-piece, a piece or cover for the heel; heel'-tap, a layer of material in a shoe-heel: a small quantity of liquor left in the glass after drinking.—at, on, upon, a person's heels, close behind; back on one's heels, driven back by an opponent: on the defensive; come to heel, come in behind: to obey or follow like a dog: to submit to authority; cool or kick one's heels, to be kept waiting for some time; down at heel, having the heels of one's shoes trodden down: slovenly: in poor circumstances; heel and toe, with strict walking pace, as opposed to running; heel of Achilles (see under Achillean); heels o'er gowdy (*Scot.*), heels over head, upside down; kick up one's heels, to frisk; lay, set, clap, by the heels, to fetter: to put in confinement; out at heel, having one's heels showing through holes in the socks or stockings: shabby; show a clean pair of heels, to run off; take to one's heels, to flee; tread on one's heels, to come crowding behind; trip up one's heels, to trip up or overthrow; turn on (upon) one's heel, to turn sharply round, to turn back or away; two for his heels, in cribbage, a score for turning up the knave; under the heel, crushed, tyrannised over. [O.E. *hēla*; Du. *hiel.*]

heel, *hēl*, *v.i.* to incline: to lean on one side, as a ship.—*v.t.* to tilt. [Earlier *heeld*, *hield*; O.E. *hieldan*, to slope; cf. Du. *hellen.*]

heel. Same as hele.

heeze, *hēz*, (*Scot.*) *v.t.* a form of hoise.—*n.* a lift: a heave upward.—*n.* heez'ie, a lift.

heft, *heft*, *n.* heaving (*obs.*): retching (*Shak.*): weight (*U.S.*): the greater part (*arch.*).—*v.t.* to lift: to try the weight of.—*adj.* heft'y, rather heavy: muscular: sizeable: vigorous: violent: abundant.—*adv.* very. [heave.]

heft, hefte (*Spens.*), obsolete forms of heaved.

heft, *heft*, (*Scot.*) *v.t.* to restrain: to retain (milk or urine). [Cf. O.N. *hefta*, to bind.]

heft, *heft*, *n.* a number of sheets fastened together: an instalment of a serial publication. [Ger.]

Hegelian, *hā-gēl'i-ən*, *adj.* of or pertaining to Wilhelm Friedrich Hegel (1770-1831) or his philosophy.—*n.* a follower of Hegel.—*n.* Hegel'ianism.

hegemony, *hi-gem'ən-i*, or *-jem'*, *n.* leadership: preponderant influence, esp. of one state over others.—*adjs.* hegemonic (*hē-gi-mon'*, or *-ji-*), -al. [Gr. *hēgemoniā*—*hēgemōn*, leader—*hēgeesthai*, to lead.]

hegira, hejira, hejra, hijra, *hej'*, *hij'(i)-rə*, *hi-ji'rə*, *n.*

the flight of Mohammed from Mecca, A.D. 622, from which is dated the Mohammedan era: any flight. [Ar. *hijrah*, flight, *hajara*, to leave.]

he-he, *hē-hē*, *interj.* representing a high-pitched or gleeful laugh.—*n.* such a laugh.—*v.i.* to laugh so. [Imit.]

heifer, *hef'ər*, *n.* a young cow. [O.E. *hēahfore*, *hēahfru*, *-fre*; lit. prob. high-goer—*faran*, to go.]

heigh, *hā* (or *hi*), *interj.* a cry of enquiry, encouragement, or exultation—also hey, ha.—*interj.* heigh'-ho, an exclamation expressive of weariness.—*n.* (*Scot.* also heich-how, *hēhh'-how'*) routine: familiar jog-trot. [Imit.]

height, *hit*, *n.* the condition of being high: degree of highness: distance upwards: angle of elevation: that which is elevated: a hill: a high place: elevation in rank or excellence: utmost degree.—*v.t.* and *v.i.* height'en, to make or become higher: to make or become brighter or more conspicuous, or (*fig.*) stronger or more intense: to elate (*obs.*).—height of land, a watershed, esp. if not a range of hills; height to paper, the standard height (11/12 inch) of type, blocks, etc., from foot to face. [From highth—O.E. *hiehtho*, *hēahthu*—*hēah*, high.]

heil!, *hil*, (Ger.) hail!

heimweh, *him'vā*, (Ger.) home-sickness.

heinous, *hā'nəs*, sometimes *hē'nəs*, *adj.* wicked in a high degree, enormous, odious, atrocious.—*adv.* hei'nously.—*n.* hei'nousness. [O.Fr. *hainos* (Fr. *haineux*)—*haïr*, to hate.]

heir, *ār*, *n.* in law, one who actually succeeds to property, title, etc., on the death of its previous holder: popularly, one entitled to succeed when the present possessor dies: a child, esp. a first-born son: a successor to a position, e.g. of leadership: inheritor of qualities, or of social conditions, or the past generally.—*v.t.* (*dial.*) to inherit.—*ns.* heir'dom, heir'ship; heir'ess, a female heir: a woman who has succeeded or is likely to succeed to a considerable fortune.—*adj.* heir'less, without an heir.—heir'-appā'rent, the one by law acknowledged to be heir, no matter who may subsequently be born; heir'-at-law, an heir by legal right; heir-by-custom, one whose right as heir is determined by customary modes of descent, as gavelkind, etc.; heir'loom, any piece of furniture or personal property which descends to the heir-at-law by special custom; heir'-por'tioner (Scots law), a joint-heiress or her representative; heir'-presump'tive, one who will be heir if no nearer relative should be born. [O.Fr. *heir*—L. *hērēs* (vulgar accus. *hērem*), an heir.]

heist, *hist*, (*slang*) *v.t.* to steal: to rob.—*n.* robbery: theft: one who robs or steals.—*n.* heist'er, one who robs or steals. [Variant of hoist.]

hejira, hejra. See hegira.

Hel, hel, *n.* in Northern mythology, the goddess of the dead, sister of the wolf Fenrir, and daughter of Loki.

helcoid, *hel'koid*, *adj.* ulcerous. [Gr. *helkos*, an ulcer.]

held, *pa.t.* and *pa.p.* of hold.

hele, heel, heal, *hēl*, *v.t.* (*Spens.*; now *dial.*) to hide, conceal: to cover.—hele in (*dial.*), to cover the roots of temporarily with earth. [O.E. *helian* from *hellan* (weak vb.) blended with *helan* (strong), both meaning to hide; Ger. *hehlen*; L. *celāre*; Gr. *kalyptein.*]

heli-, *hel-i-*, in composition, helicopter (as in *ns.* hel'ibus; hel'idrome; hel'iman; hel'ipilot; hel'iport, etc.).—*ns.* hel'icopter, (Gr. *pteron*, wing) a flying-machine sustained by a power-driven screw or screws revolving on a vertical axis; hel'iscoop, a net let down from a helicopter to rescue persons in difficulty. [Gr. *helix*, screw.]

heliac, *hē'li-ak*, heliacal, *hē-li'ək-əl*, *adjs.* solar: coincident with that of the sun, or as nearly as

could be observed.—*adv.* heli'acally.—heliacal rising, the emergence of a star from the light of the sun; heliacal setting, its disappearance in it. [Gr. *hēliakos*—*hēlios*, the sun.]
Helianthemum, *hē-li-anth'ə-məm, n.* the rock-rose genus. [Gr. *hēlios*, sun, *anthemon*, flower.]
Helianthus, *hē-li-an'thəs, n.* the sunflower genus. [Gr. *hēlios*, sun, *anthos*, flower.]
helical, etc. See helix.
Heliconian, *hel-i-kō'ni-ən, adj.* pertaining to *Helicon* (Gr. *Helikōn*), a mountain-range in Boeotia, favourite seat of the Muses, by some modern poets made a fountain.
helicopter. See heli-.
helio-, *hē'li-ō-, hē-li-o'-*, in composition, sun.—*adj.* heliocen'tric (*-sen'trik*; Gr. *kentron*, centre; *astron.*), referred to the sun as centre.—*adv.* heliocen'trically.—*n.* he'liochrome (*-krōm*; Gr. *chrōma*, colour), a photograph in natural colours.—*adj.* heliochrō'mic.—*ns.* he'liochrōmy; he'liograph (Gr. *graphē*, a drawing), an apparatus for signalling by flashing the sun's rays: an engraving obtained photographically: an apparatus for photographing the sun: an instrument for measuring intensity of sunlight.—*v.t.* and *v.i.* to communicate by heliograph.—*n.* heliog'-rapher.—*adjs.* heliograph'ic, -al.—*adv.* heliograph'ically.—*ns.* heliog'raphy; heliogravure (*-grəv-ūr'*, *-grāv'yər*; Fr. *héliogravure*), photoengraving; heliol'ater, a sun-worshipper.—*adj.* heliol'atrous.—*ns.* heliol'atry (Gr. *latreiā*, worship), sun-worship; heliol'ogy, the science of the sun; heliom'eter, an instrument for measuring angular distances, as the sun's diameter.—*adjs.* heliomet'ric, -al; helioph'ilous (Gr. *phileein*, to love), fond of the sun; heliopho'bic (Gr. *phobos*, fear), fearing or shunning sunlight.—*ns.* he'liophyte (Gr. *phyton*, a plant), a plant that can live in full exposure to sunlight; heliosciophyte (*hē-li-ō-si'ō-fit*; Gr. *skiā*, shadow), a plant that can live in shade but does better in the sun; he'lioscope (*-skōp*; Gr. *skopeein*, to look at), an apparatus for observing the sun without injury to the eye.—*adj.* helioscopic (*-skop'ik*).—*ns.* heliō'sis (Gr. *hēliōsis*), exposure to the sun: spotting of leaves by raindrops or greenhouse glass flaws, etc., acting as burning-glasses; he'liostat (Gr. *statos*, fixed), an instrument on the principle of the coelostat by means of which a beam of sunlight is reflected in an invariable direction, for study of the sun or for signalling; heliotax'is (Gr. *taxis*, arrangement), response of an organism to the stimulus of the sun's rays; heliother'apy (Gr. *therapeiā*, healing), medical treatment by exposure to the sun's rays; heliotrope (*hē'li-ō-trōp, hel'i-ō-trōp*; Gr. *hēliotropion*), any plant of the genus Heliotropium of the borage family, many species with fragrant flowers, esp. the Peruvian heliotrope, with small fragrant lilac-blue flowers: the colour of its flowers: a kind of perfume imitating that of the flower: a bloodstone (*min.*): a surveyor's heliograph.—*adjs.* heliotropic (*-trop'ik*), -al.—*adv.* heliotrop'-ically.—*ns.* heliotropism (*-ot'rə-pizm*), heliot'ropy, the tendency of stem and leaves to bend towards (*positive heliotropism*), and roots from (*negative heliotropism*), the light; he'liotype (Gr. *typos*, impression), a photograph by heliotypy.—*adj.* heliotypic (*-tip'ik*).—*n.* he'liotypy (*-ti-pi*), a photomechanical process in which the gelatine relief is itself used to print from.—*n.pl.* Heliozō'a (Gr. *zōion*, an animal), sun-animalcules, an order of Protozoa, spherical with radiating processes of living matter.—*adj.* and *n.* heliozō'an.—*adj.* heliozō'ic. [Gr. *hēlios*, the sun.]
heliodor, *hēl'i-ə-dōr, -dör, n.* a variety of clear yellow beryl occurring in S.W. Africa. [Ger.]
heliograph, etc. See helio-.
helispheric, -al. See helix.
helium, *hē'li-əm, n.* an element (He; at. numb. 2),

a very light inert gas, discovered (1868) by Lockyer in the sun's atmosphere, isolated (1895) by Ramsay from cleveite, and found in certain natural gases.—helium speech, distorted speech of persons in a helium atmosphere.—liquid helium, helium in liquid form (below 4·22°K), which has remarkable qualities, undergoing a striking change at 2·19°K (see superfluidity). [Gr. *hēlios*, sun.]
helix, *hē'liks, n.* a screw-shaped coil: in math., a curve on a developable surface (esp. a right circular cylinder) which becomes a straight line when the surface is unrolled into a plane—distinguished from a *spiral*, which is a plane curve: the rim of the ear (*anat.*): a small volute or twist in the capital of a Corinthian column (*archit.*): a screw-propeller: (*cap.*; *zool.*) a genus of molluscs including the best-known land-snails:—*pl.* hē'lixes or helices (*hel'i-sēz*).—*adj.* helical (*hel'ik-əl*).—*adv.* hel'ically.—*n.pl.* Helicidae (*-is'i-dē*), a large family of terrestrial, air-breathing gasteropods, including the common snails.—*n.* hel'icograph, a drawing instrument for describing spirals on a plane.—*adjs.* hel'icoid, -al, like a helix, screw-shaped; helispher'ic, -al, loxodromic.—helicoid cyme, a bostryx. [Gr. *hēlix*, a spiral—*helissein*, to turn round.]
Hell, *hel, n.* the place of the dead in general: the place or state of punishment of the wicked after death: the abode of evil spirits: the powers of Hell: (the following meanings without *cap.*) any place of vice or misery: a place of turmoil: (a state of) supreme misery or discomfort: anything causing misery, pain or destruction: ruin, havoc: commotion, uproar: severe censure or chastisement: used in various coll. phrases expressing displeasure, emphasis, etc. (as *what in hell?*): a gambling-house: a space under a tailor's board, or other receptacle for waste: the den in certain games.—*interj.* expressing displeasure or emphasis.—*v.i.* to live or act in a wild or dissolute fashion (usually with *around*).—*ns.* hell'er, an obstreperous troublesome person; hellion (*hel'yən*), a troublesome, mischievous child: one given to diabolical conduct.—*adj.* hell'ish, pertaining to or like hell: often used to express displeasure (*coll.*).—*adv.* hell'ish(ly) in the manner of hell: often used intensively (*coll.*).—*n.* hell'ishness.—*adj.* (*coll.*) hell'uva, hell'ova (hell of a), great, terrific—*adv.* very.—*adj.* and *adv.* hell'ward, towards hell.—*adv.* hell'wards.—hell'bender, a large American salamander: a reckless or debauched person.—*adj.* and *adv.* hell'-bent, with reckless determination.—*adjs.* hell'-black (*Shak.*), black as hell; hell'-born, born in hell: of hellish origin; hell'-bred.—hell'-box, a receptacle for broken type; hell'-broth (*Shak.*), a composition boiled up for malignant purposes; hell'-cat, a malignant hag; hell'-fire, the fire of hell: punishment in hell; hell'-gate, the entrance into hell.—*adj.* hell'-hat'ed (*Shak.*), hated or abhorred as hell.—hell'-hole, the pit of hell; hell'hound, a hound of hell: an agent of hell; hell'-kite (*Shak.*), a kite of infernal breed.—for the hell of it, for fun or adventure; hell for leather, at a furious pace. [O.E. *hel, hell*; O.N. *hel*, Ger. *hölle*; cf. Hel.]
hell, *hel, n.v.t.* obs. form of hele.—*n.* (*dial.*) hell'ier, a slater: a tiler: a thatcher. [See hele.]
he'll, *hēl,* contraction for he will.
Helladic, *hel-ad'ik, adj.* Greek: of the Greek mainland Bronze Age, answering roughly to Minoan. [Gr. *Helladikos*, Greek—*Hellas*, Greece.]
hellbender. See Hell.
hellebore, *hel'i-bōr, -bör, n.* any plant of the genus Helleborus, of the buttercup family (as *black hellebore* or Christmas rose, *stinking hellebore*, *green hellebore*): any plant of the genus Veratrum

Neutral vowels in unaccented syllables: *el'ə-mənt*; for certain sounds in foreign words, see p. viii

of the lily family (*American, false*, or *white helle-bore*, known also as Indian poke or itchweed): the winter aconite (*winter hellebore*): the rhizome and roots of these prepared as a drug.—*n.* **hell′-eborine** (-*in*, -*in*), an orchid of the genus Epipactis. [Gr. *helleboros*.]

**Hellene**, *hel′ēn*, *n.* a Greek.—*adj.* **Hellēn′ic** (or -*en′*), Greek.—*v.i.* **hell′enise**, -**ize** (-*in*-*iz*), to conform, or tend to conform, to Greek usages.—*v.t.* to make Greek.—*ns.* **Hell′enism**, a Greek idiom: the Greek spirit: Greek nationality: conformity to Greek ways, esp. in language; **Hell′enist**, one skilled in the Greek language: one who adopted Greek ways and language, esp. a Jew.—*adjs.* **Hellenist′ic**, -**al**, pertaining to the Hellenists: pertaining to the Greeks, the Greek language and Greek culture, affected by foreign influences after the time of Alexander.—*adv.* **Hellenist′ically**. [Gr. *Hellēn*, a Greek: also the son of Deucalion.]

**heller**, *hel′ər*, *n.* a small coin probably first made at Hall in Swabia, in Austria and Czechoslovakia once worth a hundredth part of a crown.

**hellgrammite, hellgramite**, *hel′grə-mit*, *n.* a large American neuropterous larva, used as bait by bass-fishers. [Origin unknown.]

**hellicat**, *hel′i-kat*, (*Scot.*) *adj.* giddy-headed: flighty.—*n.* a wicked creature. [Origin obscure.]

**hellier.** See hell.

**hellion**, etc. See **H**ell.

**hello.** Same as hallo.

**helm**, *helm*, *n.* steering apparatus.—*v.t.* to direct, steer.—*adj.* **helm′less**—**helms′man**, a steersman. [O.E. *helma*; O.N. *hjālm*, a rudder, Ger. *helm*, a handle.]

**helm**, *helm*, **helmet**, *hel′mit*, *ns.* a covering for armour for the head: anything resembling a helmet, as a cloud on a mountain top, the top of a guinea-fowl's head, the hooded upper lip of certain flowers.—*adjs.* **helmed**, **hel′meted.**—**hel′met-shell**, a gasteropod of the genus Cassis, having a thick heavy shell with bold ridges. [O.E. *helm*; Ger. *helm*; cf. **hele**.]

**helminth**, *hel′minth*, *n.* a worm.—*n.* **helminthi′-asis**, infestation with worms.—*adjs.* **helmin′thic**; **helmin′thoid**, worm-shaped; **helminthol′og′ic, -al.**—*ns.* **helminthol′ogist**; **helminthol′ogy**, the study of worms, esp. parasitic.—*adj.* **helminth′-ous**, infested with worms. [Gr. *helmins, -inthos*, a worm.]

**helot**, *hel′ət*, *n.* one of a class of serfs among the ancient Spartans, deliberately humiliated and liable to massacre (*hist.*): a serf (*hist.*): a plant or animal living symbiotically with another in a subject relationship (*biol.*).—*ns.* **hel′otage**, the state of a helot; **hel′otism**; **helotry**, the whole body of the helots: any class of slaves. [Gr. *Heilōtēs*, also *Heilōs, -ōtos*.]

**help**, *help*, *v.t.* to contribute towards the success of, aid, or assist: to give means for doing anything: to relieve the wants of: to provide or supply with a portion: to deal out: to remedy: to mitigate: to prevent, to keep from.—*v.i.* to give assistance: to contribute:—*pa.t.* **helped**, *arch.* **hōlp**; *pa.p.* **helped**, *arch.* **hōlp′en**.—*n.* means or strength given to another for a purpose: assistance: relief: one who assists: a hired servant, esp. domestic: an employee.—*n.* **help′er**, one who helps: an assistant: an assistant minister (*arch.*).—*adj.* **help′ful**, giving help: useful.—*n.* **help′fulness.**—*adj.* **help′ing**, giving help or support.—*n.* a portion served at a meal.—*adj.* **help′less**, without ability to do things for oneself: wanting assist-ance: destitute of (*obs.*): giving no help (*Shak.*): that cannot be helped (*Spens.*).—*adv.* **help′-lessly.**—*n.* **help′lessness.**—**helping hand**, as-sistance; **help′mate**, a modification of **help′-meet**, itself formed from the phrase in Gen. ii. 18, 'an help meet for him', *specif.* a wife.—cannot help (be helped), cannot avoid (be avoided);

**help off with**, to aid in taking off, disposing or getting rid of; **help on with**, to help to put on; **help oneself (to)**, to take for oneself without waiting for offer or authority; **help out**, to eke out: to supplement: to assist; **more than one can help**, (illogically but idiomatically) more than is necessary; **so help me (God)**, a form of solemn oath: on my word. [O.E. *helpan*, pa.t. *healp* (pl. *hulpon*), pa.p. *holpen*; O.N. *hjālpa*; Ger. *helfen*.]

**helter-skelter**, *hel′tər-skel′tər*, *adv.* in a confused hurry: tumultuously.—*n.* a confused medley: disorderly motion: a fair-ground spiral slide.—*adj.* confused.—*n.* **hel′ter-skel′teriness**. [Imit.]

**helve**, *helv*, *n.* the handle of an axe or similar tool.—*v.t.* to furnish with a helve.—**helve′-hamm′er**, a trip-hammer. [O.E. *helfe* (*hielfe*), a handle.]

**Helvetic**, *hel-vet′ik*, **Helvetian**, *hel-vē′shən*, *adjs.* Swiss.—*n.* **helvē′tium**, a superseded name for astatine.—**Helvetic Confessions**, two confessions of faith drawn up by the Swiss theologians in 1536 and 1566. [L. *Helvētia*, Switzerland.]

**hem**, *hem*, *n.* an edge or border: a border doubled down and sewed.—*v.t.* to form a hem on: to edge:—*pr.p.* **hemm′ing**; *pa.t.* and *pa.p.* **hemmed**.—**hem′-stitch**, the ornamental finishing of the inner side of a hem, made by pulling out several threads adjoining it and drawing together in groups the cross-threads by successive stitches.—*v.t.* to embroider with such stitches.—**hem in**, to surround. [O.E. *hemm*, a border.]

**hem**, *hem*, *hm*, *n.* and *interj.* a sort of half-cough to draw attention.—*v.i.* to utter the sound *hem*:—*pr.p.* **hemm′ing**; *pa.t.* and *pa.p.* **hemmed**. [Sound of clearing the throat.]

**hem**, (*h*)*əm*, (*obs.*) them: to them. See **'em**.

**hem-.** See **haem-**.

**he-man.** See **he**.

**hematite**, etc. See **haematite**, etc.

**hemato-.** See **haemato-** (under **haem-**).

**heme**, *hēm*, (*Spens.*) *adv.* Same as home.

**hemeralopia**, *hem-ər-ə-lō′pi-ə*, *n.* day-blindness: vision requiring dim light: sometimes misapplied to night-blindness. [Gr. *hēmerā*, day, *alaos*, blind, *ōps*, eye.]

**Hemerobaptist**, *hem-ər-ō-bap′tist*, *n.* a member of an ancient Jewish sect that practised daily baptism: also a Mandaean. [Gr. *hēmerā*, day, *baptistēs*, a baptiser.]

**Hemerocallis**, *hem-ər-ō-kal′is*, *n.* a day-lily. [Gr. *hēmerā*, day, *kallos*, beauty.]

**hemi-**, *hem′i-*, in composition, half.—*n.* **hemian-ops′ia** (Gr. *an-*, priv., *opsis*, sight), blindness in half of the field of vision.—Also **hemianōp′ia**, **hemiō′pia**, **hemiop′sia**.—*adjs.* **hemianop′tic**, **hemi-op′ic**.—*ns.pl.* **Hemichordata** (-*kör-dā′tə*), **hemi-chorda** (-*kör′də*), a group of worm-like marine animals with rudimentary notochord, including Balanoglossus, believed by many to represent the ancestors of the vertebrates.—*n.* **hemicrania** (-*krā′ni-ə*; Gr. *hēmikrāniā—krānion*, skull, head), headache confined to one side.—*adj.* **hemicrys′talline** (*petrol.*), consisting of crystals in a glassy or partly glassy groundmass.—*n.* **hem′icycle** (Gr. *kyklos*, wheel), a semicircle: a semicircular structure.—*adj.* **hemicy′clic** (*bot.*), having some parts in whorls, some in spirals.—*ns.* **hemihē′drism**, **hemihē′dry** (-*dri*; Gr. *hedrā*, a seat), a property of crystals of being **hemihē′dral**, or having half the number of symmetrically arranged planes occurring on a holohedron.—*n.* **hemihē′dron**.—*adj.* **hemimorph′ic** (Gr. *morphē*, form) having a polar axis, dissimilar at the two ends.—*ns.* **hemimorph′ism**; **hemimorph′ite**, the mineral electric calamine, hydrous zinc silicate, which forms crystals whose ends are different in form and pyroelectric property; **hemiō′lia** (Gr. *hēmiōlios*, half as much again—*holos*, whole) in mediaeval music, a perfect fifth: also, a triplet.—*adj.* **hemiolic** (-*ol′*), in or based on the ratio of

3 to 2, as the paeonic foot.—*ns.* **hemionus** (*hi-mī'-on-əs*), **hemione** (*hem'i-ōn*; Gr. **hēmionos**, mule—*onos*, an ass), an Asiatic wild ass, the kiang or the dziggetai; **hemipar'asite**, an organism that is partly parasitic, partly independent: a saprophyte capable of living parasitically.—*adj.* **hemiparasīt'ic.**—*adv.* **hemiparasīt'ically.**—*n.* **hemiplegia** (*-plē'ji-a*, or *-gi-a*; Gr. **plēgē**, a blow), paralysis of one side only.—*adj.* **hemiplegic** (*-plej'* or *-plēj'*).—*n.pl.* **Hemip'tera** (Gr. **pteron**, a wing), an order of insects, variously defined, with wings (when present) often half leathery, half membranous—the bugs, cicadas, greenfly, cochineal insect, etc.—*adjs.* **hemip'teral, hemip'-teran, hemip'terous.**—*n.* **hem'isphere** (Gr. **hēmi-sphairion**—**sphaira**, a sphere), a half-sphere divided by a plane through the centre: half of the globe or a map of it: one of the two divisions of the cerebrum.—*adjs.* **hemisphĕr'ic, -al.**—*n.* **hemisphē'roid**, the half of a spheroid.—*adj.* **hemisphĕroi'dal.**—*n.* **hemistich** (*hem'i-stik*; Gr. **hēmistichion**—**stichos**, a line), one of the two divisions of a line of verse: half a line, an incomplete or unfinished line: an epodic line or refrain.—*adj.* **hem'istichal** (or *-is'*).—*n.* **hem'itrope** (Gr. **tropos**, a turn), a form of twin crystal in which one twin is as if rotated through two right angles from the position of the other.—*adjs.* **hem'itrope, hemitropal** (*hem-it'rə-pl*), **hemitropic** (*-trop'*), **hemit'ropous.**—Eastern and Western hemispheres, the eastern and western halves of the terrestrial globe, the former including Europe, Asia and Africa; the latter, the Americas. [Gr. **hēmi-**, half.]

**hemlock,** *hem'lok*, *n.* a poisonous spotted umbelliferous plant (*Conium maculatum*): the poison got from it: extended to other umbelliferous plants, e.g. water-hemlock (*Cicuta*): a N. American tree (hemlock spruce, *Tsuga*) whose branches are fancied to resemble hemlock leaves. [O.E. **hymlīce** (Kentish **hemlīc**).]

**hemo-.** See **haemo-** (under **haem-**).

**hemp,** *hemp*, *n.* a plant (*Cannabis sativa*) of the mulberry family, yielding a coarse fibre, a narcotic drug, and an oil: the fibre itself: the drug: a similar fibre got from various other plants (e.g. Manila, sisal, sunn hemp).—*adjs.* **hemp'en**, made of hemp: pertaining to the hangman's noose or hanging (*arch.*); **hemp'y**, like hemp: roguish: romping.—*n.* (*Scot.*) a rogue: a romp: a tomboy.—**hemp'-ag'rimony**, a composite plant (*Eupatorium cannabinum*) with hemp-like leaves; **hemp'bush**, an Australian fibre-plant (Plagianthus) of the mallow family; **hempen widow,** the widow of a man who has been hanged; **hemp'-nett'le,** a coarse bristly labiate weed (Galeopsis); **hemp'-palm,** a palmetto (yielding fibre); **hemp'-seed,** the oil-yielding seed of hemp, a bird's food: gallows-bird (*Shak.*). [O.E. **henep, hænep;** cf. Gr. **kannabis**.]

**hen,** *hen, n.* a female bird: a female domestic fowl: applied loosely to any domestic fowl: the female of certain fishes and crustaceans: (facetiously, disrespectfully, or endearingly) a woman or girl: a faint-hearted person.—*v.i.* (*Scot.*) to lose courage or resolution: to balk.—*v.t.* (*Scot.*) to challenge to an act of daring.—*adj.* female: composed of females.—*ns.* **henn'er** (*Scot.*), a challenge to an act of daring; **henn'ery,** a place where fowls are kept; **henn'y,** a hen-like cock.—*adj.* **hen-like.**—**hen-and-chick'ens,** a name for various plants, esp. a garden daisy with small heads surrounding the main head; **hen'bane,** a poisonous plant (*Hyoscyamus niger*) of the nightshade family; **hen'-bit,** the ivy-leaved speedwell: a species of dead-nettle; **hen'-coop,** a coop for a hen; **hen'-court,** an enclosure for fowls; **hen'-driv'er, hen-harrier,** the hen-harrier; **hen-flesh,** gooseflesh; **hen'-harr'ier,** the common harrier.—*adj.* **hen'-heart'ed,** faint-hearted: timid.—**hen'-house,** a

house for fowls; **hen'-huss'y,** a man who meddles with women's affairs; **hen'-pad(d)'le, -paid'le** (see **paddle** (2)); **hen'-par'ty,** a gathering of women only.—*v.t.* **hen'peck,** to domineer over (said of a wife).—**hen'peck, henpeck'ery; hen'-pen'** (*Scot.*), fowl-house manure; **hen'-roost,** a roosting-place for fowls; **hen'-run,** an enclosure for fowls.—*adj.* **hen'-toed,** with toes turned in.—**hen'-wife,** a woman with charge of poultry.—*adj.* **hen'-witted,** brainless, silly.—**hen on a hot girdle** (chiefly *Scot.*), one who is in a jumpy or nervous state. [O.E. **henn,** fem. of *hana,* a cock; Ger. **henne** (*hahn,* cock).]

**hence, hens,** *adv.* from this place: from this time onward: in the future: from this cause or reason: from this origin.—*interj.* away! begone!—*advs.* **hence'forth, hencefor'ward,** from this time forth or forward. [M.E. **hennes,** formed with genitive ending from *henne*—O.E. **heonan,** from the base of her; Ger. **hinnen, hin,** hence: so L. **hinc,** hence—*hic,* this.]

**henchman, hench', hensh'man,** *n.* a servant: a page: a right-hand man: an active political partisan, esp. from self-interest: a thick-and-thin supporter:—*pl.* **hench'men.** [O.E. **hengest,** a horse (Ger. **hengst**), and *man;* not connected with **haunch.**]

**hend, hend,** (*obs.*) *adj.* convenient: skilful: gracious: courteous. [App. O.E. **gehende,** handy—*hand.*]

**hend, hend,** (*Spens.*) *v.t.* to seize, to grasp. [O.E. **gehendan** or O.N. **henda;** cf. **hand.**]

**hendecagon, hen-dek'ə-gon,** *n.* a plane figure of eleven angles and eleven sides.—*adj.* **hendecagonal** (*-ag'ən-l*). [Gr. **hendeka,** eleven, *gōniā,* an angle.]

**hendecasyllable, hen'dek-ə-sil'ə-bl,** *n.* a metrical line of eleven syllables.—*adj.* **hendecasyllabic** (*-ab'ik*). [Gr. **hendeka,** eleven, *syllabē,* a syllable.]

**hendiadys, hen-di'ə-dis,** *n.* a rhetorical figure in which one and the same notion is presented in two expressions, as *with might and main.* [Gr. **hen dia dyoin,** lit. one by two.]

**henequen, hen'ə-kən,** *n.* a Mexican agave: its leaf-fibre, sisal-hemp used for cordage.—Also **hen'equin, hen'iquin.** [Sp. **henequén, jeniquén.**]

**henge, henj,** (*Spens.*) *n.* axis. [hinge.]

**henge, henj,** *n.* a megalithic circular, oval, or horseshoe-shaped structure of wood or stone, often surrounded by a bank or ditch. [Back-formation from *Stonehenge,* a famous example.]

**henna, hen'ə,** *n.* a small Oriental shrub (Lawsonia) of the loosestrife family, with fragrant white flowers: a red or reddish-orange pigment made from its leaves for dyeing the nails and hair and for skin decoration.—*adj.* **hennaed** (*hen'əd*), dyed with henna. [Ar. **hinnā'.**]

**henotheism, hen'ō-thē-izm,** *n.* belief in one god, supreme or specially venerated but not the only god—a stage between polytheism and monotheism.—*n.* **henothē'ist.**—*adj.* **henotheist'ic.** [Gr. **heis, henos,** one, *theos,* god.]

**henotic, hen-ot'ik,** *adj.* tending to unify or reconcile. [Gr. **henōtikos**—*heis, henos,* one.]

**henpeck.** See **hen.**

**henry, hen'ri,** (*elect.*) *n.* the unit of inductance, such that an electromotive force of one volt is induced in a circuit by current variation of one ampere per sec. [Joseph **Henry,** American physicist (1797-1878).]

**hent, hent,** (*obs.*) *v.t.* to grasp: to snatch away, carry off: to reach:—*pa.t.* and *pa.p.* **hent.**—*n.* a grasp (*obs.*): perh. a conception, intention, perh. an opportunity (*Shak.*). [O.E. **hentan;** to seize.]

**heortology, hē-ört-ol'ə-ji,** *n.* the study of religious feasts.—*adj.* **heortological** (*-ə-loj'i-kl*).—*n.* **heortol'ogist.** [Gr. **heortē,** a feast, *logos,* discourse.]

**hep, hep,** *n.* See **hip** (2).

hep, *hep*, (*obsolescent slang*) *adj.* knowing, informed, well abreast of fashionable knowledge and taste, esp. in the field of jazz.—hep'-cat, hep'ster (*slang*), a hipster (*q.v.*).—be, get, hep to, to be, become informed about. [Perh. *hep*, left (command in drilling)—with ideas of being in step.]

hepar, *hē'pär, n.* old name for liver-coloured compounds of sulphur.—*ns.* heparin (*hep'ə-rin*), complex substance formed in tissues of liver, lung, etc., that delays clotting of blood, used in medicine and surgery; hepatec'tomy, excision of the liver.—*adj.* hepatic (*hi-pat'ik*), pertaining to, or acting on, the liver: pertaining to liverworts: liver-coloured.—*n.* a liverwort: a hepatic medicine.—*n.* Hepat'ica, a genus of plants with slightly liver-like leaf once classed as a section of the Anemone genus: the common liverwort *Marchantia polymorpha*: (in *pl.*) Hepat'icae (*-sē*), liverworts.—*adjs.* hepat'ical; hepaticolog'ical.—*ns.* hepaticol'ogist, a student of liverworts; hepaticol'ogy; hepatisation, -z- (*-ət-i-zā'shən*), a liver-like solidification of tissue as of the lungs in pneumonia.—*v.t.* hep'atise, -ize, to convert into a substance resembling liver: to impregnate with sulphuretted hydrogen (*obs.*).—*ns.* hep'atite, a variety of barytes with a sulphureous stink; hepati'tis, inflammation of the liver; hepatol'ogist, a specialist in liver diseases; hepatol'ogy; hepatos'copy, divination by inspection of the livers of animals. [Gr. *hēpar, hēpatos*, liver.]

hephthemimer, *hef-thi-mim'ər, (Gr.* and *Lat. pros.) n.* seven half-feet.—*adj.* hophthemim'eral, of a caesura, occurring in the middle of the fourth foot. [Gr. *hepta*, seven, *hēmi-*, half, *meros*, part.]

Hepplewhite, *hep'l-(h)wit, adj.* belonging to a light and graceful school of furniture design that began with George Hepplewhite (d. c. 1786).

hept, *hept,* (*Spens.*) for heaped.

hepta-, *hep'tə-, hep-ta', in* composition, seven.—*ns.* hep'tachord (Gr. *chordē*, string), in Greek music, a diatonic series of seven tones, containing five whole steps and one half-step: an instrument with seven strings: an interval of a seventh; hep'tad (Gr. *heptas, heptados*), a group of seven: an atom, radical, or element having a combining power of seven (*chem.*).—*adj.* hep'taglot (Gr. *heptaglōttos—glōtta*, tongue), in seven languages.—*n.* a book in seven languages.—*n.* hep'tagon (Gr. *heptagōnos—gōniā*, an angle), a plane figure with seven angles and seven sides.—*adj.* heptag'onal.—*n.pl.* Heptagynia (*-jin'i-ə*; Gr. *gynē*, woman, female), in Linnaean classification an order of plants (in various classes) having seven styles.—*adj.* heptag'ynous.—*n.* Heptam'eron (Gr. *hēmerā*, a day), a book containing the transactions of seven days, esp. the collection of stories told in seven days bearing the name of Queen Margaret of Navarre (1492-1549).—*adj.* heptam'erous (Gr. *meros*, part), having parts in sevens.—*n.* hepta'meter (Gr. *metron*, measure), a verse of seven measures or feet.—*n.pl.* Heptan'dria (Gr. *anēr, andros*, a man, male), a Linnaean class of plants having seven stamens.—*adj.* heptan'drous, with seven stamens.—*n.* hep'tane, a hydrocarbon (C₇H₁₆), seventh of the methane series.—*adj.* heptapod'ic.—*ns.* heptap'ody (Gr. *pous, podos*, foot), a verse of seven feet; hep'tarch, heptarchist, ruler in a heptarchy.—*adj.* heptar'chic.—*n.* heptarchy (*hep'tär-ki*; Gr. *archē*, sovereignty), a government by seven persons: a country governed by seven: a misleading term for a once supposed system of seven English kingdoms—Wessex, Sussex, Kent, Essex, East Anglia, Mercia, and Northumbria.—*adj.* heptasyllab'ic, seven-syllabled.—*n.* Hep'-tateuch (*-tūk*; Gr. *teuchos*, instrument, volume), the first seven books of the Old Testament.—*adj.* heptaton'ic (Gr. *tonos*, tone; *mus.*), of a

scale, consisting of seven notes. [Gr. *hepta*, seven.]

her, *hûr, pron., gen.* (or *poss. adj.*), *dat.,* and *acc.* of the *pron.* she: herself (*refl.*, *poetic* only): she (*coll. nom.*). [O.E. *hire*, gen. and dat. sing. of *hēo*, she.]

her, *hûr,* (*obs.*; *Spens.) pron.* or *poss. adj.* their. [O.E. *hiera, hira, heora*, gen. pl. of he.]

Heraclean, Heracleian, *her-ə-klē'ən, adj.* pertaining to Heracles (Gr. *Hēraklēs*).—*adj.* Heracli'dan, Heraclei'dan, pertaining to the Heracleidae or descendants of Heracles (Hercules), the aristocracy of Sparta.—*n.* Her'aclid, one claiming such descent.

herald, *her'əld, n.* in ancient times, an officer who made public prcclamations and arranged ceremonies: in mediaeval times, an officer who had charge of all the etiquette of chivalry, keeping a register of the genealogies and armorial bearings of the nobles: an officer whose duty is to read proclamations, to blazon the arms of the nobility, etc.: a proclaimer: a forerunner: a name given to many newspapers: the redbreasted merganser, usually her'ald-duck.—*v.t.* to usher in: to proclaim.—*adj.* heraldic (*her-, hər-al'dik*), of or relating to heralds or heraldry.—*adv.* heral'dically.—*ns.* her'aldry, the art or office of a herald: the science of recording genealogies and blazoning coats of arms; her'aldship. [O.Fr. *herault*; of Gmc. origin.]

herb, *hûrb* (old-fashioned *ûrb*), *n.* a plant with no woody stem above ground, distinguished from a tree or shrub: a plant used in medicine: an aromatic plant used in cookery.—*adj.* herbā'ceous, pertaining to, composed of, containing, or of the nature of, herbs: like ordinary foliage leaves: usu. understood as of tall herbs that die down in winter and survive in underground parts (*hort.*).—*n.* herb'age, herbs collectively: herbaceous vegetation covering the ground: right of pasture.—*adjs.* herb'aged, covered with grass; herb'al, composed of or relating to herbs.—*n.* a book containing descriptions of plants with medicinal properties, orig. of all plants.—*ns.* herb'alist, one who studies, collects, sells, or administers herbs or plants: an early botanist; herb'ar (*Spens.*; see arbour); herbā'rian, a herbalist; herbārium, a classified collection of preserved plants:—*pl.* herbā'riums, herbā'ria; herb'ary, a garden of herbs.—*adj.* herbicid'al.—*ns.* herb'icide (*-i-sid*), a substance for killing weeds, etc., esp. a selective weedkiller; herb'ist, a herbalist.—*n.pl.* herbiv'ora (*ə-rə*), grass-eating animals, esp. ungulates.—*n. sing.* herb'ivore (*-vōr, -vör*).—*adjs.* herbiv'orous, eating or living on grass or herbage; herbless.—*ns.* herb'let, herb'elet (*Shak.*), a small herb; herborisa'tion.—*v.i.* herb'orise, -ize, to botanise.—*n.* herb'orist, a herbalist.—*adjs.* herb'ous, herb'ose, abounding with herbs; herb'y, of or pertaining to herbs.—herb'-beer, a substitute for beer made from herbs; herb'-benn'et (L. *herba benedicta*, blessed herb), avens; herb'-Chris'topher, baneberry; herb'-(of-)grace', or of-repent'ance, the common rue; herb'-Par'is, a tetramerous plant (*Paris quadrifolia*) of the lily family; herb'-Pē'ter, cowslip; herb'-Rob'ert, stinking crane'sbill (*Geranium robertianum*), a plant with small reddish-purple flowers; herb'-tea', a drink made from aromatic herbs; herb'-trin'ity, the pansy. [Fr. *herbe*—L. *herba*.]

Herbartian, *har-bärt'i-ən, adj.* of Johann Friedrich Herbart (1776-1841), German philosopher and paedagogic psychologist.

hercogamy, herkogamy, *hər-kog'ə-mi,* (*bot.*) *n.* an arrangement of the flower preventing self-pollination.—*adj.* hercog'amous. [Gr. *herkos*, fence, *gamos*, marriage.]

Herculean, *hûr-kū-lē'ən, -kū'li-ən, adj.* of or pertaining to Hercules (*hûr'kū-lēz*); Greek Hēraklēs):

(without *cap.*) extremely difficult or dangerous, as the twelve labours of Hercules: (without *cap.*) of extraordinray strength and size.—**Hercules beetle**, a gigantic S. American lamellicorn beetle, 6 inches long, with a long horn on the thorax of the male and a smaller one on the head; **Hercules' choice**, toil and duty chosen in preference to ease and pleasure—from a famous story in Xenophon's *Memorabilia*; **Hercules' club**, a stick of great size and weight: a West Indian tree (Xanthoxylum): a kind of gourd: a species of Aralia.—**Pillars of Hercules**, two rocks flanking the entrance to the Mediterranean at the Strait of Gibraltar.

**Hercynian**, *hûr-sin'i-ən*, *adj.* of or pertaining to the forest-covered mountain region between the Rhine and the Carpathians or the mountain chains running NW. and SE. between Westphalia and Moravia, of Upper Carboniferous to Cretaceous date.—*n.* **her'cynite**, black spinel, aluminate of iron. [L. *Hercynia (silva)*, the Hercynian (forest).]

**herd**, *hûrd*, *n.* a company of animals, esp. large animals, that habitually keep together: a group of domestic animals, esp. cows or swine, with or without a guardian: a stock of cattle: the people regarded as a mass, as acting from contagious impulse, or merely in contempt: the rabble.—*v.i.* to associate as in herds: to live like a beast in a herd.—*v.t.* to put in a herd: to drive together.—**herd'-book**, a pedigree book of cattle or pigs; **herd'-in'stinct**, the instinct that urges men or animals to act upon contagious impulses or to follow the herd; **herds'man**, keeper of a herd. [O.E. *heord*; Ger. *herde*; cf. **herd** (2).]

**herd**, *hûrd*, *n.* keeper of a herd or flock.—*v.t.* to tend: harbour.—*v.i.* to act as herd.—*n.* **herd'ess** (*rare*).—**herd'boy**, boy who acts as shepherd, cowherd, etc.: a cowboy; **herd'-groom** (*arch.*), a herdsman: shepherd boy; **herd'man** (*obs.*), a herdsman. [O.E. *hirde, hierde*; Ger. *hirte*; cf. **herd** (1).]

**herden**, *hûrd'ən*. See under **hards**.

**herd grass, herd's grass**, (*U.S.*) *hûrd(z) gräs*, timothy: redtop. [From John *Herd*, who observed timothy in New Hampshire, 1700.]

**herdic**, *hûr'dik*, *n.* a low-hung two- or four-wheeled carriage with back entrance and side seats. [From the inventor, P. *Herdic* (1824-88), Pennsylvania.]

**herdwick**, *hûrd'wik*, (*obs.*) *n.* a grazing ground: breed of Lake District sheep. [**herd** and **wick** (2).]

**here**, *hēr*, *adv.* in this place: hither: in the present life or state.—*advs.* **here'about, -s**, about this place; **hereaf'ter**, after this, in some future time, life, or state.—*n.* a future state.—*advs.* **hereat'**, at or by reason of this; **here'away** (*coll.*), hereabout; **hereby'**, not far off: by this; **here-from'**, from this: from this place; **herein'**, in this; **hereinaf'ter**, afterward in this (document, etc.)—opp. to **hereinbefore'**.—*n.* **here'ness**, fact of being here.—*advs.* **hereof'**, of this; **hereon'**, on or upon this; **hereto'**, to this: till this time (*Shak.*): for this object; **here'tofore'**, before this time: formerly; **hereund'er**, under this; **here'unto** (also *-un'*), to this point or time; **here'upon'**, on this: immediately after this; **herewith'**, with this.—**here and there**, in this place, and then in that: thinly: irregularly; **here goes!**, an exclamation indicating that the speaker is about to do something; **here's to**, I drink the health of; **here you are** (*coll.*), this is what you want: this is something for you: this way; **neither here nor there**, of no special importance. [O.E. *hēr*, from base of *hē*, he; Du. and Ger. *hier*, Sw. *här*.]

**heredity**, *hi-red'i-ti*, *n.* transmission of characters to descendants: heritability.—*n.* **hereditabil'ity**.—*adj.* **hered'itable**, that may be inherited.—*n.* **heredit'ament** (*her-id*-), any property that may pass to an heir.—*adv.* **hered'itarily**.—*n.* **hered'-itariness**, the quality of being hereditary.—*adj.*

**hered'itary**, descending or coming by inheritance: transmitted to offspring: succeeding by inheritance: according to inheritance. [L. *hērēditās, -ātis—hērēs, -ēdis*, an heir.]

**Hereford**, *her'i-fərd*, *adj.* of a breed of white-faced red cattle, originating in *Hereford*shire.]

**Herero**, *hə-re'rō, he'rə-rō*, *n.* a Bantu people of South West Africa: a member of this people: its language:—*pl.* Hereros, Hereroes.—*adj.* of or pertaining to the Herero people or their language.

**heresy**, *her'i-si*, *n.* belief contrary to the authorised teaching of one's natural religious community: an opinion opposed to the usual or conventional belief: heterodoxy.—*ns.* **heresiarch** (*he-rē'zi-ärk*), a leader in heresy; **heresiog'rapher**, one who writes about heresies; **heresiog'raphy**; **heresiol'ogist**, a student of, or writer on, heresies; **heresiol'ogy**; **heretic** (*her'ə-tik*), the upholder of a heresy.—*adj.* **heretical** (*hi-ret'i-kl*).—*adv.* **heret'i-cally**.—*v.t.* **heret'icate**, to denounce as heretical.—**her'esy-hunt**, vexatious pursuit of a supposed heretic; **her'esy-hunt'er**. [O.Fr. *heresie*—L. *haeresis*—Gr. *hairesis*, the act of taking, choice, set of principles, school of thought—*haireein*, to take.]

**heriot**, *her'i-ət*, *n.* a fine due to the lord of a manor on the death of a tenant—originally his best beast or chattel.—*adj.* **her'iotable**. [O.E. *heregeatu*, a military preparation—*here*, an army, *geatwe*, equipment.]

**herisson**, *her'i-sən*, *n.* a spiked beam turning on a pivot, for defence: a hedgehog (*her.*).—*adj.* **hérissé** (*her'is-ā, ā'-rē-sā; her.*), bristled. [Fr.; see **urchin**.]

**heritable**, *her'i-tə-bl*, *adj.* that may be inherited.—*n.* **heritabil'ity**.—*adv.* **her'itably**.—*n.* **her'itor**, one who inherits: in Scotland, a landholder in a parish, liable to public burdens:—*fem.* **her'itress**, **her'itrix** (*pl.* her'itrixes, heritri'cēs).—*n.* **heritage**, *her'it-ij*, that which is inherited: inherited lot, condition of one's birth: anything transmitted from ancestors or past ages: the children (of God; *B.*).—**heritable property** (*Scots law*), real property, as opposed to movable property or chattels; **heritable security**, same as English mortgage. [O.Fr. *(h)eritable, (h)eritage*—L.L. *hērēditāre*, to inherit—*hērēditas*; see **heredity**.]

**herkogamy**, *her'kə-gam-i*. See **hercogamy**.

**herl**. Same as **harl** (1).

**herling, hirling**, *hûr'ling*, (*dial.*) *n.* a young seatrout, a finnock.

**herm, herma**, *hûrm, -ə*, *n.* a head or bust (originally of *Hermes*) on a square base, often double-faced:—*pl.* herms, hermae (*-ē*).

**hermandad**, *ûr-män-däd'*, *n.* a confederation of the entire burgher class of Spain for police and judicial purposes, formed in 1282, and formally legalised in 1485. [Sp., brotherhood—*hermano*, brother—L. *germānus.*]

**hermaphrodite**, *hûr-maf'rod-it*, *n.* an animal or plant with the organs of both sexes, whether normally or abnormally: a compound of opposite qualities.—*adj.* uniting the characters of both sexes: combining opposite qualities.—*n.* **hermaph'roditism**, the union of the two sexes in one body.—*adjs.* **hermaphrodit'ic, -al.**—**hermaphrodite brig**, a brig square-rigged forward and schooner-rigged aft. [Gr. *Hermaphroditos*, the son of *Hermes* and *Aphroditē*, who grew together with the nymph Salmacis into one person.]

**hermeneutic, -al**, *hûr-mə-nū'tik, əl*,—*adjs.* interpreting: concerned with interpretation.—*adv.* **hermeneu'tically.**—*ns.* **hermeneu'tics**, the science of interpretation (treated as *sing.*); **hermeneu'-tist**. [Gr. *hermēneutikos—hermēneus*, an interpreter, from *Hermēs.*]

**Hermes**, *hûr'mēz*, *n.* the herald of the Greek gods, patron of herdsmen, arts, eloquence, and thieves: the Egyptian Thoth, identified with the Greek

Neutral vowels in unaccented syllables: *el'ə-mənt*; for certain sounds in foreign words, see p. viii

Hermes: a herm. [Gr. *Hermēs*, identified by the Romans with Mercury.]

hermetic, -al, *hûr-met'ik*, *-əl*, adjs. belonging in any way to the beliefs current in the Middle Ages under the name of *Hermes*, the Thrice Great: belonging to magic or alchemy, magical: perfectly close.—*adv.* hermet'ically.—*n.* (treated as *sing.*) hermet'ics, the philosophy wrapped up in the hermetic books, esoteric science: alchemy.—hermetically sealed, closed completely: made air-tight by melting the glass. [From *Hermēs Trismegistos*, Hermes the thrice-greatest, the Greek name for the Egyptian Thoth, god of science, esp. alchemy.]

hermit, *hûr'mit*, *n.* a solitary religious ascetic: one who lives a solitary life: a beadsman: a kind of humming-bird: a hermit-crab.—*ns.* her'mitage, a hermit's cell: a retired abode: a wine produced near Valence (Drôme) in France, where there was a supposed hermit's cell; her'mitess, a female hermit.—*adj.* hermit'ical.—her'mit-crab, a soft-bodied crustacean that inhabits a mollusc shell. [M.E. *eremite*, through Fr. and L. from Gr. *erēmitēs*—*erēmos*, solitary.]

hern, *hûrn.* Same as heron.

hern, *ûrn*, a dialect form for hers. [App. from her, on the analogy of mine, thine.]

hernia, *hûr'ni-ə*, *n.* a protrusion through a weak place of part of the viscera, rupture.—*adjs.* her'nial; her'niated.—*n.* herniot'omy (Gr. *tomē*, a cut), cutting for hernia. [L.]

hernshaw, *hûrn'shō*, *n.* See heronshaw.

hero, *hē'rō*, *n.* a man of distinguished bravery: any illustrious person: a person reverenced and idealised: the principal male figure, or the one whose career is the thread of the story, in a history or work of fiction: orig. a man of superhuman powers, a demigod:—*pl.* hē'roes (formerly, as *Spens.*, who never uses the singular, hērō'es, from which a singular form, hērō'e, was formed); *fem.* heroine (*her'ō-in*).—*adj.* heroic (*hi-rō'ik*), befitting a hero: of or pertaining to heroes: epic: supremely courageous.—*n.* a heroic verse: (in *pl.*) extravagant phrases, bombast.—*adj.* herō'ical.—*adv.* herō'ically (*Milt.* herō'icly).—*ns.* herō'icalness, herō'icness; heroism (*her'ō-izm*), the qualities of a hero: courage: boldness; herō'on, a temple dedicated to a hero: a temple-shaped tomb or monument; hē'roship, the state of being a hero.—heroic age, any semi-mythical period when heroes or demigods were represented as living among men; heroic couplet, a pair of rhyming lines of heroic verse.—*adj.* herō'i-com'ic, -al, consisting of a mixture of heroic and comic: high burlesque.—heroic poem, an epic: a compromise between epic and romance which flourished in the 16th and 17th centuries; heroic remedy, one that may kill or cure; heroic size, in sculpture, larger than life, but less than colossal; heroic verse, the form of verse in which the exploits of heroes are celebrated (in classical poetry, the hexameter; in English, the iambic pentameter, esp. in couplets; in French, the alexandrine); hē'ro-worship, the worship of heroes: excessive admiration of great men, or of anybody. [Through O.Fr. and L. from Gr. *hērōs*; akin to L. *vir*, O.E. *wer*, a man, Sans. *vīra*, a hero.]

heroin, *her'ō-in*, *hi-rō'in*, *n.* a derivativ' of morphine used in medicine and by drug-addicts. [Said to be from Gr. *hērōs*, a herc, from its effect.]

heron, *her'ən*, *hûrn*, *hern*, *n.* a large screaming wading-bird (Ardea or kindred genus).—*n.* her'onry, a place where herons breed. [O.Fr. *hairon*—O.H.G. *heigir.*]

heronshaw, heronsew, hernshaw, *her'ən-* or *hern'-*, *hûrn'-shō*, *-shōo*, *n.* a young heron: a heron. [O.Fr. *herounçel*, confounded with shaw (wood).]

herpes, *hûr'pēz*, *n.* a skin disease of various kinds,

with spreading clusters of vesicles on an inflamed base—esp. herpes *zoster* or shingles.—*adj.* herpetic (*-pet'ik*), relating to or resembling herpes: creeping. [Gr. *herpēs*—*herpein*, to creep.]

Herpestes, *hər-pes'tēz*, *n.* the ichneumon or mongoose genus. [Gr. *herpēstēs*—*herpein*, to creep.]

herpetology, *hûr-pi-tol'ə-ji*, *n.* the study of reptiles.—*adjs.* her'petoid, reptile-like; herpetolog'ic, -al.—*adv.* herpetolog'ically.—*n.* herpetol'ogist, [Gr. *herpeton*, a reptile—*herpein*, to creep.]

herr, *her*, *n.* lord, master, the German term of address equivalent to sir, or (prefixed) Mr:—*pl.* herr'en.—*n.* herrenvolk, *her'en-fōlk*, master race, fitted and entitled by their superior qualities to rule the world. [Ger.]

herring, *her'ing*, *n.* a common small sea-fish (*Clupea harengus*) of great commercial value, found moving in great shoals or multitudes.—*n.* herr'inger (*-ing-ər*), a man or boat employed in herring fishing.—*adj.* herr'ing-bone, like the spine of a herring, applied to a kind of masonry in which the stones slope in different directions in alternate rows, to a zigzag stitch crossed at the corners, to a crossed strutting, etc.: in skiing, of a method of climbing a slope, the skis being placed at an angle and leaving a herring-bone-like pattern in the snow.—*v.t.* to make in herring-bone work, or mark with herring-bone pattern: to climb a slope on skis by herring-bone steps.—herr'ing-buss (*hist.*; see buss (2)); herr'ing-fish'ery; herr'ing-gull, a large white gull with black-tipped wings; herr'ing-pond (*facet.*), the ocean, esp. the Atlantic.—dead as a herring, quite certainly dead—a herring out of water soon dies; neither fish nor flesh nor good red herring (see fish); packed like herring (in a barrel), very closely packed; red herring (see red). [O.E. *hǣring*, *hēring*; cf. Ger. *häring* (mod. *hering*).]

Herrnhuter, *hûrn'hōōt-ər*, *n.* one of the Moravians or United Brethren, so called from their settlement in 1722 at Herrnhut in Saxony.

herry. See hery.

herry, *her'i*, (*Scot.*) *v.t.* to harry.—*n.* herr'iment, herr'yment, spoliation: plunder. [harry.]

hers, *hûrz*, *pron.* possessive of she (used without a noun).

hersall, *hûr'səl*, (*Spens.*) *n.* rehearsal.

herse, *hûrs*, (*obs.*) *n.* a harrow: a spiked portcullis: a form of battle-array: a hearse in various senses.—*adj.* hersed, arranged in harrow form. [hearse.]

herself, *hûr-self'*, *pron.* an emphatic form for she or her: in her real character: reflexive for her: predicatively (or *n.*) one having the command of her faculties, sane, in good form or (*Scot.*) alone, by herself: the mistress of a house, owner of an estate, etc. (*Scot.*). [See her, self.]

hership, *hûr'ship*, (*Scot.*) *n.* plundering: plunder. [O.E. *here*, army, and *hergan*, to harry; cf. O.N. *herskap*, warfare.]

hertz, *hûrts*, *n.* the unit of frequency, that of a periodic phenomenon of which the periodic time is one second—sometimes called cycle per second in U.K.—*adj.* Hertz'ian, connected with Heinrich Hertz (see below).—Hertzian waves, electromagnetic waves used in communicating information through space. [After Heinrich Hertz (1857-94), German physicist.]

hery, herye, herry, *her'i*, (*Spens.*) *v.t.* to praise, to regard as holy. [O.E. *herian*, to praise.]

Heshvan. See Hesvan.

hesitate, *hez'i-tāt*, *v.i.* to hold back or delay in making a decision: to be in doubt: to stammer.—*v.t.* (*rare*) to express or utter with hesitation.—*ns.* hes'itancy, hesitā'tion, wavering: doubt: stammering: delay.—*adj.* hes'itant, hesitating.—*adv.* hes'itātingly.—*adj.* hes'itātive, showing hesitation.—*n.* hes'itātor.—*adj.* hes'itātory, hesitating.—**hesitation waltz**, a kind of waltz into which a pause and gliding step are introduced at intervals. [L. *haesitāre, -ātum*, freq. of *haerēre, haesum*, to stick.]

**hesp**, *hesp*, a Scots form of **hasp**.

**Hesper**, *hes'pər*, **Hesperus**, *-əs*, *ns.* Venus as the evening star.—*adj.* **Hesperian** (*-pē'ri-ən*), western: Italian (from the Greek point of view): Spanish (from the Roman): of the Hesperides: of the skipper butterflies.—*n.* a westerner: a skipper butterfly.—*ns.* **hes'perid** (*-pər-id*) one of the Hesperides: a skipper butterfly:—*pl.* **Hesperides** (*-per'i-dēz*), the sisters who guarded in their delightful gardens in the west the golden apples which Hera, on her marriage with Zeus, had received from Gaea; **hesperid'ium** (*bot.*), a fruit of the orange type.—*pl.* **Hesperiidae** (*-i'i-dē*), a family of moth-like butterflies, the skippers.—*n.* **Hes'peris**, the dame's violet genus of Cruciferae, generally fragrant in the evening. [Gr. *hesperos*, evening, western.]

**Hessian**, *hes'i-ən*, sometimes *hesh'(i)ən*, *adj.* of or pertaining to Hesse: mercenary (from the use of Hessian mercenaries by the British against the Revolutionaries) (*U.S.*).—*n.* a native or citizen of Hesse: (without *cap.*) a cloth made of jute: short for **Hessian boot**, a kind of long boot first worn by Hessian troops.—**Hessian fly**, a midge whose larva attacks wheat stems in America, once believed to have been introduced in straw for the Hessian troops. [*Hesse*, Ger. *Hessen*, in Germany.]

**hessonite**, an amended form of **essonite**.

**hest**, *hest*, (*arch.*) *n.* behest, command: vow.— Also (*Spens.*) **heast** (*hēst*). [O.E. *hǣs*, a command —*hātan*, to command.]

**hesternal**, *hes-tûr'nəl*, *adj.* of yesterday. [L. *hesternus*.]

**Hesvan**, *hes'vän*, **Heshvan**, *hesh'*, *n.* the second month of the Jewish civil year and the eighth month of the Jewish ecclesiastical year. [Heb.]

**Hesychast**, *hes'i-kast*, *n.* one of a 14th-century quietist sect of the Greek Church.—*n.* **Hes'y-chasm**, their doctrines and practice. [Gr. *hēsy-chastēs—hēsychos*, quiet.]

**het**, *het*, a Scots form of **hot**. [O.E. *hāt*.]

**het**, *het*, (*U.S.* and *dial.*) *pa.p.* for **heated**.—**het up**, agitated.

**hetaira**, *he-tī'rə*, *n.* in Greece, a woman employed in public or private entertainment, as flute-playing, dancing, etc.: a paramour: a concubine: a courtesan, esp. of a superior class:—*pl.* **hetai'rai** (*-rī*).—*ns.* **hetai'ria** (*hist.*), a club or society; **hetai'rism**, concubinage: the system of society that admitted hetairai: a supposed primitive communal marriage; **hetai'rist.**— Also (Latinised) **hetaera** (*-tē'*; L. *-ti'*), etc. [Gr. *hetairā*, fem. of *hetairos*, companion; *hetair(e)iā*, a club.]

**heter-**, **hetero**, *het'ər-, -ō-*, or *-o'-*, in composition, other, different: one or other (often opposed to *homo-, auto-*).—*n.* **heterauxē'sis** (Gr. *auxēsis*, growth; *bot.*), unsymmetrical growth.—*adj.* **heteroblast'ic** (Gr. *blastos*, bud, germ), derived from different kinds of cells: showing indirect development.—*n.* **het'eroblasty**, heteroblastic condition.—*adj.* **heterocarp'ous** (Gr. *karpos*, fruit), bearing fruit of more than one kind.—*n.pl.* **Heterocera** (*-os'ər-ə*; Gr. *keras*, horn), a loose term for moths, distinguished from *Rhopalocera* (butterflies).—*adj.* **heterocercal** (*-sûr'kəl*; Gr. *kerkos*, tail), having the vertebral column passing into the upper lobe of the tail, which is usually larger than the lower, as in sharks.—*ns.* **hetero-cercal'ity, het'erocercy.**—*adjs.* **heterochlamydeous** (*-klə-mid'i-əs*; Gr. *chlamys, -ydos*, mantle), having calyx and corolla distinctly different; **heterochromous** (*-krō'məs*; Gr. *chrōma*, colour), having different or varying colours; **hetero-chron'ic.**—*n.* **heteroch'ronism.**—*adjs.* **hetero-**

chronist'ic; **heteroch'ronous.**—*n.* **heterochrony** (*ok'rə-ni*; Gr. *chronos*, time; *biol.*), divergence from the normal time sequence in development. —*adj.* **het'eroclite** (*-klit*; Gr. *heteroklitos—klitos*, inflected—*klinein*, to inflect; *gram.*), irregularly inflected: irregular: having forms belonging to different declensions.—*n.* a word irregularly inflected: anything irregular.—*adjs.* **heteroc'litous; heterocyclic** (*-si'klik*; Gr. *kyklos*, wheel), having a closed chain in which the atoms are not all alike (*chem.*): having different numbers of parts in different whorls (*bot.*).—*n.* **heterodactyl** (*-dak'til*; Gr. *daktylos*, toe), a heterodactylous bird.—*adj.* **heterodactylous.**—*adjs.* **heterodac'tylous**, having the first and second toes turned backwards (as trogons—not the first and fourth as parrots); **het'erodont** (Gr. *odous, odontos*, a tooth), having different kinds of teeth; **het'erodox** (Gr. *heterodoxos—doxa*, opinion—*dokeein*, to think), holding an opinion other than or different from the one generally received, esp. in theology: heretical.—*n.* **het'ero-doxy**, heresy.—*adjs.* **het'erodyne** (*-ō-din*; Gr. *dynamis*, strength), in radio communication, applied to a method of imposing on a continuous wave another of slightly different length to produce beats; **heteroecious** (*-ē'shəs*).—*n.* **hetero-ecism** (*-ē'sizm*; Gr. *oikos*, a house), parasitism upon different hosts at different stages of the life-cycle.—*adj.* **heterog'amous.**—*ns.* **heterog'amy** (Gr. *gamos*, marriage), alternation of generations (*biol.*): reproduction by unlike gametes (*biol.*): presence of different kinds of flower (male, female, hermaphrodite, neuter, in any combination) in the same inflorescence (*bot.*): indirect pollination (*bot.*); **heterogenē'ity.**—*adj.* **hetero-geneous** (*-jē'ni-əs*; Gr. *heterogenēs—genos*, a kind), different in kind: composed of parts of different kinds—opp. to *homogeneous.*—*adv.* **heteroge'neously.**—*ns.* **heteroge'neousness; het-erogenesis** (*-jen'i-sis*; Gr. *genesis*, generation; *biol.*), spontaneous generation: alternate genera-tion.—*adj.* **heterogenetic** (*-ji-net'ik*).—*n.* **hetero-geny** (*-oj'ən-i*), a heterogeneous assemblage: heterogenesis.—*adj.* **heterogonous** (*-og'ə-nəs*; Gr. *gonos*, offspring, begetting), having flowers differing in length of stamens (*bot.*): having alternation of generations (*biol.*).—*ns.* **heterog'-ony; het'erograft**, a graft of tissue from a member of one species to a member of another species; **het'erokont, het'erocont** (Gr. *kontos*, a punt-ing pole), any member of the **Heterocont'ae** or yellow-green algae (e.g. the common Con-ferva), a class usually characterised by the pair of unequal cilia on the motile cells.—*adjs.* **heterokont'an; heterologous** (*-ol'ə-gəs*), not homologous: different: of different origin: abnormal.—*n.* **heterol'ogy**, lack of correspon-dence between apparently similar structures due to different origin.—*adjs.* **heterom'erous** (Gr. *meros*, part), having different numbers of parts in different whorls (*bot.*): (of lichens) having the algal cells in a layer (*bot.*): having unlike seg-ments (*zool.*); **heteromor'phic** (Gr. *morphē*, form), deviating in form from a given type: of different forms—also **heteromor'phous.**—*ns.* **het-eromor'phism, het'eron.orphy.**—*adj.* **heteron'o-mous** (Gr. *nomos*, law), subject to outside rule or law: subject to outside rule or law—opp. to *autonom-ous.*—*ns.* **heteron'omy; het'eronym**, a word of the same spelling as another but of different pro-nunciation and meaning.—*adjs.* (often *cap.*) **het-erousian** (*het-ər-ō-ōō'si-ən*, or *-ow'*; Gr. *ousiā*, being), **heterousian** (*-ōō'*, *-ow'*, or *-ō-ōō'*), of unlike essence: holding with the Father and Son to be of different substance.—*n.* (often *cap.*) a holder of such belief.—*adj.* **heterophyllous** (*-fil'əs*; Gr. *phyllon*, a leaf), having different kinds of foliage leaf.—*ns.* **het'erophylly; hetero-plasia** (*-plā'z(h)i-ə, -si-ə*; Gr. *plasis*, a forming),

Neutral vowels in unaccented syllables: *el'ə-mənt*; for certain sounds in foreign words, see p. viii

development of abnormal tissue or tissue in an abnormal place.—*adj.* heteroplastic (-*plas'tik*).—*ns.* het'eroplasty, heteroplasia: grafting of tissue from another person; heteropod.—*ns.pl.* Heterop'oda (Gr. *pous, podos,* foot), pelagic gasteropods in which the foot has become a swimming organ; Heterop'tera (Gr. *pteron,* a wing), a suborder of insects, the bugs, Hemiptera with fore and hind wings (when present) markedly different.—*adj.* heterop'terous.—*n.* heteroscian (*het-ər-osh'i-ən*; Gr. *skiā,* a shadow), a dweller in a temperate zone, whose noon-shadow is always thrown one way, either north or south.— *adj.* heterosex'üal, having, or pertaining to, sexual attraction towards the opposite sex.—*ns.* heterosexual'ity; heterö'sis, cross-fertilisation.— *n.pl.* Heterosö'mata (Gr. *sōma,* pl. *sōmata,* a body), the flat-fishes.—*adj.* heterosö'matous; heterosporous (-*os'por-əs,* or -*pōr',* -*pör'*), having different kinds of asexually produced spores.— *n.* heteros'pory.—*adj.* heterostroph'ic (Gr. *strophē,* a turning), consisting of unequal strophes: coiled contrary to the usual direction.—*n.* heteros'trophy.—*adjs.* het'erostyled, heterosty'lous, having styles of different length in different flowers.—*ns.* heterostyl'ism; het'erostyly.—*adj.* heterotact'ic.—*ns.* heterotax'is, het'erotaxy (Gr. *taxis,* arrangement), anomalous arrangement of, e.g. parts of the body, etc.—*adj.* heterothall'ic (Gr. *thallos,* a shoot; *bot.*), having (as certain fungi) two 'physiologically different types of mycelium, called plus and minus, comparable to male and female.—*ns.* heterothall'ism, het'erothally.—*adj.* heterothcr'mal (Gr, *thermos,* heat), taking the temperature of the surroundings.—*n.* het'erotroph, a heterotrophic organism.—*adj.* heterotroph'ic.—*n.* heterot'rophy (Gr. *trophē,* livelihood; *bot.*), dependence (immediate or ultimate) upon green plants for carbon (as in most animals, fungi, etc.).—*adjs.* heterotyp'ic, differing from the normal condition: pertaining to the first (reductional) cell division in meiosis (*biol.*), see homotypic; heterousian (see heteroousian).—*n.* heterozygote (-*zī'gōt*; Gr. *zygōtos,* yoked—*zygon,* yoke), a zygote or individual formed from gametes differing with respect to some pair of alternative characters (one dominant and one recessive).—*adj.* heterozy'gous. [Gr. *heteros,* other, one or other.]

hether, hetherward (*Spens.*). Same as hither, hitherward.

hetman, het'man, (*hist.*) *n.* a Polish officer: the head or general of the Cossacks:—*pl.* het'mans. —*ns.* het'manate, het'manship. [Pol.,—Ger. *hauptmann,* captain.]

heugh, heuch, *hühh,* (*Scot.*) *n.* a crag: a ravine or steep-sided valley: a quarry-face: an excavation, esp. for coal. [O.E. *hōh,* heel; cf. hoe (2).]

heulandite, *hū'lan-dit, n.* a zeolite like stilbite. [After H. *Heuland,* an English mineralogist.]

heuristic, *hū-ris'tik, adj.* serving or leading to find out: encouraging desire to find out: (of method, argument) depending on assumptions based on past experience: consisting of guided trial and error.—*n.* the art of discovery in logic: the method in education by which the pupil is set to find out things for himself: (in *pl.*) principles used in making decisions when all possibilities cannot be fully explored.—*adv.* heuris'tically.—*ns.* heuret'ic (*logic*), heuristic; heur'ism, the heuristic method or principle in education. [Irreg. formed from Gr. *heuriskein,* to find; cf. eureka.]

hevea rubber, *hē'vē-ə rub'ər,* rubber from the *Hevea brasiliensis* tree, used in electrical insulators for its good electrical and mechanical properties.

hew, *hū, v.t.* to cut with blows: to shape, fell or sever with blows of a cutting instrument.—*v.i.* to deal blows with a cutting instrument:—*pa.t.*

hewed; *pa.p.* hewed, or hewn.—*n.* (*Spens.*) hacking.—*n.* hew'er, one who hews.—*n.* and *adj.* hew'ing.—*adj.* hewn. [O.E. *hēawan;* Ger. *hauen.*]

hew (*Spens.*). See hue (1).

hewgh, *hū,* (*Shak.*) *interj.* imitating the whistling of an arrow.

hex, *heks, n.* a witch: a wizard: a spell: something which brings bad luck. [Ger. *hexe* (*fem.*), *hexer* (*masc.*).]

hex, *heks, n.* coll. for uranium hexafluoride, a compound used in separating uranium isotopes by gaseous diffusion.

hex-, hexa-, *heks-, heks'ə-, heks-a'-,* in composition, six.—*n.* hex'achord (-*körd*), a diatonic series of six notes having a semitone between the third and fourth.—*adj.* hex'act (-*akt*; Gr. *aktis,* -*inos,* ray), six-rayed.—*n.* a six-rayed sponge spicule.—*adj.* hexacti'nal (or -*akt'i-nl*), six-rayed.—*n.* and *adj.* hexactinell'id.—*n.pl.* Hexactinell'ida, a class of sponges whose spicules have three axes and therefore (unless some are suppressed) six rays.—*n.* hexad (*heks'ad*; Gr. *hexas,* -*ados*), a series of six numbers: a set of six things: an atom, element, or radical with a combining power of six units (*chem.*).—*adjs.* hexad'ic; hexadactyl'ic, hexadact'ylous (Gr. *daktylos,* finger, toe), six-fingered: six-toed.—*n.* hexaëmeron (*heks-ə-ē'mer-on*; Gr. *hēmerā,* day), a period of six days, esp. that of the creation, according to Genesis: a history of the six days of creation.—*adj.* hex'aglot (Gr. *glōtta,* tongue), in six languages.—*n.* hex'agon (Gr. *hexagōnon—gōniā,* an angle), a figure with six sides and six angles.—*adj.* hexagonal (-*ag'ən-əl*), of the form of a hexagon: of the hexagonal system, a crystal system with three axes at 60° to each other and a fourth perpendicular to their plane (*cryst.*).— *adv.* hexag'onally.—*n.* hex'agram (Gr. *gramma,* figure), a figure of six lines, esp. a stellate hexagon.—*n.pl.* Hexagynia (-*jin'i-ə*; Gr. *gynē,* woman), a Linnaean order of plants (in various classes) having six styles.—*adjs.* hexagyn'ian, hexagynous (-*aj'i-nəs*); hexahē'dral.—*n.* hexahē'dron (Gr. *hēdrā,* a base), a solid with six sides or faces, esp. a cube.—*adj.* hexam'erous (Gr. *meros,* part), having six parts, or parts in sixes. —*n.* hexam'eter (Gr. *metron,* measure), a verse of six measures or feet: in Greek and Latin verse such a line where the fifth is almost always a dactyl and the sixth a spondee or trochee, the others dactyls or spondees.—*adj.* having six metrical feet.—*adjs.* hexamet'ric, -al.—*v.i.* hexam'etrise, -ize, to write hexameters.—*n.* hexam'etrist, a writer of hexameters.—*n.pl.* Hexan'dria (Gr. *anēr, andros,* a man, male), a Linnaean class of plants having six stamens.—*adjs.* hexan'drian; hexan'drous, having six stamens.— *ns.* hexane (*heks'ān*), a hydrocarbon (C₆H₁₄), sixth member of the methane series; hex'apla (Gr. *hexaplā,* contracted pl. neut. of *hexaploos,* sixfold), an edition (esp. of the Bible) in six versions.—*adjs.* hex'aplar, hexaplār'ian, hexaplāric; hex'aploid, of, or having, six times the ordinary number of chromosomes.—*n.* a hexaploid cell, individual, species, etc.—*n.* hex'apod (Gr. *pous, podos,* a foot), an animal with six feet.—*n.pl.* Hexap'oda, insects.—*n.* hexap'ody, a line or verse of six feet.—*adj.* hexarch (*heks'ärk*; Gr. *archē,* beginning; *bot.*), having six vascular strands.—*n.* hexastich (*heks'ə-stik*; Gr. *hexastichos,* adj.—*stichos,* a line), a poem or stanza of six lines.—*adjs.* hexastichal (*as-'tik-l*), having six lines or rows; hexastyle (*heks'ə-stil*; Gr. *hexastylos—stÿlos,* a pillar), having six columns.—*n.* a building or portico having six columns in front.—*n.* Hexateuch (*heks'ə-tūk*; Gr. *teuchos,* tool, afterwards book), the first six books of the Old Testament.—*adj.* hexateuch'al.—*ns.* hexylene (*heks'i-lēn,* or *hÿlē,* matter), hex'ene, an unsaturated hydrocarbon ($C_6H_{12}$) of the ethylene series; **hex'ose**, a sugar (of various kinds) with six carbon atoms to the molecule. [Gr. *hex*, six; cf. L. *sex*, and **six**.]

**hexobarbitone sodium**, *heks-ō-bär'bi-tōn*. See **Evipan**.

**hey**, *hā*, *interj*. expressive of joy or interrogation, or calling attention.—*interjs*. **hey'day** (*arch*.), expressive of frolic, exultation, or wonder; **hey'-go-mad** (*dial*.), expressing a high degree of excitement.—Also *n*., as like **hey-go-mad**, helter-skelter.—*interjs*. and *ns*. **hey'-pass, hey'-pres'to**, a conjuror's command in passing objects.—**hey for**, now for: off we go for. [Imit.]

**hey, hay,** *hā*, *n*. a winding country dance.—*v.i.* to dance the hay.—*n*. **hey'-** or **hay-de-guy** (-*gi*), -**guise,-guyes**, a hay popular in the 16th and 17th centuries. [Obs. Fr. *haye*.]

**heyday,** *hā'dā, n.* high spirits (*arch*.): culmination or climax of vigour, prosperity, gaiety, etc.: flush or full bloom. [Origin obscure.]

**heyduck.** See **haiduck**.

**hi!,** *hī, interj.* calling attention: hey. [Cf. **hey** (1).]

**hiant,** *hi'ənt, adj.* gaping. [L. *hiāns, -antis,* pr.p. of *hiāre*, to gape.]

**hiatus,** *hi-ā'təs, n.* a gap: an opening: a break in continuity, a defect: a concurrence of vowel sounds in two successive syllables (*gram*.):—*pl.* **hiā'tuses**.—**hiatus hernia**, one in which a part of a viscus protrudes through a natural opening, esp. through that in the diaphragm intended for the oesophagus. [L. *hiātus, -ūs*—*hiāre, hiātum,* to gape.]

**hibernate,** *hi'bər-nāt, v.i.* to winter: to pass the winter in a resting state.—*ns.* **hi'bernacle**, winter quarters: a hibernaculum; **hibernac'ulum**, a winter retreat: a bud in Polyzoa that regenerates the colony after winter (*zool*.): a winter-bud, bulb, etc., by which a plant survives the winter (*bot*.):—*pl.* **hibernac'ula**.—*adj.* **hiber'nal**, belonging to winter: wintry.—*n.* **hibernā'tion**.—**hibernation anaesthesia**, freezing-down. [L. *hibernāre, -ātum*—*hibernus*, wintry—*hiems*, winter.]

**Hibernian,** *hi-bûr'ni-ən*, relating to Hibernia or Ireland: Irish: characteristic of Ireland.—*n.* an Irishman.—*ns.* **Hiber'nianism, Hiber'nicism** (-*sizm*), an Irish idiom or peculiarity: a bull in speech.—*adv.* **Hiber'nically**.—*v.t.* **hiber'nicise, -ize** (-*sīz*), to render Irish.—*n.* **hibernisā'tion**, -**z-**, a making Irish.—*v.t.* **hi'bernise, -ize**, to hibernicise. [L. *Hibernia,* Ireland.]

**Hibiscus,** *hib-is'kəs, n.* a genus of malvaceous plants, mostly tropical. [L.,—Gr. *ibiskos*, marshmallow.]

**hic,** *hik, interj.* representing a hiccup.

**hic,** *hik, hēk,* (L.) this (*demons. pron*.).—**hic et ubique** (*et ū-bi'kwē, ōō-bē'kwe*), here and everywhere; **hic jacet** (*jā'set, yä'ket*), here lies; **hic sepultus** (*sə-pul'tus, se-pōōl'tōōs*), here buried.

**hiccatee, hicatee,** *hik-ə-tē', n.* a West Indian freshwater tortoise. [From a native name.]

**hiccup,** *hik'əp, n.* the involuntary contraction of the diaphragm while the glottis is spasmodically closed: the sound caused by this.—*v.i.* to make a hiccup.—*v.t.* to say with a hiccup:—*pr.p.* **hicc'-uping;** *pa.t.* and *pa.p.* **hicc'uped**.—*adj.* **hicc'upy**, marked by hiccups. [Imit.; an early form was **hicket**; cf. Du. *hik*, Dan. *hik*, Bret. *hik*. The spelling *hiccough* is due to a confusion with *cough*.]

**hick,** *hik, n.* a lout: a booby.—*adj.* pertaining to, or suggestive of, a hick: rural and uncultured. [A familiar form of *Richard*.]

**hickery-pickery,** *hik'ər-i-pik'ər-i.* See **hiera-picra**.

**hickory,** *hik'ər-i, n.* a North American genus (*Carya*) of the walnut family, yielding edible nuts and heavy strong tenacious wood. [Earlier *pohickery*; of Indian origin.]

**hickwall,** *hik'wöl,* (*dial*.) *n.* the green woodpecker. [Origin obscure.]

**hid, hidden.** See **hide** (1).

**hidage.** See **hide** (3).

**hidalgo,** *hi-dal'gō, n.* a Spanish nobleman of the lowest class: a gentleman:—*pl.* **hidal'gōs;** *fem.* **hidal'ga,** *pl.* **hidal'gas**.—*adj.* **hidal'gōish**.—*n.* **hidal'gōism.** [Sp. *hijo de algo*, son of something.]

**hiddenite,** *hid'ən-it, n.* a green spodumene, discovered by W. E. *Hidden* (1853-1918).

**hidder,** *hid'ər,* (*Spens*.) *n.* a young male sheep:—*fem.* **shidder**. [Perh. **he**, and **deer**.]

**hide,** *hid, v.t.* to conceal: to keep in concealment: to keep secret or out of sight.—*v.i.* to go into, or to stay in, concealment:—*pa.t.* **hid,** *hid; pa.p.* **hidden,** *hid'n,* **hid.**—*n.* a hiding-place: a concealed place from which to observe wild animals, etc.—*adj.* **hidd'en,** concealed: unknown.—*adv.* **hidd'enly,** in a hidden or secret manner.—*n.* **hidd'enness**.—*adj.* **hidd'enmost**, most hidden.—*n.* **hid'ing,** concealment: a place of concealment. --**hide'-and-(go-)seek,** a game in which one seeks the others, who have hidden themselves; **hide'-away,** a fugitive: a place of concealment: a refuge.—*adj.* that hides away.—**hide'out,** a retreat; **hid'ing-place; hid'y-hole** (*Scot.* and *U.S.*), a hiding-place. [O.E. *hȳdan;* cf. M.L.G. *hūden,* and (doubtfully) Gr. *keuthein*.]

**hide,** *hid, n.* the skin of an animal, esp. the larger animals, sometimes used derogatorily for human skin.—*v.t.* to flog or whip: to skin.—*n.* **hid'ing,** a thrashing.—*adj.* **hide'-bound,** of animals, having the hide attached so closely to the back and ribs that it is taut, not easily moved: in trees, having the bark so close that it impedes the growth: stubborn, bigoted, obstinate.—**tan someone's hide** (*coll*.), to whip him. [O.E. *hȳd;* Ger. *haut,* L. *cutis*.]

**hide,** *hid, n.* in old English law, a variable unit of area of land, enough for a household.—*n.* **hid'age,** a tax once assessed on every hide of land. [O.E. *hid,* contracted from *higid;* cf. *hīwan, higan,* household.]

**hide,** *hid,* (*Spens*.) *pa.t.* of **hie** (1).

**hideous,** *hid'i-əs, adj.* frightful: horrible: ghastly: extremely ugly: huge (*obs*.).—*ns.* **hideos'ity,** **hid'eousness**.—*adv.* **hid'eously.** [O.Fr. *hideus, hisdos*—*hide, hisde,* dread, poss.—L. *hispidus,* rough, rude.]

**hid'lings, hid'lins, hid'ling,** *hid'lin(g)s,* (*Scot*.) *adv.* in secrecy.—*adj.* secret.—*n.* a hiding-place or hiding-places: secrecy. [**hid,** and adv. suff. *-ling*.]

**hidrosis,** *hid-rō'sis, n.* sweating, esp. in excess.—*n.* and *adj.* **hidrotic** (-*rot'ik*), sudorific. [Gr. *hidrōs, -ōtos,* sweat.]

**hie,** *hī, v.i.* to hasten.—*v.t.* to urge on (with *on*): pass quickly over (one's way):—*pr.p.* **hie'ing;** *pa.t.* and *pa.p.* **hied**.—*n.* (*obs*.) haste. [O.E. *hīgian*.]

**hie,** *hī, hi,* (*Scot*.) *n.* and *interj.* the call to a horse to turn to the left—opp. to *hup*.—*v.t.* and *v.i.* to turn to the left (of or to a horse or plough-ox.)

**hielaman,** *hē'lə-man, n.* the native Australian narrow shield of bark or wood. [Native word *hilaman*.]

**Hieland,** *hēl'ən(d), -ənt, adj.* a Scots form of Highland.—*n.* sae **Hielant**, not altogether absurd: not so bad as might be.

**hiems,** *hi'emz,* (*Shak*.) *n.* winter.—*adj.* **hi'emal.** [L. *hiems*.]

**Hieracium,** *hi-ər-ā'shi-əm, n.* the hawkweed genus of Compositae. [Latinised from Gr. *hierākion,* hawkweed—*hierāx,* hawk.]

**hiera-picra,** *hi'ər-ə-pik'rə, n.* a purgative drug from aloes and canella bark.—Also **hick'ery-pick'ery,** **hig'ry-pig'ry.** [Gr. *hierā* (fem.), sacred, *pikrā* (fem.), bitter.]

**hierarch,** *hi'ər-ärk, n.* a ruler in holy things: a chief priest: a prelate: an archangel (*Milt*.): one in a high position.—*adjs.* **hi'erarchal, -arch'ic,** **-al.**—*adv.* **hierarch'ically.**—*ns.* **hi'erarchism;**

hi'erarchy, the collective body of angels, grouped in three divisions and nine orders of different power and glory; (1) seraphim, cherubim, thrones; (2) dominations or dominions, virtues, powers; (3) principalities, archangels, angels: each of the three main classes of angels: classification in graded subdivisions: a body classified in successively subordinate grades: priestly government. [Gr. *hierarchēs—hieros,* sacred, *archein,* to rule.]

hieratic, *hi-ar-at'ik, adj.* priestly: applying to a certain kind of ancient Egyptian writing which consisted of abridged forms of hieroglyphics; also to certain styles in art bound by religious convention.—*n.* hierat'ica, the finest papyrus. [L. *hierāticus*—Gr. *hierātikos—hieros,* sacred.]

hierocracy, *hi-ar-ok'ra-si, n.* priestly government. —*n.* hi'erocrat.—*adj.* hierocrat'ic. [Gr. *hieros,* sacred, *krateein,* to rule.]

hierodule, *hi'ar-ō-dūl, n.* a temple slave. [Gr. *hieros,* sacred, *doulos,* a slave.]

hieroglyph, *hi'ar-ō-glif, n.* a sacred character used in ancient Egyptian picture-writing or in picture-writing in general.—*v.t.* to represent by hieroglyphs.—*adjs.* hieroglyph'ic, -al.—*n.* hieroglyph'ic, a hieroglyph: any written character difficult to read.—*adv.* hieroglyph'ically.—*n.* hieroglyphist (-*og'*), one skilled in hieroglyphics. [Gr. *hieroglyphikon—hieros,* sacred, *glyphein,* to carve.]

hierogram, *hi'ar-ō-gram, n.* a sacred or hieroglyphic symbol.—*n.* hierogramm'at(e), a writer of sacred records.—*adjs.* hierogrammat'ic, -al.—*ns.* hierogramm'atist; hi'erograph, a sacred symbol; hierog'rapher, a sacred scribe.—*adjs.* hierograph'ic, -al, pertaining to sacred writing. —*n.* hierog'raphy, a description of sacred things. [Gr. *hieros,* sacred, *gramma,* a character, *graphein,* to write.]

hierolatry, *hi-ar-ol'a-tri, n.* the worship of saints or sacred things. [Gr. *hieros,* sacred, *latreiā,* worship.]

hierology, *hi-ar-ol'a-ji, n.* the science of sacred matters, esp. ancient writing and Egyptian inscriptions.—*adj.* hierologic (*-ō-loj'ik*).—*n.* hierol'-ogist. [Gr. *hieros,* sacred, *logos,* discourse.]

hieromancy, *hi-ar-ō-man'si, n.* divination by observing the objects offered in sacrifice. [Gr. *hieros,* sacred, *manteiā,* divination.]

Hieronymic, *hi-ar-on-im'ik, adj.* of or pertaining to St Jerome.—Also Hieronym'ian.—*n.* Hieron'-ymite, a member of any of a number of hermit orders established in the 13th and 14th centuries. [L. *Hierōnymus,* Gr. *Hierōnymos,* Jerome.]

hierophant, *hi'ar-ō-fant, n.* one who shows or reveals sacred things: a priest: an expounder.—*adj.* hierophant'ic. [Gr. *hierophantēs—hieros,* sacred, *phainein,* to show.]

hieroscopy, *hi-ar-os'ka-pi, n.* hieromancy. [Gr. *hieros,* sacred, *skopeein,* to look at.]

Hierosolymitan, *hi-a-rō-sol'i-mi-tan, adj.* of or pertaining to Jerusalem. [L. and Gr. *Hierosol-yma,* Jerusalem.]

hierurgy, *hi'ar-ûr-ji, n.* a sacred performance.—*adj.* hierur'gical. [Gr. *hierourgiā—hieros,* sacred, *ergon,* work.]

Hi-Fi, hi-fi, *hi-fī.* See high.

higgle, higg'l, *v.i.* to make difficulty in bargaining: to chaffer.—Also higg'le-hagg'le (reduplicated variant).—*n.* higg'ler.—*n.* and *adj.* higg'ling. [Prob. a form of haggle.]

higgledy-piggledy, *hig'l-di-pig'l-di, adv.* and *adj.* haphazard: in confusion. [Origin obscure.]

high, *hī, adj.* elevated: lofty: tall: far up from a base, as the ground, sea-level, low-tide, the mouth of a river, the zero of a scale, etc.: advanced in a scale, esp. the scale of nature: reaching far up: expressible by a large number: of a height specified or to be specified: of advanced degree of intensity: advanced, full (in time, e.g. *season, summer*): of grave importance: advanced: exalted: excellent: eminent: dignified: chief: noble: haughty: arrogant: extreme in opinion: powerful: angry: loud: violent: tempestuous: acute in pitch: luxurious: elated: drunk: over-excited, nervy: under the influence of a drug: standing out: difficult, abstruse: dear: for heavy stakes: remote in time: of meat, etc., slightly tainted: pronounced with some part of the tongue much raised in the mouth (*phon.*): of latitude, far from the equator: of an angle, approaching a right angle: florid.—*adv.* at or to an elevated degree: aloft: shrilly: arrogantly: eminently: powerfully: luxuriously: dear: for heavy stakes.—*n.* that which is high: an elevated region: the highest card: the maximum, high level.—*adj.* high'er, *comp.* of high.—*v.t.* to raise higher: to lift.—*v.i.* to ascend. —*adjs.* high'ermost (*rare*), high'est, *superl.* of high.—*n.pl.* High'ers (*coll.*), school examinations leading to the Scottish Certificate of Education at higher level: passes in these.—*adj.* high'ish, somewhat high.—*adv.* high'ly, in a high degree: in a high position.—*adj.* high'most.—*ns.* high'-ness, the state of being high: dignity of rank: a title of honour given to princes; hight (*hit*), highth (*hīth*), obsolete forms of height.—high ad'miral, a high or chief admiral of a fleet; high altar (see altar); high bailiff, an officer who serves writs, etc., in certain franchises, exempt from the ordinary supervision of the sheriff; high'ball (*U.S.*), whisky and soda or the like with ice in a tall glass.—*adj.* high'-batt'led (hye-battel'd; *Shak.*), app. in command of proud battalions.—high'binder (*U.S.*), a member of a Chinese criminal secret society: a conspirator: a rowdy, ruffian, blackmailer.—*adjs.* high-blest (*Milt.*), supremely blest or happy; high'blood'ed, of noble lineage: high'-blown, swelled with wind: inflated, as with pride (*Shak.*); high'-born, of noble birth; high'boy (*U.S.*), a tallboy; high'-bred, of noble breed, training, or family.—high'brow, an intellectual.—Also *adj.*—high'-browism; hign camp (see camp); high'-chair, child's tall chair.—*adj.* High Church, of a party within the Church of England that exalts the authority of the episcopate and the priesthood, the saving grace of sacraments, etc.: of similar views in other churches.—*ns.* High-Church'ism; High-Churchman.—*adjs.* high'-class, superior; high-col'oured, having a strong or glaring colour: ruddy: over-vivid.—high court, a supreme court; high cross, a town or village cross; high day, a holiday or festival: (*-dā'*) broad daylight: (*hī'*) heyday (erroneously).—*adj.* befitting a festival.—*adj.* high'-dried, brought to an advanced stage of dryness: of fixed and extreme opinions.—High Dutch, High German: pure Dutch of Holland (opp. to former *Cape Dutch*); high'er-up, one occupying an upper position; high'-explos'ive, a detonating explosive (e.g. dynamite, T.N.T.) of great power and exceedingly rapid action—also *adj.*; high-falutin(g) (*-lōōt'*), bombastic discourse.—*adj.* affected: pompous.—high feather, high spirits: happy trim.—*adj.* high'-fed, fed highly or luxuriously: pampered.—high'-feed'ing.—*adj.* high-fidel'ity, good in reproduction of sound (also Hi-Fi, hi-fi). —high'-fli'er, -fly'er, a bird that flies high: one who runs into extravagance of opinion or action: an ambitious person, or one naturally equipped to reach prominence: (*cap.*) (*hist.*), a High-Churchman, or, in Scotland, an Evangelical.—*adjs.* high'-flown, extravagant: elevated: turgid; high'-fly'ing, extravagant in conduct or opinion. —high frequency (see frequency).—*adj.* high'-gear (see gear).—High German, of upper or southern Germany: that form of German language affected by the second consonant shift, including the literary language of Germany.

—*adj.* high′-grade, superior: rich in metal.—*v.t.* to steal rich ore from.—*adj.* high′-grown (*Shak.*), covered with a high growth.—high hand, arbitrary arrogance.—*adj.* high′-hand′ed, overbearing: arbitrary.—high′-hand′edness; high′-hat′, orig. a wearer of a top-hat: a snob or aristocrat: one who puts on airs.—*adj.* affectedly superior. —*v.i.* to put on airs.—*v.t.* to adopt a superior attitude towards or to ignore socially.—*adjs.* high′-heart′ed, full of courage; high′-heeled, having, wearing, high-heels.—high′jack, -er (see hijack, -er); high jinks, boisterous play, jollity: an old Scottish tavern game in which persons played various parts under penalty of a forfeit; high jump, (a field event consisting of) a jump for height.—*adj.* high′-kilt′ed, having the skirt much kilted up: indecorous.—high′land, a mountainous district, esp. (in *pl.* Highlands) the north-west of Scotland, bordered geologically by the great fault running from Dumbarton to Stonehaven, or, ethnologically, the considerably narrower area in which Gaelic is or was recently spoken.—*adj.* belonging to or characteristic of a highland, esp. the Highlands of Scotland.— High′lander, High′landman, an inhabitant or native of a mountainous region, esp. the Highlands of Scotland; Highland cattle, a shaggy breed with very long horns; Highland dress, or costume, kilt, plaid, and sporran; Highland fling, a lively dance of the Scottish Highlands, danced by one person.—*adj.* high′-lev′el, at a high level, esp. involving very important people.—high life, the life of fashionable society: the people of this society; high′light, outstanding feature: (in *pl.*) the most brightly lighted spots.—*v.t.* to throw into relief by strong light: also *fig.*—high living, luxurious living.— *adv.* high′-lone (*Shak.*), quite alone.—high′-low (*arch.*; often *pl.*), an ankle-high shoe fastened in front.—*adj.* high′ly-strung, high-strung.— high′-man, a loaded die:—*pl.* high′men.—high mass, a mass celebrated with music, ceremonies, and incense.—*adjs.* high′-mett′led, high-spirited, fiery; high′-mind′ed, having a high, proud, or arrogant mind (*rare*): having lofty principles and thoughts.—*n.* high′-mind′edness.—*adj.* high′-necked, of a garment, covering the shoulders and neck.—high noon, exactly noon: the peak (*fig.*):—*adjs.* high-oc′tane (of petrol) of high octane number and so of high efficiency; high′-pitched, acute in sound, tending towards treble: steep (as a roof): lofty-toned.—high′-place (*B.*), an eminence on which idolatrous rites were performed by the Jews—hence the idols, etc., themselves.—*adj.* high′-placed, having a high place: placed high.—high polymer, a polymer of high molecular weight.—*adjs.* high′-pow′ered, very forceful and efficient; high′-press′ure, making or allowing use of steam or other gas at a pressure much above that of the atmosphere: involving intense activity; high′-priced, costly.— high priest (see priest); high priestess; high-priest′hood.—*adjs.* high-priest′ly; high′-prin′-cipled, of high, noble, or strict principle; high′-proof, proved to contain much alcohol: highly rectified; high′-raised, -reared, raised aloft: elevated. — high′-ranker. — *adj.* high′-ranking, senior: eminent.—*(adj.* high′-reach′ing, reaching upwards: ambitious.—high relief, bold relief, standing out well from the surface.—*adj.* high-rise, (of flats, office blocks, etc.) containing a large number of storeys.—high′road, one of the public or chief roads: a road for general traffic; high′-roll′er, a plunging spendthrift; high′-roll′ing; high school, a secondary school; high seas, the open ocean.—*adjs.* high′- or high′ly-sea′soned, made rich or piquant with spices or other seasoning; high′-set, placed or pitched high.—high shoe (*arch.*), a boot not reaching far above the ankle.—*adj.* high′-sight′ed (*Shak.*),

looking upwards, supercilious.—high society, fashionable, wealthy society.—*adjs.* high′-souled, having a high or lofty soul or spirit; high′-sound′ing, pompous: imposing; high′-speed, working, or suitable for working, at a great speed; high′-spir′ited, having a high spirit or natural fire: bold: daring.—high spot, an outstanding feature; high′-stepp′er, a horse that lifts its feet high from the ground: a person of imposing bearing or fashionable pretensions.— *adjs.* high′-stepp′ing; high′-stom′ached (*Shak.*), proud-spirited, lofty, obstinate; high′-strung, nervously sensitive, excitable.—High Street, a common name for the main, or former main street of a town; high table, the don's table in a college dining-hall; high′-ta′per, hag-taper.— *v.i.* high′tail, to hightail it (see below).— *adj.* high′-tast′ed, having a strong, piquant taste or relish.—high tea, a tea with meat, etc., as opposed to a plain tea.—*adj.* high-test, (of petrol) boiling at comparatively low temperature and so of high performance.—high tide, high water: a tide higher than usual: a great festival (*rare*); high time, quite time (that something were done): a time of jollity; high toby (*thieves'* *slang*), (see toby).—*adj.* high′-toned, high in pitch: morally elevated: superior, fashionable. —high′-top (*Shak.*), a mast-head; high treason, treason against the sovereign or state; high′-up, one in high position (also *adj.*).—*adjs.* high-veloc-ity, (of shells) propelled at high speed with low trajectory; high′-viced (*Shak.*), enormously wicked.—high wa′ter, the time at which the tide or other water is highest: the greatest elevation of the tide; high′-wa′ter-mark, the highest line so reached: a tide-mark; high′way, a public road on which all have right to go: the main or usual way or course; high′wayman, a robber who attacks people on the public way; high wire, a tightrope stretched exceptionally high above the ground; high words, angry altercation.—*adj.* high′wrought, wrought with exquisite skill: highly finished: elaborate: worked up, agitated. —for the high jump (*coll.*), about to be hanged: about to be reprimanded or chastised; high and dry, up out of the water, stranded; high and low, rich and poor: up and down: everywhere; high and mighty (*ironically*), exalted: arrogant; high life below stairs, servants' imitation of the life of their employers; high-speed steel, an alloy that remains hard when red-hot, suitable for metal-cutting tools; high (old) time (*coll.*), a time of special jollity or enthusiasm; hightail it (*coll.*), hurry away; hit the high spots, to go to excess: to reach a high level; on high, aloft: in heaven; on one's high horse, in an attitude of fancied superiority: very much on one's dignity; on the high ropes (*coll.*), in an elated or highly excited mood; how's that for high? (*U.S.*), beat that if you can (from a card game). [O.E. *hēah*.]— Goth. *hauhs*, O.N. *hār*, Ger. *hoch*.]

hight, *hīt*, *Scot.* hecht, *hehht*, *obs.* hete, *hēt*, *v.t.* to command (*obs.*): to promise, assure, vow (*Scot.*): to call, name (*arch.*): to mention (*Spens.*): to commit (*Spens.*): to direct, deter-mine, intend (*Spens.*); senses not found elsewhere. —*v.i.* (*arch.*, and only in pa.p.; orig. *passive*) to be called or named, to have as a name:—*pa.t.* (*arch.*) hight, (*Scot.*) hecht, (*Spens.*) hete; *pa.p.* (*arch.*) hight, (*Scot.*) hecht, (*obs.*) ho′ten. [O.E. *hēht* (*hēt*), redup. pa.t. of *hātan* (pa.p. *hāten*) substituted for the present and for the last surviving trace of the inflected passive in English, *hātte*, is or was called; cf. Ger. *ich heisse*, I am named, from *heissen*, to call, be called, com-mand.]

highty-tighty, *hī′ti-tī′ti*. Same as hoity-toity. higry-pigry, *hig′ri-pig′ri*. See hiera-picra. hijacker, highjacker, *hī′jak-ər*, *n.* a highwayman (*hist.*): a robber or blackmailer of rum-runners and bootleggers: one who hijacks.—*v.t.* hi'jack, high'jack, to stop and rob (a vehicle): to steal in transit: to force a pilot to fly (an aeroplane) to an unscheduled destination: to force the driver to take (a vehicle) to a destination of the hijacker's choice.—Also *v.i.* [Origin obscure.]

hijinks. Same as high jinks.

hijra, hijrah. Same as hegira.

hike, *hik*, *v.t.* (usually with *up*; *coll.*) to raise up with a jerk: to increase (e.g. prices) sharply and suddenly.—*v.i.* to hitch: to tramp: to go walking and camping with equipment on back: (of shirts, etc.) to move up out of place.—*ns.* hike, a walking tour, outing or march; hi'ker. [Perh. hitch.]

hilar. See hilum.

hilarious, *hi-lā'ri-əs*, *adj.* gay: extravagantly merry.—*adv.* hilā'riously.—*n.* hilarity (*hi-lar'*), gaiety: pleasurable excitement. [L. *hilaris*—Gr. *hilaros*, cheerful.]

Hilary, *hil'ər-i*, *adj.* a term or session of the High Court of Justice in England: also one of the university terms at Oxford and Dublin—from St *Hilary* of Poitiers (d. *c*. 367; festival, Jan. 13).

hilch, *hilsh*, (*Scot.*) *v.t.* to hobble.—*n.* a limp.

hild, *hild* (*Shak.*, *Spens.*). Same as held.

Hildebrandism, *hil'də-brand-izm*, *n.* the spirit and policy of *Hildebrand* (Pope Gregory VII, 1073-1085), unbending assertion of the power of the Church, etc.—*adj.* Hildebrand'ic.

hilding, *hild'ing*, (*arch.*) *n.* a mean, cowardly person, a dastard: a worthless beast.—*adj.* cowardly, spiritless. [Prob. conn. with heel (2).]

hill, *hil*, *n.* a high mass of land, less than a mountain: a mound: an incline on a road.—*v.t.* to form into a hill: to bank up (sometimes for hele).—*adj.* hilled, having hills.—*ns.* hill'iness; hill'ock, a small hill.—*adjs.* hill'ocky; hill'y, full of hills.—hill'-billy (*U.S.*), a rustic of the hill country.—Also *adj.*—hill'-digg'er, a rifler of sepulchral barrows, etc.; hill'folk, hill'men, people living or hiding among the hills: the Scottish sect of Cameronians: the Covenanters generally; hill'-fort, a fort on a hill: a prehistoric stronghold on a hill; hill'-pasture; hill'side, the slope of a hill; hill'top, the summit of a hill.—old as the hills (*coll.*), immeasurably old; over the hill, past one's highest point of efficiency: on the downgrade: past the greatest difficulty; up hill and down dale, vigorously and persistently. [O.E. *hyll*; cf. L. *collis*, a hill, *celsus*, high.]

hillo. Same as hallo.

hilt, *hilt*, *n.* the handle, esp. of a sword or dagger (sometimes in *pl.*).—*v.t.* to furnish with a hilt.— up to the hilt, completely, thoroughly, to the full. [O.E. *hilt*; M.Du. *hilte*; O.H.G. *helza*; not conn. with hold.]

hilum, *hi'ləm*, *n.* the scar on a seed where it joined its stalk (*bot.*): the depression where ducts, vessels, etc., enter an organ (*anat.*).—*adj.* hi'lar. [L. *hīlum*, a trifle, 'that which adheres to a bean'.]

him, *him*, *pron.* the dative and accusative (objective) case of he: the proper character of a person. [O.E. *him*, dat. sing. of *hē*, he, he, *hit*, it.]

Himalaya(n), *him-ə-lā'ə(n)*, *hi-mäl'yə(n)*, *adjs.* pertaining to the Himalaya(s), the mountain range along the border of India and Tibet.

himation, *hi-mat'i-on*, *n.* the ancient Greek outer garment, oblong, thrown over the left shoulder, and fastened either over or under the right. [Gr.]

himself, *him-self'*, *pron.* the emphatic form of he, him: in his real character: having command of his faculties: sane: in normal condition: in good form: alone; by himself (*Scot.*): the head of an institution or body of people (e.g. husband; *Scot.*): the reflexive form of him (*dat.* and *accus.*). [See him, self.]

Himyarite, *him'yär-it*, *n.* a member of an ancient South Arabian people.—*n.* and *adj.* Himyaritic

(-*it'ik*). [*Himyar*, a traditional king of Yemen.]

hin, *hin*, *n.* a Hebrew liquid measure containing about four or six English quarts. [Heb. *hin*.]

hind, *hind*, *n.* the female of the stag or red-deer.— *n.* hind'berry, the raspberry. [O.E. *hind*; Du. and Ger. *hinde*.]

hind, *hind*, (now *Scot.*) *n.* a farm-servant, with cottage on the farm, formerly bound to supply a female field-worker (*bondager*): a rustic. [O.E. *hina*, *hiwna*, gen. pl. of *hiwan*, members of a household.]

hind, *hind*, *adj.* placed in the rear: pertaining to the part behind: backward—opp. to *fore*.—*adj.* hinder (*hin'dər*; *Scot*. *hin'ər*), hind: last (*Scot.*; as *this hinder nicht*, last night).—*n.pl.* hind'erlin(g)s, less correctly hinderlan(d)s (*hin'ər-lənz*; *Scot.*), the buttocks.—*adjs.* hind'ermost, hind'-most, superlative of hind, farthest behind.—*adj.* and *adv.* hind'ward.—hind'-brain', the cerebellum and medulla oblongata; hin'der-end (*Scot*. *hin'ər-en'*, *-end'*) the latter end: buttocks; hind'-foot.—*adv.* hindfore'most, with the back part in the front place.—hind'-gut, the posterior part of the alimentary canal; hind'head, the back of the head, the occiput; hind'leg.—*n.pl.* hind-quar'ters, the rear parts of an animal.—hind'-sight, wisdom after the event; hind'-wheel; hind'-wing. [O.E. *hinder*, backwards; Goth. *hindar*, Ger. *hinter*, behind; cf. O.E. *hindan* (adv.), back; behind.]

hinder, *hin'dər*, *v.t.* to keep back: to stop, or prevent, progress of.—*v.i.* to be an obstacle.—*ns.* hin'derer; hin'drance, act of hindering: that which hinders: prevention: obstacle.—Also hin'derance. [O.E. *hindrian*; Ger. *hindern*.]

hinderland, *hin'dər-land*, an Anglicised form of hinterland. See also under hind-.

Hindi, *hin'dē*, *n.* an Indo-Germanic language of Northern India: a recent literary form of it, with terms from Sanskrit. [Hindi *Hindī*—*Hind*, India.]

Hindu, Hindoo, *hin-dōō'*, or *hin'*, *n.* a member of any of the races of Hindustan or India (*arch.*): a believer in a form of Brahmanism.—*v.t.* and *v.i.* Hin'duise, -ize.—*n.* Hindu'ism (or *hin'*), the religion and customs of the Hindus. [Pers. *Hindū*—*Hind*, India.]

Hindustani, Hindoostanee, *hin-dōō-stä'nē*, *n.* a form of Hindi containing elements from other languages.—Also *adj.*

hing, *hing*, *n.* asafoetida. [Hindi *hig̃*—Sans. *hiṅgu*.]

hinge, *hinj*, *n.* the hook or joint on which a door or lid turns: a joint as of a bivalve shell: the earth's axis (*Milt.*): a cardinal point: a principle or fact on which anything depends or turns.—*v.t.* to furnish with hinges: to bend.— *v.i.* to hang or turn as on a hinge: to depend (with *on*):—*pr.p.* hinging (*hinj'ing*); *pa.t.* and *pa.p.* hinged (*hinjd*).—*adj.* hinge'-bound, unable to move easily on a hinge.—hinge'-joint (*anat.*), a joint that allows movement in one plane only.—off the hinges, disorganised: out of gear. [Related to hang.]

hinny, *hin'i*, *n.* the offspring of a stallion and she-ass. [L. *hinnus*—Gr. *ginnos*, later *hinnos*, a mule.]

hinny, *hin'i*, *n.* a Scottish or N. Eng. variant of honey.

hinny, *hin'i*, *v.i.* to neigh, whinny. [Fr. *hennir*—L. *hinnire*.]

hint, *hint*, *n.* moment, opportunity (*obs.*): a distant or indirect indication or allusion: slight mention: insinuation: a helpful suggestion, tip.—*v.t.* to intimate or indicate indirectly.—*v.i.* to give hints.—*adv.* hint'ingly.—hint at, to give a hint, suggestion, or indication of. [O.E. *hentan*, to seize.]

hinterland, *hint'ər-land*, *-länt*, *n.* a region lying inland from a port or centre of influence. [Ger.]

hip, *hip*, *n.* the haunch or fleshy part of the thigh:

the hip-joint: in archit., the external angle formed by the sides of a roof when the end slopes backwards instead of terminating in a gable.—*v.t.* to sprain or hurt the hip of: to throw over the hip: to carry on the hip (*U.S.*): to construct with a hip (*archit.*):—*pr.p.* **hipp′ing**; *pa.t.* and *pa.p.* **hipped, hipt.**—*adj.* **hipped,** having a hip or hips: of a roof, sloping at the end as well as at the sides.—*n.* **hipp′ing** (*Scot.*), a napkin wrapped about an infant's hips.—*adj.* **hipp′y,** having large hips.—*n.* **hip′sters,** trousers (for men or women) from the hips, not the waist.—**hip′-bath,** a bath to sit in; **hip′-belt,** the 14th-century sword-belt, passing diagonally from waist to hip; **hip′-bone,** the innominate bone; **hip′-flask,** a flask carried in a hip-pocket; **hip′-gir′dle,** the pelvic girdle: a hip-belt; **hip′-gout,** sciatica; **hip′-joint,** the articulation of the head of the thigh-bone with the ilium; **hip′-knob,** an ornament placed on the apex of the hip of a roof or of a gable; **hip′-lock,** in wrestling, a form of cross-buttock; **hip′-pock′et,** a trouser pocket behind the hip; **hip′-roof′,** a hipped roof.—*adj.* **hip′-shot,** having the hip out of joint.—**have, catch, on the hip,** to get an advantage over someone (from wrestling); **hip-joint disease,** a disease of the hip-joint with inflammation, fungous growth, caries, and dislocation. [O.E. *hype*; Goth. *hups,* Ger. *hüfte.*]

**hip,** *hip,* **hep,** *hep, n.* the fruit of the dog-rose or other rose. [O.E. *hēope.*]

**hip, hyp,** *hip, n.* (*arch.*) hypochondria.—*v.t.* to render melancholy or annoyed: to offend. *adjs.* **hipped,** melancholy: peevish, offended, annoyed: obsessed; **hipp′ish.** [hypochondria.]

**hip,** *hip, interj.* an exclamation to invoke a united cheer—**hip′-hip′-hurrah′.**

**hip,** *hip, adj.* a later form of **hep.**—*ns.* **hipp′y,** one of the hippies, successors of the beatniks as rebels against the values of middle-class society, who stress the importance of love, organise to some extent their own communities, and wear colourful clothes; **hipster,** *hip′stər,* one who knows and appreciates up-to-date jazz: a member of the beat generation (1950s and early 1960s).

**Hipparion,** *hi-pā′ri-on, n.* a fossil genus of Equidae. [Gr. *hipparion,* dim. of *hippos,* a horse.]

**hippety-hoppety,** *hip′ə-ti-hop′ə-ti, adv.* hopping and skipping.—*n.* and *adv.* **hipp′ety-hop′.**

**hippiatric,** *hip-i-at′rik, adj.* relating to the treatment of the diseases of horses.—*n.pl.* **hippiat′rics.**—*ns.* **hippiatrist** (*-i′ət-rist*); **hippiatry** (*-i′ət-ri*). [Gr. *hippiātrikos—hippos,* horse, *iātros,* a physician.]

**hippic,** *hip′ik, adj.* relating to horses. [Gr. *hippikos—hippos,* horse.]

**hippo,** *hip′ō, n.* a shortened form of **hippopotamus.**

**hippocampus,** *hip-ō-kam′pəs, n.* a fish-tailed horse-like sea-monster (*myth.*): a genus of small fishes (family Syngnathidae) with horse-like head and neck, the sea-horse: a raised curved trace on the floor of the lateral ventricle of the brain (*anat.*):—*pl.* **hippocamp′i.** [Gr. *hippokampos—hippos,* a horse, *kampos,* a sea-monster.]

**Hippocastanaceae,** *hip-ō-kast-ə-nā′si-ē, n.pl.* the horse-chestnut family. [Gr. *hippos,* horse, *kastanon,* chestnut tree.]

**hippocentaur,** *hip-ō-sent′ör, n.* Same as **centaur.** [Gr. *hippokentauros—hippos,* a horse, and *kentauros.*]

**hippocras,** *hip′ō-kras, n.* spiced wine, formerly much used as a cordial. [M.E. *ypocras,* Hippocrates.]

**Hippocratic,** *hip-ō-krat′ik, adj.* pertaining to the Greek physician *Hippocrates* (*Hippokratēs*; born about 460 B.C.).—*v.i.* **Hippocratise, -ize,** (*-ok′rə-tiz*), to imitate, follow, Hippocrates.—*n.* **Hippoc′ratism.—Hippocratic face,** look, etc.,

sunken, livid appearance, e.g. near death, described by Hippocrates.—**Hippocratic oath,** an oath taken by a doctor binding him to observe the code of medical ethics contained in it—first drawn up (perhaps by Hippocrates) in the 4th or 5th century B.C.

**Hippocrene,** *hip-ō-krē′nē, hip′ō-krēn,* (*myth.*) *n.* a fountain on the northern slopes of Mount Helicon, sacred to the Muses and Apollo, attributed to a kick of Pegasus. [Gr. *hippokrēnē—hippos,* a horse, *krēnē,* a fountain.]

**hippocrepian,** *hip-ō-krē′pi-ən, adj.* horseshoe-shaped. [Gr. *hippos,* a horse, *krēpis,* a shoe.]

**hippodame,** *hip′ō-dām, n.* (*Spens.,* wrongly) the sea-horse.—*n.* **hippodamist** (*hip-od′ə-mist*), a horse-tamer.—*adj.* **hippod′amous,** horse-taming. [Gr. *hippos,* horse, *damaein,* to tame.]

**hippodrome,** *hip′ə-drōm, n.* a racecourse for horses and chariots (*ant.*): a circus: a variety theatre.—*adj.* **hippodromic** (*-drom′*). [Gr. *hippodromos—hippos,* a horse, *dromos,* a course.]

**hippogriff, hippogryph,** *hip′ō-grif, n.* a fabulous mediaeval animal, a griffin-headed winged horse. [Fr. *hippogriffe*—Gr. *hippos,* a horse, *gryps,* a griffin.]

**hippomanes,** *hip-om′ən-ēz, n.* an ancient philtre obtained from a mare or foal. [Gr. *hippos,* a horse, *maniā,* madness.]

**hippophagy,** *hip-of′ə-ji, -gi, n.* feeding on horse-flesh.—*n.* **hippoph′agist,** an eater of horse-flesh.—*adj.* **hippoph′agous** (*-gəs*), horse-eating. [Gr. *hippos,* a horse, *phagein* (aor.), to eat.]

**hippopotamus,** *hip-ō-pot′ə-məs, n.* a large African artiodactyl ungulate of aquatic habits, with very thick skin, short legs, and a large head and muzzle:—*pl.* **-muses** or **-mi,** sometimes **-mus.**—*adjs.* **hippopotamian** (*-tām′*), **hippopotamic** (*-tam′,* also *-pot′*), like a hippopotamus, clumsy. [L.,—Gr. *hippopotamos—hippos,* a horse, *potamos,* a river.]

**hippuric,** *hip-ū′rik, adj.* denoting an acid, first obtained from the urine of horses, occurring in the urine of many animals, particularly in that of herbivores and rarely in that of human beings. [Gr. *hippos,* a horse, *ouron,* urine.]

**Hippuris,** *hi-pū′ris, n.* the mare's-tail genus of Haloragidaceae.—*n.* **hipp′ūrite,** a Cretaceous fossil lamellibranch (*Hippuri′tes*) with a conical valve and a flat one.—*adj.* **hippurit′ic.** [Gr. *hippos,* a horse, *ourā,* a tail.]

**hippus,** *hip′əs, n.* clonic spasm of the iris. [Gr. *hippos.*]

**hippy.** See **hip** (5).

**hipster, hipsters.** See **hip** (5), (1).

**hircine,** *hûr′sin, adj.* goat-like: having a strong goatish smell.—*n.* **hircos′ity,** goatishness.—**hircocervus** (*hûr-kō-sûr′vəs*), a fabulous creature, half goat, half stag. [L. *hircus,* a he-goat.]

**hirdy-girdy,** *hûr′di-gûr′di,* (*Scot.*) *adv.* in confusion or tumult.

**hire,** *hir, n.* wages for service: the price paid for the use of anything: an arrangement by which use or service is granted for payment.—*v.t.* to procure the use or service of, at a price: to engage for wages: to grant temporary use of for compensation (often with *out*).—*adjs.* **hir′able, hire′able; hired.**—*n.* **hire′ling,** a hired servant: a mercenary: one activated solely by material considerations.—Also *adj.*—*ns.* **hir′er,** one who obtains use or service for payment: (now *Scot.* or *obs.*) one who lets out on hire; **hir′ing,** the act or contract by which an article or service is hired: a fair or market where servants are engaged (*arch.*).—Also *adj.*—**hire′-pur′chase,** a system by which a hired article becomes the hirer's property after a stipulated number of payments.—Also *adj.*—**on hire,** for hiring: for hire. [O.E. *hӯr,* wages, *hӯrian,* to hire.]

**hirple,** *hûr′, hir′pl,* (*Scot.*) *v.i.* to walk or run as if lame.—*n.* a limping gait.

**hirrient,** *hir'i-ənt, adj.* roughly trilled.—*n.* a trilled sound. [L. *hirriēns, -entis,* pr.p. of *hirrīre,* to snarl.]

**hirsel,** *hûr', hir'sl, (Scot.) n.* a stock of sheep: a multitude: the ground occupied by a hirsel of sheep.—*v.t.* to put in different groups. [O.N. *hirzla,* safe-keeping—*hirtha,* to herd.]

**hirsle,** *hûr', hir'sl, (Scot.) v.i.* to slide, wriggle, or hitch on the hams: to move forward with a rustling sound. [Cf. O.N. *hrista,* to shake.]

**hirstie,** *hirs', hûrs'ti, (obs. Scot.) adj.* dry: barren.

**hirsute,** *hûr'sūt,* or *hər-sūt', adj.* hairy: rough: shaggy: having long, stiffish hairs *(bot.).—n.* **hirsute'ness.** [L. *hirsūtus—hirsus, hirtus,* shaggy.]

**hirudin,** *hir-ōōd'in, n.* a substance present in the salivary secretion of the leech which prevents blood-clotting.—*n. pl.* **Hirudinea** (-*in'i-ə*), a class of worms, the leeches.—*n.* and *adj.* **hirudin'ean.**—*adjs.* **hirud'inoid; hirud'inous.** [L. *hirūdō, -inis,* a leech.]

**hirundine,** *hi-run'din, -din, adj.* of or pertaining to the swallow. [L. *hirundō, -inis,* a swallow.]

**his,** *hiz, pron., gen.* of **he,** or *(obs.)* of **it** (or *possessive adj.).—*hisn,* dialectal forms on the analogy of *mine, thine.* [O.E. *his, gen.* of *hē, he,* he, and of *hit,* it.]

**hish,** *hish,* a by-form of **hiss.**

**Hispanic,** *his-pan'ik, adj.* Spanish.—*adv.* **Hispan'ically.**—*vs.t.* **hispan'icise, -ize,** (*-i-siz*), **hispan'iolise, -ize,** to render Spanish.—*n.* **hispan'icism,** a Spanish phrase. [L. *Hispānia,* Spain.]

**Hispano-,** *his-pā'nō-,* in composition, Spanish, as *Hispano-American,* Spanish-American. [L. *Hispānus.*]

**hispid,** *his'pid, (bot.* and *zool.) adj.* rough with, or having, strong hairs or bristles.—*n.* **hispid'ity.** [L. *hispidus.*]

**hiss,** *his, v.i.* to make a sibilant sound like that represented by the letter *s,* as a goose, snake, gas escaping from a narrow hole, a disapproving audience, etc.—*v.t.* to condemn by hissing: to drive by hissing.—*n.* a sibilant.—*n.* and *adj.* **hiss'ing.**—*adv.* **hiss'ingly.** [Imit.]

**hist,** *hist, st, interj.* demanding silence and attention: hush: silence.—*v.t. (hist.)* to urge or summon, as by making the sound.—*v.i.* to be silent. [Imit.]

**hist-, histio-,** histo-, *hist-, -(i-)ō-, -o'-,* in composition, tissue: sail.—*ns.* **hist'amine** (*ə-mēn*), a base used in medicine obtained from ergot, from histidine, etc.; present also in all tissues of the body, being liberated into the blood, e.g. when the skin is cut or burnt; **hist'idine** (*-i-dēn*), an amino-acid derived from proteins.—*adjs.* **hist'ioid, hist'oid,** like ordinary tissue.—*ns.* **histiol'ogy** (same as **histology**); **Histioph'orus, Istioph'orus** (Gr. *phoros,* bearer), a genus of sword-fishes with sail-like dorsal fin.—*adj.* **histioph'oroid.**—*ns.* **hist'oblast,** a cell or group of cells, forming the primary element or unit of tissue; **histochem'istry,** the chemistry of living tissues; **hist'ogen** *(bot.),* a more or less well-defined region within a plant where tissues undergo differentiation; **histogenesis** (*-jen'i-sis*), the formation or differentiation of tissues *(biol.).* —*adj.* **histogenetic** (*-ji-net'ik*).—*adv.* **histogenet'ically.**—*adj.* **histogen'ic.**—*ns.* **histogeny** (*his-toj'i-ni*), **histog**ensis; **hist'ogram,** a statistical graph in which frequency distribution is shown by means of rectangles.—*adjs.* **histolog'ic, -al.**—*ns.* **histologist** *(tol');* **histol'ogy,** the study of the minute structure of the tissues of organisms; **histol'ysis** (Gr. *lysis,* loosing), the breakdown of organic tissues.—*adj.* **histolytic** (*-ō-lit'ik*).—*ns.* **histopathol'ogist,** a pathologist who studies effects of disease on tissues of the body; **histopathol'ogy.** [Gr. *histos* and *histion,* a web.]

**histie,** same as **hirstie.**

**history,** *hist'ər-i, n.* an account of an event: a systematic account of the origin and progress

of the world, a nation, an institution, a science, etc.: the knowledge of past events: a course of events: a life-story: an eventful life, a past of more than common interest: a drama representing historical events.—*v.t.* to record *(Shak.).* —*n.* **historian** (*his-tō'ri-ən, -tö'),* a writer of history (usu. in the sense of an expert, an authority, on).—*adjs.* **histo'riāted,** adorned with figures; **historic** (*-tor'ik),* famous or important in history; **histor'ical,** pertaining to history: containing history: derived from history: associated with history: according to history: authentic. (Formerly historic and historical were often used interchangeably.)—*adv.* **histor'ically.**—*v.t.* **histor'icise, -ize,** (*-siz),* to make or represent as, historic.—*n.* **histor'icism,** a theory that all sociological phenomena are historically determined: a strong or excessive concern with, and respect for, the institutions of the past.—*n.* and *adj.* **histor'icist.**—*ns.* **historicity** (*hist-ər-is'i-ti),* historical truth or actuality; **historiette',** a short history or story.—*v.t.* **histor'ify,** to record in history.—*n.* **historiog'rapher,** a writer of history (esp. an official historian).—*adjs.* **historiograph'ic, -al.**—*adv.* **historiograph'ically.**—*ns.* **historiog'raphy,** the art or employment of writing history; **historiol'ogy,** the knowledge or study of history.—**historical method,** the study of a subject in its historical development; **historical novel,** a novel having as its setting a period in history and involving historical characters and events; **historical painting,** the painting of historic scenes in which historic figures are introduced; **historical present,** the present tense used for the past, to add life and reality to the narrative.—**make history,** to do that which will mould the future or have to be recognised by future historians: to do something never previously accomplished. [L. *historia*—Gr. *historiō—histōr,* knowing.]

**histrionic, -al,** *his-tri-on'ik, -əl, adjs.* relating to the stage or actors: stagy, theatrical: affected: melodramatic: hypocritical.—*adv.* **histrion'ically.**—*ns.* **his'trio** (L.), **his'triōn** (Fr.), an actor.—*adv.* **histrion'ically.**—*ns.* **histrion'icism,** **his'triouism,** acting: theatricality.—*n.pl.* **histrion'ics,** play-acting: stagy action or speech: insincere exhibition of emotion. [L. *histriōnicus—histriō,* an actor.]

**hit,** *hit, v.t.* to strike: to reach with a blow or missile (also *fig.):* to come into forceful contact with: to knock (e.g. oneself, one's head): to inflict (a blow): to drive by a stroke: to move onto (a road), reach (a place): (of news) to be published in *(coll.):* to light upon, or attain, by chance: to imitate exactly: to suit, fit, conform to: to hurt, affect painfully *(fig.).—v.i.* to strike: to make a movement of striking: to come in contact: to arrive suddenly and destructively: to come, by effort or chance, luckily (upon): to suit (with) *(obs.):* (of an internal combustion engine) to ignite the air and fuel mixture in the cylinders:—*pr.p.* **hitt'ing;** *pa.t.* and *pa.p.* **hit.**—*n.* an act or occasion of striking: a successful stroke or shot: a lucky chance: a surprising success: an effective remark, e.g. a sarcasm, witticism: something that pleases the public or an audience: at backgammon, a move that throws one of the opponent's men back to the entering point, or a game won after one or two men are removed from the board.—*n.* **hitt'er.**—*adjs.* **hit'-and-miss',** hitting or missing, according to circumstances; **hit'-and-run',** (e.g. of an air raid) lasting only a very short time: (of a driver) causing injury and running away without reporting the incident: (of an accident) caused by a hit-and-run driver: **hit'-or-miss',** random.—**hit'-parade,** a list of currently popular songs.—*adj.* **hitt'y-miss'y,** random, haphazard.—**a hit or a miss,** a case in which either success or complete failure is possible; **hard hit**, gravely affected by some trouble, or by love; **hit a blot**, to capture an exposed man in backgammon: to find a weak place; **hit at**, to aim a blow, sarcasm, jibe, etc., at; **hit below the belt** (see **belt**); **hit it**, to find, often by chance, the right answer; **hit off**, to agree, be compatible and friendly; **hit off**, to imitate or describe aptly (someone, something); **hit on** or **upon**, to come upon, discover, devise: to single out; **hit out**, to strike out, esp. with the fist: to attack strongly (*absol.* or with *at*); **hit the ceiling** or **roof**, to be seized with, express, violent anger; **hit the high spots** (see **high**); **hit the nail on the head** (see **nail**); **hit wicket**, the act, or an instance, of striking the wicket with bat or part of the body, (and thus being out; *cricket*): **make a hit with**, to become popular with: **make a good impression on**. [O.E. *hyttan*, app. O.N. *hitta*, to light on, to find; Sw. *hitta*, to find, Dan. *hitte*, to hit upon.]

**hitch**, *hich*, *v.i.* to move jerkily: to hobble or limp: to catch on an obstacle: to connect with a moving vehicle so as to be towed (*orig. U.S.*): to travel by getting lifts.—*v.t.* to jerk: to hook: to catch: to fasten: to tether: to harness to a vehicle: to make fast: to throw into place: to bring in (to verse, a story, etc.), esp. with obvious straining or effort.—*n.* a jerk: a limp or hobble: a catch or anything that holds: a stoppage owing to a small or passing difficulty: a species of knot by which one rope is connected with another, or to some object (*naut.*): a means of connecting a thing to be dragged: a mode or act of harnessing a horse or horses, a team, or a vehicle with horses (*U.S.*): a lift in a vehicle: a slight fault or displacement in a bed of sedimentary rock (*mining*): a recess cut in rock to support a timber (*mining*).—*n. hitch'er.—adv. hitch'ily.—adj. hitch'y.—v.i. hitch'-hike*, to hike with the help of lifts in vehicles.—**hitch'-hike; hitch'-hi'ker.—hitch and kick**, a technique in high jumping whereby the athlete springs from, kicks with, and lands on, the same foot; **hitch up**, to harness a horse to a vehicle: to jerk up: to marry (*slang*). [Ety. obscure.]

**hithe**, *hidh*, *n.* a small haven or port, esp. a landing-place on a river. Now *obs.* except in historical use or in place names. [O.E. *hyth*.]

**hither**, *hidh'ər*, *adv.* to this place.—*adj.* on this side or in this direction: nearer.—*v.i.* to come —chiefly in phrase *to hither and thither*, i.e. to go to and fro.—*adj.* **hith'ermost**, nearest on this side.—**hith'erside**, the nearer side.—*advs.* **hith'er to**, up to this time: to this point or place (*arch.*); **hith'erward(s)**, towards this place.—**hither and thither**, to and fro: this way and that. [O.E. *hider*; Goth. *hidrē*, O.N. *hethra*.]

**Hitlerism**, *hit'lər-izm*, *n.* the principles, policy, and methods of Adolf *Hitler* (1889-1945), German Nazi dictator, i.e. militant anti-Semitic nationalism, subordinating everything to the state.—*ns.* and *adjs.* **Hit'lerist, Hit'lerite**.

**Hitopadesa**, *hē-tō-pä-dā'shä*, *n.* a collection of fables and stories in Sanskrit literature, a popular summary of the *Panchatantra*. [Sans. *Hito-padeśa*.]

**Hittite**, *hit'it*, *n.* one of the Khatti or Heth, an ancient people of Syria and Asia Minor: an extinct language belonging to the Anatolian branch of Indo-European and discovered from documents in cuneiform writing.—Also *adj.* [Heb. *Hitti*; Gr. *Chettaios*.]

**hive**, *hiv*, *n.* a box or basket in which bees live and store up honey: a colony of bees: a scene of great industry: a teeming multitude or breeding-place: a hat of plaited straw shaped like an old beehive (*obs.*).—*v.t.* to collect into a hive: to lay up in store.—*v.i.* of bees, to enter

or take possession of a hive: to take shelter together: to reside in a body.—*adjs.* **hive'less; hive'like.**—*n.* **hiv'er**, one who hives.—*adj.* and *adv.* **hive'ward.**—*adv.* **hive'wards.**—**hive'-bee**, common honey-producing bee, *Apis mellifica*; **hive'-hon'ey; hive'-nest**, large nest built and occupied by several pairs of birds in common. —**hive off**, withdraw as if in a swarm: to assign (work) to a subsidiary company: to divert (assets or sections of an industrial concern) to other concerns. [O.E. *hyf*.]

**hives**, *hivz*, *n.* a popular term for nettlerash and similar diseases or for laryngitis. [Origin unknown.]

**hizz**, *hiz*, *v.i.* (*Shak.*) to hiss. [Echoic.]

**ho, hoa**, *hō*, *interj.* a call to excite attention, to announce destination or direction, to express exultation, surprise, or (repeated) derision: **hullo**: hold: stop.—*n.* cessation: moderation. *v.i.* (*obs.*) to stop. [Cf. O.N. *hō*, Fr. *ho.*]

**hoactzin**. See **hoatzin**.

**hoar**, *hōr, hör, adj.* white or greyish-white, esp. with age or frost: mouldy (*obs.*)—*n.* hoariness: age.—*v.i.* (*Shak.*) to become mouldy.—*v.t.* (*Shak.*) to make hoary.—*adv.* **hoar'ily.**—*n.* **hoar'iness.**—*adj.* **hoar'y**, white or grey with age: ancient: covered with short, dense, whitish hairs (*bot.*).—**hoar'-frost**, rime or white frost, the white particles formed by the freezing of the dew; **hoar'head**, a hoary-headed old man. —*adj.* **hoar'-head'ed.**—**hoar-stone** (*Scot.* **hare'-stane**), an old hoary stone: a standing-stone or ancient boundary stone. [O.E. *hār*, hoary, grey; O.N. *hārr.*]

**hoard**, *hōrd, hörd, n.* a store: a hidden stock: a treasure: a place for hiding anything (*obs.*).— *v.t.* to store, esp. in excess: to treasure up: to amass and deposit in secret.—*v.i.* to store up: to collect and form a hoard.—*n.* **hoard'er**. [O.E. *hord*; O.N. *hodd*, Ger. *hort.*]

**hoard**, *hōrd, hörd, hoarding, hōrd'ing, hörd', ns.* a screen of boards, esp. for enclosing a place where builders are at work, or for display of bills. [O.Fr. *hurdis*—*hurt, hourt, hourd*, a palisade.]

**hoarhound**. See **horehound.**

**hoarse**, *hōrs, hörs, adj.* rough and husky: having a rough husky voice, as from a cold: harsh: discordant.—*adv.* **hoarse'ly.**—*v.t.* and *v.i.* **hoars'en.**—*n.* **hoarse'ness**. [M.E. *hors, hoors*— O.E. *hās*, inferred *hārs.*]

**hoast**, *hōst*, (*dial.*) *n.* a cough.—*v.i.* to cough. [O.N. *hōste*; cf. O.E. *hwōsta*; Du. *hoest.*]

**hoastman**, *hōst'man, n.* a member of an old merchant guild in Newcastle, with charge of coal-shipping, etc. [O.Fr. *hoste*—L. *hospes*, stranger, guest.]

**hoatzin**, *hō-at'sin*, **hoactzin**, -*akt'*, *n.* the stink-bird (Opisthocomus), a S. American bird forming an order by itself, with occipital crest, great crop, peculiar sternum, and, in the tree-climbing and swimming young, clawed wings. [Nahuatl *uatsin.*]

**hoax**, *hōks*, *n.* a deceptive trick played as a practical joke.—*v.t.* to trick, by a practical joke or elaborated tale, for sport, or without malice. —*n.* **hoax'er**. [App. **hocus.**]

**hob**, *hob*, *n.* a hub: a surface beside a fireplace, on which anything may be laid to keep hot: a game in which stones are thrown at coins on the end of a short stick—also the stick used: a gear-cutting tool.—**hob'nail**, a nail with a thick strong head, used in horseshoes, heavy workshoes, etc.—*v.t.* to furnish with hobnails: to trample upon with hobnailed shoes.—*adj.* **hob'nailed**. [Cf. **hub.**]

**hob**, *hob*, *n.* a lout: a fairy or brownie (as Robin Goodfellow): a clownish fellow: a male ferret: mischief.—*adj.* **hobb'ish**, clownish.—*ns.* **Hobb'inoll**, a rustic (from Spenser's

*Shepheards Calender*); hob′goblin, a mischievous fairy: a frightful apparition; hobgob′linism, hobgob′linry.—play hob, raise hob, to make confusion. [For *Robert*.]

hob-a-nob, hob-and-nob. Same as hobnob.

Hobbesian, *hobz′i-ən*, Hobbian, *hob′i-ən*, *adjs.* relating to Thomas *Hobbes* (1588-1679) or his political philosophy.—*ns.* a follower of Hobbes.—*ns.* Hobbes′ianism, Hobb′ianism, Hobb′ism; Hobb′ist, a Hobbian.—*adjs.* Hobb′ist, Hobbist′-ical.

hobble, *hob′l*, *v.i.* to walk with short unsteady steps: to walk awkwardly: (of action, verse, speech, etc.) to move irregularly.—*v.t.* to fasten the legs of (a horse) loosely together: to hamper: to perplex.—*n.* an awkward hobbling gait: a difficulty, a scrape (*arch.*): anything used to hamper the feet of an animal, a clog or fetter.—*ns.* hobb′ler, one who hobbles: an unlicensed pilot, a casual labourer in docks, etc.: a man who tows a canal-boat with a rope; hobb′ling.—*adv.* hobb′lingly.—hobble-bush, the N. American wayfaring-tree (*Viburnum alnifolium*), a small shrub with white flowers and straggling branches that impede movement among them; hobble skirt, a narrow skirt that hampers walking. [Cf. Du. *hobbelen*, *hobben*, to toss: and hopple.]

hobbledehoy, *hob′l-di-hoi′*, *n.* an awkward youth, a stripling, neither man nor boy.—*ns.* hobbledehoy′dom, hobbledehoy′hood, hobbledehoy′ism.—*adj.* hobbledehoy′ish. [Origin obscure.]

hobbler, *hob′lər*, (*obs.*) *n.* one bound to keep a hobby (horse) for military service: a horseman employed for light work, as reconnoitring, etc.: a horse. [O.Fr. *hobeler*—*hobin*, a small horse.]

hobby, *hob′i*, *n.* a small or smallish strong, active horse: a pacing horse: a subject on which one is constantly setting off, as in *to ride* or *to mount a hobby*(*-horse*): a favourite pursuit followed as an amusement: a hobby-horse: an early form of bicycle.—*ns.* hobb′yism; hobb′yist, one who rides a hobby.—*adj.* hobb′yless.—hobb′y-horse, a stick or figure of a horse straddled by children: one of the chief parts played in the ancient morris-dance: the wooden horse of a merry-go-round: a rocking-horse: a dandy-horse: a loose and frivolous person, male or female (*Shak.*): a hobby.—*adj.* hobby-hors′ical, whimsically given to a hobby. [M.E. *hobyn*, *hoby*, prob. *Hob*, a by-form of *Rob*. O.Fr. *hobin*, *hobi* (Fr. *aubin*), is from the English.]

hobby, *hob′i*, *n.* a small species of falcon. [O.Fr. *hobé*; *hobet*—L.L. *hobētus*; prob. O.Fr. *hober*, to move.]

hobday, *hob′dā*, *v.t.* to cure a breathing impediment in (a horse) by surgical operation.—*adj.* hob′dayed. [After Sir Frederick Hobday (1869-1939).]

hobgoblin. See hob (2).

hobjob, *hob′job*, (*dial.*) *n.* an odd job.—*v.i.* to do odd jobs.—*ns.* hob′jobber; hob′jobbing.

hobnail. See hob (1).

hobnob, *hob′nob*, *adv.* at a venture: hit-or-miss: with alternate or mutual drinking of healths.—*v.i.* to associate or drink together familiarly: to talk unreservedly (with):—*pr.p.* hob′nobbing.—*n.* a sentiment in drinking (*obs.*): mutual health-drinking: a familiar private talk.—*adj.* hob′-nobby. [Prob. *hab nab*, have or have not (ne-have); cf. *Twelfth Night*, III, iv. 'Hob, nob, is his word; give 't or take 't'.]

hobo, *hō′bō*, *n.* a vagrant workman: a tramp, esp. of the arrogant type: *pl.* ho′boes.—*v.t.* to travel as a hobo.—*ns.* ho′bodom, ho′boism. [Origin unknown.]

Hobson-Jobson, *hob′sən-job′sən*, *n.* festal excitement, esp. at the Moharram ceremonies: the modification of names and words introduced from foreign languages, which the popular ear assimilates to already familiar sounds, as in the case of the word Hobson-Jobson itself. [Ar. *Yā Hasan! Yā Hosain!* a typical phrase of Anglo-Indian argot at the time adopted as an alternative title for Yule and Burnell's *Glossary of Anglo-Indian Colloquial Words and Phrases* (1886).]

Hobson's choice. See choice.

hoc, *hok*, *hōk*, (L.) this (*adj. pron.*).—hoc anno (*an′o*), in this year; hoc genus omne (*jĕn′əs*, *gen′oōs*, *om′ne*), all that sort; hoc loco (*lōk′*, *lok′ō*), in this place; hoc tempore (*tem′pə-rē*, *-po-re*), at this time.

hock, *hok* (*Scot.* hough, *hohh*), *n.* joint on hind-leg of a quadruped, between the knee and fetlock, corresponding to the ankle-joint in man: a piece of meat extending from the hock-joint upward: in man, the back part of the knee-joint: the ham.—*v.t.* to hamstring.—*n.* hock′er. [O.E. *hōh*, the heel.]

hock, *hok*, (*slang*) *v.t.* to pawn. [Perh. *hawk* (see hawker).]

hock, *hok*, *n.* properly, the wine made at *Hochheim*, on the Main, in Germany; now applied to all white Rhine wines. [Obs. *Hockamore*—Ger. *Hochheimer*.]

hock, *hok*, *v.t.* to subject to Hock-tide customs.—*v.i.* to observe Hock-tide.—Hock′-day (Hock Tuesday), an old English festival held on the second Tuesday after Easter Sunday, one of the chief customs being the seizing and binding of men by women until they gave money for their liberty: (in *pl.*) Hock Tuesday and the preceding day (Hock Monday) on which the men seized the women in like manner; Hock′-tide, the two Hock-days. [Origin unknown.]

hockey, *hok′i*, *n.* a ball game played with a club or stick curved at one end, a development of shinty: a hockey stick (*U.S.*): ice hockey.—Also hook′ey. [Prob. O.Fr. *hoquet*, a crook.]

hockey, *hok′i*, (*dial.*) *n.* harvest-home, the harvest-supper.—Also hawk′ey, hork′ey.—hock′-cart, the cart that brings home the last load of the harvest. [Origin unknown.]

hocus-pocus, *hō′kəs-pō′kəs*, *n.* a juggler (*obs.*): a juggler's trick or formula: jugglery: deception: mumbo-jumbo.—*v.i.* to juggle.—*v.t.* to play tricks on.—*v.t.* hoc′us, to cheat: to stupefy with drink: to drug (drink):—*pr.p.* hoc′us(s)ing; *pa.t.* and *pa.p.* hō′cus(s)ed. [Sham Latin.]

hod, *hod*, *n.* a V-shaped stemmed trough for carrying bricks or mortar on the shoulder: a coal-scuttle: a pewterer's blowpipe.—hod′man, a man who carries a hod: a mason's labourer. [Cf. dial. *hot*, *hott*, Ger. *hotte*, obs. Du. *hodde*, Fr. *hotte*, a basket.]

hod, *hod*, (*Scot.*) *v.i.* to bob: to jog.—*v.i.* hodd′le (*Scot.*), to waddle.

hodden, *hod′n*, *n.* coarse, undyed homespun woollen cloth.—*adj.* of or clad in hodden: rustic.—hodd′en-grey, hodden made of mixed black and white wool.—Also *adj.* [Origin unknown.]

Hodge, *hoj*, *n.* a countryman, rustic. [For *Roger*.]

hodgepodge, *hoj′poj*, *n.* see hotchpotch.—hodge′-pudd′ing (*Shak.*), a pudding made of a mass of ingredients mixed together.

hodiernal, *hō-di-ûrn′əl*, *adj.* of or pertaining to the present day. [L. *hodiernus*—*hodiē*, to-day = *hōc diē*, on this day.]

hodmandod, *hod′mən-dod*, *n.* a shelled snail.—(*obs.*) hodd′y-dodd′y, a dumpy person: a duped husband: a noodle. [Cf. dodman.]

hodograph, *hod′ə-gräf*, (*math.*) *n.* a curve whose radius vector represents the velocity of a moving point. [Gr. *hodos*, a way, *graphein*, to write.]

hodometer, odometer, *hod-om′i-tər*, *od-*, *n.* an instrument attached to a wheel for measuring distance travelled. [Gr. *hodos*, a way, *metron*, a measure.]

hoe, *hō*, *n.* an instrument for scraping or digging

up weeds and loosening the earth.—*v.t.* to scrape, remove, or clean with a hoe: to weed. —*v.i.* to use a hoe:—*pr.p.* **hoe′ing**; *pa.t.* and *pa.p.* **hoed.**—*n.* **hō′er.**—**hoe′-cake** (*U.S.*), a thin cake of Indian meal (originally baked on a hoe-blade); **hoe′down**, a country-dance, esp. a square dance: hillbilly or other music for it: a party at which such dances are performed. [O.Fr. *houe* —O.H.G. *houwâ* (Ger. *haue*), a hoe.]

**hoe, hō,** *n.* a promontory or projecting ridge (now only in place-names). [O.E. *hōh*, heel; cf. **heugh.**]

**hof,** *hof, hōf,* (Ger.) yard: manor: court.

**hog,** *hog, n.* a general name for swine: a castrated boar: a pig reared for slaughter: a yearling sheep not yet shorn (also **hogg**): the wool from such a sheep: a yearling of other species: formerly slang for a shilling: a low filthy fellow: a greedy person: an inconsiderate boor: a person of coarse manners.—*v.t.* and *v.i.* to eat hoggishly: to arch or hump like a hog's back. —*v.t.* to cut like a hog's mane: to behave like a hog or a road-hog towards: to take or use selfishly:—*pr.p.* **hogg′ing**; *pa.t.* and *pa.p.* **hogged.** —*adj.* **hogged** (*hogd*).—*ns.* **hogg′erel**, a yearling sheep; **hogg′ery**, hogs collectively: hoggishness of character: coarseness; **hogg′et**, a yearling sheep or colt.—*adj.* **hogg′ish**.—*adv.* **hogg′ishly.**— *ns.* **hogg′ishness**; **hog′hood**, the nature of a hog. —**hog′back, hog′s-back**, a hill-ridge, an ancient monument, or other object, shaped like a hog's back, i.e. curving down towards the ends; **hog′-chol′era**, swine-fever; **hog′-deer**, a small Indian deer; **hog′-fish**, a fish having bristles on the head; **hog′-frame**, a frame built to resist vertical flexure; **hog′-mane**, a mane clipped short or naturally short and upright.—*adj.* **hog′-maned.** —**hog′-nose**, an American snake (*Heterodon*; various species); **hog′-pen**, a pig-sty; **hog′-plum**, a West Indian tree (*Spondias*) of the cashew family, the fruit relished by hogs; **hog′-rat**, the hutia, a West Indian rodent (*Capromys*); **hog′-reeve, -con′stable**, an officer whose duty was to round up stray swine; **hog′-ring′er**, one who puts rings into the snouts of hogs.—*v.t.* **hog′-shouther** (*shōō′dhər*; *Scot.*), to jostle with the shoulder.—**hog′-skin**, leather made of the skin of swine; **hog′s pudding**, a hog's entrails stuffed with various ingredients; **hog′wash**, the refuse of a kitchen, brewery, etc., given to pigs: thin worthless stuff: insincere nonsense; **hog′ward**, a swine-herd; **hog′weed**, the cow-parsnip: applied also to many other coarse plants.— **bring one's hogs to a fine market**, to make a complete mess of something; **go the whole hog** (see whole); **hog in armour**, a boor in fine clothes; **hog it** (*slang*), to eat greedily: to live in a slovenly fashion. [O.E. *hogg*.]

**hog,** *hog, n.* in curling, a stone that does not pass the hog-score.—*v.t.* to play a hog.—**hog′-score**, a line drawn across the rink short of which no stone counts. [Perh. **hog** (1).]

**hog,** *hog,* (*dial.*) *n.* a mound of earth and straw in which potatoes, etc., are stored.—*v.t.* to store (potatoes, etc.) in such a heap. [Origin obscure.]

**hogen-mogen,** *hō′gən-mō′gən,* (*obs.*) *n.* haughtiness: (usu. in *pl.*) the Dutch States General. —*adj.* high and mighty: Dutch: (of liquor) strong.—*n.* **ho′gan, ho′gen**, strong liquor. [Du. *hoog en mogend*, high and mighty.]

**hogg, hoggerel, hogget.** See under **hog** (1).

**hogger,** *hog′ər,* (*Scot.*) *n.* a footless stocking worn as a gaiter: a short connecting-pipe. [Origin obscure.]

**hoggin, hogging,** *hog′in, n.* sifted gravel: a mixture containing gravel. [Origin uncertain.]

**hogh,** a Spenserian spelling of **hoe** (2).

**Hogmanay,** *hog-mə-nā′,* (*Scot.*) *n.* the last day of the year: a refection or gift begged or bestowed then. [Prob. from North Fr. dial.

*hoginane*—16th cent. *agiullanneuf* (*-l'an neuf*) a gift at the New Year.]

**hogshead,** *hogz′hed, n.* a large cask (*Shak.*): a measure of capacity = 52½ imperial gallons, or 63 old wine gallons; *of beer* = 54 gallons; *of claret* = 46 gallons; *of tobacco* (*U.S.*), 750 to 1200 lb. [App. **hog's**, and **head**; reason unknown.]

**ho-hum,** *hō′-hum′,* (*coll.*) *adj.* dull, apathetic: boring, routine.

**hoick, hoik,** *hoik, n.* a jerk.—*v.t.* and *v.i.* to hitch up: (esp. of aeroplanes) to jerk upwards. [Cf. **hike.**]

**hoicks, hoiks,** *interj.* a cry to urge hounds.—*v.t.* to urge on with cries.—*v.i.* to shout hoicks: to hark back.

**hoiden.** See **hoyden.**

**hoi polloi,** *hoi′-pə-loi′,* (Gr.) the many: the rabble, the vulgar.

**hoise, hoiz,** (*arch.*) *v.t.* to hoist:—*pa.t.* and *p.p.* **hoised, hoist.**—**hoist with his own petar(d)** (*Shak.*), blown up with his own explosive device, caught in his own trap. [Perh. Old Du. *hijssen*, Du. *hijschen*, to hoist.]

**hoist,** *hoist, v.t.* to lift: to heave upwards: to raise or move with tackle.—*n.* act of lifting: the height of a sail: that part of a flag next to the mast: a lift for heavy goods.—**hoist′man**, one who works a hoist; **hoist′way**, a hoist shaft. [Pa.t. and p.p. of **hoise** (q.v.).]

**hoisting,** *hōst′ing* (*Scott*). Same as **hosting.**

**hoity-toity,** *hoi′ti-toi′ti, interj.* an exclamation of surprise or disapprobation.—*adj.* giddy, noisy: huffy: superciliously haughty.

**hokku.** See **haiku.**

**hokum,** *hō′kəm,* (*U.S. slang*) *n.* something done for the sake of applause: claptrap. [App. **hocus-pocus** combined with **bunkum.**]

**hoky-poky, hokey-pokey,** *hō′ki-pō′ki,* *n.* hocus-pocus: a kind of ice-cream sold on the streets.

**Holarctic,** *hol-ärk′tik,* *adj.* of the north temperate and Arctic biological region, including Palae-arctic and Nearctic. [Gr. *holos*, whole, *arktikos*, northern—*arktos*, a bear, the Great Bear constellation.]

**hold,** *hōld, v.t.* to keep: to have: to grasp: to have in one's possession, keeping, or power: to sustain: to defend successfully: to maintain: to assert authoritatively: to think, believe: to occupy: to derive title to: to bind: to contain: to have a capacity of: to enclose: to confine: to restrain: to detain: to retain: to keep the attention of: to catch: to stop: to continue: to persist in: to celebrate, observe: to conduct: to carry on: to convoke and carry on: to esteem or consider: to aim, direct: to endure: to bet (*arch.*).—*v.i.* to grasp: to remain fixed: to be true or unfailing: to continue unbroken or unsubdued: to remain valid: to continue, to persist: to adhere: to derive right:— *pr.p.* **hold′ing**; *pa.t.* **held**; *pa.p.* **held,** *obs.* **hōld′en.**—*n.* act or manner of holding: grip: power of gripping: tenacity: a thing held: a place of confinement: custody: stronghold: a (sign for) a pause (*mus.*): a reservation (*U.S.*): means of influencing.—*ns.* **hold′er**; **hold′ing**, anything held: a farm held of a superior: hold: influence: tenure (Scots *law*): the burden of a song (*Shak.*).—**hold′-all**, an accommodating receptacle for clothes, etc., e.g. a canvas wrapper; **hold′-back**, a check: a strap joining the breeching to the shaft of a vehicle; **hold′erbat** (*building*), a metal collar formed of two semicircular parts which can be clamped together round a pipe, with a projecting piece for fixing to a wall; **hold′-fast**, that which holds fast: a long nail: a catch: a plant's fixing organ other than a root; **holding company**, an industrial company that owns and controls part or all of one or more other companies, usu. without having a direct hand in production; **hold'-up,** an attack with a view to robbery: a highwayman: an act or state of holding up: a stoppage.—**get hold of,** to obtain: to get in touch with; **hold against** (*coll.*), to remember as a failing or as a misdemeanour on the part of; **hold back,** to restrain: to hesitate: to keep in reserve; **hold by,** to believe in: to act in accordance with; **hold down,** to restrain; to keep (a job) by carrying out its duties efficiently, esp. in spite of difficulties; **hold forth,** to put forward: to show: to speak in public, to declaim; **hold good,** to remain the case; **hold hard!,** stop; **hold in,** to restrain, check: to restrain oneself; **hold it!,** keep the position exactly!; **hold of** (*Pr. Bk.*), to regard; **hold off,** to keep at a distance; **hold on,** to persist in something: to continue: to cling: stop (*imper.*): wait a bit; **hold one in hand,** to amuse in order to gain some advantage; **hold one's own,** to maintain one's position; **hold one's peace, tongue,** to keep silence; **hold out,** to endure, last: to continue resistance: to offer; **hold out on** (*coll.*), to keep information from; **hold over,** to postpone: to keep possession of (land or a house beyond the term of agreement); **hold to, hold one to,** to keep, make one keep (a promise), adhere to (a decision), etc.; **hold together,** to remain united: to cohere; **hold up,** to raise: to keep back: to endure: to bring to, or keep at, a standstill: to stop and rob: to rob by threatening assault; **hold up one's head,** to face the world with self-respect; **hold water** (see **water**); **hold with,** to take sides with: to approve of; **no holds barred,** not observing any rules of fair play. [O.E. *haldan* (W.S. *healdan*); O.H.G. *haltan,* Goth. *haldan.*]

**hold,** *hōld, n.* the interior cavity of a ship used for the cargo. [**hole,** with excrescent *d.*]

**hole,** *hōl, n.* a hollow place: a cavity: an aperture: a gap: a breach: a pit: a subterfuge: a means of escape: a difficult situation: a scrape: a place of hiding, a mean lodging, a secret room for some disreputable business: an animal's excavation or place of refuge: a miserable or contemptible place: a cavity 4½ inches in diameter, into which golf-balls are played: the distance, or the part of the game, between tee and hole: the score for playing a hole in fewest strokes: a vacancy in an energy band, caused by removal of an electron, which moves and is equivalent to a positive charge (*electronics*).—*v.t.* to form holes in: to put, send, play into a hole.—*v.i.* to go, play, into a hole.—*adj.* holey (*hōl'i*), full of holes.—*n.* and *adj.* **hol'ing.**—*adj.* **hole'-and-cor'ner,** secret: underhand: in obscure places.—**hōl'ing-axe,** a narrow axe for cutting holes in posts; **hol'ing-pick,** a pick used in under-cutting coal.—**a hole in one's coat,** a stain on a person's reputation; **hole out** (*golf*), to play the ball into the hole; **hole in the heart,** imperfect separation of the left and right sides of the heart; **in holes,** full of holes; **make a hole in** (e.g. one's pocket), to use up a large amount of (e.g. money); **pick holes in** (see **pick**); **toad in the hole,** meat baked in batter, etc. [O.E. *hol,* a hole, cavern; Du. *hol,* Dan. *hul,* Ger. *hohl,* hollow; conn. with Gr. *koilos,* hollow.]

**hole,** an earlier (and etymological) spelling (*Spens.*) of whole.—*adj.* **hole'som(e),** wholesome.

**Holi,** *hō'lē, n.* a Hindu spring festival characterised by boisterous revelry. [Hind. *holī*—Sans. *holikā.*]

**holiday.** See **halibut.**

**holiday,** *hol'i-dā, n.* orig., a religious festival: a day or season of idleness and recreation.—*adj.* befitting a holiday: cheerful.—**hol'idaymaker,** one on holiday away from home: a tourist. [**holy, day.**]

**holism,** *hol'izm, hōl'izm, n.* the theory that the fundamental principle of the universe is the creation of wholes, i.e. complete and self-contained systems from the atom and the cell by evolution to the most complex forms of life and mind.—*n.* **hol'ist.**—*adj.* **holist'ic.** [Gr. *holos,* whole; coined by General Smuts.]

**holla,** *hol'a, interj.* ho, there! attend! the usual response to *ahoy!* (*naut.*).—*n.* a loud shout.—*interj.* **holl'a-ho(a)!** [Fr. *hola*—*ho* and *là*—L. *illāc,* there.]

**holland,** *hol'ənd, n.* a coarse linen fabric, unbleached or dyed brown, which is used for covering furniture, etc.: orig., a fine kind of linen first made in *Holland.*—*n.* **Holl'ander,** a native or citizen of *Holland:* a Dutch ship.—*adj.* **Holl'andish.**—*n.* **holl'ands,** gin made in Holland.—**sauce hollandaise** (*sōs ol-ā-dez;* Fr.), a sauce made of the yolk of an egg with melted butter and lemon juice.

**holler,** *hol'ər,* (*U.S.* and *dial.*) *n.* and *vb.* **hollo.**

**hollo,** *hol'ō, n.* and *interj.* a shout of encouragement or to call attention: a loud shout.—*v.t.* and *v.i.* to shout. [Cf. **holla, hallo.**]

**holloa,** *hol-ō'.* Same as **hallo.**

**hollow,** *hol'ō, n.* a hole: a cavity: a depression: a vacuity: a groove: a channel.—*adj.* having an empty space within or below: concave: sunken: unsound, unreal, fleeting, deceptive: insincere: muffled, as if coming from a hollow.—*v.t.* to make a hole in: to make hollow: to excavate.—*adv.* completely: clean.—*adv.* **holl'owly,** with a hollow sound: in a hollow or insincere manner.—*n.* **holl'owness,** the state of being hollow: cavity: insincerity: treachery.—*adjs.* **holl'ow-eyed,** having sunken eyes; **holl'ow-ground,** ground so as to have concave surface(s); **holl'ow hearted,** having a hollow heart: faithless: treacherous.—**holl'ow-ware,** trade name for hollow articles of iron, as pots and kettles. [O.E. *holh,* a hollow place—*hol;* see **hole.**]

**holly,** *hol'i, n.* an evergreen shrub (*Ilex aquifolium;* family Aquifoliaceae) having leathery, shining, and spinous leaves and scarlet or yellow berries, much used for Christmas decorations. —**holl'y-fern,** a spiny-leaved fern; **holl'y-oak,** the holm-oak. [O.E. *holegn;* cf. W. *celyn,* Ir. *cuileann.*]

**hollyhock,** *hol'i-hok, n.* a plant (Althaea) of the mallow family brought into Europe from the Holy Land. [M.E. *holihoc*—*holi,* holy, and O.E. *hoc,* mallow.]

**Hollywood,** *hol'i-wŏŏd, adj.* of or belonging to *Hollywood,* a suburb of Los Angeles in California, a centre of the American cinema: typical of or resembling films made there, brash and romantic, presenting the image of an affluent or artificial society.

**holm,** *hōm, n.* an islet, esp. in a river: rich flat land beside a river. [O.E. *holm;* Ger. *holm,* etc.]

**holm,** *hōm,* (*Spens.*) *n.* holly: the holm-oak.— **holm'-oak',** the evergreen oak (*Quercus ilex*), not unlike holly. [M.E. *holin;* see **holly.**]

**holmium,** *hōl'mi-əm, n.* a metallic element (Ho; at. numb. 67).—*n.* **hol'mia,** its oxide. [Mod. L. *Holmia,* Stockholm.]

**holo-,** *hol'ō-, hol-,* *hol-,* in composition, whole: wholly.—*adj.* **holoblast'ic** (Gr. *blastos,* a bud), (of egg) segmenting completely.—*n.* **hol'ocaust** (-*köst;* Gr. *holokauston*—*kaustos,* burnt), a sacrifice, in which the whole of the victim was burnt: a huge slaughter or destruction of life.— *adj.* **holocrys'talline,** wholly crystalline in structure—without glass.—*ns.* **hol'ogram,** a photographic negative made on a plate without use of lens by means of interference between two parts of a split laser beam, the picture appearing as a meaningless pattern until suitably illuminated, when it shows as a 3-D image (a number of pictures can be 'stored' on the same plate); **hol'ograph** (-*gräf*), a document wholly written by the person from whom it proceeds.—Also

*adj.—adj.* **holographic** (*-graf'ik*).—*n.* **holog'raphy**, (the technique or process of) making or using holograms.—*adj.* **holohe'dral** (Gr. *hedrā*, base). —*ns.* **holohē'drism** (*math.*), the property of having the full number of symmetrically arranged planes crystallographically possible; **holohē'dron**, a form possessing this property.— *adj.* **holometabol'ic**,—*n.* **holometab'olism**, complete metamorphosis.—*adj.* **holophōt'al** (Gr. *phōs, phōtos*, light).—*ns.* **hol'ophote**, an apparatus by which all the light from a lighthouse is thrown in the required direction; **hol'ophrase**, a single word expressing a sentence or phrase.— *adj.* **holophytic** (*-fit'ik*; Gr. *phyton*, a plant), obtaining nutriment wholly in the manner of a green plant.—*n.* **holophytism** (*-fit'izm*).—*adj.* **holop'tic**, having the eyes meeting in front.— *n.pl.* **Holostei** (*hol-os'ti-ī*; Gr. *osteon*, bone), an order of fishes including Lepidosteus.—*adjs.* **holosteric** (*-ster'ik*; Gr. *stereos*, solid), wholly solid: having no liquids (as an aneroid barometer): holozoic (*-zō'ik*; Gr. *zōion*, an animal), obtaining nutrition wholly in the manner of an animal, i.e. from other organisms live or dead. [Gr. *holos*, whole.]
**holothurian**, *hol-ō-thōō'ri-ən*, *n.* any member of the Holothuroid'ea, a class of wormlike unarmoured echinoderms—the sea-cucumbers.— Also *adj.* [Gr. *holothourion*, a kind of sea animal.]
**holozoic.** See holo-.
**holp, hōlp, holpen**, *-ən*, old *pa.t.* and *pa.p.* of help.
**hols, holz**, (*school slang*) *n.pl.* holidays.
**holster, hōl'stər,** *n.* a pistol-case, on saddle or belt.—*adj.* **hol'stered.** [Perh. Du. *holster*, pistol-case; cf. O.E. *heolster*, hiding-place.]
**holt, hōlt,** *n.* a wood or woody hill: an orchard. [O.E. *holt*, a wood; O.N. *holt*, a copse, Ger. *holz*.]
**holt, hōlt,** (*U.S.* and *dial.*) *n.* a hold (*obs.*): a refuge: an otter's den. [hold (1).]
**holus-bolus, hōl'əs-bōl'əs,** *adv.* all at a gulp: altogether. [Sham L.; perh.—Eng. *whole bolus* or Gr. *holos* and *bōlos*, lump, bolus.]
**holy, hō'li,** *adj.* perfect in a moral sense: pure in heart: religious: set apart to a sacred use: regarded with awe (often ironically): saintly: sanctimonious.—*n.* holy object, place, or (*obs.*) person.—*adv.* **ho'lily.**—*ns.* **ho'liness,** sanctity: a title of the pope; **holydam(e), hollidam** (*Shak.*), for halidom.—*adj.* **holier-than-thou,** offensively sanctimonious and patronising.—*n.* such an attitude: one who has such an attitude.—**ho'ly-ale,** (conjectured in Shak., *Pericles*, Prol., 9, for rhyme's sake) a church festival; **Holy Alliance,** a league formed after the fall of Napoleon (1815) by the sovereigns of Austria, Russia, and Prussia, professedly to regulate all national and international relations in accordance with the principles of Christian charity; **holy city,** Jerusalem: Rome: Mecca: Benares: Allahabad, etc.; **holy coat,** the seamless coat of Jesus, claimed to be kept at Trier.—*adj.* **ho'ly-cru'el** (*Shak.*), cruel through holiness.— **holy day,** a religious festival (see also holiday); **Holy Family,** the infant Christ with Joseph, Mary, etc.; **Holy Ghost, Spirit,** the third person of the Christian Trinity; **holy grail** (see grail, 3); **holy grass,** a sweet-smelling grass sometimes strewed on church floors on festival days; **holy Joe** (*slang*), a parson: a pious person; **Holy Land,** Palestine; **Holy Office,** the Inquisition; **Holy One,** God: Christ: the one who is holy, by way of emphasis: one separated to the service of God; **holy orders** (see order); **ho'lyrood** (as a place-name, *hol'*), Christ's cross: a cross, esp. in R.C. churches over the entrance to the chancel (for **Holy-rood Day,** see rood); **ho'lystone,** a sandstone used by seamen for cleansing the decks, said to be named from

cleaning the decks for Sunday, or from kneeling in using it.—*v.t.* to scrub with a holystone.— **holy terror** (*coll.*), a formidable person, or one given to causing commotion or agitation; **Holy Thursday, Maundy Thursday: Ascension Day; holy war,** a war for the extirpation of heresy or a rival religion: a Crusade; **holy water,** water blessed for religious uses; **Holy Week,** the week before Easter; **Holy Willie,** a religious hypocrite (after Burns's poem); **holy writ,** the Scriptures.—**holy of holies,** the inner chamber of the Jewish tabernacle; **Holy Roman Empire,** the official denomination of the German Empire from 962 to 1806. [O.E. *hālig,* lit. *whole—hāl,* sound; conn. with **hail, heal, whole.**]
**homage, hom'ij,** *n.* a vassal's acknowledgment that he is the man of his feudal superior: anything done or rendered as such an acknowledgment: reverence, esp. shown by outward action: a body of vassals or tenants.—*v.t.* to do homage to.—*n.* **hom'ager,** one who does homage. [O.Fr. *homage*—L.L. *hominǎticum*—L. *homō*, a man.]
**homaloid, hom'əl-oid,** *n.* Euclidean space, analogous to a plane.—*adj.* **homaloid'al,** flat: of the nature of a plane. [Gr. *homalos,* even, *eidos,* form.]
**hombre, ōm-brā,** (Sp.) man.
**Homburg (-hat), hom'bûrg** (*-hat'*), *n.* a man's hat, of felt, with narrow brim and crown, dinted in at the top. [First worn at *Homburg.*]
**home, hōm,** *n.* habitual abode, or the place felt to be such: residence of one's family: the scene of domestic life, with its emotional associations: a separate building occupied by a family (*U.S.*): one's own country: the mother-country: seat: habitat: natural or usual place of anything: the den or base in a game: the goal: the inner table in backgammon: the plate in baseball: an institution affording refuge, asylum, or residence for strangers, the afflicted, poor, etc.: a private hospital: a place where cats, dogs, etc., are received and boarded.—*adj.* pertaining or belonging to or being in one's own dwelling, country, or playing-ground: domestic: near the dwelling or headquarters: coming or reaching home: effective, searching.—*adv.* to home: to the innermost or final position: effectively.—*v.i.* to go home: to find the way home: to dwell: to be guided to a target or destination.—*v.t.* to send home: to set up in a home: to guide to a target or destination.— *adj.* **home'less,** without a home.—*n.* **home'lessness.**—*adj.* **home'like,** like a home: familiar: easy: comfortable.—*adv.* **home'lily** (*-li-li*).—*n.* **home'liness.**—*adj.* **home'ly,** pertaining to home: familiar: plain: unpretentious: ugly (*U.S.*).— *n.* **hom'er,** a pigeon of a breed that can readily be trained to find its way home from a distance: any person or animal so skilled: a stroke in itself enabling a baseball-player to make a complete circuit.—*advs.* **home'ward, home'wards.**—*adjs.* **home'ward,** in the direction of home; **home'y, hom'y,** home-like; **hom'ing,** returning home: trained to return home: guiding home: guiding to target or destination.—Also *n.*—*adjs.* **home'-and-home', home'-and-away',** of sports events, played alternately on one's own and one's opponents home grounds; **home'-born,** originating at home or in the home: native, not foreign; **home'-bound,** homeward bound: fixed to the home; **home'-bred,** bred at home: native: domestic: plain: unpolished; **home'-brewed,** brewed at home or for home use: also *fig.*—**home circuit,** the south-eastern circuit of Assize with boundaries changed at various times; **home'-com'er;** **home'-com'ing,** arrival at home: return home. —Also *adj.*—**home counties,** the counties over and into which London has extended—Middlesex, Essex, Kent, Surrey (Herts, Sussex);

home'craft, household arts: arts practised at home or concerned with home life; home'-croft, a cottage with a small piece of land for an industrial worker to grow his own food; home'-croft'er; home'-croft'ing; home'-defence', defence of a country by a force of its own people within it; Home Department, that part of government which is concerned with the maintenance of the internal peace of England—its headquarters the Home Office, its official head the Home Secretary; home'-farm, the farm attached to and near a great house.—adj. home'felt, felt in one's own breast: inward: private.—home'-fire, the domestic hearth, with its activities and connections.—adj. home'-grown, produced in one's own country.—home-guard', a member of a volunteer force for home-defence: a force of the kind (first in war of 1939-45, Home Guard); home help, a woman hired part-time to help with housework.—adj. home'-keeping, staying at home.—home'land, native land, fatherland: mother-country; home'-life, domestic life.—adj. home'-made, made at home: made in one's own country: plain.—home market, the market for goods in the country that produces them.—adj. home'-produced', produced within the country, not imported.—Home Rule, self-government, as that claimed by Irish (hist.), Scottish, Welsh Nationalists, including a separate parliament to manage internal affairs; home'-rul'er, an advocate of Home Rule.—adj. home'sick, pining for home.—home'sickness; home'-sig'nal, a signal at the beginning of a section of railway line showing whether or not the section is clear.—adj. home'-spun, spun or wrought at home: not made in foreign countries: plain: inelegant.—n. cloth made at home: an unpolished person (Shak.).—home'stall (obs.), a homestead: a farmyard; home'stead, a dwelling-house with outhouses and enclosures immediately connected with it: a piece of public land allotted under special laws to a settler (U.S.); home'steader; home'-stretch', the last stretch of a racecourse; home'-thrust', in fencing, a hit that goes home where it is aimed: a pointed remark that goes home; home'-town, the town where one's home is or was; home'-truth, a pointed, usually unanswerable, typically wounding, statement that strikes home.—adj. home'ward-bound, bound homeward or to one's native land.—home'work, work or preparation to be done at home, esp. for school.—at home, in one's own house: ready to receive a visitor: feeling the ease of familiarity with a place or situation; at-home', a reception (not at home, out of one's house or not receiving a visitor); bring home to, to prove to, in such a way that there is no way of escaping the conclusion: to impress upon; do one's home-work, to prepare oneself, e.g. for a discussion by acquainting oneself with the relevant facts; eat out of house and home, to live at the expense of another so as to ruin him; long home, the grave; make one's self at home, to be as free and unrestrained as in one's own house; nothing to write home about (coll.), not very exciting; pay home, to strike to the quick: to retaliate. [O.E. hām; Du. and Ger. heim, Goth. haims.]

homelyn, hom'əl-in, hōm'lin, n. the spotted ray. [Origin unknown.]

homeopathy, etc. Same as homoeopathy, etc., under homo-.

homer, hō'mər, n. a Hebrew measure of capacity, roughly 11 bushels. [Heb. khōmer, a heap—khāmar, to swell up.]

Homeric, hō-mer'ik, adj. pertaining to Homer, the great poet of Greece (c. 850 B.C.): attributed to Homer: resembling Homer or his poetry: worthy of Homer: in the heroic or epic manner.—n. Homerid (hō'mər-id), one of the Homer'idae

(-i-dē), Chian reciters of the Homeric poems, claiming descent from him.—Homeric laughter, loud inextinguishable laughter (see asbestos gelōs (Gr.), in the Appendices; Homeric question, the question of Homer's authorship of the Iliad and the Odyssey, disputed by Wolf (1795). [Gr. hōmērikos—Hŏmēros, Homer.]

homicide, hom'i-sid, n. manslaughter: one who kills another.—adj. homici'dal, pertaining to homicide: murderous: bloody. [L. homicidium, manslaughter, and homicida, a man-slayer—homō, a man, caedĕre, to kill.]

homily, hom'i-li, n. a plain expository sermon, practical rather than doctrinal: a hortatory discourse.—adjs. homilet'ic, -al.—n. homilet'ics, the art of preaching.—n. hom'ilist. [Gr. homīliā, an assembly, a lecture or sermon—homos, the same, ilē, a company.]

hominid, hom'in-id, (zool.) n. an animal of the family (Homin'idae) comprising man and his ancestors.—n. and adj. hom'inoid. [L. homō, -inis, man.]

hominy, hom'i-ni, n. maize hulled, or hulled and crushed, boiled with water—a kind of Indian-corn porridge. [Amer. Ind. origin.]

homme, om, (Fr.) man.—homme d'affaires (da-fer), a business man: an agent, steward; homme de bien (də byē), a man of worth, a good man; homme de lettres (də letr'), a man of letters; homme d'épée (dā-pā), a military man; homme d'esprit (des-prē), a man of wit; homme d'état (dā-tä), a statesman; homme du monde (dü mōd), a man of fashion; homme moyen sensuel (mwa-yē sā-sü-el), the ordinary man: the man in the street; homme sérieux (sā-ryø), a serious, earnest man.

hommock. See hummock.

homo, hō'mō, n. man generically: (cap.; zool.) the human genus.—Homo erectus, a name given to a type of erect hominid between Australopithecus and Homo sapiens, represented by Java man and Peking man; Homo habilis, a name given to a much earlier hominid, thought also to walk upright; Homo Neanderthalensis (see Neanderthal); Homo sapiens, the one existing species of man. [L. homō, -inis, man being.]

homo-, hom'ō, hom-o', in many cases alternatively pronounced hōm-, in composition, same.—homoeo-, homeo-, homoio-, hom'i-ō-, -oi'ō-, or -o'-, like, similar.—n. and adj. homo (hō'mō; slang), abbreviation of homosexual.—adj. homo-blast'ic (Gr. blastos, a germ; zool.), derived from similar cells: showing direct embryonic development.—n. hom'oblasty.—adjs. homocentric (-sen'trik; Gr. homokentros—kentron, centre, point), concentric: proceeding from or diverging to the same point: of rays, either parallel or passing through one focus (phys.); homocercal (-sür'kəl; Gr. kerkos, tail), having the upper and lower lobes of the tail-fin alike; homochlamydeous (-klə-mid'i-əs; Gr. chlamys, -ydos, cloak; bot.), with calyx and corolla similar; homochromous (-krō'məs; Gr. chrōma, colour), alike in colour.—n. homochromy (-ok', or -krōm'), protective coloration.—adjs. homocyclic (-sik'lik; Gr. kyklos, a ring; chem.), having a closed chain of like atoms; homodont (hom'ə-dont; Gr. odous, odontos, tooth), having teeth all alike; homodyne (hom'ə-din; Gr. dynamis, power; radio telephony), applied to the reception of waves strengthened by the imposition of a locally generated wave of the same length; hom(o)eom'erous, hom(o)eom'erous (Gr. meros, part), composed of similar parts: of lichens, having the algal cells distributed throughout the thallus: in metameric animals, having all the somites alike—also hom(o)eomeric (-mer'ik).—ns. hom(o)eom'ery; hom(o)eomorph (Gr. morphē, form), a thing similar in form to another but essentially different, esp. a different chemical substance with similar crystalline form. —*adj.* hom(o)eomorph′ic, of or pertaining to a homoeomorph: of two geometrical figures, such that one can be converted into the other·by distortion (*math.*).—*n.* hom(o)eomorph′ism.— *adj.* hom(o)eomorph′ous.—*ns.* hom(o)eomorph′y; hom(o)eopath (*hom′* or *hōm′i-ə-path*; Gr. *pathos*, feeling), hom(o)eopathist (*-op′ə-thist*), one who believes in or practises homoeopathy.—*adj.* hom(o)eopathic (*-path′*).—*adv.* hom(o)eopath′i-cally.—*ns.* hom(o)eopathy (*-op′ə-thi*), the system of treating diseases by small quantities of drugs that excite symptoms similar to those of the disease; hom(o)eosis (*hom-i-ō′sis*; Gr. *homoiōsis*, a becoming like; *biol.*), assumption of the character of a corresponding member of another whorl or somite; hom(o)eostasis (*hom-i-os′tə-sis*; Gr. *stasis*, a standing still), the tendency for the internal environment of the body to remain constant in spite of varying external conditions: a tendency towards stable conditions.—*adj.* hom(o)eostat′ic.—*n.* hom(o)eoteleuton (*hom-i-ō-tel-ū′ton*; Gr. *homoioteleuton*—*teleutē*, ending), the use, or occurrence, of similar endings.—*adjs.* hom(o)eotherm′al, -ic, -ous, homothermous.— Also homoi′other′mal, etc.; homogamic (*-gam′ik*), homogamous (*hom-og′ə-məs*).—*ns.* homogamy (*hom-og′ə-mi*; Gr. *gamos*, marriage), breeding of like with like: inbreeding: the condition of having all the flowers of an inflorescence sexually alike (*bot.*): simultaneous ripening of stamens and stigmas (*bot.*); homogeneity (*hom-ō-ji-nē′i-ti*), the state or fact of being homogeneous.— *adj.* homogeneous (*hom-ō-jēn′i-əs*, also *hōm-*, *-jen′*; Gr. *homogenēs*—*genos*, kind), of the same kind or nature: having the constituent elements similar throughout: of the same degree or dimensions in every term (*math.*).—*n.* homo-gē′neousness.—*adj.* homogenous (*hom-oj′ən-əs*), similar owing to common descent.—*n.* homo-genesis (*-jen′i-sis*; Gr. *genesis*, birth; *biol.*), a mode of reproduction in which the offspring is like the parent, and passes through the same cycle of existence.—*adjs.* homogenet′ic, -al, homo-genous.—*v.t.* homog′enise (or *hom′ō-jən-iz*), to make homogeneous: to make (milk) more digestible by breaking up fat globules, etc.: to produce (milk) synthetically by mixing its con-stituents.—*ns.* homogenisation, -z-; homogeniser; homog′eny, similarity owing to common descent; hom′ograft (*hom′ō-gräft*), a graft from one individual to an unrelated member of the same species; homograph (*hom′ō-gräf*; Gr. *graphein*, to write), a word of the same spelling and pronunciation as another, but of different meaning and origin.—*adj.* homoiousian (*hom-oi-ōō′si-ən*, or *-ow′*; Gr. *ousiā*, being), of similar (as distinguished from identical) essence: believing the Father and Son to be of similar essence.—*n.* a holder of such belief, a semi-Arian.—*v.t.* homol′ogate (L.L. *homologāre*, *-ātum*—Gr. *homo-logeein*, to agree—*logos*, speech), to confirm: to approve: to consent to: to ratify.—*v.i.* to agree.—*n.* homologā′tion (Scots law), confirming and ratifying by subsequent act.—*adj.* homo-logical (*-loj′*).—*v.t.* and *v.i.* homol′ogise, -ize (*-jiz*).—*adj.* homologous (*hom-ol′ə-gəs*), agreeing: of the same essential nature, corresponding in relative position, general structure, and descent. —*n.* hom′ologue (*-ə-log*), that which is homolo-gous to something else, as a man's arm, a whale's flipper, a bird's wing.—*n.pl.* homolog(o)umena (*hom-ol-o-gōō′mi-nə*; Gr. *homologoumena*, things granted, neut. pl. of pr.p. pass. (contracted) of *homologeein*), the books of the New Testament whose authenticity was universally acknowledged in the early Church—opp. of *antilegomena*.—*ns.* homol′ogy (*-ə-ji*; Gr. *homologos*), the quality of being homologous: affinity of structure and

origin, apart from form or use; hom′omorph (Gr. *morphē*, form), a thing having the same form as another.—*adjs.* homomorph′ic, homomorph′-ous, alike in form, esp. if essentially different: uniform.—*ns.* homomorph′ism; homomorphō′sis, regeneration of a lost part in the original form; hom′onym (Gr. *homōnymos*—*onyma*, *onoma*, name), a word having the same sound and perhaps the same spelling as another, but a different meaning and origin: a name rejected as preoccupied by another genus or species (*biol.*): a namesake.—*adjs.* homonym′ic, per-taining to homonyms; homon′ymous, having the same name: having different significations and origins but the same sound: ambiguous: equivocal.—*adv.* homon′ymously.—*n.* homon′-ymy.—*adj.* homoousian, homousian (*hom-(ō-)ōō′si-ən*, or *-ow′*; Gr. *ousiā*, being), of the same essence: believing the Son to be of the same essence as the Father.—*n.* a holder of such belief (according to the Nicene Creed).—*n.* homophone (*hom′ə-fōn*; Gr. *phōnē*, sound), a character representing the same sound as another: a word pronounced alike with another but different in spelling and meaning.—*adjs.* homophonic (*-fon′*), sounding alike in unison: in the monodic style of music; homophonous (*-of′*). —*n.* homoph′ony.—*adj.* homoplast′ic (Gr. *plas-tikos*, plastic, *plasma*, a mould; *biol.*), similar in structure and development owing to parallel or convergent evolution but not descended from a common source.—*ns.* hom′oplasmy (*-plaz-mi*), homop′lasy.—*n.pl.* Homoptera (*-op′*; Gr. *pteron*, a wing), an order of insects (or suborder of Hemiptera) having the wings alike—cicadas, frog-hoppers, green-fly, scale-insects, etc.—*adjs.* homop′terous; homosex′ūal, having, or pertain-ing to, sexual propensity to one's own sex.— Also *n.*—*ns.* homosex′ualist; homosexual′ity.— *adjs.* homosporous (*-os′por-əs*, or *-ō-spō′rəs*, *-spō′*; Gr. *sporos*, seed; *bot.*), having spores all of one kind; homotax′ial, homotax′ic.—*n.* homotax′is (Gr. *taxis*, arrangement; *geol.*), coincidence in order of organic succession but not necessarily in time: similarity in geological age, while not necessarily strict contemporaneity.—*adj.* homo-thall′ic (*bot.*), having only one type of mycelium (opp. to *heterothallic*).—*ns.* homothall′ism, hom′othally.—*adjs.* homotherm′ic, homotherm′-ous (Gr. *thermē*, heat), keeping the same tempera-ture, warm-blooded; homotonic (*-ton′*), homo′-tonous (Gr. *tonos*, tone), of the same tenor or tone.—*n.* homot′ony.—*adjs.* homotypal (*-tip′l*), homotypic (*-tip′ik*), conforming to normal type: (homotypic; *biol.*) pertaining to the second (equational) cell division in meiosis (cf. hetero-typic).—*ns.* hom′otype (*ō-tip*; Gr. *typos*, type), that which has the same fundamental structure as something else; homotypy (*hom′ō-ti-pi*, *hom-ot′i-pi*); homozygōs′is, the condition of having inherited a given genetical factor from both parents, so producing gametes of only one kind as regards that factor: genetical stability as regards a given factor; homozy′gote, a zygote which is formed as a result of homozygosis. —*adj.* homozy′gous. [Gr. *homos*, same, *homoios*, like, similar.]

homunculus, hō-mung′kū-ləs, *n.* a tiny man capable of being produced artificially according to Para-celsus, endowed with magical insight and power: a dwarf, manikin: a dwarf of normal propor-tions (*med.*): a minute human form believed by the spermatist school of preformationists to be contained in the spermatozoon.—Also homunc′-ūle, homunc′le.—*adj.* homunc′ūlar. [L., dim. of *homō*.]

hond, *hond*, an obs. form of hand.

hone, *hōn*, *n.* a smooth stone used for sharpening instruments.—*v.t.* to sharpen as on a hone.— hone′-stone, a hone: any hard fine-grained stone

suitable for honing, esp. novaculite. [O.E. *hān*; O.N. *hein*; allied to Gr. *kōnos*, a cone.]
**hone**, *hōn*, (*dial.*) *v.i.* to pine, moan, grieve. [Perh. Fr. *hogner*, to grumble.]
**honest**, *on'ist*, *-əst*, *adj.* full of honour: just: fair-dealing: upright: the opposite of thievish: free from fraud: candid: truthful: ingenuous: seemly: respectable (now only patronisingly): chaste (*arch.*): honourable.—*adv.* **hon'estly**, in an honest way: in truth.—*interj.* expressing annoyance, disbelief, etc.—*n.* **hon'esty**, the state of being honest: integrity: candour: a cruci-ferous garden-plant (*Lunaria biennis*) with shin-ing silvery or satiny white dissepiments: de-corum (*obs.*): chastity (*Shak.*).—*adj.* **hon'est-to-God'**, **hon'est-to-good'ness**, genuine, out-and-out.—Also *adv.*—**honest Injun** (Indian), upon my honour; **make an honest woman of**, to marry, where the woman has first been seduced. [O.Fr. *honeste*—L. *honestus*—*honor*.]
**honey**, *hun'i*, *n.* a sweet, thick fluid elaborated by bees from the nectar of flowers: nectar of flowers: anything sweet like honey: a term of endearment: anything pleasant or delightful (*coll.*):—*v.t.* to sweeten: to make agreeable.—*v.i.* (*Shak.*) to talk endearingly:—*pr.p.* **hon'eying**; *pa.t.* and *pa.p.* **hon'eyed**, *-id.*—*adj.* (*Shak.*) sweet.—*adjs.* **hon'eyed**, **hon'ied**, covered with honey: sweet: seductive: flattering; **hon'eyless.**—**hon'ey-ant**, one of several types of ant, esp. of the genus *Myrmecocystus*, that feed on honey, and store it in the worker-ants, who disgorge it as necessary; **hon'ey-badg'er**, the ratel; **hon'ey-bag**, an enlargement of the alimentary canal of the bee in which it carries its load of honey; **hon'ey-bear**, the kinkajou, which robs the nests of wild bees: the sloth-bear: the Malayan bear; **hon'ey-bee**, the hive-bee; **hon'ey-bird**, a honey-guide: a honey-sucker; **hon'ey-blob** (*dial.*), a sweet yellow gooseberry; **hon'ey-buzz'ard**, a buzzard or falcon (*Pernis apivora*) that feeds on larvae of bees, wasps, etc.; **hon'ey-cart**,-**wag(g)on**, truck for offensive refuse; **hon'ey-chile** (*U.S. dial.*), a term of endearment; **hon'eycomb** (*-kōm*), a comb or mass of waxy cells formed by bees, in which they store their honey: anything like a honeycomb: a bewildering maze of rooms, cavities, etc.—*v.t.* to make like a honey-comb.—*adj.* **hon'eycombed** (*-kōmd*).—**hon'ey-comb-moth'**, a bee-moth; **hon'ey-crock**, a crock or pot of honey; **hon'ey-dew**, a sugar secretion from aphides or plants: ambrosia: a fine sort of tobacco moistened with molasses; **honeydew melon**, a sweet-flavoured melon with smooth green or orange rind; **hon'ey-eat'er**, a honey-sucker; **hon'ey-guide**, a bird of a mainly African family (Indicatoridae) supposed to guide men to honey by hopping from tree to tree with a peculiar cry: a marking on a flower showing the way to the nectaries; **hon'ey-lo'cust**, an orna-mental N. American tree (Gleditschia); **hon'ey-moon** (*obs.* **hon'eymonth**), the first weeks after marriage, commonly spent on holiday, before settling down to the business of life.—Also *v.i.*—**hon'eymooner**; **hon'ey-mouse**, a long-snouted Australian marsupial (Tarsipes) that feeds on honey and insects.—*adj.* **hon'ey-mouthed**, having a honeyed mouth or speech: soft or smooth in speech.—**hon'eypot**, a container for honey: (in *pl.*) a children's game: see also hanepoot (*S. Afr.*); **hon'ey-stalk** (*Shak.*), prob. the stalk or flower of the clover; **hon'ey-stone**, mellite, a very soft yellow mineral found with lignite; **hon'ey-suck'er**, any bird of a large Australian family, Meliphagidae; **hon'eysuckle**, a climbing shrub (Lonicera) with beautiful cream-coloured flowers, so named because honey is readily sucked from the flower (by long-tongued insects only): applied also to clover and many other plants.—*adj.* **hon'(e)y-suckle**, and *adj.* and *n.*

**hon'(e)y-seed** (*Shak.*; *Henry IV part* 2), the Hostess's blunders for homicidal, homicide.—*adjs.* **hon'ey-sweet**, sweet as honey; **hon'ey-tongued**, soft, pleasing, persuasive, or seductive in speech: eloquent.—**virgin honey**, honey that flows of itself from the comb; **wild honey**, honey made by wild bees. [O.E. *hunig*; Ger. *honig*; O.N. *hunang.*]
**honeypot**, *hun'i-pot*. See honey, hanepoot.
**hong**, *hong*, *n.* a Chinese warehouse: foreign mer-cantile house in China. [Chin. *hang*, row, range.]
**hong**, *hong*, obs. form of hang, hung.
**honied.** See honeyed.
**Honiton**, *hon'i-tən*, local *hun'*, *adj.* applied to a kind of pillow lace with sprigs, made at *Honiton*, Devon.
**honk**, *hongk*, *n.* the cry of the wild goose: the noise of a motor horn.—Also *v.i.* [Imit.]
**honky-tonk**, *hongk'i-tongk*, (*slang*) *n.* a low drink-ing haunt: cheap entertainment: jangly piano music. [Ety. dub.]
**honorarium**, *hon-ə-rā'ri-əm*, *n.* a voluntary fee paid, esp. to a professional man for his services.—*adj.* **honorary** (*on'(ə-)rə-ri*), conferring honour: holding a title or office without performing services or without reward.—*n.* an honorary fee. [L. *honōrārius*, *honōrārium* (*dōnum*), honorary (gift)—*honor*, *-ōris*, honour.]
**honorific**, (*h*)*on-ə-rif'ik*, *adj.* attributing or doing honour.—*n.* an honorific form of title, address or mention.—*adj.* **honorif'ical.**—*adv.* **honorif'ically.** [L. *honōrificus*—*honor*, *-ōris*, honour, and *facēre*, to do, make.]
**honorificabilitudinity**, *hon-or-if-ik-ab-il-i-tū-din'i-ti*, *n.* honourableness. [L.L. *honōrificābilitū-dinitās*, preserved in the abl. pl. *honōrificābilitū-dinitātibus* as a superlatively long word, in *Love's Labour's Lost*, V, i. 44 and elsewhere; the gen. sing. is used by Albertino Mussato (early 14th cent.).]
**honoris causa** or **gratia**, *hon-ōr'is* (*-ör'*) *kö'zə*, *kow' zä*, or *grä'shi-ə*, *grä'ti-ä*, (L.L.) as an honour, a token of respect.
**honour**, in U.S. **honor**, *on'ər*, *n.* the esteem due or paid to worth: respect: high estimation: venera-tion: that which rightfully attracts esteem: that which confers distinction or does credit: self-respecting integrity: a fine and scrupulous sense of what is due: chastity: virginity: distinction: exalted rank: any mark of esteem: privilege: a title or decoration: a title of respect in addressing or referring to judges, etc. (in Ireland quite generally): a prize or distinction: (in *pl.*) privileges of rank or birth: an ornament or decoration (*poet.*): (in *pl.*) civilities paid: (in *pl.*) in universities, etc., a higher grade of distinction for meritorious, advanced, or specialised work: the right to play first from the tee (*golf*): any one of four (in whist) or five (in bridge) best trumps, or an ace in a no-trump hand: (in *pl.*) a score for holding these: a group of manors held by one lord.—*v.t.* to hold in high esteem: to respect: to adorn (*obs.*): to exalt: to do honour to: to confer honour upon: to grace: to accept and pay when due.—*adj.* **hon'ourable**, worthy of honour: illustrious: actuated by principles of honour: conferring honour: befitting men of exalted station: (*cap.*; written Hon.), prefixed to the names of various persons as a courtesy title.—*n.* **hon'ourableness**, eminence: conform-ity to the principles of honour: fairness.—*adv.* **hon'ourably.**—*adjs.* **hon'oured**; **hon' oured**; **hon'ourless.**—*n.* **hon'ourer.**—**hon'our-point** (*her.*), the point just above the fesse-point; **hon'ours-man**, one who has taken a university degree with honours.—**affair of honour**, a duel; **birthday honours**, honours granted to mark the monarch's birthday; **Companions of Honour**, an order instituted in 1917 for those who have rendered conspicuous service of national importance; **Court of Honour**,

a court regulating affairs of honour; **debt of honour** (see **debt**); **do the honours,** to render civilities, esp. as host; **honour bright,** a kind of interjectional minor oath or appeal to honour; **honours easy** (see **ease**); **honours of war,** the privileges granted to a capitulating force of marching out with their arms, flags, etc.; **last honours,** funeral rites; **laws of honour,** the conventional rules of honourable conduct, esp. in the conduct of duels; **maid of honour,** a lady in the service of a queen or princess: a kind of cheese-cake: a bridesmaid (*U.S.*); **person of honour** (*obs.*), a titled person; **point of honour,** any scruple caused by a sense of duty: the obligation to demand and to receive satisfaction for an insult, esp. in the duel; **upon my honour,** an appeal to one's honour in support of a statement; **word of honour,** a promise which cannot be broken without disgrace. [A.Fr. (*h*)*onour*—L. *honor, honōs, -ōris.*]
**hoo, hōō,** (*Shak.*) *interj.* expressing boisterous emotion.—Also **hoo-oo′.**
**hooch, hōōhh,** *interj.* a Highland dancer's shout.
**hooch, hōōch.** See **hootch.**
**hood, hōōd,** *n.* a flexible covering for the head and back of the neck: a covering for a hawk's head: a distinctive ornamental fold worn on the back over an academic gown: a folding roof for a carriage, etc.: a chimney-cowl: an overhanging or protective cover: the expansion of a cobra's neck: a hood-moulding: a motor-car bonnet (*U.S.*).—*v.t.* to cover with a hood: to blind.—*adjs.* **hood′ed; hood′less,** having no hood.—**hood′ie-crow,** the hooded crow (*Corvus cornix*); **hood′man** (*obs.*), the person blind-folded in blindman's buff; **hood′man-blind** (*Shak.*), blindman's buff; **hood′-mould, hood′-mould′ing,** an uppermost projecting moulding over a door, window, or arch. [O.E. *hōd*; Du. *hoed*, Ger. *hut.*]
**hood, hōōd,** (*slang*) *n.* a hoodlum.
**hood, hōōd,** (*Spens.*) *n.* condition. [O.E. *hād.*]
**-hood, -hōōd,** *n. suff.* indicating state, nature, as *hardihood, manhood.*—Also **-head** (*-hed*), as *Godhead.* [O.E. *hād*, Ger. *-heit*, state.]
**hoodlum, hōōd′ləm,** *n.* a rowdy, street bully: a small-time criminal or gangster.
**hoodoo, hōō′dōō,** *n.* voodoo: a bringer of bad luck: foreboding of bad luck: bad luck: a rock-pinnacle (*geol.*).—*v.t.* to bewitch: to bring bad luck to. [App. **voodoo.**]
**hoodwink, hōōd′wingk,** *v.t.* to blindfold: to cover up, hide (*Shak.*): to deceive, impose on. [**hood, wink.**]
**hooey, hōō′i,** (*slang*) *n.* nonsense.
**hoof, hōōf,** *n.* the horny part of the feet of certain animals, as horses, etc.: a hoofed animal: a foot (*coll.*):—*pl.* **hoofs, hooves.**—*v.t.* to strike with the hoof, to kick: to expel.—*v.i.* (with *it*) to walk: dance (*slang*).—*adjs.* **hoofed; hoof′less.**—*adj.* **hoof′-bound,** having a contraction of the hoof causing lameness; **hoof′-mark, hoof′print,** the mark of a hoof on the ground, etc.; **hoof′rot, foot-rot.**—**on the hoof,** alive (of cattle). [O.E. *hōf*; Ger. *huf*; O.N. *hōfr.*]
**hoo-ha, hōō′hä′,** (*slang*) *n.* noisy fuss. [Imit.]
**hook, hōōk,** *n.* an object of bent form, such as would catch or hold anything: a sharply bent line: a snare: an advantageous hold: a curved instrument for cutting grain, branches, etc.: a spit of land with hooked end: a boxer's blow with bent elbow: the curve of a ball in flight (*sport*): an act of hooking.—*v.t.* to catch, fasten, or hold with or as with a hook: to form into or with a hook: to ensnare: to pull abruptly (*golf* and *cricket*): to obtain possession of (the ball) in the scrum (*rugby*).—*v.i.* to bend: to be curved: to pull abruptly: to act as hooker (*rugby*).—*pa.p.* or *adj.* **hooked** (*hōōkt*), physically dependent on drugs: (with *on, by*) addicted to a drug,

activity, or indulgence.—*ns.* **hook′edness; hook′er,** one who hooks: one whose part it is to hook the ball (*rugby*).—*adj.* **hook′y,** full of, or pertaining to, hooks.—**hook′-climber,** a climbing plant that clings to its support by means of hooks.—*adj.* **hook′-nosed.**—**hook′-pin,** an iron pin with hooked head used for pinning the frame of a floor or roof together; **hook′-up,** a connection: a temporary linking up of separate broadcasting stations for a special transmission; **hook′-worm,** a parasitic nematode with hooks in the mouth: the disease it causes, ankylostomiasis or miner's anaemia.—**by hook or by crook,** one way if not another; **hook and eye,** a contrivance for fastening garments by means of a hook that catches in a loop or eye; **hook it** (*slang*), to decamp, make off; **hook, line and sinker,** complete(ly); **off the hook,** ready-made: out of difficulty or trouble; **off the hooks,** out of gear: superseded: dead; **on one's own hook,** on one's own responsibility, initiative, or account; **sling,** or **take, one's hook** (*slang*), to get out, away, make off. [O.E. *hōc*; Du. *hoek*.]
**hookah, hooka, hōōk′a,** *n.* the water tobacco-pipe of Arabs, Turks, etc. [Ar. *huqqah*, bowl, casket.]
**hooker, hōōk′ər,** *n.* a two-masted Dutch vessel: a small fishing-smack. [Du. *hoeker.*]
**hookey, hooky, hōōk′i,** (*U.S.*) *n.* truant (in the phrase *play hookey*).—**blind hookey,** a gambling card-game; **hookey walker** (see under **walk**).
**hookey.** See **hockey** (1).
**hooligan, hōōl′i-gan,** *n.* a street rough.—*n.* **hool′-iganism.** [Said to be the name of a leader of a gang.]
**hoolock, hōō′lək,** *n.* a small Assamese gibbon. [Said to be native name, *hulluk.*]
**hooly, hül′i, hūl′i,** (*Scot.*) *adv.* softly, carefully.—Also *adj.*—**hooly and fairly,** fair and soft, gently. [Perh. O.N. *hōfliga,* fitly, or *hōgliga,* gently.]
**hoop, hōōp,** *n.* a ring or circular band, esp. for holding together the staves of casks, etc.: a large ring of metal, etc., for a child to trundle, for leaping through, for expanding a skirt, or other purpose: a ring: a croquet arch.—*v.t.* to bind with hoops: to encircle.—*n.* **hoop′er,** one who hoops casks: a cooper.—**hoop′-ash,** a kind of ash used for making hoops: the nettle-tree (Celtis); **hooped′-pot,** a drinking-pot with hoops to mark the amount each man should drink.—*interj.* **hoop′-la,** orig. used at a circus when a performer jumped through a hoop.—*n.* a fairground game in which small hoops are thrown over prizes: great activity, excitement or disturbance; **hoop′-snake,** any of several harmless snakes, popularly believed to have formed themselves into a hoop and rolled over the ground.—**to go through the hoop,** suffer an ordeal, undergo punishment. [O.E. *hōp*; Du. *hoep.*]
**hoop, hooper, hooping-cough.** See under **whoop.**
**hoopoe, hōōp′ōō,** *n.* a crested bird (*Upupa epops*), an occasional visitor in Britain. [Earlier *hoop*—O.Fr. *huppe,* partly remodelled on L. *ŭpŭpa*; cf. Gr. *epops.*]
**hoord,** an obs. form of **hoard.**
**hoos(e)gow, hōōs′gow,** *n.* (*U.S. slang*), a prison, jail. [Sp. *juzgado,* tribunal, courtroom—*juzgar,* to judge—L. *jūdicāre.*]
**hoosh, hōōsh,** *interj.* used in driving away animals.—*v.t.* to drive or shoo away. [Imit.]
**hoosh, hōōsh,** *n.* a thick soup.
**hoot, hōōt,** *v.i.* (of an owl) to give a hollow cry: to make a sound like an owl, usually expressing hostility or scorn: to laugh loudly: to sound a motor-horn, siren, or the like.—*v.t.* to greet or drive with such sounds.—*n.* the sound of hooting: the note of an owl, motor-horn, etc.: a whit (often *two hoots*).—*interj.* (*sing.* or *pl.*; *Scot.*) expressing incredulity, irritation, annoyance, etc. (also **hoot′-toot′, hoots′-toots′**).—*n.*

Neutral vowels in unaccented syllables: *el′ə-mənt*; for certain sounds in foreign words, see p. viii

hoot'er, one who hoots: a factory or mine siren or steam whistle. [Imit., prob. immediately Scand.; cf. Sw. *hut*, begone.]

hootch, hooch, *hōōch*, *n.* a drink made by the Indians of N.W. America from fermented dough and sugar: whisky: liquor, esp. if illicitly got or made. [Said to be from *Hootchino*, an Alaskan tribe.]

hoot(e)nanny, hoota-, -ie, *hōōt'nan-ē*, *n.* thingummy (*U.S.*, *dial.*): a party with folk-singing and sometimes dancing: an informal concert with folk music.

hoove, *hōōv*, *n.* a disease of cattle and sheep, marked by distension of the abdomen by gas—also *wind-dropsy*, *drum-belly.—adjs.* hoov'en, hō'ven. [Cf. heave.]

hoove. See hove (2).

hooves. See hoof.

hop, hop, *v.i.* to leap on one leg: to move in jumps like a bird: to walk lame: to limp: to fly (in aircraft).—*v.t.* to cause to hop: to jump or fly over: to jump from: to board when in motion (*U.S.*):—*pr.p.* hopp'ing; *pa.t.* and *pa.p.* hopped.—*n.* a leap on one leg: a jump: a spring: a dance, dancing-party: a stage in a flying journey.—*ns.* hopp'er, one who hops: a hopping or leaping animal, esp. (*U.S.*) a grasshopper: a jack or sticker of a piano: a shaking or conveying receiver, funnel, or trough (originally a shaking one) in which something is placed to be passed or fed, as to a mill: a barge with an opening in its bottom for discharging refuse: a vessel in which seed-corn is carried for sowing; hopp'ing.—hop-off', the start of a flight; hop'-o'-my-thumb (i.e. on my thumb), a pygmy; hop'-scotch, a game in which children hop over lines scotched or traced on the ground.—hop it (*slang*), to take oneself off; hop, skip and jump, a leap on one leg, a skip, and a jump with both legs; hop the twig (*slang*), to escape one's creditors: to die; on the hop, in a state of restless activity: in the act, unawares, at the very moment. [O.E. *hoppian*, to dance; Ger. *hopfen*, *hüpfen*.]

hop, hop, *n.* a plant (*Humulus lupulus*) of the mulberry family with a long twining stalk: (in *pl.*) its bitter catkin-like fruit-clusters used for flavouring beer and in medicine: opium (*slang*): any narcotic (*slang*).—*v.t.* to mix or flavour with hops.—*v.i.* to gather hops:—*pr.p.* hopp'ing; *pa.t.* and *pa.p.* hopped.—*adj.* hopped, impregnated with hops.—*ns.* hopp'er, hop'-pick'er, one who picks hops: a mechanical contrivance for stripping hops from the bines; hopp'ing, the act of gathering hops: the time of the hop harvest.—*adj.* hopp'y, tasting of hops.—hop'bind, hop'bine, the stalk of the hop; hop'-bitt'ers, a drink like ginger-beer, flavoured with hops; hop'dog, the tussock-moth caterpillar: a tool for pulling out hop-poles; hop'-flea, a small beetle injurious to hops; hop'-fly, a greenfly injurious to hops; hop'-garden, a field of hops; hop'-head (*slang*), a drug addict; hop'-oast, a kiln for drying hops.—*adj.* hopped'-up (*slang*), drugged: under an exhilarating drug: excited, agitated: artificially stimulated: made to seem exciting: given added power.—hop'-pick'er, a hopper; hop'-pock'et, coarse sack for hops: about 1½ cwt. of hops; hop'-pole, pole supporting hop-bine; hop'(-)sack, sack for hops: (also -sacking) coarse fabric of hemp and jute, or woollen fabric with roughened surface; hop'-tree, American rutaceous shrub (*Ptelea trifoliata*) with bitter fruit, substitute for hops; hop'-tre'foil, a yellow clover; hop'-vine, hop-plant: its stem; hop'-yard, field where hops are grown.—hop up (*slang*), to excite, artificially stimulate: to drug. [Du. *hop.*]

hope, *hōp*, *v.i.* to cherish a desire of good with some expectation of fulfilment: to have confidence:

to be hopeful.—*v.t.* to desire with belief in the possibility of fulfilment: to expect, fear (*obs.*).—*n.* a desire of some good, with a certain expectation of obtaining it: confidence: anticipation: that on which hopes are grounded: an embodiment of hope: that which is hoped for.—*adj.* hope'ful, full of hope: having qualities which excite hope: promising good or success.—*n.* a promising young person.—*adv.* hope'fully, in a hopeful manner: it is hoped, if all goes well (*coll.*).—*n.* hope'fulness.—*adj.* hope'less, without hope: giving no ground to expect good or success: incurable: unhoped-for (*Spens.*).—*adv.* hope'lessly.—*n.* hope'lessness.—*adv.* hōp'ingly.—hope'-chest (*U.S.*), a repository of things stored by a woman for her marriage—a bottom drawer.—hope against hope, to continue to hope when all ground for hoping is gone. [O.E. *hopian*—*hopa*, hope; Du. *hopen*, Ger. *hoffen.*]

hope, hōp, *n.* an enclosure: the upper end of a narrow mountain-valley: a combe—common in Border place-names (usu. pron. -*əp*): an inlet. [O.E. *-hop* (in compounds), or O.N. *hōp.*]

hope. See forlorn hope.

hoplite, *hop'lit*, *n.* a heavy-armed Greek footsoldier. [Gr. *hoplitēs.*]

hoplology, *hop-lol'ə-ji*, *n.* the study of weapons.—*n.* hoplol'ogist. [Gr. *hoplon*, tool, weapon.]

hopple, *hop'l*, *v.t.* to restrain by tying the feet together.—*n.* (chiefly in *pl.*) a fetter for horses, etc., when left to graze. [Cf. obs. Flem. *hoppelen*; also hop, hobble.]

hoppus (cubic) foot, *hop'əs*, a unit of volume for round timber. [E. *Hoppus.*]

horae canonicae, hō', hō'rē kən-on'i-kē, hō'ri kan-on'i-ki (L.), the canonical hours.

horal, hō'rəl, hō'rəl, *adj.* relating to hours: hourly.—*adj.* ho'rary, pertaining to an hour: noting the hours: hourly: continuing an hour. [L. *hōra*, an hour.]

Horatian, hor-ā'shən, *adj.* pertaining to Horace, the Latin poet (65-8 B.C.), or to his manner or verse.

horde, hōrd, hörd, *n.* a migratory or wandering tribe or clan: a multitude.—*v.i.* to live together as a horde: to come together to form a horde.—Golden Horde (see golden). [Fr.,—Turk. *ordu*, camp.]

Hordeum, hör'di-əm, *n.* the barley genus.—*ns.* hordein (hör'di-in), a protein found in barley grains; hordeolum (-dē'), a sty on the eyelid. [L., barley.]

hore (*Spens.*). Same as hoar.

horehound, hoarhound, hōr', hör'hownd, *n.* a hoary labiate plant (*Marrubium vulgare*) once popular as a remedy for coughs.—Also called white horehound.—black horehound, stinking horehound, a darker-coloured kindred weed (*Ballota nigra*); water horehound, gypsywort. [O.E. *hār*, hoar, *hūne*, horehound.]

horizon, *har-i'zən*, *n.* the circle in which earth and sky seem to meet (*sensible*, *apparent*, or *visible horizon*): a plane through the earth's centre parallel to the sensible horizon (*rational horizon*), or the great circle in which it meets the heavens: a horizontal reflecting surface, as of mercury, used as a substitute for the horizon in taking an observation (*artificial horizon*): a stratigraphical level, characterised generally by some particular fossil or fossils (*geol.*): a level line or surface (*anat.*): the limit of one's experience or apprehension.—*adj.* horizontal (hor-i-zont'l), pertaining to the horizon: parallel to the horizon: level: near the horizon: measured in the plane of the horizon.—*n.* a horizontal line, position, or object: a large Tasmanian shrub, whose stem and branches ascend and then grow horizontally to form a dense mass of boughs and foliage, also horizontal scrub.—*n.* horizontal'ity.—*adv.* horizon'tally. [Fr.,—L.,—Gr. *horizōn* (*kyklos*), bounding (circle); *horizōn, -ŏntos,* pr.p. of *horizein,* to bound—*horos,* a limit.]

**horkey.** See hockey (2).

**horme,** *hör'mē (psychol.), n.* goal-directed or purposive behaviour.—**hormic** theory, theory stressing the importance of instinctive impulses and purposive striving. [Gr. *hormē,* animal impulse.]

**hormone,** *hör'mōn, n.* an internal secretion which on reaching some part of a plant or animal body exercises a specific physiological action.—*adjs.* **hor'monal** (or *-mōn'*), **hormon'ic** (or *-mōn'*). [Gr. *hormōn,* contracted pr.p. of *hormaein,* to stir up.]

**horn,** *hörn, n.* a hard outgrowth on the head of an animal, sometimes confined to the hollow structure on an ox, sheep, goat, etc., sometimes extended to a deer's antler, the growth on a giraffe's head, on a rhinoceros's snout, etc.: a beetle's antenna: a snail's tentacle: any projection resembling a horn: a cusp: a crescent tip: an outgrowth visible only to the eye of faith on a cuckold's forehead: the material of which horns are composed, keratin: an object made of or like a horn, as a drinking vessel: a funnel-shaped mouthpiece: a wind instrument orig. made from a horn, now of brass, etc.: a sounding apparatus on motor vehicles: a Jewish symbol of strength.—*adj.* made of horn. —*v.t.* to furnish with horns, real or visionary: to dishorn: to outlaw (*obs. Scots law*): to gore: to butt or push.—*v.i.* to play or blow the horn: to butt.—*adj.* **horned,** having a horn or horns: curved like a horn.—*ns.* **horn'er,** one who works or deals in horns: a horn-player: a cuckold-maker (*obs.*); **horn'ful; Horn'ie** (*Scot.*), the devil, usu. represented with horns; **horn'iness; horn'ing,** appearance of the moon when in its crescent form: a mock serenade with tin horns and any discordant instruments (*U.S. dial.*): putting to the horn (*obs. Scots law*): cuckold-making (*obs.*).—*adj.* **horn'ish,** like horn: hard.— *n.* **horn'ist,** a horn-player.—*adj.* **horn'less,** without horns.—*n.* **horn'let,** a little horn.—*adj.* **horn'y,** like horn: of horn: hard: callous.— **horn'beak** (*dial.*), the garfish; **horn'beam,** a tree (Carpinus) resembling a beech, with hard tough wood; **horn'bill,** a bird (of family Bucerotidae) with a horny excrescence on its bill; **horn'book** (*hist.*), a first book for children, which consisted of a single leaf set in a frame, with a thin plate of transparent horn in front to preserve it; **horn'bug** (*U.S.*), a stag-beetle; **horned cairn** (*archaeol.*), a long barrow with a pair of curved projecting arms at one end, or at both; **horned horse,** the gnu; **horned owl, horn owl,** an owl with hornlike tufts of feathers on its head; **horned poppy,** a poppy (Glaucium) with horned seed-vessel; **horned toad,** a spiny American lizard (Phrynosoma): a S. American toad (Cerato-phrys) with a bony shield on the back; **horn'fels** (*-fels*; Ger. *fels,* rock), a compact rock composed of lime silicates produced by contact meta-morphism:—*pl.* **hornfels, hornfelses.**—*adj.* **horn'-foot'ed,** hoofed.—**horn gate,** gate of horn (see gate (1)); **horn'geld** (*hist.*), cornage.—*adj.* **horn'-mad** (*arch.*), mad to the point of goring anybody: enraged like a cuckold.—**horn'-mad'ness** (*Browning*); **horn'-mak'er** (*Shak.*), a cuckold-maker; **horn mercury,** native mercurous chloride or calomel; **horn'-nut,** water-chestnut.—*adj.* **horn'-rimmed,** having rims of horn, or material resembling horn.—**horn'-rims,** dark horn-rimmed spectacles; **horn silver,** cerargyrite; **horn spoon,** a spoon made of a sheep's horn; **horn'stone,** a flinty chalcedony; **horn'tail,** a hymenopterous insect, often with a stout ovipositor; **horn'work,** an outwork having angular points or horns, and composed of two demi-bastions joined by a curtain (*fort.*): work in horn: cuckoldry (*obs.*); **horn'worm,** a hawk-moth caterpillar; **horn'wort,**

a rootless water-plant (Ceratophyllum) with much-divided submerged leaves that turn trans-lucent and horny; **horn'wrack,** the sea-mat.— *adj.* **horn'y-hand'ed,** with hands hardened by toil.—**horn'yhead,** an American cyprinoid fish with hornlike processes on its head.—**horn in,** to interpose, butt in; **horn in plenty** (see cornu-copia); **horns of a dilemma** (see dilemma); **horns of the altar,** the projections at the four corners of the Hebrew altar; **letters of horning** (*Scots law*), letters running in the sovereign's name, and passing the signet, instructing messengers-at-arms to charge the debtor to pay, on his failure a caption or warrant for his apprehension being granted; **make a spoon or spoil a horn,** to attempt something at the risk of failure; **pull,** or **draw, in one's horns,** to abate one's ardour or pre-tensions: to curtail or restrict one's activities, spending, etc.; **put to the horn** (*obs. Scots law*), to outlaw by three blasts of the horn at the Cross of Edinburgh. [O.E. *horn;* Scand. and Ger. *horn,* Gael. and W. *corn,* L. *cornū,* Gr. *keras.*]

**hornblende,** *hörn'blend, n.* a rock-forming mineral, one of the amphiboles, essentially silicate of calcium, magnesium and iron, generally green to black, with cleavage angle about 56°. [Ger.; cf. **horn, blende.**]

**hornet,** *hörn'it, n.* a large kind of wasp. [O.E. *hyrnet,* app.—*horn,* horn.]

**hornito,** *hör-nē'tō, n.* a low oven-shaped fumarole. [Sp., dim. of *horno*—L. *furnus,* an oven.]

**hornpipe,** *hörn'pip, n.* an old Welsh musical instrument like a clarinet, prob. sometimes with a horn mouthpiece or bell: a lively English dance, usually by one person, popular amongst sailors: a tune for the dance. [horn, pipe (1).]

**horography,** *hor-og'ra-fi, n.* the art of constructing sundials, clocks, etc.—*n.* **horog'rapher.** [Gr. *hōrā,* an hour, *graphein,* to describe.]

**horologe,** *hor'a-loj, n.* any instrument for telling the hours.—*ns.* **horologer** (*-ol'a-jar*), **horol'ogist,** a maker of clocks, etc.—*adjs.* **horolog'ic, -al.**— *ns.* **horolog'ium,** a horologe (*obs.*): (*cap.*) a southern constellation (*astron.*); **horol'ogy,** the science of time measurement: the art of clock-making: the office-book of the Greek Church for the canonical hours, also **horologium.** [L. *hōrologium*—Gr. *hōrologion*—*hōrā,* an hour, *legein,* to tell.]

**horometry,** *hor-om'it-ri, n.* time measurement.— *adj.* **horometrical** (*-met'*). [Gr. *hōrā,* an hour, *metron,* a measure.]

**horoscope,** *hor'a-skōp, n.* an observation of the heavens at the hour of a person's birth, by which the astrologer predicted the events of his life: a representation of the heavens for this purpose: any similar prediction about a person's future.— *adj.* **horoscopic** (*-skop'*).—*ns.* **horoscopist** (*-os'ka-pist*), an astrologer; **horos'copy,** the art of pre-dicting the events of a person's life from his horoscope: aspect of the stars at the time of birth. [Gr. *hōroskopos*—*hōrā,* an hour, *skopeein,* to observe.]

**horrendous,** *hor-end'as, (coll.) adj.* dreadful: fright-ful: horrible. [L. *horrendus,* ger. of *horrēre,* to bristle.]

**horrent,** *hor'ant, adj.* bristling. [L. *horrēns, -entis,* pr.p. of *horrēre,* to bristle.]

**horrible,** *hor'i-bl, adj.* exciting horror: dreadful: detestable (*coll.*).—*n.* **horr'ibleness.**—*adv.* **horr'-ibly.** [L. *horribilis*—*horrēre,* to shudder.]

**horrid,** *hor'id, adj.* shaggy, bristling, rough (*arch.* or *poet.*): horrible (*arch.*): repellent, detestable (*coll.*).—*adv.* **horr'idly.**—*n.* **horr'idness.** [L. *horridus*—*horrēre,* to bristle.]

**horrify,** *hor'i-fī, v.t.* to strike with horror:—*pr.p.* **horr'ifying;** *pa.t.* and *pa.p.* **horr'ified.**—*adj.* **horrif'ic,** exciting horror: frightful. [L. *horrificus* —root of *horrēre,* to shudder, *facĕre,* to make.]

**horripilation,** *hor-i-pi-lā'shan, n.* a contraction

Neutral vowels in unaccented syllables: *el'a-mant;* for certain sounds in foreign words, see p. viii the cutaneous muscles causing erection of the hairs and goose-flesh.—*adj.* **horrip'ilant.**—*v.t.* and *v.i.* **horrip'ilate.** [L. *horripilātiō, -ōnis*—root of *horrēre*, to bristle, *pilus*, a hair.]

**horrisonant,** *hor-is'ən-ant*, *adj.* sounding dreadfully.—Also **horris'onous** (*arch.*). [From root of L. *horrēre*, to bristle, *sonāns, -antis*, sounding.]

**horror,** *hor'ər*, *n.* shagginess, raggedness (*obs.*): a shuddering: intense repugnance: power of exciting such feeling: a source of such feeling: anything mildly objectionable, ridiculous, grotesque, or distasteful (*coll.*).—*adj.* of a comic (i.e. strip cartoon),. film, novel, etc., having gruesome, violent, horrifying, or bloodcurdling themes.—*adjs.* **horr'or-stricken, -struck.**—**the horrors,** extreme depression: delirium tremens. [L. *horror*, a shudder, bristling, etc.]

**hors,** *or*, (Fr.) out of, outside; **hors concours** (*kɔ̄-kōōr*), not in competition; **hors de combat** (*də kɔ̄-ba*), unfit to fight, disabled; **hors de saison** (*də se-zɔ̄*), out of season; **hors d'œuvre** (*pl.* **d'œuvre, d'œuvres;** *də-vr'*), savoury, e.g. olives, sardines, etc., to whet the appetite before a meal; **hors la loi** (*la lwa*), in outlawry, outlawed; **hors série** (*sā-rē*), excluded from a series, added later; **hors texte** (*tekst*), an illustration inset separately into a book.

**horse,** *hörs,'n.* a solid-hoofed ungulate (*Equus caballus*) with flowing tail and mane: any member of the genus Equus (horse, ass, zebra, etc.) or the family Equidae: a male adult of the species: *'(collec.)* cavalry: a wooden frame on which soldiers used to be mounted as a punishment—also *timber-mare*: a gymnastic apparatus for vaulting, etc.: a horselike apparatus or support of various kinds (as *saw-horse, clothes-horse*): a crib or translation (*U.S.* slang): a mass of barren country interrupting a lode: heroin (*slang*):—*pl.* **horses,** sometimes **horse.**— *v.t.* to mount or set as on a horse: to provide with a horse: to sit astride: to carry on the back: (of a stallion) to cover: to urge at work tyrannically.—*v.i.* to get on horseback: to travel on horseback: to charge for work before it is done (with *it*).—*adj.* **horse'less,** without a horse: mechanically driven.—*ns.* **hors'iness; hors'ing** (*arch.*), birching of a person mounted on another's back.—*adj.* **hors'y,** of or pertaining to horses: horselike: devoted to horses, horse-racing, or breeding.—*adj.* **horse'-and-bugg'y,** hopelessly out of date.—**horse artillery,** field artillery with comparatively light guns and the gunners mounted; **horse'back,** the back of a horse; **horse bean,** a variety of broad bean: applied also to other beans; **horse block,** a block or stage for mounting and dismounting by; **horse boat,** a boat for carrying horses, or towed by a horse; **horse bot,** a botfly; **horse box,** a railway car for horses: a stall on shipboard: a high-sided church pew (*facet.*); **horse'-boy,** a stable boy; **horse brass,** a brass ornament orig. for hanging on the harness of a horse; **horse'-bread,** a coarse bread for feeding horses; **horse'-break'er, -tam'er,** one who breaks or tames horses, or teaches them to draw or carry: a courtesan who appears on horseback (*obs.*); **horse'car** (*U.S.*), a streetcar drawn by horses; **horse chestnut,** a smooth, brown, bitter seed or nut, perh. so called from its coarseness contrasted with the edible chestnut: the tree that produces it (*Aesculus hippocastanum*); **horse'-cloth,** a cloth for covering a horse; **horse'-collar,** a stuffed collar for a draught-horse, carrying the hames; **horse'-cop'er or** (*Scot.*) **horse'-couper** (*kow', kōō'*), **horse'-deal'er,** one who deals in horses; **horse'-courser** (*obs.*), a jobbing dealer in horses; **horse'-doc'tor,** a veterinary surgeon; **horse'-drench,** a dose of medicine for a horse.— *adj.* **horse'-faced,** having a long horselike face.— **horse fair,** a fair or market for sale of horses;

**horse'flesh,** the flesh of a horse: horses collectively.—*adj.* of reddish-bronze colour.— **horseflesh ore,** bornite or erubescite, from its colour; **horse'fly,** the forest-fly or other large fly that stings horses; **horse'-foot,** coltsfoot (*obs.*): a kingcrab; **horse'-god'mother** (*dial.*), a fat clumsy woman; **horse'-gow'an** (*Scot.*), the ox-eye daisy.—*n.pl.* **horse guards,** horse soldiers employed as guards: (*cap.*) the cavalry brigade of the British household troops, esp. the *Royal Horse Guards*, or *Blues*, a regiment raised in 1661: (*cap.*) their headquarters in Whitehall, London, once seat of the departments of the army commander-in-chief: the military authorities.—**horse'hair,** a hair from a horse's mane or tail: a mass of such hairs: a fabric woven from horsehair.—*adj.* made of or stuffed with horsehair.—**horse'hide; horse hoe,** a hoe drawn by horses; **horse'-knack'er,** one who buys and slaughters worn-out horses; **horse latitudes,** two zones of the Atlantic Ocean (about 30°N and 30°S, esp. the former) noted for long calms; **horse'laugh,** a harsh, boisterous laugh; **horse'-leech,** a horse-doctor (*obs.*): a large species of leech, so named from its fastening on horses: a bloodsucker (Prov. xxx. 15); **horseless carriage** (*arch.*), a motor-car; **horse'-litt'er,** a litter or bed borne between two horses: bedding for horses; **horse mackerel,** the scad or allied fish: the tunny: applied to various other fishes; **horse'man,** a rider: one skilled in managing a horse: a mounted soldier: one who has charge of horses: a kind of carrier pigeon: a kind of land-crab; **horse'manship,** the art of riding and of training and managing horses; **horse marine,** a person quite out of his element: a member of an imaginary corps; **horse'meat,** food for horses; **horse mill,** a mill turned by horses; **horse'-mill'iner** (*arch.*), one who provides the trappings for horses; **horse'mint,** any wild mint: the American *Monarda punctata* (**sweet horsemint,** the common dittany); **horse mushroom,** a large coarse mushroom; **horse mussel,** a mollusc (*Modiolus*) akin to the common mussel but much bigger; **horse nail,** a nail for fastening a horseshoe to the hoof; **horse opera,** a Wild West film; **horse pistol,** a large pistol formerly carried in a holster by horsemen; **horse'play,** rough, boisterous play; **horse'pond,** a pond for watering horses at; **horse'power,** the power a horse can exert, or its conventional equivalent (taken as 746 watt); **horse race,** a race by horses; **horse racing,** the practice of racing or running horses in matches; **horse'radish,** plant allied to scurvy-grass with a pungent root, used as a condiment; **horse'radish tree,** a tree, *Moringa pterygosperma*, cultivated in tropical countries for its edible capsules and its seeds, ben-nuts, which yield oil of ben—the roots tasting like horseradish: an Australian tree, *Codonocarpus cotinifolius*, with leaves of horseradish flavour; **horse rake,** a rake drawn by horses; **horse'-rid'ing; horse sense** (*coll.*), plain common sense; **horse'shoe,** a shoe for horses, consisting of a curved piece of iron: anything of like shape.— *adj.* shaped like a horseshoe.—**horse'shoer** (*-shōō'ər*), one who makes or affixes horseshoes; **horse'shoe'ing;** (African) **horse'-sick'ness,** a serious disease of horses, due to a virus; **horse soldier,** a cavalry soldier; **horse'tail,** a horse's tail: a Turkish standard, marking rank by number: any plant of the genus Equisetum (scouring-rush) with hollow rush-like stems, constituting with kindred fossils a class of fern-allies, Equisetinae; **horse'-thief; horse'-trading,** hard bargaining; **horse'-train'er,** one who trains horses for racing, etc.; **horse'way,** a road by which a horse may pass; **horse'whip,** a whip for driving horses.—*v.t.* to thrash with a horsewhip: to lash.—**horse'-wom'an,** a woman who rides on horseback, or who rides well.—**dark horse** (see **dark**); **flog a dead horse**, to try to work up excitement about a threadbare subject; **gift horse** (see **gift**); **high horse** (see **on one's high horse** (under **high**)); **hold your horses**, not so fast: wait a moment; **horse and hattock** (see **hattock**, at **hat**); **horse around** (*slang*), to fool about; **horses for courses**, phrase expressing the view that each racehorse will do best on a certain course which peculiarly suits it: also *fig.*; **horse of a different colour**, another thing altogether; **put the cart before the horse** (see **cart**); **(straight) from the horse's mouth**, from a very trustworthy source; **take horse**, to mount on horseback; **white horse** (see **white**); **willing horse**, a willing, obliging, worker. [O.E. *hors*; O.N. *hross*; O.H.G. *hros* (Ger. *ross*).]

**horson** (*Shak.*). Same as **whoreson**.

**horst**, *hörst*, (*geol.*) *n.* a block of the earth's crust that has remained in position while the ground around it has either subsided or been folded into mountains by pressure against its solid sides. [Ger.]

**hortative**, *hört'ə-tiv*, *adj.* inciting: encouraging: giving advice.—Also **hort'atory**.—*n.* **hortā'tion**. [L. *hortārī*, *-ātus*, to incite.]

**horticulture**, *hör'ti-kul-chər*, *n.* the art of gardening.—*adj.* **horticul'tural**.—*n.* **horticul'turist**, one versed in the art of cultivating gardens. [L. *hortus*, a garden, *cultūra—colĕre*, to cultivate.]

**hortus siccus**, *hör'təs sik'əs, hor'tŏŏs sik'ŏŏs*, (L.), a collection of dried plants: a herbarium.

**hosanna**, *hō-zan'ə*, *n.* an exclamation of praise to God. [Gr. *hōsanna*—Heb. *hōshi'āh nnā, hōshiā'*, save, *nā*, I pray.]

**hose**, *hōz*, *n.* a covering for the legs or feet: stockings: socks (*half-hose*): close-fitting breeches or drawers (*obs.*): a flexible pipe for conveying water, etc., so called from its shape: a socket for a shaft:—*pl.* **hose**; **hos'en** (*arch.*); in some of pipe, *pl.* **hos'es**.—*v.t.* to provide with hose (*arch.*): to play a hose on.—*adj.* **hosed**.—*ns.* **hosier** (*hōzh'(y)ər, hōz'yər*), a dealer in or a maker of hosiery; **hō'siery**, hose collectively: knitted goods.—**hose'man**, a fireman who directs the stream of water; **hose'-net** (*Scot.*), a stocking-shaped net; **hose'pipe**; **hose'-reel**, a large revolving drum for carrying hose. [O.E. *hosa*, pl. *hosan*, Du. *hoos*, Ger. *hose*.]

**hospice**, *hos'pis*, *n.* a house of entertainment for strangers, esp. one kept by monks: a hostel: a home of refuge. [Fr.,—L. *hospitium—hospes*, *-itis*, a stranger, guest.]

**hospitable**, *hos'pit-ə-bl*, or *hos-pit'*, *adj.* kind to strangers: welcoming and generous towards guests.—*n.* **hos'pitableness** (or *-pit'*).—*adv.* **hos'pitably** (or *-pit'*).—*ns.* **hospitage** (*hos'pit-ij*; *Spens.*), that which is due from a guest; **hospitality** (see under **hospital**). [L.L. *hospitāgium*—L. *hospes*, *-itis*, stranger, guest.]

**hospital**, *hos'pit-l*, *n.* a hostel for travellers (*obs.*): formerly, a charitable institution for the old or destitute, or for reception (and education) of the needy young: an institution for treatment of sick or injured: a building for any of these purposes.—*ns.* **hos'pitale** (*-āl*; *Spens.*), lodging; **hospitalisā'tion**, *-z-*.—*v.t.* **hos'pitalise**, **-ize**, to send to hospital.—*ns.* **hospitality** (*-al'i-ti*), (friendly welcome and) entertainment of guests; —also *fig.*; **hos'pitaller** (*U.S. -pitaler*), one of a charitable brotherhood for the care of the sick in hospitals: one of the Knights of St John (otherwise called Knights of Rhodes, and afterwards of Malta), an order which built a hospital for pilgrims at Jerusalem.—**hos'pital-ship'**, a ship fitted out exclusively for the treatment and transport of the sick and wounded. [O.Fr. *hospital*—L.L. *hospitāle—hospes*, *-itis*, a guest.]

**hospitium**, *hos-pish'i-əm*, *n.* a hospice:—*pl.* **hospit'ia**. [L.; cf. **hospice**.]

**hospodar**, *hos'po-där*, (*hist.*) *n.* a prince or governor, esp. of Moldavia or Wallachia.—Also **gos'podar**. [Rum. *hospodár*, of Slav. origin.]

**hoss**, *hos*, (*U.S.* and *coll.*) *n.* a horse.

**host**, *hōst*, *n.* one who entertains a stranger or guest at his house without (or with) reward—*fem.* **host'ess**: an innkeeper—*fem.* **host'ess**: an organism on which another lives as a parasite. —*v.t.* (*Spens.* and *U.S.*), to receive and entertain as one's guest.—*v.i.* (*Spens., Shak.*) to lodge, to be a guest.—*ns.* **host'ess**, see **host**: a paid female partner at a dance-hall, nightclub, etc.:—also *v.t.* (*obs.* and *U.S.*) and *v.i.* (*obs.*); **host'ess-ship**, the character or office of a hostess.—*adj.* **host'esse** (*Spens.*), inhospitable.—*n.* **host'ry** (*Spens.*), lodging.—**air'-hostess**, one appointed to look after the comfort of the passengers in an aircraft; **lie at host** (*Shak.*), to be lodged; **reckon**, or **count, without one's host**, to count up one's bill without reference to the landlord: fail to take account of some important possibility, as the action of another. [O.Fr. *hoste*—L. *hospes, hospitis*.]

**host**, *hōst*, *n.* an army (*arch.*): a great multitude.—*n.* **host'ing**, a battle (*Milt.*): a muster, a military expedition (*Spens.*).—**a host in himself**, one of great strength, skill, or resources, within himself; **heavenly host**, the angels and archangels; **Lord of hosts**, a favourite Hebrew term for Jehovah, considered as head of the hosts of angels, the hosts of stars, etc. [O.Fr. *host*—L. *hostis*, an enemy.]

**host**, *hōst*, *n.* a sacrificial victim (*obs.*): (often *cap.*) in the R.C. Church, the consecrated wafer of the eucharist. [L. *hostia*, a victim.]

**Hosta**, *hōst'ə*, *n.* a genus of decorative perennial herbaceous plants (fam. *Liliaceae*) from Asia with ribbed basal leaves and blue, white, and lilac flowers. [After Austrian botanist N. T. *Host*.]

**hostage**, *hos'tij*, *n.* one kept in the hands of an enemy as a pledge.—**hostages to fortune**, the people and things one most values most (Bacon's *Essays*: Of Marriage and Single Life). [O.Fr. *hostage* (Fr. *ôtage*)—L. *obses, obsidis*, a hostage.]

**hostel**, *hos'tal*, *n.* an inn: in some universities an extra-collegiate hall for students: a residence for students or for some class or society of persons, esp. one not run commercially: a youth hostel.—*ns.* **hos'teler**, **hos'teller**, hospitaller (*arch.*): keeper of a hostel: one who lives in, or uses, a hostel; **hos'telling**, making sojourns in youth hostels; **hos'telry**, an inn. [O.Fr. *hostel*, **hostellerie**—L. *hospitāle*; cf. **hospital**.]

**hostile**, *hos'til*, in *U.S.* *-təl*, *adj.* pertaining to an enemy: showing enmity or unfriendliness, or angry opposition: resistant (to; esp. to new ideas, changes): (of place, conditions) inhospitable, harsh: engaged in hostilities: pertaining to hostilities.—*adv.* **hos'tilely**.—*n.* **hostility** (*-til'*), enmity:—*pl.* **hostil'ities**, acts of warfare. [L. *hostilis—hostis*.]

**hostler.** See **ostler**.

**hot**, *hot*, *adj.* having a high temperature: very warm: fiery: pungent: giving a feeling suggestive of heat: animated: ardent: vehement: violent: passionate: sexually excited: lustful: dangerously charged with electricity: dangerous: near the object sought: of news, fresh, exciting: of jazz, etc., music which is intensely played with complex rhythms and exciting improvisations: skilful (*coll.*): recently obtained dishonestly (*coll.*): highly radioactive (*coll.*).—*adv.* **hotly**.—*v.t.* (*coll.*) to heat.—*n.* **hot'ness**.—*adj.* **hott'ish**.—**hot air**, empty talk.—*adjs.* **hot'-air**, making use of heated air: boastful, empty; **hot'-and-hot'**, cooked and served up at once in hot dishes.—Also *n.*—**hot'bed**, a glass-covered bed heated by a layer of fermenting manure for bringing forward plants rapidly: a place favourable to rapid growth or development, usu. of a bad kind (*fig.*); **hot blast**, a blast of heated air.—*adj.* **hot'-blood'ed**, having hot blood: homothermous: passionate: ardent: high-spirited: irritable.—**hot'-brain** (*arch.*), a hot-head.—*adj.* **hot'-brained** (*arch.*).—**hot'-cock'les**, an old game in which one with eyes covered guesses who strikes him; **hot coppers** (see **copper**); **hot dog**, a hot sausage sandwich; **hot flue** (*obs.*), a drying-room.—*adv.* **hot'foot**, in haste.—**hot gospeller**, a revivalist preacher; **hot'head**, an impetuous headstrong person.—*adj.* **hot'head'ed.**—**hot'house**, a house kept hot for the rearing of tropical or tender plants: any heated chamber or drying-room, esp. that where pottery is placed before going into the kiln: a hot-bathing establishment (*obs.*): a brothel (*Shak.*); **hot line**, special telephone and tele-printer link with Kremlin, orig. one from Washington: any line of speedy communication ready for an emergency.—*adj.* **hot'-liv'ered** (*Milt.*), hot-tempered.—**hot money**, funds trans-ferred suddenly from one country to another because conditions make transfer financially advantageous.—*adj.* **hot'-mouthed** (*obs.*), restive, as when the bit hurts.—**hot plate**, the flat top surface of a stove for cooking: a similar plate, independently heated, for keeping things hot; **hot'pot**, a dish of chopped mutton seasoned and stewed in a pot, with sliced potatoes, or similar mixture.—*v.t.* **hot'-press**, to press between hot plates to produce a glossy surface.—**hot rod** (*U.S. slang*), a motor-car converted for speed by stripping off non-essentials and heightening in power; **hot rodder** (*U.S. slang*), the owner of a hot rod: a reckless youth; **hot seat**, the electric chair (*U.S. slang*): any uncomfortable situation (*fig.*).—*adjs.* **hot'-short**, brittle when heated; **hot'-spir'ited**, having a fiery spirit.—**Hot'spur**, a violent, brash man like Henry Percy (1364-1403), so nicknamed; **hot stuff** (*slang*), any person, thing, or performance that is outstandingly remarkable, excellent, vigorous, or reprehensible.—*adj.* **hot'-tem'pered**, having a quick temper.—**hot'-trod** (*Scot.*), the hot pursuit in old Border forays; **hot wall**, a wall enclosing passages for hot air, affording warmth to fruit-trees; **hot war**, real war, not cold war; **hot water** (*coll.*), a state of trouble; **hot well**, a spring of hot water: in a condensing engine, a reservoir for the warm water drawn off from the condenser.—**go, sell, like hot cakes**, to sell off or disappear promptly; **hot cross-bun**, a bun bearing a cross, customarily eaten on Good Friday; **hot on** (*coll.*), ford of, interested in: good at, well-informed about; **hot under the collar**, indignant, embar-rassed; **make it hot for**, to make it unpleasant or impossible for. [O.E. *hāt*; Ger. *heiss*, Sw. *het*.]

**hot**, *hot*, **hote**, *hōt*, (*Spens.*), named: was called. [Pa.t. active and passive of **hight**.]

**hotch**, *hoch*, (*Scot.*) *v.t.* and *v.i.* to hitch, jog: to fidget with eagerness. [Cf. Du. *hotsen*, Fr. *hocher*.]

**hotchpotch**, *hoch'poch*, **hotchpot**, *hoch'pot*, **hodge-podge**, *hoj'poj*, *n.* a confused mass of ingredients shaken or mixed together in the same pot: a kind of mutton-broth with vegetables of many kinds: a jumble.—*n.* **hotchpot**, a commixture of property in order to secure an equable division amongst children. [Fr. *hochepot*—*hocher*, to shake, and *pot*, a pot; cf. Du. *hutspot*.]

**hotel**, *hō-tel'* (old-fashioned *ō-tel'*), *n.* a house for the accommodation of strangers: an inn: in France, also a public office, a private town-house, a palace.—**hôtel de ville** (Fr. *ō-tel də vēl*), a town hall; **hôtel-Dieu** (Fr. *ō-tel-dyø*), a hos-pital; **hotelier**, *hō-tel'yər* (Fr. *hôtelier*; *ōt-ə-lyä*), **hotel'-keeper**. [Fr. *hôtel*—L. *hospitālia*, guest-chambers—*hospes*.]

**Hottentot**, *hot'n-tot*, *n.* one of a dwindling,

nomad, pastoral, pale-brown race in S.-W. Africa (resembling Bushmen and Bantu), calling themselves *khoi-khoin* (men of men): their language: a barbarian: (without *cap.*) a small fish *Pachymetopon blochii*.—Also *adj.*—**Hotten-tot fig**, the edible fruit of a Mesembrianthemum; **Hottentot's bread**, elephant-foot; **Hottentot's god**, praying mantis. [Du. imit.; the language was unintelligible to them and sounded staccato.]

**hotter**, *hot'er*, (*Scot.*) *v.i.* to vibrate: to tremble: to clatter: to totter: to jolt: to swarm.—*n.* vibration: commotion: swarming. [Cf. Flem. *hotteren*.]

**houdah.** See **howdah.**

**houdan**, *hōō'dan*, *n.* a black and white five-toed domestic fowl of a breed orig. from *Houdan* in Seine-et-Oise.

**hough**, *hok* (*Scot. hohh*). See **hock** (1).

**hound**, *hownd*, *n.* a dog (*arch., coll.*): a dog of a kind used in hunting: a pursuer in a paper-chase: a contemptible scoundrel: a hunter, tracker, or assiduous seeker of anything: an addict, devotee—often in composition.—*v.t.* to set on in chase: to drive by harassing.—**hound'-fish**, a dog-fish; **hounds'-berry**, dogwood; **hounds'-foot** (Ger. *hundsfott*, *-futt*, vulva can-ina), a scoundrel.—*adj.* (*Scott*) scoundrelly.—**hound's'-tongue**, a plant (Cynoglossum) of the borage family (from its leaf); **hound's'-tooth**, a textile pattern of broken checks.—Also *adj.*—**hound'-trailing**, speed competition between hounds trained to follow an aniseed trail.—**Gabriel('s) hounds** (*coll.*), the yelping noise made by flights of wild-geese, ascribed to damned souls whipped on by the angel Gabriel; **master of hounds**, the master of a pack of hounds. [O.E. *hund*; Gr. *kyōn, kynos*, L. *canis*, Sans. *śva*.]

**hour**, *owr*, *n.* 60 minutes, or the 24th part of a day: the time as indicated by a clock, etc.: an hour's journey, or three miles: a time or occasion: an angular unit (15°) of right ascension: (in *pl.*) the goddesses of the seasons and the hours (*myth.*): set times of prayer, the *canonical hours*, the offices or services prescribed for these, or a book containing them, often illustrated (also **book of hours**): (*pl.*) the prescribed times for doing business.—*adj.* **hour'ly**, happening or done every hour: frequent.—*adv.* every hour: frequently.—**hour'-ang'le** (*astron.*), the angle (usu. measured as time) between the declination circle of a body observed and the observer's meridian; **hour'-cir'cle**, a great circle passing through the celestial poles: the circle of an equatorial which shows the right ascension; **hour'-glass**, an instrument for measuring the hours by the running of sand through a narrow neck.—*adj.* having the form of an hour-glass: constricted.—**hour'-hand**, the hand which shows the hour on a clock, etc.; **hour'plate**, a time-piece dial.—**at all hours**, at irregular hours, esp. late hours; **at the eleventh hour**, at the last moment (Matt. xx. 6, 9); **in a good, or evil, hour**, under a fortunate, or an unfortunate, impulse—from the old belief in astrological influences; **keep good hours**, to go to bed and to rise early: to lead a quiet and regular life. [O.Fr. *hore* (Fr. *heure*)—L. *hora*—Gr. *hōrā*.]

**houri**, *hōō'ri*, *how'ri*, *n.* a nymph of the Moham-medan paradise: a voluptuously alluring woman. [Pers. *hūrī*—Ar. *hūriya*, a black-eyed girl.]

**house**, *hows*, *n.* a building for dwelling in: a building in general: a dwelling-place: an inn: a public-house: a household: a family in line of descent: kindred: a trading establishment: one of the twelve divisions of the heavens in astrology: a legislative or deliberative body or its meeting-place: a convent: school boarding-house: pupils of such collectively: section of a school where no such boarding-house exists:

an audience, auditorium, or performance: the workhouse (*old. coll.*): (the House) at Oxford, Christ Church (*Aedes Christi*): in London, the Stock Exchange, the Houses of Parliament: a gambling form of lotto, bingo:—*pl.* houses, *howz'iz.—adj.* domestic.—*v.t.* house (*howz*), to protect by covering: to shelter: to store: to provide houses for.—*v.i.* to take shelter: to reside.—*n.* house'ful (*pl.* house'fuls).—*adj.* house'less, without a house or home: having no shelter.—*n.* housing (*howz'ing*), houses, accommodation, or shelter, or the provision thereof: a cavity into which a timber fits: housing joint.— Also *adj.*—house'-a'gent, one who arranges the buying, selling, and letting of houses; house'-arrest', confinement, under guard, to one's house, or to a hospital, etc., instead of imprisonment; house'-boat, a barge with a deck-cabin that may serve as a dwelling-place; house'-bote, a tenant's right to wood to repair his house; house'-break'er, one who breaks into and enters a house for the purpose of stealing: one whose work is demolishing old houses; house'-break'-ing; house'-carl (*hist.*), member of a king's or noble's bodyguard; house'-coat, a woman's long dress, formed like a coat, worn at home; house'craft, skill in domestic activities; house'-dog, a dog kept in a house: a watch-dog; house'-dū'ty, -tax, a tax laid on inhabited houses; house'-fac'tor (*Scot.*), a house-agent; house'-fa'ther, the male head of a household or community: a man in charge of children in an institution; house'-flag, the distinguishing flag of a shipowner or shipping company; house'-fly, the common fly universally distributed; house'-hold, those who are held together in the same house, and compose a family.—*adj.* pertaining to the house and family.—house'holder, the holder or tenant of a house; household gods, (see god, lar, penates); household suffrage, or franchise, the right of householders to vote for members of parliament; household troops, Guards regiments whose peculiar duty is to attend the sovereign and defend the metropolis; household word, a familiar saying or name; house'keeper, a person employed to keep house: one who has the chief care of a house: one who stays much at home: a dispenser of hospitality (*obs.*): a watch-dog (*obs.*); house'keeping, the keeping or management of a house or of domestic affairs: hospitality (*obs.*).—*adj.* domestic.—house'-leek, a plant (*Sempervivum tectorum*) of the stonecrop family with succulent leaves, often growing on roofs; house lights (*theatre*), the lights illuminating the auditorium; house'-line (*naut.*), a small line of three strands, for seizings, etc.; house'maid, a maid employed to keep a house clean, etc.; housemaid's knee, an inflammation of the sac between the knee-pan and the skin, to which those whose work involves frequent kneeling are specially liable; house'man, a recent graduate in medicine holding a junior resident post in a hospital; house'master, the head of a boarding-house in connection with a public school; house'-mate, one sharing a house with another; house'-moth'er, the mother of a family, the female head of a family: a woman in charge of children in an institution; house'-par'ty, a company of guests spending some days in a country-house. —*adj.* house'-proud, taking a pride in the condition of one's house.—house'-room, room or place in a house; house'-stew'ard, a steward who manages the household affairs of a great family; house'-sur'geon, a resident surgeon in a hospital—so also house'-physi'cian.—*adj.* house'-to-house, performed or conducted by calling at house after house.—house'top, the top or roof of a house.—*adj.* house'-trained, of animals, taught to be cleanly indoors: of

human beings, well-mannered (*coll.*).—house'-warm'ing, an entertainment given after moving into a new house; housewife (*hows'wif*, formerly *huz'if*), the mistress and manager of a house: (*huz'if*) a pocket sewing-outfit.—*adj.* house'-wifely.—*ns.* housewifery (*hows'wif-ri, -wif-ri, huz'if-ri*).—*ns.* house'wifeship, (*Scot.*) -skep; house'work, domestic work; house'y-house'y (*gambling*), house.—housing estate, a planned residential area, esp. one built by a local authority; hous'ing (joint), a joint where the end of one board fits into a groove cut across another board; housing scheme, a plan for the designing, building, and provision of houses, esp. by a local authority: sometimes applied to an area coming under such a plan.—bring down the house, to evoke very loud applause in a place of entertainment; house longhorn beetle (see long); house of call, a house where the journeymen of a particular trade call when out of work: a house that one often visits; house of correction, a jail; house of God, prayer, or worship, a place of worship; house of ill-fame, a brothel; House of Commons, Lords, Peers, Representatives (see common, lord, peer, represent); House of the People, the lower house of the Indian parliament; Inner House, the higher branch of the Court of Session, its jurisdiction chiefly appellate; Outer House, the lower branch of the Court of Session; keep a good house, to keep up a plentifully supplied table; keep house, to maintain or manage an establishment; keep open house, to give entertainment to all comers; keep the house, to remain indoors: to take charge of the house or be on watch for the time being: to be confined to the house; like a house on fire, afire, with astonishing rapidity; on the house, of drinks, at the publican's expense; set up house, to start a domestic life of one's own; the Household, the royal domestic establishment. [O.E. *hūs*; Goth, *hūs*, Ger. *haus*.]

housel, *howz'əl*, *n.* the eucharist: the act of taking or administering it.—*v.t.* to administer the eucharist to:—*pa.p.* hous'elled.—*n.* hous'elling.—*adj.* (*Spens.*) hous'ling, sacramental. [O.E. *hūsel*, sacrifice.]

housing, *howz'ing*, *n.* an ornamental covering for a horse: a saddle-cloth: (in *pl.*) the trappings of a horse. [O.Fr. *houce*, a mantle, of Gmc. origin.]

hout, hout-tout, houts-touts. Same as hoot, etc.

Houyhnhnm, (h)*win'əm*, *n.* one of the noble and rational race of horses in Swift's *Gulliver's Travels*. [Perh. whinny.]

Hova, huv'ə, hōv'ə, *n.* one of the dominant race in Madagascar, esp. of the middle class:—*pl.* Hova, Hovas.

hove, hōv, hōōv, Scot. hüv, *v.t.* to swell.—*v.i.* to swell: to rise (*Spens.*). [Perh. a form of heave.]

hove, hoove, hōōv, (*Spens.*) *v.i.* to hover: to loiter, linger. [Origin unknown.]

hove, *pa.t.* and *pa.p.* of heave.

hovel, *hov'əl, huv'əl, n.* a small or wretched dwelling: a shed: a framework for a corn-stack (*dial.*).—*v.t.* to put in a hovel: to shelter: to build like a hovel or shed, as a chimney with side opening.—hov'el-post, a post for supporting a corn-stack. [Origin doubtful.]

hoveller, *hov', huv'(ə-)lər, n.* a boatman acting as an uncertificated pilot or doing any kind of occasional work on the coast: a small coasting-vessel. [Origin doubtful.]

hoven, *hō'vən.* See hoove.

hover, *hov'ər, huv'ər, v.i.* to remain aloft flapping the wings: to remain suspended: to linger: to move about near.—*v.t.* to brood over.—*n.* act or state of hovering: a helicopter (*U.S.*): an apparatus for keeping chicks warm: in composition, describing vessels, vehicles, or stationary objects, resting on a cushion of air, e.g.

Neutral vowels in unaccented syllables: el'ə-mənt; for certain sounds in foreign words, see p. viii

hov′ercraft (a craft able to move at a short distance above the surface of sea or land supported by a down-driven blast of air); hov′erbarrow, -bus, -car, -train, hover-bed (which supports patient on film of warm air).—*adv.* hov′eringly.—hov′er-fly, a syrphid or other wasp-like fly that hovers and darts. [Perh.— hove (2).]

how, *how, adv.* in what manner: to what extent: by what means: in what condition: for what reason: to what an extent, in what a degree: that.—*n.* manner, method.— and how (*U.S. slang*), yes, certainly: very much indeed: I should think so indeed; how are you, a conventional greeting to an acquaintance: sometimes specifically referring to his or her state of health; how about, what do you think of; how come, how does that come about; how-do-you-do (see do); how now, what is this: why is this so; how's that (*how-zat′*; *cricket*), the appeal of the fielding side to the umpire to give the batsman out; the how and the why, the manner and the cause. [O.E. *hū*, prob. an adverbial form from *hwā*, who.]

how, howe, *how,* (*Scot.*) *n.* a hollow. [hole.]
how, *how,* (*dial.*) *n.* a low hill. [O.N. *haugr*; cf. O.E. *hēah*, high.]

howbeit, *how-bē′it, conj.* be it how it may: notwithstanding: yet: however—(*Spens.*) howbe′. [how, be, it.]

howdah, houdah, *how′da, n.* a pavilion or seat fixed on an elephant's back. [Ar. *haudaj.*]

howdie, howdy, *how′di,* (*Scot.*) *n.* a midwife. [Poss. O.E. *hold*, gracious.]

howdy, *how′di, interj.* a colloquial form of the common greeting, *How do you do?*—how′-d′ye-do′, how′dy-do′, a troublesome state of matters.

however, *how-ev′ər, adv.* and *conj.* in whatever manner or degree: nevertheless: at all events. [how, ever.]

howff, houff, *howf,* (*Scot.*) *n.* a haunt, resort.—*v.i.* to resort to a place. [Poss. O.E. *hof*, a house.]

howitzer, *how′its-ər, n.* a short, squat gun, used for shelling at a steep angle, esp. in siege and trench warfare. [Ger. *haubitze*—Czech *houfnice*, a sling.]

howk, *howk,* (*Scot.*) *v.t.* and *v.i.* to dig, burrow. [Earlier *holk*; cf. L.G. *holken.*]

howker, *how′kər, n.* Same as hooker.

howl, *howl, v.i.* to yell or cry, as a wolf or dog: to utter a long, loud, whining sound: to wail: to roar.—*v.t.* to utter with outcry:—*pr.p.* howl′ing; *pa.t.* and *pa.p.* howled.—*n.* a loud, prolonged cry of distress: a mournful cry: a loud sound like a yell, made by the wind, a wireless receiver, etc.—*n.* howl′er, one who howls: a S. American monkey, with prodigious power of voice: a glaring and amusing blunder (*slang*).— *adj.* howl′ing, filled with howlings, as of the wind, or of wild beasts: tremendous (*slang*).—*n.* a howl. [O.Fr. *huller*—L. *ululāre*, to shriek or howl—*ulula*, an owl; cf. Ger. *heulen*, Eng. owl.]

howlet, *how′lit, n.* an owlet: (*Scot. hōōl′it*) an owl. [owlet.]

howre, an obs. form of hour.

howso, *how′sō,* (*obs.*) *adv.* howsoever.

howsoever, *how-sō-ev′ər, adv.* in what way soever: although: however.—Provincial forms are howsomev′er and howsomdev′er. [how, so, ever; and M.E. *sum*, as.]

hox, *hoks,* (*Shak.*) *v.t.* to hock or hamstring. [O.E. *hōhsinu*, hock-sinew.]

hoy, *hoi, n.* a large one-decked boat, commonly rigged as a sloop. [M.Du. *hoei*; Du. *heu*, Flem. *hui.*]

hoy, *hoi, interj.* ho! stop!—*v.t.* to incite, drive on.

hoyden, hoiden, *hoi′dən, n.* a tomboy, a romp: formerly also *masc.*—*ns.* hoy′denhood, hoy′denism.—*adj.* hoy′denish. [Perh. Du. *heiden*, a heathen, a gypsy, *heide*, heath.]

huanaco. Same as guanaco.

hub, *hub, n.* the nave of a wheel: a mark at which quoits, etc. are cast.—hub′-brake, a brake acting on the hub of a wheel; hub′-cap, a metal covering over the end of an axle.—hub of the universe, Boston, U.S.A. [Prob. a form of hob (1); origin unknown.]

hubble-bubble, *hub′l-bub′l, n.* a bubbling sound: tattle: confusion: a crude kind of hookah. [Reduplic. from bubble.]

hubbub, *Shak.* whoobub, *hub′ub, n.* a confused sound of many voices: riot: uproar.—Also hubb′uboo. [App. of Irish origin.]

hubby, *hub′i,* (*coll.*) *n.* a diminutive of husband.

hubris, *hū′bris,* hybris, *hī′bris, n.* insolence: arrogance, such as invites disaster: overweening. —*adj.* hubris′tic.—*adv.* hubris′tically. [Gr. *hybris.*]

huckaback, *huk′ə-bak, n.* a coarse linen or cotton with raised surface, used for towels, etc. [Origin unknown.]

huckle, *huk′l, n.* the haunch: the hip.—Also huck. —*adjs.* huck′le-backed, -shoul′dered, having the back or shoulders round.—huckle′-bone, the hip-bone: the astragalus. [Poss. conn. with hook.]

huckleberry, *huk′l-bər-i, -ber-i, n.* a N. American shrub (Gaylussacia) akin to whortleberry: its fruit: extended to species of whortleberry.—*n.* huck′leberrying. [App. for hurtleberry.]

huckster, *huk′stər, n.* a retailer of smallwares, a hawker or pedlar: a mean, haggling fellow.— *v.i.* to deal in small articles: to higgle meanly. —*ns.* huck′sterage; huck′steress, huck′stress; huck′stery. [Origin obscure.]

hudden. See haud.

huddle, *hud′l, v.t.* to hustle out of sight, hush up (*obs.*): to jumble: to hustle, bundle: to drive, draw, throw or crowd together in disorder: to put hastily: to perform perfunctorily and hastily.—*v.i.* to crowd in confusion.—*n.* a confused mass: a jumble: confusion: perfunctory haste: a gathering of the team behind their line of scrimmage so as to receive instructions, signals, etc. (*U.S. football*): a secret conference: a period of deep consideration of a problem.— *adj.* hudd′led, jumbled: crowded: in a heap: crouching. [Poss. conn. with hide.]

huddup, *hud-up′,* (*U.S.*) *interj.* get up (to a horse).

Hudibrastic, *hū-di-bras′tik, adj.* similar in style to *Hudibras*, a metrical burlesque on the Puritans by Samuel Butler (1612-80).—*n.pl.* Hudibras′tics, verses of the form used in *Hudibras*, a burlesque cacophonous octosyllabic couplet with extravagant rhymes.

hue (*Spens.* hew), *hū, n.* appearance: colour: tint: dye.—*adjs.* hued, having a hue; hue′less. [O.E. *hiow, hēow* (W.S. *hiw, hiew*); Sw. *hy*, complexion.]

hue, *hū, n.* a shouting, clamour.—*n.* hu′er, a pilchard fishermen's lookout man.—hue and cry, an outcry calling upon all to pursue one who is to be made prisoner: a proclamation or publication to the same effect: the pursuit itself: a loud clamour about something. [Imit.; perh. Fr. *huer.*]

huff, *huf, n.* a puff of wind (*obs.*): bluster (*obs.*): a blusterer (*obs.*): a fit of anger, sulks, or offended dignity: an act of huffing in draughts. —*v.t.* to puff up (*obs.*): to hector: to give offence: (in draughts) to remove from the board for omitting capture.—*v.i.* to blow, puff, swell (*obs.*): to take offence: to bluster.—*n.* a bully, blusterer (*obs.*).—*adjs.* huff′ish, huff′y, given to huff: touchy: ready to take offence.— *advs.* huff′ishly, huff′ily.—*ns.* huff′ishness, huff′iness.—*adj.* huff′-cap (*obs.*), of liquor, heady: blustering. [Imit.]

hug, *hug, v.t.* to clasp close with the arms: to cherish: to keep close to, skirt:—*pr.p.* hugg′ing;

*pa.t.* and *pa.p.* **hugged**.—*n.* a close embrace: a particular grip in wrestling.—**hug'-me-tight**, a close-fitting knitted garment.—**hug oneself**, to congratulate oneself. [Ety. obscure.]

**huge**, *hūj*, *adj.* vast: enormous.—*adv.* **huge'ly**.— *n.* **huge'ness**.—*adj.* **huge'ous** (*arch.*), huge.—*adv.* **huge'ously**.—*n.* **huge'ousness**.—*adj.* **hug'y** (*arch.*). [O.Fr. *ahuge.*]

**hugger-mugger**, *hug'ər-mug'ər*, *n.* secrecy: confusion.—*adj.* secret: disorderly.—*adv.* in secrecy or disorder. [Origin obscure.]

**Huguenot**, *hū'gə-not*, or *-nō*, (*hist.*) *n.* a French Protestant.—Also *adj.* [Fr.,—earlier *eiguenot*— Ger. *eidgenoss*, confederate, assimilated to the name *Hugues*, Hugh.]

**huia**, *hōō'yə*, *n.* a New Zealand bird (*Heteralocha acutirostris*) akin to the crows and starlings, now prob. extinct. [Maori; imit.]

**huissier**, *wē-syā*, (Fr.) a doorkeeper, usher: a bailiff.

**huitain**, *wē-tān'*, *n.* a group of eight lines of verse. [Fr.,—*huit*, eight.]

**hula-hula**, *hōō'lə-hōō'lə*, *n.* a Hawaiian women's dance.—Also **hu'la**.—**hu'la-hoop**, a light hoop used in the diversion of keeping the hoop in motion about the waist by swinging movement of the hips. [Hawaiian.]

**hule**. Same as ule.

**hulk**, *hulk*, *n.* an unwieldy ship: a dismantled ship: a big lubberly fellow: anything unwieldy: often by confusion, a hull:—*pl.* (with *the*) old ships formerly used as prisons.—*adjs.* **hulk'ing**, **hulk'y**, clumsy. [O.E. *hulc*, perh. Gr. *holkas*, a towed ship—*helkein*, to draw.]

**hull**, *hul*, *n.* a husk or outer covering.—*v.t.* to separate from the hull: to husk.—*adj.* **hull'y**, having husks or pods. [O.E. *hulu*, a husk, as of corn—*helan*, to cover; Ger. *hülle*, a covering, *hehlen*, to cover.]

**hull**, *hul*, *n.* the frame or body of a ship: part of a flying-boat in contact with the water: the heavily-armoured body of a tank.—*v.t.* to pierce the hull of.—*v.i.* (*Shak.*) to float or drift, as a mere hull, to float about.—*adv.* **hull'-down'**, so far away that the hull is below the horizon. [Perh. same word as above, modified in meaning by confusion with Du. *hol*, a ship's hold, or with hulk.]

**hullabaloo**, *hul-ə-bə-lōō'*, *n.* an uproar. [Perh. halloo.]

**hullo**, *hu-lō'*, *vb.*, *n.*, and *interj.* Same as hallo.

**Hulsean**, *hul'si-ən*, *adj.* of or pertaining to John *Hulse* (1708-90), founder of the Hulsean divinity lectures at Cambridge.

**hum**, *hum*, *v.i.* to make a sound like bees or that represented by *m*: to sing with closed lips without words or articulation: to pause in speaking and utter an inarticulate sound: to stammer through embarrassment: to be audibly astir: to have a strong, unpleasant smell (*slang*): to be busily active.—*v.t.* to render by humming: to applaud (*obs.*):—*pr.p.* **humm'ing**; *pa.t.* and *pa.p.* **hummed**.—*n.* the noise of bees: a murmurous sound: an inarticulate murmur: the sound of humming.—*n.* **humm'er**, a person or thing that hums, as a bee, a humming-bird, a top: one who makes things hum.—*n.* and *adj.* **humm'ing**. —**humming ale**, ale that froths up well, or that makes the head hum; **humm'ing-bird**, any member of the tropical family Trochilidae, very small birds of brilliant plumage and rapid flight (from the humming sound of the wings); **humm'ing-top**, a top that gives a humming sound as it spins.—**hum and haw** (or **ha**), to make inarticulate sounds when at a loss: to shilly-shally; **make things hum**, to set things going briskly. [Imit.; cf. Ger. *hummen*, *humsen*.]

**hum**, *hum*, *v.t.* to impose on: to hoax.—*n.* an imposition: a hoax. [Contr. of humbug.]

**hum**, *hum*, *interj.* expressing doubt or reluctance to agree.

**huma**, *hōō'mə*, *n.* a fabulous restless bird. [Pers. *humā*, phoenix.]

**human**, *hū'mən*, *adj.* belonging or pertaining to or of the nature of man or mankind: having the qualities of a man or the limitations of man: humane: not invidiously superior: genial, kind. —*n.* a human being.—*adj.* **humane** (*hū-mān'*), having the feelings proper to man: kind: tender: merciful: humanising, as *humane letters*, classical, elegant, polite.—*adv.* **humane'ly**.—*n.* **humane'ness**.—*v.t.* **humanise**, **-ize** (*hū'mən-īz*), render human or humane: soften: impart human qualities to, make like that which is human or of mankind.—*v.i.* become humane or civilised.—*ns.* **humanisā'tion**, -z-; **hū'manist**, student of polite literature: at the Renaissance, a student of Greek and Roman literature: a student of human nature: advocate of any system of humanism: a pragmatist.—Also *adj.* —*n.* **hū'manism**, literary culture: any system which puts human interests and the mind of man paramount, rejecting the supernatural: pragmatism (*phil.*): a critical application of the logical method of pragmatism to all the sciences. —*adj.* **hūmanist'ic**.—*n.* **hu'mankind**, the human species.—*adj.* **hū'manlike**.—*adv.* **hū'manly**, in a human manner: by human agency: having regard to human limitations: humanely.—*ns.* **hū'manness**; **hū'manoid**, one of the immediate kindred of man (closer than *anthropoid*).— **human nature**, the nature of man: the qualities of character common to all men that differentiate them from other species: irrational, or, less than saintly, behaviour (often *facet.*). [Fr. *humain*—L. *hūmānus*—*homō*, a human being.]

**humanity**, *hū-man'it-i*, *n.* the nature peculiar to a human being: humanness: humaneness: the kind feelings of man: mankind collectively: in Scottish universities, Latin language and literature: (in *pl.*) grammar, rhetoric, Latin, Greek, and poetry, so called from their humanising effects.—*n.* **humanitarian** (*hū-man'i-tā'ri-ən*), one who denies Christ's divinity, and holds him to be a mere man: a philanthropist.—*adj.* of or belonging to humanity, benevolent.—*n.* **humanitā'rianism**. [Fr. *humanité*—L. *hūmānitās*—*hūmānus*—*homō*, a man.]

**humble**, *hum'bl* (old-fashioned *um'bl*), *adj.* low: lowly: modest: unpretentious: having a low opinion of oneself or of one's claims: abased. —*v.t.* to bring down to the ground: to lower: to abase: to mortify: to degrade.—*ns.* **hum'bleness**; **hum'blesse** (*Spens.*).—*adj.* and *n.* **hum'bling**. —*advs.* **hum'blingly**, **hum'bly**.—*adj.* **hum'blemouthed**, humble in speech.—**your humble servant**, an old formula used in subscribing a letter. [Fr.,—L. *humilis*, low—*humus*, the ground.]

**humble**, *hum'bl*. Same as hummel.

**humble-bee**, *hum'bl-bē*, *n.* the bumble-bee (Bombus). [Perh. from *humble*, freq. of hum; cf. Ger. *hummel*.]

**humbles**, see umbles.—**hum'ble-pie'**, a pie made from the umbles of a deer.—**eat humble-pie**, punningly, to humble, abase oneself, eat one's words, etc.

**humbug**, *hum'bug*, *n.* an imposition under fair pretences: hollowness, pretence: one who so imposes: a lump of toffee, peppermint drop, or the like.—*v.t.* to deceive: to hoax: to cajole.— *v.i.* to potter about:—*pr.p.* **hum'bugging**; *pa.t.* and *pa.p.* **hum'bugged**.—*adj.* **humbugg'able**.— *ns.* **hum'bugger**; **hum'buggery**. [Appears about 1750; origin unknown.]

**humbuzz**, *hum'buz*, (*dial.*) *n.* a cockchafer: a bullroarer. [hum, buzz.]

**humdinger**, *hum-ding'ər*, (*slang*) *n.* an exception-

ally excellent person or thing: a smooth-running engine: a swift vehicle or aircraft. [Prob. hum, and ding (1).]
**humdrum**, *hum'drum'*, *adj.* dull: droning: monotonous: commonplace.—*n.* a stupid fellow: monotony: tedious talk. [hum, and perh. drum.]
**humdudgeon**, *hum-duj'ən*, (*Scot.*) *n.* an unnecessary outcry. [hum and dudgeon (1).]
**Humean, Humian**, *hū'mi-ən*, *adj.* pertaining to David *Hume*, or his philosophy.—*n.* a follower of Hume.—*ns.* Hūm'ism, Hūm'ist.
**humect**, *hū-mekt'*, *v.t.* and *v.i.* to make or become moist.—Also **humect'ate**.—*adjs.* and *ns.* **humect'-ant, humect'ive.**—*n.* **humectā'tion.** [L. (*h)ūmec-tāre—ūmēre*, to be moist.]
**humerus**, *hū'mar-əs*, *n.* the bone of the upper arm: —*pl.* **hū'meri.**—*adj.* **hū'meral,** belonging to the shoulder or the humerus.—*n.* an oblong vestment worn on the shoulders. [L. (*h)umerus*, shoulder.]
**humgruffin**, *hum-gruf'in,* **humgruffian,** *-i-ən, n.* a terrible person. [App. hum and griffin.]
**humhum,** *hum'hum, n.* a kind of plain, coarse cotton cloth used in the East Indies.
**humic.** See under humus.
**humid,** *hū'mid, adj.* moist: damp: rather wet.— *ns.* **humidificā'tion; humid'ifier,** a device for increasing or maintaining humidity.—*v.t.* **humid'-ify,** to make humid.—*n.* **humid'ity,** moisture: a moderate degree of wetness.—*adv.* **hu'midly.**— *ns.* **hu'midness; hum'idor,** a chamber, etc., for keeping anything moist, as cigars: a contrivance for keeping the air moist. [L. (*h)ūmidus—*(*h)ūmēre*, to be moist.]
**humify,** *hū'mi-fī, v.t.* to moisten.—Also (*obs.*) **hu'mefy.**—*n.* **humificā'tion.** [L. (*h)ūmificāre*.]
**humify,** *hū'mi-fī, v.t.* and *v.i.* to make or turn into humus.—*n.* **humificā'tion.** [humus.]
**humiliate,** *hū-mil'i-āt, v.t.* to humble: to mortify. —*adjs.* **humil'iant,** humiliating; **humil'iāting;** humil'iative; humil'iatory (*-ə-tər-i*).—*ns.* **humil-iā'tion; humil'iātor.** [L. *humiliāre, -ātum.*]
**humility,** *hū-mil'i-ti, n.* the state or quality of being humble: lowliness of mind: modesty. [O.Fr. *humilite*—L. *humilitās—humilis,* low.]
**humite,** *hū'mit, n.* an orthorhombic magnesium orthosilicate also containing magnesium hydroxide, found in impure marbles. [Sir Abraham *Hume,* 19th-century mineral collector.]
**humlie.** See under hummel.
**hummaum.** Same as hammam.
**hummel,** *hum'l,* **humble,** *hum'(b)l* (*Scot.*), *adj.* hornless: awnless.—*n.* a hornless stag.—*v.t.* to make hummel.—*ns.* **hum'lie** (*Scot.*), a polled or hornless cow, etc.: **humm'eller** (*dial.*), a machine for removing barley awns.—**hummel** (usu. **hummle**) **bonnet,** a type of Scotch cap worn by Highland regiments before the introduction (1851) of the glengarry. [Cf. L.G. *hummel, hommel*.]
**hummer, humming.** See under hum (1, 2).
**hummock,** *hum'ək, n.* a hillock: a pile or ridge of ice.—*adjs.* **humm'ocked, humm'ocky.** [Origin unknown: at first nautical.]
**hummum.** Same as hammam.
**humogen,** *hū'mō-jən, n.* a fertiliser composed of peat treated with a culture of nitrogen-fixing bacteria. [L. *humus,* soil, Gr. *gennaein,* to produce.]
**humour,** in U.S. **humor,** *hū'mər, ū'mər, n.* moisture (*arch.*): a fluid: a fluid of the animal body, esp. formerly any one of the four that in an old physiology were held to determine temperament: temperament or disposition of mind: state of mind (*good, ill humour*): disposition: caprice: in Corporal Nym's vocabulary in *The Merry Wives* and *Henry V* (also as *adj.* and *v.t.,* and *adj.* **humoured**) a word of any meaning, down to no meaning at all (*Shak.*): a mental quality which apprehends and delights in the !udicrous and mirthful: that which causes mirth and amusement: playful fancy.—*v.t.* to go along with the humour of: to gratify by compliance.—*adj.* **hū'moral,** pertaining to or proceeding from a body fluid.—*ns.* **hū'moralism,** the state of being humoral: the old doctrine that diseases have their seat in the humours; **hū'moralist,** one who favoured the doctrine of humoralism; **hūmoresk', hūmoresque',** a musical caprice; **hū'morist,** one whose conduct and conversation are regulated by humour or caprice (*arch.*): one who studies or portrays the humours of people: one possessed of humour: a writer of comic stories. —*adjs.* **hūmoris'tic,** humorous; **hū'morous,** governed by humour (*arch.*): capricious (*arch.*): irregular (*arch.*): full of humour: exciting laughter.—*adv.* **hū'morously.**—*n.* **hū'morous-ness.**—*adjs.* **hū'mourless; hū'moursome,** capricious, petulant.—*n.* **hū'moursomeness.**—comedy of humours, the comedy of Ben Jonson and his school in which the characters instead of being conceived in the round are little more than personifications of single qualities: out of humour, out of temper, displeased. [O.Fr. *humor* (Fr. *humeur*)—L. (*h)ūmor—*(*h)ūmēre,* to be moist.]
**humous.** See under humus.
**hump,** *hump, n.* a hunch on the back: a protuberance: a walk with swag on back (*Austr.*): despondency (*slang*): sulks (*slang*).—*v.t.* to bend in a hump: to exert oneself (*slang*): to hurry (*slang*): to vex or annoy (*slang*): to shoulder, to carry on the back (*Austr.*).—*v.i.* to put forth effort.—*adjs.* **humped,** having a hump; **hump'y,** full of humps or protuberances.—**hump'back,** a back with a hump or hunch: a person with a humpback: a Pacific species of salmon: a whale with a humplike dorsal fin.—*adjs.* **hump'-back, hump'-backed,** having a humpback. —**hump the bluey** (*Austr.*), to be itinerant; over the hump, past the crisis or difficulty. [Origin obscure.]
**humph, hmh, huh, hmf,** *interj.* expressive of reserved doubt or dissatisfaction.
**Humphrey, to dine with Duke.** See dine.
**Humpty-dumpty,** *hum(p)'ti-dum(p)'ti, n.* a short, squat, egg-like being of nursery folklore: a gypsy drink, ale boiled with brandy.—*adj.* short and broad.
**humpy,** *hum'pi,* (*Austr.*) *n.* a hut. [Native *oompi.*]
**humstrum,** *hum'strum,* (now *dial.*) *n.* a hurdy-gurdy or other musical instrument. [hum, strum, with imit. effect.]
**humus,** *hūm'əs, n.* decomposed organic matter in the soil.—*adjs.* **hū'mic, hū'mous.** [L. *humus;* cf. Gr. *chamai,* on the ground.]
**Hun,** *hun, n.* one of a powerful squat, swarthy, and savage nomad race of Asia who moved westwards, and under Attila (433-453) overran Europe: in U.S. formerly a Hungarian: a barbarian: a German (*war slang* of 1914).— *adjs.* **Hunn'ic, Hunn'ish.** [O.E. (pl.) *Hūne, Hūnas;* L. *Hunni;* Gr. *Ounnoi, Chounnoi.*]
**hunch,** *hunch, hunsh, n.* a hump: a lump: a premonition: a hint.—*v.t.* to hump, bend.—*n.* **hunch'back,** one with a hunch or lump on his back.—*adj.* **hunch'backed.**—play one's hunch, to act on one's hunch (as a gambler might). [Origin obscure.]
**hundred,** *hun'drəd, n.* the number of ten times ten: applied also to various other numbers used in telling: a set of a hundred things: a hundred pounds, dollars, etc.: a division of a county in England orig. supposed to contain a hundred families (chiefly *hist.*):—*pl.* **hundreds,** or, preceded by a numeral, **hundred.**—*adj.* to the number of a hundred: hundredth (*obs.* or *dial*): also used indefinitely, very many (*coll.*).— *n.* **hun'dreder, -or** (*hist.*), the bailiff, or an

inhabitant, of a hundred.—*adj.*, *adv.*, and *n.* **hun′dredfold**, folded a hundred times: in a hundred divisions: a hundred times as much.—*adj.* **hun′dredth**, last of a hundred: equal to one of a hundred equal parts.—*n.* one of a hundred equal parts.—*adj.* **hun′dred-per-cent′**, out-and-out: thorough-going.—*n.* **hun′dred-percent′er** (*U.S.*), an uncompromising patriot.—*n.pl.* **hun′dreds-and-thou′sands**, little sweets used as an ornamental dressing.—**hun′dredweight**, 1/20 of a ton, or 112 lb. avoirdupois (50·80 kg.) orig. and still in U.S., 100 lb., abbrev. *cwt.* (*c* standing for L. *centum*, *wt.* for weight).—**Chiltern Hundreds**, a district of Bucks, whose stewardship is a nominal office under the Crown, the temporary acceptance of which by a member of parliament enables him to vacate his seat; **great**, or **long hundred**, usually six score: sometimes some other number greater than ten tens (as of herrings, 132 or 126); **Hundred Years′ War**, the struggle between England and France, from 1337 down to 1453; **not a hundred miles from**, at, very near; **Old Hundred** (see old); **one, two, etc. hundred hours**, one, two, etc., o′clock, from the method of writing hours and minutes 1.00, 2.00, etc.; **the Hundred Days**, time between Napoleon′s return from Elba and his final downfall after Waterloo (the reign lasted exactly 95 days, March 20-June 22, 1815). [O.E. *hundred*—old form *hund*, a hundred, with the suffix *-red*, a reckoning.]

**hung**, *pa.t.* and *pa.p.* of **hang** (*q.v.*).

**Hungarian**, *hung-gā′ri-ən*, *adj.* pertaining to *Hungary* or its inhabitants.—*n.* a person of Hungarian birth, descent, or citizenship: the Magyar or Hungarian language.—**Hungary** (*hung′gə-ri*) **water**, oil of rosemary distilled with alcohol (said to have been used by a queen of Hungary). [Cf. Ugrian.]

**hunger**, *hung′gər*, *n.* craving for food: need or lack of food: strong desire for anything.—*v.i.* to crave food: to long.—*adjs.* **hung′erful**, hungry; **hung′erly** (*Shak.*), hungry.—*adv.* (*Shak.*) hungrily.—*adv.* **hung′rily**.—*adj.* **hung′ry**, having eager desire for food (or anything else): greedy: lean: poor.—*adj.* **hung′er-bitten**, bitten, pained, or weakened by hunger.—**hunger march**, a procession of unemployed or others in need, as a demonstration; **hunger′-march′er**; **hunger strike**, prolonged refusal of all food by a prisoner as a form of protest, or a means to ensure release.—Also *v.i.*—*n.* **hung′er-strik′er**. [O.E. *hungor* (n.), *hyngran* (vb.); cf. Ger. *hunger*, Du. *honger*, etc.]

**hunk**, *hungk*, *n.* a lump. [Same as **hunch**.]

**hunk**, *hungk* (*U.S.*), *n.* goal or base in boys′ games.—*adjs.* **hunk′y**, **hunk′y-do′ry**, in good position or condition: all right. [Du. *honk*.]

**hunker**, *hungk′ər*, (*U.S.*) *n.* orig. a member of the conservative section of the New York Democratic party (1845-48): a conservative person. [Origin obscure.]

**hunker**, *hungk′ər*, *v.i.* to squat down.—*n.pl.* **hunk′ers**, the hams. [Origin obscure; perh. conn. with O.N. *hūka*, to squat.]

**hunks**, *hungks*, *n.sing.* a miserly curmudgeon. [Origin unknown.]

**hunky**, *hungk′i*, (*U.S.*) *n.* a derogatory name for an unskilled workman, orig. for one of East European descent. [For Hungarian.]

**hunt**, *hunt*, *v.t.* to chase or go in quest of for prey or sport: to seek or pursue game over: to ransack: to use in the hunt: to search for: to pursue: to hound, drive.—*v.i.* to go out in pursuit of game: to search: to oscillate or vary in speed (*mech.*).—*n.* a chase of wild animals: search: a pack of hunting hounds: an association of huntsmen: the district hunted by a pack: game killed in a hunt (*Shak.*): a

huntsman (*obs.*).—*ns.* **hunt′er**, one who hunts:—*fem.* **hunt′ress**: a horse used in the chase: a watch whose face is protected with a metal case (a half-hunter, if that case has a small circle of glass let in); **hunt′ing**, the pursuit of wild game, the chase.—Also *adj.*—**hunt′-count′er** (*Shak.*), perh. one who hunts counter (q.v.); **hun′ter′s-moon**, full moon following harvest-moon; **hunt′ing-box**, -lodge, -seat, a temporary abode for hunting; **hunt′ing-cap**, a form of cap much worn in the hunting-field; **hunt′ing-cog**, an extra cog in one of two geared wheels, by means of which the order of contact of cogs is changed at every revolution; **hunt′ing-crop**, -whip, a short whip with a crooked handle and a loop of leather at the end, used in the hunting-field; **hunt′ing-field**, the scene or sphere of hunting, esp. fox-hunting: the assemblage of huntsmen; **hunt′ing ground**, a place or region for hunting; **hunt′ing-horn**, a horn used in hunting, a bugle; **hunt′ing-knife**, -sword, a knife or short sword used to despatch the game when caught, or to skin and cut it up; **hunt′ing-mass** (*hist.*), hasty and abridged mass said for impatient hunters; **hunt′ing-song**, a song about hunting; **hunt′ing-tide**, the season of hunting; **hunts′man**, one who hunts: one who manages the hounds during the chase; **hunts′manship**, the qualifications of a huntsman; **hunt′s′-up** (*Shak.*), a tune or song intended to arouse huntsmen in the morning—hence, anything calculated to arouse; **hunt′-the-gowk**, the making of an April fool: a fool′s errand, a deception, or a hoax, appropriate to the First of April.—Also *adj.*—*v.t.* to make an April fool of.—**hunt-the-slipp′er**, a game in which one in the middle of a ring tries to catch a shoe passed around by the others.—*interj.* **good hunting!**, good luck! (*coll.*); **hunt after**, **for**, to search for; **hunt counter**, to follow the scent backwards; **hunt down**, to pursue to extremities: to persecute out of existence; **hunt out**, or **up**, to seek out; **hunt the letter**, to affect alliteration. [O.E. *huntian*; prob. conn. with *hentan*, to seize.]

**Hunterian**, *hun-tē′ri-ən*, *adj.* of or pertaining to the surgeon John *Hunter* (1728-93), to his anatomical collection, nucleus of the Hunterian Museum in London, or to the annual Hunterian Oration at the Royal College of Surgeons: of or pertaining to his elder brother, William *Hunter* (1718-83), anatomist and obstetrician, or his museum in Glasgow.

**Huntingdonian**, *hun-ting-dō′ni-ən*, *n.* a member of the Countess of Huntingdon′s Connection, a denomination of Calvinistic Methodists founded by Whitefield with Selina, Countess of *Huntingdon* (1707-91).—Also *adj.*

**Huon-pine**, *hū′on-pin′*, *n.* a Tasmanian conifer (*Dacrydium franklinii*), found first on the *Huon* river.

**hup**, *hup*, *v.i.*, to shout hup: of a horse, to go on, to go faster: to turn to the right.—*v.t.* to turn (a horse) to the right.—*n.* a cry of ′hup′.—*interj.* (to a horse) to go faster or to turn to the right.—**neither hup nor wind** (*Scot.*), do neither one thing nor another, be unmanageable.

**hupaithric**, *hū-pāth′rik*, *adj.* hypaethral.

**hurcheon**, *hûr′chən*, Scots form of **urchin**.

**hurdies**, *hûr′diz*, (*Scot.*) *n.pl.* the buttocks. [Origin unknown.]

**hurdle**, *hûr′dl*, *n.* a frame of twigs or sticks interlaced: a movable frame of timber or iron for gates, etc. (*agri.*): in certain races, a portable barrier over which runners jump: a rude sledge on which criminals were drawn to the gallows (*hist.*): an obstacle (*fig.*): (in *pl.*) a hurdle-race.—*v.t.* to enclose with hurdles.—*v.i.* to jump as over a hurdle: to run a hurdle-race.—*ns.* **hurd′ler**, a maker of hurdles: a hurdle-racer; **hur′dling**—**hur′dle-race**, a race in which hurdles have to be cleared; hur'dle-rac'er; hur'dle-rac'ing. [O.E. *hyrdel*; Ger. *hürde*.]

**hurds, hurden.** Same as hards, harden (see hards).

**hurdy-gurdy,** *hûr'di-gûr'di, n.* a musical stringed instrument, whose strings are sounded by the turning of a wheel: a hand-organ. [Imit.]

**hurl,** *hûrl, v.t.* to fling with violence: to wheel (*Scot.*): to convey in a wheeled vehicle (*Scot.*). —*v.i.* to dash: to travel in a wheeled vehicle (*Scot.*): to play hurley.—*n.* act of hurling: a trip or journey in a wheeled vehicle (*Scot.*).—*ns* **hurl'er; hurl'ey,** Irish form of hockey (also **hurl'ing**): a kind of hockey stick for playing it; **hurl'y** (*Scot.*), large two-wheeled barrow.—**hurl'-barrow** (*Scot.*), a wheelbarrow; **hurl'ey-house** (*Scott*), a house in a state of disrepair; **hurl'y-hack'et** (*Scot.*), a carriage, gig: an improvised sledge: sledging. [Cf. L.G. *hurreln,* to hurl, precipitate; influenced by hurtle and whirl.]

**hurly,** *hûr'li, n.* commotion: tumult.—*n.* **hurly-burly** (*hûr'li-bûr'li*), tumult: confusion.—Also *adj.* and *adv.* [Perh. from hurl.]

**Huronian,** *hū-rō'ni-ən,* (*geol.*) *n.* and *adj.* upper Pre-Cambrian of Canada, well exemplified north of lake *Huron.*

**hurrah, hurra,** *hŏŏr-ä', hur-ä', hurray, -ä', interj.* an exclamation of approbation or joy.—Also *n.* and *v.i.* [Cf. Norw., Sw., Dan. *hurra,* Ger. *hurrah,* Du. *hoera.*]

**hurricane,** *hur'i-kin, -kăn, n.* a West Indian cyclonic storm of great violence: a wind of extreme violence (over 75 miles an hour): anything tempestuous (*fig.*): a social party, a rout (*obs.*): (*cap.*) a type of fighting aeroplane used in World War II.—*n.* **hurricā'nō** (*obs.*), a hurricane: a waterspout (*Shak.*).—**hurr'icane-deck,** a light partial deck over the saloon of some steamers; **hurr'icane-lamp,** an oil lamp encased so as to defy strong wind: also a protected electric lamp. [Sp. *huracán,* from Carib.]

**hurry,** *hur'i, v.t.* to urge forward: to hasten.—*v.i.* to move or act with haste, esp. perturbed or impatient haste:—*pr.p.* **hurr'ying;** *pa.t.* and *pa.p.* **hurr'ied.**—*n.* a driving forward: haste: flurried or undue haste: commotion: a rush: need for haste: in mus., a tremolo passage for strings, or drum roll, in connection with an exciting situation.—*adj.* **hurr'ied.**—*adv.* **hurr'iedly.**—*n.* **hurr'iedness.**—*n.* and *adj.* **hurr'ying.**—*adv.* **hurr'y-ingly.**—**hurr'y-skurr'y, -scurr'y,** confusion and bustle.—*adv.* confusedly.—**in a hurry,** in haste, speedily: soon: willingly; **hurry up,** make haste. [Prob. imit.; cf. Old Sw. *hurra,* to whirl round.]

**hurst,** *hûrst, n.* a wood, a grove. [O.E. *hyrst.*]

**hurt,** *hûrt, v.t.* to cause pain to: to damage: to injure: to wound, as the feelings.—*v.i.* to give pain: to be the seat of pain: to be injured:—*pa.t.* and *pa.p.* **hurt.**—*n.* a wound: injury.—*adj.* injured: pained in body or mind.—*n.* **hurt'er,** that which hurts: a beam, block, etc., to protect a wall from wheels: the shoulder of an axle against which the hub strikes.—*adj.* **hurt'-ful,** causing hurt or loss: harmful.—*adv.* **hurt'-fully.**—*n.* **hurt'fulness.**—*adj.* **hurt'less,** without hurt or injury, harmless.—*adv.* **hurt'lessly.**—*n.* **hurt'lessness.** [O.Fr. *hurter* (Fr. *heurter*), to knock, to run against.]

**hurtle,** *hûrt'l, v.t.* to dash: to hurl: to brandish (*Spens.*).—*v.i.* to clash (*arch.*): to rattle: to move rapidly with a clattering sound. [Freq. of hurt in its original sense.]

**hurtleberry,** a form of whortleberry.

**husband,** *huz'bənd, n.* a man to whom a woman is married: a husbandman (*obs.*): a manager: a thrifty manager.—*v.t.* to supply with a husband (*arch.*): to become, be, or act as, a husband to (*arch.*): to manage with economy: to conserve: to cultivate (*arch.*).—*n.* **hus'bandage,** allowance

or commission of a ship's husband.—*adjs.* **hus'bandless; hus'bandlike; hus'bandly,** frugal, thrifty, pertaining to or befitting a husband.—*n.* **hus'bandry,** the business of a farmer: tillage: economical management: thrift.—**hus'bandland** (*hist.*), a manorial tenant's holding: two oxgangs; **hus'bandman,** a working farmer: one who labours in tillage.—**ship's husband,** an owner's agent who manages the affairs of a ship in port. [O.E. *hūsbonda,* O.N. *hūsbōndi—hūs,* a house, *būandi,* inhabiting, pr.p. of O.N. *būa,* to dwell; cf. boor, bower, and Ger. *bauen,* to till.]

**hush,** *hush, interj.* or *imper.* silence: be still.—*n.* a silence, esp. after noise: a rush of water or its sound (*dial.*): the washing away of surface soil to lay bare bedrock (*min.*).—*adj.* silent (*arch.*): quiet (*arch.*): for the purpose of concealing information (e.g. *hush money*).—*v.i.* to become silent or quiet.—*v.t.* to make quiet: to calm: to procure silence or secrecy about (sometimes with *up*): to pour in a stream (*dial.*): to wash away or to pour in order to expose bedrock (*min.*).—*n.* **hush'aby** (*-ə-bi*), a lullaby used to soothe babies to sleep.—Also *v.t.* and *interj.*—*adj.* **hushed,** silent, still.—*adj.* **hush'-hush** (*coll.*), secret.—**hush'-boat** (1920s), a mystery-ship.—**hush up,** to stifle, suppress: to be silent. [Imit.; cf. hist and whist.]

**husher,** *hush'ər.* Form of usher.

**husk,** *husk, n.* the dry, thin covering of certain fruits and seeds: a case, shell, or covering, esp. one that is worthless or coarse: (in *pl.*) refuse, waste: huskiness: bronchitis in cattle caused by parasitic nematodes: a supporting frame.—*v.t.* to remove the husk or outer integument from.—*adj.* **husked,** covered with a husk: stripped of husks.—*n.* **husk'er,** one who husks Indian corn, esp. at a husking-bee: apparatus (as a glove) for the same purpose.—*adv.* **husk'ily.**—*ns.* **husk'i-ness; husk'ing,** the stripping of husks: a festive gathering to assist in husking Indian corn (maize) —also **husk'ing-bee.**—*adj.* **husk'y,** full of husks: of the nature of husks: like a husk: dry: sturdy like a corn-husk: with a dry, almost whispering voice, as if there were husks in the throat.—*n.* (*U.S.*) a sturdy fellow. [Perh. conn. with house.]

**husky,** *hus'ki.* See husk.

**husky,** *hus'ki, n.* an Eskimo sledge-dog: an Eskimo: the Eskimo language. [App.—*Eskimo.*]

**huso,** *hū'sō, n.* the great sturgeon. [O.H.G. *hūso.*]

**hussar,** *hə-, hŏŏ-zär', n.* a soldier of a light cavalry regiment: orig. a soldier of the national cavalry of Hungary in the 15th century. [Hung. *huszar,* through Old Serb.—It. *corsaro,* a freebooter.]

**hussif.** Dial. form of housewife (*q.v.*).

**Hussite,** *hus'īt, hŏŏs'it, n.* a follower of the Bohemian reformer John *Hus,* martyred in 1415.

**hussy,** *hus'i, huz'i, n.* a pert girl: a worthless wench: a housewife (*obs.*): a hussif (*obs.*). [housewife.]

**hustings,** *hus'tingz, n.sing.* the principal court of the city of London: formerly the booths where the votes were taken at an election of an M.P., or the platform from which the candidates gave their addresses: electioneering. [O.E. *hūsting,* a council (used in speaking of the Danes)—O.N. *hūsthing—hūs,* a house, *thing,* an assembly.]

**hustle,** *hus'l, v.t.* to shake or push together: to crowd with violence: to jostle: to thrust hastily: to hasten roughly: to exert pressure on: to sell (esp. aggressively): to obtain (money) illicitly (*slang*).—*v.i.* to act strenuously or aggressively: to earn money illicitly (as a prostitute; *slang*).—*n.* frenzied activity.—*n.* **hus'tler,** an energetic fellow: a swindler (*slang*): a prostitute (*slang*). [Du. *hutselen,* to shake to and fro; cf. hotchpotch.]

**huswife.** Obs. form of housewife.

**hut,** *hut, n.* a small or mean house: a small

*fāte, fär; mē, hûr* (her); *mīne; mōte, fōr; mūte, mōōn, fŏŏt; dhen* (then temporary dwelling or similar structure.—*v.t.* to quarter in or furnish with a hut or huts.— *v.i.* to dwell in a hut or huts:—*pr.p.* **hutt′ing**; *pa.t.* and *pa.p.* **hutt′ed**.—*ns.* **hut′ment**, an encampment of huts: lodging in huts; **hutt′ing**, material for making huts.—**hut′-cir′cle** (*ant.*), the remains of a prehistoric circular hut, a pit lined with stones, etc. [Fr. *hutte*—O.H.G. *hutta* (Ger. *hütte*); cf. **hide**.]

**hutch,** *huch, n.* a box, a chest: a coop for rabbits: a baker's kneading-trough: a trough used with some ore-dressing machines: a low wagon in which coal is drawn up out of the pit.—*v.t.* (*Milt.*) to hoard up. [Fr. *huche*, a chest—L.L. *hūtica*, a box; prob. Gmc.]

**Hutchinsonian,** *huch-in-sōn′i-ən, n.* a follower of John Hutchinson (1674-1737), who held that the Hebrew Scriptures contain typically the elements of all rational philosophy, natural history, and true religion.

**hutia,** *hōō-tē′a, n.* the hog-rat. [Sp. *hutía*, from Taino.]

**Huttonian,** *hut-ō′ni-ən, adj.* relating to the teaching of James Hutton (1726-97), esp. expounding the importance of geological agencies still at work, and the igneous origin of granite and basalt.—*n.* a follower of Hutton.

**huzoor,** *huz-ōōr′, n.* an Indian potentate, or (loosely) any person of rank or importance. [Ar. *hudūr*, the presence.]

**huzza,** *hōōz-ä′, huz-ä′, interj.* and *n.* hurrah: a shout of joy or approbation.—*v.t.* to attend with shouts of joy.—*v.i.* to utter shouts of joy or acclamation:—*pr.p.* **huzza′ing**; *pa.t.* and *pa.p.* **huzzaed, huzza′d** (-*zäd′*). [Perh. Ger. *hussa*; cf. **hurrah**.]

**huzzy,** *huz′i,* dial. variant of **hussy**.

**hwyl,** *hū′il, n.* divine inspiration in oratory: emotional fervour. [W.]

**hyacine,** *hi′ə-sin,* (*Spens.*) *n.* hyacinth (the stone).

**hyacinth,** *hi′ə-sinth, n.* a flower that sprang from the blood of Hyacinthus, a youth accidentally killed by Apollo (*myth.*): a bulbous genus (Hyacinthus) of the lily family, much cultivated: extended to others of the family, as **wild hyacinth** (the English bluebell), **grape hyacinth** (Muscari): a blue stone of the ancients (perh. aquamarine): a red, brown, or yellow zircon—jacinth: cinnamon-stone: a purple colour, of various hues.—*adj.* **hyacin′thine,** consisting of or resembling hyacinth: very beautiful, like Hyacinthus: of a colour variously understood as golden, purple-black, or a blue or purple of some kind. [Gr. *hyakinthos*, a species of Scilla, blue larkspur, a blue stone; cf. **jacinth**.]

**Hyades,** *hi′ə-dēz,* **Hyads,** *hi′adz, n.pl.* a cluster of five stars in the constellation of the Bull, supposed by the ancients to bring rain when they rose with the sun. [Gr. *Hyădĕs, Hyădĕs,* explained by the ancients as from *hyein*, to rain; more prob. little pigs, *hys*, a pig.]

**hyaena.** See **hyena**.

**hyaline,** *hi′ə-lin, -lin, adj.* glassy: of or like glass: clear: transparent: free from granules.—*n.* (*Milt.*) a glassy transparent surface.—*n.* **hy′alite,** transparent colourless opal.—*adj.* **hy′aloid,** hyaline, transparent.—*ns.* **hyalom′elan(e)** (-*ăn,* -*an*; Gr. *melăs, -ănos,* black), tachylite; **hyalonē′ma** (Gr. *nēma,* thread), the glass-rope sponge; **hy′alophane** (root of Gr. *phainesthai,* to seem), a feldspar containing barium; **hy′aloplasm,** the clear fluid part of protoplasm. [Gr. *hyalos,* glass.]

**Hyblaean,** *hi-blē′ən, adj.* pertaining to ancient *Hybla* in Sicily, noted for its honey.

**hybrid,** *hi′brid, n.* an organism which is the offspring of a union between different races, species, genera or varieties: a mongrel: a word formed of elements from different languages.—*adjs.* **hy′brid, hyb′ridous,** produced from different

species, etc.: mongrel.—*adj.* **hybridis′able, -z-.**— *n.* **hybridisā′tion, -z-.**—*v.t.* **hy′bridise, -ize,** to cause to interbreed.—*v.i.* to interbreed.—*ns.* **hybridis′er, -z-; hy′bridism, hybrid′ity,** state of being hybrid. [L. *hibrida,* offspring of a tame sow and wild boar; with associations of Gr. *hybris,* insolence, overweening.]

**hybris.** Same as **hubris**.

**hydathode,** *hi′dath-ōd,* (*bot.*) *n.* an epidermal water-excreting organ. [Gr. *hydōr, hydatos,* water, *hodos,* way.]

**hydatid,** *hi′də-tid, n.* a water cyst or vesicle in an animal body, esp. one containing a tapeworm larva: the larva itself.—*adj.* **hydatid′iform,** resembling a hydatid.—**hydatidiform mole** (*med.*), an affection of the vascular tufts of the foetal part of the placenta whereby they become greatly enlarged. [Gr. *hydatis, -idos,* a watery vesicle—*hydōr, hydatos,* water.]

**hydatoid,** *hi′də-toid, adj.* watery. [Gr. *hydōr, -atos,* water, *eidos,* form.]

**Hydnocarpus,** *hid-nō-kär′pəs, n.* a genus of trees akin to the chaulmoogra, yielding an oil containing chaulmoogric acid. [Gr. *hydnon,* a truffle, *karpos,* a fruit.]

**hydr-.** See **hydro-**.

**Hydra,** *hi′drə, n.* a water-monster with many heads, which when cut off were succeeded by others (*myth.*): any manifold evil: a freshwater hydrozoon remarkable for power of multiplication on being cut or divided: a large southern constellation.—*adj.* **hy′dra-head′ed,** difficult to root out, springing up vigorously again and again. [Gr. *hydrā*—*hydōr,* water, akin to Sans. *udra,* an otter.]

**hydraemia, hydragogue, Hydrangea,** etc. See **hydro-**.

**hydrargyrism,** *hi-drär′jir-izm, n.* mercurial poisoning.—*adj.* **hydrar′gyral.**—*n.* **hydrar′gyrum,** mercury. [Gr. *hydrargyros,* mercury—*argyros,* silver; *hydrargyrum* is mod. L. on analogy of *argentum,* etc., L. *hydrargyrus.*]

**hydrate, hydraulic,** etc. See **hydro-**.

**hydrazine,** *hi′drə-zēn, n.* a fuming corrosive liquid, $H_2N\cdot NH_2$, a powerful reducing agent, used as a rocket fuel: any of a class of organic bases derived from it.—*n.pl.* **hy′drazides,** a class of chemical compounds derived from hydrazine. [**hydr-, az**(o)-.]

**hydria,** *hi′dri-ə, hid′ri-ə, n.* a large Greek watervase. [Gr. *hydriā.*]

**hydro-,** *hi′drō-, -dro′-,* **hydr-,** in composition, of, like, by means of, water (see also **hydrogen**). —*n.* **hydraemia,** in U.S. **hydremia** (*hi-drē′mi-ə*; Gr. *haima,* blood), wateriness of the blood.— *adj.* **hydragogue** (*hi′drə-gog, -gōg;* Gr. *agōgos,* bringing; *med.*), removing water or serum.—*n.* a drug with that effect.—*ns.* **Hydrangea** (*hi-drān′jə, -jyə;* Gr. *angeion,* vessel), a genus of shrubby plants of or akin to the saxifrage family with large globular clusters of showy flowers, natives of China and Japan; **hydrant** (*hi′drənt*), a connection for attaching a hose to a watermain or a fire-plug; **hydranth** (*hi′dranth;* Gr. *anthos,* flower), a nutritive polyp in a hydroid colony; **hy′drate,** a compound containing water chemically combined yet somehow retaining its identity: an old word for a *hydroxide* (see under **hydrogen**).—*v.t.* to combine with water.—*ns.* **hydrā′tion.**—*adj.* **hydraulic** (*hi-dröl′ik, -drol′;* Gr. *aulos,* a pipe), relating to hydraulics: conveying water: worked by water or other liquid in pipes: setting in water.—*v.t.* (*mining*), to excavate and wash out by powerful jets of water: —*pr.p.* **hydraul′icking**; *pa.t.* and *pa.p.* **hydraul′-icked.**—*adv.* **hydraul′ically.**—*n.pl.* **hydraul′ics,** used as *sing.,* the science of hydrodynamics in general, or its practical application to waterpipes, etc.—*n.* **hydrē′mia,** mainly U.S. form of **hydraemia.**—*adj.* **hy′dric,** pertaining to an abundance of moisture.—*adv.* hy'drically.—*ns.* hy'drŏ, an abbreviation of hydroelectric (*adj.*) and of hydropathic (establishment); hydroae'roplane (in U.S. hydro-air'plane), a seaplane; hy'drocele (-*sēl*; Gr. *kēlē*, a swelling; *med.*), a swelling containing serous fluid, esp. in the scrotum; hydrocephalus (-*sef'ə-ləs*, or -*kef'*; Gr. *kephalē*, head), an accumulation of serous fluid within the cranial cavity, either in the subdural space or the ventricles: water in the head: dropsy of the brain.—*adjs.* hydrocephal'ic, hydroceph'alous.—*ns.* Hydrocharis (*hī-drok'ə-ris*; Gr. *charis*, -*itos*, grace), the frogbit genus, giving name to the Hydrocharitā'ceae, a family of water-plants akin to the pondweeds; hy'drochore (-*kōr*, -*kör*; Gr. *chōreein*, to make room, spread about), a plant disseminated by water.— *adj.* hydrochoric (-*kor'ik*).—*n.pl.* Hydrocoralli'nae, an order of Hydrozoa, massive reef-builders, the millepores, etc.—*n.* and *adj.* hydrocor'alline.—*adj.* hydrodynamic (-*din-am'ik*; Gr. *dynamis*, power), -al.—*n.* hydrodynam'icist. —*n.* (treated as *sing.*) hydrodynam'ics, the science of the motions and equilibrium of a material system partly or wholly fluid (called *hydrostatics* when the system is in equilibrium, *hyd'okinetics* when it is not).—*adj.* hydroelec'tric.—*ns.* hydroelectric'ity, electricity produced by means of water, esp. by water-power; hydroextract'or, a drying-machine that works centrifugally; hy'drofoil, a device on a boat for raising it from the water as its speed increases: a corresponding device on a seaplane to aid its take-off, also hy'drovane: a craft with hydrofoils; hydrog'-rapher (Gr. *graphein*, to write).—*adjs.* hydrographic (-*graf'ik*), -al.—*adv.* hydrograph'ically.— *n.* hydrog'raphy, the investigation of seas and other bodies of water, including charting, sounding, study of tides, currents, etc.—*adj.* hy'droid, like a Hydra: polypoid.—*n.* a hydrozoan: a hydrozoan in its asexual generation.—*n.* (treated as *sing.*) hydrokinet'ics, a branch of *hydrodynamics* (*q.v.*).—*adjs.* hydrolog'ic, -al.—*ns.* hydrol'ogist; hydrol'ogy, the study of water resources in land areas of the world—(*U.S.*) esp. underground water.—*v.t.* hydrolyse, -yze (*hī'drō-līz*), to subject to hydrolysis.—*ns.* hydrolysis (*hī-drol'i-sis*; Gr. *lysis*, loosing), chemical decomposition or ionic dissociation caused by water; hy'drolyte (-*līt*), a body subjected to hydrolysis.—*adj.* hydrolytic (-*lit'ik*).—*n.* hy'dromancy (Gr. *manteiā*, divination), divination by water.—*adj.* hydromant'ic.—*n.* (treated as *sing.*) hydromechan'ics, hydrodynamics.—*n.* hydromedū'sa, a hydrozoan in its sexual generation: —*pl.* Hydromedū'sae, the class Hydrozoa.—*adjs.* hydromedū'san, hydromedū'soid (also *ns.*).—*ns.* hy'dromel (Gr. *hydromeli*—*meli*, honey), a beverage made of honey and water; hydromē'teor (Gr. *meteōron*, a meteor), any weather phenomenon depending on the moisture content of the atmosphere; hydrometeorol'ogy; hydrom'-eter (Gr. *metron*, a measure), a float for measuring specific gravity.—*adjs.* hydrometric (-*met'*), -al.—*ns.* hydrom'etry; Hydromys (*hī'drō-mis*; Gr. *mŷs*, mouse), an Australasian genus of aquatic rodents; hydronephrō'sis, distension of the kidney with urine held up as a result of obstruction in the urinary tract.—*adj.* hydronephrō'tic.—*n.* hydrop'athy, the treatment of disease by water, externally and internally.— *adj.* hydropathic (*hī-drō-path'ik*; Gr. *pathos*, suffering), of, for, relating to, practising, hydropathy.—*n.* (in full hydropathic establishment; *coll.* hy'dro), a hotel (with special baths, etc.) where guests can have hydropathic treatment.— *adj.* hydropath'ical.—*adv.* hydropath'ically.—*ns.* hydrop'athist, one who practises hydropathy; hydrophane (*hī'drō-fān*; Gr. *phānos*, bright), a translucent opal transparent in water.—*adj.*

hydrophanous (-*drof'ən-əs*), transparent on immersion.—*n.pl.* Hydrophidae (*hī-drof'i-dē*; Gr. *ophis*, snake), a family of venomous sea-snakes. —*n.* hydroph'ilite, native calcium chloride (a very hygroscopic substance).— *adjs.* hydrophil'ic (*chem.*), attracting water; hydroph'ilous, water-loving: pollinated by agency of water (*bot.*).— *ns.* hydroph'ily (Gr. *phileein*, to love), water-pollination; hydrophō'bia (Gr. *phobos*, fear), horror of water: inability to swallow water owing to a contraction in the throat, a symptom of rabies: rabies itself.—*adjs.* hydrophobic (-*fob'ik*), pertaining to hydrophobia: repelling water (*chem.*); hydrophobous (-*drof'ə-bəs*) (*obs.*). —*ns.* hy'drophone (-*fōn*; Gr. *phōnē*, voice), an apparatus for listening to sounds conveyed by water; hy'drophyte (-*fīt*; Gr. *phyton*, plant), a water-plant.—*adj.* hydrophytic (-*fit'ik*).—*n.* hydrophyton (*hī-drof'i-ton*), the coenosarc of a hydroid colony.—*adjs.* hydroph'ytous; hydrop'ic (erroneously hydrop'tic, see hydropsy), dropsical: thirsty: charged or swollen with water.—*ns.* hy'droplane, a light, flat-bottomed motor-boat which, at high speed, skims along the surface of the water: (erroneously) a *hydro-aeroplane* or seaplane; hydropol'yp, a hydrozoan polyp.—*n.* (treated as *sing.*) hydroponics (*hī-drō-pon'iks*; Gr. *ponos*, toil), the art or practice of growing plants in a chemical solution without soil.— *n.* hy'dropsy (Gr. *hydrōps*, dropsy), dropsy.—*n.pl.* Hydropterid'eae (-*i-ē*; Gr. *pteris*, -*idos*, male-fern), the water-ferns or heterosporous ferns.— *ns.* hy'dropult (modelled on catapult), a hand force-pump; hydroquinone (-*kwin-ōn'*, or -*kwin'*, or -*kwin'*), quinol; hy'droscope (Gr. *skopeein*, to view), a kind of water-clock, a graduated tube, from which the water escaped (*hist.*): an instrument for viewing under water; hy'droski, a kind of hydrofoil used on seaplanes as a source of hydrodynamic lift, on aeroplanes to make them amphibious; hydroso'ma, hy'drosome (-*sōm*; Gr. *sōma*, body), a hydroid colony:—*pl.* hydroso'mata, hy'drosomes.—*adjs.* hydrosō'mal, hydrosō'matous.—*ns.* hydrosphere (*hī'drō-sfēr*; Gr. *sphaira*, sphere), the water on the surface of the earth—the seas and oceans; hy'-drostat (Gr. *statos*, standing), a contrivance for indicating the presence of water.—*adjs.* hydrostat'ic, hydrostat'ical.—*adv.* hydrostat'i-cally.—*n.* (treated as *sing.*) hydrostat'ics, a branch of *hydrodynamics* (*q.v.*).—*adj.* hydrotac'tic.—*ns.* hydrotax'is (Gr. *taxis*, arrangement), response of an organism to the stimulus of water; hydrothē'ca (Gr. *thēkē*, case), the horny cup of a hydranth; hydrother'apy, hydrotherapeu'tics, treatment of disease by the external use of water, e.g. treatment of disability by developing movement in water.—*adjs.* hydrotherapeu'tic; hydrother'mal, pertaining to, or produced by, action of heated or super-heated water, esp. in dissolving, transporting, and redepositing mineral matter.— *n.* hydrothorax (-*thō'*, -*thō'*; Gr. *thōrax*, chest), dropsy in the chest.—*adj.* hydrotrop'ic.—*n.* hydrot'ropism (Gr. *tropos*, a turn), the turning of an organ towards (*positive*) or away from (*negative*) moisture.—*adj.* hydrous (*hī'drəs*; *chem.*, *min.*), containing water.—*n.* hydrozincite (-*zingk'it*), basic zinc carbonate.—*n.pl.* Hydro-zō'a (Gr. *zōion*, an animal), a class of Coelenterata, chiefly marine organisms in which alternation of generations typically occurs, the hydroid phase colonial, giving rise to the medusoid phase by budding—the zoophytes, millepores, etc.: sometimes extended to include the true jellyfishes.—*sing.* hydrozo'on.—*n.* and *adj.* hydrozō'an.—hydrated electron, very reactive free electron released in aqueous solutions by the action of ionising radiations; hydrated ion, ion surrounded by molecules of water which it holds in a degree of orientation; hydraulic belt, an endless belt of absorbent material for raising water; **hydraulic jack**, a lifting apparatus in which oil, etc., is pumped against a piston; **hydraulic mining**, hydraulicking; **hydraulic press**, a press operated by forcing water into a cylinder in which a ram or plunger works; **hydraulic ram**, a device whereby the pressure head produced when a moving column of water is brought to rest is caused to deliver some of the water under pressure; **hydraulic seeding**, sowing seed by spraying it, mixed with nutrients, etc., on the ground; **hydrostatic balance**, a balance for weighing bodies in water to determine their specific gravity; **hydrostatic drive, transmission**, in vehicle, drive consisting of system transmitting power through oil, under pressure; **hydrostatic extrusion** (*metallurgy*), form of extrusion in which the metal to be shaped is preshaped to fit a die forming the lower end of a high-pressure container which is filled with a pressure-transmitting liquid; pressure is built up in the liquid by a plunger until the metal is forced through the die; **hydrostatic paradox**, the principle that—disregarding molecular forces—any quantity of fluid, however small, may balance any weight, however great; **hydrostatic press**, a hydraulic press; **hydrostatic transmission** (see **hydrostatic drive**). [Gr. *hydōr*, water.]

**hydrogen**, hi'dro-jən, *n.* a gas (symbol H, atomic number 1) which in combination with oxygen produces water, the lightest of all known substances, and very inflammable, of great importance in the moderation (slowing down) of neutrons.—*adj.* **hy'dric**, of or containing hydrogen.—*n.* **hy'dride**, a compound of hydrogen with an element or radical.—*adjs.* **hydriodic** (*hi-dri-od'ik*), of an acid composed of hydrogen and iodine, hydrogen iodide; **hydrobrō'mic**, applied to an acid composed of hydrogen and bromine, hydrogen bromide.—*n.* **hydrocar'bon**, a compound of hydrogen and carbon with nothing else.—*adj.* **hydrochloric** (-*klor'ik*, -*klōr'*, -*klōr'*), applied to an acid composed of hydrogen and chlorine, hydrogen chloride, still sometimes called **muriatic acid**.—*ns.* **hydrochlor'ide**, a compound of hydrochloric acid with an organic base; **hy'drocracking**, cracking of petroleum, etc., in the presence of hydrogen.—*adjs.* **hydrocyanic** (-*si-an'ik*), denoting an acid (*prussic acid*) composed of hydrogen and cyanogen; **hydroferricyanic** (-*fer-i-si-an'ik*), **hydroferrōcyan'ic**, applied to two acids composed of hydrogen, iron, and cyanogen, hydroferricyanic acid, $H_3Fe(CN)_6$, having an atom of hydrogen less than hydroferrocyanic, $H_4Fe(CN)_6$; **hydrofluor'ic**, applied to an acid composed of fluorine and hydrogen, hydrogen fluoride.—*v.t.* **hydrogenate** (*hi'drō-jən-āt* or *hi-droj'ən-āt*), to cause to combine with hydrogen, as in the hardening of oils by converting an olein into a stearin by addition of hydrogen in the presence of a catalyst such as nickel or palladium. —*n.* **hydrogenā'tion**.—*adj.* **hydrog'enous**.—*ns.* **hydrosul'phide**, a compound formed by action of hydrogen sulphide on a hydroxide; **hydrosul'phite**, a hyposulphite (esp. sodium hyposulphite).—*adj.* **hydrosulphū'ric**, formed by a combination of hydrogen and sulphur.—*ns.* **hydrox'ide**, a chemical compound which contains one or more hydroxyl groups; **hydrox'yl** (Gr. *hȳlē*, matter), a compound radical consisting of one atom of oxygen and one of hydrogen: sometimes loosely applied to *hydrogen peroxide*; **hydroxyl'amine**, a basic substance composed of a hydroxyl group and an amino group ($NH_2OH$). —**hydrogen bomb**, or *H-bomb*, a bomb in which an enormous release of energy is achieved by converting hydrogen nuclei into helium nuclei—a fusion, not fission, process started by great heat; the first H-bomb was exploded by the U.S.A. in November 1952; **hydrogen ion**, an

atom or molecule of hydrogen having a positive charge, esp. an atom formed in a solution of acid in water—strong acids being highly ionised and weak acids only slightly; **hydrogen peroxide** (see **peroxide**); **hydronium ion**, a hydrated hydrogen ion, as $H_3O^+$.—**heavy hydrogen** (see **heavy**); **hydrogenation of coal**, conversion of coal to liquid fuels by hydrogenation. [Coined by Cavendish (1766) from Gr. *hydōr*, water, and *gennaein*, to produce.]

**hydyne**, hi'din, *n.* an American rocket-launching fuel.

**hye** (*Spens.*) for **hie, high**.

**hyena, hyaena**, hi-ē'nə, **hyen** (*Shak.*), hi'en, *n.* a carrion-feeding carnivore (genus **Hyae'na**, constituting a family **Hyae'nidae**) with long thick neck, coarse mane, sloping body, and hysterical-sounding laugh.—**hyena dog**, an African wild dog, blotched like a hyena. [L. *hyaena*—Gr. *hyaina*—*hȳs*, a pig.]

**hyetal**, hi'i-tl, *adj.* rainy: pertaining to rain or rainfall.—*n.* hy'etograph, a rain chart: a self-registering rain gauge.—*adjs.* hyetograph'ic, -al. —*ns.* hyetog'raphy; hyetol'ogy, a branch of meteorology dealing with rainfall; **hyetom'eter**, a rain-gauge; **hyetomet'rograph**, a self-registering rain gauge, hyetograph. [Gr. *hȳetos*, rain.]

**Hygeian**, hi-jē'ən, *adj.* relating to Hygeia or to health and its preservation. [Gr. *Hygieia*, later *Hygeia*, goddess of health, daughter of Asklēpios (Aesculapius).]

**hygiene**, hi'jēn, *n.* the science or art of preserving health: sanitary principles.—*adj.* **hygienic** (*hi-jēn'ik*).—*adv.* **hygien'ically**.—*n.* (treated as *sing.*) **hygien'ics**, principles of hygiene.—*n.* **hygienist** (*hi'jēn-ist*), one skilled in hygiene. [Fr. *hygiène* —Gr. *hygieinē* (*technē*), hygienic (art)—*hygieiā*, health, *hygiēs*, healthy.]

**hygro-**, hi'grō-, -gro', in composition, wet, moist. —*n.* **hygrochasy** (*hi-grok'ə-si*; Gr. *chasis*, a gape), dehiscence on moistening.—*adj.* **hygrochas'tic**.—*ns.* hy'grodeik (-*dīk*; Gr. *deiknynai*, to show), a psychrometer with an index and scale; **hy'grograph**, an instrument, a development of a hygroscope, for recording the humidity of the air.—*adjs.* **hygrograph'ic, -al**.—*n.* **hygrom'eter**, an instrument for measuring the humidity of the air or of other gases.—*adjs.* **hygrometric** (*-met'-rik*), -al, belonging to hygrometry: hygroscopic. —*n.* **hygrom'etry**, measurement of the humidity of the air or of other gases.—*adjs.* **hy'grophil**, **hygrophilous** (*-grof'*; Gr. *phileein*, to love), moisture-loving: living where there is much moisture; **hy'grophobe** (Gr. *phobeein*, to fear), growing best where moisture is scanty.—*n.* **hy'grophyte** (*-fit*; Gr. *phyton*, plant), a plant adapted to plentiful water-supply.—*adj.* **hygrophytic** (*-fit'ik*).—*n.* **hy'groscope**, an instrument that shows, without measuring, changes in the humidity of the air.—*adjs.* **hygroscopic** (*-skop'ik*), -al, relating to the hygroscope: readily absorbing moisture from the air: indicating or caused by absorption or loss of moisture, as some movements of plants.—*ns.* **hygroscopicity** (*-skop-is'i-ti*); hygro'stat, an apparatus which produces constant humidity.—**hygroscopic salt**, any salt, esp. chloride of calcium, used to withdraw moisture from other substances. [Gr. *hygros*, wet.]

**hyke, hik**, *n.* See **haik**.

**Hyksos**, hik'sos, -sōs, *n.* a foreign line of kings (the xv and xvi dynasties, called the shepherd kings) who ruled Egypt for centuries. [Gr. *Hyksōs*— Egyptian *Hiku-khasut*, princes of the desert, app. misunderstood as shepherd princes.]

**hylding** (*Spens.*). Same as **hilding**.

**hyle**, hi'lē, *n.* wood, matter.—*adj.* hy'lic, material: corporeal.—*ns.* hy'licism, hy'lism, materialism; hy'licist, hy'list (wrongly hy'loist); hy'lobate, a gibbon (genus **Hylob'atēs**; from the root of

Neutral vowels in unaccented syllables: *el'ə-mənt*; for certain sounds in foreign words, see p. viii

Gr. *bainein*, to go); hylogen'esis, the origin of matter; hylog'athism (Gr. *pathos*, feeling), the doctrine that matter is sentient; hylog'athist.— *adj.* hyloph'agous (Gr. *phagein*, to eat), woodeating.—*ns.* hy'lophyte (Gr. *phyton*, plant), a woodland plant; hy'lotheism (Gr. *theos*, god), the doctrine that there is no God but matter and the universe; hy'lotheist.—*adjs.* hylot'omous (Gr. *tomē*, a cut), wood-cutting; hylozō'ical, hylozoist'ic.—*ns.* hylozō'ism (Gr. *zōē*, life), the doctrine that all matter is endowed with life; hylozō'ist. [Gr. *hȳlē*, wood, matter.]

**hyleg,** *hī'leg, n.* the ruling planet at the hour of birth. [Origin obscure; cf. Pers. *hailāj*, nativity.]

**Hymen,** *hī'men, n.* the god of marriage (*myth.*): marriage (*arch.*).—*adjs.* hymenē'al, hymenē'an (also -ae'al, -ae'an).—*n.* hymenē'al, wedding hymn: (in *pl.*) nuptials (*arch.*). [Gr. weddingcry, perh. also a god.]

**hymen,** *hī'men, n.* a membrane: a thin membrane partially closing the virginal vagina.—*adjs.* hy'menal, pertaining to the hymen; hymē'nial, pertaining to the hymenium.—*n.* hymē'nium, the spore-bearing surface in fungi.—*ns.pl.* Hymenomycetes (*hī-mən-ō-mi-sē'tēz*), an order of fungi with exposed hymenium from an early stage—toadstools, etc.; Hymenophyllā'ceae, the filmy ferns.—*adj.* hymenophyllā'ceous.—*n.pl.* Hymenop'tera, an order of insects with four transparent wings—ants, bees, wasps, etc.—*adj.* hymenop'terous. [Gr. *hȳmēn*, membrane.]

**hymn,** *him, n.* a song of praise.—*v.t.* to celebrate in song: to worship by hymns.—*v.i.* to sing in adoration:—*pr.p.* hymning (*him'ing, him'ning*); *pa.t.* and *pa.p.* hymned (*himd, him'nid*).—*ns.* hym'nal, hym'nary, a hymn-book.—*adj.* hym'nic.—*ns.* hym'nist; hym'nody, hymns collectively: hymn-singing: hymnology; hymnog'rapher; hymnog'raphy, the art of writing hymns: the study of hymns; hymnol'ogist; hymnol'ogy, the study or composition of hymns. [Gr. *hymnos.*]

**hynde,** a Spenserian spelling of hind (2).

**hyoid,** *hī'oid, adj.* having the form of the Greek letter upsilon (υ), applied to a bone at the base of the tongue. [Gr. *hȳoeidēs*—*hȳ*, the letter upsilon and *eidos*, form.]

**hyoplastron,** *hi-ō-plas'tron, n.* in a turtle's plastron a plate between the hypoplastron and the entoplastron:—*pl.* hyoplas'tra.—*adj.* hyoplas'tral. [Gr. *hȳ*, the letter upsilon.]

**Hyoscyamus,** *hi-ō-sī'ə-məs, n.* the henbane genus. —*ns.* hy'oscine (*-sēn, -sən*; also called scopolamine; used as a truth drug, for travel sickness, etc.), and hyoscy'amine, two poisonous alkaloids similar to atropine, got from henbane. [Gr. *hyoskyamos.*]

**hyp.** See hip (3).

**hypabyssal,** *hip-ə-bis'l, (petr.) adj.* moderately deep-seated, not quite abyssal, intermediate between plutonic and eruptive. [Gr. *hypo*, beneath.]

**hypaethral,** *hip-ē'thrəl,* or hip-, *adj.* roofless, open to the sky.—*n.* hypae'thron, an open court. [Gr. *hypo*, beneath, *aithēr*, upper air, sky.]

**hypalgesia,** *hip-al-jē'si-a, -zi-a,* or hip', *n.* diminished susceptibility to pain.—Also hypal'gia.—*adj.* hypalgē'sic. [Gr. *hypo*, under, *algēsis, algos*, pain.]

**hypallage,** *hip-, hip-al'ə-jē, (rhet.) n.* a figure in which the relations of words in a sentence are mutually interchanged.—*adj.* hypallact'ic. [Gr. *hypo*, under, *allassein*, to exchange.]

**hypanthium,** *hip-, hip-an'thi-əm, n.* the flat or concave receptacle of a perigynous flower. [Gr. *hypo*, under, *anthos*, flower.]

**hypate,** *hip'ə-tē, (Gr. mus.) n.* the lowest string of the lyre or its tone. [Gr. *hypatē*, highest (fem.), prob. as having the longest string.]

**hype,** *hip, (slang) n.* short for hypodermic.—hyped up, artificially stimulated.

**hyper-,** *hī'pər-, hī-pûr'-,* in composition, over: excessive: more than normal.—*ns.* hyperacid'ity, excessive acidity, esp. in the stomach; hyperacusis (*-ə-kū'sis*; Gr. *akousis,* hearing), abnormally increased power of hearing.—*adj.* hyperacute'.—*ns.* hyperacute'ness; hyperadrē'nalism, excessive activity of the adrenal gland; hyperaemia, in U.S. hyperemia (*-ē'mi-ə*; Gr. *haima,* blood), congestion or excess of blood in any part.—*adj.* hyperae'mic.—*n.* hyperaesthesia, in U.S. hyperesthesia (*-ēs-* or *-es-thē'si-ə, -zi-ə*; Gr. *aisthēsis,* perception), excessive sensitivity to stimuli: an abnormal extension of the bodily senses assumed to explain telepathy and clairvoyance: exaggerated aestheticism. — *adjs.* hyperaesthē'sic, hyperaesthetic (*-thet'ik*), overaesthetic: abnormally or morbidly sensitive.—*n.* hyperalgē'sia (*si-ə, -zi-ə*; Gr. *algēsis,* pain), heightened sensitivity to pain.—*adj.* hyperalgē'sic.—*adjs.* hyperbar'ic, having specific gravity greater than that of cerebrospinal fluid (*spinal anaesthesia*): pertaining to conditions of high atmospheric pressure with a greater concentration of oxygen than normal, as in a hyperbaric chamber, a chamber containing oxygen at high pressure; hyperbat'ic.—*adv.* hyperbat'ically.—*ns.* hyperbaton (Gr., —root of *bainein,* to go; *rhet.*), a figure by which words are transposed from their natural order; hyper'bola (Gr. *hyperbolē,* overshooting —*ballein,* to throw; *pl.* usu. in -s; *geom.*), one of the conic sections, the intersection of a plane with a cone when the plane cuts both branches of the cone; hyperbole (*hī-pûr'bo-lē*), a rhetorical figure which produces a vivid impression by extravagant and obvious exaggeration.—*adjs.* hyperboli'c, -al, of a hyperbola or hyperbole; hyperbolic functions, in math., a set of six functions (sinh, cosh, tanh, etc.) analogous to the trigonometrical functions; hyperbolic geometry, that involving the axiom that through any point in a given plane there can be drawn more than one line that does not intersect a given line; hyperbolic logarithms, natural logarithms; hyperbolic paraboloid, a saddle-shaped surface represented by the equation $x^2/a - y^2/b = z$; hyperbolic spiral, a spiral of polar equation $\rho\theta = k^2$—*adv.* hyperbol'ically.—*v.t.* hyper'bolise, -ize, to represent hyperbolically.—*v.i.* to speak hyperbolically or with exaggeration.—*ns.* hyper'bolism; hyper'boloid, a solid figure certain of whose plane sections are hyperbolas.—*adj.* hyperborean (*-bō', -bö'*; Gr. *Hyperboreoi,* a people supposed to live in sunshine beyond the north wind—*Boreas,* the north wind), belonging to the extreme north. —*n.* an inhabitant of the extreme north.—*n.* hypercalc(a)e'mia, abnormal rise in the calcium content of the blood.—*adj.* hypercatalect'ic (*pros.*), having an additional syllable or half-foot after the last complete dipody.—*ns.* hypercatalex'is; hy'percharge, the strangeness of a particle plus its baryon number; hypercrit'ic, one who is over-critical: a carper.—*adjs.* hypercrit'ic, -al.—*adv.* hypercrit'ically.—*v.t.* hypercrit'icise, -ize (*-siz*).—*n.* hypercrit'icism.—*adj.* hyperdac'tyl (Gr. *daktylos,* finger, toe).—*n.* hyperdac'tyly, possession of more than five fingers or toes.—*adj.* hyperdorian (*-dō', dö'*; Gr. *hyperdōrios; mus.*), above the Dorian mode: applied in ancient Greek music to a mode having as its lower tetrachord the upper tetrachord of the Dorian (as: *b c d e; e f g a; b*).—*ns.* hyperdulia (*-dōō-lī'ə*) (see dulia); hyperem'esis (Gr. *emesis,* vomiting), excessive vomiting.—*adj.* hyperemet'ic.—*ns.* hyperemia, hyperesthesia (see hyperaemia, hyperaesthesia).—*adj.* hyper'gamous, pertaining to hypergamy.—*ns.* hypergamy (*hī-pûr'gə-mi;* Gr. *gamos,* marriage), a custom that allows a man but forbids a woman to marry a person of lower social standing: now sometimes more generally as marriage of a man with a woman of higher social rank; **hyperglyc(a)emia** (*-gli-sē′mi-ə*), abnormal rise in the sugar content of the blood.—*adj.* **hypergolic** (*-gol′ik*), of two or more liquids, spontaneously explosive on mixing.—*ns.* **hyper(h)idrō′sis**, excessive sweating; **hyperinō′sis** (Gr. *is*, *inos*, strength, fibre), excess of fibrin in the blood.—*adj.* **hyperinöt′ic**; **hyperlydian** (*-lid′i-ən*; Gr. *hyperlÿdios*), above the Lydian mode: applied in ancient Greek music to a mode having as its lower tetrachord the upper tetrachord of the Lydian (as: *g a b c*; *c d e f*; *g*).—**hy′permarket**, a very large self-service store with a wide range of goods.—*adj.* **hypermet′rical**, beyond or exceeding the ordinary metre of a line: having or being an additional syllable.—*n.* **hypermetrō′pia** (Gr. *metron*, measure, *ōps*, eye), long-sightedness.—Also **hyperō′pia**.—*adjs.* **hypermetrōp′ic**.—*ns.* **hy′peron**, any particle with mass greater than that of a proton or neutron; **hyperphagia** (*-fā′ji-ə*), bulimia.—*adjs.* **hyperphrygian** (*-frij′i-ən*, *-frij′ən*; Gr. *hyperphrÿgios*), above the Phrygian: applied to a mode of ancient Greek music having as its lower tetrachord the upper tetrachord of the Phrygian (as: *a b c d*; *d e f g*; *a*); **hyperphys′ical**, beyond physical laws: supernatural.—*n.* **hyperplasia** (*-plā′zi-ə*, *-zhə*; Gr. *plasis*, a forming; *path.*), overgrowth of a part due to excessive multiplication of its cells.—*adjs.* **hyperplastic** (*-plas′*); **hyperpyretic** (*-pir-et′ik*; Gr. *pyretikos*, feverish).—*ns.* **hyperpyrex′ia**, abnormally high body temperature; **hypersarcō′ma**, **hypersarcō′sis** (Gr. *hypersarkōma*, *hypersarkōsis—sarx*, flesh; *path.*), proud or fungous flesh.—*v.t.* **hypersens′itise**, *-ize*, to increase the sensitivity of.—*adj.* **hypersens′itive**, excessively sensitive.—*ns.* **hypersens′itiveness**; **hypersensitiv′ity**.—*adjs.* **hypersen′sual**, beyond the scope of the senses; **hyperson′ic** (L. *sonus*, sound), (of speeds) greater than Mach 5.—*ns.* **hyperson′ics**; **hypersthene** (*hī′pər-sthēn*; Gr. *sthenos*, strength, because harder than hornblende), rock-forming orthorhombic pyroxene, anhydrous silicate of magnesium and iron, generally dark green, brown, or raven-black with metallic lustre; **hypersthē′nia** (*path.*), a morbid condition marked by excessive excitement of all the vital phenomena.—*adj.* **hypersthenic** (*-sthen′ik*), of hypersthene or of hypersthenia.—*ns.* **hypersthē′nite**, a rock consisting almost entirely of hypersthene: an aggregate of labradorite and hypersthene (*obs.*); **hyperten′sion**, blood pressure higher than normal; **hyperthermia**, (dangerous) overheating of the body; **hyperthyroidism** (*-thī′roid-izm*), overactivity of the thyroid gland, and the resulting condition.—*adjs.* **hypertroph′ic**, *-al*, **hyper′trophied**, **hyper′trophous** (Gr. *trophē*, nourishment).—*ns.* **hyper′trophy**, overnourishment: abnormal enlargement; **hypervitaminos′is**, the condition resulting from too much of any vitamin (esp. vitamin D). [Gr. *hyper*, over.]

**Hypericum**, *hi-per′i-kəm*, *n.* the St John's wort genus of plants, giving name to a family **Hypericā′ceae**. [Gr. *hyperikon* or *hypereikos—hypo*, under, *ereikē*, heath.]

**Hyperion**, *hi-pēr′i-on*, *n.* a Titan, son of Uranus and Ge, and father of Helios, Selene, and Eos: Helios himself, the incarnation of light and beauty. [Gr. *Hypĕriōn*.]

**hypha**, *hī′fa*, *n.* a thread of fungus mycelium:—*pl.* **hy′phae** (*-fē*).—*adj.* **hy′phal**. [Gr. *hyphē*, web.]

**hyphen**, *hī′fən*, *n.* a short stroke (-) joining two syllables or words.—*v.t.* to join by a hyphen.—*v.t.* **hy′phenate**, to hyphen.—*adj.* **hyphened**: hyphenated.—*n.* a hyphenated American.—*adj.* **hy′phenated**, hyphened: of nationality expressed by a hyphened word, as Irish-American: of divided, or alien, national sympathies.—*n.* a hyphenated American.—*n.* **hyphena′tion**.—*adj.*

**hyphenic** (*-fen′ik*).—*v.t.* **hy′phenise**, *-ize*.—*ns.* **hyphenisā′tion**, *-z-*, **hyphening**; **hy′phenism**, state of being a hyphenate. [Gr. *hÿphĕn—hypo*, under, *hen*, one.]

**hypinosis**, *hip-i-nō′sis*, *n.* defect of fibrin in the blood; opposite of *hyperinosis* (under **hyper-**). [Gr. *hypo*, under, *is*, *inos*, fibre.]

**hypnagogic**, **hypnogogic image**. See under Hypnos.

**Hypnos**, *hip′nos*, *n.* the Greek god of sleep.—*adjs.* **hypnagogic** (*-goj′ik*, *-gog′ik*; Gr. *agōgos*, bringing), sleep-bringing: ushering in sleep; **hyp′nic**, pertaining to or inducing sleep.—*n.* a soporific.—*ns.* **hypno-anaesthē′sia**, hypnotic sleep; **hyp′noanal′ysis**, analysis of a patient's psychological troubles by obtaining information from him while he is in a state of hypnosis; **hypnogen′esis**, **hypnogeny** (*-noj′i-ni*), production of the hypnotic state.—*adjs.* **hypnogenet′ic**, **hypnog′enous**, **hypnogen′ic**, inducing the hypnotic state, or sleep; **hyp′noid**, *-al*, like sleep: like hypnosis: esp. of a state between hypnosis and waking.—*v.t.* **hyp′noidise**, *-ize*, to put in the hypnoidal state.—*ns.* **hypnol′ogy**, the scientific study of sleep; **hyp′none**, an aromatic ketone used in medicine as a hypnotic; **hypnopae′dia**, learning or conditioning, by repetition of recorded sound during sleep (or semiwakefulness).—*adj.* **hypnopomp′ic** (Gr. *pompē*, a sending), dispelling sleep.—*ns.* **hypnō′sis**, a sleeplike state in which the mind responds to external suggestion and can recover forgotten memories; **hypnother′apy**, the treatment of illness by hypnotism.—*adj.* **hypnot′ic**, of or relating to hypnosis: soporific.—*n.* a soporific: a person subject to hypnotism or in a state of hypnosis.—*adv.* **hypnot′ically**.—*adj.* **hypnotis′able**, *-z-*.—*ns.* **hypnotisabil′ity**; **hypnotisā′tion**, *-z-*.—*v.t.* **hyp′notise**, *-ize*, to put in a state of hypnosis: fascinate, dazzle, overpower the mind of (*fig.*).—*ns.* **hyp′notiser**, *-z-*; **hyp′notism**, the science of hypnosis: the art or practice of inducing hypnosis: hypnosis; **hyp′notist**, one who hypnotises.—*adjs.* **hypnotist′ic**; **hyp′notoid**, like hypnosis.—**hypnagogic**, **hypnogogic**, **image**, hallucination experienced when falling asleep or fatigued. [Gr. *hypnos*, sleep.]

**Hypnum**, *hip′nəm*, *n.* a large genus (often divided) of mosses, with capsules on special lateral branches. [Latinised from Gr. *hypnon*, a kind of lichen.]

**hypo-**, *hī′pō-*, *hip′ō-*, or *-o′-*, in composition, under: defective: inadequate.—*n.* **hy′po** (*phot.*), an abbreviation of *hypo*sulphite, in the sense of sodium thiosulphate.—*adj.* **hypoaeolian** (*hī-pō-ē-ō′li-ən*), below the Aeolian mode: applied in old church music to a plagal mode extending from *e* to *e*, with *a* for its final.—*n.* **hypoblast** (*hip′*, *hip′ō-blast*; Gr. *blastos*, bud; *zool.*), the inner germ-layer of a gastrula.—*adj.* **hypoblast′ic**.—*ns.* **hypobole** (*hip-ob′o-lē*; Gr. *hypobolē*, throwing under, suggestion—*ballein*, to throw; *rhet.*), anticipation of objections; **hypocaust** (*hip′*, *hip′ō-köst*; Gr. *hypokauston—hypo*, under, *kaiein*, to burn), a space under a floor for heating by hot air or furnace gases, esp. in ancient Roman villas; **hypochlorite** (*hi-pō-klō′rit*, *-klō′*), a salt of **hypochlō′rous acid**, an acid (HClO) with less oxygen than chlorous acid; **hypochondria** (*hip-*, *hip-ō-kon′dri-a*), originally the *pl.* of **hypochondrium** (see below): morbid anxiety about health: imaginary illness: a nervous malady, often arising from indigestion, and tormenting the patient with imaginary fears (once supposed to have its seat in the abdomen (*obs.*).—*adj.* **hypochon′driac**, relating to or affected with hypochondria: melancholy.—*n.* a sufferer from hypochondria.—*adj.* **hypochondri′acal**.—*ns.* **hypochondri′asis**, **hypochondri′acism**, **hypochon′driasm**, hypochondria; **hypochon′driast**, one suffering from hypochondria; **hypochon′drium** (Gr. *hypochondrion—chondros*, cartilage; *anat.*), the region of the abdomen on either side, under the costal cartilages and short ribs; hypocist (*hī'pō-sist*; Gr. *hypokistis—kistos*, cistus), an inspissated juice from fruit of *Cytinus hypocistis* (Rafflesiaceae), a plant parasitic on cistus roots; hypocorism (*hip-*, *hip-ok'ər-izm*), hypocorisma (*-iz'ma*; Gr. *hypokorisma—hypokorizesthai*, to use child-talk—*koros*, boy, *korē*, girl), a pet-name: a diminutive or abbreviated name.— *adjs.* hypocorist'ic, -al.—*adv.* hypocorist'ically. —*n.* hypocotyl (*hip-*, *hip-ō-kot'il*), that part of the axis of a plant which is between the cotyledons and the primary root.—*adj.* hypocotylē'donary.— *ns.* hypocrisy (*hī-pok'ri-si*; Gr. *hypokrisiā*, acting, playing a part), a feigning to be better than one is, or to be what one is not: concealment of true character or belief (not necessarily conscious): an instance or act of hypocrisy; hypocrite (*hip'ə-krit*; Gr. *hypokritēs*, actor), one who practises hypocrisy.—*adj.* hypocrit'ical (also hypocrit'ic), practising hypocrisy: of the nature of hypocrisy.—*adv.* hypocrit'ically.—*n.* hypocycloid (*hī-pō-sī'kloid*), a curve generated by a point on the circumference of a circle which rolls on the inside of another circle.—*adj.* hypocycloid'al.—*ns.* hypoderm (*hip'* or *hip'ō-dûrm*), hypoder'ma, hypoder'mis (Gr. *derma*, skin; *bot.*), the tissue next under the epidermis.—*adjs.* hypoderm'al; hypoderm'ic, pertaining to the hypodermis: under the epidermis: under the skin, subcutaneous, esp. of a method of injecting a drug in solution under the skin by means of a fine hollow needle to which a small syringe is attached.—*n.* hypoder'mic, a hypodermic injection: a drug so injected: a syringe for the purpose.—*adv.* hypoder'mically.—*adjs.* hypodorian (*hī-pō-dō'ri-ən*, -dō'*; Gr. *hypodōrios*), below the Dorian: applied in ancient Greek music to a mode whose upper tetrachord is the lower tetrachord of the Dorian (as: *a*; *b c d e*; *e f g a*): in old church music to a plagal mode extending from *a* to *a*, with *d* as its final; hypogastric (*hip-* or *hip-ō-gas'trik*; Gr. *gastēr*, belly), belonging to the lower median part of the abdomen.—*n.* hypogas'trium, the hypogastric region.—*adjs.* hypogeal, -gaeal (-*jē'əl*), -ge'an, -gae'an, -ge'ous, -gae'ous (Gr. *hypogeios*, -*gaios* —*gē* or *gaia*, the ground; *bot.*), underground: germinating with cotyledons underground; hypogene (*hip'* or *hip'ō-jēn*; Gr. *gennaein*, to engender; *geol.*), of or pertaining to rocks formed, or agencies at work, under the earth's surface, plutonic—opp. to *epigene*).—*n.* hypogeum, hypogaeum (*hip-*, *hip-ō-jē'əm*), an underground chamber: a subterranean tomb:—*pl.* hypoge'a, -gae'a.—*adj.* hypoglossal (*hip-* or *hip-ō-glos'əl*; Gr. *glōssa*, the tongue), under the tongue.—*ns.* hypoglyc(a)emia (*hī-po-gli-sē'mi-a*; *med.*), abnormal reduction of sugar content of the blood; hypog'nathism.—*adjs.* hypognathous (*hip-* or *hip-og'nə-thəs*), having the lower jaw or mandible protruding; hypogynous (*hī-poj'i-nəs*; Gr. *gynē*, a woman, female; *bot.*), growing from beneath the ovary: having the other floral parts below the ovary.—*n.* hypog'yny.—*adjs.* hypolydian (*hī-pō-lid'i-ən*), below the Lydian mode: applied in ancient Greek music to a mode having as its upper tetrachord the lower tetrachord of the Lydian (as: *f*; *g a b c*; *c d e f*): in old church music to a plagal mode extending from *c* to *c* with *f* as its final; hypomixolydian (*hī-pō-mik-sō-lid'i-ən*), applied in old church music to a mode extending from *d* to *d* with *g* as its final.— *n.* hypomania (*hip-*, *hip-ō-mā'ni-ə*; *med.*), simple mania, a condition marked by overexcitability. —*adj.* hypomā'nic (or *-man'ik*).—*ns.* hyponasty (*hip'* or *hip'ō-nas-ti*; Gr. *nastos*, pressed close; *bot.*), increased growth on the lower side causing an upward bend—opp. to *epinasty*; hypophosphite (*hī-pō-fos'fīt*), a salt of hypophos'phorous

acid, an acid ($H_3PO_2$) with less oxygen than phosphorous acid.—*adj.* hypophrygian (*-frij'i-ən*), below the Phrygian mode: applied in ancient Greek music to a mode having its upper tetrachord the lower tetrachord of the Phrygian (as, *g*; *a b c d*; *d e f g*); in old church music to a plagal mode extending from *b* to *b*, with *e* for its final.—*ns.* hypophysis (*hip-*, *hip-of'i-sis*; Gr. *hypophysis*, an attachment underneath—*phyein*, to grow), a down-growth (*zool.*): the pituitary body of the brain: an inflated part of the pedicel under the capsule, in mosses (*bot.*): in flowering plants, a cell between the suspensor and the embryo proper; hypoplastron (*hip-*, *hip-ō-plas'tron*; *zool.*), the plate behind the hypoplastron in a turtle's plastron; hypostasis (*hip-*, *hip-os'tə-sis*; Gr. *hypostasis—stasis*, setting), orig. basis, foundation: substance, essence (*metaph.*): the essence or real personal subsistence or substance of each of the three divisions of the Trinity: sediment, deposit: passive hyperaemia in a dependent part owing to sluggishness of circulation (*med.*).—*adjs.* hypostatic (-*stat'ik*), -al.—*adv.* hypostat'ically.— *v.t.* hypos'tatise, -ize, to treat as hypostasis: to personify.—*n.* hypostrophe (*hip-*, *hip-os'trə-fi*; Gr. *hypostrophē*, turning back), relapse (*med.*): reversion after a parenthesis (*rhet.*).—*adj.* hypostyle (*hip'*, *hip'ō-stil*; Gr. *stylos*, a pillar; *archit.*), having the roof supported by pillars.— Also *n.*—*ns.* hyposul'phate, a dithionate; hyposul'phite, a salt of hyposul'phurous acid ($H_2S_2O_4$; also, in older usage $H_2S_2O_3$).—*adjs.* hyposulphūr'ic, dithionic; hypotac'tic.—*ns.* hypotaxis (*hip-*, *hip-ō-tak'sis*; Gr. *taxis*, arrangement; *gram.*), dependent construction—opp. to *parataxis*; hypotenuse (*hip-*, *hip-ot'ən-ūs*, or -*ūz*), hypothenuse (*-oth'*; Fr. *hypoténuse*—L. *hypotēnūsa*—Gr. *hypoteinousa*, fem. part., subtending or stretching under—*teinein*, to stretch), the side of a right-angled triangle opposite to the right angle; hypoten'sion, low blood-pressure; hypothalamus (*hip-*, *hip-ō-thal'ə-məs*; L.L.; *med.*), the part of the brain which makes up the floor and part of the lateral walls of the third ventricle.—*adj.* hypothalam'ic.—*n.* hypothec (*hip-*, *hip-oth'ik*; Gr. *hypothēkē*, a pledge), in Scots law, a lien or security over goods in respect of a debt due by the owner of the goods —the whole (hale) hypothec (*Scot.*), the whole affair, collection, concern—everything.—*adj.* hypoth'ecary, pertaining to hypothecation or mortgage.—*v.t.* hypoth'ecate, to place or assign as security under an arrangement: to mortgage. —*ns.* hypothecā'tion; hypoth'ecātor; hypothermia (*hip-*, *hip-ō-thûr'mi-ə*; Gr. *thermē*, heat), subnormal body temperature, esp. that induced for purposes of heart and other surgery (see freeze-down); hypothesis (*hī-poth'i-sis*; Gr. *hypothesis—thesis*, placing), a supposition: a proposition assumed for the sake of argument: a theory to be proved or disproved by reference to facts: a provisional explanation of anything: —*pl.* hypoth'esēs.—*vs.t.* and *vs.i.* hypoth'esise, -ize, hypoth'etise, -ize.—*adjs.* hypothet'ic, -al. —*adv.* hypothet'ically.—*ns.* hypotrochoid (*hip-*, *hip-ō-trō'koid*; Gr. *trochos*, wheel, *eidos*, form), the curve traced by a point on the radius, or radius produced, of a circle rolling within another circle; hypotyposis (*hip-*, *hip-ō-tip-ō'sis*; *rhet.*), vivid description of a scene. [Gr. *hypo*, under.] hypo. See hypo.

hypso-, *hip'sō-*, in composition, height.—*ns.* hypsometry (*hip-som'ə-tri*; Gr. *metron*, a measure), the art of measuring the heights of places on the earth's surface; hypsom'eter, an instrument for doing this by taking the boiling point of water.— *adj.* hypsomet'ric.—*ns.* hypsophobia (*hip-sō-fō'bi-ə*; Gr. *phobos*, fear), fear of (falling from) high places; hypsophyll (*hip'sō-fil*; Gr. *phyllon*, leaf; *bot.*), a bract.—*adj.* hypsophyll'ary. [Gr. *hypsos*, height.]

hypural, *hī-pū'rəl, adj.* situated beneath the tail. [Gr. *hypo*, under, *ourā*, tail.]

**Hyrax, *hī'raks, n.*** a genus (also called Procavia) of mammals superficially like marmots but really closer akin to the ungulates, living among rocks in Africa and Syria—the daman, the dassie or rock-rabbit, the cony of the Bible—constituting the order Hyracoid'ea. [Gr. *hȳrax*, a shrew.]

hyson, *hī'son, n.* a very fine sort of green tea.— hy'son-skin, the refuse of hyson tea removed by winnowing. [From Chin.]

hyssop, *his'əp, n.* an aromatic labiate (*Hyssopus officinalis*): an unknown wall-plant used as a ceremonial sprinkler (*B.*): a holy-water sprinkler. [L. *hyssōpus, -um*—Gr. *hyssōpos, -on*; cf. Heb. *'ēzōb*.]

hyster-, hystero-, *his'tər-(o-)*, in composition, womb.—*ns.* hysterec'tomy (Gr. *ektomē*, a cutting out), surgical removal of the uterus; hysteri'tis, inflammation of the uterus; hysterot'omy (Gr. *tomē*, a cut), surgical incision of the uterus. [Gr. *hysterā*, the womb.]

hysteranthous, *his-tər-an'thəs, adj.* having the leaves appearing after the flowers. [Gr. *hysteros*, later, *anthos*, flower.]

hysteresis, *his-tə-rē'sis, n.* the retardation or lagging of an effect behind the cause of the effect: the influence of earlier treatment of a body on its subsequent reaction.—*adjs.* hysterēs'-

ial, hysterĕt'ic.—high-hysteresis rubber, rubber with less than normal bounce. [Gr. *hysterēsis*, a deficiency, coming late—*hysteros*, later.]

hysteria, *his-tē'ri-ə, n.* a psychoneurosis in which repressed complexes become split off or dissociated from the personality, forming independent units, partially or completely unrecognised by consciousness, giving rise to hypnoidal states (amnesia, somnambulisms), and manifested by various physical symptoms, such as tics, paralysis, blindness, deafness, etc., general features being an extreme degree of emotional instability and an intense craving for affection: an outbreak of wild emotionalism.—*adjs.* hysteric (*his-ter'ik*), -al, pertaining to, of the nature of, or affected with, hysterics or hysteria: like hysterics: fitfully and violently emotional.—*adv.* hyster'ically.—*adj.* hyster'icky (*coll.*).—*n.pl.* hyster'ics, hysteric fits: popularly, alternate paroxysms of laughing and crying.—*adjs.* hys'teroid, -al, like hysteria.—*n.* hysteromän'ia, hysterical mania, often marked by erotic delusions and an excessive desire to attract attention.—hysterical pregnancy (see pseudocyesis). [Gr. *hysterā*, the womb, with which hysteria was formerly thought to be connected.]

hysteron-proteron, *his'tər-on-prot'ər-on, n.* a figure of speech in which what would ordinarily follow comes first: an inversion. [Gr., lit. latter-former.]

hythe. Same as hithe.

Neutral vowels in unaccented syllables: *el'ə-mənt*; for certain sounds in foreign words, see p. viii

**I, i, ī,** *n.* the ninth letter of our alphabet, answering to Greek *iōta*, has various sounds (as in *dip, mind, bird, machine*). In Roman numerals I represents one; in mathematics *i* represents the imaginary square root of −1.

**I, ī,** *pron.* the nominative singular of the first personal pronoun: the word used in mentioning oneself.—*n.* the object of self-consciousness, the ego. [M.E. *ich*—O.E. *ic*; Ger. *ich*, O.N. *ek*, L. *ego*, Gr. *egō*.]

**I, ī,** *adv.* same as ay.

**i', i,** *prep.* a form of in.

**-ia,** *-ē′ə, -yə, suff.* used in naming (1) a pathological condition, (2) a genus of plants or animals, (3) (as L. or Gr. *neut. pl.*) a taxonomic division, (4) (as *pl.*) things pertaining to (something specified).

**iambus,** *i-am′bəs, n.* a foot of two syllables, a short followed by a long, or an unstressed by a stressed:—*pl.* **iam′buses, iam′bi.**—Also **i′amb.**—*adj.* **iam′bic,** consisting of iambuses: of the nature of an iambus: using iambic verse: satirical in verse.—*n.* an iambus: (in *pl.*) iambic verse, esp. satirical.—*adv.* **iam′bically,** in the manner of an iambic.—*ns.* **iam′bist, iambo′grapher,** a writer of iambics. [L. *iambus*—Gr. *iambos*—*iaptein,* to assail, this metre being first used by satirists.]

**ianthine,** *i-an′thin, adj.* violet-coloured. [Gr. *ianthinos*—*ion,* violet, *anthos,* flower.]

**Iastic,** *i-ast′ik, (mus.) adj.* Ionian.—**Iastic mode,** the Ionian, hypophrygian, or hyperdorian mode of ancient Greek music. [Gr. *Iastikos,* Ionian.]

**iatric, -al,** *i-at′rik, -əl, adj.* relating to medicine or physicians.—*adj.* **iatrochem′ical.**—*ns.* **iatrochemist; iatrochem′istry,** an application of chemistry to medical theory introduced by Franciscus Sylvius (1614-72) of Leyden.—*adj.* **iatrogen′ic,** (of disease) caused by treatment, esp. for some other ailment.—*n.* **iatro′geny.** [Gr. *iātros, iātros,* a physician.]

**Iberian,** *i-bē′ri-ən, adj.* of Spain and Portugal: of Iberia (now Georgia) in the Caucasus: of the ancient inhabitants of either of these, or their later representatives: of a Mediterranean people of Neolithic culture in Britain, etc.—*n.* a member of any of these peoples. [L. *Ibēria*—Gr. *Ibēriā.*]

**Iberis,** *i-bē′ris, n.* the candytuft genus of Cruciferae. [Gr. *ibēris,* pepperwort.]

**ibex,** *i′beks, n.* a large-horned mountain wild-goat:—*pl.* **i′bexes,** also **ibices** (*i′bi-sēz*). [L. *ibex, -icis.*]

**ibidem,** *ib-i′dəm, ib′i-dəm, i-bē′dem,* (L.) in the same place.—Abbrev. **ib., ibid.**

**ibis,** *i′bis, n.* a wading bird with curved bill, akin to the spoonbills, one species worshipped by the ancient Egyptians. [L. and Gr. *ibis,* prob. Egyptian.]

**Iblis.** See Eblis.

**Icarian,** *i-kā′ri-ən, i-, adj.* of or like Icarus (*ī-* or *i-*; Gr. *Ikăros*), who flew from Crete on wings made by Daedalus—made partly of wax which melted as he passed too near the sun, plunging him into the sea. See also **daedal.**

**ice,** *īs, n.* frozen water: any substance resembling this: concreted sugar on a cake, etc.: a frozen confection of fruit-juice, etc.: ice-cream: reserve, formality: coldness of manner: diamond(s) (*slang*).—*adj.* of ice.—*v.t.* to cover with ice: to freeze: to cool with ice: to cover with concreted sugar.—*v.i.* to freeze: to become covered with ice (with *up*):—*pr.p.* ic′ing; *pa.t.* and *pa.p.* iced.—*adj.* **iced** (*īst*), covered with or cooled with ice; encrusted with sugar.—*n.* **i′cer,** one who makes icing.—*adv.* **ic′ily.**—*ns.* **ic′iness; ic′ing,** covering with or of ice or concreted sugar.—*adjs.* **ic′y,** composed of, abounding in, or like ice: frosty: cold: chilling: without warmth of affection.—**ice′-action,** the work of land-ice in grinding the earth's surface; **ice age** (*geol.*), any time when a great part of the earth's surface has been covered with ice, esp. that in Pleistocene times; **ice′-anchor,** a one-armed anchor for mooring to an ice-floe; **ice′-ā′pron,** a structure on the up-stream side of a bridge pier to break or ward off floating ice; **ice′-axe,** an axe used by mountain climbers to cut steps in ice; **iceberg** (from Scand. or Du.), a huge mass of floating ice; **ice′-bird,** the little auk or sea-dove; **ice′blink,** a gleam reflected from distant masses of ice; **ice′-boat,** a boat for forcing a way through or sailing or being dragged over ice.—*adj.* **ice′-bound,** bound, surrounded, or fixed in with ice.—**ice′-box,** the freezing compartment of a refrigerator: a refrigerator (*U.S.*); **ice′-breaker,** ship for breaking channels through ice: anything for breaking ice; **ice′-bucket,** a receptacle with ice for cooling bottles of wine; **ice′-cap,** a covering of ice over a convexity, as a mountain top, the polar regions of a planet.—*adj.* **ice′-cold,** cold as, or like, ice.—**ice′-craft,** skill in travelling over or through ice; **ice′-cream′,** cream, or a substitute, sweetened or flavoured, and frozen (**ice′-cream soda,** soda-water with ice-cream added); **ice′-fall,** a fall of ice: a steep broken place in a glacier; **ice′-fern,** a fern-like encrustation on a window in frost; **ice′-field,** a large area covered with ice, esp. floating ice; **ice′-floe,** a large sheet of floating ice; **ice′-foot,** a belt of ice forming round the shores in Arctic regions—also **ice′-belt, ice′-ledge.**—*adj.* **ice′-free,** without ice.—**ice′-front,** the front face of a glacier; **ice′-hill;** a slope of ice for tobogganing; **ice′-hill′ing; ice′-hock′ey,** a form of hockey played on ice with a puck by skaters; **ice′-house,** a house for keeping ice in; **ice′man,** a man skilled in travelling upon ice: a dealer in ice: a man who looks after an ice-rink; **ice′pack,** drifting ice packed together: a pack prepared with ice; **ice′-pan,** a slab of floating ice; **ice′-plant,** a plant (Mesembrianthemum) whose leaves glisten like ice in the sun; **ice′-rink,** a skating rink of ice; **ice′-run,** a tobogganing slide; **ice′-sheet,** land-ice covering a whole region; **ice′-show,** an entertainment or exhibition provided by skaters on ice; **ice′-spar,** a clear glassy orthoclase; **ice′-stone,** cryolite; **ice′-water,** water from melted ice: iced water; **ice′-worm,** a species of oligochaete stated by some to be found on glaciers in Alaska, etc.; **ice′-yacht,** a ship on runners and with sails for sailing over smooth ice; **ice′-yacht′ing.**—*adj.* **ic′y-pearl′ed** (*Milt.*), studded with pearls or spangles of ice.—**break the ice** (see break); **cut no ice,** to count for nothing; **dry ice,** solid carbon dioxide; **on ice** (*fig.*), kept or waiting in readiness. [O.E. *is*; O.N. *iss*; Ger. *eis*, Dan. *is.*]

**Iceland,** *īs′lənd, adj.* belonging to, originating in, Iceland.—*n.* **Ice′lander,** a native or citizen of Iceland: an Iceland falcon.—*adj.* **Icelandic**

*fāte, fär; mē, hûr* (her); *mīne; mōte, for; mūte; mōōn, fōōt; đhen* (then) (*island'ik*), of Iceland.—*n.* the modern language of the Icelanders: Old Norse.—Ice'land-dog', a shaggy white dog, sharp-eared, imported from Iceland; Iceland falcon, a white gerfalcon of Iceland; Iceland moss, a lichen of northern regions, used as a medicine and for food; Iceland poppy, a dwarf poppy (*Papaver nudicaule*) with grey-green pinnate leaves and flowers varying from white to orange-scarlet; Iceland spar, a transparent calcite with strong double refraction.

ich, *ich*, (*Shak.*) *v.t.* Same as eke.

ichabod, *ik'ə-bod, interj.* the glory is departed. [From Heb.; see 1 Sam. iv. 21.]

ichneumon, *ik-nū'mən, n.* any animal of the mongoose genus (Herpestes) of the civet family, esp. the Egyptian species that destroys crocodiles' eggs: (in full ichneu'mon-fly) any insect of a large family of Hymenoptera whose larvae are parasitic in or on other insects. [Gr. *ichneumōn,* lit. tracker, *ichneuein,* to hunt after—*ichnos,* a track.]

ichnography, *ik-nog'raf-i, n.* a ground plan: the art of drawing ground plans.—*adjs.* ichnographic (*-nō-graf'ik*), -al.—*adv.* ichnograph'ically. —*n.* ichnol'ogy, footprint lore: the science of fossil footprints. [Gr. *ichnos,* a track, footprint.]

ichor, *i'kör, n.* the ethereal juice in the veins of the gods (*myth.*): a watery humour: colourless matter from an ulcer.—*adj.* i'chorous. [Gr. *ichōr.*]

ichthy(o)-, *ik'thi-(ō-),* in composition, fish.—*adj.* ich'thic.—*ns.* ichthyocoll'a (Gr. *kolla,* glue), fishglue: isinglass; ichthyodor'ūlite, -dor'ylite (*-i-līt*; Gr. *dory,* a spear, *lithos,* a stone), a fossil fishspine; ichthyog'raphy, a description of fishes. —*adjs.* ich'thyoid, -al, fishlike.—*n.* ichthyol'atry (Gr. *latreiā,* worship), fish-worship.—*adj.* ichthyol'atrous.—*n.* ich'thyolite (Gr. *lithos,* a stone), a fossil fish or fish-fossil.—*adjs.* ichthyolitic (*-lit'ik*); ichthyolog'ical.—*ns.* ichthyol'ogist; ichthyol'ogy, the branch of natural history that treats of fishes; ichthyophagist (*-of'ə-jist;* Gr. *phagein,* to eat), a fish-eater.—*adj.* ichthyoph'-agous (*-ə-gəs*).—*ns.* ichthyophagy (*-of'ə-ji*), the practice of eating fish; ichthyop'sid, -an (Gr. *opsis,* appearance).—*ns.pl.* Ichthyop'sida, a group of vertebrates in Huxley's classification comprising amphibians, fishes, and fishlike vertebrates; Ichthyopterygia (*-op-tar-ij'i-ə;* Gr. *pterygion,* a fin, dim. of *pteryx,* wing), the Ichthyosauria.—*ns.* Ichthyor'nis (Gr. *ornis,* a bird), a Cretaceous fossil bird with vertebrae like those of fishes, and with teeth set in sockets; ichthyosaur (*ik'thi-ō-sör;* Gr. *sauros,* lizard), any member of the genus Ichthyosaur'us or of the order Ichthyosaur'ia, gigantic Mesozoic fossil fishlike marine reptiles.—*adj.* ichthyosaur'ian.—*n.* ichthyō'sis, a disease in which the skin becomes hardened, thickened, and rough. —*adj.* ichthyŏt'ic.—*n.* ich'thys, an emblem or motto (ΙΧΘΥΣ), supposed to have a mystical connection with Jesus Christ, being the first letters of the Greek words meaning 'Jesus Christ, Son of God, Saviour'. [Gr. *ichthys,* fish.]

icicle, *is'i-kl, n.* a hanging, tapering piece of ice formed by the freezing of dropping water. [O.E. *isesgicel—ises,* gen. of *is,* ice, *gicel,* icicle.]

icker, *ik'ər,* (*Scot.*) *n.* an ear of corn. [O.E. (Northumbrian) *eher, æhher* (W.S. *ēar*).]

icon, *i'kon, n.* a figure: image: a portrait, carved, painted, etc.: in the Greek Church a figure representing Christ, or a saint, in painting, mosaic, etc. (not sculpture).—*adj.* icon'ic, of images or icons: conventional in type.—*ns.* icon'oclasm (Gr. *klaein,* to break), act of breaking images: opposition to image-worship; icon'oclast, a breaker of images: one opposed to image-worship, esp. those in the Eastern Church, from the 8th century: one who assails old cherished errors and superstitions.—*adj.* iconoclast'ic.—*ns.* iconog'raphy (Gr. *graphiā,* a writing), the art of illustration: the study, description, cataloguing, or collective representation of portraits; iconol'ater, an image-worshipper; iconol'atry (Gr. *latreiā,* worship), image-worship; iconol'ogist; iconol'ogy, the study of icons: symbolism; iconomachist (*-om'ə-kist*), one who contends against the use of icons in worship; iconom'achy (Gr. *machē,* fight), opposition to image-worship.—*adj.* iconomat'ic, using pictures of objects to represent not the things themselves but the sounds of their names, as in a transition stage between picture-writing and a phonetic system.—*ns.* iconomat'icism (*-i-sizm*); iconom'eter, an instrument for inferring distance from size or size from distance of an object, by measuring its image: a direct photographic view-finder; iconom'etry; icono'-philism, a taste for pictures, etc.; iconoph'ilist, a connoisseur of pictures, etc.; icon'oscope, a form of electron camera; iconos'tasis (Gr. eikonostasis—*stasis,* placing), in Eastern churches, a screen shutting off the sanctuary, on which the icons are placed. [L. *icōn*—Gr. *eikōn,* an image.]

icosahedron, *i-kos-ə-hē'dron,* (*geom.*) *n.* a solid with twenty plane faces:—*pl.* icosahē'dra.—*adj.* icosahē'dral.—*n.* icositetrahē'dron (*geom.*), a solid figure with twenty-four plane faces. [Gr. *eikosi,* twenty, *hedrā,* a seat.]

Icosandria, *i-kos-an'dri-ə, n.pl.* a Linnaean class of plants with twenty or more free stamens.—*adjs.* icosan'drian, icosan'drous. [Gr. *eikosi,* twenty, *anēr, andros,* a man (male).]

icterus, *ik'tər-əs, n.* jaundice: (*cap.*) a genus of birds with much yellow in their plumage, including the Baltimore oriole, giving name to the American family Icteridae (*-ter'i-dē*); hangnests, bobolinks, troupials, grackles).—*adjs.* icteric (*-ter'ik*), -al, relating to or affected with jaundice.—*ns.* a medicine for jaundice.—*adjs.* ic'terine (*-tər-in, -in*), of or like the family Icteridae: yellowish or marked with yellow; icteritious (*ik-tər-ish'əs*), jaundiced: yellow. [Gr. *ikteros,* jaundice, also a yellowish bird (acc. to Pliny the golden oriole) the sight of which cured jaundice.]

ictus, *ik'təs, n.* a stroke: rhythmical or metrical stress: a pulsation:—*pl.* ic'tuses (or L. *pl.* ic'tūs, *-tōōs*).—*adj.* ic'tic. [L., a blow.]

I'd, *id,* contracted from I would, or I had: also used for I should.

id, *id,* ide, *id, n.* a fish of the same family as the carp, inhabiting fresh water in Northern Europe. [Sw. *id.*]

id, *id,* (*biol.*) *n.* in Weismann's theory, an element in a chromosome carrying all the hereditary characters.—*n.* idant (*i'dant*), an aggregation of ids: a chromosome. [Gr. *idios,* own, private; appar. suggested by idioplasm.]

id, *id,* (*psych.*) *n.* the sum total of the primitive instinctive forces in an individual subserving the pleasure-pain principle. [L. *id,* it.]

Idaean, *i-dē'ən, adj.* of Mount Ida in Crete, or that near Troy.—Idaean vine, the cowberry.

Idalian, *i-dā'li-ən, adj.* pertaining to Idalium (Gr. *Idálion*), in Cyprus, or to Aphrodite, to whom it was sacred.

ide. See id (1).

idea, *i-dē'ə, n.* an image of an external object formed by the mind: a notion, thought, impression, any product of intellectual action, of memory and imagination: plan: an archetype of the manifold varieties of existence in the universe, belonging to the supersensible world, where reality is found and where God is (*Platonic*): one of the three products of the reason (the Soul, the Universe, and God) transcending the conceptions of the understanding—*transcendental ideas*, in the functions of mind concerned with unification of existence (*Kantian*): the ideal realised, the absolute truth of which everything that exists is the expression (*Hegelian*). —*adjs.* idē'aed, idē'a'd, provided with an idea or ideas; idē'al, existing in idea: conceptual: existing in imagination only: highest and best conceivable: perfect, as opposed to the real, the imperfect: theoretical, conforming absolutely to theory.—*n.* the highest conception of anything, or its embodiment: a standard of perfection: that which exists in the imagination only: a subring of a ring, any member of which when multiplied by any member of the ring, whether in the subring or not, results in a member of the subring (*math.*).—*adj.* idē'aless, devoid of ideas.—*n.* idēalisā'tion, -z-.—*v.t.* idē'alise, -ize, to regard or represent as ideal.—*v.i.* to form ideals: to think or work idealistically.—*ns.* idē'aliser, -z-; idē'alism, the doctrine that in external perceptions the objects immediately known are ideas, that all reality is in its nature psychical: any system that considers thought or the idea as the ground either of knowledge or existence: tendency towards the highest conceivable perfection, love for or search after the best and highest: the habit or practice of idealising: impracticality: the imaginative treatment of subjects; idē'alist, one who holds the doctrine of idealism: one who strives after the ideal: an impractical person.—*adj.* idēalist'ic, pertaining to idealists or to idealism.—*adv.* idēalist'ically.—*n.* idēality (-*al'i-ti*), ideal state: ability and disposition to form ideals of beauty and perfection.—*adj.* idē'alless, having no ideals.—*adv.* idē'ally, in an ideal manner: mentally.—*n.* idē'alogue (a misspelling of ideologue).—*v.t.* idē'ate, to form or have an idea of: to imagine: to preconceive.— *v.i.* to form ideas.—*adj.* produced by an idea.— *n.* the correlative or object of an idea.—*n.* idēā'tion, the power of the mind for forming ideas: the exercise of such power.—*adjs.* idēā'tional, idē'ative.—*adv.* idēā'tionally. [L. *idēa*—Gr. *idēā*; cf. *idein* (aor.), to see.]

idée, ē-dā, (Fr.) idea; idée fixe (*fēks*) a fixed idea, a monomania: a recurring theme in music; idée reçue (*rə-sü*), accepted idea: conventional outlook.

idem, i'dem, i'dem, (L.) the same.—Abbrev. id.; idem sonans (*sō'nanz, so'näns*), sounding the same (used of a word in a legal document which, though misspelt can be accepted as that for which it clearly stands).

identify, *i-den'ti-fī, v.t.* to make, reckon, ascertain or prove to be the same: to ascertain or establish the identity of: to assign to a species: to bind up or associate closely: to regard, or wish to regard, (oneself) as sharing (with a person or group) interests and experiences, or (because of an emotional tie, usu. abnormal) attitudes, characteristics and behaviour.—*v.i.* to become the same:—*pr.p.* iden'tifying; *pa.p.* iden'tified.— *adj.* iden'tifiable.—*n.* identificā'tion, act of identifying: state of being identified: anything which proves one's identity: a process by which a person assumes the behaviour, ideas, etc., of someone else, particularly someone whom he admires (*psych.*). [L.L. *identificāre*— *idem*, the same, *facĕre*, to make.]

identity, *i-den'ti-ti, n.* state of being the same: sameness: individuality: personality: who or what a person or thing is: an equation true for all values of the symbols involved (*math.*).— *adj.* iden'tical, the very same: not different: expressing or resulting in identity.—Also iden'tic. —*adv.* iden'tically.—*n.* iden'ticalness.—identical twins, twins developing from one zygote; identic note, action (*diplomacy*), identical note, action,

sent by, carried out by, two or more governments in dealing with another, others; identikit (orig. *U.S. Identi-Kit*), a device for building up a composite portrait from a large number of different features on transparent slips (also *fig.*); identity card, disk, a card, disk, etc., bearing the owner's or wearer's name, etc., used to establish his identity; identity element (*math.*), an element (*e*) in a system of elements such that $e*x = x*e = x$, for every value of $x$—where * denotes a binary operation. In the ordinary number system, for addition $e = 0$, for multiplication $e = 1$.—law or principle of identity (*logic*), law stating that A is A, that a thing is the same as itself. [L.L. *identitās, -ātis*—L. *idem*, the same.]

ideogram, *id'i-ō-gram*, or *id'*, ideograph, -gräf, *ns.* a written character or symbol that stands not for a word or sound but for the thing itself directly.—*adjs.* ideographic (-*graf'ik*), -al.—*adv.* ideograph'ically.—*n.* ideography (-*og'rə-fi*). [Gr. *idēā*, idea, *gramma*, a drawing, *graphein*, to write.]

ideology, *id-, id-i-ol'ə-ji, n.* the science of ideas, metaphysics: abstract speculation: visionary speculation: body of ideas: way of thinking.— *adjs.* ideologic (-*loj'*), -al, of or pertaining to an ideology: arising from, concerned with, rival ideologies.—*n.* ideol'ogist, one occupied with ideas or an idea: a mere theorist or visionary— also ideologue (*i-dē'ō-log*). [Gr. *idēā*, idea, *logos*, discourse.]

ideopraxist, *id-, id-i-ō-prak'sist, n.* one who is impelled to carry out an idea. [Gr. *idēā*, idea, *prāxis*, doing.]

Ides, *idz, n.pl.* in ancient Rome, the 15th day of March, May, July, October, and the 13th of the other months. [Fr. *ides*—L. *idūs* (pl.).]

id est, *id est*, (L.) that is.—Abbrev. i.e.

idiocy. See idiot.

idioglossia, *id-i-ō-glos'i-a, n.* a condition in which pronunciation is so bad as to be quite unintelligible. [Gr. *idios*, own, private, *glōssa*, tongue.]

idiograph, *id'i-ō-gräf, n.* a private mark: trademark.—*adj.* idiographic (-*graf'ik*). [Gr. *idios*, own, private, *graphein*, to write.]

idiolect, *id'i-ō-lekt, n.* an individual's own distinctive form of speech. [Gr. *idios*, own, *legein*, to speak.]

idiom, *id'i-əm, n.* a mode of expression peculiar to a language: an expression characteristic of a particular language not logically or grammatically explicable: a form or variety of language: a dialect: a characteristic mode of expression.—*adjs.* idiomat'ic, -al.—*adv.* idiomat'ically.—*ns.* idioticon (-*ot'i-kon*), a vocabulary of a particular dialect or district; id'iotism (-*ə-tizm*), an idiom: an idiomatic expression: idiomatic character: (see also under idiot). [Gr. *idiōma, idiōtikon—idios*, own.]

idiomorphic, *id-i-ō-mör'fik, adj.* having the faces belonging to its crystalline form, as a mineral that has had free room to crystallise out. [Gr. *idios*, own, *morphē*, form.]

idiopathy, *id-i-op'ə-thi, n.* a state or experience peculiar to the individual: a primary disease, one not occasioned by another (*med.*).—*adj.* idiopathic (-*path'ik*).—*adv.* idiopath'ically. [Gr. *idios*, own, *pathos*, suffering.]

idioplasm, *id'i-ō-plazm, n.* that part of the protoplasm that determines hereditary character. [Gr. *idios*, own, private, *plasma*, mould.]

idior(r)hythmic, *id-i-ō-ridh'mik*, or *rith'*, *adj.* self-regulating: allowing each member to regulate his own life. [Gr. *idios*, own, *rhythmos*, order.]

idiosyncrasy, *id-i-ō-sing'krə-si, n.* peculiarity of temperament or mental constitution: any characteristic of a person.—*adjs.* idiosyncratic (-*krat'ik*), -al. [Gr. *idios*, own, *synkrāsis*, a mixing together—*syn*, together, *krāsis*, a mixing.]

idiot, id′i-ət, id′yət, n. a person so defective in mind from birth as to be unable to protect himself against ordinary physical dangers: one afflicted with the severest grade of feeble-mindedness: a flighty fool: a blockhead: a foolish or unwise person.—adj. afflicted with idiocy: idiotic.—ns. id′iocy (-ə-si), id′iotcy (rare), state of being an idiot: imbecility: folly. —adjs. idiotic (ot′ik), -al, pertaining to or like an idiot: foolish.—adv. idiot′ically.—adj. id′iotish, idiotic.—n. id′iotism, the state of being an idiot: (see also under idiom).—idiot board, a mechanical device used to prompt a speaker on television; idiot card, a large card with words, etc., for the same purpose. [Fr.,—L. idiōta—Gr. idiōtēs, a private person, ordinary person, one who holds no public office or has no professional knowledge—idios, own, private.] idiothermous, id-i-ō-thûr′məs, adj. warm-blooded, i.e. having a temperature of one's own, independent of surroundings. [Gr. idios, own, thermē, heat.]
idioticon. See under idiom.
idle, i′dl, adj. vain: baseless: trifling: unemployed: averse to labour: not occupied: useless: unimportant: unedifying.—v.t. to spend in idleness: to cause to be idle.—v.i. to be idle or unoccupied: of machinery, to run without doing work.—ns. i′dlehood (arch.), i′dleness; i′dler; id′lesse (poet.), idleness.—adv. i′dly.—adj. i′dle-head′ed, foolish.—i′dle-wheel, a wheel placed between two others for transferring the motion from one to the other without changing the direction.—i′dle-worms (coll.), worms once jocularly supposed to be bred in the fingers of lazy maid-servants. [O.E. idel; Du. ijdel, Ger. eitel.]
Ido, ē′dō, n. an auxiliary international language developed (since 1907) from Esperanto.—ns. Id′ist, I′doist. [Ido, offspring.]
idocrase, id′, id′ō-krās, -krāz, n. the mineral vesuvianite. [Gr. eidos, form, krāsis, mixture.]
idol, i′dl, n. a figure (arch.): an image, a semblance: a phantom: a counterfeit (Spens.): an image of a god: an object of worship: an object of love, admiration, or honour in an extreme degree: (also Idō′lon, Idō′lum; pl. Idō′la) a false notion or erroneous way of looking at things to which the mind is prone, classified by Bacon (Novum Organum, i. § 39) as Idols of the tribe (due to the nature of man's understanding); Idols of the den or cave (due to personal causes); Idols of the forum (due to the influence of words or phrases); Idols of the theatre (due to misconceptions of philosophic system or demonstration).—v.t. i′dolise, -ize, to make an idol of.—ns. idolis′er, -z-, i′dolism, idol-worship: idolising: a false notion (Milt.); i′dolist (Milt.), an idolater; idoloclast (-dol′), a breaker of images. [L. idōlum—Gr. eidōlon—eidos, form—idein (aor.), to see.]
idolater, i-dol′ə-tər, n. a worshipper of idols: a great admirer:—fem. idol′atress.—v.t. and v.i. idol′atrise, -ize, to worship as an idol: to adore. —adj. idol′atrous.—adv. idol′atrously.—n. idol′-atry, the worship of an image held to be the abode of a superhuman personality: excessive love. [Fr. idolâtre—Gr. eidōlolatrēs—eidōlon, idol, latreuein, to worship.]
idyll, id′il, id′il, -əl, n. a short pictorial poem, chiefly on pastoral subjects: a story, episode, or scene of happy innocence or rusticity: a work of art of like character in any medium.— Also idyl.—adjs. idyll′ian, idyll′ic.—n. i′dyllist. [L. idyllium—Gr. eidyllion, dim. of eidos, image.]
if, if, conj. on condition that: provided that: in case that: supposing that: whether.—n. a condition: a supposition.—as if, as it would be if. [O.E. gif; cf. Du. of, O.N. ef.]

igad, i-gad′. Same as egad.
igapó. Same as gapó.
igarapé, ē-gä-rä-pä′, n. a canoe waterway in Brazil. [Tupí.]
igloo, ig′lōō, n. orig. a dome-shaped hut of snow: now usu. a dwelling of other materials: a dome-shaped place of storage or container for goods: a hollow in the snow made by a seal over its breathing hole in the ice. [Eskimo.]
ignaro, ig-nä′rō, ēn-yä′rō, n. an ignorant person. [Prob. from Spenser's character (Faerie Queene, I, viii) whose only answer is 'He could not tell' —It. ignaro—L. ignārus, ignorant.]
Ignatian, ig-nä′shən, adj. of or pertaining to St Ignatius, first-century bishop of Antioch (applied to the Epistles attributed to him): or Ignatius Loyola.—n. a Jesuit.—Ignatius's bean (see under Saint).
igneous, ig′ni-əs, adj. of or like fire: produced by solidification of the earth's internal molten magma (geol.).—adj. ignip′otent (Pope), presiding over fire. [L. ignis, fire.]
ignescent, ig-nes′ənt, adj. emitting sparks when struck.—n. an ignescent substance. [L. ignēscēns, -entis, pr.p. of ignēscĕre, to catch fire.]
ignis-fatuus, ig′nis-fat′ū-əs, -fat′ōō-ōōs, n. Will-o'-the-wisp—the light of combustion of marsh-gas, apt to lead travellers into danger: any delusive ideal that leads one astray:—pl. ignes-fatui (ig′nēz-fat′ū-i; ig′nās-fat′ōō-ē). [L. ignis, fire, fatuus, foolish.]
ignite, ig-nit′, v.t. to set on fire: to heat to the point at which combustion occurs.—v.i. to take fire.—adj. ignit′able (also ignit′ible).—ns. ignitabil′ity (ignitibil′ity); ignit′er, one who ignites: apparatus for firing an explosive or explosive mixture; ignition (-nish′ən), act of igniting: means of igniting: state of being ignited: the firing system of an internal-combustion engine; ig′nitron (or ig-ni′tron), a device for conducting current in which an electrode dips into a pool of mercury and draws up an arc to start ionisation. [L. ignire, ignitum, to set on fire, to make red-hot—ignis, fire.]
ignoble, ig-nō′bl, adj. of low birth: mean or worthless: unworthy: base: dishonourable.— v.t. to degrade.—ns. ignōbil′ity, ignō′bleness.— adv. ignō′bly. [Fr.,—L. ignōbilis—in-, not, (g)nōbilis, noble.]
ignominy, ig′nə-min-i, or -nō-, n. loss of good name: public disgrace: infamy—formerly also (as Shak.) ig′nomy.—adj. ignomin′ious, deserving or marked with ignominy.—adv. ignomin′iously. [L. ignōminia, in-, not, (g)nōmen, -inis, name.]
ignoramus, ig-nō-rā′məs, -nə-, n. the word formerly written by a grand jury on the back of a rejected indictment: an ignorant person, esp. one pretending to knowledge:—pl. ignorā′-muses. [L. ignōrāmus, we are ignorant, in legal use, we ignore, take no notice, 1st per. pl. pres. indic. of ignōrāre.]
ignorant, ig′nər-ənt, adj. without knowledge, in general or particular: uninstructed: uninformed: unaware: showing, arising from, want of knowledge: keeping back knowledge (Shak.): unknown (obs.).—n. an ignorant person.— ig′norance, want of knowledge—in R.C. theol. vincible or wilful ignorance is such as one may be fairly expected to overcome; invincible ignorance is that which cannot help or abate: the time of ignorance, i.e. before Mohammed: an instance of ignorance: an act committed in ignorance.—adv. ig′norantly. [Fr.,—L. ignōrāns, -antis, pr.p. of ignōrāre; see ignore.]
Ignorantine, ig-nō-ran′tin, -nō-, -tin, (R.C.) n. a member of a religious congregation of men devoted to the instruction of the poor—inaccurately applied to Brethren of the Christian Schools.
ignoratio elenchi, ig-nə-rā′shō il-eng′-kī, ig-nō-rät′i-ō

Neutral vowels in unaccented syllables: el′ə-mənt; for certain sounds in foreign words, see p. viii

# ignore 650 illict

*el-eng'kē*, (L.) ignoring the point in question; the fallacy of arguing to the wrong point.

**ignore**, *ig-nōr'*, *-nör'*, *v.t.* wilfully to disregard: to set aside.—*adj.* **ignor'able.**—*ns.* **ignorā'tion,** ignoring; **ignor'er.** [L. *ignōrāre,* not to know—*in-*, not, and the root of (g)*nōscĕre,* to know.]

**Iguana,** *i-gwä'nə, n.* a genus of large thick-tongued arboreal lizards in tropical America: loosely extended to others of the same family (**Iguan'idae**): (without *cap.*) in South Africa a monitor lizard. [Sp., from Carib.]

**Iguanodon,** *i-gwä'nə-don, n.* a large Jurassic and Cretaceous herbivorous dinosaur, with teeth like those of the iguana. [iguana, and Gr. *odous, odontos,* tooth.]

**Iguvine,** *ig'ū-vīn, adj.* Eugubine.

**ihram,** *ē-räm', ēhh'räm, n.* the scanty garb worn by Mohammedan pilgrims on drawing near Mecca: the holy state it betokens. [Ar. *ihrām.*]

**ikebana,** *ē'ke-bä'nə, n.* Japanese art of flower arrangement.

**ikon.** Same as **icon.**

**ilang-ilang.** Same as **ylang-ylang.**

**ileac.** See **ileum, ileus.**

**ileum,** *il', il'i-əm, n.* the posterior part of the small intestine.—*adj.* **il'eac, il'iac.**—*n.* **ileitis** (*il-, īl-ə-ī'tis*), inflammation of the ileum. [L.L. *īleum,* L. *ilia* (pl.), the groin, flank, intestines.]

**ileus,** *il'-, il'i-əs, n.* obstruction of the intestine with severe pain, vomiting, etc.—Also **ileac** or **iliac passion.**—*adj.* **il'eac, il'iac.** [L. *ileos*—Gr. *īleos* or *eileos,* colic.]

**ilex,** *i'leks, n.* the holm-oak (*Quercus ilex*): (*cap.*) the holly genus:—*pl.* **i'lexes, ilices** (*i'li-sēz*). [L. *īlex,* holm-oak.]

**Iliac, iliac.** See **ileum, ileus, Ilium, ilium.**

**Iliad,** *il'i-ad, -əd, n.* a Greek epic ascribed to Homer, on the siege of Troy: a long story or series of woes. [Gr. *Īlias, -ados—Īlios* or *Īlion,* Ilium, Troy.]

**Ilium,** *il'i-əm, il', n.* Troy.—*adjs.* **Il'iac, Il'ian.** [L. *Īlium*—Gr. *Īlion,* Troy.]

**ilium,** *il', il'i-əm, n.* the bone that unites with the ischium and pubis to form the innominate bone:—*pl.* **il'ia,** the flanks.—*adj.* **il'iac.** [L. *ilium* (in classical L. only in pl. *ilia*); see **ileum.**]

**ilk,** *ilk, adj.* same.—**of that ilk,** of that same, i.e. of the estate of the same name as the family—often used ignorantly for 'of that kind'. [O.E. *ilca,* same.]

**ilk,** *ilk,* (*Scot.*) *adj.* each: usu. compounded with the article as **ilk'a** (*-ə, -a*).—*n., adj., adv.* **ilk'aday,** every day, every day but Sunday. [O.E. *ælc,* each, *ān,* one.]

**ill,** *il, adj.* (*comp.* **worse;** *superl.* **worst**) evil, bad: wicked: producing evil: hurtful: unfortunate: unfavourable: difficult: reprehensible: sick: diseased: incorrect: cross, as temper: grieved, distressed (*Scot.*): severe (*Scot.*).—*adv.* (*comp.* **worse;** *superl.* **worst**) badly: not well: not rightly: wrongfully: unfavourably: amiss: with hardship: with difficulty.—*n.* evil: wickedness: misfortune: harm: ailment.—*ns.* **ill'ness,** sickness: disease; **illth** (*Ruskin,* etc.), the contrary of wealth or well-being.—*adv.* **illy** (*il'li; rare*), ill.—*adjs.* **ill'-advised',** imprudent: ill-judged; **ill'-affect'ed,** not well disposed.—**ill'-be'ing,** the state of being poor or in bad health.—*adj.* **ill'-beseem'ing** (*Shak.*), unbecoming.—**ill'-blood',** **ill'-feel'ing,** resentment, enmity.—*adjs.* **ill'-bod'ing,** inauspicious; **ill'-bred',** badly bred or educated: uncivil.—**ill'-breed'ing.**—*adjs.* **ill'-condit'ioned,** in bad condition: churlish; **ill'-deed'y** (*Scot.*), mischievous; **ill'-disposed',** unfriendly: inclined to evil; **ill'-faced** (*Spens.* **ill-faste**), ugly-faced.—**ill'-fame',** disrepute (see **house**).—*adjs.* **ill'-fat'ed,** unlucky; **ill'-faurd'** (*Scot.*), **ill'-fā'voured,** ill-looking: deformed: ugly.—*adv.* **ill'-fā'vouredly.**—**ill'-fā'vouredness.**—*adjs.* **ill'-got',** **-gott'en,** procured by bad means;

**ill'-haired'** (*Scot.*), cross-grained; **ill'-head'ed** (*Spens.* **-hedd'ed**), not clear in the head; **ill'-hu'moured,** bad-tempered; **ill'-judged',** not well judged; **ill'-look'ing,** having an evil look: ugly; **ill'-manned',** provided with too few men; **ill'-mann'ered,** rude: ill-bred; **ill'-nā'tured,** of a bad temper: cross: peevish.—*adv.* **ill'-nā'turedly.**—**ill'-nā'turedness.**—*adjs.* **ill'-off',** in bad circumstances; **ill'-ō'mened** having bad omens: unfortunate; **ill'-spent,** spent amiss; **ill'-starred',** born under the influence of an unlucky star: unlucky; **ill'-tem'pered,** having a bad temper: morose: badly tempered, ill-mixed, distempered (*Shak.*); **ill'-timed',** said or done at an unsuitable time.—*v.t.* **ill-treat',** to treat ill: to abuse.—**ill-treat'ment;** **ill'-turn',** an act of unkindness or enmity; **ill-us'age.**—*v.t.* **ill'-use,** to ill-treat.—*adj.* **ill-used',** badly used or treated.—**ill'-will',** unkind feeling: enmity; **ill'-wisher,** one who wishes harm to another.—*adj.* **ill'-wrest'ing,** misinterpreting to disadvantage.—**go ill with,** to result in danger or misfortune to; **take it ill,** to be offended. [O.N. *illr;* not connected with O.E. *yfel,* evil but formerly confused with it, so that *ill* is often (esp. in Scots) to be read where *evil* is written.]

**illapse,** *il-aps', n.* a sliding in.—*v.i.* to glide in. [L. *illāpsus—il-* (*in-*), in, *lābī,* to slip, to slide.]

**illaqueate,** *i-lak'wi-āt, v.t.* to ensnare.—*adj.* **illaq'ueable.**—*n.* **illaqueā'tion.** [L. *illaqueāre, -ātum—il-* (*in-*), into, *laqueus,* a noose.]

**illation,** *il-ā'shən, n.* act of inferring from premises: inference: conclusion.—*adj.* **illative** (*il'ə-tiv,* also *il-ā'tiv*), pertaining to, of the nature of, expressing, or introducing an inference: of a case in some Finno-Ugric languages expressing direction into or towards (*gram.*).—*n.* the illative case: a word in this case.—*adv.* **ill'atively.** [L. *illātiō, -ōnis—illātus,* used as pa.p. of *inferre,* to infer—*il-* (*in-*), in, *lātus,* carried.]

**illaudable,** *il-ö'də-bl, adj.* not praiseworthy.—*adv.* **illau'dably.** [Pfx. **il-** (in- (2)).]

**Illecebrum,** *il-es'i-brəm, n.* a genus of plants of one species found in Devon and Cornwall, giving name in some classifications to a family **Illecebrā'ceae,** corresponding more or less to the Paronychiaceae or Corregiolaceae of others, by others again placed in Caryophyllaceae. [Said to be from L. *illecebra,* allurement, 'as enticing the simpler into bogs and marshes'.]

**illegal,** *il-ē'gl, adj.* contrary to law.—*v.t.* **illē'galise, -ize,** to render unlawful.—*n.* **illegality** (*-gal'i-ti*), the quality or condition of being illegal.—*adv.* **illē'gally.** [Pfx. **il-** (in- (2)).]

**illegible,** *il-ej'i-bl, adj.* that cannot be read: indistinct.—*ns.* **illeg'ibleness, illegibil'ity.**—*adv.* **illeg'ibly.** [Pfx. **il-** (in- (2)).]

**illegitimate,** *il-i-jit'i-mit, adj.* not according to law: not in the legal position of those born in wedlock or legitimised: not properly inferred or reasoned: not recognised by authority or good usage: (of racing) other than flat-racing.—*n.* a bastard.—*v.t.* (*-māt*) to pronounce or render illegitimate.—*n.* **illegit'imacy** (*-mə-si*).—*adv.* **illegit'imately.**—*n.* **illegitimā'tion,** the act of pronouncing or rendering, or state of being, illegitimate.—**illegitimate pollination,** in dimorphic flowers, pollination of long style from short stamen, or short from long. [Pfx. **il-** (in- (2)).]

**illiad,** a Shakespearian form of **oeillade.**

**illiberal,** *il-ib'ər-əl, adj.* niggardly: mean, narrow in opinion or culture.—*v.t.* **illib'eralise, -ize.**—*n.* **illiberality** (*-al'i-ti*).—*adv.* **illib'erally.** [Pfx. **il-** (in- (2)).]

**illicit,** *il-is'it, adj.* not allowable: unlawful: unlicensed.—*adv.* **illic'itly.**—*n.* **illic'itness.**—**illicit process of the major,** or **minor** (*log.*), the fallacy of distributing the major or minor term in the conclusion when it is not distributed in the

*fāte, fär; mē, hûr* (her); *mīne; mōte, för; mūte; mōōn, fōōt; dhen* (then)

premise. [L. *illicitus*—*il*- (*in*-), not, *licitus*, pa.p. of *licēre*, to be allowed.]

illimitable, *il-im'it-ə-bl*, *adj.* that cannot be bounded: infinite.—*n.* illim'itableness.—*adv.* illim'itably.—*n.* illimitā'tion.—*adj.* illim'ited. [Pfx. il- (in- (2)).]

illinium, *il-in'i-əm*, *n.* a name proposed for element No. 61.—See promethium. [*Illinois* University, where its discovery was claimed.]

illipe, *il'i-pi*, illupi, *il-ōō'pi*, *n.* the mahwa tree (Sapotaceae) yielding illipe nuts and oil. [Tamil *illuppai*.]

illiquation, *il-i-kwā'shən*, *n.* the melting of one thing into another. [Pfx. il- (in- (1)).]

illision, *il-izh'ən*, *n.* the act of striking against something. [L. *illisiō*, *-ōnis*—*illidēre*—*in*, into, *laedēre*, to strike.]

illiterate, *il-it'ər-it*, *adj.* unacquainted with literature: without book-learning: uneducated: ignorant: unable to read: of or characteristic of those who are without literary education.— *n.* an illiterate person: one who cannot read. —*adv.* illit'erately.—*ns.* illit'erateness, illit'eracy (*-ə-si*). [Pfx. il- (in- (2)).]

illogical, *il-oj'i-kəl*, *adj.* contrary to the rules of logic: regardless or incapable of logic.—*adv.* illog'ically.—*n.* illog'icalness. [Pfx. il- (in- (2)).]

illude, *il-ōōd'*, *-ūd'*, *v.t.* to trick. [L. *illūdēre*— *in*, on, *lūdēre*, *lūsum*, to play.]

illume, *il-ūm'*, *ōōm'*, *v.t.* a shortened poetic form of illumine.—*v.t.* illum'inate (*in-āt*), to light up: to enlighten: to illustrate: to adorn with coloured lettering or illustrations: to confer power of vision upon.—*adj.* (*-āt*, *-it*) enlightened: pretending to enlightenment: admitted to a mystery.—*n.* an initiate.—*adj.* illu'minable, that may be illuminated.—*adj.* illu'minant, enlightening.—*n.* a means of lighting.—*n.pl.* Illuminā'ti (L. *il-lōō-mi-nä'tē*), the enlightened, a name given to various sects, and especially to a society of German Free-thinkers at the end of the 18th century.—*n.* illuminā'tion, lighting up: enlightenment: intensity of lighting up: splendour: brightness: a decorative display of lights: adorning of books with coloured lettering or illustrations: divine inspiration or instance of it: the luminous flux per unit area expressed in lux (also illuminance).—*adj.* illu'minative (*-ə-tiv*, *-ā-tiv*), giving light: illustrative or explanatory.—*n.* illu'minātor.—*v.t.* illu'mine, to make luminous or bright: to enlighten: to adorn.— *ns.* illu'miner, an illuminator; illu'minism, the principles of the Illuminati: belief in or claim to an inward spiritual light. [L. *illūmināre*, *-ātum*, *in*, in, upon, *lūmināre*, to cast light.]

illupi. Same as illipe.

illusion, *il-ōō'zhən*, *-ū'*, *n.* a mocking (*obs.*): deceptive appearance: an apparition: false conception: delusion: a false sense-impression of something actually present (*psych.*).—*ns.* illu'sionism, the doctrine that the external world is illusory: the production of illusion; illu'sionist, a believer in or practitioner of illusionism: one who produces illusions, a conjurer, prestidigitator.—*adjs.* illu'sive (*-siv*), illu'sory (*-sər-i*), deceiving by false appearances: false.—*adv.* illu'sively.—*n.* illu'siveness. [See illude.]

illustrate, *il'əs-trāt* (old-fashioned *il-us'trāt*), *v.t.* to make bright, adorn (*obs.*): to show in a favourable light (*obs.*): to give distinction or honour to (*obs.*): to make clear to the mind (*arch.*): to exemplify: to explain and adorn by pictures: to execute pictures for.—*adj.* (*-lus'*; *Shak.*) illustrious: renowned.—*n.* illustrā'tion, act of making lustrous or clear: lighting up (*obs.*): act of explaining: that which illustrates: exemplification, example: a picture or diagram elucidating, or at least accompanying, letterpress.—*adj.* ill'ustrated (or *-us'*), having pictorial illustrations.—*n.* an illustrated periodical.—

adjs. illustrā'tional, illustrative (*il'əs-trā-tiv* or *-trə-*, or *il-us'trə-tiv*), illus'tratory, having the quality of making clear or explaining.—*adv.* ill'ustratively (or *il-us'*).—*n.* ill'ustrātor.—*adj.* illus'trious, luminous (*obs.*): highly distinguished: noble: conspicuous.—*adv.* illus'-triously.—*n.* illus'triousness. [L. *illūstris*; *illū-strāre*, *-ātum*, *lūstrāre*, to light up, prob.—*lūx*, light.]

illustrious, etc. See illustrate.

illustrious, *il-us'tri-əs*, (*Shak.*) *adj.* dull. Perh. for *illustrous*, not lustrous.

illustrissimo, *ēl-lōōs-trē'sē-mō*, (It.) most illustrious.

ilmenite, *il'mən-it*, *n.* a black mineral composed of iron, titanium, and oxygen. [From the *Ilmen* Mountains in the Urals.]

il penseroso, *ēl* pen-se-rō'zō, (It. *pensieroso*) the pensive man.

I'm, *īm*, a contraction of I am.

image, *im'ij*, *n.* likeness: a statue: an idol: a representation in the mind, an idea: a picture or representation (not necessarily visual) in the imagination or memory: an appearance: that which very closely resembles anything: a type: a figure got from another figure by joining every point in it with a fixed point, or dropping a perpendicular from it to a fixed straight line or plane, and producing to the same distance (*geom.*): the figure of any object formed by rays of light reflected or refracted (*real* if the rays converge upon it, *virtual* if they appear to diverge from it) (*opt.*): an analogous figure formed by other rays (*opt.*): a metaphor or simile (*rhet.*): public image (see public).—*v.t.* to form an image of: to form a likeness of in the mind: to mirror: to imagine: to portray: to typify.—*adjs.* im'ageable; im'ageless, having no image.—*ns.* imagery (*im'ij-ri*, *-ə-ri*), the work of the imagination: mental pictures: figures of speech: images in general or collectively; im'agism; im'agist, one of a twentieth-century school of poetry aiming at concentration, exact and simple language, and freedom of form and subject.—Also *adj.*—im'age-breaker, an iconoclast; im'age-wor'ship. [O.Fr.,—L. *imāgō*; image; cf. *imitāri*, to imitate.]

imagine, *im-aj'in*, *v.t.* to form an image of in the mind: to conceive: to think: to think vainly or falsely: to conjecture: to contrive or devise. —*v.i.* to form mental images: to exercise imagination.—*adj.* imag'inable.—*n.* imag'inableness.—*adv.* imag'inably.—*adj.* imag'inary, existing only in the imagination: not real: non-existent.—*n.* imaginā'tion, act of imagining: the faculty of forming images in the mind: the artist's creative power: that which is imagined: contrivance.—*adj.* imag'inative (*-ə-tiv*, or *-ā-tiv*), full of imagination: suffused with imagination. —*ns.* imag'inativeness, imag'iner; imag'ining, that which is imagined; imag'inist (*Jane Austen*), a person of active imagination and speculative temper.—imaginary point, line, etc., a non-existent point, etc., whose co-ordinates are imaginary quantities, non-existent quantities involving the square roots of negative quantities. [O.Fr. *imaginer*—L. *imāgināri*—*imāgō*, an image.]

imago, *i-mā'gō*, *-mä'*, *n.* the last or perfect state of insect life: an image or optical counterpart of a thing: an elaborated type, founded on a parent or other, persisting in the unconscious as an influence (*psych.*):—*pl.* imagines (*i-mā'jin-ēz*, *-mä'gin-*), imā'gōs.—*adj.* imaginal (*i-maj'*). [L. *imāgō*, *-inis*, image.]

imâm, *i-mäm'*, imaum, *i-möm'*, *n.* the officer who leads the devotions in a mosque: (*cap.*) a title for various Mohammedan potentates, founders, and leaders.—*n.* imam'ate. [Ar. *imām*, chief.]

imb-, for many words see emb-.

imbalance, im-bal'əns, *n.* a lack of balance, as

between the ocular muscles or between the activities of the endocrines, or between the parts of the involuntary nervous system, or between the elements of a diet (*med.*): temporary lack of balance in a self-adjusting system: lack of balance in a sphere of a nation's economy. [Pfx. im- (in- (2)).]
**imbark**, *im-bärk'*, *v.t.* to enclose in bark. [Pfx. im- (in- (1)).]
**imbecile**, *im'bi-sēl*, *-sil*, *-sil*, formerly *im-bi-sēl'*, *im-bes'il*, *adj.* feeble (now generally in mind): fatuous.—*n.* one who is imbecile: one whose defective mental state (from birth or an early age) does not amount to idiocy, but who is incapable of managing his own affairs: loosely, a foolish, unwise or stupid person.—*n.* imbecil'ity. [Fr. *imbécille* (now *imbécile*)—L. *imbēcillus*; perh. *in-*, not and *bēcillus*, variant of *bacillus*, dim. of *baculus*, a stick.]
**ịmbibe**, *im-bīb'*, *v.t.* to drink in: to absorb: to receive into the mind.—*v.i.* to drink, absorb.— *ns.* imbib'er; imbibition (*im-bib-ish'ən*). [L. *imbībĕre*—*in*, in, into, *bibĕre*, to drink.]
**imbrast**, (*Spens.*) for embraced.
**imbrex**, *im'breks*, *n.* orig. in Roman buildings, one of a series of usu. curved tiles fixed over the joins of flat tiles:—*pl.* im'brices (*-bri-sēz*). —*v.t.* imbricate, *im'bri-kāt*, to lay one overlapping another, as tiles on a roof.—*v.i.* to be so placed.—*adj.* (*-kit*, *kāt*) (of fish-scales, birdscales, layers of tissue, teeth), overlapping like roof-tiles.—*n.* imbricā'tion. [L. *imbrex*, a tile, *imbricāre*, *-ātum*, to tile—*imber*, a shower of rain.]
**imbroccata**, *im-bro-kä'ta*, *n.* in fencing, a thrust. [It.]
**imbroglio**, *im-brōl'yō*, *n.* a confused mass: a tangle: an embroilment: an ordered confusion (*mus.*). [It., confusion—*imbrogliare*, to confuse, embroil.]
**imbrue**, *im-brōō'*, *v.t.* to wet or moisten: to soak: to drench: to stain or dye.—Also **embrue**.— *n.* **imbrue'ment**. [O.Fr. *embreuver*—*bevre* (Fr. *boire*)—L. *bibĕre*, to drink.]
**imbrute**, *im-brōōt'*, *v.t.* or *v.i.* to reduce, or sink, to the state of a brute.—Also **embrute**. [Pfx. im- (in- (1)).]
**imbue**, *im-bū'*, *v.t.* to moisten: to tinge deeply: to fill, permeate (e.g. the mind; with *with*). [O.Fr. *imbuer*—L. *imbuĕre*—*in*, and root of *bibĕre*, to drink.]
**imburse**, *im-bûrs'*, *v.t.* to put in a purse or in one's purse: to pay: to repay. [Pfx. im- (in- (1)), and L. *bursa*, a purse.]
**imitate**, *im'i-tāt*, *v.t.* to strive to be like or produce something like: to copy, not necessarily exactly: to mimic.—*n.* imitability (*-ə-bil'i-ti*).— *adj.* im'itable, that may be imitated or copied: inviting or worthy of imitation (*obs.*).—*ns.* im'itancy, the tendency to imitate; im'itant, a counterfeit; imitā'tion, act of imitating: that which is produced as a copy, or counterfeit: a performance in mimicry: the repeating of the same passage, or the following of a passage with a similar one in one or more of the other parts or voices (*mus.*).—*adj.* sham, counterfeit: machine-made (as lace).—*adj.* im'itātive, inclined to imitate: formed after a model: mimicking.—*adv.* im'itātively.—*ns.* im'itātiveness; im'itātor. [L. *imitāri*, *-ātus*.]
**immaculate**, *im-ak'ū-lit*, *adj.* spotless: unstained: pure.—*n.* immac'ulacy, state of being immaculate.—*adv.* immac'ulately.—*n.* immac'ulateness. —**Immaculate Conception**, the R.C. dogma that the Virgin Mary was conceived without original sin—first proclaimed an article of faith in 1854 —not the same as the Virgin Birth. [L. *immaculātus*—*in-*, not, *maculāre*, to spot.]
**immanacle**, *im-(m)an'ə-kl*, (*Milt.*) *v.t.* to put in manacles, to fetter or confine. [Pfx. im- (in- (1)).]

**immanation**, *im-ə-nā'shən*, *n.* inflow. [L. *in*, in, *mānāre*, *-ātum*, to flow.]
**immane**, *im-ān'*, *adj.* huge: cruel, savage.—*adv.* immane'ly.—*n.* immanity (*im-an'i-ti*), cruelty. [L. *immānis*, huge, savage.]
**immanent**, *im'ə-nənt*, *adj.* indwelling: pervading: inherent.—*ns.* imm'anence, imm'anency, the pervasion of the universe by the intelligent and creative principle—a fundamental conception of Pantheism.—*adj.* immanental (*-ent'l*).—*ns.* imm'anentism, belief in an immanent God; imm'anentist. [L. *in*, in, *manēre*, to remain.]
**immantle**, *im-(m)an'tl*, *v.t.* to envelop in a mantle. [Pfx. im- (in- (1)).]
**Immanuel, Emmanuel**, *i-man'ū-el*, *n.* a name given to Jesus (Matt. i. 23) in allusion to Is. vii. 14. [Gr. *Emmanouēl*—Heb. *'Immānūēl*, God-withus.]
**immarcescible**, *im-är-ses'i-bl*, *adj.* never-fading: imperishable.—Less correctly immarcess'ible. [L. *in-*, not, *marcēscĕre*, to languish.]
**immarginate**, *im-är'jin-āt*, *-it*, *adj.* without distinct margin. [Pfx. im- (in- (2)).]
**immask**, *im-mäsk'*, (*Shak.*) *v.t.* to mask, disguise. [Pfx. im- (in- (1)).]
**immaterial**, *im-ə-tē'ri-əl*, *adj.* not consisting of matter: incorporeal: unimportant.—*v.t.* immatē'rialise, *-ize*, to separate from matter.—*ns.* immatē'rialism, the doctrine that there is no material substance; immatē'rialist; immaterial ity (*-al'*), the quality of being immaterial or of not consisting of matter.—*adv.* immatē'rially. [Pfx. im- (in- (2)).]
**immature, immatured**, *im-ə-tyoōr(d)'*, *-choōr(d)'*, *adjs.* not ripe: not perfect: come before the natural time.—*adv.* immature'ly.—*ns.* immature'-ness, immatur'ity. [Pfx. im- (in- (2)).]
**immeasurable**, *im-ezh'ər-ə-bl*, *adj.* that cannot be measured: very great.—*n.* immeas'urableness.—*adv.* immeas'urably.—*adj.* immeas'ured (*Spens.*), beyond the common measure, immeasurable. [Pfx. im- (in- (2)).]
**immediate**, *im-ē'di-it*, *-dyət*, *-dyit*, *-jət*, *adj.* with nothing between: not acting by second causes: direct: present: without delay.—*n.* immē'diacy, state of being immediate: direct appeal to intuitive understanding.—*adv.* immē'diately.—*ns.* immē'diateness; immē'diatism, immediateness: the policy of action at once, esp. (*U.S. hist.*) in abolition of slavery. [Pfx. im- (in- (2)).]
**immedicable**, *im-(m)ed'i-kə-bl*, *adj.* incurable. [Pfx. im- (in- (2)).]
**immemorial**, *im-i-mōr'i-əl*, *-mör'*, *adj.* ancient beyond the reach of memory.—*adv.* immemō'-rially. [Pfx. im- (in- (2)).]
**immense**, *i-mens'*, *adj.* that cannot be measured: vast in extent: very large: fine, very good (*slang*).—*adv.* immense'ly.—*ns.* immense'ness; immens'ity, an extent not to be measured: infinity: greatness. [Fr.,—L. *immēnsus*—*in-*, not, *mēnsus*, pa.p. of *metīri*, to measure.]
**immensurable**, *im-(m)en'shoōr-ə-bl*, *-syoōr-*, *-syər-*, *adj.* that cannot be measured.—*n.* immensurabil'ity. [Pfx. im- (in- (2)).]
**immerge**, *im-(m)ûrj'*, *v.t.* and *v.i.* to plunge in. [Pfx. im- (in- (1)).]
**immeritous**, *im-mer'it-əs*, (*Milt.*) *adj.* undeserving. [L. *immeritus*—*in-*, not, *meritus*, deserving.]
**immerse**, *im-(m)ûrs'*, *v.t.* to dip under the surface of a liquid: to baptise by dipping the whole body: to engage or involve deeply.—*adj.* immersed' (*bot.*), embedded in the tissues.—*ns.* immer'sion, act of immersing: state of being immersed: deep absorption or involvement: baptism by immersing: entry into a position of invisibility as in eclipse or occultation (*astron.*): application of liquid to a microscope objectglass; immer'sionism; immer'sionist, one who favours or practices baptism by immersion.— **immersion heater**, an electrical apparatus directly

immersed in the liquid, used for heating water; immersion lens, a microscope object-glass that works with a drop of oil or water between it and the cover-glass. [See immerge.]
immesh. See enmesh.
immethodical, *im-(m)i-thod'ik-əl, adj.* without method or order: irregular.—*adv.* immethod'ically. [Pfx. im- (in- (2)).]
immew. See emmew.
immigrate, *im'i-grāt, v.i.* to migrate or remove into a country with intention of settling in it.—*ns.* imm'igrant, one who immigrates; immigrā'tion. [L. *immigrāre*—*in*, into, *migrāre*, *-ātum*, to remove.]
imminent, *im'i-nənt, adj.* overhanging: intent: threatening: impending.—*ns.* imm'inence, fact or state of being imminent: impending evil (*Shak.*); imm'inency.—*adv.* imm'inently. [L. *imminēns, -entis*—*in*, upon, *minēre*, to project, jut.]
immingle, *im-(m)ing'gl, v.t.* and *v.i.* to mingle together, to mix. [Pfx. im- (in- (1)).]
immiscible, *im-(m)is'i-bl, adj.* not capable of being mixed.—*n.* immiscibil'ity. [Pfx. im- (in- (2)).]
immit, *im-(m)it', v.t.* to insert: to introduce: to inject:—*pr.p.* immitt'ing; *pa.t.* and *pa.p.* immitt'ed.—*n.* immission (*-ish'ən*). [L. *immittēre*—*in*, into, *mittēre, missum*, to send.]
immitigable, *im-it'i-gə-bl, adj.* incapable of being mitigated.—*adv.* immit'igably. [Pfx. im- (in- (2)).]
immix, *im-(m)iks', (Milt.) v.t.* to mix in: to involve in mixture. [Pfx. im- (in- (1)).]
immobile, *im-(m)ō'bil, -bēl*, in U.S. *-bil, adj.* immovable: not readily moved: motionless: stationary.—*n.* immobilisā'tion, *-z-.*—*v.t.* immob'ilise, -ize, to render immobile: to put or keep out of action or circulation.—*n.* immobil'ity. [Pfx. im- (in- (2)).]
immoderate, *im-od'ər-it, adj.* exceeding due bounds: extravagant: unrestrained.—*ns.* immod'eracy, immod'erateness.—*adv.* immod'erately.—*n.* immoderā'tion, want of moderation: excess. [Pfx. im- (in- (2)).]
immodest, *im-od'ist, adj.* wanting restraint: exceeding in self-assertion: impudent: wanting shame or delicacy: indecent.—*adv.* immod'estly.—*n.* immod'esty. [Pfx. im- (in- (2)).]
immolate, *im'ō-lāt, im'əl-āt, v.t.* to offer in sacrifice: to dedicate to the church or church uses (*obs.*)—*ns.* immolā'tion, the act of sacrificing: the state of being sacrificed: that which is offered in sacrifice; imm'olātor. [L. *immolāre, -ātum*, to sprinkle meal (on a victim), hence to sacrifice—*in*, upon, *mola*, meal.]
immoment, *im-mō'mənt, (Shak.) adj.* of no value. [Pfx. im- (in- (2)).]
immoral, *im-(m)or'əl, adj.* inconsistent with or disregardful of morality: sometimes esp. of sexual morality: wicked: licentious.—*ns.* immor'alism, denial or rejection of morality; immor'alist; immorality (*im-or-, im-ər-al'i-ti*), quality of being immoral: an immoral act or practice.—*adv.* immor'ally. [Pfx. im- (in- (2)).]
immortal, *im-ör'tl, adj.* exempt from death: imperishable: never to be forgotten (as a name, poem, etc.).—*n.* one who will never cease to exist: one whose works will always retain their supremacy: one of the forty members of the French Academy.—*n.* immortalisā'tion, *-z-.*—*v.t.* immor'talise, -ize, to make immortal.—*n.* immortality (*im-ör-, im-ər-tal'i-ti*).—*adv.* immor'tally. [Pfx. im- (in- (2)).]
immortelle, *im-ör-tel', n.* an everlasting flower. [Fr. (*fleur*) *immortelle*, immortal (flower).]
immovable, *im-ōōv'ə-bl, adj.* impossible to move: steadfast: unyielding: impassive: motionless: unalterable: not liable to be removed (*law*): commonly immove'able): real, not personal (*law*).—*n.* (*law*) usu. in *pl.* immove'ables) immoveable

property.—*ns.* immov'ableness, immovabil'ity.—*adv.* immov'ably. [Pfx. im- (in- (2)).]
immune, *im-ūn', adj.* exempt: not liable to danger, esp. infection: free from obligation.—*n.* one who is immune.—*n.* immunisā'tion, *-z-.*—*v.t.* imm'unise, -ize, to render immune, esp. to make immune from a disease by injecting disease germs, or their poisons (either active or rendered harmless).—*n.* immun'ity.—immuno-, in composition, immune, immunity, as in immunochem'istry (the chemistry of antibodies, antibody reactions, etc.).—*ns.* immunol'ogist; immunol'ogy, the scientific study of immunity.—*adj.* immunosuppress'ive, applied to drugs which lessen the body's rejection of e.g. transplanted organs.—immune body, antibody. [L. *immūnis*—*in-*, not, *mūnis*, serving.]
immure, *im-ūr', v.t.* to wall in: to shut up: to imprison (also *fig.*).—*n.* (*Shak.* emure') an enclosing wall.—*n.* immure'ment, imprisonment: walling up. [L. *in*, in, *mūrus*, a wall.]
immutable, *im-ūt'ə-bl, adj.* unchangeable.—*ns.* immūtabil'ity, immūt'ableness.—*adv.* immūt'ably. [Pfx. im- (in- (2)).]
imp, *imp, n.* a shoot, scion, graft (*obs.*): a scion of a family (*obs.*): a young man (*obs.*): a child: a teasing or taunting mischievous child: a little devil or wicked spirit.—*v.t.* to graft, engraft (*arch.*): to engraft feathers in (to mend a wing; *falconry*).—*adj.* imp'ish, like or characteristic of an imp, teasing: mischievous.—*adv.* imp'ishly.—*n.* imp'ishness. [O.E. *impa*—L.L. *impotus*, a graft—Gr. *emphytos*, engrafted.]
imp-, for words beginning thus see also emp-.
impacable, *im'pak-ə-bi, (Spens.) adj.* not to be quieted or appeased. [L. *in-*, not, *pācāre*, to quiet.]
impact, *im-pakt', v.t.* to press firmly together: to drive close: to strike or collide.—*ns.* im'pact, the blow of a body in motion impinging on another body: the impulse resulting from collision: the impulse resulting from a new idea or theory: strong effect, influence; impac'tion, act of pressing together, or of fixing a substance tightly in a body cavity: condition so produced.—impacted fracture (see fracture); impacted tooth, one wedged between the jawbone and another tooth and thus unable to come through the gum. [L. *impactus*, pa.p. of *impingēre*; see impinge.]
impaint, *im-pānt', (Shak.) v.t.* to paint, depict. [Pfx. im- (in- (1)).]
impair, *im-pār', (Spens.* empaire') *v.t.* to diminish in quantity, value, or strength: to injure: to weaken.—*v.i.* to become worse: to decay.—*n.* impairing.—*n.* impair'ment. [O.Fr. *empeirer* (Fr. *empirer*), from L. *im-* (*in-*), intensive, *pējōrāre*, to make worse—*pējor*, worse.]
impair, *im-pār', (Shak.) adj.* perhaps, unsuitable, unfit, inferior. [Fr.,—L. *impār*—*in-*, not, *pār*, equal.]
impala, *im-pä'lə, n.* a large African antelope (*Aepyceros melampus*). [Zulu *i-mpālaj.*]
impale, *im-pāl', v.t.* to shut in, esp. to fence in with stakes (*arch.*): to surround with a border (*rare*): to put to death by spitting on to a stake: to transfix: to combine palewise (*her.*).—Also empale'.—*n.* impale'ment, an enclosed space (*arch.*): the act or punishment of impaling: the marshalling side by side of two escutcheons combined in one (*her.*). [Fr. *empaler*—L. *in*, in, *pālus*, a stake.]
impalpable, *im-pal'pə-bl, adj.* not perceivable by touch: extremely fine-grained: eluding apprehension.—*n.* impalpabil'ity.—*adv.* impal'pably. [Pfx. im- (in- (2)).]
impanation, *im-pə-nā'shən*, or *-pā-, n.* local union of the body of Christ with the consecrated bread in the Eucharist: later specially used of Luther's consubstantiation.—*adj.* impanate

(*im-pān'āt,im'pən-āt*), embodied in bread. [From L.L. *impānāre, -ātum—in*, in, *pānis*, bread.]
**impanel, impannel.** See **empanel**.
**imparadise,** *im-par'ə-dīs,* (*Milt.*) *v.t.* to put in a paradise or state of extreme felicity: to make a paradise of.—Also **empar'adise.** [Pfx. im-in- (1)).]
**impar(i)-,** *im-par-(i)-,* in composition, unequal. —*n.* **imparity,** *im-par'i-ti,* inequality: oddness (*arith., obs.*).—*adjs.* **imparipinn'ate** (*bot.*), pinnate with a terminal leaflet; **imparisyllab'ic,** having a syllable more in the other cases than in the nominative. [L. *impār—in-,* not, *pār,* equal.]
**impark,** *im-pärk',* *v.t.* to enclose in, or as, a park. —*n.* **imparkā'tion.** [Pfx. im- (in- (1)).]
**imparl,** *im-pärl',* (*arch.* except *law*) *v.i.* to hold a consultation.—*v.t.* to talk over.—*n.* **imparl'ance** (*Spens.* **emparlaunce**), parleying, conference: delay in pleading, ostensibly for amicable adjustment. [Obs. Fr. *emparler—em-* (L. *in-*), *parler,* to talk.]
**impart,** *im-pärt'* (*Spens.* **empart'**), *v.t.* to bestow a part of, or share out (*arch.*): to give (something abstract): to communicate, make known. —*v.i.* to give a part (of).—*ns.* **impartā'tion;** **impart'ment;** **impart'ment** (*Shak.*). [O.Fr. *empartir*—L. *impartīre—in,* on, *pars, partis,* a part.]
**impartial,** *im-pär'shl, adj.* not favouring one more than another: just: partial (*Shak.*).—*ns.* **impartiality** (*-shi-al'i-ti*), **impar'tialness.**—*adv.* **impar'tially.** [Pfx. im- (in- (2)).]
**impartible,** *im-pärt'i-bl, adj.* capable of being imparted.—*n.* **impartibil'ity.** [impart.]
**impartible,** *im-pärt'i-bl, adj.* not partible: indivisible.—*n.* **impartibil'ity.** [Pfx. im- (in- (2)).]
**impassable,** *im-päs'ə-bl, adj.* not capable of being passed.—*ns.* **impassabil'ity, impass'ableness.**—*adv.* **impass'ably.**—*n.* **impasse** (*am-pas', ē-pas;* Fr.), a place from which there is no outlet: a deadlock. [Pfx. im- (in- (2)).]
**impassible,** *im-pas'i-bl, adj.* incapable of suffering, injury, or emotion.—*ns.* **impassibil'ity,** **impass'ibleness.** [Church L. *impassibilis—in-,* not, *pati, passus,* to suffer.]
**impassion,** *im-pash'ən, v.t.* to move with passion: to make passionate.—*adjs.* **impass'ionate** (*Spens.* **empass'ionate**), impassioned: dispassionate; **impass'ioned** (*Spens.* **empass'ioned**), moved by or charged with passion: animated. [It. *impassionare—*L. *in,* in, *passiō, -ōnis,* passion.]
**impassive,** *im-pas'iv, adj.* not susceptible of feeling: not showing feeling; imperturbable.—*adv.* **impass'ively.**—*ns.* **impass'iveness, impassiv'ity.** [Pfx. im- (in- (2)).]
**impaste,** *im-pāst', v.t.* to form into, or enclose in, a paste: to lay colours thick on.—*ns.* **impastation** (*im-pas-tā'shən*); **impasto** (*im-päs'tō;* It.), in painting and pottery, the thick laying on of pigments.—*adj.* **impast'oed, impast'o'd.** [L.L. *impastāre—in,* into, *pasta,* paste.]
**Impatiens,** *im-pā'shi-enz, n.* the balsam genus of plants, whose ripe capsules burst at a touch. [L., impatient.]
**impatient,** *im-pā'shənt, adj.* not able to endure or to wait: fretful: restless: intolerant (of).—*n.* **impā'tience.**—*adv.* **impā'tiently.** [L. *impatiēns, -entis,* impatient—*in,* not, *patiēns,* patient.]
**impave,** *im-pāv',* (*Wordsworth*) *v.t.* to depict in pavement, as mosaic. [Pfx. im- (in- (1)).]
**impavid,** *im-pav'id,* (*rare*) *adj.* fearless.—*adv.* **impav'idly.** [L. *impavidus—im-* (in-), not, *pavidus,* fearing.]
**impawn,** *im-pön', v.t.* to put in pawn: to pledge: to risk. [Pfx. im- (in- (1)).]
**impeach,** *im-pēch',* (*Spens.* **empeach**) *v.t.* to hinder, impede (*obs.*): to beset (*obs.*): to impair (*obs.*): to disparage: to find fault with: to call in question: to arraign (esp. when a lower legislative house charges a high officer with grave

offences before the upper house as judges): to turn king's evidence against, peach upon.—*n.* hindrance (*Spens.*): damage, injury, impairment, detriment (*Spens.*): calling in question (*Shak.*). —*adj.* **impeach'able.**—*ns.* **impeach'er; impeach'ment.** [O.Fr. *empech(i)er,* to hinder (Fr. *empêcher*)—L. *impedicāre,* to fetter—*in,* in, *pēdica,* fetter—*pēs, pĕdis,* foot.]
**impearl,** *im-pûrl', v.t.* to adorn with or as with pearls: to make like pearls. [Pfx. im- (in- (1)).]
**impeccable,** *im-pek'ə-bl, adj.* not liable to sin: faultless.—*n.* one who is impeccable.—*ns.* **impeccabil'ity, impecc'ancy.**—*adj.* **impecc'ant,** without sin. [Pfx. im- (in- (2)).]
**impecunious,** *im-pi-kū'ni-əs, -nyəs, adj.* without money: short of money.—*n.* **impecunios'ity.** [Pfx. im- (in- (2)).]
**impede,** *im-pēd', v.t.* to hinder or obstruct.—*n.* **impē'dance,** hindrance: an apparent increase of resistance to an alternating current owing to induction in a circuit (*elect.*).—*n.* **impediment** (*-ped'*), obstacle: a defect preventing fluent speech.—*n.pl.* **impediment'a** (L. *impedimenta*), military baggage: baggage generally: encumbrances.—*adjs.* **impedimen'tal, imped'itive,** hindering. [L. *impedīre—in,* in, *pēs, pedis,* a foot.]
**impel,** *im-pel', v.t.* to urge forward: to excite to action: to instigate:—*pr.p.* **impell'ing;** *pa.t.* and *pa.p.* **impelled'.**—*adj.* **impell'ent,** impelling or driving on.—*n.* an impelling agent or power.—*n.* **impell'er** one who, or that which, impels: a rotor for transmitting motion. [L. *impellĕre, impulsum—in,* on, *pellĕre,* to drive.]
**impend,** *im-pend', v.i.* to overhang: to threaten: to be about to happen.—*ns.* (*obs.*) **impend'ence,** **impend'ency.**—*adjs.* **impend'ent, impend'ing.** [L. *impendēre—in,* on, *pendēre,* to hang.]
**impenetrable,** *im-pen'i-trə-bl, adj.* not to be penetrated: impervious: inscrutable: occupying space exclusively (*phys.*).—*n.* **impenetrabil'ity.**—*adv.* **impen'etrably.** [Pfx. im- (in- (2)).]
**impenetrate,** *im-pen'i-trāt, v.t.* to permeate: penetrate thoroughly.—*n.* **impenetrā'tion.** [Pfx. im- (in- (1)).]
**impenitent,** *im-pen'i-tant, adj.* not repenting.—*n.* one who does not repent: a hardened sinner.—*ns.* **impen'itence; impen'itency.**—*adv.* **impen'itently.** [Pfx. im- (in- (2)).]
**imperative,** *im-per'ə-tiv, adj.* expressive of command, advice, or request: authoritative: peremptory: obligatory: urgently necessary: calling out for action.—*n.* that which is imperative: the imperative mood: a verb in the imperative mood.—*adv.* **imper'atively.**—**imperative mood,** the form of a verb expressing command, advice, or request.—**categorical imperative** (see under **category**). [L. *imperātīvus—imperāre,* to command—*in,* in, *parāre,* to prepare.]
**imperator,** *im-pər-ā'tər;* L. *im-per-ä'tor,* *n.* a commander: a ruler: an emperor.—*adj.* **imperatorial** (*im-per-ə-tō'ri-əl, -tō'*). [L. *imperātor,* a general, later an emperor—*imperāre,* to command.]
**imperceable,** *im'pûrs-ə-bl,* (*Spens.*) *adj.* unpierceable. [Pfx. im- (in- (2)).]
**imperceptible,** *im-pər-sep'ti-bl, adj.* not discernible by the senses: very small, slight or gradual.—*n.* an imperceptible thing.—*ns.* **impercep'tibleness, imperceptibil'ity.**—*adv.* **impercep'tibly.**—*adjs.* **impercep'tive, impercip'ient,** not perceiving: having no power to perceive. [Pfx. im- (in- (2)).]
**imperfect,** *im-pûr'fikt, adj.* incomplete: defective: wanting any normal part, or the full normal number of parts: incapable of being enforced (*legal*): expressing continued or habitual action in past time (*gram.*): diminished, less by a semitone (*mus.*): duple (*old mus.*).—*n.* the imperfect tense: a verb in the imperfect tense.—*adj.* **imperfect'ible,** that cannot be made perfect.—*ns.* **imperfectibil'ity;**

imperfection (-*fek'shən*), state of being imperfect: a defect.—*adv.* imper'fectly.—*n.* imper'fectness. —imperfect cadence, any cadence other than a perfect cadence, esp. one passing from tonic to dominant chord. [Pfx. im- (in- (2)).]

imperforate, *im-pûr'fə-rit*, -d, -*rā-tid, adjs.* not pierced through or perforated: having no opening: abnormally closed (*med.*): without perforations for tearing apart, as a sheet of postage stamps.—*adj.* imper'forable.—*n.* imperforā'tion. [Pfx. im- (in- (2)).]

imperial, *im-pē'ri-əl, adj.* pertaining to, or of the nature of, an empire or emperor: sovereign, supreme: commanding, august.—*n.* an emperor or empress: a supporter of an emperor: tuft of hair on lower lip (earlier than Napoleon III): a pointed dome of ogee section (*build.*): the top of a coach, carriage, or a trunk for carrying on it: a British size of paper before metrication, 22 × 30 in. (a U.S. size 23 × 33): a size of slates, 33 × 24 in. (838 × 610 mm.): an obs. Russian gold coin.—*v.t.* impē'rialise, -ize, to make imperial.—*ns.* impē'rialism, the power or authority of an emperor: the policy of making or maintaining an empire: the spirit of empire; impē'rialist, a soldier or partisan of an emperor: a believer in the policy of developing and utilising the spirit of empire.—*adj.* impērialist'ic.—*n.* impēriality (-*al'i-ti*), imperial power, right, or privilege.— *adv.* impē'rially.—*adj.* impē'rious, assuming command: haughty: tyrannical: domineering: peremptory: authoritative: imperial (*obs.*).— *adv.* impē'riously.—*ns.* impē'riousness; impē'rium (L. *impērium*), a military chief command: empire.—imperial cap, a size of brown paper, 22 × 29 in. (558 × 760 mm.); imperial city, Rome: in the older German Empire a city that owed allegiance only to the emperor, exercised suzerainty within its own bounds, and had the right of voting in the imperial diet; Imperial Conference, a former periodical conference (orig. *Colonial Conference*) of the prime ministers and other representatives of the United Kingdom and the self-governing Dominions; imperial measure, weight, standard of measure, weight (imperial gallon, yard, pound) as fixed by parliament for the United Kingdom (final act 1963); imperial octavo, a book size, 7⅛ × 11 in. in Britain, 8¼ × 11½ in U.S.; Imperial Parliament, the parliament of the United Kingdom; imperial preference (*hist.*), the favouring of trade within the British Empire by discriminating tariffs. [L. *impērium*, sovereignty.]

imperil, *im-per'il, v.t.* to endanger:—*pa.p.* imper'illed.—*n.* imper'ilment. [Pfx. im- (in- (1)).]

imperishable, *im-per'ish-ə-bl, adj.* indestructible: everlasting.—*ns.* imper'ishableness, imperishabil'ity.—*adv.* imper'ishably. [Pfx. im- (in- (2)).]

imperium, *im-pēr'i-əm, -per'*, (L.) absolute sovereignty, command: area, or extent, of absolute sovereignty.—imperium in imperio (*in im-pēr'i-ō, -per'*), absolute authority within the sphere of higher authority.

impermanence, *im-pûr'man-əns, n.* want of permanence.—*n.* imper'manency.—*adj.* imper'manent. [Pfx. im- (in- (2)).]

impermeable, *im-pûr'mi-ə-bl, adj.* not permitting passage, esp. of fluids: impervious.—*ns.* impermeabil'ity, imper'meableness.—*adv.* imper'meably. [Pfx. im- (in- (2)).]

imperseverant, *im-pər-sev'ər-ənt*, (*Shak.*) *adj.* perh. unseeing, wanting in power to perceive what is before one, or perh. stubborn. [Pfx. im- (in- (2)), and perceive, or persevere.]

impersistent, *im-pər-sis'tənt, adj.* not persistent: not enduring. [Pfx. im- (in- (2)).]

impersonal, *im-pûr'sən-əl, adj.* not having personality: used only in the third person singular (in English usu. with *it* as subject) (*gram.*): without reference to any particular person: objective, uncoloured by personal feeling.—*v.t.* imper'sonalise, -ize.—*n.* impersonality (*al'i-ti*).—*adv.* imper'sonally. [Pfx. im- (in- (2)).]

impersonate, *im-pûr'sən-āt, v.t.* to invest with personality or the bodily substance of a person: to ascribe the qualities of a person to (*obs.*): to personify: to assume the person or character of, esp. on the stage.—*adj.* (-*it, -āt*) personified.— *ns.* impersonā'tion; imper'sonātor. [L. *in*, in, *persōna*, person; see personate.]

impertinent, *im-pûr'ti-nənt, adj.* not pertaining to the matter in hand: trifling: intrusive: saucy: impudent.—*n.* an impertinent person: one whose presence is interfering or intrusive.—*ns.* imper'-. tinence, imper'tinency, that which is impertinent: intrusion: impudence, overforwardness: matter introduced into an affidavit, etc., not pertinent to the matter (*law*).—*adv.* imper'tinently. [Pfx. im- (in- (2)).]

imperturbable, *im-pər-tûr'bə-bl, adj.* that cannot be disturbed or agitated: permanently quiet. —*n.* imperturbabil'ity.—*adv.* impertur'bably.— *n.* imperturbā'tion. [L. *imperturbābilis*—*in*-, not, *perturbāre*, to disturb; see perturb.]

impervious, *im-pûr'vi-ə-bl*, impervious, *im-pûr'vi-əs, adjs.* not to be penetrated: not easily influenced by ideas, arguments, etc., or moved or upset (with *to*).—*ns.* imper'viableness, imperviabil'ity, imper'viousness.—*adv.* imper'viously. [Pfx. im- (in- (2)).]

impeticos, *im-pet'i-kos*, (*Shak.*) *v.t.* a word coined by the fool in *Twelfth Night* (II, iii) perh. meaning *impocket*, or perh. bestow on (the wearer of) a petticoat.

impetigo, *im-pi-ti'gō, n.* a skin disease characterised by thickly-set clusters of pustules:—*pl.* impetigines (-*tij'i-nēz*).—*adj.* impetiginous (-*tij'*). [L. *impetigō*—*impetĕre*, to rush upon, attack.]

impetrate, *im'pi-trāt, v.t.* to obtain by entreaty or petition.—*n.* impetrā'tion.—*adjs.* im'petrā-tive, im'petrātory. [L. *impetrāre, -ātum*—*in*, on, *patrāre*, to bring about.]

impetus, *im'pi-təs, n.* momentum: impulse: incentive:—*pl.* im'petuses.—*adj.* impetuous (*im-pet'ū-əs*), rushing on with impetus or violence: vehement: acting with headlong energy.—*n.* impetuosity (-*os'i-ti*).—*adv.* impet'uously.—*n.* impet'uousness. [L. *impetus* (pl. *impetūs*)—*in*, into, on, *petĕre*, seek.]

impi, *im'pi, n.* a body of southern African native warriors. [Zulu.]

impictured, *im-pik'chərd*, (*Spens.*) *adj.* painted. [Pfx. im- (in- (1)).]

impierceable, *im-pērs'ə-bl* (*Spens.* imperceable, *im'pərs-ə-bl*), *adj.* incapable of being pierced. [Pfx. im- (in- (2)).]

impiety, *im-pi'ə-ti, n.* want of piety or veneration. [L. *impietās, -ātis*—*in*, not; cf. piety.]

impignorate, *im-pig'nər-āt, v.t.* to pledge or pawn. —*n.* impignorā'tion. [L. *in*, in, into, *pignus, -ōris, -ēris*, pledge.]

impinge, *in-pinj', v.i.* (with *on, upon, against*) to strike: to encroach.—*v.t.* to drive, strike:—*pr.p.* imping'ing.—*n.* impinge'ment.—*adj.* imping'ent. [L. *impingĕre*—*in*, against, *pangĕre*, to fix, drive in.]

impious, *im'pi-əs, adj.* irreverent: wanting in veneration, as for gods, parents, etc. [L. *impius* —*im*- (*in*-), not, *pius*; cf. pious.]

impish. See imp.

implacable, *im-plak'ə-bl, -plāk'* (*Spens.* im'), *adj.* not to be appeased: inexorable: irreconcilable. —*ns.* implac'ableness, implacabil'ity.—*adv.* im-plac'ably. [Pfx. im- (in- (2)).]

implacental, *im-plə-sen'tl, adj.* having no placenta. [Pfx. im- (in- (2)).]

implant, *im-plänt', v.t.* to engraft: to plant firmly: to fix in: to insert: to instil or inculcate: to plant (ground, etc., with).—*n.* something implanted in body tissue, as a graft, a pellet containing a

hormone, a tube containing a radioactive substance.—*n.* implantā′tion. [Pfx. im- (in- (1)).]
implate, *im-plāt′*, *v.t.* to put a plate or covering upon: to sheathe. [Pfx. im- (in- (1)).]
implausible, *im-plöz′i-bl*, *adj.* not plausible.—*n.* implausibil′ity. [Pfx. im- (in- (2)).]
impleach, *im-plēch′*, (*Shak.*) *v.t.* to intertwine. [Pfx. im- (in- (1)).]
implead, *im-plēd′*, *v.t.* to sue (a person; *arch.*).—*n.* implead′er. [Pfx. im- (in- (1)).]
impledge, *im-plej′*, *v.t.* to pledge. [Pfx. im- (in- (1)).]
implement, *im′pli-mənt*, *n.* a piece of equipment, a requisite: a tool or instrument of labour: fulfilment (*Scots law*).—*v.t.* (often -*ment′*) to give effect to: to fulfil or perform.—*adj.* implemen′tal, instrumental: effective.—*n.* implementā′tion. [L.L. *implēmentum*—L. *in*, in, *plēre*, to fill.]
implete, *im-plēt′*, *v.t.* to fill.—*adj.* replete.—*n.* impletion (-*plē′shən*), filling: fulness: fulfilment. [L. *implēre*, -*ētum*—in, in, *plēre*, to fill.]
implex, *im′pleks*, *adj.* not simple: complicated.—*n.* (*zool.*) in Arthropoda, an in-turning of the integument for attachment of muscles.—*n.* implexion (*im-plek′shən*).—*adj.* implex′ūous. [L. *implexus*—in, into, *plectēre*, to twine.]
implicate, *im′pli-kāt*, *v.t.* to entwine together: to enfold: to involve: to entangle: to imply: to show to be, to′ have been, a participator.—*n.* a thing implied.—*adj.* (-*kit*) intertwined.—*n.* implicā′tion, the act of implicating or implying: entanglement: that which is implied.—*adj.* im′-plicātive (or *im-plik′ə-tiv*), tending to implicate. —*adv.* im′plicatively.—*adj.* implicit (*im-plis′it*), implied: relying entirely, unquestioning: entangled, involved (*rare*).—*adv.* implic′itly.—*n.* implic′itness. [L. *implicāre*, -*ātum*, also -*itum*—in, in, *plicāre*, -*ātum* or -*itum*, to fold.]
implode, *im-plōd′*, *v.t.* and *v.i.* to burst inwards: to sound by implosion.—*ns.* implōd′ent, an implosive sound; implosion (-*plō′zhən*), bursting inward: in the formation of voiceless stops, compression of enclosed air by simultaneous stoppage of the mouth parts and the glottis (*phon.*): inrush of air in suction stop (*phon.*). —*adj.* implosive (-*plōs′iv*, or -*plōz′*).—*n.* an implosive consonant: a suction stop or click. [L. *in*, in, *plōdēre* (*plaudēre*), to clap.]
implore, *im-plōr′*, -*plör′*, *v.t.* to ask earnestly: to entreat.—Also *v.i.*—*n.* (*Spens.*) entreaty.—*ns.* implorā′tion; implor′ator (*Shak.*), one who implores or entreats.—*adj.* imploratory (-*plor′ə-tə-ri*).—*n.* implōr′er.—*adv.* implōr′ingly, in an imploring manner. [L. *implōrāre*, to invoke with tears—*in*, in, *plōrāre*, to weep.]
implosion. See implode.
implunge, *im-plunj′*, *v.t.* to plunge, submerge.— Also (*Spens.*) emplonge. [Pfx. im- (in- (1)).]
impluvium, *im-plōō′vi-əm*, *n.* in ancient Roman houses, the square basin in the atrium that received the rain-water:—*pl.* implu′via. [L. *implŭvium*—in, in, into, *pluěre*, to rain.]
imply, *im-plī′*, *v.t.* to enfold (*Spens.*): to involve the truth or reality of: to express indirectly: to insinuate: to mean: to signify:—*pr.p.* imply′ing; *pa.t.* and *pa.p.* implied′.—*adv.* impli′edly. [O.Fr. *emplier*—L. *implicāre*.]
impocket, *im-pok′it*, *v.t.* to put in the pocket. [Pfx. im- (in- (1)).]
impolder, *im-pōl′dər*, *v.t.* to make a polder of. [Du. *impolderen*; see polder.]
impolite, *im-pə-līt′*, *adj.* of unpolished manners: uncivil.—*adv.* impolite′ly.—*n.* impolite′ness. [Pfx. im- (in- (2)).]
impolitic, *im-pol′i-tik*, *adj.* not politic: inexpedient.—Also (*obs.*) impolit′ical.—*n.* impol′icy. —*advs.* impolit′ically (*rare*); impol′iticly. [Pfx. im- (in- (2)).]
imponderable, *im-pon′dər-ə-bl*, *adj.* not able to be

weighed or estimated: without weight, immaterial: without sensible weight.—Also *n.*—*ns.* impon′derableness, imponderabil′ity.—*n.pl.* im-pon′derables, once-supposed fluids without sensible weight, as heat, light, electricity, magnetism: factors in a situation whose influence cannot be gauged.—Also (L.) imponderabil′ia.—*adj.* impon′derous, weightless: very light. [Pfx. im- (in- (2)).]
impone, *im-pōn′*, *v.t.* and *v.i.* to impose: to lay on: to stake, as a wager (*Shak.*—perh. an error for *impawn*).—*adj.* impōn′ent, competent to impose an obligation.—*n.* one who imposes. [L. *impōněre*—in, on, *pōněre*, to place.]
import, *im-pōrt′*, -*pört′*, *v.t.* to bring in: to bring from abroad: to convey, as a word: to signify: to betoken: to portend: (*impers.*; *arch.*) to be of consequence to, also to behove.—Also *v.i.* —*n.* im′port (formerly -*pōrt′*, -*pört′*), that which is brought from abroad: meaning: importance: tendency.—*adj.* import′able, that may be imported or brought into a country.—*ns.* import′-ance, the fact of being important: extent of value or significance: weight, consequence: appearance of dignity: import, significance (*Shak.*): importunity (*Shak.*); import′ancy (*Shak.*).—*adj.* import′ant, of great import or consequence: momentous: pompous: urgent, importunate (*Shak.*).—*adv.* import′antly.— *ns.* importā′tion, the act of importing: a commodity imported; import′er.—*adj.* import′less (*Shak.*), without consequence.—invisible imports, such items in a national trade balance as money spent by tourists abroad, etc.; opp. to visible imports, goods bought from foreign countries by traders. [L. *importāre*, -*ātum*—in, in, *portāre*, to carry.]
importable, *im-pōrt′ə-bl*, -*pört′*, (*Spens. im′*; *obs.*), *adj.* unbearable: irresistible. [L. *impor-tābilis*—im- (*in-*), not, *portāre*, to bear.]
importune, *im-pōr-tūn′*, -*pör′*, *adj.* inopportune, untimely (*obs.*): burdensome (*obs.*): importunate: urgent, resistless (*Spens.*).—*v.t.* to be troublesome to (*obs.*): to urge or crave with troublesome application: to solicit for immoral purposes, make improper advances to: to import, signify (*Spens.*; wrongly).—*v.i.* to be importunate.—*ns.* impor′tunacy (*Shak.* -*tūn′*), import′unateness.—*adj.* impor′tunate (-*it*, -*āt*), inopportune (*obs.*): burdensome (*obs.*): troublesomely urgent: pressing: pertinacious.—*v.i.* to solicit pertinaciously.—*advs.* impor′tunately; im-portune′ly (or -*pör′*).—*ns.* importun′er; importun′-ing; importun′ity. [L. *importūnus*, inconvenient —im- (in-), not, *portus*, a harbour; cf. opportune.]
impose, *im-pōz′*, *v.t.* to place upon something: to lay on: to enjoin: to set as a burden or task: to set up in or by authority: to pass off unfairly: to arrange or place in a chase, as pages of type (*print.*).—*v.i.* (with *on*, *upon*) to mislead, deceive: to lay a burden, as by encroaching, taking undue advantage of one's good nature: act with constraining effect.—*n.* (*Shak.*) command, injunction.—*adj.* impos′able, capable of being imposed or laid on.—*n.* impos′er.—*adj.* impos′ing, commanding, impressive: adapted to impress forcibly: specious: deceptive.—*adv.* impos′ingly.— *n.* impos′ingness. [Fr. *imposer*; see compose.]
imposition, *im-pəz-ish′ən*, *n.* a laying on: laying on of hands in ordination: a tax, a burden: a deception: a punishment task: assembling of pages and locking them into a chase (*print.*). [L. *impositiō*, -*ōnis*—in, on, *pōněre*, *pōsitum*, to place.]
impossible, *im-pos′i-bl*, *adj.* that cannot be: that cannot be done or dealt with: that cannot be true: out of the question: hopelessly unsuitable: beyond doing anything with.—*n.* a person or thing that is impossible.—*ns.* imposs′ibilism, belief in or advocacy of an impracticable policy;

*ʼāte, fär; mē, hûr (her); mīne; mōte, för; mūte; mōōn, fŏŏt; dhen (then)*

imposs'ibilist; impossibil'ity. [Pfx. im- (in- (2)).]
impost, im'pōst, n. a tax, esp. on imports: the weight carried by a horse in a handicap race (coll.). [O.Fr. impost (Fr. impôt)—L. impōnĕre, impŏsitum, to lay on.]
impost, im'pōst, (archit.) n. the upper part of a pillar in vaults and arches, on which the weight of the building is laid: a horizontal block resting on uprights. [Fr. imposte—It. imposta—L. impōnĕre, impŏsitum.]
impostor, im-pos'tər, n. one who assumes a false character or personates another.—Also impost'er.—n. impos'ture (-chər), an imposition, fraud. [L.L.,—L. impōnĕre, impŏsitum, to impose.]
impostume, imposthume, im-pos'tūm, (arch.) n. an abscess.—v.t. and v.i. impos't(h)ūmate.—n. impost(h)ūmā'tion.—adj. impos't(h)ūmed. [O.Fr. empostume from aposteme—Gr. apostēma, abscess—apo, from, and the root of histanai, to set; the form due to confusion with posthumous, which itself is due to confusion.]
impot, im'pot, (school slang) n. an imposition.
impotent, im'pə-tənt, adj. powerless: helpless: without sexual power: without self-control (obs.): ungovernable (Spens.).—ns. im'potence, im'potency.—adv. im'potently. [Pfx. im- (in- (2)).]
impound, im-pownd', v.t. to confine, as in a pound: to restrain within limits: to hold up in a reservoir: to take legal possession of.—adj. impound'able.—ns. impound'age; impound'er; impound'ment. [Pfx. im- (in- (1)), and pound (2).]
impoverish, im-pov'er-ish, v.t. to make poor (lit. or fig.).—n. impov'erishment. [From O.Fr. empovrir, -iss- from L. in. in, pauper, poor.]
impracticable, im-prak'tik-ə-bl, adj. not able to be done: not able to be used or traversed: unmanageable (arch.).—ns. impracticabil'ity, imprac'ticableness.—adv. imprac'ticably. [Pfx. im- (in- (2)).]
impractical, im-prak'ti-kl, adj. unpractical.—ns. impracticality (-kal'); imprac'ticalness. [Pfx. im- (in- (2)).]
imprecate, im'pri-kāt, v.t. to call down by prayer (esp. something evil): pray for or to: invoke evil upon.—v.i. to curse.—n. imprecā'tion.—adj. im'precatory (-kə-tə-ri, or -kā or -kā'). [L. imprecāri—in, upon, precāri, -ātus, to pray.]
imprecise, im-pri-sis', adj. not precise.—n. im precis'ion. [Pfx. im- (in- (2)).]
impregn, im-prēn', (Milt.) v.t. to impregnate.—adj. impregnant (-preg'nənt), impregnating: impregnated (obs.).—v.t. impreg'nate, to make pregnant: to fecundate: to fill or imbue (with the particles or qualities of another thing): to saturate (also fig.).—n. impregnā'tion. [L.L. impraegnāre, -ātum—in, in, praegnāns, pregnant.]
impregnable, im-preg'nə-bl, adj. that cannot be taken: proof against attack.—n. impregnabil'ity.—adv. impreg'nably. [Fr. imprenable—L. in-, not, prendĕre, prehendĕre, to take; g, a freak of spelling, has come to be pronounced.]
impregnate. See impregn.
impresa, im-prā'za, (obs.) n. an emblematic device, often with a motto: a motto.—Also imprese (im'prēz, or as Milt. -prēz'). [It.]
impresario, im-pre-sä'ri-ō, or -zä', n. the manager of an opera company, etc.:—pl. impresa'rios, impresa'ri (-rē). [It.,—impresa, enterprise.]
imprescriptible, im-pri-skrip'ti-bl, adj. not liable to be lost by prescription, or lapse of time: inalienable.—n. imprescriptibil'ity. [Pfx. im- (in- (2)).]
impress, im-pres', v.t. to press: to apply with pressure, esp. so as to leave a mark: to mark by pressure: to produce by pressure: to stamp or print: to fix deeply in the mind: to affect the mind: to produce a profound effect upon, or upon the mind of.—ns. im'press, that which is made by pressure: stamp: distinctive mark;

impressibil'ity.—adj. impress'ible, susceptible.—ns. impression (im-presh'ən), the act or result of impressing: pressure: a difference produced in a thing by action upon it: a single printing of a book: the effect of anything on the mind: a profound effect on the emotions: a vague uncertain memory or inclination to believe: belief, generally ill-founded; impressionabil'ity.—adj. impress'ionable, able to receive an impression: very susceptible to impressions.—n. impress'ionism, a nineteenth-century movement in painting, originating in France, aiming at the realistic representation of the play of light in nature, purporting to render faithfully what the artist actually saw, dispensing with the academic rules of composition and colouring: any similar tendency in other arts.—n. and adj. impress'ionist.—adj. impressionis'tic.—adv. impressionist'ically.—adj. impressive (-pres'), exerting or tending to exert pressure: capable of making a deep impression on the mind: solemn.—adv. impress'ively.—ns. impress'iveness; impressure (impresh'ər; Shak.), impression.—be under the impression, to think or believe without certainty. [L. imprimĕre, -pressum—in, premĕre; see press (1).]
impress, im-pres', v.t. to force into service, esp. the public service.—ns. im'press (Shak. im-pres'); impress'ment, the act of impressing or seizing for service, esp. in the navy. [Pfx. im- (in- (1)), and prest (2); cf. press (2).]
impress, impresse, im'pres, (Shak.) n. an impresa.
impress, a variant of imprest.
imprest, im'prest, n. earnest-money: money advanced.—v.t. imprest', to advance on loan. [Pfx. im- (in- (1)) and prest (2).]
imprimatur, im-pri-mā'tər, n. a licence or permission to print a book, etc. [L. imprimātur, let it be printed, subj. pass. of imprimĕre—in, on, premĕre, to press.]
imprimis, im-prī'mis, adv. in the first place. [L. imprimis—in primis (abl. pl.), in, in, primus, first.]
imprint, im-print', v.t. to print: to stamp: to impress: to fix in the mind.—n. (im'print) that which is imprinted: the name of the publisher, time and place of publication of a book, etc., printed usu. on the title-page: the printer's name on the back of the title-page or at the end of the book.—n. imprint'ing, a learning process in young animals in which their social preferences become restricted to their own species, or a substitute for this. [Pfx. im- (in- (1)).]
imprison, im-priz'n, v.t. to put in prison: to shut up: to confine or restrain.—n. impris'onment. [Pfx. im- (in- (1)).]
improbable, im-prob'ə-bl, adj. unlikely.—n. improbabil'ity.—adv. improb'ably. [Pfx. im- (in- (2)).]
improbation, im-prō-bā'shən, n. in Scots law, an action for the purpose of declaring some instrument false or forged.—adj. improbative (-prob'ətiv), disapproving—also improb'atory. [Pfx. im- (in- (2)).]
improbity, im-prōb'i-ti, -prob', n. want of probity. [Pfx. im- (in- (2)).]
impromptu, im-promp'tū, adv. and adj. impromptu: offhand.—adv. without preparation: on the spur of the moment.—n. an extempore witticism or speech: an improvised composition: a musical composition with the character of an extemporisation. [L. impromptū for in promptū (abl.), in, in, promptus, readiness.]
improper, im-prop'ər, adj. not strictly belonging: not properly so called: not suitable: unfit: unbecoming: unseemly: indecent.—adv. improp'erly.—n. improp'riety.—improper fraction, a fraction not less than unity. [L. im- (in-), not, proprius, own.]
impropriate, im-prō'pri-āt, v.t. to appropriate to

private use: to place (ecclesiastical property) in the hands of a layman.—*adj.* (*-it*) devolved into the hands of a layman.—*ns.* **impropriā'tion;** **imprō'priātor,** a layman who is in possession of a benefice or its revenues. [L.L. *impropriātus*—L. *in*, in, *proprius*, one's own.]

**improve,** *im-prōōv'*, *v.t.* to turn to good use (*rare*): to make use of, occupy (*U.S.*): to increase (whether good or ill) (*obs.*): to raise in value (esp. by cultivating or building): to raise in price (*obs.*): to make better.—*v.i.* to increase (*obs.*): to grow in price or value: to grow better: to make progress: to make improvements: to follow up with something better (with *on*).—*ns.* **improvabil'ity, improv'ableness.**—*adj.* **improv'-able.**—*adv.* **improv'ably.**—*ns.* **improve'ment,** the act of improving: a change for the better: a thing changed, or introduced in changing, for the better: a better thing substituted for or following one not so good (often with *on*); **improv'er,** one who, that which, improves: worker who is in part learner: one who sets himself to the improvement of land: a pad or bustle.—*pr.p.* and *adj.* **improv'ing,** tending to cause improvement: instructive: edifying: uplifting.—*adv.* **improv'ingly.**—**improve the occasion,** to seize an opportunity for edification or other purpose: to draw a moral from what has happened. [A.Fr. *emprower*—O.Fr. *en prou, preu,* into profit.]

**improvident,** *im-prov'i-dənt, adj.* not provident or prudent: wanting foresight: thoughtless.—*adj.* **improvided** (*im-prə-vī'did*), unprovided: unforeseen (*Spens.*).—*n.* **improv'idence.**—*adv.* **improv'idently.** [Pfx. im- (in- (2)).]

**improvise,** *im-prō-, -prə-vīz', or im', improvisate, im-prov'i-zāt, vs.t.* to compose and recite, to perform, without preparation: to bring about on a sudden: to make or contrive off'hand or in emergency.—*v.i.* to perform extempore: to do anything off'hand. (The spelling with *z* is wrong.)—*ns.* **improvisā'tion** (or *prov'iz-*), act of improvising: that which is improvised; **improvisator** (*im-prov'iz-ā-tər, or im'prov-īz*); It. **improvvisatore,** *im-prov-vē-sä-tō'rä*); sometimes *fem.* **improv'isātrix** (It. **improvvisatrice,** *-trē'chä*), one who improvises: one who composes and performs or speaks without preparation.—*adjs.* **improvisatō'rial** (*-iz-ə-*), **improvisatory** (*-iz'* or *-iz'*).—*n.* **improvis'er.** [Fr. *improviser*—L. *in-*, not, *prōvīsus*, foreseen; see **provide.**]

**imprudent,** *im-prōō'dənt, adj.* wanting foresight or discretion: incautious: inconsiderate.—*n.* **impru'dence.**—*adv.* **impru'dently.** [Pfx. im- (in- (2)).]

**impudent,** *im'pū-dənt, adj.* wanting shame or modesty: brazen-faced: shamelessly bold: pert: insolent.—*n.* **im'pudence.**—*adv.* **im'pudently.**—*n.* **impudicity** (*-dis'i-ti*). [L. *im-* (*in-*), not, *pudēns, -entis,* pr.p. of *pudēre,* to be ashamed; and *pudīcus,* modest.]

**impugn,** *im-pūn', v.t.* to oppose: to attack by words or arguments: to call in question.—*adj.* **impugnable** (*-pūn'*; distinguished from obs. or rare impug'nable, unassailable, from L. *in-*, not).—*ns.* **impugn'er; impugn'ment.** [L. *impugnāre*—*in*, against, *pugnāre,* to fight.]

**impuissant,** *im-pū'is-ənt, -pū-is', -pwis', -pwēs', (arch.) adj.* powerless.—*n.* **impuiss'ance** (or *-pū'*; *arch.*). [Pfx. im- (in- (2)).]

**impulse,** *im'puls, n.* the act of impelling: effect of an impelling force: force suddenly and momentarily communicated: a beat: a single blow, thrust, or wave: a disturbance travelling along a nerve (**nervous impulse**) or a muscle: an outside influence on the mind: a sudden inclination to act.—*n.* **impul'sion** (*-shən*), impelling force: instigation.—*adj.* **impuls'ive,** having the power of impelling: acting or actuated by impulse: not continuous: given to acting upon impulse.—

*adv.* **impuls'ively.**—*ns.* **impuls'iveness; impulsiv'-ity.**—*adj.* **impuls'ory.** [L. *impulsus,* pressure—*impellĕre;* see **impel.**]

**impunity,** *im-pūn'i-ti, n.* freedom or safety from punishment or ill consequences. [L. *impūnitās, -ātis*—*in,* not, *poena,* punishment.]

**impure,** *im-pūr', adj.* mixed with something else: defiled: unholy: unchaste: unclean materially, morally, or ceremonially.—*adv.* **impure'ly.**—*ns.* **impure'ness, impur'ity.** [Pfx. im- (in- (2)).]

**impurple,** *im-pûr'pl.* Same as **empurple.**

**impute,** *im-pūt', v.t.* to ascribe (usually evil): to charge: to attribute vicariously (*theol.*): to reckon (*obs.*): to impart (*obs.*).—*adj.* **imput'able,** capable of being imputed or charged: open to accusation: attributable.—*ns.* **imput'ableness, imputabil'ity.**—*adv.* **imput'ably.**—*n.* **imputā'tion,** act of imputing or charging: censure: reproach: the reckoning as belonging.—*adj.* **imput'ative,** imputed.—*adv.* **imput'atively.**—*n.* **imput'er.** [Fr. *imputer*—L. *imputāre, -ātum*—*in,* in, *putāre,* to reckon.]

**imshi, imshy,** *im'shi,* (*mil. slang*), *interj.* go away! [Ar.]

**in,** *in, prep.* expressing the relation of a thing to that which surrounds, encloses, includes, or conditions it, with respect to place, time, or circumstances, or to that which is assumed, held, maintained, or the relation of a right or possession to the person who holds or enjoys it: at: among: into: within: during: consisting of: by way of: because of: by or through: by the medium or method of: with (*obs.*): among the characteristics or possibilities of: wearing: belonging to: being a member of.—*adv.* within: not out: at home: on the spot: in or to a position within or inward: in or into office, parliament, etc.: in favour: in mutual favour: in intimacy: in fashion: in the market: in season: at the bat: as an addition: alight: in pocket.—*n.* a member of the party in office or the side that is having its innings: a re-entrant or inward turn.—*adj.* **inward:** proceeding inwards: that is fashionable, much in use, as **in-word, in-thing:** within a small group.—*v.t.* to take in: to enclose: to gather in harvest.—*adj.* and *adv.* **in'-and-in',** (of breeding) from parents that are near akin: with constant and close interaction.—*n.* a game with four dice.—*adj.* **in-and-out,** by turns good and bad.—**in'-fighting,** fighting or bitter rivalry, between individuals or within a group, that goes on more-or-less secretly (see **infighting**—separate article); **in'group,** a social group of people having the same interests and attitudes; **in'-joke,** a joke to be fully appreciated only by members of a particular limited group; **in'-off** (*billiards*), a losing hazard; **in'-patient,** one lodged, fed and treated in a hospital.—*adjs.* **in'-ser'vice,** carried out while continuing with one's ordinary employment as *in-service training*; **in'shore,** close to the shore: moving towards the shore.—**in'-tray,** a shallow container for letters, etc., still to be dealt with.—**in as far as, in so far as, insofar as,** to the extent that; **in as much as, inasmuch as,** considering that; **in for,** doomed to receive (esp. unpleasant consequences): involved to the extent of: entered for: (see also **go**): **in for it,** in for trouble: committed to a certain course; **in it,** in enjoyment of success: in the running; **in itself,** intrinsically, apart from relations; **in on** (*slang*), participating in; **ins and outs** (or **outs and ins),** turning this way and that: nooks and corners: the whole details of any matter: those who repeatedly enter and leave; **in that,** for the reason that; **in with,** friendly with, associating much with: enjoying the favour of; **nothing in it,** no truth, no importance, no difficulty in the matter: no important difference—six of one and half a dozen of the other. [O.E. *in;* Du., Ger.]

*in*, O.N. *i*; W. *yn*, L. *in*, Gr. *en*. O.E. also had *innan*, within; cf. O.H.G. *innana*, Sw. *innan*.]

**in**, *in*, (*Spens.*) *n*. See **inn**.

**in-**, *in-*, *pfx.*, (1) in words derived from L. and O.E., used to form verbs with the sense in, into; sometimes used to form other parts of speech with this sense; sometimes used as an intensive or almost meaningless pfx.; (2) in words derived from L., used to form negatives.

**inability**, *in'ə-bil'i-ti*, *n.* want of sufficient power: incapacity. [Pfx. **in-** (2).]

**in absentia**, *in ab-sensh'yə, ab-sent'i-ä*, (L.) in absence.

**inabstinence**, *in-ab'sti-nəns*, *n.* want of abstinence. [Pfx. **in-** (2).]

**in abstracto**, *in ab-strak'tō*, (L.) in the abstract.

**inaccessible**, *in-ak-ses'i-bl*, or *-ək-*, *adj.* not to be reached, obtained, or approached.—*ns.* **inaccessibil'ity**, **inaccess'ibleness**.—*adv.* **inaccess'ibly**. [Pfx. **in-** (2).]

**inaccurate**, *in-ak'ūr-it*, *adj.* not accurate: incorrect: erroneous.—*n.* **inacc'uracy** (-*ə-si*), want of exactness: mistake.—*adv.* **inacc'urately**. [Pfx. **in-** (2).]

**inactive**, *in-akt'iv*, *adj.* not active: inert: having no power to move: sluggish: idle: lazy: having no effect: not showing any action (*chem.*): not rotating the plane of polarised light.—*n.* **inac'tion**, absence of action: idleness: rest.—*v.t.* **inact'ivate**, to render inactive.—*n.* **inactivā'tion**.—*adv.* **inact'ively**.—*n.* **inactiv'ity**, inaction: inertness: idleness. [Pfx. **in-** (2).]

**inadaptable**, *in-ə-dap'tə-bl*, *adj.* that cannot be adapted.—*n.* **inadaptā'tion** (-*ad-*).—*adj.* **inadap'tive**. [Pfx. **in-** (2).]

**inadequate**, *in-ad'i-kwit*, *adj.* insufficient: short of what is required: incompetent.—*ns.* **inad'equacy** (*-kwə-si*), **inad'equateness**, insufficiency.—*adv.* **inad'equately**. [Pfx. **in-** (2).]

**inadmissible**, *in-əd-mis'i-bl*, *adj.* not allowable.—*n.* **inadmissibil'ity**.—*adv.* **inadmiss'ibly**. [Pfx. **in-** (2).]

**inadvertent**, *in-əd-vúrt'ənt*, *adj.* inattentive: unintentional.—*ns.* **inadvert'ence**, **inadvert'ency**, negligence: oversight.—*adv.* **inadvert'ently**. [Pfx. **in-** (2).]

**inadvisable**, *in-ad-vi'zə-bl*, *adj.* not advisable, unwise.—**unadvisable** (*q.v.*) was formerly preferred and still is by some.—*ns.* **inadvisabil'ity**, **inadvis'ableness**.

**inaidable**, *in-ād'ə-bl*, (*Shak.*) *adj.* that cannot be aided. [Pfx. **in-** (2).]

**inalienable**, *in-āl'yən-ə-bl*, *-i-ən-ə-bl*, *adj.* not capable of being transferred or removed.—*n.* **inalienabil'ity**.—*adv.* **inal'ienably**. [Pfx. **in-** (2).]

**inalterable**, **-ability**. Same as **unalterable**, etc.

**inamorata**, *in-am-o-rä'tə*, *n. fem.* a woman in love or beloved:—*masc.* **inamora'to**. [It. *innamorata*, *-to*—L.L. *inamorāre*, to cause to love—L. *in*, in, *amor*, love.]

**inane**, *in-ān'*, *adj.* empty, void: vacuous: senseless: characterless.—*n.* the void of space.—*ns.* **inanition** (*in-ə-nish'ən*), exhaustion from want of food; **inanity** (*in-an'i-ti*), senselessness: mental vacuity: emptiness: an insipid empty-headed utterance. [L. *inānis*.]

**inanimate**, *in-an'i-mit*, **-d**, *-māt-id*, *adjs.* without animation: without life: dead: spiritless: dull.—*ns.* **inan'imateness**, **inanimā'tion**. [Pfx. **in-** (2).]

**inappeasable**, *in-ə-pēz'ə-bl*, *adj.* that cannot be appeased. [Pfx. **in-** (2).]

**inappetent**, *in-ap'i-tənt*, *adj.* lacking desire.—*ns.* **inapp'etence**, **inapp'etency**. [Pfx. **in-** (2).]

**inapplicable**, *in-ap'lik-ə-bl*, *in-əp-lik'*, *adj.* not applicable.—*n.* **inapplicabil'ity**. [Pfx. **in-** (2).]

**inapposite**, *in-ap'ə-zit*, *adj.* not apposite, suitable, or pertinent.—*adv.* **inapp'ositely**.—*n.* **inapp'ositeness**. [Pfx. **in-** (2).]

**inappreciable**, *in-ə-prē'shə-bl*, *-shy-əbl*, *adj.* too small or slight to be noticed, or to be important:

priceless (*arch.*).—*n.* **inappreciation** (*-shi-ā'shən*).—*adj.* **inapprē'ciative** (*-shi-ə-tiv*, or *-shi-ā-tiv*), not valuing justly or at all. [Pfx. **in-** (2).]

**inapprehensible**, *in-ap-ri-hen'si-bl*, *adj.* not apprehensible or intelligible.—*n.* **inapprehen'sion**.—*adj.* **inapprehen'sive**. [Pfx. **in-** (2).]

**inapproachable**, *in-ə-prōch'ə-bl*, *adj.* unapproachable: inaccessible.—*adv.* **inapproach'ably**. [Pfx. **in-** (2).]

**inappropriate**, *in-ə-prō'pri-it*, *adj.* not appropriate, not suitable.—*adv.* **inappro'priately**.—*n.* **inappro'priateness**. [Pfx. **in-** (2).]

**inapt**, *in-apt'*, *adj.* not apt: unfit, or unqualified.—*ns.* **inapt'itude**, **inapt'ness**, unfitness, awkwardness.—*adv.* **inapt'ly**. [Pfx. **in-** (2).]

**inarable**, *in-ar'ə-bl*, *adj.* not arable. [Pfx. **in-** (2).]

**inarch**, *in-ärch'*, (*rare*) *v.t.* to graft by uniting without separating from the original stem.—Also **enarch'**. [Pfx. **in-** (1).]

**inarm**, *in-ärm'*, *v.t.* to embrace. [Pfx. **in-** (1).]

**inarticulate**, *in-är-tik'ū-lit*, *adj.* not jointed or hinged: not uttered with the distinct sounds of spoken language: indistinctly uttered or utter ing: incapable of clear and fluent expression.—*n.* **inartic'ulacy**.—*adv.* **inartic'ulately**.—*ns.* **inartic'ulateness**, **inarticulā'tion**, indistinctness of sounds in speaking. [Pfx. **in-** (2).]

**in articulo mortis**, *in ärt-ik'ū-lō mör'tis, ärt-ik'ōō-lō*, (L.) at the point of death.

**inartificial**, *in-ärt-i-fish'əl*, *adj.* not done by art: simple.—*adv.* **inartific'ially**. [Pfx. **in-** (2).]

**inartistic**, **-al**, *in-är-tis'tik*, *-əl*, *adjs.* not artistic: deficient in appreciation of art.—*adv.* **inartis'tically**. [Pfx. **in-** (2).]

**inasmuch**, *in-az-much'*, *-əz-*. See **in**.

**inattentive**, *in-ə-ten'tiv*, *adj.* careless: not fixing the mind to attention: neglectful.—*ns.* **inatten'tion**, **inatten'tiveness**.—*adv.* **inatten'tively**. [Pfx. **in-** (2).]

**inaudible**, *in-öd'i-bl*, *adj.* not able to be heard.—*ns.* **inaudibil'ity**, **inaud'ibleness**.—*adv.* **inaud'ibly**. [Pfx. **in-** (2).]

**inaugurate**, *in-ö'gūr-āt*, *v.t.* to induct formally into an office: to cause to begin: to make a public exhibition of for the first time.—*adj.* **inau'gural**, pertaining to, or done at, an inauguration.—*n.* an inaugural address.—*ns.* **inaugurā'tion**; **inau'gurator**.—*adj.* **inau'guratory** (*-ə-tər-i*). [L. *inaugurāre*, *-ātum*, to inaugurate with taking of the auspices; see **augur**.]

**inaurate**, *in-ö'rāt*, (*rare*) *adj.* gilded: having a golden lustre. [L. *inaurāre*, *-ātum*, to gild—*in*, in, on, *aurum*, gold.]

**inauspicious**, *in-ö-spish'əs*, *adj.* not auspicious: ill-omened: unlucky.—*adv.* **inauspic'iously**.—*n.* **inauspic'iousness**. [Pfx. **in-** (2).]

**in banco regis**, *in bang'kō rē'jis, rä'gis*, (L.L.) in The King's Bench.

**inbeing**, *in'bē-ing*, *n.* inherent existence: inherence: inner nature. [Pfx. **in-** (1).]

**inbent**, *in'bent*, *adj.* bent inwards. [Pfx. **in-** (1).]

**in bianco**, *in byang'kō, bē-äng'kō*, (It.) in blank, in white.

**in-between**, *in-bi-twēn'*, *adj.* intervening: intermediate.—*n.* an interval: an intermediary: any thing or person that is intermediate.

**inboard**, *in'bōrd*, *-börd*, *adv.* and *adj.* within the hull or interior of a ship: toward or nearer to the centre. [Pfx. **in-** (1).]

**inborn**, *in'börn*, *adj.* born in or with one: innate: implanted by nature. [Pfx. **in-** (1).]

**inbreak**, *in'brāk*, (*rare*) *n.* a violent rush in: irruption. [Pfx. **in-** (1).]

**inbreathe**, *in-brēdh'*, *in'brēdh*, *v.t.* to breathe in. [Pfx. **in-** (1).]

**inbreed**, *in'brēd*, *in-brēd'*, *v.t.* to breed or generate within: to breed in-and-in:—*pa.p.* and *adj.* **in'bred**, innate: bred in-and-in.—*n.* **in'breeding** (*obs.*). [Pfx. **in-** (1).]

**inbring**, *in-bring'*, (*obs.*) *v.t.* to bring in: to bring into court:—*pa.p.* and *adj.* **inbrought'**.—*n.* **in'-bringing**. [Pfx. **in-** (1).]

**inburning**, *in-bûrn'ing*, (*Spens.*) *adj.* burning within. [Pfx. **in-** (1).]

**inburst**, *in'bûrst*, (*rare*) *n.* an irruption. [Pfx. **in-** (1).]

**inby, inbye**, *in-bī'*, (*Scot.*) *adv.* toward the interior: near: near the house: towards the coal face (*mining*).—Also *adj.* [Pfx. **in-** (1).]

**Inca**, *ing'kə*, *n.* an Indian of Peru: a member of the old royal family of Peru: a Peruvian king or emperor.—Also *adj.* [Quechua, prince.]

**incage**, *in-kāj'* (*obs.*). Same as **encage**.

**incalculable**, *in-kal'kū-lə-bl*, *adj.* not calculable or able to be reckoned: too great to calculate: unpredictable.—*ns.* **incalculabil'ity**, **incal'culableness**.—*adv.* **incal'culably**. [Pfx. **in-** (2).]

**incalescent**, *in-ka-les'ənt*, or *-kə-*, *adj.* growing warm.—*n.* **incalesc'ence**. [L. *incalēscēns*, *-entis*, pr.p. of *incalēscēre*—*in*, in, *calēscēre*, inceptive of *calēre*, to be warm.]

**in-calf**, *in-käf'*, *adj.* pregnant (with calf). [in, calf.]

**in camera**, *in kam'ər-a*, *kam'er-ä*, (L.L.) in a (judge's private) room: in secret.

**incandesce**, *in-kan-des'*, *v.i.* to be luminous by heat.—*n.* **incandesc'ence**, a white heat.—*adj.* **incandesc'ent**, white-hot.—*n.* **incandescent lamp**, one whose light is produced by heating something to white heat, as a filament resisting an electric current in a glow-lamp, or a mantle heated by a flame. [L. *in*, in, *candēscēre*—*candēre*, to glow.]

**incantation**, *in-kan-tā'shən*, *n.* a formula of words said or sung for purposes of enchantment: the use of spells.—*n.* **in'cantātor**.—*adj.* **incan'tatory** (*-tə-tə-ri*). [L. *incantāre*, to sing a magical formula over.]

**incapable**, *in-kāp'ə-bl*, *adj.* not capable: unable to receive or take in (*obs.*): unable (with *of*): incompetent: helplessly drunk: disqualified.—*n.* an incompetent person: one who is helplessly drunk.—*n.* **incapabil'ity**.—*adv.* **incap'ably**. [Pfx. **in-** (2).]

**incapacious**, *in-kə-pā'shəs*, *adj.* not large, narrow: of small capacity.—*n.* **incapā'ciousness**.—*v.t.* **incapacitate** (*-pas'*), to disable: to make unfit (for): to disqualify legally.—*ns.* **incapacitā'tion**, a disqualifying; **incapac'ity**, want of capacity: inability: disability: legal disqualification. [L. *incapāx*, *-ācis*.]

**in capite**, *in kap'it-ē*, *kap'it-e*, (L.L.) in chief: holding or held immediately of the crown.

**incapsulate**, *in-kap'sūl-āt*, *v.t.* to enclose as in a capsule: to enclose (a modifying element) between other elements of a word. [Pfx. **in-** (1).

**incarcerate**, *in-kär'sər-āt*, *v.t.* to imprison: to confine.—*n.* **incarcerā'tion**, imprisonment: obstinate constriction or strangulation (*surg.*). [L. *in*, in, *carcer*, a prison.]

**incardinate**, *in-kär'di-nāt*, *v.t.* to attach as a cardinal part, as a priest to his church.—*adj.* Sir Andrew Aguecheek's blunder for *incarnate* (*Twelfth Night* V, i). [L. *in*, in, into, *cardo*, *-inis*, a hinge.]

**incarnadine**, *in-kär'nə-dīn*, *-din*, *v.t.* to dye red. —*adj.* carnation-coloured: flesh-colour: blood-red. [Fr. *incarnadin*—It. *incarnadino*, carnation, flesh-colour.]

**incarnate**, *in-kär'nāt*, or *in'*, *v.t.* to embody in flesh, give human form to: to personify (*fig.*).—*v.i.* to form flesh, heal.—*adj.* (*-kär'nit*, *-nat*) invested with flesh: personified.—*n.* **incarnā'tion**, (often *cap.*) act of embodying in flesh, esp. of Christ: an incarnate form: manifestation, visible embodiment: the process of healing, or forming new flesh (*surg.*) [L.L. *incarnāre*, *-ātum*—L. *in*, in, *carō*, *carnis*, flesh.]

**incase, incasement**. See **encase, encasement**.

**incatenation**, *in-kat-i-nā'shən*, *n.* harnessing:

**chaining** together: linking. [L. *in*, *catēna*, chain.]

**incautious**, *in-kö'shəs*, *adj.* not cautious or careful. —*ns.* **incau'tion**, **incau'tiousness**.—*adv.* **incau'-tiously**. [Pfx. **in-** (2).]

**incave**. Same as **encave**.

**incavo**, *in-kä'vō*, *n.* the incised part in an intaglio. [It.,—L. *in*, in, *cavus*, hollow.]

**incede**, *in-sēd'*, (*rare*), *v.i.* to advance majestically. —*adv.* **incēd'ingly**. [L. *incēdēre*; see Virg. *Aen.* I, 46.]

**incendiary**, *in-sen'di-ər-i*, *n.* one who maliciously sets fire to property: one who inflames passions or promotes strife: an incendiary bomb.—*adj.* relating to incendiarism: adapted or used for setting buildings, etc., on fire: tending to excite strife.—*n.* **incen'diarism**—**incendiary bomb**, a bomb containing a highly inflammable substance and designed to burst into flames on striking its objective. [L. *incendiārius*—*incendium*—*incendēre*, to kindle.]

**incendivity**, *in-sen-div'i-ti*, *n.* power of causing ignition. [L. *incendēre*, to set on fire.]

**incense**, *in-sens'*, *v.t.* to kindle (*obs.*): to inflame with anger: to incite, urge.—*ns.* **incense'ment** (*Shak.*), anger; **incens'or**, instigator: inciter. [O.Fr. *incenser*—L. *incendēre*, *incēnsum*, to kindle.]

**incense**, *in'sens*, *n.* material burned or volatilised to give fragrant fumes, esp. in religious rites—usu. a mixture of resins and gums, etc. (olibanum, benzoin, styrax, cascarilla bark): the fumes so obtained: any pleasant smell: homage, adulation (*fig.*).—*v.t.* to perfume or fumigate with incense: to offer incense to.—*ns.* **in'censer**; **in'sensor** (or *-sens*), a burner or offerer of incense: a flatterer; **in'sensory** (or *-sens'*), a censer or thurible.—**in'cense-boat**, a boat-shaped vessel for feeding a censer with incense.—*adj.* **in'cense-breathing**, exhaling fragrance.—**in'cense-burner**, a stationary vessel for burning incense. [O.Fr. *encens*—L. *incēnsum*—*incendēre*, to set on fire.]

**incentive**, *in-sent'iv*, *adj.* inciting, encouraging: igniting (*Milt.*).—*n.* that which incites to action. [L. *incentivus*, striking up a tune—*incinēre*—*in*, in, *canēre*, to sing.]

**incentre**, *in'sen-tər*, *n.* the centre of the inscribed circle or sphere. [Pfx. **in-** (1).]

**incept**, *in-sept'*, *v.t.* to begin (*obs.*): to take into the body.—*v.i.* at Cambridge, to complete the taking of a master's or doctor's degree.—*n.* **incep'tion**, beginning.—*adj.* **incep'tive**, beginning or marking the beginning: inchoative (*gram.*).—*n.* (*gram.*) an inchoative verb.—*n.* **incep'tor**. [L. *incipēre*, *inceptum*, to begin—*in*, in, on, *capēre*, to take.]

**incertain**, *in-sûr'tən*, *adj.* (*Shak.*) uncertain.—*ns.* **incer'tainty** (*Shak.*), **incer'titude**. [Pfx. **in-** (2).]

**incessant**, *in-ses'ənt*, *adj.* uninterrupted: continual.—*adv.* **incess'antly**, unceasingly: immediately (*obs.*). [L. *incessāns*, *-antis*—*in-*, not, *cessāre*, to cease.]

**incest**, *in'sest*, *n.* sexual intercourse within the prohibited degrees of kindred.—*adj.* **incest'ūous**, pertaining to, or characterised by, incest: turned inward on itself, or of, or within, a small closely-knit group (*fig.*).—*adv.* **incest'uously**.—*n.* **incest'-uousness**. [L. *incestum*—*in-*, not, *castus*, chaste.]

**inch**, *inch*, *insh*, *n.* the twelfth part of a foot, equal to 2·54 cm.: amount of e.g. rainfall that will cover a surface to the depth of one inch (now measured in millimetres): amount of atmospheric pressure to balance the weight of a column of mercury one inch high (now measured in millibars): proverbially, a small distance or degree: (in *pl.*) stature.—*v.t.* and *v.i.* to move by slow degrees.—*adj.* **inched**, containing inches: marked with inches.—*adv.* **inch'meal**, inch by inch.—**inch'-tape**, a measuring tape divided into inches; **inch'-worm,** a looper caterpillar.—**at an inch** (*Shak.*), ready at hand; **by inches, inch by inch,** by small degrees; **every inch,** entirely, thoroughly. [O.E. *ynce,* an inch—L. *uncia,* a twelfth part; cf. ounce.]

**inch,** *insh,* (*Scot.*) *n.* an island: a low-lying meadow beside a river. [Gael. *innis,* island.]

**incharitable,** *in-char'it-ə-bl,* (*Shak.*) *adj.* uncharitable. [Pfx. in- (2).]

**inchase,** *in-chās'.* Same as **enchase.**

**inchoate,** *in-kō'āt, in'kō-āt, adj.* only begun: unfinished, rudimentary: not established.—*v.t.* (*arch.*) (*in'*) to begin.—*adv.* **inchoately** (*-kō'*, or *in'*).—*n.* **inchoā'tion,** beginning: rudimentary state.—*adj.* **inchoative** (*in-kō'ə-tiv* or *in-kō-ā'tiv*), incipient: denoting the beginning of an action, inceptive (*gram.*).—*n.* (*gram.*) an inchoative verb. [L. *inchoāre* (for *incohāre*), *-ātum,* to begin.]

**inchpin,** *inch', insh'pin,* (*obs.*) *n.* a deer's sweetbread. [Perh. inch, pin.]

**incident,** *in'si-dənt, adj.* falling upon something: liable to occur: naturally belonging (to): consequent.—*n.* that which happens: an event: a subordinate action: an episode: that which naturally belongs to or is consequent on something else: a minor event showing hostility and threatening more serious trouble: a brief violent action, e.g. a raid, a bomb explosion.—*n.* **in'cidence,** the frequency or range of occurrence: the fact or manner of falling: bearing or onus, as of a tax: the falling of a ray on a surface: the falling of a point on a line, or a line on a plane (*geom.*).—*adj.* **incidental** (*-dent'l*), incident: striking or impinging: liable to occur: naturally attached: accompanying: concomitant: occasional, casual.—*n.* anything that occurs incidentally.—*adv.* **incident'ally,** in an incidental way: loosely, by the way, parenthetically, as a digression.—*n.* **incident'alness.**—**incidental music,** music accompanying the action of a play.—**angle of incidence,** the angle between an incident ray and the normal to the surface it falls on. [L. *incidēns, -entis—in,* on, *cadĕre,* to fall.]

**incinerate,** *in-sin'ər-āt, v.t.* to reduce to ashes.—*ns.* **incinerā'tion; incin'erātor,** a furnace for consuming anything. [L. *incinerāre, -ātum—in,* in, *cinis, cineris,* ashes.]

**incipient,** *in-sip'i-ənt, adj.* beginning: nascent.—*ns.* **incip'ience, incip'iency.**—*adv.* **incip'iently.** [L. *incipiēns, -entis,* pr.p. of *incipĕre,* to begin.]

**incise,** *in-sīz', v.t.* to cut into: to cut or gash: to engrave.—*adj.* **incised',** cut: engraved: cut to about the middle (*bot.*); **incis'iform,** shaped like an incisor tooth.—*n.* **incision** (*in-sizh'ən*), the act of cutting in, esp. (*surg.*) into the body: a cut: a gash: a notch: trenchancy.—*adj.* **incisive** (*-sīs'*), having the quality of cutting in: trenchant: acute: sarcastic.—*adv.* **inci'sively.**—*ns.* **inci'siveness; incisor** (*-sīz'ər*), a cutting or fore-tooth.—*adjs.* **incisorial** (*-sis-ō'ri-əl, -siz-, -ō'*), **incisory** (*-sis', -siz'ər-i*).—*n.* **incisure** (*-sizh'ər*), a cut, incision. [Fr. *inciser*—L. *incīdĕre, incīsum—in,* into, *caedĕre,* to cut.]

**incite,** *in-sīt', v.t.* to move to action: to instigate.—*ns.* **incitant** (*in'sit-ənt, in-sīt'ənt*), that which incites: a stimulant; **incitā'tion** (*-sit-, -sīt-*), the act of inciting or rousing: an incentive.—*adj.* and *n.* **incitative** (*-sīt'ə-tiv*).—*ns.* **incite'ment;** **incit'er.**—*adv.* **incit'ingly.** [Fr.,—L. *incitāre—in,* in, *citāre,* to rouse—*ciĕre,* to put in motion.]

**incivil,** *in-siv'il, adj.* (*Shak.*) uncivil.—*n.* **incivil'ity,** want of civility or courtesy: impoliteness: an act of discourtesy (in this sense *pl.* **incivil'ities**). [Pfx. in- (2).]

**incivism,** *in'siv-izm, n.* neglect of duty as a citizen, conduct unbecoming a good citizen. [Fr. *incivisme.*]

**inclasp,** *in-kläsp'.* Same as **enclasp.**

**inclement,** *in-klem'ənt, adj.* severe: stormy:

harsh.—*n.* **inclem'ency.**—*adv.* **inclem'ently.** [Pfx. in- (2).]

**incline,** *in-klīn', v.i.* to lean forward or downward: to bow or bend: to deviate or slant: to slope: to tend: to be disposed: to have some slight desire.—*v.t.* to cause to bend downwards: to turn: to cause to deviate: to slope: to tilt: to direct: to dispose.—*n.* (*in'klīn, in-klīn'*) a slope: a sloping tunnel or shaft (*min.*).—*adj.* **inclin'able,** leaning, capable of being tilted or sloped: tending: somewhat disposed: favourably disposed.—*ns.* **inclin'ableness; inclinā'tion** (*in-klin-*), act of inclining: a bend or bow: a slope or tilt: a deviation: angle with the horizon or with any plane or line: tendency: disposition of mind: natural aptness: favourable disposition, preference, affection.—*adj.* **inclīnā'tional.**—*n.* **inclinato'rium,** the dipping-needle.—*adjs.* **inclin'-atory; inclined',** bent: sloping: oblique: having a tendency: disposed.—*n.* **inclin'ing,** inclination: side, party (*Shak.*).—*n.* **inclinom'eter** (*-klin-*), an instrument for measuring slopes (clinometer), the magnetic dip (dipping-needle), or the inclination of the axis of an aeroplane.—**inclined plane,** one of the mechanical powers, a slope or plane up which one can raise a weight one could not lift. [L. *inclīnāre,* to bend towards —*in,* into, *clīnāre,* to lean.]

**inclip,** *in-klip', (Shak.) v.t.* to embrace, enfold. [Pfx. in- (1).]

**inclose, inclosure.** See **enclose.**

**include,** *in-klōōd', v.t.* to enclose: to comprise as a part: to classify, or reckon as part: to take in: to conclude (*Shak.*).—*adj.* **includ'ed,** enclosed: comprised: not protruding (*bot.*).—*prep.* (or *pr.p.* merging in *prep.*) with the inclusion of.—*adj.* **includ'ible.**—*n.* **inclusion** (*-klōō'zhən*), act of including: that which is included: a foreign body enclosed in a crystal, or the like.—*adj.* **inclusive** (*-klōō'siv*), shutting in: enclosing: comprehensive: including everything: comprehending the stated limit or extremes, including (with *of*): included (*obs.* or *loose*).—*adv.* **inclu'sively.**—**inclusive transcription,** any phonetic transcription admitting of more than one pronunciation of the transcribed words.—**include out** (*coll.*) to exclude. [L. *inclūdĕre, in-clūsum—in,* in, *claudĕre,* to shut.]

**incoagulable,** *in-kō-ag'ū-lə-bl, adj.* incapable of coagulation. [Pfx. in- (2).]

**incoercible,** *in-kō-ûrs'i-bl, adj.* that cannot be coerced: that cannot be liquefied by pressure. [Pfx. in- (2).]

**incog,** *in-kog', adv.* an abbreviation for **incognito.**

**incogitable,** *in-koj'i-tə-bl, adj.* unthinkable.—*ns.* **incogitabil'ity, incog'itancy.**—*adjs.* **incog'itant,** unthinking: without power of thought; **incog'-itātive.** [L. *in-,* not, *cōgitāre,* to think.]

**incognisable, incognizable,** *in-kog'niz-ə-bl,* or *in-kon'iz-ə-bl, adj.* that cannot be known or distinguished.—*adj.* **incog'nisant, incog'nizant,** not cognisant.—*ns.* **incog'nisance, incog'nizance,** failure to recognise; **incognoscibil'ity** (*-kog-nos-i-*).—*adj.* **incognosc'ible.** [See **cognition,** cognosce, recognise.]

**incognito,** *in-kog'ni-tō, in-kog-nē'tō, adj.* unknown, unidentified: disguised: under an assumed title.—*adv.* under an assumed name: with concealment, or feigned concealment, of identity.—*n.* a man unknown, unidentified, or disguised (*fem.* **incognita**): concealment, real or feigned. [It.,—L. *incognitus—in-,* not, *cognitus,* known—*cognōscĕre,* to recognise, come to know.]

**incoherent,** *in-kō-hēr'ənt, adj.* not coherent: loose: rambling.—*ns.* **incohēr'ence, -ency.**—*adv.* **incohēr'ently.**—*n.* **incohē'sion.**—*adj.* **incohē'sive** (*-siv*). [Pfx. in- (2).]

**incombustible,** *in-kəm-bust'i-bl, adj.* incapable of combustion.—*ns.* **incombustibil'ity, incombust'-ibleness.**—*adv.* **incombust'ibly.** [Pfx. in- (2).]

Neutral vowels in unaccented syllables: *el'ə-mənt*; for certain sounds in foreign words, see p. viii

**income**, in′kum, in′kəm, ing′kəm, *n.* coming in, advent (*Shak.*): that which comes in: profit, or interest from anything: revenue: a disease coming without known cause (*Scot.*).—*n.* in-comer (in′kum-ər), one who comes in: one who takes possession of a farm, house, etc., or who comes to live in a place, not having been born there.—*adj.* in′coming, coming in: accruing: ensuing, next to follow.—*n.* the act of coming in: revenue.—**income tax,** a tax directly levied on income or on income over a certain amount. [Pfx. in- (1).]
**in commendam.** See commend.
**incommensurable,** in-kəm-en′shə-rə-bl, -shŏŏ-, *adj.* having no common measure: incommensurate.—*n.* a quantity that has no common measure with another, esp. with rational numbers.—*ns.* **incommensurabil′ity, incommen′surableness.**—*adv.* **incommen′surably.**—*adj.* **incommen′surate,** disproportionate: not adequate: incommensurable.—*adv.* **incommen′surately.**—*n.* **incommen′surateness.** [Pfx. in- (2).]
**incommiscible,** in-kəm-is′i-bl, *adj.* that cannot be mixed together. [L. in-, not, commiscēre, to mix.]
**incommode,** in-kəm-ōd′, *v.t.* to cause trouble or inconvenience to.—*adj.* **incommō′dious,** inconvenient: (of e.g. house) rather small: troublesome (obs.): unsuitable (with to, for; obs.)—*adv.* **incommō′diously.**—*ns.* **incommō′diousness; incommodity** (-od′), inconvenience: anything that causes inconvenience. [Fr. incommoder—L. incommodāre—in-, not, commodus, commodious.]
**incommunicable,** in-kəm-ūn′i-kə-bl, *adj.* that cannot be communicated or imparted to others.—*ns.* **incommunicabil′ity, incommun′icableness.**—*adv.* **incommun′icably.**—*adj.* **incommun′icative,** uncommunicative.—*adv.* **incommun′icatively.**—*n.* **incommun′icativeness.** [Pfx. in- (2).]
**incommunicado,** in-kəm-ūn-i-kä′dō, *adj.* and *adv.* without means of communication: in solitary confinement. [Sp. incomunicado.]
**incommutable,** in-kəm-ūt′ə-bl, *adj.* that cannot be commuted or exchanged.—*ns.* **incommutabil′ity, incommut′ableness.**—*adv.* **incommut′ably.** [Pfx. in- (2).]
**incomparable,** in-kom′pər-ə-bl, *adj.* not admitting comparison: matchless.—*ns.* **incomparabil′ity, incom′parableness.**—*adv.* **incom′parably.**—*adj.* **incompared** (in-kom-pār′ed; Spens.), peerless. [Pfx. in- (2).]
**incompatible,** in-kəm-pat′i-bl, *adj.* not consistent: contradictory: incapable of existing together in harmony or at all: incapable of combination, co-operation, functioning together: mutually intolerant or exclusive: irreconcilable.—*n.* a thing incompatible with another: (in pl.) things which cannot co-exist.—*ns.* **incompatibil′ity,** state of being incompatible: a difference, usu. physiological, which prevents completion of fertilisation (bot.): a difference in physiological properties between a host and parasite which limits the development of the latter (bot.); in-**incompat′ibleness.**—*adv.* **incompat′ibly.** [Pfx. in- (2).]
**incompetent,** in-kom′pi-tənt, *adj.* wanting adequate powers: unable to function: wanting the proper legal qualifications: grossly deficient in ability for one's work.—*n.* an incompetent person.—*ns.* **incom′petence, incom′petency.**—*adv.* **incom′petently.** [Pfx. in- (2).]
**incomplete,** in-kəm-plēt′, *adj.* imperfect: unfinished: wanting calyx, corolla, or both (bot.).—*n.pl.* **Incomplē′tae** (-tē), an artificial group of dicotyledons with perianth absent or incomplete, the Monochlamydeae.—*adv.* **incomplete′ly.**—*ns.* **incomplete′ness, incomplē′tion.** [Pfx. in- (2).]
**incompliance,** in-kəm-pli′əns, *n.* refusal to comply: an unaccommodating disposition.—*adj.* **incom-pli′ant.** [Pfx. in- (2).]

**incomposed,** in-kəm-pōzd′, (Milt.) *adj.* discomposed. [Pfx. in- (2).]
**incomposite,** in-kom′pəz-it, *adj.* simple: ill-constructed.—**incomposite numbers,** prime numbers. [Pfx. in- (2).]
**incompossible,** in-kəm-pos′i-bl, (rare), *adj.* incapable of co-existing.—*n.* **incompossibil′ity.** [Pfx. in- (2).]
**incomprehensible,** in-kom-pri-hens′i-bl, *adj.* not capable of being understood: not to be contained within limits (theol.).—*ns.* **incomprehensibil′ity, incomprehens′ibleness.**—*adv.* **incomprehens′ibly.**—*n.* **incomprehen′sion,** lack of comprehension.—*adj.* **incomprehens′ive,** not comprehensive.—*n.* **incomprehens′iveness.** [Pfx. in- (2).]
**incompressible,** in-kəm-pres′i-bl, *adj.* not to be compressed into smaller bulk.—*ns.* **incompressibil′ity, incompress′ibleness.** [Pfx. in- (2).]
**incomputable,** in-kəm-pūt′ə-bl, or in-kom′, *adj.* that cannot be computed or reckoned. [Pfx. in- (2).]
**inconceivable,** in-kən-sēv′ə-bl, *adj.* that cannot be conceived by the mind: incomprehensible: involving a contradiction in terms: physically impossible: taxing belief or imagination (coll.).—*n.* an inconceivable thing.—*ns.* **inconceivabil′ity, inconceiv′ableness.**—*adv.* **inconceiv′ably.** [Pfx. in- (2).]
**inconcinnity,** in-kən-sin′i-ti, *n.* want of congruousness or proportion.—*adj.* **inconcinn′ous.** [Pfx. in- (2).]
**inconclusive,** in-kən-klōōs′iv, *adj.* not settling a point in debate, indeterminate, indecisive.—*n.* **inconclusion** (-klōō′zhən).—*adv.* **inconclus′ively.**—*n.* **inconclus′iveness.** [Pfx. in- (2).]
**incondensable,** in-kən-dens′ə-bl, *adj.* not condensable. [Pfx. in- (2).]
**incondite,** in-kon′dit,-dīt, *adj.* not well put together, irregular, unfinished. [L. inconditus—in-, not, condĕre, conditum, to build.]
**incongruous,** in-kong′grōō-əs, *adj.* inconsistent: not fitting well together, disjointed: unsuitable.—Also **incong′ruent.**—*ns.* **incongruity** (-kong- or -kən-grōō-), **incong′ruousness.**—*adv.* **incong′ruously.** [Pfx. in- (2).]
**inconnu,** fem. **inconnue,** ē-ko-nü, (Fr.) an unknown person.
**inconscient,** in-kon′sh(y)ənt, *adj.* unconscious: abstracted: not controlled by, or arising from, consciousness.—*adv.* **incon′sciently.**—*adj.* **incon′scious,** unconscious.
**inconscionable,** in-kon′shən-ə-bl, *adj.* unconscionable. [Pfx. in- (2).]
**inconsecutive,** in-kən-sek′ū-tiv, *adj.* not succeeding or proceeding in regular order.—*n.* **inconsec′-utiveness.** [Pfx. in- (2).]
**inconsequent,** in-kon′si-kwənt, *adj.* not following from the premises: illogical: irrelevant: disconnected: unrelated: unimportant.—*n.* **incon′-sequence.**—*adj.* **inconsequential** (-kwen′shl), not following from the premises: of no consequence or value.—*advs.* **inconsequen′tially, incon′se-quently.** [Pfx. in- (2).]
**inconsiderable,** in-kən-sid′ər-ə-bl, *adj.* not worthy of notice: unimportant: of no great size.—*n.* **inconsid′erableness.**—*adv.* **inconsid′erably.** [Pfx. in- (2).]
**inconsiderate,** in-kən-sid′er-it, *adj.* not considerate: thoughtless: rash, imprudent.—*adv.* **inconsid′er-ately.**—*ns.* **inconsid′erateness, inconsiderā′tion.** [Pfx. in- (2).]
**inconsistent,** in-kən-sist′ənt, *adj.* not consistent: not suitable or agreeing: intrinsically incompatible: self-contradictory: changeable, fickle.—*ns.* **inconsist′ence, inconsist′ency.**—*adv.* **inconsist′-ently.** [Pfx. in- (2).]
**inconsolable,** in-kən-sōl′ə-bl, *adj.* not to be comforted.—*n.* **inconsol′ableness.**—*adv.* **inconsol′-ably.** [Pfx. in- (2).]
**inconsonant,** in-kon′sən-ənt, *adj.* not consonant.—

*n.* incon'sonance.—*adv.* incon'sonantly. [Pfx. in- (2).]

**inconspicuous,** *in-kən-spik'ū-əs, adj.* not conspicuous.—*adv.* inconspic'uously.—*n.* inconspic'-uousness. [Pfx. in- (2).]

**inconstant,** *in-kon'stənt, adj.* subject to change: fickle.—*n.* incon'stancy.—*adv.* incon'stantly. [Pfx. in- (2).]

**inconsumable,** *in-kən-sūm'ə-bl, adj.* that cannot be consumed or wasted.—*adv.* inconsum'ably. [Pfx. in- (2).]

**incontestable,** *in-kən-test'ə-bl, adj.* too clear to be called in question: undeniable.—*n.* incontesta-bil'ity.—*adv.* incontest'ably. [Pfx. in- (2).]

**incontiguous,** *in-kən-tig'ū-əs, adj.* not adjoining or touching.—*adv.* incontig'uously.—*n.* incontig'u-ousness. [Pfx. in- (2).]

**incontinent,** *in-kon'ti-nənt, adj.* not restraining the passions or appetites: unchaste: unable to restrain natural discharges or evacuations (*med.*).—*ns.* incon'tinence, incon'tinency.—*adv.* incon'-tinently. [L. *incontinēns, -entis—in,* not, *con-tinēns*; see continent.]

**incontinent,** *in-kon'ti-nənt,* (*arch.*) *adv.* straightway. —Also incon'tinently. [Fr.,—L.L. *in continenti* (*tempore*), in unbroken (time).]

**incontrollable,** *in-kən-trōl'ə-bl, adj.* uncontrollable. —*adv.* incontroll'ably. [Pfx. in- (2).]

**incontrovertible,** *in-kon-trə-vûrt'i-bl, adj.* too clear to be called in question.—*n.* incontrovertibil'ity. —*adv.* incontrovert'ibly. [Pfx. in- (2).]

**in contumaciam,** *in kon-tū-mā'shi-əm, in kon-tōō-mä'ki-am,* (L.) as an act of contumacy.

**inconvenient,** *in-kən-vēn'yənt, adj.* unsuitable: causing trouble or uneasiness: increasing difficulty: incommodious.—*v.t.* inconven'ience, to trouble or incommode.—*ns.* inconven'ience, inconven'iency.—*adv.* inconven'iently. [Pfx. in- (2).]

**inconversable,** *in-kən-vûrs'ə-bl, adj.* indisposed to conversation, unsocial. [Pfx. in- (2).]

**inconversant,** *in-kon'vər-sənt,* (*rare*) *-kən-vûr', adj.* not versed (with *with* or *in*). [Pfx. in- (2).]

**inconvertible,** *in-kən-vûrt'i-bl, adj.* that cannot be changed or exchanged.—*n.* inconvertibil'ity.—*adv.* inconvert'ibly. [Pfx. in- (2).]

**inconvincible,** *in-kən-vin'si-bl, adj.* not capable of being convinced. [Pfx. in- (2).]

**incony, inconie,** *in-kun'i,* (*Shak.*) *adj.* fine, delicate, pretty. [Origin unknown.]

**inco-ordinate,** *in-kō-örd'(i)-nit, adj.* not co-ordinate —*n.* inco-ordination (*-i-nā'shon*), want or failure of co-ordination. [Pfx. in- (2).]

**incoronate,** *in-kor'ə-nāt, -nit,* -d, *-nāt-id, adjs.* crowned.—*n.* incoronā'tion. [Pfx. in- (1).]

**incorporate,** *in-kör'pər-āt, v.t.* to form into a body: to combine into one mass, or embody: to take or put into the body: to merge: to absorb: to form into a corporation: to admit to a corporation: to incarnate.—*v.i.* to unite into one mass: to form a corporation.—*adj.* (*-it*) united in one body: constituted as an incorporation.—*adj.* incor'porāting (*philol.*), combining the parts of a sentence in one word.—*n.* incor-porā'tion, act of incorporating: state of being incorporated: formation of a legal or political body: an association: an incorporated society: an embodiment.—*adj.* incor'porative (*-ə-tiv, -ā-tiv*).—*n.* incor'porātor, one who incorporates: a member, or original member, of an incorporated company (*U.S.*): a member of a university admitted to membership of another. [L. *incorporāre, -ātum—in,* in, into, *corpus, -oris,* body.]

**incorporate,** *in-kör'pər-it, -āt, adj.* without a body: unembodied.—*adjs.* incor'poral(l) (*Shak.*), incor-poreal (*-pō', -pö'ri-əl*), not having a body: spiritual: intangible.—*ns.* incorpo'realism, incor-porē'ity, incorporeality (*-kör-pōr, -pör-i-al'i-ti*). —*adv.* incorpo'really. [L. *incorporātus, incor-porālis,* bodiless—*in—,* not, *corpus, -oris,* body.]

**incorpse,** *in-körps',* (*Shak.*) *v.t.* to incorporate. [Pfx. in- (1).]

**incorrect,** *in-kər-ekt', adj.* containing faults: not accurate: not correct in manner or character: not regulated (*Shak.*).—*adv.* incorrect'ly.—*n.* incorrect'ness. [Pfx. in- (2).]

**incorrigible,** *in-kor'i-ji-bl, adj.* beyond correction or reform.—Also *n.*—*ns.* incorr'igibleness, in-corrigibil'ity.—*adv.* incorr'igibly. [Pfx. in- (2).]

**incorrosible,** *in-kə-rō'si-bl,* **incorrodible,** *in-kə-rō'di-bl, adjs.* incapable of being corroded: not readily corroded. [Pfx. in- (2).]

**incorrupt,** *in-kər-upt', adj.* sound: pure: not depraved: not to be influenced by bribes.—*adj.* incorrupt'ible, not capable of decay: that cannot be bribed: inflexibly just.—*ns.* incorrupt'ibleness, incorruptibil'ity.—*adv.* incorrupt'ibly.—*ns.* incor-rup'tion, incorrupt'ness.—*adj.* incorrupt'ive.—*adv.* incorrupt'ly. [Pfx. in- (2).]

**incrassate,** *in-kras'āt, v.t.* and *v.i.* (*obs.* except in *pharm.*) to thicken.—*adjs.* incrass'ate, -d, thickened.—*n.* incrassā'tion.—*adj.* incrass'ative (*-ə-tiv*). [L.L. *incrassāre, -ātum*—L. *in,* in, *crassus,* thick.]

**increase,** *in-krēs', v.i.* to grow in size, number, or (*arch.*) wealth: to have a syllable more in the genitive than in the nominative (*L. gram.*).—*v.t.* to make greater in size, number, or (*arch.*) wealth.—*n.* in'crease, growth: increment: addition to the original stock: profit: produce: progeny (*arch.*).—*adjs.* increas'able; increase'ful (*Shak.*), abundant of produce.—*n.* increas'er.—*n.* and *adj.* increas'ing.—*adv.* increas'ingly. [M.E. *encressen*—A.Fr. *encresser*—L. *incrēscĕre—in, crēscĕre,* to grow.]

**increate,** *in-krē-āt',* (*arch.*) *adj.* uncreated. [Pfx. in- (2).]

**incredible,** *in-kred'i-bl, adj.* surpassing belief: difficult to believe in: very great: unusually good (*coll.*).—*ns.* incredibil'ity; incred'ibleness. —*adv.* incred'ibly. [Pfx. in- (2).]

**incredulous,** *in-kred'ū-ləs, adj.* hard of belief, sceptical: not believing: incredible (*Shak.*).—*ns.* incredū'lity (*-krid-*), incred'ūlousness.—*adv.* in-cred'ūlously. [Pfx. in- (2).]

**incremate,** *in'kri-māt,* (*obs.*) *v.t.* to burn: to cremate.—*n.* incremā'tion. [Pfx. in- (1).]

**increment,** *ing'* or *in'kri-mənt, n.* increase: amount of increase: an amount or thing added: the finite increase of a variable quantity (*math.*): an adding of particulars towards a climax (*rhet.*): a syllable in excess of the number of the nominative singular or the second pers. sing. present indicative (*gram.*).—*adj.* incremental (*-ment'l*).—**unearned increment,** any exceptional increase in the value of land, houses, etc., not due to the owner's labour or outlay. [L. *incrēmentum—incrēscĕre,* to increase.]

**increscent,** *in-kres'ənt,* (*her.*) *adj.* waxing (of the moon). [Pfx. in- (1).]

**incriminate,** *in-krim'in-āt, v.t.* to charge with a crime or fault, to criminate: to implicate, involve in a charge.—*adj.* incrim'inatory. [Pfx. in- (1).]

**incrust, incrustation.** See encrust, encrustation.

**incubate,** *in'* or *ing'kū-bāt, v.i.* to sit on eggs: to hatch: to undergo incubation: to brood, meditate (*fig.*).—*v.t.* to hatch: to foster the development of (as bacteria, etc.): to brood or ponder over (*fig.*).—*n.* incubā'tion, the act of sitting on eggs to hatch them: hatching (natural or artificial): fostering (as of bacteria, etc.): sleeping in a holy place to obtain dreams from the gods: meditation on schemes (*fig.*): the period between infection and appearance of symptoms (*med.*).—*adjs.* in'cubative, in'cubatory. —*n.* in'cubător, a brooding hen: an apparatus for hatching eggs by artificial heat, for rearing prematurely born children, or for developing bacteria.—*adj.* in'cubous (*bot.*), having the upper leaf-margin overlapping the leaf above. [L. *incubāre*, -*ātum* (usu. -*itum*)—*in*, on, *cubāre*, to lie, recline.]

**incubus**, *in'* or *ing'kū-bəs*, *n*. the nightmare: a devil supposed to assume a male body and have sexual intercourse with women in their sleep: any oppressive person, thing, or influence:— *pl*. in'**cubuses**, in'**cubi** (-*bī*). [L. *incŭbus*, night-mare—*in*, on, *cubāre*, to lie.]

**inculcate**, *in'kul-kāt* or -*kul'*, *v.t.* to instil by frequent admonitions or repetitions.—*n*. **incul-cā'tion**.—*adj*. **inculc'ative** (-*ə-tiv*).—*n*. in'**culcātor**. —*adj*. **inculc'atory**. [L. *inculcāre*, -*ātum*—*in*, into, *calcāre*, to tread—*calx*, heel.]

**inculpable**, *in-kul'pə-bl*, *adj*. blameless.—*adv*. in-**cul'pably**. [L. *inculpābilis*—*in*-, not, *culpābilis*; see **culpable**.]

**inculpate**, *in'kul-pāt*, or -*kul'*, *v.t.* to involve in a charge or blame: to charge.—*n*. **inculpā'tion**.— *adj*. **incul'patory** (-*pə-tə-ri*). [L.L. *inculpāre*, -*ātum*—L. *in*, in, *culpa*, a fault.]

**incult**, *in-kult'*, (*rare*) *adj*. uncultivated.

**incumbent**, *in-kum'bənt*, *adj*. lying or resting: weighing on something: overlying (*geol*.): lean-ing over (*arch*.): overhanging (*arch*.): imposed or resting as a duty: lying along a surface, as a moth's wings at rest: of a radicle, lying along the back of one cotyledon (*bot*.).—*n*. one who holds an ecclesiastical benefice.—*n*. **incum'bency**, a lying or resting on something: the state or fact of being incumbent or an incumbent: a duty or obligation: the holding of an office: an ecclesiastical benefice.—*adv*. **incum'bently**. [L. *incumbēns*, -*entis*, pr.p. of *incumbĕre*, to lie upon.]

**incunabula**, *in-kū-nab'ū-la*, *n.pl*. books printed in early period of the art, esp. before the year 1500: the cradle, birthplace, origin of a thing—*sing*. **incūnab'ūlum**, also **incūn'able**.—*adj*. **incūnab'-ūlar**.—*n*. **incūnab'ūlist**, a student or collector of incunabula. [L. *incūnābŭla*, swaddling-clothes, infancy, earliest stage—*in*, in, *cūnābula*, dim. of *cūnae*, a cradle.]

**incur**, *in-kûr'*, *v.t.* to become liable to: to bring upon oneself: to suffer:—*pr.p.* **incurr'ing**; *pa.t.* and *pa.p.* **incurred'**.—*adj*. **incurr'able**. [L. *incurrēre*, *incursum*—*in*, into, *currēre*, to run.]

**incurable**, *in-kūr'ə-bl*, *adj*. not admitting of cure or correction.—*n*. one beyond cure.—*ns*. **incur'-ableness**, **incurabil'ity**.—*adv*. **incur'ably**. [Pfx. in- (2).]

**incurious**, *in-kū'ri-əs*, *adj*. not curious or inquisi-tive: inattentive: careless: indifferent: not fastidious, uncritical (*obs*.): not exquisite (*obs*.): deficient in interest (*arch*.).—*adv*. **incū'riously**.— *ns*. **incū'riousness**, **incūrios'ity**. [Pfx. in- (2).]

**incurrent**, *in-kur'ənt*, *adj*. running in: carrying an inflowing current. [L. *in*, into, *currēns*, -*entis*, pr.p. of *currēre*, to run.]

**incursion**, *in-kûr'shən*, *n*. a hostile inroad: the action of running in: a sudden attack, invasion. —*adj*. **incur'sive**, making inroads: aggressive: invading. [L. *incursiō*, -*ōnis*—*incurrēre*.]

**incurve**, *in-kûrv'*, *v.t.* and *v.i.* to curve: to curve inward.—*n*. in'**curve**, a curve inwards: a ball that curves in, or towards the batsman (*baseball*). —*v.t.* and *v.i.* **incur'vate** (or *in'*), to bend, esp. inwards.—*adj*. curved, esp. inward—also in-**cur'vāted**.—*ns*. **incurvā'tion**, bending: bowing, kneeling, etc.: an inward bend or growth; in-**cur'vature**, curve or curvature, esp. inwaru.— *adj*. **incurved** (or *in'*), curved: curved inward.— *n*. **incur'vity**. [L. *incurvāre*, to bend in, *incurvus*, bent.]

**incus**, *ing'kəs*, *n*. one of the bones in the middle ear, so called from its fancied resemblance to an anvil:—*pl*. **incudes** (*ing-kū'dēz*, or *ing'*).—*adj*. anvil-shaped. [L. *incūs*, *incūdis*, an anvil; see **incuse**.]

**incuse**, *in-kūz'*, *v.t.* to impress by stamping, as a

coin.—*adj*. hammered.—*n*. an impression, a stamp. [L. *incūsus*, pa.p. of *incūdĕre*—*in*, on, *cūdĕre*, to strike: to work on the anvil.]

**incut**, *in'kut*, *adj*. set in by, or as if by, cutting: esp. in printing, inserted in spaces left in the text. [in, cut.]

**Ind**, *ind*, *ind*, (*poet*.) *n*. India.

**indaba**, *in-dä'ba*, *n*. an important tribal confer-ence: international Scout conference: one's affair, business (*S. Afr*.; *coll*.). [Zulu.]

**indagate**, *in'də-gāt*, (*arch*.), *v.t.* to search out.—*n*. **indagā'tion**.—*adj*. in'**dagātive**.—*n*. in'**dagātor**.— *adj*. in'**dagātory**. [L. *indāgāre*, -*ātum*, to trace.]

**indart**. See **endart**.

**indebted**, *in-det'id*, *adj*. being in debt: obliged by something received.—*ns*. **indebt'edness**, **indebt'-ment**. [Pfx. in- (1).]

**indecent**, *in-dē'sənt*, *adj*. offensive to common modesty: unbecoming: gross, obscene.—*n*. in-**dē'cency**, quality of being indecent: anything violating modesty or seemliness.—*adv*. **indē'-cently**. [Pfx. in- (2).]

**indeciduous**, *in-di-sid'ū-əs*, *adj*. not deciduous.— *adj*. **indecid'uate**, not deciduate. [Pfx. in- (2).]

**indecipherable**, *in-di-sī'fər-ə-bl*, *adj*. incapable of being deciphered. [Pfx. in- (2).]

**indecision**, *in-di-sizh'ən*, *n*. want of decision, or resolution: hesitation.—*adj*. **indecisive** (-*sī'siv*), settling nothing, inconclusive: hesitant: un-certain, indistinct.—*adv*. **indeci'sively**.—*n*. in-**deci'siveness**. [Pfx. in- (2).]

**indeclinable**, *in-di-klin'ə-bl*, (*gram*.) *adj*. not varied by inflection.—*adv*. **indeclin'ably**. [Pfx. in- (2).]

**indecomposable**, *in-dē-kəm-pōz'ə-bl*, *adj*. that can-not be decomposed. [Pfx. in- (2).]

**indecorous**, *in-dek'ə-rəs*, sometimes -*di-kō'*, or -*kō'*, *adj*. unseemly: violating good manners.— *adv*. **indec'orously**.—*ns*. **indec'orousness**, in-**decō'rum**, want of propriety of conduct: a breach of decorum. [L. *indēcōrus*.]

**indeed**, *in-dēd'*, *adv*. in fact: in truth: in reality. It emphasises an affirmation, marks a qualifying word, or clause, a concession or admission, or, used as an interj., it expresses surprise or inter-rogation, disbelief, or mere acknowledgment. [in, deed.]

**indefatigable**, *in-di-fat'i-gə-bl*, *adj*. not to be wearied out: unremitting in effort.—*n*. inde-**fat'igableness**.—*adv*. **indefat'igably**. [Fr. (obs.), —L. *indēfatigābilis*—*in*-, not, *dē*, from, *fatigāre*, to tire.]

**indefeasible**, *in-di-fēz'i-bl*, *adj*. not to be made void.—*n*. **indefeasibil'ity**.—*adv*. **indefeas'ibly**. [Pfx. in- (2).]

**indefectible**, *in-di-fekt'i-bl*, *adj*. incapable of defect: unfailing. [Pfx. in- (2).]

**indefensible**, *in-di-fens'i-bl*, *adj*. untenable, that cannot be defended (*lit*. or *fig*.): that cannot be excused or justified.—*n*. **indefensibil'ity**.—*adv*. **indefens'ibly**. [Pfx. in- (2).]

**indefinable**, *in-di-fīn'ə-bl*, *adj*. that cannot be defined.—*adv*. **indefin'ably**. [Pfx. in- (2).]

**indefinite**, *in-def'i-nit*, *adj*. without clearly marked outlines or limits: of a character not clearly distinguished: not precise: undetermined: not referring to a particular person or thing (*gram*.; see also **article**): not distinguishing between complete and incomplete active (as the Greek aorist): not fixed in number (*bot*.): not terminating in a flower (*bot*.): racemose or centripetal (*bot*.).—*adv*. **indef'initely**.—*n*. in-**def'initeness**. [Pfx. in- (2).]

**indehiscent**, *in-di-his'ənt*, (*bot*.) *adj*. not dehiscent: (of fruits) not opening when mature.—*n*. in-**dehisc'ence**. [Pfx. in- (2).]

**indelible**, *in-del'i-bl*, *adj*. that cannot be blotted out or effaced: making a mark which cannot be erased.—*ns*. **indelibil'ity**, **indel'ibleness**.—*adv*. **indel'ibly**. [L. *indēlēbilis*—*in*-, not, *dēlēre*, to destroy: influenced by words ending in -*ible*.]

indelicate, *in-del'i-kit, adj.* immodest or verging on the immodest: wanting in fineness of feeling or tact: coarse.—*n.* indel'icacy.—*adv.* indel'icately. [Pfx. in- (2).]

in deliciis, *in dəl-is'i-ēs, dāl-ik'i-ēs,* (L.) as favourites.

indemnify, *in-dem'ni-fī, v.t.* (with *against*) to secure: to compensate: (with *from*) to free, exempt:—*pr.p.* indem'nifying; *pa.t.* and *pa.p.* indem'nified.—*n.* indemnification (*-fi-kā'shən*), act of indemnifying: state of being indemnified: amount paid as compensation. [L. *indemnis,* unhurt (*—in-,* not, *damnum,* loss), and *facĕre,* to make.]

indemnity, *in-dem'ni-ti, n.* security from damage or loss: compensation for loss or injury: legal exemption from incurred liabilities or penalties.

—Act of Indemnity, an act or decree for the protection of public officers from any technical or legal penalties or liabilities they may have been compelled to incur. [Fr. *indemnité*—L. *indemnis,* unharmed—*damnum,* loss.]

indemonstrable, *in-dem'ən-strə-bl,* or *in-di-mon',* *adj.* that cannot be demonstrated or proved.—*n.* indemonstrabil'ity. [Pfx. in- (2).]

indene, *in'dēn, n.* a hydrocarbon ($H_8C_9$) got from coal-tar. [indigo.]

indent, *in-dent', v.t.* to cut into zigzags: to divide along a zigzag line: to notch: to indenture, apprentice: (as a deed, contract, etc.) to draw up in exact duplicate: to begin farther in from the margin than the rest of a paragraph: to impress: to dent or dint.—*v.t.* and *v.i.* to make out a written order with counterfoil or duplicate: to order (esp. from abroad): to requisition: (of a coastline, etc.) to penetrate, form recesses.—*v.i.* to move in a zigzag course (*Shak.*): to bargain (*obs.*): to make a compact (*obs.*).—*n.* (*in'dent,* also *in-dent'*) a cut or notch: a recess like a notch: an indenture: an order for goods (esp. from abroad): (orig. Indian) official requisition for goods: a dint.—*n.* indentā'tion, a hollow or depression: act of indenting or notching: notch: recess.—*adj.* indent'ed, having indentations: serrated: zigzag.—*ns.* indent'er, a person or thing that indents; inden'tion, indentation: blank space at the beginning of a line; indent'ure, the act of indenting, indentation: a deed under seal, with mutual covenants, where the edge is indented for future identification (*law*): a written agreement between two or more parties: a contract.—*v.t.* to bind by indentures: to indent. [Two different words fused together: (1)—L.L. *indentāre*—L. *in,* in, *dēns, dentis,* a tooth; (2)—English in and dint, dent.]

independent, *in-di-pend'ənt, adj.* (with *of*) not dependent or relying on others: not subordinate: completely self-governing: (of a business, etc.) not affiliated or merged with a larger organisaton: thinking or acting for oneself: too self-respecting to accept help: not subject to bias: having or affording a comfortable livelihood without necessity of working or help from others: not depending on another for its value, said of a quantity or function (*math.*): (*cap.*) belonging to the Independents.—*n.* (*cap.*) one who in ecclesiastical affairs holds that every congregation should be independent of every other and subject to no superior authority—a Congregationalist: a politician or other who commits himself to no party.—*ns.* independ'ence, the state of being independent: a competency; independ'ency, independence: a sovereign state: an independent income: (*cap.*) Congregationalism.—*adv.* independ'ently.—Independence Day (see Declaration of Independence), a day when a country becomes self-governing or the anniversary of this event (usu. celebrated with an annual national holiday; independent school,

a public school.—Declaration of Independence, the document (1776) proclaiming with reasons the secession of the thirteen colonies of America from the United Kingdom; reported to the Continental Congress, 4th July 1776—observed in the U.S. as a national holiday, Independence Day; Independent Labour Party, a Socialist party founded by Keir Hardie in 1893. [Pfx. in- (2).]

in deposito, *in də-poz'it-ō, dā-pos'ēt-ō,* (L.L.) for a pledge.

indescribable, *in-di-skrib'ə-bl, adj.* that cannot be described.—*n.* (*old slang,* in *pl.*) trousers.—*n.* indescribabil'ity.—*adv.* indescrib'ably. [Pfx. in- (2).]

indesignate, *in-dez'ig-nāt, (log.) adj.* without any indication of quantification. [Pfx. in- (2).]

indestructible, *in-di-struk'ti-bl, adj.* that cannot be destroyed.—*ns.* indestructibil'ity, indestruc'tibleness.—*adv.* indestruc'tibly. [Pfx. in- (2).]

indetectable, *in di-tekt'ə-bl, adj.* not to be detected.
—Also indetect'ible. [Pfx. in- (2).]

indeterminable, *in-di-tûr'min-ə-bl, adj.* not to be ascertained or fixed: of argument, etc., that cannot be settled.—*n.* indeter'minableness.—*adv.* indeter'minably.—*n.* indeter'minacy.—*adj.* indeter'minate, not determinate or fixed: uncertain: having no defined or fixed value.—*adv.* indeter'minately.—*ns.* indeter'minateness, indeterminā'tion, want of determination: want of fixed direction.—*adj.* indeter'mined, not determined: unsettled.—*ns.* indeter'minism, the theory that denies determinism; indeter'minist.—indeterminacy principle, uncertainty principle. [Pfx. in- (2).]

indew, a Spenserian form of endue.

index, *in'deks, n.* the forefinger (also in'dex-fing'er), or the digit corresponding: a pointer or hand on a dial or scale, etc.: a moving arm, as on a surveying instrument: the gnomon of a sun-dial: the finger of a finger-post: a figure of a pointing hand, used to draw attention (*print.*): the nose (*old slang*): anything giving an indication: a table of contents or other preliminary matter in a book (*obs.*): hence a preface, prologue, introduction (*Shak.; fig.*): an alphabetical register of subjects dealt with, usu. at the end of a book, with other page or folio references: a similar list of other things: a list of prohibited books: a direct, or indication of the first notes of next page or line (*mus., obs.*): a symbol denoting a power (*math.*): a number, commonly a ratio, expressing some relation (as *refractive index,* ratio of sines of angles of incidence and refraction; *cranial index,* breadth of skull as percentage of length): reciprocal of intercept with parameter as unit (*crystal.*):—*pl.* of a book usu. in'dexes; other senses indices, *in'di-sēz.*—*v.t.* to provide with or place in an index.—*n.* in'dexer.—*adjs.* index'ical; in'dexless.—in'dex-learn'ing, superficial knowledge got together from book indexes; index number, a figure showing periodic movement up or down of a variable compared with another figure (usu. 100) taken as a standard. [L. *index, indicis*—*indicāre,* to show.]

index auctorum, *in'deks ōk-tōr'əm, -tor',* owk-tōr'ōom, (L.) index of authors; index librorum prohibitorum (*lib-rōr'əm, -rōr', prō-hib-it-ōr'əm, -ōr', lib-rō'rōōm prō-hib-it-ōr'ōōm*), loosely, index expurgatorius (*eks-pūr-gə-tō'ri-əs, -tō', -pōōr-gā-tō'ri-ōōs*), a list of books prohibited (to Roman Catholic readers) either absolutely or until amended; index locorum (*lok-ōr'əm, -ōr', lok-ōr'ōōm*), rerum (*rē'rəm, rā'rōōm*), verborum (*vûr-bōr'əm, -bōr', wer-bōr'ōōm*), index of places, things, words.

indexterity, *in-deks-ter'i-ti, n.* want of dexterity. [Pfx. in- (2).]

Indian, *in'di-ən, adj.* of or belonging to India

(with various boundaries) or its native population, or to the Indies, East or West, or to the aborigines of America: made of maize.—*n.* a member of one of the races of India: form., a European long resident in India: an aboriginal of America.—*v.t.* In′dianise, -ize, to make Indian: to assimilate to what is Indian.—*v.i.* to become Indian or like an Indian.—*adj.* In′dic, originating or existing in India: of the Indian branch of the Indo-Germanic languages.—*n.* In′dianist, one who has a scholarly knowledge of Indian languages, history, etc.—In′diaman, a large ship employed in trade with India; **Indian berry**, the fruit of *Anamirta Cocculus* (see **cocculus indicus**); **Indian bread**, a Virginian fungus said to have been eaten by the Indians: maize bread; **Indian club**, a bottle-shaped block of wood, swung in various motions by the arms to develop the muscles; **Indian corn**, maize, so called because brought from the West Indies; **Indian cress**, a garden plant (*Tropaeolum majus*, popularly nasturtium) from Peru, with orange flowers; **Indian fig**, the banyan-tree: the prickly pear; **Indian file** (see **file**); **Indian fire**, a firework used as a signal-light, consisting of sulphur, realgar, and nitre; **Indian gift**, a gift that is asked back or for which a return gift is expected; **Indian hemp**, *Cannabis sativa* (*Cannabis indica* is a variety), source of drug variously known as hashish, marihuana, etc.: a species of Apocynum (*U.S.*); **Indian ink** (see **ink**); **Indian liquorice**, the jequirity or crab's-eye plant; **Indian meal**, ground maize; **Indian millet**, durra; **Indian pink** (see **pinkroot**); **Indian pipe**, an American Monotropa with a solitary drooping flower, not unlike a tobacco-pipe; **Indian poke**, an American liliaceous plant, white hellebore; **Indian red**, red ochre, or native ferric oxide, formerly imported from the East as a red pigment, also made artificially; **Indian rice** (see **Zizania**); **Indian runner**, a breed of domestic duck; **Indian shot**, a cosmopolitan tropical plant of the genus Canna, much cultivated for its flowers; **Indian summer**, (orig. in America) a period of warm, dry, calm weather in late autumn, with hazy atmosphere; **Indian tobacco**, an American lobelia; **Indian turnip**, an American araceous plant with a starchy tuber; **India Office**, a government office in London where till 1947 were managed the affairs of the Indian government; **India paper**, a thin soft absorbent paper, of chinese or Japanese origin, used in taking the finest proofs (**India proofs**) from engraved plates: a thin tough opaque paper used for printing Bibles; **in′dia-rubb′er**, an elastic gummy substance, the inspissated juice of various tropical plants: a piece of this material, esp. one used for rubbing out pencil marks; **India shawl**, a Kashmir shawl.—**East India Company**, a great chartered company formed for trading with India and the E. Indies, the English Company, incorporated in 1600 and (having lost its power by 1858) dissolved in 1874; **East Indian**, an inhabitant or native of the East Indies, usually applied to a Eurasian; **Red Indian**, one of the aborigines of America (from the coppery-brown colour of some tribes); **West Indian**, a native or an inhabitant of the West Indies. [L. *India*—*Indus* (Gr. *Indos*), the Indus (Pers. *Hind*, Sans. *sindhu*, a river).]

**Indic.** See **Indian. indican.** See **indigo.**

**indicate**, in′di-kāt, *v.t.* to point out: to show: to give some notion of: to be a mark or token of: to give ground for inferring: to point to as suitable treatment (*med.*): also (usu. in pass.) as desirable course of action in any sphere.—*adj.* **in′dicant**, indicating.—*n.* that which indicates.—*n.* **indicā′tion**, act of indicating: mark: token: suggestion of treatment: symptom.—*adj.* **indicative** (*in-dik′ə-tiv*), pointing out: giving intimation: applied to the mood of the verb that ex-

presses matter of fact (*gram.*).—*n.* the indicative mood: a verb in the indicative mood.—*adv.* **indic′atively.**—*n.* **in′dicātor**, one who or that which indicates: a pointer: a diagram showing names and directions of visible objects, as on a mountain top: a substance showing chemical condition by change of colour: a measuring contrivance with a pointer or the like: any device for exhibiting condition for the time being: (*cap.*) a genus of birds, the honey-guides.—*adj.* **in′dicatory** (or *dik′*).—**in′dicator-di′agram**, a graphical representation of the pressure and volume changes undergone by a fluid in performing a work-cycle in the cylinder of an engine on compression, the area representing, to scale, the work done during the cycle.—**indicated horse-power**, of a reciprocating engine, the horse-power developed by the pressure-volume changes of the working agent within the cylinder, exceeding the useful or brake horse-power at the crankshaft by the power lost in friction and pumping. [L. *indicāre*, *-ātum*—*in*, in, *dicāre*, to proclaim.]

**indicia**, in-dish′i-a, in-dik′i-a, (L.) marks, signs (*sing.* **indic′ium**).

**indict**, in-dīt′, *v.t.* to charge with a crime formally or in writing.—*adj.* **indict′able.**—*ns.* **indictee′**, one who is indicted; **indict′ment**, formal accusation: the written accusation against one who is to be tried by jury: the form under which one is put to trial at the instance of the Lord Advocate (*Scots law*).—**find an indictment**, of a grand jury, to be satisfied that there is a *prima facie* case, and endorse the bill *a true bill*. [With Latinised spelling (but not pronunciation) from A.Fr. *enditer*—L. *in*, in, *dictāre*, to declare, freq. of *dicēre*, to say.]

**indiction**, in-dik′shən, *n.* a proclamation: a decree of the emperor, fixing land-tax valuation (*Rom. hist.*): the tax itself (*Rom. hist.*): a cycle of fifteen years, instituted by Constantine the Great for fiscal purposes, and adopted by the popes as part of their chronological system: a year bearing a number showing its place in a fifteen years' cycle, reckoning from 24th September (or other day), A.D. 312 (*Rom. hist.*). [L. *indictiō*, *-ōnis*—*indīcēre*, to appoint.]

**indifferent**, in-dif′ər-ənt, *adj.* without importance: uninteresting: of a middle quality: not very good, inferior: in poor health (*dial.*): neutral: unconcerned.—*n.* one who is indifferent or apathetic: that which is indifferent.—*ns.* **indiff′erence**, **indiff′erency**; **indiff′erentism**, indifference: the doctrine that religious differences are of no moment (*theol.*): the doctrine of absolute identity—i.e. that to be in thought and to exist are one and the same thing (*metaph.*); **indiff′erentist.**—*adv.* **indiff′erently**, in an indifferent manner: tolerably: passably: without distinction, impartially. [Pfx. **in-** (2).]

**indigenous**, in-dij′in-əs, *adj.* native born: originating or produced naturally in a country—opp. to *exotic.*—*adj.* and *n.* **in′digene** (-*jēn*), native, aboriginal.—*adv.* **indig′enously.** [L. *indigena*, a native—*indu-*, in, and *gen-*, root of *gignēre*, to produce.]

**indigent**, in′di-jənt, *adj.* in need, esp. of means of subsistence.—*ns.* **in′digence**, **in′digency.**—*adv.* **in′digently.** [Fr.,—L. *indigēns*, *-entis*, pr.p. of *indigēre*—*indu-*, in, *egēre*, to need.]

**indigest**, in-di-jest′, *adj.* not digested, shapeless.—*n.* a crude mass, disordered state of affairs.—*adj.* **indigest′ed**, not digested: unarranged: not methodised.—*ns.* **indigestibil′ity**; **indigestion** (*in-di-jes′chən*), want of digestion: painful digestion.—*adj.* **indigest′ible**, not digestible: not easily digested: not to be received or patiently endured.—*adv.* **indigest′ibly.**—*adj.* **indigest′ive**, dyspeptic. [L. *indigestus*, unarranged—*in*, not, *digerēre*, to arrange, digest.]

indign, *in-dīn'*, (*arch.*) *adj.* unworthy: disgraceful. [L. *in-*, not, *dignus*, worthy.]

indignant, *in-dig'nant*, *adj.* feeling or showing justifiable anger (often mixed with scorn).—*n.* indig'nance (*arch.*), indignation: contemptuous impatience.—*adv.* indig'nantly.—*n.* indignā'tion, righteous anger at injustice, etc.: feeling caused by an unjustified slight, etc., to oneself: something showing anger (*Shak.*).—*v.t.* indig'nify, to treat insultingly (*Spens.*): to disgrace (with inadequate praise; *obs.*).—*n.* indig'nity, unworthiness (*obs.*): disgrace: dishonour: unmerited contemptuous treatment: incivility with contempt or insult: indignation (*Spens.*). [L. *indignus*, unworthy—*in-*, not, *dignus*, worthy.]

indigo, *in'di-gō*, *n.* a violet blue dye obtained from the leaves of the indigo plant, from woad, or synthetically: indigotin: the indigo plant, any of various species of Indigof'era, a tropical genus of Papilionaceae.—*adj.* deep blue.—*ns.* in'dican, a glucoside found in indigo leaves; in'digotin (or *in-dig'*), indigo blue, the blue colouring matter of indigo got from indican by hydrolysis; indirubin (*in-di-roō'bin*), indigo red, an isomer of indigotin, got from natural indigo.—indigo bird, an American finch, of which the male is blue. [Sp. *indico, indigo*—L. *indicum*—Gr. *Indikon*, Indian (neut. adj.).]

indirect, *in-di-rekt'*, or *-dī-*, *adj.* not direct or straight: not lineal or in direct succession: not related in the natural way, oblique: not straightforward or honest.—*adv.* indirect'ly.—*ns.* indirect'ness; indirec'tion (*Shak.*), indirect course or means, dishonest practice.—indirect evidence, or testimony, circumstantial or inferential evidence; indirect object (*gram.*), a substantive word dependent on a verb less immediately than an accusative governed by it; indirect speech (L. *ōrātiō obliqua*), speech reported with adjustment of the speaker's words to change of persons and time; indirect tax, one collected not directly from the taxpayer but through an intermediate agent, as e.g. a customs duty (passed on in the form of higher price); indirect taxation. [Pfx. in- (2).]

indiscernible, *in-di-sûrn'i-bl*, or *-zûrn'*, *adj.* not discernible.—*adv.* indiscern'ibly. [Pfx. in- (2).]

indiscerptible, *in-di-sûrp'ti-bl*, *adj.* not discerptible.—*n.* indiscerptibil'ity. [Pfx. in- (2).]

indiscipline, *in-dis'i-plin*, *n.* want of discipline.—*adj.* indisc'iplinable. [Pfx. in- (2).]

indiscoverable, *in-dis-kuv'ər-ə-bl*, *adj.* not discoverable. [Pfx. in- (2).]

indiscreet, *in-dis-krēt'*, *adj.* not discreet: imprudent: injudicious.—*adv.* indiscreet'ly.—*ns.* indiscreet'ness; indiscretion (*-kresh'ən*), want of discretion: rashness: an indiscreet act, or one seemingly indiscreet: (esp. formerly) an action breaking the moral code of society. [Pfx. in- (2).]

indiscrete, *in-dis-krēt'*, or *-dis'*, *adj.* not separated or distinguishable in parts: homogeneous.—*adv.* indiscrete'ly.—*n.* indiscrete'ness. [Pfx. in- (2).]

indiscriminate, *in-dis-krim'i-nit*, *adj.* not making distinctions: promiscuous.—*adv.* indiscrim'inately.—*adjs.* indiscrim'inating, undiscriminating; indiscrim'inative (*-ə-tiv*), not discriminative.—*n.* indiscriminā'tion. [Pfx. in- (2).]

indispensable, *in-dis-pens'ə-bl*, *adj.* that cannot be dispensed with: absolutely necessary: of a law, etc., that cannot be set aside.—*ns.* indispensabil'ity, indispens'ableness.—*adv.* indispens'ably. [Pfx. in- (2).]

indispose, *in-dis-pōz'*, *v.t.* to render indisposed, averse, or unfit.—*pa.p.* and *adj.* indisposed', averse: slightly disordered in health.—*ns.* indispos'edness; indisposition (*-pə-zish'ən*), state of being indisposed: disinclination: slight illness. [Pfx. in- (2).]

indisputable, *in-dis-pū'tə-bl*, also *-dis'*, *adj.* beyond dispute.—*n.* indisput'ableness.—*adv.* indisput'ably. [Pfx. in- (2).]

indissociable, *in-dis-ō'sh(y)ə-bl*, *adj.* incapable of being separated. [Pfx. in- (2).]

indissoluble, *in-dis-ol'ū-bl*, or *-dis'əl-*, *adj.* that cannot be broken or violated: inseparable: binding for ever.—*ns.* indissol'ubleness, indissolubility (*-ol-ū-bil'*).—*adv.* indissol'ubly. [Pfx. in- (2).]

indissolvable, *in-di-zol'və-bl*, (*arch.*) *adj.* that cannot be dissolved. [Pfx. in- (2).]

indissuadable, *in-dis-wād'ə-bl*, *adj.* not to be dissuaded.—*adv.* indissuad'ably. [Pfx. in- (2).]

indistinct, *in-dis-tingkt'*, *adj.* not plainly marked: confused: not clear to the mind: dim.—*adj.* indistinct'ive, not constituting a distinction.—*adv.* indistinct'ively, indiscriminately.—*n.* indistinct'iveness.—*adv.* indistinct'ly.—*ns.* indistinct'ness; indistinc'tion (*rare*), confusion: absence of distinction, sameness. [Pfx. in- (2).]

indistinguishable, *in-dis-ting'gwish-ə-bl*, *adj.* that cannot be distinguished.—*n.* indistin'guishableness.—*adv.* indistin'guishably. [Pfx. in- (2).]

indistributable, *in-dis-trib'ū-tə-bl*, *adj.* not distributable. [Pfx. in- (2).]

indite, *in-dīt'*, *v.t.* to compose or write: to invite (*Shak.*).—*v.i.* to compose.—*ns.* indite'ment; indit'er. [O.Fr. *enditer*; see indict.]

indium, *in'di-əm*, *n.* a soft malleable silver-white metallic element (In; at. numb. 49). [From two *indigo*-coloured lines in the spectrum.]

indivertible, *in-di-vûrt'i-bl*, *adj.* not capable of being turned aside out of a course. [Pfx. in- (2).]

individable, *in-di-vīd'ə-bl*, (*Shak.*) *adj.* that cannot be divided. [Pfx. in- (2).]

individual, *in-di-vid'ū-əl*, *adj.* not divisible without loss of identity: subsisting as one: pertaining to one only or to each one separately of a group: single, separate: inseparable (*Milt.*).—*n.* a single person, animal, plant, or thing considered as a separate member of its species or as having an independent existence: a person (*coll.*).—*n.* individualisā'tion, *-z-*.—*v.t.* individ'ualise, -ize, to stamp with individual character: to particularise.—*ns.* individ'ualism, individual character: independent action as opposed to co-operation: that theory which opposes interference of the state in the affairs of individuals, opp. to *socialism* or *collectivism*: the theory that looks to the rights of individuals not to the advantage of an abstraction such as the state: the doctrine that individual things alone are real: the doctrine that nothing exists but the individual self; individ'ualist, one who thinks and acts with independence: one who advocates individualism.—Also *adj.* individualist'ic.—*n.* individuality (*-al'i-ti*), separate and distinct existence: oneness: distinctive character.—*adv.* individ'ually.—*v.t.* individ'uate, to individualise: to give individuality to.—*adj.* undivided: inseparable: individuated.—*n.* individuā'tion, the act or process of individuating or individualising: individual existence: essence: continued identity: the sum of the processes of individual life: synthesis into a single organic whole.—*n.* individ'uum, an indivisible entity: an individual person or thing: a member of a species. [L. *individuus*—*in-*, not, *dividuus*, divisible—*dividēre*, to divide.]

indivisible, *in-di-viz'i-bl*, *adj.* not divisible.—*n.* (*math.*) an indefinitely small quantity.—*ns.* indivisibil'ity, indivis'ibleness.—*adv.* indivis'ibly. [Pfx. in- (2).]

Indo-, *in'dō-*, in composition, Indian.

Indo-Chinese, *in'dō-chī-nēz'*, *adj.* of or pertaining to Indo-China, the south-eastern peninsula of Asia.

indocile, *in-dō'sil*, or *in-dos'il*, *adj.* not docile: not disposed to be instructed.—Also **indō′cible**.—*n.* **indocil′ity**. [Pfx. in- (2).]

**indoctrinate**, *in-dok′trin-āt*, *v.t.* to instruct in any doctrine: to imbue with any opinion.—*ns.* **indoctrinā′tion**; **indoc′trinātor**. [Pfx. in- (1).]

**Indo-European**, *in′dō-ū-rō-pē′ən*, (*philol.*) *adj.* **Indo-Germanic.**

**Indo-Germanic**, *in-dō-jûr-man′ik*, (*philol.*) *adj.* of the family of languages, also called Indo-European and sometimes Aryan, whose great branches are Aryan proper or Indian, Iranian, Armenian, Greek or Hellenic, Italic, Celtic, Tocharian, Balto-Slavonic, Albanian, and Germanic.

**indole**, *in′dōl*, *n.* a substance ($C_8H_7N$) related to indigo.—Also **indol**. [indigo and L. *oleum*, oil.]

**indolent**, *in′dəl-ənt*, *adj.* indisposed to activity: not painful (*med.*).—*ns.* **in′dolence**, **in′dolency**. —*adv.* **in′dolently**. [L. *in-*, not, *dolēns*, *-entis*, pr.p. of *dolēre*, to suffer pain.]

**in Domino**, *in dom′i-nō*, (L.L.) in the Lord.

**indomitable**, *in-dom′it-ə-bl*, *adj.* not to be overcome.—*adv.* **indom′itably**. [Pfx. in- (2).]

**Indonesian**, *in-dō-nē′zi-ən*, *-zh(y)ən*, *-sh(y)ən*, *adj.* of the East Indian or Malay Archipelago, specif. of the Republic of Indonesia, covering much of this territory: of a short, mesocephalic black-haired, light-brown race distinguishable in the population of the East Indian Islands: of a branch of the Austronesian family of languages chiefly found in the Malay Archipelago and Islands (Malay, etc.).—*n.* an Indonesian national, a member of the race or speaker of one of the languages. [Gr. *Indos*, Indian, *nēsos*, island.]

**indoor**, *in′dōr*, *-dör*, *adj.* practised, used, or being within a building.—*adv.* **indoors′**, inside a building.—**indoor relief** (*hist.*), support given to paupers in the workhouse or poorhouse, as opposed to *outdoor relief*, or help given them at their own homes. [Pfx. in- (1).]

**indorse.** See endorse (1).

**Indra**, *in′dra*, *n.* the Hindu god of the firmament and of rain. [Sans.]

**indraught, indraft**, *in′dräft*, *n.* a drawing in: an inward flow of current. [in, draught.]

**indrawn**, *in′drön*, *in-drön′*, *adj.* drawn in. [in, drawn.]

**indrench**, *in-drench′*, *-drensh′*, (*Shak.*) *v.t.* to submerge in water. [Pfx. in- (1).]

**Indri(s)**, *in′drē(s)*, *n.* a genus of short-tailed lemurs found in Madagascar: (without *cap.*) a member of a species of these, *Indris brevicaudatus.*

**indubious**, *in-dū′bi-əs*, (*arch.*) *adj.* not dubious: certain. [Pfx. in- (2).]

**indubitable**, *in-dū′bit-ə-bl*, *adj.* that cannot be doubted: certain.—*ns.* **indubitabil′ity**; **indū′bitableness**.—*adv.* **indū′bitably**. [Pfx. in- (2).]

**induce**, *in-dūs′*, *v.t.* to bring in (*obs.*): to draw on: to prevail on: to bring into being: to cause, as an electric state, by mere proximity (*phys.*): to infer inductively (*log.*).—*v.i.* to reason or draw inferences inductively.—*ns.* **induce′ment**, that which induces: persuasion (*Shak., Milt.*): incentive, motive: a statement of facts introducing other important facts (*law*); **induc′er**.—*adj.* **indu′cible**.—**induced current** (*elect.*), a current set in action by the influence of the surrounding magnetic field, or by the variation of an adjacent current. [L. *indūcĕre*, *inductum*—*in*, into, *dūcĕre*, to lead.]

**induct**, *in-dukt′*, *v.t.* to introduce: to put in possession, as of a benefice, to instal: to enlist into military service (*U.S.*).—*ns.* **induct′ance**, the property of inducing an electromotive force by variation of current in a circuit: a device having inductance.—*n.* **induc′tion**, bringing or drawing in: installation in office, benefice, etc.: a prelude: introductory section or scene: the act of inducing (*arch.*): magnetising by proximity with-

out contact: the production by one body of an opposite electric state in another by proximity: production of an electric current by magnetic changes in the neighbourhood: reasoning from particular cases to general conclusions (*log.*).—*adjs.* **induc′tional**; **induct′ive.**—*adv.* **induct′ively**.—*ns.* **inductiv′ity**; **induct′or.**—**induction coil**, an electrical machine consisting of two coils of wire, in which every variation of the current in one induces a current in the other; **induction motor**, electric motor in which currents in the primary winding set up an electromagnetic flux which induces currents in the secondary winding, interaction of these currents with the flux producing rotation; **induction port, valve**, a port, valve, by which steam, or an explosive mixture, is admitted to the cylinder of an engine.—**induction by simple enumeration**, logical induction by enumeration of all the cases singly. [See induce.]

**inductile**, *in-duk′til*, or *til*, *adj.* not ductile.—*n.* **inductility** (*-til′i-ti*). [Pfx. in- (2).]

**indue.** See endue.

**indulge**, *in-dulj′*, *v.t.* to yield to the wishes of: to favour or gratify: to treat with favour or undue favour: not to restrain: to grant an indulgence to or on: to grant some measure of religious liberty to (*hist.*).—*v.i.* to gratify one's appetites freely, or permit oneself any action or expression (with *in*): to partake, esp. of alcohol (*coll.*).—*n.* **indulg′ence**, gratification: excessive gratification: favourable or unduly favourable treatment: a grant of religious liberty: forbearance of present payment: in the R.C. Church, a remission, to a repentant sinner, of the temporal punishment which remains due after the sin and its eternal punishment have been remitted (*plenary* indulgences, which remit all, *partial*, which remit a portion of the temporal punishment due; *temporal*, those granted only for a time, *perpetual* or *indefinite*, those which last till revoked; *personal*, those granted to a particular person or confraternity; *local*, those gained only in a particular place): exemption of an individual from an ecclesiastical law.—Also **indulg′ency.**—*adj.* **indulg′ent**, ready to gratify the wishes of others: compliant: not severe.—*adv.* **indulg′ently.**—*ns.* **indulg′er**; **indult′**, a licence granted by the Pope, authorising something to be done which the common law of the Church does not sanction.—**Declaration of Indulgence**, a name given to proclamations of Charles II and (esp.) James II declaring laws restraining religious liberty suspended by the king's will. [L. *indulgēre*, to be kind to, indulge—*in*, in, and prob. *dulcis*, sweet.]

**induline**, *in′dū-lin*, *-lēn*, *-lin*, *n.* any one of a class of coal-tar dyestuffs, giving blues, etc. [indigo.]

**indult.** See under indulge.

**indumentum**, *in-dū-men′təm*, *n.* a general covering of hair, feathers, etc.: woolly pubescence. [L. *indūmentum*, garment—*induĕre*, to put on.]

**induna**, *in-dōō′nə*, *n.* a tribal councillor in South Africa. [Zulu, person of rank.]

**induplicate**, *in-dū′pli-kit*, (*bot.*) *adj.* folded inwards.—*n.* **induplicā′tion**. [Pfx. in- (1).]

**indurate**, *in′dū-rāt*, *v.t.* and *v.i.* to harden.—Also *adj.*—*n.* **indurā′tion**.—*adj.* **in′durative**. [L. *indūrāre*, *-ātum*—*in*, in, *dūrāre*, to harden.]

**indusium**, *in-dū′zi-əm*, *n.* a protective membrane or scale, esp. that covering a fern sorus: an insect larva-case:—*pl.* **indu′sia**.—*adjs.* **indu′sial**, containing fossil insect indusia; **indu′siate**, having indusia. [L. *indūsium*, an under-garment.]

**industry**, *in′das-tri*, *n.* quality of being diligent: assiduity: steady application: habitual diligence: systematic economic activity: any branch of trade or manufacture, *heavy industry* relating to such basic industries as coalmining, steel-making, shipbuilding, etc., involving heavy equipment, *light* industry to smaller factory-processed goods, e.g. knitwear, glass, electronics components, etc.—*adj.* **industrial** (-*dus'*), relating to or consisting in industry.—*n.* an industrial worker: (*pl.*) stocks and shares in industrial concerns.—*n.* **industrialisā'tion**, -z-.—*v.t.* **indus'trialise**, **-ize**, to give an industrial character, or character of industrialism, to.—*ns.* **indus'trialism**, devotion to labour or industrial pursuits: that system or condition of society in which industrial labour is the chief and most characteristic feature; **indus'trialist**, one who owns, or holds a powerful position in, industrial concern(s).—*adj.* of or characterised by industry.—*adv.* **indus'trially**.—*adj.* **indus'trious**, diligent or active in one's labour: laborious: diligent in a particular pursuit.—*adv.* **indus'triously**.—**industrial action**, a strike or go-slow; **industrial council** (see Whitley Council); **industrial estate**, a planned industrial area, with factories organised to provide varied employment; **industrial melanism**, melanism (e.g. in moths) developed as response to blackening of trees, etc., by industrial pollution; **industrial relations**, relations between management and workers or labour in general; **industrial revolution**, the economic and social changes arising out of the change from industries carried on in the home with simple machines to industries in factories with power-driven machinery—esp. such changes (from about 1760) in Britain, the first country to be industrialised; **industrial school** (*hist.* in U.K.), a school in which some industrial art is taught: a school where neglected or delinquent children are taught mechanical arts. [L. *industria*, perh. from the old word *indu*, in, within, and *struĕre*, to build up.]

**induviae**, *in-dū'vi-ē*, (*bot.*) *n.pl.* withered leaves persistent on the stems of some plants.—*adjs.* **indū'vial**; **indū'viate**. [L. *induviae*, clothes.]

**indwell**, *in-dwel'*, *v.i.* and *v.t.* to dwell or abide in:—*pr.p.* **indwell'ing**; *pa.t.* and *pa.p.* **indwelt'**.—*n.* **in'dweller**, an inhabitant.—*adj.* **in'dwelling**, dwelling within, abiding permanently in the mind or soul.—*n.* residence within, or in the heart or soul. [Pfx. **in-** (1).]

**inearth**, *in-ûrth'*, (*arch.*) *v.t.* to inter. [Pfx. **in-** (1).]

**inebriate**, *in-ē'bri-āt*, *v.t.* to make drunk, to intoxicate: to exhilarate greatly.—*adj.* (-*it*, -*ət*) drunk: intoxicated.—*n.* a drunk person: a drunkard.—*adj.* **inē'briant**, intoxicating.—Also *n.*:—*ns.* **inēbriā'tion**, **inebriety** (*in-ē-brī'i-ti*, or *in-i-*), drunkenness: intoxication.—*adj.* **inē'brious**, drunk: causing intoxication (*obs.*). [L. *inēbriāre*, *-ātum*—*in-*, inten., *ēbriāre*, to make drunk—*ēbrius*, drunk.]

**inedible**, *in-ed'i-bl*, *adj.* unfit to be eaten.—*n.* **inedibil'ity**. [Pfx. **in-** (2).]

**inedited**, *in-ed'it-id*, *adj.* not edited: unpublished. [Pfx. **in-** (2).]

**ineducable**, *in-ed'ū-kə-bl*, *adj.* incapable of education.—*n.* **ineducabil'ity**. [Pfx. **in-** (2).]

**ineffable**, *in-ef'ə-bl*, *adj.* that cannot be described, inexpressible.—*n.* **ineff'ableness**.—*adv.* **ineff'ably**. [L. *ineffābilis*—*in-*, not, *effābilis*, effable.]

**ineffaceable**, *in-i-fās'ə-bl*, *adj.* that cannot be rubbed out.—*adv.* **inefface'ably**. [Pfx. **in-** (2).]

**ineffective**, *in-i-fek'tiv*, *adj.* not effective: useless.—*adv.* **ineffec'tively**.—*adj.* **ineffec'tual**, fruitless: ineffective, weak.—*ns.* **ineffectual'ity**, **ineffec'tualness**.—*adv.* **ineffect'ually**.—*n.* **inefficacious** (*in-ef-i-kā'shəs*), not having power to produce an effect, or the desired effect.—*adv.* **inefficā'ciously**.—*n.* **ineff'icacy** (-*ef'i-kə-si*), want of efficacy.—*n.* **inefficiency** (*in-i-fish'ən-si*).—*adj.* **ineffic'ient**, not efficient.—*adv.* **ineffic'iently**. [Pfx. **in-** (2).]

**inelaborate**, *in-il-ab'ər-it*, *-āt*, *adj.* unlaboured: simple.—*adv.* **inelab'orately**. [Pfx. **in-** (2).]

**inelastic**, *in-i-las'tik*, *adj.* not elastic: incom-

pressible.—*n.* **inelasticity** (*in-el-əs-tis'i-ti*). [Pfx. **in-** (2).]

**inelegance**, *in-el'i-gəns*, *n.* want of gracefulness or refinement.—Also **inel'egancy**.—*adj.* **inel'egant**.—*adv.* **inel'egantly**. [Pfx. **in-** (2).]

**ineligible**, *in-el'i-ji-bl*, *adj.* not qualified for election: not suitable for choice: not rich enough or of the right social background to be chosen as a husband: unsuitable.—Also *n.*—*n.* **ineligibil'ity**.—*adv.* **inel'igibly**. [Pfx. **in-** (2).]

**ineloquent**, *in-el'ə-kwənt*, *adj.* not eloquent.—*n.* **inel'oquence**. [Pfx. **in-** (2).]

**ineluctable**, *in-i-luk'tə-bl*, *adj.* not to be escaped from. [L. *inēluctābilis*—*in-*, not, *ē*, from, *luctārī*, to struggle.]

**inenarrable**, *in-en'ər-ə-bl*, *in-ē-nar'ə-bl*, *adj.* incapable of being narrated or told. [L. *inēnarrābilis*—*in-*, not, *ē-*, out, *narrāre*, to tell.]

**inept**, *in-ept'*, *adj.* unfit: irrelevant and futile: fatuous: void (*law*).—*ns.* **inept'itude**, **inept'ness**.—*adv.* **inept'ly** [L. *ineptus*—*in-*, not, *aptus*, apt.]

**inequable**, *in-ek'wə-bl*, *-ēk'*, *adj.* not equable, changeable. [Pfx. **in-** (2).]

**inequality**, *in-ē-kwol'i-ti*, or *in-i-*, *n.* want of equality: difference: inadequacy: incompetency: unevenness: dissimilarity: an uneven place. [Pfx. **in-** (2).]

**inequation**, *in-ə-kwā'-shən*, *n.* a mathematical sentence which expresses an inequality. [Pfx. **in-** (2).]

**inequitable**, *in-ek'wi-tə-bl*, *adj.* unfair, unjust.—*adv.* **ineq'uitably**.—*n.* **ineq'uity**, lack of equity: an unjust action. [Pfx. **in-** (2).]

**ineradicable**, *in-i-rad'i-kə-bl*, *adj.* not able to be eradicated or rooted out.—*adv.* **inerad'icably**. [Pfx. **in-** (2).]

**inerasable**, *in-i-rāz'ə-bl*, *adj.* impossible to erase.—Also **ineras'ible**.—*advs.* **ineras'ably**, **-ibly**. [Pfx. **in-** (2).]

**inerm**, *in-ûrm'*, *adj.* unarmed: without thorns. [L. *inermis*—*in-*, not, *arma* (pl.), arms.]

**inerrable**, *in-er'ə-bl*, or *-ûr'*, *adj.* incapable of erring.—*adv.* **inerr'ably**.—*n.* **inerr'ancy**, freedom from error.—*adj.* **inerr'ant**, unerring. [Pfx. **in-** (2).]

**inert**, *in-ûrt'*, *adj.* without inherent power of moving, or of active resistance to motion: passive: chemically inactive: sluggish: disinclined to move or act.—*n.* **inertia** (*in-ûr'shi-ə*, *-shyə*, *-shə*), inertness: the inherent property of matter by which it continues, unless constrained, in its state of rest or uniform motion in a straight line.—*adj.* **iner'tial**, of, or pertaining to, inertia.—*adv.* **inert'ly**.—*n.* **inert'ness**.—**inert gas**, one of several elements whose outer electron orbits are complete, rendering them inert to all the usual chemical reactions; **inertial control guidance**, **navigation**, automatic gyroscopic guidance system for aircraft, missiles, etc., using data computed from acceleration and the physical properties of the earth, but dispensing with the magnetic compass and independent of ground-based radio aids; **inertia selling**, sending unrequested goods to householders and attempting to charge for them if they are not returned. [L. *iners*, *inertis*, unskilled, idle—*in-*, not, *ars*, *artis*, art.]

**inerudite**, *in-er'ū-dīt*, or *ōō-*, *adj.* not erudite: unlearned. [Pfx. **in-** (2).]

**inescapable**, *in-is-kā'pə-bl*, *adj.* unescapable: inevitable. [Pfx. **in-** (2).]

**inesculent**, *in-es'kū-lənt*, *adj.* inedible. [Pfx. **in-** (2).]

**inescutcheon**, *in-is-kuch'ən*, (*her.*) *n.* a single shield borne as a charge. [in, escutcheon.]

**in esse**. See esse.

**inessential**, *in-is-en'shl*, *adj.* not essential: not necessary: immaterial. [Pfx. **in-** (2).]

**inessive**, *in-es'iv*, (*gram.*) *adj.* denoting, as in

Neutral vowels in unaccented syllables: *el'ə-mənt*; for certain sounds in foreign words, see p. viii

Finnish, place in which.—*n.* the inessive case. [*L. inesse*, to be in, on, or at.]

**inestimable**, *in-es'tim-ǝ-bl*, *adj.* not able to be estimated or valued: priceless.—*adv.* **ines'timably.** [Pfx. **in-** (2).]

**inevitable**, *in-ev'it-ǝ-bl*, *adj.* not to be evaded or avoided: certain to happen: exactly right, giving the feeling that the thing could not have been other than it is.—*ns.* **inevitabil'ity**; **inev'itableness.**—*adv.* **inev'itably.** [*L. inēvītābilis—in-*, not, *ē*, from, *vitāre*, to avoid.]

**inexact**, *in-igz-akt'*, *adj.* not precisely correct or true: lax.—*ns.* **inexact'itude**, lack of exactitude: an example of inexactitude; **inexact'ness.**—*adv.* **inexact'ly.** [Pfx. **in-** (2).]

**in excelsis**, *in ek-sel'sis*, *ik-*, *eks-*, *iks-chel'sis*, or *-kel'sis*, *-sēs*, (L.L.) on the heights: on high: in the highest degree.

**inexcitable**, *in-ek-sīt'ǝ-bl*, *adj.* not excitable: from which one cannot be roused (*obs.*). [Pfx. **in-** (2).]

**inexcusable**, *in-iks-kūz'ǝ-bl*, *adj.* not justifiable: unpardonable.—*ns.* **inexcusabil'ity, inexcus'ableness.**—*adv.* **inexcus'ably.** [Pfx. **in-** (2).]

**inexecrable**, *in-eks'i-krǝ-bl*, *adj.* in Shak., *Merchant of Venice* IV, i. 128, read by some as a misprint for *inexorable*, by some as an intensive form of *execrable*.

**inexecutable**, *in-igz-ek'ūt-ǝ-bl*, or *in-eks-ek'*, or *in-eks-i-kūt'ǝ-bl*, *adj.* incapable of being executed.—*n.* **inexecū'tion**, fact or state of not being executed. [Pfx. **in-** (2).]

**inexhausted**, *in-igs-ös'tid*, *adj.* (*arch.*) unexhausted, not used up or spent.—*n.* **inexhaustibil'ity.**—*adj.* **inexhaust'ible**, not able to be exhausted or spent: unfailing.—*adv.* **inexhaust'ibly.**—*adj.* **inexhaust'ive**, unfailing (*arch.*): not exhaustive. [Pfx. **in-** (2).]

**inexistence**, *in-ig-zist'ǝns*, *n.* non-existence.—*adj.* **inexist'ent.** [Pfx. **in-** (2).]

**inexistence**, *in-ig-zist'ǝns*, (*arch.*) *n.* inherence.—*adj.* **inexist'ent**, indwelling. [Pfx. **in-** (1).]

**inexorable**, *in-eks'ǝr-ǝ-bl*, *adj.* not to be moved by entreaty: unrelenting: unyielding.—*ns.* **inex'orableness**, **inexorabil'ity.**—*adv.* **inex'orably.** [L.L. *inexōrābilis—in-*, not, *exōrāre—ex*, out of, *ōrāre*, to entreat.]

**inexpansible**, *in-iks-pan'si-bl*, *adj.* incapable of being expanded. [Pfx. **in-** (2).]

**inexpectant**, *in-iks-pek'tǝnt*, *adj.* not expecting.—*n.* **inexpec'tancy.** [Pfx. **in-** (2).]

**inexpedient**, *in-iks-pē'di-ǝnt*, *adj.* contrary to expediency: impolitic.—*ns.* **inexpe'dience, inexpe'diency.**—*adv.* **inexpe'diently.** [Pfx. **in-** (2).]

**inexpensive**, *in-iks-pens'iv*, *adj.* not costly: not inclined to spend much.—*adv.* **inexpens'ively.**—*n.* **inexpens'iveness.** [Pfx. **in-** (2).]

**inexperience**, *in-iks-pē'ri-ǝns*, *n.* want of experience.—*adj.* **inexpe'rienced**, not having experience: unskilled or unpractised. [Pfx. **in-** (2).]

**inexpert**, *in-eks'pûrt*, or *in-eks-pûrt'*, *adj.* unskilled.—*n.* **inexpert'ness.** [Pfx. **in-** (2).]

**inexpiable**, *in-eks'pi-ǝ-bl*, *adj.* not able to be expiated or atoned for: not to be appeased.—*n.* **inex'piableness.**—*adv.* **inex'piably.** [Pfx. **in-** (2).]

**inexplicable**, *in-eks'pli-kǝ-bl*, *plik'*, *adj.* that cannot be disentangled (*obs.*): incapable of being explained or accounted for.—*ns.* **inexplicabil'ity, inex'plicableness.**—*adv.* **inex'plicably.** [Pfx. **in-** (2).]

**inexplicit**, *in-iks-plis'it*, *adj.* not explicit: not clear. [Pfx. **in-** (2).]

**inexpressible**, *in-iks-pres'i-bl*, *adj.* that cannot be expressed: unutterable: indescribable.—*n.* (in *pl.*) trousers (*arch. facet.*).—*adv.* **inexpress'ibly.**—*adj.* **inexpress'ive**, inexpressible (*arch.*): unexpressive.—*n.* **inexpress'iveness.** [Pfx. **in-** (2).]

**inexpugnable**, *in-iks-pug'nǝ-bl*, *adj.* not to be taken by assault: unassailable.—*adv.* **inexpug'nably.** [Pfx. **in-** (2).]

**inextended**, *in-iks-tend'id*, *adj.* not extended:

without extension.—*n.* **inextensibil'ity.**—*adj.* **inexten'sible**, that cannot be extended or stretched. —*n.* **inexten'sion.** [Pfx. **in-** (2).]

**in extenso**, *in ik-sten'sō*, or *ek-sten'*, (L.L.) at full length.

**inextinguishable**, *in-iks-ting'gwish-ǝ-bl*, *adj.* that cannot be extinguished, quenched, or destroyed. —*adv.* **inextin'guishably.** [Pfx. **in-** (2).]

**in extremis**, *in ik-strē'mis*, or *ek-strā'mēs*, (L.L.) at the point of death: at the last gasp: in desperate circumstances.

**inextricable**, *in-eks'tri-kǝ-bl*, *-trik'*, *adj.* such as one cannot extricate oneself from (*Scott*): not able to be extricated or disentangled.—*adv.* **inex'tricably.** [L. *inextricābilis*.]

**infall**, *in'föl*, *n.* an inroad: falling in: confluence, inlet, or junction. [in, fall.]

**infallible**, *in-fal'i-bl*, *adj.* incapable of error: certain to succeed: inevitable.—*ns.* **infall'ibilism**, the doctrine of the Pope's infallibility; **infall'ibilist**; **infallibil'ity.**—*adv.* **infall'ibly.**—the doctrine of **infallibility** in the R.C. Church (defined in 1870) is that the Pope, when speaking *ex cathedra*, is kept from error in all that regards faith and morals. [Pfx. **in-** (2).]

**infame**, *in-fām'*, *v.t.* to defame.—*adj.* **infamous** (*in'fǝ-mǝs*, formerly *in-fā'mǝs*), having a reputation of the worst kind: publicly branded with guilt: notoriously vile: disgraceful.—*vs.t.* **infamise**, **-ize** (*in'fǝ-mīz*), **infamonise**, **-ize** (*infam'ǝn-iz*; *Shak.*), to defame, to brand with infamy.—*adv.* **in'famously.**—*n.* **in'famy**, ill repute: public disgrace: an infamous act: extreme vileness: a stigma attaching to the character of a person so as to disqualify him from being a witness (*law*). [L. *infāmāre—in-*, not, *fāma*, fame.]

**infangthief**, *in'fang-thēf*, *n.* in old English law, the right of taking and fining a thief within the boundary of one's own jurisdiction. [O.E. *infangenethēof—in*, in, the root of *fōn*, to seize, *thēof*, thief.]

**infant**, *in'fǝnt*, *n.* a babe: a person under the age of legal maturity (*Eng. law*): a noble youth (*Spens.*): an infante or infanta.—*adj.* of or belonging to infants: of or in infancy.—*v.t.* (*obs.*) to give birth to.—*n.* **in'fancy**, the state or time of being an infant: childhood: the beginning of anything: want of distinct utterance (*Milt.*).—*adj.* **infantile** (*in'fǝn-tīl*, in U.S. *-til*, also *-fant'*), pertaining to infancy or to an infant: having characteristics of infancy: no better than that of an infant: undeveloped.—*n.* **infant'-ilism**, persistence of infantile characters: an utterance or trait worthy of an infant.—*adj.* **in'fantine** (*-īn*), of infancy or an infant: infant-like.—**infantile paralysis**, poliomyelitis; **infant school**, a school for children up to about the age of seven. [L. *infāns*, *infantis—in-*, not, *fāns*, pr.p. of *fāri*, to speak; cf. Gr. *phanai*.]

**infante**, *in-fan'tā*, (*hist.*) *n.* a prince of the blood royal of Spain or Portugal, esp. a son of the king other than the heir-apparent:—*fem.* **infant'a**, a princess likewise defined: the wife of an infante. [Sp. and Port. from the root of **infant**.]

**infanticide**, *in-fan'ti-sid*, *n.* the killing of newborn children as a social institution in some states of society: the murder of an infant by, or with consent of, a parent: the murderer of an infant.—*adj.* **infantici'dal** (or *-fant'*). [L. *infanticidium*, child-killing, *infanticīda*, child-killer—*infāns*, an infant, *caedĕre*, to kill.]

**infantry**, *in'fǝnt-ri*, *n.* foot-soldiers: a part of an army composed of such soldiers: infants or children collectively (*arch.*).—Also *adj.*—*n.* **in'fantryman.** [Fr. *infanterie*—It. *infanteria—infante*, youth, servant, foot-soldier—L. *infāns*, *-antis*.]

**infarct**, *in-färkt'*, *n.* a portion of tissue that is dying because blood supply to it has been cut off.—*n.* **infarc'tion**. [Mediaeval L. *infarctus—in*, in, *far*(*c*)*tus—farcīre*, to cram, stuff.]

**infare**, *in'fār*, *n.* entrance (*obs.*): ingoing (*obs.*): a house-warming after a wedding (*Scot.* and *U.S.*). [O.E. *innfær*; cf. **in**, **fare**.]

**infatuate**, *in-fat'ū-āt*, *v.t.* to turn to folly: to deprive of judgment: to inspire with foolish passion.—*adj.* infatuated:—*pa.p.*, *adj.* **infat'uated**, deprived of judgment: doting: besotted. —*n.* **infatuā'tion**. [L. *infatuāre*, *-ātum—in*, in, *fatuus*, foolish.]

**infaust**, *in-föst'*, *adj.* unlucky: ill-omened. [L. *infaustus—in-*, not, *faustus*, propitious.]

**infeasible**, *in-fēz'i-bl*, *adj.* not feasible.—*n.* **infeasibil'ity**. [Pfx. **in-** (2).]

**infect**, *in-fekt'*, *v.t.* to impart some quality to: to taint, especially with disease: to introduce pathogenic micro-organisms into: to corrupt: to spread to: to affect successively.—*adj.* (*Shak.*) tainted.—*n.* **infec'tion** (*-shən*), act of infecting: that which infects or taints: an infectious disease.—*adjs.* **infec'tious** (*-shəs*), **infec'tive** (*-tiv*), having the quality of infecting: corrupting: apt to spread.—*adv.* **infec'tiously.**—*ns.* **infec'tiousness**; **infect'iveness**; **infect'or.—infectious mononucleosis**, glandular fever. [L. *infícēre*, *infectum—in*, into, *facēre*, to make.]

**infecundity**, *in-fi-kun'di-ti*, *n.* want of fecundity or fertility: unfruitfulness.—*adj.* **infecund** (*-fek'*, *fēk'*). [Pfx. **in-** (2).]

**infeft**, *in-feft'*, (*Scots law*) *v.t.* to invest with heritable property:—*pa.p.* **infeft'**, rarely **infeft'ed.** —*n.* **infeft'ment** (*Scots law*), the symbolical giving possession of land in completion of the title. [enfeoff.]

**infelicitous**, *in-fi-lis'i-təs*, *adj.* not felicitous or happy: inappropriate, inapt.—*n.* **infelic'ity**. [Pfx. **in-** (2).]

**infelt**, *in'felt*, *adj.* felt deeply, heart-felt. [Pfx. **in-** (1).]

**infer**, *in-fûr'*, *v.t.* to bring on (*Spens.*, *Shak.*): to render (*Milt.*): to derive as a consequence: to arrive at as a logical conclusion: to conclude: to entail or involve as a consequence: to imply:—*pr.p.* **inferr'ing**; *pa.t* and *pa.p.* **inferred'.**—*adj.* **in'ferable** (or *-fûr'*; also **inferr'able**, **-ible**), that may be inferred or deduced.— *n.* **in'ference**, that which is inferred or deduced: the act of drawing a conclusion from premises: consequence: conclusion.—*adj.* **inferential** (*-en'-shl*), relating to inference: deducible or deduced by inference.—*adv.* **inferen'tially**. [L. *inferre—in*, into, *ferre*, to bring.]

**infere**, *in-fēr'*, *adv.* (*obs.*) for **in fere**, together. [See **fere** (1).]

**inferiae**, *in-fē'ri-ē*, *ēn-fe'ri-ī*, (L.) offerings to the manes of the dead.

**inferior**, *in-fē'ri-ər*, *adj.* lower in any respect: subordinate: poor or poorer in quality: somewhat below the line (*print.*): of an ovary, having the other parts above it (*bot.*): of the other parts, below the ovary (*bot.*): of a planet, revolving within the earth's orbit.—*n.* one lower in rank or station.—*n.* **inferiority** (*-or'*).—*adv.* **infe'riorly**, in an inferior manner.—**inferior conjunction**, conjunction when the planet is between the sun and the earth; **inferiority complex** (*psych.*), a complex involving a suppressed sense of personal inferiority: popularly, a feeling of inferiority. [L. *inferior*, comp. of *inferus*, low.]

**infernal**, *in-fûr'nəl*, *adj.* belonging to the lower regions: resembling or suitable to hell: outrageous, very unpleasant (*coll.*).—*n.* **infernality** (*-nal'*).—*adv.* **infer'nally.**—*n.* **Infer'no** (*It.*), hell (also without *cap.*): title and subject of one of the divisions of Dante's great poem, *La Divina Commedia*: (without *cap.*) a conflagration.— **infernal machine**, a contrivance made to resemble some ordinary harmless object, but

charged with a dangerous explosive. [L. *infernus—inferus*.]

**infertile**, *in-fûr'til*, in U.S. *-til*, *adj.* not productive: barren.—*n.* **infertility** (*-til'*). [Pfx. **in-** (2).]

**infest**, *in-fest'*, *v.t.* to disturb: to harass: to molest: to haunt, beset, or swarm about, in a troublesome or injurious way.—*adj.* (*obs.*) hostile: troublesome.—*n.* **infestā'tion**, molestation (*Milt.*): attack, or condition of being attacked, esp. by parasites. [L. *infestāre*, from *infestus*, hostile.]

**infeudation**, *in-fū-dā'shən*, *n.* the putting of an estate in fee: the granting of tithes to laymen. [Pfx. **in-** (1), and **feud** (2).]

**infibulate**, *in-fib'ū-lāt*, *v.t.* to fasten with a clasp. —*n.* **infibulā'tion**, act of confining, esp. the sexual organs. [Pfx. **in-** (1), and *fibula*, a clasp.]

**inficete**, *in-fi-sēt'*, (*rare*) *adj.* not facetious: rudely jesting. [L. *inficētus—in-*, not, *facētus*, courteous, witty.]

**infidel**, *in'fi-dl*, *adj.* unbelieving: sceptical: disbelieving Christianity or whatever be the religion of the user of the word.—*n.* one who rejects Christianity, etc.: loosely, one who disbelieves in any theory, etc.—*n.* **infidel'ity**, want of faith or belief: disbelief in Christianity, etc.: unfaithfulness, esp. to the marriage contract: treachery. [O.Fr. *infidèle*—L. *infidēlis—in-*, not, *fidēlis*, faithful—*fidēs*, faith.]

**infield**, *in'fēld*, *n.* in baseball, the space enclosed within the base-lines: formerly, land near the farmhouse, kept constantly manured and under tillage (also *adj.*)—opp. to **outfield** (*Scot.*).—*n.* **in'fielder**, a player on the infield. [**in**, **field.**]

**infighting**, *in'fīt-ing*, *n.* boxing at close quarters when blows from the shoulder cannot be given. —For **in-fighting**, see **in** (1). [**in** (1), **fighting**.]

**infilling**, *in'fil-ing*, *n.* filling up or in: material used to fill up or level: adding to property by building inside or alongside a house while staying within one's boundaries. [**in**, **fill**.]

**infiltrate**, *in'fil-trāt*, *-fil'*, *v.t.* to cause to percolate: to cause to percolate into: to sift into: to permeate.—*v.i.* to permeate by degrees: to sift or filter in.—*v.t.*, *v.i.* of troops, agents, to enter (hostile area) secretly and for subversive purposes.—*v.t.* **infil'ter**, to filter or sift in.— *ns.* **infiltrā'tion**, the process of infiltrating: gradual permeation or interpenetration: gradual accession or introduction of a new element, as of population or troops: a deposit or substance infiltrated; **in'filtrator**, one who gets himself accepted as a member of a group towards which he has hostile or subversive intentions. [Pfx. **in-** (1).]

**infima species**, *in'fi-mə spē'shēz*, *ēn'fi-ma spe'ki-ās*, (L.L.) the lowest species included in a genus or class.

**infinite**, *in'fin-it*, in church singing also *in'fi-nit*, *adj.* without end or limit: greater than any quantity that can be assigned (*math.*): extending to infinity: vast: in vast numbers: inexhaustible: infinitated (*log.*): (of part of verb) not limited by person or number.—*n.* that which is not only without determinate bounds, but which cannot possibly admit of bound or limit: the Absolute, the Infinite Being or God.—*adjs.* **infin'itant**, denoting merely negative attribution; **infin'itary**, pertaining to infinity.—*v.t.* **infin'itate**, to make infinite: to turn into a negative term (*log.*).—*adv.* **in'finitely.**—*n.* **in'finiteness.**—*adj.* (orig. ordinal numeral) **infinitesimal** (*-es'*), infinitely small: loosely, extremely small.—*n.* an infinitely small quantity.—*adv.* **infinites'imally**. —*ns.* **infin'itude**, **infin'ity**, boundlessness: an infinite quantity: an infinite distance: vastness, immensity: countless or indefinite number.— **infinite canon** (*mus.*), a canon that can be repeated indefinitely; **infinite set** (*math.*), one that can be put into a one-one correspondence with

part of itself; **infinitesimal calculus,** differential and integral calculus. [Pfx. **in-** (2).]
**infinitive,** *in-fin'it-iv,* (*gram.*) *adj.* expressing, in the mood that expresses, the idea without person or number.—*n.* the infinitive mood: a verb in the infinitive mood.—*adj.* **infiniti'val.**—*adv.* **infin'itively.** [L. *infinitivus—in-,* not, *finire,* to limit.]
**infirm,** *in-fûrm',* adj. feeble: sickly: weak: frail: unstable.—*ns.* **infirmā'rian,** an officer in a monastery having charge of the quarters for the sick; **infirmary** (*in-fûrm'ər-i*), a hospital or place for the treatment of the sick; **infirm'ity.** —*adv.* **infirm'ly.**—*n.* **infirm'ness.** [L. *infirmus—in-,* not, *firmus,* strong.]
**infix,** *in-fiks',* *v.t.* to fix in: to drive or fasten in: to set in by piercing: to insert an element within (a root) (*philol.*).—Also **enfix** (*Shak.*).—*n.* **in'fix** (*philol.*), an element inserted within a root, as *m* in the Gr. *lambanō,* from the root *lab.* [L. *infixus—in,* in, *fīgĕre, fixum,* to fix.]
**in flagrante delicto,** *in flə-gran'ti di-lik'tō, flä-gran'te dä-lik'tō,* (L.) in the very act of committing the crime.
**inflame,** *in-flām',* *v.t.* to cause to flame: to cause to burn: to make hot: to make red: to cause inflammation in: to arouse passions in: to excite: exacerbate.—*v.i.* to burst into flame: to become hot, painful, red or excited: to undergo inflammation.—*adjs.* **inflām'able** (*obs.*), inflammable; **inflamed'.**—*n.* **inflām'er.** [O.Fr. *enflammer*—L. *inflammāre;* see next.]
**inflammable,** *in-flam'ə-bl,* adj. that may be set on fire (see **flammable**): easily kindled or excited.—*n.* an inflammable substance.—*ns.* **flammabil'ity; inflamm'ableness.**—*adv.* **inflamm'ably.**—*n.* **inflammation** (*-flə-mā'shən*), state of being in flame: heat of a part of the body, with pain, redness, and swelling: kindling of the passions.—*adj.* **inflamm'atory,** tending to inflame: inflaming: exciting, tending to stir up trouble. [L. *inflammāre—in,* into, *flamma,* a flame.]
**inflate,** *in-flāt',* *v.t.* to swell with air or gas: to puff up: to elate: to expand unduly.—*v.i.* to become full of air or gas: to distend.—*adj., n.* **inflat'able,** (any object) that can be inflated.— *adj.* **inflat'ed,** swollen or blown out: turgid: pompous: hollow, filled with air (*bot.*).—*adv., n.* **inflat'ingly.**—*n.* **inflation** (*in-flā'shən*), the act of inflating: the condition of being inflated: afflatus, inspiration (*rare*): turgidity of style: undue increase in quantity of money in proportion to buying power, as on an excessive issue of fiduciary money.—*adj.* **infla'tionary.**—*ns.* **infla'tionism,** the policy of inflating currency; **infla'tionist.** —*adj.* **inflat'ive,** causing inflation: tending to inflate.—*ns.* **inflat'or,** one who inflates: a cycle pump; **inflat'us** (L.), inspiration. [L. *inflāre, -ātum—in,* into, *flāre,* to blow.]
**inflect,** *in-flekt',* *v.t.* to bend in: to turn from a direct line or course: to modulate, as the voice: to vary in the terminations (*gram.*).—*n.* **inflec'tion,** **inflex'ion,** a bending or deviation: modulation of the voice: the varying in termination to express the relations of case, number, gender, person, tense, etc. (*gram.*).—*adjs.* **inflec'tional; inflex'ional; inflec'tionless, inflex'ionless; inflect'ive,** subject to inflection; **inflect'ed,** bent: turned.—*n.* **inflexure** (*in-flek'shər*), an inward bend or fold. [L. *inflectĕre—in,* *flectĕre, flexum,* to bend, *flexiō, -ōnis,* a bend.]
**inflexible,** *in-flek'si-bl,* adj. that cannot be bent: unyielding: rigid: unbending.—*ns.* **inflexibil'ity, inflex'ibleness.**—*adv.* **inflex'ibly.** [Pfx. **in-** (2).]
**inflict,** *in-flikt',* *v.t.* to lay on: to impose (as punishment, pain).—*n.* **inflic'tion,** act of inflicting or imposing: that which is inflicted.—*adj.* **inflict'ive,** tending or able to inflict. [L. *infligĕre, inflictum—in,* against, *fligĕre,* to strike.]

**inflorescence,** *in-flor-es'əns, -flər-, n.* mode of branching of a flower-bearing axis: aggregate of flowers on an axis. [L. *inflōrēscĕre,* to begin to blossom.]
**inflow,** *in'flō, n.* the act of flowing in, influx: that which flows in.—*adj.* **in'flowing,** flowing in. [Pfx. **in-** (1).]
**influence,** *in'floo-əns, n.* inflow (*obs.*): the power or virtue supposed to flow from planets upon men and things (*astrol.*): a spiritual influx: power of producing an effect, esp. unobtrusively: effect of power exerted: that which has such power: a person exercising such power: ascendency, often of a secret or undue kind: exertions of friends at court, wire-pulling, and the like.—*v.t.* to have or exert influence upon: to affect.—*adj.* **in'fluent,** inflowing: exerting influence.—*n.* a tributary stream.—*adj.* **influential** (*-en'shl*), of the nature of influence: having much influence: effectively active (in bringing something about).—*adv.* **influen'tially.** [O.Fr.,—L.L. *influentia*—L. *in,* into, *fluĕre,* to flow.]
**influenza,** *in-floo-en'zə, n.* an epidemic virus disease attacking esp. the upper respiratory tract.—*adj.* **influen'zal.** [It., influence, influenza (as a supposed astral visitation)—L.L. *influentia;* see **influence.**]
**influx,** *in'fluks, n.* a flowing in: accession: that which flows in.—*n.* **influxion** (*in-fluk'shən*). [L. *influxus—influĕre.*]
**info,** *in'fō,* coll. abbrev. of **information.**
**in-foal,** *in-fōl', adj.* pregnant (with foal). [in, foal.]
**infold.** See **enfold.**
**infold,** *in'fold', n.* fold inwards. [Pfx. **in-** (1).]
**inforce.** Same as **enforce.**
**inform,** *in-förm', v.t.* to give form to (*obs.*): animate or give life to: to impart a quality to: to impart knowledge to: to tell: to direct (*Milt.*).— *v.i.* to take shape or form (*Shak.*): to give information, make an accusation (with *against* or *on*).—*ns.* **inform'ant,** one who informs or gives intelligence; **information** (*in-fər-mā'shən*), intelligence given: knowledge: an accusation given to a magistrate or court.—*adjs.* **inform'a-tive,** having power to form: instructive; **inform'atory,** instructive: giving information.—*n.* **inform'er,** one who gives information: one who informs against another: an animator.—*n.* **information theory,** mathematical analysis of efficiency with which communication channels are employed. [O.Fr. *enformer*—L. *infōrmāre—in,* into, *fōrmāre,* to form, *fōrma,* form.]
**inform,** *in-förm', adj.* without form: unformed: ill-formed.—*adj.* **inform'al,** not in proper form: irregular: unceremonious.—*n.* **informal'ity.**—*adv.* **inform'ally.**—*adj.* **informed',** unformed (*Spens.*): of stars not included within the figures of any of the ancient constellations (*astron.*). [L. *in-,* not, *fōrma,* form; *infōrmis,* formless, misshapen.]
**in forma pauperis,** *in för'mə pö'pər-is, för'mä powp'er-is,* (L.) as a poor man.
**informidable,** *in-för'mi-də-bl, (Milt.) adj.* not formidable. [Pfx. **in-** (2).]
**in foro conscientiae,** *in fö'rō kon-shi-en'shi-ē, kōn-ski-en'ti-ī,* (L.) in the court of conscience: judged by one's own conscience.
**infortune,** *in-för'tūn, n.* misfortune. [Pfx. **in-** (2).]
**infra,** *in'frə, ēn'frä,* (L.) below: lower down on the page, or further on in the book.—**infra dignitatem** (*dig-ni-tä'təm, -tä'tem*), below one's dignity (colloquially sometimes **infra dig.**).
**infracostal,** *in-frə-kos'tl, adj.* beneath the ribs. [L. *infrā,* below, *costa,* a rib.]
**infraction,** *in-frak'shən, n.* violation, esp. of law: breach.—*v.t.* **infract',** to infringe.—*adjs.* **infract'** (*obs.*), **infract'ed,** broken: interrupted: bent in. —*n.* **infrac'tor,** one who infracts. [L. *infringĕre, infrāctum—in,* *frangĕre, frāctum,* to break.]

# infragrant 673 ingredient

**infragrant**, *in-frā'grənt*, *adj.* not fragrant. [Pfx. in- (2).]

**infrahuman**, *in-frə-hū'mən*, *adj.* lower than human. [L. *infrā*, below.]

**Infralapsarian**, *in-frə-lap-sā'ri-ən*, *n.* a believer in Infralapsarianism.—Also *adj.*—*n.* **Infralapsār'- ianism**, the common Augustinian and Calvinist doctrine, that God for his own glory determined to create the world, to permit the fall of man, to elect some and leave the rest to punishment— distinct both from *Supralapsarianism* and *Sublapsarianism*: also used as equivalent to Sublapsarianism. [L. *infrā*, below, after *lāpsus*, a fall.]

**inframaxillary**, *in-frə-mak'si-lə-ri*, *adj.* situated under the jaw: belonging to the lower jaw. [L. *infrā*, below, *maxilla*, jaw.]

**infrangible**, *in-fran'ji-bl*, *adj.* that cannot be broken: not to be violated.—*ns.* **infrangibil'ity**, **infran'gibleness**. [L. *in-*, not, *frangĕre*, to break.]

**infraorbital**, *in-frə-ör'bi-təl*, *adj.* situated below the orbit of the eye. [L. *infrā*, below.]

**infra-red**, *in'frə-red'*, *adj.* beyond the red end of the visible spectrum: using infra-red radiation: sensitive to this radiation. [L. *infrā*, below.]

**infrasonic**, *in-frə-son'ik*, *(acoustics) adj.* of frequencies, below the usual audible limit.—*n.* **in'frasound**. [L. *infrā*, below.]

**infrastructure**, *in'frə-struk'chər*, *n.* inner structure, structure of component parts: a system of communications and services as backing for military or other operations. [L. *infrā*, below.]

**infrequent**, *in-frē'kwənt*, *adj.* seldom occurring: rare: uncommon.—*ns.* **infrē'quence**, **infrē'- quency**.—*adv.* **infrē'quently**. [Pfx. in- (2).]

**infringe**, *in-frinj'*, *v.t.* to violate, esp. law: to neglect to obey.—*n.* **infringe'ment**. [L. *infringĕre—in*, in, *frangĕre*, to break.]

**infructuous**, *in-fruk'tū-əs*, *adj.* not fruitful.—*adv.* **infruc'tuously**. [L. *infrūctuōsus—in-*, not, *frūctuōsus*, fruitful.]

**infula**, *in'fū-lə*, *n.* a white-and-red fillet or band of woollen stuff, worn by the ancient Romans upon the forehead in religious rites: a lappet in a mitre:—*pl.* **in'fulae** (-*ē*). [L. *infula*.]

**infundibular**, *in-fun-dib'ū-lər*, *adj.* funnel-shaped. —Also **infundib'ulate**, **infundib'uliform**. [L. *infundibulum*, a funnel—*in*, in, *fundĕre*, to pour.]

**infuriate**, *in-fū'ri-āt*, *v.t.* to enrage: to madden. —*adj.* (-*it*, -*āt*) enraged: mad. [L. *in*, in, *furiāre*, -*ātum*, to madden—*furĕre*, to rave.]

**infuscate**, *in-fus'kāt*, -*kit*, *adj.* clouded with brown. [L. *in*, in, *fuscus*, brown.]

**infuse**, *in-fūz'*, *v.t.* to pour in: to instil: to steep in liquor without boiling: to shed, to pour (*Shak.*): to imbue.—*v.i.* to undergo infusion.— *n.* (*Spens.*) infusion.—*adj.* **infus'ible**.—*n.* **infusion** (*in-fū'zhən*), pouring in: something poured in or introduced: the pouring of water over any substance in order to extract its active qualities: a solution in water of an organic, esp. a vegetable, substance: the liquor so obtained: inspiration: instilling.—*adj.* **infusive** (-*fū'siv*), having the power of infusion, or of being infused. [L. *infundĕre*, *infūsum—in*, into, *fundĕre*, *fūsum*, to pour.]

**infusible**, *in-fūz'i-bl*, *adj.* that cannot be fused: having a high melting-point. [Pfx. in- (2).]

**infusoria**, *in-fū-zō'ri-ə*, -*zö'*, -*sō'ri-ə*, -*sö'*, *n.pl.* orig., minute organisms found in stagnant infusions of animal or vegetable material: (*cap.*) the Ciliophora, a class of Protozoa with cilia throughout life (Ciliata) or in early life (Suctoria). —*adjs.* **infūsō'rial**, **infū'sory**, composed of or containing infusoria.—*n.* and *adj.* **infūsō'rian**.— **infusorial earth**, diatomite. [Neut. pl. of modern L. *infūsorius*; see **infuse**.]

**ingan**, *ing'ən*, *n.* a Scots and dialectal form of **onion**.

**ingate**, *in'gāt*, *n.* an inlet for molten metal in founding. [in, gate (1).]

**ingate**, *in'gāt*, (*Spens.*) *n.* a way in: entrance: ingress. [in, gate (2).]

**ingathering**, *in'gadh-ər-ing*, *n.* collection: securing of the fruits of the earth: harvest.—**Feast of Ingathering** (see **Tabernacles**, Feast of). [Pfx. in- (1).]

**ingeminate**, *in-jem'in-āt*, *v.t.* to reiterate: to double.—*n.* **ingeminā'tion**. [L. *ingemināre*, -*ātum—in*, in, *geminus*, twin.]

**ingener**, *in'jən-ər*, (*Shak.*) *n.* Same as **engineer**.

**ingenerate**, *in-jen'ər-āt*, *v.t.* to generate or produce within.—*adj.* (-*it*) inborn: innate. [Pfx. in- (1).]

**ingenerate**, *in-jen'ər-it*, -*āt*, *adj.* not generated, self-existent. [Pfx. in- (2).]

**ingenious**, *in-jē'nyəs*, -*ni-əs*, *adj.* of good natural abilities (*obs.*): skilful in invention or contriving: skilfully contrived.—*adv.* **ingē'niously**.—*ns.* **ingē'niousness**, power of ready invention: facility in combining ideas: curiousness in design; **ingē'nium**, bent of mind. [L. *ingenium*, mother-wit.]

**ingénue**, *ē-zhā-nü*, (Fr.) a naïve young woman, esp. on the stage.

**ingenuity**, *in-ji-nū'i-ti*, *n.* orig., ingenuousness: (by confusion with **ingenious**) ingeniousness. [L. *ingenuitās*, -*ātis*,; see next word.]

**ingenuous**, *in-jen'ū-əs*, *adj.* free-born (*obs.*): frank: honourable: free from deception.—*adv.* **ingen'uously**.—*ns.* **ingen'uousness**; **ingenu'ity** (see previous word). [L. *ingenuus*, free-born, ingenuous.]

**ingest**, *in-jest'*, *v.t.* to take into the body.—*n.pl.* **ingest'a**, materials taken into the body.—*adj.* **ingest'ible**.—*n.* **ingestion** (*in-jes'chən*).—*adj.* **ingest'ive**. [L. *ingerĕre*, *ingestum*, to carry in—*in*, *gerĕre*, to carry.]

**ingine**, *in-jin'*, (*obs.*) *n.* ability: genius. [L. *ingenium*.]

**ingle**, *ing'gl*, (Scot. *ing'l*) *n.* a fire: fireplace.— **ing'le-cheek**, the jamb of a fireplace; **ing'le-nook**, a chimney-corner; **ing'le-side**, a fireside. [Possibly Gael. *aingeal*; or L. *igniculus*, dim. of *ignis*, fire.]

**ingle**, *ing'gl*, (*obs.*) *n.* a catamite: (wrongly) a friend. [Origin obscure.]

**inglobe**, *in-glōb'*, (*Milt.*) *v.t.* to englobe, form into a sphere. [Pfx. in- (1).]

**inglorious**, *in-glō'ri-əs*, -*glö'*, *adj.* not glorious: unhonoured: shameful.—*adv.* **inglō'riously**.—*n.* **inglō'riousness**. [Pfx. in- (2).]

**ingluvies**, *in-glōō'vi-ēz*, *n.* the crop or craw of birds.—*adj.* **inglu'vial**. [L. *inglŭviēs*.]

**ingoing**, *in'gō-ing*, *n.* a going in: entrance: a reveal (*Scot.*).—*adj.* going in: entering as an occupant: thorough, penetrating. [in, go.]

**ingot**, *ing'gət*, -*got*, *n.* a mass of unwrought metal, esp. gold or silver, cast in a mould.—Also (*Spens.*, *pl.*) **ingowes**, **ingoes**. [Perh. O.E. *in*, in, and the root *got*, as in *goten*, pa.p. of *gēotan*, to pour; Ger. *giessen*, Goth. *giutan*.]

**ingraft**. See **engraft**.

**ingrain**, *in-grān'*, *v.t.* the same as **engrain**.—*adj.* (pron. *in'grān* when attributive) dyed in the yarn or thread before manufacture: deeply fixed: through and through.—*adj.* **ingrained'** (attrib. *in'grānd*). [Pfx. in- (1).]

**ingram**, **ingrum**, *ing'rəm*, (*obs.*) *adj.* ignorant. [ignorant.]

**ingrate**, *in-grāt'*, *in'grāt*, *adj.* unpleasing (*obs.*): ungrateful (*arch.*).—*n.* one who is ungrateful. —*adj.* **ingrate'ful**, unthankful. [L. *ingrātus—in-*, not, *grātus*, pleasing, grateful.]

**ingratiate**, *in-grā'shi-āt*, *v.t.* to commend to someone's grace or favour (often reflexively; followed by *with*).—*adj.* **ingra'tiating**. [L. *in*, into, *grātia*, favour.]

**ingratitude**, *in-grat'i-tūd*, *n.* unthankfulness. [L.L. *ingrātitūdō*—L. *ingrātus*, unthankful.]

**ingredient**, *in-grē'di-ənt*, *n.* that which enters into

Neutral vowels in unaccented syllables: *el'ə-mənt*; for certain sounds in foreign words, see p. viii

a compound: a component. [L. *ingrediēns, -entis*, pr.p. of *ingredī—in*, into, *gradī*, to walk.]

**in gremio**, *in' grēm', grem'i-ō*, (L.L.) in the bosom.

**ingress**, *in'gres*, *n.* entrance: power, right, or means of entrance.—*n.* **ingression** (*in-gresh'ən*). [L. *ingressus—ingredī*; see preceding.]

**ingroove.** See **engroove.**

**ingross**, *in-grōs'*, (*Shak.*) *v.t.* Same as **engross.**

**ingrowing**, *in'grō-ing*, *adj.* growing inward: growing into the flesh: growing within.—*adj.* **in'-grown.**—*n.* **in'growth**, growth within or inward: a structure so formed. [Pfx. **in-** (1).]

**inguinal**, *ing'gwin-əl*, *adj.* relating to the groin. [L. *inguinālis—inguen, inguinis*, the groin.]

**ingulf, ingulph.** See **engulf.**

**ingurgitate**, *in-gûr'ji-tāt*, *v.t.* to swallow up greedily, as in a gulf.—*n.* **ingurgitā'tion.** [L. *ingurgitāre, -ātum—in*, into, *gurges, -itis*, a whirlpool.]

**inhabit**, *in-hab'it*, *v.t.* to dwell in: to occupy—. *v.i.* (*arch.*) to dwell.—*adj.* **inhab'itable**, that may be inhabited (see also next word).—*ns.* **inhab'itance, inhab'itancy**, the act of inhabiting: abode; **inhab'itant**, one who inhabits: a resident.—*adj.* resident.—*ns.* **inhabitā'tion**, the act of inhabiting: dwelling-place: population, or perh. the inhabited world (*Milt.*); **inhab'itor**, an inhabitant (*B.*): a colonist, settler (*obs.*); **inhab'-itiveness** (*phrenol.*), love of locality and home; **inhab'itress**, a female inhabitant. [L. *inhabitāre—in*, in, *habitāre*, to dwell.]

**inhabitable**, *in-hab'it-ə-bl*, *adj.* not habitable, uninhabitable. See also under **inhabit.** [L. *inhabitābilis—in-*, not, *habitābilis.*]

**inhale**, *in-hāl'*, *v.t.* and *v.i.* to breathe in: to draw in.—*adj.* **inhā'lant**, inhaling: drawing in.—*ns.* **inhā'lant**, an inhaling organ, structure or apparatus: a medicinal preparation to be inhaled; **inhalation** (*in-hə-lā'shən*), the act of drawing into the lungs: something to be inhaled; **inhalator** (*in'hə-lā-tər*, or *-lā'*), apparatus for enabling one to inhale a gas, etc.; **inhalatorium** (*in-hāl-ə-tō'ri-əm, tōr'*), an institution or department for administering inhalations; **inhā'ler**, one who inhales; one who habitually inhales tobacco smoke: an inhalator: a respirator or gas-mask. [L. *in*, upon, *hālāre*, to breathe (L. *inhālāre* means to breathe upon).]

**inharmonious**, *in-här-mō'ni-əs*, *adj.* discordant, unmusical: disagreeing: marked by disagreement and dispeace.—*adjs.* **inharmonic** (*in-här-mon'ik*), **-al**, wanting harmony: inharmonious.—*adv.* **inharmō'niously.**—*ns.* **inharmō'niousness; inharmony** (*in-här'mən-i*). [Pfx. **in-** (2).]

**inhaust**, *in'hŏst*, *v.t.* to drink in. [L. *in*, in, *haurīre, haustum*, to draw.]

**inhearse, inherce**, *in-hûrs'*, (*Shak.*) *v.t.* to enclose as in a hearse: to bury.—Also **enhearse.** [Pfx. **in-** (1).]

**inhere**, *in-hēr'*, *v.i.* to stick, remain firm in something: to be inherent.—*ns.* **inhēr'ence, inhēr'-ency**, a sticking fast: existence in something else: a fixed state of being in another body or substance.—*adj.* **inhēr'ent**, sticking fast (*arch.*): existing in and inseparable from something else: innate: natural.—*adv.* **inhēr'ently.** [L. *inhaerēre, inhaesum—in*, in, *haerēre*, to stick.]

**inherit**, *in-her'it*, *v.t.* to make heir (*Shak.*): to be the heir of, succeed as heir (*arch.*): to get as heir: to possess by transmission from past generations: to have at second-hand from anyone (*coll.*): to have by genetic transmission from ancestors.—*v.i.* to succeed.—*adj.* **inher'itable**, same as **heritable.**—*ns.* **inher'itance**, that which is or may be inherited: hereditary descent; **inher'itor**, one who inherits or may inherit: an heir:—*fem.* **inher'itress, inher'itrix.** [O.Fr. *enhériter*, to put in possession as heir— L.L. *inhērēditāre*, to inherit—L. *in*, in, *hērēs, hērēdis*, an heir.]

**inhesion**, *in-hē'zhən.* Same as **inherence.**

**inhibit**, *in-hib'it*, *v.t.* to hold in or back: to keep back: to check.—*ns.* **inhibi'tion**, the act of inhibiting or restraining: the state of being inhibited: prohibition: a writ from a higher court to an inferior judge to stay proceedings (*obs.*): a restraining action of the unconscious will: the blocking of a mental or psychophysical process by another set up at the same time by the same stimulus: stoppage, complete or partial, of a physical process by some nervous influence; **inhib'itor**, that which inhibits: a substance that interferes with a chemical or biological process.—*adj.* **inhib'itory**, prohibitory. [L. *inhibēre, -hibitum—in*, in, *habēre*, to have.]

**inholder**, *in-hōld'ər*, (*Spens.*) *n.* an inhabitant. [Pfx. **in-** (1).]

**inhoop**, *in-hōōp'*, (*Shak.*) *v.t.* to confine, as in a hoop or enclosure. [Pfx. **in-** (1).]

**inhospitable**, *in-hos'pit-ə-bl*, *adj.* affording no kindness to strangers: (of place) barren, not offering shelter, food, etc.—*ns.* **inhos'pitableness, inhospital'ity**, want of hospitality or courtesy to strangers.—*adv.* **inhosp'itably.** [Pfx. **in-** (2).]

**inhuman**, *in-hū'mən*, *adj.* barbarous: cruel: unfeeling.—*n.* **inhumanity** (*in-hū-man'i-ti*), the state of being inhuman: barbarity: cruelty.—*adv.* **inhū'manly.** [Pfx. **in-** (2).]

**inhumane**, *in-hū-mān'*, *adj.* not humane, cruel. [Pfx. **in-** (2).]

**inhume**, *in-hūm'*, *v.t.* to bury in the earth.—Also **inhumate** (*in'*, or *-hūm'*).—*n.* **inhumā'tion**, the act of depositing in the ground: burial. [L. *inhumāre—in*, in, *humus*, the ground.]

**inimical**, *in-im'i-kl*, *adj.* unfriendly: hostile: unfavourable: opposed.—*adv.* **inim'ically.**—*adj.* **inimicitious** (*-sish'əs; Sterne*), unfriendly. [L. *inimīcālis—inimīcus*, enemy—*in-*, not, *amīcus*, friend.]

**inimitable**, *in-im'it-ə-bl*, *adj.* that cannot be imitated: surpassingly excellent.—*ns.* **inimitabil'ity, inim'itableness.**—*adv.* **inim'itably.** [Pfx. **in-** (2).]

**inion**, *in'i-ən* *n.* the external occipital protuberance:—*pl.* **in'ia.** [Gr. *īnion*, the occiput.]

**iniquity**, *in-ik'wi-ti*, *n.* want of equity or fairness (*arch.*): injustice: wickedness: a crime: (*cap.*) one of the names of the Vice, the established buffoon of the old Moralities (*hist.*).—*adj.* **iniq'uitous**, unjust: scandalously unreasonable: wicked.—*adv.* **iniq'uitously.** [Fr. *iniquité*—L. *iniquitās, -ātis—inīquus*, unequal—*in-*, not, *aequus*, equal.]

**inisle.** Same as **enisle.**

**initial** *in-ish'l*, *adj.* beginning: of, at, or serving as the beginning: original.—*n.* the letter beginning a word, esp. a name.—*v.t.* to put the initials of one's name to:—*pr.p.* **init'ialling;** *pa.t.* and *pa.p.* **init'ialled.**—*v.t.* **init'ialise, -ize,** to designate by initial letters.—*adv.* **init'ially.**—*v.t.* **initiate** (*-ish'i-āt*), to begin, start: to introduce (e.g. to knowledge): to admit esp. with rites (as to a secret society, a mystery).—*v.i.* to perform the first act or rite.—*n.* (*-it*) one who is initiated.—*adj.* initiated: belonging to one newly initiated.—*n.* **initiā'tion.**—*adj.* **init'iative** (*-i-ə-tiv*), serving to initiate: introductory.—*n.* the lead, first step, considered as determining the conditions for others: the right or power of beginning: energy and resourcefulness enabling one to act without prompting from others: the right to originate legislation, or a constitutional method of doing so.—*n.* **init'iator**, one who initiates.—*adj.* **init'iatory** (*-i-ə-tə-ri*), tending or serving to initiate: introductory.—*n.* introductory rite.—**initial cell** (*bot.*), a cell that remains meristematic and gives rise to many daughter-cells from which permanent tissues are formed; **initiation fee** (*U.S.*), entrance fee of a society.— **Initial Teaching Alphabet,** teaching alphabet of 44 characters. [L. *initiālis—initium*, a beginning, *inīre, initum—in*, into, *īre, itum*, to go.]

**inject**, *in-jekt'*, *v.t.* to throw in or on (*obs.*): to force in: to inspire or instil: to fill by injection. —*ns.* **injec'tion** (*-shən*), act of injecting or forcing in, esp. a liquid: a liquid injected into the body: a magma injected into a rock (*geol.*): see **insertion** (*space*): the spraying of oil-fuel into the cylinder of a compression-ignition engine by an injection pump; **injec'tor**, one who injects: something used for injecting, especially an apparatus for forcing water into a boiler.—**injection moulding**, moulding of thermoplastics by squirting from a heated cylinder into a water-chilled mould. [L. *injicĕre, injectum*—*in*, into, *jacĕre*, to throw.]

**injelly**, *in-jel'i*, (*Tenn.*) *v.t.* to place as if in jelly. [Pfx. **in-** (1).]

**injoint**, *in-joint'*, (*Shak.*) *v.t.* to join. [Pfx. **in-** (1).]

**injudicious**, *in-jōō-dish'əs*, *adj.* not judicious: ill-judged.—*adv.* **injudic'ial**, not according to law-forms.—*advs.* **injudic'ially, injudic'iously.**—*n.* **injudic'iousness.** [Pfx. **in-** (2).]

**Injun**, *in'jən*, (*coll.*) *n.* an (American) Indian.— Also *adj.*—**honest Injun** (see **honest**).

**injunction**, *in-jungk'shən*, *n.* act of enjoining or commanding: an order: a precept: exhortation: an inhibitory writ by which a superior court stops or prevents some inequitable or illegal act being done—called in Scotland an *interdict*: conjunction (*Milt.*). [L.L. *injunctiō, -ōnis*—*in*, in, *jungĕre, junctum*, to join.]

**injure**, *in'jər*, *v.t.* to wrong: to harm: to damage: to hurt.—*ns.* **in'jurant**, that which causes injury; **in'jurer.**—*adj.* **injurious** (*in-jōō'ri-əs*), tending to injure: wrongful: hurtful: damaging to reputation.—*adv.* **inju'riously.**—*ns.* **inju'riousness; injury** (*in'jər-i*), that which injures: wrong: damage: hurt: impairment: annoyance: insult, offence (*obs.*).—**injury time**, in ball games, extra time allowed for play to compensate for time lost as a result of injury during the game. [L. *injūria*, injury—*in*, not, *jūs, jūris*, law.]

**injustice**, *in-jus'tis*, *n.* violation or withholding of another's rights or dues: wrong: iniquity. [Pfx. **in-** (2).]

**ink**, *ingk*, *n.* a black or coloured liquid used in writing, printing, etc.: a dark liquid ejected by cuttle-fishes, etc.—*v.t.* to daub, cover, blacken, or colour with ink.—*ns.* **ink'er**, one who inks: a pad or roller for inking type, etc.; **ink'iness.** —*adj.* **ink'y**, consisting of or resembling ink: very black: blackened with ink.—**ink'-bag, -sac,** a sac in some cuttle-fishes, containing a black viscid fluid; **ink'-bottle**, a bottle for holding ink; **ink'-erā'ser**, india-rubber treated with fine sand, used for rubbing out ink-marks; **ink'-feed**, the passage by which the nib of a fountain-pen is fed with ink; **ink'holder**, a container for ink: the reservoir of a fountain-pen; **ink'horn** (*obs.*), an ink-holder, formerly of horn: a portable case for ink, etc.—*adj.* pedantic, bookish.—**ink'-horn-mate** (*Shak.*), a bookish man; **ink'ing-roll'er**, a roller covered with a composition for inking printing type; **ink'ing-ta'ble**, a table or flat surface used for supplying the inking-roller with ink during the process of printing; **ink pencil**, a copying-pencil, a pencil made from a composition whose marks when moistened look like ink and can be copied by a printing-press; **ink'pot**, an ink-bottle, or pot for dipping a pen in; **ink'-slinger** (*slang*), a professional author: a scribbler: a controversialist; **ink'stand**, a stand or tray for ink-bottles and (usually) pens; **ink'stone**, a kind of stone containing sulphate of iron, used in making ink; **ink'well**, a reservoir for ink let into a desk.—**China ink, Indian ink** (sometimes without *caps.*), a mixture of lamp-black and size or glue, kept in solid form and rubbed down in water for use; **ink-blot test** (see **Rorschach test**); **invisible** or **sympathetic ink**, a kind of ink that remains invisible on the paper

until it is heated; **mark'ing-ink** (see **mark**); **print'ing-ink** (see **print**); **sling ink** (*slang*), to write: to earn one's bread by writing: to engage in controversy. [O.Fr. *enque* (Fr. *encre*)—L.L. *encaustum*, the purple-red ink used by the later Roman emperors—Gr. *enkauston—enkaiein*, to burn in. See **encaustic**.]

**inkle**, *ingk'l*, (*Shak.*) *n.* a kind of broad linen tape. [Poss. Du. *enkel*, single.]

**inkling**, *ingk'ling*, *n.* a slight hint: intimation: a dim notion or suspicion.—*v.i.* **ink'le**, to have or give a hint of. [M.E. *inclen*, to hint at; origin unknown.]

**in-kneed**, *in'-nēd'*, *adj.* bent inward at the knees: knock-kneed. [Pfx. **in-** (1).]

**inlace.** Same as **enlace**.

**inlaid.** See **inlay**.

**inland**, *in'land*, *in'lənd*, *n.* the interior part of a country: the peopled part, or part near the capital (*arch.*).—*adj.* remote from the sea: carried on, or produced, within a country: confined to a country: refined, polished (*Shak.*).— *adv.* (also *in-land'*) landward: away from the sea: in an inland place.—*n.* **in'lander**, one who lives inland.—**inland navigation**, passage of boats or vessels on rivers, lakes, or canals within a country; **inland revenue**, internal revenue, derived from excise, stamps, income-tax, etc. [O.E. *inland*, a domain—*in* and *land*.]

**in-law**, *in-lô'*, (*coll.*) *n.* a relative by marriage, e.g. mother-in-law, brother-in-law:—*pl.* **in-laws'.**

**inlay**, *in'lā'*, *in-lā'*, *v.t.* to insert, embed: to insert for preservation in a larger page, serving as margin: to ornament by laying in or inserting pieces of metal, ivory, etc.:—*pr.p.* **in'lay'ing**; *pa.t.* and *pa.p.* **in'laid'.**—*n.* **in'lay**, inlaying: inlaid work: material inlaid.—*adj.* **in'laid'** (or *in'lād*, or *in-lād'*), inserted by inlaying: decorated with inlay: consisting of inlay: having a pattern set into the surface.—*ns.* **inlayer** (*in'lā-ər, in-lā'ər*); **inlay'ing.** [Pfx. **in-** (1).]

**inlet**, *in'let*, *n.* entrance: a passage by which anything is let in: place of ingress: a small bay or opening in the land: a piece let in or inserted. [**in, let**.]

**inlier**, *in'li-ər*, (*geol.*) *n.* an outcrop of older rock surrounded by younger. [**in, lie**.]

**in limine**, *in li'mi-nē, lē'mi-ne*, (L.) on the threshold. 

**inlock**, *in-lok'*, *v.t.* Same as **enlock**.

**in loco parentis**, *in lō'kō, lok'ō, pə , pä-ren'tis*, (L.) in the place of a parent.

**inly**, *in'li*, *adj.* inward: secret.—*adv.* inwardly: in the heart: thoroughly, entirely. [**in.**]

**in malam partem**, *in mä'ləm pär'təm, ma'lam pär'tem*, (L.) in an unfavourable manner.

**inmate**, *in'māt*, *n.* one who lodges in the same house with another (*arch.*): one of those who live in a house, esp. one confined to an institution.—*adj.* (*obs.*) dwelling in the same place. [**in** or **inn, mate**.]

**in medias res**, *in mē'di-as rēz, mä'di-, me'di-äs räs*, (L.) into the midst of things.

**in memoriam.** See **memory**.

**inmost.** See **innermost**.

**inn**, *in*, *n.* abode (*obs.*; form. often in *pl.*): a house open to the public for lodging and entertainment of travellers: a hostel: a hotel: loosely, a public-house.—*v.t.* and *v.i.* to lodge, put up. —*ns.* **inn'holder** (*Bacon; U.S.*), **inn'keeper**, one who keeps an inn; **inn'yard**, the courtyard round which an old-fashioned inn was built.—**Inns of Court**, the buildings of four voluntary societies that have the exclusive right of calling to the English bar (Inner Temple, Middle Temple, Lincoln's Inn and Gray's Inn): hence the societies themselves; the **Inns of Chancery** were the buildings of minor societies, residences of junior students of law. [O.E. *inn*, an inn, house—*in, inn*, within (adv.), from the prep. *in*, in.]

innards, *in'ərdz*, (*coll.*) *n.pl.* entrails: internal parts of a mechanism: interior. [inwards.]

innate, *in'āt, in-nāt'*, *adj.* inborn: natural to the mind: inherent: of an anther, attached by the base to the tip of the filament (*bot.*).—*adv.* inn'ately (or *-nāt'*).—*n.* inn'ateness (or *-nāt'*).—*adj.* innā'tive, native. [L. *innātus—in-*, in, *nāscī, nātus*, to be born.]

innavigable, *in-nav'i-gə-bl, adj.* unnavigable.—*adv.* innav'igably. [Pfx. in- (2).]

inner, *in'ər, adj.* (comp. of in) farther in : interior. —*n.* (a hit on) that part of a target next the bull's eye.—*adjs.* inn'ermost, in'most (superl. of in), farthest in: most remote from the outside. —inner man, soul: mind: stomach (*facet.*); inner part, voice, a voice part intermediate between the highest and the lowest; inner space, the undersea region regarded as an environment. [O.E. *in*, comp. *innera*, superl. *irnemest* = *inne-m-est*—thus a double superlative.]

innervate, *in'ûr-vāt, in-ûr'vāt, v.t.* to supply with nerves or nervous stimulus.—Also innerve'.—*n.* innervā'tion. [Pfx. in- (1).]

inning, *in'ing, n.* ingathering, esp. of crops: (in *pl.*; in U.S. sometimes in *sing.*) a team's turn of batting in cricket, etc.: hence, the time during which a person or a party is in possession of anything, a spell or turn: (in *pl.*) lands recovered from the sea.—a good innings, a long life. [in or inn.]

innocent, *in'ə-sənt, adj.* not hurtful: inoffensive: blameless: harmless: guileless: simple: ignorant of evil: imbecile (*dial.*): not legally guilty: devoid (with *of*): not malignant or cancerous (*med.*).—*n.* one free from fault: one with no knowledge of evil: a child: a simpleton: an idiot.—*ns.* inn'ocence, harmlessness: blamelessness: guilelessness: simplicity: freedom from legal guilt; inn'ocency, the quality of being innocent.—*adv.* inn'ocently.—Innocents' Day (see **Childermas**). [O.Fr.,—L *innocēns, -entis—in-*, not, *nocēre*, to hurt.]

innocuous, *in-ok'ū-əs, adj.* harmless.—*adv.* innoc'-uously.—*ns.* innoc'uousness, innocu'ity. [L. *innocuus—in-*, not, *nocuus*, hurtful—*nocēre*, to hurt.]

innominate, *i-nom'i-nāt, -nit, adj.* having no name. —*adj.* innom'inable, unnamable.—*n.* (in *pl.*; *obs. facet.*) trousers.—innominate artery, the first large branch given off from the arch of the aorta; innominate bone (*os innōminātum*), the haunch-bone, hip-bone, formed by fusion in the adult of the ilium, ischium, and pubis; innominate vein, one of two large veins on either side of the lower part of the neck formed by the union of the internal jugular and subclavian veins. [L. *in-*, not, *nōmināre, -ātum*, to name.]

innovate, *in'ō-vāt, in'ə-vāt, v.t.* to renew, alter (*rare*): to introduce as something new.—*v.i.* to introduce novelties: to make changes.—*ns.* in-novā'tion, the act of innovating: a thing introduced as a novelty: revolution (*Shak.*): substitution of one obligation for another (*Scots law*): a season's new growth (*bot.*); innovā'tionist; inn'ovātor. [L. *innovāre, -ātum—in*, in, *novus*, new.]

innoxious, *in-ok'shəs, adj.* not noxious.—*adv.* in-nox'iously.—*n.* innox'iousness. [Pfx. in- (2).]

innuendo, *in-ū-en'dō, n.* insinuation: an indirect reference or intimation: a part of a pleading in cases of libel and slander, pointing out what and who was meant:—*pl.* innuen'do(e)s.—*v.t.* to insinuate by innuendo: to interpret as insinuation. —*v.i.* to make insinuations. [L. *innuendō*, by nodding at (i.e. indicating, to wit—used in old legal documents to introduce a parenthetic indication), ablative gerund of *innuĕre*, to nod to, indicate—*in*, to, *nuĕre*, to nod.]

innumerable, *in-(n)ū'mər-ə-bl, adj.* that cannot be

numbered: countless.—*ns.* innūmerabil'ity; in-nū'merableness.—*adv.* innū'merably.—*adj.* in-nū'merous (*Milt.*), without number: innumerable. [Pfx. in- (2).]

innumerate, *in-nūm'-ər-it, adj.* having no understanding of mathematics or science.—Also *n.*—*n.* innum'eracy. [Coined 1959 by Sir Geoffrey Crowther (on analogy of *illiterate*)—L. *numerus*, number.]

innutrition, *in-(n)ū-trish'ən, n.* want of nutrition: failure of nourishment.—*adjs.* innū'trient, not nutrient; innūtritious (*-trish'əs*), not nutritious. [Pfx. in- (2).]

inobedient, *in-ō-bē'dyənt, adj.* disobedient.—*n.* inobe'dience.—*adv.* inobe'diently. [Pfx. in- (2).]

inobservant, *in-əb-zûr'vənt, adj.* unobservant: heedless.—*adj.* inobser'vable, incapable of being observed.—*ns.* inobser'vance, lack of observance; inobservā'tion (*-ob-*). [Pfx. in- (2).]

inobtrusive, *in-əb-trōō'siv, adj.* unobtrusive.—*adv.* inobtru'sively.—*n.* inobtru'siveness. [Pfx. in- (2).]

inoccupation, *in-ok-ū-pā'shən, n.* lack of occupation. [Pfx. in- (2).]

inoculate, *in-ok'ū-lāt, v.t.* to insert as a bud or graft: to graft: to imbue: to introduce (e.g. bacteria, a virus) into an organism: to give a mild form of (a disease) in this way: to make an inoculation in, esp. for the purpose of safeguarding against infection.—*v.i.* to practise inoculation.—*n.* inoculabil'ity.—*adj.* inoc'ulable.—*n.* inoculā'tion, act or practice of inoculating: insertion of the buds of one plant into another: the communication of disease by the introduction of a germ or virus, esp. that of a mild form of the disease to produce immunity: the analogous introduction of anything, e.g. nitrogen-fixing bacteria into soil, seed, a crystal into a supersaturated solution to start crystallisation.—*adjs.* inoc'ulative (*-ə-tiv*, or *-ā-tiv*); inoc'ulatory (*-ə-tər-i*).—*ns.* inoc'ulātor; inoc'ulum, material used for inoculating. [L. *inoculāre, -ātum—in*, into, and *oculus*, an eye, a bud.]

inodorous, *in-ō'dər-əs, adj.* without smell.—*adv.* ino'dorously.—*n.* ino'dorousness. [Pfx. in- (2).]

inoffensive, *in-ə-fen'siv, adj.* giving no offence: harmless.—*adv.* inoffen'sively.—*n.* inoffen'siveness. [Pfx. in- (2).]

inofficious, *in-ə-fish'əs, adj.* disobliging (*obs.*): regardless of duty (*law*): inoperative. [Pfx. in- (2).]

inoperable, *in-op'ər-ə-bl, adj.* that cannot be operated on successfully, or without undue risk.—*adj.* inop'erative, not in action: producing no effect. [Pfx. in- (2).]

inoperculate, *in-o-pûr'kū-lāt, adj.* without an operculum or lid. [Pfx. in- (2).]

inopinate, *in-op'in-āt, (obs.) adj.* unexpected. [L. *inopīnatus.*]

inopportune, *in-op'ər-tūn, -tūn', adj.* unseasonable in time.—*adv.* inopp'ortūnely (or *-tūn'*).—*ns.* inopp'ortūnist (or *-tūn'*), one who thinks a policy inopportune; inopportūn'ity. [Pfx. in- (2).]

inorb, *in-örb', v.t.* to set in an orb. [Pfx. in- (1).]

inordinate, *in-örd'(i-)nit, adj.* unrestrained: excessive: immoderate.—*ns.* inor'dinacy, inor'-dinateness.—*adj.* inor'dinately.—*n.* inordinā'tion, deviation from rule: irregularity. [L. *inordin-ātus—in-*, not, *ordināre, -ātum*, to arrange, regulate.]

inorganic, *in-ör-gan'ik, adj.* not organic: not organised: not belonging to an organism: of accidental origin, not normally developed.—*adv.* inorgan'ically.—*n.* inorganisā'tion, want of organisation.—*adj.* inor'ganised, -ized, un-organised.—inorganic chemistry, the chemistry of all substances but carbon compounds, generally admitting a few of these also (as oxides of carbon, carbonates). [Pfx. in- (2).]

inornate, *in-ör-nāt'*, or *-ör'nit*, *adj.* not ornate: simple. [Pfx. in- (2).]

inosculate, *in-os'kū-lāt*, *v.t.* and *v.i.* to unite by mouths or ducts, as two vessels in an animal body: to anastomose.—*n.* inoscula'tion. [L. *in*, in, and *osculāri*, *-ātus*, to kiss.]

inositol, *in-os'i-tol*, *n.* a member of the vitamin B complex, occurring in practically all plant and animal tissues. [Gr. *is*, *inos*, a sinew, muscle, and suffixes *-ite* and *-ol*.]

in pace, *in pā'sē*, *pä'chä*, *pä-ke*, (L.) in peace.

in partibus infidelium, *in pär'ti-bəs in-fi-dē'li-əm*, *pär'ti-boōs ēn-fi-dä'li-oōm*, (L.) in unbelieving countries—a phrase formerly applied to titular bishops in countries where no Catholic hierachy had been set up.

in-patient. See in.

in petto, *ēn*, *in pet'tō*, (It.) within the breast: in one's own mind but not yet divulged.

inphase, *in-fāz'*, *adj.* in the same phase. [in, phase.]

inpouring, *in'pōr-ing*, *-pör-*, *n.* a pouring in: addition. [in, pouring.]

in principio, *in prin-sip'i-ō*, *-kip'*, (L.) in the beginning.

in propria persona, *in prō-pri-ə pûr-sō'nə, pro'-pri-ä per-sō'nä*, (L.L.) in person.

in puris naturalibus, *in pū'ris na-tūr-āl'i-bəs, poō'rēs na-toō-räl'i-boōs*, (L.L.) quite naked.

input, *in'poōt*, *n.* contribution (*Scot.*): amount, material, or energy, that is put in: power, or energy, or coded information, stored or for storage: information available in a computer for dealing with a problem: process of feeding in data.—*adj.* relating to computer input.—*v.t.* to feed into a computer. [in, put.]

inquere, enquere, *in-kwēr'*, (*Spens.*) *v.i.* and *v.t.* to inquire. [inquire.]

inquest, *in'kwest*, formerly *in-kwest'*, *n.* act of inquiring: search (*obs.*): judicial inquiry before a jury into any matter, esp. any case of violent or sudden death: the body of men appointed to hold such an inquiry: the decision reached. [O.Fr. *enqueste*—L.L. *inquesta*—L. *inquisita* (*rēs*)—*inquirēre*, to inquire.]

inquietude, *in-kwī'i-tūd*, *n.* disturbance: uneasiness.—*adj.* inqui'et, unquiet.—*v.t.* (*rare*) to disturb. [Pfx. in- (2).]

inquiline, *in'kwi-lin*, *adj.* living in the abode of another.—*n.* an animal so living.—*adj.* inquili'-nous. [L. *inquilīnus*, tenant, lodger—*incola*, inhabitant—*in*, in, *colĕre*, to inhabit.]

inquinate, *in'kwin-āt*, *v.t.* to defile.—*n.* inquinā'-tion. [L. *inquināre*, *-ātum*.]

inquire, enquire, *in-kwīr'*, *v.i.* to ask a question: to make an investigation.—*v.t.* to ask: to seek (*obs.*): to make an examination regarding (*obs.*): to call (*Spens.*).—*n.* (*Shak.*) inquiry.—*ns.* inquirā'tion (*Dickens*), inquirā'tion, inquiry; inquiren'do (*law*), an authority to inquire; inquir'er, enquir'er.—*adj.* inquir'ing, given to inquiry: eager to acquire information: (of e.g. a look) expressing inquiry.—*adv.* inquir'ingly.—*n.* inquir'y, enquir'y (or *ing'*), act of inquiring: search for knowledge: investigation: a question. —writ of inquiry, a writ appointing an inquest. [O.Fr. *enquerre* (Fr. *enquérir*)—L. *inquirēre*—in, *quaerĕre*, *quaesitum*, to seek.]

inquisition, *in-kwi-zish'ən*, *n.* searching examination: investigation: judicial inquiry: (*cap.*) a tribunal in the R.C. church for discovery, repression, and punishment of heresy, unbelief, etc., 'the Holy Office', now the 'Congregation for Doctrine of the Faith'.—*v.t.* (*Milt.*) to subject to inquisition.—*adjs.* inquisit'ional, searching or vexatious in making inquiry: relating to inquisition or the Inquisition; inquisitive (*-kwiz'-i-tiv*), eager to know: apt to ask questions, esp. about other people's affairs: curious.—*adv.* inquis'itively.—*ns.* inquis'itiveness; inquis'itor, one

who inquires, esp. with undue pertinacity or searchingness: an official inquirer: a member of the Inquisition tribunal.—*adj.* inquisitō'rial.—*adv.* inquisitō'rially.—*n.* inquis'itress, an inquisitorial woman.—*adj.* inquisitū'rient (*Milt.*), eager to act as inquisitor.—Grand Inquisitor, the chief in a court of Inquisition. [L. *inquisitiō*, *-ōnis*. See inquire.]

in re, *in rē*, *rä*, (L.) in the matter (of).

in rerum natura, *in rē'rəm nə-tūr'rə, rä'roōm na-toō'rä*, (L.) in nature: in the natural or physical world: in the order of nature.

inro, *in'rō*, *n.* a small Japanese medicine-chest. [Jap., seal-box.]

inroad, *in'rōd*, *n.* an incursion into an enemy's country: a raid: encroachment. [in, and road, in sense of riding; cf. raid.]

inrush, *in'rush*, *n.* an inward rush. [in, rush.]

in saecula saeculorum, *in sek'yoō-lə sek-yoō-lör'-əm, si'koō-lä si'koō-lō'roōm*, (L.) for ever and ever.

insalivate, *in-sal'i-vät*, *v.t.* to mix with saliva.—*n.* insaliva'tion. [Pfx. in- (1).]

insalubrious, *in-sa-loō'bri-əs*, *-lū'*, *adj.* unhealthy. —*n.* insalu'brity. [Pfx. in- (2).]

insalutary, *in-sal'ū-tər-i*, *adj.* unwholesome. [Pfx. in- (2).]

insane, *in-sān'*, *adj.* not sane or of sound mind: crazy: mad: utterly unwise: senseless: causing insanity (*Shak.* insane root, prob. a root mentioned by Plutarch, *Life of Antony*, perh. hemlock, henbane, or belladonna).—*adv.* insane'ly. —*ns.* insane'ness, insanity: madness; insa'nie (*Shak.*; an emendation of the reading *infamie*), insanity; insanity (*in-san'i-ti*), want of sanity: mental disorder causing one to act against the social or legal demands of society: madness. [L. *insānus*.]

insanitary, *in-san'i-tər-i*, *adj.* not sanitary. [Pfx. in- (2).]

insatiable, *in-sā'sh(y)ə-bl*, *adj.* that cannot be satiated or satisfied.—*ns.* insā'tiableness, insātiabil'ity.—*adv.* insā'tiably.—*adj.* insā'tiate, not sated: insatiable.—*n.* insatiety (*in-sə-tī'i-ti*), unsated or insatiable state. [Pfx. in- (2).]

inscient, *in'sh(y)ənt*, *-shi-ənt*, *adj.* ignorant.—*n.* in'science. [L. *insciēns*, *-entis*—*in-*, not, *scire*, to know.]

inscient, *in'sh(y)ənt*, *adj.* having insight or inward knowledge. [L. *in*, in, *sciēns*, *-entis*, pr.p. of *scire*, to know.]

inscribe, *in-skrib'*, *v.t.* to engrave or otherwise mark: to engrave or mark on: to enter in a book or roll: to dedicate: in geom., to describe within another figure so as to touch all sides or faces of the bounding figure or to have all angular points on it.—*adj.* inscrib'able.—*ns.* in-scrib'er; inscription (*in-skrip'shən*), the act of inscribing: that which is inscribed: dedication: a record inscribed on stone, metal, clay, etc.—*adjs.* inscrip'tional, inscrip'tive. [L. *inscrībĕre*, *inscriptum*—in, upon, *scrībĕre*, to write.]

inscroll, *in-skrōl'*, (*Shak.*) *v.t.* to write on a scroll.

inscrutable, *in-skroōt'ə-bl*, *adj.* that cannot be scrutinised or searched into and understood: inexplicable.—*ns.* inscrutabil'ity, inscrut'able-ness.—*adv.* inscrut'ably. [L. *inscrūtābilis*—in-, not, *scrūtāri*, to search into.]

insculp, *in-skulp'*, *v.t.* to engrave, to cut or carve upon something (*Shak.*): to carve: to form by carving (*arch.*).—*adj.* insculpt', engraved (*Shak.*): having depressions in the surface (*bot.*).—*n.* insculp'ture, anything engraved (*Shak.*): inscription (*arch.*).—*v.t.* (*arch.*) to carve on something. [L. *insculpĕre*—in, in, *sculpĕre*, to carve.]

inseam. Same as enseam (3).

insect, *in'sekt*, *n.* a word loosely used for a small invertebrate creature, esp. one with a body as if cut into, or divided into sections: a member of the Insecta (*zool.*).—*adj.* of insects: like an insect: small: mean.—*n.pl.* Insec'ta, a subphylum of arthropods sharply divided into head, thorax, and abdomen, with three pairs of legs attached to the thorax, usually winged in adult life, breathing air by means of tracheae, and commonly having a metamorphosis in the life-history.—*ns.* insect**ä**r′ium, a vivarium for insects; insec′ticide (-*i-sīd*), killing of insects: an insect-killing substance: an insect-killer.— *adjs.* insec′tiform; insec′tile, having the nature of an insect.—*n.* insec′tifuge, a substance that drives away insects.—*n.pl.* Insectiv′ora, an order of mammals, mostly terrestrial, insect-eating, nocturnal in habit, and small in size—shrews, moles, hedgehogs, etc.—*n.* insect′ivore, a member of the Insectivora.—*adj.* insectiv′orous, living on insects.—*ns.* insection (*in-sek′shən*), an incision: notch: division into segments; insectol′ogist; insectol′ogy, the study of insects.—*adj.* in′secty, abounding in insects.—in′sect-net, a light hand-net for catching insects; in′sect-pow′der, powder for stupefying and killing insects: an insecticide or insectifuge. [L. *insectum,* pa.p. of *insecāre*—*in,* into, *secāre,* to cut.]

insecure, *in-si-kūr′, adj.* apprehensive of danger or loss: in anxious state because not well-adjusted to life: exposed to danger or loss: unsafe: uncertain: not fixed or firm.—*adv.* insecure′ly.—*n.* insecur′ity. [Pfx. in- (2).]

inseem (*Shak.*). Same as enseam (2).

inselberg, *in′zəl-bûrg, in′tsəl-berg,* (geol.) *n.* a steep-sided eminence arising from a plain tract; often found in the semi-arid regions of tropical countries:—*pl.* inselberge (-*gə*). [Ger.]

inseminate, *in-sem′in-āt, v.t.* to sow: to implant: to introduce: to impregnate, esp. artificially.— *n.* inseminā′tion. [L. *insēmināre*—*in,* in, *sēmen, -inis,* seed.]

insensate, *in-sen′sāt, -it, adj.* without sensation, inanimate: lacking sensibility or moral feeling: lacking in good sense.—*n.* insen′sateness. [L. *insēnsātus*—*in-,* not, *sēnsātus,* intelligent—*sēnsus,* feeling.]

insensible, *in-sen′si-bl, adj.* not having feeling: not capable of emotion: callous: dull: unconscious: imperceptible by the senses.—*ns.* insensibil′ity, insen′sibleness.—*adv.* insen′sibly. [Pfx. in- (2).]

insensitive, *in-sen′si-tiv, adj.* not sensitive. [Pfx. in- (2).]

insensuous, *in-sen′sū-əs, -shoō-əs, adj.* not sensuous. [Pfx. in- (2).]

insentient, *in-sen′sh(y)ənt, adj.* not having perception. [Pfx. in- (2).]

inseparable, *in-sep′ər-ə-bl, adj.* that cannot be separated.—*n.* (usu. in *pl.*) an inseparable companion.—*ns.* insep′arableness, inseparabil′ity.— *adv.* insep′arably.—*adj.* insep′arate (*Shak.*), not separate or separable. [Pfx. in- (2).]

insert, *in-sûrt′, v.t.* to put in: introduce (into).— *n.* in′sert, something inserted in a proof, etc.: a paper placed within the folds of a periodical or leaves of a book.—*adj.* insert′ed (*bot.*), attached to or growing out of another member.—*n.* insertion (*in-sûr′shən*), act of inserting: mode or condition of being inserted: point or place of attachment (*zool.*): that which is inserted: lace or the like suitable for letting into another material: the putting of a man-made craft or satellite into orbit (also injection). [L. *inserēre, insertum*—*in,* in, *serēre,* to join.]

Insessores, *in-ses-ō′rēz, -ō′, n.pl.* perching birds, in old classifications an order answering roughly to Passeriformes.—*adj.* insesso′rial, of the Insessores: adapted for perching. [L. *insessor,* pl. *-ōrēs,* besetter (of the roads), highwayman, adopted with the meaning percher—*insidēre*—*in,* on, *sedēre,* to sit.]

inset, *in′set, n.* something set in, an insertion or insert, a leaf or leaves inserted between the folds

of other leaves: a small map or figure inserted in a spare corner of another: a piece let in: the setting in of a current.—*v.t.* inset′, to set in, to infix or implant. [in, set.]

inseverable, *in-sev′ər-ə-bl, adj.* that cannot be severed or separated. [Pfx. in- (2).]

inshallah, *in-shä′lä, interj.* (among Mohammedans) if God will. [Ar. *in shā ′llāh.*]

inshell, *in-shel′,* (*Shak.*) *v.t.* to draw in or withdraw, as into a shell. [Pfx. in- (1).]

inshelter, *in-shel′tər, v.t.* to place in shelter. [Pfx. in- (1).]

inship, *in-ship′,* (*Shak.*) *v.t.* to ship, to embark. [Pfx. in- (1).]

inshore, *in′shōr′, -shör′, adv.* near or toward the shore.—*adj.* (*in′shōr, -shör*) situated, carried on, or operating, near the shore, as fishings, fishing, or fishermen.

inshrine, *in-shrin′.* Same as enshrine.

inside, *in′sīd′, in′sid, in′sid′, n.* the side, space, or part within: (often *pl.*) the entrails: inner nature: that which is not visible at first sight: a passenger in the interior part of a vehicle: (in *pl.*) the inner quires of a ream of paper.— *adj.* being within: interior: indoor: working indoors: from within: from a secret or confidential source: (of a criminal 'job') carried out by, or with the help of, someone trusted and/or employed by the victim (*slang*).—*adv.* in or to the interior: indoors: on the inner side: in or into prison (*slang*).—*prep.* within: into: on inner side of.—*n.* insi′der, one who is inside: inside passenger: one within a certain organisation, etc.: one possessing some particular advantage. —in′side-car, an Irish jaunting-car in which the passengers face one another; inside edge (see edge); inside left, right, in some games a forward between the centre and outside; inside track, the inner side in a race-course: the advantage in position.—inside of (esp. *U.S.*), in less than; inside out, with the inner side turned outwards. [in, side.]

insidious, *in-sid′i-əs, adj.* watching an opportunity to ensnare: intended to entrap: deceptive: underhand: advancing imperceptibly: treacherous.—*adv.* insid′iously.—*n.* insid′iousness. [L. *insidiōsus*—*insidiae,* an ambush—*insidēre*—*in, sedēre,* to sit.]

insight, *in′sīt, n.* power of seeing into and understanding things: imaginative penetration: practical knowledge: enlightenment: a view into anything: awareness, often of one's own mental condition (*psych.*): the apprehension of the principle of a task, puzzle, etc. (*psych.*).—*adj.* insight′ful.—insight learning, direct learning without process of trial and error. [in, sight.]

insight, *in′sit, in′sihht,* (*Scot.*) *n.* household goods, furniture.—Also *adj.* [Origin unknown.]

insignia, *in-sig′ni-ə, n.pl.* in U.S. treated as *sing.,* signs or badges of office, honour, membership, occupation, etc.: marks by which anything is known. [L., neut. pl. of *insignis*—*in, signum,* a mark.]

insignificant, *in-sig-nif′i-kənt, adj.* destitute of meaning: without effect: unimportant: petty. —*ns.* insignif′icance, insignif′icancy.—*adv.* signif′icantly.—*adj.* insignif′icative, not significative or expressing by external signs. [Pfx. in- (2).]

insincere, *in-sin-sēr′, adj.* not sincere.—*adv.* insincere′ly.—*n.* insincerity (-*ser′i-ti*). [Pfx. in- (2).]

insinew, *in-sin′ū, v.t.* (*Shak.*) to be joined as with sinews. [Pfx. in- (1).]

insinuate, *in-sin′ū-āt, v.t.* to introduce gently or artfully: to hint, esp. a fault: to work into favour.—*v.i.* to creep or flow in: to enter gently: to obtain access by flattery or stealth.—*adj.* insin′uating.—*adv.* insin′uatingly.—*n.* insinuā′-tion.—*adj.* insin′uative, insinuating or stealing on the confidence: using insinuation.—*n.* insin′u-

# insipid 679 instance

ator.—*adj.* insin'uatory (-ə-tər-i). [L. *insinuāre*, -*ātum*—*in*, in, *sinus*, a curve.]

**insipid**, *in-sip'id, adj.* tasteless: without satisfying or definite flavour: wanting spirit or interest: dull.—*adv.* insip'idly.—*ns.* insip'idness, insipid'ity. [L.L. *insipidus*—L. *in-*, not, *sapidus*, well-tasted —*sapĕre*, to taste.]

**insipience**, *in-sip'i-əns, n.* lack of wisdom.—*adj.* insip'ient. [L. *insipientia*—*in-*, not, *sapiēns*, wise.]

**insist**, *in-sist', v.i.* to speak emphatically and at length: to persist in pressing: to persevere (*Milt.*).—*v.t.* to maintain persistently.—*n.* insist'ence.—*adj.* insist'ent, urgent: prominent: (of bird's hind-toe) touching the ground with the tip only.—*adv.* insist'ently.—*n.* insist'ure, persistence: prob., uniformity of motion (*Shak.*). [L. *insistĕre*, in, upon, *sistĕre*, to stand.]

**in situ**, *in si'tū, si'tōō,* (L.) in the original situation.

**insnare**. Same as ensnare.

**insobriety**, *in-sō-brī'ə-ti, n.* want of sobriety, drunkenness. [Pfx. in- (2).]

**insociable**, *in-sō'shə-bl, adj.* unsociable: incompatible (*obs.*).—*n.* insociabil'ity. [Pfx. in- (2).]

**insofar**. See in (1).

**insolate**, *in'sō-lāt, in-sō'lāt, v.t.* to expose to the sun's rays: to treat by exposure to the sun's rays.—*n.* insolā'tion, exposure to the sun's rays: received solar radiation: injury caused by the sun. [L. *insōlāre*, -*ātum*—*in*, in, *sōl*, the sun.]

**insole**, *in'sōl, n.* the inner sole of a boot or shoe —opp. to *outsole*: a sole of some material placed inside a shoe for warmth or dryness. [in, sole.]

**insolent**, *in'səl-ənt, adj.* overbearing: insulting: rude.—*n.* in'solence.—*adv.* in'solently. [L. *insolēns*, -*entis*—*in-*, not, *solēns*, pa.p. of *solēre*, to be wont.]

**insolidity**, *in-so-lid'i-ti, n.* want of solidity. [Pfx. in- (2).]

**insoluble**, *in-sol'ū-bl, adj.* not capable of being dissolved: not to be solved or explained.—*v.t.* insol'ubilise, -ize, to render insoluble.—*ns.* insolubil'ity, insol'ubleness.—*adv.* insol'ubly. [Pfx. in- (2).]

**insolvable**, *in-solv'ə-bl, adj.* not solvable. [Pfx. in- (2).]

**insolvent**, *in-solv'ənt, adj.* not able to pay one's debts: bankrupt: pertaining to insolvent persons.—*n.* one unable to pay his debts.—*n.* insolv'ency, bankruptcy. [Pfx. in- (2).]

**insomnia**, *in-som'ni-ə, n.* sleeplessness: prolonged inability to sleep.—*n.* insom'niac, a person who suffers from insomnia.—*adj.* suffering from, causing, or caused by, insomnia.—*adj.* insom'nious.—*n.* insom'nolence. [L. *insomnis*, sleepless.]

**insomuch**, *in-sō-much', adv.* to such a degree: inasmuch: so.

**insooth**, *in-sōōth',* (*arch.*) *adv.* in sooth, indeed. [in, sooth.]

**insouciant**, *in-sōō'si-ənt, ĕ-sōō-sē-ā, adj.* indifferent, unconcerned: heedless.—*n.* insouciance (*in-sōō'si-əns, ĕ-sōō-sē-äs*). [Fr.,—*in-*, not, *souciant,* pr.p. of *soucier*—L. *sollicitāre*, to disturb.]

**inspan**, *in-span', in'span, v.t.* to yoke to a vehicle. —*v.i.* to prepare to depart:—*pr.p.* inspann'ing; *pa.t.* and *pa.p.* inspanned'. [Du. *inspannen*, to yoke—*in*, in, *spannen*, to tie.]

**inspect**, *in-spekt', v.t.* to look into: to examine: to look at narrowly, officially, or ceremonially. —*n.* in'spect (*obs.*), inspection.—*adv.* inspect'ingly.—*n.* inspec'tion, the act of inspecting or looking into: careful or official examination.— *adjs.* inspec'tional; inspec'tive.—*ns.* inspec'tor, one who inspects: an examining officer: a police officer ranking below a superintendent; inspec'torate, a district under charge of an inspector: the office of inspector: a body of inspectors.—*adj.* inspectō'rial.—*ns.* inspec'tor-

ship, the office of inspector; inspec'tress, a female inspector. [L. *inspectāre*, freq. of *inspicĕre, inspectum*—*in*, into, *specĕre*, to look.]

**insphere, inspheare.** See ensphere.

**inspire**, *in-spir', v.t.* to breathe or blow into (*arch.*): to breathe in or blow in (air, etc.): to draw or inhale into the lungs: to infuse into (the mind), esp. with an encouraging or exalting influence: (of divine influence, etc.): to instruct or guide: to instruct or affect with a particular emotion: to bring about, cause to occur: to animate.— *v.i.* to draw in the breath: to blow (*obs.*; *Spens.* inspyre).—*adj.* inspir'able, able to be inhaled.— *n.* inspirā'tion (*in-spər-, -spir-, -spir-*), the act of inspiring or breathing in: a breath: instruction, dictation, or stimulation by a divinity, a genius, an idea or a passion: unacknowledged prompting by authorities: an inspired condition: an object or person that inspires: an inspired thought or idea.—*adjs.* inspirā'tional; inspirative (*in-spir'ə-tiv, in'spir-ā-tiv*), tending to inspire.—*n.* inspirator (*in'spir-ā-tər*), apparatus for injecting or drawing in vapour, liquid, etc.— *adj.* inspiratory (*in-spir'ə-tər-i,* or *in-spir',* or *in'spir-*), belonging to or aiding inspiration or inhalation.—*ns.* inspirā'tionism, inspirā'tionist, one who maintains the direct inspiration of the Scriptures.—*adj.* inspired', actuated or directed by divine influence: influenced by elevated feeling: prompted by superior, but not openly declared, knowledge or authority: actually authoritative.—*n.* inspir'er.—*adv.* inspir'ingly. [L. *inspirāre*—*in*, into, *spirāre*, to breathe.]

**inspirit**, *in-spir'it, v.t.* to infuse spirit into. [Pfx. in- (1).]

**inspissate**, *in-spis'āt, v.t.* to thicken, condense.— *n.* inspissā'tion. [L. *in*, in, *spissāre*—*spissus*, thick.]

**instability**, *in-stə-bil'i-ti, n.* want of steadiness. —*adj.* instā'ble, unstable. [Pfx. in- (2).]

**install** (also **instal**), *in-stöl', v.t.* to place in a stall or official seat: to place in an office or order: to invest with any charge or office with the customary ceremonies: to set up and put in use:—*pr.p.* install'ing; *pa.t.* and *pa.p.* installed'.—*ns.* installā'tion, the act of installing or placing in an office with ceremonies: a placing in position for use: apparatus placed in position for use: the complete apparatus for electric lighting, or the like; install'ment, a knight's seat (*Shak.*): installation (*arch.*). [L.L. *installāre*—*in*, in, *stallum*, a stall—O.H.G. *stal* (Ger. *stall*, Eng. stall).]

**instalment**, in U.S. -stall-, *in-stöl'mənt, n.* one of a series of partial payments: a portion supplied or completed at one time, as of a serial story. [A.F. *estaler*, to fix, set; prob. influenced by install.]

**instance**, *in'stəns, n.* quality of being urgent (*arch.*): solicitation, urging: occurrence: occasion: example: evidence, proof (*Shak.*): process, suit (*law*).—*v.t.* to mention as an example.—*n.* in'stancy, insistency: urgency: imminence.—*n.* in'stant, urgent (*arch.*): immediate: without delay: present, current: (of food, drink) pre-prepared so that little has to be done to it before use.—*n.* the present moment of time: any moment or point of time: the present month.—*n.* instantaneity (*in-stant-ə-nē'i-ti*).—*adj.* instantaneous (*in-stənt-ā'ni-əs*), done in an instant: momentary: occurring or acting at once or very quickly: for the instant: at a particular instant.—*adv.* instantā'eously.—*n.* instantā'eousness.—*adj.* instantial (*in-stan'shl*; *rare*).—*adv.* in'stantly, at once: at this very time (*Shak.*): importunately, zealously (*B.*). —at the instance of, at the motion or solicitation of; for instance, as an example; in the first instance, firstly, originally; on the instant,

Neutral vowels in unaccented syllables: *el'ə-mənt;* for certain sounds in foreign words, see p. viii

forthwith. [L. *instāns, instantis,* pr.p. of *instāre,* to be near, press upon, urge—*in,* upon, *stāre,* to stand.]

**instar,** *in-stär',* *v.t.* to adorn with stars: to place as a star (*arch.*). [Pfx. in- (1).]

**instar,** *in'stär, n.* the form of an insect between moult and moult. [L. *instar,* image.]

**instar omnium,** *in', ēn'stär om'ni-əm, -ōōm,* (L.) example of all the rest.

**instate,** *in-stāt',* *v.t.* to put in possession: to install. [Pfx. in- (1) and state.]

**in statu pupillari,** *in stāt'ū pū-pi-lä'rī, stat'ōō pōō-pi-lä'rē,* (L.L.) in a state of wardship; **in statu quo** (*kwō*), in the former state.

**instauration,** *in-stör-ā'shan, n.* restoration: renewal. [L. *instaurātiō, -ōnis.*]

**instead,** *in-sted', adv.* in the stead, place, or room (of): as an alternative or substitute. [in, stead.]

**instep,** *in'step, n.* the prominent arched part of the human foot near its junction with the leg: the corresponding part of a shoe, stocking, etc.: in horses, the hindleg from the ham to the pastern joint.—in'step-rais'er, an arched device to support the instep and counteract a tendency to flat feet. [Origin obscure.]

**instigate,** *in'sti-gāt, v.t.* to urge on, incite: to foment.—*ns.* instiga'tion, the act of inciting: impulse, esp. to evil; in'stigātor, an inciter, generally in a bad sense. [L. *instigāre, -ātum.*]

**instil, instill,** *in-stil', v.t.* to drop in: to infuse slowly into the mind:—*pr.p.* instill'ing; *pa.p.* instilled'.—Also **instill.**—*ns.* instillā'tion, instil'ment, the act of instilling or pouring in by drops: the act of infusing slowly into the mind: that which is instilled or infused. [L. *instillāre—in,* in, *stillāre,* to drop.]

**instinct,** *in'stingkt,* formerly *in-stingkt', n.* impulse: an involuntary prompting to action: intuition: the natural impulse by which animals are guided apparently independently of reason or experience: a complex co-ordination of reflex actions which results in achievement of adaptive ends without foresight or experience.—*adj.* (*in-stingkt'*) instigated or incited: moved: animated: charged: imbued.—*adj.* instinct'ive, prompted by instinct: involuntary: acting according to or determined by natural impulse.—*adv.* instinc'tively.—*n.* instinctiv'ity (*rare*).—*adj.* instinc'tual, pertaining to instincts. [L. *instinctus—instinguēre,* instigate.]

**institorial,** *in-sti-tō'ri-əl, -tō'ri-,* (*law*) *adj.* pertaining to an agent or factor. [L. *institōrius—institor,* an agent, broker.]

**institute,** *in'sti-tūt, v.t.* to set up, establish: to set on foot: to order (*obs.*): to appoint: to educate (*obs.*).—*n.* anything instituted or formally established: the act of instituting (*obs.*): established law: precept or principle: an institution: a literary and philosophical society or organisation for education, research, etc.: the building in which such an organisation is housed: a foundation for further education, esp. in technical subjects: a temporary school, esp. for teachers (*U.S.*): the person first nominated as heir (distinguished from the *substitutes* who follow, failing the institute; *Scots law*): (in *pl.*) a book of precepts, principles, or rules.—*n.* institution (*-tū'shan*), the act of instituting or establishing: that which is instituted or established: foundation: established order: enactment: a society or organisation established for some object, esp. cultural, charitable, or beneficent, or the building housing it: a custom or usage, esp. one familiar or characteristic: that which institutes or instructs (*obs.*): a system of principles or rules (*obs.*): appointment of an heir: the act by which a bishop commits a cure of souls to a priest.—*adj.* institu'tional, pertaining to institution, institutions, or institutes: of the

nature of an institution: depending on or originating in institution: characterised by the possession of institutions.—*v.t.* institu'tionalise, -ize, to make an institution of: to confine to an institution.— *ns.* institu'tionalism, the system or characteristics of institutions or institution life: belief in the nature of institutions; institu'tionalist, a writer on institutes: one who sets a high value of institutionalism.—*adj.* institu'tionary, institutional: educational (*obs.*).—*n.* in'stitūtist, a writer of institutes or elementary rules.—*adj.* in'stitūtive, able or tending to establish: depending on an institution.—*n.* in'stitūtor, one who institutes: instructor (*obs.*).—*institutional church,* one that is active through social organisations. [L. *instituēre, -ūtum—in,* in, *statuēre,* to cause to stand—*stāre,* to stand.]

**instreaming,** *in'strēm-ing, n.* an influx.—Also *adj.* [in, streaming.]

**instruct,** *in-strukt', v.t.* to prepare (*obs.*): to inform: to teach: to direct: (of a judge) to give (a jury) guidance concerning the legal issues of a case: to order or command.—*adj.* (*Milt.*) instructed.—*adj.* instruct'ible, able to be instructed.—*n.* instruc'tion, the art of instructing or teaching: information: direction: command: (in *pl.*) special directions, commands.—*adjs.* instruc'tional, relating to instruction: educational; instruc'tive, affording instruction: conveying knowledge.—*adv.* instruc'tively.—*ns.* instruc'tiveness; instruc'tor, a teacher: a college lecturer (*U.S.*):—*fem.* instruc'tress. [L. *instruēre, instructum—in,* in, *struēre,* to pile up.]

**instrument,** *in'strōō-mant, n.* a tool or utensil: a contrivance for producing musical sounds: a writing containing a contract: a formal record: one who, or that which, is made a means or agency: a term generally employed to denote an indicating device but also other pieces of small electrical apparatus.—*v.t.* (*-ment'*) to score for instruments: to equip with indicating, measuring, or control, etc., apparatus.—*adj.* for instruments: by means of instruments (as *instrument flight*).—*adj.* instrumental (*-ment'l*), acting as an instrument or means: serving to promote an object: helpful: of, for, belonging to, or produced by, musical instruments: serving to indicate the instrument or means (*gram.*).—*n.* the instrumental case.—*ns.* instrument'alism, a form of pragmatism associated with John Dewey; instrument'alist, one who plays on a musical instrument; instrumentality (*-ment-al'i-ti*), agency.—*adv.* instrument'ally.—*n.* instrumenta'tion, use or provision of instruments: the arrangement of a composition for performance by different instruments (*mus.*).—*adj.* instrumen'ted, equipped with electronic, etc., instruments. [L. *instrūmentum—instruēre,* to instruct; see instruct.]

**insubjection,** *in-səb-jek'shən, n.* want of subjection. [Pfx. in- (2).]

**insubordinate,** *in-səb-örd'(i-)nit, adj.* not subordinate or submissive.—*n.* insubordinā'tion. [Pfx. in- (2).]

**insubstantial,** *in-səb-stan'shəl, adj.* not substantial (*Shak.*): not real.—*n.* insubstantiality (*-shi-al'i-ti*). [Pfx. in- (2).]

**insucken,** *in'suk-n,* (*Scots law; hist.*) *adj.* pertaining to a sucken. [in, sucken.]

**insufferable,** *in-suf'ər-ə-bl, adj.* that cannot be endured: detestable.—*adv.* insuff'erably. [Pfx. in- (2).]

**insufficient,** *in-səf-ish'ənt, adj.* inadequate: lacking (*obs.*).—*ns.* insuffic'ience (*rare*), insuffic'iency.—*adv.* insuffic'iently. [Pfx. in- (2).]

**insufflate,** *in'suf-lāt* (or *-suf'*), *v.t.* to blow in: to breathe on.—*ns.* insufflā'tion, the act of breathing on anything, esp. in baptism or exorcism: the act of blowing air, powder, etc., into a cavity or on a surface; in'sufflātor, an instrument for

insufflation. [L. *insufflāre—in*, in, on, *sufflāre*, to blow upon.]
insula, *in'sū-lə* (L. *ēn'sŏŏ-la*), *n.* a block of buildings (*Rom. ant.*): an apartment house (*Rom. ant.*): Reil's island, a small lobe of the cerebrum hidden in the fissure of Sylvius (*anat.*).
—*ns.* in'sūlance, resistance between electric conductors separated by insulating material; in'sūlant, insulating material.—*adj.* in'sūlar, belonging to an island: surrounded by water: standing or situated alone: narrow, prejudiced. —*ns.* in'sūlarism, insūlarity (*-lar'i-ti*), the state of being insular.—*adv.* in'sūlarly.—*v.t.* in'sūlate, to place in a detached situation: to cut off from connection or communication: to separate, esp. from the earth, by a non-conductor (*elect.*).—*ns.* insūlā'tion; insūlā'tor, one who, or that which, insulates: a non-conductor of electricity: a contrivance for insulating a conductor: a stand for a piano leg; in'sūlin, an extract got from the islands or islets of Langerhans in the pancreas of animals, used for treating diabetes and also mental diseases.—insulating board (*build.*), fibreboard of low density used for thermal insulation and acoustical control; insulin shock, a state of collapse produced by an overdose of insulin. [L. *insula*, island.]
insulse, *in-suls'*, *adj.* insipid: stupid.—*n.* insul'sity (*Milt.*), stupidity. [L. *insulsus—in-*, not, *salēre*, to salt.]
insult, *in-sult'*, *v.t.* to assail (*obs.*): to triumph insolently or exultantly over: to treat with indignity or contempt: to affront.—*v.i.* (*obs.*) to make an attack: to behave with boastful insolence.—*n.* in'sult, abuse: affront: contumely. —*adjs.* insult'able, capable of being insulted; insult'ant (*rare*), insulting.—*n.* insult'er.—*adj.* insult'ing.—*adv.* insult'ingly.—*n.* insult'ment (*Shak.*), insult. [L. *insultāre—insilīre*, to spring at—*in*, upon, *salīre*, to leap.]
insuperable, *in-sū'pər-ə-bl, -sŏŏ'*, *adj.* that cannot be overcome or surmounted.—*n.* insuperabil'ity. —*adv.* insu'perably. [L. *insuperābilis—in-*, not, *superāre*, to pass over—*super*, above.]
insupportable, *in-səp-ōrt'ə-bl, -ört'*, *adj.* unbearable: not sustainable: (*-sup'*) irresistible (*Spens.*).—*n.* insupport'ableness.—*adv.* insupport'ably. [Pfx. in- (2).]
insuppressible, *in-sə-pres'i-bl, adj.* not to be suppressed or concealed.—*adj.* insuppress'ive (*Shak.*), insuppressible. [Pfx. in- (2).]
insure, *in-shŏŏr'*, *v.t.* to make sure or secure: to guarantee: to make an arrangement for the payment of a sum of money in the event of loss or injury to: to make such an arrangement for the payment of (a sum of money) (*arch.*).—*v.i.* to effect or undertake insurance.—*adj.* insur'able, that may be insured.—*ns.* insur'ance, the act or system of insuring: a contract of insurance, a policy: the premium paid for insuring: the sum to be received; insur'ancer (*obs.*); insur'ant, an insurance policy holder; insur'er, either party to a contract of insurance (now, strictly the insurance company). [O.Fr. *enseurer—en*, and *seur*, sure; see ensure, sure.]
insurgent, *in-sûr'jənt, adj.* rising: rushing in: rising in revolt.—*n.* one who rises in opposition to established authority: a rebel.—*ns.* insur'-gence, insur'gency, a rising up or against: rebellion: insurrection. [L. *insurgēns, -entis—in*, upon, *surgĕre*, to rise.]
insurmountable, *in-sər-mownt'ə-bl, adj.* not surmountable: that cannot be overcome.—*n.* insurmountabil'ity.—*adv.* insurmount'ably. [Pfx. in- (2).]
insurrection, *in-sər-ek'shən, n.* a rising or revolt.— *adjs.* insurrec'tional, insurrec'tionary.—*ns.* insurrec'tionary, insurrec'tionist. [L. *insurrēctiō, -ōnis—insurgĕre*; see insurgent.]
insusceptible, *in-səs-ep'ti-bl, adj.* not susceptible.

Also insuscep'tive.—*n.* insusceptibil'ity. [Pfx. in- (2).]
inswathe. Same as enswathe.
inswing, *in'swing, n.* an inward swing or swerve. —*n.* inswinger (*in'swing-ər*; cricket), a ball bowled so as to swerve to leg. [in, swing.]
intact, *in-takt', adj.* untouched: unimpaired: whole: undiminished.—*n.* intact'ness. [L. *intactus—in-*, not, *tangĕre, tactum*, to touch.]
intaglio, *in-täl'yō, n.* a figure cut into any substance: a stone or gem in which the design is hollowed out—opp. to *cameo*: a countersunk die: a method of printing in which the image area is sunk into the surface of the plate—opp. to *relief.*—Also *v.t.*—*adj.* intagl'iated, incised, engraved. (See cavo-rilievo.) [It.,—*in*, into, *tagliare*, to cut—L. *tālea*, a cutting, layer.]
intake, *in'tāk, n.* that which is taken in: a tract of land enclosed: an airway in a mine: a place where water is taken in: a narrowing in a pipe: decrease in width as in a stocking-leg by knitting two stitches together: the place where contraction occurs: the setting back of a wall-face: a body of people taken into an organisation, as new recruits, or new pupils at a school: the point at which fuel mixture enters the cylinder of an internal-combustion engine: a cheat or cheater (*dial.*). [in, take.]
intangible, *in-tan'ji-bl, adj.* not tangible or perceptible to touch: insubstantial: eluding the grasp of the mind.—*n.* something intangible, e.g. a supplementary asset such as goodwill.—*ns.* intan'gibleness, intangibil'ity.—*adv.* intan'gibly. [See intact.]
intarsia, *in-tär'si-ə*, intarsio, *-ō*, (It. *ēn-tär-sē'ä, -ō*), *n.* and *adj.* a form of decorative wood inlay work, developed in Italy during the 15th cent. [It. *intarsio*.]
integer, *in'ti-jər, n.* a whole: a whole number, as opposed to a fraction (*arith.*).—*adjs.* in'tegrable (*-grə-bl*), capable of being integrated; in'tegral (*-grəl*), entire or whole: not fractional: not involving fractions: relating to integrals: unimpaired: intrinsic, belonging as a part to the whole.—*n.* a whole: the whole as made up of its parts: the value of function of a variable whose differential coefficient is known (*math.*).—*adv.* in'tegrally.—*ns.* integral'ity, wholeness, integrity, completeness; in'tegrand, expression to be integrated.—*adj.* in'tegrant, making part of a whole: necessary to form an integer or an entire thing.—*v.t.* in'tegrate, to make up as a whole: to make entire: to find the integral of (*math.*): to find the total value of.—*v.i.* to become integral: to perform integration.—*adj.* made up of parts: complete: whole.—*n.* integrā'tion, act or process of integrating (*math.*): unification into a whole, e.g. of diverse elements in a community, as white and coloured: state of being integrated: formation of a unified personality (*psych.*); integrā'-tionist, one who favours integration of a community.—*adj.* in'tegrative, integrating: tending to integrate.—*ns.* in'tegrātor, one who integrates: an instrument for finding the results of integrations; integrity (*in-teg'ri-ti*), entireness, wholeness: the unimpaired state of anything: uprightness: honesty: purity.—integral calculus (see calculus); integral function (*alg.*), a function which does not include the operation of division in any of its terms; integrated circuit, a circuit consisting of an assembly of electronic elements in a single structure which cannot be subdivided without destroying its intended function. [L. *integer—in-*, not, root of *tangĕre*, to touch.]
integument, *in-teg'ū-mənt, n.* an external covering: either of the two coats of an ovule (*bot.*).—*adj.* integumentary (*-ment'ər-i*). [L. *integumentum—in*, upon, *tegĕre*, to cover.]
intellect, *int'i-lekt, n.* the mind, in reference to its rational powers: the thinking principle:

meaning (*Shak.*): (in *pl.*) mental powers (*arch.*).
—*adj.* in'tellected (*Cowper*), endowed with
intellect.—*n.* intellec'tion, the act of understanding: apprehension or perception (*phil.*).—
*adjs.* intellec'tive, able to understand: produced
or perceived by the understanding; intellectual
(-*lek'tū-al*), of or relating to the intellect: perceived or performed by the intellect: having the
power of understanding: well endowed with
intellect.—*n.* a person of superior intellect or
enlightenment (often used to suggest doubt as to
practical sagacity): intellect (*obs.*): (in *pl.*)
mental powers (*arch.*): (in *pl.*) things of the
intellect (*obs.*).—*v.t.* intellect'ualise, -ize, to
reason intellectually: to endow with intellect:
to give an intellectual character to.—*ns.* intellect'-
ualism, the doctrine that derives all knowledge
from pure reason: the culture (esp. exclusive or
unbalanced) of the intellect; intellect'ualist;
intellectuality (-*al'i-ti*), intellectual power.—*adv.*
intellect'ually. [L. *intellēctus*, -*ūs*—*intelligĕre*,
*intellēctum*, to understand—*inter*, between,
*legĕre*, to choose.]
intelligent, *in-tel'i-jənt*, *adj.* having intellect: endowed with the faculty of reason: alert, bright,
quick of mind: well-informed: cognisant:
bringing intelligence (*obs.*): communicative
(*Shak.*).—*ns.* intell'igence, intellectual skill or
knowledge: mental brightness: information
communicated: news: intelligence department:
a footing of mutual understanding (*rare*): a
spiritual being; intell'igencer, a spy: a news-
monger: an avenue of intelligence: a newspaper.
—*adj.* intelligential (-*jen'shl*), pertaining to the
intelligence: consisting of spiritual being.—*adv.*
intell'igently.—*adj.* intell'igible, that may be
understood: clear: capable of being apprehended by the understanding only, not by senses
(*phil.*).—*ns.* intell'igibleness, -igibil'ity.—*adv.*
intell'igibly.—intelligence (department, service),
department of state or armed service for securing
information; intelligence quotient, the ratio, commonly expressed as a percentage, of a person's
mental age to his actual age; intelligence test,
a test by questions and tasks to determine a
person's mental capacity, or the age at which his
capacity would be normal. [L. *intelligēns*, -*entis*,
pr.p. of *intelligĕre*.]
intelligentsia, intelligentzia, *in-tel-i-jent'si-ə*, or
-*gent'*, *n.* the intellectual or cultured classes,
originally esp. in Russia. [Russ.,—L. *intelli-
gentia.*]
Intelsat, *in-tel'sat*, *n.* a world-wide satellite
service dealing with communications such as
television exchange, business messages, etc.
intemperance, *in-tem'pər-əns*, *n.* want of due
restraint: excess of any kind: habitual over-
indulgence in intoxicating liquor.—*n.* intem'-
perant, one who is intemperate.—*adj.* intem'-
perate, indulging to excess in any appetite or
passion: given to an immoderate use of intoxicating liquors: passionate: exceeding the usual
degree: immoderate.—*adv.* intem'perately.—*n.*
intem'perateness. [L. *intemperans*, intemperate.]
intempestive, *in-tem-pest'iv*, *adj.* unseasonable:
untimely.—*n.* intempestiv'ity. [L. *intempestivus*
—*in-*, not, *tempestās*, season—*tempus*, time.]
intenable, *in-ten'ə-bl*, *adj.* untenable. [Pfx. in-
(2).]
intend, *in-tend'*, *v.t.* to stretch forth (*Spens.*):
to expand (*Milt.*): to strain (*obs.*): to intensify
(*obs.*): to direct, turn (*Shak.*): to fix the mind
upon: to design: to purpose: to mean: to
designate (*Spens.*): superintend (*arch.*).—*v.i.* to
direct one's course (*Shak.*): to purpose a
journey: to be in attendance (*obs.*): to attend,
listen (*obs.*).—*ns.* intend'ancy, the office, term of
office, or sphere of an intendant: a body of
intendants; intend'ant, an officer who superintends some public business, a title of many

public officers in France and other countries.—
*adj.* intend'ed, purposed: stretched (*obs.*).—
*n.* (*coll.*) betrothed.—*adv.* intend'edly, with intention or design.—*ns.* intend'iment (*Spens.*),
attentive consideration, understanding, meaning;
intend'ment (*Shak.*), intention, design: meaning.
[O.Fr. *entendre*—L. *intendĕre*, *intentum* and
*intēnsum*—*in*, towards, *tendĕre*, to stretch.]
intenerate, *in-ten'ər-āt*, *v.t.* to make tender: to
soften.—*n.* intenerā'tion. [L. *in*, in, to, *tener*,
tender.]
intenible, *in-ten'i-bl*, (*Shak.*) *adj.* irretentive. [L.
*in-*, not, *tenēre*, to hold.]
intense, *in-tens'*, *adj.* strained: concentrated,
dense: extreme in degree: (of person, manner,
etc.) earnestly or deeply emotional, or affecting
to have deep feeling: of a photographic negative, opaque.—*v.t.* intens'ate (*Carlyle*), to intensify.—*adv.* intense'ly.—*ns.* and *adjs.* intens'-
ative, intens'itive, intensive.—*n.* intense'ness,
intens'ity; intensificā'tion, the act of intensifying;
intens'ifier.—*v.t.* intens'ify, to make more intense.—*v.i.* to become intense:—*pr.p.* intens'ifying; *pa.t.* and *pa.p.* intens'ified.—*n.* intension
(-*ten'shən*), straining: intentness: intensity:
intensification: the sum of the qualities implied
by a general name (*logic*).—*adj.* intens'ive,
concentrated, intense: strained: unremitting:
relating to intensity or to intension: intensifying:
intensified: giving force or emphasis (*gram.*).
—*n.* an intensive word.—*adv.* intens'ively.—*n.*
intens'iveness.—intensive culture, getting the very
most out of the soil of a limited area.—intensive
care unit, an area in a hospital where a patient's
condition is carefully monitored. [See intend.]
intent, *in-tent'*, *adj.* having the mind bent: fixed
with close attention: diligently applied.—*n.* the
thing aimed at or intended: purpose, intention,
design: intentness (*obs.*): meaning (*obs.*).—*n.*
intention (*in-ten'shən*), application or direction
of the mind (*obs.*): design: purpose: application of thought to an object: a concept: a plan
of treatment (*med.*): (in *pl.*) purpose with respect
to marriage (*coll.*).—*adj.* inten'tional, with
intention: intended: designed.—*adv.* inten'-
tionally, with intention: on purpose.—*adjs.*
inten'tioned, having such and such intention;
intent'ive (*Bacon*), attentive.—*adv.* intent'ly,
earnestly: diligently.—*n.* intent'ness.—healing
by first intention, healing of a wound by immediate union, without granulation; by second
intention, with granulation; to all intents (and
purposes), in every important respect: virtually:
well- (or ill-) intentioned, having good (or ill)
designs: meaning well (or ill). [See intend.]
inter, *in-tûr'*, *v.t.* to bury:—*pr.p.* interr'ing; *pa.t.*
and *pa.p.* interred'.—*n.* inter'ment, burial. [Fr.
*enterrer*—L.L. *interrāre*—L. *in*, into, *terra*, the
earth.]
inter-, *in'tər-*, *in-tûr'*, *pfx.* between, among, in
the midst of: mutual, reciprocal: together. [L.
*inter*.]
inter alia, *in'tər*, -*ter*, *ā'li-ə*, *a'li-a*, (L.) among
other things; inter alios (*ā'li-ōs*, *a'li-ōs*), among
other persons; inter nos (*nōs*), between ourselves; inter pocula (*pok'ū-lə*, -*oō-la*), over one's
cups; inter se (*sē*, *sā*), amongst themselves;
inter vivos (*vīv'ōs*, *wē'wōs*; *law*), from one
living person to another.
interact, *in'tər-akt*, *n.* an interlude: an entr'acte:
the interval between acts.—*v.i.* interact' to act
on one another.—*ns.* interaction (-*ak'shən*),
mutual action; interac'tionism, the theory that
mind and body act on each other (distinguished
from *psychophysical parallelism* and *epipheno-
menalism*); interac'tionist.—*adj.* interac'tive.
[Pfx. inter-.]
interallied, *in-tər-al'īd*, or -*id'*, *adj.* between or
among allies. [Pfx. inter-.]
interambulacrum, *in-tər-am-bū-lā'krəm*, *n.* in sea-

urchins, a radial band between two ambulacra:
—*pl.* interambulā'cra.—*adj.* interambulā'cral.
[Pfx. inter-.]
inter-arts, *in'tər-ärts'*, *adj.* belonging to the
examination between matriculation and B.A. of
London University. [For intermediate arts.]
interbedded, *in-tər-bed'id*, *adj.* interstratified.—*n.*
interbedd'ing. [Pfx. inter-.]
interbreed, *in-tər-brēd'*, *v.t.* and *v.i.* to breed together, esp. of different races:—*pa.t.* and *pa.p.*
interbred'.—*n.* interbreed'ing. [Pfx. inter-.]
intercalate, *in-tûr'kə-lāt*, *v.t.* to insert between
others, as a day in a calendar: to interpolate.—
*adjs.* inter'calar (-*lər; obs.*), inter'calary, inserted
between others.—*n.* intercalā'tion.—*adj.* inter'-
calative (-*lā-tiv*, -*lə-tiv*). [L. *intercalāre*, -*ātum*—
*inter*, between, *calāre*, to proclaim; see calends.]
intercede, *in-tər-sēd'*, *v.i.* to act as peacemaker
between two: to plead (for one).—*adj.* intercēd'ent.—*n.* intercēd'er. [L. *intercēdēre*, -*cēssum*
—*inter*, between, *cēdēre*, to go.]
intercellular, *in-tər-sel'ū-lər*, (*biol.*) *adj.* placed
among cells. [Pfx. inter-.]
intercensal, *in-tər-sen'səl*, *adj.* between censuses.
[Irreg., formed from L. *inter* and census.]
intercept, *in-tər-sept'*, *v.t.* to stop and seize in
passage: to cut off: to take or comprehend
between (*math.*).—*ns.* in'tercept (*math.*), that
part of a line that is intercepted; intercep'ter,
intercep'tor, one who or that which intercepts:
a light, swift aeroplane for pursuit; intercep'-
tion.—*adj.* intercep'tive. [L. *intercipēre*, -*ceptum*
—*inter*, between, *capēre*, to seize.]
intercession, *in-tər-sesh'ən*, *n.* act of interceding or
pleading for another.—*adj.* intercess'ional.—*n.*
intercessor (-*ses'ər*), one who intercedes: a
bishop who acts during a vacancy in a see.—
*adjs.* intercessō'rial (-*ōr'*, -*ör'*), intercess'ory,
interceding.—intercession of saints, prayer
offered on behalf of Christians on earth by
saints. [See intercede.]
interchain, *in-tər-chān'*, *v.t.* to chain together.
[Pfx. inter-.]
interchange, *in-tər-chānj'*, *v.t.* to give and take
mutually: to exchange.—*v.i.* to succeed alternately.—*n.* in'terchange, mutual exchange:
alternate succession.—*adj.* interchange'able, that
may be interchanged: following each other in
alternate succession (*obs.*).—*ns.* interchange'-
ableness, interchangeabil'ity.—*adv.* interchange'-
ably.—*ns.* interchange'ment (*Shak.*), exchange,
mutual transfer; interchang'er. [Pfx. inter-.]
interchapter, *in'tər-chap-tər*, *n.* an intercalary
chapter in a book, not numbered in the general
sequence. [Pfx. inter-.]
intercipient, *in-tər-sip'i-ənt*, (*obs.*) *adj.* intercepting.
—*n.* the person or thing that intercepts. [L.
*intercipiēns*, -*entis*, pr.p. of *intercipēre*; see
intercept.]
intercity, *in-tər-sit'i*, *adj.* between cities. [Pfx.
inter-.]
interclavicular, *in-tər-klə-vik'ū-lər*, *adj.* situated
between clavicles. [Pfx. inter-.]
interclude, *in-tər-klōōd'*, *v.t.* to block: to enclose:
to cut off.—*n.* interclusion (-*klōō'zhən*). [L.
*interclūdēre*—*inter*, between, *claudēre*, to shut.]
intercollegiate, *in-tər-kə-lē'ji-āt*, -*ət*, *adj.* between
colleges. [Pfx. inter-.]
intercolline, *in-tər-kol'in*, *adj.* lying between hills.
[Pfx. inter-.]
intercolonial, *in-tər-kə-lō'ni-əl*, *adj.* between
colonies.—*adv.* intercolo'nially. [Pfx. inter-.]
intercolumniation, *in-tər-kə-lum-ni-ā'shən*, (*archit.*)
*n.* spacing of, or distance between, columns,
measured in terms of the lower diameter.—*adj.*
intercolum'nar, placed between columns. [Pfx.
inter-.]
intercom, *in'tər-kom*, *n.* a telephone system
within a building, aeroplane, tank, etc. [*Internal*
communication.]

intercommune, *in-tər-kə-mūn'*, *v.i.* to commune
mutually or together: to hold intercourse, have
dealings.—*adj.* intercommun'icable.—*v.t.* and *v.i.*
intercommun'icāte, to communicate mutually or
together: to have free passage from one to
another.—*ns.* intercommunicā'tion; intercommun'ion, mutual communion or relation, esp.
between churches; intercommun'ity, state of
being or having in common.—letters of inter-
communing, an ancient writ issued by the
Scottish Privy Council warning persons not to
harbour or have any dealings with those named,
on pain of being held accessory. [Pfx. inter-.]
interconnect, *in-tər-kə-nekt'*, *v.t.* to connect
mutually and intimately, or by a multitude of
ways.—*v.i.* to be mutually connected.—*n.* inter-
connec'tion, interconnex'ion. [Pfx. inter-.]
intercontinental, *in-tər-kon-ti-nen'tal*, *adj.* between
or connecting different continents. [Pfx. inter-.]
interconvertible, *in-tər-kən-vûrt'i-bl*, *adj.* mutually
convertible: interchangeable: exactly equivalent. [Pfx. inter-.]
intercostal, *in-tər-kost'əl*, *adj.* between the ribs or
the leaf-veins. [L. *inter*, between, *costa*, a rib.]
intercourse, *in-tər-kōrs*, -*körs*, *n.* connection by
dealings: communication: commerce: communion: coition. [O.Fr. *entrecours*—L. *inter-
cursus*, a running between—*inter*, between,
*currēre*, *cursum*, to run.]
intercrop, *in-tər-krop'*, *v.t.* and *v.i.* to grow or
cultivate in alternate rows:—*pr.p.* intercropp'ing;
*pa.t.* and *pa.p.* intercropped'.—*n.* in'tercrop.
[Pfx. inter-.]
intercross, *in-tər-kros'*, *v.t.* and *v.i.* to cross and
recross: to cross mutually: to place or lie crosswise: to interbreed.—*n.* in'tercross, a crossing of
breeds. [Pfx. inter-.]
intercrural, *in-tər-krōōr'əl*, *adj.* situated between
the crura or legs. [Pfx. inter-.]
intercurrent, *in-tər-kur'ənt*, *adj.* running between,
intervening: supervening.—*n.* intercurr'ence.
[L. *inter*, between, *currēre*, to run.]
interdash, *in-tər-dash'*, *v.t.* to intersperse with
dashes. [Pfx. inter-.]
interdeal, *in'tər-dēl*, (*arch.*) *n.* mutual dealings:
intercourse: negotiations.—Also (*Spens.*) enterdeale.—*v.i.* interdeal' (*arch.*), to have mutual
dealings.—*n.* interdeal'er. [Pfx. inter-.]
interdenominational, *in-tər-di-nom-i-nāsh'(ə-)nl*,
*adj.* common to, with participation of, various
religious denominations: independent of denomination. [Pfx. inter-.]
interdental, *in-tər-dent'əl*, *adj.* between the teeth:
pronounced with the tip of the tongue between
upper and lower teeth.—*adv.* interdent'ally. [Pfx.
inter-.]
interdepartmental, *in-tər-dē-pärt-ment'l*, *adj.* between departments.—*adv.* interdepartment'ally.
[Pfx. inter-.]
interdependence, *in-tər-di-pend'əns*, *n.* mutual
dependence: dependence of parts one on
another.—*adj.* interdepend'ent. [Pfx. inter-.]
interdict, *in-tər-dikt'*, *v.t.* to prohibit: to forbid
to forbid communion.—*n.* in'terdict, prohibition:
a prohibitory decree: a prohibition of the pope
restraining the clergy from performing divine
service.—*n.* interdic'tion (-*shən*).—*adjs.* interdic'tive, interdic'tory, containing interdiction:
prohibitory. [L. *interdīcēre*, -*dictum*—*inter*,
between, *dicēre*, to say.]
interdigital, *in-tər-dij'i-tl*, *adj.* between digits.—
*v.t.* and *v.i.* interdig'itate, to interlock by finger-
like processes.—*n.* interdigitā'tion. [Pfx. inter-.]
interdine, *in-tər-din'*, *v.i.* to eat together. [Pfx.
inter-.]
interess, interesse, *in'tər-es*, or -*es'*, (*obs.*) *n.*
interest.—*v.t.* to interest:—*pa.p.* (*Shak.*) interest'.
[A.Fr. *interesse*—L.L. *interesse*, compensation,
interest—L. *interesse* (inf.), to concern.]
interest, *int'(ə-)rest*, -*rist*, *n.* advantage, benefit:

Neutral vowels in unaccented syllables: *el'ə-mənt*; for certain sounds in foreign words, see p. viii

premium paid for the use of money: any increase: concern, importance: personal influence: a right to some advantage: claim to participate or be concerned in some way: stake: share: behalf: partisanship or side: the body of persons whose advantage is bound up in anything: regard to advantage: a state of engaged attention and curiosity: disposition towards such a state: power of arousing it: that in which one has interest or is interested.—*v.t.* to concern deeply: to cause to have an interest: to engage the attention of: to awaken concern in: to excite (on behalf of another).—*adj.* in'terested, having an interest or concern: affected or biased by personal considerations, self-interest, etc.—*adv.* in'terestedly.—*n.* in'terestedness.—*adj.* in'teresting (old-fashioned *-est'*), engaging or apt to engage the attention or regard: exciting emotion or passion.—*adv.* in'terestingly.—*n.* in'terestingness.—compound interest (see compound); in an interesting condition, state, situation, oldfashioned euphemisms for pregnant; in the interest(s) of, with a view to furthering or to helping; make interest for, secure favour for. [From **interess**, influenced by O.Fr. *interest*, L. *interest*, it concerns, 3rd pers. sing. pres. ind. of *interesse—inter*, between, among, and *esse*, to be.]

**interface**, in'tər-fās, *n.* a surface forming a common boundary: the surface of separation between phases (*chem.*).—*adj.* **interfacial** (*-fā'shl*), between plane faces: of an interface. [Pfx. **inter-**.]

**interfascicular**, in-tər-fə-sik'ū-lər, *adj.* between vascular bundles. [Pfx. **inter-**.]

**interfemoral**, in-tər-fem'ər-əl, *adj.* situated between the thighs, connecting the hind limbs. [Pfx. **inter-**.]

**interfenestration**, in-tər-fen-is-trā'shən, *n.* spacing of windows. [L. *inter*, between, *fenestra*, a window.]

**interfere**, in-tər-fēr', *v.i.* (of horse) to strike foot against opposite leg in walking: to intervene: to come in the way: to interpose: to intermeddle: to act reciprocally—said of waves, rays of light, etc.—*n.* interfer'ence, the act of interfering: the effect of combining similar rays of light, etc.: the spoiling of a wireless or television signal by others or by natural disturbances.—*adj.* interferential (*-fər-en'shl*).—*n.* interfer'er.—*adv.* interfer'ingly.—*n.* interfêrom'eter, an instrument which, by observing interference fringes, makes precision measurements, mainly of wavelengths.—*adj.* interfêromet'ric.—*ns.* interfêrom'etry; interfer'on, a protein produced naturally in the body, active against many viruses.—interference figure, a figure observed when a crystal section is viewed between crossed nicols; interference fringes, alternate light and dark bands seen when similar beams of light interfere; interfere with, to meddle in: to get in the way of, hinder: to assault sexually. [O.Fr. *entreférir* —L. *inter*, between, *ferire*, to strike.]

**interflow**, in'tər-flō, *n.* intermingling.—*v.i.* interflow', to flow into one another or between. [Pfx. **inter-**.]

**interfluent**, in-tûr'floo-ənt, *adj.* flowing between or together.—Also **inter'fluous**.—*n.* inter'fluence. [L. *interfluēns*, *-entis—inter*, between, *fluēre*, to flow.]

**interfold**, in-tər-fōld', *v.t.* to fold one into the other. [Pfx. **inter-**.]

**interfoliate**, in-tər-fō'li-āt, *v.t.* to interleave. [L. *inter*, between, *folium*, a leaf.]

**interfretted**, in-tər-fret'id, (*her.*) *adj.* interlaced. [Pfx. **inter-**.]

**interfrontal**, in-tər-frun'tl, *-fron'tl, adj.* between the frontal bones. [Pfx. **inter-**.]

**interfuse**, in-tər-fūz', *v.t.* to pour between or through: to permeate: to fuse together: to

**associate.**—*v.i.* to fuse together: to blend.—*n.* **interfusion** (*-fū'zhən*). [Pfx. **inter-**.]

**intergalactic**, in-tər-gal-ak'tik, *adj.* between, or among, galaxies. [Pfx. **inter-**.]

**intergatory**, in-tûr'gə-tə-ri, (*obs.*; *usu.* in *pl.*) *n.* a shortened form of **interrogatory**. [Pfx. **inter-**.]

**interglacial**, in-tər-glā'sh(y)əl, (*geol.*) *adj.* occurring between two periods of glacial action.

**Interglossa**, in'tər-glos'ə, *n.* an international language largely based on well-known Greek roots, devised by Lancelot Hogben (1943). [L. *inter*, between, Gr. *glōssa*, tongue.]

**intergrade**, in-tər-grād', *v.i.* to merge in or shade off into something else through a series of intermediate forms.—*n.* in'tergrade, an intermediate grade.—*n.* intergradation (*-grə-dā'shən*). [Pfx. **inter-**.]

**intergrow**, in-tər-grō', *v.t.* to grow into or among each other.—*adj.* intergrown'.—*n.* in'tergrowth. [Pfx. **inter-**.]

**interim**, in'tər-im, *n.* the time between or intervening: the meantime: (*cap.*) in the history of the Reformation, the name given to certain edicts of the German emperor for the regulation of religious and ecclesiastical matters, till they could be decided by a general council—as the Augsburg Interim (1548), etc.—*adj.* temporary.—*adv.* (*rare*), meanwhile. [L.]

**interior**, in-tē'ri-ər, *adj.* inner: remote from the frontier or coast: inland: situated within or further in (sometimes with *to*): devoted to mental or spiritual life.—*n.* the inside of anything: the inland part of a country: a picture of a scene within a house: home affairs of a country: inner nature or character.—*n.* interiority (*-or'i-ti*).—*adv.* inter'iorly.—interior decoration, design, the construction and furnishing of the interior of a building; interior grate, an open grate with built-in boiler. [L., comp. of assumed *interus*, inward.]

**interjacent**, in-tər-jā'sənt, *adj.* lying between: intervening.—*n.* interjā'cency. [L. *interjacēns*, *-entis*, pr.p. of *interjacēre—inter*, between, *jacēre*, to lie.]

**interjaculate**, in-tər-jak'ū-lāt, *v.t.* to ejaculate in interruption.—*adj.* interjac'ulatory (*-ū-lə-tə-ri*). [L. *inter*, between, *jaculāri*, to throw.]

**interject**, in-tər-jekt', *v.t.* to throw between: to interpose: to exclaim in interruption or parenthesis: to insert.—*v.i.* to throw oneself between. —*n.* interjec'tion (*-shən*), a throwing between: a word thrown in to express emotion (*gram.*).—*adjs.* interjec'tional, interjec'tionary, interjec'tural.—*adv.* interjec'tionally. [L. *inter(j)icēre*, *interjectum—inter*, between, *jacēre*, to throw.]

**interjoin**, in-tər-join', (*Shak.*) *v.t.* to join together. [Pfx. **inter-**.]

**interknit**, in-tər-nit', *v.t.* to knit into each other. [Pfx. **inter-**.]

**interlace**, in-tər-lās', *v.t.* to lace, weave, or entangle together.—*v.i.* to intermix.—*n.* interlace'ment.—interlaced scanning, in television, the alternate scanning of an image in two sets of alternate lines. [Pfx. **inter-**.]

**interlard**, in-tər-lärd', *v.t.* to mix in, as fat with lean: to diversify by mixture. [Pfx. **inter-**.]

**interleave**, in-tər-lēv', *v.t.* to put a leaf between: to insert blank leaves in.—*n.* in'terleaf, a leaf so inserted:—*pl.* in'terleaves. [Pfx. **inter-**.]

**interline**, in-tər-līn', *v.t.* to write in alternate lines: to insert between lines: to write between the lines of.—*adj.* **interlinear** (*-lin'i-ər*), written between lines.—*ns.* interlineation (*-lin-i-ā'shən*), interlin'ing. [Pfx. **inter-**.]

**Interlingua**, in-tər-ling'gwə, *n.* an international language based on the living Latin roots in European languages. [L. *inter*, between, *lingua*, tongue.]

**interlink**, in-tər-lingk', *v.t.* and *v.i.* to link together. [Pfx. **inter-**.]

**interlobular**, *in-tǝr-lob'ū-lǝr*, *adj.* between lobes. [Pfx. **inter-**.]

**interlocation**, *in-tǝr-lō-kā'shǝn*, *n.* a placing between. [Pfx. **inter-**.]

**interlock**, *in-tǝr-lok'*, *v.t.* to lock or clasp together: to connect so as to work together.—*v.i.* to be locked together.—*n.* in'terlock, an interlocked condition: synchronising mechanism. [Pfx. **inter-**.]

**interlocution**, *in-tǝr-lo-kū'shǝn*, *n.* conference: an intermediate decree before final decision.—*n.* **interlocutor** (*-lok'ū-tǝr*), one who speaks in dialogue: a judge's decree (*Scots law*).—*adj.* **interloc'utory**.—*ns.* **interloc'utress, interloc'utrice, interloc'utrix**, a female interlocutor. [L. *interlocūtiō, -ōnis—inter*, between, *loqui, locūtus*, to speak.]

**interloper**, *in'tǝr-lō-pǝr*, *n.* one who trades without licence: an intruder.—*v.t.* and *v.t.* **interlope'** (or *in'*), to intrude into any matter in which one has no fair concern. [Prob. L. *inter*, between, and **lope**.]

**interlude**, *in'tǝr-lōōd, -lūd, n.* a short piece introduced between the acts of the mysteries and moralities, etc., unconnected with the main theme and light in character: an early form of modern drama: a short piece of music played between the parts of a drama opera, hymn, etc.: an interval, any period of time or any happening different in character from what comes before or after.—*v.t.* and *v.i.* to interrupt, as an interlude.—*adj.* **interlu'dial.** [L. *inter*, between, *lūdus*, play.]

**interlunar**, *in-tǝr-lōō'nǝr, -lū'*, *adj.* belonging to the moon's monthly time of invisibility.—Also **interlu'nary**.—*n.* **interlunā'tion** (*-lōō-*), the dark time between old moon and new. [L. *inter*, between, *lūna*, the moon.]

**intermarry**, *in-tǝr-mar'i*, *v.i.* to marry, esp. of different races or groups, or of near kin: to mingle by repeated marriages.—*n.* **intermarr'iage**. [Pfx. **inter-**.]

**intermaxilla**, *in-tǝr-maks-il'ǝ*, *n.* the premaxilla.—*adj.* **intermax'illary** (or *-il'*), of the intermaxilla: between the maxillaries.—*n.* the intermaxilla. [L. *inter*, between, *maxilla*, a jawbone.]

**intermeddle**, *in-tǝr-med'l*, *v.i.* to meddle: to interfere improperly.—*n.* **intermedd'ler**. [Pfx. **inter-**.]

**intermediate**, *in-tǝr-mē'dyit, -di-it, adj.* placed, occurring, or classified between others, extremes, limits, or stages: of igneous rocks, between acid and basic in composition: intervening.—*n.* that which is intermediate: any compound manufactured from a primary that serves as a starting material for the synthesis of some other product (*chem.*).—*v.i.* (*-di-āt*) to interpose: to act between others.—*n.* **intermē'diacy** (*-ǝ-si*), state of being intermediate.—*adjs.* **intermē'dial** (*rare*), intermediate: intermediary; **intermē'diary**, acting between others: intermediate.—*n.* an intermediate agent.—*adv.* **intermē'diately**.—*ns.* **intermēdiā'tion**, act of intermediating; **intermē'diātor**.—*adj.* **intermē'diatory** (*-ǝ-tǝ-ri*).—*n.* **intermē'dium**, an intervening agent or instrument. [Pfx. **inter-**.]

**interment**. See **inter** (1).

**intermezzo**, *in-tǝr-met'sō*, sometimes *-med'zō, n.* a short dramatic or musical entertainment as entr'acte: a short intermediate movement or the like (*mus.*):—*pl.* **intermez'zi** (*-zē*), or *-os*. [It.,—L. *intermedius*.]

**intermigration**, *in-tǝr-mi-grā'shǝn, n.* reciprocal migration. [Pfx. **inter-**.]

**interminable**, *in-tûr'min-ǝ-bl*, **interminate**, *in-tûr'min-āt, -it, adjs.* without termination or limit: boundless: endless.—*n.* **inter'minableness**.—*adv.* **inter'minably**.—**interminate decimal**, a decimal fraction that runs to an infinity of places. [Pfx. **in-** (2).]

**intermingle**, *in-tǝr-ming'gl*, *v.t.* and *v.i.* to mingle or mix together. [Pfx. **inter-**.]

**intermit**, *in-tǝr-mit'*, *v.t.* and *v.i.* to stop for a time. —*v.t.* (*obs.*) to interpose.—*n.* **intermission** (*-mish'ǝn*), act of intermitting: interval: music played during a theatre or similar interval: pause: respite: perh., occupation, recreation interposed, something to do (*Shak.*).—*adj.* **intermissive** (*-mis'iv*), coming and going: intermittent.—*ns.* **intermitt'ence; intermitt'ency**.— *adj.* **intermitt'ent**, intermitting or ceasing at intervals.—*advs.* **intermitt'ently; intermitt'ingly**. [L. *intermittĕre*, *-missum—inter*, between, *mittĕre*, to cause to go.]

**intermix**, *in-tǝr-miks'*, *v.t.* and *v.i.* to mix together. —*n.* **intermix'ture**, a mass formed by mixture: something added and intermixed. [L. *intermiscēre*, *-mixtum—inter*, among, *miscēre*, to mix.]

**intermolecular**, *in-tǝr-mol-ek'ū-lǝr*, *adj.* between molecules. [Pfx. **inter-**.]

**intermundane**, *in-tǝr-mun'dān, adj.* between worlds. [Pfx. **inter-**.]

**intermure**, *in-tǝr-mūr'*, (*obs.*) *v.t.* to wall in. [L. *inter*, within, *mūrus*, a wall.]

**intern, interne**, *in-tûrn'*, *adj.* internal.—*n.* an inmate, as of a boarding-school: a resident assistant surgeon or physician in a hospital (*U.S.*).—*v.t.* to send into the interior of a country: to confine within fixed bounds without permission to leave the district, camp, port, or like limits.—*ns.* **internee'**, one so restricted; **intern'-ment**, confinement of this kind. [Fr. *interne*—L. *internus*, inward.]

**internal**, *in-tûr'nǝl, adj.* in the interior: domestic as opposed to foreign: intrinsic: pertaining to the inner nature or feelings—opp. to *external*.—*n.* (in *pl.*) inner parts.—*n.* **internality** (*-nal'i-ti*).— *adv.* **inter'nally**.—**internal evidence**, evidence afforded by the thing itself; **internal student**, one who has studied at the university that examines him.—**internal-combustion engine**, an engine in which the fuel is burned within the working cylinder. [L. *internus—inter*, within.]

**international**, *in-tǝr-nash'ǝn-ǝl, adj.* between nations or their representatives: transcending national limits: extending to several nations: pertaining to the relations between nations.—*n.* (*cap.*) a short-lived association formed in London in 1864 to unite the working classes of all countries in efforts for their economic emancipation: (*cap.*) a second organisation of socialists of all countries formed in 1889 as a successor to the first International—also (Fr.) **Internationale**: (*cap.*) a rival organisation (third International) operating from Moscow from 1919 to 1943: a game or contest between players chosen to represent different nations (*coll.*): a player who takes (or has taken) part in an international match.—*n.* **Internationale** (*ĕ-ter-na-syō-näl'*), an international communist song, composed in France in 1871.—*v.t.* **interna'tionalise, -ize**, to make international: to put under international control.—*ns.* **interna'tionalism; interna'tionalist**, one who favours the common interests, or action, of all nations: one who favours the principles of the International: one who represents his country in international contests: a specialist in international law.—*adv.* **interna'tionally**.—**international law**, the law regulating the relations of states (**public international law**), or that determining what nation's law shall in any case govern the relations of private persons (**private international law**); **international pitch**, since 1939, 440 cycles per second at 20°C for A in the treble clef; **international units**, internationally recognised units in terms of which pure, or impure, vitamin material can be assayed.— **International Bible Students' Association** (see **Russellite**); **international match point**, a scoring unit in tournament contract bridge; **international**

standard atmosphere, a standardised atmosphere adopted internationally for comparing aircraft performance; **international system of units** (see S.I. units); **international temperature scale**, a scale differing slightly from the absolute (thermodynamic) scale, with fixed points ranging from −182·970° Celsius, the boiling-point of oxygen, to 1063·0° Celsius, the freezing-point of gold. [Pfx. inter-.]
**internecine**, *in-tər-nē′sin*, *adj.* deadly: murderous: loosely, mutually destructive: involving conflict within a group.—Also **interne′cive**. [L. *internecīnus*, *-īvus*—*internecāre*—*inter*, between (used intensively), *necāre*, to kill.]
**internee**. See intern.
**interneural**, *in-tər-nū′rəl*, (*anat.*) *adj.* situated between the neural spines or spinous processes of successive vertebrae. [Pfx. inter-.]
**internode**, *in′tər-nōd*, *n.* the space between two nodes.—*adjs.* **interno′dal**, **internō′dial** (*obs.*). [L. *internōdium*—*inter*, between, *nōdus*, a knot.]
**internuncio**, *in-tər-nun′shi-ō*, *n.* a messenger between two parties: the Pope's representative at minor courts.—*adj.* **internun′cial**, relating to an internuncio: interconnecting, as the neurone linking the afferent and efferent neurones of the central nervous system. [It. *internunzio*, Sp. *internuncio*, L. *internuntius*—*inter*, between, *nuntius*, a messenger.]
**interoceanic**, *in-tər-ō-shi-an′ik*, *adj.* between oceans. [Pfx. inter-.]
**interocular**, *in-tər-ok′ū-lər*, *adj.* between the eyes. [Pfx. inter-.]
**interorbital**, *in-tər-ör′bit-əl*, *adj.* between the orbits. [Pfx. inter-.]
**interosculation**, *in-tər-os-kū-lā′shən*, *n.* interconnection by, or as if by, osculation: possession of characters common to different groups: dovetailing into one another.—*adj.* **interos′culant**.—*v.t.* **interos′culate**. [Pfx. inter-.]
**interosseous**, *in-tər-os′i-əs*, *adj.* situated between bones.—Also **inteross′eal**. [Pfx. inter-.]
**interpage**, *in-tər-pāj′*, *v.t.* to insert on intermediate pages. [Pfx. inter-.]
**interparietal**, *in-tər-pə-rī′ə-təl*, *adj.* situated between the right and left parietal bones of the skull. [Pfx. inter-.]
**interpellation**, *in-tər-pel-ā′shən*, *n.* a question raised during the course of a debate: interruption (*obs.*): intercession (*obs.*): a summons (*obs.*).—*v.t.* **inter′pellate** (or *-pel′*), to question by interpellation. [Fr.,—L. *interpellāre*, *-ātum*, to disturb by speaking—*inter*, between, *pellēre*, to drive.]
**interpenetrate**, *in-tər-pen′i-trāt*, *v.t.* to penetrate thoroughly.—*v.t.* and *v.i.* to penetrate mutually.—*n.* **interpenetrā′tion**.—*adj.* **interpen′etrātive**. [Pfx. inter-.]
**interpetiolar**, *in-tər-pet′i-ō-lər*, (*bot.*) *adj.* between the petioles. [Pfx. inter-.]
**interphase**, *in′tər-fāz*, *n.* an interface (*chem.*): an interval between stages of mitosis (*biol.*). [Pfx. inter-.]
**interphone**, *in′tər-fōn*, *n.* intercom. [Gr. *phōnē*, voice.]
**interpilaster**, *in-tər-pil-as′tər*, (*archit.*) *n.* space between two pilasters. [Pfx. inter-.]
**interplanetary**, *in-tər-plan′it-ə-ri*, *adj.* between planets. [Pfx. inter-.]
**interplant**, *in-tər-plänt′*, *v.t.* to plant among another crop. [Pfx. inter-.]
**interplay**, *in′tər-plā*, *n.* mutual action: interchange of action and reaction. [Pfx. inter-.]
**interplead**, *in-tər-plēd′*, (*law*) *v.i.* to discuss adverse claims to property by bill of interpleader.—*n.* **interplead′er**, one who interpleads: a form of process in the English courts, by a bill in equity, intended to protect a defendant who claims no interest in the subject matter of a suit, while at the same time he has reason to know

that the plaintiff's title is disputed by some other claimant. [Pfx. inter-.]
**interpleural**, *in-tər-plōō′rəl*, *adj.* situated between the right and left pleural cavities. [Pfx. inter-.]
**Interpol**, *in′tər-pol*, the *Inter*national Criminal *Pol*ice Commission, directed to international co-operation in the suppression of crime.
**interpolar**, *in-tər-pō′lər*, *adj.* between or connecting the poles. [Pfx. inter-.]
**interpolate**, *in-tûr′pō-lāt*, *-pə-lāt*, *v.t.* to insert unfairly, as a spurious word or passage in a book or manuscript: to tamper with, to corrupt by spurious insertions: to insert, intercalate, interject: to fill in as an intermediate term of a series (*math.*).—*adj.* **inter′polable**.—*n.* **interpolā′tion**.—*adj.* **inter′polātive**.—*n.* **inter′polātor**. [L. *interpolāre*, *-ātum*—*inter*, between, *polīre*, to polish.]
**interpone**, *in-tər-pōn′*, (*Scots law*) *v.t.* to interpose. [L. *interpōnere*.]
**interpose**, *in-tər-pōz′*, *v.t.* to place between: to thrust in: to offer, as aid or services: to put in by way of interruption.—*v.i.* to come between: to mediate: to interfere.—*ns.* **interpos′al**; **interpos′er**; **interposition** (*in-tər-poz-ish′ən*), act of interposing: intervention: mediation: in U.S., the right of a state to oppose the federal government for encroachment on the prerogatives of the state: anything interposed. [Fr. *interposer*—L. *inter*, between, Fr. *poser*, to place; see pose.]
**interpret**, *in-tûr′prit*, *v.t.* to explain the meaning of, to elucidate, unfold, show the purport of: to translate into intelligible or familiar terms.—*v.i.* to practise interpretation.—*adj.* **inter′pretable**, capable of being explained.—*v.t.* and *v.i.* (*arch.*) **inter′pretate**.—*n.* **interpretā′tion**, act of interpreting: the sense given by an interpreter: the power of explaining (*obs.*): the representation of a dramatic part, performance of a piece of music, or the like, according to one's conception of it.—*adj.* **inter′pretative** (*-āt-iv*, *-ət-iv*), inferred by or containing interpretation.—*adv.* **inter′pretatively**.—*ns.* **inter′preter**, one who translates orally for the benefit of two or more parties speaking different languages: an expounder: a translator (*obs.*); **inter′pretership**; **inter′pretress**, a female interpreter (sometimes **inter′pretess**). [L. *interpretārī*, *-ātus*—*interpres*, *-etis*.]
**interprovincial**, *in-tər-prə-vin′shl*, *adj.* between provinces. [Pfx. inter-.]
**interpunction**, *in-tər-pungk′shən*, *n.* the insertion of points in writing.—Also **interpunctuā′tion**.—*v.t.* **interpunc′tuate**. [Pfx. inter-.]
**interracial**, *in-tər-rā′sh(y)əl*, *-shi-əl*, *adj.* between races. [Pfx. inter-.]
**interradial**, *in-tər-rā′di-əl*, *adj.* between radii or rays: pertaining to an interradius.—*adv.* **interrā′dially**.—*n.* **interrā′dius**, an interradial part: a radius midway between primary radii or perradii. [Pfx. inter-.]
**interramal**, *in-tər-rā′məl*, *adj.* situated between the rami or branches, esp. of the lower jaw.—*n.* **interramifica′tion** (*-ram-*), interweaving of branches. [L. *inter*, between, *rāmus*, a branch.]
**interregal**, *in-tər-rē′gəl*, *adj.* between kings. [Pfx. inter-.]
**interregnum**, *in-tər-reg′nəm*, *n.* the time between two reigns: the time between the cessation of one and the establishment of another government: any breach of continuity in order, etc.:—*pl.* **interreg′na**, **interreg′nums**.—*n.* **in′terreign** (*Bacon*). [L. *inter*, between, *regnum*, rule.]
**interrelation**, *in-tər-ri-lā′shən*, *n.* reciprocal relation.—*n.* **interrelā′tionship**. [Pfx. inter-.]
**interrex**, *in′tər-reks*, *n.* one who rules during an interregnum: a regent:—*pl.* **interreges** (*-rē′jēz*). [L. *inter*, between, *rēx*, a king.]
**interrogate**, *in-ter′ə-gāt*, *v.t.* to question: to examine by asking questions: of a radar set, etc., to send out signals to (a radio-beacon) in order to ascertain position.—*v.i.* to ask questions.—

# 687 — in terrorem / interview

**adj. interr'ogable.**—*ns.* **interr'ogant**, a questioner; **interroga'tion**, act of interrogating: a question put: the mark placed after a question (?).—*adj.* **interrogative** (*in-tər-og'ə-tiv*), denoting a question: expressed as a question.—*n.* a word used in asking a question.—*adv.* **interrog'atively.**—*ns.* **interr'ogator**; **interrog'atory**, a question or inquiry.—*adj.* expressing a question. [L. *interrogāre*, *-ātum*—*inter*, between, *rogāre*, to ask.]

**in terrorem**, *in te-rōr'em* or *-rör'*, (L.) as a warning.

**interrupt**, *in-tər-upt'*, *v.t.* to break in between: to stop or hinder by breaking in upon: to break continuity in.—*v.i.* to make an interruption.—*adj.* **interrupted** (*obs.*): gaping apart (*Milt.*).—*adj.* **interrupt'ed**, broken in continuity: irregular in spacing or size of parts (*biol.*).—*adv.* **interrupt'edly**, with interruptions: irregularly.—*ns.* **interrup'ter** (also **interrup'tor**), one who interrupts: apparatus for interrupting, e.g. for breaking an electric circuit, for preventing the firing of a gun from an aircraft when the screw is in the line of fire; **interrup'tion**, act of interrupting: hindrance: temporary cessation.—*adj.* **interrup'tive**, tending to interrupt.—*adv.* **interrup'tively.** [L. *interrumpĕre*, *-ruptum*—*inter*, between, *rumpĕre*, to break.]

**interscapular**, *in-tər-ska'pū-lər*, (*anat.*) *adj.* between the shoulder-blades. [Pfx. **inter-.**]

**interscholastic**, *in-tər-skə-las'tik*, *adj.* between schools. [Pfx. **inter-.**]

**inter-science**, *in-tər-sī'əns*, *adj.* belonging to the examination between matriculation and B.Sc. of London University. [Pfx. **inter-.**]

**interscribe**, *in-tər-skrīb'*, (*obs.*) *v.t.* to write between. [L. *interscribĕre*—*inter*, between, *scribĕre*, to write.]

**intersect**, *in-tər-sekt'*, *v.t.* to cut across: to cut or cross mutually: to divide into parts.—*v.i.* to cross each other.—*ns.* **in'tersect**, point of intersection; **intersec'tion**, intersecting: the point or line in which lines or surfaces cut each other (*geom.*): the set of elements which two or more sets have in common (*math.*): a crossroads.—*adj.* **intersec'tional.** [L. *inter*, between, *secāre*, *sectum*, to cut.]

**interseptal**, *in-tər-sep'tl*, *adj.* between septa. [Pfx. **inter-.**]

**intersert**, *in-tər-sûrt'*, *v.t.* (*obs.*) to insert between other things, interpolate.—*adj.* **intersert'al** (*petr.*), having interstitial crystalline or glassy matter between feldspar laths. [L. *interserĕre*, *-sertum*, to interpose—*inter*, between, *serĕre*, to plant.]

**interservice**, *in-tər-sûr'vis*, *adj.* between the armed forces. [Pfx. **inter-.**]

**intersex**, *in'tər-seks*, (*biol.*) *n.* an individual developing some characters of the other sex.—*adj.* **intersex'ual**, between the sexes: intermediate between the sexes.—*n.* **intersexual'ity.** [Pfx. **inter-.**]

**intersidereal**, *in-tər-sī-dē'ri-əl*, (*rare*) *adj.* interstellar. [Pfx. **inter-.**]

**interspace**, *in'tər-spās*, *n.* an interval.—*v.t.* (*-spās'*) to put intervals between.—*adj.* **interspatial** (*-spā'shl*).—*adv.* **interspa'tially.** [Pfx. **inter-.**]

**interspecific**, *in-tər-spis-if'ik*, *adj.* between species. [Pfx. **inter-.**]

**intersperse**, *in-tər-spûrs'*, *v.t.* to scatter or set here and there: to diversify.—*ns.* **interspers'al** (*rare*); **interspersion** (*-spûr'shən*). [L. *interspergĕre*, *-spersum*—*inter*, among, *spargĕre*, to scatter.]

**interspinal**, *in-tər-spī'nəl*, *adj.* between spines of the vertebrae.—Also **interspi'nous.** [Pfx. **inter-.**]

**interstate**, *in'tər-stāt*, or *-stāt'*, *adj.* pertaining to relations, esp. political and commercial, between states. [Pfx. **inter-.**]

**interstellar**, *in-tər-stel'ər*, *adj.* beyond the solar system or among the stars: in the intervals between the stars.—Also **interstell'ary.** [L. *inter*, between, *stella*, a star.]

**interstice**, *in-tûr'stis*, *n.* a small space between

things closely set, or between the parts which compose a body: the time interval required by canon law before receiving higher orders (*R.C.*): a space between atoms in a lattice where other atoms can be located.—*adj.* **interstitial** (*-stish'l*), occurring in interstices.—*n.* an extra atom in a crystal lattice, causing a defect. [L. *interstitium*—*inter*, between, *sistĕre*, *stătum*, to stand, set.]

**interstratification**, *in-tər-strat-i-fi-kā'shən*, *n.* the state of lying between, or alternating with, other strata.—*adj.* **interstrat'ified.**—*v.t.* and *v.i.* **interstrat'ify.** [Pfx. **inter-.**]

**intertangle**, *in-tər-tang'gl*, *v.t.* and *v.i.* to tangle together.—*n.* **intertang'lement.** [Pfx. **inter-.**]

**intertarsal**, *in-tər-tär'sl*, *adj.* between tarsal bones. [Pfx. **inter-.**]

**intertentacular**, *in-tər-ten-tak'ū-lər*, *adj.* between tentacles. [Pfx. **inter-.**]

**interterritorial**, *in-tər-ter-i-tō'ri-əl*, *-tö'*, *adj.* between territories. [Pfx. **inter-.**]

**intertexture**, *in-tər-teks'chər*, *n.* interwoven state. [Pfx. **inter-.**]

**intertidal**, *in-tər-tī'dl*, *adj.* between low-water and high-water mark. [Pfx. **inter-.**]

**intertie**, *in'tər-tī*, *n.* in roofing, etc., a short timber binding together upright posts. [Origin obscure.]

**intertissued**, *in-tər-tish'ūd*, *adj.* interwoven.—Also (*Shak.*) **entertiss'ued.** [Pfx. **inter-.**]

**intertraffic**, *in-tər-traf'ik*, *n.* traffic between two or more persons or places. [Pfx. **inter-.**]

**intertribal**, *in-tər-trī'bl*, *adj.* between tribes. [Pfx. **inter-.**]

**intertrigo**, *in-tər-trī'gō*, *n.* an inflammation of the skin from chafing or rubbing. [L. *intertrīgō*—*inter*, between, *terĕre*, *tritum*, to rub.]

**intertropical**, *in-tər-trop'i-kl*, *adj.* between the tropics. [Pfx. **inter-.**]

**intertwine**, *in-tər-twīn'*, *v.t.* and *v.i.* to twine or twist together.—*ns.* **in'tertwine**, intertwining; **intertwine'ment.**—*n.* and *adj.* **intertwin'ing.**—*adv.* **intertwin'ingly.** [Pfx. **inter-.**]

**intertwist**, *in-tər-twist'*, *v.t.* to twist together.—*adv.* **intertwist'ingly.** [Pfx. **inter-.**]

**interunion**, *in-tər-ūn'yən*, *n.* a blending together. [Pfx. **inter-.**]

**interurban**, *in-tər-ûr'bən*, *adj.* between cities. [L. *inter*, between, *urbs*, *urbis*, a city.]

**interval**, *in'tər-vəl*, *n.* time or space between: any dividing tract in space or time: a break between lessons, acts of a play, etc.: difference of pitch between any two musical tones (*mus.*).—*n.* **in'tervāle** (*U.S. dial.*; influenced by vale (1)), a level tract along a river.—*adj.* **intervallic** (*-val'ik*).—*n.* **intervall'um** (*obs.*), an interval. [L. *intervallum*—*inter*, between, *vallum*, a rampart.]

**intervein**, *in-tər-vān'*, *v.t.* to intersect, as with veins. [Pfx. **inter-.**]

**intervene**, *in-tər-vēn'*, *v.i.* to come or be between: to occur between points of time: to happen so as to interrupt: to interpose: to interpose in an action to which one was not at first a party (*law*).—*v.t.* (*obs.*) to separate.—*n.* **interven'er**, one who intervenes.—Also (*law*) **interven'or.**—*adj.* **intervenient** (*-vēn'yənt*), being or passing between: intervening.—*ns.* **intervention** (*-ven'shən*), intervening: interference: mediation: interposition; **interven'tionism**; **interven'tionist**, one who advocates interference; **interven'tor**, a mediator in ecclesiastical controversies. [L. *inter*, between, *venīre*, to come.]

**interview**, *in'tər-vū*, *n.* a mutual view or sight (*obs.*): a formal meeting: a meeting between employer, board of directors, etc., and a candidate to ascertain by questioning and discussion the latter's suitability for a post, etc.: a meeting between journalist, or radio or TV broadcaster, and a notable person to discuss the latter's views, etc., for publication or broadcasting: an article or programme based on such a meeting.—*v.t.* to have an interview with.—*ns.* **interviewee'**,

Neutral vowels in unaccented syllables: *el'ə-mənt*; for certain sounds in foreign words, see p. viii

one who is interviewed; **in'terviewer**, one who interviews. [O.Fr. *entrevue—entre*, between, *voir*, to see.]

**intervital**, *in-tər-vī'tl*, *adj.* between lives, between death and resurrection. [L. *inter*, between, *vita*, life.]

**intervocalic**, *in-tər-vō-kal'ik*, *adj.* between vowels. [Pfx. **inter-**.]

**intervolve**, *in-tər-volv'*, *v.t.* and *v.i.* to entwine or roll up one with or within another. [L. *inter*, within, *volvĕre*, to roll.]

**interwar**, *in-tər-wör'*, *adj.* between wars. [Pfx. **inter-**.]

**interweave**, *in-tər-wēv'*, *v.t.* and *v.i.* to weave together: to intermingle. [Pfx. **inter-**.]

**interwind**, *in-tər-wīnd'*, *v.t.* and *v.i.* to wind together or around and among one another:—*pa.t.* and *pa.p.* **interwound** (-*wownd'*). [Pfx. **inter-**.]

**interwork**, *in-tər-wûrk'*, *v.t.* and *v.i.* to work together: to work into another or one another. —*adj.* **interwrought** (-*röt'*). [Pfx. **inter-**.]

**interwreathe**, *in-tər-rēdh'*, *v.t.* to wreathe together or into one another. [Pfx. **inter-**.]

**interzone**, *in-tər-zōn'*, **interzonal**, -*zōn'əl*, *adjs.* between zones (as of occupied country).—*n.* **in'terzone**. [Pfx. **inter-**.]

**intestate**, *in-tes'tāt*, -*tit*, *adj.* dying without having made a valid will: not disposed of by will.—*n.* a person who dies without making a valid will.—*n.* **intes'tacy** (-*tə-si*), the state of one dying without having made a valid will. [L. *intestātus—in-*, not, *testāri*, -*ātus*, to make a will.]

**intestine**, *in-tes'tin*, *adj.* internal: contained in the animal body (*obs.*): domestic, not foreign.—*n.* (commonly in *pl.*) a part of the digestive system, divided into the smaller intestine (comprising duodenum, jejunum, and ileum) and the greater intestine.—*adj.* **intes'tinal** (also -*tīn'*), pertaining to the intestines of an animal body. [L. *intestinus —intus*, within.]

**inthral, inthrall.** See **enthrall.**

**intil**, *in-til'*, (*Scot.*) *prep.* into, in, or unto. [in, till.]

**intimate**, *in'ti-mit*, -*māt*, *adj.* innermost: internal: close: deep-seated: private: personal: closely acquainted: familiar: in illicit sexual connection: encouraging informality and closer personal relations through smallness, exclusiveness. —*n.* a familiar friend: an associate.—*v.t.* (-*māt*) to hint: to announce.—*n.* **in'timacy** (-*mə-si*), state of being intimate: close familiarity: illicit sexual intercourse.—*adv.* **in'timately.** —*ns.* **intimā'tion**, indication: hint: announcement; **in'timism**, a genre of French impressionist painting of the early 20th cent., based on subjectmatter from everyday life.—*n.* and *adj.* **in'timist** (Fr. *intimiste*, *ē-tēm-ēst*).—*n.* **intim'ity** (*arch.*), intimacy. [L. *intimāre*, -*ātum—intimus*, innermost—*intus*, within.]

**intime**, *ē-tēm*, *adj.* intimate: small and cosy. [Fr.]

**intimidate**, *in-tim'i-dāt*, *v.t.* to strike fear into: to influence by threats or violence.—*n.* **intimidā'tion**, act of intimidating: use of violence or threats to influence the conduct or compel the consent of another: state of being intimidated.— *adj.* **intim'idatory.** [L. *in*, into, *timidus*, fearful.]

**intinction**, *in-tingk'shən*, *n.* an Eastern mode of administering communion by dipping the bread into the wine. [L.L. *intinctiō*, -*ōnis—*L. *intingĕre*, *intinctum*, to dip in.]

**intine**, *in'tin*, -*tēn*, -*tin*, *n.* the inner membrane of a pollen grain or spore. [L. *intus*, within.]

**intire**, an obsolete form of **entire.**

**intitule**, *in-tit'ūl.* Same as **entitle.**

**into**, *in'tōō*, *prep.* to a position within: to a state of: used to indicate the dividend in dividing (*math.*).—**multiply into** (*rare*), to find the product of two quantities. [in, to.]

**intoed**, *in-tōd'*, *adj.* having the toes more or less turned inwards. [Pfx. **in-** (1).]

**intolerable**, *in-tol'ər-ə-bl*, *adj.* not to be endured. —*ns.* **intolerabil'ity**, **intol'erableness.**—*adv.* **intol'erably.**—*ns.* **intol'erance**, **intolerā'tion**, state of being intolerant.—*adj.* **intol'erant**, not able or willing to endure: not enduring difference of opinion: persecuting.—*n.* one opposed to toleration.—*adv.* **intol'erantly.** [Pfx. **in-** (2).]

**intomb**, *in-tōōm'*, obsolete form of **entomb.**

**intonate**, *in'tōn-āt*, (*obs.*) *v.t.* and *v.i.* to thunder. [L. *intonāre*, -*ātum*, to thunder; cf. next word.]

**intonate**, *in'tōn-āt*, *v.t.* and *v.i.* to intone.—*ns.* **intonā'tion**, the opening phrase of any plainsong melody, sung usually either by the officiating priest alone, or by one or more selected choristers: pitching of musical notes: modulation or rise and fall in pitch of the voice: intoning; **in'tonātor**, a monochord.—*v.t.* **intone** (*in-tōn'*), to chant, read, or utter in musical tones, singsong, or monotone: to begin by singing the opening phrase: to utter with a particular intonation.—*n.* **intōn'er.**—*n.* and *adj.* **intōn'ing.** —*adv.* **intōn'ingly.** [L.L. *intonāre*, -*ātum—*L. *in*, in, *tonus*, tone.]

**intorsion**, **intortion**, *in-tör'shən*, *n.* a twist: a twine. —*adj.* **intort'ed**, twisted inwards: involved. [Fr. *intorsion*, L. *intortiō*, -*ōnis—in*, in, *torquēre*, *tortum*, to twist.]

**in toto**, *in tō'tō*, (L.) entirely.

**intown**, *in'tōōn*, (*Scot.*) *adj.* infield, near the farmhouse.—**intown multure**, payment to the miller by those who are compelled to have their grain ground at the mill. [in, (*Scot.*) **town.**]

**intoxicate**, *in-toks'i-kāt*, *v.t.* to poison (*obs.*): to make drunk: to excite to enthusiasm or madness: to elate excessively.—*adj.* **intox'icant**, intoxicating.—*n.* an intoxicating agent.—*adj.* **intox'icāting.**—*n.* **intoxicā'tion**, poisoning (*med.*): state of being drunk: high excitement or elation. [L.L. *intoxicāre*, -*ātum—in*, in, *toxicum—*Gr. *toxikon*, arrow-poison—*toxon*, a bow.]

**intra**, *in'trə*, *in'trä*, (L.) within.—**intra muros** (*mū'rōs*, *mōō'rōs*), within the wall; **intra vires** (*vi'rēz*, *wē'* or *vē'rās*), within the legal power of.

**intra-**, *in'trä-*, -*trə-*, in composition, within, as in **intra-abdom'inal**, situated within the cavity of the abdomen; **intra-artē'rial**, within an artery; **intracap'sular**, lying within a capsule; **intracar'-diac**, within the heart; **intracell'ular**, inside a cell; **intramercū'rial**, within Mercury's orbit; **intramolec'ular**, within the limits of the molecule; **intramun'dane**, within the world; **intramū'ral**, within walls: included within the college; **intramus'cular**, within a muscle· **intrapari'etal**, within walls, private: situated in the parietal lobe of the brain; **intrapet'iolar**, between petiole and stem; **intraterrito'rial**, within a territory; **intrathē'cal**, within, or introduced into, the sheath of the spinal cord or brain; **intratrop'ical**, within the tropics; **intraur'ban**, within a city; **intra-ū'terine**, within the uterus; **intravē'nous**, within, or introduced into, a vein or veins. [L. *intrā*, within.]

**intractable**, *in-trakt'ə-bl*, *adj.* unmanageable: obstinate.—*ns.* **intractabil'ity**, **intract'ableness.**— *adv.* **intract'ably.** [Pfx. **in-** (2).]

**intrados**, *in-trä'dos*, (*archit.*) *n.* the soffit or under surface of an arch. [Fr.,—L. *intrā*, within, *dorsum*, the back.]

**intramercurial . . . to . . . intramuscular.** See **intra-**.

**intransigent**, *in-tran'si-jənt*, -*trän'*, -*zi-*, *adj.* refusing to come to any understanding, irreconcilable.—*n.* one who is intransigent.—*ns.* **intran'-sigence** or **intran'sigency**; **intran'sigentism**; **intran'sigentist**, one who practices such a method of opposition.—Also **intransigeant**, etc. (Fr.). [Fr. *intransigeant—*Sp. *intransigente—*L. *in-*, not, *transigĕns*, -*entis*, pr.p. of *transigĕre*, to transact; see **transact.**]

**intransitive**, *in-tran'si-tiv*, -*trän'*, -*zi-*, *adj.* nopassing over or indicating passing over: representing action confined to the agent, i.e. having no object (*gram*.).—*adv*. intran′sitively. [Pfx. in- (2).]

in transitu, *in tran′* or *trän′si-tōō*, (L.) in passage, in transit.

intransmissible, *in-trans-mis′i-bl*, *-tranz-*, *-tränz-*, *adj*. that cannot be transmitted. [Pfx. in- (2).]

intransmutable, *in-trans-mūt′ə-bl*, *-tranz-*, *-tränz-*, *adj*. that cannot be changed into another substance.—*n*. intransmutabil′ity. [Pfx. in- (2).]

intrant, *in′trənt*, *adj*. entering: penetrating.—*n*. one who enters, esp. on membership, office, or possession. [L. *intrāns*, *-antis—intrāre*, to enter.]

intraparietal ... to ... intravenous. See intra-.

intreat, etc., *in-trēt′*. Same as entreat, etc.

intrench, intrenchment. See entrench.

intrenchant, *in-trensh′ənt*, *-trench′*, (*Shak*.) *adj*. not able to be cut or wounded, indivisible. [Pfx. in- (2).]

intrepid, *in-trep′id*, *adj*. without trepidation or fear: undaunted: brave.—*n*. intrepid′ity, firm, unshaken courage.—*adv*. intrep′idly. [L. *intrepidus* —*in-*, not, *trepidus*, alarmed.]

intricate, *in′tri-kit*, *-kāt* (also *-trik′it*), *adj*. involved: entangled: complex.—*ns*. in′tricacy (*-kə-si*; also *-trik′*), intricateness.—*adv*. intricately. [L. *intricātus—in-*, in, *tricāre*, to make difficulties—*tricae*, hindrances.]

intrigue, *in-trēg′*, *n*. indirect or underhand scheming or plot: a private scheme: the plot of a play or romance: a secret illicit love affair.—*v.i.* to engage in intrigue.—*v.t.* to puzzle, to fascinate (a Gallicism).—*n*. intrigu′er.—*ns*. and *adjs*. intrig(u)ant (*in′tri-gant*, *ĕ-trē-gā*), (*fem*.) intrig(u)ante (*in-tri-gant′*, *ĕ-trē-gät*).—*adj*. intrigu′-ing.—*adv*. intrigu′ingly. [Fr.; see intricate.]

intrince, *in-trins′*, (*Shak*.) *adj*. intricate. [See intrinsicate.]

intrinsic, -al, *in-trin′sik*,*-əl*, *adjs*. inward: genuine: inherent: essential, belonging to the point at issue: (of muscles) entirely contained within the limb and girdle.—*n*. intrinsicality (*-al′i-ti*) (*rare*).—*adv*. intrin′sically.—*n*. intrin′sicalness (*rare*). [Fr. *intrinsèque*—L. *intrinsecus—intrā*, within, suff. *-in*, *secus*, following.]

intrinsicate, *in-trins′i-kāt*, (*Shak*.) *adj*. intricate. [App. It. *intrinsecato*, familiar, confused with intricate.]

intro, *in′trō*, *n*. contraction of introduction, used esp. of the opening passage of a jazz or popular music piece.

intro-, *in′trō-*, *in-tro′-*, *pfx*. within, into. [L. *intrō*.]

introduce, *in-trə-dūs′*, *v.t.* to lead or bring in: to conduct into a place: formally to make known or acquainted: to bring into notice or practice: to preface.—*n*. introduc′er.—*adj*. introduc′ible.—*n*. introduction (*-duk′shən*), act of introducing: preliminary matter to a book: preliminary passage or section leading up to a movement (*mus*.): a treatise introductory to a science or course of study.—*adj*. introductive (*-duk′tiv*), promoting introduction.—*adv*. introduc′torily.—*adj*. introduc′tory, serving to introduce: preliminary: prefatory. [L. *intrōdūcĕre*, *-ductum—intrō*, inward, *dūcĕre*, to lead.]

introit, *in-trō′it*, or *in′*, *-troit*, *n*. anthem sung at the beginning of Mass, immediately after the *Confiteor*, and when the priest has ascended to the altar (*R.C.*): in other churches, an introductory hymn, psalm, or anthem.—*n*. intrō′itus, an entrance to a cavity, esp. the vagina: an introit. [L. *introitus—introīre—intrō*, inwards, *īre*, *itum*, to go.]

introjection, *in-trō-jek′shən*, *n*. the endowment of inanimate objects with the attributes of living creatures: a taking into the self of persons or things from the outer world so as to experience a oneness with them and to feel personally

touched by their fate.—*v.t.* and *v.i.* introject′. [L. *intrō*, within, *jacĕre*, to throw.]

introld. See entrold.

intromit, *in-trō-mit′*, or *-trə-*, *v.t.* to send within: to admit: to permit to enter: to insert.—*v.i.* to have dealings (*Scots law*): to interfere, esp. with the effects of another (esp. *Scots law*):—*pr.p.* intromitt′ing; *pa.t.* and *pa.p.* intromitt′ed.—*ns*. intromission (*-mish′ən*), sending within: insertion: in Scots law, the assumption of authority to deal with another's property (*legal*, where the party is expressly or impliedly authorised to interfere, vicious, where an heir or next of kin, without any authority, interferes with a deceased person's estate): proceeds of such interference.—*adjs*. intromiss′ive, pertaining to intromission: intromitting; intromitt′ent, intromitting: adapted for insertion, esp. (*zool*.) in copulation.—*n*. intromitt′er. [L. *intrō*, inward, *mittĕre*, *missum*, to send.]

introrse, *in-trörs′*, *adj*. turned or facing inward: (of an anther) opening towards the centre of the flower.—*adv*. introrse′ly. [L. *introrsus*, toward the middle, inward—*intrō*, inward and *versus*—*vertĕre*, to turn.]

introspect, *in-trō-spekt′*, or *-trə-*, *v.t.* to look into (esp. the mind).—*v.i.* to practise introspection.—*ns*. introspection (*-spek′shən*), a viewing of the inside or interior: the act of observing directly the processes of one's own mind; introspec′-tionist.—*adj*. introspec′tive. [L. *intrō*, within, *specĕre*, to look at.]

introsusception, *in-trō-sə-sep′shən*, *n*. intussusception. [L. *intrō*, inwards.]

introvert, *in-trō-vûrt′*, or *-trə-*, *v.t.* to turn inwards: to turn in upon itself: to turn inside out: to withdraw part within the rest of.—*n*. in′trovert, anything introverted: a person interested mainly in his own inner states and processes—opp. to *extravert*, *extrovert* (psych.).—*adj*. introvers′ible.—*n*. introver′sion (*-shən*).—*adjs*. introver′sive; introver′tive. [L. *intrō*, inwards, *vertĕre*, *versus*, to turn.]

intrude, *in-trōōd′*, *v.i.* to thrust oneself in: to enter uninvited or unwelcome.—*v.t.* to force in.—*ns*. intrud′er, one who or that which intrudes: a military aircraft which raids enemy territory alone; intrusion (*-trōō′zhən*), act of intruding: encroachment: an injection of rock in a molten state among and through existing rocks: a mass so injected; intru′sionist, one who intrudes, esp. of those who, before the Scottish Disruption of 1843, refused a parish the right of objecting to the settlement of an obnoxious minister by a patron—opp. to *non-intrusionist*.—*adj*. intru′-sive (*-siv*), tending or apt to intrude: intruded: inserted without etymological justification: entering without welcome or right: of a rock which has been forced while molten into cracks and fissures in other rocks.—*n*. an intrusive rock.—*adv*. intru′sively.—*n*. intru′siveness. [L. *in*, in, *trūdĕre*, *trūsum*, to thrust.]

intrust. A variant of entrust.

intubate, *in′tū-bāt*, *v.t.* to insert a tube into: to treat by insertion of a tube into, e.g. the larynx (*med*.).—*n*. intūbā′tion, insertion of tube. [L. *in*, in, *tubus*, a tube.]

intuition, *in-tū-ish′ən*, *n*. the power of the mind by which it immediately perceives the truth of things without reasoning or analysis: a truth so perceived, immediate knowledge in contrast with mediate.—*v.t.* and *v.i.* intuit (*in′tū-it*), to know intuitively.—*adj*. intu′ited.—*adj*. intuitional (*-ish′-ən-əl*).—*ns*. intuit′ion(al)ism, doctrine that the perception of truth is by intuition: a philosophical system which stresses intuition and mysticism as opposed to the idea of a logical universe; intuit′ion(al)ist.—*adj*. intu′itive, perceived, perceiving, by intuition: received or known by simple inspection and direct

Neutral vowels in unaccented syllables: *el′ə-mənt*; for certain sounds in foreign words, see p. viii

apprehension.—*adv.* intu'itively.—*n.* intu'itivism. [L. *in*, into or upon, *tuĕrī, tuitus*, to look.]

intumesce, *in-tū-mes'*, *v.i.* to swell up.—*n.* intumesc'ence.—*adj.* intumesc'ent. [L. *in*, in, *tumēscĕre*, to swell.]

inturbidate, *in-tûr'bi-dāt*, *v.t.* to render turbid. [L. *in*, in, *turbidāre, -ātum*, to trouble.]

intuse, *in'tūs*, (*Spens.*) *n.* a bruise. [L. *in*, in, *tundĕre, tūsum*, to thump.]

intussusception, *in-təs-sə-sep'shən, n.* the passing of part of a tube (esp. the intestine) within the adjacent part: growth by intercalation of particles.—*v.t.* intussuscept', to receive or take in thus.—*adjs.* intussuscept'ed, intussuscep'tive. [L. *intus*, within, *susceptiō, -ōnis—suscipĕre*, to take up.]

intwine, intwist. Same as entwine, entwist.

Inula, *in'ū-lə, n.* the elecampane genus of Compositae.—*ns.* in'ulase (*-lās*), an enzyme that forms fructose from inulin; in'ulin, a carbohydrate got from elecampane roots. [L. *inula*, prob.—Gr. *helenion*, elecampane.]

inumbrate, *in-um'brāt*, *v.t.* to cast a shadow upon: to shade. [L. *inumbrāre, -ātum—in*, on, *umbrāre*, to shade—*umbra*, a shadow.]

inunction, *in-ungk'shən, n.* anointing: smearing or rubbing with an ointment or liniment. [L. *inunctiō, -ōnis—inunguĕre*, to anoint—*in*, in on, *ung*(*u*)*ĕre*, to smear.]

inundate, *in'un-dāt*, formerly *in-un'dāt, v.t.* to flow upon or over in waves (said of water): to flood: to overwhelm (*fig.*): to fill with an overflowing abundance.—*adj.* inun'dant, overflowing.—*n.* indundā'tion. [L. *inundāre, -ātum—in*, in, *undāre*, to rise in waves—*unda*, a wave.]

inurbane, *in-ûr-bān'*, *adj.* not urbane.—*adv.* inurbane'ly.—*n.* inurbanity (*-ban'i-ti*). [Pfx. in- (2).]

inure, *in-ūr'*, *v.t.* to use or to exercise (*obs.*): to accustom: to habituate: to harden: to put into operation (*Spens., Milt.* in the form enure'): commit.—*v.i.* (*law*) to come into use or effect: to serve to one's use or benefit.—Also enure'.—*n.* inure'ment, act of inuring: state of being inured: habituation. [Pfx. in- (1), and *ure.*]

inure, *in-ūr'*, (*obs.*) *v.t.* to burn in. [L. *inūrĕre—in*, in, *urĕre*, to burn.]

inurn, *in-ûrn'*, *v.t.* to place in an urn: to entomb. [Pfx. in- (1).]

inusitate, *in-ū'zi-tāt*, (*obs.*) *adj.* unwanted.—*n.* inusita'tion (*-ā'shən; obs.*), disuse. [L. *inūsitātus —in*, not, *ūsitātus*, familiar.]

inust, *in-ust'*, (*obs.*) *adj.* burned in.—*n.* inustion (*in-us'chən; obs.*), burning in: cauterisation. [L. *inūrĕre, inūstum*; see inure (2).]

in usum Delphini, *in ūz'əm del-fī'nī, ōōs'ōōm del-fē'nē*, (L.) for the use of the Dauphin: toned down to suit the young person.

inutility, *in-ū-til'i-ti, n.* want of utility: uselessness: unprofitableness: something useless. [Pfx. in- (2).]

in utrumque paratus, *in ū-trōōm'kwi pə-rä'təs, ōō-trōōm'kwe pa-rä'tōōs*, (L.) prepared for either.

inutterable, *in-ut'ər-ə-bl, adj.* unutterable. [Pfx. in- (2).]

in vacuo, *in vak'ū-ō, vak'ōō-ō, wak'*, (L.) in a vacuum.

invade, *in-vād'*, *v.t.* to enter as an enemy: to attack: to encroach upon: to violate: to seize or fall upon: to enter: to penetrate: to come upon: to rush into.—*ns.* invad'er; invasion (*-vā'zhən*), the act of invading: an attack: an incursion: an attack on the rights of another: an encroachment: a violation.—*adj.* invasive (*vā'siv*), making invasion: aggressive: encroaching: infringing another's rights. [L. *invādĕre, invāsum—in*, in, *vādĕre*, to go.]

invaginate, *in-vaj'in-āt*, *v.t.* to ensheath: to dint inwards, push or withdraw within, introvert.— *v.i.* to be introverted: to form a hollow in-

growth.—*n.* invaginā'tion. [Pfx. in- (1), and L. *vāgina*, a sheath.]

invalid, *in-val'id, adj.* without validity, efficacy, weight, or cogency: having no effect: void: null.—*adj.* invalid (*in'və-lid, -lēd*), deficient in health, sick, weak: disabled: suitable for invalids.—*n.* in'valid (*-id, -ēd, -ēd'*), one who is weak: a sickly person: one disabled for active service, esp. a soldier or sailor.—*v.t.* in'valid (*-id, -ēd, -ēd'*), to make invalid or affect with disease: to enrol or discharge as an invalid.—*v.i.* (*arch.*) to become an invalid: to be discharged as an invalid.—*v.t.* invalidate (*-val'*), to render invalid: to make of no effect —*ns.* invalidā'tion; invalidhood (*in'və-lid-hōōd*, or *-lēd-*, or *-lēd'*); in'-validing, the sending or return home, or to a more healthy climate, of those rendered incapable of active duty by wounds, sickness, etc.— *adj.* in'validish (*-id-, -ēd-*, or *-ēd'*).—*ns.* in'validism (*-id-, -ēd-*, or *-ēd'*); invalid'ity, inval'idness, want of cogency or force.—*adv.* inval'idly. [Pfx. in- (2).]

invaluable, *in-val'ū-ə-bl, adj.* that cannot have a value set upon it: priceless: valueless (*obs.*).— *adv.* inval'uably. [Pfx. in- (2).]

Invar, *in'vär, in-vär'*, *n.* an alloy of iron, nickel and carbon, very slightly expanded by heat, used in the making of scientific instruments. [Trademark, from invariable.]

invariable, *in-vā'ri-ə-bl, adj.* not variable: without alteration or change: unalterable: constantly in the same state.—*ns.* invā'riableness, invāriabil'ity.—*adv.* invā'riably.—*n.* invā'riant, that which does not change: an expression or quantity that is unaltered by a particular procedure (*math.*).—Also *adj.*—*n.* invar'iance, invariableness: the theory of the constancy of physical laws. [Pfx. in- (2).]

invasion, invasive. See invade.

inveagle. Same as inveigle.

invecked, *in-vekt'*, *adj.* invected.

invected, *in-vek'tid*, (*her.*) *adj.* having or consisting of a border-line of small convex curves—opp. to engrailed. [L. *invehĕre, invectum*, to enter.]

invective, *in-vek'tiv, n.* a severe or reproachful accusation brought against anyone: an attack with words: a violent utterance of censure: sarcasm or satire.—*adj.* railing: abusive: satirical.—*adv.* invec'tively (*Shak.*). [See inveigh.]

inveigh, *in-vā'*, *v.i.* to make an attack with words: to rail: to revile. [L. *invehĕre, invectum—in*, in, *vehĕre*, to carry.]

inveigle, *in-vē'gl, in-vā'gl, v.t.* to entice: to ensnare by cajolery: to wheedle—older forms invea'gle, envei'gle.—*ns.* invei'glement; invei'gler. [Prob. altered from A.Fr. *enveogler* (Fr. *aveugler*), to blind—L. *ab.* from, *oculus*, the eye.]

invendible, *in-ven'di-bl, adj.* unsaleable.—*n.* invendibil'ity. [Pfx. in- (2).]

invenit, *in-vēn'it, in-wān'it, -vān'*, (L.) devised (this).

invent, *in-vent'*, *v.t.* to find (*Spens.*): to devise or contrive: to design for the first time, originate: to frame by imagination: to fabricate (something false).—*adj.* inven'tible.—*n.* inven'tion, that which is invented: contrivance: a deceit: faculty or power of inventing: ability displayed by any invention or effort of the imagination: a short piece working out a single idea (*mus.*).— *adj.* inven'tive, able to invent: ready in contrivance.—*adv.* inven'tively.—*ns.* inven'tiveness; inven'tor;—*fem.* inven'tress.—Invention of the Cross, a festival observed on 3rd May in commemoration of the alleged discovery of the true cross at Jerusalem in 326 by Helena, mother of Constantine the Great. [L. *invenire, inventum— in*, upon, *venire*, to come.]

inventory, *in'vən-tər-i, n.* a list or schedule of

*fāte, fär; mē, hûr* (her); *mīne; mōte, för; mūte; mōōn, fŏŏt; dhen* (then)

articles comprised in an estate, etc.: a catalogue: stock, equipment: stock of a commodity (*U.S.*): stocktaking (*U.S.*): the total quantity of material in a nuclear reactor.—*v.t.* to make an inventory of: to amount to.—*v.i.* to sum up.—*adj.* inventō'rial.—*adv.* inventō'rially. [L.L. *inventōrium* for L. *inventārium*, a list of things found—*invenīre*, to find.]

inveracity, *in-vər-as'i-ti, n.* want of veracity: an untruth. [Pfx. in- (2).]

Inverness, *in-vər-nes', in'vər-nes, adj.* of or named after the town of *Inverness*, as a cloak or overcoat with cape or tippet.

inverse, *in'vûrs, in-vûrs', adj.* inverted: upside down: in the reverse or contrary order: opposite—opp. to *direct*: opposite in effect, as subtraction to addition, etc. (*math.*): related by inversion.—*n.* an inverted state: the result of inversion: a direct opposite: a proposition formed by immediate inference from another, its subject being the negative of the original subject (*log.*): a point so related to another point that the rectangle contained by their distances from a fixed point collinear with them is constant, or related in some analogous manner (*geom.*).—*v.t.* inverse', to invert.—*adv.* inverse'ly.—*n.* inver'- sion (-*shən*), the act of inverting: the state of being inverted: a change or reversal of order or position: that which is got by inverting.—*adj.* inver'sive.—inverse proportion (*math.*), process by which one quantity decreases while another increases, their product remaining constant; inverse ratio, the ratio of reciprocals. [L. *inversus*, pa.p. of *invertĕre, inversum—in*, in and *vertĕre*, to turn.]

invert, *in-vûrt', v.t.* to turn in or about: to turn upside down: to reverse: to change the customary order or position of: to form the inverse of: to change by placing the lowest note an octave higher (*mus.*): to modify by reversing the direction of motion: to break up (cane-sugar) into dextrose and laevulose, thereby (the laevulose prevailing) reversing the direction of rotation of polarised light (*chem.*).—*n.* in'vert, an inverted arch: inverted sugar: a homosexual. —*n.* in'vertase (or -*vûr'*), an enzyme that inverts cane-sugar.—*adj.* inver'ted, turned inwards: upside down: reversed: pronounced with tip of tongue turned up and back (as *r* in S.W. England).—*adv.* inver'tedly.—*n.* inver'ter, inver'tor.—inverted arch, an arch with its curve turned downwards; inverted commas (see comma); invert sugar, the mixture got by hydrolysis of cane-sugar. [L. *invertĕre, inversum—in*, in, *vertĕre*, to turn.]

invertebrate, *in-vûrt'i-brit, -brāt, adj.* without a vertebral column or backbone: weak, irresolute: characterless: formless.—*n.* a member of the Invertebrata: an indecisive person.—*n.pl.* Invertebra'ta, a collective name for all animals other than vertebrates. [Pfx. in- (2).]

invest, *in-vest', v.t.* to clothe: to envelop: to put on (*Spens.*): to clothe with insignia of office: to settle or secure: to place in office or authority (with *with* or *in*): to adorn: to surround: to block up: to lay siege to: to lay out for profit, as by buying property, shares, etc.—*v.i.* (*coll.*) to lay out money, make a purchase (with *in*).—*adj.* inves'titive.—*ns.* inves'titure, investing: ceremony of investing: in feudal and ecclesiastical history, the act of giving corporal possession of a manor, office, or benefice, accompanied by a certain ceremonial, such as the delivery of a branch, a banner, etc., to signify the authority which it is supposed to convey; invest'ment, the act of investing: putting on: clothes (*arch.*): covering: investiture: a blockade: act of surrounding or besieging: any placing of money to secure income or profit: that in which money is invested; inves'tor, one who invests, esp. money.

—investment trust (see trust). [L. *investīre, -ītum—in*, on, *vestīre*, to clothe.]

investigate, *in-vest'i-gāt, v.t.* to search or inquire into with care and accuracy.—*v.i* to make investigation.—*adj.* invest'igable, able to be investigated.—*n.* investigā'tion, act of examining: research.—*adjs.* invest'igātive, invest'igātory.—*n.* invest'igātor. [L. *investigāre, -ātum—in*, in, *vestigāre*, to track.]

inveterate, *in-vet'ər-it, adj.* firmly established by long continuance: deep-rooted, confirmed in any habit: stubborn: rootedly hostile.—*adv.* invet'erately.—*ns.* invet'erateness, invet'eracy (-*ə-si*), firmness produced by long use or continuance. [L. *inveterātus*, stored up, long continued—*in*, in, *vetus, veteris*, old.]

invexed, *in-vekst', (her.) adj.* arched: concave. [L. *in*, in, and the root of *vehĕre*, to carry.]

inviable, *in-vī'ə-bl, adj.* not viable: unable to survive.—*n.* inviabil'ity. [Pfx. in- (2).]

invidious, *in-vid'i-əs, adj.* likely to incur or provoke ill-will: likely to excite envy, enviable: offensively discriminating.—*adv.* invid'iously.—*n.* invid'iousness. [L. *invidiōsus—invidia*, envy.]

invigilate, *in-vij'i-lāt, v.t.* and *v.i.* to supervise, esp. at examinations.—*ns.* invigilā'tion; invig'ilātor. [L. *in*, on, *vigilāre, -ātum*, to watch.]

invigorate, *in-vig'ər-āt, v.t.* to give vigour to: to strengthen: to animate.—*ns.* invig'orant, an invigorating agent; invigorā'tion; invig'orātor. [Pfx. in- (1).]

invincible, *in-vin'si-bl, adj.* that cannot be overcome: insuperable.—*ns.* invin'cibleness, invincibil'ity.—*adv.* invin'cibly.—invincible ignorance (see ignorance).—the Invincible Doctor, William of Occam (d. *c.* 1349). [Pfx. in- (2).]

in vino veritas, *in vī'nō ver'it-as, wē'nō wār'it-äs, vē'nō vär'it-äs,* (L.) in wine is truth.

inviolable, *in-vī'ə-lə-bl, adj.* that must not be profaned: that cannot be injured.—*ns.* inviolabil'ity, invī'olableness, the quality of being inviolable.—*adv.* invī'olably.—*adjs.* invī'olate (-*lit, -lāt*), -d (-*lāt-id*), not violated: unprofaned: uninjured.—*adv.* invī'olately.—*n.* invī'olateness. [Pfx. in- (2).]

invious, *in'vi-əs, (rare) adj.* impassable: trackless. [L. *invius—in-*, not, *via*, a way.]

invis'd, *in'vizd, (Shak.) adj.* prob., unseen or inscrutable. [L. *invisus*, unseen.]

invisible, *in-viz'i-bl, adj.* incapable of being seen: unseen: not shown in regular statements, as *invisible assets* (see export, import; *finance*).—*ns.* invisibil'ity, invis'ibleness.—*adv.* invis'ibly.— Invisible Church (see visible); invisible green, green that is almost black; invisible ink (see ink). [Pfx. in- (2).]

invite, *in-vīt', v.t.* to ask hospitably or politely to come: to express affable willingness to receive or to have done: to be of such a kind as to encourage or tend to bring on: to offer inducement: to attract.—*n.* (*coll.*) an invitation.—*n.* invitation (*in-vi-tā'shən*), the act of inviting: an asking or solicitation: the written or verbal form with which a person is invited: the brief exhortation introducing the confession in the Anglican communion office.—*adj.* invitatory (*in-vīt'ə-tə-ri*), using or containing invitation.—*n.* a form of invitation to worship, esp. the antiphon to the Venite or 95th Psalm.—*ns.* invite'ment (*Lamb*), allurement, temptation; invit'er.—*adj.* invit'ing, alluring: attractive.—*n.* (*Shak.*) invitation.—*adv.* invit'ingly.—*n.* invit'ingness, attractiveness. [L. *invītāre, -ātum*.]

in vitro, *in vit'rō, wit'rō, vit',* (L.) in glass: in the test tube—opp. to in vivo.

in vivo, *in vī'vō, wē'wō, vē'vō,* (L.) in the living organism.

invocate, *in'vō-kāt, v.t.* to invoke.—*n.* invocā'tion, the act or the form of invoking or addressing in prayer or supplication: an appellation under which one is invoked: any formal invoking of the blessing or help of a god, a saint, etc.: an opening prayer in a public religious service or in the Litany: a call for inspiration from a Muse or other deity as at the beginning of a poem: an incantation or calling up of a spirit: a call or summons, esp. for evidence from another case (*law*).—*adj.* invocatory (*in-vok′ə-tə-ri*), making invocation. [See invoke.]

invoice, *in′vois*, *n.* a letter of advice of the despatch of goods, with particulars of their price and quantity.—*v.t.* to make an invoice of. [Prob. pl. of Fr. *envoi*.]

invoke, *in-vōk′*, *v.t.* to call upon earnestly or solemnly: to implore assistance of: to address in prayer: to conjure up: to call to help, resort to. [Fr. *invoquer*—L. *invocāre*, *-ātum*—*in*, on, *vocāre*, to call.]

involucre, *in′və-lōō-kər*, *-lū-*, *n.* an envelope (*anat.*): a ring or crowd of bracts around a capitulum, umbel, etc. (*bot.*).—Also involū′crum. —*n.* involucel (*in-vol′ū-sel*), the group of bracts below a partial umbel.—*adjs.* involūcell′ate, having an involucel; involu′cral, of the nature of, pertaining to, an involucre; involu′crate, having an involucre. [L. *involūcrum*—*involvēre*, to involve.]

involuntary, *in-vol′ən-tər-i*, *adj.* not voluntary: not having the power of will or choice: not under control of the will: not done voluntarily. —*adv.* invol′untarily.—*n.* invol′untariness. [Pfx. in- (2).]

involute, *in′vol-ōōt*, *-ūt*, *adj.* involved: rolled inward at the margins (*bot.*): turned inward: closely rolled.—*n.* that which is involved or rolled inward: a curve traced by the end of a string unwinding itself from another curve (the *evolute*).—*v.t.* and *v.i.* to make or become involute.—*adj.* in′voluted.—*n.* involu′tion, the action of involving: state of being involved or entangled: complicated grammatical construction: raising to a power (*math.*): the condition satisfied by a system of pairs of points in a straight line such that the rectangle contained by their distances from a fixed point in that line (the *centre of involution*) is constant (*geom.*): retrograde development, return to normal size (*zool.*).—*adj.* involu′tional.—involutional psychosis, melancholia, a psychosis occurring in middle life, with feelings of anxiety, futility, guilt, and, in some cases, with delusions of persecution. [See involve.]

involve, *in-volv′*, *v.t.* to coil: to wrap up: to envelop: to entangle: to complicate: to implicate: to comprehend: to entail or imply, bring as a consequence: to be bound up with: to concern: to raise to a power (*math.*): to make (oneself) emotionally concerned (in, with): to engage the emotional interest of.—*n.* involve′-ment. [L. *involvēre*—*in*, in, *volvēre*, *volūtum*, to roll.]

invulnerable, *in-vul′nər-ə-bl*, *adj.* that cannot be wounded: not vulnerable (as in bridge).—*ns.* invulnerabil′ity, invul′nerableness.—*adv.* invul′-nerably. [Pfx. in- (2).]

invultuation, *in-vul-tū-ā′shən*, *n.* the making or use of an image of a person for purpose of witchcraft. [L.L. *invultuātiō*, *-ōnis*.—L. *in*, in, *vultus*, the face.]

inwall. See enwall.

inward, *in′wərd*, *adj.* placed or being within: internal: seated in the mind or soul, not perceptible to the senses: uttered as if within, or with closed mouth: confidential (*arch.*): secret, private (*arch.*).—*n.* inside (*Shak.*): interior (*obs.*): an intimate friend (*Shak.*): (in *pl.*): often *in′ərdz*) entrails (also innards).—*adv.* toward the interior: into the mind or thoughts.—*adv.* in′-wardly, within: in the heart: privately: toward the centre.—*n.* in′wardness, internal state: inner

meaning or significance: intimacy, familiarity (*Shak.*).—*adv.* in′wards, same as inward. [O.E. *inneweard* (adv.).]

inweave, *in-wēv′*, *v.t.* to weave in: to complicate: —*pa.t.* inwove′; *pa.p.* inwo′ven (*Milt.*, etc., inwove′). [Pfx. in- (1).]

inwick, *in′wik*, *n.* in curling, a stroke in which the stone glances off the edge of another stone, and then slides close to the tee.—*v.i.* inwick′, to make an inwick. [in, wick (4).]

inwit, *in′wit*, (*obs.*) *n.* inward knowledge: conscience. [in, wit.]

inwith, *in′with*, in-widh′, (*Scot.*) prep. and adv. within. [in, with.]

inwork, *in-wûrk′*, *v.t.* and *v.i.* to work in.—*n.* in′-working, energy exerted inwardly.—*adj.* in′-wrought (as pa.p. *in-röt′*), wrought in or among other things: adorned with figures. [Pfx. in- (1).]

inworn, *in′wörn*, in-wörn′, *-wörn*, *adj.* worn or worked in, inwrought. [Pfx. in- (1).]

inwrap. Same as enwrap.

inwreathe. Same as enwreathe.

inyala, *in-yä′lə*, *n.* a S. African antelope. [Bantu.]

io, *i′ō*, *interj.* of invocation, or expressing joy or triumph or grief.—*n.* a cry of 'Io':—*pl.* i′os. [Gr. *iō*.]

iodine, *i′ə-dēn*, or *i′ō-dēn*, also *-din*, *-din*, *n.* a halogen element (I; atomic number 53) giving a violet-coloured vapour.—*n.* i′odate, a salt of iodic acid.—*adj.* iodic (*i-od′ik*), pertaining to or caused by iodine: applied to an acid ($HIO_3$) and its anhydride ($I_3O_5$).—*n.* i′odide, a salt of hydriodic acid.—*v.t.* i′odise, -ize, to treat with iodine.—*ns.* i′odism, a morbid condition due to iodine; iodoform (*i-od′*, *-ōd′ə-förm*), a lemon-yellow crystalline compound of iodine ($CHI_3$) with a saffron-like odour, used as an antiseptic. —*adjs.* iodomet′ric (*chem.*), measured by iodine; iod′ophile (*-fil*, *-fil*), staining intensely with iodine.—*n.* iod′üret (*obs.*), an iodide.—iodine-131, a short-lived radioactive isotope of iodine present in fall-out, widely used in medicine. [Gr. *ioeidēs*, violet-coloured—*ion*, a violet, *eidos*, form.]

iodyrite, *i-od′ir-it*, *n.* a mineral, silver iodide. [iodine, argyrite.]

iolite, *i′ō-lit*, *n.* cordierite or dichroite, a strongly dichroic transparent gem, a silicate of aluminium, magnesium, and iron, violet-blue, grey, or yellow according to direction of view by transmitted light. [Gr. *ion*, violet, *lithos*, stone.]

ion, *i′ən*, *i′on*, *n.* electrically charged particle formed by loss or gain by an atom of electrons, effecting by its migration the transport of electricity.—*adj.* ionic (*i-on′ik*).—*v.t.* ionise, -ize (*i′ən-iz*), to produce ions in: to turn into ions. —*ns.* ionisā′tion; ionophoresis, electrophoresis, esp. of small ions; ion′osphere, the region of the upper atmosphere that includes the highly ionised Appleton and Kennelly-Heaviside layers.—*adj.* ionospher′ic.—*n.* iontophoresis, the migration of ions into body tissue through electric currents: electrophoresis.—*adj.* iontophoret′ic.—ion engine, a space engine in which the thrust is produced by a stream of ionised particles; ion-exchange, transfer of ions from a solution to a solid or another liquid, used in water-softening and many industrial processes. [Gr. *iŏn*, neut. pr.p. of *ienai*, to go.]

Ionic, *i-on′ik*, *adj.* relating to the Ionians, to one of the main divisions of the ancient Greeks, to their dialect, to Ionia, the coastal district of Asia Minor settled by them, to a foot of two long and two short syllables (*Ionic a majore*) or two short and two long (*Ionic a minore*), to verse characterised by the use of that foot, to a style of Greek architecture characterised by the volute of its capital, to a mode of ancient Greek music (the same as the Iastic, Hypophrygian, or Hyperlydian), or to an old ecclesiastical mode extending from C to C with C for its final.—*n.* the Ionic dialect: an Ionic foot or verse: an Ionic philosopher.—*adj.* and *n.* **Ionian** (*ī-ō´ni-ən*), **Ionic**: an Ionic Greek.—*vs.t.* and *vs.i.* **Ionicise, -ize** (*ī-on´i-sīz*), **Ionise, -ize** (*i´ən-īz*), to make or become Ionian: to use the Ionic dialect.—*ns.* I´onism; I´onist.—Ionic dialect, the most important of the three main branches of the ancient Greek language (Ionic, Doric, Aeolic), the language of Homer and Heródotus, of which Attic is a development; Ionic school, the representative philosophers of the Ionian Greeks, such as Thales, Anaximander, Heraclitus, Anaxagoras, who debated the question what was the primordial constitutive principle of the cosmic universe. [Gr. *Iōnikos, Iōnios.*]

**ionium,** *ī-ōn´i-əm, n.* a radioactive isotope of thorium. [ion.]

**ionosphere.** See ion.

**iota,** *ī-ō´tə, n.* the Greek letter I, ι, answering to I: as a numeral ι´ = 10, ͵ι = 10,000: a jot.—*n.* **iot´acism,** excessive use of the Greek letter iota or i or of its sound: the conversion of other vowel sounds into that. (Eng. *ē*) of iota, as in modern Gr. of η, υ, ει, η, οι, υι. [Gr. *iōta,* the smallest letter in the alphabet, I, ι; Heb. *yōd.*]

**I O U,** *ī-ō-ū´, n.* a memorandum of debt given by a borrower, requiring no stamp, but holograph, and usually dated, and addressed to the lender, [Pronunciation of *I owe you.*]

**ipecacuanha,** *ip-i-kak-ū-an´ə, n.* a valuable medicine or the Brazilian plant (Cephaelis or Uragoga; fam. Rubiaceae) whose root produces it—used as an emetic: applied to other roots used as substitutes.—Familiarly abbrev. **ipecac´.** [Port. from Tupí.]

**Ipomoea,** *ip-ō-mē´ə, n.* the jalap and morning-glory genus of the Convolvulus family. [Gr. *ips, ipos,* a worm, *homoios,* like.]

**ipse dixit,** *ip´sē dik´sit, ip´se dēk´sit,* (L.) he himself said it: his mere word: a dogmatic pronouncement.

**ipsissima verba,** *ip-sis´ə-mə vûr´bə, ip-sis´-i-ma ver´, wer´ba,* (L.) the very words.

**ipso facto,** *ip´sō fak´tō,* (L.) by that very fact: thereby.

**iracund,** *i´rə-kund, adj.* inclined to anger.—*n.* **iracund´ity.**—*adj.* **iracund´ulous,** somewhat iracund. [L. *irācundus—ira,* anger.]

**irade,** *i-rä´de, n.* a written decree of the Sultan of Turkey. [Turk.,—Ar. *irādah,* will.]

**Iranian,** *i-, i-rän´i-ən,* or *-rän´, adj.* and *n.* Persian: (of) a branch of the Indo-Germanic tongues including Persian.—Also **Iranic** (*i-ran´ik*). [Pers. *Irān,* Persia.]

**Iraqi,** *i-rä´kē, n.* a native of Iraq: the form of Arabic spoken in Iraq.—*adj.* pertaining to the country of Iraq, its inhabitants or language. [Ar. *'Irāqi.*]

**irascible,** *ir-as´i-bl,* or *ir-, adj.* susceptible of ire or anger: irritable.—*n.* **irascibil´ity.**—*adv.* **irasc´-ibly.** [Fr.,—L. *irāscibilis—irāsci,* to be angry —*ira,* anger.]

**ire,** *ir, n.* anger: rage: keen resentment.—*adjs.* **irate** (*i-rāt´* or *ir´āt*), enraged, angry; **ire´ful,** full of ire or wrath: resentful.—*advs.* **irate´ly; ire´fully.**—*n.* **ire´fulness.** [L. *ira,* anger.]

**irenic,** *i-rēn´ik, adj.* tending to create peace: pacific.—Also **irēn´ical.**—*ns.* **irēn´icon** (same as eirenicon); **irēn´ics,** (treated as *sing.*) irenical theology—opp. to *polemics.* [Gr. *eirēnē,* peace.]

**iridectomy, iridescence, iridium,** etc. See iris.

**iris,** *i´ris, n.* the rainbow: an appearance resembling the rainbow: the contractile curtain perforated by the pupil, and forming the coloured part of the eye: the fleur-de-lis, or flagflower (Iris): an iris diaphragm:—*pl.* **i´rides, i´rises:** (*cap.*) the Greek rainbow goddess, messenger of the gods.—*v.t.* to make iridescent: to form

into a rainbow: to work an iris diaphragm.— *n.* **i´rid,** the iris of the eye: any plant of the iris family.—*n.pl.* **Iridā´ceae** (*-si-ē*), the iris family, distinguished from lilies by their inferior ovary and single whorl of stamens.—Also **Irid´eae.**— *adjs.* **iridaceous** (*-ā´shəs*), **irid´eal,** belonging to the Iridaceae; **i´ridal, irid´ial, irid´ian,** pertaining to the rainbow or the iris of the eye: rainbow-like.—*ns.* **iridec´tomy,** surgical removal of part of the iris; **iridescence** (*ir-i-des´əns*), play of rainbow colours, caused by interference, as on bubbles, mother-of-pearl, some feathers.—*adjs.* **iridesc´ent, i´risated,** coloured like the rainbow: glittering with changing colours.—*n.* **iridisation, -z-** (*i-rid-iz-ā´shən,* or *ir-id-,* or *-iz-*), iridescence. —*v.t.* **iridise, -ize** (*ir´* or *ir´*), to make iridescent: to tip with iridium.—*ns.* **irid´ium** (*ir-* or *ir-*), a very heavy steel-grey metallic element (Ir; atomic number 77), with very high melting-point; **iridosmine** (*ir-id-oz´min,* or *ir-,* or *-os´*), a native alloy of iridium and osmium used for pen-points, also called *osmiridium.*—*v.t.* **i´risate,** to make iridescent.—*n.* **irisation** (*i-ri-sā´shən*).— *adjs.* **irised** (*i´rist*), showing colours like the rainbow; **irit´ic,** having iritis: affecting the iris. —*n.* **irit´is,** inflammation of the iris of the eye. —**iris diaphragm,** an adjustable stop for a lens, giving a continuously variable hole. [Gr. *Iris, -idos,* the rainbow goddess.]

**iriscope,** *i´ri-skōp, n.* an instrument for exhibiting the prismatic colours. [Gr. *iris,* and *skopeein,* to see.]

**Irish,** *i´rish, adj.* relating to, or produced in, or derived from Ireland: Highland Scottish (*obs.*): characteristic of Ireland, esp. blundering, self-contradictory, bull-making.—*n.* the Celtic language of Ireland or (*obs.*) of the Scottish Highlands (Gaelic): an Irish commodity, esp. whiskey: temper, passion (*coll.*): (as *pl.*) the natives or people of Ireland.—*ns.* **I´risher** (*Scot.,* often slightly contemptuous), an Irishman; **I´rishism** (also **I´ricism,** *-sizm,* a faulty form), a Hibernicism, an Irish phrase, idiom or characteristic, esp. a bull; **I´rishman; I´rishry,** the people of Ireland collectively; **I´rishwoman.**— **Irish bridge,** a ford or watersplash treated so as to be permanent; **Irish car,** a jaunting car; **Irish coffee,** a beverage made of sweetened coffee and Irish whiskey and topped with cream; **Irish Guards,** a regiment formed in 1900 to represent Ireland in the Foot Guards; **Irish moss,** carragheen; **Irish stew,** mutton, onions, and potatoes stewed with flour; **Irish terrier,** a breed of dog with rough, wiry, reddish-brown coat.

**irk,** *ûrk, v.t.* (now used only impersonally) to weary: to disgust: to distress.—*adj.* **irk´some,** causing uneasiness (*arch.*): tedious: burdensome.—*adv.* **irk´somely.**—*n.* **irk´someness.** [M.E. *irken.*]

**iron,** *i´ərn, n.* the most widely used of all the metals, the element (Fe) of atomic number 26: a weapon, instrument, or utensil made of iron, as a hand-harpoon, flat-iron, branding instrument, etc.: a pistol or revolver (*slang*): a golf-club with an iron head (formerly limited to certain types): strength: a medicinal preparation of iron: (in *pl.*) fetters, chains: the safety curtain in a theatre (orig. made of iron and thus called the **iron curtain**): a stirrup.—*adj.* formed of iron: resembling iron: harsh, grating: stern: fast-binding: not to be broken: robust: insensitive: inflexible.—*v.t.* to smooth with a flat-iron: to arm with iron: to fetter: to smooth, clear up (with *out; fig.*).—*ns.* **i´roner,** one who irons; **i´roning,** the act or process of smoothing with hot irons: clothes to be ironed. —*adj.* **i´rony,** made, consisting of, rich in iron: like iron: hard.—**Iron Age,** the age in which the ancient Greeks and Romans themselves lived,

Neutral vowels in unaccented syllables: *el´ə-mənt*; for certain sounds in foreign words, see p. viii

regarded by them as a third step in degeneracy from the Golden Age (*myth*.): the stage of culture of a people using iron as the material for their tools and weapons (*archaeol*.); i'ron-bark, eucalyptus of various species.—*adjs*. i'ron-bound, bound with iron: rugged, as a coast; i'ron-cased; i'ron-clad, clad in iron: covered or protected with iron.—*n*. a ship defended by iron plates.—i'ron-clay, clay ironstone; Iron Cross, a Prussian war medal instituted in 1813, revived in 1870 and 1914 and reinstated by Hitler as a German war medal in 1939; Iron Crown, the crown of Lombardy, so named from a thin band of iron said to be made from one of the nails of the Cross; iron curtain, an impenetrable barrier to observation or communication, esp. between communist Russia with its satellites and the West; i'ron-founder, one who founds or makes castings in iron; i'ron-foundry; i'ron-glance, specular iron.—*adj*. i'ron-gray', -grey', of a grey colour like that of iron freshly cut or broken.—*n*. this colour.—iron hand, strict, despotic control (the iron hand is sometimes hidden in the *velvet glove*, *q.v*.).—*adjs*. i'ron-hand'ed; i'ron-heart'ed, having a heart as hard as iron: unfeeling.—iron horse, a worn-out circumlocution for a railway engine; i'roning-board, a smooth board covered with cloth, on which clothes are ironed; i'ron-liq'uor, iron acetate, a dyers' mordant; iron lung, an apparatus consisting of a chamber that encloses a patient's chest, the air pressure within the chamber being varied rhythmically so that air is forced into and out of the lungs; i'ron-master, a proprietor of ironworks; i'ron-mine; i'ron-miner; i'ron-mining; i'ronmonger, a dealer in ironmongery: loosely, in household goods and equipment generally; i'ronmongery, articles made of iron: hardware; i'ron-mould (earlier -mole, *Scot*. -mail; O.E. *māl*, mole, spot), a spot left on wet cloth after touching iron; i'ron-ore; i'ron-pan', a hard layer in sand or gravel, due to percolation of water precipitating iron salts; iron pyrites, common pyrites, sulphide of iron; iron ration, a ration of concentrated food, esp. for an extreme emergency; i'ron-sand, sand containing particles of iron-ore: steel filings used in fireworks.—*adj*. i'ron-sick (*naut*.), having the iron bolts and spikes much corroded.—*n*. I'ronside, I'ronsides, a nickname for a man of iron resolution (as King Edmund, Oliver Cromwell): a Puritan cavalryman: a Puritan: (in *pl*.) a name given to Cromwell's irresistible cavalry.—*adj*. i'ron-sid'ed, having a side of, or as hard as, iron: rough: hardy.—i'ronsmith, a worker in iron, blacksmith; i'ron-stone, any iron-ore, esp. carbonate; i'ronware, wares or goods of iron.—*adj*. i'ron-witt'ed (*Shak*.), unfeeling, insensible.—i'ronwood, timber of great hardness, and many kinds of trees producing it.—*adj*. i'ron-word'ed (*Tenn*.), in words as strong as iron.—i'ronwork, the parts of a building, etc., made of iron: anything of iron, esp. artistic work: (often in *pl*.) an establishment where iron is smelted or made into heavy goods.—rule with a rod of iron, to rule with stern severity; strike while the iron is hot, to seize one's opportunity while the circumstances are favourable to one; too many irons in the fire, too many things on hand at once. [O.E. *iren* (*isern*, *īsen*); Ger. *eisen*.]

irony, ī'rən-i, *n*. the Socratic method of discussion by professing ignorance: conveyance of meaning (generally satirical) by words whose literal meaning is the opposite: a situation or utterance (as in a tragedy) that has a significance unperceived at the time, or by the person involved: a condition in which one seems to be mocked by fate or the facts.—*adjs*. ironic (ī-ron'ik), iron'ical.—*adv*. iron'ically.—*n*. i'ronist. [L.

*irōnia*—Gr. *eirōneiā*, dissimulation—*eirōn*, a dissembler, perh.—*eirein*, to talk.]

Iroquoian, ir-ō-kwoi'ən, *adj*. of, belonging to, the *Iroquois*, a confederation of American Indian tribes: of the group of languages spoken by these tribes.—Also *n*.

irradiate, i-rā'di-āt, *v.t*. to shed light or other rays upon or into: to treat by exposure to rays: to light up: to brighten: to radiate.—*v.i*. to radiate: to shine.—*adj*. adorned with rays of light or with lustre.—*ns*. irra'diance, irra'diancy.—*adj*. irra'diant.—*n*. irradiā'tion, act of irradiating: exposure to rays: that which is irradiated: brightness: apparent enlargement of a bright object by spreading of the excitation of the retina, or in a photograph by reflections within the emulsion: spread of a nervous impulse beyond the usual area affected: intellectual light.—*adj*. irra'diative. [Pfx. ir- (in- (1)).]

irradicate, i-rad'i-kāt, *v.t*. to fix firmly. [Pfx. ir- (in- (1)).]

irrational, ir-ash'ən-əl, *adj*. not rational: not commensurable with natural numbers: long treated as short, or having such a syllable (indicated > ; *pros*.).—*n*. an irrational being or number.—*v.t*. irra'tionalise, -ize, to make irrational.—*ns*. irra'tionalism, an irrational system: irrationality; irra'tionalist.—*adj*. irrationalist'ic.—*n*. irrational'ity.—*adv*. irra'tionally. [Pfx. ir- (in- (2)).]

irrealisable, -izable, ir-ē-ə-līz'ə-bl, *adj*. not realisable.—*n*. irreality (-al'-i-ti), unreality. [Pfx. ir- (in- (2)).]

irrebuttable, ir-i-but'ə-bl, *adj*. not to be rebutted. [Pfx. ir- (in- (2)).]

irreceptive, ir-i-sep'tiv, *adj*. not receptive. [Pfx. ir- (in- (2)).]

irreciprocal, ir-i-sip'rə-kəl, *adj*. not reciprocal.—irreciprocity (ir-es-i-pros'i-ti). [Pfx. ir- (in- (2)).]

irreclaimable, ir-i-klām'ə-bl, *adj*. that cannot be claimed back, brought into cultivation, or reformed: incorrigible.—*n*. irreclaim'ableness.—*adv*. irreclaim'ably. [Pfx. ir- (in- (2)).]

irrecognisable, -izable, ir-ek-əg-nīz'ə-bl, or ir-ek', *adj*. unrecognisable.—*n*. irrecognition (-nish'ən), lack of recognition. [Pfx. ir- (in- (2)).]

irreconcilable, ir-ek-ən-sil'ə-bl, or ir-ek', *adj*. incapable of being brought back to a state of friendship or agreement: inconsistent.—*n*. an irreconcilable opponent: an intransigent.—*ns*. irreconcil'ableness, irreconcilabil'ity.—*adv*. irreconcil'ably.—*adj*. irrec'onciled, not reconciled, esp. (*Shak*.) with God: not brought into harmony.—*n*. irreconcile'ment. [Pfx. ir- (in- (2)).]

irrecoverable, ir-i-kuv'ər-ə-bl, *adj*. irretrievable: not reclaimable: beyond recovery.—*n*. irrecov'erableness.—*adv*. irrecov'erably. [Pfx. ir- (in- (2)).]

irrecusable, ir-i-kū'zə-bl, *adj*. that cannot be rejected.—*adv*. irrecūs'ably. [Fr.—L.L. *irrecūsābilis*.]

irredeemable, ir-i-dēm'ə-bl, *adj*. not redeemable: not subject to be paid at the nominal value.—*ns*. irredeem'ableness, irredeemabil'ity.—*n.pl*. irredeem'ables, undated government or debenture stock.—*adv*. irredeem'ably. [Pfx. ir- (in- (2)).]

Irredentist, ir-e-den'tist, *n*. one of an Italian party formed in 1878, its aims to gain or regain for Italy various regions claimed on language and other grounds: one who makes similar claims for any nation.—Also *adj*.—*n*. Irredent'ism, the programme of the Irredentist party: the doctrine of 'redeeming' territory from foreign rule.—Often irredentist, irredentism. [It. (*Italia*) *irredenta*, unredeemed (Italy)—L. *in-*, not, *redemptus*, pa.p. of *redimĕre*, to redeem.]

irreducible, ir-i-dūs'i-bl, *adj*. that cannot be reduced or brought from one degree, form, or state to another: not to be lessened: not to be overcome: not to be reduced by manipulation, as a hernia, etc.—*n*. irreduc'ibleness.—*adv*. irreduc'ibly.—*ns.* irreducibil'ity, irreductibility (*-duk-ti-bil'i-ti*); irreduction (*-duk'shən*). [Pfx. ir- (in- (2)).]

**irreflective,** *ir-i-flek'tiv, adj.* not reflective.—*n.* irreflec'tion, irreflex'ion. [Pfx. ir- (in- (2)).]

**irreformable,** *ir-i-förm'ə-bl, adj.* not reformable: not subject to revision or improvement. [Pfx. ir- (in- (2)).]

**irrefragable,** *ir-ef'rə-gə-bl, adj.* that cannot be refuted: unanswerable.—*ns.* irrefragabil'ity, irrefragableness.—*adv.* irrefragably.—the Irrefragable Doctor, Alexander Hales (died 1245) who prepared a system of instruction for the schools of Christendom. [L. *irrefrăgābilis—in-,* not, *re-,* backwards, *frangĕre,* to break.]

**irrefrangible,** *ir-i-fran'ji-bl, adj.* incapable of refraction. [Pfx. ir- (in- (2)).]

**irrefutable,** *ir-ef'ūt-ə-bl,* also *-ūt', adj.* that cannot be refuted.—*adv.* irref'utably (also *-ūt'*). [Pfx. ir- (in- (2)).]

**irregular,** *ir-eg'ū-lər, adj.* not regular: not conforming to rule or to the ordinary rules: disorderly: uneven: unsymmetrical: variable: (of troops) not trained under authority of a government: (of a marriage) not celebrated by a minister after proclamation of banns or of intention to marry.—*n.* an irregular soldier.—*n.* irregularity (*-lar'i-ti*).—*adv.* irreg'ularly.—*adj.* irreg'ulous (*Shak.*), lawless. [Pfx. ir- (in- (2)).]

**irrelative,** *ir-el'ə-tiv, adj.* not relative: irrelevant.—*adj.* irrelated (*ir-i-lā'tid*).—*n.* irrelā'tion.—*adv.* irrel'atively. [Pfx. ir- (in- (2)).]

**irrelevant,** *ir-el'ə-vənt, adj.* not relevant.—*ns.* irrel'evance, irrel'evancy.—*adv.* irrel'evantly. [Pfx. ir- (in- (2)).]

**irreligious,** *ir-i-lij'əs, adj.* destitute of religion: regardless of religion: opposed to religion: false in religion (*Shak.*): ungodly.—*adv.* irrelig'iously.—*ns.* irrelig'iousness, irrelig'ion, want of religion: hostility to or disregard of religion. [Pfx. ir- (in- (2)).]

**irremeable,** *ir-em'i-ə-bl,* or *-ēm', adj.* not admitting of return. [L. *irremeābilis—in-,* not, *re-,* back, *meăre,* to go, come.]

**irremediable,** *ir-i-mē'di-ə-bl, adj.* beyond remedy or redress.—*n.* irremē'diableness.—*adv.* irremē'diably. [Pfx. ir- (in- (2)).]

**irremissible,** *ir-i-mis'i-bl, adj.* not to be remitted or forgiven.—*ns.* irremiss'ibleness, irremission (*-mish'ən*).—*adj.* irremiss'ive, unremitting. [Pfx. ir- (in- (2)).]

**irremovable,** *ir-i-mōōv'ə-bl, adj.* not removable: not liable to be displaced.—*ns.* irremovabil'ity, irremov'ableness.—*adv.* irremov'ably. [Pfx. ir- (in- (2)).]

**irrenowned,** *ir-i-nown'id,* (*Spens.*) *adj.* inglorious. [Pfx. ir- (in- (2)).]

**irrepairable,** *ir-i-pār'ə-bl, adj.* beyond repair. [Pfx. ir- (in- (2)).]

**irreparable,** *ir-ep'ər-ə-bl, adj.* that cannot be made good or rectified: beyond repair.—*ns.* irreparabil'ity, irrep'arableness.—*adv.* irrep'arably. [Pfx. ir- (in- (2)).]

**irrepealable,** *ir-i-pēl'ə-bl, adj.* that cannot be repealed or annulled.—*adv.* irrepeal'ably. [Pfx. ir- (in- (2)).]

**irreplaceable,** *ir-i-plās'ə-bl, adj.* whose loss cannot be made good: without possible substitute. [Pfx. ir- (in- (2)).]

**irreprehensible,** *ir-ep-ri-hens'i-bl, adj.* beyond blame.—*n.* irreprehens'ibleness.—*adv.* irreprehens'ibly. [Pfx. ir- (in- (2)).]

**irrepressible,** *ir-i-pres'i-bl, adj.* not to be put down or kept under.—*adv.* irrepress'ibly. [Pfx. ir- (in- (2)).]

**irreproachable,** *ir-i-prōch'ə-bl, adj.* free from blame: faultless.—*n.* irreproach'ableness.—*adv.* irreproach'ably. [Pfx. ir- (in- (2)).]

**irreproducible,** *ir-ē-prō-dūs'i-bl, adj.* that cannot be reproduced. [Pfx. ir- (in- (2)).]

**irreprovable,** *ir-i-prōōv'ə-bl, adj.* blameless.—*n.* irreprov'ableness.—*adv.* irreprov'ably. [Pfx. ir- (in- (2)).]

**irresistance,** *ir-i-zist'əns, n.* want of resistance: passive submission.—*adj.* irresist'ible, not to be opposed with success: resistless: overpowering: overmastering.—*ns.* irresist'ibleness, irresistibil'ity.—*adv.* irresist'ibly. [Pfx. ir- (in- (2)).]

**irresoluble,** *ir-ez'əl-ū-bl, -ōō-bl, adj.* that cannot be resolved into parts: that cannot be solved: that cannot be loosed or got rid of. [Pfx. ir- (in- (2)).]

**irresolute,** *ir-ez'əl-ūt, -ōōt, adj.* not firm in purpose.—*adv.* irres'olutely.—*ns.* irres'oluteness, irresolution (*-ū'shən, -ōō'shən*), want of resolution. [Pfx. ir- (in- (2)).]

**irresolvable,** *ir-i-zolv'ə-bl, adj.* that cannot be resolved.—*ns.* irresolvabil'ity, irresolv'ableness.

**irrespective,** *ir-i-spek'tiv, adj.* not having regard (with *of*).—Also *adv.*—*adv.* irrespec'tively. [Pfx. ir- (in- (2)).]

**irrespirable,** *ir-es'pir-ə-bl,* or *-pir', adj.* unfit for respiration. [Pfx. ir- (in- (2)).]

**irresponsible,** *ir-i-spons'i-bl, adj.* not responsible: without sense of responsibility: free from feeling of responsibility, light-hearted, carefree: done without feeling of responsibility.—*n.* irresponsibil'ity.—*adv.* irrespons'ibly.—*adj.* irrespons'ive, not responding: not readily responding.—*n.* irrespons'iveness. [Pfx. ir- (in- (2)).]

**irrestrainable,** *ir-i-strān'ə-bl, adj.* not restrainable. [Pfx. ir- (in- (2)).]

**irresuscitable,** *ir-i-sus'i-tə-bl, adj.* incapable of being resuscitated or revived.—*adv.* irresusc'itably. [Pfx. ir- in- (2)).]

**irretention,** *ir-i-ten'shən, n.* absence of retention or power to retain.—*adj.* irreten'tive. [Pfx. ir- (in- (2)).]

**irretrievable,** *ir-i-trēv'ə-bl, adj.* not to be recovered: irreparable.—*adv.* irretriev'ableness.—*adv.* irretriev'ably. [Pfx. ir- (in- (2)).]

**irreverent,** *ir-ev'ər-ənt, adj.* not reverent: proceeding from irreverence.—*n.* irrev'erence, want of reverence or veneration, esp. for God.—*adj.* irreverential (*-en'shəl*).—*adv.* irrev'erently. [Pfx. ir- (in- (2)).]

**irreversible,** *ir-i-vûrs'i-bl, adj.* not reversible: that cannot proceed in the opposite direction or in both directions: incapable of changing back: not alike both ways: that cannot be recalled or annulled.—*ns.* irreversibil'ity, irrevers'ibleness.—*adv.* irrevers'ibly. [Pfx. ir- (in- (2)).]

**irrevocable,** *ir-ev'ək-ə-bl, adj.* that cannot be recalled or revoked.—*ns.* irrevocabil'ity, irrev'ocableness.—*adv.* irrev'ocably. [Pfx. ir- (in- (2)).]

**irrigate,** *ir'i-gāt, v.t.* to wet or moisten: to water by means of canals or watercourses: to cause a stream of liquid to flow upon.—*v.i.* (*slang*) to drink.—*adj.* irr'igable.—*ns.* irrigā'tion; irr'igător, one who, or that which, irrigates: an appliance for washing a wound, etc.—*adj.* irrig'ŭous, watered: wet: irrigating. [L. *irrigāre, -ātum,* to water, and *irriguus,* watering, watered—*in,* upon, *rigāre,* to wet.]

**irrision,** *ir-izh'ən, n.* act of laughing at another.—*adj.* irrisory (*ir-i'sər-i*), mocking, derisive. [L. *irrisiō, -ōnis—in,* on, at, *ridēre, risum,* to laugh.]

**irritate,** *ir'i-tāt, v.t.* to excite or stimulate: to rouse: to provoke: to make angry or fretful: to excite a painful, uncomfortable, or unhealthy condition (as heat and redness) in.—*n.* irritabil'ity, the quality of being easily irritated: the peculiar susceptibility to stimuli possessed by living matter.—*adj.* irr'itable, that may be irritated: easily annoyed: susceptible of excitement or irritation.—*n.* irr'itableness.—*adv.* irr'itably.—*n.* irr'itancy.—*adj.* irr'itant, irritating.—*n.* that which causes irritation.—*n.* irritā'tion, act of irritating or exciting: anger, annoyance:

stimulation: the term applied to any morbid excitement of the vital actions not amounting to inflammation, often, but not always, leading to that condition (*med.*).—*adj.* irr'itātive, tending to irritate or excite: accompanied with or caused by irritation. [L. *irritāre, -ātum*.]

irritate, ir'i-tāt, (*Scots law*) *v.t.* to make void.—*n.* irr'itancy.—*adj.* irr'itant, rendering void. [L. *irritāre—in-*, not, *ratus*, valid.]

irrupt, ir-upt', *v.i.* to break in: to make irruption.—*n.* irruption (*ir-up'shən*), a breaking or bursting in: a sudden invasion or incursion.—*adj.* irrup'tive, rushing suddenly in.—*adv.* irrup'tively. [L. *irrumpĕre, irruptum—in*, in, *rumpĕre*, to break.]

Irvingite, ûr'ving-īt, *n.* a popular name for a member of the Catholic Apostolic Church.—Also *adj.*—*n.* Ir'vingism, the doctrine and practice of the Irvingites. [From Edward *Irving* (1792-1834).]

is, iz, used as third pers. sing. pres. indic. of be. [O.E. *is*; Ger. *ist*, L. *est*, Gr. *esti*, Sans. *asti*.]

isabel, iz'ə-bel, *n.* and *adj.* dingy yellowish-grey or drab.—Also isabell'a, isabell'ine (*-in, -in*). [Origin unknown: too early in use to be from *Isabella*, daughter of Philip II, who did not change her linen for three years until Ostend was taken.]

isagogic, i-sa-goj'ik, -gog'ik, *adj.* introductory.—*n.pl.* (treated as *sing.*) isagog'ics, that part of theological study introductory to exegesis. [Gr. *eisagōgē*, an introduction—*eis*, into, *agein*, to lead.]

isallobar, is-, iz-al'-ə-bär, (*meteor.*) *n.* the contour line on a weather chart, signifying the location of equal changes in the barometer over a specified period. [Gr. *isos*, equal, *allos*, other, different, *baros*, weight.]

isapostolic, i-sap-əs-tol'ik, *adj.* equal to the apostles, as bishops of apostolic creation, the first preachers of Christ in a country, etc. [Gr. *isos*, equal, *apostolikos*, apostolic.]

Isatis, i'sə-tis, *n.* the woad genus of Cruciferae.—*n.* i'satin, -tine, substance (C₈H₅O₂N) got by oxidising indigo. [Gr. *isatis*, woad.]

isch(a)emia, is-kē'mi-ə, *n.* deficiency of blood in a part of the body.—*adj.* isch(a)em'ic. [Gr. *ischein*, to restrain, *haima*, blood.]

ischium, is'ki-əm, *n.* a posterior bone of the pelvic girdle.—*adjs.* ischiad'ic, is'chial, ischiat'ic. [Latinised from Gr. *ischion*, the hip-joint.]

ischuria, is-kū'ri-ə, *n.* a stoppage of urine.—*adj.* and *n.* ischuretic (*is-kū-ret'ik*). [Gr. *ischein*, to hold, *ouron*, urine.]

-ise, -ize, suffix forming verbs from adjs. (meaning to make), as equal*ise*, or from nouns, as botan*ise*, satir*ise*. [L. *-izāre*, from Gr. *-izein*; Fr. *-iser*.]

isenergic, is-en-ûr'jik, *adj.* in physics, denoting equal energy. [Gr. *isos*, equal, *energeia*, energy.]

Isengrim, i'zən-grim, Isegrim, i'zə-grim, *n.* the wolf in the beast epic of *Reynard the Fox*.

isentropic, i-sen-trop'ik, (*phys.*) *adj.* of equal entropy. [Gr. *isos*, equal, *entropē*, a turning about —*en*, in, *trepein*, to turn.]

-ish, *adj.* suffix signifying somewhat, as brown*ish*, old*ish*; sometimes implying deprecation, as outland*ish*, child*ish*. [O.E. *-isc*.]

ish, *ish*, (*Scots law*) *n.* issue, liberty of going out: expiry. [O.Fr. *issir*, to go out—L. *exire—ex*, out of, *ire*, to go.]

Ishmael, ish'mā'əl, *n.* one like Ishmael (Gen. xvi. 12), at war with society.—*n.* Ish'maelite, a descendant of Ishmael: a Bedawi Arab: an Ishmael.—*adj.* Ishmaelit'ish.

Isiac, i'si-ak, *adj.* relating to Isis.

Isidorian, is-, iz-i-dō', dō', ri-ən, *adj.* of or pertaining to St *Isidore* of Seville (*c.* 560-636), or the collection of canons and decretals adopted by him; but esp. applying to the forged *Pseudo-Isidorian* or *False Decretals*, published (*c.* 845)

by *Isidore* Mercator, and fathered upon St Isidore.

isinglass, i'zing-gläs, *n.* a material, mainly gelatine, got from sturgeons' air-bladders and other sources. [App. from obs. Du. *huizenblas—huizen*, a kind of sturgeon, *blas*, a bladder; Ger. *hausenblase*; cf. huso.]

Isis, i'sis, *n.* an Egyptian goddess, wife and sister of Osiris.—*adjs.* I'siac; Isi'acal. [Gr. *Isis*.]

Islam, iz'läm, or *is*', or *-läm*', Is'lamism, *ns.* the Mohammedan religion: the whole Mohammedan world.—*adjs.* Islamic (*-lam'ik*), Islamitic (*-lə-mit'ik*).—*n.* Is'lamite.—*v.t.* and *v.i.* Islamise', -ize', to convert or conform to Mohammedanism. [Ar. *islām*, surrender (to God).]

island, i'lənd, *n.* a mass of land (not a continent) surrounded with water: anything isolated, detached, or surrounded by something of a different nature, e.g. a wood among prairies, a hill in a marsh or plain, a show-case, a building or building-site with a clear space around it: a small raised traffic-free area in a street for pedestrians: tissue or cells detached and differing from their surroundings.—*adj.* of an island: forming an island.—*v.t.* to cause to appear like an island: to isolate: to dot as with islands.—*n.* islander (i'lənd-ər), an inhabitant of an island.—island universe, a spiral nebula regarded as forming a separate stellar system.—Reil's island (see insula). [M.E. *iland*—O.E. *iegland, igland, ēgland—ieg, ig, ēg*, island (from a root which appears in Angles-*ea*, Aldern-*ey*, etc., O.E. *ēa*, L. *aqua*, water) and *land*. The *s* is due to confusion with *isle*.]

isle, *il*, *n.* an island.—*v.t.* to make an isle of: to set in an isle.—*v.i.* to dwell in an isle.—*ns.* isles'man, an islander, esp. an inhabitant of the Hebrides—also isle'man; islet (i'lit), a little isle. —Isle of Wight disease, a disease of bees caused by a mite in the spiracles, that appeared in the Isle of Wight in 1906, and spread to other regions; islets of Langerhans (läng'ər-häns), groups of epithelial cells discovered by Paul *Langerhans*, a German anatomist (1847-88), in the pancreas, producing a secretion whose want causes diabetes. [M.E. *ile, yle*—O.Fr. *isle* (Fr. *île*)—L. *insula*.]

-ism, -asm, or (with -ic) -icism, suffix forming abstract nouns signifying condition, system, as egoism, deism, Calvinism, laconism, pleonasm, Anglicism, witticism. [L. *-ismus, -asmus*—Gr. *-ismos, -asmos*.]

ism, izm, *n.* any distinctive doctrine, theory, or practice—usually in disparagement.—*adjs.* ismat'ic, -al, ism'y, addicted to isms or faddish theories.—*n.* ismat'icalness. [From the suffix *-ism*.]

Ismaili, is-mä-ē'lē, or is-mä'i-li, *n.* one of a sect of Shiite Mohammedans whose imâm or spiritual head is the Aga Khan.—Also *adj.*—*n.* and *adj.* Ismailian (*is-mä-il'i-ən*).—Is'mailism.—*adj.* Ismailit'ic.

iso-, i'sō-, *pfx.* equal: in chem. denoting an isomeric substance—e.g. iso-oc'tane, one of the isomers of normal octane. [Gr. *isos*, equal.]

isobar, i'sō-bär, *n.* a curve running through places of equal pressure: esp. one connecting places, or their representations on a map, of equal barometric pressure (*meteor.*): (see isobare; *chem.*).—*adjs.* isobaric (*-bar'ik*), isobaromet'ric. [Pfx. iso-, and Gr. *baros*, weight.]

isobare, i'sō-bär, *n.* either of two atoms of different chemical elements but of identical atomic mass (e.g. an isotope of titanium and an isotope of chromium both of atomic mass 50).—Also i'sobar. [Same as isobar above.]

isobase, i'sō-bās, (*geol.*) *n.* a contour line of equal upheaval of the land. [Pfx. iso-, and Gr. *basis*, step.]

isobath, i'sō-bäth, *n.* a contour line of equal

**depth.**—*adj.* **isobath'ic.** [Pfx. iso-, and Gr. *bathos*, depth.]

**isobilateral,** *i-sō-bī-lat'ər-əl, adj.* bilaterally symmetrical with upper and under surfaces alike: symmetrical about two planes (*bot.*): having the flanks of the organ flattened surfaces. [Pfx. iso-, and **bilateral.**]

**isobront,** *i'sō-bront, n.* a contour line marking simultaneous development of a thunderstorm. [Pfx. iso-, and Gr. *brontē*, thunder.]

**isochasm,** *i'sō-kazm, n.* a contour line of equal frequency of auroral displays.—*adj.* **isochasm'ic.** [Pfx. iso-, and Gr. *chasma*, a gap, expanse.]

**isocheim,** *i'sō-kīm, n.* a contour line of mean winter temperature.—*adjs.* and *ns.* **isocheim'al,** **isocheim'enal.**—*adj.* **isocheim'ic.** [Pfx. iso-, and Gr. *cheima*, winter weather, *cheimainein*, to be stormy.]

**isochor, isochore,** *i'sō-kōr, -kör, n.* a curve representing variation of some quantity under conditions of constant volume.—*adj.* **isochoric** (*-kor'ik*). [Pfx. iso-, and Gr. *chōrā*, space.]

**isochromatic,** *i-sō-krō-mat'ik, adj.* having the same colour (*optics*): orthochromatic (*phot.*). [Pfx. iso-, and Gr. *chrōma, -atos*, colour.]

**isochronal,** *i-sok'rən-əl,* **isoch'ronous, -əs,** *adjs.* of equal time: performed in equal times: in regular periodicity.—*advs.* **isoch'ronally, isoch'ronously.**—*ns.* **is'ochrone,** a line on a chart or map joining points associated with a constant time difference, e.g. in reception of radio signals; **isoch'ronism.** [Pfx. iso-, and Gr. *chronos*, time.]

**isoclinal,** *i-sō-kli'nəl, adj.* folded with nearly the same dip in each limb (*geol.*): in terrestrial magnetism, having the same magnetic dip.— *n.* an isoclinical line, or contour line of magnetic dip.—*adj.* and *n.* **isoclinic** (-*klin'ik*), **isoclinal.** [Pfx. iso-, and Gr. *klinein*, to bend.]

**isocryme,** *i'sō-krīm, n.* a contour line of equal temperature during the coldest time.—*adj.* and *n.* **isocrym'al.** [Pfx. iso-, and Gr. *krȳmos*, cold.]

**isocyclic,** *i'sō-sī-klik, adj.* homocyclic. [iso-, cyclic.]

**Isodia,** *i-sō'di-ə, n.pl.* the feast of the presentation of the Virgin in the temple at the age of three. [Gr., neut. pl. of adj. *eisodios—eisodos,* entrance.]

**isodiametric, -al,** *i-sō-di-ə-met'rik, -əl, adjs.* of equal diameters: about as broad as long. [Pfx. iso-.]

**isodicon,** *i-sod'i-kon,* (*Gr. Ch.*) *n.* a troparion or short anthem sung while the Gospel is being carried through the church. [Dim. of Gr. *eisodos*, entrance.]

**isodimorphism,** *i-sō-di-mörf'izm,* (*crystal.*) *n.* isomorphism between each of the two forms of a dimorphous substance and the corresponding forms of another dimorphous substance.—*adjs.* **isodimorph'ic, isodimorph'ous.** [Pfx. iso-.]

**isodomon,** *i-sod'o-mon, n.* masonry of uniform blocks in courses of equal height, the vertical joints placed over the middle of the blocks below.—Also (Latinised) **isod'omum**:—*pl.* **isod'-oma.**—*adj.* **isod'omous.** [Gr., neut. of *isodomos,* equal-coursed—*isos,* equal, *domos,* a course—*demein,* to build.]

**isodont,** *i'sō-dont,* (*zool.*) *adj.* having all the teeth similar in size and form.—Also **isodont'al.**—*n.* an isodontal animal. [Gr. *isos,* equal, *odous, odontos,* tooth.]

**isodynamic,** *i-sō-din-am'ik,* or *-din-, adj.* of equal strength, esp. of magnetic intensity.—*n.* an isodynamic line on the earth or the map, a contour line of magnetic intensity. [Pfx. iso-, and Gr. *dynamis,* strength.]

**isoelectric,** *i-sō-i-lek'trik, adj.* having the same potential.—**isoelectric point,** the pH-value at which the ionisation of an ampholyte is at a minimum. [Pfx. iso-, electric.]

**Isoetes,** *i-sō'e-tēz, n.* the quillwort genus consti-

tuting a family (**Isoetā'ceae**) of pteridophytes, with short stem, a bunch of quill-shaped leaves in which the sporangia are sunk, and branching roots. [Gr. *isoetes,* houseleek (an evergreen)— *isos,* equal, *etos,* a year.]

**isogamy,** *i-sog'ə-mi,* (*biol.*) *n.* the conjugation of two gametes of similar size and form.—*n.* **isogamete** (*i-sō-gam'ēt,* or *-ēt'*).—*adjs.* **isogam'ic, isog'amous.** [Pfx. iso-, and Gr. *gamos,* marriage.]

**isogeny,** *i-sōj'ə-ni, n.* likeness of origin.—*adjs.* **isogenetic** (*i-sō-ji-net'ik*), **isog'enous.** [Pfx. iso-, and Gr. *genos,* kind.]

**isogeotherm,** *i-sō-jē'ō-thûrm, n.* a subterranean contour of equal temperature.—*adj.* **isogeotherm'al.**—*n.* an isogeotherm. [Pfx. iso-, and Gr. *gē,* the earth, *thermē,* heat—*thermos,* hot.]

**isogloss,** *i'sō-glos, n.* a line separating one region from another region which differs from it in a particular feature of dialect.—*adjs.* **isogloss'al,** **-glott'al.** [Pfx. iso-, and Gr. *glōssa,* tongue.]

**isogonic,** *i-sō-gon'ik,* **isogonal,** *i-sog'ən-əl, adj.* of equal angles, esp. of magnetic declination. —*n.* an isogonic line or contour line of magnetic declination. [Pfx. iso-, and Gr. *gōniā,* an angle.]

**isogram,** *i'sō-gram, n.* a line drawn on a map or diagram showing all points which have an equal numerical value with respect to a given climatic or other variable. [Pfx. iso-, and Gr. *gramma,* a letter.]

**isohel,** *i'sō-hel, n.* a contour line of equal amounts of sunshine. [Pfx. iso-, and Gr. *hēlios,* sun.]

**isohyet,** *i-sō-hi'ət, n.* a contour line of equal rainfall.—*adj.* **isohy'etal.**—*n.* an isohyet. [Pfx. iso-, and Gr. *hyetos,* rain—*hyein,* to rain.]

**Isokontae,** *i-sō-kont'ē, n.pl.* the green algae, whose zoospores have usually equal cilia.—*n.* **i'sokont.**—*adj.* and *n.* **isokont'an.** [Pfx. iso-, and Gr. *kontos,* a (punting) pole.]

**isolate,** *i'sō-lāt, v.t.* to place in a detached situation, like an island: to detach: to insulate: to separate (esp. those who might be infected; *med.*): to seclude: to segregate: to obtain in an uncompounded state.—*adj.* **is'olable.**—*ns.* **isolā'tion; isolā'tionism,** the policy of avoiding political entanglements with other countries; **isolā'tionist.**—*adj.* **i'solātive,** tending towards isolation: occurring without influence from outside.—*n.* **i'solātor.**—**isolating languages,** those in which each word is a bare root, not inflected or compounded. [It. *isolare—isola*—L. *insula,* an island.]

**isomer,** *i'sō-mər,* (*chem.*) *n.* a substance, radical, or ion isomeric with another: an atomic nucleus having the same atomic number and mass as another or others but a different energy state.—*n.* **i'somère** (*zool.*), an organ or segment corresponding to or homologous with another. —*adj.* **isomeric** (*-mer'ik; chem.*), identical in percentage composition and molecular weight but different in constitution or the mode in which the atoms are arranged: of nuclei, differing only in energy state and half-life.—*v.t.* and *v.i.* **isomerise, -ize,** (*i-som'ər-iz*), to change into an isomer.—*ns.* **isomerisā'tion, -z-;** **isom'erism,** the property of being isomeric: the existence of isomers.—*adj.* **isom'erous** (*bot.*), having the same number of parts (esp. in floral whorls). [Pfx. iso-, and Gr. *meros,* part.]

**isometric, -al,** *i-sō-met'rik, -əl, adjs.* having equality of measure: pertaining to isometrics: having the plane of projection equally inclined to three perpendicular axes: of the cubic system, or referable to three equal axes at right angles to one another (*crystal.*).—*adv.* **isomet'rically.**—*ns.* **isomet'rics,** system of strengthening the muscles and tuning up the body by opposing one muscle to another or to a resistant object; **isom'etry,** equality of measure. [Pfx. iso-, and Gr. *metron,* measure.]

Neutral vowels in unaccented syllables: *el'ə-mənt*; for certain sounds in foreign words, see p. viii

**isomorph**, *i'sō-mörf*, *n.* that which shows isomorphism.—*adj.* **isomorph'ic**, showing isomorphism.—*n.* **isomorph'ism**, similarity in unrelated forms (*biol.*): close similarity in crystalline form combined with similar chemical constitution (*crystal.*).—*adj.* **isomorph'ous**.—**isomorphous mixture**, a mixed crystal or solid solution in which isomorphous substances are crystallised together by vicarious substitution. [Pfx. **iso-**, and Gr. *morphē*, form.]

**isoniazid(e)**, *i-sō-ni'ə-zid, -zid*, *n.* a drug, a pyridine derivative, used against tuberculosis; sold under several proprietary names.

**isonomy**, *i-son'ə-mi*, *n.* equal law, rights, or privileges. [Gr. *isonomiā—isos*, equal, *nomos*, law.]

**isoperimeter**, *i-sō-pər-im'i-tər*, *n.* a figure with perimeter equal to another.—*adj.* **isoperimetrical** (*i-sō-per-i-met'ri-kəl*).—*n.* **isoperim'etry**. [Pfx. **iso-**, and Gr. *perimetron*, circumference.]

**isopleth**, *i'sō-pleth*, *n.* an isogram, esp. one on a graph showing variations of a climatic element as a function of two variables. [Pfx. **iso-**, and Gr. *plēthos*, great number.]

**isopod**, *i'sō-pod*, *n.* a member of the Isopoda.—*n.pl.* **Isopoda** (*i-sop'ə-də*), an order of Crustacea with no carapace, depressed body, sessile eyes, seven pairs of nearly equal thoracic legs, and usually lamellar uropods—woodlice, fishlice, etc.—*adj.* **isop'odous**. [Pfx. **iso-**, and Gr. *pous, podos*, a foot.]

**isopolity**, *i-sō-pol'i-ti*, *n.* reciprocity of rights of citizenship in different communities. [Pfx. **iso-**, and Gr. *politeiā*, citizenship.]

**isoprene**, *i'sō-prēn*, *n.* a hydrocarbon of the terpene group, which may be polymerised into synthetic rubber. [Etymology obscure.]

**Isoptera**, *i-sop'tər-ə*, *n.pl.* an order of insects having the two pairs of wings (when present) closely alike—the termites.—*adj.* **isop'terous**. [Pfx. **iso-**, and Gr. *pteron*. a wing.]

**isorhythmic**, *i-sō-ridh'mik, -rith'mik*, *adj.* in ancient prosody, equal in the number of time-units for thesis and arsis, as dactyl, spondee, anapaest. [Pfx. **iso-**, and Gr. *rhythmos*, rhythm.]

**isosceles**, *i-sos'i-lēz*, (*geom.*) *adj.* having two equal sides, as a triangle. [Gr. *isoskelēs—isos*, equal, *skelos*, a leg.]

**isoseismal**, *i-sō-sis'məl*, *n.* a curve or line connecting points at which an earthquake shock is felt with equal intensity.—*adjs.* **isoseis'mal, isoseis'-mic**. [Pfx. **iso-**. and Gr. *seismos*, a shaking.]

**isosporous**, *i-sos'pər-əs*, or *i-sō-spō'rəs, -spō'*, *adj.* having spores of one kind only—opp. to *heterosporous*.—*n.* **isos'pory**. [Pfx. **iso-**, and Gr. *sporos*, seed.]

**isostasy**, *i-sos'tə-si*, (*geol.*) *n.* a condition of equilibrium held to exist in the earth's crust, equal masses of matter underlying equal areas, whether of sea or land down to an assumed level of compensation.—*adj.* **isostatic** (*i-sō-stat'ik*), in hydrostatic equilibrium from equality of pressure: in a state of isostasy: pertaining to isostasy.—*adv.* **isostat'ically**. [Gr. *isos*, equal, *stasis*, setting, weighing, *statikos*, pertaining to weighing.]

**isostemonous**, *i-sō-stēm'ən-əs*, *adj.* having as many stamens as petals. [Pfx. **iso-**, and Gr. *stēmōn*, a thread.]

**isothere**, *i'sō-thēr*, *n.* a contour line of equal mean summer temperature.—*adj.* **isotheral** (*i-soth'ər-əl, i-sō-thēr'əl*).—*n.* an isothere. [Gr. *theros*, summer—*therein*, to make warm.]

**isotherm**, *i'sō-thûrm*, *n.* a contour line of equal temperature.—*adj.* **isotherm'al**, at constant temperature: pertaining to isotherms.—*n.* an isothermal line, isotherm.—*adv.* **isotherm'ally**. [Pfx. **iso-**, and Gr. *thermē*, heat—*thermos*, hot.]

**isotone**, *i'sō-tōn*, *n.* one of a number of nuclides having the same number of neutrons in the nucleus with differing numbers of protons. [Pfx. **iso-**, and prob. Gr. *tonos*, tension.]

**isotonic**, *i-sō-ton'ik*, *adj.* having the same tone, tension, or osmotic pressure. [Pfx. **iso-**, and Gr. *tonos*, tension, tone.]

**isotope**, *i'sō-tōp*, *n.* one of a set of chemically identical species of atom which have the same atomic number but different mass numbers; a natural element is made up of isotopes, always present in the same proportions.—*adj.* **isotopic** (*-top'ik*).—*n.* **isotopy** (*i-sot'ə-pi*), fact or condition of being isotopic.—**isotopic number**, the excess number of neutrons over protons in a nuclide.—**stable isotope**, a non-radioactive isotope found in nature. [Pfx. **iso-**, and Gr. *topos*, place (*scil.* in the periodic table).]

**isotron**, *i'sō-tron*, *n.* a device for separating isotopes by accelerating ions by means of an electric field—the velocities attained are in inverse proportion to the masses. [**iso(tope)** and suff. **-tron**.]

**isotropic**, *i-sō-trop'ik*, *adj.* having the same properties irrespective of direction: without predetermined axes (*biol.*).—Also **isotropous** (*i-sot'rə-pəs*).—*ns.* **isot'ropism, isot'ropy**. [Pfx. **iso-**, and Gr. *tropos*, turn, direction.]

**isotype**, *i'sō-tīp*, *n.* a presentation of statistical information by a row of diagrammatic pictures each representing a particular number of instances. [Pfx. **iso-**, and Gr. *typos*, form.]

**I-spy**, *i'-spi'*, *n.* a children's game of hide-and-seek, so called from the cry when one is spied: a word-game, in which one guesses objects in view, whose names begin with a certain letter of the alphabet. [**I, spy**.]

**Israeli**, *iz-rā'lē*, *n.* a citizen of the modern state of Israel.—Also *adj.* [See **Israelite**.]

**Israelite**, *iz'ri-əl-it, -rē-*, *n.* a descendant of Israel or Jacob: a Jew: one of the elect (*fig.*): a member of a Christian sect that observes the Jewish law.—*adjs.* **Israelit'ic, Israclit'ish**. [Gr. *Isrāēlitēs—Isrāēl*, Heb. *Yisrāēl*, perh. contender with God—*sara*, to fight, *El*, God.]

**issei**, *ēs'sā'*, *n.* a Japanese immigrant in the U.S.A.—cf. **nisei**. [Jap., first generation.]

**issue**, *ish'ū, -ōō, is'ū*, *n.* a going or flowing out: an outlet: act of sending out: that which flows or passes out: fruit of the body, children: produce, profits: a fine (*obs.*): a putting into circulation, as of banknotes: publication, as of a book: a giving out for use: a set of things put forth at one time: a single thing given out or supplied (chiefly *mil.*): ultimate result, outcome: upshot: critical determination: luck or success in conclusion (*Shak.*): an act, deed (*Shak.*): point in dispute: a point on which a question depends: a question awaiting decision or ripe for decision: a discharge or flux (*med.*): an ulcer produced artificially.—*v.i.* (in *Spens.* usu. **issue'**) to go, flow, or come out: to proceed, as from a source: to spring: to be produced: to come to a point in fact or law (*law*): to turn out, result, terminate.—*v.t.* to send out: to put forth: to put into circulation: to publish: to give out for use: to supply (*mil. jargon*).—*adj.* **iss'uable**, capable of issuing, admitting of an issue.—*n.* **iss'uance**, act of giving out, promulgation.—*adjs.* **iss'uant** (*her.*), issuing or coming up from another, as a charge or bearing; **iss'ueless**, without issue: childless.—*n.* **iss'uer**, one who issues or emits.—**at issue**, in quarrel or controversy: in dispute; **feigned issue** (*law*), an issue made up for trial by agreement of the parties or by an order of court, instead of by the ordinary legal procedure; **general issue** (*law*), a simple denial of the whole charge, as 'Not guilty', instead of a **special issue**, an issue taken by denying a particular part of the allegations; **immaterial issue**, an issue which is not decisive of any part of the litigation, as opp. to

a **material issue**, one which necessarily involves some part of the rights in controversy; **join**, or **take**, **issue**, to take an opposite position, or opposite positions, in dispute: to enter into dispute: to take up a point as basis of dispute; **side issue**, a subordinate issue arising from the main business. [O.Fr. *issue—issir*, to go or flow out—L. *exire—ex*, out, *īre*, to go.]
**-ist**, *-ist*, *suff.* denoting the person who holds a doctrine or practises an art, as Calvin*ist*, chem*ist*, novel*ist*, art*ist*, royal*ist*. [L. *-ista*—Gr. *-istēs*.]
**isthmus**, *is(th)'məs*, *n.* a narrow neck of land connecting two larger portions: a constriction.— *adj.* **isth'mian**, pertaining to an isthmus, esp. the Isthmus of Corinth.—**The Isthmian Games** were on that isthmus, near the Saronic Gulf shore. [L.,—Gr. *isthmos*, from root of *ienai*, to go.]
**Istiophorus.** Same as **Histiophorus** (see under hist-).
**istle**, *ist'li*, **ixtle**, *ikst'li*, *n.* a valuable fibre obtained from Agave, Bromelia, and other plants. [Mexican Sp. *ixtle*—Nahuatl *ichtli*.]
**it**, *it*, *pron.* the neut. of **he**, **him** (and formerly **his**), applied to a thing without life, a lower animal, a young child, rarely (except as an antecedent or in contempt) to a man or woman: used as an impersonal, indefinite, or anticipatory or provisional subject or object, as the object of a transitive verb that is normally an intransitive, or a noun: as gen., its (*obs.* and *dial.*): in children's games, the player chosen to oppose all others: the *ne plus ultra*, that which answers exactly to what one is looking for (*coll.*): an indefinable crowning quality by which one carries it off—personal magnetism: sex-appeal (*slang*):—*gen.* **its** (*obs.* **his**, **it**; see also **its**); *pl.* **they, them.** [O.E. *hit*, neut. (nom. and acc.) of *hē*; Du. *het*, Goth. *hita*, this; akin to Goth. *ita*, Ger. *es*, L. *id*, Sans. *i*, pronominal root = here. The *t* is an old neuter suffix, as in *that*, *what*, and cognate with *d* in L. *illud*, *istud, quod*.]
**it.** Abbreviation for Italian vermouth.
**ita**, *ē'tə, it'ə, n.* the mīriti palm. [Arawak *ité*.]
**itacism**, *ē'tə-sizm, n.* the pronunciation of Greek *ēta* as in Modern Greek, like English long *e* (opp. to *etacism*): iotacism in pronunciation of various vowels and diphthongs. [Gr. *ēta*, eta, η.]
**itacolumite**, *it-ə-kol'ūm-īt, n.* a schistose quartzite containing scales of mica, talc, and chlorite, often having a certain flexibility. [*Itacolumi* mountain, Brazil.]
**itaconic acid**, *it-ə-kon'ik*, or *īt-*, a white crystalline solid got by fermentation of sugar with Aspergillus mould, used in plastics manufacture. [Anagram of *aconitic*.]
**Italian**, *i-tal'yən, adj.* of or relating to Italy or its people or language.—*n.* a native or citizen of Italy, or person of the same race: the language of Italy.—*adj.* **Ital'ianate**, Italianised.—*vs.t.* **Ital'ianate**, **Ital'ianise**, **-ize**, to make Italian: to give an Italian character to.—*vs.i.* to become Italian: to play the Italian: to speak Italian: to use Italian idioms: to adopt Italian ways.— *ns.* **Ital'ianism**, **Ital'icism** (*-sizm*), an Italian idiom or habit: Italian sympathies; **Ital'ianist**, one who has a scholarly knowledge of Italian: a person of Italian sympathies.—*adj.* **Ital'ic**, pertaining to Italy, esp. ancient Italy: (without *cap.*) of a sloping type introduced by the Italian printer Aldo Manuzio in 1501, used esp. for emphasis or other distinctive purpose, indicated in MS. by single underlining.—*n.* (usu. in *pl.*) an italic letter.—*n.* **italicisā'tion**, *-z-.*—*v.t.* **ital'icise**, **-ize**, to put in, or mark for, italics.—*n.* **Ital'iot**, **Ital'iote**, a Greek of ancient Italy.—Also *adj.*— **Italian architecture**, the style practised by Italian architects of the 15th-17th centuries, which orig-

inated in a revival of the ancient architecture of Rome; **Italianate Englishman**, an Englishman of the Renaissance, full of Italian learning and vices, proverbially equivalent to a devil incarnate; **Italian garden**, a formal garden with statues; **Italian iron**, a smoothing iron for fluting; **Italian sixth**, a chord of a note with its major third and augmented sixth; **Italian warehouseman**, a dealer in such groceries as macaroni, olive oil, dried fruits, etc.; **Italic dialects**, languages of ancient Italy akin to Latin; **Italic version**, or **It'ala**, a translation of the Bible into Latin, based on the 'Old Latin' version, and made probably in the time of Augustine. [L. *Italiānus* and Gr. *Italikos*—L. *Italia*, Gr. *Italiā*, Italy.]
**italic.** See **Italian**.
**Italo-**, *i-tal'ō*, *i'təl-o*, in composition, Italian.
**itch**, *ich*, *n.* an irritating sensation in the skin: scabies, an eruptive disease in the skin, caused by a parasitic mite: a constant teasing desire.— *v.i.* to have an uneasy, irritating sensation in the skin: to have a constant, teasing desire.—*n.* **itch'iness.**—*adj.* **itch'y**, pertaining to or affected with itch or itching.—**itching palm**, a greed for gain; **itch'-mite**, a mite that burrows in the skin causing itch or scabies; **itch'weed**, Indian poke. [O.E. *giccan*, to itch; Scot. *youk, yuck*, Ger. *jucken*, to itch.]
**-ite**, *-īt*, *suff.* used to form (1) names of persons, indicating their origin, place of origin, affiliations, loyalties, etc. (e.g. *Semite, Durhamite, Jacobite, Buchmanite, Janeite*); (2) names of fossil organisms (e.g. *ammonite*); (3) names of minerals (e.g. *calcite*); (4) names of salts of acids with suff. *-ous* (e.g. *sulphite*, salt of sulphurous acid); (5) names of bodily parts (e.g. *somite*). The nouns may be used also as adjs.
**item**, *i'tam*, *adv.* likewise: also.—*n.* a separate article or particular in an enumeration: a piece of news or other matter in a newspaper.—*v.t.* to set down in enumeration: to make a note of. —*v.t.* **i'temise**, **-ize**, to give by items. [L. *ītem*, likewise.]
**iterate**, *it'ar-āt*, *v.t.* to do again: to say again, repeat.—*ns.* **it'erance**, **iterā'tion**, repetition.— *adjs.* **it'erant**, **it'erative** (*-ə-tiv* or *-ā-tiv*), repeating. [L. *iterāre*, *-ātum—iterum*, again.]
**iterum**, *it'ə-rəm, -e-room*, (L.) again.
**ithyphallus**, *ith-i-fal'əs*, *n.* an erect phallus: (*cap.*) the stinkhorn genus of fungi.—*adj.* **ithyphall'ic**, of or with an ithyphallus: pertaining to the processions in honour of Dionysos in which an ithyphallus was carried, or to the hymns sung or the metres used: shameless. [Gr. *ithyphallos—ithys*, straight, *phallos*, a phallus.]
**itinerant**, *i-tin'ər-ənt*, also *ī-*, *adj.* making journeys from place to place: travelling.—*n.* one who travels from place to place, esp. a judge, a Methodist preacher, a strolling musician, (or a peddler: a wanderer.—*ns.* **itin'eracy** (*-ə-si*), **itin'erancy.**—*adv.* **itin'erantly.**—*adj.* **itin'erary**, travelling: relating to roads or journeys.—*n.* a plan or record of a journey: a road-book: a route: an itinerant.—*v.i.* **itin'erate**, to travel from place to place, esp. for the purpose of judging, preaching, or lecturing. [L. *iter, itineris*, a journey.]
**-itis**, *-i'tis*, *n. suff.* denoting a disease (now inflammation), as bronch*itis*: also jocularly imputing an imaginary disease, as jazz*itis*. [Gr. *-ītis*.]
**its**, *its*, possessive or genitive of **it**. (The old form was **his**, **its** not being older than the end of the 16th century. *Its* does not occur in the English Bible of 1611 (inserted in 1660 in Leviticus xxv. 5) or in Spenser, rarely in Shakespeare, and is not common until the time of Dryden.)—*pron.* **itself**, *it-self'*, the emphatic and reflexive form of **it**.—**by itself**, alone, apart; **in itself**, by its own nature.

**ivory,** *i'və-ri, n.* dentine, esp. the hard white substance composing the tusks of the elephant, walrus, hippopotamus, and narwhal: an object of that material, as a billiard-ball, a piano-key: a tooth or the teeth (*slang*).—*adj.* made of, or resembling, ivory.—*adj.* **i'voried,** made like ivory: furnished with teeth.—*n.* **i'vorist,** a worker in ivory.—**i'vory-black,** a black powder, originally made from burnt ivory, but now from bone; **i'vory-gate'** (*myth.*; see **gate**); **i'vory-nut,** the nut of Phytelephas or other palm, yielding **vegetable ivory,** a substance like ivory; **i'vory-palm; i'vory-por'celain,** a fine ware with an ivory-white glaze; **ivory tower** (*fig.*), a place of retreat from the world and one's fellows; **i'vory-tree,** the palay.—**show one's ivories,** to show the teeth. [O.Fr. *ivurie* (Fr. *ivoire*)—L. *ebur, eboris,* ivory; Coptic *ebu,* elephant, ivory.]

**ivresse,** *ē-vres', (Fr.)* drunkenness.

**ivy,** *i'vi, n.* an araliaceous evergreen plant (*Hedera helix*) that climbs by roots on trees and walls. —*adjs.* **i'vied** (also **i'vy'd**), **i'vy-mant'led,** overgrown or mantled with ivy.—**i'vy-bush,** a bush or branch of ivy, esp. formerly one hung at a tavern-door, the ivy being sacred to Bacchus.— *adjs.* **i'vy-leaved,** having five-lobed leaves like ivy (as the *ivy-leaved* toadflax); **ivy-man'tled,** ivied. —**i'vy-tod',** a bush of ivy.—**ground-ivy,** poison-ivy (see **ground, poison**). [O.E. *ifig,* O.H.G. *ebah.*]

**iwis, ywis,** *i-wis', (obs.) adv.* certainly—sometimes ignorantly written *I wis,* as if 'I know'. [M.E. *ywis, iwis*—O.E. *gewis,* certain; Ger. *gewiss* (adv.).]

**ixtle.** See **istle.**

**iynx.** Same as **jynx.**

**Iyyar,** *ē'yär, n.* the eighth month of the Jewish year (second of the ecclesiastical year). [Heb.]

**izard,** *iz'ərd, n.* the Pyrenean ibex. [Fr. *isard.*]

**izzard,** *iz'ərd,* **izzet,** *iz'it, (arch.* or *dial.) n.* the letter Z.

**-ize.** See **-ise.**

# J

**J, j,** *jā, n.* the tenth letter in our alphabet, developed from I, specialised to denote a consonantal sound (*dzh* in English, *y* in German and other languages, *zh* in French, an open guttural in Spanish), I being retained for the vowel sound—a differentiation not general in English books till about 1630: as numeral, used in old MSS. and in medical prescriptions instead of *i* final, as *vj,* six: used equally with *i* for $\sqrt{-1}$: J represents the mechanical equivalent of heat.—**J-pen,** a pen with a short broad nib.

**jab,** *jab, v.t.* and *v.i.* to poke, stab.—*n.* a sudden thrust or stab. [Cf. **job** (1).]

**jabber,** *jab'ər, v.i.* to gabble or talk rapidly.—*v.t.* to utter indistinctly.—*n.* rapid indistinct speaking.—*n.* **jabb'erer.**—*n.* and *adj.* **jabb'ering.**—*adv.* **jabb'eringly.** [Imit.]

**jabble,** *jab'l,* (*Scot.*) *n.* an agitation in liquid: a rippling: a quantity of liquid enough to dash about or splash.—*v.t.* and *v.i.* to splash: to ripple: to dash: to jumble (*fig.*). [Imit.]

**jabers,** *jā'bərz, n.* in the Irish oath *be jabers,* prob. for **Jesus.**

**jabiru,** *jab'i-rōō, -rōō', n.* a large Brazilian stork: extended to other kinds. [Tupí *jabirú.*]

**jaborandi,** *jab-ə-ran'di, jab-ŏ-, n.* a Brazilian drug with sialagogue and diaphoretic properties, got from the leaflets of rutaceous shrubs (Pilocarpus) and other sources. [Tupí.]

**jabot,** *zha'bō, n.* a frill of lace, etc., worn in front of a woman's dress or on a man's shirtfront, esp. (now) as part of full Highland dress. [Fr.]

**jacamar,** *jak'ə-mär, n.* any one of a South American family (Galbulidae) of long-billed insect-catching birds with reversible fourth toe and usu. metallic green or bronze plumage. [Fr.,—Tupí *jacamá-ciri.*]

**jaçana,** *zhä-sə-nä', jacana, jak'ə-nə, n.* a long-toed swamp bird of the tropics. [Port., from Tupí.]

**jacaranda,** *jak-ə-ran'də, n.* a South American tree of the Bignoniaceae, with hard, heavy, brown wood. [Port. and Tupí *jacarandá.*]

**jacchus,** *jak'əs, n.* a South American marmoset (Callithrix). [L. *Iacchus*—Gr. *Iakchos,* Bacchus.]

**jacent,** *jā'sənt,* (*obs.*) *adj.* lying flat: sluggish. [L. *jacēns, -entis,* pr.p. of *jacēre,* to lie.]

**jacinth,** *jas'inth, jās', n.* originally, a blue gemstone, perhaps sapphire: a reddish-orange variety of transparent zircon—hyacinth (*min.*): a variety of garnet, topaz, quartz, or other stone (*jewellery*): a reddish-orange colour: a slaty-blue fancy pigeon. [hyacinth.]

**jack,** *jak, n.* (with *cap.*) a familiar form or diminutive of John: (with *cap.*) the common man (*obs.*): (with *cap.*) contemptuously, a fellow (*obs.*): (usu. with *cap.*) an ill-mannered, vulgar or boorish fellow (*obs.*): (sometimes with *cap.*) an attendant, servant or labourer: (often with *cap.*) a sailor: (with *cap.*) man, fellow, used in addressing a man whose name is unknown to the speaker (*U.S. slang*): a detective (*U.S. slang*): money (*U.S. slang*): a machine or device which orig. took the place of a servant, as a boot-jack for taking off boots, a contrivance for turning a spit (smoke-jack, roasting-jack), an apparatus for raising heavy weights: a winch: a figure that strikes the bell in clocks: the male of some animals: a jackass: a jack-rabbit: a jackdaw: a young pike: in keyboard instruments, part of the action that moves the hammer or carries the quill or tangent: the key itself (*Shak.*): a contrivance for guiding threads in a loom: a saw-horse: a small flag indicating nationality, flown by a ship, usu. at the bow or the bowsprit: a leather pitcher or bottle: a knave in cards: the small white ball aimed at in bowls.—*v.t.* to raise with, or as if with, a jack (with *up*): to act upon with a jack: to throw up or abandon promptly (also with *up* or *in*) (*slang*): to increase (as prices) (with *up*).—*v.i.* to give up (with *up*) (*slang*).—**Jack'-a-dan'dy,** a dandy or fop, esp. if diminutive; **Jack'-a-lan'tern, Jack'-o'-lan'tern,** Will-o'-the-wisp; **Jack'-a-Lent** (*Shak.*), a boy (for Jack of Lent, a kind of puppet formerly thrown at in sport at Lent); **jack'-block,** a block of pulleys used for raising and lowering topgallant-masts; **jack'-boot,** a large boot reaching above the knee, to protect the leg, orig. covered with iron plates and worn by cavalry: military rule, esp. when brutal (*fig.*); **Jack'-by-the-hedge',** garlic-mustard; **jack'-cross'tree,** the crosstree at the head of a topgallant-mast; **Jack'-fool',** a fool; **Jack Frost,** frost personified; **Jack'-go-to-bed-at-noon',** the plant goat's-beard.—*adj.* and *adv.* **jack'-high,** in bowls, as far as the jack.—**Jack'-in-off'ice,** a vexatiously self-important petty official; **Jack'-in-the-box',** a figure that springs up from a box when the lid is released; **Jack'-in-the-green',** a May-Day dancer enclosed in a green shrubby framework; **Jack'-in-the-pul'pit,** a N. American plant (*Arisaema triphyllum*) like cuckoo-pint: also applied to various other plants, esp. of the genus Arisaema; **Jack Ketch,** a public hangman—from one so named under James II; **jack'-knife,** a large clasp-knife: a dive in which the performer doubles up in the air and straightens out again.—*v.i., v.t.* to double up as a jack-knife does: (of connected vehicles or parts) through faulty control, to form, or cause to form, an angle of 90° or less.—**Jack Nasty,** a sneak: a sloven; **Jack'-of-all'-trades,** one who can turn his hand to anything; **jack'-pine,** a name for several N. American species of pine; **jack'-plane,** a large strong plane used by joiners; **jack'pot,** a poker game, played for the pot or pool (consisting of equal stakes from all the players), which must be opened by a player holding two jacks or better: a money pool in card games, competitions, etc., that can be won only on certain conditions being fulfilled and accumulates till such time as they are: a prize-money fund: a mess, an awkward situation (*U.S. slang*); **Jack'-priest',** (in contempt) a parson; **Jack'-pudd'ing** (*arch.*), a merry-andrew, buffoon; **jack'-rabb'it,** a long-eared American hare; **jack'-raft'er,** a rafter shorter than the rest, as in a hip-roof; **Jack'-sauce** (*Shak.*), an impudent fellow; **Jack'-slave** (*Shak.*), a low servant, a vulgar fellow; **jack'smith** (*obs.*), a maker of jacks for the kitchen; **jack'-snipe,** a small species of snipe; **Jack Sprat,** a diminutive fellow; **jack'-staff,** the staff on which the jack is hoisted.—*n.pl.* **jack'-stays,** ropes or strips of wood or iron stretched along the yards of a ship to bind the sails to.—**Jack'-straw', jack'-straw,** a straw effigy: a man of straw, of no real significance: a straw or slip used in the game of **jack'-straws',** or spillikins; **Jacktar** (also without *cap.*), a sailor; **jack towel,** a long endless towel passing over a roller—**before you**

can say **Jack Robinson**, very quickly; **cheap Jack** (see **cheap**); **every man Jack**, one and all; **hit the jackpot**, to win a jackpot: to have a big success; **jack easy**, indifferent, not caring one way or the other; **poor Jack**, poor-John; **steeplejack** (see **steeple**); **Union Jack** (not properly a jack; see **union**); **yellow Jack** (*slang*), yellow fever. [App. Fr. *Jacques*, the most common name in France, hence used as a substitute for *John*, the most common name in England; really = *James* or *Jacob*—L. *Jacōbus*; but possibly partly from *Jackin, Jankin*, dim. of *John*.]

**jack**, *jak*, *n*. a mediaeval defensive coat, esp. of leather.—**jack'man**, a soldier clad in a jack: a retainer. [Fr. *jaque*, perh. from *Jacques*, James.]

**jack**, **jak**, *jak*, *n*. a tree of the East Indies of the breadfruit genus (*Artocarpus*): its fruit.—**jack'-fruit**; **jack'-tree**. [Port. *jaca*—Malayalam *chakka*.]

**jackal**, *jak'öl*, *n*. a wild, gregarious animal closely allied to the dog—erroneously supposed to act as a lion's provider or hunting scout: hence, one who does another's dirty work: a drudge: one who would share the spoil without sharing the danger.—*v.i.* to play the jackal:—*pa.p.* **jack'alled.** [Pers. *shaghāl*.]

**jackanapes**, *jak'ə-nāps*, *n*. an ape or monkey (*arch*.): an impudent fellow: a coxcomb: a forward child. [Origin uncertain.]

**jackaroo, jackeroo**, *jak-ə-rōō', (Austr.) n*. a newcomer, or other person, gaining experience on a sheep-station.—*v.i.* to be a jackaroo. [App. an imitation of kangaroo with Jack.]

**jackass**, *jak'as*, *n*. a he-ass: a blockhead, fool.—**laughing jackass**, an Australian kingfisher which has a laughter-like call, the kookaburra. [jack (1), ass.]

**jackdaw**, *jak'dö*, *n*. a daw, a small species of crow with greyish neck. [jack (1), daw (2).]

**jackeroo**. See jackaroo.

**jacket**, *jak'it*, *n*. a short coat: an animal's coat: skin (of potatoes): a loose paper cover: outer casing of a boiler, pipe, etc., as a steam-jacket, water-jacket: the aluminium or zirconium alloy covering of the fissile elements in a reactor.—*v.t.* to furnish or cover with a jacket: to beat (*slang*).—*adj.* **jack'eted**, wearing a jacket.—**dust one's jacket**, to beat one. [O.Fr. *jaquet*, dim. of *jaque*; see jack (2).]

**Jacobean**, *jak-ō-bē'ən, adj*. of or characteristic of the period of James I of England (1603-25). —**Jacobean lily**, (*Sprekelia formosissima*), a Mexican bulbous plant named after St James. [L. *Jacōbus*, James.]

**Jacobin**, *jak'ō-bin*, *n*. a French Dominican monk, so named from their original establishment being that of St *Jacques*, Paris: one of a society of revolutionists in France, so called from their meeting in the hall of the Jacobin convent: a demagogue: an extremist or radical, esp. in politics: a hooded pigeon.—*adjs.* **Jacobin'ic, -al.** —*v.t.* **Jac'obinise.**—*n.* **Jac'obinism**, the principles of the Jacobins or French revolutionists. [Fr.,—L. *Jacōbus*, James.]

**Jacobite**, *jak'ō-bīt*, *n*. an adherent of James II and his descendants: in Church history, a Syrian monophysite, named after the 6th-century monk *Jacobus* Baradaeus.—*adjs.* **Jac'obite, Jacobit'ic, -al.**—*n.* **Jac'obitism**. [L. *Jacōbus*, James.]

**Jacob's-ladder**, *jā'kəbz-lad'ər*, *n*. a ladder of ropes with wooden steps (*naut*.): a wild or garden plant (Polemonium) with ladder-like leaves: an endless chain of buckets used as an elevator. [From the *ladder* seen by Jacob in his dream, Gen. xxviii. 12.]

**Jacob's-staff**, *jā'kəbz-stäf*, *n*. a pilgrim's staff: a staff with a cross-head used in surveying: a sword-cane. [Prob. from the pilgrimage to St James (L. *Jacōbus*) of Compostela.]

**jacobus**, *jə-kō'bəs*, *n*. a gold coin of James I worth 20s. to 25s. [L. *Jacōbus*, James—Gr. *Iakōbos*—Heb. *Ya'aqōb*.]

**jaconet**, *jak'ə-net*, *n*. a cotton fabric, rather stouter than muslin—different from the fabric orig. so-named which was imported from *Jagannāth* (same word as Juggernaut), Puri in India: a thin material with waterproof backing used for medical dressings.

**jacquard**, *jak'ärd*, *jak-ärd'*, (*often cap.*) *n*. an apparatus with perforated cards for controlling the movement of the warp threads in weaving a pattern: a fabric so woven.—**Jacq'uard-loom**, a loom with jacquard. [Joseph Marie *Jacquard* (1752-1834), the inventor.]

**Jacqueminot**, *jak'mi-nō*, *n*. a deep-red hybrid perpetual rose.—Also **Jacque** and **Jack**. [From General *Jacqueminot* of Paris.]

**Jacquerie**, *zhäk'rē*, *n*. the revolt of the French peasants in 1358: any peasant revolt. [From *Jacques* Bonhomme, Goodman Jack, a name applied in derision to the peasants.]

**jactation**, *jak-tā'shən*, *n*. act of throwing: extreme restlessness in disease: bodily agitation: boasting. [L. *jactātiō*, *-ōnis*, tossing, boasting—*jactāre*, to throw.]

**jactitation**, *jak-ti-tā'shən*, *n*. restless tossing in illness: twitching or convulsion: tossing or bandying about (*obs*.): bragging: public assertion, esp. ostentatious and false.—**jactitation of marriage**, pretence of being married to another. [L.L. *jactitātiō*, *-ōnis*—L. *jactitāre*, *-ātum*, to toss about, put about, make a display of, freq. of *jactāre*, to throw.]

**jaculation**, *jak-ū-lā'shən*, *n*. the act of throwing or hurling, as a dart.—*v.t.* **jac'ulate**, to dart, throw.—*n.* **jac'ulātor**, a dart-thrower: an archer-fish.—*adj.* **jac'ulatory** (*-ət-ər-i*), darting or throwing out suddenly: ejaculatory. [L. *jaculāri*, *-ātus*, to throw as a dart—*jaculum*, a dart—*jacēre*, to throw.]

**jade**, *jād*, *n*. a sorry horse: a worthless nag: a woman, esp. perverse, ill-natured, or not to be trusted, often in irony.—*v.t.* to make a jade of: to weary, dull, cause to flag: to play the jade with.—*v.i.* to become weary.—*adj.* **jad'ed.**—*adv.* **jad'edly.**—*n.* **jad'ery**, the tricks of a jade.—*adj.* **jad'ish.** [Origin unknown; cf. O.N. *jalda*, a mare; Scot. *yaud*.]

**jade**, *jād*, *n*. a hard ornamental stone of varying shades of green and sometimes almost white—esp. *nephrite* (silicate of calcium and magnesium) and jade'ite (silicate of aluminium and sodium)—once held to cure side pains.—*adj.* **jade**, of jade: of the colour of jade. [Fr.,—Sp. *ijada*, the flank—L. *ilia*.]

**j'adoube**, *zha-dōōb'*, (Fr.), I adjust (in chess: a warning that only an adjustment is intended, not a move).

**Jaeger**, *yā'gər*, woollen material which contains no vegetable fibre. [Dr Gustav *Jaeger*, the original manufacturer.]

**jaeger**. Same as **jäger**.

**Jaffa**, *jaf'ə*, *n*. an orange from *Jaffa* in Israel (**Jaffa orange**).

**jag**, *jag*, *n*. a notch, slash, or dag in a garment, etc.: a ragged protrusion: a cleft or division (*bot*.): a prick (*Scot*.): an inoculation, injection. —*v.t.* to cut into notches: to prick or pierce:—*pr.p.* **jagg'ing**; *pa.p.* **jagged** (*jagd*).—*adj.* **jagg'ed**, notched, rough-edged, uneven.—*adv.* **jagg'edly.** —*ns.* **jagg'edness**; **jagg'er**, a brass wheel with a notched edge for cutting cakes, etc., into ornamental forms—also **jagg'ing-i'ron.**—*adj.* **jagg'y**, notched: slashed: prickly (*Scot*.). [Origin unknown.]

**jag**, *jag*, *n*. a load: a saddle-bag or other bag: a quantity: a thrill: a spree, bout of indulgence: one's fill of liquor or narcotics: a spell, fit.— *v.t.* to cart: to transport by pack-horse.—*adj.*

jagged (*jagd*; *U.S.*), drunk.—*n.* jagg'er, a carter: a pack-horseman: a pedlar.

**Jagannath**, *jug-un-üt'*, *n.* a corrected form of **Juggernaut.**

jäger, *yā'gər, n.* a (German) huntsman: a German rifleman or sharpshooter: an attendant upon an important or wealthy person, clad in huntsman's costume: a skua that chases and robs other gulls. [Ger., hunter—*jagen*, to hunt.]

jaggery, *jag'ə-ri, n.* a coarse, dark sugar made from palm-sap or otherwise. [Hindi *jāgrī*, Sans. *śarkarā*; cf. **sugar, Saccharum.**]

jaghir, jaghire, jagir, *jä-gēr', n.* the government revenues of a tract of land assigned with power to administer.—*n.* jaghir'dar, the holder of a jaghir. [Hind. and Pers. *jāgīr.*]

jaguar, *jag'wär,* or *jag'ū-är, n.* a powerful beast of prey, allied to the leopard, found in South America. [Tupi *jaguāra.*]

jaguarundi, jaguarondi, *jä-gwə-run'dē,* or *-ron', n.* a South American wild cat. [Tupi—Guaraní.]

Jah, yä, jä, *n.* Jehovah.—*n.* Jah'veh (same as Yahwe). [Heb. *Yah.*]

jai alai, hi' (*ə-*)*lī,* or *-lī'*, a game resembling handball but played with a long curved basket strapped to the wrist. [Sp.—Basque—*jai,* festival, *alai,* merry.]

jail, gaol, *jāl, n.* a prison.—*ns.* jail'er, jail'or, gaol'er, one who has charge of a jail or of prisoners: a turnkey:—*fem.* jail'eress, etc.— jail'-bird, gaol'-bird, a humorous name for one who is, has been, or should be much in jail; jail'-deliv'ery, gaol'-deliv'ery, clearing of jail by sending all prisoners to trial: delivery from jail; jail'-fē'ver, gaol'-fē'ver, typhus fever, once common in jails.—break jail, to force one's way out of prison; Commission of Jail Delivery (*obs.* from 1972), one of the commissions issued to judges of assize and judges of the Central Criminal Court in England. [O.Fr. *gaole* (Fr. *geôle*)—L.L. *gabiola,* a cage—L. *cavea,* a cage—*cavus,* hollow.]

Jain, jin, jän, Jaina, ji'na, *n.* an adherent of an Indian religion allied to Brahmanism and Buddhism.—Also *adjs.*—*n.* Jain'ism. [Hind. *jina,* a deified saint.]

jak, jak, *n.* Same as jack (3).

jake, *jāk,* (*U.S.*) *n.* a country lout: a yokel. [Perh. from the name *Jacob.*]

jake, *jāk,* (*coll.*) *adj.* honest: correct: first-rate.

jakes, *jāks,* (*Shak.*) *n.* a privy. [Origin unknown.]

jalap, *jal'ap, n.* the purgative root of an Ipomoea or Exogonium, first brought from *Jalapa* or Xalapa, in Mexico.—*adj.* jalap'ic.—*n.* jal'apin, a glucoside resin, one of the purgative principles of jalap.—false jalap, marvel of Peru, formerly used as a substitute.

jalop(p)y, *jə-lop'i, n.* an old motor-car or aeroplane. [Origin obscure.]

jalouse, *jə-lōōz', (Scot.) v.t.* to suspect.—Also jealouse, same root as jealous.

jalousie, *zhal-ōō-zē',* or *zhal', n.* an outside shutter with slats.—*adv.* jal'ousied. [Fr., *jalousie,* jealousy.]

jam, *jam, n.* a conserve of fruit boiled with sugar: good luck (*coll.*).—*v.t.* spread with jam: make into jam.—*adj.* jamm'y, smeared or sticky with jam: like jam: lucky, excellent. (*coll.*).—jam'pot, a jar for jam: a high collar, esp. a clergyman's [Perh. from next.]

jam, *jam, v.t.* to press or squeeze tight: to crowd full: to block by crowding: to bring to a standstill by crowding or interlocking: to interfere with by emitting signals of similar wavelength (*wireless*).—*v.i.* to become stuck, wedged, etc.: to become unworkable: to press or push (as into a confined space): in jazz, to play enthusiastically, interpolating and improvising freely: —*pr.p.* jamm'ing; *pa.t.* and *pa.p.* jammed.—*n.* a crush, squeeze: a block or stoppage due to

crowding or squeezing together: a jammed mass (as of logs in a river): a jamming of wireless messages: a difficult or embarrassing situation (*coll.*).—jam session, a gathering of jazz musicians (orig. an informal one) at which jazz as described at *v.i.* is played. [Cf. champ.]

jamadar, *jum'ä-där.* Same as jemadar.

Jamaica, *jə-mā'kə,* Jamaican, *-kən, adjs.* of the island of Jamaica.—*n.* Jamai'can, a native or inhabitant of Jamaica.—Jamaica bark, Caribbee bark; Jamaica cedar, bastard Barbados cedar; Jamaica ebony, cocus-wood; Jamaica pepper, allspice; Jamaica plum, hog-plum; Jamaica rum, slowly-fermented, full-bodied pungent rum.

jamb, *jam, n.* the sidepiece or post of a door, fireplace, etc.: leg-armour (in this sense also jambe, *jam*).—*ns.* jambeau (*jam'bō; obs.*), leg-armour: legging:—*pl.* jambeaux, jambeux (*Spens.* giambeux); jam'ber, jam'bier (*obs.*), leg-armour. [Fr. *jambe,* leg; cf. gamb.]

jambee, *jam-bē', n.* an 18th-century light cane. [*Jambi* in Sumatra.]

jambok. See sjambok.

jambolan(a). See jambu.

jambone, *jam'bōn, n.* a lone hand in euchre, played only by agreement, in which the player lays his cards on the table and must lead one chosen by his opponent, scoring 8 points if he takes all the tricks. [Origin unknown.]

jamboree, *jam-bə-rē', n.* in euchre, a lone hand of the 5 highest cards, by agreement scoring 16 points for the holder: a boisterous frolic, a spree (*slang*): a great Scout rally. [Origin unknown.]

jambu, *jum', jam'bōō, n.* the rose-apple tree or other Eugenia.—Also jambul, jambool (*jumbōōl'*), jam'bolan, jambolana (-*bō-lä'nə*). [Sans. *jambu, jambū, jambūla.*]

jamdani, *jäm'dä-nē, n.* a variety of Dacca muslin woven in design of flowers. [Pers. *jämdānī.*]

james. Same as jemmy (1).

Jamesian, *jāmz'i-an, adj.* relating to William *James* (1842-1910), American psychologist, or other of the name of James.

Jamesonite, *jim'i-sən-it,* or *jäm'sən-it, n.* a mineral compound of lead, antimony, and sulphur. [Robert *Jameson* (1772-1854), Scottish mineralogist.]

Jamestown-weed. See Jimson-weed.

jampan, *jam'pan, n.* an Indian sedan-chair.—*n.* jampanee, jampani (-*ē'*), its bearer. [Beng. *jhāmpān.*]

jane, *jän, n.* a small silver Genoese coin (*Spens.*): jean (cloth). [L.L. *Janua,* L. *Genua,* Genoa.]

jane, *jän,* (*slang*) *n.* a woman. [The name, *Jane.*]

Janeite, *jān'īt, n.* a devotee of *Jane* Austen.

jangle, *jang'gl, v.t.* and *v.i.* to sound with unpleasant tone, as bells.—*v.i.* to wrangle or quarrel.—*n.* dissonant clanging: contention.— *ns.* jang'ler; jang'ling.—*adj.* jang'ly. [O.Fr. *jangler.*]

janitor, *jan'i-tər, n.* a doorkeeper: attendant or caretaker:—*fem.* jan'itrix, jan'itress.—*adj.* janitorial (-*tō', -tö'*).—*n.* jan'itorship. [L. *jānitor*—*jānua,* a door.]

janizary, *jan'i-zər-i, n.* a soldier of the old Turkish footguards (*c.* 1330-1826), formed originally of renegade prisoners and of a tribute of Christian children.—Also jan'issary (-*zər-i*), jan'izar.—*adj.* janizā'rian.—janizary music, military music with much percussion. [Fr. *Janissaire,* supposed to be—Turk. *yeni,* new, *tsheri,* soldiery.]

janker, *jang'kər,* (*Scot.*) *n.* a long pole on wheels for transporting large logs suspended from it. [Origin unknown.]

jankers, *jang'kərz,* (*mil. slang*) *n.pl.* defaulters: punishment: detention. [Ety. dub.]

jann, *jän, n.pl.* the least powerful order of jinn: (*sing.*) a jinni. [Ar. *jänn.*]

Neutral vowels in unaccented syllables: *el'ə-mənt*; for certain sounds in foreign words, see p. viii

**jannock**, *jan'ək*, (*dial.*) *adj.* straightforward. [Origin obscure.]

**jannock**, *jan'ək*, (*N. of England*) *n.* oaten bread: a cake thereof. [Origin obscure.]

**Jansenism**, *jan'sən-izm*, *n.* a system of evangelical doctrine deduced from Augustine by Cornelius Jansen (1585-1638), Roman Catholic Bishop of Ypres, essentially a reaction against the ordinary Catholic dogma of the freedom of the will and that of merely sufficient grace, maintaining that interior grace is irresistible, and that Christ died for all.—*n.* **Jan'senist**, a believer in Jansenism.

**jantee, janty.** See **jaunty.**

**January**, *jan'ū-ər-i*, *n.* the first month of the year, dedicated by the Romans to Janus. [L. *Jānuārius.*]

**Janus**, *jā'nəs*, *n.* the ancient Italian two-faced god of doors, whose temple in Rome was closed in time of peace.—*adjs.* **Jān'iform** (wrongly **Jān'uform**), two-faced; **Jān'ian**, **Jān'us-faced**, two-faced. [L. *Jānus.*]

**Jap**, *jap*, *n.* and *adj.* coll. for *Japanese.*—**Jap'-silk**, a thin kind of silk.

**jap.** Same as **jaup.**

**japan**, *jə-pan'*, *adj.* of Japan: japanned.—*n.* Japanese ware or work: a glossy black varnish or lacquer: japanned work.—*v.t.* to varnish with Japan, esp. in imitation of Japanese work: to make black: to ordain (a clergyman; *old slang*). —*pr.p.* **japann'ing**; *pa.t.* and *pa.p.* **japanned'.**— *adj.* **Japanese** (*jap-ə-nēz'*, or *jap'*), of Japan, of its people, or of its language.—*n.* a native or citizen of Japan: the language of Japan:—*pl.* **Japanese** (formerly **Japaneses**).—*ns.* **Japanēs'ery**, Japanese decoration: a Japanese ornament: Japanese bric-à-brac; **Japanesque** (*-esk'*), a design in Japanese style.—*adjs.* **Japanesque'**, **Japanēs'y**, savouring of the Japanese.—*n.* **japann'er.**—**Japan Current**, Kuroshio; **japan'-earth**, or terra-japonica, gambier; **Japanese cedar**, a very tall Japanese conifer (*Cryptomeria japonica*), often dwarfed by Japanese gardeners; **Japanese medlar**, the loquat; **Japanese paper**, a fine soft paper made from paper-mulberry bark; **Japan lacquer** (see **Japan varnish**); **Japan laurel**, a shrub (*Aucuba japonica*) of the dogwood family, with spotted yellow leaves; **japanned leather**, patent leather (see **patent**); **Japan varnish**, a varnish got from a species of sumach (*Rhus vernicifera*), extended to various other similar varnishes; **Japan wax**, a fat got from the berries of species of sumach.

**jape**, *jāp*, *v.i.* to jest, joke.—*v.t.* to mock: to seduce (*obs.*).—*n.* a jest, joke, trick. [O.Fr. *japer*, to yelp.]

**Japhetic**, *jə-fet'ik*, (*obs.*) *adj.* of European race: Indo-European in language. [From supposed descent from *Japhet.*]

**Japonic**, *jə-pon'ik*, *adj.* Japanese.—*n.* **japon'ica**, the Japanese quince (*Pyrus*, or *Cydonia, japonica*), camellia, or other Japanese plant.

**jar**, *jär*, *v.i.* to make a harsh discordant sound or unpleasant vibration: to give an unpleasant shock: to grate: to be discordant or distasteful: to tick (*Shak.*): to clash: to quarrel: to be inconsistent.—*v.t.* to shake, as by a blow: to cause to vibrate unpleasantly: to grate on: to make dissonant:—*pr.p.* **jarr'ing**; *pa.t.* and *pa.p.* **jarred**.—*n.* a harsh sudden vibration: a dissonance: a grating sound or feeling: a tick of a clock (*Shak.*): clash of interests or opinions: dispeace, conflict.—*n.* **jarr'ing**, the act of jarring: severe reproof.—Also *adj.*—*adv.* **jarr'ingly.** [*Imit.*]

**jar**, *jär*, *n.* a wide-mouthed wide vessel: as much as a jar will hold: a Leyden jar (q.v.).—*v.t.* to put in jars.—*n.* **jar'ful**:—*pl.* **jar'fuls.** [O.Fr. *jarre* or Sp. *jarra*—Ar. *jarrah.*]

**jar**, *jär*, *n.* a turn, used only in the phrase *on the*

**jar**, ajar. [Earlier *char*—O.E. *cerr*; cf. *char* (3), ajar.]

**jararaca** or **jararaka**, *jär-ər-äk'ə*, *n.* a venomous South American snake of the family *Crotalidae.* [Tupí—Guaraní.]

**jardinière**, *zhär'dē-nyer'*, *n.* a vessel for the display of flowers, growing or cut: a dish including a mixture of vegetables: a lappet forming part of an old head-dress. [Fr., gardener (fem.).]

**jargon**, *jär'gən*, *n.* chatter, twittering: confused talk: slang: artificial or barbarous language: the terminology of a profession, art, group, etc. —*v.i.* to twitter, chatter: to speak jargon.—*ns.* **jargoneer'**, **jar'gonist**, one who uses jargon. [Fr. *jargon.*]

**jargonelle.** See next word.

**jargoon**, *jär'gōōn*, **jargon**, *jär'gən*, *n.* a brilliant colourless or pale zircon.—*n.* **jargonelle'**, an early pear (orig. a gritty kind). [Fr. *jargon*; prob. conn. with **zircon.**]

**jark**, *järk*, (*cant*) *n.* a seal on a document (usu. counterfeit document): a pass, safe-conduct.— **jark'man**, a swindling beggar, a begging-letter writer.

**jarl**, *yärl*, *n.* a noble, chief, earl. [O.N.; conn. with **earl.**]

**jarrah**, *jar'ə*, *n.* a Western Australian timber tree, *Eucalyptus marginata.* [From a native name.]

**jarta, yarta**, *yär'tə*, (*Shetland*) *n.* lit. heart, used as an endearment.—Also *adj.*—Also (*Scott*) **yar'to.** [O.N. *hjarta*, heart.]

**jarul, jarool**, *jə-rōōl'*, *n.* the Indian bloodwood (Lagerstroemia), a lythraceous tree. [Beng. *jarūl.*]

**jarvey**, *jär'vi*, (*slang*) *n.* a hackney-coach driver: a jaunting-car driver. [Earlier *Jarvis*, poss. from St *Gervase*, whose emblem is a whip.]

**jasey, jasy, jazy**, *jā'zi*, *n.* a wig, orig. of worsted. [jersey.]

**Jasher, Jashar**, *jäsh'ər*, *n.* one of the lost books of the ancient Hebrews, quoted twice (Josh. x. 13; 2 Sam. i. 18), most probably a collection of heroic ballads.

**jasmine**, *jas'min* or *jaz'*, **jessamine**, *jes'ə-min*, *ns.* a genus (*Jasminum*) of oleaceous shrubs, many with very fragrant flowers.—**red jasmine**, a tropical American shrub akin to periwinkle— frangipani (*Plumeria*). [Fr. *jasmin, jasemin*— Ar. *yāsmin, yāsamin*—Pers. *yāsmin.*]

**jasp**, *jasp* (*Spens.*), **jasper**, *jas'pər*, *ns.* a precious stone (*obs.*): an opaque quartz containing clay or iron compounds: a fine hard porcelain (also **jas'perware**).—*adj.* of jasper.—*adjs.* **jaspe, jaspé** (*jasp, -ā*), mottled, variegated, or veined.—*n.* cotton or rayon cloth with a shaded effect used for bedspreads, curtains, etc.—*v.t.* **jasp'erise, -ize**, to turn into jasper.—*adjs.* **jasp'erous, jasp'ery.** —*n.* **jas'pis**, jasper.—*adjs.* **jaspid'ean, jaspid'eous.** [O.Fr. *jaspe, jaspre*—L. *iaspis, -idis*; from Gr. *iaspis, -idos*, of Eastern origin.]

**Jat**, *jät*, *n.* one of a tribe situated in north-west India. [Hindi *jāt.*]

**jataka**, *jä'tə-kə*, *n.* a nativity, the birth-story of Buddha. [Sans. *jātaka*—*jāta*, born.]

**jato**, *jā'tō*, *n.* (*aero.*), a jet assisted take-off, using a *jato* unit consisting of one or more rocket motors, usu. jettisoned after use.

**jaunce**, **jaunse**, *jöns*, *jäns*, *v.i.* (*Shak.*) to prance: to cause a horse to prance.—*n.* prancing (*Shak.*): a wearisome journey (*dial.*). [Perh. from a doubtful O.Fr. *jancer*, to cause to prance.]

**jaundice**, *jön'dis* (rarely *jän'dis*), *n.* a disease in which there is yellowness of the eyes, skin, etc., by excess of bile pigment, the patient in rare cases seeing objects as yellow: a disease showing this condition: state of taking an unfavourable, prejudiced view.—*v.t.* to affect with jaundice, in any sense.—*adj.* **jaun'diced**, affected with jaundice: feeling, or showing, prejudice, jaunt 705 jelly

distaste, or jealousy. [Fr. *jaunisse—jaune*, yellow—L. *galbinus*, yellowish, *galbus*, yellow.]
**jaunt**, *jönt* (also *jänt*), *v.i.* to go from place to place, formerly with fatigue, now chiefly for pleasure: to make an excursion.—*n.* an excursion: a ramble.—*adj.* jaunt'ing, strolling: making an excursion.—jaunt'ing-car, a low-set, two-wheeled, open vehicle used in Ireland, with side-seats usu. back to back. [Origin obscure; cf. jaunce.]
**jaunty**, **janty**, *jön'ti* (also *jän'ti*), *adj.* gentlemanly (formerly **jantee**, **jauntee**) (*obs.*): having an airy or sprightly manner approaching swagger.—*adv.* jaunt'ily.—*n.* jaunt'iness. [Fr. *gentil*.]
**jaunty.** See jonty.
**jaup**, *jöp*, or *jäp*, **jap**, *jäp*, (*Scot.*) *v.t.* and *v.i.* to spatter: to splash.—*n.* a splash: a spattering. [Origin unknown]
**Java**, *jä'və*, *adj.* of the island of Java.—*adjs.* and *ns.* Ja'van, Javanese'.—Java man, Pithecanthropus; Java plum, the jambolana (*Eugenia jambolana*); Java sparrow, a kind of weaver-bird.
**javel**, *jav'əl*, (*Spens.*) *n.* a worthless fellow. [Origin unknown.]
**Javel(le) water**, *zha-* or *zhə-vel' wö'tər*, **eau de** (*ō də*) **Javel(le)**, a solution of potassium chloride and hypochlorite used for bleaching, disinfecting, etc. [After *Javel*, former town, now part of the city of Paris.]
**javelin**, *jav'(ə-)lin*, *n.* a throwing-spear.—**jav'elin-man**, an armed member of a sheriff's retinue or a judge's escort at assizes: a soldier armed with a javelin. [Fr. *javeline*; prob. Celt.]
**jaw**, *jö*, *n.* a mouth-structure for biting or chewing: one of the bones of a jaw: one of a pair of parts for gripping, crushing, cutting, grinding, etc.: (in *pl.*) a narrow entrance: talkativeness, scolding (*slang*).—*v.t.* (*slang*) to scold.—*v.i.* to talk, esp. in excess.—*adj.* jawed, having jaws. —*n.* jaw'ing (*slang*), talk, esp. unrestrained, abusive, or reproving.—jaw'bone, the bone of the jaw; jaw'-break'er, -twist'er (*slang*), a word hard to pronounce; jaw'fall, a falling of the jaw (*arch.*): depression of spirits (*rare*).—*adj.* jaw'-fallen (*rare*), depressed in spirits: dejected. —jaw'-foot, a foot-jaw, maxilliped; jaw lever, an instrument for opening the mouth of a horse or cow to admit medicine; jaw'-tooth, a molar. —hold one's jaw, to cease from talking or scolding. [Perh. chaw, modified by Fr. *joue*, cheek.]
**jaw**, *jö*, (*Scot.*) *n.* a dash or surge of liquid: a portion of liquid so dashed.—*v.t.* and *v.i.* to pour suddenly in a body.—jaw'box, a sink; jaw'hole, a cesspool: an entrance to a sewer. [Origin unknown.]
**jawan**, *jə-wän'*, *n.* an Indian common soldier. [Urdu *javān*.]
**jawbation**, *jö-bā'shən*, *n.* for jobation. [Influenced by jaw (1); see Job.]
**ja wohl**, *ya võl'*, (Ger.) yes indeed.
**jay**, *jā*, *n.* a bird of the crow family with gay plumage: a wanton woman (*arch. slang*): an indifferent actor (*arch. slang*): a stupid or awkward fellow (*U.S. slang*).—*adj.* (*U.S. slang*), stupid, inferior.—*v.i.* jay'walk.—jay'walker, a careless pedestrian whom motorists are expected to avoid running down; jay'walking. [O.Fr. *jay*.]
**jay**, *jā*, *n.* tenth letter of the alphabet (J, j): object or mark of that shape.
**jazerant**, *jaz'ə-rənt*. See jesserant.
**jazy.** Same as jasey.
**jazz**, *jaz*, *n.* style of American Negro folk music with improvisation, syncopation, etc.: an art form and also various types of popular dance music derived from it: garish colouring, lively manner, vivid quality: insincere or lying talk (*slang*).—Also *adj.*—*v.t.* to impart a jazz character to (often with *up*).—*adv.* jazz'ily.—*n.* jazz'i-

ness.—*adj.* jazz'y.—jazz age, the decade following World War I, esp. in America. [Origin uncertain.]
**jealous**, *jel'əs*, *adj.* suspicious of, or incensed at, rivalry: envious: solicitous: anxiously heedful: mistrustfully vigilant: brooking no unfaithfulness.—*v.t.* jealouse (*jə-lōōz'*; *obs.* except *Scot.*; see jalouse).—*adv.* jeal'ously.—*ns.* jeal'ousy, jeal'oushood (*Shak.*), jeal'ousness. [O.Fr. *jalous* —L. *zēlus*—Gr. *zēlos*, emulation.]
**Jeames**, *jēmz*, *n.* a flunkey. [From Thackeray's *Jeames* (James) de la Pluche.]
**jean**, *jēn*, (esp. formerly) *jān*, *n.* a twilled-cotton cloth (also in *pl.*): (in *pl.*) trousers or overalls of jean: (in *pl.*) close-fitting, sometimes three-quarter length, casual trousers of jean or similar material.—*n.* jeanette (*ja-net'*), a light or coarse jean.—satin jean, a smooth, glossy fustian. [O.Fr. *Janne*—L. *Genua*, Genoa.]
**jeat**, *jet* (*Milt.*). Same as jet.
**Jebusite**, *jeb'ū-zit*, *n.* one of a Canaanitish people, predecessors of Israelites at Jerusalem: 17th-century nickname for Roman Catholic.—*adj.* **Jebusitic** (-*zit'ik*).
**Jeddart**, *jed'ərt*, **Jethart**, *jedh'ərt*, *n.* Jedburgh. —**Jethart justice**, hanging first and trying afterwards; **Jethart staff**, a sort of battle-axe with a long head. [O.E. *Gedwearde*.]
**jee.** Same as gee (1 and 3).
**jee**, *jē*, (*Scot.*) *v.i.* to stir: to budge.—*v.t.* to disturb: to set on one side or ajar.—*n.* a displacement to the side: a condition of being ajar.—
**jee** or **jow** one's ginger, to bestir oneself, show perturbation.
**jeel**, *jēl*, **jeely**, *-i*, (*Scot.*) *ns.* and *vs.i.* jelly: to jelly.—jeely nose (*coll.*), a bleeding nose.
**jeep**, *jēp*, *n.* a light military vehicle with great freedom of movement. [From G.P., for general purpose; perh. with reminiscence of a comic-strip animal character.]
**jeer**, *jēr*, *v.t.* to make sport of: to treat with derision.—*v.i.* to scoff: to deride: to make a mock.—*n.* a railing remark: biting jest: mockery.—*n.* jeer'er.—*n.* and *adj.* jeer'ing.—*adv.* jeer'ingly. [Origin unknown.]
**jeff**, *jef*, *v.i.* to gamble with printer's quadrats thrown like dice.
**jeff**, *jef*, *n.* a rope, in circus slang.
**Jeffersonian**, *jef-ər-sōn'i-an*, *adj.* pertaining to Thomas *Jefferson* (1743-1826), U.S. President 1801-09: of the American Democratic party.— *n.* a Democrat.
**jehad.** See jihad.
**Jehovah**, *ji-hō'və*, *n.* Yahweh, the Hebrew God, a name used by Christians.—*n.* Jehō'vist, one who held that the vowel-points annexed to the word *Jehovah* in the Hebrew are the proper vowels of the word (*obs.*): a writer of passages in the Pentateuch in which the name applied to God is Yahweh, a Yahwist.—*adj.* Jehovist'ic.—
**Jehovah's Witnesses**, international Bible Students' Association (see Russellite). [Heb.; for *Yĕhōwāh*, i.e. Yahweh with the vowels of *Adōnāi*.]
**Jehu**, *jē'hū*, (*coll.*) *n.* a driver, esp. a furious whip. [A reference to 2 Kings ix. 20.]
**jeistiecor**, *jēs'ti-kōr*, *-kör*, (*Scot.*) *n.* (*obs.*) a close-fitting garment. [Fr. *juste au corps*, close-fitting to the body.]
**jejune**, *ji-jōōn'*, *adj.* empty: spiritless, meagre, arid: showing lack of information or experience: naïve, immature, callow.—*adv.* jejune'ly.—*ns.* jejune'ness; jeju'num, the part of the small intestine between the duodenum and the ileum. [L. *jejūnus*, hungry.]
**Jekyll and Hyde**, *jēk'il* (or *jek'il*) and *hid*, the good side and the bad side of a human being— from R.L. Stevenson, *The Strange Case of Dr Jekyll and Mr Hyde* (1886).
**jelly**, *jel'i*, *n.* anything gelatinous: the juice of

Neutral vowels in unaccented syllables: *el'ə-mənt*; for certain sounds in foreign words, see p. viii

fruit boiled with sugar: a gelatinous preparation for the table (in U.S. jell′o, formerly a trademark): a glass for jelly: a jellyfish.—*v.i.* to set as a jelly: to congeal.—*v.t.* to make into a jelly.—*v.i.* and *v.t.* jell, to jelly: to take distinct shape (*coll.*).—*adjs.* jell′ied, in a state of jelly: enclosed in jelly; jell′iform.—*v.t.* jell′ify, to make into a jelly.—*v.i.* to become gelatinous.— jelly bag, a bag through which fruit juice is strained for jelly; jell′yfish, a marine coelenterate with jelly-like body: a person who lacks firmness of purpose; jell′ygraph, a copying appliance that uses a plate of jelly.—*v.t.* to copy by this means. [Fr. *gelée*, from *geler*—L. *gelāre*, to freeze; cf. gel.]

jelutong, *jel′ōō-tong, n.* pontianac, a substitute for gutta-percha: the Bornean apocynaceous tree (*Dyera costulata*) yielding it. [Malay.]

jemadar, *jem′a-där, n.* an Indian army officer below a subahdar: an officer of police, customs, etc.—Also jamadar (*jum′*), jem′idar. [Urdu *jama'dār.*]

jemima, *ji-mi′mə,* (*coll.*) *n.* an elastic-sided boot. [An appropriate woman's name.]

jemmy, *jem′i, n.* a burglar's short crowbar: a baked sheep's head (*slang*): an overcoat (*dial.*). [A form of the name *James.*]

jemmy, *jem′i,* (*dial.*) *adj.* neat, smart, handy.— Also gemm′y.—*n.* jemm′iness, neatness. [Cf. jimp.]

Jena glass, *yā′nə gläs,* a special type of glass containing borates and free silica, resistant to chemical attack. [From *Jena,* Germany.]

je ne sais quoi, *zhə nə se kwa,* an indefinable something. [Fr., I don't know what.]

Jenkins, *jengk′inz,* (*coll.*) *n.* a society reporter: a toady.

jennet, *jen′it, n.* a small Spanish horse.—Also genn′et, gen′et. [O.Fr. *genet*—Sp. *jinete,* a light horseman, perh. of Arab origin.]

jenneting, *jen′it-ing, n.* a kind of early apple. [Prob. St John's apple—Fr. *Jeannet,* dim. of *Jean,* John; not from *June-eating.*]

Jenny, *jen′i, n.* generic name for a country lass (*Scot.*): a womanish man (*Scot.*): a wren or owl regarded as female: a she-ass: a travelling crane: a spinning-jenny: an in-off into a middle pocket from near the cushion (*billiards*). —Jenny-long′-legs (*Scot.*), Jenn′y-spinner (*dial.*), a crane-fly; Jenny-wren′, a wren. [From the name *Jenny.*]

jeofail, *jef′āl,* (*obs.*) *n.* an error in pleadings, or the acknowledgment of a mistake. [A.Fr. *jeo fail,* I mistake.]

jeopardy, *jep′ər-di, n.* hazard, danger: the danger of trial and punishment faced by the accused on a criminal charge (*U.S. law*).—*vs.t.* jeop′ard (*rare* and *U.S.*), jeop′ardise, -ize, jeop′ardy (*rare*), to put in jeopardy.—*n.* jeop′arder.—*adj.* jeop′-ardous (*obs.*), dangerous: venturesome.—*adv.* jeop′ardously. [Fr. *jeu parti,* a divided or even game—L.L. *jocus partitus*—L. *jocus,* a game, *partitus,* divided—*partiri,* to divide.]

jequirity, *jə-kwir′i-ti, n.* Indian liquorice: its seed, otherwise jequirity bean, crab's-eye, prayer-bead. [Origin obscure.]

jerboa, *jər-bō′ə, n.* a desert rodent (family *Dipodidae*) that jumps like a kangaroo. [Ar. *yarbūʻ.*]

jeremiad, *jer-i-mī′ad, n.* a lamentation: a tale of grief: a doleful story. [From *Jeremiah,* reputed author of the *Book of Lamentations.*]

jerfalcon. Same as gerfalcon.

Jericho, *jer′i-kō, n.* a remote place, to which one is humorously consigned. [Supposed to refer to 2 Sam. x. 4, 5.]

jerid, jereed, *jer-ēd′, n.* a blunt Oriental javelin: a tournament in which it is used. [Ar. *jarīd.*]

jerk, *jûrk, n.* a stroke (*obs.*): a short movement begun and ended suddenly: a twitch: an involuntary spasmodic contraction of a muscle:

a movement in physical exercises: a short burst of bird-song (*obs.*): a useless person (*slang*).— *v.t.* to thrash (*obs.*): to throw or move with a jerk.—*v.i.* to move with a jerk: to utter abruptly. —*ns.* jerk′er, one who jerks: a hornyhead (fish); jerk′iness.—*adj.* jerk′y, moving or coming by jerks or starts, spasmodic.—jerk′inhead (*archit.*), the combination of a truncated gable with a lipped roof. [An imit. word, akin to yerk.]

jerk, etc. See jerque, etc.

jerk, *jûrk, v.t.* to make into charqui.—*n.* charqui. —Also jerk′ed-meat, jerk′y. [charqui.]

jerkin, *jûr′kin, n.* a jacket, a short coat or close waistcoat.—*n.* jirkinet′ (*Scot.*), a woman's bodice. [Origin unknown.]

jeroboam, *jer-ō-bō′əm, n.* a very large bowl or bottle. [Allusion to 1 Kings xi. 28.]

jerque, jerk, *jûrk, v.t.* to search (as a vessel) for concealed or smuggled goods: to examine (as a ship's papers).—*ns.* jerqu′er, jerk′er; jerqu′-ing, jerk′ing. [Poss. It. *cercare,* to search.]

jerrican, jerrycan, *jer′i-kan, n.* a kind of petrol-can, orig. German.

Jerry, Gerry, *jer′i,* (*war slang*) *n.* a German.

jerry, *jer′i* (*slang*), *n.* a chamber-pot. [jeroboam.]

jerry, *jer′i, n.* (*coll.*) a jerry-builder.—*adj.* hastily made of bad materials.—jerr′y-builder, one who builds flimsy houses cheaply and hastily.—jerr′y-building.—*adj.* jerr′y-built.—jerr′y-come-tum′ble (*dial.*), a tumbler, circus performer; jerr′y-shop, a low dram-shop. [Prob. the personal name.]

jerrymander, a mistaken form of gerrymander.

jersey, *jûr′zi, n.* the finest part of wool: combed wool: a close-fitting woollen upper garment: a cow of Jersey breed.—*n.* Jer′sian, a hybrid obtained by mating a Jersey bull and a Friesian cow. [From the island of *Jersey.*]

Jerusalem artichoke, *jər-ōōs′ə-ləm,* see artichoke. —Jerusalem cross, a cross potent: Jerusalem letters, tattooed letters on one who has made a pilgrimage to Jerusalem; Jerusalem pony, an ass; Jerusalem sage, a perennial plant, *Phlomis fruticosa* found in south Europe, with dense yellow flowers.

jess, *jes, n.* a short strap round the leg of a hawk. —*adj.* jessed, having jesses on. [O.Fr. *ges*—L. *jactus,* a cast—*jacĕre,* to throw.]

jessamine. See jasmine.

jessamy, *jes′ə-mi,* (*obs.*) *n.* jasmine: a dandy.

jessant, *jes′ənt,* (*her.*) *adj.* overlying: also app. for issuant. [App. O.Fr. *gesant,* pr.p. of *gesir*— L. *jacĕre,* to lie.]

Jesse, *jes′i, n.* a genealogical tree of Christ's descent from *Jesse:* a large branched church candlestick.—Jesse window, one showing Christ's genealogy in stained glass or carved on the mullions.

jesserant, *jes′ə-rənt,* jazerant, *jaz′,* (*hist.*) *n.* splint armour. [O.Fr. *jaseran*(*t*), *jazeran*—Sp. *jacerina.*]

Jessie, *jes′i,* (*Scot.*) *n.* an effeminate man.

jest, *jest, n.* something ludicrous: object of laughter: joke: fun: something uttered in sport.—*v.i.* to make a jest: to joke.—*v.t.* to jeer at, ridicule: to utter as a jest.—*ns.* jestee′ (*Sterne*), the object of a jest; jest′er, one who jests: a reciter of romances (*arch.*): a buffoon: a court-fool.—*adj.* jest′ful, given to jesting.—*n.* and *adj.* jest′ing.—*adv.* jest′ingly.—jest′book, a collection of funny stories; jest′ing-stock (*obs.*), a butt for jests. [Orig. a deed, a story, M.E. *geste*—O.Fr. *geste*—L. *gesta,* things done, doings —*gerĕre,* to do.]

Jesuit, *jez′ū-it, n.* a member of the famous religious order, the Society of *Jesus,* founded in 1534 by Ignatius Loyola: (opprobriously) a crafty person, an intriguer, a prevaricator.— *adjs.* Jesuit′ic, -al.—*adv.* Jesuit′ically.—*ns.* Jes′uitism, Jes′uitry, the principles and practices of or ascribed to the Jesuits.—Jesuits' bark, cinchona (brought to Rome by Jesuit missionaries); **Jesuits' drops,** friar's balsam.

**Jesus,** *jē'zəs, n.* the founder of Christianity—also (in hymns, etc., esp. in the vocative) **Jesu** (*jē'zū*). [Gr. *Iēsous* (voc. and oblique cases *Iēsou*)—Heb. *Yēshūa'*, contr. of *Yehōshūa'*, Joshua.]

**jésus,** *zhā'zü, n.* a size of paper in France, approximately super-royal.—**grand jésus,** imperial size.

**jet, jet,** *n.* a rich black variety of lignite, very hard and compact, taking a high polish, used for ornaments: jet-black.—*adj.* of jet: jet-black.—*n.* **jett'iness.**—*adj.* **jett'y,** of the nature of jet, or black as jet.—*adj.* **jet'-black,** black as jet.—Also *n.* [O.Fr. *jaiet*—L. and Gr. *gagatēs*—*Gagas* or *Gangai,* a town and river in Lycia, where it was obtained.]

**jet, jet,** *n.* a narrow spouting stream: a spout, nozzle or pipe emitting a stream or spray of fluid: a strutting movement (*obs.*): a jet-plane.—*v.t.* and *v.i.* to spout.—*v.i.* to jut (*obs.*): to encroach (*Shak.*): to strut (*obs.*): to travel by jet-plane.—**jet'-drive.**—*adj.* **jet'-driven,** driven by the backward emission of a jet of gas, etc.—**jet'(-)plane,** a jet-driven aeroplane.—*adj.* **jet'-propelled.**—**jet'-propulsion; jet'(-)stream,** very high winds more than 20,000 feet above the earth: the exhaust of a rocket engine.—**the jet set,** moneyed social set able to spend much of their time at fashionable resorts all over the world. [O.Fr. *jetter*—L. *jactāre,* to fling.]

**jet d'eau,** *zhe dō,* (Fr.) jet of water, e.g. in an ornamental fountain.

**jeté,** *zhə-tā, (ballet) n.* a leap from one foot to the other in which the free leg usu. finishes extended forward, backward, or sideways. [Fr., thrown.]

**jetsam,** *jet'səm, n.* jettison (*obs.*): goods jettisoned from a ship and washed up on shore: according to some, goods from a wreck that remain under water (see flotsam).—Also **jet'som** (*arch.*), **jet'son** (*arch.*).—*n.* **jett'ison,** the act of throwing goods overboard.—*v.t.* to throw overboard, as goods in time of danger: to abandon, reject (*fig.*).—**flotsam and jetsam,** often, unclaimed odds and ends. [A.Fr. *jetteson*—L. *jactātiō, -ōnis,* a casting—*jactāre,* freq. of *jacēre,* to cast.]

**jettatura,** *jet-ə-tōō'rə, n.* the spell of the evil eye. [It. *iettatura,* a Neapolitan word—L. *ējectāre*—*jactāre,* freq. of *jacēre,* to throw.]

**jettison.** See jetsam.

**jetton, jeton,** *jet'ən, n.* a piece of stamped metal used as a counter in card-playing, casting accounts, etc. [Fr. *jeton—jeter,* to throw—L. *jactāre,* freq. of *jacēre,* to throw.]

**jetty,** *jet'i, n.* a projection: a pier. [O.Fr. *jettee,* thrown out; see jet (2).]

**jeu,** *zhə,* (Fr.) a game.—**jeu de mots:**—*pl.* **jeux de mots** (*də mō*), a play on words, a pun; **jeu d'esprit:**—*pl.* **jeux d'esprit** (*des-prē*), a witticism.

**jeune,** *zhœn,* (Fr.) young.—**jeune amour** (*a-mōōr*), young love; **jeune fille** (*fē-y'*), a girl; **jeune premier** (*prə-myā*):—*fem.* **première,** (*prə-myer*), (*theat.*) a juvenile lead.

**jeunesse dorée,** *zhœ-nes do-rā,* (Fr.) gilded youth: luxurious, stylish, sophisticated young people.

**Jew,** *jōō, n.* a person of Hebrew descent or religion: an Israelite: (*offensively*) a usurer, miser, etc.:—*fem.* **Jew'ess.**—*v.t.* (*offensively*) to overreach, or to cheat.—*adj.* **Jew'ish,** of the Jews or their religion.—*adv.* **Jew'ishly.**—*n.* **Jew'ishness.**—**Jew'-bait'ing,** the persecuting of Jews; **jew'fish,** a name for several very large American and Australian fishes; **Jew's'-ear,** an ear-like fungus (Auricularia) parasitic on elder and other trees; **Jew's eye,** formerly, something of very high value (*Shak.* 'worth a Jewe's eye'; from the practice of torturing Jews for money); **Jew's'-frank'incense,** benzoin; **Jew's'-harp**

**harp', -trump',** a small lyre-shaped instrument played against the teeth by twitching a metal tongue with the finger; **Jews' houses, leavings,** in Cornwall, remains of prehistoric miners' dwellings, mine refuse, and tin furnaces; **Jew's'-mall'ow,** a kind of jute cultivated as a pot-herb in Syria; **Jew's'-myr'tle,** butcher's broom; **Jew's'-pitch,** asphaltum; **Jew's'-stone,** a large fossil sea-urchin spine; **Jews' thorn,** Christ's thorn.—**wandering Jew** (see wander). [O.Fr. *Jueu*—L. *Jūdaeus*—Gr. *Ioudaios*—Heb. *Yehūdāh,* Judah.]

**jewel,** *jōō'əl, n.* a precious stone: a personal ornament of precious stones, gold, etc.: a hard stone (ruby, etc.) used for pivot bearings in a watch: an imitation of a gemstone: a glass boss: anything or anyone highly valued.—*v.t.* to adorn with jewels: to fit with a jewel:—*pr.p.* **jew'elling;** *pa.t.* and *pa.p.* **jew'elled.**—*ns.* **jew'eller,** one who deals in, or makes, jewels; **jewellery** (*jōō'əl-ri*), **jew'elry,** jewels in general.—**jew'el-case,** a casket for holding jewels; **jew'el-house,** a room in the Tower of London where the crown-jewels are kept; **jewel-weed,** any plant of the genus Impatiens. [O.Fr. *jouel* (Fr. *joyau*); either a dim. of Fr. *joie,* joy, from L. *gaudium,* joy—*gaudēre,* to rejoice—or derived through L.L. *jocāle,* from L. *jocāri,* to jest.]

**Jewry,** *jōō'ri, n.* Judaea: a district inhabited by Jews: the Jewish world, community, or religion.

**jezail,** *jez'il, -āl', n.* a heavy Afghan gun. [Pers. *jazā'il.*]

**Jezebel,** *jez'ə-bəl, n.* a shameless painted woman. [From Ahab's wife, 2 King's ix. 30.].

**jib, jib,** *n.* a triangular sail borne in front of the foremast in a ship: the boom of a crane or derrick: the under-lip (*dial.*): the face: a jibbing horse: an act of jibbing: a standstill.—*v.t.* to cause to gybe.—*v.i.* to gybe: (of a horse) to balk or shy: to refuse, show objection, boggle (*fig.*):—*pr.p.* **jibb'ing;** *pa.t.* and *pa.p.* **jibbed.**—*n.* **jibb'er,** a jibbing horse.—**jib'-boom',** a boom or extension of the bowsprit, on which the jib is spread; **jib'-crane',** a crane with an inclined arm fixed to the foot of a rotating vertical post, the upper ends connected.—**the cut of one's jib,** one's appearance. [Origin obscure; perh. several different words; cf. **gibbet, gybe;** the j sound stands in the way of connecting with Dan. *gibbe,* Du. *gijpen.*]

**jib, jib,** (*Scot.*) *v.t.* to milk closely, strip: to fleece.—*n.pl.* **jibb'ings,** the last milk drawn from a cow.

**jibbah, jib'ə.** See jubbah.

**jibber.** See gibber.

**jib-door,** *jib'-dōr, -dör, n.* a disguised door, flush with the wall. [Origin unknown.]

**jibe.** See gybe.

**jibe.** Same as gibe, usu. *U.S.*

**jiffy,** *jif'i, (coll.) n.* an instant.—Also **jiff.** [Origin unknown.]

**jig, jig,** *n.* a jerky movement: a lively dance usu. in 6-8 time: a dance-tune of like kind—a giga or gigue: a mocking ballad (*obs.*): a jingle or piece of doggerel (*obs.*): a farcical afterpiece or interlude sung and danced to popular tunes (*obs.*): a jest (*obs.*): a contrivance of various kinds, esp. one for catching fish by jerking hooks into its body, an appliance for guiding a tool, a miner's jigger.—*v.t.* and *v.i.* to jerk: to perform as a jig.—*v.t.* to work upon with a jig:—*pr.p.* **jigg'ing;** *pa.t.* and *pa.p.* **jigged.**—*ns.* **jigamaree', jigg'umbob,** a what's-its-name: a gadget; **jigg'er,** one who jigs in any sense: anything that jigs: one of many kinds of subsidiary appliances, esp. with reciprocating motion, as an oscillation transformer, an apparatus for separating ores by jolting in sieves in water, a simple potter's wheel or a template or profile used with it, a warehouse crane, the bridge or rest for the cue in billiards: a golf-club, used esp. formerly, with narrow lofted iron head: old fashioned sloop-rigged boat: a jigger-mast (*naut.*): a sail on a jigger-mast (*naut.*): odd person: odd or despised contrivance: a small measure for drinks.—*v.t.* to jerk or shake: to form with a jigger: to ruin.—*v.i.* to tug or move with jerks.—*n.* jigg′ing.—*adj.* jigg′ish.—*v.t.* and *v.i.* jigg′le, to move with vibratory jerks.—*n.* a jiggling movement.— jigg′er-mast, a four-masted ship's aftermost mast: a small mast astern; jig′saw, a narrow reciprocating saw: a jigsaw puzzle.—*v.t.* and *v.i.* to cut with a jigsaw.—jigsaw puzzle, a picture cut up into pieces, as by a jigsaw, to be fitted together.—jiggered up (*slang*), exhausted. [Origin obscure.]

jigger, *jig′ər, n.* a form of chigoe.

jiggered, *jig′ərd*, (*coll.*) *adj.* confounded. [Origin doubtful.]

jiggery-pokery, *jig′ə-ri-pō′kə-ri, n.* trickery: deception. [Cf. joukery-pawkery.]

jig-jog, *jig′-jog′, adv.* with a jolting, jogging motion.—*n.* a jolting motion: a jog.—Also jick′ajog′, jig′jig′, jig′ajig′, jig′ajog′, jigg′ety-jog′. [jig, jog.]

jigot. Same as gigot.

jihad, jehad, *jē-had′, n.* a holy war (for the Mohammedan faith): a stunt campaign. [Ar. *jihād*, struggle.]

jill, jillet, etc. See gill (3).

jilt, *jilt, n.* one, esp. a woman, who encourages and then rejects a lover.—*v.t.* to discard (a lover) after encouragement. [Possibly jillet or gillet.]

jimcrack. See gimcrack.

Jim Crow, *jim krō,* a generic name for the Negro (derogatory): racial discrimination against Negroes.—jim′-crow, a tool for bending or straightening iron rails or bars: a plane or other tool that works in both directions.—Jim Crow car, school, etc., one for Negroes only. [From a Negro minstrel song with the refrain 'Wheel about and turn about and jump Jim Crow'.]

jiminy, *jim′in-i.* See geminate.

jimjam, *jim′jam, n.* a gimcrack: a gadget: an oddity: (in *pl.*) delirium tremens: (in *pl.*) the fidgets. [Origin unknown.]

jimmy, *jim′i,* (chiefly *U.S.*) *n.* a burglar's jemmy. [James.]

jimp, *jimp,* (*Scot.*) *adj.* slender: elegant: scant.— *advs.* jimp, jimp′ly, neatly: hardly: scant.—*n.* jimp′ness.—*adj.* jimp′y, neat. [Origin unknown.]

Jimson-weed, Jimpson-weed, Jamestown-weed, *jim′san-wēd, n.* thorn-apple. [*Jamestown*, Virginia, where it established itself.]

jingal, gingall, gingal, *jin(g)′gōl, -gōl′, n.* a large Chinese or Indian swivel-musket. [Hind. *janjāl.*]

jingbang, *jing-bang′, jing′,* (*slang*) *n.* company: collection: lot. [Origin unknown.]

jingle, *jing′gl, n.* a succession of clinking sounds: that which makes a tinkling sound, esp. a metal disk on a tambourine: a thin or paltry correspondence of sounds in verse: a verse or set of verses of such a kind: a covered two-wheeled vehicle.—*v.t.* and *v.i.* to sound with a jingle.— *ns.* jing′ler; jing′let, a ball serving as the clapper of a sleigh-bell; jing′ling, a game in which blindfolded players within a ring try to catch a player with a bell tied to him.—*adj.* jing′ly.—jing′le-jang′le, a dissonant continued jingling: a jingling trinket; jingling Johnny, a Chinese pavilion, or musical percussion instrument. [Imit.]

jingo, Jingo, *jing′gō, n.* used in the mild oaths 'By jingo!', 'By the living jingo!' (*Scot.* 'By jing!', 'By jings!'): from its occurrence in a music-hall song of 1878 that conveyed a threat against Russia, a (British) chauvinist.—*adjs.* jing′o, jing′oish, chauvinist: jingois′tic, charac-

teristic of jingoism.—*n.* jing′oism, (British) chauvinism. [Appears first as a conjurer's summoning call; possibly from Basque *Jinkoa, Jainko,* God.]

jingo-ring, *jing′gō-ring, n.* a children's game in which the players dance round one of their number singing 'Here we go round the jingo-ring'. [Conn. with jink.]

jinjili. See gingili.

jink, *jingk,* (*Scot.*) *v.i.* to dodge nimbly.—*v.t.* to elude: to cheat.—*n.* a quick, illusory turn.— high jinks (see high). [Perh. a natural expression of the movement.]

jinn, *jin, n.pl.* (*sing.* jinnee, jinni, djinni, genie (*jin-ē′, jēn′i*)) a class of spirits in Mohammedan mythology, formed of fire, living chiefly on the mountains of Káf which encircle the world, assuming various shapes, sometimes as men of enormous size and portentous hideousness.— Also djinn, ginn. The *jinn* are often called *genii* by a confusion. A plural jinns is sometimes erroneously used. [Ar. *jinn,* sing. *jinni.*]

jinricksha, jinrickshaw, jinrikisha. See ricksha.

jinx, *jingks, n.* a bringer of bad luck.

jirble, *jir′, jûr′bl,* (*Scot.*) *v.t.* and *v.i.* to pour splashingly or unsteadily.

jirkinet. See jerkin.

jitney, *jit′ni,* (*U.S. slang*) *n.* five-cent piece: a bus, etc., with low fares: anything cheap or paltry. —*adj.* cheap: paltry. [Perh. Fr. *jeton,* counter.]

jitter, *jit′ər,* (orig. *U.S.*) *v.i.* to behave in a flustered way.—*n.pl.* jitt′ers, a flustered state.— *adj.* jitt′ery.—jitt′erbug (*U.S.*), a violent spasmodic type of dancing to jazz music: one who dances so: (in Britain, by misunderstanding or extension) a scaremonger, alarmist.—*v.i.* to dance wildly and grotesquely.

jiu-jitsu. Same as ju-jitsu.

jive, *jiv, n.* a style of jazz music: dancing thereto: jargon (*slang*).—*v.i.* to play or dance jive: talk jargon (*slang*).

jiz. See gizz.

jo, joe, *jō,* (*Scot.*) *n.* a beloved one. [An old form of joy.]

Job, *jōb, n.* a person of great patience—from *Job* in the *Book of Job.*—*n.* jōbā′tion (also jawbā′-tion), a tedious scolding.—*v.t.* jobe (*jōb*), to reprimand tediously.—Job's comforter, one who aggravates the distress of the unfortunate man he has come to comfort; Job's news, bad news; Job's post, the bearer of bad news; Job's tears, the stony involucres of an Indian grass, *Coix lachryma,* used as beads: round grains of chrysolite.

job, *job, n.* a sudden thrust with anything pointed, as a beak.—*v.t.* and *v.i.* to prod or peck suddenly: —*pr.p.* jobb′ing; *pa.t.* and *pa.p.* jobbed. [App. imit.; cf. jab.]

job, *job, n.* any definite piece of work, esp. of a trifling or temporary nature: any undertaking or employment with a view to profit: an appointment or situation: state of affairs (*coll.*): a transaction in which private gain is sought under pretence of public service: an end accomplished by intrigue or wire-pulling: a criminal enterprise, esp. theft: a hired horse or carriage: a job-lot.—*adj.* employed, hired, or used by the job or for jobs: bought or sold lumped together.—*v.i.* to work at jobs: to buy and sell, as a broker: to practise jobbery.—*v.t.* to perform as a job: to put or carry through by jobbery: to deal in, as a broker: to hire or let out, esp. horses.—*ns.* jobb′er, one who jobs: one who buys and sells, as a broker: one who turns official actions to private advantage: one who engages in a mean lucrative affair: a wholesale merchant, esp. if selling to retailers (*U.S.*); jobb′ery, jobbing: unfair means employed to secure some private end.—*adj.* jobb′ing, working by the job.—*n.* the doing of jobs: miscellaneous

printing-work: buying and selling as a broker: stock-jobbing: jobbery.—job'-lot, a collection of odds and ends, esp. for sale as one lot: any collection of inferior quality; job'-mas'ter, a livery-stable keeper who jobs out horses and carriages.—a bad, good, job, a piece of work ill, or well, done: an unlucky, or lucky, fact; have a job to (coll.), to have difficulty in; job of work, a task, bit of work; jobs for the boys, jobs given to or created for associates or adherents; just the job (coll.), exactly what is wanted; odd jobs, occasional pieces of work; on the job, at work, in activity. [Origin unknown.]
**jobation.** See Job.
**jobe.** See Job.
**jobernowl,** job'ər-nōl, n. a dull head: a stupid person. [App. Fr. jobard, a noodle, and nowl, noll.]
**Jock,** jok, n. Jack (Scot.): the jack or knave in cards (Scot.): a yokel: a Scottish soldier (slang). [Jack.]
**jockey,** jok'i, n. a man (orig. a boy) who rides in a horse-race: a horse-dealer: one who takes undue advantage in business.—v.t. to jostle by riding against: to manoeuvre: to trick by manoeuvring.—v.i. to seek advantage by manoeuvring.—ns. jock'eyism, jock'eyship, the art or practice of a jockey.—Jockey Club, an association for the promotion and ordering of horse-racing: a perfume composed of rose, orris, cassia, tuberose, bergamot, etc; jockey strap (see jockstrap). [Dim. of Jock.]
**jocko,** jok'ō, n. a chimpanzee. [Fr., from a W. African word nchɛko.]
**Jock Scott,** jok skot, n. a kind of artificial fly.
**jockstrap,** jok'strap, n. genital support worn by men participating in athletics.—Also jock, jockey strap. [Dial. jock, the male organ, strap.]
**jockteleg,** jok'tə-leg, (Scot.) n. a large clasp-knife. [The suggested Jacques de Liège lacks confirmation.]
**joco,** jō-kō', (Scot.) adj. cheerfully complacent [jocose.]
**jocorous,** jō-kō'rəs, -kö', (Anglo-Ir.) adj. jocose. [jocose.]
**jocose,** jō-kōs', adj. full of jokes: facetious: merry.—adv. jocose'ly.—ns. jocose'ness, jocosity (-kos'i-ti), the quality of being jocose.—adj. jocose'rious, half in jest, half in earnest. [L. jocōsus—jocus, a joke.]
**jocular,** jok'ū-lər, əd. given to jokes: inclined to joke: of the nature of, intended as, a joke. —n. jocularity (-lar'i-ti).—adv. joc'ularly.—n. joc'ulātor, a professional jester or minstrel. [L. joculāris—jocus.]
**jocund,** jōk'und, jok'und, -ənd, adj. mirthful: merry: cheerful: pleasant.—ns. jocundity (kund'i-ti), joc'undness.—adv. joc'undly. [O.Fr. —L.L. jocundus for L. jūcundus, pleasant, modified by association with jocus.]
**jodel,** yō'dl. Same as yodel.
**jodhpurs,** jod'pûrz, n.pl. riding-breeches with a tight extension to the ankle (also jodhpur breeches): ankle-high boots worn with jodhpur breeches for riding (also jodhpur boots, shoes). [Jodhpur in India.]
**joe,** jō, joey, jō'i, (slang) n. fourpenny-bit (Joseph Hume, M.P., 1836): threepenny bit—n. Joey jō'i, a circus clown, esp. in the English tradition (Joseph Grimaldi).—Joe Miller, an old or stale jest, a jest-book; J oe Millerism, the habit of retailing stale jests—from Joe Miller (1684-1738), a comedian but a notoriously dull fellow, on whom a jest-book was fathered; Joe Soap, or merely Joe (airman's slang), one imposed on to perform unpleasant tasks.—not for Joe (see Joseph).
**joe.** Same as jo.

**joey,** jō'i (Austr.) n. a young animal, esp. kangaroo. [Australian joe.]
**jog,** jog, v.t. to shake: to push with the elbow or hand: to stimulate, stir up, as the memory.— v.i. to move by jogs: to trudge:—pr.p. jogg'ing; pa.t. and pa.p. jogged.—n. a slight shake: a push or nudge.—ns. jogg'er, (Dryden) one who moves slowly and heavily; jogg'ing, exercising by running with a slow bouncing movement. —jog'-trot', a slow jogging trot: humdrum routine.—be jogging, to move on: to depart. [Perh. akin to shog.]
**joggle,** jog'l, n. a tooth, notch, or pin to prevent sliding of surfaces in contact: a joint so made. —v.t. to join with a joggle. [Perh. conn. with jag, a projection.]
**joggle,** jog'l, v.t. to jog or shake slightly: to jostle.—v.i. to shake:—pr.p. jogg'ling; pa.t. and pa.p. jogg'led. [App. dim. or freq. of jog.]
**johannes,** jō-(h)an'ēz, n. a gold coin of John V of Portugal.—Also joann'es.—adjs. Johann'ean, Johann'ine, of or pertaining to John, esp. the Apostle. [L. Jōhannēs from Jōannēs—Gr. Iōannēs—Heb. Yōchānān, John.]
**Johannisberger,** jō-han'is-bûrg-ər, n. a white Rhenish wine grown at Johannisberg ('St John's Mountain'), near Wiesbaden.
**John,** jon, n. a proper name of whose diminutives Johnny, Johnn'ie, is sometimes used in slang for a simpleton, an empty-headed man about town or fellow generally: lavatory (slang). —n. Johnian (jōn'i-ən), a member of St John's College, Cambridge.—John'-a-dreams' (Shak.), a dreamy fellow; John a-Nokes, John a-Stiles, -Styles, fictitious persons in English law-suits, or generally; John'-apple, a kind of apple, otherwise apple-John; John Barleycorn, malt liquor personified; John Bull, a generic name for an Englishman, from Arbuthnot(t)'s History of John Bull, 1712; John Bullism, the typical English character, or any act or word expressive of it; John Chinaman, a Chinaman: the Chinese generically; John Citizen, a typical citizen; John Collins, an alcoholic drink based on gin; John Company, the East India Company; John Doe (see doe); John Dory (see dory, 1); John'-go-to-bed-at-noon', the goat's-beard (from its early closing); Johnn'y-cake, a cake of Indian meal toasted; Johnn'y-come-late'ly, a newcomer; Johnn'y-head'-in-air, John o'dreams, a dreamy, impractical person; Johnn'y-raw, a beginner: a greenhorn. [L. Jōhannēs; see johannes.]
**Johnsonian,** jon-sō'ni-ən, adj. of, in the manner of, Dr Samuel Johnson, the lexicographer (1709-1784).—ns. Johnsō'nianism, John'sonism (-sən-izm); John'sonese, Johnsonian style, idiom, diction, or an imitation of it—ponderous English, full of antitheses, balanced triads, and words of classical origin.—n.pl. Johnsōniana (-ä'nə, -ä'nə), matters, miscellaneous items, connected with Johnson.
**joie de vivre,** zhwa də vē-vr', (Fr.) joy of living.
**join,** join, v.t. to connect: to unite: to associate: to add or annex: to become a member of: to come into association with or the company of: to go to and remain with, in, or on: to draw a straight line between (geom.).—v.i. to be connected: to combine, unite: to run into one: to grow together: to be in, or come into, close contact.—n. a joining: a place where things have been joined: a mode of joining.—ns. joind'er, joining; join'er, one who joins or unites: a worker in wood, esp. one who makes smaller structures than a carpenter: one who joins many societies; join'ery, the art of the joiner: joiner's work; join'ing, the act of joining: a seam: a joint; joint, a joining: the place where, or mode in which, two or more things join: a place where two things (esp. bones) meet with power of movement as of a hinge:

a node, or place where a stem bears leaves, esp. if swollen: a segment: a piece of an animal's body as cut up for the table: the flexible hinge of cloth or leather connecting the back of a book with its sides: a crack intersecting a mass of rock (*geol.*): the place where adjacent surfaces meet: condition of adjustment at a joint (in the phrase *out of joint*): a place of resort for tramps: a low resort: a place, esp. a public house or hotel.—*adj.* joined, united, or combined: shared among more than one: sharing with another or others.—*v.t.* to unite by joints: to fit closely: to provide with joints or an appearance of joints: to fill the joints of: to divide into joints.—*v.i.* to fit like or by joints.—*adj.* joint′ed, having joints: composed of segments: constricted at intervals.—*n.* joint′er, the largest kind of plane used by a joiner: a bricklayer's tool for putting mortar in joints.—*adj.* joint′less. —*adv.* joint′ly, in a joint manner: unitedly or in combination: together.—*ns.* joint′ness; joint′ure, property settled on a woman at marriage to be enjoyed after her husband's death.—*v.t.* to settle a jointure upon.—*ns.* joint′uress, joint′ress, a woman on whom a jointure is settled.—join′-hand, running hand; jointed cactus, a plant (*Opuntia pusilla*) of the prickly-pear genus, a serious pest in S. Africa; joint′-fir, any plant of the family Gnetaceae; joint′-heir, one who inherits jointly with another or others; joint′ing-rule, a long straight-edged rule used by bricklayers for keeping their work even; joint′-oil, synovia; joint′-stock, stock held jointly or in company (joint′-stock company, one in which each shareholder can transfer shares without consent of the rest); joint′-stool (*Shak.*), a stool made of parts inserted in each other; joint′-ten′ancy; joint′-ten′ant, one who is owner of land or goods along with others; joint′-worm (*U.S.*), a hymenopterous larva that attacks grain-stalks near the first joint.—join battle, to begin a fight or contest; join issue, to begin to dispute: to take up the contrary view or side; join up, to enlist, esp. in participation in a general movement; out of joint, dislocated: disordered (*fig.*); put one's nose out of joint, to supplant in another's love or confidence: to disconcert: to rebuff; second joint, the middle piece of a fly fishing-rod: the thigh of a fowl—opp. to the leg or drumstick, the first joint; universal joint, a contrivance by which one part is able to move freely in all directions, as in the ball-and-socket joint. [O.Fr. *joindre*—L. *jungĕre, junctum*, to join.]

joist, *joist, n.* a beam supporting the boards of a floor or the laths of a ceiling.—*v.t.* to fit with joists. [O.Fr. *giste—gesir*—L. *jacēre*, to lie.]

joke, *jōk, n.* a jest: a witticism: anything said or done to excite a laugh: anything provocative of laughter: an absurdity.—*v.t.* to cast jokes at: to banter: to make merry with.—*v.i.* to jest: to be merry: to make sport.—*n.* jok′er, one who jokes or jests: a fifty-third card in the pack, used at euchre, poker, etc.: an innocent-looking clause insidiously introduced to cripple the effect of a bill or document (*U.S.*): an unforeseen factor affecting a situation: a fellow (*slang*).—*adj.* joke′some.—*adv.* jok′ingly, in a joking manner.—*n.* joke′smith, a maker of jokes. —no joke, a serious or difficult matter. [L. *jocus.*]

jokol, *yō′köl,* (*Shetland*; *obs.*) *adv.* yes (lit. yes carl).—Also yo′kul. [Shetland Norn *jo*, yes, and (inferred) *koll*—O.N. *karl*, carl.]

jole, joll, other forms of jowl (1 and 2).

jolie laide, *zho-lē led,* (Fr.) a woman whose ugliness by conventional standards is part of her charm.

jolly, *jol′i, adj.* merry: expressing or exciting mirth, jovial: robust: used as an in-

definite expression of approbation (*coll.*).—*v.t.* to make fun of: put or keep in good humour, beguile.—*adv.* (*coll.*) uncommonly.—*n.* a marine (*slang*): a jollification (*coll.*).—*n.* jollificā′tion, a making jolly: noisy festivity and merriment. —*adv.* joll′ily.—*ns.* joll′iment (*Spens.*), merriment; joll′iness, joll′ity, joll′yhead (*Spens.*).— Jolly Roger, the pirates' black flag with white skull and crossbones. [O.Fr. *jolif, joli*, very doubtfully referred to O.N. *jōl*, Yule.]

jollyboat, *jol′i-bōt, n.* a ship's boat. [Origin obscure.]

jolt, *jōlt, v.i.* to shake or proceed with sudden jerks.—*v.t.* to shake with a sudden shock.—*n.* a sudden jerk: a shock: a stimulating shock.— *n.* jolt′er.—*adv.* jolt′ingly, in a jolting manner. [Ety. obscure.]

jolterhead, *jōlt′ər-hed,* jolthead, *jōlt′hed, ns.* a large clumsy head: a blockhead. [Ety. obscure.]

jomo, or dsomo. See zho.

Jonah, *jō′na, n.* a bringer of ill-luck on shipboard or elsewhere. [From the prophet *Jonah.*]

Jonathan, *jon′a-than, n.* the people of the United states, collectively, or a typical specimen (*Brother Jonathan*): an American variety of apple. [Perh. from the sagacious Governor *Jonathan* Trumbull, 1710-85.]

jongleur, *zhō-glœr′, n.* a wandering minstrel: a mountebank. [Fr.,—O.Fr.*jogleor*—L.*joculātor*; cf. juggler.]

jonquil, *jong′kwil,* formerly *jung-kwil′, n.* a name given to certain species of narcissus with rush-like leaves. [Fr. *jonquille*—L. *juncus*, a rush.]

jonty, *jon′ti,* jaunty, jauntie, janty, *jön′ti, jän′ti,* (*slang*) *n.* a naval master-at-arms.

Jordan, *jör′dn, n.* country in S.-W. Asia.—Also *adj.*—*adj.* Jordan′ian, (-*dān′*).—*n.* a native or citizen of Jordan. [See next.]

Jordan, *jör′dn, n.* the great river of Palestine: death (*fig.*; as a passage into the Promised Land, Numb. xxxiii. 51): a chamber-pot (*Shak.*; according to some, from *Jordan*-bottle, a pilgrim's bottle containing *Jordan* water).

jordeloo, *jör-di-lōō′.* See gardyloo.

jorum, joram, *jör′əm, jör′, n.* a large drinking-bowl: a great drink. [Ety. unknown; poss. from *Joram* in 2 Sam. viii. 10.]

Joseph, *jō′zif, n.* one whose chastity is above temptation—from the story of *Joseph* and Potiphar's wife in Gen. xxxix.: a caped overcoat worn by women in the 18th century for riding—possibly in allusion to *Joseph's* coat, Gen. xxxvii.—not for Joseph (or Joe), not on any account (the particular Joseph, if any, is unknown).

josh, *josh, v.t.* to ridicule.—*n.* a hoax: a derisive jest: a fool.—*n.* josh′er.

joskin, *jos′kin, n.* a clown, yokel. [Thieves' cant.]

joss, *jos, n.* a Chinese idol: luck: fate.—*n.* joss′er, a clergyman (*Austr.*): a fellow (*slang*): a blunderer (*slang*).—joss′-house, a temple; joss′-stick, a stick of gum burned by the Chinese as incense to their gods. [Port. *deos*, god—L. *deus.*]

joss-block, *jos′-blok,* (*dial.*) *n.* a horse-block.

jostle, *jos′l,* justle, *jus′l, v.i.* to tilt, joust (*obs.*). —*v.t.* and *v.i.* to shake or jar by collision: to hustle: to elbow.—*n.* an act of jostling.—*ns.* jos′tlement, jos′tling. [Freq. of joust, just.]

jot, *jot, n.* an iota, a whit, a tittle.—*v.t.* to set down briefly: to make a memorandum of:— *pr.p.* jott′ing; *pa.t.* and *pa.p.* jott′ed.—*ns.* jott′er, one who jots: a book or pad for rough notes; jott′ing, a memorandum: a rough note. [L. *iōta* (read as *jōta*)—Gr. *iōta*, the smallest letter in the alphabet, equivalent to i; Heb. *yōd.*]

jota, *hhō′tä, n.* a Spanish dance in triple time. [Sp.]

jotun, *yō′tən,* jötunn, *yæ′tən, n.* a giant. [O.N. *jötunn.*]

**jougs,** jōōgz, jugz, n.pl. an iron neck-ring—the old Scottish pillory. [Prob. O.Fr. joug, a yoke—L. jugum.]

**jouisance, jouysaunce,** jōō'is-əns, (Spens.) n. joyousness. [Fr. jouissance—jouir, to enjoy—L. gaudēre, to rejoice.]

**jouk, jook,** jōōk, (Scot.) v.i. to duck: to dodge: to bow.—n. an elusive duck or dodging movement: a bow.—ns. jouk'ery, jook'ery, jouk'ery-pawk'ery (Scot.), trickery, roguery. [Ety. obscure.]

**joule,** jōōl, jowl, n. orig. unit of energy, now of energy, work and heat in the M.K.S. system, equal to work done when a force of 1 newton advances its point of application 1 metre (1 joule = $10^7$ ergs). [After the physicist J. P. Joule (said to be pronounced jowl; 1818-89).]

**jounce, jowns,** v.t. and v.i. to jolt, shake. [Origin unknown.]

**jour, zhōōr** (Fr.), a day.—jour de fête (də fet), a feast day, esp. a saint's day.

**journal,** jûr'nəl, n. a daily register or diary: a book containing a record of each day's transactions: a newspaper published daily (or otherwise): a magazine: the transactions of any society.—adj. (Shak.) diurnal.—n. journalese', the jargon of bad journalism.—v.i. jour'nalise, -ize, to write for or in a journal.—v.t. to enter in a journal.—ns. journ'alism, the profession of conducting or writing for public journals: writing of fleeting interest or hasty character; jour'nalist, one who writes for or conducts a newspaper or magazine: one who keeps a journal.—adj. journalist'ic. [Fr.,—L. diurnālis; see diurnal.]

**journal,** jûr'nəl, (mech.) n. that part of a shaft or axle which rests in the bearings.—v.t. to provide with or fix as a journal.—jour'nal-box, a box or bearing for a journal. [Origin unexplained.]

**journal intime,** zhōōr-nal ĕ-tēm (Fr.), a diary.

**journey,** jûr'ni, n. a day's work or travel (obs.): a campaign (obs.): any travel: tour: excursion: movement from end to end of a fixed course: the weight of finished coins delivered at one time to the Master of the Mint (also jour'ney-weight): a train of colliery trucks:—pl. jour'-neys.—v.i. jour'ney, to travel:—pr.p. jour'-neying; pa.t. and pa.p. jour'neyed (-nid).—n jour'neyer.—adj. jour'ney-bat'ed (Shak.), way-worn.—jour'neyman, one who works by the day: any hired workman: one whose apprenticeship is completed: an electrically controlled clock or dial; jour'ney-work, work done by a journeyman or for hire: necessary, routine work. [Fr. journée—jour, a day—L. diurnus.]

**joust, just,** just (jōōst and jowst are recent pronunciations due to the spelling), n. the encounter of two knights on horseback at a tournament.—v.i. to tilt. [O.Fr. juste, jouste, joste—L. juxtā, nigh to.]

**jovial,** jō'vi-əl, adj. joyous: full of jollity and geniality: (cap.) of Jupiter: (cap.) influenced by Jupiter.—ns. joviality (-al'i-ti), jo'vialness.—adv. jo'vially. [L. joviālis—Jovis (in the nom. usu. Juppiter, Jupiter), the god Jove or Jupiter, or the planet Jupiter, an auspicious star.]

**jovysaunce,** a misreading of jouysaunce. See jouisance.

**jow, jow,** (Scot.) v.t. and v.i. to ring, toll: to rock. —n. a stroke of a bell.—n. and adj. jow'ing-in', ringing in.—jow one's ginger (see jee one's ginger). [jowl (2).]

**jowar, jow-är', jowari, jawari,** -ē, n. durra. [Hind. jawār, jawāri.]

**jowl,** jowl, jōl, n. the jaw: the cheek: a pendulous double chin: a dewlap: a head: the head and shoulders of a salmon, sturgeon, or ling.—n. jowl'er, a heavy-jawed hound. [Prob. several different words. The development and relations of M.E. chaul, O.E. ceafl, jaw, M.E. chol, O.E.

ceolu, ceolur, etc., and the modern forms with j are difficult to make out. Fr. joue, cheek, or some other word may have added to the confusion.]

**jowl, joll, jole, joule,** jōl, (dial.) v.t. and v.i. to bump: to beat: to toll.—n. a stroke: a knock. [Ety. obscure.]

**joy, joi,** n. intense gladness: rapture: mirth: a cause of joy: a beloved one.—v.i. to rejoice: to be glad: to exult.—v.t. to give joy to: to enjoy (Milt.):—pr.p. joy'ing; pa.t. and pa.p. joyed.—n. joy'ance (Spens.), gaiety, festivity.—adj. joy'ful, full of joy: feeling, expressing, or giving joy.—adv. joy'fully.—n. joy'fulness.—adj. joy'less, without joy: not giving joy.—adv. joy'lessly.—n. joy'-lessness.—adj. joy'ous, joyful.—adv. joy'ously. —n. joy'ousness.—joy'-ride (slang), a pleasure-drive, esp. reckless or surreptitious, often in a stolen car; joy'-riding; joy'-stick (slang), the control-lever of an aeroplane; joy'-wheel, a great wheel that carries passengers high in the air in pleasure-grounds.—no joy (slang), no news, reply, information, luck. [Fr. joie (cf. It. gioja) —L. gaudium.]

**Joycean,** joi'sē-ən, adj. of, or in the manner of, James Joyce (1882-1941), Irish writer.—n. a student or imitator of James Joyce.

**juba,** jōō'bə, n. a Negro breakdown or rustic dance, in which the spectators clap hands, slap their thighs, and sing verses with juba as a refrain.

**jubate,** jōō'bāt, adj. maned. [L. jubātus—juba, mane.]

**jubbah,** jōōb'ə, jub'ə, n. a long loose outer garment worn by Mohammedans.—Also jibbah, djibbah. [Ar. jubbah.]

**jube,** jōō'bē, n. a rood-loft. [L., imper. of jubēre, to command.]

**jubilant,** jōō'bi-lənt, adj. shouting for joy: uttering songs of triumph: rejoicing.—n. ju'bilance, exultation.—adv. ju'bilantly.—v.i. ju'bilate, to exult, rejoice.—ns. jubilate (jōō-bi-lä'tē, yōō-bi-lä'te), the third Sunday after Easter, so called because the church service began on that day with the 66th Psalm, 'Jubilate Deo', etc.: also the 100th Psalm, which in the English Prayer Book is a canticle used as an alternative for the Benedictus; jubilā'tion, a shouting for joy: the declaration of triumph. [L. jūbilāre, to shout for joy. Not conn. with jubilee.]

**jubilee,** jōō'bi-lē, n. among the Jews, every fiftieth year, a year of release of slaves, cancelling of debts, return of property to its former owners, proclaimed by the sound of a trumpet: the celebration of a fiftieth anniversary—e.g. of a king's accession, a bishop's consecration, etc.: in the R.C. Church, a year (every twenty-fifth—ordinary jubilee) of indulgence for pilgrims and others, an extraordinary jubilee being specially appointed by the Pope: any season or condition of great joy and festivity: joyful shouting: exultant joy.—silver, golden, diamond jubilee, respectively a twenty-fifth, fiftieth, sixtieth anniversary. [Fr. jubilé—L. jūbilaeus—Heb. yōbēl, a ram, ram's horn.]

**jud, jud,** n. a mass of coal holed or undercut so as to be thrown down by wedges. [Origin unknown.]

**Judaean, Judean,** jōō-dē'ən, adj. of Judaea or the Jews.—n. a native of Judaea: a Jew. [L. Judaea.]

**Judaic, -al,** jōō-dā'ik, -əl, adjs. pertaining to the Jews.—adv. Judā'ically.—n. Judāisā'tion, -z-.— v.t. Ju'dāise, -ize, to conform to, adopt, or practise Jewish customs or Judaism.—ns. Judāi'-ser, -z-; Ju'dāism, the doctrines and rites of the Jews: conformity to the Jewish rites; Ju'dāist, one who holds the doctrines of Judaism.—adj. Judāist'ic.—adv. Judāist'ically. [L. Jūdaicus—Jūda, Judah, a son of Israel.]

**Judas,** jōō'dəs, n. a traitor: (also without cap.) a

spy-hole in a door.—*adj.* **Ju′das-coloured,** red, of hair (*Judas* traditionally being red-haired).— **Ju′das-hole,** a spy-hole; **Ju′das-kiss,** any act of treachery under the guise of kindness (Matt. xxvi. 48, 49); **Ju′das-tree,** a tree (Cercis) of the Caesalpinia family, with rose-coloured flowers that appear before the leaves (*Judas* having traditionally hanged himself on one): also the elder (for the same reason). [*Judas* Iscariot.]

**judder,** *jud′ər, n.* a vibratory effect in singing produced by alternations of greater or less intensity of sound: aircraft or other vibration.— Also *v.i.* [Prob. jar and shudder.]

**judenhetze,** *yōō′den-het-sə* (Ger.), Jew-baiting.

**judge,** *juj, v.i.* to exercise the office of judge: to point out or declare what is just or law: to try and decide questions of law or guiltiness, etc.: to pass sentence: to compare facts to determine the truth: to form or pass an opinion: to distinguish.—*v.t.* to hear and determine authoritatively: to sit in judgment on: to pronounce on the guilt or innocence of: to sentence: to decide the merits of: to be censorious towards: to condemn (*B.*): to decide: to award: to estimate: to form an opinion on: to conclude.—*n.* one who judges: one appointed to hear and settle causes, and to try accused persons: one chosen to award prizes, to decide doubtful or disputed points in a competition, etc.: an arbitrator: one who can decide upon the merit of anything: in Jewish history, a supreme magistrate having civil and military powers: one capable of discriminating well: (*cap.*; *pl.*), title of 7th book of the O.T.—*ns.* **judge′ship,** the office of a judge; **judg′ment** (also **judge′ment**), act of judging: the comparing of ideas to elicit truth: faculty by which this is done, the reason: opinion formed: discrimination: good taste: sentence: condemnation: doom: a misfortune regarded as sent by Providence in punishment.— **judge′-ad′vocate,** the crown-prosecutor at a court-martial.—*adj.* **judge′-made′,** based on decisions of judges (as law).—**judg′ment-day,** a day of final judgment on mankind; **judg′ment-debt,** a debt evidenced by legal record; **judg′-ment-hall,** a hall where a court of justice meets; **judg′ment-seat,** seat or bench in a court from which judgment is pronounced.—**judgment reserved,** decision delayed after the close of a trial (in Scotland, 'avizandum made'); **judgment respited,** execution of sentence delayed. [A.Fr. *juger*—L. *jūdicāre*—*jūs,* law, and *dīcĕre,* to say, to declare.]

**Judica,** *jōō′di-kə, n.* Passion Sunday—from the opening words of the introit, '*Judica* me, Deus' (43rd Psalm).

**judicature,** *jōō′di-kə-chər, n.* power of dispensing justice by legal trial: jurisdiction: the office of judge: the body of judges: a court: a system of courts.—*adj.* **ju′dicable,** that may be judged or tried.—*n.* **judicā′tion,** judgment.—*adj.* **ju′dicative,** having power to judge.—*ns.* **ju′dicātor,** one who judges; **ju′dicatory** (-kə-tər-i), judicature: a court.—*adj.* pertaining to a judge: distributing justice. [L. *jūdicāre,* -ātum, to judge.]

**judicial,** *jōō-dish′əl, adj.* pertaining to a judge or court of justice: established by statute: arising from process of law: of the nature of judgement: judge-like, impartial: critical.—*adv.* **judic′ially.— judicial astrology,** the would-be science of the influence of the planets on human affairs; **judicial combat,** trial by battle; **Judicial Committee,** an offshoot of the Privy Council, forming a court of appeal; **judicial separation,** the separation of two married persons by order of the Divorce Court; **judicial trustee** (or **factor,** in Scotland), an administrator appointed by the courts to manage the estate of someone under some imperfection. [L. *jūdiciālis*—*jūdicium.*]

**judiciary,** *jōō-dish′ər-i, -i-ər-i, adj.* pertaining to

judgmen t,judges, or courts of law.—*n.* a body of judges: a system of courts. [L. *jūdiciārius.*]

**judicious,** *jōō-dish′əs, adj.* according to sound judgment: possessing sound judgment: discreet. —*adv.* **judic′iously.**—*n.* **judic′iousness.** [Fr. *judicieux*—L. *jūdicium.*]

**judo,** *jōō′dō, n.* a modern variety of ju-jitsu. [Jap. *jiu,* gentleness, *do,* way.]

**Judy,** *jōō′di, n.* Punch's wife in the puppet-show: a frump, an odd-looking woman: (without *cap.*) a girl (*dial.* or *slang*). [From the name Judith.]

**jug,** *jug, n.* a vessel with a handle and a spout or lip for pouring liquids: a jugful.—*v.t.* to boil or stew as in a closed jar:—*pr.p.* **jug′ging;** *pa.t.* and *pa.p.* **jugged.**—*n.* **jug′ful,** as much as a jug will hold:—*pl.* **jug′fuls.**—**jugged hare,** hare cut in pieces and stewed with wine and other seasoning. [Origin unknown.]

**jug,** *jug,* (*slang*) *n.* prison. [Cf. **jougs.**]

**jug,** *jug, n.* a note of the nightingale.—*v.i.* to utter the sound.—Also **jug′-jug′.** [Imit.]

**jugal,** *jōō′gəl, adj.* relating to a yoke, esp. that of marriage: malar.—*n.* the malar bone. [L. *jugālis*—*jugum,* a yoke.]

**jugate,** *jōō′gāt, adj.* paired (*bot.*): having the leaflets in pairs (*bot.*): joined side by side or overlapping, as heads shown on a coin, etc. [L. *jugāre,* -ātum, to join—*jugum,* a yoke.]

**Juggernaut,** *jug′ər-nöt,* **Jagannath,** *jug′ə-nät, n.* an incarnation of Vishnu, beneath whose car devotees were supposed by Europeans to immolate themselves; hence the 'car of Juggernaut' stands metaphorically for any relentless destroying force or object of devotion and sacrifice. [Sans. *Jagannātha,* lord of the world.]

**juggins,** *jug′inz,* (*slang*) *n.* a simpleton. [Origin unknown.]

**juggle,** *jug′l, v.i.* to perform as an entertainer (*obs.*): to amuse by sleight-of-hand, conjure— now usu. to manipulate balls or other objects with great dexterity: to practise artifice or imposture: to tamper or manipulate.—*v.t.* to transform, render, put by jugglery.—*n.* a trick by sleight-of-hand: an imposture.—*ns.* **jugg′ler; jugg′lery** (-lə-ri), art or act of a juggler: legerdemain: trickery.—*n.* and *adj.* **jugg′ling.**—*adv.* **jugg′lingly,** in a deceptive manner. [O.Fr. *jogler* —L. *joculāri,* to jest—*jocus,* a jest.]

**Juglans,** *jōō′glanz, n.* the walnut genus. [L. *jūglāns*—*Jovis glāns,* Jove's acorn.]

**Jugoslav.** Same as **Yugoslav.**

**jugular,** *jug′,* *jōōg′ū-lər, adj.* pertaining to the neck. —*n.* one of the large veins on each side of the neck.—*v.t.* **jug′ūlate,** to cut the throat of: to strangle, check by drastic means (*fig.*). [L. *jugulum,* the collar-bone—*jungĕre,* to join.]

**juice,** *jōōs, n.* the sap of vegetables: the fluid part of animal bodies: interesting quality: piquancy: electric current, petrol vapour, or other source of power (*slang*).—*adj.* **juice′less.**—*n.* **juic′iness.— adj. juic′y.**—**step on the juice,** to accelerate a motor-car. [Fr. *jus,* broth, lit. mixture.]

**ju-jitsu, jiu-jitsu,** *jōō-jit′sōō, n.* a system of fighting barehanded developed by the samurai in Japan: a system of wrestling as sport founded on it. [Jap. *jū-jutsu.*]

**ju-ju,** *jōō′jōō, n.* an object of superstitious worship in West Africa: a fetish or charm. [App. Fr. *joujou,* a toy.]

**jujube,** *jōō′jōōb, n.* a spiny shrub or small tree (Zizyphus) of the buckthorn family: its fruit, which is dried as a sweetmeat: a lozenge made of sugar and gum in imitation of the fruit. [Fr. *jujube* or L.L. *jujuba*—Gr. *zizyphon.*]

**juke,** *jōōk,* (*slang*) *v.i.* to dance.—**juke′-box,** a slot machine that plays gramophone records; **juke′-joint,** a resort for dancing and drinking. [Poss. —African *dzug,* to lead a careless life.]

**julep,** *jōō′ləp, n.* a sweet drink, often medicated: an American drink of spirits, sugar, ice, and mint (also mint'-julep). [Fr.,—Sp. julepe—Ar. julāb—Pers. gulāb—gul, rose, āb, water.]

Julian, jōōl'yən, adj. pertaining to Julius Caesar (100-44 B.C.).—Julian year (see year).

julienne, jōō-li-en', zhü-lyen, n. a clear soup, with shredded herbs: any foodstuff which has been shredded. [Fr. name.]

July, jōō-lī', formerly and still by some jōō'li, n. the seventh month of the year. [L. Jūlius, from Gaius Julius Caesar, who was born in it.]

July-flower, a mistaken form of gillyflower.

jumart, jōō'märt, -mərt, n. the fabled offspring of a bull and a mare, or stallion and cow. [Fr.]

jumbal, jumble, jum'bl, n. a thin, crisp, sweet cake, formerly made in the shape of a ring. [Perh. gimmel, gimbal.]

jumble, jum'bl, v.t. to mix confusedly: to throw together without order: to shake up, jolt.—v.i. to be mixed together confusedly: to be agitated: to flounder.—n. a confused mixture: confusion: jolting.—adv. jum'blingly, in a confused or jumbled manner.—adj. jum'bly.—jum'ble-sale, a sale of miscellaneous articles, rubbish, etc., often for charity. [Origin obscure.]

jumbo, jum'bō, n. anything very big of its kind: an elephant (after a famous large one so named). —adj. huge: colossal.—v.t. jum'boise, -ize (-bō-īz), to enlarge (a ship) by adding a prefabricated section, e.g. amidships. [Prob. mumbojumbo; earlier than Jumbo the elephant.]

jumby, jumbie, jum'bi, n. a West Indian Negro's word for a ghost or evil spirit. [Congolese zumbi.]

jumelle, jōō-mel', zhü-mel, n. a paired or twinned article, esp. opera-glasses. [Fr., twin; cf. gemel, gimmal.]

jump, jump, v.i. to spring or bound: to move suddenly: to bounce: to rise suddenly: to pass discontinuously: to throb: to agree, coincide (with).—v.t. to cause or help to leap: to toss: to leap over, from, or on to: to skip over: to spring or start, as game: to risk (Shak.): to appropriate, as when the owner has failed to satisfy conditions or has abandoned his claim: to make up hastily, patch up (obs.):—pr.p. jump'ing; pa.t. and pa.p. jumped.—n. act of jumping: a bound: an obstacle to be jumped over: height or distance jumped: a sudden rise or movement: a start: (in pl.) convulsive movements, chorea, delirium tremens, or the like: a bounce: a discontinuity: a venture, a hazard (Shak.).—adv. (Shak.) exactly.—ns. jump'er, one who jumps: a long iron drill used in quarries, etc.: one of certain Welsh Methodists (c. 1760), who jumped about in worship; jump'iness.—adj. jump'y, nervy, inclined to start.—adj. jumped'-up (coll.), upstart.—jump'ing-bean, the seed of a Mexican euphorbiaceous plant (Sebastiania), which an enclosed larva causes to move or jump; jump'ing-deer', the black-tailed American deer; jump'ing-hare', a South African rodent akin to the jerboa; jump'ing-jack, a toy figure whose limbs can be moved by pulling a string; jump'ing-mouse', a genus (Zapus) of jumping rodents, American and Chinese; jump'-jet, a fighter plane able to fly straight up or down; jump'-off (U.S.), the start: starting-place; jump'-seat, a movable carriage-seat: a carriage with a movable seat: a folding seat; jump suit, a one-piece, trouser and jacket or blouse, garment for either sex.—for the high jump (see high); jump at, to accept with eagerness; jump down one's throat, to assail with violent rating; jumping-off place, the terminus of a route: the point where one sets forth into the wilds, the unknown, etc.; jump on, to jump so as to come down heavily upon: to censure promptly and vigorously; jump one's bail, to abscond, forfeiting one's bail; jump the gun (i.e. the starting-gun in a race), to get off one's mark too soon, act

prematurely, take an unfair advantage; jump the queue, to get ahead of one's turn (lit. and fig.); jump to conclusions, to form inferences prematurely; jump to it! hurry! [Prob. onomatopoeic.]

jump, jump, n. a short coat: (in pl.) stays: clothes. —n. jump'er, an overall, slipped over the head: a woman's knitted upper garment, originally one loose at the waist: a pinafore dress (U.S.). [Perh. from Fr. juppe, now jupe, a petticoat.]

juncate, (Spens.) a form of junket.

junco, jung'kō, n. the reed-bunting (obs.): a North American snow-bird. [Sp. junco—L. juncus, rush.]

junction, jung'shən, jungk', n. a joining, a union or combination: place or point of union, esp. of railway lines. [L. junctiō, -ōnis; see join.]

juncture, jungk'chər, n. a joining, a union: a critical or important point of time. [L. junctūra; see join.]

Juncus, jungk'əs, n. the typical genus of rushes, giving name to the Juncāceae, the rush family. adj. juncā'ceous. [L. juncus, a rush.]

June, jōōn, n. the sixth month.—June'berry, the fruit of the shad-bush. [L. Jūnius.]

juneating, jōōn'ēt-ing, an erroneous form of jenneting.

Jungermanniales, yōōng-ər-man-i-ā'lēz, n.pl. one of the main divisions of the Hepaticae, with thallus or leafy stem, and usually capsule opening by four valves. [Ludwig Jungermann (1572-1653), German botanist.]

jungle, jung'gl, n. originally waste ground: a dense tropical growth of thickets, brushwood, etc.: dense tropical forest: a jumbled assemblage of large objects: a confusing mass of, e.g. regulations: a place or situation where there is ruthless competition, or cruel struggle for survival.—adj. jungli (jung'gli; Ind.), inhabiting a jungle: wild and boorish.—n. an inhabitant of a jungle: an uneducated peasant.—adj. jung'ly.—jungle fever, a severe malarial fever; jungle fowl, the wild parent of the barndoor fowl.—adj. jun'gle-green, very dark green. [Sans. jāṅgala, desert.]

junior, jōōn'yər, adj. younger: less advanced: of lower standing.—n. one younger, less advanced, or of lower standing: a young person: a bridgeplayer on the declarer's right: an American student in his third year (of four).—n. juniority (-i-or'i-ti).—junior optime (see optime); junior service, the Army; junior soph, an undergraduate of the second year at Cambridge. [L. jūnior, compar. of jūvenis, young.]

juniper, jōō'ni-pər, n. an evergreen coniferous shrub (Juniperus), whose berries are used in making gin. [L. jūniperus.]

junk, jungk, n. a Chinese vessel, with high forecastle and poop, sometimes large and three-masted. [Port. junco, app.—Javanese djong.]

junk, jungk, n. pieces of old cordage (arch.): rubbish generally: a chunk: salt meat, perh. because it becomes as hard as old rope (orig. naut.): nonsense (fig.): a narcotic.—v.t. to cut into junks: treat as junk.—n. junk'er, junk'ie, a narcotics addict.—junk'-bottle (U.S.), a thick strong bottle of green or black glass; junk'-dealer, a man, a dealer in junk; junk'-ring, a metal ring confining the packing of a piston; junk'-shop, a place where junk is sold. [Origin doubtful.]

junker, yōōngk'ər, n. a young German noble or squire: an overbearing, narrow-minded, reactionary aristocrat.—ns. junk'erdom; junk'erism. [Ger.,—jung, young, herr, lord.]

junket, junk'it, n. a rush-basket (dial.): a cream cheese: any sweetmeat or delicacy (obs.): curds mixed with cream, sweetened and flavoured: a feast or merrymaking, a picnic, an outing, a spree.—v.i. to feast, banquet, take part in a convivial entertainment or spree.—*v.t.* to feast, regale, entertain:—*pr.p.* junk'eting; *pa.p.* junk'eted.—*n.* junk'eting, a merry feast or entertainment, picnicking. [A.Fr. *jonquette*, rush-basket—L. *juncus*, a rush.]

Juno, *jōō'nō, n.* in Roman mythology, the wife of Jupiter, identified with the Greek Hera, special protectress of marriage and guardian of woman from birth to death: a queenly woman.—*adjs.* Junō'nian, pertaining to Juno; Junoesque (-*esk'*), large, buxom, and (usu.) beautiful. [L. *Jūnō, -ōnis.*]

junta, *jun'tə, n.* a meeting, council: a Spanish grand council of state: (in the following meanings also jun'to), *pl.* jun'tos), a body of men joined or united for some secret intrigue: a confederacy: a cabal or faction: a government formed by a usu. small group following a coup d'état. [Sp., L. *jungĕre, junctum,* to join.]

jupati, *jōō'pə-tē* or -*tē', n.* a species of raphia palm. [Tupí.]

Jupiter, *jōō'pi-tər, n.* the chief god among the Romans, the parallel of the Greek Zeus—also Jove: the largest and, next to Venus, the brightest of the planets.—Jupiter's beard, the house-leek: a kidney-vetch: a fungus (*Hydnum barba-jovis*). [L. *Jūpiter, Juppiter,* Father (*pater*) Jove.]

jupon, *jōō'pən, n.* a sleeveless jacket or close-fitting coat, extending down over the hips: a petticoat. [Fr.]

jural, *jōō'rəl, adj.* pertaining to natural or positive right.—*adv.* ju'rally. [L. *jūs, jūris,* law.]

jurant, *jōō'rənt, adj.* taking an oath.—*n.* one who takes an oath.—*adj.* ju'ratory, pertaining to an oath. [L. *jūrāre, -ātum,* to swear.]

Jurassic, *jōō-ras'ik,* (geol.) *adj.* of the middle division of the Mesozoic rocks, well-developed in the *Jura* Mountains.—*n.* the Jurassic period or system.—Also Ju'ra.

jurat, *jōō'rat, n.* the official memorandum at the end of an affidavit, showing the time when and the person before whom it was sworn. [L. *jūrātum,* sworn—*jūrāre,* to swear.]

jurat, *jōō'rat, n.* a sworn officer, as a magistrate. [Fr.,—L. *jūrāre, -ātum,* to swear.]

jure, *jōō'rē, yōō're* (L.) by law.—jure divino (*di-vī'nō, dē-wē'nō*), by divine law; jure humano (*hū-mā'nō,* (h)*ōō-mā'nō*), by human law.

juridical, *jōō-rid'ik-əl, adj.* relating to the distribution of justice: pertaining to a judge: used in courts of law.—*adv.* jurid'ically. [L. *jūridicus* —*jūs, jūris,* law, *dicĕre,* to declare.]

jurisconsult, *jōō'ris-kon-sult', n.* one who is consulted on the law: a lawyer who gives opinions on cases put to him: one learned in law. [L. *jūris cōnsultus*—*jūs, jūris,* law, *cōnsulĕre, cōnsultus,* to consult.]

jurisdiction, *jōō-ris-dik'shən, n.* the distribution of justice: legal authority: extent of power: district over which any authority extends.—*adjs.* jurisdic'tional, jurisdic'tive. [L. *jūrisdictiō, -ōnis.*]

jurisprudence, *jōō-ris-prōō'dəns, n.* the science or knowledge of law.—*adj.* jurispru'dent, learned in law.—*n.* one who is learned in law.—*adj.* jurisprudential (-*den'shl*).—medical jurisprudence, forensic medicine (see forensic). [L. *jūrisprū-dentia*—*jūs, jūris,* law, *prūdentia,* knowledge.]

jurist, *jōō'rist, n.* one who is versed in the science of law, esp. Roman or civil law: a student of law: a graduate in law: a lawyer (*U.S.*).—*adjs.* jurist'ic, -al.—*adv.* jurist'ically. [Fr. *juriste.*]

juris utriusque doctor, *jōō'ris ū-tri-us'kwē, yōō'ris ōō-tri-ōōs'kwe, dok'tor,* (L.) doctor both of canon and of civil law.

jury, *jōō'ri, n.* a body of persons sworn to declare the truth on evidence before them: a committee of adjudicators or examiners.—*n.* ju'ror, one who serves on a jury (also ju'ryman, ju'rywoman;

—*pl.* ju'rymen, ju'rywomen).—ju'ry-box, the place in which the jury sit during a trial; ju'ry-pro'cess, a writ summoning a jury.—jury of matrons, a jury of women empanelled to give a decision in a case of alleged pregnancy. [A.Fr. *juree—jurer*—L. *jūrāre,* to swear.]

jurymast, *jōō'ri-mäst, -məst, n.* a temporary mast raised instead of one lost.—*adj.* ju'ry-rigged, rigged in a temporary way.—ju'ry-rudd'er, a temporary rudder for one lost. [Not *injury-mast,* but perh. O.Fr. *ajurie,* aid—L. *adjūtāre,* to aid.]

jus, *jus, yōōs,* (L.) law: legal right.—jus civile (*si-vī'lē, kē-wē'le, -vē'*), civil law; jus divinum (*di-vī'nəm, di-wē'nōōm, -vē'*), divine right; jus gentium (*jen'shi-əm, gen'ti-ōōm*), law of nations; jus mariti (*ma'ri-tī, -tē*), right of a husband; jus naturale, (*nat'ū-rā'lē, nat'ōō-räl'e*), law of nature: common sense of justice; jus primae noctis (*prī'mē, prē'mī, nok'tis*), formerly alleged right of a feudal superior to deflower a vassal's bride.

jusqu'au bout, *zhüs-kō bōō,* (Fr.) to the very end.

jussive, *jus'iv, adj.* expressing command.—*n.* a grammatical form of construction expressing command. [L. *jubēre, jussum,* to command.]

just, *just.* Same as joust.

just, *just, adj.* righteous (*B.*): fair: impartial: according to justice: due: in accordance with facts: well-grounded: accurately true: exact: normal (*obs.*): close-fitting (*obs.*).—*adv.* precisely: exactly: so much and no more: barely: only: merely: quite (*coll.*).—*adv.* just'ly, in a just manner: equitably: accurately: by right.—*n.* just'ness, equity: fittingness: exactness.—just intonation, observance of the true mathematical theoretical pitch, without compromise or temperament.—just now, precisely at this moment: hence, a little while ago, or very soon. [Fr. *juste,* or L. *jūstus—jūs,* law.]

juste milieu, *zhüst mēl-yə,* (Fr.) the just mean, the happy medium.

justice, *jus'tis, n.* the quality of being just: integrity: impartiality: rightness: the awarding of what is due: a judge: a magistrate.—*ns.* jus'ticer, a vindicator or administrator of justice; jus'ticeship, the office or dignity of a justice or judge.—*adj.* justiciable (*jus-tish'i-ə-bl*), liable to trial.—*ns.* justiciar (-*tish'i-ər; hist.*), an administrator of justice: a chief-justice; justiciary (-*tish'i-ə-ri*), a judge: a chief-justice: jurisdiction of a justiciar or justiciary.—*adj.* pertaining to the administration of justice.— justices' justice, the kind of justice sometimes administered by the unpaid and amateur magistracy of England.—High Court of Justice, a section of the English Supreme Court, comprising Chancery and King's (Queen's) Bench Divisions; High Court of Justiciary, the supreme criminal court in Scotland; Justice of the Peace (J.P.), a local minor magistrate commissioned to keep the peace; Lord Chief-justice, the chief judge of the King's (or Queen's) Bench Division of the High Court of Justice; Lord Justice-clerk, the Scottish judge ranking next to the Lord Justice-general, presiding over the Second Division of the Inner House of the Court of Session, vice-president of the High Court of Justiciary; Lord Justice-general, the highest judge in Scotland, called also the Lord President of the Court of Session. [Fr.,—L. *jūstitia.*]

justify, *jus'ti-fī, v.t.* to make just: to prove or show to be just or right: to vindicate: to absolve: to punish, esp. to hang (*obs.*): to adjust by spacing (*print.*):—*pr.p.* jus'tifying; *pa.t.* and *pa.p.* jus'tified.—*adj.* jus'tifiable (or -*fī*), that may be justified or defended.—*n.* jus'tifiableness (or -*fī*).—*adv.* jus'tifiably (or -*fī'*).—*n.* justification (*jus-ti-fi-kā'shən*), act of justifying: that which justifies: vindication:

absolution: a plea of sufficient reason.—*adjs.* **jus′tificãtive, justificatory** (*jus-tif′i-kə-tə-ri* or *jus′ti-fi-kā-tə-ri*, or *-kā′*), having power to justify.—*ns.* **jus′tificãtor, jus′tifier,** one who defends or vindicates: he who pardons and absolves from guilt and punishment.—**justifiable homicide,** the killing of a person in self-defence, or to prevent an atrocious crime.—**justification by faith,** the doctrine that men are justified by faith in Christ. [Fr. *justifier* and L. *jūstificāre*—*jūstus,* just, *facĕre,* to make.]

**justle.** See jostle.

**jut,** *jut, n.* a projection: a jerking movement (*obs.*).—*v.i.* to project:—*pr.p.* **jutt′ing;** *pa.t.* and *pa.p.* **jutt′ed.**—*adj.* **jutt′ing.**—*adv.* **jutt′ingly.**— **jut′-win′dow,** a bay window. [A form of jet (2).]

**jute,** *jōōt, n.* the fibre of *Corchorus capsularis* and *C. olitorius* (fam. Tiliaceae) plants of Pakistan, etc., used for making sacks, mats, etc.: the plant itself.—Also *adj.*—**China jute,** a species of Abutilon: its fibre. [Bengali *jhuto*—Sans. *jūṭa,* matted hair.]

**jutty,** *jut′i, n.* a projecting part of a building: a pier, a jetty.—*v.t.* (*Shak.*) to project beyond.— *v.i.* to jut. [Cf. jetty.]

**juvenal,** *jōō′vən-əl,* (*Shak.*) *n.* a youth. [L. *juvenālis,* belonging to youth—*juvenis,* young.] **Juvenalian,** *jōōv-i-nā′li-ən, adj.* of the Roman satirist *Juvenal* (Decimus Junius Juvenalis, 1st-2nd cent. A.D.): lurid and denunciatory rather than humorous.

**juvenescent,** *jōō-vən-es′ənt, adj.* becoming youthful.—*n.* **juvenesc′ence.** [L. *juvenēscĕre,* to grow young.]

**juvenile,** *jōō′və-nil, adj.* young: pertaining or suited to youth or young people: having or retaining characteristics of youth: childish.—*n.* a young person: a book written for the young: an actor who plays youthful parts.—*n.* **ju′venile-ness.**—*n.pl.* **juvenilia** (*-il′yə*), writings or works of one's childhood or youth.—*n.* **juvenility** (*-il′i-ti*), juvenile character.—**juvenile delinquent,** a young law-breaker, in Britain under the age of seventeen; **juvenile hormone,** a hormone necessary to an insect in immature stages, which must be absent when it changes to adult form. [L. *juvenilis*—*juvenis,* young.]

**juxtaposition,** *juks-tə-pə-zish′ən, n.* a placing or being placed close together.—*v.t.* **jux′tapose** (or *-pōz′*), to place side by side.—**juxtaposition twin,** crystals twinned as if set together face to face without interpenetration. [L. *juxtā,* near, and position, pose.]

**jymold.** See gimmal.

**Jynx,** *jingks, n.* the wryneck genus: a wryneck [L. *iynx*—Gr. *iynx* or *iynx.*]

Neutral vowels in unaccented syllables: *el′ə-mənt*; for certain sounds in foreign words, see p. viii

# K

**K, k,** *kā, n.* the eleventh letter in our alphabet, derived from Greek kappa, representing a back voiceless stop, formed by raising the back of the tongue to the soft palate: as a mediaeval numeral, K = 250: in mathematics *k* often stands for a constant quantity: in thermometry K stands for the Kelvin scale.

**ka,** *kä, n.* in ancient Egyptian religion, the double or genius, or individuality. [Egypt.]

**ka, kae,** *kā, (obs.) v.t.* serve (in the phrase *ka me, ka thee,* one good turn deserves another). [Origin unknown.]

**Kaaba,** *kä'bə, n.* the holy building at Mecca into which the Black Stone is built. [Ar. *ka'bah*— *ka'b,* cube.]

**kaama,** *kä'mə, n.* the hartebeest. [Of Hottentot or Bantu origin.]

**kabala.** Same as **cabbala.**

**kabaya,** *kä-bä'ya, n.* a loose tunic. [Malay, from Pers. or Ar.]

**kabeljou, kabeljouw,** *kob', kub'l-yō, n.* a large South African fish, *Johnius Hololepidotus.* [Afrik.]

**kabob, kebab, kabab, kebob, cabob,** *kə-bob', n.* (also used in *pl.*) small pieces of meat cooked with vegetables, etc., esp. (from Turkish **shish kebab**) when on a skewer. [Ar. *kabāb.*]

**kabuki,** *kä-bōō-kē', n.* a popular Japanese dramatic form, historical, classical, eclectic, with music.

**Kabyle,** *ka-bil', n.* one of a branch of the great Berber people of North Africa: a dialect of Berber. [Fr.,—Ar. *qabā'il,* pl. of *qabīlah,* a tribe.]

**kacha, kachcha.** Same as **cutcha.**

**kachahri, kacheri,** *kuch'ə-ri, kuch-er'i, n.* an Indian magistrate's office or courthouse.—Also **cutcherry.** [Hindi *kacahrī.*]

**Kaddish,** *kad'ish, n.* a Jewish form of thanksgiving and prayer, used at funerals, etc. [Aramaic *qaddish.*]

**kade.** See **ked.**

**kadi,** *kä'di, n.* Same as **cadi.**

**kae,** *kā, (Scot.) n.* a jackdaw.—Also **ka.** [Cf. M.Du. *ka,* Dan. *kaa.*]

**kae.** See **ka** (2).

**Kaffir, Kaffer,** *kaf'ər, kuf'ər, n.* name applied to certain indigenous peoples of S. Africa including the Xhosa (*hist.*): now often used derogatorily: any of the languages spoken by them (*hist.*): (*pl.*) S. African mining shares.—Earlier **Caffre, Kaf'ir.**—Also *adj.*—**kaff'ir-boom** (Du. *boom,* tree) the coral-tree (*Erythrina caffra*); **kaffir bread,** the pith of S. African cycads (*Encephalartos*); **kaffir corn,** sorghum. [**Kafir** (*q.v.*).]

**kaffiyeh,** *käf-ē'ye, n.* a Bedouin shawl for the head. [Ar. *kaffiyah.*]

**kafila,** *käf'i-la, n.* a camel train, caravan. [Ar. *qāfilah.*]

**Kafir,** *käf'ər, n.* an infidel (also **Caffre**): a native of Kafiristan (in Afghanistan): a Kaffir. [Ar. *kāfir,* unbeliever.]

**kaftan.** Same as **caftan.**

**kago,** *käg'ō, n.* a Japanese basketwork palanquin. [Jap. *kango.*]

**kai,** *kä'ē, ki, n.* (*N. Zealand,* etc.) *n.* food.—*n.* **kai'kai,** food: feast.—*v.t.* to eat. [Maori.]

**kaiak.** Same as **kayak.**

**kaid,** *kä-ēd', kād, n.* a North African chief. [Ar. *qā'id;* cf. **alcaid.**]

**kaie,** *kā,* an obsolete form of **key.**

**kaif,** *kif, n.* an undisturbed quiescence. [Ar.]

**kail,** *kāl, n.* a ninepin: (in *pl.*) the game of ninepins: (in *pl.*) skittles. [Cf. Du. and Ger. *kegel.*]

**kail, kaim.** See **kale, kame.**

**kaimakam,** *ki-mä-käm', n.* a Turkish lieutenant-colonel or lieutenant-governor. [Turk. *qāima-qām.*]

**kain.** Same as **cain.**

**kainite,** *ki'nīt, kā'nit, kä'in-īt, n.* hydrous magnesium sulphate with potassium chloride, found in salt deposits, used as a fertiliser. [Ger. *kainit*—Gr. *kainos,* new, recent.]

**Kainozoic.** Same as **Cainozoic.**

**kaisar-i-Hind,** *ki'sar-ı-hind', n.* title from 1876 to 1947 of the British monarch as emperor of India. [Pers. *qaysari-Hind*—L. *Caesar.*]

**kaiser,** *ki'zər, n.* an emperor, esp. a German Emperor.—Also (as *Spens.*) **kesar, keasar** (*kē'zər*).—*ns.* **kai'serdom; kai'serism; kai'sership.**—**the Kaiser's war,** the war of 1914-18 (Kaiser Wilhelm II). [Ger.,—L. *Caesar.*]

**kajawah,** *kä-jä'wa, n.* a camel litter or pannier. [Pers.]

**kaka,** *kä'kə, n.* a New Zealand parrot (*Nestor meridionalis*).—**ka'ka-beak, -bill,** the New Zealand glory-pea (Clianthus); **ka'kapo,** the New Zealand owl-parrot, large-winged but almost flightless. [Maori *kaka,* parrot, *po,* night.]

**kakemono,** *kak-i-mō'nō, n.* a Japanese wall-picture with roller. [Jap. *kake,* to hang, *mono,* thing.]

**kaki,** *kä'kē, n.* the Japanese persimmon, or Chinese date-plum. [Jap.]

**kakistocracy,** *kak-is-tok'rə-si, n.* government by the worst. [Gr. *kakistos,* superl. of *kakos,* bad, *kratos,* power.]

**kakodyl.** Same as **cacodyl.**

**kala-azar,** *kä'lä-ä-zär', n.* a tropical fever, characterised by bloodlessness, and ascribed to a protozoan parasite. [Assamese *kālā,* black, *āzār,* disease.]

**kalamdan,** *kal'am-dan, n.* a Persian writing-case. [Pers. *qalamdān*—*qalam,* a pen, *dān,* holding.]

**kalamkari,** *kal-am-kä'rē, n.* a method of colouring and decorating by several dyeings or printings: a chintz so treated. [Pers. *qalamkāri,* writing, painting, etc.—*qalam,* pen.]

**kale, kail,** *kāl, n.* a cabbage with open curled leaves: cabbage generally: broth of which kale is a chief ingredient, and also dinner (*Scot.*).—**kail'-pot** (*Scot.* -**pat'**); **kail'-runt',** a cabbage stem; **kail'yard', -yaird',** a cabbage-patch.—**kailyard school,** a set of Scottish sentimental story-writers (one of these, Ian Maclaren, used the title *Beside the Bonnie Brier Bush,* 1894, in allusion to the Jacobite song 'There grows a bonnie brier bush in our Kailyard').—**give one one's kale through the reek** (*Scot.*), to reprimand one severely. [Northern form of **cole.**]

**kaleidophone,** *kə-li'də-fōn, n.* an instrument for exhibiting sonorous vibrations by lines of light on a screen. [Gr. *kalos,* beautiful, *eidos,* form, *phōnē,* voice.]

**kaleidoscope,** *kə-li'də-skōp, n.* an optical toy in which one sees an ever-changing variety of beautiful colours and forms.—*adj.* **kaleidoscopic** (-*skop'ik*), pertaining to a kaleidoscope: showing constant change. [Gr. *kalos,* beautiful, *eidos,* form, *skopeein,* to look.]

**kalendar, kalends = calendar, calends.**

**Kalevala,** *kä'le-vä-lə, n.* the great Finnish epic, in eight-syllabled trochaic verse (from which

*fāte, fär; mē, hûr (her): mīne; mōte, för; mūte; mōōn, fŏŏt; dhen (then)*

Longfellow's *Hiawatha* is imitated) pieced together from oral tradition by Dr. Elias Lönnrot in 1835-49. [Finnish *kaleva*, a hero, *-la*, denoting place.]

**kali**, *kal'i*, or *ka̅'li̅*, *n.* the prickly saltwort or glasswort (*Salsola kali*): its ash (*obs.*): alkali, esp. potash (*obs.*).—*ns.* **kalinite** (*kal'in-it*), native potash alum; **kā'lium**, potassium. [Ar. *qili* as in root of **alkali**.]

**kali**, *kä'lē*, *n.* a carpet with long nap: the large carpet covering the centre of a Persian room. [Pers. *kāli̅*.]

**Kali**, *kä'lē*, *n.* a Hindu goddess, Durga, wife of Siva, as goddess of destruction. [Sans.]

**kalian**, *käl-yän'*, *n.* a Persian hookah. [Pers.]

**kalif.** See **caliph**.

**Kaliyuga**, *käl-i-yōō'gə*, *n.* in Hindu mythology, the present (fourth) age of the world, of universal degeneracy. [Sans.]

**Kallima**, *kal'i-mə*, *n.* an Oriental genus of butterflies, mimicking dead leaves. [Gr. *kallimos*, beautiful.]

**kallitype**, *kal'i-tip*, *n.* a photographic process in which ferric are reduced to ferrous salts. [Gr. *kallos*, beauty, *typos*, type.]

**Kalmia**, *kal'mi-ə*, *n.* a genus of North American evergreen shrubs of the heath family, including the mountain laurel or calico-bush. [From Peter *Kalm*, pupil of Linnaeus.]

**Kalmuck**, *kal'muk*, *n.* a member of a Mongolian race in China and Russia: their language.—Also *adj.* [Turki and Russ.]

**kalong**, *kä'long*, *n.* a large fruit-bat. [Malay *kālong*.]

**kalotype.** Same as **calotype**.

**kalpa**, *kal'pə*, *n.* a day of Brahma, a period of 4320 million years.—Also **cal'pa**. [Sans., formation.]

**kalpak**, *käl'päk*, or *-päk'*, *n.* a triangular Turkish or Tatar felt cap.—Also **calpac**, **calpack**. [Turk. *qālpāq*.]

**kalpis**, *kal'pis*, *n.* a water-vase. [Gr.]

**kalsomine**, a wrong form of **calcimine**. See **calcium**.

**kalumpit**, *kä-lōōm-pēt'*, *n.* a Philippine tree of the myrobalan genus: its edible fruit. [Tagálog.]

**kalyptra**, *ka-lip'trə*, *n.* a veil worn by Greek women. [Gr.; see also **calyptra**.]

**kam, kamme, cam**, *kam*, (*Shak.*) *adj.* and *adv.* awry. [Cf. W., Gael., Ir. *cam*.]

**Kama**, *kä'ma*, *n.* the god of love in the Puranas: impure desire.—Also **Cama**, **Ka'madeva** (*-dä-vä*). [Sans. *Kāma*.]

**kamala**, *kä'mä-la*, *n.* an orange dyestuff got from the fruit-hairs of an East Indian tree of the spurge family (*Mallotus philippinensis*): the tree itself.—Also **kamela**, **kamila** (*kä-mä'la*, *-mē'la*). [Sans. *kamala*; Hind. *kamēlā*, *kamilā*.]

**kame, kaim**, *kām*, *n.* a comb (*Scot.*): a low irregular ridge like a cock's comb: an esker, a bank or ridge of gravel, sand, etc., associated with the glacial deposits of Scotland (*geol.*): a fortified site (*Scott*). [Northern form of **comb**.]

**kame, came**, *kām*, *n.* a lead rod for framing a pane in a lattice or stained-glass window.

**kamees**, *ka-mēs'*. Same as **camise**.

**kamela.** See **kamala**.

**kamerad**, *kam-ər-äd'*, *interj.* comrade (said to have been a German form of surrender or appeal for quarter).—*v.i.* to surrender. [Ger.,—Fr. *camarade*, comrade.]

**kami**, *kä'mi*, *n.* a Japanese lord, national god, demigod, or deified hero, or any of their supposed descendants, as the mikados and the imperial family. [Jap., superior.]

**kamichi**, *kä'mē-shē*, *n.* the horned screamer, a South American bird. [Fr., from Carib.]

**kamikaze**, *kä-mi-kä'zē*, *n.* (a Japanese airman, or plane, making) a suicidal attack. [Jap., divine wind.]

**kamila.** See **kamala**.

**kamis**, *ka-mēs'*. Same as **camise**.

**kampong**, *kam'pong*, *kam-pong'*, *n.* an enclosed space: a village. [Malay.]

**kamsin.** Same as **khamsin**.

**kana**, *kä'na*, *n.* Japanese syllabic writing, as distinguished from Japanese written in Chinese characters. [Jap.]

**kanaka**, *kən-ak'a*, *kan'ə-kä*, *n.* a South Sea Islander, esp. an indentured or forced labourer. [Hawaiian, a man.]

**Kanarese, Canarese**, *kan-ər-ēz'*, *adj.* of *Kanara* in western India.—*n.* one of the people thereof: their Dravidian language, akin to Telugu.

**kandy**, *kan'di*, *n.* Same as **candy** (2).

**kaneh, caneh**, *kä'ne*, *n.* a Hebrew measure of 6 cubits' length. [Heb. *qāneh*, reed, cane.]

**kang, kang**, *n.* a large Chinese water-jar: a platform (e.g. of brick) for sleeping on that can be warmed by a fire underneath. [Chin.]

**kangaroo**, *kang-gə-rōō'*, *n.* a large marsupial of Australia, with very long hind-legs and great power of leaping: (in *pl.*) Australian mining shares.—**kangaroo'-app'le**, the edible fruit of a species of Solanum: the plant that yields it; **kangaroo closure**, the method of allowing the chairman to decide which clauses shall be discussed and which passed or leaped over; **kangaroo court**, a court operated by a mob, by prisoners in jail, by any improperly constituted body: a tribunal before which a fair trial is impossible: a comic burlesque court; **kangaroo'-grass**, a valuable Australian fodder grass (Anthistiria or Themeda); **kangaroo justice**, the kind of justice dispensed by a kangaroo court; **kangaroo'-rat'**, a North American rodent (Dipodomys) akin to the jerboa: sometimes used for rat-kangaroo; **kangaroo'-thorn'**, a prickly Australian acacia (*Acacia armata*). [Supposed to be a native name.]

**Kannada**, *kän'ə-da*, *n.* an important Dravidian language. [Kanarese, *Kannada*.]

**kans**, *käns*, *n.* an Indian grass which is allied to sugar-cane.

**kant.** Same as **cant** (2).

**kantar, cantar**, *kan-tär'*, *n.* a varying weight in Turkey, Egypt, etc., approximately a hundred-weight. [Ar. *qintār*; see **quintal**.]

**kanten**, *kan'tən*, *n.* agar-agar jelly. [Jap.]

**Kantian**, *kant'i-ən*, *adj.* pertaining to the great German philosopher Immanuel *Kant* (1724-1804) or his philosophy.—*ns.* **Kan'tianism**, **Kant'ism**, the doctrines or philosophy of Kant; **Kant'ist**, one who is a disciple or follower of Kant.

**kantikoy, canticoy**, *kan'ti-koi*, **cantico**, *-kō*, *n.* an American Indian religious dance: a dancing-match.—*v.i.* to dance as an act of worship. [From Algonquian.]

**Kanuck.** Same as **Canuck**.

**Kanzu**, *kan'zōō*, *n.* a long white garment worn by men in central East Africa. [From Swahili.]

**kaoliang**, *kä-ō-li-ang'*, *n.* sorghum grain of various varieties: a spirituous liquor made from it. [Chin., tall grain.]

**kaolin**, *kä'ō-lin*, *n.* China clay, esp. that composed of kaolinite.—*v.t.* and *v.i.* **ka'olinise**, **-ize**, to turn into kaolin.—*n.* **ka'olinite**, a hydrated aluminium silicate occurring in minute monoclinic flakes, a decomposition product of feldspar, etc. [From the mountain *Kao-ling* (high ridge) in China.]

**kaon**, *kä'on*. See under **meson**.

**kapellmeister**, *kə-pel'mis'tər*, *n.* the director of an orchestra or choir, esp. formerly of the band of a ruling prince in Germany. [Ger. *kapelle*, chapel, orchestra, *meister*, master.]

**kapok**, *kap'*, *käp'ok*, *n.* very light, waterproof, oily fibre covering the seeds of a species of silk-cotton tree, used for stuffing pillows, life-belts, etc. [Malay *kāpoq*.]

Neutral vowels in unaccented syllables: *el'ə-mənt*; for certain sounds in foreign words, see p. viii

**kappa,** *kap'ə, n.* the tenth (earlier eleventh) letter of the Greek alphabet (Κ, κ): as a numeral κ' =20, ͵κ =20,000.

**kaput, kaputt,** *kə-pŏŏt', (slang),* ruined: broken: smashed. [Ger.]

**karabiner,** *ka-rə-bēn'ər, (mountaineering) n.* a steel link with a spring clip in one side. [Ger.]

**karait,** *kär-it'.* Same as **krait.**

**Karaite,** *kā'rā-īt, n.* one of a stricter sect of Jews who cling to the literal interpretation of Scripture as against oral tradition. [Heb. *qārā,* to read.]

**karaka,** *ka-ra'ka, kä'rə-kə, n.* a New Zealand tree with edible orange fruit whose seeds are poisonous until treated. [Maori.]

**karakul, caracul,** *kär'ə-kōōl, -kŏŏl', n.* an Asiatic breed of sheep: a fur prepared from the skin of very young lambs of the Karakul or Bukhara breed, or of kids: a cloth imitating it. [Russ. *Kara Kul,* a lake near Bukhara.]

**karat,** U.S. spelling of **carat.**

**karate,** *ka-rä'tä, n.* a Japanese combative sport using blows and kicks.—**karate chop,** a sharp downward blow with the side of the hand.

**Karen,** *kə-ren', n.* (one of) a people of eastern and southern Burma: the language of the Karens.—Also *adj.*—*n.* **Karenn'i,** (one of) a group of eastern Karen peoples whose women stretch their necks by wearing brass collars.

**karite,** *kar'i-ti, n.* the shea-tree. [Native African name.]

**Karling,** *kär'ling, n.* and *adj.* Carlovingian. [Ger. *Karl,* Charles, and patronymic suffix *-ing.*]

**karma,** *kär'ma, n.* the conception (Buddhist, etc.) of the quality of actions, including both merit and demerit, determining the future condition of all sentient beings: the theory of inevitable consequence generally: the result of the actions of a life.—*adj.* **kar'mic.** [Sans. *karma,* act.]

**Karmathian,** *kär-mä'thi-ən, n.* a member of a pantheistic socialistic Mohammedan sect which arose in Turkey about the close of the 9th century. [*Karmat,* its founder.]

**Karoo, Karroo,** *kä-rōō', n.* a high inland pastoral tableland (*S. Afr.*): a series of strata in South Africa of Permian and Trias age (*geol.*). [Believed to be of Hottentot origin.]

**kaross,** *kä-ros', n.* a S. African skin blanket. [Perh. a Hottentot modification of Du. *kuras,* cuirass.]

**karri,** *kar'ē, n.* a Western Australian gum-tree (*Eucalyptus diversicolor*): its red timber. [Native name.]

**karst,** *kärst, n.* rough limestone country with underground drainage. [From the *Karst* district, east of the Adriatic.]

**kart,** *kärt, n.* go-kart (*q.v.*).—*n.* **kart'ing,** go-kart racing.

**kartell,** *kär-tel', n.* a German form of **cartel.**

**karyokinesis,** *ka-ri-ō-kin-ē'sis, (biol.) n.* mitosis—a complicated process of division of the cell-nucleus, involving the arrangement of protoplasmic fibres in definite figures. [Gr. *karyon,* kernel, and *kinēsis,* movement.]

**karyoplasm,** *ka'ri-ō-plazm, n.* the protoplasm of a cell-nucleus. [Gr. *karyon,* kernel, and *plasma,* that which is formed.]

**kasba(h), casbah,** *kaz'ba, n.* a castle or fortress in a N. African town or the area round it, esp. in Algiers.

**Kashmir.** Same as **Cashmere** (which is the usual English spelling when reference is to the fabric). [Country in north-west of Indian subcontinent.]

**kat, kat,** *n.* a shrub (*Catha edulis*) of the spindle-tree family, used like tea by the Arabs. [Ar. *qat.*]

**kat, khat,** *kät, n.* the chief ancient Egyptian unit of weight, 1/50 lb. avoirdupois.

**katabasis,** *kat-ab'ə-sis, n.* a going down.—*adj.* **katabatic** (*-ə-bat'ik*). [Gr.]

**katabolism, catabolism,** *kat-ab'ə-lizm, (biol.) n.* the disruptive processes of chemical change in organisms—destructive metabolism, opposed to *anabolism*—*adj.* **katabolic** (*kat-ə-bol'ik*). [Gr. *katabolē—kataballein,* to throw down—*kata,* down, *ballein,* to throw.]

**katabothron, katavothron,** *kat-ə-both'ron, kat-av'oth-ron, n.* an underground water-channel. [Mod. Gr. *katabothron*—Gr. *kata,* down, *bothros,* hole.]

**katadromous.** Same as **catadromous.**

**katakana,** *kat-ä-kä'na, n.* a Japanese syllabary. [Jap.]

**katathermometer,** *ka-tə-thər-mom'i-tər, n.* an alcohol thermometer for measuring the cooling power of the air. [Gr. *kata,* down, and **thermometer.**]

**kathakali,** *käth-ə-kä'li, n.* a classical dance drama of Southern India. [Malayalam, drama.]

**katharsis, kathode, kation.** Same as **catharsis, cathode, cation.**

**katydid,** *kä'ti-did, n.* an American insect akin to the grasshopper. [Imit. of its note.]

**katzenjammer,** *kat'sən-jam-er,* or *-jam', n.* a hangover: a similar state of emotional distress (*fig.*): an uproar, clamour. [Ger., meaning 'cats' misery'.]

**kaugh.** See **kiaugh.**

**kauri,** *kow'ri,* or **kauri-pine,** *n.* a splendid coniferous forest-tree of New Zealand (*Agathis australis*), source of **kau'ri-gum,** a resin used in making varnish. [Maori.]

**kava,** *kä'və, n.* a species of pepper (*Piper methysticum*): a narcotic drink prepared from its root and stem.—Also **a'va.** [Polynesian.]

**kavass,** *kä-väs', n.* an armed attendant in Turkey. [Ar. *qawwās.*]

**kay,** *kā, n.* the eleventh letter of the alphabet (K, k).

**kayak,** *kī'ak, n.* an Eskimo seal-skin canoe. [Eskimo.]

**kayf.** Spelling of **café** to represent a (*vulg.*) pronunciation *käf.*

**kayo(e).** Stands for K.O. (knockout (*q.v.*)) *n.* and *v.t.*

**kayle.** Same as **kail** (1).

**kazoo,** *kä-zōō', n.* a would-be musical instrument, a tube with a strip of catgut, etc., that resonates to the voice. [Prob. imit.]

**kea,** *kā'ä, kē'ä, n.* a New Zealand parrot that sometimes kills sheep. [Maori.]

**keasar,** *kēz'ər.* See **kaiser.**

**keb,** *keb, (Scot.) v.i.* to cast a lamb prematurely.—*n.* a ewe that has cast its lamb. [Cf. Ger. *kibbe, kippe,* ewe.]

**kebab.** See **kabob.**

**kebbie,** *keb'i, (Scot.) n.* a shepherd's crook: a crook-handled walking-stick.

**kebbock, kebbuck,** *keb'ək, (Scot.) n.* a cheese. [Origin unknown; Gael. *cabag,* a cheese, may be derived from this word.]

**keblah.** See **kiblah.**

**keck,** *kek, v.i.* to retch, feel loathing.—*n.* a retching. [Imit.]

**keck, kecksy.** See **kex.**

**keckle,** *kek'l, v.t.* to protect by binding with rope or chains.—*n.* **keck'ling,** rope, chains, etc., used to keckle cables or hawsers. [Origin unknown.]

**keckle,** *kek'l, (chiefly Scot.) v.i.* a form of **cackle.**

**ked, ked, kade, käd,** *n.* a sheep-tick. [Origin unknown.]

**keddah.** Same as **kheda.**

**kedge,** *kej, n.* a small anchor for keeping a ship steady, and for warping the ship.—*v.t.* to move by means of a kedge, to warp.—*n.* **kedg'er,** a kedge. [Origin doubtful.]

**kedge,** *kej, (dial.) adj.* brisk, lively: pot-bellied.—Also **kedg'y, kidge.** [Cf. **cadgy.**]

**kedgeree,** *kej'ə-rē, n.* an Indian dish of rice, cooked with butter and dal, flavoured with spice, shred onion, etc.: a similar European dish made with fish, rice, etc. [Hind. *khichri*.]

**keech, *kēch*, (***Shak.****) n.* a lump of fat. [Perh. conn. with **cake**.]

**keek, *kēk*, (***Scot.****) v.i.* to peep.—*n.* a peep.—*n.* **keek′er,** one who peeps or spies: an inspector of coal: an eye: a black eye.—**keek′ing-glass,** a mirror. [M.E. *kyke*; cf. Du. *kijken*, Ger. *kucken*.]

**keel, *kēl*, *n.*** the part of a ship extending along the bottom from stem to stern, and supporting the whole frame: a longitudinal member running along the under side of an airship's hull or gasbag: the two lowest petals of a papilionaceous flower, arranged like a ship's keel (*bot.*): any narrow prominent ridge.—*v.t.* or *v.i.* to navigate: to turn keel upwards.—*n.* **keel′age,** dues for a keel or ship in port.—*adj.* **keeled,** keel-shaped (*bot.*): having a ridge on the back.—*v.t.* **keel′-haul,** to punish by hauling under the keel of a ship by ropes from the one side to the other: to rebuke severely.—**keel′hauling.** [O.N. *kjölr.*]

**keel, *kēl*, *n.*** a low flat-bottomed boat: a coal-lighter: a ship.—*ns.* **keel′er, keel′man,** one who works on a barge. [Du. *kiel*, ship, prob.—O.E. *cēol*, ship.]

**keel, *kēl*, (***Shak.****) v.t.** to cool. [O.E. *cēlan*, to chill.]

**keel, *kēl*, (***Scot.****) n.** red ochre, ruddle.—*v.t.* to mark with ruddle. [Origin obscure: Gael. *cil*, ruddle, may be from this word.]

**keelie, *kē′li*, (***Scot.****) n.** the kestrel or other hawk: a town rough, particularly one belonging to Glasgow and surrounding district: a boorish vulgarian. [Perh. imit.; some connect with **gillie**.]

**keeling, *kē′ling*, (***Scot.****) n.** a codfish. [Origin unknown.]

**keelivine, keelyvine, *kē′li-vīn*, (***Scot.****) n.** a lead pencil. [**keel** (4); ety. otherwise unknown.]

**keelson, kelson, *kel′sən*, *n.*** a ship's inner keel, which binds the floor-timbers to the outer keel. [**keel** (1); the forms in kindred languages suggest that the second syllable is equivalent either to **sill**, or to **swine**, animal names being sometimes used in similar ways.]

**keen, *kēn*, *adj.*** eager: sharp, having a fine edge: piercing: acute of mind: penetrating: intense.—*adv.* **keen′ly.**—*n.* **keen′ness.**—**keen prices,** very low prices.—**keen on** (*coll.*), devoted to: fond of: much interested in: very desirous of. [O.E. *cēne*, bold, fierce, keen; Ger. *kühn*, bold; O.N. *kœnn*, expert.]

**keen, *kēn*, *n.*** a lamentation over the dead.—*v.i.* to wail over the dead.—*n.* **keen′er,** a professional mourner. [Ir. *caoine*.]

**keep, *kēp*, *v.t.*** to reck of, care for (*obs.*): to tend: to have the care of: to guard: to maintain: to manage, conduct, run: to attend to the making of records in: to retain: to retain as one's own: to have in one's custody: to have habitually in stock for sale: to support, supply with necessaries: to have in one's service: to remain in or on: to adhere to: to continue to follow or hold to: to continue to make: to maintain hold upon: to restrain from departure, to hold back: to prevent: to reserve: to preserve in a certain state: to observe: to celebrate: to conform to the requirements of: to fulfil.—*v.i.* to care, reck (*obs.*): to remain: to continue to be or go: to be or remain in a specified condition: to remain fresh or good: to last or endure: to continue: to lodge (*obs.*): to have rooms at college (Cambridge): to refrain: to confine or restrict oneself: to keep wicket:—*pr.p.* **keep′ing;** *pa.t.* and *pa.p.* **kept, kept.**—*n.* care (*arch.*): a charge: condition: that which keeps or protects: subsistence: food: the innermost and strongest part of a castle, the donjon: a stronghold.—*ns.* **keep′er,** one who or that which keeps, in any sense: an attendant,

esp. upon the insane, or upon animals in captivity: a custodian: a gamekeeper: the title of certain officials as *Lord Keeper* (*of the Great Seal*), whose office since 1757 has been merged in that of Lord Chancellor: one who keeps a mistress (*obs.*): a wicket-keeper: the socket that receives the bolt of a lock: the armature of a magnet: a guard-ring; **keep′ership,** office of a keeper; **keep′ing,** care: preservation: reservation: retention: observance: custody: charge: maintenance, support (*Shak.*): maintenance of, or as, a mistress: just proportion: harmonious consistency.—**keep′ing-room** (*dial.*), a sitting-room, parlour; **keep′sake,** something given to be kept for the sake of the giver: an annual gift-book (such as *The Keepsake* itself, 1827-56).—*adj.* (also **keep′saky**) sumptuously inane.—**for keeps,** as a permanent possession: for good: permanently: with serious intent: defensively (in cricket, *Austr.*); **how are you keeping?** how are you?; **keep an act,** formerly, to hold an academical disputation; **keep an eye on, keep chapel, company, counsel, distance, hours, house, the peace, a term,** etc. (see the nouns); **keep at it,** to persist in anything; **keep back,** to withhold: to keep down, repress; **keep body and soul together,** to maintain life; **keep down,** to restrain: to repress: to remain low: to set in lower-case type, avoiding capitals; **keep from,** to abstain from: to remain away from: **keep going in** (a thing), to keep one supplied with it; **keep in,** to prevent from escaping: to confine in school after school hours: to conceal: to restrain; **keep in with,** to maintain the confidence or friendship of someone, often with the suggestion of unworthy means; **keep off,** to hinder from approaching or making an attack; **keep one's breath to cool one's porridge,** to hold one's peace when further talk is clearly in vain; **keep one's countenance,** to avoid showing one's emotions; **keep one's hand in,** to retain one's skill by practice; **keep one's powder dry,** to keep one's energies ready for action: to observe all practical precautions; **keep tab(s) on,** to keep a check on, to keep account of; **keep time,** to observe rhythm accurately, or along with others: to go accurately (as a clock); **keep to,** to stick closely to: to confine oneself to; **keep under,** to hold down in restraint; **keep up,** to retain one's strength or spirit: to support, prevent from falling: to continue, to prevent from ceasing: to maintain in good condition: to continue to be in touch (with): to keep pace (with; also *fig.*, as **keep up with the Joneses,** to keep on social equality with one's neighbours, e.g. by having possessions of like quality in like quantity): to stop (*obs.*); **keep wicket,** to act as a wicket-keeper. [O.E. *cēpan.*]

**keeshond, *kās′hond*, -nt, *n.*** a medium-sized dog of the spitz group once common on Dutch barges. [Du.,—*kees*, terrier, *hond*, dog.]

**keeve, kieve, *kēv*, *n.*** a large tub. [O.E. *cȳf*, vat.]

**kef, *käf*, *n.*** a state of dreamy repose: something, as Indian hemp, smoked to produce this. [Ar. *kaif*, pleasure.]

**keffel, *kef′l*, (***dial.****) n.** a horse, nag. [W. *ceffyl*; cf. **caple**.]

**kaffiyeh.** Same as **kaffiyeh.**

**kefir, kephir, *ke′fər*, *n.*** an effervescent drink of low alcoholic content, made from fermented cow's milk. [Native name in the Caucasus.]

**kefuffle.** See **carfuffle.**

**keg, *keg*, *n.*** a small cask. [Earlier *cag*—O.N. *kaggi.*]

**keight, *kīt*, (***Spens.****) v.t.** for **caught** (*pa.t.* of **catch**).

**keir.** See **kier.**

**keitloa, *kāt′lō-ə*, *n.*** a two-horned rhinoceros. [Tswana *kgetlwa.*]

**kell, *kel*, (***Northern****) n.** a woman's head-dress or hair-net: a film, network: a caul. [**caul.**]

Neutral vowels in unaccented syllables: *el′ə-mənt*; for certain sounds in foreign words, see p. viii

**kellaut.** See **killut.**

**kelp,** *kelp*, *n.* any large brown seaweed, wrack: the calcined ashes of seaweed, a source of soda, iodine, etc.—Also **kilp.** [M.E. *culp*; origin unknown.]

**kelpie, kelpy,** *kel'pi*, *(Scot.) n.* a malignant watersprite haunting fords in the form of a horse: a kind of collie *(Austr.)*. [Origin uncertain.]

**kelson.** Same as **keelson.**

**kelt,** *kelt*, *n.* a salmon, etc., that has just spawned. [Origin unknown.]

**kelt,** *kelt*, *(Scot.) n.* coarse cloth usu. made of black and white wool mixed and not dyed.—*n.* and *adj.* **kelt'er.** [Origin obscure.]

**Kelt, Keltic.** Same as **Celt, Celtic.**

**kelter,** *kelt'ər*, **kilter,** *kilt'ər*, (mainly *dial.* and *U.S.) n.* good condition. [Origin unknown.]

**keltie, kelty,** *kel'ti*, *(Scot.) n.* a bumper, esp. one imposed as a penalty on one who does not drain his glass completely.

**Kelvin,** *kel'vin*, *adj.* applied to a thermometer scale with absolute zero for zero and centigrade degrees.—*n.* **kel'vin** (SI units), the unit of temperature (formerly 'degree Kelvin'): kilowatthour *(rare)*. [Sir William Thomson, Lord *Kelvin* (1824-1907), physicist.]

**kemb, kem,** *(obs.* and *dial.) v.t.* to comb.—*adj.* **kempt** *(kemt, kempt)*, combed. [O.E. *cemban.*]

**kembo.** Same as **kimbo.**

**kemp,** *kemp*, *n.* the coarse, rough hairs of wool: *(pl.)* knotty hair that will not felt. [O.N. *kampr*, beard.]

**kemp,** *kemp*, *n.* a champion *(arch.)*: a contest in reaping or other work *(Scot.)*.—*v.i.* to strive for mastery.—*ns.* **kem'per, kem'pery-man,** a champion, a knight-errant; **kemp'ing.** [O.E. *cempa*, a warrior; cf. **champion.**]

**kemple,** *kem'pl*, *(Scot.) n.* forty bottles of hay or straw. [Origin obscure.]

**ken,** *ken*, *v.t.* to cause to know, direct *(obs.)*: to see and recognise at a distance *(arch.)*: to know (mainly *Scot.)*:—*pa.t.* and *pa.p.* **kenned, kent.**—*n.* range of sight or knowledge.—*ns.* **kenn'er; kenn'ing,** range of vision: a small portion, a little bit *(Scot.)*: a periphrastic formula in Old Norse or other old Germanic poetry; **kenno** *(ken'ə; Scot.,* know not), a cheese prepared in ostensible secrecy for the gossips at a birth.—*adj.* **kent,** known. [O.E. *cennan*, causative of *cunnan*, and O.N. *kenna*; cf. **can** (1), **con** (2).]

**ken,** *ken*, *(slang) n.* a house, esp. disreputable. [Perh. Pers. *khān*, a caravansarai; or **kennel**; or conn. with preceding word.]

**Kendal-green,** *ken'dl-grēn*, *n.* green cloth for foresters made at *Kendal* in Westmorland.

**kendo,** *ken'dō*, or *dō'*, *n.* Japanese art of swordsmanship practised with bamboo staves, in 18th-cent. armour, and observing strict ritual. [Jap. *kendō*.]

**kennel,** *ken'l*, *n.* a house for dogs: a pack of hounds: the hole of a fox, etc.: a haunt.—*v.t.* to keep in a kennel.—*v.i.* to live in a kennel:—*pr.p.* **kenn'elling;** *pa.t.* and *pa.p.* **kenn'elled.**—*n.* (in *pl.,* treated as *sing.)* an establishment where dogs are boarded.—**kenn'el-maid, kenn'el-man,** an attendant upon dogs. [From an O.N.Fr. form answering to Fr. *chenil*—L. *canile*—*canis*, a dog.]

**kennel,** *ken'l*, *n.* a street gutter. [M.E. *canel*—O.N.Fr. *canel*—L. *canālis*; see **canal.**]

**kennel-coal.** Same as **cannel-coal.**

**Kennelly-Heaviside layer** or **region,** *ken'ə-li-hev'i-sid*, a strongly ionised region of the upper atmosphere about 60 miles up, in which wireless waves are deflected.—Also **Heaviside layer; E-layer.** [From A. E. *Kennelly* and O. *Heaviside*, who inferred its existence.]

**kennet,** *ken'it*, *(obs.) n.* a small hunting dog. [O.N.Fr. *kennet*, dim.—L. *canis*, dog.]

**Kennick,** *ken'ik*, *n.* the jargon of tramping tinkers.

**kenning, kenno.** See **ken** (1).

**kenosis,** *ken-ō'sis*, *n.* the self-limitation of the Logos in incarnation.—*adj.* **kenotic** *(-ot'ik)*.—*n.* **kenot'icist** *(-i-sist)*, a believer in kenosis. [Gr. *kenōsis*, emptying, from Phil. ii. 7.]

**Kensington,** *ken'zing-tən*, *adj.* (of person) interested exclusively in an artificial city life and in material values. [Part of a London borough.]

**kenspeckle,** *ken'spek-l*, *adj.* easily recognised: conspicuous.—Also *(N. of England)* **ken'speck.** [Appar. O.N. *kennispeki*, power of recognition.]

**kent,** *kent*, *(Scot.) n.* a leaping or punting pole.—*v.t.* and *v.i.* to punt or pole. [Cf. **quant.**]

**kent.** See **ken** (1).

**kent-bugle,** *kent'-bū'gl*, *n.* an obsolete key-bugle. [Supposed to be named after a Duke of Kent.]

**kente cloth,** *ken'ti*, a silk cloth made in Ghana by sewing together long narrow handwoven strips. [Origin uncertain.]

**Kentish,** *kent'ish*, *adj.* of *Kent*.—*n.* the dialect of Kent, Essex, etc.—**Kent'ish-fire',** synchronised volleys of applause—probably from anti-Catholic demonstrations in Kent, 1828-29; **Kent'ish-man,** a native of W. Kent (one born east of the Medway being a *Man of Kent*); **Kent'ish-rag',** a rough limestone in the Lower Greensand of Kent.

**kentledge,** *kent'lij*, *n.* pig-iron in a ship's hold for ballast.—Also **kint'ledge.** [Origin unknown.]

**kep,** *kep*, *(Scot.) v.t.* to catch (an approaching object):—*pa.t.* and *pa.p.* **kepp'it.**—*n.* a catch: act or opportunity of catching. [keep.]

**kephalic,** *ki-fal'ik*. Same as **cephalic.**

**kepi,** *kāp'ē*, *n.* a flat-topped forage-cap with a straight peak. [Fr. *képi*.]

**Keplerian,** *kep-lē'ri-ən*, *adj.* pertaining to the German astronomer Johann *Kepler*. See **law** (1).

**kept,** *pa.t.* and *pa.p.* of **keep.**

**keramic,** *ki-ram'ik*. Same as **ceramic.**

**keratin,** *ker'ə-tin*, *n.* a nitrogenous compound, the essential ingredient of horny tissue, as of horns, nails, etc.—*v.t., v.i.* **ker'atinise, -ize,** to make or become horny.—*n.* **keratinisā'tion, -z-,** formation of keratin: becoming horny.—*adj.* **keratinous** *(kə-rat'i-nəs)*, horny.—*n.* **kerati'tis,** inflammation of the cornea.—*adj.* **keratogenous** *(-oj'i-nəs)*, producing horn or keratin.—*n.* **ker'atoplasty,** grafting of part of a healthy cornea to replace a piece made opaque by disease, etc. [Gr. *keras, -atos*, a horn.]

**keratophyre,** *ker'ət-ō-fīr*, *n.* a fine-grained soda trachyte. [Gr. *keras, -atos*, horn, and *-phyre* from **porphyry.**]

**keraunograph,** *kə-ron'ō-gräf*, *n.* an instrument for recording distant thunderstorms. [Gr. *keraunos*, a thunderbolt, *graphein*, to write.]

**kerb.** See **curb.**

**kerchief,** *kûr'chif*, *n.* a square piece of cloth worn to cover the head, neck, etc.: a handkerchief.—*v.t.* to cover with a kerchief.—*adj.* **ker'chiefed.** [O.Fr. *cuevrechief* (Fr. *couvrechef*)—*covrir*, to cover, *chef*, the head.]

**kerf,** *kûrf*, *n.* a cut: a notch: the groove made by a saw: a cut place, face of a cut: the place where a cut is made: a quantity cut at once, as of wool, etc.: a single layer of hay, turf, etc., cut. [O.E. *cyrf*, a cut.]

**kermes,** *kûr'mēz*, *n.* the female bodies of a coccus insect *(Kermes,* or *Coccus, ilicis*), used as a red dyestuff: the oak **(kermes oak;** *Quercus coccifera)* on which they breed: a cherry-red mineral, antimony oxysulphide (also **kermes mineral,** ker'mesite). [Pers. and Ar. *qirmiz.*]

**kermis,** *kûr'mis*, *n.* a fair in the Low Countries: in America, an indoor fair.—Also **ker'mess,** **kir'mess.** [Du. *kermis*—*kerk*, church, *mis*, mass.]

**kern.** See **quern** and **kirn** (1).

kern(e), *kûrn, n.* an Irish foot-soldier: a boor.— *adj.* ker′nish. [From Ir.—O. Gael; see cateran.]

kern, *kûrn, v.i.* to granulate. [Cf. corn.]

kern, *kûrn, (print.) n.* part of a type that projects beyond the body and rests on an adjoining letter. [Fr. *carne,* a projecting angle—L. *cardō, -inis.*]

kernel, *kûr′nl, n.* a seed within a hard shell: the edible part of a nut: a gland *(rare):* a nucleus: the important part of anything.—*adj.* ker′nelly, full of, or resembling, kernels. [O.E. *cyrnel—corn,* grain, and dim. suffix *-el;* Ger. *kern,* a grain.]

kernite, *kûrn′it, n.* hydrated oxide of sodium and boron. [*Kern* Co., California, where much is mined.]

kerogen, *ker′ō-jen, n.* the organic matter in oil-shale that gives oil on distillation. [Gr. *kēros,* wax, and root of *gennaein,* to generate.]

kerosine, *ker′o-sēn, n.* paraffin-oil obtained from shale or by distillation of petroleum. This spelling is now used commercially; *kerosene* is the older spelling. [Gr. *kēros,* wax.]

kersantite, *kûr′sən-tit, n.* a dyke-rock of black mica and plagioclase. [*Kersanton,* a locality in Brittany.]

kersey, *kûr′zi, n.* a coarse woollen cloth. [Perh. from *Kersey* in Suffolk.]

kerseymere, *kûr′zi-mēr,* or *-mēr′, n.* twilled cloth of the finest wools. [For cassimere, cashmere.]

kerve, *kûrv′, v.t. (Spens.)* a form of carve.

kerygma, *kə-rig′mə, n.* (preaching of) the Christian gospel, esp. in the way of the early Church. —*adj.* kerygmat′ic. [Gr. *kērygma,* proclamation, preaching.]

kesar, *kē′zər, n.* See kaiser.

kest, *kest,* an obs. form of cast.

kestrel, *kes′trəl, n.* a small species of falcon. [O.Fr. *quercerelle.*]

ket, *ket, (Scot.) n.* carrion. [O.N. *kjöt.*]

ket, *ket, (Scot.) n.* matted wool. [A.Fr. *cot.*]

keta, *kē′tə, n.* a Pacific salmon, the dog-salmon. [Russ. *keta.*]

ketch, *kech, n.* a small two-masted vessel. [Earlier *catch,* perh. from the vb. catch.]

ketch, *kech,* an obs. form of catch.

ketchup, *kech′əp, n.* a sauce made from tomatoes, mushrooms, etc.—Also catch′up, cat′sup. [Malay *kēchap,* perh. from Chinese.]

ketone, *kē′tōn, n.* an organic compound consisting of a carbonyl group united to two like or unlike alkyl radicals. [Modified from acetone.]

kettle, *ket′l, n.* a vessel for heating or boiling liquids, esp. one with a spout and a lid for domestic use: a cauldron: a cavity like a kettle in rock (see giant's kettle): a kettledrum *(Shak.).*—*n.* kett′leful.—kett′ledrum, a musical instrument, consisting of a hollow metal hemisphere with a parchment head, tuned by screws: a large tea-party; kett′ledrumm′er; kett′leholder, a little cloth, etc., for lifting a hot kettle. —a kettle of fish (cf. kiddle), a riverside picnic at which new-caught salmon are cooked on the spot: (ironically—often a pretty kettle of fish) an awkward mess. [O.E. *cetel;* Ger. *kessel,* Goth. *katils;* all perh. from L. *catillus,* dim. of *catinus,* a deep cooking-vessel.]

kettle-pins. Same as kittle-pins.

Keuper, *koi′pər, (geol.) n.* the uppermost division of the Trias.—Also *adj.* [Ger. miners' term.]

kevel, *kev′l.* Same as cavel.

kewpie doll, *kū′pi dol,* a plump baby doll with a top-knot of hair. [Cupid.]

kex, *keks, n.* a dry, often hollow, herbaceous (usu. umbelliferous) stalk: any tall umbelliferous plant.—Also kecks, and (false singulars) keck, kecks′y, keks′ye. [Origin unknown.]

key, *kē,* formerly *kā, n.* an instrument for locking or unlocking, winding up, turning, tuning, tightening or loosening: a wedge: a piece in-serted to prevent relative motion: a tapered piece of metal for fixing the boss of a wheel, etc., to a shaft: a spanner: the middle stone of an arch: a piece of wood let into another piece crosswise to prevent warping: in musical instruments, a lever or piston-end pressed to produce the sound required: a similar part in other instruments for other purposes, as in a typewriter or calculating machine: a lever to close or break an electrical circuit: a dry winged fruit, as of ash or maple, often hanging with others in bunches: a fret pattern: preparation of a surface to take plaster, glue, or the like: a keynote *(obs.):* a system of tones definitely related to one another in a scale: that which gives command of anything or upon which success turns: a scheme or diagram of explanation or identification: a set of answers to problems: a crib translation: that which leads to the solution of a problem: a leading principle: general tone of voice, emotion, morals, etc.— *v.t.* to lock or fasten with a key: to furnish with a key: to give an advertisement a feature that will enable replies to it to be identified: to attune (with *to):* to stimulate (to a state of nervous tension and excitement), raise (in pitch or standard), increase (with *up).*—*adj.* vital: essential: crucial.—*adjs.* keyed, furnished with a key or keys: set to a particular key: in a state of tension or readiness; key′less, without a key: not requiring a key.—key′board, a range of keys or levers in a musical or other instrument; key′bugle, a bugle with keys, giving a chromatic scale of two octaves.—*adj.* key′-cold *(Shak.),* cold as a key, lifeless.—key′-desk, the frame enclosing keyboards, stops, etc., of an organ; key′-fruit, a winged fruit; key′hole, the hole in which a key of a lock is inserted; key′holelim′pet, a mollusc (Fissurella) with perforated conical shell; key industry, an industry indispensable to others and essential to national economic welfare and independence; key man, an indispensable worker, essential to the continued conduct of a business, etc.; key money, a premium, fine, or sum additional to rent, demanded for the grant, renewal, or continuance of a tenancy; key′note, the fundamental note or tonic: any central principle or controlling thought; key′-pin, the pivot on which a pipe-key turns: a pin serving as fulcrum for a key of an organ, etc.; key′-plate, a keyhole escutcheon; key′-ring, a ring for holding a bunch of keys; key′-seat, a groove for receiving a key, to prevent one piece of machinery from turning on another; key signature, the indication of key by marking sharps, flats or naturals where the key changes or at the beginning of a line; key′stone, the stone at the apex of an arch: the chief element or consummation: that on which all else depends; key′-way, a groove cut in a shaft or boss to accommodate a key.—have the key of the street *(coll.),* to be locked out: to be homeless; power of the keys, the power to loose and bind, conferred by Christ on Peter (Matt. xvi. 19), and claimed by the Popes. [O.E. *cǣg.*]

key, an old spelling of quay.

key, *kē, n.* a low island or reef.—Also cay. [Sp. *cayo.*]

Keynesian, *kānz′i-ən, adj.* relating to John Maynard *Keynes* (1883-1946) or to his economic teaching, esp. his advocacy of a measure of public control within capitalism of the unrestricted play of economic forces both national and international.

Keys, *kēz, n.pl.* in full House of Keys, the lower house of the Manx Court of Tynwald. [App. key (1), not Manx *kiare-as-feed,* four-and-twenty.]

kgotla, *kgot′la, n.* an assembly of tribal elders in Botswana: the place of such assembly. [Bantu.]

**khaddar**, *kud'ər*, *n.* in India, hand-spun, hand-woven cloth.—Also **khadi**. [Hind. *khādar, khādi*.]

**khaki**, *kä'ki*, *adj.* dust-coloured, dull brownish or greenish yellow: militaristically imperialist (*hist*.).—*adv.* (*hist*.) with war-spirit.—*n.* a light drab cloth used for military uniforms. [Urdu and Pers. *khākī*, dusty.]

**khalat**, *kal'ət*. Same as **killut**.

**khalif**. See **caliph**.—*ns.* **khalifa, khalifah**, *kä-lē'fä*, a caliph: a Senusi leader: the Mahdi's successor; **khalifat, khalifate**, *käl'i-fat, -fāt*, the caliphate. [Ar. *khalīfah*.]

**khamsin**, *kam'sin, -sēn'*, *n.* a hot S. or S.E. wind in Egypt, blowing for about fifty days from mid-March. [Ar. *khamsīn—khamsūn*, fifty.]

**khan**, *kän, n.* an Eastern inn, a caravanserai. [Ar. *khān*.]

**khan**, *kän, n.* in N. Asia, a prince or chief: in Persia, a governor.—*ns.* **khan'ate**, a khan's dominion or jurisdiction; **khan'um** (*-ōōm*), lady: Mrs. [Turki (and thence Pers.) *khān*, lord or prince.]

**kharif**, *kə-rēf'*, (*India*) *n.* crop sown before the monsoon to ripen in autumn. [Hind. *kharīf—*Ar., gathered.]

**khat**. Same as **kat** (1).

**Khaya**, *kä'yə, n.* a genus of African trees akin to mahogany. [Wolof *khaye*.]

**kheda, keddah**, *ked'a, n.* an enclosure for catching wild elephants: the operation of catching wild elephants. [Hindi *khedā*.]

**khedive**, *ke-dēv', n.* the title (1867-1914) of the viceroy of Egypt.—*ns.* **khedi'va**, his wife; **khedi'v**(i)ate, the khedive's office or territory.—*adjs.* **khedi'v**(i)al. [Fr. *khédive—*Turk. *khidiv, hudiv—*Pers. *khidīw*, prince.]

**khidmutgar**, *kid'mut-gär*, **khitmutgar**, *kit', n.* a table-servant. [Hind.,—Pers. *khidmat*, service, and agent suffix *-gär*.]

**khilafat**, *kil'ä-fat, kil-ä'fat, n.* caliphate.—*adj.* of an anti-British agitation among Muslims in India after Treaty of Sèvres, 1920. [Ar. *khilāfat*; cf. **caliph**.]

**khilat**, *kil'ət*. Same as **killut**.

**Khmer**, *kmûr, n.* a member of a people inhabiting Cambodia: their language, the official language of Cambodia.—Also *adj.* (See **Mon-Khmer**.)

**khoja, khodja**, *kō'ja*, also **hodja**, *hō', n.* an Eastern title of respect: a professor or teacher. [Turk. and Pers., *khōjah, khwājah*.]

**khor**, *kōr, kör, n.* a dry watercourse: a ravine. [Ar. *khurr, khorr*.]

**khud**, *kud, n.* a pit, hollow: a ravine. [Hindi *khaḍ*.]

**khuskhus**. Same as **cuscus** (3).

**khutbah**, *kōōt'ba, n.* a Mohammedan prayer and sermon delivered in the mosques on Fridays.—Also **khot'bah, khot'beh**. [Ar.]

**kiang, kyang**, *kyang, ki-ang', n.* a Tibetan wild ass. [Tibetan *rkyang*.]

**kia-ora**, *ke'ä-ō'rə, -ö', (N. Zealand), interj.* good health. [Maori.]

**kiaugh**, *kyöhh, kyähh, (Scot.) n.* care, trouble.—Also **kaugh** (*köhh, kähh*).

**kibble**, *kib'l, n.* the bucket of a draw-well.—**kibbl'e-chain**, the chain for drawing up a bucket. [Cf. Ger. *kübel*.]

**kibble**, *kib'l, v.t.* to grind cereal, etc., fairly coarsely. [Origin obscure.]

**kibbutz**, *kē-bōōts', n.* a Jewish communal agricultural settlement in Israel:—*pl.* **kibbutzim** (*kē-bōōts-ēm'*). [Heb.]

**kibe**, *kib, n.* chilblain, esp. on heel. [Cf. W. *cibwst*.]

**kibitka**, *ki-bit'ka, n.* a Russian covered wagon or sledge: a Central Asian felt tent. [Russ.]

**kibitzer**, *kib'it-sər, n.* onlooker (at cards, etc.) who gives unwanted advice. [Yiddish.]

**kiblah**, *kib'la, n.* the point toward which Moham-

medans turn in prayer.—Also **keb'lah**. [Ar. *qiblah*.]

**kibosh**, *ki'bosh, ki-bosh', (coll.) n.* nonsense, rot.—*v.t.* to dispose of finally.—**put the kibosh on**, to kibosh. [Ety. obscure.]

**kick**, *kik, v.t.* to hit with the foot: to put or drive by blows with the foot: to start or work by foot on a pedal: to achieve by a kick or kicking: to free oneself from (e.g. a habit).—*v.i.* to thrust out the foot with violence: to show opposition or resistance: to recoil violently: to jerk violently: to move as if kicked: to be exposed to kicking, lie around (often with *about*): to flourish (usu. in *pr.p.*).—*n.* a blow or fling with the foot: the recoil of a gun: a jerk: kicking power: resistance: resilience: fashion (*arch. slang*): the depression in the bottom of a bottle: stimulus, pungency (*coll.*): thrill (*coll.*): dismissal (esp. with *the; slang*): sixpence (*slang*): an enthusiastic but short-lived interest: a phase of such interest.—*adj.* **kick'able**.—*n.* **kick'er**, one who kicks, esp. a horse.—**kick'back** (*U.S.*), part of a sum received paid to another by confidential agreement for favours past or to come: money paid in return for protection; **kick'ing-strap'**, a strap behind a draught-horse's hindquarters to prevent kicking; **kick'-off**, the first kick in a game of football; **kick'-start'**, the starting of an engine by a treadle; **kick'-up'**, a disturbance: a dance: a depression in the bottom of a bottle.—**for kicks**, for thrills; **kick around**, move around from place to place; **kick in** (*slang*), to contribute: to die; **kick one's heels** (see **heel**); **kick out** (*coll.*), to eject with force: to dismiss; **kick over the traces**, to throw off control; **kick, or strike, the beam**, to rise, as the lighter scale of a balance, so as to strike against the beam—hence to be of little weight or importance; **kick the bucket** (see **bucket**); **kick up a dust or row**, to create a disturbance; **kick upstairs**, to promote (usu. to a less active or less powerful position). [M.E. *kiken*: origin unknown: W. *cicio*, to kick, comes from Eng.]

**kickie-wickie**, *kik'i-wik'i, (Shak.) n.* a wife. [Altered by editors to **kicksy-wicksy**; perh. conn. with **kickshaws**.]

**kickshaws**, *kik'shöz*, **kickshaw**, *-shö, n.* something fantastical: a fantastical dish (*cook*.). [Fr. *quelque chose*, something.]

**kid**, *kid, n.* a young goat: extended to young antelope, etc.: a child or young person (*coll.*): leather of kidskin, or a substitute: a glove, shoe, or boot of kid.—*adj.* made of kid leather or imitation kid leather.—*v.t.* and *v.i.* to bring forth (of a goat):—*pr.p.* **kidd'ing**; *pa.t.* and *pa.p.* **kidd'ed**.—*ns.* **kidd'y**, dim. of kid: a flashy thief (*thieves' slang*):—*pl.* **kiddi'es**; **kid'ling**, a young kid.—**kid'-fox** (*Shak*.), a young fox; **kid'-glove'**, a glove of kid.—*adj.* as if done by one wearing kid-gloves: overnice, delicate.—**kid'-skin**. [O.N. *kith*; cf. Dan. *kid*; Ger. *kitze*, a young goat.]

**kid**, *kid, n.* a small tub. [Perh. a variant of **kit**.]

**kid**, *kid, n.* a faggot. [Origin unknown: W. *cedys*, faggots, is prob. from Eng.]

**kid**, *kid, (coll.) v.t.* and *v.i.* to hoax: to pretend, esp. banteringly (also **kidd'y**): to tease.—*n.* a deception.—*n.* **kidd'er**. [Perh. conn. with **kid**, a child.]

**kidder**, *kid'ər*, **kiddier**, *-i-ər, ns.* a forestaller: a huckster. [Origin obscure.]

**Kidderminster**, *kid'ər-min-stər, n.* a two-ply or ingrain carpet formerly made at *Kidderminster*.

**kiddle**, *kid'l, n.* a stake-fence set in a stream for catching fish.—Also **kid'el, kett'le**. [O.Fr. *quidel*; cf. Bret. *kidel*.]

**kidnap**, *kid'nap, v.t.* to steal (a human being), often for ransom:—*pr.p.* **kidnapping**; *pa.t.* and *pa.p.* **kidnapped**.—*n.* **kidnapper**. [**kid**, a child, **nap** (4).]

**kidney**, *kid′ni*, *n*. one of two flattened glands that secrete urine: temperament, humour, disposition—hence, sort or kind.—**kid′ney-bean′**, the French bean; **kidney machine**, an artificial kidney (q.v.); **kid′ney-ore′**, haematite in kidney-shaped masses; **kid′ney-potā′to**, a kidney-shaped variety of potato; **kid′ney-stone′**, nephrite: a septarian nodule: a hard deposit in the kidney; **kid′ney-vetch**, any plant of the papilionaceous genus Anthyllis, including lady's fingers. [M.E. *kidenei* (pl. *kideneiren*), perh. a comp. of *ei* (pl. *eiren*), egg, confused sometimes with *nere*, kidney.]

**kie-kie**, *kē′ā-kē-ā, kē′kē*, *n*. a New Zealand high-climbing shrub (*Freycinetia banksii*) of the screw-pine family. [Maori.]

**kier, keir,** *kēr*, *n*. a bleaching vat. [Cf. O.N. *ker*, tub.]

**kierie,** *kē′rē*, (*S.Afr.*) *n*. a stick. [Prob. Hottentot.]

**kieselguhr,** *kē′zl-gōōr, n.* diatomite. [Ger.,—*kiesel*, flint, *guhr*, fermentation.]

**kieserite,** *kēz′ər-īt, n.* a mineral, hydrated magnesium sulphate (MgSO$_4$H$_2$O), a source of Epsom salts. [After D. G. *Kieser* (1779-1862) of Jena.]

**kieve.** See keeve.

**kight** (*Spens.*). Same as kite (1).

**kikumon,** *kik′ōō-mon, n.* the chrysanthemum badge of the Japanese imperial family. [Jap. *kiku*, chrysanthemum, *mon*, badge.]

**Kikuyu,** *ki-, kē-kōō′ū, n.* an agricultural Negro tribe of Kenya: a member thereof.—**kikuyu** (**grass**), an African grass (*Pennisetum clandestinum*) grown in Australia and S. America.

**kild,** *kild,* a Spenserian form of killed.

**kilderkin,** *kil′dər-kin, n.* a small barrel: a liquid measure of 18 gallons. [Old Du. *kindeken*, *kinneken* (Scot. *kinken*), dim. of *kintal*—L.L. *quintāle*, quintal, associated with Du. *kind*, child.]

**kilerg,** *kil′ûrg, n.* a thousand ergs. [Gr. *chilioi*, thousand, erg.]

**kiley.** Same as kylie.

**kilfud-yoking,** *kil-fud′-yōk′ing,* (*Scot.*) *n.* a fireside disputation. [Scot. *kilfuddie*, the aperture for feeding a kiln, and yoking.]

**kill,** *kil, v.t.* to put to death, to slay: to deprive of life: to destroy: to nullify or neutralise, to render inactive, to weaken or dilute: to reject, discard, defeat: to fascinate, overcome: to injure seriously (*Ir.*): to spoil: to muffle or still: to cause to stop (as machinery, etc.): to exhaust: to cause severe pain: to consume completely (*coll.*): to mark for cancellation (*print.*): to order (the distribution of) type (*print.*): to play (a return shot) so hard that opponent cannot play it back again (*lawn tennis*).—*v.i.* to murder, slaughter.—*n.* the act of killing: prey or game killed: a ball impossible to return (*lawn tennis*).—*n.* **kill′er**, one who kills: one who murders readily or habitually: a slaughterer or butcher: an instrument for killing: a neutralising agent: the grampus or other ferocious delphinid (also **killer whale**). —*adj.* **kill′ing**, depriving of life: destructive: deadly, irresistible: exhausting: fascinating: irresistibly funny (*coll.*).—*n.* slaughter: a severe handling.—**kill′-court′esy** (*Shak.*), a discourteous person; **kill′cow**, a butcher: a bully; **killing time**, the days of the persecution of the Covenanters; **kill′joy**, a spoil-sport.—*adj.* austere.— **kill by inches**, to kill gradually, as by torture; **kill off**, to exterminate; **kill the fatted calf**, to prepare an elaborate feast, etc., for a homecoming or welcome; **kill time**, to occupy oneself with amusements, etc., in order to pass spare time or to relieve boredom; **kill two birds with one stone**, to effect one thing by the way, or by the same means with which another thing is done; **kill up** (*Shak.*), to exterminate; **to kill** (*coll.*), in an irresistible manner. [M.E. *killen* or *cullen.*]

**kill,** *kil,* (U.S. *dial.*) *n.* a stream, brook: a river: a channel (used chiefly in place-names, particularly in areas originally settled by Dutch). [Du. *kil* from M.Du. *kille*, a channel.]

**killadar,** *kil′ə-där, n.* the commandant of a fort or garrison. [Hind. (Pers.) *qil‘adār.*]

**killas,** *kil′əs, n.* clay slate. [Cornish miners' term.]

**killcrop,** *kil′krop, n.* an insatiate child: a changeling. [L.G. *kilkrop*; Ger. *kielkropf.*]

**killdee,** *kil′dē, n.* the largest North American ringplover.—Also **kill′deer.** [Imit.]

**killick, killock,** *kil′ik, -ək, n.* a small anchor: its fluke. [Origin obscure.]

**killogie,** *ki-lō′gi,* (*Scot.*) *n.* the space before the fireplace of a kiln. [**kiln**, **logie.**]

**killut,** *kil′ut, n.* in India, a robe of honour or other ceremonial present.—Also **kell′aut, khal′at** **khil′at.** [Hind. and Pers. *khil‘at.*]

**Kilmarnock,** *kil-mär′nək, n.* a kind of closely woven broad blue cap, originally made at *Kilmarnock*.—**Kilmarnock cowl**, kind of nightcap.

**kiln,** *kiln, kil, n.* a large oven for drying, baking, or calcining corn, hops, bricks, pottery, limestone, etc.—*v.t.* **kiln′-dry**, to dry in a kiln:— *pa.p.* and *adj.* **kiln′-dried.**—**kiln′-hole**, the mouth of a kiln. [O.E. *cyln, cylen*—L. *culina*, a kitchen.]

**kilo,** *kēl′ō, n.* a shortened form of **kilogram(me)** or sometimes of other word with the prefix **kilo-.**

**kilo-,** *kil′ə-, kil′ō-, pfx.* denoting 1000 times the unit to which it is attached, e.g. **kil′obar** = 1000 bars; **kil′ocalorie,** Calorie, 1000 calories, used to measure energy content of food; **kil′ocycle per second,** kilohertz (q.v.); **kil′ogram(me),** SI base unit of mass, the mass of a platinum-iridium cylinder at BIPM, Paris, 2·205 lb; **kil′ohertz,** 1000 cycles of oscillation per second, used to measure frequency of sound and radio waves; **kil′omega,** *pfx.* now replaced by giga-, one thousand million times; **kil′ometre** (also *-om′-*), 1000 metres, 0·6214 or about ⅝ mile; **kil′oton,** a measure of explosive force equivalent to that of 1000 tons of TNT; **kil′owatt,** 1000 watts, the power dissipated by one bar of the average electric fire; **kil′owatt hour,** the energy consumed by a load of one kilowatt in one hour of use (3·6 megajoules), the unit by which electricity is charged to the consumer. [Gr. *chilioi*, a thousand.]

**kilp, kilp.** Same as kelp.

**kilt,** *kilt, n.* a man's short pleated skirt, usu. of tartan, forming part of Highland dress.—*v.t.* to tuck up (skirts): to truss up (*arch.*): to hang, string up (*arch.*): to pleat vertically.—*v.i.* to move lightly and quickly, to trip.—*adj.* **kilt′ed,** dressed in a kilt: tucked up: vertically pleated. —*n.* **kilt′y, kilt′ie,** a wearer of a kilt. [Scand.; cf. Dan. *kilte*, to tuck up; O.N. *kilting*, a skirt.]

**kilt,** *kilt,* (*Spens.* and *Ir.*, esp. hyperbolically) *pa.p.* of kill.

**kilter,** *kil′tər.* Same as kelter.

**kimberlite,** *kim′bər-līt, n.* a mica-peridotite, an eruptive rock, the matrix of the diamonds found at *Kimberley* and elsewhere in South Africa.

**kimbo,** *kim′bō, v.t.* to set akimbo:—*p.adj.* **kim′boed.**

**Kimeridgian,** *kim-ə-rij′i-ən,* (*geol.*) *adj.* of the lowest division of the Upper Jurassic, named from a clay well developed at *Kimmeridge* in Dorset.—Also *n.*

**kimmer.** See cummer.

**kimono,** *ki-mō′nō, n.* a loose robe with wide sleeves, fastening with a sash, an outer garment in Japan: a dressing-gown of similar form.— **kimono sleeve,** a magyar sleeve. [Jap.]

kin, *kin*, *n.* persons of the same family: relatives: relationship: affinity.—*adj.* related.—*adj.* kin'-less, without relations.—next of kin, the relatives (lineal or collateral) of a deceased person, among whom his personal property is distributed if he dies intestate: the person(s) most closely related to an individual by blood or marriage, or a legal ruling: of kin, of the same kin. [O.E. *cynn*; O.N. *kyn*, Goth. *kuni*, family, race; cog. with L. *genus*, Gr. *genos*.]

kin, *kin*, *n.* a Japanese and Chinese weight, the catty. [Jap. *kin*, Chin. *chin*.]

-kin, a noun suffix denoting a diminutive, as lamb*kin*, mani*kin*; also in proper names, as Jen*kin* (*John*), Wil*kin* (*William*). [Prob. Du. or L.G.; cf. Ger. *-chen*.]

kina, kinakina. See quina.

kinaesthesis, in U.S. kinesthesis, *kīn-ēs-thē'sis*, *kin-*, *-es-*, *n.* sense of movement or of muscular effort.—Also kinaesthē'sia (*-zi-ə*, *-zyə*).—*adj.* kinaesthetic (*-thet'ik*), pertaining to kinaesthesis. [Gr. *kineein*, to move, *aisthēsis*, sensation.]

kinchin, *kin'chin*, *n.* a child in thieves' slang.—kin'chin-cove (*obs.*), a boy; kin'chin-lay, the robbing of children; kin'chin-mort (*obs.*), a girl. [Appar. Ger. *kindchen*, little child.]

kincob, *king'kəb*, *n.* a rich silk fabric embroidered with gold or silver thread, made in India. [Hind. and Pers. *kimkhāb*.]

kind, *kind*, *n.* those of kin, a race: sort or species, a particular variety: nature, the material universe (*arch.*): innate character (of a person) (*arch.*): fundamental qualities (of a thing): sex (*obs.*): produce, as distinguished from money: a eucharistic element.—*adj.* having or springing from the feelings natural for those of the same family: disposed to do good to others: benevolent.—*adj.* kind'less (*Shak.*), unnatural, destitute of kindness.—*adv.* kind'ly, in a kind manner: a (rather peremptory) substitute for please (for the *adj.*, see sep. art.).—*n.* kind'ness, the quality or fact of being kind: a kind act.—*adj.* kind'-heart'ed. — kind'-heart'edness. — *adj.* kind'-spok'en, spoken kindly: given to speaking kindly.—after (its) kind, according to (its) nature; do one's kind (*Shak.*), to act according to one's nature; in a kind, in a way, to some extent; in kind, in goods instead of money: tit for tat; kind of (*coll.*), of a kind, somewhat, to some extent, as it were—used adjectivally and adverbially. [O.E. (*ge*)*cynde*—*cynn*, kin.]

kind, *kīnd*, (*obs.*) *v.t.* to beget:—*Spens.*, *pa.p.* kynd'ed.

kindergarten, *kin'dər-gär-tn*, *n.* an infant school on Froebel's principle (1826), in which object-lessons and games figure largely.—*n.* kindergart'ener, a teacher in a kindergarten: a pupil of a kindergarten (*U.S.*).—Also kindergärtner (*-gert'nər*). [Ger.,—*kinder*, children, *garten*, garden.]

kinderspiel, *kin'dər-spēl*, *n.* a children's cantata or play. [Ger., children's sport, child's play—*kinder*, children, *spiel*, game, play.]

kindle, *kin'dl*, *v.t.* to set fire to: to light: to inflame, as the passions: to provoke: to incite.—*v.i.* to take fire: to begin to be excited: to be roused.—*ns.* kin'dler; kin'dling, the act of causing to burn: materials for starting a fire. [Cf. O.N. *kyndill*, a torch—L. *candēla*, candle.]

kindle, *kin'dl*, (*Shak.*) *v.t.* and *v.i.* to bring forth young.—*n.* brood, litter.—in kindle, with young. [M.E. *kindlen*: cf. kind.]

kindly, *kind'li*, *adj.* natural (*obs.*): orig., belonging to the kind or race: native: native-born (*arch.*): inclined to kindness: benign: genial: comfortable.—*adv.* in a kind or kindly manner (see also under kind).—*adv.* kind'lily (*rare*).—*n.* kind'liness.—*adj.* kind'ly-nā'tured.—kindly tenant (*Scot*; *obs.*), a tenant of the same stock as his landlord, or one whose family has held lands in succession, from father to son, for several

generations; take it kindly, feel it as a kindness; take kindly to, (often with *neg.*) to take a favourable view of, or to adopt (a practice) with enthusiasm. [O.E. *gecyndelic*; cf. kind.]

kindred, *kin'drid* (*Spens.* kin'red), *n.* relationship by blood, less properly, by marriage: relatives: a group of relatives, family, clan.—*adj.* akin: cognate: congenial.—*ns.* kin'dredness; kin'-dredship. [M.E. *kinrede*—O.E. *cynn*, kin, and the suffix *-rǣden*, expressing mode or state.]

kine, *kīn*, (*B.*) *n.pl.* cows. [M.E. *kyen*, a doubled plural of O.E. *cū*, a cow, the plural of which is *cȳ*; cf. Scots kye.]

kinema, kinematograph. See cinematograph.

kinematics, *kin-i-mat'iks*, or *kīn-*, *n.* the science of motion without reference to force.—*adjs.* kinemat'ic, -al. [Gr. *kinēma*, motion—*kineein*, to move.]

kinesipathy, *kin-ē-sip'ə-thi*, *n.* a mode of treating disease by muscular movements, movement-cure—also kinesither'apy.—*adjs.* kinesiat'ric, kinesipath'ic.—*ns.* kine'sipath, kinesip'athist. [Gr. *kinēsis*, movement.]

kinesis, *ki-nē'sis*, or *kī-*, *n.* movement, change of position, *specif.* under stimulus and with direction not precisely determined.—*ns.* kinē'sics (*pl.* treated as *sing.*), (study of) body movements which convey information in the absence of speech; kinesiol'ogist; kinesiol'ogy, scientific study of human movement, relating mechanics and anatomy. [Gr. *kinēsis*, movement.]

kinesthesis, etc. U.S. spelling of kinaesthesis, etc.

kinetheodolite, *kin-*, *kin-i-thi-od'ə-līt*, *n.* an improved form of theodolite used in tracking missiles and artificial satellites.

kinetics, *ki-net'iks* or *ki-*, *n.* the science of the action of force in producing or changing motion.—*adjs.* kinet'ic, -al, pertaining to motion or to kinetics: due to motion.—*ns.* kinet'ograph, a camera for taking motion-pictures; kinet'oscope, an early form of cinematograph: an instrument for the production of curves by combination of circular movements. — kinetic art, sculpture, art, sculpture, in which movement (produced by air currents, or electricity, or sound, etc.) plays an essential part; kinetic energy, energy possessed by a body in virtue of its motion. [Gr. *kinetikos*—*kineein*, to move.]

king, *king*, *n.* a hereditary chief ruler or titular head of a nation: a monarch: a queen bee (*obs.*): a playing-card having the picture of a king: the most important piece in chess: a crowned man in draughts: one who is pre-eminent among his fellows: (*cap.*; *pl.*) the title of two historical books of the Old Testament:—*fem.* queen.—king, in composition, most important.—*v.t.* to make king: to furnish with a king: to play king (with object *it*).—*n.* king'-dom, the state or attributes of a king: a monarchical state: a region that was once a monarchical state: one of the three grand divisions of natural history (animal, vegetable, mineral).—*adj.* king'domed (*Shak.*), constituted like a kingdom.—*n.* king'hood, kingship: kingliness.—*adj.* king'less.—*ns.* king'let, a little or petty king: the golden-crested wren; king'lihood.—*adj.* king'-like.—*ns.* king'liness; king'ling, a petty king.—*adj.* king'ly, belonging or suitable to a king: royal: king-like.—Also *adv.*—*n.* king'ship, the state, office, or dignity of a king.—king'-app'le, a large red variety of apple; king'-archon, the second of the nine archons in Athens, successor to the abolished kings in religious functions; king'-bird, an American tyrant-flycatcher; king'-bolt, -rod, a metal rod in a roof connecting the tie-beam and the ridge; king'-co'bra, a large Asiatic species of cobra; king'-crab (Limulus), a curious large marine arachnoid, with convex horseshoe-shaped buckler, the last of its race (Xiphosura); king'craft, the art of governing, mostly in a bad sense; **king'-crow**, a kind of drongo; **king'cup**, the buttercup: the marsh-marigold; **king'fish**, the opah; **king'-fisher**, a fish-eating bird with very brilliant plumage, the halcyon; **King Log**, a do-nothing king, as opp. to **King Stork**, one who devours his frog-subjects—from Aesop's fable; **king'-maker**, one who has the creating of kings in his power; **king mob**, the vulgar multitude; **king'-of-arms'** (sometimes **-at-arms'**), a principal herald (those of England having the designations Garter, Clarencieux, and Norroy and Ulster (includes N. Ireland), of Scotland, Lyon); **king'-penguin**, a large penguin, smaller than the emperor; **king'-pin**, a tall pin, or one prominently placed: a pin on which swivels an axle of the type of that of an automobile front-wheel: the most important person of a group engaged in an undertaking; **king'post**, a perpendicular beam in the frame of a roof rising from the tie-beam to the ridge; **king'-sal'mon**, the largest Pacific salmon, the quinnat; **King's Bench (Queen's Bench** in a queen's reign), formerly a court in which the king sat: now a division of the High Court of Justice; **king's'-chair, -cush'ion**, a seat formed by two persons clasping wrists; **king's counsel** (or **queen's counsel**), an honorary rank of barristers and advocates; **king's English**, correct standard speech; **king's'-e'vil**, a scrofulous disease formerly supposed to be healed by the touch of the king; **king's'-hood**, the second stomach of a ruminant, sometimes humorously for the human stomach.—*adj.* **king'-size(d)**, of large size.— **king's'-man**, a royalist: a custom-house officer; **king's peace**, orig. the peace secured by the king for certain persons (as those employed on his business): the peace of the kingdom generally; **king's'-spear**, an asphodel; **king's speech** (or **queen's speech** in a queen's reign), the sovereign's address to parliament at its opening and closing; **king's'-yell'ow**, orpiment as a pigment; **king'-vul'ture**, a large brilliantly-coloured tropical American vulture; **king'wood**, a beautiful Brazilian wood—also *violet-wood*: the papilionaceous tree yielding it, a species of Dalbergia.—**King Charles's head**, a matter that persists in obtruding itself as did King Charles's head in the thoughts of Mr Dick in *David Copperfield*; **King Charles spaniel** (see **spaniel**); **kingdom come** (*slang*), the state after death; **king of beasts**, the lion; **king of birds**, the eagle; **king of kings**, a powerful monarch with other monarchs subject to him: (*cap.*) God, Christ; **king of metals**, gold; **king of terrors**, death; **king of the forest**, the oak; **king of the herrings**, the shad: the oarfish: applied also to various other fishes, as the opah, the rabbit-fish or chimaera; **take the king's shilling** (see **shilling**); **three kings of Cologne**, the three Wise Men of the East, Gaspar, Melchior, and Balthazar; **turn king's (queen's) evidence** (see **evident**). [O.E. *cyning*—*cynn*, a tribe, with suffix *-ing*; cog. with **kin**.]

**kingle**, *king'l*, (*Scot.*) *n.* very hard rock, esp. sandstone.

**kink**, *kingk*, *n.* a twisted loop in a string, rope, etc.: a mental twist: a crick: a whim: an imperfection.—*v.i.* to form a kink.—*v.t.* to cause a kink in.—*n.* **kink'le**, a slight kink.—*adj.* **kink'y**, twisted: curly: eccentric (*coll.*): mad (*coll.*): out of the ordinary in an attractive and sophisticated way (*coll.*): homosexual, or sexually perverted (*coll.*). [Prob. Du. *kink*; but cf. Ger., Sw., and Norw. *kink*.]

**kink**, *kingk*, (*Scot.*) *v.i.* to cough loudly: to gasp for breath.—*n.* a convulsive cough or gasp.— **kink'-cough, kink'-ho(a)st** (*Scot.*), whooping-cough, chincough. [Northern form of **chink** (3).]

**kinkajou**, *king'ka-jōō*, *n.* a South American animal allied to the raccoon. [App. from a North Amer. Indian word misapplied.]

**kinnikinick**, *kin-i-kin-ik'*, *n.* a mixture used by American Indians as a substitute for tobacco· a species of cornel or other plant entering into it. [From Algonquian, mixture.]

**kino**, *kē'nō*, *n.* an astringent exudation from various tropical trees. [App. of W. African origin.]

**kinsfolk**, *kinz'fōk*, *n.* folk or people kindred or related to one another.—Also **kins'folks**.—*ns.* **kin'ship**, relationship; **kins'man**, a man of the same kin or race with another:—*fem.* **kins'-woman**. [See **kin**.]

**kintledge**. See **kentledge**.

**kiosk**, *kē'osk, ki-osk'*, *n.* an Eastern garden pavilion: a small roofed stall for sale of papers sweets, etc., either out-of-doors or inside a public building: a bandstand: a public telephone box. [Turk. *kiöshk, keushk*—Pers. *kūshk*.]

**kip**, *kip*, (*Scot.*) *v.i.* to play truant.—Also *n.* in the phrase *to play the kip*, to play truant. [Origin uncertain.]

**kip**, *kip*, *n.* the skin of a young animal.—**kip'-skin**, leather made from the skin of young cattle, intermediate between calfskin and cowhide. [Obs. Du., bundle of hides, is suggested.]

**kip**, *kip*, *n.* a level or slight incline at the end of an underground way, on which the tubs of coal stand till hoisted up the shaft.

**kip**, *kip*, (*slang*) *n.* a house of ill-fame: a lodging-house: a bed: a nap.—*v.i.* to go to bed: to lie.—**kip'-shop**, a brothel: a tramps' lodging-house.—**kip down**, to go to bed. [Cf. Dan. *kippe*, a low alehouse.]

**kip**, *kipp, kip*, (*Scot.*) *n.* anything beaked: a pointed hill. [Cf. Ger. (L.Ger.) *kippe*, point, tip.]

**kip**, *kip*, (*Austr.*) *n.* a short flat stick used to throw up pennies in the game of two-up. [Origin unknown.]

**kipe**, *kip*, (*dial.*) *n.* an osier basket for catching pike. [O.E. *cȳpe*.]

**kipp**, *kip*, *n.* a form of generator for hydrogen sulphide or other gas.—Also **Kipp's apparatus**. [P. J. *Kipp* (19th cent.), Dutch founder of a firm of manufacturers of scientific apparatus.]

**kippage**, *kip'ij*, (*Scot.*) *n.* a state of displeasure or anger. [Fr. *équipage*; see **equipage**.]

**kipper**, *kip'ər*, *n.* a male salmon during the spawning season after spawning: a salmon or (esp.) herring split open, seasoned, and dried: a person (often *giddy kipper*; *slang*).—*v.t.* to cure or preserve, as a salmon or herring.—*n.* **kipp'erer**. [Perh. O.E. *cypera*, a spawning salmon: or perh. from **kip** (5), from the beaked lower jaw of the male salmon after spawning.]

**kirbeh**, *kir'be*, *n.* a skin for holding water. [Ar. *qirba*.]

**kiri**, *kir'i*. Older form of **kierie**.

**kirimon**, *kē'ri-mon*, *n.* one of the two imperial crests of Japan, bearing three leaves and three flowers of Paulownia. [Jap.]

**kirk**, *kirk, kûrk*, (*Scot.*) *n.* church, in any sense: by English Episcopalians sometimes specially applied to the Church of Scotland.—*v.t.* to church.—*ns.* **kirk'ing, kirk'in'**, the first attendance of a pair after marriage, of a magistrate after election.—*adj.* and *adv.* **kirk'ward.**—**kirk'-sess'ion**, the lowest court in Presbyterian churches, minister(s) and elders as the governing body of a particular congregation; **kirk'ton, -town**, (*Scot.*) the village in which the parish church stands; **kirkyard, -yaird** (*-yārd'*; or *kirk'*), a churchyard.—**Auld Kirk**, in Scotland the Established Church: by association of ideas the whisky bottle, whisky (*coll.*); **make a kirk or, and, a mill of it**, do what you please or can

Neutral vowels in unaccented syllables: *el'ə-mənt*; for certain sounds in foreign words, see p. viii

with it. [A Northern Eng. form of church.—O.N. *kirkja*—O.E. *cirice*.]

**kirn,** *kirn,* kern, *kern, kûrn, (Scot.) n.* the cutting of the last sheaf or handful of the harvest: a harvest-home.—**kirn'-ba'by, corn'-ba'by, kirn'-doll'ie, corn'-maid'en,** a dressed-up figure made of the last handful of corn cut. [Origin unknown.]

**kirn,** *kirn, n.* a Northern form of churn.—**kirn'-milk',** buttermilk.

**kirschwasser,** *kērsh'väs-ər, n.* a liqueur made from the wild cherry.—Also **kirsch.** [Ger., cherry water.]

**kirtle,** *kûr'tl, n.* a sort of gown or outer petticoat: a mantle.—*adj.* **kir'tled.** [O.E. *cyrtel*; Dan. *kjortel*; O.N. *kyrtill*; app.—L. *curtus*, short.]

**kisan,** *kē'sän, (India) n.* a peasant. [Hindi *kisān.*]

**Kislev, Chislev,** *kis'lef,* **Kisleu,** *kis'li-ōō, n.* the third (ecclesiastically ninth) Jewish month, parts of November and December. [Heb.]

**kismet,** *kiz'met,* or *kis', n.* fate, destiny. [Turk. *qismet*—Ar. *qisma.*]

**kiss,** *kis, v.t.* to caress or salute with the lips: to touch gently.—*v.i.* to salute with the lips: to collide.—*n.* a caress or salute with the lips: a drop of sealing-wax.—*n.* **kiss'er,** one who kisses: the mouth (*pugilistic slang*).—**kiss'-curl,** a small curl at the side of the forehead; **kiss'ing-com'fit,** a perfumed comfit for sweetening the breath; **kissing cousin,** a more or less distant relation with whom one is on terms familiar enough to kiss on meeting; **kiss'ing-crust,** that part of the upper crust of the loaf which overhangs and touches another.—*n.pl.* **kiss'ing-strings,** cap or bonnet strings tied under the chin.—**kiss'-in-the-ring',** an old game in which one kisses another after a chase round a ring of players; **kiss'-me,** the wild pansy or other plant: a short veil: a small bonnet—also **kiss'-me-quick.**—**kiss hands,** to kiss the sovereign's hands on acceptance of office; **kiss of life,** a mouth-to-mouth method of restoring breathing: a means of restoring vitality or vigour (*fig.*); **kiss of peace,** a kiss of greeting between the members of the early Church; **kiss the book,** to kiss a Bible or New Testament, in England, after taking a legal oath; **kiss the gunner's daughter,** to get a flogging, tied to the breech of a cannon; **kiss the rod,** to submit to punishment. [O.E. *cyssan,* to kiss—*coss,* a kiss; Ger. *küssen,* Dan. *kys*; allied to **choose** and **gust** (2).]

**kist,** *kist, (Scot.) n.* a chest.—*v.t.* to coffin.—**kist o' whistles,** an organ. [O.E. *cist,* chest, or O.N. *kista.*]

**kistvaen,** *kist'vin, n.* a chest-shaped burial-chamber made of flat stones. [W. *cist,* chest, and form of *maen,* stone.]

**kit,** *kit, n.* a small wooden tub: an outfit: a set of persons (*coll.* or *slang*): equipment: a container and/or the material, tools, instructions, assembled in it for some specific purpose.—*v.t.* (sometimes with *out*) to provide with kit.—**kit'-bag,** a strong canvas bag for holding one's kit or outfit (*mil.*): a knapsack: a strong canvas grip; **kit'-boat, -car,** a boat, car, put together, from standard components, by an amateur builder [Prob. Middle Du. *kitte,* a hooped beer-can.]

**kit,** *kit, n.* a small pocket violin. [Origin obscure; cf. O.E. *cytere,* Gr. *kithara.*]

**kit,** *kit, n.* a contraction of **kitten.**—**kit'-cat,** the game of tip-cat (see also below).

**Kitcat,** *kit'kat, n.* the name of a London Whig literary club, which existed from about 1688 or 1703 to about 1720, meeting for some time at the pie-shop of Christopher (*Kit*) *Cat* (or Catling): a portrait 36 by 28 inches in size, like those of the Kitkat Club painted by Kneller to fit their later low-ceilinged clubroom.

**kitchen,** *kich'ən, n.* a place where food is cooked: cooking department or equipment: a tea-urn

(*obs. Scot.*): anything eaten as a relish with other food (chiefly *Scot.*).—*v.t.* to regale in the cook-room (*Shak.*): to serve as relish to (*Scot.*): to make palatable (*Scot.*): to use sparingly, make to last (*Scot.*).—*ns.* **kitch'endom,** the domain of the kitchen; **kitch'ener,** a person employed in the kitchen: a cooking-stove; **kitchenette',** a tiny kitchen: a compact combined kitchen and pantry.—**kitchen Dutch, kitchen Kaffir** (*arch. S.Afr.*), a mixture of Dutch or Kaffir with English, used in speaking to native servants; **kitch'en-fee,** the fat that falls from meat in roasting—the cook's perquisite; **kitch'en-fur'niture,** the furniture of a kitchen: the percussion instruments of an orchestra; **kitch'en-gar'den,** a garden where vegetables are cultivated for the kitchen; **kitch'en-knave,** a scullion; **kitch'en-maid,** a maid or servant whose work is in the kitchen; **kitch'en-midd'en** (Dan. *kjökkenmödding*), a prehistoric rubbish-heap; **kitchen physic** (*Milt.*), substantial fare; **kitch'en-range,** a kitchen grate with oven, boiler, etc., attached, for cooking.—*adj.* **kitch'en-sink',** (of plays, etc.) dealing with sordid real-life situations.—**kitch'en-stuff,** material used in kitchens: kitchen refuse, esp. fat from pots, etc.; **kitchen unit,** a set of up-to-date kitchen fitments; **kitch'en-wench,** a kitchen-maid. [O.E. *cycene*—L. *coquina*—*coquĕre,* to cook.]

**kite,** *kit, n.* a rapacious bird of the hawk kind: a rapacious person: a light frame covered with paper or cloth for flying in the air: a more complicated structure built of boxes (*box-kite*) for carrying recording instruments or a man in the air: a light and lofty sail: a rumour or suggestion given out to see how the wind blows, test public opinion, or the like: an accommodation bill, esp. a mere paper credit: an aircraft (*airman's slang*).—**kite'-balloon',** an observation-balloon designed on the principle of the kite to prevent revolving, etc.; **kite'-flying,** sending up and controlling a kite: the dealing in fictitious accommodation paper to raise money: testing public opinion by circulating rumours, etc. (**fly a kite,** to take part in **kite-flying**); **kite'-mark,** a kite-shaped mark on goods indicating conformity in quality, size, etc., with the specifications of the British Standards Institution. [O.E. *cyta*; cf. W. *cud,* Bret. *kidel,* a hawk.]

**kite, kyte,** *kit, (Scot.) n.* a paunch, belly. [Ety. obscure.]

**kith,** *kith, n.* knowledge: native land: acquaintance—obs. except in **kith and kin,** friends (originally home-country) and relatives. [O.E. *cȳth*—*cunnan,* to know.]

**kithara,** *kith'ə-rə.* Same as **cithara.** [Gr.]

**kithe.** Same as **kythe.**

**kitsch,** *kich, n.* trash: work in any of the arts that is pretentious and inferior or in bad taste. [Ger.]

**kitten,** *kit'n, n.* a young cat: sometimes the young of another animal.—*v.t.* and *v.i.* (of a cat) to bring forth.—*n.* **kit'ling** (*Scot.*), a kitten.—*adjs.* **kitt'enish, kitt'eny,** frolicsome: skittish: affectedly playful.—*v.t.* and *v.i.* **kitt'le** (*Scot.*), to kitten: to come into being.—**kitt'en-moth,** any of the smaller kindred of the puss-moth.—**have kittens,** to be in a state of excitement or anger. [M.E. *kitoun,* dim. of **cat.**]

**kittiwake,** *kit'i-wāk, n.* a species of gull with long wings and rudimentary hind-toe. [Imit.]

**kittle,** *kit'l,* (orig. *Scot.*) *adj.* ticklish, intractable.—*v.t.* to tickle: to puzzle.—*adj.* **kitt'ly** (*Scot.*), easily tickled, sensitive.—**kitt'ly-bend'ers** (*Amer.*), running on thin bending ice. [Ety. obscure].

**kittle-pins,** *kit'l-pinz, n.pl.* skittles.—Also **kett'le-pins.** [Origin obscure.]

**kittul,** *kit-ōōl', n.* the jaggery palm (*Caryota urens*): its fibre. [Sinhalese *kitūl.*]

# kitty 727 kneel

**kitty,** *kit'i,* (*Northern* and *slang*) *n.* a jail: a pool or fund: the jack (*bowls*).

**kiwi,** *kē'wi, n.* the Apteryx: a New Zealander (*slang*): a non-flying member of an airfield staff (*slang*). [Maori, from its cry.]

**klang,** *klang,* (*mus.*) *n.* a complex tone, composed of fundamental and harmonics: timbre.—Also **clang.**—**klang'farbe** (*-fär-bə*), tone-colour, timbre. [Ger.]

**klavier,** *klä-vēr', n.* clavier. [Ger.—Fr. *clavier.*]

**klaxon,** *klaks'ən, n.* orig., a mechanical horn with rasping sound: (*cap.*) electric horn (registered trademark).

**Kleig light.** Same as Klieg light.

**Klein bottle,** *klin,* (*math.*) *n.* a one-sided surface obtained by pulling the narrow end of a tapering cylinder through the wall of the cylinder and then stretching the narrow end and joining it to the larger end. [Felix *Klein,* Ger. mathematician.]

**klendusic,** *klen-dū'sik, adj.* of plants, able to withstand disease by means of some protective mechanism.—*n.* **klendū'sity.** [Gr. *kleidoein,* to lock up—*kleis,* a key.]

**klepht,** *kleft, n.* a Greek or Albanian brigand.—*adj.* **klepht'ic.**—*n.* **klepht'ism.** [Mod. Gr. *klephtēs*—anc. Gr. *kleptēs,* thief—*kleptein,* to steal.]

**kleptomania,** *klep-tō-mā'ni-ə, n.* a mania for stealing: a morbid impulse to secrete things.—*n.* **kleptomā'niac.** [Gr. *kleptein,* to steal, *maniā,* madness.]

**kletterschuhe,** *klet'ər-shōō-ə, n.pl.* felt-soled rock-climbing boots. [Ger. — *kletter-,* climbing, *schuh* (pl. *-e*), shoe.]

**Klieg light, Kleig light,** *klēg lit,* a type of incandescent floodlighting lamp for film studio use.—**klieg eyes,** the effect of strain on the eyes caused by the brilliance of floodlights in film production. [From *Kliegl* brothers, the inventors.]

**klinker,** *klingk'ər, n.* a very hard paving-brick. [Du.]

**klinostat,** *kli'nō-stat, n.* a revolving stand for experimenting with growing plants. [Gr. *klinein,* to incline, *statos,* standing.]

**klipdas,** *klip'dus, n.* the Cape hyrax. [Du., lit. rock-badger.]

**klipspringer,** *klip'spring-ər, n.* a small South African antelope. [Du. *klip,* rock, *springer,* jumper.]

**Klondike, Klondyke,** *klon'dik, n.* a very rich source of wealth: a card game, a form of patience.—*v.t.* and *v.i.* to export (fresh herring) direct from Scotland to the Continent. [From the gold-rush to *Klondike* in the Yukon, in 1896, etc.]

**kloof,** *klōōf, n.* a mountain ravine. [Du., cleft.]

**Klystron,** *klis', klis'tron, n.* any of a number of electron tubes (amplifiers, oscillators, etc.) in which the velocity of the electron beam is modulated by an ultra-high-frequency field and subsequently imparts energy to it or other u.h.f. fields. [Gr. *klystēr,* syringe.]

**knack,** *nak, n.* a petty contrivance: a toy: a nice trick: dexterity, adroitness.—*n.* **knack'iness.**—*adjs.* **knack'ish, knack'y,** cunning, crafty. [Orig. imit.; cf. Du. *knak,* a crack, Ger. *knacken,* to crack.]

**knacker,** *nak'ər, n.* anything that makes a snapping or cracking sound: (*pl.*) castanets or clappers, bones. [Imit.]

**knacker,** *nak'ər, n.* a horse-slaughterer: one who buys and breaks up old houses, ships, etc.: a worn-out horse.—*n.* **knack'ery,** a knacker's yard. [Origin obscure.]

**knag,** *nag, n.* a knot in wood: a peg.—*n.* **knagg'iness.**—*adj.* **knagg'y,** knotty: rugged. [Cf. Dan. *knag,* Ger. *knagge.*]

**knap,** *nap, v.t.* to snap or break with a snapping

noise: to break in pieces with blows, as stones: to pronounce with a snapping effect: to rap: bite off, nibble: to steal:—*pr.p.* **knapp'ing;** *pa.t.* and *pa.p.* **knapped.**—*v.i.* **knapp'le,** to nibble.—*n.* **knapp'er,** one who breaks stones, esp. one who breaks up flint-flakes for gun-flints.—**knap'-bottle;** the bladder-campion; **knapp'ing-hammer** (*Scot.*), a hammer for breaking stones. [Du. *knappen,* to crack or crush.]

**knap,** *nap,* (*obs.* except *dial.*) *n.* a protuberance: a hillock: a hill-crest. [O.E. *cnæpp.*]

**knapsack,** *nap'sak, n.* a case for necessaries borne on the back: a rucksack. [Du. *knappen,* to crack, eat.]

**knapskull, knapscull, knapscal,** *nap'skəl,* (*Scot. obs.*) *n.* a kind of helmet. [Origin unknown.]

**knapweed,** *nap'wēd, n.* a composite plant of the genus Centaurea, like a spineless thistle. [Earlier *knopweed;* see **knop.**]

**knar, gnar,** *när, n.* a knot on a tree.—*adj.* **knarred, gnarred,** gnarled, knotty. [Cf. L.G. *knarre,* Du. *knar;* also **knur.**]

**knar,** *när.* Same as **gnar.**

**knave,** *nāv, n.* orig., as in *Shak.,* a boy: a serving-boy: a false, deceitful fellow: a playing-card bearing the picture of a servant or soldier.—*ns.* **knav'ery,** dishonesty; **knave'ship** (*Scot.*), a certain quantity of grain, the due of the miller's servant.—*adj.* **knav'ish,** fraudulent: rascally.—*adv.* **knav'ishly.**—*n.* **knav'ishness.**—**knave'-bairn** (*Scot.*), a male child. [O.E. *cnafa, cnapa,* a boy, a youth; Ger. *knabe, knappe.*]

**knawel,** *nö'əl, n.* a cornfield weed (Scleranthus) of the chickweed family. [Ger. *knauel* or *knäuel.*]

**knead,** *nēd, v.t.* to work and press together into a mass, as flour into dough: to operate upon in massage.—*n.* **knead'er—knead'ing-trough,** a trough for kneading. [O.E. *cnedan;* O.N. *knotha,* Ger. *kneten,* to knead.]

**knee,** *nē, n.* the joint between the thigh and shin bones: in a horse's foreleg, the joint answering to the wrist: in a bird the joint answering to the ankle: part of a garment covering the knee: a root upgrowth by which swamp-growing trees breathe: a piece of timber or metal like a bent knee: a genuflection (*Shak.*).—*v.t.* to kneel to (*Shak.*): to achieve by kneeling, or pass over on the knees (*Shak.*): to furnish with a knee: to press with the knee: to make baggy at the knee.—*v.i.* to kneel.—*adj.* **kneed, knee'd,** having knees or angular joints: baggy at the knees, as trousers.—*n.pl.* **knee'-breech'es,** breeches extending to just below the knee, as in court-dress.—**knee'-cap,** the kneepan: a cap or strong covering for the knees, used chiefly for horses to save their knees in case of a fall.—*n.pl.* **knee'-cords,** knee-breeches of corduroy.—*adjs.* **knee'-crooking,** obsequious: fawning; **knee'-deep,** rising to the knees: sunk to the knees.—**knee'-drill,** directed devotional exercises.—*adj.* **knee'-high,** rising or reaching to the knees.—**knee'-holl'y,** butcher's broom; **knee'-jerk,** a reflex throwing forward of the leg when tapped below the knee-cap; **knee'-joint,** the joint of the knee: a joint with two pieces at an angle, so as to be very tight when pressed into a straight line; **knee'-pan,** the patella, a flat round bone on the front of the knee-joint; **knee'-stop, -swell,** a lever worked by the performer's knee, for regulating the wind-supply of a reed-organ, etc.; **knee'-tim'ber,** timber bent into a shape suitable for a knee in shipbuilding, etc.; **knee'-trib'ute** (*Milt.*), the homage of kneeling.—**give,** or **offer, a knee** (Thackeray, etc.), to act as second in a fight, it being usual for the principal to rest on the second's knee between the rounds; **on the knees of the gods,** awaiting the decision of fate (after Homer). [O.E. *cnēow, cnēo;* Ger. *knie,* L. *genu,* Gr. *gony.*]

**kneel,** *nēl, v.i.* to rest or fall on the bended knee:

*Neutral vowels in unaccented syllables: el'ə-mənt; for certain sounds in foreign words, see p. viii*

—*pa.t.* and *pa.p.* **kneeled, knelt** (*nelt*).—*n.* **kneel′er,** one who kneels: a flat cushion to rest the knees on while kneeling: a hassock. [O.E. *cnēowlian.*]

**kneipe,** *knī′pə,* (Ger.) a tavern, a student's beer-house or drinking party.

**knell,** *nel, n.* the stroke of a bell: the sound of a bell at a death or funeral.—*v.i.* to sound as a bell: toll.—*v.t.* to summon as by a tolling bell. [O.E. *cnyllan,* to beat noisily; Du. and Ger. *knallen.*]

**knelt,** *nelt, pa.t.* and *pa.p.* of **kneel.**

**Knesset,** *knes′it, n.* the one-chamber parliament of Israel. [Heb., assembly.]

**knevell,** a form of **nevel.**

**knew,** *nū, pa.t.* of **know.**

**knicker.** Same as **nicker** (3).

**knickerbocker,** *nik′ər-bok-ər,* (*cap.*) *n.* descendant of one of the original Dutch settlers of New York: (*cap.*) a New Yorker: (in *pl.*) loose breeches gathered in at the knee.—Also *n.pl.* **knick′ers, knicks** (*coll.*), knickerbockers: a woman's under-garment of similar form, covering the thigh and not always gathered in.—*adj.* **knick′ered,** clad in knickers. [From the wide-breeched Dutchmen in Knickerbocker's (Washington Irving's) humorous *History of New York.*]

**knick-knack,** *nik′-nak, n.* a small, trifling ornamental or would-be ornamental article—*dim.* **knick-knack′et.**—*ns.* **knick-knack′atory,** a collection of knick-knacks; **knick-knack′ery,** knick-knacks collectively.—*adj.* **knick′-knacky.** —Also **nick′-nack,** etc. [A doubling of **knack.**]

**knife,** *nīf, n.* an instrument for cutting:—*pl.* **knives,** *nīvz.*—*v.t.* to cut: to convey, or apply with a knife: to stab: to try to defeat by treachery e.g. within the party.—*adj.* **knife′-less,** without a knife: without use of the knife. —**knife′-and-fork′,** a trencherman.—*adj.* involving or relating to use of knife and fork.—**knife′-board,** a board on which knives are cleaned: a seat running along the top of an old form of bus (*coll.*); **knife′-box,** a box for keeping table cutlery in; **knife′-boy,** a boy employed in cleaning knives; **knife′-edge,** a sharp-edged ridge: a sharp piece of steel like a knife's edge serving as the axis of a balance, etc. (also *fig.*); **knife′-grinder,** one who grinds or sharpens knives; **knife′-money,** a knife-shaped bronze currency formerly used in China; **knife′-rest,** a rest for a carving knife or fork.—**have one's knife in,** to be persistently hostile or vindictive towards; **under the knife,** undergoing a surgical operation; **war to the knife,** unrelenting conflict. [M.E. *knif*—O.E. *cnif.*]

**knight,** *nīt, n.* orig. a lad, servant: one of gentle birth and bred to arms, admitted in feudal times to a certain honourable military rank: one of the rank, with the title 'Sir', next below baronets: a member of the equestrian order in ancient Rome: one devoted to the service of a lady, her 'servant' or champion: a chessman, usu. with a horse's head, that moves one square forward, backward, or to either side, and one diagonally, at each move.—*v.t.* to make a knight.—*ns.* **knight′age,** knights collectively; **knight′hood,** the rank, title, or status of knight: the order or fraternity of knights.—*adj.* **knight′less** (*Spens.*), unbecoming a knight.—*n.* **knight′liness.**—*adj.* **knight′ly,** like a knight: befitting a knight: chivalrous: of a knight or knights.—Also *adv.*— **knight′-bach′elor,** a knight not a member of any order; **knight′-bann′eret,** a knight who carried a banner and who was superior in rank to the knight-bachelor; **knight′-err′ant,** a knight who travelled in search of adventures: a man or boy who behaves in a quixotic fashion:—*pl.* **knights-errant; knight′-err′antry; knight′hood-err′ant** (*Tenn.*), the body of knights-errant; **knight′-mar′shal,** formerly an officer who had cognis-

ance of offences within twelve miles of the king's abode; **knight′-service,** tenure by a knight on condition of military service; **knight's fee,** a holding of land for which knight-service was required; **knight's progress,** a series of moves in which a knight may visit every square on the chess-board; **Knights Templars** (see temple).—*The following are jocular titles used formerly (excluding* knight of the shire, *which is hist.*):—**knight of industry,** a footpad, thief, or sharper; **knight of St Crispin,** a shoemaker; **knight of the pestle,** an apothecary; **knight of the post** (i.e. possibly the whipping-post), a professional false witness and offerer of bail; **knight of the rainbow,** a flunkey (from his livery); **knight of the road,** a highwayman: a commercial traveller: a tramp; **knight of the shears,** a tailor; **knight of the shire,** a member of parliament for a county; **knight of the spigot,** a tapster, a publican; **knight of the stick,** a compositor; **knight of the whip,** a coachman.—**Knights of Labour,** in the United States, a national labour organisation; **Knights of Malta** (see hospital). [O.E. *cniht,* youth, servant, warrior; Ger. and Du. *knecht,* servant.]

**Kniphofia,** *nip-hōf′i-ə, n.* an African genus of the lily family, otherwise called *Tritoma,* the red-hot poker or torch-lily. [Named after J. H. *Kniphof* (1704-65), German botanist.]

**knit,** *nit, v.t.* to form into a knot (*arch.*): to tie together (*arch.*): to intertwine: to unite into network by needles or machinery: to make by means of knitting-needles or knitting-machine: to unite closely, to draw together: to contract. —*v.i.* to interweave with needles: to grow together:—*pr.p.* **knitt′ing;** *pa.t.* and *pa.p.* **knitt′ed** or **knit.**—*n.* (*Shak.*) a style of knitting.—*ns.* **knitt′er; knitt′ing,** the work of a knitter: union, junction: the network formed by knitting.— Also *adj.*—**knitt′ing-machine′,** a machine for knitting; **knitt′ing-needle,** a long needle or wire used for knitting; **knit′wear,** knitted clothing. [O.E. *cnyttan—cnotta,* a knot.]

**knitch,** *nich,* (*dial.*) *n.* a faggot. [O.E. *gecnycc,* bond.]

**knittle,** *nit′l, n.* a small line made of two or three yarns twisted with the fingers (*naut.*): (in *pl.*) the halves of two yarns in a rope, twisted for pointing. [O.E. *cnyttels,* sinew, string.]

**knive,** *nīv, v.t.* to knife.—**knives,** *pl.* of **knife.**

**knob,** *nob, n.* a hard protuberance: a hard swelling: a round ornament or handle.—*adj.* **knobbed,** containing or set with knobs.—*ns.* **knobb′er,** a stag in its second year; **knobb′iness; knobb′le,** a little knob.—*adjs.* **knobb′ly, knobb′y,** having, full of knobs: knotty.—**knob′-stick,** a stick with knobbed head: a blackleg or scab (*slang*).—**with knobs on,** with interest, more so. [Cf. Low Ger. *knobbe; knop.*]

**knobkerrie,** *nob′ker-i, n.* a round-headed stick used as a club and a missile by S. African natives. [knob and kiri, on the model of Afrik. *knopkierie.*]

**knock,** *nok, v.i.* to strike with something hard or heavy: to drive or be driven against something: to strike for admittance: to rap: to make a noise by, or as if by, striking: (of machinery) to rattle: (of internal-combustion engine) to give noise of detonation.—*v.t.* to strike: to drive against: to render, put, make, or achieve by blows: to impress strongly, stun, daze, confound (*slang*): to arrest (*slang*): to disparage, criticise in a carping way (*coll.*).—*n.* a sudden stroke: a rap: the noise of detonation in an internal-combustion engine: a clock (*Scot.*): a reversal, shock (*coll.*): a criticism (*coll.*).—*ns.* **knock′er,** one who knocks: a hammer suspended to a door for making a knock: a goblin inhabiting a mine who points out the presence of ore by knocks (*dial.*): a carper (*coll.*); **knock′ing,**

a beating on a door: a rap: a noise as if of something that knocks: knock in an internal-combustion engine: a piece knocked off.—knock'about, a boisterous performance with horseplay: a performer of such turns: a doer of odd jobs (*Austr.*): a small yacht without bowsprit: a small motor-car suitable for doing short journeys.—*adj.* of the nature of knock-about: suitable for rough use.—*adj.* knock'-down, such as to overthrow: adapted for being taken to pieces: (of prices) very low.—knock'er-up, a person employed to rouse workers in the morning; knock'ing-shop (*slang*), a brothel; knock'-knee, state of being knock-kneed.—*adj.* knock'-kneed, having knees that knock or touch in walking: weak (*fig.*).—knock'out', the act of knocking out: a blow that knocks out: a combination among dealers at an auction: any person or thing of outstanding attraction or excellence (*coll.*).—*adj.* (of a competition) eliminating losers at each round.—knockout auction, an auction where the bidders are largely swindling confederates; knockout drops, a drug put in a drink to render the drinker unconscious; knock'-rating, the measurement of freedom from detonation of a fuel in an internal-combustion engine in terms of the percentage of octane in an octane-heptane mixture of equivalent knock-proneness; knock'-up', (in tennis, etc.) practice immediately before a match.—knock about, around, to mistreat physically: to saunter, loaf about: to travel about, roughing it and having varied experiences; knock back (*slang*), to drink, eat; knock cold, to fell: to shock violently; knock copy, to disparage a rival's wares; knock down, to fell with a blow: to demolish: to assign with a tap of the auctioneer's hammer (to): to reduce in price: to embezzle (*U.S.*); knock into a cocked hat (see cock, 1); knock off, to stop (work): to accomplish hastily: to deduct: to steal (*slang*): to kill (*slang*); knock on (*Rugby football*), to knock forward with the hand (an infringement of the rules; *n.* knock'-on'); knock on the head, to suppress, put an end to; knock out, to dislodge by a blow: to strike insensible or incapable of recovering in time, in boxing; for technical knockout see under technical: to overcome, demolish: to produce, esp. quickly or roughly (*coll.*): to tire (oneself) out (*slang*); knock sideways, to put off one's usual course; knock together, to get together or construct hastily; knock the bottom out of, to make, or show to be, invalid: to make ineffectual, bring to nothing; knock under (*arch.*), to give in, yield; knock up, to rouse by knocking: to weary out: to be worn out: to construct or arrange hastily: to score (so many runs) (*cricket*): to get with child (*slang*); up to the knocker (*slang*), up to the required standard of excellence or fashion. [O.E. cnocian; perh. imit.]

knoll, *nōl* (*Scot.* knowe, *now*), *n.* a round hillock: the top of a hill (*dial.*). [O.E. cnol; Ger. knollen, a knob, lump.]

knoll, *nōl.* Arch. form of knell.

knop, *nop, n.* a knob: a bud: a loop: a tuft. [Cf. O.N. knappr; Du. knop, Ger. knopf.]

knosp, *nosp, n.* the unopened bud of a flower: an architectural ornament resembling that. [Ger. knospe.]

knot, *not, n.* a snipe-like shore bird of the sand-piper family. [Origin unknown: the connection with King Cnut is a fancy of Camden's.]

knot, *not, n.* an interlacement of parts of a cord or cords, etc., by twisting the ends about each other, and then drawing tight the loops thus formed: a piece of ribbon, lace, etc., folded or tied upon itself in some particular form, as *shoulder-knot*, *breast-knot*, etc.: anything like a knot in form: a bond of union: an elaborately designed

flower-bed (*dial.*): a tangle: a difficulty: the main point or central part of a tangle, intricacy, problem, or difficulty: a complex of lines, mountains, etc.: the base of a branch buried in a later growth of wood: a node or joint in a stem, esp. of a grass: a lump: a concretion: a swelling: a knob: a boss: a bud: a hill: a clump or cluster: a measured quantity of yarn: a division of the knot-marked log-line: a nautical mile per hour, used in navigation and meteorology: (loosely) a nautical mile.—*v.t.* to tie in a knot: to unite closely: to make knotty: to make by knotting: to remove knots from: to cover knots in (before painting wood).—*v.i.* to form a knot or knots: to knit knots for a fringe: —*pr.p.* knott'ing; *pa.t.* and *pa.p.* knott'ed.—*adjs.* knot'less, without knots; knott'ed, full of, or having, knots.—*ns.* knott'er, a person or contrivance that makes or removes knots; knott'iness, the quality of being knotty; knott'ing, formation or removal of knots: covering of knots before painting: material for the purpose: fancywork done by knitting threads into knots.—*adj.* knott'y, containing knots: hard, rugged: difficult: intricate.—knot'grass, a much-jointed species of Polygonum, a common weed: applied also to various grasses; knot'-hole, a hole in wood where a knot has fallen out; knot'work, ornamental work made with knots: carving or decoration in interlaced forms.—bowline knot (see bowline); granny knot (see granny); porters' knot, a shoulder-pad with loop for the forehead. [O.E. cnotta; Ger. knoten, Dan. knude, L. nōdus.]

knotenschiefer, *knō'tən-shē-fər, n.* spotted slate, spotted schist, slightly altered argillaceous rock spotted with little concretions. [Ger., knot slate or schist.]

knout, *knōōt,* also nowt, *n.* whip formerly used as an instrument of punishment in Russia: punishment inflicted by the knout.—*v.t.* to flog. [French spelling of Russ. knut.]

know, *nō, v.t.* to be informed of: to be assured of: to be acquainted with: to recognise: to approve (*B.*): to have sexual commerce with (*arch.*).—*v.i.* to possess knowledge:—*pr.p.* know'ing; *pa.t.* knew, nū, *U.S.* noō; *pa.p.* known, nōn.—*n.* knowledge (*Shak.*): possession of the relevant facts.— *adj.* know'able, capable of being known, discovered, or understood.—*ns.* know'ableness; know'er.—*adj.* know'ing, intelligent: skilful: cunning.—*adv.* know'ingly, in a knowing manner: consciously: intentionally.—*n.* know'-ingness, the quality of being knowing or intelligent: shrewdness.—know'-all, one who thinks he knows everything; know'-how, the faculty of knowing the right thing to do in any contingency: specialised skill; know'-noth'ing, one who is quite ignorant: a member of the native American party (1854-56), originally secret.—*adj.* completely ignorant.—know-noth'ingism.—in the know, in possession of private information: initiated; I wouldn't know, I am not in a position to know; know all the answers, to be completely informed on everything, or to think one is; know better, to be too wise, well-instructed (to do this or that); knowing to (*obs.* and *U.S.*), aware, informed, of; known as, going by name of; know the ropes, to understand the detail or procedure, as a sailor does his rigging; know what's o'clock, know what's what, to be wide awake; know which side one's bread is buttered on, to be fully alive to one's own interest; what do you know?, what is the news?: a greeting or expression of incredulity. [O.E. cnāwan; O.N. knā, L. (g)nōscere, Gr. gignōskein.]

knowe. See knoll (1).

knowledge, *nol'ij, n.* assured belief: that which is known: information, instruction: enlightenment, learning: practical skill: acquaintance:

cognisance (*law*): sexual intimacy (*arch*.).—*v.t.* (*obs.*) to acknowledge.—*adj.* **knowl'edgeable**, possessing knowledge: intelligent.—**knowledge box** (*slang*), the head.—**to one's knowledge**, so far as one knows. [M.E. *knowleche*, where -*leche* is unexplained; see **know**.]

**knub, nub,** *nub, n.* a knob: a small lump: the waste or refuse of silk-cocoons.—*n.* **knubb'le,** **nubb'le,** a small lump. — *adjs.* **knubb'ly, nubb'ly, knubb'y, nubby.** [Cf. Low Ger. *knubbe*.]

**knubble, nubble,** *nub'l,* **knobble,** *nob'l, v.t.* to beat with the fists: to knock. [**knob**.]

**knuckle,** *nuk'l, n.* projecting joint of a finger: the knee-joint of a calf or pig (*cook*.).—*v.i.* (in marbles) to touch the ground with the knuckles (usu. with *down*): to touch the forehead as a mark of respect: to yield (usu. with *down* or *under*): to bend the knuckles or knee.—*v.t.* to touch with the knuckle: to shoot from the thumb knuckle.—**knuck'le-bone**, any bone with a rounded end: (in *pl.*) the game of dibs; **knuck'le-bow**, the curved part of a sword-guard that covers the fingers; **knuck'leduster**, a metal covering for the knuckles, like a cestus, for attack or defence; **knuck'le-joint**, a joint where the forked end of a connecting-rod is joined by a bolt to another piece of the machinery.—**near the knuckle**, on the verge of the indecent. [M.E. *knokel*, not recorded in O.E.; cf. Du. *knokkel* (dim. of *knok*), Ger. *knöchel*, ankle-bone, knuckle (dim. of *knochen*, bone).]

**knur, knurr, nur, nurr,** *nûr, n.* an excrescence on a tree: a hard ball or knot of wood.—**knur and spell**, a game played with a knur, trap (*spell*), and stick, in vogue chiefly in the North of England. [M.E. *knurre*; cf. Du. *knor*, Ger. *knorre*, *knorren*.]

**knurl, nurl,** *nûrl, n.* a small excrescence or protuberance: a ridge or bead, esp. in series, as in the milling of a screw-head: a kink: a dwarfish person (*Burns*).—*v.t.* to make knurls on, to mill. —*adj.* **knurled** (spelt **gnarled,** *Shak*., *Measure for Measure*, folio 1623) covered with knurls. —*n.* **knurl'ing**, mouldings or other woodwork elaborated into a series of knobs. [Prob. a dim. of **knur**.]

**knut, nut, (slang).** See **nut.**

**koa,** *kō'ə, n.* a Hawaiian acacia. [Hawaiian.]

**koala,** *kō-ä'la, kōō'lə, n.* an Australian marsupial, like a small bear, called also **koala bear, native bear.** [Australian *kūlā*.]

**kob,** *kob, n.* an African water-antelope. [Wolof.]

**koban,** *kō'ban,* **kobang,** *kō'bang, n.* an obsolete Japanese oblong gold coin, rounded at the corners. [Jap. *ko-ban*.]

**kobold,** *kō'bold, n.* in German folklore, a spirit of the mines: a domestic brownie. [Ger.]

**Kodak,** *kō'dak, n.* a small portable photographic camera with a continuous roll of sensitised film. —*v.t.* and *v.i.* to photograph with a Kodak. [The trademark name of the Eastman *Kodak* Company.]

**koff,** *kof, n.* a small Dutch sailing-vessel. [Du. *kof*.]

**koftgar,** *koft'gär, n.* one who inlays steel with gold.—*n.* **koftgari** (*koft-gur-ē'*), such work— sometimes **koft'work.** [Hind. from Pers. *koftgar*.]

**kohl,** *kōl, n.* a fine powder of native stibnite (formerly known as antimony) which is black in colour, used in the East for staining the eyelids. [Ar. *koh'l*.]

**kohlrabi,** *kōl'rä'bi, n.* a cabbage with a turnip-shaped stem. [Ger.,—It. *cavolo rapa*, cole-turnip.]

**Koine,** *koi'nē, n.* a Greek dialect developed from Attic, in use in the Eastern Mediterranean in Hellenistic and Byzantine times: (often without *cap*.) any dialect which has spread and become

the common language of a larger area. [Gr. *koinē* (*dialektos*), common (dialect).]

**kokra,** *kok'rə, n.* the wood of an Indian tree (*Aporosa*) of the spurge family, used for making flutes, clarinets, etc.

**kok-sagyz,** *kok'-sä'gēz, n.* a species of dandelion (*Taraxacum kok-saghyz*) from the Tien Shan, grown in Russia, etc., for rubber-making.

**kokum,** *kō'kəm, n.* an East Indian tree (*Garcinia indica*).—**kokum butter,** an edible fat got from its nuts. [Marathi *kokamb*, mangosteen.]

**kola.** See **cola.**

**Kolarian,** *kō-lä'ri-ən, n.* and *adj.* Munda (language).

**kolinsky,** *ko-lin'ski, n.* the fur of the polecat or mink. [Russ. *kolinski*, of the Kola Peninsula.]

**kolkhoz,** *kol-hhoz', n.* a collective or co-operative farm. [Russ. abbrev. of *kollektivnoe khozyaistvo*.]

**kolo,** *kō'lō, n.* a Serbian dance or dance-tune. [Serb., wheel.]

**Kominform, Komintern.** Russian forms of **Cominform, Comintern.**

**komissar.** See **commissar.**

**komitaji,** *kō-mē-tä'jē, n.* orig. a member of the Bulgarian Revolutionary Committee in Macedonia: any Balkan guerrillero. [Turk. *qomitaji*, committee-man, bandit—*qomite*—Fr. *comité*, committee.]

**kommers,** *kom-ers', n.* a German students' gathering.—*n.* **kommers'buch** (-*bōōhh*), a songbook for such occasions. [Ger.,—L. *commercium*, commerce.]

**Komodo dragon** or **lizard,** *kə-mō'dō drag'ən, liz'ərd,* a very large monitor lizard (*Varanus komodoensis*) of some Indonesian islands. [From *Komodo* Island, Indonesia.]

**Komsomol,** *kom'sō-mol, n.* the Communist youth organisation of Russia. [Russ. abbrev. of *Kommunisticheskii Soyuz Molodezhi*.]

**kon,** (*Spens*.) form of con (know):—*pa.t.* **kond.**

**konfyt,** *kon-fit', n.* a preserve of fruit, in syrup or candied: jam. [Afrik.—Du. *konfijt*.]

**konimeter,** *kon-im'i-tər, n.* an instrument for measuring dust in air.—*n.* **kon'iscope,** an instrument for estimating the dustiness of air. [Gr. *konis,* dust, *metron,* measure, *skopeein,* to look at.]

**konk.** Same as **conk.**

**koodoo.** See **kudu.**

**kook,** *kōōk,* (*slang*) *n.* a person who is mad, foolish, or eccentric and amoral.—*adj.* **kook'ie, kook'y,** with the qualities of a kook: (of clothes) smart and eccentric.

**kookaburra,** *kōōk'ə-bur'ə, n.* the laughing jackass. [Native Australian name.]

**koolah,** *kōō'la.* Same as **koala.**

**kop,** *kop,* (*S.Afr.*) *n.* a hill, generally round-topped. [Du.; lit. head.]

**kopeck, copeck,** *kō-pek', kō'pek, n.* a Russian coin, the hundredth part of a ruble. [Russ. *kopeika*.]

**kopje,** older form of **koppie.**

**koppa,** *kop'ə, n.* a Greek letter (ϙ) between Pi and Rho in the alphabet, answering to Q, dropped by most dialects but retained as a numeral ϙ′ =90, ϙ =90,000. [Gr.; cf. Hebr. *qōph.*]

**koppie,** *kop'i, n.* a low hill. [Cape Du. *kopje*— kop, head.]

**kora,** *kō'rə, kō', n.* the water-cock (Gallicrex).

**Koran,** *kō-rän', kō-,* sometimes *kō'rən, kō', n.* the Mohammedan Scriptures.—*adj.* **Koranic** (*rän'ik*). [Ar. *qurān,* reading.]

**korfball,** *körf'böl, körf', n.* a game of Dutch origin resembling basket-ball played by teams of six men and six women a side. [Du. *korfbal*— *korf,* basket, *bal,* ball.]

**korkir.** Same as **corkir.**

**kos, koss.** Same as **coss.**

**kosher,** *kō'shər, adj.* pure, clean, according to the Jewish ordinances—as of meat killed and prepared by Jews. [Heb. *kāshēr,* right.]

kosmos. Same as cosmos.

koto, *kō'tō, n.* a Japanese musical instrument consisting of a long box with thirteen silk strings. [Jap.]

kotow, *kō-tow', n.* the Chinese ceremony of prostration.—*v.i.* to perform that ceremony: to abase oneself before (with *to*).—Usually kowtow'. [Chin. *k'o*, knock, *t'ou*, head.]

kottabos, *kot'ə-bos.* Same as cottabus.

kotwal, cotwal, *kōt'wäl, n.* a chief constable or magistrate of an Indian town. [Hind. *kotwāl.*]

Kotytto, *kot-it'ō,* or Kotys, *kot'is, ns.* a Thracian goddess worshipped with wild orgies. [Gr. *Kotyttō, Kotys.*]

koulan, koumiss, kourbash, kouskous. See kulan, kumiss, kurbash, couscous.

kowhai, *kō'hi,* -(*h*)*wi, n.* a papilionaceous shrub (*Sophora tetraptera*) of New Zealand, etc.: the New Zealand glory-pea (Clianthus). [Maori.]

kowtow, *kow-tow',* the more usual form of kotow.

kraal, *kräl, n.* a S. African native village: loosely, a single hut: a corral.—*v.t.* to pen. [Du. *kraal* —Port. *curral*—L. *currēre*, to run.]

krait, *krit, n.* a deadly Indian rock snake (*Bungarus caeruleus*). [Hind. *karait.*]

kraken, *krä'kən, n.* a fabled sea-monster. [Norw.; the -*n* is the def. art.]

krakowiak. See cracovienne (under Cracovian).

Krameria, *krä-mē'ri-a, n.* the rhatany genus of Caesalpiniaceae, or according to some, constituting a family Krameriā'ceae. [J. G. H. and W. H. *Kramer*, 18th-century German botanists.]

krang, *krang.* Same as kreng.

krantz, *kränts, (S.Afr.) n.* a crown of rock on a mountain-top: a precipice.—Also krans, kranz. [Du. *krans*, a wreath.]

kraut, *krowt,* (often *cap.*; *slang*) *n.* a German. [From sauerkraut.]

kreasote, kreatine. Same as creosote, creatine.

kreese. Same as kris.

kremlin, *krem'lin, n.* a citadel, specially that of Moscow: the Russian government. [Russ. *kreml'.*]

kreng, *kreng, n.* the carcass of a whale after the blubber has been removed.—Also krang. [Du.]

kreosote. Same as creosote.

kreutzer, *kroit'sər, n.* an obs. copper coin of Austria, South Germany, etc., 100 to the florin or gulden. [Ger. *kreuzer*—*kreuz*, cross, because at one time stamped with a cross.]

k'ri, *krē, n.* a marginal reading in the Hebrew Bible. [Heb. *qerē*, read (imper.).]

kriegspiel, kriegsspiel, *krēg'spēl, n.* a war-game played on a map to train officers. [Ger. *kriegsspiel*—*krieg*, war, *spiel*, game.]

Krilium, *kril'i-əm, n.* improver of soil structure, consisting of synthetic polymers. [Trademark.]

krill, *kril, n.* whaler's name for species of Euphausia (fam. Euphausiaceae), phosphorescent shrimps.

kris, *krēs, n.* a Malay dagger with wavy blade:— *pl.* kris'es.—*v.t.* to stab with a kris.—Also crease, creese, kreese. [Malay.]

Krishna, *krish'na, n.* a deity in later Hinduism, a form of Vishnu.

kromesky, *krō'mis-ki, n.* a croquette fried in bacon or calf's udder. [Russ. *kromochka.*]

krone, *krō'nə, n.* (*pl.* kro'ner) in Denmark and Norway, and krona, *krōō'na* (*pl.* kro'nor), in Sweden, a silver coin and monetary unit equal to 100 öre.—*n.* krone (*krō'nə; pl.* kro'nen), a former silver coin of Austria, equal to 100 heller: in Germany a former gold coin of 10 marks. [Cf. crown.]

Kronos, *kron'os, n.* a supreme god of the Greeks, son of Ouranos and Gaia, dethroned by his son Zeus.

Kru, Kroo, *krōō, n.* one of a West African people of the coast of Liberia noted as seamen.—Also *adj.*—Kru'- or Kroo'-boy, -man.

krummhorn, krumhorn, *krōōm'hörn, n.* an old double-reed wind instrument with curved end: an organ reed-stop. [Ger., curved horn.]

kryometer, etc. Same as cryometer, etc.

krypsis, *krips'is, n.* the 17th cent. doctrine that Christ secretly exercised divine powers. [Gr., concealment.]

krypton, crypton, *krip'ton, n.* an inert gas discovered in the air (where it is present in extremely small quantity) by Sir W. Ramsay in 1898 (Kr; atomic number 36). [Gr. *kryptein,* to hide.]

ksar, *ksär, n.* a Miltonic form of tsar.

Kshatriya, *kshat'ri-ya, n.* a member of the second or military caste among the Brahmanic Hindus. [Sans.]

k'thibh, *kthēv, n.* a textual reading in the Hebrew Scriptures: originally a marginal note calling attention to the textual form. [Heb. *kethibh,* written.]

kuchcha. Same as cutcha.

kuchen, *kōōhh'ən,* (Ger.) cake.

kudos, *kū'dos,* Gr. *kü'dos, n.* credit, fame, renown, prestige. [Gr. *kȳdos*, glory.]

kudu, koodoo, *kōō'dōō, n.* an African antelope with long spiral horns. [From Hottentot.]

kudzu, *kood'zōō, n.* an ornamental papilionaceous plant of China and Japan (*Pueraria thunbergiana*) with edible root tubers and a stem yielding a fibre. [Jap.]

Kufic, Cufic, *kū'fik, adj.* of Al *Kūfa*, south of Babylon: esp. of the lettering of its coins, inscriptions, and MSS., mainly early copies of the Koran.

kuh-horn, *kōō'hörn, n.* an alpenhorn. [Ger.]

Ku-Klux Klan, *kōō', kü'kluks klan,* or Ku-Klux, *n.* a secret organisation in several Southern U.S. states after Civil War of 1861-65, to oppose Northern influence, and prevent Negroes from enjoying their rights as freemen—revived in 1916 to deal drastically with Jews, Catholics, Negroes, etc. [Gr. *kyklos*, a circle, and clan.]

kukri, *kook're, n.* a sharp, curved Gurkha knife or short sword. [Hindi *kukṛi.*]

kulak, *kōō-lak', n.* a rich peasant: an exploiter. [Russ., fist.]

kulan, koulan, *kōō'län, n.* the onager, or a nearly related wild ass of the Kirghiz Steppe. [Kirghiz.]

kultur, *kōōl-tōōr', n.* culture: civilisation: a type of civilisation: sometimes used ironically.—*ns.* kultur'geschichte (*-gə-shēhh'tə*), history of civilisation; kultur'kampf (*-kampf*), the war of culture (said by Virchow in 1873 of the conflict between Bismarck and the Catholic Church); kultur'kreis (*-krīs*), an area regarded as a centre of diffusion of culture elements. [Ger.]

kumara, *kōō-mä'ra, n.* sweet potato. [Maori.]

kumari, *kōō-mär'i,* (*India*) *n.* Miss (title of respect).

kumiss, koumiss, *kōō'mis, n.* fermented mares' milk. [Russ. *kumis*—Tatar, *kumiz.*]

kümmel, *küm'l, kim'l, kōōm'l, n.* a liqueur flavoured with cumin and caraway seeds. [Ger., —L. *cuminum*—Gr. *kyminon*, cumin.]

kumquat, *kum'kwot, n.* a small kind of orange. [Cantonese, gold orange.]

kunkur or kunkar, *kung'kür, kung'kər, n.* a concretionary limestone in India: a laterite found in Ceylon. [Hindi *kaṇkar*, stone.]

kunstlied, *koonst'lēt,* (Ger.) an art-song.

Kuomintang, *kwō'min-tang, gwō'min-däng, n.* the Chinese nationalist people's party. [Chin.]

Kuo-yü, *kwō', gwō'yü, n.* lit. 'national language', a form of Mandarin taught all over China.

kupferschiefer, *kōōp'fər-shē-fər, n.* a shale rich in copper in the Permian of Germany. [Ger., copper shale.]

kurbash, kourbash, *kōōr'bash, n.* a hide whip used in the East.—*v.t.* to whip with a kurbash. [Ar. *qurbāsh.*]

kurchatovium, *kûr-chə-tō'vi-əm, n.* element 104

named by Russians (who claimed its discovery in 1966) after a Russian physicist.

**Kurd**, *kōōrd*, *kûrd*, *n.* one of the people of Kurdistan, Iranian in speech, often blond, Xenophon's *Kardouchoi*.—*adj.* and *n.* **Kurd'ish**.

**kurgan**, *kōōr-gän'*, *n.* a sepulchral barrow. [Russ. from Tatar.]

**kurhaus**, *kōōr'hows*, *n.* a building in which a spa is housed. [Ger., lit. cure-house.]

**Kuroshio**, *kōō-rō'shi-ō*, *n.* a warm current flowing north along the western edge of the Pacific. [Jap., black stream.]

**kurrajong**, *kur'ə-jong*, *n.* an Australian name for various trees with fibrous bark. [Native name.]

**kurre** (*Spens.*). Same as **cur**.

**kursaal**, *kōōr'zäl*, *n.* the reception-room of a spa. [Ger., lit. cure-saloon.]

**kurvey**, *kûr-vā'*, (*rare S.Afr.*) *v.i.* to transport goods.—*n.* **kurvey'or**, transport rider. [Du. *karwei*, work—Fr. *corvée*; cf. **corvée**.]

**kutch**. Same as **cutch** (2).

**kutcha**. Same as **cutcha**.

**kvass**, *kväs*, *n.* rye-beer. [Russ. *kvas*.]

**kwashiorkor**, *kwä-shi-ör'kör*, or *kwosh'*, *n.* a widespread nutritional disease of children in tropical and subtropical regions due to deficiency of protein. [Ghanaian name.]

**kwela**, *kwä'la*, *n.* a Zulu folk-music of jazz type. [Bantu, lift, from the leaping upward in dancing to the music.]

**kyang**. See **kiang**.

**kyanise**, **-ize**, *ki'ə-nīz*, *v.t.* to preserve from dry-rot by injecting corrosive sublimate into the pores of (wood). [From John H. *Kyan* (1774-1830).]

**kyanite**, *ki'ə-nit*, *n.* a mineral, an aluminium silicate, generally sky-blue.—Also **cyanite** (*si'*). [Gr. *kyanos*, blue.]

**kyat**, *kyät*, *kē-ät'*, *n.* the monetary unit of Burma.

**kye**, **ky**, *kī*, (*Scot.*) *n.pl.* cows. [See **kine**.]

**kyle**, *kil*, *n.* a narrow strait. [Gael. *caol.*]

**kylie**, **kiley**, **kyley**, *ki'li*, *n.* a boomerang. [Western Australian word.]

**kylin**, *kē'lin*, *n.* a fabulous animal figured in the decoration of Chinese pottery. [From Chinese *ch'i lin.*]

**kylix**, *kil'* or *kil'iks*. Same as **cylix**.

**kyllosis**, *kil-ō'sis*, *n.* club-foot. [Gr. *kyllōsis.*]

**kyloe**, *ki'lō*, *n.* one of the cattle of the Hebrides. [Origin unknown.]

**kymograph**, *ki'mō-gräf*, *n.* an instrument for recording the pressure of fluids, esp. of blood in a blood-vessel.—*adj.* **kymographic** (*-graf'ik*). [Gr. *kȳma*, a wave, *graphein*, to write.]

**kynd**, **kynde**, *kind*, (*Spens.*) *n.*, *adj.*, and *v.t.* Same as **kind** (1) and (2).

**kyne** (*Spens.*). Same as **kine**.

**kyphosis**, *ki-fō'sis*, *n.* a hunchbacked condition.—*adj.* **kyphotic** (*-fot'ik*). [Gr. *kȳphōsis*—*kȳphos*, a hump.]

**Kyrie eleison**, *kēr'i-e el-ā'i-son*, *kir'*, *kir'i-e el-e-ē'son*, *el-e-ā'son*, etc., abbrev. **Kyrie**, *n.* a form of prayer in all the ancient Greek liturgies, retained in the R.C. mass, following immediately after the introit (including both words and music): one of the responses to the commandments in the Anglican ante-communion service. [Gr. *Kyrie*, *eleēson*, Lord, have pity.]

**kyrielle**, *kēr-i-el'*, *n.* a string of short lines in stanzas all ending with the same word. [Fr., litany, rigmarole, kyrielle—Gr. *Kyrie eleēson*; see preceding.]

**kyte**, *kit*, (*Scot.*) *n.* a paunch, belly. [Origin obscure.]

**kythe**, **kithe**, *kidh*, (*Scot.*) *v.t.* to make known:—2nd pers. sing. **kydst**, in Spenser blunderingly used in the sense of knowest.—*v.i.* to show oneself, to appear. [O.E. *cȳthan*, to make known. See **uncouth**.]

*fāte, fär; mē, hûr* (her); *mīne; mōte, för; mūte; mōōn, fōōt; dhen* (then)

# L

**L, l,** *el, n.* the eleventh letter in the Roman, the twelfth in our alphabet, representing a lateral liquid sound, the breath passing the side or sides of the tongue: anything shaped like the letter: used as a sign for pound (L. *libra*): as a Roman numeral L = 50, L̄ = 50,000: an elevated railway, or train (*U.S.*).

**la,** *lä, interj.* lo! see! behold! ah! indeed! [Cf. **lo, law** (5).]

**la,** *lä, n.* the sixth note of the scale in sol-fa notation—also spelt **lah.** [See Aretinian.]

**laager,** *lä'gər,* Afrik. form **laer,** not used in S. Afr. Eng., *n.* in South Africa, a defensive ring of ox-wagons: any extemporised fortification: an encampment.—*v.t.* and *v.i.* to arrange or camp in a laager. [Cape Du. *lager*—Ger. *lager,* a camp; Du. *leger*; cf. **lair, layer, leaguer.**]

**lab,** *lab, n.* a familiar contraction of **laboratory.**

**labanotation,** *läb-ə-nō-tā'shən, n.* the Laban system of ballet notation. [Rudolf von *Laban,* who proposed it.]

**labarum,** *lab'ə-rəm, n.* orig. a Roman military standard, the imperial standard after Constantine's conversion—with a monogram of the Greek letters XP (ChR), for Christ: a similar ecclesiastical banner borne in processions: any moral standard or guide. [L.,—Late Gr. *labaron,* origin unknown.]

**labda, labdacism, labdanum.** See **lambda, lambdacism, ladanum.**

**labefactation,** *lab-i-fak-tā'shən,* **labefaction,** *-fak'-shən, ns.* a weakening decay: overthrow. [L. *labefactātiō, -ōnis—labāre,* to totter, *facĕre,* to make.]

**label,** *lā'bl, n.* an attached band or strip (*arch.*): a small slip placed on or near anything to denote its nature, contents, ownership, destination, etc.: a paper annexed to a will, as a codicil (*law*): a fillet with pendants (an eldest son's cadency mark; *her.*): a dripstone (*archit.*): a character-ising or classificatory designation (*fig.*).—*v.t.* to affix a label to: to describe by or on a label:—*pr.p.* **lā'belling;** *pa.t.* and *pa.p.* **lā'belled.**—**labelled atom,** a tagged atom. [O.Fr. *label,* perh.—O.H.G. *lappa* (Ger. *lappen*), flap.]

**labellum,** *lə-bel'əm, n.* the lower petal, morphologically the upper, of an orchid: applied also to other lip-like structures in flowers:—*pl.* **labell'a.**—*adj.* **labell'oid.** [L., dim. of *labrum,* lip.]

**labial,** *lā'bi-əl, adj.* of or formed by the lips: sounded by impact of air on a lip-like projection, as an organ flue-pipe (*mus.*).—*n.* a sound formed by the lips.—*v.t.* **lā'bialise, -ize,** to make labial: to pronounce with lip action.—*n.* **lā'bialism,** a tendency to labialise.—*adv.* **lā'bially.**—*n.pl.* **Lābiātae** (*-ā'tē*), a family of sympetalous dicotyledons with lipped flowers, four-cornered stems, and opposite branches—the dead-nettles, mints, etc.—*adj.* **lā'biate,** lipped: having a lipped corolla: belonging to the Labiatae.—*n.* any plant of the Labiatae.—*n.* **lā'bium,** a lip or lip-like part: in insects the underlip, formed by the partial fusion of the second maxillae:—*pl.* **lā'bia.**—*adj.* and *n.* **lābiodent'al,** (a sound) pronounced both by the lips and teeth. [L. *lābium,* a lip.]

**labile,** *lā'bīl,* in U.S. *-əl, adj.* unstable: apt to slip or change. [L. *lābilis—lābī,* to slip.]

**labis,** *lā'bis, n.* the cochlear or eucharistic spoon. Gr. *labis,* handle—root of *lambanein,* to take.]

**labium.** See **labial.**

---

**lablab,** *lab'lab, n.* a tropical bean (*Dolichos lablab*) with edible pods. [Ar. *lablāb.*]

**laboratory,** *lə-bor'-ə-tə-ri, lab'ə-rə-tə-ri, n.* orig. a chemist's workroom: a place for experimental work or research. [L. *labōrāre—labor,* work.]

**labor improbus,** *lā'bör im-prō'bəs, la'bor im-pro'bŏos,* (L.) persistent, dogged labour.

**labour,** in U.S. **labor,** *lā'bər, n.* toil: work: bodily work: pains: duties: a task requiring hard work: effort toward the satisfaction of needs: workers collectively: supply or services of workers, esp. bodily workers: the Labour Party or its cause, principles, or interest: the outcome of toil (*arch.*): trouble taken (*arch.*): exertion of influence (*arch.*): the pangs and efforts of childbirth: heavy pitching or rolling of a ship.—*adj.* of labour or the Labour Party.—*v.i.* to undergo labour: to work: to take pains: to be oppressed: to move slowly: to be in travail: to pitch and roll heavily (*naut.*).—*v.t.* to spend labour on (*arch.*): to cultivate (*dial.*): to elaborate, work out in detail: to strain, over-elaborate.—*adj.* **laborious** (*lə-bō', -bō'ri-əs*), involving or devoted to labour: strenuous: arduous.—*adv.* **labo'riously.**—*n.* **labo'riousness.**—*adj.* **lā'boured,** cultivated (*dial.*): worked (*arch.*): bearing marks of effort in execution: strained: over-elaborated.—*ns.* **lā'bourer,** one who labours: one who does work requiring little skill; **lā'bourism;** **lā'bourist,** one who contends for the rights of workers.—*adjs.* **lā'bour-sav'ing,** intended to supersede or lessen labour; **lā'boursome** (*Shak.*), laborious.—**Labour Day,** in many countries the 1st of May, a day of labour demonstrations: in U.S., the first Monday in September; **Labour Exchange** (see **employment exchange**); **Labour Party,** a party aiming at securing for workers by hand or brain the fruits of their industry and equitable distribution thereof: its representatives in parliament: a local organisation of the party.—**hard labour,** compulsory work imposed in addition to imprisonment, abolished in U.K. in 1948; **labour of love,** work undertaken without hope of emolument; **labour with,** to take pains to convince. [O.Fr. *labour, labeur*—L. *labor.*]

**Labrador,** *lab'rə-dör,* or *lab-rə-dör', n.* a mainland region of Newfoundland and Quebec.—Also *adj.*—*n.* **lab'radorite** (or *-dör'*), a plagioclase feldspar with fine play of colours found on the Labrador coast.—**Labrador (dog, retriever),** a sporting dog about twenty-two inches in height, either black or (yellow, or golden, Labrador) from red to fawn in colour; **Labrador tea,** a shrub of the heather family (Ledum) used in Labrador as a substitute for tea.

**labrum,** *lā'brəm, n.* a lip: a lip-like part:—*pl.* **lā'bra.**—*n.* **lā'bret,** a lip ornament.—*adj.* **lā'brose,** thick-lipped. [L. *lābrum,* a lip.]

**Labrus,** *lā'brəs, n.* the wrasse genus of fishes, of the family **La'bridae.**—*adj.* **la'broid.** [L. *lābrus, lābros,* a kind of fish.]

**labrys,** *lab'ris, lāb'ris, n.* the double-headed axe, a religious symbol of ancient Crete, etc. [Gr., from Lydian; perh. conn. with **labyrinth.**]

**laburnum,** *lə-bûr'nəm, n.* a small poisonous papilionaceous tree, a native of the Alps. [L.]

**labyrinth,** *lab'i-rinth, n.* orig. a building with intricate passages: an arrangement of tortuous paths or alleys (usually between hedges) in

---

which it is difficult to find the way out: a maze: a tangle of intricate ways and connections: a perplexity: the cavities of the internal ear (*anat*.).—*adjs*. labyrinth′al, labyrinth′ian, labyrinth′ic, -al, labyrinth′ine (-*in*, -*in*).—*ns*. labyrinthi′tis, inflammation of the inner ear; labyrinth′odont, an extinct stegocephalian amphibian of Carboniferous, Permian, and esp. Triassic times, so called from the mazy pattern of a section of the teeth (Gr. *odous, odontos*, tooth) in some. [Gr. *labyrinthos*, perh. conn. with *labrys*, the double axe; see labrys.]

lac. Same as lakh.

lac, *lak, n.* a dark-red transparent resin produced on the twigs of trees in the East by coccid insects.—lac′-dye, lac′-lake, scarlet colouring matters obtained from it. [Hind. *lākh*—Sans. *lākṣā*, 100,000 hence the (teeming) lac insect.]

laccolite, *lak′ō-līt, n.* a mass of igneous rock that has risen in a molten condition and bulged up the overlying strata to form a dome.—Also lacc′olith (-*lith*).—*adjs*. laccolitic (-*lit′ik*), laccolith′ic. [Gr. *lakkos*, a reservoir, *lithos*, a stone.]

lace, *lās, n.* a string for passing through holes: an ornamental fabric made by looping, knotting, plaiting, or twisting threads into definite patterns.—*v.t.* to fasten with a lace: to compress or pinch by lacing: to adorn with lace: to streak: to thrash: to reprimand severely: to intermix, as coffee with brandy, etc.: to intertwine.—*v.i.* to have lacing as mode of fastening: to practise tight-lacing.—*adj*. laced.—*n*. lacet (*lās-et′*), a kind of braidwork.—*n*. and *adj.* lac′ing.—*adj.* lac′y (also lac′ey), like lace.—lace′bark, a lofty West Indian tree of the Daphne family, the inner bark like coarse lace; lace′-boot, a boot fastened by a lace; laced mutton (*Shak.*), a prostitute; lace′-frame, a machine used in lace-making; lace′-leaf (see lattice-leaf); lace′-man, a dealer in lace; lace′-paper, paper stamped or cut like lace; lace′-pill′ow, a cushion held on the knees by lace-makers; lace-ups, boots or shoes having laces; lace′-wing, the golden-eye, a neuropterous insect with gauzy wings and brilliant golden eyes; lacy glass, early form of pressed glass with lacy design (also lace glass). [O.Fr. *las*, a noose—L. *laqueus*.]

lacerate, *las′ə-rāt, v.t.* to tear: to rend: to wound: to afflict.—*adjs*. lac′erable; lac′erant, harrowing; lac′erate, -d, rent, torn: with edges cut into irregular segments (*bot*.).—*n*. lacerā′tion. —*adj.* lac′erative, tearing: having power to tear. [L. *lacerāre*, -*ātum*, to tear—*lacer*, torn.]

Lacerta, *la-sûr′tə, n.* a genus of lizards, including the common lizard: one of the northern constellations, the Lizard.—*adj*. lacertian (-*sûr′shyən*), of lizards: lizard-like.—*n.pl.* Lacertil′ia, the lizard order or suborder of reptiles.—*adjs*. lacertil′ian; lacer′tine. [L.]

laches, *lach′iz*, (*law*) *n.* negligence or undue delay, esp. such as to disentitle to remedy. [A.Fr. *lachesse*.]

Lachesis, *lak′i-sis, n.* in myth. that one of the three Fates who assigned to each mortal his destiny—she spun the thread of life from the distaff held by Clotho: a genus of snakes including the bushmaster. [Gr.]

lachrymal, *lak′ri-məl, adj.* of or for tears.—*n*. a tear-bottle: a bone near the tear-gland: (in *pl.*) lachrymal organs: (in *pl.*) weeping fits.—*adjs*. lach′rymary, lach′rymatory, lachrymal: causing tears to flow.—*ns*. a tear-bottle.—*n*. lach′rymător, a substance that causes tears to flow, as tear-gas: a contrivance for letting it loose.—*adj.* lach′rymose, shedding tears: given to weeping: lugubrious.—*adv.* lach′rymosely.—Also lacrymal, lacrimal, etc.—lachryma Christi (*lak′ri-mə kris′tē*; L., Christ's tear), a sweet but piquant wine from grapes grown on Vesuvius;

lachrymal duct, a duct that conveys tear-water from the inner corner of the eye to the nose; lachrymal gland, a gland at the outer angle of the eye that secretes tears; lachrymal urn, a tear-bottle. [From *lachryma*, a mediaeval spelling of L. *lacrima*, tear; cf. Gr. *dakry*; Eng. tear; Gr. *dakrȳma* may have influenced the spelling.]

lacinia, *lə-sin′i-ə, n.* a long narrow lobe in a leaf, etc.: the inner lobe of the maxilla (*entom*.):—*pl*. lacin′iae (-*ē*).—*adjs*. lacin′iate, -d, cut into narrow lobes, slashed.—*n*. laciniā′tion. [L., a lappet, tag.]

lack, *lak, n.* want, deficiency: a thing absent or in short supply.—*v.t.* to be without: to be short of or deficient in: to need: to miss (*obs.*).—*v.i.* (now usu. in *pr.p.*) to be wanting, absent: to be deficient: to be in want (*obs.*).—*adj*. lack′ing. —lack′-all, one who is destitute; lack′-beard; lack′-brain (*Shak.*), a fool; lack′land.—Also *adj*.—lack′-Latin (*obs.*; often *Sir John Lack-Latin*), an ignorant priest.—*adj.* uneducated, ignorant.—*adj*. lack′-linen (*Shak.*), wanting linen. —lack′-love, one who is deficient in love.—Also *adj*.—*adj*. lack′-lus′tre, dull, without brightness, sheen or vitality.—Also *n*. [Cf. M.L.G. and Du. *lak*, blemish.]

lack, *lak, n.* See good-lack under good.

lackadaisical, *lak-ə-dā′zi-kl, adj.* affectedly pensive: vapidly sentimental: listless: languishing. —*interjs*. (*arch.*) lack′adai′sy, lack′aday. [See alack-a-day.]

lacker. See lacquer.

lackey, lacquey, *lak′i, n.* a footman or valet: a servile follower:—*pl*. lack′eys, lacqu′eys.—*v.t.* and *v.i.* to serve or attend as or like a footman. —lackey moth, a moth (*Malacosoma neustria*) of the egger group with gaudily striped caterpillar, like a footman in livery. [O.Fr. *laquay* (Fr. *laquais*)—Sp. *lacayo*, a lackey; perh. Ar. *luka′*, servile.]

lacmus, *lak′məs, n.* Same as litmus.

Laconian, *lə-kō′nyən, -ni-ən*, Laconic, *lə-kon′ik, adjs*. of Laconia or Lacedaemonia, Spartan.—*adjs*. laconic, -al, expressing or expressed in few words after the manner of the Laconians: sententiously brief.—*adv*. lacon′ically.—*ns*. laconism (*lak′*), lacon′icism, a concise style: a short, pithy phrase. [Gr. *lakōnikos*.]

lacquer, lacker, *lak′ər, n.* a solution of film-forming substances in a volatile solvent, esp. a varnish of lac and alcohol: a similar substance sprayed on the hair to hold it in place: the juice of the lacquer-tree (*Japan lacquer*) or similar product: a covering of one of these: an article, or ware, so coated.—*v.t.* to cover with lacquer: to varnish.—*ns*. lacq′uerer; lacq′uering, varnishing with lacquer: a coat of lacquer varnish.—lacq′uer-tree′, a tree of the genus Rhus. [Fr. *lacre*—Port. *lacre, laca*; see lac (2).]

lacrimal, etc. Variants of lachrymal, etc.

lacrosse, *lə-, lä-kros′, n.* a team game (orig. N. American) in which the ball is driven through the opponents' goal by means of a crosse. [Fr.]

lacteal, *lak′ti-əl, adj.* of milk: conveying chyle. —*n*. a lymphatic conveying chyle from the intestines to the thoracic ducts.—*ns*. lactase (*lak′tās*), an enzyme that acts on lactose; lac′-tate, a salt of lactic acid; lactā′tion, secretion or yielding of milk: the period of suckling.—*adj*. lac′teous, milky.—*n*. lactesc′ence.—*adjs*. lactesc′ent, turning to milk: producing milky juice; lac′tic, pertaining to milk; lactif′erous, conveying or producing milk or milky juice; lactif′ic, producing milk or milky juice; lactif′luous, flowing with milk.—*n*. lac′tose, milk-sugar $C_{12}H_{22}O_{11} + H_2O$, obtained by evaporating whey.—lactic acid, an acid obtained from milk, $CH_3CH(OH)COOH$. [L. *lac, lactis*, milk; Gr. *gala, galaktos*, milk.]

**lactoflavin**, *lak-tō-flā'vin*, *n.* an earlier name of riboflavin. [L. *lac, lactis*, milk, *flāvus*, yellow.]

**Lactuca**, *lak-tū'kə*, *n.* the lettuce genus of composite plants, with milky juice. [L. *lactūca—lac, lactis*, milk.]

**lacuna**, *lə-*, *la-kū'nə*, *n.* a gap or hiatus: an intercellular space (*biol.*): a cavity: a depression in a pitted surface:—*pl.* **lacū'nae** (*-nē*).—*adj.* **lacūn'al**, lacunary.—*n.* **lacū'nar**, a sunken panel or coffer in a ceiling or a soffit: a ceiling containing these:—*pl.* **lacū'nars**, **lacunaria** (*lak-ū-nā'ri-ə*).—Also *adj.—adjs.* **lacūn'ary**, **lacūn'ate**, pertaining to, or including, lacunae: **lacū'nose**, having lacunae: pitted. [L. *lacūna*, hollow, gap, and *lacūnar, -āris*, a fretted ceiling.]

**lacustrine**, *lə-kus'trin*, *adj.* pertaining to lakes: dwelling in or on lakes: formed in lakes. [L. *lacus*, a lake.]

**lacy.** See lace.

**lad**, *lad*, *n.* a boy: a youth: a stable-man: a dashing fellow: a lover (*Scot.*).—*n.* **ladd'ie**, a little lad: a boy.—**lad's love** (*dial.*), southernwood. [M.E. *ladde*, youth, servant; origin obscure.]

**lad**, obs. form of led.

**ladanum**, *lad'ə-nəm*, *n.* a resin exuded from Cistus leaves in Mediterranean countries.—Also **lab'danum**. [L. *lādanum, lēdanum*—Gr. *lādanon, lēdanon—lēdon*, the Cistus plant, prob.—Pers. *lādan*.]

**ladder**, *lad'ər*, *n.* a contrivance, generally portable, with rungs between two supports, for going up and down: anything of similar form, as a run in knitwear where the breaking of a thread gives an appearance of rungs: a contrivance for enabling fish to ascend a waterfall (*fish-ladder, salmon-ladder*): means of attaining a higher status (*fig.*).—*v.t.* to furnish with a ladder: to scale with a ladder.—*v.i.* to develop a ladder.—*adjs.* **ladd'ered**, **ladd'ery**. [O.E. *hlǣder*; Ger. *leiter*.]

**lade**, *lād*, *v.t.* to load: to burden: to put on board: to ladle or scoop: to empty, drain, as with a ladle.—*v.i.* to take cargo aboard:—*pa.t.* **lād'ed**; *pa.p.* **lād'en**, **lād'ed**.—*adj.* **lād'en**, loaded: burdened.—*n.* **lād'ing**, the act of loading: that which is loaded: cargo: freight. [O.E. *hladan*, pa.t. *hlōd*; pa.p. *hlæden, hladen*, load, draw water.]

**lade**, laid, *lād* (*Scot.*). See load.

**lade**, *lād*, (*Scot.*) *n.* a mill-stream. [Perh. O.E. *lād*, way, course; cf. lode, lead (1).]

**la-di-da, lah-di-dah**, *lä-di-dä'*, (*slang*), *adj.* affectedly fine, esp. in speech or bearing.

**Ladin**, *lä-dēn'*, *n.* a Romance tongue spoken in the upper Inn valley: a general name for the Rhaeto-Romanic languages or dialects.—Also **Ladi'no**.—*n.* **Ladinity** (*-din'i-ti*). [L. *Latīnus*, Latin.]

**Ladino**, *lä-dē'nō*, *n.* the old Castilian tongue: the Spanish jargon of Macedonian Jews: a Spanish-American of mixed white and Indian blood. [Sp.,—L. *Latīnus*, Latin.]

**Ladino.** See Ladin.

**ladle**, *lād'l*, *n.* a large spoon for lifting liquid: the float-board of a mill-wheel: a long-handled pan or bowl for holding molten metal: a church collection-box on a long handle (*Scot.*).—*v.t.* to transfer or distribute with a ladle.—*n.* **lad'leful**, as much as a ladle will hold:—*pl.* **lad'lefuls**. [O.E. *hlædel—hladan*, to lade.]

**ladrone**, *lə-drōn'*, *n.* a robber. [Sp. *ladrón*—L. *latrō, -ōnis*.]

**lady**, (*cap.* when prefixed), *lā'di*, *n.* the mistress of a house: used as the feminine of lord and of gentleman, and ordinarily as a less formal substitute for dame: any woman of refinement of manners and instincts: a consort, a term formerly preferred to wife by some who like to stand upon their dignity (*arch.*): a lady-love

or object of chivalric devotion: a size of slates, 16 × 8 inches: used also as a feminine prefix: —*pl.* **ladies** (*lā'diz*); old genitive **la'dy**.—*n.* **ladies'**, **ladies' public lavatory.**—*adj.* **la'dyfied**, **la'dified**, inclined to affect the manners of a lady.—*v.t.* **la'dyfy**, **la'dify**, to make a lady of: to call My Lady or Your Ladyship.—*n.* **la'dyhood**, condition, character of a lady.—*adj.* **la'dyish**, having the airs of a fine lady.—*n.* **la'dyism**, affectation of the airs of a fine lady.—*n.* **la'dykin**, an endearing dim. of lady.—*adj.* **la'dylike**, like a lady in manners: refined: soft, delicate: often implying want of touch with reality and sincerity—genteel.—*n.* **la'dyship**, the title of a lady.—**ladies' companion**, a small bag used for a woman's needlework; **ladies' gallery**, a gallery in the House of Commons, once screened off by a grille; **ladies' man**, one fond of women's society; **la'dybird**, any member of the family Coccinellidae, little round beetles, often brightly spotted, preying on greenfly, etc.—also **la'dybug**, **la'dycow**, **la'dyfly**; **La'dy-chap'el**, a chapel dedicated to the Virgin Mary, usually behind the high altar, at the end of the apse; **Lady Day**, 25th March, the day of the annunciation of the Virgin; **la'dy-fern**, a pretty British fern (*Athyrium filix-foemina*), with long bipinnate fronds (imagined by the old herbalists to be the female of the male-fern); **la'dy-help**, one paid to assist in housework, but treated more or less as one of the family; **la'dy-in-wait'ing**, an attendant to a lady of royal status; **la'dy-killer**, a man who is, or fancies himself, irresistible to women; **la'dy-love**, a lady or woman loved: a sweetheart; **la'dy's-cu'shion**, the mossy saxifrage; **la'dy's-fing'er**, **-fing'ers**, a name for many plants, esp. the kidney-vetch: a finger-shaped cake; **la'dy's-maid**, a female attendant on a lady, esp. for the toilet; **la'dy's-mantle**, a genus (*Alchemilla*) of rosaceous plants with small, yellowish-green flowers and leaves like folded drapery; **la'dy's-slipp'er**, a genus(Cypripedium) of orchids with large slipper-like lip; **la'dy's-smock**, the cuckoo-flower (*Cardamine pratensis*), a cruciferous meadow-plant, with pale lilac-coloured flowers; **la'dy's-thist'le**, the milk thistle; **la'dy-trifles** (*Shak.*), trifles befitting a lady.—**her, your ladyship, my lady**, forms of expression used in speaking of, or to, one who has the title of Lady; **our Lady**, the Virgin Mary; (**Our**) **Lady's bedstraw** (see bedstraw). [O.E. *hlǣfdige*, lit. app. the bread-kneader—*hlāf*, loaf, and a lost word from the root of dough.]

**laeotropic**, *lē-ō-trop'ik*, *adj.* turning to the left. [Gr. *laios*, left, *tropos*, a turn.]

**laesa majestas**, *lē'zə mə-jes'tas*, *li'sa mä-yes'täs* (L.) injured majesty, lese majesty (q.v.).

**laesie**, (*Spens.*) for lazy.

**laetare**, *lē-tā'ri*, *lī-tär'e*, *n.* the fourth Sunday in Lent. [*Laetāre* (first word of the introit), imper. sing. of L. *laetāri*, to rejoice—*laetus*, joyful.]

**laevigate**, a faulty spelling of levigate.

**laevo-, levo-**, *lē-vō-*, in composition, on, or to, the left. [L. *laevus*, left.]

**laevorotatory, levorotatory**, *lē-vō-rō'tə-tə-ri, -rō-tā'*, *adj.* counterclockwise: rotating the plane of polarisation of light to the left.—*n.* **laevorotā'-tion.** [L. *laevus*, left, *rotāre*, to rotate.]

**laevulose**, *lēv'ū-lōs*, or *lev'*, *n.* fructose, a laevorotatory sugar (C₆H₁₂O₆).—Also **levulose**. [L. *laevus*, left.]

**lag**, *lag*, *adj.* hindmost: behindhand: late: tardy. —*n.* he who, or that which, comes behind: the fag-end: (esp. in *pl.*) dregs: a retardation or falling behind: the amount by which one phenomenon is delayed behind another: delay.—*v.i.* to move or walk slowly: to loiter: to fall behind:—*pr.p.* **lagg'ing**; *pa.t.* and *pa.p.* **lagged.**—*adj.* **lagg'ard**, lagging.—*ns.* **lagg'ard**, **lagg'er**, one who lags behind.—*n.* and *adj.* **lagg'ing.**—*adv.*

**lagg'ingly.**—**lag'-end** (*Shak.*), the last or long-delayed end.—**lag of the tides,** the progressive lengthening of the interval between tides as neap-tide is approached—opp. to *priming.* [Origin unknown.]

**lag,** *lag, n.* a stave: a lath: boarding: a wooden lining: a non-conducting covering: a perforated wooden strip used instead of a card in weaving.—*v.t.* to furnish with a lag.—*n.* **lagg'ing,** boarding, as across the framework of a centre for an arch, or in a mine to prevent ore falling into a passage: a non-conducting covering for pipes, etc. [Prob. O.N. *lögg,* barrel-rim; cf. Sw. *lagg,* stave.]

**lag,** *lag,* (*slang*) *v.t.* to steal: to carry off: to arrest: to transport or send to penal servitude.—*n.* a convict: an old convict: a term of penal servitude or transportation. [Origin unknown.]

**lagan,** *lag'ən, n.* wreckage or goods at the bottom of the sea: later taken to mean such goods attached to a buoy with a view to recovery.—Also **ligan** (*lī'gən*). [O.Fr. *lagan,* perh. Scand. from the root of **lay, lie;** falsely associated with L. *ligāmen,* a tying.]

**lagena,** *lə-jē'nə,* (*ant.*) *n.* a narrow-necked bottle. —*adj.* **lage'niform,** flask-shaped. [L. *lagēna*—Gr. *lagÿna.*]

**lager,** *lä'gər, n.* (in full **lager beer**) a light beer kept for up to six months before use. [Ger. *lager-bier*—*lager,* a storehouse.]

**laggen, laggin,** *lag', läg'ən,* (*Burns*) *n.* the angle between the side and bottom of a wooden dish. —**lagg'en-gird,** a hoop at the bottom of a wooden vessel. [Cf. **lag** (2), **leglin.**]

**lagniappe,** *lan'yap, n.* something given beyond what is strictly required: a gratuity. [Louisiana Fr., from Amer. Sp. (Quechua *yápa,* addition).]

**lagoon,** *lə-gōōn', n.* a shallow lake, esp. one near or communicating with the sea or a river.—Also (old-fashioned) **lagune.** [It. *laguna*—L. *lacūna.*]

**lagrimoso,** *läg-ri-mō'sō,* (*mus.*) *adj* and *adv.* plaintive(ly). [It.,—L. *lacrimōsus,* tearful—*lacrima,* a tear.]

**Lagthing, Lagting,** *läg'ting,* (*obs.*) *n.* the upper house of the Norwegian parliament. [Norw. *lag,* law, *ting* (*thing*), court, parliament.]

**lagune.** Same as **lagoon.**

**lah.** Same as **la** (2).

**lahar,** *lä'här, n.* a mud-lava or other mud-flow.

**laic, laical, laicise.** See **lay** (6).

**laid,** *lād, pa.t.* and *pa.p.* of **lay.**—*adj.* put down, prostrate: pressed down.—**laid paper,** such as shows the marks of the close parallel wires on which the pulp was laid—opp. to *wove;* **laid work,** in embroidery, couching of the simplest kind.

**laidly,** *lād'li, adj.* Northern (*Scot.*) form of **loathly.**

**laigh,** *lähh, adj.* and *adv.* a Scots form of **low:** low-lying: sunken.—*n.* a tract of low-lying or sunken land.

**laik.** Same as **lake** (4).

**laika,** *lī'kə, n.* any of several similar breeds of working dog, originating in Finland, small and reddish-brown.

**lain,** *pa.p.* of **lie,** to rest.

**lair,** *lār, n.* a lying-place, esp. the den or retreat of a wild beast: an enclosure for beasts: the ground for one grave in a burying-place (*Scot.*). —*v.t.* to put in a lair.—*v.i.* to lie: to go to a lair.—*n.* **lair'age,** a place where cattle are housed or laired, esp. at markets and docks. [O.E. *leger,* a couch—*licgan,* to lie down; Du. *leger,* Ger. *lager.*]

**lair,** *lār,* (*Scot.*) *v.t.* and *v.i.* to mire.—*n.* mire.—*adj.* **lair'y** (*Scot.*). [O.N. *leir,* mud.]

**lair,** *lār, n.* Scots form of **lore.**

**lair,** *lār,* (*Austr. slang*) *n.* a flashily dressed man. —*adj.* **lair'y.**—*v.i.* **laired up,** dressed flashily.

**laird,** *lārd,* (*Scot.*) *n.* a landed proprietor.—*n.* **laird'ship.** [Northern form of **lord.**]

**laisse,** *les, n.* a tirade or string of verses on one rhyme. [Fr.]

**laissez-aller,** *les'ā-al'ā, n.* unconstraint.—Also **laiss'er-all'er.** [Fr., let go.]

**laissez-faire,** *les'ā-fer', n.* a general principle of non-interference.—Also **laiss'er-faire'.** [Fr., let do.]

**laissez-passer,** *les'ā-päs'ā, n.* pass, special passport. [Fr., let pass.]

**laith,** *lāth,* a Scots form of **loth.**—*adj.* **laithfu'** (*lāth'fə*), bashful.

**laity.** See **lay** (6).

**lake,** *lāk, n.* a reddish pigment originally got from lac: a coloured substance got by combination of a dye with a metallic hydroxide: its colour: carmine.—*v.t.* and *v.i.* to make or become lake-coloured.—*adj.* **lak'y.** [lac (2).]

**lake,** *lāk, n.* a large or considerable body of water within land: a large quantity, an excess, as of wine, etc.—*ns.* **lake'let,** a little lake; **lāk'er,** a fish found in lakes: a boat for lakes: one who sails on lakes: a Lake poet: a visitor to the Lake District.—*adjs.* **lāk'ish,** savouring of the Lake school; **lāk'y.**—**lake'-basin,** a hollow now or once containing a lake: the area drained by a lake; **Lake District,** a picturesque and mountainous region in Cumberland, Westmorland, and Lancashire, with many lakes; **lake'-dweller; lake'-dwelling,** a settlement, esp. prehistoric, built on piles in a lake; **lake herring** (see **cisco**); **lake'-law'yer** (*U.S.*), the bowfin: the burbot; **Lake poets, Lake school,** Wordsworth, Coleridge, and Southey, dwellers in the Lake District. [M.E. *lac,* either—O.E. *lacu,* stream (see next word), confused in sense with L. *lacus,* lake, or from *lacus* itself, directly or through Fr. *lac.*]

**lake,** *lāk,* (*obs.*) *n.* a small stream or water-channel. [O.E. *lacu.*]

**lake, laik,** *lāk,* (*N.England*) *v.i.* to sport, play. [O.E. *lācan.*]

**lakh, lac,** *lak, n.* the number 100,000: 100,000 rupees. [Hind. *lākh*—Sans. *laksa,* 100,000.]

**lakin,** *lā'kin,* (*Shak.*) *n.* a shortened form of **ladykin,** dim. of **lady.**

**Lakshmi,** *luksh'mē, n.* in Hindu mythology, Vishnu's consort. [Sans.]

**lalang,** *lä'läng, n.* a coarse grass, *Imperata arundinacea,* of the Malay archipelago. [Malay.]

**lallan,** *lal', läl'ən, adj.* and *n.* a form of **lawland, lowland.**—*n.* (*cap.; pl.*) Broad Scots: a form of Scots developed by modern Scottish writers.

**lallation,** *lal-ā'shən, n.* childish speech: pronouncing of *r* like *l.*—*n.* **lall'ing,** babbling. [L. *lallāre,* to sing lullaby.]

**l'allegro,** *lä-lā'grō,* (It.) the merry, cheerful man.

**lallygag, lolly-,** *lal', lol'i-gag,* (*coll.*), *v.i.* to idle, loiter: to caress, esp. publicly. [Ety. dub.]

**lam,** *lam, v.t.* to beat.—*n.* **lamm'ing,** a thrashing. [Cf. O.E. *lemian,* to subdue, lame, O.N. *lemja,* to beat, lit. lame.]

**lama,** *lä'ma, n.* a Buddhist priest in Tibet.—*ns.* **Lamaism** (*lä'mä-izm*), the religion prevailing in Tibet and Mongolia, being Buddhism corrupted by Sivaism, and by Shamanism or spirit-worship; **La'maist;** **la'masery** (or *lä-mä'sa-ri*), **lamaserai** (*-rī*), a Tibetan monastery. [Tibetan, *blama,* the *b* silent.]

**lamantin,** *lä-man'tin, n.* the manatee. [Fr.]

**Lamarckism,** *lä-märk'izm, n.* the theory of the French naturalist J. B. P. A. de Monet de *Lamarck* (1744-1829) that species have developed by the efforts of organisms to adapt themselves to new conditions—also **Lamarck'ianism.**—*adj.* and *n.* **Lamarck'ian.**

**lamb,** *lam, n.* the young of a sheep: its flesh as a food: lambskin: one simple, innocent or gentle as a lamb.—*v.t.* and *v.i.* to bring forth as sheep: to tend at lambing.—*ns*. lamb'kin, lamb'ling, lamb'ie (*Scot*.), a little lamb.—*adj*. lamb'-like, like a lamb: gentle.—lamb'-ale, a feast at lamb-shearing; lamb'skin, the skin of a lamb dressed with the wool on: the skin of a lamb dressed as leather: a woollen cloth resembling this: a cotton cloth with raised surface and deep nap; lamb's'-lett'uce, corn-salad; lamb's'-wool, fine wool: an old English beverage composed of ale and the pulp of roasted apples, with sugar and spices.—the Lamb, Lamb of God, applied to Christ, in allusion to the paschal lamb and John i. 29. [O.E. *lamb*; Ger. *lamm*, Du. *lam*.]

lambast, *lam-bast'*, *v.t.* to thrash.—Also lambaste (*lam-bāst'*). [Perh. lam and baste.]

lambda, *lam'də*, also (more correctly) labda, *lab'də*, *n*. the Greek letter (Λ, λ) corresponding to Roman *l*: as a numeral, λ' = 30, ,λ = 30,000: used as a symbol for wavelength: the meeting of the sagittal and lambdoid sutures of the skull.—*ns*. lamb'dacism, lab'dacism, a too frequent use of words containing *l*-sounds: faulty pronunciation of the sound of *l*: a defective pronunciation of *r*, making it like *l*.—*adjs*. lamb'doid, -al, shaped like the Greek capital Λ —applied in anatomy to the suture between the occipital and the two parietal bones of the skull.—lambda particle, a subatomic particle, the lightest of the hyperons. [Gr. *lambda*, properly *labda*—Heb. *lāmedh*.]

lambent, *lam'bənt*, *adj*. licking: moving about as if touching lightly: gliding over: flickering.— *n*. lam'bency, the quality of being lambent: a flicker.—*adv*. lam'bently.—*adj*. lam'bitive (*obs*.), taken by licking.—*n*. a medicine so taken. [L. *lambĕre*, to lick.]

lambert, *lam'bərt*, *n*. a unit of brightness, one lumen per square centimetre. [After J. H. Lambert (1728-77), German physicist, etc.]

Lambeth degree, *lam'bəth*, a degree conferred by the Archbishop of Canterbury, whose palace is at *Lambeth*.

lamboys, *lam'boiz*, (*ant*.) *n.pl*. kilted flexible steelplates worn skirt-like from the waist. [Perh. Fr. *lambeaux*, flaps; or a blunder for *jambeaux*.]

lambrequin, *lam'bər-kin*, or -*bri-kin*, *n*. a veil over a helmet: mantling: a strip of drapery over a window, doorway, from a mantelpiece, etc. [Fr.]

lame, *lām*, *adj*. disabled, esp. in the use of a leg: hobbling: unsatisfactory: imperfect.—*v.t.* to make lame: to cripple: to render imperfect.— *adv.* lame'ly.—*n*. lame'ness.—*adj*. lam'ish, a little lame: hobbling.—lame duck (see duck, 3). [O.E. *lama*, lame; Du. *lam*, Ger. *lahm*.]

lame, *lām*, *n*. a thin plate, esp. of metal, as in armour.—*n*. lamé, *lä'mā*, a fabric in which metal threads are interwoven. [Fr.,—L. *lāmina*, a thin plate.]

lamella, *lə-mel'ə*, *n*. a thin plate or layer:—*pl*. lamell'ae (-*ē*).—*adjs*. lamell'ar (or *lam'i-lər*), lam'ellate (or -*el'*), -d, lamell'iform, lamell'oid, lamell'ose.—*n*. lamell'ibranch (-*brangk*; L. *branchiae*, gills), any member of the Lamellibranchiā'ta, Pelecypoda, or bivalve molluscs, from their plate-like (nutritive) gills.—*adj*. lamellibranch'iate.—*n*. lamell'icorn (L. *cornū*, horn), a member of the Lamellicor'nes, a very numerous group of beetles—the cockchafer, etc., with the ends of the antennae expanded in flattened plates.—*adj*. lamelliros'tral (L. *rōstrum*, beak), having transverse lamellae within the edge of the bill. [L. *lāmella*, dim. of *lāmina*.]

lament, *lə-ment'*, *v.i.* to utter grief in outcries: to wail: to mourn.—*v.t.* to mourn for: to deplore.—*n*. sorrow expressed in cries: an elegy or dirge: a musical composition of like character.—*adj*. lamentable (*lam'ənt-ə-bl*), deserving of expressing sorrow: sad: pitiful: worthless

(*coll*.).—*adv*. lam'entably.—*n*. lamentā'tion, act of lamenting: audible expression of grief: wailing: (*cap*.; *pl*.) a book of the Old Testament traditionally attributed to Jeremiah.—*adj*. lament'ed.—*n*.and *adj*. lament'ing.—*adv*. lament'ingly. [L. *lāmentāri*.]

lameter, lamiter, *lām'i-tər*, (*Scot*.) *n*. a cripple. [Obscurely derived from lame.]

lamia, *lā'mi-ə*, *n*. in Greek and Roman mythology, a blood-sucking serpent-witch. [Gr. and L. *lāmiā*.]

lamiger, lammiger, *lam'i-jər*, (*dial*.) *n*. a cripple. [Cf. lameter.]

lamina, *lam'i-nə*, *n*. a thin plate or layer: a leafblade: a thin plate of bone: a plate of sensitive tissue within a hoof:—*pl*. laminae (-*nē*).—*adjs*. lam'inable, suitable for making into thin plates; lam'inar, lam'inary, consisting of or like thin plates or layers: of or relating to a fluid, streamlined flow.—*n*. Laminā'ria, the tangle genus of brown seaweeds, with large expanded leathery fronds.—*adj*. laminār'ian.—*v.t.* lam'inarise, -ize, to make (a surface, etc.) such that a flow over it will be laminar.—*adj*. lam'inate, -d, in laminae or thin plates: consisting of scales or layers, over one another: made by laminating.—*v.t.* lam'inate, to make into a thin plate: to separate into layers: to make by putting layers together. —*n*. a laminated plastic, or other material similarly made.—*n*. laminā'tion, arrangement in thin layers: a thin layer.—laminar flow, viscous flow: a fluid flow in which the particles move smoothly without turbulence, esp., as in aircraft, such a non-impeding flow over a streamlined surface (*phys*.); laminated plastic, sheets of paper, canvas, linen, or silk, impregnated with a resin, dried and pressed together. [L. *lāmina*, a thin plate.]

Lammas, *lam'əs*, *n*. the feast of first fruits on 1st August.—Lamm'as-tide, season of Lammas. [O.E. hlāf-mæsse, hlāmmæsse—hlāf, loaf, mæsse, feast.]

lammer, *lam'*, *lam'ər*, (*Scot*.) *n*. amber. [Fr. *l'ambre*, the amber.]

lammergeier, lammergeyer, *lam'ər-gī-ər*, *n*. the great bearded vulture of southern Europe, etc. [Ger. *lämmergeier—lämmer*, lambs, *geier*, vulture.]

lammy, lammie, *lam'i*, *n*. a thick quilted jumper worn in cold weather by sailors. [Perh. lamb.]

lamp, *lamp*, *n*. a vessel for burning oil with a wick, and so giving light: any structure containing a source of artificial light: any source of light: an eye (*arch*. and *slang*).—*v.i.* (*Spens*.) to shine.—*v.t.* to illumine: to supply with lamps. —*ns*. lamp'ad, a lamp, candlestick, or torch; lamp'adary, in the Greek Church, one who looks after the lamps and carries a lighted taper before the patriarch: a candelabrum; lampaded'romy, lampadephor'ia (Gr. *lampadēdromiā*, *lampadēphoriā*), an ancient Greek torch-race; lamp'adist, a runner in a torch-race; lamp'adomancy (Gr. *manteiā*, divination), divination by flame.—*adj*. lamp'ing, shining.—*n*. lamp'ion, an oil lamp, often in a coloured glass pot for illuminations.—lamp'-black, soot from a lamp, or from the burning of bodies rich in carbon (mineral oil, turpentine, tar, etc.) in a limited supply of air: a pigment made from it.—*v.t.* to blacken with lamp-black.—lamp'-burner, that part of a lamp from which the flame proceeds; lamp'-chimney, lamp'-glass, a glass funnel placed round the flame of a lamp; lamp'-fly (*Browning*), perh. a glow-worm, or a firefly; lamp'holder, a socket for an electric bulb; lamp'hole, a shaft for lowering a lamp into a sewer; lamp'-hour, the energy required to maintain a lamp for an hour; lamp'light, the light shed by a lamp or lamps; lamp'lighter, a person employed to light street-lamps: a spill or other means of

founded in Ireland in 1879, to procure reduction of rents and to promote peasant-proprietorship—suppressed 1881; land'-line, overland line of communication or transport.—*adj.* land'-locked, almost or quite shut in by land: cut off from the sea.—land'lord, a man who has tenants or lodgers: the master of an inn; land'lordism, the authority, policy, behaviour, or united action of the landowning class: the system of land-ownership; land'-lubber, (*naut.*; in contempt) a landsman.—*adj.* land'lubberly.—land'-man, a countryman: a landsman; land'mark, any land-boundary mark: any conspicuous object on land marking a locality or serving as a guide: an event of outstanding moment in history, thought, etc.; land'-measure, a system of square measure used in measuring land; land'-measuring, determination of superficial extent of land; land'-mine, a mine laid on or near the surface of the ground, to explode when an enemy is over it: a large bomb dropped by parachute; land'owner, one who owns land; land'-ownership.—*adj.* land'-owning.—land'-pilot (*Milt.*), one skilled in finding his way by land; land'-pirate, a highway robber: one who swindles sailors in port: a piratical publisher (*obs.*); land'-plane, an aeroplane that rises from and alights on land; land'rail, the corncrake; land'-rat, a rat properly so called, not a water-rat: a thief by land, distinguished from a pirate; land'-reeve, a land-steward's assistant; land'-roll, a clod-crusher; land'-rover, Ⓡ sturdy motor-vehicle used for driving over rough ground; land'-scrip (*U.S.*), negotiable government certificate entitling to acquisition of public land; land'-shark, a land-grabber: one who plunders sailors on shore: a lean breed of hog (*U.S.*); land'-ship, a land vehicle having certain properties of a ship—e.g. a tank; land'skip, (same as landscape); land'slide, a landslip (orig. *U.S.*): a great transference of votes; land'slip, a fall of land or rock from a hillside or cliff: a portion so fallen; lands'man, one who lives or serves on land: one inexperienced in seafaring; land'-spring, a shallow intermittent spring; land'-steward, a person who manages a landed estate; land'-survey'ing, measurement and mapping of land; land'-survey'or; land'-tax, a tax upon land; land'-val'ue, (usu. in *pl.*) the economic value of land, a basis of taxation; land'-waiter, a custom-house officer who attends on the landing of goods from ships; land'wind, a wind blowing off the land; land-yacht(ing) (see yacht).—land with, to encumber with (a burden, difficult situation, etc.); see how the land lies, find out in advance how matters stand. [O.E. *land*; Du., Ger. *land*.]

land, *land*, (*obs.*) *n.* Same as laund.

land, *land*, (*U.S.*) *n.* and *interj.* euphemism for lord.

landamman(n), *land'am-an*, (Ger. *länt'äm-än*), *n.* the chief magistrate in some Swiss cantons. [Ger. *landammann*—*land*, land, and *amtmann*, bailiff—*amt*, office, and *mann*, man.]

landau, *lan'dö*, *n.* a carriage with folding top.—*n.* landaulet', -ette', a motor-car whose enclosed part can be uncovered: a small landau. [*Landau* in Germany, where it is said to have been first made.]

landdamne, *land-dam'*, (*Shak.*) *v.t.* said to mean to abuse with violence (perh. a misprint for *lamdamn* or *lame-damn*).

landdros(t), *lunt'dros(t)*, (*S.Afr.*) *n.* a district magistrate or sheriff. [Du.,—*land*, land, *drost*, a bailiff.]

lande, *läd*, *n.* a heathy plain or sandy tract (now forested) along the coast in S.W. France. [Fr.]

landgrave, *land'gräv*, *n.* a German count with jurisdiction over a territory: later a mere title:—*fem.* landgravine (*land'grə-vēn*).—*n.* landgrä'-

viate, the territory of a landgrave. [Ger. *landgraf*—*land*, land, *graf*, count.]

ländler, *lent'lər*, *n.* a South German dance, or its tune, like a slow waltz. [Ger.,—*Landl*, a nickname for Upper Austria.]

land-louper, *land'lowp-ər*, landloper. land-loper, *-löp-ər*, *n.* a vagabond or vagrant. [Du. *land-looper*—*land*, land, *loopen*, to ramble; cf. Ger. *landläufer*.]

landscape, *land'skäp*, *n.* the appearance of that portion of land which the eye can view at once: the aspect of a country, or a picture representing it: the painting of such pictures.—*v.t.* to improve by landscape-gardening.—Also *v.i.*—land'scape-gar'dening, the art of laying out grounds so as to produce the effect of a picturesque landscape; land'scape-mar'ble, a limestone with dendritic markings; land'scape-paint'er, land'scapist, a painter of landscapes; land'scape-paint'ing. [Du. *landschap*, from *land* and *-schap*, suffix = *-ship*.]

landsknecht, *länts'knehht*, (*hist.*) *n.* a mercenary foot-soldier of the 16th century. [Ger.,—*lands*, gen. of *land*, country, *knecht*, servant, soldier.]

Landsmaal, -mål, *läns'möl*, *n.* a literary language based on Norwegian dialects by Ivar Aasen (1850), now called Nynorsk, new Norse. [Norw.,—*land*, land, *maal*, speech.]

Landsting, Landsthing, *läns'ting*, *n.* the upper house of the Danish Rigsdag or parliament: a Swedish provincial council. [Dan. and Sw.—*land*, land, *t(h)ing*, parliament.]

Landsturm, *länt'shtŏŏrm*, *n.* a general levy in time of national emergency: the force so called out. [Ger.,—*land*, land, country, *sturm*, alarm.]

Landtag, *länt'tähh*, *n.* the legislative assembly of a German state or land: the Diet of the Holy Roman Empire, or of the German Federation: formerly the provincial assembly of Bohemia or Moravia. [Ger.,—*land*, country, *tag*, diet, day.]

Landwehr, *länt'vär*, *n.* an army reserve. [Ger.,—*land*, land, *wehr*, defence.]

lane, *län*, *n.* a narrow passage or road: a narrow street: a passage through a crowd or among obstructions: a division of a road for a single stream of traffic: a channel: a sluggish stream (*Scot.*): a prescribed course.—Red Lane, the throat, gullet. [O.E. *lane*, *lone*.]

lane, *län*, a Scottish form of lone.—my lane, his lane, etc., alone.

lang, a Scottish form of long.—*adv.* lang syne (*sin*), long since, long ago.—*n.* time long past.

langaha, *läng-gä'ha*, *n.* a Madagascan woodsnake, with a long flexible snout. [Perh. Malagasy.]

langlauf, *läng'lowf*, *n.* cross-country skiing. [Ger. *lang*, long and *lauf*, race, run, leap.]

Langobard, *lang'gō-bärd*. See Lombard.

langouste, *lä-gōōst*, *n.* the spiny lobster. [Fr.]

langrage, langridge, *lang'grij*, *n.* shot consisting of a canister containing irregular pieces of iron, formerly used to damage sails and rigging.—Also langrel (*lang'grəl*) (*obs.*). [Origin unknown.]

Langshan, *lang'shan*, *n.* a small black Chinese hen. [From a place near Shanghai.]

langspel, langspiel, *läng'späl*, *-spēl*, *n.* an old Shetland cithern. [Norw. *langspill*—*lang*, long, *spill*, play, instrument.]

language, *lang'gwij*, *n.* human speech: a variety of speech or body of words and idioms, esp. that of a nation: mode of expression: diction: any manner of expressing thought or feeling: an artificial system of signs and symbols, with rules for forming intelligible communications, for use in e.g. a computer: a national branch of one of the religious and military Orders, e.g. the Hospitallers.—*v.t.* (*arch.*) to express in language.—*adjs.* lang'uaged, skilled or rich in or having language; **lang′uageless** (*Shak.*), speechless, silent.—**language laboratory**, a room in which pupils in separate cubicles are taught a language by means of material recorded on tapes.—**bad language**, swearing; **dead language**, one no longer spoken, as opp. to **living language**; **the language**, Gaelic; **to speak the same language**, to come within one's range of understanding: to have the same tastes or habit of mind. [Fr. *langage*—*langue*—L. *lingua*, the tongue.]

**langued**, *langd*, (*her.*) *adj.* having a tongue (of this or that tincture). [Fr. *langue*—L. *lingua*, tongue.]

**Langue d'oc**, *läg dok*, a collective name for the Romance dialects of southern France—the tongue of the troubadours, often used as synonymous with Provençal, one of its chief branches. The name itself survived in the province *Languedoc*, giving name to a class of wines.—*adj.* **Languedocian** (*lang-gə-dō′shi-ən*).—**Langue d'oïl** (*läg do-ēl, doïl*), also **Langue d'oui** (*dwē*), the Romance dialect of northern France, the language of the trouvères, the main element in modern French. [O.Fr. *langue*—L. *lingua*, tongue; *de*, of; Prov. *oc*, yes—L. *hŏc*, this; O.Fr. *oïl, oui*, yes—L. *hŏc illud*, this (is) that, yes.]

**languet, languette**, *lang′gwet*, *-get*, *-get′*, *n.* a tongue-like object or part. [Fr. *languette*, dim. of *langue*, tongue.]

**languid**, *lang′gwid*, *adj.* slack: flagging: inert: listless: faint: relaxed: spiritless.—*adj.* **languescent** (*-gwes′ənt*), growing languid.—*adv.* **lang′uidly**.—*n.* **lang′uidness**. [L. *languidus*—*languēre*, to be weak.]

**languish**, *lang′gwish*, *v.i.* to become or be languid, inert, depressed: to lose strength and animation: to pine: to flag, droop: to look languishingly.—*n.* (*Shak.*) languishing: languishment.—*adj.* **lang′uished**, sunken in languor.—*ns.* **lang′uisher; lang′uishing**.—*adj.* expressive of languor, or merely sentimental emotion: lingering.—*adv.* **lang′uishingly**.—*n.* **lang′uishment**, the act or state of languishing: tenderness of look. [Fr. *languiss-* (serving as part. stem of *languir*) —L. *languēscēre*—*languēre*, to be faint.]

**languor**, *lang′gər*, *n.* affliction (*obs.*): pining: languidness: listlessness: lassitude: dreamy inertia: tender softness.—*adj.* **lang′uorous**, full of or expressing languor: languishing. [L. *languor, -ōris*.]

**langur**, *lung-gōōr′*, *n.* the entellus monkey or other of its genus. [Hindi *lāgūr*.]

**laniary**, *lä′ni-ər-i*, *adj.* fitted for tearing. [L. *laniārius*, of a butcher—*lanius*, a butcher.]

**laniferous**, *lan-if′ər-əs*, *adj.* wool-bearing.—Also **lanigerous** (*-ij′*). [L. *lānifer, lāniger*—*lāna*, wool, *ferre, gerĕre*, to bear.]

**lank**, *langk*, *adj.* flabby: drooping: flaccid: limp: thin: (of hair) straight and flat.—*v.t.* and *v.i.* (*Shak.*) to make or become lank.—*n.* **lank′iness**.—*adv.* **lank′ly**.—*n.* **lank′ness**.—*adj.* **lank′y**, lean, tall, and ungainly: long and limp. [O.E. *hlanc*.]

**lanner**, *lan′ər*, *n.* a kind of falcon, esp. the female. —*n.* **lann′eret**, the male lanner. [Fr. *lanier*, possibly—L. *laniārius*, tearing, or from *lānārius*, a weaver (a mediaeval term of reproach).]

**lanolin(e)**, *lan′ō-lin, -lēn*, *n.* fat from wool, a mixture of palmitate, oleate, and stearate of cholesterol. [L. *lāna*, wool, *oleum*, oil.]

**lansquenet**, *lans′kə-net*, *n.* a landsknecht: a card game. [Fr.,—Ger. *landsknecht*.]

**lant**, *lant*, *n.* stale urine, used in wool-scouring. [O.E. and O.N. *hland*.]

**lant**, *lant*. Same as **launce** (3).

**Lantana**, *lan-tä′nə*, or *-tä′*, *n.* a showy-flowered genus of shrubs of the vervain family.

**lanterloo**, *lant′ər-lōō*, (*obs.*) *n.* a card game, an-

cestral form of loo. [Fr. *lanturlu* (a meaningless refrain).]

**lantern**, *lant′ərn*, *n.* a case for holding or carrying a light: the light-chamber of a lighthouse: a **magic lantern**: an open structure like a lantern, esp. one surmounting a building, giving light and air.—*v.t.* to furnish with a lantern.—*n.* **lant′ernist**, one who works a magic lantern.— **lantern fly**, any insect of the homopterous family Fulgoridae, with a lantern-like proboscis, formerly thought to give out light.— *adj.* **lan′tern-jawed**, hollow-faced.—**lantern jaws**, thin long jaws; **lantern slide**, a transparent slip with a picture to be projected by a magic lantern or slide projector.—**lantern of the dead**, a lighted tower, once common in French cemeteries. [Fr. *lanterne*—L. *lanterna*—Gr. *lamptēr*—*lampein*, to give light.]

**lanthanum**, *lan′thə-nəm*, *n.* the metallic element of atomic number 57 (La).—*n.pl.* **lan′thanides**, the rare-earth elements.—**lanthanum glass**, optical glass used for high-quality photographic lenses, etc. [Gr. *lanthanein*, to escape notice, because it lay hid in rare minerals till 1839.]

**lanthorn**, *obs.* spelling of **lantern**, based on folk etymology, from the old use of horn for lanterns.

**lantskip**, *lant′skip*, (*Milt.*) *n.* Same as **landscape**.

**lanugo**, *lan-ū′gō*, *n.* down: an embryonic woolly coat of hair.—*adjs.* **lanū′ginose** (*-jin-*), **lanū′ginous**, downy: covered with fine soft hair. [L. *lānūgō, -inis*, down—*lāna*, wool.]

**lanx**, *langks*, (*ant.*) *n.* a platter:—*pl.* **lances** (*lan′sēz*). [L.]

**lanyard, laniard**, *lan′yərd*, *n.* a short rope used as a fastening or handle (*naut.*): a cord for hanging a knife, whistle, or the like about the neck. [Fr. *lanière*, origin doubtful; confused with **yard**.]

**lanzknecht**, an erroneous form of **landsknecht** (as if from Ger. *lanze*, lance.)

**Laodicean**, *lā-od-i-sē′ən*, *adj.* lukewarm in religion, like the Christians of *Laodicea* (Rev. iii. 14-16).—*n.* **Laodicē′anism**. [Gr. *Lāodikeia*, Laodicea.]

**Laotian**, *la-ō′shən*, *adj.* of Laos or its people.—*n.* a native of Laos.

**lap**, *lap*, *v.t.* to scoop up with the tongue (often with *up*): to take in greedily or readily (*fig.*) (usu. with *up*): to wash or flow against.—*v.i.* to drink by licking up: to make a sound or movement as of lapping:—*pr.p.* **lapp′ing**; *pa.t.* and *pa.p.* **lapped**.—*n.* a motion or sound of lapping: that which may be lapped: thin liquor.—*n.* and *adj.* **lapp′ing**. [O.E. *lapian*; L.G. *lappen*; L. *lambĕre*, to lick; Gr. *laptein*.]

**lap**, *lap*, *n.* a flap: a lobe (of the ear): a fold: part of a garment disposed to hold or catch: the fold of the clothes and body of a person sitting: place where one is nurtured (*fig.*; in phrases): a round, as of a race-course, or of anything coiled: an overlap: amount of overlap (in slating, over the next but one): in a steamengine, the distance the valve has to move from mid position to open the steam or exhaust port: in euchre, etc., points carried over to another game: a polishing disk, cylinder, or the like.— *v.t.* to wrap, enfold, surround: to lay overlappingly: to polish with a lap: to unite accurately: to get or be a lap ahead of: to traverse as a lap or in laps: to hold in the lap.—*v.i.* to lie with an overlap: to overlap: to extend beyond some limit.—*ns.* **lap′ful; lapp′er**, one who wraps or folds: a machine that compacts scutched cotton into a fleece upon a roller called a **lap-roller**.—*n.* and *adj.* **lapp′ing.—lap′board**, a flat wide board resting on the lap, used by tailors and seamstresses; **lap′dog**, a small dog fondled in the lap: a pet dog.—*adj.* **lap′-joint′ed**, having joints formed by overlapping edges.—**lap'stone**, a stone held in the lap to hammer leather on; **lap'streak**, a clinker-built boat.—Also *adj.*—**lap'work**, lap-jointed work. —**lap of honour**, a ceremonial circuit of field, track, show ring, made by the victor(s) in a contest; **the lap of luxury**, luxurious conditions; **in the lap of the gods**, of a situation, such that the result cannot be predicted. [O.E. *læppa*, a loosely hanging part; Ger. *lappen*, a rag.]

**lap**, *läp* or *lap*, Scots *pa.t.* of **leap** (1).

**lap, lappie**, form. **lapje**, *lap*, *lap'i*, (*S.Afr.*) *n.* a rag or clout. [Afrik.,—Du. *lap*, rag, patch.]

**laparotomy**, *lap-ə-rot'ə-mi*, *n.* surgical cutting of the abdominal wall. [Gr. *laparā*, flank, *tomē*, cutting.]

**lapel** (*obs.* **lappel**), *la-*, *lə-pel'*, *n.* part of a coat folded back continuing the collar.—*adj.* **lapelled'**. [Dim. of **lap** (2).]

**lapis**, *lap'is*, *n.* a stone (the Latin word, used in certain phrases only, as *lapis philosophicus*, the philosophers' stone, *lapis ollaris*, potstone).—*adj.* **lapidār'ian**, pertaining to stones: inscribed on stones: learned in stones.—*ns.* **lap'idarist** (*-ə-rist*), an expert in gems; **lap'idary** (*-ə-ri*), a cutter of stones, esp. gem-stones: a treatise on gems (*obs.*): an expert in gems (*obs.*).—*adj.* pertaining to stones: dwelling in stone-heaps (as a kind of bee): inscribed on stone: suitable for inscription.—*v.t.* **lap'idate** (*arch.*), to pelt with stones. — *n.* **lapidā'tion**, stoning. — *adj.* **lapid'eous**, stony.—*n.* **lapidesc'ence** (*arch.*).—*adj.* **lapidesc'ent** (*arch.*), becoming stone: petrifying.—*adjs.* **lapidic'olous** (L. *colēre*, to inhabit), living under or among stones; **lapidif'ic** (*arch.*). —*n.* **lapidificā'tion** (*arch.*).—*v.t.* and *v.i.* **lapid'ify** (*arch.*), to turn into stone:—*pr.p.* **lapid'ifying**; *pa.t.* and *pa.p.* **lapid'ified**.—*n.pl.* **lapilli** (*lä-pil'lē*), small fragments (in size from a pea to a walnut) of lava ejected from a volcano (*pl.* of It. *lapil'lo*; also of L. *lapill'us*).—*adj.* **lapill'iform**.—**lap'is-laz'üli**, a beautiful stone consisting of calcite and other minerals coloured ultramarine by lazurite, haüyne, and sodalite, commonly spangled with iron pyrites (see **azure, lazulite, lazurite**).— **lapis-lazuli blue**, a deep blue, sometimes veined with gold, used in decoration and in porcelain; **lapis-lazuli ware**, a pebble ware veined with gold upon blue. [L. *lapis*, *-idis*, a stone.]

**Lapith**, *lap'ith*, *n.* one of a people of Thessaly who fought with the Centaurs:—*pl.* **-ae** or **-s**.

**lapje**. See **lap** (4).

**Lapp**, *lap*, **Lap'lander**, *-ləndər*, *ns.* a native or inhabitant of Lapland: one of the race or people inhabiting Lapland.—*adjs.* **Lapp, Lap'landish; Lapp'ish**.—*ns.* the language of the Lapps.

**lapper**. See **lopper**.

**lappet**, *lap'it*, *n.* a little lap or flap.—*adj.* **lapp'eted**. —**lapp'et-head** (*obs.*), a head-dress with lappets; **lappet moth**, a moth of the Sasiocampidae whose caterpillar has lappets on its sides. [Dim. of **lap** (2).]

**lappie**. See **lap** (4).

**lapse**, *laps*, *v.i.* to slip or glide: to pass by degrees: to fall away by cessation or relaxation of effort or cause: to fall from the faith: to fail in virtue or duty: to pass into disuse: to pass or fail owing to some omission or non-fulfilment: to become void.—*v.t.* (*Shak.*), to catch in a lapse (perh. with associations of *lap* or *latch*).—*n.* a slip: a gliding (*arch.*): passage (of time): a falling away: a failure (in virtue, attention, memory, etc.): a vertical gradient as of atmospheric temperature.—*adjs.* **laps'able**, liable to lapse; **lapsed**, having slipped or passed or been let slip: fallen away (esp. in the Christian Church, from the faith).—**lapse rate** (*meteor.*), rate of change in temperature in relation to height in the atmosphere. [L. *lāpsāre*, to slip, *lāpsus*, *lāpsus*, to slip.]

**lapsus**, *lap'səs*, *lap'soūs*, (L.) a slip.—**lapsus calami** (*kal'ə-mi*, *ka'la-mē*), a slip of the pen; **lapsus linguae** (*ling'gwē*, *'gwi*), a slip of the tongue; **lapsus memoriae** (*me-mōr'i-ē* or *mör'* or *'ri-i*), a slip of the memory.

**Laputa**, *lä-pū'tə*, *n.* a flying island in Swift's *Gulliver's Travels*, inhabited by people who engaged in ridiculous projects.—*ns.* **Lapu'tan, Lapu'tian** (*-shən*), an inhabitant of Laputa.— *adjs.* absurd: chimerical.

**lapwing**, *lap'wing*, *n.* a bird of the plover family, the peewit. [M.E. *lappewinke*—O.E. *læpewince*, *hlēapewince*, *hlēapewince*: modified by folk ety.]

**lar**, *lar*, *n.* the god of a house (orig. prob. a field god):—*pl.* **lares** (*lā'rēz*; L. *lä'räs*). [L. *lar*.]

**larboard**, *lär'bōrd*, *-börd*, *läb'ərd*, (*obs.*) *n.* and *adj.* port or left. [M.E. *laddeborde*, influenced by **starboard**; origin unknown.]

**larceny**, *lär'sə-ni*, *n.* the legal term in England and Ireland for stealing: theft.—*ns.* **lar'cener**, **lar'cenist**, a thief.—*adj.* **lar'cenous**.—*adv.* **lar'cenously**.—**grand larceny**, in England before 1827, larceny of property of the value of one shilling or more, as opposed to **petty larceny**, larceny of property less in value than one shilling; **simple larceny**, as opposed to **compound larceny**, is larceny uncombined with aggravating circumstances. [O.Fr. *larrecin* (Fr. *larcin*)—L. *latrōcinium—latrō*, a robber.]

**larch**, *lärch*, *n.* any tree of the coniferous genus Larix, distinguished from cedar by the deciduous leaves.—*adj.* (*rare*) **larch'en**. [Ger. *lärche*—L. *larix*, *-īcis*.]

**lard**, *lärd*, *n.* the rendered fat of the hog.—*v.t.* to smear or enrich with lard: to stuff with bacon or pork: to fatten: to mix with anything: to stuff or load: to interlard, interpenetrate: to garnish, strew.—*v.i.* (*Shak.*) to be intimately mixed.—*adj.* **lardā'ceous**.—*n.* **lar'don, lardoon'**, a strip of bacon used for larding.—*adj.* **lar'dy**. [O.Fr.,—L. *lāridum*, *lārdum*; cf. Gr. *lārinos*, fat, *lāros*, pleasant to taste.]

**lardalite**. See **laurdalite**.

**larder**, *lärd'ər*, *n.* a place where food is kept: stock of provisions.—*n.* **lard'erer**, one in charge of a larder. [O.Fr. *lardier*, bacon-tub; see **lard**.]

**lare**, *lär*, a Northern form of **lore**; also a Spenserian form of **lair** (pasture).

**lares et penates**, *lä'rēz et pe-nä'tēz*, *lä'räs et pe-nä'täs*. (L.) household gods: valued personal or household objects.

**Largactil**, *lär-gak'til*, Ⓡ *n.* a tranquillising drug, chlorpromazine.

**large**, *lärj*, *adj.* great in size: extensive: bulky: broad: copious: abundant: generous: magnanimous: loftily affected or pretentious: in a great way: diffuse (*obs.*): (of language) free, licentious (*Shak.*): (of the wind) having a favouring component (*naut.*).—*adv.* before the wind (*naut.*): ostentatiously.—*n.* (*mus.*) an obsolete note, equal to two (or in 'perfect' time three) longs.—*adv.* **large'ly**, in a large manner: in great measure.—*n.* **large'ness**.—*adj.* **larg'ish**, fairly large, rather big.—*adjs.* **large'-hand'ed**, having large hands: grasping (*Shak.*): profuse; **large'-heart'ed**, having a large heart: of liberal disposition or comprehensive sympathies: generous; **large'-mind'ed**, magnanimous: characterised by breadth of view.—**as large as life**, actually, really; **at large**, at liberty: at random: in general: in full: representing the whole area, not a division (*U.S.*); **large paper edition**, a special edition with wider margins. [Fr.,— L. *largus*, abounding.]

**largess, largesse**, *lärj'es*, *n.* a bestowal or distribution of gifts.—*n.* **largition** (*lär-jish'ən*), giving of largess. [Fr. *largesse* and L. *largitiō*, *-ōnis—largus*.]

**largo**, *lär'gō*, (*mus.*) *adj.* broad and slow.—Also

*adv.*—*n.* a movement to be so performed.— *adj.* **larghet′to,** somewhat slow: not so slow as largo.—*n.* a somewhat slow movement. [It.,— L. *largus.*]

**lariat,** *lar′i-ət, n.* a picketing rope, a lasso. [Sp. *la,* the, *reata,* picketing rope.]

**lark,** *lärk, n.* a well-known bird (Alauda) that flies high as it sings: extended to various similar birds.—*v.i.* to catch larks.—*adj.* **lark′-heeled,** having a long hind-claw.—**lark′ing-glass,** an instrument with mirrors used by bird-catchers to dazzle larks; **lark's′-heel,** the Indian cress: the larkspur; **lark′spur,** any plant of the genus Delphinium, from the spurred flowers. [M.E. *laverock*—O.E. *lǣwerce, lāwerce;* Ger. *lerche.*]

**lark,** *lärk, n.* a frolic: a piece of mischief.—*v.i.* to frolic.—*ns.* **lark′er; lark′iness.**—*adjs.* **lark′ish; lark′y** (*coll.*). [Perh. from the preceding (cf. skylarking); some connect it with lake (4).]

**larmier,** *lär′mi-ər, n.* a corona or other course serving as a dripstone (*archit.*): a tear-pit (*zool.*). [Fr.,—*larme*—L. *lacrima,* a tear.]

**larrikin,** *lar′i-kin,* (*Austr.*) *n.* a rough or hooligan. —Also *adj.*—*n.* **larr′ikinism.** [Origin doubtful.]

**larrup,** *lar′əp,* (*coll.*) *v.t.* to flog, thrash. [Cf. Du. *larpen,* thresh vith flails.]

**larum,** *lar′əm, n.* alarm: a noise giving notice of danger.—**lar′um-bell.** [alarm.]

**Larus,** *lār′əs, lär′əs, n.* the principal genus of the gull family (**Laridae,** *lar′i-dē*).—*adj.* **lar′oid.** [L., —Gr. *lāros,* a bird, prob. a gull.]

**larva,** *lär′va, n.* a spectre or ghost: an animal in an immature but active state markedly different from the adult, e.g. a caterpillar:—*pl.* **larvae** (*lär′vē;* L. *-vi*). — *adjs.* **lar′val; lar′vate, -d,** clothed as with a mask; **larvici′dal,** destroying larvae.—*n.* **lar′vicide.**—*adjs.* **lar′viform; larvip′-arous,** giving birth to larvae. [L. *lārva, lārua,* a spectre, a mask.]

**larvikite.** See laurvikite.

**larynx,** *lar′ingks, n.* the upper part of the wind-pipe:—*pl.* **larynges** (*lar′in-jēz,* or *lar′in′jēz*) or **lar′ynxes.**—*adjs.* **laryngal** (*lar-ing′gl*), **laryngeal** (*lar-in′ji-əl*).—*n.* **laryngismus** (*-jiz′məs*), spasm of the larynx.—*adj.* **laryngitic** (*-jit′ik*).—*n.* **laryngitis** (*-ji′tis*), inflammation of the larynx.—*adj.* **laryngological** (*-ing-gə-loj′*).—*ns.* **laryngol′ogist; laryngology** (*-gol′ə-ji*), the science of the larynx; **laryngophony** (*-gof′*), the sound of the voice as heard through the stethoscope applied over the larynx; **laryng′oscope,** a mirror for examining the larynx and trachea.—*adj.* **laryngoscop′ic.** —*ns.* **laryngos′copist; laryngos′copy; laryngot′omy,** the operation of cutting into the larynx. [Gr. *larynx, -yngos.*]

**lasagne,** *lä-zän′yə, n.pl.* flat pieces of pasta: a baked dish of this with tomatoes, cheese, meat. —Also **lasagna.** [It.; sing. *lasagna.*]

**lascar,** *las′kər, -kär,* or *las-kär′, n.* an Oriental (originally Indian) sailor or camp-follower. [Hind. and Pers. *lashkar,* army, or *lashkarī,* a soldier.]

**lascivious,** *lə-siv′i-əs, adj.* wanton: inclining or tending to libidinousness.—*adv.* **lasciv′iously.**— *n.* **lasciv′iousness.** [L.L. *lasciviōsus*—L. *lascivus,* playful.]

**laser,** *lās′ər, n.* silphium (*hist.*): (now) the juice of laserwort.—*ns.* **Laserpicium** (*las-ər-pish′i-əm*), a genus of umbelliferous perennial herbs of Europe, Asia and North Africa; **laserwort,** (*läs′ər-wûrt*), any plant of the genus, esp. herb frankincense (L. *latifolium*): also applied to species of Ferula and Thapsia. [L. *lāser,* the juice of *lāserpicium,* the silphium plant.]

**laser,** *lāz′ər, n.* a device which amplifies an input of light, producing an extremely narrow and intense, monochromatic beam.—*v.i.* **lase** (of a crystal, etc.), to be, or become, suitable for use as a laser. [*Light amplification by stimulated emission of radiation.*]

**lash,** *lash, n.* the flexible part of a whip, or its terminal piece of whipcord: a scourge: an eye-lash: a stroke with a whip or anything pliant: a sweep or flick: a stroke of satire.—*v.t.* to strike with, or as if with, a lash: to dash against: to drive, urge, or work by blows of anything flexible, or figuratively: to whisk or flick with a sweeping movement: to secure with a rope or cord: to scourge with sarcasm or satire: to lavish, squander (*obs.*).—*v.i.* to dash: to make a rapid sweeping movement or onset: to use the whip.—*ns.* **lash′er,** one who lashes or whips: a rope for binding one thing to another; **lash′-ing,** act of whipping: a rope for making things fast: (colloquial, esp. in *pl.*) an abundance of anything.—**lash′-up** (*slang*), a mess, fiasco: an improvisation.—**lash out,** to kick out, fling out, hit out without restraint: to spend extravagantly. [Perh. several different words, with possible connections with latch, lash (2), and lace.]

**lash,** *lash, adj.* slow, slack (*obs.*): soft: insipid. —*n.* **lash′er,** a weir: a waterfall from a weir: a pool below a weir. [M.E. *lasche,* slack— O.Fr. *lasche* (Fr. *lâche,* cowardly)—L. *laxus,* lax.]

**lashkar,** *lash′kär, n.* a camp of Indian soldiers (*obs.*): a body of armed Indian tribesmen, a force. [Hind., army, camp; cf. lascar.]

**Lasiocampidae,** *lā-zi-ō-kamp′i-dē,* or *lā-si-, n.pl.* a family of moths including eggers and lackey-moths. [Gr. *lasios,* woolly, *kampē,* a caterpillar.]

**lasket,** *las′kit, n.* a loop at the foot of a sail, to fasten an extra sail. [Perh. **latchet.**]

**lass,** *las, n.* a girl: a sweetheart: a maid-servant (*Scot.*).—*ns.* (dims.) **lassie** (*las′i*), the ordinary Scots word for a girl; **lass′ock.**—*adj.* **lass′lorn** (*Shak.*), forsaken by one's mistress. [Origin obscure; the association with lad may be accidental.]

**lassitude,** *las′i-tūd, n.* faintness: weakness: weariness: languor. [L. *lassitūdō*—*lassus,* faint.]

**lasso,** *la-sōō′, la′sō, n.* a long rope with a running noose for catching wild horses, etc.:—*pl.* **lasso(e)s′** (or *las′*)—*v.t.* to catch with the lasso: —*pr.p.* **lasso′ing** (or *las′*); *pa.p.* **lassoed** (*las-ōōd′* or *las′*). [S. Amer. pron. of Sp. *lazo*—L. *laqueus,* a noose.]

**lassu,** *losh′ōō, n.* the slow movement of a csárdás. [Hung.]

**last,** *läst, n.* a shoemaker's model of the foot on which boots and shoes are made or repaired.— *v.t.* to fit with a last.—*n.* **last′er,** one who fits the parts of shoes to lasts: a tool for doing so. [O.E. *lǣste,* last, *lāst,* footprint.]

**last,** *läst, v.i.* to continue, endure: to escape failure: remain fresh, unimpaired: to hold out: to survive.—*n.* **last′er,** one who has staying power: a thing that keeps well.—*adj.* **last′ing,** enduring: durable.—*n.* **endurance.**—*adv.* **last′-ingly.**—*n.* **last′ingness.**—**last out,** to last as long as or longer than: to last to the end or as long as is required. [O.E. *lǣstan,* to follow a track, keep on, suffice, last; see foregoing word.]

**last,** *läst, n.* a load, cargo: a varying weight, generally about 4000 lb.—*n.* **last′age,** the lading of a ship: room for stowing goods in a ship: a duty formerly paid for the right of carrying goods, etc. [O.E. *hlæst*—*hladan,* to lade; Ger. *last,* O.N. *hlass.*]

**last,** *läst, adj.* latest: coming or remaining after all the others: final: immediately before the present: utmost: ending a series: most unlikely, least to be preferred.—Also *adv.*—*adv.* **last′ly,** finally.—**last heir,** the person to whom lands escheat for want of other heirs; **last post** (*mil.*), second of two bugle-calls denoting the hour of retiring for the night: farewell bugle-call at military funerals; **last straw** (the straw that

*fāte, fär; mē, hûr (her); mīne; mōte, fôr; mūte; mōōn, fōōt; then (then)* breaks the camel's back), that beyond which there can be no endurance; **last word**, final remark in an argument: final decision: the most up-to-date of its kind (*coll.*).—**at last**, in the end; **at long last**, after long delay; **breathe one's last**, to die; **die in the last ditch**, to fight to the bitter end; **first and last**, altogether; **on one's last legs**, on the verge of utter failure or exhaustion; **put the last hand to**, to finish, put the finishing touch to; **see (hear) the last of**, see (hear) for last time; **the Last Day**, the Day of Judgment; **the Last Supper**, the supper partaken of by Christ and his disciples on the eve of the crucifixion; **the last trump**, the trumpet that will sound at the Last Day (1 Cor. xv. 52); **to the last**, to the end: till death. [O.E. *latost*, superl. of *læt*, slow, late.]

**lat**, *lät, n.* in India an isolated pillar. [Hindi *laṭ.*]

**Latakia**, *lat-ä-kē'a, n.* a Syrian tobacco from *Latakia.*

**latch**, *lach, v.t.* (*Shak.*) probably to moisten, but possibly to fasten (next word).—*n.* (*Scot.*) a mire: a boggy water-channel. [**leach.**]

**latch**, *lach, n.* a door catch lifted from without by a lever or string: a light door-lock, opened from without by a key.—*v.t.* (*obs.*) to seize, take, receive.—*v.t.* and *v.i.* to fasten with a latch.—*ns.* **latch'key**, **latch'-string**, a key, string, for opening a latched door.—**latchkey child**, one who regularly returns home to an empty house; **latch on to** (*coll.*), attach oneself to: gain comprehension of; **on the latch**, not locked, but to be opened by a latch. [O.E. *læccan*, to catch.]

**latchet**, *lach'it,* (*obs.*) *n.* a loop: a thong or lace. [O.Fr. *lachet*, a form of *lacet*, dim. of *laz*; see **lace.**]

**late**, *lāt, adj.* (*comp.* **lāt'er**; *superl.* **lāt'est**) slow (*dial.*): tardy: behindhand: coming, remaining, flowering, ripening, producing, etc., after the due, expected, or usual time: long delayed: far advanced towards the close: deceased: departed: out of office: former: not long past.— Also *adv.*—*adj.* **lāt'ed** (*Shak.*), belated.—*adv.* **late'ly**, recently.—*v.t.* and *v.i.* **lāt'en**, to make or grow late.—*n.* **late'ness**.—*adj.* and *adv.* **lāt'ish**.— **of late**, recently. [O.E. *læt*, slow; Du. *laat*, O.N. *latr*, Ger. *lass*, weary; L. *lassus*, tired.]

**lateen**, *lə-tēn', adj.* applied to a triangular sail, common in the Mediterranean, the Lake of Geneva, etc. [Fr. (*voile*) *latine*—L. *Latinus*, Latin.]

**La Tène**, *la ten, adj.* of a division of the Iron Age exemplified at *La Tène* near Neuchâtel, later than Hallstatt.

**latent**, *lā'tənt, adj.* hid: concealed: not visible or apparent: dormant: undeveloped, but capable of development.—*ns.* **lā'tence**, **lā'tency.**—*adv.* **lā'tently.**—*n.* **lātesc'ence.**—*adj.* **lātesc'ent**, becoming latent.—**latent heat** (see **heat**); **latent period**, the time between stimulus and reaction: that between contracting a disease and appearance of symptoms. [L. *latēns*, -*entis*, pr.p. of *latēre*, to lie hid; Gr. *lanthanein*, to be hidden.]

**lateral**, *lat'ə-rəl, adj.* belonging to the side.—*n.* **laterality** (-*ral'i-ti*), state of belonging to the side: physical one-sidedness, either right or left. —*adv.* **lat'erally.**—**lateral line**, in fishes, a line along the side of the body, marking the position of a sensory organ; **lateral thinking**, thinking which seeks new ways of looking at a problem and does not merely proceed by logical steps from the starting-point of what is known or believed. [L . *laterālis*—*latus, latĕris*, a side.]

**Lateran**, *lat'ə-rən, adj.* pertaining to the Church of St John *Lateran* at Rome, the Pope's cathedral church, on the site of the splendid palace or basilica of Plautius Lateranus (executed A.D. 66). —**Lateran Councils**, five general councils of the Western Church, held in the Lateran basilica (1123, 1139, 1179, 1215, and 1512-17), regarded by Roman Catholics as œcumenical; **Lateran**

**Treaty**, restored the papal state (1929). [L. *Laterānus.*]

**laterigrade**, *lat'ə-ri-grād, adj.* running sideways, like a crab. [L. *latus*, -*eris*, side, *gradus*, step.]

**laterite**, *laʹə-rit, n.* a clay formed by weathering of rocks in a tropical climate, composed chiefly of iron and aluminium hydroxides.—*n.* **laterisā'-tion**, **-izātion**, conversion into laterite. [L. *later*, *latĕris*, a brick.]

**lateritious**, *lat-ə-rish'əs, adj.* brick-red. [L. *latericius*—*later, latĕris*, a brick.]

**latewake**, *lāt'wāk, n.* a mistaken form of **lykewake.**

**latex**, *lā'teks*, (*bot.*) *n.* the milky juice of some plants, e.g. rubber trees.—*adj.* **laticiferous** (*lat-i-sif'ə-rəs*), containing or conveying latex. [L. *lātex, lāticis.*]

**lath**, *läth, n.* a thin slip of wood: a substitute for such a slip, used in slating, plastering, etc.: anything long and thin:—*pl.* **laths** (*lädhz, läths*).—*v.t.* to cover with laths.—*adj.* **lathen** (*läth'ən*).—*n.* **lath'ing**, the act or process of covering with laths: a covering of laths.—*adj.* **lath'y**, like a lath.—**lath'-splitter**, one who splits wood into laths.—**dagger of lath**, the Vice's weapon in the old morality plays. [O.E. *lætt.*]

**lathe**, *lādh, n.* a machine for turning and shaping articles of wood, metal, etc.: the swing-frame of a loom carrying the reed for separating the warp threads and beating up the weft. [Origin doubtful.]

**lathe**, *lādh, n.* a division of Kent. [O.E. *læth*, a district; O.N. *lāth*, landed property.]

**lather**, *läth'ər, lädh'ər, n.* a foam made with water and soap: froth from sweat: state of agitation (*coll.*).—*v.t.* to spread over with lather: to thrash (*coll.*).—*v.i.* to form a lather.—*adj.* **lath'ery**. [O.E. *lēathor*; O.N. *lauthr.*]

**lathi, lathee**, *lä-tē', n.* a heavy stick. [Hind. *lāthī.*]

**Lathyrus**, *lath'i-rəs, n.* the sweetpea genus of Papilionaceae.—*n.* **lath'yrism**, a disease with stiffness and paralysis of the legs among eaters of chickling, but apparently due to admixture of seeds of cultivated vetch. [L.,—Gr. *lathyros*, the chickling vetch.]

**laticlave**, *lat'i-klāv, n.* a broad stripe on a Roman senator's tunic. [L. *lātus*, broad, *clāvus*, a stripe.]

**latifundia**, *lat-i-fun'di-ə, n.pl.* great landed estates. —Also in *sing.* **latifun'dium**, and as It. *pl.* **latifondi** (*lä-tē-fon'dē*). [Pl. of L. *lātifundium*—*lātus*, wide, *fundus*, an estate.]

**Latin**, *lat'in, adj.* pertaining to ancient Latium (esp. Rome) or its inhabitants, or its language, or to those languages that are descended from Latin, or to the peoples speaking them: written or spoken in Latin: Roman Catholic.— *n.* an inhabitant of ancient Latium: the language of ancient Latium, and esp. of Rome: a speaker of a language derived from ancient Latin: a Roman Catholic.—*adj.* **Latian** (*lā'shyən, -shən*) of Latium.—*n.* **Lat'iner**, one who knows Latin: an interpreter (*obs.*).—*v.t.* **Lat'inise**, -**ize**, to turn into or make Latin or like to Latin.—*v.i.* to use Latin idioms or derivatives.—*ns.* **Lat'inism**, a Latin idiom: use or inclination towards use of Latin idioms, words, or ways; **Lat'inist**, one skilled in Latin; **Latin'ity**, the quality of one's Latin.—**Latin America**, those parts of America where Spanish, Portuguese, and French are spoken; **Latin Church**, the Church that uses Latin and recognises the primacy of Rome—the Roman Catholic Church; **Latin cross**, an upright cross with the lowest limb longest; **Latin Empire**, that portion of the Byzantine Empire seized in 1204 by the Crusaders (French and Venetian), and overthrown by the Greeks in 1261; **Latin Kingdom**, the Christian kingdom of Jerusalem ruled by French or Latin kings, and lasting from 1099 to 1187; **Latin Quarter**, the educational and students' quarter of Paris

---

Neutral vowels in unaccented syllables: *el'ə-mənt*; for certain sounds in foreign words, see p. viii

around the Sorbonne (where Latin was spoken in the Middle Ages; Fr. *quartier latin*), famous for its unconventional way of life; **Latin Union**, a monetary union (1865-1926) of France, Belgium, Italy, and Switzerland, with Greece from 1868.—classical Latin, the Latin of the writers who flourished from about 75 B.C. to about A.D. 200; **dog Latin**, barbarous Latin; **Late Latin**, the Latin written by authors between A.D. 200 and *c.* 600; **Low Latin**, Mediaeval, or Late and Mediaeval, Latin; **Middle** or **Mediaeval Latin**, the Latin of the Middle Ages between A.D. 600 and 1500; **New, Modern, Latin**, Latin as written between 1500 and the present time, mostly used as a scientific medium; **thieves' Latin**, thieves' cant. [L. *Latinus*, belonging to *Latium*, the district round Rome.]

**latirostral**, *lat-i-ros'trəl*, *adj.* broad-billed.—Also **latiros'trate**. [L. *lātus*, broad, *rōstrum*, beak.]

**latiseptate**, *lat-i-sep'tāt*, *adj.* having a broad partition. [L. *lātus*, broad, *saeptum*, a fence (used in pl.).]

**latitant**, *lat'i-tənt*, *adj.* lurking: lying in wait: hibernating: dormant.—*n.* **lat'itancy.**—*ns.* **lat'i-tat**, a writ based on the supposition that the person summoned is in hiding; **latitā'tion**. [L. *latitāre*, *-ātum* (3rd pers. sing. *latitat*), freq. of *latēre*, to be in hiding.]

**latitude**, *lat'i-tūd*, *n.* (now chiefly playful) width: a wide extent: range: scope: allowance: breadth in interpretation: extent of signification: freedom from restraint: laxity: angular distance from the equator (*geog.*): a place of specified angular distance from the equator (*geog.*): angular distance from the ecliptic (*celestial latitude*; *astron.*).—*adjs.* **latitūd'inal**, pertaining to latitude: in the direction of latitude; **latitūdinā'rian**, broad or liberal, esp. in religious belief: lax.—*n.* a member of a school of liberal and philosophical theologians within the English Church in the later half of the 17th century: one who regards specific creeds, methods of church government, etc., with indifference.—*n.* **latitūdinā'rianism.**—*adj.* **latitūd'inous**, broad, wide, esp. in interpretation. [L. *lātitūdō*, *-inis*—*lātus*, broad.]

**latration**, *lə-trā'shən*, *n.* barking.—*adj.* **latrant** (*lā'trənt*). [L. *lātrāre*, *-ātum*, to bark.]

**la trenise**. See trenise.

**latria**, *lā-trī'ə*. See dulia. [Gr. *latreiā*—*latreuein*, to serve.]

**latrine**, *lə-trēn'*, *n.* a lavatory, esp. in barracks, etc. [L. *lātrina*—*lavātrina*—*lavāre*, to wash.]

**latrocinium**, *lat-rō-sin'i-əm*, **latrociny**, *lat'rō-sin-i*, (*obs.*) *ns.* highway-robbery: Pope Leo I's name for the 'Robber-Council' at Ephesus in 449, which upheld Eutychianism. [L. *latrōcinium*, robbery.]

**latron**, *lā'tron*, *n.* a robber. [L. *latrō*, *-ōnis.*]

**latten**, *lat'ən*, *n.* brass or similar alloy in former use: tin-plate: metal in thin plates. [O.Fr. *laton* (Fr. *laiton*); of Gmc. origin; cf. **lath.**]

**latter**, *lat'ər*, *adj.* later: coming or existing after: second-mentioned of two: modern: recent: last (*Shak.*).—*adv.* **latt'erly**, towards the latter end, of late.—*adj.* **latt'ermost**, last (O.E. *lætemest*).—*adjs.* **latt'er-born** (*Shak.*), younger; **latt'er-day**, modern: recent.—**latter end**, the final part: the end of life; **latt'ermath**, aftermath; **latt'er-mint** (*Keats*), apparently a late kind of mint; **latt'er-wit** (*U.S.*), a witty thought after the occasion has passed.—**Latter-day Saint**, a Mormon. [O.E. *lætra*, compar. of *læt*, slow, late.]

**lattice**, *lat'is*, *n.* a network of crossed laths or bars, called also **latt'ice-work**: anything of like pattern: a window with lozenge-shaped panes set in lead: a space-lattice: the geometrically regular, three-dimensional arrangement of

fissionable and non-fissionable material in an atomic pile: the regular arrangement of atoms in crystalline material: a system of lines for position-fixing overprinted on a navigational chart: a partially-ordered set in which any two elements have a least upper bound and a greatest lower bound (*math.*).—*v.t.* to form into open work: to furnish with a lattice.—**latt'ice-bridge**, a bridge of lattice-girders; **latt'ice-gird'er**, a girder composed of upper and lower members joined by a web of crossing diagonal bars; **latt'ice-leaf**, the lace-leaf or ouvirandra (*Aponogeton fenestrale*), a water-plant of Madagascar with leaves like open lattice-work.—**red lattice** (*Shak.*), the sign of an ale-house. [Fr. *lattis*—*latte*, a lath.]

**latus rectum**, *lā'tas rek'təm*, *la'tōos rek'tŏom*, a focal chord parallel to the directrix of a conic. [L. *lătus rectum*, right or perpendicular side.]

**Latvian**, *lat'vi-ən*, *adj.* Lettish.—*n.* a native or citizen of Latvia or Lettland. [Lettish *Latvija*, Latvia, Lettland.]

**lauch**, *löhh*, a Scots form of **law** (*Scott*) and of **laugh**, *n.* and *vb.*:—*pa.t.* **leuch**, **leugh** (*lūhh*) *pa.p.* **leuch'en**, **leugh'en**.

**laud**, *löd*, *v.t.* to praise: to celebrate.—*n.* praise: (in *pl.*) in the R.C. Church, the prayers immediately following matins.—*adj.* **laud'able**, praiseworthy.—*n.* **laud'ableness.**—*adv.* **laud'ably.**—*n.* **laudā'tion**, praise: honour paid.—*adjs.* **laud'-ative**, **laud'atory**, containing praise: expressing praise.—*ns.* (*obs.*) eulogy.—*n.* **laud'er.** [L. *laud-āre*—*laus*, *laudis*, praise.]

**laudanum**, *löd'(ə-)nəm*, *n.* tincture of opium. [Coined by Paracelsus; perh. **ladanum**, transferred to a different drug.]

**laugh**, *läf*, *v.i.* to emit explosive inarticulate sounds of the voice, generally, with a smile, heaving of the sides, and other bodily movements, under the influence of amusement, joy, scorn, etc., or of bodily stimulus as tickling: to be amused, make merry about (with *at*): to make fun of (with *at*): to flout (with *at*): to have a cheerful appearance (*fig.*).—*v.t.* to render, put, or drive with laughter: to express by laughter: to laugh at, deride (*Spens.*).—*n.* an act or sound of laughing.—*adj.* **laugh'able**, ludicrous.—*n.* **laugh'ableness.**—*adv.* **laugh'ably.**—*n.* **laugh'er**, one who laughs: a breed of pigeon with laughing note.—*adj.* **laugh'ful**, mirthful.—*n.*, *adj.* **laugh'ing.**—*adv.* **laugh'ingly.**—*adj.* **laugh'-some**, inclined to laugh: provocative of laughter.—*n.* **laugh'ter**, the act or sound of laughing.—*adj.* **laugh'y**, inclined to laugh.—**laugh'ing-gas**, nitrous oxide, which may excite laughter when breathed, used as an anaesthetic, esp. in dentistry; **laugh'ing-jack'ass**, the great kingfisher of Australia; **laugh'ing-stock**, an object of ridicule.—*adj.* **laugh'worthy**, deserving to be laughed at.—**have the laugh of**, to best; **laugh and lie (or lay) down**, an old card-game in which a player lays down his hand on attaining his object; **laugh in one's sleeve**, to laugh inwardly; **laugh on the wrong side of the mouth**, on the other side of the face, be made to feel disappointment or sorrow, esp. after boasting, etc.; **laugh to scorn**, to deride or jeer at. [O.E. (Anglian) *hlæhhan* (W.S. *hliehhan*); Ger. *lachen*, Goth. *hlahjan*.]

**launce**, *löns*, *läns* (*Spens.*). Same as **lance** (1).

**launce**, *löns*, *läns*, (*Spens.*) *n.* a balance. [L. *lanx*, *lancis*, a plate, a scale of a balance.]

**launce**, **lance**, *löns*, *läns*, *n.* a sand eel (*Ammodytes*), an eel-like fish that buries itself in wet sand at ebb-tide.—Also **lant**. [Perh. conn. with **lance** (1).]

**launcegaye**, *löns'gā*, *läns'gā*. Same as **lancegay**.

**launch**, **lanch**, *lönch*, *lönsh*, *länch*, *länsh*, *v.t.* to throw or hurl: to dart: to send forth: to set going: to initiate: to cause or allow to slide into water or to take off from land: to pierce (*Spens.*):

fāte, fär; mē, hûr (her); mīne, mōte, för; mūte, mōōn, fŏŏt; dhen (then) to lance (*obs.*).—*v.i.* to rush, dart, plunge, fling oneself: to be launched: to take off: to throw oneself freely or venturesomely into some activity.—*n.* the act or occasion of launching: a lancing (*Spens.*).—*n.* launch′er, a device for launching, esp. for sending off a rocket.—launch′ing-pad, a platform from which a rocket can be launched.—*n.pl.* launch′ing-ways, the timbers on which a ship is launched.—launch vehicle (see vehicle). [O.Fr. *lanchier, lancier* (Fr. *lancer*); see lance (1).]

launch, *lönch, lönsh, länch, länsh, n.* the largest boat carried by a man-of-war: a large power-driven boat for pleasure or short runs. [Sp. *lancha*, perh. from Malay *lanchār*, swift.]

laund, *lönd*, (*Shak.*) *n.* a glade: a grassy place. [O.Fr. *launde, lande*; prob. Celt.; see lawn.]

launder, *lön′dər, län′, n.* a washerwoman or washerman (*obs.*): a trough for conveying water. —*v.t.* and *v.i.* to wash and iron, as clothes.—*v.i.* to admit of laundering.—*ns.* laund′erer; laun′-dress, a woman who washes and irons clothes; laun′dry, a place where clothes are washed and dressed: clothes for or from the laundry, a wash. —laund′ry-maid; laun′dry-man, a male worker in a laundry: one who runs a laundry. [M.E. *lavander*—O.Fr. *lavandier*—L. *lavandārius*, from the ger. of *lavāre*, to wash.]

launderette, *lön-dər-et′, n.* a shop where customers wash clothes in washing machines. [Orig. trademark.]

Laundromat, *lön′drō-mat, n.* launderette. [Trademark.]

laura, *lö′rə*, lavra, *läv′rə, n.* a group of recluses' cells. [Gr. *laurā* (mod. *labra*, with *b* as *v*), alley, lane, monastery.]

laurdalite, lardalite, *lör′, lär′dəl-it, n.* a coarse nepheline syenite. [*Laurdal* or *Lardal* in Norway.]

laureate, *lö′ri-it, adj.* crowned with laurel.—*n.* one crowned with laurel: a poet-laureate.—*v.t.* (-*āt*) to crown with laurel, in token of literary merit: to confer a degree upon.—*ns.* lau′reate-ship; laurea′tion, crowning with laurel: graduation.—Poet Laureate, formerly one who received a degree in grammar (i.e. poetry and rhetoric) at the English universities: a poet bearing that title in the royal household or in a society. [L. *laureātus*, laurelled—*laurus*, laurel.]

laurel, *lor′əl, n.* sweet bay tree (*Laurus nobilis*), used by the ancients for making honorary wreaths: another species of Laurus found in Madeira and the Canaries: the cherry-laurel: in America any species of Rhododendron or of Kalmia: extended to various trees and shrubs of similar appearance: a crown of laurel: honours gained (often in *pl.*).—*adjs.* lau′rel; lau′relled, crowned, adorned or covered with laurel.—lau′rel-wa′ter, a sedative and narcotic water distilled from cherry-laurel leaves; lauric acid, an acid, $CH_3 \cdot (CH_2)_{10} \cdot COOH$, occurring in the berries of *Laurus nobilis*, etc.; lauryl alcohol, a liquid made by the reduction of coconut oil or its fatty acids, used in the manufacture of detergents; lauryl thiocyanate, a salt of lauryl alcohol used as a disinfectant.—cherry-laurel, Japan laurel, spurge-laurel (see under cherry, Japan, spurge). [Fr. *laurier*—L. *laurus*.]

Laurentian, *lö-ren′sh(y)ən, adj.* pertaining to *Lorenzo* or *Laurentius* de' Medici, or to the library founded by him at Florence: of or pertaining to the river St *Lawrence*: applied to a series of Pre-Cambrian rocks covering a large area in the region of the Upper Lakes of North America.

lauric. See under laurel.

Laurus, *lö′rəs, n.* the laurel genus, giving name to the family Laurā′ceae, leathery-leaved archichlamydeous dicotyledons.—*adj.* laurā′ceous. [L.]

laurustine, laurustinus, *lö′rəs-tin, -ti′nəs, ns.* a winter-flowering shrub (*Viburnum tinus*). [L. *laurus*, laurel, *tinus*, laurustine.]

laurvikite, larvikite, *lör′, lär′vik-it, n.* a soda syenite composed mainly of feldspar with schiller structure. [*Laurvik* or *Larvik* in Norway.]

lauryl. See under laurel.

laus Deo, *lös dē′ō, lows dā′ō*, (L.) praise to God.

lauwine, *lö′win*, (*Byron*) *n.* an avalanche. [Ger. *la(u)wine*, perh.—*lau*, tepid.]

lava, *lä′və, n.* matter discharged in a molten stream from a volcano or fissure, whether still molten or subsequently solidified:—*pl.* la′vas.—*adj.* la′va-form, in the form of lava. [It., poss.—L. *lavāre*, to wash, or from L. *lābes*, a falling down. —*lābi*, to slide, fall.]

lava-lava, *lä′və-lä′və, n.* a rectangular piece of printed cloth worn by both sexes in Polynesia as a kind of skirt. [Samoan, clothing.]

lavallière, lavaliere, *la-va-lyer, lav′ə-lēr, n.* a loosely-tied bow: a jewelled pendant worn round the neck on a chain. [After the Duchesse de *la Vallière* (1644–1710).]

lave, *läv, v.t.* and *v.i.* to wash: to bathe.—*ns.* lavabo (*lav-ä′bō*), in the mass, the ritual act of washing the celebrant's fingers while he says *Lavabo inter innocentes*: a monastic lavatory: a fixed basin or washstand; lavage (*lav′ij, läv-äzh′*; *med.*), irrigation or washing out; lavation (*lav-ä′shən*), washing; lav′atory, a place, room, fixture, or vessel for washing: a laundry: a bowl, usu, with a wooden or plastic seat and flushed by water, used for urination and defecation: a room containing a lavatory and often a wash-basin: a ritual washing: a lotion (*obs.*). —*adj.* lavator′ial.—*ns.* lavement (*läv′*), a washing: a lavage; läv′er, a large vessel for washing, esp. ritual washing: the basin of a fountain (*Spens.*): an ablution (*Milt.*). [L. *lavāre, -ātum*; Gr. *louein*, to wash.]

lave, *läv*, (*Scot.*) *n.* remainder. [O.E. *läf*; O.N. *leif*; see leave.]

lave, *läv, v.t.* to pour out: to bale. [O.E. *lafian*, to pour; fused with L. *lavāre*, to wash.]

laveer, *lä-vēr′*, (*arch.*) *v.i.* to beat to windward. [Du. *laveeren*; cf. luff.]

lavender, *lav′ən-dər, n.* a labiate plant (*Lavandula vera*) with fragrant pale-lilac flowers, yielding a volatile oil: sprigs of it used for perfuming and preserving linen, etc.: the colour of its blossoms. —*adj.* of the colour of lavender flowers.—*v.t.* to sprinkle with lavender.—lav′ender-cott′on, a species of Santolina; lav′ender-wa′ter, a perfume composed of spirits of wine, essential oil of lavender, and ambergris.—lay in lavender, to lay by carefully, with sprigs of lavender: to pawn (*coll.*); oil of lavender, an aromatic oil distilled from lavender flowers and stems, used as a stimulant and tonic. [A.Fr. *lavendre* (Fr. *lavande*)—L.L. *lavandula*, earlier *livendula*, perh. conn. with *lividus*, livid.]

laver. See lave (1).

laver, *läv′ər, n.* edible seaweed of various kinds, esp. Porphyra (*purple laver*) and Ulva (*green laver*). [L. *laver*, a kind of water-plant.]

laverock, *lav′ə-rək*, Scot. *läv′(ə-)rək*, an archaic and dialectal form of lark.

lavish, *lav′ish, n.* (*obs.*) profusion: over-abundance: extravagant outpouring.—*v.t.* to expend or bestow profusely: to waste.—*adj.* bestowing profusely: prodigal: extravagant: unrestrained. —*adv.* lav′ishly.—*ns.* lav′ishment; lav′ishness. [O.Fr. *lavasse, lavache*, deluge of rain—*laver*—L. *lavāre*, to wash.]

lavolt, *lä-volt′*, lavolta, -*ə*, (*Shak.*) *n.* an old dance in which there was much turning and high leaping.—*v.i.* to dance the lavolta. [It. *la volta*, the turn.]

lavra. See laura.

law, *lö, n.* a rule of action established by authority: statute: the rules of a community or state: jurisprudence: established usage: that which is lawful: the whole body of persons connected professionally with the law: litigation: a rule or code in any department of action, as morality, art, honour, arms (including heraldry), a game: a theoretical principle educed from practice or observation: a statement or formula expressing the constant order of certain phenomena: the Mosaic code or the books containing it (*theol.*): a start (*sport*): indulgence (*obs.*).—*v.t.* to go to law with: to determine (*Burns*): to expeditate (*obs.*).—*v.i.* (*obs.*) to go to law.—*adj.* law'ful, allowed by law: rightful.—*adv.* law'fully.—*ns.* law'fulness; law'ing, going to law (*arch.*): expeditation (*obs.*).—*adj.* law'less, not subject to or controlled by law: unruly.—*adv.* law'lessly.—*ns.* law'lessness; law'yer, a practitioner in the law, esp. a solicitor: one learned or skilled in law: an interpreter of the Mosaic law (*N.T.*): a brier, bramble, or other tenacious trailing or climbing plant (see also **Penang-lawyer**).—*adj.* law'yerly.—*adj.* law'-abiding, obedient to the law.—law'-agent (*Scots law*), a solicitor; law'-book, a book treating of law or law cases; law'-breaker, one who violates a law; law'-burrows (*Scots law*), a writ requiring a person to give security against doing violence to another; law'-calf, a book-binding in smooth, pale-brown calf; law'-court, court of justice; law'-day, a day of open court; lawful day, one on which business may be legally done—not a Sunday or a public holiday; law'giver, one who enacts or imposes laws.—*adj.* law'giving.—law Latin, Latin as used in law and legal documents, being a mixture of Latin with Old French and Latin-ised English words; law'-list, an annual book of information about lawyers, courts, etc.; law'-lord, a peer in parliament who holds or has held high legal office: in Scotland, a judge of the Court of Session; law'-maker, a legislator; law'-man, one of a select body with magisterial powers in some of the Danish towns of early England; law'-mer'chant, the customs that have grown up among merchants in reference to mercantile documents and business; law'monger, a low pettifogging lawyer; law'-officer, a legal functionary and adviser of the government, esp. Attorney-General, Solicitor-General, or Lord Advocate; law'-stā'tioner, one who sells parchment and other articles needed by lawyers; law'suit, a suit or process in law; law'-writer, a writer on law: a copier or engrosser of legal papers.—**Boyle's, or Mariotte's, law,** the law that, for a gas at a given temperature, pressure varies inversely as volume—announced by Robert *Boyle* in 1662, and confirmed by Mariotte; **Charles's law,** the law that all gases have the same value for the coefficient of expansion at constant pressure, stated by J. A. C. *Charles* (Fr. physicist, 1746-1823)—also called **Gay-Lussac's law; go to law with,** resort to litigation against; **Gresham's law,** the law that of two forms of currency the inferior or more depreciated tends to drive the other from circulation, owing to the hoarding and exportation of the better form; **Grimm's law,** the law formulating certain changes undergone by Indo-Germanic stopped consonants in Germanic, stated by Jacob *Grimm* (1785-1863); **have the law of, have the law on** (*coll.*), to enforce the law against; **Kepler's laws,** three laws of planetary motion discovered by Johann *Kepler* (1571-1630)—(1) the orbits of the planets are ellipses with the sun at one focus; (2) the areas described by their *radii vectores* in equal times are equal; (3) the squares of their periodic times vary as the cubes of their mean distances from the sun; **law of nations,** now international law, originally applied to those

ethical principles regarded as obligatory on all communities; **law of nature,** the invariable order of nature: natural law; **law of octaves** (see octave); **law of the land,** the established law of a country; **laws of motion** (see motion); **lay down the law,** to state authoritatively or dictatorially; **the law** (*coll.*), the police: a policeman; **Verner's law,** a law stated by Karl *Verner* in 1875, showing the effect of accent in the shifting of Indo-Germanic stopped consonants and *s* in Germanic, and explaining the most important anomalies in the application of Grimm's law. [M.E. *lawe*—late O.E. *lagu,* of O.N. origin, from the same root as lie, lay.]

law, *lö,* (*obs.*) *n.* score, share of expense.—*n.* law'ing (*Scot.*), a tavern reckoning. [O.N. *lag,* market-price.]

law, *lö,* (*Scot.*) *n.* a hill, esp. rounded or conical. [Northern form of low (3), O.E. *hlāw.*]

law, *lö,* (*Scot.*) *adj.* low.—*n.* and *adj.* law'land, lowland. [Northern form of low (2).]

law, *lö, interj.* expressing asseveration (*obs.*): expressing surprise (*dial.*). [Partly for la or lo, partly lord.]

lawk, *lök,* lawks, *löks,* (*dial.*) *interj.* implying surprise. [lord or lack.]

lawn, *lön, n.* a sort of fine linen or cambric: extended to some cottons.—*adj.* made of lawn.—*adj.* lawn'y.—lawn sleeves, wide sleeves of lawn worn by Anglican bishops. [Prob. from *Laon,* near Rheims.]

lawn, *lön, n.* an open space between woods (*arch.*): a smooth space of ground covered with grass, generally beside a house.—*adj.* lawn'y.—lawn'-mower, a machine for cutting grass on a lawn; lawn'-par'ty (*U.S.*), a garden-party; lawn'-sprink'ler, a machine for watering a lawn by sprinkling; lawn-tenn'is, a game derived from tennis, played by one or two a side on an un-walled court (hard or of turf), the aim being to hit the ball over the net and within the court, if possible so as to prevent like return. [laund.]

lawrencium, *lö-ren'si-əm, n.* name given to element 103 (symbol Lr) whose production at Berkeley, California, is claimed. [Ernest O. *Lawrence,* scientist.]

lax, *laks, adj.* slack: loose: soft, flabby: not strict in discipline or morals: loose in the bowels.—*adj.* lax'ative, having the power of loosening the bowels: giving freedom (*arch.*): speaking, expressing itself, freely (*obs.*).—*n.* a purgative or aperient medicine.—*ns.* lax'ativeness; laxā'tor, a muscle that relaxes an organ or part; lax'ism, the view that in morals an opinion only slightly probable may be safely followed; lax'ist, one holding loose notions of moral laws, or of their application; lax'ity, lax'ness.—*adv.* lax'ly. [L. *laxus,* loose.]

lay, *lā, n.* a form of lea (1, 2, 3).

lay, *lā, pa.t.* of lie (2).

lay, *lā, v.t.* to cause to lie: to place or set down: to beat down: to deliver of a child (*obs.*): to spread on a surface: to spread something on: to cover: to apply: to cause to subside: to exorcise: to put below the horizon by sailing away: to deposit: to set on the table: to wager: to put forward: to cause to be: to set: to produce and deposit: to station: to locate: to set in position: to waylay: to beset (*Shak.*): to impose: to attribute, impute: to set material in position for making: to form by setting in position and twisting (as a rope): to design, plan: to layer (*hort.*): to have sexual intercourse with (*slang.*).—*v.i* to produce eggs: to wager, bet: to deal blows: to lie (*arch., naut.,* and *illit.*):—*pr.p.* lay'ing; *pa.t.* and *pa.p.* laid.—*n.* situation, a lying-place: an oyster-bed: mode of lying: disposition, arrangement or plan: a layer: mode of twisting: laying activity: a bet (*Shak.*): a share of profit, esp. in whaling: a field or method of operation, esp. in thieving (*slang*): act of sexual intercourse (*slang*): a partner, usually female, in sexual intercourse (*slang*). —*n*. layer (*lā'ər*), one who or that which lays— e.g. a hen, a bricklayer: (*lār*) a course, bed, or stratum: a distinctively coloured space between contour-lines on a map: a shoot bent down to earth in order to take root.—*v.t.* and *v.i.* to propagate by layers.—*v.t.* to put in layers.—*v.i.* to be laid flat, lodge.—*adj.* lay'ered, in or with layers.—*ns.* lay'ering; lay'ing, the first coat of plaster: the act or time of laying eggs: the eggs laid.—lay'about, a lounger, loafer; lay'away, goods on which a deposit has been paid, kept for a customer until he completes payment (as *vb.* lay away); lay'back, a method of climbing a sharp-edged crack in a horizontal position.— Also *v.i.*—lay'-by, an expansion of a roadway to allow vehicles to draw up out of the stream of traffic:—*pl.* lay'-bys: a deposit against future purchase (also lay'-bye; *S.Afr.*); lay'er-cake, a cake built up in layers; lay'-off, an act or time of discontinuing work; lay'-out, that which is laid out: a display: an outfit: disposition, arrangement, plan, esp. of buildings or ground: the general appearance of a printed page: a set, unit, organisation; lay'-shaft, auxiliary geared shaft in a machine, esp. the secondary shaft in automobile gear-box; lay'-stall, place for depositing dung, rubbish, etc.; lay'-up, time or condition of being laid up.—lay aboard, to run alongside, esp. in order to board; lay about one, to deal blows vigorously or on all sides; lay a course, to succeed in sailing to the place required without tacking; lay aside, away, to discard: to put apart for future use; lay at, to endeavour to strike; lay away (*Scot.*, etc.), to lay eggs in out-of-the-way places; lay bare, to make bare, disclose; lay before, to submit to, as of plans; lay by, to keep for future use: to dismiss: to put off; lay by the heels (see heel); lay down, to give up: to deposit, as a pledge: to apply, as embroidery (*arch.*): to formulate: to assert (law, rule): to store: to plant: to lay on (*print.*); lay hands on (see hand); lay heads together, to confer together; lay hold of, or on, to seize; lay in, to get in a supply of; lay into, to beat thoroughly; lay it on, to charge exorbitantly: to do anything, as to exaggerate, or to flatter, with profuseness; lay off, to mark off: to doff: to harangue volubly: to hedge (*betting*): to discontinue work or activity: to dismiss temporarily: to cease (*coll.*); lay on, to install a supply of: to provide: to deal blows with vigour: to arrange made-up pages in the correct order on the imposing surface (also lay down) (*print.*); lay on hands (see hand); lay oneself out to, to make it one's professed object or practice, take great pains, to; lay on load (*Spens.*), to belabour; lay on the table (see table); lay open, to make bare, to show, expose: to cut open; lay out, to display: to expend: to plan: to dispose according to a plan: to prepare for burial: to fell: to take measures, seek; lay siege to, to besiege: to importune; lay to, to apply with vigour: to bring a ship to rest; lay to heart (see heart); lay under, to subject to; lay up, to store up, preserve: (usu. in *pass.*) to confine to bed or one's room: to put in dock after dismantling; lay upon, to wager upon; lay wait, to lie in wait, or in ambush; lay waste, to devastate; on a lay, on shares instead of wages. [O.E. *lecgan*, to lay, causative of *licgan*, to lie; cf. O.N. *leggja*, Ger. *legen*.]

lay, *lā*, *n*. a short narrative poem: a lyric: a song. [O.Fr. *lai*; origin obscure.]

lay, *lā*, (*arch*.) *n*. law: religious faith. [O.Fr. *lei* (Fr. *loi*)—L. *lēx*, *lēgis*, law.]

lay, *lā*, *adj*. pertaining to the people: not clerical: non-professional: not trumps (*cards*).—*n*. the

laity: a layman (*obs.*).—*adj*. laic (*lā'ik*), lay.—*n*. a layman.—*adj*. lā'ical.—*v.t.* laicise, -ize (*lā'isiz*), to make laical: to open to the laity.—*n*. lā'ity, the people as distinguished from some particular profession, usu. the clerical.—lay baptism, baptism administered by a layman; lay brother, sister, one under vows of celibacy and obedience, who serves a religious house, but is exempt from the studies and choir duties of monks or nuns; lay communion, the state of being in the communion of the church as a layman; lay impropriator, an impropriator who is a layman; lay'man, one of the laity: a non-professional man: one not an expert; lay reader, in the Anglican Church, a layman authorised to read part of the service; lay vicar, a layman who is vicar-choral in an Anglican cathedral. [O.Fr. *lai*—L. *lāicus*—Gr. *lāikos*—*lāos*, the people.]

lay-day, *lā'-dā*, *n*. one of a number of days allowed for loading and unloading of cargo. [Perh. delay, and day.]

layer. See lay (3).

layette, *lā-et'*, *n*. a baby's complete outfit. [Fr.]

lay-figure, *lā'-fig'ər*, *n*. a jointed model used by painters: a living person or a fictitious character wanting in individuality.—Also (earlier) lay'man. [Du. *leeman*—*led* (now *lid*), joint, *man*, man.]

laylock, *lā'lək*, *n*. an obsolete form of lilac.

lazar, *laz'ər*, *n*. one afflicted with a loathsome and pestilential disease like *Lazarus*, the beggar.—*n*. Laz'arist, a member of the Roman Catholic Congregation of the Priests of the Mission, founded by St Vincent de Paul in 1624.—*adj*. or *adv*. la'zar-like.—lazar house, a lazaretto.

lazaretto, *laz-ə-ret'ō*, *n*. a hospital for infectious diseases, esp. leprosy: a place of quarantine: a place for keeping stores on a ship.—Also laz'aret. [It. *lazzaretto*.]

lazuli, *laz'ū-lī*. See lapis-lazuli.

lazulite, *laz'ū-līt*, *n*. a blue mineral, hydrated phosphate of aluminium, magnesium, and iron. [L.L. *lazulum*—Pers. *lājward*; cf. azure, lapis-lazuli, lazurite.]

lazurite, *laz'ū-rīt*, *n*. a blue cubic mineral, sodium aluminium silicate with some sulphur, a constituent of lapis-lazuli. [L.L. *lazur*—Pers. *lājward*; cf. azure, lapis-lazuli, lazulite.]

lazy, *lā'zi*, *adj*. disinclined to exertion: averse to labour: sluggish.—*v.i.* laze, to be idle (backformation).—*adv*. la'zily.—*n*. la'ziness.—la'zy-bed, a bed for growing potatoes, the seed being laid on the surface and covered with earth dug out of trenches along both sides; la'zy-bones (*coll.*), a lazy person, an idler; la'zy-jack, a jack constructed of compound levers pivoted together. —*n.pl.* la'zy-tongs, a series of diagonal levers pivoted together at the middle and ends, capable of being extended by a movement of the scissors-like handles so as to pick up objects at a distance. —*adj*. constructed on the model of lazy-tongs. [Origin unknown.]

lazzarone, *läd-zä-rō'nā*, or *laz-ə-rō'ni*, *n*. a Neapolitan beggar:—*pl.* lazzaro'ni (-*nē*). [It.]

lea, *lē*, *n*. open country—meadow, pasture, or arable.—Also lay, lee, ley (*lā*, *lē*). [O.E. *lēah*; dial. Ger. *lohe*, *loh*; perh. Flem. *-loo* in place-names, as Waterloo; confused with lease (4).]

lea, *lē*, *adj*. and *n*. fallow: arable land under grass or pasture.—Also lay (*lā*), ley (*lē*, *lā*).—lea'-rig, an unploughed rig or grass field; ley'-farm'ing, pasturing and cropping in alternating periods. [O.E. *lǣge*, found in *lǣghrycg*, lea-rig.]

lea, *lē*, lay, ley, *lā*, *n*. a measure of yarn—80 yards of worsted, 120 of cotton, 300 of linen. [Perh. conn. with Fr. *lier*—L. *ligāre*, to bind.]

leach, *lēch*, *v.t.* to allow (a liquid) to percolate through something: to subject (something) to percolation so as to separate soluble constituent(s): to drain away by percolation.—Also letch.—*n.* leach'ing.—*adj.* leach'y, liable to be leached.—leach'-trough, -tub, a trough or tub in which ashes are leached.—bacterial leaching, the use of selected strains of bacteria to accelerate the leaching acid of sulphide materials. [O.E. *leccan,* to water, irrigate, moisten.]

leach, leachour (*Spens.*), for leech, lecher.

lead, *lēd, v.t.* to show the way by going first: to precede: to guide by the hand: to direct: to guide: to conduct: to convey: to cart (*dial.*): to induce: to live: to cause to live or experience: to adduce (*Scots law*): to have a principal or guiding part or place in: to play as the first card of a round (*cards*).—*v.i.* to be first or among the first: to be guide or chief: to act first: to cart crops to the farmyard (often with *in*): to afford a passage (to), or (*fig.*) tend towards:—*pa.t.* and *pa.p.* led.—*n.* first place: precedence: amount by which one is ahead: direction: guidance: indication: precedent or example: chief rôle: the player of a chief rôle: leadership: initiative: the act or right of playing first, or the play of him who plays first: the first player of a side (*curling,* etc.): a leash: a watercourse leading to a mill: a channel among ice: the course of a running rope from end to end: a main conductor in electrical distribution.—*ns.* lead'er, one who leads or goes first: a chief: the principal first violin: the head of a party, expedition, etc.: the leading editorial article in a newspaper (also **leading article**): the principal upward-growing shoot of a tree: a horse in a front place in a team: a tendon: a translucent connection between a fishing-line and bait: a line of dots to guide the eye (*print.*): principal wheel in any machinery: alternative name for conductor (of orchestra, etc.) (*U.S.*); leaderette', a brief newspaper leader; lead'ership, office of leader or conductor: ability to lead; lead'ing, guidance: spiritual guidance: leadership: carting (crops, etc.).—*adj.* acting as leader: directing, controlling: principal: preceding.—lead'er-ca'ble, a cable on the sea-bottom by which ships with induction-receiving apparatus can find their way into port; lead'-in', the part of the groove on a disk before the start of the recording (opp. to *lead-out*): the cable connecting the transmitter or receiver to the elevated part of an aerial: introduction to telecast advertisement; leading business, the acting of the principal parts or rôles in plays (by the leading lady and the leading man); leading case (*leg.*), case serving as a precedent; leading counsel, counsel who takes precedence of another in conducting a case; leading edge, the edge first met: the foremost edge of an aerofoil or propeller blade: rising amplitude portion of a pulse signal (*telecommunications*); leading light, a very influential member; leading note, the seventh tone of a major or minor scale, which leads the hearer to expect the tonic to follow; leading question, a question so put as to suggest the desired answer.—*n.pl.* lead'ing-strings, strings used to lead children beginning to walk: vexatious care or custody.—lead apes in hell (see ape); lead astray, to draw into a wrong course, to seduce from right conduct; lead by the nose, to make one follow submissively; lead in (*Scot.*), to house the harvest; lead in prayer, to offer up prayer in an assembly, uniting the prayers of others; lead off, to begin or take the start in anything; lead on, to persuade to go on, to draw on: to persuade to a foolish course: to hoax in jest; lead one a dance (see dance); lead out, to conduct to execution or a dance: to proceed to play out (*cards*); lead the way, to go first and guide others; lead up to, to bring about by degrees, to prepare for by steps or stages: to play in challenge to, or with a view to weakness in (*cards*). [O.E. *lǣdan,* to lead, *lād,* a way; Ger. *leiten,* to lead.]

lead, *led, n.* a heavy soft bluish-grey metal (symb. Pb; at. numb. 82): a plummet for sounding: a thin plate of lead separating lines of type: a pan or cauldron of lead, or of a kind once made of lead: a leaden frame for a window-pane: extended loosely to blacklead: a stick of blacklead for a pencil: (*pl.*) sheets of lead for covering roofs, a flat roof so covered.—*adj.* made of lead.—*v.t.* to cover, weight, or fit with lead: to separate the lines of with leads (*print.*).—*adjs.* lead'ed, fitted or weighted with or set in lead: separated by leads (*print.*); lead'en, made of lead: lead-coloured: inert: depressing: heavy: dull.—*v.t.* and *v.i.* to make or become leaden.—*adv.* lead'enly.—*n.* lead'enness.—*adjs.* lead'less; lead'y, like lead.—lead'-arm'ing, tallow, etc., placed in the hollow of a sounding-lead to ascertain the nature of the bottom.—*adj.* lead'en-stepp'ing (*Milt.*), moving slowly.—lead'-glance', galena; lead'-line, a sounding-line; lead'-paint', paint with white lead as base; lead'-pencil, a blacklead pencil for writing or drawing; lead'-poi'soning, plumbism, poisoning by the absorption of lead into the system, its commonest form lead colic, or painter's colic: death by shooting (*slang*); leads'man, a seaman who heaves the lead.—red lead, white lead (see red, white); swing the lead (*naut.* and *mil. slang*), to invent specious excuses to evade duties; tree of lead (see Saturn). [O.E. *lēad;* Ger. *lot.*]

leaf, *lēf, n.* one of the lateral organs developed from the stem or axis of the plant below its growing-point, esp. one of those flat green structures that perform the work of transpiration and carbon-assimilation, but also more generally any homologous structure, as a scale, a petal: condition of having leaves: leaves collectively: anything beaten thin like a leaf: two pages of a book on opposite sides of the same paper: a broad thin part or structure, hinged, sliding, or inserted at will, as of folding doors, windowshutters, table-tops, drawbridges, etc.:—*pl.* leaves, *lēvz.*—*v.t.* to turn the pages of (a book etc.).—*v.i.* (also leave) to produce leaves:—*pr.p.* leaf'ing; *pa.p.* leafed.—*adj.* in the form of leaves.—*n.* leaf'age, foliage.—*adj.* leafed (*lēft*), having leaves (also leaved, *lēvd*).—*n.* leaf'iness.—*adj.* leaf'less, destitute of leaves.—*n.* leaf'let, a little leaf: a division of a compound leaf: a single unstitched leaf of printed matter: a tract.—*adj.* leaf'-like.—*adjs.* leaf'y, leav'y, covered with or abounding in leaves: leaf-like.–leaf'-base, the base of a leaf-stalk, where it joins the stem; leaf'-bridge, a drawbridge with rising leaves swinging on hinges; leaf'bud, a bud producing a shoot with foliage leaves only (not flowers); leaf'-climb'er, a plant that climbs by means of its leaves (petioles or tendrils); leaf'-curl, a plant disease of various kinds characterised by curling of the leaves; leaf'-cushion, a swollen leaf-base: a pulvinus that serves as a hinge for leaf movements: a raised scar marking the position of a leaf; leaf'-cutter, an insect (ant or bee) that cuts pieces out of leaves; leaf'-cutt'ing, a leaf used as a cutting for propagation; leaf'-fall, the shedding of leaves: the time of the shedding of leaves, usu. autumn: premature fall of leaves; leaf'-green, chlorophyll; leaf'-hopper, a name for various hopping orthopterous insects that suck plant juices; leaf'-in'sect, an orthopterous insect of family Phasmidae with wing-covers like leaves; leaf'-met'al, metal, especially alloys imitating gold and silver, in very thin leaves, for decoration; leaf'-mosa'ic, the arrangement of leaves so as to avoid shading one another: a name for various virus diseases of potato, tobacco, etc., in which the leaf is mottled; leaf'-mould, earth formed from decayed leaves, used as a soil for plants.—*adj.* leaf'-nosed, having a leaf-like structure on the nose, as certain bats.—**leaf'-roll**, a potato disease; **leaf'-scar**, a scar left by the fall of a leaf; **leaf'-sheath**, a leaf-base more or less completely enveloping the stem; **leaf'-stalk**, the petiole of a leaf; **leaf'-trace'**, a branch from the vascular system of the stem destined to enter a leaf.—**take a leaf out of one's book** (see **book**); **turn over a new leaf**, to begin a new and better course of conduct. [O.E. *lēaf*; Ger. *laub*, Du. *loof*, a leaf.]

**league**, *lēg, n.* a nautical measure, 1/20th of a degree, 3 international nautical miles, 3·456 statute miles (5·556 km.): an old measure of length, varying from the Roman league, 1·376 mod. Eng. miles (2·215 km.), to the French, 2·764 miles (4·448 km.), and the Spanish, 4·214 miles (6·781 km.). [L.L. *leuga*, *leuca*, a Gallic mile of 1500 Roman paces; said to be Gaulish.]

**league**, *lēg, n.* a bond or alliance: union for mutual advantage: an association or confederacy: an association of clubs for games: a class or group.—*v.t.* and *v.i.* to join in league.—*n.* **lea'guer**, a member of a league, esp. (*cap.*) that against the Huguenots in the time of Henry III of France, the Anti-Corn-Law League, or the Irish Land League.—**league match**, a match between two clubs in the same league.—**League of Nations**, an international body, under a covenant drawn up in 1919, to secure peace, justice, scrupulous observance of treaties, and international co-operation generally—superseded in 1945 by the United Nations; **top, bottom, of the league**, (*fig.*) highest, lowest, in a particular field of achievement, or in quality. [Fr. *ligue*—L.L. *liga*—L. *ligāre*, to bind.]

**leaguer**, *lēg'ər*, (*arch.*) *n.* a camp, esp. of a besieging army: siege: (by confusion with **ledger**) an ambassador.—*v.t.* to beleaguer.—**lea'guer-la'dy**, **lea'guer-lass'**, a female camp-follower. [Du. *leger*, a lair.]

**leaguer**, *lēg'ər*, (*obs.*) *n.* an old Dutch liquid measure: a large cask. [Du. *ligger*, a tun.]

**leak**, *lēk, n.* a crack or hole in a vessel through which liquid may pass: passage through such an opening: place, means, instance, of unintended or undesirable admission or escape (*lit.* and *fig.*): a high resistance, esp. serving as a discharging path for a condenser (*elect.*).—*adj.* (*obs.*) leaky.—*v.i.* to have a leak: to pass through a leak.—*v.t.* to cause a leak: to let out or in by, or (*fig.*) as if by, a leak.—*ns.* **leak'age**, a leaking: that which enters or escapes by leaking: an allowance for leaking: unauthorised divulgation; **leak'iness**.—*adj.* **leak'y**.—**leak out**, to find vent: to get to the public ears; **spring a leak**, to become leaky. [O.E. *hlec*, leaky; or perh. reintroduced from Du. or L.G. *lek*, leak; or O.N. *leka*, to leak.]

**leal**, *lēl, adj.* true-hearted, faithful.—*n.* **lealty** (*lē'əl-ti*).—**Land o' the Leal**, the home of the blessed after death—heaven. [O.F. *leel*, *leiel*; doublet of **loyal**.]

**leam**, **leme**, *lēm*, (*arch.*) *n.* a gleam of light, a glow.—*v.i.* to shine. [O.E. *lēoma*.]

**leam**, *lēm*. Same as **lyam**.

**lean**, *lēn, v.i.* to incline: to be or become inclined to the vertical: to rest sideways against something: to bend over: to swerve: to abut: to have an inclination: to rely.—*v.t.* to cause to lean:—*pa.t.* and *pa.p.* **leaned**, *lēnd*, or **leant**, *lent*.—*n.* an act or condition of leaning: slope: a thing to lean on (*arch.*).—*n.* and *adj.* **lean'ing**.—**lean'-to**, a shed or penthouse propped against another building or wall.—**lean on** (*slang*), to put pressure on, to use force on (a person); **lean over backwards** (see **backwards**). [O.E. *hlēonian*, *hlinian*, and causative *hlǣnan*; Du. *leunen*.]

**lean**, *lēn, adj.* thin, wanting flesh: not fat: without fat: unproductive: unprofitable, taking extra time—a printer's word.—*n.* flesh without fat.—*adv.* **lean'ly**.—*n.* **lean'ness**.—*adj.* **lean'** (*Spens.*), lean.—**lean concrete**, a non-load-bearing concrete of low cement content.—*adjs.* **lean'-faced**, having a thin face: slender and narrow, as letters (*print.*); **lean'-witt'ed**, of little sense. [O.E. *hlǣne*; L.G. *leen.*]

**leap**, *lēp, v.i.* to move with bounds: to spring upward or forward: to jump: to rush with vehemence: to pass abruptly or over a wide interval.—*v.t.* to bound over: to cause to take a leap: to cover (of male animals):—*pr.p.* **leap'ing**; *pa.t.* and *pa.p.* **leaped**, *lēpt*, or **leapt**, *lept*.—*n.* act of leaping: bound: space passed by leaping: a place of leaping: an abrupt transition: a wide gap or interval.—*n.* **leap'er**, steeplechaser: one who leaps.—**leap'-day**, an intercalary day in the calendar (29th February); **leap'-frog**, a sport in which one places his hands on the back of another stooping in front of him, and vaults over him.—*v.t.* to advance by passing each other alternately.—**leap'ing-house** (*Shak.*), a brothel; **leap'ing-time** (*Shak.*), active youth; **leap'-year**, a year with an intercalary day (perh. because any anniversary after that day misses or leaps over a day of the week).—**leap in the dark**, an act of which we cannot foresee the consequences. [O.E. *hlēapan*; cf. **lope**, **loup**, Ger. *laufen*, to run.]

**leap**, *lēp, n.* a basket: a wicker net. [O.E. *lēap.*]

**leaprous**, **leaperous**, **leaporous**, old spellings of **leprous**.

**lear**, **leare**, **lere**, **leir**, *lēr, v.t.* to teach (*arch.* and *Scot.*): to learn (*Spens.*).—*n.* that which is learned, a lesson: lore: learning (*Scot.*). [O.E. *lǣran*, to teach.]

**lear**, **leer**, **lehr**, *lēr, n.* a glass-annealing oven. [Origin unknown.]

**learn**, *lûrn, v.t.* to be informed: to get to know: to gain knowledge, skill, or ability in: to teach (now *illit.*).—*v.i.* to gain knowledge or skill:—*pa.t.* and *pa.p.* **learned** (*lûrnd*) or **learnt** (*lûrnt*).—*adjs.* **learn'able**, that may be learned; **learned** (*lûrn'id*), having learning: versed in literature, etc.: skilful.—*adv.* **learn'edly**;—*ns.* **learn'edness**; **learn'er**, one who learns: one who is yet in the rudiments; **learn'ing**, what is learned: knowledge: scholarship: skill in languages or science.—**New Learning**, the awakening to classical learning in the 16th century, led (in England) by Colet, Erasmus, Warham, More, etc. [O.E. *leornian*; Ger. *lernen*; cf. O.E. *lǣran* (Ger. *lehren*), to teach.]

**lease**, *lēs, n.* a contract letting a house, farm, etc., for a term: tenure or rights under such a contract: duration of such tenure: a hold upon, or prospect of continuance of, life, enjoyment, health, etc.—*v.t.* to grant or take under lease.—*adj.* **leas'able**.—*ns.* **leas'er**, a lessee.—**lease'hold**, a tenure by lease: land, etc., so held.—*adj.* held by lease.—**lease'holder**.—*n.* and *adj.* **lease'-lend** (see **lend-lease**). [Fr. *laisser*, to leave—L. *laxāre*, to loose, *laxus*, loose.]

**lease**, *lēz*, (*dial.*) *v.i.* to glean.—*n.* **leas'ing**, gleaning. [O.E. *lesan*, to gather.]

**lease**, *lēs, n.* place or mode of separating warp threads at the ends.—**lease'-band**, **lease'-rod**, a band, rod, above and below which the warp threads are placed. [Perh. conn. with **leash**.]

**lease**, **leaze**, *lēz*, (*dial.*) *n.* pasture. [See **leasow**.]

**leash**, *lēsh, n.* a line for holding a hawk or hound: control by a leash, or as if by a leash: a set of three, especially animals.—*v.t.* to hold by a leash: to bind. [O.Fr. *lesse* (Fr. *laisse*), a thong to hold a dog by—L. *laxus*, loose.]

**leasing**, *lēz'ing*, (*dial.*) *n.* falsehood, lies: lying.—**leas'ing-mak'er**, a speaker of seditious words; **leas'ing-mak'ing**. [O.E. *lēasung*—*lēasian*, to lie—*lēas*, false, loose; Goth. *laus*, O.H.G. *los.*]

**leasow**, **leasowe**, *lē'sō, -zō*, (*dial.*) *n.* pasture.—*v.t.* and *v.i.* to pasture. [Same word as **lease** (4)—O.E. *lǣs*, a meadow, in oblique cases *lǣswe*; cf. **mead**, **meadow**.]

**least**, *lēst, adj.* (serving as superl. of **little**) little beyond all others: smallest.—*adv.* in the smallest or lowest degree.—*n.* the smallest amount: the lowest degree.—*advs.* least′aways, least′ways (*dial.*), -wise (*rare*), at least: however—used to tone down a preceding statement.—at least, or at the least, at the lowest estimate: at any rate. [O.E. *lǣst* (adj. and adv.); compar. *lǣssa* (adj.), *lǣs* (adv.); no positive.]

least, *lēst, conj.* (*Spens.*). Same as lest.

leasure, (*Spens.*) an obsolete spelling of leisure.

leat, leet, (*dial.*) *n.* a trench for bringing water to a mill-wheel, etc. [O.E. *gelǣt.*]

leather, *ledh′ər, n.* a tanned, tawed, or otherwise dressed skin: a strap or other piece of leather: the ball in certain games: human skin (*slang*): (in *pl.*) riding breeches made from leather.—*adj.* of leather.—*v.t.* to apply leather to: to thrash (*coll.*).—*ns.* leatherette′, cloth or paper made to look like leather; leath′ering (*coll.*), a thrashing. —*adjs.* leath′ern, of or like leather; leath′ery, resembling leather: tough.—leath′er-back, a large variety of sea-turtle; leath′er-cloth, a fabric coated on one face so as to resemble leather —called also *American cloth*; leath′er-coat (*Shak.*), an apple with a rough coat, the golden russet; leath′er-head, a blockhead: an Australian friar-bird with a bare head; leath′er-jacket, one of various fishes: a grub of the crane-fly; leath′er-knife, a curved knife for cutting leather. —*adjs.* leath′er-lunged, strong-lunged, able to shout vigorously; leath′er-mouthed (-*mowdhd*), of certain fish, having a mouth like leather, smooth, and toothless.—leath′er-neck, sailor's name for a soldier or marine (from the leather stock he once wore).—*adj.* leath′er-winged (*Spens.*), having wings like leather.—artificial leather, any of certain plastic materials treated so as to simulate leather; fair leather, leather not artificially coloured; morocco leather (see morocco); patent leather—also japanned or lacquered leather (see patent); Russia leather (see Russia); split leather, leather split by a machine, for trunk-covers, etc.; white leather, tawed leather, having its natural colour. [O.E. *lether*, leather; Du. and Ger. *leder.*]

leave, *lēv, n.* permission: liberty granted: formal parting: farewell: permission to depart or be absent: permitted absence from duty: time of this: holidays.—leave′-taking, bidding farewell. —French leave (see French); take leave, assume permission: part, say farewell; take leave of one's senses, to become irrational. [O.E. *lēaf*, permission, cog. with *lēof*, dear; see lief.]

leave, *lēv, v.t.* to allow to remain: to abandon, resign: to quit or depart from: to have remaining at death: to bequeath: to refer for decision. —*v.i.* to desist: to cease: to depart:—*pr.p.* leav′ing; *pa.t.* and *pa.p.* left.—*n.pl.* leav′ings, things left: relics: refuse.—leav′ing-shop, an unlicensed pawnshop.—leave alone, to let remain undisturbed; leave off, to desist, to terminate: to give up using; leave out, to omit. [O.E. *lǣfan.*]

leave, *lēv* (*Spens.*) *v.t.* to levy, to raise. [Fr. *lever.*]

leave, leaved, leaves, leavy. See leaf.

leaven, *lev′n, n.* the ferment that makes dough rise: anything that makes a general change.— *v.t.* to raise with leaven: to permeate with an influence.—*n.* leav′ening.—*adj.* leav′enous, containing leaven. [Fr. *levain*—L. *levāmen*—*levāre*, to raise—*levis*, light.]

leaze. Same as lease (4).

lebbek, *leb′ek, n.* an Old World tropical mimosaceous timber tree (*Albizzia Lebbek*). [Origin unknown.]

lebensraum, *lāb′-əns-rowm,* (Ger.) space inhabited by living things: room to live (and, if necessary, expand).

Lecanora, *lek-ə-nō′ra, -nö′, n.* a genus of lichens,

including the edible manna lichen of the steppes and deserts of Asia and Africa. [Gr. *lekanē*, a dish.]

lecher, *lech′ər, n.* a man addicted to lewdness.— *v.i.* to practise lewdness.—*adj.* lech′erous, lustful: provoking lust.—*adv.* lech′erously.—*ns.* lech′-erousness, lech′ery. [O.Fr. *lecheor*—*lechier*, to lick; O.H.G. *leccôn*, Ger. *lecken*, Eng. lick.]

Lecher wires, *lehh′ər wirz,* two insulated parallel stretched wires, forming a microwave electro-magnetic transmission line. [Ernst *Lecher*, Austrian physicist.]

lecithin, *les′i-thin, n.* a very complex substance containing phosphorus, found in yolk of egg, brain, blood, etc. [Gr. *lekithos*, egg-yolk.]

lectern, *lek′tərn, n.* a church reading-desk from which the lessons are read.—Also (*obs.*) lec′turn, lett′ern. [L.L. *lectrinum*—*lectrum*, a pulpit— Gr. *lektron*, a couch.]

lection, *lek′shən, n.* a reading: a lesson read in Church.—*n.* lec′tionary, a book of church lessons for each day. [L. *lectiō, -ōnis*—*legĕre*, *lectum*, to read.]

lectisternium, *lek-ti-stûr′ni-əm, n.* an ancient Roman religious observance at which images of gods were placed on couches as at a feast. [L., —*lectus*, a couch, *sternĕre*, to spread.]

lector, *lek′tör, -tər, n.* a reader, esp. in a college: an ecclesiastic in one of the minor orders, lowest in the Orthodox, next above doorkeeper, in the Roman Catholic.—*ns.* lec′torate, lec′torship; lec′tress, a female reader.—lector benevole (*bi-nev′ə-li, be-nev′o-le*), kind reader. [L. *lector*, *-ōris*—*legĕre*, *lectum*, to read.]

lecture, *lek′chər, n.* reading (*arch.*): a lesson or period of instruction: a discourse on any subject, esp. a professorial or tutorial discourse: an expository and discursive religious discourse: an endowed lectureship, as the Bampton, Hulsean, etc.: a formal reproof.—*v.t.* to instruct by discourses: to instruct authoritatively: to reprove.—*v.i.* to give a lecture or lectures.—*ns.* lec′turer, one who lectures: a college or university instructor of lower rank than a professor: one of a class of preachers in the Church of England, supported by voluntary contributions; lec′tureship, the office of a lecturer: the foundation of a course of lectures. [L. *lectūra*—*legĕre*, *lectum*, to read.]

lecythus, *les′i-thəs, n.* the Latinised form of lekythos.—*n.* Lec′ythis, the monkey-pot genus of Lecythidā′ceae, a family of tropical trees, including Brazil-nut, cannon-ball tree, and anchovy-pear. [See lekythos.]

led, led, *pa.t.* and *pa.p.* of lead, to show the way.— *adj.* under leading or control, esp. of a farm or place held along with another by a non-resident. —led captain, an obsequious attendant, a henchman; led horse, a spare horse led by a servant, a sumpter-horse or pack-horse.

ledden, *led′n,* (*Spens.*) *n.* language, dialect, speech. [O.E. *lēden, lēoden*, language—*lēode*, people, confused with *lǣden*, Latin—L. *Latinum*, Latin.]

lederhosen, *lā′dər-hōz-ən,* (Ger.) short leather trousers with braces.

ledge, *lej, n.* an attached strip: a raised edge (*obs.*): a shelf-like projection: a ridge or shelf of rocks: a lode.—*adj.* ledg′y, abounding in ledges. [M.E. *legge*, prob. from the root of lay (3).]

ledger, *lej′ər,* formerly also lidger, lij′ər, *n.* a book that lies permanently in one place (*obs.*): a register (*U.S.*): the principal book of accounts among merchants, in which the entries in all the other books are entered: a horizontal timber in scaffolding: a flat grave-slab: (also leidger, lieger, leiger) a resident, esp. an ambassador (*obs.*).—*adj.* resident, stationary.—*v.i.* to fish with a ledger-line.—ledg′er-bait, fishing bait that lies on the bottom, the ledg′er-tackle being weighted; **ledger-line,** a line fixed in one place (*angling*): a short line added above or below the stave where required (often **leger-line;** *mus.*). [App. from O.E. *licgan,* to lie, *lecgan,* to lay.]

**Ledum,** *lē'dəm, n.* the Labrador tea genus of ericaceous plants. [Latinised from Gr. *lēdon,* ladanum.]

**lee,** *lē, n.* shelter: the sheltered side: the quarter toward which the wind blows: tranquillity (*obs.*).—*adj.* (opp. to *windward* or *weather*) sheltered: on or towards the sheltered side.— **lee'-board,** a board lowered on the lee-side of a vessel, to lessen drift to leeward; **lee'-gage,** position to leeward—opp. to *weather-gage;* **lee shore,** a shore on a ship's lee side; **lee side,** the sheltered side; **lee tide,** a tide in the same direction as the wind; **lee'way,** leeward drift.— **lee licht of the mune,** (in Scottish ballads) perh. the pleasant moonlight; **make up leeway,** to make up for lost time, ground, etc. [O.E. *hlēo*(*w*), gen. *hlēowes,* shelter; O.N. *hlē,* L.G. *lee;* see also **lew.**]

**lee,** *lē,* (*Spens.*) *n.* a river. [Poss. from the River *Lee.*]

**lee.** See **lea** (1), **lees, lie** (1).—*n.* **leear,** *lē'ər,* Scots form of **liar.**

**leech,** *lēch, n.* the side edge of a sail. [Cf. O.N. *lik;* Dan. *lig;* Sw. *lik,* a bolt-rope.]

**leech,** *lēch, n.* a blood-sucking worm: a physician (*arch.*): one who attaches himself to another for personal gain.—*v.t.* to apply leeches to: to cling to like a leech: to drain.—*v.i.* (usually with *on*) to cling to.—*ns.* **leech'craft** (*arch.*), the art of medicine; **leech'dom** (*arch.*), a remedy or prescription. [O.E. *lǣce,* perh. orig. two different words.]

**leechee.** Same as **litchi.**

**leek,** *lēk, n.* a vegetable (*Allium porrum*) of the onion genus—national emblem of Wales.—**eat the leek** (*Shak.—Henry V,* V, i.), to be compelled to take back one's words or put up with insulting treatment. [O.E. *lēac,* leek, plant; cf. **charlock, garlic, hemlock.**]

**lee-lane,** *lē'-lān'* (*Scot.*) *n.* used only in phrases (**by**) **my, his,** etc., **lee-lane,** quite alone.—Also **lee'some-lane.** [lee of obscure origin; see **lone.**]

**leer,** *lēr, n.* a sly, sidelong, or lecherous look: complexion, colour (*Shak.*).—*v.i.* to glance sideways: to look lecherously.—*n.* and *adj.* **leer'ing.**—*adv.* **leer'ingly.**—*adj.* **leer'y,** cunning: wary (with *of*). [O.E. *hlēor,* face, cheek.]

**leer.** Same as **lear** (2).

**Leerie,** *lē'ri,* (*Scot.*) *n.* a nickname for a lamplighter—in full **Lee'rie-licht'-the-lamp.**

**lees,** *lēz, n.pl.* sediment or dregs of liquor.—*sing.* (*rare*) **lee.** [Fr. *lie*—L.L. *lia.*]

**leese,** *lēz,* (*Spens., Shak.*) *v.t.* to lose:—*pa.t.* **lore** (*lōr, lör*); *pa.p.* **lore, lorn** (in *Spens.,* in the sense of left). [O.E. *lēosan* (in compounds), to lose.]

**leet,** *lēt,* (*Scot.*) *n.* a selected list of candidates for an office.—**short leet,** a select list for the final choice. [Origin uncertain.]

**leet,** *lēt,* (*hist.*) *n.* a court-leet: its jurisdiction or district: the right to hold it. [A.Fr. *lete* or Anglo-Latin *leta,* possibly—O.E. *lǣth,* lathe (of a county).]

**leet.** See **leat.**

**leetle,** *lē'tl,* an old-fashioned affectation for **little.**

**leeze.** See under **lief.**

**left,** *left, pa.t.* and *pa.p.* of **leave.**—*adjs.* **left'-off,** laid aside, discarded; **left'-o'ver,** remaining over from a previous occasion.—*n.* a thing left over: a survival: food uneaten at a meal (usu. in *pl.*).

**left,** *left, adj.* on, for, or belonging to that side which in man has normally the weaker and less skilful hand (opposed to *right*): on that side from the point of view of a person looking downstream, a soldier looking at the enemy, a president looking at an assembly, an actor looking

at the audience: relatively liberal, democratic, progressive, innovating in politics.—*n.* the left side: the region to the left side: the left hand: a blow with the left hand: a shot on the left side or a bird so killed: a glove, shoe, etc., for the left hand or foot, etc.: the more progressive or actively innovating party or wing (from its sitting in some legislatures to the president's left).— *adv.* on or towards the left.—*ns.* **left'ism,** principles of the political left; **left'ist.**—*adj.* and *adv.* **left'ward,** towards the left: on the left side. —*advs.* **left'wardly, left'wards.**—**Left Bank,** artistic quarter of Paris on the south bank of the Seine.—*adjs.* **left'-bank; left'-footed,** performed with the left foot: having more skill or strength in the left foot; **left'-hand,** on the left side: performed with the left hand; **left'-hand'ed,** having the left hand stronger and readier than the right: for the left hand: counter-clockwise: forming a mirror-image of the normal or right-handed form: awkward: unlucky: dubious (as *a left-handed compliment*): morganatic.— *adv.* **left'-hand'edly.**—**left'-hand'edness; left'-hand'er,** a blow with the left hand: a left-handed person; **left'-hand'iness,** awkwardness. —*adj.* **left'-wing,** playing on the left wing: belonging to the more leftwardly inclined section.—**left-hand drive,** a driving mechanism on the left side of a vehicle which is intended to be driven on the right-hand side of the road; **over the left (shoulder)** (*obs. slang*), contrariwise. [M.E. *lift, left*—O.E. (Kentish) *left,* weak, worthless; cf. O.E. *lyftādl,* paralysis.]

**lefte,** *left,* (*Spens.*) *pa.t.* lifted.

**leg,** *leg, n.* a walking limb: the human hind-limb, or sometimes the part between knee and ankle: a long, slender support of anything, as of a table: in cricket, that part of the field, or that fielder, on or behind a line straight out from the batsman on the on side (also *adj.*): a branch or limb of anything forked or jointed, as a pair of compasses: part of a garment that covers the leg: a backward movement of the leg in bowing (*arch.*): a turf-swindler (for *blackleg*): a distinct part or stage of any course, e.g. of a flight: in sports, one event or part in a contest consisting of two or more parts or events.—*v.t.* (with *it*) and *v.i.* to walk vigorously: to propel through a canal tunnel by pushing with the feet on wall or roof.—*adj.* **legged,** having legs.—*ns.* **legg'er,** a bargeman who legs: a worker or machine that makes stocking-legs; **legg'iness; legg'ing,** an outer and extra gaiter-like covering for the lower leg; **legg'ism** (*arch.*), character of a black-leg.—*adj.* **legg'y,** having noticeably long and lank legs.—*ns.* **leg'lessness; leg'let,** a leg ornament.—**leg'-bail** (see **bail** (1)); **leg'-break,** a ball that breaks inwards from the leg side; **leg'-bus'iness** (*slang*), ballet-dancing; **leg'-bye,** in cricket, a run made when the ball touches any part of the batsman's person except his hand; **leg'-guard,** a cricketer's pad; **leg'-iron,** a fetter for the leg; **leg'-man,** one whose share in the business of an organisation involves journeys outside the office: a newspaper reporter. —*adj.* **leg-of-mutt'on,** shaped like a leg of mutton, as a triangular sail, a sleeve tight at the wrist and full above.—**leg'-pull,** a bantering attempt to impose on one's credulity; **leg'-puller; leg'-pulling; leg'-rest,** a support for the legs; **leg'-show,** an entertainment depending mainly on the exhibition of women's legs; **leg side** (or **the leg;** *cricket*), that half of the field nearest the batsman's legs (opp. to *off side*); **leg theory** (*cricket*), the policy of bowling on the striker's legs with a trap of leg-side fielders: body-line.—**a leg up,** a help or hoist in mounting, climbing, or generally; **change the leg** (of a horse), to change the gait; **feel one's legs,** to begin to support oneself on the legs; **find one's**

legs, to become habituated, to attain ease; **fine, long, short, square leg** (*cricket*), fielding positions respectively fine from, far from, near to, square to, the batsman on the leg side; **in high leg** (*arch.*), in great excitement; **leg before (wicket)**, in cricket, a way of being given out as penalty for stopping with the leg (or any part of the body except the hands) a straight or off-break ball that would have hit the wicket (**l.b.w.**); **not a leg to stand on**, no case at all; **on one's last legs** (see *last*); **on one's legs**, standing, esp. to speak; **pull one's leg**, to make a playful attempt to impose upon one's credulity; **shake a leg** (*coll.*), hurry up; **show a leg**, make an appearance: get up; **upon one's legs**, in an independent position. [O.N. *leggr*, a leg; Dan. *læg*, Sw. *lägg*.]

**legacy**, *leg'ə-si*, *n.* that which is left to one by will: a bequest of personal property.—*ns.* **leg'atary**, a legatee; **legatee'**, one to whom a legacy is left; **legator** (*li-gā'tər*), a testator.—**legacy duty**, a duty levied on legacies, varying according to degree of relationship, abolished in 1950; **leg'acy-hunter**, one who courts those likely to leave legacies.—**cumulative legacy**, an additional legacy to the same person; **demonstrative legacy**, a general legacy with a particular fund named from which it is to be satisfied; **general legacy**, a sum of money payable out of the assets generally; **residuary legatee**, the person to whom the remainder of the property is left after all claims are discharged; **specific legacy**, a legacy of a definite thing, as jewels, pictures, a sum of stock in the funds, etc.; **substitutional legacy**, a second legacy to the same person instead of the first. [L. *lēgāre*, *-ātum*, to leave by will.]

**legal**, *lē'gl*, *adj.* pertaining to, or according to, law: lawful: created by law: according to the Mosaic law or dispensation (*theol.*).—*n.* **lēgālisā'tion**, *-z-*. —*v.t.* **lē'galise**, **-ize**, to make lawful.—*ns.* **lē'galism**, strict adherence to law: in theol., the doctrine that salvation depends on strict adherence to the law, as distinguished from the doctrine of salvation by grace: the tendency to observe letter or form rather than spirit, or to regard things from the point of view of law; **lē'galist**, one inclined to legalism: one versed in law; **lēgality** (*-gal'i-ti*).—*adv.* **lē'gally.**—**legal tender**, that which a creditor cannot refuse in payment of a debt. [L. *lēgālis*—*lēx*, *lēgis*, law.]

**legate**, *leg'it*, *n.* an ambassador, esp. from the Pope: a delegate, deputy, esp. orig. a Roman general's lieutenant: the governor of a Papal province (*hist.*).—*n.* **leg'ateship.**—*adj.* **leg'atine** (*-ə-tin*), of or relating to a legate.—*n.* **legation** (*li-gā'shən*), a diplomatic mission, body of delegates, or its official abode: the office or status of legate: a Papal province (*hist.*). [L. *lēgātus*—*lēgāre*, to send with a commission.]

**legatee.** See **legacy.**

**legato**, *le-gä'tō*, (*mus.*) *adj.* and *adv.* smooth, smoothly, the notes running into each other without a break (*superl.* **legatis'simo**).—*n.* a legato passage or manner. [It., bound, tied—L. *ligāre*, *-ātum*, to tie.]

**legend**, *lej'ənd*, *n.* a story of a saint's life: a traditional story: a body of tradition: an untrue or unhistorical story: a person having a special place in public esteem because of striking qualities or deeds, real or fictitious: the body of fact and fiction gathered round such a person: a motto, inscription, or explanatory words (with, e.g. a picture): a book of readings from the Bible and saints' lives (*obs.*).—*n.* **leg'endary**, a book or writer of legends.—*adj.* pertaining to, of the nature of, consisting of, legend: romantic: fabulous.—*ns.* **leg'endist**, a writer of legends; **leg'endry.** [Fr. *légende*—L.L. *legenda*, to be read.]

**legend**, *lej'ənd*, *n.* Shak. for **legion.**

**leger**, *lej'ər*, (*obs. cant*) *n.* one who sells short

weight in charcoal: one who swindles by scamping work, using bad materials, or the like.—*n.* **leg'ering.** [Poss. Fr. *léger*, light.]

**legerdemain**, *lej-ər-də-mān'*, *n.* sleight-of-hand: jugglery.—*adj.* juggling: tricky. [Lit. light of hand—Fr. *léger*, light, *de*, of, *main*, hand.]

**legerity**, *li-jer'i-ti*, *n.* lightness: nimbleness. [Fr. *légèreté*—*léger*, light—assumed L.L. *leviārius*—L. *levis*, light.]

**leger-line**—better **ledger-line.** See **ledger.**

**legge**, *leg*, (*Shak.*) *n.* dregs of the people. [**lag** (1).]

**leghorn**, *leg'hörn*, *li-görn'*, *n.* fine straw plait made in Tuscany: a hat made of it: (*li-görn'*) a small breed of domestic fowl. [*Leghorn* (It. *Legorno*, now *Livorno*, L. *Liburnus*) in Italy.]

**legible**, *lej'i-bl*, *adj.* clear enough to be deciphered: easy to read: readable (*rare*).—*ns.* **leg'ibleness**, **legibil'ity**.—*adv.* **leg'ibly.** [L. *legibilis*—*legēre*, to read.]

**legion**, *lē'jən*, *n.* in ancient Rome, a body of three to six thousand soldiers: a military force: applied especially to several in French history: a great number—*adj.* (*rare*) multitudinous. —*adj.* **le'gionary**, of, relating to, or consisting of, a legion or legions: containing a great number. —*n.* a member of a legion.—*adj.* **le'gioned**, arrayed in legions.—**British Legion**, ex-servicemen's association; **Foreign Legion**, a body of foreigners, esp. that in the French army organised in 1831; **Legion of Honour**, an order instituted in 1802 by Napoleon I; **their name is Legion**, they are beyond numbering (from Mark v. 9); **Thundering Legion**, in Christian tradition a body of soldiers under Marcus Aurelius, whose prayers brought down a thunder-storm and destroyed the enemy. [L. *legiō*, *-ōnis*—*legēre* to levy.]

**legislate**, *lej'is-lāt*, *v.i.* to make laws.—*n.* **legislā'tion.**—*adj.* **leg'islātive** (or *-lə-tiv*), law-making: having power to make laws: pertaining to legislation.—*n.* law-making power: the law-making body.—*adv.* **leg'islatively.**—*n.* **leg'islator**, a lawgiver: a member of a legislative body: —*fem.* (*rare*) **leg'islatress.**—*adj.* **legislatorial** (*-lə-tō'ri-əl*, *-tö'*), of or pertaining to, or of the nature of, a legislator, legislature, or legislation. —*ns.* **leg'islatorship**; **leg'islature**, a law-making body. [L. *lēx*, *lēgis*, law, *latum*, serving as supine to *ferre*, to bear.]

**legist**, *lē'jist*, *n.* one skilled in the laws. [Fr. *légiste*.]

**legitim**, *lej'i-tim*, (*Scots law*) *n.* that which children are entitled to out of a deceased father's moveable estate—also *bairn's-part*. [L. *lēgitima* (*pars*), lawful (part)—*lēx*, law.]

**legitimate**, *le-jit'i-mit*, *-māt*, *adj.* lawful: lawfully begotten, born in wedlock, or having the legal status of those born in wedlock: related, derived, or transmitted by birth in wedlock or subsequently legitimated: as used by believers in the theory of divine right, according to strict rule of heredity and primogeniture: logically inferred: following by natural sequence: genuine: conforming to an accepted standard: of, or pertaining to, legitimate drama (*theat.*).—*v.t.* (*-māt*) to make lawful: to give the rights of a legitimate child to.—*n.* **legit'imacy** (*-mə-si*), fact or state of being legitimate.—*adv.* **legit'imately.** —*ns.* **legit'imateness**; **legitimā'tion**, act of rendering legitimate, esp. of conferring the privileges of lawful birth.—*v.t.* **legit'imise**, **-ize**, to legitimate. —*n.* **legit'imist**, one who believes in the right of royal succession according to the principle of heredity and primogeniture.—**legitimate drama**, drama of permanent value: drama of typical form, normal comedy and tragedy, distinguished from opera, play with music, variety, etc. as well as cinema and television; **legitimate pollination**, in heterostyled plants, pollination

# leglin · 753 · length

of long styles from long stamens, short from short. [L.L. *lēgitimāre*, *-ātum*—L. *lēgitimus*, lawful—*lēx*, law.]

**leglin, leglan, leglen,** *leg'lən*, (*Scot.*) *n.* a milking-pail.—**to cast a leglin girth,** to have an illegitimate child. [Cf. **laggen**.]

**legume,** *leg'ūm*, *li-gūm'*, *n.* a pod (as in pea, bean, etc.) of one carpel: a vegetable used as food.—*n.* legū'min, a globulin got in peas, beans, etc.—*n.pl.* Legūminō'sae (*-sē*), an order of angiosperms characterised by the legume, including Papilionaceae, Mimosaceae, and Caesalpiniaceae.—*adj.* legū'minous, pertaining to pulse: of or pertaining to the Leguminosae: bearing legumes. [L. *legūmen*, pulse, prob.—*legēre*, to gather.]

**lehr.** See **lear** (2).

**lei.** See **leu**.

**lei,** *lā'ē*, *n.* a garland, wreath. [Hawaiian.]

**Leibni(t)zian,** *lib-nit'si-an*, *adj.* pertaining to the great German philosopher and mathematician Gottfried Wilhelm *Leibniz* (1646-1716).—*n.* **Leibni(t)z'ianism,** the philosophy of Leibniz— the doctrine of primordial monads, pre-established harmony, fundamental optimism on the principle of sufficient reason.

**Leicester,** *les'tər*, *adj.* of a long-woolled breed of sheep that originated in *Leicestershire*.—*n.* a sheep of that breed.—**Leicester(shire) plan,** a comprehensive school system, started in Leicestershire in 1957, which avoids the use of very large schools and also makes full use of free modern methods of learning.

**leidger, leiger.** Forms of **ledger**.

**leiotrichous,** *lī-ot'ri-kəs*, *adj.* straight-haired.—*n.* **leiot'richy** (*-ki*), straight-hairedness. [Gr. *leios*, smooth, *thrix*, *trichos*, hair.]

**Leipoa,** *li-pō'ə*, *n.* a genus of Australian mound-birds. [Gr. *leipein*, to leave, forsake, and *ōon*, an egg.]

**leir.** See **lear** (1).

**Leishmania,** *lēsh-mān'i-ə*, *-man'i-ə*, *n.* a genus of Protozoa.—*ns.* **leishmaniasis** (*lēsh-mən-ī'ə-sis*), **leishmaniō'sis,** kala-azar, due to infection with Leishmania. [Named after Sir William *Leishman* (1865-1926), who discovered the cause of the disease.]

**leister,** *lēs'tər*, (*Scot.*) *n.* a salmon-spear.—*v.t.* to spear with a leister. [O.N. *ljōstr*; Dan. *lyster*.]

**leisure,** *lezh'ər*, (*U.S.* and old-fashioned) *lēzh'ər*, *n.* time free from employment: freedom from occupation: convenient opportunity.—*adj.* free from necessary business.—*v.i.* to have leisure.—*v.t.* to make leisurely.—*adj.* **leis'urable,** leisured: leisurely.—*adv.* **leis'urably.**—*adj.* **leis'ured,** having much leisure.—*adj.* and *adv.* **leis'urely,** not hasty or hastily.—**at** (one's) **leisure,** free from occupation: at one's ease or convenience. [O.Fr. *leisir*—L. *licēre*, to be permitted.]

**leitmotiv,** *līt'mō-tēf'*, *n.* a theme associated with a person or a thought, recurring when the person appears on the stage or the thought becomes prominent in the action: a recurring theme (*fig.*).—Also **leitmotif**. [Ger., —*leiten*, to lead, and *motiv*, a motif.]

**leke.** Spens. form of **leak** (*adj.*).

**lekythos,** *lē'ki-thos*, (*ant.*) *n.* a narrow-necked Greek flask. [Gr. *lēkythos.*]

**lem,** or **LEM,** *lem*, *n.* abbrev. for **lunar excursion module**.

**leman,** *lem'ən*, or *lēm'*, (*arch.*) *n.* a lover: a sweet-heart: a paramour: later chiefly *fem.* and in a bad sense:—*pl.* **lem'ans.** [O.E. *lēof*, lief, *mann*, man.]

**lemma,** *lem'ə*, *n.* a preliminary proposition (*math.*): a premise taken for granted (*math.*): a theme, argument, heading, or head-word:—*pl.* **lemm'as, lemm'ata.** [Gr. *lēmma*, *-atos*, from the root of *lambanein*, to take.]

**lemming,** *lem'ing*, *n.* a northern rodent (Lemmus

and other genera) near allied to voles. [Norw. *lemming*.]

**Lemna,** *lem'nə*, *n.* the duckweed genus, giving name to the family **Lemnā'ceae,** free-floating spathifloral monocotyledons. [Gr. *lemna*, water starwort.]

**Lemnian,** *lem'ni-ən*, *adj.* pertaining to *Lemnos* in the Aegean Sea.—**Lemnian earth,** a bole from Lemnos; **Lemnian ruddle,** a red ochre found in Lemnos.

**lemniscate,** *lem-nis'kāt*, *n.* the locus of the foot of the perpendicular from the centre of a conic upon the tangent. [L. *lēmniscātus*, ribboned— Gr. *lēmniskos*, a ribbon, bandage.]

**lemon,** *lem'ən*, *n.* a pale yellow oval citrus fruit with acid pulp: the tree that bears it: a pale yellow colour: something disappointing, worthless, unattractive, unpleasant (*slang*).—*adj.* flavoured with lemon: (coloured) pale yellow.—*v.t.* to flavour with lemon.—*n.* **lemonade',** a drink (still or aerated) made with lemon juice or more or less flavoured with lemon.—*adj.* **lem'ony.**— **lemon cheese, curd,** a soft paste of lemons, eggs, and butter.—*adj.* **lem'on-coloured.**—**lemon drop,** a hard lemon-flavoured sweet; **lem'on-grass,** a fragrant perennial grass (Cymbopogon or Andropogon) of India, etc., smelling like lemon and yielding an essential oil; **lemon peel,** the skin of lemons, candied or not; **lemon squash,** a highly concentrated lemon drink; **lemon squeezer,** a small hand-press for extracting the juice of lemons; **lem'on-weed,** sea-mat.—*n.* and *adj.* **lem'on-yell'ow.**—**hand one a lemon** (*slang*), to swindle one. [Fr. *limon* (now the lime); cf. Pers. *līmūn*; cf. **lime** (2).]

**lemon,** *lem'ən*, *n.* a species of sole differing in its markings from the common sole (**lem'on-sole**, or sand sole): a kind of dab resembling a sole (**lem'on-dab'**, **lem'on-sole'**, also called smear-dab or smooth dab). [Fr. *limande*.]

**lemur,** *lē'mər*, *n.* any member of the Lemuroidea (*lem-ū-roid'i-ə*) or Prosimiae, a group of mammals akin to the monkeys, forest dwellers, mainly nocturnal in habits, common in Madagascar: an ancient Roman ghost of the dead:— *pl.* **lē'murs** (animals), **lemures** (*lem'ū-rēz*; spectres).—*n.* **Lemuria** (*li-mū'ri-ə*; *pl.*), an ancient Roman festival (9th, 11th, and 13th of May) when ghosts were exorcised: (*sing.*) a hypothetical vanished continent where the Indian Ocean now is, posited to explain the distribution of lemurs.—*ns.* and *adjs.* **lemurian** (*li-mū'ri-ən*), **lemurine** (*lem'ū-rin*), **lem'ūroid**. [L. *lēmūrēs*, ghosts.]

**lend,** *lend*, *v.t.* to give the use of for a time: to afford, grant, or furnish, in general: to let for hire.—*v.i.* to make a loan:—*pr.p.* **lend'ing**; *pa.t.* and *pa.p.* **lent.**—*n.* (*Scot.*) a loan (often **len'**).— *ns.* **lend'er**; **lend'ing,** the act of giving in loan: that which is lent or supplied (*Shak.*).—**lend'-lease,** an arrangement authorised by Congress in 1941 by which the President could supply war materials to other countries whose defence he deemed vital to the United States.—Also *adj.* [O.E. *lænan*—*læn*, *lān*, a loan.]

**leng,** *leng*, (*obs.*) *v.t.* to lengthen: to tarry: to long (*Spens.*). [O.E. *lengan*.]

**lenger, leng'gər,** *adj.* and *adv.* (*Spens.*), longer.— *adj.* and *adv.* **leng'est** (*obs.*), longest. [O.E. *lengra*, compar. of *lang* (adj.), *lengest*, superl. of *lang* and of *lange* (adv.).]

**length,** *length*, *n.* quality of being long: extent from end to end: the longest measure of anything: long continuance: prolixity: time occupied in uttering a vowel or syllable: the quantity of a vowel: any definite portion of a known extent: a stretch or extent: distance (chiefly *Scot.*): a suitable distance for pitching a cricket ball: the lengthwise measurement of a horse, boat, etc. (*racing*).—*v.t.* and *v.i.* **length'en,** to

Neutral vowels in unaccented syllables: *el'ə-mənt*; for certain sounds in foreign words, see p. viii

increase, in length.—*adj.* (*obs.*) length'ful.—*adv.*
length'ily.—*n.* length'iness.—*advs.* length'ways,
length'wise, in the direction of the length.—*adj.*
length'y, of great or tedious length: rather long.
—at length, in full: fully extended: at last;
go (to) great lengths, go to all lengths, any length(s)
to do everything possible (sometimes more than
is ethical) to achieve a purpose; length of days,
prolonged life. [O.E. *lengthu—lang*, long.]
lenient, *lēn'yənt, -ni-ənt, adj.* softening (*arch.*):
soothing (*arch.*): mild: merciful.—*n.* (*med.,
arch.*) that which softens: an emollient.—*ns.*
lē'nience, lē'niency.—*adv.* lē'niently.—*v.t.* lenify
(*len', lēn'*), (*arch.*) to mitigate, to assuage.—*adj.*
lenitive (*len'*), mitigating: laxative.—*n.* any
palliative: an application for easing pain (*med.*):
a mild purgative (*arch.*).—*n.* lenity (*len'*), mildness: clemency. [L. *lēniēns, -entis*, pr.p. of
*lēnīre*, to soften—*lēnis*, soft.]
Leninism, *len'in-izm, n.* the political, economic and
social principles and practices of the Russian
revolutionary leader, *Lenin* (Vladimir Ilyich
Ulyanov; 1870-1924), esp. his theory of government by the proletariat.—*ns.* Len'inist, Len'inite.
leno, *lē'nō, n.* a thin muslin-like fabric. [Perh. Fr.
*linon.*]
lenocinium, *lē-nō-sin'i-əm,* (*Scots law*) *n.* conniv-
ance at one's wife's adultery. [L. *lēnōcinium*,
enticement—*lēnō*, a pander.]
lens, *lenz, n.* a piece of transparent matter causing
regular convergence or divergence of rays
passing through it (*opt.*): the refracting structure
(*crystalline lens*) between the crystalline and
vitreous humours of the eye: a device to
influence the direction of sound waves (*acoustic
lens*): (*cap.*), the lentil genus:—*pl.* lens'es.—
*adjs.* lent'iform, lent'oid.—electron lens, any
arrangement of electrodes designed to influence
the direction of cathode rays. [L. *lēns, lentis*,
lentil.]
Lent, *lent, n.* spring (*obs.*): the time from Ash
Wednesday to Easter observed as a time of
fasting in commemoration of Christ's fast in
the wilderness (Matt. iv. 2).—*adj.* Lent'en, of
Lent: sparing: fleshless.—lent'-lil'y, the daffodil.
[O.E. *lencten*, the spring; Du. *lente*, Ger. *lenz.*]
lent, *pa.t.* and *pa.p.* of lend.
Lentibulariaceae, *len-tib-ū-lā-ri-ā'si-ē, n.pl.* the
bladderwort and butterwort family of tubifloral
dicotyledons. [Origin obscure.]
lenticel, *lent'i-sel, n.* a breathing pore in bark.—
*adj.* lenticell'ate.—*n.* lent'icle (*geol.*), a lenticular
mass.—*adj.* lentic'ūlar, shaped like a lens or
lentil seed: double-convex.—*adv.* lentic'ūlarly.
[L. *lēns, lentis,* a lentil.]
lentigo, *len-ti'gō, n.* a freckle: (usu.) freckles:—*pl.*
lentigines (*len-tij'i-nēz*).—*adjs.* lentig'inose, lentig'inous (*bot.*), minutely dotted. [L. *lentigō,
-inis,* a freckle—*lēns,* a lentil.]
lentil, *len'til, n.* an annual papilionaceous plant
(*Lens esculenta*, or *Ervum lens*) common near
the Mediterranean: its seed used for food.
[O.Fr. *lentille*—L. *lēns, lentis,* the lentil.]
lentisk, *len'tisk, n.* the mastic tree. [L. *lentiscus.*]
lento, *len'tō,* (*mus.*) *adj.* slow.—*adv.* slowly.—*n.* a
slow passage or movement.—*adv.* lentamen'te
(*-tā*).—*adj.* and *adv.* lentan'do, slowing. [It.,—
L. *lentus,* slow.]
lentor, *len'tör,* (*arch.*) *n.* sluggishness: viscidity.—
*adj.* len'tous. [L. *lentus,* slow.]
lenvoy, *len-voi'.* Same as envoy (2). [Fr. *l'* for *le,*
the.]
Leo, *lē'ō, n.* the Lion, a constellation between
Cancer and Virgo: the 5th sign of the zodiac, in
which it used to be (the constellation is now in
the sign Virgo).—*n.* Lē'onid (*-ə-nid*), a meteor of
a swarm whose radiant is in the constellation Leo.
—*adj.* Lē'onine, pertaining to any of the Popes
named Leo: of a kind of Latin verse, generally
alternate hexameter and pentameter, rhyming

at the middle and end (prob. from some unknown
poet named Leo, Leoninus, or Leonius): (without *cap.*) lionlike. [L. *leō, -ōnis,* lion.]
leontiasis, *lē-ont-i'ə-sis, n.* a form of leprosy giving
a lionlike appearance. [Gr. *leontiāsis—leōn,
-ontos,* lion.]
leopard, *fem.* leop'ardess, *lep'ərd, -es, n.* a large
spotted animal of the cat kind found in Africa
and Asia: in America, the jaguar: a lion passant
gardant (also, *rarely,* leop'ardess; *her.*).—
leop'ard-cat, a spotted wild cat of India;
leop'ard's-bane, a composite plant, Doronicum;
leop'ard-wood, letter-wood.—hunting leopard,
the cheetah; snow leopard, the ounce. [O.Fr.,—
L. *leopardus*—Gr. *leopardos* (for *leontopardos*)—
*leōn,* lion, *pardos,* pard.]
leotard, *lē'o-tärd, n.* a skin-tight garment worn by
dancers and acrobats, sleeveless or long-sleeved,
legs varying from none at all to ankle-length.
[Jules *Léotard,* 19th-century French trapeze
artist.]
lep, *lep, v.i.* (*dial.,* esp. *Ir.*) for leap: also *dial.* for
the *pa.t.*—*pa.t.* (*Spens.*) lepp'ed.
leper, *lep'ər, n.* leprosy (*obs.*): one affected with
leprosy: a tainted person (*fig.*): an outcast.—*n.*
lep'ra, leprosy: a scurfy, mealy substance on
some plants (*bot.*).—*adj.* lep'rose (*-rōs*), scaly:
scurfy.—*ns.* leprosā'rium, a hospital for lepers;
leprosity (*-ros'i-ti*), scaliness; lep'rosy (*-rə-si*), a
name formerly widely applied to chronic skin
diseases: now to one caused by a bacillus and
occurring in two forms, tubercular, beginning
with spots and thickenings of the skin, and
anaesthetic, attacking the nerves, with loss of
sensation in areas of skin: corruption (*fig.*).—
*adj.* lep'rous, of or affected with leprosy: scaly:
scurfy. [O.Fr. *lepre* and Gr. *leprā—lepros,* scaly
—*lepos,* or *lepis,* a scale, *lepein,* to peel.]
lepid, *lep'id, adj.* pleasant, jocose. [L. *lepidus.*]
lepid-, lepido-, *lep'id-, -ō-, -o',* in composition,
scale.—*n.* Lepidoden'dron (Gr. *dendron,* tree), a
genus of fossil trees, mainly Carboniferous of the
Lepidodendrā'ceae, akin to Lycopodiaceae, the
stem covered with ovate leaf-scars arranged
spirally.—*adj.* and *n.* lepidoden'droid.—*ns.* lepid'olite (Gr. *lithos,* stone), a lithia mica, usu. pink;
lepidomelane' (Gr. *melās, -ănos,* black), a black
mica rich in iron, occurring in scales.—*n.pl.*
Lepidop'tera (Gr. *pteron,* wing), an order of
insects, with four wings covered with fine scales
—butterflies and moths.—*n.* lepidop'terist, a
student of butterflies and moths.—*adj.* lepidop'-
terous.—*ns.* Lepidosi'ren (Gr. *Seirēn,* a Siren),
an Amazon mudfish; Lepidos'teus (Gr. *osteon,* a
bone), a genus of fishes with rhomboid scales
hard like bone, the bony pike; Lepidos'trobus
(Gr. *strobos,* twist), the fossil fructification of
Lepidodendron.—*adj.* lep'idote (Gr. *lepidōtos*),
scaly: scurfy. [Gr. *lepis, -idos,* a scale.]
leporine, *lep'ə-rin, adj.* pertaining to or resembling
the hare. [L. *leporinus—lepus, lepŏris,* the hare.]
lepped. See lep.
leprechaun, leprechawn, *lep-rə-hhön', n.* a little
brownie who helps Irish housewives, mends
shoes, grinds meal, etc. [Prob. Old Ir. *luchorpán,
lu,* small, *corpan, corp,* a body.]
leproserie, leprosery, *lep'rə-sər-i, n.* a leper
hospital. [Fr. *léproserie.*]
leprosy. See leper.
lepton, *lep'ton, n.* the smallest ancient Greek coin,
translated mite in the N.T.: a modern Greek
coin, 1/100th of a drachma:—*pl.* lep'ta: any
of a group of subatomic particles with weak
interactions, electrons, negative muons and
neutrinos (*pl.* lep'tons).—*adj.* leptocephal'ic
(Gr. *kephălē,* head), narrow-skulled.—*n.* lep-
toceph'alus, the larva of an eel.—*adj.* lep-
tocerc'al (Gr. *kerkos,* tail), slender-tailed.—
*n.* leptodac'tyl (Gr. *daktylos,* finger, toe).—
*adj.* leptodac'tylous, slender-toed.—*n.* lep'tome,

phloem or bast.—*adjs.* lep'torrhine (Gr. *rhis, rhinos*, nose), narrow-nosed; lep'tosome (Gr. *sōma*, body), slender-bodied: asthenic.—*n.* leptospirō'sis (Gr. *speira*, a coil), a disease of animals or man caused by bacteria of the genus Leptospira.—*adj.* leptosporan'giate, having each sporangium derived from a single cell (opposed to *eusporangiate*). [Gr. *leptos*, neut. *lepton*, slender.]

lere. Same as lear (1).

Lerna, *lûr'nə*, Lerne, *lûr'nē, n.* a swamp near Argos, supposed to be the home of the Hydra killed by Hercules.—*adjs.* lernaean, lernean (*lûr-nē'ən*).

Lesbian, *lez'bi-ən, adj.* of the island of *Lesbos,* Mitylene, or Mytilene, home of Alcaeus and Sappho: amatory, erotic: (of women) homosexual.—*n.* a woman homosexual.—*n.* Les'bianism.—Lesbian rule, an adaptable standard, from the pliable leaden rule of Lesbian masons.

lese-majesty, leze-majesty, *lēz'-maj'is-ti, n.* an offence against the sovereign power, treason.—lese, leze, treated as if it had verbal force, has also been used to form compounds such as lese'-human'ity, leze-liberty. [Fr. *lèse majesté,* transl. of L. *laesa mājestās,* injured majesty—*laedĕre,* to hurt.]

lesion, *lē'zhən, n.* a hurt: an injury or wound (*med.*). [Fr. *lésion*—L. *laesiō, -ōnis*—*laedĕre, laesum,* to hurt.]

less, *les, adj.* (used as *comp.* of little) smaller (not now used of material things): in smaller quantity: minor: fewer (*arch.* and *coll.*): inferior, lower in estimation: younger: more (*Shak.*, with an expressed or implied negative).—*adv.* not so much: in a lower degree.—*n.* a smaller portion or quantity.—*conj.* (*Milt.*) unless (often written 'less).—*prep.* without: with diminution of, minus.—much less, often used by confusion for much more; nothing less than, (formerly) anything rather than: (now) quite as much as. [O.E. *lǣssa,* less, *lǣs* (adv.); apparently not conn. with little.]

-less, *adj.* suffix, free from, wanting, as guilt*less,* god*less.* [O.E. *-lēas,* Ger. *-los,* Goth. *-laus.*]

lessee, *les-ē', les'ē, n.* one to whom a lease is granted. [lease.]

lessen, *les'n, v.t.* to make less, in any sense: to lower in estimation: to disparage: to belittle.—*v.i.* to become less, shrink. [less.]

lesser, *les'ər, adj.* less: smaller: inferior: minor. —*adv.* (*Shak.*) less. [Double comp. from less.]

lesson, *les'n, n.* a portion of Scripture read in divine service: a spell, instalment, or prescribed portion of instruction: an exercise: a piece or performance of music (*obs.*): an instructive or warning experience or example: a severe reproof.—*v.t.* to instruct: to train: to rebuke.—*n.* less'oning. [Fr. *leçon*—L. *lectiō, -ōnis*—*legĕre,* to read.]

lessor, *les'ör, n.* one who grants a lease. [lease.]

lest, *lest, conj.* that not: for fear that. [M.E. *leste*—O.E. *thў lǣs the,* the less that—*thў* instrum. case; see the (2).]

lest, *lest,* (*Spens.*) *v.i.* for list, to listen.

let, *let, v.t.* to leave (*Shak.*): to omit (*Shak.*): to allow to escape (*arch.*): to allow to go or come: to give leave or power to, to allow, permit, suffer (usu. with infin. without *to*): to grant to a tenant or hirer: in the imper. with accus. and infin. without *to,* often used virtually as an auxiliary with imperative or optative effect: to behave so as to give an impression, make it appear (*obs.*; also *v.i.*):—*pr.p.* lett'ing; *pa.t.* and *pa.p.* let.—*n.* a letting for hire.—*n.* lett'er, one who lets, esp. on hire; lett'ing.—let'-alone (*Shak.*), absence of restraint, freedom. —*adj.* refraining from interference: leaving things to themselves.—let'-down, an act or occasion of letting down: a disappointment; let'-off, a festivity: an outlet: (in games) a

failure to take advantage of an opportunity; lett'er-gae' (*Scot.*), one who lets go, a precentor; let'-up, cessation: abatement: alleviation.—let alone, not to mention, much less: to refrain from interference with: (*imper.*) trust (*arch.*); let be (*dial.* let-a-be), to leave undisturbed: not to mention, to say nothing of (*Scot.*); let blood, to bleed; let down, to allow to fall: to lower: to leave in the lurch, fail to back up at need; let drive, to aim a blow: to discharge a missile; let fall, to drop; let fly, to fling, discharge, shoot; let go, to cease holding: to slacken (*naut.*); let in, to allow to enter: to take in or swindle: to betray into or involve in (*for*) anything vexatious: to insert: to leak inwards; let into, to admit to the knowledge of: to throw into one with; let off, to allow to go free or without exacting all: to fire off, discharge; let on (*dial.*), to allow to be believed, to pretend: to betray awareness: to reveal, divulge; let one know, to inform one; let oneself loose, to let go restraint, to indulge in extravagant talk or conduct; let out, to allow to get free, or to become known: to strike out or kick out: to widen, slacken, enlarge: to put out to hire: to leak outwards; let up, to become less: to abate; let up on, to cease to have to do with; let well alone, to let things remain as they are from fear of making them worse. [O.E. (Anglian) *lētan* (W.S. *lǣtan*), to permit, pa.t. *lēt;* pa.p. *lǣten;* Ger. *lassen.*]

let, *let, v.t.* (*arch.*) to hinder: to prevent:—*pa.t.* and *pa.p.* lett'ed, let.—*adj.* let (*arch.*), obstructed. —*n.* hindrance, obstruction (*arch.*): delay (*arch.*): obstruction by the net, or other ground for cancelling a service (*lawn-tennis,* etc.): a service so affected.—*n.* lett'er. [O.E. *lettan,* to hinder—*lǣt,* slow.]

-let, *-lit, -lət,* noun suff., used to form diminutives, as brace*let,* leaf*let,* stream*let.*

letch, *lech.* See latch (1), leach (1).

lethal, *lē'thəl, adj.* death-dealing: deadly: mortal. —*ns.* lethal'ity; le'thee (*Shak.*), app. life-blood, or death; prob. with some reminiscence of Lethe (see below).—*adj.* lethif'erous, carrying death. [L. *lēt(h)ālis*—*lēt(h)um,* death.]

lethargy, *leth'ər-ji, n.* heavy unnatural slumber: torpor.—*adjs.* lethargic (*-är'*), -al, pertaining to lethargy: unnaturally sleepy: torpid.—*adv.* lethar'gically.—*adj.* leth'argied.—*v.t.* leth'argise, -ize. [Gr. *lēthārgiä,* drowsy forgetfulness—*lēthē,* forgetfulness, *ärgos,* idle.]

Lethe, *lē'thē, n.* a river of the underworld causing forgetfulness of the past to all who drank of it: oblivion.—*adjs.* lethe'an; leth'ied (*Shak.*). [Gr. *lēthē,* forgetfulness (*lēthēs hydōr,* the water or river of forgetfulness)—*lēthein,* a collateral form of *lanthanein,* to be hidden.]

Lett, *let, n.* a member of a people inhabiting Lett'-land (Latvia): native or citizen of Latvia.—*adjs.* Lett'ic, of the group (also called *Baltic*) of languages to which Lettish belongs, incl. Lithuanian and Old Prussian; Lett'ish.—*n.* language of Letts. [Ger. *Lette*—Lettish *latvis* (now *latvietis*).]

letter, *let'ər, n.* a conventional mark primarily used to express a sound of speech: often loosely applied to the sound itself: a written or printed message: literal meaning: printing-type: (in *pl.*) learning, literary culture.—*v.t.* to stamp letters upon: to mark with a letter or letters.—*adj.* lett'ered, marked with letters: educated: versed in literature: literary.—*ns.* lett'erer; lett'ering, the act of impressing or marking with letters: the letters impressed: their style or mode of formation.—*adj.* lett'erless, without letters: illiterate.—lett'er-board, a board on which matter in type is placed for keeping or convenience in handling; lett'er-book, a book in which letters or copies of letters are kept; lett'er-box, a box for receiving letters for or from the post; **lett′er-card**, a card folded and gummed like a letter, with perforated margin for opening; **letter-carrier**, postman: mail-carrier; **lett′er-clip**, an appliance for gripping letters or papers to keep them together; **lett′er-file**, arrangement for holding letters for reference; **lett′er-founder**, one who casts type; **letterhead**, a printed heading on notepaper, etc.: a piece of notepaper with such heading.—*adj.* **lett′er-perfect**, (of actor, etc.) having the words of the part committed accurately to memory.—**lett′erpress**, printed reading matter: a copying-press.—*ns.pl.* **lett′ers-pat′ent**, a writing conferring a patent or privilege, so called because written on open sheets of parchment; **letters requisitory**, or **rogatory**, an instrument by which a court of one country asks that of another to take certain evidence on its behalf.—**lett′er-stamp**, an instrument for cancelling postage-stamps: a stamp for imprinting dates, etc.; **lett′er-weight**, a paper-weight; **lett′er-wood**, leopard-wood, a South American tree of the bread-nut genus, with dark brown mottled heart-wood; **lett′er-writer**, one who writes letters, esp. for hire: a book of forms for imitation in writing letters.—**letter of credit**, a letter authorising credit or cash to a certain sum to be given to the bearer; **letter of indication**, a banker's letter requesting foreign bankers to accept the bearer's circular notes; **letter of the law**, literal interpretation of the law. [Fr. *lettre*—L. *littera, litera*.]

**lettern**, *let′ərn.* Same as **lectern**.

**lettre**, *le-tr′*, (Fr.) a letter.—**lettre de cachet** (*də ka-she*), a letter under the royal signet: a royal warrant for arrest and imprisonment; **lettre de change** (*də shäzh*), a bill of exchange; **lettre de marque** (*də märk*), a letter of marque or of reprisal.

**lettuce**, *let′is, n.* a composite plant (*Lactuca sativa*) with milky juice: its leaves used as a salad: extended to other (inedible) plants of the genus.—**frog's lettuce**, a kind of pondweed; **lamb's lettuce**, corn-salad. [Appar. from some form (perh. the pl.) of A.Fr. *letue* (Fr. *laitue*)— L. *lactūca*—*lac*, milk.]

**leu**, *le′ōō, n.* the monetary unit or franc of Rumania.—Also **ley** (*lā*):—*pl.* **lei** (*lā*). [Rum., lion.]

**leuc-, leuco-, leuk-, leuko-**, *lūk-, lōōk-, lūs-, lōōs-, lū′kō, lōōk′ō-, -ko′-,* (-c- and -k- are in most cases interchangeable, and, except in the first case, -k- forms have not been given below), in composition, white.—*ns.* **leucaemia, leukaemia** (or, more strictly formed) **leuchaemia,** (*lū-kē′mi-ə,* Gr. *haima,* blood), **leucocythaemia; leucocyte** (*-kō-sit;* Gr. *kytos,* container, used as if cell), a white corpuscle of the blood or lymph.—*adj.* **leucocytic** (*-sit′ik*).—*ns.* **leucocythaemia** (*-sī-thē′mi-ə;* Gr. *haima,* blood), a disease in which there is a great increase (in some forms a decrease) of white corpuscles in the blood, associated with changes in the lymphatic system and enlargement of the spleen; **leucocytol′ysis** (Gr. *lysis,* dissolution), breaking down of the leucocytes; **leucocytopē′nia** (Gr. *peniā,* poverty), poverty in leucocytes; **leucocytō′sis,** the presence of an excessive number of white corpuscles in the blood; **leucoplast** (*lū′, lōō′kō-plāst;* Gr. *plastos,* formed—*plassein,* to form; *bot.*), a starch-forming body in protoplasm; **leucorrhoea** (*lū-, lōō-kō-rē′ə;* Gr. *rhoiā—rheein,* to flow), an abnormal mucous or muco-purulent discharge from the vagina, the whites; **leucotomy** (*lū-, lōō-kot′ə-mi;* Gr. *tomē,* a cutting), a surgical scission of the white association fibres between the frontal lobes of the brain and the thalamus to relieve cases of severe schizophrenia and manic-depressive psychosis; **leu′cotome** (*-kō-tōm*), a needle used for the purpose.—**leu′co-base,** **leu′co-compound,** a colourless reduction

product of a dye that can be converted back to the dye by oxidation. [Gr. *leukos,* white.]

**leuch.** See **lauch.**

**leucin(e),** *lū′, lōō′sin, -sēn, n.* a decomposition product of proteins. [Gr. *leukos,* white.]

**Leuciscus,** *lū-, lōō-sis′kəs, n.* a genus of fresh-water cyprinoid fishes, including the roach, dace, chub, minnow, etc. [Gr. *leukiskos,* white mullet.]

**leucite,** *lū′, lōō′sit, n.* a whitish mineral (silicate of aluminium and potassium).—*adj.* **leucitic** (*-sit′ik*). —*ns.* **leucitohē′dron,** the cubic icositetrahedron, simulated by typical leucite crystals. [Gr. *leukos,* white.]

**Leucojum,** *lū-, lōō-kō′jəm, n.* the snowflake genus of amaryllids. [Gr. *leukoīon,* snowdrop, etc. —*leukos,* white, *ion,* violet.]

**leucoma,** *lū-, lōō-kō′mə, n.* a white opacity of the cornea. [Gr. *leukōma—leukos.*]

**leuk(o)-.** Alternative form of **leuc(o)-.** See **leuc-.**

**lev, lew,** *lef, n.* the monetary unit or franc of Bulgaria:—*pl.* **leva** (*lev′ä*). [Bulg., lion.]

**Levant,** *li-vant′, n.* the East (*obs.*): the eastern Mediterranean and its shores: (without *cap.*) the levanter wind: (without *cap.*) a kind of morocco leather.—*adj.* (without *cap.*) (*lev′ənt*), eastern.—*n.* **Levant′er,** an inhabitant of the Levant: (without *cap.*) a boisterous easterly wind in the Levant.—*adj.* **Levant′ine** (or *lev′ən-tin*), of the Levant. [Fr. *levant* or It. *levante,* east, lit. rising—L. *levāre,* to raise.]

**levant,** *li-vant′, v.i.* to decamp.—*n.* **levant′er,** one who absconds, esp. with bets unpaid. [Sp. *levantar,* to move.—L. *levāre,* to raise.]

**levator,** *le-vā′tər, -tōr, n.* a muscle that raises—opp. to *depressor.* [L. *levātor,* a lifter—*levāre.*]

**levee,** *lev′i,* also *li-vē′, n.* getting out of bed (*arch.*): a morning (or comparatively early) reception of visitors, esp. by a person of distinction.—*v.t.* to attend the levee of. [Fr. *levée, lever*—L. *levāre,* to raise.]

**levee,** *lev′i, li-vē′, n.* a natural or artificial riverside embankment, esp. on the Lower Mississippi: a quay. [Fr. *levée,* raised; see the foregoing.]

**levée en masse,** *lə-vā ä mas,* (Fr.). See **levy.**

**level,** *lev′l, n.* an instrument for testing horizon-tality: a horizontal position: a condition of horizontality: a horizontal plane or line: a nearly horizontal surface or region with no con-siderable inequalities: the horizontal plane, literal or figurative, that anything occupies or reaches up to: height: a horizontal mine-gallery: the act of aiming (*Shak.*): the thing aimed at (*Spens.*): an ascertainment of relative elevation: a levelling survey: natural or approp-riate position or rank: a condition of equality: a ditch or channel for drainage, esp. in flat country. —*adj.* horizontal: even, smooth: even with anything else: uniform: well-balanced, sound of judgment: in the same line or plane: filled to a level with the brim: equal in position or dignity.—*adv.* in a level manner: point-blank.— *v.t.* to make horizontal: to make flat or smooth: to lay low: to raze: to aim: to make equal: to direct: survey by taking levels.—*v.i.* to make things level: to aim: to guess, estimate.—*v.t.* and *v.i.* to change in spelling or pronunciation, making one word, form, the same as another: —*pr.p.* lev′elling; *pa.t.* and *pa.p.* lev′elled.—*ns.* **lev′eller,** one who levels in any sense: one who would remove all social or political inequalities, esp. (*cap.*) one of an ultra-republican party in the parliamentary army, crushed by Cromwell in 1649; **lev′elling,** act of making level: change in spelling or pronunciation making one word, form, the same as another.—**level best** (*coll.*), one's utmost; **lev′el-cross′ing,** a place at which a road crosses a railway at the same level.—*adj.* **lev′el-head′ed,** having sound common sense.— **lev′elling-rod, -staff,** a graduated rod used in levelling.—**level down** or **up,** to lower or raise

*fāte, fär; mē, hûr* (her); *mīne; mōte, för; mūte; mōōn, fōōt; dhen* (then)

to the same level or status; **level off**, to make flat or even: to reach and maintain equilibrium; **find one's level**, come to equilibrium in one's natural position or rank; **on the level**, fair: honestly speaking. [O.Fr. *livel, liveau* (Fr. *niveau*)—L. *libella*, a plummet, dim. of *libra*, a balance.]

**level-coil**, *lev'l-koil,* (*arch.*) *n.* an old Christmas game in which the players changed seats: a hubbub. [Fr. *lever le cul*, to lift the buttocks.]

**lever**, *lē'vər, n.* a bar turning on a support or fulcrum for imparting pressure or motion from a source of power to a resistance.—*v.t.* to move with a lever.—*n.* **le'verage**, the mechanical power gained by the use of the lever: advantage gained for any purpose.—**le'ver-watch**, a watch having a vibrating lever in the mechanism of the escapement. [O.Fr. *leveor—lever*—L. *levāre*, to raise.]

**lever de rideau**, *lə-vă də rē-dō,* (Fr.) curtain-raiser.

**leveret**, *lev'ə-rit, n.* a hare in its first year. [O.Fr. *levrette* (Fr. *lièvre*)—L. *lepus, lepŏris*, a hare.]

**leviable.** See levy.

**leviathan**, *le-vī'ə-thən, n.* a water animal, in Job xli, apparently a crocodile (*B.*): a huge sea-monster: anything of huge size, esp. a ship or a man: (after Hobbes's book, 1651) the state: Satan (*obs.*).—*adj.* gigantic, formidable. [Heb. *livyāthān.*]

**levigate**, *lev'i-gāt, v.t.* to smooth: to grind to fine powder, esp. with a liquid.—*adj.* smooth.—*adj.* **lev'igable.**—*n.* **leviga'tion.** [L. *lēvigāre, -ātum—lēvis*, smooth; Gr. *leios*; akin to level.]

**levigate**, *lev'i-gāt, v.t.* to lighten. [L. *lēvigāre, -ātum—lēvis*, light.]

**levin**, *lev'in,* (*arch.*) *n.* lightning. [M.E. *leuen(e)*, prob.—O.N.]

**levirate**, *lēv'* or *lev'i-rāt, n.* the (ancient Hebrew and other) custom of compulsory marriage with a childless brother's widow.—*adjs.* **lev'irate**, **leviratical** (*-rat'i-kl*).—*n.* **levirā'tion.** [L. *lēvir*, a brother-in-law.]

**Levis**, *lē'viz, n.pl.* heavy, close-fitting denim, etc., trousers, with low waist, reinforced at points of strain with copper rivets. [Trademark.]

**levitation**, *lev-i-tā'shən, n.* the act of rising by virtue of lightness: act of rendering light: the floating of heavy bodies in the air, according to spiritualists: raising and floating on a cushion of air.—*v.t., v.i.* **lev'itate**, to (cause to) float. [On the model of *gravitate*—L. *levis*, light.]

**Levite**, *lē'vīt, n.* a descendant of *Levi*: an inferior priest of the ancient Jewish Church: a clergyman (*slang*).—*adjs.* **levitic** (*li-vit'ik*), **-al.**—*adv.* **levit'ically.**—*n.* **Levit'icus**, the third book of the Old Testament.—**Levitical degrees**, the degrees of kindred within which marriage was forbidden in Lev. xviii. 6-18.

**levity**, *lev'it-i, n.* lightness of weight: lightness of temper or conduct: thoughtlessness: disposition to trifle: vain quality. [L. *levitās, -ātis*—*levis*, light.]

**levo-.** Same as laevo-.

**levulose.** Same as laevulose.

**levy**, *lev'i, v.t.* to raise, collect, as an army or tax: to call for: to impose: to begin to wage:—*pr.p.* **lev'ying**; *pa.t.* and *pa.p.* **lev'ied.**—*n.* the act of levying: a contribution called for from members of an association: a tax: the amount collected: troops levied.—*adj.* **leviable** (*lev'i-ə-bl*), able to be levied or assessed.—**to levy war**, to make war; **levy in mass** (Fr. **levée en masse**), a levy of all able-bodied men for military service. [Fr. *levée*—*lever*—L. *levāre*, to raise.]

**lew**, *lū, lōō, adj.* tepid, lukewarm. [O.E. *hlēow.*]

**lewd**, *lōōd, lūd, adj.* ignorant (*obs.*): bare (*B.*): bad (*obs.*): lustful: unchaste.—*adv.* **lewd'ly.**—*ns.* **lewd'ness**; **lewds'by**, **lewd'ster**, one addicted to lewdness. [O.E. *lǣwede*, ignorant.]

**lewis**, *lōō'is, n.* a dovetail iron tenon for lifting

blocks of stone (also **lew'isson**): a freemason's son. [Ety. dub.]

**Lewis gun**, *lōō'is gun*, a light machine-gun invented by Col. Isaac Newton *Lewis*.

**Lewisian**, *lōō-iz'i-ən,* or *-is',* adj. of *Lewis* in the Outer Hebrides: Pre-Cambrian (*geol.*).

**lewisite**, *lōō'is-it, n.* a yellow cubic mineral, calcium titanium antimonate. [Named after W. J. *Lewis* (1847-1926), English mineralogist.]

**lewisite**, *lōō'is-it, n.* a vesicant liquid, an arsine derivative, used in chemical warfare. [Named after W. L. *Lewis*, American chemist.]

**lex**, *leks,* (L.) law.—**lex non scripta** (*non skrip'tə, nōn skrēp'ta*), unwritten law—i.e. the common law; **lex scripta** (*skrip'tə, skrēp'ta*), statute law; **lex talionis** (*ta-li-ō'nis, tä-*), the law of talion.

**lexicon**, *leks'i-kən, n.* a word-book or dictionary.—*adj.* **lex'ical**, belonging to a lexicon: pertaining to the words of a language as distinct from its grammar and constructions.—*adv.* **lex'ically.**—*n.* **lexicographer** (*-kog'rə-fər*).—*adjs.* **lexicographic** (*kə-graf'ik*), **-al.**—*ns.* **lexicog'raphist**; **lexicog'raphy**, dictionary-making; **lexicol'ogist**; **lexicol'ogy**, the study of the history and meaning of words.—**lexical meaning**, the meaning of the base word when not inflected. [Gr. *lexikon*, a dictionary—*lexis*, a word, *legein*, to speak.]

**lexigraphy**, *leks-ig'rə-fi, n.* a system of writing in which each sign represents a word.—*adjs.* **lexigraphic** (*-graf'ik*), **-al.** [Gr. *lexis*, word, *graphein*, to write.]

**ley**, *lā, lē.* Same as lea.—**ley'-farming** (see lea (2)).

**Leyden jar**, *lā'dən jär*, a condenser for electricity, a glass jar coated inside and outside with tin-foil or other conducting material. [*Leyden* in Holland, where it was invented.]

**leze-majesty.** See lese-majesty.

**lhasa apso**, *lä'sə ap'sō, n.* a Tibetan (breed of) small, long-haired terrier:—*pl.* apsos. [*Lhasa*, the capital of Tibet.]

**lherzolite**, *lûr'zə-līt, n.* peridotite, consisting essentially of olivine with monoclinic and ortho-rhombic pyroxenes. [From Lake *Lherz* in the Pyrenees (Ariège).]

**li**, *lē, n.* a Chinese unit of distance, about one-third of a mile. [Chin.]

**liable**, *lī'ə-bl, adj.* subject to an obligation: exposed to a possibility or risk: subject (*Shak.*): responsible: tending: apt: fitting, suitable (*Shak.*): likely.—*n.* **liabil'ity**, state of being liable: that for which one is liable, a debt, etc.—**employers' liability**, responsibility of employers to their servants for the negligence of those to whom they have delegated their authority; **limited liability**, a principle of modern statute law which limits the responsibilities of shareholders in a partnership, joint-stock company, etc., by the extent of their personal interest therein. [App.—Fr. *lier*—L. *ligāre*, to bind.]

**liaison**, *lē-ā'zn, -zŏ, lyez-ŏ, n.* union, or bond of union: connection: illicit union between the sexes: in French, the linking in pronunciation of a final (and otherwise silent) consonant to a vowel beginning the next word: effective conjunction with another unit or force (*mil.*).—*v.i.* **liaise** (*lē-āz'*; back-formation), to form a link: to be or get in touch.—**liaison officer**, an officer forming a link with another unit or force. [Fr.,—L. *ligātiō, -ōnis—ligāre*, to bind.]

**liana**, *lē-ä'nə,* **liane**, *lē-än', n.* any climbing plant, especially any contorted woody kind festooning tropical forests. [Fr. *liane*, Latinised or Hispanicised as *liana*, app.—*lier*—L. *ligāre*, to bind.]

**liang**, *lyang, n.* a Chinese ounce or tael. [Chin.]

**liar.** See lie. (1).

**liard**, *lī'ərd, adj.* grey: dapple-grey (*Scot.* **li'art**, **ly'art**).—*n.* (*lyär*) an old French coin of little worth. [O.Fr. *liard, liart.*]

**Lias**, *lī'əs,* (geol.) *n.* and adj. Lower Jurassic.—*adj.* **Liassic** (*lī-as'ik*). [A Somerset quarryman's word, app.—O.Fr. *liois* (Fr. *liais*), a kind of limestone.]

**lib**, *lib*, (now *dial*.) *v.t.* to geld. [Cf. Du. *lubben*.]

**libation**, *li-bā′shən, li-*, *n.* the pouring forth of wine or other liquid in honour of a god, or (*facet*.) for other purpose: the liquid poured.—*adj.* **li′bant**, sipping: lightly touching.—*v.t.* **li′bate** (*rare*), to make a libation to.—*adj.* **li′batory**. [L. *libāre, -ātum*, to pour, sip, touch; Gr. *leibein*, to pour.]

**libbard**, *lib′ərd*, (*arch*.) *n.* Same as **leopard**.

**libeccio**, *li-bet′chō*, *n.* the south-west wind.—Also (*Milt*.) **libecchio**. [It.,—L. *Libs*; Gr. *Lips, Libos*.]

**libel**, *lī′bl*, *n.* a written accusation: any malicious defamatory publication or statement: written defamation (*English law*): distinguished from *slander* or spoken defamation; in Scots law both are slander): the statement of a plaintiff's grounds of complaint.—*v.t.* to defame by libel: to satirise unfairly: to proceed against by producing a written complaint (*law*):—*pr.p.* **li′belling**; *pa.t.* and *pa.p.* **li′belled**.—*ns.* **li′bellant**, one who brings a libel; **li′beller**, a defamer; **li′belling**.—*adj.* **li′bellous**, containing a libel: defamatory.—*adv.* **li′bellously**. [L. *libellus*, dim. of *liber*, a book.]

**liber**, *lī′bər*, *n.* bast. [L. *līber*, bast, book.]

**liberal**, *lib′ə-rl*, *adj.* befitting a freeman or a gentleman: directed towards the cultivation of the mind for its own sake, disinterested (opposed to *technical* and *professional*): generous: noble-minded: broad-minded: not bound by authority or traditional orthodoxy: looking to the general or broad sense rather than the literal: candid: free: free from restraint: licentious in speech or action (*obs*.): ample: (*cap*.) of the Liberal Party (see below).—*n.* one who advocates greater freedom in political institutions: one whose views are liberal.—*n.* **liberalisā′tion**.—*v.t.* and *v.i.* **lib′eralise**, **-ize**, to make or become liberal, or enlightened.—*ns.* **lib′eralism**, the principles of a liberal in politics or religion; **lib′eralist**.—*adj.* **liberalist′ic**.—*n.* **liberality** (*-al′i-ti*), the quality of being liberal: generosity: largeness or nobleness of mind: candour: freedom from prejudice.—*adv.* **lib′erally**.—**liberal arts**, the studies that make up a liberal education: in the Middle Ages, the *trivium* and *quadrivium*; **Liberal Party**, successors of the Whigs, including the Radicals, advocates of democratic reform and liberty; **Liberal Unionists**, a section of the Liberal Party that opposed Gladstone's Home Rule policy (1886) and joined the Conservatives. [L. *liberālis*, befitting a freeman—*liber*, free.]

**liberate**, *lib′ə-rāt*, *v.t.* to set free: to release from restraint, confinement, or bondage: to give off.—*ns.* **liberā′tion**; **liberā′tionism**; **liberā′tionist**, one who is in favour of church disestablishment; **lib′erātor**.—*adj.* **lib′eratory** (*ə-tə-ri*), tending to liberate. [L. *liberāre, -ātum—liber*, free.]

**liberty**, *lib′ər-ti*, *n.* freedom from constraint, captivity, slavery, or tyranny: freedom to do as one pleases: the unrestrained enjoyment of natural rights: power of free choice: privilege: permission: free range: leisure: disposal: the bounds within which certain privileges are enjoyed: (often in *pl*.) a limited area outside a prison in which prisoners were allowed to live: presumptuous or undue freedom: speech or action violating ordinary civility.—*ns.* **libertā′rian**, a believer in free-will; **libertā′rianism**; **liber′ticide**, a destroyer of liberty: destruction of liberty; **lib′ertinage** (also *-ûrt′*), debauchery; **lib′ertine** (*-tēn, -tin, -tin*), originally, a freedman: formerly one who professed free opinions, esp. in religion: one who leads a licentious life, a rake or debauchee.—*adj.* belonging to a freedman: unrestrained: licentious.—*n.* **lib′ertinism**.

—**lib′erty-boat**, a boat for liberty-men; **liberty cap** (see **cap**); **Liberty Hall**, a place where one may do as one likes; **liberty horse**, a circus horse that, as one of a group and without a rider, carries out evolutions on command; **liberty-man**, a sailor with permission to go ashore; **liberty ship**, a prefabricated all-welded cargo-ship mass-produced in the U.S.A. during World War II.—**at liberty**, free: unoccupied: available; **civil liberty**, freedom of an individual within the law: individual freedom as guaranteed by a country's laws; **liberty of indifference**, freedom of the will; **liberty of the press**, freedom to print and publish without government permission; **take liberties with**, to treat with undue freedom or familiarity, or indecently: to falsify; **take the liberty**, venture, presume. [Fr. *liberté*—L. *libertās, -ātis*, liberty: L. *libertinus*, a freedman—*liber*, free.]

**libido**, *li-bē′dō, li-bi′dō*, *n.* vital urge, either in general or as of sexual origin (*psych*.): sexual impulse.—*adjs.* **libidinal** (*-bid′*), pertaining to the libido; **libid′inous**, lustful, lascivious, lewd.—*ns.* **libid′inist**, a lewd person; **libidinos′ity**, **libid′inousness**.—*adv.* **libid′inously**. [L. *libidō, -inis*, desire—*libet, lubet*, it pleases.]

**libken**, *lib′ken*, (*old slang*) *n.* a place of abode. [Old slang *lib*, to sleep, **ken** (2).]

**libra**, *lī′brə*, L. *lē′*, *n.* a Roman pound (*ant*.; used in contraction lb. for the British pound, and £ for a pound in money): (*cap*.) the Balance, a constellation between the Virgin and the Scorpion: the seventh sign of the zodiac in which it used to be (it is now in Scorpio). [L. *libra*.]

**libraire**, *lē-brer*, (Fr.) bookseller; **librairie** (*lē-bre-rē*), book-trade: bookshop.

**library**, *lī′brə-ri*, *n.* a collection of books: a building or room containing it: a publisher's series: also a collection of gramophone records, computer programmes, etc.—*ns.* **librā′rian**, the keeper of a library; **librā′rianship**.—**lending library**, one from which people may take books away on loan. [L. *librārium*, a bookcase—*liber*, a book.]

**librate**, *lī′brāt*, *v.t.* to poise: to balance.—*v.i.* to oscillate: to be poised.—*n.* **librā′tion**, balancing: a state of equipoise: a slight swinging motion.—*adj.* **lī′bratory**.—**libration of the moon**, a slight turning of the moon to each side alternately so that more than half of its surface is visible one time or other. [L. *librāre, -ātum—libra*, balance.]

**libretto**, *li-bret′ō*, *n.* the text or book of words of an opera, oratorio, or ballet:—*pl.* **librett′i** (*-ē*), **librett′os**.—*n.* **librett′ist**, a writer of libretti. [It., dim. of *libro*—L. *liber*, a book.]

**Librium**, *lib′ri-əm*, *n.* proprietary name for chlordiazepoxide, a tranquilliser. [Tradename.]

**Libyan**, *lib′i-ən*, *adj.* of Libya in North Africa.—*n.* a native thereof. [Gr. *Libyē*, Libya.]

**lice**, *līs*, plural of **louse**.

**licence**, in U.S. **license**, *lī′səns*, *n.* a being allowed: leave: grant of permission, as for manufacturing a patented article, selling intoxicants, driving a motor vehicle, piloting an aeroplane, using a television set, keeping a dog, owning a gun: the document by which authority is conferred: excess or abuse of freedom: licentiousness, libertinage, debauchery: a departure for effect from a rule or standard in art or literature: tolerated freedom.—*v.t.* **li′cense**, to grant licence to: to permit to depart, dismiss: to authorise or permit.—Also **licence**.—*adjs.* **li′censable**; **li′censed**, holding a licence: permitted, tolerated.—*ns.* **licensee′**, one to whom a licence is granted; **li′censer**, one who grants licence or permission: one authorised to license; **li′censure**, act of licensing; **licentiate** (*lī-sen′shi-āt*), among Presbyterians, a person authorised by a Presbytery to preach: a holder of an academic diploma of various kinds: in some European universities, a graduate ranking between bachelor and doctor.—*adj.* **licentious** (*-sen'shəs*), indulging in excessive freedom: given to the indulgence of the animal passions: dissolute. — *adv.* **licen'tiously.** — *n.* **licen'tiousness.**—**licensed victualler,** a victualler who holds a licence to sell intoxicating liquors.— **special licence,** licence given by the Archbishop of Canterbury permitting the marriage of two specified persons without banns, and at a place and time other than those prescribed by law— loosely used in Scotland in speaking of marriage by consent registered by warrant of the sheriff. [Fr. *licence*—L. *licentia*—*licēre,* to be allowed.]

**licentia vatum,** *li-sen'shyə vā'təm, li-ken'ti-a wā'toōm, vä'*, (L.) poetic licence.

**lich,** *lich,* (*Spens.*) *adj.* a Southern form of **like.**

**lich,** *lich, n.* a body, living or dead (*obs.*).—**lich'-gate,** a roofed churchyard gate to rest the bier under; **lich'-owl,** a screech-owl, deemed a death-portent; **lich'wake** (see **lykewake**); **lich'way,** a path by which the dead are carried to burial. [M.E. *lich, liche* (Southern), *like* (Northern)—O.E. *lic;* Ger. *leiche,* corpse.]

**lichanos,** *lik'a-nos,* (*anc. Gr. mus.*) *n.* the string or the note struck by the forefinger. [Gr. *lichanos,* forefinger, lichanos—*leichein,* to lick.]

**lichee.** Same as **litchi.**

**lichen,** *li'kən, lich'ən, n.* a compound plant consisting of a fungus and an alga living symbiotically, forming crusts and tufts on stones, trees, and soil: an eruption on the skin.—*adj.* **li'chened,** covered with lichens.—*ns.* **li'chenin,** a starch got from Iceland moss; **li'chenism,** the consorting of fungus and alga as a lichen; **li'chenist, lichenol'ogist,** one versed in **lichenol'ogy,** the study of lichens.—*adj.* **li'chenous,** abounding in, or pertaining to, of the nature of, lichens, or lichen. [L. *lichēn*—Gr. *leichēn, -ēnos.*]

**lichgate,** etc. See **lich.**

**licht,** *lihht,* the Scots form of **light** (1, 2, 3).

**licit,** *lis'it, adj.* lawful, allowable.—*adv.* **lic'itly.** [L. *licitus.*]

**lick,** *lik, v.t.* to pass the tongue over: to take in by the tongue: to lap: to put or render by passing the tongue over: to pass over or play upon in the manner of a tongue: to smear: to beat (*slang*).—*v.i.* (*slang*) to go at full speed.—*n.* an act of licking: a quantity licked up, or such as might be imagined to be licked up: a slight smearing or wash: a place where animals lick salt: a blow, flick (esp. *Scot.* in *pl.,* a thrashing): vigorous speed (*coll.*): a wag (*Scot.*).—*ns.* **lick'er; lick'ing,** a thrashing.—**lick'er-in',** a toothed cylinder that takes in material to a carding engine; **lick'penny,** that which licks up, or is a drain upon, one's money; **lick'-platter, lick'spittle,** a toady; **lick'-trencher,** a parasite.— **a lick and a promise,** a perfunctory wash; **lick into shape,** to mould into due form, from the notion that the she-bear gives form to her shapeless young by licking them; **lick one's boots,** to toady; **lick the dust,** to be slain: to be abjectly servile. [O.E. *liccian;* Ger. *lecken,* L. *lingĕre,* Gr. *leichein.*]

**lickerish, liquorish,** *lik'ər-ish, adj.* dainty: tempting: eager to taste or enjoy: lecherous.—*adv.* **lick'erishly.**—*n.* **lick'erishness.** [Variant of **lecherous.**]

**licorice.** Same as **liquorice.**

**lictor,** *lik'tör, -tər, n.* an officer who attended a Roman magistrate, bearing the fasces. [L. *lictor.*]

**lid,** *lid, n.* a cover, hinged or separate, for the opening of a receptacle: the movable cover of the eye: an effective restraint (*fig.*): a hat (*slang*).— *adjs.* **lidd'ed,** having a lid or lids; **lid'less.**—**put the lid on it,** to end the matter: to be a culminating injustice, misfortune, etc. [O.E. *hlid* (Du. *lid*)—*hlidan,* to cover.]

**lidger.** See **ledger.**

**lido,** *lē'dō, n.* a bathing beach: an open-air swimming-pool. [From the *Lido* at Venice— L. *litus,* shore.]

**lie,** *lī, n.* a false statement made with the intention of deceiving: anything misleading or of the nature of imposture: (with *the*) an accusation of lying.—*v.i.* to utter falsehood with an intention to deceive: to give a false impression:— *pr.p.* **ly'ing;** *pa.t.* and *pa.p.* **lied.**—(*Scot.*) **lee** (*lē*), *n.* and *v.i.* often of an unintentional false statement.—(*dial.*) **lig.**—*n.* **li'ar,** one who lies, esp. habitually.—**lie detector,** an instrument claimed to detect lying by recording abnormal involuntary bodily reactions in a person not telling the truth.—**give one the lie (in one's throat),** to charge one to one's face of lying; **give the lie to,** to charge with lying: to prove false; **lie in one's throat,** to lie shamelessly; **white lie,** a conventional phrase not strictly true: a well-meant falsehood. [O.E. *lyge* (noun), *lēogan* (strong vb.): Du. *liegen,* Goth. *liugan,* Ger. *lügen,* to lie.]

**lie,** *lī, v.i.* to be in a horizontal or nearly horizontal posture: to assume such a posture: to lean: to press: to be situated: to have a position or extent: to remain: to be or remain passively: to abide: to be still: to be incumbent: to depend: to consist: to be sustainable (*law*): to be imprisoned (*Shak.*): to lodge, pass the night (*arch.*):—*pr.p.* **ly'ing;** *pa.t.* **lay;** *pa.p.* **lain,** (*B.*) **li'en**—erroneously **laid,** by confusion with **lay.**—*n.* mode or direction of lying: slope and disposition: relative position: general situation: a spell of lying: an animal's lurking-place or favourite station: position from which a golf-ball is to be played: a layer: a railway siding.—*n.* **li'er.**—**lie'-abed',** one who lies late —also *adj.*—**lie along,** to be extended at full length (*arch.*); **lie at one's door,** to be directly imputable to one: **lie at one's heart,** to be an object of interest or affection to one; **lie back,** to lean back on a support: to rest after a period of hard work; **lie by,** to be inactive: to keep out of the way: to lie to (*naut.*); **lie by the heels,** to be in prison; **lie hard** or **heavy on, upon, to,** to oppress, burden; **lie in,** to be in childbed: to stay in bed late; **lie in one,** to be in one's power; **lie in the way,** to be ready, at hand: to be an obstacle; **lie in wait,** to lie in ambush; **lie low,** to keep quiet or hidden: to conceal one's actions or intentions; **lie on, upon,** to be incumbent on; **lie on one's hands,** to remain unwanted, unclaimed, or unused; **lie on the oars** (see **oars**); **lie out of,** to remain without the good of, without payment of; **lie over,** to be deferred to a future occasion; **lie to,** to be or become nearly stationary with head to wind; **lie under,** to be subject to or oppressed by; **lie up,** to abstain from work: to take to or remain in bed: of a ship, to go into or be in dock; **lie with,** to lodge or sleep with (*arch.*): to have sexual intercourse with: to rest with as a choice, duty, etc.; **lying-in hospital,** a maternity hospital; **take it lying down,** to endure tamely. [O.E. *licgan;* Ger. *liegen;* Goth. *ligan.*]

**Lie algebra,** *lē,* that dealing with groups (**Lie groups**) of quantities subject to relationships reducing the number which are independent. [(Marius) Sophus *Lie* (1842-99), Norwegian mathematician.]

**Liebig,** *lē'big, n.* a beef extract first prepared by the German chemist J. von *Liebig* (1803-73).— **Liebig condenser,** the ordinary water-cooled glass condenser used in laboratory distillations.

**lied,** *lēt, n.* a German lyric or song, esp. an art-song:—*pl.* **lieder** (*lē'dər*).—**lied ohne worte** (*ō'nə vör'ta*), song without words. [Ger.; cf. O.E. *lēoth,* a song.]

**lief,** *lēf,* (*arch.*) *adj.* and *n.* beloved, dear.—*adv.*

willingly.—Also *adj.* and *adv.* **lieve, leve** (*lēv*):—
*compar.* **lief'er, liev'er** (*Scot.* **loor**); *superl.*
**lief'est, liev'est.**—**had as lief,** should like as
well to; **had liefer, liever,** had rather; **leeze me,**
(*Scot.*) for *lief is me,* an expression of affection
(usu. with *on*). [O.E. *lēof*; Ger. *lieb.*]
**liege,** *lēj, adj.* free except as within the relations
of vassal and feudal lord: under a feudal tenure.—*n.* one under a feudal tenure: a vassal:
a loyal vassal, subject: a lord or superior (also
in this sense, **liege'-lord**).—*n.* **liege'dom,** allegiance.—*adj.* **liege'less,** not subject to a superior.
—**liege'man,** a vassal: a subject. [O.Fr. *lige,*
prob. from O.H.G. *ledic,* free, *lidan,* to depart.]
**lien,** *lē'ən, lēn,* (*law*) *n.* a right to retain possession of another's property until the owner
pays a debt. [Fr.,—L. *ligāmen,* tie, band.]
**lien,** *li'ən,* (*B.*) *pa.p.* of **lie** (2).
**lien,** *li'ən, n.* the spleen.—*adj.* **li'enal.** [L. *liēn.*]
**lientery,** *li'ən-tə-ri, n.* a form of diarrhoea with
liquid evacuations of undigested food.—*adj.*
**lienteric** (*-ter'ik*). [Gr. *leios,* smooth, *enteron,*
an intestine.]
**lierne,** *li-ûrn', n.* a cross-rib or branch-rib in
vaulting.
**lieu,** *lū, lōō, n.* place, stead, chiefly in the phrase
'in lieu of'. [Fr.,—L. *locus,* place.]
**lieutenant,** *lef-, lif-, ləf-ten'ənt,* also *le-, lə-, arch.*
naval, *lōō-ten'-, lōōt'nənt,* in U.S., *lōō-, n.* one
representing, or performing the work of a
superior (form. also *fig.*): an officer holding the
place of another in his absence: a commissioned
officer in the army next below a captain, or in
the navy next below a lieutenant-commander
and ranking with captain in the army: one holding a place next in rank to a superior, as in
the compounds **lieuten'ant-col'onel, lieuten'ant-
command'er, lieute.₁'ant-gen'eral.**—*ns.* **lieuten'-
ancy, lieuten'antship,** (*Shak.*) **lieuten'antry,** office
or commission of a lieutenant: the body of
lieutenants; **lieuten'ant-col'onelcy; lieuten'ant-
command'ership; lieuten'ant-gen'eralship; lieuten'ant-gov'ernancy,** a State governor's deputy
(*U.S., Austr.*): a governor subordinate to a
governor-general: a governor (Isle of Man,
Jersey, Guernsey); **lieuten'ant-gov'ernorship.**—
**Lord Lieutenant,** the title of the viceroy of
Ireland (till 1922): a permanent governor of a
county, head of the magistracy and the chief
executive authority:—*pl.* **lords lieutenant, lord
lieutenants, lords lieutenants.** [Fr.; see **lieu** and
**tenant.**]
**life,** *līf, n.* state of being alive: conscious existence: animate or vegetative existence: the sum
of the activities of plants and animals: continuation or possession of such a state: continued existence, activity, or validity of anything: vitality: union of soul and body: the
period between birth and death: a continued
opportunity of remaining in the game: career:
present state of existence: manner of living:
moral conduct: animation: liveliness: appearance of being alive: a living being: living things:
social state: human affairs: narrative of a life:
eternal happiness: a quickening principle: that
on which continued existence depends: one
who imparts animation: the living form and
expression, living semblance: an insured person:—*pl.* **lives** (*līvz*).—*interj.* used as an oath,
abbreviated from *God's life.*—*adj.* (and in composition) for the duration of life: of life.—
*adjs.* **life'ful** (*Spens.*) **lyfull, lifull**), full of vital
energy; **life'less,** dead: insensible: without
vigour: insipid: sluggish.—*adv.* **life'lessly.**—*n.*
**life'lessness.**—*adjs.* **life'like,** like a living person
or the original; **life'some,** full of life: gay,
lively.—*n.* **lif'er,** a person sentenced for life:
a life sentence.—*adj.* **life'-and-death',** critical:
determining between life and death.—**life'-
annū'ity,** a sum paid to a person yearly during

life; **life'-assur'ance, life'-insur'ance,** insurance
providing a sum of money for a specified bene-
ficiary in the event of the policy-holder's death,
and for the policy-holder if he reaches a specified
age; **life'belt,** a buoyant belt for sustaining
a person in the water; **life'-blood,** the blood
necessary to life: that which gives strength or
life: a twitching, as of the eyelid; **life'boat,** a
boat for saving shipwrecked persons; **life'-buoy,**
a buoy for supporting a person in the water till
he can be rescued; **life'-cycle** (*biol.*), the round
of changes in the life and generations of an
organism, from zygote to zygote; **life'-estate',**
an estate held during the life of the possessor;
**life'-force',** a directing principle supposed to be
immanent in living things, turning their activities
to nature's own purposes.—*adj.* **life'-giving,** imparting life: invigorating.—**life'guard,** a bodyguard: one employed to rescue bathers in difficulties: (*cap., pl.,*) two horse regiments formed
in 1660; **life'-his'tory,** the history of a life: the
succession of changes from zygote to maturity
and death: the life-cycle.—*adj.* **life'hold,** held for
life.—**life'-in'terest,** an interest lasting during a
life; **life'-jack'et,** a buoyant jacket, a lifebelt;
**life'-line,** a rope for saving or safeguarding
life: a vital line of communication.—*adj.* **life'-
long,** lasting throughout life.—**life'manship**
(*facet.—Stephen Potter*), the art of making the
other fellow feel inferior; **life'-mor'tar,** a mortar for throwing a line to a ship in distress;
**life'-peer,** a peer whose title is not hereditary;
**life'-peer'age; life'-peeress,** a woman who receives a peerage which cannot be handed down
to heirs; **life'-preserv'er,** an apparatus for
saving from drowning: a loaded cane.—*adj.*
**life'-ren'dering** (*Shak.*), yielding up life.—**life'-
rent** (*Scots law*), a right to use for life; **life'-
renter,** one who enjoys a liferent:—*fem.* **life'-
rentrix; life'-rock'et,** a rocket for carrying a
line to a ship in distress; **life'-saver,** one who
saves from death, esp. from drowning: one
employed to rescue bathers in difficulty: something, or someone, that comes to one's aid at
a critical moment (*fig.*); **life'-sav'ing.**—*adj.*
designed to save life, esp. from drowning.—
**life'-school,** a school where artists work from
living models.—*adj.* **life'-size(d),** of the size of
the object represented.—**life'-table,** a table of
statistics of probability of life; **life'-tenant,** the
holder of a life-estate; **life'time,** time during
which one is alive.—*adj.* **life'-wear'y** (*Shak.*),
weary of life: wretched.—**life'-work,** the work
to which one's life is or is to be devoted.—
**bring to life,** to confer life upon: to reanimate;
**come to life,** to become alive: to be reanimated;
**for life,** for the whole period of one's existence:
(as if) to save one's life; **for the life of him,**
though it were to save his life: do what he
might; **high life,** fashionable society or its manner of living; **line of life,** a crease in the palm
in which palmists see a promise of longevity;
**not on your life** (*coll.*), on no account; **see life,**
to see how other people live, esp. the disreputable; **take one's life,** to kill one; **to the life,**
very closely like the original: exactly drawn.
[O.E. *līf*; O.N. *līf,* Sw. *lif,* Du. *lijf,* body, life;
Ger. *leib,* body, *leben,* to live, life.]
**lift,** *lift,* (*Scot.*) *n.* the air, heavens, sky. [O.E.
*lyft*; Ger. *luft,* O.N. *lopt,* Goth. *luftus,* the air.]
**lift,** *lift, v.t.* to bring to a higher position: to
elevate: to take up: to take up for burial
(*Scot.*): to increase (*U.S.*): to elate: to take
and carry away: to hold up, support: to arrest
(*slang*): to steal: to plagiarise.—*v.i.* to rise.—
*n.* act of lifting: lifting power: vertical distance
of lifting: the component of the aerodynamic
force on an aircraft acting upwards at right
angles to the drag: that which is to be raised:
that which assists to lift: an enclosed platform

moving in a well to carry persons or goods up and down: the well in which it works: one of the layers of material in a shoe heel: a contrivance for raising or lowering a vessel to another level of a canal: a step in advancement: help on one's way by taking upon a vehicle.—*adj.* lift′able.—*n.* lift′er, one who, or that which, lifts: a thief (*Shak.*).—lift′ing-bridge, a bridge whose roadway can be raised bodily; lift′-off, the take-off of an aircraft or rocket: the moment when this occurs; lift′-pump, any pump that is not a force-pump.—lift one's hand, to raise it in hostility; have one's face lifted, to undergo an operation for smoothing and firming it. [O.N. *lypta*—*lopt*, the air.]

lig, ligge, *lig*, (*Spens.* and *Northern dialect*) *v.i.* a form of lie (2).—*infin.* and *pl.* (*Spens.*) also ligg′en. Lig is also a dialect form of lie (1).

ligament, *lig′ə-mənt*, *n.* anything that binds: the bundle of fibrous tissue joining bones or cartilages (*anat.*): a bond of union.—*adjs.* ligamental (*-ment′l*), ligament′ary, ligament′ous.—*v.t.* ligate (*li′gāt*), to tie up.—*ns.* liga′tion, act of binding: state of being bound; ligature (*lig′ə-chər*), anything that binds: a bandage: a tie or slur (*mus.*): a type of two or more letters (e.g. ff, ffi) (*print.*): a cord for tying the blood-vessels, etc. (*med.*): impotence produced by magic.—*v.t.* to bind with a ligature. [L. *ligāre*, to bind.]
ligan. See lagan.

liger, *li′gər*, *n.* cross between *li*on and female ti*ger*.

ligger, *lig′ər*, *n.* the horizontal timber of a scaffolding: a nether millstone: a plank bridge: a coverlet for a bed: a kelt or spent salmon: a night-line with float and bait for pike-fishing. [lig, Northern form of lie (2).]

light, *lit*, *n.* the agency by which objects are rendered visible: electromagnetic radiation capable of producing visual sensation: that from which it proceeds, as the sun, a lamp: a high degree of illumination: day: a gleam or shining from a bright source: a gleam or glow in the eye or on the face: the power of vision: an eye (*arch.*): the brighter part of a picture: means of igniting or illuminating: a lighthouse: mental or spiritual illumination (*fig.*): enlightenment: a hint, clue, keyword, help towards understanding: knowledge: open view: aspect: a conspicuous person: an aperture for admitting light: a vertical division of a window.—*adj.* not dark: bright: whitish: well lighted.—*v.t.* to give light to: to set fire to: to attend with a light.—*v.i.* to become light or bright:—*pr.p.* light′ing; *pa.t.* and *pa.p.* light′ed or lit.—*n.* light′er, one who sets alight: a spill, mechanical device, or other means of igniting.—*adj.* light′ful, full of light.—*n.* light′ing, illumination: ignition, kindling: disposal or quality of lights.—Also *adj.*—*adjs.* light′ish; light′less.—*n.* light′ness.—*adj.* light′some, full of light.—light′-ball (*hist.*), a combustible ball used to give light in warfare.—*n.pl.* light′-dues, tolls from ships, for maintenance of lighthouses.—light′house, a building with a light to guide or warn ships or aircraft; light′-houseman, light(house)keep′er, the keeper of a lighthouse.—*n.* and *adj.* light′ing-up (lighting-up time, the time from which vehicles must show lights).—light′-mill, a radiometer; light′-or′gan, a keyboard instrument that gives a play of light as an organ gives sound.—*adj.* light′proof, light-tight.—light′ship, ship serving the purpose of a lighthouse.—*adj.* light′-tight, impervious to light.—light time, the time taken by light to travel from a heavenly body to the observer; light′-tower; light′-year, distance light travels in a year (about 6,000,000,000,000 miles).—according to one's lights, as far as one's knowledge, spiritual illumination, etc., enable one to judge; between the lights, in the twilight; between two

lights, under cover of darkness; bring to light, to reveal; come to light, to be revealed; fixed light, in lighthouses, an unchanging light; floating light, a light at the masthead of a lightship; inner light, spiritual illumination, light divinely imparted; in one's, the, light, between one and the source of illumination or chance of success, etc.; light of nature, intellectual perception or intuition: man's capacity of discovering truth unaided by revelation (*theol.*); lights out (*mil.*), bugle or trumpet call for extinction of lights; light up, to light one's lamp, pipe, etc.: to turn on the light: to make or become light or bright; lit (up), drunk; northern (southern) lights, aurora borealis (australis); see the light, to come into view or being: to be converted; stand in one's own light, to hinder one's own advantage. [M.E. *liht*—O.E. (Anglian) *leht*, *lēht* (W.S. *lēoht*); Ger. *licht*.]

light, *lit*, *adj.* not heavy: of short weight: easily suffered or performed: easily digested: well risen, as bread: containing little alcohol: not heavily armed: active: not heavily burdened: unimportant: not dense or copious or intense: slight: scanty: gentle: delicate: nimble: facile: frivolous: unheeding: gay, lively: amusing: unchaste: loose, sandy: giddy, delirious: idle: worthless: delivered of a child (in *compar.*; *obs.*): short of contract (*bridge*).—*adv.* lightly.—*v.t.* (*obs.*) to lighten (see also next article).—*v.t.* lighten, to make lighter.—*v.i.* to become lighter.—*ns.* light′er, a large open boat used in unloading and loading ships; light′erage, unloading by lighters: the payment for such unloading; light′erman.—*adj.* light′ish.—*adv.* light′ly, in a light manner: slightly: easily, readily, unthinkingly (*Shak.*): not improbably (*arch.*): promptly.—*v.t.* (esp. in Scots form lichtly (*lihht′li*), to slight.—*n.* light′ness.—*n.pl.* lights, the lungs of an animal (as lighter than adjoining parts).—*adj.* light′some, light, gay, lively, cheering.—*n.* light′someness.—*adj.* light′-armed, armed in a manner suitable for activity.—light engine, one without coaches or trucks attached.—*adjs.* light′er-than-air, of aircraft, sustained by a gas-bag; light′-faced, of type, having thin lines; light′-fing′ered, light or active with one's fingers: thievish; light′-foot, -ed, nimble, active; light′-hand′ed, with light, delicate, or dexterous touch: having little in the hand: empty-handed: insufficiently manned; light′-head′ed, giddy in the head: delirious: thoughtless: unsteady. — light′-head′edness.—*adj.* light′-heart′ed, unburdened or merry of heart: free from anxiety: cheerful: inconsiderate.—*adv.* light′-heart′edly.—light′-heart′edness.—*adj.* light′-heeled, swift of foot: loose, unchaste (*obs.*).—light′-horse, light-armed cavalry; light′-horse′man; light industry (see industry); light′-in′fantry, light-armed-infantry.—*adj.* light′-legged, swift of foot.—light literature, music, etc., such as calls for little mental effort.—*adj.* light′-mind′ed, frivolous or unstable: inconsiderate.—light′-mind′edness; light′-o′-love, a fickle or wanton woman: in *Shak.* the name of an old dance tune; light railway, a railway of light construction.—*adj.* light′-spir′ited, having a cheerful spirit.—light′weight, a man or animal between the middleweight and the featherweight, as a boxer over 9 st. and not over 9 st. 9 lb. (amateur 7 lb.): a person of little importance or influence: a light article of any kind, esp. a motor-cycle.—*adj.* light in weight.—*adj.* light′-winged, having light wings: volatile.—make light of, to treat as of little consequence. [O.E. (Anglian) *liht* (W.S. *lioht*, *lēoht*); Ger. *leicht*, O.N. *lēttr*; L. *lēvis*.]

light, *lit*, *v.i.* dismount: to come down as from a horse or vehicle or from fall or flight: to alight: to settle: to rest: to come by chance:—*pr.p.* light′ing; *pa.t.* and *pa.p.* light′ed or lit.

—Also (*Pr. Bk.*) light'en.—light out, to decamp. [O.E. *lihtan*, to dismount, lit. make light; see preceding.]

**lighten,** *līt'n, v.t.* to make light or lighter, or brighter: to illuminate.—*v.i.* to become light, lighter, or brighter: to flash as lightning.— *ns.* light'ening, a making or becoming lighter or brighter; light'ning, the electric flash usually followed by thunder: a revival or exhilaration supposed to precede death (*Shak.*).—*adj.* characterised by speed and suddenness.—light'ning-arrest'er, apparatus for protecting electrical apparatus in thunderstorms; light'ning-bug, a firefly; light'ning-conduc'tor, -rod, a metallic rod for protecting buildings from lightning; lightning strike, an industrial strike without warning; light'ning-tube', a fulgurite. [light (1).]

**lighten.** See light (2 and 3).

**lightsome.** See light (1 and 2).

**lignage,** *lin'ij* (*Spens.*). Same as lineage.

**lign-aloes, lignaloes,** *līn-al'ōz, lig-nal'ōz,* (*B.*) *n.* aloes-wood. [L. *lignum*, wood, and *aloēs*, gen. of L. and Gr. *aloē*, aloe.]

**ligne,** *lin,* (Fr. *lēn-y*'), *n.* a measure of watch movement (Swiss ligne = 2·256 mm.). [Fr.]

**lignocaine,** *lig'nō-kān, n.* a local anaesthetic much used in dentistry.

**lignum,** *lig'nəm, n.* wood.—*adj.* lig'neous, woody: wooden.—*n.* lignificā'tion.—*v.t.* and *v.i.* lig'nify, to turn into wood or woody:—*pr.p.* lig'nifying; *pa.t.* and *pa.p.* lig'nified.—*n.* lig'nin, a complicated mixture of substances deposited in thickened cell-walls of plants.—*adj.* ligniper'dous (L. *perdĕre*, to destroy), destructive of wood.—*n.* lig'nite (-*nīt*), brown coal, a stage in the conversion of vegetable matter into coal.—*adjs.* lignitic (-*nit'ik*); ligniv'orous (L. *vorāre*, to devour), feeding on wood.—lig'num-vitae (*vī'tē*; L. lig'num *wē'ti, vē'*; wood of life), the wood of Guaiacum. [L. *lignum*, wood.]

**lignum,** *lig'nəm*, (*Austr.*) *n.* a wiry shrub (*Muehlenbeckia cunninghamii*) or other shrub of the Polygonum family, forming dense masses in swamps and plains in Australia.—lig'num-scrub'; lig'num-swamp'. [For Polygonum.]

**ligroin,** *lig'rō-in, n.* a petroleum fraction boiling between 80° and 120°C. [Origin unknown.]

**ligule,** *lig'ūl, n.* (*bot.*) a scale at the top of the leaf-sheath in grasses: a similar scale on a petal: a strap-shaped corolla in composite plants.— *n.* lig'ula, a tongue-like part or organ: the anterior part of an insect's labium, or lower lip. —*adjs.* lig'ular; lig'ulate (*bot.*), like a strap: having ligules.—*n.pl.* Liguliflo'rae, a division of the Compositae having all flowers ligulate.— *adj.* liguliflo'ral. [L. *ligula*, dim. of *lingua*, a tongue.]

**Liguorian,** *li-gwō'ri-ən, -gwō', n.* and *adj.* Redemptorist.

**ligure,** *lig'ūr, -yər,* (*B.*) *n.* an unknown precious stone—jacinth or amber according to R.V. (New English Bible says turquoise). [Gr. *ligȳrion*.]

**like,** *līk, adj.* identical, equal, or nearly equal in any respect: similar, resembling: suiting, befitting (often in compound *adjs.* as *ladylike*): characteristic of (sometimes in compound *adjs.*): inclined, likely, probable (*dial.*).—*n.* one of the same kind: the same thing: a stroke bringing the total to the same as the other side's (*golf*): an exact resemblance.—*adv.* in the same manner: probably (*dial.*): as it were (*dial.*): as if about (*dial.*): nearly (*coll.*): to some extent (*dial.*): sometimes used meaninglessly (*dial.*).— *conj.* (*Shak.*; another reading *as*; now *illit.*) as: as if.—*prep.* in the same manner as: to the same extent as.—*v.t.* (*Shak.*) to compare, liken. —*v.i.* (*obs.*) to be or seem likely (to), come near (to).—*ns.* like'lihood, similitude (*obs.*): semblance (*obs.*): resemblance (*obs.*): probability:

promise of success or of future excellence; like'liness, likelihood: likeness (*Spens.*).—*adj.* like'ly, similar (*Spens.*): like the thing required: promising: probable: credible: pleasing (*dial.*): comely (*dial.*).—*adv.* probably.—*v.t.* lik'en, to represent as like or similar: to compare.—*n.* like'ness, resemblance: semblance: guise: one who or that which has a resemblance: a portrait.—*adv.* like'wise, in the same or similar manner: moreover: too.—feel like, to be disposed or inclined towards; had like, was likely, came near to; look like, to show a likelihood of: to appear similar to; something like a, a fine specimen, a model of what the thing should be; such like, of that kind; the likes of (them), people like (them). [O.E. *līc*, seen in *gelīc*; O.N. *līkr*, Du. *gelijk*, Ger. *gleich* ( = *geleich*).]

**like,** *līk, v.t.* to please (*obs.*): to be pleased with: to approve: to enjoy.—*n.* a liking, chiefly in phrase 'likes and dislikes'.—*adj.* lik(e)'able, lovable: amiable.—*ns.* lik'er, one who likes; lik'ing, affection, inclination: taste: satisfaction: beloved (*Milt.*): condition, plight (*obs.*). —*adj.* (*obs.*) pleasing: in good condition (also good'-liking, well'-liking).—on liking (*arch.*), on approval. [Orig. impersonal—O.E. *līcian*, to please, to be suitable—*līc*, like, suitable, likely.]

**like,** *līk,* (*Scot.*) *n.* a corpse: a lykewake.—*n.* like'-wake, -walk (see lykewake). [Northern form of lich.]

**likin,** *lē-kēn', n.* formerly, a Chinese transit duty. [Chin.]

**lilac,** *lī'lək, n.* a European tree (*Syringa vulgaris*) of the olive family, with light-purple or white flowers, or other species of the genus: a light-purple colour.—*adj.* of that colour. [Fr. (*obs.*; now *lilas*) and Sp.,—Ar. *līlāk, lilāk*—Pers. *lilak, nīlak*, bluish.]

**liliaceous, etc.** See lily.

**lill,** *lil,* (*Spens.*) *v.t.* to loll (the tongue). [Cf. loll.]

**lill,** *lil,* (*Scot.*) *n.* a finger-hole of a wind instrument. [Cf. Du. *lul.*]

**Lillibullero,** *lil-i-boo-lē'rō, n.* the famous ballad in mockery of the Irish Catholics, which 'sung James II out of three kingdoms'.—Also Lilliburlē'ro. [From the meaningless refrain.]

**Lilliputian,** *lil-i-pū'sh(y)ən, n.* an inhabitant of Lilli'put (-*put*), an imaginary country described by Swift in his *Gulliver's Travels*, inhabited by pygmies: a midget, pygmy.—*adj.* diminutive.

**lilt,** *lilt, v.i.* to do anything briskly or adroitly, as to hop about (*dial.*): to sing or play, esp. merrily, or vaguely and absent-mindedly, giving the swing or cadence rather than the structure of the melody: to hum.—*v.t.* to sing or play in such a manner.—*n.* a cheerful song or air: cadence, movement of a tune or the like: a lill (*obs.*). [M.E. *lulte*; origin unknown.]

**lily,** *lil'i, n.* any plant or flower of the genus Lil'ium, typical genus of Liliā'ceae, a family of monocotyledons differing from rushes chiefly in the large conspicuous flowers: extended to others, of the same family, of the kindred Amaryllidaceae, or unrelated: the fleur-de-lis: a person or thing of great purity or whiteness (*fig.*).—*adj.* white: pale.—*adjs.* liliā'ceous; lil'ied, adorned with lilies: resembling lilies.—*adjs.* lil'y-liv'ered, white-livered: cowardly; lil'y-white.— lily of the Nile, Richardia or Zantedeschia; lily of the valley, Convallaria. [O.E. *lilie*—L. *lilium*—Gr. *leirion*, lily.]

**lima,** *lē'mə, n.* (in full Lima bean) a bean (*Phaseolus lunatus*) akin to the French bean.—li'ma-wood, a kind of brazil-wood. [*Lima* in Peru.]

**limation,** *lī-mā'shən, n.* filing. [L. *līma*, a file.]

**Limax,** *lī'maks, n.* the common genus of slugs, giving name to the slug family Limā'ceae:—*pl.* limaces (*lī-mā'sēz*).—*adj.* limaceous (*lī-mā'shəs*). —*n.* limacel (*lim-ə-sel'*), a slug's reduced, usually embedded, shell.—*adj.* limaciform (*lim-as'*, or *li-mäs'*), slug-like.—*n.* **limaçon** (*lim'ə-son*; Fr. *lē-mä-sɔ̃*), a curve whose polar equation is *r* = *a* cos θ + *b*. [L. *limāx*, a slug.]

**limb**, *lim*, *n.* a member or organ of the body, now only an arm, leg, or wing: a prudish euphemism for leg: a projecting part: a main branch of a tree or of anything else: a member of a body of people, as 'a limb of the law': an imp, scapegrace, as 'a limb of Satan'.—*v.t.* to supply with limbs (*Milt.*): to dismember.—*adjs.* **limbed**, furnished with limbs; **limb'less.**—*adv.* **limb'meal** (*Shak.*), limb by limb.—**limb'-girdle**, a bony arch with which a limb articulates.—**out on a limb**, in a hazardous position on one's own (*fig.*). [O.E. *lim*; O.N. *limr*, Sw. *lem*.]

**limb**, *lim*, *n.* an edge or border, as of the sun, etc.: the edge of a sextant, etc.: the free or expanded part of a floral or other leaf (*bot.*).—*adjs.* **limb'ate**, bordered; **limb'bous**, overlapping. [L. *limbus*, a border.]

**limbeck, limbec,** *lim'bek*, (*Spens., Shak.*) *n.* aphetic for alembic.

**limber,** *lim'bər*, *n.* the shaft of a vehicle (*dial.*): the detachable fore-part of a gun-carriage (*mil.*). —*v.t.* to attach to the limber. [Poss. Fr. *limonière.*]

**limber,** *lim'bər*, *adj.* pliant, flexible.—*v.t.* to make limber.—**lim'ber-neck,** botulism in birds.—**limber up,** to tone up the muscles in preparation for physical effort of some sort.

**limber,** *lim'bər*, (*naut.*) *n.* (usu. *pl.*) channel or hole on either side of the keelson for drainage. [Fr. *lumière*—L. *luminària,* windows.]

**Limbo, limbo,** *lim'bō, n.* the borderland of Hell, assigned to the unbaptised (*Limbus patrum* for the righteous who died before Christ, *Limbus infantum* for children): any unsatisfactory place of consignment or oblivion: prison.—Also **Lim'bus** (*-bəs*). [From the Latin phrase *in limbo, in,* in, and abl. of *limbus,* border.]

**limbo,** *lim'bō, n.* a West Indian dance in which the dancer bends backwards and passes under a bar which is progressively lowered. [Perh. **limber** (1).]

**limburgite,** *lim'bər-gīt, n.* a volcanic rock composed of olivine and augite, etc., in a fine-grained or glassy groundmass. [*Limburg* in Baden, a typical locality.]

**Limbus patrum, infantum.** See **Limbo.**

**lime,** *lim, n.* any slimy or gluey material (*dial.*): bird-lime: the white caustic earth (calcium oxide, quicklime, caustic lime) got by calcining calcium carbonate (as limestone): calcium hydroxide (slaked lime) got by adding water to quicklime: loosely, limestone or calcium carbonate.—*adj.* of lime.—*v.t.* to cover with lime: to cement (*dial.*): to treat with lime: to manure with lime: to ensnare (also *fig.*).—*v.i.* (*Shak.*) to adulterate wine with lime.—*ns.* **lim'iness;** **lim'ing,** the soaking of skins in limewater to remove hair: application of lime.—*adj.* **lim'y,** glutinous, sticky (*dial.*): smeared with, containing, like, of the nature of, lime.—**lime'-burner,** one who calcines limestone, etc., to form lime; **lime'kiln,** a kiln or furnace in which calcium carbonate is calcined to lime; **lime'light,** Drummond light, light produced by a blowpipe-flame directed against a block of quicklime: the glare of publicity (*fig.*); **lime'stone,** a sedimentary rock of calcium carbonate, sometimes (*magnesian* limestone) with much dolomite; **lime'-twig,** a twig smeared with bird-lime: a snare; **lime'wash,** a milky mixture of slaked lime and water, used for coating walls, etc.; **lime'water,** a suspension of calcium hydroxide in water. [O.E. *lim*; Ger. *leim,* glue, L. *limus,* slime.]

**lime,** *lim, n.* a kind of lemon tree: its small nearly globular fruit.—*n.* **lime'y** (*slang*), a British sailor of any sort (from the use of lime-juice on British ships to prevent scurvy): any

British person.—**lime'-juice,** the acid juice of the lime. [Fr.,—Sp. *lima*; cf. **lemon.**]

**lime,** *lim, n.* the linden tree (*Tilia europaea*), or other of the genus.—**lime'-tree; lime'-wood.** [**lind.**]

**lime.** See **lyam.**

**limen,** *li'men,* (*psych.*) *n.* the threshold of consciousness: the limit below which a stimulus is not perceived.—*adj.* **liminal** (*lim', lim'in-əl*). [L. *limen, -inis,* threshold.]

**limerick,** *lim'ə-rik, n.* a form of humorous verse in a five-line jingle. [Said to be from a refrain formerly used, referring to *Limerick* in Ireland.]

**limes,** *li'mēz, lē'mes, n.* a boundary or boundary work, esp. of the Roman Empire:—*pl.* **limites** (*li'mit-ēz, lē'mi-tās*). [L. *limes, -itis.*]

**limicolous,** *li-mik'ə-ləs, adj.* living in mud.—*adj.* **lim'ous** (*arch.*), muddy: slimy. [L. *limus,* mud, *colĕre,* to dwell.]

**limit,** *lim'it, n.* boundary: that which may not be passed: restriction: a value, position, or figure, that can be approached indefinitely (*math.*): a prescribed time (*Shak.*): that which is bounded, a region or division: the unspeakable extreme of endurability (*coll.*).—*v.t.* to appoint, specify (*Shak.*): to confine within bounds: to restrict.—*adj.* **lim'itable.**—*n.* **limitā'rian,** one who limits salvation to part of mankind.—*adj.* **lim'itary** (*-ə-ri*), of a boundary: placed at the boundary: confined within limits: licensed as a limiter (*hist.*).—*n.* **limitā'tion.**—*adjs.* **lim'itative,** tending to limit; **lim'ited,** within limits: narrow: restricted.—*n.* a limited company.—*adv.* **lim'itedly.**—*ns.* **lim'itedness; lim'iter,** person or thing that limits or confines: a friar who had a licence to beg within certain bounds (*hist.*).—*n.* and *adj.* **lim'iting.**—*adj.* **lim'itless,** having no limits: boundless: immense: infinite.—*adv.* **lim'itlessly.**—*n.* **lim'itlessness.**—**limited liability** (see **liability**); **limited (liability) company; limited express** (*U.S.*), a railway train carrying a limited number of passengers; **limited monarchy,** one in which the monarch shares the supreme power with others. [L. *limes, -itis,* boundary.]

**limitrophe,** *lim'i-trōf, adj.* near the frontier: border. [L. *limitrophus*—*limes, -itis,* border, Gr. *trophos,* feeder.]

**limma,** *lim'ə, n.* a pause of one mora (*pros.*): in Pythagorean music, the difference between two whole tones and a perfect fourth: applied also to other minute intervals. [Gr. *leimma,* a remnant.]

**limmer,** *lim'ər, n.* a rogue or thief (*obs.*): a hussy, a jade (*Scot.*). [Origin obscure.]

**limn,** *lim, v.t. v.i.* (*arch.*) to draw or paint, esp. in water-colours: orig. to illuminate with ornamental letters, etc.:—*pr.p.* **limning** (*lim'ing, lim'ning*).—*n.* **limner** (*lim'nar*), a painter on paper or parchment: a portrait-painter. [O.Fr. *luminer* or *enluminer*—L. *lūmināre* or *illūmināre.*]

**Limnaea,** *lim-nē'ə, n.* a genus of pond-snails.—*n.* **limnae'id,** any member of the family **Limnae'idae,** to which it belongs.—*adjs.* **limnetic** (*-net'ik*), living in fresh water; **limnolog'ical.**—*ns.* **limnol'ogist; limnol'ogy,** the scientific study (embracing physical, geographical, biological, etc., characteristics) of lakes and other freshwater bodies.—*adj.* **limnoph'ilous,** living in ponds or marshes. [Gr. *limnē,* a pool or marsh.]

**limonite,** *li'mən-it, n.* brown iron ore, hydrated ferric oxide, a deposit in bogs and lakes (*bog-iron*), or a decomposition product in rocks.—*adj.* **limonitic** (*-it'ik*). [Gr. *leimōn,* a meadow.]

**limosis,** *li-mō'sis, n.* a morbidly ravenous appetite. [Gr. *limos,* hunger.]

**limous.** See under **limicolous.**

**Limousin,** *lē-mōō-zɛ̃, n.* a breed of cattle.—*n.* **limousine,** *lim'ōō-zēn,* large closed motor-car (orig. with the driver's seat outside but covered by the roof) which has a partition separating driver and passengers: loosely, any large motor-car (sometimes used ironically). [*Limousin*, a district in France.]

**limp**, *limp*, *adj.* wanting stiffness: flaccid: drooping. [Origin obscure.]

**limp**, *limp*, *v.i.* to halt: to drag a leg: (of damaged ship, aircraft) to proceed with difficulty.—*n.* a limping gait: a halt.—*n.* and *adj.* **limp'ing.**—*adv.* **limp'ingly.** [There is an O.E. adj. *lemphealt*, halting.]

**limpet**, *lim'pit*, *n.* a gasteropod (Patella, etc.) with conical shell, that clings to rocks: one not easily ousted. [O.E. *lempedu*, lamprey.]

**limpid**, *lim'pid*, *adj.* clear: transparent.—*n.* **limpid'ity.**—*adv.* **lim'pidly.** [L. *limpidus*.]

**Limulus**, *lim'ū-ləs*, *n.* the king-crab genus. [L. *limulus*, dim. of *limus*, looking sideways.]

**lin**, *lin*, *v.i.* (*Spens.*) to cease, to give over.—*v.t.* (*obs.*) to cease from. [O.E. *linnan*, to cease.]

**lin.** See linn.

**linac.** Abbrev. for *linear accelerator.*

**linage.** See under line (2).

**linch**, *linch*, *linsh*, (*dial.*) *n.* a boundary ridge or unploughed strip: a terrace or ledge.—Also **linch'et**, **lynch'et.** [O.E. *hlinc*, ridge; cf. link (3).]

**linchpin**, *linch'*, *linsh'pin*, *n.* a pin used to keep a wheel on its axle. [O.E. *lynis*, axle, and **pin.**]

**Lincoln-green**, *lingk'ən-grēn*, *n.* a bright green cloth once made at *Lincoln*: its colour.

**linctus**, *lingk'təs*, *n.* a syrup-like medicine:—*pl.* **linc'tuses.**—*n.* **linc'ture.** [L. *linctus*, *-ūs*, a licking.]

**lind**, *lind*, **linden**, *lin'dən.* Same as lime (3). [O.E. *lind*; cf. O.N. *lind*, Ger. *linde*.]

**lindane**, *lin'dān.* Same as Gammexane.

**lindworm**, *lind'wûrm*, (*myth.*) *n.* a wingless dragon. [Adapted from Sw. and Dan. *lindorm*.]

**line**, *lin*, *n.* flax, its fibre, or its seed (*obs.*): heckled flax: yarn spun from good flax: linen thread or cloth (*obs.*).—*v.t.* to cover on the inside: to fill, stuff: to reinforce, strengthen (esp. books): to be placed along the side of: to serve as a lining. —*adj.* **lined**, having a lining.—*ns.* **lin'er**, that which serves as a lining: one who lines; **lin'ing**, the action of one who lines: material applied to a surface, esp. material on the inner surface of a garment, etc.: contents: (in *pl.*) underclothing, esp. drawers (*obs.* or *dial.*). [O.E. *līn*, flax, cognate with or derived from L. *līnum*; cf. next word.]

**line**, *lin*, *n.* a thread, string, cord, rope, esp. one for fishing, sounding, hanging clothes, or guidance: that which has length without breadth or thickness (*math.*): a long narrow mark: a streak, stroke, or narrow stripe: draughtsmanship: a row: a row of printed or written characters, ships, soldiers, etc.: a verse, such as is usu. written in one row: a series or succession, as of progeny: a service of ships, buses, etc. or a company running them: a course, route, system: a railway or tramway track or route: a stretch or route of telegraph, telephone, or power wires or cables: an order given to an agent for goods: such goods received: trade in, or the stock on hand of, any particular goods: a lineament: a rank: a short letter or note: a wrinkle: a trench: limit: method: policy: a rule or canon: the equator: lineage: direction: occupation: course: province or sphere of life, interest, or taste: regular army: line of battle (see below): the twelfth part of an inch: relevant information (*coll.*): glib talk (*slang*): in TV, the path traversed by the electron beam or scanning spot in moving once from side to side (horizontal scanning) or from top to bottom (vertical scanning) of the picture: in *pl.* **lines**, marriage or church membership certificate: words of an actor's part: lot in life (*rare*): outlines: military field-works: rows of huts (*mil.*): a school imposition: fits of bad temper (*Shak.*).—*v.t.* to mark out with lines: to cover with lines: to put in line: to form a line along: to give out for public singing, as a hymn, line by line: to delineate, sketch (sometimes verbally): to measure with a line (*arch.*). —*v.i.* to take a place in line.—*ns.* **linage, lineage** (*lin'ij*), aligning (*arch.*): measurement or payment by the line; **lineage** (*lin'i-ij*), earlier **linage, lignage, lynage** (*lin'ij*), ancestry.—*adj.* **lineal** (*lin'i-əl*), of or belonging to a line or lines or one dimension: composed of lines: in the direction of a line: in, of, or transmitted by, direct line of descent, or legitimate descent.—*n.* **lineality** (*-al'i-ti*).—*adv.* **lin'eally.**—*n.* **lineament** (*lin'i-ə-mənt*), feature: distinguishing mark in the form, esp. of the face.—*adj.* **linear** (*lin'i-ər*), of or belonging to a line: of one dimension: consisting of, or having the form of, lines: long and very narrow, with parallel sides: capable of being represented on a graph by a straight line: of a system, in which doubling the cause doubles the effect.—*n.* **linearity** (*lin-i-ar'i-ti*).—*adv.* **lin'early.**—*adjs.* **lin'eate, -d,** marked with lines.—*n.* **lineā'tion**, marking with lines: arrangement of or in lines.—*adj.* **lined** (*līnd*), marked with lines: having a line.—*adj.* **lineolate** (*lin'i-ə-lāt*), marked with fine lines.—*ns.* **lin'er**, one who makes, marks, draws, paints, or writes lines: a paint-brush for making lines: a line-fisher: a line-fishing boat: a vessel or aircraft of a line: colouring matter used to outline the eyes; **lin'ing**, alignment: the making of a line: use of a line: marking with lines.—**linear A**, a script, essentially the same as linear B, used with an earlier Semitic language of Crete; **linear accelerator**, apparatus in which electrons are accelerated while travelling down (a) metal tube(s), e.g. by means of electromagnetic waves; **linear B**, an ancient script (*c.* 1400 B.C.) found in Crete, deciphered with all but general acceptance as a form of Greek seven centuries earlier than any previously known; **linear perspective**, that part of perspective which regards only the positions, magnitudes, and forms of the objects delineated; **linear programming**, that which enables a computer to give an optimum result when fed with a number of unrelated variables, used in determining the most efficient arrangement of e.g. an industrial process; **line'-engrav'er**; **line'-engrav'ing**, the process of engraving in lines, steel or copperplate engraving: an engraving so done; **line'-fence** (*U.S.*), a farm-boundary fence; **line'-fish**, one taken with the line; **line'-fish'er**, **-fish'erman**; **line'-fish'ing**; **line'man**, one who attends to the line of railway, telegraph, telephone, or electric-light wires, etc.; **line'-of-batt'le-ship**, a ship fit for the line of battle, a battleship; **line'-out**, a formation of Rugby football players when the ball is thrown from touch; **line'-shooter** (*slang*), one who shoots a line; **linesman** (*līnz'*), **lineman**: a soldier in a regiment of the line: in Association football, one who marks the spot at which the ball goes into touch: in lawn-tennis, one who decides on which side of a line the ball falls; **line'-squall**, one of a chain of squalls occurring along a travelling line, with rise and sudden change of wind, rise of pressure and fall of temperature; **line'-storm** (*U.S.*), an equinoctial storm; **line'-up'**, an arrangement in line: putting or coming into line: a queue.—**bring into line**, to cause to conform; **draw the line** (see **draw**); **Fraunhofer's lines**, dark lines crossing the spectrum—from the Bavarian optician Joseph von *Fraunhofer* (1787-1826); **get a line on** (*slang*), to get information about; **give line**, (from angling) to allow apparent freedom in order to secure at last; **in line**, in a straight line: in agreement or harmony: in the running; **line of battle**, arrangement in line to meet the enemy; **line of beauty** (Hogarth's), a curve like a drawn-out S; **line up**, to bring into alignment: to make a stand (in support of, or against): to gather together in readiness: to secure, arrange (for a person); **one's line of country**, one's field of study or interest; **on the line** (*paint.*), hanging on the level of the eyes; **read between the lines**, infer what is not explicitly stated; **shoot a line** (see **shoot**); **toe the line** (see **toe**). [Partly from O.E. *line*, cord (from or cognate with L. *līnum*, flax), partly through Fr. *ligne*, and partly directly from L. *linea*; cf. preceding word.]

**line**, *līn*, *v.t.* (esp. of a dog or wolf) to copulate with. [Fr. *ligner*.]

**line**, *līn*, *n.* a form of **lind.**—*n.* (*Shak.*) **line-grove.**

**lineage, lineal, linear,** etc. See **line** (2).

**lined.** See **line** (1 and 2).

**linen**, *līn'ən*, *n.* cloth made of lint or flax: under-clothing, orig. of linen: articles of linen, or of other materials as cotton, rayon, etc.—**table-linen,** bed-linen, body-linen.—*adj.* of or like linen.—**lin'en-draper,** a dealer in linens; **lin'enfold, lin'en-scroll',** a decoration in mouldings like parallel folds of linen.—**wash one's dirty linen at home, in public,** to keep secret, to expose, sordid family affairs. [O.E. *linen* (adj.)—*līn,* flax; see **line** (1).]

**-ling,** noun suffix denoting a diminutive as duck*ling*, hence expressing affection as dar*ling* (O.E. *dēorling*), sometimes implying depreciation, as under*ling*.

**ling,** *ling*, *n.* a fish (*Molva*) of the cod family. [Prob. conn. with **long.**]

**ling,** *ling*, *n.* heather.—*adj.* **ling'y.** [O.N. *lyng*.]

**ling,** *ling*, *n.* Scots form of **line** (2).—**sting and ling** (see **sting** (2)).

**lingam,** *ling'gam*, *n.* the Hindu phallus, a symbol of Siva.—Also **ling'a.** [Sans.]

**lingel, lingle,** *ling'gl* (chiefly *Scot.*, *ling'l*), *n.* a shoemaker's waxed thread. [O.Fr. *lignoel*—a dim. from L. *linea*.]

**linger,** *ling'gər*, *v.i.* to remain long: to delay in reluctance: to tarry: to loiter: to be protracted: to remain alive, although gradually dying.—*v.t.* to prolong, protract (*Shak.*): to pass in tedium or dawdling.—*n.* **ling'erer.**—*n.* and *adj.* **ling'ering.** —*adv.* **ling'eringly.** [Freq. from O.E. *lengan,* to protract—*lang,* long.]

**lingerie,** *lēzh-ə-rē, n.* linen goods: women's under-clothing. [Fr.,—*linge,* linen—L. *līnum,* flax, thread, linen.]

**lingo,** *ling'gō, n.* language, esp. one despised or not understood. [Prov. *lengo, lingo,* or some other form of L. *lingua,* language.]

**lingoa geral,** *ling'gwä zher-äl',* a trade jargon used in Brazil based on Tupí-Guaraní. [Port., general language.]

**lingot,** *ling'gət, n.* an ingot. [Fr. *lingot*—Eng. *ingot,* with the def. art. *l'.*]

**lingua,** *ling'gwə, n.* the tongue: a tongue-like structure.—*adj.* **ling'ual.**—*adv.* **ling'ually.**—*adj.* **ling'uiform,** tongue-shaped.—*ns.* **ling'uist,** one who has a good knowledge of languages; **ling'-uister** (*U.S.*), an interpreter.—Also **link'ster, ling'ster.**—*adjs.* **linguist'ic, -al,** pertaining to languages or knowledge or study of languages. —*adv.* **linguist'ically.**—*n.* (treated as *sing.*) **linguist'ics,** the study of language in its widest sense, in every aspect and in all its varieties.— *ns.* **ling'uistry; lingula** (*ling'gū-lə*), a little tongue-like part: (*cap.*) a narrow-shelled genus of brachiopods: extended loosely to kindred genera, as **Lingulell'a,** the characteristic fossil of the Upper Cambrian *Lingula Flags.*—*adjs.* **ling'ular,** pertaining to a lingula; **ling'ulate,** tongue-shaped.—**lingua franca** (*ling'gwə frangk'ə*; It., Frankish language), a mixed Italian trade

jargon used in the Levant: any international jargon; **linguistic philosophy,** a term loosely used to cover methods of analysis of philosophically puzzling concepts by meticulous assembly and scrutiny of the widely-varying expressions of these concepts in ordinary discourse; later extended to a systematic study of the working of language itself.—Also **linguistic analysis.** [L. *lingua* (for *dingua*), the tongue.]

**linhay, linny,** *lin'i,* (*dial.*) *n.* a shed, open in front. [Origin obscure.]

**liniment,** *lin'i-mənt, n.* a thin ointment: an embro-cation. [L. *linimentum*—*linire, linĕre,* to smear.]

**linin,** *lī'nin, n.* a substance which forms the net-work of a cell nucleus. [L. *līnum,* thread, net.]

**lining.** See **line** (1 and 2).

**link,** *lingk, n.* a ring of a chain, chain-mail, etc.: anything connecting (also *fig.*): a unit in a communications system: the 1/100th part of the surveyor's chain, 7·92 inches: a segment or unit in a connected series: a winding of a river (*Scot.*).—*v.t.* to connect.—*v.i.* to be or become connected: to go arm-in-arm.—*ns.* **link'age,** an act or mode of linking: the fact of being linked: a system of links: a chemical bond: product of magnetic flux by number of coils (*elect.*): a system of lines pivoted together, describing definite curves (*math.*): a tendency of certain characters to be inherited together (*biol.*).—**linked verse,** a form of Japanese verse alternating three lines of respectively 3, 7, 5 syllables with two lines of 7, 7 syllables, different poets supplying succeeding verses; **link man,** one who provides a connection as by passing on information, or by holding together separate items of a programme: **link'-mo'tion,** reversing gear of a steam-engine: a system of pieces moving as a linkage; **link'-up,** a connection, union; **link'work.**—**missing link,** any point or fact needed to complete a series or a chain of argument: an intermediate form in the evolution of man from simian ancestors. [Prob. from an O.N. form cog. with O.E. *hlence* (pl.), armour; Ice. *hlekkr,* Ger. *gelenk,* a joint.]

**link,** *lingk, n.* a torch of pitch and tow: burnt links used as blacking (*Shak.*).—**link'boy, link'-man,** an attendant carrying a link in dark streets. [Origin doubtful.]

**link,** *lingk, n.* a bank (*obs.*): (in *pl.* often treated as *sing.*) a stretch of flat or gently undulating ground along a seashore, hence a golf-course. [O.E. *hlinc,* a ridge of land, a bank; cf. **linch.**]

**link,** *lingk,* (*Scot.*) *v.i.* to move nimbly: to trip along briskly. [Cf. Norw. *linke,* to hobble, limp.]

**linkster.** See **lingua.**

**linn, lin,** *lin, n.* a waterfall: a cascade pool: a deep ravine. [O.E. *hlynn,* a torrent, combined with Gael. *linne,* Ir. *linn,* W. *llyn,* pool.]

**Linnaean, Linnean,** *lin-ē'ən, adj.* pertaining to *Linnaeus* or *Linné,* the Swedish botanist (1707-1778), or to his artificial system of classification.

**linnet,** *lin'it, n. Linota cannabina,* a common finch, feeding on flax-seed.—**green linnet,** the greenfinch. [O.Fr. *linette, linot*—*lin,* flax—L. *līnum;* cf. O.E. *linece* or *linete,* and **lintie.**]

**linoleic,** *lin-ō-lē'ik,* **linolenic,** *lin-ō-lēn'ik* (or *-len'*), **acid,** highly unsaturated fatty acids obtained from the glycerides of certain fats and oils, as linseed oil, and constituting Vitamin F.

**linoleum,** *lin-ō'li-əm, -lyəm, n.* floor-covering made by impregnating a fabric with a mixture of oxidised linseed-oil, resins, and fillers (esp. cork). —Also *adj.*—Also **lino** (*lī'nō*) (*coll.*).—*n.* **linocut** (*lī'nō-kut*), a design cut in relief in linoleum: a print from such a block. [L. *līnum,* flax, *oleum,* oil.]

**Linotype,** *lin'ō-tīp, n.* a machine for producing stereotyped lines: a slug or line of printing-type cast in one piece. [line o' type (trademark).]

**linsang,** *lin'sang, n.* a civet-like animal of Borneo and Java: applied also to kindred animals of the Himalayas, Burma, and West Africa. [Javanese *linsan.*]

**linseed,** *lin'sēd, n.* lint or flax seed—also **lint'seed.** —**lin'seed-cake,** the cake remaining when the oil is pressed out of lint or flax seed, used as a food for sheep and cattle; **lin'seed-meal,** the meal of linseed, used for poultices and as a cattle-food; **lin'seed-oil,** oil from flax seed. [O.E. *lin,* flax, *sǣd,* seed.]

**linsey,** *lin'zi, n.* cloth made of linen and wool.— Also *adj.*—**lin'sey-woolsey** (*-wool'zi*), a thin coarse stuff of linen and wool mixed, or inferior wool with cotton: gibberish (*Shak.*).—*adj.* of linen and wool: neither one thing nor another. [Perh. **line** (1), **wool,** and possibly **say** (3).]

**linstock,** *lin'stok, n.* a staff to hold a lighted match for firing cannon.—Also **lint'stock.** [Du. *lontstok—lont,* a match (cf. **lunt**), *stok,* a stick.]

**lint,** *lint, n.* flax (*Scot.*): scraped linen or a cotton substitute for dressing wounds: cotton fibre: raw cotton.—*n.* **lint'er** (*U.S.*), a machine for stripping off short cotton fibre from the ginned seeds: (in *pl.*) the fibre so removed.— **lint'seed** (*Scot.*), flax seed for sowing.—*adj.* **lint'-white,** flaxen. [M.E. *lynt, lynet,* perh.—L. *linteus,* of linen—*linum,* flax.]

**lintel,** *lint'l, n.* a timber or stone over a doorway or window.—*adj.* **lint'elled.** [O.Fr. *lintel* (Fr. *linteau*)—a dim. of L. *limes, -itis,* border.]

**lintie,** *lin'ti,* **lintwhite,** *lint'(h)wit,* (now chiefly *Scot.*) *ns.* a linnet. [O.E. *linetwige,* lit. perh. flax-twitcher.]

**lion,** *li'ən, n.* a large, fierce, tawny, loud-roaring animal of the cat family, the male with shaggy mane: a man of unusual courage (*fig.*): the constellation or the sign Leo (*astron.*): any object of interest, esp. a famous or conspicuous person much sought after (from the lions once kept in the Tower, one of the sights of London): an old Scots coin, with a lion on the obverse, worth 74 shillings Scots (James VI):—*fem.* **li'oness.**—*ns.* **li'oncel, li'oncelle, li'onel** (*her.*), a small lion used as a bearing: **li'onet,** a young lion.—*v.t.* **li'onise, -ize,** to treat as a lion or object of interest: to go around the sights of: to show the sights to.—*n.* **li'onism,** lionising: lion-like appearance in leprosy.—*adjs.* **li'on-like, li'only.**—**li'on-heart,** one with great courage.— *adj.* **li'on-heart'ed.**—**li'on-hunt'er,** a hunter of lions: one who runs after celebrities; **lion's provider,** the jackal, supposed to attend upon the lion, really his hanger-on; **lion's share,** the whole or greater part.—**twist the lion's tail,** to harass Great Britain. [A.Fr. *liun*—L. *leō, -ōnis* —Gr. *leōn, -ontos.*]

**lip,** *lip, n.* either of the muscular flaps in front of the teeth: any similar structure, as each of the two divisions of a labiate corolla: the edge or rim of an orifice, cavity, or vessel: part of such a rim bent outwards like a spout: impudent talk, insolence (*slang*).—*v.t.* to touch with the lips: to kiss: to wash, overflow, or overrun the edge of: to lap or lave: to form a lip on: to edge: to turn or notch the edge of (*Scot.*): to utter with the lips.—*v.i.* to manage the lips in playing a wind-instrument: to lap at the brim: to have water lapping over:—*pr.p.* **lipp'ing;** *pa.t.* and *pa.p.* **lipped.**—*adj.* of the lip: formed or sounded by the lips: (in composition) from the lips only, not sincere.—*adjs.* **lip'less; lipped** (*lipt*), having a lip or lips: labiate; **lipp'y,** with hanging lip: saucy (*slang*).—*adj.* **lip'-deep,** insincere: immersed to the lips.—*v.i.* **lip'-read.**— **lip'-reader; lip'-read'ing,** gathering what a person says by watching the movement of the lips; **lip'-rounding,** rounding of the lips, as in pronouncing *o;* **lip'salve,** ointment for the lips: blandishment; **lip'-service,** insincere professions

or worship; **lip'stick,** colouring for the lips in the form of a stick.—*v.t.* and *v.i.* to paint with lipstick.—**in Lipsburie pinfold** (*Shak.*), perh. between the teeth; (**keep) a stiff upper lip,** (to show) a face of resolution, with no yielding to emotion; **make a lip** (*Shak.*), to pout in sullenness or derision. [O.E. *lippa;* Du. *lip,* Ger. *lippe,* L. *labium.*]

**liparite,** *lip'ə-rīt, n.* rhyolite. [From the *Lipari* Islands, where it occurs.]

**lip-, lipo-, lip-** (*lip-*), **lip-** (*ō-*), in composition, fat.—*ns.* **lip'ase** (*-ās, -āz*), an enzyme that breaks up fats; **lipochrome** (*-krōm;* Gr. *chrōma,* colour), a pigment of butter fat, etc.—*adj.* **lip'oid,** fat-like.— *n.* a fat-like substance: a lipid.—*ns.* **lip'id(e),** a fat or wax, etc., found in living cells; **lipō'ma,** a fatty tumour:—*pl.* **lipō'mata; lipomatō'sis,** the excessive growth of fat.—*adj.* **lipō'matous.** [Gr. *lipos,* fat.]

**Lipizzaner,** *lip-it-sä'nər, n.* a breed of horses (usu. grey or white in colour) particularly suited for displays of haute école.—Also **Lippizaner, Lipizzaner, Lippizana** (*-nə*), **Lippizzana.** [*Lipizza* (*Lippiza, Lippizza*), near Trieste, where orig. bred.]

**lipogram,** *lip'ō-gram,* or *lip',* *n.* a writing, esp. in verse, from which all words are omitted which contain a particular letter.—*adj.* **lipogrammat'ic.**—*ns.* **lipogramm'atism; lipogramm'atist; lipog'raphy,** accidental omission of a letter or letters in writing. [Gr. *leipein,* to leave, *gramma,* a letter, *graphein,* to write.]

**lippen,** *lip'n,* (*Scot.*) *v.i.* to trust, rely, depend (with *to, on*).—*v.t.* to expect.—*adj.* **lipp'ening** (*Scott*), unguarded. [Origin obscure.]

**lippitude,** *lip'i-tūd,* (*arch.*) *n.* soreness of the eyes. [L. *lippitūdō—lippus,* blear-eyed.]

**lippy, lippie,** *lip'i, n.* an old Scottish dry measure, the fourth part of a peck. [Dim. from O.E. *lēap,* a basket; cf. **leap** (2).]

**liquate,** *lik'wāt, v.t.* to melt: to subject to liquation.—*adj.* **liq'uable.**—*n.* **liquā'tion,** melting: separation of metals with different melting-points. [L. *liquāre, -ātum,* to liquefy.]

**liquefy,** *lik'wi-fī, v.t.* to make liquid.—*v.i.* to become liquid: to drink (*facet.*):—*pr.p.* **liq'uefying;** *pa.t.* and *pa.p.* **liq'uefied.**—*n.* and *adj.* **liquefacient** (*-fā'shant*).—*n.* **liquefaction** (*-fak'-shən*).—*adj.* **liq'uefiable.**—*n.* **liq'uefier.**—**liquefied petroleum gas,** propane or butane under moderate pressure, used in vehicles in place of petrol or diesel oil. [L. *liquefacĕre—liquēre,* to be liquid, *facĕre,* to make.]

**liquesce,** *lik-wes', v.i.* to become liquid: to merge. —*ns.* **liquesc'ence, liquesc'ency.**—*adj.* **liquesc'ent.** [L. *liquēscĕre—liquēre,* to be liquid.]

**liqueur,** *lik-ūr',* or *lē-kər', n.* an alcoholic preparation flavoured or perfumed and sweetened—as chartreuse, cherry brandy, curaçao, benedictine, kümmel, maraschino.—*v.t.* to flavour with a liqueur.—*adj.* (of brandy or whisky) that may be drunk as a liqueur.—**liqueur'-glass,** a very small drinking-glass. [Fr.,—L. *liquor;* see **liquor.**]

**liquid,** *lik'wid, adj.* flowing: fluid: watery: in phys., in a state between solid and gas, in which the molecules move freely about one another but do not fly apart: clear: moist: of sound, etc., free from harshness: indisputable: unfixed: readily converted into cash.—*n.* a liquid substance: a flowing consonant sound, as *l, r.*—*v.t.* **liq'uidate,** to clear up or off: to arrange or wind up: to dispose of: to wipe out, do away with (*slang*): to kill off (*slang*).—*v.i.* to go into liquidation.—*ns.* **liquidā'tion; liq'uidator.**—*v.t.* **liq'uidise, -ize,** to render liquid.—*n.* **liquid'ity.**—*adv.* **liq'uidly.**—*n.* **liq'uidness.** [L. *liquidus,* liquid, clear—*liquēre,* to be clear.]

**Liquidambar,** *lik-wid-am'bər, n.* a genus of balsamiferous trees of the family Hamamelidaceae, found in North America and Asia. [L. *liquidus*, liquid, L.L. *ambar*, amber.]

**liquor**, *lik'ər*, *n*. anything liquid, esp. the product of cooking or other operation: a liquid secretion: a beverage, esp. alcoholic: strong drink: a strong solution: any prepared solution.—*v.t.* to apply liquor or a solution to: to rub with oil or grease (*Shak.*).—*v.i.* (*slang*) to drink (esp. with *up*).—**in liquor**, also **liquored** (*slang*), drunk; **liquor laws**, laws controlling the sale of intoxicating drinks. [O.Fr. *licur*, *licour* (Fr. *liqueur*)—L. *liquor*, *-ōris*.]

**liquorice, licorice**, *lik'ə-ris*, (in U.S. also *-rish*), *n*. a papilionaceous plant (*Glycyrrhiza glabra*, or other species) of Europe and Asia: its long sweet root used in medicine: an extract from the root: confectionery made from it.—**Indian liquorice**, Abrus (also *liquorice-vine*); **wild liquorice**, a kind of milk-vetch (*Astragalus glycyphyllus*—also *liquorice-vetch*): rest-harrow. [A.Fr. *lycorys*—L.L. *liquirītia*, a corr. of Gr. *glykyrrhiza*—*glykys*, sweet, *rhiza*, root.]

**liquorish**, another spelling of **lickerish**: also used to mean inclined towards liquor.

**lira**, *lē'ra*, *n*. Italian monetary unit (coins of 5, 10, etc., lire being in circulation):—*pl*. **lire** (*lē'rā*), **lir'as**. [It.,—L. *libra*, a pound.]

**Liriodendron**, *lir-i-ō-den'dron*, *n*. the tulip-tree genus. [Gr. *leirion*, a lily, *dendron*, a tree.]

**liripoop**, *lir'i-pōōp*, (*obs.*) *n*. the long tail of a graduate's hood: a part or lesson committed to memory: a silly person.—Also **lir'ipipe** (*-pīp*). [L.L. *liripipium*; origin unknown.]

**lirk**, *lirk*, (*Scot.*) *n*. a fold: a wrinkle.—*v.i.* to wrinkle. [Origin unknown.]

**lis**, *lēs*, (*her.*) *n*. a fleur de-lis:—*pl*. **lis**, **lisses** (*lēs'iz*). [Fr.].

**Lisbon**, *liz'bən*, *n*. a light-coloured wine from Estremadura in Portugal, shipped from *Lisbon*.

**lisle**, *lil*, *n*. a long-stapled, hard-twisted cotton yarn.—Also *adj*. [Old spelling of *Lille*, France.]

**lisp**, *lisp*, *v.i.* to speak with the tongue against the upper teeth or gums, as in pronouncing *th* for *s* or *z*: to articulate as a child: to utter imperfectly.—*v.t.* to utter with a lisp.—*n*. the act or habit of lisping: a defect of speech by which one lisps.—*n*. **lisp'er**.—*adj*. and *n*. **lisp'ing**.—*adv*. **lisp'ingly**. [O.E. *wlisp* (adj.), stammering; Du. *lispen*, Ger. *lispeln*.]

**lispound, lispund**, *lis'pownd*, *pōnd*, (*Orkney* and *Shetland*) *n*. a varying weight, 12 to 34 pounds. [L.G. or Du. *lispund*, for *livschpund*, Livonian pound.]

**lissencephalous**, *lis-ən-sef'ə-ləs*, *adj*. with smooth cerebral hemispheres. [Gr. *lissos*, smooth, *enkephalon*, brain.]

**lissome, lissom**, *lis'əm*, *adj*. lithesome, nimble, flexible.—*n*. **liss'om(e)ness**. [lithesome.]

**lissotrichous**, *lis-ot'ri-kəs*, *adj*. smooth-haired. [Gr. *lissos*, smooth, *thrix*, *trichos*, hair.]

**list**, *list*, *n*. the selvage on woven textile fabrics: a border: a stripe: a strip: a ridge or furrow made with a lister (*U.S.*): a strip cut from an edge: material composed of cut-off selvages: a boundary (*obs.*): a destination (*Shak.*): (in *pl*.) the boundary of a tilting-ground or the like, hence the ground itself, combat.—*adj*. made of strips of woollen selvage.—*v.t.* to border: to put list on: to remove the edge from: to plough with a lister (*U.S.*).—*adj*. **list'ed**, enclosed for tilting or the like: fought in lists.—*n*. **list'er** (*U.S.*), a double-mould-board plough.—**enter the lists**, to come forward for contest. [O.E. *liste*; Ger. *leiste*; affected in some senses by O.Fr. *lisse* (Fr. *lice*, It. *lizza*)—L.L. *liciae*, barrier.]

**list**, *list*, *n*. a catalogue, roll, or enumeration.—*v.t.* to place in a list or catalogue: to enroll (as soldiers).—*v.i.* to enlist (also *'list*, as if for enlist).—**active list**, the roll of those liable for

active service. [O.F. *liste*, of Gmc. origin, ultimately same word as above, from the sense of a strip of paper.]

**list**, *list*, *n*. a fillet (*archit.*): a division of parted hair.—*n*. **list'el**, a small fillet. [It. *lista*, *listello*; ult. the same as **list** (1 and 2).]

**list**, *list*, *v.t.* to please (*impers.*, *arch.*): to have pleasure in (*pers.*): to desire: to like or please: to choose: to cause to heel over (*naut.*).—*v.i.* to heel over:—*pa.t.* **list'ed**, **list**; *pa.p.* **list'ed**; *3rd pers. sing. pr.t.* **list**, **lists**, **listeth**.—*n*. joy (*obs.*): desire: inclination: choice: heeling over.—*adj*. **list'less**, having no desire or wish: uninterested: languid.—*adv*. **list'lessly.**—*n*. **list'lessness**. [O.E. *lystan*, impers., to please—*lust*, pleasure.]

**list**, *list*, (*arch.* or *poet.*) *v.i.* to listen.—*v.t.*to listen to.—*adj*. **list'ful**, attentive. [O.E. *hlystan*.]

**listen**, *lis'n*, *v.i.* to give ear or hearken: to follow advice.—*n*. act of listening.—*n*. **listener** (*lis'nər*), one who listens or hearkens.—**list'ener-in** (*pl*. **list'eners-in**); **list'ening-in**; **list'ening-post**, a post where men are stationed to hear what the enemy is doing.—**listen in**, to listen to a wireless broadcast: to overhear intentionally a message intended for another. [O.E. *hlysnan*, recorded in the Northumbrian form *lysna*.]

**Listerism**, *lis'tər-izm*, *n*. antiseptic treatment of surgical wounds introduced by the English surgeon Lord *Lister* (1827-1912).—*adj*. **Listerian** (*-tē'ri-ən*), pertaining to Lister or his system.—*v.t.* **Lis'terise, -ize**, to treat by Listerism.

**lit**, *pa.t.* and *pa.p.* of **light** (1 and 3).

**litany**, *lit'ə-ni*, *n*. a prayer of supplication, esp. in processions: an appointed form of responsive prayer in public worship in which the same thing is repeated several times.—**lit'any-desk, -stool**, in the English Church, a movable desk at which a minister kneels, facing the altar, while he recites the litany.—**lesser litany**, the common formula, 'Kyrie eleison, Christe eleison, Kyrie eleison'. [L.L. *litania*—Gr. *litaneiā*—*litesthai*, to pray.]

**litchi, leechee, lychee**, *lē'chē', li'*, *n*. a Chinese fruit, a nut or berry with a fleshy aril: the tree (*Litchi chinensis*; fam. Sapindaceae) that bears it. [Chin. *li-chi*.]

**lit de justice**, *lē də zhüs-tēs*, (Fr.). See **bed-of-justice**, under **bed** (1).

**lite, lyte**, *līt*, (*dial.*, also **leet**, otherwise *obs.*) *n*., *adj*., *adv*. little. [O.E. *lȳt*.]

**lite** (*Spens.*). Same as **light** (3): also as **light** (2) in phrase *lungs and lites*.

**lite pendente**, *li'tē pen-den'tē*, *lē'te pen-den'te*, (L.) pending the suit.

**liter**, American spelling of **litre**.

**literae, litterae, humaniores**, *lit'ər-ē hū-mān-i-ōr'ēz*, *-ör'*, *lit'ə-rī (h)ōō-män-i-ōr'ās*, (L.) polite letters, the humanities, Latin and Greek: name of school and examination at Oxford University.

**literal**, *lit'ə-rəl*, *adj*. pertaining to letters of the alphabet: of the nature of a letter: according to the letter: not figurative or metaphorical: following word for word: inclined to use or understand words in a matter-of fact sense.—*n*. a wrong letter in printed or typed matter: a misprint of a letter.—*v.t.* **lit'eralise, -ize**.—*ns*. **lit'eraliser, -z-**; **lit'eralism**, strict adherence to the letter: interpretation that is merely verbal: exact and unimaginative rendering (*art*); **li'teralist**; ' **literality** (*-al'i-ti*).—*adv*. **lit'erally** (often used by no means literally).—*n*. **lit'eralness**. [L. *litterālis*—*littera* (*lītera*), a letter.]

**literary**, *lit'ər-ər-i*, *adj*. pertaining to letters of the alphabet (*obs.*): epistolary (*obs.*): pertaining to, of the nature of, versed in, or practising literature or the writing of books: bookish.—*adv*. **lit'erarily**.—*ns*. **lit'erariness**; **lit'eraryism**, a bookish expression. [L. *literārius*—*litera* (*littera*), a letter.]

**literate**, *lit'ər-it*, *-āt*, *adj*. learned: able to read and write.—*n*. one who is literate: an educated person without a university degree, esp. a candidate for orders, or formerly a woman holding a certificate from St Andrews University (*L.L.A.*, *Lady Literate in Arts*).—*n*. lit′eracy, condition of being literate.—*n.pl.* literā′ti (L., *obs*. It., -ä′tē), men of letters, the learned:—*sing*. literā′tus (L.), literato (-ä′tō; It.).—*adv*. literā′tim (L. -ä′), letter for letter: without the change of a letter.— *n*. lit′erātor, a dabbler in learning: a man of letters, a literary man.—*adj*. lit′erose, affectedly or spuriously literary.—*n*. literos′ity. [L. *litera*, līterātus, literātim, literōsus—*litera* (*littera*), letter.]

literature, *lit*′(*ə*-)*rə-chər*, *n*. the art of composition in prose and verse: the whole body of literary compositions universally, or in any language, or on a given subject, etc.: literary matter: printed matter: humane learning: literary culture or knowledge.—*adj*. lit′eratured (*Shak*.), learned, having literary knowledge. [L. *literātūra—litera* (*littera*), a letter.]

lith, *lith*, (*arch*. and *Scot*.) *n*. a joint or segment. [O.E. *lith*, a member; Ger. *glied*.]

lith-, litho-, *lith-*, -*ō*-, -*ə*-, -*o*-, in composition, stone: calculus.—*ns*. lith′ate (*obs*.), a urate; lithi′asis (Gr. *lithiāsis*), formation of calculi in the body.—*adj*. lith′ic, pertaining to or got from stone or calculi.—*ns*. lithist′id, any of the Lithist′ida, hard stony sponges; lith′ite, a calcareous body secreted in an animal cell, esp. with a sensory function.—*adj*. lithochromatic (-*ə-krō-mat′ik*, or -*krə-*).—*n*. (treated as *sing*.) lithochromat′ics.—*ns*. lith′ochromy (-*krō-mi*; Gr. *chrōma, -atos*, colour), painting on stone: chromolithography; lith′oclast (Gr. *klaein*, to crush), an instrument for crushing bladderstones; lith′ocyst (-*ō-sist*; Gr. *kystis*, a bladder), a sac containing a lithite.—*adj*. lithodomous (-*od′ə-məs*; Gr. *lithodomos*, a mason—*domos*, a dwelling), living in burrows in rocks.—*n*. Lithod′omus, the date-shell genus.—*adj*. lithogenous (*oj′i-nəs*), rock-building.—*ns*. lith′oglyph (-*ə-glif*; Gr. *glyphein*, to carve), an engraving on stone, esp. a precious stone; lith′ograph (-*gräf*; Gr. *graphein*, to write), a print from stone (lithographic stone or slate, a fine-grained slaty limestone), or a substitute (as zinc or aluminium), with greasy ink.—*v.t.* and *v.i.* to print so.—*n*. lithographer (-*og′rə-fər*).—*adjs*. lithographic (-*ə-graf′ik*), -al.—*adv*. lithograph′ically.—*n*. lithog′raphy.—*adjs*. lith′oid, lithoid′al, like stone.—*n*. lith′olapaxy (Gr. *lapaxis*, evacuation), the operation of crushing stone in the bladder and working it out.—*adj*. lithol′atrous (-*ol′ə-tri*; Gr. *latreiā*, worship), stone-worship.—*adjs*. litholog′ic, -al.—*ns*. lithol′ogist; lithol′ogy, the science of rocks as mineral masses: the department of medicine concerned with calculi; lith′omancy (-*man-si*; Gr. *manteiā*, divination), divination by stones; lith′omarge (-*ō-märj*; L. *marga*, marl), a compact china-clay.—*adj*. lithophagous (-*of′ə-gəs*; Gr. *phagein*, to eat), stone-swallowing: rock-boring.—*n*. lith′ophane (-*ō-fān*; Gr. *phainesthai*, to appear), porcelain with pictures showing through transparency.— *adj*. lithophilous (-*of′i-ləs*; Gr. *philos*, friend), growing, living, or sheltering among stones.— *ns*. lithophysa (-*ō-fi′sə*; Gr. *physa*, bubble), a bladder-like spherulite (also lith′ophyse):—*pl*. lithophy′sae (-*sē*); lith′ophyte (-*fit*; Gr. *phyton*, plant), a plant that grows on rocks or stones: a stony organism, as coral.—*adj*. lithophytic (-*fit′ik*).—*ns*. lith′opone (-*ō-pōn*; perh. L. *pōnĕre*, to set, apply), a white pigment of barium sulphate and zinc sulphide; lith′osphere (-*ō-sfēr*; Gr. *sphaira*, sphere), the rocky crust of the earth; lith′otome (-*ō-tōm*; Gr. *tomos*, cutting), an instrument for lithotomy.—*adjs*. lithotomic (-*tom′*), -al.—*n*. lithotomist (-*ot′əm-ist*), one who cuts for stone in the bladder.—*adj*. lithot′omous, boring in rocks, as some molluscs.—*n*. lithot′omy, cutting for stone in the bladder. [Gr. *lithos*, stone.]

litharge, *lith*′*ärj*, *n*. lead monoxide, such as is got in refining silver. [Fr.,—Gr. *lithargyros—lithos*, a stone, *argyros*, silver.]

lithe, *lidh*, *adj*. supple, limber.—*adv*. lithe′ly.—*n*. lithe′ness.—*adj*. lithe′some.—*n*. lithe′someness. [O.E. *lithe*, soft, mild; Ger. *lind* and *gelinde*.]

lithe, *lidh*, (*obs*.) *v.i.* to listen. [O.N. *hlýtha*, to listen.]

lither, *lidh′ər*, *adj*. bad (*obs*.): lazy (*obs*.): soft, yielding (*Shak*.).—*adj*. lith′erly, mischievous.— *adv*. idly. [O.E. *lythre*, bad; influenced by lithe.]

lithia, *lith′i-ə*, *n*. oxide of lithium (from its mineral origin, unlike soda and potash).—Also *adj*.—*adj*. lith′ic, pertaining to or got from lithium.—*n*. lithium (*i-əm*), the lightest metallic element (Li; at. numb. 3). [Gr. *lithos*, stone.]

Lithospermum, *lith-ō-spûr′məm*, *n*. a genus of plants of the borage family. [Gr. *lithospermon*, gromwell—*lithos*, stone, *sperma*, seed.]

lithotrity, *lith-ot′ri-ti*, lithotripsy, *lith′ō-trip-si*, *ns*. the operation of crushing a stone in the bladder, so that its fragments may be removed through the urethra.—*ns*. lith′otrite, lithotri′tor, lithotrip′tor, lithontrip′tor, an instrument for the purpose.—*adjs*. lithotritic (-*trit′ik*), lithotrip′tic, lithontrip′tic, lithonthryp′tic.—*ns*. a medicine producing the like result.—*v.t.* lithot′ritise, -ize.—*ns*. lithot′ritist, lithotrip′tist, lithontrip′tist, one who performs the operation. [Gr. *lithōn* (gen. pl.) *thryptika*, breakers of stones; reconstructed as from Gr. *tripsis*, rubbing, or L. *tritus*, rubbing.]

litigate, *lit′i-gāt*, *v.t.* and *v.i.* to dispute, esp. by a lawsuit.—*adjs*. lit′igable; lit′igant, contending at law: engaged in a lawsuit.—*n*. a person engaged in a lawsuit.—*n*. litigā′tion.—*adj*. litigious (-*ij′əs*), pertaining to litigation: inclined to engage in lawsuits: disputable: open to contention: perh. depending on results of negotiation (*Shak*.).—*adv*. litig′iously.—*n*. litig′iousness. [L. *litigāre, -ātum—lis, litis*, strife, *agĕre*, to do.]

litmus, *lit′məs*, *n*. a substance obtained from certain lichens, turned red by acids, blue by alkalies. —litmus paper, a test-paper dipped in litmus solution. [O.N. *litr*, colour, *mosi*, moss.]

litotes, *lit′* or *lit′ō-tēz*, (*rhet*.) *n*. meiosis or understatement: esp. affirmation by negation of the contrary. [Gr. *litotēs*, simplicity—*litos*, plain.]

litre, *lē′tər*, *n*. the metric unit of capacity, orig. intended to be 1 cubic decimetre: (1901) volume of a kilogram of water at 4°C, under standard atmospheric pressure (1·00028 cu. dm.): (1964) 1 cubic decimetre. [Fr.,—L.L. *litra*—Gr. *lītrā*, a pound.]

litter, *lit′ər*, *n*. a heap of straw, bracken, etc., used for animals to lie upon: materials for a bed: any scattered or confused collection of objects, esp. of little value: a state of confusion and untidiness with things strewn about: wastage, rubbish: a couch carried by men or beasts: a stretcher: a brood of animals: an occasion of birth of animals.—*v.t.* to cover or supply with litter: to scatter carelessly about: to give birth to (said of animals).—*v.i.* to produce a litter or brood.— *adj*. litt′ered.—*adj*. litt′ery, in condition of litter: addicted to litter.—litt′er-bin, a receptacle for rubbish; litt′er-bug, -lout, one who wilfully drops litter. [O.Fr. *litiere*—L.L. *lectāria*—L. *lectus*, a bed.]

literae humaniores. See literae humaniores.

littérateur, *lē-tä-rä-tœr′*, *n*. a literary man. [Fr.]

little, *lit′l*, *adj*. small in size, extent, quantity, or significance: petty: small-minded.—*n*. (or *adj*. with a noun understood) that which is small in quantity or extent: a small quantity: a small thing.—*adv*. in a small quantity or degree: not much.—**less**, **least**, serve as comp. and superl. to the adv. and to some extent, along with **lesser**, to the adj.—*ns.* **litt'leness**; **litt'ling** (*Scot.* **litt'-lin**, **litt'leane**; O.E. *lȳtling*), a child.—**litt'le-ease**, a confined space in which a prisoner can neither sit, stand nor lie: the pillory: the stocks; **Litt'le-end'ian**, one of the Lilliputian party who opposed the *Big-endians*, maintaining that boiled eggs should be cracked at the little end; **little Englander**, an opponent of British imperialism and empire-building; **litt'le-go** (see go); **little magazine**, a small high-brow magazine; **little man**, a man of no importance, an underdog; **little Mary** (*J. M. Barrie*), the stomach; **little office**, a short service of psalms, hymns, collects, etc.; **little people**, the fairies, or a traditional race of pygmies; **little theatre**, a small theatre in which experimental plays, and other plays not likely to be a great commercial success, are produced.—*adj.* **litt'leworth**, worthless.—**by little and little**, **little by little**, by degrees; **in little**, on a small scale; **little green men**, type of men imagined as originating in parts of the universe other than our earth; **make little of**, to treat as of little consequence, belittle: to comprehend only slightly. [O.E. *lȳtel*.]

**littoral**, *lit'ər-əl*, *adj.* belonging to the seashore, to lands near the coast, the beach, the space between high and low tidemarks, or water a little below low-water mark.—*n.* the strip of land along it. [L. *littorālis* for *litorālis*—*litus*, *litoris*, shore.]

**liturgy**, *lit'ər-ji*, *n.* the form of service or regular ritual of a church—strictly, that used in the celebration of the eucharist: in ancient Greece, personal service to the state.—*adjs.* **liturgic** (-*ûrj'ik*), -**al**.—*adv.* **litur'gically**.—*ns.* **litur'gics**, the doctrine of liturgies; **liturgiol'ogist**; **liturgiol'ogy**, the study of liturgical forms; **lit'urgist**, a leader in public worship: one who adheres to, or who studies, liturgies. [Gr. *leitourgiā*.]

**lituus**, *lit'ū-əs*, *n.* an augur's curved staff: a J-shaped Roman trumpet: a curve of similar form with the polar equation $r^\theta_0 = a$. [L. *lituus*.]

**live**, *liv*, *v.i.* to have, or continue in, life, temporal, spiritual, or figurative: to last: to enjoy life: to direct one's course of life: to be supported, subsist, get a living: to escape destruction or oblivion: to dwell.—*v.t.* to spend or pass: to act in conformity to: to express by one's life, make one's life the same thing as:—*pr.p.* **liv'ing**; *pa.t.* and *pa.p.* **lived** (*livd*).—*adjs.* **liv'able**, **live'able**, worth living, capable of being lived: habitable.—*n.* **liv'er**.—*adj.* **liv'able-with**, such as one could endure to live with.—**live and let live**, give and expect toleration or forbearance; **live down**, live so as to allow to be forgotten; **live in**, **out**, dwell in, away from, one's place of employment; **live it up**, to go on the spree: to live rather too intensely; **live on**, live by feeding upon, or with expenditure limited to; **live out**, to survive: to be in domestic service (*U.S.*); **live to**, live long enough to, come at last to; **live under**, to be tenant to; **live up to**, to rule one's life in a manner worthy of: to spend up to the scale of; **live with**, to cohabit with: to accept and adapt to as an inescapable part of one's life; **the living theatre**, the live theatre. [O.E. *lifian* (W.S. *libban*).]

**live**, *liv*, *adj.* having life: alive, not dead: active: stirring: unquarried or unwrought: charged with energy (as by electricity, explosives or other chemicals, etc.) and still capable of discharge: burning: vivid: of the theatre, etc., concerned with living performance as distinct from filming, broadcasting, or televising: of a broadcast, made directly from the actual event, not from a recording: a fishmonger's word for very fresh. —**lived** (*livd*; sometimes *livd*) in composition, having life (as *long-lived*).—*v.t.* **liv'en**, to enliven.

—*v.i.* to become lively.—**live'-ax'le**, driving-axle; **live'-bait**, a living animal as bait; **live'-birth'**, birth in a living condition (opposed to *still-birth*).—*adj.* **live'-born**.—**live'-box**, a glass box for examining living objects under the microscope: a box for live fish; **live cartridge**, one containing a bullet, opposed to a *blank* or a *spent* cartridge; **live circuit**, a circuit through which an electric current is flowing.—*n.pl.* **live'-feath'ers**, those plucked from the living fowl; **live'-oak**, an American evergreen oak, with durable wood; **live'-rail**, **live'-wire**, one carrying electric current; **live'-wire** (*fig.*) a person of intense energy or alertness; **live shell**, a shell still capable of exploding; **live'stock**, domestic animals, esp. horses, cattle, sheep, and pigs: domestic or body vermin (*slang*); **live'-weight**, weight of living animals; **live'-well**, the well in a fishing-boat where fish are kept alive. [**alive**.]

**livelihood**, *liv'li-hŏŏd*, *n.* means of living: support. —Also (*Spens.*) **live'lod**, **live'lood**. [O.E. *liflād*—*lif*, life, *lād*, course.]

**livelong**, *liv'long*, also *liv'long*, *adj.* very long: protracted: enduring. [lief, used intensively, long.]

**livelong**, *liv'long*, *n.* the orpine, a plant difficult to kill. [live (v.), long.]

**lively**, *liv'li*, *adj.* vital (*obs.*): lifelike: oral (*obs.*): brisk: active: sprightly: spirited: vivid.—*adv.* vivaciously: vigorously.—*n.* **live'lihead** (*obs.*), liveliness: life: living form: likelihood.—*adv.* **live'lily**.—*n.* **live'liness**. [O.E. *liflic*—*lif*, life.]

**liver**, *liv'ər*, *n.* a large gland that secretes bile, formerly regarded as seat of courage, love, etc.: its substance as food: a disordered state of the liver (*coll.*): in old chemistry a sulphide or other liver-coloured substance (*liver of sulphur*, mixture got by heating potassium carbonate with sulphur).—*adj.* **liver-colour**.—*adjs.* **liv'ered**, having a liver, as *white-livered*, *lily-livered*, cowardly; **liv'erish**, **liv'ery**, suffering from disordered liver: irritable.—*n.* and *adj.* **liv'er-col'our**, dark reddish brown.—*adj.* **liv'er-coloured**.—**liv'er-fluke**, a trematode worm that infects the bile-ducts of sheep and other animals.—*adj.* **liv'er-grown**, having a swelled liver.—**liv'er-rot**, a disease caused by liver-flukes; **liv'er-wing**, a fowl's right wing, which is cooked with the liver; **liv'erwort** (-*würt*), any plant of the Hepaticae, some kinds having once been used medicinally in diseases of the liver. [O.E. *lifer*; Ger. *leber*, O.N. *lifr*.]

**liver**. See live (1).

**liver**, *li'vər*, *n.* a fanciful bird on the arms of the city of Liverpool. [Formed from *Liverpool*.]

**Liverpudlian**, *liv-ər-pud'li-ən*, *adj.* belonging to Liverpool.—*n.* a native of Liverpool. [*Liverpool*, influenced by *puddle*.]

**livery**, *liv'ər-i*, *n.* a delivery or handing over (*obs.*): a dispensing or allowance of food or clothes to servants and retainers (*hist.*): the feeding, care, and stabling of a horse at a certain rate: the distinctive dress or badge of a great man's household (*hist.*): the distinctive garb of a person's servants, esp. men-servants, or of a body, e.g. a trade-guild: any characteristic garb: a body of liverymen or of livery-servants: a livery-servant (*arch.*).—*adj.* **liv'eried**, clothed in livery. —**liv'ery-com'pany**, a guild of the city of London; **liv'eryman**, a man who wears a livery: a freeman of the city of London entitled to wear the livery and enjoy other privileges of his company: one who keeps or works at a livery-stable; **liv'ery-servant**, a servant who wears a livery; **liv'ery-stable**, a stable where horses are kept at livery and for hire.—**sue one's livery** (*Shak.*), to ask for the writ delivering a freehold into the possession of its heir. [A.Fr. *liveré*, lit. handed over—*livrer*—L. *liberāre*, to free.]

**lives**, *livz*, *n.* plural of **life**.

**livid**, *liv'id*, *adj.* black and blue: of a lead colour: discoloured: pale, ashen: extremely angry (*coll.*).—*ns.* livid'ity, liv'idness, livor (*li'vər*, *-vör*). [L. *lividus—livēre*, to be of a lead colour.]

**living**, *liv'ing*, *adj.* live: alive: having vitality: lively: in present life, existence, activity, or use. —*n.* means of subsistence: manner of life: a property: a benefice.—liv'ing-room, a sitting-room for all-round use; living memory, the memory of anybody or somebody still alive; living rock, rock still in its natural position; living wage, a wage on which it is possible for a workman and his family to live fairly. [Pr.p. of live (1).]

**livraison**, *lē-vrez-ɔ̃*, *n.* a number of a book published in parts. [Fr.,—L. *liberātiō*, *-ōnis*, delivery.]

**livre**, *lēvr'*, *n.* an old French coin, superseded by the franc in 1795: an old French weight about 1 lb. avoirdupois. [Fr.,—L. *libra*, a pound.]

**lixiviation**, *liks-iv-i-ā'shən*, *n.* leaching.—*adjs.* lixiv'ial, lixiv'ious.—*v.t.* lixiv'iate.—*n.* lixiv'ium, lye. [L. *lixivium*, lye.]

**lizard**, *liz'ərd*, *n.* any member of the Lacertilia, an order of scaly reptiles, usually differing from snakes in having four legs, movable eyelids, and non-expansible mouths (*cap.*) the constellation Lacerta. [O.Fr. *lesard* (Fr. *lézard*)—L. *lacerta*.]

**llama**, *lä'ma*, *n.* a S. American transport animal of the camel family, a domesticated guanaco: its wool: cloth made thereof. [Sp., from Quechua.]

**llano**, *lyä'nō*, or *lä'nō*, *n.* one of the vast steppes or plains in the northern part of South America:—*pl.* lla'nos.—*n.* llanero (*lyä-nā'rō*), an inhabitant of the llanos. [Sp.,—L. *plānus*, plain.]

**lo**, *lō*, *interj.* look: behold. [O.E. *lā*.]

**loach**, *lōch*, *n.* a small river-fish of a family (Cobitidae) akin to the carps. [Fr. *loche*.]

**load**, *lōd*, *n.* that which is carried: that which may or can be carried at one time or journey: a burden: a charge: a freight or cargo: a definite quantity, varying according to the goods: weight carried: power output of an engine, etc.: work imposed or expected: power carried by an electric circuit: a large quantity borne: a burden sustained with difficulty: that which burdens or grieves: a weight or encumbrance: weight of blows (*Spens.*): abundance (*coll.*, esp. in *pl.*).—*v.t.* to lade or burden: to charge: to put a load on or in: to put on or in anything as a load: to put film in (a camera): to put on overmuch: to weigh down: to overburden: to supply, present, or assail overwhelmingly or lavishly: to weight: to give weight or body to, by adding something: to mix with white: to lay on in masses (*painting*): to add charges to (*insurance*): (of wine) to doctor, drug, adulterate, or fortify.—*v.i.* to put or take on a load: to charge a gun: to become loaded or burdened:—*pa.t.* load'ed; *pa.p.* load'ed or (*arch.*) load'en.—*adj.* load'ed, rich, wealthy: under the influence of drink or drugs (*slang*): weighted in discussion in a certain direction: charged with contentious material.—*v.t.* load'en (*obs.* or *dial.*), to load.—*ns.* load'er; load'ing, the act of lading: that with which anything is loaded.—loaded question, a question designed to make an unwilling answerer commit himself to some opinion, action, or course; loading coil, a coil inserted in an electric circuit to increase inductance; loading gauge, a suspended bar that marks how high a railway truck may be loaded; load'-line, a line on a ship's side to mark the depth to which her cargo may be allowed to sink her; load shedding, temporarily reducing the amount of electricity sent out by a power station.—get a load of (*slang*), listen to, look at, pay attention to; load dice, to make one side heavier than the other so as to influence their fall for purposes of cheating; load the dice against one (*fig.*), to deprive one of any chance of

success. [O.E. *lād*, course, journey, conveyance; meaning affected by the unrelated lade; cf. lode, lead.]

**loadstar, loadstone.** Same as lodestar, lodestone.

**loaf**, *lōf*, *n.* bread (formerly, still *Scot.*): a portion of bread baked in one mass, esp. of standard weight: a moulded portion of food, esp. bread or meat: a conical mass of sugar: any lump (*obs.*): a cabbage-head: the head, or brains (*slang*):—*pl.* loaves (*lōvz*).—*v.i.* loaf, loave (*lōv*), to form a head, as a cabbage.—loaf'-bread (*Scot.*), ordinary plain bread; loaf'-cake (*U.S.*), a plain cake like a loaf in form; loaf'-sug'ar, refined sugar moulded in the form of a great cigar.—half loaf, a loaf of half the standard weight; loaves and fishes, temporal benefits, the main chance (John vi. 26). [O.E. *hlāf*, bread.]

**loaf**, *lōf*, *v.i.* to loiter or stand idly about, pass time idly.—*n.* loaf'er, one who loafs: a casual shoe, often resembling a moccasin.—*adj.* loaf'erish.—*n.* and *adj.* loaf'ing. [Origin obscure.]

**loam**, *lōm*, *n.* a soil consisting of a natural mixture of clay and sand, with animal and vegetable matter: a composition basically of moist clay and sand used in making bricks.—*v.t.* to cover with loam.—*adj.* loam'y. [O.E. *lām*; Ger. *lehm*; cf. lime.]

**loan**, *lōn*, (*Scot.*) *n.* a lane: an open space for passage left between fields of corn: a place for milking cows.—Also loan'ing. [O.E. *lone, lane*; see lane.]

**loan**, *lōn*, *n.* anything lent, esp. money at interest: the act of lending: the condition of being lent: an arrangement for lending: permission to use. —*v.t.* to lend.—*adj.* loan'able.—loan'-office, a public office at which loans are negotiated, received, or recorded: a pawnshop; loan'-shark, a usurer; loan'-society, a society organised to subscribe money to be lent; loan'-word, one borrowed from another language. [O.N. *lān*; cf. lend, O.E. *lǣnan*; Dan. *laan*.]

**loast**, *lōst*, (*Spens.*) *pa.p.* of loose.

**loath.** Same as loth.

**loathe**, *lōdh*, *v.t.* to dislike intensely: to feel disgust at.—*adj.* loathed.—*ns.* loath'edness; loath'er.—*adj.* loath'ful, exciting loathing or disgust: (*Spens.*) lothefull, lothfull) loathsome: reluctant.—*ns.* loath'fulness; loath'ing, extreme hate or disgust: abhorrence.—*adj.* hating.—*adv.* loath'ingly.—*n.* loath'liness.—*adjs.* loath'ly (*arch.*), hideous; loathsome; loathsome (*lōth'*, *lōdh'səm*), exciting loathing or abhorrence: detestable.—*adv.* loath'somely.—*n.* loath'someness.—*adj.* loathy (*lōdh'i; arch.*). [O.E. *lāthian*; cf. loth.]

**loave, loaves.** See loaf (1).

**lob**, *lob*, *n.* a lump: a clumsy person: a lout: something thick and heavy: a pollack: a lob-worm: in cricket, a slow, high underhand ball: in lawn-tennis, a ball high overhead, dropping near the back of the court.—*v.t.* to droop (*Shak.*): to bowl or strike as a lob:—*pa.p.* lobbed.—Lob'-lie'-by-the-fire, a brownie who works by night for his bowl of cream: a Puck; Lob's pound (*dial.*), prison: difficulty. [Cf. Fris. and Du. *lob*.]

**lobby**, *lob'i*, *n.* a small hall or waiting-room: a passage serving as a common entrance to several apartments: the ante-chamber of a legislative hall: a corridor into which members pass as they vote: a group of persons who campaign to persuade legislators to make regulations favouring their particular interests.—*v.t.* to seek to influence in the lobby.—*v.i.* to frequent the lobby in order to influence members or to collect political intelligence.—*ns.* lobb'ying; lobb'yist. —lobby correspondent, reporter on parliamentary affairs; lobb'y-member (*U.S.*), formerly, one who frequented a lobby in the interest of some cause.

[L.L. *lobia*—M.H.G. *loube* (Ger. *laube*), a portico, arbour—*laub*, a leaf; cf. **lodge**.]
**lobe**, *lōb, n.* a broad, esp. rounded, segmental division, branch, or projection: the soft lower part of the ear: a division of the lungs, brain, etc.: a division of a leaf.—*adjs.* **lōb′ar, lōb′ate**, **lōbed, lōb′ose**.—*n.* lōbā′tion, lobing.—**lōbe′-foot**, a phalarope.—*adjs.* **lōbe′-foot′ed,** lō′biped, having lobate feet, i.e. with lobes along the sides of the toes, as a coot.—*ns.* **lōbe′let, lobule** (*lob′ūl*), small lobe; **lōb′ing,** division into lobes: formation of, possession of, or provision with, lobes; **lobot′omy,** leucotomy.—*adjs.* **lōb′ular, -ulate(d)**.—*ns.* **lōbulā′tion; lōb′ulus,** a small lobe or lobe-like structure:—*pl.* **lōb′uli** (*-i*); **lō′bus,** a lobe:—*pl.* **lō′bi**.—**lobar pneumonia,** inflammation of a whole lobe of the lungs, as distinguished from **lobular pneumonia,** which attacks the lungs in patches. [Gr. *lobos*, lobe.]
**Lobelia,** *lō-bē′lya, n.* a genus of plants giving name to a family, **Lobeliā′ceae,** differing from Campanulaceae in having two carpels and zygomorphic flowers, twisted upside-down, including favourite blue-flowered garden plants; **lobeline** (*lō′bə-lēn, -lin*), a poisonous alkaloid obtained from *Lobelia inflata,* used as a respiratory stimulant and to discourage tobacco-smoking. [Named after the botanist Matthias de *Lobel* (1538–1616).]
**loblolly,** *lob′lol-i, n.* thick gruel, hence ship's medicine (*dial.*): a lout (*dial.*): a puddle (*U.S.*): a name for various American pines (also **loblolly pine**).—**lob′lolly-bay,** an American tree of the tea family (*Gordonia lasianthus*), its bark used in tanning; **lob′lolly-boy** (*obs.*), a ship-surgeon's attendant; **lob′lolly-tree,** a name for several American leathery-leaved trees. [Perh. **lob** and **lolly**.]
**lobscouse,** *lob′skows, n.* a stew or hash with vegetables or biscuit, a sea dish.—Also **lob's course**. [Origin obscure; cf. **lob, loblolly**.]
**lobster,** *lob′stər, n.* a large strong-clawed edible crustacean (Homarus), red when boiled: extended to kindred kinds, as the **Norway lobster** (Nephrops), **spiny** or **rock lobster** (Palinurus): a British soldier (*obs. slang*).—**lob′ster-pot,** a basket for trapping lobsters. [O.E. *loppestre*—L. *locusta,* a lobster; cf. **locust**.]
**lobworm,** *lob′wûrm, n.* a lugworm: sometimes an earthworm. [**lob, worm**.]
**local,** *lō′kl, adj.* pertaining to position in space: of or belonging to a place: confined to a place or places.—*n.* someone or something local, as an inhabitant, a public-house, an examination, an item of news, a railway train, in U.S. a trade union branch: a place (*lō-kâl′*; erroneously **locale,** for Fr. *local*) the scene of some event.—*n.* localisā′tion, -z-.—*v.t.* lo′calise, -ize, assign, limit, to a place.—*n.* lo′caliser, -z-, something that localises, esp. a radio transmitter used in effecting a blind landing.—Also *adj.* as *localiser beam,* etc.—*ns.* lo′calism, the state of being local: affection for a place: provincialism; **locality** (*lō-kal′i-ti*), place: position: district.—*adv.* lo′cally.—*v.t.* **locate′,** to place: to set in a particular position: to designate or find the place of.—*v.i.* to settle, take up one's abode (*U.S.*).—*n.* locā′tion, act of locating: a farm: a claim or place marked off (for native occupation, etc.): position, site: site for filming outside the studio (*cinema*): a leasing on rent (*law*).—*adj.* **locative** (*lok′ə-tiv*), pertaining to location: denoting place where (*gram.*).—*n.* the locative case: a word in the locative case.—**local authorities,** elected bodies for local government, e.g. town councils, county councils; **local colour,** colour of individual items as apart from general colour-scheme in a picture: faithful, characteristic details of particular scenery, manners, etc., giving verisimilitude in works of

art and fiction; **local examinations,** examinations of school pupils held in various local centres by universities; **local government,** self-administration (in local affairs) by towns, counties, and the like, as opp. to *national* or *central government;* **local option,** the right of a town or district to decide whether liquor licences shall be granted within its bounds, or to decide whether or not to enforce (locally) permissive laws and regulations; **local preacher,** a Methodist layman authorised to preach in his district; **local time,** the time of a place as shown by the sun; **local veto,** the power of a district to prohibit the sale of liquors in its own area. [L. *locālis*—*locus,* a place.]
**locellate,** *lō-sel′āt, adj.* divided into small compartments. [L. *locellus,* dim. of *locus,* a place.]
**loch,** *lohh, n.* a lake: an arm of the sea.—*n.* **loch′an** (*Gael.*), a lakelet. [Gael. *loch;* O.E. (Northumbrian) *luh.*]
**Lochaber-axe,** *lohh-ä′bər-aks, n.* a long-handled Highland variety of halberd. [*Lochaber* district in Inverness-shire.]
**lochia,** *lok′i-a,* or *lōk′, n.pl.* a discharge after childbirth.—*adj.* lō′chial. [Gr. *lochia* (pl.).]
**lock,** *lok, n.* a fastening device, esp. one in which a bolt is moved by mechanism, with or without a key: an enclosure for raising or lowering boats: the part of a firearm by which it is discharged: a grapple in wrestling: a state of being jammed, or immovable: an assemblage of things mutually engaged: a lockful: a lock-keeper: any narrow, confined place: a lock-hospital: locking up: the full extent of the turning arc of the front wheels of a motor vehicle.—*v.t.* to fasten (door, chest, etc.) with a lock: to fasten so as to impede motion: to engage: to jam: to shut up: to close fast: to embrace closely: to furnish with locks.—*v.i.* to become fast: to unite closely: to become locked.—*ns.* **lock′age,** the locks of a canal: the difference in the levels of locks: materials used for locks: water lost by use of a lock: tolls paid for passing through locks; **lock′er,** box, small cupboard, properly one that may be locked; **locket** (*lok′it*), a little ornamental case usually containing a miniature or memento, and hung from the neck.—*adj.* **lock′fast,** firmly fastened by locks.—*n.* **lock′ful,** enough to fill a lock.—**lock′-chain,** a chain for fastening the wheels of a vehicle by tying the rims to some part which does not rotate; **lock′-gate,** a gate for opening or closing a lock in a canal, river, or dock-entrance; **lock′-hos′pital,** a hospital for venereal diseases (from one in Southwark, originally a lazar-house, probably as specially isolated); **lock′house,** a lock-keeper's house; **lock′-jaw,** tetanus: loosely, trismus; **lock′-keeper,** the attendant at a lock; **lock′man,** a lock-keeper: a hangman (*Scot., obs.*): an under-sheriff, or a coroner's summoner (*Isle of Man*); **lock′out′,** the act of locking out, esp. used of the locking out of a teacher by the pupils, pupils by teacher, or employees by employer; **locks′man,** a turnkey: a lock-keeper; **lock′smith,** one who makes and mends locks; **lock′step,** a style of marching in which each individual is as close as possible to the one immediately in front; **lock′stitch,** a stitch formed by the locking of two threads together; **lock′-up,** a place for locking up prisoners, motor-cars, etc.: a locking up.—*adj.* capable of being locked up.—**a shot in the locker** (see **shot**); **Davy Jone's locker.** See under **Davy Jones; lock in, out,** to confine, keep out, by locking doors; **lock, stock, and barrel,** the whole: altogether; **lock up,** to confine: to lock securely: to lock whatever is to be locked: to make inaccessible or unavailable (*fig.*). [O.E. *loc.*]
**lock,** *lok, n.* a tuft or ringlet of hair, wool, etc.: a small quantity, as of hay: a quantity of meal, the perquisite of a mill-servant (*Scots law*): a

lovelock (*Shak.*). [O.E. *locc*; O.N. *lokkr*, Ger. *locke*, a lock.]

Lockian, *lok'i-ən*, *adj.* pertaining to the philosophy of John Locke (1632-1704).—*ns.* Lock'ian, Lock'ist.

lockram, *lok'rəm*, *n.* a coarse linen said to have been made at *Locronan* (Ronan's cell) in Brittany.

loco, *lō'kō*, (*U.S.*) *adj.* mad.—*n.* (also lo'co-plant, -weed) Astragalus or other leguminous plant.— *adj.* locoed (*lō'kōd*), poisoned by loco: mad. [Sp. *loco*, mad.]

loco citato, *lō'kō si-tā'tō, ki-tä'tō*, (L.) in the passage cited—abbrev. loc. cit.

locofoco, *lō-kō-fō'kō*, (*U.S.*) *n.* a friction match: (usu. *cap.*) one of the extreme section of the Democratic party of 1835, known as the Equal Rights Party. [Origin unknown.]

locomotive, *lō-kə-mō'tiv*, *adj.* moving from place to place: capable of, or assisting in, locomotion. —*n.* a locomotive machine: a railway engine.— *adj.* locomo'bile (-*bil*), having power of changing place: self-propelling.—*n.* a locomobile vehicle. —*v.i.* lo'comote, to move from place to place (back formation).—*ns.* locomotion (-*mō'shən*); locomotiv'ity; locomo'tor.—*adjs.* locomo'tor, locomo'tory.—locomotor ataxy, tabes dorsalis, a chronic degenerative disease of the nervous system of which want of power to co-ordinate the muscles is a characteristic symptom. [L. *lŏcus*, a place, *movēre, mōtum*, to move.]

locorestive, *lō-kō-res'tiv*, (*Lamb*) *adj.* staying in one place. [Humorously modelled on preceding —L. *restāre*, to stay still.]

Locrian, *lō'kri-ən*, *adj.* of *Locris* in Greece, or its people, the *Locri.*—*n.* one of the Locri.— Locrian mode, in ancient Greek music, the same as the Hypodorian. [Gr. *Lokros*, Locrian.]

loculus, *lok'ū-ləs*, *n.* a small compartment (*bot., anat., zool.*): in ancient catacombs, a small recess for holding an urn:—*pl.* loc'uli (-*li*).—*n.* loc'ulament (*bot.*), loculus.—*adjs.* loc'ular, loc'ulate, having loculi; loculicidal (*lok-ū-li-si'dl*; L. *caedĕre*, to cut), dehiscing along the back of the carpel. [L. *loculus*, dim. of *locus*, a place.]

locum (tenens), *lō'kəm (tēn', ten'enz)*, *n.* a deputy or substitute, esp. for a clergyman or doctor.—*n.* lō'cum-ten'ency, the holding by a temporary substitute of a post. [L. *lŏcum*, accus. of *lŏcus*, a place, *tĕnēns*, pr.p. of *tenēre*, to hold.]

locuplete, *lok'ū-plēt*, *adj.* well-stored. [L. *locuplēs, -ētis*.]

locus, *lō'kəs, lok'ōōs*, *n.* a place, locality, location: a passage in a writing: the position of a gene in a chromosome: the line or surface constituted by all positions of a point or line satisfying a given condition (*math.*):—*pl.* loci (*lō'si*; *lok'ē*).—locus classicus (*klas'i-kəs, -kōōs*), the classical passage, the stock quotation; locus paenitentiae (*pē-ni-ten'shi-ē, pi-ni-ten'ti-i*), room for penitence: time for repentance; locus standi (*stan'dī, -dē*), a place for standing: a right to interfere. [L. *lŏcus*, place.]

locust, *lō'kəst*, *n.* a name for several kinds of migratory winged insects of the family Acrididae, akin to grasshoppers, highly destructive to vegetation: extended to various similar insects: a devourer or devastator (*fig.*): a locust-bean: a locust-tree.—*v.i.* (rare) to lay waste like locusts.—*n.* locust'a, a grass spikelet: (*cap.*) a genus of grasshoppers of the family Locust'idae (not usually reckoned locusts):—*pl.* locust'ae (-*ē*).—lo'cust-bean', the carob-bean; lo'cust-tree', the carob: the false acacia (*Robinia pseudo-acacia*): a large West Indian tree (*Hymenaea courbaril*) of the Caesalpinia family, with buttress roots, valuable wood, bark exuding animé. [L. *locusta*, lobster, locust; cf. lobster.]

locution, *lok-ū'shən*, *n.* act or mode of speaking: expression, word, or phrase.—*n.* loc'utory, a room for conversation, esp. in a monastery. [L. *loqui, locūtus*, to speak.]

lode, *lōd*, *n.* a vein containing metallic ore: a reach of water: an open ditch.—lodes'man, a pilot; lode'star, load'star, the star that guides, the Pole Star—often used figuratively; lode'-stone, load'stone, a form of magnetite which exhibits polarity, behaving, when freely suspended, as a magnet: a magnet—often figuratively. [O.E. *lād*, a course; cf. load.]

lodge, *loj*, *n.* an abode, esp. if secluded, humble, small, or temporary: a house in the wilds for sportsmen: a gate-keeper's cottage: a college head's residence: a porter's room: the meeting-place of a branch of some societies, as freemasons: the branch itself: an American Indian's abode: the dwelling-place of a beaver, otter, etc.: a retreat: often, a villa (as part of its name): an accumulation (*obs.*): a loggia: a box in a theatre.—*v.t.* to furnish with a temporary dwelling: to place: to deposit: to infix: to vest: to settle: to drive to covert: to lay flat, as grain. —*v.i.* to dwell, esp. for a time, or as a lodger: to pass the night: to take covert: to come to rest in a fixed position: to lie flat, as grain.—*ns.* lodg'er, one who lodges: one who lives in a hired room or rooms; lodg'ing, temporary habitation: (often in *pl.*) a room or rooms hired in the house of another: harbour; lodg'ment (also lodge'ment), act of lodging, or state of being lodged: accumulation of something that remains at rest: the occupation of a position by a besieging party, and the works thrown up to maintain it (*mil.*).—lodge'-gate', a gate with a lodge; lodge'-keeper; lodge'pole, a pole used in making an Amer. Indian lodge; lodg'ing-house, a house where lodgings are let: a house other than a hotel where travellers lodge: a house where vagrants may lodge; lodging turn, a turn of railway work that requires sleeping away from home. [O.Fr. *loge*—O.H.G. *lauba*, shelter; cf. lobby, loggia.]

lodicule, *lod'i-kūl*, *n.* a small scale in a grass flower.—Also lodic'ula:—*pl.* lodic'ulae (-*ē*). [L. *lōdicula*, dim. of *lōdix, -īcis*, coverlet.]

lo'e, *lōō*, Scots form of love (verb).

loess, löss, *læs*, or *lō'es*, *n.* a loamy deposit of aeolian origin. [Ger. *löss*.]

loft, *loft*, *n.* upper region, sky, height (*Spens.*): a room or space immediately under a roof: a gallery in a hall or church: an upper room: an upper floor (*U.S.*): a floor or ceiling (*Spens.*): a room for pigeons: a layer (*Milt.*): a stroke that causes a golf-ball to rise: a backward slope on a golf-club head for the purpose of lofting: a lifting action.—*v.t.* to furnish with a loft (*obs.*): to put or keep in a loft (*obs.*): to strike up (*golf*): to toss.—*n.* loft'er, a golf iron for lofting.— *adv.* loft'ily.—*n.* loft'iness.—*adj.* loft'y, very high in position, character, sentiment, manner, or diction: stately: haughty: of wool, bulky, springy, supple, and soft.—cock of the loft, the head or chief of a set; lofted house (*Scot.*), a house of more than one storey. [Late O.E. *loft*—O.N. *lopt*, sky, an upper room; O.E. *lyft*, Ger. *luft*, the air.]

log, *log*, *n.* abbreviation for logarithm.

log, *lŏg, log*, *n.* a Hebrew liquid measure, believed to be very nearly an English pint. [Heb. *lōg*.]

log, *log*, *n.* a bulky piece of wood: a clog or impediment: an inert or insensitive person (*fig.*): an apparatus (originally a block of wood) for ascertaining a ship's speed: a record of a ship's, or other, performance and experiences, a log-book.—*adj.* consisting of logs—*v.t.* to cut or haul in the form of logs: to enter in a log-book: to cover a distance of, according to the log: to record the name and punishment of:

to punish.—*n.* **logg′at**, a small log or piece of wood: a stake: (in *pl.*) old game of throwing loggats at a stake.—*adj.* **logged** (*logd*), reduced to the inactivity or helplessness of a log: waterlogged: cleared of logs.—*ns.* **logg′er**, a lumberman: (also **data logger**) a device which automatically records data; **logging**.—**log′board**, a hinged board for noting particulars for the logbook; **log′-book**, a book containing an official record of a ship's progress and proceedings on board, or of a journey made by an aircraft or car, or of any progress: a headmaster's record of attendances, etc.; **log′-cab′in**, a hut built of hewn or unhewn logs; **log′-canoe′**, a boat made by hollowing out the trunk of a tree; **log′-chip**, the quadrant-shaped board attached to a log-line; **logg′erhead**, a blockhead: a dunce: a round piece of timber in a whale-boat, over which the line is passed (*naut.*): a large sea-turtle: a round mass of iron with a long handle, heated for various purposes.—*adj.* **logg′erheaded.**—**log′-glass**, a 14- or 28-second sand-glass, used with the logline to ascertain the speed of a ship; **log′-head**, a blockhead; **log′-house**, a log-cabin: a prison (*U.S.*); **log′-hut′**; **log′-jam**, jamming that brings floating logs to a standstill; **log′-juice** (*slang*), bad port wine, as if coloured with logwood; **log′line**, the line fastened to the log, and marked for finding the speed of a vessel; **log′-man**, a man who carries logs (*Shak.*): one who cuts and removes logs; **log′-reel**, a reel on which the logline is wound.—*v.t.* and *v.i.* **log′-roll.**—**log′-roller**; **log′-rolling**, a combination for facilitating the collection of logs after the clearing of a piece of land, or for rolling logs into a stream: mutual aid among politicians or reviewers; **log′-slate**, a double slate used as a logboard; **log′wood**, a tropical American tree (*Haematoxylon campechianum*) of the Caesalpinia family, exported in logs: its dark-red heartwood: an extract from it used in dyeing.—**at loggerheads**, at issue, quarrelling. [Origin obscure.]

**logan**, *log′ən*, *n.* a rocking-stone.—Also **log′anstone**, **logg′an-stone**, **logg′ing-stone**. [Dialect word *log*, to rock; poss. conn. with Dan. *logre*, to wag the tail.]

**loganberry**, *lō′gan-ber-i*, *n.* a supposed hybrid between raspberry and Pacific coast blackberry, obtained by Judge J. H. *Logan*.

**Logania**, *lō-gā′ni-ə*, *n.* a genus of Australian plants giving name to the **Loganiä′ceae**, akin to the gentians. [Named after James *Logan* (1674–1751), American botanist, scholar, and statesman.]

**logaoedic**, *log-ə-ē′dik*, (*ancient prosody*) *adj.* combining dactyls with trochees. [Gr. *logos*, prose, *aoidē*, song.]

**logarithm**, *log′-ə-rithm*, *-ridhm*, *n.* the power of a fixed number (called the base of the system, usu. 10 or *e*) that equals the number in question.—*adjs.* **logarith′mic**, *-al*.—*adv.* **logarith′mically.**—**logarithmic sine**, **cosine**, etc., the logarithm of the sine, cosine, etc.; **logarithmic spiral**, the path of a point travelling along a radius vector with a velocity increasing as its distance from the pole, its polar equation being *r = aθ*, or *θ = k* log *r*. [Gr. *logos*, ratio, reckoning, *arithmos*, number.]

**loge**, *lozh*, (Fr.) a box in the theatre.

**loggat**, **logger**, etc. See log (3).

**loggia**, *loj′(y)ə*, *n.* a covered open arcade:—*pl.* **loggie** (*loj′ā*), **loggias**. [It.; cf. lodge.]

**logia**, *log′i-ə*, *n.pl.* sayings, esp. early collections of those attributed to Christ:—*sing.* **log′ion**. [Gr.]

**logic**, *loj′ik*, *n.* the science and art of reasoning correctly: the science of the necessary laws of thought: the principles of any branch of knowledge: sound reasoning: individual method of reasoning: convincing and compelling force (as of facts, events): basis of operation as designed and effected in a computer, comprising **logical elements**, which perform specified elementary arithmetical functions.—*adj.* **log′ical**, of or according to logic: rightly reasoning.—*ns.* **logical′ity**, **log′icalness**.—*adv.* **log′ically.**—*n.* **logician** (*loj-ish′ən*), one skilled in logic.—*v.i.* **log′icise**, *-ize* (*-siz*), to argue.—**logical analysis**, (*phil.*) analysis, the process of stating clearly what our concepts comprise and imply; **logical designer**, one engaged in the scientific construction of computers; **logical positivism** (or **empiricism**)—see **positive**; **logic diagram** (*computers*), a diagram showing logical elements and interconnections without engineering details.—**chop logic** (see **chop**). [Gr. *logikē* (*technē*), logical (art)—*logos*, speech, reason.]

**logie**, *lō′gi*, (*Scot.*) *n.* the space before a kiln fire. [Origin unknown; cf. **killogie**.]

**logistic**, *-al*, *loj-is′tik*, *-əl*, *adjs.* pertaining to reasoning, to calculation, or to logistic: proportional.—*n.* **logis′tic**, the art of calculation: sexagesimal arithmetic: (in *pl.*) art of movement and supply of troops.—**logistics vessel**, a ship designed for the transport of troops and vehicles, and for their landing directly on to beaches. [Gr. *logistikos*—*logizesthai*, to compute; influenced by Fr. *loger*, to lodge.]

**loglog**, *log′log*, *n.* the *log*arithm of a *log*arithm.—Also **lō′log**.

**logo**. See **logotype**.

**logodaedalus**, *log-ō-dē′də-ləs*, *n.* an artificer in words.—*n.* **logodae′daly**, verbal legerdemain. [Latinised from Gr. *logodaidalos*—*logos*, word, *Daidalos*, Daedalus; see **Daedal**.]

**logogram**, *log′ō-gram*, *n.* a single sign for a word: a logogriph. [Gr. *logos*, word, *gramma*, letter.]

**logographer**, *log-og′rə-fər*, *n.* in Greek literature, one of the earliest annalists, esp. those before Herodotus: a professional speech-writer.—*adjs.* **logographic** (*-graf′ik*), *-al*.—*adv.* **logograph′ically.**—*n.* **logog′raphy**, a method of printing with whole words cast in a single type. [Gr. *logos*, word, *graphein*, to write.]

**logogriph**, *log′ō-grif*, *n.* a riddle in which a word is to be found from other words made up of its letters, or from synonyms of these. [Gr. *logos*, word, *griphos*, a net, riddle.]

**logomachy**, *log-om′ə-ki*, *n.* contention about words or in words merely.—*n.* **logom′achist**. [Gr. *logomachiä*—*logos*, word, *machē*, fight.]

**logorrhoea**, *log-ō-rē′ə*, *n.* excessive flow of words. [Gr. *rhoiä*, flow.]

**Logos**, *log′os*, *n.* in the Stoic philosophy, the active principle living in and determining the world: the Word of God incarnate (*Christian theol.*). [Gr. *logos*, word.]

**logothete**, *log′ō-thēt*, *n.* a chancellor, esp. in the Byzantine Empire and in Norman Sicily. [Gr. *logothetēs*, an auditor.]

**logotype**, *log′ō-tip*, *n.* a type of a word or several letters cast in one piece: a single piece of type comprising a name and/or address, trademark, or design.—Also **logo**. [Gr. *logos*, word, *typos*, an impression.]

**-logy**, *-lo-ji*, *suffix* indicating science, theory: discourse, treatise. [Gr. *logos* word, reason.]

**loid**, *loid*, (*slang*) *n.* abbrev. for **celluloid**.—*v.t.* to open, (a lock) with a strip of celluloid.

**loin**, *loin*, *n.* the back of a beast cut for food: (usu. in *pl.*) the reins, or the lower part of the back: (in *pl.*) generating source.—**loin′-cloth**, a piece of cloth for wearing round the loins.—**gird up the loins**, to prepare for energetic action, as if by tucking up one's clothes. [O.Fr. *loigne*—L. *lumbus*, loin.]

**loiter**, *loi′tər*, *v.i.* to proceed lingeringly: to dawdle: to linger.—*n.* **loi′terer**.—*n.* and *adj.* **loi′tering.**—*adv.* **loi′teringly**. [Du. *leuteren*, to dawdle; Ger. dial. *lottern*, to waver.]

**Loki**, *lō′ki*, *n.* an evil god in Norse mythology.

**Loligo**, *lō-li′gō*, *n.* the typical genus of **Loliginidae**

(*lol-i-jin'i-dē*) including the common squid. [L. *lōligō, -inis.*]

**Lolium,** *lō'li-əm,* n. a genus of grasses including darnel and rye-grass. [L. *lōlium,* darnel, 'tares'.]

**loll,** *lol, v.i.* to lie lazily about, to lounge, sprawl: to dangle, hang (now mainly of the tongue).— *v.t.* to let hang out.—*n.* loll'er.—*adv.* loll'ingly. —*v.i.* loll'op, to lounge, idle: to bound clumsily along. [Perh. imit.; cf. Du. *lollen,* to sit over the fire.]

**Lollard,** *lol'ərd,* n. a follower of Wycliffe: an idler.—*ns.* Loll'ardy, Loll'ardry, Loll'ardism. [M.Du. *lollaerd,* mutterer, droner—*lollen,* to mew, bawl, mutter; combined with loller (see loll).]

**lollipop,** *lol'i-pop,* n. a sweetmeat made with sugar and treacle: a large hard sweetmeat impaled on a stick: (usu. in *pl.*) a sweetmeat in general (also *fig.*).—Also loll'y—as *slang,* money. —**lollipop man,** woman, one appointed to conduct children across a busy street, distinguished by carrying a pole with a disk on the end. [Perh. Northern dial. *lolly,* tongue.]

**lollop.** See loll.

**loll-shraub, loll-shrob,** *lol'-shrob', -shrob',* (*India*) n. claret. [Hind. *lāl sharāb*—Pers. *lāl,* red, Ar. *sharāb,* wine.]

**lolly.** See lollipop.

**loma,** *lō'mə,* (*zool.*) n. a membranous fringe or flap. [Gr. *lōma, -atos.*]

**Lombard,** *lom'bərd, lum'bərd,* n. an inhabitant of *Lombardy* in Italy: one of the Langobardi, or Longobardi, a Germanic tribe, which founded a kingdom in Lombardy (568), overthrown by Charlemagne (774): a banker or money-lender, so called from the number of Lombard bankers in London (*obs.*).—*adjs.* Lom'bard, Lombardic (*-bär'dik*).—**Lombard architecture,** the Romanesque style of Northern Italy, superseded by the Gothic in the 13th century; **Lombardic script,** a mediaeval Italian style of handwriting; **Lombard Street,** the chief centre of the banking interest in London; **Lombardy poplar,** a variety of black poplar with erect branches. [O.Fr., — L. *Langobardus, Longobardus.*]

**lome,** (*Spens.*) for loam.

**lomentum,** *lō-ment'əm,* n. a pod that breaks in pieces at constrictions between the seeds:— *pl.* loment'a.—Also lō'ment (*-mənt*). [L. *lōmentum,* bean-meal (used as a cosmetic)— *lavāre, lōtum,* to wash.]

**lompish,** (*Spens.*) for lumpish.

**Londoner,** *lun'dən-ər,* n. a native or citizen of *London.*—*adjs.* Londonese', Londonian (*-dō'ni-ən*), Lon'donish, Lon'dony.—*n.* Londonese', cockney speech.—*v.t.* and *v.i.* Lon'donise, -ize.— *n.* Lon'donism, a mode of speech, etc., peculiar to London.—**London Clay,** a Lower Eocene formation in south-eastern England; **London ivy,** smoke; **London pride,** a hardy perennial saxifrage (*Saxifraga umbrosa*)—also *none-so-pretty* and *St Patrick's cabbage*: formerly applied to other plants.

**lone,** *lōn, adj.* isolated: solitary: unfrequented, uninhabited: unmarried, or widowed.—*ns.* lone'-ness; lon'er, a lone wolf.—*adj.* lone'some, solitary: feeling lonely.—Also *n.*—*adv.* lone'-somely.—*n.* lone'someness.—**lone wolf** (*fig.*), one who prefers to act on his own and not to have close friends or confidential relationships. [alone.]

**lonely,** *lōn'li, adj.* unaccompanied: isolated: uninhabited, unfrequented: uncomfortably conscious of being alone. [alone.]

**long,** *long,* (*Shak.* and *dial.*) *adj.* and *adv.* on account. [along (2).]

**long,** *long,* (*arch.*) *v.i.* to belong, pertain, be fitting. [Not found as a vb. in O.E.; perh.— *gelang,* along, beside (as if to go along with).]

**long,** *long, adj.* not short: of a specified (or to be

specified) length: extended in space in the direction of greatest extension: far-extending: extended in time: of extended continuance: distant in time (*rare*): of distant date: requiring much time in utterance or performance: loosely, accented: loosely, in a long syllable: numerically extensive: of more than average number (as a suit of cards): exceeding the standard value (see dozen, hundred): tedious:—*comp.* longer (*long'-gər*), *obs.* leng'er; *superl.* longest (*long'gist*), *obs.* leng'est.—*n.* a long time: a long syllable (*pros.*): the long summer university vacation (*coll.*): an obsolete note equal to two (in 'perfect' time three) breves (*mus.*; L. *longa*): (in *pl.*) long trousers.—*adv.* for, during, or by, a great extent of time: throughout the whole time: far in space (*rare*);—*comp.* and *superl.* as for *adj.*— *v.i.* to yearn.—*ns.* long'a (*mus.*), a long; long'ing, an eager desire, craving.—*adj.* yearning.—*adv.* long'ingly.—*adj.* longish (*long'ish, -gish*).—*adv.* long'ly (*Shak.*), long.—*n.* long'ness (*rare*).— *adj.* long'some, long and tedious.—*advs.* long'-ways, -wise, lengthwise.—*adj.* long'-ago', of the far past.—*n.* the far past.—**long'boat,** the largest and strongest boat of a ship; **long'bow,** a bow drawn by hand—opp. to *crossbow.*—*adj.* long'-breathed (*bretht'*), able to continue violent exercise of the lungs for a long time.—**long'-cloth,** a cotton made in long pieces.—*ns.pl.* long'-clothes, (*obs.*) -coats, long garments for a baby.— *adjs.* long'-descend'ed, of ancient lineage; long'-dist'ance, going or extending to or over a long distance or time.—**long'-divi'sion,** division in which the working is shown in full.—*adjs.* long'-drawn (*-out'*), prolonged: unduly protracted; long'-eared, with long ears or earlike feather-tufts; long'-faced, dismal-looking.—**long'-field** (*cricket*), a fielder or station near the boundary on the bowler's side; **long'-firm,** a company of swindlers who get goods on pretence of being established in business, and then decamp without payment; **long'-hair,** a highbrow.—Also *adj.*— *adj.* long'-haired, highbrow.—**long'hand,** ordinary writing—opp. to *shorthand;* **long'-head,** a dolichocephal.—*adj.* long'-head'ed, dolichocephalous: shrewd: sagacious.—**long'-head'edness;** **long home,** the grave; **long hop** (*cricket*), a short-pitched, and so long-bounding, ball, easy to hit; **long'horn,** an animal with long horns or antennae, as a longicorn beetle (**house longhorn beetle,** a beetle whose larvae are very destructive to house timbers): a long-eared owl; **long'-house,** a long communal house, esp. of American Indians; **long johns,** long underwear; **long jump,** a jump for distance along the ground; **long'-leg** (*cricket*), a fieldsman, or his station, far out behind the batsman and a little to his left.—*adj.* long'-legged, having long legs.—**long'-legs,** a crane-fly.—*adj.* long'-lived (*-livd';* also *-līvd'*), having a long life.—**long'-meas'ure,** lineal measure: quatrains of eight-syllable lines; **long moss,** a tropical American rootless epiphyte (*Tillandsia usneoides*) of the pineapple family, resembling bunches of hair; **long'-nine'** (*U.S.*), a cheap cigar; **long odds,** in betting, unfavourable odds; **long'-off, long'-on** (*cricket*), the fielders in the long-field to the off and on of the batsman respectively: their position; **long oil** (see oil length); **long'-pig'** (from cannibal term), human flesh as food.—*adj.* long'-playing, of a gramophone record, giving length in reproduction because of the extremely fine groove.— **long'prim'er,** a size of type intermediate between small pica and bourgeois; **long'-pur'ples,** the early purple orchis: purple loosestrife.—*adj.* long'-range, long in range: covering a long future time or long distance.—**long robe** (see robe).— *n.pl.* longs'-and-shorts', Greek or Latin verses: masonry of alternate vertical and horizontal blocks, as in quoins and jambs.—**long sheep,** a long-wooled sheep; **long′ship** (*hist.*), a long vessel of the old Norsemen; **long shot**, (a bet, entry, venture, etc., with) a remote chance of success.—*adj.* **long′-sight′ed**, able to see far but not close at hand: hypermetropic: presbyopic: having foresight: sagacious.—**long′-sight′edness.** —*n.pl.* **long′-six′es**, candles weighing six to a pound.—**long′-slip** (*cricket*), a fielder some distance behind the batsman on the off side.— *adjs.* **long′-spun**, long-drawn, tedious; **iong′-stand′ing**, of long existence or continuance; **long′-sta′ple**, having a long fibre.—**long′-stop** (*cricket*), one who stands behind the wicket-keeper to stop balls missed by him.—*v.i.* to field as **long-stop.**—*adj.* **long′-suff′ering**, enduring long and patiently.—*n.* long endurance or patience.—**long′-tail**, an animal, esp. a dog, with uncut tail: a greyhound.—Also *adj.*—*adj.* **long′-term**, extending over a long time: of a policy, concerned with time ahead as distinct from the immediate present.—**long Tom**, **long ton** (see **Tom, ton**).—*adjs.* **long′-tongued**, having a long tongue: talkative, babbling; **long′-vis′aged**, long-faced: of rueful countenance; **long′-waist′ed**, having a long waist: long from the armpits to the hips.—**long′wall**, a long working face in a coal-mine.—*adj.* **long′-wave** (*radio*), of, or using, wavelengths over 1000 metres.—**long whist** (see **whist**).—*adj.* **long′-wind′ed**, long-breathed: tediously wordy and lengthy.—**long′-wind′edness.**—**a long figure** (*slang*), a high price or rate; **a long purse**, abundance of money; **before long**, ere long, soon; **draw the long bow** (see **bow** (2)); **in the long run** (see **run**); **make a long arm** (*coll.*), to help oneself freely at table; **make a long nose**, to cock a snook or put a thumb to the nose; **no longer**, not now as formerly; **not long for this world**, near death; **so long!** (*coll.*), good-bye; **so long as**, provided only that; **the long and the short (of it)**, or (*Shak.*) **the short and the long (of it)**, the sum of the matter in a few words. [O.E. *lang*, *long* (adj.), *lange*, *longe* (adv.); Ger. *lang*, O.N. *langr*; L. *longus*.]

**longa**, *long′ga*, *n.* See **long** (3).

**longan**, *long′gan*, *n.* a tree (*Nephelium longana*) akin to the litchi: its fruit. [Chin. *lung-yen*, dragon's eye.]

**longanimity**, *long-ga-nim′i-ti*, *n.* forbearance.— *adj.* **longanimous** (-*gan′*). [L. *longanimitās*, -*ātis* —*longus*, long, *animus*, spirit.]

**longe**. Same as **lunge** (2).

**longeron**, *lon′jə-*, *lon′zhə-ron*, *l5-zhə-r5̃*, *n.* a longitudinal member of an aeroplane. [Fr.]

**longevity**, *lon-jev′i-ti*, *n.* great length of life.— *adjs.* **longaeval**, **-geval**, **longaevous**, **-gevous** (-*jēv′*). [L. *longaevitās*, -*ātis*—*longus*, long, *aevum*, age.]

**longicaudate**, *lon-ji-kö′dāt*, (*zool.*) *adj.* long-tailed. [L. *longus*, long, *cauda*, tail.]

**longicorn**, *lon′ji-körn*, *n.* any beetle of the family Cerambycidae, with very long antennae (the larvae feed on wood).—Also *adj.* [L. *longus*, long, *cornū*, horn.]

**longinquity**, *lon-jingk′wi-ti*, *n.* remoteness. [L. *longinquitās*, -*ātis*—*longus*, long.]

**longipennate**, *lon-ji-pen′āt*, (*zool.*) *adj.* having elongate wings or feathers. [L. *longus*, long, *penna*, feather, wing.]

**longitude**, *lon′ji-tūd*, *long′gi-*, *n.* length: arc of the equator between the meridian of a place and a standard meridian (usually that of Greenwich) expressed in degrees E. or W.: the arc of the ecliptic between a star's circle of latitude and the first point of Aries or vernal equinox, measured eastwards (*astron.*).—*adj.* **longitud′inal**, of or in length or longitude: lengthwise.—*adv.* **longitūd′inally.** [L. *longitūdō*, -*inis*, length—*longus*, long.]

**Longobard.** See **Lombard** (second meaning).

**longshore**, *long′shōr*, *-shôr*, *adj.* existing or employed along the shore.—**long′shoreman**, a

stevedore: one who makes a living along the shore. [alongshore.]

**longueur**, *l5̃-ger*, (Fr.) a tedious passage, e.g. in a book: prolixity:—often in *pl.*

**Lonsdale belt**, *lonz′dāl*, award (see **belt**) for gaining the same boxing title three times in succession. [Lord *Lonsdale*.]

**loo**, *lōō*, (*coll.*) *n.* a lavatory. [Ety. dub.]

**loo**, *lōō*, *n.* a card game.—*v.t.* to subject to a forfeit at loo.—**loo′-table**, a form of round table, orig. one for playing loo. [See **lanterloo**.]

**loo**, *lōō*, Scots form of **love** (verb).

**looby**, *lōōb′i*, *n.* a clumsy, clownish fellow.—*adv.* **loob′ily.** [Cf. **lob**.]

**loof**, *lōōf*. Same as **luff**.

**loof**, *lōōf*, *Scot.* *lüf*, *n.* the palm of the hand:—*pl.* **loofs, looves.**—*n.* **loof′ful** (*Scot. lüf′fə*), an open handful. [O.N. *lōfi*.]

**loofa, loofah.** See **luffa**.

**look**, *lōōk*, *v.i.* to direct the sight with attention: to give attention: to face: to seem: to seem to be: to have an appearance: to tend.—*v.t.* to make sure: to see to it: to ascertain by a look: to look at: to expect: to seem likely: to render by a look: to express by a look: to refer to, turn up (with *up*): give (a look, as cognate object).—*n.* the act of looking: view: air: appearance: (in *pl.*) beauty, comeliness (also *good looks*).—*imper.* or *interj.* see: behold.—*ns.* **look′er**, one who looks: an observer: one who has good looks; **look′ing.**—*adj.* (in composition) having the appearance of.—**look′er-in′**, a television viewer; **look′er-on′**, an onlooker: a mere spectator (*pl.* **look′ers-on′**); **look′-in′**, a chance of doing anything effectively or of sharing: a short casual call; **look′ing-for** (*B.*), expectation; **look′ing-glass**, a mirror; **look′out′**, a careful watch: a place to observe from: one set to watch: prospect: concern; **look′-see** (*slang*), a look around.—**look after**, take care of: seek: expect (*B.*); **look alive** (*coll.*), to bestir oneself; **look down on**, to despise; **look down one's nose**, to regard with contempt; **look for**, to search for: to expect; **look forward to**, to anticipate with pleasure; **look here!** I say! attend to this!; **look in**, to make a short call: to watch television; **look into**, to inspect closely: to investigate; **look on**, to regard, view, think: to be a spectator; **look out**, to be watchful: to be on one's guard: to look for and select: to show, appear (*Shak.*); **look over**, to examine cursorily: to overlook or pass over; **look sharp** (*coll.*), be quick about it; **look to**, to look at, towards; to watch: to take care of: to depend on (for): to expect (to do); **look up**, to search for, refer to: to take courage: to improve, to have taken a turn for the better: to seek out and call upon, visit (*coll.*); **look up to**, feel respect or veneration for; **look you** (*arch.* and *Welsh*), observe, take notice of this. [O.E. *lōcian*, to look.]

**loom**, *lōōm*, *n.* a tool, implement (*obs.*): a receptacle (*Scot.*): a machine for weaving: the shaft of an oar. [O.E. *gelōma*, a tool.]

**loom**, *lōōm*, *v.i.* to appear indistinctly or as in a mirage, esp. in an exaggerated or magnified form: to take shape, as an impending event.—*n.* an indistinct or mirage-like appearance. [Origin obscure.]

**loon**, *lōōn*, also **lown(e)**, *lown*, (*Shak.*) *n.* a low-born fellow (*arch.*): a rascal: a harlot: in north-east of Scotland, a boy (also **loon′ie**). [Origin unknown.]

**loon**, *lōōn*, *loom*, *lōōm*, *n.* any of an order of northern diving birds.—*n.* **loon′ing**, their cry. [O.N. *lōmr*.]

**loony**, *lōōn′i*, *n.* and *adj.* for **lunatic**.—**loon′y-bin** (*slang*), a lunatic asylum.

**loop**, *lōōp*, *n.* a doubling of a cord, chain, etc., leaving a space: an ornamental doubling in fringes: anything of like form, as an element in fingerprints: a branch of anything that returns to the main part.—*v.t.* to fasten in or with a loop: to ornament with loops: to make a loop of.—*v.i.* to travel in loops.—*adj.* looped.—*n.* loop'er, a geometrid caterpillar, from its mode of walking by forming the body in a loop and planting its hinder legs close behind the six 'true' legs: one who loops the loop in an aeroplane.—*n.* and *adj.* loop'ing.—*adj.* loop'y, having loops: crafty (*Scot.*): slightly crazed (*slang*).—loop'-line, a branch railway that returns to the main line.— loop the loop, to move in a complete vertical loop or circle, head downwards at the top of the curve. [Ety. dub.]

loop, *lōōp*, loophole, *lōōp'hōl*, *n.* a slit in a wall: a means of escape or evasion.—*adjs.* looped (*Shak.*), full of small openings.—*v.t.* loop'hole, to make loopholes in.—loop'-light, a small narrow window. [Perh. M.Du. *lûpen*, to peer.]

loor. See lief.

loord, *lōōrd*, (*Spens.*) *n.* a lout. [Fr. *lourd*, heavy.]

loos (*Spens.*). See los.

loose, *lōōs*, *adj.* slack: free: unbound: not confined: not compact: unattached: untied: not close-fitting: not tight: relaxed: inexact: indefinite: vague: not strict: unrestrained: lax: licentious: inattentive: dispersedly or openly disposed: not serried.—*adv.* loosely.—*n.* an act or mode of loosing, esp. an arrow: the loose state: unrestraint: freedom: abandonment: an outbreak of self-indulgence: a course or rush (*obs.*): event, upshot, end (as in *at the very loose*) (*Shak.*).—*v.t.* to make loose: to set free: to unfasten: to untie: to disconnect: to relax: to slacken: to discharge: to solve (*Spens.*).—*v.i.* to shoot: to weigh anchor (*arch.*).—*adv.* loose'ly.—*v.t.* loos'en, to make loose: to relax: to make less dense: to open, as the bowels.—*v.i.* to become loose: to become less tight.—*ns.* loos'ener, a laxative; loose'ness, the state of being loose: diarrhoea.—*adj.* loose'-bod'ied, flowing, loose-fitting: loose in behaviour.— loose'-box, a part of a stable where horses are kept untied; loose'-cover, a detachable cover, as for a chair; loose fish, one of irregular, esp. lax habits: a prostitute.—*adj.* loose'-leaf, having a cover such that leaves may be inserted or removed.—at a loose end (see end); break loose, to escape from confinement; give a loose to, to give rein or free vent to; let loose, to set at liberty; on the loose, indulging in a bout of unrestraint. [O.N. *lauss*; O.E. *lēas*; see less.]

loosestrife, *lōōs'strif*, *n.* a plant (*Lysimachia vulgaris*) of the primrose family, or other member of the genus (as yellow pimpernel, creeping Jenny): a tall waterside plant (*Lythrum salicaria*, purple loosestrife). [Intended as a translation of Gr. *lysimacheion*, common loosestrife (as if from *lyein*, to loose, *machē*, strife), which may be from the personal name *Lysimachos*.]

loot, *lōōt*, *n.* plunder: money (*slang*).—*v.t.* or *v.i.* to plunder. [Hindi *lūt*.]

loot, *lüt*, *lōōt*, *Scots* *pa.t.* of let:—*pa.p.* loot'en, litt'en, lutt'en.

loot, *lōōt*, (*coll.*) *n.* abbrev. for lieutenant.

lop, *lop*, *v.i.* to hang down loosely.—*adj.* lop'-eared, having drooping ears.—lop'grass (or lop), soft brome-grass.—*adj.* lop'-sid'ed, ill-balanced: heavier, bigger, on one side than the other. [Perh. conn. with lob.]

lop, *lop*, *v.t.* to cut off the top or ends of, esp. of a tree: to cut away, as superfluous parts:—*pr.p.* lopp'ing; *pa.t.* and *pa.p.* lopped.—*n.* twigs of trees cut off: an act of lopping.—*ns.* lopp'er; lopp'ing, a cutting off: that which is cut off. [O.E. *loppian*.]

lope, *lōp*, *v.i.* to leap: to run with a long stride. [O.N. *hlaupa*; cf. leap, loup.]

lope, *lōp*, (*Spens.*) *pa.t.* of leap.

lophobranch, *lōf'* or *lof'ō-brangk*, *n.* any fish of the seahorse and pipefish group, characterised by tufted gills.—Also *adj.*—*adjs.* lophobranch'iate; loph'odont, having transversely ridged molar teeth. [Gr. *lophos*, a crest, *branchia*, gills, *odous, odontos*, a tooth.]

lopper, *lop'ər* (*dial.*; *Scot.* lapper, *läp'ər*), *v.i.* to curdle.—*v.t.* to curdle: to clot.—*n.* a clot: slush.—*n.* (*Scot.*) lapp'er(ed)-milk'. [O.N. *hlōypa*, to curdle.]

lopper, lopping. See lop (2).

loquacious, *lō-kwā'shəs*, *adj.* talkative.—*adv.* loquā'ciously.—*ns.* loquā'ciousness, loquacity (-*kwas'*). [L. *loquāx, -ācis—loqui*, to speak.]

loquat, *lō'kwot, -kwat*, *n.* a Chinese and Japanese tree (*Eriobotrya japonica*) of the rose family: its fruit. [Chinese *luh kwat*.]

loran, *lō'*, *lö'rän*, *n.* a long-range radio-navigation system. [Long-range navigation.]

lorcha, *lör'chə*, *n.* a light vessel of European build, but rigged like a Chinese junk. [Port.]

lord, (Lord, when prefixed), *lörd*, *n.* a master: a feudal superior (also lord'-supe'rior; *hist.*): a ruler: the proprietor of a manor (*hist.*): an owner (*arch.*): a dominant person: a husband (*arch.*, or *facet.*): a titled nobleman—duke (not prefixed), marquess, earl, viscount or (esp.) baron: a peer: by courtesy the son of a duke or marquis, or the eldest son of an earl: a bishop, esp. if a member of the House of Lords: a judge of the Court of Session: used as part of various official titles: God: Christ.—*v.t.* to make a lord (*arch.*): to address as lord: (with *it*) to play the lord, tyrannise.— *interj.* expressing surprise (*coll.* lor', law).—*n.* lord'ing (*arch.*), sir (usu. in pl., gentlemen): a petty lord.—*adj.* lord'less.—*ns.* lord'liness; lord'-ling, a little lord: a would-be lord—also lord'kin. —*adj.* lord'ly, like, becoming, or of a lord: magnificent: lavish: lofty: haughty: tyrannical. —Also *adv.*—*ns.* lordol'atry (*jocular*), worship of nobility; lord'ship, state or condition of being a lord: the territory of a lord (*hist.*): dominion: authority: used in referring to, addressing, a lord (with *his, your*), or a woman sheriff or judge (with *her, your*).—Lord's Day, Sunday; Lord Lieutenant (see lieutenant); Lord Mayor (see mayor); Lord Provost (see provost); lords ordinary, the judges forming the Outer House of the Court of Session; Lord's Prayer, prayer Christ taught his disciples (Matt. vi. 9-13); lords spiritual, the archbishops and bishops (and formerly mitred abbots) in the House of Lords; Lord's Supper, holy communion; Lord's table, the communion table; lords temporal, the lay peers.—drunk as a lord, extremely drunk; House of Lords, upper house of British parliament; live like a lord, live in luxury; Lord knows (who, what, etc.), I don't know, and I question if anybody does; Lord of Misrule (see misrule); lords and ladies, common arum; Lord of Session, a judge of the Court of Session; My Lord (*mi-lörd', mi-lud'*), used in addressing a judge or other lord: formerly also prefixed. [M.E. *loverd, laverd*—O.E. *hláford*—*hláf*, bread, *ward* (W.S. *weard*), keeper, guardian.]

lordosis, *lör-dō'sis*, *n.* abnormal curvature of the spinal column, the convexity towards the front. —*adj.* lordot'ic, affected with, relating to lordosis. [Gr. *lordōsis—lordos*, bent back.]

lore, *lōr, lör, n.* that which is learned: teaching (*arch.*): doctrine (*arch.*): learning: now esp. learning of a special, traditional, or out-of-the-way miscellaneous kind.—*n.* lor'ing (*Spens.*), teaching. [O.E. *lár*.]

lore, *lōr, lör, n.* a thong (*obs.*): the side of the head between eye and bill (*ornith.*).—*adjs.* lor'al; lor'ate, strap-like. [L. *lōrum*, thong.]

lore. See leese.

lorel. See losel.

lorette, *lör-et'*, *n.* a courtesan. [Fr., from the

church of their district in Paris, Notre Dame de Lorette.]

**lorgnette**, *lörn-yet'*, *n.* eyeglasses with a handle: an opera-glass.—*n.* **lorgnon** (*lörn'yɔ̃*) an eyeglass: eyeglasses. [Fr. *lorgner*, to look sidelong at, to ogle.]

**lorica**, *lō-*, *lö-*, *lə-ri'kə*, *n.* a leather corslet: the case of a protozoan, rotifer, etc.:—*pl.* **lori'cae** (*-sē*).—Also **loric** (*lö'*, *lö'rik*).—*v.t.* **loricate** (*lor'i-kāt*), to coat or armour protectively.—*adj.* armoured with plates or scales.—*n.* **lorica'tion**. [L. *lōrica*, a leather corslet—*lōrum*, a thong.]

**lorikeet**, *lor-i-kēt'*, *n.* a small lory. [From **lory**, on analogy of para*keet*.]

**lorimer**, *lor'i-mər*, **loriner**, *-nər*, *n.* a maker of the metal parts of horse-harness. [O.Fr. *loremier*, *lorenier*—L. *lōrum*, a thong.]

**loriot**, *lö'ri-ət*, *lö'*, *n.* the golden oriole. [Fr. *loriot* —*l'*, the, O.Fr. *oriol*—L. *aureolus*, dim. of *aureus*, golden—*aurum*, gold.]

**loris**, *lö'*, *lö'ris*, *n.* the slender lemur of Ceylon: an East Indian lemur (*Nycticebus* or *Bradycebus tardigradus*, the *slow loris*). [Fr. *loris*; said to be from Du.]

**lorn**, *lörn*, (*arch.*) *adj.* lost: forsaken: left (*Spens.*). [O.E. *loren*, pa.p. of *lēosan* (found in compounds), to lose; see **leese**.]

**lorrell.** See **losel**.

**lorry**, *lor'i*, *n.* a long wagon without sides, or with low sides.—*v.i.* (or *v.t.* with *it*) **lorr'y-hop**, to proceed by help of lifts on lorries.—**lorr'y-hopping**. [Origin uncertain.]

**lory**, *lö'*, *lö'ri*, *n.* any parrot of a family with brushlike tongues, natives of New Guinea, Australia, etc.: in South Africa a turaco. [Malay *lūri*.]

**los, loos**, *lōs*, (*arch.*) *n.* praise, reputation. [O.Fr., —L. *laudēs*, pl. of *laus*, praise.]

**lose**, *lōōz*, *v.t.* to fail to keep or get possession of: to be deprived or bereaved of: to cease to have: cease to hear, see or understand: to mislay: to waste, as time: to miss: to be defeated in: to cause the loss of: to cause to perish: to bring to ruin.—*v.i.* to fail, to be unsuccessful: to suffer waste or loss: of a clock or watch, to go too slowly:—*pr.p.* **los'ing**; *pa.t.* and *pa.p* **lost** (*lost*).—*adj.* **los'able**.—*n.* **los'er**.—*n.* and *adj.* **los'ing**.—*adj.* **los'ingly**.—*adj.* **lost** (*lost*), parted with: no longer possessed: missing: thrown away: squandered: ruined: confused, unable to find the way (*lit.*, and *fig.*).—**losing game**, a game that is going against one: a game played with reversal of the usual aim; **lost tribes**, the tribes of Israel that never returned after deportation by Sargon of Assyria in 721 B.C. —**lose face** (see face); **lose oneself**, to lose one's way: to become rapt or bewildered; **lose out** (*coll.*), to suffer loss or disadvantage: to fail to acquire something desired; **lost to**, insensible to. [O.E. *losian*, to be a loss; apparently influenced in sense by **leese** and in pronunciation by **loose**.]

**lose**, *lōz*, *v.t.* Spens. for **loose**.—Also **los'en**:—*pa.p.* **loast, los'te** (both *lōst*).

**losel**, *lö'zl*, *lōō'zl*, **lorel**, *lö'*, *lö'rəl* (*Spens.* **lozell**, **lorrell**), *n.* a sorry, worthless fellow: a scamp. —*adj.* good-for-nothing. [Apparently from the past participle *losen, loren*, of **leese**.]

**losh**, *losh*, (*Scot.*) *interj.* lord.

**loss**, *los*, *n.* losing: diminution: default (*Shak.*): bereavement: destruction: defeat: deprivation: detriment: that which is lost.—**loss adjuster**, an assessor employed by an insurance company, usu. in fire damage claims; **loss'-leader**, a thing sold at a loss to attract other custom.—**at a loss**, off the scent: at fault: nonplussed: perplexed. [O.E. *los*, influenced by **lost**.]

**löss.** See **loess**.

**lost.** See **lose**.

**los'te**, *lōst*, a Spens. *pa.p.* of **loose**.

**lot**, *lot*, *n.* an object, as a slip of wood, a straw, drawn or thrown out from among a number in order to reach a decision by chance: decision by this method: sortilege: a prize so to be won: destiny: that which falls to any one as his fortune: a separate portion: a parcel of ground: a set: a set of things offered together for sale: the whole: a plot of ground allotted or assigned to any person or purpose, esp. for building: a turn (*obs.*): a tax or due (*hist.*; see **scot**): a large quantity or number.—*v.t.* to allot: to separate into lots: to cast lots for (*obs.*):—*pr.p.* **lott'ing**; *pa.t.* and *pa.p.* **lott'ed**.—**across lots** (*U.S.*), by short cuts; **bad 'ot**, a person of bad moral character; **cast, or throw, in one's lot with**, share the fortunes of; **cast, or draw, lots**, to draw from a set alike in appearance in order to reach a decision; **lots of** (*coll.*), many; **lots to blanks** (*Shak.*), any odds. [O.E. *hlot, lot*—*hlēotan*, to cast lots.]

**lota, lotah**, *lö'tä*, *n.* in India, a small brass or copper pot. [Hindi *loṭä*.]

**lote.** See **lotus**.

**loth, loath**, *lōth*, *adj.* hateful, repulsive, ugly (*obs.*): reluctant, unwilling.—**nothing loth**, not at all unwilling. [O.E. *lāth*, hateful; cf. **loathe**.]

**Lothario**, *lō-thä'ri-ō*, *-thä'*, *n.* a gay seducer. [From *Lothario*, in Rowe's play, *The Fair Penitent*.]

**lotion**, *lö'shən*, *n.* a washing (*obs.*): a liquid preparation, medicinal or cosmetic. [L. *lōtiō*, *-ōnis*, a washing—*lavāre, lōtum*, to wash.]

**lottery**, *lot'ər-i*, *n.* an arrangement for distribution of prizes by lot: a matter of chance: a card game of chance.—*n.* **lott'o, lö'to**, a game played by covering on a card each number drawn till a line of numbers is completed. [It. *lotteria, lotto*, of Gmc. origin; cf. **lot**.]

**lotus**, *lö'təs*, *n.* an Egyptian or Indian water-lily of various species of Nymphaea and Nelumbium: a tree (possibly the jujube) in North Africa, whose fruit induced in the eater a state of blissful indolence and forgetfulness: an architectural ornament like a water-lily: (*cap.*) the bird's-foot trefoil genus.—Also **lote** (*lōt*), **lö'tos** (*Gr.*).— **Lot'us-eat'ers, Lotophagi** (*lö-tof'ə-ji*; Gr. *phagein*, to eat), a people who ate the fruit of the lotus, among whom Ulysses lived for a time: (without *cap.*) an eater of the lotus, one given up to indolence; **Lo'tus-land**, the country of the Lotus-eaters. [Latinised Gr. *lōtos*.]

**louche**, *lōōsh*, (Fr.) squinting: ambiguous: shady.

**loud**, *lowd*, *adj.* making a great sound: noisy: obtrusive: vulgarly showy.—*advs.* **loud, loud'ly**. —*v.t.* and *v.i.* **loud'en**, to make or grow louder.— *adj.* **loud'ish**.—*n.* **loud'ness**.—*adjs.* **loud'-lunged**; **loud'-mouthed**.—**loud'speaker**, an electro-acoustic device, which amplifies sound.—*adj.* **loud'-voiced**. [O.E. *hlūd*; Ger. *laut*; L. *inclytus, inclutus*, Gr. *klytos*, renowned.]

**lough**, *lohh*, *n.* the Irish form of **loch**.

**louis**, *lōō'i*, *n.* a French gold coin superseded in 1795 by the 20-franc piece:—*pl.* **lou'is** (*-iz*).—*n.* **lou'is-d'or'**, a louis: a 20-franc piece:—*pl.* **louis-d'or** (*lōō-i-dör'*).—*adjs.* **Louis-Quatorze** (*-kä-törz*), characteristic of the reign (1643-1715) of Louis XIV, as in architecture and decoration; **Lou'is-Quinze** (*kēz*), of that of Louis XV (1715-1774); **Lou'is-Seize** (*-sez*), of that of Louis XVI (1774-92); **Lou'is-Treize** (*-trez*), of that of Louis XIII (1610-43).

**loun, lound.** See **lown**.

**lounder**, *lōōn'dər*, *lown'dər*, (*Scot.*) *v.t.* to beat, to bethump.—*n.* a heavy blow.—*n.* **loun'dering**, a beating.

**lounge**, *lownj*, *v.i.* to loll: to idle.—*v.t.* to idle (away).—*n.* an act, spell, or state of lounging: an idle stroll: a resort of loungers: a sitting-room in a private house: a room in a public building for sitting or waiting, often providing refreshment facilities: a kind of sofa, esp. with back and one raised end: an easy chair suitable for lolling in.—*n.* loung′er.—*n.* and *adj.* loung′ing.—*adv.* loung′ingly.—lounge′-liz′ard, one who loafs with women in hotel lounges, etc.; lounge′-suit′, a suit worn on informal occasions. [Origin doubtful.]

**loup**, *lowp*, (*Scot.*) *n.* a leap.—*v.i.* to leap: to dance: to flee: to burst:—*pa.t.* loup′it; *pa.p.* loup′en, loup′it.—loup′ing-ill, a disease causing sheep to spring up in walking, due to a virus transmitted by ticks; loup′ing-on′-stane′, a stone to mount a horse from; loup′-the-dyke, runaway: flighty: wayward. [O.N. *hlaup*; cf. lope, leap.]

**loup**, a variant (*Scott*) of loop (1), and (*Spens.*) of loop (2).

**lour**, lower, *lowr*, *low′ər*, *v.i.* to look sullen or threatening: to scowl.—*n.* a scowl, glare: a gloomy threatening appearance.—*n.* and *adj.* lour′ing, lower′ing.—*adv.* lour′ingly, lower′ingly.—*adj.* lour′y, lower′y. [M.E. *louren*; cf. Du. *loeren.*]

**loure**, *lōor*, *n.* an old slow dance, or its tune, usu. in 6-4 time, sometimes included in suites. [Fr., bagpipe.]

**louse**, *lows*, *n.* a wingless parasitic insect (Pediculus), with a flat body, and short legs: extended to similar animals related and unrelated (see bird-louse, fish-louse, etc.): a person worthy of contempt (*slang*; *pl.* in -es):—*pl.* lice, *līs.*—*v.t.* (*lowz*) to remove lice from: to spoil, make a mess of (with *up*; *slang*).—*adv.* lou′sily (*-zi-*).—*n.* lous′iness.—*adj.* lousy (*low′zi*), infested with lice: swarming or full (with *with*; *slang*): inferior, bad, unsatisfactory (*slang*).—louse′-wort, any plant of the genus Pedicularis, marsh-growing scrophulariaceous herbs popularly supposed to cause grazing animals to become lousy. [O.E. *lūs*, pl. *lȳs*; Ger. *laus.*]

**lout**, (*obs.* lowt) *lowt*, *n.* a bumpkin: an awkward boor.—*v.t.* (*Shak.*) to treat with contempt, to flout.—*v.i.* to play the lout.—*adj.* lout′ish, clownish: awkward and boorish.—*adv.* lout′ishly.—*n.* lout′ishness. [Perh. conn. with next word.]

**lout**, (*obs.* lowt) *lowt*, (*arch.*) *v.i.* to bow: to stoop.—*n.* a bow. [O.E. *lūtan*, to stoop.]

**louvre, louver**, *lōo′vər*, *n.* a turret-like structure on a roof for escape of smoke or for ventilation: a dovecote (*obs.*): an opening or shutter with louvre-boards: a louvre-board.—louvre′-, lou′ver-board, a sloping slat placed across an opening; lou′vre-, lou′ver-door, -win′dow, a door, open window crossed by a series of sloping boards. [O.Fr. *lover, lovier*; origin obscure.]

**lovage**, *luv′ij*, *n.* an umbelliferous salad plant (*Levisticum officinale*) of Southern Europe akin to Angelica: a liquor made from its roots and seeds: any plant of the kindred genus Ligusticum, including *Scottish lovage.* [O.Fr. *luvesche*—L.L. *levisticum*, L. *ligusticum*, lit. Ligurian.]

**love**, *luv*, *n.* fondness: charity: an affection of the mind caused by that which delights: strong liking: devoted attachment to one of the opposite sex: sexual attachment: a love-affair: the object of affection: used as a term of endearment or affection: the god of love, Cupid, Eros: a kindness, a favour done (*Shak.*): the mere pleasure of playing, without stakes: in some games, no score.—*v.t.* to be fond of: to regard with affection: to delight in with exclusive affection: to regard with benevolence.—*v.i.* to have the feeling of love.—*adjs.* lov′able, worthy of love: amiable; love′less.—*n.* love′lihead (*rare*), loveliness.—*adv.* love′lily (*rare*).—*n.* love′liness. — *adj.* love′ly, loving, amorous (*Shak.*): exciting admiration: attractive: extremely beautiful: delightful (*coll.*).—*adv.* lovingly (*Spens.*): beautifully (*obs.*): delightfully, very well (*coll.*).—*n.* (*coll.*) a beautiful woman, esp. showgirl, model.—*n.* lover, one who loves, esp. one in love with a person of the opposite sex (in the singular usually of the man): a paramour: one who is fond of anything: a friend (*Shak.*).—*adjs.* lov′ered (*Shak.*), having a lover; lov′erless; lov′erly, like a lover; love′some, lovely: loving: love′worthy, worthy of being loved.—*n.* and *adj.* lov′ing.—*adv.* lov′ingly.—*n.* lov′ingness.—love′-affair′, an amour, honourable or dishonourable; love′-apple, the tomato; love′-arrow, a hair-like crystal of rutile enclosed in quartz: a calcareous dart protruded by a snail, supposed to have a sexual function; love′bird, a small African parrot (Agapornis), strongly attached to its mate: extended to other kinds; love′-bro′ker (*Shak.*), a go-between in love-affairs; love′-charm, a philtre, love′-child, a bastard; love′-day (*Shak.*), a day for settling disputes; love′-drug, dagga; love′-favour, something given to be worn in token of love; love′-feast, the agape, or a religious feast in imitation of it; love′-feat, an act of courtship; love′-game (*lawn-tennis*), a game in which the loser has not scored (poss. from Fr. *l'œuf*, egg—cf. duck, in cricket); love′-in-a-mist′, a fennel-flower (*Nigella damascena*): a West Indian passion-flower; love′-in-i′dleness, the pansy; love′-juice, a concoction dropped in the eye to excite love; love′-knot, lover′s-knot, an intricate knot, used as a token of love; love′-letter, a letter of courtship; love′-lies-bleed′ing, a kind of amaranth with drooping red spike; love′light, a lustre in the eye expressive of love; love′lock, a long or prominent lock of hair, esp. one hanging at the ear, worn by men of fashion in the reigns of Elizabeth and James I.—*adj.* love′lorn, forsaken by one's love: pining for love.—love′-lornness; love′-maker; love′-making, amorous courtship: sexual intercourse; love′-match, a marriage for love, not money; love′-monger, one who deals in affairs of love; love′-nest, a place where lovers, often illicit, meet or live; love′-potion, a philtre; love′-seat, an armchair for two; love′-shaft, a dart of love from Cupid's bow.—*adj.* love′sick, languishing with amorous desire.—love′-song, a song expressive of or relating to love; love′-story, a story whose subject-matter is love; love′-suit (*Shak.*), courtship; love′-token, a gift in evidence of love; lov′ing-cup, a cup passed round at the end of a feast for all to drink from; lov′ing-kind′ness (*B.*), kindness full of love: tender regard: mercy.—fall in love, become enamoured of; for love or money, in any way whatever; for the love of it, for the sake of it: for the pleasure of it; for the love of Mike (*slang*), for any sake; in love, enamoured; make love to, to try to gain the affections of: to have sexual intercourse with; of all loves (*Shak.*), for any sake, by all means; play for love, to play without stakes; there's no love lost between them, they have no liking for each other. [O.E. *lufu*, love; Ger. *liebe*; cf. L. *libet, lubet*, it pleases.]

**Lovelace**, *luv′lās*, *n.* a well-mannered libertine. [From *Lovelace*, in Richardson's *Clarissa.*]

**lover**, an obsolete form of louver (louvre).

**low**, *lō*, *v.i.* to make the noise of oxen.—*n.* sound made by oxen.—*n.* low′ing. [O.E. *hlōwan*; Du. *loeien.*]

**low**, *lō*, *adj.* occupying a position far downward or not much elevated: of no great upward extension: not reaching a high level: depressed: not tall: of type or blocks, below the level of the forme surface: reaching far down: of clothes, cut so as to expose the neck (and bosom): quiet, soft, not loud: grave in pitch, as sounds produced by slow vibrations: produced with part of the tongue low in the mouth (*phon.*): in shallow relief: expressed in measurement by a small number: of numbers, small: of small value, intensity, quantity, or rank: weak in vitality or nutrition: scanty, deficient: attributing lowness: for stakes of no great value: dejected: debased: base: mean: vulgar: humble: socially depressed: little advanced in organisation or culture: of latitude, near the equator: of dates, comparatively recent (*arch.*): attaching little value to priesthood, sacraments, etc.:—*comp.* **lower** (*lō'ər*); *superl.* **lowest** (*lō'ist*), **low'ermost.**—*n.* that which is low or lowest: an area of low barometrical pressure: a low or minimum level: low gear.—*adv.* in or to a low position, state, or manner: humbly: with a low voice or sound: at low pitch: at a low price: late (*arch.*): in small quantity or to small degree.—*v.t.* **low'er**, to make lower: to let down: to lessen: to dilute (*obs.*).—*v.i.* to become lower or less.—*n.* **low'ering**, the act of bringing low or reducing.—*adj.* letting down: sinking: degrading.—*adj.* **low'ermost**, lowest.—*n.* **low'lihead** (*arch.*), humility.—*adv.* **low'lily** (*-li-li*).—*n.* **low'liness.**—*adj.* **low'ly**, humble: modest: low in stature or in organisation.—*n.* **low'ness.**—*adj.* **low'-born**, of humble birth.—**low'boy**, a low-churchman (*obs.*): a short-legged dressing-table with drawers (*U.S.*).—*adj.* **low'-bred**, ill-bred: unmannerly.—**low'-brow**, one who is not intellectual or makes no pretensions to intellect.— Also *adj.*—*adj.* **Low Church**, of a party within the Church of England setting little value on sacerdotal claims, ecclesiastical constitutions, ordinances, and forms, holding evangelical views of theology—opp. to *High Church.*—**Low-Church'ism**; **Low-Church'man**; **low comedy**, comedy of farcical situation, slapstick, low life.— *adjs.* **low'-country**, lowland (**the Low Countries,** Holland and Belgium); **low'-down** (*coll.*), base: dishonourable.—*n.* (*slang*) information, esp. of a confidential or damaging nature.—**low-down'er** (*U.S.*), a poor white; **Low Dutch** (*obs.*), Low German including Dutch.—*adjs.* **low'er-brack'et**, in a low grouping in a list; **low'er-case** (*print.*), lit. kept in a lower case, small as distinguished from capital; **low'er-class**, pertaining to persons of the humbler ranks.—**low'er-deck**, deck immediately above the hold: ship's crew (as opposed to officers).—Also *adj.*—**lower house,** chamber, the larger more representative of two legislative chambers; **lower regions,** Hades, hell.— *adjs.* **low-frequency**, **low'-gear**, **Low German** (see **frequency**, **gear**, **German**).—**low'land**, land low with respect to higher land (also *adj.*); **low'lander** (also *cap.*), a native of lowlands, esp. **the Lowlands** of Scotland; **Low Latin** (see **Latin**); **low life**, sordid social circumstances: persons of low social class.—*adjs.* **low'-life**; **low'-lived** (*-livd*), vulgar: shabby.—**low'-loader**, a low sideless wagon for very heavy loads; **low mass**, mass without music and incense.—*adjs.* **low'-mind'ed**, moved by base or gross motives: vulgar; **low'-necked**, cut low in the neck and away from the shoulders, décolleté; **low'-paid'**, (of worker) receiving, (of job) rewarded by, low wages; **low'-pitched**, of sound, low in pitch: of a roof, gentle in slope: having a low ceiling; **low'-press'ure**, employing or exerting a low degree of pressure (viz. less than 50 lb. to the sq. inch), said of steam and steam-engines: having low barometric pressure; **low'-slung'**, (of vehicle, etc.) with body close to the ground: (of building) not tall; **low'-spir'ited**, having the spirits low or cast down: not lively: sad.— **low'-spir'itedness**; **Low Sunday**, the first Sunday after Easter, so called in contrast to the great festival whose octave it ends.—*adj.* **low'-thought'ed**, having the thoughts directed to low pursuits.— **low tide, water**, the lowest point of the tide at ebb; **low toby** (see **toby**); **low wines**, the weak spirit produced from the first distillation of substances containing alcohol.—**in low water,**

short of money; **lay low,** to overthrow, fell, kill; **lie low** (see **lie** (2)); **low side window,** a narrow window (or lower part of a window) near the ground, sometimes found in old churches, esp. in the chancel; **low temperature physics,** study of physical phenomena at temperatures near absolute zero. [O.N. *lāgr*, Du. *laag*, low; allied to O.E. *licgan*, to lie.]

**low,** *lō*, (*arch.* except in place-names) *n.* a hill: a tumulus. [O.E. *hlāw*; cf. **law** (3).]

**low, lowe,** *low*, (*Scot.*) *n.* a flame.—*v.i.* to blaze.—

**low-bell** (*low'*, *lō'*, *lōō'bel*; *dial.*), a small bell: a bell used by night along with a light, to frighten birds into a net. [O.N. *logi*; cf. Ger. *lohe.*]

**lower, lowr.** See **lour. lower,** *lō'ər.* See **low** (2).

**lown, lowne,** *lown*, *n.* variants of **loon** (1).

**lown, lownd, loun, lound,** *lown(d)*, (*Scot.*) *adj.* sheltered: calm: quiet.—*adv.* quietly.—*n.* calm: quiet: shelter.—*v.i.* to calm. [O.N. *logn* (noun).]

**Lowrie,** *low'ri*, (*Scot.*) *n.* a nickname for the fox. —Also **Low'rie-tod, Tod-low'rie.** [Laurence.]

**lowse, lows,** (*Scot.*) *adj.* loose.—*v.t.* (*lows*, or *lowz*) to loose: to unyoke: to redeem.—*v.i.* to unyoke the horses: to knock off work:—*pa.t.* and *pa.p.* **lows'it.** [See **loose.**]

**lox, loks,** *n.* liquid oxygen, used as a rocket propellant.—Also **loxygen.**

**loxodrome,** *loks'ə-drōm*, *n.* a line on the surface of a sphere which makes equal oblique angles with all meridians, a rhumb-line—also **loxodromic curve, line,** or **spiral.**—*adjs.* **loxodromic** (*-drom'ik*), **-al.**—*n.* **loxodrom'ics,** the art of sailing on rhumb-lines. [Gr. *loxos*, oblique, *dromos*, a course.]

**loy,** *loi*, *n.* a long, narrow spade with footrest on one side of the handle.

**loyal,** *loi'əl*, *adj.* faithful: true as a lover: firm in allegiance: personally devoted to a sovereign or would-be sovereign: legitimate (*Shak.*): manifesting loyalty.—*n.* **loy'alist,** a loyal adherent, esp. of a king or of an established government: in English history, a partisan of the Stuarts: in the American war of Independence, one that sided with the British.—*adv.* **loy'ally.**—*n.* **loy'alty.** [Fr.,—L. *lēgālis—lēx, lēgis,* law.]

**lozenge,** *loz'inj*, *n.* a diamond-shaped parallelogram or rhombus: a small sweetmeat, medicated or not, originally diamond-shaped: a diamond-shaped shield for the arms of a widow, spinster, or deceased person (*her.*).—*n.* **loz'en** (*Scot.*), a window-pane.—*adjs.* **loz'enged,** divided into lozenges; **loz'engy** (*her.*), divided into lozenge-shaped compartments.—*adj.* **loz'enge-shaped.** [Fr. *losange* (of unknown origin).]

**LSD.** See under **lysis.**

**lubber,** *lub'ər*, **lubbard,** *lub'ərd*, *n.* an awkward, clumsy fellow: a lazy, sturdy fellow.—*adj.* **lubberly.**—*adj.* and *adv.* **lubb'erly.**—**lubber fiend,** a beneficent goblin or drudging brownie, Lob-lie-by-the-fire; **lubber's hole,** a hole in a mast platform saving climbing round the rim; **lubber's line,** a line on the compass bowl marking the position of the ship's head. [Origin doubtful.]

**lubfish,** *lub'fish*, *n.* a kind of stockfish. [**lob.**]

**lubra,** *lōō'brə*, (*Austr.*) *n.* an aboriginal woman. [Tasmanian.]

**lubricate,** *lōō'*, *lū'bri-kāt*, *v.t.* to make smooth or slippery: to supply with oil or other matter to overcome friction: to supply with liquor: bribe.—*adjs.* **lu'bric, -al, lubricious** (*-brish'əs*), **lu'bricous** (*-kəs*), slippery: lewd.—*adj.* **lu'bricant,** lubricating.—*n.* a substance used to reduce friction.—*n.* **lubrica'tion.**—*adj.* **lu'bricative.**—*ns.* **lu'bricātor; lubricity** (*-bris'i-ti*), slipperiness: smoothness: instability: lewdness.—**lubricated water,** water with certain additives which make it flow more smoothly. [L. *lūbricus,* slippery.]

**lucarne,** *lōō-,* *lū-kärn',* *n.* a dormer-window, esp. in a church spire. [Fr. (of unknown origin).]

**luce,** *lōōs,* *lūs,* *n.* a freshwater fish, the pike. [O.Fr. *lus*—L.L. *lūcius.*]

**lucent,** *lōō',* *lū'sənt,* *adj.* shining: bright.—*n.* **lu'cency.** [L. *lūcēns,* *-entis,* pr.p. of *lūcēre,* to shine—*lūx,* *lūcis,* light.]

**lucerne,** *lōō-,* *lū-sûrn',* *n.* purple medick (in U.S. called alfalfa), a valuable forage-plant.—Also **lucern'** (*Browning* **lu'zern**); formerly often **la lucerne.** [Fr. *luzerne.*]

**lucid,** *lōō',* *lū'sid,* *adj.* shining: transparent: easily understood: intellectually bright: not darkened with madness.—*ns.* **lucid'ity,** **lu'cidness.**—*adv.* **lu'cidly.**—**lucid intervals,** times of sanity in madness, of quietness in fever, turmoil, etc. [L. *lūcidus—lūx,* *lūcis,* light.]

**Lucifer,** *lōō',* *lū'si-fər,* *n.* the planet Venus as morning-star: Satan: (without *cap.*) a match of wood tipped with a combustible substance to be ignited by friction—also **lu'cifer-match'.** —*adj.* **Luciferian,** pertaining to Lucifer.—*ns.* **lucif'erase,** an oxidising enzyme in the luminous organs of certain animals that acts on luciferin to produce luminosity; **lucif'erin,** a protein-like substance in the luminous organs of certain animals.—*adj.* **lucif'erous,** light-bringing: light-giving. [L. *lūcifer,* light-bringer—*lūx,* *lūcis,* light, *ferre,* to bring.]

**lucifugous,** *lōō-,* *lū-sif'ū-gəs,* *adj.* shunning light. [L. *lūx,* *lūcis,* light, *fugēre,* to flee.]

**lucigen,** *lōō',* *lū'si-jen,* *n.* a lamp burning oil mixed with air in a spray. [L. *lūx,* *lūcis,* light, and root of L. *gignēre,* *genitum,* to beget.]

**Lucina,** *lōō-,* *lū-sī'nə,* *n.* the Roman goddess of childbirth, Juno: also Diana: hence, the moon: a midwife (*arch.*). [L. *Lūcīna,* thought by the Romans to be from *lūx,* *lūcis,* light, as if the bringer to light.]

**luck,** *luk,* *n.* fortune: good fortune: an object with which a family's fortune is supposed to be bound up.—*adv.* **luck'ily.**—*n.* **luck'iness.**—*adj.* **luck'less,** without good luck: unhappy.—*adv.* **luck'lessly.**—*n.* **luck'lessness.**—*adj.* **luck'y,** having, attended by, portending, or bringing good luck.—**luck'-penny,** a trifle returned for luck by a seller: a coin carried for luck; **luck'y-bag,** a bag sold without disclosing its contents: a bag in which one may dip and draw a prize (also **luck'y-dip**): a receptacle for lost property on board a man-of-war; **lucky charm,** an object which is supposed to promote good fortune; **luck'y-piece,** a coin: the illegitimate child of a prosperous father (*coll.*); **lucky stone,** a stone with a natural hole through it (carried for good fortune); **lucky strike,** a stroke of luck.—**down on one's luck** (*coll.*; see **down**); **push one's luck** (*coll.*), to try to make too much of an advantage, risking total failure; **touch lucky** (*coll.*), to have good luck; **worse, tough luck,** more's the pity. [Prob. L.G. or Du. *luk;* cf. Ger. *glück,* prosperity.]

**lucken,** *luk'ən,* (*Scot.*) *adj.* closed.—**luck'engow'an,** the globe-flower. [O.E. *locen,* pa.p. of *lūcan,* to lock.]

**lucky, luckie** (prefixed or vocative, **Lucky**), *luk'i,* (*Scot.*) *n.* an elderly woman: a woman who keeps an ale-house.—**luck'ie-dad,** a grandfather. [Perh. from adj. **lucky.**]

**lucky,** *luk'i,* (*slang*) *n.* departure.—**cut,** or **make, one's lucky,** to bolt.

**lucre,** *lōō',* *lū'kər,* *n.* sordid gain: riches.—*adj.* **lu'crative** (*-krə-tiv*), profitable.—*adv.* **lu'cratively.** [L. *lucrum,* gain.]

**luctation,** *luk-tā'shən,* *n.* struggle. [L. *luctātiō,* *-ōnis.*]

**lucubrate,** *lōō',* *lū'kū-brāt,* *v.i.* to study by lamplight: to discourse learnedly or pedantically.—*ns.* **lucubra'tion,** study or composition protracted late into the night: a product of such study: a composition that smells of the lamp; **lu'cubrātor.** [L. *lūcubrāre,* *-ātum—lūx,* light.]

**luculent,** *lōō',* *lū'kū-lənt,* *adj.* bright: clear: convincing.—*adv.* **lu'culently.** [L. *lūculentus—lūx,* light.]

**Lucullan,** *lōō-,* *lū-kul'ən,* *adj.* in the style of the Roman L. Licinius Lucullus, famous for his banquets.—Also **Lucullē'an, Lucull'ian, Lucull'ic.**

**Lucuma,** *lōō'kū-ma,* *n.* genus, mostly S. American, of sapotaceous trees with edible fruit. [Quechua.]

**lucumo,** *lōō',* *lū'kū-mō,* *n.* an Etruscan prince and priest. [L. *lūcūmō,* from Etruscan.]

**lud,** *lud,* *n.* a minced form of **lord** (trivial and forensic).—*n.* **lud'ship.**

**Luddite,** *lud'it,* *n.* one of a band of destroyers of machinery in northern England about 1812-18.—Also *adj.*—*n.* **Ludd'ism.** [Said to be from one Ned *Ludd,* who had smashed stocking-frames at a slightly earlier date.]

**ludicrous,** *lōō',* *lū'di-krəs,* *adj.* sportive (*obs.*): humorous (*obs.*): adapted to excite laughter: laughable.—*adv.* **lu'dicrously.**—*n.* **lu'dicrousness.** [L. *lūdicrus—lūdēre,* to play.]

**ludo,** *lōō',* *lū'dō,* *n.* a game in which counters are moved on a board according to the fall of dice. [L. *lūdō,* I play.]

**lues,** *lōō',* *lū'ēz,* *n.* a pestilence: now confined to syphilis.—*adj.* **luetic** (*-et'ik;* a bad formation). [L. *lūēs.*]

**luff,** *luf,* *n.* the windward side of a ship: the act of sailing a ship close to the wind: the loof, or the after-part of a ship's bow where the planks begin to curve in towards the cut-water.—*v.i.* to turn a ship towards the wind.—*v.t.* to turn nearer to the wind: to move (the jib of a crane) in and out.—**luffing'(-jib) crane,** a jib crane with the jib hinged at its lower end to the crane structure so as to permit of alteration of its radius of action. [Origin obscure.]

**luffa, loofah, loofa,** *luf'ə,* *lōōf'ə,* *n.* a tropical genus (Luffa) of the gourd family: the fibrous network of its fruit, used as flesh-brush. [Ar. *lūfah.*]

**luffer-board,** *luf'ər-bōrd,* *-börd.* Same as **louvreboard.**

**luftwaffe,** *lōōft'vä-fə,* (Ger.) air force.

**lug,** *lug,* *v.t.* to pull: to drag heavily.—*v.i.* to pull:—*pr.p.* **lugg'ing;** *pa.t.* and *pa.p.* **lugged.**—*n.* **lugg'age,** the trunks and other baggage of a traveller.—**lugg'age-carrier,** a structure fixed to a bicycle, motor-car, etc., for carrying luggage; **lugg'age-van,** a railway wagon for luggage.—**lug in,** to introduce without any apparent connection or relevance. [Cf. Sw. *lugga,* to pull by the hair; perh. conn. with **lug** (4).]

**lug,** *lug,* **lugsail,** *lug'sāl,* *lug'sl,* *ns.* a square sail bent upon a yard that hangs obliquely to the mast.—*n.* **lugg'er,** a small vessel with lugsails.

**lug,** *lug,* *n.* a pole or stick: a perch or rod of land (*Spens.*). [Origin obscure.]

**lug,** *lug,* *n.* the flap or lappet of a cap: the ear (chiefly *Scot.*): an earlike projection or appendage: a handle: a loop: a chimney corner (*Scot.*).—*adj.* **lugged** (*lugd*), having lugs or a lug.—*n.* **lugg'ie** (*Scot.*), a hooped dish with one long stave.—**lug'-chair,** an easy-chair with side headrests. [Perh. conn. with **lug** (1).]

**lug,** *lug,* **lugworm,** *lug'wûrm,* *ns.* a sluggish worm found in the sand on the seashore, much used for bait. [Origin doubtful.]

**luge,** *lōōzh,* *lüzh,* *n.* a light hand-sledge for one.—*v.i.* to glide on such a sledge.—*pa.p.* and *n.* **lug'ing, luge'ing.** [Swiss Fr.]

**luggage,** see **lug** (1).

**lugger.** See **lug** (2). **luggie.** See **lug** (4).

**lugubrious,** *lōō-gū'bri-əs,* *adj.* mournful: dismal.—*adv.* **lugū'briously.** [L. *lūgubris—lūgēre,* to mourn.]

**Luing cattle,** *ling kat'l,* a breed of hardy beef cattle. [*Luing,* island off west Scotland.]

**luit**, *lüt, lit*, **luit′en**, *Scots. pa.t.* and *pa.p.* of **let** (1).

**luke**, *lōōk*, (*dial.*) *adj.* moderately warm: tepid.— *adjs.* **luke′warm**, luke: half-hearted; **luke′-warmish.**—*adv.* **luke′warmly.**—*ns.* **luke′warmness, luke′warmth.** [M.E. *luek, luke*; doubtful whether related to **lew**, or to Du. *leuk.*]

**lull**, *lul*, *v.t.* to soothe: to compose: to quiet.— *v.i.* to become calm: to subside.—*n.* an interval of calm: a calming influence.—*n.* **lull′aby** (*-ǝ-bi*), a song to lull children to sleep, a cradle-song. —*v.t.* to lull to sleep. [Cf. Sw. *lulla.*]

**lulu**, *lōō′lōō*, (*slang*) *n.* thing, person, that is remarkable, wonderful.

**lum**, *lum*, (*Scot.*) *n.* a chimney: a chimney-pot hat (also **lum′-hat**).—**lum′-head′**, the top of a chimney. [Origin obscure; O.Fr. *lum*, light, and W. *llumon*, chimney, have been suggested.]

**lumbago**, *lum-bā′gō*, *n.* a rheumatic affection of the muscles or fibrous tissues in the lumbar region.—*adjs.* **lumbaginous** (*-baj′i-nǝs*); **lumbar** (*lum′bǝr*), of, or near, the loins. [L. *lumbāgō*, lumbago, *lumbus*, loin.]

**lumbang**, *lōōm-bäng′*, *n.* the candle-nut tree or other species of Aleurites, whose nuts yield **lumbang′-oil′.** [Tagálog.]

**lumber**, *lum′bǝr*, *n.* furniture stored away out of use: anything cumbersome or useless: timber, esp. sawed or split for use (*U.S.* and *Canada*). —*v.t.* to fill with lumber: to heap together in confusion: to cumber: to cut the timber from.— *v.i.* to work as a lumberman.—*ns.* **lum′berer**, a lumberjack; **lum′bering**, felling, sawing and removal of timber.—**lum′ber-camp**, a lumberman's camp; **lum′berjack, lum′berman**, one employed in lumbering; **lum′ber-jacket**, a man's longish, loose-fitting sometimes belted jacket fastened right up to the neck and usu. in bold-patterned heavy material: a woman's cardigan of like fastening; **lum′ber-mill**, a sawmill; **lum′ber-room**, a room for storing things not in use; **lum′ber-yard**, a timber-yard. [Perhaps from **lumber** (2), or from **lumber** (3) influenced by **lumber** (2).]

**lumber**, *lum′bǝr*, (*arch. slang*) *n.* pawn: a pawnshop: prison.—*v.t.* to pawn: to imprison.—*n.* **lum′berer**, a pawnbroker.—**lum′ber-pie′**, a pie of meat or fish, with eggs. [See **Lombard.**]

**lumber**, *lum′bǝr*, *v.i.* to move heavily and clumsily: to rumble.—*n.* **lum′berer.**—*adjs.* **lum′berly, lum′-bersome.**—*n.* **lum′bersomeness.** [M.E. *lomeren*, perh. a freq. formed from *lome*, a variant of **lame**; but cf. dial. Sw. *lomra*, to resound.]

**Lumbricus**, *lum-bri′kǝs*, *n.* a very common genus of earthworms, giving name to the family **Lumbricidae** (*-bris′i-dē*) to which all British earthworms belong.—*adj.* **lum′brical** (or *-brī′*), worm-like.—*n.* (for **lumbrical muscle**) one of certain muscles of the hand and foot used in flexing the digits.—*adjs.* **lumbriciform** (*-bris′*), **lum′bricoid** (or *-brī′*), worm-like. [L. *lumbricus.*]

**lumen**, *lōō′*, *lū′men*, *n.* a unit of luminous flux— the light emitted in one second in a solid angle of one steradian from a point-source of uniform intensity of one candela: the cavity of a tube: the space within the cell-wall (*bot.*):—*pl.* **lū′mina, lu′mens.**—*adj.* **lu′minal**, of a lumen.—*n.* **lu′min-ance,** luminousness: the measure of brightness of a surface, measured in candela/cm² of the surface radiating normally.—*adj.* **lu′minant,** giving light. —*n.* an illuminant.—*ns.* **lu′minarism; lu′minarist**, one who paints luminously, or with skill in lights: an impressionist or plein-airist; **lu′min-ary,** a source of light, esp. one of the heavenly bodies: one who illustrates any subject or instructs mankind; **luminā′tion,** a lighting up.— *v.t.* **lumine** (*-in*), to illumine.—*n.* **luminescence** (*-es′ǝns*), emission of light otherwise than by incandescence.—*adj.* **luminesc′ent.**—*adj.* **lumin-if′erous,** giving, yielding, being the medium of,

**light.**—*ns.* **lu′minist**, a luminarist; **luminosity** (*-os′i-ti*), luminousness: quantity of light emitted.—*adj.* **lu′minous,** giving light: shining: lighted: clear: lucid.—*adv.* **lu′minously.**—*n.* **lu′minousness.**—**luminous paint,** a paint that glows in the dark, those that glow continuously having radioactive additives. [L. *lūmen, -inis,* light—*lūcēre,* to shine.]

**luminaire**, *lü-mēn-er*, *n.* light-fitting. [Fr.]

**lumme, lummy**, *lum′i, interj.* (Lord) love me.

**lummy**, *lum′i*, (*slang; Dickens*) *adj.* excellent.

**lump**, *lump*, *n.* a shapeless mass: a protuberance: a swelling: a feeling as if of a swelling in the throat: a considerable quantity: the whole to-gether: the gross: an inert, dull, good-natured, or fair-sized person: a lumpfish.—*v.t.* to throw into a confused mass: to take in the gross: to include under one head: to endure willy-nilly: to put up with: to be lumpish about: to dislike. —*v.i.* to be lumpish: to gather in a lump: to stump along.—*ns.* **lump′er**, a labourer employed in the lading or unlading of ships: a militiaman (*dial.*): one inclined to lumping in classifica-tion—opp. to *hair-splitter.*—*adv.* **lump′ily.**—*n.* **lump′iness.**—*adjs.* **lump′ing**, in a lump: heavy: bulky; **lump′ish**, like a lump: heavy: gross: dull: sullen.—*adv.* **lump′ishly.**—*ns.* **lump′ishness; lump′kin**, a lout.—*adj.* **lump′y**, full of lumps: like a lump.—**lump′fish, lump′sucker,** a clumsy sea-fish (Cyclopterus) with pectoral fins trans-formed into a sucker; **lump′-su′gar,** loaf-sugar broken in small pieces or cut in cubes; **lump sum,** a single sum of money in lieu of several; **lump′y-jaw′,** actinomycosis affecting the jaw in cattle.—**if you don't like it you may lump it,** take it as you like, but there is no remedy; **in the lump,** in gross; **the lump,** system of using for a particular job non-union workmen hired by a middleman. [Origin doubtful; found in various Gmc. languages.]

**lumpen**, *lum′pǝn*, *adj.* pertaining to a dispossessed and/or degraded section of a social class, as in **lumpen proletariat** (also as one word), the very poor, low-class ne'er-do-wells, etc. [Ger., rag.]

**lunar, lunate, lunatic**, etc. See **lune**.

**lunch**, *lunch, lunsh*, *n.* a thick slice, a lump (*dial.*): a slight repast between breakfast and midday meal: midday meal: snack at any time of day (*U.S.*).—*v.i.* to take lunch.—*v.t.* to provide lunch for.—*n.* **lunch′eon**, lunch.—*v.i.* to lunch (also *v.t.*).—*n.* **lunch′er.**—**lunch′eon-bar,** a counter where luncheons are served; **lunch′eon-basket,** basket for carrying lunch, with or without cutlery, etc.; **lunch′eon-meat,** a type of pre-cooked meat containing preservatives, usually served cold; **lunch(-eon) voucher,** a ticket or voucher given by employer to employee to be used to pay for the latter's lunch; **lunch′-hour, lunch′-time,** the time of, or time set apart for, lunch: an interval allowed for lunch. [Perh. altered from **lump;** or from Sp. *lonja,* a slice of ham, etc.]

**lune**, *lōōn, lūn,* *n.* anything in the shape of a half-moon: a lunule: a fit of lunacy (*Shak.*).—*n.* **lunacy** (usu. *lōō′nǝ-si*), a form of insanity once believed to come with changes of the moon: insanity generally: extreme folly.—*adj.* **lunar** (usu. *lōō′nǝr*), belonging to the moon: measured by the moon's revolutions: caused by the moon: like the moon: of silver (*old chem.*).—*n.* a lunar distance.—*ns.* **lunā′rian**, an inhabitant of the moon: a student of the moon; **lu′narist**, one who thinks the moon affects the weather; **lu′nary,** the moonwort fern: the plant honesty. —*adj.* **lunar.**—*adjs.* **lu′nate, -d,** crescent-shaped; **lunatic** (*lōō′nǝ-tik*), affected with lunacy.—*n.* a person so affected: a madman.—*ns.* **lunā′tion,** a synodic month; **lunette′,** a crescent-shaped ornament: a semi-circular or crescent-shaped space where a vault intersects a wall or another vault, often occupied by a window or by decoration: an arched opening in a vault: a detached bastion (*fort.*): a small horseshoe: a watch-glass flattened more than usual in the centre: in the R.C. Church, a moon-shaped case for the consecrated host.—*adj.* luniso′lar, pertaining to the moon and sun jointly.—*n.* lu′nūla, a lunule: a crescent-like appearance, esp. the whitish area at the base of a nail.—*adjs.* lu′nūlar; lu′nūlate, -d (*bot.*), shaped like a small crescent.—*n.* lu′nule, anything in form like a small crescent: a geometrical figure bounded by two circular arcs.—lunar caustic, fused crystals of silver nitrate, applied to ulcers, etc.; lunar cycle (see metonic cycle); lunar distances, a method of finding the longitude by comparison of the observed angular distance of the moon from a star at a known local time, with the tabulated angular distance at a certain Greenwich time; Lunar Excursion Module (LEM, lem), module for use in the last stage of the journey to land on the moon; lunar month (see month); lunar theory, the *a priori* deduction of the moon's motions from the principles of gravitation; lunar year (see year); lunatic fringe, the more nonsensical, extreme-minded, or eccentric members of a community or of a movement. [L. *lūna*, the moon—*lūcēre*, to shine.]

lung, *lung, n.* a respiratory organ in animals that breathe atmospheric air: an open space in a town (*fig.*).—*adj.* lunged.—lung′-book, a breathing organ in spiders and scorpions, constructed like the leaves of a book; lung′-fish, one of the Dipnoi, having lungs as well as gills.—*adj.* lung′-grown, having an adhesion of the lung to the pleura.—lung′wort, a genus (Pulmonaria) of the borage family, once thought good for lung diseases because of its spotted leaves: a lichen (*Lobaria pulmonaria*) on tree-trunks, used as a domestic remedy for lung diseases.—iron lung (see iron). [O.E. *lungen.*]

lunge, *lunj, n.* a sudden thrust as in fencing: a forward plunge.—*v.i.* to make a lunge: to plunge forward.—*v.t.* to thrust with a lunge:—*pr.p.* lunge′ing, lung′ing. [Fr. *allonger*, to lengthen—L. *ad*, to, *longus*, long.]

lunge, longe, *lunj, n.* a long rope used in horse-training: training with a lunge: a training-ground for horses.—*v.t.* to train or cause to go with a lunge. [Fr. *longe*—L. *longus*, long.]

lungi, *lōōn′gē, n.* a long cloth used as loincloth, sash, turban, etc. [Hind. and Pers. *lungī.*]

lungie, *lung′i*, (*Scot.*) *n.* the guillemot. [Norw. dial. *lomgivie.*]

lungie, lunyie, *lung′i, lun′yi, n.* Scottish forms of loin.

lunisolar, lunulate, lunule, etc. See lune.

lunt, *lunt*, (*Scot.*) *n.* a slow-match or means of setting on fire: a sudden flame, blaze: smoke.—*v.t.* to kindle: to smoke.—*v.i.* to blaze up: to emit smoke: to smoke tobacco. [Du. *lont*, a match; cf. Ger. *lunte.*]

Lupercal, *lōō′par-kal, -kl,* or *lū′, n.* the grotto, or the festival (Feb. 15), of *Lŭpercus*, Roman god of fertility and flocks.—Also (*pl.*) Luperca′lia. [Perh. *lupus*, wolf, *arcēre*, to ward off.]

lupin, lupine, *lōō′, lū′pin, n.* a genus (Lupinus) of Papilionaceae, with flowers on long spikes: its seed. [L. *lupinus.*]

lupine, *lōō′, lū′pin, adj.* of a wolf: like a wolf: wolfish. [L. *lupinus*—*lupus,* a wolf.]

luppen, *lup′n,* Scots. *pa.p.* of leap.

lupulin, *lōō′pū-lin, n.* a yellow powder composed of glands from hop flowers and bracts.—*adjs.* lu′puline, lupulinic (-*lin′ik*). [L. *lupus*, hop-plant.]

lupus, *lōō′, lū′pəs, n.* a chronic tuberculosis of the skin, often affecting the nose. [L. *lupus*, a wolf.]

lur. See lure (2).

lurch, *lûrch, n.* an old game, probably like back-gammon: in various games, a situation in which one side fails to score at all, or is left far behind: a discomfiture.—*v.t.* to defeat by a lurch: to outdo so as to deprive of all chance (*Shak.*): to leave in the lurch.—leave in the lurch, to leave in a difficult situation without help. [O.Fr. *lourche.*]

lurch, *lûrch, n.* wait, ambush.—*v.i.* to lurk, prowl about.—*v.t.* to get the start of, forestall (*arch.*): to defraud, to overreach (*arch.*): to filch (*arch.*).—*n.* lurch′er, one who lurches: a glutton (*obs.*): a dog with a distinct cross of grey-hound, esp. a cross of greyhound and collie. [Connection with lurk difficult; influenced apparently by foregoing.]

lurch, *lûrch, v.i.* to roll or pitch suddenly forward or to one side. *n.* a sudden roll or pitch. [Origin obscure.]

lurdan, lurdane, lurden, *lûr′dən, n.* a dull, heavy, stupid or sluggish person.—Also *adj.* [O.Fr. *lourdin*, dull—*lourd*, heavy.]

lure, *lōōr, lūr, n.* any enticement: bait: decoy: a bunch of feathers used to recall a hawk.—*v.t.* to entice: decoy. [O.Fr. *loerre* (Fr. *leurre*)—M.H.G. *luoder* (Ger. *luder*), bait.]

lure, lur, *lōōr, n.* a long curved Bronze Age trumpet still used in Scandinavian countries for calling cattle, etc. [O.N. *lūthr*; Dan. and Norw. *lur.*]

Lurgi, *lōōr′gi, adj.* pertaining to a German plant that enables coal-gas to be made from low-grade coal.

lurid, *lōō′, lū′rid, adj.* glaringly, wanly, or dingily reddish-yellow or yellowish-brown: dingy brown or yellow (*bot.*): gloomily threatening: ghastly pale, wan: ghastly: melodramatically sensational: brimstony.—*adv.* lu′ridly.—*n.* lu′-ridness. [L. *lūridus.*]

lurk, *lûrk, v.i.* to lie in wait: to be concealed: to skulk: to go or loaf about furtively.—*n.* a prowl: a lurking-place: a swindling dodge.—*n.* lurk′er.—*n.* and *adj.* lurk′ing.—lurk′ing-place. [Perh. freq. from lour.]

lurry, *lur′i,* (*Milt.*) *n.* gabbled formula: confusion. [liripoop.]

luscious, *lush′əs, adj.* sweet in a great degree: delightful: fulsome: voluptuous.—*adv.* lusc′-iously.—*n.* lusc′iousness. [Origin unknown; delicious, influenced by lush, has been suggested.]

lush, *lush, adj.* rich and juicy: luxuriant.—*adv.* lush′ly.—*n.* lush′ness. [Perh. a form of lash (2).]

lush, *lush,* (*arch. slang*) *n.* liquor: a drink: a drinking bout: a drinker or drunkard.—*v.t.* to ply with liquor.—*v.t.* and *v.i.* to drink.—*n.* lush′er.—*adj.* lush′y, tipsy.—lush′-house, a low public house. [Perh. from foregoing.]

Lusiad, *lōō′, lū′si-ad, n.,* and Lusiads (-*adz*), *n.pl.* a Portuguese epic by Camoens, celebrating Vasco da Gama's voyage to India by the Cape. —*n.* and *adj.* Lusitā′nian, Portuguese.—Lusitano-American, Brazilian of Portuguese descent.—*pfx.* Luso-, Portuguese. [Port. *Os Lusiadas*, the Lusitanians; L. *Lūsitānia*, approximately, Portugal.]

lusk, *lusk,* (*obs.*) *n.* a lazy fellow.—*adj.* lazy.—*v.i.* to skulk: to lie about lazily.—*adj.* lusk′ish.—*n.* lusk′ishness. [Origin obscure.]

lust, *lust, n.* pleasure (*Spens., Shak.*): appetite: relish: longing: eagerness to possess: sensual desire: sexual desire, now always of a degraded kind.—*v.i.* to desire eagerly (with *after, for*): to have carnal desire: to have depraved desires.—*n.* lust′er.—*adj.* lust′ful, having lust: inciting to lust: sensual.—*adv.* lust′fully.—*n.* lust′fulness.—*adj.* lust′ick, lust′ique (*Shak.* 'as the Dutchman says'; for Du. *lustig*), lusty, healthy, vigorous.—*ns.* lust′ihead, lust′ihood, lust′iness. —*adv.* lust′ily.—*adjs.* lust′less (*Spens.*), listless, feeble; lust′y, vigorous: healthful: stout: bulky: lustful (*Milt.*): pleasing, pleasant (*obs.*).

—*adjs.* **lust'-breathed** (*-brēdh'id*; *Shak.*), animated by lust; **lust'-di'eted** (*Shak.*), pampered by lust. [O.E. *lust*, pleasure.]

**lustre**, *lus'tər*, *n.* characteristic surface appearance in reflected light: sheen: gloss: brightness: splendour: renown (*fig.*): a candlestick, vase, etc., ornamented with pendants of cut-glass: a dress material with cotton warp and woollen weft, and highly finished surface: a metallic pottery glaze.—*v.t.* to impart a lustre to.—*v.i.* to become lustrous.—*adj.* **lus'treless.**—*n.* **lus'tring.**—*adj.* **lus'trous**, bright: shining: luminous. —*adv.* **lus'trously.** [Fr.,—L. *lūstrāre*, to shine on.]

**lustre**, *lus'tər*, **lustrum**, *lus'trəm*, *n.* a purification of the Roman people made every five years, after the taking of the census: a period of five years:—*pl.* **lus'tres**, **lus'tra**, **lus'trums.**—*adj.* **lus'tral.**—*v.t.* **lus'trate**, to purify by sacrifice: perambulate (*obs.*).—*n.* **lustrā'tion**, purification by sacrifice: act of purifying. [L. *lūstrum*, prob. —*luēre*, to wash, to purify.]

**lustring**, *lus'tring*, *n.* a glossy silk cloth.—Also **lus'trine**, **lutestring** (*lōōt'*, *lūt'string*). [Fr. *lustrine*—It. *lustrino*.]

**lusty.** See **lust.**

**lusus naturae**, *lōō'səs na-tū'rē*, *lōō'sŏŏs na-tōōr'ī*, (L.) a sport or freak of nature.

**lute**, *lōōt*, or *lūt*, *n.* an old stringed instrument shaped like half a pear.—*v.i.* to play on the lute. —*v.t.* and *v.i.* to sound as if on a lute.—*ns.* **lut'anist**, **lut'enist**, **lut'er**, **lut'ist**, player on lute; **luthier** (*lūt'i-ər*), maker of lutes, etc.—**lute'-string**, string of lute (see also **lustring**). [O.Fr. *lut* (Fr. *luth*); like Ger. *laute*, from Ar. *al*, the, *'ūd*, wood, the lute.]

**lute**, *lōōt*, *lūt*, *n.* clay, cement or other material used as a protective covering, an airtight stopping, or the like: a rubber packing-ring for a jar.—*v.t.* to close or coat with lute.—*n.* **lut'ing.** [L. *lutum*, mud—*luēre*, to wash.]

**lute**, *lōōt*, *lūt*, *n.* a straight-edge for scraping off excess of clay in a brick mould. [Du. *loet*.]

**lutecium.** Same as **lutetium.**

**lutein**, *lōōt'ē-in*, *lūt'*, *n.* a yellow colouring-matter in yolk of egg.—*n.* **lutē'olin**, the yellow colouring-matter of weld or dyer's weed.—*adjs.* **lutē'olous**, yellowish; **lu'teous** (*-i-əs*), golden-yellow; **lutescent** (*es'ənt*), yellowish. [L. *lūteus*, yellow, *lūteum*, egg-yolk, *lūtum*, weld.]

**lutestring.** See **lustring**, **lute.**

**Lutetian**, *lū-tē'shən*, *adj.* Parisian. [L. *Lutetia Parisiōrum*, the mud town of the Parisii, Paris—*lutum*, mud.]

**lutetium**, *lōō-tē'shi-əm*, *lū-*, *n.* metallic element (Lu; at. numb. 71) first separated from *ytterbium* by Georges Urbain, a Parisian. [L. *Lutetia*, Paris.]

**Lutheran**, *lōō'thər-ən*, *adj.* pertaining to Martin *Luther*, the great German Protestant reformer (1483-1546), or to his doctrines.—*n.* a follower of Luther.—*ns.* **Lu'ther(an)ism**; **Lu'therist.**

**lux**, *luks*, *n.* a unit of illumination, one lumen per square metre:—*pl.* **lux**, **luxes**, **luces** (*lōō'sēs*).—**lux'meter**, instrument for measuring illumination. [L. *lūx*, light.]

**luxate**, *luks'āt*, *v.t.* to put out of joint: to displace.—*n.* **luxā'tion**, a dislocation. [L. *luxāre*, *-ātum*—*luxus*—Gr. *loxos*, slanting.]

**lux mundi**, *luks mun'dī*, *lōōks mŏŏn'dē*, (L.) light of the world.

**luxulyanite**, **luxul(l)ianite**, *luks-ūl'yən-īt*, *n.* a tourmaline granite found at *Luxulyan*, Cornwall.

**luxury**, *luk'shə-ri*, also *lug'zhə-ri*, *n.* abundant provision of means of ease and pleasure: indulgence, esp. in costly pleasures: anything delightful, often expensive, but not necessary: a dainty: wantonness (*Shak.*).—*adj.* relating to or providing luxury.—*ns.* **luxuriance** (*lug-zhŏŏ'ri-əns*, *-zū'*, *-zhū'*, or *luk-*, etc.), **luxu'riancy**, growth in rich abundance or excess: exuberance: over-

growth: rankness.—*adj.* **luxu'riant**, exuberant in growth: overabundant: profuse: erroneously, for luxurious.—*adv.* **luxu'riantly.**—*v.i.* **luxu'riate**, to be luxuriant (*obs.*): to live luxuriously: to enjoy luxury: to enjoy free indulgence.—*n.* **luxuriā'tion.**—*adj.* **luxu'rious**, of luxury: given to luxury: ministering to luxury: furnished with luxuries: softening by pleasure: luxuriant (*Milt.*): lustful (*Shak.*).—*adv.* **luxu'riously.**—*ns.* **luxu'riousness**; **luxurist** (*luk'shə-rist*, *-sū-*), one given to luxury. [O.Fr. *luxurie*—L. *luxuria*, *luxury*—*luxus*, excess.]

**luz**, *luz*, *n.* a bone supposed by Rabbinical writers to be indestructible, probably the sacrum.

**Luzula**, *lōō'*, *lū'zū-lə*, *n.* the woodrush genus, with flat generally hairy leaves. [Old It. *luzziola* (mod. *lucciola*), firefly, glow-worm, from its shining capsules.]

**lyam**, *li'əm*, **lime**, **lyme**, **līm**, *n.* a leash: a lyam-hound.—*n.* **ly'am-hound**, **lime'-hound**, **lyme'-hound**, a bloodhound. [O.Fr. *liem* (Fr. *lien*)— L. *ligāmen*—*ligāre*, to tie.]

**lyart.** See **liard.**

**Lycaena**, *li-sē'na*, *n.* a genus of butterflies giving name to the family **Lycae'nidae**, usu. small and blue or coppery. [Gr. *lykaina*, she-wolf.]

**lycanthropy**, *li-*, *li-kan'thrə-pi*, *n.* power of changing oneself into a wolf: a kind of madness, in which the patient fancies himself to be a wolf. —*ns.* **lycanthrope** (*li'kan-thrŏp*, or *-kan'*), **lycan'-thropist**, a wolf-man or werewolf: one affected with lycanthropy.—*adj.* **lycanthropic** (*-throp'*). [Gr. *lykos*, a wolf, *anthrōpos*, a man.]

**lycée**, *lē'sā*, *n.* a state secondary school in France. [Fr., lyceum.]

**Lyceum**, *li-sē'əm*, *n.* a gymnasium and grove beside the temple of Apollo at Athens, in whose walks Aristotle taught: (without *cap.*) a college: (without *cap.*) a place or building devoted to literary studies and lectures: (without *cap.*) an organisation for instruction by lectures (*U.S.*): (without *cap.*) a lycée:—*pl.* **lyce'ums.** [L. *Lȳcēum*—Gr. *Lykeion*—*Lykeios*, an epithet of Apollo (perh. wolf-slayer, perhaps the Lycian).]

**lychee.** Same as **litchi.**

**lychgate.** Same as **lichgate.**

**Lychnic**, *lik'nik*, *n.* the first part of the vespers of the Greek Church.—*ns.* **Lychnap'sia** (Gr. *haptein*, to touch, light), a series of seven prayers in the vespers of the Greek Church; **lych'noscope**, a low side window (named on the theory that it was intended to let lepers see the altar lights). [Gr. *lychnos*, a lamp.]

**Lychnis**, *lik'nis*, *n.* the campion genus of the pink family. [Gr. *lychnis*, rose-campion.]

**lycopod**, *li'kə-pod*, *n.* a club-moss, any plant of the genus Lycopodium or of the Lycopodiales. —*ns.pl.* **Lycopōdiā'ceae**, a homosporous family of Lycopodiales; **Lycopōdiā'lēs**, **Lycopodi'nae**, **Lycopodin'eae**, one of the main branches of the Pteridophytes, usually with dichotomously branched stems and axillary sporangia, commonly in cones.—*n.* **Lycopō'dium**, the typical genus of Lycopodiaceae, club-moss, or stag's horn: (without *cap.*) a powder consisting of the spores of Lycopodium. [Gr. *lykos*, a wolf, *pous*, *podos*, a foot.]

**Lycosa**, *li-kō'sa*, *n.* a genus of hunting spiders, including the true tarantula, typical of the family **Lycosidae** (*-kos'i-dē*) or wolf-spiders. [L. *lykos*, a wolf, also a kind of spider.]

**lyddite**, *lid'īt*, *n.* a powerful explosive made in Kent from picrate of potash. [Tested at *Lydd*.]

**Lydford law**, *lid'fərd*, the same kind of law as that called Jeddart justice. [*Lydford* in Devon.]

**Lydian**, *lid'i-ən*, *adj.* pertaining to *Lydia* in Asia Minor: of music, soft and slow, luxurious and effeminate.—*n.* native of Lydia: the language of ancient Lydia, apparently akin to Hittite.— **Lydian mode**, in ancient Greek music, a mode of two tetrachords with a semitone between the two highest notes in each and a whole tone between the tetrachords (as: *c d e f*; *g a b c*): but reckoned downwards by the Greeks): in old church music, an authentic mode, extending from *f* to *f*, with *f* for its final; **Lydian stone,** touchstone. [Gr. *Lȳdiā*, Lydia.]

**lye,** *lī*, *n.* a short side-branch of a railway. [lie (2).]

**lye,** *lī*, *n.* a strong alkaline solution: a liquid used for washing: a solution got by leaching. [O.E. *lēah*, *lēag*; Ger. *lauge*; allied to L. *lavāre*, to wash.]

**lying,** *lī'ing*, *adj.* addicted to telling lies.—*n.* the habit of telling lies.—*adv.* **ly'ingly.** [lie (1).]

**lying,** *lī'ing*, *adj.* being in a horizontal position. —**ly'ing-in'**, confinement during child-bearing.— Also *adj.*—**take it lying down,** to make no resistance or protest. [lie (2).]

**lyke-wake,** *līk'-wāk*, (*Scot.*) *n.* a watch over the dead, often with merrymaking. [Northern form of lich, and wake.]

**lym,** *lim*, *n.* a conjectural Shakespearian form of **lyme,** a lyme-hound. See **lyam.**

**Lymantriidae,** *lī-man-trī'i-dē*, *n.pl.* the tussock-moths, a family akin to the eggers. [Gr. *lȳmantēr*, destroyer.]

**lyme-grass,** *līm'-gräs*, *n.* a coarse sand-binding grass, *Elymus arenarius* or other of the genus. [Origin unknown.]

**lymiter** (*Spens.*). Same as **limiter.**

**Lymnaea.** See **Limnaea.**

**lymph,** *limf*, *n.* pure water: a colourless or faintly yellowish fluid in animal bodies, of a rather saltish taste, and with an alkaline reaction: a vaccine.—*n.* **lymphangitis** (*-an-jī'tis*), inflammation of a lymphatic vessel.—*adj.* **lymphat'ic,** mad (*obs.*): pertaining to lymph: of a temperament or bodily habit once supposed to result from excess of lymph: disposed to sluggishness and flabbiness.—*n.* a vessel that conveys lymph. —*ns.* **lymphocyte** (*-ō-sīt*), a kind of leucocyte formed in the lymph-glands and spleen; **lymphō'ma,** a tumour consisting of lymphoid tissue. [L. *lympha*, water; *lymphāticus*, mad.]

**lymphad,** *lim'fad*, *n.* a Highland galley. [Gael. *longfhada*.]

**lynage** (*Spens.*). Same as **lineage.**

**lynch,** *linch*, *linsh*, *v.t.* to judge and put to death without the usual forms of law.—**lynch'-law.** [Captain William *Lynch* of Virginia.]

**lynchet.** See **linch.**

**lyne** (*Spens.*). Same as **line** (linen).

**lynx,** *lingks*, *n.* an animal (genus Lynx) of the cat family, high at the haunches, with short tail and tufted ears:—*pl.* **lynx'es.**—*adjs.* **lyncean** (*lin-sē'an*), lynx-like: sharp-sighted; **lynx'-eyed.** [L., —Gr. *lynx*, *lynkos*.]

**lyomerous,** *lī-om'ə-rəs*, *adj.* relating to the **Lyom'eri,** soft-bodied fishes. [Gr. *lyein*, to loosen, *meros*, part.]

**Lyon,** *lī'ən*, *n.* the chief herald of Scotland.— Also **Lord Lyon, Lyon King-of-arms** (or -at-arms).—**Lyon Court,** the court over which he presides, having jurisdiction in questions of coat-armour and precedency. [From the heraldic *lion* of Scotland.]

**lyophil, lyophile,** *lī'ō-fil*, *-fil*, **liophilic,** *-fil'ik*, *adjs.*

of a colloid, readily dispersed in a suitable medium.—*n.* **lyophilisā'tion,** -z-, freeze-drying.—*v.t.* **lyoph'ilise,** -ize, to dry by freezing.—*adjs.* **ly'o-phobe** (*-fōb*), **lyophobic** (*-fob'*), of a colloid, not readily dispersed. [Gr. *lȳē*, separation, *phileein*, to love, *phobeein*, to fear.]

**lyre,** *līr*, *n.* a musical instrument like the harp, anciently used as an accompaniment to poetry —a convex sound-chest with a pair of curved arms connected by a cross-bar, from which the strings were stretched over a bridge to a tail-piece.—*n.* **Ly'ra,** one of the northern constellations.—*adjs.* **ly'rate, -d,** lyre-shaped: having the terminal lobe much larger than the lateral ones (*bot.*).—*advs.* **ly'ra-way, ly'ra-wise,** according to lute tablature.—*adjs.* **lyric, -al,** (*lir'*), pertaining to the lyre: fitted to be sung to the lyre: of poetry, expressing individual emotions: song-like: that composes lyrics: effusive.—*ns.* **lyric** (*lir'*), a lyric poem: a song: (*pl.*) the words of a popular song: a composer of lyric poetry (*obs.*); **lyricism** (*lir'i-sizm*), a lyrical expression: lyrical quality; **lyr'ism** (*lir'*, *lir'*), lyricism: singing; **lyrist** (*līr'* or *lir'*), a player on the lyre or harp: (*lir'*) a lyric poet.—**ly'ra-vi'ol,** an obsolete instrument like a viola da gamba adapted for playing from lute tablature; **lyre'-bird,** an Australian passerine bird about the size of a pheasant, having the 16 tail-feathers of the male arranged in the form of a lyre. [L. *lyra*—Gr. *lyrā*.]

**Lysenkoism,** *li-sen'kō-izm*, *n.* the teaching of the Soviet geneticist T. D. *Lysenko* (born 1898) that acquired characters are inheritable.

**lysis,** *lī'sis*, *n.* the gradual abatement of a disease, as distinguished from *crisis*: breaking down as of a cell (*biol.*): the action of a lysin.—*v.t.* **lyse** (*līz*), to cause to undergo lysis.—*adjs.* **lysigenic** (*li-* or *li-sī-jen'ik*), **lysigenet'ic, lysigenous** (*-sij'i-nas*), caused by breaking down of cells.— *ns.* **lysim'eter,** an instrument for measuring percolation of water through the soil; **lysin** (*lī'sin*), a substance that causes breakdown of cells; **ly'sine** (*-sin*, *-sēn*), an amino-acid, a decomposition product of proteins; **ly'sol,** a solution of cresol in soap, a poisonous disinfectant (a trademark in some countries); **ly'sozyme** (*-zim*), a bacteriolytic enzyme present in some plants, animal secretions (e.g. tears), egg-white, etc.— **lysergic acid** (*li-sûr'jik*), a substance, $C_{16}H_{16}O_2N_2$, got from ergot, causing (in the form of lysergic acid diethylamide—LSD) a schizophrenic condition, with hallucinations and thought processes outside the normal range. [Gr. *lysis*, dissolution—*lyein*, to loose.]

**lyte.** Form of **light** (3).

**lythe** (*Spens.*). Form of **lithe.**

**lythe,** *lidh*, (*Scot.*) *n.* the pollack.

**Lythrum,** *lith'rəm*, *n.* the purple loosestrife genus, giving name to a family of archichlamydeous dicotyledons, **Lythrā'ceae,** commonly hexamerous, heterostyled, with epicalyx. [Latinised from Gr. *lythron*, gore, from the colour of its flowers.]

**lytta,** *lit'a*, *n.* a cartilaginous or fibrous band on the under surface of the tongue in carnivores— the worm of a dog's tongue. [Gr.]

*fāte, fär; mē, hûr* (her); *mīne; mōte, för; mūte; mōōn, fōōt; dhen* (then)

# M

**M, m,** *em, n.* the twelfth letter of the Roman, the thirteenth of our alphabet, representing a labial nasal consonant: an object or figure shaped like the letter: as a Roman numeral M = 1000; M̄ = 1,000,000; in chem. *m* = *meta-*, or *meso-*, and it is used as a symbol in chem. and other sciences, with a number of meanings.—**M′-roof,** a roof formed by the junction of two common roofs, so that its section is like the letter M. See also **em.**

**ma,** *mä, n.* a childish contraction for **mamma.**

**ma'am,** *mäm, mam, məm, n.* a colloquial contraction of **madam**—vulgarly **marm** (*mäm*), **mum.**

**Mab,** *mab, n.* the name of a female fairy, bringer of dreams: the queen of the fairies.

**Mabinogion,** *mab-i-nō′gi-on, n.* a title applied to four tales in the *Red Book of Hergest*, a Welsh MS. of the 14th century: extended to the whole collection in Lady Charlotte Guest's edition and translation in 1838. [W., juvenilities.]

**Mac,** *mak, mək,* a Gaelic prefix in names, meaning *son* (of). [Gael. and Ir. *mac*, son; W. *mab,* O.W. *map.*]

**macabre,** *ma-, mə-kä′br′, -bər, adj.* gruesome: like the Dance of Death.—*adj.* **macaberesque** (*-bər-esk′*). [Fr. *macabre*, formerly also *macabré,* app.—Heb. *meqaber,* grave-digger.]

**macadamise, -ize,** *mək-ad′əm-iz, v.t.* to cover with small broken stones, so as to form a smooth, hard surface.—*ns.* **macad′am,** macadamised road surface: material for macadamising; **macadamisā′tion, -izā′tion.** [From John Loudon *McAdam* (1756-1836).]

**macahuba.** See **macaw-tree.**

**macaque,** *mə-käk′, n.* a monkey of genus Macacus, to which belong the rhesus and the Barbary ape. [Fr.,—Port. *macaco,* a monkey.]

**macarise, -ize,** *mak′ə-riz, v.t.* to declare to be happy or blessed.—*n.* **mac′arism,** a beatitude. [Gr. *makar,* happy.]

**macaroni,** *mak-ə-rō′ni, n.* a paste of hard wheat flour pressed through perforations into long tubes, and dried: a medley: something fanciful and extravagant: in the 18th century, a dandy: a rock-hopper or crested penguin:—*pl.* **macarō′-ni(e)s.**—*adj.* **macaronic** (*-ron′ik*), in a kind of burlesque verse, intermixing modern words Latinised, or Latin words modernised, with genuine Latin—loosely, verse in mingled tongues. —*n.* (often in *pl.*) macaronic verse.—**macaroni cheese,** macaroni cooked with cheese. [It. *maccaroni* (now *maccheroni*), pl. of *maccarone,* prob.—*maccare,* to crush.]

**macaroon,** *mak-ə-rōōn′, n.* a sweet biscuit made of almonds. [Fr. *macaron*—It. *maccarone* (see above).]

**macassar-oil,** *mə-kas′ər-oil, n.* an oil once used for the hair, got from the seeds of a sapindaceous tree *Schleichera trijuga,* or from ylang-ylang flowers, or other Eastern source. [*Macassar* or Mangkasara in Celebes.]

**macaw,** *mə-kö′, n.* any of the large, long-tailed, showy tropical American parrots of the genus Ara. [Port. *macao.*]

**macaw-tree, -palm,** *mə-kö′-trē, -päm, ns.* a South American palm (Acrocomia) whose nuts yield a violet-scented oil.—Also **maco′ya, macahuba** (*mä-kä-ōō′ba*). [Sp. *macoya,* from Arawak; Port. *macauba,* from Tupi.]

**Maccabaean, Maccabean,** *mak-ə-bē′ən, adj.* pertaining to Judas *Maccabaeus,* or to his family the Hasmonaeans or *Macc′abees,* who freed the Jewish nation from the persecutions of Antiochus Epiphanes, king of Syria, about 166 B.C.—as related in two *Books of Maccabees* of the Apocrypha.

**McCarthyism,** *mə-kär′thi-izm, n.* the hunting down and removal from public employment of all suspected of Communism. [From Joseph *McCarthy* (1909-1957), U.S. politician.]

**macchie,** *mak′kyä, n.pl.* Italian form of **maquis** (in sense (1), i.e. thicket).

**mace,** *mäs, n.* a metal or metal-headed war-club, often spiked: a somewhat similar staff used as a mark of authority: a mace-bearer: a light, flat-headed stick formerly used in billiards: a mallet used by a currier in dressing leather.—*n.* **mac′er,** a mace-bearer: in Scotland, an usher in a law-court.—**mace′-bearer,** one who carries the mace in a procession, or before men in authority. [O.Fr. *mace* (Fr. *masse*)—hypothetical L. *matea,* whence L. dim. *mateola,* a kind of tool.]

**mace,** *mäs, n.* a spice which is ground from the dried layer immediately within a nutmeg drupe and outside shell and kernel.—**mace′-ale,** ale flavoured with mace. [M.E. *macis* (mistakenly supposed to be a plural)—Fr.; of uncertain origin.]

**macédoine,** *ma-sā-dwän′, -sə-, n.* a mixture, esp. of vegetables or fruit embedded in jelly: a medley. [Fr., lit. Macedonia.]

**maceranduba.** Same as **massaranduba.**

**macerate,** *mas′ər-āt, v.t.* to steep: to soften, or remove the soft parts of, by steeping: to wear down, esp. by fasting: to mortify.—*v.i.* to undergo maceration: to waste away.—*ns.* **macerā′-tion; mac′erātor,** one who macerates: a paper-pulping apparatus. [L. *mācerāre, -ātum,* to steep.]

**machair,** *ma′hhər, n.* a low-lying sandy beach or boggy links affording some pasturage. [Gael.]

**Machairodus,** *ma-kī′rə-dəs,* **Machaerodus,** *-kē′, n.* the sabre-toothed tiger of prehistoric times.—*n.* and *adj.* **machair′odont.** [Gr. *machaira,* a sword, *odous, odontos,* a tooth.]

**machan,** *ma-chän′, n.* a shooting-platform up a tree. [Hindi *macān.*]

**machete,** *ma-chā′tä, n.* a heavy knife or cutlass used by the Cubans, etc. [Sp.]

**Machiavellian,** *mak-i-ə-vel′yən, adj.* destitute of political morality, ruled by expediency only: crafty, perfidious in conduct, activity.—*n.* one who imitates Niccolo *Machiavelli,* statesman and writer, of Florence (1469-1527): any cunning and unprincipled statesman.—*ns.* **Machiavell′ianism, Machiavell′ism,** the principles taught by Machiavelli, or conduct regulated by them: cunning statesmanship.

**machicolation,** *ma-chik-ō-lā′shən, (archit.) n.* a space between the corbels supporting a parapet, or an opening in the floor of a projecting gallery, for dropping solids or liquids on an attacking enemy: a structure with such openings: the provision of such openings or structures.—*v.t.* **machic′olate,** to provide or build with machicolations.—*adj.* **machic′olated.** [Fr. *mâchicoulis.*]

**machinate,** *mak′i-nāt, mash′, v.i.* to form a plot or scheme esp. for doing harm.—*ns.* **machinā′tion,** act of machinating: an intrigue or plot; **mach′inātor,** one who machinates. [L. *māchinārī, -ātus*—*māchina*—Gr. *mēchanē,* contrivance.]

**machine,** *mə-shēn′, n.* any artificial means or

contrivance: any instrument for the conversion of motion: an engine: a vehicle (*obs.* or *Scot.*): one who can do only what he is told: a contrivance by which a god might descend upon the stage: a supernatural agent employed in carrying on the action of a poem: an organised system: a political party organisation (*U.S.*).—*v.t.* to use machinery for: to print, sew, or make by machinery.—*ns.* **machin´ery**, machines in general: the working parts of a machine: combined means for keeping anything in action, or for producing a desired result: supernatural agents in a poem: **machin´ist**, a constructor of machines: one well versed in machinery: one who works a machine.—**machine´-gun**, an automatic quick-firing gun on a stable but portable mounting.—*v.t.* to shoot at with a machine-gun; **machine´-gunner.**—*adj.* **machine´-made**, made by machinery.—**machine´man**, a man who manages the working of a machine; **machine´-rul´er**, an instrument for ruling lines on paper; **machine´ shop**, a workshop where metal, etc., is machined to shape; **machine´-tool**, a power-driven machine, as lathe, milling machine, drill, press, for shaping metal, wood, or plastic material; **machine´-work**, work done by a machine. [Fr., —L. *māchina*—Gr. *mēchanē*, akin to *mēchos*, contrivance.]

**Mach number**, *mähh, mahh, num´bər*, the ratio of the air speed (i.e. speed in relation to the air) of an aircraft to the velocity of sound under the given conditions.—*n.* **mach´meter**, an instrument for measuring Mach number. [Named after Ernst *Mach*, Austrian physicist and philosopher (1838-1916).]

**machtpolitik**, *mähht´pō-lē-tēk´*, (Ger.) power politics, esp. the doctrine that a state should use force to attain its ends.

**mackerel**, *mak´ər-əl*, *n.* a food fish (*Scomber*), bluish green, with wavy cross-streaks above, and silvery below: a bawd (*obs.*).—**mack´erel-breeze´**, a breeze that ruffles the surface of the sea and so favours mackerel fishing; **mack´erel-guide´**, the common garfish, which visits the coasts just before the mackerel; **mack´erel-midge´**, a small rockling; **mack´erel-shark´**, the porbeagle; **mack´erel-sky´**, a sky with clouds broken into long, thin, white, parallel masses. [O.Fr. *makerel* (Fr. *maquereau*).]

**mackinaw**, *mak´in-ö*, *n.* an American Indian's blanket: a short heavy woollen coat: a flat-bottomed lake-boat. [*Mackinaw*, an island between Lakes Huron and Michigan.]

**mac(k)intosh**, *mak´in-tosh*, *n.* waterproof cloth: a waterproof overcoat:—*contr.* **mac(k).** [From Charles *Macintosh* (1766-1843), a Scottish chemist, the patentee.]

**mackle**, *mak´l*, *n.* a spot or blemish in printing, by a double impression, wrinkling, etc.—*v.t.* to spot, blur. [See next.]

**macle**, *mak´l*, *n.* a dark spot in a crystal: chiastolite: a twin crystal.—*adj.* **macled** (*mak´ld*), spotted. [Fr. *macle*—L. *macula*, spot.]

**Macmillanite**, *mək-mil´ən-it*, *n.* a Cameronian or Reformed Presbyterian. [From Rev. John *Macmillan* (1670-1753), who helped to form the church.]

**McNaghten rules**, *mək-nö´tn*, (*Eng. law*) rules dating from Rex v. *McNaghten* (1843), under which mental abnormality relieves from criminal responsibility only if the person did not know what he was doing or did not know that what he was doing was wrong.

**Mâcon**, *mä-kɔ̃*, *n.* a burgundy from Mâcon district.

**maconochie**, *mə-kon´ə-hhi*, (*mil.*) *n.* tinned meat and vegetable stew: tinned food. [Packer's name.]

**macoya.** See macaw-tree.

**macramé, macrami**, *mə-krä´mi*, *n.* a fringe or

trimming of knotted thread: knotted thread-work. [App. Turk. *maqrama*, towel.]

**macro-**, *mak-rō-, -ro-*, in composition, long, great, sometimes interchanging with *mega-*.—*n.* **macro-axis** (*mak´rō-aks´is*; *crystal.*), the longer lateral axis.—*adj.* **macrō´bian** (Gr. *bios*, life), long-lived.—*n.pl.* **macrobiō´ta**, the larger organisms in the soil.—*n.* **macrobiote** (*-bi´ōt*), a long-liver.—*adj.* **macrobiotic** (*-bi-ot´ik*), prolonging life: long-lived: (of a seed) able to remain alive in dormant state for years: relating to longevity, or to macrobiotics.—*n.* (*pl.* in form) **macrobiot´ics**, the art or science of prolonging life: a cult partly concerned with diet, foods regarded as pure being vegetable substances grown and prepared without chemicals or processing.—*adjs.* **macrocephalic** (*-si-fal´ik*), **macrocephalous** (*-sef´ə-ləs*).—*ns.* **macrocephaly** (*-sef´ə-li*; Gr. *kephalē*, head), largeness, or abnormal largeness, of head; **mac´rocopy**, an enlarged copy of printed material for use by people with weak sight; **mac´rocosm** (*-kozm*; Gr. *kosmos*, world), the great world: the whole universe—opp. to *microcosm*.—*adj.* **macrocos´mic.**—*n.* **mac´rocyte** (*-sit*; Gr. *kytos*, a vessel), a large uninuclear leucocyte with great powers of mobility and phagocytosis.—*adjs.* **macrodactyl** (*-dak´til*), **macrodactylic** (*-til´ik*), **macrodactylous** (*-dak´til-əs*; Gr. *daktylos*, finger, toe), long-fingered, long-toed.—*ns.* **macrodac´tyly**, condition of being macrodactylous; **macrodiag´onal** (*crystal.*), the longer lateral axis; **mac´rodome**, **macropin´akoid**, **mac´roprism**, a dome, pinakoid, prism, parallel to the macrodiagonal; **macrogamete´** (or *-gam´ēt*), a female gamete; **macrol´ogy**, much talk with little to say; **macromol´ecule**, a large molecule, esp. one formed from a number of simpler molecules; **mac´ron** (U.S. *mä´*; Gr., *makros*), a straight line placed over a vowel to show it is long (as in *ē*)—opp. to *breve*, the mark of a short vowel (*ĕ*).—*adjs.* **macrop´terous** (Gr. *pteron*, a wing), long-winged: long-finned; **macroscop´ic**, visible to the naked eye—opp. to *microscopic.*—*adv.* **macroscop´ically.**—*ns.* **macrosporan´gium**, **mac´rospore** (same as megasporangium, -spore).—*n.pl.* **Macrura** (*mak-rōō´ra*; Gr. *ourā*, tail), a group of decapod crustaceans including lobsters, shrimps, prawns, etc.—*adjs.* **macru´ral**, **macru´rous**, long-tailed. [Gr. *makros*, long, also great.]

**mactation**, *mak-tā´shən*, *n.* slaying, esp. of a sacrificial victim. [L. *mactātiō, -ōnis.*]

**macula**, *mak´ū-la*, *n.* a spot, as on the skin, the sun, a mineral, etc.:—*pl.* **maculae** (*-lē*).—*v.t.* **mac´ulate**, to spot, to defile.—*adj.* spotted: soiled.—*ns.* **macula´tion**, act of spotting, a spot; **mac´ulāture**, an impression taken from an engraved plate to remove the ink before inking afresh; **mac´ule**, a macula: a mackle.—*adj.* **mac´ulose**, spotted. [L. *macula*, a spot.]

**mad**, *mad*, *adj.* (*comp.* **madd´er**; *superl.* **madd´est**) disordered in intellect: insane: proceeding from madness: extremely and recklessly foolish: infatuated: frantic with pain, violent passion, or appetite: furious with anger (*coll.*, orig. *U.S.*): extravagantly playful or exuberant: rabid.—*v.t.* (*Shak.*) to drive mad.—*v.i.* (*arch.*) to be mad: to act madly.—*v.t.* **madd´en**, to make mad: to enrage.—*v.i.* to become mad: to act as one mad.—*adj.* **madd´ening**, driving to madness: making very angry: extremely annoying.—*adv.* **madd´eningly.**—*adj.* **madd´ing**, distracted, acting madly.—*advs.* **madd´ingly**, **mad´ly.**—*ns.* **mad´ling**, a mad person; **mad´man.**—*adjs.* **mad´brain**, **mad´-brained** (*Shak.*), disordered in brain or mind: rash: hot-headed; **mad´-bred** (*Shak.*), bred in madness or heat of passion.—**mad´cap**, a person who acts madly: a wild, rash, hot-headed person: an exuberantly frolicsome person.—*adj.* fond of wild and reckless or extravagantly merry action.—**mad'-doc'tor**, formerly, one who studied and treated diseases of mad people; **mad'house**, formerly, a house for mad persons, an asylum: a place where there is noise, confusion, and unpredictable behaviour; **mad'man**, a man who is mad: a foolish and reckless man; **mad'wort**, a plant believed to cure canine madness—Alyssum, Asperugo, etc.—**go mad**, to become demented; **like mad**, madly, furiously. [O.E. *gemǣd(e)d*; O.Sax. *giméd*, foolish.]

**madam**, *mad'əm, n.* a courteous form of address to a lady, esp. an elderly or a married one: word of address to a woman in a formal letter: a woman of rank, station, or pretension: the mistress of a household (*arch.*): a formidable woman: a general term of opprobrium for a woman: a concubine (*obs.*): the woman in charge of a brothel: prefixed to a name instead of Mrs or Miss in U.S. to distinguish mother-in-law from daughter-in-law (*obs.*):—*pl.* **mad'-ams**; in sense (2) above, **mesdames**, *mā-däm'.*—*v.t.* to address as madam.—*n.* **madame** (*ma-däm', mad'əm;* usu. *cap.*), prefixed instead of Mrs to a French or other foreign woman's name: used also of palmists, milliners, and musicians:—*pl.* **mesdames.** [Fr. *ma*, my, *dame*, lady—L. *mea domina.*]

**mad-apple**, *mad'-ap-l, n.* the fruit of the eggplant: the Dead Sea apple: a gall produced by a gall-wasp (*Cynips insana*) on an oak in the East. [From some form of mod. L. *melongēna*, It. *melanzana*; *mālum insānum*, transl. as mad apple.]

**madarosis**, *mad-ə-rō'sis, n.* loss of hair, esp. of the eyebrows or eyelashes. [Gr. *madarōsis—madaros*, bald, *madaein*, to fall off.]

**madder**, *mad'ər, n.* a plant (*Rubia tinctorum*) whose root affords a red dye, or other species of Rubia.—**madd'er-lake**, a colour mixed either with oil or water, made from madder.—**field madder**, a minute lilac-flowered plant (*Sherardia arvensis*) of the same family. [O.E. *mæddre, mædere*; O.N. *mathra*, Du. *mede*, later *meed, mee.*]

**made**, *mād, pa.t.* and *pa.p.* of make, and *adj.*—**made dish**, a dish of various ingredients, often recooked; **made ground**, ground formed by artificial filling in; **made man**, one whose prosperity is assured; **made road**, one with deliberately made surface, not merely formed by traffic: a road with a metalled surface as opposed to a gravel surface.—**made to measure, order,** made to individual requirements; **made up**, put together, finished: parcelled up: dressed for a part, disguised: painted and powdered: meretricious: artificial, invented: consummate (*Shak.*).

**madefy**, *mad'i-fī, v.t.* to moisten.—*n.* **madefac'-tion.** [L. *madefacĕre, -factum—madēre*, to be wet.]

**Madeira**, *mə-dē'ra, ma-dā'ra, n.* a rich wine of the sherry class produced in *Madeira*.—**Madei'racake**, a variety of sponge-cake.

**madeleine**, *mad-len*, (Fr.) a small, shell-shaped rich cake.

**Madelenian.** Same as Magdalenian.

**mademoiselle**, *mad-mwə-zel', n.* a form of address to an unmarried French or other foreign woman: (with capital) prefixed to a name, Miss (*pl.* **Mesdemoiselles**, *mād-*): a French governess. [Fr. *ma*, my, and *demoiselle*; see damsel.]

**madge**, *maj, n.* a leaden hammer. [Woman's name.]

**madge**, *maj, n.* the barn owl: the magpie. [App. from the woman's name.]

**madid**, *mad'id, adj.* wet, dank. [L. *madidus—madēre*, to be wet; akin to Gr. *madaein*.]

**Madonna**, *mə-don'a, n.* my lady (*Shak.*): the Virgin Mary, esp. as seen in works of art.—*adj.* **madonn'aish.**—*adv.* **madonn'awise**, after the fashion of the Madonna, esp. in the arrangement of a woman's hair.—**Madonn'a-lil'y**, the white lily. [It., lit. my lady—L. *mea domina.*]

**madoqua**, *mad'ō-kwa, n.* a very small Abyssinian antelope. [Amharic *midaqua.*]

**madras**, *mə-dräs', n.* a large, usu. bright, handkerchief worn on the head by Negroes, formerly exported from *Madras*: a fine cotton fabric: sunn.

**madrasa, madrasah, madrassah, medresseh,** *madras'a, mə-dres'ə, n.* a Mohammedan college: a mosque school. [Ar. *madrasah*.]

**madrepore**, *mad'ri-pōr, -pör, n.* a coral of the common reef-building type.—*adj.* **madreporic** (*-por'ik*).—*n.* **mad'reporite**, or **madreporic plate**, in echinoderms, a perforated plate serving as opening to the stone canal. [It. *madrepora—madre*, mother—L. *māter*, and Gr. *pōros*, a soft stone, stalactite, etc., or L. *porus*, a pore.]

**madrigal**, *mad'ri-gəl, n.* an unaccompanied song in several parts in counterpoint (*mus.*): a lyrical poem suitable for such treatment.—*adj.* **madrigā'lian.**—*n.* **mad'rigalist.** [It. *madrigale*, perh. from *mandr(i)a*, a cattle-shed—Gr. *mandrā.*]

**madroño**, *ma-drō'nyō, n.* a handsome evergreen Arbutus tree of North California.—Also **madrō'ña.** [Sp. *madroño.*]

**Maecenas**, *mē-sē'nas, n.* a Roman knight who befriended Virgil and Horace: any rich patron of art or literature. [L. *Maecēnās, -ātis.*]

**maelstrom**, *māl'strom, n.* a fabled whirlpool off the coast of Norway (also *cap.*): a confused, disordered state of affairs: any resistless overpowering influence for destruction. [Du. (now *maalstroom*), a whirlpool.]

**maenad**, *mē'nad, n.* a female follower of Bacchus: a woman beside herself with frenzy.—*adj.* **maenad'ic**, bacchanalian: furious. [Gr. *mainas, -ados*, raving—*mainesthai*, to be mad.]

**Maeonian**, *mē-ō'ni-ən, adj.* and *n.* Lydian.—*n.* **Maeonides** (*mē-on'i-dēz*), Homer, as a supposed native of Lydia. [Gr. *Maiōnia*, an old name for Lydia.]

**maestoso**, *mä-es-tō'sō, mī-stō'sō, (mus.) adj.* and *adv.* with dignity or majesty. [It.]

**maestro**, *mä-es'trō, mī'strō, n.* a master, esp. an eminent musical composer or conductor. [It.]

**Mae West**, *mā-west', n.* an airman's pneumatic life-jacket. [From a supposed resemblance, when inflated, to an American actress of that name.]

**maffick**, *maf'ik, v.i.* to rejoice with hysterical boisterousness.—*ns.* **maff'icker, maff'icking.** [By back-formation from *Mafeking*, treated jocularly as a gerund or participle, from the scenes in the streets of London on the news of the relief of the town (1900).]

**maffled**, *maf'ld, (coll.) adj.* confused in the intellect.—*n.* **maff'lin(g)**, a simpleton.

**Mafia, Maffia**, *mä'fē-a, n.* a spirit of opposition to the law in Sicily, hence a preference for private and unofficial rather than legal justice: a secret criminal society originating in Sicily, controlling many illegal activities, e.g., gambling, narcotics, etc., in many parts of the world, and particularly active in the U.S.—Also called **Cosa Nostra.** [Sicilian Italian *mafia*.]

**ma foi**, *ma fwa*, (Fr.) my goodness (*lit.* upon my faith).

**mag**, *mag*, (*arch. slang*) *n.* a halfpenny.—Also **maik, make** (*māk*).

**mag**, *mag*, (*dial.*) *v.i.* to chatter.—*v.t.* to tease: (*Scott* magg) to steal.—*n.* chatter: the magpie: the long-tailed titmouse.—*n.pl.* **mag(g)s** (*Scot.*; perh. mag (1)), a gratuity: the free allowance granted to some workers, esp. drinks for brewery employees.—**mags'man**, a street swindler. [From the name *Margaret*.]

**mag**, abbrev. of **magazine** (periodical publication).

**magazine**, *mag-ə-zēn', also mag', n.* a storehouse:

a place for military stores: a ship's powder-room: a compartment in a rifle for holding extra cartridges: a periodical publication or broadcast containing articles, stories, etc., by various people.—magazine'-gun, -rifle, one from which a succession of shots can be fired without reloading. [Fr. *magasin*—It. *magazzino* —Ar. *makhāzin*, pl. of *makhzan*, a store-house.]

**Magdalen, Magdalene,** *mag'də-lən, -lēn* (in the names of Oxford and Cambridge colleges, *möd'lin*) *n.* (without *cap.*) a repentant prostitute: an institution for receiving such persons (abbrev. for *Magdalene hospital, asylum*). [From Mary *Magdelene*, i.e. (Gr.) *Magdalēnē*, of Magdala (Luke viii. 2), on the assumption that she was the woman of Luke vii. 37-50.]

**Magdalenian, Madelenian,** *ma(g)d-ə-lē'ni-ən, adj.* belonging to an upper Palaeolithic culture that succeeded the Solutrean and preceded the Azilian. [La *Madeleine*, a cave on the Vézère.]

**Magdeburg hemispheres,** *mag'de-bûrg hem'i-sfērz,* two hemispherical cups held together by atmospheric pressure when the air is pumped out from between them. [Invented at *Magdeburg* in Germany.]

**mage,** *māj.* See **Magus.**

**Magellanic clouds,** *mag-el-an'ik,* or *maj-,* two galaxies in the southern hemisphere, appearing to the naked eye like detached portions of the Milky Way, the nearest galaxies to the earth.

**magenta,** *mə-jen'ta, n.* the dyestuff fuchsin: its colour, a reddish purple.—*adj.* reddish purple. [From its discovery about the time of the battle of *Magenta* in North Italy, 1859.]

**magg.** See **mag** (2).

**maggot,** *mag'ət, n.* a legless grub, esp. of a fly: a fad or crotchet: a whimsical tune or impromptu (*obs.*).—*adj.* **magg'oty,** full of maggots: crotchety: very drunk (*slang*).—*n.* **maggotorium** (-*tō', -tō'*), a place where maggots are bred for sale to fishermen. [Poss. a modification of M.E. *maddok, mathek,* dim., see **mawk.**]

**maggs.** See **mag** (2).

**Magi, Magian.** See **Magus.**

**magic,** *maj'ik, n.* the art of producing marvellous results by compelling the aid of spirits, or by using the secret forces of nature, such as the power supposed to reside in certain objects as 'givers of life': enchantment: sorcery: art of producing illusions by legerdemain: a secret or mysterious power over the imagination or will.—*v.t.* to affect by, or as if by, magic.— *adjs.* **mag'ic, -al,** pertaining to, used in, or done by, magic: causing wonderful or startling results.—*adv.* **mag'ically.**—*n.* **magician** (*mə-jish'ən*), one skilled in magic: a wizard: an enchanter: a wonder-worker.—**magic eye,** a miniature cathode ray tube in a radio receiver which helps in tuning the receiver by indicating, by means of varying areas of luminescence and shadow, the accuracy of the tuning; **magic lantern,** an apparatus for projecting pictures on slides upon a screen; **magic square,** a square filled with rows of figures so arranged that the sums of all the rows will be the same, perpendicularly or horizontally—as the square formed from the three rows 2, 7, 6; 9, 5, 1; 4, 3, 8; **magic circles, cubes, cylinders, spheres,** are similarly arranged.—**black magic,** the black art, magic by means of evil spirits; **natural magic,** the art of working wonders by a superior knowledge of the powers of nature: power of investing a work of art with an atmosphere of imagination: legerdemain; **sympathetic magic,** magic aiming at the production of effects by mimicry, as bringing rain by libations, injuring a person by melting his image or sticking pins in it; **white magic,** magic without the aid of the devil. [Gr. *magikē (technē),* magic (art). See **Magus.**]

**magilp, megilp,** *mə-gilp', n.* a vehicle used by oil-painters, consisting of linseed-oil and mastic varnish. [Origin unknown.]

**Maginot-minded,** *mä'zhē-nō-mind'id, adj.* over-concerned with the defensive (*mil.*): static in ideas. [From the abortive French Maginot Line fortifications (1927-35) along the German border (war minister André *Maginot;* 1877-1932).]

**magister,** *mə-jis'tər, n.* one licensed to teach in a mediaeval university: still used in the degree titles of *Magister Artium,* etc.—*adj.* **magisterial** (*maj-is-tē'ri-əl*), pertaining or suitable to, or in the manner of, a teacher, master artist, or magistrate: of the rank of a magistrate: authoritative: dictatorial: of a magistery.—*adv.* **magis-tē'rially.**—*ns.* **magistē'rialness; magistē'rium,** the philosopher's stone: teaching authority or function; **magistery** (*maj'is-tə-ri*), in alchemy, a transmuting agent, as the philosopher's stone: a product of transmutation: a precipitate: any sovereign remedy: magisterium; **mag'istracy** (-*trə-si*), the office or dignity of a magistrate: a body of magistrates.—*adj.* **magistral** (*mə-jis'trəl,* or *maj'is-*), of or pertaining to a master: masterly: authoritative: specially prescribed for a particular case as a medicine: effectual: guiding or determining the other positions (*fort.*).—Also *n.*—*ns.* **magistrand** (*maj'*), at Scottish universities, an arts student ready to proceed to graduation, now only at St Andrews and Aberdeen; **mag'istrate,** one who has power of putting the law in force, esp. a justice of the peace, a provost, or a bailie, or one who sits in a police court.— *adjs.* **magistratic** (-*trat'ik*), **-al.**—*n.* **mag'istrature.** —**Magister Artium,** *mə-jis'tər är'shi-əm,* Master of Arts. [L. *magister,* master.]

**Maglemosian,** *mag-li-mō'zi-ən,* (*archaeol.*) *adj.* of a culture represented by finds at *Maglemose* in Denmark, transitional between Palaeolithic and Neolithic.

**magma,** *mag'ma, n.* a pasty or doughy mass: molten or pasty rock material: a glassy base of a rock:—*pl.* **mag'mata** (-*mə-ta*), **mag'mas.**—*adj.* **magmatic** (-*mat'ik*). [Gr. *magma, -atos,* a thick unguent.]

**Magna Carta (Charta),** *mag'nə kär'tə,* the Great Charter obtained from King John, 1215, the basis of English political and personal liberty: any document establishing rights. [L.]

**magnalium,** *mag-nā'li-əm, n.* a light, strong, easily-worked, and rust-resisting alloy of *magne-*sium and *alumin*ium used in aircraft construction, etc.

**magnanimity,** *mag-nə-nim'i-ti, n.* greatness of soul: that quality of mind which raises a person above all that is mean or unjust: generosity.— *adj.* **magnanimous** (-*nan'*).—*adv.* **magnan'imously.** [L. *magnanimitās*—*magnus,* great, *animus,* mind.]

**magnate,** *mag'nāt, -nit, n.* a noble: a man of rank or wealth, or of power. [L. *magnās, -ātis*— *magnus,* great.]

**magnes,** *mag'nēz,* (*arch.*) *n.* lodestone.—*n.* **mag'-nesstone** (*Spens.*). [L. and Gr. *magnēs.*]

**magnesium,** *mag-nē'z*(h)*i-əm, -z*(h)*yəm, -shi-em, -shyəm, n.* manganese (*obs.*): a metallic element (Mg; at. numb. 12) of a bright, silver-white colour, burning with a dazzling white light.—*n.* **magnē'sia,** an imagined substance sought by the alchemists (*obs.*): manganese (*obs.*): a light white powder, oxide of magnesium: basic magnesium carbonate, used as a medicine.—*adj.* **magnē'sian,** belonging to, containing, or resembling magnesia.—*n.* **magnesite** (*mag'nəs-it*), native magnesium carbonate.—**Magnesian Limestone,** dolomite rock: a division of the Permian of England. [See **magnet.**]

**magnet,** *mag'nit, n.* the lodestone (**natural magnet**): a bar or piece of steel, etc., to which the properties of the lodestone have been imparted: anything or anyone that attracts (*fig.*).—*adjs.*

magnetic (*mag-net'ik*), **-al**, pertaining to the magnet: having, or capable of acquiring, the properties of the magnet: attractive: strongly affecting others by personality: hypnotic.—*adv.* magnet'ically.—*n.* magnetician (*-ish'ən*), one versed in magnetism.—*n.pl.* (or *sing.*) magnet'ics, the science of magnetism.—*adj.* magnetis'able, -iz'able.—*n.* magnetisā'tion, -izā'tion.—*v.t.* mag'-netise, -ize, to render magnetic: to attract as if by a magnet: to hypnotise.—*ns.* mag'netiser, -z-; mag'netism, the cause of the attractive power of the magnet: the phenomena connected with magnets: the science which treats of the properties of the magnet: attraction: influence of personality: mag'netist, one skilled in magnetism; mag'netite, magnetic iron ore ($Fe_3O_4$), called lodestone when polar; magneto (*mag-nē'tō*; for *magneto-electric machine*), a small generator with permanent magnet, used for ignition in an internal-combustion engine, etc.—magneto-, in composition, magnetic: pertaining to magnetism: magneto-electric.—*adjs.* magnē'to-elec'tric, -al, pertaining to magneto-electricity.—*ns.* magnē'to-electric'ity, electricity produced by the action of magnets: the science thereof; magnē'tograph, an instrument for recording the variations of the magnetic elements; magnē'to-hydrodynam'ics, a branch of mathematical physics dealing with interactions between an electrically-conducting fluid (such as an ionised gas) and a magnetic field: the practical application of such interactions to producing **magneto-hydrodynamic** power by means of a **magneto-hydrodynamic generator**; magnetometer (*mag-ni-tom'i-tər*), an instrument for measuring the strength of a magnetic field, esp. the earth's.—*adj.* magnētomō'tive, producing a magnetic flux.—*ns.* magnē'ton (or *mag'ni-ton*), a natural unit of magnetic moment; magnēto-op'tics, study of the influence of magnetism on light; magnet'osphere, the region surrounding the earth corresponding to the earth's magnetic field; magnēto-stric'tion (or *-net-*), the change in dimensions produced in a magnetic material, esp. nickel, when it is magnetised; mag'netron, a vacuum tube combined with a magnetic field to deflect electrons.—animal magnetism, Mesmer's name for hypnotism: power to hypnotise: sexual power of attraction due entirely to physical attributes; artificial magnet, a magnet made by rubbing with other magnets; bar magnet, a magnet in the form of a bar; horse-shoe magnet, a magnet bent like a horse-shoe; magnetic battery, several magnets placed with their like poles together, so as to act with great force; magnetic bottle, the containment of a plasma during thermonuclear experiments by applying a specific pattern of magnetic fields; magnetic curves, the curves formed by iron-filings around the poles of a magnet; magnetic equator, the line round the earth where the magnetic needle remains horizontal; magnetic field, the space over which magnetic force is felt; magnetic fluid, a hypothetical fluid formerly assumed to explain the phenomena of magnetism; magnetic flux, the surface integral of the product of the permeability of the medium and the magnetic field intensity perpendicular to the surface; magnetic flux density, the product of the field intensity and the permeability of the medium; magnetic forming, use of magnetic fields to shape metal; magnetic induction, induced magnetisation in magnetic material: magnetic flux density; magnetic ink, ink with magnetic quality used, e.g. in printing cheques that are to be sorted by machine; magnetic meridian, the vertical plane through the magnetic needle; magnetic mine, a mine sunk to the sea-bottom, detonated by a pivoted magnetic needle when a ship approaches; magnetic needle, the

light bar in the mariner's compass which, because it is magnetised, points always to the north; magnetic north, the direction indicated by the magnetic needle; magnetic poles, two nearly opposite points on the earth's surface, where the dip of the needle is 90°; magnetic storm, a disturbance in the magnetism of the earth; magnetic tape, flexible plastic tape, coated on one side with magnetic material, used to register for later reproduction television images, or sound, or computer data; permanent magnet, a magnet that keeps its magnetism after the force which magnetised it has been removed; personal magnetism, power of a personality to make itself felt and to exercise influence; terrestrial magnetism, the magnetic properties possessed by the earth as a whole. [Through O.Fr. or L., from Gr. *magnētis* (*lithos*), Magnesian (*stone*), from *Magnēsiā*, in Lydia or Thessaly.]

magnific, *mag-nif'ik*, magnifical, *-əl*, *adjs.* magnificent: exalted: pompous.—*adv.* magnif'ically.—*n.* magnifico (It. *adj.*), a Venetian noble: a grandee. [L. *magnificus*; cf. magnify.]

Magnificat, *mag-nif'i-kat*, *n.* the song of the Virgin Mary, Luke i. 46-55, beginning in the Vulgate with this word. [L. '(my soul) doth magnify', 3rd pers. sing. pres. ind. of *magnificāre*.]

magnificence, *mag-nif'i-səns*, *n.* well-judged liberality (*arch.*): the quality of being magnificent.—*adj.* magnif'icent, great in deeds or in show: noble· pompous: displaying greatness of size or extent: very fine (*coll.*).—*adv.* magnif'icently. [L. *magnificēns*, *-entis*, lit. doing great things.]

magnify, *mag'ni-fī*, *v.t.* to make great or greater: to enlarge: to cause to appear greater: to exaggerate: to praise highly.—*v.i.* to signify (*old slang*):—*pr.p.* mag'nifying; *pa.t.* and *pa.p.* mag'nified.—*adj.* mag'nifiable, that may be magnified.—*ns.* magnification (*-fi-kā'shon*), act or power of magnifying: state of being magnified: enlarged appearance or state or copy: extolling; mag'nifier (*-fī-ər*), one who, or that which, magnifies or enlarges, esp. a pocket-lens (magnifying glass): one who extols. [L. *magnificāre*—*magnus*, great, *facĕre*, to make.]

magniloquent, *mag-nil'ə-kwənt*, *adj.* speaking in a grand or pompous style: bombastic.—*n.* magnil'oquence.—*adv.* magnil'oquently. [L. *magnus*, great, *loquēns*, *-entis*, pr.p. of *loquī*, to speak.]

magnitude, *mag'ni-tūd*, *n.* greatness: size: extent: importance: brightness, according to a scale in which the brightest stars are of the first magnitude (*astron.*).—absolute magnitude (see absolute). [L. *magnitūdō*—*magnus*.]

Magnolia, *mag-nōl'i-a*, or *-ya*, *n.* an American and Asiatic genus of trees with beautiful foliage, and large solitary flowers, giving name to the family Magnoliā'ceae, with petaloid perianth and spirally arranged stamens and carpels.—*adj.* magnoliā'ceous. [From Pierre *Magnol* (1638-1715), a Montpellier botanist.]

magnum, *mag'nəm*, *n.* a two-quart bottle or vessel: two quarts of liquor:—*pl.* mag'nums.—*n.* mag'num bōn'um, a large good variety, esp. of plums or potatoes:—*pl.* mag'num bōn'ums. [L. *magnum* (neut.), big, *bōnum* (neut.), good.]

magnum opus, *mag'nəm ōp'əs*, *mag'nōōm op'ōōs*, (L.) a great work, esp. of literature or learning, esp. a person's greatest achievement.

Magog. See Gog and Magog.

magot, *mag'ət*, *mä-gō'*, *n.* the Barbary ape, a macaque, the only European monkey: a small grotesque figure, in Chinese or Japanese workmanship. [Fr.]

magpie, *mag'pī*, *n.* the pie (*Pica rustica*), a black-and-white chattering bird allied to the crow: extended to other black-and-white or pied birds (in Australia a piping crow): a chattering person: an Anglican bishop (*obs.*): a hit on the penultimate outermost division of a target: one

Neutral vowels in unaccented syllables: *el'ə-mənt*; for certain sounds in foreign words, see p. viii

who hoards or steals trifles (*fig.*): a halfpenny (*obs. slang*).—(*Shak.*) mag'ot-pie, magg'ot-pie.— **magpie moth**, the moth of the gooseberry caterpillar. [*Mag*, *Magot*, shortened forms of *Margaret*, and pie (1).]

**magsman.** See mag (2).

**maguey,** *mag'wä*, *mä-gä'i*, *n.* agave. [Sp.]

**Magus,** *mä'gəs*, *n.* ancient Persian priest or member of a priestly class: an Eastern magician: (without *cap.*) a magician: a Wise Man of the East:—*pl.* **Ma'gi** (-*ji*).—*ns.* **mage** (*mäj*), a magus or sorcerer; **mage'ship.**—*adj.* **Ma'gian,** pertaining to the Magi or to a sorcerer.—*n.* a magus: a sorcerer.—*ns.* **Ma'gianism, Ma'gism,** philosophy or teaching of the Magi. [L.,—Gr. *magos*—O.Pers. *magus.*]

**Magyar,** *mag'yär*, *mod'yor*, *n.* one of the prevailing people of Hungary: the Finno-Ugric speech of Hungary.—*adj.* (without *cap.*) of a garment, cut with the sleeves in a piece with the rest.—*v.t.* and *v.i.* **Mag'yarise, -ize,** to make or become Magyar.—*n.* **Mag'yarism,** Hungarian national spirit. [Magyar.]

**Mahabharata,** *mu-hä-bä'ru-tu*, *n.* one of the great epics of ancient India. [Sans.]

**Mahadeva,** *mu-hä-dä'vu*, *n.* Siva. [Sans. *mahat*, great, *deva*, god.]

**maharaja, maharajah,** *mä-hä-rä'jä*, *mu-hä-rä'ju*, *n.* a great Indian prince:—*fem.* **maharani, maharanee** (-*rä'nē*). [Hind., from Sans. *mahat*, great, *räjan*, king, *räni*, queen.]

**mahatma,** *mə-hät'mä*, *-hat'*, *n.* one skilled in mysteries or religious secrets: an adept: a wise and holy leader. [Sans. *mahätman*, high-souled.]

**Mahdi,** *mä'dē*, *n.* the great leader of the faithful Mohammedans, who is to appear in the last days: a title of various insurrectionary leaders, esp. one who overthrew the Egyptian power in the Sudan in 1884-85.—*ns.* **Mah'diism, Mah'dism; Mah'diist, Mah'dist.** [Ar. *mahdiy.*]

**mah-jongg,** *mä-jong'*, *n.* an old Chinese table game for four, played with small painted bricks or 'tiles'. Also **mah-jong.** [Chin.]

**mahlstick.** See **maulstick.**

**mahmal,** *mä'mäl*, *n.* the empty litter sent to Mecca in the hadj.

**mahogany,** *mə-hog'ə-ni*, *n.* a tropical American tree (*Swietenia mahogoni*) of the Meliaceae: its timber, valued for furniture-making: the colour of the timber, a dark reddish brown: a dining-table (*coll.*): gin and treacle (*obs. slang* or *dial.*): brandy and water (*obs. slang*).—Also *adj.* [Origin unknown.]

**Mahommedan, Mahometan.** See **Mohammedan.**

**Mahonia,** *mə-hō'ni-a*, *n.* a pinnate-leaved genus (or section of *Berberis*) of the barberry family. [Named after Bernard *McMahon*, Irish-American gardener and botanist (*d.* 1816).]

**Mahoun, Mahound,** *mə-hown(d)'*, *-hōōn(d)'*, or *mä'*, *n. Mohammed*, imagined in the Middle Ages to be a pagan god (*arch.*): the devil (*Scot. mə-hōōn'*).

**mahout,** *mä-howt'*, *n.* the keeper and driver of an elephant. [Hind. *mahäut, mahäwat.*]

**Mahratta.** See **Maratha.**

**mahseer, mahsir,** *mä'sēr*, *n.* a large fish found in the rivers of Northern India. [Hind. *mahäsir.*]

**mahwa, mahua,** *mä'(h)wä*, *n.* a kind of butter-tree (*Bassia*, or *Illipe, latifolia*) with edible flowers.— **mahwa butter,** a fat got from its seeds.—Also **mowa, mowra.** [Hindi *mahūä.*]

**maid,** *mäd*, *n.* an unmarried woman, esp. one who is young: a virgin: a female servant: a young skate.—*v.i.* to work as a maid-servant.—*n.* **maid'hood.**—*adjs.* **maid'ish; maid'less,** without a maid.—*adj.* **maid'-pale** (*Shak.*), pale, like a sick girl.—**maid'-child** (*B., Shak.*), a female child; **maid'-servant,** a female servant.—**maid of all work,** a maid who does general housework; **maid of honour** (see **honour**); **old maid,** a woman

left unmarried: a card game. [Shortened from **maiden.**]

**maidan,** *mī-dän'*, *n.* an open plain: an open space, an esplanade or parade-ground near a town, in Persia and India. [Pers. *maidän.*]

**maiden,** *mäd'n*, *n.* a maid: a corn-maiden (*Scot.*): washing dolly: clothes-horse: Scottish beheading machine (*hist.*).—*adj.* unmarried: virgin: female: pertaining to a virgin or young woman: consisting of maidens: unpolluted (*fig.*): fresh: new: unused: in the original or initial state: grown from a seed: that has never been captured, climbed, trodden, penetrated, pruned, etc.: that has never won a race (of a horse): first.—*ns.* **maid'enhead** (pron. *-hed*; M.E. suff. *-hēd*(*e*), *-hood*), virginity: the first assay, experience, or use of anything (*obs.*): the hymen; **maid'enhood,** the state or time of being a maiden: maidenhead. —*adjs.* **maid'enish** (*depreciatorily*), like a maiden; **maid'enlike.**—Also *adv.*—*n.* **maid'enliness.**— *adj.* **maid'enly,** maidenlike: becoming a maiden: gentle: modest.—Also *adv.*—**maiden assize,** an assize at which there are no criminal cases; **maiden battle,** a first contest; **maiden castle,** a common name for a prehistoric earthwork (term prob. orig. having some other meaning): a castle never taken; **maiden fortress,** a fortress that has never been captured; **maid'enhair,** a fern (*Adiantum*), with fine footstalks: extended to species of spleenwort (**maid'enhair-spleenwort**); **maid'enhair-tree,** the ginkgo.—*adj.* **maid'en-meek,** meek as a maiden.—**maiden name,** the family name of a married woman before her marriage; **maiden over,** in cricket, an over in which no runs are made; **maiden pink,** a wild species of pink, *Dianthus deltoides*; **maiden speech,** one's first speech, esp. in Parliament; **maiden stakes,** in horse-racing, the prize in a race between horses that have not won before the date of entry.—*adj.* **maid'en-tongued,** gentle in voice like a girl.—**maiden voyage,** a first voyage; **maid'enweed,** mayweed.—*adj.* **maid'en-wid'owed,** widowed while still a virgin. [O.E. *mægden.*]

**maidism,** *mä'id-izm*, *n.* pellagra (attributed to a maize diet). [maize.]

**maieutic,** *mī-* or *mä-ūt'ik*, *adj.* helping birth, esp. of thoughts.—*n.* (treated as *sing.*) **maieut'ics,** the Socratic art. [Gr. *maieutikos—maia*, good woman, a midwife; Socrates, son of a midwife, called himself a midwife to men's thoughts.]

**maigre,** *mä'gər*, *meg'r'*, *adj.* made without flesh: belonging to a fast-day or to a fast.—*adv.* without using flesh (*obs.*).—*n.* (also **meagre,** *mē'gər*) a large Mediterranean fish (*Sciaena aquila*) noted for the sound it emits. [Fr. *maigre*, lean—L. *macer.*]

**maik,** *mäk*, *n.* Same as mag (1), or make (3).

**mail,** *mäl*, *n.* defensive armour for the body, formed of steel rings or network: armour generally: protective covering of an animal.— *v.t.* to clothe in mail.—*adj.* **mailed,** protected by mail.—*adj.* **mail'-clad,** clad with a coat of mail.— **mailed fist,** physical force. [Fr. *maille*—L. *macula*, a spot or a mesh.]

**mail,** *mäl*, *n.* a travelling bag (*obs.*): a bag for the conveyance of letters, etc.: the contents of such a bag: post (esp. for long distances): correspondence: a batch of letters, etc.: the person or the carriage by which the mail is conveyed.—*v.t.* to post: to send by post.—*adj.* **mail'able,** capable of being sent by mail.—**mail'-bag,** a bag in which letters are carried; **mail'-boat,** a boat that carries the public mails; **mail'-box** (*U.S.*), a letter-box; **mail'-cart,** a cart in which mails are carried: a small hand-cart, with long handles, for the conveyance of children; **mail'-catcher,** an apparatus for catching up mail-bags by a train in motion; **mail'-coach, -car, -carriage, -drag, -gig, -van,** a conveyance that carries the public mails; **mail'ing-card** (*U.S.*), a postcard;

**mail'man**, also **mail'-carrier**, a postman; **mail order**, an order for goods to be sent by post (also *adj.* as in *mail-order firm, house*); **mail'-plane**, **mail'-train**, one that carries the public mails. [O.Fr. *male*, a trunk, a mail—O.H.G. *malha, malaha*, a sack.]

**mail**, *māl*, (*Scot.*) *n.* payment: rent.—*ns.* **mail'er**, one who pays rent: a cottager; **mail'ing**, a rented farm: rent. [Late O.E. *māl*—O.N. *māl*, speech, agreement; cf. O.E. *mǣl*.]

**mail**, **maile**, *māl*, (*obs.*) *n.* a halfpenny. [A.Fr. *mayle*—assumed L.L. *metallea*; see **medal**.]

**mail**, *māl*, (*Scot.*) *n.* a spot, esp. one caused by ironing cloth.—*v.t.* to spot. [O.E. *māl*; see **mole** (1).]

**mail**, *māl*, (*Shak.*) *v.t.* to wrap up (a hawking word).

**maillot**, *mä-yō*, *n.* tights for ballet-dancer, etc.: one-piece close-fitting swimsuit. [Fr., *lit.* swaddling-clothes.]

**maim**, *mām*, *n.* serious bodily injury: a lameness: the loss of any essential part.—*v.t.* to disable: to mutilate: to lame or cripple: render defective. —*adj.* **maimed**.—*adj.* **maimed**.—*ns.* **maimedness** (*māmd'* or *mām'id-nis*); **maim'ing**. [O.Fr. *mahaing*.]

**main**, *mān*, *n.* might: strength: the principal part: the mainland: the high sea: a great expanse (*Shak., Milt.*): a principal pipe or conductor in a branching system: that which is essential: the most part: purpose (*obs.*).—*adj.* **strong** (*Milt.*): sheer (as in *main force*): great: extensive: important: chief, principal: first in importance or extent: leading: general.—*adv.* (*dial.*) exceedingly.—*adv.* **main'ly**, chiefly, principally: much (*obs.* or *dial.*).—**main'boom**, the spar that extends the foot of a fore-and-aft mainsail; **main'brace**, the brace attached to the mainyard (see **splice**); **main chance** (see **chance**); **main'-course**, mainsail; **main'-deck**, the principal deck of a ship; **main'door**, a door giving independent access to a house, distinguished from one opening upon a common passage: a ground-floor house in a tenement building or villa-block, entered from the front by a door of its own (*Scot.*); **main'land** (*-land, -land*), the principal or larger land, as opposed to neighbouring islands; **main'lander**; **main line**, a railway line between important centres: an important vein (*slang*).—*adj.* **main'line**.—*v.i.* (*slang*) to take narcotics intravenously.—**main'liner**; **main'-lining**; **main'mast** (*-mast, -mäst*), the principal mast, usually second from the prow; **main'sail** (*-sl, -sāl*), the principal sail, generally attached to the mainmast; **main'sheet**, the sheet or rope attached to the lower corner of the mainsail; **main'spring**, the spring that gives motion to any piece of machinery, esp. that of a watch or a clock: principal motive (*fig.*); **main'stay**, a rope stretching forward and down from the top of the mainmast: chief support; **main stream**, a river with tributaries: the chief direction or trend in any historical development, including that of an art.—*adj.* **main'stream**, pertaining to the main stream (*lit.* and *fig.*): of swing, coming in the line of development between early and modern (*jazz*).—**main'top**, a platform on the top of the lower mainmast; **maintop-gall'ant-mast**, the mast above the maintopmast; **maintop'mast**, the mast next above the lower mainmast; **maintop'sail**, the sail above the mainsail, in square-rigged vessels; **main'yard**, the lower yard on the mainmast.—**in the main**, for the most part: on the whole; **might and main**, utmost strength; **Spanish Main** (see **Spanish**). [Partly O.E. *mægen*, strength, partly O.N. *meginn*, strong; influence of O.Fr. *maine, magne* (—L. *magnus*), great, is questioned.]

**main**, *mān*, *n.* a banker's shovel. [O.Fr. *main*— L. *manus*, hand.]

**main**, *mān*, *n.* in hazard, a number (5 to 9) called before throwing the dice: a game of hazard: a cockfighting match: a set of cocks engaged in a match: a match in some other sports. [Perh. same as preceding.]

**main**, *mān*, (*dial.; Shak.*) *v.t.* to lame, maim.

**mainor**, **mainour**, **manner**, *mān'ər*, *man'ər*, (*arch.; hist.*) *n.* act or fact, esp. of theft: that which is stolen.—**in**, **with**, **the manner**, in the act: in possession of the thing stolen. [A.Fr. *meinoure*, *mainoure*, *mainoevere*; see **manoeuvre**.]

**mainprise**, *mān'priz*, (*arch.; law*) *n.* suretyship, esp. for the appearance of a prisoner.—*n.* **mainpernor** (*-pûr'nər*), one who gives mainprise. [A.Fr. *mainprise*, *mainpernour*—*main*, hand, *prendre*, to take.]

**mains**, *mānz*, (*Scot.*) *n.pl.* a home farm. [demesne, domain.]

**maintain**, *mān-tān'*, *mən-*, *men-*, *v.t.* to observe or practise: to keep in existence or in any state: to preserve from capture, loss, or deterioration: to uphold: to carry on: to keep up: to support: to make good: to support by argument: to affirm: to defend: to support in an action in which one is not oneself concerned (*law*).—*adj.* **maintain'able**.—*ns.* **maintain'er**; **maintenance** (*mān'tən-əns*), the act of maintaining, supporting, or defending: continuance: the means of support: defence, protection: illegal outside interference in a lawsuit, etc., in favour of one of the parties (*law*).—*v.t.* to keep in working order. —**main'tenance-man**, one keeping machines, etc., in working order.—**cap of maintenance**, a cap of dignity borne by or before a noble or other person of rank. [Fr. *maintenir*—L. *manū* (abl.) *tenēre*, to hold in the hand.]

**maire**, *mer*, (Fr.) *n.* mayor.

**maise**, *māz*. Same as **mease** (of herrings).

**maison de ville**, *me-zō də vēl*, (Fr.) a town house, residence in town.

**maisonnette**, **maisonette**, *mez-on-et'*, *n.* a small house or flat. [Fr. *maisonnette*.]

**maister**, *mās'tər*, (*obs.* and *Scot.*). Same as **master**. —*ns.* **mais'terdome**; **mais'tring** (both *Spens.*).

**maître**, (*fem.* **maîtresse**) **de ballet**, *metr' (me-tres) də bal-e*, *n.* one who trains dancers and takes rehearsals (formerly one who acted also as choreographer). [Fr., ballet master, mistress.]

**maître d'hôtel**, *metr' dō-tel*, a house-steward, major domo: manager or head-waiter of a hotel. See **à la**.

**maize**, *māz*, *n.* a staple cereal (*Zea mays*) in America, etc., with large ears (corncobs)—called also *Indian corn*, or *mealies*: the yellow colour of maize.—Also *adj.*—**water maize**, *Victoria regia*. [Sp. *maiz*—from Haitian.]

**maize**, *māz*. Same as **mease** (of herrings).

**majesty**, *maj'is-ti*, *n.* greatness and glory of God: grandeur: dignity: elevation of manner or style: royal state: a title of monarchs (*His, Her, Your, Majesty, Their, Your, Majesties*): a representation of God (sometimes Christ) enthroned: the canopy of a hearse.—*adjs.* **majestic** (*mə-jes'tik*), **-al**, having or exhibiting majesty: stately: sublime.—*adv.* **majes'tically**, in a majestic manner.—*ns.* **majes'ticalness**, **majes'ticness** (*obs.*), majesty. [Fr. *majesté*—L. *mājestās, -ātis*—*mājor*, *mājus*, comp. of *magnus*, great.]

**Majlis**, *mäj-lis'*, *n.* the Persian parliament: the assembly.—Also **Mejlis'**. [Pers. *majlis*.]

**majolica**, *mə-jol'i-kə*, or *-yol'*, *n.* glazed or enamelled earthenware. [Perh. from *Majorca*.]

**major**, *mā'jər*, *adj.* greater in number, quantity, size, value, importance, dignity: in boys' schools, senior: greater (than minor) by a semitone (*mus.*): involving a major third (see below, *mus.*).—*n.* a person of full legal age (in U.K., before 1970, 21 years; from 1970, 18 years): an officer in rank between a captain and lieutenant-colonel: by courtesy, a sergeant-major: anything that is major opposed to minor: a student's special subject (*U.S.*): a kind of wig (*obs.*).—*v.i.* to play the major, strut: to specialise at college (*U.S.*).—*ns.* majorat (*mä-zhō-rä*; Fr.), primogeniture; majorette', drum majorette; majority (*mə-jor'i-ti*), pre-eminence: the greater number: the difference between the greater and the less number: full age (see major, above): the office or rank of major.—Also *adj.*—*n.* mā'jorship.— major axis, in conic sections, that passing through the foci; mā'jor-dōmō (Sp. *mayor-domo*, L. *mājor domūs*), an official who has the general management in a large household: a general steward; mā'jor-gen'eral, an officer in the army next in rank below a lieutenant-general; mā'jor-gen'eralcy, mājor gen'eralship; major key, mode, scale, one with its third a major third above the tonic; major premise (*log.*), that in which the major term occurs; major suit (*bridge*), spades or hearts, valued more highly than diamonds or clubs; major term, the term which is the predicate of the conclusion; major third, an interval of four semitones; major tone, an interval of vibration ratio 8 : 9.—go over to, or join, the majority, to die. [L. *mājor*, comp. of *magnus*.]

majoritaire, *mä-zhor-ē-ter*, (Fr.) a member of a majority section of a party, esp. of socialists.

majuscule, *mə-jus'kūl*, or *maj'əs-kūl*, (*palaeog.*) *n.* a large letter whether capital or uncial.—Also *adj.*—*adj.* majus'cular. [L. (*littera*) *mājuscula*, somewhat larger (letter).]

mak, *mäk*, Scots form of make.—*n.* makar (see maker).

make, *māk*, *v.t.* to fashion, frame, construct, compose, or form: to create: to bring into being: to produce: to conclude, contract: to bring about: to perform: to force: to cause: to result in: to cause to be: to convert or turn: to appoint: to render: to represent as doing or being: to reckon: to get as result or solution: to occasion: to bring into any state or condition: to establish: (in the navy) to promote: to prepare: to shut (as a door) (*Shak.*): to shuffle (*cards*): to declare as trumps (*cards*): to obtain, gain, earn: to score: to constitute: to amount to: to count for: to turn out: to be capable of turning or developing into or serving as: to arrive in sight of: to reach, succeed in reaching: to accomplish, achieve: to attempt, offer, or start: to be occupied with: to do: to cause, assure, success of: to persuade (a woman) to have sexual intercourse with one (*slang*): to have sexual intercourse with (*slang*).—*v.i.* to behave (as if), esp. in order to deceive: to proceed: to tend: to contribute: to flow: to versify (*arch.*): to be in condition for making: to matter (as *it maksna*, it does not matter; *Scot.*):—*pr.p.* māk'ing; *pa.t.* and *pa.p.* māde.—*n.* form or shape: structure, texture: build: formation: manufacture: brand: type: making: quantity made: establishment of an electric circuit or contact: trump declaration.—*ns.* māk'er, one who makes: (*cap.*) the Creator: (*arch.*; esp. in Scots form, makar, *mak'*, *māk'ər*) a poet: the declarer (*bridge*): a knave in cards (*obs.*): a calker's tool; māk'ing, the act of forming: structure: form: (in *pl.*) gains: (in *pl.*) that from which something can be made.—*adj.* make'-and-break', making and breaking a circuit.—make'bate, a mischiefmaker.—*v.i.* make'-believe, to pretend, feign: to play at believing.—*n.* feigning (also make'belief).—*adj.* feigned.—*adj.* make'-do, makeshift.—make'-peace (*Shak.*), a peace-maker; make-ready, preparation of a letterpress sheet for printing, so as to obtain evenness of impression; make'shift, a temporary expedient or substitute.—*adj.* of the nature of or characterised by temporary expedient.—make'-up, the way anything is arranged, composed, or constituted,

or the ingredients in its constitution: one's character, temperament, mental qualities: an actor's materials for personating a part or a woman's, esp. cosmetics, for self-beautification: the effect produced thereby: the arrangement of composed types into columns or pages (*print.*); make'-weight, that which is thrown into a scale to make up the weight: something of little value added to supply a deficiency.—make account of (see account); make a face, to grimace, contort the features; make a figure, to be conspicuous; make after, to follow or pursue; make a fool of (see fool); make against, to militate, tell, against; make a (good) meal, dinner, etc., to dine, etc. (plentifully or heartily); make amends, to render compensation or satisfaction; make an ass of oneself, to behave like a fool; make a night (day) of it, to pass a night (day) in enjoyment; make as if, or though, to act as if, to pretend that; make at, to make a hostile movement against; make away (with), to put out of the way, get rid of, destroy, kill; make believe (see makebelieve above); make bold (see bold); make do (with), to manage (with the means available— usually inferior or inadequate); make down, to refashion so as to fit a smaller person: to turn down the sheets and blankets of (*Scot.*); make eyes at (see eye); make for, to set out for, seek to reach: to favour; make free with (see free); make friends, to become friendly: to acquire friends; make good, make light of, make little of, make love to, make merry (see good, etc.); make head or tail of, to find any sense in; make it, to reach an objective: to succeed in a purpose; make much of, to treat with fondness, to cherish, to foster: to turn to great account: to find much sense in, succeed in understanding; make no doubt, to have no doubt, to be confident; make nothing of, to think it no great matter, have no hesitation or difficulty: to be totally unable to understand; make of, to construct from (as material): to understand by: to make much of, to pet (*obs.* and *Scot.*): to esteem (*obs.*); make off, to decamp; make off with, to run away with; make on (*Shak.*), to make much of; make one's way, to proceed: to succeed; make or meddle with, to have to do with, interfere with; make out, to descry: to discern: to decipher: to comprehend, understand: to prove: to seek to make it appear: to draw up: to achieve (*obs.*): to fill up: to make shift, get along somehow: to succeed; make over, to remake, reconstruct: to transfer; make sail, to increase the quantity of sail: to set sail; make sure (of), to ascertain: to put beyond doubt or risk: to secure: to feel certain: to betroth (*obs.*); make the best of, to turn to the best advantage: take in the best spirit; make the most of, to use to the best advantage; make up, to fabricate: to feign: to collect: to put together: to parcel: to put into shape: to arrange: to compose (quarrels): to constitute: to repair: to complete, supplement: to adjust one's appearance (as an actor for a part): to apply paint and powder, etc., to the face: to put type, etc., into columns and pages: to make good: to compensate: to decide (*Shak.*); make up one's mind, to come to a decision; make up to, to make friendly, adulatory, or amorous approaches to: to compensate; make way (see way); on the make (*coll.*), bent on self-advancement or promotion. [O.E. *macian*; Ger. *machen*.]

make, *māk*, *n.* Same as mag (1).

make, *māk*, (*obs.* or *dial.*) *n.* a mate, consort, equal.—*adj.* make'less (*obs.* or *dial.*), without a make or mate. [O.E. (*ge*)*mæcca*; see match.]

makimono, *mäk-i-mō'nō*, *n.* a roll, as of silk, esp. a long picture or writing rolled up and not hung. [Jap.]

mal, *mal*, (Fr.) pain, sickness.—mal de mer (*də*

*mer*), sea-sickness; **mal du pays** (*dü pā-ē*), homesickness, nostalgia; **mal du siècle** (*dü syekl'*), depression about the state of the world; used by Sainte-Beuve (1833) and current in the 20th cent.

**mal-**, *mal-*, *pfx.* bad, badly. [Fr.,—L. *male*, badly.]

**Malabar-rat**, *mal'ə-bär-rat'*, *n.* the bandicoot rat. [*Malabar* in India.]

**Malacca-cane**, *mal-ak'ə-kān*, *n.* a brown walking-cane made from a rattan. [*Malacca*, a centre of the trade.]

**malachite**, *mal'ə-kīt*, *n.* a green mineral, basic copper carbonate. [Gr. *malachē*, mallow, as of the colour of a mallow leaf.]

**malacia**, *mal-ā'shi-ə*, *n.* pathological softening: perverted appetite. [Gr. *malakiā*, softness.]

**malacology**, *mal-ə-kol'ə-ji*, *n.* the study of molluscs.—*adj.* **malacological** (*-kə-loj'*).—*n.* **malacol'ogist.** [Gr. *malakos*, soft, *logos*, discourse.]

**malacophilous**, *mal-ə-kof'i-ləs*, (*bot.*) *adj.* pollinated by snails. [Gr. *malakos*, soft, *phileein*, to love.]

**Malacopterygii**, *mal-ə-kop-tər-ij'i-ī*, *n.pl.* a soft-finned suborder of bony fishes—herrings, salmon, etc.—*adj.* and *n.* **malacopteryg'ian.** [Gr. *malakos*, soft, *pteryx*, *pterygos*, a wing, fin.]

**Malacostraca**, *mal-ə-kos'trə-ka*, *n.pl.* the best-known class of crustaceans—crabs, lobsters, shrimps, prawns, etc.—*adj.* and *n.* **malacos'tracan.**—*adj.* **malacos'tracous.** [Gr. *malakos*, soft, *ostrakon*, a shell.]

**maladaptation**, *mal-ad-ap-tā'shən*, *n.* faulty adaptation.—*adjs.* **maladap'ted; maladap'tive.** [Pfx. **mal-.**]

**maladdress**, *mal-ə-dres'*, *n.* awkwardness: clumsiness: tactlessness. [Fr. *maladresse*.]

**maladjusted**, *mal-ə-just'id*, *adj.* poorly or inadequately adjusted, esp. to one's environment or circumstances.—*n.* **maladjust'ment.** [Pfx. **mal-.**]

**maladministration**, *mal-əd-min-is-trā'shən*, *n.* bad management, esp. of public affairs. [Pfx. **mal-.**]

**maladroit**, *mal'ə-droit* (or *-droit'*), *adj.* not dexterous: unskilful: clumsy.—*adv.* **maladroit'ly.**—*n.* **maladroit'ness.** [Fr.]

**malady**, *mal'ə-di*, *n.* illness: disease, either of the body or of the mind: a faulty condition. [Fr. *maladie*—*malade*, sick—L. *male habitus*, in ill condition—*male*, badly, *habitus*, pa.p. of *habēre*, to have, hold.]

**mala fide**, *mā'lə fī'dē*, *ma'lä fē'dä*, (L.) in bad faith, treacherously.

**Malaga**, *mal'ə-gə*, *n.* a white wine imported from *Málaga*.

**Malagasy**, *mal-ə-gas'i*, *adj.* of or pertaining to Madagascar or its inhabitants.—*n.* a native of Madagascar: the language of Madagascar.—Also **Malagash'** (or *mal'*).

**malaguetta**, *mal-ə-get'ə*, *n.* grains of paradise (also **malaguetta pepper**). [Origin obscure.]

**malaise**, *mal-āz'*, *n.* uneasiness: a feeling of discomfort or of sickness. [Fr. *malaise*.]

**malakatoone.** Same as **melocoton.**

**malander, mallender,** *mal'ən-dər*, *n.* an eruption of the skin behind a horse's knee—often *pl.* [Fr. *malandre*—L. *malandria* (sing. or pl.).]

**malapert**, *mal'ə-pûrt*, *adj.* bold: forward: saucy: impudent.—*adv.* **mal'apertly.**—*n.* **mal'apertness.** [O.Fr., unskilful—*mal* (L. *malus*), bad, *appert* for *espert* (L. *expertus*; see **expert**), but understood in English as if—Fr. *apert*, open, outspoken—L. *apertus*, open.]

**malappropriate**, *mal-ə-prō'pri-āt*, *v.t.* to misuse.—*n.* **malappropriā'tion.** [Pfx. **mal-.**]

**malapropism**, *mal'ə-prop-izm*, *n.* misapplication of words without mispronunciation, from Mrs *Malaprop* in Sheridan's play, *The Rivals*, who uses words *malapropos*.

**malapropos**, *mal'a'prō-pō*, *mal-a-prō-pō'*, *adj.* out of place: unsuitable: inapt.—*adv.* inappropriately: unseasonably. [Pfx. **mal-.**]

**malar**, *mā'lər*, *adj.* pertaining to the cheek.—*n.* the

cheek-bone. [L. *māla*, the cheek—*mandēre*, to chew.]

**malaria**, *mə-lā'ri-ə*, *n.* poisonous air arising from marshes, once believed to produce fever: miasma: the fever once attributed thereto, actually due to a protozoan parasite transmitted by mosquitoes.—*adjs.* **malā'rial, malā'rian, malā'rious.**—*ns.* **malario'logist; malario'logy,** the study of malaria. [It. *mal' aria*—L. *malus*, bad, *āēr, āēris*, air.]

**malark(e)y**, *ma-lär'ki*, (*U.S.*) *n.* unfounded story: nonsense.

**malassimilation**, *mal-ə-sim-i-lā'shən*, *n.* imperfect assimilation or nutrition. [Pfx. **mal-.**]

**malate.** See **malic.**

**malax, malaxate,** *mal'aks*, *-āt*, *vs.t.* to soften by kneading, rubbing or mixing.—*ns.* **mal'axage; malaxā'tion; mal'axator.** [L.L. *malaxāre*, to soften.]

**Malay, -an,** *mə-lā'*, *-ən*, *ns.* a member of a race inhabiting Malaysia, Singapore and Indonesia (formerly known as the Malay Archipelago): the language of the Malays.—*adjs.* of the Malays, their language, or their countries.—*adj.* **Malay'-sian** (*-si-ən*, *-zhən*, *-shən*), relating to the Malay Archipelago or esp. to Malaysia.—Also *n.* [Malay *malāyu*.]

**Malayalam**, *mä-lä-yä'läm*, *n.* the Dravidian language of Malabar.—Also *adj.*

**malconformation**, *mal-kon-för-mā'shən*, *n.* bad conformation or form. [Pfx. **mal-.**]

**malcontent**, *mal'kən-tent*, *adj.* discontented, dissatisfied, esp. in political matters.—*n.* one discontented.—*adj.* **malcontent'ed.**—*adv.* **malcontent'edly.**—*n.* **malcontent'edness.** [O.Fr. *malcontent*.]

**maldistribution**, *mal-dis-tri-bū'shən*, *n.* uneven, unfair, or inefficient, distribution. [Pfx. **mal-.**]

**male**, *māl*, (*Spens.*) *n.* for **mail** (armour).

**male**, *māl*, *adj.* masculine: of or pertaining to the sex that begets (not bears) young, or produces relatively small gametes: staminate (*bot.*): adapted to fit into a corresponding hollow part (*mach.*).—*n.* one of the male sex: apparently, a father (*Shak.*).—**male'-fern,** an elegant woodland fern once fancied to be the male of the lady-fern; **male orchis,** the early purple orchis (cf. **Orchis**); **male order,** in architecture, the Doric order; **male rhymes,** those in which only the final syllables correspond; **male screw** (see **screw**). [O.Fr. *male*—L. *masculus*, male—*mās*, a male.]

**Malebolge**, *mä-lä-bol'jä*, *n.* the eighth circle of Dante's Hell. [It., bad holes or pits, lit. pockets.]

**malediction**, *mal-i-dik'shən*, *n.* evil-speaking: a calling down of evil.—*adjs.* **maledicent** (*-di'sənt*), cursing; **mal'edict** (*-dikt*), accursed.—*v.t.* and *v.i.* to curse.—*adj.* **maledic'tory.** [L. *maledicēre*, *-dictum*—*male*, ill, *dīcēre*, to speak.]

**malefactor**, *mal'i-fak-tər*, *n.* an evil-doer: a criminal.—*n.* **malefac'tion** (*Shak.*), a crime, an offence.—*adjs.* **malefac'tory, malefic** (*məl-ef'ik*), doing mischief: producing evil.—*adv.* **malef'-ically.**—*ns.* **mal'efice** (*-i-fis; arch.*), an evil deed: enchantment; **maleficence** (*-ef'i-səns*).—*adjs.* **malef'icent, maleficial** (*mal-i-fish'l; rare*), hurtful: wrong-doing. [L. *malefacēre*, to do evil.]

**maleic.** See under **malic.**

**malemute**, *mäl'ə-mūt*, *n.* an Eskimo dog.—Also **mal'amute.** [From a tribe on the Alaskan coast.]

**malengine**, *mal-en'jin*, (*Spens.*) *n.* evil device: deceit. [O.Fr. *malengin*—L. *malus*, *-um*, bad, *ingenium*, ingenuity.]

**malentendu**, *mal-ä-tä-dü*, (Fr.) a misunderstanding.

**malevolent**, *mal-ev'ə-lənt*, *adj.* wishing evil: ill-disposed towards others: rejoicing in another's misfortune.—*n.* **malev'olence.**—*adv.* **malev'ol-ently.** [L. *malevolēns*, *-entis*, ill disposed, wishing evil.]

**malfeasance**, *mal-fē'zəns, n.* evil-doing (*rare*): the doing of what one ought not to do (*rare*): an illegal deed, esp. of an official (*law*).—*adj.* **malfea'sant.** [Fr. *malfaisance*—L. *male*, ill, *facēre*, to do.]

**malformation**, *mal-för-mā'shən, n.* faulty structure: deformity.—*adj.* **malformed'.** [Pfx. **mal-**.]

**malfunction**, **-ing**, *mal-fungk'shən, -ing, ns.* act or fact of working imperfectly. [Pfx. **mal-**.]

**malgrado**, *mal-grä'dō,* (*obs.*) *prep.* in spite of. [It.]

**malgre.** Same as **maugre**.

**malgré**, *mal-grā,* (Fr.) in spite of.—**malgré lui**, **moi**, etc., in spite of his, my, etc., efforts: willy-nilly; **malgré tout** (*tōō*), nevertheless, all things considered.

**mali**, **mallee**, ·*mä'lē, n.* one of the gardener class in India. [Hindi *mālī.*]

**Malibu board**, *mal'i-bōō, n.* a long, light surfing board equipped with fins. [*Malibu*, California.]

**malic**, *mä'lik, mal'ik, adj.* obtained from apple juice—applied to an acid ($H_6C_4O_5$) found in unripe fruits.—*n.* **ma'late**, a salt of malic acid.—*adj.* **maleic** (*mə-lē'ik*).—**maleic acid**, an acid, isomeric with fumaric acid, got from malic acid; **maleic hy'drazide**, a chemical used in retarding plant growth; **malon'ic acid**, a white crystalline acid $CH_2(COOH)_2$. [L. *mālum*, an apple; Gr. *mēlon*.]

**malice**, *mal'is, n.* ill-will: spite: disposition or intention to harm another or others: a playfully mischievous attitude of mind.—*v.t.* to have ill-will against: to wish to injure (*pa.p.* in *Spens.* **mal'ist**).—*adj.* **malicious** (*mə-lish'əs*), bearing ill-will or spite: moved by hatred or ill-will: mischievous.—*adv.* **malic'iously.**—*n.* **malic'iousness.** [Fr.,—L. *malitia*—*malus*, bad.]

**malicho**, *mal'i-chō,* (*Shak.*) *n.* mischief. [Conjectured to be for Sp. *malhecho*, mischief.]

**malign**, *mə-līn', adj.* baleful: injurious: malignant.—*v.t.* to speak evil of, especially falsely and rancorously, to defame: to regard with malice or hatred (*obs.*): to grudge (*obs.*).—*ns.* **malign'er**; **malignity** (*mə-lig'ni-ti*), state or quality of being malign: great hatred, virulence: deadly quality.—*adv.* **malign'ly.**—*n.* **malign'ment.** [Fr. *malin*, fem. *maligne*—L. *malignus* for *maligenus*, of evil disposition—*malus*, bad, and *gen-*, root of *genus.*]

**malignant**, *mə-lig'nənt, adj.* disposed to do harm: baleful: actuated by great hatred: Royalist or Cavalier (also *cap.*, *hist.*): rebellious, disaffected (*obs.*): tending to cause death, or to go from bad to worse (*med.*): esp. cancerous.—*n.* (usu. *cap.*) a Royalist or Cavalier.—*ns.* **malig'nance**, **malig'nancy.**—*adv.* **malig'nantly.** [L. *malignāns, -antis,* pr.p. of *malignāre*, to act maliciously.]

**Malines**, *me-lēn'.* Same as **Mechlin**.

**malinger**, *mə-ling'gər, v.i.* to feign sickness in order to avoid duty.—*ns.* **maling'erer**; **maling'ery**, feigned sickness. [Fr. *malingre*, sickly.]

**malison**, *mal'i-zn, -sn, n.* a curse—opp. to **benison**. [O.Fr. *maleison*; a doublet of **malediction**.]

**malkin**, *mö'kin, n.* a dirty or lewd woman (*Shak.*): a mop (*dial.*): a scarecrow (*dial.*): a hare (*Scot.*).—Also **maw'kin**. [Dim. of *Matilda, Maud.*]

**mall**, *möl,* or *mal, n.* a maul, large wooden beetle or hammer: a mallet for the old game of pall-mall: the game itself: a pall-mall alley: (from a former alley of the kind in London) a level shaded walk: a public walk.—*v.t.* to maul or beat. [See **maul** and **pall-mall**.]

**mallard**, *mal'ərd, n.* the male of the common wild duck. [O.Fr. *mallart, malart*; origin obscure.]

**malleate**, *mal'i-āt, v.t.* to hammer: beat thin.—*adj.* **mall'eable**, able to be beaten, rolled, etc., into a new shape (also *fig.*).—*ns.* **mall'eableness**, **malleabil'ity**; **mallea'tion**, hammering: a hammer-mark.—*adj.* **malleiform** (*mal'ē-i-förm*), hammer-shaped.—*n.* **malleus** (*mal'i-əs*), one of the

small bones of the middle ear in mammals. [L. *malleus*, a hammer.]

**mallecho**, an editorial emendation of **malicho** (*Shak.*).

**mallee**, *mal'ē, n.* dwarf Eucalyptus, esp. *E. dumosa.*—**mall'ee-fowl**, **-fowl**, **-hen**, an Australian mound-bird; **mall'ee-scrub'**, a thicket formation of mallee. [Australian word.]

**mallee.** Same as **mali**.

**mallemaroking**, *mal'i-mə-rō'king, n.* carousing of seamen in icebound ships. [Obs. Du. *mallemerok*, a romping woman—*mal*, foolish, *marok*—Fr. *marotte*, a favoured object.]

**mallemuck**, *mal'i-muk, n.* the fulmar or similar bird. [Du. *mallemok*—*mal*, foolish, *mok*, gull; Ger. *mallemuck.*]

**malleolus**, *mə-lē'ə-ləs, n.* a bony protuberance on either side of the ankle.—*adj.* **mallē'olar** (or *mal'i-*). [L. *malleolus*, dim. of *malleus*, hammer.]

**mallet**, *mal'it, n.* a small wooden hammer: a long-handled hammer for playing croquet or polo. [Fr. *maillet*, dim. of *mail*, a mall.]

**Mallophaga**, *mal-of'ə-ga, n.pl.* an order of wingless parasitic insects, bird-lice or biting-lice.—*adj.* **malloph'agous.** [Gr. *mallos*, a flock of wool, *phagein*, to eat.]

**mallow**, *mal'ō, n.* any plant of the genus Malva, from its emollient properties or its soft downy leaves: extended to other genera of Malvaceae: a mauve colour. [O.E. *m(e)alwe*—L. *malva*; Gr. *malachē*—*malassein*, to soften.]

**malm**, *mäm, n.* calcareous loam, earth specially good for brick: an artificial mixture of clay and chalk. [O.E. *m(e)alm* (*-stän*), a soft (stone).]

**malmag**, *mal'mag, n.* the tarsier. [Philippine word.]

**malmsey**, *mäm'zi, n.* a sort of grape: a strong and sweet wine, first made in Greece and exported from *Monembasia.*—Also **malvasia** (*mäl-vä-sē'ə*), **malvesie**, **malvoisie** (*mäl'və-zi, -voi-zi*). [L.L. *malmasia*; cf. O.Fr. *malvesie*, Fr. *malvoisie*, It. *malvasia*, Sp. *malvasía.*]

**malnutrition**, *mal-nū-trish'ən, n.* imperfect or faulty nutrition. [Pfx. **mal-**.]

**malodour**, *mal-ō'dər, n.* an ill smell.—*adj.* **malo'-dorous.**—*n.* **malo'dorousness.** [Pfx. **mal-**.]

**malonic acid.** See **malic**.

**Malpighia**, *mal-pig'i-a, n.* the Barbados cherry genus of tropical American trees, shrubs, and lianes, giving name to the family **Malpighiā'ceae**, of the geranium cohort.—*adj.* **Malpigh'ian**, applied to several structures, esp. in the kidney, investigated by Marcello *Malpighi* (1628-94).

**malposition**, *mal-pō-zish'ən, n.* a wrong position, misplacement. [Pfx. **mal-**.]

**malpractice**, *mal-prak'tis, n.* an evil or improper practice: professional misconduct: treatment falling short of reasonable skill or care: illegal attempt of a person in position of trust to benefit himself at others' cost.—*n.* **malpractitioner** (*-tish'ən-ər*). [Pfx. **mal-**.]

**malpresentation**, *mal-prez-ən-tā'shən, n.* abnormal presentation in childbirth. [Pfx. **mal-**.]

**mal soigné**, *mal swa-nyā,* (Fr.) badly groomed, unkempt.

**malstick.** See **maulstick**.

**malt**, *mölt, n.* barley or other grain steeped in water, allowed to sprout, and dried in a kiln, used in brewing ale, etc.: malt liquor.—*v.t.* to make into malt: to treat or combine with malt.—*v.i.* to become malt: to drink malt liquor (*facet.*).—*adj.* containing or made with malt.—*ns.* **malt'ase**, an enzyme that produces grape-sugar from maltose; **malt'ing**, a building where malt is made; **malt'ose**, a hard, white crystalline sugar, formed by the action of malt or diastase on starch; **malt'ster**, a maltman.—*adj.* **malt'y.**—**malt'-dust**, grain-sprouts produced and 'screened off' in malt-making; **malt'-ex'tract**, a fluid medicinal food made from malt; **malt'-floor**, a perforated floor in the chamber of a malt-kiln, through which heat rises; **malt'-horse**, a heavy horse, such as is used by brewers—hence (*Shak.*) a dull, stupid person; **malt'-house, malt'-kiln; malt liquor**, a liquor, as ale or porter, formed from malt; **malt'-mill**, a mill for grinding malt; **malt'man**, one whose occupation it is to make malt; **malt tea**, the liquid infusion of the mash in brewing; **malt'worm** (*Shak.*), a lover of malted liquors, a tippler. [O.E. *m(e)alt*; cf. Ger. *malz*.]

**Malta**, *mol'*, *möl't*, *adj.* of the island of Malta.—*adj.* **Maltese** (*-tēz'*), of Malta, its people, or language.—*n.* one of the people of Malta (*pl.* **Maltese**): an official language of Malta—Arabic with a strong Italian infusion.—**Malta fever**, undulant fever, once common in Malta (see also **brucellosis**); **Maltese cross**, the badge of the Knights of Malta, a cross with two-pointed expanding limbs; **Maltese dog**, a very small spaniel with long silky hair. [L. *Melita*, Gr. *Melitē*.]

**maltalent**, *mal'tal-ant*, (*Spens.*) *n.* ill-will. [Fr. *mal*, ill, *talent*, disposition; see **talent**.]

**maltha**, *mal'tha*, *n.* a thick mineral pitch: an ancient cement. [Gr.]

**Malthusian**, *mal-thūz'i-an*, *adj.* relating to Thomas Robert Malthus (1766-1834), or to his teaching that the increase of population tends to outstrip that of the means of living.—*n.* a disciple of Malthus.—*n.* **Malthus'ianism.**

**maltreat**, *mal-trēt'*, *v.t.* to use roughly or unkindly.—*n.* **maltreat'ment.** [Fr. *maltraiter*—L. *male*, ill, *tractāre*, to treat.]

**Malva**, *mal'va*, *n.* the mallow genus, giving name to the family **Malvā'ceae**, including hollyhock, cotton, etc., akin to the lime family.—*adj.* **malvā'ceous.** [L.; cf. **mallow**.]

**malvasia.** Same as **malmsey.**

**malversation**, *mal-vər-sā'shən*, *n.* misbehaviour in office as by bribery, extortion, embezzlement: corrupt administration (of funds). [Fr.,—L. *male*, badly, *versārī*, *ātus*, to occupy oneself.]

**malvesie, malvoisie.** Same as **malmsey.**

**mal vu**, *mal vü*, (Fr.) looked upon with disapproval.

**mama.** See **mamma.**

**mamba**, *mam'ba*, *n.* a large, deadly African snake (*Dendraspis*), black or green. [Kaffir *im mamba*, large snake.]

**mambo**, *mam'bō*, *n.* a voodoo priestess: a West Indian dance, or dance-tune, like the rumba.

**mamelon**, *mam'a-lan*, *n.* a rounded hill or protuberance. [Fr., nipple.]

**mameluco**, *mam-e-loō'kō*, *n.* in Brazil, the offspring of a person of European stock and an Indian. [Port.; cf. **Mameluke**.]

**Mameluke**, *mam'a-loōk*, *n.* one of a military force originally of Circassian slaves—afterwards the ruling class and sultans of Egypt: a slave, esp. white. [Ar. *mamlūk*, a purchased slave—*malaka*, to possess.]

**mamilla, mammilla**, *mam-il'a*, *n.* the nipple of the mammary gland: a nipple-shaped protuberance:—*pl.* **mamill'ae** (*-ē*).—*adjs.* **mam'illar, mam'illary**, pertaining to the breast: nipple-shaped: studded with rounded projections; **mam'illate, mam'illated**, having mamillae: nipple-shaped.—*n.* **mamilla'tion.**—*adj.* **mamill'iform.** [L. *mam(m)illa*, dim. of *mamma*.]

**mamma, mama**, *mä-mä'* (in U.S. *mä'ma*), *n.* mother—once considered genteel, now used chiefly by young children.—*n.* **mammy** (*mam'i*), a child's word for mother: a coloured nurse (*U.S.*).—**mammy-wagon**, in West Africa, an open-sided bus. [Repetition of *ma*, a child's natural utterance.]

**mamma**, *mam'a*, *n.* the milk gland: the breast:—*pl.* **mammae** (*-ē*).—*adjs.* **mamm'ary**, of the nature of relating to, the mammae or breasts; **mamm'ate**, having breasts.—*n.* **mamm'ifer**, a mammal.

—*adjs.* **mammif'erous**, having mammae; **mamm'iform**, having the form of a breast.—*n.* **mammill'a** (see **mamilla**).—*adj.* **mammogen'ic**, of hormones, promoting growth of the duct and alveolar systems of the milk gland.—*n.* **mammog'raphy**, radiological examination of the breast. [L. *mamma*.]

**mammal**, *mam'al*, *n.* a member of the **Mammalia** (*ma-mā'li-a*), the class of animals that suckle their young.—*adjs.* **mammā'lian; mammalif'erous** (*geol.*), bearing remains of mammals; **mammalog'ical.**—*ns.* **mammalogist** (*-al'a-jist*); **mammal'ogy**, the scientific knowledge of mammals. [L. *mammālis*, of the breast—*mamma*, the breast.]

**mammee**, *mam-ē'*, *n.* a highly esteemed fruit (also **mammee apple**) of the West Indies, etc., having a sweet taste and aromatic odour: the tree producing it (*Mammea americana*; family Guttiferae). —**mammee'-sapo'ta**, the marmalade tree or its fruit. [Sp. *mamey*, from Haitian.]

**mammer**, *mam'ar*, (*Shak.*) *v.i.* to hesitate, to stand muttering and in doubt. [Prob. imit.]

**mammet**, *mam'it*, **maumet, mawmet**, *möm'it*, **mommet**, *mom'it*, *n.* an idol: a puppet, a figure dressed up (*Shak.*).—*ns.* **mamm'etry, maum'etry, maw'metry**, idolatry: idols collectively: Mohammedanism. [**Mohammed**; cf. **Mahound**.]

**mammilla.** Same as **mamilla.**

**mammock**, *mam'ak*, *n.* a shapeless piece, shred.—*v.t.* (*Shak.*) to tear to pieces, to mangle. [Origin obscure.]

**mammon**, *mam'an*, *n.* riches: (*cap.*) the god of riches.—*adj.* **mamm'onish**, devoted to money-getting.—*ns.* **mamm'onism**, devotion to gain; **mamm'onist, mamm'onite**, a person devoted to riches: a worldling.—*adj.* **mammonist'ic.** [L.L. *mam(m)ōna*—Gr. *mam(m)ōnās*—Aramaic *māmōn*, riches.]

**mammoth**, *mam'ath*, *n.* an extinct species of elephant.—*adj.* resembling the mammoth in size: gigantic.—**mamm'oth-tree'**, a Sequoia. [Former Russ. *mammot* (now *mamant* or *mamont*).]

**man**, *man*, *n.* a human being: mankind: a grown-up human male: a male attendant or servant: a workman employed by a master: a vassal: a common soldier: one possessing a distinctively manly character: a husband: a piece used in playing chess or draughts or similar game: a cairn or rock pillar: a hill with such a man: a ship, as in *man*-of-war: a word of familiar address: formerly in the Scottish Highlands, a layman of peculiar holiness and austerity:—*pl.* **men.**—*adj.*, also in composition (as **man'-cook'**), male.—*v.t.* to furnish with a man or men: to strengthen or put manhood into:—*pr.p.* **mann'-ing**; *pa.t.* and *pa.p.* **manned** (*mand*).—*n.* **man'dom** (*rare*), humanity: men collectively.—*adj.* **man'ful**, having the good qualities of a man: manly: bold: courageous: vigorous: stout: noble-minded. — *adv.* **man'fully.** — *ns.* **man'fulness; man'hood**, state of being a man: manly quality: human nature; **man'kind'**, the human race, the mass of human beings: (*man'kind*) human males collectively.—*adj.* (*Shak.*) man-like, viragoish.—*adj.* **man'-like**, having the appearance or qualities of a human being or of an adult human male.—*adv.* in the manner of a man: in a way that might be expected of a male person: manfully.—*n.* **man'liness.**—*adjs.* **man'ly**, befitting a man: brave: dignified: noble: pertaining to manhood: not childish or womanish; **manned** (*mand*); **mann'ish**, like or savouring of a male or grown-up man (usu. depreciatory): masculine.—*n.* **mann'ishness.**—**man-about-town**, a fashionable, sophisticated man; **man'-at-arms'**, a soldier, esp. mounted and heavy-armed; **man'-body** (*Scot.*), a man; **man'-child**, a male child: a boy:—*pl.* **men'-children; man'-day**, a day's work of one man:—*pl.* man'-days; man'-eater, a cannibal: a tiger or other animal that has acquired the habit of eating men.—*adj.* man'-en'tered (*Shak.*), entered upon manhood. —*v.t.* man'handle, to move by manpower: to handle, treat, roughly (orig. *slang*).—man'-hole, a hole large enough to admit a man, esp. to a sewer, cable-duct, or the like; manhood suffrage, right to vote accorded to male citizens; man'-hour', an hour's work of one man:—*pl.* man'-hours; man'-jack', man jack', individual man (as *every man-jack*).—*adj.* man'-made, made by man: humanly made or originated.—man'-mill'iner, a man engaged in millinery—often in contempt.—*adj.* man'-mind'ed, having the mind or qualities of a man.—man'-of-war', a warship: a soldier (*arch.* or *facet.*): (in full man-of-war bird) the frigate-bird: (Portuguese man-of-war, see Physalia); man'-of-war's'-man, a man who serves on board a warship; man'-or'chis, an orchid (*Aceras anthropophora*) whose flowers are like little men; man'power, the agency or energy of man in doing work: the rate at which a man can work: available resources in population or in able-bodied men; man'-queller (*Shak.*), a man-killer, a murderer; man'-servant, a male servant:—*pl.* men'-servants.—*adjs.* man'-size(d), suitable for, or requiring, a man.—man'-slaughter, the slaying of a man: criminal or culpable homicide—without malice aforethought (*law*); man'-slayer, one who kills a man; man'-stealer, one who steals human beings, especially to make slaves of them; man'trap, a trap for catching trespassers: any source of potential danger; man'-week, man'-year, a week's, year's work of one man:—*pl.* man'-weeks, man'-years; men'folk(s), male people.—man alive!, an exclamation of surprise; Man Friday, a factotum or servile attendant—from Robinson Crusoe's man; man in the moon, a fancied semblance of a man seen in the moon; man in the street, the ordinary, everyday man—Tom, Dick, or Harry; man of business, an agent or a lawyer; man of God, a holy man: a clergyman; man of his hands, a man of prowess; man of law, a lawyer; man of letters, a scholar: a writer; man of sin, the devil: Antichrist; man of straw, a person of no substance (esp. financially): one nominally, but not really, responsible; man of the moment, the man (most capable of) dealing with the present situation; man of the world, one accustomed to the ways and dealings of men; man to man, one man to another as individuals in fight or talk: frank and confidential; old man of the sea (see old); to a man, without exception. [O.E. *mann*; Ger. *mann*, Du. *man*.]

mana, *mä'nä*, (*anthrop.*) *n.* a mysterious power associated with persons and things. [Maori.]

manacle, *man'ə-kl*, *n.* a handcuff.—*v.t.* to handcuff: to shackle. [O.Fr. *manicle*—L. *manicula*, dim. of *manica*, sleeve, glove, handcuff—*manus*, hand.]

manage, *man'ij*, *n.* manège.—*v.t.* to train by exercise, as a horse: to handle: to wield: to conduct: to control: to administer, be at the head of: to deal tactfully with: to husband, use sparingly (*arch.*): to contrive successfully: to be able to cope with: to manipulate: to contrive: to bring about.—*v.i.* to conduct affairs: to get on, contrive to succeed.—*n.* manageabil'ity, the quality of being manageable. —*adj.* man'ageable, that can be managed: governable.—*n.* man'ageableness.—*adv.* man'-ageably.—*ns.* man'agement, art or act of managing: manner of directing or of using anything: administration: skilful treatment: a body of managers; man'ager, one who manages: a person who controls a business or other concern: one who organises other people's doings:

a domestic contriver: a party leader (*U.S.*):—*fem.* man'ageress; man'agership.—*adjs.* mana-gē'rial, of or pertaining to a manager, or to management; man'aging, handling: controlling: administering: contriving: domineering.—management consultant, one who advises firms on the most efficient procedures applicable to particular businesses or industries. [It. *maneggio*—L. *manus*, the hand.]

manakin, *man'ə-kin*, *n.* a small tropical American bird of various species of or akin to the Cotinga family: a manikin. [See manikin.]

mañana, *män-yä'nä*, (Sp.) tomorrow: an unspecified time in the future (*n.* and *adv.*).

manatee, manati, *man-ə-tē'*, *n.* a sirenian (*Manatus* or *Trichechus*) of the warm parts of the Atlantic and the rivers of Brazil. [Sp. *manatí*—Carib *manatoui*; not connected with L. *manus*, hand.]

mancando, *mangk-an'dō*, (*mus.*) *adj.* and *adv.* fading away. [It., lacking.]

manche, *mänsh*, (*her.*) *n.* a sleeve. [Fr.]

Manchester, *man'chis-tər*, *adj.* belonging to or made in *Manchester*, or similar to goods made in Manchester, applied esp. to cotton cloths.—Manchester school, the followers of Bright and Cobden, advocates of free-trade and of individual freedom of action.

manchet, *man'chit*, (*arch.*) *n.* the finest bread of wheat: a loaf of manchet. [Origin obscure.]

manchineel, *manch-i-nēl'*, *n.* a tropical American tree (*Hippomane*) of the spurge family, with poisonous latex. [Sp. *manzanilla*, dim. of *manzana*, apple.]

Manchu, Manchoo, *man-chōō'*, or *man'*, *n.* one of the race from which Manchuria took its name, and which governed China from the 17th to the 20th century: their language.—*adj.* of or pertaining to Manchuria or to its inhabitants.—*n.* Manchu'ria (Jap. Manchukuo, *-kwō'*).—*adj.* Manchur'ian. [Manchu, pure.]

mancipation, *man-si-pā'shən*, (*Rom. hist.*) *n.* a legal transfer by actual or symbolic sale.—*v.t.* man'cipate.—*adj.* man'cipatory (*-pə-tə-ri*). [L. *mancipātiō*, *-ōnis*—*manus*, hand, *capĕre*, to take.]

manciple, *man'si-pl*, *n.* a steward: a purveyor, particularly of a college or an inn of court. [O.Fr.,—L. *manceps*, *-cipis*, a purchaser: see foregoing.]

Mancunian, *man*(g)*-kūn'i-ən*, *adj.* belonging to Manchester.—*n.* a Manchester man. [Doubtful L. *Mancunium*, a Roman station in Manchester. *Mamucium* is probably right.]

mancus, *mang'kəs*, (*hist.*) *n.* an old English coin or its value, thirty pence:—*pl.* manc'uses. [O.E. *mancus*.]

mand, Spens. for manned. See man.

Mandaean, *man-dē'ən*, *n.* and *adj.* one of an ancient and surviving sect in southern Babylonia, their religion a corrupt Gnosticism, with many Jewish and Parsee elements.—Also *Mendaites, Nasoraeans, Sabians*, or (misleadingly) *Christians of St John*: the Aramaic dialect of their sacred books.—Also *adj.* [Mandaean *mandayyā*, knowledge, gnosis.]

mandala, *mun'də-lə*, *n.* in Buddhism, etc., a symbol of the universe, varying a little but having an enclosing circle, usu. images of deities, and a tendency to arrangement in fours, used as an aid to religious meditation: in the psychology of Jung, symbol of the wholeness of the self (in imperfect form shows lack of harmony in the self). [Sans. *maṇḍala*.]

mandamus, *man-dā'məs*, *n.* a writ or command issued by a higher court to a lower:—*pl.* manda'-muses. [L. *mandāmus*, we command.]

mandarin, *man'də-rin*, *-rēn*, *n.* a member of any of nine ranks of officials under the Chinese Empire (*hist.*): a statuette of a seated Chinese figure, often with a movable head (a nodding mandarin): (*cap.*) the most important form of the Chinese language: a man in office, bureaucrat: a person of standing in the literary world, often one who tends to be reactionary or pedantic or express himself *ore rotundo*: (also man'darine) a small kind of orange (of Chinese origin): its colour: a liqueur.—*adj.* pertaining to a mandarin: of style or language, formal and ornate.—*n.* man'darinate, office of mandarin: mandarins as a group.—mandarii. collar, a high, narrow, stand-up collar the front ends of which do not quite meet; mandarin duck, a crested Asiatic duck (*Aix galericulata*); mandarin orange, a mandarin (mandarine). [Port. *mandarim*—Malay (from Hind.) *mantri*, counsellor—Sans. *mantra*, counsel.]

mandate, *man'dāt*, *n.* a charge: a command from a superior official or judge to an inferior, ordering him how to act, esp. from the Pope to a legate, etc.: a right given to a person to act in name of another: a rescript of the Pope: the sanction held to be given by the electors to members of parliament to deal with a question that was before the country at the election: power conferred upon a state by the League of Nations in 1919 to govern a region elsewhere.— *v.t.* to assign by mandate.—*ns.* man'datary, man'datory (-*də-tə-ri*), the holder of a mandate: a mandate; mandā'tor, the giver of a mandate.— *adj.* man'datory, containing a mandate or command: of the nature of a mandate: bestowed by mandate: compulsory: allowing no option. [L. *mandātum*—*mandāre*—*manus*, hand, *dāre*, give.]

mandible, *man'di-bl*, *n.* a jaw or jaw-bone, esp. the lower: either part of a bird's bill: an organ performing the functions of a jaw in the lower animals, as one of the first pair of mouth appendages in insects or crustaceans.—*adjs.* mandib'ular, relating to the jaw; mandib'ulate, -d. [L. *mandibula*—*mandēre*, to chew.]

Mandingo, *man-ding'gō*, *n.* an African people of the Niger valley: a member of this people: their language:—*pl.* Mandingo, -goes, -gos.— Also *adj.*

mandioc, mandiocca. See manioc.

mandira, mandir, *mun'dər*(-*a*), *n.* a Hindu temple. [Hind.]

mandoline, mandolin, *man'də-lin*, -*lēn*, *n.* a round-backed instrument like a guitar.—*ns.* mandō'la, mandō'ra, a large mandoline. [It. *mandola*, *mandora*, dim. *mandolino*.]

mandorla, *man'dör-lə*, *n.* an oval panel, or a work of art filling one: the *vesica piscis*. [It., almond.]

mandrake, *man'drāk*, *n.* a poisonous plant (*Mandragora*) of the potato family, subject of many strange fancies: extended to various other plants, as white bryony.—(*Shak.*) mandr**a**gora (-*drag'ə-rə*). [L. *mandragora*—Gr. *mandragorās*.]

mandrel, mandril, *man'drəl*, *n.* a bar of iron fitted to a turning-lathe on which articles to be turned are fixed: the axle of a circular saw. [Fr. *mandrin*.]

mandrill, *man'dril*, *n.* a large West African baboon. [Prob. man, and drill (baboon).]

manducate, *man'dū-kāt*, *v.t.* to chew or eat.—*adj.* man'ducable.—*n.* manducā'tion.—*adj.* man'ducatory (-*kə-tə-ri*). [L. *manducāre*—*mandēre*, to chew.]

mane, *mān*, *n.* long hair on the back of the neck and neighbouring parts, as in the horse and the lion: a long bushy head of hair.—*adjs.* maned; mane'less.—mane'-sheet, a covering for the upper part of a horse's head. [O.E. *manu*; O.N. *mön*; Ger. *mähne*.]

manège, *man-ezh'*, *n.* the managing of horses: the art of horsemanship or of training horses: a horse's actions and paces as taught him: a riding-school.—*v.t.* to train, as a horse. [Fr.; cf. manage.]

maneh. Same as myna.

manes, *mā'nēz*, (*Roman myth.*) *n.pl.* the spirits of the dead. [L. *mānēs*.]

manet, *ma'net* (L.) remains (on the stage):—*pl.* manent.

maneuver. U.S. spelling of manoeuvre.

mangabeira, *mang-ga-bā'rə*, *n.* a Brazilian apocynaceous rubber tree (*Hancornia speciosa*). [Port.,—Tupi *mangaba*.]

mangabey, *mang'gə-bā*, *n.* the white-eyelid monkey, any species of the mainly West African genus *Cercocebus*, esp. the sooty mangabey. [From a district in Madagascar, where, however, they are not found.]

mangal, *mang-gäl'*, *n.* a brazier. [Turk.]

manganese, *mang-gə-nēz'*, *mang'*, *n.* a hard brittle greyish-white metallic element (Mn; at. numb. 25): (originally and commercially) its dioxide (*black manganese*) or other ore.—*n.* mang'anate, a salt of manganic acid.—*adjs.* manganic (-*gan'ik*), of manganese of higher valency; manganif'erous, containing manganese.—*ns.* mang'anin, an alloy of copper with manganese and some nickel; mang'anite, a salt of manganous acid (*chem.*): a grey ore, hydrated oxide of manganese (*min.*). —*adj.* mang'anous, of manganese of lower valency.—manganese bronze, a bronze or brass with a little manganese; manganese spar, rhodochrosite. [Fr. *manganèse*—It. *manganese*—L. *magnēsia*.]

mange. See mangy.

mangel-wurzel, mangold-wurzel, *mang'gl-wûr'zl*, *n.* a variety of beet cultivated as cattle food.—Also mang'el, mang'old. [Ger. *mangold*, beet, *wurzel*, root.]

manger, *mānj'ər*, *n.* a trough in which food is laid for horses and cattle.—dog in the manger, (see dog (1)). [O.Fr. *mangeoire*—L. *mandūcāre*, to chew, eat.]

mangle, *mang'gl*, *v.t.* to hack to raggedness: to tear in cutting: to mutilate: bungle (*fig.*): distort.—*n.* mang'ler. [A.Fr. *mangler*, *mahangler*, prob. a freq. of O.Fr. *mahaigner*, to maim— *mahaing*, a hurt.]

mangle, *mang'gl*, *n.* a rolling-press for smoothing linen.—*v.t.* to smooth with a mangle: to calender.—*n.* mang'ler. [Du. *mangel*—Gr. *manganon*; cf. mangonel.]

mango, *mang'gō*, *n.* a tropical, orig. East Indian, tree (*Mangifera indica*) of the cashew-nut family: its fleshy fruit: a green musk-melon pickled:— *pl.* mang'oes.—wild mango, an African tree of the Simarubaceae with edible fruit, oil-giving seed, and termite-resistant wood. [Port. *manga*— Malay manggā—Tamil *mān-kāy*, mango-fruit.]

mangold, mangold-wurzel. See mangel-wurzel.

mangonel, *mang'gə-nel*, *n.* a mediaeval engine for throwing stones, etc. [O.Fr.,—L.L. *mangonum* —Gr. *manganon*.]

mangosteen, *mang'gə-stēn*, *n.* a tree, *Garcinia mangostana*, or its dark brown, orange-shaped fruit, with thick rind and delicious rose-coloured pulp.—Also mang'ostan. [Malay *mangustan*.]

mangouste. See mongoose.

mangrove, *mang'grōv*, *n.* a tree, esp. species of Rhizophora, that grows in muddy swamps covered at high tide or on tropical coasts and estuary shores. [Origin obscure.]

mangy, mangey, *mānj'i*, *adj.* scabby: affected with mange, shabby, seedy: mean.—*ns.* mange (*mānj*), a back-formation), inflammation of the skin of animals caused by mites; mang'iness. [Fr. *mangé*, eaten, pa.p. of *manger*—L. *mandūcāre*, to chew.]

Manhattan, *man-hat'ən*, *n.* an American cocktail containing vermouth, whisky, bitters, etc. [*Manhattan*, New York.]

mania, *mā'ni-ə*, *n.* a mental illness characterised by euphoria, excessively rapid speech and violent, destructive actions (*psychiat.*): the elated phase of manic-depressive psychosis (*psychiat.*):

Neutral vowels in unaccented syllables; *el'ə-mənt*; for certain sounds in foreign words, see p. viii excessive or unreasonable desire: a craze.—*n.* mā′niac, a person affected with mania: a madman.—*adj.* raving mad.—*adj.* maniacal (*mə-ni′ə-kl*).—*adv.* mani′acally.—*adj.* manic (*mān′ik* or *man′ik*), of or affected by mania.—man′ic-depress′ive, one suffering from manic-depressive psychosis.—Also *adj.*—manic-depressive psychosis, a form of mental illness characterised by phases of depression and elation, either alone or alternately, with lucid intervals. [L.,—Gr. *maniă.*]

Manichaean, Manichean, *man-i-kē′ən, adj.* pertaining to followers of *Manes* or *Manichaeus*, a native of Ecbatana (*c.* A.D. 216-*c.* 276), who taught that everything sprang from two chief principles, light and darkness, or good and evil.—*n.* a believer in Manichaeanism—also Man′ichee. —*ns.* Manichae′anism, Man′ichaeism, Maniche′anism, Man′icheism.

manicure, *man′i-kūr, n.* the care of hands and nails: professional treatment for the hands and nails: one who practises this.—*v.t.* to apply manicure to.—*n.* man′icurist. [L. *manus*, hand, *cūra*, care.]

manifest, *man′i-fest, adj.* that may be easily seen by the eye or perceived by the mind.—*v.t.* to make clear or easily seen: to put beyond doubt: to reveal or declare.—*n.* an open or public statement: a list or invoice of the cargo of a ship or aeroplane to be exhibited at the customhouse: a list of passengers carried by an aeroplane.—*adj.* manifest′able, manifest′ible, that can be manifested or clearly shown.—*n.* manifestā′tion, act of disclosing what is dark or secret: that by which something is manifested: display: mass-meeting, procession, demonstration.—*adj.* manifest′ative.—*adv.* man′ifestly. —*n.* man′ifestness, state of being manifest. [L. *manifestus*, prob. *manus*, the hand, *festus*, pa.p. of obs. *fendĕre*, to strike, to dash against (as in *offendĕre*).]

manifesto, *man-i-fest′ō, n.* a public written declaration of the intentions, opinions, or motives of a sovereign or of a leader, party, or body:—*pl.* -o(e)s.—*v.i.* (*rare*) to issue a manifesto. [It.; see manifest.]

manifold, *man′i-fōld, adj.* various in kind or quality: many in number: having many features: performing several functions.—*n.* a pipe with several lateral outlets to others: aggregate (*math.*): a carbon-copy: manyplies (*dial.*; also in *pl.*).—*v.t.* to multiply: to make simultaneous copies of.—*n.* man′ifolder.—*adv.* man′ifoldly.—*n.* man′ifoldness—man′ifold-pa′per, thin paper for making copies; man′ifold-writ′er, a copying apparatus. [many, and suff. -fold.]

maniform, *man′i-förm, adj.* having the form of a hand. [L. *manus*, the hand, *förma*, a shape.]

Manihot, *man′i-hot, n.* a tropical American genus of the spurge family, including manioc. [manioc.]

manikin, mannikin, *man′i-kin, n.* a dwarf: an anatomical model: a mannequin: a manakin. [Du. *manneken*, a double dim. of *man*; Eng. man.]

manil(l)a, *mə-nil′ə, n.* cheroot made in *Manila*: abaca: strong paper orig. made from abaca.— Manil(l)a hemp, abaca.

manilla, *mə-nil′ə, n.* a West African bracelet, serving as money [Sp.,—L.L. *manilia*, a bracelet —L. *manus*, the hand, or L. *monilia* (pl. of *monile*), necklace, influenced by *manus*.]

manille, *mə-nil′, n.* in ombre and quadrille, the highest card but one. [Sp. *malilla*.]

manioc, *man′i-ok, n.* manihot or cassava: meal therefrom.—Also man′dioc, mandio′c(c)a, man′-ihoc. [Tupí *mandioca*.]

maniple, *man′i-pl, n.* a company of foot-soldiers in the Roman army (*hist.*): in the Western Church, a eucharistic vestment, a narrow strip worn on the left arm.—*adj.* and *n.* manipular

(*mə-nip′ū-lər*). [L. *manipulus*—*manus*, the hand, *plēre*, to fill.]

maniplies. Same as manyplies.

manipulate, *mə-nip′ū-lāt, v.t.* to work with the hands: to handle or manage: to give a false appearance to: to turn to one's own purpose or advantage.—*n.* manipulā′tion.—*adjs.* manip′ul-(at)able, capable of being manipulated; manip′-ular, manip′ulative, manip′ulatory.—*n.* manip′ul-ātor, one who manipulates: a mechanical device for handling small, remote, or radioactive objects. —See also master-slave manipulator. [L.L. *manipulāre, -ātum*; see maniple.]

Manis, *mā′nis, n.* the pangolin or scaly ant-eater. [App. intended as sing. of manes.]

manito, *man′i-tō, n.* a spirit or object of reverence among American Indians.—Also manitou (-*tōō*). [Algonkin.]

manjack, *man′jack, n.* a West Indian boraginaceous tree (*Cordia macrophylla*): its fruit.

mankind, manly. See man.

manna, *man′ə, n.* the food miraculously provided for the Israelites in the wilderness (*B.*): delicious food for body or mind: anything advantageous falling one's way as by divine bounty: a sugary exudation from the mann′a-ash (*Fraxinus ornus*), -larch (Briançon manna), and other trees, from a species of tamarisk, from Alhagi, etc.: edible fragments of the mann′a-li′chen (*Lecanora*): float-grass seeds: honey-dew.— *adj.* mannif′erous.—*ns.* mann′ite, mann′itol, a sweet alcohol, $C_6H_8(OH)_6$, got from manna, from seaweeds of the genus Laminaria, etc.; mann′ose, a sugar ($C_6H_{12}O_6$) got by oxidising mannitol.—mann′a-croup (*krōōp*; Russ. *krupa*), -groats, grains of manna-grass; mann′a-dew, manna imagined to be solidified dew; mann′a-grass′, an aquatic grass (*Glyceria*) with edible seeds, float-grass. [Heb. *män hū*, what is it? or from *man*, a gift.]

mannequin, *man′i-kin, n.* a dummy figure: a person, usu. a woman, employed to wear and display clothes. [Fr.,—Du.; see manikin.]

manner, *man′ər, n.* the way in which anything is done: method: fashion: personal style of acting or bearing: custom: style of writing or of thought: sort (of; formerly often with omission of following *of*): style: (*pl.*) morals (*arch.*): (*pl.*) social conduct: (*pl.*) good behaviour.—*adj.* mann′ered, having manners (esp. in compounds, as *well-* or *ill-mannered*): affected with mannerism: artificial: stilted.—*ns.* mann′-erism, a constant sameness of manner: stiltedness: a marked peculiarity or trick of style or manner, esp. in literary composition: manner or style becoming wearisome by its sameness: a late 16th-cent. art style characterised by distortion esp. of the human figure, bright harsh colours, etc.: mann′erist, one addicted to mannerism.—*adj.* manneris′tic.—*adv.* manner-is′tically.—*n.* mann′erliness.—*adj.* mann′erly, showing good manners: well-behaved: not rude.—*adv.* with good manners: civilly: respectfully: without rudeness.—by no manner of means, under no circumstances whatever; in a manner, in a sense; make one's manners (*arch.*), to salute a person on meeting by a bow, curtsy, etc.; shark's manners, rapacity; to the manner born, accustomed from birth. [Fr. *manière*—*main*—L. *manus*, the hand.]

manner, *man′ər, n.* Same as mainor (in or with the manner).

manning. See man.

mannikin. See manikin.

mannitol. See manna.

manoeuvre, in U.S. maneuver, *mə-nōō′vər*. or -*nū′, n.* a piece of dexterous management: a stratagem: a skilful and clever movement in military or naval tactics: (usu. *pl.*) a large-scale battle-training exercise of armed forces.—*v.i.*

and *v.t.* to perform a manoeuvre: to manage with art: to change the position of troops or of ships: to effect or to gain by manoeuvres.— *ns.* manoeu'vrer; manoeuvrabil'ity.—*adj.* manoeu'vrable.—In U.S. maneuverer, etc. [Fr. *manœuvre*—L. *manū*, by hand, *opera*, work; cf. manure.]

manometer, *man-om'i-tər, n.* an instrument for measuring the pressure of fluids.—*adjs.* manometric (*man-ō-met'rik*), -al. [Gr. *manos*, rare, thin, *metron*, measure.]

manor, *man'ər, n.* the land belonging to a nobleman, or so much as he formerly kept for his own use: the district over which the court of the lord of the manor had authority (*hist.*): a tract of land in America for which a fee-farm rent was paid: a police district (*slang*).—*adj.* manorial (*ma-nō'ri-əl, -nō'*), pertaining to a manor.— man'or-house, -seat, the house or seat belonging to a manor. [O.Fr. *manoir*—L. *manēre, mānsum*, to stay.]

manqué, *mä-kā,* (Fr.) unsuccessful, not having realised promise or hope—placed after the noun.

manred, *man'red,* (*obs.*) *n.* homage: a body of vassals.—(*Scot.*) man'rent. [O.E. *mannrǣden*; man and suff. *-rǣden*, expressing mode or state.]

mansard, *man'särd, n.* a roof having the lower part steeper than the upper.—Usually man'sard-roof'. [Employed by François *Mansard* or *Mansart* (1598-1666).]

manse, *mans, n.* an ecclesiastical residence, esp. that of a parish minister of the Church of Scotland.—son of the manse, a minister's son. [L.L. *mansus, mansa*, a dwelling—*manēre, mānsum*, to remain.]

mansion, *man'shən, n.* abode, stay (*obs.*): a resting-place on a journey (*obs.*): a dwelling-place (*arch.*; often in *pl.*): an apartment, separate lodging in a building (*obs.*): a large house: a manor-house: a house (*astrol.*): (in *pl.*) a large building let in flats.—*n.* man'sionry (*Shak.* man'sonry), residence: mansions.—man'sionhouse, a mansion (Mansion House, the official residence of the Lord Mayor of London). [O.Fr., —L. *mānsiō, -ōnis*—*manēre, mānsum*, to remain, to stay.]

mansuete, *man'swēt,* (*arch.*) *adj.* gentle: mild: tame.—*n.* man'suetude (-*swi-tūd*). [L. *mānsuētus*—*manus*, hand, *suēscēre*, to accustom.]

mansworn, *man'swōrn, -swōrn,* (*arch.*) *adj.* perjured. [O.E. *mānswerian*—*mān*, evil, *swerian*, to swear.]

manta, *man'tə, n.* a blanket: a cloak: a horse-cloth: (*cap.*) a genus of gigantic rays or sea-vampires. [Sp.]

manteau, manto, *man'tō, n.* (17th-18th cent.) a woman's loose gown. [Fr. *manteau*—L. *mantellum.*]

manteel, *man-tēl',* (*obs.*) *n.* a soldier's cloak: a lady's cape. [Fr. *mantille*—Sp. *mantilla.*]

mantel, *man'tl, n.* a manteltree: a mantelpiece: a mantelshelf.—man'telet, a mantlet.—man'telpiece, the ornamental structure over and in front of a fireplace: a mantelshelf; man'telshelf, the ornamental shelf over a fireplace; man'teltree, the lintel or arch of a fireplace. [mantle.]

mantic, *man'tik, adj.* relating to divination: prophetic. [Gr. *mantikos*—*mantis*, a prophet.]

manticore, *man'ti-kōr, -kör,* manticora, *-kō', -kö'rə, n.* a fabulous compound of lion and scorpion with a human head. [L. *manticora*— Gr. *mantichōrās*, a wrong reading for *martichōrās*, from an Old Persian word for man-eater.]

mantilla, *man-til'ə, n.* a small mantle: a kind of veil covering the head and falling down upon the shoulders. [Sp.; dim. of *manta.*]

Mantis, *man'tis, n.* a genus of orthopterous insects carrying their large spinous forelegs in the attitude of prayer.—mantis shrimp, a stomatopod

crustacean with claws like the mantis. [Gr. *mantis, -eōs*, prophet.]

mantissa, *man-tis'ə, n.* the fractional part of a logarithm. [L., make-weight.]

mantle, *man'tl, n.* a cloak or loose outer garment: a covering: symbol of the spirit or authority (of; in allusion to Elijah, 1 Kings xix. 19 ff.): a fold of the integument of a mollusc or a brachiopod secreting the shell: the back and folded wings of a bird: a scum on a liquid (*arch.*): a hood or network of refractory material that becomes incandescent when exposed to a flame: the part of the earth immediately beneath the crust, constituting the greater part of the earth's bulk, and presumed to consist of solid heavy rock.— *v.t.* to cover: to obscure: to form a scum upon (*arch.*): to suffuse: to disguise.—*v.i.* to spread like a mantle: to develop a scum (*arch.*): to froth: to be suffused: to stretch the wings over the legs, as a hawk.—*ns.* man'tlet, man'telet, a small cloak for women: a movable shield or screen (*fort.*); man'tling, cloth suitable for mantles: the drapery of a coat-of-arms (*her.*).— mantle rock, loose rock at the earth's surface. [Partly through O.E. *mentel*, partly through O.Fr. *mantel* (Fr. *manteau*)—L. *mantellum.*]

manto. See manteau.

mantra, *man'trə, n.* a Vedic hymn: a sacred text used as an incantation: extended to music having mystical effect.—Also mantram. [Sans., instrument of thought.]

mantua, *man'tū-ə, n.* (17th-18th cent.) a woman's loose outer gown—(*Scot.*) mant'y.—*n.* man'tua-mak'er, a dressmaker. [manteau, confused with *Mantua*, in Italy.]

Mantuan, *man'tū-ən, adj.* of Mantua in Italy.—*n.* a native or inhabitant of Mantua, esp. Virgil.— Also the name of the Latin pastoral poet Baptista *Mantuanus* (1448-1516).

manual, *man'ū-əl, adj.* of the hand: done, worked, or used by the hand: working with the hands.— *n.* drill in the use of weapons, etc.: a handbook or handy compendium of a large subject or treatise: an old office-book like the modern R.C. *Rituale*: a key or keyboard played by hand: a primary feather. — *adv.* man'ually. — manual alphabet, the signs for letters made by the deaf and dumb; manual exercise, drill in handling arms. [L. *manuālis*—*manus*, the hand.]

manubrium, *mā-nū'bri-əm, n.* any handle-like structure: the presternum or anterior part of the breast-bone in mammals:—*pl.* manū'bria.—*adj.* manū'brial. [L. *manūbrium*, a handle.]

manufacture, *man-ū-fak'chər, v.t.* to make, originally by hand, now usu. by machinery and on a large scale: to fabricate, concoct: to produce unintelligently in quantity.—*v.i.* to be occupied in manufacturing.—*n.* the practice, act, or process of manufacturing: anything manufactured.—*n.* manufact'ory, a factory or place where goods are manufactured.—*adj.* manufact'ural.—*n.* manufact'urer, one who works in a factory (*obs.*): one who owns a factory: one who makes, concocts, or invents.—*adj.* manufact'uring, pertaining to manufactures. [Fr.,—L. *manū* (abl.), by hand, *factūra*, a making, from *facēre, factum*, to make.]

manuka, *mä'nōō-kä, n.* an Australian and New Zealand tree (*Leptospermum*) of the myrtle family, with hard wood, its leaves a substitute for tea. [Maori.]

manul, *mä'nōol, n.* a Central Asian wild cat. [Mongolian.]

manumit, *man-ū-mit', v.t.* to release from slavery: to set free:—*pr.p.* manumitt'ing; *pa.t.* and *pa.p.* manumitt'ed.—*n.* manumission (*-mish'ən*). [L. *manūmittēre* or *manū mittēre* or *ēmittēre*, to send from one's hand or control—*manus*, the hand, *mittēre, missum*, to send.]

manure, *mən-ūr'*, formerly *man'ūr, v.t.* to hold,

occupy (*obs.*): to manage (*obs.*): to cultivate (*obs.*): to enrich with any fertilising substance.— *n.* any substance applied to land to make it more fruitful.—*ns.* manur'ance (*arch.*), cultivation; manur'er.—*adj.* manur'ial.—*n.* manur'ing. [A.Fr. *maynoverer* (Fr. *manœuvrer*); see manoeuvre.]

manus, *mā'nəs, mä'nōōs, n.* the hand or corresponding part of an animal. [L. *mănus*, pl. *-ūs.*]

manuscript, *man'ū-skript, adj.* written by hand or typed, not printed.—*n.* a book or document written by hand before invention of printing: copy for a printer, in handwriting or typed: handwritten form.—Abbrev. MS. [L. *manū* (abl.), by hand, *scribĕre, scriptum,* to write.]

Manx, *mangks, n.* the language of the Isle of *Man,* belonging to the Gadhelic branch of Celtic.—*adj.* pertaining to the Isle of Man or to its inhabitants. —Manx cat, a breed of cat with only a rudimentary tail; Manx'man:—*fem.* Manx'woman.

many, *men'i, adj.* (*comp.* more, *mōr, mŏr*; *superl.* most, *mōst*) consisting of a great number: numerous.—*n.* many persons: a great number (usu. with omission of *of*): company, retinue (*Spens.*; perh. for meinie).—*adjs.* man'y-coloured, man'y-eyed', having many colours, eyes; man'y-fold'ed (*Spens.*), having many layers: having many folds; man'y-head'ed, having many heads: consisting of many.—man'y-root, Ruellia.—*adj.* man'y-sid'ed, having many qualities or aspects: having wide interests or varied abilities.—man'y-sid'edness.—*adj.* man'y-tongued'.—many a, many (with singular noun and verb); many-headed beast, monster, the people (see *belua multorum capitum* in *Appendices*); the many, the crowd. [O.E. *manig.*]

manyplies, *men'i-plīz, n. sing.* and *pl.* the third stomach of a ruminant—the *omasum* or *psalterium.*—Also man'iplies and (*dial.*) moniplies, mony-plies (*mon', mun'*). [many, ply.]

manzanilla, *man-zə-nil'ə, -nē'yə, n.* a very dry, light sherry. [Sp.; also meaning camomile; same root as manchineel.]

manzanita, *man-zə-nē'tə, n.* bearberry of Californian species. [Sp., dim. of *manzana,* apple.]

Maoist, *mow'ist, n.* one who adheres to the Chinese type of communism as set forth by Mao Tse-tung.—*n.* Mao'ism.

Maori, *mow'ri, mä'ō-ri, n.* a member of the brown race of New Zealand: the language of this race: —*pl.* Mao'ris.—Also *adj.*—Maori hen, the weka. [Maori.]

maormor, *mär'mŏr, -mōr,* a wrong form of mormaor.

map, *map, n.* a representation in outline of the surface features of the earth, the moon, etc., or of part of it, usu. on a plane surface: a similar plan of the stars in the sky: a representation, scheme, or epitome of the disposition or state of anything.—*v.t.* to make a map of: to place (the elements of a set) in one-to-one correspondence with the elements of another set (*math.*):—*pr.p.* mapp'ing; *pa.t.* and *pa.p.* mapped. —*ns.* mapp'er; mapp'ery (*Shak.*), perh. working with, or making, maps, or planning out; mapp'ist.—map'-measurer, an instrument for measuring distances on a map; map'-mounter, one who mounts maps, or backs them with cloth and fixes them on rollers, etc.; map'-reading, the interpretation of what one sees in a map.—*adv.* map'wise, in the manner of a map.— map out, to plan, divide up, and apportion; off the map, out of existence: negligible; on the map, to be taken into account. [L. *mappa,* a napkin, a painted cloth, orig. Punic.]

maple, *mā'pl, n.* any tree of the genus *Acer,* from the sap of some species of which sugar and syrup can be made; its timber.—*adj.* of maple.— maple sugar; maple syrup; maple leaf, the emblem of Canada. [O.E. *mapul,* maple.]

mappemond, *map'ə-mŏnd, map-mŏnd', n.* a map of the world (*hist.*): the world itself (*obs.*). [L.L. *mappa mundī.*]

mapstick. See mopstick.

maquette, *ma-ket', n.* a small model of something to be made, esp. a model in clay or wax of a piece of sculpture. [Fr.]

maqui, *mä'kē, n.* a Chilean evergreen shrub (*Aristotelia maqui*; fam. Elaeocarpaceae) whose berry yields a medicinal wine. [Araucan.]

maquillage, *ma-kē-yäzh, n.* (art of using) cosmetics, make-up. [Fr.]

maquis, *mä'kē', n.sing.* and *pl.* a thicket formation of shrubs, as in Corsica and on Mediterranean shores (*bot.*): (often *cap.*) French guerrilla bands (1940-45), or a member of one.—*n.* (often *cap.*) maquisard (*mä-kē-zär*), a member of the maquis. [Fr.,—It. *macchia*—L. *macula,* mesh.]

mar, *mär, v.t.* to interfere with (*obs.*): to spoil: to impair: to injure: to damage: to disfigure:— *pr.p.* marr'ing; *pa.t.* and *pa.p.* marred (*Spens.* mard).—*n.* mar'dy (*dial.*), a spoilt child: a timid or petulant cry-baby.—Also *adj.* and *v.t.*— mar'plot, one who defeats or mars a plot by unwarranted interference; mar'-sport, a spoil-sport; mar'-text, an ignorant preacher. [O.E. *merran.*]

mara, *mä'rä, n.* the so-called Patagonian hare or Dolichotis.

marabou(t), *mar'ə-bōō(t), n.* an adjutant bird, esp. an African species: its feathers: a plume or trimming of its feathers: a feather necklet: a very white raw silk. [Same as next word.]

marabout, *mar'ə-bōōt, n.* a Mohammedan hermit, esp. in N. Africa: a Moslem shrine. [Fr.,—Ar. *murābit,* hermit.]

maraca, *mä-rä'ka, n.* a dance-band instrument, a gourd or substitute, containing beans, beads, shot, or the like. [Carib.]

marah, *mä'rä, n.* bitterness: something bitter. [Heb.]

maranatha, *mar-ə-nä'tha.* See anathema.

Maranta, *mä-ran'ta, n.* the arrowroot genus of monocotyledons giving name to the family Maranta'ceae, akin to the banana and ginger families. [After Bartolommeo *Maranta,* 16th-cent. Italian herbalist.]

maraschino, *mar-ə-skē'nō, -shē'nō, n.* a liqueur distilled from a cherry grown in Dalmatia.— maraschino cherry, a cherry preserved in real or imitation maraschino and used for decorating cocktails, etc. [It.,—*marasca, amarasca,* a sour cherry—L. *amārus,* bitter.]

marasmus, *mə-raz'məs, n.* a wasting away of the body.—*adj.* maras'mic.—*n.* Maras'mius, a common genus of toadstools, including the fairy-ring champignon, drying up in sunshine but recovering in damp. [Latinised—Gr. *marasmos*—*marainein,* to decay.]

Maratha, Mahratta, *mə-rät'ə, n.* a member of a once dominant people of S.W. India.—*n.* Marathi (*mə-rät'ē*), their Sanskritic language. [Hindi *marhaṭa*—Sans. *mahārāṣṭra,* great kingdom.]

Marathon, *mar'ə-thon, -thən, n.* scene of the Greek victory over the Persians, 490 B.C., 22 miles from Athens: a marathon race (without *cap.*): a test of endurance (without *cap.*).—*adj.* (without *cap.*), of great length in time, or distance, etc.: displaying powers of endurance and stamina.—*n.* mar'athoner.—*adj.* and *n.* Marathōn'ian.— marathon race, a long-distance foot-race (usually 26 miles 385 yards), commemorating the tradition that a Greek ran from Marathon to Athens with news of the victory: used loosely of long-distance race in other sports, e.g. swimming. [Gr. *Marathōn.*]

Marattia, *ma-rat'i-a, n.* a genus of ferns giving name to the Marattia'ceae, a tropical family of very large primitive eusporangiate ferns. [Named after G. F. *Maratti* (d. 1777), Italian botanist.]

maraud, *mə-röd', v.i.* to rove in quest of plunder.

—*v.t.* to harry.—*n.* raiding: plundering.—*n.* **maraud′er**. [Fr. *maraud*, rogue; origin obscure.]

**maravedi**, *mar-ə-vā′di*, *n.* an obsolete Spanish copper coin of little value. [Sp. *maravedi*—Ar. *Murābitin*, the dynasty of the Almoravides (11th and 12th cent.).]

**marble**, *mär′bl*, *n.* a granular crystalline limestone: loosely, any rock of similar appearance taking a high polish: a slab, work of art, tombstone, tomb, or other object made of marble: a little hard ball (originally of marble) used by boys in play: marbling: anything hard, cold, polished, white, or otherwise like marble (*fig.*): (in *pl.*) a game played with little balls.—*adj.* composed of marble: shining: unyielding: hard: insensible: marbled.—*v.t.* to stain or vein like marble.—*adj.* **mar′bled**, irregularly mottled and streaked like some kinds of marble: wrought in marble: furnished with marble.—*ns.* **mar′bler**; **mar′bling**, a marbled appearance or colouring: the act of veining or painting in imitation of marble.—*adv.* **mar′bly**, like marble.—*adjs.* **mar′ble-breast′ed**, hard-hearted, cruel; **mar′ble-con′stant**, constant or firm as marble, immovable. —**mar′ble-cutter**, one who hews marble: a machine for cutting marble; **mar′bled-white′**, a butterfly of the Satyridae.—*adjs.* **mar′ble-edged**, having the edges marbled, as a book; **mar′ble-heart′ed**, hard-hearted, insensible.—**mar′ble-paper**, paper coloured in imitation of variegated marble.—**Elgin marbles**, a collection of marbles obtained chiefly from the Parthenon by Lord *Elgin* in 1811, now in the British Museum. [O.Fr. *marbre*—L. *marmor*; cf. Gr. *marmaros*—*marmairein*, to sparkle.]

**marc**, *märk*, Fr. *mär*, *n.* fruit-refuse in wine- or oil-making.—**marc brandy**, brandy made from marc. [Fr.]

**marcantant**, *mär′kən-tant*, (*Shak.*) *n.* a merchant. [It. *mercatante*.]

**marcasite**, *mär′kə-sit*, *n.* sulphide of iron in orthorhombic crystals (in the gem trade can be pyrite, polished steel, etc.). [L.L. *marcasita*—Ar. *marqashit(h)ā*; origin unknown.]

**marcato**, *mär-kä′tō*, *adj.* marked: emphatic: strongly accented:—*superl.* **marcatis′simo**.—Also *adv.* [It.,—*marcare*, to mark.]

**Marcel, marcel**, *mär-sel′*, *n.* (in full **Marcel wave**), an artificial wave imparted to hair by a hot iron, a comb, and manipulation.—*v.t.* to make a marcel in.—*adj.* **marcelled′**. [*Marcel*, a French hairdresser, the inventor (1872).]

**marcella**, *mär-sel′ə*, *n.* a type of cotton or linen fabric, in twill weave. [Anglicisation of *Marseilles*.]

**marcescent**, *mär-ses′ənt*, *adj.* withering without falling off.—*adj.* **marcesc′ible**. [L. *marcēscēns*, *-entis*, pr.p. of *marcēscĕre*—*marcĕre*, to fade.]

**Marcgravia**, *märk-grä′vi-a*, *n.* a tropical American genus of climbing epiphytic shrubs, with pitcher-like bracts developed as nectaries, visited by hummingbirds, giving name to the family **Marcgraviā′ceae**, akin to the tea family. [After Georg *Markgraf* (1610-44), German traveller.]

**March**, *märch*, *n.* the third month of the year (in England until 1752 the year began on 25th March).—**March beer**, strong beer brewed in March; **March hare**, a hare gambolling in the breeding season, proverbially mad. [L. *Martius* (*mēnsis*), (the month) of Mars.]

**march**, *märch*, *n.* a boundary: border: a border district—used chiefly in *pl.*—*v.i.* to have a common boundary.—*n.* **march′er**.— **march′-dyke, -dike**, a boundary wall, usu. of turf; **march′man**, a borderer; **march′-stone**, a boundary stone; **march′-trea′son**, an offence against the laws of the marches, e.g. raiding the neighbouring country in time of peace.—**Lord marcher** (*hist.*), a lord who had royal prerogative in, and jurisdiction over, lands in the marches;

**riding the marches**, a ceremony of riding round the bounds of a municipality. [Fr. *marche*; of Gmc. origin; cf. mark, O.E. *mearc*.]

**march**, *märch*, *v.i.* to walk in a markedly rhythmical military manner, or in a grave, stately, or resolute manner: to advance steadily or irresistibly.—*v.t.* to cause to march: to force to go. —*n.* a marching movement: an act of marching: distance traversed at a stretch by marching: regular advance: a piece of music fitted for marching to, or similar in character and rhythm, usu. with a trio.—**marching orders**, orders to march: (as from employment, etc.) dismissal (*coll.*); **marching regiment**, one without permanent quarters; **march past**, the march of a body in front of one who reviews it.—**forced march**, a march vigorously pressed forward for combative purposes; **on the march**, afoot and journeying; **rogue's march**, music played in derision of a person expelled; **steal a march on**, to gain an advantage over, esp. in a sly or secret manner. [Fr. *marcher*, to walk, prob.—L. *marcus*, a hammer.]

**Marchantia**, *mär-kan′shi-a*, *-ti-a*, *n.* a genus of liverworts with flat, lobed and branched thallus, growing in damp places, giving name to the family **Marchantiā′ceae**. [Named after Nicolas *Marchant* (d. 1678), French botanist.]

**märchen**, *mer′hhyən*, *n. sing.* and *pl.* a story or fable, a folk-tale. [Ger.]

**marchioness**, *mär′shən-es*, *-is*, *n.* the wife of a marquis, marquess: a woman who holds a marquisate in her own right: a size of roofing slate 22 × 12 in.—*n.* **marchesa** (*mär-kā′za*), It. fem. of **marchese** (*mär-kā′ze*), a marquis. [L.L. *marchiōnissa*, fem. of *marchiō*, *-ōnis*, a lord of the marches.]

**marchpane**, *märch′pān*, (*Shak.*) *n.* until 19th cent., name of marzipan (*q.v.*). [It. *marzapane*.]

**Marcionite**, *mär′shən-it*, *n.* a follower of *Marcion* of Sinope (d. A.D. 165), who, partly under Gnostic influences, constructed an ethico-dualistic philosophy of religion.—Also *adj.*—*ns.* **Mar′cionist**; **Mar′cionitism**.

**Marcobrunner**, *mär′kō-broōn-ər*, *n.* a fine white wine produced in Erbach, near Wiesbaden. [From the *Markbrunnen* fountain hard by.]

**Marconi**, *mär-kō′ni*, *adj.* connected with Guglielmo *Marconi* (1874-1937), or his system of wireless telegraphy.—*v.t.* and *v.i.* (without *cap.*) to communicate by wireless telegraphy.—*n.* **marco′nigram**, a message so transmitted.—*v.t.* and *v.i.* **marco′nigraph**.

**mard, mardy**. See under mar.

**Mardi Gras**, *mär-de grä*, (Fr.) Shrove Tuesday.

**mare**, *mär*, *n.* the female of the horse.—**mare's′-nest**, a supposed discovery that turns out to have no reality; **mare's′-tail**, a tall marsh plant of the genus Hippuris: also applied to the horse-tail: (in *pl.*) long straight fibres of grey cirrus cloud.—**the grey mare is the better horse**, the wife rules her husband, or is the abler. [O.E. *mere*, fem. of *mearh*, a horse; cog. with Ger. *mähre*, O.N. *merr*, W. *march*, a horse.]

**mare**, *mär*, (*Shak.*) *n.* the nightmare (q.v.).

**mare**, *mä′rē*, *ma′re*, *n.* any of various darkish level areas in (*a*) the moon, (*b*) Mars:—*pl.* **maria** (*mä′ri-a*, *ma′*). [L., sea.]

**mare clausum**, *mä′rē klö′səm*, *ma′re klow′soōm*, (L.) a closed sea—a sea within the jurisdiction of one state.

**maremma**, *mär-em′a*, *n.* seaside marshland. [It., —L. *maritima*, seaside.]

**mareschal**, *mär′shl*. Same as **marshal**.

**margarin**, *mär′gər-in*, *n.* a mixture of palmitin and stearin once thought a compound: a glyceryl ester of margaric acid.—*ns.* **margarine** (*mär′gər-ēn*; pop. pron. *mär′jər-ēn*; contr. **marge**, *märj*), a butterlike substance made from vegetable oils and fats, etc.; **mar′garite**, a pearly-lustred mineral sometimes reckoned a lime-alumina mica.—*adjs.* **margaric** (-*gar'*); **margarit'ic; margaritif'erous,** pearl-bearing.—**margar(it)ic acid,** an acid intermediate between palmitic and stearic. [Gr. *margarītēs,* a pearl.]

**margay,** *mär'gä, n.* a spotted S. American tiger-cat. [Fr. (or Sp.),—Tupi *mbaracaïa.*]

**marge,** *märj, n.* margin, brink. [Fr.,—L. *margō, -inis.*]

**margin,** *mär'jin, poet.* **margent,** *mär'jənt, n.* an edge, border: the blank edge on the page of a book: something allowed more than is needed: a deposit to protect a broker against loss: difference between selling and buying price.—*v.t.* to furnish with margins: to enter on the margin.—*adj.* **mar'ginal,** pertaining to a margin: in or on the margin: barely sufficient.—*n.* **margina'lia,** notes written on the margin.—*v.t.* **mar'ginalise, -ize,** to furnish with notes.—*adv.* **mar'ginally.**—*adjs.* **mar'ginate, -d,** having a well-marked border; **mar'gined.**—**marginal constituency,** a constituency that does not provide a safe seat for any of the political parties; **marginal land,** less fertile land which will be brought under cultivation only if economic conditions justify it; **marginal seat.** [L. *margō, marginis*; cf. **mark, march** (2).]

**margosa,** *mär-gō'sa, n.* the tree that yields nim oil. [Port. *amargosa* (fem.), bitter.]

**margrave,** *mär'grāv, n.* a German nobleman of rank equivalent to an English marquis:—*fem.* **margravine** (*mär'grə-vēn*).—*ns.* **mar'gravate, margrä'viate,** the jurisdiction or dignity of a margrave. [M.Du. *markgrave* (Du. *markgraaf*; Ger. *markgraf*)—*mark,* a border, *grave* (mod. *graaf*), a count; cf. Ger. *graf,* O.E. *gerēfa,* Eng. **reeve, sheriff.**]

**marguerite,** *mär-gə-rēt', n.* the ox-eye daisy or other single chrysanthemum. [Fr., daisy—Gr. *margarītēs,* pearl.]

**maria.** See **mare** (3).

**mariage de convenance,** *ma-rē-äzh də kɔ̄-v-nās,* (Fr.), marriage for reasons of material advantage rather than love.

**marialite,** *mā'ri-ə-līt, n.* a variety of scapolite rich in sodium, chlorine, and silica, poor in calcium. [*Maria* Rose vom Rath, a mineralogist's wife.]

**Marian,** *mā'ri-ən, adj.* relating to the Virgin *Mary* or to Queen *Mary* (Tudor or Stewart).—*n.* a devotee, follower, or defender of Mary: an English Roman Catholic of Mary Tudor's time. [L. *Maria.*]

**Marian,** *mar'i-ən, mā'ri-ən, adj.* relating to the great Roman general Gaius *Marius* (d. 86 B.C.).

**marid,** *mar'id, mä-rēd', n.* a jinni of the most powerful class. [Ar. *mārid, marid.*]

**marigold,** *mar'i-gōld, n.* a yellow-flowered composite (*Calendula*) or its flower: extended to other yellow flowers (see **corn, marsh**).—**African, French marigold,** Mexican composites (*Tagetes*). [From the Virgin *Mary* and **gold** (flower).]

**marigraph,** *mar'i-gräf, n.* a recording tide-gauge.—*n.* **mar'igram,** a record given by one. [L. *mare,* sea, Gr. *graphein,* to write.]

**marijuana, marihuana,** *mä-ri-(hh)wä'na, n.* hemp: its dried flowers smoked as an intoxicant. [Amer. Sp.]

**marimba,** *mə-rim'bə, n.* an African xylophone, adopted by Central Americans and jazz musicians. [Of African origin.]

**marine,** *mə-rēn', adj.* of, in, near, concerned with, or belonging to, the sea: done or used at sea: inhabiting, found in or got from the sea.—*n.* a soldier serving on shipboard: shipping, naval or mercantile, fleet: nautical service: naval affairs: a sea-piece in painting.—*ns.* **marina** (*ma-rē'na*), a yacht station, prepared with every kind of facility for a yachting holiday; **marinade** (*mar-i-nād'*), a liquor or pickle in which fish or meat is steeped before cooking, to improve the

flavour.—*vs.t.* **mar'inade, mar'inate,** to steep in wine, oil, herbs, etc.—*n.* **mar'iner,** a sailor.—**marine acid,** hydrochloric acid; **marine boiler,** a steamship boiler; **marine engine,** a ship's engine; **marine glue** (see **glue**); **marine insurance,** insurance of ships or cargoes; **marine soap,** a coconut-oil soap, for washing with sea-water; **marine store,** a place where old ships' materials are dealt in; **marine stores,** old ships' materials: supplies for ships; **marine trumpet,** the tromba marina.—**tell that to the marines,** a phrase expressive of disbelief and ridicule, from the sailor's contempt for the marine's ignorance of seamanship. [Fr.,—L. *marinus—mare,* sea.]

**Marinist,** *mə-rē'nist, n.* a follower or imitator of the Italian poet Giambattista *Marini* (1569-1625).—*n.* **Marin'ism,** his manner, full of strained conceits.

**Mariolatry,** *mā-ri-ol'ə-tri, n.* (excessive) worship of the Virgin *Mary*—the veneration duly paid to her being properly *hyperdulia.*—*n.* **Mariol'ater,** one who practises Mariolatry.—*adj.* **Mariol'-atrous.** [Gr. *Maria,* Mary, *latreiä,* worship.]

**marionette,** *mar-i-ə-net', n.* a puppet moved by strings. [Fr., dim. of the name *Marion,* itself a dim. of *Marie,* Mary.]

**Mariotte's law.** See **law.**

**marischal,** a Scots spelling of **marshal.**

**marish,** *mar'ish, n.* and *adj.* Same as **marsh.**

**Marist,** *mar'ist, n.* a member of a modern R.C. congregation for teaching, preaching, and foreign missions.—*adj.* devoted to the service of the Virgin. [Fr. *Mariste.*]

**maritage,** *mar'it-ij, (hist.) n.* the feudal superior's right to dispose of a vassal's heiress (or heir) in marriage, or exact a fine. [L.L. *maritāgium.*]

**marital,** *mar'i-təl, mə-ri'təl, adj.* pertaining to a husband, or to a marriage: of the nature of a marriage.—*adv.* **mar'itally** (or *mə-ri'*). [L. *maritālis—maritus,* a husband.]

**maritime,** *mar'i-tim, adj.* pertaining to the sea: relating to sea-going or sea-trade: having a sea-coast: situated near the sea: living on the shore, littoral: having a navy and sea-trade. [L. *maritimus—mare,* sea.]

**Marivaudage,** *mä-rē-vō-däzh, n.* preciosity in writing. [Fr., from Pierre de *Marivaux* (1688-1763), French author.]

**marjoram,** *mär'jə-ram, n.* an aromatic labiate plant (*Origanum*) used as a seasoning. [O.Fr. *majorane;* origin doubtful.]

**mark,** *märk, n.* a boundary (*arch.*): a limit (*arch.*): a standard: a territory, esp. a border territory (*arch.*): a tract of common land belonging to a village community (*hist.*): a boundary stone, post, or the like: an object indicating position or serving as a guide: an object to be aimed at, striven for, or attained, as a butt, a goal, the jack at bowls, the pit of the stomach in boxing: a hawk's quarry (*obs.*): a suitable victim (*slang*): that which exactly suits one (*slang*): a visible indication or sign: a symbol: a distinctive device: a brand: a set, group, or class, marked with the same brand: a stamp: a token: a substitute for a signature: a distinguishing characteristic: an impression or trace: a dis-coloured spot, streak, smear, or other local modification of appearance: note: distinction: noteworthiness: a point awarded for merit: a footprint: the impression of a Rugby football player's heel on the ground on making a fair catch: the starting-line in a race: a groove indicative of youth in a horse's incisor (as in *mark of mouth*): a tag on a lead-line indicating so many fathoms, feet, etc.—*v.t.* to make a mark on: to indicate: to record: to make emphatic, distinct, or prominent: to impress with a sign: to note: to regard.—*v.i.* to take particular notice.—*adj.* **marked,** having marks: indicated: noticeable: prominent: emphatic: watched and suspected: doomed.—*adv.* **mark′edly**, noticeably.—*ns.* **mark′er**, a person or tool that marks: something that marks a position, as a stationary light, a flare: one who marks the score at games, as at billiards: a counter or other device for scoring: a bookmark: a recorder of attendances: a kind of school monitor: a memorial tablet (*U.S.*): the soldier who forms the pivot round which a body of soldiers wheels; **mark′ing**, act of making a mark: (esp. in *pl.*) disposition of marks.—Also *adj.*— **mark′er-bea′con**, **-bomb**, **-flag**; **mark′ing-ink**, indelible ink, used for marking clothes; **mark′-ing-nut**, the fruit of an East Indian tree (Seme-carpus) of the cashew family, yielding a black juice used in marking clothes; **mark′man**, one of the community owning a mark: a marksman; **marks′man**, **marks′woman**, one good at hitting a mark: one who shoots well; **mark′-white** (*Spens.*), the centre of a target.—**beside the mark** (see under **beside**); (**God**) **bless**, or **save, the mark**, a phrase expressing ironical astonishment or scorn, from the usage of archery; **make one′s mark**, to make a notable impression: to gain great influence; **mark down**, set down in writing: to label at a lower price: lower the price of: to note the position of: to destine for one′s own; **mark off**, to lay down the lines of: to graduate: to mark as attended to, disposed of; **mark of the Beast** (see under **beast**); **a mark on** (*arch. slang*), (one having) a preference for; **mark out**, to lay out the plan or outlines of: to destine; **mark time**, to move the feet alternately in the same manner as in marching, but without changing ground: to keep things going without progressing; **mark up**, to raise the price of; **off the mark**, well away from the start in a race; **pass the mark**, pass on the badge of demerit to the next offender (as formerly in some schools); **soft mark**, an easy dupe: one easy to cope with; **up to the mark**, satisfactory, up to standard: fit and well. [O.E. (Mercian) *merc* (W.S. *mearc*), a boundary, a limit; Ger. *mark*, Goth. *marka*.]

**mark**, *märk*, *n.* a weight of 8 ounces (for gold and silver; *obs.*): its value in money at 20 pennies to an ounce = 13s. 4d. (*obs.*): a coin of Germany (in 1924 officially named the reichs-mark; in 1948 the Deutsche mark), of Finland (the *markka*, *pl.* *markkaa*, originally equivalent to a franc), and formerly of various countries. [O.E. *marc*, of doubtful origin.]

**market**, *mär′kit*, *n.* a periodic concourse of people for the purposes of buying and selling: a build-ing, square, or other public place used for such meetings: a shop (orig. *U.S.*): a region in which there is a demand for goods: buying and selling: opportunity for buying and selling: demand: state of being on sale: bargain: sale: rate of sale: value.—*v.i.* to deal at a market: to buy and sell. —*v.t.* to put on the market:—*pr.p.* **mar′keting**; *pa.t.* and *pa.p.* **mar′keted**.—*adj.* **mar′ketable**, fit for the market: saleable.—*ns.* **marketabil′ity**, **mar′ketableness**; **marketer**, one who goes to mar-ket, buys or sells at a market; **marketing**, the act or practice of buying and selling in market.— **mar′ket-bell** (*Shak.*), a bell to give notice of the time of market; **mar′ket-cross′**, a cross or similar structure anciently set up where a market was held; **mar′ket-day**, the fixed day on which a market is held; **mar′ket-gar′den**, a garden in which fruit and vegetables are grown for market; **mar′ket-gar′dener**; **mar′ket-gar′dening**; **mar′ket-hall**, **mar′ket-house**, a building in which a market is held; **mar′ket-man**, one who sells, buys, or works in a market; **mar′ket-place**, **mar′ket-square**, the open space in a town where markets are held; **mar′ket-price**, **mar′ket-val′ue**, the current price; **market research,** research to determine consumers′ preferences and what they

can afford to buy; **mar′ket-town**, a town having the privilege of holding a public market; **mar′ket-woman**.—**in the market for**, desirous of buying; **on the market**, available for buying: on sale. [Late O.E. *market*—O.N.Fr. *market* (Fr. *marché*, It. *mercato*), from L. *mercātus*, trade, a market —*merx*, merchandise.]

**markhor**, *mär′kör*, *n.* a wild goat of the mountains of Asia. [Pers. *märkhör*.]

**marl**, *märl*, *n.* a limy clay often used as manure: the ground (*poet.*).—*v.t.* to cover with marl.— *adj.* **mar′ly**, like marl: abounding in marl.— **marl′-pit**, a pit where marl is dug; **marl′stone**, a Middle Lias series of argillaceous limestones with ironstones, etc. [O.Fr. *marle* (Fr. *marne*)— L.L. *margila*, a dim. of L. *marga*, marl.]

**marl**, *märl*, *v.t.* to bind with marline. [Du. *marlen*, app. a freq. of *marren*, to bind.]

**marl**, **marle**, *märl*, an obs. form of **marvel**.

**marl**, *märl*, a dial. form of **marble**.—*adj.* mottled. —*adj.* **marled**, marbled.—*n.* **marl′ing**.—*adj.* **marl′y**, **mirl′y**, marbled.

**marlin**, *mär′lin*, *n.* a large oceanic fish of the genus *Makaira* akin to the swordfishes. [**marline-spike**.]

**marline**, *mär′lin*, *n.* a small rope for winding round a larger one to keep it from wearing.—**mar′line-spike**, a spike for separating the strands of a rope in splicing.—Also spelt **marlin**, **marlinspike**. [Du. *marling*, vbl. n. from *marlen* (see **marl** (2)), or *marlijn*—*marren*, and *lijn*, rope (cf. **moor**, line).]

**marm.** See **ma′am**.

**marmalade**, *mär′mə-lād*, *n.* a jam or preserve generally made of the pulp (and rind) of oranges, originally of quinces.—**marmalade tree**, a tropical American sapotaceous tree (*Vitellaria*, or *Lucuma*, *mammosa*) cultivated for its fruit, the marmalade plum. [Fr. *marmelade*—Port. *marme-lada*—*marmelo*, a quince—L. *melimēlum*—Gr. *melimēlon*, a sweet apple—*meli*, honey, *mēlon*, an apple.]

**marmarosis**, *mär-mə-rō′sis*, *n.* conversion of lime-stone into marble.—*v.t.* **mar′marise**, **-ize**. [Gr. *marmaros*, crystalline rock—*marmairein*, to sparkle.]

**marmoreal**, *mär-mōr′i-əl*, *-mōr′*, *adj.* of, or like, marble. [L. *marmor*, marble; Gr. *marmaros*; see preceding.]

**marmose**, *mur′mōs*, *n.* a small South American opossum. [Fr., app. from *marmouset*; see next.]

**marmoset**, *mär′mə-zet*, *n.* a very small American monkey. [Fr. *marmouset*, grotesque figure.]

**marmot**, *mär′mət*, *n.* a genus of stout burrowing rodents (*Marmota* or *Arctomys*), in America called woodchuck. [It. *marmotto*—Romansch *murmont*—L. *mūs*, *mūris*, mouse, *mōns*, *montis*, mountain.]

**marocain**, *mar′ə-kān*, *n.* a dress material finished with a grain surface like morocco-leather. [Fr. *maroquin*, morocco-leather; cf. **maroquin**.]

**Maronian**, *ma-rō′ni-ən*, *adj.* Virgilian. [Publius Vergilius *Marō* (*-ōnis*).]

**Maronite**, *mar′ə-nit*, *n.* one of a former Mono-thelite sect, now Uniats, living around Lebanon. [St *Marōn*, about A.D. 400, or John *Marōn*, a patriarch of the sect in the 7th century.]

**maroon**, *mə-rōōn′*, *n.* a brownish crimson: a detonating firework.—*adj.* of the colour maroon. [Fr. *marron*, a chestnut—It. *marrone*, a chestnut.]

**maroon**, *mə-rōōn′*, *n.* a fugitive slave: a marooned person.—*v.t.* to put and leave ashore on a desolate island: to isolate uncomfortably.—*ns.* **maroon′er**; **maroon′ing**. [Fr. *marron*—Sp. *cimarrón*, wild.]

**maroquin**, *mar′ə-kēn′*, *mar′ə-k(w)in*, *n.* goat-leather: morocco-leather. [Fr.; cf. **marocain**.]

**marplot.** See **mar.**

**marque**, *märk*, *n.* reprisals (*obs.*): a privateer.—

letter(s)-of-marque, a privateer's licence to commit acts of hostility. [Fr.]

marque, märk, (Fr.) a brand, mark.

marquee, mär-kē', n. a large tent. [From marquise, as if pl.]

marquess, etc. See marquis.

marquetry, marqueterie, märk'i-tri, n. work inlaid with pieces of various-coloured wood. [Fr. marqueterie—marqueter, to inlay—marque, a mark.]

marquis, or (spelling used by some holders of the title) marquess, mär'kwis, n. a title of nobility next below that of a duke:—fem. marchioness (mär'shan-es, -is).—ns. mar'quisate, -quessate, the lordship of a marquis; marquise (mär-kēz'), in France, a marchioness: a style of parasol about 1850: entrance canopy: marquee: ring set with gems arranged to form a pointed oval; mar'quisette, a woven clothing fabric, used also for curtains and mosquito nets. [O.Fr. marchis, assimilated later to Fr. marquis—L.L. marchēnsis, a prefect of the marches.]

marram, marrum, mar'əm, n. a seaside grass (Ammophila, or Psamma, arenaria), a binder of sand-dunes. [O.N. marr, sea, halmr, haulm.]

marriage, mar'ij, n. the ceremony, act, or contract by which a man and woman become husband and wife: the union of a man and a woman as husband and wife: a declaration of king and queen in bezique, etc.: a close union (fig.).—adj. marr'iageable, suitable for marriage.—n. marr'iageableness.—marr'iage-bed, the bed of a married couple: marital intercourse: the rights and obligations of marriage; marr'iage-bone, a merrythought; marr'iage-broker, one who, for a fee, arranges a marriage contract; marr'iage-con'tract, an agreement to be married: an agreement respecting property by persons about to marry; marr'iage-fa'vour, a knot or decoration worn at a marriage; marr'iage-li'cence, a licence to marry without proclamation of banns in a church.—n.pl. marr'iage-lines, a certificate of marriage.—marr'iage-por'tion, a dowry; marr'iage-ring', a wedding ring; marr'iage-sett'lement, an arrangement of property, etc., before marriage, by which something is secured to the wife or her children if the husband dies. [O.Fr. mariage; see marry.]

marrons glacés, ma-rɔ̃ gla-sā, (Fr.) chestnuts coated with sugar.

marrow, mar'ō, n. the soft tissue in the hollow parts of the bones: pith or pulp of plants (obs.): a vegetable marrow (see under vegetable): the essence or best part of anything: the inner meaning or purpose.—adjs. marr'owish, of the nature of, or resembling, marrow; marr'owless, having no marrow; marr'owy, full of marrow: strong: forcible: pithy.—marr'ow-bone, a bone containing marrow: (pl.) the knees or the bones of the knees; marr'owfat, a rich kind of pea, called also Dutch admiral pea.—n.pl. marr'ow-men, those who in the Church of Scotland supported the teaching of The Marrow of Modern Divinity (1645) after its republication in 1718.—marr'ow-squash (U.S.), vegetable marrow.—spinal marrow, the spinal cord. [O.E. (Anglian) merg, mærh (W.S. mearg); Ger. mark.]

marrow, mar'ō, (arch.) n. a mate: a companion: a match, equal, like: one of a pair.—v.i. to be a marrow.—v.t. to be a marrow to: to couple.—adj. marr'owless. [Origin unknown.]

marrowsky, mar-ow'ski, n. a spoonerism.—v.i. to utter a spoonerism. [Said to be from the name of a Polish count.]

marry, mar'i, v.t. to take for husband or wife: to give in marriage: to unite in matrimony: to unite, join, put together.—v.i. to take a husband or a wife:—pr.p. marr'ying; pa.t. and pa.p. marr'ied.—adj. marr'ied.—n. marr'ier, one who marries in any sense: the sort of person likely to

marry.—n. and adj. marr'ying. [Fr. marier—L. maritāre, to marry, maritus, a husband—mās, maris, a male.]

marry, mar'i, (arch.) interj. indeed! forsooth!—marry come up, an exclamation of defiant protest. [By Mary.]

Mars, märz, n. the Roman god of war: the planet next after the earth in the order of distance from the sun: iron (old chem.). [L. Mārs, Mārtis.]

Marsala, mär-sä'lə (It. mär-sä'lä), n. a light wine resembling sherry, from Marsala in Sicily.

Marseillaise, mär-sə-lāz', -sä-ez', n. French revolutionary hymn composed by Rouget de Lisle in 1792, sung by the volunteers of Marseilles as they entered Paris, 30th July, and when they marched to the storming of the Tuileries.

marsh, marsh, n. a tract of wet land: a morass, swamp, or fen.—adj. inhabiting or found in marshes.—n. marsh'iness.—adj. marsh'y, of the nature of marsh: abounding in marshes.—marsh'-fe'ver, malaria; marsh'-gas, methane; marsh'-harr'ier, a harrier frequenting marshes; marsh'land, marshy country; marsh'lander; marsh'locks, a marsh-growing species of cinquefoil (Potentilla or Comarum)—also marsh'-cinq'uefoil; marsh'-mall'ow, a maritime marsh-growing plant (Althaea officinalis) close akin to hollyhock: a gelatinous sweetmeat, originally made from its root; marsh'-man, a marsh-dweller; marsh'-mar'igold, the kingcup (Caltha palustris), a marsh plant of the buttercup family with flowers like big buttercups; marsh'-sam'phire, a plant of the genus Salicornia, glasswort; marsh'wort, a small umbelliferous marsh plant akin to celery. [O.E. mersc, merisc, orig. adj.; see mere (1).]

marshal, mär'shl, n. a farrier (obs.): an officer in a royal household, originally the king's farrier, later having care of military arrangements, the regulation of ceremonies, preservation of order, points of etiquette, etc.: any official with like functions: a law-court officer with charge of prisoners: a prison-keeper: (Oxford) a proctor's attendant or bulldog: the chief officer who regulated combats in the lists (hist.): in France, etc., an officer of the highest military rank: a civil officer appointed to execute the process of the courts (U.S.): a police or fire-brigade head (U.S.).—v.t. to arrange in order: to usher: to combine in one coat of arms, or with a coat.—v.i. to come together in order:—pr.p. mar'shalling; pa.t. and pa.p. mar'shalled.—ns. mar'shalcy, the rank, office, or department of a marshal: esp. (in the form Mar'shalsea) till 1842 a prison in Southwark, under the marshal of the royal household; mar'shaller; mar'shalling; mar'shalship.—marshalling yard, a place where railway wagons are sorted out and made up into trains. —air-marshal, etc. (see air); field-marshal (see field); marshal of the Royal Air Force, an officer of supreme rank in the Royal Air Force, ranking with an admiral of the fleet or a field-marshal. [O.Fr. mareschal (Fr. maréchal); from O.H.G. marah, a horse, schalh (Ger. schalk), a servant.]

Marsilea, mär-sil'i-a, n. a genus of aquatic leptosporangiate ferns, with four-lobed leaves and bean-like stalked sporocarps, giving name to a family Marsileä'ceae.—Also Marsilia. [Named after L. F. Marsigli (1658-1730), Italian naturalist.]

Marsipobranchii, mär'sip-ō-brangk'i-ī, n.pl. the Cyclostomata.—n. mar'sipobranch.—adj. marsipobranch'iate. [Gr. marsipos, pouch, branchia, gills.]

marsupium, mär-sū'pi-əm, (zool.) n. a pouch.—adj. marsū'pial, pertaining to a pouch or to the Marsupialia: of the nature of a pouch: of the Marsupialia.—n. a member of the Marsupialia.—n.pl. Marsupiä'lia, an order of mammals coextensive with the subclass Metatheria, animals whose young are born in a very imperfect state and are usually carried in a pouch by the female. [L. *marsūpium*—Gr. *marsip(p)ion, marsyp(p)ion,* a pouch.]

**mart,** *märt, n.* a place of trade.—*v.i.* (*Shak.*) to traffic.—*v.t.* (*Shak.*) to vend. [Du. *markt,* mart; cf. **market.**]

**mart,** *märt,* (*Scot.*) *n.* a cow or ox fattened, killed (usu. about Martinmas), and salted for winter use. [Gael. *mart,* cow, ox.]

**martagon,** *mär'tə-gən, n.* the Turk's-cap lily. [Turk. *martagān,* a kind of turban.]

**martel,** *mär'təl, n.* a war-hammer.—*v.i.* (*Spens.*) to hammer:—*pa.t.* **mar'telled.** [O.Fr. *martel.*]

**martellato,** *mär-tel-lä'tō,* (*mus.*) *adj.* played with a hammering touch, or with short quick detached strokes of the bow.—Also *adv.* [It., hammered.]

**martello,** *mär-tel'ō, n.* (in full **martello tower**) a circular fort for coast defence. [From Cape *Mortella* in Corsica, where one resisted for some time a British cannonade in 1794.]

**marten,** *mär'tən, n.* an animal (**pine-marten**) close akin to the weasels, or other species of *Mustela.* [Fr. *martre,* from the Gmc. root seen in Ger. *marder,* and O.E. *mearth,* marten.]

**martenot,** *mär'tən-ō, n.* an electronic musical instrument resembling a spinet in appearance, invented by the Frenchman Maurice *Martenot* (born 1898).

**martial,** *mär'shl, adj.* belonging to Mars, the god of war, or to the planet Mars: of or belonging to war, or to the army and navy: warlike.—*ns.* **mar'tialism; mar'tialist,** a soldier.—*adv.* **mar'-tially.**—**martial law,** exercise of arbitrary power by the supreme authority in time of emergency (war, riot, etc.), ordinary administration ceasing to operate. [Fr. *martial*—L. *mārtiālis*—*Mārs.*]

**Martian,** *mär'shən, adj.* of Mars (god or planet): of battle.—*n.* an imagined inhabitant of Mars. [L. *Mārtius*—*Mārs.*]

**martin,** *mär'tin, n.* a bird of the swallow genus (*Delichon* or *Chelidon*).—Also **mar'tinet** (*obs.*). [The name *Martin.*]

**martinet,** *mär-ti-net',* or *mär', n.* a system of drill drawn up by *Martinet,* an officer of Louis XIV (*obs.*): a strict disciplinarian.—*n.* **martinet'ism.**

**martingale,** *mär'tin-gäl, n.* a strap passing between a horse's forelegs, fastened to the girth and to the bit, noseband, or reins, to keep his head down: a short spar under the bowsprit: in gambling, the policy of doubling the stake on losing. [Fr., perh. from a kind of breeches worn at *Martigues* in Provence.]

**Martini,** *mär-tē'nē, n.* a cocktail of vermouth, gin, bitters, etc. [Trademark of a type of vermouth.]

**Martini (-Henry),** *mär-tē'nē (-hen'ri), n.* a 19th-cent. rifle with action as designed by Frederic *Martini* and barrel by *Henry,* a gunsmith.

**Martinmas,** *mär'tin-məs, n.* the *mass* or feast of St *Martin,* 11th Nov., a term-day in Scotland.— Also (*obs.*) **Mar'tlemas.**

**martlet,** *märt'lit, n.* the martin: a martin or swallow without feet, used as a bearing, a crest, or a mark of cadency for a fourth son (*her.*). [From Fr. *martinet,* dim. of *martin,* martin.]

**martyr,** *mär'tər, n.* one who by his death bears witness to his belief: one who suffers for his belief: one who suffers greatly from any cause, a victim.—*v.t.* to put to death for one's belief: to torture.—*n.* **mar'tyrdom,** state of being a martyr: the sufferings or death of a martyr: torment generally.—*v.t.* **mar'tyrise, -ize,** to offer as a sacrifice: to cause to suffer martyrdom: to make a martyr of: to torture.—*adj.* **martyrolog'ical.**— *ns.* **martyrol'ogist; martyrol'ogy,** a history of martyrs: a discourse on martyrdom. [O.E.,— L.,—Gr., a witness.]

**marvel,** *mär'vl, n.* a wonder: anything astonishing or wonderful: astonishment (*arch.*).—*v.i.* to wonder: to feel astonishment.—*v.t.* to wonder

at (*obs.*):—*pr.p.* **mar'velling;** *pa.t.* and *pa.p.* **mar'velled.** — *adj.* **mar'vellous,** astonishing: almost or altogether beyond belief: improbable, very good, extremely pleasing (*coll.*).—*adv.* **mar'vellously.**—*n.* **mar'vellousness.**—**marvel of Peru** (*pə-rōō'*), a shcwy garden flower (*Mirabilis jalapa;* family Nyctaginaceae) from Mexico, open and scented in the evening. [Fr. *merveille* —L. *mīrābilis,* wonderful—*mīrāri,* to wonder.]

**Marxian,** *märks'i-ən, adj.* pertaining to Karl *Marx* (1818-83) or his socialism, esp. as interpreted in Russia.—*n.* a follower of Marx.—*ns.* **Marx'ianism, Marx'ism.**—*n.* and *adj.* **Marx'ist.**

**marybud,** *mā'ri-bud, n.* a marigold bud.

**marzipan,** *mär-zi-pan', n.* a sweet almond paste, formerly called marchpane. [Ger.,—It. *marzapane.*]

**Masai,** *mä'sī, n.,* an African people of the high-lands of Kenya and Tanzania.—Also *adj.*

**mascara, mascaron.** See **mask.**

**mascle,** *mas'kl, n.* a bearing, lozenge-shaped and perforated (*her.*): a lozenge-shaped plate for scale-armour.—*adjs.* **mas'cled, mas'cūly.** [App. O.Fr. *mascle*—L.L. *mascula*—L. *macula,* mesh, influenced by O.H.G. *masca,* mesh.]

**mascon,** *mas'kon, n.* any of several mass con-centrations of dense material, of uncertain origin, lying beneath the moon's surface. [*mass concentration.*]

**mascot,** *mas'kət, n.* a talisman: a supposed bringer of good luck. [Fr. *mascotte.*]

**masculine,** *mäs', mas'kū-lin, -lin, adj.* male (*rare*): characteristic of, peculiar to, or appropriate to, a man or the male sex: mannish: of that gender to which belong words denoting males and, in some languages, various associated classes of words (*gram.*).—*n.* the male sex or nature: a male: a word of masculine gender.— *adv.* **mas'culinely.**—*n.* **mas'culineness.**—*v.t.* **mas'-culinise, -ize,** to cause to develop masculine characters.—*v.i.* to develop such characters.—*n.* **masculin'ity.**—**masculine rhyme,** a rhyme on a final stressed syllable: in French one without a final mute e. [Fr.,—L. *masculīnus*—*masculus,* male—*mās,* a male.]

**maser,** *māz'ər, n.* a device used to amplify long range radar and radio astronomy signals (very small when not amplified) while generating little unwanted noise within itself. [*M*icrowave *a*mpli-fication by *s*timulated *e*mission of *r*adiation.]

**mash,** *mash, n.* in brewing, a mixture of crushed malt and hot water: a mixture, as of bran with meal or turnips, beaten and stirred as a food for animals: any material beaten or crushed into a soft or pulpy state: crushed condition: a muddle, hash, or bungle.—*v.t.* to make into a mash: to pound down or crush: to infuse (*dial.*). —*ns.* **mash'er; mash'ing.**—*adj.* **mash'y,** produced by mashing: of the nature of a mash.—**mash'-tub, -tun, -vat, mash'ing-tub,** a vessel in which the mash in breweries is mixed. [O.E. *masc*(*-wyrt*), *mash*(*-wort*).]

**mash,** *mash,* (*obsolescent slang*) *v.t.* to seek to fascinate (one of the other sex): to treat as a sweetheart.—*v.i.* to flirt.—*n.* one who mashes or is mashed: a masher: mashing.—*n.* **mash'er,** a fellow who dresses showily to attract the attention of silly young women: a dandy.— **mashed on,** enamoured of.

**mashallah,** *mä-shä'lä, interj.* (among Moham-medans) what God will. [Ar. *mā shā'llāh.*]

**mashie, mashy,** *mash'i, n.* an iron golf-club for lofting, a number five iron.—**mash'ie-nib'lick,** a club between mashie and niblick, a number six iron. [Perh. Fr. *massue,* club.]

**mashlam, mashlin,** etc. See **maslin.**

**masjid,** *mus'jid, n.* a mosque. [Ar.]

**mask,** *mäsk, n.* a covering for the face, or the upper part of it, for concealment, disguise, or pro-tection: a false-face: a grotesque representation of a face worn in the ancient drama, or used as an architectural ornament, etc.: a fox's (or other beast's) face or head: a mould of a face: a masque: a disguise, pretence, or concealment (*fig.*): any means of screening or disguising: a screen to cover part of a sensitive surface (*phot.*).—*v.t.* to cover the face of with a mask: to hide, cloak, screen, or disguise.—*v.i.* to masquerade: to be disguised in any way.—*ns.* **mascara** (*mas-kä′ra*; Sp. *máscara*), colouring for the eyelashes; **mas′caron** (*archit.*), a grotesque face on a keystone, door-knocker, etc. —*adj.* **masked**, wearing a mask: concealed: personate (*bot.*).—*n.* **mask′er**, one who wears a mask: a masquerader.—**masked′-ball**, a ball in which the dancers wear masks. [Fr. *masque*—Sp. *máscara* or It. *maschera*, of doubtful origin, app. conn. in some way with L.L. *mascus*, *masca*, a ghost, and with Ar. *maskharah*, a jester, man in masquerade.]

**mask**, *mäsk*, (*Scot.*) *v.t.* to steep, infuse.—*v.i.* to be infusing. [See mash.]

**maslin**, *mas′lin*, *n.* a mixed grain, esp. rye and wheat.—Also (*Scot.*) **mash′lam**, **mash′lim**, **mash′-lin**, **mash′loch** (*-lohh*), **mash′lum**. [O.Fr. *mesteillon*—L.L. *mistiliō*, *-ōnis*—L. *mistus*, mixed —*miscēre*, to mix.]

**masochism**, *maz′ə-kizm*, *n.* a sexual perversion with pleasure in being dominated or treated cruelly by the other sex: (*loosely*) morbid gratification in suffering pain, physical or mental. —*n.* **mas′ochist**.—*adj.* **masochist′ic**. [From the novelist Sacher-*Masoch*, who described it.]

**mason**, *mā′sn*, *n.* one who cuts, prepares, and lays stones: a builder in stone: a member of the society of freemasons.—*v.t.* to build in or repair stonework, brickwork, etc.—*adjs.* **masonic** (*məson′ik*), relating to freemasonry; **mā′sonried**, constructed of masonry.—*n.* **mā′sonry**, the art, skill, or practice of a mason: the work of a mason: building-work in stone: freemasonry. —*adj.* consisting of mason-work.—**mason's mark**, a device carved on stones by a mason to identify his share in the work.—**mas′ter-mā′son** (see under master). [O.Fr. *masson* (Fr. *maçon*)— L.L. *maciō*, *-ōnis*, prob. Gmc.; cf. M.H.G. *mezzo*, a mason, whence *steinmetz*, a stone-mason; O.H.G. *meizan*, to hew, whence Ger. *meissel*, a chisel.]

**masoolah**, **massoola**, **masula**, *mä-sōō′la*, *n.* a high many-oared Indian surf-boat. [Origin obscure.]

**Masora**, **Masorah**, *mä-sō′ra*, *-sō′*, *n.* a collection of critical notes on the text of the Old Testament.— Also **Massora(h)**, **Maso′reth**.—*n.* **Mas(s)′orete** (*-rēt*), a compiler of the Masora.—*adj.* **Mas(s)oretic** (*-ret′ik*). [Heb. *māsoreth*, mod. *māsōrāh*.]

**masque**, *mäsk*, *n.* a masked person: a company of maskers: a masquerade or masked ball: a form of courtly spectacle in vogue in the 16th and 17th centuries, in which masked performers danced and acted, developing into a form of drama with scenery and music: a literary composition for the purpose: a mask (*obs.*).—*n.* **masqu′er**, a masker. [See mask.]

**masquerade**, *mäsk-ər-ād′*, *n.* an assembly of persons wearing masks, generally at a ball: disguise.— *v.i.* to wear a mask: to join in a masquerade: to go in disguise: to pretend to be (with *as*).—*n.* **masquerad′er**. [Fr. *mascarade*; see mask.]

**mass**, *mas*, *n.* a lump of matter: matter, material (*obs.*): a quantity: a collected or coherent body: an unbroken expanse: the aggregate: the main body: the greater part: the principal part: quantity of matter in any body, measured by its resistance to change of motion: (in *pl.*) the lower classes of the people.—*adj.* pertaining to a mass, or to large numbers or quantities, or to ordinary people as a whole.—*v.t.* to form into mass: to bring together in masses.—*v.i.* to assemble in masses.—*adj.* **massive** (*mas′iv*),

bulky: weighty: giving an impression of weight: not separated into parts or elements: without crystalline form: (*loosely*) great in quantity: on a very large scale, or of great size or power (*fig.*). —*adv.* **mass′ively.**—*ns.* **mass′iveness**, **mass′iness**. —*adj.* **mass′y**, massive, made up of masses.— **mass defect**, the difference between the sum of the masses of the neutrons and protons in a nucleus and the mass of the nucleus itself; **mass medium**, any medium of communication (e.g. newspapers, television) reaching very large numbers of people:—*pl.* **mass media**; **mass′-meet′ing**, a large meeting for a public protest or assertion; **mass number**, the atomic weight of an isotope, the number of nucleons in the nucleus; **mass observation**, study of the habits, opinions, etc., of the general body of a community.—*v.t.* **mass′-produce′**, to produce in great quantity by standardised process.—*adj.* **mass′-produced′.**— **mass′-produc′tion**; **mass radiography**, taking of large numbers of chest X-ray photographs by mobile units; **mass spectrograph**, an instrument by means of which a positive ray spectrum can be obtained, the images due to particles of different masses being spaced according to the masses, so that the atomic weights of the particles can be deduced; **mass spectrometer**, an instrument like the mass spectrograph but measuring not the masses of particles but the relative number of particles of each mass present; **mass spectrometry.**—**in mass**, as a body: all together; **in the mass**, in the aggregate: as a whole: indiscriminately; **law of mass action** (*chem.*), rate of chemical change is proportional to the product of the concentrations of the reacting substances; **mass-energy equivalence** (*phys.*), the fundamental principle that mass and energy are equivalent and interconvertible. [Fr. *masse*—L. *massa*, a lump, prob.—Gr. *māza*, a barley cake—*massein*, to knead.]

**mass** (often with *cap.*), *mas*, *mäs*, *n.* the celebration of the Lord's Supper or Eucharist in R.C. churches: the office for it: a musical setting of certain parts of the R.C. liturgy: a church service (*Shak.*): a church festival or feast-day, as in *Candlemas*, *Christmas*, *Martinmas*, etc.— **mass′-bell**, a sacring bell; **mass′-book**, the R.C. missal or service-book; **mass′-priest**, formerly a R.C. secular priest, as distinct from one living under a rule—later, a priest retained in chantries, etc., to say masses for the dead: a R.C. priest generally. [O.E. *mæsse*—L.L. *missa*—L. *mittĕre*, to send away, perh. from the phrase at the close of service, *ite, missa est* (*ecclesia*), go, (the congregation) is dismissed.]

**Mass, Mas, mäs, Mess, Mes, mes, (obs.) n.** shortened forms of Master.—**Mas(s)-John, Mes(s)-John**, (*obs.*) a contemptuous name for a Scottish parish minister.

**massa**, *mas′ə*, *n.* a Negro corruption of master.

**massacre**, *mas′ə-kər* (*Spens.* sometimes *-ak′*), *n.* indiscriminate slaughter, esp. with cruelty: carnage.—*v.t.* to kill with violence and cruelty: to slaughter. [Fr.; origin doubtful.]

**massage**, *ma′säzh*, *mə-säzh′*, *n.* a system of treatment by stroking, pressing, tapping, kneading, friction, etc.—*v.t.* to subject to massage.—*ns.* **massa′gist**, **masseur** (*-sær′*, or *-sür′*):—*fem.* **masseuse** (*-sæz′*). [Fr., from Gr. *massein*, to knead.]

**massaranduba**, *mas-ə-ran-dōō′ba*, *n.* the Brazilian milk-tree (*Mimusops elata*).—Also **masseranduba**, **maceranduba**. [Port. *maçaranduba*, from Tupí name.]

**massé**, *mas′ā*, *n.* in billiards, a sharp stroke made with the cue vertical or nearly so. [Fr.]

**masseter**, *mas-ē′tər*, *n.* a muscle that raises the under jaw. [Gr. *masētēr* (not *massētēr*), chewer —*masaesthai*, to chew.]

**masseur**, **masseuse**. See massage.

**massicot,** *mas'i-kot, n.* yellow lead monoxide. [Fr.]
**massif,** *ma-sēf'*, *mas'if, n.* a central mountain-mass: an orographic fault-block. [Fr.]
**Massora(h).** See Masora.
**massymore,** *mas-i-mōr'*, *-mör'*, *(Scott) n.* a subterranean prison. [Perh. Sp. *mazmorra.*]
**mast,** *mäst, n.* a long upright pole, esp. one for carrying the sails of a ship.—*v.t.* to supply with a mast or masts.—*adjs.* mast'ed; mast'less.—mast'head, the top of a mast: the name of a newspaper or periodical in the typographical form in which it normally appears, or a similar block of information regularly used as a heading. —*v.t.* to raise to the masthead: to punish by sending to the masthead.—mast'house, the place where masts are made or stored.—before the mast, as a common sailor (whose quarters are in the forecastle). [O.E. *mæst*; Ger. *mast.*]
**mast,** *mäst, n.* the fruit of the oak, beech, chestnut, and other forest trees, on which swine feed: nuts, acorns.—*adjs.* mast'ful; mast'less; mast'y, of the nature of mast: as if well fed on mast.—*adj.* mast'-fed. [O.E. *mæst*; Ger. *mast,* whence *mästen,* to feed.]
**mastaba,** *mas'tə-bə, n.* an ancient Egyptian tomb in which offerings were made in an outer chamber communicating with an inner one where was the figure of the dead man, with a shaft descending to the actual grave. [Ar. *mastabah,* a bench.]
**mastectomy.** See mastoid.
**master,** *mäs'tər, n.* one who commands or controls: a lord or owner: a leader or ruler: a teacher: an employer: the commander of a merchant ship: formerly the navigator or sailing-master of a ship-of-war: one eminently skilled in anything, esp. art: one who has complete knowledge: a workman who has set up on his own account, or is qualified to do so: formerly prefixed to a name or designation as Mr is now: now only of a boy in this use: a title of dignity or office—a degree conferred by universities, as *Master of Arts,* etc., the title of the heir apparent of a Scottish viscount or baron, the head of some corporations, as Balliol College, etc., of a lodge of freemasons, etc.: a husband *(dial.).*—*adj.* chief: controlling: predominant: of a master: of the rank of a master.—*v.t.* to become master of: to overcome: to gain control over: to acquire a thorough knowledge of: to become skilful in: to rule as master: to temper, to season: to treat with lye *(tanning).*—*v.i. (arch.);* also *v.t.* with *it)* to act the master or be a schoolmaster. —*ns.* mas'terate, degree, title, or rank, of master; mas'terdom, power of control: masterfulness.—*adj.* mas'terful, exercising the authority or power of a master: imperious: masterly *(rare).*—*adv.* mas'terfully.—*ns.* mas'terfulness; mas'terhood; mas'tering, action of verb *master:* lye.—*adj.* mas'terless, without a master or owner: ungoverned: unsubdued: beyond control.—*n.* mas'terliness.—*adj.* mas'terly, like a master: with the skill of a master: overbearing *(obs.).*—*adv.* with the skill of a master.—*ns.* mas'tership, the condition, authority, status, office, or term of office of master: rule or dominion: superiority; mas'tery, the power or authority of a master: upper hand: control: masterly skill or knowledge.—mas'ter-at-arms', a ship's chief police officer; mas'ter-build'er, a chief builder· one who directs or employs others; mas'ter-card, the card that commands a suit; mas'ter-clock, that regulates other clocks electrically; mas'ter-hand, the hand of a master: a person highly skilled; mas'ter-joint, a joint of the most marked system of those by which a rock is intersected; mas'ter-key, a key that opens many locks: a clue able to guide one out of many difficulties *(fig.);* masterly

inactivity, the position or part of a neutral or a Fabian combatant, carried out with diplomatic skill, so as to preserve a predominant influence without risking anything; mas'ter-mar'iner, the captain of a merchant-vessel or fishing-vessel; mas'ter-ma'son, a freemason who has attained the third degree; mas'ter-mind, a mind, or a person having a mind, of very great ability: the person conceiving or directing a project.—*v.t.* to originate, think out, and direct.—mas'ter-pass'ion; mas'terpiece, piece of work worthy of a master: one's greatest achievement; master race (see herrenvolk); mas'terstroke, a stroke or performance worthy of a master: superior performance: an effective, well-timed act; master-switch, a switch for controlling the effect of a number of other switches or contactors; mas'ter-wheel, the wheel in a machine which imparts motion to other parts: mas'ter-work, work worthy of a master: masterpiece; mas'ter-wort, a plant *(Peucedanum,* or *Imperatoria, ostruthium)* akin to parsnip, once used as a pot-herb and in medicine: applied also to Astrantia, etc.—little masters, 16th-17th cent. group of followers of Dürer, notable for fine work on wood and copper; master of ceremonies, of the rolls, etc. (see ceremonies, rolls, etc.); master of the horse, the Roman *Magister Equitum,* an official appointed by the dictator to act next under himself: an equerry, esp. a high official of the British court; Master of the Temple, the preacher of the Temple Church in London; master-slave manipulator, a manipulator, esp. one used to handle, from behind a protective screen, radioactive material; masters of the schools, at Oxford, the conductors of the first examination *(Responsions)* for the degree of B.A.; old masters, a term applied collectively to the great painters about the time of the Renaissance, esp. the Italians; passed master, one who has passed as a master: a thorough proficient (see pastmaster, under past). [Partly O.E. *mægester,* partly O.Fr. *maistre* (Fr. *maître),* both from L. *magister,* from root of *magnus,* great.]
**mastic, mastich,** *mas'tik, n.* a pale yellow gumresin from the lentisk and other trees, used for varnish, cement, liquor: a tree exuding mastic, esp. the lentisk *(Pistachia lentiscus);* cashew-nut family): a bituminous or oily cement of various kinds. [Fr. *mastic*—L.L. *mastichum*—Gr. *mastichē.*]
**masticate,** *mas'ti-kāt, v.t.* to chew: to knead mechanically, as in rubber manufacture.—*adj.* mas'ticable, that may be chewed.—*ns.* mastică'tion; mas'ticātor, one who masticates: a tooth or jaw *(facet.):* a machine for grinding: a machine for kneading india-rubber.—*adj.* mas'-ticatory *(-kə-tə-ri),* chewing: adapted for chewing.—*n.* a substance chewed to increase the saliva. [L. *masticāre, -ātum;* cf. Gr. *mastax,* jaw, *mastichaein,* to grind the teeth.]
**masticot.** Same as massicot.
**mastiff,** *mas'tif, n.* a thick-set and powerful variety of dog used as a watch-dog. [O.Fr. *mastin,* app.—L. *mansuētus,* tame; perh. confused with O.Fr. *mestif,* mongrel.]
**Mastigophora,** *mas-ti-gof'ə-rə, (zool.) n.pl.* the flagellates in a wide sense.—*adjs.* mastigophoric *(-gə-for'ik);* mastigophorous *(-gof'ə-rəs),* of the Mastigophora: whip-carrying. [Gr. *mastix, -igos,* whip, *phoreein,* to carry.]
**mastitis.** See mastoid.
**Mastodon,** *mas'tə-don, n.* a genus of extinct elephants, so named from the teat-like prominences of the molar teeth of some species. [Gr. *mastos,* breast, *odous, odontos,* a tooth.]
**mastoid,** *mas'toid, adj.* like a nipple or a teat.—*n.* a process of the temporal bone behind the ear (also mastoid bone, process): mastoiditis *(coll.).* —*ns.* mastect'omy, surgical removal of a breast;

masti′tis, inflammation of the mammary gland. —*adj.* mastoid′al.—*n.* mastoidi′tis, inflammation of the air cells of the mastoid processes. [Gr. *mastos*, a nipple.]

masturbation, *mas-tər-bā′shən*, *n.* stimulation, usually by oneself, of the sexual organs by manipulation, etc., so as to produce orgasm.—*v.i.* mas′turbate.—*n.* mas′turbator. [L. *masturbāri*.]

masu, *mä′soō*, *n.* a Japanese salmon (*Oncorhynchus masou*). [Jap.]

masula. See masoolah.

masurium, *mə-soō′ri-əm*, *-sū′*, *n.* a name proposed for element No. 43 when its discovery was prematurely claimed—see technetium. [*Masurenland*, in East Prussia.]

mat, *mat*, *n.* a piece of fabric of sedge, rushes, straw, coarse fibre, etc., or of rubber, wire, or other material, for cleaning shoes, for covering a floor, hearth, threshold, for protection, packing, for standing, sleeping, etc., on, or for other purpose: a rug: a small piece of strawplait, cloth, slab of cork or wood, etc., for placing under a vase, dish, or other object: a sack of matting used to cover a chest of tea, coffee, etc.: a certain weight held by such a sack: a closely interwoven or tangled mass, as of hair, of vegetation, of brushwood protecting a river-bank: a web of rope-yarn.—*v.t.* to cover with mats: to interweave: to tangle closely.—*v.i.* to become tangled in a mass:—*pr.p.* matt′ing; *pa.t.* and *pa.p.* matt′ed.—*n.* matt′ing, mat-making: becoming matted: covering with mats: material used as mats.—mat′grass, mat′weed, a small, tufted, rushlike moorland grass (*Nardus stricta*): marram.—on the mat, on the carpet (*fig.*). [O.E. *matt*(*e*), *meatte*—L. *matta*, a mat; perh. of Punic origin.]

mat, *mat*, *adj.* dull or lustreless.—Also matt, matte.—*n.* mat, a dull uniform finish or surface: a border of dull gold or of white or colour round a picture: a punch for roughening a surface.—*v.t.* to produce a dull surface on: to frost (glass). [Fr. *mat*; Ger. *matt*, dull; cf. checkmate; amate (2), mate (2).]

mat. Abbrev. for matrix.

matachin, *mat-ə-chēn′*, *-shēn′*, (*arch.*) *n.* a masked sword-dancer or sword-dance. [Fr. (cbs.) *matachin* and Sp. *matachín*, perh.—Ar. *mutawajjihin*, masked.]

matador, matadore, *mat′ə-dör*, *-dōr*, *n.* the man who kills the bull in bullfights: one of the three chief cards at ombre and quadrille: a form of dominoes. [Sp. *matador*—*matar*, to kill—L. *mactāre*, to kill, to honour by sacrifice—*mactus*, honoured.]

matamata, *ma-tə-mä′tə*, *n.* a South American river-turtle. [Port., from Tupi *matamatá*.]

match, *mach*, *n.* a piece of inflammable material which easily takes or carries fire: a prepared cord for firing a gun, an explosive, etc.: a short stick of wood or other material tipped with an easily ignited material.—match′box, a box for holding matches; match′lock, the lock of a musket containing a match for firing it: a musket so fired; match′-maker; match′wood, touch-wood: wood suitable for matches: splinters. [O.Fr. *mesche* (Fr. *mèche*); origin obscure.]

match, *mach*, *n.* that which tallies or exactly agrees with another thing: an equal: one able to cope with another: a condition of exact agreement or close resemblance, esp. in colours: equality in contest: a compact (*obs.*): a formal contest or game: a pairing: a marriage: one to be gained in marriage.—*v.i.* to be exactly or nearly alike: to correspond: to form a union: to compete or encounter (esp. on equal terms).—*v.t.* to be equal to: to be a counterpart to: to be exactly like in colour, etc.: to be able to compete with: to find an equal or counterpart to: to pit or set against another in contest or as equal: to treat as equal: to fit in with: to suit: to join in marriage.—*adj.* match′able.—*n.* match′er.—*adj.* match′less, having no match or equal: superior to all: peerless: not matching (*Spens.*).—*adv.* match′lessly.—*n.* match′lessness. —match′board, a board with a tongue cut along one edge and a groove in the opposite edge; matchboard′ing; match′-joint, the junction of matchboards; match′maker, one who plans to bring about marriages; match′making; match′-point, the stage at which another point wins the match: the point that wins the match.—to match, in accordance, as in colour. O.E. *gemæcca*; cf. make (3).]

match-maker. See match (1).

matchmaker. See match (2).

mate, *māt*, *n.* a companion: an equal: a fellow-workman: a friendly or ironic form of address: a husband or wife: an animal with which another is paired: one of a pair: a ship's officer under the captain or master: in the navy, formerly a rank to which a warrant-officer might be promoted: an assistant, deputy (as *plumber's mate*). —*v.t.* to be equal to, to rival (*arch.*): to marry: to pair (esp. animals): to couple: to fit.—*v.i.* to claim equality (*arch.*): to marry: to pair: to consort (*arch.*).—*adjs.* mate′less, without a mate or companion; mat(e)′y (*coll.*), friendly and familiar, esp. in a studied or overdone manner. [Prob. M.L.G. *mate* or earlier Du. *maet* (now *maat*); cf. O.E. *gemetta*, a messmate, and meat.]

mate, *māt*, *adj.* (*arch.*) checkmated: confounded: baffled: exhausted: daunted.—*v.t.* to checkmate: to subdue (*arch.*): to baffle (*arch.*): to confound (*arch.*).—*n.* and *interj.* checkmate. [O.Fr. *mat*, checkmated; see checkmate, mat (2).]

mate, maté, *ma′tā*, *n.* a South American species of holly (*Ilex paraguayensis*): an infusion of its leaves and green shoots (Paraguay tea). [Sp. *mate*—Quechua *mati*, a gourd (in which it is made).]

matelassé, *mat-lä-sä*, *adj.* and *n.* (of silks) having a raised pattern as if quilted.—Also matel(l)asse. [Fr.,—*matelas*, a mattress.]

matelot. See matlo.

matelote, *mat′ə-lōt*, *n.* fish stewed with wine sauce, onions, etc.: a sort of hornpipe. [Fr.,—*matelot*, a sailor.]

mater, *mā′tər*, *mā′ter*, *n.* a mother (*slang*): either of the two membranes of the brain, outer and inner, separated by the arachnoid—the dura mater, or dura, and pia mater, or pia. [L. *māter*; cf. Gr. *mētēr*; mother.]

materfamilias, *mā′tər-fa-mil′-i-as*, *mä′ter-*, (L.) the mother of a family.

material, *mə-tē′ri-əl*, *adj.* relating to matter: consisting of matter: being the substance of the thing (*Shak.*): matterful (*Shak.*): corporeal, not spiritual: bodily: physical: gross, lacking spirituality: relating to subject-matter: relevant: of serious importance, esp. of legal importance: pertaining to matter as opposed to form (*phil.*).— *n.* that out of which anything is or may be made: that which may be made use of for any purpose: a fabric.—*n.* materialisā′tion, *-z-*.—*v.t.* mate′rialise, -ize, to render material: to cause to assume bodily form: to reduce to or regard as matter: to render materialistic.—*v.i.* to take bodily form: to become actual (*coll.*).—*ns.* mate′rialism, the doctrine that denies the independent existence of spirit, and maintains that there is but one substance—matter: the explanation of history as the working out of economic conditions: blindness to the spiritual: excessive devotion to bodily wants or financial success; mate′rialist.—Also *adj.*—*adjs.* materialist′ic, *-al.*— *advs.* materialist′ically; mate′rially, in material manner: in respect of matter or material conditions, or material cause: in a considerable or important degree.—*ns.* mate′rialness, materiality (-*al′i-ti*).—material distinction, the distinction between individuals of the same species; material evidence, evidence tending to prove or to disprove the matter under judgment; material fallacy, a fallacy in the matter or thought, rather than in the logical form.—dialectical materialism, Karl Marx's view of history as a conflict between two opposing forces, thesis and antithesis, which is resolved by the forming of a new force, synthesis; present conditions are due to a class struggle between the capitalists, whose aim is private profit, and the workers, who resist exploitation. [L. *māteriālis—māteria*, matter.]

materia medica, *mǝ-tē′ri-ǝ med′i-kǝ*, substances used in medicine: the science of their properties and use. [L.L., medical material.]

matériel, *ma-tā-ri-el′, -ryel′, n.* material: equipment: the baggage and munitions of an army. [Fr.]

maternal, *mǝ-tûr′nǝl, adj.* of a mother: motherly: on the mother's side: of the nature, or in the person, of a mother.—*adv.* mater′nally.—*n.* mater′nity, the fact of being in the relation of mother: motherhood: maternal nature: a maternity hospital.—*adj.* of or for women at or near the time of childbirth. [Fr. *maternel* (It. *maternale*) and *maternité*—L. *māternus—māter*, mother.]

matfelon, *mat′fel-ǝn, n.* the greater knapweed. [O.Fr. *matefelon*; cf. mate (2) and felon.]

math, *math,* (*dial.*) *n.* a mowing. [O.E. *mǣth*.]

mathematic, -al, *math-i-mat′ik, -ǝl, adjs.* pertaining to, or done by, mathematics: very accurate.—*adv.* mathemat′ically.—*ns.* mathematician (-*mǝ-tish′ǝn*), one versed in mathematics; mathemat′ics (treated as *sing.*; *coll.* maths, in U.S. math), the science of magnitude and number, and of all their relations. [Gr. *mathēmatikē* (*epistēmē*), skill, knowledge) relating to learning—*mathēma*—root of *manthanein*, to learn.]

mathesis, *mǝ-thē′sis* (*obs.* math′i-sis), *n.* mental discipline, esp. mathematical. [Gr. *mathēsis*.]

Mathurin, Mathurine, *math′ū-rin, -rēn, n.* a Trinitarian canon. [Perh. from their house near St *Mathurin's* chapel in Paris.]

matico, *mä-tē′kō, n.* a Peruvian pepper shrub, used as a styptic. [Sp. dim. of *Mateo*, Matthew.]

matin, *mat′in, n.* morning (*Shak.*): a morning song (*Milt.*): (in *pl.*; often *cap.*) one of the seven canonical hours of the R.C. Church, usually sung between midnight and daybreak, or now by anticipation the afternoon or evening before: (in *pl.*) the daily morning service of the Church of England.—*adj.* of the morning: of matins.—*adj.* mat′inal.—*n.* matinée, matinee (*mat′i-nā*, mat(-ǝ)-nā′; Fr.), a public entertainment or reception usually held in the afternoon: a woman's dress for morning wear.—matinée coat, jacket, a baby's coat or jacket made of wool or similar material. [Fr. *matines* (fem. pl.)—L. *mātūtinus*, belonging to the morning—*Mātūta*, goddess of morning, prob. akin to *mātūrus*, early.]

matlo, matlow, *mat′lō,* (*slang*) *n.* a seaman, sailor.—Also matelot (*mat′lō*). [Fr. *matelot*.]

matrass, *mat′ras, n.* a long-necked chemical flask: a hard-glass tube closed at one end. [Fr. *matras*.]

matriarchy, *mā′tri-är-ki, n.* government by a mother or by mothers: an order of society in which descent is reckoned in the female line.—*n.* ma′triarch, a patriarch's wife: a woman of like status to a patriarch: an elderly woman who dominates her family or associates: an old woman of great dignity.—*adj.* matriar′chal.—*ns.* matriar′chalism, a condition of society with matriarchal customs: the theory of such a

society; matriar′chate, the position of a matriarch: a matriarchal condition or community. [Formed on the analogy of patriarchy —L. *māter*, mother.]

matrice, *mā′tris, mat′ris, n.* Same as matrix.

matricide, *māt′* or *mat′ri-sid, n.* a murderer of his (or her) own mother: the murder of one's own mother.—*adj.* matrici′dal. [L. *mātricīda, mātricīdium—māter*, mother, *caedere*, to kill.]

matricula, *mǝ-trik′ū-lǝ, n.* a register of members, students, etc.—*adj.* matric′ular, pertaining to a register: contributed to the federal fund (as formerly by German states).—*v.t.* matric′ulate, to admit to membership by entering one's name in a register, esp. in a college.—*v.i.* to become a member of a college, university, etc., by being enrolled.—*n.* one admitted to membership in a society.—*n.* matriculā′tion, act of matriculating: state of being matriculated: an entrance examination (familiarly matric′). [L.L. *mātricula*, a register, dim. of L. *mātrix*.]

matrilineal, *mat-ri-lin′i-ǝl,* matrilinear, *-ǝr, adjs.* reckoned through the mother or through females alone.—*adv.* matrilin′eally.—*n.* mat′-riliny (*or -li′ni*). [L. *māter,* a mother, *linea,* a line.]

matrilocal, *mat-ri-lō′kl, adj.* of a form of marriage, in which the husband goes to live with the wife's group. [L. *māter,* mother, *locālis—locus,* place.]

matrimony, *mat′ri-mǝn-i, n.* wedlock: a card game of chance in which one of the winning combinations is that of king and queen: the combination of king and queen in that and in various other games.—*adj.* matrimonial (-*mō′ni-ǝl*).—*adv.* matrimo′nially. [L. *mātrimōnium—māter, mātris,* mother.]

matrix, *mā′triks,* or *mat′riks, n.* the womb (*anat.*): the cavity in which anything is formed: that in which anything is embedded, as ground-mass, gangue, intercellular substance, cementing material: the bed on which a thing rests, as the cutis under a nail, the hollow in a slab to receive a monumental brass: a mould: a rectangular array of quantities or symbols (*math.*):—*pl.* ma′trices (-*tris-ēz,* or *-iz*): by strict adherence to L. quantities it would be *mā-tri′sēz*), or ma′trixes. —Abbrev. mat. [L. *mātrix, -icis,* a breeding animal, later, the womb—*māter,* mother.]

matroclinic, *mat-rō-klin′ik,* matroclinous, *-klī′nǝs, adjs.* inherited from the mother: more like the mother than the father.—*n.* matrocli′ny. [L. *māter* (or Doric Gr. *mātēr*), mother, and Gr. *klīnein,* to lean.]

matron, *mā′trǝn, n.* a married woman: an elderly lady of staid and sober habits: one in charge of nursing and domestic arrangements in a hospital school, or other institution.—*ns.* ma′tronage, ma′tronhood, state of being a matron: a body of matrons.—*adj.* ma′tronal, pertaining or suitable to a matron: motherly: grave.—*v.t.* ma′tronise, -ize, to render matronly: to act as matron to: to chaperon.—*v.i.* to become a matron or matronly.—*adj.* ma′tronly, like, becoming, or belonging to a matron: elderly: sedate: plump. --*n.* ma′tronship.—*adj.* ma′tron-like. [Fr. *matrone*—L. *mātrōna—māter,* mother.]

matronymic. See metronymic.

matross, *mǝ-tros′,* (*obs.*) *n.* a gunner's assistant in artillery. [Du. *matroos,* app.—Fr. *matelot,* a sailor.]

matt. Same as mat (2).

mattamore, *mat-ǝ-mōr′, -mōr′* or *mat′, n.* a subterranean chamber. [Fr. *matamore*—Ar. *mat-mūrah*.]

matte, mat, *n.* a product of the smelting of sulphide ores.—Also *regulus* and *coarse metal.* [Fr.]

matte, matt, *adj.* Same as mat (2).

matter, *mat′ǝr, n.* that which occupies space, and with which we become acquainted by our bodily senses: that out of which anything is made, material: subject or material of thought, speech, writing, dispute, etc.: substance (opp. to *form*): good sense (*Shak.*): anything engaging the attention: affair: subject: thing: that with which one has to do: cause or ground: thing of consequence: something that is amiss: that with which a court is concerned, something to be tried or proved: importance: an approximate amount: material for work, type set up, copy, etc. (*print.*): that which may be sent by post (*postal matter*): pus.—*v.i.* to be of importance: to signify: to form or discharge pus.—*v.t.* (*obs.*) to mind, concern oneself about.—*adjs.* matt′er-ful, full of matter, pithy; matt′erless; matt′ery, purulent: containing, discharging, or covered with pus.—matter′-of-fact′, adhering to literal, actual or pedestrian fact: not fanciful: prosaic.—as a matter of fact, really; for that matter, as for that: indeed; matter of course, a thing occurring in natural time and order, as to be expected; no matter, it does not matter: it makes no difference. [O.Fr. *matiere*—L. *māteria*, matter.]

matting. See mat (1).

mattins. Same as matins, *pl.* of matin.

mattock, *mat′ək, n.* a kind of pickaxe for loosening the soil, with cutting end instead of a point. [O.E. *mattuc.*]

mattoid, *mat′oid, n.* a person on the borderline between sanity and insanity. [It. *mattoide—matto,* mad.]

mattress, *mat′ris, n.* a bed made of a stuffed bag, or a substitute or supplementary structure of wire, hair, etc.: a mass of brushwood, etc., used to form a foundation for roads, etc., or for the walls of embankments, etc. [O.Fr. *materas* (Fr. *matelas*)—Ar. *matrah,* a place where anything is thrown.]

mature, *mə-tūr′,* U.S. also *-tōōr′, adj.* fully developed: perfected: ripe: well thought out: due: in due time (*Milt.*): suppurating.—*v.t.* to bring to ripeness, full development, or perfection: to bring to a head: to cause to suppurate.—*v.i.* to come to or approach ripeness, full development, or perfection: to become due.—*adj.* matur′able, capable of being matured.—*v.t.* maturate (*mat′*), to make mature: to promote the suppuration of (*med.*).—*v.i.* (*med.*) to suppurate perfectly.—*n.* maturā′tion, a bringing or a coming to maturity: the process of suppurating fully: the final stage in the production of a germ-cell, at which the reducing division occurs.—*adj.* matur′ative (or *mat′*), promoting ripening: promoting suppuration.—*adv.* mature′ly.—*ns.* mature′ness; matur′ity, ripeness: full development: the time of becoming due, as of a bill. [L. *mātūrus,* ripe.]

matutinal, *mat-ū-tī′nl* (or *mə-tūt′i-nəl), adj.* pertaining to the morning: happening ear.y in the day.—Also matutine (*mat′ū-tin*). [L. *mātūtinālis, mātūtīnus;* see matin.]

matzo, *mat′sə, -sō, n.* unleavened bread: a wafer of it:—*pl.* (with verb *sing.* or *pl.*) mat′zoth, -zos.—Also mat′zoh, mat′za(h):—*pls.* mat′zot(h), mat′za(h)s. [Yiddish *matse;* from Heb.]

maud, *möd, n.* a Scottish shepherd's woollen plaid. [Origin unknown.]

maudlin, *möd′lin, adj.* silly: sickly-sentimental: fuddled, half-drunk: tearful (*obs.*).—*n.* maud′linism, the tearful stage of drunkenness. [M.E. *Maudelein,* through O.Fr. and L. from Gr. *Magdalēnē,* (woman) of Magdala, from the assumption that Mary Magdalene was the penitent woman of Luke vii. 38.]

maugre, maulgre, *mö′gər,* also *-gri, mö(l)-grē′* (*arch.*) *prep.* in spite of, notwithstanding: a curse upon (*Spens.,* with dative).—*adv.* in despite.—*n.* ill-will, spite (*obs.*). [O.Fr. *malgré*—L. *male grātum—male,* badly, *grātum,* agreeable.]

maul, *möl, n.* a war-club or mace (*obs.*): a heavy wooden hammer or beetle, a mall: a scrimmage (*Rugby football*): in goal, a struggle for the ball

when carried across the goal-line, but not yet touched down (*Rugby football*).—*v.t.* to beat with a maul or heavy stick: to handle roughly, batter, maltreat: to split with a maul (*U.S.*).—*v.i.* to thrust forward in a close mass. [mall.]

maulstick, *möl′stik, n.* a stick used by painters as a rest for the hand.—Also mahl′stick. [Du. *maalstok—malen,* to paint, *stock,* stick, assimilated to stick.]

maumet, mawmet. Same as mammet.

maun, *mön, män, mun,* (*Scot.*) *v.t.* must.—maunna (*mön′a, mun′ə*), must not. [See mun.]

maund, *mönd,* (*Shak.*) *n.* a basket. [O.E. *mand.*]

maund, *mönd, n.* a measure of weight in India, its value varying in different places from about 25 to 85 pounds avoirdupois. [Hind. and Pers. *man.*]

maund, *mönd,* (*obs. slang*) *v.t.* and *v.i.* to beg.—*n.* maund′er, a beggar.—*v.i.* to beg. [Poss. Fr. *mendier,* to beg—L. *mendicāre.*]

maunder, *mön′dər, v.i.* to grumble: to mutter: to drivel: to wander idly.—*ns.* maun′derer; maun′dering, drivelling talk. [Origin unknown.]

maundy, *mön′di, n.* the religious ceremony of washing the feet of the poor, in commemoration of Christ's washing the disciples' feet (John xiii) —long practised by some monarchs.—maundy money, the dole given away on Maundy Thursday, the day before Good Friday, by the royal almoner, usu. a silver penny for each year of sovereign's age—the small silver coins specially minted since 1662. [Fr. *mandé*—L. *mandātum,* command (John xiii. 34).]

Maurist, *mö′rist, n.* a member of the reformed Benedictine Congregation of St *Maur,* settled from 1618 at the abbey of St *Maur*-sur-Loire, near Saumur, notable for its great services to learning.—Also *adj.*

Mauritius, *mo-, mö-rish′əs, adj.* of the island of *Mauritius* (named after Maurice (1567-1625), Prince of Orange).—Mauritius hemp, the fibre of an amaryllidaceous plant, *Furcraea gigantea.*

Mauser, *mow′zər, n.* series of German rifles, esp. a magazine rifle of 1897. [Inventor's surname.]

mausoleum, *mö-so-lē′əm, n.* a magnificent tomb or monument.—*adj.* mausole′an. [L. *mausōlēum*—Gr. *Mausōleion,* the magnificent tomb of *Mausōlos* (d. 353 B.C.), satrap of Caria, erected by his widow Artemisia at Halicarnassus.]

mauther, mawther, *mö′dhər,* (*dial.* esp. E. Anglia) *n.* a girl: a great awkward girl.—Also (esp. vocatively) mawr, mor. [Origin obscure.]

mauvais, *mo-ve,* (Fr.) bad, worthless:—*fem.* mauvaise, *-vez.*—mauvais goût (*gōō*), bad taste, lack of taste; mauvaise honte (*mo-vez ōt*), false modesty, bashfulness; mauvais moment (*mo-mä*), a bad, unpleasant moment—also mauvais quart d'heure (*kär dær*), bad quarter of an hour; mauvais sujet (*sü-zhä*), a worthless fellow; mauvais ton (*tō*), bad style, bad form.

mauve, *möv, möv, n.* a purple aniline dye: its colour, that of mallow flowers.—*adj.* of the colour of mauve.—*n.* mauve(e)′in(e), mauve dye. [Fr.,—L. *malva,* mallow.]

maverick, *mav′ər-ik,* (*U.S.*) *n.* a stray animal without an owner's brand, esp. a calf: one who does not conform: anything dishonestly obtained.—*v.t.* to seize without legal claim. [From Samuel *Maverick,* a Texas cattle-raiser.]

mavis, *mā′vis, n.* the song-thrush. [Fr. *mauvis.*]

mavourneen, *ma-vōōr′nēm,* (Ir.) *n.* and *interj.* my dear one. [Ir. *mo mhurnín.*]

maw, *mö, n.* the stomach, esp. in the lower animals: the craw in birds: the fourth stomach in ruminants: inward parts: any insatiate gulf or receptacle (*fig.*).—*adj.* maw′bound, (of cattle) constipated by impaction of the rumen.—maw′-worm, a worm infesting the stomach or intestines. [O.E. *maga;* Ger. *magen.*]

maw, *mö, n.* a mew or gull. [O.N. *mär.*]

maw, *mö, n.* an old card-game. [Origin unknown.]

mawk, *mök,* (now *dial.) n.* a maggot.—*adj.* mawk'ish, (orig.) maggoty: loathesome, disgusting: squeamish: insipid: sickly: sickly-sentimental, maudlin.—*adv.* mawk'ishly.—*n.* mawk'ishness. [O.N. *mathkr,* maggot.]

mawkin. Same as malkin.

mawmet, mawther. See mammet, mauther.

mawseed, *mö'sēd, n.* poppy seed as cage-bird food, etc. [Ger. *mahsaat—mah,* poppy.]

max, *maks,* (*obs.) n.* gin. [Origin obscure.]

maxilla, *maks-il'a, n.* a jawbone, esp. the upper: in arthropods an appendage close behind the mouth, modified in connection with feeding:—*pl.* maxill'ae (*-ē*).—*adj.* maxill'ary (or *maks'*), pertaining to a jaw or maxilla.—*n.* a bone forming the posterior part of the upper jaw.—*ns.* maxill'iped, -pede (*-ped, -pēd*), in Crustacea, a jaw-foot, an appendage behind the mouth, adapted to help in passing food to the mouth; maxill'ūla, in crustaceans, a maxilla of the first pair:—*pl.* maxill'ūlae (*-lē*). [L. *maxilla,* jawbone.]

maxim, *maks'im, n.* a general principle, serving as a rule or guide: a pithy saying: a proverb.—*ns.* max'imist, max'im-mong'er, maker of maxims. [Fr. *maxime*—L. *maxima* (*sententia,* or some other word), greatest (opinion, etc.), fem., superl. of *magnus,* great.]

Maxim, *maks'im, n.* often put for Max'im-gun', an automatic machine-gun invented by Hiram *Maxim* (1840-1916).

maxima cum laude, *maks'i-ma kum löd'ē, koom lowd'e,* (L.) with distinction, with the greatest praise (of attainment of high standard in degree examinations).

maximal, etc. See maximum.

maximum, *maks'i-məm, adj.* greatest.—*n.* the greatest number, quantity, or degree: the highest point reached: the value of a variable when it ceases to increase and begins to decrease (*math.*):—*pl.* max'ima.—opp. to *minimum.*—*adj.* maxi'mal, of the highest or maximum value.—*n.* max'imalist, one who makes the fullest demands: a Bolshevik: one who demands the maximum programme.—*adv.* max'imally.—*v.t.* max'imise, -ize, to raise to the highest degree.—*v.i.* to give greatest scope to a doctrine.—maximum and minimum thermometer, a thermometer that shows the highest and lowest temperatures that have occurred since last adjustment. [L., superl. neut. of *magnus,* great.]

maxixe, *mä-shē'shā, n.* a Brazilian dance: a tune for it. [Port.]

maxwell, *maks'wəl, n.* the cgs unit of magnetic flux, equal to $10^{-8}$ weber. [James Clerk-*Maxwell* (1831-79), Scottish physicist.]

may, *mā, vb.* expressing ability, permission, freedom, possibility, contingency, chance, competence, or wish, or softening a blunt question—used with infin. without *to:*—infin. and participles obsolete: *2nd pers. sing.* mayst, mayest; *3rd* may; *pa.t.* might (*mit*), (*obs.*) mought (*mowt*); *2nd pers.* mightest, mightst.—*adv.* may'be, perhaps, possibly.—*n.* a possibility.—*adv.* may'hap (or *-hap'*), perhaps. [O.E. *mæg,* pr.t. (old pa.t.) of *magan,* to be able, pa.t. *mihte;* cog. with Goth. *magan,* Ger. *mögen.*]

May, *mā, n.* now the fifth month of the year (see March): the early or gay part of life: (*without cap.*) may-blossom.—*v.i.* to gather may on Mayday: to participate in May sports.—*n.* may'ing, the observance of Mayday customs.—May'-app'le, *Podophyllum* or its egg-shaped fruit; may'-bee'tle, may'-bug, the cockchafer; may'-bloom', -bloss'om, the hawthorn flower; May'day, the first day of May, given to sports and to socialist and labour demonstrations.—Also *adj.*—May'-dew', the dew of May, esp. that of the morning of the first day of May, said

to whiten linen, and beautify faces; may'-duke, a variety of sour cherry; May'fair, the aristocratic West End of London, at one time scene of a fair in May; may'flower, the hawthorn or other flower that blooms in May; may'fly, a short-lived plectopterous insect (Ephemera) that appears in May: the caddis-fly; May'-game, sport appropriate to Mayday: frolic generally; May'-lā'dy, the queen of the May; May laws, Prussian laws passed in three successive Mays (1873-75) restricting the power of the Church; may'-lil'y, the lily of the valley; May'-lord', a youth directing May-games: one enjoying transitory dignity.—*n.pl.* May'-meet'ings, meetings of various religious and philanthropic societies held in London in May.—May'-morn', -morn'-ing, a morning in May: youthful freshness as of May (*Shak.*); may'pole, a pole erected for dancing round on Mayday; May'-queen', a young woman crowned with flowers as queen on Mayday; May'-time, the season of May. [O.Fr. *Mai*—L. *Māius* (*mēnsis*), prob. (month) sacred to *Māia,* mother of Mercury.]

may, *mā, n.* a maid. [Prob. O.E. *mæg,* a kinswoman.]

maya, *mä'ya, n.* illusion. [Sans. *māyā.*]

Maya, *mä'ya, n.* one of an Indian people of Central America and Southern Mexico who developed a remarkable civilisation.—*adjs.* Ma'ya, Ma'yan.—*ns.* Mayol'ogist, Mayol'ogy.

mayday, *mä'dā,* the international radiotelephonic distress signal for ships and aircraft. [Fr. *m'aidez,* pron. *mä-dā,* help me.]

Mayday. See May.

mayhem, *mā'hem, mā'əm, n.* maiming: malicious damage (*legal* and *U.S.*). [maim.]

mayonnaise, *mā-ə-nāz', or mā', n.* a sauce composed of the yolk of eggs, salad-oil, and vinegar or lemon-juice, seasoned: any cold dish of which it is an ingredient. [Fr.]

mayor, *mā'ər, mār, n.* the chief magistrate of a city or borough in England, Ireland, etc., whether man or woman.—*adj.* may'oral.—*ns.* may'oralty, may'orship, the office of a mayor; may'oress, a mayor's wife, or other lady who performs her social and ceremonial functions.—Lord Mayor, the chief magistrate of certain English, Welsh, Irish and Australian cities and boroughs; Mayor of the Palace, in Merovingian France, the king's major-domo or prime minister, the real ruler. [Fr. *maire*—L. *mājor,* comp. of *magnus,* great.]

mayster, *mās'ter,* maysterdome, etc., Spenserian forms of master, etc.

mayweed, *mā'wēd, n.* stinking camomile (*Anthemis cotula*): corn feverfew (*Matricaria inodora*; a scentless mayweed): applied to various similar plants. [O.E. *mægtha,* mayweed, and weed.]

mazard, mazzard, *maz'ərd, n.* a head or skull (*Shak.*): a wild European cherry. [Prob. mazer.]

mazarine, *maz-ə-rēn', n.* a rich blue colour: a blue gown or stuff.—Also *adj.*—*n.* mazarinade', a satire or pamphlet against Cardinal *Mazarin* (1602-61).—Mazarin(e) Bible, the first printed Bible, printed by Gutenberg and Fust about 1450, of which the Cardinal had twenty-five copies; mazarine hood, a hood of a form said to have been worn by the Duchesse de *Mazarin.*

mazarine (dish), (plate), *maz-ə-rēn' (dish), (plāt),* a 17th-cent. deep, usu. metal, plate: a cooking and serving dish set inside a larger dish. [Origin uncertain.]

Mazdaism, *maz'dä-izm,* Mazdeism, *maz'dē-izm, ns.* the religion of the ancient Persians.—*adj.* Mazdē'an. [See Ormuzd.]

maze, *māz, n.* bewilderment: a labyrinth: a set of intricate windings.—*v.t.* to bewilder: to confuse.—*adj.* maze'ful (*Spens.*).—*n.* maze'ment.—*adv.* maz'ily.—*n.* maz'iness.—*adj.* maz'y. [Prob.

from a lost O.E. word; the compound *āmasod*, amazed, occurs.]

**maze**, *māz*. Same as **mease** (of herrings).

**mazer**, *mā'zər*, *n.* a hard wood, probably maple: a cup of maple wood (*Spens.*): a similar cup of other material. [O.Fr. *masere*, of Gmc. origin; cf. O.H.G. *masar*, O.N. *mösurr*, a maple-tree.]

**mazurka**, *mə-zoōr'ka*, or *-zûr'*, *n.* a lively Polish dance: music for it, in triple time. [Pol., Masurian woman.]

**mazut**, **mazout**, *mə-zoōt'*, *n.* petroleum residue after distillation. [Russ. *mazat'*, to daub, smear.]

**me**, *mē*, *mi*, *pers. pron.* the accusative and dative of I. [O.E. *mē*.]

**me**, an anglicised spelling of **mi**.

**meacock**, *mē'kok*, (*Shak.*) *adj.* timorous, effeminate, cowardly.—*n.* a milksop. [Origin unknown.]

**mea culpa**, *mē'ə kul'pə*, *mā'ä koōl'pä*, (L.) by my own fault.

**mead**, *mēd*, *n.* honey and water fermented and flavoured. [O.E. *meodu*; Ger. *met*, W. *medd*.]

**mead**, *mēd*, (*poet.*), and **meadow**, *med'ō*, *ns.* a level tract producing grass to be mown down: a rich pasture-ground, esp. beside a stream.—*adj.* **mead'owy**.—**mead'ow-brown'**, a butterfly of the Satyridae; **mead'ow-grass**, any grass of the genus Poa (**floating meadow-grass**, manna-grass, float-grass); **mead'ow-lark'** (*U.S.*), a name for various species of birds of the genus *Sturnella* (family Icteridae); **mead'ow-rue'**, a genus (*Thalictrum*) of the buttercup family with rue-like leaves; **mead'ow-saff'ron**, *Colchicum autumnale*—also autumn-crocus, or *naked lady*; **mead'ow-sax'ifrage**, a saxifrage (*Saxifraga granulata*) that grows on banks and dry meadows: applied also to umbelliferous plants of the genera Seseli and Silaus. [O.E. *mǣd*, in oblique cases *mǣdwe—māwan*, to mow; Ger. *matte*.]

**meadow-sweet**, *med'ō-swēt*, *n.* the rosaceous plant queen of the meadows (*Spiraea ulmaria*), a tall fragrant plant of watery meadows. [Earlier **mead-sweet**, which may be from **mead** (1) or from **mead** (2), as the obs. **mead'wort** is in O.E. *meduwyrt*.]

**meagre**, *mē'gər*, *adj.* having little flesh: lean: poor: without richness or fertility: barren: scanty: without strength: jejune: maigre.—*n.* the maigre.—*adv.* **mea'grely**.—*n.* **mea'greness**. [Fr. *maigre*—L. *macer*, *macra*, *-rum*, lean; cf. Ger. *mager*.]

**meal**, *mēl*, *n.* the food taken at one time: the act or occasion of taking food, as a breakfast, dinner, or supper.—*n.* **meal'er**, one who takes his meals at a boarding-house, lodging elsewhere. —**meals-on-wheels**, a welfare service taking cooked, usu. hot, meals to old people in need of such help; **meal ticket**, a ticket that can be exchanged for a meal (esp. at reduced price): someone or something that is the source of one's expenses or income: someone who can be depended upon; **meal'-tide** (*arch.*) *Scot.* **meltith**, *mel'tith*, a meal), **meal'-time**, the time for a meal. [O.E. *mǣl*, time, portion of time; Du. *maal*, Ger. *mahl*.]

**meal**, *mēl*, *n.* grain ground to powder: other material in powder: a powdery surface-covering. —*v.t.* to cover with meal: to grind into meal.— *v.i.* to yield or be plentiful in meal.—*n.* **meal'iness**. —*adj.* **meal'y**, like meal: covered with meal or with something like meal: spotty: whitish.— **meal'-ark** (*Scot.*), a large chest for holding meal; **meal'-man**, or **meal'-monger**, one who deals in meal; **Meal Monday**, the second Monday in February, a St Andrews (and formerly, Edinburgh) University holiday, originally to allow the students to go home and replenish their stock of meal; **meal'-poke**, a beggar's meal-bag; **meal'-tree**, the wayfaring tree, from its mealy

leaves and shoots; **meal'-worm**, the larva of a beetle (Tenebrio) abounding in granaries and flour-stores; **meal'y-bug**, a hothouse pest, a coccus insect with a white powdery appearance. —*adj.* **meal'y-mouthed** (-*mowdhd*), smooth-tongued: over-squeamish in choice of words.— **meal'y-mouth'edness**. [O.E. *melu*, *melo*; Ger. *mehl*, Du. *meel*, meal.]

**meal**, *mēl*, (*Shak.*, in *pa.p.* **meal'd**) *v.t.* to stain, spot. [O.E. *mǣlan*.]

**mealie**, *mēl'i*, (*S.Afr.*) *n.* an ear of maize: esp. in *pl.*) maize. [S.Afr. Du. *milie*, millet.]

**mean**, *mēn*, *adj.* low in rank or birth: base: sordid: low in worth or estimation: of little value or importance: poor, humble: low: inconsiderable: despicable: shabby: paltry: small-minded: ungenerous: stingy: malicious: out of sorts, uncomfortable (*U.S.*).—*n.* **mean'ie**, -**y**, (*coll.*) an ungenerous, ungracious, small-minded, or malicious person.—*adv.* **mean'ly**.—*n.* **mean'ness**.—*adjs.* **mean'-born**; **mean'-spir'ited**. —**mean'-spir'itedness**. [O.E. *gemǣne*; Ger. *gemein*; L. *communis*, common.]

**mean**, *mēn*, *adj.* intermediate: average: moderate (*obs.*).—*n.* that which is between or intermediate: an average amount, or value: a middle state or position: an intermediate term in a progression: meantime (*Spens.*): a middle or intermediate part (*mus.*): an instrument or medium: a mediator or intercessor (*obs.*):—*pl.* in form **means**, that by whose instrumentality anything is caused or brought to pass: (treated as *sing.* or *plur.*) way to an end: (treated as *pl.*) pecuniary resources: what is required for comfortable living.—*ns.* **mean'time**, **mean'while**, the intervening time.—*advs.* in the intervening time.— **means test**, the test of private resources, determining or limiting claim to concession or allowance; **mean sun**, an imaginary sun moving uniformly in the equator, its position giving mean time (coinciding with true sun time four times a year); **mean'-tone** (*mus.*), an interval of mean value between a major and a minor second, formerly used in a system of temperament.—**arithmetic(al) mean**, the sum of a number of quantities divided by their number; **by all means**, certainly; **by any means**, in any way; **by means** (*Spens.*), because; **by no means**, certainly not; **geometric(al) mean**, the *n*th root of the product of *n* quantities; **golden mean**, the middle course between two extremes: a wise moderation; **harmonic mean**, the reciprocal of the arithmetical mean of the reciprocals of two quantities; **in the mean** (*Spens.*), in the meantime; **quadratic mean**, the square root of the arithmetical mean of the squares of the given quantities. [O.Fr. *meien* (Fr. *moyen*)—L. *mediānus—medius*, middle.]

**mean**, *mēn*, *v.t.* to have in mind as signification: to intend, to purpose: to destine, design: to signify.—*v.i.* (with *well*, *ill*) to have good, bad, intentions or disposition: (with *much*, *little*, etc.) to be of much, little, importance (to):—*pr.p.* **mean'ing**; *pa.t.* and *pa.p.* **meant** (*ment*).—*n.* **mean'ing**, that which is in the mind or thoughts: signification: the sense intended: purpose.—*adj.* significant.—*adjs.* **mean'ingful**; **mean'ingless**, senseless: expressionless: without significance. —*adv.* **mean'ingly**, significantly: intentionally. [O.E. *mǣnan*; Ger. *meinen*, to think.]

**mean**, **meane**, **mein**, **mene**, *mēn*, (*Shak.* and *Scot.*) *v.t.* and *v.i.* to lament, to moan: to complain. [O.E. *mǣnan*; cf. **moan**.]

**meander**, *mi-an'dər*, *n.* a sinuosity: a winding course: a maze: an intricate fret pattern: perplexity.—*v.i.* to wind about: to be intricate: to wander listlessly (with some reminiscence of **maunder**).—*adjs.* **mean'dered**, formed into or covered with many passages or patterns; **mean'-dering**, **mean'drian** (*obs.*), **mean'drous**, winding.

[L. *Maeander*—Gr. *Maiandros*, a winding river in Asia Minor.]

**meant**, *ment*, *pa.t.* and *pa.p.* of **mean** (*vb.*).

**meare**, *mēr*, Spenser's spelling of **mere** (2 and 3).
—**mear'd** (*Spens.*) *pa.t.* of **mere** (3).

**mease**, *mēz*, maze, maize, maise, *māz*, (*dial.*) *n.* a measure of five 'hundreds' of herrings—varying from 500 to 630. [O.Fr. *meise*, receptacle for herrings; O.N. *meiss*, box, basket; O.H.G. *meisa*.]

**mease**, *mēz*, (*Scot.*) *v.t.* to assuage: to mitigate. [O.Fr. *amesir*—L. *ad*, to, *mitis*, mild.]

**measles**, *mē'zlz*, *n.* (*pl.* in form, treated as *sing.*) an infectious fever accompanied by eruptions of small red spots upon the skin: a disease of swine and cattle, caused by larval tapeworms: a blister or a disease of trees (*obs.*).—*n.* **mea'sle**, a tapeworm larva.—*v.t.* (*arch.*) to infect with measles.—*v.i.* (*arch.*) to take measles.—*adj.* **mea'sled**, measly.—*n.* **meas'liness**.—*adj.* **mea'sly**, infected with measles, or with tapeworm larvae: spotty: paltry, miserable.—**German measles**, rubella. [M.E. *maseles*; cf. Du. *mazelen*, measles, O. H. G. *masala*, blister; Ger. *masern*, measles.]

**measure**, *mezh'ər*, *n.* ascertainment of extent by comparison with a standard: a system of expressing the result of such ascertainment: amount ascertained by comparison with a standard: that by which extent is ascertained or expressed: size: a standard or unit: a quantity by which another can be divided without remainder: an instrument for finding the extent of anything, esp. a graduated rod or tape for length, or a vessel of known content for capacity: the quantity contained in a vessel of known capacity—often a bushel: adequacy or due amount: some amount or degree, a portion: proportion: moderation: restraint: limit (*Milt.*): extent: that which is meted out to one, treatment: means to an end: an enactment or bill: rhythm: a unit of verse—one foot or two feet: metre: strict time: a bar of music: a strain: a dance, esp. a slow and stately one: the width of a page or column, usually in *ems* (*print.*): (in *pl.*) a series of beds or strata (*geol.*).—*v.t.* to ascertain or show the dimensions or amount of: to mark out or lay off: to mete out: to proportion: to pit: to traverse: to sing or utter in measure (*Spens.*).—*v.i.* to be of the stated size: to take measurements.—*adj.* **meas'urable**, that may be measured or computed: moderate: in small quantity or extent.—*n.* **meas'urableness**.—*adv.* **meas'urably**.—*adj.* **meas'ured**, determined by measure: mensurable: rhythmical: with slow, heavy, steady rhythm: considered: restrained.—*adv.* **meas'uredly**.—*adj.* **meas'ureless**, boundless.—*ns.* **meas'urement**, the act of measuring: quantity found by measuring (**measurement goods**, light goods carried for charges according to bulk, not weight); **meas'urer**.—*n.* and *adj.* **meas'uring**.—**meas'uring-rod**, **-tape**, one for measuring with; **meas'uring-worm'**, a looper caterpillar.—**above**, or **beyond**, or (*arch.*) **out of**, **measure**, to an exceedingly great degree; **be the measure of** (something), to be the standard by which its quality, etc., may be judged; **hard measures**, harsh treatment; **in a measure**, **in some measure**, to some degree; **measure one's length**, to fall or be thrown down at full length; **measure up to**, to be adequate for; **measure strength**, to engage in a contest; **measure swords**, orig. to compare lengths of swords before a duel: to fight; **out of measure** (see above measure); **short measure**, less than the due and professed amount; **take measures**, to adopt means to gain an end; **take one's measure**, to estimate one's character and abilities; **tread a measure**, to go through a dance; **within measure**, moderately; **without measure**, immoderately. [O.Fr. *mesure*—L.

*mēnsūra*, a measure—*mētīrī*, *mēnsum*, to measure.]

**meat**, *mēt*, *n.* anything eaten as food: a meal (*obs.*): the edible part of anything (now chiefly *U.S.*): the flesh of animals used as food—sometimes beef, mutton, pork, veal, etc., as opposed to poultry, fish, etc.: proleptically, game, destined prey: food for thought, substance, pith (*fig.*).—*n.* **meat'iness**.—*adjs.* **meat'less**, foodless: without butcher's meat; **meat'y**, full of meat: fleshy: flesh-like in taste or smell: pithy.—**meat'-eater**, one who eats butcher's meat; **meat'-fly**, a blowfly: a flesh-fly; **meat'-man**, a seller of butcher's meat; **meat'-mar'ket**, a flesh-market; **meat'-off'ering**, a Jewish sacrificial offering of fine flour or first-fruits with oil and frankincense; **meat'-pie**; **meat'-safe**, a receptacle for storing meat; **meat'-sales'man**, one who sells meat, esp. to the retail butchers; **meat'screen**, a metal screen behind roasting meat, to throw back the fire's heat upon it; **meat'-tea'**, a high tea with meat; **meat'-tub**, a pickling-tub. [O.E. *mete*.]

**meath(e)**, *mēdh*, *n.* an obs. form of **mead** (1).

**meatus**, *mi-ā'tas*, (*anat.*) *n.* a passage or canal:—*pl.* **mea'tuses**.—*adj.* **mea'tal**. [L. *meātus* (pl. *-ūs*) —*meāre*, to go.]

**meawes**, a Spenserian spelling of (sea-) **mews** (see **mew** (1)).

**meazel**. See **mesel**.

**mebos**, *mā'bos*, (*S.Afr.*) *n.* salted or sugared dried apricots. [Perh. Japanese *umeboshi*, a kind of plum.]

**Mecca**, *mek'a*, *n.* the birthplace of Mohammed, a place of pilgrimage for Moslems: any outstanding place reverenced or resorted to—e.g. St Andrews, Mecca of golf.

**mechanic**, *mi-kan'ik*, *adj.* mechanical.—*n.* a handicraftsman: a skilled worker, esp. one who makes or maintains machinery: an air-mechanic: a term of contempt for one of the lower orders (*obs.*).—*adj.* **mechan'ical**, pertaining to machines: dynamical: worked or done by machinery or by mechanism: acting or done by physical not chemical means: machine-like: of the nature of a machine or mechanism: without intelligence or conscious will: performed simply by force of habit: reflex: skilled in mechanism: manual (*arch.*): manually employed: technical (*obs.*): mechanistic.—*n.* (*Shak.*) a mechanic.—*adv.* **mechan'ically**.—*ns.* **mechanician** (*mek-an-ish'ən*), a machine-maker: one skilled in the structure of machines; **mechan'ics** (treated as *sing.*), dynamics, the science of the action of forces on bodies, including kinetics and statics: the art or science of machine construction: the details of making or creating by manual or other process: system on which something works: routine procedure; **mechanisā'tion**, **-izā'tion**.—*v.t.* **mech'anise**, **-ize**, to make mechanical: to adapt to mechanical working: to provide with armoured armed vehicles.—*ns.* **mech'anism**, the construction of a machine: arrangement and action by which a result is produced: a philosophy that regards the phenomena of life as explainable by mechanical forces: the means adopted unconsciously towards a subconscious end (*psych.*); **mech'anist**, a mechanician: a believer in philosophical mechanism.—*adj.* **mechanist'ic**.—*adv.* **mechanist'ically**.—**mechanical powers**, the elementary forms or parts of machines—three *primary*, the lever, inclined plane, and pulley; and three *secondary*, wheel-and-axle, the wedge, and the screw; **mechanical tissue**, any tissue that gives a plant power of resisting stresses; **mechanics' institute**, an institution for the education of mechanics, with lectures, library, etc. [Gr. *mēchanikos*—*mēchanē*, a contrivance.]

**Mechitharist**. See **Mekhitarist**.

**Mechlin,** *mek'* or *mehh'lin, adj.* produced at *Mechlin* or Malines.—*n.* lace made at Mechlin.

**meconic,** *mi-kon'ik, adj.* denoting an acid obtained from poppies.—*ns.* **meconate** (*mek'ɔn-āt,* or *mēk'*), a salt of meconic acid; **mec'onin,** a white, fusible, neutral substance (C₁₀H₁₀O₄) existing in opium; **mecō'nium,** the first faeces of a new-born child, or of a newly emerged insect imago: opium; **Meconops'is** (Gr. *opsis,* appearance). a genus of largely Asiatic poppies. [Gr. *mēkōn,* the poppy.]

**Mecoptera,** *mē-kop'tɔ-ra, n.pl.* an order of insects linking the Hymenoptera with the Trichoptera—the scorpion-flies. [Gr. *mēkos,* length, *pteron,* wing.]

**medaewart,** *med'ē-wärt, n.* meadow-sweet (*Spens.*). [O.E. *meduwyrt*; see **meadow-sweet.**]

**medal,** *med'l, n.* a piece of metal in the form of a coin bearing some device or inscription, struck or cast usually in commemoration of an event or as a reward of merit.—*v.t.* to decorate with a medal:—*pr.p.* **med'alling;** *pa.t.* and *pa.p.* **med'alled.**—*n.* **med'alet,** a small medal, esp. the representation of saints, worn by Roman Catholics.—*adj.* **medallic** (*mi-dal'ik*).—*n.* **medallion** (*mi-dal'yɔn*), a large medal: a bas-relief of a round (sometimes a square) form: a round ornament, panel, tablet, or design of similar form. —*v.t.* to ornament, decorate, with medallions: to make in the form of a medallion.—*n.* **med'allist,** one with expert knowledge of medals, or a collector of medals: a designer or maker of medals: one who has gained a medal.—**medal play,** golf scored by strokes for the round, not by holes. [Fr. *médaille*—It. *medaglia*; through L.L. from L. *metallum,* metal.]

**meddle,** *med'l, v.t.* and *v.i.* (*arch.*) to mix.—*v.i.* to concern oneself (with; *arch.*): to engage in fight (*Shak.*): to interfere unnecessarily, temerariously, (with, in): to tamper (with).—*n.* **medd'ler.**—*adj.* **medd'lesome,** given to meddling.—*n.* **medd'lesomeness.**—*n.* and *adj.* **medd'ling.** [O.Fr. *medler,* a variant of *mesler* (Fr. *mêler*)—L.L. *misculāre*—L. *miscēre,* to mix.]

**Mede.** See **Median** (2).

**media,** *mē'di-ɔ, n.* a voiced stop consonant, or letter representing it: the middle coat of a blood-vessel: a middle primary vein of an insect's wing.—See also **medium.** [L. *media* (*littera, tunica, vena*), middle (letter, coat, vein), fem. of *medius,* middle.]

**mediacy.** See **mediate.**

**mediaeval, medieval,** *med-i-ē'vl,* U.S. *mē-d(ē-)ē, adj.* of the Middle Ages.—*ns.* **medi(a)e'valism,** spirit of Middle Ages: devotion to mediaeval ideals; **medi(a)e'valist,** one versed in the history, art, etc., of the Middle Ages: one who follows mediaeval practices.—*adv.* **medi(a)e'vally.** [L. *medius,* middle, *aevum,* age.]

**medial,** *mē'di-ɔl, adj.* intermediate: occurring within a word: median: pertaining to a mean or average.—*n.* (*phon.*; *obs.*) a media.—*adv.* **me'dially.** [L.L. *mediālis*—L. *medius,* middle.]

**median,** *mē'di-ɔn, adj.* in the middle, running through the middle: situated in the straight line or plane (*median line, plane*) that divides anything longitudinally into symmetrical halves.—*n.* a straight line joining an angular point of a triangle with the middle point of the opposite side: a middle nervure of an insect's wing: in a series of values, the value middle in position (not usu. in magnitude). [L. *mediānus*—*medius,* middle.]

**Median,** *mē'di-ɔn, adj.* pertaining to Media, ancient kingdom north-west of Persia, its people, or their Indo-Germanic language (also *n.*).—*n.* **Mede,** one of the people of Media, fused as a nation with the Persians about 500 B.C.—*adj.* **Me'dic.**—*v.i.* **Me'dise, -ize,** to become Median, or as the Medians: to favour the Persians (called Medes by the Greeks).—*v.t.* to make

**Median.**—*n.* **Me'dism,** the adoption of Persian interests—to a Greek, treachery.—**law of the Medes and Persians,** the type of 'that which altereth not' (Dan. vi. 12). [Gr. *Mēdos,* a Mede.]

**mediant,** *mē'di-ɔnt, n.* the third tone of a scale, about midway between tonic and dominant. [L.L. *mediāns, -antis,* pr.p. of *mediāre,* to be in the middle.]

**mediastinum,** *mē-di-as-tī'nɔm, n.* a membranous septum, or a cavity, between two principal portions of an organ, esp. the folds of the pleura and the space between the right and left lungs.— *adj.* **mediasti'nal.** [Neut. of L.L. *mediastinus,* median (in classical L. *mediastinus* is a drudge)— *medius.*]

**mediate,** *mē'di-it, adj.* middle: intervening: indirect: related or acting through something intervening.—*v.i.* (-*āt*) to interpose between parties as a friend of each: to act as intermediary: to intercede: to be or act as a medium: to hold a mediate position.—*v.t.* to bring about, end, promote, obtain, or communicate by friendly intervention, or by intercession, or through an intermediary: to be the medium or intermediary of: to transmit, convey, pass on.—*n.* **me'diacy** (-*ɔ-si*), mediateness.—*adv.* **me'diately.**—*ns.* **me'diateness,** state of being mediate; **media'tion,** the act of mediating or coming between: entreaty for another; **mediatisā'tion, -z-.**—*v.t.* **me'diatise, -ize,** to cause to act in a subordinate position or through an agent: to reduce from immediate to mediate vassal (of the empire) without loss of dignity: to annex, or to subordinate, as a smaller state to a larger neighbouring one.—*adj.* **me'diative** (-ɔ-tiv).—*n.* **me'diātor,** one who mediates between parties at strife:—*fem.* **me'diātress, media'trix:**—*pl.* **mediātrices** (-trī'sēz).—*adj.* **mediatō'rial.**—*adv.* **mediatō'rially.**—*n.* **me'diatorship.**—*adj.* **me'diatory.** [L.L. *mediāre, -ātum,* to be in the middle—L. *medius.*]

**medic,** *med'ik, adj.* medical (*poet.*).—*n.* a physician (*rare*): a medical student (*slang*).—*n.* **medicas'ter,** a quack.—*adjs.* **med'ico-chirur'gical,** relating to both medicine and surgery; **med'ico-le'gal,** relating to the application of medicine to questions of law. [L. *medicus.*]

**medical,** *med'i-kl, adj.* relating to the art of healing: relating to the art of the physician, distinguished from surgery.—*n.* (*coll.*) a student of medicine: a medical examination to ascertain the state of one's physical health.—*adv.* **med'ically.** [L.L. *medicālis*—L. *medicus,* a physician —*medēri,* to heal.]

**medicament,** *med-ik'ɔ-mɔnt,* or *med', n.* a substance used in curative treatment, esp. externally. —*v.t.* to treat with medicaments.—*adjs.* **medicamental** (-*ment'l*), **medicament'ary.**—*adv.* **medicament'ally.** [L. *medicāmentum*—*medicāre.*]

**medicate,** *med'i-kāt, v.t.* to treat with medicine: to impregnate with anything medicinal: to drug, doctor, tamper with.—*adj.* **med'icable,** that may be healed.—*adj.* **med'icated.**—*n.* **medicā'tion.**—*adj.* **med'icative.** [L. *medicāre, -ātum,* to heal—*medicus.*]

**Medicean,** *med-i-sē'ɔn, adj.* relating to the *Medici,* a distinguished Florentine family which attained to sovereign power in the 15th century.

**medicine,** *med'sin, -sn,* also (esp. U.S.) *med'i-sin, -sn, n.* any substance used (esp. internally) for the treatment or prevention of disease: a drug: the art or science of prevention and cure of disease, esp. non-surgically: remedial punishment: a charm: anything of magical power: a physician (*Shak.*).—*v.t.* to treat or cure by medicine.—*adjs.* **medicinable** (*med'sin-ɔ-bl*), having a healing power; **medicinal** (*med-is'i-nl,* sometimes *med-i-si'nl*; in *Shak.,* etc., *med'si-nl*; *Milt.* **med''cinal**), used in medicine: curative: relating to medicine: like medicine.—*adv.* **medic'inally.**—*ns.* **med'icine-ball,** a heavy ball tossed and caught for exercise; **med'icine-bott'le**; **med'icine-chest**, a chest for keeping a selected set of medicines; **med'icine-dropp'er**; **med'icine-man**, among savages, a witch-doctor or magician; **med'iciner** (*arch.*), a physician. [L. *medicina—medicus*.]

**medick**, *med'ik*, *n.* any species of *Medicago*, a genus distinguished from clover by its spiral or sickle-shaped pods and short racemes—including lucerne. [L. *mēdica*—Gr. *Mēdikē* (*poā*), Median (herb), i.e. lucerne.]

**medico**, *med'ik-ō*, (*slang*) *n.* a medical practitioner or student. [It. *medico*, or Sp. *médico*—L. *medicus*, a physician.]

**medieval.** Same as **mediaeval.**

**medio-**, *mē'di-ō-*, (in compounds) middle. [L. *medius*, middle.]

**mediocre**, *mē'di-ō-kər*, or *-ō'*, *adj.* of middling goodness (usu. disparagingly).—*n.* **medioc'rity** (*-ok'*), a middling degree: a mediocre person. [Fr. *médiocre*—L. *mediocris—medius*, middle.]

**Medise, Medism.** See **Median** (2).

**meditate**, *med'i-tāt*, *v.i.* to consider thoughtfully (with *on*, *upon*): to engage in contemplation, esp. religious.—*v.t.* to consider deeply, reflect upon: to revolve in the mind: to intend.—*adj.* **med'i-tated.**—*n.* **meditā'tion**, the act of meditating: deep thought: serious continuous contemplation esp. on a religious or spiritual theme: a meditative discourse: a meditative treatment of a literary or musical theme.—*adj.* **med'itātive.**—*adv.* **med'itātively.**—*n.* **med'itātiveness.**—**meditate the muse** (Latinism, after Milton), to give one's mind to composing poetry. [L. *meditāri*, prob. cog. with L. *medēri*, to heal.]

**mediterranean**, *med-i-tə-rā'ni-ən*, *adj.* situated in the middle of earth or land: land-locked: of the **Mediterranean Sea** (so called from being in the middle of the land of the Old World), or its shores.—**Mediterranean fever**, Malta or undulant fever; **Mediterranean race**, a long-headed dark race of white men, of medium stature, inhabiting south Europe and north Africa. [L. *mediterrāneus—medius*, middle, *terra*, earth.]

**medium**, *mē'di-əm*, *n.* the middle: the middle place or degree: a middle course: a mean (*obs.*): any intervening means, instrument, or agency: instrumentality: a substance through which any effect is transmitted: that through which communication is maintained: a channel (as newspapers, radio, television) through which information is transmitted: an enveloping substance or element in which a thing exists or lives: environment: a vehicle for paint, etc.: a nutritive substance on which a culture (as of bacteria, tissue, etc.) may be fed: in spiritualism, the person through whom spirits are said to communicate with the material world: a person of supernormal sensibility:—*pl.* **me'dia** or **me'diums.**—*adjs.* **me'dium**, intermediate: mean, average (*obs.*): of a standard size of paper between demy and royal, now 18 in. by 23 in.; **mediumis'tic**, of or pertaining to spiritualistic mediums.—**medium waves** (*radio*), electro-magnetic waves of between 200 and 1000 metres.—**circulating medium**, money passing from hand to hand, as coin, banknotes, etc. [L. *medium*, neutr. of *medius*, middle.]

**medius**, *mē'di-əs*, *n.* the middle finger. [L. *medius*, middle.]

**Medjidie**, *me-jēd'i-e*, *n.* a Turkish order of knighthood founded by Sultan Abdu'l Majid.

**medlar**, *med'lər*, *n.* a small tree (*Mespilus*, or *Pyrus, germanica*) akin to the apple: its fruit. [O.Fr. *medler, mesler*—L. *mespilum*—Gr. *mespilon*.]

**medle**, an old spelling (*Shak.* and *Spens.*) of **meddle.**

**medley**, *med'li*, *n.* a mingled and confused mass: a miscellany: a song or piece of music made up of bits from various sources: a cloth woven from

yarn of different colours: a mêlée, fight (*obs.*). [O.Fr. *medler, mesler*, to mix.]

**Médoc**, *mā-dok'*, *n.* a French wine produced in the district of *Médoc*, department of Gironde.

**medulla**, *me-dul'ə*, *n.* the inner portion of an organ, hair, or tissue: bone-marrow: pith: a loose or spongy mass of hyphae.—*adjs.* **medull'ar**, **-y**, consisting of, or resembling, marrow or pith; **medull'ate**, having medulla; **med'ullated**, provided with a medullary sheath.—**medulla oblongā'ta**, that part of the brain that tapers off into the spinal cord; **medullary ray** (*bot.*), a band of cells (appearing as a ray in cross-section) cutting radially through wood and bast; **medullary sheath**, a thin layer surrounding the pith (*bot.*): a whitish fatty membrane covering an axis-cylinder (*anat.*). [L. *medulla*, marrow.]

**Medusa**, *me-dū'zə*, *n.* one of the three Gorgons, whose head, with snakes for hair, turned beholders into stone, but was cut off by Perseus, and placed in Athena's aegis: (without *cap.*) a jellyfish: (without *cap.*) an individual of the free-swimming sexual generation of jellyfishes and Hydrozoa:—*pl.* **medu'sae** (*-zē*).—*adj.* **medu'-san.**—*n.* a medusa.—*adjs.* **medu'siform**, like a jellyfish; **medu'soid**, like a medusa.—*n.* a sexual hydrozoan that remains attached to the parent hydroid colony. [L. *Medūsa*—Gr. *Medousa*, the Gorgon Medusa (lit. ruler).]

**meed**, *mēd*, *n.* wages (*arch.*): reward: what is bestowed for merit: measure, portion. [O.E. *mēd*; Ger. *miete*.]

**meek**, *mēk*, *adj.* mild and gentle of temper: submissive.—*v.t.* **meek'en**, to render meek.—*v.i.* to become meek.—*adv.* **meek'ly.**—*n.* **meek'ness**, state or quality of being meek. [O.N. *mjūkr*; early mod. Du. *muik*, soft.]

**meer**, *mēr*, *n.* an obsolete spelling of **mere.**—*adj.* **meer'ed** (*Shak.*), possibly, set up as a *mere* or division, dividing: according to some, sole. [mere (3) or **mere** (2).]

**meerkat**, *mēr'kat*, *n.* a monkey (*obs.*): a South African carnivore (*Cynictis penicillata*), akin to the ichneumon: the suricate: a ground-squirrel: a lemur.—Also **meercat**. [Du. *meerkat*, monkey, as if 'overseas cat', from *meer*, sea, *kat*, cat, but perh. really an Eastern word.]

**meerschaum**, *mēr'shəm*, *n.* a fine light whitish clay, sepiolite—once supposed to be a petrified sea-scum: a tobacco-pipe made of it. [Ger.,—*meer*, sea, *schaum*, foam.]

**meet**, *mēt*, *adj.* fitting: qualified: even, quits (*Shak.*).—*adv.* fittingly (*Shak.*).—*adv.* **meet'ly.**—*n.* **meet'ness**. [Prob. from an O.E. (Anglian) form answering to W.S. *gemǣte—metan*, to measure.]

**meet**, *mēt*, *v.t.* to come face to face with: to come into the company of: to become acquainted with, be introduced to: to encounter in conflict: to find or experience: to refute: be suitable to: satisfy, as by payment: to receive, as a welcome: to cause to meet, bring into contact: await arrival of, keep an appointment with.—*v.i.* to come together from different points: to assemble: to have an encounter: to balance, come out correct:—*pa.t.* and *pa.p.* **met.**—*n.* a meeting, as of huntsmen: an assembly for racing.—*n.* **meet'ing**, a coming face to face for friendly or hostile ends: an interview: an assembly: an organised assembly for transaction of business: an assembly for religious worship, esp. (in England) of Dissenters: place of meeting: junction.—**meet'ing-house**, house or building where people, esp. Dissenters, meet for public worship.—**race'-meet'ing**, a stated occasion for horse-racing; **give the** (or **a**) **meeting** (*arch.*), appoint or come to a rendezvous, for a duel or other purpose; **meet half-way**, to make concessions in compromise; **meet in with, wi'** (*Scot.*), to meet with, come across; **meet the ear**, or **eye**, to be readily apparent; **meet with**, to come to or upon, esp. unexpectedly: to undergo, chance to experience: to obviate (as an objection) (*Bacon*); **well met**, an old complimentary greeting. [O.E. *mētan*, to meet—*mōt, gemōt*, a meeting.]

**meg(a)-, megalo-,** *meg-ə-(lō-)*, in composition, big: in names of units, a million.—**megamega-,** *pfx.* a million million (better **tera-**).—*adj.* **megacephalous** (-*sef'ə-ləs*; Gr. *kephalē*, head), largeheaded.—*n.pl.* **Megacheiroptera** (-*kir-op'tər-a*), the fruit-bats.—*ns.* **meg'acycle,** a million cycles; **meg'adeath,** death of a million people, unit in estimating casualties in nuclear war; **megafar'ad,** a million farads; **meg'afog,** a fog-signal with megaphones pointing in several directions; **meg'alith** (Gr. *lithos*, stone), a huge stone, as in prehistoric monuments.—*adj.* **megalith'ic.**—*n.* **megaloma'nia,** the delusion that one is great or powerful: a mania, or passion, for big things.—*n.* and *adj.* **megaloma'niac.**—*ns.* **megalop'olis,** a wide-spreading, thickly-populated urban area.—**meg'alosaur** (Gr. *sauros*, a lizard), a gigantic Jurassic and Cretaceous dinosaur (Megalosaurus), carnivorous in mode of life.—*adj.* **megalosau'rian.**—*ns.* **meg'anewton, meg'awatt,** etc., a million times a newton, watt, etc.; **meg'aphone** (Gr. *phōnē*, voice), a funnel-shaped device for directing, or increasing volume of, sound.—*v.t.* and *v.i.* to communicate by megaphone.—*ns.* **meg'apode** (Gr. *pous, podos*, foot), a mound-bird; **meg'aron** (Gr. *megaron*), the principal hall of an ancient Greek house; **meg'ascope** (Gr. *skopeein*, to view), an instrument for projecting an enlarged image.—*adj.* **megascopic** (-*skop'ik*), enlarged: visible to the naked eye.—*ns.* **megasporangium** (-*spor-an'ji-əm*), a sporangium producing only megaspores:—*pl.* **megasporan'gia; meg'aspore,** the larger of two forms of spore: a spore giving rise to a female gametophyte; **megasporophyll** (-*spor'ə-fil*), a sporophyll that carries or subtends only megasporangia; **Megathē'rium** (Gr. *thērion*, wild beast), a gigantic extinct S. American groundsloth; **meg'ohm,** a million ohms.—**megaton bomb** (*meg'ə-tun*), a bomb of explosive force equal to one million tons of TNT; **megawatt day,** the unit of energy used in speaking of nuclear power reactors (day = 24 hours). [Gr. *megas*, fem. *megalē*, neut. *mega*, big.]

**Megaera,** *mə-jē'ra, me-gī'ra, n.* one of the Furies. [L.,—Gr. *Megaira*.]

**megass(e),** *mə-gäs'.* Same as **bagasse.**

**megilp,** *mə-gilp'.* See **magilp.**

**megrim,** *mē'grim.* See **migraine.**

**megrim,** *mē'grim, n.* the scald-fish.

**meinie, mein(e)y,** *n.* a retinue (*Shak.*): a herd. [O.Fr. *mesnie*—L. *mānsio, -ōnis*, a dwelling.]

**meint.** See **ming.**

**meionite,** *mī'ən-it, n.* a scapolite with less sodium and silica than marialite. [Gr. *meiōn*, less, from the short vertical axis of its crystal.]

**meiosis,** *mi-ō'sis, n.* understatement as a figure of speech (*rhet.*): litotes: cell-division with reduction of the number of chromosomes towards the development of a reproductive cell (*biol.*).—*adj.* **meiotic** (-*ot'ik*). [Gr. *meiōsis*, diminution.]

**Meissen** (**china, porcelain, ware**). Same as **Dresden.**

**meistersinger,** *mis'tər-zing-ər, -sing-ər, n.* one of the burgher poets and musicians of Germany in the 14th-16th centuries, the successors of the Minnesingers:—*pl.* **meistersinger, -s.** [Ger., master-singer.]

**meith,** *mēth*, (*Scot.*) *n.* a landmark: a boundary. [Prob. O.N. *mith*, a fishing-bank found by landmarks.]

**Meilis.** Same as **Majlis.**

**me judice,** *mē jōō'di-sē, mā yōō'di-ke*, (L.) I being judge, in my opinion.

**Mekhitarist, Mechitharist,** *mehh-, mek-i-tär'ist, n.* an Armenian Uniat monk of a congregation founded by *Mekhitar* (1676-1749) at Constantinople in 1701, since 1717 with headquarters near Venice.—Also *adj.*

**mekometer,** *mə-kom'ə-tər, n.* device for accurate measurement of distances by means of a light beam. [Gr. *mēkos*, length.]

**melaconite,** *mel-ak'ən-it, n.* tenorite. [Gr. *melās,* black, *konis*, dust.]

**melamine,** *mel'ə-mēn, n.* a white crystalline organic substance used in forming **melamine resins,** thermosetting plastics used as adhesives, coatings, etc. [Ger. *melamin*.]

**melampode,** *mel-am'pōd, mel'*, (*Spens.*) *n.* the black hellebore. [Gr. *melampodion*.]

**melanaemia,** *mel-ən-ē'mi-ə, n.* presence of melanin in the blood. [Gr. *melās, -ānos*, black, *haima*, blood.]

**melancholy,** *mel'ən-kol-i, -kəl-i*, formerly *mel-ang'-kol-i, n.* black bile, an excess thereof, or the mental condition or temperament supposed to result (*obs.*): surliness (*obs.*): continued depression of spirits: dejection: melancholia: indulgence in thoughts of pleasing sadness: pensiveness.—*adj.* prone to, affected by, expressive of, or causing, melancholy: depressed: pensive: deplorable.—*ns.* **melancho'lia,** a mental state characterised by dejection and misery; **melancho'liac,** a sufferer from melancholia.—Also *adj.*—*adj.* **melancholic** (-*kol'ik*), affected with, or caused by, melancholy or melancholia: dejected: mournful.—*n.* a melancholiac.—*adj.* **melancho'lious.** [Gr. *melancholiā—melās, -ānos,* black, *cholē*, bile.]

**Melanesian,** *mel-ən-ēz'i-ən, -ēz'yən, -ēzh'(y)ən, adj.* pertaining to *Melanesia*, a group of islands lying N.E. of Australia, in which the dominant race is dark-skinned.—*n.* a native, or a language, of these islands.—**Neo-Melanesian** (see **neo-**). [Gr. *melās, -ānos*, black, *nēsos*, an island.]

**mélange,** *mā-lāzh', n.* a mixture: a medley. [Fr.]

**melanic,** *mi-lan'ik, adj.* black or dark in pigmentation.—*ns.* **melanin** (*mel'ə-nin*), dark pigment in skin, hair, etc.; **mel'anism,** more than normal development of dark colouring matter.—*adj.* **melanist'ic.**—*ns.* **mel'anite,** a black garnet; **melano** (*mi-lä'nō, mel'ə-nō*; on the analogy of *albino*), a person or animal abnormally dark; **mel'anophore** (-*fōr, -för*), a chromatophore containing melanin; **melanō'sis,** an abnormal deposit of melanin: the associated condition of body.—*adjs.* **melanōt'ic; mel'anous,** dark-complexioned.—*n.* **melanū'ria,** the presence of a dark pigment in the urine.—*adj.* **melanū'ric.**—*n.* **melaphyre** (*mel'ə-fir*; after *porphyry*), orig. a dark porphyritic rock: applied very loosely to an altered basalt. [Gr. *melās, -ānos*, black.]

**Melanochroi,** *mel-ən-ō-krō'ī, n.pl.* a race or type of man with dark hair and pale skin—darkhaired Caucasian type.—*adjs.* **melanochro'ic, melanochroous** (-*ok'rō-əs*). [Gr. *melās, -ānos,* black, and either *ōchros,* pale, or *chroā*, skin.]

**melanterite,** *mi-lan'tə-rit, n.* native copperas. [Gr. *melantēriā*, a black pigment.]

**Melastomaceae,** *mel-ə-stō-mā's(h)i-ē, n.pl.* a tropical family of plants akin to the myrtles, very abundant in South America, characterised by the leaf-veins diverging from the base and meeting at the tip, named from the Old World genus **Melastoma** (*mi-las'tō-ma*). [Gr. *melās,* black, *stoma,* mouth, from the fruit of some staining the lips.]

**meld, meld,** (*obs.* except in cards) *v.t.* and *v.i.* to declare: to announce. [O.E. *meldan,* or Ger. *melden.*]

**meld, meld,** (*U.S. slang*) *v.t.* and *v.i.* to merge.

**melder,** *mel'dər,* (*Scot.*) *n.* the quantity of meal ground at one time. [O.N. *meldr.*]

mêlée, *mel´ā, n.* a fight in which the combatants are mingled together: a confused conflict: an affray. [Fr.,—*mêler*, to mix; cf. **meddle, mell.**]

**Melia,** *mē´li-a, n.* the nim tree genus, giving name to the family **Meliā´ceae** (mahogany, *Cedrela,* etc.).—*adj.* **meliā´ceous** (*-shəs*). [Gr. *meliā*, ash-tree (from a resemblance in leaves).]

**Meliboean,** *mel-i-bē´ən, adj.* in poetry, amoebaean. [From *Meliboeus,* in Virgil's first eclogue.]

**melic,** *mel´ik, adj.* to be sung: lyric: strophic. [Gr. *melikos*—*melos,* song.]

**melic,** *mel´ik, n.* a grass (*Melica*) of the fescue tribe.—Also **mel´ic-grass´.** [Origin obscure.]

**melicotton.** See melocoton.

**melilite,** *mel´i-līt, n.* a tetragonal mineral, calcium aluminium magnesium silicate, often honey-yellow. [Gr. *meli,* honey, *lithos,* stone.]

**melilot,** *mel´i-lot, n.* a genus (*Melilotus*) of clover-like plants with racemes of white or yellow flowers and a peculiar sweet odour. [Gr. *melilōtos*—*meli,* honey, *lōtos,* lotus.]

**melinite,** *mel´in-īt, n.* an explosive made from picric acid. [Fr. *mélinite*—Gr. *mēlinos,* quince yellow—*mēlon,* quince.]

**meliorate,** *mē´li-ə-rāt, v.t.* to make better.—*v.i.* to grow better.—*n.* **meliora´tion.**—*adj.* **me´liorātive,** tending towards improvement.—*ns.* **me´liorātor; me´liorism,** the doctrine that the world is capable of improvement, as opposed to *optimism* and *pessimism;* **me´liorist; meliority** (*-or´i-ti*), better-ness. [L.L. *meliōrāre, -ātum*—L. *melior,* better.]

**meliphagous,** *mel-if´ə-gəs, adj.* feeding upon honey. [Gr. *meli,* honey, *phagein* (aor.), to eat.]

**melisma,** *mel-iz´mə, n.* a song: a tune: a melodic embellishment.—*adj.* **melismatic,** *-mat´ik,* florid in melody, esp. where one syllable is sung to a number of notes. [Gr. *melisma, -matos,* a song tune.]

**mell,** *mel, v.t.* and *v.i.* to mix, mingle.—*v.i.* to have to do (with *with*): to have intercourse: to join in fight: to be concerned: to meddle. [O.F. *meller;* cf. **meddle, medley.**]

**mell,** *mel, n.* a Northern form of **mall, maul.**

**mellay,** *mel´ā, n.* another form of **mêlée.**

**melliferous,** *mel-if´ə-rəs, adj.* honey-producing.—*ns.* **mellifica´tion,** honey-making; **mellif´luence** (L. *fluĕre,* to flow), a flow of sweetness: a smooth sweet flow.—*adjs.* **mellif´luent, mellif´luous,** flowing with honey or sweetness: smooth.—*advs.* **mellif´luently, mellif´luously.**—*n.* **mell´ite,** honey stone.—*adjs.* **mellit´ic; melliv´orous** (L. *vorāre* to devour), eating honey. [L. *mel, mellis,* honey.]

**mellow,** *mel´ō, adj.* soft and ripe: well matured: soft to the touch, palate, ear, etc.: genial: half-tipsy.—*v.t.* to soften by ripeness or age: to mature.—*v.i.* to become soft: to be matured, ripened: to become gentler and more tolerant.—*adv.* **mell´owly.**—*n.* **mell´owness.**—*adj.* **mell´owy,** mellow. [Prob. O.E. *melu,* meal, influenced by *mearu,* soft, tender.]

**melocoton, melocotoon,** *mel-ō-kot-ōn´, -ōōn´,* (*obs.*) *n.* a large kind of peach.—Also **malakatoone´, melicott´on.** [Sp. *melocotón*—It. *melocotogna,* quince, peach—L.L. *mēlum cotōneum*—Gr. *mēlon Kȳdōnion,* Cydonian (Cretan) apple, quince.]

**melodrama,** *mel´ō-drä-mə,* or *-drä´, n.* a play with musical accompaniment to the action and spoken dialogue, with or without songs (*obs.*): a kind of romantic and sensational drama, crude, sentimental, and conventional, with strict attention to poetic justice and happy endings—also **mel´odrame** (*-dräm*).—*adj.* **melodramat´ic** (*-drə-mat´ik*), of the nature of melodrama: over-strained: sensational.—*n.* **melodramatist** (*-dram´-ə-tist*), a writer of melodramas. [Gr. *melos,* a song, *drāma,* action.]

**melody,** *mel´ə-di, n.* an air or tune: music: an agreeable succession of single musical sounds, as distinguished from *harmony.*—*n.* **melodeon** (*mi-lō´di-ən*), a small reed organ: an improved

accordion.—*adj.* **melodic** (*mi-lod´ik*).—*n.* **melod´ics,** the branch of music concerned with melody.—*adj.* **melō´dious,** full of melody: agreeable to the ear.—*adv.* **melō´diously.**—*n.* **melō´diousness.**—*v.i.* **mel´odise, -ize,** to make melody: to perform a melody.—Also *v.t.*—*n.* **mel´odist.**—**melodic minor,** a minor scale with major sixth and seventh ascending and minor sixth and seventh descending. [Fr., through L.L.,—Gr. *melōidiā.*]

**melomania,** *mel-ō-mā´ni-ə, n.* a craze for music.—*n.* **meloma´niac.**—*adj.* **melomanic** (*-man´*). [Gr. *melos,* song, *maniā,* madness.]

**melon,** *mel´ən, n.* any of several juicy gourds: the plant bearing it: profits to be divided (*slang*). [Fr.,—L. *mēlō, -ōnis*—Gr. *mēlon,* an apple.]

**Melpomene,** *mel-pom´i-nē, n.* the Muse of tragedy. [Gr. *Melpomēnē,* lit. songstress.]

**melt,** *melt, v.i.* to become liquid from the solid state, esp. by heat: to fuse: to dissolve: to stream with liquid: to lose distinct form: to blend: to shade off: to become imperceptible: to be dispersed or dissipated: to be softened emotionally.—*v.t.* to cause to melt in any sense: —*pa.t.* **melt´ed,** *arch.* **mōlt;** *pa.p.* **melt´ed,** *arch.* **mōlt´en, ymōlt´en, ymōlt´.**—*n.* the act of melting: state of being melted: molten material: quantity melted.—*n.* and *adj.* **melt´ing.**—*adv.* **melt´ingly.**—*n.* **melt´ingness.**—*adj.* **molt´en,** melted: made of melted metal.—*adv.* **molt´enly.**—**melt´ing-point,** the temperature at which a given solid begins to become liquid; **melt´ing-pot,** a vessel for melting things in: a state of dissolution preparatory to shaping anew (*fig.*); **melt-water,** water running off melting ice or snow.—**molten salt reactor,** one in which uranium is dissolved in a molten mixture of fluoride salts. [O.E. *meltan* (intrans. strong vb.), and *mæltan, meltan* (causative weak vb., W.S. *mieltan*); O.N. *melta,* to digest, to malt, Gr. *meldein.*]

**meltith,** *mel´tith,* (*Scot.*) *n.* a meal: a cow's yield at one milking. [meal-tide.]

**melton,** *mel´tən, n.* a strong cloth for overcoats. [*Melton* Mowbray.]

**member,** *mem´bər, n.* a distinct part of a whole, esp. a limb of an animal: a clause (*gram.*): one of a society: a representatve in a legislative body.—*adj.* **mem´bered,** having limbs.—*n.* **mem´bership,** the state of being a member or one of a society: the members of a body regarded as a whole.—*adj.* **mem´bral,** pertaining to the limbs rather than the trunk.—**member of parliament,** a member of the House of Commons, M.P. [Fr. *membre*—L. *membrum.*]

**membrane,** *mem´brān, -brin, n.* a thin flexible solid sheet or film: a thin sheet-like structure, usually fibrous, connecting other structures or covering or lining a part or organ (*biol.*): a skin of parchment.—*adjs.* **membranaceous** (*-brə-nā´shəs*), **membrān´eous** (*rare*), **mem´branous** (*-brə-nəs*), like or of the nature of a membrane: thin, translucent, and papery (*bot.*).—**membrane bone,** one formed directly from connective tissue without passing through a stage of cartilage. [L. *membrāna*—*membrum.*]

**membrum virile,** *mem´brum vir-i´lē, -brōōm wir-ē´le,* (L.) penis.

**memento,** *mi-men´tō, n.* something kept or given as a reminder: a brown study (*obs.*):—*pl.* **memen´tos** or **-toes.**—**memento mori,** *mō´ri, mo´rē,* remember that you must die: anything to remind one of mortality. [L., imper. of *meminisse,* to remember.]

**Memnon,** *mem´non, n.* an Ethiopian king who fought for the Trojans: a statue of Amenoph III at Thebes in Egypt, thought by the Greeks to be of Memnon and to give out a musical sound at sunrise in salutation of his mother Eos (the Dawn).—*adj.* **Memnō´nian.** [Gr. *Memnōn.*]

**memo,** *mem´ō, n.* a contraction for **memorandum.**

**memoir**, *mem'wär, -wör, n.* (usu. *pl.*) a written record set down as material for history or biography: a biographical sketch: a record of a study of some subject investigated by the writer: (in *pl.*) the transactions of a society.—*ns.* **mem'oirism**, the act or art of writing memoirs; **mem'oirist**, a writer of memoirs. [Fr. *mémoire*—L. *memoria*, memory—*memor*, mindful.]

**memorabilia, memorable, etc.** See **memory.**

**memorandum**, *mem-ə-ran'dəm, n.* something to be remembered: a note to assist the memory: a brief note of some transaction (*law*): a summary of the state of a question (*diplomacy*): —*pl.* **memoran'dums, memoran'da.** [L., a thing to be remembered, neut. gerundive of *memorāre*, to remember.]

**memory**, *mem'ə-ri, n.* the power of retaining and reproducing mental or sensory impressions: an impression so reproduced: a having or keeping in the mind: time within which past things can be remembered: commemoration: a religious service in commemoration: remembrance: of computers, a store.—*n.pl.* **memorabil'ia** (L.), things worth remembering: noteworthy points. —*adj.* **mem'orable**, deserving to be remembered: remarkable.—*adv.* **mem'orably.**—*adjs.* **mem'orative** (*obs.*), pertaining to memory: aiding the memory; **memorial** (*-ōr', -ör'*), serving or intended to preserve the memory of anything: pertaining to memory: remembered (*obs.*).—*n.* that which serves to keep in remembrance: a monument: a note to help the memory: a written statement of facts: a record: memory (*obs.*): (in *pl.*) historical or biographical notices. —*v.t.* **memor'ialise, -ize,** to present a memorial to: to petition by a memorial.—*n.* **memorialist,** one who writes, signs, or presents a memorial.—*v.t.* **mem'orise, -ize,** to commit to memory: to cause to be remembered (*Shak.*): to record, celebrate (*arch.*).—*adv.* **memor'iter** (L.), from memory: by heart.—**Memorial Day,** a day (Monday nearest 30th May) kept in honour of U.S. servicemen killed in war (orig. known as *Decoration Day* and kept, in most parts of U.S. on 30th May, in honour of men killed in the U.S. Civil War, 1861-65); **memo'ria tech'nica** (L.), artificial memory—a mnemonic device.—**in memor'iam,** to the memory of: in memory. [L. *memoria*, memory.]

**Memphian**, *mem'fi-ən, adj.* relating to *Memphis*, an ancient capital of Egypt.—Also **Mem'phite** (*-fīt*), **Memphitic** (*-fit'*).

**mem-sahib**, *mem'-sä-ib, n.* in India, a married European lady. [ma'am and sahib.]

**men,** plural of **man.**

**menace**, *men'əs, -is, n.* a threat or threatening: a show of an intention to do harm: a threatening danger.—*v.t.* to threaten.—*v.i.* to act in a threatening manner.—*adj.* **men'acing.**—*adv.* **men'acingly.** [Fr.,—L. *mināciae* (pl.), threats—*minae*, overhanging parts, threats.]

**menadione,** *men-ə-di'ōn, n.* vitamin K₃. [*methyl naphthoquinone, -dione,* suff. denoting a compound containing two carbonyl groups.]

**menage,** obsolete form of **manage.**

**ménage**, *mä-näzh', n.* a household: management of a house: benefit society (*Scot.*): arrangement for selling on instalment (*Scot.*).—**ménage à trois** (*a trwa*), a household composed of a husband and wife and the lover of one of them. [Fr.,— L. *mānsiō,* dwelling.]

**menagerie**, *mi-naj'ə-ri, n.* a collection of wild animals in cages for exhibition: place where these are kept. [Fr. *ménagerie*—*ménage*.]

**menarche**, *mə-när'kē, n.* the first menstruation. [Gr. *mēn,* month, *archē,* beginning.]

**mend**, *mend, v.t.* to remove a fault from: to repair: to make better: to correct: to improve: to improve upon: to supplement (*obs.*).—*v.i.* to grow better: to reform.—*n.* a repair: a repaired place: an act of mending: (in *pl.*) amends (*arch.*).—*ns.* **mend'er; mend'ing,** the act of repairing: a repair: things requiring to be mended.—**mend one's pace,** to go quicker; **mend one's ways,** to reform one's behaviour; **on the mend,** improving, recovering. [amend.]

**mendacious**, *men-dā'shəs, adj.* lying.—*adv.* **menda'ciously.**—*n.* **mendacity** (*-das'i-ti*), lying: a falsehood. [L. *mendāx, -ācis,* conn. with *mentiri*, to lie.]

**mendelevium**, *men-de-lē', -lä'vi-əm, n.* the element (symbol Md) of atomic number 101, artificially produced in 1955 and named after the Russian D. I. *Mendeleev* (1834-1907), who developed the periodic table of elements.

**Mendelian**, *men-dēl'i-ən, adj.* pertaining to the Austrian-German Gregor *Mendel* (1822-84), or his teaching on heredity.—*n.* a believer in Mendel's theory.—*n.* **Men'delism** (*-də-lizm*).

**mendicant**, *men'di-kənt, adj.* begging.—*n.* a beggar: a begging friar (*hist.*).—*ns.* **men'dicancy, mendicity** (*-dis'i-ti*), the condition of a beggar: begging. [L. *mendicāns, -antis,* pr.p. of *mendicāre,* to beg—*mendicus,* a beggar.]

**mene,** obs. form of **mean.**

**Menevian**, *men-ē'vi-ən,* (*geol.*) *adj.* and *n.* Middle Cambrian. [L.L. *Menevia,* St David's, in Pembrokeshire.]

**meng, menge.** See **ming.**

**menhaden**, *men-hā'dn, n.* an oily fish (*Brevoortia tyrannus*) of the herring family, found off the east coast of the United States. [From an Indian name.]

**menhir**, *men'hēr, n.* an ancient monumental standing stone. [Breton *men,* stone, *hir,* long.]

**menial**, *mē'ni-əl, adj.* of or pertaining to a train of servants or work of a humiliating or servile nature: servile.—*n.* a domestic servant: one performing servile work: a person of servile disposition. [A.Fr. *menial*; cf. meinie.]

**meninx**, *mē'ningks, n.* any of three membranes that envelop the brain and spinal cord:—*pl.* **meninges** (*men-in'jēz*).—*adj.* **mening'eal.**—*ns.* **meningiō'ma**, a tumour of the meninges of the brain and, more rarely, of the spinal cord; **meningitis** (*-jī'*), inflammation of the meninges; **meningocele** (*men-ing'gō-sēl;* Gr. *kēlē,* tumour), protrusion of the meninges through the skull. [Gr. *mēninx, -ingos,* a membrane.]

**Menippean**, *men-ip-ē'ən, adj.* pertaining to, or in imitation or emulation of, the Greek satirist *Menippos* (3rd cent. B.C.) of Gadara.

**meniscus**, *men-is'kəs, n.* a crescent-shaped figure: a crescentic fibrous cartilage in a joint: a convexo-concave lens: a liquid surface curved by capillarity:—*pl.* **menisci** (*-kī;* L. *-kē*).—*adj.* **menis'coid** (*bot.*), watchglass-shaped.—**meniscus telescope,** a telescope in which the spherical aberration of a concave spherical mirror is corrected by a meniscus lens. [Gr. *mēniskos,* dim. of *mēnē,* the moon.]

**Menispermum**, *men-i-spûr'məm, n.* the moonseed genus, giving name to a family **Menispermā'ceae** akin to the buttercup family. [Gr. *mēnē,* moon, *sperma,* seed.]

**Mennonite**, *men'ən-it, n.* one of a Protestant sect combining some of the distinctive characteristics of the Baptists and Friends. [From *Menno* Simons (d. 1559), their chief founder.]

**menology**, *mē-nol'ə-ji, n.* a register or calendar of Saints' days, esp. of the Greek Church:—*pl.* **menologies.** [Late Gr. *mēnologion—mēn,* month, *logos,* account.]

**menominee**, *mi-nom'i-nē, n.* a whitefish of N. American lakes. [From an Indian tribe.]

**meno mosso,** *mā'nō mos'sō,* (It.) not so quick.

**menopause**, *men'ō-pöz, n.* the ending of menstruation, change of life. [Gr. *mēn,* month, *pausis,* cessation.]

**menopome,** *men'ə-pōm, n.* the hellbender—from

its persistent gill-aperture. [Gr. *menein*, to remain, *pōma*, lid.]

**Mensa**, *men'sə*, *n.* one of the southern constellations, the Table. [L. *mēnsa*, table.]

**mensal**, *men'səl*, *adj.* monthly.—Also **men'sual**. [L. *mēnsis*, month.]

**mensal**, *men'səl*, *adj.* belonging to the table. [L. *mēnsa*, table.]

**mense**, *mens*, (*Scot.*) *n.* propriety: ornament: credit.—*v.t.* to grace or set off (something).— *adjs.* **mense'ful** (*Scot.*), decorous: respectable: gracious: generous; **mense'less** (*Scot.*), graceless, uncivil. [O.N. *mennska*, humanity; cf. O.E. *menniscu*, humanity, *mennisc*, human.]

**menses**, *men'sēz*, *n.pl.* the monthly discharge from the uterus. [L. *mēnsēs*, pl. of *mēnsis*, month.]

**Menshevik**, *men'shə-vik*, *n.* (*hist.*) a moderate or minority socialist in Russia—as opp. to *Bolshevik*. [Russ. *menshye*, smaller, -(*v*)*ik*, agent suffix.]

**menstruum**, *men'strōō-əm*, *n.* a solvent (from a fancy of the alchemists):—*pl.* **men'strua**, the menses.—*adj.* **men'strual**, monthly: pertaining to the menses.—*v.i.* **men'struate**, to discharge the menses.—*n.* **menstrua'tion**.—*adj.* **men'struous**. [L. neut. of *mēnstruus*, monthly—*mēnsis*.]

**mensur**, *men-sōōr'*, *n.* a German students' duel, a form of sport:—*pl.* **mensur'en**. [Ger., measurement (from the measured distance of the participants)—L. *mēnsūra*.]

**mensurable**, *men'sh(y)ər-ə-bl*, or -*sūr*-, *adj.* measurable: having a fixed relative time-value for each note (*mus.*).—*n.* **mensurabil'ity**.—*adj.* **mens'-ural**, pertaining to measure: measurable (*mus.*). —*n.* **mensura'tion**, the act or art of finding by measurement and calculation the length, area, volume, etc., of bodies.—*adj.* **men'surative**. [L. *mēnsūrāre*, to measure.]

**ment.** See **ming.**     **mental.** See **mentum.**

**mental**, *men'tl*, *adj.* pertaining to the mind: done in the mind, esp. in the mind alone, without outward expression: suffering from, or provided for, or involved in the care of, disease or disturbance of the mind: mentally unbalanced (*slang*).—*ns.* **men'talism**, process of mental action: idealism; **men'talist**; **mentality** (-*tal'i-ti*), mind: mental endowment: cast of mind: way of thinking; **mentā'tion**, mental activity.—*adv.* **men'tally.**—*n.* **menticide** (*men'ti-sid*), the systematic reduction of a person's mind by psychological or other pressure to a point where views formerly repugnant will be accepted.—**mental age**, the age in years, etc., at which an average child would have reached the same stage of mental development as the individual under consideration.—**mental cruelty**, conduct in marriage, not involving physical cruelty or violence, that wounds feelings or personal dignity—in U.S., grounds for separation or divorce; **mental deficiency**, mental retardation; **mental home**, **hospital**; **mental patient**; **mental retardation**, retarded development of learning ability, whether arising from innate defect or from some other cause. [Fr.,—L. *mēns*, *mentis*, the mind.]

**menthol**, *men'thol*, *n.* a camphor got from oil of peppermint, used as a local analgesic.—*adj.* **men'tholated**, containing menthol. [L. *mentha*, mint.]

**mention**, *men'shən*, *n.* a brief notice: occurrence or introduction of name or reference.—*v.t.* to notice briefly: to remark: to name.—*adj.* **men'tionable**, fit to be mentioned: worth mentioning.—**honourable mention**, an award of distinction not entitling to a prize; **not to mention**, to say nothing of—a parenthetical rhetorical pretence of refraining from saying all one might say. [L. *mentiō*, *-ōnis*.]

**mentonnière**, *men-ton-i-er'*, (*hist.*) *n.* a piece of armour for the chin and throat. [Fr.,—*menton*, chin—L. *mentum*.]

**mentor**, *ment'ər*, -*tōr*, *n.* a wise counsellor.—*adj.*

**mentorial** (-*tōr'*, *tör'ri-əl*). [Gr. *Mentōr*, the tutor by whom (or Athena in his form) Telemachus was guided.]

**mentum**, *men'təm*, *n.* the chin: the central part of the labium in insects.—*adj.* **men'tal** (*anat.*), pertaining to the chin. [L. *mentum*, the chin.]

**menu**, *men'ū*, *n.* a bill of fare. [Fr.,—L. *minūtus*, small.]

**menuisier**, *mə-nwē-zyā*, (Fr.) a joiner.

**meo periculo**, *mē'ō pe-rik'ū-lō*, *mā'ō pe-rēk'ōō-lō*, (L.) at my own risk.

**mepacrine**, *mep'ə-krēn*, *n.* a bitter yellow powder derived from acridine dye compounds, formerly used against malaria—also *atabrin*, *atebrin*.

**Mephistopheles**, *mef-is-tof'i-lēz*, *n.* the devil in the *Faust* story.—Also **Mephistoph'ilis**, **Mephostoph'ilus**, etc.: abbrev. **Mephis'tō**.—*adjs.* **Mephistophelē'an**, **Mephistophē'liau**, **Mephistophelic** (-*fel'*), cynical, scoffing, fiendish. [Ety. unknown; prob. influenced by Gr. *mē*, not, *phōs*, *phōtos*, light, *philos*, loving.]

**mephitis**, *me-fī'tis*, *n.* a poisonous exhalation: a foul stink.—*adjs.* **mephitic** (-*fit'*), -**al**.—*n.* **meph'-itism** (-*it-izm*), mephitic poisoning. [L. *mephitis*.]

**meprobamate**, *mep-rō-bam'āt*, *n.* a drug used as a muscle relaxant and as a sedative.

**mercantile**, *mûr'kən-til*, *adj.* pertaining to merchants: having to do with trade: commercial: mercenary.—*ns.* **mer'cantilism**; **mer'cantilist**.— **mercantile agency**, a means of getting information about the circumstances of merchants for those who sell to them; **mercantile law**, the law relating to the dealings of merchants with each other; **mercantile marine**, the ships and crews of any country employed in commerce; **mercantile system** (*economics*), the system of encouraging exportation and restricting importation, so that more may be received than is paid away. [Fr.,—It. *mercantile*—L. *mercāri*; cf. **merchant**.]

**mercaptan**, *mər-kap'tan*, *n.* a substance analogous to an alcohol, with sulphur instead of oxygen.— *n.* **mercap'tide**, a compound in which a metal takes the place of a hydrogen atom of a mercaptan. [L. *mercūrium captāns*, laying hold of mercury, from the readiness with which it forms mercury mercaptide.]

**mercat**, *mer'kət*, a Scottish form of **market**.

**Mercator**, *mər-kā'tər*, *mer-kā'tör*, *n.* a Latin translation of the name of the Flemish-born German cartographer Gerhard Kremer (lit. shopkeeper; 1512-94).—**Mercator's projection**, a representation of the surface of the globe in which the meridians are parallel straight lines, the parallels straight lines at right angles to these, their distances such that everywhere degrees of latitude and longitude have the same ratio to each other as on the globe itself.

**mercenary**, *mûr'sin-ər-i*, *adj.* hired for money: actuated by the hope of reward: too strongly influenced by desire of gain: sold or done for money.—*n.* one who is hired: a soldier hired into foreign service.—*adv.* **mer'cenarily**. [L. *mercēnārius*—*mercēs*, hire.]

**mercer**, *mûr'sər*, *n.* a dealer in textiles, esp. the more costly: a dealer in small wares.—*n.* **mer'cery**, the trade of a mercer: the goods of a mercer. [Fr. *mercier*.]

**mercerise**, **-ize**, *mûr'sər-īz*, *v.t.* to treat (cotton) so as to make it appear like silk.—*ns.* **mercerisā'tion**; **mer'ceriser**. [From John *Mercer* (1791-1866), the inventor of the process.]

**merchant**, *mûr'chant*, *n.* a trader, esp. wholesale: a shopkeeper: a supercargo (*obs.*): a merchantman: a fellow, esp. one who specialises in some specified way (*slang*).—*adj.* commercial.—*v.i.* to trade.—*v.t.* to trade in.—*n.* **mer'chandise** (-*dīz*), goods bought and sold for gain: trade (*B.* and *Shak.*): dealing.—*v.t.* (also -**ize**) to traffic in (*Shak.*): to buy and sell: to plan the advertising of, selling campaign for.—Also *v.i.* (also -ize).—*n.* mer'chandising, -z-.—*adj.* mer'chantable, fit or ready for sale: marketable.—*adj.* and *adv.* mer'chantlike (*Shak.*), like a merchant.—*n.* mer'chantry, the business of a merchant: merchants collectively.—merchant bank (see bank (3)); mer'chantman, a trading ship: a merchant (*B.*):—*pl.* mer'chantmen; merchant prince, a merchant of great wealth, power, and consequence; merchant service, mercantile marine; merchant ship, a ship that carries merchandise; merchant tailor, a tailor who supplies the cloth for the clothes which he makes.—speed merchant (*slang*), one whose main interest in driving is in moving fast. [Fr. *marchand.*]

**merchet**, *mûr'chit*, (*hist.*) *n.* a fine paid to a lord for the marriage of a daughter. [A.Fr. *merchet*; see **market.**]

**mercury**, *mûr'kū-ri*, *n.* a silvery metallic element (Hg; atomic number 80) liquid at ordinary temperatures, also called *quicksilver*: the column of mercury in a thermometer or barometer: a plant (dog's mercury, Mercurialis) of the spurge family: the plant Good King Henry: a preparation of mercury: a messenger: a common title for newspapers: mercurial character (*obs.*) (*cap.*), the Roman god of merchandise, theft, and eloquence, messenger of the gods, identified with the Greek Hermes: (*cap.*) the planet nearest the sun.—*adj.* mercu'rial, containing mercury: of or like mercury: caused by mercury: (*cap.*) of or pertaining to Mercury the god or the planet: (sometimes *cap.*) having the qualities attributed to persons born under the planet—eloquent, etc.: active, sprightly, often changing.—*n.* a drug containing mercury: the plant mercury (*obs.*): (sometimes *cap.*) one born under the planet (*obs.*).—*v.t.* mercu'rialise, -ize, to treat with mercury or a drug containing mercury (*med.*): to make mercurial.—*ns.* mercu'rialism, a morbid condition due to mercury; mercu'rialist (*obs.*), a believer in the medical use of mercury: a mercurial person.—*adv.* mercu'rially.—*adjs.* mercu'ric, containing bivalent mercury; mer'curous, containing univalent mercury. [L. *Mercūrius*, prob. *merx, mercis*, merchandise.]

**mercy**, *mûr'si*, *n.* forbearance towards one who is in one's power: a good thing regarded as derived from God: a happy chance (*dial.*): a forgiving disposition: clemency: compassion for the unfortunate.—*interj.* of thanks (now *obs.*) or surprise (for God *have mercy*).—Also mercy on us.—*adjs.* mer'ciable (*Spens.*), merciful; mer'ciful, full of, or exercising, mercy.—*adv.* mer'cifully. — *n.* mer'cifulness. — *v.t.* mer'cify (*Spens.*, in *pa.p.* mer'cifide), to deal mercifully with, to pity.—*adj.* mer'ciless, without mercy: unfeeling: cruel.—*adv.* mer'cilessly.—*ns.* mer'cilessness.—mercy killing, killing, esp. painlessly, to prevent incurable suffering; mer'cyseat, the seat or place of mercy: the covering of the Jewish Ark of the Covenant: the throne of God.—at the mercy of, wholly in the power of; for mercy! (*obs.*), for mercy's sake!, an earnest conjuration in the form of an appeal to pity; sisters of mercy, members of female religious communities who tend the sick, etc. [Fr. *merci*, grace—L. *mercēs, -ēdis*, the price paid, wages, later favour.]

**mere**, *mēr*, *n.* a pool or lake.—Also (*obs.*) meer.—mere'swine (*obs.*), a porpoise: a dolphin. [O.E. *mere*, sea, lake, pool; Ger. and Du. *meer*, L. *mare*, the sea.]

**mere**, *mēr*, *adj.* unmixed (*obs.*): pure (*obs.*): only what is said and nothing else, nothing more, nothing better: absolute (*obs.*).—*adv.* (*obs.*) absolutely.—*adj.* meered (*Shak.*), perh. entire.—*adv.* mere'ly, purely (*obs.*): entirely (*obs.*):

simply: only: without being more or better. [L. *merus*, unmixed.]

**mere**, *mēr*, (*dial.*) *n.* a boundary.—*v.t.* to bound: to mark off.—meres'man (*dial.*), a man appointed to ascertain boundaries; mere'stone (*dial.*), a boundary stone. [O.E. *gemǣre.*]

**mere, meri**, *mer'i*, *n.* a war-club: a greenstone trinket in the form of a war-club. [Maori.]

**merel, merell**. Same as meril.

**meretricious**, *mer-i-trish'as*, *adj.* of the nature of harlotry: characteristic or worthy of a harlot: flashy: gaudy.—*adv.* meretric'iously.—*n.* meretric'iousness. [L. *meretrix, -icis*, a harlot—*merēre*, to earn.]

**merganser**, *mûr-gan'sar*, *n.* any bird of the genus Mergus (goosander, smew, etc.). [L. *mergus*, a diving bird, *ānser*, a goose.]

**merge**, *mûrj*, *v.t.* to dip or plunge (*arch.*): to cause to be swallowed up or absorbed in something greater or superior: to cause to coalesce, combine, or amalgamate.—*v.i.* to be swallowed up, or lost: to coalesce: to lose identity in something else: to combine or amalgamate.—*n.* mer'ger (*law*), a sinking of an estate, title, etc., in one of larger extent or of higher value: a combine or absorption. [L. *mergěre, mersum.*]

**mericarp**, *mer'i-kärp*, *n.* a separating one-seeded part of a schizocarp, esp. half of a cremocarp. [Gr. *meros*, a part, *karpos*, fruit.]

**meridian**, *ma-rid'i-an*, *adj.* of or at midday: on the meridian: pertaining to a meridian or the sun or other body on the meridian: at culmination or highest point.—*n.* midday: a midday dram or nap (*Scot.*): an imaginary great circle through the poles of the earth, the heavens, or any spherical body or figure, or its representation on a map: in particular, that cutting the observer's horizon at the north and south points, which the sun crosses at local noon: culmination or highest point, as of success, splendour, power, etc.—*adj.* merid'ional, pertaining to the meridian: in the direction of a meridian: midday: culminating: southern: characteristic of the south.—*n.* a southerner, esp. in France.—*n.* meridional'ity.—*adv.* merid'ionally.—magnetic meridian (see magnetic); meridian altitude, arc of a meridian between a heavenly body and the horizon; meridian circle, a telescope mounted to revolve in the plane of the meridian; meridian passage, the transit or passage of a heavenly body across the observer's meridian.—prime (or first) meridian, the meridian from which longitudes are measured east or west, specif. that through Greenwich. [L. *meridiānus, meridionālis—meridiēs* (for *medidiēs*), midday—*medius*, middle, *diēs*, day.]

**meril, merel, merell**, *mer'al*, *n.* a counter used in the game of merils: (in *pl.*) a rustic game played by two persons with counters on a figure marked on the ground, a board, etc., consisting of three squares, one within another, the object to get three counters in a row at the intersection of the lines joining the corners and the mid-points of the sides.—Also marls, marr'els, mor'als, morr'is, mir'acles.—fivepenny morris, the game as played with five pieces each; ninepenny morris, nine men's morris, with nine: the figure cut in the ground for the game (*Shak.*). [O.Fr. *merel*, counter.]

**merimake**, *mer'i-māk*, (*Spens.*) *n.* merrymaking: sport.

**meringue**, *ma-rang'*, *n.* a crisp cake or covering made of a mixture of sugar and white of eggs. [Fr.; origin unknown.]

**merino**, *ma-rē'nō*, *n.* a sheep of a fine-woolled Spanish breed: a fine dress fabric, originally of merino wool: a fine woollen yarn, now mixed with cotton: knitted goods of this: waste from fine worsted clothes:—*pl.* merinos.—*adj.* belonging to the merino sheep or its wool: made of merino. [Sp., a merino sheep, also a governor —L. *mājōrinus*, greater, also (L.L.) a head-man— L. *mājor*, greater.]

merism, *mer'izm*, (*biol.*) *n.* repetition of parts.—*adj.* merist'ic. [Gr. *meros*, part.]

meristem, *mer'is-tem*, *n.* the formative tissue of plants, distinguished from the permanent tissues by the power its cells have of dividing and forming new cells.—*adj.* meristematic (*-sti-mat'ik*). [Gr. *meristos*, divisible, *merizein*, to divide—*meros*, a part.]

merit, *mer'it*, *n.* excellence that deserves honour or reward: worth: value: desert: that which one deserves, whether reward or punishment (*arch.*): (in *pl.*, esp. in *law*) the intrinsic right or wrong.—*v.t.* to earn: to have a right to claim as a reward: to deserve.—*v.i.* (*obs.*), to acquire merit.—*n.* meritoc'racy, (government by) the class of persons who are in prominent positions because of their ability, real or apparent.—*adj.* meritorious (*tōr'*, *tör'*), possessing merit or desert: deserving of reward, honour, or praise.—*adv.* meritor'iously. —*n.* meritor'iousness.—order of merit, arrangement in which the best is placed first, the next best second, and so on: (*caps.*) a strictly limited British order (O.M.), instituted in 1902, for eminence in any field. [L. *meritum—merēre*, *-itum*, to obtain as a lot, to deserve.]

merk, *merk*, *n.* the old Scots mark or 13s. 4d. Scots, 13⅓d. sterling. [mark (2).]

merle, *mûrl*, *n.* the blackbird. [Fr.,—L. *merula*.]

merlin, *mûr'lin*, *n.* a species of small falcon. [A.Fr. *merilun—*O.Fr. *esmerillon*.]

merling, *mûr'ling*, (*obs.*) *n.* the whiting. [O.Fr. *merlanke*—L. *merula*, a sea-carp.]

merlon, *mûr'lən*, (*fort.*) *n.* the part of a parapet between embrasures. [Fr. *merlon*—It. *merlone* —*merlo*, battlement.]

mermaid, *mûr'mād*, *n.* a sea-woman, a woman to the waist, with fish's tail.—*mer'maid'en; mer'-man; mer'child; mer'folk; mer'people; mer'maid's-glove'*, the largest kind of British sponge; *mer'maid's-purse'*, egg-case of skate, etc. [O.E. *mere*, lake, sea, *mægden*, maid.]

meroblastic, *mer-ō-blast'ik*, (*zool.*) *adj.* undergoing or involving cleavage in part of the ovum only, as where there is much yolk.—*adv.* meroblast'ically. [Gr. *meros*, part, *blastos*, a shoot, bud.]

merogenesis, *mer-ō-jen'i-sis*, (*biol.*) *n.* segmentation.—*adj.* merogenetic (*-ji-net'ik*). [Gr. *meros*, part, *genesis*, production.]

merogony, *mer-og'ə-ni*, *n.* production of an embryo from a fertilised fragment of an ovum without a nucleus. [Gr. *meros*, part, *gonē*, birth.]

meroistic, *mer-ō-ist'ik*, (*entom.*) *adj.* of an ovary, producing yolk-forming cells as well as ova. [Gr. *meros*, part, *ōion*, egg.]

merome, *mer'ōm*, *n.* a merosome. [Gr. *meros*, part.]

Merops, *mer'ops*, *n.* the bee-eater genus.—*n.* merop'idan, a bird of the bee-eater family (Merop'idae). [Gr. *merops*, bee-eater.]

merosome, *mer'ō-sōm*, *n.* one of the serial segments of which a body is composed, as the ring of a worm, a metamere, a somite. [Gr. *meros*, part, *sōma*, body.]

Merovingian, *mer-ō-vin'ji-ən*, *adj.* pertaining to the first dynasty of Frankish kings in Gaul, founded by Clovis.—*n.* a member of this family. [L. *Merovingi—Merovaeus* or *Merovech*, king of the Salian Franks (448-457), grandfather of Clovis.]

merry, *mer'i*, *adj.* pleasant (*obs.*): sportive: cheerful: noisily gay: causing laughter: enlivened by drink: lively.—*adv.* merr'ily.—*ns.* merr'iment, gaiety with laughter and noise: mirth: hilarity; merr'iness.—*merr'y-an'drew*, a quack's zany: a buffoon: one who makes sport for others; *merry dancers*, the aurora;

merry England, idealistically jovial picture of life in England in the past, esp. in Elizabethan times; *merr'y-go-round*, a revolving ring of hobby-horses, etc.; *merr'y-make*, a merrymaking.—*v.i.* to make merry.—*merr'ymaker*; *merr'ymaking*, a merry entertainment: a festival; *merr'yman*, a zany: a jester: (in *pl.*; *merry men*) followers, in arms or in outlawry; *merr'y-night'*, a village festival; *merr'ythought*, a fowl's furcula or wishbone, in playful divination pulled apart, the longer part indicating the first to be married or fulfilment of a wish.—*make merry*, to hold festival: to indulge in enjoyment: to turn to ridicule (with *with* or *over*); the *merry monarch*, Charles II. [O.E. *myr(i)ge*.]

merry, *mer'i*, *n.* a gean. [Fr. *merise*.]

mersalyl, *mər-sal'il*, *n.* a diuretic drug. [*mercury*, *salicyl*.]

mersion, *mûr'shən*, *n.* dipping. [L. *mersiō*, *-ōnis*; cf. merge.]

Merulius, *mə-rōō'li-əs*, *n.* the dry-rot fungus genus.

merum sal, *mer'əm*, *mer'ōōm sal*, (L.) pure salt, genuine Attic wit.

merveilleux, *mer-vā-yə*, *fem.* merveilleuse, *mer-vā-yəz*, (Fr.) marvellous.—*n.* a fantastic extremist in fashion in France during the Directorate, the women aping classical modes.

merycism, *mer'i-sizm*, *n.* rumination, a disease symptom in man. [Gr. *mērȳkismos*.]

mesa, *mā'sa*, *n.* a table-shaped hill. [Sp.,—L. *mēnsa*, table.]

mesail, mezail, *mes'*, *mez'āl*, *n.* a vizor, esp. one made in two parts. [Fr. *mézail*.]

mésalliance, *mā-zal-yäs*, (Fr.) an unsuitable marriage: marriage with one of lower station.

mesaraic, *mes-ə-rā'ik*, *adj.* mesenteric. [Gr. *mesaraikos*—*mesos*, middle, *araiā*, flank, belly.]

mesaticephalic, *mes-ə-ti-sef-al'ik*, mesaticephalous, *-sef'ə-ləs*, *adjs.* intermediate between dolichocephalic and brachycephalic.—*n.* mesaticeph'aly. [Gr. *mesatos*, midmost, *kephalē*, head.]

mescal, *mes-kal'*, *n.* the peyote cactus, chewed or drunk in infusion as an intoxicant in Mexico: an intoxicant distilled from Agave.—*ns.* mescalin (*mes'kəl-in*), the principal alkaloid ($C_{11}H_{17}NO_3$) in mescal, producing hallucinations and schizophrenia; mescal'ism, addiction to mescal. [Sp. *mescal*, *mezcal—*Nahuatl *mexcalli*.]

mesdames. See madam.

mese, *mes'ē*, (*Gr. mus.*) *n.* the middle string of the lyre: its note: the keynote. [Gr. *mesē* (*chordē*), middle (string).]

meseems, *mi-sēmz'*, (*poet.*) *v.impers.* it seems to me:—*pa.t.* meseemed'. [me (dat.) and seem.]

mesel, meazel, *mēz'l*, (*obs.*) *n.* a leper: leprosy (*Shak.*).—*adj.* leprous.—*adj.* mes'eled. [O.Fr. *mesel*—L. *misellus*, dim. of *miser*, wretched.]

Mesembrianthemum, conventionally Mesembryanthemum, *mi-zem-bri-an'thi-məm*, *n.* a genus of succulent plants (family Aizoaceae) mostly South African (Hottentot fig, ice-plant). [Gr. *mesēmbriā*, midday—*mesos*, middle, *hēmerā*, day, *anthemon*, a flower: some are open only about midday.]

mesencephalon, *mes-en-sef'ə-lon*, *n.* the mid-brain. —*adj.* mesencephalic (*-si-fal'ik*). [Gr. *mesos*, middle, and encephalon.]

mesentery, *mes'ən-tər-i*, or *mez'*, *n.* a fold of the peritoneum, keeping the intestines in place: in coelenterates a vertical inward fold of the body-wall.—*adjs.* mesenterial (*-tē'ri-əl*), mesenteric (*-ter'ik*).—*n.* mesenteron (*-en'tər-on*), the mid-gut. [Gr. *mesos*, middle, *enteron*, intestines.]

mesh, *mesh*, *n.* the opening between the threads of a net: the threads and knots bounding the opening: network: trap: engagement of geared wheels or the like.—*v.t.* to catch in a net: to provide or make with meshes.—*v.i.* to become engaged, as gear-teeth: to become entangled.

Neutral vowels in unaccented syllables: *el'ə-mənt*; for certain sounds in foreign words, see p. viii

—*n.* **mesh'ing.**—*adj.* **mesh'y,** formed like network.—**mesh'-work,** a network, web. [Perh. M.Du. *maesche*; cf. O.E. *max*, net; Ger. *masche.*]

**mesial,** *mē′zi-əl, adj.* middle: in or towards the median plane or line—also **me′sian.**—*adv.* **me′sially.** [Gr. *mesos,* middle.]

**mesic.** See meson.

**mesic,** *me′zik, mē′, -sik, adj.* pertaining to, or adapted to life with, a moderate supply of moisture. [Gr. *mesos,* middle.]

**mesmerise, -ize,** *mez′mər-iz, v.t.* to hypnotise: loosely, to fascinate, dominate the will or fix the attention of.—*adjs.* **mesmeric** (*-mer′ik*), **-al.** —*ns.* **mesmerisā′tion, -z-;** **mes′meriser, -z-, mes′merist;** **mes′merism,** hypnotism as expounded, with some fanciful notions, from 1775 by Friedrich Anton or Franz *Mesmer,* a German physician (1734-1815): hypnotic influence.

**mesne,** *mēn,* (*law*) *adj.* intermediate. [Law Fr. *mesne,* middle; cf. mean (2).]

**mes(o)-,** *mes(-ō)-,* in composition, middle.—*n.* **mes′oblast** (Gr. *blastos,* shoot), the middle germinal layer.—*adj.* **mesoblas′tic.**—*n.* **mes′ocarp** (Gr. *karpos,* fruit), middle layer of a pericarp.— *adjs.* **mesocephalic** (*-si-fal′ik*), **-cephalous** (*-sef′ə-ləs*) **mesaticephalic:** mesencephalic—*ns.* **mesoceph′alism, mesoceph′aly;** **mes′oderm** (Gr. *derma,* skin), mesoblast or tissues derived from it; **mesogloea** (*-glē′a*; Gr. *gloiā,* glue), in coelenterates and sponges, a structureless gelatinous layer between ectoderm and endoderm; **mes′-olite** (Gr. *lithos,* stone), a zeolite intermediate in composition between natrolite and scolecite.— *adj.* **Mesolith′ic,** intermediate between Palaeolithic and Neolithic.—*ns.* **mesom′erism** (*chem.*), resonance: a type of tautomerism; **mes′-omorph** (*mes′-, mez′o-mörf;* Gr. *morphe,* form), of muscular, bodily type.—*adj.* **mesomor′phic.**—*ns.* **mes′omorphy;** **mes′ophyll** (Gr. *phyllon,* leaf), the spongy tissue within a leaf; **mes′ophyte** (*-fīt;* Gr. *phyton,* plant), a plant intermediate between a xerophyte and a hydrophyte.—*adj.* **mesophytic** (*-fit′ik*).—*n.* **mes′oscaphe** (*-skāf;* Gr. *skaphos,* ship), a submersible observation chamber for use at less great depths than the bathyscaphe.—*adj.* **mesothoracic** (*-thō-, -thoras′ik*).—*n.* **mesothor′ax,** the middle one of the three segments of an insect's thorax.—*n.pl.* **Mesozō′a** (Gr. *zōion,* animal), minute animals once thought intermediate between Protozoa and Metazoa, prob. Metazoa reduced by parasitism.—*adj.* **Mesozo′ic** (Gr. *zoē,* life), of the Secondary geological period, including the Triassic, Jurassic, and Cretaceous systems. [Gr. *mesos,* middle.]

**meson,** *mēz′on, mes′on, n.* a short-lived subatomic particle of smaller mass than a proton (η-mesons, π-mesons (*pions*), and κ-mesons (*kaons*); the *muon,* formerly classified as the μ-meson is now known to be a lepton).—*adjs.* **mes′ic, meson′ic.**— *n.* (after *electron*) **mes′otron** (*obs.*), formerly a meson, then a μ-meson.—**mesic, mesonic, atom,** a nucleus with an orbital meson. [Gr. *meson,* neut. of *mesos,* middle.]

**mesprise, mesprize.** See misprise (1 and 2).

**mesquin,** *mes-kē̃,* (Fr.) mean:—*fem.* **mesquine,** *-kēn.*—*n.* **mesquinerie,** *-kēn-ə-rē,* meanness.

**mesquite,** *mes-kēt′, mes′kēt, n.* a leguminous tree or shrub (Prosopis) of America, with nutritious pods. [Mex. Sp. *mezquite.*]

**mess,** *mes, n.* dish of food, course, or meal (*arch.*): a set of usually four persons served together at a banquet (*arch.*): a set of four (*Shak.*): a number of persons who take their meals together, esp. in the fighting services: a place where a group of persons in a fighting service take their meals together: a cow's yield at one milking (*dial.*): a quantity (*U.S.*): a take or haul of fish (*U.S.*): a dish of soft, pulpy or liquid stuff: liquid,

pulpy or smeary dirt: a mixture disagreeable to the sight or taste: a medley: disorder: confusion: embarrassment: a bungle.—*v.t.* to supply with a mess: to make a mess of: to muddle: to befoul.—*v.i.* to eat of a mess: to eat at a common table: to belong to a mess: to make a mess: to potter (often with *about; coll.*). —*adv.* **mess′ily.**—*n.* **mess′iness.**—*adj.* **mess′y,** confused, untidy (also *fig.*): involving, or causing, dirt or mess: bungling.—**mess deck** (*naut.*), crew's living-quarters on board ship: crew's dining-hall (*U.S.*); **mess′mate,** a member of the same mess: a commensal; **mess′-room;** **mess′-tin,** a soldier's utensil serving as plate, cup, and cooking-vessel; **mess′-up′,** a mess, muddle, bungle, or confusion.—**mess of pottage,** a material advantage accepted in exchange for something of higher worth, as by Esau (Gen. xxv. 29 ff.); **mess or mell** (*Scot.*), to associate, have to do. [O.Fr. *mes* (Fr. *mets*), a dish—L. *mittĕre, missum,* to send, in L.L. to place.]

**mess,** *mes, n.* obs. form of mass (2 and 3).

**message,** *mes′ij, n.* any communication sent from one person to another: an errand: an official communication of a president, governor, etc., to a legislature or council: the teaching that a poet, sage, prophet, has to communicate to the world: domestic shopping, a journey for the purpose, or the goods bought (*Scot.*).—*v.t.* to send as a message: to transmit as by signalling.— *v.i.* (*Dickens*) to carry a message.—*n.* **mess′enger** (*-ən-jər*), one who carries messages or a message: a forerunner: a light scudding cloud preceding a storm: a small object sent along a line, as a paper up a kite string: the secretary-bird: a rope or chain connecting a cable with the capstan for heaving up the anchor: an officer who executes the summonses of the Court of Session, called a **mess′enger-at-arms** (*Scots law*).—**mess′age-boy, -girl,** errand boy or girl; **mess′-enger-wire,** a wire supporting an overhead cable.—**get the message** (*slang*), understand; **king's,** or **queen's, messenger,** an officer who carries official despatches. [Fr.,—L.L. *missāticum*—L. *mittĕre, missum,* to send.]

**messan,** *mes′ən,* (*Scot.*) *n.* a lap-dog: a cur. [Perh. Gael. *measan.*]

**messerschmitt,** *mes′ər-shmit, n.* German fighter aircraft used by the Luftwaffe in World War II, esp. the M.E.-109. [Willy *Messerschmitt,* b. 1898, aircraft designer.]

**Messiah,** *mə-si′a, n.* the expected deliverer of the Jews: by Christians, applied to Jesus: a hoped-for deliverer, saviour, or champion generally— also **Messias.**—*adj.* **Messianic** (*mes-i-an′ik*).—*ns.* **Messi′anism,** belief in a Messiah; **Messi′anist; Messi′ahship.** [Gr. *Messīās*—Aram. *m'shīhā,* Heb. *māshīah,* anointed—*māshah,* to anoint.]

**Messidor,** *mes-i-dör′, n.* the tenth month of the French revolutionary calendar, about June 19th–July 18th. [Fr.,—L. *messis,* harvest, Gr. *dōron,* a gift.]

**messieurs,** *mes-yø;* contracted and anglicised as **Messrs** (*mes′ərz*), *pl.* of **monsieur.**

**messuage,** *mes′wij,* (*law*) *n.* a dwelling and offices with the adjoining lands appropriated to the household: a mansion-house and grounds. [A.Fr.; poss. orig. a misreading of *mesnage;* cf. ménage.]

**mestee,** *mes-tē′,* **mustee,** *mus-tē′, n.* the offspring of a white person and a quadroon.—*n.* **mestizo** (*mes-tē′zō;* Sp. *-thō*), a half-caste, esp. of Spanish and American Indian parentage:—*pl.* **mesti′zos;** *fem.* **mesti′za,** *pl.* **mesti′zas.** [Sp. *mestizo*—a L.L. derivative of L. *mixtus,* mixed.]

**mesto,** *mes′tō,* (*mus.*) *adj.* sad. [It.]

**met,** *pa.t.* and *pa.p.* of **meet.**

**met., met.** Abbrev. for *meteorology.*—**met′cast,** weather forecast; **met man,** a weather forecaster.

**met(a)-,** *met(-ə)-,* in composition, among, with:

after, later: often implies change, as *metamorphose*: beyond, above, as *metamathematics*. In *chem.* meta- indicates (1) a derivative of, or an isomer or polymer of, the substance named, or (2) an acid or hydroxide derived from the ortho- form of the substance by loss of water molecules, or (3) a benzene substitution product in which the substituted atoms or groups are attached to two carbon atoms which are themselves separated by one carbon atom (in this sense commonly represented by *m*).—*adj.* **metacarp′al** (Gr. *karpos*, wrist).—*ns.* **metacarp′us**, the part of the hand (or its bones) between the wrist and the fingers, or its corresponding part, e.g. the foreleg of a horse between 'knee' and fetlock; **met′acentre** (Gr. *kentron*, point), the point of intersection of a vertical line through the centre of gravity of a body floating in equilibrium and that through the centre of gravity of the displaced liquid when the body is slightly displaced.—*adj.* **metacen′tric.**—*ns.* **metachro′sis** (-*krō′sis*; Gr. *chrōsis*, colouring), ability to change colour in animals; **metagal′axy**, the whole universe outside our own galaxy; **metagen′esis** (Gr. *genesis*, generation; *biol.*), alternation of generations.—*adjs.* **metagenet′ic**; **metagnathous** (*met-ag′nə-thəs*; Gr. *gnathos*, jaw), of birds, having crossed mandibles: of insects, having biting jaws in the larvae, sucking in the adult state.—*ns.* **metalang′uage**, a language or a system of symbols used to discuss another language or symbolic system; **metal′dehyde**, a polymer of acetaldehyde.—*ns.pl.* (treated as *sing.*) **meta-linguis′tics**, study of the relation between a language and other features of behaviour in a particular culture, of language structure in relation to meaning, of expression or gesture accompanying spoken language, etc.; **metamathemat′ics**, the philosophy of the higher mathematics.—*ns.* **met′amer** (Gr. *meros*, a part; *chem.*), a compound metameric with another; **met′amere** (-*mēr*; *zool.*), a segment, merosome, or somite.—*adj.* **metamer′ic.**—*ns.* **metam′erism**, a particular form of isomerism in which different groups are attached to the same central atom (*chem.*): segmentation of the body along the primary axis, producing a series of homologous parts (*zool.*); **met′aphase**, the stage of mitosis at which the chromosomes form the equatorial plate; **metaphos′phate**, a salt of metaphosphoric acid.—*adj.* **metaphosphor′ic**, applied to an acid (HPO₃) containing a molecule less of water than orthophosphoric acid; **metapsychic, -al** (*met-ə-si′kik, -əl*; from *psychic*, on the analogy of *metaphysics*).—*n.pl.* **metapsych′ics** (treated as *sing.*) the study of psychic phenomena beyond the limits of ordinary or orthodox psychology— 'psychical research'.—*n.* **metasil′icate** (-*i-kāt*), a salt of metasilicic acid.—*adjs.* **metasilic′ic** (-*is′ik*), applied to an acid (H₂SiO₃) containing a molecule less of water than orthosilicic acid; **metasōmat′ic** (Gr. *sōma, -atos*, body; *geol.*).— *ns.* **metasōm′atism**, metamorphism by chemical changes in minerals; **metastabil′ity**, state which appears to be chemically stable, often because of the slowness with which equilibrium is attained—said of, e.g., a supersaturated solution. —*adjs.* **metastable** (*met′ə-stā-bl*; **metastable state**, excited state, esp. of an atom which has, however, insufficient energy to emit radiation); **metatarsal** (-*tär′səl*; Gr. *tarsos*, the flat of the foot).—*n.* **metatar′sus**, that part of the foot, or its bones, between the tarsus and the toes.—*n.pl.* **Metatheria** (-*thē′ri-a*; Gr. *thērion*, a wild beast), the marsupials.—*adj.* **metathoracic** (-*thō-ras′ik*).—*n.* **metathorax** (-*thō′raks*), the third and last segment of an insect's thorax.— *n.pl.* **Metazoa** (*met-ə-zō′a*; Gr. *zōion*, animal), many-celled animals—opp. to single-celled **Protozoa**:—*sing.* **metazo′on.**—*adjs.* **metazo′an**,

**metazo′ic**; **metempiric, -al** (*met-em-pir′ik, -əl*), beyond the scope of experience.—*ns.* **metempir′icism** (-*i-sizm*); **metempir′icist**. [Gr. *meta*, among, with, beside, after.] **metabasis**, *met-ab′ə-sis*, *n.* a transition.—*adj.* **metabatic** (*met-ə-bat′ik*). [Gr. *metabasis—bainein*, to go.] **metabolism**, *met-ab′əl-izm*, *n.* the sum-total of chemical changes of living matter: metamorphosis.—*n.pl.* **metab′ola**, insects that undergo metamorphosis.—*adj.* **metabolic** (-*bol′ik*), exhibiting or relating to metabolism.—*v.t.* **metab′-olise, -ize.**—*n.* **metab′olite**, a product of metabolism. [Gr. *metabolē*, change.] **metacarpus**, etc., **metacentre**, etc. See **met(a)-.** **metachronism**, *met-ak′ron-izm*, *n.* the error of dating an event too late. [Gr. *metachronios, metachronos*, anachronistic, out of date— *chronos*, time.] **metachrosis.** See **met(a)-.** **metage**, *mēt′ij*, *n.* official weighing of coal, grain, etc.: charge for such weighing. [**mete**.] **metagenesis, -etic, metagnathous.** See **met(a)-.** **metagrobolise, -ize**, *met-ə-grob′əl-iz*, **metagrabo-lise, -ize**, *-grab′*, *v.t.* to mystify: to puzzle out. [Obs. Fr. *metagrabouilzer* (Rabelais).] **métairie**, *mā-ter-ē*, *n.* a piece of land cultivated for a share of the produce. [Fr.; see **métayer**.] **metal**, *met′l*, *n.* an opaque elementary substance, possessing a peculiar lustre, fusibility, conductivity for heat and electricity, readiness to form positive ions, etc., such as gold, etc.: an alloy: that which behaves chemically like a true metal: courage or spirit (now spelt *mettle*): intrinsic quality: guns of a ship-of-war: or or argent as a tincture (*her.*): molten material for glass-making: country-rock (*mining*): broken stones used for macadamised roads or as ballast for railways: (*pl.*) the rails of a railroad.—*adj.* made of metal.—*v.t.* to furnish or cover with metal.—*adjs.* **met′alled**, covered with metal, as a road; **metallic** (*mi-tal′ik*), pertaining to, or like, a metal: consisting of metal.—*adv.* **metall′ically**. —*n.* **met′alliding**, a high-temperature electrolytic technique for creating metal alloys on the surface of metals.—*adjs.* **metallif′erous**, bearing or yielding metal; **met′alline**, of, like, consisting of, or mixed with, metal.—*ns.* **met′alling**, road-metal, broken stones; **metallisā′tion, -izā′-.**—*v.t.* **met′allise, -ize**, to make metallic: to deposit thin metal films on glass or plastic.—*ns.* **met′allist**, a worker in metals; **metallog′rapher.**—*adj.* **metal-lograph′ic.**—*ns.* **metallog′raphy**, the study of the structure and constitution of metals; **met′alloid**, a non-metal: an element resembling a metal in some respects, as selenium, tellurium.—*adjs.* **met′alloid, metalloid′al**, pertaining to, or of the nature of, the metalloids.—*n.* **metall′ophone**, an instrument like a xylophone with metal bars, the hammers being operated by hand or by means of a keyboard.—*adj.* **met′ally**, suggestive of metal. —**met′al-work, -er, -ing.** [O.Fr.,—L. *metallum*— Gr. *metallon*, a mine.] **metalepsis**, *met-ə-lep′sis*, (*rhet.*) *n.* metonymy, esp. of a double, complicated, or indirect kind.— *adjs.* **metalep′tic, -al.** [Gr. *metalēpsis*, substitution.] **metallurgy**, *met′əl-ûr-ji, met-al′ər-ji*, *n.* art and science applied to metals, including extraction from ores, refining, alloying, shaping, treating, and the study of structure, constitution, and properties.—*adjs.* **metallur′gic, -al**, pertaining to metallurgy.—*n.* **met′allurgist** (or -*al′-*). [Gr. *metallourgeein*, to mine—*metallon*, a mine, *ergon*, work.] **metamere, metamerism.** See **met(a)-.** **metamorphosis**, *met-ə-mör′fəs-is*, sometimes *-fōs′is*, *n.* change of shape, transformation: transformation of a human being to a beast, stone, tree, etc (*folklore*): the marked change which some living beings undergo in the course of growth, as caterpillar to butterfly, tadpole to frog:—*pl.* metamor′phoses (*-sēz*, or *-fō′sēz*).— *adj.* metamor′phic, showing or relating to change of form: formed by alteration of existing rocks by heat, pressure, or other processes in the earth's crust (*geol.*).—*ns.* metamor′phism, transformation of rocks in the earth's crust (*contact metamorphism*, by contact with or neighbourhood of igneous material; *regional*, owing to general conditions over a wide region); metamor′phist, one who believes that Christ's body merged into the Deity at the Ascension.—*v.t.* metamor′phose (*-fōz*, *-fōs*), to transform: to subject to metamorphism or metamorphosis: to develop in another form. [Gr. *metamorphōsis—morphē*, form.]

metaphase. See met(a)-.

metaphor, *met′ə-fər, n.* a figure of speech by which a thing is spoken of as being that which it only resembles, as when a ferocious man is called a tiger.—*adjs.* metaphoric (*-for′ik*), -al.—*adv.* metaphor′ically.—*n.* met′aphorist.—mixed metaphor, an expression in which two or more metaphors are confused, as *to take arms against a sea of troubles.* [Gr. *metaphorā—pherein*, to carry.]

metaphosphoric, -phosphate. See met(a)-.

metaphrase, *met′ə-frāz, n.* a turning of prose into verse or verse into prose: a rendering in a different style or form: an altered wording: a word for word translation—also metaphrasis (*-af′rə-sis*).—*n.* met′aphrast (*-frast*), one who produces a metaphrase.—*adj.* metaphrast′ic. [Gr. *metaphrasis—phrasis*, a speaking.]

metaphysics, *met-ə-fiz′iks, n.* (treated as *sing.*) the science which investigates the first principles of nature and thought: ontology or the science of being: loosely and vaguely applied to anything abstruse, abstract, philosophical, subtle, transcendental, occult, supernatural, magical.—*n.* metaphys′ic, metaphysics: philosophical groundwork.—*adj.* metaphysical.—*adj.* metaphys′ical, pertaining to metaphysics: abstract: beyond nature or the physical: supernatural: fanciful: addicted to far-fetched conceits (applied by Johnson to Donne, Cowley, and others).—*adv.* metaphys′ically.—*n.* metaphysician (*-ish′ən*), one versed in metaphysics. [Originally applied to those writings of Aristotle which in the accepted order came after (Gr. *meta*) those dealing with natural science (*ta physika—physis*, nature).]

metaplasia, *met-ə-plā′si-a, n.* tissue transformation, as of cartilage into bone.—*ns.* metaplasis (*-ap′lə-sis*), metaplasia: period of maturity in the life-cycle; met′aplasm (*-plazm*), cell-contents other than protoplasm: change in a word by addition, dropping, or exchange of parts.—*adj.* metaplast′ic. [Gr. *metaplasis, metaplasmos*, a moulding afresh—*plassein*, to form.]

metapsychic(s), metasilicate, etc., metasomatic, etc., metastability, etc. See met(a)-.

metastasis, *met-as′tə-sis, n.* removal from one place to another: transition: transformation: paramorphic change in rocks: metabolism:—*pl.* metas′tases.—*v.i.* metas′tasise, -ize, to pass to another part of the body, as a tumour.—*adj.* metastatic (*-stat′ik*). [Gr. *metastasis*, change of place—*stasis*, a standing.]

metatarsus, -al, Metatheria. See met(a)-.

metathesis, *met-ath′ə-sis, n.* transposition or exchange of places, esp. between the sounds or letters of a word:—*pl.* metath′eses.—*adjs.* metathetic (*met-ə-thet′ik*), -al. [Gr.,—*metatithenai*, to transpose—*tithenai*, to place.]

metathoracic, -thorax. See met(a)-.

métayer, *mā-tā-yā, n.* a farmer who pays, instead of money rent, a fixed proportion of the crops.— *n.* métayage (*-yäzh*), this system. [Fr.,—L.L. *medietārius*—L. *medietās*, half—*medius*, middle.]

Metazoa, etc. See met(a)-.

metcast. See met (2).

mete, *mēt, v.t.* to measure: to apportion (*pa.t.* mēt′ed, in Spens. mott).—*n.* measure.—mete′-stick, mete′wand, mete′yard, a measuring-rod. [O.E. *metan*; Ger. *messen.*]

mete, *mēt, n.* a boundary or limit. [L. *mēta*, a goal or boundary.]

metempiric, etc. See met(a)-.

metempsychosis, *met-emp-si-kō′sis, n.* the passing of the soul after death into some other body:— *pl.* metempsychō′ses. [Gr. *metempsychōsis*— *en*, in, *psychē*, soul.]

meteor, *mē′tyər, mē′ti-ər, n.* orig., now rarely, any atmospheric phenomenon: a luminous appearance: one of numberless small bodies travelling through space, revealed to observation when they enter the earth's atmosphere as aerolites, fireballs, or shooting-stars: anything brilliant or dazzling but short-lived.—*adj.* meteoric (*mē-ti-or′ik*), above the earth's surface: atmospheric: influenced by weather: of or pertaining to meteors in any sense: of the nature of a meteor: transiently flashing like a meteor.—*adv.* meteor′-ically, in manner of a meteor.—*ns.* me′teorist, one versed in meteors; me′teorite, a fallen meteor: a meteor.—*adj.* meteorit′ic, me′teorital (*-it-l*).—*ns.* meteorit′ics, science of meteors; me′teorogram, a meteorograph record; me′teorograph, an instrument by which several meteorological elements are recorded in combination; me′teoroid, a meteor that has not reached the earth's atmosphere; me′teorolite (Gr. *lithos*, stone), a meteoric stone.—*adjs.* meteorolog′ic, -al.—*ns.* meteorol′ogist; meteorol′ogy, study of weather and climate.—*adj.* me′teorous (or, usu. in poetry, *mē-tē′ər-əs*), like a meteor, meteoric.—meteor crater, a crater formed by the fall of a meteor; meteoric iron, iron as found in meteorites; meteoric showers, showers of meteors; meteoric stones, aerolites; meteor streams, streams of dust revolving about the sun, whose intersection by the earth causes meteor showers. [Gr. *ta meteōra*, things on high—*meta* and the root of *aeirein*, to lift.]

meter, *mē′tər, n.* a measurer: an apparatus for measuring, esp. quantity of a fluid, or of electricity, used: a gauge or indicator: a parking meter.—*v.t.* to measure by a meter. [mete (1).]

meter, American spelling of metre (1 and 2).

methadone, *meth′ə-dōn, n.* a synthetic addictive drug similar to morphine, longer-acting than heroin. [di*methyl*amino-, diphenyl, heptan*one*.]

methane, *meth′ān, n.* marsh-gas ($CH_4$), the simplest hydrocarbon, found wherever the decomposition of vegetable matter is taking place under water, also in coal-mines, forming when mixed with air the deadly fire-damp. [methyl.]

methanol, *meth′ə-nol, n.* methyl alcohol, wood spirit. [methane, -*ol*, suffix—L. *oleum*, oil.]

methedrine, *meth′ə-drēn, n.* an amphetamine, a soft drug, but used by drug addicts.

metheglin, *meth-eg′lin, n.* a Welsh fermented liquor made from honey. [W. *meddyglyn*— *meddyg*, medicinal (—L. *medicus*, physician), *llyn*, liquor.]

methinks, *mi-thingks′*, methink′eth, methink′, *v.impers.* it seems to me: I think:—*pa.t.* methought (*mi-thöt′*). [O.E. *mē thyncth*, it seems to me; *thyncan*, to seem, has been confused with *thencan*, to think; cf. Ger. *dünken*, to seem, *denken*, to think.]

method, *meth′əd, n.* the mode or rule of accomplishing an end: orderly procedure: manner: orderly arrangement: classification: system, rule: manner of performance: an instruction-book systematically arranged.—*adjs.* methodic (*mi-thod′ik*), -al, arranged with method: disposed in a just and natural manner: observing method: formal.—*adv.* method′ically.—*v.t.* meth′odise, -ize, to reduce to method: to dispose in due order.—*ns.* Meth'odism, the principles and practice of the Methodists; meth'odist, one who observes method: (*cap.*) a follower of the Wesleys—a name given first to a group of students at Oxford 'for the regularity of their lives as well as studies'.—*adjs.* Methodist'ic, -al, resembling the Methodists, esp. as viewed by opponents: strict in religious matters.—*adv.* Methodist'ically.—*ns.* methodol'ogy, a system of methods and rules applicable to research or work in a given science or art: evaluation of subjects taught and principles and techniques of teaching them; Meth'ody, a disrespectful nickname for a Methodist.—method acting, acting as a personal living of a part, contrasted with mere technical performance (also called the method). [Gr. *methodos*—*meta*, after, *hodos*, a way.]

methomania, *meth-ō-mā'ni-ə, n.* an intermittent morbid craving for alcohol. [Gr. *methē*, strong drink, *maniā*, madness.]

methought. See methinks.

methoxamine hydrochloride, *meth-oks'ə-mēn hī-drō-klōr'īd, -klōr'*, a drug used in slowing down the action of the heart.

meths. Abbrev. for methylated spirit.

Methuselah, *mi-thū'zə-la, -thoō', n.* a patriarch said to have lived 969 years (Gen. v. 27): any very aged person: a very large wine-bottle (holding about 6½ quarts).

methyl, *meth'il,* (*chem.*) *n.* the radical $(CH_3)$ of wood (or methyl) alcohol $(CH_3 \cdot OH)$.—*n.* methylamine (*-a-mēn'*), an inflammable gas $(CH_3 \cdot NH_2)$ which can be got from herring brine.—See also dimethylamine and trimethylamine.—*v.t.* meth'ylate, to mix or impregnate with methyl alcohol: to introduce the radical $CH_3$ into.—*n.* methyl alcohol derivative: compound with methyl group.—*ns.* methylā'tion; meth'ylene, hypothetical compound $CH_2$.—*adj.* methyl'ic.—methylated spirit, alcohol made unpalatable with methyl alcohol, and usually other things; methyl chloride, a refrigerant and local anaesthetic.—methyl-propyl ether, an inhalation anaesthetic. [Gr. *meta, hȳlē*, wood.]

methysis, *meth'i-sis,* (*path.*) *n.* drunkenness.—*adj.* methys'tic, intoxicating. [Gr.]

metic, *met'ik, n.* a resident alien. [Gr. *metoikos*—*meta,* indicating change, and *oikos,* a house.]

meticulous, *me-tik'ū-ləs, adj.* timid (*obs.*): scrupulously careful: (popularly) overcareful.—*adv.* metic'ulously.—*n.* metic'ulousness. [L. *meticulōsus,* frightened—*metus,* fear.]

métier, *mā-tyā, n.* one's calling or business: that in which one is specially skilled. [Fr.,—L. *ministerium.*]

metif, *mā'tēf, n.* the offspring of a white and a quadroon.—*n.* metis (*mā-tēs*), a person of mixed descent, esp., in Canada, a half-breed of French and Indian parentage:—*fem.* métisse. [Fr.; cf. mestizo.]

Metis, *mē'tis, n.* a Greek personification of prudence. [Gr. *mētis.*]

Metol, *mē'tol, n.* *p*-methylaminophenol sulphate, the basis of a rapid developer for photographic negatives. [Trademark.]

Metonic, *mi-ton'ik, adj.* pertaining to the Athenian astronomer *Mētōn* or his cycle (433 B.C.) of 19 years after which the moon's phases recur on the same days of the year.

metonym, *met'ə-nim, n.* a word used in a transferred sense.—*adjs.* metonym'ic, -al.—*adv.* metonym'ically.—*n.* metonymy (*mi-ton'i-mi*), a trope in which the name of one thing is put for that of another related to it, the effect for the cause, etc., as 'the bottle' for 'drink'. [Gr. *metōnymiā*—*meta,* indicating change, and *onyma* =*onoma,* a name.]

metope, *met'o-pē,* also *met'ōp,* (*archit.*) *n.* the slab, plain or sculptured, between the triglyphs of a Doric frieze. [Gr. *metōpē*—*meta* and *ōpē,* an opening for a beam-end.]

metope, *met'ōp, n.* the face, forehead, frontal surface generally.—*adj.* metopic (*mit-op'ik*).—*ns.* metopism (*met'ə-pizm*), the condition of having a persistent metopic or frontal suture; metoposcopy (*met-ə-pos'kə-pi*; Gr. *skopeein,* to look), the study of character from the physiognomy.—*adjs.* metoposcop'ic, -al.—*n.* metopos'copist. [Gr. *metōpon,* forehead, lit. between the eyes—*meta,* and *ōps,* eye.]

metopon, *met'ō-pon, n.* a pain-relieving drug derived from opium but less habit-forming than morphine.

metopryl, *met'ō-pril, n.* an anaesthetic related to ether, but more powerful and less disturbing in after-effects.

metre, *mē'tər, n.* that regulated succession of certain groups of syllables (long and short, stressed and unstressed) in which poetry is usually written: verse, or poetry generally: a scheme of versification, the character of a stanza as consisting of a given number of lines composed of feet of a given number, arrangement, and kind: musical time.—*v.t.* and *v.i.* to versify.—*adjs.* metred (*mē'tərd*), rhythmical; metric (*met'rik*), -al, pertaining to metre: in metre: consisting of verses.—*adv.* met'rically.—*n.* metrician (*me-trish'ən*), a metricist.—*v.t.* met'ricise, -ize (*-sīz*), to analyse the metre of.—*ns.* met'ricist (*-sist*), one skilled in metres: one who writes in metre; met'ric(s), the art or science of versification; metrificā'tion, metrical structure: the act of making verses; met'rifier, a versifier; met'rist, one skilled in the use of metres: a student of metre; metromā'nia, a mania for writing verses.—common metre, a quatrain in eights and sixes, of four and of three iambic feet alternately—also service metre, from its use in the metrical psalms, etc., and ballad metre, from its use in old ballads; long metre, an octosyllabic quatrain, the four lines with four feet each; short metre, the quatrain in sixes, with the third line octosyllabic. [O.E. *mēter* and O.Fr. *metre,* both—L. *metrum*—Gr. *metron,* measurement, metre; and partly directly.]

metre, *mē'tər, n.* the fundamental unit of length in the metric system—orig. intended to be one ten-millionth of distance from pole to equator: later the distance between two marks on a platinum-iridium bar in Paris: defined more recently in terms of the wavelength in vacuo of the orange radiation of the krypton-86 atom: by British Act of Parliament (1963) 1 yard equals 0·9144 metre.—*adj.* metric (*met'rik*), pertaining to the metre, or to the metric system.—*v.t., v.i.* met'ricate, to convert, change to the metric system.—*n.* metricā'tion.—metre-kilogram(me)-second (contr. M.K.S. or MKS) system, a system of scientific measurement having the metre, etc., as units of length, mass, time (with the addition of ampere—M.K.S.A., or more usually MKSA—forming the Giorgi system of units); metric system, a decimal system of weights and measures; metric ton (see tonne).—to go metric, to metricate. [Fr. *mètre*—Gr. *metron,* measure.]

metric, *met'rik, adj.* quantitative.—*adj.* met'rical, pertaining to measurement.—*n.pl.* met'rics, the theory of measurement.—*n.* metrol'ogy, the science of weights and measures. [Gr. *metron,* measure.]

metric. See metre (1 and 2).

metr(o)-, *pfx.* of the uterus (used as hystero- is used).

métro, *mā-trō, n.* (often *cap.*) an underground railway, esp. the Paris subway. [Fr. *métro.* Abbrev. for *chemin de fer métropolitain,* metropolitan railway.]

metronome, *met'rə-nōm, n.* an instrument with an

inverted pendulum that can be set to beat so many times a minute, the loud ticking giving the right speed of performance for a piece of music. —*adj.* **metronomic** (*-nom'ik*). [Gr. *metron*, measure, *nomos*, law.]

**metronymic**, *met-rə-nim'ik, adj.* derived from the name of one's mother or other female ancestor: indicating the mother: using such a system of naming.—*n.* an appellation so derived (cf. *patronymic*).—Also **matronymic** (prob.—L. *māter*, though Doric Greek is *mātēr*). [Gr. *mētēr*, *-tros*, mother, *onyma* = *onoma*, name.]

**metropolis**, *mi-tròp'ə-lis, n.* the capital of a country, county, etc.: the chief cathedral city, as Canterbury of England: the mother-city of an ancient Greek colony: a chief centre, seat or focus: the main habitat (*biol.*):—*pl.* **metrop'- olises.**—*adj.* **metropolitan** (*met-rə-pol'i-tən*), of a metropolis: of the mother-church.—*n.* the bishop of a metropolis, presiding over the other bishops of a province: an archbishop.—*n.* **metropol'itanate.**—*adj.* **metropolit'ical.** [Gr. *mētropolis*—*mētēr*, mother, *polis*, a city.]

**metrostyle**, *met'rə-stil, n.* a device for regulating speed in a player-piano. [Gr. *metron*, measure, *stȳlos*, a pillar.]

**mettle**, *met'l, n.* temperament: ardent temperament: spirit: sprightliness: courage.—*adj.* (*Scot.*) **mettlesome.**—*adjs.* **mett'led, mett'lesome,** high-spirited: ardent.—*n.* **mett'lesomeness.—** **put on his mettle,** to rouse (a person) to put forth his best efforts. [metal.]

**meu**, *mū, n.* baldmoney or spignel. [L. *mēum*— Gr. *mēon.*]

**meum et tuum**, *mē'əm et tū'əm, me'ōom et tōō'- ōom,* (L.) mine and thine.

**meuse, muse, mews,** *mūs, mūz, n.* a way of escape through a hedge, etc.—*v.i.* to pass through a meuse. [O.Fr. *muce*, a place for hiding things.]

**meuse.** See mew (3).

**meve**, *mēv,* an obs. form of move (*vb.*).

**mew**, *mū, n.* a gull. [O.E. *mǣw;* Du. *meeuw,* O.N. *mār,* Ger. *möwe.*]

**mew**, *mū, v.i.* to cry as a cat.—*n.* the cry of a cat.— *interj.* expressing derision. [Imit.]

**mew**, *mū, v.t.* to shed, moult, or cast: to change, as the covering or dress: to confine, as in a cage. —*v.i.* to cast the antlers or feathers: to moult.— *n.* process of moulting: a cage for hawks, esp. while mewing: a coop: a place of confinement: a retreat: a hiding-place.—*n.* **mews, meuse** (*mūz, mūs;* orig. *pl.* of **mew,** now commonly as *sing.* with new *pl.* **mews'es**), a street or yard of stabling (often converted into dwelling-houses or garages)—from the king's mews at Charing Cross when hawks were succeeded by horses. [O.Fr. *muer*—L. *mūtāre,* to change.]

**mewl**, *mūl, v.i.* and *v.t.* to mew: to cry feebly, as a child. [Imit.]

**Mexican**, *meks'i-kən, adj.* of Mexico and its people.—*n.* a native or citizen of Mexico: an Aztec: the Nahuatl language: a Mexican dollar: a coarse cotton cloth.—**Mexican hog,** the peccary; **Mexican tea,** a kind of goosefoot, used as an anthelmintic. [Sp. *Mexicano,* now *Mejicano.*]

**meynt.** See ming.

**mezereon**, *me-zē'ri-on, n.* a European shrub (*Daphne Mezereum*) whose flowers appear in early spring: its extremely acrid bark used in medicine. [Ar. and Pers. *māzaryūn.*]

**mezuza(h)**, *mə-zōōz'ə, n.* a parchment scroll containing scriptural texts which is placed in a case and fixed to the doorpost by some Jewish families as a sign of their faith:—*pl.* -zuzahs, -zuzoth (*-zōō-zōt'*). [Heb., (lit.) doorpost.]

**mezzanine**, *mez'ə-nēn, n.* an entresol (*archit.*): a small low window (*archit.*): a room below the stage.—Also *adj.* [Fr.,—It. *mezzanino*—*mezzano*—L. *mediānus*—*medius,* middle.]

**mezza voce**, *met'sa võ'chä, med'zä, (mus.) adj.* and *adv.* with medium volume, tone. [It.]

**mezzo-forte**, *met'sa-, med'zō-för'tä, adj.* and *adv.* rather loud. [It.]

**mezzo-rilievo**, *met'sō-, med'zō-ril-yā'vō, n.* a degree of relief in figures half-way between high and low relief. [It.]

**mezzo-soprano**, *met'sō-, med'zō-so-prä'nō, n.* a voice between soprano and contralto: low soprano: a part for such a voice: a person possessing it. [It. *mezzo,* middle, and *soprano.*]

**mezzotint**, *met'sō-, med'zō-tint,* **mezzotinto**, *-tint'ō, n.* a method of copperplate engraving giving an even gradation of tones by roughening a plate and removing the bur for lights: an impression from a plate so produced. [It. *mezzotinto*— *mezzo,* middle, half, *tinto,* tint—L. *tingĕre, tinctum,* to dye.]

**mho**, *mō, n.* formerly a unit of electric conductance, that of a body with a resistance of one ohm (now **siemens**). [ohm spelt backwards.]

**mhorr**, *mör, n.* a West African gazelle. [Ar.]

**mi**, *mē, n.* the third note of the scale in sol-fa notation—also anglicised in spelling as me. [See Aretinian.]

**miaow, mi-ow', myow'.** Same as mew (2).

**miarolitic**, *mi-a-rō-lit'ik, (geol.) adj.* having irregular cavities into which the constituent minerals of the rock project with perfectly terminated crystals. [It. *miarolo,* local name of a granite.]

**miasma**, *mi-* or *mi-az'mə, n.* an unwholesome exhalation—also mi'asm:—*pl.* mias'mata, mias'- mas, mi'asms.—*adjs.* mias'mal, miasmat'ic, mias'matous, mias'mic, mias'mous. [Gr. *miasma,* *-atos,* pollution—*miainein,* to stain, pollute.]

**miaul**, *mi-öl', mi-owl', v.i.* to cry as a cat.—*n.* a mew. [Fr. *miauler;* imit.]

**mica**, *mi'kə, n.* a rock-forming mineral (muscovite, biotite, lepidolite, etc.) with perfect basal cleavage, the laminae flexible and elastic, and usu. transparent, of various colours, used as an electric insulator and as a substitute for glass:— *pl.* mi'cas.—*adj.* **micaceous** (*-kā'shəs*).— *n.* mi'cate, to furnish with mica.—mi'ca-schist', -slate', a metamorphic rock consisting of alternate folia of mica and quartz. [L. *mica,* a crumb; use probably influenced by association with *micāre,* to glitter.]

**Micawberish**, *mi-kö'bər-ish, adj.* like Wilkins *Micawber* in Dickens's *David Copperfield,* jaunty and improvident, always 'waiting for something to turn up'.—*n.* Micaw'berism.

**mice**, *mis,* plural of mouse.

**micelle**, *mi-sel',* **micella**, *mi-sel'a, ns.* a group of molecular chains, a structural unit found in colloids: a hypothetical unit of living matter.— *adj.* micell'ar. [Dim. of L. *mica,* crumb, grain.]

**Michaelmas**, *mik'əl-məs, n.* the festival of St *Michael,* Sept. 29: a quarterly rent-day in England.—**Mich'aelmas-dai'sy,** a wild aster: any of several garden plants of the genus Aster with clusters of small purple flowers; **Michael-mas term,** the autumn term at Oxford and Cambridge and some other universities. [mass (2).]

**miche**, *mich, (dial.) v.i.* to mouch, skulk, slink: to loaf: to play truant.—*v.t.* to pilfer.—*n.* mich'er. —*n.* and *adj.* mich'ing. [Poss. same as mooch.]

**Michurinism**, *mē-chōō'rin-izm, n.* Lysenkoism. [I. V. *Michurin,* Russian horticulturalist.]

**mick, mickey, micky**, *mik'(i), n.* an Irishman (*rather offensive*): a wild young bull (*Austr.*).— **Mickey (Finn),** a doped drink (*slang*); **Mickey Mouse,** an animated cartoon character created by Walt Disney, 1928 (*adj.* mickey, of music or band, trite, corny; *U.S. slang*).—**take the mick, mickey (micky),** or **mike (or a mike), out of** (*slang;* perhaps with different origin), to annoy: to make game of. [*Michael.*]

**mickle**, *mik'l, (arch.) adj.* much: great.—*n.* a

great quantity.—*adv.* much.—*Scot.* muck'le.— many a little (or pickle) makes a mickle (*often* absurdly many a mickle makes a muckle), every little helps. [O.E. *micel, mycel.*]

**micky.** See mick.

**Micmac,** *mik'mak, n.* an Indian tribe of eastern Canada: a member of it: its language.

**mico,** *mē'kō, n.* a marmoset, esp. the black-tailed. [Port.,—Carib *meku,* monkey.]

**micr(o)-,** *mi-kr(ō)-, mi-kr(ə)-,* in composition, (1) (a) abnormally small: (b) using, or used in, or prepared for, microscopy: (c) dealing with minute quantities, objects or values: (d) dealing with a small area: (e) magnifying, amplifying: (f) reducing, or reduced, to minute size: (2) a millionth part, as in mi'croampere, a millionth part of an ampere, one-millionth of a bar of pressure, mi'crofarad, mi'crogram, and others, including those listed below but not defined. [Gr. *mikros,* little.]

**microanalysis,** *mī-krō-ə-nal'i-sis, n.* chemical analysis of minute quantities.—*adj.* micro-analyt'ical. [micro- (1c).]

**microbalance,** *mi'krə-bal-əns, n.* balance for measuring very small weights. [micro- (1c).]

**microbar,** *mi-krə-bär.* See micro- (2).

**microbe,** *mi'krōb, n.* a microscopic organism, esp. a disease-causing bacterium.—*adjs.* microˈbial, micro'bian, microˈbic.—*ns.* mi'crobiology, biology of microscopic or ultramicroscopic organisms, as bacteria, viruses, fungi; mi'crobiota, the smallest soil organisms. [Fr.,—Gr. *mikros,* little, *bios,* life.]

**microcapsule,** *mi'krō-kap-sūl, n.* an extremely small, thin-walled capsule of plastic or wax, formed around liquid, powder, etc., which, when fractured, releases its contents to fulfil some purpose; such capsules have been used e.g. to make copying paper without carbon.—*n.* microencapsulāˈtion. [micro- (1a).]

**microcard,** *mi'krə-kärd, n.* card reproducing some 200 or more pages of a book in microscopic print for later reading by enlargement. [micro- (1f).]

**microcephalous,** *mī-krō-sef'ə-ləs, adj.* abnormally small-headed.—Also microcephalic (*-si-fal'ik*). —*ns.* microceph'al, an abnormally small-headed person; microceph'aly, abnormal smallness of head. [Gr. *mikros,* little, *kephalē,* head.]

**Microcheiroptera** (*U.S.* -chir-), *mī-krō-ki-rop'tə-ra, n.pl.* bats other than fruit-bats (which are large). [micro- (1a), Cheiroptera.]

**microchemistry,** *mī-krō-kem'is-tri, n.* chemistry dealing with very small quantities. [micro- (1c).]

**microcircuit,** *mī-krə-sûr'kit, n.* an electronic circuit with components formed in one unit of semiconductor crystal. [micro- (1f).]

**Microchiroptera.** See Microcheiroptera.

**microclimate,** *mi'krō-kli-māt, -kli-mit, n.* the climate of a small or very small area, esp. if different from that of the surrounding area.—*n.* microclimatol'ogy, study of a microclimate or microclimates. [micro- (1d).]

**microcline,** *mi'krə-klin, n.* an anorthic potash-feldspar with cleavage-angle differing very slightly from a right angle. [Gr. *mikros,* little, *klinein,* to slant.]

**micrococcus,** *mī-krə-kok'əs, n.* a rounded bacillus: —*pl.* micrococci (*-kok'si*).—*adj.* micrococc'al. [micro- (1a) and Gr. *kokkos,* a grain.]

**microcomponent,** *mī-krō-kəm-pō'nənt, n.* a minute component of e.g. a microcircuit. [micro- (1a).]

**microcopying,** *mi-krə-kop'i-ing, n.* copying on microfilm. [micro- (1f).]

**microcosm,** *mi'krə-kozm, n.* a little universe or world: man, who was regarded by ancient philosophers as a model or epitome of the universe.—*adjs.* microcos'mic, -al, pertaining to the microcosm.—*n.* microcosmog'raphy.— micro-

**cosmic salt,** sodium ammonium hydrogen phosphate, used as a blowpipe flux (orig. got from human urine). [Gr. *mikros,* small, *kosmos,* world.]

**microcrystalline,** *mī-krə-kris'təl-in, -in, adj.* having a crystalline structure visible only under the microscope. [micro- (1a).]

**microcyte,** *mi'krə-sit, n.* a small red blood corpuscle. [Gr. *kytos,* a container (used as if = cell).]

**microdetector,** *mi-krō-di-tekt'ər, n.* an instrument for detecting minute amounts or changes.—*n.* microdetec'tion. [micro- (1c).]

**microdissection,** *mi-krō-di-sek'shən, n.* dissection under the microscope. [micro- (1b).]

**microdot,** *mi'krə-dot, n.* photograph of usu. secret material reduced to size of large dot. [micro- (1f).]

**microelectronics,** *mi-krō-i-lek-tron'iks, n.pl.* (treated as *sing.*) the technology of electronic systems involving microminiaturisation. [micro- (1f).]

**microencapsulation.** See microcapsule.

**microfarad,** *mi-krə-far'ad, n.* one millionth of a farad.—*n.* mi'cromicrofarad, one millionth of a microfarad, a picofarad. [micro- (2).]

**microfelsitic,** *mi-krə-fel-sit'ik, adj.* of the crypto-crystalline texture of a quartz-felsite groundmass. [micro- (1a).]

**microfiche,** *mi'krə-fēsh, n.* a sheet of microfilm suitable for filing. [micro- (1f), and Fr. *fiche,* slip of paper, etc.]

**microfilm,** *mi'krə-film, n.* a photographic film for preserving a microscopic record of a document, which can be enlarged in projection. [micro- (1f).]

**microgamete,** *mi-krə-gam'ēt,* or *-ēt', n.* the smaller, generally the male, gamete. [micro- (1a).]

**microgram,** *mi'krə-gram, n.* one millionth of a gram. [micro- (2).]

**microgram,** *mi'krə-gram, n.* a micrograph—a picture or drawing of an object under the microscope: a message typed, photographed and printed on a card, or the card concerned. [micro- (1f).]

**microgranite,** *mi-krə-gran'it, n.* a completely but minutely crystalline rock of the composition of granite.—*adj.* microgranit'ic. [micro- (1a).]

**micrograph,** *mi'krə-gräf, n.* a pantograph instrument for minute writing or drawing: a minute picture: a delineation of a microscopic object.— *n.* micrographer (*mi-krog'rə-fər*), one who draws or describes microscopic objects.—*adj.* micrographic (*mi-krə-graf'ik*), pertaining to micrography: minutely written or delineated: showing intergrowth of crystalline constituents on a microscopic scale (*geol.*).—*n.* microg'raphy, study with the microscope: the description of microscopic objects. [micro- (1f), and Gr. *graphein,* to write.]

**microgroove,** *mi'krə-grōōv, n.* the fine groove of long-playing gramophone records. [micro- (1a).]

**microhenry,** *mi-krə-hen'ri.* See micro- (2).

**microhm,** *mi'krōm.* See micro- (2).

**Microlepidoptera,** *mi-krō-lep-id-op'tər-a, n.pl.* small moths of various kinds. [micro- (1a).]

**microlite,** *mi'krə-lit, n.* a mineral composed of calcium, tantalum, and oxygen, occurring in very small crystals: an incipient crystal, detected under the microscope by polarised light.—*n.* mi'crolith, a microlite: a very small stone implement of the Stone Age.—*adjs.* microlith'ic; microlitic (*-lit'ik*). [micro- (1a), and Gr. *lithos,* a stone.]

**micrology,** *mi-krol'ə-ji, n.* the study of microscopic objects: study or discussion of trivialities. —*adjs.* micrologic (*-loj'*), -al.—*adv.* microlog'-ically.—*n.* microl'ogist. [Gr. *mikros,* little, *logos,* discourse.]

**microlux,** *mi'krə-luks.* See micro- (2).

**micro-manipulation,** *mī-krō-mə-nip-ū-lā'shən, n.* the technique of using delicate instruments, as microneedles and micropipettes, to work on cells, bacteria, etc. under high magnifications, or of working with extremely small quantities in microchemistry. [micro- (1b, c).]

**micrometer,** *mī-krom'i-tər, n.* an instrument for measuring minute distances or angles.—*adj.* **micrometric** (*mī-krə-met'rik*), **-al.**—*n.* **microm'etry,** measuring with a micrometer. [micro- (1c).]

**micro-meteorite,** *mī-krō-mē'tē-ə-rīt, n.* a particle of meteoric dust too small to be consumed by friction in the atmosphere.—*n.* **micro-meteorol'ogy,** the study of atmospheric conditions over a small area, and usu. to a very limited height above the ground. [micro- (1d).]

**micromicr(o)-,** *mī-krō-mī-kr(ō)-* (better pico-), in composition, a millionth of a millionth part, as in **micromicrocurie** (used in measuring the quantity of a radioactive substance present in stable material) **micromicrofarad,** etc. [micro- (2).]

**micromillimetre,** *mī-krə-mil'i-mēt-ər, n.* one millionth of a millimetre: one thousandth of a millimetre, or one micron (*bot.*). [micro- (2).]

**microminiature,** *mī-krō-min'i-ə-chər, adj.* made on an extremely small scale.—*n.* **mi'crominiaturisā'-tion, -z-,** reduction to extremely small size of scientific or technical equipment or any part of it.—*v.t.* **mi'cromin'iaturise, -ize.** [micro- (1f).]

**micron, mikron,** *mī'kron, n.* one millionth of a metre (denoted by μ). [Gr. *mikron,* neut. of *mikros,* little.]

**Micronesian,** *mī-krə-nē'zh(y)ən, -zyən, -zi-ən adj.* pertaining to *Micronesia,* a group of small islands in the Pacific, north of New Guinea.—*n.* a native of the group. [Gr. *mikros,* little, *nēsos,* an island.]

**micronutrient,** *mī-krə-nū'tri-ənt, n.* a nutritive substance required in minute quantities by a plant.—Also *adj.* [micro- (1a).]

**micro-organism,** *mī-krō-ôr'gən-izm, n.* a microscopic (or ultramicroscopic) organism. [micro- (1a).]

**micropegmatite,** *mī-krə-peg'mə-tīt, n.* a micrographic intergrowth of quartz and feldspar.—*adj.* **micropegmatitic** (-*tit'ik*). [micro- (1a).]

**microphone,** *mī'krə-fōn, n.* an instrument for intensifying sounds: a sensitive instrument (pop. contracted **mike,** *mīk*), similar to a telephone transmitter, for picking up sound-waves to be broadcast or amplified and translating them, e.g. by means of a diaphragm and carbon granules, into a fluctuating electric current.—*adj.* **microphonic** (-*fon'ik*). [Gr. *mikros,* small, *phōnē,* voice.]

**microphotograph,** *mī-krə-fōt'ə-gräf, n.* strictly, a photograph reduced to microscopic size: loosely, a photomicrograph, or photograph of an object as magnified by the microscope.—*n.* **microphotographer** (-*og'rə-fər*)—*adj.* **microphotographic** (-*ə-graf'ik*).—*n.* **microphotog'raphy.** [micro- (1f).]

**microphyllous,** *mī-krō-fil'əs,* (*bot.*) *adj.* small-leaved. [Gr. *mikros,* little, *phyllon,* leaf.]

**microphysics,** *mī-krə-fiz'iks, n.* physics dealing with subatomic particles. [micro- (1c).]

**microphyte,** *mī'krō-fīt, n.* a microscopic plant.—*adj.* **microphyt'ic.** [micro- (1b).]

**micropsia,** *mī-krop'si-ə, n.* a condition in which objects look smaller than usual. [Gr. *mikros,* little, *opsis,* appearance.]

**micropterous,** *mī-krop'tər-əs, adj.* with reduced fins or hind-wings. [Gr. *mikros,* little, *pteron,* wing.]

**micropyle,** *mī-krə-pīl, n.* the orifice in the coats of the ovule leading to the apex of the nucellus, through which the pollen-tube commonly enters (*bot.*): an opening by which a spermatozoon may enter an ovum (*zool.*).—*adj.* **micropy'lar.** [Gr. *mikros,* little, *pylē,* gate.]

**microscope,** *mī'krə-skōp, n.* an instrument for magnifying minute objects.—*adjs.* **microscopic** (-*skop'ik*), **-al,** pertaining to a microscope or to microscopy: magnifying: able to see minute objects: invisible or hardly visible without the aid of a microscope: minute.—*adv.* **microscop'ically.**—*ns.* **microscopist** (*mī-kros'kop-ist, mī-krə-skō'pist*); **micros'copy.**—**acoustic microscope,** one in which ultrasonic waves passed through the specimen are scanned by a laser beam; **compound microscope, simple microscope,** microscopes with respectively two and a single lens; **electron, proton, ultraviolet microscope,** one using a beam of electrons, protons, or ultraviolet rays; **phase-contrast, phase-difference, microscope** (see phase); **reflecting microscope** (see reflect). [Gr. *mikros,* little, *skopeein,* to look at.]

**microsecond,** *mī'krə-sek-ənd.* See micro- (2).

**microseism,** *mī'krə-sīzm, n.* a slight earth-movement detectable only instrumentally.—*adjs.* **microseis'mic, -al.**—*ns.* **microseis'mograph,** an instrument for recording microseisms and distant earthquakes; **microseismom'eter,** an instrument for measuring microseisms; **microseismom'etry.** [Gr. *mikros,* little, *seismos,* earthquake.]

**microsome,** *mī'krə-sōm, n.* a minute granule or drop in cytoplasm. [Gr. *mikros,* little, *sōma,* body.]

**microspore,** *mī'krə-spōr, -spör, n.* the smaller of two forms of spore: a spore giving rise to a male gametophyte.—*ns.* **microsporangium** (-*spör-an'ji-əm*), a sporangium producing only microspores:—*pl.* **microsporan'gia;** **microsporophyll** (-*spör', -spōr'ə-fil*), a sporophyll that carries or subtends only microsporangia. [micro- (1a).]

**microstructure,** *mī-krō-struk'chər, n.* structure, especially of metals and alloys, as revealed by the microscope. [micro- (1a, b).]

**microtome,** *mī'krə-tōm, n.* an instrument for cutting thin sections of objects for microscopic examination.—*adjs.* **microtomic, -al** (-*tom'ik, -al*).—*ns.* **microtomist** (-*krot'ə-mist*); **microt'omy.** [Gr. *mikros,* little, *tomē,* a cut.]

**microtone,** *mī'krə-tōn, (mus.) n.* an interval less than a semitone.—*n.* **microtonal'ity.** [micro- (1a).]

**microwatt,** *mī'krə-wot.* See micro- (2).

**microwave,** *mī'krə-wāv, n.* in radio communication, one of very short wavelength: now usu. a wave in the radiation spectrum between normal radio waves and infrared.—Also *adj.* [micro- (1a).]

**microwire,** *mī'krō-wīr, n.* a very strong, very fine filament of metal or other material. [micro- (1a).]

**micrurgy,** *mī'krûr-ji, n.* micro-manipulation. [micro- (1b, c), and Gr. -*ourgos* (as in *metallourgos,* working a mine)—*ergon,* work.]

**micturition,** *mik-tū-rish'ən, n.* the frequent desire to pass urine: (loosely) the act of urinating.—*n.* **mic'tion** (*obs.*), voiding urine.—*v.i.* **mic'turate** (irregularly formed), to urinate. [L. *micturīre, -ītum,* desiderative of *mingĕre, mi(n)ctum,* to pass urine, *mi(n)ctiō, -ōnis,* urination.]

**mid-, mid-,** in composition, the middle part of: of or in the middle of. [From mid, adj.; not always hyphened.]

**mid,** *mid, adj.* middle: situated between extremes: uttered with the tongue in a position between high and low (*phon.*).—*n.* middle.—*adj.* **midd'est** (*Spens.*), middle: middlemost.—*n.* **midst.**—*adj.* **mid'most,** middlemost.—*n.* the very middle.—*adv.* in the very middle.—*prep.* in the very middle of.—**mid-age'** (*Shak.*), middle age; **mid-air',** a region somewhat above the ground: the midst of a course through the air; **mid'brain,** the part of the brain derived from the second brain vesicle of the embryo; **mid'day,** noon.—*adj.* of,

at, or pertaining to, noon.—**mid'-gut**, that part of the alimentary canal formed from the original gastrula cavity and lined with endoderm: also, the small intestine; **mid'-heav'en**, the middle of the sky or of heaven: the meridian; **mid'-hour**, the middle time: an intervening hour.—*adj.* **mid'land**, in the middle of, or surrounded by, land: distant from the coast: inland.—*n.* the interior of a country: (*pl.*) esp. (*cap.*) the central parts of England.—**mid'-leg'**, the middle of the leg.—*adv.* as high or deep as the middle of the leg.—**mid'-Lent'**, the middle of Lent: the fourth Sunday in Lent; **mid'night**, the middle of the night: twelve o'clock at night: pitch darkness.—*adj.* of or at midnight: dark as midnight. —**midnight sun**, the sun visible at midnight in the polar regions; **mid'noon'**, noon; **mid-off'**, **mid-on'** (*cricket*), a fieldsman on the *off*, or *on*, side nearly in line with the bowler: his position; **mid'rib**, the rib along the middle of a leaf; **mid'-sea'**, the open sea; **mid'-seas'on** (also *adj.*).—*adj.* **mid'ship**, in the middle of a ship.—**mid'shipman**, once the title of a young officer (orig. quartered *amidships*) entering the navy, thereafter a junior ranking below a sub-lieutenant, but above a naval cadet, now, since 1957, only a shore ranking during training—abbrev. (by landsmen) **mid**, **midd'y**, jocularly **mid'shipmite**.—*adv.* **mid'-ships**, amidships.—**mid-sky'**, the middle of the sky; **midstream'**, the middle of the stream.— *adv.* in the middle of the stream.—**mid'summer** (also *-sum'*), the middle of the summer: the summer solstice, about the 21st of June; **Midsummer day**, the 24th of June, a quarter-day; **midsummer madness**, madness attributed to the hot sun of midsummer; **midsummer moon**, a season when madness was supposed to be rife.— *adj.* **mid-Victo'rian**, of or characteristic of the middle part of Queen Victoria's reign.—**mid'way**, the middle of the way or distance: a middle course: a central avenue in an American fair or exhibition.—*adj.* in the middle of the way or distance.—*adv.* half-way along.—*prep.* half-way along or across.—**Mid'-week**, Wednesday (cf. Ger. *Mittwoch*).—*adj.* **mid'-week**, in the middle of the week.—**Mid'west**, Middle West; **mid'-wick'et**, mid-off or mid-on; **mid-win'ter**, the middle of winter: the winter solstice (21st or 22nd December), or the time near it.—*adj.* **mid'-year**, in the middle of the (academic) year. [O.E. *midd*; cf. Ger. *mitte*, L. *medius*, Gr. *mesos*.]
**'mid**, **mid**, for **amid**.
**Midas**, *mī'das*, *n.* a king of Phrygia whose touch turned all to gold, and on whom Apollo bestowed ass's ears: a genus of marmosets.— **Midas's ear**, a shell of the genus Auricula.
**midden**, *mid'ən*, *n.* a dunghill: a refuse-heap: a kitchen-midden (*ant.*).—**midd'en-cock'**; **midd'en-stead**, a place where dung is heaped up. [Scand., as Dan. *mödding*—*mög*, dung; cf. **muck**.]
**middle**, *mid'l*, *adj.* equally distant (in measurement or in number of steps) from the extremes: intermediate: intervening: intermediate between active and passive, reflexive or expressing an action in some way affecting the agent (*gram.*): (*cap.*; of languages), between Old and Modern (as *Middle English*, *Middle High German*).—*n.* the middle point, part, or position: midst: central portion, waist: middle voice (*gram.*): middle term (*log.*): a middle article.— **midd'le-age**.—*adj.* **midd'le-aged** (*-ājd'*), between youth and old age, variously reckoned to suit the reckoner.—**Middle Ages**, the time between the fall of the Western Roman empire and the Renaissance (5th-15th cent.); **middle article**, a newspaper article of literary or general rather than topical interest.—*adjs.* **midd'le-brack'et**, in a midway grouping in a list; **midd'lebrow**, midway between highbrow and lowbrow.—Also *n.*— **middle C**, the C in the middle of the piano key-

board: the first line below the treble or above the bass stave; **middle class**, that part of the people which comes between the aristocracy and the working-class.—Also *adj.*—**middle distance** (same as **middle ground**); **midd'le-earth'**, the earth, considered as placed between the upper and lower regions; **Middle East**, the countries of Asia west of India (or of China); **Middle English** (see **English**); **middle ground**, the part of a picture between the foreground and background; **Middle Kingdom**, China; **midd'leman**, one occupying a middle position: an intermediary, esp. between producer and consumer: in Ireland, one who rents land in large tracts, and lets it in small portions.—*adjs.* **middl'emost**, nearest the middle; **middle-of-the-road**, midway between extremes.—**middle passage**, the voyage across the Atlantic from Africa to the West Indies on board a slave-ship.—*adj.* **midd'le-sized**, of average size.—**Middle States**, New York, New Jersey, Pennsylvania, Delaware; **midd'le-stitch'ing**, monk's-seam; **middle term** (*log.*), that term of a syllogism which appears in both premises but not in the conclusion; **middle watch**, that from midnight to 4 a.m.; **midd'le-weight**, a boxer (over 10 st 7 lb. and not over 11 st. 6 lb.—professional only) or jockey of intermediate weight (**light-middleweight**, a boxer, amateur only, not over 11 st. 2 lb.); **Middle West**, the Mississippi basin as far south as Kansas, Missouri, and the Ohio River; **midd'le-world**, middle-earth. [O.E. *middel* (adj.); Du. *middel*, Ger. *mittel*; see **mid**.]
**middling**, *mid'ling*, *adj.* intermediate (*obs.*): moderate (*coll.*): indifferent: mediocre: fairly good.—*adv.* (*coll.*) fairly: fairly well.—*n.* (usu. in *pl.*) goods of a middle quality: the coarser part of ground wheat: partially concentrated ore. [Orig. Scots—**mid** and suff. *-ling*.]
**Midgard**, *mid'gärd*, (*Scand. myth.*) *n.* the abode of men, middle-earth. [O.N. *mithgarthr*, mid-yard.]
**midge**, *mij*, *n.* a small gnat-like fly, esp. of the family Chironomidae: a very small person.—*n.* **midg'et**, something very small of its kind: a very small person. [O.E. *mycg*, *mycge*; Ger. *mücke*.]
**Midi**, *mē-dē*, *n.* the south (of France).—*n.* **midinette** (*-net*), a Paris work-girl (noticeable at lunch-hour). [Fr. *midi*, midday; *midinette* is said to be from *midi* and *dînette*, lunch.]
**midi-**, *mid'i-*, in composition, of middle size, length, etc., as *midi-skirt*. [**mid**; cf. **mini-**.]
**midland**, **midmost**, **midnight**, etc. See **mid**.
**Midrash**, *mid'rash*, *n.* the Hebrew exposition of the Old Testament—its two divisions, *Haggada* and *Halachah*:—*pl.* **Midrashim** (*mid-rä'shēm*), commentaries on individual books or sections of the Old Testament. [Heb., exposition.]
**midriff**, *mid'rif*, *n.* the diaphragm: the part of a woman's garment that fits over the diaphragm. [O.E. *mid*, middle, *hrif*, belly.]
**midst**, *midst*, *n.* middle.—*adv.* in the middle.— *prep.* (also '**midst** as if for **amidst**) amidst. [M.E. *middes*, from gen. of *mid*, with excrescent *t* (cf. **whilst**); perh. partly a superl.]
**midwife**, *mid'wīf*, *n.* a woman who assists others in childbirth:—*pl.* **midwives** (*mid'wīvz*).—*v.t.* to help in bringing forth (a child): also *fig.*:— *pr.p.* **-wifing**, **-wiving**; *pa.t.*, *pa.p.* **-wifed**, **-wived**. —*n.* **mid'wifery** (*-wif-ə-ri*, *-wif-ri*, *-if-ri*, *-wif'ri*), art or practice of a midwife: assistance at childbirth: obstetrics. [O.E. *mid*, with (Ger. *mit*, Gr. *meta*), *wif*, woman.]
**mien**, *mēn*, *n.* air or look, manner, bearing (*literary*): expression of face (*obs.*). [Perh. **demean**, influenced by Fr. *mine*, of unknown origin.]
**mieve**, *mēv*, (*Spens.*) *v.t.* Same as **move**.
**miff**, *mif*, (*coll.*) *n.* a slight feeling or fit of resentment.—*v.t.* to put out of humour.—*v.i.* to take offence: to wither away.—*adj.* **miff'y**, ready to

take offence or to wither away: touchy.—Also (*obs.*) **mift'y**. [Cf. Ger. *muffen*, to sulk.]

**might**, *mit, pa.t.* of **may** (1).—**might'-have-been**, one who, or that which, might have been, or might have come to something.

**might**, *mit, n.* power: ability: strength: energy or intensity of purpose or feeling.—*adj.* **might'-ful** (*Shak.*), mighty: powerful.—*adv.* **might'ily**. —*n.* **might'iness**, state of being mighty: power: greatness: great amount: a title of dignity: excellency.—*adj.* **might'y**, having greater power: strong: valiant: very great: important: exhibiting might: wonderful.—*adv.* (now *coll.*, usu. with a tinge of irony) very.—**might and main**, utmost strength. [O.E. *miht, meaht;* Ger. *macht;* cf. **may** (1).]

**mignon**, *mē-nyɔ̃*, (Fr.) small and dainty:—*fem.* **mignonne** (*mē-nyon*).

**mignonette**, *min-yə-net', n.* a sweet-scented Reseda: a fine kind of lace. [Fr. *mignonette*, fem. dim. of *mignon*, daintily small, a darling.]

**migraine** (from 18th cent.), *mē'grän*, **megrim** (from 14th cent.), *mē'grim, n.* a pain affecting only one half of the head or face and usu. accompanied by nausea: a condition marked by recurring migraines: (for the fol. meanings, megrim) vertigo: (*pl.*) lowness of spirits: a caprice (*arch.*). [Fr. *migraine*—Gr. *hēmikrāniā*—*hēmi*, half, *krānion*, skull.]

**migrate**, *mī-grāt', v.i.* to pass from one place to another: to change one's abode to another country, college, etc.: to change habitat periodically: to move (as parasites, phagocytes, etc.) to another part of the body: to pass in a stream (as ions, particles).—*n.* **mi'grant**, a person or animal that migrates or is migrating.—Also *adj.*—*adj.* **mi'gratory** (*-grə-tə-ri*), migrating or accustomed to migrate: wandering.—*ns.* **migrā'-tion**, a change of abode: a removal from one country or climate to another, esp. in a body: a number removing together; **migrā'tionist**, one who emigrates: one who explains facts by a theory of migration; **mi'grātor**. [L. *migrāre, -ātum;* cf. *meāre*, to go.]

**mihrab**, *mē-räb', n.* a niche or slab in a mosque marking the direction of Mecca. [Ar. *mihrāb*.]

**mikado**, *mi-kä'dō, n.* a title given by foreigners to the Emperor of Japan. [Jap., exalted gate.]

**mike**, *mik, n.* a contraction of **microphone** and **microscope**.

**mike**. Variant of **mick**.

**mil**, *mil, n.* a unit (1/1000 in.) in measuring the diameter of wire: a proposed coin = £1/1000: in Cyprus, a coin of this value: in pharmacy, a millilitre. [L. *mille*, a thousand.]

**milady**, **miladi**, *mi-lād'i, n.* a French-English term for an English lady of quality. [Fr. modification of **my lady**.]

**milch**, *milch, milsh, adj.* giving milk.—**milch'-cow**, a cow yielding milk or kept for milking: a ready source of gain or money (*fig.*). [O.E. **milce** (found in the compound *thri-milce*, May, when cows can be milked thrice a day); cf. **milk**.]

**mild**, *mild, adj.* gentle in temper and disposition: not sharp or bitter: acting gently: gently and pleasantly affecting the senses: soft: calm.—*v.t.* **mild'en**, to render mild.—*v.i.* to become mild.—*adv.* **mild'ly**.—*n.* **mild'ness**.—**mild ale**, formerly, new ale, without the taste that comes from keeping: now ale with less hop flavouring than pale ale.—*adj.* **mild'-spok'en**, having a mild manner of speech.—**mild steel**, steel with little carbon. [O.E. *milde*, mild; cf. Ger. *mild*, O.N. *mildr*, gracious, etc.]

**mildew**, *mil'dū, n.* honey-dew (*obs.*): a disease on plants, caused by the growth of minute fungi (Erysiphe, Oidium, etc.): a similar appearance on other things or of another kind: a fungus causing the disease.—*v.t.* to taint with mildew.—

*adj.* **mil'dewy**. [O.E. *meledēaw, mildēaw*, from a lost word for honey and *dēaw*, dew; influenced by *melu*, meal.]

**mile**, *mil, n.* a Roman unit of length, 1000 (double) paces (*mille passūs* or *passuum*; about 1611 English yards): applied to various later units, now in Britain and U.S. to one of 1760 yards or 5280 feet (1·61 km.)—*statute mile,*—*ns.* **mil'age**, **mile'age**, length in miles: travelling allowance at so much a mile; **mil'er**, runner of a mile race.—**mile-castle**, a castellum, one of a series placed at intervals along a Roman wall; **mile'stone**, a stone or mark showing distance in miles: a stage or reckoning point.—**geographical** or **nautical mile**, one minute of longitude measured along the equator—6082·66 feet: in British practice, *Admiralty measured mile*, 6080 feet (1·85 km.); *international nautical mile*—official unit in U.S. since 1954—6076·1033 feet, or 1·852 km; Irish mile (*obs.*), 2240 yards; Scots mile (*obs*), about 1976 yards. [O.E. *mil*—L. *milia*, pl. of *mille* (*passuum*), a thousand (paces).]

**Milesian**, *mi-lē'zyən, -zhyən, -zhən*, or *mi-*, *adj.* of **Miletus**, an Ionian Greek city of Asia Minor.—*n.* a native or citizen of Miletus.—**Milesian tales**, witty voluptuous tales, from a lost book so called, by Aristides 'of Miletus' (2nd cent. B.C.). [Gr. *Milēsios*—*Milētos*.]

**Milesian**, *mi-lē'shyən, -shən, -zhyən, -zhən*, or *mi-*, *adj.* of **Milesius** or **Miledh**, a mythical king of Spain, or his sons and their followers who seized Ireland: Irish.—*n.* (usu. jocular) an Irishman.

**milfoil**, *mil'foil, n.* yarrow or other species of Achillea: extended to other plants with finely divided leaves, as **wat'er-mil'foil** (Myriophyllum, family Haloragidaceae). [O.Fr.,—L. *millefolium*—*mille*, a thousand, *folium*, a leaf.]

**miliary**, *mil'i-ər-i, adj.* like a millet-seed: characterised by an eruption like millet-seeds. [L. *miliārius*—*milium*, millet.]

**milieu**, *mēl-yɵ, n.* environment, setting, medium, element. [Fr., middle.]

**militant**, *mil'it-ənt, adj.* fighting: engaged in warfare: actively contending: combative: using violence: militaristic.—*n.* one who takes active part in a struggle: one who seeks to advance a cause by violence.—*n.* **mil'itancy**.—*adv.* **mil'itantly**.—*adj.* **mil'itar** (*obs.*), military.—*n.* **militarisā'tion**, *-z-*.—*v.t.* **mil'itarise**, **-ize**, to reduce or convert to a military model or method: to make militaristic: to subject to military domination.—*ns.* **mil'itarism**, an excess of the military spirit: domination by an army, or military class or ideals: belief in such domination: tendency to overvalue military power or to view things from the soldier's point of view; **mil'itarist**, a soldier (*Shak.*): a student of military science: one imbued with militarism.—*adjs.* **militarist'ic**; **mil'itary**, pertaining to soldiers, armies, or warfare: warlike.—*n.* soldiery: the army: a soldier (*obs.*).—*v.i.* **mil'itate**, to serve as a soldier (*arch.*): to contend: to have weight, tell (esp. with *against*): to fight for a cause.—**military band**; a band of brasses, woodwinds, and percussion; **military cross**, a decoration (M.C.) awarded since 1914 to army officers (below major) and warrant officers; **military medal**, a medal awarded since 1916 to non-commissioned and warrant officers and serving men.—**church militant** (see **church**). [L. *miles, -itis*, a soldier, *militāris*, military, *militāre, -ātum*, to serve as a soldier.]

**militaria**, *mil-it-ā'ri-ə, n.* weapons, uniforms, and other things connected with wars past and present. [*military*, and noun suffix *-ia*.]

**militarise**, etc. See **militant**.

**militia**, *mi-lish'ə, n.* a body of men enrolled and drilled as soldiers, but only liable to home service (transformed in 1908 into the Special Reserve;

again called militia, 1921): the National Guard and its reserve (*U.S.*): a general levy: a territorial force: troops of the second line.— **milit′iaman**. [L. *militia*, military service or force—*miles*, a soldier.]

**milk**, *milk*, *n*. a white liquid secreted by female mammals for the nourishment of their young: a milklike juice or preparation: lactation.—*v.t.* to squeeze or draw milk from: to supply with milk: to extract money, venom, etc., from: to extract: to manipulate as if milking a cow.—*v.i.* to yield milk.—*adj*. **milk′en** (*rare*), of or like milk.—*n*. **milk′er**, one who milks: a machine for milking cows: a cow that gives milk.—*adv*. **milk′ily**.—*ns*. **milk′iness**, cloudiness: mildness; **milk′ing**, the act or art of obtaining milk (*lit*. or *fig*.): the amount of milk drawn at one time.—Also *adj*.—*adjs*. **milk′less**; **milk′like**; **milk′y**, made of, full of, like, or yielding, milk: clouded: soft: gentle.—*adj*. **milk′-and-wa′ter**, insipid: wishy-washy.—**milk′-bar**, a shop where milk, milk-shakes, and the like are sold for drinking on the spot; **milk′-choc′olate**, eating chocolate made from cocoa, cocoa-butter, sugar, and condensed or dried milk; **milk′-cow**, a milch-cow; **milk-denti′tion**, the first set of teeth; **milk′en-way** (*Bacon*), the Milky Way; **milk′-fe′ver**, a fever accompanying the secretion of milk shortly after childbirth: in cows, a congestion of the brain (without fever) after calving; **milk′-float**, vehicle in which milk-bottles are carried; **milk′-gland**, a mammary gland; **milk′-house**, place for keeping milk; **milking-parlour** (see **parlour**); **milk′ing-stool**, a stool on which the milker sits; **milk′ing-time**; **milk′ing-machine**, an apparatus by which a cow is milked; **milk′-kin′ship**, the bond arising from fostering; **milk′-leg**, white-leg.—*adj*. **milk′-liv′ered** (*Shak*.), white-livered.—**milk′-loaf**, a loaf of a sweetish kind of bread; **milk′maid**, a woman who milks; **milk′man**, a man who sells or delivers milk; **milk′-mō′lar**, a grinding milk-tooth, shed and superseded by a premolar; **milk′-porr′idge**, porridge made with milk instead of water; **milk′-pudd′ing**, rice, tapioca, etc., cooked with milk; **milk′-punch**, a drink made of milk, rum or whisky, sugar, and nutmeg; **milk′-run**, a milkman's morning round: a routine flight (*U.S. airmen's slang*); **milk′-shake′**, milk shaken up with a flavouring; **milk′-sop**, a piece of bread sopped or soaked in milk: a soft, unadventurous, effeminate fellow; **milk′-su′gar**, lactose; **milk′-this′tle**, lady's thistle (*Silybum Marianum*), with white-veined leaves; **milk′-tooth**, one of the first or deciduous set of teeth; **milk′-tree**, a tree yielding a milklike nourishing juice, as the cow-tree of Venezuela, the massaranduba of Pará; **milk′-vetch**, a plant of the genus Astragalus, cultivated as fodder and supposed to increase yield of milk; **milk′-walk**, a milkman's round.—*adj*. **milk′-warm**, warm as new milk.—**milk′-weed**, a plant of the genus Asclepias, from its milky juice.—*adj*. **milk′-white**.—**milk′wood**, any of various trees with latex; **milk′wort**, a plant (Polygala) supposed by some to promote production of milk (**sea′-milkwort**, Glaux); **Milky Way**, the Galaxy.—**milk and honey**, abundance, plenty: luxury; **milk of human kindness** (*Shak*.), compassionate nature; **milk of lime**, **of magnesia**, a suspension of calcium hydroxide, magnesium hydroxide, in water; **milk of sulphur**, precipitated sulphur. [O.E. (Mercian) *milc* (W.S. *meolc*), milk; Ger. *milch*, milk; L. *mulgēre*, Gr. *amelgein*, to milk.]

**mill**, *mil*, *n*. a machine for grinding by crushing between hard, rough surfaces, or for more or less similar operations: a building or factory where corn is ground, or manufacture of some kind is carried on, as spinning and weaving, paper-making, sawing of timber: a snuff-box

(commonly **mull**), orig. one with grinding apparatus (*Scot*.): a contest at boxing (*slang*).—*v.t.* to grind: to press, stamp, roll, cut into bars, full, furrow the edges of, or otherwise treat in a mill: to froth up: to beat severely with the fists (*slang*): to revolve in the mind.—*v.i.* to move round in a curve: to practise the business of a miller: to box (*slang*): (often with *about*, *around*; of crowd) to move in an aimless and confused manner.—*adj*. **milled**, prepared by a grinding-mill or a coining-press: transversely grooved on the edge (as a coin or screw-head): treated by machinery, esp. smoothed by calendering rollers in a paper-mill.—*ns*. **mill′er**, one who owns or works a mill; **mill′ing**, the business of a miller: the act of passing anything through a mill: the act of fulling cloth: the process of turning and ridging the edge of a screw-head or coin: a gruelling: aimless and confused movement of a crowd; **milloc′racy** (*obs*.), a governing class of mill-owners, or their rule; **mill′ocrat**.—**mill′-board**, stout pasteboard, used esp. in binding books; **mill′dam**, the dam of a millpond: a millpond: a millrace or tail-race (*Scot*.); **miller's dog**, tope (3); **mill′er's-thumb′**, the bull-head; **mill′-eye′**, the opening by which meal comes from a mill; **mill′-girl**; **mill′-hand′**, a factory worker; **mill′-horse**, a horse that turns a mill; **mill′-owner**; **mill′pond**, a pond to hold water for driving a mill (proverbially smooth): the Atlantic Ocean (*facet*.); **mill′race**, the current of water that turns a mill-wheel, or the channel in which it runs; **mill′-six′pence** (*Shak*.), a milled sixpence; **mill′stone**, one of the two stones used in a mill for grinding corn: a very heavy burden (*fig*.); **mill′stone-grit′**, a hard, gritty sandstone suitable for millstones: (*cap*.) a series of grits, sandstones, shales, underlying the British Coal Measures; **mill′-stream**, the stream of water that turns a mill-wheel; **mill′-tail**, a tail-race; **mill′-tooth**, a molar; **mill′-wheel**, a water-wheel used for driving a mill; **mill′-work**, the machinery of a mill: the planning and putting up of machinery in mills; **mill′wright**, a wright or mechanic who builds and repairs mills.—**gastric mill**, in Malacostraca, a digestive organ, sometimes known as the stomach, provided with muscles and ossicles for trituration of food; **go**, **put**, **through the mill**, to undergo, subject to, probationary hardships, suffering or experience, or severe handing; **run of the mill** (see **run**); **see through a millstone**, to see far into or through difficult questions. [O.E. *myln*—L.L. *molina*—L. *mola*, a mill—*molēre*, to grind.]

**mill**, *mil*, *n*. the thousandth part of a dollar (not coined) (*U.S.*): a mil. [L. *mille*, a thousand.]

**mill**, *mil*, (*slang*) *v.t.* and *v.i.* to rob: to steal.

**mille**, *mēl*, (Fr.) thousand.—**millefeuilles** (*mēl-fœy′*), a layered cake made with puff-pastry; **millefleurs** (*mēl-flœr*), a perfume prepared from many kinds of flowers.

**millefiori**, *mēl-e-fē-ō′rē*, (It.) ornamental glass made by fusing coloured rods together.

**millenary**, *mil′in-ər-i* (also *-ēn′*, or *-en′*), *n*. a thousand: a thousand years: a thousandth anniversary: a signatory of the Millenary Petition (*hist*.): a believer in the millennium.—*adj*. consisting of a thousand, or a thousand years: pertaining to the millennium or to belief in it.—*adj*. **millenā′rian**, pertaining to the millennium.—*n*. a believer in the millennium.—*ns*. **millenā′rianism**, **mill′enārism**. — **Millenary Petition**, a petition of Puritan tendency, signed by nearly a thousand clergymen, presented to James I in 1603. [L. *millēnārius*, of a thousand —*mille*.]

**millennium**, *mil-en′i-əm*, *n*. a thousand years: a thousandth anniversary, millenary: the thousand years after the second coming of Christ: (usu. ironical) a coming golden age:—*pl*. **millenn′ia**.—

*adj.* **millenn'ial.**—*ns.* **millenn'ialist,** a believer in the millennium; **millenn'ianism, millenn'iarism.** [L. *mille,* a thousand, *annus,* a year.]

**millepede.** See millipede.

**millepore,** *mil'i-pōr, -pör, n.* a hydrozoan coral with many pores or polyp-cells. [L. *mille,* a thousand, *porus*—Gr. *poros,* a passage.]

**Millerian,** *mil-ēr'i-ən, adj.* pertaining to W. H. *Miller* (1801-80), mineralogist, or to the crystallographic notation used by him, by which a plane is represented by indices which are the reciprocals of its intercepts on the axes (expressed as fractions of the parameters).—*n.* **mill'erite,** native nickel sulphide, crystallising in needles, named in his honour.

**millesimal,** *mil-es'im-əl, adj.* thousandth: consisting of thousandth parts.—*adv.* **milles'imally.** [L. *millēsimus*—*mille,* a thousand.]

**millet,** *mil'it, n.* a food-grain (*Panicum miliaceum*): extended to other species and genera (*Setaria, Panicum,* etc.).—**mill'et-grass,** a tall panicled woodland grass (*Milium effusum*); **mill'et-seed'.**—*adj.* of the size or appearance of seeds of millet: miliary. [Fr. *millet*—L. *milium.*]

**milli-,** *mil'i-,* in composition, in names of units, a thousandth part.—*ns.* **mill'iampere, mill'iare** (*-är*), **mill'ibar,** etc., a thousandth part of an *ampere, are, bar,* etc.—**millimicro-,** in composition, **nano-** (the preferred term); **millimilli-,** in composition, (better) **micro-.** [L. *mille,* a thousand.]

**milliard,** *mil'yärd, n.* a thousand millions. [Fr.,—L. *mille,* a thousand.]

**milliary,** *mil'i-ər-i, adj.* pertaining to a Roman mile.—*n.* a Roman milestone. [L. *milliārius, -a, -um.*]

**millième,** *mēl-yem, n.* a coin representing one thousandth of the basic unit of currency, as in Egypt. Also **millime** (*mē-lēm*) in Tunisia. [Fr.,—L. *mille,* a thousand.]

**milliner,** *mil'in-ər, n.* orig. a dealer in goods made in *Milan*—'fancy goods': one who makes or sells women's headgear, trimmings, etc.—*n.* **mill'inery,** the articles made or sold by milliners: the industry of making them.—**horse'-mill'iner** (see **horse**). [*Milaner,* a trader in Milan wares, esp. silks and ribbons.]

**million,** *mil'yən, n.* a thousand thousands (1,000,000): a very great number: a million pounds, dollars, etc.: (in *pl.*) the guppy.—Also *adj.*—*n.* **millionaire** (*-ār'*), a man worth a million pounds, dollars, etc. (more or less):—*fem.* **millionair'ess.**—*adj.* **mill'ionary,** pertaining to, or consisting of, millions.—*adj.* and *adv.* **mill'ionfold** (usu. preceded by *a* or a numeral).—*adj.* and *n.* **mill'ionth,** the ten hundred thousandth.—**the million,** the great body of the people generally. [Fr.,—L.L. *milliō, -ōnis*—L. *mille,* a thousand.]

**millipede, millepede,** *mil'i-pēd, n.* any myriapod of the class Chilognatha, vegetarian cylindrical animals with many joints, most of which bear two pairs of legs: a woodlouse (*rarely*).—Also **mill'iped, mill'eped** (*-ped*). [L. *millepeda,* a woodlouse—*mille,* a thousand, *pēs, pedis,* a foot.]

**mill-mountain,** *mil'mownt'ən, n.* purging flax (see **flax**). [Origin unknown.]

**milor, milord,** *mi-lör(d)', n.* a rich Englishman. [Fr. modification of *my lord.*]

**milreis,** *mil'rās, n.* 1000 reis: a Port. coin superseded by the escudo: a coin of Brazil (now cruzeiro). [Port., thousand reis.]

**milsey,** *mil'si,* (*Scot.*) *n.* a milk-strainer. [milk, and either sye or sile.]

**milt,** *milt, n.* the spleen (*anat.*): the soft roe of male fishes.—*v.t.* (of fishes) to impregnate.—*n.* **milt'er,** a male fish. [O.E. *milte,* spleen.]

**Miltonic,** *mil-ton'ik, adj.* relating to *Milton* (1608-1674), or to his poetry, or in his manner.—*adj.* **Miltonian** (*-tōn'i-ən*).—*n.* **Mil'tonism** (*-tən-izm*).

**Miltown,** *mil'town, n.* meprobamate. [Trademark.]

**Milvus,** *mil'vəs, n.* the kite genus.—*adj.* **mil'vine.** [L. *milvus,* a kite.]

**mim,** *mim,* (*Scot.* and *dial.*) *adj.* demure, prim.—*adj.* **mim'-mou'd'** (*-mōōd;* Scots form of **mouthed**). [Imit.]

**mimbar,** *mim'bär,* **minbar,** *min', ns.* a mosque pulpit. [Ar. *minbar.*]

**mime,** *mīm, n.* an ancient farcical play of real life, with mimicry (esp. in its Latin form): an actor in such a farce: a play without dialogue, relying solely on movement, expression, etc.: an actor in such a play: mimicry without words: a mimic: a buffoon.—*v.t.* and *v.i.* to act as a mime: to act with mimicry; to mimic.—*ns.* **mim'er;** **mimesis** (*mim-* or *mīm-ē'sis*), imitation or representation in art: the rhetorical use of a person's supposed or imaginable words: simulation of one disease by another (*med.*): mimicry (*biol.*); **mime'ster.**—*adjs.* **mimet'ic, -al** (*mim-* or *mīm-*), imitative: mimic: pertaining to, showing mimicry or miming.—*adv.* **mimet'ically.**—*ns.* **mimetite** (*mīm', mim'*), a mineral, lead arsenate and chloride (from its resemblance to pyromorphite); **mimic** (*mim'ik*), a mime-actor (*obs.*): one who imitates, esp. one who performs in ludicrous imitation of others' speech and gestures: an unsuccessful imitator or imitation: a plant or animal exemplifying mimicry.—*adj.* **miming** (*obs.*): imitative: mock or sham.—*v.t.* to imitate, esp. in ridicule or so as to incur ridicule: to ape: to produce an imitation of: to resemble deceptively:—*pr.p.* **mim'icking;** *pa.t.* and *pa.p.* **mim'icked.**—*adj.* (*obs.*) **mimical** (*mim'*).—*ns.* **mim'icker;** mimicry (*mim'*), act of mimicking: an advantageous superficial resemblance to some other species or object (*biol.*); **mimog'rapher,** a writer of mimes; **mimog'raphy; Mimus,** the mocking-bird genus. [Gr. *mimos,* a mime, *mīmēsis,* imitation, *mīmētēs,* an imitator.]

**Mimeograph,** *mim'i-ō-gräf, n.* an apparatus for making copies of stencils. [Trademark.]

**mimic, mimmick.** See **minnick.**

**Mimosa,** *mim-ō'zə, n.* the sensitive plant genus: popularly extended to *Acacia* and other genera of the **Mimosā'ceae,** a regular-flowered family of Leguminosae. [Gr. *mīmos,* a mimic.]

**Mimulus,** *mim'ū-ləs, n.* the musk and monkey-flower genus of the figwort family. [Gr. *mīmos,* a mime, with L. dim. suffix *-ulus,* from the grinning corolla.]

**mina,** *mī'nə, n.* a Greek weight, or sum of money, 100 drachmas: a weight of money valued at fifty shekels (*B.*).—Also **maneh** (*mä'ne*), **mna** (*mnä*). [L. *mīna*—Gr. *mnā;* cf. Heb. *māneh.*]

**mina.** Same as **myna.**

**minacious,** *min-ā'shəs, adj.* threatening.—*n.* **minacity** (*-as'*). [L. *mināx, -ācis*—*minārī,* to threaten.]

**minar,** *min-är', n.* a tower.—*n.* **min'aret,** a mosque tower, from which the call to prayer is given. [Ar. *manār, manārat,* lighthouse—*nār,* fire.]

**minatory,** *min'ə-tə-ri* (or *mīn'*), *adj.* threatening. [L. *minārī, -ātus,* to threaten.]

**minauderie,** *mēn-ō-də-rē, n.* a display of affectation. [Fr.]

**mince,** *mins, v.t.* to cut into small pieces: to chop fine: to diminish or suppress a part of in speaking: to pronounce affectedly.—*v.i.* to walk with affected nicety: to speak affectedly:—*pr.p.* **minc'ing;** *pa.t.* and *pa.p.* **minced,** *minst.*—*n.* minced meat: mincemeat.—*n.* **minc'er,** one who minces: a machine for mincing.—*adj.* **minc'ing,** not speaking fully out: speaking or walking with affected nicety.—Also *n.*—*adv.* **minc'ingly.**—**minced collops** (see **collop**); **mince'meat,** meat chopped small—hence anything thoroughly broken or cut to pieces: a chopped mixture of raisins, peel, and other ingredients; **mince-pie',** a

*fāte, fär; mē, hûr* (her); *mīne; mōte, för; mūte; mōōn, fŏŏt; dhen* (then)

pie made with mincemeat, esp. in latter sense. —**make mincemeat of**, destroy utterly (esp. *fig.*); **mince matters, words**, to speak of things with affected delicacy, or to soften an account unduly. [O.Fr. *mincier, minchier*—L. *minūtus*; cf. **minute**.]

**mind**, *mīnd, n.* memory: commemoration (*arch.* or *R.C.*): record, mention (*obs.*): thought: judgment: opinion: purpose (*Shak., Milt.*): inclination: attention: direction of the will: state of thought and feeling: wits, right senses, sanity: consciousness: intellect: that which thinks, knows, feels, and wills: soul: personality: a thinking or directing person.—*v.t.* to remind (*arch.* and *Scot.*): to bring to mind (*Spens.*): to remember (*Scot.*): (*refl.*) to remember (with *of*; *arch.*): to attend to: to tend, have care or oversight of: to be careful about: to beware of: to purpose (*Shak.*): to have a mind to (*dial.*): to apply oneself to: to be troubled by, object to, dislike: to notice (*obs.* or *dial.*).—*v.i.* to remember (with *of*; *dial.*): to attend: to care: to look out, take heed: to be troubled, object.—*adj.* **mind´ed**, inclined: disposed: (in composition) having a mind of such-and-such a kind or inclined towards this or that.—*ns.* **mind´edness**, (in composition) inclination; **mind´er**, one who minds a machine, child, etc.: a child left to be minded (*arch.*).—*adj.* **mind´ful**, bearing in mind: taking thought or care: attentive: observant: having memory (*arch.*): inclined (*obs.*).—*adv.* **mind´fully.**—*n.* **mind´fulness.**—*adj.* **mind´less**, without mind: stupid: unmindful.—*adv.* **mind´lessly.**—*n.* **mind´lessness.**—*adjs.* **mind´-bending**, influencing the mind so that it becomes permanently inclined towards certain beliefs, (also *n.*); **mind´-blowing**, (of a drug) producing a state of ecstasy.—**mind´-cure, mind´-healing**, cure or healing of a diseased mind, or of bodily ailment through the mind or by the supposed influence of a mind; **mind´-curer, -healer; mind´-reading**, thought-reading; **mind´s eye**, visual imagination, mental view, contemplation.—**absence of mind**, inattention to what is going on owing to absorption of the mind in other things; **bear in mind** (see **bear**); **break one's mind** (*obs.*), to make known, confide, or divulge one's thoughts; **change one's mind**, to come to a new resolution or opinion; **cross one's mind** (see **cross**); **do you mind?**, interjection expressing annoyance or disagreement; **do, or would you mind?**, please do: do you object?; **have a (good, great) mind**, to wish or to be inclined strongly; **have half a mind**, to be somewhat inclined; **if you don't mind**, if you have no objection; **in two minds**, wavering; **know one's own mind**, to be sure of one's intentions and opinions: to be self-assured; **make up one's mind**, to come to a decision; **mind one's p's and q's**, to be watchfully accurate and punctilious; **mind your eye** (*slang*), look out; **mind your own business**, this is none of your affair; **month's mind**, commemoration by masses one month after death or burial: strong desire or inclination; **never mind**, do not concern yourself: it does not matter: you are not to be told; **of one (or a) mind**, agreed; **of two minds**, uncertain what to think or do; **on one's mind**, weighing upon one's spirit; **out of mind**, forgotten: out of one's thoughts; **out of one's mind**, mad; **piece of one's mind** (see **piece**); **presence of mind**, a state of calmness in which all the powers of the mind are on the alert and ready for action; **put in mind**, to remind; **set one's mind on**, to fix a settled desire upon; **speak one's mind**, to say plainly what one thinks; **take one's mind off**, to distract from; **time out of mind**, from time immemorial; **to my mind**, to my thinking, in my opinion: to my liking; **year's mind**, a commemorative service on the anniversary of a

death or burial. [O.E. *gemynd*—*munan*, to think; Dan. *minde*, memorial, L. *mēns*, the mind.]

**Mindel**, *min´dl, (geol.) n.* the second glaciation in the Alpine region.—*adjs.* **Min´del, Mindelian** (-*dē´li-ən*). [*Mindel*, a tributary of the Danube, in Bavaria.]

**Mindererus**, *min-dər-ē´rəs, n.* Latinised name of the German physician R. M. *Minderer* (*c.* 1570-1621).—**Mindererus spirit**, ammonium acetate solution, a diaphoretic.

**mine**, *mīn, pron.*, genitive of **I**, used predicatively or absolutely, belonging to me: my people: that which belongs to me: (adjectivally, esp. before a vowel or *h* or after its noun) my (*arch.*). [O.E. *mīn*.]

**mine**, *mīn, n.* a place from which minerals are dug —not usually including building-stone, and legally distinguished from a quarry by being artificially lighted: a cavity in the earth (*arch.*): a burrowing animal's gallery, as an insect's in a leaf: an excavation dug under a position to give secret ingress, to subvert it, or to blow it up (*mil.*): an explosive charge therefor: a submerged or floating charge of explosives in a metal case to destroy ships: a land-mine: a rich source.—*v.t.* to excavate, tunnel, make passages in or under: to obtain by excavation: to work as a mine: to bring down or blow up by a mine: to beset with mines: to lay mines in or under.—*v.i.* to dig or work a mine or mines: to tunnel: to burrow: to lay mines: to proceed secretly, insidiously (*fig.*).—*n.* mi´ner, one who works in a mine: a soldier who lays mines: an insect or other animal that makes galleries in the earth, leaves, etc.—*n.* and *adj.* min´ing.—*adj.* min´y, pertaining to mines: like a mine.—**mine´-captain**, overseer of a mine; **mine´-field**, an area beset with mines; **mine´-layer**, a ship for laying mines; **mine´-owner**; **miner's anaemia**, ankylostomiasis; **miner's inch**, the amount of water that will flow in twenty-four hours through an opening of one square inch at a pressure of six inches of water; **miner's lamp**, a lamp carried by a miner, commonly on his cap; **miner's phthisis**, phthisis caused by breathing dusty air in mines; **miner's worm**, the hookworm that causes ankylostomiasis; **mine´-sweeper**, a vessel for removing mines; **mine´-thrower** (a transl. of Ger. minenwerfer, *mē´nən-ver-fər*, in soldiers' slang minnie, *min´i*), a trench-mortar; **mine´-worker**, a miner. [Fr. *mine* (noun), *miner* (verb), of doubtful origin.]

**mine**, *mīn*, (*Shak., Merry Wives*, I, iii. at end) *n.* perhaps for **mind** (disposition), or **mien**.

**mineral**, *min´ər-l, n.* a substance produced by processes of inorganic nature: a substance got by mining: ore: a substance neither animal nor vegetable: a mine (*Shak.*): a poison (*Shak.*): a mineral water (in a wide sense).—*adj.* relating to minerals: having the nature of minerals: impregnated with minerals, as water: of inorganic substance or nature.—*n.* **mineralisā´tion, -z-.** —*v.t.* **min´eralise, -ize**, to make into a mineral: to give the properties of a mineral to: to go looking for and examining minerals.—*ns.* **mineralis´er, -z-**, one who, that which, mineralises: an element that combines with a metal to form an ore, as sulphur: a gas or vapour that promotes the crystallising out of minerals from an igneous magma; **min´eralist**, one versed in or employed about minerals.—*adj.* **mineralog´ical**, pertaining to mineralogy. — *adv.* **mineralog´ically.** — *v.i.* **mineralogise, -ize** (-*al´*), -to collect or study minerals.—*ns.* **mineral´ogist**, one versed in mineralogy; **mineral´ogy**, the science of minerals. —**mineral al´kali** (*obs.*), sodium carbonate; **mineral caoutchouc**, elaterite; **mineral coal**, coal in the ordinary sense, distinguished from charcoal; **mineral jelly**, a soft yellow substance resembling soft soap, got from the less volatile residue of petroleum; **mineral kingdom,** that department of nature which comprises substances that are neither animal nor vegetable; **mineral oil,** any oil of mineral origin; **mineral pitch,** natural asphalt; **mineral spring, well,** a spring of mineral water; **mineral tallow,** a soft yellowish natural hydrocarbon; **mineral tar, pissasphalt; mineral water,** spring water impregnated with minerals: an artificial imitation thereof: loosely, an effervescent non-alcoholic beverage; **mineral wax,** ozokerite; **mineral wool,** a mass of fibres got by blowing steam through molten slag. [Fr. *minéral—miner,* to mine; cf. **mine** (2).]

**Minerva,** *min-ûr′va, n.* the Roman goddess of wisdom, identified with the Greek Athena.— **Minerva Press,** a London printing-house that issued sentimental novels about 1800. [L., prob. from root of *mēns,* the mind.]

**minestrone,** *min-i-strōn′ē, n.* a thick vegetable soup with pieces of pasta, etc. [It.]

**minette,** *min-et′, n.* an intrusive rock of orthoclase and biotite in a close-grained ground-mass. [Fr.]

**ming,** *ming, meng, meng, menge, menj,* (*arch.*) *v.t.* and *v.i.* to mix: *to unite, couple: to work up: —*pa.t.* and *pa.p.* **minged, menged,** older forms **meint, meynt** (*ment, mănt*), **ment.** [O.E. *mengan;* Ger. *mengen.*]

**Ming,** *ming, n.* a Chinese dynasty (1368-1643).— *adj.* of the dynasty, its time, or esp. its pottery and other art.

**mingle,** *ming′gl, v.t.* and *v.i.* to mix.—*n.* a mixture: a medley.—*ns.* **ming′lement; ming′ler; ming′ling.—***adv.* **ming′lingly.—ming′le-mang′le,** a medley, jumble.—*adj.* jumbled.—*v.t.* to confuse, jumble together. [Freq. of **ming.**]

**mingy,** *min′ji,* (*coll.*) *adj.* niggardly. [Perh. a portmanteau-word from **mangy** or **mean** and **stingy.**]

**mini-,** *min′i-,* in composition, small (abbrev. of **miniature**), as in e.g. the following:—**mini(-) buffet,** a snack-bar on a train; **mini-bus,** a small motor bus; **mini-cab,** a small motor vehicle plying for hire; **mini-car; mini-motorway,** one with two lanes; **mini-skis,** short, slightly thick, skis for learners; **mini-skirt,** a skirt whose hem-line is well above the knees; **mini-sub(marine); mini-track,** a system for tracking an earth satellite or a rocket by radio signals from it to a series of ground stations.—**mini-rocket launcher,** a handgun firing tiny rockets.

**mini.** Abbrev. for **mini-car, mini-skirt.**

**miniate.** See **minium.**

**miniature,** *min′i(-ə)-chər, min′yə-tūr, -tyər, n.* rubrication (*obs.*): manuscript illumination: a painting on a very small scale, on ivory, vellum, etc.: the art of painting in this manner: a small or reduced copy of anything: a chess problem with few pieces or moves.—*adj.* on a small scale: minute.—*v.t.* to represent on a small scale.—*n.* **miniaturisā′tion, -z-.—***v.t.* **min′iaturise, -ize,** to make very small.—*n.* **min′iaturist,** one who paints miniatures. [It. *miniatura—*L. *minium,* red lead; meaning affected by association with L. *minor, minimus,* etc., and their derivatives.]

**minibus,** *min′i-bəs,* (*obs.*) *n.* a light passenger horse-drawn vehicle.—**mini-bus** (see **mini-**). [L. *minor,* less, *minimus,* least, and **omnibus.**]

**Minié,** *min′i-ā, adj.* invented by C. E. *Minié* (died 1879)—applied to a bullet and a rifle adapted to it.

**minify,** *min′i-fī, v.t.* to diminish, in appearance or reality.—*n.* **minificā′tion.** [Ill-formed (after **magnify**) from L. *minor,* less.]

**minikin,** *min′i-kin, n.* a little darling: a diminutive or undersized person or thing: a small sort of pin: the treble string of a lute.—*adj.* diminutive:

dainty: affected: mincing. [Obs. Du. *minneken,* dim. of *minne,* love; cf. **minnesinger.**]

**minim,** *min′im, n.* a least part: a note, formerly the shortest, equal to two crotchets (*mus.*): apothecaries′ measure, one-sixtieth of a fluid drachm: apothecaries weight, a grain: a short down-stroke in handwriting: a diminutive creature (*Milt.*): a friar, sister, or lay member of any of three orders founded by St Francis of Paula (1416-1507)—so called as if humbler than even the Friars Minor.—*adj.* extremely minute. —*adj.* **min′imal,** of, least, or least possible, size, amount, or degree: of the nature of a minimum. —*ns.* **min′imalist,** a Menshevik; **minimisā′tion.— ***v.t.* **min′imise, -ize,** to reduce to the smallest possible amount: to make as light as possible: to estimate at the lowest possible: loosely, to lessen, diminish: loosely, to belittle.—*ns.* **min′imism,** inclination to reduce a dogma to the least possible; **min′imist; min′imum,** the least quantity or degree, or the smallest possible: the lowest point or value reached: in math., a value of a variable at which it ceases to diminish and begins to increase—opp. of *maximum:—pl.* **min′ima.—***adj.* smallest or smallest possible.— *n.* **min′imus,** a being of the smallest size (*Shak.*): in boys′ schools, youngest of the surname.— **minimal art,** art whose practitioners reject such traditional elements as composition and interrelationship between parts of the whole; **minimising glass,** a diminishing glass; **minim rest,** a rest of the duration of a minim; **minimum wage,** the lowest wage permitted by law or regulation for certain work: a fixed bottom limit to workers′ wages in various industries. [L. *minimus, -a, -um,* smallest.]

**miniment,** *min′i-mənt, n.* obs. form of **muniment.**

**minion,** *min′yən, n.* a darling, a favourite, esp. of a prince: a flatterer: a servile dependent: a small kind of type, about 10½ lines to the inch, between nonpareil and brevier (*print.*). [Fr. *mignon, mignonne.*]

**minish,** *min′ish,* (*Spens.*) *v.t.* to make little or less: to diminish. [Fr. *menuiser,* to cut small, said of a carpenter—L. *minūtia,* smallness.]

**minister,** *min′is-tər, n.* a servant (*arch.*): one who administers or proffers, in service or kindness: one who serves at the altar: a clergyman (not now usually, as in *Pr. Bk.,* of the Church of England): the head, or assistant to the head, of several religious orders: one transacting business for another: the responsible head of a department of state affairs: the representative of a government at a foreign court.—*v.i.* to give attentive service: to perform duties: to supply or do things needful: to conduce.—*v.t.* (*arch.*) to furnish.—*adj.* **ministē′rial,** pertaining to a minister or ministry (in any sense): on the government side: administrative: executive: instrumental: conducive.—*n.* **ministē′rialist,** a supporter of the government in office.—*adv.* **ministē′rially.—***adj.* **min′istering,** attending and serving.—*n.* **ministē′rium,** the body of the ordained Lutheran ministers in a district.—*adj.* **min′istrant,** administering: attendant.—*n.* **ministrā′tion,** the act of ministering or performing service: office or service of a minister.—*adj.* **min′istrative** (*-trə-tiv,* or *-trā-tiv*), serving to aid or assist: ministering.—*ns.* **min′istress,** a female who ministers; **min′istry,** act of ministering: service: office or duties of a minister: the clergy: the clerical profession: the body of ministers who manage the business of the country: a department of government, or the building it occupies: term of office as minister.— **Minister of State,** an additional, non-Cabinet, minister in an exceptionally busy government department. [L. *minister—minor,* less.]

**minium,** *min′i-əm, n.* vermilion: red lead: its colour.—*adj.* **min′iate,** of the colour of minium.

—*v.t.* to paint with minium: to illuminate.—*n.*
**miniä'tion.** [L. *minium*, red-lead, also cinnabar.]
**miniver, minever,** *min'i-vər, n.* white fur, orig. a
mixed or variegated fur: the ermine in winter
coat. [O.Fr. *menu*, small—L. *minūtus*, and *vair*,
fur—L. *varius*, particoloured.]
**minivet,** *min'i-vet, n.* a brightly coloured shrike-
like bird (Pericrocotus of several species) of
India, etc. [Etymology unknown.]
**mink,** *mingk, n.* a small animal (of several species)
of the weasel kind: its fur. [Perh. from Sw.
*mänk.*]
**Minkstone,** *mink'stōn, n.* a cast concrete with a
very smooth finish.
**minnesinger,** *min'i-sing-ər,* Ger. *-zing-ər, n.* one
of a 12th-13th cent. school of German amatory
lyric poets, mostly of noble birth. [Ger. *minne*,
love, *singer*, singer.]
**minnick, minnock, minnock, -ək, mimmick, mim',**
(*dial.*) *n.* an affected person.—*v.i.* to be over-
dainty in eating: to behave with affected primness.—In Shak. *Mid. N.D.*, III, ii. 19 by some
amended to *mimic*.
**minnie,** *min'i,* (*Scot.*; *hypocoristic*) *n.* mother.
**minnie.** See under mine (2).
**minnow,** *min'ō, n.* a very small freshwater fish
(*Phoxinus phoxinus*) close akin to chub and dace:
loosely extended to other small fish. [Prob. an
O.E. form related to extant *myne*.]
**mino,** *mē'nō, n.* a raincoat of hemp, etc. [Jap.]
**Minoan,** *min-ō'ən, min-, adj.* pertaining to prehistoric Crete and its culture.—*n.* a prehistoric
Cretan. [Gr. *Minōs*, a legendary king of Crete.]
**minor,** *mi'nər, adj.* lesser: inferior in importance,
degree, bulk, etc.: inconsiderable: lower:
smaller (than major) by a semitone (*mus.*): in
boys' schools, junior: Franciscan.—*n.* a person
under age: the minor term, or minor premise
(*log.*): anything that is minor opposed to major.
—*ns.* minoritaire (*mē-nor-ē-ter'*; Fr.), a member
of a minority section of a party, esp. of socialists;
mi'norite, a Franciscan friar:—*fem.* mi'noress.—
*adj.* Franciscan.—*n.* minority (*min-* or *min-
or'i-ti*), the condition or fact of being little
or less: the state or time of being under age
(also mi'norship): the smaller number: less than
half: the party of smaller numbers: the number
by which it falls short of the other party—opp. to
majority.—*adj.* of the minority.—minor axis, in
conics, that perpendicular to the major axis;
**minor canon** (see canon); **minor key, mode, scale,**
one with its third a minor third above the tonic;
**minor planet,** a small planet, any one of many
hundreds with orbits between those of Mars
and Jupiter; **minor poet,** a genuine but not
great poet; **minor premise** (*log.*), that in which
the minor term occurs; **minor prophets,** the
twelve from Hosea to Malachi in the Old Testament; **minor suit,** in bridge, clubs or diamonds;
**minor term** (*log.*), the term which is the subject
of the conclusion; **minor third** (*mus.*), an interval
of three semitones; **minor tone,** an interval with
a vibration ratio of 9/10. [L. *minor*, less; cf.
minus.]
**Minorca,** *min-ör'ka, n.* a black variety of laying
poultry of Mediterranean family. [From the
island of *Minorca*, Sp. *Menorca*.]
**Minotaur,** *min'* or *min'ə-tör, n.* the bull-headed
monster in the Cretan Labyrinth, offspring of
Pasiphae, wife of Minos. [Gr. *Minōtauros*—
*Minōs*, Minos, *tauros*, bull.]
**minster,** *min'star, n.* a monastery (*obs.*): an abbey
church or priory church: often applied to a
cathedral or other great church without any
monastic connection. [O.E. *mynster*—L. *monas-
tērium*, a monastery.]
**minstrel,** *min'stral, n.* orig. a professional entertainer: a musician: now generally a mediaeval
harper who sang or recited his own or others'
poems: a poet (*poet.*): one of a troupe of

entertainers with blackened faces.—*n.* **min'strelsy**
(*-si*), the art or occupation of a minstrel: music:
a company or body of minstrels: a collection
of songs. [O.Fr. *menestrel*—L.L. *ministeriālis*—
L. *minister*, attendant.]
**mint,** *mint, n.* a place where money is coined, esp.
legally: a source or place of fabrication: a vast
sum of money.—*v.t.* to coin: to invent: to
stamp.—*adj.* in mint condition.—*ns.* **mint'age,**
coining: coinage: stamp: duty for coining;
**mint'er.**—**mint condition, state,** the condition of
a new-minted coin: of books, etc., perfect
condition, as if unused; **mint'-man,** one skilled
in coining or coinage; **mint'-mark,** a mark
showing where a coin was minted; **mint'-master,**
the master of a mint: one who invents. [O.E.
*mynet*, money—L. *monēta*; see **money**.]
**mint,** *mint, n.* any plant of the aromatic labiate
genus Mentha, as spearmint, peppermint, pennyroyal: any labiate (*U.S.*).—*adj.* **mint'y.**—**mint'-
ju'lep** (see julep); **mint'-sauce',** chopped spearmint or other mint mixed with vinegar and sugar,
used as a sauce for roast lamb: punningly,
money. [O.E. *minte*—L. *mentha*—Gr. *minthē*,
*mintha.*]
**mint,** *mint,* (*Scot.*) *v.t.* and *v.i.* to purpose: to
attempt: to aim: to threaten by movement: to
venture: to aspire (with *at*): to hint.—*n.* attempt:
aim: threatening gesture: an incipient movement. [O.E. *myntan*, to mean.]
**minuend,** *min'ū-end, n.* the number from which
another is to be subtracted. [L. *minuendus*
(*numerus*)—*minuĕre*, to lessen.]
**minuet,** *min-ū-et', n.* a slow, graceful dance in
triple measure, invented in Poitou about the
middle of the 17th century: the music for such a
dance: a sonata movement in the same form.
[Fr. *menuet*—*menu*, small—L. *minūtus*, small.]
**minus,** *mi'nəs, prep.* diminished by (*math.*):
deficient in respect of, deprived of, without
(*coll.*).—*adj.* negative.—*n.* a deficiency or subtraction: a negative quantity or term: the
sign (also minus sign) of subtraction or negativity
(−) opposed to *plus*.—**minus strain** (*bot.*), one
of two strains in heterothallism. [L. *minus*,
neut. of *minor*, less.]
**minuscule,** *min'əs-kūl,* or *-us', n.* a small cursive
script, originated by the monks in the 7th-9th
centuries: a manuscript written in it: a lower-
case letter (*print.*): opposed to *majuscule*.—*adj.*
very small, very unimportant.—*adj.* **minus'cular.**
[L. (*littera*) *minuscula*, smallish (letter).]
**minute,** *min-ūt',* or *min-ūt', adj.* extremely small:
having regard to the very small: exact.—*adv.*
**minute'ly.**—*n.* **minute'ness.** [L. *minūtus*, pa.p.
of *minuĕre*, to lessen.]
**minute,** *min'it, n.* the sixtieth part of an hour: the
sixtieth part of a degree: an indefinitely small
space of time: a particular moment: a brief
jotting or note: (in *pl.*) a brief summary of the
proceedings of a meeting: a minute's walk, or
distance traversed in a minute.—*v.t.* to make a
brief jotting or note of: to record in the minutes.
—*adj.* **minutely** (*min'it-li*; *Shak.*), happening once
a minute.—**min'ute-bell,** a bell sounded every
minute, in mourning; **min'ute-book,** a book of
minutes or short notes: **min'ute-drop,** a drop
falling at a minute's interval; **min'ute-glass,** a
sand-glass that runs for a minute; **min'ute-gun,**
a gun discharged every minute, as a signal of
distress or mourning; **min'ute-hand,** the hand
that indicates the minutes on a clock or watch;
**min'ute-jack** (*Shak.*), time-server, or a flighty,
unstable person; **min'uteman** (often *cap.*), a
man ready to turn out at a minute's warning, as
in the American war of independence (*hist.*): a
member of an armed right-wing organisation
in the U.S., formed to take prompt action
against Communist activities; **minute steak,** a
small thin piece of steak which can be cooked

Neutral vowels in unaccented syllables: *el'ə-mənt*; for certain sounds in foreign words, see p. viii

quickly; **min'ute-watch,** a watch that marks minutes; **min'ute-while** (*Shak*.), a minute's time. —up to the minute, right up to date. [Same word as foregoing.]

**minutia,** *mi-nū'shi-ə, n.* a minute particular or detail:—*pl.* **minū'tiae** (*-ē*).—*adj.* minū'tiose (*-shi-ōs*). [L. *minūtia,* smallness.]

**minx,** *mingks, n.* a pert young girl: a jade. [Poss. from minikin; or L.Ger. *minsk, minske,* a wench, jade, cognate with Ger. *mensch,* man, human being.]

**Miocene,** *mi'ō-sēn,* (*geol*.) *adj.* of the Tertiary period preceding the Pliocene and having a smaller proportion of molluscan fossils of species now living.—*n.* the Miocene system, period, or strata. [Gr. *meiōn,* smaller, *kainos,* recent.]

**miosis,** *mī-ō'sis, n.* Same as meiosis.

**mir,** *mēr, n.* a Russian village community. [Russ.]

**Mira,** *mī'rə, n.* a variable star in the constellation Cetus. [L. *mira* (fem.), wonderful.]

**mirable,** *mir'ə-bl, adj.* (*Shak*.) wonderful.—*n.pl.* **mirabi'lia** (L.), wonders.—*n.* Mirabilis (*mir-* or *mir-ab'il-is*), the marvel of Peru genus: (without *cap.*), short for aqua mirabilis. [L. *mirābilis,* wonderful.]

**miracle,** *mir'ə-kl, n.* a supernatural event: hyperbolically, a marvel, a wonder: a miracle play.— *adj.* **miraculous** (*-ak'ū-ləs*), of the nature of a miracle: done by supernatural power: very wonderful: able to perform miracles.—*adv.* **mirac'ulously.** — *n.* **mirac'ulousness.** — **mir'acle-mong'er,** one who pretends to work miracles; **miracle play,** a mediaeval form of drama founded on Old or New Testament history, or the legends of the saints. [Fr.,—L. *mīrāculum*— *mīrāri, -ātus,* to wonder at.]

**mirador,** *mir-ə-dōr', -dör', n.* a belvedere or watchtower. [Sp.]

**mirage,** *mi-räzh', n.* an appearance of objects raised or depressed, erect or inverted, single or double, owing to the varying refractive index of layers of hot and cold air, the sky often simulating the appearance of water: something illusory (*fig*.). [Fr. *mirer,* to look at—L. *mīrāri,* to wonder at.]

**mirbane,** *mûr'bān, n.* apparently meaningless word, used in naming essence, oil of mirbane, nitrobenzene, as used in perfumery.

**mire,** *mir, n.* deep mud.—*v.t.* to plunge and fix in mire: to soil with mud—*v.i.* to sink in mud.— *n.* **mir'iness.**—*adj.* **mir'y,** consisting of mire: covered with mire.—**mire'-drum,** the bittern; **mire'-snipe,** the common snipe. [O.N. *mȳrr,* bog.]

**mirific, -al,** *mir-if'ik, -əl, adjs.* wonder-working: marvellous.—*adv.* **mirif'ically.** [L. *mirificus* —*mirus,* wonderful, *facĕre,* to do.]

**miriti,** *mi-ri-tē', mir'i-ti, n.* any palm of the genus Mauritia. [Tupí.]

**mirk, mirksome.** See murk.

**mirligoes,** *mûr'li-gōz,* (*Scot*.) *n.pl.* dizziness.

**mirliton,** *mûr'li-tən, mēr-lē-tō, n.* a toy reed-pipe. [Fr.]

**mirly.** See marl (4).

**mirror,** *mir'ər, n.* a looking-glass: a reflecting surface: a faithful representation (*fig*.): an example, good or bad.—*v.t.* to reflect an image of, as in a mirror: to furnish with a mirror.— *pr.p.* **mirr'oring;** *pa.p.* **mirr'ored.**—*adj.* and *adv.* **mirr'orwise,** with interchange of left and right.— **mirr'or-im'age,** an image with right and left reversed as in a mirror; **mirror machine,** a device for experimentation in the controlled production of thermonuclear energy, in which gas is tossed to and fro between magnetic mirrors; **mirror nuclides,** pairs of nuclides each containing the same number of protons as the other of neutrons; **mirr'or-writer,** one who writes mirrorwise; **mirr'or-writing,** writing which is like ordinary

writing as seen in a mirror. [O.Fr. *mireor, mirour*—L. *mirāri, -ātus,* to wonder at.]

**mirth,** *mûrth, n.* merriness: pleasure: delight: noisy gaiety: jollity: laughter.—*adj.* **mirth'-ful,** full of mirth: causing mirth: merry: jovial. —*adv.* **mirth'fully.**—*n.* **mirth'fulness.**—*adj.* **mirth'-less.**—*adv.* **mirth'lessly.**—*n.* **mirth'lessness.** [O.E. *myrgth*—*myrige,* merry.]

**MIRV,** *mûrv, n.* a missile containing many thermonuclear warheads, able to attack separate targets. [**M**ultiple **I**ndependently **T**argeted **Re**entry **V**ehicle.]

**Mirza,** *mûr'zə, mēr'zə, n.* as a Persian title (after a name) Prince: (before) official or learned man. [Pers. *mirzā, mīrzā.*]

**mis-,** *mis-, pfx.* wrong, ill, e.g. *misbehave, misdeed, mislead.* [O.E. *mis-;* O.N. *mis-,* Goth. *missa-,* Ger. *miss-;* cf. miss (1).].

**mis,** *mis,* (*Spens*.) *v.i.* to do amiss: to fail. [miss (1).]

**misacceptation,** *mis-ak-sep-tā'shən, n.* understanding in a wrong sense. [Pfx. mis-.]

**misadventure,** *mis-əd-ven'chər, n.* ill-luck: mishap: accidental killing.—*adjs.* misadvent'ured (*Shak*.), unfortunate: misadvent'urous.—*n.* misadvent'-urer. [M.E.—O.Fr., *mesaventure.*]

**misadvertence,** *mis-əd-vûrt'əns, n.* inadvertence. [Pfx. mis-.]

**misadvise,** *mis-əd-vīz', v.t.* to advise ill.—*adj.* **misadvised'.**—*adv.* misadvi'sedly.—*n.* misadvis'-edness. [Pfx. mis-.]

**misaim,** *mis-ām', v.t.* to aim ill. [Pfx. mis-.]

**misallege,** *mis-ə-lej', v.t.* to allege wrongly. [Pfx. mis-.]

**misalliance,** *mis-ə-li'əns, n.* an unsuitable alliance, esp. marriage with one of a lower rank.—*adj.* **misallied'.** [Fr. *mésalliance.*]

**misallot,** *mis-ə-lot', v.t.* to allot wrongly.—*n.* misallot'ment. [Pfx. mis-.]

**misanthrope,** *mis'ən-thrōp, n.* a hater of mankind, one who distrusts everyone else—also misanthropist (*mis-an'throp-ist*).—*adjs.* misanthropic, **-al** (*mis-an-throp'ik, -əl*), hating or distrusting mankind—*adv.* misanthrop'ically.—*ns.* misan'thropos (*Shak*.), a misanthrope; misan'thropy, hatred or distrust of mankind. [Gr. *mīsanthrōpos*— *mīseein,* to hate, *anthrōpos,* a man.]

**misapply,** *mis-ə-plī', v.t.* to apply wrongly: to use for a wrong purpose.—*n.* misapplicā'tion (*-ap-*). [Pfx. mis-.]

**misappreciate,** *mis-ə-prē'shi-āt, v.t.* to fail to appreciate rightly or fully.—*n.* misappreciā'tion. —*adj.* misappre'ciative. [Pfx. mis-.]

**misapprehend,** *mis-ap-ri-hend', v.t.* to apprehend wrongly: to take or understand in a wrong sense. —*n.* misapprehen'sion.—*adj.* misapprehen'sive.— *adv.* misapprehen'sively, by or with misapprehension or mistake.—*n.* misapprehen'siveness. [Pfx. mis-.]

**misappropriate,** *mis-ə-prō'pri-āt, v.t.* to put to a wrong use: to take dishonestly for oneself.—*n.* misappropriā'tion. [Pfx. mis-.]

**misarrange,** *mis-ə-rānj', v.t.* to arrange wrongly: to put in wrong order.—*n.* misarrange'ment. [Pfx. mis-.]

**misarray,** *mis-ə-rā', n.* want of proper order. [Pfx. mis-.]

**misassign,** *mis-ə-sīn', v.t.* to assign wrongly. [Pfx. mis-.]

**misaunter,** *mis-ön'tər,* (*obs*.) *n.* misadventure. [O.Fr. *mesaventure,* see aunter.]

**misavised,** *mis-ə-vīz'id,* (*Spens*.) *adj.* ill-advised.

**misbecome,** *mis-bi-kum', v.t.* to be unbecoming or unsuitable to.—*adj.* misbecom'ing.—*n.* mis-becom'ingness. [Pfx. mis-.]

**misbegot, misbegotten,** *mis-bi-got', -got'n, adj.* unlawfully begotten (*Shak*.): monstrous. [Pfx. mis-, and *pa.p.* of beget.]

**misbehave,** *mis-bi-hāv', v.t.* (*refl*.) and *v.i.* to behave ill or improperly.—*adj.* **misbehaved'**

(*Shak.*), badly behaved: ill-bred.—*n.* misbe-hav′iour. [Pfx. mis-.]

**misbelieve,** *mis-bi-lēv′*, *v.t.* to believe wrongly or falsely.—*ns.* misbelief′ (or *mis′*), belief in false doctrine; misbeliev′er.—*adj.* misbeliev′ing. [Pfx. mis-.]

**misbeseem,** *mis-bi-sēm′*, *v.t.* to suit ill. [Pfx. mis-.]

**misbestow,** *mis-bi-stō′*, *v.t.* to bestow improperly, or on the wrong person.—*n.* misbestow′al. [Pfx. mis-.]

**misborn,** *mis′börn*, or *mis-börn′*, *adj.* abortive: deformed from birth: base-born.—*n.* misbirth′, an abortion. [Pfx. mis-.]

**miscalculate,** *mis-kal′kū-lāt*, *v.t.* and *v.i.* to cal-culate wrongly.—*n.* miscalculā′tion. [Pfx. mis-.]

**miscall,** *mis-köl′*, *v.t.* to call by a wrong name: (*Spens.*; now mainly *Scots*—also misca′) to call by an ill name: to abuse or revile. [Pfx. mis-.]

**miscarriage,** *mis-kar′ij*, *n.* an act or instance of miscarrying: failure: failure to reach the in-tended result or destination: ill-conduct (*obs.*): act of bringing forth prematurely, esp. of ex-pelling a fetus between the third and seventh months.—*v.i.* miscarr′y, to be unsuccessful: to fail of the intended effect: to bring forth before the proper time: to be born prematurely.—*v.t.* (*obs.*) to lead astray.—miscarriage of justice, failure of the courts to do justice. [Pfx. mis-.]

**miscast,** *mis-käst′*, *v.t.* and *v.i.* to cast (in any sense) amiss or blameworthily. [Pfx. mis-.]

**miscegenation,** *mis-i-jin-ā′shan*, *n.* mixing of race: interbreeding, intermarriage, or sexual inter-course between different races.—*v.i.* misc′egen-ate, to practise miscegenation.—*v.t.* to produce by miscegenation.—*adj.* mixed in race.—*ns.* miscegenā′tionist, misc′egenātor, miscegenist (*mis-ej′in-ist*), one who favours or practises misce-genation; miscegen (*mis′i-jən*), misc′egene (*-jēn*), misc′egine (*-jin*, *-jin*), an individual of mixed race. [L. *miscēre*, to mix, *genus*, race.]

**miscellaneous,** *mis-əl-ān′i-əs*, *adj.* mixed or mingled: consisting of several kinds.—*adj.* mis-cellanarian (*-ən-ā′ri-ən*).—*n.* a writer of mis-cellanies.—*adv.* miscellān′eously.—*ns.* miscel-lān′eousness; miscellanist (*mis-el′ən-ist*, or *mis′əl-*), a writer of miscellanies; miscellany (*mis-el′*, or *mis′əl-*), a mixture of various kinds: a collection of writings on different subjects or by different authors.—*n.pl.* miscellā′nea (L. *neut. pl.*), a miscellany. [L. *miscellāneus*—*miscēre*, to mix.]

**mischallenge,** *mis-chal′ənj*, (*Spens.*) *n.* a wrongful challenge. [Pfx. mis-.]

**mischance,** *mis-chäns′*, *n.* ill-luck: mishap.—*v.i.* to chance wrongly: to come to ill-luck.—*adjs.* mischance′ful; mischan′cy (*chiefly Scot.*), un-lucky: dangerous. [M.E.—O.Fr. *meschance*.]

**mischanter,** *mis-chän′tər*, mishanter, *mi-shän′*, (*Scot.*) *n.* an unlucky chance, misfortune. [aunter; perh. influenced by obs. *mischant*, *meschant*—O.Fr. *mescheant* (Fr. *méchant*), un-lucky, wicked.]

**mischarge,** *mis-chärj′*, *v.t.* to charge wrongly.—*n.* a mistake in charging. [Pfx. mis-.]

**mischief,** *mis′chif*, *n.* an ill consequence: evil: injury: damage, hurt: the troublesome fact: a source of harm: petty misdeeds or annoyance: pestering playfulness: a mischievous person: the devil (*coll.*).—Also *v.t.*—*adj.* mischievous (*mis′chiv-əs*; *Spens.* usu. *-chēv′*), causing mischief: injurious: prone to mischief.—*adv.* mis′chievously.—*n.* mis′chievousness.—mis′chief-maker, one who stirs up strife.—*n.* and *adj.* mis′chief-making. [O.Fr. *meschef*, from *mes*- (from L. *minus*, less) and *chef*—L. *caput*, the head.]

**mischmetal,** *mish′met-l*, *n.* an alloy of cerium with rare-earth metals and iron, used to produce the spark in cigarette and other lighters. [Ger. *mischen*, to mix, and metal.]

**miscible,** *mis′si-bl*, *adj.* that may be mixed.—*n.* miscibil′ity. [L. *miscēre*, to mix.]

**miscolour,** *mis-kul′ər*, *v.t.* to colour falsely: to give a wrong meaning to: to misrepresent. [Pfx. mis-.]

**miscomprehend,** *mis-kom-pri-hend′*, *v.t.* to mis-understand.—*n.* miscomprehen′sion. [Pfx. mis-.]

**miscompute,** *mis-kəm-pūt′*, *v.t.* to reckon wrongly. —*n.* miscomputā′tion (*-kom-*), wrong com-putation: false reckoning. [Pfx. mis-.]

**misconceit,** *mis-kən-sēt′*, (*Spens.*) *n.* misconception. —*v.t.* to have wrong conception of. [Pfx. mis-.]

**misconceive,** *mis-kən-sēv′*, *v.t.* and *v.i.* to conceive wrongly: to mistake: to suspect (*obs.*).—*n.* misconcep′tion. [Pfx. mis-.]

**misconduct,** *mis-kon′dukt*, *n.* bad conduct: wrong management: adultery.—*v.t.* misconduct (*-kən-dukt′*). [Pfx. mis-.]

**misconjecture,** *mis-kən-jek′chər*, *n.* a wrong con-jecture or guess.—*v.t.* or *v.i.* to guess or con-jecture wrongly. [Pfx. mis-.]

**misconster,** *mis-kon′stər*, obs. form of miscon-strue.

**misconstruction,** *mis-kən-struk′shən*, *n.* wrong con-struction, construing, or interpretation: faulty construction.—*v.t.* misconstruct′. [Pfx. mis-.]

**misconstrue,** *mis-kən-strōō′*, or *-kon′strōō*, *v.t.* to construe or to interpret wrongly. [Pfx. mis-.]

**miscontent,** *mis-kən-tent′*, (*arch.*) *n.*, *adj.*, and *v.t.*, discontent.—*adj.* miscontent′ed.—*n.* miscontent′-ment. [Pfx. mis-.]

**miscopy,** *mis-kop′i*, *v.t.* to copy wrongly or imper-fectly.—*n.* an error in copying. [Pfx. mis-.]

**miscorrect,** *mis-kə-rekt′*, *v.t.* to alter or mark wrongly in would-be correction.—*n.* miscor-rec′tion. [Pfx. mis-.]

**miscounsel,** *mis-kown′sl*, *v.t.* to advise wrongly. [Pfx. mis-.]

**miscount,** *mis-kownt′*, *v.t.* to count wrongly: to misjudge.—*n.* a wrong counting. [Pfx. mis-.]

**miscreant,** *mis′kri-ənt*, *n.* orig. a misbeliever, a heretic or infidel: a vile wretch, a detestable scoundrel.—*adj.* unbelieving (*arch.*): depraved, ill-doing.—*n.* mis′creance, mis′creaunce (*Spens.*), false religious belief. [O.Fr. *mescreant*—*mes*- (from L. *minus*, less) and L. *crēdēns*, *-entis*, pr.p. of *crēdēre*, to believe.]

**miscreate, -d,** *mis-krē-āt′*, *-id*, *adjs.* created amiss: deformed.—*n.* miscreā′tion.—*adj.* miscreā′tive, inclining towards wrong creation.—*n.* mis-creā′tor. [Pfx. mis-.]

**miscredit,** *mis-kred′it*, *v.t.* to disbelieve. [Pfx. mis-.]

**miscreed,** *mis-krēd′*, *n.* a false creed. [Pfx. mis-.]

**miscue,** *mis-kū′*, *n.* at billiards, a stroke spoiled by the slipping off of the cue. [Pfx. mis-, or miss (2).]

**misdate,** *mis-dāt′*, *v.t.* to date wrongly.—*n.* a wrong date. [Pfx. mis-.]

**misdeal,** *mis-dēl′*, *n.* a wrong deal, as at cards.—*v.t.* and *v.i.* to deal wrongly: to divide improp-erly:—*pa.t.* and *pa.p.* misdealt (*-delt′*). [Pfx. mis-.]

**misdeed,** *mis-dēd′*, *n.* wrong-doing, an evil deed. [O.E. *misdǣd*.]

**misdeem,** *mis-dēm′*, *v.t.* and *v.i.* to think ill (of): to think or judge wrongly (of): to suspect:—*pa.p.* misdeemed′, (*Spens.*) misdempt′.—*adjs.* mis-deem′ful; misdeem′ing, misjudging: suspicious: deceiving (*Spens.*).—*n.* misjudgment: suspicion. [Pfx. mis-.]

**misdemean,** *mis-di-mēn′*, *v.t.* (*refl.*) and *v.i.* to misbehave.—*ns.* misdemean′ant, one guilty of petty crime, or misconduct; misdemean′our, bad conduct: a misdeed: formerly a legal offence of less gravity than a felony. [Pfx. mis-, demean (1).]

**misdesert,** *mis-di-zùrt′*, (*Spens.*) *n.* ill-desert. [Pfx. mis-.]

**misdevotion,** *mis-di-vō′shən*, *n.* ill-directed devo-tion. [Pfx. mis-.]

**misdid.** See misdo.

**misdiet,** *mis-di'ət,* (*Spens.*) *n.* improper feeding. [Pfx. mis-.]

**misdight,** *mis-dit',* (*Spens.*) *adj.* ill-arranged: in sorry plight. [Pfx. mis-.]

**misdirect,** *mis-di-rekt',* *v.t.* to direct wrongly.—*n.* **misdirec'tion.** [Pfx. mis-.]

**misdo,** *mis-dōō',* *v.t.* to do wrongly or badly: to injure (*obs.*): to kill (*obs.*).—*v.i.* to act amiss: —*pa.t.* **misdid'**; *pa.p.* **misdone'**; old *infin.* (*Spens.*) **misdonne'.**—*ns.* misdo'er; misdo'ing. [Pfx. mis-.]

**misdoubt,** *mis-dowt',* *v.t.* to have a doubt, suspicion, misgiving, or foreboding of or about: to suspect.—*n.* suspicion: hesitation: misgiving.—*adj.* **misdoubt'ful.** [Pfx. mis-.]

**misdraw,** *mis-drö',* *v.t.* to draw or draft badly.—*n.* misdraw'ing. [Pfx. mis-.]

**misdread,** *mis-dred',* (*Shak.*) *n.* dread of evil to come. [Pfx. mis-.]

**mise,** *mēz, miz, n.* expenditure, outlay (*obs.*): in Wales and the county palatine of Chester, a payment to a new king, prince, Lord of the Marches, or earl, to secure certain privileges: the issue in a writ of right: the adjustment of a dispute by agreement (*hist.*): a stake in gambling: the layout of cards.—**mise(-)en(-)scène** (*mē-zä-sen*), act, result, or art, of setting a stage scene or arranging a pictorial representation. [O.Fr. *mise*, placing or setting—L. *mittĕre, missum.*]

**misease,** *mis-ēz',* (*arch.*) *n.* distress: uneasiness. [O.Fr. *mesaise.*]

**miseducation,** *mis-ed-ū-kā'shən, n.* improper or hurtful education. [Pfx. mis-.]

**misemploy,** *mis-im-ploi',* *v.t.* to employ wrongly or amiss: to misuse.—*n.* misemploy'ment. [Pfx. mis-.]

**misentreat,** *mis-in-trēt',* *v.t.* to ill-treat. [Pfx. mis-, and **entreat** (to treat).]

**misentry,** *mis-en'tri, n.* a wrong entry. [Pfx. mis-.]

**miser,** *mī'zər, n.* a wretch (*Spens., Shak.*): one who lives miserably in order to hoard wealth: a niggard.—*adj.* like a miser.—*n.* mi'serliness.—*adj.* mi'serly. [L. *miser,* wretched.]

**miser,** *miz'ər, n.* a well-boring instrument. [Origin doubtful.]

**miserable,** *miz'ə-rə-bl, adj.* wretched: exceedingly unhappy: causing misery: extremely poor or mean: contemptible.—*n.* a wretch: very weak tea.—*n.* mis'erableness.—*adv.* mis'erably. [Fr. *misérable*—L. *miserābilis*—*miser.*]

**misère,** *mē-zer', mis-ār', n.* in card games, an undertaking to take no tricks. [Fr. *misère,* misery.]

**Miserere,** *miz-e-rē'ri, mis-e-rā're, n.* the 50th Psalm of the Vulgate (51st in A.V.)—from its first word (*R.C.*): a musical setting of it: (without *cap.*) a misericord in a church stall. [L., 2nd pers. sing. imper. of *miserēri,* to have mercy, to pity—*miser,* wretched.]

**misericord, misericorde,** *miz-er'i-körd,* or *miz'ər-,* or *-körd', n.* mercy, forgiveness, pity (*obs.*): a relaxation of monastic rule: a room in a monastery where some relaxation of rule was allowed: a bracket on a turn-up seat in a choirstall, allowing the infirm some support when standing: a narrow-bladed dagger for killing a wounded foe. [O.Fr. *misericorde*—L. *misericordia*—*misericors, -cordis,* tender-hearted.]

**misery,** *miz'ər-i, n.* wretchedness: extreme pain: miserable conditions: misère (*cards*): avarice (*Shak.*): very unhappy experience: a doleful person (*coll.*). [O.Fr.,—L. *miseria.*]

**misesteem,** *mis-es-tēm',* *n.* disrespect.—*v.t.* to value wrongly.—*v.t.* mises'timate, to estimate wrongly. [Pfx. mis-.]

**misfaith,** *mis-fāth', n.* distrust. [Pfx. mis-.]

**misfall,** *mis-föl',* (*obs.*) *v.t.* to befall unluckily:—*pa.t.* misfell'; *pa.p.* misfall'en (*Spens.* misfalne'). [Pfx. mis-.]

**misfare,** *mis-fār',* (*Spens.*) *n.* misfortune.—*v.i.*

to fare ill.—*n.* misfar'ing (*Spens.*), wrong-doing. [O.E. *misfaran.*]

**misfeasance,** *mis-fēz'əns,* (*law*) *n.* the doing of a lawful act in a wrongful manner, as distinguished from *malfeasance.*—*n.* misfeas'or. [O.Fr. *mesfaisance*—pfx. *mes-* (from L. *minus,* less) *faisance*—*faire*—L. *facĕre,* to do.]

**misfeature,** *mis-fē'char, n.* ill feature, trait, or aspect: deformity.—*adjs.* misfeat'ured, ill-featured; misfeat'uring, distorting the features. [Pfx. mis-.]

**misfeign,** *mis-fān', v.i.* to feign with bad design. [Pfx. mis-.]

**misfire,** *mis-fīr', v.i.* to fail to go off, explode, or ignite, at all or at the right time: to fail to have the effect intended (*fig.*).—*n.* a failure to fire, or to achieve effect. [miss, fire.]

**misfit,** *mis'fit, n.* a bad fit: a thing that fits badly: a person who cannot adjust himself to his social environment, or his job, etc.—*v.t.* and *v.i.* (*mis-fit'*) to fit badly. [Pfx. mis-.]

**misform,** *mis-förm', v.t.* to form or shape badly or improperly.—*n.* misformā'tion. [Pfx. mis-.]

**misfortune,** *mis-för'tūn, n.* ill-fortune: an evil accident: calamity: an illegitimate child, or the having of one (*coll.*).—*adj.* misfor'tuned (*arch.*), unfortunate. [Pfx. mis-.]

**misgive,** *mis-giv', v.t.* to suggest apprehensions to fill with forebodings: to give amiss.—*v.i.* to have, apprehensive forebodings: to fail (*Scot.*).—*pa.t.* misgave'; *pa.p.* misgiv'en.—*n.* misgiv'ing, mistrust: a feeling that all is not well. [Pfx. mis-.]

**misgo,** *mis-gō',* (*obs.* or *dial.*) *v.i.* to go astray or amiss:—*pa.t.* wanting (**miswent,** supplied from **miswend**); *pa.p.* misgone (*mis-gon'*; *obs.,* now illit., **miswent**). [Pfx. mis-.]

**misgotten,** *mis-got'n,* (*Spens.*) *adj.* ill-gotten: misbegotten. [Pfx. mis-.]

**misgovern,** *mis-guv'ərn, v.t.* to govern badly or unjustly.—*ns.* misgov'ernauce (*Spens.*), mismanagement; misgov'ernment. [Pfx. mis-.]

**misgraff,** *mis-gräf,* (*Shak.*) **misgraft,** *mis-gräft', v.t.* to graft unsuitably. [Pfx. mis-.]

**misgrowth,** *mis-grōth', n.* an irregular growth: an excrescence: a sport of nature. [Pfx. mis-.]

**misguggle,** *mis-gug'l,* **mishguggle,** *mish-,* (*Scot.*) *v.t.* to bungle, mar. [Pfx. mis-.]

**misguide,** *mis-gīd', v.t.* to guide wrongly: to lead into error: to ill-treat (*Scot.*).—*n.* (*obs.*) misbehaviour.—*n.* misguid'ance.—*adj.* misguid'ed, erring: misdirected: ill-judged.—*adv.* misguid'edly. [Pfx. mis-.]

**mishallowed,** *mis-hal'ōd, adj.* consecrated to evil. [Pfx. mis-.]

**mishandle,** *mis-han'dl, v.t.* to handle amiss or unskilfully: to maltreat. [Pfx. mis-.]

**mishanter.** Same as mischanter.

**mishap,** *mis-hap', n.* ill chance: unlucky accident: misfortune.—*v.i.* to happen unfortunately.—*v.i.* mishapp'en (*Spens.*), to happen ill. [Pfx. mis-.]

**mishappt** (*Spens.*), for misshaped.

**mishear,** *mis-hēr', v.t.* and *v.i.* to hear wrongly. [Pfx. mis-.]

**mishit,** *mis-hit', v.t.* to hit faultily.—*n.* (*mis'hit*), a faulty hit. [Pfx. mis-.]

**mishmash,** *mish'mash, n.* a hotch-potch, medley. [Redup. of mash (1).]

**mishmee, mishmi,** *mish'mē, n.* the bitter tonic rootstock of an Assamese gold-thread (*Coptis teeta*). [Said to be Assamese *mishmitita.*]

**Mishnah, Mishna,** *mish'nä, n.* the Jewish oral law, finally redacted A.D. 220:—*pl.* Mishnayōth'.—*adjs.* Mishnā'ic, Mish'nic. [Heb. *mishnāh*—*shānāh,* to repeat, teach, learn.]

**misimprove,** *mis-im-prōōv', v.t.* to turn to bad use: to make worse by would-be improvement.—*n.* misimprove'ment. [Pfx. mis-.]

**misinform,** *mis-in-förm', v.t.* to inform or tell incorrectly.—*ns.* misinform'ant; misinformā'-tion; misinform'er. [Pfx. mis-.]

misinstruct, *mis-in-strukt'*, *v.t.* to instruct amiss.— *n.* misinstruc'tion, wrong instruction. [Pfx. mis-.]

misintelligence, *mis-in-tel'i-jəns*, *n.* wrong or false information: misunderstanding: want of intelligence. [Pfx. mis-.]

misintend, *mis-in-tend'*, (*obs.*) *v.t.* to intend or aim in malice. [Pfx. mis-.]

misinterpret, *mis-in-tûr'prit*, *v.t.* to interpret wrongly: to explain wrongly.—*ns.* misinterpretā'tion; misinter'preter. [Pfx. mis-.]

misjoin, *mis-join'*, *v.t.* to join improperly or unfitly. —*n.* misjoin'der (*law*), an incorrect union of parties or of causes of action in a suit. [Pfx. mis-.]

misjudge, *mis-juj'*, *v.t.* and *v.i.* to judge wrongly.— *n.* misjudg'ment—also misjudge'ment. [Pfx. mis-.]

misken, *mis-ken'*, (*Scot.*) *v.t.* to be, or to appear, ignorant of: to fail or refuse to recognise. [Pfx. mis-.]

misknow, *mis-nō'*, *v.t.* to misapprehend.—*n.* misknowledge (*mis-nol'ij*). [Pfx. mis-.]

mislay, *mis-lā'*, *v.t.* to place amiss: to lay in a place not remembered: to lose:—*pa.t.* and *pa.p.* mislaid'. [Pfx. mis-, and lay (3).]

mislead, *mis-lēd'*, *v.t.* to draw into error: to cause to mistake:—*pa.t.* and *pa.p.* misled'.—*n.* mislead'er.—*adj.* mislead'ing, deceptive.—*adv.* mislead'ingly. [Pfx. mis-.]

misleared, *mis-lērd'*, (*Scot.*) *adj.* mistaught: unmannerly: ill-conditioned. [Pfx. mis-.]

misleeke, *mis-lēk'*, (*Spens.*) *v.i.* for mislike.

misletoe. A former spelling of mistletoe.

mislight, *mis-līt'*, *v.t.* to lead astray by a light. [Pfx. mis-.]

mislike, *mis-līk'*, (*arch.*) *v.t.* to dislike: to displease.—*v.i.* to disapprove.—*n.* dislike: disapprobation. [Pfx. mis-.]

mislippen, *mis-lip'n*, (*Scot.*) *v.t.* to distrust: to suspect: to disappoint, deceive: to neglect, overlook. [Pfx. mis-.]

mislive, *mis-liv'*, *v.i.* to live a bad life. [Pfx. mis-.]

misluck, *mis-luk'*, *n.* ill-luck.—*v.i.* to meet with bad luck, to fail. [Pfx. mis-.]

mismake, *mis-māk'*, *v.t.* to make amiss, shape ill. —*pa.p.* and *adj.* mismade'. [Pfx. mis-.]

mismanage, *mis-man'ij*, *v.t.* to conduct badly: to conduct carelessly.—*n.* misman'agement. [Pfx. mis-.]

mismanners, *mis-man'ərz*, *n.pl.* bad manners. [Pfx. mis-.]

mismarry, *mis-mar'i*, *v.t.* and *v.i.* to marry unsuitably.—*n.* mismarr'iage. [Pfx. mis-.]

mismatch, *mis-mach'*, *v.t.* to match unsuitably.— *n.* a bad match.—*n.* mismatch'ment. [Pfx. mis-.]

mismate, *mis-māt'*, *v.t.* and *v.i.* to mate unsuitably.—*adj.* mismat'ed. [Pfx. mis-.]

mismeasure, *mis-mezh'ər*, *v.t.* to measure wrongly. —*n.* mismeas'urement. [Pfx. mis-.]

mismetre, *mis-mēt'ər*, *v.t.* to spoil the metre of. [Pfx. mis-.]

misname, *mis-nām'*, *v.t.* to call by an unsuitable or wrong name. [Pfx. mis-.]

misnomer, *mis-nō'mər*, *n.* a misnaming: a wrong or unsuitable name.—*v.t.* to misname. [O.Fr. from *mes-* (from L. *minus*, less) and *nommer*— L. *nōmināre*, to name.]

miso-, *mis-ō-*, *mis-ō-*, in composition, hater of, hating.—*adjs.* misocap'nic (Gr. *kapnos*, smoke), hating smoke, esp. that of tobacco; mis'oclere (-*klēr*; Gr. *kleros*, clergy; *Fuller*), hating the clergy.—*ns.* misogamist (-*og'ə-mist*; Gr. *gamos*, marriage), a hater of marriage; misog'amy; misogynist (-*oj'i-nist*, -*og'*; Gr. *gynē*, a woman), a woman-hater.—*adjs.* misogynist'ical, misog'ynous.—*ns.* misog'yny; misology (-*ol'ə-ji*; Gr. *logos*, reason), hatred of reason, reasoning, or knowledge; misol'ogist; misoneism (-*nē'izm*; Gr. *neos*, new), hatred of novelty; misonē'ist.— *adj.* misonēist'ic. [Gr. *mīseein*, to hate.]

misobserve, *mis-ob-zûrv'*, *v.t.* and *v.i.* to fail to observe: to observe amiss or incorrectly.—*n.* misobserv'ance. [Pfx. mis-.]

misocapnic . . . to . . . misoneistic. See miso-.

misorder, *mis-ör'dər*, *n.* and *v.t.* disorder. [Pfx. mis-.]

mispersuasion, *mis-pər-swā'zhən*, (*rare*), *n.* a wrong persuasion or notion: a false opinion.—*v.t.* mispersuade'. [Pfx. mis-.]

mispickel, *mis'pik-əl*, *n.* arsenical pyrites, a mineral composed of iron, arsenic, and sulphur. [Ger.]

misplace, *mis-plās'*, *v.t.* to put in a wrong place: to mislay: to set on an improper object (*fig.*), or indulge in in unsuitable circumstances (*fig.*).— *n.* misplace'ment. [Pfx. mis-.]

misplay, *mis-plā'*, *n.* a wrong play.—Also *v.t.* and *v.i.* [Pfx. mis-.]

misplead, *mis-plēd'*, *v.t.* and *v.i.* to plead wrongly. —*n.* misplead'ing, an error in pleading. [Pfx. mis-.]

misplease, *mis-plēz'*, *v.t.* to displease. [Pfx. mis-.]

mispoint, *mis-point'*, *v.t.* to punctuate wrongly. [Pfx. mis-.]

mispraise, *mis-prāz'*, *v.t.* to praise amiss: to dispraise. [Pfx. mis-.]

misprint, *mis-print'*, *v.t.* to print wrong.—*v.i.* to make footprints in unusual positions.—*n.* (*mis'-print*, *mis'print'*) a mistake in printing. [Pfx. mis-.]

misprise, misprize, *mis-prīz'*, *v.t.* to scorn: to slight: to undervalue.—*n.* (*Spens.* mesprise, mesprize, misprize) scorn: slighting: failure to value. [O.Fr. *mespriser*—pfx. *mes-* (from L. *minus*, less), L.L. *pretiāre*—L. *pretium*, price, value.]

misprise, misprize, *mis-prīz'*, *v.t.* to mistake.— *n.* (*Spens.* mesprize) error.—*adj.* misprised', mistaken. [O.Fr. *mespris*, pa.p. of *mesprendre*, to commit an offence; cf. misprision (1).]

misprision, *mis-prizh'ən*, *n.* mistake: criminal oversight or neglect in respect to the crime of another (*law*): any serious offence, failure of duty—*positive* or *negative*, according as it is maladministration or mere neglect.—misprision of heresy, treason, etc., knowledge of and failure to give information about heresy, treason, etc. [O.Fr. *mes-* (from L. *minus*, less), L.L. *prēnsiō, -ōnis*—L. *praehendere*, to take.]

misprision, *mis-prizh'ən*, *n.* failure to appreciate. [misprise (1), after the model of misprision (1).]

mispronounce, *mis-prə-nowns'*, *v.t.* to pronounce incorrectly.—*n.* mispronunciation (-*nun-si-ā'-shən*), wrong or improper pronunciation. [Pfx. mis-.]

misproportion, *mis-prə-pōr'shən*, -*pör'*, *n.* lack of due proportion.—*adj.* mispropor'tioned. [Pfx. mis-.]

misproud, *mis-prowd'*, *adj.* unduly proud. [Pfx. mis-.]

mispunctuate, *mis-pungk'tū-āt*, -*pungk'chōō-*, *v.t.* and *v.i.* to punctuate wrongly.—*n.* mispunctuā'tion. [Pfx. mis-.]

misquote, *mis-kwōt'*, *v.t.* to quote wrongly.—*n.* misquotā'tion. [Pfx. mis-.]

misrate, *mis-rāt'*, *v.t.* to value wrongly. [Pfx. mis-.]

misread, *mis-rēd'*, *v.t.* to read wrongly.—*n.* mis'-read'ing. [Pfx. mis-.]

misreckon, *mis-rek'n*, *v.t.* and *v.i.* to reckon or compute wrongly.—*n.* misreck'oning. [Pfx. mis-.]

misregard, *mis-ri-gärd'*, (*Spens.*) *n.* inattention. [Pfx. mis-.]

misrelate, *mis-ri-lāt'*, *v.t.* to relate incorrectly.— *n.* misrelā'tion.—misrelated participle, a participle which the grammatical structure of the sentence insists on attaching to a word it is not intended to qualify (e.g. *Lost in thought, the bus passed me without stopping*). [Pfx. mis-.]

misremember, *mis-ri-mem'bər*, *v.t.* and *v.i.* to

remember wrongly or imperfectly: to forget (*dial.*). [Pfx. mis-.]

**misreport,** *mis-ri-pōrt'*, *-pŏrt'*, *v.t.* to report falsely, misleadingly, or wrongly: to speak ill of (*Shak.*).—*n.* false reporting or report: ill repute (*obs.*). [Pfx. mis-.]

**misrepresent,** *mis-rep-ri-zent'*, *v.t.* to represent falsely: to give a misleading interpretation to the words or deeds of: to be an unrepresentative representative of.—*n.* misrepresentā'tion. [Pfx. mis-.]

**misrule,** *mis-rōōl'*, *n.* disorder: bad or disorderly government.—*v.t.* and *v.i.* to govern badly.—**Lord of Misrule,** a leader of Christmas revels. [Pfx. mis-.]

**Miss,** *mis*, *n.* a title prefixed to the name of an unmarried (formerly, and now *dial.* and *U.S. illit.*, also a married) woman or girl (at first less respectful than *Mrs*): also prefixed to a representational title, esp. in beauty contests, e.g. *Miss World*: (without the name) an eldest daughter, young lady of the house (*obs.*): vocatively used alone in displeasure, real or assumed, otherwise *coll.* (esp. in addressing a waitress): (without *cap.*) a schoolgirl, or girl or woman with the faults attributed to schoolgirls: person between a child and a woman: a kept mistress (*obs.*):—*pl.* **miss'es**—either 'the Miss Hepburns' or 'the Misses Hepburn' may be said, but the latter is more formal.—*n.* **miss'-hood.**—*adj.* **miss'ish,** schoolgirlish: having the faults attributed to schoolgirls—sentimental, insipid, namby-pamby, squeamish, silly, etc.—*ns.* **miss'ishness; miss'y** (usu. subservient) the little girl.—*adj.* **missish.**—**Miss Nancy** (*coll.*), a very effeminate man. [Shortened form of **mistress.**]

**miss,** *mis*, *v.t.* (or *v.i.*, *arch.*, with *of*) to fail to hit, reach, find, meet, touch, catch, get, have, take advantage of, observe, see: to avoid (a specified danger): to fail (to do; *arch.*): to omit: to discover the absence of: to feel the want of: to leave out: to do without (*Shak.*).—*v.i.* to fail to hit or obtain: to fail: to go wrong (*obs.*): to miss fire.—*n.* the fact or condition or an act or occasion of missing: failure to hit the mark: loss: feeling of loss or absence: wrong-doing (*Shak.*).—*adj.* **miss'ing,** not to be found: not in the expected place: wanting: of unascertained fate (*mil.*).—*adv.* **miss'ingly** (*Shak.*), with sense of loss.—**give a miss,** in billiards, to allow an opponent to score by intentionally missing: to leave out, omit, avoid anything; **miss fire,** to fail to go off or explode (cf. **misfire**): **miss one's tip** (*slang*), to fail in one's plan or attempt; **miss stays** (*naut.*), to fail in going about from one tack to another; **miss the bus** (or **boat**) (*coll.*), to lose one's opportunity; **near miss,** (*lit.* and *fig.*; see under **near**). [O.E. *missan*; Du. *missen*, to miss.]

**miss.** See **Miss.**

**missa** (also *cap.*) *mis'ə*, *-a*, (L.) the Mass (*R.C.*).—**missa, Missa solemnis** (*sol-em'nis*), high mass.

**missal,** *mis'l*, *n.* a book containing the complete service for mass throughout the year. [L.L. *missāle*, from *missa*, mass.]

**missay,** *mis-sā'*, (*arch.*) *v.t.* and *v.i.* to say or speak amiss, wrongly, falsely, or in vain: to slander: to revile:—*pa.t.* and *pa.p.* **missaid** (*-sed'*).—*n.* **missay'ing.** [Pfx. mis-.]

**missee,** *mis-sē'*, *v.t.* and *v.i.* to see wrongly. [Pfx. mis-.]

**misseem,** *mis-sēm'*, (*Spens.*) *v.t.* to misbecome.—*adj.* **misseem'ing,** unbecoming.—*n.* false appearance. [Pfx. mis-.]

**missel,** *mis'l*, *miz'l*, *n.* mistletoe (*obs.*): the missel-thrush.—**miss'el-thrush,** a large thrush fond of mistletoe berries.—Also **miss'el-bird.** [O.E. *mistel*, *mistil*, mistletoe.]

**missel-tree,** *mis'l-trē*, *n.* a melastomaceous tree

(*Bellucia aubletii*) of northern South America, with edible berries.

**missend,** *mis-send'*, *v.t.* to send by mistake: to send to the wrong person or place:—*pa.t.* and *pa.p.* **missent'.** [Pfx. mis-.]

**misset,** *mis-set'*, *v.t.* to set or place wrongly or unfitly: to put out of humour (*Scot.*). [Pfx. mis-.]

**misshape,** *mis-shāp'*, *v.t.* to shape ill: to deform.—*n.* deformity.—*adjs.* **misshap'en,** **misshaped'** (*Spens.* mishapt), ill-shaped.—*n.* **misshap'enness.** [Pfx. mis-.]

**missheathed,** *mis-shēdh'id*, (*Shak.*) *adj.* wrongly sheathed. [Pfx. mis-.]

**missile,** *mis'il*, *mis'l*, *adj.* capable of being thrown or projected: pertaining to a missile.—*n.* a weapon or object for throwing by hand or shooting from a bow, gun, or other instrument, esp. a rocket-launched weapon, often nuclear-powered. [L. *missilis*—*mittēre*, *missum*, to throw].

**missing.** See **miss** (*vb.*).

**mission,** *mish'ən*, *n.* an act of sending, esp. to perform some function: a flight with a specific purpose, as a bombing raid or a task assigned to an astronaut or astronauts: the errand or purpose for which one is sent: that for which one has been or seems to have been sent into the world, vocation: a sending out of persons on a political or diplomatic errand, for the spread of a religion, or for kindred purpose: an organisation that sends out missionaries: its activities: a station or establishment of missionaries: any particular field of missionary enterprise: the body of persons sent on a mission: an embassy: a settlement for religious, charitable, medical, or philanthropic work in a district: a religious organisation or district not fully developed as a parish: a series of special religious services conducted by a missionary.—*adj.* of a mission or missions, esp. characteristic of the old Spanish missions in California.—*v.t.* (*rare*) to commission.—*v.t.* and *v.i.* **miss'ionarise, -ize,** to act as missionary (to, among, or in).—*n.* **miss'ionary,** one sent upon a mission, esp. religious.—*adj.* pertaining to missions.—*n.* **miss'ioner,** one who conducts a series of special mission services.—*v.t.* and *v.i.* **miss'ionise, -ize,** to do missionary work (upon, in, among).—**mission architecture,** the style of the old Spanish missions in California, etc.; **miss'ionary-bish'op,** one having jurisdiction in an unconverted country, or in districts not yet formed into dioceses. [L. *missiō, -ōnis*—*mittēre*, to send.]

**missis, missus,** *mis'is*, *-iz*, *n.* (*illit.*, *coll.*) mistress of the house: wife. [**mistress.**]

**missive,** *mis'iv*, *adj.* sent: missile (*obs.*).—*n.* that which is sent, as a letter: messenger (*Shak.*): a missile (*obs.*):—*n.pl.* letters sent between two parties in which one makes an offer and the other accepts it (*Scots law*).—**letter missive,** a missive, esp. from a sovereign or authority to a particular person or body, as one giving *congé d'élire*. [L.L. *missivus*—L. *mittēre*, *missum*, to send.]

**misspeak,** *mis-spēk'*, *v.t.* and *v.i.* to speak wrongly. [Pfx. mis-.]

**misspell,** *mis-spel'*, *v.t.* and *v.i.* to spell wrongly:—*pa.t.* and *pa.p.* **misspelt', misspelled'.**—*n.* **misspell'ing,** a wrong spelling. [Pfx. mis-.]

**misspend,** *mis-spend'*, *v.t.* to spend ill: to waste or squander:—*pa.t.* and *pa.p.* **misspent'.** [Pfx. mis-.]

**misstate,** *mis-stāt'*, *v.t.* to state wrongly or falsely.—*n.* **misstate'ment.** [Pfx. mis-.]

**misstep,** *mis-step'*, *v.i.* to make a false step: to make a mistake.—*n.* a mistake in conduct, etc. [Pfx. mis-.]

**missuit,** *mis-sōōt'*, *-sūt'*, *v.t.* to be unbecoming to. [Pfx. mis-.]

**missummation,** *mis-sum-ā'shən, n.* wrong addition. [Pfx. mis-.]

**missus.** See missis.

**mist,** *mist, n.* watery vapour seen in the atmosphere: cloud in contact with the ground: thin fog: rain in very fine drops: a suspension of liquid in a gas: a dimness or dim appearance: anything that dims or darkens the sight or the judgment.—*v.t.* to obscure or veil with mist or as with mist.—*v.i.* to become misty or veiled.— *adj.* mist'ful, misty.—*adv.* mist'ily.—*ns.* mist'iness; mist'ing, mist.—*adj.* misty: hazy: dimming.—*adj.* mist'y, full of, covered with, obscured by, mist: like mist: dim: obscure: clouded: vague: not perspicuous.—*mist'-flower,* a North American hemp-agrimony, with clusters of blue or violet flowers.—**Scotch mist,** a thick wetting mist: a drizzle. [O.E. *mist,* darkness, dimness; Ice. *mistr,* Du. *mist.*]

**mistake,** *mis-tāk', v.t.* to remove wrongfully (*obs.*): (app.) to take or come upon to his loss (*Spens.*): to understand wrongly: to take for another thing or person: to be wrong about: to think wrongly: to believe wrongly to be (*Spens.*).— *v.i.* to err in opinion or judgment: to do amiss: —*pa.t.* mistook'; *pa.p.* mistak'en, also mista'en'. —*n.* a taking or understanding wrongly: an error: (*mis'*) a faulty shot in cinematography. —*adjs.* mistak'able; mistak'en, understood wrongly: guilty of or under a mistake: erroneous: incorrect: ill-judged.—*adv.* mistak'enly.—*ns.* mistak'enness; mistak'ing (*Shak.*), a mistake.— **and no mistake** (*coll.*), assuredly: be mistaken, to make or have made a mistake: to be misunderstood; **mistake one's man,** think too lightly of the man one has to deal with; **mistake one's way,** take the wrong road. [M.E. *mistaken*—O.N. *mistaka,* to take wrongly—*mis-,* wrongly, *taka,* to take.]

**misteach,** *mis-tēch', v.t.* to teach wrongly:—*pa.t.* and *pa.p.* mistaught (*mis-töt'*). [Pfx. mis-.]

**mistell,** *mis-tel', v.t.* to count, narrate, or inform, wrongly:—*pa.t.* and *pa.p.* mistold'. [Pfx. mis-.]

**mistemper,** *mis-tem'pər,* (*obs.*) *n.* and *v.t.* disorder. —*adj.* mistem'pered, tempered or mixed ill (*Shak.*): tempered for an evil purpose (*Shak.*). [Pfx. mis-.]

**mister,** *mis'tər, n.* craft, trade, profession (*obs.*): manner, kind (Spens.; without *of*—what mister man, orig. = man of what class, hence what kind of man): need, necessity (*Scot.*).—*v.i.* (*Spens.*) to be necessary: to have need.—*v.t.* to need.—*n.* mis'tery (see mystery (2)). [O.Fr. *mestier* (Fr. *métier*), trade—L. *ministerium,* service.]

**Mister,** *mis'tər, n.* a title prefixed to a man's name, and to certain designations (as Mr Justice, Mr Speaker), written Mr: sir (*coll., illit.*).—*v.t.* mis'ter (*illit.*), to address as 'mister'. [master.]

**misterm,** *mis-tûrm', v.t.* to name wrongly or unsuitably. [Pfx. mis-.]

**mistery.** Same as mystery (2).

**misthink,** *mis-thingk', v.t.* to think ill of (*Shak.*): to think wrongly.—*v.i.* to have wicked or mistaken thoughts (*obs.*):—*pa.t.* and *pa.p.* misthought (*mis-thöt'*).—*n.* misthought', a wrong notion. [Pfx. mis-.]

**mistico,** *mis'ti-kō, n.* a small Mediterranean coaster, between a xebec and a felucca. [Sp. *místico,* prob. from Ar.]

**mistigris,** *mis'ti-gris, n.* a variation of poker in which a joker or blank card can be given any value: the card so used. [Fr. *mistigri,* knave of clubs.]

**mistime,** *mis-tīm', v.t.* to time wrongly.—*adj.* mistimed', unseasonable. [Pfx. mis-.]

**mistitle,** *mis-ti'tl, v.t.* to call by an unsuitable title. [Pfx. mis-.]

**mistle.** Same as mizzle or missel.

**mistletoe,** *mis'l-tō,* or *miz', n.* a hemiparasitic evergreen shrubby plant (*Viscum album*) with white viscous fruits, growing on the apple, apricot, etc. (very rarely on the oak): extended to other species of its genus or family (Loranthaceae). [O.E. *misteltān*—*mistel, mistil,* mistletoe, *tān,* twig; see missel.]

**mistook,** *mis-töök', pa.t.* of mistake.

**mistral,** *mis'tral, n.* a violent cold dry north-west wind in southern France. [Fr.,—Prov. *mistral*— L. *magistrālis,* masterful, *magister,* master.]

**mistranslate,** *mis-trans-lāt', v.t.* and *v.i.* to translate incorrectly.—*n.* mistranslā'tion. [Pfx. mis-.]

**mistrayned,** *mis-trānd',* (*Spens.*) *pa.p.* drawn away, misled. [Pfx. mis-; see train (1).]

**mistreading,** *mis-tred'ing,* (*Shak.*) *n.* a false step, misdeed. [Pfx. mis-.]

**mistreat,** *mis-trēt', v.t.* to treat ill.—*n.* mistreat'ment. [Pfx. mis-.]

**mistress,** *mis'tris, n.* (*fem.* of master) a woman employer of servants or head of a house or family: a woman (or anything personified as a woman) having power of ownership: a woman teacher, esp. in a school: a woman well skilled in anything: a woman loved and courted: a concubine: vocatively madam (*arch.* and *dial.*): the jack at bowls (*Shak.*): (*cap.*; *mis'iz*; now usu. written Mrs; *fem.* of Mister, Mr), a title prefixed to the name, once of any woman or girl, now ordinarily of a married woman, sometimes also prefixed to a designation.—*adj.* principal: leading: ruling.—*v.t.* to make a mistress of, pay court to as a mistress: to address as mistress: to become or be mistress of or over: (with *it*) to play the mistress.—*adjs.* mis'tressless; mis'tressly.—*n.* mis'tress-ship. [O.Fr. *maistresse* (Fr. *maîtresse*)—L.L. *magistrissa,* fem. from L. *magister,* master.]

**mistrial,** *mis-trī'əl, n.* a trial void because of error: an inconclusive trial (*U.S.*). [Pfx. mis-.]

**mistrust,** *mis-trust', n.* distrust.—*v.t.* to distrust: to suspect.—*v.i.* to have suspicion.—*adj.* mistrust'ful.—*adv.* mistrust'fully.—*n.* mistrust'fulness.—*adv.* mistrust'ingly.—*adj.* mistrust'less. [Pfx. mis-.]

**mistryst,** *mis-trīst',* (*Scot.*) *v.t.* to disappoint by not keeping an engagement.—*adj.* mistryst'ed, disturbed, put out. [Pfx. mis-.]

**mistune,** *mis-tūn', v.t.* to tune wrongly or falsely: to put out of tune. [Pfx. mis-.]

**misunderstand,** *mis-und-ər-stand', v.t.* to take in a wrong sense: to fail to appreciate the true nature, motives, etc. of:—*pa.t.* and *pa.p.* misunderstood'. —*n.* misunderstand'ing, a mistake as to meaning: a slight disagreement.—*adj.* misunderstood'. [Pfx. mis-.]

**misuse,** *mis-ūs', n.* improper use: application to a bad purpose: evil usage or behaviour (*Shak.*). —*v.t.* misuse (*mis-ūz'*), to use for a wrong purpose or in a wrong way: to treat ill: to speak ill of (*Shak.*): to deceive (*Shak.*):—*pa.t.* (*Spens.*) misust (*ūst'*).—*n.* misus'age, misconduct, evil practice (*Spens.*): ill-usage: wrong use. [Pfx. mis-.]

**misventure,** *mis-ven'chər, n.* a misadventure.— *adj.* misvent'urous. [Pfx. mis-.]

**miswandered,** *mis-won'dərd,* (*Spens.*) *adj.* strayed over. [Pfx. mis-.]

**misween,** *mis-wēn', v.t.* and *v.i.* to judge wrongly, have a wrong opinion of (*Spens.*). [Pfx. mis-.]

**miswend,** *mis-wend',* (*Spens.*) *v.i.* to go astray or amiss: to come to grief, miscarry:—*pa.t.* and *pa.p.* miswent' (see misgo).

**misword,** *mis-wûrd', n.* (*dial.*) an angry or harsh word.—*v.t.* to word incorrectly.—*n.* misword'ing. [Pfx. mis-.]

**misworship,** *mis-wûr'ship, v.t.* to worship wrongly. —*n.* worship of a wrong object. [Pfx. mis-.]

**miswrite,** *mis-rit', v.t.* to write incorrectly. [Pfx. mis-.]

**misyoke,** *mis-yōk', v.t.* to yoke or marry unsuitably. [Pfx. mis-.]

**mite**, *mīt*, *n.* a very small acaridan arachnid.—*adj.* **mit'y**, infested with mites. [O.E. *mīte*.]

**mite**, *mīt*, *n.* orig. an old Flemish coin of very small value: used to translate the Gr. *lepton* of which two make a *kodrantēs* or 'farthing' (Mark xii. 42) (*B*): vaguely, a very small amount: a small contribution proportionate to one's means: a minute portion or fragment: a jot: a diminutive person: a small child. [M.Du. *mite* (Du. *mijt*); perh. ult. the same as the preceding.]

**miter**, American spelling of **mitre**.

**Mithras**, *mith'ras*, **Mithra**, *-rä*, *n.* the ancient Persian light-god, whose worship became popular in the Roman Empire.—*n.* **Mithraeum** (*-rē'əm*), a grotto sacred to Mithras:—*pl.* **Mithrae'a**.—*adj.* **Mithrä'ic**.—*ns.* **Mithrä'icism**, **Mith'raism** (*-rä-izm*); **Mith'raist**. [L. and Gr. *Mithrās*—O.Pers. *Mithra*.]

**mithridate**, *mith'ri-dāt*, *n.* an antidote to poison, *Mithridates* (better, *Mithradātēs*), king of Pontus (reigned *c.* 120-63 B.C.), having traditionally made himself proof against poisons.—*adj.* **Mithridatic**, **Mithradatic** (*-dat'ik*), pertaining to Mithridates, esp. of his wars against Rome.—*n.* **mith'ridatism** (*-dāt-izm*), acquired immunity to a poison.— **mithridate mustard**, field penny-cress (*Thlaspi arvense*); **mithridate pepperwort**, field cress (*Lepidium campestre*).

**mitigate**, *mit'i-gāt*, *v.t.* to mollify, appease: to make more easily borne: to lessen the severity, violence, or evil, of: to temper.—*adjs.* **mit'igable** and **mit'igant**, mitigating.—*n.* **mitigā'tion**.—*n.* and *adj.* **mit'igative**.—*n.* **mit'igātor**.—*adj.* **mit'igātory**. [L. *mitigāre*, *-ātum*—*mitis*, mild.]

**mitochondria**, *mit-*, *mit-ō-kon'dri-ə*, *n.pl.* thread-like bodies in cytoplasm. [Gr. *mitos*, thread, *chondros*, granule.]

**mitosis**, *mī-*, *mi-tō'sis*, *n.* an elaborate process of cell-division involving the arrangement of proto-plasmic fibres in definite figures—karyokinesis. —*adj.* **mitotic** (*-tot'ik*). [Gr. *mitos*, fibre.]

**mitraille**, *mē'trī-y'*, *n.* small shot or projectiles sent in a shower, esp. from a mitrailleuse.—*ns.* **mitrailleur** (*yœr'*), a machine-gunner: a mitrailleuse; **mitrailleuse** (*-yœz'*), a machine-gun that discharges a stream of small missiles. [Fr.]

**mitre**, *mī'tər*, *n.* a Greek (or later) woman's head-fillet: a girdle (*Pope*, following *Homer*): an eastern hat or turban: a high head-dress, cleft on top, worn by archbishops and bishops, and by some abbots: episcopal dignity (*fig.*): a gasteropod of the genus *Mitra* or its conical shell (**mit're-shell**): a gusset in sewing, etc.—*v.t.* to adorn with a mitre.—*adjs.* **mi'tral**, of or like a mitre: of the mitral valve; **mit'riform** (*mit'*, or *mīt'*), mitre-shaped.—**mitral valve**, a mitre-shaped valve of the heart. [Fr.,—Gr. *mitrā*, fillet.]

**mitre**, *mī'tər*, *n.* a joint (also **mi'tre-joint**) in which each piece is cut at an angle of 45° to its side, giving a right angle between the pieces: sometimes applied to any joint where the plane of junction bisects the angle: an angle of 45°: a gusset, a tapered insertion.—*v.t.* to join with a mitre: to turn a corner in, by cutting out a triangular piece and joining (*needlework*).—*v.i.* to meet in a mitre.—**mi'tre-wheel**, a bevel-wheel having its face inclined 45° to its axis. [Prob. same as above.]

**mitt**, *mit*, *n.* a mitten: a hand (*slang*). [Abbrev. of **mitten**.]

**mitten**, *mit'n*, *n.* a kind of glove, without a separate cover for each finger: a glove for the hand and wrist, but not the fingers: a boxing-glove: dismissal (*slang*): (in *pl.*) handcuffs (*slang*).— *adj.* **mitt'ened**, covered with a mitten or mittens. —**mitt'en-crab**, a Chinese crab that can do damage to river banks.—**frozen mitten** (*slang*), chilly reception, the cold shoulder; **get the**

**mitten** (*slang*), to be dismissed, esp. as a suitor. [O.Fr. *mitaine*; origin obscure.]

**mittimus**, *mit'i-mas*, *n.* a warrant granted for sending to prison a person charged with a crime (*law*): a writ by which a record is transferred out of one court to another (*law*): dismissal, discharge (*coll.*): a nickname for a magistrate. [L., we send—*mittĕre*, to send.]

**Mitty** (**Walter Mitty**), a nobody who lives a life of imaginary roles as a somebody: an intrepid day-dreamer. [From the hero of a short story by James Thurber.]

**mitzvah**, *mits'və*, *mits-vä'*, *n.* a good deed:—*pl.* **-voth** (*-vōt'*), **-vahs**. [Heb., (lit.) commandment.]

**miurus**, *mi-ū'ras*, *n.* a hexameter with short pen-ultimate syllable. [Latinised from Gr. *meiouros*, curtailed—*meiōn*, less, *ourā*, a tail.]

**mix**, *miks*, *v.t.* to combine so that the parts of one thing or things of one set are diffused among those of another: to prepare or compound in like manner: to blend: to mingle: to join: to combine in one film (*cinematography*): to confound: to associate: to interbreed, cross: to involve.—*v.i.* to become mixed: to be joined: to associate: to have intercourse.—*n.* a mixing: a mixture, esp. a standard mixture: a formula giving constituents and proportions: a jumble, a mess.—*adj.* **mixed** (*mikst*), mingled: promiscuous: of or for both sexes: miscellaneous: confused: not select: combining characters of two or more kinds: between front and back (*phon.*).—*adj.* **mix'edly** (or *mikst'li*).—*ns.* **mixed'-ness**; **mix'er**, one who mixes: that by which or in which things are mixed: one who is easily sociable in all sorts of company: one who mixes drinks; **mix-in'**, a fight (*U.S.*).—*adj.* **mixt** (same as **mixed**).—Also *pa.p.* and *pa.t.*— *ns.* **mix'ter-max'ter**, **mix'tie-max'tie**, **mix'ty-max'ty**, **mix'y-max'y** (all *Scot.*), a confused jumble.—*adjs.* and *advs.* in a confused jumble.— *ns.* **mixtion** (*miks'chən*), a mixture of amber, mastic, and asphaltum used as a mordant for gold-leaf: mixture (*obs.*); **mix'ture** (*-chər*), act of mixing: state of being mixed: the product of mixing: a product of mixing in which the in-grēdients retain their properties—distinguished from *compound* (*chem.*): in an organ, a compound-stop giving harmonics: a mixture of petrol vapour and air (*motoring*).—*adj.* **mix'y**, mixed.—**mixed chalice**, the chalice prepared for the eucharist, containing the wine mixed with water; **mixed doubles**, tennis matches with a male and a female player as partners on each side; **mixed foursome**, a golf match with a male and female player as partners on each side; **mixed marriage**, one between persons of different religions or races.—*adj.* **mixed'-mē'dia**, of a work in the arts, combining traditional forms, e.g. acting, dance, painting, and electronic media, e.g. tape recording.—**mixed metaphor** (see **metaphor**); **mixed train**, railway train made up partly of passenger carriages and partly of goods wagons.—*adj.* **mixed'-up'**, socially confused, bewildered, and ill-adjusted.—**mix'-up'**, confusion: a confused jumble.—**mix it** (*slang*), to fight forcefully. [L. *miscēre*, *mixtus*, to mix; exact relation to O.E. *miscian*, Ger. *mischen*, uncertain.]

**mixen**, *miks'n*, *n.* a dunghill. [O.E. *mixen*—*mix*, *meox*, dung.]

**mixo-**, *miks-ō-*, in composition, mixed.—*adjs.* **mixobarbar'ic**, part barbaric, part Greek; **mixo-lyd'ian**, in ancient Greek music the same as hyperdorian: in old church music applied to an authentic mode extending from *g* to *g*, with *g* for its final; **mixotroph'ic** (*biol.*), combining different modes of nutrition. [Gr. *mixis*, mixing, *misgein*, to mix.]

**mizmaze**, *miz'māz*, *n.* a labyrinth: bewilderment. [**maze**.]

**mizzen, mizen**, *miz'n*, *n.* in a three-masted vessel,

the hindmost of the fore-and-aft sails: the spanker or driver.—*adj.* belonging to the mizzen: nearest the stern.—mizz'en-course; mizz'en-mast; mizz'en-sail. [Fr. *misaine*, foresail, foremast—It. *mezzana*, mizzen-sail—L.L. *mediānus*, middle—L. *medius*, middle; the development of meaning is puzzling.]

mizzle, *miz'l*, *v.i.* to rain in small drops.—*n.* fine rain.—*n.* mizz'ling.—*adj.* mizz'ly. [Cf. L.Ger. *miseln*, mist.]

mizzle, *miz'l*, (*slang*) *v.i.* to decamp. [Origin obscure.]

mizzle, *miz'l*, *v.t.* to confuse. [Origin obscure.]

mizzonite, *miz'ən-it*, *n.* a scapolite richer in sodium than meionite. [Gr. *meizōn*, greater, from its longer vertical axis.]

Mjöllnir, Mjölnir, *myœl'nir*, *n.* Thor's terrible hammer. [O.N.]

mna. See mina (1).

mneme, *nē'mē*, *n.* a memory-like capacity of living matter for after-effect of stimulation of the individual or an ancestor.—*adj.* mnē'mic, pertaining to the mneme.—*ns.* mne'mon, a hypothetical unit of memory; mnemonic (*nimon'ik*), a device, e.g. verse, to help memory: (in *pl.*, treated as *sing.*) art of assisting memory. —*adj.* pertaining to the mneme.—*adj.* mnemon'-ical.—*ns.* mnē'monist, a teacher or practitioner of mnemonics: one from whose memory nothing is erased; Mnemosyne (*nē-mos'i-nē*, or *-moz'*), the Greek Goddess of memory, mother of the Muses.—*adj.* mnemotechnic (*nē-mō-tek'nik*), mnemonic.—*ns.* mnemotech'nics, mnemonics; mnemotech'nist. [Gr. *mnēmē*, memory, *mnēmōn*, mindful, *Mnēmosynē*, Mnemosyne.]

mo, *mō*, (*arch.*) *adv.* and *adj.* more.—Also moe; (*Scot.*) mae (*mā*), more (in number, not quantity). [O.E. *mā* (adv.); cf. more, most.]

mo. See moment.

moa, *mō'ə*, *n.* a gigantic extinct bird (Dinornis) of New Zealand. [Maori.]

Moabite, *mō'ə-bit*, *n.* one of the ancient people of *Moab*, living east of the lower Jordan and the Dead Sea.—*adj.* of or pertaining to Moab.— Moabite stone, a basalt slab found (1868) at Dibon in Moab, with a long inscription in Hebrew-Phoenician letters, about the revolt of Mesha, king of Moab, against Israel (9th cent. B.C.; 2 Kings iii.).

moan, *mōn*, *n.* lamentation: a lament: a complaint: a grumble (*coll.*): a low murmur of pain: a sound like a murmur of pain.—*v.t.* to lament: to bemoan: to utter with moans: to condole with (*obs.*).—*v.i.* to make or utter a moan: to grumble (*coll.*).—*adj.* moan'ful, expressing sorrow: lamentable.—*adv.* moan'fully. [Unrecorded O.E. *mān* (noun) answering to the verb *mǣnan*.]

moat, *mōt*, *n.* a deep trench round a castle or fortified place, sometimes filled with water: a mote-hill.—*v.t.* to surround with a moat.—*adj.* moat'ed. [O.Fr. *mote*, mound.]

mob, *mob*, *n.* the mobile or fickle common people: the vulgar: the rabble: a disorderly crowd: a riotous assembly: a gang: a crowd, mixed collection, large herd or flock (*Austr.*).—*v.t.* to attack in a disorderly crowd: to crowd around with vexatious curiosity or attentions: to drive by mob action.—*v.t.* and *v.i.* to form into a mob: —*pr.p.* mobb'ing; *pa.t.* and *pa.p.* mobbed.—*adj.* mobb'ish.—*ns.* mobile (*mō'bi-li*; 17th cent.), the mob; moboc'racy (*slang*), rule or ascendency exercised by the mob; mob'ocrat.—*adj.* mobo-crat'ir.—*n.* mob'ster, gangster.—mob'-law, lynch-law: the will of the mob; mobs'man, member of a mob: swell-mobsman (*q.v.*). [L. *mōbile* (*vulgus*), fickle (multitude): *movēre*, to move.]

mob, *mob*, (*obs.*) *n.* a loose woman: a négligé dress: a mob-cap.—*v.t.* to muffle the head of.— *adj.* mobbed, in dishabille: muffled up.—mob'-

cap, a woman's indoor morning cap with puffy crown, a broad band, and frills (*hist.*).—mob it (*obs.*), to go unobtrusively to an unfashionable part of the theatre. [Perh. *Mab*, for *Mabel*; but cf. O.Du. *mop*; mod. Du. *mopmuts*, a woman's nightcap.]

mobby, mobbie, *mob'i*, *n.* a spirituous beverage made from sweet-potatoes (*West Indies*): fruit-juice for brandy-making, or brandy made therefrom (*U.S. arch.*). [Carib *mabi*.]

mobile, *mō'bil*, *-bēl*, *-bil*, *adj.* movable: able to move about: easily, speedily moved: not fixed: changing rapidly: of a liquid, characterised by great fluidity.—*n.* with great, principal, etc., translation of primum mobile (*obs.*): a moving or movable body or part: an artistic structure, orig. consisting of dangling forms, now sometimes having a base, in which movement is caused by air currents.—*ns.* mobile (*mō'bi-li*; see mob (1)); mobilisation.—z- (*mō-* or mo-bil-i-zā'shən*, or *-i-*).—*v.t.* mō'bilise, -ize, to make movable, mobile, or readily available: to put in readiness for service in war: to call into active service, as troops.—*v.i.* to make armed forces ready for war: to undergo mobilisation.—*n.* mobility (*mō-bil'i-ti*), quality of being mobile: description of the drift of ions (including electrons and holes in semiconductors) under applied electric fields, additional to thermal agitation (*electronics*): the mob (*slang*).—mobile shop, one set up in a motor vehicle, driven to customers' homes. [Fr.,—L. *mōbilis—movēre*, to move.]

Möbius strip, *mœ'bē-əs strip*, (*maths.*) *n.* the one-sided surface formed by joining together the two ends of a long rectangular strip, one end being twisted through 180 degrees before the join is made. [August F. *Möbius*, 1790-1868, mathematician.]

moble, mobble, *mob'l*, (*obs.*) *v.t.* to muffle, as in a mob.—*adj.* mob'led (*Shak.*), muffled: other suggestions are, richly endowed (cf. Fr. *meuble*), set in motion, violently agitated (L. *mōbilis*), or that there is no meaning at all. [Freq. of mob (2).]

moccasin, mocassin, *mok'ə-sin*, *n.* a North American Indian's shoe of deerskin or other soft leather: a lady's slipper more or less resembling it: a venomous North American pit-viper.—mocc'asin-flow'er, a lady's-slipper or-chid. [American Indian.]

Mocha, *mok'a*, *mō'ka*, *n.* a fine coffee.—Mocha stone, a moss agate or similar stone. [Both first brought from *Mocha*, on the Red Sea.]

mochell. Same as muchel.

mock, *mok*, *v.t.* to deride: to scoff at derisively: to make sport of: to mimic in ridicule: to simulate: to defy, set at naught, tantalise, dis-appoint, deceive, befool, as if in mockery (*fig.*). —*v.i.* to jeer: to scoff: to speak or behave as one not in earnest.—*n.* ridicule: a bringing into ridicule: a scoff: a mockery: a thing mocked. —*adj.* sham: false: resembling, or accepted as a substitute for, the true or real.—*adj.* mock'-able, worthy of derision.—*ns.* mock'age (*obs.*); mock'er; mock'ery, derision: ridicule: subject of ridicule: mimicry: imitation, esp. a contemptible or insulting imitation: false show: insulting or ludicrous futility.—*n.* and *adj.* mock'ing.—*adv.* mock'ingly.—*adj.* mock'-hero'ic, burlesquing the heroic style.—*n.* a mock-heroic composition (in *pl.*) mock-heroic verses: sham heroic utterances or pose.—*adj.* mock-hero'ical. — *adv.* mock'-hero'ically. — mock'ing-bird, an American bird (Mimus) of the thrush family, that mimics other birds' songs and other sounds; mock'ing-thrush', a thrasher.—*adj.* mock'-mod'est.—mock'-mod'esty, sham mod-esty; mock moon, a paraselene, or bright spot in the moon's halo, 22° to right or left of the moon, due to refraction from ice crystals floating vertically; **mock'-or'ange**, a tall shrub (Philadelphus, commonly called syringa) of the saxifrage family with strong-scented flowers: a kind of cherry-laurel (*U.S.*); **mock'-priv'et**, a shrub (Phillyrea) akin to privet; **mock sun**, a parhelion or spot in the sun's halo; **mock'-up**, a full-size dummy model: a fabrication.—**mocks the pauses** (*Shak.*, *Ant. and Cleo.*, V, i. 2), perh. throws away the opportunities given by the pauses; **mock turtle soup**, an imitation of turtle soup, made of calf's head or veal. [O.Fr. *mocquer*; origin uncertain.]

**mockado**, *mok-ä'dō*, (*obs.*) *n.* an inferior cloth of Flemish origin: trumpery. [Prob. It. *mocaiardo*, haircloth.]

**mocker-nut**, *mok'ər-nut*, *n.* a kind of hickory-nut with kernel difficult to extract.

**mocock**, *mō-kok'*, **mocuck**, *mō-kuk'*, *n.* an American Indian birch-bark box or basket. [Of Algonquian origin.]

**mod**, *mod*, *mōd*, *mōd*, *n.* a Highland literary and musical festival. [Gael, *mòd*—O.N. *mōt*; cf. *moot*.]

**Mod**, *mod*, *n.* a member of a teenage faction in the 1960s distinguished by special dress (typically neat), etc., from their rivals, the Rockers.

**mod. con.**, *mod kon*, **modern** con**venience**, any item of up-to-date plumbing.

**mode**, *mōd*, *n.* way or manner of acting, doing, happening, or existing: kind: form: manifestation: state of being: that which exists only as a quality of substance: a mood (*gram.*): character as necessary, contingent, possible or impossible (*log.*): a mood (*log.*): actual percentage mineral composition (*petr.*): the value of greatest frequency (*statistics*): modality: fashion: that which is fashionable: fashionableness: a model of fashion (*obs.*): alamode, or a garment made of it: open-work between the solid parts of lace: the method of dividing the octave according to the position of its steps and half-steps (*mus.*): in old music, the method of time-division of notes (*perfect* into three, *imperfect* into two; *major*, division of large into longs, *minor* of long into breves).—*adj.* **modal** (*mōd'l*), relating to mode.—*ns.* **mod'alism**, the doctrine first set forth by Sabellius that the Father, the Son, and the Holy Spirit are not three distinct personalities but only three different modes of manifestation; **mod'alist**, one who holds this theory.—*adj.* **modalist'ic**.—*n.* **modality** (*mōd-al'i-ti*), fact or condition of being modal: mode: method, terms, style: any of the primary methods of sensation: classification of propositions as to whether true, false, necessary, possible or impossible (*log.*): the quality of being limited by a condition (*law*).—*adv.* **mod'ally**.—*adj.* **modish** (*mōd'ish*), fashionable: affectedly, foolishly, or absurdly fashionable.—*adv.* **mod'ishly**.—*ns.* **mod'ishness**; **mod'ist**, a follower of the fashion; **modiste** (*mō-dēst'*; Fr.), a professedly fashionable dressmaker or milliner.—**Greek modes** consist each of two disjunct tetrachords with a whole tone (diazeuctic tone) between them, or two conjunct tetrachords with a whole tone above (where the prefix is *hyper-*) or below them (*hypo-*); **Gregorian, mediaeval, or ecclesiastical modes** have the same names as Greek modes but do not correspond to them (use **authentic**, *plagal*: also **Aeolian, Locrian, Ionian, Dorian, Phrygian, Lydian, Mixolydian**, and names under *hyper-, hypo-*); **major mode**, modern mode, consisting of two steps, a half-step, three steps, and a half-step; **minor mode**, a modern mode consisting of a step, a half-step, two steps, a half-step, and two steps. [L. *modus*; partly through Fr. *mode*.]

**model**, *mod'l*, *n.* plan, design (*obs.*): a preliminary solid representation, generally small, or in plastic material, to be followed in construction: something to be copied: a pattern: an imitation of something on a smaller scale: a person or thing closely resembling another: one who poses for an artist: one who exhibits clothes for a shop by wearing them: a pattern of excellence: an article of standard design or a copy of one: structural type: a medal (*obs.*): a close covering or mould (*Shak.*).—*adj.* of the nature of a model: set up for imitation: completely suitable for imitation, exemplary.—*v.t.* to form after a model: to shape: to make a model or copy of: to form in some plastic material: of a mannequin, to display (a garment) by wearing it.—*v.i.* to practise modelling:—*pr.p.* **mod'elling**; *pa.t.* and *pa.p.* **mod'elled**.—*ns.* **mod'eller**; **mod'elling**, the act or art of making a model of something, a branch of sculpture: rendering of solid form. [O.Fr. *modelle*—It. *modello*, dim. of *modo*—L. *modus*, a measure.]

**modena**, *mod'i-na*, *n.* a shade of crimson. [*Modena* in Italy.]

**moderate**, *mod'ə-rāt*, *v.t.* to keep within measure or bounds: to regulate: to reduce in intensity: to make temperate or reasonable: to pacify: to preside as moderator over or at: to decide as an arbitrator (*obs.*).—*v.i.* to become less violent or intense: to preside or act as a moderator.—*adj.* (*-rit*) kept within measure or bounds: not excessive or extreme: temperate: of middle rate.—*n.* one whose views are far from extreme: one of a party in the Scottish Church in the 18th century and early 19th, broad in matters of doctrine and discipline, opposed to Evangelicalism and popular rights.—*adv.* **mod'erately**.—*ns.* **mod'erateness**; **modera'tion**, act of moderating: state of being moderated or moderate: freedom from excess: self-restraint: the process of slowing down neutrons in an atomic pile: (in *pl.*) the first public examination for B.A. at Oxford (*coll.* **mods**); **mod'eratism**, moderate opinions in religion or politics; **mod'erātor**, one who, or that which, moderates: a president, esp. in Presbyterian church courts: formerly an officer at Oxford and Cambridge who superintended degree examinations: one of two presiding over Mathematical Tripos at Cambridge: a moderations examiner at Oxford: oil-lamp with regulated flow of oil: the material in which neutrons are slowed down in an atomic pile:—*fem.* **mod'erātrix**; **mod'erātorship**.—**moderate (in) a call**, of a presbytery, to act with the congregation in calling the minister it has chosen. [L. *moderāri, -ātus*—*modus*, a measure.]

**moderato**, *mod-ə-rä'tō*, (*mus.*) *adj.* and *adv.* at a moderate speed. [It.]

**modern**, *mod'ərn*, *adj.* of or characteristic of present or recent time: not ancient or mediaeval: in education, mainly or wholly concerned with subjects other than Greek and Latin: of a style of type with contrasting thick and thin strokes, serifs at right-angles, curves thickened in the centre (*print.*): everyday, commonplace (*Shak.*): (*cap.*), of a language, of or near the form now spoken and written, distinguished from *Old* and *Middle*.—*n.* one living in modern times, esp. distinguished from the ancient Greeks and Romans: a modernist: a modern printing type.—*n.* **modernisā'tion**, **-z-**.—*v.t.* **mod'ernise**, **-ize**, to adapt to the present time, conditions, needs, language, or spelling.—*v.i.* to adopt modern ways.—*ns.* **mod'erniser**, **-z-**; **mod'ernism**, modern usage, expression, or trait: modern spirit or character: a tendency to adjust Christian dogma to the results of science and criticism; **mod'ernist**, an admirer of modern ideas, ways, literature, studies, etc.: one who favours modernism; **modernis'tic**; **modern'ity**.—*adv.* **mod'ernly**.—*n.* **mod'ernness**. [L.L. *modernus*—*modo*, just now, orig. abl. of *modus*.]

**modest**, *mod'ist*, *adj.* restrained by a sense of seemliness: unobtrusive: unpretentious: unassuming: diffident: decent: chaste: pure and delicate, as thoughts or language: not excessive or extreme: moderate.—*adv.* **mod'estly.**—*n.* **mod'esty**, the quality or fact of being modest: a slight covering for a low neck. [L. *modestus*—*modus*, a measure.]

**modicum**, *mod'i-kəm*, *n.* a small quantity: a small person (*obs.*): (disrespectfully) a woman (*obs.*): —*pl.* **modicums.** [L. neut. of *modicus*, moderate —*modus.*]

**modify**, *mod'i-fī*, *v.t.* to moderate: to determine the mode of (*philos.*): to change the form or quality of: to alter slightly: to vary: to differentiate: of an adverb, to limit or qualify the sense of (*gram.*): to subject to umlaut (*philol.*): to assess, decree, or award (a payment) (*Scots law*):—*pr.p.* **mod'ifying;** *pa.t.* and *pa.p.* **mod'ified.**—*adj.* **mod'ifiable.**—*n.* **modification** (*-fi-kā'shən*), act of modifying or state of being modified: result of alteration or change: changed shape or condition: a change due to environment, lasting only as long as the operative conditions (*biol.*).—*adjs.* **mod'ificative, mod'ificatory,** tending to modify: causing change of form or condition.—*adj.* **mod'ified** (*-fīd*), altered by modification: homologous but developed in a different direction (*biol.*).—*n.* **mod'ifier** (*-fī-ər*), one who modifies: a modifying agent: a diacritic indicating modification, esp. umlaut. [Fr. *modifier*—L. *modificāre, -ātum*—*modus*, a measure, *facēre*, to make.]

**modillion**, *mod-il'yən*, (*archit.*) *n.* an ornamental bracket under a Corinthian or other cornice. [It. *modiglione*—L. *modulus*—*modus*, a measure.]

**modiolus**, *mo-di'ə-ləs*, *n.* the axis of the cochlea of the ear: (*cap.*; also **Modiola**) the horse-mussel genus.—*adj.* **modi'olar.** [L. *mŏdĭŏlus*, nave of a wheel, water-wheel bucket, drinking-vessel, etc., dim. of *modus.*]

**modish, modist, modiste.** See **mode.**

**modius**, *mō'di-əs*, *mod'i-ŏŏs*, *n.* a Roman dry measure, about a peck: a cylindrical head-dress of the gods:—*pl.* **mō'dii** (*-ī*). [L. *mŏdius.*]

**mods.** See **moderations.**

**modulate**, *mod'ū-lāt*, *v.t.* to regulate, adjust: to inflect: to soften: to vary the pitch or frequency of: to impress characteristics of signal wave on (carrier wave) (*radio*): to vary velocity of electrons in electron beam.—*v.i.* (*mus.*) to pass from one key into another.—*adj.* **mod'ular**, of or pertaining to mode or modulation, or to a module.—*ns.* **modulā'tion; mod'ulātor**, one who, or that which, modulates: any device for effecting modulation (*radio*): a chart used in the tonic sol-fa notation on which modulations are shown; **mod'ule**, a small measure or quantity: a unit of size, used in standardised planning of buildings and design of components: a self-contained unit forming part of a spacecraft: an assembly within a geometrical framework of electronic units functioning as a system: a measure, often the semidiameter of a column, for regulating proportions of other parts (*archit.*): a model, image (*Shak.*).—*adv.* **mod'ulo** (*math.*), with respect to a (specified) modulus.—*n.* **mod'ulus**, a constant multiplier or coefficient (*math.*): a quantity used as a divisor to produce classes of quantities, each class distinguished by its members yielding the same remainders (*math.*): the positive square root of the sum of the squares of the real and imaginary parts of a complex number (*math.*): a quantity expressing the relation between a force and the effect produced: —*pl.* **moduli** (*mod'ū-lī*). [L. *modulārī, -ātus*, to regulate, *modulus*, dim. of *modus*, a measure.]

**modus**, *mō'dəs, mo'dŏŏs*, *n.* manner, mode: the way in which anything works: a fixed payment instead of tithes:—*pl.* **mō'di.**—**modus operandi,**

(*op-ər-an'dī, -an'dē*), mode of operation, way of working; **modus vivendi** (*vi-ven'dī, dē, wē-wen'-dē*), way of life or living: an arrangement or compromise by means of which those who differ may get on together for a time: such an arrangement between states or between a state and the Pope. [L. *mŏdus*, manner.]

**moe**, *mō* (*Shak.*). See **mo** (1), **mow** (1).

**moellon**, *mō'ə-lon*, *n.* rubble in mason-work. [Fr.]

**Moeso-gothic**, *mē-sō-goth'ik*, *adj.* relating to the *Goths* who settled in *Moesia.*—*n.* their language.

**mofette**, *mō-fet'*, *n.* an opening in the earth giving out carbon dioxide with some nitrogen and oxygen—the last stage of volcanic activity. [Fr., —It. *mofeta*, perh. L. *mephitis*, foul exhalation.]

**mofussil**, *mō-fus'l*, *n.* in India, all outside the capital or great towns.—*adj.* provincial: rural. [Hind. *mufassil*—Ar. *mufassal*, distinct, separate, pa.p. of *fassala*, to separate.]

**moggan**, *mog'ən*, (*Scot.*) *n.* a footless stocking. [Origin unknown.]

**moggy, mog,** *mog'i, mog*, *ns.* a cat (*slang*): a pet name for a cow, etc. (*dial.*). [Perh. *Maggie.*]

**Mogul**, *mō'gul, mō-gul'*, *n.* a Mongol or Mongolian, esp. one of the followers of Baber, the conqueror of India (1483-1530): a name applied to the best quality of playing-cards: (without *cap.*) an influential person, magnate.—*adj.* pertaining to the Mogul Empire, architecture, etc.—**Great Mogul,** the title by which Europeans knew the Emperors of Delhi. [Pers. *Mughul*, properly a Mongol.]

**mohair**, *mō'hār*, *n.* the long, white, fine silken hair of the Angora goat: other hair as a substitute for it: cloth made of it. [Ar. *mukhayyar*; influenced by **hair.**]

**Mohammedan,** *mō-ham'i-dən*, **Mohommedan,** *mə-hom'*, **Mahometan,** *mə-hom'it-ən*, **Muhammadan, Muhammedan,** *mŏŏ-ham'ə-dən, -i-dən*, *adj.* pertaining to Mohammed (formerly popularly rendered as Mahomet) or to his religion.—*n.* a follower of Mohammed: one who professes Mohammedanism.—*v.t.* and *v.i.* **Mohamm'edanise, -ize,** etc., to convert to, or conform to, Mohammedanism.—*ns.* **Mohamm'edanism, Mohamm'edism,** etc., the religion of Mohammed, contained in the Koran.—See also **Mahoun, mammet.** [Ar. *Muhammad*, the great prophet of Arabia (*c.* 570-632); lit. praised.]

**Moharram, Muharram, Muharrem,** *mō-, mŏŏ-hur'um*, *n.* the first month of the Mohammedan year: a great fast in commemoration of Hasan and Hosain (grandsons of Mohammed) during its first ten days: a public procession during the fast. [Ar. *muharram*, sacred.]

**Mohawk**, *mō'hök*, *n.* an Indian of an Iroquois tribe of New York State: a Mohock: a skating movement consisting of a stroke on the edge of one skate followed by a stroke in the opposite direction on the same edge of the other skate. [From an Algonquian name.]

**Mohican**, *mō-hē'kən*, **Mohegan,** *-gən*, *n.* an Indian of a former tribe in Connecticut.—Also *adj.* [From a native name.]

**Moho, Mohorovicic(ian), discontinuity,** *mō'hō, mō-hō-rō'və-chich(-i-ən)*, the boundary between the rocks of the earth's crust and the different rock of the mantle. [A. *Mohorovičić*, who deduced a difference of rock nature from the behaviour of earthquake shocks.]

**Mohock**, *mō'hok*, *n.* one of a band of aristocratic ruffians of early 18th-century London. [**Mohawk.**]

**mohr.** Same as **mhorr.**

**mohur**, *mō'hər*, *n.* a former Persian and Indian gold coin, in India fifteen rupees. [Pers. *mohr.*]

**moider**, *moi'dər*, **moither,** *-dhər*, *v.t.* to confuse: to stupefy, overcome.—*v.i.* to work hard: to wander in mind. [Dialect word; origin obscure.]

**moidore,** *moi'dōr, -dör, n.* a disused gold coin of Portugal. [Port. *moeda d'ouro,* lit. money of gold—L. *monēta, dē, aurum.*]

**moiety,** *moi'ə-ti, n.* half: one of two parts or divisions: a small share (*Shak.*). [O.Fr. *moite*—L. *medietās, -tātis,* middle point, later half—*medius,* middle.]

**moil,** *moil, (arch.) v.t.* to wet: to bedaub: to defile.—*v.i. (dial.)* to toil: to drudge.—*n. (dial.* and *arch.)* a spot: a defilement: labour: trouble: turmoil.—*n.* moil'er. [O.Fr. *moillier* (Fr. *mouiller*), to wet—L. *mollis,* soft.]

**moineau,** *moi'nō, n.* a small flat bastion to protect a fortification while being erected. [Fr.]

**Moira,** *moi'ra, n.* a Fate (goddess): fate, destiny.—*pl.* Moirai (*-ri*). [Gr. *Moirā.*]

**moire,** *mwär,* also *mwör, mör, moir, n.* orig. watered mohair: now watered silk or other fabric with watered appearance.—*adj.* moiré (*m:wär'ā, moi'ri*), watered.—*n.* a watered appearance on cloth or metal surface: sometimes for moire, the material. [Fr., from English mohair.]

**moist,** *moist, adj.* damp: humid: rainy: watery: juicy (*Shak.*).—*v.t.* (*Shak.*) to moisten.—*vs.t.* **moisten** (*mois'n*), to make moist: to wet slightly; **moist'ify,** (jocular) to make moist.—*adv.* **moist'ly.**—*ns.* moist'ness; moist'ure, moistness: that which makes slightly wet: liquid, esp. in small quantity.—*adj.* moist'ureless.—*v.t.* moist'-**urise, -ize,** to add or restore moisture to.—Also *v.i.*—*n.* moist'uriser. [O.Fr. *moiste* (Fr. *moite*), perh.—L. *mustum,* juice of grapes, new wine, perh. L. *mūcidus,* mouldy.]

**moither.** See moider.

**moke,** *mōk, (slang) n.* a donkey: a variety performer on several instruments: a Negro (*U.S. slang*). [Origin unknown.]

**mol, molal, etc., molar, etc.** See mole (1).

**molar,** *mō'lar, adj.* used for grinding: pertaining to a grinding tooth.—*n.* a grinding tooth, or back tooth. [L. *molāris*—*mola,* a millstone—*molēre,* to grind.]

**Molasse,** *mō-läs', n.* a series of Oligocene or Miocene sandstones and sandy marls in Switzerland, France, and Germany. [Fr.]

**molasses,** *mo-las'iz, n.sing.* a thick treacle that drains from sugar. ¬[Port. *melaço* (Fr. *mélasse*)—L.L. *mellāceum*—*mel, mellis,* honey.]

**mold.** See mould (1, 2, 3), mole (2).

**moldwarp.** See mouldwarp.

**mole,** *mōl, n.* the amount of substance that contains as many (specified) entities (e.g. atoms, molecules, ions, photons) as there are atoms in 12 grams of carbon-12 (abbrev. mol, *mōl*): formerly defined as equal to gram-molecule.—*adj.* mol'al, of, relating to, or containing, a mole.—*n.* molal'ity, the concentration of a solution expressed as the number of moles of dissolved substance per thousand grams of solvent.—*adj.* mol'ar, of, or relating to, a mole: per mole: per unit amount of substance: of, or relating to molecules: of or pertaining to mass or masses or to large masses (L. *mōlēs,* mass).—*ns.* molar'ity, the concentration of a solution expressed as the number of moles of dissolved substance per litre of solution; mole'-electronics (also molecular electronics), technique of growing solid-state crystals so as to form transistors, etc., for microminiaturisation. [Ger.,—*molekül,* molecule; both words (Ger. and Eng.) ult. from L. *mōlēs,* mass.]

**mole,** *mōl, n.* a spot, esp. one caused by iron on linen (*obs.* except in Scots form mail and in iron-mould): a small spot or elevation on the skin, often coloured and hairy.—*Spens.* mōld. [O.E. *māl.*]

**mole,** *mōl, n.* a small insectivorous animal (Talpa) with very small eyes and soft fur, which burrows in the ground and casts up little heaps of mould:

extended to kindred or similar animals: one who works in darkness or underground (*fig.*): one who sees badly (*fig.*).—mole'cast, a molehill; **mole'catcher,** one whose business it is to catch moles; **mole'-crick'et,** a burrowing insect (Gryllotalpa) of the cricket family, with forelegs like a mole's; **mole drainer** (*agri.*), a pointed cylinder on the lower edge of a blade, which is drawn longitudinally through soil to form a drainage channel.—*adj.* mole'-eyed, having eyes like those of a mole: seeing imperfectly.—mole'-**hill,** a little hill or heap of earth cast up by a mole; **mole'rat,** a name for several burrowing rodents (Spalax, Bathyergus, etc.); mole'skin, the skin of a mole: mole's fur: a superior kind of fustian, double-twilled, cropped before dyeing: (in *pl.*) clothes, esp. trousers, made of this fustian; **mole'-spade,** a small spade used by mole-catchers.—**make a mountain out of a molehill,** to magnify a trifling matter; **mole out,** to seek, or elicit, bit by bit, as if by burrowing. [M.E. *molle, mulle;* cf. Du. *mol,* L.G. *mol, mul;* poss. shortened from mouldwarp.]

**mole,** *mōl, n.* a massive breakwater: an ancient Roman mausoleum. [Fr. *môle*—L. *mōlēs,* mass.]

**molecule,** *mol'i-kūl,* or *mōl', n.* the smallest particle of any substance that retains the properties of that substance: a gram-molecule.—*adj.* **molecular** (*mol-ek'ū-lər*).—*n.* molecularity (*mol-ek-ū-lar'i-ti*).—*adv.* molec'ularly.—molecular biology, study of the molecules of the substances involved in the processes of life; molecular electronics (see mole (1)); molecular weight, weight of a molecule relatively to that of an atom of carbon-12 taken as 12. [Fr. *molécule.*—L. *mōlēs,* mass.]

**molendinar,** *mol-en'din-ar, (pedantically facet.) adj.* pertaining to a mill or a miller.—*n.* a molar tooth.—*adj.* molen'dinary (*pedantically facet.*), relating to a mill.—*n.* a mill. [L.L. *molendīnum,* a mill—L. *molēre,* to grind.]

**molest,** *mə-, mō-lest', v.t.* to vex: to interfere with in a troublesome or hostile way: to annoy.—*n.* annoyance.—*ns.* molesta'tion (*mo-, mō-*); molest'er.—*adj.* molest'ful. [Fr. *molester*—L. *molestāre*—*molestus,* troublesome.]

**molimen,** *mō-li'men, n.* a great effort, esp. any periodic effort to discharge a natural function.—*adj.* **moliminous** (*-lim'in-əs*). [L. *mōlimen*—*mōliri,* to toil—*mōlēs,* mass.]

**moline,** *mō'lin, -lin', (her.) adj.* like a millstone rind—applied to a cross with each arm ending in two outward curving branches.—*n.* a moline cross. [L. *mola,* a mill.]

**Molinism,** *mol'in-izm, n.* the doctrine of the 16th-cent. Spanish Jesuit Luis *Molina,* reconciling predestination and free will by God's foreknowledge, the efficacy of grace depending on the co-operation of the will.—*n.* Mol'inist.

**Molinism,** *mol'in-izm, n.* the quietism of Miguel de *Molinos* (17th cent.).—*n.* Mol'inist.

**moll,** *mol, n.* (with *cap.*) a familiar form of *Mary:* a gangster's girl-friend: a prostitute.

**mollah, molla.** See mullah.

**mollie,** *mol'i, n.* an abbreviation of mallemaroking.

**mollify,** *mol'i-fi, v.t.* to soften: to assuage: to cause to abate: to appease.—*v.i.* to become soft: to relax in severity or opposition:—*pr.p.* moll'ifying; *pa.t.* and *pa.p.* moll'ified.—*ns.* **mollification** (*-fi-kā'shən*); moll'ifier. [Fr. mollifier—L. *mollificāre*—*mollis,* soft, *facēre,* to make.]

**mollities,** *mol-ish'i-ēz, n.* (L.) softness, softening.—*adj.* **mollitious** (*-ish'əs*), luxurious. [L. *mollitiēs*—*mollis,* soft.]

**mollusc, mollusk,** *mol'əsk, n.* one of the Mollusca (*-us'ka*), a large phylum of invertebrates, without segments or limbs, usually having a mantle or fold of skin that secretes a shell—lamellibranchs, gasteropods, cephalopods, and some smaller

*fāte, fär; mē, hûr* (her); *mīne; mōte, för; mūte; mōōn, fŏŏt; dhen* (then)

groups: a person of inert habit.—*adjs.* **mollus'-can, mollus'cous,** of or belonging to the Mollusca.
—*n.* **mollus'cicide** (*-ki-sīd*), an agent for destroying molluscs, e.g. snails responsible for spread of disease.—*adj.* **mollus'cicidal.**—*n.* **mollus'coid,** a member of a now abandoned division of invertebrates of the **Molluscoid'ea,** Polyzoa and brachiopods.—*adj.* of the Molluscoidea: like a mollusc. [L. *molluscus,* softish—*mollis,* soft.]

**molly,** *mol'i, n.* (with *cap.*) dim. of *Mary:* a milksop.—*n.* **moll'ycoddle,** an effeminate fellow. *v.t.* to coddle.—**Molly Maguire,** a member of an Irish society formed in 1843 to resist government evictions, who disguised themselves as women: a member of a Pennsylvanian secret society formed to resist oppressive conditions in the mines, and crushed in 1877.

**mollymawk,** *mol'i-mök.* Same as **mallemuck.**

**Moloch,** *mō'lok, n.* a Semitic god to whom children were sacrificed (also **Mo'lech**): any cause to which dreadful sacrifice is made or destruction due: an exceedingly spiny harmless Australian lizard.—*v.t.* **mo'lochise, -ize,** to sacrifice as to Moloch. [Gr. and L. *Moloch*—Heb. *Mōlek.*]

**Molossian,** *mol-os'i-ən, adj.* of *Molossia* or *Molossis* in Epirus, famous in ancient times for its great dogs, a kind of mastiff.—*n.* **moloss'us,** a metrical foot of three long syllables:—*pl.* **moloss'i.**

**Molotov cocktail,** *mol'ə-tof,* a crude form of hand-grenade consisting of a bottle with inflammable liquid, and a wick to be ignited just before the missile is thrown. [V. M. *Molotov,* Russian statesman.]

**molt.** See **moult.**

**molt, molten.** See **melt.**

**molto,** *mol'tō, (mus.) adv.* very: much. [It.]

**Molucca bean,** *mo-luk'ə,* nicker nut, bonduc.

**moly,** *mō'li, n.* a magic herb given by Hermes to Odysseus as a counter-charm against the spells of Circe: a species of wild onion, *Allium moly.* [Gr. *mōly.*]

**molybdenum,** *mol-ib'din-əm* (also *mol-ib-dē'nəm*), *n.* silvery-white metal (Mo; atomic number 42). —*ns.* **molyb'date,** a salt of molybdic acid; **molybdēn'ite** (or *-ib'dən-īt*), a mineral, molybdenum disulphide.—*adj.* **molyb'dic.**—*n.* **molybdō'sis,** lead-poisoning.—**molybdic acid,** H₂MoO₄. [Latinised neuter—Gr. *molybdaina,* a lump of lead, a leadlike substance—*molybdos,* lead.]

**mome,** *mōm, (obs.) n.* a buffoon: a carper. [*Momus.*]

**mome,** *mōm, (Spens.) n.* a blockhead. [Origin obscure.]

**moment,** *mō'mənt, n.* a point of time: a time so short that it may be considered as a point: a very short time (abbrev. in slang, mo): a second: a precise instant: the present, or the right, instant: moving cause or motive (*Shak.*): importance, consequence: an infinitesimal change in a varying quantity (*math.*; *obs.*): a stage or turning-point: an element or factor (as in *psychological moment,* rightly used): a measure of turning-effect—the *moment of a force* about a point is the product of the force and the perpendicular on its line of action from the point.—*adjs.* **momentān'eous,** momentary: instantaneous; **mo'mentary** (*Shak.*), momentary.—*adv.* **mo'mentarily,** for a moment: every moment: at any moment.—*n.* **mo'mentariness.**—*adj.* **mo'mentary,** lasting for a moment: short-lived.—*adv.* **mo'mently,** every moment: for a moment.—*adj.* occurring every moment: of a moment.—*adj.* **momentous** (*-ment'*), of great consequence.—*adv.* **moment'ously.**—*ns.* **moment'ousness; moment'um,** the quantity of motion in a body measured by the product of mass and velocity: force of motion gained in movement, impetus (*coll.*):—*pl.* **moment'a.—moment of truth,** the climax of

the bullfight: a moment when, suddenly and dramatically, one is face to face with stark reality—often a testing moment (*fig.*). [L. *mōmentum,* for *movimentum—movēre, mōtum,* to move.]

**mommet.** See **mammet.**

**Momus,** *mō'məs, n.* the god of ridicule. [Latinised from Gr. *mōmos,* blame, reproach, personified.]

**mon-.** See **mon(o)-.**

**mona,** *mō'nə, n.* a West African monkey, *Cercopithecus mona.* [It., Sp., or Port. *mona,* monkey.]

**monachism,** *mon'ək-izm, n.* monasticism.—*adjs.* **mon'achal, mon'achist.**—*n.* **Mon'achus,** the monk-seal genus. [Gr. *monachos,* solitary—*monos,* single, alone.]

**monacid,** *mon-as'id,* **monoacid,** *mon-ō-as'id, adj.* having one replaceable hydrogen atom: capable of replacing one hydrogen atom of an acid. [**mon(o)-.**]

**monact,** *mon'akt, adj.* one-rayed.—*adjs.* **monact'-inal** (*-i-nəl* or *-i'nəl*), **monact'ine** (*-in*). [Gr. *monos,* single, alone, *aktis, -inos,* a ray.]

**monad,** *mon'ad, n.* the number one: a unit: an ultimate unit of being, material and psychical: a spirit: God: a hypothetical primitive living organism or unit of organic life: a flagellate of the genus Monas or akin to it: a univalent element, atom, or radical.—Also *adj.*—*adjs.* **monad'ic, -al; monad'iform,** like a monad.—*ns.* **mon'adism, monadol'ogy,** a theory or doctrine of monads, esp. Leibniz's; **mon'as,** a monad: (with *cap.*), a genus of flagellates. [Gr. *monas -ados,* a unit—*monos,* single, alone.]

**monadelphous,** *mon-ə-del'fəs, adj.* of stamens, united by the filaments in one bundle: of a flower or plant, having all the stamens so united. —*n.pl.* **Monadel'phia,** in Linnaeus's system, a class of plants with stamens united in one bundle. [Gr. *monos,* single, alone, *adelphos,* brother.]

**monandrous,** *mon-an'drəs, adj.* having or allowing one husband or male mate (at a time): having one stamen or one antheridium (*bot.*).—*n.pl.* **Monan'dria,** in Linnaeus's system, a class of plants with one stamen.—*n.* **monan'dry,** the condition or practice of being monandrous. [Gr. *monos,* single, alone, *anēr, andros,* a man, male.]

**monarch,** *mon'ərk, n.* a sole hereditary head of a state, whether titular or ruling.—*adjs.* **monarchal** (*-ärk'əl*), **monarch'ial, monarch'ic, -al.**—*ns.* **Monarch'ian,** a Christian who denied the personal independent subsistence of Christ—*dynamic,* when regarding the divinity of Christ as only a power (*dynamis*) communicated to him; *modalistic,* when regarding Christ as the Father who had assumed flesh, a mere *modus* of the Godhead; **Monarch'ianism.**—*adj.* **Monarchianis'tic.**—*v.t.* **mon'archise, -ize,** to rule over as a monarch: to convert into a monarchy.—*v.i.* (also *v.t.* with *it*) to play the monarch.—*n.* **mon'archism,** the principles of monarchy: love of monarchy; **mon'archist,** an advocate of monarchy: a believer in monarchy: a Monarchian.—Also *adj.*—*adj.* **monarchist'ic.**—*ns.* **Monarch'o** (*Shak.*), a foppish fantastic megalomaniac (from a crazy Italian about Elizabeth's court); **mon'archy,** a kind of government of which there is a monarch: a state with monarchical government: the territory of a monarch. [Gr. *monarchēs—monos,* single, alone, *archein,* to rule.]

**monarch,** *mon'ärk, (bot.) adj.* having one xylem strand. [Gr. *monos,* single, alone, *archē,* origin.]

**monastery,** *mon'as-tər-i, -tri, n.* a house for monks, or (*rarely*) nuns.—*adjs.* **monastē'rial, monastic** (*-as'tik*), **-al,** pertaining to monasteries, monks, and nuns: recluse: solitary.—*n .* **monas'tic,** a monk.—*adv.* **monas'tically.**—*n.* **monas'ticism** (*-sizm*), the corporate monastic life or system of living. [Late Gr. *monastērion—monastēs,* a monk—*monos,* single, alone.]

**Monastral blue, green,** tradename for certain phthalocyanine pigments.

**monatomic,** *mon-ə-tom'ik, adj.* consisting of one atom: having one replaceable atom or group: univalent. [**mon(o)-.**]

**monaul, monal,** *mon'öl, n.* a magnificent Himalayan pheasant (*Lophophorus*). [Nᴇpali *munāl*.]

**monaural,** *mon-ö'rəl, adj.* having or using only one ear: pertaining to one ear: of a gramophone record, giving the effect of sound from a single direction—not stereophonic. [**mon(o)-.**]

**monaxial,** *mon-aks'i-əl, adj.* having only one axis.—*adj.* **monax'on,** monaxial.—*n.* a monaxonic sponge spicule.—*adj.* **monaxon'ic.**—*n.pl.* **Monaxon'ida,** an order of sponges with monaxon spicules only. [**mon(o)-.**]

**monazite,** *mon'əz-īt, (min.) n.* a phosphate of cerium, lanthanum, neodymium, praseodymium, and usually thorium, a source of thorium. [Gr. *monazein,* to be solitary—on account of its rarity.]

**monchiquite,** *mon'shi-kīt, n.* a fine-grained lamprophyric rock, composed of olivine and augite with little or no feldspar, in an analcite groundmass. [From the Serra de *Monchique,* in S.W. Portugal.]

**Monday,** *mun'di, n.* the second day of the week.—*adj.* **Mon'dayish,** having the feelings normal after Sunday's activities or inactivities with the prospect of the week's work.—**black Monday, Handsel Monday, Meal Monday, Plough Monday** (see **black,** etc.). [O.E. *mōnandæg, mōnan,* gen. of *mōna,* moon, *dæg,* day.]

**monecious.** Same as **monoecious.**

**Monel metal,** *mō-nel', n.* a nickel-base alloy with high strength and resistance to corrosion. [Trademark.]

**moner,** *mōn'ər,* **moneron,** *mon-ēr'on, n.* Haeckel's hypothetical simplest protozoan:—*pl.* **monēr'a.** [Gr. *monērēs,* single.]

**monergism,** *mon'ər-jizm, (theol.) n.* the doctrine that regeneration is entirely the work of the Holy Spirit, the natural will being incapable of co-operation. [Gr. *monos,* single, alone, *ergon,* work.]

**monetary,** *mon'* or *mun'i-tər-i, adj.* of or relating to money: consisting of money.—*n.* **monetisā'-tion,** *-z-.*—*v.t.* **mon'etise, -ize,** to give the character of money to, to coin as money. [L. *monēta* (see **money**).]

**moneth,** *munth (Spens.).* Same as **month.**

**money,** *mun'i, n.* coin: pieces of stamped metal used in commerce: any currency used in the same way: wealth:—*pl.* **mon'eys, mon'ies** (*arch.* and *legal*), sums of money: money.—*adj.* **mon'eyed, mon'ied,** having money: rich in money: consisting in money.—*n.* **mon'eyer,** one who coins money legally (*arch.*): a capitalist (*obs.*).—*adj.* **mon'eyless,** having no money.—**money'-bag,** a bag for or of money: (*pl.*) a rich man; **mon'ey-bill,** a bill introduced into parliament or congress for raising revenue or otherwise dealing with money.—*adj.* **mon'ey-bound,** unable to move for want of money.—**money'-box,** a box for collecting or saving money, usu. with a slit for insertion; **mon'ey-broker,** one who carries out transactions in money for others; **mon'ey-changer,** one who exchanges one currency for another; **mon'ey-grubber,** a sordid accumulator of wealth; **mon'ey-lender,** a professional lender of money at interest; **mon'ey-lending; mon'ey-maker,** one who acquires riches: anything that brings profit; **mon'ey-making,** act of gaining wealth.—*adj.* lucrative, profitable.—**mon'ey-mar'ket,** the market or field for the investment of money; **mon'ey-or'der,** an order for money deposited at one post-office, and payable at another; **mon'ey-scriv'ener,** one who does financial business for clients; **mon'ey-spi'der,** a small spider supposed to bring luck;

**mon'ey-spinner,** a money-spider: a successful speculator: anything that brings much money: **mon'ey's-worth,** something as good as money: full value; **mon'ey-taker,** one who receives payments of money, esp. at an entrance-door: one who can be bribed; **mon'eywort,** a round-leaved loosestrife, creeping Jenny.—**for my, our, money,** if I, we, were to choose, express an opinion, etc.; **hard money,** coin; **in the money,** among the prize-winners (*racing,* etc.): well-off; **make money,** to acquire wealth: to make a profit; **money down,** money paid on the spot; **money for jam, old rope,** etc., money obtained without effort; **money of account,** a monetary unit (not represented by current coins) used in keeping accounts; **money talks,** the wealthy have much influence; **pot(s) of money,** a large amount of money; **ready money,** money paid for a thing at the time at which it is bought: money ready for immediate payment. [O.Fr. *moneie* (Fr. *monnaie*)—L. *monēta,* money, a mint, *Monēta* (the reminder) being a surname of Juno, in whose temple at Rome money was coined.]

**mong,** *mung,* (now *dial.*) *n.* a mixture: a crowd.—**mong'corn, mung'corn,** maslin. [O.E. *gemang.*]

'**mong, 'mongst,** aphetic for **among, amongst.**

**monger,** *mung'gər, n.* (chiefly in composition) a dealer—except in a few instances, as *ironmonger,* one who trafficks in a petty, or discreditable way.—*ns.* **mong'ering, mong'ery.** [O.E. *mangere*—L. *mangō, -ōnis,* a furbisher, slave-dealer—Gr. *manganeuein,* to use trickery.]

**Mongol,** *mong'gol, n.* a member of Genghis Khan's clan, or of the various populations under him: one of the people of Mongolia: their language: a member of a broad-headed, yellow-skinned, straight-haired, small-nosed human race, often with an epicanthic fold of skin (otherwise called Tungus): a Mongoloid idiot.—*adj.* of the Mongols, Mongolia, or Mongolian.—*adj.* **Mongolian** (*mong-gō'li-ən*) of Mongolia, the Mongols, or their language.—*n.* the language of Mongolia.—*adj.* **Mongolic** (*-gol'ik*), Mongolian: of Mongolian type: of the division of the Ural-Altaic languages to which Mongolian, Buriat, and Kalmuck belong.—*v.t.* **Mong'olise, -ize,** to make Mongolian.—*n.* **Mong'olism,** a condition of mental deficiency combined with a Mongol-like appearance.—*adj.* **Mong'oloid,** of Mongolian race or type: affected with Mongolism.—*n.* a person of Mongolian type: a Mongolian idiot.—**Mongoloid eye,** an eye with an epicanthic fold. [Said to be from Mongol *mong,* brave.]

**mongoose,** *mong', mung'gōōs, n.* an Indian animal of the civet family, a great slayer of snakes and rats: any other species of the genus (*Herpestes*), including the ichneumon: a Madagascan lemur:—*pl.* **mong'ooses.**—Also **mung'oose, mangouste** (Fr.). [Marathi *mangūs.*]

**mongrel,** *mung'grəl, n.* an animal, esp. a dog, of a mixed breed (usu. in contempt): a person, thing, or word of mixed or indefinite origin or nature: that which is neither one thing nor another.—*adj.* mixed in breed: ill-defined.—*v.t.* **mong'relise, -ize.**—*n.* **mong'relism.**—*adj.* **mong'-relly.** [Prob. from root of O.E. *mengan,* to mix.]

**monial,** *mōn'i-əl, n.* a mullion. [O.Fr., of unknown origin.]

**moni(c)ker,** *mon'i-kər, (slang;* orig. tramps') *n.* an alias, nickname, or real name.

**monied, monies.** See **money.**

**Monilia,** *mon-il'i-ə, n.* a genus of fungi with conidia in branched chains.—*n.* **moniliasis** (*-i'ə-sis*), a disease of the mouth and digestive tract in birds, animals, and man (**thrush,** 2), caused by fungi of the genus *Monilia.*—*adj.* **monil'iform,** like a string of beads. [L. *monile,* a necklace.]

**moniment,** *mon'i-ment.* See **monument.**

**moniplies,** *mun', mon'i-plīz.* See **manyplies.**

**monism**, *mon'izm*, *n.* a philosophical theory that all being may ultimately be referred to one category; thus *idealism, pantheism, materialism* are monisms—as opposed to the dualism of matter and spirit.—*n.* mon'ist.—*adjs.* monist'ic, -al. [Gr. *monos*, single, alone.]

**monition**, *mon-ish'ən*, *n.* a reminding or admonishing: warning: notice: a summons to appear and answer (*law*.).—*adj.* mon'itive, conveying admonition.—*n.* mon'itor, one who admonishes: an adviser: a senior pupil who assists in school discipline: a back-board (*obs.*): apparatus for testing transmission in electrical communication: a person employed to monitor: a low ironclad with revolving gun-turrets (from an American ship so named, the first of its kind, 1862): a genus (Varanus) of very large lizards of Africa, Asia, and Australia (from a fancy that they give warning of the presence of a crocodile): a detector for radioactivity: an instrument used in a production process to keep a variable quantity within prescribed limits by transmitting a controlling signal: a screen in a television studio showing the picture being transmitted: —*fem.* mon'itress.—*v.t.* to act as monitor to: to check (as the body and clothing of persons working with radioactive materials) for radioactivity: to track, or to control (an aeroplane, guided missile, etc.): to watch, check, supervise. —*v.i.* (*radio*), to tap on to a communication circuit, usu. in order to ascertain that the transmission is that desired: to listen to foreign broadcasts in order to obtain news, code messages, etc.—*adj.* monitorial (-*ōr'*, -*ör'*), relating to a monitor.—*adv.* monito'rially.—*n.* mon'itorship.—*adj.* mon'itory, giving admonition or warning. [L. *monēre*, -*itum*, to remind.]

**monk**, *mungk*, *n.* formerly, a hermit: a man (other than a friar, but loosely often applied to a friar also) of a religious community living together under vows: a bullfinch: an inky blotch or over-inked place in print: formerly, touchwood for firing mines.—*ns.* monk'ery (*contemptuous*), monasticism: behaviour of monks: monks collectively; monk'hood, the state or character of a monk.—*adj.* monk'ish (*depreciatory*), pertaining to a monk: like a monk: monastic.— monk'-fish, the angel fish (shark); monk'-seal, a seal (*Monachus albiventer*) of the Black Sea, Mediterranean, and N.W. Africa, dark grey above, light underneath; monks'hood, wolfs-bane, a poisonous ranunculaceous plant (Aconitum) with a large hoodlike posterior sepal; monk's rhubarb, patience-dock; monk's seam (*naut.*), a strong seam formed by overlapping two pieces and stitching on each side and down the middle.—also *middle-stitching*. [O.E. *munuc* —L. *monachus*—Gr. *monachos*—*monos*, alone.]

**monkey**, *mungk'i*, *n.* any mammal of the Primates except man and (usually) the anthropoid apes: an ape: a name of contempt, esp. for a mischievous person, also of playful endearment: the falling weight of a pile-driver: a large hammer for driving bolts: 500 pounds, or dollars (*slang*): anger (*slang*): a liquor-vessel of various kinds:— *pl.* monk'eys.—*v.i.* to meddle with anything, to fool.—*v.t.* to imitate as a monkey does.—*adj.* monk'eyish.—*n.* monk'eyism, monkey-like behaviour.—monk'ey-bag, a small money-bag, hung round the neck; monk'ey-block, a small swivel-block, used to guide running rigging; monk'ey-board, a foot-board behind a vehicle; monk'ey-boat, a narrow, half-decked river-boat; monk'ey-bread, the baobab-tree or its fruit; monkey business, underhand dealings: mischievous behaviour; monk'ey-en'gine, a pile-driving engine; monk'ey-flow'er, Mimulus; monk'ey-gaff, a small gaff above the spanker-gaff for the flag; monk'ey-gland, ape's testicle, grafted experimentally on man (1920-30s) to effect

rejuvenescence; monk'ey-grass, a coarse fibre from the leaf-stalks of *Attalea funifera*, used for brooms, etc.; monk'ey-hammer, a drop-press with a ram, which is raised and let drop freely; monk'ey-jacket, a close-fitting jacket; monk'ey-jar, a water-monkey; monk'ey-nut, the pea-nut or ground-nut (Arachis); monk'ey-pot, the round-lidded outer shell of the sapucaia nut; monk'ey-pump, a straw let through a gimlet-hole for sucking liquor from a cask; monk'ey-puzz'le, the so-called Chile pine, *Araucaria imbricata*, with close-set prickly leaves; monk'ey-rail, a light rail above the quarter-rail; monk'ey-rope, a forest creeper or liana: a rope round a sailor's waist for working in a dangerous place; monk'ey-run, a favourite place of parade and striking up of acquaintance; monk'ey-shine (*U.S. slang*), a monkeyish trick; monk'ey-suit, a man's evening suit; monk'ey-tail, a vertical scroll at the end of a hand-rail; monk'ey-trick; monk'ey-wheel, a tackle-block over which runs a hoisting-rope; monk'ey-wrench, a screw-key with a movable jaw.—have a monkey on one's back, to be addicted to drugs; have, get, one's monkey up, to be angry; make a monkey (out) of, to make a fool of; suck the monkey, to drink from a cask through an inserted tube: to drink rum, etc., from a coconut. [Origin doubtful.]

**Mon-Khmer**, *mōn'kmer'*, *adj.* of a group of Austroasiatic languages that includes *Mon*, spoken in Pegu (Burma), and *Khmer* in Cambodia.

**mon(o)-**, *mon(-ō)-*, in composition, single. [Gr. *monos*, single, alone.]

**mono**, *mon'ō*, (*coll.*) *n.* a monaural gramophone record.—Also *adj.*

**monoacid.** Same as monacid.

**monobasic**, *mon-ō-bā'sik*, *adj.* capable of reacting with one equivalent of an acid: (of an acid) having one replaceable hydrogen atom. [mon(o)-.]

**monoblepsis**, *mon-ō-blep'sis*, *n.* a condition in which vision is more distinct when one eye only is used. [Gr. *monos*, single, *blepsis*, sight.]

**monocardian**, *mon-ō-kär'di-ən*, *adj.* having an undivided heart. [Gr. *monos*, single, alone, *kardiā*, heart.]

**monocarpellary**, *mon-ō-kär'pəl-ə-ri*, or -*pel'*, *adj.* of or with only one carpel. [mon(o)-.]

**monocarpic**, *mon-ō-kärp'ik*, *adj.* fruiting once only. —*adj.* monocarp'ous, monocarpic: having only one ovary: producing one fruit. [Gr. *monos*, single, alone, *karpos*, fruit.]

**monoceros**, *mo-nos'ər-os*, *n.* a one-horned animal: the unicorn: perhaps the swordfish, or the narwhal (*Spens.*).—*adj.* monoc'erous. [Gr. *monokerōs*—*monos*, single, alone, *keras*, a horn.]

**monochasium**, *mon-ō-kā'zi-əm*, *n.* a cymose inflorescence in which each axis in turn produces one branch:—*pl.* monocha'sia.—*adj.* monocha'sial. [Gr. *monos*, single, alone; apparently on the analogy of *dichasium*, as if that were from Gr. *di-*, twice, and *chasis*, separation.]

**monochlamydeous**, *mon-ō-klə-mid'i-əs*, (*bot.*) *adj.* having a one-whorled perianth.—*n.pl.* Monochlamyd'eae, a division of the Archichlamydeae or Choripetalae, usually with perianth in one whorl. [mon(o)-.]

**monochord**, *mon'ō-körd*, *n.* an acoustical instrument with one string, sound-board and bridge: a similar instrument with more than one string and bridge: a clavichord: a tromba marina. [mon(o)-.]

**monochroic**, *mon-ō-krō'ik*, *adj.* of one colour. [Gr. *monochroos*—*monos*, *chrōs*, colour.]

**monochromatic**, *mon-ō-krō-mat'ik*, *adj.* of one colour or wavelength only: completely colour-blind: done in monochrome.—*ns.* monochro'-masy, complete colour-blindness; monochro'-mate, one who sees all colours as differing

in brilliance only; **monochro'matism,** monochromatic vision; **mon'ochrome,** representation in one colour: a picture in one colour: monochromy; **monochro'mist,** one who practises monochrome; **mon'ochromy,** the art of monochrome. [Gr. *monochrōmatos—monos,* single, alone, *chrōma, -atos,* colour.]
**monocle,** *mon'ə-kl, n.* a single eyeglass. [Fr. *monocle*—Gr. *monos,* L. *oculus,* eye.]
**monocline,** *mon'ō-klīn, (geol.) n.* a fold in strata followed by resumption of the original direction. —*adj.* **monoclin'al.** [Gr. *monos,* single, alone, *klīnein,* to cause to slope.]
**monoclinic,** *mon'ō-klīn-ik, (crystal.) adj.* referable to three unequal axes, two intersecting each other obliquely and at right angles to the third. [Gr. *monos,* single, alone, *klīnein,* to incline.]
**monoclinous,** *mon'ō-klī-nəs,* or *-klī', (bot.) adj.* hermaphrodite. [Gr. *monos,* single, alone, *klīnē,* bed.]
**mono-compound,** *mon-ō-kom'pownd, (chem.) n.* a compound containing one atom or group of that which is indicated. [mon(o)-.]
**monocoque,** *mon-ō-kok', -kōk', (aero.) n.* a fuselage or nacelle in which all, or nearly all, structural loads are carried by the skin: a motor vehicle structure in which body and chassis are in one and share stresses: the hull of a boat made in one piece. [Fr., lit. single shell.]
**monocotyledon,** *mon-ō-kot-i-lē'dən* (botanists' slang, **mon'ocot),** *n.* a plant of the **Monocotylē'dones** *(-ēz),* or **Monocot'ylae,** one of the two great divisions of the Angiosperms, the embryos with one cotyledon, leaves commonly parallel-veined, the parts of the flower usually in threes, the vascular bundles scattered and (with exceptions) without cambium.—*adj.* **monocotylē'donous.** [mon(o)-.]
**monocracy,** *mon-ok'rə-si, n.* government by one person.—*n.* **mon'ocrat** *(-ō-krat).*—*adj.* **monocrat'ic.** [Gr. *monos,* single, alone, *kratos,* power.]
**monocular,** *mon-ok'ū-lər, adj.* one-eyed: of, for, or with, one eye.—Also **monoc'ulous.** [Gr. *monos,* single, alone, L. *oculus,* an eye.]
**monoculture,** *mon'ō-kul-chər, n,* the growing of one kind of crop only, or a large area, over which it is grown [mon(o)-.]
**monocyclic,** *mon-ō-sik'lik, adj.* having one whorl or ring. [mon(o)-.]
**monodactylous,** *mon-ō-dak'ti-ləs, adj.* one-toed or one-fingered. [Gr. *monos,* single, alone, *daktylos,* finger, toe.]
**Monodelphia,** *mon-ō-del'fi-a, n.pl.* one of the three primary divisions of mammals, the placental mammals or Eutheria.—*adjs.* **monodel'phian, monodel'phic, monodel'phous.** [Gr. *monos,* single, alone, *delphys,* womb.]
**Monodon,** *mon'ō-don, n.* the narwhal.—*adj.* **mon'odont,** one-tusked: of the monodon. [Gr. *monos,* single, alone, *odous, odontos,* tooth, tusk.]
**monodrama,** *mon'ō-drä-mə, n.* a dramatic piece for a single performer.—*adj.* **monodramatic** *(-drə-mat'ik).* [mon(o)-.]
**monody,** *mon'ə-di, n.* a mournful ode or poem in which a single mourner bewails: a song for one voice: a manner of composition in which one part or voice carries the melody, the others accompanying.—*adjs.* **monodic** *(-od'),* **-al.**—*n.* **mon'odist,** one who writes monodies. [Gr. *monōidiā—monos,* single, alone, *ōidē,* song.]
**monoecious,** *mon-ē'shəs, adj.* having separate male and female flowers on the same plant.—*n.pl.* **Monoe'cia,** in the Linnaean system, a class so characterised.—*n.* **monoecism** *(-ē'sizm).* [Gr. *monos,* single, alone, *oikos,* a house.]
**monofil,** *mon'ō-fil, n.* a single strand of synthetic fibre.—Also **monofil'ament.** [Gr. *monos,* single, alone, L. *filum,* a thread.]
**monogamy,** *mon-og'ə-mi, n.* the rule, custom, or

condition of marriage to one wife or husband at a time, or (now rarely) in life.—*adjs.* **monogamic** *(mon-ō-gam'ik),* **monogamous** *(-og'əm-).*—*n.* **monog'amist.** [Gr. *monos,* single, alone, *gamos,* marriage.]
**monogenesis,** *mon-ō-jen'i-sis, n.* development of offspring from a parent like itself: asexual reproduction: community of origin.—*adj.* **monogenet'ic.**—*ns.* **monogenism** *(-oj'ən-izm),* the doctrine of the common descent of all living things, or of any particular group (esp. mankind) from one ancestor or pair; **monog'enist.**—*adjs.* **monogenist'ic;** **monog'enous.**—*n.* **monog'eny,** descent from one common ancestor or pair: asexual reproduction. [mon(o)-.]
**monoglot,** *mon'ō-glot, n.* one who knows only one language.—Also *adj.* [Gr. *monos,* single, alone, *glōtta,* tongue.]
**monogony,** *mon-og'ən-i, n.* asexual reproduction. [Gr. *monos,* single, alone, *gonos,* begetting.]
**monogram,** *mon'ə-gram, n.* a figure consisting of several letters interwoven or written into one.— *adj.* **monogrammatic** *(-grə-mat'ik).* [Gr. *monos,* single, alone, *gramma, grammatos,* a letter.]
**monograph,** *mon'ə-gräf, n.* a treatise written on one particular subject or any branch of it: a systematic account.—*v.t.* to write a monograph upon.—*ns.* **monographer** *(mon-og'rə-fər),* **monog'-raphist,** a writer of monographs.—*adjs.* **monographic** *(-graf'),* **-al,** pertaining to a monograph or a monogram: drawn in lines without colours. —*n.* **monog'raphy** *(rare),* a monograph. [Gr. *monos,* single, alone, *graphein,* to write.]
**monogyny,** *mon-oj'i-ni,* or *-og', n.* the custom, practice, or condition of having only one wife: marriage with one wife: the habit of mating with one female.—*n.pl.* **Monogynia** *(mon-ō-jin'i-ə),* in various Linnaean classes of plants an order having one style.—*adjs.* **monogyn'ian; monog'ynous,** having one wife: practising monogyny: mating with one female: having one style: monogynian. [Gr. *monos,* single, alone, *gynē,* woman.]
**monohull,** *mon'ō-hul, n.* a vessel with one hull, as opp. to catamaran, trimaran. [mon(o)-.]
**monohybrid,** *mon-ō-hī'brid, n.* a cross between parents differing in one heritable character. [mon(o)-.]
**monohydric,** *mon-ō-hī'drik, adj.* containing one hydroxyl group. [mon(o)-.]
**monolatry,** *mon-ol'ə-tri, n.* the worship of one god without excluding belief in others.—*n.* **monol'ater.** —*adj.* **monol'atrous.** [Gr. *monos,* single, alone, *latreiā,* worship.]
**monolith,** *mon'ō-lith, n.* a pillar, or column, of a single stone: anything resembling a monolith in uniformity, massiveness or intractability.—*adj.* **monolith'ic,** pertaining to or resembling a monolith: of a state, an organisation, etc., massive, and undifferentiated throughout: intractable for this reason.—**monolithic integrated circuit** (see integer). [Gr. *monos,* single, alone, *lithos,* a stone.]
**monologue,** *mon'ə-log, n.* a composition put into the mouth of one person, or intended to be spoken by one person: a harangue that engrosses conversation.—*adjs.* **monologic** *(-loj'),* **-al.**—*v.i.* **monologise, -ize** *(mon-ol'ə-jiz),* to indulge in this. —Also **monologuise, -ize** *(-giz).*—*ns.* **monol'ogist,** one who talks in monologue (also **mon'ologuist);** **monol'ogy,** the habit of doing so. [Gr. *monos,* single, alone, *logos,* speech.]
**monomachy,** *mon-om'ə-ki, n.* single combat: a duel.—Also **monomā'chia.** [Gr. *monos,* single, alone, *machē,* a fight.]
**monomania,** *mon-ō-mā'ni-ə, n.* madness confined to one subject: an unreasonable interest in any particular thing.—*n.* **monomā'niac,** one affected with monomania.—*adjs.* **monomā'niac, monomaniacal** *(-mə-nī'ə-kl).* [Gr. *monos,* single, alone, *maniā,* madness.]

monomer, *mon'*, *mōn'ə-mər*, *n.* the simplest of any series of compounds having the same empirical formula—opp. to *polymer*. [Gr. *monos*, single, alone, *meros*, part.]

monometallic, *mon-ō-mi-tal'ik*, *adj.* involving or using but one metal as a standard of currency.—*ns.* monometallism (*-met'əl-izm*); monomet'-allist. [mon(o)-.]

monometer, *mon-om'i-tər*, (*pros.*) *adj.* consisting of one measure.—*n.* a verse of one measure. [mon(o)-, and meter (1).]

monomial, *mon-ō'mi-əl*, *n.* an algebraic expression of one term only: a name consisting of one word.—Also *adj.* [Ill-formed from Gr. *monos*, single, alone, L. *nōmen*, name.]

monomorphic, *mon-ō-mör'fik*, *adj.* existing in one form only.—*adj.* monomor'phous. [Gr. *monos*, single, alone, *morphē*, form.]

monomyarian, *mon-ō-mi-ā'ri-ən*, *adj.* having one adductor muscle. [Gr. *monos*, single, alone, *mȳs*, *myos*, muscle.]

mononuclear, *mon-ō-nū'kli-ər*, *adj.* having a single nucleus: monocyclic.—*n.* (*med.*) mono-nucleosis (*mon-ō-nūk-li-ō'sis*), the presence in the blood of an abnormally large number of a type of leucocytes.—See also infectious mono-nucleosis under infect. [mon(o)-.]

monopetalous, *mon-ō-pet'ə-ləs*, (*bot.*) *adj.* having petals united. [mon(o)-.]

monophagous, *mon-of'ə-gəs*, *adj.* having only one kind of food.—*n.* monoph'agy (*-ji*), feeding on one food: eating alone. [Gr. *monos*, single, alone, *phagein* (aor.), to eat.]

monophasic, *mon-ō-fāz'ik*, *adj.* (of electric current) single-phase (also mon'ophase): having one period of rest and one of activity during the 24 hours (*biol.*). [mon(o)-.]

monophobia, *mon-ō-fō'bi-ə*, *n.* morbid dread of being alone. [mon(o)-.]

monophthong, *mon'of-thong*, *n.* a simple vowel-sound.—*adj.* monophthongal (*-thong'gəl*).—*v.t.* mon'ophthongise, -ize (*-gīz*), to turn into a mono-phthong. [Gr. *monophthongos*—*monos*, single, alone, *phthongos*, sound, vowel.]

monophyletic, *mon-ō-fi-let'ik*, or *-fi-*, *adj.* derived from a single stock. [Gr. *monos*, single, alone, *phȳletikos*, pertaining to a tribesman—*phȳlē*, tribe.]

monophyodont, *mon-ō-fi'ō-dont*, *adj.* having only one set of teeth.—*n.* an animal with but one set of teeth. [Gr. *monophyēs*, of simple nature, *monos*, single, *odous*, *odontos*, tooth.]

Monophysite, *mō-nof'i-zit*, *-sit*, *n.* one who holds that Christ had but one composite nature.—*adj.* monophysitic (*-sit'ik*, *-zit'ik*).—*n.* monoph'ysit-ism. [Gr. *monos*, single, alone, *physis*, nature.]

Monoplacophora, *mon-ō-plak-of'ə-rə*, *n.pl.* a very primitive limpet-like class of molluscs, believed, till the discovery (1952) of the living Neopilina off the W. coast of Mexico, to have been extinct since early Silurian times. [Gr. *monos*, single, alone, *plax*, *plakos*, plate, *phoros*, bearing, from the single piece of shell.]

monoplane, *mon'ə-plān*, *n.* an aeroplane or glider with one set of planes or wings. [mono-.]

monoplegia, *mon-ō-plē'ji-ə*, *n.* paralysis limited to a single part. [Gr. *monos*, single, alone, *plēgē*, stroke.]

monopode, *mon'ə-pōd*, *n.* a one-footed man, esp. a member of a fabled tribe with single foot large enough to be used by its owner as a sunshade (Pliny, *Naturalis Historia*): a one-footed table, etc.—*adj.* one-footed.—*adj.* monopo'dial, pertaining to or of the nature of a monopodium.—*adv.* monopo'dially.—*n.* monopo'dium (*bot.*), an axis that continues to grow without being supplanted, as in the sympodium, by a lateral branch. [L. *monopodius*, *-um*—Gr. *monos*, single, alone, and *pous*, *podos*, foot.]

monopoly, *mon-op'ə-li*, *n.* sole power, or privilege,

of dealing in anything: exclusive command or possession: that of which one has such a sole power, privilege, command, or possession.—*v.t.* monop'olise, -ize, to have a monopoly of: to keep to oneself: to engross.—*ns.* monop'oliser, -z-, monop'olist.—*adj.* monopolis'tic. [L. *mono-pōlium*—Gr. *monopōlion*—*monos*, single, alone, *pōleein*, to sell.]

monoprionidian, *mon-ō-pri-ə-nid'i-ən*, *adj.* serrated on one side (of graptolites). [Gr. *monos*, single, alone, *priōn*, a saw.]

monopteros, *mon-op'tər-os*, monopteron, *-on*, *n.* a circular Greek temple with one ring of columns.—*adj.* monop'teral. [Gr. *monos*, single, alone, *pteron*, a wing.]

monoptote, *mon'op-tōt*, *n.* a word with but one case-form. [Gr. *monoptōtos*—*monos*, single, alone, and *ptōtos*, fallen; cf. *ptōsis*, case (see case).]

monorail, *mon'ō-rāl*, *n.* a railway with carriages running astride of, or suspended from, one rail.—Also *adj.* [mon(o)-.]

monorchid, *mon-ör'kid*, *adj.* having only one testicle.—*n.* monorch'ism. [Faultily formed from Gr. *monorchis*—*monos*, single, alone, *orchis*, *-eōs*, testicle.]

monorhine, *mon'ō-rin*, *adj.* having one nostril.—Also monorhin'al. [Gr. *monos*, single, alone, *rhis*, *rhinos*, nose.]

monorhyme, *mon'ə-rim*, *n.* a series or tirade of lines all rhyming together.—Also *adj.*—*adj.* mon'orhymed. [mon(o)-.]

monosaccharide, *mon-ō-sak'ə-rid*, *n.* a simple sugar that cannot be hydrolysed. [mon(o)-.]

monosepalous, *mon-ō-sep'ə-ləs*, (*bot.*) *adj.* having the sepals all united. [mon(o)-.]

monosodium glutamate, *mon-ō-sō'di-əm gloō'tə-māt*, a white crystalline salt which brings out the flavour of meat (*glutamate*, a salt of glutamic acid).

monostich, *mon'ə-stik*, *n.* a poem of one line.—*adj.* monostichous (*-os'tik-əs*), in one line: in one row. [Gr. *monos*, single, alone, *stichos*, row, line.]

monostrophic, *mon-ə-strof'ik*, *adj.* not divided into strophe, antistrophe, and epode: having the same strophic or stanzaic structure throughout.—*n.pl.* monostroph'ics, monostrophic verses. [Gr. *monostrophikos*—*monos*, single, alone, *strophē*, a strophe.]

monostyle, *mon'ō-stil*, (*archit.*) *adj.* consisting of a single shaft.—*adj.* monostyl'ar. [Gr. *monos*, single, alone, *stylos*, a pillar.]

monosy, *mon'os-i*, (*biol.*) *n.* separation of parts normally fused.—Also monō'sis. [Gr. *monōsis*, solitariness—*monos*, single, alone.]

monosyllable, *mon-ə-sil'ə-bl*, *n.* a word of one syllable.—*adj.* monosyllabic (*-ab'ik*).—*n.* mono-syll'abism. [mon(o)-.]

monosymmetric, *-al*, *mon-ō-sim-et'rik*, *-əl*, *adjs.* having only one plane of symmetry. [mon(o)-.]

monotelephone, *mon-ō-tel'i-fōn*, *n.* a telephone that transmits sounds of one pitch only. [mon(o)-.]

monothalamous, *mon-ō-thal'ə-məs*, *adj.* single-chambered: with but one cavity: (of fruit) formed from a single flower.—Also monothal-amic (*-am'ik*). [Gr. *monos*, single, alone, *thalamos*, a chamber.]

monothecal, *mon-ō-thē'kl*, *adj.* having only one theca.—Also monothe'cous. [Gr. *monos*, single, alone, *thēkē*, case.]

monotheism, *mon'ō-thē-izm*, *n.* the belief in only one God.—*n.* mon'otheist.—*adjs.* monotheist'ic, *-al.* [Gr. *monos*, single, alone, *theos*, God.]

Monotheletism, *mon-ō-thel'i-tizm*, *n.* the doctrine that Christ had but one will—opp. to *Ditheletism*.—Also Monothelism (*mon-oth'əl-izm*), Mono-thel'itism.—*ns.* Monoth'elēte, Monoth'elite.—*adjs.* Monothelēt'ic, *-al.* [Gr. *monos*, single, alone, *thelētēs*, a willer—*thelein*, to will.]

**monotint**, *mon'ə-tint, n.* drawing or painting in a single tint. [mon(o)-.]

**monotocous**, *mon-ot'ə-kəs, adj.* producing single offspring at a time: fruiting once only. [Gr. *monos*, single, alone, *tokos*, birth, offspring.]

**monotone**, *mon'ə-tōn, n.* a single, unvaried tone or utterance: a succession of sounds having the same pitch: continued or extended sameness: sameness in colour.—*adj.* in monotone.—*v.t.* and *v.i.* to sing, declaim, speak, utter, in monotone.—*adjs.* **monotonic** (-*ton'ik*), in monotone: of a function or sequence, having the property of either never increasing or never decreasing; **monotonous** (*mon-ot'ə-nəs*), uttered in one unvaried tone: marked by dull uniformity.— *adv.* **monot'onously.**—*ns.* **monot'onousness; monot'ony,** dull uniformity of tone or sound: want of modulation in speaking or reading: irksome sameness or want of variety (*fig.*). [Gr. *monos*, single, alone, *tonos*, a tone.]

**Monotremata**, *mon-ō-trē'mə-ta, n.pl.* the lowest order of Mammalia, having a single opening for the genital and digestive organs.—*adj.* **monotre'matous**—also **mon'otreme.**—*n.* **mon'o-treme,** a member of the Monotremata. [Gr. *monos*, single, alone, *trēma, -atos*, a hole.]

**monotroch,** *mon'ō-trok,* (*Scott, facet.*) *n.* a wheelbarrow. [Gr. *monos*, single, alone, *trochos*, wheel.]

**Monotropa,** *mon-ot'rə-pa, n.* a genus akin to wintergreen—the bird's-nest and Indian-pipe, nourished by a fungal mycorrhiza in humus. [Gr. *monotropos*, solitary—*monos*, single, alone, *tropos*, turn.]

**monotype,** *mon'ə-tip, n.* a sole type, a species forming a genus by itself: (*cap.*) proprietary name of a machine that casts and sets type, letter by letter.—Also *adj.*—*adj.* **monotypic** (-*tip'ik*). [mon(o)-.]

**monovalent,** *mon-ō-vā'lənt, mon-ov'əl-ənt, adj.* univalent. [mon(o)-.]

**monoxide,** *mon-ok'sid, n.* an oxide with one oxygen atom in the molecule. [mon(o)-.]

**monoxylon,** *mon-oks'i-lon, n.* a canoe made from one log.—*adj.* **monox'ylous.** [Gr.,—*monos*, single, alone, *xylon*, wood.]

**monozygotic,** *mon-ō-zī-got'ik, adj.* developed from one zygote. [mon(o)-.]

**Monroeism,** *mən-rō'izm, n.* (or **Monroe doctrine**) President Monroe's principle (1823) that Europe must refrain from intervention in the affairs of independent countries in the American continents.

**Monseigneur,** *m3-sen-yœr, n.* my lord: a title in France given to a person of high birth or rank, esp. to bishops, etc. (written *Mgr*): the Dauphin: —*pl.* **Messeigneurs** (*me-sen-yœr*).—*n.* **Monsieur** (*mə-syø*), sir: a title of courtesy in France = *Mr* in English (printed *M.* or in full): the eldest brother of the king of France: a Frenchman generally—arch. and illiterate or grotesque, **moun'seer** (or -*sēr'*): a French gentleman:—*pl.* **Messieurs** (Fr. *mes-yø*, written *MM.*; Eng. *mes'ərz*, written Messrs).—**Monsieur de Paris,** the public executioner. [Fr. *mon seigneur, sieur,* my lord—L. *meum seniōrem* (accus.), my lord.]

**Monsignor,** *mon-sēn'yər*; It. *mon-sēn-yōr'*; **Monsignore** (-*yō'rā*), *n.* a title conferred on prelates and on dignitaries of the papal household—*pls.* **Monsignors** (-*sēn'*), **Monsigno'ri** (-*rē*). [It.—Fr.]

**monsoon,** *mon-sōōn', n.* a periodical wind of the Indian Ocean, S.W. from April to October, and N.E. the rest of the year: a similar wind elsewhere: in N. and W. India, the rains accompanying the S.W. monsoon.—*adj.* **monsoon'al.**— **break of the monsoon,** the first onset of the monsoon rain. [Port. *monção*—Malay *mūsim*—Ar. *mausim*, a time, a season.]

**monster,** *mon'stər, n.* anything out of the usual course of nature: a prodigy: a fabulous animal: an abnormally formed animal or plant: a grotesque animal: a gigantic animal: anything gigantic: anything horrible from ugliness or wickedness.—*adj.* gigantic, huge.—*n.* **monstrosity** (-*stros'i-ti*; *obs.* **monstruos'ity**), the state or fact of being monstrous: marked abnormality: an abnormally formed animal, plant, part, or object: anything outrageously constructed.— *adj.* **mon'strous** (*obs.* **mon'struous**), out of the common course of nature: enormous: wonderful: horrible: outrageous: preposterous.—*adv.* (*arch.*) exceedingly. — *adv.* **mon'strously.** — *n.* **mon'strousness.** [Fr. *monstre*—L. *mōnstrum,* an evil omen, a monster—*monēre, monitum,* to warn.]

**monstrance,** *mon'strəns, n.* the receptacle in which the consecrated host is exposed in R.C. churches for the adoration of the people. [O.Fr.,—L. *mōnstrāre,* to show.]

**monstre sacré,** *m3-str' sak-rā,* a person (esp. in the world of theatre or cinema) whose appeal to the public is increased by his eccentricity [Fr., sacred monster.]

**montage,** *m3-täzh', n.* selection and piecing together of material for a cinematograph film with a view to effect: (act or process of making) a composite photograph: setting-up, assemblage, superimposition: a picture made partly by sticking objects on the canvas. [Fr.,—*monter,* to mount.]

**Montagnard,** *m3-tä-nyär,* one of the Mountain or the extreme democratic wing of the French Legislative Assembly (1st Oct. 1791 to 21st Sept. 1792), so called because sitting on the topmost benches. [Fr., mountaineer.]

**montane,** *mon'tān, adj.* mountainous: mountain-dwelling. [L. *montānus—mōns, montis,* a mountain.]

**Montanism,** *mon'tən-izm, n.* a 2nd-century heresy founded by the prophet and 'Paraclete' *Montānus* of Phrygia—an ascetic reaction in favour of the old discipline and severity.—*n.* and *adj.* **Mon'tanist.**—*adj.* **Montanist'ic.**

**montant,** *mont'ənt, n.* a vertical member in panelling or framing: in fencing, apparently an upward blow (also, as if Sp., **montant'o**; *Shak.*). [Fr.,—*monter,* to rise.]

**montaria,** *mont-ä-rē'ə, n.* in Brazil, a light canoe made of one log. [Port.]

**Montbretia,** *mon(t)-brēsh'yə, n.* a plant (Tritonia) of the iris family bearing bright orange-coloured flowers. [After a French botanist, Coquebert de *Montbret* (1780-1801).]

**mont-de-piété,** *m3-də-pyä-tā* (Fr.), **monte di pietà** (*mon'tä dē pyä-tä'*; It.), *n.* a state pawnshop. [Fund (lit. mount) of pity or piety.]

**monte,** *mon'tā, -ti, n.* a shrubby tract, a forest: a Spanish-American gambling card-game.—**three-card monte,** a Mexican three-card trick. [Sp., mountain, scrub, cards remaining after a deal— L. *mōns, montis,* a mountain.]

**monteith,** *mən-, mon-tēth', n.* a large 17th- or 18th-century bowl, usually of silver, fluted and scalloped, for cooling punch-glasses (said to be named from 'a fantastical Scot' who wore his cloak so scalloped): a cotton handkerchief with white spots on a coloured ground (from Glasgow manufacturers).

**montem,** *mon'tem, n.* a former custom of Eton boys to go every third Whit-Tuesday to a hillock on the Bath road and exact 'salt-money' from passers-by, for the university expenses of the senior scholar or school captain. [L. *ad montem,* to the hill.]

**montero,** *mon-tā'rō, n.* a huntsman: a Spanish horseman's helmet-like cap with a flap.—Also **monte'ro-cap'.** [Sp. *montero,* a huntsman— *monte*—L. *mōns, montis,* a mountain.]

**Montessorian,** *mon-tes-ōr'i-ən, -ör', adj.* pertaining to Dr Maria *Montessori* or her method (*c.* 1900) of education, insisting on spontaneity and freedom from restraint.

**montgolfier,** *mon*(t)-*gol′fi-ər, n.* a fire-balloon. [From the brothers *Montgolfier,* of Annonay, who sent up the first in 1783.]

**month,** *munth, n.* the moon's period: one of the twelve conventional divisions of the year, or its length—a *calendar* month.—*n.* **month′ling,** a month-old child.—*adj.* **month′ly,** performed in a month: done, recurring, or appearing once a month.—*n.* a monthly publication: a monthly rose: (*pl.*) the menses.—*adv.* once a month: in every month.—**monthly nurse,** a nurse attending a woman in the first month after childbirth; **monthly rose,** a rose supposed to bloom every month; **month's mind** (see **mind**).—**anomalistic month,** the interval between the moon's perigee passages = 27·5545 days; **lunar month,** a month reckoned by the moon: a synodic month; **month of Sundays,** a tediously long time; **sidereal,** or **stellar, month,** the time in which the moon passes round the ecliptic to the same point among the stars = 27·3217 days; **solar month,** one-twelfth of a solar year; **synodic month,** the period of the moon's phases = 29·5306 days; **tropical,** or **periodic, month,** from the moon's passing the equinox till she again reaches it = 27·3216 days. [O.E. *mōnath-mōna,* moon.]

**monticellite,** *mon-ti-sel′it, n.* an orthorhombic calcium magnesium silicate. [After the Italian mineralogist Teodoro *Monticelli* (1759-1845).]

**monticolous,** *mon-tik′ə-ləs, adj.* mountain-dwelling. [L. *monticola,* a mountain-dweller—*mōns, montis,* mountain, *colĕre,* to inhabit.]

**monticulus,** *mon-tik′ū-ləs, n.* a little elevation—also **mon′ticle** and **mon′ticule.**—*adjs.* **montic′ulate, montic′ulous,** having small projections. [L. *monticulus,* dim. of *mōns,* mountain.]

**montre,** *mōtr′, n.* the visible pipes of an organ, usually the open diapason. [Fr., sample, show.]

**monture,** *mon′tūr, mō-tür, n.* a mounting, setting, frame. [Fr.]

**monument,** *mon′ū-mənt* (*obs.* **mon′iment**), *n.* anything that preserves the memory of a person or an event, a building, pillar, tomb, tablet, statue, etc.: any structure, natural or artificial, considered as an object of beauty or of interest as a relic of the past: a historic document or record (sometimes confused with **muniment**): a relic, indication, or trace: a notable or enduring example: a warning token or admonition (*Spens.*): a prodigy (*Shak.*).—*v.t.* to commemorate by or on a monument.—*adj.* **monumental** (*-ment′əl*), of or relating to or of the nature of a monument, tomb, memento, or token: memorial: massive and lasting: vast: impressive: amazing: loosely, very large.—*adv.* **monument′ally.** [L. *monumentum, monimentum—monēre,* to remind.]

**mony,** *mun′i,* a Scots form of **many.**

**monyplies,** *mun′i-pliz.* See **manyplies.**

**monzonite,** *mon′zən-it, n.* a coarse-grained intermediate igneous rock. [Monte *Monzoni* in the Dolomite Mountains.]

**moo,** *mōō, v.i.* to low.—*n.* a cow's low. [Imit.]

**mooch, mouch,** *mōōch, v.i.* to play truant: to go blackberrying: to slouch about: to skulk: to loiter: to sponge.—*v.t.* to pilfer.—*n.* the act of mooching.—*n.* **mooch′er, mouch′er.** [Perh. O.Fr. *muchier,* to hide; cf. **miche.**]

**mood,** *mōōd, n.* a form of the verb to express the mode or manner of an action or of a state of being (*gram.*): the form of the syllogism as determined by the quantity and quality of its three constituent propositions (*log.*): in mediaeval music, mode in the sense of relative time value. [**mode.**]

**mood,** *mōōd, n.* temporary state of the motions or of attitude: state of gloom or sullenness: anger

heat of temper (*obs.*).—*adv.* **mood′ily.**—*n.* **mood′iness,** sullenness.—*adjs.* **mood′y,** indulging in moods: sullen: angry (*obs.*); **mood′y-mad** (*Shak.*), mad with anger. [O.E. *mōd,* mind; cf. Ger. *mut,* courage.]

**mooi,** *mō′i,* (*Afrik.*) *adj.* fine—a general word of commendation. [From Du.]

**mooktar.** See **mukhtar.**

**mool,** *mōōl,* a Scots form of **mould.**

**moola(h).** See **mulla(h).**

**moon,** *mōōn, n.* the earth's satellite: a satellite: a month: anything in the shape of a moon or crescent: a crescent-shaped outwork (*fort.*).—*v.t.* to adorn with moons or crescents.—*v.i.* to wander about or gaze vacantly at anything.—*adj.* **mooned,** marked with the figure of a moon.—*n.* **moon′er,** one who moons about.—*adjs.* **moon′ish,** like the moon: variable: inconstant; **moon′less,** destitute of moonlight; **moon′y,** of or relating to the moon: moon-like: crescent-shaped: bearing a crescent: round and shining: moonlit: inclined to moon: fatuous: tipsy (*slang*).—*n.* a noodle.—**moon′beam,** a beam of light from the moon.—*adj.* **moon′-blind,** affected with moon-eye: blinded by the moon: night-blind: dim-sighted, purblind.—**moon′-bow,** a rainbow cast by the moon; **moon′calf,** a false conception or fleshy mass formed in the womb: a monster: a deformed creature: a dolt; **moon′-eye,** a disease affecting horses' eyes: an American freshwater shad-like fish; **moon′face,** a full, round face—a point of beauty in the East.—*adj.* **moon′-faced.**—**moon′-fish,** the opah or other silvery disk-shaped fish; **moon′-flower,** the ox-eye daisy; **moon′-glade,** the track of moonlight on water; **moon′-god, -goddess,** a god or goddess representing or associated with the moon; **moon′-knife,** a leather-worker's crescent-shaped knife; **moon′light,** the light of the moon—sunlight reflected from the moon's surface: smuggled spirit.—*adj.* lighted by the moon: occurring in moonlight.—**moon′lighter,** in Ireland, one who committed agrarian outrages by night about 1880: a moonshiner: one who takes work in the evening in addition to his normal day's work; **moonlight flitting,** a removal by night, with rent unpaid; **moon′lighting.**—*adjs.* **moon′lit,** lit or illumined by the moon; **moon′-loved,** loved by the moon.—**moon′-mad′ness,** lunacy, once thought to be connected with the moon's changes.—*adj.* (*Scott*) **moon′-raised,** excited or maddened by the moon.—**moon′raker,** a moon-sail: a Wiltshireman (from a Gotham story); **moon′-raking,** the following of crazy fancies; **moon′rise,** the rising of the moon; **moon′sail,** a small sail, sometimes carried above the sky-scraper; **moon′scape,** the physical appearance of the surface of the moon, or a representation of it; **moon′seed,** a plant (*Menispermum*) with lunate seeds; **moon′set,** the setting of the moon; **moon′shine,** moonlight: show without reality (*fig.*): nonsense (*coll.*): a month (*Shak.*): spirits illicitly distilled or smuggled.—*adj.* lighted by the moon: made of moonshine, bodiless.—**moon′shiner,** a smuggler or illicit distiller of spirits.—*adj.* **moon′shiny,** lighted by the moon: visionary, unreal.—**moon′shot,** act or process of launching an object or vehicle to orbit, or land on, the moon; **moon′stone,** an opalescent orthoclase feldspar, perh. sometimes selenite; **moon′strike,** the act or process of landing a spacecraft on the surface of the moon.—*adj.* **moon′struck** (also **moon′-stricken**), affected by the moon, lunatic, crazed.—**moon′wort,** a eusporangiate fern (*Botrychium lunaria*) with lunate pinnae, or other of the genus: the plant honesty (from its silvery septum).—**eggs in moonshine,** an old dish, fried eggs with onions and various flavourings. [O.E. *mōna;* cf. Ger. *mond,* L. *mēnsis,* Gr. *mēn.*]

Neutral vowels in unaccented syllables: *el′ə-mənt;* for certain sounds in foreign words, see p. viii

**moonshee.** Same as **munshi.**

**Moon-type,** $m\overline{oo}n'$-*tip*, *n.* a system of embossed lettering for the blind, invented by Dr William *Moon* (1847).

**moop.** Same as **moup.**

**moor,** $m\overline{oo}r$, *n.* a wide tract of untilled ground, often covered with heath, and having a poor, peaty soil: a heath: (*Scot.*) **muir** (*mûr, mār, mür*).—*adjs.* **moor'ish, moor'y,** resembling a moor: sterile: marshy: boggy.—**moor'-band,** a hard ferruginous layer formed under moorland soil (also **moor'-band pan, moor'-pan**); **moor'-buzz'ard,** the marsh-harrier; **moor'cock, moor'-fowl,** red, or black, grouse; **moor'hen,** water-hen: female moorfowl; **moor'-ill** (Scot.), a cattle disease of moorland districts, marked by haemoglobin in the urine; **moor'land,** a tract of moor: moorish country.—*adj.* of moorland.—**moor'log,** a deposit of decayed woody material under a marsh, etc.; **moor'man,** a dweller in moors; **moor'-pout, muir'-pout, -poot** (-*powt*, -$p\overline{oo}t$), a young grouse. [O.E. *mōr.*]

**moor,** $m\overline{oo}r$, *v.t.* to fasten by cable or anchor.—*v.i.* to make fast a ship, boat, etc.: to be made fast.—*ns.* **moor'age,** condition of being moored: act of mooring: a due paid for mooring: a place for mooring; **moor'ing,** act of mooring: that which serves to moor or confine a ship: (in *pl.*) the place or condition of a ship thus moored.—**moor'ing-mast.** [Prob. from an unrecorded O.E. word answering to M.Du. *māren.*]

**Moor,** $m\overline{oo}r$, *n.* a Mauretanian: a member of the mixed Arab and Berber people of Morocco and the Barbary coast: one of the Arab and Berber conquerors and occupants of Spain from 711 to 1492: in some countries, a Mohammedan: a dark-coloured person generally, a Negro:—*fem.* **Moor'ess.**—*n.* **Moor'ery,** a Moorish quarter.—*adj.* **Moor'ish.** [Fr. *More, Maure*—L. *Maurus,* doubtfully connected with Byzantine Gr. *mauros,* black.]

**moorva.** Same as **murva.**

**moose,** $m\overline{oo}s$, *n.* the American elk: a member of an American secret fraternity:—*pl.* **moose.**—**moose'yard,** an area where the moose tread down the snow and spend the winter. [Algonquian *mus, moos.*]

**moot,** $m\overline{oo}t$, *n.* orig. a meeting: a deliberative or administrative assembly or court (*hist.*): its meeting-place: discussion: a law students' discussion of a hypothetical case.—*v.t.* to argue, dispute: to propose for discussion.—*v.i.* to dispute, plead.—*adj.* debatable.—*adj.* **moot'able.** —*ns.* **moot'er; moot'ing.**—**moot case,** a case for discussion: a case about which there may be difference of opinion; **moot'court,** a meeting for discussion of hypothetical cases; **moot'-hall, -house,** a town-hall or council chamber: a hall for moot-courts; **moot'-hill,** a hill of meeting on which the moot was held (often confused with **mote-hill**); **moot'man,** a law student who argues in moots; **moot point,** an undecided or disputed point. [O.E. (*ge*)*mōt* (n.), *mōtian* (vb.), akin to *mētan,* to meet.]

**moove,** an old spelling of **move.**

**mop,** *mop*, *n.* a bunch of rags, yarn, or the like, on the end of a stick, for washing, removing dust, soaking up liquid, etc.: any similar instrument, as for cleansing a wound, polishing, etc.: a thick or bushy head of hair: an act of mopping: a hiring-fair (probably from the custom of carrying a badge of occupation; *dial.*).—*v.t.* to wipe, dab, soak up, or remove with a mop or as if with a mop: to clear away or dispose of as residue:—*pr.p.* **mopp'ing;** *pa.t.* and *pa.p.* **mopped.**—*ns.* **mopp'er; mopp'et,** a rag-doll: a little woolly dog: a doll-like woman: a term of endearment or contempt, esp. for a girl or child.—*adj.* **mopp'y** (*slang*), drunk.—*n.* **mop'sy,** a dowdy: a slattern: a term of endearment.—

*adj.* **mop'-head'ed,** having a shaggy, unkempt head of hair.—**mop'stick,** the handle of a mop: a hand-rail nearly circular in section: (also **map'stick**) a rod for raising a piano damper; **mop'-up',** an action of mopping up.—**mops and brooms,** half-drunk: out of sorts; **mop up,** to clear away or clean up with a mop: to clear away, dispose of, what is left of the enemy; **Mop(p), Mrs,** a cleaner, charwoman. [Possibly from O.Fr. *mappe*—L. *mappa,* a napkin; or possibly from the name *Mabel.*]

**mop,** *mop*, *n.* a grimace.—*v.i.* to grimace—*n., v.i.* often **mop and mow.** [Cf. Du. *moppen,* to pout.]

**mope,** *mōp, v.i.* to go aimlessly and listlessly: to yield to low spirits.—*v.t.* to make spiritless.—*n.* a listless person: (esp. in *pl.*) moping.—*adv.* **mop'ingly.**—*adj.* **mop'ish,** dull: spiritless.—*adv.* **mop'ishly.**—*ns.* **mop'ishness; mop'us,** one who mopes.—*adj.-adv.* **mop'y.** [Origin obscure.]

**moped,** $m\overline{o}'ped$, a *mo*tor-assisted *ped*al cycle.

**mopoke,** $m\overline{o}'p\overline{o}k$, *n.* an Australian frogmouth: a New Zealand owl: a silly.—Also **mope'hawk, more'-pork.** [From the cry of the owl and of a kindred Australian species, mistakenly attributed to the frogmouth.]

**Mopp, Mrs.** Same as **Mop, Mrs.**

**mopus,** $m\overline{o}'pas$, **mawpus,** $m\ddot{o}'pas$, (*slang*) *n.* a small coin.

**moquette,** $m\overline{o}$-*ket'*, *n.,* a carpet and soft furnishing material with a loose velvety pile—the back, thick canvas, etc. [Fr.]

**mora, morra,** $m\overline{o}'ra$, *mo', n.* delay, esp. unjustifiable (*law*): the duration of a short syllable or half that of a long (*pros.*). [L., delay.]

**mora, morra,** $mor'a$, *n.* the game of guessing how many fingers are held up. [It. *mora.*]

**moraceous.** See under **morus.**

**moraine,** $mo$-*rān'*, *n.* a continuous marginal line of débris borne on or left by a glacier: a garden imitation of this.—*adj.* **morain'ic.** [Fr.]

**moral,** $mor'al$, *adj.* of or relating to character or conduct considered as good or evil: ethical: conformed to or directed towards right, virtuous: esp. virtuous in matters of sex: capable of knowing right and wrong: subject to the moral law: supported by evidence of reason or probability —opp. to *demonstrative*: moralising (*Shak.*).—*n.* in *pl.* writings on ethics: the doctrine or practice of the duties of life: moral philosophy or ethics: principles and conduct, esp. sexual: in *sing.* the practical lesson that can be drawn from anything: an exposition of such lesson by way of conclusion: a symbol: (sometimes *mor-äl'*, after Ger. *moral* or Fr. *morale*) morality: a certainty (*slang*): an exact counterpart (*slang*): (spelt **morale** to look French and to suggest the Fr. pron. *mor-äl'*—the French word in this sense is *moral*) condition with respect to discipline and confidence, pride, fixity of purpose, faith in the cause fought for, etc. (usu. *mil.*).—*v.t.* and *v.i.* to moralise.—*ns.* **morale,** *mor-äl'* (Fr. *morale*), morality: see above (*mil.*; **moral**); **moralisā'-tion, -z-,** act of moralising, explanation in a moral sense.—*v.t.* **mor'alise, -ize,** to apply to a moral purpose: to explain in a moral sense: to make moral: to furnish with matter of morality. —*v.i.* to speak or write on moral subjects: to make moral reflections.—*ns.* **mor'aliser; mor'-alism,** a moral maxim: moral counsel: morality as distinct from religion; **mor'alist,** one who teaches morals, or who practises moral duties: a moral as distinguished from a religious man: one who prides himself on his morality.—*adj.* **moralist'ic.**—*n.* **morality** (*mor-al'i-ti*), quality of being moral: that which renders an action right or wrong: the practice of moral duties apart from religion: virtue: the doctrine of actions as right or wrong: ethics: a mediaeval allegorical drama in which virtues and vices appear as characters (also **moral'ity-play**).—*n.*

mor'aller (*Shak.*), a moralist.—*adv.* mor'ally, in a moral manner: in respect of morals: to all intents and purposes, practically.—moral agent, one who acts under a knowledge of right and wrong; moral certainty, a likelihood great enough to be acted on, although not capable of being certainly proved; moral courage, power of facing disapprobation and ridicule; moral defeat, a success so qualified as to count as a defeat, or to point towards defeat; moral faculty, moral sense; moral law, a law or rules for life and conduct, founded on what is right and wrong: the law of conscience: that part of the Old Testament which relates to moral principles, esp. the ten commandments; moral philosophy, ethics; Moral Rearmament, a movement succeeding the Oxford Group in 1938, advocating absolute private and public morality (abbrev. M.R.A.); moral sense, that power of the mind which knows or judges actions to be right or wrong, and determines conduct accordingly: (or moral interpretation, etc.) tropological interpretation of e.g. the Bible, finding of secondary meaning; moral support, the help afforded by approbation; moral theology, ethics treated with reference to a divine source; moral victory, a defeat in appearance, but in some important sense a real victory. [L. *mōrālis*—*mōs*, *mōris*, manner, custom, (esp. in *pl.*) morals.]

morall, (Shak., *Mids. N. Dr.*) *n.* emended by editors to mural, but possibly a misprint for wall.

morass, *mə-ras'*, *n.* a tract of soft, wet ground: a marsh.—*adj.* morass'y.—morass ore, bog-iron ore. [Du. *moeras*—O.Fr. *maresc*, influenced by Du. *moer*, moor.]

morat, *mō'rat*, *mō'*, *n.* a drink made of honey and mulberry juice. [L.L. *mōrātum*—*mōrum*, mulberry.]

moratorium, *mor-ə-tō'ri-əm*, *-tō'*, *n.* an emergency measure authorising the suspension of payments of debts for a given time: the period thus declared: a temporary ban on, or decreed cessation of, an activity:—*pl.* morator'ia, morator'iums.—*adj.* moratory (*mor'ə-tə-ri*), delaying: deferring. [Neut. of L.L. *morātōrius*, adj. from *mora*, delay.]

Moravian, *mo-rā'vi-ən*, *adj.* pertaining to *Moravia* or the Moravians.—*n.* one of the people of Moravia: one of the *Unitas Fratrum* or *United Brethren*, a small body of Protestants of extraordinary missionary energy, founded in the 15th century.—*n.* Morā'vianism. [L. *Moravia*, Moravia—*Morava*, the river March.]

Moravian, *mo-rā'vi-ən*, *adj.* of the old province or the modern county of Moray.—*n.* a Moray man. [L.L. *Moravia*, Moray.]

moray, murray, murrey, murry, *mō'rā*, *mō-rā'*, *mur'i*, *mur-ā'*, *n.* an eel of the family Muraenidae. [Port. *moreia*—L. *mūraena*—Gr. (*s*)*mȳraina*, fem. of (*s*)*mȳros*, eel.]

morbid, *mōr'bid*, *adj.* sickly: unwholesome: inclined to dwell on unwholesome or horrible thoughts: relating to, or of the nature of, disease.—*n.* morbid'ity, sickliness: unwholesomeness: ratio of sickness.—*adv.* mor'bidly.—*n.* mor'bidness. [L. *morbidus*—*morbus*, disease.]

morbidezza, *mōr-bi-det'sa*, *n.* that quality of flesh-painting which gives the impression of life. [It.]

morbilli, *mōr-bil'ī*, *n.pl.* measles.—*adjs.* morbill'iform, morbill'ous. [L.L. dim. of L. *morbus*, disease.]

morbus, *mōr'bəs*, *n.* disease (Lat., used in phrases).—*adjs.* morbif'erous, disease-bringing; morbi'fic, disease-causing.—morbus gallicus, the French disease, syphilis. [L.]

morceau, *mōr-sō*, *n.* a morsel: a fragment: a piece of music: a short literary composition: *pl.* morceaux (*-sō*).—morceau de salon (*də sä-*

*lɔ̄*; *mus.*), a drawingroom piece. [Fr.; see morsel.]

mordacious, *mōr-dā'shəs*, *adj.* given to biting: biting in quality (*lit.* or *fig.*).—*adv.* mordā'ciously.—*ns.* mordacity (*-das'i-ti*), mordancy (*mōr'dən-si*).—*adj.* mor'dant, biting: incisive: serving to fix dyes, paints, gold-leaf.—*n.* a corroding substance: any substance that combines witn and fixes a dyestuff in material that cannot be dyed direct: a substance used to cause paint or gold-leaf to adhere.—*v.t.* to treat with a mordant.—*adv.* mor'dantly. [L. *mordēre*, to bite.]

mordent, *mōr'dənt*, (*mus.*) *n.* a grace in which the principal note is preceded in performance by itself and the note below (twice in the double mordent): the character indicating it: sometimes extended to other graces.—inverted mordent, the pralltriller. [Ger.,—It. *mordente*.]

more, *mōr*, *mōr*, *adj.* (serving as *comp.* of many and much) in greater number or quantity: greater in size or importance (now *rare*): additional: other besides.—*adv.* to a greater degree: rather: again: longer: further: moreover.—*n.* a greater thing: something further or in addition:—*superl.*, *adj.* and *adv.* most (*mōst*).—*adj.* mo'rish, more'ish, such that one wants more.—any more, anything additional: further; more and more, continually increasing; more by token, in proof of this, besides; more or less, about: in round numbers; no more, nothing in addition: never again: no longer in existence: dead. [O.E. *māra*, greater; as an adv. more has superseded mo.]

more, *mōr*, *mōr*, *n.* a root: a stump: a plant (*Spens.*). [O.E. *moru*, more, carrot, parsnip; Ger. *möhre*.]

more, *mōr'ē*, *mōr'ē*, *mōr'e* (L.), in the manner; more majorum (*mə-jōr'əm*, *-jör'əm*, *mä-yōr'ōom*), after the manner of our (their) ancestors; more suo (*sū'*, *sōō'ō*), in his (her) own way, in characteristic fashion.

moreen, *mo-rēn'*, *n.* a stout corded stuff, woollen, cotton, or both, often watered. [Poss. conn. with moire.]

morel, *mor-el'*, *n.* any edible discomycete fungus of the genus Morchella. [Fr. *morille*; cf. O.H.G. *morhila* (Ger. *morchel*), a mushroom; more (2).]

morel, *mor-el'*, *n.* a nightshade, esp. black nightshade: (also *mor'əl*), a dark-coloured horse (*obs.*).—*adj.* blackish. [L.L. *morellus*, blackish, perh.—L. *mōrum*, a mulberry, perh. Late Gr. *mauros*, black.]

morel, *mor-el'*, *mor'əl*, morell'o, *-ō*, *n.* a dark-red cherry, much used in cooking and for cherry brandy. [Possibly—It. *morello*, dark-coloured (see preceding); possibly—Flem. *marelle*—It. *amarella*, a dim. from L. *amārus*, bitter.]

morendo, *mo-ren'dō*, (*mus.*) *adj.* and *adv.* dying away, in speed and tone. [It., dying.]

moreover, *mōr-ō'vər*, *mōr-*, *adv.* more over or beyond what has been said: further: besides: also. [more, over.]

morepork. See mopoke.

mores, *mō'*, *mō'rēz*, *mō'rās*, (L.) *n.pl.* customs, manners.

Moresco, *mor-es'kō*, *n.* a Moorish dance or morris-dance (It. *Moresca*): a Moor or Morisco.—*adj.* Moorish. [It., Moorish.]

Moresque, *mor-esk'*, *adj.* in the Moorish manner.—*n.* an arabesque. [Fr.,—It. *Moresco*.]

Moreton Bay, *mōr'tən bä*, *mōr'*, the first settlement in Queensland.—Moreton Bay chestnut, an Australian papilionaceous tree (*Castanospermum australe*): its chestnut-flavoured seed.

morganatic, *mōr-gən-at'ik*, *adj.* of, by, or of the nature of, a left-handed marriage, that is, a marriage (in some countries) between persons of unequal rank (latterly only where one is of a reigning or mediatised house), the marriage being valid, the children legitimate, but unable to inherit the higher rank, the wife (if the lower-born) not being granted the husband's title.— *adv.* morganat'ically. [L.L. *morganātica*, a gift from a bridegroom to his bride; cf. Ger. *morgengabe*, O.E. *morgengifu*, a morning gift.]

morgay, *mör'gā, n.* the small spotted dogfish or bounce. [Cornish and Welsh *morgi*—*mör*, sea, *ci*, dog.]

morgen, *mör'gən, n.* a unit of land-measurement—in Holland, S. Africa, and parts of the U.S.A., a little over two acres; in Norway, Denmark, and Prussia, about two-thirds of an acre. [Du. and Ger.; perh. *morgen*, morning, hence a morning's ploughing.]

morgenstern, *mör'gən-stûrn, -shtern, n.* a morning-star (weapon). [Ger.]

Morglay, *mör'glā, n.* Sir Bevis of Hampton's sword: hence, a sword. [Cf. claymore.]

morgue, *mörg, n.* a place where dead bodies are laid out for identification: a place, as in a news-paper office, where miscellaneous material for reference is kept. [Fr.]

morgue, *mörg, n.* hauteur. [Fr.]

moria, *mō'ri-ə, mö', n.* folly. [Gr. *möriā.*]

moribund, *mor'i-bund, adj.* about to die: in a dying state.—*n.* moribund'ity. [L. *moribundus*—*mori*, to die.]

moriche, *mor-ē'chā, n.* the miriti palm. [Carib.]

morigeration, *mō-rij-ə-rā'shən, mö-, n.* deferential behaviour.—*adjs.* morig'erate, morig'erous. [L. *mōrigerātiō, -ōnis*—*mōs, mōris*, custom, humour, *gerĕre*, to bear.]

Moringa, *mor-ing'ga, n.* the horse-radish tree genus, constituting a family Moringā'ceae, apparently linking the poppies with the Leguminosae. [Perh. Sinh. *murungā.*]

morion, morrion, *mör'* or *mör'i-ən, n.* an open helmet, without visor or beaver. [Fr., prob. from Sp. *morrión*—*morra*, crown of the head.]

morion, *mor'i-ən, n.* black quartz. [Fr.]

Morisco, *mo-ris'kō, n.* a Moor, esp. a Christian-ised Moor in Spain after the fall of Granada in 1492: the Moorish language (*obs.*): (without *cap.*) a morris-dance or dancer: an arabesque.— *adj.* Moorish.—Morisk' (*obs.*).

Morisonian, *mor-i-sō'ni-ən, n.* a member of the Evangelical Union, formed in 1843 by the Rev. James *Morison* (1816-93), after his separation from the United Secession Church—incorporated with the Congregational Union of Scotland in 1896.—*n.* Morisō'nianism.

morkin, *mor'kin, n.* a beast that has died by accident.—*n.* mor'ling, mort'ling, a sheep dead of disease: its wool. [A.Fr. *mortekine*—L. *morticīna* (fem. adj.), carrion—*mors*, death.]

mormaor, *mör-mā'ər*, (*hist.*) *n.* a high steward. [Gael. *mormaer*, now *mòrmhaor*—*mòr*, great, *maor*, steward.]

Mormon, *mör'mən, n.* one of a religious sect with headquarters since 1847 in Salt Lake City, polygamous till 1890, calling itself *The Church of Jesus Christ of Latter-day Saints*, founded in 1830 by Joseph Smith, whose *Book of Mormon* was given out as translated from the golden plates of *Mormon*, a prophet.—*ns.* Mor'monism; Mor'monite.

Mormops, *mör'mops, n.* a genus of repulsive-looking American leaf-nosed bats. [Gr. *mormō*, a bugbear, *ōps*, face.]

morn, *mörn, n.* the first part of the day: morning. —the morn (*Scot.*), tomorrow; the morn's morn or morning (*Scot.*), tomorrow morning; the morn's nicht (*Scot.*), tomorrow night. [M.E. *morwen*—O.E. *morgen*; Ger. *morgen.*]

mornay (sauce), *mör'nā, n.* a cream sauce with cheese flavouring. [Perh. Philippe de *Mornay*, Fr. Huguenot leader.]

morne, *mörn, n.* the blunt head of a jousting-lance. —*adjs.* morné (*mör-nā'*), of a lion rampant, without teeth or claws; morned (*her.*), blunted. [Fr. *morner* (pa.p. *morné*), to blunt.]

morne, *mörn, adj.* dismal, gloomy, sombre. [Fr.]

morning, *mörn'ing, n.* the first part of the day: the early part of anything: an early dram (chiefly *Scot.*): a slight repast before recognised breakfast (*dial.*).—*adj.* of the morning: taking place or being in the morning.—*adv.* morn'ings, (now *rare* or *dial.*) in the morning.—morn'ing-dress, dress, esp. formal dress, worn in early part of day, as opp. to *evening-dress*; morn'ing-gift, a gift made by the husband to the wife on the morning after marriage; morn'ing-glo'ry, a plant of the genus *Ipomoea* (esp. *Ipomoea purpurea*) or *Convolvulus*, with showy flowers of various colours; morn'ing-gown, a gown for wearing in the morning; morn'ing-land, the east; morn'ing-prayer, prayer in the morning: matins; morn'ing-room, a sittingroom for use in the morning; morn'ing-sick'ness, nausea and vomiting in the morning, common in the early stages of pregnancy; morn'ing-star, a planet, esp. Venus, when it rises before the sun: a precursor: a mediaeval weapon, a spiky ball attached directly or by a chain to a handle; morn'ing-tide, the morning time: early part; morn'ing-watch, the watch between 4 and 8 a.m. [Contr. of M.E. *morwening*; cf. morn.]

Moro, *mör'ō, mör'ō, n.* one of any of the tribes of Muslim Malays in the Philippine Islands. [Sp., lit. moor, L. *Maurus.*]

morocco, *mə-rok'ō, n.* a fine goat-skin leather tanned with sumac, first brought from *Morocco*: a sheep-skin leather imitation of it: a very strong ale, anciently brewed in Westmorland.— *adj.* consisting of morocco.—French morocco, an inferior kind of Levant morocco, with small grain; Levant morocco, a fine quality of morocco, with large grain; Persian morocco, a morocco finished on the grain side.

moron, *mör'on, mör', n.* a somewhat feeble-minded person: one who remains throughout life at the mental age of eight to twelve.—Also *adj.*—*adj.* moron'ic. [Gr. *mōros*, foolish.]

morose, *mə-rōs', adj.* sour-tempered: gloomy: severe.—*adv.* morose'ly.—*ns.* morose'ness; morosity (*-os'i-ti*; *obs.*). [L. *mōrōsus*, peevish—*mōs, mōris*, manner.]

Morpheus, *mör'fūs, -fyəs, -fi-əs, n.* Greek god of dreams, son of Hypnos (sleep).—*adjs.* morphē'an (also *mör*)', morphet'ic (irreg. formed). [Gr. *Morpheus*, lit. moulder, shaper—*morphē*, shape.]

morphew, *mör'fū, n.* a skin eruption. [It. *morfea.*]

morphia, *mör'fi-ə, n.* morphine.—*ns.* mor'phine (*-fēn*), the principal alkaloid in opium, used as a hypnotic; mor'phinism, the effect of morphine on the system: the habit of taking morphine; morphinomā'nia; morphinomā'niac. [Gr. *Morpheus*, god of dreams.]

morphic, *mör'fik, adj.* relating to form, morpho-logical.—*ns.* morphallax'is, regeneration in a changed form (Gr. *allaxis*, change); morpheme (*mör'fēm*), a linguistic unit (word or part of word) that has meaning.—*adj.* morphēm'ic.—*ns.* morphēm'ics, study of morphemes; morpho-genesis (*-fə-jen'i-sis*), the origin and development of a part, organ, or organism.—*adj.* morpho-genet'ic.—*ns.* morphogeny (*-foj'i-ni*), morpho-genesis; morphographer (*-fog'rə-fər*); mor-phog'raphy, descriptive morphology.—*adjs.* mor-pholog'ic, -al.—*ns.* morphol'ogist; morphol'ogy, the science of form, esp. that of the outer form, inner structure, and development of living organisms and their parts: also of the external forms of rocks and land-features: also of the forms of words; morphophon'ēme, a phoneme whose variants belong to one morpheme.—*adj.* morphophonēm'ic.—*ns.* morphophonēm'ics; mor-phō'sis, morphogenesis.—*adjs.* morphŏt'ic, per-taining to morphosis; morphotrop'ic.—*n.* mor-phot'ropy, the effect on crystalline form of the addition or substitution of an element or radical. [Gr. *morphē*, form.]

Morpho, *mör'fō, n.* a tropical American genus of brilliant and gigantic butterflies, often bright blue. [Gr. *Morphō*, a name of Aphrodite.]

morrhua, *mor'ōō-ə, n.* an old generic, now specific, name of the cod (*Gadus morrhua*). [L.L. *morrua*.]

morris, morrice, *mor'is*, morr'is-dance, *ns.* a dance, according to some of Moorish origin, which came to be associated with May games, with (latterly) Maid Marian, Robin Hood, the hobby-horse, and other characters, who had bells attached to their dress: a tune for the dance.—*v.i.* morr'is, to perform by dancing.—*ns.* morr'is-dancer; morr'is-pike (*Shak.*), a Moorish pike. [Moorish.]

morris. See meril (for nine men's morris, etc.).

Morris-tube, *mor'is-tūb, n.* a small-bore rifle-barrel inserted in the breech of a larger, for short-range practice. [R. *Morris* (d. 1891), the inventor.]

morrow, *mor'ō, n.* the day following the present: tomorrow: the next following day: the time immediately after any event. [M.E. *morwe* for *morwen*; cf. morn.]

morse, *mörs, n.* the walrus. [Lappish *morsa*, or Finn. *mursu*.]

morse, *mörs, n.* the fastening of a cope. [L. *morsus*, a bite, catch.]

Morse, *mörs, n.* signalling by a code in which each letter is represented by a combination of dashes and dots or their equivalents, invented by Sam F. B. *Morse* (1791-1872).—Also *adj.*

morsel, *mör'səl, n.* a bite or mouthful: a small piece of food: a choice piece of food, a dainty: a small piece of anything: a small person.—*v.t.* to divide into morsels: to apportion in small parcels. [O.Fr. *morsel* (Fr. *morceau*, It. *morsello*), dim. from L. *morsus*—*mordēre, morsum,* to bite.]

morsing-horn, *mör'sing-hörn, n.* the small horn that used to hold the fine powder used for priming. [Fr. *amorcer*, to prime (a gun).]

morsure, *mörs'ūr, n.* a bite.—*adj.* mors'al. [L. *morsus*, bite.]

mort, *mört, n.* death (*obs.*): a flourish sounded at the death of a buck, etc., in hunting: a sheep that has died a natural death (see also under morkin—morling, mortling): a dead body.—mort'bell, a funeral bell; mort'cloth, a pall; mort'-head, a death's-head; mort'-safe, a heavy grating used to guard a corpse against resurrectionists; mort'-stone, a wayside stone on which the bearers lay the bier for a rest. [Fr. *mort,* death, dead.]

mort, *mört, (dial.) n.* a great deal. [Origin obscure.]

mort, *mört, (cant) n.* a woman: a loose woman. [Origin obscure.]

mort, *mört, n.* a salmon, 3 years old. [Origin obscure.]

mortal, *mör'tl, adj.* liable to death: causing death: deadly: fatal: punishable with death: involving the penalty of spiritual death, as opposed to venial: to the death: implacable: human: very great (*coll.*): tediously long (*coll.*): without exception (*coll.*): very drunk (*slang*).—*n.* a human being.—*adv.* (*dial.* or *coll.*) extremely: confoundedly.—*v.t.* mor'talise, -ize, to make mortal.—*n.* mortality (*-tal'i-ti*), condition of being mortal: death: frequency or number of deaths, esp. in proportion to population: the human race, nature, or estate.—*adv.* mor'tally.—*adj.* mor'tal-star'ing (*Shak.*), deadly-visaged.—bills of mortality (see bill). [L. *mortālis*—*mori,* to die.]

mortar, *mör'tər, n.* a vessel in which substances are pounded with a pestle: a short piece of artillery for throwing a heavy shell, a bomb, a

life-line, etc.: a cement of lime, sand, and water.—*v.t.* to join or plaster with mortar: to bombard with a mortar.—mor'tar-board, a square board, with a handle beneath, for holding mortar: a square-topped college cap. [O.E. *mortere*—L. *mortārium,* a mortar, matter pounded.]

mortgage, *mör'gij, n.* a conditional conveyance of, or lien upon, land or other property as security for the performance of some condition (as the payment of money), becoming void on the performance of the condition: the act of conveying, or the deed effecting it.—*v.t.* to pledge as security for a debt.—*ns.* mortgagee', one to whom a mortgage is made or given; mort'gagor (*-jər*), one who mortgages his property.—Also (sometimes) mort'gager. [O.Fr.,—*mort,* dead, *gage,* a pledge.]

mortice. See mortise.

mortician, *mör-tish'ən,* (*U.S.*) *n.* an undertaker. [L. *mors, mortis,* death.]

mortiferous, *mör-tif'ər-əs, adj.* death-bringing: fatal.—*n.* mortif'erousness. [L. *mors, mortis,* death, *ferre,* to bring.]

mortify, *mör'ti-fī, v.t.* to kill (*obs.*): to destroy the vital functions of: to deaden: to subdue by severities and penance: to vex in a humiliating way: to dispose of by mortification (*Scots law*).—*v.i.* to lose vitality: to gangrene: to be subdued: to practise asceticism:—*pr.p.* mor'tifying; *pa.t.* and *pa.p.* mor'tified.—*adj.* mortif'ic, death-bringing: deadly.—*n.* mortification (*mör-ti-fi-kā'shən*), act of mortifying or state of being mortified: the death of part of the body: a bringing under of the passions and appetites by a severe or strict manner of living: humiliation: chagrin: that which mortifies or vexes: a bequest to some charitable institution (*Scots law*).—*adj.* mor'tified.—*n.* mor'tifier.—*adj.* and *n.* mor'tifying. [Fr. *mortifier*—L.L. *mortificāre,* to cause death to—*mors, mortis,* death, *facĕre,* to make.]

mortise, *mör'tis, n.* a hole made to receive a tenon—also mor'tice.—*v.t.* to cut a mortise in: to join by a mortise and tenon.—mor'tise-lock, mor'tice-lock, a lock whose mechanism is covered by being sunk into the edge of a door, etc. [Fr. *mortaise*; ety. unknown.]

mortmain, *mört'mān,* (*law*) *n.* the transfer of property to a corporation, which is said to be a dead hand, i.e. one that can never part with it again.—statutes of mortmain, acts of parliament restricting or forbidding the giving of property to religious houses. [Fr. *morte* (fem.), dead, *main*—L. *manus,* hand.]

mortuary, *mört'ū-ər-i, adj.* connected with death or burial.—*n.* a place for the temporary reception of the dead: a payment to the parish priest on the death of a parishioner or to a bishop or archdeacon on the death of a priest. [L. *mortuārius*—*mortuus,* dead, *mori,* to die.]

morula, *mör'ū-lə, n.* a solid spherical mass of cells resulting from the cleavage of an ovum: framboesia.—*adj.* mor'ular. [L. *mōrum,* a mulberry.]

Morus, *mō'rəs, mö', n.* the mulberry genus, giving name to the family Morā'ceae, including fig, breadfruit, Ceará rubber.—*adj.* morā'ceous. [L. *mōrus,* a mulberry tree; cf. Gr. *mōreā*.]

morwong, *mör'wong, n.* an Australian and N.Z. food fish. [Native name.]

Mosaic, *mō-zā'ik, adj.* pertaining to *Moses,* the great Jewish lawgiver.—*n.* Mō'saism.—Mosaic Law, the law of the Jews given by Moses at Mount Sinai.

mosaic, *mō-zā'ik, n.* the fitting together in a design of small pieces of coloured marble, glass, etc.: a piece of work of this kind: anything of similar appearance, or composed by the piecing together of different things: a leaf-mosaic: leaf-mosaic disease (or mosaic disease): a hybrid with the parental characters side by side and not blended.—*adj.* relating to, or composed of, mosaic.—*adv.* mosā′ically.—*ns.* mosā′icism (*-i-sizm*), presence side by side of patches of tissue of unlike constitution; mosā′icist (*-i-sist*), a worker in mosaic.—**mosaic gold**, an alloy of copper and zinc, ormolu, a stannic sulphide; **mosaic map**, a composite photographic map made from aerial photographs. [Fr. *mosaïque*—L.L. *mosaicum, mūsaicum*—*mūsa*—Gr. *mousa*, a muse; cf. L.L. *mūsaeum* or *mūsivum* (*opus*), mosaic (work).]

**Mosasauros,** *mō-sə-sö′rəs, n.* a gigantic Cretaceous fossil pythonomorph reptile. [L. *Mosa*, the Maas, near which the first was found, Gr. *sauros*, a lizard.]

**moschatel,** *mos-kə-tel′, n.* a small plant (*Adoxa moschatellina*), constituting in itself the Adoxaceae (by some included in the honeysuckle family), with pale-green flowers and a supposed musky smell. [Fr. *moscatelle*—It. *moschatella*—*moscato*, musk.]

**moschiferous,** *mos-kif′ər-əs, adj.* producing musk. [L.L. *moschus*, Gr. *moschos*, musk, L. *ferre*, to bring.]

**mose,** *mōz, v.i.* only in Shak., *Taming of the Shrew*, III, ii. 51—**to mose in the chine**, to have glanders. [Supposed to be for *mourn in the chine*, perh.—Fr. *morve d'eschine*, glanders, running from the spine: the morbid matter of glanders was thought to come from the spine. Another suggestion is that *mose* is for *pose*, catarrh, turned into a verb.]

**Moselle,** *mō-zel′, n.* white wine from the district of the river *Moselle*, with an aromatic flavour.

**Moses basket,** *mō′zəz*, a portable cot for babies. [Story of Moses in the bulrushes, Ex. ii. 3.]

**mosey,** *mō′zi, (slang) v.i.* to move along gently: to jog: to make off: to hurry. [Perh. for *vamoose*.]

**moshava,** *mō-shä′vä*, an agricultural settlement in Israel.

**Moslem,** *moz′lem, ləm, n.* a Mohammedan (*pl.* -ms, -min).—*adj.* of, belonging to, Mohammedans. —Also **Mus′lim.**—*n.* **Mos′lemism.** [Ar. *muslim*, pl. *muslimin*—*salama*, to submit (to God); cf. **Mussulman, Islam.**]

**moslings,** *moz′lingz, n.pl.* the thin shavings taken off by the currier in dressing skins. [Perh. **morsellings.**]

**mosque,** *mosk, n.* a Mohammedan place of worship. [Fr. *mosquée*—It. *moschea*—Ar. *masjid* (in N. Africa pron. *masgid*)—*sajada* (*sagada*), to pray.]

**mosquito,** *mos-kē′tō, n.* loosely, any small biting or stinging insect: any of several long-legged insects of the family *Culicidae*, the females of which have their mouth-parts adapted for blood-sucking and can therefore transmit diseases incl. malaria:—*pl.* **mosqui′to(e)s.**—**mosquito canopy, curtain, net**, an arrangement of netting to keep out mosquitoes; **mosquito-weight**, a light featherweight boxer. [Sp. dim. of *mosca*, a fly —L. *musca*.]

**moss,** *mos, n.* a bog (now chiefly *Scots*): boggy ground or soil: any of the Musci, a class of Bryophyta, small plants with simply constructed leaves, and no woody material, attached by rhizoids, the zygote growing into a small spore-bearing capsule that grows parasitically on the parent plant: a mass of such plants: a moss-like growth, covering, or excrescence: loosely extended to plants of similar appearance to true mosses: a moss-rose.—*v.t.* to cover with moss: to clear of moss.—*v.i.* to gather moss.—*n.* **moss′iness.**—*adj.* **moss′y,** overgrown or abounding with moss: like moss: boggy.—**moss′-ag′ate,** chalcedony with moss-like inclusions of chlorite, manganese oxide, etc.; **moss′-back**, a person of antiquated views; **moss′bluiter** (*-blüt′ər, -blit′ər; Scot.*), the bittern; **moss′-**

**cheep′er** (*Scot.*), the titlark; **moss′-crop** (*Scot.*), cotton-grass; **moss′-flow** (*Scot.*), a watery bog. —*adj.* **moss′-grown**, covered with moss.—**moss′-hag′, -hagg′** (*Scot.*), a pit or slough in a bog; **moss′land**, wet, peaty land; **moss′-litt′er**, a loose mass of lumps of peaty material; **moss′-plant**, a plant of moss: the sexual generation in the life-history of a moss, on which the asexual generation is parasitic; **moss′-rose**, a variety of rose having a moss-like growth on and below the calyx; **moss′-troop′er**, one of the freebooters that used to infest the mosses of the Border.—*n.* and *adj.* **moss′-troop′ing.**—**club-moss** (see lycopod); **Iceland moss** (see **Iceland**). [O.E. *mōs*, bog; Du. *mos*, Ger. *moos*, moss, bog.]

**mossbunker,** *mos′bung-kər, n.* the menhaden. [Du. *mars-banker*, the scad or horse-mackerel.]

**most,** *mōst, adj.* (*superl.* of **more**) greatest: in greatest quantity or number.—*adv.* in the highest degree: almost (*U.S.* and *dial.*; perhaps aphetic).—*n.* the greatest number or quantity.—*advs.* **most′ly**, for the most part; **most′what** (*Spens.*), for the most part, mostly.—**at (the) most**, at the utmost computation; **for the most part**, chiefly: in the main; **make the most of** (see **make**). [The Northumbrian form *māst* (*Scot.* maist) may have occurred in O.E. beside the ordinary form *mǣst*; or the vowel may come from analogy with the comparative; cf. Ger. *meist.*]

**mot,** *mot, (obs.) n.* a motto: a hunter's horn-call. [Fr.,—L. *muttum*, a murmur.]

**mot,** *mot, (Fr.) n.* a word: a pithy or witty saying.— **le mot juste** (*la mō zhüst*), the word which fits the context exactly.

**mote,** *mōt, (arch.) v.t.* may: must:—*3rd pers. sing. pres. tense* **mote**; *pa.t.* (*Spens.*) **mote**, **mot** (*mot*), in *pl.* **mot′en** (but see also **must**, 1).—so **mote I thee**, so may I prosper (see **thee**, 2). [O.E. *mōt*, may, pa.t. *mōste*; confused with **mought**; Ger. *muss*, must.]

**mote,** *mōt, n.* a particle of dust: a speck: a seed or other foreign particle in wool or cotton (Yorkshire **moit**): a stain or blemish: anything very small.—*adjs.* **mōt′ed**, **mote′y** (*Scot.* **motty**, *mot′i*), containing a mote or motes. [O.E. *mot*; Du. *mot.*]

**mote,** *mōt*, **motte**, *mot, (arch.) n.* a mound, esp. with a castle: a tumulus.—**mote′-hill**. [O.Fr. *mote* (Fr. *motte*); often confused with **moot, moot-hill**.]

**motel,** *mō-tel′, n.* hotel made up of units, each accommodating a car and occupants: a hotel with accommodation and servicing facilities for cars. [mo(tor), (ho)tel.]

**motet, motett,** *mō-tet′, n.* a polyphonic choral composition, usually unaccompanied, with biblical or similar prose text: loosely, an anthem or church cantata.—*n.* **motett′ist**. [Fr. *motet*, dim. of *mot*; cf **mot** (2).]

**moth,** *moth, n.* the cloth-eating larva of the clothes-moth: the imago of the same kind: any member of the Heterocera, a popular and un-scientific division of the Lepidoptera, broadly distinguished from butterflies by duller colouring, thicker body, antennae not clubbed, wings not tilted over the back in rest, and by the habit of flying by night: that which eats away gradually and silently: various kinds of insect vermin (*obs.*): a fragile, frivolous creature, readily dazzled into destruction (*fig.*): a light aeroplane: —*pl.* **moths** (*moths*).—*adjs.* **mothed** (*motht*), moth-eaten; **moth′y**, full of moths: moth-eaten.—**moth-ball**, a ball of naphthalene or other substance for keeping away clothes-moths.—*v.t.* to lay up in mothballs: to spray with a plastic and lay up (a ship, etc.).—*v.t.* **moth′-eat** (back formation), to prey upon, as a moth eats a garment.—*adj.* **moth′-eaten**, eaten or cut by moths. —**moth′-flower**, a flower pollinated by moths;

**moth'-hunter**, a goatsucker. [O.E. *moththe, mohthe*; Ger. *motte*.]

**mother**, *mudh'ǝr*, *n.* a female parent: a matron: that which has produced anything: the female head of a religious house or other establishment: a familiar term of address to, or prefix to the name of, an old woman; extended to an ancestress, a stepmother, mother-in-law, foster-mother, an apparatus for chicken-rearing: the womb (*obs.*): hysteria (*obs.*).—*adj.* received by birth, as it were from one's mother: being a mother: acting the part of a mother: originating: used to produce others from.—*v.t.* to give birth to: to acknowledge, to adopt, to treat (especially irksomely) as a son or daughter: to foster: to attribute the maternity of authorship of (with *on* or *upon*): to find a mother for.—*ns.* **moth'erhood**, state of being a mother; **moth'ering**, a rural English custom of visiting the mother church or one's parents on Mid-Lent Sunday (**Mothering Sunday**).—*adj.* **moth'erless**, without a mother.—*n.* **moth'erliness**.—*adj.* **moth'erly**, pertaining to, or becoming, a mother: like a mother.—**moth'er-cell'** (*biol.*), a cell that gives rise to others by division; **moth'er-church**, the church from which others have sprung: a principal church; **moth'er-cit'y**, one from which another was founded as a colony; **moth'er-coun'try, -land**, the country of one's birth: the country from which a colony has gone out; **moth'ercraft**, knowledge and skill required for care of child; **moth'er-fig'ure**, an older woman who symbolises for one the qualities and authority of one's mother; **moth'er-in-law**, the mother of one's husband or wife: a stepmother (*obs.*):—*pl.* **mothers-in-law.**—**moth'er-liq'uor, moth'er-lye, mother-water.**—*adj.* **moth'erna'ked**, naked as at birth.—**moth'er-of-mill'ions**, ivy-leaved toadflax; **moth'er-of-pearl'**, the nacreous internal layer of the shells in some molluscs (also *adj.*); **moth'er-right**, succession in the female line: matriarchy; **Mother's Day**, a day for honouring of mothers, as second Sunday in May; also used for Mothering Sunday; **moth'er-ship**, a ship having charge of torpedo-boats or small craft; **moth'er's-mark, moth'er-spot**, a birthmark; **mothers' meeting**, a periodical meeting of mothers connected with a church; **mother's** (or **mothers'**) **ruin**, gin; **moth'er-tongue**, native language: a language from which another has its origin; **moth'er-wa'ter**, residual liquid, still containing certain chemical substances, left after others have been crystallised or precipitated from it; **moth'er-wit**, native wit: common sense; **moth'erwort**, a labiate (*Leonurus cardiaca*) or other plant supposed to help womb disease.—**every mother's son**, every man without exception; **fits of the mother** (*obs.*), hysteria; **Mother Carey's chicken**, goose, the storm petrel, or similar bird; **Mother Hubbard**, a woman's loose flowing gown, like that proper to the nursery heroine. [O.E. *mōdor*; Du. *moeder*, O.N. *mōthir*, Ger. *mutter*, Ir. and Gael. *mathair*, L. *māter*, Gr. *mētēr*, Sans. *mātṛ*.]

**mother**, *mudh'ǝr*, *n.* dregs: scum: a slimy mass of bacteria that oxidises alcoho! into acetic acid (in full, **mother of vinegar**).—*v.i.* to become mothery.—*adj.* **moth'ery**, like or containing mother. [Poss. the same as the foregoing; or poss.—Du. *modder*, mud; cf. **mud**.]

**motif**, *mō-tēf'*, *n.* a theme or subject: an element in a composition, esp. a dominant element: a figure, subject, or leitmotif (*mus.*): an ornament added to a woman's garment, often symbolic. [Fr. *motif*; see **motive**.]

**motile**, *mō'til*, in U.S. *-til*, *adj.* capable of moving spontaneously as a whole: characterised by motion: imagining most readily in terms of muscular action.—*n.* one whose imagery naturally takes the form of feelings of action.—*n.* **motility** (*-til'i-ti*). [L. *mōtus*, movement.]

**motion**, *mō'shǝn*, *n.* the act, state, manner, of changing place: a single movement: change of posture: power of moving or of being moved: agitation: a natural impulse: a working in the mind: a feeling: an emotion: a prompting: an instigation: a formal proposal put before a meeting: an application to a court, during a case before it, for an order or rule that something be done, esp. something incidental to the progress of the cause rather than its issue: evacuation of the intestine: a piece of mechanism: progression of a part (*mus.*): a puppet show (*obs.*): a puppet (*Shak.*): (in *pl.*) faeces.—*v.t.* to direct or indicate by a gesture: to move, propose: to make a movement indicating as one's intention (*obs.*): to give motion to.—*v.i.* to offer a proposal.—*adj.* **mō'tional.**—*n.* **mō'tionist**, one who is skilled in motions.—*adj.* **mō'tionless**, without motion. — **mō'tion-man** (*obs.*), a puppet-showman; **mō'tion-pic'ture**, a cinematograph film.—**angular motion**, change of angle between a standard direction and a line joining the moving object and a fixed point; **go through the motions**, to make a half-hearted attempt: to pretend; **laws of motion**, Newton's three laws: (1) Every body continues in its state of rest, or of uniform motion in a straight line, except so far as it may be compelled by force to change that state; (2) Change of motion is proportional to force applied, and takes place in the direction of the straight line in which the force acts; (3) To every action there is always an equal and contrary reaction. [Fr. *motion*—L. *mōtiō, -ōnis—movēre, mōtum*, to move.]

**motive**, *mō'tiv, adj.* causing motion: having power to cause motion: concerned with the initiation of action: moving (*obs.*).—*n.* an incitement of the will: a consideration or emotion that excites to action: a motif: a moving part of the body (*Shak.*).—*v.t.* to motivate.—*v.t.* **mo'tivāte**, to provide with a motive: to induce.—*n.* **motivā'tion**, motivating force, incentive.—*adjs.* **motivā'tional**, pertaining to motivation; **mo'tiveless.**—*ns.* **mo'tivelessness**; **motiv'ity**, power of moving or of producing motion.—**motivated art**, art produced under the influence of drugs; **motivation(al) research**, research into motivation, esp. into consumer reaction, carried out scientifically; **motive power**, the energy or source of the energy by which anything is operated. [L.L. *mōtīvus*—L. *movēre, mōtum*, to move.]

**motley**, *mot'li, adj.* particoloured: variegated: made of, or dressed in, motley: jester-like: heterogeneous.—*n.* a cloth of mixed colours (*obs.*): a particoloured garb, such as a jester wore (*obs.*): a patchwork (*obs.*): a jester (*Shak.*).—*adj.* **mot'ley-mind'ed** (*Shak.*), having a mind of heterogeneous and inconsistent contents. [Origin obscure.]

**motmot**, *mot'mot, n.* a tropical American bird (*Momotus*), akin to rollers and kingfishers, that nibbles its tail-feathers into racquet-shape. [Said to be Mexican name.]

**motocross**, *mō'tō-kros, n.* a form of scrambling, racing round a very rough circuit. [**motor**.]

**moto perpetuo**, *mō'tō per-pet'ŏo-ō*, (It.) perpetual motion: a piece of music that goes swiftly without stop from beginning to end.

**motor**, *mō'tǝr, n.* a mover: that which gives motion: a machine whereby some source of energy is used to give motion or perform work, esp. an internal-combustion engine or a machine for converting electrical into mechanical energy: a motor-car: a muscle, or a nerve, concerned in bodily movement.—*adj.* giving or transmitting motion: driven by a motor: of, for, with, relating to, motor vehicles: concerned with the transmission of impulses: initiating bodily movement:

pertaining to muscular movement or the sense of muscular movement.—*v.t.* and *v.i.* to convey, traverse, or travel by a motor vehicle.—*adj.* **moto′rial,** motory.—*n.* **motorisā′tion,** -z-.—*v.t.* **mo′torise, -ize,** to furnish with, or adapt to the use of, a motor or motors: to interpret or imagine in terms of motor sensation.—*ns.* **mo′torist,** one who drives a motor-car, esp. for pleasure; **moto′rium,** that part of the nervous system concerned in movement.—*adj.* **mo′tory,** causing, conveying, imparting motion: motor.—**mo′tor-ban′dit,** a robber who uses a motor-car; **mo′tor-bi′cycle, -boat, -bus, -car, -coach, -cy′cle, -launch, -lorr′y, -ship,** one driven by a motor; **motorcade** (*mō′tər-kād*; after **cavalcade**), a procession of motor-cars; **mo′tor-cy′cling; mo′tor-cy′clist.—***adjs.* **mo′tor-driven,** driven by a motor; **mo′tor-jet,** a reciprocating engine with a fan for jet-propulsion; **mo′torman,** a man who controls a motor, esp. that of a tram-car; **mo′tor-trac′tion,** the conveyance of loads, including passengers, by motor vehicles; **mo′tor-trac′tor,** an internal-combustion engine for hauling loads, esp. for drawing agricultural implements; **mo′torway,** a road for motor traffic, esp. one for fast traffic with no crossings on the same level. [L. *mōtor*—*movēre*, to move.]

**motorail,** *mō′tō-rāl,* n. a system of carrying cars and passengers by train on certain routes. [motor.]

**motoscafo,** *mō-tō-skä′fō,* (It.) a motor-boat:—*pl.* **motoscafi** (-*fē*).

**mott,** *mot* (Spens.), *pa.t.* of **mete.**

**motte, mott, mot,** *n.* (S.W. *U.S.*) a clump of trees, esp. in prairie country. [Mex. Sp. *mata.*]

**motte.** Same as **mote** (3).

**mottle,** *mot′l,* v.t. to variegate blotchily.—*n.* a blotched appearance, condition, or surface: yarns of two colours folded together.—*adj.* **mott′led.** — *n.* **mott′ling.** — *adj.* **mott′le-faced.** [Prob. from **motley.**]

**motto,** *mot′ō,* n. a short sentence or phrase adopted as representative of a person, family, etc., or accompanying a coat of arms: a passage prefixed to a book or chapter shadowing forth its matter: a scrap of verse or prose enclosed in a cracker or accompanying a sweetmeat:—*pl.* **mott′oes** (-*ōz*).—*adj.* **mott′ō′d, mott′oed.** [It.,— L. *muttum,* a murmur.]

**motty.** See **mote** (2).

**motuca,** *mō-tōō′kə,* **mutuca,** *mōō-tōō′kə,* n. a large Brazilian biting fly of the Tabanidae. [Tupí *mutuca* (Port. *motuca*).]

**motu proprio,** *mō′tū prō′pri-ō, mō′tōō pro′pri-ō,* (L.) of his own accord.

**mou′, mou,** *mōō,* n. a Scots form of **mouth.**

**mouch, moucher.** Same as **mooch,** etc.

**moucharaby,** *mōō-shar′ə-bi,* n. a balcony enclosed with lattice-work. [Fr.,—Ar. *mashrabiyyah.*]

**mouchard,** *mōō-shär,* n. a police spy. [Fr.]

**mouchoir,** *mōō-shwär,* n. a pocket-handkerchief. [Fr.]

**moudi(e)wart, -wort,** Scots forms of **mouldwarp.**

**moue,** *mōō,* n. a grimace of discontent, pout. [Fr.]

**moufflon, mouflon, muflon,** *mōōf′lon,* n. a wild sheep of the mountains of Corsica, etc.: extended to large big-horned wild sheep of other kinds:—*pl.* **moufflon.** [Fr. *mouflon*—L.L. *mufrō,* -*ōnis.*]

**mought,** *mōt, mowt* (Spens. *möt*), (obs. and dial.) *pa.t.* of **may.** See also **mote** (1).

**mouillé,** *mōō-yā,* adj. (of *l* and *n*) sounded in a liquid manner, palatalised—as *ll* in 'mouillé', *gl* in 'seraglio', *ñ* in 'Señor'. [Fr. moistened.]

**moujik,** *mōō-zhik′, mōō′zhik,* n. Same as **muzhik.**

**mould** (*U.S.* mold), *mōld, n.* loose soft earth: earth, considered as the material of which the body is formed or to which it turns: the earth of the grave: the ground, the land, the world (obs. or arch.): (in *pl.*) clods, esp. in allusion to the grave (Scot. **mouls, mools,** *mōōlz*): soil rich in decayed matter.—*v.t.* to cover with soil.—*v.i.* (obs.) to moulder.—*v.i.* **mould′er,** to crumble to mould: to turn to dust: to waste away gradually.—*v.t.* to turn to dust.—*adj.* **mould′y,** like, or of the nature of, mould.—**mould′-board,** the curved plate in a plough which turns over the soil. [O.E. *molde*; Ger. dialect *molt, molten,* Goth. *mulda.*]

**mould** (*U.S.* mold), *mōld,* n. a woolly growth on bread, cheese, or other vegetable or animal matter: any one of various small fungi (Mucor, Penicillium, etc.) of different classes, forming such growths.—*v.i.* to become mouldy.—*v.t.* to cause or allow to become mouldy.—*n.* **mould′iness.**—*adj.* **mould′y,** overgrown with mould: like mould: stale: musty. [M.E. *mowle*; cf. O.N. *mygla.*]

**mould** (*U.S.* mold), *mōld, n.* a templet: matrix in which a cast is made: a formed surface from which an impression is taken: the foundation upon which certain manufactured articles are built up: a thing formed in a mould, esp. a jelly or blancmange: nature: form: model: a pattern: that which is or may be moulded: a set of mouldings (*archit.*).—*v.t.* to knead: to mix (obs.): to shape: to model: to form in a mould.—*adj.* **mould′able.**—*ns.* **mould′er; mould′ing,** the process of shaping, esp. any soft substance: anything formed by or in a mould: an ornamental edging or band projecting from a wall or other surface, as a fillet, astragal, bead, etc.: a strip of wood that can be applied for the purpose.—**mould′-candle,** a candle made in a mould, not dipped; **mould′-fac′ing,** a fine powder or wash applied to the face of a mould to ensure a smooth casting; **mould′ing-board,** a baker's board for kneading dough; **mould′-loft,** a room in which the several parts of a ship's hull are laid off to full size from the construction drawings. [O.Fr. *modle, molle* (Fr. *moule*)—L. *modulus,* a measure.]

**mouldwarp,** *mōld′wörp,* n. a mole: (Scot.) **modiwort,** *mow′di-würt,* **moudi(e)wart, -wort,** *mōō′di-.* [O.E. *molde,* mould, earth, *weorpan,* to throw; cf. O.H.G. *multwurf* (Ger. *maulwurf*), Dan. *muldvarp.*]

**moulin,** *mōō-lě,* n. a shaft in a glacier worn by water running down a crack.—*n.* **moulinet** (*mōō-li-net′,* or *mōō′*), a machine for bending a crossbow. [Fr. *moulin,* mill, and dim. *moulinet*—L.L. *molinum.*]

**moult,** (*U.S.* molt) *mōlt, v.i.* to cast feathers or other covering: to be shed.—*v.t.* to shed.—*n.* the act, process, condition, or time of moulting.—*adj.* **moult′en** (Shak.), having moulted.—*n.* **moult′ing.** [O.E. (*bi)mūtian,* to exchange—L. *mūtāre*; the *l,* first a freak of spelling, afterwards sounded.]

**mound,** *mownd,* n. a boundary-fence or hedge (obs.): a bank of earth or stone raised as a protection: a hillock: a heap.—*v.t.* to enclose with a fence or an embankment (obs.): to fortify with an embankment: to heap in a mound.—**mound′-bird,** a megapode, or bird of the Australian family Megapodidae, gallinaceous birds that build large mounds as incubators; **mound′-builder,** one of the Indians who in early times built great mounds in the eastern United States: a mound-bird. [Origin obscure; O.E. *mund* means guardianship.]

**mound,** *mownd,* n. a king's orb. [Fr. *monde*—L. *mundus,* the world.]

**mounseer,** *mown′sēr,* or -*sěr′,* (arch., illit., or derisive) n. for **monsieur,** a Frenchman.

**mount,** *mownt;* n. (arch. except **Mount,** as prefix to a name) a mountain: a small hill or mound, natural or artificial: a fleshy protuberance on the hand. [O.E. *munt* and O.Fr. *mont,* both— L. *mōns, montis,* mountain.]

**mount,** *mownt, v.i.* to go up: to climb: to get upon horseback, bicycle, or the like: to extend upward: to extend backward in time: to rise in level or amount: to amount (*obs.*).—*v.t.* to climb, ascend: to get up on: to cover or copulate with: to cause to rise, to lift, raise, erect: to place upon anything high: to put on horseback, or the like: to furnish with an animal, bicycle, etc., to ride on: to fix in a setting, on a support, stand, or mount: to furnish with accessories: to put in position and state of readiness for use or exhibition: to stage: to be armed with: to carry, wear, or put on: to put into operation, carry out.—*n.* a rise: an act of mounting: manner of mounting: a step to mount by: a signal for mounting: a riding animal or cycle: that upon which a thing is placed or in which it is set for fixing, strengthening, embellishing, esp. the card surrounding a picture, or the slide, cover-glass, etc., used in mounting an object for the microscope.—*adj.* mount'ed, on horseback: furnished with horses: set on high: raised on steps, generally three, as a cross (*her.*): set up: set.—*ns.* mount'er; mount'ing; mount'y, mount'ie (*coll.*), a Canadian mounted policeman.—mount'ing-block, a block or stone to enable one to mount a horse.— mount guard (see guard). [Fr. *monter*, to go up— L. *mōns, montis*, mountain.]

mountain, *mownt'in*, *n.* a high hill: a wine made from mountain grapes: in Ireland, wild pasture land: a large quantity, excess: (*cap.*) the extreme party in the French Revolution (see Montagnard). —*adj.* of a mountain: growing, dwelling, etc. on or among mountains.—*adj.* mount'ained. —*n.* mountaineer', an inhabitant of mountain country: a climber of mountains: a member of the Mountain.—*v.i.* to climb mountains.—*n.* mountaineer'ing, mountain climbing. —*adj.* mount'ainous, full of, characterised by, mountains: large as a mountain: huge. —mount'ain-ash', the rowan-tree; mount'ain-beav'er, the sewellel or Haplodon; mount'-ain-blue', blue carbonate of copper; mount'ain-bram'ble, the cloudberry; mount'ain-cat', a catamount, a wild-cat; mount'ain-chain', a range of mountains forming a long line; mount'ain-cork', mount'ain-leath'er, a matted mass of a fibrous amphibole, cork-like or leathery; mount'ain-dew', whisky; mount'ain-flax, amianthus; mount'ain-everlast'ing, the cat's-foot (*Antennaria dioica*), a small woolly composite plant of the hills and seashore; mount'ain-hare', a smaller species of hare, grey in summer, usually white in winter.—*adv.* and *adj.* mount'ain-high', mount'ains-high', high as a mountain (hyperbolically).—mount'ain-lau'rel, kalmia; Mountain Limestone, the lowest division of the Carboniferous in England, the Carboniferous Limestone; mount'ain-li'on, the puma; mount'ain-marr'ow, lithomarge; mount'-ain-meal, bergmehl; mount'ain-rail'way, a light narrow-gauge railway for mountainous regions, usually a rack-railway; mount'ain-sheep', the bighorn of the Rocky Mountains; mount'ain-sick'ness, sickness brought on by breathing rarefied air; mount'ain-side, the slope of a mountain; mount'ain-soap', a greasy kind of halloysite; mount'ain-tall'ow, hatchettite; mount'ain-tea', the American evergreen *Gaultheria procumbens*; mount'ain-top; mount'ain-wood', a fibrous wood-like asbestos.—Old Man of the Mountain, a popular name for the chief of the *Hashshāshin* (see assassin). [O.Fr. *montaigne* —L. *mōns, montis*, mountain. In some compounds *mountain* is used like Ger. *berg*, as if = mine.]

mountant, *mownt'ǝnt*, *n.* an adhesive paste for mounting photographs, etc.—*adj.* (*Shak.*) rising on high. [Fr. *montant*, pr.p. of *monter*, to mount.]

mountebank, *mown'ti-bangk*, *n.* a quack who

harangues and plays the fool: a buffoon: a charlatan.—*v.t.* to win, effect, render, by mountebankery.—*v.i.* (or *v.t.* with *it*) to play the mountebank.—*ns.* moun'tebankery, moun'te-banking, moun'tebankism. [It. *montimbanco, montambanco—montare*, to mount, *in*, on, *banco*, bench.]

mountenance, mountenaunce, *mount'ǝn-ans, -äns*, (*Spens.*) *n.* amount: distance. [App. O.Fr. *montance*, assimilated to maintenance; cf. mount, mountant.]

moup, moop, *mōōp*, (*Scot.*) *v.t.* to nibble: to mumble.—*v.i.* to consort. [Origin obscure.]

mourn, *mōrn, mörn*, (*rare*) *mōōrn*, *v.i.* to grieve: to be sorrowful: to wear mourning: to murmur as in grief.—*v.t.* to grieve for: to utter in a sorrowful manner.—*n.* mourn'er, one who mourns: one who attends a funeral, especially a relative of the deceased: a person hired to lament or weep for the dead: a penitent at a revival meeting (*U.S.*).—*adj.* mourn'ful, causing, suggesting, or expressing sorrow: feeling grief. — *adv.* mourn'fully.—*n.* mourn'fulness. — *adj.* mourn'ing, grieving: lamenting.—*n.* the act of expressing grief: the dress of mourners, or other tokens of mourning—also (*Scot.*) in *pl.*— *adv.* mourn'ingly.—mourn'ing-bord'er, a black margin used on notepaper, etc., by those in mourning: a dirty edge on a finger-nail (*coll.*); mourn'ing-bride, the sweet scabious (*Scabiosa atropurpurea*); mourn'ing-cloak', an undertaker's cloak, formerly worn at a funeral; mourn'ing-coach', a closed carriage for carrying mourners to a funeral; mourn'ing-dove', an American pigeon with plaintive note; mourn'ing-piece, a picture intended to be a memorial of the dead; mourn'ing-ring', a ring worn in memory of a dead person; mourn'ing-stuff, a lustreless black dress fabric, as crape, cashmere, etc., for making mourning clothes.—half-mourning (see half); in mourning, wearing black (in China white) in token of mourning: of a ship, painted blue: with eyes blackened (*slang*). [O.E. *murnan*; O.H.G. *mornēn*, to grieve.]

mournival, *mōr'ni-vǝl, mör'*, *n.* in gleek, a set of four aces, kings, etc. [Fr. *mornifle*.]

mouse, mows, *n.* a little rodent animal (Mus) found in houses and in the fields: extended to various voles and other animals more or less like the mouse, the *flitter*-mouse, *shrew*-mouse: a term of endearment (*obs.*): a muscle (*obs.*): part of a hindleg of beef. next the round (*dial.*): (also mouse'-butt'ock and mouse'-piece): a match for firing a cannon or mine: a knot or knob to prevent slipping (*naut.*): a black eye, or discoloured swelling (*slang*): a timid, shy, colourless person:—*pl.* mice (*mīs*).—*v.i.* (mowz) to hunt for mice or as if for mice: to prowl.—*v.t.* to treat or to tear as a cat does a mouse: to paw or handle amorously: to secure with a mouse (*naut.*).—*ns.* mouse'kin, mous'ie, a young or little mouse; mouser (*mowz'er*), a cat good at catching mice: a prying person: mousery (*mows'ǝr-i*), a resort of mice.—*n.* and *adj.* mousing (*mowz'ing*).—*v.t.* mousle (*mowz'l*), to pull about roughly or disrespectfully.—*adj.* mousy (*mows'i*), like a mouse in colour or smell: abounding with mice: noiseless, stealthy: of hair, limp and dull greyish-brown: of person, uninteresting, too unassertive.—mouse'-colour, the grey colour of a mouse.—*adjs.* mouse'-colour, -ed.—mouse'-deer, a chevrotain.—*adj.* mouse'-dun, mouse-coloured.—mouse'-ear, a name of several plants with soft leaves shaped like a mouse's ear, esp. forget-me-not: (mouse'-ear chick'weed, any plant of the genus Cerastium, akin to chickweed); mouse'-hole, a hole made or used by mice: a small hole or opening; mouse-hunt (*Shak.*), a mouser; mouse'-sight, myopia; mouse'-tail, a small ranunculaceous plant

(Myosurus) with a spike of seed-vessels very like the tail of a mouse; **mouse'-trap**, a trap for mice: any cheese of indifferent quality. [O.E. *mūs*, pl. *mȳs*; Ger. *maus*, L. *mūs*, Gr. *mȳs*, mouse, muscle.]

**mousmee, mousmé**, *mōōs'mā*, *n.* a Japanese girl, esp. a waitress. [Jap. *musume*.]

**mousquetaire**, *mōōs-kə-ter'*, *n.* a musketeer: a woman's cloak trimmed with ribbons, with large buttons, fashionable about 1855: a broad turn-over linen collar worn a few years earlier.— **mousquetaire glove**, a woman's glove, long-armed, loose at top, without slit lengthwise. [Fr.]

**moussaka**, *mōō-sä'kə*, *n.* a Greek dish consisting of minced meat, aubergines, tomatoes and cheese.

**mousse**, *mōōs*, *n.* an ice or other dish made from whipped cream. [Fr., moss.]

**mousseline**, *mōōs-lēn'*, *n.* fine French muslin: a very thin glassware: a claret-glass made of it.— **mousseline-de-laine** (-*də-len'*), an all-wool muslin; **mousseline-de-soie** (-*də-swä*), a silk muslin. [Fr.]

**moust.** See must (5).

**moustache, mustache**, *məs-*, *mus-*, *mōōs-täsh'*, *n.* the hair upon the upper lip—also **mustachio** (-*tä'shō*).—Also in *pl.*—*adj.* **moustached'**, **mustach'ioed**; **moustach'ial.**—**moustache'-cup**, a cup with the top partly covered, formerly used to keep the moustache from getting wet.—**old moustache**, an old soldier. [Fr. *moustache*— It. *mostaccio*—Doric Gr. *mystax*, *-ǎkos*, the upper lip, moustache.]

**Mousterian**, *mōōs-tē'ri-ən*, *adj.* of an early Palaeolithic culture between Acheulean and Aurignacian. [Le *Moustier*, a cave on the Vézère which has yielded implements of this age.]

**moutan**, *mōō'tan*, *n.* a tree-peony. [Chin.]

**mouter**, *mōōt'ər*, a Scots form of multure.

**mouth**, *mowth*, *n.* the opening in the head of an animal by which it eats and utters sound: opening or entrance, as of a bottle, river, etc.: a consumer of food: a speaker: a spokesman: cry, voice, utterance: a wry face, a grimace:— *pl.* **mouths**, *mowdhz*.—*v.t.* (*mowdh*) to utter: to utter with exaggerated, affectedly pompous, or self-conscious action of the mouth: to declaim or spout: to take in the mouth: to feel, mumble, or mangle with the mouth: to train to the bit.— *v.t.* to declaim, rant (also *v.t.* with *it*): to apply mouths (*Shak.*): to grimace: to debouch.— *adjs.* **mouthable** (*mowdh'ə-bl*), lending itself to elocutionary utterance; **mouthed** (*mowdhd*), having a mouth.—*ns.* **mouther** (*mowdh'ər*), one who mouths; **mouth'ful** (*mowth'fəl*), as much as fills the mouth: a small quantity: a big word: a momentous utterance (*slang*):—*pl.* **mouth'fuls.** — *adjs.* **mouth'less**; **mouthy** (*mowdh'i*), ranting: affectedly over-emphatic.—**mouth-breather** (*mouth'-brē'dhar*), one who habitually breathes through the mouth; **mouth'-breeder**, a cichlid fish that carries its young in its mouth for protection.—*adj.* **mouth-filling** (*mowth'*), full-sounding.—**mouth'-friend** (*Shak.*), one who only professes friendship; **mouth'-hon'our** (*Shak.*), insincere civility.—*adj.* **mouth-made** (*Shak.*), insincere.—**mouth music**, music (usually accompanying dance) sung not played on instrument(s); **mouth'-organ**, a small musical instrument encasing metallic reeds, played by the mouth—a harmonicon or harmonica: Pan-pipes; **mouth'-piece**, the piece of a musical instrument, tobacco-pipe, mask, etc., held to or in the mouth: a cigarette-holder: a spokesman.—**by word of mouth** (see word); **down in the mouth** (see down, 3); **make a poor mouth**, to profess poverty; **shut, stop, the mouth of**, to silence. [O.E. *mūth*; Ger. *mund*, Du. *mond*.]

**move**, *mōōv*, *v.t.* to cause to change place or posture: to set in motion: to impel: to excite to action: to persuade: to instigate: to arouse: to provoke: to provoke to anger (*obs.*; now *move to anger, move anger in*): to touch the feelings of: to propose formally before a meeting: to recommend.—*v.i.* to go from one place to another: to change place or posture: to walk, to carry oneself: to change residence: to make a motion as in an assembly: to bow or salute on meeting (*arch.*): to begin to act: to take action: to go about one's activities, live one's life, pass one's time: in chess, draughts, etc., to transfer a man in one's turn to another square:—*pr.p.* **mov'ing**; *pa.t.* and *pa.p.* **moved.**— *n.* an act of moving: a beginning of movement: a proceeding or step: play in turn, as at chess: turn to play, in chess, draughts, etc.: advantage depending on whose turn it is to play: the manner in which a chess-man, or the like, can be moved.—*adj.* **movable** (*moov'ə-bl*), mobile: changeable: not fixed: other than heritable (*Scots law*).—Also (esp. *law*) **move'able.**—*n.* (esp. in *pl.*) a portable piece of furniture: a piece of movable or moveable property.—*ns.* **mov'ableness** (**move'ableness**), **movabil'ity.**—*adv.* **mov'ably** (**move'ably**).—*adj.* **move'less**, motionless: immovable.—*adv.* **move'lessly.**—*ns.* **move'-lessness**; **move'ment**, act or manner of moving: change of position: activity: impulse: motion of the mind, emotion: the moving parts in a mechanism, esp. the wheelwork of a clock or watch: melodic progression: accentual character: tempo or pace: a main division of an extended musical composition, with its own more or less independent structure: the suggestion of motion conveyed by a work of art: a general tendency or current of thought, opinion, taste or action, whether organised and consciously propagated or a mere drift; **mov'er**; **mov'ie**, **mov'y** (*slang*), a moving picture, a cinematograph film: a showing of such: (in *pl.*, **movies**, usu. with **the**) motion pictures in general, or the industry that provides them.—Also *adj.*—*adj.* **mov'ing**, causing motion: changing position: affecting the feelings: pathetic.—*adv.* **mov'ingly.**— **movable feast**, a church feast whose date depends on that of Easter, as Shrove-Tuesday, Good-Friday, etc.; **moving pictures**, the cinematograph films.—**moving staircase**, an escalator.—**get a move on**, hurry up: make progress; **know a move or two**, to be sharp or knowing; **move heaven and earth** (see heaven); **on the move**, changing or about to change one's place. [A.Fr. *mover*, O.Fr. *movoir* (Fr. *mouvoir*)—L. *movēre*, to move. The obsolete **meve**, **mieve**, represent those forms in Fr. with accented root-syllable, as *meuvent* (3rd pl.).]

**mow**, *mow*, also *mō*, *n.* a wry face.—*v.i.* to make grimaces.—**nae mows** (*nā mowz*, *Scot.*), no laughing matter. [O.Fr. *moue*, *moe* (Fr. *moue*), or M.Du. *mouwe*, both meaning grimace.]

**mow**, *mow*, also *mō*, *n.* a pile of hay, corn in sheaves, pease, etc., esp. in a barn: a place for such a heap in a barn.—*v.t.* to heap in a mow:— *pr.p.* **mow'ing**; *pa.t.* and *pa.p.* **mowed** (*mowd*).— *v.i.* **mow'burn**, to heat and ferment in the mow.— *adj.* **mow'burnt.** [O.E. *mūga*, heap; O.N. *mūgi*, swath, crowd, mob.]

**mow**, *mō*, *v.t.* to cut down, or cut the grass upon, with a scythe or a grass-cutting machine: to cut down in great numbers:—*pr.p.* **mow'ing**; *pa.t.* **mowed** (*mōd*); *pa.p.* **mowed** or **mown** (*mōn*).—*adjs.* **mowed**, **mown.**—*ns.* **mow'er**, one who mows grass, etc.: a machine with revolving blades for mowing grass; **mow'ing**, the act of cutting: land from which grass is cut.—**mow'ing-machine'.** [O.E. *māwan*; Ger. *mähen*; L. *metēre*, to reap.]

**mowa**, *mow'ə*, **mowra**, *mow'rə.* Same as mahwa.

**mowdi(e)wart, -wort**, Scots forms of mouldwarp.

**moxa**, *mok'sə*, *n.* a cauterising cone of the leaf-down of a wormwood (*Artemisia moxa*), or sun-flower pith, cotton-wool, or other material.—*n.* moxibustion (-*bust'yэn*; modelled on *combustion*), cauterisation by moxa: burning of a herbal moxa as a counter-irritant. [Jap. *mogusa*.]

**moy**, *moi*, (*Shak.*) *n.* supposed by Pistol (misunderstanding a Frenchman's *moi*, me) to be the name of a coin, or possibly a measure (Fr. *muid*—L. *modius*) of corn.

**moyity**, **moyle**, Spens. for **moiety**, **moil**.

**moyl**, **moyle**, *moil*, (*obs.*) *n.* a mule. [O.Fr. *mul*, *mule*.]

**Mozarab**, *mō-zar'ab*, *n.* a privileged Christian Spaniard under Moorish rule.—*adj.* **Mozar'abic**. [Sp. *Mozárabe*—Ar. *musta'rib*, would-be Arab.]

**moze**, *mōz*, *v.t.* to gig, raise a nap on. [Origin obscure.]

**mozetta**, *mō-tset'tэ*, *n.* a short cape to which a hood may be attached, worn by popes, cardinals, bishops, abbots. [It., dim. from *mozzo*, docked.]

**mozzarella**, *mot-sэ-rel'э*, *n.* a softish Italian cheese. [It.]

**mpret**, *bret*, *n.* a former title of the ruler of Albania. [Albanian,—L. *imperâtor*, emperor.]

**M-roof.** See under **M**.

**Mr, Mrs.** See **Mister, Mistress**.

**MS.** See **manuscript**.

**mu**, *mū*, *mōō*, *mü*, *n.* the Greek letter M, μ, equivalent to M: as a numeral, μ' = 40, ‚μ = 40,000: used as a symbol for *micron*.—**mu-** (or μ-) **meson**, a subatomic particle, classed formerly as the lightest type of meson, now as the heaviest type of lepton, having unit negative charge.—Abbrev. **mu'on** (*mū'* or *mōō'*). [Gr. *my̆*.]

**much**, *much* (*comp.* **more**; *superl.* **most**), *adj.* in great quantity: great (*obs.*): many (*Shak.*).— *adv.* in a great degree: to a great extent: in nearly the same way: by far: in old ironical use, like the modern slang 'not much', I don't think.—*n.* a great deal: anything of importance or worth.—Also in unshortened form (*arch.*) **much'el**, *adj.*, *adv.*, and *n.* (*Spens.* **much'ell**, **moch'ell**; Northern form **mick'le**, **muck'le**).— *adv.* (*arch.* and *jocular*) **much'ly**.—*n.* **much'ness** (*arch.*), greatness: magnitude.—**make much of** (see **make**); **much about it**, something like what it usually is; **much of a muchness**, just about the same value or amount; **too much for**, more than a match for; **too much of a good thing**, more than can be tolerated. [M.E. *muche*, *muchel*— O.E. *micel*, *mycel*.]

**mucic**, **mucid**, **mucilage**. See under **mucus**.

**muck**, *muk*, *n.* dung: manure: wet or clinging filth: anything contemptible or worthless: gold (*poet*.; *arch*.): rubbishy reading matter: a mess.—*v.t.* to clear of muck: to manure with muck: to befoul: to make a mess of, to bungle (with *up*).—*v.i.* (usu. with *about*; *coll*.) to potter: to act the fool.—*n.* **muck'er**, one who mucks: a money-grubber (*obs*.): a mess: a mishap, disaster (orig. a fall in the mire): a coarse, unrefined person: a young townsman, not a student (*U.S.*).—*v.t.* to hoard (*obs*.): to squander: to vitiate.—*v.i.* to come to grief: to make a muddle of anything.—*n.* **muck'iness**.— *adj.* **muck'y**, nasty, filthy: of the nature of muck: like muck.—**muck'-heap**, a dunghill; **muck'-midd'en**; **muck'-rake**, a rake for scraping filth.— *v.i.* to seek out and expose scandals or supposed scandals, whether for worthy or unworthy motives.—**muck'-raker**; **muck'-raking**; **muck'-sweat**, profuse sweat; **muck'-worm**, a worm or grub that lives in muck: one who acquires money by mean devices: a miser.—**make a muck of** (*coll*.), to make dirty: to mismanage; **muck in with** (*coll*.), to share with. [Prob. Scand.; cf. O.N. *myki*, Dan. *mög*, dung.]

**muck.** See **amok**.

**muckender**, *muk'эn-dэr*, (*obs*.) *n.* a handkerchief: a table-napkin. [Apparently from some Languedocian dialect; cf. Fr. *mouchoir*, Sp. *mocador*.]

**Mucker**, *mook'эr*, *n.* a nickname for a member of a Königsberg sect (1835) of dualistic theosophists: (without *cap*.; *muk'эr*), a fanatical reformer: a hypocrite. [Ger.]

**muckle**, *muk'l*, a Scottish form of **mickle**.

**muckluck**, **mukluk**, **mucluc**, *muk'luk*, *n.* an Eskimo sealskin boot. [Eskimo.]

**Mucor**, *mū'kэr*, *n.* a genus of zygomycete fungi including some of the commonest moulds, giving name to order or family **Mūcorā'les** or **Mūcorin'eae**. [L., mould.]

**mucro**, *mū'krō*, *n.* a short stiff sharp point forming an abrupt end.—*adjs.* **mu'cronate**, **-d** (-*krэn-āt*, -*id*). [L. *mūcrō*, -*ōnis*, a sharp point.]

**mucus**, *mū'kэs*, *n.* the slimy fluid secreted by the mucous membrane of the nose or other parts.— *n.* **mu'cate**, a salt of mucic acid.—*adjs.* **mucedinous** (-*sed'*, -*sēd'*), mouldy, mildewy; **mu'cic** (-*sik*), applied to an acid got by oxidation of gums; **mu'cid**, mouldy, musty; **muciferous** (-*sif'*), secreting or conveying mucus.—*n.* **mu'cigen** (-*si-jen*), a substance secreted by the cells of mucous membrane, converted into mucin.—*n.* **mu'cilage** (-*si-lij*), a gluey mixture of carbohydrates in plants: any sticky substance: gum used as an adhesive.—*adj.* **mucilaginous** (-*laj'*).—*ns.* **mucilag'inousness**; **mu'cin**, any one of a class of albuminous substances in mucus.—*adj.* **mucoid** (*mū'koid*), like mucus.—*n.* **mucos'ity**.— *adjs.* **mu'cous**, like mucus: slimy: viscous: producing mucus; **mu'cŭlent**, like mucus; **mucopū'rulent**, of mucus and pus.—*n.* **mucovisci-dō'sis**, cystic fibrosis.—**mucous membrane**, a lining of various tubular cavities of the body, with glands secreting mucus. [L. *mūcus*, nose mucus; cf. *mungĕre*, to wipe away.]

**mud**, *mud*, *n.* wet soft earth: a mixture of earthy or clayey particles with water: something worthless or contemptible.—*v.t.* to bury in mud: to clog with mud: to plaster with mud: to befoul: to make turbid: to supply with mud.—*v.i.* to hide in the mud.—*adv.* **mudd'ily**.—*n.* **mudd'iness**.—*adj.* **mudd'y**, foul with mud: containing mud: covered with mud: of the nature of mud: like mud: mud-coloured: confused: stupid.—*v.t.* and *v.i.* to make or become muddy:—*pr.p.* **mudd'ying**; *pa.t.* and *pa.p.* **mudd'ied**.—**mud'-bath**, a bath in mud, esp. as a remedy; **mud'-boat**, a board or sled for conveyance over mud-flats or swamps: a boat for carrying away dredged mud; **mud'-cat** (*U.S.*), a name given to several species of catfish; **mud'-clerk** (*U.S.*), an assistant purser; **mud'-cone**, a cone formed by a mud-volcano.—*adjs.* **mudd'y-head'ed**; **mudd'y-mett'led** (*Shak.*), spiritless.—**mud'-fish**, a fish that burrows in mud, esp. a lung-fish; **mud'-flap**, a flap fixed behind the wheels of a vehicle to prevent mud, etc., being thrown up behind; **mud'-flat**, a muddy stretch submerged at high water; **mud'-guard**, a screen to catch mud-splashes from a wheel; **mud'-hole**, a hole with mud in it: an opening for removing sediment from a boiler, etc.; **mud'-hook** (*slang*), an anchor; **mud'lark**, a name for various birds that frequent mud: one who picks up a living along the banks of tidal rivers: a street-arab.—*v.i.* to work or play in mud.—**mud'-la'va**, a stream of mud from a volcano; **mud'-lump'**, an upstanding area of mud, often exhaling gases, as in the Mississippi delta; **mud'-minn'ow**, a small fish (Umbra) akin to the pikes; **mud'pack**, a cosmetic paste one ingredient of which is fuller's earth; **mud'-pie'**, a moulded mass of mud made by children in play; **mud'-pupp'y** (*U.S.*), the axolotl: a hellbender; **mud'scow**, a flat mud-boat; **mud'-skipper**, a goby that can skip about on bare mud; **mud'-slinger**; **mud'-slinging**, vilification; **mud'stone**, an argillaceous rock not distinctly fissile; **mud'-volca'no**, a vent that emits mud; **mud'wort**, a small mud-growing scrophulaceous plant (*Limosella aquatica*).—**his, her**, etc., **name is mud**, he, she, etc., is out of favour; **mud in your eye**, good health! (used as a toast); **throw mud at** (see **throw**). [Cf. Old Low Ger. *mudde*, Du. *modder*.]

**muddle**, *mud'l*, *v.t.* to render muddy: to confuse: to bungle: to mix.—*v.i.* to wallow, dabble, or grub in mud (*arch.*): to potter about: to blunder.—*n.* confusion, mess: mental confusion, bewilderment.—*n.* **mudd'lehead**, a blockhead.—*adj.* **muddlehead'ed**.—*adv.* **muddlehead'edly**.—*n.* **muddlehead'edness**.—**muddle away**, to squander or fritter away confusedly; **muddle through**, to get through difficulties blunderingly. [Freq. of **mud.**]

**mudir**, *mōō-dēr'*, *n.* a local governor.—*n.* **mudir'ieh**, **mudir'ia**, a mudir's province or office. [Ar. *mudir*.]

**muezzin**, *mōō-ez'in*, *n.* the Mohammedan official who calls to prayer.—Also **muedd'in.** [Ar. *mu'adhdhin.*]

**muff**, *muf*, *n.* a cylinder of fur or the like for keeping the hands warm: a similar contrivance for the feet, ear, etc.: a mitt (*obs.*).—*n.* **muffettee'** (*obs.*), a muffler: a woollen cuff. [Prob. from Du. *mof*; cf. Ger. *muff*, a muff.]

**muff**, *muf*, *n.* one who is awkward or unskilful, esp. in sport: a duffer: a bungler: an unpractical person: one who lacks savoir-faire: a failure, esp. to hold a ball.—*v.t.* to perform awkwardly: to bungle: to miss.—*v.i.* to act clumsily, esp. in letting a ball slip out of the hands. [Poss. **muff** (1).]

**muffin**, *muf'in*, *n.* a soft, porous cake, eaten hot, with butter: a small plate: one who dangles after a young woman: a poor ball-player.—*n.* **muffineer'**, a dish for keeping muffins hot: a castor for sprinkling salt or sugar on muffins.—**muff'in-bell'**, a bell rung by a muffin-man; **muff'in-cap**, a round flat cap for men; **muff'in-fight'**, -worr'y (*coll.*), a tea-party; **muff'in-man**, one who goes round selling muffins. [Origin unknown.]

**muffle**, *muf'l*, *n.* the thick naked upper lip and nose, as of a ruminant. [Fr. *mufle*.]

**muffle**, *muf'l*, *v.t.* to envelop, for warmth, concealment, stifling of sound, etc.: to blindfold (*arch.*): to deaden or dull the sound of.—*n.* a boxing-glove (*obs.*): a means of muffling: a receptacle, oven, or compartment in which things can be heated in a furnace without contact with the fuel and its products: a muffled state: a muffled sound.—*adj.* **muff'led**.—*n.* **muff'ler**, a scarf for the throat: any means of muffling: one who muffles: a silencer (*U.S.*). [App. Fr. *mouffle*, mitten.]

**mufti**, *muf'ti*, *n.* an expounder of Mohammedan law: the civilian dress of one who wears a uniform when on duty: plain clothes: a civilian. [Ar. *muftī*.]

**mug**, *mug*, *n.* a cup with more or less vertical sides: its contents.—*ns.* **mug'ful** (-*fəl*):—*pl.* **mug'fuls**; **mugg'er**, a hawker of earthenware.—**mug'-house** (*obs.*), an alehouse; **mug'-hunter** (*games*), a pot-hunter. [Origin unknown; cf. Norw. *mugga*, Sw. *mugg*.]

**mug**, *mug*, *n.* the face: the mouth.—*v.i.* (*theat.*) to grimace. [Poss. from the grotesque face on a drinking-mug.]

**mug**, *mug*, (*coll.*) *n.* a simpleton: an easy dupe.—**a mug's game**, something only fools would do. [Origin unknown.]

**mug**, *mug*, (*coll.*) *n.* a sap or swot: an exam.—*v.t.* and *v.i.* (often with *up*) to study hard: to swot up. [Origin unknown.]

**mug**, *mug*, *n.* a woolly-faced sheep.—**mug'-ewe**, -lamb, -sheep.

**mug**, *mug*, (*slang*) *v.t.*, *v.i.* to attack from behind, seizing by the throat.—*n.* **mugg'er**. [Perh. **mug** (2).]

**mugearite**, *mōō-gēr'it*, *n.* a dark finely crystalline basic igneous rock composed mainly of oligoclase, orthoclase, and olivine, with iron oxides, developed at *Mugeary* in Skye.

**mugger**, *mug'ər*, *n.* a broad-snouted Indian crocodile. [Hind. *magar*.]

**mugger**. See **mug** (1 and 6).

**muggins**, *mug'inz*, *n.* a children's card-game: a form of dominoes: a simpleton. [Ety. dub.]

**Muggletonian**, *mug-l-tō'ni-an*, *n.* a member of a sect founded by John Reeve and Lodowick *Muggleton* (1609-98), who claimed to be the two witnesses of Rev. xi. 3-6.

**muggy**, *mug'i*, *adj.* foggy: close and damp, as weather: wet or mouldy, as straw.—Also **mugg'-ish**. [Perh. O.N. *mugga*, mist.]

**mugwort**, *mug'wûrt*, *n.* a common British wormwood. [O.E. *mucgwyrt*, lit. midge-wort.]

**mugwump**, *mug'wump*, *n.* an Indian chief: a person of great importance, or one who thinks himself so: one who dissociates himself from political parties, a smug Independent. [Algonquian *mugquomp*, a great man.]

**Muhammedan, Muharram.** See **Mohammedan, Moharram.**

**muid**, *mü-ē*, *n.* an old French measure of capacity: a hogshead: a dry measure for corn, etc.: (*S.Afr.*; *mā'id*) a sack of 3 bushels. [Fr.,—L. *modius*; cf. Du. *mud*.]

**muil.** See **mule** (2). **muir.** See **moor** (2).

**muist.** See **must** (5).

**mujik.** See **muzhik**.

**mukhtar**, *mōōk'tär*, *n.* an Indian lawyer. [Ar. *mukhtār*, chosen.]

**mulatto**, *mū-lat'ō*, *n.* the offspring of a Negro and a person of European stock:—*pl.* **mulatt'os**:—*fem.* **mulatt'a, mulatt'ress.** [Sp. *mulato*, dim. of *mulo*, mule; Fr. *mulâtre*.]

**mulberry**, *mul'bər-i*, *n.* the edible multiple fruit of any tree of the genus Morus (family Moraceae): the tree bearing it, with leaves on which silkworms feed: extended to various fruits or plants more or less similar superficially or really: the colour of the fruit, dark purple.—*adj.* **mulberry-coloured**.—*adj.* **mul'berry-faced**, having a face blotched with purple.—**mul'berry-fig**, the true sycamore (sycamore), a fig-tree with leaves like those of mulberry; **Mulberry harbour**, a preconstructed harbour (code name *Mulberry*) towed across the Channel for the 1944 landings in Normandy in World War II. [Prob. O.H.G. *mulberi* (Mod. Ger. *maulbeere*)—L. *mōrum*; cf. morus, berry.]

**mulch, mulsh**, *mulch, mulsh*, *n.* loose material, strawy dung, etc., laid down to protect the roots of plants.—*v.t.* to cover with mulch.—*adj.* soft. [Cf. Ger. dial. *molsch*, soft, beginning to decay; O.E. *melsc*.]

**Mulciber**, *mul'si-bər*, *n.* Vulcan.—*adj.* **Mulcibē'rian.** [L.]

**mulct**, *mulkt*, *n.* a fine: a penalty.—*v.t.* to fine: to swindle: to deprive (with *of*):—*pa.p.* **mulct'ed, mulct.** [L. *mulcta*, a fine.]

**mule**, *mūl*, *n.* the offspring of the ass and horse (esp. he-ass and mare): a hybrid: a cross between a canary and another finch: a cotton-spinning machine: an obstinate person.—*adj.* hybrid.—*n.* **muleteer** (*mūl-i-tēr'*), a mule-driver.—*adj.* **mul'ish**, like a mule: obstinate.—*adv.* **mul'ishly**.—*n.* **mul'ishness**.—**mule'-deer**, a long-eared deer, black-tail of N. America. [O.E. *mūl*—L. *mūlus* was superseded by O.Fr. *mul* (masc.; in Mod. Fr. the dim. *mulet* is used), *mule* (fem.)—L. *mūlus, mūla*.]

**mule**, *mūl* (Scot. muil, *mül*), *n.* a loose slipper. [Fr. *mule*.]

**muley, mulley, mooly**, *mōōl'i, mūl'i*, *adj.* hornless.

—*n.* a hornless cow: any cow. [Gael. *maol* or W. *moel*, bald.]

**mulga**, *mul'gə*, *n.* an Australian acacia. [Native word.]

**muliebrity**, *mū-li-eb'ri-ti*, *n.* womanhood. [L. *muliebritās*, *-tātis*—*mulier*, a woman.]

**mull**, *mul*, *n.* a muddle.—*v.t.* to bungle. [Origin obscure.]

**mull**, *mul*, (*Scot.*) *n.* a promontory. [Prob. Gael. *maol* or O.N. *mūli*, snout; cf. Ger. *maul*.]

**mull**, *mul*, (*Scot.*) *n.* a snuff-box. [See mill (1).]

**mull**, *mul*, *n.* a soft muslin.—Also mul'mul(l). [Hind. *malmal*.]

**mull**, *mul*, *v.i.* (often with *over*) to cogitate, ponder, turn over in the mind. [Origin obscure.]

**mull**, *mul*, *v.t.* to crumble. [Cf. O.E. *myl*, dust.]

**mull**, *mul*, *v.t.* to warm, spice, and sweeten (wine, ale, etc.).—*adj.* mulled.—*n.* mull'er. [Origin obscure.]

**mull**, *mul*, (*Shak.*) *v.t.* to dull, stupefy. [Origin obscure; perh. from the mulling of wine.]

**mullah**, **moolah**, **mollah**, *mul'ə*, *mōōl'ə*, *mol'ə*, *n.* a Mohammedan learned in theology and law: a Moslem schoolmaster or teacher: a fanatical preacher of war on the infidel. [Pers., Turk., and Hind. *mullā*—Ar. *maulā*.]

**mullein**, *mul'in*, *n.* a tall, stiff, yellow-flowered woolly plant (Verbascum) of the Scrophulariaceae—popularly known as *hag-taper*, *Adam's flannel*, *Aaron's rod*, *shepherd's club*. [A.Fr. *moleine*.]

**muller**, *mul'ər*, *n.* a pulverising tool. [Perh. O.Fr. *moloir*—*moldre* (Fr. *moudre*), to grind.]

**mullet**, *mul'it*, *n.* a fish of the genus Mugil, palatable, nearly cylindrical: another fish (Mullus), slightly compressed—red mullet. [O.Fr. *mulet*, dim.—L. *mullus*, red mullet.]

**mullet**, *mul'it*, (*her.*) *n.* a five-pointed star—cadency mark of a son. [O.Fr. *molette*, rowel of a spur—L. *mola*, a millstone.]

**mulligatawny**, *mul-i-gə-tö'ni*, *n.* an East Indian curry-soup. [Tamil *milagu-tannir*, pepperwater.]

**mulligrubs**, *mul'i-grubz*, (*coll.*) *n.pl.* colic: sulkiness.

**mullion**, *mul'yən*, *n.* an upright division between the lights of windows, etc.—*adj.* mull'ioned. [Apparently from monial.]

**mullock**, *mul'ək*, *n.* rubbish, esp. mining refuse. [From obs. or dial. *mull*, dust; cf. O.E. *myl*.]

**mulsh**. Same as mulch.

**mult(i)-**, *mult-*, *mul-ti-*, in composition, much, many.—*adjs.* **multang'ular**, having many angles; **multan'imous** (L. *animus*, mind), having a many-sided mind; **mult(i)artic'ulate**, many-jointed; **multicam'erate** (L. *camera*, chamber), having many chambers or cells; **multicap'itate** (L. *caput*, *-itis*, head), many-headed; **multicau'line** (L. *caulis*, stem), having many stems; **multicell'ular**, having or made up of many cells; **multicen'tral**, having or proceeding from many centres; **multicipital** (*mul-ti-sip'i-təl*; L. *caput*, *-itis*, head), having many heads, multicapitate.—*n.* **multicolour** (*mul'ti-kul-ər*), diversity or plurality of colour.— *adj.* many-coloured.—*adjs.* mul'ticoloured; multicos'tate (L. *costa*, rib), many-ribbed; multicus'pid, having more than two cusps.—*n.* a multicuspid tooth.—*adj.* multicus'pidate.—*n.* mul'ticycle (*obs.*), a velocipede with more than three wheels: one intended to carry several men. —*adjs.* **multiden'tate** (L. *dēns*, *dentis*, tooth), many-toothed; **multidentic'ulate**, having many denticulations or fine teeth; **multidigitate** (*-dij'i-tāt*; L. *digitus*, finger), many-fingered; **multidimen'sional** (*math.*), of more than three dimensions; mul'tifaced, many-faced; mul'tifid, also multif'idous, cleft into many lobes.—*n.* mul'tifil, a multiple strand of synthetic fibre (also multifil'ament).—*adjs.* **multiflo'rous**, many-flowered; mul'tifoil, having more than five foils or arcuate

divisions.—*n.* multifoil ornament.—*adjs.* **multifo'liate** (L. *folium*, leaf), with many leaves; **multifo'liolate**, with many leaflets; mul'tiform, having many forms, polymorphic.—*n.* that which is multiform.—*n.* multiform'ity.—*adjs.* **multiju'gate**, **multiju'gous** (L. *jugum*, yoke), consisting of many pairs of leaflets; **multilat'eral** (L. *latus*, *lateris*, side), many-sided: with several parties or participants; **multilineal** (*-lin'*), **multilin'ear**, having many lines; **multilingual** (*-ling'gwəl*; L. *lingua*, tongue), in many languages: speaking several languages: (of a country, state, or society) in which several languages are spoken; **multilo'bate**, **mul'tilobed**, many-lobed; **multilobular** (*-lob'ū-lər*), **multilob'ulate**, having many lobules; **multilocular** (*-lok'ū-lər*), **multiloc'ulate**, many-chambered.—*n.* **multil'oquence**, much speaking.—*adjs.* **multil'oquent**, **multil'oquous**.—*n.* **multil'oquy**; **mul'timēd'ia**, simultaneous presentation in one place of several visual and/or sound entertainments; **multimillionaire'**, one who is a millionaire several times over.—*adj.* **multino'mial** (*alg.*), consisting of more than two terms: relating to multinomials.—*n.* a multinomial expression.—*adjs.* **multinu'clear**, **multinū'cleate**, **-d**, having several nuclei; **multinū'cleolate**, having several nucleoli; **multipar'tite** (L. *partitus*, divided), divided into many parts: much cut up into segments.—*ns.* **mul'tiped** (L. *pēs*, *pedis*, foot), a many-footed animal: a woodlouse (*obs.*; also **multipede**, *-pēd*); **mul'tiplane**, an aeroplane with more than two sets of supporting planes; **multi-ply** (*mul'ti-plī'*), ply-wood of more than three thicknesses.—*adjs.* **multip'lar**, having several poles or axons; **multip'otent** (L. *potēns*, *-entis*, powerful; *Shak.*), having power to do many things.—*n.* **multipres'ence**, the power of being in many places at once.—*adjs.* **multipres'ent**; **mul'tipur'pose**; **multirac'ial**, embracing, consisting of, many races.—*n.* **multirac'ialism**, the policy of recognising the rights of all in a multiracial society.—*adj.* **multiram'ified** (L. *rāmus*, branch, *facēre*, to make), having many branches; **multisep'tate**, having many septa; **multisē'rial**, **multisē'riate**, in many rows; **multisonant** (*multis'ən-ənt*; L. *sonāns*, *-antis*, pr.p. of *sonāre*, to sound), having many sounds: sounding much; **multispi'ral**, having many coils; **mul'ti-stage**, in a series of distinct parts: of a rocket, consisting of a number of parts that fall off in series at predetermined places on its course; **mul'tistor(e)y**; **multisulc'ate** (L. *sulcus*, furrow), having many furrows; **multituber'culate**, **-d**, having many tubercles, as teeth.—*ns.* **multivāl'ence** (or *-tiv'ə-*), **multivāl'ency** (or *-tiv'ə-*).—*adjs.* **multivāl'ent** (or *-tiv'ə-*; *chem.*), having a valency greater than one; **multivar'iate**, consisting of, concerned with, many variables; **multivar'ious**, differing widely.—*n.* **multiver'sity**, a large university made up of several campuses.—*adjs.* **multiv'-ious** (L. *via*, way), going many ways; **multiv'ocal** (L. *vōx*, *vōcis*, voice), of many meanings.—*n.* a word of many meanings.—*adjs.* **multivoltine** (*-vol'-tin*; It. *volta*, turn, winding), having several annual broods—of silkworm moths; **mul'ti-wall**, made of three or more layers of special paper; **multungulate** (*mul-tung'gū-lāt*; L. *ungula*, hoof), having the hoof divided into more than two parts.—*n.* a multungulate mammal. [L. *multus*, much.]

**multangular ... to ... mult(i)articulate.** See mult(i)-.

**multeity**, *mul-tē'i-ti*, *n.* manifoldness, very great numerousness. [L. *multus*, much, many, *-eity* as in *haecceity*.]

**multicamerate ... to ... multifaced.** See mult(i)-.

**multifarious**, *mul-ti-fā'ri-əs*, *adj.* having great diversity: made up of many parts: manifold: in many rows or ranks (*bot.*).—*adv.* multifā'riously.—*n.* multifā'riousness, the state of being multifarious: multiplied variety: the fault of improperly joining in one bill distinct and independent matters, and thereby confounding them (*law*). [L. *multifārius*; poss. from *fāri*, to speak.]

**multifid** . . . to . . . **multinucleolate.** See mult(i)-.

**multipara,** *mul-tip′ər-ə,* a woman who has given birth to a child for the second or later time, or is about to do so—opp. to *primipara.*—*n.* **multiparity** (*-par′i-ti*), condition of being a multipara: condition of being multiparous.—*adjs.* **multip′arous,** pertaining to a multipara: producing more than one at a birth (*zool.*): giving rise to several lateral axes (*bot.*). [**multi-,** *-para*—L. *parēre,* to bring forth.]

**multipartite** . . . to . . . **multiplane.** See mult(i)-.

**multiple,** *mul′ti-pl,* adj. consisting of many elements or components, esp. of the same kind: manifold: compound: multiplied or repeated: allowing many messages to be sent over the same wire (*teleg.*).—*n.* a quantity which contains another an exact number of times: an object for display, claimed to be art but designed for reproduction in numbers industrially.—*n.* **mul′-tiplet,** an optical spectrum line having several components: a group of subatomic particles.—*adv.* **multiply** (*mul′ti-pli*).—**multiple fruit,** a single fruit formed from several flowers in combination, as a pineapple, fig, mulberry; **multiple sclerosis,** disseminated sclerosis; **multiple shop, store,** one of many shops belonging to the same firm, often dispersed about the country; **multiple star,** group of stars so close as to seem one—**common multiple,** number or quantity that can be divided by each of several others without a remainder; **least common multiple,** the smallest number that forms a common multiple. [Fr.,—L.L. *multiplus*—root of L. *plēre,* to fill.]

**multiplepoinding,** *mul-ti-pl-pind′ing,* (*Scots law*) n. a process by which a person who has funds claimed by more than one, in order not to have to pay more than once, brings them all into court that one of them may establish his right.

**multiplex,** *mul′ti-pleks, adj.* multiple. [L. *multiplex*—*plicāre,* to fold.]

**multiply,** *mul′ti-pli, v.t.* to increase the number of: to accumulate: to magnify (*obs.*): to reproduce: to obtain the product of (*math.*).—*v.i.* to become more numerous: to be augmented: to reproduce: to perform the mathematical process of multiplication:—*pr.p.* **mul′tiplying;** *pa.t.* and *pa.p.* **mul′tiplied.**—*adjs.* **mul′tipliable, mul′tiplicable** (or *-plik′*).—*n.* **mul′tiplicand** (or *-kand′*), a quantity to be multiplied by another.—*adj.* **mul′tiplicate** (or *-tip′*), consisting of more than one: in many folds.—*n.* the condition of being in many copies: one of these copies.—*n.* **multiplica′tion,** the act of multiplying or increasing in number: increase of number of parts by branching (*bot.*): the rule or operation by which quantities are multiplied.—*adj.* **mult′iplicative** (or *-plik′ə-tiv*), tending or having power to multiply: indicating how many times (*gram.*).—*ns.* **mul′tiplicātor** (*math.*), a multiplier; **multiplicity** (*-plis′i-ti*), the state of being manifold: a great number; **mul′tiplier,** one who multiplies: a quantity by which another is multiplied: a device or instrument for intensifying some effect: a geared fishing-reel for drawing in the line quickly.—**multiplication table,** a tabular arrangement giving the products of pairs of numbers usually up to 12; **multiplying glass** (*obs.*), a magnifying glass: a faceted glass for multiplying reflexions.—**multiply words,** to say much: to be wordy. [Fr. *multiplier*—L. *multiplicāre*—*plicāre,* to fold.]

**multiply,** *mul′ti-pli.* See under **multiple.**

**multi-ply** . . . to . . . **multiramified.** See under mult(i)-.

**multiscience,** *mul-tish′əns, adj.* knowledge of

many things. [L.L. adj. *multiscius*—L. *scientia,* knowledge.]

**multiseptate** . . . to . . . **multituberculate.** See mult(i)-.

**multitude,** *mul′ti-tūd, n.* the state of being many: a great number or (*rare*) quantity: a crowd: the mob.—*adjs.* **multitud′inary** (*rare*); **multitud′inous.**—*adv.* **multitud′inously.**—*n.* **multitud′inousness.** [L. *multitūdō, -inis*—*multus.*]

**multivalence** . . . to . . . **multiwall.** See mult(i)-.

**multum,** *mul′təm, n.* an adulterant in brewing. [Prob. neut. of L. *multus,* much.]

**multum in parvo,** *mul′təm, mōōl′tōōm in pär′vō, -wō,* (L.) much in little, a large amount in a small space; **multum non multa** (*non mul′tə, nōn mōōl′ta*), much, not many things.

**multungulate.** See mult(i)-.

**multure,** *mul′tyər,* (*Scot.*) **mouter** (*mōōt′ər*), *n.* a fee, generally in kind, for grinding grain: the right to such a fee.—*v.t.* and *v.i.* to take multure (for).—*n.* **mul′turer** (**mou′terer**), one who receives multures: a miller: one who pays multures. [O.F. *molture, moulture*—L. *molitūra,* a grinding.]

**mum,** *mum, adj.* silent.—*n.* silence.—*interj.* not a word.—*v.i.* to act in dumb show: to act in a mummers′ play: to masquerade:—*pr.p.* **mumm′ing;** *pa.t.* and *pa.p.* **mummed.**—*ns.* **mumm′er,** an actor in a folk-play, usu. at Christmas: a masquerader: an actor; **mumm′ery,** mumming: great show without reality: foolish ceremonial; **mumm′ing.**—*n.* and *interj.* **mum′-bud′get** (*obs.*), mum.—*n.* **mum′chance′,** a silent game with cards or dice (*obs.*): a fool (*dial.*).—*adj.* silent. —**mum′s the word,** not a word. [An inarticulate sound with closing of the lips; partly O.Fr. *momer,* to mum, *momeur,* mummer; cf. Du. *mommen,* to mask.]

**mum,** *mum, n.* a wheatmalt beer, sometimes with oat and bean meal. [Ger. *mumme.*]

**mum,** *mum,* **mummy,** *mum′i, ns.* childish words for mother. [Cf. **mamma.**]

**mum,** *mum.* See **ma′am.**

**mumble,** *mum′bl, v.t.* and *v.i.* to say, utter, or speak indistinctly, softly, or perfunctorily: to mouth with the lips, or as with toothless gums.— *ns.* **mum′blement** (*Carlyle*), mumbling speech; **mum′bler.**—*n.* and *adj.* **mum′bling.**—*adv.* **mum′-blingly.**—**mum′ble-news** (*Shak.*), a tale-bearer. [Frequentative from **mum.**]

**Mumbo-jumbo,** *mum′bō-jum′bō, n.* a god or bug-bear of West Africa: (without *cap.*), any object of foolish worship or fear: mummery or hocus-pocus. [Said to be Mandingo.]

**mummock,** *mum′ək.* Same as **mammock.**

**mummy,** *mum′i, n.* an embalmed or otherwise preserved dead body: the substance of such a body, formerly used medicinally: dead flesh: anything pounded to a formless mass: a bituminous drug or pigment.—*v.t.* to mummify:—*pr.p.* **mumm′ying;** *pa.t.* and *pa.p.* **mumm′ied.**—*ns.* **mumm′ia,** mummy as a drug; **mummificā′tion.**—*adj.* **mumm′iform.**—*v.t.* **mumm′ify,** to make into a mummy:—*pr.p.* **mumm′ifying;** *pa.t.* and *pa.p.* **mumm′ified.** — **mumm′y-case;** **mumm′y-cloth,** cloth for wrapping a mummy: a similar fabric used as a basis for embroidery: a fabric like crape with cotton or silk warp and woollen weft; **mumm′y-wheat,** a variety of wheat alleged (incredibly) to descend from grains found in Egyptian mummy-cases. [O.Fr. *mumie*—L.L. *mumia* —Ar. and Pers. *mūmiyā*—Pers. *mūm,* wax.]

**mummy.** See **mum** (3).

**mump,** *mump, v.t.* to mumble or mutter (*dial.*): to mumble or munch (*dial.*): to get by, or visit for the purpose of, begging or sponging (*dial.*): to cheat (*obs.*).—*v.i.* (*dial.*) to mumble: to sponge: to sulk: to mope: to grimace: to play the beggar.—*n.* **mump′er,** one who mumps: a beggar (*old cant*).—*adj.* **mump′ish,** having mumps: dull: sullen.—*adv.* mump'ishly.—*n.* mump'ishness.—*n.* (*pl.* treated as *sing.*) mumps, an acute infectious disease characterised by a painful swelling of the parotid gland: gloomy silence.—mump'ing-day, St Thomas's Day, 21st Dec., when the poor used to go around begging corn, money, etc. [Cf. mum and Du. *mompen*, to cheat.]

mumpsimus, *mump'si-məs, n.* an error cherished after exposure: stubborn conservatism: an antiquated person. [An ignorant priest's blunder (in an old story) for L. *sūmpsimus*, we have received, in the mass.]

mun, *mun,* (*dial.*) *v.t.* must—used in pres. indic. only; *3rd pers.* mun.—Also maun, man. [O.N. *mon, mun,* or *man* (inf. *monu, munu*), a preterite-present verb.]

mun, *mun, n.* a dialect form of man.

munch, *munch, munsh, v.t.* and *v.i.* to chew with marked action of the jaws.—*n.* munch'er. [Prob. imit.]

Munda, *mōōn'da, n.* any member of a group of peoples of eastern India, or speaker of their group of languages (also called Kolarian), a division of the Austroasiatic family of languages. —Also *adj.*

mundane, *mun'dān, adj.* worldly: earthly: cosmic: ordinary, banal.—*adv.* mun'danely.—*n.* mundanity (*-dan'i-ti*). [L. *mundānus—mundus,* the world.]

mundic, *mun'dik, n.* iron pyrites. [From Cornish.]

mundify, *mun'di-fī, v.t.* to cleanse, purify.—*n.* mundificā'tion.—*adj.* mundif'icative. [L.L. *mundificāre*—L. *mundus,* clean, *facēre,* to make.]

mundungus, *mun-dung'gəs,* (*arch.*) *n.* a rank-smelling tobacco. [Sp. *mondongo,* black pudding.]

mungo, *mung'gō, n.* the waste produced in a woollen-mill from hard spun or felted cloth, or from tearing up old clothes, used in making cheap cloth. [Origin obscure.]

mungoose. Same as mongoose.

Munich, *mū'nik, -nihh, n.* a buying off by concession.—*n.* Mu'nichism. [From the pact signed at *Munich* (1938) yielding the Sudetenland of Czechoslovakia to Hitler.]

municipal, *mū-nis'i-pl, adj.* pertaining to home affairs: pertaining to the government of a borough.—*n.* municipalisā'tion,-z-.—*v.t.* munic'i-palise, -ize, to erect into a municipality: to bring under municipal control or ownership.—*ns.* munic'ipalism, concern for the interests of one's municipality: belief in municipal control; municipality (*-pal'i-ti*), a self-governing town: a district governed like a city: in France, a division of the country.—*adv.* munic'ipally. [L. *mūnicipālis—mūniceps, -ipis,* an inhabitant of a *mūnicipium,* a free town—*mūnia,* official duties, *capēre,* to take.]

munificence, *mū-nif'i-səns, n.* magnificent liberality in giving: bountifulness.—*adj.* munif'icent. —*adv.* munif'icently. [L. *mūnificentia—mūnus,* a present, *facēre,* to make.]

munify, *mū'ni-fī, v.t.* to fortify.—*n.* munifience (*-nif'i-əns*; Spens.), defence, fortification. [Irregularly formed from L. *mūnire,* to fortify, *facēre,* to make.]

muniment, *mū'ni-mənt, n.* a means of defence: a record fortifying or making good a claim: (in *pl.*) furnishings, equipment, things provided.—*v.t.* munite' (*Bacon*), to fortify, strengthen.—*ns.* munition (*-nish'ən;* commonly in *pl.*), fortification: defence: material used in war: military stores; munitioneer', munit'ion-work'er, a worker engaged in making munitions.—*fem.* (*obs. coll.*) munitionette'. [L. *mūnire, -itum,* to fortify; *mūnimentum,* fortification, later, title-deeds—*moenia,* walls.]

munnion, *mun'yən.* Same as mullion.

Munro, *mun-rō', n.* a Scottish mountain over 3000 feet. [Orig. list of these made by H. T. *Munro.*]

munshi, moonshee, *mōōn'shē,* (*India*) *n.* a secretary: an interpreter: a language teacher. [Hind. *munshī*—Ar. *munshī*'.]

muntin, munting, *munt'in(g), n.* the vertical framing piece between door panels. [montant.]

muntjak, muntjac, *munt'jak, n.* a name for a group of small deer of the Oriental region. [From the Malay name.]

Muntz metal, *muntz met'l, n.* alpha-beta brass, 60% copper and 40% zinc. [G. F. *Muntz,* 19th cent. English metallurgist.]

muon. See mu.—*n.* muonium, *mū-ōn'i-əm,* an isotope of hydrogen.—muonic atom (*mū-on'ik*), a hydrogen-like atom, formed by the slowing-down of an energetic muon by ionisation as it traverses matter.

muqaddam, mokaddam, mocuddum, *mōō-kud'um, mō-, n.* a head-man. [Ar.]

muraena, murena, *mū-rē'na, n.* a favourite food-fish of the Romans, a moray: Muraena, the moray genus, giving name to a family of eels, Murae'nidae. [L. *mūraena;* see moray.]

mural, *mū'rəl, adj.* of, on, attached to, or of the nature of, a wall.—*n.* (*obs.*) a wall (in *Shak.* only a conjectural emendation; see morall): mural decoration, esp. painting.—mural circle, a large graduated circle, fixed to a wall, for measuring arcs of the meridian; mural crown, an embattled crown given among the ancient Romans to him who first mounted the wall of a besieged city; mural painting, a painting executed, especially in distemper colours, upon the wall of a building. [L. *mūrālis—mūrus,* a wall.]

murder, *mûr'dər, n.* the act of putting a person to death intentionally and unlawfully: excessive or reprehensible slaughter not legally murder: hyperbolically, torture, excessive toil or hardship.—*v.t.* to kill (ordinarily a person) unlawfully with malice aforethought: to slaughter: hyperbolically, to torture: to mangle in performance.—Also (now only *dial.*) murther (*-dhər*).—*n.* mur'derer (*obs.* or *dial.* mur'therer), one who murders, or is guilty of murder: a small cannon (also mur'dering-piece) (*obs.*):—*fem.* mur'deress.—*adj.* mur'derous.—*adv.* mur'derously.—murder will out, murder cannot remain hidden: the truth will come to light. [O.E. *morthor—morth,* death; Ger. *mord,* Goth. *maurthr;* cf. L. *mors, mortis,* death.]

mure, *mūr, n.* (*Shak.*) a wall.—*v.t.* to wall in or up: to confine: to close.—*n.* mur'age, a tax for the building or upkeep of town-walls.—*adj.* mur'iform (*bot.*), with cells arranged like bricks in a wall. [Fr. *mur* and L. *mūrus,* a wall.]

Murex, *mū'reks, n.* a genus of gasteropod molluscs, some of which yielded the Tyrian purple dye:—*pl.* mu'rexes, mu'rices (*-ri-sēz*). [L. *mūrex, -icis.*]

murgeon, *mûr'jən,* (*Scot.*) *n.* a grimace.—*v.t.* and *v.i.* to mock with grimaces. [Origin obscure.]

muriate, *mūr'i-āt, n.* (*arch.*) a chloride.—*adjs.* mur'iāted, impregnated or combined with chlorine or a chloride; muriatic (*-at'ik*), briny: hydrochloric (not in scientific use). [L. *muria,* brine.]

muricate, *mūr'i-kāt,* (*bot.*) *adj.* rough or warty with short sharp points.—Also mur'icated. [L. *mūri-cātus—mūrex, -icis,* a murex, a sharp stone.]

Muridae, *mū'ri-dē, n.pl.* the mouse family. [L. *mūs, mūris,* a mouse.]

murine, *mūr'in, -in, adj.* mouselike: of the mouse family or subfamily.—*n.* a murine animal. [L. *mūrinus—mūs, mūris,* mouse.]

murk, mirk, mûrk, (*Scot.*) mirk, *n.* darkness (*lit., fig.*).—*adj.* dark: gloomy: obscure.—*adv.* murk'ily.—*n.* murk'iness.—*adj.* murk'ish.—*adjs.* mirk'-some; murk'y, mirk'y, dark: obscure: gloomy. [O.E. *mirce* (n. and adj.), O.N. *myrkr,* Dan. and

Sw. *mörk*; the forms with *i* are chiefly due to Spenserian and Scottish influence.]

**murken**, *mûr'kən*, (*Austr. slang*) *adj.* out of season (applied to game in the close time).

**murl**, *mûrl*, (*Scot.*) *v.t.* and *v.i.* to crumble.—*adj.* **murl'y**. [Origin obscure.]

**murlain, murlan, murlin**, *mûr'lən*, (*Scot.*) *n.* a round, narrow-mouthed basket. [Gael. *mùrlan.*]

**murmur**, *mûr'mər*, *n.* a low, indistinct sound, like that of running water: a rustling sound from the heart, lungs, etc.: a glide-vowel: a muttered or subdued grumble or complaint: rumour (*Shak.*).—*v.i.* to utter a murmur: to grumble.—*v.t.* to say or utter in a murmur.— *ns.* **murmurā'tion**, murmuring: a doubtful word for a flock of starlings; **mur'murer**.—*n.* and *adj.* **mur'muring**.—*adv.* **mur'muringly**.—*adj.* **mur'- murous**.—*adv.* **mur'murously**. [Fr. *murmure*— L. *murmur*; cf. Gr. *mormȳrein*, to surge.]

**murphy**, *mûr'fi*, (*coll.*) *n.* a potato:—*pl.* **mur'phies**. [From the common Irish name *Murphy.*]

**murra, murrha**, *mur'a*, *n.* an unknown precious material for vases, etc., first brought to Rome by Pompey (61 B.C.) from the East, conjectured to be agate.—*adjs.* **murrhine, murrine** (*mur'in, -in*), **myrrhine** (*mir'in, -in*). [L. *murra*; Gr. *morria* (pl.).]

**murrain**, *mur'in, -ən, n.* a pestilence (*obs.*): now only a cattle-plague, esp. foot-and-mouth disease.—*adj.* affected with murrain: confounded.—*adv.* confoundedly.—Also **murr'en** (*Shak., Milt.*), **murr'ion** (*Shak.*), **murr'in** (*Spens.*). —*adj.* **murr'ained**. [O.Fr. *morine*, pestilence, carcass.]

**murram**, *mur'əm*. Same as **marram**.

**murre**, *mûr*, *n.* a guillemot: a razorbill.—*n.* **murrelet** (*mûr'lit*), a name for various small birds akin to the guillemot. [Origin obscure.]

**murrey**, *mur'i*, *n.* and *adj.* mulberry-colour, dark purplish red. [O.Fr. *moré*—L. *mōrum*, mulberry.]

**murr(h)ine.** See **murra**.

**murry**. Same as **moray**.

**murther, murtherer.** Same as **murder, murderer**.

**murva, moorva**, *mōōr'va*, *n.* bowstring hemp. [Sans. *mûrvā*.]

**Musa**, *mū'za*, *n.* the banana genus, giving name to a family **Musā'ceae**, order Musa'les, of (mostly), gigantic treelike herbs.—*adj.* **musā'ceous**. [Latinised from Ar. *mauz*.]

**musang**, *mū-*, *mōō-sang'*, *n.* a paradoxure, or kindred animal. [Malay *mūsang*.]

**Musca**, *mus'ka*, *n.* the house-fly genus: a small constellation in the south, between the Crux and the Chamaeleon:—*pl.* **muscae**, *mus'ē*.—*n.* **musca- tō'rium**, (*Eastern Church*) a flabellum.—*adj.* **muscid** (*mus'id*), of the house-fly family Muscidae (*mus'i-dē*).—*n.* a member of the family.—**muscae volitantes** (*mus'ē vol-i-tan'tēz, mōōs'ki wo-li-tan'- tās*; L., fluttering flies), ocular spectra like floating black spots before the eyes. [L. *musca*, a fly.]

**muscadel**, *mus-kə-del'. mus'.* Same as **muscatel**.

**muscadin**, *müs-ka-dē̃*, (*hist.*) *n.* a fop or dandy: a middle-class moderate revolutionary. [Fr.]

**muscadine**, *mus'kə-din, -din*, (*arch.*) *n.* muscatel (wine, grape, or pear). [Perh. Prov. *muscat*, fem. *muscade*.]

**muscardine**, *mus'kär-din, -dēn, -din, n.* a silkworm disease caused by a fungus (Botrytis). [Fr.]

**muscat**, *mus'kat, n.* muscatel wine: a musky grape or its vine. [Prov. *muscat*.]

**muscatel**, *mus-kə-tel'*, or *mus', n.* a rich spicy wine, of various kinds: a grape of musky smell or taste: the vine producing it: a raisin from the muscatel grape: a variety of pear.—Also **mus- cadel**. [O.Fr. *muscatel, muscadel*—Prov. *muscat*, musky.]

**Muschelkalk**, *mōōsh'əl-kälk, n.* the middle member of the Trias in Germany, largely shelly limestone

—wanting in Britain. [Ger. *muschel*, shell, *kalk*, lime.]

**Musci**, *mus'ī, n.pl.* mosses, one of the two great divisions of the Bryophytes, the other being the Hepaticae or liverworts.—*n.* **muscology** (*-kol'ə- ji*), bryology.—*adjs.* **mus'coid** (*-koid*), **mus'cose**, moss-like. [L. *muscus*, moss.]

**muscle**, *mus'l, n.* a contractile structure by which bodily movement is effected: the tissue forming it: bodily strength.—*v.i.* to make one's way, thrust.—*adj.* **muscled** (*mus'ld*), having muscles. —*n.* **musc'ling**, delineation of muscles, as in a picture.—*adj.* **muscular** (*mus'kū-lər*), pertaining to a muscle: consisting of muscles: having strong muscles: brawny: strong: vigorous.— *n.* **muscularity** (*-lar'i-ti*).—*adv.* **mus'cularly**.—*ns.* **musculā'tion**, muscular action: musculature; **mus'culāture**, provision, disposition and system of muscles.—*adj.* **mus'culous** (*obs.*), muscular.— *adj.* **musc'le-bound**, having the muscles stiff and enlarged by over-exercise.—**musc'le-man**, man of extravagant physical development; **musc'le- reading**, interpretation of slight involuntary muscular movements; **muscle, muscular, sense** (see **kinaesthesis**); **muscular Christianity**, a vigorous combination of Christian living with devotion to athletic enjoyments, associated with Charles Kingsley (who repudiated the name); **muscular dystrophy** (*dis'trə-fi*), any of the forms of a hereditary disease in which muscles progressively deteriorate.—**muscle in** (*coll.*), to push in: to grab a share. [Fr. *muscle*, or directly—L. *mūsculus*, dim. of *mūs*, a mouse, a muscle.]

**muscovado**, *mus-kō-vä dō, n.* unrefined sugar, after evaporating the cane-juice and draining off the molasses. [Sp. *mascabado*.]

**Muscovy**, *mus'kə-vi*, (*hist.*) *n.* the old principality of Moscow: extended to Russia in general.— *ns.* and *adjs.* **Muscovian** (*-kō'vi-ən*), Muscovite; **Mus'covite**, of Muscovy: Russian: a Russian: **muscovite** (*min.*), common white mica, first got in Russia, a silicate of aluminium and potassium: its thin transparent plates, still used as glass— also **Muscovy glass**.—*adj.* **Muscovitic** (*-vit'ik*).— **mus'covy-duck** (see **musk**). [*Moscovia*, Latinised from Russ. *Moskva*, Moscow.]

**muscular**. See **muscle**.

**muse**, *mūz, v.i.* to study in silence: to be absent-minded: to meditate.—*v.t.* to meditate on: to wonder at (*Shak.*): to say musingly.—*n.* deep thought: contemplation: a state or fit of absence of mind.—*adjs.* **mused**, bemused, muzzy, fuddled; **muse'ful**, meditative.—*adv.* **muse'fully**. —*n.* **mus'er**.—*n.* and *adj.* **mus'ing**.—*adv.* **mus'- ingly**. [Fr. *muser*, to loiter, in O.Fr. to muse; perh. orig. to hold the muzzle (O.Fr. *muse*) in the air, as a dog that has lost the scent; perh. influenced by next word.]

**Muse**, *mūz, n.* one of the nine goddesses of the liberal arts—daughters of Zeus and Mnemosyne (**Calliope**, of epic poetry; **Clio**, of history; **Erato**, of love poetry; **Euterpe**, of music and lyric poetry; **Melpomene**, of tragedy; **Poly- hymnia**, of sacred lyrics; **Terpsichore**, of dancing; **Thalia**, of comedy; **Urania**, of astronomy): an inspiring goddess more vaguely imagined: poetic character: poetry or art: an inspired poet (*Milt.*). [Fr.,—L. *Mūsa*—Gr. *Mousa*.]

**muset.** Same as **musit**.

**musette**, *mū-zet'*, *n.* an old French bagpipe: a simple pastoral melody or gavotte trio for, or in imitation of, the bagpipe. [Fr., dim. of *muse*, a bagpipe.]

**museum**, *mū-zē'əm, n.* orig. a temple, home, or resort of the Muses: a place of study: a resort of the learned: an institution or repository for the collection, exhibition, and study of objects of artistic, scientific, historic, or educational interest: an art gallery (*U.S.*): a collection of curiosities:—*pl.* **muse′ums.**—**muse′um-piece,** a fine specimen, suitable for exhibit in a museum, or unsuitable for anything else. [L. *mūsēum*—Gr. *mouseion*; see **Muse.**]

**mush,** *mush, n.* meal boiled in water, esp. Indian meal: anything pulpy: sloppy sentimentality (*coll.*): rubbish· background of noise from a wireless receiver: an umbrella (*slang*; see also **mushroom**).—*v.t.* to reduce to mush: to crush the spirit of, wear out (*dial.*).—*adv.* **mush′ily.**—*n.* **mush′iness.**—*adj.* **mush′y.** [Prob. **mash.**]

**mush,** *mush,* (*Scot.*) *v.t.* to notch or scallop the edges of. [Perh. Fr. *moucher,* to trim.]

**mush,** *mush,* (*Canada*) *v.i.* to travel on foot with dogs over snow.—*n.* a journey of this kind.—*n.* **mush′er.** [Prob. Fr. *marcher,* to walk.]

**musha,** *mush′ə,* (*Irish*) *interj.* expressing surprise. [Ir. *maiseadh.*]

**mushroom,** *mush′rōōm, n.* an edible fungus (*Agaricus,* or *Psalliota, campestris,* or kindred species) of toadstool form: any edible fungus: any fungus of umbrella shape whether edible or not: any fungus: an object shaped like a mushroom: a hat with drooping brim: an umbrella (*slang*): anything of rapid growth and decay (*fig.*): one who rises suddenly from a low condition (*fig.*): an upstart.—*adj.* of or like a mushroom.—*v.i.* to expand like a mushroom cap: to gather mushrooms: to increase, spread with disconcerting rapidity.—*n.* **mush′roomer.**—**mush′room-anch′or,** an anchor with mushroom-shaped head. [O.Fr. *mousseron,* perh. *mousse,* moss, which may be of Germanic origin.]

**music,** *mū′zik, n.* the art of expression in sound, in melody, and harmony, including both composition and execution: sometimes specially of instrumental performance to the exclusion of singing: the science underlying it: a musical composition (*obs.*): the performance of musical compositions: compositions collectively: a connected series of (sweet) sounds: melody or harmony: pleasing sound: sound of definite pitch, not mere noise: a band of musicians (*arch.*): musical instruments (*obs.* or *dial.*): written or printed representation of tones, expression, etc., or of what is to be played or sung: sheets or books of parts or scores collectively: harmonious character: fun (*U.S.*).—*adj.* of or for music.—*v.i.* to perform music:—*pr.p.* **mu′sicking.**—*adj.* **mu′sical,** pertaining to, of, with, or producing, music: pleasing to the ear: of definite pitch (unlike mere noise): melodious: having skill in, or aptitude or taste for, music.—*n.* a musical person, party, or performance, esp. a theatrical performance or film in which singing and usu. dancing play an important part—a successor to musical comedy with less frivolous plot.—*ns.* **musicale** (*mū-zi-kal′,*—Fr. *soirée musicale*), a social gathering with music, or the programme of music for it; **musicality** (*-al′i-ti*).—*adv.* **mu′sically.**—*ns.* **mu′sicalness;** **musician** (*mū-zish′ən*), one skilled in music: a performer or composer of music, esp. professional; **musi′cianer, mu′sicker** (*obs.* or *dial.*).—*adj.* **musi′cianly,** characteristic of, or becoming, a musician.—*n.* **musi′cianship.**—*adj.* **musicolog′ical.**—*ns.* **musicol′ogist; musicol′ogy,** academic study of music in its historical, scientific, and other aspects.—**musical box,** a toy that plays tunes automatically, by projections from a revolving barrel twitching a comb; **musical chairs,** the game of prancing round a diminishing row of chairs and securing one when the music stops; **musical comedy,** a light dramatic entertainment with sentimental songs and situations held together by a minimum of plot; **musical director,** the conductor of an orchestra (in a theatre, etc.); **musical flame,** a flame that gives a musical tone when surrounded by an open tube; **musical glasses** (see **harmonica**);

**musical sand,** sand of nearly uniform size of grain that gives out a definite note when walked on; **mu′sic-box,** a barrel-organ (*obs.*): a musical box: jocularly, a piano; **mu′sic-case, -fō′lio,** a roll, portfolio, etc., for carrying sheet music; **mu′sic-demy′,** a size of writing-paper, 20⅜ in. × 14⅜ in.; **mus′ic-dra′ma,** that form of opera introduced by Wagner in which the relations of music and drama are reformed; **mu′sic-hall,** orig. and still sometimes a concert-hall, usu. now a hall for variety entertainments; **mu′sic-holder,** a music-case: a clip, rack, or desk for holding music during performance; **mu′sic-house,** a concert-hall: a firm dealing in music or musical instruments; **mu′sic-master, -mistress,** a teacher of music; **mu′sic-paper,** paper ruled for writing music; **mu′sic-pen,** a five-channelled pen for drawing the stave; **mu′sic-rack,** a rack attached to a musical instrument for holding the player's music; **mu′sic-roll′,** a case for carrying music rolled up: a roll of perforated paper for mechanical piano-playing; **mu′sic-room,** a room in which music is performed: a room beside the stage in which the musicians were stationed (*obs.*); **mu′sic-seller,** a dealer in printed music; **mu′sic-shell,** a volute shell with markings like music; **mu′sic-stand,** a light adjustable desk for holding music during performance; **mu′sic-stool,** a piano-stool.—**face the music** (see **face**); **music of the spheres** (see **spheres**); **rough music,** uproar: charivari. [Fr. *musique*—L. *mūsica*—Gr. *mousikē* (*technē*), musical (art)—*Mousa,* a Muse.]

**musimon,** *mūs′* or *mus′-i-mon,* **musmon,** *mus′mon, n.* the moufflon. [L. *mus*(*i*)*mō, -ōnis.*]

**musique concrète,** *mü-zēk kō-kret,* (Fr.) a kind of mid-20th cent. music, made up of odds and ends of recorded sound variously handled.

**musit,** *mū′zit,* (*Shak.*) *n.* a gap in a fence or thicket through which an animal passes. [**meuse** (1).]

**musive,** *mū′siv, adj.* Same as **mosaic** (1).

**musk,** *musk, n.* a strong-smelling substance, used in perfumery, got chiefly from the male musk-deer: the odour thereof: the musk-deer: a species of Mimulus, said once to have smelt of musk.—*adj.* or prefix to the names of many animals and plants, supposed to smell of musk.—*v.t.* to perfume with musk.—*adj.* **musked** (*muskt*), smelling, or tasting, like musk.—*adv.* **musk′ily.**—*n.* **musk′iness.**—*adj.* **musk′y,** having the odour of musk.—**musk′-bag, -cod, -pod, -pouch, -sac,** a musk-gland; **musk′-bag, -ball,** a bag, ball, containing musk, as a perfuming sachet; **musk′-beet′le,** a longicorn beetle that smells of attar of roses; **musk′-cat,** a musk-yielding animal, usu. the musk-deer, prob. confused with the civet-cat: a scented effeminate dandy: a courtesan; **musk′-ca′vy,** the hog-rat; **musk′-deer,** a hornless deer (*Moschus moschiferus*) of Asia, chief source of musk; **musk′-duck** (also by confusion **muscovy-duck**), a large musky-smelling South American duck (*Cairina moschata*); **musk′-gland,** a skin-pit in some animals producing musk; **musk′-mall′ow,** a species of mallow with faint odour of musk; **musk′-mel′on,** the common melon (apparently transferred from a musky-scented kind); **musk′-ox,** a long-haired ruminant (*Ovibos moschatus*) of northern Canada, exhaling a strong musky smell; **musk′-pear,** a fragrant variety of pear; **musk′-plant,** *Mimulus moschatus*; **musk′-plum,** a fragrant kind of plum; **musk′-rat,** the musquash: a musk-shrew: its skin; **musk′-rose,** a fragrant species of rose; **musk′-sheep,** the musk-ox; **musk′-shrew,** the desman: a musky-smelling Indian shrew; **musk′-thist′le,** a thistle (*Carduus nutans*) with large drooping scented heads. [Fr. *musc*—L. *muscus,* Gr. *moschos,* prob.—Pers. *mushk,* perh.—Sans. *muṣka,* a testicle (for which the gland has been mistaken).]

**muskeg**, *mus-keg'*, (*Canada*) *n*. swamp, bog, marsh. [Cree Indian word.]

**musket**, *mus'kit*, *n*. a male sparrow-hawk: a military hand firearm, esp. of an old-fashioned smooth-bore kind.—*ns*. **musketeer'**, a soldier armed with a musket; **musketoon'**, **musquetoon'**, a short musket: a soldier armed with one; **mus'ketry**, muskets collectively: practice with, or the art of using, small arms: fire of muskets: a body of troops armed with muskets.—*adj*. **mus'ket-proof**, capable of resisting the force of a musket-ball.—**mus'ket-rest**, a forked support for the heavy 16th-century musket; **mus'ket-shot**, shot for or from a musket: the discharge of a musket: the range of a musket. [O.Fr. *mousquet*, musket, formerly a hawk—It. *moschetto*, perh.—L. *musca*, a fly.]

**Muslim**, *muz'*, *mus'lim*, *n*. and *adj*. Same as **Moslem**.

**muslin**, *muz'lin*, *n*. a fine soft cotton fabric, gauzy in appearance, but woven plain: cotton cloth for shorts, etc. (*U.S.*): womankind (*slang*): sails, canvas (*naut. slang*): a collector's name for several different moths.—*adj*. made of muslin.—*adj*. **mus'lined**, clothed with muslin.—*n*. **muslinet'**, a coarse kind of muslin.—**mus'lin-kale** (*Scot.*), thin broth made without meat. [Fr. *mousseline*—It. *mussolino*, from It. *Mussolo*, the town of Mosul in Mesopotamia.]

**musquash**, *mus'kwosh*, *n*. a large aquatic American animal akin to the voles, very destructive to dams and waterways (also *musk-rat*): its fur. [From an Amer. Ind. word.]

**musrol**, *muz'rōl*, (*obs.*) *n*. the nose-band of a bridle. [Fr. *muserolle*—It. *museruola*—*muso*, muzzle.]

**muss**, **musse**, *mus*, *n*. a scramble (*Shak.*): disturbance: confusion, disorder: confused conflict (*U.S.*): a mess.—*v.t.* and *v.i.* to disarrange: to mess.—*n*. **muss'iness**—*adj*. **muss'y**, disordered. [Perh. different words; cf. **mess**.]

**mussel**, *mus'l* (formerly also **muscle**, **muskle**, *mus'l*, *mus'kl*), a marine lamellibranch shellfish of the family Mytilidae: a freshwater lamellibranch of the Unionidae: the shell of any of these: a mussel-plum.—*adj*. **muss'elled**, poisoned by eating infected mussels.—**muss'el-plum**, a dark purple plum not unlike a mussel-shell; **muss'el-scalp'** (*Scot*. -scaup), a bed of mussels; **muss'el-shell'**. [O.E. *mūs*(*c*)*le*; cf. Ger. *muschel*, Fr. *moule*; all from L. *mūsculus*, dim. of *mūs*, mouse.]

**mussitation**, *mus-i-tā'shən*, *n*. low muttering: speaking movement without sound.—*v.t.* **muss'itate**, to mutter. [L. *mussitāre*, freq. of *mussāre*, to mutter.]

**Mussulman**, **Musulman**, *mus'l-mən*, -*män'*, *n*. a Mohammedan:—*pl*. **Muss'ulmans**; blunderingly or facetiously **Mussulmen**.—Similarly **Muss'ulwoman**. [Pers. *musulmān*—Ar. *muslim, moslim*, Moslem.]

**must**, *must*, *v.t.* am, is, are obliged physically or morally: cannot but: insist upon (with *inf*. without *to*):—used only in the present (orig. past) indic.:—*3rd pers. sing*. **must**.—*n*. an essential, a necessity: a thing that should not be missed or neglected. [Orig. pa.t. of **mote**—O.E. *mōste*, pa.t. of *mōt*; cf. Ger. *müssen*.]

**must**, *must*, *n*. new wine: unfermented, or only partially fermented, grape-juice or other juice or pulp for fermentation: process of fermentation.—*adj*. **must'y**. [O.E. *must*—L. *mustum* (*vīnum*), new (wine).]

**must**, *must*, *n*. mustiness: mould. [App. back formation—**musty**.]

**must**, *must*, *n*. dangerous frenzy in some male animals, as elephants.—*adj*. in such a state.—*adj*. **must'y**, in a frenzy. [Pers. and Hind. *mast*, intoxicated.]

**must**, **muist**, **moust**, *müst*, *mōōst*, (*obs. Scot.*) *n*. musk: hair-powder.—*v.t.* to powder. [O.Fr. *must*, a form of *musc*: see **musk**.]

**mustache**, **mustachio**. Same as **moustache**.

**mustang**, *mus'tang*, *n*. the feralised horse of the American prairies. [Sp. *mestengo*, now *mesteño*, belonging to the *mesta* or graziers' union, combined with *mostrenco*, homeless, stray.]

**mustard**, *mus'tərd*, *n*. the powdered seeds of various species of the Sinapis section of the genus Brassica: a pungent condiment made from it: the plant yielding it.—**mus'tard-gas**, the vapour from a poisonous blistering liquid, $(CH_2Cl\cdot CH_2)_2S$, got from ethylene and sulphur chloride; **mus'tard-oil**, a volatile oil got from black mustard seeds; **mus'tard-plas'ter**, a plaster made from black and white mustard flour, deprived of their fixed oil; **mus'tard-tree**, a name given to a shrub *Salvadora persica* (family Salvadoraceae, prob. akin to Oleaceae) on the theory that it is the plant referred to in the N.T., which others think is only black mustard grown tall, as it does in Palestine.—**black mustard**, *Brassica nigra*; **French mustard**, mustard prepared for table by adding salt, sugar, vinegar, etc.; **garlic-mustard**, **hedge-mustard** (see **garlic**, **hedge**); **mustard and cress**, a salad of seedlings of white mustard and garden cress; **Sarep'ta mustard**, *Brassica juncea*; **white mustard**, *Brassica alba*; **wild mustard**, charlock.—**keen as mustard** (*slang*), intensely enthusiastic. [O.Fr. *mo*(*u*)*starde* (Fr. *moutarde*)—L. *mustum*, must (2) (because the condiment was prepared with must).]

**mustee**. Same as **mestee**.

**Mustela**, *mus-tē'la*, *n*. the marten genus, giving name to the family Muste'lidae (otters, badgers, and weasels) and the subfamily Musteli'nae (weasels and martens).—*adj*. and *n*. **mus'teline** (-*tal-in*). [L. *mustēla*, weasel.]

**muster**, *mus'tər*, *n*. a display, demonstration (*obs.*): an example (*arch.*): a commercial sample: an assembling or calling together, esp. of troops, as for inspection, verification, etc.: inspection: an assembly: a register: a round-up (*Austr.*): (perh. orig. a misunderstanding) a company of peacocks.—*v.t.* and *v.i.* to show forth (*obs.*): to assemble: to enroll: to number.—*v.t.* to summon up (often with *up*).—*v.i.* to pass muster.—**mus'ter-book** (*Shak.*), a book in which military forces or a ship's crew are registered; **mus'ter-file** (*Shak.*), a muster-roll; **mus'ter-master**, one who has charge of the muster-roll; **mus'ter-party** (*Austr.*), a rounding-up party; **mus'ter-roll**, a register of the officers and men in each company, troop, regiment, ship's crew, etc.: roll-call (*naut.*).—**muster in** (*U.S.*), to enroll, receive as recruits; **muster out** (*U.S.*), to discharge from service; **pass muster**, to bear examination, be well enough. [O.Fr. *mostre*, *moustre*, *monstre*—L. *mōnstrum*—*monēre*, to warn.]

**musty**. See **must** (2 and 4).

**musty**, *must'i*, *adj*. mouldy: spoiled by damp: stale in smell or taste: deteriorated from disuse.

**Musulman**. Same as **Mussulman**.

**mutable**, *mū'ta-bl*, *adj*. that may be changed: subject to change: variable: inconstant, fickle.—*ns*. **mutabil'ity**, **mu'tableness**.—*adv*. **mu'tably**.—*n*. **mu'tagen** (*biol.*), a substance that produces mutations.—*adj*. **mutagen'ic**.—*ns*. **mutan'dum**, something to be altered:—*pl*. **mutan'da**; **mu'tant**, a form arising from mutation.—*v.t.* and *v.i.* **mutate'**, to cause or undergo mutation.—*ns*. **mutā'tion**, change: umlaut: in Celtic languages a change of initial consonant depending on the preceding word: in old music a change of syllable for the same note in passing to another hexachord: discontinuous variation or sudden inheritable divergence from ancestral type (*biol.*); **mutā'tionist**, a believer in evolution by mutation.—*adjs*. **mu'tative**, **mu'tatory**, changing: mutable.

—*n.* mū′ton, the smallest element of a gene capable of giving rise to a new form by mutation. —**mutation mink**, a much valued shade of mink produced by selective breeding; **mutation stop**, an organ-stop whose tones differ from those the keys indicate by an interval other than a whole number of octaves. [L. *mūtāre*, *-ātum*, to change—*movēre*, *mōtum*, to move.]

**mutatis mutandis**, *mū-tā′tis mū-tan′dis*, *mōō-tä′tēs mōō-tan′dēs*, (L.) with necessary changes.— **mutato nomine** (*mū-tä′tō nom′i-nē*, *mōō-tä′tō nōm′i-ne*), the name being changed.

**mutch**, *much*, (*Scot.*) *n.* a woman's close cap. [M.Du. *mutse*; Du. *muts*, Ger. *mütze*.]

**mutchkin**, *much′kin*, *n.* a Scottish liquid measure, three-fourths of an imperial, one-fourth of a Scottish pint. [Obsolete Du. *mudseken*.]

**mute**, *mūt*, *adj.* dumb: silent: refusing to plead (*law*): without vocal utterance: unpronounced or faintly pronounced: pronounced by stoppage of the breath-passage.—*n.* a dumb person: a silent person: one who refuses to plead (*law*): a funeral attendant: a dumb servant in an Eastern house: an actor with no words to speak: a stop-consonant: a clip, pad, or other device for subduing the sound of a musical instrument. —*v.t.* to deaden the sound of with a mute: to silence.—*adj.* mut′ed, (of e.g. sound, colour) softened, not loud, harsh, or bright.—*adv* mute′ly.—*ns.* mute′ness; mut′ism, dumbness.— **mute swan**, the common swan.—**mute of malice** (*law*), refusing to plead. [L. *mūtus*.]

**mute**, *mūt*, *v.i.* to dung, as birds.—*n.* birds' dung: an act of muting. [O.Fr. *mutir*, *esmeutir*; prob. Germanic; cf. smelt.]

**mutessarif**, *mōō-tes-ä′rif*, *n.* the head of a Turkish sanjak.—*n.* mutessa′rifat, his office or jurisdiction. [Turk. *mutesarif*—Ar. *mutasarrif*.]

**muticous**, *mūt′i-kəs*, *adj.* awnless: spineless: pointless. [L. *muticus*, awnless.]

**mutilate**, *mū′ti-lāt*, *v.t.* to maim: to remove a material part of: to deform by slitting, boring, or removing a part.—*adj.* mutilated.—*ns.* mutilā′-tion; mu′tilātor. [L. *mutilāre*, *-ātum*—*mutilus*.]

**mutine**, *mū′tin*, *n.* mutiny (*obs.*): a mutineer, rebel (*Shak.*).—*v.i.* (*Shak.*, *Milt.*) to mutiny, rebel.—*n.* mutineer′, one who mutinies.—*v.i.* to mutiny.—*adj.* mu′tinous, disposed to mutiny: unsubmissive: of the nature of, or expressing, mutiny.—*adv.* mu′tinously.—*n.* mu′tinousness. —*n.* mu′tiny, insurrection against constituted authority, esp. naval or military: revolt, tumult, strife.—*v.i.* to rise against authority, esp. in military or naval service:—*pr.p.* mu′tinying; *pa.t.* and *pa.p.* mu′tinied.—**Mutiny Act**, an act passed by the British parliament from year to year, to regulate the government of the army, from 1689 down to 1879, when it was superseded. [Fr. *mutin*, riotous—L. *movēre*, *mōtum*, to move.]

**muton.** See mutable.

**mutoscope**, *mū′tō-skōp*, *n.* an early form of cinematograph. [L. *mūtāre*, to change, Gr. *skopeein*, to look at.]

**mutt**, *mut*, (*slang*, orig. *U.S.*) *n.* a blockhead: a mongrel dog. [Perh. for mutton-head.]

**mutter**, *mut′ər*, *v.i.* to utter words in a low, indistinct voice: to murmur, esp. in hostility, grumbling, mutiny, or menace: to sound with a low rumbling.—*v.t.* to utter indistinctly.—*n.* a murmuring (*Milt.*): indistinct utterance: low rumbling: subdued grumbling.—*ns.* mutterā′-tion (*Richardson*), complaining; mutt′erer.—*n.* and *adj.* mutt′ering.—*adv.* mutt′eringly. [Prob. imit., like dial. Ger. *muttern*; L. *muttire*.]

**mutton**, *mut′n*, *n.* a sheep (*obs.* or *jocular*): sheep's flesh as food: women as food for lust, hence a prostitute (*obsolete* [*slang*).—*adj.* mutt′ony.— **mutt′on-bird**, an Australasian shearwater, esp. the short-tailed, said by some to taste like mutton; **mutt′on-chop.**—*adj.* shaped like a

mutton-chop (of whiskers).—**mutt′on-cut′let.**— *n.pl.* mutt′on-dum′mies (*slang*), white plimsolls.— mutt′on-fist, a coarse, big hand: a printer's index-hand; **mutt′on-ham**, a salted leg of mutton; **mutt′on-head**, a heavy, stupid person. —*adj.* mutt′on-head′ed, stupid.—**mutt′on-su′et**, the fat about the kidneys and loins of sheep; mutt′on-thump′er, a clumsy bookbinder.—**mutton dressed as lamb**, (*coll.*) elderly woman dressing or behaving in style suitable to a young one; **return to our muttons** (*coll.*), return to the subject of discussion—a playful translation of the judge's 'Revenons à nos moutons' in the old French farce of *Maitre Pathelin*, in which the witnesses wander from the matter in dispute, some sheep. [O.Fr. *moton* (Fr. *mouton*), a sheep —L.L. *multo*, *-ōnis*; perh. of Celt. origin.]

**mutual**, *mū′tū-əl*, *adj.* interchanged: reciprocal: given and received: common, joint, shared by two or more (*Shak.*; now regarded by many as incorrect).—*n.* mutualisā′tion, *-z-*.—*v.t.* mu′tualise, *-ize*, to put upon a mutual footing.—*ns.* mu′tualism, symbiosis: theory that mutual dependence is necessary for the welfare of the individual and society: practice based on this; **mutuality** (*-al′i-ti*).—*adv.* mu′tually.—**mutual friend** (*Dickens*), a common friend; **mutual funds** (*U.S.*), unit trusts; **mutual insurance**, the system of a company in which the policy-holders are the shareholders; **mutual wall**, a wall equally belonging to each of two houses.—**mutual-admiration society**, a group of persons supposed, generally satirically or humorously, to overestimate one another's and their own merits; **mutual-improvement society**, a society whose members meet to hear lectures, read essays, hold debates, etc., in order to stimulate each other to improve in knowledge and in public speaking. [Fr. *mutuel*—L. *mūtuus*—*mūtāre*, to change.]

**mutule**, *mūt′ūl*, *n.* a kind of square, flat bracket, in Doric architecture, above each triglyph and each metope, with guttae. [L. *mūtulus*, a mutule, modillion.]

**mutuum**, *mū′tū-əm*, *n.* a bailment consisting of a loan of goods for consumption, as corn, coal, etc., to be returned in goods of the same amount. [L. neut. of *mūtuus*, lent.]

**mutuus consensus**, *mū′tū-as kon-sen′sas*, *mōō′tōō-ōōs kōn-sän′sōōs*, (L.) mutual consent.

**muu-muu**, *mōō′mōō*, *n.* a simple loose dress worn chiefly in Hawaii. [Hawaiian *mu′u mu′u*.]

**mux**, *muks*, (*U.S.* and *dial.*) *v.t.* to spoil, botch.— *n.* a mess. [Origin obscure.]

**Muzak**, *mū′zak*, ® *n.* one of the kinds of piped music (q.v.).

**muzhik, moujik, mujik**, *mōō-zhik′*, *mōō′zhik*, *n.* a Russian peasant. [Russ. *muzhik′*.]

**muzzle**, *muz′l*, *n.* the projecting jaws and nose of an animal: a strap or a cage for the mouth to prevent biting: the extreme end of a gun, etc.— *v.t.* to put a muzzle on: to keep from hurting: to gag or silence.—*v.t.* and *v.i.* to touch, thrust, or investigate with the muzzle.—*n.* muzz′ler, one who muzzles: a blow on the mouth: a muzzle-loader, a direct head-wind.—**muzz′le-bag**, a canvas bag fixed to the muzzle of a gun at sea, to keep out water; **muzz′le-load′er**, a firearm loaded through the muzzle—opp. to *breech-loader*.—*adj.* muzz′le-load′ing.—**muzz′le-veloc′-ity**, the velocity of a projectile the moment it leaves the muzzle of a gun. [O.Fr. *musel* (Fr. *museau*)—L.L. *mūsellum*, dim. of *mūsum* or *mūsus*, beak.]

**muzzy**, *muz′i*, *adj.* dazed, bewildered: tipsy: blurred: hazy.—*adv.* muzz′ily.—*n.* muzz′iness. [Origin unknown.]

**mvule**, *mvōō′le*, *n.* a huge tropical African timber tree (*Chlorophora excelsa*) of the mulberry family.

**my**, *mī* (sometimes *mi*), *poss. adj.* or *gen.* of *pron.*

I, of or belonging to me.—*interj.* expressing surprise (perh. for my word, or my God). [mine —O.E. *min* (gen.), of me.]

**Mya**, *mī'a*, *n.* a genus of lamellibranch molluscs, the gapers, including the American soft or long clam. [Gr. *mȳs* or *myax*, a mussel.]

**myalgia**, *mī-al'ji-ə*, *n.* pain in muscle.—*adj.* **myal'gic**. [Gr. *mȳs*, muscle, *algos*, pain.]

**myalism**, *mī'əl-izm*, *n.* West Indian Negro witchcraft.—*adj.* **my'al**. [Prob. of West African origin.]

**myall**, *mī'öl*, *n.* a wild Australian aboriginal.—*adj.* **wild**. [Australian *mail*, the black people.]

**myall**, *mī'öl*, *n.* an Australian acacia of various species with hard, scented wood: their wood. [Australian *maiăl*.]

**mycelium**, *mī-sē'li-əm*, *n.* the white thread-like mass of hyphae forming the thallus of a fungus: —*pl.* **mycē'lia**.—*adj.* **mycē'lial**. [Gr. *mȳkēs*, a mushroom.]

**Mycenaean**, *mī-sē-nē'ən*, *adj.* of the ancient city state of *Mȳcēnae* (Gr. *Mȳkēnai*) in Argolis, Agamemnon's kingdom, or its culture culminating in the Bronze Age.

**Mycetes**, *mī-sē'tēz*, *n.* the howler genus of South American monkeys. [Gr. *mȳkētēs*, bellower.]

**mycetes**, *mī-sē'tēz*, *n.pl.* (*rare* except in composition) fungi.—*ns.* **mycetol'ogy**, mycology; **mycetō'ma**, Madura foot, a disease of foot and leg in India, caused by a fungus.—*n.pl.* **Mycetozō'a**, the Myxomycetes or slime-fungi (when regarded as animals).—*n.* and *adj.* **mycetozō'an**. [Gr. *mȳkēs*, -*ētos*, pl. *mȳkētēs*, a mushroom.]

**myc(o)-**, *mīk-*, *mī-kō-*, in composition, fungus: mushroom. See also terms under **mycetes**.—*n.* **mycodomatium** (-*dō-mā'shyəm*, -*shi-əm*), a fungusgall:—*pl.* **mycodomā'tia**.—*adjs.* **mycologic** (*mī-ke-loj'ik*), **-al**.—*ns.* **mycologist** (-*kol'*); **mycol'ogy**, the study of fungi; **mycophagist** (*mī-kof'e-jist*; Gr. *phagein*, to eat), a toadstool-eater; **mycoph'agy**; **Mycoplas'ma** (-*plaz'mə*), a genus of pathogenic agents apparently neither viruses nor true bacteria, including the cause of socalled 'virus' pneumonia: (without *cap.*) any member of the genus:—*pl.* **-plas'mas**, **-plasmata** (-*mā'tə*).—*ns.* **mycorrhiza**, **mycorhiza** (*mī-kō-rī'zə*; Gr. *rhiza*, root), a fungal mycelium investing or penetrating the underground parts of a higher plant and supplying it with material from humus instead of root-hairs.—*adj.* **mycor(r)hi'zal**.—*n.* **mycosis** (-*kō'sis*), a disease due to growth of a fungus.—*adjs.* **mycotic** (-*kot'ik*); **mycotroph'ic** (-*trof'ik*; Gr. *trophē*, food), (of a plant) living in symbiosis with a fungus. [Gr. *mȳkēs*, -*ētos*, pl. *mȳkētēs*, a mushroom.]

**mydriasis**, *mī-drī'ə-sis*, *n.* morbid dilatation of the pupil of the eye.—*adj.* **mydriatic** (*mid-ri-at'ik*).—*n.* a drug causing this. [Gr. *mydriāsis*.]

**myelitis**, *mī-ə-lī'tis*, *n.* inflammation of the spinal cord, or sometimes of the bone-marrow.—*n.* **my'elin**, the substance forming the medullary sheath of nerve-fibres.—*adj.* **my'eloid**, like, pertaining to, of the nature of, marrow.—*n.* **my'elon**, the spinal cord. [Gr. *myelos*, marrow.]

**mygale**, *mig'ə-lē*, *n.* an American bird-catching spider. [Gr. *mȳgalē*, a field-mouse, a shrew— *mȳs*, mouse, *galeē*, weasel.]

**myiasis**, *mī'i-ə-sis*, *mī-ī-ā'sis*, *n.* disease caused by presence of flies or their larvae. [Gr. *myīa*, fly.]

**Mylodon**, *mī'lə-don*, *n.* a genus of gigantic Pleistocene ground-sloths.—*adj.* **my'lodont**. [Gr. *mylē*, a mill, *odous*, *odontos*, a tooth.]

**mylohyoid**, *mī-lō-hī'oid*, *adj.* pertaining to or near the jawbone and the hyoid bone.—*n.* a muscle so placed. [Gr. *mylē*, a mill.]

**mylonite**, *mī'lən-it*, *n.* a hard compact often streaky granular rock produced by crushing.—*adj.* **mylonitic** (-*it'ik*).—*n.* **mylonitisā'tion**, **-z-**.—*v.t.* **my'lonitise**, **-ize**, to turn into mylonite. [Gr. *mylōn*, a mill.]

**myna**, **mynah**, **mina**, *mī'na*, *n.* a common black brown and white Indian bird of the starling family: applied also to several allied kinds, including some that can be taught to talk. [Hind. *mainā*.]

**mynheer**, *mīn-hār'*, Du. *mən-ār'*, *n.* my lord: Dutch for *Mr* or *sir*: a Dutchman. [Du. *mijn*, my, *heer*, lord.]

**myo-**, *mī'ō-*, *mī-o'-*, in composition, muscle.—*n.* **my'oblast**, a cell producing muscle-tissue.—*adj.* **myoblast'ic**.—*ns.* **myocardi'tis**, inflammation of the myocardium; **myocar'dium**, the muscular substance of the heart; **my'ogen**, an albumin, soluble in water, found in muscle.—*adj.* **myogen'ic**, (of contraction) arising spontaneously in a muscle, independent of nervous stimuli.—*ns.* **my'ogram**, a myographic record; **my'ograph**, an instrument for recording muscular contractions. —*adjs.* **myograph'ic**, **-al**.—*ns.* **myog'raphist**; **myog'raphy**.—*adjs.* **my'oid**, like muscle; **myolog'ical**.—*ns.* **myol'ogist**; **myol'ogy**, the study of muscles; **myō'ma**, a tumour composed of muscular tissue; **my'osin**, a globulin of muscle whose formation is the cause of rigor mortis; **myosi'tis** (irregularly formed), inflammation of a muscle. [Gr. *mȳs*, *myos*, muscle.]

**myomancy**, *mī'ō-man-si*, *n.* divination from the movements of mice.—*adj.* **myoman'tic**. [Gr. *mȳs*, a mouse, *manteiā*, divination.]

**myopia**, *mī-ō'pi-ə*, *n.* shortness of sight.—*adj.* **myopic** (-*op'*), short-sighted.—*n.* a short-sighted person.—*ns.* **my'ops** (-*ops*), **my'ope** (-*ōp*), a short-sighted person. [Gr. *myōps*, short-sighted— *mȳein*, to shut, *ōps*, the eye.]

**myosis**, *mī-ō'sis*, *n.* abnormal contraction of the pupil of the eye.—*adjs.* **myosit'ic**; **myotic** (-*ot'*).—Also *n.* [Gr. *mȳein*, to close, blink.]

**Myosotis**, *mī-os-ō'tis*, *n.* the forget-me-not genus of the borage family. [Gr. *myosōtis*, madwort, (Asperugo), etc.—*mȳs*, *myos*, a mouse, *ous*, *ōtos*, an ear.]

**myrbane**. Same as **mirbane**.

**myria-**, *mir'i-a-*, in composition, ten thousand: a very large number. See **myriad**, **myriapod**.

**myriad**, *mir'i-ad*, *n.* any immense number.—*adj.* numberless.—*adj.* and *n.* (or *adv.*) **myr'iadfold**. —*n.* and *adj.* **myr'iadth**. [Gr. *mȳrias*, -*ados*, ten thousand.]

**myriapod**, *mir'i-ə-pod*, *n.* a member of the Myriapoda.—*n.pl.* **Myriapoda** (-*ap'ə-da*), a class of Arthropoda with many legs, centipedes and millipedes.—Also **myriopod**, etc. [Gr. *mȳriopous*, -*podos*, many-footed—*mȳrios*, numberless, *pous*, *podos*, a foot.]

**Myrica**, *mi-rī'ka*, *n.* orig., the tamarisk: the sweet-gale or bog-myrtle genus, constituting the family **Myricā'ceae**. [Gr. *myrikē* (*myrīkē*), tamarisk.]

**myringa**, *mir-ing'gə*, *n.* the eardrum.—*ns.* **myringitis** (-*in-ji'tis*), inflammation of the eardrum; **myringoscope** (-*ing'gə-skōp*), an instrument for viewing the eardrum. [L.L. *miringa*—Gr. *mēninx*, membrane.]

**myriorama**, *mir-i-ō-rä'mə*, *n.* a picture composed of interchangeable parts that can be variously combined. [Gr. *mȳrios*, numberless, *horāma*, a view.]

**myrioscope**, *mir'i-ə-skōp*, *n.* a variety of kaleidoscope. [Gr. *mȳrios*, numberless, *skopeein*, to view.]

**Myristica**, *mir-* or *mīr-is'ti-ka*, *n.* the nutmeg genus, giving name to the family **Myristicā'ceae**. —*adjs.* **myris'tic**; **myristicivorous** (-*is-ti-siv'ə-rəs*), feeding upon nutmegs.—**myristic acid**, a fatty acid (C₁₃H₂₇·COOH) got from nutmegs. [Gr. *mȳrizein*, to anoint.]

**myrmecoid**, *mûr'mik-oid*, *adj.* ant-like.—*adjs.* **myrmecolog'ic**, **-al**.—*ns.* **myrmecol'ogist**; **myrmecol'ogy**, the study of ants.—*adjs.* **myrmecoph'-agous**, feeding on ants: of the anti-bear genus

**Myrmecoph'aga; myrmecoph'ilous,** having a symbiotic relation with ants.—*n.* **myrmecoph'ily.** [Gr. *myrmēx, -ēkos,* ant.]
**Myrmidon,** *mûr'mi-dən, n.* one of a tribe of warriors who accompanied Achilles to Troy: (without *cap.*) one of a ruffianly band under a daring leader: one who carries out another's orders without fear or pity.—*adj.* **myrmidō'nian.**— **myrmidons of the law,** policemen, bailiffs, etc. [Gr. *Myrmidŏnĕs* (pl.).]
**myrobalan,** *mī-rob'ə-lən,* or *mi-, n.* the astringent fruit of certain Indian mountain species of Terminalia (Combretaceae): a variety of plum. —**emblic myrobalan** (see **emblic**). [Gr. *myrobalanos,* bito—*myron,* an unguent, *balanos,* an acorn.]
**myrrh,** *mûr, n.* a bitter, aromatic, transparent gum, exuded from the bark of Commiphora: sweet cicely.—*adj.* **myrrh'ic.**—*n.* **myrrh'ol,** the volatile oil of myrrh. [O.E. *myrra*—L. *myrrha*—Gr. *myrrā;* an Eastern word; cf. Ar. *murr.*]
**myrrhine.** See under **murra.**
**myrtle,** *mûr'tl, n.* an evergreen shrub (Myrtus) with beautiful and fragrant leaves: extended to various other plants, some near akin, others not, e.g. a kind of beech in Australia (see also under **bog, wax**).—**myr'tle-wax,** wax from the candle-berry. [O.Fr. *myrtil,* dim. of *myrte*—L. *myrtus* —Gr. *myrtos.*]
**Myrtus,** *mûr'təs,* the myrtle genus, giving name to the family **Myrtā'ceae.**—*adj.* **myrtā'ceous.** [L., —Gr. *myrtos.*]
**myself,** *mi-self',* or *mi-self', pron.* I or me, in person (used for emphasis, almost always in apposition): me (reflexively). [**me, self.**]
**mysophobia,** *mi-sō-fō'bi-ə, n.* morbid fear of con-tamination. [Gr. *mȳsos,* defilement, *phobos,* fear.]
**mystagogue,** *mis'tə-gog, -gōg, n.* an initiator into religious mysteries—also **mystagō'gus.**—*adj.* **mystagog'ic** (*-goj', -gog'*).—*n.* **mys'tagogy** (*-goj-, -gog-*). [Gr. *mystēs,* one initiated, *agōgos,* a leader.]
**mystery,** *mis'tər-i, n.* a secret doctrine: (usu. in *pl.*) in ancient religions, rites known only to the initiated, as the Eleusinian mysteries: (in *pl.*) the secrets of freemasonry, etc.: anything very obscure: that which is beyond human knowledge to explain: anything artfully made difficult: a sacrament: a miracle play (also **mys'tery-play'**): a shiftless, drifting girl (*slang*).—*pl.* **mysteries.** —*adj.* **mystē'rious,** containing mystery: having an air of mystery: obscure: secret: incompre-hensible.—*adv.* **mystē'riously.**—*n.* **mystē'rious-ness.**—**mys'tery-man',** a conjurer: a medicine-man; **mys'tery-mong'er,** a dealer in mysteries; **mys'tery-ship',** a Q-boat; **mys'tery-tour',** an excursion to a destination which remains secret until the journey's end. [L. *mystērium*—Gr. *mystērion*—*mystēs,* one initiated—*myeein,* to initiate—*myein,* to close the eyes.]
**mystery, mistery,** *mis'tər-i, n.* office, service, duty (*obs.*): craft, art, trade (*arch.*): skill (*Shak.*): a trade guild (*hist.*). [L.L. *misterium*—L. *mini-stērium*—*minister,* servant; confused with *mystē-rium* and prob. with *maistry,* **mastery.**]
**mystic, -al,** *mis'tik, -əl, adjs.* relating to mystery, the mysteries, or mysticism: mysterious: sacredly obscure or secret: involving a sacred or a secret meaning hidden from the eyes of the ordinary person, only revealed to a spiritually enlightened mind: allegorical.—*n.* **mys'tic,** one who seeks or attains direct intercourse with God in elevated religious feeling or ecstasy.—*adv.* **mys'tically.**— *ns.* **mys'ticalness; mys'ticism** (*-sizm*), the habit or tendency of religious thought and feeling of those who seek direct communion with God or the divine: fogginess and unreality of thought (with suggestion of mist); **mystifi-cā'tion; mys'tifier,** one who or that which

**mystifies:** a hoaxer.—*v.t.* **mys'tify,** to make mysterious, obscure, or secret: to involve in mystery: to bewilder: to puzzle: to hoax:— *pr.p.* **mys'tifying;** *pa.t.* and *pa.p.* **mys'tified.**— **mystic recitation,** the recitation of parts of the Greek liturgy in an inaudible voice. [L. *mysticus*—Gr. *mystikos*—*mystēs,* an initiate; cf. **mystery.**]
**mystique,** *mis-tēk', mēs-tēk, n.* incommunicable spirit, gift, or quality: secret (of an art) as known to its inspired practitioners: sense of mystery, remoteness from the ordinary, and power or skill surrounding a person, activity, etc. [Fr.]
**myth,** *mith* or (old-fashioned) *mīth, n.* an ancient traditional story of gods or heroes, esp. one offering an explanation of some fact or phenom-enon: a story with a veiled meaning: mythical matter: a figment: a commonly-held belief that is untrue, or without foundation.—*adjs.* **myth'ic, -al,** relating to myths: fabulous: untrue.—*adv.* **myth'ically.**—*v.t.* **myth'icise, -ize** (*-i-sīz*), to make the subject of myth: to explain as myth.— *ns.* **myth'icism** (*-sizm*), theory that explains miraculous stories as myth; **myth'iciser, -z-, myth'icist.**—*v.t.* **myth'ise, -ize,** to mythicise.—*ns.* **myth'ism,** mythicism; **myth'ist,** a maker of myths: a mythicist; **mythogen'esis,** the produc-tion or origination of myths; **mythog'rapher,** a writer or narrator of myths; **mythog'raphy,** representation of myths in art: collection or description of myths; **mythol'oger, mytholō'gian,** a mythologist.—*adjs.* **mytholog'ic, -al,** relating to mythology, fabulous.—*adv.* **mytholog'ically.** —*v.t.* **mythol'ogise, -ize,** to interpret or explain the mythological character of: to render mythical.—*ns.* **mythol'ogiser, -z-; mythol'ogist; mythol'ogy,** a body of myths: the scientific study of myths: symbolical meaning (*obs.*); **mytho-mā'nia** (*psychiat.*), lying or exaggerating to an abnormal extent; **mythomā'niac.**—*adjs.* **mytho-poeic** (*mith-ō-pē'ik;* Gr. *poieein,* to make), **mythopoetic** (*-pō-et'ik*), mythmaking.—*ns.* **mytho-poe'ist,** a myth-maker; **mythopō'et,** a myth-maker: a writer of poems on mythical subjects; **mythus** (*mīth'əs;* L.), **mythos** (*mith'os;* Gr.), myth: mythology: theme, scheme of events: the characteristic or current attitudes of a culture or group, expressed symbolically (through poetry, art, drama, etc.).—**mythical theory,** the theory of D. F. Strauss (1808-74) and his school, that the Gospels are mainly a collection of myths, developed during the first two centuries, from the imagination of the followers of Jesus. —**comparative mythology,** the science that investigates myths and seeks to relate those of different peoples. [Gr. *mȳthos,* talk, story, myth.]
**Mytilus,** *mit'i-ləs, n.* the common mussel genus.— *adjs.* **mytil'iform, myt'iloid.** [L. *mȳtilus, mitulus, mūtulus.*]
**myxoedema,** *mik-sē-dē'mə, n.* a diseased condition due to deficiency of thyroid secretion, character-ised by loss of hair, increased thickness and dry-ness of the skin, increase in weight, slowing of mental processes, and diminution of metabolism. —Also **myxedema.** [Gr. *myxa,* mucus, *oidēma,* swelling.]
**myxoma,** *mik-sō'mə, n.* a tumour of jelly-like substance:—*pl.* **myxō'mata.**—*adj.* **myxō'matous.** —*n.* **myxomatō'sis,** a contagious virus disease of rabbits. [Gr. *myxa,* mucus.]
**Myxomycetes,** *mik-sō-mi-sē'tēz, n.pl.* slime-fungi, a class of very simple plants, by some reckoned animals (Mycetozoa), forming in the vegetative stage naked masses of protoplasm with many nuclei, creeping on wet soil, on rotten wood, etc. —*n.sing.* **myxomycete** (*-sēt'*). [Gr. *myxa,* mucus, *mykētēs,* pl. of *mykēs,* a mushroom.]
**Myxophyceae,** *mik-sō-fish'i-ē, n.pl.* the Cyanophy-ceae. [Gr. *myxa,* slime, *phȳkos,* seaweed.]

# N

**N, n,** *en, n.* the fourteenth letter of our alphabet, thirteenth of the Greek, representing a point nasal consonant sound, or before g or k a back nasal (as in *sing, sink*): anything having the shape of the letter: an indefinite number, esp. in a series_ (*math.*): as a mediaeval numeral, N = 90, and N = 90,000: a unit of measurement (**en**) = half an em (*print.*).—**to the nᵗʰ (nth)**, to any power: hence (*coll.*) unlimited.

**na,** *nä, adv.* a Scottish form of no (1): (*ni, nä,* enclitically; *Scot.*) not.

**Naafi,** *nä′fi, n.* an organisation for providing canteens for servicemen and -women: one of the canteens.—Also **NAAFI.** [From the initials of Navy, Army, and Air-Force Institute(s).]

**naam, nam,** *näm,* (*hist.*; *law*) *n.* distraint. [O.E. *näm,* related to *niman,* to take.]

**naartje.** Same as **nartjie.**

**nab,** *nab, v.t.* to seize:—*pr.p.* **nabb′ing**; *pa.t.* and *pa.p.* **nabbed.**—*n.* **nabb′er.** [Origin obscure; cf. **nap.**]

**nab,** *nab, n.* a hilltop: a promontory: a projection: the keeper of a door-lock. [O.N. *nabbr* or *nabbi.*]

**nab,** *nab* (*obs. slang*) *n.* the head: a hat.

**Nabataean,** *nab-ə-tē′ən,* **Nabathaean,** *-thē′, n.* and *adj.* (one) of an ancient powerful Arab people about Petra. [Gr. *Nabat(h)aios.*]

**nabk,** *nabk, nubk, n.* the Christ's-thorn. [Ar. *nebq.*]

**nabob,** *nä′bob, n.* a nawab (*obs.*): a European who has enriched himself in the East (*arch.*; used in Europe only): in Europe, any man of great wealth, an important person. [Hind. *nawwäb;* see **nawab.**]

**nabs,** *nabz,* (*slang*) *n.* a personage, in such phrases as **his nabs,** himself. [Cf. **nob** (2), **nib** (2).]

**nacarat,** *nak′ə-rat, n.* a bright orange-red: a fabric so coloured. [Fr.]

**nacelle,** *nä-sel′, n.* a little boat (*obs.*): the car of a balloon: a body on an aircraft housing engine(s), etc. [Fr.,—L.L. *nävicella,*—L. *nävis,* ship.]

**nache, *näch, n.** the rump. [See **aitchbone.**]

**nachschlag,** *nähh′shlähh,* (*mus.*) *n.* a grace-note whose time is taken off the preceding note. [Ger., —*nach,* after, *schlag,* stroke.]

**nachtmaal,** *nähht′mäl.* Older form of **nagmaal.**

**nacket,** *nak′it,* **nocket,** *nok′it, n.* a snack, light lunch. [Origin obscure.]

**nacre,** *nä′kər, n.* mother-of-pearl or a shellfish yielding it.—*adj.* **nä′creous.**—Also **nä′crous.**—*n.* **nä′crite,** a clay mineral, identical in composition to kaolinite but differing in optical characteristics and atomic structure. [Fr.; prob. of Eastern origin.]

**nadir,** *nä′dēr, -dər, n.* the point of the heavens diametrically opposite to the zenith: the lowest point of anything. [Fr.,—Ar. *nadir* (*nazir*), opposite to.]

**nae,** *nä, adj.* a Scots form of **no** (2): also for **no** (1), esp. with a comparative.—**nae′body,** nobody; **nae′thing,** nothing.

**naevus,** *nē′vəs,* L. *ni′voŏs, n.* a birthmark: a pigmented spot or an overgrowth of small blood-vessels in the skin—*obs.* **naeve:**—*pl.* **naevi** (*nē′vī,* L. *ni′vē*).—*adj.* **nae′void.** [L.]

**nag,** *nag, n.* a horse, esp. a small one: a riding-horse, or an inferior horse: a jade (*Shak.*). [M.E. *nagge;* origin obscure; cf. M.Du. *negge, negghe* (mod. Du. *neg, negge*).]

**nag,** *nag, v.t.* or *v.i.* to find fault with, urge (to do something), cause pain to, or worry, constantly:

(with *at*) to worry or annoy continually:—*pr.p.* **nagg′ing**; *pa.t.* and *pa.p.* **nagged.**—*n.* **nagg′er.** [Cf. Norw. *nage,* to grow, rankle, Sw. *nagga,* to gnaw.]

**naga,** *nä′ga, n.* a snake, esp. the cobra (*Ind.*): a divine snake (*Hind. myth.*). [Sans. *nāga.*]

**nagana,** *nä-gä′nə, n.* a disease of horses and cattle caused by a trypanosome transmitted by tsetse flies. [Zulu *nakane.*]

**nagari,** *nä′gə-rē, n.* devanagari: the group of alphabets to which devanagari belongs. [Sans *nägari,* town-script—*nägaran,* town (perh. referring to a particular town); addition of *deva-* to form *devanagari* was a later development.]

**nagmaal,** *nähh′mäl, näk′, n.* (*South Africa*) Dutch Reformed Church Sacrament, Lord's Supper. [Earlier *nachtmaal,* night meal; from Du.]

**Nahuatl,** *nä′wät-l, n.* the language of the Aztecs.— Also *adj.*

**naiad,** *nī′ad, nä′əd, n.* a river or spring nymph:— *pl.* **nai′adēs, nai′ads.**—*n.* **Nai′as,** a genus of water-plants, giving name to a family **Naiadā′ceae** akin to or including the pondweeds. [Gr. *nāias, -ados,* pl. *-adēs,* from *naein,* to flow.]

**naiant,** *nä′ənt,* (*her.*) *adj.* swimming horizontally [Prob. from an A.Fr. form of O.Fr. *noiant, pr.p.* —L. *natāre,* to swim.]

**naïf,** *nä-ēf′,* **naïve,** *nä-ēv′, adj.* with natural or unaffected simplicity, esp. in thought, manners, or speech: artless: ingenuous.—*adv.* **naïve′ly.**— *ns.* **naïveté** (*nä-ēv′tä*), **naïvety** (*nä-ēv′ti*), natural simplicity and unreservedness of thought, manner, or speech.—**naïve painting,** primitive painting. [Fr. *naïf,* fem. *naïve*—L. *nātivus,* native— *nāscī, nātus,* to be born.]

**naik,** *nä′ik, n.* a lord or governor: a corporal of Indian infantry. [Urdu *nä′ik*—Sans. *näyaka,* leader.]

**nail,** *nāl, n.* a horny plate at the end of a finger or toe, usu. distinguished from a claw as being flattened: a claw: a small spike, usu. of metal, and with a head, used for fastening wood, etc.: a nail-shaped excrescence, esp. one at the tip of a bird's bill: a measure of length (2¼ inches).— *v.t.* to fasten, pierce, or stud with nails: to fix: pin down, hold fast (*fig.*): to catch or secure (*slang*).—*adj.* **nailed,** having nails: fastened with nails.—*ns.* **nailer,** a maker of nails: **nail′ery,** a place where nails are made; **nail′ing,** nail-making: fastening with nails.—**nail′-bed,** that portion of the true skin on which a finger-, toe-nail rests; **nail′-bomb,** an explosive device containing gelignite and packed with long nails; **nail′-brush,** a brush for cleaning the nails; **nail′-file,** a file for trimming finger- or toe-nails; **nail gun,** an implement used to put in nails; **nail′-head,** the head of a nail: an ornament shaped like it—*adjs.* **nail′-head′(ed),** having a head suggesting that of a nail: having nail-head ornaments.—**nail′-head-spar′,** calcite crystallised in a scalenohedron terminated by a rhombohedron; **nail′-hole,** a hole made by or for a nail: a notch for opening a pocket-knife; **nail′-rod,** a strip of iron to be made into nails: iron in that form: strong coarse tobacco (*Austr.*): a stick of liquorice; **nail′-scissors,** small scissors designed especially for trimming the finger and toe-nails; **nail′-varnish,** varnish for finger- or toe-nails.— **hit the nail on the head,** to touch the exact point; **nail a lie to the counter,** expose it and put it out of currency, from the old custom of shopkeepers with counterfeit coins; **on the nail**, on the spot. [O.E. *nægel*; Ger. *nagel*.]

**nain**, *nān*, (*Scot*.) *adj*. own.—*n*. **nainsel''**, **nainsell'**, own self: a Highlander (from the Highlander's formerly alleged habit of referring to himself as *her nainsel'*). [mine ain, my own.]

**nainsook**, *nān'sŏok*, *n*. a kind of muslin like jaconet. [Hind. *nainsukh*—*nain*, eye, *sukh*, pleasure.]

**Nair**, *nā'ir*, **Nayar**, *n*. a people of Kerala who were formerly a noble and military caste of the Malabar coast and who practised a peculiar system of polyandry and matriliny.

**naissant**, *nās'∂nt*, *adj*. nascent: rising or coming forth (*her*.). [Fr., *pr.p.* of *naître*—L. *nāscī*, *nātus*, to be born.]

**naïve**. See **naïf**.

**Naja**, *nā'ja*, *-ya*, *n*. the cobra genus.—Also **Naia**. [App. Linnaeus's misreading of **naga**, or of Sinh. *naiā*, *nayā*.]

**naked**, *nā'kid*, *adj*. without clothes: uncovered: bare: exposed: open to view: unconcealed: undisguised: evident: unarmed: defenceless: unprovided: without ornament: simple: artless: without the usual covering.—*adv*. **na'kedly**. —*n*. **na'kedness**.—**naked bed** (*obs*.), a bed in which one is (orig.) entirely naked, (later) without ordinary day clothes; **naked eye**, the eye unassisted by glasses of any kind; **naked lady**, meadow-saffron. [O.E. *nacod*; Ger. *nackt*.]

**naker**, *nā'k∂r*, *n*. a kettledrum. [O.Fr. *nacre*—Ar. *naqāra*.]

**nala**, **nalla**, **nallah**. Same as **nulla(h)**.

**nam**, *pa.t.* of **nim**. See also **naam**.

**namby-pamby**, *nam'bi-pam'bi*, *adj*. feebly wishy-washy: prettily or sentimentally childish.—*n*. namby-pamby writing or talk: a namby-pamby person.—*adj*. **nam'by-pam'bical**.—*n.pl.* **nam'by-pam'bies**.—*n*. **nam'by-pam'biness**.—*adj*. **nam'-by-pam'byish**.—*n*. **nam'by-pam'byism**. [Nickname given by Carey or by Swift to *Ambrose Philips* (1674-1749), whose simple odes to children were despised by 18th-century Tories.]

**name**, *nām*, *n*. that by which a person or a thing is known or called: a designation: reputation: fame: a celebrity: family or clan: seeming or pretension without reality: authority: behalf: assumed character (of).—*v.t.* to give a name to: to mention the name of: to designate: to speak of or to call by name: to state or specify: to utter (with cognate object): to mention for a post or office: to nominate: to mention formally by name in the House of Commons as guilty of disorderly conduct.—*adjs*. **nam'able**, **name'able**, capable, or worthy, of being named; **named**; **name'less**, without a name: anonymous: undistinguished: indescribable: unspeakable.—*adv*. **name'lessly**.—*n*. **name'lessness**.—*adj*. **name'ly** (*Scot*.), famous (for).—*adv*. especially (*obs*.): by name: that is to say.—*ns*. **nam'er**; **nam'ing**.— **name brand**, a make of an article bearing a manufacturer's distinguishing name; **name'-calling**, abuse; **name'-child**, a person called after one; **name'-day**, the day of the saint of one's name: the day when a ticket bearing the buyer's name, etc., is given to the seller (*Stock Exchange*): the day on which a name is bestowed; **name'-dropping**, trying to impress by casual mention of important or well-known persons as if they were one's friends; **name'-dropper**.—*v.i.* **name'-drop**.—**name'-part**, the part that gives title to a play, title-rôle; **name'-plate**, an attached plate bearing the name of occupant, owner, manufacturer, etc.; **name'sake**, one bearing the same name as another; **name'-son**, a male namechild.—*adj*. **name'worthy**, worth naming: distinguished.—**call names**, to bestow abuse upon; **in name**, fictitiously, as an empty title; ⸱**in name of**, on behalf of: by the authority of; **name after a person** (*U.S.* **name for**), to give the same name to in honour of a person; **name the day**, to fix

a day, esp. for a marriage; **proper name**, a name given to a particular person, place, or thing; **take a name in vain**, to use a name lightly or profanely. [O.E. *nama*; Ger. *name*; L. *nōmen*.]

**nana**. See **nanny**.

**Nancy**, *nan'si*, *n*. an effeminate young man: a homosexual (also without *cap.*)—also **Nance** (also without *cap.*), **Nan'cy-boy**, **Miss Nan'cy**.— Also *adj*. [From the girl's name.]

**nancy-pretty**, *nan'si-prit'i*, *n*. the plant *Saxifraga umbrosa*, London pride. [Prob. for none so **pretty**.]

**Nandi bear**, *nan'di*, a great fierce animal reputed to live in E. Africa, perh. the spotted hyena. [From the *Nandi* Forest, Kenya.]

**nandine**, *nan'din*, *n*. a West African palm-civet. [Prob. a native name.]

**nandu**, **nandoo**, *nan'dŏŏ*, *n*. the rhea. [Tupí *nandú*.]

**nanism**, *nān'* or *nan'izm*, *n*. condition of being dwarfed.—*n*. **nanisā'tion**, **-izā'tion**, artificial dwarfing. [Gr. *nānos*, *nannos*, dwarf.]

**nankeen**, *nan'kēn*, or *-kēn'*, *n*. a buff-coloured cotton cloth first made at *Nanking* in China: (*pl*.) clothes, esp. breeches, made of nankeen.—Also **nan'kin** (or *-kin'*).

**nanny**, *nan'i*, *n*. a she-goat (also **nann'y-goat**): a children's nurse, esp. one trained to take care of children: a pet name for a grandmother.—Also **nana**, **nanna**.—*v.t.* to nurse. [From the woman's name.]

**nano-**, *nān-ō-*, *nan-ō-*, in composition, one thousand-and millionth, $10^{-9}$, as in **nan'ogram**, **nan'o-second**: of microscopic size, as in **nanoplankton**. [Gr. *nānos*, a dwarf.]

**Nantz**, *nants*, (*arch*.) *n*. brandy. [*Nantes* in France.]

**naos**, *nā'os*, *n*. a temple: the inner cell of a temple. [Gr. *nāos*, temple.]

**nap**, *nap*, *v.i.* to take a short or casual sleep:—*pr.p.* **napp'ing**; *pa.p.* **napped**.—*n*. a short or casual sleep.—**catch napping**, to detect in error that might have been avoided: to take off one's guard or unprepared. [O.E. *hnappian*.]

**nap**, *nap*, *n*. a woolly surface on cloth, now (distinguished from *pile*) such a surface raised by a finishing process, not made in the weaving: the woolly surface removed in the process: a cloth with such a surface: a downy covering or surface on anything.—*v.t.* to raise a nap on: to remove nap from.—*adj*. **nap'less**, without nap, threadbare.—*n*. **napp'iness**.—*adj*. **napp'y**, downy: shaggy. [M.E. *noppe*; app.—M.Du. or M.L.G. *noppe*.]

**nap**, *nap*, *n*. the card-game *Napoleon*: in that game a call of five: the winning of five tricks: a racing tip that professes to be a certainty—one that one may 'go nap' on.—*v.t.* to name (a particular horse) as certain to win.—**go nap**, to undertake to win all five tricks: to risk all.

**nap**, *nap*, *v.t.* to seize: to steal. [Cf. Sw. *nappa*, Dan. and Norw. *nappe*, to catch, snatch; relation to **nab** uncertain.]

**napalm**, *nā'päm*, *na'*, *n*. a petroleum jelly, highly inflammable, used in bombs and flame-throwers. [*naphthenate palm*itate.]

**nape**, *nāp*, *n*. the back of the neck. [Ety. dub.]

**napery**, *nāp'∂-ri*, (*arch*. and *Scot*.) *n*. linen, esp. for the table. [O.Fr. *naperie*—L.L. *napāria*—*napa*, a cloth—L. *mappa*, a napkin.]

**naphtha**, *naf'th∂* (sometimes *nap'th∂*), *n*. rock-oil: a vague name for the liquid inflammable distillates from coal-tar, wood, etc., esp. the lighter and more volatile.—*n*. **naph'thalene**, an ill-smelling hydrocarbon ($C_{10}H_8$) got by distillation of coal-tar, crystallising in plates, used for killing moths, etc.—*adj*. **naphthal'ic** (*naf-thal'ik*), pertaining to, or derived from, naphthalene.— *v.t.* **naph'thalise**, **-ize**, to treat with naphtha. — *ns*. **naph'thol**, a hydroxyl derivative of naphthalene ($C_{10}H_7OH$), of two kinds; **naphthyl′amine** (or **-mēn′**), an amino-derivative of thalene ($C_{10}H_7NH_2$), of two kinds, used in dyeing. [Gr. *naphtha*.]

**Napierian, Naperian,** *nä-pē′ri-ən, adj.* pertaining to John *Napier* of Merchiston (1550-1617), or to his system of logarithms: now applied to natural logarithms, logarithms to the base *e*, the limit of $\left(1+\frac{1}{m}\right)^m$ when *m* approaches infinity, Napier's own base being a quantity depending on $e^{-1}$.—Napier's bones, or rods, an invention of Napier's for multiplying and dividing mechanically by means of rods.

**napiform,** *näp′i-förm, adj.* turnip-shaped. [L. *näpus,* a turnip.]

**napkin,** *nap′kin, n.* a small square of linen, paper, etc., used at table or otherwise: a handkerchief (*Scot.*).—**nap′kin-ring,** a ring in which a table-napkin is rolled. [Dim. of Fr. *nappe*—L. *mappa.*]

**Naples-yellow,** *nä′plz-yel′ō, n.* a light-yellow pigment, lead antimoniate, originally an Italian secret.

**napoleon,** *nə-pōl′yən,* or *-i-ən, n.* a twenty-franc gold coin issued by *Napoleon:* a French modification of the game of euchre, each player receiving five cards and playing for himself (commonly **nap**): a kind of rich iced cake.—*adj.* **Napoleonic** (*-i-on′ik*), relating to *Napoleon* I or III, the Great or the Little.—*ns.* **Napol′eonism; Napol′eonist; napol′eonite,** an orbicular diorite found in Corsica, Napoleon's native island.

**napoo,** *nä-pōō′,* (slang of 1914 war) *adj.* and *interj.* no more: used up: good for nothing: dead.—*v.t.* to kill. [Fr. *il n'y en a plus,* there is no more.]

**nappe, nap,** *n.* a sheet of rock brought far forward by recumbent folding or thrusting (*geol.*): a sheet (*math.*): one of the two sheets on either side of the vertex forming a cone (*math.*). [Fr. *nappe,* tablecloth—L. *mappa.*]

**napper,** *nap′ər,* (slang) *n.* the head.

**nappy,** *nap′i, n.* a baby's napkin.

**nappy,** *nap′i, adj.* of liquor, having a head: heady, strong: tipsy.—*n.* strong ale. [Perh. from *nappy,* shaggy; see nap (2).]

**napron,** *nä′prən, n.* earlier form (*Spens.*) of apron.

**naras.** See narras.

**Narcissus,** *när-sis′əs, n.* the daffodil genus of the Amaryllis family: esp. *N. poeticus* (the poet's narcissus):—*pl.* **narciss′uses** or **narciss′i:** in Greek myth., a youth who pined away for love of his own image, and was transformed into the flower.—*ns.* **narciss′ism,** sensual gratification found in one's own body, whether as a normal stage of development or a pathological condition; **narciss′ist.** [L.,—Gr. *Narkissos;* the connection with *narkē,* numbness, seems to be fanciful.]

**narco-analysis.** See narcotic.

**narcolepsy,** *när′kō-lep-si, n.* a condition marked by short attacks of irresistible drowsiness. [Gr. *narkē,* numbness, and *lēpsis,* seizure.]

**narcotic,** *när-kot′ik, adj.* producing torpor, sleep, or deadness: affecting the central nervous system so as to produce dizziness, euphoria, loss of memory and of neuromuscular co-ordination, and eventually unconsciousness.—*n.* anything having a narcotic effect, e.g. a drug, alcohol, an inert gas.—*n.* **narcosis** (*-kō′sis*), drowsiness, unconsciousness or other effects to the central nervous system produced by a narcotic:—*pl.* **narco′ses** (*-sēz*).—*adv.* **narcot′ically.**—*n.* **nar′cotine** (*-kə-tēn*), one of the alkaloids in opium. —*v.t.* **nar′cotise, -ize,** to subject to the influence of a narcotic.—*ns.* **nar′cotism,** the influence of narcotics; **nar′cotist.**—**nar′co-analysis,** hypno-analysis when narcotics are used in producing the hypnotic state; **nar′cocathar′sis,** narco-analysis; **nar′cohypno′sis,** the use of narcotics to produce hypnosis; **nar′cosyn′thesis,** the bringing out of repressed emotions by narcotics so that they become freely accepted into the self; **nar′co-therapy′,** treatment of disturbed mental states by prolonged drug-induced sleep. [Gr. *narkōtikos—narkē,* numbness, torpor.]

**nard, närd, n.** spikenard: an inappropriate name for matweed (*Nardus stricta*).—*v.t.* to anoint with nard. [L. *nardus*—Gr. *nardos.*]

**nardoo,** *när-dōō′, n.* an Australian Marsilea: its sporocarps, eaten by aboriginals. [Native word.]

**nare, när, n.** (*arch.*) a nostril, esp. a hawk's.—*n.pl.* **när′ēs** (L.) nostrils.—*adjs.* **när′ial, när′ine** (*-in*). —*n.* **när′icorn,** a horny termination of a bird's nostril. [L. *näris,* pl. *-ēs,* nostril.]

**narghile,** *när′gil-i, n.* a hookah.—Also **nargile(h), narg(h)il(l)y.** [Pers. *närgileh—närgil,* a coconut (from which it used to be made).]

**nark, närk,** (slang) *n.* an informer: a police spy (*copper's nark*): one who curries favour, a pick-thank: a spoil-sport: a persistent fault-finder: an annoying or baffling circumstance: an expert. —*v.i.* to grumble.—*v.t.* and *v.i.* to watch: to spy: to annoy: to tease.—*adjs.* **nark′y,** irritable; **narked,** annoyed.—**nark at,** to fret with persistent criticism. [Romany *nāk,* nose.]

**narks, the.** See nitrogen narcosis.

**narquois,** *när-kwä,* (Fr.) mocking, malicious.

**narras, naras,** *när′əs, n.* edible melon-like fruit of a S.-W. African long-rooted thorny cucurbitaceous shrub (*Acanthosicyos horrida*). [Hottentot *qnaras.*]

**narrate,** *nə-* or *na-rāt′, v.t.* to tell of (a series of events).—*v.i.* to recount or relate events.—*adj.* **narrāt′able.**—*n.* **narrā′tion,** act of telling: that which is told: an orderly account of a series of events.—*adj.* **narrative** (*nar′ə-tiv*), narrating: giving an account of any occurrence: inclined to narration: story-telling.—*n.* that which is narrated: a continued account of any series of occurrences: story.—*adv.* **narr′atively.**—*n.* **narrā′tor.**—*adj.* **narr′atory,** like narrative: consisting of narrative. [L. *narrāre, -ātum,* prob.— *gnārus,* knowing.]

**narre, när,** (*Spens.*) *adv.* an old comparative of nigh.

**narrow,** *nar′ō, adj.* of little breadth: of small extent from side to side: closely confining: limited: contracted in mind: bigoted: not liberal: parsimonious: with little to spare: close: strict, precise: detailed: keen: tense (*phon.*).—*n.* a narrow part or place: (usu. in *pl.*) narrow passage, channel, or strait.—*adv.* **narrowly.**—*v.t.* make narrow: contract or confine.—*v.i.* become narrow: reduce the number of stitches in knitting.—*n.* **narr′owing,** the act of making less in breadth: the state of being contracted: the part of anything which is made narrower.—Also *adj.*—*adv.* **narr′owly.**— *n.* **narr′owness.**—*adj.* **narrow-gauge,** of a railway, less than 4 ft 8½ in. in gauge; **narr′owmind′ed,** of a narrow or illiberal mind.—**narr′owmind′edness; narrow seas,** the seas between Great Britain and the Continent. [O.E. *nearu.*]

**narrow.** See nary.

**Narthex,** *när′theks, n.* a former genus of umbelliferous plants, now included in Ferula: (without *cap.*) a western portico or vestibule in an early Christian or Oriental church or basilica, to which women and catechumens were admitted: (without *cap.*) a vestibule between the church porch and the nave. [Gr. *narthēx,* giant fennel, a cane or stalk, a casket, a narthex.]

**nartjie,** (orig. naartje) *när′chi,* (*Afrik.*) *n.* a small sweet orange like the mandarin. [Prob. conn. with orange.]

**narwhal,** *när′wəl, n.* a kind of whale (Monodon) with one large projecting tusk (occasionally two tusks) in the male. [Dan. *narhval;* O.N. *náhvalr,* may be from *när,* corpse, *hvalr,* whale, from its pallid colour.]

nary, *nār'i*, (*U.S.* and *dial.*) for ne'er a, never a, not one.—Also narrow a, *nar'ō*.

nas, *naz*, *näz*, *obs.* for ne has (*Spens.*) and for ne was.

nasal, *nā'zl*, *adj.* belonging to the nose: affected by, or sounded through, the nose.—*n.* a sound uttered through the nose: a letter representing such a sound: a paired bone that forms the bridge of the nose: the nose-piece in a helmet.—*ns.* Nasalis (*naz-ā'lis*), the proboscis monkey genus; nasalisation, -z- (*nā-zə-lī-zā'shən*).—*v.i.* na'salise, -ize, to render nasal, as a sound.—*n.* nasality (*nā-zal'i-ti*).—*adv.* na'sally.—*n.* nasion (*nā'zi-on*), the median point of the nasofrontal suture. [L. *nāsus*, the nose.]

nasard, *naz'ərd*, *n.* an organ mutation-stop. [Fr.]

nascent, *nas'ənt*, *nās'ənt*, *adj.* coming into being.—*ns.* nasc'ence (*rare*), nasc'ency. [L. *nāscēns*, *-entis*, pr.p. of *nāscī*, *nātus*, to be born.]

naseberry, *nāz'bər-i*, *-ber'i*, *n.* the sapodilla plum: the tree bearing it.—Also neesberry (*nēz'*), nisberry (*niz'*). [Sp. *néspera*, *níspero*, medlar tree—L. *mespilus*, medlar; cf. medlar.]

nashgab, *nash'gab*, *näsh'gäb*, (*Scot.*) *n.* prattle: chatter: a pert chatterer.—Also gab'nash.

Nasik, *nä'sik*, *n.* a town of Bombay.—Also *adj.* esp. of an elaborate form of magic square devised there.

naso-, *nā'zō-*, in composition, nose: of the nose (and something else), as *adjs.* nasofront'al, pertaining to the nose and the frontal bone; nasolac'rymal, pertaining to the nose and tears, as the duct that carries tears from the eye and the nose. [L. *nāsus*, nose.]

nastic, *näs'tik*, *nas'*, *adj.* (of plant movements) not related to the direction of the stimulus. [Gr. *nastos*, close-pressed.]

Nasturtium, *nas-tûr'shəm*, *n.* the water-cress genus of Cruciferae: (without *cap.*; in popular use) the Indian cress (*Tropaeolum majus*), a garden climber. [L. *nāsus*, nose, *torquēre*, to twist (from its pungency).]

nasty, *näs'ti*, *adj.* disgustingly foul: nauseous: filthy: obscene: threatening: threatening danger: spiteful: ill-natured: difficult to deal with: awkward: unpleasant: objectionable.—*adv.* nas'tily.—*n.* nas'tiness.—a nasty piece, bit, of work, a person very objectionable in character and conduct. [Perh. for earlier *nasky* (cf. Sw. dial. *naskug*, *nasket*); or perh. connected with Du. *nestig*, dirty.]

nasute, *nā'zūt*, *-sūt*, or *-zūt'*, *-sūt'*, *adj.* keen-scented: critically discriminating: beaked.—*n.* a beaked soldier white-ant. [L. *nāsūtus* —*nāsus*, nose.]

natal, *nā'tl*, pertaining to the nates.

natal, *nā'tl*, *adj.* of or connected with birth: native.—*adj.* natalitial (*nat-* or *nāt-ə-lish'l*), pertaining to a birthday.—*n.* natality (*nə-*, *nātal'i-ti*), birth: birth-rate. [L. *nātālis*—*nāscī*, *nātus*, to be born.]

natale solum, *na-tā'lē sō'ləm*, *nä-tä'le sol'ōōm*, (L.) native soil.

natant, *nāt'ənt*, *adj.* floating: swimming.—*n.* natation (*nat-* or *nāt-ā'shən*), swimming.—*adjs.* nātato'rial, nā'tatory, pertaining to swimming: having the habit of swimming: adapted or used for swimming.—*n.* nātato'rium (*U.S.*), a swimming-pool. [L. *natāns*, *-antis*, pr.p. of *natāre*, freq. of *nāre*, to swim.]

natch, *nach*, (*dial.*) *n.* the rump. [See aitchbone.]

nates, *nā'tēz*, *n.pl.* (L.) the buttocks.—*adjs.* nā'tal; nā'tiform. [L. *natis*, pl. *-ēs*.]

natheless(e). See nathless.

nathemore, *nā-thə-mōr'*, *-mōr'*, nathemo, *-mō'*, (*Spens.*) *advs.* not or never the more. [O.E. *nā thȳ mā*, never the more (cf. following).]

nathless, natheless, nathelesse, naythles, *nāth'*, *nath'*, *näth'*, *nādh'*, *nadh'*, *nādh'(ə)-les*, or (as *Spens.*) *-les'*, (*arch.*) *adv.* and *prep.* notwith-standing. [O.E. *nā*, never, *thȳ*, by that (instrum. case), *læs*, less.]

nation, *nā'shən*, *n.* a body of people marked off by common descent, language, culture, or historical tradition: the people of a state: an American Indian tribe: a set of people, animals, etc.: a great number: an old division of students in universities: (in *pl.*) the heathen or Gentiles.—*adj.* national (*nash'nəl*, *-ə-nəl*), pertaining to a nation or nations: belonging or peculiar to a nation: characteristic of, or controlled by, a nation: public: general: attached to one's own country.—*n.* a member or fellow-member of a nation.—*n.* nationalisā'tion, -izā'.—*v.t.* nat'ionalise, -ize, to make national: to make the property of the nation: to bring under national management: to naturalise: to make a nation of.—*ns.* nat'ionalism; nat'ionalist, one who favours or strives after the unity, independence, interests, or domination of a nation: a member of a political party specially so called, e.g. the Irish Nationalist party who aimed at Home Rule: an advocate of nationalisation.—*adj.* nationalist'ic.—*n.* nationality (*-al'it-i*), membership of, fact or state of belonging to, a particular nation: nationhood: a group or set having the character of a nation: national character.—*adv.* nat'ionally.—*n.* nationhood (*nā'*), state or fact of being a nation.—*adj.* nationless (*nā'*), without nationality or nations.—national air, anthem, an official song or hymn of a nation, sung or played on ceremonial occasions; national church, a church established by law in a country; National Convention, the sovereign assembly in France from 21st Sept. 1792 to 26th Oct. 1795; national debt, money borrowed by the government of a country and not yet paid back; National Guard, a force which took part in the French Revolution, first formed in 1789: organised militia of individual States (*U.S.*); national park, area owned by or for the nation, set apart for preservation and enjoyment of the beautiful or interesting; national school, in England, formerly, a school connected with the National Society, established in 1811, to promote elementary education; national service, compulsory service in the armed forces.—*adj.* na'tion-wide, covering the whole nation.—National Socialist party, an extreme nationalistic fascist party in Germany, led by Adolf Hitler. [L. *nātiō*, *-ōnis*—*nāscī*, *nātus*, to be born.]

nation, *nā'shən*, (*U.S.*) *n.*, *adj.*, *adv.*, *interj.* for damnation.

native, *nā'tiv*, *adj.* belonging naturally: innate: inherent: natural: in a natural state: unsophisticated: occurring in a natural station: occurring naturally as a mineral (not manufactured), or naturally uncombined (as an element): belonging by birth: having a right by birth: born or originating in the place: being the place of birth or origin: belonging to the people originally or at the time of discovery inhabiting the country, esp. when they are coloured or uncivilised: connected by birth: born a thrall (*obs.*): applied to Australian plants and animals to which the name of an already known different kind has been transferred: (of an oyster) raised in a (British) artificial bed.—*n.* one born in any place: (*disparagingly*) one born and long dwelling in a place: one born under a particular planet or sign: a member of a native race: vaguely, a coloured person (*coll.*): a white person born in Australia: an indigenous species, variety, or breed, or an individual of it: a native oyster: a born thrall (*obs.*).—*adv.* na'tively.—*ns.* na'tiveness; na'tivism, the belief that the mind possesses some ideas or forms of thought that are inborn and not derived from sensation: the disposition to favour the natives of a country in preference to immigrants; na'tivist.—*adj.* nativis'tic.—*n.* nativity (*nə-tiv'i-ti*), state or fact of being born: time, place, and manner of birth: nationality by birth: fact or status of being native: the birth of Christ, hence the festival commemorating it—Christmas, or a picture representing it: a horoscope: bondage by birth (*obs.*).—**native bear**, the koala. —*adj.* **na'tive-born**, born in the country: having a status by virtue of birth (*Scot.*; *obs.*).—**native rock**, unquarried rock.—**go native** (see **go**). [L. *nātivus*—*nāscī*, *nātus*, to be born.]

**Nato**, *nä'tō*, *n.* the North Atlantic Treaty Organisation (see **north**).

**natrolite**, *nät'* or *nat'rə-līt*, *n.* a common fibrous zeolite, hydrated sodium aluminium silicate. [**natron**, and Gr. *lithos*, stone.]

**natron**, *nä'trən*, *n.* a hydrated carbonate of sodium found on some lake borders.—*n.* **na'trium**, chemists' Latin for sodium. [Ar. *natrūn*—Gr. *nitron*.]

**natter**, *nat'ər*, *v.i.* to be peevish (*N. of England*): rattle on in talk, esp. grumblingly: to chatter, talk much about little (*coll.*).—Also *n.*—*adjs.* **natt'ered**, **natt'ery**, peevish. [Origin obscure.]

**natterjack**, *nat'ər-jak*, *n.* a toad with a yellow stripe down the back. [Origin unknown.]

**nattier blue**, *nat'i-ər*, a soft azure. [J. M. *Nattier* (d. 1766), French painter.]

**natty**, *nat'i*, *adj.* dapper: spruce.—*adv.* **natt'ily**.— *n.* **natt'iness**. [Possibly connected with **neat**.]

**natura**, *nə-tūr'ə*, *na-tōō'ra*, (L.) nature; **natura naturans**, *nat'ūr-əns*, *na-tōō'räns*, creative nature; **natura naturata**, *na-tūr-ā'tə*, *na-tōō-rä'ta*, created nature.

**natural**, *nach'(ə)ral*, *adj.* pertaining to, produced by, or according to nature: furnished by or based on nature: not miraculous: not the work of man: not interfered with by man: inborn: having the feelings that may be expected to come by nature, kindly: normal: happening in the usual course: spontaneous: not far-fetched: not acquired: without affectation: not fictitious: physical: life-like, like nature: related by actual birth (not adoption, etc.): hence (now rarely) legitimate: (now usually) illegitimate: natural-born, or having the status of the natural-born: in a state of nature, unregenerate: according to the usual diatonic scale, not sharp or flat (*mus.*). —*n.* an idiot: one having a natural aptitude (for), or being an obvious choice (for): a thing assured by its very nature of success, a certainty: a tone that is neither sharp nor flat (*mus.*): a character (♮) cancelling a preceding sharp or flat (*mus.*): a white key in keyboard musical instruments.—*n.* **naturalisā'tion**, **-z-**.—*v.t.* **nat'uralise**, **-ize**, to make natural or easy: to adapt to a different climate or to different conditions of life: to grant the privileges of natural-born citizens to: to adopt into the language: to admit among accepted institutions, usages, etc.: to explain naturalistically.—*v.i.* to acquire citizenship in another country: to study natural history in the field.—*ns.* **nat'uralism**, following of nature: a close following of nature without idealisation: the theory that this should be the aim of literature, esp. the form of realism advocated or practised by Emile Zola: a world-view that rejects the supernatural: the belief that natural religion is of itself sufficient: deism; **nat'uralist**, one who studies nature, more particularly zoology and botany, esp. zoology, and esp. in the field: a dealer in live animals and articles of use and interest to students of nature, often a taxidermist: a believer in naturalism.—*adj.* **naturalist'ic**, pertaining to, or in accordance with, nature, natural history, or naturalism.— *adv.* **nat'urally**, in a natural manner: by nature: according to nature or one's own nature: in a life-like manner: normally: in the ordinary course: of course. — *n.* **nat'uralness**. — *adj.* **nat'ural-born**, native.—**natural death**, death

owing to disease or old age, not violence or accident; **natural gas**, gases issuing from the earth, whether from natural fissures or bored wells; **natural history**, originally the description of all that is in nature, now used of the sciences that deal with the earth and its productions— botany, zoology, and mineralogy, esp. field zoology; **natural law**, a law of nature: the sense of right and wrong which arises from the constitution of the mind of man, as distinguished from the results of revelation or legislation; **natural logarithm**, one to the base *e*; **natural magic** (see **magic**); **natural numbers**, the whole numbers 1, 2, 3, and upwards; **natural order**, in botany, a category now usually called a family; **natural philosophy**, the science of the physical properties of bodies: physics, or physics and dynamics; **natural scale**, a scale of music written without sharps or flats; **natural science**, the science of nature, as distinguished from mental and moral science and from mathematics; **natural selection**, evolution by the survival of the fittest with inheritance of their fitness by next generation; **natural system**, a classification of plants and animals according to presumed relationship by descent, distinguished in botany from the artificial system of Linnaeus; **natural theology**, or **natural religion**, religion derived from reason without revelation. [L. *nātūrālis*— *nātūra*, nature.]

**nature**, *nä'chər*, *n.* the power that creates and regulates the world: the power of growth: the established order of things: the cosmos: the external world, esp. as untouched by man: the qualities of anything which make it what it is: essence: being: constitution: kind or order: naturalness: normal feeling: kindliness: conformity to truth, or reality: inborn mind, character, instinct, or disposition: vital power of man, animal (*obs.*): course of life: nakedness: a primitive undomesticated condition: the strength or substance of anything.—*adjs.* **na'tured**, having a certain temper or disposition (esp. in compounds, as *good-natured*); **na'turing**, creative.—*ns.* **na'turism**, nudism: nature-worship; **na'turist**.—*adj.* **naturist'ic**.—*n.* **nat'uropath**, one who practises naturopathy.—*adj.* **naturopath'ic**. —*n.* **naturop'athy**, treatment of disease by diet, exercise, electricity, etc., the aim being to aid natural means of recovery.—**na'ture-cure**, treatment of disease by trusting mainly to nature; **na'ture-god'**, a deity personifying some force of physical nature; **na'ture-knowl'edge**, **na'ture-study**, a branch of school work intended to cultivate the powers of seeing and enjoying nature by the observation of natural objects, e.g. plants, animals, etc.; **na'ture-myth'**, a myth symbolising natural phenomena; **na'ture-printing**, printing from plates that have been impressed with some natural object; **na'ture-wor'-ship**, **na'turism**, worship of the powers of nature. —**debt of nature**, death; **ease**, or **relieve**, **nature**, to evacuate the bowels. [Fr.,—L. *nātūra*— *nāscī*, *nātus*, to be born.]

**naturopath**, **-pathy**. See **nature**.

**naught**, *nöt*, *n.* nothing: a nought (q.v.): wickedness, evil (*obs.*).—*adj.* (*arch.*) good for nothing: worthless: bad: immoral: hurtful: foiled: ruined.—*adv.* ill: not at all.—**be naught** (*obs.*), keep out of the way: efface yourself: go to the devil; **come to naught**, to come to nothing, to fail; **set at naught**, to treat as of no account, to despise.—Also **nought**. [O.E. *nāht*, *nāwiht*— *nā*, never, *wiht*, whit.]

**naughty**, *nöt'i*, *adj.* worthless (*obs.*): wicked (*Shak.*): bad: ill-behaved: verging on the indecorous: now chiefly applied to children, or used playfully in feigned censure.—*adv.* **naught'-ily**.—*n.* **naught'iness**.—**naughty nineties** (*joc.*), the 1890s, renowned for gaiety and high living;

naughty pack (*obs.*), a person, esp. a woman, of loose life, a 'bad lot'. [naught.]

naumachy, *nö'mə-ki,* naumachia, *nö-mā'ki-a, ns.* a sea-fight, esp. one got up as a spectacle among the Romans: a place for the purpose. [Gr. *naumachiā—naus,* a ship, *machē,* a fight.]

naunt, *nänt,* (*arch.*) *n.* aunt. [For mine aunt.]

nauplius, *nö'pli-əs, n.* a larval form in many Crustacea, with one eye and three pairs of appendages:—*pl.* nau'plii.—*adjs.* nau'pliiform, nau'plioid. [L., a kind of shellfish—Gr. *Nauplios,* a son of Poseidon, *naus,* a ship, *pleein,* to sail.]

nausea, *nö'si-ə, -shi-ə, -zhə, n.* sea-sickness (*orig.*): a feeling of inclination to vomit: sickening disgust or loathing.—*adj.* nau'seant, producing nausea.—*n.* a substance having this quality.—*v.i.* nau'seate, to feel nausea or disgust.—*v.t.* to loathe: to strike with disgust—*adj.* nau'seating, causing nausea or (*fig.*) disgust.—*adjs.* nau'seative (*obs.*) inclined to or causing nausea; nau'seous (*-shəs, -shi-əs, -si-əs*), producing nausea: disgusting: loathsome.—*adv.* nau'seously.—*n.* nau'seousness. [L.,—Gr. *nausiā,* seasickness—*naus,* a ship.]

nautch, *nöch,* nach, natch, *näch, n.* in India, a performance of professional dancing women known as nautch'-girls. [Hind. *nāch,* dance.]

nautic, *nöt'ik* (*rare*), -al, *-əl, adjs.* of or pertaining to ships, to sailors, or to navigation.—*adv.* nau'tically.—*n.* nau'tics, (as *sing.*) science of navigation: (as *pl.*) water sports.—**Nautical Almanac,** a periodical book of astronomical tables specially useful to sailors; **nautical mile** (see mile). [L. *nauticus*—Gr. *nautikos—nautēs,* sailor, *naus,* a ship.]

nautilus, *nö'ti-ləs, n.* a tetrabranchiate cephalopod (*pearly nautilus*) of southern seas, with a chambered external shell: a Mediterranean dibranchiate cephalopod (*paper nautilus,* or argonaut) wrongly believed by Aristotle to use its arms as sails:—*pl.* nau'tiluses, or nau'tili. [L.,—Gr. *nautilos,* a sailor, a paper nautilus—*naus,* ship.]

naval, *nā'vl, adj.* pertaining to warships or a navy: nautical (*obs.*).—*n.* nav'alism, cult of naval supremacy or sea-power.—**Naval Brigade,** a body of seamen organised to serve on land; **naval crown,** a garland awarded to a Roman who had distinguished himself in a sea-fight; **naval officer,** an officer in the navy: a custom-house officer of high rank (*U.S.*). [L. *nāvālis—nāvis,* a ship.]

navarch, *nāv'ärk, n.* an admiral in ancient Greece. —*n.* nav'archy, the office of navarch: a fleet. [Gr. *nauarchos—naus,* ship, *archē,* rule.]

navarho, *nav'ə-rō, n.* low-frequency, long-range radio navigation system for aircraft. [*navigation*; *aid;* *rho* (ρ), a navigational symbol for distance.]

nave, *nāv, n.* the middle or main body of a basilica, rising above the aisles: the main part of a church, generally west of the crossing, including or excluding its aisles. [L. *nāvis,* a ship.]

nave, *nāv, n.* the hub or central part of a wheel, through which the axle passes: the navel (*Shak.*). [O.E. *nafu;* cf. Du. *naaf,* Ger. *nabe.*]

navel, *nā'vl, n.* the umbilicus or depression in the centre of the abdomen: a central point: nombril (*her.*).—na'vel-or'ange, a variety of orange with a navel-like depression, and a smaller orange enclosed; na'vel-string, the umbilical cord; na'velwort, pennywort (Cotyledon). [O.E. *nafela,* dim. of *nafu,* nave of a wheel.]

navew, *nā'vū, n.* a rape or coleseed with carrot-shaped root: a wild Swedish turnip. [Fr. *naveau,* dim.—L. *nāpus.*]

navicert, *nav'* or *nāv'i-sûrt, n.* a certificate granted by a belligerent to a neutral ship testifying that she carries no contraband of war. [navigational certificate.]

navicula, *nav-ik'ū-lə, n.* an incense-boat: (*cap.*) a genus of diatoms.—*adj.* navic'ūlar, boat-shaped: pertaining to the navicular bone.—*n.* the navicular bone.—**navicular bone,** the scaphoid bone; **navicular disease,** inflammation of the navicular bone in horses. [L. *nāvicula,* dim. of *nāvis,* a ship.]

navigate, *nav'i-gāt, v.i.* to conduct or manage a ship, aircraft, motor vehicle, etc., in sailing, flying or moving along: to find one's way and keep one's course, esp. by water or air: to sail. —*v.t.* to direct the course of: to sail, fly, etc., over, on, or through.—*n.* navigability (*-gə-bil'i-ti*).—*adj.* nav'igable, that may be passed by ships, etc.: dirigible.—*ns.* nav'igableness; naviga'tion, the act, science, or art of conducting ships or aircraft, etc., esp. the finding of position and determination of course by astronomical observations and mathematical computations: travel or traffic by water or air: a voyage (*arch.*): shipping generally: a navigable route: a canal or artificial waterway.—*adj.* naviga'tional, pertaining to navigation.—*n.* nav'igator, one who navigates or sails: one who directs the course of a ship, etc.: one (usu. co-driver) who describes the route to, and directs, the driver in car rally or race: an explorer by sea: a navvy: an instrumental or other aid to navigation. [L. *nāvigāre, -ātum—nāvis,* a ship, *agĕre,* to drive.]

navvy, *nav'i, n.* a labourer—originally a labourer on a navigation or canal: a machine for digging out earth, etc.—*steam navvy, steam shovel.—v.i.* to work as a navvy, or like a navvy.—*v.t.* to excavate:—*pr.p.* navv'ying; *pa.t.* and *pa.p.* navv'ied. [navigator.]

navy, *nā'vi, n.* a fleet of ships: the whole of a nation's ships-of-war: the officers and men belonging to a nation's warships.—*adj.* of, used by, such as is supplied to, the navy.—*n.* and *adj.* na'vy-blue', dark blue as in naval dress.— na'vy-list', a list of officers and ships of a navy; na'vy-yard (*U.S.*), a government dockyard. [O.Fr. *navie*—L. *nāvis,* a ship.]

nawab, *nə-wäb', -wöb', n.* a deputy or viceroy in the Mogul empire: a Mohammedan prince or noble: an honorary title bestowed by the Indian government: a nabob (*rare*). [Hind. *nawwāb*—Ar. *nawwāb,* respectful pl. of *nā'ib,* deputy.]

nay, *nā, adv.* no: not only so, but: yet more: in point of fact.—*n.* a denial: a vote against.— nay'-say, a refusal.—*v.t.* to refuse: to deny.— nay'ward (*Shak.*), the negative side. [M.E. *nay, nai*—O.N. *nei;* Dan. *nei;* cog. with no.]

naya paisa. See paisa.

nayword, *nā'wûrd, n.* a catchword or watchword (*Shak.*): a proverbial reproach, a byword (*Shak.*). ayword). [Origin obscure.]

Nazarene, *naz'ə-rēn, n.* an inhabitant of Nazareth, in Galilee: a follower of Jesus of Nazareth, originally used of Christians in contempt: an early Jewish Christian: any of a group of German painters who, in the early 19th cent., tried to restore the quality of religious art.— Also Nazare'an, Naz'arite.

Nazarite, *naz'ə-rit, n.* a Jewish ascetic under a vow (see Numb. vi.)—also Naz'irite.—*adj.* Nazaritic (*-it'ik*).—*n.* Naz'aritism (*-it-izm*). [Heb. *nāzar,* to consecrate.]

naze, *nāz, n.* a headland or cape. [O.E. *næs;* cf. ness.]

Nazi, *nä'tsē, n.* and *adj.* for Ger. *National-sozialist,* National Socialist, Hitlerite.—*ns.* Naz'ism, Naz'iism.—*v.t.,* *v.i.* Naz'ify. [Ger.]

nazir, *nä'zir, n.* formerly, an Indian court official who served summonses, etc.: an official of various kinds. [Ar. *nāzir,* overseer.]

ne, *nē,* ni, (*obs.*) *adv.* not.—*conj.* nor. [O.E. *ne.*]

neafe, neaffe (*Shak.*). See nieve.

neal, *nēl, v.t.* and *v.i.* an aphetic form of anneal.

**Neanderthal,** *ni-an'dər-täl, adj.* of a Palaeolithic species of man whose remains were first found in 1857 in a cave in the *Neanderthal,* a valley between Düsseldorf and Elberfeld (1930, part of Wuppertal).—*n.* Nean'derthaler.—*adj.* Nean'derthaloid.

**neanic,** *nē-an'ik,* (*zool.*) *adj.* pertaining to the adolescent period in the life-history of an individual. [Gr. *neanikos,* youthful.]

**neap,** *nēp, adj.* of tides, of smallest range.—*n.* a neap tide.—*v.i.* to tend towards the neap.—*adj.* neaped, left aground between spring tides.— **neap'tide, neap tide,** a tide of minimum amplitude, occurring when the sun and moon are working against each other. [O.E. *nēp,* app. meaning helpless; *nēpflōd,* neap-tide.]

**Neapolitan,** *nē-ə-pol'i-tən, adj.* of the city or the former kingdom of Naples.—*n.* a native, citizen, or inhabitant of Naples: (without *cap.*) a small rectangular chocolate.—**Neapolitan ice,** layered combination of different ices; **Neapolitan sixth,** a chord of the subdominant with its minor third and minor sixth; **Neapolitan violet,** a scented double variety of sweet violet. [L. *Neāpolitānus*—Gr. *Neāpolis,* new town—*neos, -ā, -on,* new, *polis,* city.]

**near,** *nēr, adv.* (*orig.,* as compar. of *nigh*) nigher, more closely, to or at a shorter distance: (now as positive) to or at no great distance: close: closely: nearly: almost: narrowly: (new double *compar.* near'er; *superl.* near'est).—*prep.* close to (near'er, near'est also are *preps.*).—*adj.* nigh: not far away in place or time: close in kin, friendship, imitation, approximation, or in any relation: close, narrow, so as barely to escape: short, as a road: stingy: of horses, vehicles, etc., left, left-hand (*compar.* near'er; *superl.* near'est).—*v.t.* and *v.i.* to approach: to come nearer.—*adv.* near'ly, at or within a short distance: closely: intimately: scrutinisingly, parsimoniously: almost: approximately but rather less.—*n.* near'ness.—*adjs.* near'-begaun, near'-gaun (*Scot.*), niggardly; near'-by, neighbouring.—*adv.* (usu. near-by'), close at hand.— *prep.* (also near by), close to.—**Near East,** the countries of south-eastern Europe, as distinguished from the Middle East (Asia Minor to India) and the Far East or eastern Asia.—*adj.* near'-hand (*Scot.*), near.—*adv.* nearly.—*adj.* near'-legged (*Shak.*), walking so that the legs interfere.— **near miss** (*lit.* and *fig.*), a miss that is almost a hit; **near point,** the nearest point the eye can focus.—*adj.* near'-sight'ed, short-sighted.—*n.* near'-sight'edness.—**near as a touch, as ninepence, as dammit,** very nearly. [O.E. *nēar,* compar. of *nēah,* nigh (*adv.*), and O.N. *nǣr,* compar. (but also used as positive) of *nā,* nigh; cf. Ger. *näher.*]

**near-,** *nēr-,* in composition, almost, as *adj.* near'-white': a substitute closely resembling, as *ns.* near'-beer', near'-silk'.

**Nearctic,** *nē-ärk'tik, adj.* of the New World part of the Holarctic region. [Gr. *neos,* new *arktikos,* northern—*arktos,* bear, the Great Bear.]

**neat,** *nēt,* an ox, cow, bull, etc.—*pl.* neat.—*ns.* neat'-cattle; neat'-herd; neat'-house; neat'-stall; neat's leather, leather made of the hides of neat.—**neat's-foot oil,** an oil obtained from the feet of oxen. [O.E. *nēat,* cattle, a beast— *nēotan, niotan,* to use; cf. Scot. nowt from O.N. *naut.*]

**neat,** *nēt, adj.* clean (*obs.*): unmixed: undiluted: undiminished, net: clear, shining (*Spens.*): elegant: trim: tidy: finished, adroit: deft: well and concisely put: ingenious, effective, economical in effort or method.—*adv.* neatly.—*v.t.* neat'en, to make neat, tidy.—*adv.* neat'ly.—*n.* neat'ness.—*adj.* neat'-hand'ed, dexterous. [Fr. *net,* clean, tidy—L. *nitidus,* shining, bright— *nitēre,* to shine.]

**neath, 'neath,** *nēth,* (*dial.* and *poet.*) *prep.* beneath. [Aphetic for **aneath,** or for **beneath.**]

**neb,** *neb, n.* a beak or bill: the mouth (*obs.*): the nose: a nib: the sharp point of anything.—*v.i.* to bill.—*v.t.* to put a neb on.—*adj.* nebbed (*nebd*), having a neb. [O.E. *nebb,* beak, face; cog. with Du. *neb,* beak.]

**nebbish,** *neb'ish, n.* a colourless, insignificant, incompetent person, a perpetual victim.—Also *adj.* [Invented by H. Gardner, cartoonist.]

**nebbuk, nebek, nebeck,** *neb'ək.* Same as **nabk.**

**nebel,** *nē'bəl, n.* a Hebrew instrument, apparently a harp. [Heb. *nēbel.*]

**neb-neb,** *neb'-neb, n.* bablah pods. [Prob. an African word.]

**nebris,** *neb'ris, n.* a fawn-skin worn by Bacchus and his votaries. [Gr. *nebris.*]

**nebula,** *neb'ū-lə, n.* a little cloudiness: a slight opacity of the cornea: a liquid for spraying: a faint, misty appearance in the heavens produced either by a group of stars too distant to be seen singly, or by diffused gaseous matter:—*pl.* neb'ulae (*-lē*).—*adjs.* neb'ular, pertaining to nebulae: like or of the nature of a nebula; neb'ulé (*-lā*), neb'uly (*her.*), wavy.—*ns.* nebule (*neb'ūl*), wavy moulding; nebulisā'tion, *-z-.*—*v.t.* neb'ulise, -ize, to reduce to spray.—*ns.* nebulis'er, *-z-,* spraying apparatus, atomiser; nebu'lium, an element formerly assumed in order to explain certain lines in the spectra of gaseous nebulae—lines now known to be due to states of oxygen, and also nitrogen, not possible under earthly conditions; nebulos'ity.—*adj.* neb'ulous, hazy, vague, formless (*lit., fig.*): cloudlike: like, of the nature of, or surrounded by, a nebula.— *adv.* neb'ulously.—*n.* neb'ulousness.—**nebular hypothesis,** the theory of Laplace that the solar system was formed by the contraction and breaking up of a rotating nebula. [L. *nebula,* mist; cf. Gr. *nephelē,* cloud, mist.]

**nécessaire,** *nā-ses-er,* (Fr.) a dressing-case, work-box.

**necessary,** *nes'is-ə-ri, adj.* that must be: that cannot be otherwise: unavoidable: indispensable: enforced (*arch.*): (of agent) not free.—*n.* that which cannot be left out or done without (food, etc.)—used chiefly in *pl.*: a privy: money (*coll.*).—*n.* and *adj.* necessā'rian.—*n.* necessā'rianism, the doctrine that the will is not free, but subject to causes without, which determine its action.—*adv.* nec'essarily.—*n.* nec'essariness.— **necessary truths,** such as cannot but be true. [L. *necessārius.*]

**necessity,** *ni-ses'i-ti, n.* a state or quality of being necessary: that which is necessary or unavoidable: unavoidable compulsion: great need: poverty.—*n.* and *adj.* necessitā'rian.—*n.* necessitā'rianism, necessarianism.—*v.t.* necess'itate, to make necessary: to render unavoidable: to compel.—*n.* necessitā'tion.—*adjs.* necess'itied (*Shak.*), subject by need; necess'itous, in necessity: very poor: destitute.—*adv.* necess'itously. —*n.* necess'itousness.—**natural necessity,** the condition of being necessary according to the laws of nature, logical or mathematical, according to those of human intelligence, moral, according to those of moral law; **of necessity,** necessarily; **works of necessity,** work so necessary as to be allowable on the Sabbath. [L. *necessitās, -ātis.*]

**neck,** *nek, n.* the part connecting head and trunk (often in allusion to the halter or the yoke; *fig.*): the flesh of that part regarded as food: anything resembling that part: the part connecting head and body of anything, e.g. a violin: the plain lower part of the capital of a column: any narrow connecting part, e.g. an isthmus: anything narrow and throatlike, as the upper part of a bottle: a plug of igneous or fragmental rock filling a volcanic vent: a col: the part of a garment on or nearest the neck: a neck's

length: impudence, audacity (slang).—v.t. to strike, pull, or chop the neck of, esp. so as to kill: to catch or fasten by the neck: to embrace (slang): to make a neck on: to drink (slang). —v.i. (slang) to embrace.—n. neck'atee (obs.), a neckerchief.—adj. necked, having a neck.—ns. neck'ing, the neck of a column: a neck-moulding: embracing, petting (slang); neck'let, a simple form of necklace: a pendant strung for the neck: a small boa or fur for the neck.— neck'-band, the part of a shirt, etc., encircling the neck: a band worn on the neck; neck'beef, the coarse flesh of the neck of cattle: inferior stuff; neck'-bone, a cervical vertebra; neck'-cloth, a piece of folded cloth worn round the neck by men as a band or cravat, the ends hanging down often of lace; neck'erchief, a kerchief for the neck; neck'gear, apparel for the neck; neck'-herr'ing (obs.), a heavy blow on the neck; necking party, petting party; neck'lace (-lis, -ləs), a lace, chain, or string of beads or precious stones worn on the neck; neck'line, the boundary-line of a garment at the neck; neck'-moulding, a moulding where the capital of a column joins the shaft; neck'-piece, a piece forming, covering, or bordering a neck; neck'-sweet'bread, the thymus gland of veal or lamb; neck'tie, a scarf or band tied round the neck; neck'verse, the test of ability to read for those who claimed benefit of clergy, usually Psalm li. 1, success giving the privilege of being branded on the hand instead of hanging; neck'wear, apparel for the neck; neck'weed, hemp, source of the hangman's rope (old slang): a kind of speedwell, from its reputed medicinal virtue (U.S.).—get it in the neck, to be severely dealt with, hard hit; harden the neck, to grow more obstinate; neck and crop, completely: bodily: in a heap: summarily and unceremoniously; neck and neck, exactly equal: side by side; neck or nothing, risking everything; stick one's neck, chin, out, to put oneself at risk, expose oneself to trouble, danger, or contradiction; talk through (the back of) one's neck, to talk wildly or absurdly wide of the truth; tread on the neck of, to oppress or tyrannise over. [O.E. hnecca; Ger. nacken.]
necro-, nek'rō-, -ro', in composition, dead: dead body.—ns. necrōbiō'sis, degeneration of living tissue; necrog'rapher, an obituary writer; necrol'ater; necrol'atry, worship of, or morbid or sentimental reverence for, the dead, or dead bodies.—adjs. necrolog'ic, -al.—ns. necro'-logist; necrol'ogy, an obituary list; nec'rō-mancer, a sorcerer; nec'rōmancy, the art of revealing future events by calling up and questioning the spirits of the dead: enchantment.—adjs. necrōman'tic, -al.—adv. necrōman'-tically.—adj. necroph'agous, feeding on carrion. —ns. nec'rophile (-fīl), one who is morbidly attracted to corpses; necrophilia (-fil'), necrophilism.—adjs. necrophil'iac, -phil'ic.—ns. nec-roph'ilism, necroph'ily, a morbid liking for dead bodies.—adj. necroph'ilous.—n. necrōphō'bia, a morbid horror of corpses.—adj. necroph'orous, carrying away and burying dead bodies, as burying beetles.—ns. necrop'olis, a cemetery:— pl. -lises (-lis-əz), -leis (-līs); nec'ropsy (or -rop'), a post-mortem examination.—adjs. necrōscop'ic, -al.—n. necros'copy, a post-mortem examination, autopsy. [Gr. nekros, dead body, dead.]
necrosis, nek-rō'sis, n. death of part of the living body.—v.t. and v.i. necrose (nek-rōs'), to affect with or undergo necrosis.—adj. necrōt'ic.—v.t. and v.i. nec'rōtise, -ize, to necrose. [Gr. nekros, dead body.]
nectar, nek'tər, n. the name given by Homer, Hesiod, Pindar, etc., to the beverage of the gods, giving life and beauty: a delicious beverage: the honey of the glands of plants.—adjs. nectā'real, nectā'rean, nectā'reous, nec'tarous, of

or like nectar; nec'tared, imbued with nectar: mingled, filled, or abounding with nectar.—n. nectā'reousness.—adjs. nectā'rial, of the nature of a nectary; nectarif'erous, producing nectar; nec'tarine (-in), sweet as nectar.—n. (-ēn, -in), a variety of peach with a smooth skin.—n. nec'tary, a glandular organ that secretes nectar.—nec'tar-guide', a marking that guides insects to the nectary of a flower. [Gr. nektar; etymology dubious.]
nectocalyx, nek-tō-kā'liks, n. a hydrozoan swimming-bell:—pl. nectocā'lyces (-li-sēz). [Gr. nēktos, swimming, kalyx, shell, flower-cup.]
neddy, ned'i, n. a donkey. [From Edward.]
née, nā, (Fr.), born (fem.)—used in stating a woman's maiden name.
need, nēd, n. want of something which one cannot well do without: necessity: a state that requires relief: want of the means of living.—v.t. to have occasion for: to want: to require.— v.i. to be necessary: to be obliged to (used as an auxiliary).—ns. needcess'ity, a dialect or illiterate combination of need and necessity; need'er.—adj. need'ful, full of need: having need: needy: necessary: requisite.—adv. need'-fully.—n. need'fulness.—adv. need'ily.—n. need'i-ness.—adj. need'less, having no need (Shak.): not needed: unnecessary.—adv. need'lessly.— n. need'lessness.—adv. need'ly (Shak.), necessarily.—n. need'ment (Spens.), something needed —adv. needs, of necessity: indispensably.—adj. need'y, very poor: necessary (Shak.).—n. need'y-hood (Herrick).—need'-be, a necessity; need'-fire, fire produced by friction, to which a certain virtue is superstitiously attached: a beacon.—the needful (slang), ready money. [O.E. nēd, nied, nȳd, Du. nood, Ger. noth (mod. not).]
needle, nēd'l, n. a small, sharp instrument for sewing: any similar slender, pointed instrument, as for knitting, etching, playing gramophone records, dissection, (hooked) for crochet: suspended magnet of a compass or galvanometer: a pointer on a dial: the pointed end of a hypodermic syringe: a hypodermic injection (coll.): anything sharp and pointed: a pinnacle of rock: an obelisk: a long slender crystal: a strong beam passed through a wall as a temporary support: a long, narrow, stiff leaf: irritation (fig.).—adj. (of a contest) intensely keen and acutely critical.—v.t. to sew: pierce: penetrate: thread: pass through: underpin with needles: irritate, goad, heckle.—v.i. to pass out and in: sew.—ns. need'leful, as much thread as will serve conveniently for one threading of a needle; need'ler, a needlemaker.—adj. need'ly, like needles.—need'le-bath, a shower-bath with very fine strong jets; need'le-book, a needle-case in book form; need'le-case, a case for holding needles; need'lecord, a cotton material with closer ribs and flatter pile than corduroy; need'le-craft, the art of needlework; need'le-fish, a pipe-fish: a garpike; need'le-furze, the petty whin; need'le-gun, a gun in which the cartridge is exploded by the impact of a spike; need'le-paper, black paper used for wrapping needles; need'le-point, the point of a needle: a very sharp point: point-lace made with a needle.—adj. need'le-point'ed, pointed like a needle, round in section: without a barb, as a fish-hook.—need'le-tin, cassiterite in slender crystals; need'lewoman, a woman who does needlework: a seamstress; need'lework, work done with a needle: the business of a seamstress.—get the needle (coll.), to be irritated; give the needle to, to irritate; look for a needle in a haystack, bottle of hay, to engage in a hopeless search. [O.E. nǣdl; Ger. nadel; cog. with Ger. nähen, to sew; L. nēre, to spin.]
neeld, nēld, neele, nēl, obsolete forms of needle.
neem. Same as nim (3).

**neep**, *nēp*, (*Scot.*) *n.* a turnip. [O.E. *nǣp*—L. *nāpus.*]

**ne'er**, *nār*, *adv.* contr. of never.—*adj.* and *n.*

**ne'er'-do-well** (*Scot.* -*weel*), good-for-nothing.

**Ne'erday**, *nār'-dā*, (*chiefly Scot.*) *n.* New Year's Day: (without *cap.*) a gift on New Year's Day.

**neesberry.** Same as naseberry.

**neeze, neese,** *nēz, v.i.* and *n.* sneeze. [Cf. O.N. *hnjōsa*, and sneeze.]

**nef,** *nef, n.* a church nave (*obs.*): a mediaeval, usually shiplike, piece of plate for the great man's napkin, table utensils, etc. [Fr. *nef*, ship, nave— L. *nāvis.*]

**nefandous,** *ni-fan'dəs, adj.* abominable. [L. *nefandus*, unspeakable—*ne-*, not, *fandus*, to be spoken—*fāri*, to speak.]

**nefarious,** *ni-fā'ri-əs, adj.* extremely wicked: villainous.—*adv.* nefā'riously.—*n.* nefā'riousness. —*adj.* **nefast** (*ni-fast'*), abominable. [L. *nefārius*, *nefāstus*—*nefās*, wrong, crime—*ne-*, not, *fās*, divine law, prob. from *fāri*, to speak.]

**negate,** *ni-gāt', v.t.* to deny: nullify: imply non-existence of.—*ns.* negation (-*gā'shən*), act of saying no: denial: a negative proposition (*log.*): something that is the opposite (of a positive quality, state, etc.): a thing characterised by the absence of qualities; nega'tionist, one who merely denies, without offering any positive assertion.—*adj.* **negative** (*neg'ə-tiv*), denying: expressing denial, refusal, or prohibition—opp. to *affirmative*: denying the connection between a subject and a predicate (*log.*): lacking positive quality: failing to affirm: opposite, contrary to, neutralising, that which is regarded as positive: censorious (*U.S.*): defeatist (*U.S.*): less than nothing (*math.*): reckoned or measured in the opposite direction to that chosen as positive (*math.*): at relatively lower potential (*elect.*): of, having, or producing negative electricity (*elect.*; see below): having dark for light and light for dark (*opt., phot.*): in complementary colours (*opt., phot.*): acid (*chem.*): laevorotatory (*opt.*): having the index of refraction for the extraordinary ray less than for the ordinary in double refraction (*opt.*): in a direction away from the source of stimulus (*biol.*).—*n.* a word or statement by which something is denied: a word or grammatical form that expresses denial: a negative proposition or term: the right or act of saying no, or of refusing assent: the side of a question or the decision which denies what is affirmed: an image in which the lights and shades are reversed: a photographic plate bearing such an image: a negative quantity.—*v.t.* to prove the contrary of: to reject by vote: to veto: to reject by veto: to deny: to neutralise.—*adv.* **neg'atively.**—*ns.* **neg'ativeness;** **neg'ativism,** the doctrine or attitude of a negationist: a tendency to do the opposite of what one is asked to do; **negativ'ity,** the fact of being negative.—*adj.* **neg'atory,** expressing denial.—*n.* negatron (*neg'ə-tron*), a negative electron, as opp. to a positron.— **negative angle,** one generated by a straight line moving clockwise; **negative electricity,** electricity arising from the excess of electrons; **negative pole,** that pole of a magnet which turns to the south when the magnet swings freely; **negative proton,** an antiproton; **negative sign,** the sign (−, read *minus*) of subtraction. [L. *negāre*, -*ātum*, to deny.]

**neglect,** *ni-glekt', v.t.* to treat carelessly: to pass by without notice: to omit by carelessness: to fail to bestow due care upon.—*n.* disregard: slight: omission: uncared-for state.—*adj.* **neglect'able** (*rare*), negligible.—*ns.* **neglect'edness; neglect'er.**—*adj.* **neglect'ful,** careless: accustomed to omit or neglect things: slighting. —*adv.* **neglect'fully.**—*n.* **neglect'fulness.**—*adv.* **neglect'ingly,** carelessly: heedlessly.—*n.* **neglection** (-*glek'shən*; *Shak.*), negligence.—*adj.*

**neglect'ive** (now *rare*), neglectful. [L. *neglegĕre*, *neglectum*—*neg-* or *nec-*, not, *legĕre*, to gather.]

**négligé,** *nā'glē-zhā, n.* easy undress.—*adj.* carelessly or unceremoniously dressed: careless.—*n.*

**negligee** (*neg'li-jē, neg'li-zhā*), a loose gown worn by women in the 18th century: a woman's loose decorative dressing-gown of flimsy material: a necklace, usually of red coral. [Fr., neglected.]

**negligence,** *neg'li-jəns, n.* fact or quality of being negligent: want of proper care: habitual neglect: an act of carelessness or neglect (*arch.*): a slight: carelessness about dress, manner, etc.: omission of duty, esp. such care for the interests of others as the law may require.—*adj.* **neg'li-gent,** neglecting: careless: inattentive: disregarding ceremony or fashion.—*adv.* **neg'li-gently.**—*n.* **negligibil'ity.**—*adj.* **neg'ligible** (sometimes **neg'ligeable**), such as may be ignored because very little or very unimportant.—*adv.* **neg'ligibly.** [L. *negligentia* for *neglegentia* —*neglegĕre*, to neglect.]

**negotiate,** *ni-gō'shi-āt, v.i.* to traffic: to bargain: to confer for the purpose of mutual arrangement.—*v.t.* to arrange for by agreement: to manage: to transfer or exchange for value: to cope with successfully (*coll.*).—*n.* **negotiabil'ity.** —*adj.* **nego'tiable.**—*ns.* **negotiā'tion;** **nego'tiātor;** —*fem.* **nego'tiatress** (-*shyə-*), **negotiatrix** (*ni-gō'shyə-triks,* or *ni-gō-shi-ā'triks*). [L. *negōtiārī,* -*ātus*—*negōtium*, business—*neg-*, not, *ōtium,* leisure.]

**Negrillo,** *ni-gril'ō, n.* an African Negrito:—*pl.* **Negrill'os.** [Sp., dim. of *negro*, black.]

**Negrito,** *ni-grē'tō, n.* a member of any of a number of pygmy negroid peoples of S.-E. Asia and Africa:—*pl.* **Negri'tos.** [Sp., dim. of *negro*, black.]

**negritude, négritude.** See Negro.

**Negro,** *nē'grō, n.* a member of the black-skinned race of mankind in Africa or originating in Africa, esp. one characterised by woolly hair, protruding lips and a broad, flat nose:—*pl.* **Negroes.**—*adj.* of or pertaining to Negroes.— *ns.* **Ne'gress** (sometimes *derog.*), a Negro woman or girl; **nē'gritude,** translation of French négritude (J. P. Sartre), the essential quality of the Negro genius.—Also **nigritude.**—*adj.* **ne'groid,** of Negro type: like a Negro.—*n.* one who is of Negro type: one who is a Negro in a broad sense only.—*adj.* **negroid'al.**—*ns.* **ne'grōism,** any peculiarity of speech among Negroes, esp. in the southern U.S.: devotion to the cause of the Negroes; **ne'grophil, ne'grophile,** a friend of the Negro, and a supporter of his cause; **negrophilism** (*ni-grof'*); **negroph'ilist; ne'grophobe,** one who dislikes Negroes; **negropho'bia.**—**ne'gro-corn** (*W.Indies*), durra; **ne'grohead,** tobacco soaked in molasses and pressed into cakes, so called from its blackness: an inferior rubber. [Sp. *negro*—L. *niger, nigra, nigrum*, black.]

**negus,** *nē'gəs, n.* port or sherry with hot water, sweetened and spiced. [Said to be from Colonel *Negus,* its first maker, in Queen Anne's time.]

**negus,** *nē'gəs, n.* the king of Abyssinia. [Amharic.]

**neif.** Same as nieve.

**neigh,** *nā, v.i.* to utter the cry of a horse.—*n.* the cry of a horse. [O.E. *hnǣgan.*]

**neighbour,** *nā'bər, n.* a person who dwells near another: a person or thing that is near another: one of a pair (*Scot.*).—*adj.* (*arch.* and *U.S.*) neighbouring.—*v.t.* and *v.i.* to live or be near.— *n.* **neigh'bourhood,** state of being neighbours, kindly feeling: a set of neighbours: a district, esp. with reference to its inhabitants: a district: a region lying near: a near position: nearness: all the points that surround a given point in a specified degree of closeness (*math.*).—*adj.* **neigh'bouring,** being near: adjoining.—*n.* **neigh'-bourliness.**—*adj.* **neigh'bourly,** like or becoming a neighbour: friendly: social.—Also *adv.*—*adj.*

neigh'bour-stained (*Shak.*), stained with neighbours' blood.—good neighbours, the fairies; in the neighbourhood of, approximately, somewhere about. [O.E. *nēahgebūr*—*nēah*, near, *gebūr* or *būr*, a farmer.]

neist, *nēst*, a dialectal form of nighest, next.

neither, *nī'dhər*, or *nē'dhər*, *adj.* and *pron.* not either.—*conj.* not either: and not: nor yet.— *adv.* not at all: in no case. [O.E. *nāther*, *nāwther*, abbrev. of *nāhwæther*—*nā*, never, *hwæther*, whether; the vowel assimilated to either.]

neive. Same as nieve.

nek, *nek*, (*S.Afr.*) *n.* a col. [Du., neck.]

nekton, *nek'ton*, *n.* the assemblage of actively swimming organisms in a sea, lake, etc. [Gr. *nēkton* (neut.), swimming.]

nelis, nelies, *nel'is*, *n.* a winter pear:—*pl.* nel'is, nel'ies. [Fr. *nélis*.]

nellie, nelly, not on your (*nel'i*; *slang*), not on any account—said to be from *not on your Nellie Duff*, rhyming with *puff*, meaning 'life'.

nelly, *nel'i*, *n.* a large petrel. [Perh. the woman's name.]

nelson, *nel'sən*, *n.* a wrestling hold in which the arms are passed under the opponent's arms, and the hands joined at the back of his neck.

Nelumbium, *ni-lum'bi-əm*, Nelumbo, *-bō*, *ns.* a genus of water-lilies including the Egyptian bean of Pythagoras, and the sacred lotus. [Prob. Tamil.]

Nemathelminthes, *nem-ə-thel-min'thēz*, *n.pl.* according to some, a group including nematodes, Nematomorpha, and Acanthocephala.—*n.sing.* nemathel'minth.—*adj.* nemathelmin'thic. [Gr. *nēma*, *-atos*, a thread, *helmins*, *-minthos*, worm.]

nematocyst, *nem'ət-ō-sist*, or *-at'*, *n.* a stinging organ in jellyfishes, etc., a sac from which a stinging thread can be everted. [Gr. *nēma*, *-atos*, a thread, *kystis*, a bladder.]

nematode, *nem'ə-tōd*, *n.* a round-worm or thread-worm.—Also *adj.*—*ns.pl.* Nematōd'a, Nematoid'ea, the nematodes.—*adj.* nem'atoid. [Gr. *nēma*, *-atos*, thread, *eidos*, form.]

Nematomorpha, *nem-ət-ō-mör'fə*, *n.pl.* the hairworms. [Gr. *nēma*, *-atos*, thread, *morphē*, form.]

nematophore, *nem'ət-ō-fōr*, *-för*, *n.* a mouthless type of hydrozoan polyp that engulfs food by pseudopodia. [Gr. *nēma*, *-atos*, thread, *phoros*, carrying.]

Nembutal, *nem'bū-təl*, *n.* proprietary name for sodium ethylmethylbutyl barbiturate, used as a sedative, hypnotic, and antispasmodic.

Nemean, *nem-ē'ən*, *nem'i-ən*, *nēm'i-ən*, *adj.* of Nemea (Gr. *Nēmēä*), valley of Argolis, famous for its games held in the second and fourth years of each Olympiad, and for the lion slain by Herakles.

Nemertinea, *nem-ər-tin'i-ə*, *n.pl.* a phylum of worm-like animals mostly marine, ciliated, often brightly coloured with protrusile proboscis.— Also Nemer'tea.—*ns.* and *adjs.* nemer'tean, nemer'tine, nemer'tian. [Gr. *Nēmertēs*, one of the nereids.]

Nemesia, *nem-ē'zh(y)ə*, *-sh(y)ə*, *-si-ə*, *n.* a S. African genus of the figwort family, including some brightly coloured garden flowers. [Gr. *nemesion*, a kind of catchfly.]

Nemesis, *nem'i-sis*, (*myth.*) *n.* the Greek goddess of retribution: (without *cap.*) retributive justice. [Gr. *nemesis*, retribution—*nemein*, to deal out, dispense.]

nemine contradicente, *nem'ə-nē kon-trə-di-sen'tē*, *nä'mi-ne kon-trä-dē-ken'te*, (L.; often abbrev. nem. con.) without opposition: no one speaking in opposition; nemine dissentiente (*di-sen-shi-en'tē*, *-ti-en'te*), no one dissenting.

Nemophila, *nem-of'i-lə*, *n.* a N. American genus of Hydrophyllaceae, favourite garden annuals,

esp. one with blue, white-centred flowers. [Gr. *nemos*, a glade, wooded pasture, *phileein*, to love.]

nemoral, *nem'ə-rəl*, *adj.* of a wood or grove.— *adj.* nem'orous, wooded. [L. *nemus*, *-ōris*, a grove.]

nempt, nemt, (*Spens.*) named, called:—*pa.p.* of obs. nemn, to name. [O.E. *nemnan*.]

nenuphar, *nen'ū-fär*, *n.* a water-lily, esp. the common white or yellow: (*cap.*) a synonym of Nuphar. [L.L. *nenuphar*—Ar. and Pers. *nīnūfar*, *nīlūfar*—Sans. *nīlotpala*—*nīla*, blue, *utpala*, lotus.]

Neo, *nē'ō*, *nä'ō*, *n.* an artificial language launched by an Italian in 1960.

neo-, *nē'ō-*, in composition, new, young, revived in a new form.—*adj.* and *n.* Neo-Cath'olic, of, or a member of the school of, liberal Catholicism that followed Lamennais, Lacordaire and Montalembert about 1830: Anglo-Catholic with extreme leanings towards Rome.—*adj.* and *n.* Neo-Chris'tian, of, or a believer in, a liberalised and rationalised Christianity.—*n.* Neo-Christian'-ity.—*adjs.* neoclass'ic, -al, belonging to a revival of classicism, or classicism as understood by those who would revive it, e.g. in the 18th century.—*ns.* neoclass'icism (*-i-sizm*); neoclass'i-cist; neocolōn'ialism, the policy of a strong nation of obtaining control over a weaker through economic pressure, etc.—*adj.* and *n.* Neocom'ian (*-kō'mi-ən*; *geol.*; L. *Neocōmium*, Neuchâtel—Gr. *kōmē*, a village), Lower Cretaceous.—*n.* Neo-Dar'winism, a later development of Darwinism, laying greater stress upon natural selection and denying the inheritance of acquired characters.—*ns.* and *adjs.* Neo-Darwin'-ian; Neo-Dar'winist.—*ns.* neodymium, (*-dim'i-əm*) a metal (Nd; at. numb. 60), the chief component of the once-supposed element *didymium*; Neogaea, (*-jē'ə*; *biol.*; Gr. *gaia*, the earth), the Neotropical region.—*adj.* Neogae'an.—*n.* and *adj.* Neogene (*-jēn*; *geol.*; Gr. *neogenēs*, new-born), Miocene and Pliocene.—*n.* and *adj.* Neo-Goth'ic, revived Gothic of the 19th century.—*ns.* neogrammā'rian, philologist of the 19th-century German school that introduced scientific exactitude into the study of sound change; Neohell'enism, the modern Hellenism inspired by the ancient: the devotion to ancient Greek ideals in literature and art, esp. in the Italian Renaissance; Neo-Impress'ionism, a style of painting which aimed at producing greater luminosity of colour by applying pure unmixed colours in small dots; Neo-Kant'ian-ism, the philosophy of *Kant* as taught by his successors.—*n.* and *adj.* Neo-Kan'tian.—*n.* Neo-Lamarck'ism, a modern adaptation of Lamarck-ism.—*n.* and *adj.* Neo-Lamarck'ian.—*n.* and *adj.* Neo-Lat'in, Romance, i.e. Italian, Rhaeto-Romanic, French, Provençal, Spanish, Portuguese, and Rumanian.—*adj.* Neolithic (*-lith'ik*; Gr. *lithos*, a stone), of the later or more advanced Stone Age—opp. to *Palaeolithic*.—*ns.* ne'olith, a Neolithic artefact; neol'ogy (Gr. *logos*, a word), the introduction of new words, or new senses of old words: a neologism: new doctrines, esp. German rationalism (*theol.*); neolō'gian.—*adjs.* neologic (*-loj'*), -al.—*adv.* neolog'ically.—*v.i.* neol'ogise, -ize, to introduce new words or doctrines.—*ns.* neol'ogism, a new word, phrase, or doctrine: the use of old words in a new sense; neol'ogist.—*adjs.* neologis'tic, -al.—*ns.* Neo-Malthus'ianism, doctrine of the necessity for birth-control to control population; Neo-Melanē'sian, a language based on English, developed in Melanesia; neomycin (*-mi'sin*; Gr. *mykēs*, a fungus), an antibiotic effective against certain infections, esp. infections of the skin, eyes.—*adj.* neonāt'al, pertaining to the newly born.—*adj.* and *n.* ne'onate, (one) newly born. — *ns.* neonō'mianism (Gr. *nomos*, law), the doctrine that the gospel is a new law and that faith has abrogated the old moral obedience; **neonō'mian; neopā'ganism**, a revival of paganism, or its spirit.—*n*. and *adj*. **neopa'gan.**—*v.t.*, *v.i*. **neopa'ganise, -ize**.—*ns*. **neophobia** (-*fō'bi-ə*); Gr. *phobos*, fear), dread of novelty; **neophyte** (*nē'ō-fīt*; Gr. *neophytos*, newly planted—*phyein*, to produce), a new convert: one newly baptised: a newly ordained priest: a novice in a religious order: a tiro or beginner.—*adj*. **neophytic** (-*fīt'ik*).—*ns*. **Neopilina** (-*pil-i'nə*; *Pilina*, a Palaeolithic genus of similar appearance), a genus of Monoplacophora (q.v.); **neo'plasm** (Gr. *plasma*, form, mould), a morbid new growth or formation of tissue.—*adj*. **neoplas'tic**.—*ns*. **Neo-Plas'ticism** (or **neoplasticism**), a style of abstract painting in which geometrical patterns are formed of patches of flat colour enclosed by intersecting vertical and horizontal lines (see **plastic**); **Neoplā'tonism**, a combination of Platonism with Oriental elements, developed by Plotinus, Porphyry, Proclus, etc.—*adj*. **Neoplatonic** (-*plə-ton'ik*).—*n*. **neoplā'tonist**; **neoprene** (*nē'ō-prēn*), an oil-resisting and heat-resisting synthetic rubber made by polymerising chloroprene; **Neopythagorē'anism**, a revived Pythagoreanism of Alexandria beginning in the first century B.C.—*n*. and *adj*. **Neopythagorē'an**.—*ns*. **neoteny, neoteinia** (*nē-ot'ən-i*; *nē-ō-ti'ni-ə*; Gr. *teinein*, to stretch), prolonged retention of larval or immature character or characters.—*adjs*. **neotenic** (*nē-ō-ten'ik*), -**tein'ic**; **Neotrop'ical** (*biol*.), of tropical America.—*ns*. **neovi'talism**, the theory or belief that complete causal explanation of vital phenomena cannot be reached without invoking some extra-material concept; **neovi'talist**.—*adj*. **Neozoic**, (*nē-ō-zō'ik*; Gr. *zōikos*, of animals), later than Palaeozoic: later than Mesozoic. [Gr. *neos*, new.]

**neon**, *nē'on*, *n*. a gas (Ne; at. numb. 10) found in the atmosphere by Sir Wm. Ramsay (1852-1916).—**neon lamp, light**, an electric discharge lamp containing neon, giving a red glow, used e.g. for advertising signs: loosely, one of a variety of tubular fluorescent lamps giving light of various colours; **neon lighting**. [Neuter of Gr. *neos*, new.]

**neoteric, -al**, *nē-ō-ter'ik*, -*əl*, *adjs*. of recent origin, modern.—*adv*. **neoter'ically**.—*v.i*. **neoterise, -ize** (*ni-ot'ə-rīz*).—*ns*. **neot'erism**, the introduction of new things, esp. new words; **neot'erist**. [Gr. *neōterikos—neōteros*, comp. of *neos*, new.]

**Neotropical** . . . to . . . **Neozoic**. See **neo-**.

**nep, nep, nip**, *nip*, *n*. catmint. [L. *nepeta*.]

**nepenthe**, *ni-pen'thē*, *n*. a sorrow-lulling drink or drug (*poet*.): the plant yielding it.—*adj*. **nepen'thean**.—*n*. **Nepen'thes** (-*thēz*), nepenthe: the pitcher-plant genus, constituting a family **Nepenthā'ceae** akin to the Sarracenias and sundews. [Gr. *nepenthēs*, -*es*—pfx. *nē*-, not, *penthos*, grief.]

**neper**, *nā'pər*, *nē'*, *n*. a unit for expressing the ratio of two currents, or two voltages, etc., the number of nepers being equal to the natural logarithm of the ratio. (Cf. **decibel, bel.**) [John *Napier*; see **Napierian**.]

**nephalism**, *nef'ə-lizm*, *n*. total abstinence from alcoholic drinks.—*n*. **neph'alist**. [Gr. *nēphalios*, sober; *nēphein*, to be sober.]

**nepheline**, *nef'ə-lēn*, *n*. a rock-forming mineral, silicate of sodium, potassium, and aluminium, colourless, usually crystallising in hexagonal prisms.—Also **neph'elite**.—*n*. **neph'elinite**, a basalt-like rock compound of nepheline and pyroxene, with no feldspar or olivine.—**neph'elinebas'alt**, a basalt with nepheline instead of (or in addition to) feldspar. [Gr. *nephelē*, a cloud (from the effect of acid).]

**nephelometer**, *nef-ə-lom'i-tər*, *n*. an instrument for measuring cloudiness, esp. in liquids.—*adj*.

**nephelomet'ric**. [Gr. *nephelē*, cloud, *metron*, measure.]

**nephew**, *nev'ū*, or *nef'ū*, *n*. the son of a brother or sister: extended to a like relation by marriage: a grandson or descendant (*obs*.): a pope's or priest's son (*euphemistically*):—*fem*. **niece**. [(O.)Fr. *neveu*—L. *nepōs, nepōtis*, grandson; cf. O.E. *nefa*, Ger. *neffe*, nephew.]

**nepho-, nef-o-, -ō-**, in composition, cloud.—*ns*. **neph'ograph** (-*gräf*), an instrument for photographing clouds in order to determine their position; **nephology** (*nef-ol'ə-ji*), the study of clouds in meteorology.—*adjs*. **nephologic** (-*ə-loj'*) -**al**.—*ns*. **nephol'ogist; neph'ōscope**, an apparatus which determines the altitude, and direction and velocity of movement, of clouds. [Gr. *nephos*, cloud, *logos*, discourse.]

**nephr(o)-, nef-ro-, -rō-**, in composition, kidney.—*ns*. **nephralgia** (*nef-ral'ji-ə*), **nephral'gy**, pain in the kidneys; **nephrec'tomy**, surgical removal of a kidney.—*adj*. **neph'ric**.—*ns*. **nephrid'ium**, in invertebrates and lower chordates, an organ serving the function of a kidney; **neph'rite**, the mineral jade, in the narrower sense—an old charm against kidney disease; **nephrit'ic**, a medicine for the kidneys, or nephritis, or jade.—*adjs*. **nephrit'ic, -al**, pertaining to the kidneys, or nephritis, or jade. —*n*. **nephri'tis**, inflammation of the kidneys.— *adj*. **neph'roid**, kidney-shaped.—*ns*. **nephrol'ogist; nephrology**, the science concerned with structure, functions, diseases, of the kidneys; **neph'ropexy** (Gr. *pēxis*, fixing), fixation of a floating kidney; **nephropto'sis** (Gr. *ptōsis*, fall), floating kidney; **nephrō'sis**, a disease of the kidney characterised by non-inflammatory degeneration of the tubules; **nephrot'omy**, incision into the kidney. [Gr. *nephros*, a kidney.]

**nepionic**, *nep'i-on-ik*, *nēp'i-on-ik*, (*biol*.) *adj*. pertaining to the embryonic period in the life-history of an individual. [Gr. *nēpios*, infant.]

**ne plus ultra**, *nē plus ul'tra, nā ploos ōol'trä*, (L.) nothing further: the uttermost point or extreme perfection of anything.

**nepotism**, *nep'o-tizm*, *n*. undue patronage to one's relations, esp. by a pope.—*adj*. **nepot'ic**.—*n*. **nep'otist**. [L. *nepōs, nepōtis*, a grandson.]

**Neptune**, *nep'tūn*, *n*. the Roman sea-god, identified with the Greek Poseidon: a remote planet of the solar system, discovered in 1846.—*adj*. **Neptū'nian**, pertaining to Neptune or to the sea: formed by water (*geol*.).—*n*. an inhabitant of Neptune: a Neptunist.—*ns*. **Nep'tūnist**, a believer in the origin of rocks generally as chemical precipitates from the sea—opp. to **Plutonist** or **Vulcanist**; **neptū'nium**, an element (Np; at. numb. 93) named as next after uranium, as Neptune is next after Uranus. [L. *Neptūnus*.]

**nereid**, *nē'rē-id*, *n*. a sea-nymph, or daughter of the sea-god *Nereus* (Gr. *myth*.): a marine polychaete worm (**Nereis**, or kindred genus) superficially like a long myriapod. [Gr. *nērēis* or *nērēis—Nēreus*.]

**Nerine**, *ni-ri'nē*, *n*. a South African amaryllid genus, with scarlet or rose-coloured flowers, including the Guernsey lily. [L. *nērinē*, a nereid.]

**Nerita**, *ni-ri'tə*, *n*. a round-shelled genus of gasteropods of warm seas.—*n*. **nerite** (*nē'rīt*), a sea-snail of the genus Nerita or its family **Nerit'idae**.—*adj*. **neritic** (*nē-rit'ik*), belonging to the shallow waters near land.—*n*. **Neritina** (*ner-it-i'nə*), a brackish and freshwater genus akin to Nerita. [Gr. *nērēitēs, nēritēs*, a sea-snail (of various kinds).]

**Nerium**, *nē'ri-əm*, *n*. the oleander genus. [Latinised from Gr. *nērion*.]

**nerka**, *nûr'ka*, *n*. the sockeye salmon. [Origin unknown.]

**Nernst**, *närnst*, *adj*. invented by or due to the German chemist and physicist Walter *Nernst*

(1864-1941), applied esp. to an electric lamp with a filament or rod of rare-earth oxides whose conductivity is greatly increased by heating.

**nero-antico,** *nā-rō-an-tē′kō, n.* a deep-black marble found in Roman ruins. [It., black ancient.]

**neroli,** *ner′ə-lē, n.* an oil distilled from orange flowers. [Said to be named from its discoverer, an Italian princess.]

**Neronian,** *nē-rō′ni-ən, adj.* pertaining to Nero, Roman emperor from A.D. 54 to 68: excessively cruel and tyrannical.—*adj.* **Neronic** (-*ron′ik*). [L. *Nērō, -ōnis.*]

**nerve,** *nûrv, n.* a sinew (now chiefly *fig.*): a bowstring (*poet.*): strength: a cord that conveys impulses between the brain or other centre and some part of the body (*anat.*): a leaf-vein or rib (*bot.*): a nervure in an insect's wing (*entom.*): a vault rib: self-possession: cool courage: impudent assurance, audacity (*coll.*): (in *pl.*) nervousness.—*v.t.* to give strength, resolution, or courage to.—*adjs.* **nerv′al,** of the nerves; **ner′vate,** (of leaf) having veins: nerved.—*ns.* **nervā′tion, nerv′ature,** disposition of nerves, esp. in leaves.—*adjs.* **nerved,** furnished with nerves; **nerve′less,** without nerves or nervures: without strength: inert: slack, flabby: unnerved.—*ns.* **nerve′lessness; nerve′let,** a little nerve: a tendril; **nerv′er,** one who, or that which, nerves.—*adj.* **nerv′ine** (-*ēn, -īn*), acting on the nerves: quieting nervous excitement.—*n.* a medicine that soothes nervous excitement.—*n.* **nerv′iness.**—*adj.* **nerv′ous,** having nerve: sinewy: strong, vigorous, showing strength and vigour: pertaining to the nerves: having the nerves easily excited or weak, agitated and apprehensive: shy: in a jumpy state.—*adv.* **nerv′ously.**—*n.* **nerv′ousness.** —*adj.* **nerv′ūlar.**—*ns.* **nerv′ūle,** a small branch of a nervure; **nervūrā′tion; nerv′ure,** a leaf-vein: a chitinous strut or rib supporting and strengthening an insect's wing (*entom.*): a rib of a groined vault.—*adj.* **nerv′y,** nervous: cool: calling for nerve: jumpily excited or excitable. —**nerve′-cell,** any cell forming part of the nervous system; **nerve′-cen′tre,** an aggregation of nerve-cells from which nerves branch out: in an organisation, the centre from which control is exercised (*fig.*); **nerve′-end′, -end′ing,** the free end of a nerve, generally with accessory parts forming an end-organ; **nerve′-fi′bre,** an axon; **nerve gas,** any of a number of gases, prepared for use in war, having a deadly effect on the nervous system, esp. on nerves controlling respiration.—*adj.* **nerve′-rack′ing,** distressfully straining the nerves.—**nervous breakdown,** loose term indicating nervous debility following prolonged mental or physical fatigue: euphemism for any mental illness; **nervous system,** the brain, spinal cord, and nerves collectively.—**get on one's nerves,** to become oppressively irritating; **war of nerves,** (see **war**). [L. *nervus,* sinew; cf. Gr. *neuron.*]

**nescience,** *nesh′i-əns, nesh′əns, nes′i-əns, -yəns, n.* want of knowledge.—*adj.* **nesc′ient.** [L. *nescientia*—*nescīre,* to be ignorant—*ne-,* not, *scīre,* to know.]

**nesh,** *nesh, (dial.) adj.* soft, crumbly: tender.— —*n.* **nesh′ness.** [O.E. *hnesce.*]

**Neshki, Neski,** *nes′ki, n.* cursive handwriting. [Ar. *naskhī.*]

**Nesiot, Nēsiōt,** *nē′si-ōt, (anthrop.) n.* an Indonesian. [Gr. *nēsiōtēs,* an islander—*nēsos,* an island.]

**ness,** *nes, n.* a headland. [O.E. *næs, næss.*]

**nest,** *nest, n.* a structure prepared for egg-laying, brooding, and nursing, or as a shelter: a place of retreat, resort, residence, or lodgment: a den: a comfortable residence: a place where anything teems, prevails, or is fostered: the occupants of a nest, as a brood, a swarm, a gang: a set of things (as boxes, tables) fitting one within

another: a set of buildings, as advance factories, divided into blocks and units: an accumulation: a tangled mass.—*v.i.* to build or occupy a nest: to go bird's-nesting.—*v.t.* and *v.i.* to lodge, settle.—**nest′-egg,** an egg, real or sham, left or put in a nest to encourage laying: something laid up as the beginning of an accumulation: money saved; **nest′ing-box,** a box set up for birds to nest in; **nest′ing-place.**— **feather one's nest** (see **feather**). [O.E. *nest*; Ger. *nest,* L. *nīdus.*]

**nestle,** *nes′l, v.i.* to nest (*arch.*): to lie or press close or snug as in a nest: to settle comfortably or half hidden.—*v.t.* to cherish, as a bird does her young: to thrust close: to provide a nesting-place.—*n.* **nestling** (*nes′ling*), a young bird in the nest.—also *adj.* [O.E. *nestlian*—*nest.*]

**Nestor,** *nes′tör, -tər, n.* an old king of Pylos, a Greek hero at Troy remarkable for eloquence, wisdom, and long life: an old counsellor: an old man: the kea parrot genus. [Gr. *Nestor.*]

**Nestorian,** *nes-tō′ri-ən, -tō′, adj.* pertaining to Nestorius, patriarch of Constantinople (428-31), or to his teaching, that the divinity and humanity of Christ were not united in a single self-conscious personality.—*n.* a follower of Nestorius.—*n.* **Nesto′rianism.**

**net,** *net, n.* an open fabric, knotted into meshes: a piece or bag, or a screen or structure, of such fabric used for catching fish, butterflies, etc., carrying parcels, stopping balls, retaining back-hair, excluding pests: a network: machine-made lace of various kinds: a snare: a difficulty: a let (*lawn-tennis*): the shape of a three-dimensional figure when laid out flat (*math.*).— *adj.* of or like net or network.—*v.t.* to form into network: to mark or cover with network: to set with nets: to fish with nets: to form by making network: to take with a net: to capture: to send into the net.—*v.i.* to form network:— *pr.p.* **nett′ing;** *pa.t.* and *pa.p.* **nett′ed.**—*n.* **net′ful,** enough to fill a net.—*adj.* **nett′ed,** made into a net: reticulated: caught in a net: covered with a net.—*n.* **nett′ing,** act or process of forming network: a piece of network: any network of ropes or wire.—*adj.* **nett′y,** like a net.—**net′ball,** a game in which the ball is thrown into a net hung from a pole; **net′-cord,** a string supporting a lawn-tennis net; **net′-fish,** any fish, like the herring, usually caught in nets—opp. to *trawl-fish* and *line-fish*; **net′-fish′ery,** a place for net-fishing: the business of net-fishing; **net′-fishing,** fishing with nets; **net′-play,** play near the net; **net′-player; net′-prac′tice,** cricket practice with nets; **nett′ing-need′le,** a kind of shuttle used in netting.—*adjs.* **net′-veined,** having veins that branch and meet in a network; **net′-winged,** having net-veined wings.—**net′work,** any structure in the form of a net: a system of lines, e.g. railway lines, resembling a net: system of units, as, e.g. buildings, agencies, groups of persons, constituting a widely spread organisation and having a common purpose: an arrangement of electrical components: a system of stations connected for broadcasting the same programme (*radio* and *TV*).—**dance in a net,** to act in imagined concealment. [O.E. *net, nett;* Du. *net,* Ger. *netz.*]

**net, nett,** *net, adj.* clean (*obs.*): bright (*obs.*): unmixed, pure (*obs.*): neat, trim (*rare*): clear of all charges or deductions—opp. to *gross*: of weight, not including that of packaging: lowest, subject to no further deductions.—*v.t.* to gain or produce as clear profit:—*pr.p.* **nett′ing;** *pa.t.* and *pa.p.* **nett′ed.** [neat.]

**nete,** *nē′tē, (Gr. mus.) n.* the highest string or note of the lyre. [Gr. *nētē* or *neatē* (*chordē*), lit. lowest (string).]

**netheless,** *nedh′(ə-)les, adv.* Spens. for **nathless.**

**nether,** *nedh′ər, adj.* lower.—*n.pl.* **neth′erlings**

(*Dickens*), stockings.—*adjs.* neth′ermore (*rare*), lower; neth′ermost, lowest.—*advs.* neth′erward, -s, (*rare*) downwards.—neth′erstock (*hist.*), a stocking. [O.E. *neothera*, adj.—*nither*, adv., from the root *ni*-, down; Ger. *nieder*, low.]

**Netherlander**, *nedh′ər-land-ər, n.* an inhabitant of the *Netherlands* or Low Countries, now Holland, formerly also Belgium.—*adj.* Neth′erlandish, Dutch.

**Nethinim**, *neth′in-im, n.pl.* the old Jewish temple servants. [Heb. *něthinim*.]

**netsuke**, *net′skē, skă, ne′tsoō-ke′, n.* a small Japanese carved ornament, used to fasten small objects to a sash. [Jap.]

**nettle**, *net′l, n.* a common weed (Urtica) with stinging hairs.—*v.t.* to sting: to sting with annoyance.—nett′le-cell, a nematocyst; nett′le-cloth, cloth of nettle-fibre: thick japanned cotton; nett′le-fish, a jellyfish; nett′lerash, a rash of red or white weals with irritation like nettle-stings; nett′le-tree, a tree (Celtis) of the elm family, with nettle-shaped leaves, edible drupes, and wood good for turning: a tropical and Australian genus (Laportea) of the nettle family, with virulently stinging leaves.—dead-nettle, hemp-nettle (see dead, hemp). [O.E. *netele*; Ger. *nessel*.]

**nettle.** Same as knittle.

**neuk**, *nūk, nük,* a Scots form of nook.

**neume**, *nūm, n.* in mediaeval music, a succession of notes sung to one syllable: a sign giving a rough indication of rise or fall of pitch.—Also **neum.** [O.Fr.,—Gr. *pneuma,* breath.]

**neur-,** *nūr-,* **neuro-,** *nū′rō-,* in composition, pertaining to a nerve-cell, to a nerve-fibre, to nerve-tissue, or to the nervous system (esp. the brain and spinal cord): pertaining to the nerves and some other system (e.g. *adj.* neurovas′cular): concerned with, dealing with, the nervous system (e.g. neuroanat′omist, -anat′omy; neurobiol′ogy; neuropsychi′atry; neurosur′geon, -sur′-gery).—*adj.* neu′ral, of, or relating to, nerves: dorsal (opp. to *haemal*).—*n.* neuralgia (*nū-ral′jə, -jyə;* Gr. *algos,* pain), paroxysmal intermittent pain along the course of a nerve: pain of a purely nervous character.—*adj.* neural′gic.—*ns.* neurasthenia (*nū-ras-thē′ni-ə;* Gr. *astheneia,* weakness), nervous debility; neurasthē′niac, one suffering from neurasthenia.—*adj.* neurasthenic (*-then′ik,* or *-thēn′ik*).—Also *n.* a neurastheniac. —*ns.* neurā′tion, nervation; neurilemm′a, neurolemm′a (Gr. *eilēma,* covering), the external sheath of a nerve-fibre; neuril′ity, the essential character of nerve; neur′ine (*-ēn, -in, -īn*), a very poisonous ptomaine formed in putrefying flesh. —*adj.* neuritic (*-it′ik*), relating to, of the nature of, or having, neuritis,—*n.* one suffering from neuritis.—*ns.* neuri′tis, inflammation of a nerve; neurog′lia (Gr. *gliă,* glue), the supporting tissue of the brain and spinal cord, etc.; neurohypnol′ogy, neurypnol′ogy, old names for the science of hypnotism.—*adj.* neurolog′ical.—*ns.* neurol′-ogist; neurol′ogy, study of the nervous system; neurol′ysis, breaking down of nerve tissue, or exhaustion of a nerve; neurōm′a, a tumour consisting of nerve tissue; neu′ron, neu′rone, a nerve-cell with its processes; neur′opath (*-path;* Gr. *pathos,* suffering), one whose nervous system is diseased or abnormal.—*adjs.* neuropathic (*-path′*), -al.—*ns.* neuropathist (*nū-rop′ə-thist*), a specialist in nervous diseases; neuropathol′ogy, the pathology of the nervous system; neurop′-athy, nervous disease generally; neur′oplasm, the protoplasm of a nerve cell; neurō′sis, *orig.,* nervous activity, distinguished from or associated with mental: functional derangement through disordered nervous system, esp. without lesion of parts: mental disturbance characterised by a state of unconscious conflict, usually accompanied by anxiety and obsessional

fears (also called *psychoneurosis*): loosely, an obsession:—*pl.* neurōses (*-sēz*).—*adj.* neurotic (*-rot′ik*), of the nature of, characterised by, or affected by, neurosis: loosely, obsessive: hyper-sensitive.—*n.* a person with neurosis: a medicine for nerve diseases (*arch.*).—*ns.* neurot′icism (*-sizm*); neurotox′in, a substance poisonous to nerve-tissue.—*adj.* neurotrop′ic, having a special affinity for nerve cells.—neural arch, the arch of a vertebra protecting the spinal cord. [Gr. *neuron,* a nerve.]

**Neuroptera,** *nū-rop′tə-rə, n.* a former order of insects, comprising those now placed in a super-order, **Neuropteroidea** (*nū-rop-tə-roi′di-ə*), the insects have generally four net-veined wings—alder-flies, snake-flies, lace-wings, etc.—*adj.* neurop′terous.—*n.* neurop′terist, a student of the Neuropteroidea. [Gr. *neuron,* a nerve, *pteron,* a wing, *eidos,* form.]

**neuston,** *nū′ston, n.* minute organisms on the surface of water. [Gr. neut. of *neustos,* swimming.]

**neuter,** *nū′tər, adj.* neither one thing nor another: neutral: neither masculine nor feminine (*gram.*): neither active nor passive (*gram.*): intransitive (*gram.*): sexless: apparently sexless: sexually undeveloped: castrated: without functional, or any, androecium or gynaeceum.—*n.* a neutral: a neuter word, plant, or animal: esp. a worker bee, ant, etc.: a castrated cat.—*v.t.* to castrate. [L. *neuter,* neither—*ne,* not, *uter,* either.]

**neutral,** *nū′trəl, adj.* indifferent: taking no part on either side: not siding with either party: pertaining to neither party: not involved in a war or dispute: belonging to neither, esp. of two adjoining countries: of no decided charac-ter: having no decided colour: indistinct in sound: with no noticeable smell: belonging to neither of two opposites, as acid and alkaline, electrically positive and negative: neuter: with-out transmission of motion.—*n.* a person or nation that takes no part in a contest: a citizen or ship of a neutral state: an electric conductor ordinarily at zero potential: a position of gear in which no power is transmitted: a neuter.—*n.* neutralisā′tion, -z-.—*v.t.* neu′tralise, -ize, to de-clare neutral: to make inert: to render of no effect: counteract.—*ns.* neu′traliser, -z-; neutral-ism, policy of not entering into alliance with other nations or taking sides ideologically; neu′tralist, one who takes or favours a neutral position; neutrality (*-tral′i-ti*), fact or state of being neutral: those who are neutral.—*adv.* neu′trally. [L. *neutrālis*—*neuter,* neither.]

**neutron,** *nū′tron,* (*phys.*) *n.* an uncharged particle of about the same mass as the proton.—*ns.* neutrett′o, name suggested for neutral meson: type of neutrino; neutrino (*-trē′nō*), uncharged particle with zero mass.—neutron radiography, radiography using beam of neutrons; neutron star, a supposed heavenly body of very small size and very great density, an almost burnt out and collapsed star, whose existence has not, however, been confirmed. [L. *neuter,* neither.]

**névé,** *nā-vā, n.* firn. [Fr.,—L. *nix, nivis,* snow.]

**nevel,** *nev′əl,* (*Scot.*) *v.t.* to pound with the nieves. [nieve.]

**never,** *nev′ər, adv.* not ever: at no time: in no degree: not.—*adjs.* nev′er-end′ing; nev′er-fad′ing; nev′er-fail′ing.—*adv.* nev′ermore, at no future time.—*n.* nev′er-nev′er, the hire-purchase system (*coll.*): (-land) remote, thinly peopled or desolate area, esp. (*cap.*) north and west Queens-land: (-land) imaginary place, imaginary con-ditions, too fortunate ever to exist in reality.—*advs.* nevertheless′, notwithstanding: in spite of that; nevermore′ (*obs.*), none the more.—*n.* nev′er-was′, one who never was of any account. —never so (*arch.*), ever so. [O.E. *næfre*—*ne,* not, *æfre,* ever.]

**new,** *nū, adj.* lately made or produced: young:

fresh: not much used: having lately happened or begun to be: recent, modern: not before seen or known: only lately discovered or experienced: other than the former or preceding, different: additional: strange, unaccustomed: lately begun: beginning afresh: renewed: reformed or regenerated: restored or resumed: not of an ancient family: fresh from anything: uncultivated or only recently cultivated.—*n.* that which is new: newness.—*adv.* (often joined by hyphen to its adj.) newly: anew.—*v.t.* (*arch.*) to renew.—*v.i.* (*arch.*) to be renewed.—*adj.* new′-ish, somewhat new: nearly new.—*adv.* new′ly, very lately: afresh (*rare*): in a new way (*rare*). —*n.* new′ness.—new birth, renewal, esp. spiritual. —*adjs.* new′-blown, just come into bloom; new′-born, newly born.—new chum, a new arrival from the old country in Australia; New Church, New Jerusalem Church, the Swedenborgian Church.—*adj.* new′come, recently arrived.—new′comer, one who has lately come.—*adj.* new′-Commonwealth, of, belonging to, members of the Commonwealth who have joined more recently than the orig. self-governing dominions. —*v.t.* new′-create (*Shak.*), to create anew.—New Englander, a native or citizen of any of the New England states.—*adjs.* new′-fallen, newly fallen; newfangled (see separate article); new′-fash′ioned, made in a new way or fashion: lately come into fashion; new′-fledged, having just got feathers; new′-found, newly discovered or devised.—New Jerusalem, the heavenly city.—*adj.* new′-laid, newly laid.—New Learning, the new studies of the Renaissance; New Light, a member of a relatively more advanced religious school—applied esp. to the party within the 18th-century Scottish Secession Church which adopted voluntaryist views of the relations of Church and State, also sometimes to the Socinianising party in the Church of Scotland in the 18th century, etc.; new look, a change in women's fashions (1947), notably to longer and fuller skirts: a radical modification in the appearance of something.—*adjs.* new′-made, recently made; new′-marr′ied, newly married.—*v.t.* new′-mod′el, to model or form anew.—new moon, the moment when the moon is directly in line between the earth and sun, and therefore invisible: the time when the waxing moon becomes visible.—*adjs.* new′-mown, newly mown; new′-old′, old but renewed: at once new and old.—new poor, those who have come to think themselves poor by loss of advantages; new rich, the recently enriched: parvenus.—*adjs.* new′-risen, having newly risen; new′-sad (*Shak.*), recently made sad.—new′speak, a type of English described by George Orwell in his book, *Nineteen Eighty-four* (1949), developed by reducing vocabulary to such a point, and forming new words of such ugliness and so little emotive value, that literature and even thought will be impossible; New Style (see style); New Wave (see Nouvelle Vague): a slightly later movement in jazz aiming at freedom from set patterns and styles; new woman, a name applied, esp. by scoffers, in the late 19th century to such women as actively sought freedom and equality with men; New World, North and South America; New Year, the first few days of the year.—New Jersey tea, red-root; New Model Army, the Parliamentary army as remodelled by Cromwell (1645); New Red Sandstone (*geol.*), an old name for the Permian and Trias; New Year's Day, the first day of the year; of new (*arch.*), anew: of late. [O.E. *níwe*, *néowe*; Ger. *neu*, Ir. *nuadh*, L. *novus*, Gr. *neos*.]

newel, *nū′əl*, *n.* the upright column about which the steps of a circular staircase wind: an upright post at the end or corner of a stair handrail.—*adj.* new′elled. [O.Fr. *nual* (Fr. *noyau*),

fruitstone—L.L. *nucālis*, nutlike—L. *nux*, *nucis*, a nut.]

newell, *nū′əl*, (*Spens.*) *n.* a new thing. [A combination of novel and new.]

newfangled, *nū-fang′gld*, earlier newfangle, -gl, *adj.* unduly fond of new things: newly but superfluously devised.—*adv.* newfang′ledly.—*n.* newfang′ledness, newfang′leness. [M.E. *newefangel—newe* (O.E. *níwe*), new, *fangel*, ready to catch—*fang-*, the stem of O.E. *fón*, to take.]

Newfoundland, *nū-fownd′lənd*, *adj.* of *Newfoundland* (*nū′fənd-land*).—*n.* a very large, intelligent breed of dog from Newfoundland, originally black, a strong swimmer.

Newgate, *nū′gāt*, *n.* a famous prison in London, originally housed in the *new gate* of the city, the latest building demolished in 1902-3.—Newgate Calendar, a record of Newgate prisoners, with their crimes; Newgate frill, or fringe, a beard under the chin and jaw.

newmarket, *nū-mär′kit*, or *nū′*, *n.* a card game in which the stakes go to those who succeed in playing out cards whose duplicates lie on the table: a close-fitting coat, originally a riding-coat, for men or women. [*Newmarket*, the racing town.]

news, *nūz*, *n.* (*orig.pl.*) tidings: a report of a recent event: something one had not heard before: matter suitable for newspaper readers: newspaper: newsprint.—*v.t.* to report.—*n.* news′iness.—*adj.* news′y, gossipy.—*n.* (*U.S.*) a newsboy.—news′agent, one who deals in newspapers; news′boy, a boy who delivers or sells newspapers; news′cast, a news broadcast or telecast; news′casting; news′caster, one who gives newscasts: an apparatus which gives a changing display of news headlines, etc.; news′-dealer (*U.S.*), a newsagent; news′hawk (*U.S.*), a newsboy; news′hound, a reporter in search of news for, e.g. a newspaper; news′letter, orig. a written or printed letter containing news sent by an agent to his subscribers—the predecessor of the newspaper: a sheet of news supplied to members of a particular group; news′man, a bringer, collector, or writer of news: a seller of newspapers; news′monger, one who deals in news: one who spends much time in hearing and telling news; news′paper, a paper published periodically for circulating news, etc.; news′-paperdom; news′paperism; news′paper-man′, a journalist; news′print, paper for printing newspapers; news′-reader, one who reads news on radio or television; news′reel, film showing, or programme commenting on, news items; news′-room, reading-room with newspapers: room, etc., where news is made ready for newspaper, newscast, etc.; news′-sheet, a printed sheet of news, esp. an early form of newspaper; news′-stand, stall for sale of newspapers; news′-theatre, cinema showing chiefly newsreels; news′-value, interest to the general public as news; news′-vendor, a seller of newspapers.—*adj.* news′-worthy, sufficiently interesting to be told as news.—news′worthiness; news′-writer, a reporter or writer of news. [Late M.E. *newes*; Fr. *nouvelles*.]

newt, *nūt*, *n.* a tailed amphibian (Triturus, Molge, or Triton) of the salamander family. [Formed with initial *n*, borrowed from the article an, from ewt, a form of evet or eft—O.E. *efeta*, *efete*.]

newton, *nū′tən*, *n.* the SI unit of force—it is equal to the force which, acting on a mass of one kilogramme, produces an acceleration of one metre per second per second.—*adj.* Newtonian, *nū-tō′niən*, relating to, according to, formed or discovered by, Sir Isaac *Newton* (1642-1727) —also Newtonic (-*ton′ik*).—Newtonian telescope, a form of reflecting telescope.

next, *nekst*, *adj.* (*superl.* of nigh) nearest in place,

in kinship or other relation: nearest following (or preceding if explicitly stated) in time or order.—*adv.* nearest: immediately after: on the first occasion that follows: in the next place.—*prep.* nearest to.—*adv.* next′ly.—*n.* next′ness (*rare*).—next best, biggest, etc., next in order after the best, biggest, etc.—*adj.* next′-door, dwelling in or occupying the next house, shop, etc.: at or in the next house: neighbouring.—*adv.* next-door′.—next friend, a person appointed, or permitted, by a court of law to act on behalf of a minor or other person under legal disability; next Saturday, etc., (on) the first Saturday after the present day: in Scotland often (on) the Saturday of next week.—next door to, in the next house to: near, bordering upon, very nearly; next to, adjacent to: almost: thoroughly acquainted with (*U.S.*); next to nothing, almost nothing at all. [O.E. *nēhst* (*niehst*), superl. of *nēh* (*nēah*), near; Ger. *nächst*.]

nexus, nek′səs, *n.* a bond: a linked group. [L. *nexus*, pl. *-ūs*—*nectĕre*, to bind.]

ngaio, ni′ō, *n.* a New Zealand tree with white wood. [Maori.]

niacin, ni′ə-sin, *n.* nicotinic acid.

niaiserie, nyez-(ə-)rē, (Fr.) simplicity, foolishness.

nib, nib, *n.* something small and pointed: a pen-point: a bird's bill: a peak: a projecting point or spike: a timber carriage pole: a handle on a scythe's shaft (*dial.*): (in *pl.*) crushed cocoa-beans: (in *pl.*) included particles in varnish, wool, etc.—*v.t.* to furnish with a nib: to point: to mend the nib of: to reduce to nibs.—*adj.* nibbed, having a nib. [neb.]

nib, nib, (*slang*) *n.* a person of the upper classes: a person of importance or appearance of importance.—his nibs, himself: his mightiness. [Cf. nabs, nob.]

nibble, nib′l, *v.t.* to bite gently or by small bites: to eat a little at a time.—*v.i.* to bite gently: to show signs of accepting, as an offer, or of yielding, as to temptation (with *at*): to find fault.—*n.* act of nibbling: a little bit.—*ns.* nibb′ler; nibb′ling.—*adv.* nibb′lingly. [Origin obscure; cf. L.G. *nibbelen*, Du. *knibbelen*.]

Nibelung, nē′bəl-oŏng, *n.* one of a supernatural race in German mythology, guardians of a treasure wrested from them by Siegfried, the hero of the *Nibelungenlied*, an epic of *c.* 1190-1210:—*pl.* Ni′belungen. [Ger.]

niblick, nib′lik, *n.* a golf-club with a heavy head with wide face, used for lofting—a number eight or nine iron. [Origin uncertain.]

niccolite, nik′əl-īt, *n.* a hexagonal mineral, nickel arsenide, also called kupfernickel, copper-nickel. [See nickel.]

nice, nis, *adj.* foolishly simple (*obs.*): wanton (*Shak.*): coy (*Milt.*): over-particular: hard to please: fastidious: forming or observing very small differences: calling for very fine discrimination: done with great care and exactness, accurate: critical, hazardous (*obs.*): easily injured (*obs.*): delicate: dainty: loosely, agreeable, delightful, respectable (sometimes *ironic*).—*adj.* nice′ish, somewhat nice.—*adv.* nice′ly.—*ns.* nice′ness, quality of being nice; nicety (nīs′i-ti), quality of being nice: delicate management: exactness of treatment: degree of precision: fineness of perception or feeling: critical subtlety: a matter of delicate discrimination or adjustment: a refinement: coyness (*Spens.*, *Shak.*): fastidiousness: a delicacy.—nice and, used almost adverbially—commendably, pleasantly; to a nicety, with great exactness. [O.Fr. *nice*, foolish, simple—L. *nescius*, ignorant—*ne*, not, *scire*, to know.]

Nicene, nī′sēn, *adj.* pertaining to the town of *Nicaea*, in Bithynia, where an ecumenical council in 325 dealt with the Arian controversy, and another in 787 condemned the Iconoclasts.

—*n.* and *adj.* Nicaean (nī-sē′ən).—Nicene Creed, the creed based on the results of the first Nicene Council.

niche, nich, nēsh, *n.* a recess in a wall: a suitable or actual place or condition in life or public estimation or the system of nature.—*v.t.* to place in a niche.—*adj.* niched, placed in a niche. [Fr.,—It. *nicchia*, niche, of doubtful origin.]

Nichrome, ni′krōm, *n.* trademark for a nickel-chromium alloy with high electrical resistance and ability to withstand high temperatures.

nick, nik, *n.* a notch: a score for keeping an account (*arch.*): a cut: a fraudulent dint in the bottom of a beer-can (*obs.*): the precise point aimed at: the precise moment of time: at hazard, a throw answering to a main: a prison, a police-office (*slang*).—*v.t.* to notch: to cut in notches (as the hair of a fool; *Shak.*): to cut off: to defraud: to mark by cutting, carve out: to cut: to snip: to score, as on a tally: to tally with (*obs.*): to hit with precision: to hit off (*obs.*): to catch in the nick of time: to catch (*slang*): to arrest (*slang*): to steal (*slang*): to rob: to cheat at hazard, to defeat by throwing a nick: at hazard, to throw the nick of.—*n.* nick′er, one who, or that which, nicks: in the early 18th century, a brawler who broke windows with coppers.—nick′stick (*arch.*), a tally.—in (very) good nick (*coll.*), in (very) good health or condition; in the nick, (now usu.) nick of time, just in time: at the critical moment; out of all nick (*Shak.*), out of all reckoning, exceedingly. [Possibly connected with nock, notch.]

Nick, nik, *n.* the devil, esp. Old Nick.—Also (*Scot.*) Nickie-ben′. [Apparently for *Nicholas*.]

nick, nik, (*arch.*) *v.t.* to deny (in the phrase *to nick with nay*). [Origin unknown; possibly O.E. *ne ic*, not I.]

nickel, nik′l, *n.* a white magnetic metal (Ni; at. numb. 28), very malleable and ductile, largely used in alloys: a 5-cent piece (of copper and nickel; *U.S.*).—*adj.* of nickel.—*v.t.* to plate with nickel:—*pr.p.* nick′elling; *pa.t.* and *pa.p.* nick′elled.—*adjs.* nick′elic, of trivalent nickel; nickelif′erous, containing nickel.—*n.* nick′eline (*obs.*), niccolite.—*v.t.* nick′elise, -ize, to plate with nickel.—*adj.* nick′elous, of bivalent nickel.—nick′el-bloom, earthy annabergite; nick′el-ochre, earthy annabergite; nick′el-plat′ing, the plating of metals with nickel; nick′el-sil′ver, German silver; nick′el-steel′, a steel containing some nickel. [Ger. *kupfer-nickel*, niccolite—*kupfer*, copper, *nickel*, a mischievous sprite, goblin, because the ore looked like copper-ore but yielded no copper.]

nickelodeon, nik-ə-lō′di-on, *n.* a five-cent entertainment: a juke-box. [See nickel, odeum.]

nicker, nik′ər, (*Scot.*) *v.i.* to neigh: snigger.—*n.* a neigh: snigger: loud laugh.—Also nicher (nihh′ər).

nicker, nik′ər, (*arch.*) *n.* a water-monster or water-demon. [O.E. *nicor*.]

nicker, nik′ər, *n.* a clay marble (also knicker): the round seed of a Caesalpinia (or Guilandina), used for playing marbles (also nick′ar). [Cf. Du. *knikker*, North Ger. *knicker*.]

nicker, nik′ər, (*slang*) *n.* £1.

nicknack, etc. Same as knick-knack, etc.

nickname, nik′nām, *n.* a name given in contempt or sportive familiarity.—*v.t.* to give a nickname to. [M.E. *neke-name*, for *eke-name*, with *n* from the indefinite article; see an, eke, name.]

nickum, nik′əm, (Scot.) *n.* a mischievous boy.

nicky-tam, nik′i-tam′, (Scot.) *n.* a piece of string, etc., worn below the knee to keep the bottom of the trouser-leg lifted clear in dirty work or to exclude dust, etc.

nicol, nik′l, *n.* a crystal of calcium carbonate so cut and cemented as to transmit only the extraordinary ray, used for polarising light.—Also Nicol('s) prism. [From William *Nicol* (*c.* 1768-1851) of Edinburgh, its inventor.]

**nicotian,** *ni-kō'sh*(*y*)*ən, adj.* of tobacco.—*n.* a tobacco smoker.—*n.* Nicotiana (*-shi-ä'nə, -ā'nə*), the tobacco genus of Solanaceae.—*n.pl.* the literature of tobacco.—*ns.* nicotinamide (*-tin'*), a member of the vitamin B complex; nicotine (*nik'ə-tēn*), a poisonous alkaloid (C$_{10}$H$_{14}$N$_2$) got from tobacco leaves.—*adj.* nicotinic (*-tin'ik*).—*n.* nic'otinism, a morbid state induced by excessive use of tobacco.—nicotinic acid, a white crystalline substance, a member of the vitamin B complex, deficiency of which is connected with the development of pellagra. [Jean *Nicot*, who sent tobacco to Catherine de Medici.]

**nicotine.** See nicotian.

**nicrosilal,** *nik-rō'sil-əl, n.* a cast-iron alloy containing nickel, chromium, and silicon, used in high-temperature work.

**nictate,** *nik'tāt, v.i.* to wink—also nic'titate.—*ns.* nictā'tion, nictitā'tion.—nictitating membrane, the third eyelid, developed in birds, etc., a thin movable membrane that passes over the eye. [L. *nictāre, -ātum* and its L.L. freq. *nictitāre, -ātum*, to wink.]

**nid,** *nid,* nide, *nid, n.* a pheasant's nest or brood. [L. *nidus,* nest.]

**niddering,** nidderling, nidering, niderling, niding. See nithing.

**niddle-noddle,** *nid'l-nod'l, adj.* and *adv.* with nodding head.—*v.i.* to noddle the head: to waggle.—*v.t.* and *v.i.* nid'-nod', to keep nodding. [nod.]

**nide.** See nid.

**nidget,** *nij'it,* (*arch.* or *illit.*) *n.* an idiot. [idiot, with *n* from the indefinite article.]

**nidicolous,** *nid-ik'ə-ləs, adj.* (of young birds) staying long in the nest. [L. *nīdus,* a nest, *colĕre,* to inhabit.]

**nidifugous,** *nid-if'ū-gəs, adj.* (of young birds) leaving the nest soon after hatching. [L. *nīdus,* nest, *fugĕre,* to flee.]

**nidify,** *nid'i-fī, v.i.* to build a nest.—Also **nidificate** (*nid'i-fi-kāt*).—*n.* nidificā'tion. [L. *nīdus,* nest, *facĕre,* to make.]

**nidor,** *nī'dör, n.* a strong smell or fume, esp. of animal substances cooking or burning.—*adv.* ni'dorous. [L. *nidor, -ōris.*]

**nidus,** *nī'dəs, n.* a nest or breeding-place: a place where anything is originated, harboured, developed, or fostered: a place of lodgment or deposit: a point of infection: a nerve-centre:—*pl.* ni'di.—*adjs.* ni'dal, pertaining to a nest or nidus; nidament'al, nest-forming: (of glands) secreting material for the formation of a nest or of an egg-covering.—*ns.* nidament'um, an egg-capsule; nidā'tion, renewal of the lining of the uterus.—*adj.* nidūlā'tion (*nid-*), nest-building. [L. *nidus,* a nest.]

**nie,** an obsolete spelling of nigh.

**niece,** *nēs, n. orig.* a granddaughter, or any female descendant: now, a brother's or sister's daughter: extended to a like relation by marriage: euphemistically, a pope's or priest's daughter: —*masc.* nephew. [O.Fr.,—L.L. *neptia*—L. *neptis.*]

**niello,** *ni-el'ō, n.* a method of ornamenting metal by engraving, and filling up the lines with a black composition: a work so produced: an impression taken from the engraved surface before filling up: the compound used in niello-work:—*pl.* niell'i, *-ē,* niell'os.—*v.t.* to decorate with niello:—*pr.p.* niell'oing; *pa.t.* and *pa.p.* niell'oed.—*adj.* niellāted (*nē'*).—*n.* niell'ist. [It. *niello*—L.L. *nigellum,* a black enamel—L. *nigellus,* dim. of *niger,* black.]

**Niersteiner,** *nēr's*(*h*)*tīn-ər, n.* a Rhine wine, named from *Nierstein,* near Mainz.

**Nietzschean,** *nēch'i-ən, adj.* of Friedrich *Nietzsche*

(1844-1900) or his philosophy.—*n.* a follower of Nietzsche.—*n.* Nietzsch'eanism.

**nieve,** neive, *nēv,* neif, nief (*Shak.* neafe, neaffe), *nēf,* (*arch.* except *dial.*) *n.* the fist.—*ns.* nieve'ful, a closed handful; nie'vie-(nie'vie-)nick'-nack, a Scottish children's pastime, a mode of assigning by lot, by guessing which hand contains something, the holder repeating a rhyme. [M.E. *nefe*—O.N. *hnefi, nefi;* cf. Sw. *näfve,* fist.]

**nife,** *nī'fi, n.* the earth's hypothetical core of nickel and iron. [Chemical symbols *Ni* and *Fe.*]

**niff,** *nif,* (*dial.* or *slang*) *n.* a stink.—*adj.* niff'y.

**niffer,** *nif'ər,* (*Scot.*) *v.t.* to barter.—*v.i.* to haggle. —*n.* an exchange: hazard. [Possibly nieve.]

**niffnaff,** *nif-naf',* (*dial.*) *n.* a trifle: a diminutive person.—*v.i.* to trifle.—*adjs.* niff-naff'y, niff'y-naff'y, fastidious.

**Niflheim,** *niv'l-hām,* (*Scand. myth.*) *n.* a region of mist, ruled over by Hel. [O.N. *Niflheimr*—*nifl,* mist, *heimr,* home.]

**nifty,** *nif'ti,* (*slang*) *adj.* fine: spruce: smart: quick: agile.—*n.* nift'iness.

**Nigella,** *ni-jel'ə, n.* a genus of ranunculaceous plants, with finely dissected leaves, and whitish, blue, or yellow flowers, often almost concealed by their leafy involucres.—*Nigella damascena* is called love-in-a-mist, devil-in-a-bush, and ragged lady. [Fem. of L. *nigellus,* blackish—*niger,* black, from the black seeds.]

**niger,** *nī'jər,* (*obs.*) *n.* a Negro.—**ni'ger-oil,** an oil got from the black seeds (ni'ger-seeds) of an East African composite, *Guizotia abyssinica,* cultivated also in India. [L. *niger,* black.]

**niggard,** *nig'ərd, n.* one who grudges to spend or give away: a false bottom or side in a fire-grate.—*adj.* niggardly.—*v.t.* and *v.i.* (*Shak.*) to treat or behave as a niggard.—*ns.* nigg'ardise, -ize (*-iz; arch.*), nigg'ardliness, meanness, stinginess.—*adj.* nigg'ardly, stingy.—*adv.* stingily: grudgingly. [Origin obscure.]

**nigger,** *nig'ər, n.* derogatorily, a Negro, or a member of any very dark-skinned race: a black insect larva of various kinds.—*adj.* Negro: blackish brown.—*v.t.* to exhaust by overcropping: to char: to blacken.—*n.* nigg'erdom, niggers collectively.—*adj.* nigg'erish.—*ns.* nigg'erism, an idiom or expression characteristic of niggers: African blood; nigg'erling, a little nigger.—*adj.* nigg'ery.—nigg'er-head, a nodule, boulder, or boss of dark-coloured rock: an American river-mussel (Quadrula), a source of mother-of-pearl: negrohead tobacco: a tussock in a swamp (*U.S.*).—nigger in the wood-pile, a hidden evil influence; work like a nigger, to toil hard. [Fr. *nègre*—Sp. *negro;* see Negro.]

**niggle,** *nig'l, v.i.* to trifle, potter: to busy oneself with petty scrupulosity: to move in a fidgety or ineffective way: to gnaw: to criticise in a petty way.—*v.t.* to work, make, perform, with excessive detail: to befool.—*n.* small cramped handwriting.—*ns.* nigg'ler; nigg'ling, fussiness, finicking work: petty elaboration.—*adj.* over-elaborate: petty: fussy: cramped.—*adj.* nigg'ly. [Cf. Norw. *nigle.*]

**nigh,** *nī, adj.* near.—*adv.* nearly.—*prep.* near to. —*v.t.* and *v.i.* to approach, draw near: to touch (*obs.*).—*adv.* and *prep.* nigh'-hand, near hand: almost, nearly.—*adv.* nigh'ly (*obs.*), almost: closely: singly (*Spens.*).—*n.* nigh'ness. [O.E. *nēah, nēh;* Du. *na,* Ger. *nahe.*]

**night,** *nīt, n.* the end of the day: the time from sunset to sunrise: the dark part of the twenty-four-hour day: darkness: obscurity, ignorance, evil, affliction, or sorrow (*fig.*): death (*fig.*): the experience of a night: a night set apart for some purpose, esp. receiving visitors.—*adj.* belonging to night: occurring or done in the night: working or on duty by night.—*adjs.* night'ed, benighted: darkened, clouded (*Shak.*); night'less, having no night.—*adj.* and *adv.*

night'long, lasting all night.—adj. night'ly, done or happening by night or every night: dark as night (Shak.).—adv. by night: every night.—adv. nights (orig. gen. of n.; dial.), at, by night.—adj. night'ward, occurring towards night.—n. night'y, night'ie, a nightgown.—night air, the air at night: a peculiarly unwholesome gas, formerly imagined by some to circulate at night; night'-attire', garments worn in bed; night'-bell, a door-bell for use at night; night'-bird, a bird that flies or that sings at night: a person who is active or about at night; night'-blind'ness, inability to see in a dim light, nyctalopia; night'-brawl'er, one who raises disturbances in the night; night'cap, a cap worn at night in bed: a drink taken before going to bed; night'-cart (hist.), a cart used to remove the contents of privies before daylight; night'-cellar (arch.), a disreputable resort or tavern, open by night; night'-chair, a night-stool; night'-churr, the goatsucker, so called from its cry.—n.pl. night'-clothes, garments worn in bed.—night'-cloud, stratus; night'-club, a club open between nightfall and morning for amusement or dissipation; night'-crawl'er, a large earthworm which comes to the surface at night, used as bait for fishing; night'-crow (Shak.), undefined bird of ill omen that cries in the night; night'-dog (Shak.), a dog that hunts in the night; night'-dress, attire for the night, esp. a nightgown; night'fall, the fall or beginning of the night: the close of the day: evening.—adj. night'faring, travelling by night.—night'fire, a fire burning in the night: a Will-o'-the-wisp; night'-fish'ery, a mode or place of fishing by night; night'-flower, a flower that opens by night.—adj. night'flower'ing.—night'-fly, a moth or fly that flies at night.—adj. night'-fly'ing, flying by night (also n.).—night'-foe, one who makes his attack by night; night'-foss'icker (Austr.), one who robs a digging by night.—adj. night'-foun'dered, lost in the night.—night'-fowl, a night-bird; night'-gear, night-clothes; night'-glass, a spy-glass with concentrating lenses for use at night; night'(-)gown, a loose robe for sleeping in, for men or women: a dressing-gown (obs.); night'-hag, a witch supposed to be abroad at night; night'-hawk, a goatsucker: a prowler by night; night'-her'on, a heron of nocturnal habit, of various kinds; night'-house (obs.), a tavern open during the night; night'-hunter, one who hunts, poaches, or prowls about the streets for prey by night; night'jar, a goatsucker; night'-latch, a door-lock worked by a key without and a knob within; night life, activity in the form of entertainments at night; night'-light, lamp, candle that gives a subdued light all night: the faint light of the night; the light of phosphorescent sea-animals; night'-line, a fishing-line set overnight; night'-man, a night watchman, worker, or scavenger; night'mare (O.E. mære, M.E. mare, the nightmare incubus; cf. O.H.G. mara, O.N. mara), an unpleasant dream: a dream accompanied by pressure on the breast and a feeling of powerlessness to move or speak—personified as an incubus or evil spirit: a horrifying experience (fig.).—adjs. night'marish; night'mary (rare).—night out, a domestic, or other, servant's night of freedom to be absent: a festive night away from home, work, and restrictions; night'-owl, an exclusively nocturnal owl: one who sits up very late; night'-pal'sy (arch.), a numbness of the legs, incidental to women; night'piece, a picture or literary or musical description of a night-scene: a painting to be seen by artificial light; night'-por'ter, a porter in attendance during the night; night'-rail (hist.), a loose wrap or dressing-jacket; night'-rav'en (Shak.), a bird that cries at night, supposed to be of ill-omen; night'-rest, the repose of the night; night'-rider (U.S.), a participant in a lynching, etc.: a member of the Ku-Klux Klan; night'-robe, a nightgown: a dressing-gown; night'-rule (Shak.), a revel at night; night'-school, a school held at night, esp. for those at work during the day; night'-sea'son, the night-time; night'-shift, a gang or group of workers that takes its turn by night: the time it is on duty: a nightdress (arch.); night'shirt, a man's shirt for sleeping in; night'-shriek, a cry in the night; night'-side, the dark, mysterious, or gloomy side of anything; night'-sight, power of vision by night; night'-soil, the contents of privies, cesspools, etc., generally carried away at night and sometimes used for fertiliser; night'-spell, a charm against harm by night; night'-steed, one of the horses in the chariot of Night; night'-stick, an American policeman's truncheon; night'-stool, a close-stool for use in a bedroom; night'-ta'per, a night-light burning slowly.—n.pl. night'-terr'ors, the sudden starting from sleep in fright.—night'-tide, night-time: a flood-tide in the night; night'-time, the time when it is night.—adjs. night'-tripp'ing (Shak.), tripping about in the night; night'-wak'ing, watching in the night.—night'-walk, a walk in the night; night'-walk'er, a somnambulist: one who walks about at night, usu. for bad purposes, esp. a prostitute.—n. and adj. night'-wan'derer, one who wanders by night.—adjs. night'-wan'dering; night'-war'bling, singing in the night.—night'-watch, a watch or guard at night: one who is on watch by night: time of watch in the night; night'-watch'man, one who is on watch by night, esp. on industrial premises and building sites: a batsman, not himself a high scorer, put in to defend a wicket until the close of play so that his partner may have a chance to score (cricket).—night'-work, work done at night; night'-work'er.—make a night of it, to spend the night, or a large part of it, in amusement or celebration; of a night, of nights, in the course of a night: some time at night. [O.E. niht, Ger. nacht, L. nox; Gr. nyx.]

nightingale, nīt'ing-gāl, n. a small bird of the thrush family celebrated for the rich love-song of the male heard chiefly at night: a person with a beautiful singing voice. [O.E. nihtegale—niht, night, galan, to sing, Ger. nachtigall.]

nightingale, nīt'ing-gāl, n. a flannel scarf with sleeves, worn by invalids sitting up in bed. [Florence Nightingale (1820-1910), Crimean hospital nurse.]

nightmare. See night.

nightshade, nīt'shād, n. a name given to various plants, chiefly of the Solanaceae and chiefly poisonous or narcotic.—deadly nightshade, belladonna; woody nightshade, bittersweet; black nightshade, Solanum nigrum; see also enchanter. [O.E. nihtscada, app.—niht, night, scada, shade.]

nig-nog, nig'-nog, n. a fool: a raw recruit to army or to a civilian service. [Origin uncertain.]

nigrescence, nī- or ni-gres'əns, n. blackness: dark colouring or pigmentation: blackening.—adjs. nigresc'ent, growing black or dark: blackish; nigricant (nig'ri-kənt), black: blackish.—v.t. nig'rify, to blacken.—n. nig'ritude, blackness. [L. niger, black.]

Nigritian, ni-grish'ən, adj. of Nigritia, or Sudan, esp. Western Sudan, the home of the Negroes in the narrow sense.—n. a true Negro. [L. niger, black.]

nigritude. See Negro, nigrescence.

nigromancy, nig'rō-man-si, n. an old form of necromancy, the black art. [From association with L. niger, black.]

nigrosine, nig'rō-sēn, -ro-sin, n. a blackish coal-tar colour dye. [L. niger, black.]

nihil, nī'hil, n. nothing.—ns. ni'hilism (-hil- or -il-izm), belief in nothing: denial of all reality, or of all objective growth of truth: extreme scepticism: nothingness: in tsarist Russia a terrorist movement aiming at the overturn of all the existing institutions of society in order to build it up anew on different principles; ni'hilist.—*adj.* nihilist'ic.—*n.* nihility (-*hil'*), nothingness: a mere nothing. [L. *nihil*, nothing.]

nihil ad rem, *nī'*, *ni'hil ad rem*, (L.) nothing to the point; ni'hil obstat (*ob'stat*), nothing hinders —a book censor's form of permission to print.

Nike, *nī'kē*, *n.* the Greek goddess of victory. [Gr. *nikē*, victory.]

nikethamide, *nik-eth'a-mīd*, *n.* a drug used as a heart stimulant—also called coramine. [*nico*tinic acid, di*ethyl*, *amide*.]

niks-nie. See under nix.

nil, *nil*, *n.* nothing: zero. [L. *nil*, *nīhil*, nothing.]

nilgai, *nēl'* or *nil'gī*, nilgau, nylghau, *-gow*, *-gō*, *n.* a large Indian antelope, the male slaty-grey, the female tawny. [Pers. and Hind. *nīl*, blue, Hind. *gāī*, Pers. *gāw*, cow.]

nill, n'ill, *nil*, (*Spens.*) *v.t.* will not: refuse:—*pa.t.* nould, n'ould (*nōōd*), also nilled. [O.E. *nylle*—*ne*, not, *willan*, to wish.]

Nilometer, *ni-lom'i-tər*, *n.* a gauge for measuring the height of the *Nile*. [Gr. *neilometrion*.]

Nilot, *nil'ot*, Nilote, *-ōt*, *n.* an inhabitant of the banks of the Upper Nile: a Hamitised Negro of the Upper Nile.—*adj.* Nilotic (*-ot'ik*), of the Nile. [Gr. *Neilōtēs*.]

nim, *nim*, *v.t.* to take (*obs.*): to steal, pilfer (*arch.* *slang*):—*pa.t.* (*obs.*) nam, (now) nimmed.—*n.* nimm'er. [O.E. *niman*, to take.]

nim, *nim*, *n.* an old and widespread game, perh. orig. Chinese, in which two players take alternately from heaps or rows of objects (now usu. matches).

nim, *nēm*, *n.* margosa, a species of Melia, yielding nim'-oil.—Also neem. [Hind. *nīm*.]

nimble, *nim'bl*, *adj.* light and quick in motion: active: swift. — *ns.* nim'bleness, nim'blesse (*Spens.*), quickness of motion either in body or mind.—*adv.* nim'bly.—*adjs.* nim'ble-fing'ered, skilful with the fingers: thievish; nimbl'e-foot'ed, swift of foot; nim'ble-witt'ed, quick-witted. [App. O.E. *nǣmel*, *numol*—*niman*, to take; cf. Ger. *nehmen*.]

nimbus, *nim'bəs*, *n.* a cloud or luminous mist investing a god or goddess: a halo: a rain-cloud:—*pl.* nim'bi, nim'buses.—*adjs.* nimbed (*nimd*); nim'bused. [L.]

nimiety, *ni-mī'i-ti*, *n.* excess.—*adj.* nimious (*nim'i*-*əs*; *Scots law*), excessive. [L. *nimis*, too much.]

niminy-piminy, *nim'i-ni-pim'i-ni*, *adj.* affectedly fine or delicate.—*n.* affected delicacy. [Imit.]

Nimrod, *nim'rod*, *n.* any great hunter. [From the son of Cush, Gen. x. 8-10.]

nincompoop, *nin*(*g*)*'kəm-pōōp*, *n.* a simpleton: a booby—earlier nic'ompoop, nick'umpoop—shortened to nin'com, nin'cum, and also poop. [Origin unknown; not from L. *nōn compos* (*mentis*), not in possession of his wits).]

nine, *nīn*, *n.* the cardinal number next above eight: a symbol representing it (9, ix, etc.): a set of that number of things or persons (as a baseball team): a shoe or other article of a size denoted by 9: a card with nine pips: a score of nine points, tricks, etc.: the ninth hour after midday or midnight: (*cap.*; with *the*) the nine Muses.—*adj.* of the number nine.—*adj.* and *adv.* nine'fold, in nine divisions: nine times as much.—*adj.* ninth (*ninth*), the last of nine: next after the eighth: equal to one of nine equal parts.—*n.* a ninth part: an octave and a second (*mus.*): a tone at that interval (*mus.*).—*adv.* ninth'ly, in the ninth place.—nine'-eyes, a lamprey (from its seven pairs of gill-pouches): a butterfly (from its spots).—*adjs.* nine'-foot, -inch, -mile, etc., measuring 9 feet, etc.; nine'-hole, having nine holes.—nine'holes, a game in which a

ball is to be bowled into nine holes in the ground or in a board: a difficulty, fix (*U.S.*); nine'pence, the value of nine pennies: a coin of that value: a high standard of niceness, nimbleness, etc.—*adj.* nine'penny, costing, offered at, or worth ninepence.—*n.* a ninepence. —nine'-pin, a bottle-shaped pin set up with eight others for the game of nine'pins, in which players bowl a ball at these pins (see skittles). —*n.* and *adj.* nine-score, nine times twenty.— nine worthies (see worth).—naughty nineties (see naughty); nine days' wonder (see wonder); nine-penny marl or morris, nine men's morris (see meril); nine points of the law, worth nine-tenths of all the points that could be raised (proverbially of possession); to the nines, to perfection, fully, elaborately. [O.E. *nigon*, Du. *negen*, L. *novem*, Gr. *ennea*, Sans. *nava*.]

nineteen, *nin-tēn'*, or *nin'tēn*, *n.* and *adj.* nine and ten.—*n.* and *adj.* nine'teenth (or *-tēnth'*).—*adv.* nineteenth'ly.—nineteenth hole, a golf club-house, esp. the bar or restaurant.—nineteen to the dozen, with great volubility. [O.E. *nigontēne* (-*tiene*); see nine, ten.]

ninety, *nin'ti*, *n.* and *adj.* nine times ten:—*pl.* nine'ties, the numbers ninety to ninety-nine: the years so numbered in a life or a century.— *adj.* nine'tieth, last of ninety: equal to one of ninety equal parts.—*n.* a ninetieth part. [O.E. *nigontig* (*hundnigontig*).]

ninny, *nin'i*, *n.* a simpleton.—Also ninn'y-hammer. [Possibly from innocent; poss.—It. *ninno*, child; Sp. *niño*.]

ninon, *nē-nɔ̄*, *n.* a silk voile or other thin fabric. [Fr. *Ninon*, a woman's name.]

Niobe, *nī'ō-bē*, *n.* a daughter of Tantalus, turned into stone as she wept for her children, slain by Artemis and Apollo.—*adj.* Niobē'an. [Gr. *Niobē*.]

niobium, *ni-ō'bi-əm*, *n.* a metallic element (Nb; at. numb. 41) discovered in the mineral tantalite— also, but not now officially, called columbium. [See Niobe.]

nip, *nip*, *n.* a small quantity of spirits—also nipp'er (*U.S.*).—*v.i.* to take a dram.—*n.* nipp'erkin, a small measure of liquor. [Origin obscure.]

nip, *nip*, *v.t.* to pinch: to press between two surfaces: to remove or sever by pinching or biting: to check the growth or vigour of: to give a smarting or tingling feeling to: to concern closely and painfully (*obs.*): to reprehend sharply (*obs.*): to snatch: to steal (*coll.*): to arrest (*slang*).—*v.i.* to pinch: to smart: to go nimbly:—*pr.p.* nipp'ing; *pa.t.* and *pa.p.* nipped (*nipt*).—*n.* an act or experience of nipping: the pinch of cold: a nipping quality: pungency or bite (*Scot.*): a sharp reprehension (*obs.*): a more or less gradual thinning out of a stratum (*min.*): a short turn in a rope, the part of a rope at the place bound by the seizing or caught by jambing (*naut.*): a small piece, such as might be nipped off: a cut-purse (*old slang*).—*n.* nipp'er, one who, or that which, nips: a chela or great claw, as of a crab: a horse's incisor, esp. of the middle four: a pickpocket or cut-purse (*slang*): a boy assistant to a costermonger, carter, etc.: a little boy: (in *pl.*) small pincers: various pincer-like tools: handcuffs.—*v.t.* to seize (two ropes) together.—*adv.* nipp'ingly.— *adj.* nipp'y, pungent, biting: nimble (*coll.*): niggardly.—nip'-cheese, a stingy fellow (*slang*): a purser (*obs. naut.*).—nip and tuck (*U.S.*), full speed: neck and neck; nip in, to cut in; nip in the bud, to cut off in the earliest stage. [Prob. related to Du. *nijpen*, to pinch.]

nip. See nep.

Nip. See Nippon.

Nipa, *nē'*, *ni'pa*, *n.* a low-growing East Indian palm of brackish water (*Nipa fruticans*): an alcoholic drink made from it. [Malay *nipah*.]

**nipperkin.** See nip (1).

**nipperty-tipperty,** *nip'ər-ti-tip'ər-ti,* (*Scot.*) *adj.* finical: mincing: fiddle-faddle.

**nipple,** *nip'l, n.* the pap of the breast: a teat: a small projection with an orifice, esp. for regulating flow or lubricating machinery.—*v.t.* to furnish with a nipple.—**nipp'le-shield,** a defence for the nipple worn by nursing women; **nipp'le-wort,** a tall composite weed (*Lapsana communis*) with small yellow heads, once esteemed as a cure for sore nipples. [A dim. of neb or nib (1).]

**Nippon,** *nip-on', n.* Japanese name of Japan.—*n.* and *adj.* **Nipp'onese.**—Nip (*slang*), a Japanese.

**nipter,** *nip'tər, n.* the ecclesiastical ceremony of washing the feet—the same as *maundy.* [Gr. *niptēr,* a basin—*niptein,* to wash.]

**nirl,** *nirl,* (*Scot.*) *n.* a lump: a crumb: a stunted person.—*v.t.* to stunt: to shrink or shrivel: to pinch with cold.—*adjs.* **nirled, nirl'it; nirl'y, nirl'ie,** knotty: stumpy: stunted: niggardly. [Perh. **knurl;** perh. conn. Icel. *nyrfill,* niggard.]

**nirvana,** *nûr-vä'nə, n.* the cessation of individual existence—the state to which a Buddhist aspires as the best attainable: loosely, a blissful state. [Sans. *nirvāṇa,* a blowing out.]

**nis, n'is, nys,** *nis, niz,* (*Spens.*) a contraction for **ne is,** is not.

**nis,** *nis, n.* in Scandinavian folklore, a brownie or friendly goblin. [Dan. and Sw. *nisse.*]

**Nisan,** *ni'san, nē-sän', n.* the seventh civil, first ecclesiastical, month of the Jewish calendar (March to April)—called Abib before the Captivity. [Heb. *Nisān.*]

**nisberry.** Same as naseberry.

**nisei,** *nē-sā', n.* a resident in the Americas born of Japanese immigrant parents—cf. **issei.** [Jap., second generation.]

**nisi,** *ni'sī, adj.* to take effect unless, after a time, some condition referred to, be fulfilled. [The L. conj. *nisi,* unless.]

**nisi prius,** *ni'sī pri'əs, ni'si pri'ōōs,* (L.) unless previously—a name (from the first words of the writ) given to the jury sittings in civil cases.

**nisse.** Same as nis (2).

**Nissen,** *nis'ən, adj.* designed by Col. P. N. *Nissen* (1871–1930), applied to a semi-cylindrical corrugated-iron hut.

**nisus,** *ni'səs, n.* effort: striving: impulse. [L. *nisus,* pl. *-ūs.*]

**nit,** *nit, n.* the egg of a louse or other vermin: a young louse: a term of contempt, (*Shak.* etc.). —*adj.* **nitt'y,** full of nits.—**nit'-grass,** a rare grass (Gastridium) with nit-like flowers. [O.E. *hnitu;* Ger. *niss.*]

**nit,** *nit,* (*coll.*) *n.* a fool. [Poss. foregoing, or an abbrev. of nitwit.]

**nit,** *nit, n.* unit of luminance, one candela per square metre. [L. *nitor,* brightness.]

**nit,** *nit,* (*computers*) *n.* unit of information (1·44 bits). [Napierian dig*it.*]

**nithing,** *ni', ni'dhing,* (*hist.*) *n.* an infamous person: an abject coward: a traitor.—*adj.* cowardly: dastardly: niggardly—wrongly **nid(d)ering, nid-(d)erling** (*nid'*), **nid'ing.** [O.N. *nithingr* (in O.E. as *nithing*)—*nith,* contumely; Ger. *neiding.*]

**Nithsdale,** *niths'dāl, n.* an 18th-century woman's riding-hood. [From the Countess of *Nithsdale,* who contrived her husband's escape from the Tower in her clothes in 1716.]

**nitid,** *nit'id, adj.* shining: gay. [L. *nitidus—nitēre,* to shine.]

**niton,** *ni'ton, n.* a former name for radon. [L. *nitēre,* to shine.]

**nitre,** *ni'tər, n.* sodium carbonate (*obs.*): potassium nitrate or saltpetre (**cubic nitre** is sodium nitrate, or Chile saltpetre): a supposed nitrous substance in the air, etc. (*obs.*).—*n.* **ni'trate,** a salt of nitric acid: a fertiliser—natural (potassium or sodium) or synthetic (calcium) nitrate.— *v.t.* to treat with nitric acid or a nitrate: to con-

vert into a nitrate or nitro-compound.—*ns.* **nitratine** (*ni'trə-tin*), sodium nitrate as a mineral; **nitrā'tion.**—*adj.* **ni'tric.**—*n.* **ni'tride,** a compound of nitrogen with another element.—*v.t.* to turn into a nitride: to case-harden by heating in ammonia gas.—*ns.* **ni'triding; ni'trile** (*-tril, -trēl, -tril*), any of a group of organic cyanides (general formula R·C : N); **nitrificā'tion,** treatment with nitric acid: conversion into nitrates, esp. by bacteria through the intermediate condition of nitrites.—*v.t.* and *v.i.* **ni'trify,** to subject to or suffer nitrification:—*pr.p.* **ni'trifying;** *pa.t.* and *pa.p.* **ni'trified.**—*ns.* **ni'trite,** a salt of nitrous acid; **nitrom'eter,** an apparatus for estimating nitrogen or some of its compounds; **nitrosā'tion,** conversion of ammonium salts into nitrites.— *adjs.* **ni'trous; ni'try** (*obs.*), applied to the air, as supposed to contain nitre (see above).—*n.* **ni'tryl,** nitroxyl (see nitro-).—**nitric acid,** HNO₃; **nitric anhydride,** N₂O₅; **nitric oxide,** NO; **nitrous acid,** HNO₂; **nitrous anhydride,** N₂O₃; **nitrous oxide,** laughing gas, N₂O. [Fr.,—L. *nitrum*—Gr. *nitron,* sodium carbonate; prob. of Eastern origin; cf. Egyptian *ntr(j),* Heb. *nether,* Ar. *nitrún.*]

**Nitrian,** *nit'ri-ən, adj.* belonging to *Nitriae* (Nitriai), a region of ancient Egypt west of the Nile delta, including the Natron lakes and a great assemblage of hermit settlements. [Gr. *nitriā,* a soda pit—*nitron,* soda.]

**nitro-,** *ni-trō-,* in composition, indicating nitration. —*n.* **nitro-an'iline, nitran'iline,** any nitro-derivative of aniline.—*n.pl.* **ni'trobactē'ria,** bacteria that convert ammonium compounds into nitrites, and (esp.) those that convert nitrites into nitrates.—*ns.* **nitroben'zene,** a yellow oily liquid (C₆H₅NO₂) got from benzene and nitric and concentrated sulphuric acid; **nitrocell'ulose,** cellulose nitrate, used as an explosive, in lacquers, glues, etc.; **ni'tro-com'pound, ni'tro-deriv'ative,** a compound in which one or more hydrogens of an aromatic or aliphatic compound are replaced by nitro-groups; **nitroglyc'erine,** a powerfully explosive compound produced by the action of nitric and sulphuric acids on glycerine; **ni'tro-group,** the radical NO₂; **ni'tro-silk,** an artificial silk in which fibres of cellulose nitrate are made and then turned into cellulose; **nitrō'sō-group,** the group NO; **nitrotoluene,** a nitro-derivative of toluene; **nitrox'yl,** the group NO₂.

**nitrogen,** *ni'trō-jən, n.* a gas (N; at. numb. 7) forming nearly four-fifths of common air, a necessary constituent of every organised body, so called from its being an essential constituent of nitre.—*v.t.* **nitrogenise, -ize** (*-troj'*), to combine or supply with nitrogen.—*adj.* **nitro'genous,** of or containing nitrogen.—**nitrogen cycle,** the sum total of the transformations undergone by nitrogen and nitrogenous compounds in nature —from free nitrogen back to free nitrogen; **nitrogen fixation,** the bringing of free nitrogen into combination; **nitrogen narcosis,** intoxicating and anaesthetic effect of too much nitrogen in the brain, experienced by divers at considerable depths—also called **rapture of the deep, depth,** and (*slang*) **the narks.** [Gr. *nitron,* sodium carbonate (but taken as if meaning nitre), and the root of *gennaein,* to generate.]

**nitwit,** *nit'wit,* (*slang*) *n.* a blockhead.—*adj.* **nit'-witted.** [Poss. Ger. dial. *nit,* not, and wit.]

**nival,** *ni'vəl, adj.* growing among snow.—*adj.* **niveous** (*niv'i-əs*), snowy, white.—*n.* **Nivôse** (*nē-vōz*), the 4th month of the French revolutionary calendar, about 21st Dec. to 19th Jan. [L. *nix, nivis,* snow.]

**nix,** *niks,* (*Gmc. myth.*) *n.* a water-spirit, mostly malignant:—*fem.* **nix'ie, nix'y.** [Ger. *nix,* fem. *nixe;* cf. nicker (2).]

**nix,** *niks,* (*slang*) *n.* nothing: short for 'nothing doing, you'll get no support from me': postal matter addressed amiss (*U.S.* usu. in *pl.*).—*n.*

**nix-nie, niks-nie** (*niks'nē; S.Afr.*), nothing at all. —**nix my dolly** (*obs. slang*), never mind. [Colloquial Ger. and Du. for Ger. *nichts*, nothing.]

**nix,** *niks, interj.* a cry to give warning of an approaching policeman, master, etc.

**nizam,** *ni-zäm'*, or *ni-zam'*, *n.* the title of the prince of Haidarabad in India: a Turkish soldier. [Hind. *nizām*, regulator.]

**no,** *nō, adv.* not so: not: (with *compar.*) in no degree, not at all.—*n.* a denial: a refusal: a vote or voter for the negative:—*pl.* **noes.**—**no more,** destroyed: dead: never again. [O.E. *nā*—*ne*, not, *ā*, ever; cf. **nay.**]

**no,** *nō, adj.* not any: not one: by no means properly called.—*adj.* **no-account'** (*U.S.*), worthless: insignificant.—**no'-ball'** (*cricket*), a ball bowled in such a way that it is disallowed by rules; **no-fines,** concrete from which the fine aggregate (i.e. sand) has been omitted; **no'-man,** one ready to say 'no'; **no'-meaning,** want of meaning: something said that is deficient in meaning; **no-side',** the termination of a game at Rugby football; **no'-trump', no'-trumps'** (*bridge*), a call for the playing of a hand without any trump suit.—*adj.* **no'-trump'.**—**no-trump'er,** a no-trump call: a hand suitable for this: one addicted to calling no-trumps.—*advs.* **no'way, no'ways, no'wise,** in no way, manner, or degree. —**no doubt,** surely; **no end, no go** (see **end, go**); **no joke,** not a trifling matter; **no one, no single; no time,** a very short time. [O.E. *nān,* none. See **none.**]

**no,** *nō,* (*mod. Scot.*) *adv.* not. [Perh. from *nocht*; see **not, nought.**]

**no,** *nō,* **noh,** *nō, n.* (often *cap.*) the Japanese drama developed out of a religious dance. [Jap. *nō.*]

**Noachian,** *nō-ā'ki-ən, adj.* of *Noah* or his time—also **Noachic** (-*ak'*, -*āk'*).—**Noah's ark,** a child's toy in imitation of the Ark with its occupants.

**nob,** *nob, n.* head (*coll.*): knave of turn-up suit in cribbage.—**one for his nob,** point scored for holding the nob: blow on the head. [Perh. **knob.**]

**nob,** *nob, n.* a superior person.—*adv.* **nobb'ily.**—*n.* **nobb'iness.**—*adj.* **nobb'y,** smart. [Origin obscure; cf. **nabs, nib** (2).]

**nobble,** *nob'l,* (*slang*) *v.t.* to get hold of, esp. dishonestly: to win over, as by bribery: to swindle: to injure, or drug (a racehorse) to prevent it from winning: to seize.—*n.* **nobb'ler** (*slang*), a finishing-stroke: a thimble-rigger's confederate: a dram of spirits. [Perh. **nab.**]

**nobbut,** *nob'ət,* (*dial.*) *adv.* only.—*prep.* except.—*conj.* except that. [**no, but.**]

**Nobel prize,** *nō-bel',* one of the annual prizes for work in physics, chemistry, medicine, literature, and the promotion of peace instituted by Alfred B. *Nobel* (1833-96), Swedish discoverer of dynamite.

**nobelium,** *nō-bel'i-əm,* -*bēl', n.* name (symbol No) given to the element of atomic number 102 in 1957 when its production at the *Nobel* Institute, Stockholm, was claimed.

**nobility,** *nō-bil'i-ti, n.* the quality of being noble: high rank: dignity: excellence: greatness of mind or character: noble descent: nobles as a body.—*adj.* **nobil'iary,** of nobility.—*v.t.* **nobil'itate,** to ennoble.—*n.* **nobilitā'tion.** [See next word.]

**noble,** *nō'bl, adj.* illustrious: high in rank or character: of high birth: impressive: stately: generous: excellent.—*n.* a person of exalted rank: a peer: an obsolete gold coin = 6s. 8d. sterling.—*n.* **no'bleness.**—*adv.* **no'bly.**—**noble art,** boxing; **noble gas,** an inert gas; **no'bleman,** a man who is noble or of rank: a peer:—*pl.* **no'blemen;** *fem.* **no'blewoman; noble metal,** one that does not readily tarnish on exposure to air, as gold, silver, platinum—opposed to *base metal.*—*adj.* **no'ble-mind'ed.**—**no'ble-mind'-**

edness; **noble opal,** precious opal, a translucent or semi-transparent bluish or yellowish white variety with brilliant play of colours.—**most noble,** the style of a duke. [Fr. *noble*—L. (*g*)*nōbilis*—(*g*)*nōscĕre*, to know.]

**noblesse,** *nō-bles', n.* nobility: nobleness: a body of nobility.—(*Spens.*) **no'blesse,** **no'bilesse.**—**noblesse oblige** (*ō-blēzh*), rank imposes obligations. [Fr.]

**nobody,** *nō'ba-di, n.* no person: no one: a person of no account.—**nobody's business** (*slang*), a thing nobody could hope to deal with or nobody troubles about.—**like nobody's business,** very energetically or intensively. [**no, body.**]

**nocake,** *nō'kāk, n.* meal made of parched Indian corn. [Amer. Ind. word *nookik*, etc.]

**nocent,** *nō'sənt,* (*rare*) *adj.* hurtful: guilty.—*n.* one who is hurtful or guilty.—*adv.* **no'cently.** [L. *nocēns, -entis,* pr.p. of *nocēre,* to hurt.]

**nock,** *nok, n.* a notch, or a part carrying a notch, esp. on an arrow or a bow: the forward upper end of a sail that sets with a boom.—*v.t.* to notch: to fit (an arrow) on the string. [Origin obscure; appar. not the same as **notch.**]

**nocket.** See **nacket.**

**noctambulation,** *nok-tam-bū-lā'shən, n.* sleepwalking.—*ns.* **noctam'bulism; noctam'bulist.** [L. *nox, noctis,* night, *ambulāre, -ātum,* to walk.]

**Noctilio,** *nok-til'i-ō, n.* a South American genus, the hare-lipped bat. [L. *nox, noctis,* night, and the ending of *vespertiliō,* bat.]

**Noctiluca,** *nok-ti-lōō'ka, -lū', n.* a phosphorescent marine flagellate infusorian, abundant around the British coasts.—*n.* **noctilu'cence.**—*adjs.* **noctilu'cent** (-*sənt*), **noctilu'cous** (-*kəs*), phosphorescent: shining in the dark. [L. *noctilūca,* the moon, a lantern—*nox, noctis,* night, *lūcēre,* to shine.]

**noctivagant,** *nok-tiv'a-gənt, adj.* wandering in the night.—*n.* **noctivagā'tion.**—*adj.* **noctiv'agous.** [L. *nox, noctis,* night, *vagāri,* to wander.]

**Noctua,** *nok'tū-a, n.* a generic name sometimes used as a general name for any member of the **Noctū'idae,** a large family (or group of families) of mostly nocturnal, strong-bodied moths, the owlet-moths.—*n.* **noc'tüid.** [L. *noctūa,* an owl—*nox,* night.]

**noctuary,** *nok'tū-ə-ri, n.* a record of the events or thoughts of night. [L. *nox, noctis,* night, on the analogy of **diary.**]

**noctule,** *nok'tūl, n.* the great bat, the largest British species. [Fr.,—It. *nottola,* L. *nox, noctis,* night.]

**nocturn,** *nok'tərn, n.* any one of the three sections of the office of Matins: a daily portion of the psalter used at nocturns (*obs.*).—*adj.* **nocturn'al** (*tûrn'*), belonging to night: happening, done, or active by night.—*n.* an astronomical instrument for finding the hour by night: a person, animal, or spirit active by night.—*adv.* **nocturn'ally.**—*n.* **nocturne** (*nok'tûrn* or -*tûrn'*), a dreamy or pensive piece, generally for the piano, esp. associated with the name of its inventor John Field (1782-1837) and Chopin, who developed it: a moonlight or night scene (*paint.*). [L. *nocturnus*—*nox,* night.]

**nocuous,** *nok'ū-əs, adj.* hurtful.—*adv.* **noc'uously.** —*n.* **noc'uousness.** [L. *nocuus*—*nocēre,* to hurt.]

**nod,** *nod, v.i.* to give a quick forward motion of the head, esp. in assent, salutation, or command: to let the head drop in weariness: to lean over as if down to fall: to bend or curve downward, or hang from a curved support: to make a careless slip.—*v.t.* to incline: to signify or direct by a nod:—*pr.p.* **nodd'ing;** *pa.t.* and *pa.p.* **nodd'ed.**—*n.* a quick bending forward of the head: a slight bow: a movement of the head as a gesture of assent or command.—*n.* **nodd'er.**—*n.* and *adj.* **nodd'ing.**—*v.t.* and *v.i.* **nodd'le,** to nod slightly: to keep nodding.—*n.* **nodd'y,** an inverted pendulum with a spring, used to test oscillation.—**nodding acquaintance**, slight acquaintance: someone with whom one is only slightly acquainted: superficial, incomplete knowledge or understanding.—**Land of Nod**, sleep (in punning allusion to the biblical land, Gen. iv. 16); **on the nod** (*slang*), on tick. [M.E. *nodde*, not known in O.E.]

**noddle**, *nod'l*, *n.* the back of the head (*obs.*): the nape of the neck (*dial.*): now jocular, the head. [Origin obscure.]

**noddy**, *nod'i*, *n.* a noodle: an oceanic bird (Anous) akin to the terns, unaccustomed to man and therefore easily taken and deemed stupid: an old game like cribbage: the knave in this and other games: an old form of cab with a door at the back. [Origin obscure: connection among meanings doubtful.]

**node**, *nōd*, *n.* a knot: a knob or lump: a swelling: a place, often swollen, where a leaf is attached to a stem: a point of intersection of two great circles of the celestial sphere, esp. the orbit of a planet or the moon and the ecliptic: a point at which a curve cuts itself, and through which more than one tangent to the curve can be drawn (*geom.*): a similar point on a surface, where there is more than one tangent-plane (*geom.*): a point of minimum displacement in a system of stationary waves: a meeting-place of lines, roads, or parts: a complication in a story (*fig.*).—*adj.* **nō'dal**, of a node or nodes.—*v.t.* **nōd'alise, -ize,** to make nodal.—*n.* **nōdal'ity,** knottedness: state of being nodal.—*adj.* **nōd'āted,** knotted.—*n.* **nōdā'tion,** knottiness: a knotty place.—*adjs.* **nodical** (*nōd'* or *nod'*), pertaining to the nodes: from a node round to the same node again: **nodose** (*nōd-ōs'*, *nōd'ōs*), having nodes, knots or swellings: knotty.—*n.* **nodosity** (*nō-dos'i-ti*), knottiness: a knotty swelling.—*adjs.* **nōd'ous,** knotty; **nodular** (*nod'ū-lər*), of or like a nodule: in the form of nodules: having nodules or little knots; **nōd'ulāted,** having nodules.—*ns.* **nōdū-lā'tion; nōd'ūle,** a little rounded lump: a swelling on a root inhabited by symbiotic bacteria.—*adjs.* **nōd'ūled; nōd'ūlose, nōd'ūlous.** —*n.* **nōd'us** (L.), a knotty point, difficulty, complication: a swelling at the junction of nervures in an insect's wing:—*pl.* **nōd'i** (*-ī*). [L. *nōdus*; dim. *nōdulus*.]

**Noël.** See Nowel.

**noesis,** *nō-ē'sis*, *n.* the activity of the intellect.—*adj.* **noemat'ical.**—*adv.* **noemat'ically.**—*adj.* **noetic** (*nō-et'ik*), purely intellectual. [Gr. *noēsis—noeein,* to perceive, think.]

**Noetian,** *nō-ē'shən*, *n.* a Patripassian or follower of *Noëtus* of Smyrna (3rd cent.).—Also *adj.*—*n.* **Noe'tianism.**

**nog,** *nog*, *n.* Norwich strong ale (*obs.*): egg-nog or similar drink. [Origin unknown.]

**nog,** *nog*, *n.* a stump or snag: a wooden peg, pin, or cog: a brick-sized piece of wood inserted in a wall to receive nails.—*n.* **nogg'ing,** a brick filling between timbers in a partition. [Origin unknown.]

**noggin,** *nog'in*, *n.* a small mug or wooden cup: its contents, a dram of about a gill. [Origin unknown; Ir. *noigin,* Gael. *noigean,* are believed to be from English.]

**noh.** Same as no (4).

**nohow,** *nō'how, adv.* not in any way, not at all: in no definable way: (*coll.*—also **no'howish**) out of sorts.

**noils,** *noilz*, *n.pl.* short pieces of wool or other fibre separated from the longer fibres by combing.— Also *sing.* **noil,** the wool so separated. [Origin unknown.]

**noint, 'noint,** an aphetic form of anoint.

**noise,** *noiz*, *n.* sound of any kind: an unmusical sound: an over-loud or disturbing sound: din: frequent or public talk: rumour (*obs.*): report (*Shak.*): a band of musicians (*obs.*): interference

in a communication channel, as detected by hearing or (**visual noise**—e.g. snow on a television screen) sight.—*v.t.* to spread by rumour.—*v.i.* to talk or call out loud.—*adjs.* **noise'ful; noise'less.**—*adv.* **noise'lessly.**—*n.* **noise'lessness.**—*adv.* **nois'ily.**—*n.* **nois'iness.**—*adj.* **nois'y,** making a loud noise or sound: attended with noise: clamorous: turbulent.—**a big noise,** a person of great importance; **make a noise in the world,** to achieve great notoriety. [Fr. *noise,* quarrel; perh. from L. *nausea,* disgust; but possibly from L. *noxia,* hurt—*nocēre,* to hurt.]

**noisette,** *nwa-zet'*, *n.* a hybrid between China and moss rose. [From Philippe *Noisette,* its first grower.]

**noisette,** *nwa-zet'*, *n.* a small choice piece of meat specially cooked: a nutlike sweet. [Fr., hazelnut.]

**noisome,** *noi'səm*, *adj.* injurious to health: disgusting to sight or smell.—*adv.* **noi'somely.**—*n.* **noi'someness.** [noy.]

**nolens volens,** *nō'lenz vō'lenz, nō'lāns vō', wō'lāns,* (L.) willynilly.

**noli-me-tangere,** *nō-li-mē-tan'jə-ri* (**noli me tangere,** *nō-lē mā tang'ge-rā;* Vulgate John xx. 17) *n.* a warning against touching: lupus, etc., of the face: a species of balsam, *Impatiens noli-(me-)tangere,* that ejects its ripe seeds at a light touch. —*adj.* warning off. [L. *nōli* (imper. of *nōlle*), be unwilling, do not, *mē,* me, *tangēre* to touch.]

**nolition,** *nō-lish'ən, n.* unwillingness: absence of willingness: a will not to do. [L. *nōlle,* to be unwilling.]

**noll, noul, nowl** (*Spens.* **noule,** *Shak.* **nole**), *nōl, n.* the top of the head. [O.E. *hnoll.*]

**nolle prosequi,** *no'le pros'ə-kwī,* (L.; *law*) (entry on record to the effect that) plaintiff or prosecutor will proceed no further with (part of) suit.

**nolo episcopari,** *nōl'ō e-pis-ko-pär'ī,* (L.) I do not wish to be a bishop (*lit.*): refusal of responsible position.

**nom,** *nō,* (Fr.) name.—**nom de guerre** (*də ger*), an assumed name: pseudonym (**nom de plume** is not French).

**nomad, nomade,** *nōm'ad, -əd,* also *nom', n.* one of a wandering pastoral community: a rover.— Also *adj.*—**nomadic** (*nōm- or nom-ad'ik*).—*adv.* **nomad'ically.**—*n.* **nomadisā'tion, -z-.**—*v.i.* **nom'a-dise, -ize,** lead a nomadic or vagabond life.—*v.t.* make nomadic.—*n.* **nom'adism.** [Gr. *nomas, nomados—nemein,* to drive to pasture.]

**no-man's-land,** *nō'manz-land, n.* a waste region to which no one has a recognised claim: a debatable land, esp. between entrenched hostile forces.

**nomarch.** See nome.

**nombril,** *nom'bril,* (her.) *n.* a point a little below the centre of a shield. [Fr., navel.]

**nom de plume,** *nō də plüm', plōōm',* or *nom,* a pen-name, pseudonym. [Would-be Fr.—Fr. *nom,* name, *de,* of, *plume,* pen.]

**nome,** *nōm, n.* a province or department, esp. in ancient Egypt or modern Greece.—*ns.* **nomarch** (*nom'ärk*), the governor of a nome; **nom'archy,** a nome of modern Greece; **nom'os** (Gr.), a nome. [Gr. *nomos.*]

**nomen,** *nō'men,* (L.) a name, esp. of the *gens* or clan, a Roman's second name, as Gaius *Julius* Caesar.—**nomen nudum** (*nū'dəm, nōō'dōōm*), in biology, a mere name published without a description.

**nomenclator,** *nō'mən-klā-tər, n.* one who bestows names, or draws up a classified scheme of names: one who announces or tells the names of persons, esp. (*hist.*) in canvassing for a Roman election; a book containing a list of words, a vocabulary (*obs.*).—*adjs.* **no'menclātive, nomenclatorial** (*nō-men-klə-tō'ri-əl, -tō'*), **nomenclā'tural.**—*n.* **nō'men-clāture** (or *nō-men'klə-chər*), a system of names: terminology: a list of names: a vocabulary (*obs.*): mode of naming: (now considered loose) a name. [L. *nōmenclātor—nōmen*, a name, *calāre* to call.]

nomic, *nom'ik, adj.* customary: conventional, esp. of spelling. [Gr. *nomikos—nomos*, custom.]

nominal, *nom'in-əl, adj.* pertaining to, or of the nature of, a name or noun: of names: by name: only in name: so-called, but not in reality: inconsiderable, hardly more than a matter of form: nominalistic (*rare*).—*ns.* nom'inalism, the doctrine that general terms have no corresponding reality either in or out of the mind, being mere words; nom'inalist.—*adj.* nominalist'ic.—*adv.* nom'inally, by name: as a noun: in name only. [L. *nōminālis—nōmen, -inis*, a name.]

nominate, *nom'in-āt, v.t.* to name: to mention by name: to appoint: to propose formally for election.—*adj.* (chiefly *Scots law*) nominated: elect.—*adj.* nom'inable, namable: fit to be named.—*adv.* nom'inately, by name.—*n.* nominā'tion, the act or power of nominating: state of being nominated: naming.—*adj.* nominatival (*nom-in-ə-tī'vl*, or *nom-nə-*).—*adv.* nominati'vally. —*adj.* nominative (*nom'in-ə-tiv, nom'nə-tiv; gram.*), naming the subject: in the case in which the subject is expressed: (also *nom'in-ā-tiv*) nominated, appointed by nomination.—*n.* the nominative case: a word in the nominative case. —*adv.* nom'inatively.—*n.* nom'inātor, one who nominates.—nominative absolute, a nominative combined with a participle, but not connected with a finite verb or governed by any other word. [L. *nōmināre, -ātum*, to name—*nōmen*.]

nominee, *nom-in-ē', n.* one who is nominated by another: one on whose life an annuity or lease depends: one to whom the holder of a copyhold estate surrenders his interest. [L. *nōmināre, -ātum*, to nominate, with -*ee* as if from Fr.]

nomism, *nōm'izm, nom'izm, n.* religious legalism: the view that moral conduct consists in the observance of a law.—*adj.* nomist'ic (*nom-*), based on law, or on a sacred book. [Gr. *nomisma*, established custom, *nomos*, a law.]

nomocracy, *nom-ok'rə-si*, or *nōm-, n.* government according to a code of laws. [Gr. *nomos*, law, *kratos*, power.]

nomogeny, *nom-* or *nōm-oj'ə-ni, n.* the origination of life according to natural law, not miracle— opp. to *thaumatogeny.* [Gr. *nomos*, law, and the root *gen-*, as in *genesis*, origination.]

nomography, *nom-* or *nōm-og'rə-fi, n.* the art of drawing up laws.—*ns.* nomog'rapher; nom'ogram, a chart or diagram of scaled lines or curves used to help in calculations, comprising three scales in which a line joining values on two determines a third.—Also called nom'ograph, isopleth. [Gr. *nomos*, law, *graphein*, to write.]

nomology, *nom-* or *nōm-ol'ə-ji, n.* the science of law: the science of the laws of the mind.—*adj.* nomological (-ə-loj').—*n.* nomol'ogist. [Gr. *nomos*, law, *logos*, discourse.]

nomothete, *nom'ō-thēt*, or (Gr.) nomothetes (*nom-oth'i-tēz*), *n.* a lawgiver: a legislator: in ancient Athens, one of a body charged with revision of the laws.—*adj.* nomothetic (-*thet'ik*). [Gr. *nomothetēs—nomos*, law, and the root *the-*, as in *tithenai*, to set.]

non, *non*, a Latin word used as a prefix, not: sometimes used of someone or something with pretensions who, which, is ludicrously unworthy of the name mentioned, e.g. non-hero, non-event. The words given below include the most common words with *non-* but the prefix is living and many other words using it may be formed. —*ns.* non-abil'ity, incapacity: inability: non-accept'ance, want of acceptance: refusal to accept; non-ac'cess (*law*), want of opportunity for sexual intercourse; non-admiss'ion, refusal of admission: failure to be admitted; non-aggress'ion, abstention from aggression.—*adjs.*

non-alcohol'ic, not alcoholic: not containing alcohol; non-aligned', not aligned: not taking sides in international politics.—*ns.* non-align'-ment; non-appear'ance, failure or neglect to appear, esp. in a court of law; non-arri'val, failure to arrive; non-attend'ance, a failure to attend: absence; non-atten'tion, inattention; non-Chris'tian, other than Christian (also *adj.*); non'-claim, a failure to make claim within the time limited by law.—*adjs.* non-cog'nisable, of an offence, that cannot be judicially investigated; non-collē'giate, not belonging to a college (also *n.*).—*ns.* non-com' (*coll.*), a non-commissioned officer; non-com'batant, any one connected with an army who is there for some purpose other than that of fighting, as a surgeon, a chaplain: a civilian in time of war.—*adjs.* non-commiss'-ioned, not having a commission, as an officer in the army below the rank of commissioned officer; non-committ'al, not committing one or refraining from committing oneself, to any particular opinion or course of conduct: free from any declared preference or pledge: implying nothing, one way or the other.—*n.* a non-committal state or utterance.—*ns.* non-commun'icant, one who does not take communion on any particular occasion or in general, esp. formerly according to the rites of the Church of England: one who has not yet communicated; non-commun'ion; non-compear'ance (*Scots law*), failure to appear in a court of law; non-compli'ance, neglect or failure of compliance.—*adj.* non-comply'ing.—*ns.* non-compound'er, one who does not compound or make composition: a Jacobite who would restore James II unconditionally (*hist.*); non-con' (*coll.*), a Nonconformist (also *adj.*); non-concurr'ence, refusal to concur.—*adj.* non-conduct'ing, not readily conducting, esp. heat or electricity.—*n.* non-conduct'or, a substance or object that does not readily conduct heat or electricity.—*adj.* non-conform'ing, not conforming, esp. to an established church.—*ns.* non-conform'ity; non-conform'ist, one who does not conform: esp. one who refused to conform or subscribe to the Act of Uniformity in 1662: usu. applied in England (*cap.*) to a Protestant separated from the Church of England (also *adj.*); nonconform'ity, want of conformity, esp. to the established church; non'-content, one not content: in House of Lords, one giving a negative vote.—*adjs.* non-conten'tious, not subject to contention; non-contrib'utory, not based on contributions.—*ns.* non-co-operā'tion, failure or refusal to co-operate, esp. (in India before 1947) with the government; non-deliv'ery, failure or neglect to deliver: the fact of not having been delivered.—*adj.* non-effect'ive, having no effect: not efficient or serviceable: unfitted or unavailable for service: relating to those so unfitted or unavailable.—*n.* a member of a force who is unfitted or unavailable for active service.—*adj.* non-effic'ient, not up to the standard required for service.—*n.* a soldier who has not yet undergone the full number of drills.—*n.* non-e'go, in metaphysics, the not-I, the object as opposed to the subject, whatever is not the conscious self.—*adj.* non-elect', not elect.—*n.* non-elec'tion, state of not being elect: fact of not having elected or been elected.—*adjs.* non-elec'tive, not chosen by election; non-elec'tric (*obs.*), conducting electricity.—*n.* a conductor.—*ns.* non-elec'trolyte, a substance, such as sugar, that gives a non-conducting solution; non-en'try (*Scots law, hist.*), a vassal's heir's failure to renew investiture: a casualty that was due to the superior on such failure.—*adj.* non-essen'tial, not essential: not absolutely required.—*n.* something that is not essential, or is not of extreme importance.—*adj.* non-Euclid'ean, not according to Euclid's axioms and postulates.—*n.* non-exist'ence, the condition

of not being: a thing that has no existence.—
*adjs.* non-exist′ent; non-ferr′ous, containing no
iron: other than iron: relating to metals other
than iron; non-fic′tion, of a literary work,
without any deliberately fictitious element
(non-fiction novel, one whose material is entirely
drawn from people and events in real life); non-
flamm′able, not capable of supporting flame,
though combustible; non-for′feiting, of a life
insurance policy, not forfeited by reason of non-
payment.—*ns.* non-fulfil′ment, the fact of not
fulfilling or not being fulfilled; non-gre′mial, a
non-resident member, esp. of Cambridge University.—*adj.* applied to the examinations afterwards called local.—*ns.* non-interven′tion, a
policy of systematic abstention from interference
in the affairs of other nations; non-intru′sion, in
Scottish Church history, the principle that a
patron should not force an unacceptable minister
on an unwilling congregation; non-intru′sionist;
non-involve′ment, the fact of not involving or not
being involved.—*adj.* non-iss′uable, not capable
of being issued: not admitting of issue being
taken on it.—*n.* non-join′der, omission to join
all the parties to an action or suit.—*adj.* non-
jur′ing, not swearing allegiance.—*n.* Nonjur′or,
one of the clergy in England and Scotland who
would not swear allegiance to William and Mary
in 1689, holding themselves still bound by the
oath they had taken to the deposed king, James
II.—*adjs.* non-lin′ear, not linear; non-marr′ying,
not readily disposed to marry.—*ns.* non-
mem′ber, one who is not a member; non′-
met′al, an element that is not a metal.—*adjs.*
non-metall′ic, not metallic: not of metal or like
metal; non-mor′al, unconcerned with morality:
involving no moral considerations; non-nat′ural,
not natural: forced or strained.—*n.* in old
medicine (usu. in *pl.*) anything not considered of
the essence of man, but necessary to his well-
being, as air, food, sleep, rest, etc.—*adjs.* non-
nu′cleated, not nucleated; non-objec′tive (*paint.*),
non-representational.—*n.* non-observ′ance, neglect or failure to observe: disregard.—*adjs.* non-
opera′tional, not operational; non-partisan′
(or -*pärt′*), not partisan: impartial; non-par′ty,
independent of party politics.—*ns.* non-pay′ment;
non-perform′ance, neglect or failure to perform;
non′-per′son, one previously of political, etc.,
eminence, now out of favour: a complete nonentity.—*adjs.* non-play′ing, (of e.g. the captain of
a team) not taking active part in the game(s);
non-prior′ity, without privilege of priority.—*n.*
non-produc′tion.—*adj.* non-profess′ional, not professional or of a profession: not done in professional capacity.—*n.* non-profi′cient, one who
has made no progress in the art or study in which
he is engaged.—*adjs.* non-prof′it-making, not
organised or engaged in with the purpose of
making a profit.—*n.* non-prolifera′tion (see
proliferate); non-provi′ded, (of an elementary
school or education in England and Wales)
maintained but not provided by the local
education authority, and managed by a committee in which the trustees form the majority;
non-quo′ta, not included in a quota.—*n.* non-
regard′ance (*Shak.*), want of due regard.—*adj.*
non-representa′tional, not aiming at the depicting
of objects.—*n.* non-res′idence, fact of not residing
at a place, esp. where one's official or social
duties require one to reside or where one is
entitled to reside.—*adj.* and *n.* non-res′ident.—
*n.* non-resist′ance, the principle of not resisting
violence by force, or of not resisting authority:
passive submission.—*adjs.* non-resist′ant, non-
resist′ing; non-rig′id, of airships, having a
balloon or gasbag with no internal framework to
brace it, and no rigid keel; non-skid′, non-slip′,
designed to reduce chance of slipping to a
minimum.—*n.* non-smo′ker, one who does not

smoke: a railway compartment in which smoking is supposed to be forbidden.—*adjs.* non-smok′-
ing; non-soci′ety, not belonging to a society,
esp. not a member of a trade union: employing
men who are not members of a trade union;
non-spec′ialist, not devoting oneself to one
particular subject, task, etc.—also *n.*—*adj.*
non-specif′ic, not specific: of a disease, not caused
by any specific agent.—*n.* non-start′er, a horse
which, though entered for a race, does not run:
a person who has no chance at all of success.—
*adj.* non-stick′, of e.g. a pan, treated so that food
or other substance will not stick to it.—*adj.* and
*adv.* non′-stop′, uninterrupted(ly): without any
stop or halt.—*n.* non′-term (*obs.*), a vacation
between terms: a time of inactivity.—*adjs.*
non-U (see U); non-u′nion, not attached to a
trade union: employing, or produced by, non-
union workers.—*ns.* non-u′nionist; non-u′sager,
a Nonjuror who rejected the usages; non-u′ser
(*law*), omission to take advantage of a right.—
*adj.* non-util′ity, not of the special kind made or
sold for utility's sake.—*n.* non-vi′olence, (the ideal
or practice of) refraining from violence on
grounds of principle.—*adj.* non-vi′olent.—*n.* non′-
white′, (a member of) a race other than the white
race (also *adj.*). [L. *nōn*, not.]

non, *non*, *nōn*, (L.) not.—non obstante (*ob-stan′tē*,
*ob-stan′te*), not hindering: notwithstanding.

nonage, *non′ij*, *nōn′ij*, *n.* legal infancy, minority:
time of immaturity generally.—*adj.* non′aged.
[O.Fr. *nonage*—pfx. *non*- (L. *nōn*) and *age*, age.]

nonagenarian, *nōn-* or *non-ə-ji-nā′ri-ən*, *n.* one
who is ninety years old or between ninety and a
hundred.—*adj.* of that age. [L. *nōnāgēnārius*,
relating to ninety—*nōnāgintā*, ninety.]

nonagesimal, *nōn-* or *non-ə-jes′i-məl*, *adj.* ninetieth.
—*n.* point of the ecliptic 90° from its intersection
by the horizon. [L. *nōnāgēsimus*, ninetieth.]

nonagon, *non′ə-gon*, *n.* an enneagon. [L. *nōnus*,
ninth, Gr. *gōniā*, angle.]

nonane, *nōn′ān*, *n.* a hydrocarbon ($C_9H_{20}$), ninth
in the methane series. [L. *nōnus*, ninth.]

nonary, *nōn′ə-ri*, *adj.* based on nine. [L. *nōnārius*.]

nonce, *nons*, *n.* (almost confined to the phrase *for
the nonce*, which in M.E. is sometimes a mere tag
for rhyme's sake) the particular or express
purpose (*Shak.*): the occasion: the moment,
time being.—nonce′-word, a word coined for
use at the moment. [From *for the nones*, i.e.
*for then ones*, for the once, *then* being the dative
(O.E. *tham*) of *the* and *ones* the genitive (O.E.
*ānes*) of *one* substituted for the dative.]

nonchalance, *non′sha-ləns*, *n.* unconcern: coolness: indifference.—*adj.* non′chalant.—*adv.* non′-
chalantly. [Fr.,—*non*, not, *chaloir*, to matter,
interest—L. *calēre*, to be warm.]

non-come, *non-kum′*, *-kom′*, (*Shak.*) *n.* one of
Dogberry's blundering words, perh. a confusion
of *nonplus* and *non compos mentis*.

nonconformist, -ity. See non (1).

nondescript, *non′di-skript*, *adj.* not described (*obs.*):
not easily classified: not distinctive enough to be
described: neither one thing nor another.—*n.*
a person or thing not yet, or not easily, described
or classed. [L. *nōn*, not, *dēscrībĕre*, *-scriptum*,
to describe.]

none, *nun*, *pron.* (*pl.* or *sing.*) not one: no person
or persons: not the thing in question: not any:
no portion or amount.—*adj.* (separated from the
noun; otherwise *arch.*); formerly esp. before a
vowel or *h*) no.—*adv.* in no degree: by no means:
not at all.—none′-so-prett′y, Nan′cy-prett′y,
London Pride (*Saxifraga umbrosa*).—*adj.* none′-
spar′ing (*Shak.*), all-destroying.—*adv.* none′-the-
less′ (or none the less), nevertheless. [O.E. *nān*
—*ne*, not, *ān*, one.]

nonentity, *non-en′ti-ti*, *n.* the state of not being:
a thing not existing: a person or thing of no
importance. [L. *nōn*, not, *entitās* (see entity).]

**Nones,** *nōnz, n.pl.* in the Roman calendar, the ninth day before the Ides (both days included)— the 7th of March, May, July, and October, and the 5th of the other months: a church office originally for the ninth hour, or three o'clock, afterwards earlier. [L. *nōnae*—*nōnus,* ninth.]

**non(e)such,** *non', nun'such, n.* a unique, unparalleled, or extraordinary thing: black medick. [none, such.]

**nonet, nonette,** *nō-net', (mus.) n.* a composition for nine performers.—Also **nonet'to.** [It. *nonetto.*]

**non-feasance,** *non-fē'zəns, n.* omission of something which ought to be done. [Pfx. *non-,* not, O.Fr. *faisance,* doing—*faire*—L. *facĕre,* to do.]

**nonillion,** *nō-nil'yən, n.* a million raised to the ninth power: one thousand raised to the tenth power *(U.S.).—adj.* **nonill'ionth.** [L. *nōnus,* ninth, in imitation of **million, billion.**]

**Nonjuror.** See non (1).

**nonny,** *non'i, n.* a meaningless word in old ballad refrain, etc., usually 'hey, nonny', 'hey nonny nonny', or 'hey nonny no'—once a cover for obscenity.

**nonpareil,** *non-pə-rel', non'pə-rel, n.* a person or thing without equal: a fine variety of apple: a kind of comfit: a six-point printing-type.—*adj.* unequalled: matchless. [Fr. *non,* not, *pareil,* from a L.L. dim. of L. *pār,* equal.]

**nonplus,** *non'plus, n.* a state in which no more can be done or said: great difficulty.—*v.t.* to perplex completely, make uncertain what to say or do: —*pr.p.* **non'plussing;** *pa.t.* and *pa.p.* **non'plussed.** [L. *nōn,* not, *plūs,* more.]

**nonsense,** *non'səns, n.* that which has no sense: language without meaning: absurdity: trifling: foolery: humbug: trivial things: that which is manifestly false: absurd, illogical, or unintelligible statement or action.—Also *interj.—adj.* **nonsensical (-*sens'*),** without sense: absurd.—*ns.* **nonsensicality** (*non-sens-i-kal'i-ti*), **nonsens'icalness.**—*adv.* **nonsens'ically.**—**nonsense verse,** verse deliberately written to convey an absurd meaning, or without obvious meaning at all. [Pfx. *non-,* not, and **sense.**]

**non-sequitur,** *non-sek'wi-tər, n.* (the drawing of) a conclusion that does not follow logically from the premises: loosely, a remark, action, that has no relation to what has gone before.—Also *non* **sequitur.** [L. *nōn,* not and *sequitur,* follows, 3rd sing. pres. ind. of *sequi,* to follow.]

**nonsuit,** *non'sūt, -sŏŏt, n.* in England, the stopping of a suit by voluntary withdrawal of the plaintiff, or by the judge when the plaintiff has failed to make out cause of action or to bring evidence.— *v.t.* to subject to a nonsuit. [A.Fr. *no(u)nsute,* does not pursue.]

**nonuplet,** *non'ūp-let, n.* a group of nine: esp. a group of nine notes played in the time of six or eight. [L. *nōnus,* ninth; *nonuplus,* not in L., formed on the analogy of *duplus, quadruplus,* etc.]

**noodle,** *nōōd'l, n.* a simpleton: a blockhead.—*n.* **nood'ledom.** [Cf. **noddy.**]

**noodle,** *nōōd'l, n.* a flat, usu. ribbon-shaped, paste, usu. made with eggs. [Ger. *nudel.*]

**nook,** *nōōk, n.* a corner: a narrow place formed by an angle: a recess: a secluded retreat.—*adj.* **nook'y.**—*adj.* **nook'-shott'en** (*arch.*), shot out into nooks and corners. [M.E. *nok, noke;* prob. Scand.; Gael. and Ir. *niuc* is prob. from the Northern form **neuk.**]

**noology,** *nō-ol'ə-ji, n.* the science of the intellect. —*ns.* **nŏogen'esis,** evolution of mind; **nŏom'etry,** mind-measurement; **nŏ'osphere** (*Teilhard de Chardin*), the sphere of the mind, the collective memory and intelligence of the human race. [Gr. *noos,* the mind, *logos,* discourse, *metron,* measure, *sphaira,* sphere.]

**noon,** *nōōn, n.* the ninth hour of the day in Roman and ecclesiastical reckoning, three o'clock p.m.: afterwards (when the church service called *Nones* was shifted to midday) midday: middle: greatest height.—*adj.* belonging to midday: meridional. —*v.i.* to rest at noon.—*n.* **noon'ing** (esp. *U.S.*), a repast or rest about noon.—**noon'day,** midday: the time of greatest prosperity.—*adj.* pertaining to midday: meridional.—**noon'tide,** the time of noon, midday.—*adj.* pertaining to noon: meridional. [O.E. *nōn*—L. *nōna* (*hōra*), the ninth (hour).]

**no-one,** *nō'-wun, n.* and *pron.* nobody.—Also **no one.**

**noop,** *nōōp, (Scott) n.* a knob, tip (of the elbow). [Cf. **knop.**]

**noose,** *nōōs,* also *nōōz, n.* a loop with running knot which ties the firmer the closer it is drawn: a snare or bond generally, esp. hanging or marriage.—*v.t.* to tie or catch in a noose. [Perh. O.Fr. *nous,* pl. of *nou* (Fr. *nœud*)—L. *nōdus,* knot.]

**nopal,** *nō'pal, pəl, n.* a Central American cactus (Nopalea) used for rearing cochineal insects. [Sp. *nopal*—Mex. *nopalli.*]

**nope,** *nōp, adv.* an emphatic, originally American, form of **no,** pronounced with a snap of the mouth.

**nor,** *nör, conj.* and not: neither—used esp. in introducing the second part of a negative proposition—correlative to *neither.* [App. from *nother,* a form of **neither.**]

**nor,** *nör, (Scot.* and *dial.) conj.* than. [Origin obscure.]

**nor',** *nör,* a shortened form of **north.**

**noradrenalin,** *nör-ə-dren'ə-lin, n.* a drug related to adrenalin, used as a heart resuscitant.

**Norbertine,** *nör'bərt-īn, -in, n.* and *adj.* Premonstratensian. [From *Norbert,* the founder (1119).]

**Nordic,** *nör'dik, adj.* of a tall, blond, dolichocephalic type of (generally Germanic) peoples in N.W. Europe: loosely used by Nazis.—Also *n.* [Fr. *nord,* north.]

**Norfolk,** *nör'fək, adj.* belonging to the English county of *Norfolk.*—**Norfolk capon,** a red herring; **Norfolk dumpling** or **turkey,** a native or inhabitant of Norfolk; **Norfolk jacket,** a loose pleated coat with a waistband.—**Norfolk Island pine,** a lofty Araucaria of Norfolk Island (in the Pacific, named after the ducal family of *Norfolk*). [O.E. *northfolc,* north folk.]

**noria,** *nō'ri-ə, nō', n.* an endless chain of buckets on a wheel for water-raising. [Sp. *noria*—Ar. *nā'ūrah.*]

**norimon,** *nor'i-mon, n.* a Japanese palanquin. [Jap. *nori,* to ride, *mono,* thing.]

**norite,** *nō'rīt, n.* a gabbro with a rhombic pyroxene. [Norway.]

**norland, norlan',** *nör'lən(d), (Scot.* and *poet.), n.* the north country.—*adj.* belonging to or coming from the north. [north, land.]

**norm,** *nörm, n.* a rule: a pattern: an authoritative standard: a type: the ordinary or most frequent value or state.—*n.* **nor'ma,** a rule: a standard: a square for measuring right angles.—*adj.* **nor'mal,** according to rule: not deviating from the standard: ordinary: well adjusted: functioning regularly: having an unbranched chain of carbon atoms (*chem.*): (of a solution) having one gramme-equivalent of dissolved substance to a litre: perpendicular (*geom.*).—*n.* a perpendicular: a normal instance or specimen.— *ns.* **nor'malcy** (an ill-formed word), normality, often of political, economic, etc., conditions; **normalisā'tion, -z-.**—*v.t.* **nor'malise, -ize,** to make normal: of steel, to heat it in order to refine the crystal structure and to relieve internal stress.—*v.i.* become normal, regular.—*n.* **nor'mal'ity.**—*adv.* **nor'mally,** in a normal manner: usually.—*adj.* **nor'mative,** of, or pertaining to, a norm: establishing a standard: prescriptive.— **normal school,** a training-college for teachers; **normal solution** (see above and also **standard solution**). [L. *norma,* a rule.]

**Norma,** *nör'mə, n.* the Rule, a small southern constellation. [L. *norma,* a rule.]

**Norman,** *nör'mən, n.* a native or inhabitant of Normandy: one of that Scandinavian people which settled in northern France about the beginning of the 10th century, founded the Duchy of Normandy, and conquered England in 1066:—*pl.* **Nor'mans:** the Norman-French dialect.—*adj.* pertaining to the Normans or to Normandy.—*v.t.* **Nor'manise, -ize,** to give a Norman character to. — *n.* **Nor'manism.** — **Norman architecture,** a massive Romanesque style, prevalent in Normandy (10th-11th cent.) and England (11th-12th), the churches with semicircular apse and a great tower, deeply recessed doorways, small, round-headed windows, zigzag, billet, nailhead, and other characteristic ornaments; **Norman Conquest,** the conquest of England by Duke William of Normandy (1066); **Norman cross,** an elaborate memorial cross like a Gothic turret with niches for figures and pinnacles.—*n.* and *adj.* **Nor'man-French',** French as spoken by the Normans. [O.Fr. *Normanz, Normans,* nom. and accus. pl. of *Normant,* Northman, from Scand.]

**norman,** *nör'mən,* (*naut.*) *n.* a bar inserted in a windlass to fasten or veer a rope or cable on.

**Norn,** *nörn,* (*Scand. myth.*) *n.* one of the three Fates—Urd, Verdande, and Skuld.—Also (Latinised) **Norn'a.** [O.N. *norn.*]

**Norn,** *nörn, n.* the old Norse dialect of Orkney and Shetland.—Also *adj.* [O.N. *norræna.*]

**Norroy,** *nor'oi,* (*her.*) *n.* an English king-of-arms whose jurisdiction lies north of the Trent.—Since 1943, **Norroy and Ulster.** [O.Fr. *nord,* north, *roy,* king.]

**Norse,** *nörs, adj.* Norwegian: ancient Scandinavian.—*n.* the Norwegian language: the language of the ancient Scandinavians—also **Old Norse.**—*n.* **Norse'man,** a Scandinavian or Northman. [Perh. Du. *noor(d)sch;* cf. Ice. *Norskr;* Norw. *Norsk.*]

**north,** *nörth, adv.* in the direction of that point of the horizon or that pole of the earth or heavens which at equinox is opposite the sun at noon in Europe or elsewhere on the same side of the equator, or towards the sun in the other hemisphere: in the slightly different direction (*magnetic north*) in which a magnetic needle points.— *n.* the point of the horizon in that direction: the region lying in that direction: the part placed relatively in that direction: the north wind.— *adj.* lying towards the north: forming the part, or that one of two, that is towards the north: blowing from the north: (of a pole of a magnet, usually) north-seeking.—*v.i.* to turn or move towards the north.—*n.* **norther** (*nörth'ər*), a wind or gale from the north, esp. applied to a cold wind that blows in winter over Texas and the Gulf of Mexico.—*v.i.* (*nördh'ər*), shift or veer to north.—*n.* **north'erliness** (*dh*).—*adj.* **north'erly** (*dh*), being toward the north: blowing from the north.—*adv.* toward or from the north.—*adj.* **north'ern** (*dh*), pertaining to the north: being in the north or in the direction toward it: proceeding from the north.—*n.* a native of the north: a north wind.—*n.* **north'erner** (*dh*), a native of, or resident in, the north, esp. of the northern United States.—*v.t.* **north'ernise, -ize** (*dh*), to give a northern character to.—*n.* **north'ernism** (*dh*), northern idiom.—*adjs.* **north'ermost** (*dh; obs.*), **north'ernmost** (*dh*), **north'most** (*th*), most northerly.—*ns.* **north'ing** (*th*), motion, distance, or tendency northward: distance of a heavenly body from the equator northward: difference of latitude made by a ship in sailing: deviation towards the north.—*adj., adv.,* and *n.* **north'ward, nor'ward, norward** (*nörth'ward, nör'-ward, nor'əd*).—*adj.* and *adv.* **north'wardly.**—*adv.* **north'wards.**—*adjs.* **north'-bound,** bound for the

north: travelling northwards; **north'-country,** belonging to the northern part of the country, esp. of England.—**north-coun'tryman.**—*adj.* and *adv.* **north-east,** **nor'-east'** (also *nörth', nör'*), midway between north and east.—*n.* the direction midway between north and east: the region lying in that direction: the wind blowing from that direction.—**north-east'er, nor'-east'er,** a strong wind from the north-east.—*adj.* and *adv.* **north-east'erly,** towards or from the north-east.—*adj.* **north'-east'ern,** belonging to the north-east: being in the north-east, or in that direction.—*adj.* and *adv.* **north-east'ward,** toward the north-east.—*n.* the region to the north-east. —*adj.* and *adv.* **north-east'wardly.**—*adv.* **north-east'wards.**—**northern fern,** the hard fern (Lomaria); **northern lights,** the aurora borealis; **north'land** (also *adj.*), land, or lands, of the north; **North'man,** an ancient Scandinavian.— *ns., adjs.,* and *advs.* **north-north-east';** **north-north-west',** (in) a direction midway between north and north-east or north-west.—*adj.* **north pol'ar.**—**north pole,** the end of the earth's axis in the Arctic regions: its projection on the celestial sphere: (usually) that pole of a magnet which when free points to the earth's north magnetic pole (logically the other end).—*adj.* **north'-seeking,** turning towards the earth's magnetic north pole.—**North Star,** a star very near the north pole of the heavens, the Pole Star; **north water,** the space of open sea left by the winter pack of ice moving southward.—*adj.* and *adv.* **north-west', nor'-west'** (also *nörth', nör'*), midway between north and west.—*n.* the direction midway between north and west: the region lying in that direction: the wind blowing from that direction.—**north-, nor'-west'er,** a strong north-west wind.—*adjs.* and *advs.* **north'-west'erly,** toward or from the north-west; **north'-west'ern,** belonging to the north-west: being in the north-west or in that direction.—*adj., adv.,* and *n.* **north-west'ward.**—*adj.* and *adv.* **north-west'wardly.** — *adv.* **north-west'wards.** — **North Atlantic Treaty Organisation,** a political alliance linking the United States and Canada to a group of European States, established by the **North Atlantic Treaty,** 4th April 1949 (abbrev. **N.A.T.O.**); **North-east Passage,** a passage for ships along the north coasts of Europe and Asia to the Pacific, first made by Baron Nordenskjöld in 1878-79; **North-west Passage,** a seaway from the Atlantic into the Pacific north of North America, first made (partly on the ice) by Sir Robert McClure, 1850-54. [O.E. *north;* cf. Ger. *nord.*]

**Northumbrian,** *nör-thum'bri-ən, n.* a native of the modern *Northumberland,* or of the old kingdom of *Northumbria* (O.E. *Northhymbre, North-hymbraland*) stretching from the Humber to the Forth: the dialect of Old English spoken in Northumbria, later Northern English (including Scots).—*adj.* of Northumberland or Northumbria.

**norward,** etc. Same as **northward,** etc.

**Norway,** *nör'wā, adj.* Norwegian.—*n.* (*obs.*) a Norwegian:—*pl.* (*Spens.*) **Norueyses.—Norway haddock,** the rose-fish or bergylt; **Norway lobster** (see **lobster**); **Norway pine,** the red pine, *Pinus resinosa:* its wood; **Norway rat,** the brown rat; **Norway spruce,** *Picea excelsa.*

**Norwegian,** *nör-wē'j(y)ən, adj.* of Norway, its people, or its language.—*n.* a native or citizen of Norway: the language of Norway: a kind of fishing-boat on the Great Lakes of America.— *adj.* (*Shak.*) **Norweyan** (*-wā'ən*), Norwegian. —**Norwegian oven, nest,** a haybox. [L.L. *Norvegia,* Norway—O.N. *Norvegr* (O.E. *Northweg*)—O.N. *northr,* north, *vegr,* way.]

**nosce teipsum,** *nō'sē tē-ip'səm, nōs'ke tā-ip'-sōōm,* (L.) know thyself. See **gnōthi seauton.**

**nose,** *nōz, n.* the projecting part of the face used in breathing, smelling, and to some extent in speaking: the power of smelling: flair, a faculty for tracking out, detecting, or recognising (*fig.*): a projecting fore-part of anything: a projection: a beak: a nozzle: the projecting edge of a step, a moulding, or a mullion: the withered remains of the flower on a gooseberry, apple, etc., opposite the stalk: the connecting part of a pair of spectacles: an informer (*slang*).—*v.t.* to smell: to examine by smelling or as if by smelling: to track out, detect, or recognise: to touch, press, or rub with the nose: to thrust the nose into: to make (way) by feeling or pushing with the nose: to come or be face to face with: to oppose rudely face to face: to furnish with a nose: to remove the nose from (a gooseberry, etc.): to sound through the nose.—*v.i.* to sniff: to pry: to nuzzle: to move nose-first: to taper away in a noselike form.—*adj.* **nosed,** having a nose—esp. in composition, as *bottle-nosed, long-nosed,* etc.—*adj.* **nose′less.**—*n.* **nos′er,** a blow on the nose: a bloody nose: a severe rebuff: a strong head-wind: a prying person.—*adj.* **nos′ey, nos′y,** long-nosed: large-nosed: prying: ill-smelling: fragrant: sensitive to smells: nasal in sound.—*n.* a nickname for a nosey person.—*adv.* **nos′ily.**—*n.* **nos′iness,** tendency to pry.—*n.* **nos′ing,** the act of nosing: the projecting rounded edge of the step of a stair or of a moulding.—**nose′bag,** a bag for food, hung on a horse's head: a picnicker's bag; **nose′-band,** the part of the bridle coming over the nose, attached to the cheek-straps; **nose′-bleed,** a bleeding at the nose: yarrow or other plant (*obs.* or *U.S.*); **nose′-bleeding; nose′-dive,** a headlong plunge.—*v.i.* to plunge nose-first.— **nose′-flute,** a flute blown by the nose; **nose′-herb** (*Shak.*), a herb valued for its smell.—*adj.* **nose′-led,** led by the nose, ruled and befooled completely.—**nose′-leaf,** a membranous appendage on some bats' snouts:—*n.pl.* **nose′-nippers,** pince-nez.—**nose′-painting,** colouring of the nose by drinking; **nose′-piece,** a nozzle: the end of a microscope tube carrying the objective: a nose-band: the nasal in armour; **nose′-rag** (*slang*), a handkerchief; **nose′-ring,** an ornament worn in the septum of the nose or in either of its wings: a ring in the septum of the nose for controlling a bull, swine, etc.; **Nos′ey Parker,** (*coll.*) a prying person.—**cut off one's nose to spite one's face,** to injure oneself rather than fail to injure another; **follow one's nose,** to go straight forward; **lead by the nose** (see **lead**); **make a long nose, thumb one's nose** (see **long**); **nose to the grindstone** (see **grindstone**); **put one's nose out of joint** (see **joint**); **snap off one's nose,** to speak snappily; **through the nose,** exorbitantly; **thrust one's nose into,** to meddle officiously with; **turn up one's nose at,** to refuse or receive contemptuously; **under one's very nose,** in full view: close at hand. [O.E. *nosu;* Ger. *nase,* L. *nāsus.*]

**nosean,** *nōz′i-ən, n.* a cubic mineral, aluminium sodium silicate and sulphate.—Also **nos′elite.** [Named after the German mineralogist K. W. *Nose* (d. 1835).]

**nosegay,** *nōz′gā, n.* a bunch of fragrant flowers: a posy or bouquet. [**nose, gay.**]

**nosh,** *nosh,* (*slang*) *v.i.* to nibble, eat between meals: to eat.—*n.* food. [Yiddish.]

**nosocomial,** *nos-ō-kō′mi-əl, adj.* relating to a hospital. [Gr. *nosokomeion,* hospital—*nosos,* sickness, *komeein,* to tend.]

**nosography,** *nos-og′rə-fi, n.* the description of diseases.—*n.* **nosog′rapher.**—*adj.* **nosographic** (*nos-ə-graf′ik*). [Gr. *nosos,* disease, *graphein,* to write.]

**nosology,** *nos-ol′ə-ji, n.* the science of diseases: the branch of medicine which treats of the classification of diseases.—*adj.* **nosological** (*-ə-loj′*).—*n.*

**nosol′ogist.** [Gr. *nosos,* disease, *logos,* discourse.]

**nosophobia,** *nos-ə-fō′bi-ə, n.* morbid dread of disease. [Gr. *nosos,* a disease, *phobos,* fear.]

**nostalgia,** *nos-tal′ji-ə, n.* home-sickness: sentimental longing for past times.—*adj.* **nostal′gic.** —*adv.* **nostal′gically.** [Gr. *nostos,* a return, *algos,* pain.]

**nostalgie de la boue,** *nos-tal-zhē də la bōō,* (Fr.) nostalgia for mud, craving for a debased physical life without civilised refinements or fastidiousness.

**Nostoc,** *nos′tok, n.* a genus of blue-green Algae, beaded filaments forming gelatinous colonies on damp earth, etc., once thought derived from stars. [Appar. coined by Paracelsus.]

**nostology,** *nos-tol′ə-ji, n.* the study of senility or return to childish characteristics.—*adjs.* **nostologic** (*-ə-loj′*), **-al.** [Gr. *nostos,* return, *logos,* discourse.]

**nostomania,** *nos-tō-mā′ni-ə, n.* an abnormal desire to go back to familiar places. [Gr. *nostos,* return, and **mania.**]

**nostopathy,** *nos-top′ə-thi, n.* an abnormal fear of going back to familiar places. [Gr. *nostos,* return, *pathos,* suffering.]

**nostos,** *nos′tos,* (Gr.) a poem describing a return or a return journey.

**Nostradamus,** *nos-trə-dā′məs, n.* one who professes to foretell the future.—*adj.* **nostradamic** (*-dam′ik*). [From the French astrologer (1503-1566).]

**nostril,** *nos′tril, n.* one of the openings of the nose. [M.E. *nosethirl*—O.E. *nosthyr(e)l*—*nosu,* nose, *thyrel,* opening; cf. **drill,** to pierce, and **thrill.**]

**nostrum,** *nos′trəm, n.* any secret, quack, or patent medicine: any favourite remedy or scheme. [L. *nostrum* (neut.), our own—*nōs,* we.]

**not,** *not, adv.* a word expressing denial, negation, or refusal.—**not′-being,** the state or fact of not existing; **not′-I,** that which is not the conscious ego.—*adj.* and *adv.* **not-out′** (*cricket*), still in: at the end of the innings without having been put out. [Same as **naught, nought.**]

**not, nott,** *not, adj.* with close-cut hair: polled.— *adjs.* **not′-head′ed; not′-pat′ed** (*Shak.*). [O.E. *hnot.*]

**nota bene,** *nō′tə ben′i, bēn′, no′tä ben′e,* (L.) mark well, take notice—often abbrev. **N.B.**

**notabilia.** See **notable.**

**notable,** *nō′tə-bl, adj.* worthy of being known or noted: remarkable: memorable: distinguished: noticeable: considerable: (*arch.;* sometimes with old pronunciation *not′*) housewifely: capable, clever, industrious (*arch.*).—*n.* a person or thing worthy of note, esp. in *pl.* for persons of distinction and political importance in France in pre-Revolution times.—*n.pl.* **notabil′ia** (L.), things worthy of notice: noteworthy sayings.— *ns.* **notabil′ity,** the fact of being notable: a notable person or thing; **no′tableness.**—*adv.* **no′tably.** [L. *notābilis*—*notāre,* to mark.]

**notaeum,** *nō-tē′əm, n.* the upper surface of a bird's trunk—opp. to *gastraeum.* [Latinised from Gr. *nōtaion* (neut.), adj.—*nōtos* or *nōton,* the back.]

**notandum,** *nō-tan′dəm, n.* something to be specially noted or observed:—*pl.* **notan′da.** [L., ger. of *notāre,* to note.]

**notary,** *nō′tə-ri, n.* an officer authorised to certify deeds, contracts, copies of documents, affidavits, etc. (generally **notary public**): anciently, one who took notes or memoranda of others' acts.—*adj.* **notā′rial.**—*adv.* **notā′rially.**—**apostolical notary,** the official who despatches the orders of the pope; **ecclesiastical notary,** in the early church, a secretary who recorded the proceedings of councils, etc. [L. *notārius.*]

**notation,** *nō-tā′shən, n.* a system of signs or symbols: annotation (*rare*). [L. *notātiō, -ōnis* —*notāre, -ātum,* to mark.]

**notch,** *noch, n.* a nick: an indentation: a narrow

pass.—*v.t.* to make a nick in: to cut unevenly, as hair (*obs.*): to form, fix, or remove by nicking: to fit arrow to bowstring (also **nock**): to record by a notch: (with *up*) to score.—*adj* **notched**, **nicked.**—*n.* **notch'ing**, a method of joining timbers, by fitting into a groove or grooves.—**notch'-board**, a board that receives the ends of the steps of a staircase. [Supposed to be from Fr. *oche* (now *hoche*) with *n* from the indefinite article; not conn. with **nock.**]

**notchel**, **nochel**, *noch'l, n.* (*coll.*) notice that one will not be responsible for another's debts.—*v.t.* to repudiate the debts of (someone). [Origin unknown.]

**note**, *nōt, n.* a significant or distinguishing mark: a characteristic: that by which a person or thing is known: a mark or sign calling attention: a written or printed symbol other than a letter: a stigma or mark of censure: an observation or remark: a comment attached to a text, explanatory, illustrative, critical, or recording textual variants: a jotting set down provisionally for use afterwards: an impression: a short statement or record: a bill or account (*obs.*): a memorandum: a short informal letter: a diplomatic paper: a small size of paper used for writing: a mark representing a sound (**whole note**, a semibreve) (*mus.*): a key of a piano or other instrument: the sound or tone represented by the printed or written note: the song, cry, or utterance of a bird or other animal: a tune (*obs.*): music (*poet.*): a paper acknowledging a debt and promising payment, as a bank-note, a note of hand or promissory note: a voucher or receipt (*obs.*): notice: attention: cognisance: distinction: reputation: eminence: importance: consequence: notability: intimation (*Shak.*).—*v.t.* to make a note of: to notice: to attend to: to indicate: to mark: to stigmatise (*obs.*): to mention: to record in writing or in musical notation: to add musical notation to: to set to music: to annotate: to denote.—*adjs.* **nōt'al**; **nōt'ed**, marked: well known: celebrated: eminent: notorious.—*adv.* **not'edly.**—*n.* **nōt'edness.**—*adj.* **note'less**, not attracting notice: unmusical.—*ns.* **note'let**, a short annotation or letter; **nōt'er**, one who notes or observes: one who makes notes, an annotator.—**note'book**, a book for keeping notes or memoranda: a billbook; **note'-case**, a pocket-book for bank-notes; **note'paper**, writing-paper intended for letters; **note'-shav'er** (*U.S.*), one who discounts bills at an exorbitant rate: a usurer; **note'worthiness.**—*adj.* **note'-worthy**, worthy of note or of notice.—**note a bill**, to record a refusal of acceptance, as a ground of protest; **note of hand**, promissory note. [Fr.,—L. *nota*, a mark.]

**note**, **n'ote**, **no'te**, *nōt*, (*Spens.*) *v.t.* wot not: (wrongly) could not. [O.E. *nāt*, for *ne wāt*; see **ne**, **wot.**]

**nothing**, *nuth'ing, n.* no thing: the non-existent: zero number or quantity: the figure representing it, a nought: a thing or person of no significance or value: an empty or trivial utterance: a low condition: a trifle: no difficulty or trouble.—*adv.* in no degree: not at all.—*ns.* **nothingā'rian**, one who has no particular belief, esp. in religion; **nothingā'rianism**; **noth'ingism**, **nothingness**: triviality; **noth'ingness**, non-existence: state of being nothing: worthlessness: insignificance: vacuity: a thing of no value.—**noth'ing-gift** (*Shak.*), a gift of no value.—**come to nothing**, to have little or no result: to turn out a failure; **for nothing**, in vain: free of charge; **make nothing of** (see **make**); **next to nothing**, almost nothing; **nothing but**, only; **nothing doing**, an emphatic refusal; **nothing for it but**, no alternative but; **nothing on** (*slang*), no claim to superiority over: no information about (used esp. by police of criminals): no engagement; **nothing to it**,

having nothing in it worth while: easy. [**no**, **thing.**]

**Nothofagus**, *noth-ō-fā'gəs, n.* a genus of timber-trees of the southern hemisphere, close allied to beech. [Gr. *nothos*, spurious, L. *fāgus*, beech.]

**notice**, *nō'tis, n.* intimation: announcement: information: warning: a writing, placard, board, etc., conveying an intimation or warning: time allowed for preparation: cognisance: observation: heed: mention: a short book, dramatic or artistic review: civility or respectful treatment: a notion (*obs.*).—*v.t.* to mark or observe: to regard or attend to: to mention: to make observations upon: to write or publish a notice of: to show sign of recognition of: to treat with civility.—*adj.* **no'ticeable**, that can be noticed: worthy of notice: likely to be noticed.—*adv.* **no'ticeably.**—**no'tice-board**, a board for fixing a notice on.—**give notice**, to warn beforehand: to inform: to intimate, esp. the termination of an agreement. [Fr. *notifier*—L. *nōtitia*—*nōscĕre, nōtum*, to get to know.]

**notify**, *nō'ti-fī, v.t.* to make known: to declare: to give notice or information of:—*pr.p.* **no'tifying**; *pa.t.* and *pa.p.* **no'tified.**—*adj.* **no'tifiable**, that must be made known: (of diseases) that must be reported to public health authorities.—*n.* **notification** (*-fi-kā'shən*), the act of notifying: the notice given: the paper containing the notice. [Fr. *notifier*—L. *nōtificāre, -ātum—nōtus*, known, *facĕre*, to make.]

**notion**, *nō'shən, n.* a concept in the mind of the various marks or qualities of an object: an idea: an opinion, esp. one not very well founded: a caprice or whim: a liking or fancy: (*Shak., Milton*) a mind: any small article ingeniously devised or invented, usually in *pl.*—*adj.* **no'tional**, of the nature of a notion: having a full meaning of its own, not merely contributing to the meaning of a phrase: theoretical: ideal: fanciful.—*n.* **no'tionalist**, a theorist.—*adv.* **no'tionally**, in notion or mental apprehension: in idea, not in reality.—*n.* **no'tionist**, one who holds ungrounded opinions. [Fr.,—L. *nōtiō, -ōnis—nōscĕre, nōtum*, to get to know.]

**notitia**, *nō-tish'i-ə, n.* a roll, list, register: a catalogue of public functionaries, with their districts: a list of episcopal sees. [L. *nōtitia*; cf. **notice.**]

**notochord**, *nō'tō-körd, n.* a simple cellular rod, foreshadowing the spinal column, persisting throughout life in many lower vertebrates, as the amphioxus, etc.—*adj.* **notochord'al.** [Gr. *nōtos*, back, *chordē*, a string.]

**Notodonta**, *nō-tō-dont'ə, n.* a genus of moths whose larvae have toothlike humps, giving name to the family **Notodont'idae.**—*n.* **notodont'id**, a member of the family. [Gr. *nōtos*, back, *odous, odontos*, tooth.]

**Notogaea**, *nō-tō-jē'ə, n.* a zoological realm including Australia, the islands north of it, New Zealand, and Polynesia.—*adjs.* **Notogae'an**, **Notogae'ic.** [Gr. *notos*, south, *gaia*, land.]

**notonectal**, *nō-tō-nek'təl, adj.* swimming on the back, as certain insects: of the water-boatman genus (**Notonec'ta**) or family (**Notonec'tidae**) of hemipterous insects. [Gr. *nōtos*, back, *nēktēs*, a swimmer.]

**notorious**, *nō-tō'ri-əs, -tö', adj.* publicly known (now only in a bad sense): infamous.—*n.* **notori'ety**, state of being notorious: publicity: public exposure.—*adv.* **noto'riously.**—*n.* **noto'riousness.** [L.L. *nōtōrius—nōtus*, known.]

**Notornis**, *nō-tör'nis, n.* a genus of flightless rails, long thought extinct, but found surviving in New Zealand in 1948. [Gr. *notos*, south, *ornis*, a bird.]

**Notoryctes**, *nō-tō-rik'tēz, n.* a blind burrowing marsupial of South Australia, the marsupial mole. [Gr. *nōtos*, south, *oryktēs*, digger.]

**Nototherium**, *nō-tō-thē'ri-əm, n.* a genus of Tertiary

Australian fossil marsupials. [Gr. *notos*, south, *thērion*, a wild beast.]

**Nototrema**, nō-tō-trē'mə, *n.* the pouch-toad, a South American genus of tree frogs, with a brood-pouch on the female's back. [Gr. *nōtos*, the back, *trēma*, a hole.]

**notour**, nō'tər, (*Scot.*; now only legal) *adj.* well known, notorious. [L.L. *nōtōrius*.]

**Notre-Dame**, *not-r' däm*, (Fr.) Our Lady.

**nott.** Same as **not** (2).

**notum**, nō'təm, *n.* the dorsal aspect of the thorax in insects. [Latinised from Gr. *nōton*, back.]

**Notus**, nō'təs, *n.* the south or south-west wind. [L. *nōtus*—Gr. *nŏtos*.]

**notwithstanding**, *not-with-stand'ing*, or -*widh*-, *prep.* in spite of.—*conj.* in spite of the fact that, although.—*adv.* nevertheless, however, yet. [Orig. a participial phrase in nominative absolute = L. *non obstante*.]

**nougat**, nōō'gä, *n.* a confection made of a sweet paste filled with chopped almonds or pistachio-nuts. [Fr. (cf. Sp. *nogado*, an almond-cake),— L. *nux*, *nucis*, a nut.]

**nought**, nöt, *n.* not anything: nothing: the figure 0.—*adv.* in no degree.—**noughts and crosses**, a game in which one seeks to make three noughts, the other three crosses, in a row in the spaces of crossed parallel lines; **set at nought**, to despise, disregard, flout. [Same as **naught**.]

**noul, noule,** nōl, (*Spens.*) *n.* Same as **noll.**

**nould, noulde,** n'ould, (*Spens.*) *pa.t.* of **nill.**

**noumenon**, nōō' or now'mi-non, *n.* an unknown and unknowable substance or thing as it is in itself:—*pl.* **nou'mena.**—*adj.* **nou'menal.** [Gr. *nooumenon* (contraction for *noeomenon*), neuter of pr.p. pass. of *noeein*, to think—*noos* (*nous*), the mind.]

**noun**, nown, (*gram.*) *n.* a word used as a name: formerly including the adjective.—*adj.* **noun'al.**—**noun clause**, a clause equivalent to a noun. [A.Fr. *noun* (O.Fr. *non*; Fr. *nom*)—L. *nōmen, nōminis*, a name.]

**nouns**, nownz, (*obs.*) *n.pl.* used as a minced oath, in full *odds nouns*, for (*God's*) **wounds.**

**noup**, nōōp, nōōp, (*obs. Shetland*; *Scott*) *n.* a crag: a steep headland. [O.N. *gnúpr*.]

**nourice**, nur'is, (*obs.*) *n.* a nurse.—**nour'ice-fee'**, payment for a nurse. [O.Fr. *nurice*; see **nurse.**]

**nourish**, nur'ish, *v.t.* to suckle (*obs.*): to feed: to furnish with food: to support: to help forward the growth of in any way: to allow to grow: to bring up: to cherish (*fig.*): to educate.—*adj.* **nour'ishable**.—*n.* **nour'isher.**—*adj.* **nour'ishing**, affording nourishment or much nourishment.— *n.* **nour'ishment**, the act of nourishing: the state of being nourished: that which nourishes: nutriment. [O.Fr. *norir, nourir*, -*iss*- (Fr. *nourrir*)—L. *nūtrīre*, to feed.]

**nouriture, nourriture**, nur'i-chər, *n.* nourishment: food: bringing up, nurture (*obs.*). [See **nurture.**]

**noursle**, nûrs'l, (*Spens.*) *v.t.* to bring up: to foster. —Also **nousle, nousell, nuzzle.** [A form of *nuzzle* influenced by **nurse.**]

**nous**, nōōs, nows, *n.* intellect: talent: commonsense (*slang*; *nows*). [Gr. *nous*, contracted from *noos*.]

**nouveau**, nōō-vō, fem. **nouvelle,** -*vel*, (Fr.) new.—*n.* **nouvelle**, a long short-story.—**nouveau riche** (*rēsh*), one who has only lately acquired wealth, but who has not acquired good taste or manners: an upstart:—*pl.* **nouveaux riches; Nouvelle Vague** (*väg*), movement in the French cinema (beginning just before 1960) aiming at imaginative quality in films in preference to size, expense, box-office appeal.—As *adj.* applied to movements in other arts.—**art nouveau**, a style fashionable at the end of the 19th cent., using long sinuous curves to represent mainly naturalistic forms.

**nova**, nō'və, *n.* a star that suddenly flares up with explosive violence:—*pl.* **no'vae** (-vē). [L. *nŏva* (*stella*), new (star); fem. of *novus*, new.]

**novaculite**, nō-vak'ū-lit, *n.* a hone-stone, a very hard fine-grained silicious rock, sometimes containing minute garnets. [L. *novācula*, razor.]

**novalia**, nō-vā'li-ə, (Scots law) *n.pl.* waste lands newly reclaimed. [L. *novālia*.]

**Novatian**, nō-vā'sh(y)ən, *adj.* of or pertaining to the antipope *Novatianus* (251), or his party or sect, who favoured severity against the lapsed.— *ns.* **Nova'tianism; Nova'tianist.**

**novation**, nō-vā'shən, *n.* the substitution of a new obligation for the one existing: innovation. [L. *novātiō, -ōnis*—*novus*, new.]

**novel**, nov'l, nuv'l, *adj.* new (*obs.*): new and strange: of a new kind: felt to be new.—*n.* that which is new (earlier *no-vel'*; *obs.*): a piece of news (*obs.*): a new constitution or decree of Justinian or other Roman emperor, supplementary to the Codex: a fictitious prose narrative or tale presenting a picture of real life, esp. of the emotional crises in the life-history of the men and women portrayed.—*ns.* **nov'eldom**, the world of fiction; **novelette'**, a short novel, esp. one that is feeble, trite, and sentimental: Schumann's name for a short piano piece in free form.—*adj.* **novelett'ish.**—*n.* **novelett'ist.**—*v.t.* **nov'elise, -ize**, to make new or novel: to turn into a novel or novels.—*v.i.* to innovate: to write as a novelist.—*n.* **novelisā'tion, -z-.**—*adj.* **nov'elish**, savouring of a novel.—*ns.* **nov'elism**, innovation, novelty (*obs.*): favouring of innovation: novel-writing; **nov'elist**, an innovator (*obs.*): a news-monger or news-writer (*obs.*): a novel-writer.—*adj.* **novelist'ic.**—*ns.* **novella** (-el'a; L.) a Roman Emperor's decree (*pl.* **novellae** (-ē)): (*el'la*; It.), a tale, short story: in recent times, a short novel (*pl.* **novelle, novellas** -*lā*, -*əs*); **nov'elty**, newness: unusual appearance: anything new, strange, or different from what was known or usual before: a small, usually cheap, manufactured article of unusual or gimmicky design:—*pl.* **nov'elties.** [Partly through O.Fr. **novelle** (Fr. **nouvelle**), partly through It. *novella*, partly direct, from L. *novellus*. fem. *novella*—*novus*, new.]

**November**, nō-vem'bər, *n.* the eleventh month, ninth of the most ancient Roman year. [L. *November*—*novem*, nine.]

**novena**, nō-vē'nə, *n.* a devotion lasting nine days, to obtain a particular request, through the intercession of the Virgin or some saint. [L. *novēnus*, nine each, *novem*, nine.]

**novenary**, nov'ə-nə-ri (or -ē'nər-i), *adj.* pertaining to the number nine.—*n.* a set of nine things. [L. *novēnārius*—*novem*, nine.]

**novennial**, nō-ven'yəl, *adj.* recurring every ninth year. [L. *novennis*—*novem*, nine, *annus*, a year.]

**novercal**, nō-vûr'kl, *adj.* pertaining to or befitting a stepmother. [L. *novercālis*—*noverca*, a stepmother.]

**noverint**, nōv'e-rint, *n.* a writ—beginning with the words *noverint universi*, let all men know. [L. *nōverint*, 3rd pers. pl. perf. subj. of *nōscĕre*, to get to know.]

**Novial**, nō'vi-əl, nō-vi-äl', *n.* an artificial language devised by Otto Jespersen (1860-1943). [L. *novus*, new, and the initials of *international auxiliary language*.]

**novice**, nov'is, *n.* one new in anything: a beginner: a new convert or church member: an inmate of a religious house who has not yet taken the vows: a competitor that has not yet won a recognised prize.—*ns.* **nov'icehood; nov'iceship; noviciate, novitiate** (-ish'i-āt), the state of being a novice: the period of being a novice: a novice. [Fr.,—L. *novicius*—*novus*, new.]

**novity**, nov'i-ti, (*obs.*) *n.* innovation: newness. [L. *novitās, -ātis*—*novus*, new.]

**novum**, nō'vəm, (*Shak.*) *n.* a game at dice in which

the chief throws were nine and five. [Poss. L. *novem*, nine.]

**novus homo,** *nō̆v'əs hō'mō, nov'ŏŏs ho'mō*, (L.) a Roman magistrate whose ancestors had never held office: a new man.

**now,** *now, adv.* at the present time, or the time in question, or a very little before or after: as things are: used meaninglessly, or with the feeling of time lost or nearly lost, in remonstrance, admonition, or taking up a new point.—*adj.* present.—*n.* the present time or the time in question.—*conj.* at this time when and because it is the fact: since at this time.—*interj.* expressing admonition, warning or (when repeated) reassurance.—**now and then,** or **again,** sometimes: from time to time; **now** . . . **now,** at one time . . . at another time; **now of late** (*arch.*), lately; **now then!**, interjection expressing admonition or rebuke; **the now** (*Scot.*), at present: presently: very lately. [O.E. *nū*; Ger. *nun*, L. *nunc*, Gr. *nȳn*.]

**nowadays,** *now'ə-dāz, adv.* in these times.—*Spens.* **now a** (or **of**) **dayes.** [now and **days,** O.E. *dæges*, gen. of *dæg*, day, to which the prep. **a** (O.E. *on*, which governed the dative) was later added.]

**noway, noways, nowise.** See no.

**nowed,** *nowd,* (*her.*) *adj.* knotted. [Fr. *noué*.]

**Nowel(l), Noël,** *nō-el',* (*obs.* except in Christmas carols) *n.* Christmas. [O.Fr. (Fr. *noël*; cf. Sp. *natal,* It. *natale*),—L. *nātālis,* belonging to a birthday.]

**nowhere,** *nō'(h)wär, adv.* in or to no place: out of the running.—*n.* a non-existent place.—*adv.* **nō'-whither,** to no place: in no direction.—**nowhere near,** not nearly. [no, where, whither.]

**nowl,** *nōl,* (*Shak.*) *n.* Same as noll.

**nown,** *nōn,* (*obs.*) *adj.* own. [Orig. by wrong division of mine own, thine own.]

**nowt, nout,** *nowt,* (*Scot.*) *n.* cattle.—**nowt'-herd.** [O.N. *naut.*; cognate with neat (1), O.E. *nēat.*]

**nowy,** *nō'i, now'i,* (*her.*) *adj.* having a convex curvature near the middle. [O.Fr. *noé* (Fr. *noué*) —L. *nōdātus,* knotted.]

**noxious,** *nok'shəs, adj.* hurtful.—*adj.* **noxal** (*noks'l*), relating to wrongful injury by an object or animal belonging to another.—*adv.* **nox'iously.**—*n.* **nox'iousness.** [L. *noxius—noxa,* hurt—*nocēre,* to hurt.]

**noy,** *noi,* (*Spens.*) *v.t.* to vex, hurt, annoy.—*n.* (*obs.* or *dial.*) vexation, hurt, trouble.—*ns.* **noy'ance,** (*Spens., Shak.*) annoyance; **noyes** (*noiz; Spens.*), noise (see noise).—*adjs.* **noy'ous,** (*Spens.*) vexatious: grievous: injurious; **noy'some,** noisome: hurtful. [Aphetic forms of annoy, etc.; see also noisome.]

**noyade,** *nwä-yäd', n.* wholesale drowning, as by Carrier at Nantes, 1793-94. [Fr.,—*noyer,* to drown.]

**noyau,** *nwä-yō', n.* a liqueur flavoured with bitter almonds or peach-kernels. [Fr., fruit-stone—L. *nucālis,* nutlike—*nux, nucis,* a nut.]

**nozzle,** *noz'l, n.* a little nose: the snout: a projection: an outlet tube, or spout: an open end of a tube. [Dim. of nose.]

**nu,** *nū, nü, n.* the thirteenth letter (N, ν) of the Greek alphabet, answering to N: as a numeral ν′ = 50, ,ν = 50,000. [Gr. *nȳ.*]

**nuance,** *nü-äs, nwäs, nū-äns', n.* a delicate degree or shade of difference. [Fr.,—L. *nūbēs, nūbis,* a cloud.]

**nub, nubble, nubbly, nubby.** See knub, etc.

**nub,** *nub,* (*obs. slang*) *n.* the gallows.—*v.t.* to hang. —**nubb'ing-cheat,** the gallows; **nubb'ing-cove,** a hangman.

**nub,** *nub, n.* the point or gist. [Prob. knub.]

**nubecula,** *nū-bek'ū-lə, n.* a cloudiness:—*pl.* **nu-bec'ulae** (*-lē*), the Magellanic Clouds. [L. *nūbēcula,* dim. of *nūbēs,* cloud.]

**nubia, nubiferous,** etc. See nubilous.

**nubile,** *nū'bīl, bil, adj.* marriageable (esp. of a

woman).—*n.* **nubility** (*-bil'i-ti*). [L. *nūbilis—nūbĕre,* to veil oneself, hence to marry.]

**nubilous,** *nū'bi-ləs, adj.* cloudy.—*n.* **nu'bia,** a fleecy head-wrap formerly worn by women.— *adjs.* **nubif'erous,** cloud-bringing; **nu'biform,** cloudlike; **nubigenous** (*-bij'i-nəs*), cloud-born. [L. *nūbēs,* a cloud.]

**nucellus,** *nū-sel'əs, n.* the mass of tissue within the integuments of the ovule, containing the embryo-sac.—*adj.* **nucell'ar.** [A modern dim. from L. *nux, nucis,* a nut; L. has dim. *nucella,* a little nut.]

**nucha,** *nū'kə, n.* the nape of the neck.—*adj.* **nū'chal.** [L.L. *nucha*—Ar. *nukhā',* spinal marrow.]

**nuciferous,** *nū-sif'ər-əs, adj.* nut-bearing. [L. *nux, nucis,* nut, *ferre,* to bear.]

**nucivorous,** *nū-siv'ə-rəs, adj.* nut-eating. [L. *nux, nucis,* nut, *vorāre,* to devour.]

**nucleal, nuclear,** etc. See nucleus.

**nucleus,** *nū'kli-əs, n.* a central mass or kernel: that around which something may grow: a core of flint from which pieces have been flaked off: the densest part of a comet's head or a nebula: a nut kernel (*obs.*): a nucellus (*obs.*): a rounded body in the protoplasm of a cell, the centre of its life (*biol.*): the massive part of an atom, distinguished from the outlying electrons (*phys.*): a stable group of atoms to which other atoms may be attached so as to form series of compounds (*phys.*):—*pl.* **nuclei** (*nū'kli-i*).—*adjs.* **nū'cleal** (*-kli-əl; rare*), **nu'clear** (*-kli-ər*), of, or of the nature of, a nucleus (also **nucleary**): pertaining to the nucleus of an atom, nuclei of atoms: pertaining to, or derived from, fission or fusion of atomic nuclei.—*n.* **nu'cleäse,** any of a number of enzymes inducing hydrolysis in nucleic acids.—*v.t.* and *v.i.* **nu'cleate** (*-kli-āt*), to form into, or group around, a nucleus.—*v.t.* to act, in a process of formation, as a nucleus for (e.g. *to nucleate crystals*).—*adjs.* **nu'cleate, -d,** having a nucleus.—*ns.* **nucleā'tion,** action or process of nucleating: seeding clouds to control rainfall and fog formation; **nu'clein** (*-kli-in*), a colourless amorphous substance of varying composition, got from cell-nuclei.—*adjs.* **nuclē'olar,** of, or of the nature of, a nucleolus: **nu'cleolate, -d,** having a nucleus or a nucleolus: (of a spore) containing one or more conspicuous oil-drops.— *ns.* **nu'cleole,** a nucleolus; **nuclē'olus,** a body (sometimes two bodies) observed within a cell-nucleus, indispensable to growth:—*pl.* **nuclē'oli** (*-lī*); **nu'cleon,** a general name for a neutron or a proton; **nucleon'ics** (treated as *sing.*), nuclear physics, esp. its practical applications; **nu'cleo-pro'tein,** any of a group of compounds containing a protein molecule combined with a nuclein—important constituents of the nuclei of living cells; **nuclide,** *nū'klīd, -klid,* species of atom of any element distinguished by number of neutrons and protons in its nucleus, and its energy state:—also sometimes **nucleide.**—**nuclear energy,** a more exact term for *atomic energy,* energy released or absorbed during reactions taking place in atomic nuclei; **nuclear fission,** spontaneous or induced splitting of atomic nucleus; **nuclear** (or **atomic**) **fuel,** material, as uranium or plutonium, consumed to produce atomic energy; **nuclear fusion,** creation of new nucleus by merging two lighter ones, with release of energy; **nuclear physics,** the science of forces and transformations within the nucleus of the atom; **nuclear power,** power obtained from a controlled nuclear reaction (*adj.* **nuclear-powered**); **nuclear reactor,** an assembly of uranium, with moderator, in which a nuclear chain reaction can develop; **nuclear sexing,** testing a person's sex by examining cells from inside the cheek which, in females, have a material near the nucleus that can be stained blue; **nuclear warfare; nuclear warhead; nuclear weapon;**

# nucule — 903 — numerable

**nucleic acid,** any of the complex acid components of nucleo-proteins.—**nuclear magnetic resonance,** resonance which can be produced in nuclei of most isotopes of the elements and from which a clue can be obtained to the particular atoms involved. [L. *nucleus*—*nux, nucis,* a nut.]

**nucule,** *nūk′ūl, n.* a nutlet. [L. *nucula,* dim. of *nux, nucis,* a nut.]

**nude,** *nūd, adj.* naked: bare: undraped: without consideration (*law*).—*n.* a nude figure or figures: undraped condition.—*n.* nudā′tion, act of making bare.—*adv.* nude′ly.—*n.* nude′ness.—*adjs.* nu′dibranch (-*brangk*), having naked gills (also *n.*): belonging to the **Nudibranchiā′ta,** shell-less marine gasteropods with gills exposed on the back and sides of the body; **nudicau′date,** having a hairless tail, as a rat; **nu′dicaul, -ous,** having a leafless stem.—*ns.* nu′dism; nu′dist, one who goes naked, or approves of going naked.—Also *adj.*—*n.* nu′dity, the state of being nude: a nude figure:—*pl.* nu′dities, naked parts usually covered. [L. *nūdus,* naked.]

**nudge,** *nuj, n.* a gentle poke, as with the elbow. [Origin obscure; perh. connected with Norw. *nugge,* to rub, or with **knock, knuckle.**]

**nuée ardente,** *nü-ā är-dāt,* a cloud of hot gas, lava, etc., from a volcano, spreading horizontally. [Fr., burning cloud.]

**nugae,** *nū′gē, -jē, nōō′gī,* (L.) trifles.

**nugatory,** *nū′gə-tə-ri, adj.* trifling: worthless: inoperative: unavailing: futile.—*n.* nu′gatoriness. [L. *nūgātōrius*—*nūgae,* trifles, trumpery.]

**nugget,** *nug′it, n.* a lump, esp. of gold. [Origin unknown; there is a Sw. dialect word *nug,* a lump, block.]

**nuisance,** *nū′səns, n.* hurt or injury (*obs.*): that which annoys or hurts, esp. if there be some legal remedy: that which is offensive to the senses: a person or thing that is troublesome or obtrusive in some way.—*n.* nui′sancer. [Fr.,—L. *nocēre,* to hurt.]

**null,** *nul, adj.* of no legal force: void: invalid: empty of significance: amounting to nothing.—*n.* something of no value or meaning, a cipher or nought (*obs.*).—*v.t.* to annul, nullify: to wipe out (*obs.*).—*ns.* null′ity, the state of being null or void: nothingness: want of existence, force, or efficacy: null′ness—decree of nullity, a decree that a marriage has never existed. [L. *nūllus,* not any, from *ne,* not, *ūllus,* any.]

**null,** *nul, n.* a knurl: a kink.—*v.i.* to kink.—*n.* null′ing, knurling. [**knurl.**]

**nulla(h),** *nul′a, n.* a ravine: a water-course, not necessarily a dry one. [Hind. *nālā.*]

**nulla-nulla,** *nul′a-nul′a, n.* an Australian aborigine's hard-wood club.—Also **null′a.** [Native word.]

**nullifidian,** *nul-i-fid′iən, adj.* having no faith, esp. religious.—*n.* one who has no faith. [L. *nūllus,* none, *fidēs,* faith.]

**nullify,** *nul′i-fī, v.t.* to make null: to annul: to render void or of no force:—*pr.p* null′ifying; *pa.t.* and *pa.p.* null′ified.—*ns.* nullification (-*fi-kā′shən*), a rendering void or of none effect, esp. (*U.S.*) of a contract by one of the parties, or of a law by one legislature which has been passed by another; null′ifier (-*fī-ər*). [Late L. *nūllificāre*—*nūllus,* none, *facēre,* to make.]

**nullipara,** *nul-ip′ə-ra, n.* a woman who has never given birth to a child, esp. if not a virgin.—*adj.* nullip′arous.—*n.* nulliparity (-*i-par′i-ti*). [L. *nūllus,* none, *parĕre,* to bring forth.]

**nullipore,** *nul′i-pōr, -pōr, n.* a coralline seaweed. [L. *nūllus,* none, *porus,* a passage, pore.]

**nulli secundus,** *nul′ī si-kund′əs, nōōl′ē se-kōōn′dōōs,* (L.) second to none.

**numb,** *num, adj.* having diminished power of sensation or motion: powerless to feel or act: stupefied: causing (*Shak.*) or of the nature of (*Milt.*) numbness.—*v.t.* to make numb: to

deaden:—*pr.p.* **numbing** (*num′ing*); *pa.t.* and *pa.p.* **numbed** (*numd*). [O.E. *numen,* pa.p. of *niman,* to take.]

**number,** *num′bər, n.* that by which single things are counted or reckoned: quantity reckoned in units: a particular value or sum of single things or units: a representation in arithmetical symbols of such a value or sum: a full complement: a specified or recognised set, class, or group: the multitude (*obs.*): some or many of the persons or things in question (often in *pl.*): more than one: numerousness: (in *pl.*) numerical superiority: numerability: a numerical indication of a thing's place in a series, or one assigned to it for reference, as in a catalogue: a label or other object bearing such an indication: a person or thing marked or designated in such a way: an item: an issue of a periodical or serial publication: an integral portion of an opera or other composition: arithmetical faculty: (in *pl.*) rhythm, verses, music: the property in words of expressing singular, (in some languages, as Greek) dual, and plural (*gram.*): a single item in a programme, esp. of popular music and/or variety turns: an item of merchandise on show, usu. of clothing (*coll.*): a girl (*slang*): (*cap.,* in *pl.*) the fourth book of the Old Testament, in which an account of a census is given.—*v.t.* to count: to count out in payment (*Milt.*): to apportion: to have lived through: to reckon as one: to mark with a number or assign a number to: to amount to. —*v.i.* to be reckoned in the number: to be of like number.—*n.* num′berer.—*adj.* num′berless, without number: more than can be counted.— **number nine,** a purgative pill; **number one,** chief, most important: he or that whose number is one, the first in the numbered series: self, oneself (*slang*): lieutenant, first officer (under the rank of commander; *naut. slang*); **number plate,** the plaque on a motor vehicle showing its registration number; **number system** (*math.*), any set of elements which has two binary operations called addition and multiplication, each of which is commutative and associative, and which is such that multiplication is distributive with respect to addition.— **have,** or **get, one's number,** to size one up; **his number is up,** he is doomed, has not long to live; **number of the beast** (see **Apocalypse**); **one's (its) days are numbered, one's (its) end is imminent.** [Fr. *nombre*—L. *numerus.*]

**numbles, numble-pie.** See **umbles, humble-pie.**

**numerable,** *nū′mər-ə-bl, adj.* that may be numbered or counted.—*n.* numerabil′ity.—*adv.* nu′merably. —*n.* nu′meracy, state of being numerate.— *adj.* nu′meral, pertaining to, consisting of, or expressing number.—*n.* a figure or mark used to express a number, as 1, 2, I, V, α′, β′, etc.: a word used to denote a number (*gram.*): (in *pl.*) a badge indicating regiment, year of curriculum, etc.—*adv.* (*rare*) nu′merally, according to number.—*adj.* nu′merary, belonging to a certain number: contained within or counting as one of a body or a number—opp. to *supernumerary.* —*v.t.* nu′merate, to read off as numbers (from figures): orig. to enumerate, to number.—*adj.* having some understanding of mathematics and science (see also **innumerate**).—Also *n.*—*n.* numerā′tion, the act of numbering: the art of reading figures and expressing the value in numbers; nu′merātor, one who numbers: the upper number of a vulgar fraction, which expresses the number of fractional parts taken.— *adjs.* numeric (-*mer′ik*), -al, belonging to, expressed in, or consisting in, number: in number independently of sign: identical (*obs.*; often with *same*).—*adv.* numer′ically.—*ns.* numerol′ogy, study of numbers as supposed to show future events; numeros′ity, numerousness: condition

Neutral vowels in unaccented syllables: *el′ə-mənt*; for certain sounds in foreign words, see p. viii

in respect of number: harmonious flow.—*adj.* **nu'merous**, great in number or quantity: many: consisting of or pertaining to a large number: rhythmical.—*adv.* **nu'merously**.—*n.* **nu'merousness**.—**numerical analysis**, study of methods of approximation and their accuracy, etc.; **numerical control**, automatic control of operation of machine tools by means of numerical data stored on magnetic or punched tape or on punched cards. [L. *numerus*, number.]

**numinous**, *nū'min-ɔs, adj.* pertaining to a divinity: suffused with feeling of a divinity.—*n.* **nu'minousness**. [L. *nūmen, -inis*, divinity.]

**numismatic**, *nū-miz-mat'ik, adj.* pertaining to money, coins, or medals.—*n.sing.* **numismat'ics**, the study of coins and medals.—*ns.* **numis'matist; numismatol'ogist; numismatol'ogy**. [L. *numisma*—Gr. *nomisma*, current coin—*nomizein*, to use commonly—*nomos*, custom.]

**nummary**, *num'ɔ-ri, adj.* relating to coins or money.—*adjs.* **numm'ular**, coin-shaped; **numm'ūlary**, nummary; **numm'ūlāted**, coin-shaped. —*n.* **nummūlā'tion**, arrangement of bloodcorpuscles in rouleaux.—*adj.* **numm'ūline**, coinshaped: nummulitic.—*n.* **numm'ūlite**, a large coin-shaped fossil foraminifer, forming limestones.—*adj.* **nummūlitic** (*-lit'ik*), pertaining to, composed of, or containing nummulites. [L. *nummus*, a coin.]

**numnah**, *num'na, n.* a felt cloth or pad placed under a saddle to prevent chafing. [Hind. *namdā*.]

**numskull**, *num'skul, n.* a blockhead.—*adj.* **num'-skulled**. [numb, skull.]

**nun**, *nun, n.* a woman who, under a vow, has secluded herself in a religious house, to give her time to devotion: a kind of pigeon with feathers on its head like a nun's hood: a blue tit: a male smew: a tussock moth (*Psilura monacha*), a pest in pine-forests.—*ns.* **nun'hood**, the condition of a nun; **nunn'ery**, a house for nuns: nunship.—*adj.* **nunn'ish**.—*ns.* **nunn'ishness; nun'ship**, the condition of a nun.—**nun's-fidd'le**, a tromba marina; **nun's'-flesh'**, an ascetic temperament; **nun's'-veil'ing**, a woollen cloth, soft and thin, used by women for veils and dresses. [O.E. *nunne*—L.L. *nunna, nonna*, a nun, an old maiden lady, orig. mother; cf. Gr. *nannē*, aunt, Sans. *nanā*, a child's word for mother.]

**nun**, *nun,* (*obs.*) *n.* a spinning top.—**nun'-buoy**, a buoy that tapers conically each way.

**nunatak**, *nōō'na-tak, n.* a point of rock appearing above the surface of land-ice:—*pl.* **nu'nataks**, or (Sw.) **nu'natakkr**. [Eskimo.]

**nunc dimittis**, *nungk di-mit'tis, n.* the song of Simeon (Luke ii. 29-32) in the R.C. Breviary and the Anglican evening service. [From the opening words, *nunc dimittis*, now lettest thou depart.]

**nuncheon**, *nun'shɔn, n.* a light meal: a lunch. [M.E. *noneschenche*, noon-drink—O.E. *nōn*, noon, *scenc*, drink; cf. **noon, skink**.]

**nuncio**, *nun'shi-ō, n.* a messenger: one who brings tidings: an ambassador from the pope to an emperor or a king.—*n.* **nun'ciature**, a nuncio's office or term of office. [It. (now *nunzio*)—L. *nūntius*, a messenger, conjectured to be a contr. of *noventius*; cf. *novus*, new.]

**nuncle**, *nung'kl,* (*Shak.*) *n.* a contr. of mine uncle.

**nuncupate**, *nung'kū-pāt, v.t.* to utter as a vow: to declare orally.—*n.* **nuncūpā'tion**.—*adjs.* **nunc'-ūpātive** (of a will), oral: designative; **nunc'ū-patory** (*-pɔ-tɔ-ri*; *obs.*), nuncupative: dedicatory. [L. *nuncupāre*, to call by name—prob. from *nōmen*, name, *capēre*, to take.]

**nundine**, *nun'din, -din, n.* the ancient Roman market-day, every eighth day (ninth by Roman reckoning, counting both days).—*adj.* **nun'dinal** (*-din-*), pertaining to a fair or market. [L. *nūn-dinae*, market-day—*novem*, nine, *diēs*, a day.]

**nunnation**, *nun-ā'shɔn, n.* the addition of a final *n* in the declension of nouns. [As if L. *nunnātiō*—Ar. *nūn*, the letter n.]

**Nuphar**, *nū'fär, n.* the yellow water-lily genus. [Pers. *nūfar*, reduced form of *ninūfar*; see **Nenuphar**.]

**nuptial**, *nup'shal, adj.* pertaining to marriage: pertaining to mating (*zool.*).—*n.* (usu. in *pl.*) marriage: wedding ceremony.—*n.* **nuptiality** (*-shi-al'i-ti*), nuptial character or quality: marriage-rate: (in *pl.*) wedding ceremonies and festivities. [L. *nuptiālis*—*nuptiae*, marriage—*nubĕre, nuptum*, to marry.]

**nur, nurr.** See **knurr**.

**nuraghe**, *nōō-rä'gä*, **nurhag**, *nōō-räg', n.* a brochlike Sardinian round tower, probably of the Bronze Age:—*pl.* **nuraghi** (*-gē*), **nurhags**. [Sardinian dialect.]

**nurl.** See **knurl**.

**nurse**, *nûrs, n.* one who suckles a child: one who tends a child: one who has the care of the sick, feeble, or injured, or who is trained for the purpose: one set apart to guide an incompetent officer or other: a worker bee, ant, etc., that tends the young: a budding form in tunicates: one who or that which feeds, rears, tends, saves, fosters, or develops anything, or preserves it in any desired condition: a shrub or tree that protects a young plant (*hort.*): the state of being nursed (in the phrases *at nurse, out to nurse*).—*v.t.* to suckle: to tend, as an infant or a sick person: to bring up: to cherish: to manage with care and economy: to play skilfully, manipulate carefully, keep watchfully in touch with, in order to obtain or preserve the desired condition: to hold or carry as a nurse does a child.—*adj.* **nurse'like**.—*ns.* **nurs(e)'ling**, that which is nursed or fostered: an infant; **nurs'er; nurs'ery**, nursing (*Shak.*): place for nursing: an apartment for children: a place where young animals are reared, or where the growth of anything is promoted: a piece of ground where plants are reared for sale or transplanting: a race for two-year-old horses.—*adj.* pertaining to a nursery, or to early training.—**nurse'-child**, a child in the care of a nurse: a foster child; **nurse'hound**, a type of dogfish; **nurse'maid**, a maid servant who takes care of children; **nurs'ery-gov'erness**, a governess for children who still require a nurse's care; **nurs'ery-maid**, a maid employed in keeping a nursery: a nursemaid; **nurs'eryman**, a man who owns or works a nursery: one who is employed in cultivating plants, etc., for sale; **nurs'ery rhyme**, a traditional rhyme known to children; **nurs'ery school**, a school for very young children (aged two to five); **nurs'ery slopes**, slopes set apart for skiing novices.—*v.t.* and *v.i.* **nurse'-tend**, to attend as a sick-nurse.—**nurse'-tender; nurse'-tending; nurs'ing-fa'ther** (*B.*), a foster-father; **nurs'ing home**, a private hospital.—**put (out) to nurse**, to commit to a nurse, usu. away from home: to put (an estate) under trustees. [O.Fr. *norrice* (Fr. *nourrice*)—L. *nūtrix, -icis*—*nūtrīre*, to nourish.]

**nurse**, *nûrs, n.* a shark: a dogfish. [Earlier *nuss*, perh. for (*an*) *huss, husk*, a dogfish.]

**nursle**, *nûrs'l,* a mistaken form of **nousle, nuzzle**.

**nurture**, *nûr'chɔr, n.* upbringing: rearing: training: whatever is derived from the individual's experience, training, environment, distinguished from *nature*, or what is inherited: food.—*v.t.* to nourish: to bring up: to educate.—*adj.* **nur'-tural**.—*n.* **nur'turer**. [O.Fr. *noriture* (Fr. *nourriture*)—L.L. *nūtritūra*—L. *nūtrīre*, to nourish.]

**nut**, *nut, n.* popularly, any fruit with seed in a hard shell: a hard dry indehiscent fruit formed from a syncarpous gynaeceum (*bot.*): often the hazel-nut, sometimes the walnut: the head (*slang*): a hard-headed person, one difficult to deal with, a tough: a young blood (also knut, pron. *knut*): a crazy person (also a nut-case, *slang*): a small block, usu. of metal, for screwing on the end of a bolt: the ridge at the top of the fingerboard on a fiddle, etc. (*mus.*): the mechanism for tightening or slackening a bow (*mus.*): a small lump of coal: a small biscuit or round cake: a coconut-shell drinking-cup: a source of joy (in *pl.*; *slang*).—*v.t.* to look for and gather nuts:—*pr.p.* nutt'ing; *pa.t.* and *pa.p.* nutt'ed.—*ns.* nutā'rian, one who thinks nuts the best kind of food; nut'let, a one-seeded portion of a fruit that divides as it matures, as in labiates: the stone of a drupe.—*adj.* nuts, crazy (*slang*).— *ns.* nutt'er, one who gathers nuts: nut-butter: a crazy person (*slang*); nutt'iness; nutt'ing, the gathering of nuts.—*adj.* nutt'y, abounding in nuts: having the flavour of nuts: foolishly amorous (*slang*): mentally unhinged (*slang*).— *adj.* nut'-brown, brown, like a ripe hazel-nut.— nut'-butt'er, a butter-substitute made from nuts; nut'cracker, a bird (Nucifraga) of the crow family: (usu. in *pl.*) an instrument for cracking nuts.—*adj.* like a pair of nutcrackers, as toothless jaws.—nutcracker man, a type of early man found in Tanzania in 1959, by some distinguished as a separate species *Zinjanthropus*; nut'-gall, a nut-like gall, produced by a gallwasp, chiefly on the oak; nut'-grass, American sedges of various kinds, esp. one with edible tuberous root; nut'hatch, a bird (Sitta) that hacks nuts and seeks insects on trees like a creeper—also nut'jobber, nut'pecker; nut'-hook, a stick with a hook for pulling down nut-bearing boughs: a bailiff: a thief who uses a hook; nut-house (*slang*), a place where people are, or behaviour is, crazy; nut'meal, meal made from nuts; nut'-oil, an oil got from walnuts or other nuts; nut'-pine, the stone-pine or other species with large edible seeds; nut'shell, the hard covering of a nut; nut'-tree, any tree bearing nuts, esp. the hazel; nut'-wee'vil, a weevil (Balaninus) whose larvae live on hazelnuts; nut'-wrench, an instrument for turning nuts on screws.—a (hard) nut to crack, a difficult problem; be nuts on, about (*slang*), to be very fond of; in a nutshell, in very small space: briefly, concisely; not for nuts, not on any account. [O.E. *hnutu*; O.N. *hnot*, Du. *noot*, Ger. *nuss*.]

**nutant**, *nū'tant*, *adj.* nodding: drooping.—*v.i.* nu'tate, to nod: to droop: to perform a nutation.—*n.* nutā'tion, a nodding: a fluctuation in the precessional movement of the earth's pole about the pole of the ecliptic (*astron.*): the sweeping out of a curve by the tip of a growing axis (*bot.*).—*adj.* nutā'tional. [L. *nūtāre*, to nod.]

**nutmeg**, *nut'meg*, *n.* the aromatic kernel of an East Indian tree (Myristica), much used as a seasoning in cookery.—*adjs.* nut'megged; nut'-meggy. [M.E. *notemuge*—nut and inferred O.Fr. *mugue*, musk—L. *muscus*, musk.]

**nutria**, *nū'tri-ə*, *n.* the coypu: its fur. [Sp. *nutria*, otter—L. *lutra*.]

**nutrient**, *nū'tri-ənt*, *adj.* feeding: nourishing.—*n.* nu'triment, that which nourishes: food.—*adj.* nutrimental (*-ment'l*).—*n.* nutri'tion, act or process of nourishing: food.—*adjs.* nutri'tional; nutri'tious, nourishing.—*adv.* nutri'tiously.—*n.* nutri'tiousness.—*adj.* nu'tritive, nourishing: concerned in nutrition.—*adv.* nu'tritively. [L. *nūtrīre*, to nourish.]

**nux vomica**, *nuks vom'ik-ə*, a seed that yields strychnine: the East Indian tree (*Strychnos nux-vomica*; family Loganiaceae) that produces it. [L. *nux*, a nut, *vomĕre*, to vomit.]

**nuzzer**, *nuz'ər*, *n.* a present to a superior. [Hind. *nazr*, gift.]

**nuzzle, nousle**, *nuz'l*, *v.t.* and *v.i.* to poke, press, burrow, root, rub, sniff, caress, or investigate with the nose.—*v.t.* to thrust in (the nose or head).—*v.i.* to snuggle: to go with the nose toward the ground. [Freq. vb. from nose.]

**nuzzle**, *nuz'l*, *v.t.* to train: to bring up: to foster. [Origin obscure; confused with nurse; see noursle.]

**ny**, an obs. spelling of nigh.

**nyanza**, *nyan'za*, also *ni-* or *ni-an'za*, *n.* a lake (esp. in African proper names). [Bantu.]

**nyas**, *ni'as*, *n.* an old form of eyas (q.v.).

**nychthemeron**, *nik-thē'mə-ron*, *n.* a complete day of 24 hours, a night and a day.—*adj.* nychthē'-meral. [Gr. *nychthēmeron*—*nyx, nyktos*, night, *hēmerā*, day.]

**Nyctaginaceae**, *nik-tə-jin-ā'si-ē*, *n.pl.* a family of plants, mainly tropical American, akin to the goosefoots and the pinks, including the marvel of Peru. [Gr. *nyx, nyktos*, night.]

**nyctalopia**, *nik-tə-lō'pi-ə*, *n.* properly, night-blindness, abnormal difficulty in seeing in a faint light: by confusion sometimes, day-blindness.— *adj.* nyctalōp'ic. — *n.* nyc'talops (*-lops*), one affected with nyctalopia:—*pl.* nyctalō'pes. [Gr. *nyktalōps*, night-blind, day-blind—*nyx, nyktos*, night, *alaos*, blind, *ōps*, eye, face.]

**nyctinasty**, *nik'ti-nas-ti*, *n.* sleep-movement in plants, joint effect of changes in light and temperature.—*adj.* nyctinas'tic. [Gr. *nyx, nyktos*, night, *nastos*, pressed.]

**nyctitropism**, *nik-tit'rə-pizm*, *n.* the assumption by plants of certain positions at night.—*adj.* nyctitropic (*-trop'*). [Gr. *nyx, nyktos*, night, *tropos*, turning.]

**nyctophobia**, *nik-tō-fō'bi-ə*, *n.* morbid fear of the night or of darkness. [Gr. *nyx, nyktos*, night, and phobia.]

**nye**, an obs. spelling of nigh.

**nylghau, nilgau**. See nilgai.

**nylon**, *ni'lon*, *n.* any of numerous polymeric amides that can be formed into fibres, bristles, or sheets: any material made from nylon filaments or fibres: a stocking made of nylon. [Formerly a trademark.]

**nymph**, *nimf*, *n.* one of the divinities who lived in mountains, rivers, trees, etc. (*myth.*): a young and beautiful maiden (often ironical): an insect pupa (*obs.*): an immature insect, similar to the adult but with wings and sex-organs undeveloped.—*n.pl.* nymphae (*-ē*), the labia minora. —*ns.* Nymphaea (*-ē'ə*), the white water-lily genus, giving name to a family of dicotyledons Nymphaeā'ceae, akin to the buttercup family; nymphae'um, a temple, sanctuary, or grotto of the nymphs.—*adj.* nymph'al.—*n.* nymph'alid, a butterfly of the Nymphal'idae, a brush-footed family with useless, reduced fore-legs.—*adj.* nymphē'an.—*n.* nymph'et, a young nymph: a very young girl with strong sex-attraction.— *adjs.* nymph'ic, -al; nymph'ish; nymph'-like; nymph'ly.—*ns.* nymph'o, a nymphomaniac; nymph'olepsy, a species of ecstasy or frenzy said to have seized those who had seen a nymph: a yearning for the unattainable; nymph'olept, a person so affected.—*adj.* nympholept'ic.—*n.* nymphomā'nia, morbid and uncontrollable sexual desire in women.—*n.* and *adj.* nymphomā'niac. [L. *nympha*—Gr. *nymphē*, a bride, a nymph.]

**nys**, *nis, niz* (*Spens.*) is not. [ne, is.]

**nystagmus**, *nis-tag'mas*, *n.* a spasmodic, lateral oscillatory movement of the eyes, found in miners, etc.—*adjs.* nystag'mic; nystag'moid. [Latinised from Gr. *nystagmos*—*nystazein*, to nap.]

# O

**O, o, ō, n.** the fifteenth letter of our alphabet, derived from Greek omicron, chief sounds in English, being those in *note*, *not*, *for*, *work*, *son*, *do*: anything round or nearly so: a spangle: in telephone, etc., jargon, nought or nothing:—*pl.* **Oes, O's** (ōz): as a mediaeval Roman numeral, O = 11, Ō = 11,000: prefixed *o-* stands for *ortho-* (*chem.*).—**O'-level,** *n.*, *adj.* (examination at end of school course) requiring ordinary, i.e. less than A-level, knowledge of a school subject: a pass in an O-level.

**O, oh,** ō, *interj.* used in addressing or apostrophising, marking the occurrence of a thought, reception of information, or expressing wonder, admiration, disapprobation. surprise, protest, pain, or other emotion. The form **O** is chiefly used in verse (*O for, O that*).—**Fifteen O's,** fifteen meditations on Christ's Passion, each beginning with O, composed by St Bridget; **O's of Advent,** seven anthems each beginning with O, sung on the days before Christmas Eve.

**o', o,** ō, ə, a worn-down form of of and of on.

**O',** ō, *prefix,* in Irish patronymics, descendant of. [Ir. ó, ua—O.Ir. *an,* descendant.]

**oaf,** ōf, *n.* a changeling: a dolt: an idiot: a lout:—*pl.* **oafs,** (*rarely*) **oaves.**—*adj.* **oaf'ish,** idiotic, doltish: lubberly: loutish. [O.N. *ālfr,* elf; cf. **elf, ouphe.**]

**oak,** ōk, *n.* a genus (*Quercus*) of trees of the beech family: its timber valued in shipbuilding, etc.: extended to various other trees, as **poison-oak, she-oak** (qq.v.).—*adj.* of oak.—*adj.* **oak'en,** of oak.—*n.* **oak'ling,** a young oak.—*adj.* **oak'y,** like oak, firm: abounding in oaks.—**oak'-apple,** a gall caused by an insect on an oak leaf; **oak'-egg'er,** an egger moth whose caterpillars feed on oak; **oak'enshaw,** a little oak-wood; **oak'-fern,** a fern (*Thelypteris dryopteris*) of the polypody family (translation of Gr. *dryopteris,* name perh. given to ferns growing on oak-trees, transferred by Linnaeus to this species); **oak'-gall,** a gall produced on the oak; **oak'-leather,** a fungus mycelium in the fissures of old oaks; **oak'-lump,** the lichen lungwort; **oak'-mast,** acorns collectively; **oak'-nut,** a gall on the oak; **oak'-tree; oak'-wood.**—**Oak-apple Day,** the 29th of May, the anniversary of the Restoration in 1660, when country boys used to wear oak-apples in commemoration of Charles II hiding in the branches of an oak (the **Royal Oak**) from Cromwell's troopers after Worcester; **sport one's oak** (*university slang*), to keep one's outer door shut when one does not want visitors; **The Oaks,** a great English race (founded 1779) for three-year-old fillies—so named from an estate near Epsom. [O.E. *āc;* O.N. *eik,* Ger. *eiche.*]

**oaker,** (*Spens.*). Same as **ochre.**

**oakum,** ōk'əm, *n.* old (usu. tarred) ropes untwisted and teased out for caulking the seams of ships. [O.E. *ācumba* (*æcumbe*) from *ā-,* away from, and the root of *cemban,* to comb.]

**oar,** ōr, ör, *n.* a light bladed pole for propelling a boat: a stirring-pole: a swimming organ: an oarsman.—*v.t.* to impel as by rowing.—*v.i.* to row.—*n.* **oar'age,** oars collectively: rowing movement.—*adjs.* **oared,** furnished with oars; **oar'less; oar'y,** having the form or use of oars.—**oar'-fish,** a ribbon-fish (Regalecus).—*adj.* **oar'-footed,** having swimming feet.—**oar'-lap,** a rabbit with its ears standing out at right angles to the head; **oar'-lock,** (*rare*), a rowlock; **oars'-**

man, a rower: one skilled in rowing; **oars'man-ship,** skill in rowing; **oar'weed** (same as **oreweed**). —**lie** or **rest on one's oars,** to abstain from rowing without removing the oars from the rowlocks: to rest, take things easily: to cease from work; **put in one's oar,** to interpose when not asked. [O.E. *ār.*]

**oasis,** ō-ā'sis, sometimes ō'ə-sis, *n.* a fertile spot or tract in a sandy desert: any place of rest or pleasure in the midst of toil and gloom:—*pl.* **oases** (-sēz). [Gr. *oasis,* an Egyptian word; cf. Coptic *ouahe.*]

**oast,** ōst, *n.* a kiln to dry hops or malt.—*n.* **oast'-house.** [O.E. *āst.*]

**oat,** ōt (oftener in *pl.* **oats,** ōts), *n.* a well-known genus (Avena) of grasses, esp. *A. sativa,* whose seeds are much used as food: its seeds: a musical pipe of oat-straw: a shepherd's pipe: pastoral song generally.—*adj.* **oat'en,** consisting of an oat stem or straw: made of oatmeal.—**oat'cake',** a thin hard dry cake made with oatmeal.—**oat'-grass,** a grass of *Avena* or kindred genus used more as fodder than for the seed; **oat'-meal',** meal made of oats.—**feel one's oats,** to be frisky or assertive; **off one's oats,** without appetite, off one's food (*coll.*); **sow one's wild oats,** to indulge in youthful dissipation or excesses; **wild oats,** a wild species of oat (*A. fatua*). [O.E. *āte,* pl. *ātan.*]

**oath,** ōth, *n.* a solemn appeal to a god or something holy or reverenced as witness or sanction of the truth of a statement: the form of words used: a more or less similar expression used lightly, exclamatorily, decoratively, or in imprecation: a swear-word: a curse:—*pl.* **oaths** (ōdhz).—*adj.* **oath'able** (*Shak.*), capable of taking an oath.—**oath'-breaking** (*Shak.*), perjury.—**on, under, upon oath,** sworn to speak the truth: attested by oath; **take an oath,** to have an oath administered to one. [O.E. *āth;* Ger. *eid,* O.N. *eithr.*]

**ob,** ob, *n.* an objection (in the phrase **ob and sol,** objection and solution).—**ob-and-soll'er,** a disputant. [From the marginal note *ob* in old books of controversial divinity.]

**obang,** ō'bang, *n.* an old Japanese oblong gold coin. [Jap. *ōban.*]

**obbligato,** ob-(b)li-gä'tō, *adj.* that cannot be done without.—*n.* a musical accompaniment of independent importance, esp. that of a single instrument to a vocal piece. [It.]

**obcompressed,** ob'kəm-prest, (*bot.*) *adj.* flattened from front to back. [L. pfx. *ob-,* towards; in mod. L., in the opposite direction, reversed.]

**obconic, -al,** ob-kon'ik, -əl, (*bot.*) *adjs.* conical and attached by the point. [Pfx. *ob-,* as in **obcompressed.**]

**obcordate,** ob-kör'dāt, (*bot.*) *adj.* inversely heart-shaped, as a leaf. [Pfx. *ob-,* as in **obcompressed.**]

**obdiplostemonous,** ob-dip-lō-stē'mən-əs, (*bot.*) *adj.* having two whorls of stamens, the outer being situated opposite the petals. [Pfx. *ob-,* as in **obcompressed.**]

**obdurate,** ob'dū-rāt, sometimes (as *Shak., Milt.*) -dū', *adj.* hardened in heart or in feelings: difficult to influence, esp. in a moral sense: stubborn: hard.—*v.t.* and *v.i.* to make or become obdurate.—*n.* **ob'dūracy** (or ob-dū'rə-si), state of being obdurate: invincible hardness of heart.—*adv.* **ob'dūrately** (or dū').—*ns.* **ob'dūrateness** (or -dū'), **obdūrā'tion.**—*v.t.* and *v.i.* **obdūre',**

to obdurate. [L. *obdūrāre*, *-ātum—ob-*, intens., against, *dūrāre*, to harden—*dūrus*, hard.]

**obeah.** See **obi.**

**obeche,** *ō-bē'chē, n.* a large West African tree or its whitish wood. [Nigerian name.]

**obedience,** *ō-bē'dyəns, -di-əns, n.* the act of doing what one is told: the state of being obedient: willingness to obey commands: dutifulness: the collective body of persons subject to any particular authority: a written instruction from the superior of an order to those under him: any official position under an abbot's jurisdiction: an obeisance (*arch.*).—*adjs.* **obē'dient,** obeying: ready to obey; **obediential** (*ō-bē-di-en'shl*), pertaining to, of the nature of, obedience.—*n.* **obēdientiary** (*-en'shə-ri*), one subject to obedience: one charged with an obedience in a monastery.—*adv.* **obē'diently.**—**canonical obedience,** the obedience, as regulated by the canons, of an ecclesiastic to another of higher rank; **passive obedience,** unresisting and unquestioning obedience to authority, like that taught by some Anglican divines as due even to faithless and worthless kings like Charles II and James II. [L. *obēdientia;* see **obey.**]

**obeisance,** *ō-bā'səns, n.* obedience (*obs.*): a bow or act of reverence: an expression of respect.—*adj.* **obei'sant.** [Fr. *obéissancə—obéir*—L. root as **obey.**]

**obelus,** *ob'i-ləs, n.* a sign (− or ÷) used in ancient manuscripts to mark suspected, corrupt, or spurious words and passages: a dagger-sign (†) used esp. in referring to footnotes (**double obelus,** ‡; *print.*):—*pl.* **ob'eli** (*-lī*).—*n.* **obelion** (*ō-bē'li-on*), a point in the sagittal suture of the skull between the two parietal foramina.—*adjs.* **obelisc'al,** of, of of the nature of, an obelisk; **obelisc'oid,** of the form of an obelisk: obeliscal.—*v.t.* **ob'elise, -ize,** to mark with an obelus: to condemn as spurious, doubtful, corrupt, etc.—*n.* **ob'elisk,** a tall, four-sided, tapering pillar, usually of one stone, topped with a pyramid: an obelus. [L. *obelus*—Gr. *obelos* (dim. *obeliskos*), a spit.]

**Oberon,** *ō'bə-rən, n.* king of the fairies, husband of Titania. [O.Fr. *Auberon;* prob. Frankish.]

**obese,** *ō-bēs', adj.* abnormally fat.—*ns.* **obese'ness, obesity** (*-bēs', -bes'*). [L. *obēsus—ob-*, completely, *edēre, ēsum,* to eat.]

**obey,** *ō-bā', v.i.* to render obedience: to do what one is told: to be governed or controlled.—*v.t.* to do as told by: to comply with: to be controlled by.—*n.* **obey'er.** [Fr. *obéir*—L. *obēdīre—oboedīre—ob-*, towards, *audīre,* to hear.]

**obfuscate,** *ob-fus'kāt, v.t.* to darken: to obscure.—*adj.* **obfuscat'ed** (*coll.*), drunk.—*n.* **obfusca'tion.** [L. *obfuscāre, -ātum—ob-*, intens., *fuscus,* dark.]

**obi,** *ō'bi,* **obeah** (*obs.* **obia**), *ō'bi-a, n.* witchcraft and poisoning practised by Negroes of the West Indies, Guiana, etc.: a fetish or charm.—*v.t.* to bewitch.—*ns.* **o'beahism, o'beism, o'biism.—o'bi-man; o'bi-woman.** [Of W. African origin.]

**obi,** *ō'bi, n.* a broad, gaily embroidered sash worn by Japanese women and children. [Jap. *ōbi.*]

**obiit,** *ob'i-it, ō'bi-it,* (L.) died.—**obiit sine prole** (*sin'ē prō'lē, sin'e prō'le*), died without issue.

**obit,** *ob'it,* or *ō'bit, n.* death (*obs.*): date of death: funeral ceremonies: office for a dead person: a death anniversary: an anniversary or other commemoration of a death.—*adjs.* **ob'ital,** obit'ūal, pertaining to obits.—*n.* **obit'ūarist,** a writer of obituaries.—*adj.* **obit'ūary,** relating to or recording the death of a person or persons.—*n.* a register of deaths, orig. in a monastery: an account of a deceased person, or a notice of his death: a collection of death-notices: in a newspaper often extended to include notices of births and marriages, etc. [L.L. *obitus—obīre, -itum,* to go to meet, travel over, die—*ob,* in the way of, *īre,* to go.]

**obiter,** *ob', ōb'it-ər, ob'it-er,* (L.) by the way, cursor-

ily.—**obiter dictum** (*dik'təm, -tōōm*), something said by the way, a cursory remark:—*pl.* **obiter dicta** (*dik'ta*).

**object,** *ob'jikt, n.* a thing presented or capable of being presented to the senses: a thing observed: a material thing: that which is thought of, regarded as being outside, different from, or independent of, the mind (opposed to *subject*): that upon which attention, interest, or some emotion is fixed: an oddity or deplorable spectacle: that towards which action or desire is directed, an end: part of a sentence denoting that upon which the action of a transitive verb is directed, or standing in an analogous relation to a preposition (*gram.*): interposition (*obs.*): presentation to view or to the mind (*Shak.*).—*v.t.* **object** (*-jekt'*), to put in front or in the way of anything or anybody (*arch.*): to present to sense or mind (*arch.*): to present, bring forward, or adduce (*arch.*): to offer in opposition: to bring as an accusation: to impute (*obs.*).—*v.i.* to be opposed, feel or express disapproval (with *to, that, against*): to refuse assent.—*adj.* (*obs.*) opposed, interposed, exposed.—*n.* **objectificā'tion** (*-jekt-*).—*v.t.* **object'ify,** to make objective. —*n.* **objec'tion,** act of objecting: anything said or done in opposition: argument or reason against (with *to, against*): inclination to object, dislike, unwillingness.—*adj.* **objec'tionable,** that may be objected to: requiring to be disapproved of: distasteful.—*adv.* **objec'tionably.**—*v.t.* **object'ivate,** to render objective.—*n.* **objectivā'tion.**—*adj.* **object'ive** (also *ob'*), relating to or constituting an object: existing or considered only in relation to mind, subjective (*scholastic philos., obs.*): of the nature of, or belonging to, that which is presented to consciousness (opposed to *subjective*), exterior to the mind, self-existent, regarding or setting forth what is external, actual, practical, uncoloured by one's own sensations or emotions (*mod. philos.*): denoting the object (*gram.*): in the relation of object to a verb or preposition: objecting: (of lenses) nearest the object.—*n.* (*-jekt'*) the case of the grammatical object: a word in that case: an object-glass: the point to which the operations (esp. of an army) are directed.—*adv.* **object'ively.**—*n.* **object'iveness.**—*v.t.* **object'ivise, -ize,** to objectify.—*ns.* **object'ivism,** a tendency to lay stress on what is objective: a theory that gives priority to the objective; **object'ivist.**—*adj.* **objectivist'ic.**—*n.* **objectiv'ity.**—*adj.* **object'less,** having no object: purposeless.—*n.* **object'or.**—**ob'ject-ball,** a ball that a player aims at striking with his own ball; **ob'ject-find'er,** a device in microscopes for locating an object in the field before examination by a higher power; **ob'ject-glass,** in an optical instrument, the lens or combination of lenses at the end next to the object; **ob'ject-less'on,** a lesson in which a material object is before the class: a warning or instructive experience; **ob'ject-soul,** a vital principle attributed by the primitive mind to inanimate objects.—**money,** etc., **no object,** money, etc., not being a thing aimed at; **distance,** etc., **no object,** distance, etc., not being reckoned worth consideration (perh. by confusion with the foregoing). [L. *objectus,* pa.p. of *ob*(*j*)*icĕre,* or partly the noun *objectus, -ūs* (found in the abl.), or the freq. vb. *objectāre —ob,* in the way of, *jacĕre,* to throw.]

**objet,** *ob-zhā,* (Fr.) an object.—**objet d'art** (*där*), an article with artistic value; **objet trouvé** (*trōō-vā;* same as **found object**):—*pls.* **objets d'art, trouvés.**

**objure,** *ob-jōōr', v.i.* to swear.—*v.t.* to bind by oath: to charge or entreat solemnly.—*n.* **objurā'tion,** act of binding by oath: a solemn charge. [L. *objūrāre,* to bind by oath—*ob-*, down, *jūrāre,* to swear.]

**objurgate,** *ob'jər-gāt,* or *-jûr', v.t.* and *v.i.* to chide.

—*n.* objurgā'tion.—*adjs.* objur'gative, objur'gatory. [L. *objurgāre*, *-ātum*, to rebuke—*ob-*, intens., *jurgāre*, to chide.]

oblanceolate, *ob-län'si-ō-lāt*, (*bot.*) *adj.* like a lance-head reversed, as a leaf—about three times as long as broad, tapering more gently towards base than apex. [Pfx. *ob-*, as in obcompressed.]

oblast, *ob'ləst*, *n.* a province or district. [Russ.]

oblate, *ob'lāt*, *ob-lāt'*, *adj.* dedicated: offered up. —*n.* a dedicated person, esp. one dedicated to monastic life but not professed, or to a religious life.—*n.* oblā'tion, act of offering: a sacrifice: anything offered in worship, esp. a eucharistic offering: an offering generally. [L. *oblātus*, offered up, used as pa.p. of *offerre*, to offer; see offer.]

oblate, *ob'lāt'*, *ob-lāt'*, *ō-blāt'*, *adj.* flattened at opposite sides or poles, as a spheroid—shaped like an orange.—*n.* oblate'ness. [On analogy of prolate; L. pfx. *ob-*, against, or (mod. L.) in the opposite direction.]

oblige, *ō-blīj'*, *ə-blīj'*, formerly *-blēj'*, *v.t.* to bind morally or legally: to constrain: to bind by some favour rendered, hence to do a favour to. —*v.i.* (*coll.*) to do something as a favour.—*n.* obligant (*ob'li-gənt*; *Scots law*), one who binds himself to another to pay or to perform something.—*v.t.* ob'ligate (*-li-gāt*), to constrain (*U.S.* and *arch.*): to bind by contract or duty: to bind by gratitude (*arch.* or *coll.*).—*adj.* (*bot.*) by necessity, without option.—*n.* obligation (*ob-li-gā'shən*), act of obliging: a moral or legal bond, tie, or binding power: that to which one is bound: a debt of gratitude: a favour: a bond containing a penalty in case of failure (*law*).—*adv.* obligatorily (*ob'lig-ə-tər-i-li* or *o-blig'*).—*n.* ob'ligatoriness (or *o-blig'*).—*adj.* ob'ligatory (or *o-blig'*), binding: imposing duty: imposed as an obligation: obligate.—*ns.* obligee (*ob-li-jē'*), the person to whom another is bound by obligation (*law*): one who is under an obligation for a favour: oblige'ment, a favour conferred.—*adj.* oblig'ing, disposed to confer favours: ready to do a good turn: courteous.— *adv.* oblig'ingly.—*ns.* oblig'ingness; obligor (*ob'li-gör*; *law*), the person who binds himself to another. [Fr. *obliger*—L. *obligāre*, *-ātum*—*ob-*, down, *ligāre*, to bind.]

oblique, *ō-blēk'*, *ə-blēk'*, *adj.* slanting: neither perpendicular nor parallel: not at right angles: not parallel to an axis: not straightforward: indirect: underhand: not a right angle (*geom.*): having the axis not perpendicular to the plane of the base: skew: asymmetrical about the midrib (*bot.*): monoclinic (*crystal.*).—*n.* an oblique line, figure, muscle, etc.: an oblique movement or advance, esp. one about 45° from the original direction.—*v.i.* to deviate from a direct line or from the perpendicular, to slant: to advance obliquely by facing half right or left and then advancing.—*v.t.* to turn aslant.—*ns.* obliquation (*ob-li-kwā'shən*), obliqueness (*-blēk'*), obliquity (*ob-lik'wi-ti*), state of being oblique: a slanting direction: crookedness of outlook, thinking, or conduct, or an instance of it: irregularity (*obs.*).—*adv.* oblique'ly.—*adjs.* obliquid (*ob-lik'wid*; *Spens.*), oblique; obliqu'itous.—oblique case, any case other than nominative and vocative (see case); oblique motion (*mus.*), upward or downward motion of one part while another remains stationary; oblique narration or speech, indirect speech (see indirect).—obliquity of the ecliptic, the angle between the plane of the earth's orbit and that of the earth's equator. [L. *oblīquus* —*ob-*, intens., and the root of *līquis*, slanting.]

obliterate, *ō-blit'ə-rāt*, *v.t.* to blot out, so as not to be readily or clearly readable: to efface: to close up and do away with (as a tubular element; *med.* and *biol.*).—*adj.* oblit'erāted, effaced: without defined margins.—*n.* obliterā'tion.—*adj.*

oblit'erative. [L. *oblitterāre*, *-ātum*—*ob-*, over, *littera* (*litera*), a letter.]

oblivion, *ō-bliv'i-ən*, *n.* forgetfulness: a state of having forgotten: amnesty: a state of being forgotten.—*adj.* obliv'ious, forgetful: prone to forget: causing, or associated with, forgetfulness (*poet.*): raptly or absent-mindedly unaware (with *of, to*) forgotten (*obs.*).—*adv.* obliv'iously.— *ns.* obliv'iousness; obliviscence (*ob-li-vis'əns*), forgetfulness: forgetting. [L. *oblīviō*, *-ōnis*, from the root of *oblīvīscī*, to forget.]

oblong, *ob'long*, *adj.* long in one way: longer than broad: nearly elliptical, with sides nearly parallel, ends blunted, two to four times as long as broad (*bot.*).—*n.* a rectangle longer than broad: any oblong figure, whether angular or rounded. [L. *oblongus*—*ob-* (force obscure), and *longus*, long.]

obloquy, *ob'lə-kwi*, *n.* reproachful language: censure: calumny: disgrace. [L. *ubluquium*—*ob*, against, *loquī*, to speak.]

obmutescent, *ob-mū-tes'ənt*, *adj.* speechless: persistently silent.—*n.* obmutesc'ence. [L. *obmūtēscēns*, *-entis*, pr.p. of *obmūtēscēre*, to become dumb—*ob-*, intens., *mūtus*, dumb.]

obnoxious, *ob-nok'shəs*, *adj.* liable (to hurt, punishment, or censure; *obs.*): subject to the authority (*obs.*): exposed (*rare*): objectionable: offensive: noxious, hurtful (*erron.*).—*adv.* obnox'iously.—*n.* obnox'iousness. [L. *obnoxius*— *ob*, exposed to, *noxa*, hurt.]

obnubilation, *ob-nū-bi-lā'shən*, *n.* clouding: darkening.—*v.t.* obnū'bilate. [L. *obnūbilāre*, to cloud over—L. *ob-*, over, *nūbilus*, cloudy.]

oboe, *ō'bō*, (*arch.*) *ō'boi*, *n.* a double-reed treble woodwind instrument: an organ stop of similar tone.—*n.* o'bōist, a player on the oboe.—oboe d'amore (*ō'bō dä-mō'rä*; It., oboe of love), an old oboe a minor third lower; oboe di caccia (*dē-kat'cha*; of the chase), an obsolete alto or tenor oboe. [It. *oboe*—Fr. *hautbois*; see hautboy.]

obol, *ob'ol*, *n.* in ancient Greece, the sixth part of a drachma in weight, or in money (about 1½d.).— *adj.* ob'olary, extremely poor.—*n.* ob'olus (L.), an obol: in the Middle Ages applied to various small coins, as the English halfpenny:—*pl.* ob'oli (*-i*). [Gr. *obolos*.]

obovate, *ob-ō'vāt*, (*bot.*) *adj.* egg-shaped in outline, with the narrow end next to the base.—*adv.* obō'-vately.—*adj.* obō'void, solidly obovate. [Pfx. *ob-*, as in obcompressed.]

obreption, *ob-rep'shən*, *n.* surprising by stealth (*obs.*): obtaining or seeking to obtain a gift, etc., by false statement—different both in sense and in etymology from *subreption* (*law*).—*adj.* obreptitious (*-tish'əs*). [L. *obreptiō*, *-ōnis*—*ob*, in the way of, *rēpēre*, to creep.]

obscene, *ob-sēn'*, *adj.* filthy: offensive to the senses or the sensibility, disgusting: indecent esp. in a sexual sense: (less strongly) offending against an accepted standard of morals or taste: ill-omened (*obs.*).—*adv.* obscene'ly.—*ns.* obscene'ness, obscenity (*-sen'* or *-sēn'*). [L. *obscēnus*.]

obscure, *ob-skūr'*, *adj.* dark: not distinct: not easily understood: not clear, legible, or perspicuous: unknown: hidden: inconspicuous: lowly: unknown to fame: living or enveloped in darkness.—*n.* darkness: an obscure place: indistinctness.—*v.t.* to darken: to dim: to hide: to make less plain: to render doubtful.—*v.i.* to hide: to darken.—*ns.* ob'scūrant (*-ant*, or *ob-skūr'ənt*), one who labours to prevent enlightenment or reform; obscūrant'ism (or *-skūr'*), opposition to inquiry or reform; obscūrant'ist (or *-skūr'*), an obscurant.—*adj.* pertaining to obscurantism.—*n.* obscūrā'tion, the act of obscuring or state of being obscured.—*adv.* obscūre'ly. —*ns.* obscūre'ment; obscūre'ness; obscūr'er;

**obscūr'ity**, state or quality of being obscure: darkness: an obscure place, point, or condition. [Fr. *obscur*—L. *obscūrus*—*ob*-, over, and the root seen in L. *scūtum*, shield, Gr. *skeuē*, covering.]

**obsecrate**, *ob'si-krāt*, *v.t.* to beseech: to implore.—*n.* **obsecrā'tion**, supplication: one of the clauses in the Litany beginning with *by*. [L. *obsecrāre*, *-ātum*, to entreat; *ob*, before, *sacrāre* —*sacer*, sacred.]

**obsequent**, *ob'si-kwənt*, *adj.* flowing in a contrary direction to the original slope of the land, parallel to the *consequent* and perpendicular to the *subsequent* streams. [L. *ob*, face to face with, *sequēns*, *-entis*, pr.p. of *sequī*, to follow.]

**obsequies**, *ob'si-kwiz*, *n.pl.* funeral rites and solemnities:—*sing.* (*rare*) **ob'sequy** (*Milt.* **obsequie**). —*adjs.* **obsequial** (*-sē'kwi-əl*), **obsē'quious** (*Shak.*; see also next word). [L.L. *obsequiae*, a confusion of L. *exsequiae*, funeral rites, and *obsequium*; see next word.]

**obsequious**, *ob-sē'kwi-əs*, *adj.* orig., compliant, obedient, dutiful: now, compliant to excess: fawning.—*adv.* **obsē'quiously.**—*n.* **obsē'quiousness.** [L. *obsequiōsus*, compliant, *obsequium*, compliance—*ob*-, towards, *sequī*, to follow.]

**observe**, *ob-zûrv'*, *v.t.* to keep in view: to watch: to subject to systematic watching: to regard attentively: to direct watchful and critical attention to with a view to ascertaining a fact: to ascertain by such attention: to notice: to attend to: to remark in words: to comply with: to act according to: to heed and to carry out in practice: to keep with ceremony: to celebrate: to keep (as silence): to be deferential to, to humour (*Shak.*).—*v.i.* to take observations: to make remarks.—*n.* (*Scot.*) a remark.—*adj.* **observ'able**, discernible, perceptible: worthy of note: notable: to be observed.—*n.* something that can be observed by the senses, with or without the help of instrument(s).—*n.* **observ'ableness.**—*adv.* **observ'ably.**—*ns.* **observ'ance**, the keeping of, or acting according to, a law, duty, custom, ceremony: the keeping with ceremony or according to custom: a custom observed or to be observed: a rule of religious life: an order or company accepting it (esp. the Observants), or their house: a deferential act or treatment: watchful heed (*Shak.*): now rarely, observation; **observ'ancy**, observance: observation: a house of Observants.—*adj.* **observ'ant**, observing: having powers of observing and noting: taking notice: keeping an observance: carefully attentive.—*n.* an obsequious attendant (*Shak.*): one strict to comply with a custom, etc. —*ns.* **Observ'ant** or **Observ'antine** (*-ən-tin*, *-tēn*) a, Franciscan friar of stricter rule.—*adv.* **observ'antly.**—*n.* **observā'tion**, act of observing: habit, practice, or faculty of seeing and noting: attention: the act of recognising and noting phenomena as they occur in nature, as distinguished from *experiment*: a reading of an instrument: the result of such observing: watching: now rarely, observance: that which is observed: a remark: the fact of being observed. —*adj.* **observā'tional**, consisting of, or containing, observations or remarks: derived from observation, as distinguished from *experiment*.—*adv.* **observā'tionally.**—*adj.* **observ'ative**, observant: observational.—*ns.* **ob'servātor** (now *rare* or *obs.*), one who observes in any sense: a remarker; **observ'atory**, a building or station for making astronomical and physical observations: a viewpoint: a spying place; **observ'er**, one who observes in any sense: one whose function it is to take observations: formerly, airman who accompanied pilot to observe, now, flying officer (*q.v.*): a member of the Royal Observer Corps, a uniformed civilian organisation affiliated to the Royal Air Force: one deputed

to watch proceedings.—*adj.* **observ'ing**, habitually taking notice: attentive.—*adv.* **observ'ingly.** —**observation car**, a railway carriage designed to allow passengers to view scenery. [Fr. *observer* —L. *observāre*, *-ātum*—*ob*, towards, *servāre*, to keep.]

**obsess**, *ob-ses'*, *v.t.* to besiege (*obs.*): to beset (*arch.*): to occupy the thoughts of obstinately and persistently.—*n.* **obsession** (*-sesh'ən*), a siege (*obs.*): persistent attack, esp. of an evil spirit (*arch.*): the state of being so molested from without—opp. to *possession*, or control by an evil spirit from within (*arch.*): morbid persistence of an idea in the mind, against one's will: a fixed idea.—*adj.* **obsess'ional.**—*n.* **obsess'-ionist**, one who is obsessed by a fixed idea.—*adj.* **obsess'ive**, relating to obsession: obsessing. [L. *obsidēre*, *obsessum*, to besiege.]

**obsidian**, *ob-sid'i-ən*, *n.* a vitreous acid volcanic rock resembling bottle-glass. [From *obsidiānus*, a false reading of L. *obsiānus* (*lapis*), a stone found by one *Obsius* (wrongly *Obsidius*) in Ethiopia, according to Pliny.]

**obsidional**, *ob-sid'i-ən-əl*, *adj.* pertaining to a siege. —Also **obsid'ionary.** [L. *obsidiō*, *-ōnis*, a siege; see **obsess.**]

**obsign**, *ob-sin'*, **obsignate**, *ob-sig'nāt*, *vs.t.* to seal, confirm.—*n.* **obsignā'tion** (*-sig-*).—*adj.* **obsig'-natory.** [L. *obsignāre*, to seal up—*ob*-, over, *signāre*, to mark, seal.]

**obsolescent**, *ob-sə-les'ənt*, *adj.* going out of use: in course of disappearance: tending to become obsolete.—*v.i.* **obsolesce** (*-les'*), to be in process of going out of use.—*n.* **obsolesc'ence.**—*adj.* **ob'-solete** (*-lēt*), gone out of use: antiquated: no longer functional or fully developed.—*adv.* **ob'-soletely.**—*ns.* **ob'soleteness**; **obsolē'tion** (*rare*); **ob'solētism.**—**planned obsolescence**, the going out of date of a product according to a prearranged plan—achieved, e.g. by change of certain non-essential characteristics of the model. [L. *obsolēscĕre*, *obsolētum*, perh. from pfx. *obs*- (*ob*-, completeness) and the root of *alĕre*, to nourish.]

**obstacle**, *ob'stə-kl*, *n.* anything that stands in the way of or hinders advance.—*adj.* (*Shak.*) stubborn.—**obstacle race**, a race in which obstacles have to be passed. [Fr.,—L. *obstāculum*—*ob*, in the way of, *stāre*, to stand.]

**obstetric, -al**, *ob-stet'rik*, *-əl*, *adjs.* pertaining to midwifery.—*ns.* **obstetrician** (*ob-sti-trish'ən*), a man or woman skilled in practising, or qualified to practise, obstetrics; **obstet'rics**, the science of midwifery. [L. *obstetrīcius* (the *-īc-* confused with the suffix *-ic*)—*obstetrix*, *-īcis*, a midwife— *ob*, before, *stāre*, to stand.]

**obstinate**, *ob'sti-nāt*, *adj.* blindly or excessively firm: unyielding: stubborn: not easily subdued or remedied.—*ns.* **ob'stinacy** (*-nə-si*), **ob'stinate-ness.**—*adv.* **ob'stinately.** [L. *obstināre*, *-ātum*— *ob*, in the way of, *stanāre* (found in compounds), a form of *stāre*, to stand.]

**obstipation**, *ob-sti-pā'shən*, *n.* extreme constipation. [L. *ob*, against, *stipāre*, *-ātum*, to press.]

**obstreperous**, *ob-strep'ə-rəs*, *adj.* making a loud noise: clamorous: noisy: unruly.—*v.t.* **obstrep'-erate** (*Sterne*).—*adv.* **obstrep'erously.**—*n.* **ob'-strep'erousness.** [L. *obstreperus*—*ob*, before, against, *strepĕre*, to make a noise.]

**obstriction**, *ob-strik'shən*, *n.* obligation. [L. *ob stringĕre*, *obstrictum*, to bind up.]

**obstropalous, obstropulous**, *ob-strop'ə-ləs*, *-ū-ləs* illit. forms of **obstreperous.**

**obstruct**, *ob-strukt'*, *v.t.* to block up: to hinder from passing or progressing: to shut off: to hamper.—*v.i.* to be an obstruction: to practise obstruction.—*ns.* **obstruc'ter** (*rare*); **obstruc'tion**, act of obstructing: a state of being obstructed: that which hinders progress or action: an obstacle: opposition by dilatory tactics, as in a legislative assembly; **obstruc'tionist,** a politician who practises obstruction.—*adj.* **obstruct'ive,** tending to obstruct: hindering.—*n.* a hindrance: a hinderer of progress.—*adv.* **obstruct'ively.**—*n.* **obstruct'or.**—*adj.* **obstruent** (*ob'strōō-ənt*), obstructing: blocking up.—*n.* anything that obstructs, esp. in the passages of the body: an astringent drug: a stop or a fricative (*phon.*). [L. *obstruĕre, obstructum*—*ob*, in the way of, *struĕre, structum*, to pile up, build.]

**obtain,** *ob-tān'*, *v.t.* to get: to procure by effort: to gain: to reach (*arch.*): to hold, occupy (*obs.*). —*v.i.* to be established: to continue in use: to hold good: to prevail, to succeed (*arch.*): to attain (*obs.*).—*adj.* **obtain'able.**—*ns.* **obtain'er; obtain'ment; obtention** (*-ten'shən*), getting. [Fr. *obtenir*—L. *obtinēre,* to occupy—*ob,* against, *tenēre,* to hold.]

**obtect, obtected,** *ob-tekt', -id, adjs.* having wings and legs immovably pressed against the body in a hard chitinous case, as many insect pupae. [L. *obtegĕre, obtectum,* to cover over—*ob-,* over, *tegĕre,* to cover.]

**obtemper,** *ob-tem'pər, v.t.* to yield obedience to.— Also *v.i.* (with *to, unto*).—Also **obtem'perate.** [L. *obtemperāre, -ātum*—*ob,* before, *temperāre,* to restrain oneself.]

**obtend,** *ob-tend', (obs.) v.t.* to hold out in opposition: to put forward, allege. [L. *obtendĕre,* to stretch before—*ob,* in front of, *tendĕre,* to stretch.]

**obtest,** *ob-test', v.t.* to call to witness: to adjure.— *v.i.* to protest.—*n.* **obtestā'tion.** [L. *obtestāri,* to call as a witness—*ob,* before, *testis,* a witness.]

**obtrude,** *ob-trōōd', v.t.* to thrust forward, or upon one, unduly or unwelcomely.—*v.i.* to thrust oneself forward.—*ns.* **obtrud'er; obtrud'ing; obtrusion** (*-trōō'zhən*), an unwanted thrusting in or forward, or upon one.—*adj.* **obtrusive** (*-trōō'siv*), disposed to thrust oneself in or forward: unduly prominent or projecting.—*adv.* **obtru'sively.**—*n* **obtru'siveness.** [L. *obtrūdĕre*—*ob,* against, *trūdĕre, trūsum,* to thrust.]

**obtruncate,** *ob-trung'kāt, v.t.* to cut or lop off the head of. [L. *obtruncāre, -ātum,* to cut in pieces, mutilate—*ob-,* intens., *truncāre,* cut off.]

**obtund,** *ob-tund', v.t.* to blunt or dull: to deaden. —*adj.* **obtund'ent,** dulling.—*n.* an application to deaden irritation. [L. *obtundĕre,* to strike upon —*ob,* against, *tundĕre,* to thump.]

**obturate,** *ob'tū-rāt, v.t.* to stop up.—*ns.* **obturā'-tion,** stopping up: in gunnery, stopping of a hole to prevent the escape of gas; **ob'turātor,** a structure or device that closes a cavity: the structures closing a large opening in the hip-bone (*anat.*). [L. *obtūrāre, -ātum,* to stop up; etymology obscure.]

**obtuse,** *ob-tūs', adj.* blunt: not pointed: blunt or rounded at the tip (*bot.*): greater than a right angle (*geom.*): dull: dull-witted: insensitive.—*adv.* **obtuse'ly.**—*ns.* **obtuse'ness, obtus'ity.** —*adjs.* **obtuse'-ang'led, ang'ular,** having an angle greater than a right angle. [L. *obtūsus*— pa.p. of *obtundĕre;* cf. **obtund.**]

**obumbrate,** *ob-um'brāt, v.t.* to overshadow.—*n.* **obumbrā'tion.** [L. *obumbrāre, -ātum*—*ob,* in the way of, *umbra,* shadow.]

**obvention,** *ob-ven'shən, (obs.) n.* any incidental occurrence, or advantage, esp. a fee. [L. *obvenīre, -ventum,* to come to meet, come by chance—*ob,* face to face with, *venīre,* to come.]

**obverse,** *ob'vûrs, ob-vûrs', adj.* turned towards one: complemental, constituting the opposite aspect of the same fact: having the base narrower than the apex (*bot.*): got by obversion (*log.*).—*n.* **obverse** (*ob'vûrs*), the side of a coin containing the head, or principal symbol: the face or side of anything normally presented to view: a counterpart or opposite aspect: a proposition obtained from another by obversion (*log.*).— *adv.* **obverse'ly.**—*n.* **obver'sion,** the act of turning

a thing toward one: a species of immediate inference where the contradictory of the original predicate is predicated of the original subject, the quality of the proposition being changed— e.g. to infer from All A is B that No A is not B— also called *permutation* and *equipollence* (*log.*).— *v.t.* **obvert',** to turn in the direction of, or face to face with, something: to infer the obverse of. [L. *obversus,* turned against, or towards—*ob-,* towards, *vertĕre,* to turn.]

**obviate,** *ob'vi-āt, v.t.* to meet on the way (*obs.*): to prevent or dispose of in advance: to forestall. —*n.* **obviā'tion.** [L. *obviāre, -ātum*—*ob,* in the way of, *viāre, viātum,* to go—*via,* a way.]

**obvious,** *ob'vi-əs, adj.* meeting one in the way (*obs.*): easily discovered or understood: clearly or plainly evident.—*adv.* **ob'viously.**—*n.* **ob'vious-ness.** [L. *obvius*—*ob, via;* see foregoing.]

**obvolute, -d,** *ob'və-lūt, -lōōt,* or *-vo-, -id, (bot.) adjs.* arranged so that each leaf of a pair is conduplicate and enfolds one-half of the other.—*adj.* **obvolvent** (*-vol'vənt*), enwrapping: curved downward or inward (*entom.*). [L. *obvolūtus,* pa.p., and *obvolvēns, -entis,* pr.p., of *obvolvĕre,* to enwrap—*ob,* over, *volvĕre, volūtum,* to roll.]

**oca,** *ō'ka, n.* a South American wood-sorrel with edible tubers. [Sp., from Quechua.]

**ocarina,** *ok-ə-rē'nə, n.* a fluty-toned bird-shaped musical toy, orig. of terra-cotta. [It., dim. of *oca,* a goose.]

**Occamism,** *ok'əm-izm, n.* the doctrine of the nominalist schoolman, William of *Occam* or *Ockham* (who died about 1349).—*n.* **Occ'amist.**— Occam's razor, the principle that entities are not to be multiplied beyond necessity.

**occamy,** *ok'ə-mi, n.* a silvery alloy. [alchemy.]

**occasion,** *ə-kā'zhən, n.* a case, instance, time of something happening: events, course of events (*Shak.*): a suitable juncture: a special time or season: a chance of bringing about something desired: opportunity: an event which, although not the cause, determines the time at which another happens: a reason, pretext, or excuse: requirement: need: (usu. in *pl.*) business: (in *pl.*) necessary bodily functions (*obs.*): a special ceremony, celebration, or event: communion service (*Scot.* formerly): doing, occasioning, matter of responsibility (*Shak.*).—*v.t.* to give occasion or rise to: to cause: to accustom (*obs.*). —*adj.* **occā'sional,** happening, occurring infrequently, irregularly, now and then: resulting from accident (*obs.*): produced on or for some special event or for special occasions: constituting the occasion.—*ns.* **occā'sionalism,** the Cartesian explanation of the apparent interaction of mind and matter by the direct intervention of God on the occasion of certain changes occurring in one or the other; **occā'sionalist; occāsional'ity.** —*adv.* **occā'sionally,** casually (*obs.*): on or for an occasion: now and then.—*n.* **occā'sioner.**— **occasional cause,** the event which in the Cartesian philosophy is only the occasion, not the true cause: that by which the efficient cause comes into operation; **occasional conformist** (*hist.*), a Dissenter who qualified for office by conforming to the Church of England upon occasion; **occasional table,** a small portable ornamental table.—**occasioned by,** (which was) a consequence of (*obs.*): caused by: necessitated by; **on occasion,** in case of need: as opportunity offers: from time to time; **rise to the occasion** (see **rise**); **take occasion,** to take advantage of an opportunity (to). [L. *occāsiō, -ōnis,* opportunity —*ob,* in the way of, *cadĕre, cāsum,* to fall.]

**Occident, occident,** *ok'si-dənt, n.* the quarter of the sky where the heavenly bodies set: the west— opp. to *Orient.*—*adj.* **Occidental, occidental** (*-dent'l*), western: characteristic of the West (esp. Europe, America, the Western United States): relatively less precious, as a gem (because the best stones were presumed to come from the East).—*n.* a westerner: a language invented by Edgar de Wahl (1922).—*v.t.* occi-den'talise, -ize, to cause to conform to western ideas or customs.—*ns.* Occiden'talism, the culture and ways of Occidental peoples; Occiden'talist, a student of Occidental languages: an Oriental who favours western ideas, customs, etc.—*adv.* occiden'tally.—occidental topaz, a semiprecious yellow quartz; occidental turquoise, odontolite. [L. *occidēns, -entis*, setting, pr.p. of *occidĕre*—*ob*, towards, down, *cadĕre*, to fall.]

occiput, *ok'si-put, n.* the back of the head or skull.—*adj.* occip'ital, pertaining to the back of the head.—*n.* the occipital bone, the bone at the back of the skull.—*adv.* occip'itally. [L. *occiput*—*ob*, over against, *caput*, head.]

occlude, *o-klōōd', v.t.* to shut in or out: to cut or shut off: to stop (as a passage, cavity, or opening): to bring together (as the teeth or eyelids): to absorb or retain (as a gas by a metal or other solid).—*v.i.* to bite or close together (as the teeth).—*adj.* occlu'dent, serving to occlude: occluding.—*n.* that which occludes.—*adj.* occlu'sal (-*səl*), pertaining to occlusion of teeth.—*n.* occlu'sion (-*zhən*), a closing of an opening, passage, or cavity: the act of occluding or absorbing: the bite or mode of meeting of the teeth: the formation, or condition, of an occluded front.—*adj.* occlu'sive (-*siv*), serving to close: characterised by occlusion.—*n.* (*phon.*) a sound produced by closing the breath passage.—*n.* occlu'sor, that which closes, esp. a muscle for closing an opening.—occluded front, an advancing cold front into which a mass of warm air has been driven obliquely, forming a bulge which narrows as the warm air is lifted up and the cold air flows in beneath. [L. *occlūdĕre, -clūsum*—*ob*, in the way of, *claudĕre*, to shut.]

occult, *ok-ult', ok'ult, adj.* hidden: of a line, faint, or dotted, or to be rubbed out later (*rare*): secret: esoteric: unknown: not discovered without test or experiment (*obs.*): beyond the range of sense: transcending the bounds of natural knowledge: mysterious: magical: supernatural.—*v.t.* occult (*ok-ult'*), to hide: to hide by interposing.—*v.i.* to become temporarily invisible (as a lighthouse light).—*n.* occultā'tion, a concealing, esp. of one of the heavenly bodies by another: state of being hidden.—*adj.* occult'ed.—*ns.* occ'-ultism, doctrine or study of things hidden or mysterious—theosophy, etc.; occ'ultist, one who believes in occult things.—*adv.* occult'ly.—*n.* occult'ness.—occult sciences, alchemy, astrology, magic, palmistry, etc. [L. *occultus*, pa.p. of *occulĕre*, to hide—*ob*-, over, and the root of *celāre*, to hide.]

occupance, etc., occupation, etc. See occupy.

occupy, *ok'ū-pī, v.t.* to take possession of: to capture: to hold: to fill (post, office): to take up, as a space, time, etc.: to tenant: to busy: to lay out in trade (*B.*): to cohabit with (*obs.*).—*v.i.* to hold possession (*obs.*): to trade (*obs.*): to cohabit (*obs.*):—*pr.p.* occ'ūpying; *pa.t.* and *pa.p.* occ'ūpied.—*ns.* occ'ūpance (*rare*), occ'ū-pancy, the act or fact of occupying, or of taking or holding possession (esp. of that which previously had no owner): possession: the time during which one occupies; occ'ūpant, one who takes or has possession.—*v.t.* occ'ūpāte (*obs.*), to occupy.—*adj.* (*obs.*) occupied.—*n.* occūpā'tion, the act of occupying: possession: state of being employed or occupied: that which occupies or takes up one's attention: habitual employment, profession, craft, or trade.—*adj.* occupational.—*adjs.* occūpā'tional, connected with habitual occupation; occ'ūpātive, held by tenure based on occupation.—*n.* occ'ūpier (-*pī-ər*), one who occupies: an occupant: one who practises (*obs.*): a dealer (*obs.*).—occupational disease, a disease

common among workers engaged in a particular occupation because encouraged by the conditions of that occupation; occupational therapy, treatment of a disease (incl. a mental disease) or an injury by a regulated course of suitable work; occupation level, in an archaeological site, any of several distinct layers of debris left by successive occupations, from which the site can be dated. [Fr. *occuper*—L. *occupāre, -ātum*—*ob*-, to, on, *capĕre*, to take; the -*y* is unexplained.]

occur, *o-kûr', v.i.* to meet (*obs.*): to come into the mind of (with *to*): to be, be found: to happen: (of festivals) to fall on the same day:—*pr.p.* occurr'ing; *pa.p.* occurred'.—*n.* occurrence (-*kur'*), act or fact of occurring: anything that happens: an event, esp. one unlooked for or unplanned.—*adj.* occurr'ent, occurring: happening: turning up: to be found: incidental.—*n.* one who or that which meets or comes in contact (*obs.*): an occurrence, an item of news (*arch.*). [L. *occurrĕre*—*ob*, in the way of, *currĕre*, to run.]

ocean, *ō'shən, n.* the vast expanse of salt water that covers the greater part of the surface of the globe: any one of its great divisions (Atlantic, Pacific, Indian, Arctic, Antarctic; also Southern—i.e. the belt of water round the earth between 40° and 66½° south—and German—i.e. the North Sea): any immense expanse or vast quantity (*fig.*).—*adj.* pertaining to the great sea.—*ns.* oceanarium, *ō-shən-ār'i-əm*, an enclosed part of the sea (also called seaquarium), or a large saltwater pond, in which dolphins, porpoises, etc., are kept and tamed; oceanaut (*ō'shə-nöt*), one who lives, observes, explores, under the sea.—*adjs.* Oceanian (*ō-shi-ā'ni-ən*), pertaining to Oceania, which includes Polynesia, Micronesia, Melanesia, with or without Australasia; oceanic (*ō-shi-an'ik*), pertaining to the ocean: found or formed in the ocean or high seas, pelagic: wide like the ocean.—*ns.* oceanid (*ō-sē'ən-id*), a daughter of Oceanus: an ocean nymph:—*pl.* oceanides (*ō-sē-an'id-ēz*); oceanographer (*ō-shi-ən-og'ra-fər*, or *ō-shən-*, or *ō-si-ən-*).—*adj.* oceanographic (*ō-shi-an-ō-graf'ik*, or *ō-shən-*, or *ō-si-an-*).—*ns.* oceanog'raphy, the scientific description of the ocean; oceanol'ogy.—*o'cean-bā'sin*, the depression in which the waters of an ocean are contained; o'cean-grey'hound, a very fast steamer; oceanic islands, islands far from the mainland; o'cean-stream' (*Milt.*), the river Oceanus (Okeanos), supposed to encircle the land of the world. [O.Fr. *occean*—L. *Ōcĕănus*—Gr. *Ōkĕănos*, the river, or its god.]

ocellus, *ō-sel'əs, n.* a simple eye or eye-spot, distinguished from a compound eye, in insects and other lower animals: an eyelike or ringed spot of colour:—*pl.* ocell'i.—*adjs.* ocell'ar, of, or of the nature of, an ocellus or ocelli; ocell'ate (or *os'əl-āt*), -d, eyelike and ringed: having an eyelike spot or spots.—*n.* ocellation (*os-ə-lā'shən*). [L. *ŏcellus*, dim. of *oculus*, an eye.]

ocelot, *o'- or ō'si-lot, n.* an American cat (*Felis pardalis*), like a small leopard.—*adj.* o'celoid. [Mex. *ocelotl*, jaguar.]

och, *ohh, interj.* expressing impatience, or contemptuous dismissal—pshaw, tut (*Scot.*): in Ireland and part of Scotland, expressing regret.

ocherous, etc. See ochre.

ochidore, *ok'i-dōr, -dör, n.* Kingsley's name (not otherwise known) for a shore-crab.

ochlocracy, *ok-lok'ra-si, n.* mob-rule.—*n.* och'lo-crat (-*lō-krat*).—*adjs.* ochlocrat'ic, -al.—*adv.* ochlocrat'ically.—*n.* ochlophobia, *ok-la-fō'bi-ə*, fear of crowds (Gr. *phobos*, fear). [Gr. *ochlo-kratiā*—*ochlos*, a crowd, *kratos*, power.]

ochone. See ohone.

Ochotona, *ok-ō-tō'nə, n.* the pika genus. [Mongol *ochodona*.]

ochre, *ō'kər, n.* a native pigment composed of

fine clay and an iron oxide (limonite in yellow ochre, haematite in red): a paint manufactured from it, used for colouring walls, etc.: an earthy metallic oxide of various kinds: money, esp. gold (*slang*).—*v.t.* to mark or colour with ochre.—*adjs.* ochrā′ceous, ochreous (*ō′kri-əs*), o′chroid, o′chrous (sometimes o′cherous), o′chry (also o′chrey, o′chery), consisting of, containing, or resembling, ochre; ochroleu′cous (Gr. *leukos*, white), yellowish white. [Fr. *ocre*—L. *ōchra*—Gr. *ōchrā*—*ōchros*, pale yellow.]

ochrea. See ocrea.

o′clock. See clock.

ocrea (commonly ochrea), *ok′ri-ə*, (*bot.*) *n.* a sheath formed of two stipules united round a stem:—*pl.* oc(h)′reae (-*ē*).—*adj.* oc(h)′reāte. [L. *ocrea*, a legging.]

oct(a)-, *okt*(-*a*, -*ə*), also octo-, *q.v.*, in composition, eight.—*n.* octachord (*ok′tə-körd*; Gr. *chordē*, a gut string), an eight-stringed instrument: a diatonic series of eight tones.—*adj.* octachord′al. —*n.* octagon (*ok′tə-gon*; Gr. *gōniā*, an angle), a plane figure of eight sides and eight angles.— Also *adj.*—*adj.* octagonal (-*tag′ən-əl*).—*adv.* octag′onally.—*n.* octahedron (*ok-tə-hē′dron*; Gr. *hedrā*, a base), a solid bounded by eight plane faces:—*pl.* octahē′drons, octahē′dra.—*adj.* octahē′dral.—*n.* octahē′drite, anatase, crystallising in square bipyramids.—*adj.* octamerous (*ok-tam′*; Gr. *meros*, a part), having parts in eights.—*n.* octameter (*ok-tam′i-tər*; Gr. *metron*, a measure), a line of eight feet or measures.—*adj.* octandrous (*ok-tan′dras*; Gr. *anēr, andros*, a man; *bot.*), having eight stamens.—*n.pl.* Octan′dria, a Linnaean class of plants with eight stamens.— *adj.* octan′drian.—*adj.* octangular (*ok-tang′gū-lər*), having eight angles.—*n.* octapody (*ok-tap′ə-di*; Gr. *pous, podos*, foot; *pros.*), a line of eight feet.—*adj.* octapodic (*ok-tə-pod′ik*).—*n.* octastich (*ok′tə-stik*; Gr. *stichos*, row, line; *pros.*), a strophe of eight lines—also octastichon (*ok-tas′ti-kon*).—*adj.* octas′tichous (*bot.*), in eight rows.—*adj.* octastroph′ic (Gr. *strophē*, strophe; *pros.*), consisting of eight strophes.—*adj.* octastyle (*ok′tə-stil*; Gr. *stȳlos*, a column; *archit.*), having eight columns at the end.—*n.* a building or portico so designed.—Also oc′tostyle. [Gr. *okta-*, combining form of *oktō*, eight.]

octad, *ok′tad*, *n.* a set of eight things.—*adj.* octad′ic. [Gr. *oktas, -ados*.]

octagon . . . to . . . octahedrite. See oct(a)-.

octal, *ok′tal*, *adj.* pertaining to, or based on, the number eight. [Gr. *oktō*, eight.]

octamerous . . . to . . . octandrian. See oct(a)-.

octane, *ok′tān*, *n.* any of a group of eighteen isomeric hydrocarbons ($C_8H_{18}$), eighth in the methane series.—octane number, the percentage by volume of so-called iso-octane in a mixture with normal heptane which has the same knocking characteristics as the motor fuel under test. [Gr. *oktō*, eight, suff. *-ane*, as in methane.]

Octans, *ok′tanz*, *n.* a southern constellation containing the south celestial pole. [L. *octāns*, an eighth part.]

octant, *ok′tənt*, *n.* an arc of one-eighth of the circumference of a circle: a sector of one-eighth of a circle: an angle-measuring instrument with such an arc: a division of space or of a solid figure or body divided into eight by three planes, usu. at right angles: a position 45° distant from another position, esp. of the moon from conjunction or opposition (*astron.*).—*adj.* octantal (-*tant′əl*). [L. *octāns, -antis*, an eighth.]

octapla, *ok′tə-plə*, *n.* (treated as *sing.*) a book of eight (esp. Biblical) parallel texts. [Gr. *oktaplā* (contracted pl.), eightfold.]

octaploid, *ok′tə-ploid*, *adj.* eightfold: having eight times the basic number of chromosomes (*biol.*).—*n.* a cell, organism, or form with eight sets of chromosomes.—*n.* oc′taploidy, the con-

dition of being octaploid.—Also oc′toploid, etc. [Gr. *oktaploos*, eightfold, *eidos*, form.]

octapody, octapodic. See oct(a)-.

octaroon. See octoroon.

octastich . . . to . . . octastyle. See oct(a)-.

octave, *ok′tiv, -tāv*, *n.* a set of eight: the last day of eight beginning with a church festival: the eight days from a festival to its octave: an eighth, or an interval of twelve semitones (*mus.*): a note or sound an eighth above (or below) another (*mus.*): the range of notes or keys from any one to its octave (*mus.*): an organ stop sounding an octave higher than the keys indicate: a cask containing the eighth part of a pipe of wine: an eight-lined stanza: the first eight lines of a sonnet.—*adj.* consisting of eight (esp. lines): in octaves: sounding an octave higher.—*adj.* octāv′al, pertaining to an octave: based on the number eight.—oc′tave-flute′, the piccolo, an octave above the ordinary flute.— great octave, the bass octave, conventionally represented by capital letters, from C, on the second line below the bass stave, up; law of octaves, the relationship which arranges the elements in order of atomic weight and in groups of eight, with recurring similarity of properties; small octave, the tenor octave, from the second space in the bass. [Fr.,—L. *octāvus*, eighth.]

octavo, *ok-tā′vō*, *adj.* having eight leaves to the sheet: (conventionally) of a size so obtained, whether so folded or not.—*n.* a book printed on sheets so folded: (conventionally) a book of such a size: contracted 8vo—usually measuring a medium octavo 5¾ × 9 inches:—*pl.* octā′vōs. [L. *in octāvō*, in the eighth—*octāvus*, eighth.]

octennial, *ok-ten′yəl, -i-əl*, *adj.* happening every eighth year: lasting eight years.—*adv.* octenn′-ially. [L. *octennium*, eight years—*annus*, year.]

octet, octett, octette, *ok-tet′*, *n.* a group of eight (lines of verse, electrons, musicians, etc.): a composition for eight musicians. [On analogy of duet, as It. *ottetto*, Ger. *oktett*.]

octillion, *ok-til′yən*, *n.* a million raised to the eighth power, expressed by a unit with forty-eight ciphers: in U.S., one thousand raised to the ninth power, i.e. a unit with twenty-seven ciphers. [Modelled on million—L. *octō*, eight.]

octingenary, *ok′tin-jē′nə-ri*, *n.* an eight-hundredth anniversary.—Also octingentenary (-*jen-tē′*). [L. *octingēnārius*, 800 each.]

octo-, *ok-tō-, -to-*, also oct(a)-, *q.v.*, in composition, eight.—*n.* octocentenary (*ok-tō-sin-tēn′ə-ri* or -*sin-ten′* or -*sen′tin-*), an eight-hundredth anniversary.—*adjs.* octofid (*ok′tō-fid*; root of L. *findēre*, to cleave; *bot.*), cleft into eight segments; octogynous (*ok-toj′i-nəs*; Gr. *gynē*, wife; *bot.*), having eight pistils or styles.—*n.pl.* Octogyn′ia, in various Linnaean classes, an order with eight pistils.—*n.* octohedron, octahedron.— *adjs.* octopetalous (*ok-tō-pet′ə-ləs*), having eight petals; octopod (*ok′tō-pod*; Gr. *pous, podos*, foot), eight-footed or eight-armed.—*n.* an octopus or other member of the Octopoda (-*top′*), an order of dibranchiate cephalopods.—*adj.* octop′odous.—*ns.* octopus (*ok′tō-pəs*, formerly, *ok-tō′*), a genus (*Octopus*) of eight-armed cephalopods: any eight-armed cephalopod: (*fig.*) person, organisation, with widespread influence: —*pl.* oc′topuses, (*arch.*) octōp′odes (octopi is wrong).—*adjs.* octosepalous (*ok-tō-sep′ə-ləs*), having eight sepals; octostichous, octastichous; octostyle, octastyle; octosyllabic (*ok′tō-sil-ab′ik*), consisting of eight syllables: a line of eight syllables.—*n.* octosyllable (-*sil′ə-bl*), a word of eight syllables. [Gr. *oktō*, and L. *octō*.]

October, *ok-tō′bər*, *n.* the tenth month, eighth in the most ancient Roman calendar: strong ale brewed in that month.—*n.* Octo′brist, a member of a Russian moderate liberal party who made the tsar's manifesto of October 1905 their basis. [L. *octōber*—*octō.*]

**octodecimo**, *ok-tō-des'i-mō, adj.* having eighteen leaves to the sheet: contracted 18mo, often read eighteenmo.—*n.* a book with sheets so folded. [L. *octōdecim*, eighteen; cf. **octavo.**]

**octofid.** See **octo-**.

**octogenarian**, *ok-tō-ji-nā'ri-ən, n.* one who is eighty years old, or between eighty and ninety.—Also *adj.*—*adj.*octogenary (*ok-tō-jē'na-ri,ok-toj'-i-na-ri*). [L. *octōgēnārius*, pertaining to eighty.]

**octogynous** ... to ... **octohedron.** See **octo-**.

**octonary**, *ok'tə-nə-ri, adj.* based on the number eight.—*n.* a set of eight.—*adj.* **octonarian** (*ok-tō-nā'ri-ən*), having eight feet.—*n.* a line of eight feet. [L. *octōnārius.*]

**octonocular**, *ok-tō-nok'ū-lər, adj.* having eight eyes. [L. *octōnī*, eight at a time, *oculus*, eye.]

**octoploid.** Same as **octaploid.**

**octopod**, etc., **octopus**, etc. See **octo-**.

**octoroon, octaroon**, *ok-tə-rōōn', n.* the offspring of a quadroon and a person of European descent: one who has one-eighth Negro blood. [Modelled on **quadroon**—L. *octō*, eight.]

**octosepalous** ... to ... **octosyllable.** See **octo-**.

**octroi**, *ok-trwa, n.* formerly, and still in some European countries, a commercial privilege, as of exclusive trade: a toll or tax levied at the gates of a city on articles brought in: the place where, or officials to whom, it is paid: payment for passage of car on a road. [Fr.,—*octroyer*, to grant, from some such L.L. form as *auctōrizāre*, to authorise—L. *auctor*, author.]

**octuor**, *ok-tū-ör, n.* an octet. [L. *octo*, eight; modelled on *quatuor*, four.]

**octuple**, *ok'tū-pl, adj.* eightfold.—*v.t.* or *v.i.* to multiply by eight.—*n.* **oc'tuplet** (*mus.*), a group of eight notes to be played in the time of six.—*adj.* **octūp'licate**, eightfold: multiplied by eight.—Also *n.* [L. *octuplus*; cf. **duple, double.**]

**ocular**, *ok'ū-lər, adj.* pertaining to the eye or to vision: formed in, addressed to, or known by, the eye: received by actual sight: eyelike.—*n.* an eyepiece: an eye (*facet.*).—*adv.* **oc'ularly.**—*adjs.* **oc'ulate, -d**, having eyes, or spots like eyes.—*n.* **oc'ulist**, a specialist in diseases and defects of the eye. [L. *oculus*, the eye.]

**od**, *od* or *ōd, n.* Reichenbach's arbitrary name for a force supposed by him to manifest itself in light, magnetism, chemical action, hypnotism, etc.—*adj.* **o'dic.**—**od'-force**, od; **o'dism**, belief in od; **od'yl(e)** (Gr. *hylē*, matter), od; **od'ylism.**

**od, odd**, *od, n.* and *interj.* a minced form of god.—**od's-bobs**, God's body; **od's-bodikins**, God's body; **od's-life**, God's life; **od's nouns** (*nownz'*), God's wounds; **od's-pit'ikins** (*Shak.*), God's pity; **odzooks'** (same as **gadzooks**).—These are often written without an apostrophe.

**odal, odaller.** Same as **udal, udaller.**

**odalisque, odalisk**, *ō'də-lisk*, **odalique**, *-lik, n.* a female slave in a harem. [Fr.,—Turk. *ōdaliq*—*ōdah*, a chamber.]

**odd**, *od, adj.* unpaired: not matching (*Spens.*): left over: additional: extra: not one of a complete set: one in excess of half the number: left over after a round number has been taken: additional in lower denominations or lower powers of ten: not exactly divisible by two (opp. to *even*): strange: queer: casual: out-of-the-way: standing apart: at variance (*Shak.*).—*adv.* (*Shak.*) oddly.—*n.* one stroke above the like (*golf*): a stroke allowed in handicap (*golf*): one trick above book (*whist*):—in *pl.* **odds** (*odz*, sometimes treated as *sing.*), inequality: difference in favour of one against another: more than an even wager: the amount or proportion by which the bet of one exceeds that of another: the chances or probability: advantage: dispute: scraps: miscellaneous pieces, as in the phrase **odds and ends** (perh.

orig. meaning points and ends).—*adj.* **odd'ish.**—*n.* **odd'ity**, the state of being odd or singular: strangeness: a singular person or thing.—*adj.* **odd'-like** (*Scot.*), odd: odd-looking.—*adv.* **odd'ly.**—*ns.* **odd'ment**, something remaining over: one of a broken set—often in *pl.*; **odd'ness.**—**odd'-ball**, an eccentric person, nonconformist in some respect.—Also *adj.* (of, e.g. thing, plan, circumstance).—**odd'-come-short**, a short remnant: (in *pl.*) odds and ends; **odd'-come-short'ly**, an early day, any time.—*adj.* or *n.* **odd-e'ven** (*Shak.*), apparently, neither one thing nor another, as the time about midnight.—**odd'-fellow**, a member of a secret benevolent society called Oddfellows.—*adj.* **odd'-job.**—**odd jobs** (see **job**); **odd'-jobber, odd'-jobman.**—*adj.* **odd'-look'ing.**—**odd'-man**, odd-jobman: an umpire: one who has a casting vote; **odd'-man-out'**, the singling out or elimination of one from a number for any purpose: a man who is left out when numbers are made up: a person set apart, willingly or unwillingly, by difference of interests, etc., from a group in which he finds himself; **odds'man** (*Scot.*), an umpire or arbiter.—*adj.* **odds'-on'** of a chance, better than even.—**at odds**, at variance; **long odds, short odds** (see **long, short**); **make no odds**, to make no significant difference, **shout the odds**, (*slang*) to talk overmuch or too loudly; **what's the odds?**, what difference does it make? [O.N. *oddi*, point, a triangle, odd number; cf. O.N. *oddr*, O.E. *ord*, point.]

**odd.** See **od** (2).

**ode**, *ōd, n.* orig., a poem intended to be sung an elaborate lyric, often of some length, generally addressed to somebody or something.—*adj.* **o'dic.**—*n.* **o'dist**, a writer of odes. [Fr. *ode*—Gr. *ōidē*, contr. from *aoidē*—*aeidein*, to sing.]

**odeon**, *ō'di-ən, -dyən*, in ancient Greece a theatre for musical contests, etc.: a concert-hall.—Also **odeum.** [Gr. *ōideion*, L. *ōdēum.*]

**Odin**, *ō'din, n.* Woden. [O.N. *Ōthenn.*]

**odium**, *ō'di-əm, n.* hatred: offensiveness: blame: reproach attaching to (with *of*): quality of provoking hate.—*adj.* **o'dious**, hateful: offensive: repulsive: causing hatred.—*adv.* **o'diously.**—*n* **o'diousness.** [L. *ōdium.*]

**odium theologicum**, *ōd'i-əm thē-o-lo'ji-kəm, od'i-ōōm the-o-lo'gi-kōōm*, (L.) the hatred of theologians for each other's errors (or persons).

**odograph**, *od'ō-gräf, n.* a device for plotting automatically a course travelled: an odometer: a pedometer. [Gr. *hodos*, a way, *graphein*, to write.]

**odometer.** See **hodometer.**

**Odonata**, *ō-don-ā'tə*, (*zool.*) *n.pl.* the dragonfly order. [Ionic Gr. *odōn*, a tooth.]

**odont(o)-**, *od-ont(-o)-*, in composition, tooth.—*ns.* **odontalgia** (*-al'ji-ə*; Gr. *algos*, pain), odontal'gy, toothache.—*adjs.* **odontal'gic; odont'ic**, dental.—*ns.* **odont'ist** (*facet.*), a dentist; **odont'o-blast** (Gr. *blastos*, a shoot), a dentine-forming cell; **odon'tocete** (*-sēt*; Gr. *kētos*, whale), a toothed whale.—*adj.* **odontogenic** (*-jen'ik*).—*ns.* **odontogeny** (*-oj'i-ni*), the origin and development of teeth; **Odontogloss'um** (Gr. *glōssa*, tongue), a tropical American genus of orchids; **odont'ograph**, an instrument for obtaining approximate curves for gear-teeth; **odontog'raphy**, description of teeth.—*adj.* **odont'oid**, toothlike.—*n.* **odont'olite** (Gr. *lithos*, stone), bone turquoise or occidental turquoise, a fossil bone or tooth coloured blue with phosphate of iron.—*adjs.* **odontolog'ic, -al.**—*ns.* **odontol'ogist; odontol'ogy**, the science of the teeth; **odonto'ma**, a tumour arising in connection with the teeth.—*adjs.* **odontō'matous**, pertaining to odontoma; **odontophoral** (*-tof'ə-rəl*; Gr. *phoros*, bearing), **odontoph'oran.**—*n.* **odon'tophore** (*-to-fōr, -för*), the rasping apparatus in molluscs—the radula, its support, or the whole apparatus.—*adj.*

**odontoph'orous.**—*n.* **Odontoph'orus,** a genus of American quails.—*n.pl.* **odontornithes** (-*ör-ni'-thēz,* or -*ör'ni-thēz;* Gr. *ornis, ornithos,* bird), fossil birds with teeth (not a natural class).—*adj.* **odontostom'atous** (Gr. *stoma, -atos,* mouth), having biting or toothed jaws. [Gr. *odous, odontos,* a tooth.]

**odour,** *ō'dər, n.* smell: savour (*fig.*): repute (*fig.*).—*adjs.* **o'dorant,** **o'dorate,** **odorif'erous,** emitting a (usually pleasant) smell.—*adv.* **odorif'erously.**—*n.* **odorif'erousness.**—*adj.* **o'dorous** (*ō'də-rəs*; sometimes formerly *ōd-ō'rəs*), emitting an odour or scent: sweet-smelling: fragrant: bad-smelling (*coll.*).—*adv.* **o'dorously.**—*n.* **o'dorousness.**—*adjs.* **o'doured;** **o'dourless.**—in bad odour, in bad repute; **the odour of sanctity,** a fragrance after death alleged to be evidence of saintship: facetiously applied to the living who have denied themselves the sensual indulgence of washing: a sanctimonious manner. [A.Fr. *odour*—L. *odor, ōris.*]

**odso,** *od'sō, interj.* expressing surprise. [For gadso.]

**odyl(e).** See od (1).

**Odyssey,** *od'is-i, n.* a Greek epic poem, ascribed to Homer, describing the ten years' wanderings of *Odysseus* (Ulysses) on his way home from the Trojan war to Ithaca: a long wandering, or a tale of wandering.—*adj.* **Odyssē'an.** [Gr. *Odysseia.*]

**oe.** Same as oy.

**oecist,** *ē'sist,* **oikist,** *oi'kist,* (*hist.*) *n.* the founder of a colony. [Gr. *oikistēs—oikos,* a house.]

**oecology,** etc., **oecumenic,** etc. See ecology, ecumenic.

**oedema,** *ē-dē'mə, n.* dropsy: pathological accumulation of fluid in tissue spaces: an unhealthy mass of swollen parenchyma (*bot.*).—*adjs.* **oede'matose;** **oede'matous.**—Also **ede'ma,** etc. [Gr. *oidēma, -atos,* swelling.]

**Oedipus,** *ē'di-pəs, n.* a king of Thebes who solved the Sphinx's riddle and unwittingly killed his father and married his mother.—*adj.* (*irreg.*) **Oedipē'an.**—**Oedipus complex** (*psych.*), the attachment of a son to his mother with unconscious rivalry and hostility towards his father. [Gr. *Oidipous,* lit. Swell-foot.]

**œil-de-bœuf,** *œ'ē-də-bœf, n.* a little round window: an octagonal vestibule at the court of Versailles, hence one elsewhere:—*pl.* **œils-de-bœuf** (*œ'ē-*). [Fr., ox-eye.]

**œillade,** *œ-yäd',* formerly *äl'yad, il'yad, il'i-ad* (*Shak.* **illiad, eliad**), *n.* a glance or wink (*Shak.*): an ogle. [Fr. *œillade—œil,* eye.]

**oen(o)-,** *ēn(-ō)-,* in composition, wine.—Also **oin(o)-.**—*adjs.* **oenan'thic** (Gr. *anthos,* flower), having or imparting the characteristic odour of wine; **oenolog'ical.**—*ns.* **oenol'ogist;** **oenol'ogy,** the science of wines; **oe'nomancy,** divination from the appearance of wine poured out in libations; **oenomā'nia,** dipsomania; **oen'omel** (Gr. *meli,* honey), wine mixed with honey; **oenom'eter,** a hydrometer for measuring the alcoholic strength of wines; **oen'ophil, oenoph'-ilist,** a connoisseur of wine—also (now usu.) **oen'ophile** (-*fil*); **oenoph'ily,** love of, and knowledge of, wines. [Gr. *oinos,* wine.]

**Oenothera,** *ē-nō-thē'ra,* by some *ē-noth'ə-ra, n.* the evening primrose genus of *Onagraceae.* [Gr. *oinothēras,* perh. a wrong reading for *onothēras,* a plant whose roots smelt of wine, perh. oleander.]

**o'er,** *ōr, ör* (*Scot.* **owr;** also **owre, ower**), shortened form of over. For compounds, see **over-.**

**o'ercome,** *owr'kum,* (*Scot.*) *n.* the burden of a song: overplus.—*ns.* **o'er'lay,** a large cravat; **o'erword,** a refrain: a catchword.

**oerlikon,** *ūr'li-kon, n.* an anti-aircraft gun of Swiss origin. [*Oerlikon,* near Zürich.]

**oersted,** *ūr'sted, n.* the C.G.S. unit of magnetic field strength. [Named in honour of Hans Christian *Oersted* (1777-1851), Danish physicist and chemist.

**oes,** *ōz,* a plural of o.

**oesophagus, esophagus,** *ē-sof'ə-gəs, n.* the gullet.—*adj.* **oesophageal** (-*faj'i-əl*). [Gr. *oisophagos,* gullet; origin unknown; app. connected with *phagein,* to eat.]

**oestrus,** *ēs'trəs, n.* a gadfly or bot: a vehement stimulus or frenzy: (in the following meanings and words, also **es-**) heat or sexual impulse, esp. in female mammals: oestrous cycle.—Also **oes'-trum.**—*adj.* **oes'tral.**—*n.* **oestrogen** (*ēs'trō-jən*), any one of the female sex-hormones: a substance found in plants, or synthesised, that has similar effects.—*adjs.* **oestrogenic** (-*jen'*); **oes'-trous.**—**oestrous cycle,** series of physiological changes from the beginning of one period of oestrus to the beginning of the next. [L. *oestrus* —Gr. *oistros.*]

**œuvre,** *œ-vr',* (Fr.) work (of an artist, writer, etc.):—*pl.* **œuvres** (*œ-vr'*).

**of,** *ov, uv, əv, prep.* from: from among: out from: belonging to: among: proceeding or derived from: made from, having for material: having, or characterised by: in the manner that characterises: with respect to: owing to: with: over: concerning: during: by: on: in: specified as: constituted by: short of, to (in giving the time, e.g. *quarter of five*) (*U.S.*): measuring: aged: owning.—**of new** (*Spens.*), anew; **of purpose** (*B.*), intentionally. [O.E. *of*; Du. *af,* Ger. *ab,* L. *ab,* Gr. *apo.*]

**off,** *of, öf, adv.* away: in or to a position that is not on something: in motion: out of continuity: out of connection, supply, activity, operation, or validity: to a finish, up: no longer available: in deterioration or diminution: into freedom.—*adj.* most distant: on the opposite or farther side: on the side of a cricket-field: on the side opposite that on which the batsman stands (normally the bowler's left; *cricket*): (of a horse or vehicle) right: out of condition or form: not devoted to the particular or usual activity (as *off-day, off-season*).—*prep.* from: away from: removed from: opening out of: in or to a position or condition that is not on: disengaged from: disinclined to: out to sea from: from a dish of.—*n.* the off side.—*v.t.* to put off: to take off.—*v.i.* (or *v.t.* with *it*) to go off: to take off (with *with*; *coll.*).—*interj.* away! depart!—*n.* **off'ing,** the region some distance off-shore: a place or time some way off (**in the offing,** in sight, at hand).—*adj.* **off'ish,** aloof in manner.—*adv.* **off'-ward**(s), off, away from, esp. shore.—*adj.* and *adv.* **off'-and-on,** occasional(ly): intermittent(ly).—*adj.* **off'beat,** away from standard: out of the usual: eccentric.—**off'-break** (*cricket*), of a ball on pitching, deviation towards the stumps from the off side: a delivery with such a deviation; **off'-chance,** a remote chance.—*adjs.* **off'-colour, -ed,** unsatisfactory in colour (as a diamond) and so inferior: half-caste, not pure white: (**off-colour**) not completely healthy.—**off'-come,** a subterfuge (*Scot.*): a pretext (*Scot.*): manner of coming off, issue, success; **off'cut,** a piece cut off material (e.g. wood) in shaping an object; **off'-day,** see off **day,** above: a day when one is not at one's best or most brilliant; **off'-drive** (*cricket*), a drive to the off side.—*adv.* **offhand',** extempore: at once: without hesitating.—*adjs.* **off'hand,** without study: impromptu: free and easy: ungraciously curt or summary; **off'hand'ed.**—*adv.* **offhand'edly.** — **offhand'edness.** — *adj.* **off'-key,** out of tune (*lit.* and *fig.*): not in keeping.—**off-li'cence,** a licence to sell alcoholic liquors for consumption off the premises only: a shop having such a licence (*coll.*).—*v.t.* and *v.i.* **off'-load,** (*orig. S.Afr.*) to unload.—*adj.* **off'peak',**

not at time of highest demand.—**off′print**, a reprint of a single article from a periodical; **off′put** (*Scot.*), act of putting off (in any sense); **off′-putt′er**.—*n.* and *adj.* **off′-putt′ing**.—**off′-reck′oning** (usu. in *pl.*), a deduction: an account between army officers and governments concerning men's clothes, etc. (*obs.*).—*v.t.* and *v.i.* **off′saddle**, to unsaddle.—*n.*, *adj.*, *and adv.* **off′season**, (of, at) a time (for e.g. a holiday) other than the most popular and busy.—**off′scouring** (usu. in *pl.*), matter scoured off: refuse: anything vile or despised; **off′scum**, scum, refuse; **off′set**, a thing set off against another as equivalent or compensation: a lateral shoot that strikes root and forms a new plant: a mountain spur: a side branch of anything: a sudden change of direction in a pipe: a reduction of thickness or the (usually sloping) ledge formed where part of a wall, buttress, bank, etc., is set back from the general face: a hillside terrace (*U.S.*): a smudge on a newly printed sheet from another laid on it: offset printing (see below): in surveying, a perpendicular from the main line to an outlying point.—*v.t.* (*of-set′*, *of′set*) to set off against something as an equivalent or compensation.—*v.i.* to branch off: (*of′set*) to make an effort.—*v.t.* **off-shake′**, to shake off (*pa.p. Spens.* **off-shakt′**).—**off′shoot**, a branch or derivative of anything.—*adv.* **offshore′**, and *adj.* **off′-shore**, from the shore: at a distance from the shore.—**off′side**, far side: a horse's or vehicle's right towards the middle of the road: (*cricket*) see **off**, *adj.*: (*football*, etc.) field between the ball and the opponents' goal.—*adj.* and *adv.* on the off-side: between the ball, or the last player who had it, and the opponents' goal:—*n.pl.* **off′-sorts**, wool set aside in sorting, or unsuitable for a given purpose.—**off′spring**, a child or children: progeny: issue: ancestry (*obs.*): source (*obs.*).—*adv.* and *adj.* **off′-stage′**, not on the stage as visible to the spectators.—*adj.* **off′-street′**, of parking, in a car park.—**off′take**, the act of taking off in any sense: take-off: that which is taken off: a channel, passage, or pipe for removing a fluid.—*adj.* **off′-white′**, not quite white.—**be off**, to go away quickly; **come off, go off, show off, take off**, (see **come, go, show, take**); **from off**, from a position on; **ill off**, poor or ill provided; **off one's oats**, feed, head, rocker (see **oat, feed, head, rock**); **off the face, shoulder**, (of woman's hat, dress, etc.) so as to reveal the face, shoulder; **off the peg**, of a garment, bought ready to wear; **offset printing**, a method of printing lithographs, etc., by firstly taking an impression from a plate on a rubber cylinder and then transferring the impression to paper, or metal, etc.; **offshore purchase**, a purchase by one country in another; **off with**, take off at once; **tell off**, to count: to assign, as for a special duty: to chide; **well off**, rich, well provided: fortunate. [Same as **of**.]

**offal**, *of′l*, *n.* waste or rejected parts, esp. of a carcase: an edible part cut off in dressing a carcase: anything worthless or unfit for use: refuse. [**off, fall**.]

**offbeat**. See **off**.

**offcut**. See **off**.

**offend**, *o-fend′*, *v.t.* to make angry to do harm to: to hurt the feelings of: to affront: to cause to stumble or sin (*B.*): to violate (a law).—*v.i.* to sin: to cause anger: to be made to stumble or sin (*B.*).—*n.* **offence′**, a stumbling (*B.*): any cause of anger or displeasure: an injury: a transgression, an infraction of law: a crime: a sin: affront: assault.—*adjs.* **offence′ful** (*Shak.*), giving offence or displeasure: injurious; **offence′less** (*Milt.*), unoffending: innocent.—*ns.* **offend′er**:—*fem.* (*Shak.*) **offend′ress**; **offense′** (chiefly *U.S.*), same as **offence**.—*adj.* **offens′ive**, causing offence, displeasure, or injury:

used in attack: making the first attack.—*n.* the act or course of action of the attacking party: the posture of one who attacks: a great and sustained effort to achieve an end.—*adv.* **offens′ively**.—*n.* **offens′iveness**.—**give offence**, to cause displeasure; **take offence**, to feel displeasure, be offended. [L. *offendĕre*, *offēnsum*—*ob*, against, *fendĕre*, *fēnsum*, to strike (found in compounds); cf. **defend**.]

**offer**, *of′ər*, *v.t.* to present, esp. as an act of devotion, homage, charity, etc.: express willingness: to hold out for acceptance or rejection: to lay before one: to present to the mind: to attempt: to make a show of attempting, make as if: propose to give, pay, sell, or perform.—*v.i.* to present itself: to be at hand: to incline: to make an offer:—*pr.p.* **off′ering**; *pa.t.* and *pa.p.* **off′ered**.—*n.* act of offering: state of being offered: first advance: that which is offered: proposal made: an attempt, essay: a knob on an antler.—*adj.* **off′erable**, that may be offered.—*ns.* **off′erer**; **off′ering**, act of making an offer: that which is offered: a gift: that which is offered on an altar (*B.*): a sacrifice: (*pl.*) in Church of England, certain dues payable at Easter; **off′ertory**, act of offering: the thing offered: the verses or the anthem said or sung while the offerings of the congregation are being made: the money collected at a religious service: anciently a linen or silken cloth used in various ceremonies connected with the administration of the eucharist. [L. *offerre*—*ob*, towards, *ferre*, to bring.]

**offhand**, etc. See **off**.

**office**, *of′is*, *n.* an act of kindness or attention: a service: (with *ill*, etc.) a disservice: a function or duty: settled duty or employment: a position imposing certain duties or giving a right to exercise an employment: possession of a post in the government: business: act of worship: order or form of a religious service, either public or private: that which a thing is designed or fitted to do: a place where business is carried on: a body or staff occupying such a place: a state department: the building in which of a person is housed: a doctor's consulting-room (*U.S.*): a cockpit in an aeroplane (*slang*): a lavatory: a hint (*slang*): (*pl.*) the apartments of a house or the subsidiary buildings in which the domestic, etc., work is carried out.—*n.* **off′icer**, one who holds an office: person who performs some public duty: a person holding a commission in an army, navy, or air-force: one who holds a similar post in any force or body organised on a similar plan: a policeman: an office-bearer in a society.—*v.t.* to furnish with officers: to command, as officers.—*adj.* **official** (*of-ish′əl*), pertaining to an office: depending on the proper office or authority: done by authority: issued or authorised by a public authority or office: recognised in the pharmacopoeia (cf. **officinal**).—*n.* one who holds an office: a subordinate public officer: the deputy of a bishop, etc.—*ns.* **offic′ialdom**, officials as a body: the world of officials: officialism; **officialese′**, stilted, wordy, and stereotyped English alleged to be characteristic of official letters and documents; **offic′ialism**, official position: excessive devotion to official routine and detail: the self-importance of a Jack-in-office; **officiality** (*of-ish-i-al′i-ti*), **officialty** (*of-ish′al-ti*; *rare*), the charge, office, or jurisdiction of an official: the official headquarters of an ecclesiastical or other deliberative and governing body: officialism.—*adv.* **officially** (*of-ish′ə-li*).—*n.* **officiant** (*of-ish′i-ənt*), one who officiates at a religious service, one who administers a sacrament.—*v.i.* **offic′iate**, to perform the duties of an office.—*n.* **offic′iator**.—**off′ice-bearer**, one who holds office: one who has an appointed duty to perform in connection with some company, society, church, etc.; **office-block,** a large building in which an office or variety of offices is housed; off'ice-book, a book of forms of service; off'ice-boy, a boy employed to do minor jobs in an office:—*fem.* off'ice-girl; off'ice-holder, one who holds a government office: a civil servant (*U.S.*); off'ice-hunter, a self-seeking candidate for public employment; office-seeker, a candidate for office.—last offices, rites for the dead: the preparation of a corpse for burial. [Fr.,—L. *officium,* a favour, duty, service.]

**officinal,** *of-is'in-əl, -i-sin',* adj. belonging to, used in, a shop: used in medicine: recognised in the pharmacopoeia (now *official*): sold by druggists. [L.L. *officinālis*—L. *officina,* a workshop, later a monastic storeroom—*opus,* work, *facĕre,* to do.]

**officious,** *of-ish'əs,* adj. obliging (*obs.*): dutiful (*Shak.*): too forward in offering unwelcome or unwanted services: intermeddling: in diplomacy, informal, not official.—*adv.* offic'iously. —*n.* offic'iousness. [L. *officiōsus*—*officium.*]

**offing, offish, offload, offsaddle, offset, offside, offspring,** etc. See under **off.**

**oft, oft, öft, often,** *of'n, öf'n, of'ən, of'tən,* advs. frequently: many times.—*adj.* oft'en (*B.*), frequent.—*n.* oft'enness, frequency.—*advs.* oft'-times, oft'entimes, many times: frequently. [O.E. *oft;* Ger. *oft,* Goth. *ufta.*]

**ogam, ogham,** *og'əm. ō'əm, n.* an ancient Celtic alphabet of straight lines meeting or crossing the edge of a stone: any of its twenty characters.— *adjs.* og(h)am'ic (or *og', ō'*), og'mic. [O.Ir. *ogam,* mod. Ir. *ogham.*]

**ogdoad,** *og'dō-ad, n.* a set of eight. [Gr. *ogdoas,* *-ados*—*oktō,* eight.]

**ogee,** *ō'jē, ō-jē', n.* a moulding S-shaped in section: an S-shaped curve.—*adj.* having S-shaped curves.—*adj.* ogee'd. [Fr. *ogive;* see ogive.]

**ogive,** *ō'jiv, ō-jiv', (archit.) n.* a diagonal rib of a vault: a pointed arch or window.—*adj.* ogi'val. [Fr.; origin doubtful, poss.—Ar. *auj,* summit.]

**ogle,** *ō'gl, v.t.* to look at fondly, or impertinently, with side glances, to eye greedily.—*v.i.* to cast amorous glances: to stare impertinently.— *ns.* o'gle; o'gler; o'gling. [Cf. L.G. *oegeln,* freq. of *oegen,* to look at; Ger. *äugeln,* to leer, *auge,* eye.]

**Ogpu,** *og'pōō, og-pōō', n.* Russian secret police of 1922-34. [From the initials of *Obedinennoe Gosudarstvennoe Politicheskoe Upravlenie,* Unified State Political Directorate.]

**ogre,** *ō'gər, n.* a man-eating monster or giant of fairy tales: an ugly, cruel or bad-tempered person, or one whose sternness inspires fear:—*fem.* o'gress.—*adj.* o'gr(e)ish. [Fr. *ogre,* prob. invented by Perrault.]

**Ogygian,** *ō-gij'i-ən, ō-jij'i-ən, adj.* pertaining to the mythical Attic king *Ogȳgēs:* prehistoric, primaeval: very old: of Calypso's island, *Ogȳgiă.*—**Ogygian deluge,** a flood said to have occurred during the reign of Ogȳgēs.

**oh,** *ō, interj.* denoting surprise, pain, sorrow, etc. [See **o.**]

**ohm,** *ōm, n.* the unit of electrical resistance in the SI and the M.K.S.A. systems, the resistance in a conductor in which a potential difference of one volt produces a current of one ampere: formerly defined as the resistance of a specified column of mercury under stated conditions.— *adj.* ohm'ic.—*n.* ohmmeter (*ōm'mēt-ər*), an instrument for measuring electrical resistance. —**Ohm's law,** that strength of electric current is directly proportional to electromotive force and inversely to resistance. [Georg Simon *Ohm,* German electrician, 1787-1854.]

**oho,** *ō-hō', interj.* expressing triumphant surprise or gratification.

**ohone, ochone,** *ō-hōn', -hhōn', (Ir.* and *Highland) interj.* of lamentation. [Ir. and Gael. *ochoin.*]

**oidium,** *ō-id'i-əm, n.* the conidial stage of the vine-mildew and other fungi. [Gr. *ōion,* an egg, with dim. suffix *-idion* Latinised.]

**oil,** *oil, n.* the juice from the fruit of the olive-tree: any greasy liquid: (in *pl.*) oil-paints or painting: (in *pl.*) oilskins.—*v.t.* to smear, lubricate, or anoint with oil.—*v.i.* to take oil aboard as fuel.—*adj.* oiled, smeared, treated, lubricated or impregnated with oil: preserved in oil: tipsy (*slang*).—*ns.* oil'er, one who, or that which, oils: an oil-can: (in *pl.*) oilskins: a ship driven by oil: a ship that carries oil; oil'ery, the commodities, business or establishment of an oil-man.—*adv.* oil'ily.—*n.* oil'iness.—*adj.* oil'y, consisting of, containing, or having the qualities of, oil: greasy: unctuous.—oil'-**bath,** a receptacle containing lubricating oil through which part of a machine passes; oil'-**beetle,** a beetle (Meloe and kindred) that emits a yellowish oily liquid from the legs when disturbed; oil'-**belt,** a belt of country yielding mineral oil; oil'-**bird,** the guacharo; oil'-**burner,** a ship that uses oil as fuel: a lamp-burner for use with oil; oil'-**cake,** a cattle-food made of the residue of oil-seeds when most of the oil has been pressed out; oil'**can,** a can for carrying oil or for applying lubricating oil; oil'**cloth,** a canvas coated with linseed-oil paint; oil'-**colour,** a colouring substance mixed with oil; oil'-**engine,** an internal-combustion engine burning vapour from oil; oil'-**field,** an area which produces mineral oil.—*adj.* oil'-**fired,** burning oil as fuel.—oil'-**gas,** illuminating gas or heating gas made by destructive distillation of oil; oil'-**gland,** the uropygial gland in birds, forming a secretion used in preening the feathers; oil**length,** the ratio of drying oil to resin in e.g. a varnish (*adjs.* long-oil, having a high proportion, short-oil, a low proportion, of oil); oil'-**man,** one who deals in oils; oil'-**mill,** a grinding-mill for expressing oil from seeds, etc.; oil'**nut,** the North American butter-nut, the buffalo-nut, or other oil-yielding nut; oil'-**paint'ing,** a picture painted in oil-colours: the art of painting in oil-colours; oil'-**palm,** a palm (*Elaeis guineensis*) whose fruit-pulp yields palm-oil; oil'-**press,** a machine for expressing oils from seeds or pulp; oil'-**seed,** any seed that yields oil; oil'-**shale,** a shale containing diffused hydrocarbons in a state suitable for distillation into mineral oils; oil'-**silk,** a transparent silk fabric impregnated with oxidised oil; oil'**skin,** cloth made waterproof by means of oil: a garment made of oilskin; oil'**stone,** a whetstone used with oil; oil'-**tanker,** a vessel constructed for carrying oil in bulk; oil'-**well,** a boring made for petroleum.—oil one's palm, to bribe one; strike oil (see strike).—see also tall-oil. [O.Fr. *oile* (Fr. *huile*)—L. *oleum*—Gr. *elaion*—*elaiā,* olive-tree, olive.]

**oillet,** *oi'lit, n.* an obs. form of eyelet.

**oino-,** *oi-nō-,* in composition, an occasional variant in words beginning oeno-.

**ointment,** *oint'mənt, n.* anything used in anointing: any greasy substance applied to diseased or wounded parts (*med.*): an unguent.—*v.t.* oint (*Dryden*), to anoint. [Fr. *oint,* pa.p. of *oindre*— L. *unguĕre,* to anoint.]

**Oireachtas,** *er'əhh-thəs, n.* the legislature of the Republic of Ireland (President, Seanad, and Dáil). [Ir., assembly.]

**oiticica,** *oi-ti-sē'ka, n.* any of several South American trees, esp. *Licania rigida* and *Couepia grandiflora* (both rosaceous), whose nuts yield an oil used for quick-drying paints and varnishes. [Port.,—Tupi *oity-cica.*]

**okapi,** *ō-kä'pē, n.* an animal of Central Africa related to the giraffe:—*pl.* oka'pis. [Native name.]

**OK, okay,** *ō-kä', (slang) adj.* all correct: all

right: satisfactory.—*adv.* yes: all right, certainly.—*n.* approval: sanction: endorsement.—*v.t.* to mark or pass as right: to sanction. [Various explanations of the letters have been given, esp. that they stand for *Old Kinderhook*, used as a slogan by Van Buren's party in the 1840 presidential election (Van Buren was born at Kinderhook, near Albany in New York), but they have been found at an earlier date.

**oke**, *ōk, n.* a Turkish weight of about 2⅘ lb. [Turk. *ōqah*, appar. through Gr. from L. *uncia*, ounce.]

**oke**, *ōk, adv.* same as **OK**.

**okra**, *ok′ra, ōk′ra, n. Hibiscus esculentus*, gumbo. [From a W. African name.]

**old**, *ōld, adj.* advanced in years: having been long or relatively long in existence, use, or possession: of a specified (or to be specified) age: of long standing: worn or worn out: out of date: superseded or abandoned: former: old-fashioned: antique: ancient: early: belonging to later life: belonging to former times: (of a language) of the earliest, or earliest known, stage: long practised or experienced: having the characteristics of age: familiar, accustomed: in plenty, in excess, or wonderful (esp. in *high old; coll.*): a general word of familiar or affectionate approbation or contempt (often *good old; coll.*): reckoned according to Old Style (see **style**);—*comp.* old′er, eld′er (q.v.); *superl.* old′est, eld′est.—*adv.* (*Shak.*) of old.—*n.* an old person: olden times, eld.—*v.t.* and *v.i.* old′en, to age.—*adj.* old, ancient.—*adj.* old′ish, somewhat old.—*ns.* old′ness; old′ster, a man getting old (*coll.*): a midshipman of four years' standing, a master's mate.—**old age**, the later part of life; **old bachelor**, somewhat elderly or confirmed bachelor; **Old Bailey**, the Central Criminal Court in London; **Old Bill**, soldier with drooping moustache in First World War cartoons by Bruce Bairnsfather; **old bird** (*fig.*), an experienced person; **old boy**, one's father, husband, etc. (*coll.*): an old or oldish man, esp. one in authority, or one who has some air of youthfulness: a former pupil: an affectionately familiar term of address to a male of any age (*coll.*; also **old bean, old chap, old fellow, old man, old thing**):—*fem.* **old girl**; **Old Catholic**, a member of a body that broke away from the Roman Catholic Church on the question of papal infallibility; **old-clothesman**, one who buys cast-off garments; **old country**, the mother-country; **Old Dominion**, Virginia; **Old English** (see **English**): the form of black-letter used by 16th-century English printers.—*adj.* **olde-worlde**, self-consciously imitative of the past or supposed past.—**old face**, the early roman type such as Caslon (*coll.*); **old fashioned**, in a fashion like one of long ago: out of date: clinging to old things and old styles: with manners like those of a grown-up person (said of a child): knowing.—**old-fashionedness**.—*adjs.* old-fog(e)yish, like an old fogey; **old-gentlemanly**, characteristic of an old gentleman.—**old gang, guard**, old and conservative element in a party, etc.; **Old Glory**, the Stars and Stripes; **old gold**, a dull gold colour like tarnished gold, used in textile fabrics; **old hand**, an experienced performer: an old convict; **Old Harry, Nick, One, Poker, Scratch**, the devil. —*adj.* **old-hat**, out-of-date.—**Old Hundred (Old Hundredth)**, a famous tune set in England about the middle of the 16th century to Kethe's version of the 100th Psalm, marked 'Old Hundredth' in Tate and Brady (1696); **Old Light**, a member of a relatively less advanced religious school—applied esp. to the party in the Scottish Secession Church who continued to hold unchanged the principle of connection between Church and State; **old maid**, a spinster, esp. one who is likely to remain a spinster: a woman, or more

often a man, of the character supposed to be common among spinsters—fussy, prim, conventional, over-cautious, methodical: a simple game played by passing and matching cards: also the player left with the odd card; **old-maidhood, old-maidism**.—*adj.* **old-maidish**, like the conventional old maid, prim.—**old man**, unregenerate human nature: adult male kangaroo: one's husband, father, or employer (*coll.*): captain of a merchant ship: a familiar friendly or encouraging term of address: a southernwood; **old master** (often *caps.*), any great painter or painting of a period previous to the 19th cent. (esp. of the Renaissance); **old Norse** (see **Norse**); **old rose**, a deep soft pink; **old salt**, an experienced sailor; **old school**, those whose ways or thoughts are such as prevailed in the past.— Also *adj.*—**old soldier**, an empty bottle: an experienced person who knows how to make himself comfortable; **old song**, a mere trifle, a very small price; **old squaw** (*U.S.*), the hareld; **old story**, something one has heard before: something that happened long ago, or has happened often; **Old Style** (see **style**): a type-face in imitation of old face; **Old Testament** (see **testament**).—*adj.* old′-time, of or pertaining to times long gone by: of long standing: old-fashioned.—**old-tim′er**, one who has long been where he is: an experienced person, veteran: an old-fashioned person; **Old Tom**, a kind of sweetened gin; **old wife**, an old woman: one who has the character ascribed to old women: a chimney-cap for curing smoking (*Scot.*): the hareld: a fish of various kinds—sea-bream, file-fish, etc.; **old woman**, one's wife or mother (*coll.*): an old-womanish person.—*adjs.* **old-womanish**, like an old woman, esp. fussy; **old′-world**, belonging to earlier times: old-fashioned and quaint: (*cap.*) of the Old World.—*n.* **Old World**, the Eastern hemisphere.—**an old-fashioned look**, a knowing or quizzically critical look; **come the old soldier over one**, to impose on one; **of old**, long ago: in or of ancient times: formerly; **old age pension**, a pension for one who has reached old age, esp. under a national system (first instituted in Britain in 1908); **old man of the sea**, a person or burden that one cannot shake off—from the old man in the *Arabian Nights* who, having been carried across a stream by Sinbad the Sailor, refused to get down off his back; **old man's beard**, a name for several plants including traveller's joy; **Old Red Sandstone**, the lacustrine or continental equivalent of the (marine) Devonian, so called in contradistinction to the New Red Sandstone; **old school tie**, the emblem of minor (esp. upper-class) loyalties; **the Old Boy network**, the members of a society (usu. upper-class), closely interconnected, who share information, and secure advantages for each other: this form of association. [O.E. *ald* (W.S. *eald*); Du. *oud*, Ger. *alt.*]

**Olea**, *ō′li-a, n.* the olive genus, giving name to the family Olea′ceae, including ash, privet, and jasmine.—*adj.* olea′ceous. [L. *olea*, olive.]

**oleaginous**, *ō-li-aj′in-əs, adj.* oily.—*n.* oleag′inousness. [L. *oleāginus—oleum*, oil.]

**oleander**, *ō-li-an′dər, n.* an evergreen shrub (*Nerium oleander*) of the Apocynaceae, with lance-shaped leathery leaves and beautiful red or white flowers, the rose-bay or rose-laurel. [L.L. *oleander*; derivation from *rhododendron*, influenced by *laurus* and *olea*, has been conjectured.]

**oleaster**, *ō-li-as′tər, n.* properly the true wild olive: extended to the so-called wild olive, Elaeagnus. [L. *oleāster—olea*, an olive-tree— Gr. *elaiā.*]

**oleate**, *ō′li-āt, n.* a salt of oleic acid.—*adj.* olefiant (*ō-li-fī′ənt* or *ō-lē′fi-ənt*), oil-forming (in olefiant gas, ethylene).—*n.* o'lefin, -fine (-*fin*, -*fēn*), any hydrocarbon of the ethylene series.—*adjs.* olē'ic (or *ō'li-ik*), pertaining to or got from oil (as in oleic acid, $C_{18}H_{34}O_2$); oleif'erous, producing oil, as seeds.—*ns.* olein (*ō'li-in*), a glycerine ester of oleic acid; oleo (*ō'li-ō*), a contraction for oleograph or for oleomargarine; o'leograph, a print in oil-colours to imitate an oil-painting; oleog'raphy; oleomar'garine, margarine.—*adj.* oleophil'ic, having affinity for oils: wetted by oil in preference to water.—oleo-res'in, a solution of a resin in an oil. [L. *oleum*, oil.]

olecranon, *ō-li-krā'non*, *n.* a process forming the upper part of the ulna.—*adj.* olecrā'nal. [Gr. *ōlekrănon*—*ōlenē*, elbow, *krănion*, head.]

olefin(e), oleic, olein. See oleate.

olent, *ō'lǝnt*, *adj.* having a smell. [L. *olēns*, -*entis*, pr.p. of *olēre*, to smell.]

Olenus, *ō'len-ǝs*, *n.* a typically Upper Cambrian genus of trilobites.—*n.* Olenell'us, a similar Lower Cambrian genus. [Gr. *Ōlenos*, who was turned to stone.]

oleo. See oleate.

oleraceous, *ol-ǝr-ā'shǝs*, *adj.* of the nature of a pot-herb, for kitchen use. [L. (*h*)*oleraceus*—(*h*)*olus*, (*h*)*oleris*, a pot-herb, vegetable.]

olfactory, *ol-fak'tǝ-ri*, *adj.* pertaining to, or used in, smelling.—*v.t.* olfact' (*facet.*).—*adj.* olfact'-ible.—*n.* olfac'tion.—*adj.* olfac'tive.—*ns.* olfactol'ogist; olfactol'ogy, scientific study of smells and the sense of smell. [L. *olfacĕre*, to smell—*olēre*, to smell, *facĕre*, to make.]

olibanum, *ol-ib'ǝ-nǝm*, *n.* a gum-resin flowing from incisions in species of *Boswellia*, esp. species in Somaliland and Arabia, frankincense. [L.L., prob.—Gr. *libanos*, frankincense.]

olid, *ol'id*, *adj.* rank-smelling. [L. *olidus*—*olēre*, to smell.]

olig(o)-, *ol-ig-*, -*i-gō*, -*i-gǝ*-, in composition, little, few.—*ns.* oligaemia (*ol-i-gē'mi-ǝ*, -*jē'mi-ǝ*), abnormal deficiency of blood; ol'igarch (-*ärk*; Gr. *archē*, rule), a member of an oligarchy.—*adjs.* oligarch'al, oligarch'ic, -ical.—*ns.* ol'igarchy (-*är-ki*), government by a small exclusive class: a state so governed: a small body of men who have the supreme power of a state in their hands; oligist (*ol'i-jist*; Fr. *fer oligiste*—*fer*, iron, Gr. *oligistos*, superl. of *oligos*, little; as containing less iron than magnetite), crystallised haematite.—*adj.* Oligocene (*ol'i-gō-sēn*; *geol.*; Gr. *kainos*, new; as having few fossil molluscs of living species), between Eocene and Miocene.—*n.* the Oligocene system, period, or strata.—*n.* oligochaete (*ol'i-gō-kēt*; Gr. *chaitē*, bristle), any worm of the Oligochae'ta, chaetopods in which the locomotor organs are reduced to bristles—earthworms, etc.—*adj.* oligochrome (*ol'i-gō-krōm*; Gr. *chrōma*, colour), painted in few colours.—Also *n.*—*ns.* oligoclase (*ol'i-gō-klās*, -*klāz*; Gr. *klāsis*, cleavage, because thought to have a less perfect cleavage than albite), a soda-lime triclinic feldspar; oligocythaemia (*ol-i-gō-si-thē'mi-ǝ*; Gr. *kytos*, a vessel, *haima*, blood), defect of red cells in the blood.—*adj.* oligom'erous (Gr. *meros*, a part), having few parts: having fewer members than the other whorls of a flower.—*ns.* oligopoly (*ol-i-gop'o-li*; Gr. *pōleein*, to sell), a situation in which there are few sellers, and a small number of competitive firms control the market—opp. to oligopsony (*ol-i-gop'sǝ-ni*; Gr. *opsōnia*, purchase of food), a situation in which there are few buyers, each competitive buyer influencing the market. [Gr. *oligos*, little, few.]

olio, *ō'li-ō*, *n.* a savoury dish of different sorts of meat and vegetables: a mixture: a medley: a miscellany: a variety entertainment:—*pl.* olios. [Sp. *olla*—L. *ōlla*, a pot; cf. olla.]

oliphant, *ol'i-fǝnt*, *n.* an obsolete form of elephant: an ancient ivory hunting-horn.

olitory, *ol'i-tǝ-ri*, *adj.* pertaining to kitchen vegetables.—*n.* a kitchen-garden: a pot-herb. [L. (*h*)*olitor*, gardener—(*h*)*olus*, (*h*)*oleris*, a pot-herb, vegetable.]

olive, *ol'iv*, *n.* a tree (*Olea europaea*) cultivated round the Mediterranean for its oily fruit: extended to many more or less similar trees: the fruit of the olive-tree: peace, of which the olive was the emblem: a colour like the unripe olive: a person of olive-coloured complexion: an olive-shaped or oval object of various kinds: a gasteropod mollusc (Oliva) of warm seas with olive-shaped shell: a rolled lump of seasoned meat (usu. in *pl.*).—*adj.* of a brownish-green colour like the olive.—*adjs.* olivā'ceous, olive-coloured: olive-green; of i'vary, olive-shaped. —*ns.* olivenite (*ō-liv'ǝ-nīt*, or *ol'iv-*), a mineral, hydrated copper arsenate, often olive-coloured; ol'ivet, an olive-shaped button: an oval mock-pearl used in trade with primitive peoples in Africa; olivine (*ol'iv-ēn*), an orthorhombic rock-forming mineral, silicate of iron and magnesium, often olive-green, often altered to serpentine.—olive branch, a symbol of peace: a child (Ps. cxxviii. 3; *Pr. Bk.*); olive drab, the dull dark yellowish green of American uniforms; ol'ive-oil, oil pressed from the fruit of the olive; ol'ive-shell, the shell of the mollusc Oliva; ol'ive-yard, a piece of ground on which olives are grown; ol'ivine-rock, dunite. [Fr.,—L. *oliva*.]

Oliver, *ol'i-vǝr*, *n.* the comrade-in-arms of Roland (q.v.).

Oliver. See Bath.

oliver, *ol'i-vǝr*, *n.* a forge-hammer worked by foot. [Origin unknown.]

Oliverian, *ol-i-vē'ri-ǝn*, *n.* an adherent of the Protector, *Oliver* Cromwell (1599-1658).

Olivetan, *ol-iv-ē'tǝn*, *n.* one of an order of Benedictine monks founded in 1313, the original house at Monte *Oliveto*, near Siena.

olla, (Lat.) *ol'a*, *ōl'a*, (Sp.) *ōl'yä*, *n.* jar or urn: an olio.—*n.* olla-podrida (*ōl'yä-pō-drē'dä*; Sp., rotten pot), a Spanish mixed stew or hash of meat and vegetables: any incongruous mixture or miscellaneous collection. [L. *ōlla* and Sp. *olla*, pot, Sp. *podrida*—L. *putrida* (fem.)—*puter*, *putris*, rotten.]

ollav, ollamh, *ol'äv*, *n.* a doctor or master among the ancient Irish. [Ir. *ollamh*.]

-ology. The combining element is properly -logy (q.v.).—*n.* ology, *ol'ǝ-ji*, a science whose name ends in -ology: any science.

olpe, *ol'pē*, *n.* a Greek jug. [Gr. *olpē*.]

olykoek, olycook, *ol'i-kōōk*, (*U.S.*) *n.* a kind of doughnut. [Du. *oliekoek*, lit. oil-cake.]

Olympus, *ol-im'pǝs*, *n.* the name of several mountains, esp. of one in Thessaly, abode of the greater Greek gods: heaven.—*ns.* Olym'pia, a district in Elis, also the city of Pisa in it, where the Olympian games in honour of Olympian Zeus were celebrated; Olym'piad, in ancient Greece, a period of four years, being the interval from one celebration of the Olympic games to another, used in reckoning time (the traditional date of the first Olympiad is 776 B.C.): a celebration of the Olympic games: a celebration of the modern Olympic games: (sometimes without *cap.*) an international contest in bridge or other mental exercise; Olym'pian, a dweller on Olympus, any of the greater gods, esp. Zeus: a godlike person: a competitor in the Olympic games.—*adj.* of Olympus: godlike: of Olympia (now *rare*).—*adj.* Olym'pic, of Olympia: of Olympus (now *rare*).—*n.pl.* Olym'pics, the Olympic games.—Olympic games, the ancient games celebrated every four years at Olympia: quadrennial international athletic contests held at various centres since 1896; Olympic torch, since 1936, a lighted torch brought from Olympia, Greece, to kindle

the **Olympic flame**, which burns throughout the Olympic games. [Gr. *Olympos.*]
**-oma**, *-ō-ma, n. suff.* a tumour, as *sarcoma, glaucoma:—pl.* -ō´mas, -ō´mata. [Gr. *-ōma.*]
**omadhaun**, *om´ə-dön, n.* a fool. [Ir. *amadan.*]
**omasum**, *ō-mā´səm, n.* a ruminant's third stomach, the psalterium or manyplies.—*adj.* omā´sal. [L. *omāsum*, ox tripe; a Gallic word.]
**ombre**, *om´bər, -brā, um´bər, n.* a game played with a pack of forty cards, usually by three persons, one against the others: the solo player. [Sp. *hombre*—L. *homō, -inis*, a man.]
**ombrometer**, *om-brom´i-tər, n.* a rain-gauge.—*n.* om´brophil, -phile (*-fil*), a plant tolerant of much rain.—*adj.* ombroph´ilous.—*n.* om´brophobe, a plant intolerant of much rain.—*adj.* ombroph´obous. [Gr. *ombros*, a rain-storm, *metron*, measure, *phileein*, to love, *phobeein*, to fear.]
**ombú**, *om-bōō´, n.* a South American tree, a species of *Phytolacca*, that grows isolated in the pampas:—*pl.* ombús´.
**Ombudsman**, *om´bŏŏdz-man, n.* (orig. in Sweden and Denmark), a 'grievance man', an official who is appointed to investigate complaints against the Administration: in Britain officially 'Parliamentary Commissioner for Administration'. [Sw.]
**omega**, *ō´meg-ə, U.S. -mēg´, n.* last letter of the Greek alphabet—long o (Ω, ω): the conclusion: as a numeral ω´ = 800, ͵ω = 800,000. [Late Gr. *ō mega*, great O; opposed to omicron; the earlier Gr. name of the letter was *ō.*]
**omelet, omelette**, *om´lit, -let, n.* a pancake made of eggs, beaten up, and fried in a pan (with or without cheese, herbs, ham, jam, or other addition). [Fr. *omelette*, earlier *amelette*, apparently by change of suffix and metathesis from *alemelle* (*l'alemelle* for *la lemelle*), a thin plate—L. *lāmella, lāmina*, a thin plate.]
**omen**, *ō´mən, n.* a sign of some future event, either good or evil: threatening or prognosticating character: an event prognosticated (*Shak.*).—*v.t.* to portend.—*adj.* o´mened, affording or attended by omens, esp. in composition, as *ill-omened*. [L. *ōmen, -inis.*]
**omentum**, *ō-men´təm, n.* a fold of peritoneum proceeding from one of the abdominal viscera to another:—*pl.* omen´ta.—*adj.* omen´tal.—great omentum, the epiploon. [L. *ōmentum.*]
**omer**, *ō´mər, n.* a Hebrew dry measure containing about 2¼ litres, 1/10 ephah. [Heb. *'ōmer.*]
**omicron**, *ō-mi´krən, U.S. ōm´i-, om´, n.* fifteenth letter of the Greek alphabet—short o (O, o): as a numeral o´ = 70, ͵o = 70,000. [Late Gr. *o micron*, little O; opposed to omega; the earlier Greek name of the letter was *ou.*]
**ominous**, *om´in-əs, adj.* pertaining to, or containing, an omen: portending evil: inauspicious.—*adv.* om´inously.—*n.* om´inousness. [See omen.]
**omit**, *ō-mit´, v.t.* to leave out: to fail (to): fail to use, perfom: to disregard (*Shak.*): to leave off, let go (*Shak.*):—*pr.p.* omitt´ing; *pa.t.* and *pa.p.* omitt´ed.—*adj.* omiss´ible, that may be omitted.—*n.* omission (*-mish´n*), act of omitting: a thing omitted.—*adj.* omiss´ive, omitting, of the nature of omission.—*ns.* omitt´ance (*Shak.*), omission; omitt´er. [L. *omittĕre, omissum—ob-*, in front, *mittĕre, missum*, to send.]
**omlah**, *om´lä, n.* a staff of officials in India. [Ar. *'umalā.*]
**ommateum**, *om-ə-tē´əm, n.* a compound eye:—*pl.* ommate´a.—*ns.* ommatid´ium, a simple element of a compound eye:—*pl.* ommatid´ia; ommatophore (*-at´ō-fōr, -för*), an eye-stalk, as in snails. [Gr. *omma, -atos*, an eye.]
**omneity**, *om-nē´i-ti*, **omniety**, *om-ni´i-ti, ns.* allness, the condition of being all. [L. *omnis*, all.]
**omni-**, *om-ni-*, in composition, all.—*n.pl.* omniana (*-ä´nə, -ā´nə*), ana about all sorts of things.—*n.* omnibenev´olence, universal benevolence.—*adj.*
**omnibenev´olent.**—*n.* omnicom´petence, legal competence in all matters.—*adjs.* omnicom´petent; omnidirec´tional, acting in all directions; omnifā´rious, of all kinds; omnif´erous, bearing or producing all kinds; omnif´ic, all-creating; om´niform, of, or capable of, every form.—*n.* omniform´ity.—*v.t.* om´nify (*rare*), to make universal.—*adj.* omnigenous (*-nij´i-nəs*), of all kinds.—*n.* omnipar´ity, general equality.—*adjs.* omnip´arous, producing all things; omnipā´tient, enduring all things.—*ns.* omnip´otence, omnip´otency, unlimited power.—*adj.* omnip´otent, all-powerful.—*adv.* omnip´otently.—*n.* omnipres´ence, quality of being present everywhere at the same time.—*adj.* omnipres´ent.—*n.* omniscience (*om-nis´i-əns, -nish´əns, -yəns*), knowledge of all things.—*adj.* omnisc´ient, all-knowing.—*adv.* omnisc´iently.—*adj.* omniv´orous, all-devouring: feeding on both animal and vegetable food (*zool.*). [L. *omnis*, all.]
**omnibus**, *om´ni-bəs, n.* a large road-vehicle carrying a considerable number of passengers of the general public, or hotel guests (abbrev. bus): an omnibus box: an omnibus book: a waiter's or waitress's assistant:—*pl.* om´nibuses.—*adj.* widely comprehensive: of miscellaneous contents.—**omnibus book**, a book containing reprints of several works or items, usually by a single author, or on a single subject, or of the same type; **omnibus box**, a theatre box with room for many persons; **omnibus clause**, one that covers many different cases; **omnibus train**, one that stops at every station. [Lit. for all, dative pl. of L. *omnis.*]
**omnium**, *om´ni-əm, n.* a Stock Exchange term for the aggregate value of the different stocks in which a loan is funded.—om´nium-gath´erum (*coll.; sham Latin*) a miscellaneous collection. [L., of all; gen. pl. of *omnis*, all.]
**omohyoid**, *ō-mō-hī´oid, adj.* pertaining to shoulder-blade and hyoid.—*n.* the muscle joining these. [Gr. *ōmos*, shoulder.]
**omophagia**, *ō-mō-fāj´yə, -i-ə, n.* the eating of raw flesh, esp. as a religious observance.—Also **omophagy** (*ō-mof´ə-ji*).—*adjs.* omophagic (*-faj´ik*), omophagous (*-mof´ə-gəs*). [Gr. *ōmophagiā—ōmos*, raw, *phagein*, to eat.]
**omophorion**, *ō-mō-fō´ri-on, -för´, n.* an Eastern bishop's vestment like the pallium. [Gr. *ōmophórion—ōmos*, shoulder, *pherein*, to carry.]
**omoplate**, *ō´mō-plāt, n.* the shoulder-blade or scapula.—*n.* omoplatoscopy (*-plə-tos´ko-pi*), divination by observing the cracks in a burning shoulder-blade. [Gr. *ōmoplatē—ōmos*, shoulder, *platē*, blade, *skopeein*, to look.]
**omphacite**, *om´fə-sīt, n.* a grass-green pyroxene. [Gr. *omphax, -akos*, an unripe grape.]
**omphalos**, *om´fa-los, n.* the navel: a boss: a stone at Delphi held to mark the centre of the world: a centre.—*adjs.* omphalic (*-fal´ik*); om´phaloid, navel-like.—*n.* omphalomancy, divination of the number of future children from the knots in the navel-string. [Gr. *omphalos*, navel.]
**omrah**, *om´rä, n.* a Mohammedan lord. [Hindi *umrā*, orig. pl. of Ar. *amir.*]
**on**, *on, prep.* in contact with the upper, supporting, outer, or presented surface of: to a position in contact with such a surface of: in or to a position or state of being supported by: having for basis, principle, or condition: subject to: in a condition or process of: towards or to: directed towards: in the direction of: against: applied to: with action applied to: with inclination towards: close to, beside: exactly or very nearly at: at the time, date, or occasion of: very little short of: just after: concerning, about: with respect to: by (in oaths and adjurations): at the risk of: assigned to: in addition to: in (*obs.*): (of gaining, taking) from (*Shak.*,

*Milt.*): of (*obs.* or *dial.*): (of marriage) to (*Scot.*): (of waiting) for (*Scot.*): against (*U.S.*): at the expense of, to the disadvantage of (*coll.*).—*adv.* in or into a position on something: towards something: in advance: on the way to being drunk (*slang*): forward: in continuance: in, or into, or allowing connection, supply, activity, operation, or validity: in progress: on the stage, the table, the fire, the programme, the menu, or anything else: not off.—*interj.* forward! proceed!—*v.i.* on the side on which the batsman stands (normally the bowler's right) (*cricket*): in a condition expressed by the adverb on: agreed upon: willing to participate.—*n.* the on side.—*v.i.* to go on (*coll.*): (with *with*) to put on (*coll.*).—on'-licence, a licence to sell alcoholic liquors for consumption on the premises.—*adj.* and *adv.* on'side, not offside.—on to, to a position on (also on'to): forward to: aware of, cognisant of (*coll.*). [O.E. *on*; Du. *aan*; O.N. *ā*; Ger. *an*; Gr. *ana*.]

on-, *on-*, a dial. form of the prefix un-.

onager, *on'ə-jər*, *n.* the wild ass of Central Asia: an ancient military engine for throwing great stones. [L.,—Gr. *onagros—onos*, an ass, *agrios*, wild—*agros*, a field.]

Onagra, *on'ə-grə*, (*bot.*) *n.* an old name for Oenothera, giving name to the family Ona-grā'ceae.—*adj.* onagrā'ceous. [Gr. *onagrā*, the plant also known as *oinothēras*; see Oenothera.]

onanism, *ō'nan-izm*, *n.* coitus interruptus: masturbation.—*n.* o'nanist.—*adj.* onanist'ic. [See Gen. xxxviii. 9.]

once, *wuns*, *adv.* a single time: on one occasion: at a former time: at some time in the future: firstly (*obs.*): in short (*obs.*): at any time.—*n.* one time.—*adj.* former.—*conj.* when once: as soon as.—*n.* onc'er (*eccles. slang*), one who goes to church once on Sunday.—*adj.* once-accent'ed, marked with one accent—applied to the octave beginning with middle C.—*n.* once-o'ver, a single comprehensive survey.—at once, without delay: alike: at the same time; for once, on one occasion only; once and again, more than once: now and then; once (and) for all, once only and not again; once in a way, while, occasionally: rarely; once or twice, a few times; once upon a time, at a certain time in the past—the usual formula for beginning a fairy-tale. [O.E. *ānes*, orig. gen. of *ān*, one, used as adv.]

Oncidium, *on-sid'i-əm*, *n.* a tropical American genus of orchids. [Gr. *onkos*, a hook.]

oncology, *ong-kol'ə-ji*, *n.* the study of tumours.—*ns.* oncom'eter, an instrument for measuring variations in bulk of bodily organs; oncot'omy, incision into a tumour. [Gr. *onkos*, bulk, mass, tumour.]

oncome, *on'kum, -kəm*, (*Scot.*) *n.* coming on: a sudden fall of rain or snow: the beginning of attack by an insidious disease.—*n.* on'coming, approach.—*adj.* advancing: approaching. [on, come.]

Oncorhynchus, *ong-kō-ringk'əs*, *n.* a North Pacific genus of salmon. [Gr. *onkos*, hook, *rhynchos*, beak.]

oncost, *on'kost*, *n.* overhead expenses: an on-costman.—*adj.* paid by time: causing oncost.—*n.* on'costman, a mine-worker paid by the day. [on, cost.]

ondatra, *on-dat'rə*, *n.* the musquash. [Huron Indian.]

ondine. Same as undine.

onding, *on'ding*, (*Scot.*) *n.* onset, esp. a sudden fall of rain or snow. [on, ding.]

on-dit, *ō-dē*, *n.* rumour: hearsay:—*pl.* on-dits (*-dēz*). [Fr.]

one, *wun*, *adj.* single: of unit number: undivided: the same: a certain: a single but not specified: first.—*n.* the number unity: a symbol representing it: an individual thing or person: a thing

bearing or distinguished by the number one.—*pron.* somebody: anybody.—*ns.* one'ness, singleness: uniqueness: identity: unity; oner (*wun'ər*; all meanings *coll.* or *slang*), a person or thing unique or outstanding in any way: an expert: a heavy blow: a big lie.—Also one'-er, wunn'er.—*pron.* oneself', one's self, the emphatic and reflexive form of one.—one'-and-thir'ty, an old card-game like vingt-un, in which it was sought to make the pips add up to 31 and no more.—*adjs.* one'-eyed, having but one eye; one'fold, simple, single-minded; one'-hand'ed, with, by, or for, one hand; one'-horse, drawn by a single horse: petty, mean, inferior; one'-ide'a'd, entirely possessed by one idea; one'-legged; one'-man, of, for, or done by, one man; one'-piece, made in one piece; one'-sid'ed, limited to one side: partial: developed on one side only: turned to one side.—*adv.* one'-sid'edly.—one'-sid'edness; one'step, dance of U.S. origin danced to quick march time.—*v.i.* to dance a one-step.—*adjs.* one'-time, former, erstwhile; one'-to-one', corresponding each one uniquely to one; one'-track', incapable of dealing with more than one idea or activity at a time: obsessed with one idea to the exclusion of others.—one-up'manship (*facet.*; *Stephen Potter*), the art of being one up.—*adj.* one'-way, proceeding, or permitting, or set apart for traffic, in one direction only.— a, the, one, a person special or remarkable in some way (*coll.*); a one for, an enthusiast for; all one, just the same: of no consequence; at one, of one mind; be one up on, to score an advantage over (another); just one of those things, an unfortunate happening that must be accepted; one and all, everyone without exception; one another (see another); one-armed bandit, a fruit machine; one by one, singly in order; one day, on a certain day: at an indefinite time. [O.E. *ān*; O.N. *einn*, Ger. *ein*; L. *ūnus*; Gr. *oinē*, ace.]

oneiric, *ō-nī'rik*, *adj.* belonging to dreams.—*n.* oneirocrit'ic, an interpreter of dreams.—*adj.* oneirocrit'ical.—*ns.* oneirocrit'icism; oneiro-dynia (*-ō-din'i-ə*), troubled sleep: nightmare; oneirology (*on-ī-rol'ə-ji*), the study of dreams; oneir'omancy, divination by dreams; oneiros'copist, an interpreter of dreams; oneiros'copy.—Also oni'ric, etc. [Gr. *oneiros*, a dream, *kritikos*, judging, *odynē*, pain, *logos*, discourse, *manteiā*, divination, *skopiā*, watching.]

onely, a Spenserian spelling of only.

onerous, *on'ə-rəs, ō'nər-əs*, *adj.* burdensome: oppressive.—*adv.* on'erously.—*n.* on'erousness. [L. *onerōsus—onus*, a burden.]

oneyre, oneyer, *wun'yər*, *n.* (1 *Hen. IV* II, i) probably the same as oner. [See one.]

onfall, *on'föl*, *n.* an attack, onslaught, esp. (*Scot.*) of illness: a fall of rain or snow (*Scot.*). [on, fall.]

ongoing, *on'gō-ing*, *n.* a going on: course of conduct: event: (*pl.*) proceedings, behaviour, esp. misbehaviour. [on, go.]

onion, *un'yən*, *n.* a pungent edible bulb of the lily family: the plant yielding it (*Allium cepa*): applied also to some kindred species: a flaming rocket used against aircraft: the head (*slang*).—*v.t.* to apply an onion to: to produce by means of an onion.—*adj.* on'iony.—onion dome, a bulb-shaped dome having a sharp point, characteristic of Russian Eastern Orthodox church architecture.—*adj.* on'ion-eyed (*Shak.*), having the eyes full of tears.—on'ion-skin, a very thin variety of paper.—know one's onions, to know one's subject or one's job well (*coll.*); off one's onion (*slang*), off one's head. [Fr. *oignon*—L. *ūniō, -ōnis*, union, a large pearl, an onion; see union.]

oniric, etc. See oneiric.

Oniscus, *on-is'kəs*, *n.* a genus of woodlice.—*adj.*

onis'coid, of the family of Oniscus: like a wood-louse. [Gr. *oniskos*, dim. of *onos*, an ass.]
on-licence. See under on.
onlooker, *on'loōk-ər, n.* a looker on, observer.— *adj.* on'looking.
only, *ōn'li, adj.* single in number: without others of the kind: without others worthy to be counted.—*adv.* not more, other, or otherwise than: alone: merely: barely: just: pre-eminently (*obs.*): singly (*rare*).—*conj.* but: except that.—*prep.* (*dial.*) except.—if only, (I, he, etc.) wish (wished, etc.) ardently that; only too, very, extremely. [O.E. *ānlic* (adj.)—*ān*, one, *-lic*, like.]
onocentaur, *on-ō-sen'tör, n.* a kind of centaur, half-man, half-ass. [Gr. *onos*, ass.]
onomastic, *on-ə-mas'tik, adj.* pertaining to a name, esp. pertaining to the signature to a paper written in another hand.—*ns.* onomas'ticon, a dictionary of proper names; onomas'tics, (treated as *sing.*) study of the history of proper names. [Gr. *onomastikos, -on*—*onoma*, a name.]
onomatopoeia, *on-ō-mat-ō-pē'ə, n.* the formation of a word in imitation of the sound of the thing meant: a word so formed: the use of words whose sounds help to suggest the meaning (*rhet.*).—Also onomatopoesis (*-pō-ē'sis*), or onomatopoiesis (*-poi-ē'sis*).—*adjs.* onomatopoeic (*-pē'ik*), onomatopoetic (*-pō-et'ik*). [Gr. *onomatopoiiā, -poiēsis*—*onoma, -atos*, a name, *poieein*, to make.]
onrush, *on'rush, n.* a rushing onward. [on, rush.]
onset, *on'set, n.* violent attack: assault: storming: beginning, outset.—*ns.* on'setter (*arch.*), an assailant; on'setting, incitement. [on, set.]
onshore, *on'shōr, shör, adj.* toward the land.—*adv.* on'-shore. [on, shore.]
onslaught, *on'slöt, n.* an attack or onset: assault. [Prob. Du. *aanslag* or Ger. *anschlag*, refashioned as Eng.]
onst, *wunst, adv.* illiterate form of once.
onstead, *on'sted,* (*Scot.*) *n.* a farmstead: a farmhouse with its offices: the offices alone. [on, stead.]
onto, *on'tōō, prep.* to a place or position on.—Also on to.
ontogenesis, *on-tō-jen'i-sis, n.* the history of the individual development of an organised being as distinguished from *phylogenesis.*—Also ontogeny (*on-toj'i-ni*).—*adjs.* ontogenet'ic, ontogen'ic.—*advs.* ontogenet'ically, -gen'ically. [Gr. *ōn, ontos,* pr.p. of *einai,* to be, *genesis,* generation]
ontology, *on-tol'ə-ji, n.* the science that treats of the principles of pure being: that part of metaphysics which treats of the nature and essence of things.—*adjs.* ontologic (*-tə-loj'ik*), -al.—*adv.* ontolog'ically.—*n.* ontol'ogist. [Gr. *ōn, ontos,* pr.p. of *einai,* to be, *logos,* discourse.]
onus, *ō'nəs, n.* burden: responsibility.—onus probandi, *ō'nəs prō-ban'di,* or *ō'noōs pro-ban'dē,* the burden of proving. [L. *ŏnus, -eris.*]
onward, *on'wərd, adj.* going on: advancing: advanced.—*adv.* (also on'wards) towards a place or time in advance or in front: forward: in continuation of forward movement.—*adv.* on'-wardly (*rare*). [on, and suff. -ward.]
onymous, *on'i-məs, adj.* bearing the author's name. [anonymous.]
onyx, *on'iks, n.* an agate formed of alternate flat layers of chalcedony, white or yellow and black, brown or red, used for making cameos (*min.*): onychite, onyx-marble; a fingernail-like opacity in the cornea of the eye.—*ns.* onycha (*on'i-kə*), an ingredient in ancient Jewish incense: the nail-like operculum of a mollusc; onych'ia, inflammation of the nail-bed; on'ychite, onyx-marble; onychi'tis, inflammation of the soft parts about the nail; onych'ium, a pulvillus in insects; onychocryptō'sis, ingrowing toenail; on'ychomancy, divination by the fingernails; onychophagist (*-kof'ə-jist*), a nail-biter; ony-

choph'agy.—*n.pl.* Onychoph'ora, Prototracheata, the class to which Peripatus belongs.—on'yx-mar'ble, a banded travertine or stalagmite, also called oriental alabaster. [Gr. *onyx, onychos,* nail, claw, onyx.]
oo', *ōō,* a Scots form of wool.
oo, *ōō,* a Scots form of we.—*gen.* oor.
oo-, *ō'ə-, ō-o-,* in composition, egg.—*ns.* oocyte (*ō'ə-sit;* see cyte), an ovum before it matures and begins to divide; oogamy (*ō-og'ə-mi;* Gr. *gamos,* marriage), union of unlike gametes.—*adj.* oog'amous.—*ns.* oogenesis (*ō-ə-jen'i-sis;* Gr. *genesis,* formation), the genesis and development of the ovum—also oogeny (*ō-oj'i-ni*).—*adj.* oogenet'ic.—*n.* oogonium (*ō-ə-gō'ni-əm;* Gr. *gonos,* offspring), the female reproductive organ in seaweeds and fungi:—*pl.* oogo'nia.—*adj.* oogo'nial.—*n.* oolite (*ō'ə-lit;* Gr. *lithos,* a stone; *geol.*), a kind of limestone composed of grains like the eggs or roe of a fish: (*cap.*) stratigraphically the upper part of the Jurassic in Britain, consisting largely of oolites.—*adj.* oolitic (*ō-ə-lit'ik*).—*ns.* oology (*ō-ol'ə-ji;* Gr. *logos,* discourse), the science or study of birds' eggs; ool'ogist; o'ophyte (*ō'ə-fit;* Gr. *phyton,* plant), in ferns and mosses, the gametophyte; oosphere (*ō'ə-sfēr;* Gr. *sphaira,* sphere), an unfertilised ovum; oospore (*ō'ə-spōr, -spör;* Gr. *sporos,* seed), a zygote, esp. a resting zygote. [Gr. *oion,* egg.]
oodles, *ōō'dlz, n.pl.* abundance.—Also ood'lins. [Perh. huddle.]
oof, *ōōf,* (*slang*) *n.* money—orig. oof'tish. [Yiddish—Ger. *auf* (*dem*) *tische,* on the table.]
ooidal, *ō-oi'dəl, adj.* egg-shaped. [Gr. *ōioeidēs*—*ōion* and *eidos,* form.]
oolakan, *ōō'lə-kən.* Same as eulachon.
oolong, oulong, *ōō'long, n.* a variety of black tea with the flavour of green. [Chin. *wu-lung,* black dragon.]
oom, *ōōm,* (*S.Afr.*) *n.* uncle: used as term of respect for an elderly man. [Du.]
oomia(c)k. Same as umiak.
oomph, *ōōmf,* (*slang*), *n.* vitality: enthusiasm: sex-appeal: personal magnetism. [Origin obscure.]
oon, *ōōn, n.* a Scots form of oven.
oons, *ōōnz,* (*arch.*) *interj.* a minced oath, for God's wounds.
oont, *ōōnt, n.* in India, a camel. [Hind. *ūnt.*]
oop. See oup.
oophoron, *ō-of'ər-on, n.* (*zool.*) an ovary.—*ns.* oophorec'tomy (*surg.*), removal of an ovary; oophori'tis, inflammation of the ovary. [Gr. *ōiophoros, -on,* egg-bearing.]
oorial. Same as urial.
oorie. Same as ourie.
ooze, *ōōz, n.* sap (*obs.*): the liquor of a tan vat: gentle flow, as of water through sand or earth: slimy mud: a fine-grained, soft, deep-sea deposit, composed of shells and fragments of foraminifera, diatoms, and other organisms.—*v.i.* to flow gently: to percolate, as a liquid through pores or small openings: to leak.—*v.t.* to exude.—*adv.* ooz'ily.—*n.* ooz'iness.—*adj.* ooz'y, resembling ooze: slimy: oozing. [Partly O.E. *wōs,* juice, partly O.E. *wāse,* mud.]
ooze, *ōōz,* (*Scot.*) *n.* fluff: nap.—*adj.* ooz'y. [Prob. pl. of oe.]
op. Abbrev. for operation, opus and (in op art; see below) optical.
opacity, opacous. See under opaque.
opah, *ō'pə, n.* the kingfish (*Lampris*), a large sea-fish with laterally flattened body, constituting a family of uncertain affinities. [West African origin.]
opal, *ō'pl, n.* amorphous silica with some water, usually milky white with fine play of colour, in some varieties precious: opal-glass: the colouring of opal.—*adj.* of opal: like opal.—*adj.*

Neutral vowels in unaccented syllables: *el'ə-mənt;* for certain sounds in foreign words, see p. viii

o'paled.—*n.* opalesc'ence, a milky iridescence. —*adj.* opalesc'ent.—*adj.* o'paline (-ēn, -ĭn), relating to, like, or of, opal.—*n.* opal-glass: a photographic print fixed on plate-glass.—*adj.* o'palised, -z-, converted into opal: opalescent. —o'pal-glass', white or opalescent glass. [L. *opalus*; Gr. *opallios*, perh.—Sans, *upala*, gem.] **opaque**, ō-pāk', *adj.* shady: dark: dull: that cannot be seen through: impervious to light or to radiation of some particular kind: obscure, hard to understand (*fig.*): impervious to sense: doltish.—*v.t.* to make opaque.—*n.* **opacity** (ō-pas'i-ti), opaqueness.—*adj.* **opacous** (ō-pā'kəs).—*adv.* **opaque'ly.**—*n.* **opaque'ness**, quality of being opaque: want of transparency. [L. *opācus*.]

**op art**, *op ärt*, art using geometrical forms precisely executed and so arranged that movement of the observer's eye, or inability to focus, produces an illusion of movement in the painting. [*optical.*]

**ope**, ōp, *adj.*, (*poet.*) *v.t.* and *v.i.* a shortened form of **open**.

**opeidoscope**, *op-i'də-skōp*, *n.* an instrument for illustrating sound by means of light. [Gr. *ops* (found in the oblique cases), voice, *eidos*, form, *skopeein*, to look at.]

**open**, ō'pn, *adj.* not shut: allowing passage out or in: exposing the interior: unobstructed: free: unenclosed: exposed: uncovered: liable: generally accessible: available: ready to receive or transact business with members of the public: public: free to be discussed: obvious: unconcealed: undisguised: unfolded, spread out, expanded: unrestricted: not restricted to any class of persons, as *open championship*: (of a town) without military defences: not finally decided, concluded, settled, or assigned: not dense in distribution or texture: widely spaced: loose: much interrupted by spaces or holes: showing a visible space between (*naut.*): clear: unfrozen: not frosty: not hazy: free from trees: frank: unreserved: unstopped (*mus.*): without use of valve, crook, or key: (of an organ pipe) not closed at the top: (of a vowel sound) low, with wide aperture for the breath: (of a consonant) without stopping of the breath stream: (of a syllable) ending with a vowel.— *v.t.* to make open: to make as an opening: to make an opening in: to clear: to expose to view: to expound: to declare open: to begin. —*v.i.* to become open: to have an opening, aperture, or passage: to serve as passage: to begin to appear: to begin: to give tongue: to speak out.—*n.* a clear space: public view: open market: an opening.—*adj.* o'penable.— *ns.* o'pener; o'pening, the act of causing to be, or of becoming, open: an open place: an aperture: a gap: a street or road breaking the line of another: a beginning: a first stage: a preliminary statement of a case in court: the initial moves, or mode of beginning, in a game, etc.: a shopkeeper's first display of a new season's goods (*U.S.*): the two pages exposed together when a book is opened: opportunity for action: a vacancy.—Also *adj.*—*adv.* o'penly.—*n.* o'penness.—**open access**, public access to the shelves of a library; **open aestivation**, aestivation without overlap or meeting of the edges of the perianth leaves.—*adjs.* o'pen-air', outdoor; o'pen-and-shut', simple, obvious, easily decided; o'pen-armed', cordially welcoming.—**open book**, anything that can be read or interpreted without difficulty; **open bundle**, a vascular bundle with cambium; **open-cast**, in mining, an excavation open overhead.—Also *adj.* and *adv.*—*adj.* o'pen-chain' (*chem.*), with atoms linked together as a chain with loose ends.—**open circuit**, electrical circuit broken so that current cannot pass: in television, the customary system in which the

showing is for general, not restricted, viewing; **open court**, a court proceeding in public; **open diapason**, one of the chief foundation stops of an organ; **open door**, free and equal opportunity of trading for all.—*adjs.* open-end'(ed), not closely defined, general and adaptable to suit various contingencies: (of question, debate, etc.) allowing free unguided answers or expressions of opinion: (**open-end**; of investment trust) offering shares in unlimited numbers, redeemable on demand; o'pen-eyed, watchful (*Shak.*): astonished: fully aware of what is involved; o'pen-field, having the arable land in unenclosed strips held by different cultivators. —**open fire**, an exposed fire on a domestic hearth.—*adj.* o'pen-hand'ed, with an open hand: generous: liberal.—o'pen-hand'edness; **open harmony**, chords not in close position.—*adj.* o'pen-heart'ed, with an open heart: frank: generous. — o'pen-heart'edness. — *adj.* o'pen-hearth, making use of, or having, a shallow hearth of reverberating type.—**open house**, hospitality to all comers; **open letter**, a letter addressed to one person but intended for public reading.—*adj.* o'pen-mind'ed, free from prejudice: ready to receive and consider new ideas. —o'pen-mind'edness.—*adj.* o'pen-mouthed, gaping: expectant: greedy: clamorous.—**open note**, a note produced by an unstopped string, open pipe, or without a crook, etc.: a printed or written note without a solid black head—a semibreve or minim (*U.S.*); **open order**, spaced-out formation for drill, etc.; **open prison**, a prison without the usual close security, allowing prisoners considerably more freedom of movement than in conventional prisons; **open question**, a matter undecided; **open sandwich**, one which has no bread, etc., on top; **open score**, one with a separate stave for each part; **open sea**, unenclosed sea, clear of headlands; **open secret**, a matter known to many but not explicitly divulged; o'pen-ses'ame, a spell or other means of making barriers fly open—from the story of Ali Baba and the Forty Thieves in the *Arabian Nights*; **open shop**, a factory not confined to union labour; **open skies**, the open air: reciprocal freedom for aerial inspection of military establishments; o'pen-stitch (*Scot.* o'pen-steek), a kind of open-work stitching; **open town**, one without troops or military installations, and hence, according to international law, immune from attack of any kind; **open university** (earlier called **university of the air**), a university (1971) whose teaching is carried out by correspondence and by radio and television; **open verdict**, a verdict that a crime has been committed without specifying the criminal; o'pen-work, any work showing openings through it. —*adj.* open-cast.—**open fire**, to begin to shoot; **open out**, to make or become more widely open: to expand: to disclose: to unpack: to develop: to bring into view: to open the throttle, accelerate; **open-plan house**, one whose rooms run from front to back with windows on both faces; **open up**, to open thoroughly or more thoroughly: to lay open: to disclose: to make available for traffic, colonisation, or the like: to accelerate: to begin firing. [O.E. *open*; cf. Du. *open*, O.N. *opinn*, Ger, *offen*; prob. related to **up**.]

**opera**, *op'ə-ra*, *n.* musical drama: a company performing opera: an opera-house—*adj.* used in or for an opera.—*adj.* **operatic** (-at'ik), pertaining to or resembling opera.—*adv.* **operat'ically.**—**opera bouffa**, *boof'a*, (It.) comic opera, esp. of the 18th century—opp. to *opera seria*; **opera** (Fr. opéra) **bouffe**, *boof*, funny or farcical opera; **opéra comique**, *kom-ēk*, (Fr.) opera with some spoken dialogue—in the 18th century, opera having subjects less lofty than those of *grand opéra* (Eng. grand opera), in the 19th

*fāte, fär; mē, hûr* (her); *mīne; mōte, fŏr; mūte; mōōn, fŏŏt; dhen* (then)

century, having no restriction as to subject (either comic or tragic); **opera seria,** *se'rya,* (It.) serious opera; **comic opera,** opera comique: opera of amusing nature: an absurd emotional situation; **grand opera,** opera without dialogue, esp. if the subject is very dramatic or emotional; **light opera,** a lively and tuneful opera: an operetta (q.v.).—See also **music-drama, musical, musical comedy**—**op'era-cloak,** an elegant cloak for evening wear, esp. in the auditorium of a theatre; **op'era-danc'er,** one who dances in ballets introduced into operas; **op'era-glass,** a small binocular telescope for use in the theatre; **op'era-hat,** a collapsible tall hat; **op'era-house,** a theatre for opera; **op'era-sing'er.** [It.,—L. *opera*; cf. **operate.**]

**opera,** *op'ə-ra, pl.* of **opus.**

**operate,** *op'ə-rāt, v.i.* to work: to exert strength: to produce any effect: to exert moral power: to be in activity, act, carry on business: to take effect upon the human system (*med.*): to perform some surgical act upon the body with the hand or an instrument.—*v.t.* to effect, bring about, cause to occur: to work: to conduct, run, carry on.—*adj.* **op'erāble,** admitting of a surgical operation: able to be operated: practicable.—*n.* **op'erand,** something on which an operation is performed, e.g. a quantity in mathematics.—*adj.* **op'erant,** operative: active: effective.—*n.* an operator.—*adj.* **op'erāting.**—*n.* **operā'tion,** act or process of operating: that which is done or carried out: agency: influence: method of working: action or movements: surgical performance.—*abbrev.* **op.,** esp. in military or surgical sense.—*adjs.* **operā'tional,** relating to operations: ready for action; **operā'tions,** relating to problems affecting operations, esp. military (as in *operations research*); **op'erātive,** having the power of operating or acting: exerting force: producing effects: efficacious.—*n.* a workman in a manufactory: a labourer.—*adv.* **op'erātively.**—*ns.* **op'erativeness; op'erātor,** one who, or that which, operates: one charged with the operation of a machine, instrument, or apparatus: one who deals in stocks: a mine-owner (*U.S.*): a symbol, signifying an operation to be performed (*math.*).—**operating table, theatre,** one set apart for use in surgical operations; **operational, operations, research,** research to discover how a weapon, tactic, or strategy can be altered to give better results: similar research to promote maximum efficiency in industrial spheres; **operative words,** the words in a deed legally effecting the transaction (e.g. *devise and bequeath* in a will): (loosely) the most significant words. [L. *operāri, -ātus*—*opera,* work, closely connected with *opus, operis,* work.]

**operculum,** *ō-pûr'kū-ləm, n.* a cover or lid (*bot.*): the plate over the entrance of a shell (*zool.*): the gill-cover of fishes: a coal-hole cover in a pavement:—*pl.* **oper'cula.**—*adjs.* **oper'cular,** belonging to the operculum; **oper'culate, -d,** having an operculum. [L. *operculum*—*operīre,* to cover.]

**opere citato,** *op'ə-rē sit-ā'tō, op'er-e kit-ā'tō,* (L.) in the work cited:—*abbrev.* **op. cit.**

**operetta,** *op-ə-ret'a, n.* a short, light, rather trivial, musical drama: often esp. formerly, light opera (see **opera**).—*n.* **operett'ist,** a composer of operettas. [It., dim. of *opera.*]

**operose,** *op'ə-rōs, adj.* laborious: tedious.—*adv.* **op'erosely.**—*ns.* **op'eroseness, operosity** (*-os'i-ti*). [L. *operōsus*—*opus, operis,* work.]

**ophi(o)-,** *of-i(-o)-,* in composition, snake.—*ns.* **ophical'cite,** a marble containing green serpentine; **oph'icleide** (*-klīd*; Fr. *ophicléide*—Gr. *kleis, kleidos,* key), a keyed wind-instrument developed from the serpent, a bass or alto keybugle.—*n.pl.* **Ophid'ia** (Gr. *ophidion,* dim.), the

snakes as an order or suborder of reptiles.—*n.* and *adj.* **ophid'ian.**—*ns.* **ophidiā'rium,** a snakehouse; **Ophiogloss'um** (Gr. *glōssa,* tongue), the adder's-tongue genus, giving name to the **Ophioglossā'ceae,** a family of eusporangiate ferns; **ophiol'ater,** a snake-worshipper; **ophiol'atry** (Gr. *latreiā,* worship), snake-worship.—*adjs.* **ophiol'atrous; ophiolog'ic, -al.**—*ns.* **ophiol'ogist; ophiol'ogy,** the study of snakes; **oph'iomorph** (Gr. *morphē,* form), a caecilian amphibian.—*adjs.* **ophiomorph'ic, -ous,** snakelike; **ophioph'agous** (Gr. *phagein,* to eat), snake-eating.—*ns.* **ophioph'ilist,** a snake-lover; **Oph'ism; oph'ite,** a name given to various rocks mottled with green: at one time, serpentine-rock: later, a kind of diabase: **Ophite,** one of a Gnostic sect that reverenced snakes.—*adj.* **ophitic** (*of-it'ik*), pertaining to ophite: having pyroxene crystals enclosing feldspar laths: **Ophitic,** of the Ophites.—*ns.* **Oph'itism; Ophiuchus** (*-i-ook'əs, -ūk'*), the Serpent Bearer, a constellation between Aquila and Libra on the celestial equator; **Ophiura** (*-i-ōō'ra, -ū'ra*; Gr. *ourā,* tail), a genus of brittlestars.—*ns.* and *adjs.* **ophiu'ran; ophiu'rid; ophiu'roid.**—*ns.pl.* **Ophiu'rida, Ophiuroid'ea,** the brittle-stars, a class of echinoderms like starfish with long snaky sharply differentiated arms. [Gr. *ophis,* snake.]

**ophthalm(o)-,** *of-thal-m(o)-,* in composition, eye.—*n.* **ophthal'mia,** inflammation of the eye, esp. of the conjunctiva.—*adj.* **ophthal'mic,** pertaining to the eye.—*ns.* **ophthal'mist,** an ophthalmologist; **ophthalmi'tis,** ophthalmia.—*adj.* **ophthalmolog'ical.**—*ns.* **ophthalmol'ogist; ophthalmol'ogy,** the science of the eye, its structure, functions, and diseases; **ophthalmom'eter,** an instrument for eye-measurements; **ophthalmom'etry; ophthalmoplegia** (*-plē'jya*; Gr. *plēgē,* a stroke), paralysis of one or more of the muscles of the eye; **ophthal'moscope,** an instrument for examining the interior of the eye.—*adjs.* **ophthalmoscop'ic, -al.**—*adv.* **ophthalmoscop'ically.**—*n.* **ophthalmos'copy,** examination of the interior of the eye with the ophthalmoscope. [Gr. *ophthalmos,* eye.]

**opiate,** *ō'pi-āt, n.* a drug containing opium to induce sleep: that which dulls sensation, physical or mental.—*adj.* inducing sleep.—*v.t.* to treat with opium: to dull.—*adj.* **o'piated.** [opium.]

**opificer,** *op-if'i-sər, n.* an artificer. [L. *opifex, -icis*—*opus,* work, *facēre,* to make.]

**opine,** *ō-pīn', v.t.* to suppose: to form or express as an opinion.—*adj.* **opin'able,** capable of being thought. [Fr. *opiner*—L. *opināri,* to think.]

**opinicus,** *o-pin'i-kəs,* (her.) *n.* a half-lion, halfdragon. [Origin unknown.]

**opinion,** *ō-pin'yən, n.* what seems to one to be probably true: judgment: estimation: favourable estimation: self-confidence (*Shak.*): arrogance (*Shak.*): reputation (*Shak.*).—*adjs.* **opin'ionated, opin'ionātive, opin'ioned,** unduly attached to one's own opinions: stubborn.—*advs.* **opin'ionately** (*obs.*), **opin'ionātively.**—*ns.* **opin'ionātiveness; opin'ionist,** one who holds or gives an opinion, or (*obs.*) an unusual or heterodox opinion. [L. *opiniō, -ōnis.*]

**opisometer,** *op-i-som'i-tər, n.* a map-measuring instrument with a wheel that traces a line on the map and then runs backward along a straight scale until the wheel reaches its original position on the screw that holds it. [Gr. *opisō,* backward, *metron,* measure.]

**opisth(o)-,** *o-pisth(-ō, -ə)-,* in composition, behind.—*n.* and *adj.* **opisthobranch** (*o-pis'thō-brangk*; Gr. *branchia,* gills).—*n.pl.* **Opisthobranch'ia,** an order of gasteropods having the gills behind the heart.—*adj.* **opisthocoelian** (*-sē'li-ən*; Gr. *koilos,* hollow), hollow or concave behind, as a vertebra.—Also **opisthocoe'lous.**—*n.* **opisthodomos**

(*op-is-thod'o-mos*), a rear-chamber in a Greek temple.— *adjs.* **opisthogloss'al** (Gr. *glōssa*, tongue), having the tongue attached in front, free behind, as in frogs; **opisthog'nathous** (Gr. *gnathos*, jaw), having retreating jaws.—*n.* **opis'-thograph**, a manuscript or slab inscribed on the back as well as the front.—*adj.* **opisthograph'ic**.—*n.* **opisthog'raphy**.—**opisthot'onos**, extreme arching backwards of the spine and neck as a result of spasm of the muscles in that region.—*adj.* **opisthoton'ic**. [Gr. *opisthen*, behind.]

**opium,** *ō'pi-əm, n.* the dried narcotic juice of the white poppy.—**o'pium-den'**, a resort of opium-smokers; **o'pium-eat'er, -smoker**, one who makes a habitual use of opium. [L. *ōpium*— Gr. *opion*, dim. from *opos*, sap.]

**opobalsam,** *op-ō-böl'səm, n.* balm of Gilead. [Gr. *opobalsamon—opos*, juice, *balsamon*, balsam-tree.]

**opodeldoc,** *op-ō-del'dok, n.* a name given by Paracelsus to various local applications: soap-liniment. [Derivation unknown, apparently Gr. *opos*, juice.]

**opopanax,** *ō-pop'ə-naks, n.* a gum-resin formerly used in medicine, got from the roots of a Persian (and S. European) species of parsnip: a perfume got from *Commiphora*. [Gr. *opos*, juice, *panax*, a panacea.]

**oporice,** *ō-por'i-sē, n.* a medicine prepared from quinces, pomegranates, etc. [Gr. *opōrikē— opōrā*, late summer, summer fruits.]

**opossum,** *ō-pos'əm, n.* any member of the American genus *Didelphys*, or family Didelphyidae, small marsupials, often pouchless, mainly arboreal, with prehensile tail: in Australia, a phalanger: opossum-fur.—Also (*U.S.*) **possum, 'possum.—to play possum,** to feign death. [American Indian.]

**opotherapy,** *op-ō-ther'ə-pi, n.* treatment by administration of extracts of animal organs, especially of ductless glands. [Gr. *opos*, juice, and *therapy*.]

**oppidan,** *op'i-dən, n.* a townsman: in university towns one who is not a member of the university, or a student not resident in a college: at Eton (formerly elsewhere) a schoolboy who is not a foundationer or colleger.—*adj.* urban. [L. *oppidānus—oppidum*, town.]

**oppignorate, oppignerate,** *op-ig'-nə-rāt*, (*obs.*) *v.t.* to pawn.—*n.* **oppignorā'tion**. [L. *oppignorāre, oppignerāre—ob*, against, *pignus, -oris, -eris*, a pledge.]

**oppilate,** *op'il-āt, v.t.* to block up, stop up.—*n.* **oppilā'tion.**—*adj.* **opp'ilātive**. [L. *oppilāre, -ātum—ob*, in the way, *pilāre*, to ram down.]

**opponent,** *o-pō'nənt, adj.* opposing: antagonistic (with *to*; formerly with *with*): placed opposite or in front.—*n.* one who opposes a course of action, belief, person, etc.—*n.* **oppo'nency**. [L. *oppōnēns, -entis*, pr.p. of *oppōnēre—ob*, in the way of, *pōnēre*, to place.]

**opportune,** *op'ər-tūn*, or *-tūn'* (*Shak.* op-ör'tūn), *adj.* occurring at a fitting time: conveniently presented: timely: convenient: suitable: opportunist.—*adv.* **opportune'ly** (or *op'*).—*ns.* **opportune'ness** (or *op'*); **opportun'ism** (or *op'*), practice of regulating actions by favourable opportunities rather than consistent principles; **opportun'ist** (or *op'*), one (e.g. a politician) who waits for events before declaring his opinions, or shapes his conduct or policy to circumstances of the moment: a person without settled principles.—Also *adj.*—*n.* **opportun'ity, opportuneness** (*rare*): fitness (*obs.*): an occasion offering a possibility: advantageous conditions. [Fr. *opportun*—L. *opportūnus—ob*, before, *portus, -ūs*, a harbour.]

**oppose,** *o-pōz', v.t.* to place in front or in the way (with *to*): to place or apply face to face or front

to front: to set in contrast or balance: to set in conflict: to place as an obstacle: to face: to resist: to contend with.—*v.i.* to make objection. —*n.* **opposabil'ity**.—*adjs.* **oppos'able**, that may be opposed: capable of being placed with the front surface opposite (to—as a thumb to other fingers); **oppo'sing; oppose'less** (*Shak.*), not to be opposed, irresistible.—*n.* **oppos'er**. [Fr. *opposer*—L. *ob*, against, Fr. *poser*, to place—L. *pausāre*, to rest, stop; see **pose**.]

**opposite,** *op'ə-zit, adj.* placed, or being, face to face, or at two extremities of a line: facing on the other side: of leaves, in pairs at each node, with the stem between (*bot.*): of floral parts, on the same radius: directly contrary: diametrically opposed: opposed: corresponding.—*adv.* in or to an opposite position or positions.—*prep.* opposite to.—*n.* that which is opposed or contrary: an opponent: opposition (*Milt.*).—*adv.* **opp'ositely**.—*n.* **opp'ositeness**.—*adj.* **oppositive** (*-poz'*), characterised by opposing: adversative: inclined to oppose.—**opposite number,** one who has a corresponding place in another set: one who is allotted to another as partner, opponent, etc.—**be opposite with** (*Shak.*), to be perverse and contradictory in dealing with. [Fr.,—L. *oppositus—ob*, against, *pōnēre, positum*, to place.]

**opposition,** *op-ə-zish'ən, n.* the act of opposing or of setting opposite: the state of being opposed or placed opposite: opposed or opposite position: an opposite: contrast: contradistinction: resistance: a difference of quantity or quality between two propositions having the same subject and predicate (*logic*): a body of opposers: the party that opposes the ministry or existing administration: the situation of a heavenly body, as seen from the earth, when it is directly opposite to another, esp. the sun (*astron.*).—*adj.* of the parliamentary opposition. —*adj.* **opposi'tional**.—*n.* **opposi'tionist**, a member of the opposition. [L. *oppositiō, -ōnis*; cf. **opposite**.]

**oppress,** *o-pres', v.t.* to press against or upon: to crush (*obs.*): to smother (*obs.*): to overwhelm: to take by surprise (*obs.*): to distress: to lie heavy upon: to treat with tyrannical cruelty or injustice: to load with heavy burdens: to ravish (*obs.*).—*n.* **oppression** (*o-presh'ən*), act of oppressing: tyranny: feeling of distress or of being weighed down: dullness of spirits: pressure (*Shak.*).—*adj.* **oppress'ive**, tending to oppress: overburdensome: tyrannical: heavy: overpowering.—*adv.* **oppress'ively**.—*ns.* **oppress'iveness; oppress'or**. [Fr. *oppresser*—L.L. *oppressāre*, freq. of L. *oprimēre, oppressum—ob*, against, *premēre*, to press.]

**opprobrium,** *o-prō'bri-əm, n.* disgrace, reproach, or imputation of shameful conduct: infamy: anything that brings such reproach.—*adj.* **oppro'brious**, reproachful, insulting, abusive: infamous, disgraceful (*arch.*).—*adv.* **oppro'-briously**.—*n.* **oppro'briousness**. [L. *opprobrium— ob*, against, *probrum*, reproach.]

**oppugn,** *o-pūn', v.t.* to assail, esp. by argument: to oppose: to call in question.—*n.* **oppugnancy** (*o-pug'nan-si*; *Shak.*), antagonism.—*adj.* **oppug'-nant**, opposing: hostile.—*n.* an opponent.—*n.* **oppugner** (*o-pūn'ər*). [L. *oppugnāre*, to attack—*ob*, against, *pugna*, a fight.]

**ops.** Abbreviation for **operations**.

**opsimath,** *op'si-math, n.* one who learns late in life: —*n.* **opsim'athy**, learning obtained late in life. [Gr. *opsimathēs—opse*, late, *mathē*, learning.]

**opsiometer,** *op-si-om'i-tar, n.* an optometer. [Gr. *opsis*, sight, *metron*, measure.]

**opsonium,** *op-sō'ni-əm, n.* anything eaten with bread as a relish, esp. fish. fish.—*ns.* **opsomā'nia**, any morbid love for some special kind of food; **opsomā'niac**.—*adj.* **opsonic** (*op-son'ik*), relating to opsonin.—*n.* **op'sonin**, a constituent of blood-serum which makes bacteria more readily consumed by phagocytes. [Latinised from Gr. *opsōnion*—*opson*, cooked food, relish.]

**opt**, *opt*, *v.i.* to make a choice, esp. of nationality when territory is transferred: where there is more than one possibility, to decide (to do), to choose (with *for*).—*n.* **opt'ant**, one who opts: one who has exercised a power of choosing, esp. his nationality.—*adj.* **optative** (*opt'ə-tiv*, or *op-tā'tiv*), expressing desire or wish.—*n.* (*gram.*) a mood of the verb expressing wish.—*adv.* **op'tatively.**—opt out (of), to choose not to take part (in). [L. *optāre*, *-ātum*, to choose, wish.]

**optic, -al**, *op'tik*, *-əl*, *adjs.* relating to sight, or to the eye, or to optics: (**optical**) constructed to help the sight: acting by means of light: amplifying radiation: visual.—*n.* **op'tic**, an eye (now mainly *facet.*): a lens, telescope, or microscope (*obs.*): a device in, or attached to, a bottle, for measuring liquid poured out.—*adv.* **op'tically.**—*ns.* **optician** (*op-tish'ən*), formerly one skilled in optics: one who makes or sells optical instruments; **op'tics** (treated as *sing.*), the science of light; **optol'ogist**, an optician; **optol'ogy**; **optom'eter**, an instrument for sight-testing; **optom'etrist**, a sight-tester; **optom'etry**; **op'-tophone**, an instrument that translates printed characters into arbitrary sounds, and so enables the blind to read ordinary type.—**optical maser**, laser; **optic axis**, the axis of the eye—a line through the middle of the pupil and the centre of the eye: in a doubly refracting crystal, a direction in which no double refraction occurs; **optic lobe**, part of the mid-brain concerned with sight. [Gr. *optikos*, optic, *optos*, seen.]

**optimal**, etc. See **optimism.**

**optimate**, *op'ti-māt*, *n.* (*rare* in *sing.*) a member of the aristocracy:—*pl.* (L.) **optimā'tēs.** [L. *optimās*, *-ātis*—*optimus*, best.]

**optime**, *op'ti-mi*, *n.* formerly, in the university of Cambridge, one of those in the second or third rank of mathematical honours (*senior* or *junior optime*), next to the wranglers. [L. *optimē* (adv.), very well, best.]

**optimism**, *op'ti-mizm*, *n.* Leibniz's doctrine that the world is the best of all possible worlds: a belief that everything is ordered for the best: loosely, a disposition to take a bright, hopeful view of things: hopefulness.—Opp. to *pessimism*. —*adj.* **op'timal**, optimum.—*v.t.* **op'timalise**, **-ize**, to bring to the most desirable or most efficient state.—*n.* **optimalisā'tion**, **-z-**,—*v.i.* **op'timise**, **-ize**, to take the most hopeful view of anything.—*v.t.* to make the most or best of: to make as efficient as possible, esp. by analysing and planning processes: to prepare or revise (a computer system or programme) so as to achieve greatest possible efficiency.—*n.* **optimisā'tion**, **-z-**,—*n.* **op'timist**, one who believes in optimism: commonly, a sanguine person.—*adj.* **optimist'ic.**—*adv.* **optimist'ically.** [L. *optimus*, best.]

**optimum**, *op'ti-məm*, *n.* that point at which any condition is most favourable:—*pl.* **op'tima.**—*adj.* (of conditions) best for the achievement of an aim or result: very best. [L., neut. of *optimus*, best.]

**option**, *op'shən*, *n.* act of choosing: power or right of choosing: a thing that may be chosen: an alternative for choice: a power (as of buying at a fixed price) that may be exercised at will within a time-limit: wish (*obs.*).—*adj.* **op'tional**, left to choice: not compulsory: leaving to choice. —*adv.* **op'tionally.**—local option (see **local**). [L. *optiō*, *-ōnis*—*optāre*, to choose.]

**opto-.** See **optic.**

**opulent**, *op'ū-lənt*, *adj.* wealthy: loaded with wealth: luxuriant: over-enriched.—*n.* **op'u-lence**, riches: abounding riches.—*adv.* **op'u-lently.** [L. *opulentus.*]

**opulus**, *op'ū-ləs*, *n.* the guelder rose. [L. *opulus*, a kind of maple.]

**Opuntia**, *ō-pun'shi-a*, *n.* the prickly-pear genus of the cactus family. [L. *Opūntia* (*herba*, plant), of *Opūs* (Gr. *Opous*), a town of Locris where Pliny said it grew.]

**opus**, *ō'pəs*, *op'əs*, *op'ŏŏs*, *n.* a work, esp. a musical composition—esp. one numbered in order of publication, as opus 6 (abbrev. op. 6): used in naming various styles of Roman masonry:—*pl.* **opera** (*op'ə-ra*).—**opus latericium** (*la-ter-ish'i-əm*, *-ik'*, *-ik'i-ŏŏm*), a form of Greco-Roman brickwork; **opus musivum** (*mū-*, *mŏŏ-siv'əm*, *mŏŏ-sēv'ŏŏm*), mosaic work; **opus operantis** (*op-ər-an'tis*), the effect of a sacrament ascribed (as by Protestants) to the spiritual disposition of the recipient; **opus operatum** (*op-ər-ā'təm*, *op-er-ä'tŏŏm*), due celebration of a sacrament involving grace flowing from the sacramental act (the R.C. view); **opus reticulatum** (*ri-tik-yə-lā'təm*, *re-tik-ōō-lā'tŏŏm*), reticulated work. [L. *ŏpus*, *-eris*, work.]

**opuscule**, *o-pus'kūl*, *n.* a little work.—Also **opuscle** (*o-pus'l*), **opus'culum**:—*pl.* **-cula.** [L. dim. of *opus*.]

**or**, *ör*, *conj.* (or *adv.*) and *prep.* before (in time).—**or ever**, or **e'er**, or (by confusion) **or ere**, before ever, before even. [O.E. (Northumbrian) and O.N. *ār*, early, with the sense of O.E. *ǣr*, ere.]

**or**, *ör*, *conj.* marking an alternative. [M.E. other.]

**or**, *ör*, (*her.*) *n.* the tincture gold or yellow, indicated in engraving and chiselling by dots. [Fr., —L. *aurum*, gold.]

**-or.** Agent suff. from L., corr. to **-er** from O.E. In most words one or other ending is standard but in some both endings occur (**-or** used esp. in legal terms or in terms for a non-personal agent).

**orach, orache**, *or'ich*, *n.* a genus (*Atriplex*) of the goosefoot family, sometimes used as spinach is. [Fr. *arroche*—L. *atriplex*—Gr. *atraphaxys*.]

**oracle**, *or'ə-kl*, *n.* a medium or agency of divine revelation: a response by or on behalf of a god: the place where such responses are given: the Jewish sanctuary: the word of God: a person with the repute or air of infallibility or great wisdom: an infallible indication: a wise or seeming-wise or mysterious utterance.—*v.t.* to utter as an oracle.—*v.i.* to speak as an oracle. —*adj.* **oracular** (*or-ak'ū-lər*), of the nature of an oracle: like an oracle: seeming to claim the authority of an oracle: delivering oracles: equivocal: ambiguous: obscure—also **orac'-ulous** (now *rare*).—*ns.* **oracularity** (*-lar'i-ti*), **orac'ularness, orac'ulousness.**—*advs.* **orac'ularly, orac'ulously.**—work the oracle (see work). [L. *ōrāculum*—*ōrāre*, to speak.]

**ora et labora**, *ör'a*, *ör'ä et la-bö'ra*, *-bö'rä*, (L.) pray and work; **ora pro nobis**, *prō nō'bis*, *-bēs*, pray for us.

**oragious**, *ō-rā'jəs*, *adj.* stormy. [Fr. *orageux*.]

**oral**, *ö'rəl*, *ö'rəl*, *adj.* relating to the mouth: near the mouth: uttered by the mouth: spoken, not written: taken through the mouth: pertaining to the infant stage of development when satisfaction is obtained by sucking.—*n.* an oral examination.—*n.* **o'racy**, skill in self-expression and ability to communicate freely with others by word of mouth.—*adv.* **o'rally.**—**oral contraception**, inhibition of the normal process of ovulation and conception by taking orally, and according to a specified regimen, any of a number of hormone-containing pills; **oral contraceptive**, a pill of this type. [L. *ōs*, *ōris*, the mouth.]

**orang.** See **orang-utan.**

**orange**, *or'inj*, *n.* a gold-coloured fruit (hesperidium, a specialised type of berry) with tough skin, within which are juicy segments: the tree (*Citrus* genus of family Rutaceae) on which it grows: extended to various unrelated but superficially similar fruits and plants: a colour between red and yellow.—*adj.* pertaining to an orange: orange-coloured.—*ns.* orangeade (*or-in-jād′*), a drink made with orange juice; or′angery (*-ri, -ər-i*), a house or other place for growing orange-trees.—or′ange-bloss′om, the white blossom of the orange-tree, worn by brides: that of the mock-orange, similarly used.—*adj.* or′ange-col′oured.—or′ange-flower, orange-blossom (orange-flower water, a solution of oil of neroli); or′ange-grass′, a small American St John's-wort; or′ange-lil′y, a garden lily with large orange flowers; or′ange-peel, the rind of an orange, often candied; or′ange-root′, golden-seal; or′ange-squeez′er, an instrument for squeezing out the juice of oranges; or′ange-stick, a thin stick, esp. of orange-wood used in manicure and make-up.—*adj.* and *n.* or′ange-taw′ny (*Shak.*).—or′ange-tip′, a butterfly (Euchloe or kindred) with an orange patch near the tip of the forewing; or′ange-tree′; or′ange-wife (*Shak.*), a woman who sells oranges; or′ange-wood, wood of the orange tree.—bitter, Seville, or sour, orange, *Citrus aurantium*; sweet orange *Citrus sinensis*, native of China and south-east Asia, or any cultivated fruit derived from it. [Fr. ult. from Ar. *nāranj*; cf. L.L. *arangia, aurantia, narancum*; It. *arancia*, earlier *narancia*; Sp. *naranja*; the loss of the *n* may be due to confusion with the indef. art. (*una, une*), the vowel changes to confusion with L. *aurum*, Fr. *or*, gold.]

Orange, or′inj, *adj.* relating to the family of the princes of Orange, a former principality from the 11th century, passing by an heiress to the house of Nassau in 1531, the territory ceded to France in 1713: favouring the cause of the Prince of Orange in Holland or in Great Britain and Ireland: of or favouring the Orangemen: extreme Protestant Irish Conservative.—*n.* Or′angism (Or′angeism).—Or′angeman, a member of a society revived and organised in Ireland in 1795 to uphold Orange principles.

orang-utan, *ō-, ō-rang′-ōō-tan′, ō′, ō′rang-ōō′tan*, orang-outang, *ō-, ō-rang′-ōō-tang′*, *n.* an anthropoid ape, found only in the forests of Sumatra and Borneo, reddish-brown, arboreal in habit: erroneously, a chimpanzee.—Also orang′. [Malay *ō′rang ū′tan*, man of the woods (said not to be applied by the Malays to the ape)—*ōrang*, man, *ūtan*, wood, wild.]

orant, *ō′rant, ō′*, *n.* a worshipping figure in ancient Greek and early Christian art. [L. *ōrāns, -antis*, pr.p. of *ōrāre*, to pray.]

orarian, *ō-, ō-rā′ri-an, adj.* coastal.—*n.* a coast-dweller. [L. *ōrārius—ōra*, shore.]

orarium, *ō-, ō-rā′ri-əm, n.* a handkerchief (*ant.*): a stole (*obs.*): a scarf attached to a bishop's staff. —*n.* ora′rion, a Greek Church deacon's stole. [L. *ōrārium—ōs, ōris*, mouth.]

orarium, *ō-, ō-rā′ri-əm, n.* a book of private devotions. [L. *ōrāre*, to pray.]

oration, *ō-, ō-rā′shən, n.* a formal speech: a harangue.—*v.i.* orate′ (*facet.*), to harangue, hold forth. [L. *ōrātiō, -ōnis—ōrāre*, to pray.]

orator, or′ə-tər, *n.* a spokesman (*obs.*): a petitioner (*obs.*): a public speaker: a man of eloquence:—*fem.* or′atress, oratrix (*or-ā′triks*, or *or′ə-triks*).—*adjs.* oratorial (*or-ə-tō′ri-əl, -tō′*), of an orator, oratory, or an oratory; orato′rian, of an oratory.—*n.* a priest of an oratory; Oratorian, a member of an Oratory.—*adj.* oratorical (*-tor′*), characteristic of an orator: addicted to oratory: rhetorical: relating to or savouring of oratory. —*adv.* orator′ically.—*n.* or′atory, the art of the orator: rhetoric: rhetorical utterances or expression: a place for private prayer (*pl.* or′atories): a lectern for praying at: a place of public speaking (*obs.*); Oratory, one of various congregations in the R.C. Church, esp. the Fathers of the Oratory, established by St Philip

Neri (1515-95): a church of the Oratorians. [L. *ōrātor, -ōris—ōrāre*, to pray.]

oratorio, *or-ə-tō′ri-ō, -tō′*, *n.* a story, usually Biblical, set to music, with soloists, chorus, and full orchestra (scenery, costumes, and acting, however, being dispensed with): the form of such composition:—*pl.* orato′rios.—*adj.* orato′rial. [It. *oratorio*—L. *ōrātōrium*, an oratory, because they developed out of the singing at devotional meetings in church oratories.]

orb, *örb*, *n.* a circle: a sphere: anything round: a celestial body: an eyeball: the mound or globe of a king's regalia: the space within which the astrological influence of a planet operates: a sphere carrying a planet in its revolution: a cycle of time: an orbit: a world.—*v.t.* to surround: to form into an orb.—*adjs.* orbed, in the form of an orb: circular; orbic′ular, approximately circular or spherical: round: having the component minerals crystallised in spheroidal aggregates (*petr.*).—*n.* orbicula′ris, a muscle surrounding an opening:—*pl.* orbiculā′-rēs.—*adv.* orbic′ularly.—*adj.* orb′y, orbed. [L. *orbis*, circle.]

orb, *örb*, (*obs.*) *adj.* bereaved, esp. of children.—*n.* (*archit.*; *obs.*) an obscure term generally understood to mean a blind window or blank panel.—*n.* orb′ity (*obs.*), bereavement, esp. of children. [L. *orbus*, bereft.]

Orbilius, *ör-bil′i-əs, n.* a flogging schoolmaster (from Horace's teacher).

orbis terrarum, *ör′bis, ter-ā′rəm, ter-ä′rōōm*, the circle of lands, the whole world. [L.]

orbit, *ör′bit, n.* the path in which a heavenly body moves round another, or an electron round the nucleus of an atom (also or′bital), or the like: a path in space round a heavenly body: regular course or beat, sphere of action: loosely, an orb: the hollow in which the eyeball rests (also or′bita): the skin round a bird's eye.—*v.t.* of an aircraft, to circle (a given point): to circle (the earth, etc.) in space: to put into orbit.—*adj.* or′bital. [L. *orbita*, a wheel-track—*orbis*, a ring, wheel.]

orc, *örk*, *n.* a fierce sea-monster: a killer-whale: an ogre.—Or′ca, the killer-whale genus. [L. *orca*.]

Orcadian, *ör-kā′di-ən, adj.* of Orkney.—*n.* an inhabitant or a native of Orkney. [L. *Orcadēs*—Gr. *Orkadēs*, Orkney (Islands).]

orcein. See orcinol.

orchard, *ör′chərd, n.* an enclosed garden of fruit-trees.—*ns.* or′charding; or′chardist, or′chardman, one who grows and sells orchard fruits.—or′chard-grass (*U.S.*), cock's-foot grass; or′chard-house, a glass house for cultivating fruits without artificial heat. [O.E. *ort-geard*, prob. L. *hortus*, garden, and O.E. *geard*; see yard. Some connect the first part with O.E. *wyrt*; see wort.]

orchat, *ör′chət, n.* an obsolete form of the word orchard. [Partly *dial.*, partly due to confusion with Gr. *orchatos*, a row of trees.]

orchel, orchella. See archil.

orchestra, *ör′kis-tra*, formerly *-kes′, n.* in the Greek theatre, the place in front of the stage where the chorus danced: now the part of a theatre or concert-room in which the instrumental musicians are placed: a large company of musicians (strings, woodwinds, brasses, and percussion) playing together under a conductor: loosely applied to a small group, as in a restaurant.—*ns.* orche′sis, the art of dancing or rhythmical movement of the body; orchesog′raphy, notation of dancing.—*adj.* orchestic (*-kes′tik*), relating to dancing.—*n.* (*pl.* in form) orches′tics, the art of dancing.—*adj.* orchestral (*-kes′*), of or for an orchestra.—*n.* orches′tralist, an orchestral composer.—*v.t.* or′chestrate, to compose or arrange (music) for performance by an orchestra: (*fig.*)

to organise so as to achieve the best effect.—Also *v.i.*—*ns.* **orchestra′tion;** or**′chestrātor.**—*adj.* **orches′tric,** orchestric: orchestral.—*ns.* **orchestrina** (*-trē′nə*), **orches′trion,** names given to various keyboard or barrel-organ instruments designed to imitate an orchestra.—**orchestra stalls,** theatre seats just behind the orchestra. [Gr. *orchēstrā* —*orcheesƗhai,* to dance.]

**orchid,** *or′kid, n.* any plant, or flower, of the **Orchidā′ceae** or **Orchid′eae,** a family of monocotyledons, including many tropical epiphytes, with highly specialised, often showy, flowers, the upper petal (*labellum*; by twisting actually the lower) serving as a landing-place for insects, the one fertile stamen (or two) united with the gynaeceum as a *column,* the pollen in masses.—*adjs.* **orchidā′ceous, orchid′eous.**—*ns.* **or′chidist,** a fancier or grower of orchids; **orchidol′ogist; orchidol′ogy,** the knowledge of orchids; **orchidomā′nia,** a craze for orchids; **orchidomā′niac; Or′chis,** a genus of orchids, including several of the best-known British species: loosely applied to other genera.—**or′chid-house,** a place for growing orchids. [Gr. *orchis, -ios* or *-eōs,* a testicle (from the appearance of the root-tubers in Orchis and others); the *d* is a blunder, as if the genitive were *orchidos.*]

**orchil, orchilla.** See **archil.**

**orchitis,** *ör-ki′tis, n.* inflammation of a testicle.—*adj.* **orchitic** (*-kit′ik*).—*ns.* **orchidec′tomy, or-chiec′tomy** (*-ki-ek′*), excision of one or both testicles. [Gr. *orchis, -ios* or *-eōs,* testicle.]

**orcinol,** *ör′sin-ol, n.* a dihydric phenol got from archil and other lichens.—Also **or′cin, or′cine.**—*n.* **orcein** (*ör′si-in*), a purple dyestuff got from orcinol. [See **archil.**]

**ord,** *örd,* (*obs.*) *n.* a point, e.g. of a weapon: a beginning. [O.E. *ord;* cf. **odd.**]

**ordain,** *ör-dān′, v.t.* to arrange: to establish: to decree: to destine: to order: to assign, set apart: to appoint: to set apart for an office: to invest with ministerial functions: to admit to holy orders.—*adj.* **ordain′able.**—*ns.* **ordain′er; ordain′ment; ordinee′,** one who is being, or has just been, ordained. [O.Fr. *ordener* (Fr. *ordonner*)—L. *ordināre, -ātum—ordō, -inis,* order.]

**ordeal,** *ör′dēl,* less justifiably *or-dēl′* or *or-dē′əl, n.* an ancient form of referring a disputed question to the judgment of God, by lot, fire, water, etc.: any severe trial or examination.—Latinised as **ordalium** (*ör-dā′li-əm*).—*adj.* **ordā′lian.**—**ordeal bean,** the Calabar bean. [O.E. *ordēl, ordāl* (W.S. would be *ordǣl*)—pfx. *or-,* out, *dǣl,* deal, share; cf. Du. *oordeel,* Ger. *urteil.*]

**order,** *ör′dər, n.* arrangement: sequence: disposition: due arrangement: due condition: condition of normal or due functioning: regular or suitable arrangement: method: system: tidiness: restrained or undisturbed condition: a form of procedure or ceremony: the accepted mode of proceeding at a meeting: a practice: grade, degree, rank, or position, esp. in a hierarchy: degree of a curve or equation: command: a written instruction to pay money: a customer's instruction to supply goods or perform work: a pass for admission or other privilege: a class of society: a body of persons of the same rank, profession, etc.: a fraternity, esp. religious or knightly: a body modelled on a knightly order, to which members are admitted as an honour: the insignia thereof: a group above a family but below a class (*biol.*): one of the different ways in which the column and its entablature with their various parts are moulded and related to each other (*archit.*): one of the successively recessed arches of an archway: due action towards some end, esp. in old phrase 'to take order': the position of a weapon with butt on ground, muzzle close to the right side: a portion

or helping (*U.S.*): (*pl.*) the several degrees or grades of the Christian ministry.—*v.t.* to arrange: to set in order: to put in the position of order: to regulate: to conduct (*Shak.*): to command: to give an order for: to order to be (*U.S.*).—*v.i.* to give command.—*interj.* used in calling for order or to order.—*ns.* **or′derer; or′dering,** arrangement: management: the act or ceremony of ordaining, as priests or deacons.—*adj.* **or′derless,** without order: disorderly.—*n.* **or′-derliness.**—*adj.* **or′derly,** in good order: regular: well regulated: of good behaviour: quiet: being on duty.—*adv.* regularly: methodically.—*n.* a non-commissioned officer who carries official messages for his superior officer, formerly the first sergeant of a company: a hospital attendant: a street cleaner.—**or′der-book,** a book for entering the orders of customers, the special orders of a commanding officer, or the motions to be put to the House of Commons; **orderly bin,** a street receptacle for refuse; **orderly officer,** the officer on duty for the day; **orderly room,** a room for regimental, company, etc., business; **order paper,** paper showing order of deliberative business.—**full orders,** priesthood; **holy orders,** an institution, in the Roman and Greek Churches a sacrament, by which one is specially set apart for the service of religion: the rank of an ordained minister of religion; **in order,** with the purpose (with *to, that*): in accordance with rules of procedure at meetings: appropriate, suitable, likely; **in short order** (*U.S.*), promptly; **minor orders,** in the Roman Catholic Church those of acolyte, exorcist, reader, doorkeeper, in the Eastern Churches, reader; **order in council,** an order by the sovereign with advice of the Privy Council; **order of battle,** arrangement of troops or ships in preparation for a fight; **order of the day,** business set down for the day: a proclamation by a dictator or military commander; **sailing orders,** written instructions given to the commander of a vessel before sailing; **sealed orders,** instructions not to be opened until a specified time; **standing orders** or **rules,** regulations for procedure adopted by a legislative assembly; **take order,** to take measures or steps (*obs.*); **take orders,** to be ordained; **tall, large, order,** a very great task or demand; **to order,** according to, and in fulfilment of, an order. [Fr. *ordre*—L. *ordō, -inis.*]

**ordinal,** *ör′din-əl, adj.* indicating order of sequence: relating to an order.—*n.* an ordinal numeral (first, second, third, etc.—distinguished from *cardinal*): a book of rules (*obs.*): a service-book: a book of forms of consecration and ordination. [L.L. *ordinālis*—L. *ordō, -inis,* order.]

**ordinance,** *ör′din-əns, n.* that which is ordained by authority, fate, etc.: regulation: a bye-law (*U.S.*): artistic arrangement: planning: preparation (*obs.*): equipment (*obs.*): ordnance (*obs.*): decree: a religious practice enjoined by authority, esp. a sacrament: social class or order (*Shak.*).—*n.* **or′dinand,** a candidate for ordination.—*adj.* **or′dinant** (*Shak.*), ordaining.—*n.* one who ordains.—*n.* **or′dinate,** a straight line parallel to an axis cutting off an abscissa: the *y*-co-ordinate in analytical geometry.—*v.t.* to ordain: to co-ordinate or order.—*adv.* **ord′inately,** in an ordered manner: restrainedly: with moderation.—*n.* **ordinā′tion,** the act of ordaining: admission to the Christian ministry by the laying on of hands of a bishop or a presbytery: established order. [L. *ordināre, -ātum—ordō,* order.]

**ordinary,** *örd′(i-)nə-ri, Scot.* **ordinar,** *örd′nər, adj.* according to the common order: usual: of the usual kind: customary: of common rank: plain: undistinguished: commonplace: plain-looking (*coll.*): (of a judge or jurisdiction) by virtue of office, not by deputation: (of a judge in

Scotland) of the Outer House of the Court of Session (**Lord Ordinary**).—*n.* a judge of ecclesiastical or other causes who acts in his own right, as a bishop or his deputy: a chaplain who attended those condemned to death, esp. the chaplain of Newgate Prison (*hist.*): something settled or customary: usual fare (*obs.*): a meal provided at a fixed charge: a place where such a meal is provided: the company partaking of it (*obs.*): the common run, mass, or course: a high bicycle: one of a class of armorial charges, figures of simple or geometrical form, conventional in character (*her.*): a reference-book of heraldic charges.—*adv.* or'dinarily.—**ordinary shares**, shares which rank last for receiving dividend, but which may receive as large a dividend as the profits make possible (**preferred ordinary shares** have limited priority).—**in ordinary**, in regular and customary attendance; **ordinary of the mass**, the established sequence or fixed order for saying mass. [L. *ordinārius*—*ordō*, *-inis*, order.]

**ordinee.** See **ordain**.

**ordnance,** *ōrd'nəns, n.* orig., any arrangement, disposition, or equipment: munitions: great guns, artillery: a department concerned with supply and maintenance of artillery.—**Ordnance datum,** the standard sea-level of the Ordnance Survey, now mean sea-level at Newlyn, Cornwall; **Ordnance Survey,** a preparation of maps of Great Britain and N. Ireland by Ordnance Survey Department of Ministry of Housing and Local Government (until 1889 under the Board of Ordnance). [**ordinance**.]

**ordonnance,** *ōr'də-nəns, n.* co-ordination, esp. the proper disposition of figures in a picture, parts of a building, etc. [Fr.; cf. **ordinance**.]

**Ordovician,** *ōr-dō-vish'(y)ən, adj.* and *n.* Lapworth's word for Lower Silurian. [L. *Ordovicēs*, a British tribe of N. Wales.]

**ordure,** *ōrd'yər, n.* dirt: dung: excrement: anything unclean (*fig.*).—*adj.* or'durous. [Fr.,—O.Fr. *ord*, foul—L. *horridus*, rough.]

**ore,** *ōr, ör, n.* a solid, naturally-occurring mineral aggregate, of economic interest, from which one or more valuable constituents may be recovered by treatment: precious metal (*poet.*). [O.E. *ār*, brass, influenced by *ōra*, unwrought metal; cf. L. *aes, aeris*, bronze.]

**ore,** *ōr, (local) n.* seaweed: tangle (*Laminaria*).—Also **ore'weed, oar'weed.** [O.E. *wār.*]

**ore,** *o're, ōr, ör,* old spellings of **o'er** for **over**.—For compounds see **over-**.—**ore-wrought, -raught** (*Shak.*), for **over-reached** in the sense of **overtook**; **ore-rested** (*Shak.*), for **overwrested**.

**öre,** *æ'rə, n.* a coin and money of account in Sweden and (properly **øre**) Norway and Denmark. See **krone**.

**oread,** *ōr'i-ad, ō'ri-ad, (myth.) n.* a mountain nymph:—*pl.* o'reads, or oreʹadēs. [L. *ōrēas, -adis*—Gr. *oreias, oreiados*—*oros*, a mountain.]

**oregano,** *ə-reg'ə-nō, ö-reg'ə-nō, n.* origanum. [Amer. Sp. *orégano*, wild marjoram—L. *origanum*; see **Origanum**.]

**oreide.** See **oroide**.

**oreography, oreology,** etc. See **orography**.

**Oreopithecus,** *ō-, ö-rē-ō-pi-thēk'əs*, or *-pith'ə-kəs, n.* a hominid of which a complete skeleton was found in a lignite mine in Tuscany. [Gr. *oros*, mountain, *pithēkos*, ape.]

**ore rotundo.** See **Appendices, and orotund**.

**orexis,** *ōr-ek'sis, n.* appetite.—*adj.* orecʹtic. [Gr. *ōrexis*.]

**orfe,** *örf, n.* a golden-yellow semi-domesticated variety of id. [Ger. *orfe*—Gr. *orphōs*, the great sea-perch.]

**organ,** *ōr'gən, n.* an instrument or means by which anything is done: a part of a body fitted for carrying on a natural or vital operation: a region of the brain fancied to be concerned with

some mental or moral quality: a bump marking its position and development: a means of communicating information or opinions: a musical instrument in general (*obs.*): a keyboard wind instrument consisting of a collection of pipes made to sound by means of compressed air: a system of pipes in such an organ, having an individual keyboard, a partial organ: a musical instrument in some way similar to a pipe-organ, incl. pipeless organ: a barrel-organ.—*n.* organelle', a specialised part of a cell serving as an organ.—*adjs.* organic (*ör-gan'ik*), **-al,** pertaining to, derived from, like, of the nature of, an organ (in any sense): of an organism, organum or organisation: organised: inherent in organisation: structural: formed as if by organic process (*art*): belonging to the etymological structure of a word (*philol.*): instrumental: mechanical: containing or combined with carbon (*chem.*): concerned with carbon compounds.—*adv.* organ'ically.—*ns.* organicism (*ör-gan'i-sizm*), the conception of nature, life, or society as an organism: the theory that all disease is due to an organic lesion; **organ'icist; organisabil'ity.**—*adj.* **organis'able.**—*n.* organisāʹtion, **-z-,** act of organising: the state of being organised: the manner in which anything is organised: an organised system, body, or society: a political party machine (*U.S.*): the singing of the organum.—*adj.* organisāʹtional, **-z-.**—*v.t.* or'ganise, **-ize-,** to supply with organs: to form into an organic whole: to co-ordinate and prepare for activity: to arrange: to obtain (*slang*).—*v.i.* to become organic: to be active in organisation.—*adj.* or'ganised, **-z-,** having or consisting of parts acting in co-ordination: having the nature of a unified whole: organic.—*ns.* or'ganiser, **-z-,** one who organises: part of an embryo that influences the development of the rest; or'ganism, organic structure, or that which has it: that which acts as a unified whole: a living animal or vegetable.—*adj.* organis'mal.—*ns.* or'ganist, one who plays on an organ; organity (*-gan'*), an organised whole; or'ganon (Gr.), a method of investigation:—*pl.* or'gana; or'ganum (L.), an organon: in mediaeval music, a part in parallel motion to the canto fermo usually a fourth or fifth below or above:—*pl.* or'gana.—or'gan-builder, one who constructs organs; or'gan-gallery, a gallery where an organ is placed; or'gan-grinder, one who plays a hand-organ by a crank; or'ganharmō'nium, a large harmonium; or'gan-pipe, one of the sounding pipes of a pipe-organ (**organ-pipe coral,** a coral, Tubipora, with tubes arranged like organ-pipes); or'gan-point, a pedal-point; or'gan-screen, an ornamented stone or wood screen on which an organ is placed.—**organic chemistry,** the chemistry of carbon compounds; **organic disease,** a disease accompanied by changes in the structures involved; **organic sensation,** sensation from internal organs, as hunger; **organic vein** (*obs.*), the jugular vein. [L. *organum*—Gr. *organon*—*ergon*, work.]

**organdie,** *ör'gən-di, n.* fine muslin: book muslin.—*n.* organ'za, material transparently thin but made of silk, rayon or nylon, not cotton. [Fr. *organdi*.]

**organ(o)-,** *ör-gən(-ō)-,* in composition, organ: organic, as in organometallic compounds in which carbon atoms are linked directly with metal atoms, such as *organolead'*, *organotin'*, or in similar compounds in which the inorganic element is non-metallic, such as *organochlo'rine, organophos'phorus*.—*ns.* organogeny (*ör-gan-oj'i-ni*), organogen'esis, the development of living organs; organ'ogram, a chart showing graded arrangement of personnel in an organisation; organog'raphy, a description of the organs of plants or animals.—*adjs.* organolep'tic, affecting a bodily organ or sense: concerned with testing the effects of a substance on the senses, esp. of taste and smell (Gr. root of *lambanein*, to seize); **organometall'ic**, consisting of a metal and an organic radical.—*n.* **organother'apy**, treatment of disease by administration of animal organs or extracts of them, esp. of ductless gland extracts. [L. *organum*; see **organ**.]

**organzine**, *ör'gən-zēn*, *n.* a silk yarn of two or more threads thrown together with a slight twist. [Fr. *organsin*—It. *organzino*, poss.—*Urgenj*, Turkestan.]

**orgasm**, *ör'gazm*, *n.* immoderate excitement: culmination of sexual excitement: turgescence of any organ (*obs.*).—*adj.* **orgas'tic**. [Gr. *orgasmos*, swelling.]

**orgeat**, *ör'ji-at, -zhat, or-zhä*, *n.* a syrup made from almonds, sugar, etc., formerly from barley. [Fr. *orge*—L. *hordeum*, barley.]

**orgone (energy)**, *ör'gōn (en'ər-ji)*, according to Wilhelm Reich, a vital force permeating the universe, which, concentrated in a specially made **orgone box**, could cure certain diseases. [*orgasm*, and suff. *-one* indicating chemical derivative.]

**orgue**, *örg*, (*obs.*) *n.* a row of stakes let down like a portcullis: a weapon with several barrels in a row. [Fr., *organ*.]

**orgulous**, *ör'gū-ləs*, **orgillous**, *ör'gi-ləs*, (*Shak.*) *adj.* haughty. [O.Fr. *orguillus*; cf. Fr. *orgueil*, It. *orgoglio*, pride; prob. of Germanic origin.]

**orgy**, *ör'ji*, *n.* usu. in *pl.* **or'gies**, a secret rite, as in the worship of Bacchus: esp. a frantic unrestrained celebration: a celebration in general: a riotous, licentious, or drunken revel.—Also (properly *pl.*) **or'gia**.—*n.* **or'giast**, one who takes part in orgies.—*adjs.* **orgias'tic**, **or'gic**. [Fr. *orgies*—L.—Gr. *orgia* (pl.).]

**oribi**, *or'i-bi*, *n.* a small South African antelope, the pale buck. [Afrik., app. from some native language.]

**orichalc**, *or'i-kalk*, (*Spens.*) **oricalche** *n.* a gold-coloured alloy: brass.—*adj.* **orichalceous** (*-kal'si-əs*). [Gr. *oreichalkos—oros*, a mountain, *chalkos*, copper; sense influenced by association with L. *aurum*, gold.]

**oriel**, *ō'*, *ō'ri-əl*, *n.* a small room or recess with a polygonal window, built out from a wall, resting on the ground or (esp.) supported on brackets or corbels: the window of an oriel (in full **o'riel-win'dow**).—*adj.* **o'rielled**. [O.Fr. *oriol*, porch, recess, gallery.]

**orient**, *ō'*, *ō'ri-ənt*, *adj.* rising, as the sun: eastern: bright or pure in colour.—*n.* the part where the sun rises: sunrise: purity of lustre in a pearl: an orient pearl: (with *cap.*) the East: the countries of the East.—*v.t.* **o'rient** (or *-ent'*), to set so as to face the east: to build (lengthwise) east and west: to place in a definite relation to the points of the compass or other fixed or known directions: to determine the position of, relatively to fixed or known directions: to acquaint (someone, oneself) with the present position relative to known point(s), or (*fig.*) with the details of the situation.—*n.* **o'riency**, orient quality.—*adj.* **oriental, Oriental** (*-ent'əl*), eastern: pertaining to, in, or from the east: orient.—*n.* a native of the east: an Asiatic.—*v.t.* **orient'alise, -ize**.—*ns.* **Orient'alism**, an eastern expression, custom, etc.: scholarship in eastern languages; **Orient'alist**, one versed in eastern languages: an oriental; **orientality** (*-al'i-ti*).—*adv.* **orient'ally**.—*v.t.* **o'rientāte**, to orient.—*v.i.* to face the east: to be oriented.—*ns.* **orientā'tion**, the act of orienting or orientating: the state of being oriented: determination or consciousness of relative direction: assumption of definite direction in response to stimulus; **o'rientātor**, an instrument for orientating.—*adjs.* **o'riented** (or *-ent'*), **o'rientated**, directed (towards); often used in composition as second element of *adj.*: normally

aware of the elements of one's situation—time, place, persons (*psychiatry*; *also fig.*).—*n.* **orienteer'ing**, the sport of making one's way quickly across difficult country with the help of map and compass.—**oriental alabaster**, onyx-marble; **oriental amethyst, emerald, topaz**, varieties of corundum resembling amethyst, emerald, topaz; **oriental ruby**, the true ruby, a variety of corundum; **Oriental Region**, Southern Asia and its islands from the Persian Gulf to Wallace's Line; **oriental turquoise**, true turquoise; **orientation table**, an indicator of tabular form for showing the direction of various objects—mountains and the like. [L. *oriēns, -entis*, pr.p. of *orīrī*, to rise.]

**orifice**, *or'i-fis*, *n.* a mouth-like opening, esp. small.—*n.* **or'ifex** (*Shak.*), an orifice.—*adj.* **orificial** (*-fish'əl*). [Fr.,—L. *ōrificium—ōs, ōris*, mouth, *facĕre*, to make.]

**oriflamme**, *or'i-flam*, *n.* a little banner of red silk split into many points, borne on a gilt staff—the ancient royal standard of France. [Fr.,—L.L. *auriflamma*—L. *aurum*, gold, and *flamma*, flame.]

**origami**, *or-i-gäm'ē*, *n.* Japanese art of folding paper so as to make animal forms, etc.

**Origanum**, *or-ig'ə-nəm*, *n.* the marjoram genus of labiates: (without *cap.*) any of various aromatic herbs, of this or other genus, used in cookery.—*n.* **or'igan(e)** (*-gan*), marjoram, esp. wild marjoram. See also **oregano**. [L. *origanum*—Gr. *origanon*.]

**Origenist**, *or'i-jən-ist*, *n.* a follower of *Origen* (*c.* A.D. 185-254) in his allegorical method of scriptural interpretation, or his theology, esp. his heresies—the subordination though eternal generation of the Logos, pre-existence of all men, and universal restoration, even of the Devil.—*n.* **Or'igenism**.—*adj.* **Origenist'ic**.

**origin**, *or'i-jin*, *n.* the rising or first existence of anything: that from which anything first proceeds: the fixed starting-point or point from which measurement is made (*math.*): source: derivation.—*adj.* **orig'inal**, pertaining to the origin or beginning: existing from or at the beginning: being such from the beginning: innate: standing in relation of source: not derived, copied, imitated, or translated from anything else: originative: novel: originating or having the power to originate in oneself: creative: independent in invention: odd in character.—*n.* origin: that which is not itself, or of which something else is, a copy, imitation, or translation: a real person, place, etc., serving as model for one in fiction: an inhabitant, member, etc., from the beginning: a person of marked individuality or oddity: (in *pl.*, *Milt.*) original elements.—*n.* **original'ity**.—*adv.* **orig'inally**.—*v.t.* **orig'inate**, to give origin to: to bring into existence.—*v.i.* to have origin: to begin.—*n.* **originā'tion**.—*adj.* **orig'inātive**, having power to originate or bring into existence: originating.—*n.* **orig'inātor**.—**original sin**, innate depravity and corruption held to be transmitted to Adam's descendants in consequence of his sin. [L. *origō, -inis—orīrī*, to rise.]

**orillion**, *o-ril'yən*, *n.* a semicircular projection at the shoulder of a bastion intended to cover the guns and defenders on the flank. [Fr. *orillon—oreille*, an ear—L. *auricula*, dim. of *auris*, ear.]

**oriole**, *ōr'i-ōl*, *ör'*, *n.* a golden yellow bird (*Oriolus galbula*, the **golden oriole, loriot**), with black wings, or other member of the genus or of the Old World family **Oriol'idae**, related to the crows: in America applied to birds of the Icteridae (see **Baltimore**). [O.Fr. *oriol*—L. *aureolus*, dim. of *aureus*, golden—*aurum*, gold.]

**Orion**, *ə-, o-, ö-ri'ən*, (*astron.*) *n.* a constellation containing seven very bright stars, three of which form Orion's belt. [*Ōriōn*, a giant hunter slain by Artemis.]

orison, *or'i-zən, n.* a prayer. [O.Fr. *orison* (Fr. *oraison*)—L. *ōrātiō, -ōnis*—*ōrāre,* to pray.]

Oriya, *ō-rē'yə, ö-, n.* the language of Orissa in India, closely akin to Bengali: a member of the people speaking it.—Also *adj.*

orle, *örl, (her.) n.* a border within a shield at a short distance from the edge: a number of small charges set as a border. [O.Fr., border, from a dim. formed from L. *ōra,* border.]

orleans, *ör'li-ənz, n.* a fabric of cotton warp and worsted weft.—*n.* Or'leanist, a supporter of the family of the Duke of Orleans, brother of Louis XIV, as claimants to the throne of France.—Also *adj.*—*n.* Or'leanism. [*Orléans,* a city in France.]

orlop, *ör'lop, n.* the lowest deck in a ship, a covering to the hold. [Du. *overloop,* covering.]

ormer, *ör'mər, n.* an earshell or sea-ear, esp. the edible *Haliotis tuberculata,* common in the Channel Islands. [Channel Island Fr. *ormer* (Fr. *ormier*) for *oreille de mer,* sea ear.]

ormolu, *ör'mo-lōō, n.* an alloy of copper, zinc, and sometimes tin: gilt or bronzed metallic ware: gold-leaf prepared for gilding bronze, etc. [Fr. *or*—L. *aurum,* gold, and Fr. *moulu,* pa.p. of *moudre,* to grind—L. *molēre,* to grind.]

Ormuzd, Ormazd, *ör'muzd, n.* the chief god of the ancient Persians, the creator and lord of the whole universe: later, the good principle, as opposed to *Ahriman,* the bad. [Pers. *Ahura-Mazdāh,* the Living God or Lord (*ahu,* the living, life, or spirit, root *ah,* to be), the Great Creator (*maz, dā,* or the Wise One).]

ornament, *ör'nə-mənt, n.* anything meant to add grace or beauty or to bring credit: additional beauty: a mark of honour: (usu. in *pl.*) articles used in the services of the church (*Pr. Bk.*).—*v.t.* (*ör-nə-ment', ör'nə-ment*) to adorn: to furnish with ornaments.—*adj.* ornament'al, serving to adorn: decorative, pleasantly striking in dress and general appearance.—*n.* a plant grown for ornament or beauty.—*adv.* ornament'ally.—*ns.* ornamentā'tion, act or art of ornamenting: ornamental work; ornament'er; ornament'ist. [Fr. *ornement*—L. *ornāmentum*—*ornāre,* to adorn.]

ornate, *ör-nāt', ör'nāt, adj.* decorated: much or elaborately ornamented.—*adv.* ornate'ly (or *ör'*).—*n.* ornate'ness. [L. *ornāre, -ātum,* to adorn.]

ornery, *ör'nə-ri, adj.* an American illit. form of ordinary.

ornis, *ör'nis, n.* the birds collectively of a region, its avifauna.—*adj.* ornithic (*ör-nith'ik*), relating to birds.—*ns.* ornithichnite (*ör-nith-ik'nit*; Gr. *ichnos,* track), a fossil footprint of a bird.—*n.pl.* Ornithodel'phia (Gr. *delphys,* womb), the Prototheria or Monotremata—from the ornithic character of the urogenital organs.—*adjs.* ornithodel'phian (also *n.*), ornithodel'phic, ornithodel'phous.—*ns.* Ornithogaea (*-ni-thō-jē'a*; Gr. *gaia,* land), the New Zealand biological region; Ornithog'alum (Gr. *ornithogalon,* star-of-Bethlehem), a large genus of herbs of the family Liliaceae.—*adjs.* ornithoid (*ör'nith-oid*; Gr. *eidos,* form), bird-like; ornitholog'ical.—*adv.* ornitholog'ically.—*ns.* ornithol'ogist; ornithol'ogy, the study of birds; ornithomancy (*ör-ni'thō-man-si, ör'nith-ō-*; Gr. *manteiā,* divination), divination by means of birds, by observing their flight, etc.—*adj.* ornithoman'tic.—*n.* ornithomorph (*ör-ni'thō-mörf, ör'nith-ō-mörf*; Gr. *morphē,* form), a figure or design in the form of a bird.—*adjs.* ornithomorph'ic; ornithoph'ilous (Gr. *phileein,* to love), bird-pollinated.—*ns.* ornithoph'ily; ornithopter (*-op'tər*; Gr. *pteron,* wing), a flying-machine with flapping wings; Ornithorhynchus (*-ō-ring'kəs*; Gr. *rhynchos,* snout), the duckbill; ornithosaur (*ör-ni'thō-sör*; Gr. *sauros,* lizard), a pterodactyl; ornithoscopy (*-os'ka-pi*; Gr. *skopeein,* to view), augury by observation

of birds; ornitho'sis, psittacosis. [Gr. *ornis, ornithos,* a bird.]

Orobanche, *or-ō-bang'kē, n.* the broom-rape genus of dicotyledons, giving name to the family Orobanchā'ceae, root-parasites without green leaves.—*adj.* orobanchā'ceous. [Gr. *orobanchē,* dodder, also broom-rape—*orobos,* bitter vetch, *anchein,* to strangle.]

orogenesis, *or-ō-jen'i-sis, n.* mountain-building.—*adjs.* orogenet'ic, orogen'ic. [Gr. *oros,* mountain, *genesis,* production.]

orography, *or-og'rə-fi, n.* the description of mountains—also oreography (*or-i-og'*).—*adjs.* or(e)ographic (*-graf'ik*), -al.—*ns.* orology, oreology (*or-i-ol'*), the scientific study of mountains.—*adjs.* or(e)olog'ical.—*ns.* or(e)ol'ogist. [Gr. *oros, -eos,* mountain, *graphein,* to write, *logos,* discourse.]

oroide, *ō'rō-id, ö', n.* an alloy of copper and zinc or tin, etc., imitating gold.—*n.* o'rēide, a similar or identical alloy. [Fr. *or*—L. *aurum,* gold, Gr. *eidos,* form.]

orology, etc. See orography.

oropesa, *or-ō-pē'zə, -pā'sə, n.* a fish-shaped float used in marine mine-sweeping to support the sweeping wire. [From the name of a trawler.]

orotund, *o', ö'rō-tund, adj.* full and round in utterance: pompously mouthed or mouthing.—Also o'rorotund.—*ns.* o(ro)rotund'ity. [L. *ōs, ōris,* mouth, *rotundus,* round; see ore rotundo in Appendices.]

orphan, *ör'fən, n.* one bereft of father or mother, or (usually) of both.—Also *adj.*—*v.t.* to make an orphan.—*ns.* or'phanage, the state of being an orphan: a house for orphans; or'phanhood, or'phanism.—*n.* or'phan-asy'lum. [Gr. *orphanos,* akin to L. *orbus,* bereaved.]

orpharion, *ör-fa-ri'on, ör-fā'ri-on, n.* a large lutelike instrument with six to nine pairs of metal strings.—Also orpheō'reon. [*Orpheus, Ariōn,* mythical musicians.]

Orpheus, *ör'fūs, n.* a mythical Thracian musician and poet who could move inanimate objects by the music of his lyre, founder or interpreter of the ancient mysteries.—*adjs.* Orphē'an, pertaining to Orpheus; Or'phic, pertaining to the mysteries associated with Orpheus: esoteric.—*n.* Or'phism, the system taught in the Orphic mysteries: an early 20th-cent. style of abstract art using brilliant colour—also Orphic Cubism.—Orpheus harmonica, the panharmonicon.

orphrey, *ör'fri, n.* gold or other rich embroidery, esp. bordering a vestment. [O.Fr. *orfreis*—L. *auriphrygium,* Phrygian gold.]

orpiment, *ör'pi-mənt, n.* a yellow mineral, arsenic trisulphide, used as a pigment. [O.Fr.,—L. *auripigmentum*—*aurum,* gold, *pigmentum,* paint.]

orpine, orpin, *ör'pin, n.* a purple-flowered, broadleaved stonecrop. [Fr. *orpin.*]

Orpington, *ör'ping-tən, n.* a breed of poultry (white, black, or buff). [*Orpington* in W. Kent, where it took rise.]

orra, *or'a, -ə, (Scot.) adj.* odd: not matched: left over: occasional, casual: supernumerary: worthless.—orra man, a farm-worker kept to do any odd job that may occur. [Origin unknown.]

orrery, *or'ər-i, n.* a clockwork model of the solar system. [From Charles Boyle, fourth Earl of *Orrery* (1676-1731), for whom one was made.]

orris, *or'is, n.* the Florentine or other iris: its dried rootstock (orr'is-root), smelling of violets, used in perfumery. [Perh. iris.]

orris, *or'is, n.* a peculiar kind of gold or silver lace: upholsterers' galloon and gimp. [Perh. O.Fr. *orfreis;* see orphrey.]

orseille, *ör-sāl',* same as archil, orchil.—*adj.* orsell'ic. [Fr.]

ort, *ört, n.* a fragment, esp. one left from a meal—usually *pl.* [Cf. Low Ger. *ort,* refuse of fodder.]

ortanique, *ör'tan-ēk, n.* a cross between the

orange and the tangerine, or its fruit. [Portmanteau word and suff. *-ique*.]
**orthian,** *örth'i-ən, adj.* high-pitched. [Gr. *orthios*.]
**orthicon,** *örth'i-kon, n.* a television camera tube more sensitive than the earlier iconoscope; a further development is the **image orthicon**. [*ortho-, iconoscope*.]
**ortho-,** *ör-thō-,* in composition, straight: upright: perpendicular: right: genuine: derived from an acid anhydride by combination with the largest number of water molecules (distinguished from *meta-*; *chem.*): having substituted atoms or groups attached to two adjacent carbon atoms of the benzene ring (distinguished from *meta-* and *para-* —in this sense commonly represented by *o-*; *chem.*).— *n.* and *adj.* **or'tho,** a contraction for **orthochromatic** (**plate**).—*ns.* **orthoax'is**(*crystal.*), the orthodiagonal; **orthobo'-rate,** a salt of **orthobo'ric acid,** boric acid; **orthocaine** (*-kā'in, -kān*), a white crystalline substance used as a local anaesthetic; **or'thocentre,** the point of intersection of the altitudes of a triangle; **Orthoceras** (*ör-thos'ə-ras*; Gr. *keras,* horn), a genus of fossil cephalopods with straight shell.—*adj.* **orthochromat'ic** (Gr. *chrōma,* colour), correct in rendering the relation of colours, without the usual photographic modifications.—*ns.* **or'thoclase** (*-klās, -klāz*; Gr. *klasis,* fracture), common or potash feldspar, monoclinic, with cleavages at right angles; **or'tho-compound;** **or'thocousins,** children of two sisters or of two brothers; **orthodiag'onal,** in a monoclinic crystal, that lateral axis which is perpendicular to the vertical axis; **orthodontia** (*-don'shi-ə*; Gr. *odous, odontos,* tooth), rectification of abnormalities in the teeth. Also **orthodont'ics.**—*adj.* **orthodont'ic.**—*n.* **orthodont'ist.**—*adj.* **or'thodox** (Gr. *doxa,* opinion), sound in doctrine: believing, or according to, the received or established doctrines or opinions, esp. in religion: (*cap.*) of the Eastern Church.—*n.* **or'thodoxy.**—*adj.* **orthodrom'ic** (Gr. *dromos,* a course, run).—*n.* **orthod'romy,** great-circle sailing.—Also **orthodrom'ics.**—*adjs.* **orthoepic** (*-ep'ik*; Gr. *epos,* a word), **orthoep'ical.**—*ns.* **orthō'epist; orthō'epy,** correct pronunciation; **orthogen'esis** (Gr. *genesis,* generation), the evolution of organisms systematically in definite directions and not accidentally in many directions: determinate variation.—*adjs.* **orthogenet'ic,** relating to orthogenesis; **orthogen'ic,** orthogenetic: concerning the treatment of mentally and emotionally disturbed children.— *n.* **orthogen'ics.**—*adjs.* **orthognath'ic, orthog'nathous** (Gr. *gnathos,* jaw), having a lower jaw that neither protrudes nor recedes.—*n.* **orthog'nathism.** —*adj.* **orthog'onal** (Gr. *gōniā,* angle), right-angled (**orthogonal projection,** projection by lines perpendicular to the plane of projection).—*adv.* **orthog'-onally.**—*ns.* **or'thograph,** a drawing in orthographic projection, esp. of the elevation of a building; **orthog'rapher,** one skilled in orthography: a speller.—*adjs.* **orthograph'ic, -al,** pertaining or according to spelling: spelt correctly: in perspective projection, having the point of sight at infinity.—*adv.* **orthograph'ically.**—*ns.* **orthog'-raphist,** an orthographer; **orthog'raphy** (Gr. *orthographiā,* spelling, elevation—*graphein,* to write), the art or practice of spelling words correctly: spelling: orthographic projection: apparently for orthographer (Shak., *Much Ado*). —*adjs.* **orthopae'dic, -al, orthopē'dic, -al,**—*ns.* **orthopaedics, orthopēdics** (*-pē'diks*; Gr. *pais, paidos,* a child), the art or process of curing deformities arising from disease or injury of bones, esp. in childhood—also **or'thopaedy, or'thopēdy**—formerly **orthopedi'a** (or *-pēd'*); **orthopae'dist, -pē'dist; orthophos'phate,** an ordinary phosphate.—*adj.* **orthophosphor'ic.**—*n.* **orthophyre** (*-fīr; ortho*clase por*phyry*), a fine-

grained syenitic rock with orthoclase crystals.— *adj.* **orthophyric** (*-fir'ik*).—*ns.* **orthopin'akoid,** in monoclinic crystals, a form consisting of two faces parallel to the orthodiagonal and the vertical axis; **orthopnoea** (*-thop-nē'ə*; Gr. *orthopnoia—pneein,* to breathe), a condition in which one can only breathe when upright; **or'thopraxis, -praxy,** correct, orthodox practice esp. in religion (see **praxis**); **or'thoprism,** in monoclinic crystals, a form parallel to the orthodiagonal; **or'thopsychiatry,** the branch of psychiatry concerned with prevention and correction of incipient mental illness.—*n.pl.* **Orthop'tera** (Gr. *pteron,* wing), the cockroach order of insects with firm fore-wings serving as covers to the fan-wise folded hind-wings.—*n.* and *adj.* **orthop'teran.**—*ns.* **orthop'terist, orthopterol'ogist,** a student of the Orthoptera; **orthopterol'ogy.**—*adjs.* **orthop'teroid; orthop'terous,** pertaining to the Orthoptera; **orthop'tic** (Gr. *optikos,* optic), relating to normal vision.—*ns.* **orthop'tics,** the treatment of defective eyesight by exercises and visual training; **orthop'tist.**— *adjs.* **orthorhom'bic** (Gr. *rhombos,* rhomb; *crystal.*), referable to three unequal axes at right angles to each other; **orthoscop'ic** (Gr. *skopeein,* to look at), having or giving correct vision, true proportion, or a flat field of view.—*n.* **orthosil'-icate,** a salt of **orthosilicic** (*-sil-is'ik*) **acid,** $H_4SiO_4$.—*adjs.* **orthostat'ic** (Gr. *orthostatos—statos,* standing), standing erect: connected with the erect posture; **orthos'tichous** (Gr. *stichos,* a row), arranged in vertical rows.—*ns.* **orthos'tichy,** a straight row, as of leaves vertically over one another on an axis; **orthotonē'sis** (Gr. *tonos,* accent), accentuation of a proclitic or enclitic— opp. to *enclisis*.—*adjs.* **orthoton'ic,** taking an accent in certain positions but not in others— also **or'thotone; orthotrop'ic** (Gr. *tropos,* a turn), manifesting orthotropism: (of a material, as wood) having elastic properties varying in different planes.—*ns.* **orthot'ropism,** growth in the direct line of stimulus, esp. of gravity; **orthot'ropy** (of a material, as wood), the state of being orthotropic.—*adj.* **orthot'ropous,** (of an ovule) straight, having the nucellus in direct continuation of the funicle. [Gr. *orthos,* straight, upright, right.]
**orthros,** *ör'thros, n.* one of the Greek canonical hours, corresponding to the Western lauds. [Gr. *orthros,* dawn.]
**ortolan,** *ör'ta-lan, n.* a kind of bunting, common in Europe, and considered a great table delicacy. [Fr.,—It. *ortolano*—L. *hortulānus,* belonging to gardens—*hortulus,* dim. of *hortus,* a garden.]
**orval,** *ör'val,* (*obs.*) *n.* clary. [Cf. Fr. *orvale*.]
**Orvieto,** *ör-vyā'tō, n.* a white wine from *Orvieto* in Italy.—*n.* **Orvietan** (*ör-vi-ē'tan*), a supposed antidote to poison ascribed to an Orvieto man.
**oryctology,** *or-ik-tol'a-ji,* (*obs.*) *n.* mineralogy: palaeontology. [Gr. *oryktos,* dug, quarried.]
**Oryx,** *or'iks, n.* an African genus of antelopes. [Gr. *oryx, -ygos,* a pick-axe, an oryx antelope.]
**Oryza,** *ö-, ō-ri'za, n.* a tropical genus of grasses, including rice. [Gr. *oryza*.]
**os,** *os,* (L.) a bone.
**Osage,** *ō-sāj', n.* an Indian of a tribe living in Oklahoma, etc.—*adj.* **O'sage.**—**O'sage orange,** a hedge-tree (*Maclura*) of the mulberry family, first found in the Osage country: its orange-like inedible fruit.
**Oscan,** *os'kən, n.* one of an ancient Italic people in southern Italy: their language akin to Latin.— also *adj.*
**Oscar,** *os'kər, n.* a gold-plated statuette awarded by the American Academy of Motion Picture Arts and Sciences to a film writer, actor, director, etc., for the year's best performance in his particular line: any similar award. [Name fortuitously given.]

**oscheal**, *os'ki-əl, adj.* pertaining to the scrotum. [Gr. *oscheon*, scrotum.]

**oscillate**, *os'il-āt, v.i.* to swing to and fro like a pendulum: to vibrate: to radiate electromagnetic waves: to vary between certain limits: to fluctuate.—*v.t.* to cause to swing or vibrate.—*adj.* **osc'illating**.—*n.* **oscilla'tion**.—*adj.* **osc'illative**, having a tendency to vibrate: vibratory. —*n.* **osc'illātor**, one who oscillates: apparatus for producing oscillations.—*adj.* **oscillatory** (*os'il-ə-tə-ri*), swinging: moving as a pendulum does: vibratory.—*ns.* **oscill'ogram**, a record made by an oscillograph; **oscill'ograph**, an apparatus for producing a curve representing a number of electrical and mechanical phenomena which vary cyclically; **oscill'oscope**, an instrument which shows on a fluorescent screen the variation with time of the instantaneous values and waveforms of electrical quantities, including voltages translated from sounds or movements. [L. *ōscillāre, -ātum, to swing*,]

**Oscines**, *os'i-nēz, n.pl.* the song-birds, forming the main body of the Passeriformes.—*adj.* **osc'inine** or (faultily formed) **osc'ine**. [L. *oscen, oscinis,* a singing-bird.]

**oscitancy**, *os'i-tən-si, n.* yawning: sleepiness: stupidity.—*adj.* **osc'itant.**—*adv.* **osc'itantly.**—*v.i.* **osc'itate**, to yawn.—*n.* **oscitā'tion**, yawning: sleepiness. [L. *ōscitāre,* to yawn.]

**osculant**, *os'kū-lənt, adj.* kissing: adhering closely: intermediate between two genera, species, etc., linking (*biol.*).—*adj.* **os'cular**, pertaining to the mouth or osculum, or to kissing: osculating.—*v.t.* **os'culāte**, to kiss: to have three or more coincident points in common with (*math.*).—*v.i.* to be in close contact: to form a connecting-link.—*n.* **osculā'tion**.—*adj.* **os'culatory**, of or pertaining to kissing or osculation.—*n.* a carved tablet kissed by the priest and (now rarely) by the people at mass.—*ns.* **os'cule**, a little mouth: a small mouthlike aperture; **os'culum**, an exhalant aperture in a sponge: a sucker on a tapeworm's head. [L. *ōsculāri, -ātus—ōsculum,* a little mouth, a kiss, dim. of *ōs,* mouth.]

**oshac**, *ō'shak, n.* the ammoniac plant. [Ar. *ushshaq.*]

**osier**, *ōzh'(y)ər, ōz'i-ər, ōz'yər, n.* any willow whose twigs are used in making baskets, esp. *Salix viminalis.*—*adj.* made of or like osiers.—*adj.* **o'siered**, covered or fringed with osiers: twisted like osiers.—*n.* **o'siery**, osier-work.—**o'sier-bed**, a place where osiers grow. [Fr. *osier* of unknown origin; there is a L.L. *ausāria* or *osāria,* willow-bed.]

**Osiris**, *ō-si'ris, n.* the greatest of Egyptian gods, son of Seb and Nut, or Heaven and Earth, husband of Isis, father of Horus.—*adj.* **Osi'rian**. [Gr. *Osiris.*]

**Osmanli**, *os-man'li, adj.* of the dynasty of *Osmān,* who founded the Turkish empire in Asia, and reigned 1288-1326: of the Turkish empire: of the western branch of the Turks or their language. —*n.* a member of the dynasty: a Turk of Turkey. [Cf. **Ottoman**.]

**osmeterium**, *os-mē-tē'ri-əm,* or *oz-, n.* a forked process behind the head of certain caterpillars giving out a foul smell:—*pl.* **osmetē'ria**. [Gr. *osmē,* smell, stink, and suff. *-tērion,* denoting instrument.]

**osmidrosis**, *os-mi-drō'sis,* or *oz-, n.* the secretion of ill-smelling sweat. [Gr. *osmē,* smell, *hidrōs,* sweat.]

**osmium**, *oz', os'mi-əm, n.* a grey-coloured metal (Os; atomic number 76), the heaviest substance known, whose tetroxide has a disagreeable smell.—*ns.* **os'mate, os'miate**, a salt of the hypothetical osmic acid.—*adjs.* **os'mic**, containing osmium in higher valency; **os'mious, os'mous**, containing osmium in lower valency.—*n.* **osmirid'ium**, iridosmine.—**osmic acid**, strictly, a

supposed acid $H_2OsO_4$: usually, osmium tetroxide, an ill-smelling substance used as a stain for fats in microscope work. [Gr. *osmē,* smell.]

**osmosis**, *os-mō'sis,* or *oz-, n.* diffusion of liquids through a porous septum.—Also **os'mose.**—*v.t.* and *v.i.* **osmose'**, to (cause to) undergo osmosis.— *n.* **osmom'eter**, an apparatus for measuring osmotic pressure.—*adj.* **osmotic** (*-mot'ik*).—*adv.* **osmot'ically**. [Gr. *ōsmos* = *ōthismos,* impulse— *ōtheein,* to push.]

**Osmunda**, *os-mun'da, n.* a genus including the royal fern, giving name to a family **Osmundā'ceae**. [Origin unknown.]

**osnaburg**, *oz'nə-bûrg, n.* a coarse linen, originally brought from *Osnabrück* in Germany: a coarse cotton.—Also *adj.*

**osprey**, *os'pri, -prā, n.* a bird of prey (*Pandion haliaetus*) that feeds on fish: an egret or other plume used in millinery, not from the osprey. [Supposed to be from L. *ossifraga,* misapplied; see **ossifrage**.]

**osseous**, *os'i-əs, adj.* bony: composed of, or like, bone: of the nature or structure of bone.—*ns.* **ossā'rium**, an ossuary; **ossein** (*os'i-in*), the organic basis of bone; **osselet** (*os'ə-let, os'let*), a hard substance growing on the inside of a horse's knee; **oss'icle**, a little bone or bone-like plate.— *adjs.* **ossic'ular; ossif'erous**, yielding or containing bones; **ossif'ic.**—*n.* **ossifica'tion**, the process or state of being changed into a bony substance.—*v.t.* **oss'ify**, to make into bone or into a bone-like substance.—*v.i.* to become bone: —*pr.p.* **oss'ifying**; *pa.t.* and *pa.p.* **oss'ified.**—*adj.* **ossiv'orous**, feeding on or consuming bones. [L. *os, ossis,* bone.]

**osseter**, *os-et'ər, n.* a species of sturgeon. [Russ. *osetr.*]

**ossia**, *ō-sē'a,* (It.) or (giving an alternative in music).

**Ossian**, *os', osh'i-ən, n.* a legendary Gaelic poet whose poems James Macpherson professed to translate.—*adjs.* **Ossianesque** (*-esk'*), in the manner of Macpherson's Ossian; **Ossianic** (*-an'ik*), relating to Ossian or to Macpherson's publications. [Gael. *Oisin.*]

**ossifrage**, *os'i-frāj, n.* the lammergeier: the osprey: the bald eagle (*U.S.*).—*n.* **ossifraga** (*os-if'rə-gə*), the giant fulmar. [L. *ossifraga,* prob. the lammergeier—*os, ossis,* bone, and the root of *frangēre,* to break.]

**ossuary**, *os'ū-ə-ri, n.* a bone-house or charnel-house: a bone-urn. [L. *ossuārium—os,* bone.]

**ostensible**, *os-tens'i-bl, adj.* that may be shown (*obs.*): outwardly showing or professed.—*n.* **ostensibil'ity.**—*adv.* **ostens'ibly.**—*adj.* **ostens'ive**, showing: deictic: ostensible.—*adv.* **ostens'ively.** —*ns.* **osten'sory**, a monstrance; **ostent'**, appearance (*Shak.*): portent: ostentation; **ostentā'tion** (*-tən-*), act of showing: display to draw attention or admiration: boasting.—*adj.* **ostentā'tious**, given to show: fond of self-display: showy.— *adv.* **ostentā'tiously.**—*n.* **ostentā'tiousness**. [L. *ostendēre, ostēnsum* (*ostentum*), to show, and its freq. **ostentāre**—pfx. *obs-*, in front, *tendēre,* to stretch.]

**oste(o)-**, *os-ti(-ō)-*, in composition, bone.—*adj.* **osteal** (*os'ti-əl*), relating to bone: sounding like bone on percussion.—*ns.* **osteitis** (*os-ti-i'tis*), inflammation of a bone; **osteo-arthri'tis**, a form of arthritis in which the cartilages of the joint and the bone adjacent are worn away; **os'teoblast** (Gr. *blastos,* a shoot), a bone-forming cell; **osteoclasis** (*os-ti-ok'lə-sis*; Gr. *klasis,* fracture), fracture of a bone for correction of a deformity: absorption and destruction of bone tissue by osteoclasts; **os'teoclast**, a surgical instrument for fracturing bone: a bone-destroying cell; **osteocoll'a** (Gr. *kolla,* glue), a calcareous incrustation on roots, etc., once thought able to unite broken bones; os'teoderm (Gr. *derma*, skin), a bony dermal plate.—*adjs.* osteoderm'al, -derm'atous, osteoderm'ic, -derm'ous.—*ns.* osteogen'esis, osteo'geny, formation of bone.—*adjs.* osteogenet'ic, osteogen'ic, osteo'genous.—*n.pl.* Osteoglossidae (-*glos'i-dē*; Gr. *glōssa*, tongue), a family of bony fishes, including the arapaima. —*n.* osteog'raphy, description of bones.—*adj.* ost'eoid, bone-like.—*n.* Osteol'epis (Gr. *lepis*, scale), an Old Red Sandstone fossil fish with bone-like scales.—*adj.* osteolog'ical.—*ns.* osteol'ogist; osteol'ogy, the study of bones, part of anatomy; osteomalacia (-*ma-lā'shi-ə*; Gr. *malakos*, soft), softening of bones by absorption of their calcium salts, attributed to deficiency of vitamin D; osteomyelitis (-*mi-ə-lī'tis*; Gr. *myelos*, marrow), inflammation of bone and bone-marrow; os'teopath (-*path*), osteop'athist (-*ə-thist*), a practitioner of osteopathy.—*adj.* osteopathic (ost-*i-ō-path'ik*).—*ns.* osteop'athy, a system of healing or treatment consisting largely of massage and manipulation; os'teophyte (-*fīt*; Gr. *phyton*, plant), an abnormal bony outgrowth.—*adjs.* osteophytic (-*fit'ik*); osteoplast'ic.—*ns.* os'teoplasty, a plastic operation by which a loss of bone is remedied; osteoporo'sis (root as pore (1)), development of a porous structure in bone; os'teotome (Gr. *tomos*, cutting; *surg.*), an instrument for cutting bones; osteot'omy, the surgical cutting of a bone. [Gr. *osteon*, bone.]

ostinato, *os-tin-ä'tō*, (*mus.*) *n.* a ground-bass. [It.; root as obstinate.]

ostium, *os'ti-əm*, *n.* the mouth of a river: a mouth-like opening:—*pl.* os'tia.—*adj.* os'tial.—*n.* os'tiary, a doorkeeper: in the Roman Catholic Church, a member of the lowest of the minor orders: a river-mouth (*obs.*).—*adjs.* os'tiate, having an ostium or ostia; os'tiolate, having an opening.—*n.* os'tiole, a small opening. [L. *ostium*.]

ostler, hostler, *os'lər*, one who attends to horses at an inn:—*fem.* ost'leress. [hosteler.]

Ostmen, *ōst'men*, *n.pl.* the Danish settlers in Ireland. [O.N. *Austmenn*, Eastmen.]

-ostomy. The combining element is properly -stomy (*q.v.*).

ostrakon, ostracon, *os'trə-kon*, *n.* a potsherd or tile, esp. one used in ostracism in Greece or for writing on in ancient Egypt:—*pl.* os'traka, -ca. —*adjs.* octracean (os-*trā'shan*), ostrā'ceous, of the nature of an oyster.—*n.* Ostracion (os-*trā'shi-on*), the coffer-fish genus.—*v.t.* os'tracise, -ize (-*siz*), in ancient Greece, to banish by the vote of the people written on potsherds: to exclude from society, or from one's social group. —*ns.* os'tracism (-*sizm*), banishment by ostracising: expulsion from society; os'tracod, a member of the Ostracō'da, a class of minute crustacea with bivalve shells; os'tracoderm (Gr. *derma*, skin), any member (as *Cephalaspis*) of a group of Silurian and Old Red Sandstone fishes or fish-like animals, generally cased in bony armour with undeveloped lower jaw, with flippers but not ordinary paired fins. [Gr. *ostrakon*, a shell, tile, potsherd.]

Ostrea, *os'tri-a*, *n.* the oyster genus.—*adj.* ostreā'-ceous.—*ns.* ostreicul'ture (*os-trē-i-*), oyster-culture; os'treicul'turist.—*adj.* ostreophagous (*os-tri-of'ə-gəs*; Gr. *phagein*, to eat), oyster-eating.—*ns.* os'treophage (-*fāj*), an oyster-eater; ostreoph'agy (-*ə-ji*), oyster-eating. [L. *ostrea*— Gr. *ostreon*, oyster.]

ostreger, *os'tri-jər*. Same as austringer.

ostreophagous, etc. See Ostrea.

ostrich, *os'trich*, -*trij*, *n.* the largest living bird (*Struthio*), found in Africa, remarkable for its speed in running, and prized for its feathers.— *n.* os'trichism (*fig.*), the habit or policy of ignoring and refusing to face unpleasant facts.—*adj.* and *adv.* os'trich-like (usu. in reference to the

supposed habit of hiding its head when in danger).—os'trich-egg'; os'trich-farm'; os'trich-feath'er. [O.Fr. *ostruche* (Fr. *autruche*)—L. *avis*, bird, L.L. *struthiō*—Gr. *strouthiōn*, an ostrich, *strouthos*, a bird.]

Ostrogoth, *os'trō-goth*, *n.* an eastern Goth—one of the tribe of east Goths who established their power in Italy in 493, and were overthrown in 555.—*adj.* Os'trogothic.

Ostyak, Ostiak, *os'ti-ak*, *n.* a member of a Ugrian people of Siberia: their language.—Also *adj.*

otalgia, *ō-tal'ji-ə*, *n.* earache—also otal'gy. [Gr. *ous*, *ōtos*, ear, *algē*, pain.]

otary, *ō'tə-ri*, *n.* a sea-lion or sea-bear, a seal with external ears:—*pl.* o'taries.—*adj.* ot'arine. [Gr. *ōtaros*, large-eared—*ous*, *ōtos*, ear.]

other, *udh'ər*, *adj.* orig., one of two: second: alternate: different: different from or not the same as the one in question (often with *than*): not the same: remaining: additional: left (*prob.*; *Spens.*).—*pron.* (or *n.*) other one: another: each other (*arch.* and *Scot.*).—*adv.* otherwise.—*adj.* oth'erguess (see othergates).—*n.* oth'erness.—*advs.* oth'erwhere, elsewhere; other'-while, oth'erwhiles, at other times: sometimes; oth'erwise, in another way or manner: by other causes: in other respects: under other conditions.—*conj.* else: under other conditions.—*n.* oth'erworld, a world other than, better than, or beyond this.—Also *adj.*—*adj.* oth'erworld'ish.— *n.* otherworld'liness.—*adj.* otherworld'ly, concerned with the world to come, or with the world of the imagination, to the exclusion of practical interests.—every other, each alternate; rather ... than otherwise, rather than not; someone (something) or other, an undefined person or thing; the other day, etc., on an unspecified day, etc., not long past. [O.E. *ōther*; cf. Ger. *ander*, L. *alter*.]

othergates, *udh'ər-gātz*, (*obs.*) *adv.* in another way. —*adj.* of another kind.—Also oth'erguess (in *Fielding*, *Goldsmith*, etc., anotherguess).—Also spelt as separate words—other gates, other guess. [other, and gen. of gate (way).]

otic, *ō'tik*, *adj.* of or pertaining to the ear.—*ns.* oti'tis, inflammation of the ear; otocyst (*ō'tō-sist*), an auditory or equilibristic vesicle; ot'olith (Gr. *lithos*, stone), a calcareous concretion in the ear of various animals: an ear-bone; otol'ogist-otol'ogy, knowledge of the ear; otorhinolaryngology (-*ri-nō-lar-ing-gol'ə-ji*; Gr. *rhīs*, *rhinos*, nose, *larynx*, -*yngos*, larynx), knowledge of ear, nose, and larynx and their diseases; otorrhoea (*ō-tō-rē'ə*; Gr. *rhoiā*, flow), a discharge from the ear; otosclero'sis, formation of spongy bone in the capsule of the labyrinth; o'toscope, an instrument for examining the ear. [Gr. *ous*, *ōtos*, ear.]

otiose, *ō'shi-ōs*, *adj.* unoccupied: indolent: functionless: futile: superfluous.—*n.* otiosity (-*os'i-ti*), ease, idleness. [L. *ōtiōsus*—*ōtium*, leisure.]

-otomy. The combining element is properly -tomy (*q.v.*).

ottar, *ot'ər*. See attar.

ottava, *öt-tä'vä*, *os-tä'və*, *n.* an octave.—*n.* ottavino (-*vē'nō*), the piccolo.—ottava rima (*rē'mä*), an Italian stanza consisting of eight hendecasyllabic lines, rhyming *a b a b a b c c*. [It.; cf. octave.]

otter, *ot'ər*, *n.* an aquatic fish-eating carnivore (*Lutra vulgaris*) of the weasel family: its brown short fur: a board travelling edge-up, manipulated on the principle of the kite, to carry the end of a fishing-line in a lake, or to keep open the mouth of a trawl (also ott'er-board): a paravane. —*v.t.* or *v.i.* to fish with an otter-board.—ott'er-hound, a dog of a breed used in otter-hunting; ott'er-hunting; ott'er-shrew', a large otter-like aquatic West African insectivore (*Potamogale velox*); ott'er-trawl', a trawl fitted with

# otto 934 out

otter-boards; ott′er-trawl′ing. [O.E. *otor*, akin to water.]

**otto**, *ot′ō*. See attar.

**Ottoman**, *ot′ō-mən, adj.* pertaining to the Turkish Empire, founded by *Othmān* or *Osmān*: Osmanli.—*n.* a Turk of Turkey: a cushioned seat for several persons sitting with their backs to one another: a low, stuffed seat without a back: a variety of corded silk.—*n.* Ott′amite, Ott′omite, a Turk.

**ottrelite**, *ot′ri-līt, n.* a mineral like chlorite but harder.—**ott′relite-slate**, a clay slate with minute plates of ottrelite. [*Ottrez* in the Ardennes, and Gr. *lithos*, stone.]

**ou, ow**, *ōō,* (*Scot.*) *interj.* expressing concession.— **ou ay**, why yes: O yes.

**ouabain, wabain**, *wä-bä′in, n.* a poisonous alkaloid got from apocynaceous seeds and wood (*Strophanthus*, etc.). [French spelling—Somali *wabayo*, a tree that yields it.]

**oubit**, *ōō′bit.* See woubit.

**oubliette**, *ōō-bli-et′, n.* a dungeon with no opening but at the top: a secret pit in the floor of a dungeon into which a victim could be precipitated. [Fr.,—*oublier*, to forget—L. *oblīvīsci*.]

**ouch**, *owch, n.* a brooch: a clasped ornament: the socket of a precious stone. [O.Fr. *nouche*.]

**ouch**, *owch, interj.* expressing pain. [Ger. *autsch*.]

**Oudenarde**, *ōō′də-närd, n.* a tapestry representing foliage, etc., once made at *Oudenarde* in Belgium.

**ought**, *öt, n.* a variant of **aught**: also an illit. corr. of **naught**.—*adv.* (*Scot.*) **oughtlings** (*ohh′-linz*), at all.

**ought**, *öt, pa.t.* of **owe**: now *obs.* or *dial.* except as an auxiliary verb (with time expressed by tense of the principal verb) should: is or was proper or necessary.—*n.* **ought′ness**, rightness.

**ouglie, oughly**, old spellings of **ugly**.—*adj.* **ough′ly-headed** (*Milt.*).

**ouija**, *wē′jə, n.* a board with an alphabet, used with a planchette. [Fr. *oui*, Ger. *ja*, yes.]

**ouistiti**, a French spelling of **wistiti**.

**ouk, oulk**, *ōōk, n.* Scots forms of **week**.

**oulakan, oulachon**, *ōō′lə-kən.* See **eulachon**.

**oulong.** Same as **oolong**.

**ounce**, *owns, n.* the twelfth part of the (legally obsolete) pound troy = 480 grains: 1/16 of a pound avoirdupois: a minute quantity (*fig.*).— **fluid ounce** (no longer in use in the U.K.), volume of avoirdupois ounce of distilled water at 62° Fahr., 1/20 pint: 1/16 U.S. pint. [O.Fr. *unce* —L. *uncia*, the twelfth part; cf. **inch**.]

**ounce**, *owns, n.* originally, and still sometimes, a lynx: now generally the snow leopard (*Felis uncia*) of Central Asia: the jaguar: the cheetah: sometimes vaguely any moderate-sized wild beast of the cat kind. [Fr. *once*, perh. for *lonce* (as if *l'once*)—Gr. *lynx*.]

**oundy**, *own′di, adj.* wavy: undé (*her.*). [Fr. *ondé*; cf. **undate**.]

**oup, oop**, *ōōp,* (*Scot.*) *v.t.* to bind round with thread or cord: to join. [Appar. **whip**.]

**ouphe, ouph**, *owf, ōōf,* (*Shak.*) *n.* Same as **oaf**.

**our**, *owr, pron.* (*gen.*) or *poss. adj.* pertaining or belonging to us—when used absolutely, **ours** (*owrz*), *dial.* **ourn** (*owrn*).—*reflex.* and *emphatic* **ourself′**, myself (regally or editorially):—*pl.* **ourselves** (*-selvz′*). [O.E. *ūre*, gen. of *wē*, we.]

**ourali**, *ōō-rä′lē.* See **wourali**.

**ourang-outang.** Same as **orang-utan**.

**ourari**, *ōō-rä′rē.* See **wourali**.

**ourebi.** Same as **oribi**.

**ourie, oorie, owrie**, *ōō′ri,* (*Scot.*) *adj.* dingy: shabby: dreary: drooping: chill: inclined to shiver or shudder.

**ourology, ouroscopy**, etc. Same as **urology**, etc.—at **urine**.

**ousel.** See **ouzel**.

**oust**, *owst, v.t.* to eject or expel.—*n.* **oust′er** (*law*),

ejection, dispossession. [A.Fr. *ouster* (O.Fr. *oster*; Fr. *ôter*), to remove; of obscure origin.]

**oustiti**, *ōō-sti-tē′, n.* a lock-opening tool, outsiders (*q.v.*). [Fr., marmoset.]

**out** (see also **out-**), *owt, adv.* (shading into *adj.* predicatively), not within: forth: abroad: to, towards, or at the exterior or a position away from the inside or inner part or from anything thought of as enclosing, hiding, or obscuring: from among others: from the mass: beyond bounds: away from the original or normal position or state: at or towards the far end, or a remote position: seawards: away from home or a building: in or into the open air: in or into a state of exclusion: not in office: not in use or fashion: ruled out, not to be considered: no longer in the game: no longer in as a batsman, dismissed: not batting: out of the contest and unable to resume in time: in the condition of having won: away from the mark: at fault: in error: not in form or good condition: at a loss: in or into a disconcerted, perplexed, or disturbed state: not in harmony or amity: in distribution: in or into the hands of others or the public: on loan: to or at an end: in an exhausted or extinguished state: completely: thoroughly: subjected to loss: in or to the field: in quest of or expressly aiming at something: in rebellion: on strike: in an exposed state: no longer in concealment or obscurity: in or into the open: before the public: in or into society: on domestic service: in existence: at full length: in an expanded state: in bloom: in extension: loudly and clearly: forcibly: unreservedly.—*adj.* external: outlying: remote: played away from home: outwards: not batting: exceeding the usual: in any condition expressed by the adverb out. —*n.* one who is out: that which is outside: a projection or outward bend (as in *outs* and *ins*): an omission in setting type: a paying out, esp. (in *pl.*) rates and taxes, etc. (*dial.*): an outing (*dial.*): a disadvantage, drawback (*U.S.*): permission to go out (*U.S.*): a way out.—*prep.* forth from (now usu. *from out*): outside of (now *rare*): without (*obs.*).—*v.t.* to put out: to knock out: (with *with*) to bring out: (with *with*) to say suddenly or unexpectedly.—*v.i.* to go out. —*interj.* away, begone: you are, he is, out: alas: shame (usu. *out upon*; *arch.*).—*n.* **out′age**, amount of a commodity lost in transport or storage: amount of fuel used on a flight: stoppage of a mechanism due to failure of power: period during which electricity fails or is cut off.— *adjs.* **out′ed**, ejected; **out′er** (O.E. *ūterra*, comp.), more out or without: external—opp. to *inner* (**outer bar**, the junior barristers who plead outside the bar in court, as opposed to King's (Queen's) Counsel and others who plead within the bar).—*n.* the outermost ring of a target, a shot striking it: in an electrical distribution system either of the conductors whose potential is above or below the earth's.—*adjs.* **out′ermost**, **out′most** (*-məst, -mōst*; O.E. *ūtemest*, superl.), most or farthest out: most distant.—*ns.* **out′ing**, ejection: distance out: an outdoor excursion or airing; **out′ness**, state of being out: externality to the perceiving mind, objectiveness. —*adj., adv., prep., n.* **outside** (see separate article).—*adv.* **out′ward**, toward the outside: on the outside: outer: external: exterior: appearing externally: apparent: formal: not inherent, adventitious: worldly, carnal (*theol.*): dissolute (*dial.*).—*adv.* toward the exterior: away from port: to a foreign port: superficially.—*n.* external appearance (*Shak.*): the outside.—*adv.* **out′wardly**, in an outward manner: externally: in appearance.—*n.* **out′wardness**, externality: objectivity.—*adv.* **out′wards**, in an outward direction.—*adj.* **out′-and-out**, thorough-going:

thorough-paced: utter: absolute: unqualified.
—*adv.* **out-and-out'**, finally and completely:
definitely: unreservedly.—*n.* **out-and-out'er**, any
person or thing that is a complete or extreme
type: a thorough-going partisan: a great lie.
—*adj.* and *adv.* **out'back** (*Austr.*), in, to, or of,
the back-country.—*n.* the back-country.—**out'-
back'er**, one from the back-country.—*n.pl.*
**out'bounds** (*Spens.*), boundaries.—**out'building**,
a building separate from, but used in connection
with, a dwelling-house or a main building: an
outhouse.—*adv.* **outby, outbye** (*owt-bī'*, *ōōt-bī'*;
*Scot.*), out of doors: a little way off: outwards:
towards the shaft (*mining*).—*adj.* **out'by(e)**, outdoor: outlying.—**out'-dweller**, one who dwells
elsewhere, esp. one who owns land in a parish
but lives outside it; **out'edge**, the farthermost
bound; **outer space**, the immeasurable expanse
beyond the solar system, or, loosely, at a distance from the earth reached only by rocket;
**out'erwear**, clothes, as suits, dresses, worn over
other clothes; **out'field**, arable land continually
cropped without being manured—opp. to *infield* (*Scot.*): any open field at a distance from
the farm-steading: any undefined district or
sphere: at cricket and baseball, the outer part
of the field: the players who occupy it; **out'-
fielder**, one of such players; **out'guard**, a guard
at a distance, or at the farthest distance, from
the main body; **out'house**, a separate building
subsidiary to a main building; **outing flannel**,
a flannelette; **out'land**, a foreign land: land
granted to tenants: an outlying land or territory.—*adj.* foreign: outlying.—**out'lander**, a
foreigner: an uitlander.—*adj.* **outland'ish**, foreign (*arch.*): queer, bizarre: out-of-the-way.—
*adv.* **outland'ishly**.—*n.* **outland'ishness**; **out'line**, the
outer line: the line by which any figure or ob-
ject as seen is bounded: a sketch showing only
the main lines: representation by such lines: a
general statement without details: a statement
of the main principles: a set-line in fishing.—
*v.t.* to draw the exterior line of: to delineate
or sketch.—*adj.* **outlinear** (*owt-lin'i-ər*), like an
outline.—**out'lodging**, a lodging beyond bounds.
—*adjs.* **out-of-date'**, not abreast of the times:
obsolete: no longer valid; **out-of-door(s)'**, outdoor (see **out-**): outside of parliament.—*n.* **out-
of-doors'**, the open air.—*adv.* (see below).
—*adj.* **out-of-the-way'**, uncommon: singular:
secluded: remote.—*n.* and *adj.* **out-of-work'**,
unemployed (person).—*adv.* and *prep.* **out-o'ver,
out-owre** (*owt-owr'*, *ōōt-owr'*; *Scot.*), out over:
over.—**out'parish**, a parish associated with a
town but beyond the boundary: an outlying
parish; **out'part**, a part remote from the centre;
**out'-patient**, a hospital patient who is not an
inmate; **out'-pension**, a pension granted to one
who is not resident in an institution.—*v.t.* to
grant an out-pension to.—**out'-pensioner**, a non-
resident pensioner; **out'port**, a port out of or
remote from the chief port: a port away from
the town or customs area: a place of export;
**out'-porter**, a porter who carries luggage to and
from, and not merely in, the place where he is
employed; **out'post**, a post or station beyond
the main body or in the wilds: its occupants:
a remote settlement.—*n.pl.* **out'quarters**, quarters
situated away from headquarters.—**outrelief'**,
outdoor relief (see under **out-**); **out'ride**, an
unaccented syllable or syllables added to a foot,
esp. in sprung rhythm; **out'rider**, one who rides
abroad: a servant on horseback who attends a
carriage; **out'rigger**, a projecting spar for extending sails or any part of the rigging: a projecting contrivance ending in a float fixed to the
side of a canoe against capsizing: an iron
bracket fixed to the outside of a boat carrying

a rowlock at its extremity to increase the leverage
of the oar: a light racing-boat with projecting
rowlocks: a projecting beam for carrying a
suspended scaffold in building: a projecting
frame to support the controlling planes of an
aeroplane: an extension from the splinter-bar
of a carriage to take another horse.—*adj.* **out'-
right**, out-and-out: unqualified: unmitigated:
downright: direct.—*adv.* **outright'**, directly:
straight ahead: unreservedly: undisguisedly:
at once and completely.—**out'run**, an outlying
pasture or run; **out'-sentry**, a sentry placed at
a distance; **out'settlement**, an outlying settlement.—*adj.* and *n.* **out'size**, (a size, or a garment, etc., that is) exceptionally large.—**out'-
skirt**, (usu. in *pl.*) the border area; **out'sole**, the
outer sole of a boot or shoe which rests on the
ground; **out'-tray'**, a shallow container for
letters, etc., ready to be dispatched; **out'voter**,
a voter not resident in the constituency; **out'-
wall**, the outside wall of a building: external
appearance (*Shak.*).—*prep.* **outwith** (*owt'with*,
*ōōt'with*; *Scot.*), outside of.—*adv.* outwards.—
**out'work**, a work outside the principal wall or
line of fortification: outdoor work, field work:
work done away from the shop or factory.—
**at outs** (*U.S.*), at odds; **from out**, out from;
**murder will out** (see **murder**); **out and about**,
able to go out, convalescent: active out of
doors; **out and away**, by far: beyond competition; **out at elbow** (see **elbow**); **out for**, abroad
in quest of: aiming at obtaining, achieving:
dismissed from batting with a score of; **out
from under**, out of a difficult situation; **out
of**, from within: from among: not in: not
within: excluded from: from (as source,
material, motive, condition, possession, language, etc.): born of: beyond the bounds,
range, or scope of: deviating from, in disagreement with: away or distant from: without,
destitute or denuded of; **out of course**, out of
order; **out of doors**, in or into the open air;
**out of it**, excluded from participation: without
a chance; **out on one's feet**, as good as knocked
out: done for, but with a semblance of carrying
on; **outs and ins** (see **ins and outs**); **out to**, aiming,
working resolutely, to; **out to out**, in measurement
from outside to outside: overall; **out upon**, shame
on; **out with**, away with: not friendly with: to
utter, ejaculate, divulge: to bring out, whip
out; **out'ward-bound**, bound outwards or to a
foreign port; **out'ward-saint'ed**, appearing outwardly to be a saint.—See also **character**, **com-
mon**, **fashion**, **joint**, **place**, **pocket**, **print**, **question**,
**sight**, **sort**, **temper**, **time**, **use**, **wood**, etc. [O.E.
*ūte*, *ūt*; Goth. *ut*, Ger. *aus*, Sans. *ud*.]

**out-** (see also **out**), in composition, (1) meaning
'away from the inside or inner part', *lit.* and
*fig.*, and prefixed to, instead of following, verbs
(often *poet.*) and related nouns and adjectives,
e.g. *to outspread*, *an outpouring*, *outgoing*; (2)
with prepositional force, meaning 'outside of',
e.g. *outboard*, *outdoor*; (3) meaning 'through,
throughout', or 'beyond', or 'completely', e.g.
*outwatch*, *outflank*, *outweary*; (4) indicating the
fact of going beyond a norm, standard of comparison, or limit, 'more than', 'more successfully
than', 'farther than', 'longer than', etc., e.g. *outweigh*, *outmanoeuvre*, *outstep*, *outlast*. (Words
in which *out* has the adjectival senses of 'outside, not within', 'outlying', are given at **out**).
—*vs.t.* **out-ask'**, to proclaim the banns of for the
last time; **outbal'ance**, to outweigh; **outbar'gain**,
to get the better of in a bargain; **outbid'**, to
make a higher bid than; **outblust'er**, to exceed
in blustering: to get the better of by bluster:
to deprive (of) by bluster.—*adj.* **out'board**, outside
of a ship or boat: towards, or nearer, the ship's

side: having engines outside the boat.—*adv.* outside of, or towards the outside of.—*adj.* **out'bound**, bound for a distant port.—*vs.t.* **out-brag'**, to surpass in bragging or boasting: to excel in beauty or splendour (*Shak.*); **outbrave'**, to excel in boldness or splendour (*Shak.*): to outface.—*n.* **out'break**, a breaking out: a disturbance.—*v.i.* **outbreak'**, to burst forth.—*adjs.* **outbreath'd** (*-bretht'*; *Shak.*), out of breath; **out'bred**, resulting from outbreeding.—*ns.* **out'breed'ing**, breeding from parents not close akin: exogamy; **out'burst**, a bursting out: an eruption or explosion: a sudden violent expression of feeling; **out'cast**, one who is cast out of society or home: anything rejected, eliminated, or cast out: a quarrel (*Scot.*); **out'caste**, one who is of no caste or has lost caste.—*vs.t.* **out-caste'**, to put out of caste; **outclass'**, to surpass so far as to seem in a different class.—*adj.* **outclassed'**.—*n.* **out'come**, the issue: consequence: result.—*v.t.* **outcraft'y** (*Shak.*), to exceed in craft.—*n.* **out'crop**, the cropping out of a rock: a sudden emergence or occurrence.—*v.i.* (*-krop'*) to crop out.—*n.* **out'cry**, a loud cry of protest, distress, etc.: a confused noise: a public auction.—*vs.t.* **outdare'**, to surpass in daring: to defy; **outdate'**, to put out of date.—*adj.* **outdāt'ed**.—*vs.t.* **outdis'tance**, leave far behind: outstrip; **outdo'**, surpass: excel: overcome.—*adj.* **out'door**, outside the door or the house: in or for the open air.—*adv.* **outdoors'**, out of the house: abroad (**outdoor relief**, help formerly given to a pauper not living in the workhouse).—*vs.t.* **outdure'**, to outlast (*obs.*); **outdwell'**, to stay beyond (*Shak.*); **outface'**, to stare down: to confront boldly: to contradict (*obs.*): to force from (*Shak.*): to maintain boldly or impudently to the face of (that; *obs.*).—*ns.* **outfall** (*owt'-föl*), the outlet of a river, drain, etc.: a sortie: a quarrel (*dial.*); **out'fit**, the act of fitting out for an enterprise: complete equipment: expenses for fitting out: a company travelling, or working, together for any purpose, esp. in charge of cattle (*U.S.*): any set of persons, a gang.—*v.t.* to fit out, equip.—*v.i.* to get an outfit.—*ns.* **out'fitter**, one who furnishes outfits: one who deals in clothing, haberdashery, sporting equipment, etc.; **out'fitting.**—*v.t.* **out-flank'**, to extend beyond or pass round the flank of: to circumvent.—*ns.* **out'fling**, a sharp retort or gibe; **out'flow**, a flowing out: an outward current: outfall: amount that flows out; **out'-flush**, a sudden glow.—*vs.t.* **outfoot'**, to outstrip: to outsail; **outfrown'**, to frown down.—*n.* **out-gass'ing**, loss of, or removal of, occluded or adsorbed gas from a solid under vacuum conditions: also removal of gas from a liquid.—*v.t.* **outgas'**.—*n.* **out'gate** (*Spens.* and *Northern*), an outlet: an exit.—*v.t.* **outgen'eral**, to get the better of by generalship: to prove a better general than.—*n.* **out'giving**, a disbursement: an utterance: a declaration of policy.—*vs.t.* **outglare'**, to glare more than: to be more glaring than; **outgo'**, to outstrip: to surpass: to pass or live through: to overreach (*obs.*).—*v.i.* to go out: to come to an end.—*pa.t.* **outwent'**; *pa.p.* **outgone'**.—*ns.* **out'go**, that which goes out: expenditure—opp. to income; **out'-**

going, act or state of going out: extreme limit: expenditure.—*adj.* departing—opp. to *incoming*, as a tenant.—*v.t.* **outgrow'**, to surpass in growth: to grow out of, grow too big for: to eliminate or become free from in course of growth.—*ns.* **out'growth**, that which grows out from anything: an excrescence: a product; **out'haul**, a rope for hauling out the clew of a sail (also **out'hauler**).—*vs.t.* **out-Her'od**, to overact the part of (*Herod*) in violence (*Hamlet* III, ii): to outdo, esp. in what is bad; **outhire'** (*Spens.*), to give out as if on hire.—*v.t.* **outjest'**, to overcome by jesting (*Shak.*): to excel in jesting.—*ns.* **out'jet**, **out'jut**, a projection.—*ns.* and *adjs.* **outjett'ing**, **outjutt'ing**.—*n.* **out'lash**, a sudden burst or stroke.—*vs.t.* **outlast'**, to last longer than; **outlaunch'** (*Spens.* **outlaunce**), to launch forth; **out'lay**, that which is laid out: expenditure.—*v.t.* **outlay'**, to lay out in view: to expend: to surpass in laying.—*n.* **out'leap**, an act of leaping out: an excursion: an outburst.—*v.t.* **outleap'**, to leap beyond or over: to surpass in leaping.—*v.i.* to leap out.—*v.t.* **outlearn'**, to elicit (*Spens.*): to surpass: to excel in learning: to get beyond the study of.—*n.* **out'let**, the place or means by which anything is let out: the passage outward, vent.—*v.t.* **outlie'**, to surpass in telling lies.—*v.i.* **outlie'**, to lie in the open: to camp: to lie stretched out.—*v.t.* to lie beyond.—*n.* **out'lier**, one who lies in the open: one who lodges or lies apart from others or from a place with which he is connected: an outsider: a detached portion of anything lying some way off or out: an isolated remnant of rock surrounded by older rocks (*geol.*).—*v.t.* **outlive** (*-liv'*), to live longer than: to survive: to live through: to live down.—*n.* **out'look**, a vigilant watch: a place for looking out from: a view, prospect: a prospect for the future: mental point of view.—*v.t.* **outlook'** (*Shak. owt'*), to face courageously.—*v.i.* to look out.—*v.t.* **outlus'tre** (*Shak.*), to outshine.—*adj.* **out'lying**, lying out or beyond: lodging apart: remote: on the exterior or frontier: detached.—*vs.t.* **outman'**, to outdo in manliness: to outnumber in men; **outmanoeu'vre**, to surpass in or by manoeuvring; **outman'tle**, to excel in dress or ornament; **outmeas'ure**, to exceed in extent; **outmode'**, to put out of fashion.—*adj.* **outmod'ed**.—*vs.t.* **outmove'**, to move faster than: to get the better of by moving; **outname'**, to surpass in notoriety; **outnight'** (*Shak.*, *Merch. of Ven.* V, i), to surpass in mentioning nights; **outnum'ber**, to exceed in number; **outpace'**, to walk faster than: to outstrip; **out-par'amour** (*Shak.*), to exceed in addiction to mistresses; **outpass'ion**, to go beyond in passionateness; **outpeer'** (*Shak.*), to surpass or excel; **outplay'**, to play better than, and so defeat; **outpoint'**, to score more points than.—*n.* **out'pouring**, a pouring out: a passionate or fluent utterance.—*vs.t.* **outpower'**, to surpass in power; **outpray'**, to exceed in earnestness or length of prayer: to overcome in or by prayer; **outprize'** (*Shak.*), to exceed in estimation.—*n.* **out'put**, quantity produced or turned out: data in either printed or coded form after processing by a computer: punched tape or printed page by which pro-

| | | |
|---|---|---|
| **outbar'**, *v.t.* out- (1). | **outfight'**, *v.t.* out- (4). | **outgive'**, *v.i.* out- (1). |
| **outbreathe'**, *v.t.*, out- (1). | **outflash'**, *v.t.* out- (4).— | **out'goer**, *n.* out- (1). |
| **outburn'**, *v.t.* out- (4).— |     *v.i.* out- (1). | **outgush'**, *v.i.* out- (1). |
|     *v.i.* out- (3). | **outflow'**, *v.i.* out- (1). | **out'gush**, *n.* out- (1). |
| **outburst'**, *v.i.* out- (1). | **out'flowing**, *n.*, *adj.* out- (1). | **outmarch'**, *v.t.* out- (3), (4). |
| **outcry'**, *v.t.* out- (4).— | **outflush'**, *v.i.* out- (4). | **outmatch'**, *v.t.* out- (4). |
|     *v.i.* out- (1). | **outfly'**, *v.t.* out- (4).— | **outpeep'**, *v.i.* out- (1). |
| **outdance'**, *v.t.* out- (4). |     *v.i.* out- (1). | **outpour'**, *v.t.*, *v.i.* out- (1). |
| **outdrive'**, *v.t.* out- (4). | **outgive'**, *v.t.* out- (4).— | **outpour'er**, *n.* out- (1). |

*For many words beginning* **out-**, *see* **out** *or* **out-**.

cessed data leave a computer: signal delivered by a telecommunications instrument or system. —*vs.t.* **outrank'**, to rank above; **outreach'**, to reach or extend beyond: to overreach: to stretch forth; **outred'**, **outredd'en**, to surpass in redness; **outreign'**, to reign longer than: (*Spens.* **outraigne**) to reign to the end of; **outride'**, to ride beyond: to ride faster than: to ride safely through (a storm).—*n.* **out'rider**, a man who rides beside a carriage as a guard: one sent ahead as a scout.—*v.t.* **outrun'**, to go beyond in running: to exceed: to get the better of or to escape by running (**outrun**, or **overrun, the constable**, to run into debt: to live beyond one's means). —*n.* **out'runner**.—*vs.t.* **outsail'**, to leave behind in sailing: to sail beyond; **outscorn'** (*Shak.*), to face out with scorn; **outsell'**, to fetch a higher price than: to exceed in value: to surpass in the number or amount of sales.—*ns.* **out'set**, a setting out: beginning: an outward current; **out'setting**; **outshot** (*Scot.*), a projection in a building, or a recess made in the wall of a room; **out'sight**, power of seeing external things: (*owt'sit, ōōt'sihht*) outdoor possessions (*Scot.*)—Also *adj.*—*v.t.* **outsit'**, to sit beyond the time of: to sit longer than.—*adj.* **out'size**, over normal size.—*n.* an exceptionally large size: anything, esp. a garment, of exceptionally large size.—*adj.* **out'sized**.—*vs.t.* **outsleep'**, to sleep longer than: to sleep through: to sleep to or beyond the time of; **outsmart'** (*coll.*; *orig. U.S.*), to show more cleverness or cunning than, to outwit.—*adjs.* **outspent'**, thoroughly tired out; **outspō'ken**, frank or bold of speech: uttered with boldness.—*n.* **outspō'kenness**.—*v.t.* **outsport'** (*Shak.*), to sport beyond the limits of.—*v.t. and v.i.* **outspread'**, to spread out or over.—*adj.* **out'spread** (or *owt-spred'*), spread out.—*n.* an expanse.—*adj.* **outspread'ing**.—*v.i.* **outspring'**, to spring out.—*n.* **out'spring**, outcome.—*v.t.* **outstand'**, to withstand: to stand or endure through or beyond.—*v.i.* to stand out or project: to stand out (to sea): to stand over, remain.—*adj.* **outstand'ing**, prominent: unsettled: unpaid: still to be attended to or done. —*adv.* **outstand'ingly**.—*vs.t.* **outstare'**, to stare down (*Shak.*): to face the stare of unabashed: to gaze at without being blinded; **outstay'**, to stay beyond or throughout: to stay longer than: to endure longer than; **outstep'**, to step beyond, overstep; **outstrain'**, to stretch out; **outstretch'**, to stretch out: to reach forth: to spread out: to stretch to the end of: to stretch beyond; **outstrike** (*owt-strik'*, or *owt'*), to outdo in striking; **outstrip'**, to outrun: to leave behind: to surpass; **outstrip'**, to outdo in denuding oneself; **outsum'**, to outnumber; **outswear'**, to exceed in swearing: to overcome by swearing; **outsweet'en**, to excel in sweetness.—*ns.* **out'swing**, an outward swing or swerve; **out'swinger**, a ball bowled to swerve outwards.—*vs.t.* **outswell'**, to swell more than (*Shak.*): to overflow; **outtake'** (*obs.*), to take out: to except.—*prep.* (*obs.*) **outtāke'** (*obs.*; *orig. pa.p.*) **outtāk'en**, except.—*vs.t.* **outtell'**, to tell forth: to tell to the end: to tell or count beyond; **outtongue'** (*Shak.*), to speak louder than; **outtop'**, to reach higher than: to excel; **outven'om** (*Shak.*), to exceed in poisonousness; **outvill'ain** (*Shak.*), to exceed in villainy; **outvoice'** (*Shak.*), to exceed in clamour or noise: to drown the voice of; **outvote'**, to defeat by a greater number of votes; **outwatch'**, to watch longer than: to watch

throughout the time of; **outwear'**, to wear out: to spend, live through: to outlive, outgrow: to outlast; **outwea'ry**, to weary out completely; **outweed'** (*Spens.*), to root out; **outweep'**, to weep out, shed wholly: to surpass in weeping; **outweigh'**, to exceed in weight or importance.— *v.t. and v.i.* **outwell'**, to pour or well out.—*v.t.* **outwent'** (see **outgo**).—*v.i.* **outwick'**, in curling, to strike the outside of another stone and so send it within a circle.—*vs.t.* **outwin'** (*Spens.*), to get out of; **outwind** (-*wind'*), to unwind, extricate; **outwing'**, to outstrip in flying: to fly beyond: to outflank; **outwit'**, to surpass in wit or ingenuity: to defeat by superior ingenuity: —*pr.p.* **outwitt'ing**; *pa.t.* and *pa.p.* **outwitt'ed**; **outwork'** (*Shak.*), to surpass in work: to work out or bring to an end: to finish:—*pa.t.* and *pa.p.* **outwrought'**.—*adj.* **outworn'** (or *owt'*), worn out: obsolete.—*vs.t.* **outworth'** (*Shak.*), to exceed in value; **outwrest'** (*Spens.*), to extort. **outdacious**, *owt-dā'shəs*, *adj.* an illiterate perversion of **audacious**. **outfangthief**, *owt'fang-thēf*, *n.* the right of judging and fining thieves taken outside of one's own jurisdiction. [O.E. *ūtfangene-thēof—ūt*, out, the root of *fōn*, to take, *thēof*, thief.] **outher**, *ow'dhər*, *ö'dhər*, an old form, now *dial.*, of **either**. **outlaw**, *owt'lö*, *n.* one deprived of the protection of the law: (loosely) a bandit: an outcast: an unmanageable animal (*U.S.*).—*v.t.* to place beyond the law: to deprive of the benefit of the law: to ban.—*n.* **out'lawry**, the act of putting a man out of the protection of the law: state of being an outlaw. [O.E. *ūtlaga*—O.N. *ūtlāgi* —*ūt*, out, *lög*, law.] **outler**, *ōōt'lər*, (*Burns*) *adj.* not housed.—*n.* a beast that is not housed: one who is out of office. [Poss. **outlier**.] **outrage**, *owt'rij*, -*rāj*, *n.* excess, undue divergence from a mean (*Spens.*): violence beyond measure (*Shak.*): clamour (*Spens.*): gross or violent injury: an act of wanton mischief: an atrocious act: gross offence to moral feelings: violation: rape.—*v.t.* to treat with excessive abuse: to shock grossly: to injure by violence, esp. to violate, to ravish.—*adj.* **outrageous** (*owt-rā'jəs*), violent: furious: turbulent: atrocious: monstrous: immoderate.—*adv.* **outrā'geously**.—*ns.* **outrā'geousness**. [O.Fr. *ultrage*—*outre*, beyond —L. *ultrā*; the word is not connected with **out** and **rage**, but influenced by them.] **outrance**, *ōō-trās*, *n.* the utmost extremity: the bitter end (à **outrance**, to the bitter end of a combat—erroneously in Eng. use, à l'**outrance**). [Fr.,—*outre*, beyond.] **outré**, *ōō'trā*, *adj.* beyond what is customary or proper: extravagant, fantastic. [Fr.] **outrecuidance** (*Scott*), *ōōt-ər-kwē'dəns*, *ōōt-r'kwē'dās*, *n.* presumption, overweening. [Fr. *outre*, beyond, O.Fr. *cuider*, think, plume oneself— L. *cōgitāre*.] **outremer**, *ōō-tr'-mer*, *n.* the region beyond the sea: overseas. [Fr. *outre*, beyond, *mer*, sea.] **outroop**, *owt'rōōp*, (*obs.*) *n.* an auction sale.—*n.* **out'rooper** (*obs.*), an auctioneer: the Common Crier of the City of London. [Du. *uitroepen*, to cry out, proclaim.] **outrope, -er**, *owt'rōp*, *-er*. Same as **outroop, -er**. **outside**, *owt'sid'*, *owt'sid*, *owt-sid'*, *n.* the outer side: the farthest limit: the outer surface: the exterior: an outside passenger: the outer part:

---

---

*For many words beginning* **out-**, *see* **out** *or* **out-**.

Neutral vowels in unaccented syllables: *el'ə-mənt*; for certain sounds in foreign words, see p. viii

(in *pl.*) the top and bottom quires of a ream of paper.—*adj.* on or from the outside: carried on the outside: exterior: superficial: external: extreme: beyond the limit: not enjoying membership: (of a criminal activity) carried out by person(s) not having contacts with someone near the victim: (of broadcast or telecast) transmitted from a place outside the studio.— *adv.* **outside**' (sometimes *owt*'), on or to the outside: not within: out of prison.—*prep.* out'-side', outside of: except, apart from (*dial.*).— *n.* **outsid**'er, one who is not a member of a particular company, profession, etc., a stranger, a layman: one not considered fit to associate with: one who is not an inmate: one who is not participating: a racehorse not included among the favourites in the betting: one whose place in a game, at work, etc., is on the outside: (in *pl.*) a pair of nippers for turning a key in a keyhole from the outside.—**out'side-car**, an Irish jaunting-car in which the passengers sit back to back; **outside chance**, a remote chance; **outside country**, districts beyond the area of settlements in Australia; **outside edge** (see **edge**); **outside left, right**, in some games, a forward player on the extreme left, right; **outside novel**, the type of novel which deals with the author's thoughts and his relationship with the world. —**get outside of** (*coll.*), to eat or drink; **outside in**, turned so that outside and inside change places: intimately, thoroughly (of knowing anything); **outside of**, in or to a position external to: apart from, except (*coll., side* (1).] [out, side (1).]

**outspan**, *owt'span*, or -*span*', *v.t.* and *v.i.* to unyoke or unharness from a vehicle.—*n.* (*owt*') a stopping-place. [Du. *uitspannen.*]

**outspeckle**, *ōōt-spek'l*, (*obs. Scot.*) *n.* a laughing-stock, spectacle. [Perh. conn. with **kenspeckle**.]

**ouvert**, *ōō-ver*, *fem.* **ouverte**, -*vert*, (Fr.) open.

**ouvirandra**, *ōō-vi-ran'dra*, *n.* the lattice-leaf of Madagascar. [From the Malagasy name.]

**ouvrage**, *ōō-vräzh*, (Fr.) work.

**ouvrier**, *ōō-vrē-ā*, *fem.* **ouvrière**, *ōō-vrē-er*, (Fr.) worker, operative.

**ouzel, ousel**, *ōō'zl* (*Shak.* **woo'sel, woo'sell**), *n.* a blackbird (*arch.*): apparently, a dark-complexioned person (*Shak.*).—**ou'zel-cock**.—**ring'-ou'zel**, a blackish thrush with a broad white band on the throat; **wa'ter-ou'zel**, the dipper. [O.E. *ōsle*; cog. with Ger. *amsel.*]

**ouzo**, *ōō'zō*, *n.* an aniseed liqueur. [Mod. Gr. *ouzon.*]

**ova.** See **ovum**, under **ov(i)-**.

**oval**, *ō'val*, *adj.* strictly, egg-shaped, like an egg in the round or in projection, rounded, longer than broad, broadest near one end: loosely, elliptical or ellipsoidal, or nearly: rounded at both ends, about twice as long as broad, broadest in the middle (*bot.*): pertaining to eggs (*obs.*). —*n.* an oval figure or thing, e.g. an oval field. —*adv.* **o'vally**. [L. *ōvum*, egg; *ōvālis* is modern Latin.]

**ovary** ... **to** ... **ovate** (1). See **ov(i)-**.

**ovate**, *ov'āt*, *n.* an Eisteddfodic graduate neither a bard nor a druid. [W. *ofydd*, a philosopher, or lord; fancifully identified with the unrelated Celtic word preserved in Gr. as *ouāteis* (pl.), Gaulish soothsayers.]

**ovate.** See **ovation**.

**ovation**, *ō-vā'shon*, *n.* in ancient Rome, a lesser triumph: an outburst of popular applause, an enthusiastic reception: rejoicing (*arch.*).—*v.t.* **ovate**', (facetious back-formation) to receive with an ovation.—*n.* **ova'tor**. [L. *ōvātiō, -ōnis* —*ōvāre*, to exult.]

**oven**, *uv'n*, *n.* an arched cavity or closed chamber for baking, heating, or drying: a small furnace. —**o'ven-bird**, a name for various birds that build oven-shaped nests, esp. the South American genus *Furnarius*; **ov'en-tit**, the willow-warbler; **ov'enware**, dishes, as casseroles, that will stand the heat of an oven; **ov'enwood**, brushwood. [O.E. *ofen*; Ger. *ofen.*]

**over**, *ō'vər*, **o'er**, formerly **ore, o're, ōr, ör**, *prep.* above in place, rank, power, authority, contention, preference, value, quantity, number, etc.: in excess of: above and from one side of to the other: down from or beyond the edge of: from side to side or end to end of: along: throughout the extent of: until after: across: on or to the other side of: on, on to, about, or across the surface of, or all or much of: in discussion, contemplation, study of, or occupation with: concerning: on account of: in a sunk, submerged, or buried state beyond the level of.— *adv.* on the top; above; across; to or on the other side: from one person, party, condition, etc., to another: into a sleep: outwards so as to overhang, or to fall from: away from an upright position: through, from beginning to end, esp. in a cursory or exploratory way: throughout: into a reversed position: across the margin: again, in repetition: too much: in excess: left remaining: at an end.—*interj.* in telecommunications, indicates that the speaker now expects a reply.—*adj.* (usu. treated as a prefix) upper or superior: surplus: excessive. —*n.* the series of balls (as *six-ball, eight-ball, over*), or the play, between changes in bowling from one end to the other (*cricket*): anything that is over: a surplus copy, etc.: an excess, overplus.—*v.t.* to go, leap, or vault over.—**all over**, at an end: everywhere: at his, her, its, most characteristic: covered with, besmeared or bespattered with; **be all over** (one), to make a fuss of, fawn on (one); **over again**, anew; **over against**, opposite; **over and above**, in addition to: besides; **over and over** (again), many times: repeatedly; **over head and ears**, completely submerged; **over seas**, to foreign lands. [O.E. *ofer*; Ger. *über*, L. *super*, Gr. *hyper*; cf. **up**.]

**over-**, in composition, used with certain meanings of **over**, *prep., adv.*, or *adj.*, as (1) above, across, across the surface, (2) beyond an understood limit; (3) down, away from the upright position; (4) upper; (5) beyond what is usual or desirable; (6) completely.—*v.t.* **overact**', to act with exaggeration, to overdo the performance of.—Also *v.i.*—*adj.* **o'ver-age**', above the limiting age: too old.—*adv.* **overall'**, **over-all'**, everywhere (*Spens.*): above all: altogether: over the whole.—*adj.* **o'verall**, including everything: everything being reckoned: all-round.— *n.* **o'verall**, a protective garment worn over ordinary clothes for dirty work or weather: (*pl.*) trousers or leggings or combined shirt and trousers of this kind: cavalryman's trousers.— *adj.* **o'veralled**.—*v.t.* **overarch**', to arch over: to form above into an arch.—*v.i.* to hang over like an arch.—*n.* an overhead arch.—*adj.* and *adv.* **o'verarm**, with the arm raised above the shoulder.—*vs.t.* **overawe'**, to daunt by arousing fear or reverence; **overbal'ance**, to exceed in weight, value, or importance: to cause to lose balance.—*v.i.* to lose balance, fall over.—*n.* excess of weight or value.—*v.t.* **overbear'**, to bear down, overpower: to overwhelm: to overrule (objections, an objector).—*v.i.* to be too productive.—*adj.* **overbear'ing**, inclined to domineer: haughty and dogmatical: imperious. —*adv.* **overbear'ingly**.—*n.* **overbear'ingness**.— *v.t.* **overbid'**, to outbid: to make a bid that is

---

**overabound'**, *v.i.* over- (5).     **o'ver-anxi'ety**, *n.* over- (5).     **o'ver-anx'iously**, *adv.* over- (5).
**overabound'ing**, *adj.* over- (5).     **o'ver-anx'ious**, *adj.* over- (5).     **overbeat'**, *v.t., v.i.* over- (3).
**overabun'dance**, *n.* over- (5).

greater than or counts above: to bid more than the value of.—Also *v.i.*—*n.* a higher bid: an unduly high bid.—*ns.* **overbidd'er; overbidd'ing.** —*v.i.* **overblow'** (blow (2)), blow over, be past its violence: to blow with too much violence: to produce a harmonic instead of the fundamental tone, by excess of wind-pressure (*mus.*).—*v.t.* to blow away: blow across: overturn by blowing: to blow (an instrument) too strongly (*mus.*).— *v.t.* **overblow'** (blow (1)), to cover with blossoms. —*adjs.* **overblown'**, blown over or past: burnt by an excessive blast, in the Bessemer steel process: inflated to excess; **overblown'**, more than full-blown.—*adv.* **overboard'**, over the board or side: from on board: out of a ship (go **overboard about or for** (*slang*), to go to extremes of enthusiasm about or for).—*v.t.* **overbrow'**, to overhang like a brow; **overbuild'**, to cover with buildings: to build above: to build in excess: to build too much upon or in; **overbulk'** (*Shak.*), to oppress by bulk, or to dwarf by greater bulk; **overburd'en, overburth'en**, to burden overmuch.—*n.* (*ō'vǝr-*) an excessive burden: alluvial soil, etc., overlying a bed of clay or other substance to be dug, mined, or quarried.—*v.t.* **overburn'**, to burn too much.—*v.i.* to be too zealous.—*adj.* **overbus'y**, too busy: officious.— *v.t.* to busy too much.—*v.t.* **overbuy'**, to buy too dear (*Shak.*): to buy dearer than: to put in the position of having bought too much (*refl.*): to buy too much of.—*v.i.* to buy too much:— *pa.t.* and *pa.p.* **overbought'**.—*adv.* **overby'**, a little way over—mainly in Scots forms, **owerby, o'erby** (*owr-bī'*).—*vs.t.* **overcall'**, to outbid (*bridge*): to bid above: to bid too high on: to rank as a higher bid than; **overcan'opy**, to cover as with a canopy:—*pa.p.* **over-can'opied** (*Shak.* **over-cann'oped**).—*n.* **overcapitalisā'tion**, -z.—*v.t.* **overcap'italise**, -ize, to fix the capital to be invested in, or the capital value of, too high; **overcast'**, overthrow: to cast as a covering: to cast a covering over: to shade (*Spens.*): to sew stitches over (a raw edge): to cover with stitches: to recover, get over (*Scot.*): to compute too high, overestimate.—*v.i.* to grow dull or cloudy.—*adj.* clouded over.—*n.* a cloudy covering.—*n.* **overcast'ing.** — *vs.t.* **overcatch'** (*arch.*), to overtake (*pa.p.* **overcaught'**, *Spens.*). —*n.* **o'vercheck**, a large prominent check-pattern combined with a smaller: a cloth so checked.—*v.t.* **overcloud'**, to cover over with clouds: to cause gloom or sorrow to.—Also *v.i.*—*v.t.* **overcloy'**, to surfeit.—*ns.* **o'vercoat**, an outdoor coat worn over all else, a topcoat; **o'vercoating**, cloth for overcoats.—*vs.t.* **overcome'**, to cover, overspread (*arch.*): to come

**over:** to get the better of: to conquer or subdue: to surmount.—*v.i.* to be victorious.—*n.* (*Scot.*) **o'ercome, owrecome** (*owr'kǝm*), a crossing over: a surplus, excess: a fit or sudden access of illness: a refrain, byword, or recurring theme.—*v.t.* **overcom'pensate**, to allow too much in compensation of: to allow pursuit of compensation to become obsessive and exclusive (*psych.*).—Also *v.i.* (with *for*).—*n.* **overcompensā'tion.** — *adj.* **overcompen'satory.** — *v.t.* **overcorrect'**, to apply so great a correction to as to deviate in the opposite way: to correct beyond achromatism, so that the red rays come to a focus nearer the lens than the violet (*opt.*).—*n.* **overcorrec'tion.**—*vs.t.* **overcount'**, to outnumber: to reckon too high: to overreach. —*vs.t.* **o'vercrop**, to take too much out of by cultivation; **overcrow'**, *Spens.* **overcraw'**, *Shak.* **orecrowe'**, to crow, triumph, over.—*adjs.* **overdat'ed**, out of date: **over-determined**, too firmly resolved (to): too resolute, stubborn: having more than the necessary determining data or factors; **overdight** (-*dīt*; *Spens.*), dight or covered over: overspread.—*v.t.* **overdo'**, to do overmuch: to overact: to exaggerate: to carry too far: to harass, to fatigue: to cook too much: to excel.—*n.* **overdo'er.**—*adj.* **overdone'.**—*ns.* **o'verdraft**, the act of overdrawing: the excess of the amount drawn over the sum against which it is drawn; **o'verdraught** (-*dräft*), in U.S. **o'verdraft**, a current of air passing above or from above.—*v.t.* **overdraw'**, to exaggerate in drawing: to exaggerate: to draw beyond one's credit.—*v.t.* and *v.i.* **overdress'**, to dress too ostentatiously or elaborately.—*v.t.* **overdrive'**, to drive too hard: to outdrive.—*n.* **o'verdrive**, a gearing device which transmits to the driving shaft a speed greater than engine crankshaft speed.—*adjs.* **overdrowsed'** (*Wordsworth* **o'er-drows'ed**), overcome by drowsiness; **overdue'** (or *ō'vǝr-*), behind time for arrival: still unpaid after the time it is due.—*adj.* **overear'nest**, too earnest: severe in manner (*Shak.*).—*v.t.* **overeat'**, (often with *oneself*) surfeit with eating: perh. to nibble all over, perhaps, to surfeit on (*Shak.*).—*v.i.* to eat too much.—*v.t.* **overexpose'**, to expose too much, esp. to light.—*adj.* **over-ex'quisite**, excessively exact in imagining details (*Milt.*).—*v.t.* **overeye'**, to survey, look upon: to watch.—*n.* **o'verfall**, a rippling or race of water: a sudden increase of depth: a place or structure for overflow of surplus waters: a waterfall (*obs.*).—*v.t.* **overfall'**, to fall on or over: to assail.—*adv.* **overfar'**, too far: to too great an extent (*Shak.*). —*n.* **o'verflight**, a flight above and over.—*v.t.*

---

**overboil'**, *v.t.*, *v.i.* over- (2), (5).
**overbold'**, *adj.* over- (5).
**overbold'ly**, *adv.* over- (5).
**overbound'**, *v.t.* over- (1).
**o'verbridge**, *n.* over- (1).
**overbridge'**, *v.t.* over- (1).
**overbrimmed'** (*Scott*), *adj.* over- (5).
**overbur'densome**, *adj.* over- (5).
**overcare'ful**, *adj.* over- (5).
**overcarr'y**, *v.t.* over- (1, *obs.*), (2), (5).
**overcharge'**, *v.t.* over- (5).
**o'vercharge**, *n.* over- (5).
**overclad'**, *adj.* over- (5).
**overcol'our**, *v.t.* over- (1), (5).
**over-con'fidence**, *n.* over- (5).
**over-con'fident**, *adj.* over- (5).
**over-cool'**, *v.t.* over- (5).
**overcov'er**, *v.t.* over- (6).
**overcredu'lity**, *n.* over- (5).
**overcred'ulous**, *adj.* over- (5).
**overcrowd'**, *v.t.*, *v.i.* over- (5).
**overdar'ing**, *adj.* over- (5).
**overdevel'op**, *v.t.*, *v.i.* over- (5).

**overdevel'opment**, *n.* over- (5).
**overdos'age**, *n.* over- (5).
**o'verdose**, *n.* over- (5).
**overdose'**, *v.t.* over- (5).
**o'verdress**, *n.* over- (4).
**overdust'**, *v.t.* over- (1).
**overdye'**, *v.t.* over- (1), (5).
**overes'timate**, *v.t.*, *n.* over- (5).
**overestima'tion**, *n.* over- (5).
**overexcitabil'ity**, *n.* over- (5).
**overexcit'able**, *adj.* over- (5).
**overexcite'**, *v.t.* over- (5).
**overexert'**, *v.t.* over- (5).
**overexer'tion**, *n.* over- (5).
**overexpos'ure**, *n.* over- (5).
**overfall'**, *v.i.* over- (3).
**overfeed'**, *v.t.*, *v.i.* over- (5).
**overfed'**, *pa.t.*, *pa.p.* over- (5).
**overfill'**, *v.t.*, *v.i.* over- (5).
**o'verfine'**, *adj.* over- (5).
**o'verfine'ness**, *n.* over- (5).
**overfire'**, *v.t.* over- (5).
**overfish'**, *v.t.* over- (5).

---

o'verflour'ish, to cover with blossom, or with flourishes or ornament; overflow', to flow over the edge of: to flow over the surface of: to flood: to flow over and beyond: to cause to run over: (of e.g. people) to fill and then spread beyond (e.g. a room):—*pa.t.* overflowed'; *pa.p.* overflowed', formerly and still sometimes overflown'.—Also *v.i.*—*n.* o'verflow, a flowing over: that which flows over, *lit.* and *fig.* (over- flow meeting, a supplementary meeting of those unable to find room in the main meeting): a pipe or channel for spare water, etc.: an in- undation: a superabundance.—*adj.* overflow'ing, flowing over: running over: overfull: over- abounding: exuberant.—Also *n.*—*adv.* overflow'- ingly.—*adj.* overflush', too flush.—*n.* o'verflush, superfluity.—*v.t.* overfly', to outsoar: to fly over.—*n.* o'verfold, a fold tilted over so that the dip on both sides of the axis is in the same direction.—*v.t.* overfold', to fold over: to thrust into an overfold.—*adj.* overfond', foolish to excess (*obs.*): too fond: too fond (of).—*v.t.* over- freight', to overload:—*pa.p., adj.* overfraught'.—*n.* o'verfreight, an excessive load.—*vs.t.* overgall', to blister or inflame all over, or greatly; over- gang' (*Scot.* o'ergang, *owr-gang'*), to dominate: to overspread: to exceed; overget', to overtake (*obs.*): to get over, recover from (*dial.* or *arch.*): to overcome, possess the mind of; overgive' (*Spens.*), to give over or up; overglaze', to glaze over: to cover speciously.—*n.* o'verglaze, an additional glaze given to porcelain, etc.— *adj.* applied to, or suitable for painting on, a glazed surface.—*vs.t.* overgloom', to cover with gloom: to scowl over; overgo', to exceed: to surpass: to overpower: to go over: to pass over, traverse: to spread over: to pass over, forbear to speak of.—*v.i.* to go over: to pass on.—*n.* overgo'ing, passing over: crossing, traversing: transgression.—*v.t.* and *v.i.* over- grain', to grain over (a surface already grained). —*n.* overgrain'er, a brush for overgraining.— *vs.t.* overgrass', to grass over, conceal with grass; overgreen', to cover with green or ver- dure: conceal (*fig., Shak.*).—*adj.* overground', above ground.—*v.t.* overgrow', to grow beyond: to grow more than: to grow too great for: to rise above: to cover with growth.—*v.i.* to grow beyond the normal or suitable size.—*adj.* over- grown (*ō'vər-grōn,* or *-grōn'*), grown beyond the natural size: covered over with a growth.—*n.* o'vergrowth, excessive or abnormally great growth: excess or superfluity resulting from growth: that which grows over and covers anything: growth of a crystal around another (*crystal.*).—*v.t.* overhaile', overhale', to draw over (*Spens.*): to overtake, overpower (*obs.*): to examine.—*n.* o'verhair, the long hair over- lying the fur of many animals.—*adv.* overhand' (or *ō'*), with hand above the object: palm- downwards: with hand or arm raised above the shoulders or (in swimming) coming out of the water over the head: from below (*min.*): with stitches passing through in one direction and back round the edges (*needlework*).—*adj.* o'verhand, done or performed overhand (over- hand knot, the simplest of all knots, tied by passing the end over the standing part and through the bight).—*v.t.* to sew overhand.—*adj.* and *adv.* overhand'ed, with hand above: with

too many hands.—*adj.* overhand'led (*Shak.*), handled or discussed too much.—*v.t.* overhang', to hang over: to project over: to impend over: to cover with hangings.—*v.i.* to hang over, lean out beyond the vertical.—*n.* o'verhang, a pro- jecting part: degree of projection.—*v.t.* over- haul', to haul or draw over: to turn over for examination: to examine: to overtake or gain upon (*naut.*).—*n.* o'verhaul, a hauling over: examination, esp. with a view to repair.—*adv.* overhead', above one's head: aloft: in the zenith: in complete submergence: now *Scot.,* taking one with another, in the lump, on the average, apiece.—*adj.* o'verhead, above one's head: well above ground level: all-round, general, average.—*n.* (often in *pl.*; also overhead costs, charges) the general expenses of a business —as distinct from the direct cost of producing an article: that which is overhead (overhead pro- jector, one which, set up on a teacher's desk, projects transparencies on a screen behind him) —*v.t.* overhear', to hear without being meant to hear: to hear by accident: to hear over again or in turn (*Shak.*); overheat', to heat to excess.—*v.i.* to become too hot.—*v.t.* and *v.i.* to make or become agitated.—*n.* o'verheat, too great heat.—*vs.t.* overhent' (*Spens.*), to overtake: —*pa.t.* and *pa.p.* overhent'; overhold' (*Shak.*), to overvalue.—*adj.* overhung', overhanging: sus- pended from above: covered over, adorned with hangings.—*v.t.* overinform', to give an ex- cessive amount of information to: to animate too much.—*n.* overinsur'ance.—*vs.t.* overinsure', to insure for more than the real value; overiss'ue, to issue in excess, as bank-notes or bills of ex- change.—*n.* o'verissue, excessive issue.—*v.t.* over- joy', to fill with great joy: to transport with delight or gladness.—*n.* o'verjoy, joy to excess, transport.—*vs.t.* overjump', to jump (too far) over: jump farther than: pass over (*fig.*); overkest' (*Spens.*), for overcast (*pa.t.* and *pa.p.*). —*ns.* o'verkill, something, esp. power for destruction, in excess of what is necessary; o'verking, a king holding sovereignty over inferior kings.—*adj.* o'verknee, reaching above the knee. —*vs.t.* overla'bour, to labour excessively over: to be too nice with: to overwork; overlade', to overburden:—*pa.p.* overla'den; overlaid, *pa.p.* of overlay; overlain, *pa.p.* of overlie.—*adj.* o'ver- land, passing entirely or principally by land.— *adv.* overland' (or *ō'*), by or over land.—*v.t.* and *v.i.* (*Austr.*) to drive (flocks or herds) a long distance across country: to journey across country, esp. a long way.—*n.* o'verlander (or *-land'*).—*v.t.* overlap', to extend over and beyond the edge of: to reach from beyond, across the edge, and partly rest on: to coincide in part with: to ripple over.—*n.* o'verlap, an overlap- ping part: a disposition of strata where the upper beds extend beyond the boundary of the lower beds of the same series (*geol.*).—*vs.t.* overlard', to smear over as with lard: to over- load with fulsomeness; overlaunch', in ship- building, to unite by long splices or scarfs; overlay', to cover by laying or spreading some- thing over: to span (*Milt.*): to put an overlay or overlays on (*print.*): to cover to excess, en- cumber: to lay or place as a covering (*rare*): by confusion, to overlie:—*pa.t.* and *pa.p.* over- laid'.—*ns.* o'verlay, a piece of paper pasted on

---

---

*fāte, fär; mē, hûr* (her); *mīne; mōte, för; mūte; mōōn, fŏŏt; dhen* (then)

the impression-surface of a printing-press, so as to increase the impression in a place where it is too faint: a covering: a cravat (*Scot.*): **overlay′ing,** a superficial covering: that which overlays: plating.—*adv.* **overleaf′,** on the other side of the leaf of a book.—*v.t.* **overleap′** (*Scot.* **owerloup′**), to leap over: to pass over without notice (**overleap oneself,** to leap too far).—*n.* **o′verleather** (*Shak.*), the upper part of a shoe. —*v.t.* **overlie′,** to lie above or upon: to smother by lying on:—*pr.p.* **overly′ing;** *pa.t.* **overlay′;** *pa.p.* **overlain′.**—*n.* **o′verlier** (or *-lī′*).—*v.t.* **overlive** (*-liv′*), to survive: to outlive: to outlive the appropriate date of, or usefulness of (*refl.*).— *v.i.* to survive: to live too long: to live too fast, or so as prematurely to exhaust the fund of life: to live on too high a standard of luxury. —*v.t.* **overload′,** to load or fill overmuch.—*n.* (*ō′*) an excessive load.—*v.t.* **overlook′,** to look over: to see from a higher position: to view carefully: to oversee, superintend: to fail to notice or take into account: to pass by without cognisance or punishment: to slight: to bewitch by looking upon with the evil eye.—*ns.* **overlook′er; o′verlord,** a lord over other lords: a feudal superior: (with *cap.*) operational name for the Anglo-American invasion (1944) of Normandy in World War II.—*v.t.* **overlord′.**— *n.* **o′verlordship.**—*adv.* **o′verly** (*-li; coll.*), excessively, too: superciliously (*obs.*): casually (*Scot.*).—*adj.* supercilious, superior (*obs.*): casual (*Scot.*).—*adj.* **overly′ing,** lying on the top. —*n.* **o′verman,** an overseer in mining, the man in charge of work below ground: superman.— *v.t.* **overman′,** to furnish with too many men.— *n.* **o′vermantel,** an ornamental structure, often with a mirror, set on a mantel-shelf.—*vs.t.* **overmast′,** to furnish with a mast or masts too long or too heavy; **overmas′ter,** to gain or have the mastery of: to overpower: to dominate; **overmatch′,** to be more than a match for: to defeat, overcome.—*n.* **o′vermatch,** one who is more than a match: an overmatching (*obs.*).— *n.* **overmeas′ure** (or *ō′*), something given over the due measure.—*v.t.* (*-mezh′*) to measure above the true value.—*adj.* **overmerr′y,** extremely merry.—*v.t.* **overmount′,** to rise above: to excel in mounting.—*v.i.* to mount too high. —*adj.* and *adv.* **o′vermuch** (or *-much′*), too much. —*v.i.* **overmul′tiply,** to become too numerous. —*n.* **overmultiplicā′tion.**—*vs.t.* **overmult′itude** (*Milt.*), to outnumber; **overname′** (*Shak.*), to name over; **overnet′,** to cover with a net: to overfish with nets.—*adj.* **overnice′,** too fastidious. —*adv.* **overnice′ly.**—*n.* **overnice′ness.**—*n.* **o′vernight** (*Shak.;* now chiefly *U.S.*), the evening just past.—*adv.* **overnight′,** all night: during the night: in the course of the night: on the evening of the day just past.—*adj.* done or occurring overnight: for the time from afternoon till next morning: (**overnight bag, case,** a small case for carrying the clothes, toilet articles, etc., needed for an overnight stay).—*vs.t.* **overoff′ice** (*Shak.* **o′re-office**), apparently, to lord it over by virtue of office, or perhaps to exercise one's office over; **overpaint′,** to put too much paint on: to depict with exaggeration; **overpart′,** to assign too difficult a part to; **overpass′,** to pass over: to pass by without notice: to exceed.— *v.i.* to pass over: to elapse.—*n.* road bridging another road or railway, canal, etc.—*adj.* **over-**

**past′,** over: at an end.—*v.t.* **overpay′,** to pay too much: to be more than an ample reward for.— *n.* **overpay′ment.**—*vs.t.* **overpeer′** (partly from **peer** (1), partly **peer** (2); *Shak.*), to peer over or down upon: to look down on: to tower over: to excel; **overperch′** (*Shak.* **orepearch′**), to fly up and perch on, fly over; **overpersuade′,** to persuade against one's inclination; **overpic′ture,** to surpass pictorially: to cover with pictures; **overpitch′,** to pitch too far, or beyond the best distance.—*adjs.* **overpitched,** steeply pitched, as a roof; **overplaced′** (*Spens.* **overplast,** *-plãst′*), placed above.—*v.t.* **overplay′,** to overemphasise the importance, value, of: to play better than (an opponent): to try to gain more than one's assets (*lit.* and *fig.*) can be expected to yield (**overplay one's hand;** *fig.*).—*v.t.* and *v.i.* to exaggerate (emotion, acting rôle, etc.): to hit the ball beyond (the putting green) (*golf*).—*n.* **o′verplay.**—*n.* **o′verplus,** that which is more than enough: surplus.—*adj.* surplus.—*vs.t.* **overply′,** to ply beyond strength; **overpoise′,** to outweigh.—*n.* **o′verpoise,** a weight sufficient to weigh another down.—*vs.t.* **overpost′,** to hasten over quickly; **overpower′,** to overcome, reduce to helplessness, by force: to subdue: to overwhelm: to furnish with too much power.— *adj.* **overpower′ing,** excessive in degree or amount: irresistible.—*adv.* **overpower′ingly.**—*v.t.* **overpress′,** to oppress: to burden too heavily: to press unduly: to put too much pressure on.— *n.* **overpress′ure,** excessive pressure, esp. of work. —*v.t.* **overprint′,** to print too strongly or dark: to print too many copies of: to print over already printed matter (esp. a postage stamp).— *n.* **o′verprint,** an offprint: that which is printed over an already printed surface, as on a postage stamp.—*v.t.* **overprize′,** to value too highly: to surpass in value (*obs.*).—*v.t.* and *v.i.* **overproduce′.**—*n.* **overproduc′tion,** excessive production: production in excess of the demand.— *adj.* **overproof′** (or *ō′*), containing more alcohol than does proof-spirit.—*vs.t.* **overrack′,** to overstrain; **overrake′,** to sweep over.—*adj.* **overrank′,** too rank or luxurious.—*v.t.* **overreach′,** to reach or extend beyond: to overtake: to outwit or get the better of: (*refl.*) to defeat by one's own oversubtlety or by attempting too much.—*v.i.* to strike the hindfoot against the forefoot, as a horse:—*pa.t.* and *pa.p.* **overreached;** *arch.* **overraught′.**—*n.* **o′verreach,** the act of overreaching: the injury thereby done. —*v.t.* **overread** (*-rēd′*), to read over.—*adj.* **overread** (*-red′*), having read too much.—*v.t.* and *v.i.* **overreck′on,** to compute too highly.—*vs.t.* **overred′** (*Shak.*), to cover with a red colour; **overren′,** an arch. form of **overrun; override′,** to injure or exhaust by too much riding: to ride over: to trample down on horseback: to slide or mount on the top or back of: to pass over: to overlap: to set aside: to be valid against: to be more important than, prevai over: to outride, overtake (*obs.*).—*adj.* over rid′ing, dominant, stronger than anything else.— *v.t.* and *v.i.* **overruff′,** to trump with a higher trump.—*n.* **o′verruff,** an act of overruffing.—*v.t.* **overrule′,** to rule over (*obs.*): to modify or to set aside by greater power: to prevail over the will of, against a previous decision of: to impose an overriding decision upon: to prevail over and set aside: to annul, declare invalid (*law*):

---

---

to rule against: to disallow.—*v.i.* to prevail.—*n.* **overrul´er.**—*v.t.* **overrun´,** to run over, across, through, all about: to run over, crush underfoot or under wheel: to spread over: to flow over: to grow over: to infest, swarm over: to infect widely: to spread over and take possession of: to run beyond: to exceed the limit of: to carry beyond a limit: to carry over into another line or page: to adjust the type of by overrunning: to outdo in running: to escape from by running faster: (*refl.*) to injure or exhaust by too much running.—*v.i.* to run over, overflow: to run beyond a limit:—*pr.p.* **overrunn´ing;** *pa.t.* **overran´;** *pa.p.* **overrun´ (overrun the constable,** see **outrun).**—*ns.* **o´verrun,** an act or occasion of overrunning: an overrunning of type (*print.*); **overrunn´er.**—*v.t.* **oversail´** (Fr. *saillir*, to project), to project.—*n.* **o´versail,** projection.—*v.t.* **overscore´,** to score or draw lines across: to obliterate in this way.—*adjs.* **overscutched** (*-skucht´, -skuch´id; Scott*), worn out (after Shak., 2 *Hen. IV* III, ii, where **overschutch** is variously conjectured to mean overworn in service or whipped at the cart's tail); **o´versea, o´verseas,** across, beyond, or from beyond the sea.—*adv.* **oversea(s)´,** in or to lands beyond the sea: abroad.—*n.* **overseas´,** foreign lands.—*v.t.* **oversee´,** to see or look over: to superintend: to overlook, disregard: not to see without being meant to see.—*adj.* **overseen´** (*obs.*), mistaken, ill-advised: drunk: versed (in).—*n.* **o´verseer** (*-sēr, -sē-ər*), one who oversees: a superintendent: formerly, officer with care of poor, and other duties: the manager of a plantation of slaves: a critic or editor (*obs.*).—*vs.t.* and *vs.i.* **oversell´,** to sell too dear: to sell more of than is available; **overset´,** to oppress, press hard (*obs.*): to upset: to disorder.—*v.t.* **o´versew** (or *-sō´*), to sew together overhand.—*vs.t.* **overshade´,** to throw a shade or shadow over: to darken; **overshad´ow,** to throw a shadow over: to cast into the shade by surpassing, to outshine: to darken: to shelter or protect; **overshine´** (*Shak.*), to shine over or upon, illumine: to outshine.—*n.* **o´vershoe,** a shoe, esp. of waterproof, worn over another.—*advs.* **over-shoe´, over-shoes´,** deep enough to cover the shoes.—*v.t.* **overshoot´,** to shoot over or beyond, as a mark: to pass beyond, exceed, fail to stop at: to shoot, dart, or fly across overhead: to surpass in shooting: to injure or exhaust by too much shooting: to shoot with colour over the surface of (**overshoot oneself,** to venture too far, to overreach oneself).—Also *v.i.*—*n.* **o´vershoot** (*aero.*), a going beyond the mark in landing.—*adj.* **overshot´,** shot over: too much shot over: surpassed: overdone: in error by overshooting the mark: drunk (*obs. slang*).—*adj.* **o´vershot,** having the upper jaw protruding beyond the lower: fed from above, as a waterwheel.—*v.t.* **overshower´,** to shower over.—*adj.* **o´verside,** acting or done over the side.—*adv.* **overside´,** over the side.—*prep.* (*Spens.* **over side**), over the side of.—*n.* **o´versight,** superintendence: a failure to notice: mistake: omission.—*v.t.* **oversize´,** to cover with size.—*n.* **o´versize,** a large or larger size.—*adj.* **o´versized** (or *-sizd´*).

—*v.t.* **overskip´,** to skip, leap, or pass over: to overlook: to omit.—*ns.* **overslaugh** (*ō´vər-slö;* Du. *overslaan,* to miss, skip over; *mil.*), exemption from duty in turn when employed on something else: a sand-bar (*U.S.*).—*vs.t.* **overslaugh´,** to remit or pass over by overslaugh: to pass over in favour of another (*U.S.*): to hinder; **oversleep´,** to indulge in sleeping too long: to sleep beyond.—*v.i.* to sleep too long.—*v.t.* **overslip´,** to slip by: to escape the notice of: to slip unnoticed from: to let slip.—*v.i.* to slip by: to make a slip, error, inadvertently.—*ns.* **o´verslip,** an inadvertency: a close-fitting underbodice; **o´versman,** an overseer: an umpire (*Scot.*); **o´versoul,** the divine principle forming the spiritual unity of all being.—*vs.t.* **oversow´,** to sow after something has been already sown: to sow over; **overspend´,** to spend beyond: to exhaust or cripple by spending.—*v.i.* to spend too much.—*adj.* **overspent´,** excessively fatigued. —*ns.* **o´verspill,** that which is spilt over: population leaving a district, or displaced by changes in housing, etc.; **o´verspin,** the spinning of a flying ball in the same direction as if it were rolling on the ground.—*vs.t.* **overstand´,** to outstay; **overstare´** (*Shak.* **ore-stare´**), to outstare; **overstate´,** to state too strongly: to exaggerate. —*n.* **overstate´ment; o´versteer,** tendency of a motor-car to exaggerate the degree of turning applied by the steering-wheel.—*v.t.* **overstep´,** to step beyond: to exceed: to transgress.—*n.* **o´verstep** (*geol.*), the transgression of an overlapping stratum over the edges of underlying unconformable strata.—*v.t.* **overstink´,** to stink more than.—*pa.t.* **overstunk´;** *Shak.* **orestunck´.**—*v.t.* and *v.i.* **overstrain´,** to strain too much: to strain beyond the elastic limit.—*n.* **o´verstrain,** too great strain.—*adj.* **overstrained´,** strained to excess: exaggerated.—*vs.t.* **overstretch´,** to stretch to excess: to exaggerate; **overstride´,** to stride across: to stand astride of; **overstrike´,** to strike with a downward blow:—*pa.t.* **overstruck´;** *Spens.* **overstrooke´.**—*adjs.* **overstrung´,** too highly strung: (of a piano) having two sets of strings crossing obliquely to save space; **o´verstuffed,** covered completely with well-stuffed upholstery.—*v.t.* **oversubscribe´,** to subscribe for beyond what is offered.—*n.* **oversubscrip´tion.**—*vs.t.* **oversway´,** to overrule: to bear down; **overswear´,** to swear anew.—*v.t.* and *v.i.* **overswell´,** to overflow.—*vs.t.* **overswim´,** to swim across; **overtake´,** to come up with: to catch up with: to catch: to come upon: to take by surprise.—*adj.* **overtā´ken,** fuddled. —*vs.t.* **overtalk´,** to talk over; **overtask´,** to task overmuch: to impose too heavy a task on; **overtax´,** to tax overmuch: to require too much of.—*v.i.* **overteem´,** to teem, breed, or produce, in excess.—*v.t.* to exhaust or wear out by breeding.—*v.t.* **overthrow´,** to throw over, overturn, upset: to ruin, subvert: to defeat utterly: to throw too far or too strongly.—*v.i.* (*obs.*) to be overturned: to throw too far.—*ns.* **o´verthrow,** act of overthrowing or state of being overthrown: a ball missed at the wicket and returned from the field (*cricket*): a run scored in consequence; **overthrow´er; o´verthrust** (overthrust

overscru´pulous, *adj.* over- (5).
overscru´pulousness, *n.* over- (5).
oversexed´, *adj.* over- (5).
oversimplificā´tion, *n.* over- (5).
oversim´plify, *v.t.* over- (5).
o´verskirt, *n.* over- (4).
overspec´ialise, -ize, *v.i.* over- (5).
overspecialisā´tion, *-z-, n.* over- (5).
overspread´, *v.t.* over- (1).
overstain´, *v.t.* over- (1).
overstay´, *v.t.* over- (2).
overstock´, *v.t.* over- (5).

o´verstock, *n.* over- (5).
overstress´, *v.t.* over- (5).
o´verstress, *n.* over- (5).
overstrew´, *v.t.* over- (1).
overstrong´, *adj.* over- (5).
overstud´y, *v.t., v.i.* over- (5).
o´verstudy, *n.* over- (5).
oversubt´le, *adj.* over- (5).
oversubt´lety, *n.* over- (5).
oversupply´, *v.t.* over- (5).
o´versupply, *n.* over- (5).
overte´dious (*Shak.*), *adj.* over- (5).

fault), a reversed fault or thrust where older rocks are pushed up bodily upon the back of younger.—*v.t.* overthwart', to lie athwart: to cross.—*adj.* opposite, transverse: contrary, perverse.—*adv.* crosswise: opposite.—*prep.* across, on the other side of.—*n.* o'vertime, time employed in working beyond the regular hours: work done in such time: pay for such work.—*adj.* and *adv.*, during, for, or concerning, such time.— *v.t.* (*ō-vǝr-tīm'*), to time too long (esp. of a photographic exposure).—*adj.* and *adv.* overtime'ly (*obs.*), too early, untimely.—*ns.* o'vertimer, one who works overtime; o'vertone, a harmonic or upper partial: a subtle meaning, additional to the main meaning, conveyed by a word or statement: implicit quality, or constant association.—*v.t.* overtop', to rise over the top of: to be higher than: to surpass: to exceed.—*v.i.* to rise too high.—*v.t.* overtower', to tower above.—*v.i.* to soar too high.—*v.i.* overtrade', to trade overmuch or beyond capital: to buy in more than can be sold or paid for.— *v.t.* to involve in trade in such a way.—*n.* over-trad'ing (one's capital, etc.).—*v.t.* overtrain', to train so far as to do harm: to train too high.—*n.* o'vertrick (*bridge*), a trick in excess of those contracted for.—*vs.t.* overtrip', to trip nimbly over; overtrump', to trump with a higher card than one already played; overturn', to throw down or over: to upset: to subvert.— *ns.* o'verturn, an overturning: a turnover; overturn'er; overvalua'tion; o'vervalue.—*vs.t.* overval'ue, to set too high a value on; overveil', to veil over or cover.—*ns.* o'verview (*Shak.*), an inspection; o'verwash, a washing over: material carried by glacier-streams over a frontal moraine (*geol.*).—Also *adj.*—*vs.t.* overwatch', to watch over: to watch through: to overcome with long watching; overwear', to wear out: to outwear, outlive:—*pa.t.* overwore'; *pa.p.* overworn' (see below).—*v.t.* overwear'y, to overcome with weariness, weary out.—*adj.* excessively weary.—*v.t.* overweath'er (*Shak.*), to batter by violence of weather.—*v.i.* overween' to expect too much: to be presumptuous or arrogant: to think too highly, esp. of oneself.—*adj.* and *n.* overween'ing.—*v.t.* overweigh', to be heavier than: to outweigh: to weigh down.—*n.* o'verweight, weight beyond what is required or what is allowed: preponderance.—*adjs.* overweight', above the weight required; over-weight'ed, not fairly balanced in presentation.—*vs.t.* overweight', to weigh down: to put too heavy a burden on; overwent' (see overgo); overwhelm', to overspread and crush by something heavy or strong: to flow over and bear down: to reduce to helplessness: to overpower: to ply overpoweringly: to overhang (*obs.*).—*n.* and *adj.* overwhel'ming. —*adv.* overwhel'mingly.—*vs.t.* overwind (-*wīnd'*), to wind too far:—*pa.t.* and *pa.p.* overwound; overwing', to outflank (*obs.*): to fly over.—*v.i.* overwin'ter, to pass the winter.—*adj.* overwise', wise overmuch: affectedly wise: wise in one's own estimation.—*adv.* overwise'ly.—*n.* o'verword, o'erword (*ōr'*, *ōr'*, *Scot. owr'*; also owre'word), the burden of a song: a habitual saying.—*v.t.* and *v.i.* overwork', to work overmuch.—*n.* o'verwork, additional work: (o'verwork') excess of work.—*adj.* overworn' (-*wō'*, -*wō'*), worn out: subdued by toil: spoiled by use: threadbare: trite: exhausted of meaning or freshness by excessive use: out of date: spent or past; overwound', *pa.t.* and *pa.p.* of overwind.—*vs.t.* overwrest', to overstrain; overwrest'le (*Spens.*), to overcome by wrestling; overwrite', to cover over with writing or other writing: to superscribe: to exhaust by writing too much: to

write too much about: to write in a laboured manner.—*v.i.* to write too much or too artificially.—*adj.* overwrought' (and *pa.p.* of overwork), worked too hard: too highly excited: with highly strained nerves: worked or embellished all over: overdone.—*v.t.* overyear' (*obs.*), to keep into a second, or later, year.— *adj.* (*dial.*) kept over from one year to the next. —*adv.* (*dial.*) till next year.

overact...to...overswim. See over-.

overt, *ō'vûrt*, *ō-vûrt'*, *adj.* open to view, not concealed: public: evident.—*adv.* o'vertly.—overt act, something obviously done in execution of a criminal intent.—market overt, open or public market. [Fr. *ouvert*, pa.p. of *ouvrir*, to open.]

overtake...to...overtrump. See over-.

overture, o'vǝr-tūr, *n.* an opening, aperture (*obs.*): an opening up, disclosure (*Shak.*): an open place (*Spens.*): an opening of negotiations: an offer or proposal: an opening or opportunity: an opening or beginning: an instrumental prelude to an opera, oratorio, etc., or an independent composition in similar form (sonata form): the method in Presbyterian usage of beginning legislation and maturing opinion by sending some proposition made from the inferior courts to the General Assembly, and *vice versa*: also the proposal so sent.—*v.t.* to lay a proposal before: to put forward as an overture. [O.Fr. *overture* (Fr. *ouverture*), opening.]

overturn...to...overyear. See over-.

ovibos, *ōv'i-bos*, *ov'i-bōs*, *n.* the musk-ox.—*adj.* ovibō'vine. [L. *ōvis*, sheep, *bōs*, *bovis*, ox.]

ovicide, *ō'vi-sid*, (*jocular*) *n.* sheep-killing. [L. *ōvis*, sheep, *caedĕre*, to kill.]

Ovidian, *ō-vid'i-ǝn*, or *o-*, *adj.* of, like, or relating to, the Latin poet *Ovid* (43 B.C.–A.D. 17).

ov(i)-, *ōv-*, *ō-vi-*, in composition, egg: ovum.— *n.* ovary (*ō'vǝ-ri*), the female genital gland: the part of the gynaeceum that contains the ovules (*bot.*).—*adj.* ovā'rian, of or pertaining to the ovary.—*ns.* ovā'riole, one of the egg-tubes forming an insect's ovary; ovāriot'omist; ovāriot'omy (Gr. *tomē*, a cut; *surg.*), the cutting of an ovary: usu. the removal of ovaries because of a tumour. —*adj.* ovā'rious (*rare*), consisting of eggs—*n.* ovari'tis, inflammation of the ovary, oophoritis. —*adj.* ō'vate, egg-shaped: shaped in outline like an egg, broadest below the middle (*bot.*).— *n.* oviduct (*ō'vi-dukt*), the tube by which the egg escapes from the ovary (*zool.*; L. *ducĕre*, *ductum*, to convey).—*adjs.* ovidū'cal, oviduc'tal. *adjs.* oviferous (*ō-vif'ǝ-rǝs*), egg-carrying (L. *ferre*, to bear); oviform (*ō'vi-förm*), egg-shaped (L. *förma*, form); ovigerous (*ōv-ij'ǝ-rǝs*), egg-carrying (L. *gerĕre*, to carry); oviparous (*ō-vip'ǝ-rǝs*), egg-laying (L. *parĕre*, to bring forth).—*n.* ovipar'ity (-*par'i-ti*).—*adv.* ovip'arously.—*n.* ovipositor (*ō-vi-poz'i-tǝr*), an egg-laying organ (L. *positor—pōnĕre*, to place).—*v.i.* ovipos'it, to deposit eggs with an ovipositor.—*n.* oviposition (-*pǝ-zish'ǝn*).—*ns.* ovisac (*ōv'i-sak*), a broodpouch: an egg-capsule (L. *saccus*; see sac); ovist (*ō'vist*), believer in doctrine that ovum contains all future generations in germ.—*adj.* ovoid (*ō'void*), egg-shaped and solid in form (sometimes also of a plane figure): egg-shaped and attached by the broad end (*bot.*).—*n.* an eggshaped figure or body (Gr. *eidos*, form).—*adj.* ovoid'al, ovoid.—*adj.* ovoviviparous (*ō-vō-vivip'ǝ-rǝs*, or -*vi-*), producing eggs which are hatched in the body of the parent (L. *vivus*, living, *parĕre*, to bring forth).—*v.i.* ovulate (*ov'ūl-āt*, *ōv'-*), to release ova from the ovary: to form ova.—*adj.* ov'ular, of or pertaining to an ovule.—*n.* ovulā'tion.—*n.* ovule (*ōv'ūl*), in flowering plants, the body which on fertilisation

---

overtoil', *v.t.* over- (5).

overtrust', *v.i.* over- (5).

o'vertrust, *n.* over- (5).

overvi'olent, *adj.* over- (5).

becomes the seed, answering to the megasporangium and consisting of the nucellus and its integuments with the embryo-sac (megaspore): an undeveloped seed (from mod. L. dim. of *ovum*).—*adj.* ōvulif′erous, carrying ovules.—*n.* ovum (ō′vəm), an egg: the egg-cell, or female gamete (*biol.*):—*pl.* o′va. [L. *ŏvum*, egg.]

oviform, ov′i-förm, ō′vi-, *adj.* like a sheep: ovine. —*adj.* ovine (ō′vin), of sheep: sheep-like. [L. *ŏvis*, sheep, *fōrma*, form.]

oviform ... to ... ovoidal. See ov(i)-.

ovolo, ō′vō-lō, *n.* a moulding with the rounded part composed of a quarter of a circle, or of an arc of an ellipse with the curve greatest at the top (*archit.*). [It.,—L. *ŏvum*, an egg.]

ovoviviparous ... to ... ovum. See ov(i)-.

ow. Same as ou, ouch (2).

owche, owch, *n.* Same as ouch (1).

owe, ō, *v.t.* to own (*obs.* or *dial.*): to be indebted for: to be under an obligation to repay or render: to feel as a debt or as due: to have to thank: to concede or be bound to concede as a handicap.—*v.i.* to be in debt:—*pa.t.* and *pa.p.* owed. —The old *pa.t.* ought and *pa.p.* own, now differently used, are given separately; see also owing. [O.E. *āgan*, to own, possess, pres. indic. *āh*, preterite *āhte*, pa.p. *āgen*; O.N. *eiga*, O.H.G. *eigan*, to possess.]

owelty, ō′el-ti, (*law*) *n.* equality. [A.Fr. *owelté*— L. *aequālitās*, -*ātis*.]

Owenite, ō′in-īt, *n.* a disciple of Robert Owen (1771-1858), who proposed to establish society on a basis of socialistic co-operation.—*adj.* Owenian (ō-ēn′i-ən).—*ns.* Ow′enism; Ow′enist.

ower, owre, *owr*, Scots forms of over. For compounds see the forms in over-.

owing, ō′ing, *adj.* due: to be paid: imputable.— owing to, because of: in consequence of.

owl, owl, *n.* any member of the Strigiformes, nocturnal predaceous birds with large broad heads, flat faces, large eyes surrounded by disks of feathers, short hooked beaks, silent flight, and howling or hooting cry: one who sits up at night: one who sees badly, or who shuns light: a solemn person: a wiseacre: a dullard: an owl-like breed of pigeon.—*v.i.* to behave like an owl.— *v.t.* (*obs.*) to smuggle (esp. wool or sheep from England to France).—*ns.* owl′er (*obs.*), a smuggler (esp. of wool or sheep); owl′ery, an abode of owls: owlishness (*Carlyle*); owl′et, an owl: a young owl: a moth of the Noctuidae. —*adj.* owl′ish, like an owl: solemn: blinking: stupid: dull-looking. —*n.* owl′ishness. —*adj.* owl′y, owlish.—owl′-car (*U.S.*), a night tramcar.—*adj.* owl′-eyed, having blinking eyes like an owl.—Owl′-glass, Owle′-glass, Howle′glass, Owl′spiegle, *Tyll Eulenspiegel*, a mischievous clown hero of a folk-tale popular in Germany from the 16th century or earlier; owl′-light, dusk; owl′-moth, a gigantic South American moth of the Noctuidae; owl′-parr′ot, the kakapo; owl′-train (*U.S.*), a night train. [O.E. *ūle*; Ger. *eule*, L. *ulula*; imit.]

own, ōn, *v.t.* to possess, have belonging to one: to acknowledge as one's own: to claim as one's own (*obs.*): to confess: to allow to be true: to admit, concede: to acknowledge, recognise.— *v.i.* to confess (with *to*).—*n.* own′er, possessor, proprietor: captain of a warship (*slang*).—*adj.* own′erless.—*n.* own′ership.—own′er-dri′ver, one who drives his own car; own′er-occupa′tion.— *adj.* own′er-occ′upied.—own′er-occ′upier, one who owns the house he lives in.—own up, to confess freely. [O.E. *āgnian—āgen*, one's own; cf. own (adj.).]

own, ōn, *adj.* belonging to oneself: often used with reflexive force, *my own, his own*, etc., serving instead of a genitive to *myself, himself*, etc., or transferring the sense of *self* to the subject (e.g. *I bake my own bread = I myself bake my*

---

*bread*): sometimes used as an endearment.— come into one's own, to take possession of one's rights: to have one's talents, merits, realised; get one's own back, retaliate, get even; hold one's own (see hold); on one's own, on one's own account: on one's own initiative: by one's own efforts or resources: independently: set up in independence: alone, by oneself. [O.E. *āgen*, pa.p. of *āgan*, to possess; cf. owe.]

owre, ower, o′er, *owr*, Scots forms of over. For compounds see over-.

owre, *owr*, (*Spens.*) *n.* Same as ore (1).

owrie. Same as ourie.

owsen, ow′sən, *n.pl.* Scots form of oxen. See ox.

ox, oks, *n.* a general name for male or female of common horned cattle (bull and cow), esp. a castrated male of the species: extended to kindred animals:—*pl.* ox′en, used for both male and female.—*n.* ox′er, an ox-fence.—ox′-ant′e-lope, any antelope of the hartebeest group; ox′ bird, the dunlin: the ox-pecker: an African weaver-bird: applied also to various other birds; ox′-bot, a warble-fly larva infesting cattle; ox′-bow (-bō), a collar for a yoked ox: a river-bend returning almost upon itself (forming an *ox-bow lake* when the neck is pierced and the bend cut off); ox′eye, a name for various birds, esp. the great titmouse: a wild chrysanthemum with yellow disk and white (*oxeye daisy*) or yellow ray (*yellow oxeye*, or corn marigold): an elliptical dormer window.—*adj.* ox′-eyed, having large, ox-like eyes.—ox′-fence, a fence for confining cattle: a hedge with a rail; ox′gang, ox′gate, ox′land, a bovate or one-eighth of a carucate of ploughland, the share attributed to each ox in a team of eight (averaging about 13 acres); ox′head, the head of an ox: a blockhead; ox′-pecker, an African genus (*Buphaga*) of birds akin to starlings, that eat the parasites on cattle—also *beefeater*; ox′-tail, the tail of an ox, esp. as used for soup, stew, etc.; ox′-tongue, the tongue of an ox, used as food: a yellow-flowered milky-juiced composite (*Picris echioides*); ox′-war′ble, a swelling on the back of an ox: the fly whose larva produces it.—have the black ox tread on one's foot, to experience sorrow or misfortune. [O.E. *oxa*, pl. *oxan*; Ger. *ochse*, Goth. *auhsa*, Sans. *ukṣan*.]

Oxalis, oks′ə-lis, *n.* the wood-sorrel genus, giving name to the family Oxalidā′ceae, close akin to the Geranium family.—*adj.* oxalic (-*al′ik*), applied to an acid ($C_2H_2O_4$) obtained from wood-sorrel.—*n.* ox′alate, a salt of oxalic acid. [Gr. *oxalis—oxys*, sharp, acid.]

Oxbridge, oks′brij, *n.* and *adj.* (pertaining to) Oxford and Cambridge regarded as typifying an upper-class-oriented kind of education, or as a road to unfair advantages, e.g. in obtaining jobs, or as the home of particular academic attitudes.

Oxford, oks′fərd, *adj.* belonging to the city, county, or university of Oxford.—*n.* Oxfordian (-*förd′i-ən*), a division of the Middle Jurassic.— Also *adj.*—Oxford bags, very wide trousers; Oxford blue, a dark blue; Oxford clay, a dark blue or grey clay of the Oxfordian formation; Oxford English, a form of standard English in which certain tendencies are (sometimes affectedly) exaggerated, widely believed to be spoken at Oxford; Oxford groups, informal circles of followers of Dr Frank Buchman, who exchanged religious experiences, and sought divine guidance individually (**the Oxford group**, his followers as a body; 1921-1938); Oxford movement, the Tractarian movement; Oxford (shoe), a low shoe, usu. laced. [O.E. *Oxnaford*, lit. oxen's ford.]

oxide, oks′id, *n.* a compound of oxygen and some other element or radical.—*n.* ox′idase, any of a group of enzymes that promote oxidation in plant and animal cells.—*v.t.* ox′idate (*id-āt*), to oxidise.—*n.* oxidā′tion, oxidising.—*adj.* oxidis′-able, -z-.—*v.t.* and *v.i.* ox′idise, -ize, to combine with oxygen: to deprive (an atom or ion) of, or (*v.i.*) to lose, electrons: to make, or become, rusty: to put a protective oxide coating on (a metal surface).—*n.* oxidis′er. -z-, an oxidising agent; oximeter (*oks-im′i-tər*), a photoelectric instrument for measuring the amount of oxygen in the blood. [Fr. *oxide* (now *oxyde*), formed from *oxygène*, oxygen.]

oxlip, *oks′lip*, *n.* originally a hybrid between primrose and cowslip: now, a species of Primula (*P. elatior*) like a large pale cowslip.—Also (*Shak.*) ox′slip. [O.E. *oxanslyppe*—*oxan*, gen. of *oxa*, ox, and *slyppe*, slime, a slimy dropping; cf. cowslip.]

Oxonian, *oks-ō′ni-ən*, *adj.* of or pertaining to Oxford or to its university.—*n.* an inhabitant, native, student, or graduate of Oxford: a kind of shoe. [L. *Oxonia*, Oxford—O.E. *Oxnaford*.]

oxonium, *oks-ō′ni-əm*, *n.* a univalent basic radical, $H_3O$, in which oxygen is tetravalent, forming organic derivatives, oxonium salts. [*oxygen* and *ammonium*.]

oxter, *oks′tər*, (*Scot.*) *n.* the armpit.—*v.t.* to take under the arm: to support by taking the arm. [O.E. *oxta*.]

oxy-, *oks-i-*, in composition, sharp: pointed: acid: oxygen.—*adj.* ox′y-acet′ylene, involving, using, or by means of, a mixture of oxygen and acetylene.—*ns.* ox′y-a′cid, ox′y-com′pound, ox′y-salt, etc., an acid, compound, salt, etc., containing oxygen: one in which an atom of hydrogen is replaced by a hydroxyl-group; ox′y-bro′mide, -chlo′ride, -flu′oride, -hal′ide, -i′odide, a compound of an element or radical with oxgyen and a halogen (bromine, etc.); ox′yhaemo-glo′bin, a loose compound of oxygen and haemoglobin.—*adj.* ox′y-hy′drogen, involving or using a mixture of oxygen and hydrogen.—*n.* ox′y-cal′cium light, limelight. [Gr. *oxys*, sharp.]

oxygen, *oks′i-jən*, *n.* a gas (atomic number 8) without taste, colour, or smell, forming part of the air, water, etc., and supporting life and combustion.—*v.t.* ox′ygenāte (or *oks-ij′*), to oxidise: to impregnate or treat with oxygen.—*ns.* oxygenā′tion; ox′ygenator, an apparatus performing functions of heart and lungs during an operation.—*v.t.* ox′ygenise, -ize, to oxygenate.—*adj.* oxyg′enous.—oxygen mask, a masklike breathing apparatus through which oxygen is supplied in rarefied atmospheres to aviators and mountaineers; oxygen tent, tent-like enclosure in which there is a controllable flow of oxygen, erected round a patient to aid breathing. [Gr. *oxys*, sharp, acid, and the root of *gennaein*, to generate, from the old belief that all acids contained oxygen.]

oxymel, *oks′i-mel*, *n.* a mixture of vinegar and honey. [Gr. *oxymeli*—*oxys*, sour, *meli*, honey.]

oxymoron, *oks-i-mō′ron*, *-mō′*, *n.* a figure of speech by means of which contradictory terms are combined, so as to form an expressive phrase or epithet, as *cruel kindness*, *falsely true*,

etc. [Gr. neut. of *oxymōros*, lit. pointedly foolish—*oxys*, sharp, *mōros*, foolish.]

oxyrhynchus, *oks-i-ring′kəs*, *n.* an Egyptian fish, sacred to the goddess Hathor, represented on coins and sculptures. [Gr. *oxyrrynchos*—*oxys*, sharp, *rhynchos*, a snout.]

oxytocin, *oks-i-tō′sin*, *n.* a pituitary hormone that stimulates uterine muscle contraction. [Gr. *oxys*, sharp, *tokos*, birth.]

oxytone, *oks′i-tōn*, *adj.* having the acute accent on the last syllable.—*n.* a word so accented. [Gr. *oxys*, sharp, *tonos*, tone.]

oy, oye, oe, *oi*, *ō-i*, *ō*, (*Scot.*) *n.* a grandchild. [Gael. *ogha*, *odha*.]

oyer, *oi′ər*, *n.* a hearing in a law-court, an assize.—oyer and terminer (*tûr′min-ər*), a royal commission conferring power to hear and determine criminal causes (out of official use 1972). [A.Fr. *oyer* (Fr. *ouïr*)—L. *audire*, to hear.]

oyez, oyes, *ō-yes′*, *ō′yes*, *interj.* the call of a public crier, or officer of a law-court, for attention before making a proclamation.—*n.* (*oiz*; *Shak.*) a proclamation. [O.Fr. *oyez*, imper. of *oir* (Fr. *ouïr*), to hear.]

oyster, *ois′tər*, *n.* bivalve shellfish (*Ostrea*) used as food: secretive person: source of advantage.—oys′ter-bank, -bed, -farm, -field, -park, place where oysters breed or are bred; oys′ter-catcher, the sea pie—a black and white wading bird, with red bill and feet, feeding on limpets and mussels (not oysters); oys′ter-fish′ery, the business of catching oysters; oys′ter-knife, a knife for opening oysters; oys′ter-patt′y, a small pie or pasty made from oysters; oys′ter-plant, salsify, or a seaside boraginaceous plant, *Mertensia maritima*—both supposed to taste like oysters; oys′ter-shell, the shell of an oyster.—*n.pl.* oys′ter-tongs, a tool for gathering oysters.—oys′ter-wench, -wife, -woman (all *obs.*), a woman who sells oysters; the world is my (Shak., *Merry Wives* II, ii. 2, world's mine), his, etc., oyster, the world lies before me, etc., ready to yield profit or success. [O.Fr. *oistre* (Fr. *huitre*)—L. *ostrea*—Gr. *ostreon*, an oyster—*osteon*, a bone.]

oystrige, *oi′strij*, (*Spens.*) *n.* for ostrich.

ozaena, *ō-zē′na*, *n.* a fetid discharge from the nostrils. [Gr. *ozaina*, a fetid polypus of the nose—*ozein*, to smell.]

ozokerite, *ō-zō′kər-it*, *-kēr′it*, ozocerite, *ō-zos′ər-it*, *ō-zō-sēr′it*, *n.* a waxy natural paraffin. [Gr. *ozein*, to smell, *kēros*, wax.]

ozone, *ō′zōn*, *n.* an allotropic form ($O_3$) of oxygen present in the atmosphere, once regarded as health-giving, but harmful in concentration such as may occur in industrial areas: (see also ozonosphere).—*ns.* ozonā′tion, -isā′tion, -z-.—*adj.* ozonif′erous, bringing or producing ozone.—*v.t.* ō′zonise, -ize, to turn into, charge with, or treat with, ozone.—*ns.* ozonis′er, -z-, apparatus for turning oxygen into ozone; ozon′osphere, ozone layer, a layer of the upper atmosphere where ozone is formed in quantity, protecting earth from the sun's ultraviolet rays. [Gr. *ozōn*, pr.p. of *ozein*, to smell.]

Neutral vowels in unaccented syllables: *el′ə-mənt*; for certain sounds in foreign words, see p. viii

# P

**P, p,** pē, *n.* the sixteenth letter of our alphabet, and of the Greek (see pi), representing a voiceless labial stop: in mediaeval Roman notation, P = 400, P̄ = 400,000: in chem. *p*- is an abbreviation for para-.—P-Celt, P-Kelt (see Celt).—**mind one's p's and q's** (see mind).

**pa, pä,** *n.* a childish or vulgar word for father. [papa.]

**pa, pah,** pä, *n.* a Maori fort or settlement. [Maori.]

**pabouche,** pə-bōōsh', *n.* a slipper. [See baboosh.]

**pabulum,** pab'ū-, yə-, -ləm, *n.* food of any kind, esp. that of lower animals and of plants: provender: fuel: nourishment for the mind.—*adjs.* **pab'ular, pab'ūlous.** [L. *pābulum*—*pāscĕre,* to feed.]

**paca,** pä'kə, *n.* the so-called spotted cavy of South America, akin to the agouti. [Sp. and Port.,—Tupí *paca*.]

**pacable,** pāk'ə-bl, pak', *adj.* capable of being appeased: willing to forgive.—*n.* **pacation** (pə-kā'shən). [L. *pācāre,* to appease—*pāx, pācis,* peace.]

**pace,** pās, *n.* a stride: a step: the space between the feet in walking, about 30 inches, or (among the Romans), the space between two successive positions of the same foot, over 58 inches: gait: rate of walking, running, etc. (of a man or beast): rate of speed in movement or work, often applied to fast living: a mode of stepping in horses in which the legs on the same side are lifted together: amble: a step of a stair, or the like: a pass or passage (*obs.*).—*v.t.* to traverse with measured steps: to measure by steps: to train to perform paces: to set the pace for: to perform as a pace or paces.—*v.i.* to walk: to walk slowly and with measured tread: to amble. —*adj.* **paced,** having a certain pace or gait.—*n.* **pac'er,** one who paces: a horse whose usual gait is a pace: a horse trained to pace in harness racing.—**pace'maker,** one who sets the pace as in a race (also *fig.*): a small mass of muscle cells in the heart which control the heart-beat electrically; an electronic device (in later models, with radioactive core) used to correct weak or irregular heart rhythms; **pace'-setter,** a pacemaker, except in anatomical and electronic senses.—**go the pace,** to go at a great speed: to live a fast life; **keep, or hold, pace with,** to go as fast as: to keep up with; **make, set the pace,** to regulate the speed for others by example; **put one through one's paces,** to set one to show what one can do; **show one's paces,** to show what one can do. [Fr. *pas*—L. *passus,* a step—*pandĕre, passum,* to stretch.]

**pace,** pä'sē, *prep.* with or by the leave of (expressing disagreement courteously). [L., abl. of *pāx,* peace.]

**Pace,** päs, a Scots form of **Pasch.**—**pace egg,** an Easter egg, one hard-boiled and dyed; **pace'-egging,** begging for eggs, etc., at Easter: rolling pace eggs on the ground. See **pasha.**

**pacha, pachalic.** See **pasha.**

**pachisi,** pä-chē'sē, -zē, *n.* an Indian game like backgammon or ludo. [Hindi *pacīsī,* of twenty-five—the highest throw.]

**pachy-,** pak'i-, in combination, thick.—*adjs.* **pachycarp'ous** (Gr. *karpos,* fruit), having a thick pericarp; **pachydac'tyl, -ous** (Gr. *daktylos,* digit), having thick digits.—*n.* **pach'yderm** (Gr. *derma,* skin), any animal of the Pachydermata: an insensitive person.—*adj.* **pachyderm'al.**—*n.pl.*

**Pachyderm'ata,** in old classification, those ungulates that do not ruminate—elephant, horse, pig, etc.—*adj.* **pachyder'matous,** thick-skinned: of the pachyderms: insensitive.—*n.* **pachyderm'ia,** abnormal thickness of skin or mucous membrane.—*adjs.* **pachyderm'ic, pachyderm'ous.** —*n.* **pachym'eter,** an instrument for measuring small thicknesses. [Gr. *pachys,* thick.]

**pacify,** pas'i-fī, *v.t.* to appease: to calm: to bring peace to.—*adjs.* **pac'ifiable; pacif'ic,** peacemaking: appeasing: inclining towards peace: peaceful: mild: tranquil: (*cap.*) of, or pertaining to the ocean between Asia and America, so called by Magellan, the first European to sail on it, because he happened to cross it in peaceful weather conditions.—*n.* (*cap.*) the Pacific Ocean.—*adj.* **pacif'ical,** pacific (rare except in phrase *Letters pacifical,* letters recommending the bearer as one in peace and fellowship with the Church—also *Letters of peace, Pacificae*).—*adv.* **pacif'ically.**—*v.t.* **pacif'-icāte,** to give peace to.—*ns.* **pacificā'tion,** peacemaking: conciliation: appeasement: a peace treaty; **pacif'icātor,** a peacemaker.—*adj.* **pacif'-icatory** (-ə-tə-ri), tending to make peace.—*ns.* **pacif'icism** (-sizm), the beliefs and principles of pacifists; **pacif'icist** (-sist), one who is opposed to war, or believes all war to be wrong; **pac'ifier;** **pac'ifism, pac'ifist,** ill-formed, but generally preferred forms of **pacificism, pacificist.** [Partly through Fr. *pacifier*—L. *pācificus,* pacific—*pācificāre*—*pāx, pācis,* peace, *facĕre,* to make.]

**pack,** pak, *n.* a bundle, esp. orig. one made to be carried on the back by a pedlar or pack-animal: a collection, stock, or store: a bundle of some particular kind or quantity, as of wool, 240 lb.: the quantity packed at a time or in a season: a complete set of playing cards: a number of animals herding together or kept together for hunting: a shepherd's own sheep grazing along with his employer's as part payment (*Scot.*): the forwards in a Rugby football team: a group of cub scouts in the Scout movement: a worthless, disreputable or otherwise objectionable set of persons: a gang, as of thieves: a mass of pack-ice: a sheet for folding round the body to allay inflammation, fever, etc.: the use or application of such a sheet: a built support for a mine-roof: packing material: a cosmetic paste: a number of photographic plates or films exposed together: act of packing or condition of being packed: mode of packing: a person of worthless or bad character (*obs.*): a compact package, esp. of something for sale: a parachute folded in its fabric container: a group of e.g. submarines acting together.—*v.t.* to make into a bundled pack: to place compactly in a box, bag, or the like: to press together closely: to compress: to fill tightly or compactly: to fill with anything: to cram: to crowd: to envelop: to surround closely: to fill the spaces surrounding: to prepare (food) for preservation, transport and marketing: to send away, dismiss (usu. with *off*): to form into a pack: to load with a pack: to carry in packs: to carry, wear (a gun):—*v.i.* to form into a pack: to settle or be driven into a firm mass: to form a scrum: to admit of being put into compact shape: to put one's belongings together in boxes, bags, etc., as for a journey (often with *up*): to travel with a pack: to take oneself off, to depart in haste (usu. with

fāte, fär; mē, hûr (her); mīne; mōte, fŏr; mūte; mōōn, fŏŏt; dhen (then)

*off*): to plot, intrigue, arrange privately (*Shak.*).
—*n.* **pack'age**, the act, manner, or privilege of packing: a bundle, packet, or parcel: a case or other receptacle for packing goods in.—*v.t.* to put into a container or wrappings.—*adj.* **pack'aged** (*lit.* and *fig.*).—*ns.* **pack'er**, one who packs: one who packs goods for sending out: an employer or employee in the business of preparing and preserving food: a pack-animal (*Austr.*): one who transports goods by means of pack-animals (*U.S.*): a machine or device for packing; **pack'et**, a small package: a carton: a ship or vessel employed in carrying packets of letters, passengers, etc.: a vessel plying regularly between one port and another (also **pack'et-boat, pack'et-ship**, etc.): a large amount of money (*coll.*): a small group: a cluster of bacteria: used as equivalent to a quantum (*fig.*): a serious injury (*slang*).—*v.t.* to parcel up.—*n.* **pack'ing**, the act of putting into packs or of tying up for carriage or storing: material for packing: anything used to fill an empty space or to make a joint close.—**package deal**, a deal which embraces a number of matters and has to be accepted as a whole, the less favourable items along with the favourable; **package holiday, tour**, one whose details are arranged by the organiser before he advertises it; **pack'-an'imal**, a beast used to carry goods on its back; **pack'-cinch** (-*sinsh*), a wide girth for a pack-animal; **pack'-cloth**, a cloth in which goods are enclosed: packsheet; **pack'-drill**, a military punishment of marching about laden with full equipment; **pack'et-note**, a size of notepaper 5½ by 9 inches; **pack'-horse**, a horse used to carry goods on its back: a drudge; **pack'-ice**, a mass of large pieces of floating ice driven together by winds and currents; **pack'ing-box, -case**, a box or framework for packing goods in; **pack'ing-need'le**, a strong needle for sewing up packages; **pack'ing-paper**, a strong and thick kind of wrapping-paper; **pack'ing-press**, a press for squeezing goods into small compass for packing; **pack'ing-sheet**, or **pack'sheet**, coarse cloth for packing goods; **pack'-load**, the load an animal can carry; **pack'man**, a pedlar or a man who carries a pack; **pack'-mule**, a mule used for carrying burdens; **pack'-saddle**, a saddle for packs; **pack'staff**, a staff for supporting a pedlar's pack when he rests; **pack'-thread**, a coarse thread used to sew up packages; **pack'-train**, a train of loaded pack-animals; **pack'-twine**, thin twine for tying up parcels; **pack'way**, a narrow path fit for pack-horses.—**pack a punch**, to be capable of giving a powerful blow; **pack it in, up**, to stop, give up, doing something; **pack up**, stop: break down; **send one packing**, to dismiss summarily. [M.E. *packe, pakke*, app.—M. Flem. *pac* or Du. or L. Ger. *pak*.]

**pack**, *pak*, (*obs.*) *n.* a secret or underhand arrangement.—*v.i.* to make such an arrangement (*Shak.*).—*v.t.* (esp. in *pass.*) to bring into a plot as accomplice (*Shak.*): to shuffle (cards) esp. dishonestly (*obs.*): to fill up (a jury, meeting, etc.) with persons of a particular kind for one's own purposes.—**pack cards with** (*Shak.*, etc.), to make a dishonest arrangement with. [Prob. **pact**.]

**pack**, *pak*, (*Scot.*) *adj.* intimate, confidential. [Origin unknown.]

**packfong**, an incorrect form of **paktong**.

**paco**, *pä'kō*, *n.* alpaca:—*pl.* **pa'cos**. [Sp.,—Quechua *paco*.]

**pact**, *pakt*, *n.* that which is agreed on: an agreement, esp. informal or not legally enforceable.—*n.* **pac'tion** (chiefly *Scot.*), a pact.—*v.t.* to agree.—*adj.* **pac'tional**. [L. *pactum*—*pacīscĕre*, *pactum*, to contract.]

**pactum**, *pak'təm, 'tōōm*, (L.) a pact; **pactum illicitum** (*i-lis'i-təm, i-lik'i-tōōm*), an illegal

compact; **pactum nudum** (*nū'dəm, nōō'dōōm*), a pact without consideration.

**pad**, *pad*, *n.* a path: a thief on the high-road (usually *footpad*; *arch.*): (abbrev. from **pad'-horse**) a horse for riding on the road: an easy-paced horse.—*v.i.* to walk on foot: to trudge along: to walk with dull-sounding tread: to rob on foot (*arch.*):—*pr.p.* **padd'ing**; *pa.t.* and *pa.p.* **padd'ed**.—*ns.* **padd'ing-ken**, a thieves' or tramps' lodging-house; **pad'-nag**, an ambling nag.—**pad the hoof** (*slang*), to walk, trudge; **stand pad**, to beg by the roadside. [Du. *pad*, a path.]

**pad**, *pad*, *n.* anything stuffed with a soft material, to prevent friction, pressure, or injury, for inking, for filling out, etc.: a soft saddle: a cushion: a number of sheets of paper or other soft material fastened together in a block: a leg-guard for cricketers, etc.: the fleshy, thick-skinned undersurface of the foot of many animals, as the fox: the foot of a beast, esp. of chase: its footprint: a water-lily leaf (*U.S.*): (usu. in *pl.*) thick watered ribbon for watch-guards: a rocket-launching platform: a bed, room, or home, esp. one's own (*slang*): a device built into a road surface, operated by vehicles passing over it, controlling changes of traffic lights (**vehicle-actuated signals**) so as to give passage for longer time to the greater stream of traffic.—*v.t.* to stuff, cover, or fill out with anything soft: to furnish with padding: to track by footprints: to impregnate, as with a mordant:—*pr.p.* **padd'ing**; *pa.p.* **padd'ed**.—*ns.* **padd'er**, one who pads, or cushions; **padd'ing**, stuffing: matter of less value introduced into a book or article in order to make it of the length desired: the process of mordanting a fabric.—**pad'-cloth**, a cloth covering a horse's loins; **padded cell**, a room with padded walls in a mental hospital; **pad'-el'ephant**, a working elephant wearing a pad but no howdah; **pad'-saddle**, a treeless, padded saddle; **pad'-tree**, the wooden or metal frame to which harness-pads are attached. [Origin obscure; possibly connected with **pod**.]

**pad.** Same as **ped.**

**padang**, *pad'ang*, *n.* a field. [Malay.]

**padauk, padouk**, *pä-dowk'*, *n.* a Burmese timber tree of the red-sanders genus. [Burmese.]

**paddle**, *pad'l*, *v.i.* to wade about or dabble in liquid or semi-liquid: to walk unsteadily or with short steps: to play or toy with the fingers (*arch.*): to trifle (*obs.*).—*v.t.* (*arch.*) to toy with or finger.—*n.* **padd'ler**, one who paddles: (in *pl.*) a protective garment worn by children when paddling. [Cf. **pad** (1), and L. Ger. *paddeln*, to tramp about.]

**paddle, padle, paidle**, *päd'l, pād'l*, (*Scot.*) *n.* the lumpsucker.—Also **cock'-paid'le** (*masc.*), **hen'-paid'le** (*fem.*). [Origin unknown.]

**paddle**, *pad'l*, *n.* a small, long-handled spade: a short, broad, spoon-shaped oar, used for moving canoes: the blade of an oar: one of the boards of a paddle-wheel or water-wheel: a swimming animal's flipper: a paddle-shaped instrument for stirring, beating, etc.—*v.i.* to use a paddle, progress by use of paddles: to row gently: to swim about like a duck.—*v.t.* to propel by paddle: to slap.—*ns.* **padd'ler**, one who paddles; **padd'ling**, the act of paddling: a flock of wild duck on water.—**padd'le-boat**, a paddle-steamer; **padd'le-board**, one of the boards of a paddle-wheel; **padd'le-box**, the covering of a paddle-wheel; **padd'le-shaft**, the axle on which paddle-wheels turn; **padd'le-staff**, a small spade or paddle; **padd'le-steam'er**, a steamer propelled by paddle-wheels; **padd'le-wheel**, the wheel of a steam-vessel, which by turning in the water causes the boat to move; **padd'le-wood**, light, strong wood of a Guiana tree (Aspidosperma) of

the dogbane family.—**paddle one's own canoe,** to progress independently. [Origin obscure.]
**paddock,** *pad'ək,* (*arch.* and *Scot.*) *n.* a toad or frog.—**padd'ock-stool,** a toadstool. [Dim. from late O.E. *pade, padde,* toad; O.N. *padda.*]
**paddock,** *pad'ək, n.* an enclosed field under pasture, orig. near a house or stable: a small field in which horses are kept before a race: any enclosed field (*Austr.*). [Apparently from earlier *parrock*—O.E. *pearroc,* park.]
**paddy,** *pad'i, n.* growing rice: rice in the husk.—**padd'y-bird,** the Java sparrow or rice-bird; **padd'y-field.** [Malay *pādi,* rice in the straw.]
**Paddy,** *pad'i, n.* a familiar name for an Irishman: (without *cap.*) a rage (*coll.*).—*n.* **Padd'yism,** a hibernicism.—**Paddy's lantern,** the moon; **paddy wagon,** a black Maria; **padd'y-whack** (*slang*), an Irishman, esp. a big one: a rage: a nurse's word for a slap.
**padella,** *pa-del'ə, n.* a shallow dish of fat with a wick used in illuminations. [It., a frying-pan— L. *patella.*]
**pademelon, paddymelon, padymelon,** *pad'i-mel'ən, n.* a small wallaby (*Macropus thetidis*). [From a native Australian name.]
**paderero,** *pad-ə-rā'rō.* Same as **pederero.**
**padishah,** *pä'di-shä, n.* chief ruler: great king, a title of the Shah of Persia, and formerly of the Sultan of Turkey, the Great Mogul, or the (British) Emperor of India. [Pers. *pad,* master, *shāh,* king.]
**padlock,** *pad'lok, n.* a movable lock with a link turning on a hinge or pivot at one end, catching the bolt at the other.—Also *v.t.* [Origin uncertain, possibly dial. Eng. *pad,* a basket, and **lock.**]
**padouk.** Same as **padauk.**
**padma,** *päd'mə, n.* the sacred lotus. [Sans.]
**padre,** *pä'drä, n.* father, a title given to priests: an army chaplain: a parson.—*n.* **padrō'ne,** a shipmaster: an innkeeper: an employer: one who jobs out hand-organs, or who gets children to beg for him:—*pl.* **padrō'ni** (*-nē*). [Port. (also Sp. and It.) *padre,* It. *padrone*—L. *pater,* a father, *patrōnus,* a patron.]
**Paduan,** *pad'ū-ən, adj.* of *Padua.*—*n.* a native of Padua: a counterfeit Roman bronze coin made at Padua in the 16th century: the pavan.
**paduasoy,** *pad'ū-ə-soi, pä'də-soi, n.* a corded silk used in the 18th century: a garment made of it. [Fr. *pou-de-soie*—*pou, pout, poult* (of unknown origin), *de soie,* of silk; apparently influenced by *Padua.*]
**Paean,** *pē'ən, n.* the Homeric physician of the gods: later, an epithet of Apollo: (without *cap.*) a lyric to Apollo or Artemis (or some other god): (without *cap.*) a song of thanksgiving or triumph: (without *cap.*) exultation.—*n.* **pae'on,** a foot of four syllables, any one long, three short.—*adj.* **paeon'ic** (*-on'ik*). [L. *Paeān, paeōn*—Gr. *Paiān, -ānos, paiōn, -ōnos.*]
**paed(o)-, ped(o)-,** *pēd-, pē-dō-,* also sometimes **paid(o)-, pid-,** *pi-dō-,* in composition, child, boy.—*adj.* **paedagog'ic** (see **pedagogic**).—*ns.* **paed'-agogue** (see **pedagogue**); **paed'erast** (Gr. *erastēs,* lover), one who practises paederasty.—*adj.* **paederast'ic.**—*ns.* **paed'erasty,** sexual relations of a male with a male, esp. a boy; **paedeut'ic, paideut'ic, -s,** educational method or theory.—*adj.* **paediat'ric** (Gr. *iātrikos,* medical), relating to the medical treatment of children.—*ns.* **paediat'rics,** the treatment of children's diseases; **paediatrician** (*-ə-trish'ən*), **paedi'atrist; paedi'-atry; paedobap'tism,** infant baptism; **paedo-bap'tist.**—*adj.* **paedodont'ic.**—*ns.* **paedodont'ics,** branch of dentistry concerned with care of children's teeth; **paedogen'esis,** reproduction by an animal in the larval state.—*adj.* **paedogenet'ic.**—*ns.* **paedomorph'ism** (Gr. *morphē,* form), retention of juvenile characters in the mature stage; **paed'ophile** (*-fil*), one affected with paedo-

philia; **paedophilia** (*-fil'*), sexual desire whose object is children.—*adjs.* and *ns.* **paedophil'iac, -phil'ic.**—*ns.* **paed'otribe** (*-trib*; Gr. *paidotribēs*), a gymnastic teacher; **paedot'rophy** (Gr. *tropheiā,* nursing), the art of rearing children. [Gr. *pais, paidos,* boy, child; *paideutēs,* teacher.]
**paella,** *pī-el'ə, pä-el'ya, n.* a stew containing saffron, chicken, rice, vegetables, etc. [Sp.,— L. *patella,* pan.]
**paenula,** *pē'nū-lə, n.* a Roman travelling cloak: a chasuble, esp. in its older form. [L. *paenula.*]
**paeon.** See **Paean.**
**paeony.** Same as **peony.**
**pagan,** *pā'gən, n.* a heathen: one who is not a Christian, Jew, or Mohammedan: more recently, one who has no religion: one who sets a high value on sensual pleasures.—Also *adj.*—*v.t.* **pā'ganise, -ize,** to render pagan or heathen: to convert to paganism.—*adj.* **pā'ganish,** heathenish.—*n.* **pā'ganism,** heathenism: the beliefs and practices of the heathen. [L. *pāgānus,* rustic, peasant, also civilian (because the Christians reckoned themselves soldiers of Christ)—*pāgus,* a district.]
**page,** *pāj, n.* a boy attendant: a boy in buttons employed as a messenger in hotels, clubs, etc.: a messenger, boy or girl, in the U.S. Congress, etc.: a youth training for knighthood, receiving, education and performing services at court or in a nobleman's household (*hist.*): a contrivance for holding up a long skirt in walking (*hist.*).—*v.t.* to attend as a page: to seek or summon by sending a page around or by repeatedly calling aloud for.—*n.* **page'hood,** condition of a page. [Fr. *page*; of obscure origin.]
**page,** *pāj, n.* one side of a leaf of a book, etc.— 4 pages in a folio sheet, 8 in a quarto, 16 in an octavo, 24 in a duodecimo, 36 in an octodecimo: the type, illustrations, etc., arranged for printing one side of a leaf: rhetorically, writings, litera-ture: an incident, episode, or whatever may be imagined as matter to fill a page.—*v.t.* to num-ber the pages of: to make up into pages (*print.*).—*adj.* **paginal** (*paj'*).—*v.t.* **paginate** (*paj'*), to mark with consecutive numbers, to page.—*ns.* **paginā'tion,** the act of paging a book: the figures and marks that indicate the numbers of pages; **pā'ging,** the marking or numbering of the pages of a book.—**page'-proof,** a proof of matter made up into pages. [Fr.,—L. *pāgina,* a page.]
**pageant,** *paj'ənt,* (*arch.*) *pāj'-, n.* a dramatic perfor-mance, scene, or part (*arch.*): a movable stage or carriage for acting on (*obs.*): a stage machine (*obs.*): a spectacle, esp. one carried around in procession: a series of tableaux or dramatic scenes connected with local history or other topical matter, performed either on a fixed spot or in procession: a piece of empty show: dis-play.—*adj.* of the nature of a puppet: specious.—*n.* **page'antry,** splendid display: pompous spectacle: a fleeting show. [Origin obscure; Anglo-L. *pāgina* may be the classical word transferred from page to scene in a MS or *pāgina,* in the sense of slab, may have come to mean boarding, framework.]
**pagoda,** *pə-gō'də,* pagod, *pag'od,* formerly also *pə-god', n.* an Eastern temple, esp. in the form of a many-storied tapering tower, each story with a projecting roof: an ornamental building in imitation of this: an idol, a demigod (*obs.*): a former Indian coin, bearing the figure of a pagoda.—**pagoda sleeve,** a funnel-shaped outer sleeve turned back to show lining and inner sleeve; **pago'da-tree',** a name for various erect trees of pagoda-like form: a fabulous Indian tree that dropped pagodas when shaken. [Port. *pagode*—Pers. *but-kadah,* idol-house, or some other Eastern word.]
**pagri,** *pug'rē, n.* a turban: a light scarf worn

round the hat to keep off the sun.—Also **pugga-ree, puggree, puggery.** [Hindi *pagri*.]

**pah,** *pä, interj.* an exclamation of disgust.

**pah.** See **pa** (2).

**Pahlavi.** Same as **Pehlevi.**

**paid,** *päd, pa.t.* and *pa.p.* of **pay.**—*adj.* satisfied (*obs.*): drunk (*Shak.*): hired.—*adj.* **paid-up',** paid in full: having fulfilled financial obligations.—**put paid to,** to finish: to destroy chances of success in.

**paid-.** See **paed-.**

**paidle.** See **paddle** (2).

**paigle, pagle,** *pä'gl, n.* the cowslip. [Origin unknown.]

**paik,** *päk,* (*Scot.*) *v.t.* to thump, drub.—*n.* a blow: (in *pl.,* with *his,* etc.) a drubbing. [Origin unknown.]

**pail,** *päl, n.* an open cylindrical or conical vessel with a hooped handle, for holding or carrying liquids (also ice, coal, etc.), a bucket: a pailful.—*n.* **pail'ful,** as much as fills a pail. [O.E. *pægel,* a gill measure, apparently combined with or influenced by O.Fr. *paele,* a pan—L. *patella,* a pan, dim. of *patera*—*patēre,* to be open.]

**paillasse.** Same as **palliasse.**

**paillette,** *pal-yet', n.* a spangle.—*n.* **paillon** (*pal'yon, pä-yō*), a piece of foil, to show through enamel, etc. [Fr.]

**pain,** *pān, n.* penalty: suffering: bodily suffering: (now only in *pl.*) great care or trouble taken in doing anything: (in *pl.*) the throes of childbirth: a tiresome or annoying person (*coll.*).—*v.t.* to cause suffering to: to put to trouble (*arch.;* esp. *refl.*).—*adjs.* **pained,** showing or expressing pain: suffering pain: distressed; **pain'ful,** full of pain: causing pain: requiring labour, pain, or care: laborious, painstaking (*arch.*): distressing, irksome.—*adv.* **pain'fully.**—*n.* **pain'fulness.**—*adj.* **pain'less,** without pain.—*adv.* **pain'lessly.**—*n.* **pain'lessness.**—**pain'-killer,** anything that does away with pain: a nostrum claiming to end pain; **pains'taker,** one who takes pains or care: a careful worker.—*adj.* **pains'taking,** taking pains or care.—*n.* careful diligence.—**be at pains, take pains,** to put oneself to trouble, be assiduously careful; **for one's pains,** as reward or result of trouble taken (commonly ironical); **pain in the neck** (*fig.*), a feeling of acute discomfort: an exasperating circumstance: a thoroughly tiresome person; **under** or **on pain of,** under liability to the penalty of. [Fr. *peine*—L. *poena,* satisfaction—Gr. *poinē,* penalty.]

**painim,** *pä'nim.* See **paynim.**

**paint,** *pānt, v.t.* to cover over with colouring matter: to represent in a coloured picture: to produce as a coloured picture: to apply with a brush: to apply anything to, with a brush: to describe or present as if in paint (*fig.*): to colour: to apply coloured cosmetics to: to adorn, diversify: to represent speciously or deceptively.—*v.i.* to practise painting: to use coloured cosmetics on the face: to tipple (*slang*).—*n.* a colouring substance spread or for spreading on the surface: a cake of such matter: coloured cosmetics.—*adj.* **paint'able,** suitable for painting.—*adj.* **painted,** covered with paint: ornamented with coloured figures: marked with bright colours: feigned.—*ns.* **paint'er,** one who paints: an artist in painting: one whose occupation is painting: a house-decorator: a vivid describer; **paint'iness; paint'ing,** the act or employment of laying on colours: the act of representing objects by colours: a painted picture: vivid description in words; **paint'ress,** formerly, a woman artist who paints: a woman employed to paint pottery; **paint'ure** (*Dryden*), the art of painting: a picture.—*adj.* **paint'y,** overloaded with paint, with the colours too glaringly used: smeared with paint.—**paint'-box,** a box in which different paints are kept in compartments; **paint'-bridge,** a platform used by theatrical scene-painters; **paint'-brush,** a brush for putting on paint: the painted cup (see below); **painted cloth,** a hanging of cloth painted with figures, a substitute for tapestry, formerly common in taverns; **painted cup,** a scrophulariaceous plant (Castilleja) with brightly coloured upper leaves; **painted grass,** striped canary-grass, gardener's garters; **painted lady,** the thistle-butterfly, orange-red spotted with white and black: the painted cup: a parti-coloured pink, sweetpea, gladiolus, etc.; **painted snipe,** a genus (Rhynchaea) of birds akin to the snipes, the hen brightly coloured; **painter's colic,** lead-colic; **paint'er-stain'er,** a member of the London livery company of painters; **paint roller,** roller used in house-painting instead of a brush.—**paint the lily,** to attempt to beautify that which is already beautiful; **paint the town red,** to break out in a boisterous spree. [O.Fr. *peint,* pa.p. of *peindre,* to paint—L. *pingēre,* to paint.]

**painter,** *pānt'ər, n.* a rope for fastening a boat.—**cut the painter,** to sever ties; **lazy painter,** a small painter for use in fine weather only. [Origin obscure.]

**painter,** *pānt'ər,* (*U.S.*) *n.* the cougar. [**panther.**]

**paiock(e), pajock(e),** *pä'ok? pä'jok? n.* an obscure word in Shakespeare (*Hamlet* III, ii) conjectured to mean peacock (possibly a misprint for *pacock;* possibly *=pea-jock*).

**pair,** *pār, n.* two things equal, or suited to each other, or growing, grouped or used together: a set of two equal or like things forming one instrument, garment, etc., as a pair of scissors, tongs, trousers: a set of like things generally: a pack (of cards; *obs.*): a flight of stairs: a couple: husband and wife: two persons betrothed to or in love with each other: a male and a female animal mated together: two persons or things associated together: two horses harnessed together: two cards of like designation: two voters on opposite sides who have an agreement to abstain from voting.—*v.t.* to couple: to sort out in pairs.—*v.i.* to be joined in couples: to be a counterpart or counterparts: to mate.—*adj.* **paired,** arranged in pairs: set by twos of a like kind: mated.—*n.* **pair'ing.**—*adv.* **pair'wise,** in pairs.—*adj.* **pair'-horse,** for a pair of horses.—**pair'ing-time,** the time when birds go together in pairs; **pair'-oar,** a boat rowed by two.—Also *adj.*—**pair-roy'al,** three cards of the same denomination, esp. in cribbage and in the obs. post and pair: a throw of three dice all falling alike: a set of three (also **pairi'al, pri'al**).—**pair of colours,** two flags carried by a regiment, one the national ensign, the other the flag of the regiment: hence an ensigncy; **pair off,** to arrange, set against each other, or set aside in pairs: to become associated in pairs. [Fr. *paire,* a couple—L. *paria,* neut. pl. of *pār,* afterwards regarded as a fem. sing., equal.]

**pair, paire,** *pār.* Obs. aphetic forms of **appair.** [O.Fr.]

**pais,** *pā, n.* the people from whom a jury is drawn. [O.Fr.]

**paisa,** *pi'sä, n.* in India and Pakistan, a coin worth one one-hundredth of a rupee (in India, for a time, described officially as **naya paisa** (*nə-yä'*), new paisa or pice:—*pl.* **naye paise** -*yā', -sä*).

**paisley,** *pāz'li, n.* a woollen or other fabric with a pattern resembling Paisley pattern: an article made of this.—**paisley pattern,** a type of pattern whose most characteristic feature was an ornamental device known as a 'cone' (rather like a tree cone), used in the **Paisley shawl,** a shawl made in Paisley, Scotland in the 19th cent. in the style of Kashmir shawls.

**paitrick,** *pā'trik, n.* a Scots form of **partridge.**

**pajamas.** See **pyjamas.**

**pajock(e).** See **paiock(e).**

pakeha, *pä'kä-ha*, *n*. a white man. [Maori.]
Pakhto, Pakhtu. See Pushto.
Pakistani, *pä-kis-tän'i*, *n*. a citizen of Pakistan.
pakka, *puk'a*. Same as pucka.
paktong, *pak'tong*, *n*. nickel-silver.—Also (erroneously) pack'fong, pak'fong. [Chin. *peh*, white, *t'ung*, copper.]
pal, *pal*, (*slang*) *n*. a partner, mate: chum.—*v.i.* to associate as a pal:—*pr.p.* pall'ing; *pa.t.* and *pa.p.* palled (*pald*).—*adj.* pally (*pal'i*). [Gypsy.]
palabra, *pa-lä'bra*, *n*. a word: talk.—pocas (*pö'käs*) palabras, few words. [Sp.]
palace, *pal'is*, *n*. the house of a king or a queen: a very large and splendid house: a bishop's official residence: a large public building: a large and usually showy place of entertainment or refreshment.—pal'ace-car, a sumptuously furnished railway-car; palace revolution, a revolution within the seat of authority.—palais de danse (*pa-le dƏ däs*; Fr.), a dance-hall. [Fr. *palais*—L. *Palātium*, the Roman emperor's residence on the *Palatine* Hill at Rome.]
paladin, *pal'Ə-din*, (*hist.*) *n*. one of the twelve peers of Charlemagne's household: a knight-errant, or paragon of knighthood. [Fr.,—It. *paladino*—L. *palātinus*, belonging to the palace; cf. palatine.]
palae-, palaeo-, in U.S. also pale-, paleo-, *pa-li-*, *-ō-*, also *pāl-*, in composition, old: of, concerned with, the very distant past as palaeoclimatology, -geography, etc.—*adj.* Palaeanthrop'ic (Gr. *anthrōpos*, man), of the earliest types of man.—*n*. Palaean'thropus (or-*thrō'*), an extinct genus of man, including the Neanderthal and Heidelberg races.—*adj.* Palaearc'tic, of the Old World part of the Holarctic region.—*ns.* palaeethnol'ogy, the science of early man; palaeichthyol'ogy, the study of fossil fishes.—*adj.* palaeobotan'ical.—*ns.* palaeobot'anist; palaeobot'any, the study of fossil plants.—*adj.* palaeocrys'tic (Gr. *krystallos*, ice), consisting of ancient ice.—*n*. palaeogaea (*-jē'Ə*; Gr. *gaia*, earth), the Old World as a biological region.—*n*. and *adj.* Palaeogene (*-jēn*; Gr. *palai*(*o*)*genēs*, born long ago), early Tertiary —Eocene and Oligocene.—*n*. palaeog'rapher (Gr. *graphein*, to write), one skilled in palaeography. —*adjs.* palaeograph'ic, -al.—*ns.* palaeog'raphist; palaeog'raphy, ancient modes of writing: study of ancient modes of handwriting; palaeolimnol'ogy, the scientific study of lakes of past ages; pal'aeolith (Gr. *lithos*, stone), a Palaeolithic artefact.—*adj.* Palaeolith'ic, of the earlier or ruder Stone Age.—*n*. palaeomag'netism, a study of the magnetism of ancient rocks and fossils, and of bricks, pottery, etc., made in past ages.—*adj.* palaeontolog'ical.—*ns.* palaeontol'ogist; palaeontol'ogy (Gr. *onta*, neut. pl. of pr.p. of *einai*, to be, *logos*, discourse), the study of fossils; palaeopedol'ogy, the study of the soils of past geological ages; palaeophytol'ogy, palaeobotany; Palaeothe'rium (Gr. *thērion*, a wild beast—*thēr*), an odd-toed Eocene fossil ungulate with tapir-like snout; pal'aeotype, A. J. Ellis's phonetic adaptation of ordinary alphabetical type.—*adjs.* palaeotypic (*-tip'ik*); Palaeozo'ic (Gr. *zöē*, life), of the division of the fossiliferous rocks, from Cambrian to Permian; palaeozoolog'ical.—*ns.* palaeozool'ogist; palaeozool'ogy, the study of fossil animals. [Gr. *palaios*, old.]
palaestra, *pal-ēs'trƏ*, *-es'*, (*ant.*) *n*. a wrestling school: a gymnasium: wrestling: a training-ground.—*adjs.* palaes'tral, palaes'tric, -al. [L. *palaestra*—Gr. *palaistrā*—*palaiein*, to wrestle.]
palafitte, *pal'Ə-fit*, *n*. a prehistoric lake dwelling. [It. *palafitta*—*palo* (—L. *pālus*), a stake, *fitto*, pa.p. of *figgere* (—L. *figĕre*), to fix.]
palagonite, *pal-ag'Ə-nit*, *n*. an altered basic vitreous lava.—palag'onite-tuff, a tuff composed of fragments of palagonite. [*Palagonia*, in Sicily.]
palais de danse. See palace.

palama, *pal'Ə-mƏ*, *n*. the webbing of a water-bird's foot:—*pl.* pal'amae (*-mē*).—*adj.* pal'amate. [Latinised from Gr. *palamē*, palm.]
palamino. Same as palomino.
palampore, palempore, *pal'Əm-pōr*, *-pör*, *n*. a flowered chintz bedcover common in the East. [Ety. dub.]
palanquin, palankeen, *pal-Ən-kēn'*, *n*. a light litter for one, a box borne on poles on men's shoulders. [Port. *palanquim*; cf. Hind. *palang*, a bed—Sans. *palyaṅka*, a bed.]
palas, *pal-äs'*, *-äsh*, *n*. the dhak tree. [Hind. *palās*.]
palate, *pal'it*, *-Ət*, *n*. the roof of the mouth, consisting of the *hard palate* in front and the *soft palate* behind: the prominent part of the lower lip that closes the tube of a personate corolla: sense of taste: relish: mental liking: ability to appreciate the finer qualities of wine etc. (also *fig.*).—*v.t.* to taste, to relish (*Shak.*).—*adj.* pal'atable, pleasant to the taste: acceptable to mind or feelings.—*ns.* palatabil'ity, pal'atableness.—*adv.* pal'atably.—*adj.* pal'atal, pertaining to the palate: uttered by bringing the tongue to or near the hard palate.—*n*. a sound so produced. —*v.t.* pal'atalise, -ize, to make palatal.—*adj.* pal'atine, pertaining to the palate.—*n*. a paired bone forming part of the roof of the mouth.— cleft palate, a congenital defect of the palate, leaving a longitudinal fissure in the roof of the mouth. [L. *palātum*.]
palatial, *pƏ-lä'shl*, *adj*. of or like a palace. [See palace.]
palatine, *pal'Ə-tin*, *adj.* of the Palatine Hill or the palace of emperors there: of a palace: having royal privileges or jurisdiction: of a count or earl palatine (see below).—*n*. an officer of the palace: a noble invested with royal privileges and jurisdiction: a subject of a palatinate: a fur tippet (from the Princess Palatine of 1676): (*cap.*) one of the seven hills of Rome.—*n*. palatinate (or *pƏ-lat'*), office or rank of a palatine: province of a palatine, esp. an electorate of the ancient German Empire: at Durham University, a light purple blazer.—*adj.* at Durham, light purple or lilac.—count, earl, etc., palatine, a feudal lord with supreme judicial authority over a province; county palatine, the province of such a lord. [L. *palātīnus*; cf. palace.]
palaver, *pƏ-lä'vƏr*, *n*. a conference, esp. orig. with African or other natives: a talk or discussion: idle copious talk: talk intended to deceive.—*v.i.* to hold a palaver: to prate.—*v.t.* to flatter.—*n*. palav'erer. [Port. *palavra*, word—L. *parabola*, a parable, later a word, speech—Gr. *parabolē*; cf. parable, parabola.]
palay, *pa-lä'*, *pä-li'*, *-lä'*, *n*. the ivory-tree, a small S. Indian tree (Wrightia) of the dogbane family, with hard white wood. [Tamil.]
pale, *pāl*, *n*. a stake of wood driven into the ground for fencing: anything that encloses or fences in: a limit: the limit of what can be accepted as decent or tolerable (*fig.*): an enclosure: a marked-off district: a broad stripe from top to bottom of a shield (*her.*).—*v.t.* to enclose with stakes: to fence: to encircle, crown (*Shak.*).— *adv.* pale'wise (*her.*), vertically, like a pale.—*n*. palifica'tion (*pal-*, *pāl-*), act of strengthening by stakes.—*adj.* pāl'iform.—*n*. pāl'ing, the act of fencing: wood or stakes for fencing: a fence of stakes connected by horizontal pieces: an upright stake or board in a fence.—*adj.* pāl'y (*her.*), divided by vertical lines.—beyond the pale, intolerable: unacceptable; English Pale, the district in Ireland within which alone the English had power for centuries after the invasion in 1172; Jewish Pale, that part of S.W. Russia in which alone Jews were formerly allowed to live. [Fr. *pal*—L. *pālus*, a stake.]

pale, *pāl, adj.* whitish: not ruddy or fresh: wan: of a faint lustre, dim: wanting in colour.—*v.t.* to make pale.—*v.i.* to turn pale.—*n.* paleness.—*adv.* pale′ly.—*n.* pale′ness.—*adjs.* pal′ish, somewhat pale; pal′y, pale: palish.—pale ale, a light-coloured pleasant bitter ale; pale′buck, an antelope, the oribi.—*adjs.* pale′-dead (*S'tak.*), lustreless; pale′-eyed (*Milt.*), dim-eyed.—pale′-face, (attributed to American Indians) a white person.—*adj.* pale′-heart′ed (*Shak.*), dispirited. —*adj.* pale′-vis′aged (*Shak.*). [O.Fr. *palle*, pale (Fr. *pâle*)—L. *pallidus*, pale.]
pale, *pāl*, (*dial.*) *n.* a baker's peel: a cheese-scoop. —*v.t.* to test by inserting a cheese-pale. [L. *pāla*, spade.]
pale-. See palae-.
palea, *pā′li-ə, n.* the membranous inner bract (*inferior palea*) or bracteole (*superior palea*) of an individual grass-flower, above the glumes: a scale on a fern-leaf or stem: a scale on the receptacle of some composite plants:—*pl.* pā′leae (*-ē*).—*n.* pale (*pāl*), a grass palea.—*adj.* paleā′ceous (*bot.*), chaffy.—*n.* palet (*pāl′it*), a palea. [L. *pălea*, chaff.]
paleobotany, etc. Same as palaeobotany, etc.
Palestinian, *pal-is-tin′i-ən, adj.* pertaining to *Palestine* (Gr. *Palaistinē*).—*n.* a native or inhabitant of Palestine: a member of a guerrilla movement one of whose aims is to reclaim former Arab lands from Israelis.—Palestine soup, artichoke soup, by a quibble on *Jerusalem* (see artichoke). [Cf. Philistine.]
palestra. Same as palaestra.
paletot, *pal′tō, n.* a loose overcoat. [Fr.]
palette, *pal′it, n.* a little board with a thumb-hole on which a painter mixes his colours: the assortment or range of colours used by a particular artist or for any particular picture: a plate against which one leans in working a drill: a small plate covering a joint in armour, esp. at the armpit (*hist.*).—pal′ette-knife, a thin round-ended knife for mixing colours. [Fr.,—It. *paletta—pala*, spade—L. *pāla*, a spade.]
palfrey, *pōl′fri, n.* a saddle-horse, esp. for a lady (in *Faerie Queene* applied to Una's ass).—*n.* palfrenier (*pal-frə-nēr′*), a groom.—*adj.* palfreyed (*pōl′*), riding on, or supplied with, a palfrey. [O.Fr. *palefrei*—L.L. *paraverēdus*, prob. from Gr. *para*, beside, L.L. *verēdus*, a post-horse, app. a Celtic word; confused with L. *frēnum*, a bridle.]
Pali, *pä′lē, n.* the sacred language of the Buddhists of India, etc., close akin to Sanskrit. [Sans. *pāli*, canon.]
Palilia, *pa-lil′i-ə, n.pl.* (or *sing.*) the festival of Pales (L. *Palēs*), Roman goddess of flocks, held on 21st April, traditional date of the founding of Rome.
palillogy, *pal-il′ə-ji, n.* a repetition of a word or phrase. [Gr. *palillogiā—palin*, again, *logos*, word, speech.]
palimpsest, *pal′imp-sest, n.* a manuscript in which old writing has been rubbed out to make room for new: a monumental brass turned over for a new inscription. [Gr. *palimpsēston—palin*, again, *psāein* (contracted *psēn*), to rub.]
palindrome, *pal′in-drōm, n.* a word, verse, or sentence that reads alike backward and forward. —*adjs.* palindromic (*-drom′*, *-drōm′*), *-al.*—*n.* pal′indromist (or *pə-lin′*), an inventor of palindromes. [Gr. *palindromos*, running back—*palin*, back, *dromos*, a running.]
paling. See under pale (1).
palingenesis, *pal-in-jen′i-sis, n.* a new birth: re-incarnation: a second creation: regeneration: unmodified inheritance of ancestral characters: the new-formation of a rock by refusion.—Also palingenē′sia, palingen′esy.—*n.* palingen′esist.— *adj.* palingenet′ical.—*adv.* palingenet′ically. [Gr. *palin*, again, *genesis*, birth.]

palinode, *pal′i-nōd, n.* a poem of retraction: a recantation.—Also (*obs.*) pal′inŏdy. [Gr. *palin-ōidiā—palin*, back, *ōidē*, song.]
palisade, *pal-i-sād′, n.* a fence of stakes: a stake so used (*mil.*).—*v.t.* to surround or defend with a palisade.—Also palisā′do:—*pl.* palisā′does.— palisade tissue, a tissue occurring in leaves, composed of cells placed closely together with their long axes perpendicular to the surface. [Fr. *palissade* and Sp. *palizada*—L. *pālus*, a stake.]
palisander, *pal-i-san′dər, n.* jacaranda or other rosewood. [Fr. *palissandre*, from a name used in Guiana.]
palki, palkee, *päl′kē, n.* a palanquin. [Hind. *pālkī*.]
pall, *pöl, n.* a rich cloth (*arch.*): a covering of rich cloth: a corporal: a frontal: a chalice-cover: a cloth spread over a coffin or tomb: a cloak, mantle, outer garment: a pallium: a bearing representing a pallium (*her.*): a curtain, covering, or cloak, as of smoke, darkness (*fig.*).—*v.t.* to cover with, or as with, a pall.—pall′-bearer, one of the mourners at a funeral who used to hold up the corners of the pall. [O.E. *pæll*, a rich robe—L. *pallium*; see pallium.]
pall, *pöl, v.i.* to lose strength (*obs.*): to become vapid, insipid, or wearisome: to lose relish.— *v.t.* to daunt (*obs.*): to weaken (*obs.*): to pale (*obs.*): to make vapid: to cloy. [Prob. from appal.]
palla, *pal′ə, n.* a Roman woman's mantle:—*pl.* pall′ae (*-ē*). [L. *palla*.]
Palladian, *pə-lā′di-ən, adj.* relating to *Pallas*, wisdom, or learning.
Palladian, *pə-lā′di-ən, adj.* in the style of architecture introduced by Andrea *Palladio* (1518-80), modelled on Vitruvius.—*n.* Pallā′dianism.
Palladium, *pə-lā′di-əm, n.* a statue of *Pallas*, on whose preservation the safety of Troy depended: anything of like virtue: a safeguard. [L.,—Gr. *palladion—Pallas. Pallados*, Pallas.]
palladium, *pə-lā′di-əm, n.* a metallic element (Pd; at. numb. 46) resembling platinum, remarkable for power of occluding hydrogen.—*adjs.* palladic (*-lad′*), pallā′d(i)ous, containing palladium in smaller or greater proportion respectively. [Named by its discoverer Wollaston (1803) after the newly discovered minor planet *Pallas*.]
pallah, *pal′ə, n.* the impala. [Tswana *phala*.]
Pallas, *pal′as, n.* the Greek goddess Athēnē (also Pall′as Athē′nē): a minor planet discovered by Olbers in 1802.
pallescent, *pə-les′ənt, adj.* turning pale.—*n.* pallesc′ence. [L. *pallēscēns, -entis*, pr.p. of *pallēs-cēre*, to turn pale.]
pallet, *pal′it, n.* a palette: a flat wooden tool with a handle, as that used for shaping pottery: a flat brush for spreading gold-leaf: a tool for lettering book-bindings: in a timepiece, surface or part on which teeth of escape wheel act to give impulse to the pendulum or balance: a disk of a chain-pump: a valve of an organ wind-chest, regulated from the keyboard: a board for carrying newly moulded bricks: a piece of wood built into a wall for the nailing on of joiner-work: a platform or tray for lifting and stacking goods, used with the fork-lift truck, and having a double base into which the fork can be thrust.— *adj.* pall′eted, carried on pallet(s).—*n.* palletisa′-tion, -iza′tion, the adoption of pallets for moving goods. [palette.]
pallet, *pal′it, n.* a mattress, or couch, properly a mattress of straw: a small or mean bed. [Dial. Fr. *paillet*, dim. of Fr. *paille*, straw—L. *palea*, chaff.]
palliasse, *pal-i-as′, pal-yas′, n.* a straw mattress: an under-mattress.—Also paillasse′. [Fr. *pail-lasse—paille*, straw—L. *palea*.]
palliate, *pal′i-āt, v.t.* to cloak (*obs.*): to disguise (*obs.*): to excuse, extenuate: to soften by

pleading something in favour: to mitigate: to alleviate.—*adj.* (see **pallium**).—*n.* **palliā′tion**, act of palliating.—*adj.* **pall′iative** (*-ə-tiv*), serving to extenuate: mitigating: alleviating.—*n.* that which lessens pain, etc., or gives temporary relief.—*adj.* **pall′iatory**. [L. *palliāre, -ātum*, to cloak—*pallium*, a cloak.]

**pallid**, *pal′id, adj.* pale, wan.—*ns.* **pallid′ity**, **pall′idness**.—*adv.* **pall′idly**. [L. *pallidus*, pale.]

**pallium**, *pal′i-əm, n.* a large, square mantle, worn by learned Romans in imitation of the Greeks —the himation (*hist.*): a white woollen vestment like a double Y, embroidered with crosses, worn by the Pope, and conferred by him upon archbishops: the mantle in molluscs, brachiopods, and birds (*zool.*):—*pl.* **pall′ia**. (*zool.*) **pall′ial**.—*n.* **pall′iament** (*Shak.*), a Roman consular candidate's robe.—*adj.* **pall′iate**, having a pallium. [L. *pallium*.]

**pall-mall**, *pel′-mel′, n.* an old game, in which a ball was driven through an iron ring with a mallet: an alley for the game (hence the street in London). [Obs. Fr. *pale-maille—palmaille*— It. *pallamaglio—palla*, ball (cf. O.H.G. *pallā*), and *maglio*—L. *malleus*, a hammer; cf. **ball**; **pallone**.]

**pallone**, *päl-lō′nä, n.* an Italian game in which a ball is struck with a gauntlet or armguard. [It., augmentative of *palla*, ball.]

**pallor**, *pal′ər, n.* paleness. [L. *pallēre*, to be pale.]

**palm**, *päm, n.* the inner surface of the hand between wrist and fingers: the corresponding part of a forefoot, or of a glove: the sole of the foot (*rare*): a handsbreadth (3 inches, or 4 inches): the length of the hand from wrist to finger-tip: a sailmaker's instrument used instead of a thimble: a flat expansion, as of an antler, or the inner surface of an anchor fluke: an act of palming: an old game (also **palm′-play**) in which a ball was struck with the palm. —*v.t.* to touch, or stroke with the palm: to hold or conceal in the palm: to impose, pass off (esp. with *off*, and *on* or *upon*): to bribe.— *adjs.* **palmar** (*pal′mər*), relating to the palm; **palmate** (*ɟal′*), **-d**, hand-shaped: having lobes radiating from one centre (*bot.*): web-footed (*zool.*).—*adv.* **pal′mately**.—*adj.* **palmatifid** (*pal-mat′i-fid; bot.*), shaped like the hand, with the divisions extending about half-way down.—*n.* **palmā′tion**, palmate formation: a palmate structure or one of its parts or divisions.—*adjs.* **palmatipart′ite**, palmately divided rather more than half-way; **palmatisect** (*pal-mat′i-sekt*), deeply cut in a palmate manner; **palmed** (*pämd*), having a palm: held or concealed in the palm. —*ns.* **palm′ful**, as much as the palm will hold; **palmiped** (*pal′mi-ped*), **palmipede** (*-pēd*), a web-footed bird.—*adj.* web-footed.—*ns.* **palmist** (*päm′ist*), one who tells fortune from the lines on the palm; **palm′istry** (*päm′i; Scot.*), a stroke of the tawse on the palm.—**palm′-grease′, -oil′**, a bribe.—**grease one's palm**, to bribe one. [L. *palma*; cf. Gr. *palamē*; O.E. *folm*.]

**palm**, *päm, n.* any tree or shrub of the Palmae (*pal′mē*), a large tropical and sub-tropical family of monocotyledons, sometimes climbers but usually branchless trees with a crown of pinnate or fan-shaped leaves: a leaf of this tree borne in token of rejoicing or of victory: emblematically, pre-eminence, the prize: a branch of willow or other substitute in symbolic or ceremonial use.—*adjs.* **palmaceous** (*pal-mā′shəs*), of the palm family; **palmarian** (*pal-mā′ri-ən*); **palmary** (*pal′mər-i*), worthy of the palm: pre-eminent.—*ns.* **palmette** (*pal-met′*; Fr.), an ancient architectural ornament like a palm-leaf; **palmett′o** (*pal-*), a name for several kinds of palm, notably Sabal and the only European palm Chamaerops; **palmiet** (*pal-mēt′*), a

South African aloe-like riverside plant of the rush family (*Prionum palmita*); **palmificā′tion** (*pal-*), artificial fertilisation of dates by hanging a wild male flower-cluster on a cultivated female tree; **palmitate** (*pal′*), a salt of **palmit′ic acid**, a fatty acid ($C_{15}H_{31}$·COOH) got from palm-oil, etc.; **palmitin** (*pal′*), a white fat abundant in palm-oil: a glycerine ester of palmitic acid.— *adj.* **palm′y**, bearing palms: flourishing: palm-like.—**palm′a Christi**, the castor-oil; **palm′-branch′**, a palm-leaf; **palm′-butt′er**, palm-oil in a solid state; **palm′-cabb′age**, the bud of the cabbage-palm; **palm′-cat′, palm′-civ′et**, the paradoxure; **palm′-hon′ey**, evaporated coquito-palm sap; **palm′house**, a glass house for palms and other tropical plants; **palmitic acid** (see **palmitate**); **palm′-ker′nel**, the kernel of the oil-palm, yielding **palm-kernel oil**; **palm′-oil**, an oil or fat obtained from the pulp of the fruit of palms, esp. of the oil-palm; **palm′-su′gar**, jaggery; **Palm Sunday**, the Sunday before Easter, in commemoration of the strewing of palm-branches when Christ entered Jerusalem; **palm′-tree**; **palm′-wine**, fermented palm sap. [O.E. *palm, palma, palme*, also directly L. *palma*, palm-tree, from the shape of its leaves; see preceding.]

**palmer**, *päm′ər, n.* a pilgrim carrying a palm-leaf in token of having been in the Holy Land: a palmer-worm: a bristly artificial fly.—*n.* **palm′er-worm′**, a hairy caterpillar of various kinds, originally one of wandering habits. [palm (2).]

**Palmerin**, *pal′mər-in, n.* a knightly champion. [From *Palmerín*, a Spanish (or Portuguese) romance hero found as a child among *palm*-trees.]

**palmyra**, *pal-mi′rə, n.* an African and Asiatic palm (*Borassus flabellifer*) yielding toddy, jaggery, and **palmy′ra-nuts**.—**palmy′ra-wood**, properly the wood of the palmyra palm: any palm timber. [Port. *palmeira*, palm-tree, confused with *Palmyra* in Syria.]

**palolo**, *pa-lō′lō, n.* an edible sea-worm that burrows in coral-reefs, remarkable for its breeding swarms at a certain phase of the moon, the head remaining behind to regenerate. [Samoan.]

**palomino**, *pal-ə-mē′nō, n.* a horse of largely Arab blood, pale tan, yellow, or gold, with white or silver mane and tail. [Amer. Sp.,—Sp., of a dove.]

**palp**, *palp, n.* a jointed sense-organ attached in pairs to the mouth-parts of insects and crustaceans—also **pal′pus**:—*pl.* **pal′pi**.—*adj.* **pal′pal**. [L.L. *palpus*, a feeler (L. a stroking)—L. *palpāre*, to stroke.]

**palp**, *palp, v.t.* to feel, examine, or explore by touch: to speak fair (*obs.*).—*n.* **palpabil′ity**.— *adj.* **palp′able**, that can be touched or felt: perceptible: easy found out, as lies, etc.: obvious, gross.—*n.* **pal′pableness**.—*adv.* **palp′ably**.—*v.t.* **palp′āte**, to examine by touch.—*n.* **palpā′tion**, the act of examining by means of touch.—*adj.* **palp′able-gross′** (*Shak.*). [L. *palpāre, -ātum*, to touch softly, stroke, caress, flatter.]

**palpebral**, *palp′i-brəl, adj.* of or pertaining to the eyelid. [L. *palpebra*, the eyelid.]

**palpitate**, *pal′pi-tāt, v.i.* to throb: to beat rapidly: to pulsate: to quiver.—*v.t.* to cause to throb. —*adj.* **pal′pitant**, palpitating.—*n.* **palpitā′tion**, act of palpitating: abnormal awareness of heart-beat. [L. *palpitāre, -ātum*, freq. of *palpāre*; cf. **palp**.]

**palsgrave**, *pölz′grāv, n.* a count palatine:—*fem.* **palsgravine** (*pölz′grə-vēn*). [Du. *paltsgrave* (now *paltsgraaf*); cf. Ger. *pfalzgraf*; see **palace**, **graf**.]

**palstave**, *pöl′stāv*, **palstaff**, *-stäf, n.* a Bronze Age axe, the flanges of the head joined by a cross ridge to engage the ends of the prongs of the kneed shaft. [Du. *paalstav.*—O.N. *pálstafr.*]

**palsy,** *pöl'zi, n.* loss of control or of feeling, more or less complete, in the muscles of the body: paralysis.—*v.t.* to affect with palsy: to deprive of action or energy: to paralyse.—*adj.* **pal'sied.** [From paralysis.]

**palter,** *pöl'tər, v.i.* to trifle in talk: to use trickery: to haggle: to equivocate.—*n.* **pal'terer.** [Poss. conn. with **paltry.**]

**paltry,** *pöl'tri, adj.* mean: trashy: trumpery: not worth considering.—*adv.* **pal'trily.**—*n.* **pal'triness.** [Cf. Dan. *pialter*, rags, L.G. *paltrig*, ragged.]

**paludal,** *pal-ū'dl, -ōō', also pal', adj.* pertaining to marshes: marshy: malarial.—*adjs.* **palu'dic,** of marshes; **paludic'olous** (L. *colĕre*, to inhabit), marsh-dwelling: growing in marshes; **palu'dinal, pal'udine, palu'dinous,** of marshes: marshy.—*n.* **pal'udism,** malaria.—*adjs.* **pal'udose, pal'udous,** of marshes: marshy: inhabiting marshes: malarial.—*n.* **Pal'udrine,** a synthetic anti-malarial drug (trademark).—*adjs.* **palustral** (*-us'trəl*), **palus'trian, palus'trine** (*-trin*), of marshes: inhabiting marshes. [L. *palūs, palūdis,* a marsh; *palūster, -tris,* marshy.]

**paludament,** *pə-lū', -lōō', də-mənt, n.* a Roman general's or high military officer's cloak.—Also **paludament'um.** [L. *palūdāmentum.*]

**paly.** See under **pale** (1 and 2).

**palynology,** *pal-i-nol'ə-ji, n.* the study of spores and pollen-grains. [Gr. *palȳnein*, to sprinkle.]

**pam,** *pam, n.* the knave of clubs, highest card in loo: a game like nap, in which it is highest card. [Said to be from the Fr. *Pamphile*—Gr. *Pamphilos*, lit. beloved of all.]

**pampa,** *pam'pə* (usu. in *pl.* **pampas**), *n.* a vast treeless plain in southern S. America.—*adj.* **pampēan.**—*n.* **pampero,** *pam-pā'rō,* a violent S.W. wind on and from the Pampas.—**pam'pasgrass,** a tall, ornamental, reed-like grass (*Gynerium*, or *Cortaderia*) with large thick silvery panicles. [Sp.,—Quechua *pampa, bamba,* plain.]

**pampelmoose,** *pam'pl-mōōs, n.* See **pompelmoose.**

**pamper,** *pam'pər, v.t.* to feed with fine food (*arch.*): to gratify to the full; to over-indulge. —*ns.* **pam'peredness; pam'perer.** [A freq. from (*obs.*) *pamp, pomp;* cf. Ger. dial. *pampen,* to cram.]

**pamphlet,** *pam'flit, n.* a small book stitched but not bound: a separately published tractate, usu. controversial, on some subject of the day. —*n.* **pamphleteer',** a writer of pamphlets.—*v.i.* to write pamphlets.—*n.* and *adj.* **pamphleteer'ing.** [Anglo-L. *panfletus,* possibly from a Latin erotic poem *Pamphilus* (—Gr. *Pamphilos,* beloved of all) very popular in the Middle Ages.]

**pan,** *pan, n.* a broad, shallow vessel for use in the home or in arts or manufactures: anything of like shape, as the upper part of the skull (*brain-pan*), the patella (*knee-pan*): a hollow in the ground, a basin, in which water collects in the rainy season, leaving a salt deposit on evaporation: a salt-pan: a salt-work: the part of a firelock that holds the priming: a hard layer (*hard-pan*) in or under the soil: a small ice-floe: a panful: the face (*slang*).—*v.t.* to wash in a gold-miner's pan: to obtain by evaporating in a pan: to yield: to obtain: to cook and serve in a pan: to review, criticise, harshly. —*v.i.* to wash earth for gold: to yield gold (usu. with *out*): to result, turn out (with *out*): to come to an end, be exhausted (with *out*): to cake: to enlarge in speech.—*ns.* **pan'ful:**—*pl.* **pan'fuls; pann'ikel, pannicle; pann'ikin,** a small metal cup: a little pan or saucer: enough to fill a cup; **pann'ing,** washing for gold: the gold so got: harsh criticism.—**pan'cake,** a thin cake of eggs, flour, sugar, and milk, fried in a pan: an aeroplane descent or landing with wings

nearly horizontal.—*v.i.* to descend or alight so. —**pan drop** (*Scot.*), a hard smooth peppermint sweet made in a revolving pan; **pan'handle,** a strip of territory stretching out from the main body like the handle of a pan.—*v.i.* (*U.S.*) to beg esp. on the street.—**pan'handler; pan loaf** (*Scot.*), a loaf of a particular shape, made in a pan.—**flash in the pan,** a mere flash in the pan of a flint-lock without discharge: a fitful show of beginning without accomplishing anything; **pancake bell,** a churchbell rung on Shrove Tuesday, taken as the signal for pancake-making; **pancake ice,** polar sea ice in thin flat slabs, found as winter draws near; **pancake (make-up),** cosmetic in cake form, moist, or moistened before application; **Pancake Tuesday,** Shrove Tuesday. [O.E. *panne;* a word common to the West Germanic languages, possibly an early borrowing from L. *patina.*]

**Pan,** *pan, n.* the Greek god of pastures, flocks, and woods, worshipped in Arcadia, and fond of music—with goat's legs and feet, and sometimes horns and ears: later (from association with *pān,* the whole) connected with pantheistic thought.—**Pan'-pipes, Pan's pipes,** the syrinx, a musical instrument attributed to Pan, made of reeds of different lengths, fastened in a row. [Gr. *Pān.*]

**pan,** *pän, pawn, pön, n.* betel leaf: betel. [Hind. *pān.*]

**pan,** *pan, v.t.* and *v.i.* of a cinema or television camera, to move while taking a picture so as to follow a particular object or to produce a panoramic effect. [pan(orama).]

**pan-, pant-, panto-,** in composition, all [Gr. *pās, pāsa, pān,* gen. *pantos, pāsēs, pantos.*]

**panacea,** *pan-ə-sē'ə, n.* a universal medicine: a healing plant vaguely indicated (*Spens.* **panachaea,** *-kē'ä*). [Gr. *panakeia—akos,* cure.]

**panache,** *pa-näsh', -nash', n.* a plume: knightly splendour: swagger: grand manner, theatricality, sense of style. [Fr.,—It. *pennacchio—penna,* feather.]

**panada,** *pa-nä'da, n.* a dish made by boiling bread to a pulp in water, and flavouring: a thick binding sauce of breadcrumbs or flour and seasoning. [Sp. *pan* (L. *pānis*), bread.]

**Panadol,** *pan'ə-dol, n.* a proprietary form of paracetamol. [Trademark.]

**panaesthesia,** in U.S. **panesthesia,** *pan-ēs-thē'zi-ə, -zyə,* or *-es-, n.* totality of perception: general awareness.—*n.* **panaesthetism** (*-ēs'* or *es'thi-tizm*). [Gr. *aisthēsis,* perception.]

**Panagia.** Same as **Panhagia.**

**Panama,** *pan-ə-mä', n.* a republic, town, and isthmus of Central America.—Also *adj.*—*n.* and *adj.* **Panamanian** (*mä'ni-ən*).—**panama (hat),** a hand-plaited hat made, not in Panama but in Ecuador, of plaited strips of the leaves of a South American cyclanthaceous plant (*Carludovica palmata*): an imitation thereof. [Sp. *Panamá.*]

**Pan-American,** *pan-ə-mer'i-kən, adj.* including all America or Americans, North and South.—*n.* **Pan-Amer'icanism.** [pan- and American.]

**Pan-Anglican,** *pan-ang'gli-kən, adj.* representing or including all who hold the doctrines and polity of the Anglican Church. [pan- and Anglican (see Angle).]

**panaritium,** *pan-ə-rish'i-əm, n.* a whitlow. [L.L. *panāricium* for *parŏnychium*—Gr. *parōnychiā—para,* beside, *onyx, -ychos,* nail.]

**panarthritis,** *pan-är-thrī'tis, n.* inflammation involving all the structures of a joint. [pan- and arthritis.]

**panary,** *pan'ə-ri, adj.* of or pertaining to bread. —*n.* a bread store. [L. *pānārius—pānis,* bread.]

**Panathenaea,** *pan-ath-i-nē'ə, n.pl.* the chief national festival of ancient Athens—the lesser held annually, the greater every fourth year.—

*adjs.* Panatheniae'an, Panathenä'ic. [Gr. *Pana-thēnaia*.]

Panax, *pan'aks*, or *păn'*, *n.* a genus of the Aralia family. [Gr. *panax*, a name for various healing plants; see panacea.]

pancake. See pan.

pance. See pansy.

Panchatantra, *pun-chä-tunt'rə*, *n.* the oldest extant Sanskrit collection of beast-fables, in five books. [Sans., five books.]

panchayat, *pun-chä'yət*, *n.* a village council. [Hindi *pañcāyat*—Sans. *pañca*, five.]

Panchen Lama, *păn'chən lä'mə*, Tibetan religious leader second in importance to the Dalai Lama. [Chin. *pan ch'an*.]

pancheon, panchion, *pan'shən*, *n.* a coarse earthenware pan. [App. conn. with pan; perh. influenced by puncheon.]

panchromatic, *pan-krō-mat'ik*, *adj.* equally or suitably sensitive to all colours: rendering all colours in due intensity.—*n.* panchro'matism. [Gr. *chrōma*, *-atos*, colour.]

pancratium, *pan-krä'shi-əm*, *n.* a combination of boxing and wrestling.—*adj.* pancrä'tian.—*n.* pancrä'tiast (*-shi-ast*), a competitor or victor in the pancratium.—*adj.* pancratic (*-krat'ik*), of the pancratium: excelling all round in athletics or accomplishments: of a lens, adjustable to different degrees of magnification.—*n.* pan'-cratist. [Gr. *pankration*—*kratos*, strength.]

pancreas, *pan(g)'kri-as*, *n.* the sweetbread, a large gland discharging into the duodenum and containing islands of endocrine gland tissue.—*adj.* pancreat'ic.—*ns.* pan'creatin, the pancreatic juice; pancreatit'is, inflammation of the pancreas. [Gr. *kreas*, *-atos*, flesh.]

pand, *pand*, (*Scot.*) *n.* the valance of a bed. [Cf. O.Fr. *pandre*, to hang.]

panda, *pan'də*, *n.* a remarkable raccoon-like animal (*Ailurus fulgens*) of the Himalayas.—giant panda, a larger beast (*Ailuropus melanoleucus*) of Tibet, apparently linking the panda with the bears.—panda car, a small car used by a policeman on the beat in a residential area. [Said to be its name in Nepal.]

Pandanus, *pan-dā'nəs*, *n.* the screw-pine, the typical genus of the Pandanä'ceae, a family of trees and bushes akin to the bulrushes and bur-reeds.—*adj.* pandanä'ceous. [Malay *pandan*.]

pandar. See pander.

pandation, *pan-dā'shən*, *n.* warping. [L. *pandātiō*, *-ōnis*—*pandāre*, *-ātum*, to bend.]

Pandean, *pan-dē'ən*, *adj.* of the god Pan: of Pan-pipes.—Pandean pipes, Pan-pipes. [Irregularly formed from *Pān*.]

pandect, *pan'dekt*, *n.* a treatise covering the whole of any subject: (in *pl.*; *cap.*) the digest of Roman law made by command of the Emperor Justinian in the 6th century.—*n.* pandect'ist. [L. *pandecta*—Gr. *pandektēs*—*pās*, *pān*, all, *dechesthai*, to receive.]

pandemic, *pan-dem'ik*, *adj.* incident to a whole people, epidemic over a wide area.—*n.* a pandemic disease.—*n.* pendemia (*-dē'mi-ə*), a widespread epidemic.—*adj.* pandē'mian, vulgar: sensual. [Gr. *pandēmios*—*dēmos*, people.]

Pandemonium, Pandaemonium, *pan-di-mō'ni-əm*, *n.* the capital of Hell in Milton's *Paradise Lost*: (without *cap.*) any very disorderly or noisy place or assembly: (without *cap.*) tumultous uproar.—*adjs.* Pandemō'niac, Pandemoni'acal, Pandemō'nian, Pandemonic (*-mon'ik*). [Gr. *pās*, *pān*, all, *daimōn*, a spirit.]

pander, *pan'dər*, *n.* one who procures for another the means of gratifying his base passions: a pimp.—*v.t.* to play the pander for: to indulge, gratify (with *to*).—*v.i.* to act as a pander: to minister to the passions.—*ns.* pan'deress, a procuress; pan'derism, the employment or practices of a pander.—*adjs.* pan'derly (*Shak.*), act-

ing as a pander; pan'derous.—Also pan'dar, etc. [*Pandarus*, in the story of Troilus and Cressida as told by Boccaccio (*Filostrato*), Chaucer, and Shakespeare.]

pandermite, *pan-dûr'mit*, *n.* a hydrogen calcium borate found massive at *Panderma* (Bandirma) on the Sea of Marmora.

pandiculation, *pan-dik-ū-lā'shən*, *n.* the act of stretching and yawning. [L. *pandiculāri*, *-ātus*, to stretch oneself.]

Pandion, *pan-dī'on*, *n.* the osprey genus. [Gr. *Pandiōn*, father of Procne and Philomela.]

pandit. Same as pundit.

Pandora, *pan-dō'*, *-dō'rə*, *n.* the first woman, made for Zeus so that he might through her punish man for the theft by Prometheus of heavenly fire, given a box from which escaped and spread all the ills of human life.—Pandora's box, any source of great and unexpected troubles. [Gr. *pas*, *pān*, all, *dōron*, a gift.]

pandora, *pan-dō'*, *-dō'rə*, pandore, *pan-dōr'*, *-dōr'*, *n.* an ancient Eastern musical instrument like a long-necked lute with (commonly) three strings: a bandore.—*n.* pandū'ra, a pandora: a Neapolitan instrument like a mandoline with eight metal wires, played with a quill.—*adjs.* pan'dūrate, *-d*, pandū'riform, fiddle-shaped. [Gr. *pandoura*, a 3-stringed instrument, fancifully connected with *Pān*, but probably an Eastern word; cf. bandore, banjo, mandoline.]

pandore, *pan'dōr*, dōr, *n.* an esteemed variety of oysters formerly got at Prestonpans on the Firth of Forth. [Said to be from the *doors* of the salt-*pans*, where they were found.]

pandour, *pan'dōōr*, *n.* an 18th-century Croatian foot-soldier in the Austrian service: a robber.—Also pan'door. [Fr.,—Serbo-Croat *pàndūr*—L.L. *banderius*, follower of a banner.]

pandowdy, *pan-dow'di*, (*U.S.*) *n.* a kind of apple pie or pudding. [Origin unknown.]

pandy, *pan'di*, (*coll.*) *n.* a stroke on the palm as a school punishment.—*v.t.* to slap. [L. *pande*, hold out, imper. of *pandēre*.]

pandy, *pan'di*, (*coll.*, *obs.*) *n.* an insurgent sepoy in the Indian Mutiny. [Said to be from *Pande*, a common surname.]

pane, *pān*, *n.* a piece of cloth (*obs.*): a piece of cloth pieced together with others, or separated from others by slashing (*arch.*): a rectangular compartment: a panel: a slab of window glass: a flat side or face: a length of wall: the side of a quadrangle: a rectangular piece of ground: a large sheet of stamps issued by the Post Office.—*v.t.* to insert panes or panels in.—*adj.* paned (*pānd*), made of panes or small squares: variegated. [Fr. *pan*—L. *pannus*, a cloth, a rag.]

pane. Same as pean (1, 2), peen.

panegoism, *pan-eg'ō-izm*, *n.* solipsism. [Gr. *egō*, I.]

panegyric, *pan-i-jir'ik* (*U.S.* sometimes) *-jir'* *n.* a eulogy, esp. public and elaborate (on, upon): laudation.—*adjs.* panegyr'ic, *-al.*—*adv.* panegyr'ically.—*n.* panegyr'icon, in the Greek Church, a collection of sermons for festivals.—*v.t.* pan'egyrise, *-ize* (or *-ej'ər-*), to write or pronounce a panegyric on: to praise highly.—*ns.* pan'egyrist (or *-jir'*, or *-ej'ər-*); pan'egyry, a great assembly: a religious festival. [Gr. *panēgyrikos*, fit for a national festival—*pās*, *pān*, all, *agyris* (*agorā*), an assembly.]

paneity, *pa-nē'i-ti*, *n.* the state of being bread. [L. *pānis*, bread.]

panel, *pan'l* *n.* a cloth under a saddle (*obs.*): a crude form of saddle: a rectangular piece of any material: a compartment: a bordered rectangular area: a thin flat piece sunk below the general surface of a door, shutter, wainscot, or the like, often with a raised border: a compartment or hurdle of a fence: a strip of material inserted in a dress: a slip of parchment: such a slip containing a list of names, esp. of jurors: a jury: prior to the introduction of the national health service, a list of doctors available to treat those who paid into a national health insurance scheme: such a doctor's list of patients: an accused person or persons (in *sing.*; *Scots law*): a thin board on which a picture is painted: a large long photograph: a group of persons chosen for some purpose, as to judge a competition, serve on a brains trust, or be the guessers in radio and television guessing games (**panel games**).—*v.t.* to furnish with a panel or panels: to put on trial (*Scots law*): —*pr.p.* **pan'elling**; *pa.t.* and *pa.p.* **pan'elled**.— *n.* **pan'elling**, panel-work.—**panel doctor**, a doctor who was on the panel or had a panel; **panel heating**, indoor heating diffused from floors, walls, or ceilings; **panel pin**, a light, narrow-headed nail of small diameter used chiefly for fixing plywood or hardboard to supports; **panel saw**, a saw for cutting very thin wood; **panel working**, a method of working a coal-mine by dividing it into compartments. [O.Fr.,—L.L. *pannellus*—L. *pannus*, a cloth.]

**pang**, *pang*, *n.* a violent but not long-continued pain: a painful emotion.—*v.t.* to inflict a pang on.—*adjs.* **pang'ing** (*Shak.*), painful; **pang'less**. [Poss. **prong**; *pronge*, *prange*, have been found.]

**pang**, *pang* (*Scot.*) *v.t.* to stuff, cram.—*adj.* stuffed, crammed, crowded: tight.—*adj.* **pang'-full'**, **-fu''**, filled full. [Origin unknown.]

**panga**, *pang'gə*, *n.* a broad, heavy African knife used as a tool and as a weapon.

**pangamy**, *pan*(g)*'gə-mi*, *n.* random mating.—*adj.* **pangamic** (*pan-gam'ik*). [Gr. *gamos*, marriage.]

**pangenesis**, *pan-jen'i-sis*, *n.* Darwin's theory that every cell of the body contributes gemmules to the germ-cells and so shares in the transmission of inherited characters.—*n.* **pan'gen**, **-gene** (*-jēn*), a hypothetical unit of living matter.—*adj.* **pangenet'ic**. [Gr. *genesis*, production.]

**Pan-German**, *pan-jûr'mən*, *adj.* pertaining to or including all Germans.—*n.* **Pan-Ger'manism**, a movement for a Greater Germany or union of all German peoples. [**pan-** and **German**.]

**Panglossian**, *pan-glos'i-ən*, **Pangloss'ic**.—*adjs.* taking an over-cheerful and optimistic view of the world as did Dr **Pan'gloss** in Voltaire's *Candide*.

**pangolin**, *pang-gō'lin*, *n.* the scaly ant-eater, an edentate mammal (Manis; order Pholidota) of Asia and Africa. [Malay *peng-gōling*, roller, from its habit of rolling up.]

**pangrammatist**, *pan-gram'ə-tist*, *n.* one who contrives verses or sentences containing all the letters of the alphabet. [Gr. *gramma*, *-atos*, letter.]

**Panhagia, Panagia,** *pan-(h)ä'gi-ə*, *adj.* all-holy, an epithet of the Virgin in the Eastern Church: a cut loaf elevated in her honour: a medallion of the Virgin worn by bishops. [Gr. *hagios*, holy.]

**panhandle.** See pan (1).

**panharmonicon**, *pan-här-mon'i-kon*, *n.* a mechanical musical instrument mimicking an orchestra.

**panhellenic**, *pan-hel-ēn'ik*, or *-en'*, *adj.* pertaining to all Greece: including all Greeks.—*ns.* **panhellē'nion**, or (L.) **panhellē'nium**, a council representing all the sections of the Greeks; **panhell'enism** (*-ən-izm*), a movement or aspiration for Greek union; **panhell'enist**. [Gr. *Hellēnikos*, Greek—*Hellas*, Greece.]

**panic**, *pan'ik*, *n.* frantic or sudden fright: contagious fear: great terror without any visible ground or foundation: a state of terror about investments, impelling men to rush and sell what they possess.—*adj.* relating or due to the god Pan: of the nature of a panic: inspired by panic.—*v.t.* to throw into a panic.—*v.i.* to be struck by panic:—*pr.p.* **pan'icking**; *pa.t.* and

*pa.p.* **pan'icked**.—*adj.* **pan'icky**, inclined to, affected by, resulting from, or of the nature of, panic.—**pan'ic-bolt'**, an easily moved bolt for emergency exits; **pan'ic-mong'er**, one who creates or fosters panics.—*adjs.* **pan'ic-strick'en**, **-struck**, struck with a panic or sudden fear. [Gr. *pānikos*, belonging to Pan; *pānikon* (*deima*), panic (fear), fear associated with the god Pan.]

**panic**, *pan'ik*, *n.* any grass of the genus Panicum or of various closely related genera (also **pan'ic-grass'**): the edible grain of some species.—Also **pan'ick**, **pann'ick**.—*n.* **pan'icle**, a raceme whose branches are themselves racemes: loosely, a lax irregular inflorescence.—*adjs.* **pan'icled**, **panic'-ūlate**, **-d**, furnished with, arranged in, or like, panicles.—*adv.* **panic'ūlately**.—*n.* **Pan'icum**, a large genus of grasses having the one- or two-flowered spikelets in spikes, racemes or panicles —including several of the millets. [L. *pānicum*, Italian millet.]

**panification**, *pan-i-fi-kā'shən*, *n.* conversion into bread. [L. *pānis*, bread, *facěre*, to make.]

**panim**, a Miltonic spelling of **paynim**.

**Panionic**, *pan-i-on'ik*, *adj.* of or including all Ionians. [**pan-** and **Ionic**.]

**panisk, panisc**, *pan'isk*, *n.* an inferior god, attendant on Pan. [Gr. *Pāniskos*, dim. of *Pān*.]

**panislam**, *pan-iz'läm*, *n.* the whole Mohammedan world: panislamism.—*adj.* **panislam'ic**.—*ns.* **panis'lamism**, an aspiration or movement for the union of all Mohammedans; **panis'lamist**. [**pan-** and **Islam**.]

**Panjabi.** Same as **Punjabi**.

**panjandrum**, *pan-jan'drəm*, *n.* an imaginary figure of great power and importance, a burlesque potentate, from the Grand Panjandrum in a string of nonsense made up by Samuel Foote.—Also **panjan'darum**.

**panlogism**, *pan'lō-jizm*, *n.* the theory that the universe is an outward manifestation of the Logos. [**Logos**.]

**panmixia**, *pan-mik'si-ə*, (*biol.*) *n.* cessation of the influence of natural selection. [Gr. *mixis*, mixing.]

**pannage**, *pan'ij*, *n.* food picked up by swine in the woods, mast: the right to pasture swine in a forest. [O.Fr. *pasnage*—L.L. *pastiōnāticum*—*pascěre*, *pastum*, to feed.]

**panne**, *pan*, *n.* a fabric resembling velvet, with a long nap. [Fr.]

**pannelled**, *pan'ld*, *v.t.* (*pa.t.*) conjectured to be a misprint for *spanielled*; i.e. followed or fawned on as by a spaniel (Shak., *Ant. and Cle.* IV, xii. 26).

**pannicle**, *pan'i-kl*, **panniculus**, *pə-nik'ū-ləs*, *n.* a thin, sheet-like investment. [L. *panniculus*, dim. of *pannus*, a cloth.]

**pannier**, *pan'yər*, or *pan'i-ər*, *n.* a provision-basket: a basket carried on the back: one of a pair of baskets slung over a pack-animal's back or over the back of a motor-cycle, etc.: a sculptured basket (*archit.*): a contrivance formerly used for puffing out a woman's dress at the hips: the part so puffed out: a piece of basket-work for protecting archers, or, when filled with gravel or sand, for forming and protecting dikes, embankments, etc.: a covered basket of medicines and surgical instruments, hence (blunderingly) an ambulance (*mil.*).—*adj.* **pann'iered**. [Fr. *panier*—L. *pānārium*, a bread-basket—*pānis*, bread.]

**pannier**, *pan'yər*, *-i-ər*, *n.* a coll. name for a robed waiter in the Inns of Court. [Origin unknown.]

**pannikell**, *pan'i-kel*, (*Spens.*) *n.* the skull. [**pannicle**.]

**pannikin.** See pan (1).

**pannose**, *pan'ōs*, (*bot.*) *adj.* like felt. [L. *pannōsus* —*pannus*, cloth.]

**panocha**, *pä-nō'chə*, *n.* a Mexican coarse sugar. [Sp.]

**panoistic,** *pan-ō-is'tik,* (*entom.*) *adj.* of an ovary, producing ova only, not yolk-forming cells—opp. to *meroistic.* [Gr. *ōion,* an egg.]

**panomphaean,** *pan-om-fē'ən, adj.* all-oracular, an epithet of Zeus: applied (after Rabelais) to the word 'drink' (which is celebrated by all nations). [Gr. *omphē,* a divine voice.]

**panophobia,** *pan-ō-fō'bi-ə, n.* a form of melancholia marked by groundless fears: erroneously used for **pantophobia.** [Gr. *Pān,* the god who inspired fears, *phobos,* fear.]

**panophthalmitis,** *pan-of-thal-mī'tis, n.* inflammation of the whole eye.—Also **panophthalmia.** [Gr. *ophthalmos,* eye.]

**panoply,** *pan'ə-pli, n.* complete armour: a full suit of armour: full or brilliant covering or array.—*adj.* **pan'oplied,** in panoply. [Gr. *panopliā,* full armour of a hoplite—*pās, pān,* all, *hopla* (pl.), arms.]

**panopticon,** *pan-op'ti-kon, n.* a prison in which all prisoners can be watched from one point: an exhibition room. [Gr. *optikon* (neut. adj.), for seeing.]

**panorama,** *pan-ə-rä'mə, n.* a wide or complete view: a picture disposed around the interior of a room, viewed from within in all directions: a picture unrolled and made to pass before the spectator.—*adj.* **panoramic** (*-ram'ik*).—**panorama head,** a swivel device fitted to the head of a camera tripod to permit the sideways swinging motion of the camera when taking panning shots; **panoramic camera,** one which takes very wide angle views, generally by rotation about an axis and by exposing a roll of film through a vertical slit. [Gr. *horāma,* a view, from *horaein,* to see.]

**panpharmacon,** *pan-fär'mə-kon, n.* a universal remedy. [Gr. *pharmakon,* a drug.]

**Pan-Presbyterian,** *pan-prez-bi-tē'ri-ən, adj.* of, including, or representing, all Presbyterians. [pan- and **Presbyterian** (see **presbyter**).]

**panpsychism,** *pan-sik'izm, n.* the theory that all nature has a psychic side.—*n.* **panpsych'ist.**—*adj.* **panpsychist'ic.** [pan- and **psychism** (see **psyche**).]

**pansexualism,** *pan-seks'ū-əl-izm, n.* the view that all mental activity is derived from sexual instinct.—*adj.* **pansex'ual.**—*n.* **pansex'ualist.** [pan- and **sexualism** (see **sex**).]

**Pan-Slav,** *pan-släv', adj.* of, including, or representing, all Slavs.—*adj.* **Pan-Slav'ic.**—*ns.* **Pan-Slav'ism,** a movement for the union of all Slav peoples; **Pan-Slav'ist.**—*adj.* **Pan-Slavon'ic.** [pan- and **Slav.**]

**pansophy,** *pan'sə-fi, n.* universal knowledge.—*adjs.* **pansophic** (*-sof'ik*), **-al.**—*ns.* **pan'sophism; pan'-sophist.** [Gr. *sophiā,* wisdom.]

**panspermatism,** *pan-spûr'mə-tizm,* **panspermism,** *-mizm,* **panspermy,** *-mi,* **panspermia,** *-mi-a, ns.* the theory that life could be diffused through the universe by means of germs carried by meteorites.—*adjs.* **panspermat'ic, -sper'mic.**—*ns.* **pansper'matist, -mist.** [Gr. *sperma, -atos,* seed.]

**pansy,** *pan'zi, n.* a name for various species of violet, esp. the heart's-ease (*Viola tricolor*) and garden kinds derived from it, as well as other species with up-turned side petals and large leafy stipules: a soft bluish-purple: an effeminate or namby-pamby man: a male homosexual.—Also (*obs.*; *Spens.,* etc.) **pance, paunce, pawnce** (*päns, pöns*).—*adj.* bluish-purple: effeminate.—*adj.* **pan'sied.** [Fr. *pensée—penser,* to think—L. *pēnsāre,* to weigh.]

**pant-.** See **pan-.**

**pant,** *pant, v.i.* to gasp for breath: to run gasping: to throb: to wish ardently, to long, to yearn: to bulge and shrink successively, as ships' hulls, etc.—*v.t.* to gasp out: to yearn (with *for*).—*n.* **pant,** a gasping breath: a throb.—*n.* and *adj.* **pant'ing.**—*adv.* **pant'ingly.** [Apparently related to O.Fr. *pantoisier,* to pant.]

**pant,** *pänt,* (*Northern*) *n.* a public fountain: a puddle by a midden. [Origin obscure.]

**pantable,** *pan'tə-bl.* Same as **pantofle.**

**pantagamy,** *pan-tag'ə-mi, n.* a word that ought to mean universal bachelorhood, applied with unconscious irony to the universal marriage of the Perfectionists, in which every man in the community is the husband of every woman. [Gr. *gamos,* marriage, *agamiā,* bachelorhood.]

**pantagraph.** See **pantograph.**

**Pantagruelism,** *pan-tə-grōō'əl-izm, -tag'rōō-, n.* the theories and practice of *Pantagruel* as described by Rabelais (*d.* 1553): burlesque ironical buffoonery as a cover for serious satire.—*adj.* and *n.* **Pantagruelian** (*-el'i-ən*).—*ns.* **Pantagruel'-ion,** a magic herb, hemp; **Pantagru'elist** (or *-tag'rōō-*).

**pantaleon,** *pan-tal'i-on, n.* a very large dulcimer invented about 1700 by *Pantaleon* Hebenstreit.

**pantalets,** *pan-tə-lets', n.pl.* long frilled drawers, worn by women and children in the first half of the 19th century: a detachable ruffle for these, or one simulating these: extended to various trouser-like garments worn by women.—Also **pantalettes.**—*adj.* **pantalett'ed.** [Dim. of **pantaloons.**]

**Pantaloon,** *pan-tə-lōōn', or pan', n.* a character in Italian comedy, and afterwards in pantomime, a lean old man (originally a Venetian) more or less a dotard: (without *cap.*; *Shak.*) a feeble old man: (without *cap.*; in *pl.*) various kinds of trousers worn by or suggesting the stage pantaloon, as wide breeches of the Restoration, later combined breeches and stockings, later 18th-century trousers fastened below the calf or under the shoe, children's trousers resembling these, (usu. **pants**) trousers generally or long woollen underpants.—*n.* **pan'talon,** a movement in a quadrille.—*adj.* **pantalooned'.**—*n.* **pantaloon'ery,** buffoonery. [Fr. *pantalon*—It. *pantalone,* from St *Pantaleone,* a favourite saint of the Venetians.]

**pantechnicon,** *pan-tek'ni-kon, n.* orig., a building in London intended for the sale of all kinds of artistic work, turned into a furniture-store: a furniture-van (in full **pantech'nicon-van'**): loosely, a receptacle holding a large number of miscellaneous objects. [Gr. *technē,* art.]

**panter.** See **pantler.**

**pantheism,** *pan'thē-izm, n.* the doctrine that identifies God with the universe: the worship of all gods (*rare*).—*n.* **pan'theist.**—*adjs.* **pantheïst'ic, -al.**—*ns.* **pantheol'ogist; pantheol'ogy,** a synthesis of all religions and the knowledge of all gods; **Pantheon** (*pan'thi-on, pan-thē'on*), a temple of all the gods, esp. the rotunda erected by Hadrian at Rome (on the site of Agrippa's of 27 B.C.), now the church of Santa Maria Rotonda, a burial-place of great Italians: a building serving as a general burial-place or memorial of the great dead, as Sainte Geneviève at Paris: an 18th-century place of amusement in London (Oxford Street): all the gods collectively: a complete mythology. [Gr. *theos,* a god, *pantheion,* a Pantheon.]

**panthenol,** *pan'thin-ol, n.* a vitamin of the B-complex, affecting the growth of hair.

**pantheologist,** etc, Pantheon. See **pantheism.**

**panther,** *pan'thər, n.* a leopard, esp. a large one, formerly believed to be a different species: a puma (*U.S.*):—*fem.* **pan'theress.**—*adjs.* **pan'ther-ine** (*-in*), **pan'therish.** [Gr. *panthēr.*]

**pantile,** *pan'til, n.* a roofing tile whose cross-section forms an ogee curve: a tile concave or convex in cross-section: a flat paving tile (*obs.*).—*adj.* (*obs. slang*) dissenting—chapels being often roofed with these.—*adj.* **pan'tiled.**—*n.* **pan'tiling** (*-til-*), (pl.), **tile.**]

**pantine,** *pan'tēn,* (*obs.*) *n.* a pasteboard jumping-jack, fashionable in the 18th century. [Fr. *pantine,* afterwards *pantin.*]

**pantisocracy**, *pant-is-ok'rə-si*, or *-īs-*, *n.* a community (planned by Coleridge, Southey, and Lovell) in which all should have equal power.— *n.* **pantis'ocrat**.—*adj.* **pantisocrat'ic**. [Gr. *pās, pantos*, all, *isos*, equal, *krateein*, to rule.]

**pantler**, *pant'lər*, (*Shak.*) *n.* the officer in a great family who had charge of the bread and other provisions.—Also **pant'er**. [Fr. *panetier*—L. *pānis*, bread.]

**panto.** See **pantomime**.

**Pantocrator**, *pan-tok'rə-tər*, *n.* the ruler of the universe, esp. Christ enthroned, as in icons, etc. [Gr. *kratos*, power.]

**pantofle**, **pantoffle**, **pantoufle**, *pan'tof-l, -tof'l, tōōf'l*, *n.* a slipper: a high chopin (*hist.*): an overshoe (*arch.*).—Also **pantable** (*pan'tə-bl*).— **on one's pantables**, on one's dignity, high horse, lofty in manner. [Fr. *pantoufle*.]

**pantograph**, *pan'tə-gräf*, *n.* a jointed framework of rods, based on the geometry of a parallelogram, for copying drawings, plans, etc., on the same, or a different, scale: a similar framework for other purposes, as for collecting a current from an overhead wire.—*n.* **pantographer** (*-tog'rə-fər*).—*adjs.* **pantographic** (*-tō-graf'ik*), **-al.** —*n.* **pantog'raphy**.—Also (*faulty*) **pan'tagraph**, etc. [Gr. *graphein*, to write.]

**pantomime**, *pan'tə-mīm*, *n.* a Roman actor in dumb show (*hist.*): a play or an entertainment in dumb show: a theatrical entertainment, usu. about Christmas-time, developed out of this, no longer in dumb show, with showy scenery, topical allusions, songs of the day, buffoonery and dancing strung loosely upon a nursery story, formerly ending with a transformation scene and a harlequinade: dumb show.—*adj.* of pantomime: pantomimic.—**pan'to**, coll. for pantomime.—*adjs.* **pantomimic** (*-mim'ik*), **-al.**— *adv.* **pantomim'ically**.—*n.* **pan'tomimist**, an actor in or writer of pantomime. [L. *pantomimus*—Gr. *pantomimos*, imitator of all—*pās, pantos*, all, *mimos*, an imitator.]

**panton**, *pan'tan*, (*Scot.*) *n.* a slipper.—*n.* **pan'tonshoe'**, a horse-shoe for curing a narrow and hoofbound heel. [App. conn. with **pantofle**.]

**pantophagy**, *pan-tof'ə-ji*, *n.* omnivorousness.—*n.* **pantoph'agist**.—*adj.* **pantoph'agous** (*-gəs*). [Gr. *phagein*, to eat.]

**pantophobia**, *pan-tə-fō'bi-ə*, *n.* morbid fear of everything: (by confusion with **panophobia**) causeless fear. [Gr. *pās, pantos*, all, *phobos*, fear.]

**pantopragmatic**, *pan-tə-prag-mat'ik*, *adj.* meddling in everybody's business.—*n.* a universal busybody.—*n.* (treated as *sing.*) **pantopragmat'ics**, the science of universal benevolent interference. [From Peacock's imaginary society (*Gryll Grange*)—Gr. *pās, pantos*, all, *pragmata* (pl.), business.]

**pantoscope**, *pan'tə-skōp*, *n.* a panoramic camera: a very wide-angled photographic lens.—*adj.* **pantoscopic** (*-skop'ik*), giving a wide range of vision: bifocal. [Gr. *skopeein*, to look at.]

**pantothenic**, *pan-to-then'ik*, *adj.* lit. from all quarters: applied to an acid, a member of the vitamin B complex, so ubiquitous that the effects of its deficiency in man are not known. [Gr. *pantothen*, from everywhere.]

**pantoum**, *pan-tōōm'*, properly **pantun**, *pan-tōōn'*, *n.* a verse-form orig. Malay, quatrains rhyming *ab ab, bc bc*, etc., returning to rhyme *a* at the end. [Malay.]

**pantry**, *pan'tri*, *n.* a room or closet for provisions and table furnishings, or where plate, knives, etc., are cleaned.—*ns.* **pan'trymaid**; **pan'tryman**. [Fr. *paneterie*—L.L. *pānitāria*—L. *pānis*, bread.]

**pants**, *pants*, *n.pl.* trousers: drawers.—*n.pl.* **pant'ies**, very short drawers for children and women. [**pantaloons**.]

**pantun.** See **pantoum**.

**panzer**, *pant'sər*, (Ger.) armour: a tank.—**panzer division**, an armoured division.

**paolo**, *pä'ō-lō*, *n.* an obsolete papal silver coin, worth about fivepence:—*pl.* **pa'oli** (*-lē*). [It. *Paolo*, Paul, i.e. Pope Paul V.]

**pap**, *pap*, *n.* soft food for infants, as of bread boiled with milk (often *fig.*): mash: pulp.—*v.t.* to feed with pap.—*adj.* **papp'y**.—**pap'-boat**, a boat-shaped vessel for pap; **pap'-meat**, soft food for infants; **pap'-spoon**. [Imit.]

**pap**, *pap*, (*dial.*) *n.* a nipple: in place-names, a round conical hill. [App. Scand.]

**papa**, *pə-pä'* (*U.S. pä'pə*), *n.* father (old-fashioned hypocoristic and genteel): a pope (*pä'pä*; *obs.*): a priest of the Greek Church. [Partly through Fr. *papa*, partly directly from L.L. *pāpa*, Gr. hypocoristic *papās, pappās*, father.]

**papacy**, *pä'pə-si*, *n.* the office of pope: a pope's tenure of office: papal government. [L.L. *pāpātia*—*pāpa*, pope.]

**papain**, *pə-pā'in*, *n.* a digestive enzyme in the juice of papaw (Carica) fruits and leaves. [Sp. *papaya*, papaw.]

**papal**, *pä'pl*, *adj.* of the pope or the papacy.— *adj.* **pap'able**, likely to, or qualified to, become pope.—*v.t.* and *v.i.* **pa'palise**, *-ize*, to render or become papal or papalist.—*ns.* **pa'palism**, the papal system; **pa'palist**, a supporter of the pope and of the papal system.—*adv.* **pa'pally**.—**papal cross**, a cross with three cross-bars; **Papal States**, States of the Church (see **state**). [L.L. *pāpālis*—*pāpa*, pope.]

**papaprelatist**, *pä-pə-prel'ə-tist*, (*Scott*) *n.* a supporter of popish prelates.

**Papaver**, *pə-pä'vər*, *n.* the poppy genus, giving name to the family **Papaverā'ceae**.—*adj.* **papaveraceous** (*pə-pav-*, or *-pāv-ə-rā'shəs*), of the poppy family.—*n.* **papaverine** (*pə-pav'ə-rēn, -rin*, or *-pāv'*), an alkaloid got from poppy juice.— *adj.* **papaverous** (*-pav'* or *-pāv'*), resembling or having the qualities of the poppy. [L. *papāver*, the poppy.]

**papaw**, *pə-pö'*, *pö'pö*, *n.* the tree *Asimina triloba* (of the custard-apple family) or its fruit, native to the U.S.: the papaya.—Also **paw'paw'**. [Prob. variant of **papaya**.]

**papaya**, *pə-pä'yə*, *n.* the tree *Carica papaya*, or its fruit, native to South America but common in the tropics, the trunk, leaves, and fruit yielding papain, the leaves forming a powerful anthelmintic.—Also called **papaw**. [Sp. *papayo* (tree), *papaya* (fruit) app. from Carib.]

**pape**, *päp*, *n.* a Scots form of **pope**.—*adj.* **pāp'ish**, popish.—*n.* (*dial.* and *illit.*, by confusion with **papist**) a papist.—*n.* **pāp'isher**.

**paper**, *pä'pər*, *n.* a material made in thin sheets as an aqueous deposit from linen rags, esparto, wood-pulp, or other form of cellulose, used for writing, printing, wrapping, and other purposes: extended to other materials of similar purpose or appearance, as to papyrus, rice-paper, to the substance of which some wasps build their nests, to cardboard, and even to tinfoil ('silver paper'): a piece of paper: a written or printed document or instrument, note, receipt, bill, bond, deed, etc.: a newspaper: an essay or literary contribution, esp. one read before a society: a set of examination questions: free passes of admission to a theatre, etc., also the persons so admitted: paper-money: paperhangings for walls: a wrapping of paper: a quantity of anything wrapped in or attached to a paper.—*adj.* consisting or made of paper: papery: on paper.—*v.t.* to cover with paper: to fold in paper: to treat in any way by means of paper, as to sandpaper, etc.: to paste endpapers and fly-leaves to.—*n.* **pa'pering**, the operation of covering with paper: the paper so used.—*adj.* **pa'pery**, like paper.—**pa'perback**, a book with paper cover; **pa′per-birch′**, an American birch with papery bark; **pa′per-boy, -girl**, one who delivers newspapers; **pa′per-case**, a box for writing materials, etc.; **pa′per-chase**, the game of hare and hounds, in which some runners (*hares*) set off across country strewing paper by which others (*hounds*) track them; **pa′per-cigar′** (*obs*.), a cigarette; **pa′per-clip**, a clip of bent wire or the like, for holding papers together: a letter-clip; **pa′per-cloth**, a fabric prepared in the Pacific islands from the inner bark of the paper-mulberry; **pa′per-coal**, a lignite that splits into thin layers; **pa′per-cred′it**, credit given to a person because he shows that money is owing to him; **pa′per-cutter**, a paper-knife: a machine for cutting paper in sheets, for trimming the edges of books, etc.; **pa′per-day** (*law*), one of certain days in each term for hearing cases down in the paper or roll of business; **pa′per-enam′el**, an enamel for cards and fine note-paper.—*adj.* **pa′per-faced** (*Shak.*), having a thin face like a sheet of paper: faced with paper.—**pa′per-fastener**, a button with two blades that can be forced through papers and bent back; **pa′per-feeder**, an apparatus for delivering sheets of paper to a printing-press, etc.; **pa′per-file**, appliance for filing papers; **pa′per-folder**, folder (2nd sense); **pa′per-gauge**, a rule for measuring the typeface of matter to be printed, and the width of the margin; **pa′per-hanger**, one who papers walls; **pa′per-hangings**, paper for covering walls; **pa′per-knife**, a thin, flat blade for cutting open the leaves of books and other folded papers; **pa′per-maker**, a manufacturer of paper; **pa′per-making**; **pa′per-mar′bler**, one engaged in marbling paper; **pa′per-mill**, a mill where paper is made; **paper money**, pieces of paper stamped or marked by government or by a bank, as representing a certain value of money, which pass from hand to hand instead of the coin itself; **pa′per-mul′berry**, a tree (*Broussonetia papyrifera*) of Eastern Asia and Polynesia, of the mulberry family, whose inner bark yields tapa cloth and paper-making material; **pa′per-mus′lin**, a glazed muslin; **paper nautilus**, the argonaut (see **nautilus**); **pa′per-off′ice**, an office where state-papers are kept; **pa′per-pulp**, pulpy material for making paper; **pa′per-reed**, the papyrus; **pa′per-rul′er**, one who, or an instrument which, makes straight lines on paper; **pa′per-sail′or**, an argonaut; **pa′per-stain′er**, one who prepares paper-hangings: a poor author, scribbler; **paper tiger**, a person, organisation, that appears to be powerful but is in fact the reverse; **pa′per-wash′ing** (*phot.*), water in which prints have been washed; **pa′per-weight**, a small weight for keeping loose papers from being displaced; **paper work**, clerical work: keeping of records as part of a job.—**on paper**, planned, decreed, existing theoretically only; **paper over (the cracks)**, to create the impression that there is or has been no dissent, error, or fault; **paper the house**, fill a theatre by issuing free passes. [A.Fr. *papir*, O.Fr. (Fr.) *papier*—L. *papyrus*—Gr. *papȳros*, papyrus.]

**papeterie**, *pap-ə-trē′*, *n.* a stationery-case. [Fr., stationery, paper-trade.]

**Paphian**, *pā′fi-ən*, *adj.* pertaining to *Paphos* in Cyprus, sacred to Aphrodite: lascivious.—*n.* a native of Paphos: a votary of Aphrodite: a whore.

**papier collé**, *pä-pyā kol-ā*, scraps of paper and odds and ends pasted out as a help to cubist composition. [Fr., glued paper.]

**papier-mâché**, *pap′yä-mä′shä*, *n.* a material consisting of paper-pulp or of sheets of paper pasted together, treated so as to resemble varnished or lacquered wood or plaster.—*adj.* of papier-mâché. [Would-be French,—Fr.

*papier* (see **paper**), *mâché*, chewed—L. *masticātus*.]

**Papilio**, *pə-pil′i-ō*, *n.* the swallow-tailed butterfly genus, giving name to the family **Papilionidae** (*-on′i-dē*), in which all six legs are fully developed in both sexes.—*adj.* **papilionā′ceous**, of butterflies: butterfly-like: of a form of corolla somewhat butterfly-like, with a large posterior petal (*vexillum*), two side petals or wings (*alae*), and two anterior petals forming a keel (*carina*): of the **Papilionā′ceae**, a family of Leguminosae characterised by such a corolla, including pea, bean, clover, gorse, laburnum, etc. [L. *pāpiliō, -ōnis*, butterfly.]

**papilla**, *pə-pil′ə*, *n.* a small nipple-like protuberance: a minute elevation on the skin, esp. of the finger-tips and upper surface of the tongue, in which a nerve ends: a protuberance at the base of a hair, feather, tooth, etc.: a minute conical protuberance as on the surface of a petal:—*pl.* **papill′ae** (*-ē*).—*adjs.* **papill′ar, papill′ary**, like, of the nature of, or having, papillae; **papill′ate, -d, papillif′erous** (*pap-*), having papillae; **papill′iform**, in the form of a papilla.—*ns.* **papilli′tis**, inflammation of the head of the optic nerve; **papillō′ma**, a tumour formed by hypertrophy of a papilla or papillae, as a wart, etc.—*adjs.* **papillom′atous**; **pap′illōse**, full of papillae, warty—also **papill′ous**; **papill′ūlate**, finely papillose.—*n.* **papill′ūle**, a very small papilla. [L., dim. of *papula*.]

**papillon**, *pap-ē-yō̃*, *n.* a breed of toy spaniel with erect ears. [Fr., butterfly.]

**papillote**, *pap′il-ōt*, *n.* a curl-paper: frilled paper used to decorate the bones of chops, etc. (*cook.*): oiled or greased paper in which meat is cooked and served (*cook.*). [Fr., app.—*papillon*, butterfly—L. *pāpiliō, -ōnis*.]

**papish.** See **pape**.

**papist**, *pā′pist*, *n.* an adherent of the pope: a name slightingly given to a Roman Catholic.—*n′.* **pā′pism**, popery.—*adjs.* **pāpist′ic, -al**, pertaining to popery, or to the Church of Rome, its doctrines, etc.—*adv.* **pāpist′ically.**—*n.* **pā′pistry**, popery. [L.L. *pāpa*, pope.]

**papoose**, *pə-pōōs′*, *n.* a North American Indian child. [Narraganset *papoos*.]

**pappadom.** See **pop(p)adum**.

**pappus**, *pap′əs*, *n.* a ring or parachute of fine hair or down, respresenting the calyx limb, which grows above the seed and helps in wind-dissemination in composites and some other plants (*bot.*): the downy beginnings of a beard.—*adjs.* **papp′ōse** (or *-ōs′*), **papp′ous**. [L. *pappus* —Gr. *pappos*, a grandfather, down, a pappus.]

**paprika**, *pap′ri-kə, pa-prēk′ə*, *n.* Hungarian red pepper, a species of Capsicum. [Hung.]

**Papuan**, *pap′ū-ən*, *adj.* pertaining to *Papua* or New Guinea.—*n.* a member of the black, dolichocephalic, frizzly-haired race inhabiting Papua, etc. [Malay *papuwa*, frizzled.]

**papula**, *pap′ū-la*, **papule**, *pap′ūl*, *ns.* a pimple: a papilla:—*pl.* **pap′ūlae** (*-lē*), **pap′ules.**—*adj.* **pap′ūlar.**—*n.* **papūlā′tion**, the development of papules.—*adjs.* **pap′ūlose, pap′ūlous**. [L. *papula*, a pimple.]

**papyrus**, *pə-pī′rəs*, *n.* the paper-reed (*Cyperus papyrus*, or kindred species), a tall plant of the sedge family, once common in Egypt: its pith cut in thin strips and pressed together as a writing material of the ancients: a manuscript on papyrus:—*pl.* **papy′ri** (*-rī*).—*adj.* **papyraceous** (*pap-i-rā′shəs*), papery.—*ns.* **papyrologist** (*pap-i-rol′ə-jist*); **papyrol′ogy**, the study of ancient papyri. [L. *papȳrus*—Gr. *papȳros*: probably Egyptian.]

**par**, *pär*, *n.* state of equality: equal value: norm or standard: state or value of bills, shares, etc., when they sell at exactly the price marked on them—i.e. without *premium* or *discount*: equality of condition: the number of strokes that should be taken for a hole or a round by perfect play, two putts being allowed on each green (*golf*).— **par contest** (*bridge*), a competition in which points are awarded for the bidding of a pre-pared hand and for the playing of the hand in a directed contract; **par value,** value at par.— **above par,** at a premium, or at more than the nominal value; **at par,** at exactly the nominal value; **below par,** at a discount, or at less than the nominal value: out of sorts (*fig.*); **nominal par,** value with which a bill or share is marked, or by which it is known; **no par value,** with no stated nominal value; **par of exchange,** the value of currency of one country expressed in that of another. [L. *pär*, equal.]

**par,** *pär, n.* Same as parr.

**par,** *pär, n.* a colloquial abbreviation of para-graph.

**para,** *pär'ə, n.* a small Turkish coin: the 40th part of a piastre: in Yugoslavia the 100th part of a dinar. [Turk. *pārah*.]

**Pará,** *pä-rä', n.* a city, state, and estuary of Brazil. —**pará grass,** piassava; **pará nut,** Brazil nut; **pará rubber,** that got from *Hevea brasiliensis*.

**para-,** in composition, beside: faulty: dis-ordered: abnormal: false: a polymer of: a compound related to: closely resembling, or parallel to (as in *adjs.* **paramed'ical,** helping doctors or supplementing medical work; **para-military**): in organic chem., having substituted atoms or groups attached to two opposite car-bon atoms of the benzene ring—commonly re-presented by *p*-.—**pa'ra-compound.** [Gr. *para*, beside.]

**para-,** *pa-ra-, pfx.,* parachute, as in *ns.* **par'a-doctor,** a doctor who parachutes to patients; **par'afoil,** a form of steerable parachute, con-sisting of air-filled nylon cells; **par'aglider,** a glider with inflatable wings; **par'agliding,** the sport of being towed through the air, then allowed to drift to the ground; **par'amedic(o),** a paradoctor.—*adjs.* **par'amedic(al).**

**para-amino-salicylic acid,** *par-ə-a-mē'nō-sal-i-sil'ik as'id,* a drug used along with streptomycin in the treatment of tuberculosis:—abbrev. **PAS.**

**parabaptism,** *par-ə-bap'tizm, n.* uncanonical bap-tism. [para- (1) and baptism (see baptise).]

**parabasis,** *pə-rab'ə-sis, n.* part of the Old Comedy of Greece in which the chorus came forward and addressed the audience on behalf of the poet. [Gr., a going aside—*para*-, beside, beyond, *basis*, a going.]

**parabema,** *par-ə-bē'mə, n.* in Byzantine architec-ture, either the chapel of the prothesis or the diaconicon, when walled off from the bema:— *pl.* **parabe'mata.**—*adj.* **parabemat'ic.** [Gr. *para*, beside, beyond, *bēma*, a step.]

**parabiosis,** *par-ə-bī-ō'sis, n.* the union of similar embryos between which a functional connection exists.—*adj.* **parabio'tic.**—**parabiotic twins,** Siam-ese twins. [Gr. *para*, beside, *biōsis*, manner of life.]

**parable,** *par'ə-bl, n.* a similitude: a fable or story of something which might have happened, told to illustrate some doctrine, or to make some duty clear: a proverb (*arch.*): discourse (*arch.*). —*v.t.* to represent by a parable.—*ns.* **parabola** (*pə-rab'ə-lə*), a curve, one of the conic sections, the intersection of a cone and a plane parallel to its side, or the locus of a point equidistant from a fixed point (the *focus*) and a fixed straight line (the *directrix*)—its equation with vertex as origin $y^2 = 4ax$: generalised to include any curve whose equation is $y^n = px^m$:—*pl.* **parab'-olas; parab'ole** (*-lē*) in rhetoric, a similitude, simile, or metaphor.—*adjs.* **parabol'ic** (*par-ə-bol'ik*), **-al,** of or like a parable or a parabola or a parabole: expressed by a parable: belong-ing to, or of the form of, a parabola.—*adv.*

**parabol'ically.**—*v.t.* **parab'olise, -ize,** to set forth by parable: to treat as a parable.—*ns.* **parab'olist; parab'oloid,** a surface or solid generated by the rotation of a parabola about its axis.—*adjs.* **parab'oloid, -al.**—**parabolic geo-metry,** Euclidean geometry; **parabolic velocity** (*astron.*), the velocity which a body at a given point would require to describe a parabola about the centre of attraction. [Gr. *parabolē*, a placing alongside, comparison, parabola, etc.—*para*, be-side, beyond, *ballein*, to throw.]

**parablepsis,** *par-ə-blep'sis, n.* false vision: over-sight.—Also **par'ablepsy.**—*adj.* **parablep'tic.** [Gr., looking askant—*para*, beside, beyond, *blepein*, to see.]

**parabola.** See parable.

**parabolanus,** *par-ə-bō-lā'nəs, n.* in the early Eastern Church, a layman who tended the sick. [Gr. *parabolos*, venturesome, exposing oneself.]

**Paracelsian,** *par-ə-sel'si-ən, adj.* of or relating to the famous German Swiss philosopher and physician, *Paracelsus* (1493-1541), or resembling his theories or practice. The name was coined for himself by Theophrastus Bombastus von Hohenheim, and apparently implied a claim to be greater than Celsus.

**paracentesis,** *par-ə-sen-tē'sis,* (*surg.*) *n.* tapping. [Gr. *parakentēsis*—*para*, beside, beyond, *ken-teein*, to pierce.]

**parachronism,** *par-ak'rən-izm, n.* an error in dating, esp. when anything is represented as later than it really was. [Gr. *para*, beside, be-yond, *chronos*, time.]

**parachute,** *par'ə-shōōt, n.* an apparatus like an umbrella for descending safely from a height: any structure serving a like purpose, as a pappus, a patagium.—*v.i.* to descend by parachute.—*n.* **par'achutist.**—**parachute troops.** [Fr. *parachute* —It. *para*, imper. of *parare*, to ward—L. *parāre*, to prepare, and Fr. *chute*, fall.]

**paraclete,** *par'ə-klēt, n.* an advocate or legal helper, or intercessor—applied to the Holy Ghost (John xiv. 26). [Gr. *paraklētos*—*para-kaleein*, to call in, also to comfort—*para*, beside, beyond, *kaleein*, to call.]

**paracme,** *pər-ak'mē, n.* the stage of decline or senescence after the culmination of develop-ment. [Gr. *para*, beside, beyond, *akmē*, a point.]

**paracrostic,** *par-ə-kros'tik, n.* a poem whose initial letters reproduce its first verse. [para- (1) and acrostic.]

**paracusis,** *par-ə-kū'sis, n.* disordered hearing. [Gr. *para*, beside, beyond, *akousis*, hearing.]

**paracyanogen,** *par-ə-si-an'ə-jən, n.* a polymer of cyanogen. [para- (1) and cyanogen.]

**parade,** *pə-rād', n.* show: display: ostentation: an assembling in order for exercise, inspection, etc.: a procession: ground for parade of troops: a public promenade: a parry (*fencing*). —*v.t.* to show off: to thrust upon notice: to lead about and expose to public attention: to traverse in parade: to marshal in military order. —*v.i.* to march up and down as if for show: to pass in military order: to march in pro-cession: to show off.—**parade'-ground.** [Fr.,— Sp. *parada*—*parar*, to halt—L. *parāre, -ātum,* to prepare.]

**paradigm,** *par'ə-dim, n.* an example, exemplar: an example of the inflection of a word (*gram.*). —*adjs.* **paradigmatic** (*-dig-mat'ik*), **-al.**—*adv.* **paradigmat'ically.** [Fr. *paradigme*—Gr. *para-deigma*—*paradeiknynai,* to exhibit side by side —*para*, beside, beyond, *deiknynai,* to show.]

**paradiddle,** *par'ə-did-l, n.* a drum roll in which the principal beats are struck by the left and right sticks in succession.

**paradise,** *par'ə-dis, n.* a park or pleasure-ground esp. in ancient Persia: a park in which foreign animals were kept: the garden of Eden:

heaven: the abode (intermediate or final) of the blessed dead: any place of bliss: a parvis: a small private apartment (*arch.*).—*adjs.* **paradisaic** (*par-ə-dis-ā´ik*), **-al**, **paradisal** (-*di´səl*), **paradisean** (-*dis´i-ən*), **paradisiac** (*dis´i-ak*, *diz´i-ak*), **paradisiacal** (-*dis-i´ə-kl*), **paradisial** (-*dis´*, -*diz´*), **paradisian** (-*dis´*, -*diz´*), **paradisic** (-*dis´*, -*diz´*).—**par´adise-fish,** a Chinese freshwater fish (Macropodus), often kept in aquaria for its beauty of form and colouring.—**bird of paradise,** any bird of the family **Paradisē´idae,** inhabitants chiefly of New Guinea, close akin to the crows but extremely gorgeous in plumage: **fool's paradise** (see **fool**). [Gr. *paradeisos*, a park—O.Pers. *pairidaēza*, park.]

**parados,** *par´ə-dos*, *n.* earthworks protecting against a rear attack. [Fr.—L. *parāre*, to prepare, *dorsum*, back.]

**paradox,** *par´ə-doks*, *n.* that which is contrary to received opinion: that which is apparently absurd but is or may be really true: a self-contradictory statement: paradoxical character. —*adj.* **paradox´al.**—*n.* **par´adoxer.**—*adj.* **paradox´ical.**—*adv.* **paradox´ically.**—*ns.* **paradox´icalness;** **Paradox´ides** (-*i-dēz*), a typically Middle Cambrian genus of trilobites, some very large (2 feet).—*adj.* **paradoxid´ian.**—*ns.* **par´adoxist; paradoxol´ogy,** utterance or maintaining of paradoxes; **par´adoxy,** the quality of being paradoxical.—**paradoxical sleep,** deep sleep. [Gr. *paradoxos*, -*on*, contrary to opinion —*para*, beside, beyond, *doxa*, opinion.]

**paradoxure,** *par-ə-dok´sūr*, *n.* a civet-like carnivore of Southern Asia and Malaysia, the palm-cat of India.—*adj.* **paradoxū´rine.** [Gr. *paradoxos*, paradoxical, *para*, beside, beyond, *ourā*, tail.]

**paraenesis, parenesis,** *par-ēn´i-sis*, or -*en´*, *n.* exhortation.—*adjs.* **paraenetic** (-*net´ik*), **-al.** [Gr. *parainesis*—*para*, beside, beyond, *aineein*, to commend.]

**paraesthesia,** in U.S. **paresthesia,** *par-ēs-thē´si-ə*, or -*es*-, *n.* abnormal sensation. [Gr. *para*, beyond, *aisthēsis*, sensation.]

**paraffin,** *par´ə-fin*, *n.* originally, paraffin-wax— so named by its discoverer, Reichenbach, from its having little chemical affinity for other bodies: generalised to mean any saturated hydrocarbon of the methane series, gaseous, liquid, or solid, the general formula being $C_nH_{2n+2}$: paraffin-oil.—Also **par´affine.**—*v.t.* to treat with paraffin. —*adjs.* **paraffin´ic, par´affinoid, par´affiny.**— **par´affin-oil´,** any of the mineral burning oils associated with the manufacture of paraffin, mixtures of liquid paraffin and other hydrocarbons; **par´affin-scale´,** unrefined solid paraffin; **par´affin-wax´,** a white transparent crystalline substance got by distillation of shale, coal, tar, wood, etc., a mixture of solid paraffins. —**liquid paraffin,** a liquid form of petrolatum, used as a mild laxative. [L. *parum*, little, *affinis*, having affinity.]

**paraffle, parafle,** *pə-rä´fl*, (*Scot.*) *n.* pretentious display. [Cf. **paraph.**]

**parage,** *par´ij*, *n.* lineage (*obs.*): high birth or rank: equality among persons of whom one does homage for all, the others holding of him (*feudal law*). [Fr.]

**paraglossa,** *par-ə-glos´ə*, *n.* either of two appendages of the ligula in insects:—*pl.* **paragloss´ae** (-*ē*).—*adjs.* **paragloss´al; paragloss´ate.** [Gr. *para*, beside, beyond, *glōssa*, tongue.]

**paragnathous,** *pər-ag´nə-thəs*, *adj.* having equal mandibles.—*n.* **parag´nathism.** [Gr. *para*, beside, beyond, *gnathos*, jaw.]

**paragnosis,** *par-ə-gnō´sis*, (*psych.*) *n.* wrong perception or understanding of sense-impressions. [Gr. *para*, beside, beyond, *gnōsis*, knowing.]

**paragoge,** *par-ə-gō´jē*, -*gē*, *n.* an addition to the end of a word, as *t* in *against*, *amidst*, *amongst*, *whilst*, *d* in *drownd* (illiterate for *drown*).—*adjs.*

**paragogic** (-*goj´ik*, -*gog´ik*), **-al.**—**paragogic future,** the cohortative tense in Hebrew—a lengthened form of the imperfect or future, usually confined to the first person, giving the sense of 'let me' or 'let us'. [Gr. *paragōgē*, a leading part, addition—*para*, beside, beyond, *agein*, to lead.]

**paragon,** *par´ə-gon*, -*gən*, *n.* a model of perfection or supreme excellence: match, equal (*arch.*): mate (*Spens.*): rival (*arch.*): comparison (*Spens.*): emulation, competition (*Spens.*): a diamond of 600 carats or more: a black marble (*obs.*): a camlet used for upholstering and dress (*obs.*): 20-point printing-type, intermediate between great-primer and double-pica.—*v.t.* (*arch.* or *rare*) to compare: to match: to surpass (*Shak.*): to hold up as a paragon (*Shak.*). [O.Fr. *paragon*—It. *paragone*, touchstone; origin obscure.]

**paragonite,** *par´ə-gən-it*, or *pər-ag´*, *n.* a soda-mica, once mistaken for talc. [Gr. *puragōn*, misleading—*para*, beside, beyond, *agein*, to lead.]

**paragram,** *par´ə-gram*, *n.* a play upon words by change of initial (or other) letter.—*n.* **paragramm´atist,** a punster. [Gr. (*skōmmata*) *para gramma*, (jokes) by letter.]

**paragraph,** *par´ə-gräf*, *n.* a sign (in ancient MSS. a short horizontal line, in the Middle Ages ¶, now ¶, ‖) marking off a section of a book, etc.: a distinct part of a discourse or writing marked by such a sign or now usually by indenting: a short passage, or a collection of sentences, with unity of purpose: a short separate item of news or comment in a newspaper.—*v.t.* to form into paragraphs: to write or publish paragraphs about.—*ns.* **par´agrapher, par´agraphist,** one who writes paragraphs, esp. for newspapers.—*adjs.* **paragraphic** (-*graf´*), **-al.**— *adv.* **paragraph´ically.** [Gr. *paragraphos*, written alongside—*para*, beside, beyond, *graphein*, to write.]

**paragraphia,** *par-ə-graf´i-ə*, *n.* writing of wrong words and letters, owing to disease or injury of the brain.—*adj.* **paragraphic** (-*graf´ik*). [Gr. *para*, beside, beyond, *graphein*, to write.]

**Paraguay,** *par-ə-gwi´*, -*gwä´*, *n.* a country and river of South America.—**Paraguay tea,** maté.

**paraheliotropic,** *par-ə-hē-li-ō-trop´ik*, (*bot.*) *adj.* turning edgewise to the light.—*n.* **paraheliotropism** (-*ot´rə-pizm*). [Gr. *para*, beside, beyond, and *hēlios*, the sun, and *tropos*, a turn—*trepein*, to turn.]

**parakeet, parrakeet,** *par´ə-kēt*, *n.* a small long-tailed parrot of various kinds.—Also **paroquet, parroquet** (-*ket*), **paraquito** (*pa-ra-kē´tō*). [Sp. *periquito*, It. *parrocchetto*, or O.Fr. *paroquet* (Fr. *perroquet*); the origin and relations of these are not determined.]

**paralalia,** *par-ə-la´*, -*lā´li-ə*, *n.* a form of speech disturbance, particularly that in which a different sound or syllable is produced from the one intended. [Gr. *para*, beside, beyond, *lalia*, speech.]

**paraldehyde,** *par-al´də-hid*, *n.* a polymer, $(C_2H_4O)_3$, of acetaldehyde, used to induce sleep. [para- (1) and **aldehyde.**]

**paraleipsis, paralipsis,** *par-ə-lip´sis*, -*lip´*, *n.* a rhet. figure by which one fixes attention on a subject by pretending to neglect it, as 'I will not speak of his generosity', etc.—*n.* **paral(e)ipom´enon,** a thing left out, added in supplement:—*pl.* **paral(e)ipom´ena,** esp. (in the Septuagint, etc.) the Books of Chronicles. [Gr. *paraleipsis, paraleipomenon* (neut. pr. part. pass.)— *paraleipein*, to leave aside—*para*, beside, beyond, *leipein*, to leave.]

**paralexia,** *par-ə-lek´si-ə*, *n.* a defect in the power of seeing and interpreting written language, with meaningless transposition of words and syllables. [Gr. *para*, beside, beyond, *lexis*, a word.]

**paralipsis**, etc. See **paraleipsis**.

**parallax**, *par'ə-laks*, *n.* an apparent change in the position of an object caused by change of position in the observer: in astron. the apparent change (measured angularly) in the position of a heavenly body when viewed from different points—when viewed from opposite points on the earth's surface this change is called the *daily* or *diurnal* or *geocentric parallax*; when viewed from opposite points of the earth's orbit, the *annual* or *heliocentric parallax.—adjs.* **parallac'tic, -al**. [Gr. *parallaxis—para*, beside, beyond, *allassein*, to change—*allos*, another.]

**parallel**, *par'ə-lel*, *adj.* extended in the same direction and equidistant in all parts: analogous, corresponding: alongside in time: having a constant interval (major and minor being reckoned alike; *mus.*).—*n.* a parallel line: a line of latitude: an analogue, or like, or equal: an analogy: a tracing or statement of resemblances: a besieger's trench parallel to the outline of the place besieged: a printer's reference mark of two vertical lines: parallel arrangement.—*v.t.* to place so as to be parallel: to conform: to represent as parallel: to liken in detail: to find a parallel to: to match: to be or run parallel to.—*v.i.* to be or run parallel:—*pr.p.* **par'alleling**; *pa.t.* and *pa.p.* **par'alleled**.—*v.t.* **par'allelise, -ize**, to furnish a parallel to.—*ns.* **par'allelism**, state or fact of being parallel: resemblance in corresponding details: a balanced construction of a verse or sentence, where one part repeats the form or meaning of the other: comparison: development along parallel lines: the theory or belief (in full **psychophysical parallelism**) that mind and matter do not interact but correspond; **par'allelist**, one who draws a parallel or comparison: a believer in psychophysical parallelism. —*adj.* **parallelis'tic.—advs.** **par'allelly**; **par'allelwise.—parallel bars**, a pair of fixed bars used in gymnastics; **parallel motion**, a name given to any linkage by which circular motion may be changed into straight-line motion; **parallel ruler** or **rulers**, rulers joined by two pivoted strips, for ruling parallel lines.—*adj.* **par'allelveined** (*bot.*), having the main veins running side by side.—**in parallel**, of electrical apparatus, so arranged that terminals of like polarity are connected together. [Gr. *parallēlos*, as if *par' allēloin*, beside each other.]

**parallelepiped**, *par-ə-lel-ep'i-ped* (or *-lel'*, or *-ə-pī'*), *n.* a solid figure bounded by six parallelograms, opposite pairs being identical and parallel. —Also **parallelepip'edon** (*pl.* -a), improperly **parallelopi'ped**, **parallelopi'pedon**. [Gr. *parallēlepipedon—parallēlos*, *epipedon*, a plane surface—*epi*, on, *pedon*, ground.]

**parallelogram**, *par-ə-lel'ō-gram*, *n.* a plane four-sided figure, the opposite sides of which are parallel and equal.—*adjs.* **parallelogrammat'ic, -al**, **parallelogramm'ic, -al.—parallelogram of forces**, a figure in which the direction and amount of two component forces are represented by two sides of a parallelogram, those of their resultant by the diagonal. [Gr. *parallēlogrammon—grammē*, a line.]

**paralogia**, *par-ə-loj'i-ə*, *n.* impairment of reasoning power characterised by difficulty in expressing logical ideas in speech.—*v.i.* **paral'ogise, -ize**, to reason falsely.—*n.* **paral'ogism**, false reasoning —also **paral'ogy**. [Gr. *paralogismos—para*, beside, beyond, *logismos—logos*, reason.]

**paralysis**, *pə-ral'i-sis*, *n.* palsy, a loss of power of motion, or sensation, in any part of the body: deprivation of power of action.—*v.t.* **paralyse** (*par'ə-liz*), to afflict with paralysis: to deprive of power of action.—*n.* **paralys'er.—adj.** **paralytic** (*par-ə-lit'ik*), of or pertaining to paralysis:

afflicted with or inclined to paralysis: helplessly drunk (*slang*).—*n.* one who is affected with paralysis. [Gr. *paralysis*, secret undoing, paralysis —*lyein*, to loosen.]

**Paramaecium**. See **Paramecium**.

**paramagnetic**, *par-ə-mag-net'ik*, *adj.* magnetic in the ordinary sense—said of bodies that when freely suspended between the poles of a magnet place themselves parallel to the lines of force— opp. to *diamagnetic.—n.* **paramag'netism**. [**para-** (1) and **magnetic** (see **magnet**).]

**paramastoid**, *par-ə-mas'toid*, *adj.* situated near the mastoid, paroccipital.—*n.* a paramastoid process. [**para-** (1) and **mastoid**.]

**paramatta**, **parramatta**, *par-ə-mat'ə*, *n.* a fabric like merino made of worsted and cotton. [App. from *Parramatta* in New South Wales.]

**Paramecium**, *par-ə-mē's(h)i-əm*, *n.* the slipper-animalcule, a slipper-shaped infusorian:—*pl.* **paramē'cia.**—Often misspelled **paramoecium**, **paramaecium**. [Gr. *paramēkēs*, long-shaped— *para*, alongside, *mēkos*, length.]

**paramedical**. See **para-** (1), **para-** (2).

**parament**, *par'ə-mənt*, (*obs.*) *n.* a rich decoration, hanging, or robe. [L. *parāre*, to prepare.]

**paramese**, *pa-ram'i-sē*, (Gr. *mus.*) *n.* the string or tone next above the mese. [Gr. *paramesē*.]

**parameter**, *pə-ram'i-tər*, *n.* a line or quantity which serves to determine a point, line, figure, or quantity in a class of such things (*math.*): a constant quantity in the equation of a curve: in conic sections, a third proportional to any diameter and its conjugate diameter: the latus rectum of a parabola: the intercept upon an axis of a crystal face chosen for purpose of reference (the *parametral plane*): a quantity to which an arbitrary value may be given as a convenience in expressing performance or for use in calculations (*elect.*): variable: a variable which is given a series of arbitrary values in order that a family of curves of two other related variables may be drawn: any constant in learning or growth curves that differs with differing conditions (*psychol.*).— *adjs.* **param'etral**, **parametric** (*par-ə-met'rik*), **-al**. [Gr. *para*, beside, beyond, *metron*, measure.]

**paramilitary**, *par-ə-mil'i-tər-i*, *adj.* on military lines and intended to supplement the strictly military. [**para-** (1) and **military** (see **militant**).]

**paramnesia**, *par-am-nē'zh(y)ə*, *n.* a memory disorder in which words are remembered but not their proper meaning: condition of believing that one remembers events and circumstances which have not previously occurred. [Gr. *para*, beside, beyond, and the root of *mimnēskein*, to remind.]

**paramo**, *pä'rä-mō*, *n.* a bare wind-swept elevated plain in South America:—*pl.* **par'amos.** [Sp. *páramo.*]

**Paramoecium**. See **Paramecium**.

**paramorph**, *par'ə-mörf*, (*min.*) *n.* a pseudomorph formed by a change in molecular structure without change of chemical composition.—*adj.* **paramorph'ic.—n.** **paramorph'ism**. [Gr. *para*, beside, beyond, *morphē*, form.]

**paramount**, *par'ə-mownt*, *adj.* superior to all others: supreme:—opp. to *paravail.—n.* supreme chief: a superior.—*n.* **par'amount(c)y.—adv.** **par'amountly.—paramount chief**. [O.Fr. *paramont*, *par* (L. *per*) *à mont* (L. *ad montem*); see **amount**.]

**paramour**, *par'ə-mōōr*, (*obs.*) *adv.* by the way of love, as a lover, for love's sake, out of kindness. —*n.* a lover of either sex, formerly in an innocent, now usually in the illicit, sense. [Fr. *par amour*, by or with love—L. *per amōrem*.]

**Paraná**, *pa-ra-nä'*, *n.* river and state in Brazil.— **Paraná pine**, the tree, *Araucaria brasiliana*, native to S. Brazil, or its wood.

**paranephros**, *par-ə-nef'ros*, *n.* the suprarenal

gland, near the kidney.—*adj.* **paraneph′ric.** [Gr. *para*, beside, beyond, *nephros*, kidney.]

**paranete,** *par-a-nē′tē*, (Gr. *mus.*) *n.* the string or tone next below the nete. [Gr. *paranētē.*]

**parang,** *pär′ang*, *n.* a heavy Malay knife. [Malay.]

**paranitroaniline,** *par-a-ni-trō-an′i-lēn*, *n.* a nitro-derivative of aniline, used in dyeing. [**para-** (1) and **nitroaniline** (see **nitre**).]

**paranoia,** *par-a-noi′a*, *n.* a form of mental disorder characterised by fixed delusions, esp. of grandeur, pride, persecution.—Also (*rarely*) **paranoea** (*-nē′a*).—*adj.* **paranoi′ac**, of paranoia. —*n.* a victim of paranoia.—Also **paranoe′ic**, **paranoic** (*-nō′ik*).—*adjs.* **par′anoid**, **paranoid′al**, resembling paranoia. [Gr. *paranoiā—para*, beside, beyond, *noos*, mind.]

**paranormal,** *par-a-nör′mal*, *adj.* abnormal, esp. psychologically. [**para-** (1) and **normal.**]

**paranthelion,** *par-an-thē′li-on*, *n.* a whitish image of the sun, having the same altitude, at an angular distance of 90° to 140°:—*pl.* **paran-the′lia.** [Gr. *para*, beside, beyond, *anti*, against, *hēlios*, the sun.]

**paranymph,** *par′a-nimf*, (*ant.*; *Milt.*) *n.* a friend who went with the bridegroom to fetch the bride, a groomsman or bridesmaid: one who countenances and supports another. [Gr. *paranymphos—para*, beside, beyond, *nymphē*, a bride.]

**parapet,** *par′a-pit*, *n.* a bank or wall to protect soldiers from the fire of an enemy in front: a low wall along the side of a bridge, edge of a roof, etc.—*adj.* **par′apeted**, having a parapet. [It. *parapetto*, from pfx. *para-* (see **parachute**) and It. *petto*—L. *pectus*, the breast.]

**paraph,** *par′af*, *n.* a mark or flourish under one's signature.—*v.t.* to append a paraph to, to sign with initials. [Fr. *paraphe*; cf. **paragraph.**]

**paraphasia,** *par-a-fā′zh(y)a*, *n.* a form of aphasia in which one word is substituted for another.— *adj.* **paraphasic** (*-fā′zik*, *-sik*). [**para-** (1) and **aphasia.**]

**paraphernalia,** *par-a-far-nāl′ya*, *-i-a*, *n.pl.* formerly, property other than dower that remained under a married woman's own control, esp. articles of jewellery, dress, personal belongings: ornaments of dress of any kind: trappings: equipment: miscellaneous accessories. [Late L. *paraphernālia—parapherna—*Gr., from *para*, beside, beyond, *phernē*, a dowry—*pherein*, to bring.]

**paraphilia,** *par-a-fil′i-a*, *n.* sexual perversion.—*n.* **paraphiliac** (*-fil′i-ak*), one who indulges in abnormal sexual practices.—Also *adj.* [**para** (1) and Gr. *philia*, fondness, liking for.]

**paraphimosis,** *par-a-fi-mō′sis*, *n.* strangulation of the glans penis by constriction of the prepuce. [**para-** (1) and **phimosis.**]

**paraphonia,** *par-a-fō′ni-a*, *n.* in Byzantine music, a melodic progression by fourths and fifths: a morbid change of voice: an alteration of the voice, as at puberty.—*adj.* **paraphonic** (*-fon′ik*). [Gr. *para*, beside, beyond, *phōnē*, voice.]

**paraphrase,** *par′a-frāz*, *n.* expression of the same thing in other words: an exercise in such expression: a verse rendering of a biblical passage for church singing, esp. in the Church of Scotland.—*v.t.* to express in other words.—*v.i.* to make a paraphrase.—*ns.* **par′aphraser**, **par′aphrast** (*-frast*), one who paraphrases.—*adjs.* **paraphrast′ic**, *-al*.—*adv.* **paraphrast′ically.** [Gr. *paraphrasis—para*, beside, beyond, *phrasis*, a speaking—*phrazein*, to speak.]

**paraphraxia, -phrasis,** *par-a-fraks′i-a*, *-fraks′is*, *n.* inability to perform purposive movements properly. [**para** (1), and Gr. *phraxis*, barricade.]

**paraphysis,** *pa-raf′i-sis*, *n.* a sterile filament among spore-bearing structures in lower plants: —*pl.* **paraphyses** (*-sēz*). [Gr., a side-growth— *para*, beside, beyond, *physis*, growth.]

**parapineal,** *par-a-pin′i-al*, *adj.* beside the pineal

gland—applied to the pineal eye. [**para-** (1) and **pineal.**]

**paraplegia,** *par-a-plē′j(y)a*, *n.* paralysis of the lower part of the body.—*adjs.* **paraplectic** (*-plekt′ik*), **paraplegic** (*-plēj′* or *-plej′*). [Ionic Gr. *paraplēgiē*, a stroke on the side—*para*, beside, beyond, *plēgē*, a blow.]

**parapodium,** *par-a-pō′di-am*, *n.* one of the jointless lateral appendages of polychaete worms, etc.: a swimming organ in some molluscs, a lateral expansion of the foot:—*pl.* **parapō′dia.**—*adj.* **parapō′dial.** [Gr. *para*, beside, beyond, *pous*, *podos*, a foot.]

**parapophysis,** *par-a-pof′i-sis*, *n.* a ventral transverse process of a vertebra:—*pl.* **parapoph′yses** (*-sēz*).—*adj.* **parapophysial** (*par-ap-ō-fiz′i-al*). [**para-** (1) and **apophysis.**]

**parapsychism,** *par-a-sī′kizm*, *n.* panpsychistic parallelism.—*adjs.* **parapsy′chic**, *-al*; **parapsycholog′ical.**—*ns.* **parapsychol′ogist**; **parapsychol′ogy**, psychical research: the study of phenomena such as telepathy and clairvoyance which seem to suggest that the mind can gain knowledge by means other than the normal perceptual processes; **parapsychō′sis**, an abnormal psychosis. [**para-** (1) and **psychism.**]

**paraquadrate,** *par-a-kwod′rāt*, *n.* the squamosal. [**para-** (1) and **quadrate.**]

**paraquat,** *par′a-kwat*, *n.* a weed-killer very poisonous to human beings.

**paraquito,** *par-a-kē′tō*. See **parakeet.**

**para-red,** *par′a-red′*, *n.* an azo-dye for cottons, derived from paranitroaniline. [**para-** (1).]

**pararosaniline,** *par-a-roz-an′i-lēn*, *n.* a base entering into various dyestuffs, such as magenta. [**para-** (1) and **rosaniline.**]

**pararthria,** *par-är′thri-a*, *n.* disordered articulation of speech. [Gr. *para*, beside, beyond, *arthron*, a joint.]

**parasang,** *par′a-sang*, *n.* an old Persian measure of length, reckoned at 30 stadia, or between 3 and 4 miles. [Gr. *parasangēs*, from O.Pers. (mod. Pers. *farsang*).]

**parascenium,** *par-a-sē′ni-am*, *n.* in the Greek theatre, a wing, side-scene:—*pl.* **parascē′nia.** [Gr. *paraskēnion—para*, beside, beyond, *skēnē*, tent, stage.]

**parasceve,** *par′a-sēv*, *par-a-sē′vē*, *n.* preparation (*obs.*): the eve of the Jewish Sabbath, Friday, the day of preparation (*arch.*): Good Friday (R.C. Church). [L.L. *parascēvē—*Gr. *paraskeuē*, preparation—*para*, beside, beyond, *skeuē*, equipment.]

**paraselene,** *par-a-se-lē′nē*, *n.* a mock moon:— *pl.* **paraselē′nae** (*-nē*). [Gr. *para*, beside, beyond, *selēnē*, moon.]

**parasite,** *par′a-sit*, *n.* a hanger-on or sycophant who frequents another's table: one who lives at the expense of society or of others and contributes nothing: an organism that lives in or on another organism and derives subsistence from it without rendering it any service in return: in literary but not scientific use extended to an epiphyte.—*adjs.* **parasitic** (*-sit′ik*), *-al*, of, of the nature of, caused by, or like, a parasite.—*adv.* **parasit′ically.**—*ns.* **parasit′icalness; parasiticide** (*-sit′i-sid*), that which destroys parasites; **par′asitism** (*sit-izm*).—*adj.* **par′asitoid** (*-sit-*), parasitic in one phase of the life-history, thereafter independent.—Also *n.*—*ns.* **parasitol′ogist**; **parasitol′ogy; parasitō′sis**, infestation with parasites. [Gr. *parasitos—para*, beside, and *sitos*, corn, bread, food.]

**parasol,** *par′a-sol*, or *-sol′*, *n.* a sunshade: an aeroplane with its wings overhead. [Fr.,—It. *parasole—para*, imper. of *parare*, to ward—L. *parāre*, to prepare, and *sole—*L. *sōl*, *sōlis*, the sun.]

**parasphenoid,** *par-a-sfē′noid*, *adj.* alongside the sphenoid bone.—*n.* a bone of the skull, part of the cranial floor. [para- (1), **sphenoid** (see **sphene**).]

**parastichy,** *pər-as'ti-ki*, (*bot.*) *n.* a secondary spiral joining leaf-bases on an axis, visible where the leaves are crowded together, e.g. the scales of a pine-cone. [Gr. *para*, beside, beyond, *stichos*, a row.]

**parasympathetic,** *par-ə-sim-pə-thet'ik*, *adj.* See under **sympathy.**

**parasynthesis,** *par-ə-sin'thi-sis*, *n.* derivation of words from compounds, as *come-at-able*, where *come* and *at* are first compounded and then the derivative suffix *-able* added.—*adj.* **parasynthetic** (*-thet'ik*).—*n.* **parasyn'theton**, a word so formed:—*pl.* **parasyn'theta**. [Gr.]

**parataxis,** *par-ə-tak'sis*, (*gram.*) *n.* the arrangement of clauses or propositions without connectives.—*adjs.* **paratac'tic, -al.**—*adv.* **paratac'tically.** [Gr.,—*para*, beside, beyond, *taxis*, arrangement.]

**parathesis.** *pə-rath'i-sis*, *n.* apposition (*gram.*): compounding of words without change, as L. *rēspūblica* from *rēs* and *pūblica* (*philol.*). [Gr., placing alongside.]

**parathyroid,** *par-ə-thī'roid*, *adj.* beside the thyroid. —*n.* any of a number of small ductless glands apparently concerned with calcium metabolism. [**para-** (1) and **thyroid.**]

**paratonic,** *par-ə-ton'ik*, (*bot.*) *adj.* induced by external stimulus. [Gr. *para*, beside, beyond, *tonos*, a stretching.]

**paratroops,** *par'ə-trōops*, *n.pl.* troops carried by air, to be dropped by parachute.—*n.* **par'a-trooper.** [**para-** (2) and **troop.**]

**paratyphoid,** *par-ə-tī'foid*, *n.* a disease (of various types) resembling typhoid.—Also *adj.* [**para-** (1).]

**paravail,** *par-ə-vāl'*, *adj.* inferior: lowest, said of a feudal tenant of least account—opp. to **paramount.** [O.Fr. *par aval*, below—L. *per*, through, *ad*, to, *vallem*, accus. of *vallis*, valley.]

**paravane,** *par'ə-vān*, *n.* a fish-shaped device, with fins or vanes, towed from the bow, for deflecting mines along a wire and severing their moorings —sometimes called an 'otter': an explosive device of similar design for attacking submerged submarines. [**para-** (2) and **vane.**]

**paravant, paravaunt,** *par-ə-vänt'*, *vönt'*, *Spens. adv.* in front, first, beforehand, pre-eminently. [O.Fr. *paravant—par*, through, *avant*, before—L. *ab*, from, *ante*, before.]

**Parazoa,** *par-ə-zō'ə*, *n.pl.* a division of the animal kingdom, the sponges, co-ordinate with *Protozoa* and *Metazoa.* [Gr. *para*, beside, beyond, *zōion*, animal.]

**parboil,** *pär'boil*, *v.t.* orig., to boil thoroughly: (now, by confusion) to boil slightly. [O.Fr. *parboillir*—L.L. *perbullire*, to boil thoroughly; influenced by confusion with **part.**]

**parbreak,** *pär'brāk*, (*arch.*) *n.* a vomit.—*v.t.* and *v.i.* (*pär'* or *-brāk'*) to vomit:—*pa.p.* **parbreaked.** [M.E. *brake*, to vomit; cf. Du. *braken*; the pfx. may be Fr. *par-*.]

**parbuckle,** *pär'buk-l*, *n.* a purchase made by making fast a rope in the middle and passing the ends under and then over a heavy object to be rolled up or down: a sling made by passing both ends of a rope through its bight.—*v.t.* to hoist or lower by a parbuckle. [Earlier *parbunkel, parbuncle*; origin unknown.]

**Parca,** *pär'kə*, *n.* a Fate, any one of the Roman goddesses Nona, Decuma, and Morta, identified with the Greek Moirai:—*pl.* **Par'cae** (*-sē*). [L., prob. conn. with *parēre*, to produce, not *parcĕre*, to spare.]

**parcel,** *pär'sl*, *n.* a little part: a portion: a quantity: a group: a set: a pack (depreciatively): a lot: an item (*arch.*): a sum of money lost or won (*coll.*): a package, esp. one wrapped in paper and tied with string: a continuous stretch of land.—*adv.* (*arch.*) partly.—*adj.* (*arch.*) in

part.—*v.t.* to divide into portions (esp. with *out*): to make up into parcels or a parcel (esp. with *up*): possibly, to make up into a total, complete, round off, or to add up or detail, item by item (*Shak., Antony and Cleopatra,* V, ii): to cover with tarred canvas (*naut.*):—*pr.p.* **par'celling;** *pa.t.* and *pa.p.* **par'celled.**—*adv.* **par'celwise,** by parcels, piecemeal.—**par'cel-bawd** (*Shak.*), one partly a bawd.—*adj.* **par'cel-gilt',** partially gilded.—**parcel post** (also, formerly, **parcels post**), Post Office service forwarding and delivering parcels. [Fr. *parcelle* (It. *particella*)— L. *particula*, dim. of *pars, partis*, a part.]

**parcener,** *pär'sən-ər*, *n.* a co-heir.—*n.* **par'cenary** (*-ə-ri*), co-heirship. [A.Fr. *parcener*—L.L. *partiōnārius—pars*, part.]

**parch,** *pärch*, *v.t.* to make hot and very dry: to roast slightly: to scorch.—*v.i.* to be scorched: to become very dry.—*adj.* **parched.**—*adv.* **parch'edly.**—*n.* **parch'edness.** [Origin unknown.]

**parchment,** *pärch'mənt*, *n.* the skin of a sheep, goat, or other animal prepared for writing on, etc.: a piece of this material: a manuscript written on it: a parchment-like membrane or skin.—*adj.* of parchment.—*v.t.* **parch'mentise,** *-ize*, to make like parchment, esp. by treating with sulphuric acid.—*adj.* **parch'menty,** like parchment.—**parchment paper,** or **vegetable parchment,** unsized paper made tough and transparent by dipping in sulphuric acid.— **virgin parchment,** a fine kind of parchment made from the skins of new-born lambs or kids. [Fr. *parchemin*—L. *pergamēna* (*charta*), Pergamene (paper)—from Gr. *Pergamos*, Bergama, in Asia Minor.]

**parcimony,** an arch. spelling of **parsimony.**

**parclose,** *pär'klōz*, *n.* a screen or railing in a church enclosing an altar or tomb, or separating a chapel or other portion from the main body of the church. [O.Fr. *pa.p.* (fem.) of *parclore* —L. *per*, through, *claudēre, clausum*, to close.]

**pard,** *pärd*, *n.* the leopard.—*ns.* **pard'al** (*-əl*), **pard'ale** (*-əl, -āl*; *Spens.*), **pard'alis,** a pard: a small pard once supposed a different species.— *adjs.* **pard'ed,** spotted; **pard'ine** (*-in*). [L. *pardus* (masc.), *pardalis* (fem.)—Gr. *pardos, pardalis*; prob. of Eastern origin.]

**pard,** *pärd*, **pard'ner,** *-nər*, (*U.S.*) *ns.* slang forms of **partner.**

**pardi, pardie, pardy.** See **perdie.**

**pardon,** *pär'dn*, *v.t.* to forgive: to allow to go unpunished: to excuse: to tolerate: to grant in remission, refrain from exacting or taking: to grant remission of sentence to (even if the condemned has been found innocent).—*v.i.* to forgive: to grant pardon.—*n.* forgiveness, either of an offender or of his offence: remission of a penalty or punishment: forbearance: a warrant declaring a pardon: a papal indulgence: a festival at which indulgences are granted (*obs.*). —*adj.* **par'donable,** that may be pardoned: excusable.—*n.* **par'donableness.**—*adv.* **par'donably.** —*n.* **par'doner,** one who pardons: a licensed seller of papal indulgences (*hist.*).—*n.* and *adj.* **par'doning.**—*adj.* **par'donless,** unpardonable.— **I beg your pardon, pardon?,** what did you say? **pardon me, excuse me**—used in apology and to soften a contradiction. [Fr. *pardonner*—L.L. *perdōnāre*—L. *per*, through, away, *dōnāre*, to give.]

**pare,** *pär*, *v.t.* to cut or shave off the outer surface or edge of: to trim: to remove by slicing or shaving: to diminish by littles.—*n.* **pār'er.** [Fr. *parer*—L. *parāre*, to prepare.]

**paregoric,** *par-i-gor'ik*, *adj.* soothing, lessening pain.—*n.* a medicine that soothes pain: an alcoholic solution of opium, benzoic acid, camphor, and oil of anise. [Gr. *parēgorikos—parēgoreein*, to exhort, comfort—*para*, beside, beyond, and *agorā*, marketplace.]

**pareira**, *pə-rā'rə, n.* orig., a tropical menispermaceous climbing plant (*Cissampelos pareira*) or its root (now called **false pareira**): a South American plant of the same family (*Chondrodendron tomentosum*, **pareira brava**, *brä'və*, i.e. wild): a tonic diuretic drug derived from its root.—**white pareira** (*Abuta rufescens*), another South American plant of the same family. [Port. *parreira*, wallclimber.]

**parella**, *pə-rel'ə, n.* a crustaceous lichen (*Lecanora parella*) yielding archil: extended to others of like use.—Also **parelle'**. [Fr. *parelle*.]

**parencephalon**, *par-en-sef'ə-lon, n.* a cerebral hemisphere. [Gr. *para*, beside, beyond, *enkephalon*, brain.]

**parenchyma**, *pə-reng'ki-mə, n.* the ordinary soft thin-walled tissue of plants, not differentiated into conducting or mechanical tissue: soft spongy indeterminate tissue in animals.—*adj.* **parenchym'atous**. [Gr. *para*, beside, beyond, *enchyma*, infusion, inpouring.]

**parenesis**. See **paraenesis**.

**parent**, *pā'rənt, n.* one who begets or brings forth: a father or a mother: one who, or that which, produces: that from which anything springs or branches: an author: a cause: as a Gallicism, a relative.—*n.* **pā'rentage**, descent from parents: extraction: rank or character derived from one's parents or ancestors: relation of parents to their children: state or fact of being a parent: parents collectively, or perh. parent (*Spens.*).—*adj.* **parental** (*pə-rent'əl*).—*adv.* **parent'ally.**—*n.* **pā'renthood**, state of being a parent: duty or feelings of a parent.—*adj.* **pā'rentless**, without a parent. [Fr. *parent*, kinsman—L. *parēns*, *-entis*, old pr.p. of *parēre*, to bring forth.]

**parenteral**, *par-en'tər-əl, adj.* not intestinal: not by way of the alimentary tract (said of the administration of a drug).—*adv.* **paren'terally.** [Gr. *para*, beside, and **enteral**.]

**parenthesis**, *pə-ren'thi-sis, n.* a word or passage of comment or explanation inserted in a sentence which is grammatically complete without it: a figure of speech consisting of the use of such insertion: a digression: an interval, space, interlude: (usu. in *pl.*) a round bracket ( ) used to mark off a parenthesis:—*pl.* **paren'theses** (*-sēz*).—*v.i.* **parenth'esise, -ize.**—*adjs.* **parenthetic** (*par-ən-thet'ik*), **al**, of the nature of a parenthesis: using or over-using parenthesis.—*adv.* **parenthet'ically.** [Gr.,—*para*, beside, beyond, *en*, in, *thesis*, a placing.]

**Pareoean**, *par-ē-ē'ən, adj.* of a race inhabiting South China, Burma, etc.—otherwise called Southern Mongoloid.—Also *n.* [Gr. *para*, beside, *ēōs*, dawn.]

**parergon**, *par-ûr'gon, n.* a by-work, any work subsidiary to another:—*pl.* **parer'ga.** [Gr.,—*para*, beside, beyond, *ergon*, work.]

**paresis**, *par'i-sis, n.* a diminished activity of function—a partial form of paralysis.—*adj.* **paretic** (*-et'ik*). [Gr.,—*parienai*, to relax.]

**parfait**, *pär-fe', n.* a kind of frozen dessert containing whipped cream and eggs. [Fr., lit. perfect.]

**parfleche**, *pär-flesh', n.* a dried skin, usu. of buffalo: an article made of it. [App. Canadian Fr.]

**pargana, pergunnah**, *pər-gun'a, n.* a division of a zillah in India. [Hind. and Pers *parganah*.]

**pargasite**, *pär'gə-sit, n.* a green amphibole. [*Pargas* in Finland.]

**parget**, *pär'jit, v.t.* to plaster over: to cover with ornamental plaster-work: to decorate the surface of: to bedaub:—*pr.p.* **par'geting**; *pa.t.* and *pa.p.* **par'geted.**—*n.* plaster spread over a surface: cow-dung plaster for chimney flues: ornamental work in plaster: surface decoration.—*v.t.* **parge**, to plaster.—*ns.* **par'geter; par'geting, parge'-work.**—The irregular forms **par'getting**,

etc., are used by some. [App. O.Fr. *parjeter*, to throw all over.]

**parhelion**, *pär-hēl'i-ən, n.* a mock sun:—*pl.* **parhē'lia.**—*adjs.* **parhelic** (*-hē'lik, -he'lik*), **parheliacal** (*-hē-li'ə-kl*). [Irregularly—Gr. *parēlion—para*, beside, beyond, *hēlios*, sun.]

**parhypate**, *pär-hip'ə-tē*, (Gr. *mus.*) *n.* the lowest note but one in a tetrachord—next above the hypate. [Gr. *para*, beside, beyond; see **hypate**.]

**pariah**, *par'i-ə, pär'*, or (esp. *U.S.*) *pə-ri'ə, n.* a member of a caste in Southern India lower than the four Brahminical castes: one of low or no caste: a social outcast: an ownerless cur of Eastern towns (in full **pariah dog**), a pye-dog. [Tamil *paraiyar*.]

**parial**. Same as **pairial**; see under **pair**.

**Parian**, *pā'ri-ən, adj.* of the island of *Paros*, in the Aegean Sea.—*n.* a native or inhabitant of Paros: a fine porcelain like marble.—**Parian marble**, a fine white marble found in Paros.

**parietal**, *pə-ri'i-tl, adj.* of a wall or walls: of, attached to, or having connection with, the side, or the inside of the wall, of a cavity, esp. a plant ovary: pertaining to or near the parietal bone: residing, or relating to residence, within the walls of a college (*U.S.*).—*n.* a bone (**parietal bone**), forming with its fellow part of the sides and top of the skull, between the frontal and the occipital. [L. *parietālis—pariēs, parietis*, a wall.]

**pari-mutuel**, *par-ē-mü-tü-el, n.* a betting-machine which automatically pools stakes and distributes winnings—a totalisator. [Fr., lit. mutual bet.]

**paring**, *pär'ing, n.* act of trimming or cutting off: that which is pared off: the cutting off of the surface of grass land for tillage. [**pare**.]

**pari passu**, *pā'ri pas'ū, pa'rē, pas'oo*, (L.) with equal pace: together.

**paripinnate**, *par-i-pin'it,-āt, (bot.) adj.* pinnate without a terminal leaflet. [L. *pār*, equal.]

**Paris**, *par'is, n.* the capital of France.—*adj.* of, originating in, Paris.—*adj.* **Parisian** (*pə-ri'zyən, -zhyən, -zhən*), of or pertaining to Paris.—*n.* a native or resident of Paris:—*Fr. fem.* **Parisienne** (*pa-rē-zē-en,-zyen'*).—**Paris doll** (*obs.*), a small figure dressed in the latest fashions, sent out by Paris modistes; **Paris green**, copper arsenite and acetate, a pigment and insecticide. [L. *Parisii*, the Gallic tribe of the Paris district.]

**parish**, *par'ish, n.* a district having its own church and minister or priest of the Established Church: a district assigned by a church to a minister or priest: division of county for administrative and local government purposes (not now in Scotland): in Louisiana a county: the people of a parish: a congregation or a denomination (*U.S.*).—*adj.* belonging or relating to a parish: employed or supported by the parish: for the use of the parish.—*ns.* **par'ishen** (see **parochin**); **parishioner** (*pə-rish'ə-nər*), one who belongs to or is connected with a parish: a member of a parish church.—**parish church**, the church of the establishment for a parish; **parish clerk**, the clerk or recording officer of a parish: the one who leads the responses in the service of the Church of England; **parish council**, a body elected to manage the affairs of a parish; **parish councillor; parish minister, priest**, a minister or priest who has charge of a parish; **parish pump**, the symbol of petty local interests; **parish register**, a book in which the births, baptisms, marriages, and deaths of a parish are registered; **parish top**, a spinning-top formerly kept for the amusement of the parish.—**on the parish**, in receipt of poor-relief. [A.Fr. *paroche* (Fr. *paroisse*)—L. *parochia*—Gr. *paroikiā*, an ecclesiastical district—*para*, beside, *oikos*, a dwelling; altered by confusion with Gr. *parochos*, a purveyor.]

**parisyllabic,** *par-i-si-lab'ik, adj.* having the same number of syllables. [L. *pār*, equal.]

**paritor,** *par'i-tǝr, (Shak.) n.* aphetic for **apparitor.**

**parity,** *par'i-ti, n.* equality in status: parallelism: equivalence: a standard equivalence in currency. —**parity law,** a law that a symmetry obtains in the natural world with no distinction between right and left, long held as basic, but shown in 1957 not to apply in the field of nuclear physics. [Fr. *parité*—L. *paritās*—*pār*, equal.]

**parity,** *par'i-ti, n.* the condition or fact of having borne children. [L. *parĕre*, to bring forth.]

**park,** *pärk, n.* an enclosed piece of land for beasts of the chase: a tract of land surrounding a mansion, kept as a pleasure-ground: hence often part of the name of a house, street, or district: a piece of ground for public recreation: a piece of country kept in its natural condition as a nature-reserve or the like: a paddock, grass field (*Scot.*): a field (*Ireland*): a level valley among mountains (*U.S.*): a place occupied by artillery, wagons, etc. (*mil.*): a piece of ground where motor-cars or other vehicles may be left untended: an enclosed basin for oyster-culture.—*v.t.* to enclose in a park: to make a park of: to bring together in a body, as artillery: to place and leave in a parking-place: to deposit and leave (*coll.*).—*v.i.* to use a car park or parking-place.—*ns.* **park'er** (*obs.*), a park-keeper; **park'ing,** the action of the verb park: a turf strip, sometimes with trees, along the middle of a street (*U.S.*).—*adjs.* **park'ish; park'like; park'ly.**—*advs.* **park'ward, -s.**—**park'-ing lot** (*U.S.*), a car park; **park'ing meter,** a coin-operated meter that charges for motor-car parking-time; **park'ing-place; park'keeper,** a park officer; **park'land, -s,** park-like grassland dotted with trees; **park'-off'icer,** the keeper of a park; **park'way,** a broad road adorned with turf and trees, often connecting the parks of a town. [O.Fr. *parc*, of Gmc. origin; cf. O.E. *pearruc, pearroc.*]

**parka,** *pärk'ǝ, (Canada* and *Alaska) n.* a fur shirt with a hood, or a similar garment made of a wind-proof material.—Also **parkee, parki** (*pärk'ē*). [Aleutian Eskimo word.]

**parkin,** *pär'kin,* **perkin,** *pûr'kin, (Northern) n.* a biscuit of oatmeal and treacle. [Ety. unknown.]

**Parkinson's disease,** *pär'kin-sǝnz,* shaking palsy, a disease characterised by rigidity of muscles, tremor of hands, etc.; studied by James Parkinson (1755-1824).—Also **Par'kinsonism.**

**Parkinson's Law,** *pär'kin-sǝnz, (facet.)* any one of the laws propounded by C. Northcote Parkinson, esp. the law that in officialdom work expands so as to fill the time available for its completion.

**parkleaves,** *pärk'lēvz, n.* tutsan. [App. **park, leaf.**]

**parky,** *pär'ki, (coll.) adj.* chilly. [Origin unknown.]

**parlance.** See under **parle.**

**parlando,** *pär-län'dō, (mus.) adj.* and *adv.* in declamatory style: recitative. [It., speaking; cf. **parle.**]

**parlay,** *pär'lā, v.t.* to bet (orig. stake plus winnings), or lay out (orig. investment plus earnings), in a later venture: to succeed in converting (an asset) into something more valuable.—Also *n.* [Fr. *paroli*; from Neapolitan.]

**parle,** *pärl, (arch.) v.i.* to talk: to confer: to parley.—*n.* talk: speech: parleying.—*n.* **par'-lance** (*arch.*), speaking: conversation: diction, phraseology, jargon, mode of speech.—*v.i.* **par'-ley,** to speak with another: to confer: to treat with an enemy.—*n.* talk: a conference with an enemy: a conference.—*n.* **parleyvoo'** (*slang*), French: a Frenchman.—*v.i.* to speak French. [Fr. *parler*, to speak (*parlez-vous?* do you speak?)—L.L. *parlāre*—*parabolāre*—Gr. *parabolē*, a parable, word.]

**parliament,** *pär'lǝ-mǝnt, n.* a meeting for delibera-

tion: a legislative body: in France, down to the Revolution, one of certain superior and final courts of judicature, in which also the edicts of the king were registered before becoming law: gingerbread in the form of rectangular biscuits (also **par'liament-cake;** *Scot.* **par'ley, par'ly**).—*n.* **parliamentā'rian,** an adherent of Parliament in opposition to Charles I: one skilled in the ways of parliament.—*adj.* on the side of parliament.—*adv.* **parliamentarily** (*-ment'ǝr-i-li*).—**parliament'arism,** the principles of parliamentary government: the parliamentary system.—*adj.* **parliament'ary,** pertaining to parliament: enacted, enjoined, or done by parliament: according to the rules and practices of legislative bodies: (of language) civil, decorous: for Parliament against the Royalists.—*n.* **parliamenting** (*-ment'ing*), acting as member of parliament: debating.—**parliamentary agent,** a person employed by private persons or societies for drafting bills or managing business to be brought before parliament; **parliamentary burgh** (see **burgh**); **parliamentary train,** a railway train which, by act of parliament (1844), ran daily with sufficient accommodation for passengers at a penny a mile; **par'liament-heel',** a slight careening of a ship; **par'liament-hinge',** hinge allowing a door to be laid back along the wall; **par'liament-house,** a building where parliament sits or has sat; **par'liament-man',** a member of parliament: a parliamentarian.—**act of parliament,** a statute that has passed through both the House of Commons and the House of Lords, and received the formal royal assent; **Parliamentary Commissioner for Administration** (see **Ombudsman**). [Fr. *parlement*—*parler*, to speak.]

**parlour,** *pär'lǝr, n.* a room where conversation is allowed in a monastery or nunnery: a private room for conversation or conference in a public building, office, etc.: a more or less private room in an inn or tavern: a simple unpretentious drawing-room or dining-room, or a smaller room of similar kind: a family sitting-room or living-room: a shop fitted like a room, or a room attached to a shop, esp. for personal services to customers (*U.S.*).—*adj.* used in or suitable for a parlour.—**par'lour-board'er,** a pupil at a boarding-school who enjoys particular privileges; **par'lour-car** (*U.S.*), a luxuriously fitted railway saloon carriage; **par'lour-maid,** a maid-servant who waits at table; **parlour pink,** a rather tepid Socialist; **parlour tricks,** minor social accomplishments: performances intended to impress.—**milking parlour,** special room or building in which cows are milked.—See **beauty, funeral.** [A.Fr. *parlur* (Fr.*parloir*)—*parler,* to speak.]

**parlous,** *pär'lǝs, adj.* perilous.—*adv.* (*arch.* and *facet.*) extremely. [A form of **perilous.**]

**parmacitie,** *pär-mǝs-it'i, n. Shak.* for **spermaceti.**

**Parmesan,** *pär-mi-zan',* or *pär', adj.* pertaining to *Parma.*—*n.* Parmesan cheese.—**Parma violet,** Neapolitan violet.

**Parnassus,** *pär-nas'ǝs, n.* a mountain in Greece, sacred to Apollo and the Muses: a collection of poems.—*adj.* **Parnass'ian,** of Parnassus: of the Muses: of a school of French poetry supposed to believe in art for art's sake (from the collections published as *Le Parnasse contemporain,* 1866-76).—*n.* a poet: a member of the Parnassian school.—*n.* **Parnass'ianism.**—**grass of Parnassus,** a white-flowered plant of wet moors (*Parnassia palustris*) of the saxifrage family.

**Parnellism,** *pär'nǝl-izm, n.* the principles and policy of Charles Stewart *Parnell* (1846-91) who sought to promote Home Rule for Ireland.—*n.* **Par'nellite,** a follower of Parnell.—Also *adj.*

**paroccipital,** *par-ok-sip'i-tl, adj.* near the occiput. [**para-** (1) and **occiput.**]

**parochial**, *pə-rō'ki-əl, adj.* of or relating to a parish: restricted or confined within narrow limits—of sentiments, tastes, etc.: denominational (*U.S.*).—*v.t.* **parō'chialise, -ize,** to make parochial: to form into parishes.—*v.i.* to do parish work.—*ns.* **parō'chialism,** a system of local government which makes the parish the unit: provincialism, narrowness of view; **parōchiality** (*-al'*).—*adv.* **parō'chially.—parochial board,** (formerly, in Scotland) a board charged with poor-relief. [L. *parochiālis—parochia*; see **parish**.]

**parochin(e), parischan(e), parishen,** *pä'rish-in,* (*Scot.*) *n.* parish.

**parody,** *par'ə-di, n.* a burlesque imitation.—*v.t.* to make a parody of:—*pr.p.* **par'odying;** *pa.t.* and *pa.p.* **par'odied.**—*adjs.* **parod'ic(al).**—*n.* **par'-odist.** [Gr. *parōidiā—para,* beside, *ōidē,* an ode.]

**paroemia,** *pə-rē'mi-ə, n.* a proverb, adage.—*adj.* **paroe'miac.**—*n.* (*Gr. pros.*) the anapaestic dimeter catalectic.—*adj.* **paroe'mial.**—*ns.* **paroemiog'rapher,** a writer or collector of proverbs; **paroemiog'raphy;** **paroemiol'ogy,** the study of proverbs. [Gr. *paroimiā,* a proverb—*paroimos,* by the road—*oimos,* road.]

**parol.** See **parole.**

**parole,** *pə-rōl', n.* word of mouth: word of honour (esp. by a prisoner of war, to fulfil certain conditions; *mil.*): the condition of having given one's word of honour, or privilege of having it accepted: conditional release of a prisoner: officers' daily password in a camp or garrison.—*adj.* pertaining to parole: (usu. **parol,** usu. *par'*) given by word of mouth—opp. to *documentary,* as *parol* evidence.—*v.t.* **parole',** to put on parole: to release on parole.—*v.i.* to give parole. [Fr. *parole,* word—L. *parabola,* a parable, saying—Gr.; see **parable.**]

**paronomasia,** *par-on-o-mā'syə, -zyə, -zh(y)ə, n.* a play upon words—also **paronom'asy** (*-ə-si, -ə-zi*).—*adjs.* **paronomastic** (*-mas'tik*), **-al.**—*n.* **paronym** (*par'o-nim*), a word from the same root, or having the same sound, as another.—*adj.* **paron'ymous.**—*n.* **paron'ymy.** [Gr. *para,* beside, *onoma, onyma,* name.]

**paronychia,** *par-o-nik'i-ə, n.* a whitlow: (*cap.*) the whitlow-wort genus of plants.—*adj.* **paronych'ial.** [Gr. *para,* beside, *onyx, onychos,* nail.]

**paroquet.** See **parakeet.**

**parotid,** *pə-rot'id, -rōt', adj.* near the ear.—*n.* the parotid gland, a salivary gland in front of the ear—also **parō'tis.**—*ns.* **parotidi'tis, paroti'tis,** inflammation of the parotid gland, as in mumps. [Gr. *parōtis, -idos—para,* beside, *ous, ōtos,* ear.]

**parousia,** *pə-rōō'zi-ə,* or *-row', (theol.) n.* the second coming of Christ. [Gr. *parousiā,* presence, arrival.]

**paroxysm,** *par'oks-izm, n.* a fit of acute pain: a fit of passion, laughter, coughing, etc.: any sudden violent action.—*adj.* **paroxys'mal.** [Gr. *paroxysmos—para,* beyond, *oxys,* sharp.]

**paroxytone,** *par-ok'si-tōn, adj.* having the acute accent on the last syllable but one.—*n.* a word so accented. [Gr. *paroxytonos—para,* beside, *oxys,* acute, *tonos,* tone.]

**parpen,** *pär'pən, n.* a stone passing through a wall from face to face: a wall of such stones: a partition: a bridge parapet.—Also **par'pane, par'pend, par'pent, par'point, per'pend, per'pent.**—*ns.* **par'pen-stone; par'pen-wall.** [O.Fr. *parpain.*]

**parquet,** *pär'kā, -kit, pär-kā', -ket', n.* a floor-covering of wooden blocks fitted in a pattern: the stalls of a theatre (*U.S.*; **parquet circle,** that part of the floor behind these).—*adj.* of parquetry.—*v.t.* to cover or floor with parquetry:—*pa.p.* **par'queted, parquett'ed.**—*n.* **par'quetry** (*-ki-tri*), flooring in parquet. [Fr. *parquet,* dim. of *parc,* an enclosure.]

**parr,** *pär, n.* a young salmon. [Ety. unknown.]

**parrakeet.** See **parakeet.**

**parral.** See **parrel.**

**parramatta.** See **paramatta.**

**parrel, parral,** *par'əl, n.* a band by which a yard is fastened to a mast.—**parrel truck,** a wooden ball strung on a parrel. [Cf. O.Fr. *parail,* rigging.]

**parrhesia,** *pa-rē'syə, -zyə, n.* boldness of speech. [Gr. *parrēsiā—para,* beside, beyond, *rhēsis,* speech.]

**parricide,** *par'i-sid, n.* the murder of a parent or near relative, or the murder of anyone to whom reverence is considered to be due: one who commits such a crime.—*adj.* **parricid'al.** [Fr., —L. *parricidium, pāricidium* (the offence), *parricida, pāricida* (the offender)—*caedĕre,* to slay; the connection with *pater,* father, is apparently fanciful.]

**parritch,** *pär', par'ich, n.* Scots form of **porridge.**

**parroquet.** See **parakeet.**

**parrot,** *par'ət, n.* one of a family of tropical and subtropical birds with brilliant plumage, hooked bill, and zygodactyl feet, good imitators of human speech: an uncritical repeater of the words of others.—*v.t.* to repeat by rote: to teach to repeat by rote.—*v.i.* to talk like a parrot (also *v.t.* with *it*):—*pa.p.* **parr'oted.**—*ns.* **parr'oter; parr'otry,** unintelligent imitation.—*adj.* **parr'oty,** like a parrot or parrot-coal.—**parr'ot-beak, -bill, -jaw,** the New Zealand glory-pea, from the form of its flowers; **parr'ot-coal** (*Scot.*), cannel coal (possibly from chattering as it burns); **parr'ot-cry',** a catch-phrase senselessly repeated from mouth to mouth; **parr'ot-disease',** psittacosis; **parr'ot-fish,** a name applied to various fishes, esp. of the wrasse family and the kindred Scaridae, from their colours or their powerful jaws; **parr'ot-wrasse,** a parrot-fish, esp. that of the Mediterranean (*Scarus cretensis*), prized by the ancients. [Possibly Fr. *Perrot,* dim. of *Pierre,* Peter.]

**parry,** *par'i, v.t.* to ward or keep off: to turn aside: to avert:—*pr.p.* **parr'ying;** *pa.t.* and *pa.p.* **parr'ied.**—*n.* a turning aside of a blow or a thrust or of an attack of any kind, e.g. an argument or a jibe. [Perh. from Fr. *parez,* imper. of *parer*—L. *parāre,* to prepare, in L.L. to keep off.]

**parse,** *pärz,* also, *pärs, (gram.) v.t.* to describe (a word) fully from point of view of classification, inflexion, and syntax: to analyse (a sentence).—*ns.* **pars'er; pars'ing.** [L. *pars* (*ōrātiōnis*), a part (of speech).]

**parsec,** *pär'sek* or *pär-sek', n.* the distance (about 19 billion miles) at which half the major axis of the earth's orbit subtends an angle of one second, a unit for measurement of distances of stars. [**parallax, second.**]

**Parsee, Parsi,** *pär'sē,* or *-sē', n.* a descendant of the Zoroastrians who emigrated from Persia to India in the 8th century.—*n.* **Par'seeism, Par'sism** (or *-sē'*), **Par'sism,** their religion. [Pers. *Pärsi—Pärs,* Persia.]

**parsimony,** *pär'si-mən-i, n.* sparingness in the spending of money: praiseworthy economy in use of means to an end: avoidance of excess: frugality: niggardliness.—*adj.* **parsimonious** (*-mō'ni-əs*).—*adv.* **parsimō'niously.**—*n.* **parsimō'niousness.—law of parsimony,** the principle of Occam's razor (see **Occamism**). [L. *parsimōnia—parcĕre, parsus,* to spare.]

**parsley,** *pärs'li, n.* a bright-green umbelliferous herb (*Carum petroselinum*) with finely divided, strongly scented leaves, used in cookery.—**parsley fern,** a fern (*Cryptogramma crispa*) with bright green crisped leaves not unlike parsley. [O.E. *petersilie,* modified by Fr. *persil,* both—L. *petroselinum*—Gr. *petroselinon—petros,* a rock, *selinon,* parsley.]

**parsley-piert,** *pärs'li-pĕrt,* **parsley-pert, -pŭrt,** *n.* a dwarf species of lady's-mantle (*Alchemilla* *arvensis*), a weed of dry waste ground. [Prob. Fr. *perce-pierre*, lit. pierce-stone.]

**parsnip, parsnep,** *pärs'nip, n.* an umbelliferous plant (*Pastinaca sativa* or *Peucedanum sativum*), or its edible carrot-like root. [L. *pastināca—pastinum*, a dibble; prob. affected by neep.]

**parson,** *pär'sn, n.* the priest or incumbent of a parish: a rector: any minister of religion: one who is licensed to preach.—*ns.* **par'sonage,** the residence appropriated to a parson: orig. the house, lands, tithes, etc., set apart for the support of the minister of a parish: tithes (*Scott*).—*adjs.* **parsonic** (-*son'ik*), **-al, par'sonish.**—**par'son-bird,** a New Zealand honey-bird of glossy blue-black plumage with tufts of white at the neck, the tui; **parson's nose,** the pope's nose (q.v.). [O.Fr. *persone*—L. *persōna,* a person, prob. in legal sense, or a mouthpiece.]

**part,** *pärt, n.* something less than the whole: a portion: that which along with others makes up, has made up, or may at some time make up, a whole: a constituent: a member or organ: an equal quantity: share: region: direction, hand, or side: participation: concern: interest: side or party: character taken by an actor in a play: words and actions of a character in a play or in real life: a voice or instrument in concerted music: that which is performed by such a voice or instrument: a copy of the music for it: a constituent melody or succession of notes or harmony: a section of a work in literature, in music: a separately published portion or number: an inflected form of a verb: a quantity which taken a certain number of times (when unspecified, less than the whole) will equal a larger quantity: (in *pl.*) intellectual qualities, talents, or conduct.—*adj.* in part: partial.—*adv.* in part: partly.—*v.t.* to divide: to separate: to break: to put or keep asunder: to set in different directions: to distribute: to share: to leave, quit (*Shak.*).—*v.i.* to become divided or separated: to separate: to go different ways: to depart: to come or burst apart: to relinquish (with *with*): to share (*B.*).—*adj.* **part'ed,** divided: separated: sundered: departed: assigned a part: endowed with parts or abilities (*Shak.*): deeply cleft, as a leaf (*bot.*).—*n.* **part'er.**—*adj.* **part'ible,** that may be parted: separable.—*ns.* **partibil'ity; part'ing,** the action of the verb to part: a place of separation or division: a dividing line: leave-taking.—*adj.* separating: dividing: departing: leave-taking: of or at leave-taking.—*adv.* **part'ly,** in part: in some degree.—**part'ing-cup',** a two-handled drinking-cup; **part'-own'er,** a joint owner; **part'-pay'-ment,** payment in part; **part'-singing; part'-song,** a melody with parts in harmony, usu. unaccompanied.—*adj.* **part'-time,** for part of working time only.—**part'-tim'er; part'-writing,** composition of music in parts.—**for my part,** as far as concerns me; **for the most part,** commonly; **in bad, or ill, part,** unfavourably; **in good part,** favourably: without taking offence; **in great part,** to a great extent; **in part,** partly: so far as part is concerned: not wholly but to some extent; **on the part of,** so far as concerns: as done or performed by: in the actions of: on the side of; **part and parcel,** essentially a part; **part brass rags** (*sea slang*), to quarrel; **part company,** to separate; **parting of the ways,** a point at which a fateful decision must be made; **part of speech,** one of the various classes of words; **take part in,** to share or to assist in; **take part with,** to take the side of. [O.E. and Fr. *part*—L. *pars, partis.*]

**partake,** *pär-, pər-tāk', v.i.* to take or have a part or share (usu. with *of* or *in*): to take some, esp. of food or drink: to have something of the nature or properties (of): to make common cause (*Shak.*).—*v.t.* to have a part in: to share:

to have a share in the knowledge of: to give a share of (*Shak.*): to inform (*Spens.*):—*pr.p.* **partā'king;** *pa.t.* **partook';** *pa.p.* **partā'ken.**—*ns.* **partā'ker; partā'king.** [Back-formation from **partaker**—**part, taker.**]

**partan,** *pär'tn,* (*Scot.*) *n.* the edible crab. [Gael.]

**parterre,** *pär-ter', n.* an arrangement of flower-beds: the pit of a theatre, esp. the part under the galleries. [Fr.,—L. *per,* along, *terra,* earth, ground.]

**parthenocarpy,** *pär-then-ō-kär'pi,* (*bot.*) *n.* the production of a fruit without a preliminary act of fertilisation.—*adj.* **parthenocar'pic.** [Gr. *parthenos,* a virgin, *karpos,* a fruit.]

**parthenogenesis,** *pär-thi-nō-jen'i-sis, n.* reproduction by means of an unfertilised ovum.—*adj.* **parthenogenetic** (-*ji-net'ik*). [Gr. *parthenos,* a virgin, *genesis,* production.]

**Parthenon,** *pär'thi-non, n.* the temple of Athēnē *Parthēnos,* on the Acropolis at Athens. [Gr. *Parthenōn—parthenos,* a virgin.]

**Parthian,** *pär'thi-ən, adj.* of Parthia.—*n.* a native of Parthia.—**a Parthian shot,** a parting shot, from the Parthian habit of turning round in the saddle to discharge an arrow at a pursuer.

**parti,** *par-tē,* (Fr.) a group of people: a decision: a marriageable person considered as a match or catch.—**parti pris** (*prē*), bias, preconceived opinion.

**partial,** *pär'shl, adj.* relating to a part only: not total or entire: inclined to favour one person or party: having a preference or fondness (with *to*): of partiality (*Shak.*): component: subordinate (*bot.*).—*n.* a partial tone, one of the single-frequency tones which go together to form a sound actually heard.—*ns.* **par'tialism; par'tialist,** one who is biased: one who sees or knows only part: a particularist (*theol.*); **parti-ality** '(-*shi-al'i-ti*).—*v.t.* **par'tialize** (*Shak.*), to bias.—*adv.* **par'tially.**—**partial pressure,** the pressure exerted by any component in a mixture of gases. [Fr.,—L.L. *partiālis*—L. *pars,* a part.]

**particeps criminis,** *pär'ti-seps kri'mi-nis, par'ti-keps krē'mi-nis,* (L.) one who, though not present, helps in any way the commission of a crime or who after the deed aids those who did it.

**participate,** *pär-tis'i-pāt, v.i.* to have a share, or take part (in): to have some of the qualities (of).—*v.t.* to receive a part or share of (*arch.*).—*adjs.* **partic'ipable,** capable of being participated in or shared; **partic'ipant,** participating: sharing.—*n.* a partaker.—*adv.* **partic'ipantly.**—*n.* **participā'tion.**—*adj.* **partic'ipative,** capable of participating.—*n.* **partic'ipator,** one who participates: a person who has a share in the capital or income of a company. [L. *participāre, -ātum—pars, partis,* part, *capēre,* to take.]

**participle,** *pär'ti-sip-l, n.* a word combining the functions of adjective and verb.—**present participle, past** or **perfect participle,** referring respectively to an action roughly contemporaneous or past; the present participle is active, the past usually passive.—*adj.* **particip'ial.**—*adv.* **particip'ially.** [O.Fr. (Fr. *participe*),—L. *participium—pars, partis,* a part, *capēre,* to take.]

**particle,** *pär'ti-kl, n.* a little part: a very small portion: a clause of a document: a minute piece of matter: a little hard piece: a material point (*mech.*): a smallest amount: a short, usu. indeclinable word, as a preposition, a conjunction, an interjection: a prefix or suffix: a crumb of consecrated bread or a portion used in the communion of the laity (*R.C. Church*).—*adj.* **particular** (*pər-tik'ū-lər*), relating to a part: predicating of part of the class denoted by the subject (*log.*): pertaining to a single person or thing: individual: special: worthy of special attention: detailed: markedly and discriminatingly or intimately attentive towards a person (*obs.*): noteworthy: definite: concerned with or marking things single or distinct: minutely attentive and careful: fastidious in taste: particularist.—*n.* a distinct or minute part: a single point: a single instance: a detail: an item: personal relation (*Shak.*): a favourite (*coll.*): a favourite drink (esp. *London particular*, a Madeira wine for the London market, hence a *London fog*; *coll.*).—*n.* particularisā′tion, -z-.—*v.t.* partic′ularise, -ize, to render particular: to mention the particulars of: to enumerate in detail: to mention as a particular or particulars. —*v.i.* to mention or attend to minute details. —*ns.* partic′ularism, attention to one's own interest or party: a minute description: the doctrine that salvation is offered only to particular individuals, the elect, and not to the race: attention to the interest of a federal state before that of the confederation: policy of allowing much freedom in this way.—*n.* and *adj.* partic′ularist.—*adj.* particularist′ic.—*n.* particularity (-*lar′i-ti*), quality of being particular: minuteness of detail: a single instance or case: a detail: peculiarity: marked attention to a person (*obs.*).—*adv.* partic′ularly, in a particular manner: individually: severally: in detail: in the manner of a particular proposition: intimately: notably: in a very high degree.—*n.* partic′ularness.—*adj.* partic′ulate, having the form of or relating to particles.—**in particular**, especially: in detail: severally, individually (*obs.*). [L. *particula*, dim. of *pars*, *partis*, a part.]

**parti-coated, parti-coloured.** See under **party**.

**particular**, etc. See **particle**.

**partie carrée**, *par-tē kar-ā*, (Fr.) a party consisting of two men and two women.

**partim**, *pär′tim*, (L.) in part.

**partisan, partizan**, *pär-ti-zan′*, *pär′ti-zan*, *n.* an adherent, esp. a blind or unreasoning adherent, of a party or a faction: a light irregular soldier who scours the country and forays: in World War II, an irregular resister within the enemy occupation lines.—Also *adj.*—*n.* par′tisanship (or -*zan*′). [Fr. *partisan*, from a dialect form of It. *partigiano*—parte (L. *pars*, *partis*), part.]

**partisan**, *pär′ti-zan*, *n.* a kind of halberd or long-handled weapon, common in the Middle Ages: a man armed with one. [Fr. *partizane* (now *pertuisane*)—It. *partesana*, of doubtful origin.]

**partita**, *pär-tē′ta*, (*mus.*) *n.* (esp. 18th cent.) a suite: a set of variations. [It.]

**partite**, *pär′tit*, *adj.* divided: cut nearly to the base.—*n.* **partition** (-*tish′ən*), *n.* act of dividing: state of being divided: a separate part: that which divides: a wall between rooms: a barrier, septum or dissepiment: score (*mus.*).—*v.t.* to divide into shares: to divide into parts by walls, septa, or the like.—*ns.* parti′tioner, one who partitions property; parti′tionist, one who favours partition; parti′tionment.—*adj.* par′titive, parting: dividing: distributive: indicating that a part is meant (*gram.*).—*n.* a partitive word.—*adv.* par′titively.—*ns.* partitur (-*toor′*; Ger.), partitura (-*too′ra*; It.), score in music.— **parti′tion-wall′**, an internal wall. [L. *partitus*, pa.p. of *partiri* or *partire*, to divide—*pars*, part.]

**Partlet**, *pärt′lit*, *n.* a proper name for a hen, from Chaucer's *Pertelote* in the Nun's Priest's Tale: sometimes applied to a woman. [O.Fr. *Pertelote*, a woman's name.]

**partlet**, *pärt′lit*, (*obs.*) *n.* a neck-covering: a ruff: a kind of shirt. [App. O.Fr. *patelette*, a band.]

**partner**, *pärt′nər*, *n.* a sharer: an associate: one engaged with another in business: one who plays on the same side with another in a game: one who dances or goes in to dinner with another: a husband or wife: an associate in commensalism or symbiosis.—*v.t.* to join as a partner (*Shak.*): to be the partner of.—*n.* part′nership, state of being a partner: a contract

between persons engaged in any business. [Prob. a form of **parcener**.]

**partridge**, *pär′trij*, *n.* any member of a genus (*Perdix*) of game-birds of the pheasant family: extended to many other birds, esp. (in North America) the Virginian quail and the ruffed grouse, and (in South America) the tinamous: —*pl.* **partridge(s)**.—**par′tridge-berry**, a North American trailing plant of the madder family (*Mitchella repens*) or its fruit: applied also to the checker-berry; **par′tridge-wood**, a hard variegated tropical American cabinet-maker's wood (Andira) of the Papilionaceae: oak or other wood speckled owing to attack by a fungus. [Fr. *perdrix*—L. *perdix*—Gr. *perdix*.]

**parture**, *pärt′yər*, (*Spens.*) *n.* departure. [Prob. **part**.]

**parturient**, *pär-tū′ri-ənt*, *adj.* bringing, or about to bring, forth: of parturition.—*n.* parturi′tion, act of bringing forth. [L. *parturire*, desiderative from *parēre*, to bring forth.]

**party**, *par′ti*, *n.* a part (*obs.*): a side, in a battle, game, lawsuit, or other contest: a body of persons united in favour of a political or other cause: the spirit of faction: a small body of persons associated together in any occupation or amusement: a detachment: a company: a meeting or entertainment of guests: a game (*obs.*): one concerned in any affair: a person who enters into a contract, e.g. of marriage: a possible match in marriage: a person (*coll.*).— *adj.* pertaining to party: parted or divided (*her.*). —*n.* par′tyism, devotion to party.—*adjs.* par′ticoat′ed, par′ty-coat′ed, having on a coat of various colours; par′ti-col′oured, par′ty-col′oured, variegated.—par′ty-call′, a call upon one's host or hostess after a party; par′tycap′ital, advantage or credit to one's party derived from some contingency; par′ty-gov′ernment, government by the prevailing political party; par′ty-ju′ry, a jury half of natives and half of aliens; par′ty-line′, a telephone exchange line shared by two or more subscribers: boundary between properties: the policy rigidly laid down by the party leaders; par′ty-man′, a partisan; par′ty-pol′itics, politics viewed from a party standpoint, or arranged to suit the views or interests of a party; par′ty-spir′it, the unreasonable spirit of a party-man.—*adj.* par′tyspir′ited.—par′ty-ver′dict, a joint verdict; par′tywall, a wall between two adjoining properties or houses. [Fr. *partie*, fem. (and also *parti*, masc.), pa.p. of *partir*—L. *partire*, *partiri*, to divide— *pars*, a part.]

**parure**, *pa-rür′*, *n.* a set of ornaments, etc. [Fr.]

**parvanimity**, *pär-və-nim′i-ti*, *n.* littleness of mind. [L. *parvus*, little, *animus*, mind.]

**parvenu**, *pär′və-nü*, -*nū*, *n.* an upstart: one newly risen into wealth, notice, or power, esp. if vulgar or exhibiting an inferiority complex.—Also *adj.* [Fr. pa.p. of *parvenir*—L. *pervenire*, to arrive.]

**parvis, parvise**, *pär′vis*, *pär′vēs*, *n.* an enclosed space, or sometimes a portico, before a church: a room over a church porch (*erron.*). [O.Fr. *parevis*; same root as **paradise**.]

**pas**, *pä*, *n.* a step: a dance: action: precedence.— **pas d'armes** (-*därm*), a joust, a tilt or a tourney; **pas de deux** (-*də də*), a dance of two persons; **pas redoublé** (*rə-dōōb-lā*), a quickstep.—**have the pas of one**, to take precedence of him. [Fr.,— L. *passus*; cf. **pace**.]

**pascal**, *pas′kal*, *n.* unit of pressure, the newton per square metre, a supplementary SI unit. [Blaise *Pascal*, French philosopher and scientist.]

**Pasch, pask**, Scot. **Pace**, *päs*, *n.* the Passover: Easter (*arch.*).—*adj.* pasch′al.—pasch′al-can′dle, a large candle blessed and placed on the altar on the day before Easter; pasch′al-flow′er (same as **pasque-flower**); pasch′al-lamb, the lamb slain and eaten at the Passover; **pasch'-egg** (*Scot.* **pace'-egg**), an Easter-egg.—**Pasch of the Cross**, Good Friday. [L. *pascha*—Gr. *pascha*—Heb. *pesach*, the Passover—*pāsach*, to pass over.]

**pasear**, *pä-sā-är'* (*U.S. slang*) *v.i.* to take a walk. —*n.* a walk.—*n.* **paseo** (*pä-sā'ō*), a walk: a street or promenade. [Sp.]

**pash**, *pash*, (*Shak.*) *v.t.* to strike, to dash, to crush.—*v.i.* to dash.—*n.* a blow. [Perh. imit.]

**pash**, *pash*, (*Shak.*) *n.* the head. [Origin unknown.]

**pash**, *pash*, *n.* a slang abbreviation of **passion**.

**pasha**, *pa'sha*, *pä-shä'*, *n.* a Turkish title (abolished 1934) given to governors and high military and naval officers.—Also **pacha**.—*n.* **pash'alik** (or *pä-shä'lik*), the jurisdiction of a pasha.—Also **pachalic**. [Turk. *pāshā*; cf. **bashaw**.]

**pashm**, *push'əm*, *n.* the fine underfleece of the goats of Northern India, used for making rugs, shawls, etc.—Also **pashim** (*push'ēm*), **pashmina** (*push-mē'nə*). [Pers., wool.]

**Pashto, Pashtu.** See **Pushtu**.

**pasigraphy**, *pə-sig'rə-fi*, *n.* a system of ideographic writing.—*adjs.* **pasigraphic** (*pas-i-graf'ik*), **-al**. [Gr. *pāsi* (dat. pl.), to or for all, *graphein*, to write.]

**paso doble**, *pä'sō dō'blä*, (Sp.) a march usu. played at bullfights: a two-step: the music for this dance.

**paspalum**, *pas'pä-ləm*, *n.* an American and tropical genus of pasture grasses, a common example being pampas-grass. [Gr. *paspalos*, millet.]

**paspy**, *päs'pi*. Same as **passepied**.

**pasque-flower**, *päsk'flowr*, *n.* a species of anemone (*Anemone pulsatilla*): extended to some other species. [Fr. *passefleur*, apparently—*passer*, to surpass, modified after **pasch**, as flowering about Easter.]

**Pasquil**, *pas'kwil*, **Pasquin**, *pas'kwin*, *n.* nickname (perh. after somebody who lived near) of an ancient statue dug up in Rome in 1501, to which it became customary to attach lampoons and satires: an imaginary lampooner or satirist: a lampoon or satire.—*v.t.* and *v.i.* to lampoon or satirise.—*ns.* **pas'quilant**, **pas'quiler**, **pasquinä'der**, a lampooner; **pasquinäde'**, a lampoon.—*v.t.* to lampoon. [It. *Pasquino*, *Pasquillo*.]

**pass**, *päs*, *v.i.* to proceed: to go or be transferred from one place to another: to make one's way: to reach, extend, or have a course: to undergo change from one state to another: to be transmitted: to change ownership: to change: to shade off (*obs.*): to be astir: to circulate: to be accepted or reputed or known: to go by: to go unheeded or neglected: to elapse, to go away: to disappear, come to an end, fade out: to die: to go or get through an obstacle, difficulty, test, ordeal, examination, etc.: to get through an examination without honours: to be approved: to meet with acceptance: to be sanctioned: to be made law: to be talented: to come through: to be voided: to happen: to be communicated or transacted: to sit or serve (upon a jury): to adjudicate: to be pronounced: to care, reck (with *of* or *for*; *obs.*): to surpass or beat everything (*obs.*): to exceed bounds: to perform a pass (see noun below): to abstain from making a call or declaration (*cards*).—*v.t.* to go or get by, over, beyond, through, etc.: to undergo, experience: to undergo successfully: to spend (as time): to omit: to disregard: to exceed: to surpass: to cause or allow to pass: to transfer, transmit: to hand: to utter: to circulate: to pledge (as one's word): to emit: to perform a pass with or upon: to perform as a pass: to esteem (*obs.*):—*pa.t.* and *pa.p.* **passed**, **päst**, rarely **past**.—*n.* a way by which one may pass or cross: a narrow passage, esp. over a range of mountains: a narrow defile: an act of passing: the passing of an examination, esp. without honours: currency (*obs.*): reputation (*Shak.*):

event, issue, fulfilment, consummation: state or condition: a predicament, critical position: a passport: a written permission to go somewhere: permission to be in a certain area (*S.Afr.*): a free ticket: a thrust (*fencing*): transference of the ball to another team-member (*football*, etc.): transference in a juggling trick: a movement of the hand over anything, as by a mesmerist: perhaps trick, perhaps conduct (Shak., *Measure for Measure*).—*adj.* **pass'able**, that may be passed, travelled over, or navigated: that may bear inspection: that may be accepted or allowed to pass: tolerable.—*n.* **pass'ableness**.— *adv.* **pass'ably**.—*ns.* **pass'er**; **passimeter** (*pasim'i-tər*) an automatic ticket-issuing machine.— *adj.* **passing** (*päs'ing*), going by, through, or away: transient: fleeting: happening now: incidental: casual: surpassing (*arch.*).—*adv.* (*arch.*) exceedingly: very.—*n.* the action of the verb to pass: a place of passing: a coming to an end: death: gold or silver thread with a silk core.—*adj.* **pass'less**, having no pass: impassable.—**pass'-book**, a book that passes between a trader and his customer, in which credit purchases are entered: a bank-book: a booklet containing permission to be in a certain area, and other documents (*S.Afr.*); **pass'-check**, a pass-out ticket; **pass'er-by**, one who passes by or near:—*pl.* **pass'ers-by**; **pass'ing-bell**, a bell tolled immediately after a death, originally to invite prayers for the soul passing into eternity; **pass'ing-note** (*mus.*), a note or tone effecting a smooth passage, but forming no essential part of the harmony: one forming an unprepared discord in an unaccented place in the measure; **pass'key**, a key enabling one to enter a house: a key for opening several locks; **pass'man**, one who gains a degree without honours.—*adj.* **pass'out**, entitling one who goes out to return. —**pass'word** (*mil.*), a secret word by which a friend may pass or enter a camp, etc.—**bring to pass**, bring about, cause to happen; **come to pass**, to happen (apparently originally a noun in these expressions); **make a pass at**, to aim a short blow at, especially ineffectually (*slang*): to make an amorous advance to (*slang*); **pass away**, to come to an end, go off: to die: to elapse; **pass off**, to impose fraudulently, to palm off: to take its course satisfactorily: to disappear gradually; **pass on**, to go forward: to proceed: to die: to transmit, hand on; **pass on**, or **upon**, to give judgment or sentence upon: to practise artfully, or impose, upon: to palm off; **pass out**, to distribute: to die: to faint, become unconscious or dead drunk (*slang*): to go off; **pass over**, to overlook, to ignore; **pass the time of day**, to exchange any ordinary greeting of civility; **pass through**, to undergo, experience; **pass up**, to renounce, to have nothing to do with: to neglect (an opportunity). [Fr. *pas*, step, and *passer*, to pass—L. *passus*, a step.]

**passacaglia**, *pas-a-käl'ya*, (*mus.*) *n.* a slow solemn old Spanish dance-form, slower than the chaconne, in triple time, usually on a ground-bass. [Italianised from Sp. *pasacalle*—*pasar*, to pass, *calle*, street, appar. because often played in the streets.]

**passade**, *pä-sād'*, *n.* the motion of a horse to and fro over the same ground.—*n.* **passado** (*pä-sä'dō*; Shak.), in fencing, a thrust with one foot advanced. [Fr. *passade*, Sp. *pasada*—L. *passus*, step.]

**passage**, *pas'ij*, *n.* act of passing: transit: crossing: migration: transition: a journey (now only by water or air, or *fig.*): right of conveyance: possibility of passing: lapse, course: transmission: evacuation of the bowels: the passing of a bill: a means or way of passing: an alley: a corridor or lobby: a navigable channel or route: a crossing-place, ford, ferry, bridge, or mountain-pass: that which passes: traffic (*Shak.*): an occurrence, incident, episode: transaction, interchange of communication or intercourse, dealings together: a continuous but indefinite portion of a book, piece of music, etc., of moderate length: a run, figure, or phrase in music: an old dicing game, the object to throw doublets above (passing) ten, with three dice.—*v.i.* to make or perform a passage.—**pass´age-boat**, a boat plying regularly for passengers; **pass´age beds** (*geol.*), transitional strata; **pass´-age-money**, fare; **pass´ageway**, a way of access: a corridor: an alley.—**bird of passage**, a migratory bird: a transient visitor (*fig.*); **passage of arms**, any feat of arms: an encounter, esp. in words. [Fr. *passage*—L. *passus*, step.]

**passage**, *pas-āzh´*, *pas´ij*, *v.i.* to go sideways.—*v.t.* to cause (a horse) to go sideways. [Fr. *passager*—*passéger*—It. *passeggiare*, to walk—L. *passus*, step.]

**passamezzo.** See **passy-measure.**

**passant**, *pas´ənt*, (*her.*) *adj.* walking towards the dexter side, with dexter fore-paw raised. [Fr.]

**passé**, *fem.* **passée**, *pa-sā*, (Fr.) past one's best, faded: nearly out of date.

**passement, passment,** *pas´mənt*, **passament, -ə-mənt**, *n.* decorative trimming.—*v.t.* to adorn with passement.—*n.* **passementerie** (*päs-mä-t(ə)-rē*; Fr.). [Fr.]

**passenger**, *pas´in-jər*, *n.* one who passes: one who travels in a private or public conveyance (as opposed to one who drives or operates the vehicle, etc.): one carried along by others' efforts (*fig.*).—*adj.* of or for passengers.—**pass´enger-pig´eon**, an extinct North American pigeon that flew in vast numbers in search of food. [O.Fr. *passagier* (Fr. *passager*), with inserted *n*, as in *messenger, nightingale*.]

**passe-partout**, *päs-pär-tōō´*, *n.* a means of passing anywhere: a master-key: a card or the like cut as a mount for a picture: a kind of simple pictureframe, usually of pasteboard, the picture being fixed by strips pasted over the edges: adhesive tape or paper. [Fr., a master-key, from *passer*, to pass, *par*, over, *tout*, all.]

**passepied**, *päs-pyä*, *n.* a dance or dance-tune like the minuet, but quicker. [Fr., lit. pass-foot.]

**Passeres**, *pas´ə-rēz*, *n.pl.* an old order of birds (also called Insessores) comprising more than half of all the birds.—*n.pl.* **Passeriform´mēs**, the huge order of perching birds (sparrow-like in form) including amongst others all British songsters.—*adj.* **pass´erine** (*-in*). [L. *passer*, a sparrow.]

**passible**, *pas´i-bl*, *adj.* susceptible of suffering, or of impressions from external agents.—*ns.* **passibil´ity, pass´ibleness.**—*adv.* **pass´ibly.** [L. *passibilis*—*pati*, *passus*, to suffer.]

**Passiflora**, *pas-i-flō´ra*, *flō´ra*, *n.* the passion-flower genus, giving name to the family **Passi-florā´ceae.** [L. *passiō*, passion, *flōs, flōris*, flower.]

**passim**, *pas´im*, (L.) *adv.* everywhere: throughout: dispersedly.

**passimeter.** See **pass.**

**passion**, *pash´n*, *n.* the sufferings (esp. on the Cross) and death of Christ: martyrdom: suffering: a painful bodily ailment (as *iliac passion*): fact, condition, or manner of being acted upon: passivity: a passive quality: strong feeling or agitation of mind, esp. rage, often sorrow: a fit of such feeling, esp. rage: an expression or outburst of such feeling: ardent love: sexual desire: an enthusiastic interest or direction of the mind: the object of such a feeling.—*v.t.* to imbue with passion.—*v.i.* to exhibit passion.—*adj.* **pass´ional.**—*ns.* **pass´ional, pass´ionary**, a book of the sufferings of saints and martyrs.—*adj.* **pass´ionate**, moved by passion: showing strong and warm feeling: easily moved to

passion: intense, fervid: compassionate (*Shak.*): moving to compassion (*Spens.*).—*v.t.* to express with passion: to imbue with passion: to impassion.—*adv.* **pass´ionately.**—*n.* **pass´ionateness.**—*adj.* **pass´ioned**, moved by passion: expressing passion: expressed with passion.—*n.* **Pass´ionist**, a member of a Roman Catholic congregation devoted to the commemoration of the Passion of Christ by missions, etc.—*adj.* **pass´ionless**, free from passion: not easily excited to anger.—**pass´ion-flower**, any flower or plant of genus Passiflora, consisting mostly of climbers of tropical and warm temperate America, from a fancied resemblance of parts of the flower to the crown of thorns, nails, and other emblems of Christ's Passion: the plant itself; **pass´ion-fruit**, the granadilla: any edible passion-flower fruit; **Pass´ion-mū´sic**, music to which words describing the sufferings and death of Christ are set; **Pass´ion-play**, a religious drama representing the sufferings and death of Christ; **Pass´ion-Sunday**, the fifth Sunday in Lent; **Pass´ion-tide**, the two weeks preceding Easter; **Pass´ion-week**, Holy-week: the week before Holy-week. [O.Fr. *passiun* and L. *passiō, -ōnis*—*pati, passus*, to suffer.]

**passive**, *pas´iv*, *adj.* suffering (*obs.*): acted upon, not acting: inert: lethargic: not reacting: not actively resisting: bearing no interest: under a liability (*Scots law*): expressing the suffering of an action by the person or thing represented by the subject of the verb (*gram.*).—*n.* the passive voice: a passive verb: a passive person.—*adv.* **pass´ively.**—*ns.* **pass´iveness, passiv´ity.**—**passive obedience**, absolute submission to the ruling power: obedience to the 'divine right of kings'; **passive resistance**, deliberate refusal (from scruples of conscience) to do what law or regulation orders, and submission to the consequent penalties; **passive resister.** [L. *passivus*—*pati, passus*, suffer.]

**passman.** See **pass.**

**Passover**, *päs´ō-vər*, *n.* annual feast of the Jews, to commemorate the destroying angel passing over the houses of the Israelites when he slew the first-born of the Egyptians.—*adj.* pertaining to the Passover.

**passport**, *päs´pōrt, pört*, *n.* authorisation to leave a port either to put to sea or to proceed inland: a permit for entering a country: that which gives privilege of entry to anything (*fig.*). [Fr. *passe-port*; cf. **pass, port.**]

**passus**, *pas´us*, *n.* a section, canto, or fytte. [L. *passus*, plur. *-ūs*, a step.]

**passy-measure, passemeasure,** *pas´i-mezh´ər*, *n.* an old dance, a pavan in quicker time, called also **passamezzo** (*pas-sa-med´zō*), **passy measures pavan** (in *Shak.* app. misprinted *panin*). [It. *passemezzo.*]

**past**, *päst*, *adj.* bygone: elapsed: ended: in time already passed: expressing action or being in time that has passed, preterite (*gram.*): just before the present: past one's best: having served a term of office.—*n.* time that has passed: things that have already happened: bygone career, esp. if marked by tragedy or scandal: the past tense: a verb or verbal form in the past tense.—*prep.* after: after the time of: beyond, in place, etc.: beyond the possibility of.—*adv.* by: laid aside in store, for later use (*Scot.*).—*v.t.* and *v.i.* an unusual pa.p. of **pass.**—**past´master**, one who has held the office of master (as among freemasons): hence, a thorough proficient (distinguished from **passed master**; see **master**). [An old pa.p. of **pass.**]

**pasta**, *päs´, pas´ta*, (It.) *n.* flour dough in fresh, processed (e.g. spaghetti), and/or cooked form.

**pastance**, *pas´tans*, (*arch.*) *n.* pastime. [App. Fr. *passe-temps*, pastime.]

**paste**, *päst*, *n.* a soft plastic mass: dough for pie-crust, etc.: a doughy sweetmeat: a smooth preparation of food suitable for spreading on bread: a cement made of flour, water, etc.: material for making pottery: the basis of a man's character (*fig.*): a fine kind of glass for making artificial gems.—*adj.* of paste.—*v.t.* to fasten or cover with paste: to thrash (*slang*).—*ns.* **pāst'er,** one who pastes: a slip of gummed paper; **pāst'iness.**—*adj.* **pāst'y,** like paste.— **paste'board,** a stiff board made of sheets of paper pasted together: a visiting-card, playing-card, or ticket (*slang*).—*adj.* of pasteboard: sham: trumpery.—**paste'-eel',** a nematoid worm found in paste; **paste'-grain,** an imitation of morocco-leather, used in binding books and in making fancy goods.—*adj.* **past'y-faced',** pale and dull of complexion. [O.Fr. *paste* (Fr. *pâte*)—L.L. *pasta*—Gr. *pasta,* barley porridge (neut. pl. of *pastos,* sprinkled, salted)—*passein,* to sprinkle.]

**pastel,** *pas'tal, -tel, n.* chalk mixed with other materials and coloured for crayons: a drawing made with pastels: the process or art of drawing with pastels: woad.—*adj.* in pastel: (of colour) soft, quiet.—*n.* **pastellist** (*pas',* or *-tel'*). [Fr. *pastel*—It. *pastello*—L. *pasta,* paste.]

**pastern,** *pas'torn, n.* a hobble for a horse (*obs.*): the part of a horse's foot from the fetlock to the hoof, where the shackle is fastened. [O.Fr. *pasturon* (Fr. *paturon*)—O.Fr. *pasture,* pasture, a tether for a horse; cf. **pester.**]

**Pasteurian,** *pas-tûr'i-an, adj.* relating to Louis *Pasteur* (1822-95) or his methods.—*n.* **pasteuri-sā'tion,** -z-, sterilisation of milk, etc., by heating. —*v.t.* **pas'teurise, ize.**—*ns.* **pasteuris'er,** -z-, an apparatus for sterilising milk, etc.; **pas'teurism,** Pasteur's method of inoculation with the attenuated virus of certain diseases, esp. hydrophobia.

**pastiche,** *pas-tēsh', n.* a jumble: a pot-pourri: a composition (in literature, music, or painting) made up of bits of other works or imitations of another's style; **pasticheur** (*-ē-shœr*).—Also **pasticcio** (*pas-tit'chō; pl.* **pasticci,** *-chē*). [Fr. (from It.) and It. *pasta,* paste; see **paste.**]

**pastil,** *pas'til, n.* Same as **pastel** or **pastille.**

**pastille,** *pas-tēl', n.* a small cone of charcoal and aromatic substances, burned as incense, or for fumigation, fragrance: a small (often medicated) sweetmeat: paper tube containing a firework which causes a small wheel to rotate: the same as **pastel** (*art*). [Fr.,—L. *pāstillus,* a little loaf.]

**pastime,** *päs'tim, n.* that which serves to pass away the time: recreation. [**pass, time.**]

**pastor,** *päs'tor, n.* one who has care of a flock or of a congregation: a shepherd: a clergyman: in the Catholic Apostolic Church, a minister of the lowest grade: the rose-coloured starling (*Pastor roseus*), from its following sheep for the sake of parasites.—*adj.* **pas'toral,** relating to shepherds or to shepherd life: of the nature of pastureland: of or pertaining to the pastor of a church: addressed to the clergy of a diocese by their bishop.—*n.* a poem, play, romance, opera, piece of music, or picture depicting the life of (usually idealised or conventionalised) shepherds: such writing as a genre: a pastoral letter: a book on the care of souls: a pastoral staff.—*ns.* **pastorale** (*päs-to-rä'lä;* It.), a pastoral composition in music: a pastoral, rustic, or idyllic opera or cantata; **pas'toralism,** pastoral character, fashion, cult, mode of writing; **pas'toralist.**—*adv.* **pas'torally.**—*n.* **pas'torate,** the office of a pastor: a pastor's tenure of office: a body of pastors.— *adj.* **pas'torly,** becoming a pastor.—*n.* **pas'torship.**—**pastoral address,** or **letter,** an address or a letter by a pastor to his people, or by a bishop to his clergy; **pastoral charge,** position of a pastor: the church, etc., over which a pastor is placed: an address to a newly ordained minister; **pastoral epistles,** those in the New Testament to Timothy and Titus; **pastoral staff,** a crosier: a

tall staff forming part of a bishop's insignia, headed like a shepherd's crook; **pastoral theology,** that part of theology which treats of the duties of pastors in relation to the cure of souls. [L. *pāstor*—*pāscĕre, pāstum,* to feed.]

**pastourelle,** *päs-tōō-rel', n.* a mediaeval poetic genre, esp. Provençal and French, a dialogue between a knight and a shepherdess, or the like: a movement in a quadrille. [Fr., little shepherdess.]

**pastry,** *pās'tri, n.* articles made of paste or dough collectively: crust of pies, tarts, etc.: a small cake: a place where pastry is made (*Shak.*): the art or practice of making pastry (*obs.*).— **pas'trycook,** a maker or seller of pastry. [**paste.**]

**pasture,** *päs'char, n.* feeding (*arch.*): food (*Spens.*): grazing: growing grass for grazing: grazing land: a grazing ground, piece of grazing land.— *v.i.* to graze.—*v.t.* to put to graze: to graze on.— *adj.* **past'urable,** fit for pasture.—*n.* **past'urage,** the business of feeding or grazing cattle: pasture-land: grass for feeding: right of pasture.—*adjs.* **past'ural,** of pasture; **past'ureless.**—**past'ure-land,** land suitable for pasture. [O.Fr. *pasture* (Fr. *pâture*)—L. *pāstūra*—*pāscĕre, pāstum,* to feed.]

**pasty,** *päs'ti, adj.* See under **paste.**

**pasty,** *pas'ti, n.* a meat-pie baked without a dish. [O.Fr. *pastée*—L. *pasta;* see **paste.**]

**pat,** *pat, n.* a gentle stroke with a flat surface, as the palm of the hand: such a stroke as a caress or mark of approbation: a sound as of such a stroke: a small lump, esp. of butter, such as might be moulded by patting.—*v.t.* to strike (now only to strike gently) with the palm of the hand or other flat surface.—*v.i.* to tap: to make the sound of pats, as with the feet:—*pr.p.* **patt'ing;** *pa.t.* and *pa.p.* **patt'ed.**—*adv.* and *adj.* hitting the mark to a nicety: at the right time or place: exactly to the purpose: with or ready for fluent or glib repetition: of a hand in poker, not likely to be improved by drawing (*U.S.*).—*adv.* **pat'ly** (*rare*), fitly, conveniently: glibly, fluently. —*n.* **pat'ness.**—**pat'ball,** rounders: gentle hitting in other games.—**pat on the back,** a mark of encouragement or approbation; **stand pat,** in poker, to decide to play one's hand as it is: to refuse to change. [Prob. imit.]

**Pat,** *pat, n.* a nickname for an Irishman. [**Patrick.**]

**patagium,** *pat-a-ji'am, n.* a bat's wing-membrane: the parachute of a flying-squirrel, etc.: the fold of integument between the upper arm and the forearm of a bird: a paired scale on a moth's pronotum:—*pl.* **patagi'a.**—*adj.* **patagial** (*pa-tā'ji-al*). [L. *patagium*—Gr. *patageion,* an edging.]

**Patagonian,** *pat-a-gō'nian, n.* an Indian of Patagonia: a giant.—*adj.* of Patagonia: gigantic. [Sp. *patagón,* big foot: the tallness of the Patagonians was grossly exaggerated by travellers.]

**patamar,** *pat'a-mär, n.* a vessel, on the Bombay coast, with arched keel and great stem and stern rake. [Port.,—Konkani *pātamāri.*]

**pataphysics,** *pat'a-fiz-iks, n.* 'the science of imaginary solutions' invented by the French dramatist Alfred Jarry (1873-1907), writer of symbolic farce, from which is descended the theatre of the absurd.

**Patarin, -ine,** *pat'ar-in, -ēn, (hist.) n.* orig., an adherent of a popular party in Milan opposed to marriage of priests (11th century): later a nickname for Manichaeans, Cathari, and other heretics. [Said to be from *Pattaria,* a district in Milan.]

**Patavinity,** *pat-a-vin'i-ti, n.* the diction of the people of Padua, esp. Livy: the use of dialect, provincialism generally. [L. *patavinitās*— *Patavium,* Padua.]

**patch,** *pach, n.* a piece put on or to be put on to mend a defect: a piece of plaster for a cut or sore: a pad for a hurt eye: a small piece of ground: an overlay to obtain a stronger impression (*print*.): a small piece of black silk, etc., stuck by ladies on the face, to bring out the complexion by contrast, or as a political party badge—common in the 17th and 18th centuries: a smallish area differing in colour or otherwise from its surroundings: a plot of ground: a scrap or fragment: a scrap pieced together with others.—*v.t.* to mend with a patch: put a patch on: apply as a patch: join in patchwork: mend or construct hastily, clumsily, or temporarily (commonly with *up*): to construct as a patchwork: to mark with patches.—*adj.* **patch′able**.—*adj.* **patched**.—*n.* **patch′er**.—*adv.* **patch′ily**.—*n.* and *adj.* **patch′ing**.—*adj.* **patch′y**, covered with patches: diversified in patches: inharmonious, incongruous.—**patch′-box**, a fancy box for holding the patches worn on the face, generally having a mirror inside the lid; **patch′-pocket**, a flat, usu. square piece of material attached to the outside of a garment; **patch-up′**, a provisional repairing; **patch′work**, work formed of patches or pieces sewed together: an incongruous combination: work patched up or clumsily executed: a surface diversified in patches.—**not a patch on**, not fit to be compared with. [M.E. *pacche*; origin unknown; poss. conn. with **piece**.]

**patch**, *pach*, *n.* a fool or jester (*arch.*): a booby (*dial.*): an ill-natured person (*dial.*).—*n.* **patch′ery** (*Shak.*), knavery.—**patch′cocke, patchocke** (*Spens.*), perhaps a clown (reading and meaning doubtful; cf. **paiock**). [Perh. from preceding, from the patched coat; nickname of Cardinal Wolsey's fool, Sexton; perh. It. *pazzo*, fool.]

**patchouli, patchouly**, *pach′ōō-lē*, also *pə-chōō′lē*, *n.* a labiate shrub (*Pogostemon patchouly*) of S.E. Asia: a perfume got from its dried branches. [Tamil *patch*, green, *ilai*, leaf.]

**pate**, *pāt*, *n.* the crown of the head: the head.—*adj.* **pāt′ed**, having a pate. [Origin unknown.]

**pâté**, *pät-*, *pat-ä*, (Fr.) orig. a pie, pastry: now usu. a paste made of blended meat, herbs, etc.—**pâté de foie gras**, *də fwä grä*, orig. a pasty of fat goose liver: now usu. the goose liver paste filling.

**patella**, *pə-tel′ə*, *n.* a little pan (*ant.*): the kneepan (*anat.*): a saucer-like apothecium (*bot.*): (*cap.*) the limpet genus:—*pl.* **patell′ae** (-ē).—*adjs.* **patell′ar**, of the kneecap; **patell′ate** (or *pat′*), saucer-shaped: limpet-shaped; **patell′iform**.—**patellar reflex**, the knee-jerk. [L., dim. of *patina*, a pan.]

**paten**, *pat′ən*, *n.* a plate: a communion plate: a chalice-cover: a metal disk. [O.Fr. *patene*—L. *patena, patina*, a plate—Gr. *patanē*.]

**patent**, *pā′tənt*, or (esp. in *letters-patent* and *Patent Office*, and in U.S.) *pat′ənt*, *adj.* lying open: conspicuous, obvious, evident: generally accessible: protected by a patent: spreading (*bot.*): expanding: ingenious (*slang*).—*n.* an official document, open, and having the Great Seal of the government attached to it, conferring an exclusive right or privilege, as a title of nobility, or the sole right for a term of years to the proceeds of an invention: something invented and protected by a patent: a privilege: a certificate.—*v.t.* to secure a patent for.—*n.* **pā′tency**, openness: obviousness.—*adj.* **pā′tentable**.—*n.* **pātentee′**, one who holds a patent, or to whom a patent is granted.—*adv.* **pā′tently**, openly, obviously.—*n.* **pā′tentor**, one who grants a patent.—**pā′tent-leath′er**, finely varnished leather; **patent medicine**, strictly, a medicine protected by a patent: loosely, any proprietary medicine, esp. one liable to stamp duty, as made by secret process or for other reason; **Patent Office**, an office for the granting of patents for inventions; **patent outside, or inside**, a newspaper

printed on the outside or inside only, sold to a publisher who fills the other side with his own material, as local news, etc.; **pā′tent-right**, the exclusive right reserved by letters-patent.—*n.pl.* **pā′tent-rolls**, the register of letters-patent issued in England.—**patent still**, a still performing several operations at once, and producing a purer spirit than a pot-still.—**nothing patent** (*slang*), not very good. [L. *patēns, -entis*, pr.p. of *patēre*, to lie open.]

**pater**, *pā′tər*, (*slang*) *n.* father. [L. *păter*.]

**patera**, *pat′ə-ra*, *n.* a round flat dish, esp. for receiving a sacrificial libation among the Romans: a round flat ornament in bas-relief in friezes, etc.—often applied loosely to rosettes and other flat ornaments (*archit.*):—*pl.* **pat′erae** (-rē). [L.,—*patēre*, to lie open.]

**patercove**, *pat′ər-kōv*, *n.* Same as **patrico**.

**paterero**, *pat-ə-rā′rō*, *n.* Same as **pederero**:—*pl.* **patere′roes** (-rōz).

**paterfamilias**, *pā-tər-fə-mil′i-as*, or *pat′ər-*, *n.* the father or head of a family or household:—*pl.* (strictly) **patresfamil′ias**. [L. *păter*, a father: *familiās*, old gen. of *familia*, a household.]

**paternal**, *pə-tûr′n(ə)l*, *adj.* of a father: on the father's side: derived or inherited from the father: fatherly: showing the disposition or manner of a father.—*n.* **pater′nalism**, a system or tendency in which provident fostering care is apt to pass into unwelcome interference.—*adv.* **pater′nally**.—*n.* **pater′nity**, state or fact of being a father: fatherhood: the relation of a father to his children: origin on the father's side: origination or authorship. [L. *pater* (Gr. *patēr*), a father.]

**paternoster**, *pat-ər-nos′tər*, or *pāt′*, *n.* the Lord's Prayer: a muttered formula or spell: a harangue: a large bead in a rosary, at which, in telling, the Lord's Prayer is repeated: a rosary: anything strung like a rosary, esp. a fishing-line with hooks at intervals: an ornament shaped like beads, used in as:.agals, etc. (*archit.*): a passenger or goods lift, consisting of a series of cars moving on a continuous belt, the floors remaining horizontal at the top and bottom of travel. [L. *Pater noster*, 'Our Father', the first words of the Lord's Prayer.]

**pater patriae**, *pā′tər pā′tri-ē, pa′ter pa′tri-ī*, (L.) the father of his country.

**path**, *päth*, *n.* a way trodden out by the feet: a way for foot-passengers: course, route, line along which anything moves: course of action, conduct:—*pl.* **paths**, *pädhz*.—*v.i.* (*Shak.*) to go.—*adj.* **path′less**, without a path: untrodden.—**path′finder**, one who explores the route, a pioneer: a radar device used as an aircraft navigational aid: a radar device for guiding missiles into a target area; **path′way**, a path. [O.E. *pæth*; Ger. *pfad*.]

**Pathan**, *pə-tän′, put-(h)än′*, *n.* an Afghan proper: one of Afghan race settled in India.—Also *adj.*

**pathos**, *pā′thos*, *n.* the quality that raises pity.—*adj.* **pathetic** (*pə-thet′ik*), relating to or affecting the passions or their expressions (*obs.*): affecting the emotions of pity, grief, sorrow: touching: applied to the superior oblique muscle, which turns the eyeball downwards, and to the trochlear nerve connecting with it (*anat.*).—*n.* that which is pathetic: the style or manner fitted to excite emotion: (in *pl.*) attempts at pathetic expression.—*adj.* **pathet′ical**.—*adv.* **pathet′ically**.—*adj.* **pathic** (*path′ik*), passive.—*n.* a passive subject: a catamite.—**path(o)-**, in composition, disease, as in *ns.* **pathogen** (*path′ō-jen*), an organism or substance that causes disease; **pathogen′esis, pathogeny** (*pə-thoj′ə-ni*), mode of production or development of disease.—*adjs.* **pathogenetic** (*path-ō-ji-net′ik*), **pathogenic** (-*jen′ik*), **pathog′enous**, producing disease; **pathognomon′ic** (-*og-nō-*; Gr. *gnōmōn*, judge, index), indicative of a particular disease.—*ns.* **pathog'nomy**; **pathog'raphy**, a description of, article on, a disease: abnormality.—*adjs.* **patholog'ic, -al,** relating to pathology in either sense.—*adv.* **patholog'ically.**—*ns.* **pathol'ogist**, one skilled in pathology: one who carries out post-mortems; **pathol'ogy**, the study of diseases or abnormalities; **pathopho'bia** (Gr. *phobos*, fear), morbid fear of disease.—**pathetic fallacy**, the reading of one's own emotion into external nature. [Gr. *pathos*, experience, feeling, pathos.]

**patible,** *pat'i-bl, adj.* capable of suffering or being acted on: passible. [L. *patibilis—patī,* to suffer.]

**patibulary,** *pa-tib'ū-la-ri, adj.* of or pertaining to a gibbet or gallows. [L. *patibulum,* a gibbet.]

**patience,** *pā'shans, n.* quality of being able calmly to endure suffering, toil, delay, vexation, or the like: sufferance: a card-game of various kinds, generally for one person, the object to fit the cards as they turn up into some scheme: a species of dock (also **pa'tience-dock'**; *Rumex patientia*) used like spinach, or other species of dock: also applied to bistort.—*adj.* **pā'tient,** sustaining pain, delay, etc., without repining: not easily provoked: persevering in long-continued or minute work: expecting with calmness: long-suffering: enduring: susceptible (of an interpretation).—*n.* one who bears or suffers: a person under medical or surgical treatment: a physician's client.—*v.t.* (*Shak.*) to make patient. —*adv.* **pā'tiently.** [Fr.,—L. *patientia—patī,* to bear.]

**patin, patine.** Obs. form of **paten.**

**patina,** *pat'i-na, n.* a shallow Roman pan: a eucharistic paten: a film of basic copper carbonate that forms on exposed surfaces of copper or bronze: a similar film of oxide, etc., on other metals: a film or surface appearance that develops on other substances (wood, flint, etc.) on long exposure or burial.—*adj.* **pat'ināted.**—*n.* **patinā'tion.**—*adj.* **pat'ined.** [L. *patina,* a dish.]

**patio,** *pa'ti-ō, -tyō, n.* a courtyard. [Sp.]

**pâtisserie,** *pa-tēs'rē,* (Fr.) a pastry shop: pastry.

**patois,** *pat'wä, n.* illiterate or provincial dialect:— *pl.* **patois** (-*wäz*). [Fr.; origin unknown.]

**patonce,** *pa-tons',* (*her.*) *adj.* of a cross, having four arms expanding in curves from the centre, with floriated ends. [Origin unknown.]

**patres conscripti,** *pāt', pat'rēz, -rās, kon-skrip'tī, -tē,* (L.) the conscript fathers, those enrolled as Roman senators.

**patria potestas,** *pā', pa'tria po-tes'tās,* (L.) the authority of a Roman father over his children.

**patrial,** *pā', pa'tri-al, adj.* pertaining to one's native land: (of a word) denoting a native or inhabitant of the place from whose name the word is formed.—*n.* a patrial word: a U.K. citizen having specified qualifications entitling him, her, to be considered legally a native.—*v.t.* **pa'trialise** **(-ize).**—*ns.* **patrialisā'tion, -z-;** **pa'trialism; patrial'ity,** the condition of being a patrial. [Obs. Fr.—L. *patria.* fatherland.]

**patriarch,** *pā'tri-ärk, n.* one who governs his family by paternal right: one of the early heads of families from Adam downwards to Abraham, Jacob, and his sons (*B.*): a bishop ranking above primates and metropolitans: the head of certain Eastern Churches: a father or founder: a venerable old man: an oldest inhabitant: an old leader of a flock: the most imposing and greatest of its kind.—*adj.* **patriarch'al,** belonging or subject to a patriarch: like a patriarch: of the nature of a patriarch.—*ns.* **patriarch'alism,** the condition of tribal government by a patriarch; **pa'triarchate,** the province, dignity, office, term, or residence of a church patriarch: patriarchy; **pa'triarchism,** government by a patriarch; **pa'-triarchy,** a community of related families under the authority of a patriarch: the patriarchal

system.—**patriarchal cross,** a cross with two horizontal bars. [Gr. *patriarchēs—patriā,* family —*patēr,* father, *archē,* rule.]

**patrician,** *pa-trish'an, n.* a member or descendant by blood or adoption of one of the original families of citizens forming the Roman people— opp. to *plebeian*: a nobleman of a new order nominated by the emperor in the later Roman Empire: an imperial Roman provincial administrator in Italy or Africa: a hereditary noble: an aristocrat.—Also *adj.*—*adj.* **patri'cianly.**—*n.* **patriciate** (*pa-trish'i-āt*), the position of a patrician: the patrician order. [L. *patrïcius—pater, patris,* a father.]

**Patrician.** See **patrick.**

**patricide,** *pat'ri-sid, n.* the murder of one's own father: one who murders his father.—*adj.* **patrici'dal.** [Doubtful L. *patricïda,* as if from *pater, patris,* father, *caedēre,* to kill; prob. an error for *parricïda*; see **parricide.**]

**patrick,** *pat'rik, n.* a 17th-century Irish halfpenny. —*adj.* **Patrician** (*pa-trish'an*), of St. Patrick.— **St Patrick's cabbage,** a saxifrage, London pride; **St Patrick's cross,** a red saltire on a white ground, representing Ireland. [St. *Patrick* (L. *Patrïcius*), 5th-century christianiser of Ireland.]

**patrico,** *pat'ri-kō,* (*slang*) *n.* a hedge-priest.—Also **pat'ercove.** [First part unexplained; see **cove** (2).]

**patrilineal,** *pat-ri-lin'i-al,* **patrilinear,** -*ar, adjs.* reckoned through the father or through males alone.—*n.* **patrilineage,** (-*lin'i-ij*). [L. *pater, patris,* father, *linea,* line.]

**patrilocal,** *pat-ri-lō'kl, adj.* (of a form of marriage) in which the wife goes to live with the husband's group. [L. *pater, patris,* father, *locālis—locus,* place.]

**patrimony,** *pat'ri-man-i, n.* an inheritance from a father or from ancestors: a church estate or revenue.—*adj.* **patrimonial** (-*mō'ni-al*).—*adv.* **patrimō'nially.** [L. *patrimōnium,* a paternal estate— *pater, patris,* a father.]

**patriot,** *pā'tri-at,* sometimes *pat',* *n.* one who truly, or ostentatiously and injudiciously, loves and serves his fatherland.—*adj.* devoted to one's country.—*adj.* **patriotic** (*pat-ri-ot'ik,* or *pāt-*), like a patriot: actuated by a love of one's country: directed to the public welfare.—*adv.* **patriot'ically.**—*n.* **pā'triotism** (or *pat'*). [Gr. *patriōtēs,* fellow-countrymen—*patrios—patēr,* a father.]

**Patripassian,** *pat-ri-pas'i-an, n.* a member of one of the earliest classes of anti-Trinitarian sectaries (2nd cent.), who denied the distinction of three persons in one God, maintaining that the sufferings of the Son could be predicated of the Father.—Also *adj.*—*n.* **Patripass'ianism.** [L. *pater, patris,* father, *patī, passus,* to suffer.]

**patristic, -al,** *pa-tris'tik, -al, adjs.* pertaining to the fathers of the Christian Church.—*n.* **patris'ticism** (-*sizm*), mode of thought, etc., of the fathers.— *n.pl.* **patris'tics,** the knowledge of the fathers as a subject of study—sometimes **patrol'ogy.** [Gr. *patēr, pat(e)ros,* a father.]

**patrol,** *pa-trōl', v.i.* to go the rounds for purpose of watching, repressing, protecting, inspecting, etc.: to be on duty on a beat.—*v.t.* to go the rounds of: to perambulate:—*pr.p.* **patröll'ing;** *pa.t.* and *pa.p.* **patrölled'.**—*n.* the act or service of going the rounds: perambulation: a man or body of men going the rounds: a small reconnoitring party: a small group of Scouts or of Girl Guides.—*n.* **patroll'er.**—**patrol car,** that used by police to patrol an area; **patrol'man,** a policeman on duty on a beat (*U.S.*): a policeman without rank (*U.S.*): (or **patrol**) a man on patrol to help motorists in difficulties; **patrol'-wagon** (*U.S.*), a prison-van. [O.Fr. *patrouiller,* to patrol, orig. to paddle in the mud.]

**patrology.** See **patristic.**

**patron**, *pā'trən, n.* in ancient Rome, the former master of a freed slave, retaining certain rights: a Roman patrician who gave countenance and legal aid to his client in return for services: formerly, one who accepted a dedication and gave the author a present: protector: one who countenances or encourages: customer: habitual attender: upholder: proprietor of restaurant, etc.: one who has the right to appoint to any office, esp. to a living in the church: a guardian saint: captain of a Mediterranean vessel: a slave-owner: a pattern (*obs.*):—*fem.* **pā'troness.**—*n.* **patronage** (*pat'*), support given by a patron: protection (*Spens.*): guardianship of saints: the right of bestowing offices, privileges, or church benefices: habitual commercial dealings.—*v.t.* (*Shak.*) to countenance.—*adj.* **patronal** (*pa-, pə-trō'nl, pāt', pat'rən-l*).—*v.t.* **patronise, -ize** (*pat'*, U.S. *pāt'*), to act as a patron toward: to give encouragement to: to assume the condescending air of a patron toward: to give one's custom to, or to frequent, habitually.—*n.* **pat'roniser.**—*adj.* **pat'ronising.**—*adv.* **pat'ronisingly.**—*adj.* **pā'tronless.**—**patron saint**, a saint regarded as a protector. [L. *patrōnus*—*pater, patris*, a father.]

**patronymic**, *pat-rə-nim'ik, adj.* derived from the name of a father or an ancestor.—*n.* a name so derived. [Gr. *patrōnymikos*—*patēr*, a father, *onyma* (*onoma*), a name.]

**patroon**, *pə-trōōn', n.* captain of a ship: coxswain of a longboat: holder of a grant of land under the old Dutch government of New York or New Jersey.—**patroon'ship.** [Fr. *patron*, Sp. *patrón*, and Du. *patroon*; cf. **patron.**]

**patte**, *pat, pät, n.* a narrow band keeping a belt or sash in its place. [Fr.]

**patté, pattée**, *pa-tā', pat'i,* (*her.*) *adj.* of a cross, spreading towards the ends, or having the ends expanded in three clawlike divisions. [Fr., pawed.]

**patten**, *pat'n, n.* a wooden shoe (*obs.*): a wooden sole mounted on an iron ring to raise the shoe above the mud (*obs.*): the base of a pillar (*archit.*).—*v.i.* (*obs.*) to go on pattens.—*adj.* **patt'ened**, with pattens. [O.Fr. *patin*, clog (now *skate*), perh.—*patte*, paw.]

**patten.** An old form (*Shak.*) of **paten.**

**patter**, *pat'ər, v.i.* to pat or strike often, as hailstones: to make the sound of a succession of light pats: to run with short quick steps.—*n.* the sound of pattering. [Freq. of **pat.**]

**patter**, *pat'ər, v.i.* to repeat the Lord's Prayer (*obs.*): to gabble prayers (*obs.*): to talk or sing rapidly and glibly: to talk thus, esp. on the stage, as accompaniment to action or for comic effect.—*v.t.* to repeat hurriedly, to gabble.—*n.* **patt'erer**, one who sells articles on the street by speechifying.—**patt'er-song**, a comic song in which a great many words are sung or spoken very rapidly.—**patter flash**, to talk the jargon of thieves. [paternoster.]

**pattern**, *pat'ərn, n.* a person or thing to be copied: a model: a design or guide with help of which something is to be made (e.g. a dressmaker's paper pattern): a model of an object to be cast, from which a mould is prepared: a sample: a typical example: a decorative design: a particular disposition of forms and colours: a design or figure repeated indefinitely: the distribution of shot on a target.—*v.t.* to make or be a pattern for (*Shak.*): to match, parallel (*Shak.*): to take as a pattern: to fashion after a pattern: to make a pattern upon.—**patt'ern-maker**, one who makes the patterns for moulders in foundry-work; **patt'ern-shop**, the place in which patterns for a factory are prepared; **patt'ern-wheel**, the countwheel in a clock. [Fr. *patron*, patron, pattern; cf. **patron.**]

**pattle**, *pat', pät'l*, **pettle**, *pet'l*, (*Scot.*) *n.* a small long-handled spade for cleaning a plough. [Origin obscure; cf. **paddle.**]

**patty**, *pat'i, n.* a little pie: a small flat cake of minced beef or other food.—**patt'y-pan**, a pan for baking patties. [Fr. *pâté*; cf. **pasty.**]

**patulous**, *pat'ū-ləs, adj.* spreading.—*n.* **pat'ulin**, a drug got from the mould *Penicillium patulum.* [L. *patulus*—*patēre*, to lie open.]

**paua**, *pow'a, n.* the New Zealand name for the abalone.—Also **pawa.** [Maori.]

**paucity**, *pö'sit-i, n.* fewness: smallness of quantity. [L. *paucitās, -ātis*—*paucus*, few.]

**paughty**, *pöhh'ti,* (*Scot.*) *adj.* haughty. [Origin unknown.]

**paul.** Same as **pawl.**

**paul**, *pöl, n.* a paolo.—*ns.* **Paul'ian, Paul'ianist**, a follower of Paul of Samosata, a third-century Monarchian Unitarian of Antioch.—Also *adjs.* —*n.* **Paulician** (*-ish'ən*), a member of a seventh-century sect in Armenia and later in Thrace, with Marcionite and Adoptianist affinities (perh. from Paul of Samosata, or the apostle, or one of their founders).—Also *adj.*—*adj.* **Paul'ine** (*-īn*), of the apostle Paul.—*n.* a member of any religious order named after him: a scholar of St Paul's School, London.—*adj.* **Paulinian** (*-in'i-ən*), **Pauline.**—*ns.* **Paul'inism**, the teaching or theology of Paul; **Paul'inist.**—*adj.* **Paulinist'ic.**—**Paul Jones** (*jōnz*), a dance in the course of which each man takes another partner—perh. from the Scottish-American seaman Paul Jones (1747-92), who excelled in the capture of prizes; **Paul Pry** (*prī*), one who pries into other people's business —from a character in John Poole's play (1825) so named; **Paul's'-man**, formerly, a lounger in the middle aisle of St Paul's, London. [L. *Paulus, Paullus*, a Roman cognomen, meaning 'little'.]

**pauldron**, *pöl'drən*, **pouldron**, *pōl', n.* a separable shoulder-plate in armour. [O.Fr. *espalleron*—*espalle*, the shoulder.]

**paulo-post-future**, *pö'lō-pōst-fū'chər, adj.* and *n.* future perfect: future immediately after the present. [L. *paulō*, a little, *post*, after, *futūrum*, future.]

**Paulownia**, *pöl-ō'ni-ə, n.* a Chinese and Japanese genus of trees of the figwort family, with showy flowers. [Named after the Russian princess Anna *Pavlovna.*]

**paunce.** See **pansy.**

**paunch**, *pönch, pönsh, n.* the belly: a protuberant belly: the first and largest stomach of a ruminant: a rope mat to prevent chafing (*naut.*).—*v.t.* to eviscerate.—*adj.* **paunch'y**, big-bellied. [O.Fr. *panche* (Fr. *panse*)—L. *pantex, panticis.*]

**pauper**, *pö'pər, n.* a destitute person: one not required to pay costs in a law suit: one supported by charity or by some public provision:—*fem.* **pau'peress.**—*n.* **pauperisā'tion, -z-.**—*v.t.* **pau'perise, -ize**, to reduce to pauperism: to accustom to expect or depend on support from without.—*n.* **pau'perism**, state of being a pauper. [L., poor.]

**pause**, *pöz, n.* intermission: a temporary stop: cessation caused by doubt: hesitation: a mark for suspending the voice: a continuance of a note or rest beyond its time, or a mark indicating this (*mus.*).—*v.i.* (*Shak. v.t. reflex.*) to make a pause.—*v.t.* to cause to stop.—*adjs.* **paus'al;** **pause'ful.**—*adv.* **pause'fully.**—*adj.* **pause'less.**—*adv.* **pause'lessly.**—*n.* **paus'er.**—*n.* and *adj.* **paus'ing.**—*adv.* **paus'ingly.**—**give pause**, cause to hesitate. [Fr.,—L. *pausa*—Gr. *pausis*, from *pauein*, to cause to cease.]

**pavan**, *pav'ən,* (*Shak.*) *n.* a slow dance, much practised in Spain: music for it, in 4-4 time.— Also **pav'ane** (or *pav-än'*), **pav'en, pav'in.** [Fr. *pavane*, or Sp. or It. *pavana*, prob.—L. *pāvō, -ōnis*, peacock.]

**pave**, *pāv, v.t.* to cover with slabs or other closeset pieces, so as to form a level surface for walking on: to cover with anything close-set: to be such a covering for.—*n.* (*U.S.*) pavement.—*n.* pă'vage, a charge, or right to levy a charge, for paving streets.—*adj.* paved.—*n.* pave'ment, a paved surface, or that with which it is paved: a footway by the side of a street (sometimes even when unpaved): paved road (*U.S.*): a floor-like surface: an underlying bed, esp. of fireclay under coal.—*v.t.* to pave: to be a pavement for.—*adj.* pā'ver, paved.—*n.* and *adj.* pā'ving.—*n.* pā'viour, one who lays pavement or rams sets: a paving-stone.—Also pā'ver, pā'vior.—pavement artist, one who seeks a living by drawing coloured pictures on the pavement; pavement epithelium, epithelium in the form of a layer of flat cells; pavement light, a window of glass blocks in the pavement to light a cellar; pa'ving-stone.—on the pavement, without a lodging; pave the way for, to prepare the way for: make easier: help to bring on. [Fr. *paver*, prob. a back-formation from *pavement*—L. *pavimentum*—*pavire*, to beat hard; cog. with Gr. *paiein*, to beat.]

pavé, *pa-vā*, (Fr.) pavement: a setting of jewellery with the stones close together, covering the metal.

pavid, *pav'id*, *adj.* timid. [L. *pavidus*, afraid—*pavere*, to be frightened.]

pavilion, *pə-vil'yən*, *n.* a tent, esp. a large or luxurious one: a tent-like covering: a canopy (*obs.*): a light building for players and spectators of a game: an ornamental or showy building for pleasure purposes: a projecting section of a building, usually with a tent-like roof and much decorated: a hospital block: an exhibition building: an ornamental building often turreted or domed: the bell of a horn: the outer ear: a flag or ensign (*obs.*).—*v.t.* to furnish with pavilions: to cover, as with a tent.—pavil'ion-roof, a tent-like roof.—Chinese pavilion, a set of bells hanging from a frame on a pole. [Fr. *pavillon*—L. *pāpiliō, -ōnis*, a butterfly, a tent.]

pavior, paviour. See pave.

pavis, pavise, *pav'is*, *n.* a shield for the whole body. [O.Fr. *pavais*—It. *pavese*, prob. from *Pavia* in Italy.]

Pavo, *pā'vō*, *n.* the peacock genus: a southern constellation.—*n.* pavone (*pə-vōn'*; *Spens.*), a peacock.—*adjs.* pavō'nian, pavonine (*pav'ən-in*). [L. *pāvō, -ōnis*, peacock.]

paw, *pö*, *n.* a clawed foot: a hand, or hand-writing (*facet.* or *derog.*).—*v.i.* to draw the fore-foot along the ground: to strike the ground with the forefoot: to strike out with the paw: to feel about or over anything, esp. offensively.—*v.t.* to scrape, feel, handle, or strike with the fore-foot or hand: to handle grossly, coarsely, or clumsily. [O.Fr. *poe, powe*, prob. Gmc.; cf. Du. *poot*, Ger. *pfote*.]

paw, *pö*, (*obs.*) *interj.* pah.—*adj.* (also paw'paw) foul: obscene.

pawa. See paua.

pawk, *pök*, (*Scot.*) *n.* a trick.—*adv.* pawk'ily.—*n.* pawk'iness.—*adj.* pawk'y, drily or slyly humorous. [Origin unknown.]

pawl, *pöl*, *n.* a catch engaging with the teeth of a ratchet wheel to prevent backward movement. [Origin obscure; poss. conn. with Du. or Fr. *pal*, L. *pālus*, stake.]

pawn, *pön*, *n.* something deposited as security for repayment or performance: state of being pledged (as *in* or *at pawn*).—*v.t.* to give in pledge: to pledge.—*ns.* pawnee', one who takes anything in pawn; pawn'er, one who gives a pawn or pledge as security for money borrowed.—pawn'-broker, a broker who lends money on pawns; pawn'broking; pawn'shop, a shop of a pawn-broker; pawn'ticket, a ticket marked with the name of the article, the amount advanced, etc., delivered to the pawner of anything. [O.Fr.

pan; cf. Du. *pand*; connection with L. *pannus*, cloth, very doubtful.]

pawn, *pön*, *n.* a small piece in chess of lowest rank and range: a humble tool or lightly valued agent (*fig.*). [O.Fr. *paon*, a foot-soldier—L.L. *pedō, -ōnis*—L. *pēs, pedis*, the foot.]

pawn, *pön*, *n.* a gallery or covered walk. [Cf. Du. *pand*.]

pawn, pown, powin, *pown*, (chiefly *Scot.*) *n.* a peacock. [O.Fr. *poun*, Fr. *paon*—L. *pāvō, -ōnis*.]

pawnce. See pansy.

Pawnee, *pö'nē*, or *-nē'*, *n.* one of a tribe of Indians in Nebraska, etc., afterwards in Oklahoma.—Also *adj.*

pawnee, *pö'nē*. See under brandy.

pawnee. See under pawn (1).

pawpaw. See paw (2), papaw.

pax, *paks*, *n.* the kiss of peace: an osculatory.—*interj.* truce.—pax'-board, pax'-brede (*i.e.* board), an osculatory. [L. *pāx*, peace.]

pax, *paks*, (L.) peace.—pax vobiscum (*vo-bis'kəm*, *vō-*, *wō-bēs'kōōm*), peace be with you.

paxiuba, *päsh-ē-ōō'ba*, *n.* a Brazilian palm (*Iriartea exorrhiza*) with stilt-roots. [Port., from Tupí.]

paxwax, *paks'waks*, *n.* the strong tendon in an animal's neck. [Orig. *fax-wax*—O.E. (Anglian) *fæx* (W.S. *feax*), hair, *weaxan*, to grow.]

pay, *pā*, *v.t.* to satisfy, gratify (*obs.*): to give what is due (in satisfaction of a debt, in exchange, in compensation, in remuneration, etc.) to: to give in satisfaction of a claim, in exchange, compensation, remuneration, etc.: to settle, discharge, as a claim, bill, debt, duty: to hand over money, etc., for: to be or yield satisfactory remuneration or compensation for, or enough to discharge: to yield: to be profitable to: to render: to thrash (*Shak.* and *dial.*): of a rope, to allow or cause to run out (*naut.*).—*v.i.* to hand over money or other equivalent, compensation, etc.: to afford an equivalent or means of making payment: to be worth one's trouble: to be profitable: to suffer or be punished: to be the subject of pay-ment of:—*pr.p.* pay'ing; *pa.t.* and *pa.p.* paid, (*obs.* except in the nautical sense) payed, pād.—*n.* satisfaction (*obs.*): money given for service: salary, wages: receipt of pay, service for pay, hire (esp. for an evil purpose): payment or time of payment: remunerative yield of mineral.—*adj.* paid (see separate article).—*adj.* pay'able, that may or should be paid: due: profitable.—*ns.* payee' one to whom money is paid; pay'er.—*n.* and *adj.* pay'ing.—*n.* pay'ment, the act of paying: the discharge of a debt by money or its equivalent in value: that which is paid: re-compense: reward: punishment.—pay-as-you-earn, a method of income-tax collection in which the tax is paid by deduction from earnings before they are received:—abbrev. P.A.Y.E.—pay'-bill, -sheet, a statement of moneys to be paid to workmen, etc; pay'-box, pay'-desk, a box or desk at which a customer pays; pay'-day, a regular day for payment, as of wages; pay'-dirt, -grav'el, gravel or sand containing enough gold to be worth working; paying guest, a boarder in a private house; pay'-list, -roll, a list of persons entitled to pay, with the amounts due to each: (pay'-roll) the money for paying wages; pay'-load, the part of an aeroplane's load for which revenue is obtained: the part of a rocket's equipment that is to fulfil the purpose of the rocket, as a warhead, or apparatus for obtaining information; pay'master, the master who pays: one who pays workmen, soldiers, etc.; Pay-master General, the minister at the head of a department of the Treasury that makes payments on behalf of government departments: in the navy, an officer in charge of the Bureau dealing with payments, clothing, etc. (*U.S.*): formerly also a similar officer in the army (*U.S.*); pay-off, (time of) payment—reward or punishment: outcome: dénouement: **pay'-office**, the place where payments are made; **pay'-packet**, envelope containing one's wages: wages; **pay'-roll** (see **pay'-list**); **pay'-station** (*U.S.*), a telephone call-box.—**pay back**, to pay in return (a debt): to give tit for tat; **pay down**, to pay in cash on the spot; **pay for**, to make amends for: to suffer for: to bear the expense of; **pay in**, to contribute to a fund: to deposit money in a bank-account; **pay off**, to pay in full and discharge: to take revenge upon: to requite: to fall away to leeward (*naut.*): to yield good results, justify itself; **pay one's** or **its, way**, to have, or bring, enough to pay expenses: to compensate adequately for initial outlay; **pay out**, to cause to run out, as rope: to disburse: to punish deservedly; **pay round**, to turn the ship's head; **pay the piper** (see **pipe,** 1); **pay through the nose**, to pay dearly; **pay up**, to pay in full: to pay arrears: to accept the necessity and pay. [Fr. *payer*—L. *pācāre*, to appease; cf. *pāx*, peace.]

**pay**, *pā, v.t.* to smear with tar, etc.:—*pa.t.* and *pa.p.* **payed**. [O.Fr. *peier*—L. *picāre*, to pitch.]

**paynim**, *pā'nim*, (*obs.*) *n.* heathendom: a heathen: a non-christian, esp. a Moslem.—Also *adj.*—Also **pai'nim**, **pā'nim** (*Milt.*).—*n.* **pay'nimry**, heathendom. [O.Fr. *paienisme*, paganism—L. *pāgānismus*—*pāgānus*, a pagan.]

**payola**, *pā-ō'la, n.* secret payment to secure a favour. [**pay** (1).]

**pays**, *pā-ē,* (Fr.) country.—**les Pays Bas** (*lā pā-ē ba*), the Low Countries.

**paysage**, *pā-ē-zäzh, n.* a landscape, a landscape painting (*obs.* for a time then reborrowed).—*n.* **paysagist**, *pā-zə-jist,* a landscape-painter. [Fr.]

**paysd**, *pāzd*, (*Spens.*) for **peised**, **poised**.

**pea**, *pe, n.* a new singular formed from **pease** (q.v.), which was mistaken for a plural, with a new plural **peas**—the nutritious seed of the papilionaceous climbing plants *Pisum sativum* (garden pea) and *P. arvense* (field pea): the plant itself (also **pea'-plant**): extended to various similar seeds and plants (esp. of the genus Lathyrus), and to various rounded objects, e.g. roe of salmon and some other fish, very small pieces of coal.—**pea'berry**, a small round coffee seed, growing singly; **pea'-crab**, a little round crab (Pinnotheres) that lives symbiotically in lamellibranch shells.—*n.* and *adj.* **pea-'green** (or *-grēn'*), green like green peas.—**pea-'iron**, limonite in little round nodules; **pea'nut**, monkey-nut or ground-nut (Arachis); **peanut butter**, a paste made from ground roasted peanuts; **peanut oil**, oil expressed from peanuts; **pea'-pod'; pea'-ri'fle**, a rifle throwing a very small bullet; **pea'cod, peas'cod** (see **peasecod**); **pea'shooter**, a small metal tube for blowing peas through; **pea'-soup** (see **pease-soup**); **pea-soup'er**, a fog like pea-soup.—*adj.* **pea-soup'y.**—**pea'-stone**, pisolite; **pea'-straw** (see **pease-straw**); **pea'-trainer**, an erection for pea-plants to climb on.—**Egyptian pea**, the chickpea; **split peas**, peas stripped of their membranous covering, dried and halved; **Sturt's desert pea**, a scarlet-flowered Australian glory-pea. [See **pease**.]

**pea**, *pē, (rare; obs.) n.* a **pea'-fowl**—a male or female peacock.—*ns.* **pea'-chick**, a young pea-fowl; **pea'-hen**, the female of the peacock. [O.E. *pēa (pāwa)*—L. *pāvō.*]

**peace**, *pēs, n.* a state of quiet: freedom from disturbance: freedom from war: cessation of war: a treaty that ends a war: freedom from contention: ease of mind or conscience: tranquility: quiet: stillness: silence.—*v.i.* (*Shak.*) to be silent—passing in the *imper.* into *interj.* silence: be silent: hist.—*adj.* **peace'able**, disposed to peace: peaceful.—*n.* **peace'ableness.**—*adv.* **peace'ably.**—*adj.* **peace'ful**, enjoying peace:

tending towards or favouring peace: inclined to peace: belonging to time of peace: consistent with peace: tranquil: calm: serene.—*adv.* **peace'-fully.**—*n.* **peace'fulness.**—*adv.* **peace'less.**—*n.* **peace'lessness.**—**peace'-breaker**, one who breaks or disturbs the peace; **peace establishment**, the reduced military strength maintained in time of peace; **peace'maker**, one who makes or produces peace: one who reconciles enemies: a revolver; **peace'making; peace'-monger**, a peacemaker from the point of view of those who think him a sentimental busybody; **peace'-off'ering**, among the Jews a thank-offering to God: a gift offered towards reconciliation, propitiation, or deprecation; **peace'-off'icer**, an officer whose duty it is to preserve the peace: a police-officer.—*adj.* **peace'-part'ed** (*Shak.*), dismissed from the world in peace.—**peace'-par'ty**, a political party advocating the making or the preservation of peace; **peace'-pipe**, the calumet; **peace'time**, time when there is no war.—*adj.* of peacetime.—**peace'-warrant**, a warrant of arrest issued by a Justice of the Peace.—**at peace**, in a state of peace: not at war; **breach of the peace** (see **breach**); **hold one's peace**, remain silent; **in peace**, in enjoyment of peace; **keep the peace**, to refrain from disturbing the public peace: to refrain from, or to prevent, contention; **kiss of peace** (see **kiss**); **peace of God**, the protection from acts of private warfare formerly offered by the Church to consecrated persons and places, and on Sundays and holy days; **letter of peace** (see **pacifical**); **make one's peace with**, to reconcile or to be reconciled with; **make peace**, to end a war; **the king's or queen's peace** (see **king**); **swear the peace**, to take oath before a magistrate that a certain person ought to be put under bond to keep the peace. [O.Fr. *pais* (Fr. *paix*)—L. *pāx, pācis*, peace.]

**peach**, *pēch, v.t.* (*Shak.*) to accuse, inform against, betray.—*v.i.* to betray one's accomplice: to become informer.—*n.* **peach'er.** [Aphetic form of **appeach.**]

**peach**, *pēch, n.* a sweet, juicy, velvety-skinned stone-fruit: the tree (*Prunus,* or *Amygdalus, persica*) bearing it, close akin to the almond: extended to other fruits and fruit-trees, as the quandong: peach-brandy (*U.S.*): anything regarded as a very choice example of its kind, esp. a girl (*slang*; in *U.S.* also **peacherino**, *-ə-rē'nō*): a yellow slightly tinged with red.—*adj.* of the peach: of the colour of a peach.—*adj.* **peach'y.** —**peach'-bloom'**, the powdery bloom on a peach: a similar appearance on the face, on pottery, etc.: a peach flower (also **peach'-bloss'om**): its pinkish colour: a moth with wings so coloured (*Thyatira batis*); **peach'-blow**, a pinkish glaze on porcelain, esp. Chinese porcelain.—Also *adjs.*—**peach'-brand'y**, a spirit distilled from the fermented juice of the peach.—*adj.* **peach'-coloured**, of the colour of a ripe peach (yellowish, tinged with red) or of peach-blossom (pink).—**peach Melba**, peach with ice-cream; **peach'-palm**, the pupunha, a South American palm (Bactris or Guilielma) with edible fruit like a peach in appearance; **peach'-stone; peach'-tree; peach'-water**, a flavouring extract from peach-leaves; **peach'-wood**, the wood of the peach-tree: Nicaragua wood (Caesalpinia); **peach'-yell'ows**, a virus disease that turns peach-leaves yellow and kills the tree. [O.Fr. *pesche* (Fr. *pêche*, It. *persica, pesca*)—L. *Persicum (mālum)*, the Persian (apple). Its native country is unknown.]

**pea-coat.** Same as **pea-jacket.**

**peacock**, *pē'kok, n.* a genus (Pavo) of large birds of the pheasant kind, consisting of the common peacock (*P. cristatus*) and the Javan (*P. muticus*), noted for gay plumage, esp. in the tail-coverts: the male of either species: a vainglorious person.

—*v.t.* to make like a peacock.—*v.i.* to strut about or behave like a peacock.—*n.* peacock′ery, vainglorious ostentation.—*adjs.* pea′cockish; pea′-cock-like; pea′cocky.—pea′-chick (see **pea**, 2, above); pea′cock-blue′, the blue of the peacock's neck.—Also *adj.*—pea′cock-butt′erfly, a butterfly (*Vanessa Io*) with spots like those of the peacock's train; pea′cock-copp′er, copper-pyrites, from the colours of its tarnish; pea′cock-fish, a variegated Mediterranean wrasse; pea′cock-flower, a name for various species of Poinciana (flamboyant tree, Barbados pride); pea′cock-ore′, bornite: copper-pyrites; pea′cock-pheas′-ant, an Asiatic genus (Polyplectron) akin to the peacocks and Argus pheasants; pea′cock-stone′, a jeweller's name for the cartilaginous ligament of some molluscs; pea′cock-throne′, the throne of the kings of Delhi, carried off to Persia in 1739. [**pea** (2) and **cock**, etc.]
**pea-crab.** See under **pea** (1).
**pea-fowl.** See **pea** (2).
**peag,** *pēg,* **peak,** *pēk, n.* North American Indian shell-money. [Massachusetts *piak*.]
**peahen.** See **pea** (2).
**pea-jacket,** *pē′-jak′it, n.* a sailor's coarse thick overcoat.—Also **pea′-coat.** [Du. *pie* (now *pij*), coat of coarse stuff, and **jacket, coat.**]
**peak,** *pēk, n.* a point: the pointed end or highest point of anything: the top of a mountain, esp. when sharp: a summit: a maximum point in a curve or the corresponding value in anything capable of being represented by a curve: a sharp projection: the projecting front of a cap or (formerly) of a widow's hood: a projecting point of hair on the forehead: a pointed beard: the upper outer corner of a sail extended by a gaff or yard (*naut.*): the upper end of a gaff (*naut.*).—*adj.* maximum: of a maximum.—*v.i.* to rise in a peak.—*v.t.* (*naut.*) to tilt up.—*adj.* peaked, having a peak or peaks.—*adj.* peak′y, having a peak or peaks: like a peak.—peak′-load, the maximum demand of electricity, or load on a power-station. [Found from the 16th cent. (*peked* in the 15th); app. connected with **pike.**]
**peak,** *pēk, v.i.* to sneak or slink about (*Shak.*): to mope (*obs.*): to droop, to look thin or sickly. —*adjs.* peaked, peak′ing, peak′y, having a pinched or sickly look, sharp-featured. [Origin unknown.]
**peak.** See **peag.**
**peal,** *pēl, n.* a loud sound: a number of loud sounds one after another: a set of bells tuned to each other: a chime or carillon: the changes rung upon a set of bells.—*v.i.* to resound in peals: to appeal (*Spens.*).—*v.t.* to give forth in peals: to assail with din (*Milt.*). [Apparently aphetic for **appeal.**]
**peal, peel,** *pēl,* (*local*) *n.* a grilse: a young sea-trout. [Origin unknown.]
**pean,** *pēn, n.* a heraldic fur, differing from ermine only in the ground being sable and the spots or. [Perhaps O.Fr. *pene, panne*.]
**pean.** Same as **peen** and **paean.**
**peanut.** See **pea** (1).
**pear,** *pār, n.* an esteemed fruit, a pome tapering towards the stalk and bulged at the end: the tree (*Pyrus communis*) bearing it, of the apple genus: extended to various fruits (**alligator-, anchovy-pear, prickly-pear,** etc.).—pear′-drop, a pear-shaped pendant: a pear-shaped, pear-flavoured sweetmeat; pear′monger, a seller of pears; pear′-push, -switch, an electric push-button in a hanging pear-shaped bob; pear′-tree. [O.E. *pere, peru*—L.L. *pira*—L. *pirum* (wrongly *pyrum*), pear.]
**pearce, peare, pearst,** Spenserian spellings of **pierce, peer, pierced.**
**pearl,** *pûrl, n.* a concretion of nacre formed in a pearl-oyster, pearl mussel, or other shellfish,

around a foreign body or otherwise, prized as a gem: nacre: a paragon or finest example: a lustrous globule: a granule: a tubercle of an antler burr: cataract of the eye: a five-point type (about 15 lines to the inch) (*print.*).—*adj.* of or like pearl: granulated.—*v.t.* to set or adorn with pearls or pearly drops: to make pearly: to make into small round grains.—*v.i.* to take a rounded form: to become like pearls: to fish for pearls.—*adj.* pearl′ed.—*ns.* pearl′er, a pearl-fisher or his boat; pearl′iness.—*n.* and *adj.* pearl′ing.—*adj.* pearl′y, like pearl, nacreous: rich in pearls.—*n.* (in *pl.* pearl′ies), pearl-buttons: costermongers' clothes covered with pearl-buttons.—pearl′-ash′, partly purified potassium carbonate; pearl′-bar′ley (see **barley**); pearl′-butt′on, a mother-of-pearl button; pearl disease, bovine tuberculosis; pearl′-div′er, one who dives for pearls; pearl′-essence, a silvery preparation from fish scales used in making artificial pearls; pearl′-eye, cataract.—*adj.* pearl′-eyed.—pearl′-fisher, one who fishes for pearls; pearl′-fishery; pearl′-fishing; pearl′-gray′, -grey′, a pale grey. —Also *adj.*—pearl′-mill′et, the bulrush millet or spiked millet (*Pennisetum typhoideum*), a grain much grown in India; pearl′-muss′el, a freshwater mussel (*Unio margaritifera*) that yields pearls; pearl′-oys′ter, any oyster that produces pearls, esp. *Avicula* (or *Meleagrina*) *margaritifera*; pearl′-pow′der, a cosmetic of basic bismuth nitrate or of bismuth oxychloride; pearl′-sā′go, sago in round granules; pearl′-shell, mother-of-pearl: pearly or pearl-bearing shell; pearl′-shell′er; pearl′-shelling; pearl′-spar, a pearly-lustered pale dolomite; pearl′-stone, perlite; pearl′-tapiō′ca, tapioca granulated and graded acc. to its size: a potato-starch imitation; pearl′-white, a material made from fish-scales, used in making artificial pearls: basic nitrate of bismuth, used in medicine and as a cosmetic: bismuth trichloride, used as a pigment: lithopone: calcium sulphate; pearl′-wort, a genus (*Sagina*) of small plants akin to chickweed; pearly gates (Rev. xxi), entrance to heaven; pearly nautilus (see **nautilus**).—cultured pearl, a true pearl formed by artificial means, as by planting a piece of mother-of-pearl wrapped in oyster epidermis in the body of an oyster; false, imitation, simulated pearl, an imitation, as, for instance, a glass bulb coated with pearl essence. [Fr. *perle*, prob. from dim. of L. *perna*, leg, leg-of-mutton-shaped; cf. It. dial. *perna*, pearl, It. *pernocchia*, pearl-oyster.]
**pearl,** *pûrl, n.* a small loop on the edge of lace, ribbon, etc.: in knitting, purl.—*v.t.* to purl.— *ns.* pearl′ing, pearl′in (*Scot.*), lace of silk or of thread: (in *pl.*) edgings of such lace or clothes trimmed with it.—pearl-edge, an edging of small loops. [Cf. **purl.**]
**pearlite,** *pûr′līt, n.* a constituent of steel composed of alternate plates of ferrite and cementite. —*adj.* pearlit′ic. [**pearl** (1).]
**pearmain,** *pār′mān, n.* a variety of apple. [App. O.Fr. *parmain, permain.*]
**peart,** *pērt,* (*dial.*) *adj.* lively: saucy: in good health and spirits.—*adv.* peart′ly. [**pert.**]
**peasant,** *pez′ənt, n.* a small farmer: a tiller of the soil: a countryman: a rustic: an ignorant or low fellow.—*adj.* of or relating to peasants, rustic, rural: rude.—*n.* peas′antry, the body of peasants: the condition or quality of a peasant. —peasant proprietor, a peasant who owns and works his own farm; Peasants' Revolt, Wat Tyler's rising of 1381; Peasants' War, a popular insurrection in Germany, in 1525. [O.Fr. *paisant* (Fr. *paysan*)—*pays*—assumed L. *pāgēnsis* —*pāgus,* a district.]
**pease,** *pēz, n.* orig., a pea or pea-plant (old *pl.* **peason,** *pēz′ən*): now almost wholly superseded by the new singular **pea** (q.v.) and plural **peas,**

except in a collective sense.—**pease'-bann'ock**, a bannock of pease-meal; **pease'-blossom**; **pease'-brose'**, brose made of pease-meal; **pease'-cod, peas'cod, pea'cod**, the pod of the pea.—*adj.* **pease'cod-bell'ied**, of a doublet, peaked downwards in front.—**pease'cod-cuirass'**, a cuirass shaped like the peasecod-bellied doublet; **pease'-meal, pease'-porr'idge, pease'-pudd'ing**, meal, porridge, or pudding made from pease; **pease'-soup, pea'-soup**, soup made from pease: a thick yellow heavy-smelling fog; **pease'-straw**, the stems and leaves of the pea-plant after the peas have been picked. [M.E. *pēse*, pl. *pēsen*—O.E. *pise*, pl. *pisan*—L.L. *pisa*, L. *pisum* Gr. *pison* or *pisos*.]

**peaseweep**, *pēz'wēp*. See peewit.

**peat**, *pēt*, *n.* a shaped block dug from a bog and dried or to be dried for fuel: the generally brown or nearly black altered vegetable matter (chiefly bog-moss) found in bogs, from which such blocks are cut.—*ns.* **peat'ary, peat'ery**, **pēt'ary, peat'-bank, -bed, -bog, -moor, -moss**, a region, bog, moor, etc., covered with peat: a place from which peat is dug.—*adj.* **peat'y**, like, of the nature of, abounding in, or composed of, peat.—**peat'-caster**, one who digs peats and throws them on the bank to dry; **peat'-casting**; **peat'-creel**, a basket for carrying peats; **peat'-hag, -hagg**, a hag in a peat-bog (see hag (3)); **peat'-hole; peat'man**, a carter or seller of peats; **peat'-reek'**, the smoke of peat, imagined to add a special flavour to whisky: Highland whisky; **peat'-reek'er**, ornamental apparatus for producing the smell of peat-smoke; **peat'-smoke'; peat'-spade**, a spade having a side wing at right angles for cutting peat in rectangular blocks; **peat'-stack'**, a stack of peats, drying or stored. [From the 13th cent. in S.E. Scotland in Anglo-Latin as *peta*, a peat; possibly of British origin; cf. piece.]

**peat**, *pēt*, *(obs.)* *n.* an endearment applied to a woman or girl or friend or favourite: an advocate favoured by a judge.—*n.* **peat'ship** *(Scott)*. [Origin obscure.]

**peavey, peavy**, *pē'vi*, *(U.S.)* *n.* a lumberman's spiked and hooked lever. [Joseph *Peavey*, its inventor.]

**peaze.** See peise.

**peba**, *pē'ba*, *n.* a South American armadillo. [Tupi.]

**pebble**, *peb'l*, *n.* a small roundish stone, esp. water-worn: transparent and colourless rock-crystal: a lens made of it: a semi-precious agate: a grained appearance on leather, as if pressed by pebbles: a large size of gunpowder.—*adj.* of pebble.—*v.t.* to stone or pelt: to impart pebble to (leather).—*adjs.* **pebb'led; pebb'ly**, full of pebbles.—*n.* **pebb'ling.**—**pebble dash**, a method of coating exterior walls with small pebbles set into the mortar; **pebb'le-pow'der**, gunpowder in large cubical grains; **pebb'le-stone**, a pebble; **pebb'le-ware**, a fine pottery of mixed coloured clays. [O.E. *papol* (-*stān*), a pebble (-stone).]

**pébrine**, *pā-brēn'*, *n.* a destructive protozoan disease of silkworms. [Fr.]

**pec**, *pek*, *n.* a photoelectric cell. [From the initials.]

**pecan**, *pi-kan'*, *n.* a North American hickory (also **pecan'-tree**): its nut (**pecan'-nut'**). [Indian name; cf. Cree *pakan*.]

**peccable**, *pek'ə-bl*, *adj.* liable to sin.—*ns.* **pecca-bil'ity; pecc'ancy**, sinfulness: transgression.—*adj.* **pecc'ant**, sinning: offending: morbid.—*adv.* **pecc'antly**. [L. *peccāre*, *-ātum*, to sin.]

**peccadillo**, *pek-ə-dil'ō*, *n.* a trifling fault:—*pl.* **peccadill'os** (or **peccadill'oes**). [Sp. *pecadillo*, dim. of *pecado*—L. *peccātum*, a sin.]

**peccary**, *pek'ə-ri*, *n.* either of two species of hog-like South American animals. [Carib *pakira*.]

**pech, pegh**, *pehh*, *(Scot.)* *v.i.* to pant.—*n.* a pant. [Imit.]

**Pecht, Peght**, *pehht*, *(Scot.)* *n.* a Pict. [O.E. (Anglian) *Pehtas* (W.S. *Peohtas*), Picts.]

**peck**, *pek*, *n.* formerly a measure of capacity for dry goods, 2 gallons, or one-fourth of a bushel: a measuring vessel holding this quantity: an indefinitely great amount (as *a peck of troubles*). [M.E. *pekke, pek*—O.Fr. *pek*, generally a horse's feed of oats; origin unknown.]

**peck**, *pek*, *v.t.* to strike or pick up with the point of the beak or other sharp instrument: to make, render, or cause to be by quick movement of the beak, etc.: to eat sparingly or with affectation of daintiness or *(slang)* eat in general: to kiss with dabbing movement.—*v.i.* to strike or feed with the beak or in similar manner: to cavil.—*n.* an act of pecking: a hole made by pecking: food *(slang)*.—*ns.* **peck'er**, that which pecks: a woodpecker: a kind of hoe: a part with an up-and-down movement in a telegraph instrument: spirit (as if orig. beak, nose, as in *keep your pecker up*; *slang*); **peck'ing.**—*adj.* **peck'ish**, somewhat hungry.—**pecking order**, a social order among poultry according to which any bird may peck a less important bird but must submit to being pecked by a more important one: order of prestige or power in a human social group. [App. a form of pick (1).]

**peck**, *pek*, *v.t. (Shak.* pecke) to pitch: to jerk.—*v.i.* to incline: to stumble, esp. of a horse by failing to put the foot down flat.—*n.* **peck'ing**, stone-throwing. [A form of pitch (2); cf. pick (2).]

**Pecksniffian**, *pek-snif'i-ən*, *adj.* like, or of, the hypocrite *Pecksniff* in Dickens's *Martin Chuzzlewit*.

**Pecora**, *pek'ə-rə*, *n.pl.* the Cotylophora, or ruminants other than camels and chevrotains. [L. pl. of *pecus, -oris*, cattle.]

**pecten**, *pek'tan*, *n.* a comb-like structure of various kinds, e.g. in a bird's or reptile's eye: the pubic bone: a tactile organ in scorpions: *(cap.)* the scallop genus of molluscs, with ribbed shell:—*pl.* **pec'tines** (*-tin-ēz*).—*adjs.* **pectinaceous** (*-ā'shəs*), like the scallops; **pec'tinal**, of a comb: comb-like: having bones like the teeth of a comb; **pec'tinate, -d**, toothed like a comb: having narrow parallel segments or lobes: like the teeth of a comb.—*adv.* **pec'tinately.**—*n.* **pectinā'tion**, the state of being pectinated: a comb-like structure.—*adjs.* **pectin'eal**, of the pubic bone: comb-like; **pec'tinibranchiate** (*-brangk-i-āt*), having comb-like gills. [L. *pecten, -inis*, a comb.]

**pectic**, *pek'tik*, *adj.* of, relating to, or derived from, pectin.—*ns.* **pec'tin**, a mixture of carbohydrates found in the cell-walls of fruits, important for the setting of jellies; **pectisā'tion.**—*v.t.* and *v.i.* **pec'tise, -ize**, to congeal.—*n.* **pec'tōse**, a substance yielding pectin contained in the fleshy pulp of unripe fruit.—**pectic acid**, an insoluble substance (of several varieties) formed by hydrolysis of pectins. [Gr. *pēktikos*, congealing—*pēgnynai*, to fix.]

**pectolite**, *pek'tə-līt*, *n.* a zeolite-like monoclinic acid calcium sodium silicate. [Gr. *pēktos*, congealed, *lithos*, stone.]

**pectoral**, *pek'tə-rəl*, *adj.* of, for, on, or near, the breast or chest: coming from the heart or inward feeling *(fig.)*.—*n.* armour for the breast of man or horse: an ornament worn on the breast, esp. the breastplate worn by the ancient Jewish high-priest, and the square of gold, embroidery, etc., formerly worn on the breast over the chasuble by bishops during mass: a chest-protector: a medicine for the chest: a pectoral cross: a pectoral fin.—*adv.* **pec'torally.**—*n.* **pectoril'oquy** (L. *loqui*, to talk), the sound of the patient's voice heard through the stethoscope when applied to the chest in certain morbid conditions of the lungs.—**pectoral cross**, a gold cross worn on the breast by bishops, etc.; **pectoral fins**, the anterior paired fins of fishes; **pectoral girdle**, the shoulder-girdle, consisting of shoulder-blade, coracoid, and collar-bone; **pectoral theology**, the theology of those who make much of experience and emotion as guides to a knowledge of divine truth. [L. *pectorālis*— *pectus, pectoris*, the breast.]

**peculate**, *pek'ū-lāt*, *v.t.* and *v.i.* to appropriate dishonestly to one's own use, pilfer, embezzle. —*ns.* **pecula'tion**; **pec'ulātor**. [L. *pecūlāri, -ātus* —*pecūlium*, private property, akin to *pecūnia*, money.]

**peculiar**, *pi-kū'lyər*, *adj.* own: of one's own: belonging exclusively: privately owned: appropriated: preserved: characteristic: special: very particular: odd, strange.—*n.* private property or right (*obs.*): a parish or church exempt from the jurisdiction of the ordinary or bishop in whose diocese it is placed: anything exempt from ordinary jurisdiction: one of the Peculiar People: a type of unusual kind that has to be specially cast (*print.*).—*v.t.* **pecu'liarise, -ize**, to set apart.—*n.* **peculiarity** (*-li-ar'i-ti*), quality of being peculiar or singular: that which is found in one and in no other: that which marks anything off from others: individuality: oddity.— *adv.* **pecu'liarly.**—*n.* **pecu'lium**, private property, esp. that given by a father to a son, etc.— **Peculiar People**, the Jews, as God's chosen people (N.E. Bible 'special possession', Deut. xxvi. 18, 'a people marked out as his own', Titus ii 14): an Evangelical denomination, founded in 1838, holding inspiration of Holy Scriptures, believers' baptism, Holy Communion, and Divine healing. [L. *pecūlium*, private property.]

**pecuniary**, *pi-kū'nyə-ri, -ni-ə-ri*, *adj.* relating to money: consisting of money.—*adv.* **pecu'niarily.** —*adj.* **pecu'nious** (*rare*), rich. [L. *pecūnia*, money; from the root that appears in L. *pecudēs* (pl.), cattle, and **fee**.]

**ped**, *ped*, (*dial.*) *n.* a pannier or hamper.—Also **pad**. [Origin unknown.]

**ped**, *ped*, *n.* short for **pedestrian**.

**ped-**. See **paed(o)-**.

**pedagogue**, *ped'ə-gog*, *n.* a teacher: a pedant.— *v.t.* to teach.—*adjs.* **pedagogic** (*-gog', -goj'*), **-al**. —*adv.* **pedagog'ically.**—*ns.* **pedagog'ics** (*-gog', -goj'*; treated as *sing.*), the science and principles of teaching; **ped'agoguery** (*-gog-ə-ri*), a school: schoolmastering: pedagoguishness.— *adj.* **ped'agoguish**, like a pedagogue.—*ns.* **ped'agoguishness**; **ped'agog(u)ism** (*-gizm, -jizm*), spirit or system of pedagogy: teaching; **ped'agogy** (*-gog-i, -goj-i*), the science of teaching: instruction: training. [Partly through Fr. and L. from Gr. *paidagōgos*, a slave who led a boy to school—*pais, paidos*, boy, *agōgos*, leader— *agein*, to lead.]

**pedal**, *ped'l* (*zool.* also *pē'dəl*), *adj.* of the foot: of the feet of perpendiculars: of, with, or pertaining to, a pedal or pedals.—*n.* (*ped'l*) a lever pressed by the foot: the lower and thicker part of a straw: a plait thereof: a pedal-point: a pedal-organ: a pedal-board.—*v.i.* to use a pedal or pedals: to advance by use of the pedals.— *v.t.* to drive by the pedals:—*pr.p.* **ped'alling**; *pa.t.* and *pa.p.* **ped'alled.**—*ns.* **pedalier** (*-ēr'*), a pedal-board attached to a piano for the bass strings; **ped'aller**, one who uses pedals; **ped'alling.**—**ped'al-ac'tion**, the apparatus worked by the pedals of a musical instrument; **ped'alboard**, **ped'al-clavier'**, the keyboards of pedals of an organ or other instrument; **ped'al-bone**, a horse's coffin-bone; **pedal cycle**; **ped'alorgan**, the division of an organ played by means of pedals; **ped'al-point**, organ point, a tone or

tones (usu. tonic and dominant) sustained normally in the bass, while other parts move independently. [L. *pedālis*—*pēs, pedis*, foot.]

**Pedaliaceae**, *pi-dā-li-ā'si-ē*, *n.pl.* a family of tubifloral dicotyledons akin to the bignonias. [Gr. *pēdalion*, a rudder, from the keeled fruit.]

**pedalier, pedaller**, etc. See **pedal**.

**pedant**, *ped'nt*, *n.* a schoolmaster (*Shak.*): one who is learned without being judicious, whose learning is indigested, or allowed to appear unseasonably: one who attaches too much importance to merely formal matters in scholarship.—*adjs.* **pedantic** (*pid-ant'ik*), **-al**, schoolmasterly: of the character or in the manner of a pedant.—*adv.* **pedant'ically.**—*v.t.* **pedant'icise, -ize** (*-i-siz*), to make pedantic, give pedantic form to.—*n.* **pedant'icism** (*-i-sizm*), a pedant's expression.—*v.i.* **ped'antise, -ize**, to play the pedant.—*v.t.* to turn into a pedant.—*ns.* **ped'antism**, **pedantry**: pedanticism; **pedantoc'racy**, government by pedants; **pedant'ocrat.**—*adj.* **pedantocrat'ic.**—*n.* **ped'antry**, the character or manner of a pedant: a pedantic expression: unduly rigorous formality. [It. *pedante* (perh. through Fr. *pédant*); connection with **pedagogue** not clear.]

**pedate**, *ped'āt*, *adj.* footed: foot-like: palmately lobed with the outer lobes deeply cut, or ternately branching with the outer branches forked (*bot.*).—*adv.* **ped'ately.**—*adj.* **pedatifid** (*pi-dat'i-fid*), divided in a pedate manner, but having the divisions connected at the base. [L. *pedātus*, footed—*pēs, pedis*, foot.]

**pedder**, *ped'ər*, **pether**, *pedh'ər*, (now *Scot.*) *n.* a pedlar.—**pedd'er-coffe** (prob. *kŏv*; *Scot* after *David Lyndsay*); **cove** (2)). [App.—**ped** (1).]

**peddle**, *ped'l*, *v.i.* to go about as a pedlar: to trifle.—*v.t.* to sell or offer as a pedlar.—*n.* (esp. *U.S.*) **pedd'ler.**—*adj.* **pedd'ling**, unimportant.— *n.* the trade or tricks of a pedlar. [App. partly a back-formation from **pedlar**, partly from **piddle**.]

**pederasty**, etc. See **paed(o)-**.

**pederero**, *ped-ə-rā'rō*, *n.* an old gun for discharging stones, pieces of iron, etc., also for firing salutes.—Also **padere'ro, patere'ro, pedre'ro**, etc. [Sp. *pedrero*—L. *petra*, stone—Gr. *petrā*.]

**pedesis**, *ped-ē'sis*, *n.* Brownian movement.—*adj.* **pedetic** (*pi-det'ik*). [Gr. *pēdēsis*, jumping.]

**pedestal**, *ped'is-tl*, *n.* the support of a column, statue, vase, etc.: the fixed casting which holds the brasses in which a shaft turns, called also *axle-guard* or *pillow-block*.—*v.t.* to place on a pedestal.—*adj.* **ped'estalled.** [Fr. *piédestal*—It. *piedistallo*, for *piè di stallo*, foot of a stall—*piè*, foot (L. *pēs, pedis*), *di*, of (L. *dē*), *stallo*, stall (see **stall**).]

**pedestrian**, *pi-des'tri-ən*, *adj.* on foot: of walking: not mounted on Pegasus, hence prosaic, uninspired: flat or commonplace.—*n.* a walker: one who practises feats of walking or running. —*v.i.* **pedestrianise, -ize**, to walk.—*v.t.* to convert (street) to use by pedestrians only.—*n.* **pedestrianisā'tion, -z-.**—*n.* **pedes'trianism**, walking, esp. as an exercise or athletic performance: pedestrian quality (*fig.*). [L. *pedester, -tris*—*pēs, pedis*.]

**pedetentous**, *ped-i-ten'təs*, *adj.* proceeding slowly. [L. *pedentim, -temptim*—*pēs, pedis*, foot, *temptāre*, *-ātum*, to make trial of.]

**pediatrics**. See **paed(o)-**.

**pedicab**, *ped'i-kab*, *n.* a light vehicle consisting of a tricycle with the addition of a seat, usu. behind, covered by a hood, for passenger(s). [L. *pēs, pedis*, the foot and **cab**.]

**pedicel**, *ped'i-sel*, *n.* the stalk of a single flower in an inflorescence: the stalk of a sedentary animal: the stalk of an animal organ, e.g. a crab's eye.—*n.* **pedicellā'ria**, a stalked (or sessile) bladed snapping forceps on the surface

of a starfish or sea-urchin:—*pl.* **pedicellã´riae.**
—*adj.* **ped´icellate** (or *-dis´*, or *-sel´*), provided
with a pedicel. [Botanists' dim. of L. *pēs, pedis,*
the foot.]
**pedicle,** *ped´i-kl, n.* a little stalk.—*adjs.* **ped´icled;**
**pedic´ūlate,** stalked: belonging to the **Pedicu-
lā´tī,** the angler-fish order, whose pectoral fins
have a wrist-like articulation; **pedic´ulated.** [L.
*pediculus,* a little foot—*pēs, pedis,* foot.]
**Pediculus,** *pi-dik´ū-los, n.* the louse genus: a
louse.—*adj.* **pedic´ular,** of lice: lousy.—*ns.* **Pedi-
culā´ris,** the lousewort genus; **pediculā´tion,**
**pediculō´sis,** lousiness.—*adj.* **pedic´ulous,** lousy.
[L. *pēdiculus,* dim. of *pēdis,* a louse.]
**pedicure,** *ped´i-kūr, n.* the treatment of corns,
bunions, or the like: one who treats the feet.—
*v.t.* to apply foot-treatment to.—*n.* **ped´icurist.**
[L. *pēs, pedis,* foot, *cūra,* care.]
**pedigree,** *ped´i-grē, n.* a line of ancestors: a
scheme or record of ancestry: lineage: genealogy: distinguished and ancient lineage: derivation, descent: succession, series, set.—*adj.* of
known descent, pure-bred, and of good stock.—
*adj.* **ped´igreed,** having a pedigree. [App. Fr.
*pied de grue,* crane's-foot, from the arrow-head
figure in a stemma.]
**pediment,** *ped´i-mant, (archit.) n.* a triangular
structure crowning the front of a Greek building,
less steeply sloped than a gable: in later architecture a similar structure, triangular, rounded,
etc., over a portico, door, window, or niche.—
*adjs.* **pedimental** (*-ment´l*); **ped´imented,** furnished with a pediment: like a pediment.
[Earlier *periment,* prob. for **pyramid.**]
**pedipalp,** *ped´i-palp, n.* the second paired appendage in Arachnida (also **pedipalp´us**): a
whip-scorpion.—*ns.pl.* **Pedipalp´i, Pedipalp´ida,**
the whip-scorpions, an order of Arachnida with
large pedipalps. [L. *pēs, pedis,* foot, *palpus,*
stroking, in L.L. a feeler.]
**pedlar,** *ped´lar, n.* one who goes about with a
pack of goods for sale (technically, one who
carries it himself—distinguished from a *hawker,*
who has a horse and cart, etc.): one who peddles.
—*n.* **ped´lary,** the wares or occupation of a
pedlar. [Prob. from **pedder,** with inserted *l,* as
in **tinkler** from **tinker.**]
**pedo-.** See **paed(o)-.**
**pedology,** *ped-ol´a-ji, n.* the study of soils.—*adj.*
**pedological** (*-a-loj´*).—*n.* **pedol´ogist.** [Gr. *pedion,*
ground, *logos,* discourse.]
**pedometer,** *pid-om´i-tar, n.* an instrument for
counting paces and so approximately measuring
distance walked. [L. *pēs, pedis,* foot—Gr.
*metron,* measure.]
**pedrail,** *ped´rāl, n.* a tractor with foot-like pieces
on the circumference of its wheels: one of the
pieces so used. [L. *pēs, pedis,* foot, and **rail.**]
**pedrero,** *ped-rā´rō.* Same as **pederero.**
**peduncle,** *pi-dung´kl, n.* the stalk of an inflorescence or of a solitary flower: the stalk by which
a sedentary animal is attached: a narrow stalk-
like connecting part: a tract of white fibres
in the brain.—*adjs.* **pedun´cular, pedun´culate, -d.**
[Botanists' L. *pedunculus*—L. *pēs, pedis,* the
foot.]
**pee,** *pē, n.* the sixteenth letter of the alphabet (P,
p.).
**pee,** *pē, v.i.* to urinate.—Also *n.* [For **piss.**]
**peece,** an obsolete spelling of **piece.**
**peek,** *pēk, n.* a peep.—*v.i.* to peep.—*n.* **peek´abo(o)´,**
a child's peeping game. [Origin obscure.]
**peel,** *pēl, v.t.* to pill, pillage, plunder (*obs.*): to
strip off the skin, bark, or other covering from:
to strip off: to cause (someone else's ball) to go
through a hoop (*croquet*).—*v.i.* to come off as
the skin: to lose the skin: to undress (*coll.*).—
*n.* rind, esp. that of oranges, lemons, etc., in the
natural state or candied.—*adj.* **peeled,** pillaged:
bald: tonsured: stripped of skin, rind, or bark.

—*ns.* **peel´er,** one who peels: a plunderer: a
plant that impoverishes the soil: an instrument
or machine for peeling or decorticating; **peel´-
ing,** the act of stripping: a piece, strip, or shred
stripped off: the removing of the layers of a
paper overlay, to get a lighter impression (*print.*).
—**peel-and-eat´** (*Scot.*), potatoes served in their
jackets.—Also *adj.*—**pack and,** or, **peel,** to have
dealings (with; *Scott*); **peel off,** (*aero.*) to
leave a flying formation by a particular manoeuvre: (of ship) to veer away from a convoy.
[O.E. *pilian*—L. *pilāre,* to deprive of hair—*pilus,*
a hair; perh. influenced by Fr. *peler,* to skin; cf.
**pill** (2).]
**peel,** *pēl, n.* a stake (*obs.*): a palisaded enclosure
(*hist.*): a peel-house.—**peel´-house, peel´-tower,**
orig. a fortified dwelling-house, usually entered
by ladder to the first floor, with vaulted ground
floor for cattle, common on the Borders: now
loosely used. [A.Fr. *pel*—L. *pālus,* stake.]
**peel,** *pēl, n.* a shovel, esp. a baker's wooden
shovel: an instrument for hanging up paper to
dry: the blade of an oar (*U.S.*). [O.Fr. *pele*—
L. *pāla,* a spade.]
**peel.** Same as **peal** (fish).
**peeler,** *pēl´ar, n.* a policeman, from Sir R. *Peel*
who established the Irish police (1812-18) and
improved those in Britain (1828-30).—*n.* **Peel´ite,**
a follower of Peel in the reform of the Corn-laws
in 1846.
**peen, pean,** *pēn,* **pane, pān,** *n.* the end of a hammer-
head opposite the hammering face.—*v.t.* to
strike or work with a peen. [Origin uncertain;
cf. Norw. *pen,* Ger. *pinne,* Fr. *panne.*]
**peenge,** *pēnj, pēnzh,* (*Scot.*) *v.i.* to whine like a
peevish child. [Perh. based on **whinge.**]
**peeoy, pioy, pioye,** *pē-ō´i,* (*Scot.*) *n.* a home-made
firework, a cone of damp gunpowder.
**peep,** *pēp, v.i.* to cheep like a chicken.—*n.* a high
feeble sound.—*n.* **peep´er,** a young bird: a tree-
frog (*U.S.*). [Imit.; cf. **pipe,** L. *pipāre,* Fr.
*pépier,* Ger. *piepen, piepsen,* to cheep, Gr. *pipos,*
a young bird.]
**peep,** *pēp, v.i.* to look through a narrow opening:
to look out from concealment: to look slyly,
surreptitiously, or cautiously: to be just showing: to begin to appear.—*v.t.* to put forth from
concealment as if to take a view: to direct as
if to view.—*n.* a sly look: a beginning to appear:
a speck of light or flame: a glimpse: a slit:
an eye (*slang*).—*n.* **peep´er,** one that peeps: a
prying person: the eye (*slang*): a glass, for
various purposes (*slang*).—**peep´-hole,** a hole
through which one may look without being
seen; **peeping Tom,** a prying fellow, esp. one
who peeps in at windows; **peep´-show,** a small
show viewed through a small hole, usually
fitted with a magnifying glass; **peep´-sight,** a
back-sight with a small hole.—*adj.* **peep´-
through,** allowing of being seen through.—**peep´-
toe,** a shoe cut away so as to show the toe.—
**Peep-o'-day Boys,** an Ulster Protestant society
(1780-95) opposed to the Catholic *Defenders;*
**peep of day,** the first appearance of light in the
morning. [Origin obscure.]
**peep, peepe,** *pēp,* (*Shak.*) *n.* earlier forms of **pip**
(3).
**peer,** *pēr, n.* an equal: a fellow: an antagonist
(*Spens.*): a nobleman of the rank of baron upward: a member of the House of Lords: one
of Charlemagne's paladins: a member of any
similar body.—*fem.* **peer´ess.**—*v.t.* **peer,** to
equal: to confer a peerage on (*coll.*).—*v.i.* to
rank as equal.—*adj.* (of a group in society) like in
age or in some other unifying character: pertaining
to a peer group.—*n.* **peer´age,** the rank or dignity
of a peer: the body of peers: a book of the
genealogy, etc., of the different peers.—*adj.* **peer´-
less,** unequalled: matchless.—*adv.* **peer´lessly.**—
*n.* **peer´lessness.**—**House of Peers,** the House of

Lords; **spiritual peer,** a bishop or archbishop qualified to sit in the House of Lords; **temporal peer,** any other member. [O.Fr. (Fr. *pair*)—L. *pār, paris,* equal.]

**peer,** *pēr, v.i.* to look narrowly or closely: to look with strain, or with half-closed eyes: to peep: to appear.—*v.t.* to protrude.—*adj.* **peer′y,** inclined to peer: prying: sly. [Origin unknown: perh. partly M.E. *piren* (cf. L.G. *piren*), influenced by *pere,* aphetic form of **appear,** partly from *pere* itself.]

**peerie, peery,** *pēr′i,* (*Scot.*) *n.* a pear-shaped wooden peg-top. [App. **pear,** pron. *pēr* in Scots.]

**peesweep,** *pēz′wēp.* See **peewit.**

**peetweet,** *pēt′wēt,* (*U.S.*) *n.* the spotted sandpiper. [Imit.]

**peever,** *pē′vǝr, n.* a tile, slab, or can-lid used in playing hop-scotch: (in *pl.*) hop-scotch.

**peevish,** *pēv′ish, adj.* foolish (*obs.*): vexatious (*obs.*): perverse (*Shak.*): wayward: fretful.— *v.t.* **peeve** (back-formation), to irritate.—*v.i.* to be fretful: to show fretfulness.—*n.* a fretful mood: a grievance, grouse.—*adv.* **peev′ishly.**— *n.* **peev′ishness.** [Origin unknown.]

**peewit, pewit,** *pē′wit,* also *pū′it, n.* the lapwing: its cry.—(*Scot.*) **pees′weep, pease′weep, pee′wee.** [Imit.]

**peg,** *peg, n.* a pin (esp. of wood): a fixture for hanging a hat or coat on: a pin for tuning a string: a small stake for securing tent-ropes, marking a position, boundary, claim, etc.: a pin for scoring as in cribbage: a pin in a cup to show how far down one may drink: hence a drink, esp. of brandy and soda: a degree or step: a wooden or other pin used in shoemaking: a turtle harpoon: a clothes-peg: a peg-top: a wooden leg (*coll.*): a leg (*coll.*): a poke or thrust (*dial.* or *slang*): a theme (*fig.*).—*v.t.* to fasten, mark, score, furnish, pierce, or strike with a peg or pegs: to insert or fix like a peg: to score (as at cribbage): to keep from falling or rising by buying or selling at a fixed price (*stock-exchange*): to stabilise: to drive (*slang*): to throw.—*v.i.* to keep on working assiduously: to make one's way vigorously:—*pr.p.* **pegg′ing;** *pa.t.* and *pa.p.* **pegged.**—*adj.* **pegged.**—*n.* **pegg′-ing.**—**peg′board,** a board having holes into which pegs are placed, used for playing and scoring in games or for display purposes; **peg′-box,** part of the head of a musical instrument in which the pegs are inserted; **peg′-leg,** a simple wooden leg: a man with a wooden leg; **peg′-tank′ard,** a drinking-vessel having each one's share marked off by a knob; **peg′-top,** a top with a metal point, spun by winding a string round it and suddenly throwing it: (in *pl.*) trousers narrowing at the ankles.—*adj.* shaped like a top.—**a peg too low,** tipsy: depressed; **peg away,** to work on assiduously; **peg out,** in croquet, to finish by driving the ball against the peg: in cribbage, to win by pegging the last hole before show of hands: to mark off with pegs: to become exhausted, be ruined, or die (*slang*); **round peg in a square hole** or **square peg in a round hole,** one who is unsuited to the particular position he occupies; **take down a peg,** to take down, to humble, to snub. [Cf. L.G. *pigge,* Du. dial. *peg,* Dan. *pig.*]

**Pegasus,** *peg′ǝ-sǝs, n.* the winged horse that sprang from Medusa's blood, by later writers associated with the Muses: hence, an embodiment of the power that raises a poet's imagination above the earth: a genus of small fishes superficially like sea-horses, of the coasts of Asia and Australia, with large, wing-like, pectoral fins: one of the constellations in the northern sky.—*adj.* **Pegasē′an.** [L. *Pēgasus*— Gr. *Pēgasos.*]

**peggy,** *peg′i, n.* a small warbler of various kinds —the white-throat, etc.: a washerwoman's dolly:

a size of roofing slate, 10 by 14 in. [Hypocoristic from *Margaret.*]

**pegh, Peght.** See **pech, Pecht.**

**pegmatite,** *peg′mǝ-tit, n.* graphic granite: a very coarsely crystallised granite, as in dykes and veins: any very coarse-grained igneous rock occurring in like manner.—*adj.* **pegmatitic** (-*tit′ik*). [Gr. *pēgma,* a bond, framework, from the root of *pēgnynai,* to fasten.]

**Pehlevi,** *pā′le-vē,* **Pahlavi,** *pä′lä-vē, n.* an ancient West Iranian idiom of the Sassanide period (3rd-7th cent. A.D.), largely mixed with Semitic words: the characters used in writing it.—Also *adj.* [Pers. *Pahlavi,* Parthian.]

**peignoir,** *pen-wär, n.* a woman's dressing-gown, esp. one worn when combing the hair: loosely, a morning-gown. [Fr.,—*peigner*—L. *pectināre,* to comb.]

**peinct,** *pānt,* an obsolete spelling of **paint.**

**peine forte et dure,** *pen fört ä dür,* (Fr.) strong and severe punishment, a kind of judicial torture.

**peirastic,** *pī-ras′tik, adj.* experimental: tentative. —*adv.* **peiras′tically.** [Gr. *peirastikos*—*peira,* a trial.]

**peise, peize, pease, peaze, peyse,** *pāz, pēz,* (*obs.*) *n.* weight: a weight: a balance: a blow (*Spens.*). —*v.t.* to balance (*Spens., Shak.*): to poise (*Spens.*): to put weights on, weigh down (*Shak.*).—*v.i.* (*Spens.*) to press or settle downwards. [O.Fr. *peis,* weight, *peser,* to weigh; cf. **poise.**]

**pejorate,** *pē′jǝr-āt, pi′, v.t.* to make worse.—*n.* **pejorā′tion,** a making or becoming worse: deterioration.—*adj.* **pe′jorative** (or -*jor′*), depreciating, disparaging.—*n.* a depreciating word or suffix.—*adv.* **pē′joratively.** [L. *pējor,* worse.]

**pekan,** *pek′ǝn, n.* the wood-shock, a large North American marten. [Canadian Fr. *pékan*— Algonquin *pékané.*]

**Pekingese, Pekinese,** *pē-kin(g)-ēz′, adj.* of *Peking,* China.—*n.* a native or inhabitant of Peking: the chief dialect of Mandarin: a dwarf pug-dog of a breed brought from Peking (also abbrev. **peke).**—**Peking man,** a type of fossil man first found (1929) S.W. of Peking, related to Java man.

**pekoe,** *pēk′ō, pek′ō, n.* a scented black tea. [Chin. *pek-ho,* white down.]

**pela,** *pā′lä, n.* white wax from a scale-insect. [Chin. *peh-la,* white wax.]

**pelage,** *pel′ij, n.* a beast's coat of hair or wool. [Fr.]

**Pelagian,** *pi-lā′ji-ǝn, n.* a follower of *Pelagius,* a 5th-cent. British monk, who denied original sin.—Also *adj.*—*n.* **Pelā′gianism.**

**pelagic,** *pi-laj′ik, adj.* oceanic: of, inhabiting, or carried out in, the deep or open sea: living in the surface waters or middle depths of the sea: deposited under deep-water conditions.—*adj.* **pelagian,** *pi-lā′ji-ǝn,* pelagic.—*n.* a pelagic animal. [Gr. *pelagos,* sea.]

**Pelargonium,** *pel-ǝr-gō′ni-ǝm, n.* a vast genus of the geranium family, often cultivated under the name of geranium. [Gr. *pelargos,* stork, the beaked capsules resembling a stork's head.]

**Pelasgic,** *pe-las′jik, adj.* pertaining to the *Pelasgians* or *Pelasgi,* prehistoric inhabitants of Greece, of unknown affinities.—Also **Pelas′gian.**—**Pelasgian architecture,** cyclopean architecture.

**Pele,** *pā′lā, n.* the Hawaiian volcano goddess.— **Pele's hair,** volcanic glass drawn out into threads as it flies through the air.

**pele,** a Spenserian spelling of **peal.**

**Pelecypoda,** *pel-e-sip′ǝ-dǝ, n.pl.* the Lamellibranchs. [Gr. *pelekys,* axe, *pous, podos,* foot.]

**pelerine,** *pel′ǝ-rin, -rēn, n.* a woman's tippet or cape, esp. one with long ends coming down in front. [Fr. *pèlerine,* tippet, pilgrim (fem.); see **pilgrim.**]

**pelf,** *pelf, n.* riches (in a bad sense): money. [O.Fr. *pelfre,* booty; cf. **pilfer.**]

Neutral vowels in unaccented syllables: *el′ǝ-mǝnt;* for certain sounds in foreign words, see p. viii

**pelham,** *pel'əm* (often *cap.*), *n.* a type of bit, a combination of the curb and snaffle designs. [Perh. name *Pelham.*]

**pelican,** *pel'i-kən, n.* a large water-fowl, with enormous pouched bill, fabled in the Middle Ages to wound its breast and feed its young with its blood: an alembic with beaks that lead back to the body—used for continuous distillation: a dentist's beaked instrument: an old species of ordnance, or its shot.—**pel'ican-fish,** a deep-sea fish (Eurypharynx) with enormous mouth and very little body; **pel'ican-flower,** the goose-flower, an Aristolochia with a gigantic flower; **pel'ican's-foot',** a marine gasteropod mollusc (*Aporrhais pes-pelicani*): its shell, with a lip like a webbed foot.—**pelican in her piety** (*her.*), a pelican with wings distended, feeding her young with her blood. [L.L. *pelicānus*— Gr. *pelekan, -ānos,* pelican; cf. *pelekās, -āntos,* a woodpecker, and *pelekys,* an axe.]

**pelisse,** *pe-lēs', n.* orig. a fur-lined or fur garment, esp. a military cloak: a lady's long mantle: formerly, a young child's out-of-door coat. [Fr.,—L.L. *pellicea* (*vestis*)—L. *pellis,* a skin.]

**pelite,** *pē'lit, n.* any rock derived from clay or mud.—*adj.* **pēlitic** (-*lit'ik*).—*ns.* **pē'loid,** any naturally produced medium used in medical practice as a cataplasm; **pēlol'ogy; pēlother'apy,** treatment by mud baths and the like. [Gr. *pēlos,* clay, mud.]

**pell,** *pel,* (*obs.*) *n.* a skin or hide: a roll of parchment. [O.Fr. *pel* (Fr. *peau*)—L. *pellis,* a skin or hide.]

**pellach, pellack.** See pellock.

**pellagra,** *pel-ag'rə, -āg'rə, n.* a deadly deficiency disease marked by shrivelled skin, wasted body, and insanity.—*n.* **pellag'rin,** one afflicted with pellagra.—*adj.* **pellag'rous,** connected with, like, or afflicted with, pellagra. [Gr. *pella,* skin, *agrā,* seizure; or It. *pelle agra,* rough skin.]

**pellet,** *pel'it, n.* a little ball: a small rounded boss: a small pill: a ball of shot: a mass of undigested refuse thrown up by a hawk or owl. —*v.t.* to form into pellets (*Shak.*): to hit or pelt with pellets. [O.Fr. *pelote*—L. *pīla,* a ball.]

**pellicle,** *pel'i-kl, n.* a thin skin or film: a film or scum on liquors.—*adj.* **pellic'ūlar.** [L. *pellicula,* dim. of *pellis,* skin.]

**pellitory,** *pel'i-tə-ri, n.* a plant (*Parietaria officinalis*) of the nettle family, growing on old walls (called *pellitory of the wall*), or other member of the genus.—cf. **pellitory** (2). [L. (*herba*) *parietāria* —*parietārius—pariēs, parietis,* a wall.]

**pellitory,** *pel'i-tə-ri, n.* a North African and South European plant (*Anacyclus pyrethrum*), known as *pellitory of Spain,* akin to camomile: extended to various similar plants, as yarrow, feverfew.—cf. **pellitory** (1). [M.E. *peletre*—L. *pyrethrum*—Gr. *pyrethron,* pellitory of Spain; see **pyrethrum.**]

**pell-mell,** *pel'-mel', adv.* confusedly, promiscuously: headlong: helter-skelter: vehemently. —*adj.* confusedly mingled: promiscuous, indiscriminate: headlong.—*n.* disorder: confused mingling: a hand-to-hand fight. [O.Fr. *pesle-mesle* (Fr. *pêle-mêle*).—*mesle* being from O.Fr. *mesler* (Fr. *mêler*), to mix—L.L. *misculāre* —L. *miscēre;* and *pesle,* a rhyming addition, perh. influenced by Fr. *pelle,* shovel.]

**pellock, pellack,** *pel'ək,* **pellach,** *pel'əhh,* (*Scot.*) *n.* a porpoise. [Origin unknown.]

**pellucid,** *pe-lū'sid, -loo'sid adj.* perfectly clear: transparent.—*ns.* **pellucid'ity, pellu'cidness.**—*adv.* **pellu'cidly.** [L. *pellūcidus—per,* through, *lūcidus,* clear—*lūcēre,* to shine.]

**pelma,** *pel'mə, n.* the sole of the foot.—*adj.* **pelmatic** (-*mat'ik*).—*n.pl.* **Pelmatozō'a,** a division of the Echinodermata, typically stalked, including crinoids and the fossil blastoids and cystoids. [Gr. *pelma, -atos,* sole, stalk.]

**pelmet,** *pel'mit, n.* a fringe, valance, or other device hiding a curtain rod. [Perh. Fr. *palmette.*]

**Pelopid,** *pel'ō-pid,* a descendant of *Pelops,* son of Tantalus, and grandfather of Agamemnon and Menelaus.

**Peloponnesian,** *pel-ō-pə-nē'sh(y)ən, -zh(y)ən, -zyən, adj.* of the *Peloponnesus* or Peloponnese, the southern peninsula of Greece.—*n.* a native thereof.—**Peloponnesian War,** a war between Athens and Sparta, 431-404 B.C. [Gr. *Peloponnēsos,* Peloponnese—*Pelops* (see foregoing), *nēsos,* an island.]

**peloria,** *pi-lō'ri-ə, -lō'ri-ə, n.* regularity in a normally irregular flower.—Also **pelorism** (*pel'ərizm*), **pel'ory.**—*adjs.* **peloric** (*pi-lor'ik*), **pel'orised.** [Gr. *pelōr,* a monster.]

**pelorus,** *pel-ōr'əs, -ōr', n.* a kind of compass. [Perh. *Pelorus,* Hannibal's pilot.]

**pelota,** *pel-ō'ta, n.* a ball-game resembling fives, of Basque origin. [Sp. *pelota,* ball.]

**pelt,** *pelt, n.* a raw hide: a hawk's prey when killed, especially when torn.—*n.* **pelt'ry,** the skins of animals with the fur on them: furs.— **pelt'monger,** a dealer in skins. [App. a backformation from *peltry*—O.Fr. *pelleterie*—L. *pellis,* a skin.]

**pelt,** *pelt, v.t.* to assail (formerly with repeated blows, now usu.) with showers of missiles, or of words, reproaches, pamphlets, etc.: to drive by showers of missiles: to shower.—*v.i.* to shower blows or missiles: to beat vigorously, as rain, hail: to speak angrily: to speed.—*n.* a blow: a pelting: a downpour, as of rain: a storm of rage: a rapid pace.—*n.* **pelt'er,** one who or that which pelts: a shower of missiles: a sharp storm of rain, of anger, etc.—*v.i.* to go full pelt: to pelt (*dial.*).—*n.* and *adj.* **pelt'ing.**— **full pelt,** at full speed. [Origin obscure.]

**pelta,** *pel'ta,* (*ant.*) *n.* a light buckler.—*n.* **peltast** (*pelt'ast*), a light-armed Greek soldier with a pelta.—*adj.* **pelt'ate** (*bot.*), having the stalk attached not to the edge but near the middle of the under surface. [L.,—Gr. *peltē.*]

**pelting,** *pel'ting,* (*Shak.*) *adj.* paltry, contemptible. —*adv.* **pelt'ingly.** [App. conn. with **paltry.**]

**Pelton-wheel,** *pel'tn-(h)wēl', n.* a water-wheel with specially shaped cups around the circumference into which one or more jets of water are aimed at high speed, invented by Lester Allen *Pelton,* American engineer (1829-1908).

**pelvis,** *pel'vis, n.* the bony cavity at the lower end of the trunk, of which the part above the plane through the promontory of the sacrum and the pubic symphysis is the *false pelvis,* the part below the *true pelvis:* the bony frame enclosing it: the cavity of the kidney: the basal part of a crinoid cup:—*pl.* **pel'ves** (-*vēz*).—*adjs.* **pel'vic; pel'viform,** basin-shaped.—*ns.* **pelvim'eter,** an instrument for measuring the pelvis; **pelvim'etry.** —**pelvic fin,** a fish's paired fin homologous with a mammal's hindleg; **pelvic girdle,** or **arch,** the posterior limb-girdle of vertebrates, with which the hind-limbs articulate, consisting of the haunch-bones (ilium, pubis and ischium united), which articulate with the sacrum. [L. *pelvis,* a basin.]

**pembroke,** *pem'brŏōk, n.* (in full **pembroke table**) a small four-legged table with hinged flaps. [App. from *Pembroke,* in Wales.]

**pemmican, pemican,** *pem'i-kən, n.* a North American Indian preparation of lean flesh-meat, dried, pounded, and mixed with fat and other ingredients: highly condensed information or reading-matter (*fig.*). [Cree *pimekan.*]

**pemphigus,** *pem'fi-gəs, n.* an affection of the skin with watery vesicles.—*adjs.* **pem'phigoid, pem'-phigous.** [False Latin—Gr. *pemphix, -igos,* blister.]

**pen,** *pen, n.* a small enclosure, esp. for animals: a West Indian farm or plantation: a dam or weir: animals kept in, and enough to fill, a pen.—*v.t.* to put or keep in a pen: to confine: to dam:—*pr.p.* penn'ing; *pa.t.* and *pa.p.* penned or pent.—pen'fold, a fold for penning cattle or sheep: a pound.—submarine pen, a dock for a submarine, esp. if protected from attack from above by a deep covering of concrete. [O.E. *penn,* pen.]

pen, *pen, n.* a large feather: a flight-feather: a quill: a cuttle-bone: an instrument used for writing (with ink or otherwise), formerly made of a quill, but now of other materials: a nib: a nib with a holder: writing: literary style: an author.—*v.t.* to write, to commit to paper: —*pr.p.* penn'ing; *pa.t.* and *pa.p.* penned.—*n.* pen'ful, as much ink as a pen can take at a dip: as much as the reservoir of a fountain-pen can hold: what one can write with one dip of ink. —*adj.* penned, written: quilled.—*n.* penn'er (*arch.*), a case for carrying pens.—*n.* pen'-and-ink', writing materials: a pen drawing.—*adj.* writing: written: executed with pen and ink, as a drawing.—pen'-case, a receptacle for a pen or pens; pen'craft, penmanship: the art of composition; pen'-driver, a clerk; pen'-feather, a quill feather: pin-feather (*dial.*).—*adj.* pen'-feathered.—pen'-friend, -pal, an otherwise unknown person (*usu.* abroad) with whom one corresponds; pen'-gun, (*Scot.*), a popgun made of a quill; pen'holder, a rod on which a nib may be fixed; pen'knife, orig. a knife for making or mending pens: a small pocket-knife; pen'-man, one skilled in handwriting: a writer or author:—*fem.* pen'woman; pen'manship; pen'-name, a writer's assumed name; pen'-nib, a nib for a pen; pen'-wiper, a piece of cloth, leather, etc., for wiping ink from pens.—talk like a pen-gun, to chatter volubly. [O.Fr. *penne*—L. *penna,* a feather.]

pen, slang abbrev. of penitentiary.

pen, *pen, n.* a female swan. [Origin unknown.]

penal, *pē'nl, adj.* pertaining to, liable to, imposing, constituting, or used for, punishment: constituting a penalty: very severe.—*n.* pēnalisā'tion, -z-.—*v.t.* pē'nalise, -ize, to make punishable: to put under a disadvantage.—*adv.* pē'nally.—penal laws, laws imposing penalties, esp. (*hist.*) in matters of religion; penal servitude, hard labour in a prison under different conditions from ordinary imprisonment, substituted in 1853 for transportation, abolished 1948; penal settlement, a settlement peopled by convicts. [L. *poenālis*—*poena*—Gr. *poinē,* punishment.]

penalty, *pen'l-ti, n.* punishment: suffering or loss imposed for breach of a law: a fine or loss agreed upon in case of non-fulfilment of some undertaking: a fine: a disadvantage imposed upon a competitor for breach of a rule of the game, for want of success in attaining what is aimed at, as a handicap, or for any other reason arising out of the rules: a loss or suffering brought upon one by one's own actions or condition: a score for an opponent's failure to make his contract or for the bidder's success when the call is doubled (*bridge*).—penalty goal, one scored by a penalty kick; penalty kick, a free kick, or the privilege granted to a player to kick the ball as he pleases, because of some breach of the rules by the opposing side; penalty line, the boundary of the penalty area. —death penalty, punishment by putting to death.—under, or on, penalty of, with liability in case of infraction to the penalty of. [L.L. *poenālitās*; see foregoing.]

penance, *pen'əns, n.* repentance (*obs.*): an act of mortification undertaken voluntarily or imposed by a priest to manifest sorrow for sin: the sacrament by which absolution is conveyed (involving contrition, confession, and satisfaction; *R.C.* and *Orthodox*): expiation: punishment (*Milt.*):

hardship.—*v.t.* to impose penance on. [O.Fr.; cf. penitence.]

Penang-lawyer, *pē-nang'-lö'yər, n.* a walking stick made from the stem of a prickly dwarf palm (*Licuala acutifida*): misapplied to a Malacca cane. [*Penang,* its place of origin, and lawyer, or poss. from Malay *pinang liyar,* wild areca, or *pinang láyor,* fire-dried areca.]

penannular, *pen-an'ū-lər,* or pēn-, *adj.* in the form of an almost complete ring. [L. *paene,* almost, *annulāris,* annular.]

penates, *pe-nā'tēz, pe-nä'tāz, n.pl.* the household gods of a Roman family. [L. *penātēs,* prob. from the root found in *penus,* provisions, storeroom, *penes,* in the house of, *penetrāre,* to penetrate.]

pence, *pens, n.* a plural of penny.

penchant, *pā-shā, n.* inclination: decided taste: bias. [Fr., *pr.p.* of *pencher,* to incline—assumed L.L. *pendicāre*—L. *pendēre,* to hang.]

pencil, *pen'sl, n.* a fine paint-brush: a small tuft of hairs: a writing or drawing instrument that leaves a streak of blacklead, chalk, slate, or other solid matter, esp. one of blacklead enclosed in wood and sharpened as required: a small stick of various materials shaped like a lead-pencil, for medical, cosmetic, or other purpose: the art of painting or drawing: a system of straight lines meeting in a point (*geom.*): a set of rays of light diverging from or converging to a point: a narrow beam of light.—*v.t.* to paint, draw, write, or mark with a pencil: to apply a pencil to:—*pr.p.* pen'cilling; *pa.t.* and *pa.p.* pen'cilled.—*adj.* pen'cilled, painted, drawn, written or marked with a pencil: marked as if with a pencil: showing fine concentric streaking: having pencils of rays: radiated: tufted.—*ns.* pen'ciller; pen'cilling, the art or act of painting, writing, sketching, or marking with a pencil: marks made with a pencil: fine lines on flowers or feathers: a sketch: the marking of joints in brickwork with white paint.—pen'cil-case, a case for pencils: metal case receiving a movable piece of blacklead or the like, used as a pencil; pen'cil-ce'dar, juniper of various kinds suitable for lead-pencils; pen'cil-com'pass, a compass having a pencil on one of its legs; pen'cil-lead, graphite for pencils: a stick of it for a metal pencil-case; pen'cil-ore, radiating botryoidal graphite; pen'cil-sharpener, an instrument for sharpening lead-pencils by rotation against a blade; pen'cil-sketch; pen'cil-stone, a pyrophyllite used for making slate-pencils. [O.Fr. *pincel* (Fr. *pinceau*)—L. *pēnicillum,* a painter's brush, dim. of *pēnis,* a tail.]

pend, *pend,* (*Scot.*) *n.* a vaulted passage: a vaulted entrance to a passageway. [L. *pendēre,* to hang.]

pend, *pend, v.i.* to hang, as in a balance, to impend.—*adj.* pend'ing, hanging: impending: remaining undecided: not terminated.—*prep.* during: until, awaiting. [Fr. *pendre* or L. *pendēre* to hang; sometimes aphetic for append or for depend.]

pend, an old spelling of penned, from pen (1) or pen (2).

pendant, sometimes pendent, *pen'dənt, n.* anything hanging, especially for ornament: a hanging ornament worn on the neck: the hanging (esp. decorated) end of a waist-belt: an earring: a lamp hanging from the roof: an ornament of wood or of stone hanging downwards from a roof: a pennant: a pendant-post: anything attached to another thing of the same kind, an appendix: a companion picture, poem, etc.—*n.* pen'dency, undecided state: droop.—*adj.* pen'dent, sometimes pen'dant, hanging: dangling: drooping: overhanging: not yet decided: grammatically incomplete, left in suspense.—*n.* pendentive (*-dent'-*), a spherical triangle formed

Neutral vowels in unaccented syllables: *el'ə-mənt*; for certain sounds in foreign words, see p. viii

by a dome springing from a square base (*archit.*): part of a groined vault resting on one pier.—*adv.* pen´dently.—*ns.* pen´dicle, a pendant: a dependency or appendage: something attached to another, as a privilege, or a small piece of ground for cultivation; pen´dicler, the tenant of a pendicle.—pen´dant-post, a post placed against a wall, usu. resting on a corbel or capital, with a tie-beam or hammer-beam fixed to its upper end. [Fr. *pendant*, pr.p. of *pendre*, to hang—L. *pendēns*, *-entis*—pr.p. of *pendēre*, to hang.]

**pendente lite**, *pen-den´tē li´tē*, *pen-den´te li´te*, (L.) during the process of litigation.

**pendragon**, *pen-drag´ən*, *n.* an ancient British supreme chief.—*n.* pendrag´onship. [W. *pen*, head, *dragon*, a dragon, dragon-standard.]

**pendulum**, *pen´dū-ləm*, *n.* theoretically, a heavy material point suspended by a weightless thread, free to swing without friction (*simple pendulum*): any weight so hung from a fixed point as to swing freely (*compound pendulum*): the swinging weight which regulates the movement of a clock: anything that swings or is free to swing to and fro:—*pl.* pen´dulums.—*adj.* pen´dular, relating to a pendulum.—*v.i.* pen´dulate, to swing, vibrate.—*adj.* pen´duline, building a pendulous nest.—*n.* pendulos´ity.—*adj.* pen´dulous, hanging loosely: swinging freely: drooping: dangling: overhanging: suspended from the top: floating in air or space.—*adv.* pen´dulously.—*n.* pen´dulousness.—compensation pendulum, a pendulum so constructed that its rod is not much altered in length by changes of temperature. [Neut. of L. *pendulus*, hanging—*pendēre*, to hang.]

**Peneian**, *pē-nē´ən*, *adj.* relating to the river *Pēnēus* in the famous Vale of Tempe in Thessaly. [Gr. *Pēnēios*, now Salambria.]

**penelopise**, -ize, *pi-nel´ə-piz*, *v.i.* to act like *Penelope*, the wife of Ulysses, who undid at night the work she did by day in order to gain time. [Gr. *Pēnelopē*.]

**peneplain**, *pē´ni-plān*, or -plān´, *n.* a land surface so worn down by denudation as to be almost a plain.—Also pe´neplane. [L. *paene*, almost, and plain (2).]

**penetrate**, *pen´i-trāt*, *v.i.* to thrust or force a way into the inside of: to pierce into or through: to permeate: to reach the mind or feelings of: to pierce with the eye or understanding, see into or through (*fig.*): to understand.—*v.i.* to make way or pass inwards.—*ns.* penetrability (*-trə-bil´i-ti*), pen´etrableness.—*adj.* pen´etrable.—*adv.* pen´etrably, so as to be penetrated.—*n.pl.* penetrā´lia (*pl.* of L. *penetral* or *penetrāle*), the inmost parts of a building: the most holy place in a temple: innermost mysteries.—*n.* pen´etrancy.—*adjs.* pen´etrant, penetrating; pen´etrāting, piercing: having keen and deep insight: sharp: keen: discerning.—*adv.* pen´etrātingly.—*n.* penetrā´tion, the act or power of penetrating or entering: acuteness: discernment: the space-penetrating power of a telescope.—*adj.* pen´etrātive, tending or able to penetrate: piercing: having keen and deep insight: reaching and affecting the mind.—*adv.* pen´etrātively.—*ns.* pen´etrātiveness; pen´etrātor. [L. *penetrāre*, *-ātum*—*penes*, in the house, possession, or power of; formed on the model of *intrāre*, to enter—*intus*, within; cf. *penates*.]

**penfold.** See pen (1), and cf. pinfold.

**penguin**, *peng´gwin*, *pen´*, *n.* a former name for the great auk: now any bird of the *Sphenisciformes*, flightless sea birds of the Southern Hemisphere, of peculiar structure: a training aeroplane that cannot fly (*slang*): a member of the Women's Royal Air Force, 'flappers who did not fly' (*slang*).—Also pin´guin.—*n.* pen´guinery, pen´-guinry, a penguin rookery or breeding-place. [According to some, W. *pen*, head, *gwyn*, white,

or the corresponding Breton words, though the great auk had a black head with two white patches: conjectures are *pin-wing*, and L. *pinguis*, fat.]

**penguin.** Same as pinguin (2).

**peni.** Spenserian spelling of penny.

**penicillate**, *pen-i-sil´it*, *āt*, *pen´*, *adj.* tufted: forming a tuft: brush-shaped.—*adj.* penicill´iform, paint-brush-shaped.—*ns.* penicill´in, a group of substances that stop the growth of bacteria, extracted from moulds, esp. *Penicillium notatum*, of the genus of fungi, Penicill´ium (*Ascomycetes*; see *ascus*), which includes also the mould of jam, cheese, etc. (*P. glaucum*). [L. *pēnĭcĭllus*, paint-brush, dim. of *pēnis*, tail.]

**penie.** Spenserian spelling of penny.

**peninsula**, *pen-in´sū-lə*, *n.* a piece of land that is almost an island.—*adj.* penin´sular.—*n.* penin-sular´ity.—*v.t.* penin´sulate, to form into a peninsula.—Peninsular War, the war in Spain and Portugal carried on by Great Britain against Napoleon's marshals (1808-14).—The Peninsula, Spain and Portugal. [L. *paeninsula*—*paene*, almost, *insula*, an island.]

**penis**, *pē´nis*, *n.* the external male organ:—*pl.* pē´nes (*-nēz*).—*adj.* pē´nial. [L. *pēnis*, orig. a tail.]

**penistone**, *pen´i-stən*, *n.* a coarse frieze, formerly made at *Penistone* in Yorkshire.

**penitent**, *pen´i-tənt*, *adj.* suffering pain or sorrow for sin with will to amend: contrite: repentant: expressing sorrow for sin: undergoing penance: appropriate to penance.—*n.* one who sorrows for sin: one who has confessed sin, and is undergoing penance: a member of one of various orders devoted to penitential exercises and work among criminals, etc.—*ns.* pen´itence; pen´-itency (*rare*).—*adj.* penitential (*-ten´shl*), of the nature of, pertaining to, or expressive of, penitence.—*n.* a book of rules relating to penance: a penitent: (in *pl.*) the behaviour or garb of a penitent: black clothes (*coll.*).—*adv.* peniten´tially.—*adj.* penitentiary (*-ten´sha-ri*), relating to penance: penitential: penal and reformatory.—*n.* a penitent: an officer who deals with cases of penitence and penance: an office (under the *Grand Penitentiary*) at Rome dealing with cases of penance, dispensations, etc.: a book for guidance in imposing penances: a place for the performance of penance (*obs.*): an asylum for prostitutes (*arch.*): a reformatory prison or house of correction: a prison (*U.S.*).—*adv.* pen´itently.—penitent form, a seat for penitents at an evangelistic meeting; penitential garment, a rough garment worn for penance; penitential psalms, seven psalms suitable for singing by penitents—the 6th, 32nd, 38th, 51st, 102nd, 130th, 143rd. [L. *paenitēns*, *-entis*, pr.p. of *paenitēre*, to cause to repent, to repent.]

**penk.** Same as pink (7).

**penknife**, penman. See under pen.

**penna**, *pen´ə*, *n.* a feather, esp. one of the large feathers of the wings or tail:—*pl.* penn´ae (*-ē*).—*adjs.* pennaceous (*-ā´shəs*), featherlike; penn´ate, pinnate: winged, feathered, or like a wing in shape.—*n.* penne (*pen*; *Spens.*), a pen: a pinion.—*adjs.* penned, feathered: quilled: winged; penn´iform, feather-shaped. [L. *penna*, feather, wings.]

**pennal**, *pen´əl*, *pen-äl´*, *n.* a freshman at a German university.—*n.* penn´alism, a system of fagging once in vogue at German universities. [Ger. *pennal*—L. *pennāle*, pen-case.]

**pennant**, *pen´ənt*, (*naut.*) *pen´ən*, *n.* a dangling line with a block (*naut.*): a long narrow flag: a signalling flag: a pennon: a flag awarded for victory in a game (*U.S.*).—broad pennant, a long swallow-tailed flag flown by a commodore. [A combination of pendant and pennon.]

**Pennatula**, *pen-at´ū-lə*, *n.* the typical genus of

sea-pens.—*adj.* **pennatulā'ceous.** [Fem. of L. *pennātulus,* winged—*penna.*]

**penneeck, penneech,** *pen-ēk', (Scott) n.* an old card-game with a new trump for every trick.

**pennill,** *pen'il, n.* a form of Welsh improvised verse:—*pl.* **pennill'ion.**—**pennill'ion-sing'ing,** a Welsh mode of singing in which the singer has to change words and measure according to the variations of his accompanist on the harp. [Welsh.]

**pennine,** *pen'in, n.* a mineral of the chlorite group found in the *Pennine* Alps, a hydrous silicate of aluminium, magnesium, and iron.—Also **penn'in-ite** (*in-it*).

**Pennisetum,** *pen-i-sē'təm, n.* a genus, mainly African, of grasses with bristles around the spikelets, including bulrush millet or pearl millet. [L. *penna,* feather, *saeta,* bristle.]

**pennon,** *pen'ən, n.* a mediaeval knight-bachelor's ensign: a flag or streamer attached to a lance: a flag: a long narrow flag or streamer: a pinion or wing (*Milt.*).—*n.* **penn'oncelle, pen'oncelle, penn'oncel, pen'oncel,** a small flag like a pennon. —*adj.* **penn'oned,** bearing a pennon. [O.Fr. *penon,* streamer, arrow-feather, prob.—L. *penna,* feather.]

**penny,** *pen'i, n.* a coin, originally silver, later copper, bronze from 1860, formerly worth 1/12 of a shilling, or 1/240 of a pound, now (**new penny**) equal to a hundredth part of £1: its value: applied to various more or less similar coins: a cent (*U.S.*): a small sum: money in general: a denarius (*N.T.*): pound, in *fourpenny, sixpenny, tenpenny nails,* four, six, ten *pound* weight to the thousand: (*pl.* **pennies,** *pen'iz,* as material objects; **pence, pens,** as units of value).—*adj.* sold for a penny: costing a penny.—*adjs.* **penn'ied,** possessed of a penny; **penn'iless,** without . a penny: without money: poor.—*n.* **penn'ilessness.**—*n.* and *v.i.* **penny-a-line'.**—**penny-a-lin'er,** a hack writer of the worst, or worst-paid, kind; **penny-a-lin'erism,** a hack writer's expression; **penn'y-bank,** a savings-bank that takes pennies; **penn'y-black** (*coll.*), the first adhesive postage stamp, issued by Britain, 1840; **penn'y-cress,** a cruciferous plant of the genus Thlaspi, with round flat pods; **penn'y-dog',** the tope or miller's dog, a kind of shark; **penny dreadful** (see **dread**); **penn'y-far'thing,** a penny and a farthing: an old-fashioned 'ordinary' bicycle, with a big wheel and a little; **penn'y-fee,** wages in money: (without hyphen) a small wage (*Scot.*); **penny gaff** (*slang*), a low-class theatre.—*adj.* **penny-in-the-slot,** worked by putting a penny in a slot.—**penn'yland** (*hist.*), land valued at a penny a year; **penny mail** (*Scot.*), rent in money, not in kind: a small sum paid to the superior of land; **penn'y-piece,** a penny; **penn'y-pig** (*Scot.*), a money-box, properly of earthenware (pig); **penn'y-post',** a means of, or organisation for, carrying a letter for a penny; **penn'y-rent',** rent in money: income; **penn'y-stone, -stane** (*Scot.*), a round flat stone used as a quoit; **penn'ystone-cast',** a stone's throw for such a stone; **penn'y-wedd'ing,** a wedding at which the guests contribute money to set up the bride and bridegroom; **penn'y-weight,** twenty-four grains of troy weight (the weight of a silver penny); **penn'y-whist'le,** a tin whistle or flageolet; **penn'y-wis'dom,** prudence in petty matters.—*adj.* **penn'y-wise,** saving small sums at the risk of larger: niggardly on improper occasions.—**penn'y-wort,** a name given to various plants with round leaves, esp. Hydrocotyle (an umbelliferous marsh-plant) and navelwort (Cotyledon); **penn'yworth,** a penny's worth of anything: the amount that can be got for a penny: a good bargain—also **penn'orth** (*pen'-ərth; coll.*).—**a pretty penny,** a considerable sum of money; **in penny numbers,** a very few, or a

very little, at a time; **not a penny the worse,** never a whit the worse; **pennies from heaven,** money obtained without effort and unexpectedly; **Peter's pence,** Rome-scot, a tax or tribute of a silver penny paid to the Pope—in England perhaps from the time of Offa of Mercia, in Ireland from Henry II, abolished under Henry VIII: a similar tax elsewhere: a voluntary contribution to the Pope in modern times; **the penny drops,** now I (etc.) understand; **turn an honest penny,** to earn some money honestly; **two a penny,** in abundant supply and of little value. [O.E. *penig,* oldest form *pending;* cf. Ger. *pfennig;* Du. *penning;* O.N. *penningr.*]

**pennyroyal,** *pen-i-roi'əl, n.* a species of mint (*Mentha pulegium*) once esteemed in medicine: a related plant, *Hedeoma pulegioides* (*U.S.*). [M.E. *puliol real*—A.Fr. *puliol real*—L. *pūleium, pūlegium,* pennyroyal, and *regālis, -e,* royal.]

**pennywinkle.** Same as **periwinkle** (2).

**penology,** *pē-nol'ə-ji, n.* the study of punishment in its relation to crime: the management of prisons. —*adj.* **penological** (*-nə-loj'*).—*n.* **penologist** (*-nol'ə-jist*). [Gr. *poinē,* punishment, *logos,* discourse.]

**pensée,** *pā-sā,* (Fr.) thought.

**pensieroso,** *pen-sye-rō'sō,* (It.) melancholy: thoughtful.

**pensil,** *pen'sl, n.* a small pennon. [A.Fr. *pencel,* dim. of *penon,* pennon.]

**pensile,** *pen'sil, -sil, adj.* hanging: suspended: overhanging: building a hanging nest.—*ns.* **pen'sileness, pensility** (*-sil'i-ti*). [L. *pēnsilis—pendēre,* to hang.]

**pension,** *pen'shən, n.* a periodical payment, as tribute, wages, etc. (*obs.*): an allowance of money as a bribe for future services, as a mark of favour, or in reward of one's own or another's merit: an allowance to one who has retired or has been disabled or reached old age or has been widowed or orphaned, etc.: (now pronounced as Fr., *pä-syõ*) a Continental boarding-house: board.—*v.t.* to grant a pension to.—*adjs.* **pen'-sionable,** entitled, or entitling, to a pension; **pen'sionary,** receiving a pension: of the nature of a pension.—*n.* one who receives a pension: one whose interest is bought by a pension: the syndic or legal adviser of a Dutch town (*hist.*).— *n.* **pen'sioner,** one who receives a pension: a dependent: a gentleman-at-arms (*obs.*): one who pays out of his own income for his commons, chambers, etc., at Cambridge University = an Oxford **commoner:** a boarder, esp. in a religious house (*obs.*).—**Grand Pensionary** (*hist.*), the president of the States-general of Holland; **pension off,** to dismiss, or allow to retire, with a pension. [Fr.,—L. *pēnsiō, -ōnis—pendēre, pēnsum,* to weigh, pay.]

**pensionnat,** *pä-syo-na,* (Fr.) boarding-school.

**pensive,** *pen'siv, adj.* meditative: expressing thoughtfulness with sadness.—*adj.* **pen'siv'd** (*Shak.*), made pensive.—*adv.* **pen'sively.**—*n.* **pen'siveness.** [Fr. *pensif, -ive—penser*—L. *pēnsāre,* to weigh—*pendēre,* to weigh.]

**penstock,** *pen'stok, n.* a sluice. [pen (1), stock.]

**pensum,** *pen'səm, n.* a task: a school imposition (*U.S.*). [L. *pēnsum.*]

**pent,** *pa.t.* and *pa.p.* of pen, to shut up.

**pent,** *pent, n.* a penthouse: a sloping or overhanging covering.—**pent'roof,** a roof that slopes one way only. [From **penthouse,** app. influenced by Fr. *pente,* slope.]

**pent-, penta-,** in composition, five.—*ns.* **penta-chord** (*pen'tə-körd;* Gr. *chordē,* string), a musical instrument with five strings: a diatonic series of five notes; **pentacle** (*pent'ə-kl;* L.L. *pentaculum,* app.—Gr. *pente*): according to some O.Fr. *pentacol—pendre,* to hang, *à,* on, *col,* the neck), a pentagram or similar figure (sometimes a hexagram) or amulet used as a defence against demons; **Pentacrinus** (-*ak'rin-əs*; Gr. *krinon*, lily), a genus of fossil crinoids, in the form of a feathery five-rayed star on a long pentagonal stalk.—*adj.* **pentac'rinoid**, like, or akin to, *Pentacrinus*.—*n.* a young form of some crinoids that resembles *Pentacrinus*.—*adj.* **pent'-act** (Gr. *aktis, aktinos*, ray), five-rayed.—*n.* a five-rayed sponge spicule.—*adjs.* **pentactinal** (-*ak'tin-əl*, or -*ak-ti'nəl*); **pentacy'clic** (Gr. *kyklos*, wheel), having five whorls.—*n.* **pent'ad** (Gr. *pentas, -ados*), a set of five things: a period of five years or five days: an atom, element or radical with a combining power of five.—Also *adj.*—*adjs.* **pentad'ic**; **pentadac'tyl, pentadac'-tyle** (-*til*; Gr. *daktylos*, finger, toe), having five digits.—*n.* a person with five fingers and five toes.—*adjs.* **pentadactyl'ic, pentadac'tylous.**—*ns.* **pentadac'tylism**; **pentadac'tyly.**—*adj.* **pentadel'-phous** (Gr. *adelphos*, brother), having five bundles of stamens: united in five bundles.—*n.* **pentagon** (*pen'tə-gon*; Gr. *pentagōnon*—*gōniā*, angle), a rectilineal plane figure having five angles and five sides (*geom.*): a fort with five bastions: (*cap.*) headquarters of the U.S. armed forces at Washington—from the shape of the building.—*adj.* **pentagonal** (*pen-tag'ən-əl*).—*adv.* **pentag'onally.**—*ns.* **pen'tagram** (Gr. *pentagrammon*—*gramma*, a letter), a stellate pentagon or five-pointed star: a magic figure of that form; **pen'tagraph**, a wrong form of **pantograph.**—*n.pl.* **Pentagynia** (*jin'i-ə*; Gr. *gynē*, a woman, in the sense of female; *obs.*), a Linnaean order of plants (in various classes) with five pistils.—*adjs.* **pentagyn'ian, pentagynous** (-*aj'*).—*ns.* **pental'pha** (Gr. *alpha*, the letter alpha), a pentacle; **Pentam'eron** (It. *Pentamerone*—Gr. *pente, hēmerā*, day), a famous collection of folk-tales in Neapolitan dialect by Giambattista Basile (*d.* 1632) supposed to be told during five days; **pentam'-erism** (Gr. *meros*, part), condition of being **pentamerous.**—*adj.* **pentam'erous**, having five parts or members: having parts in fives.—*ns.* **pentam'ery**; **pentam'eter** (Gr. *pentametros*—*metron*, a measure), a verse of five measures or feet (**elegiac pentameter**, a verse of two penthemimers, the first admitting spondees instead of dactyls, the second dactyls only; **iambic pentameter**, a somewhat unsuitable name for the line used in the English heroic couplet and blank verse).—Also *adj.*—*n.pl.* (*obs.*) **Pentan'dria** (Gr. *anēr, andros*, a man, a male), in Linnaeus's classification a class of plants with five stamens.—*adjs.* **pentan'drian, pentan'drous.**—*ns.* **pentane** (*pent'ān*), a hydrocarbon (C₅H₁₂), fifth member of the methane series; **pent'angle**, a pentacle: a pentagon.—*adjs.* **pentang'ular**; **pentaploid** (*pent'-ə-ploid*; Gr. *pentaploos*, five-fold, *eidos*, form), five-fold: having five times the haploid number of chromosomes (*biol.*).—*n.* a cell, organism, or form with five sets of chromosomes.—*n.* **pent'-aploidy**, the condition of having five sets of chromosomes.—*adj.* **pentapodic** (*pent-ə-pod'ik*).—*ns.* **pentapody** (*pen-tap'ə-di*; Gr. *pous, podos*, foot), a measure of five feet; **pentap'olis** (Gr. *polis*, a city), a group of five cities, esp. those of Cyrenaica—Cyrene, Berenice, Arsinoe, Ptolemais, and Apollonia.—*adjs.* **pentapolitan** (*pent-ə-pol'i-tən*); **pentarch** (*pent'ärk*; Gr. *archē*, beginning), (of roots) having five vascular strands.—*ns.* **pent'arch** (Gr. *archē*, rule), a ruler or governor in a pentarchy; **pentarchy** (*pent'ärk-i*), government by five persons: a group of five kings, rulers, states, or governments; **pentastich** (*pent'ə-stik*; Gr. *stichos*, row, line), a group of five lines of verse:—*pl.* **pentastichs** (-*stiks*).—*adjs.* **pentastichous** (*pen-tas'ti-kəs*), five-ranked; **pen'-tastyle** (Gr. *stȳlos*, a pillar), having five columns in front.—*n.* a building or portico with five columns.—*adj.* **pentasyllab'ic**, five syllabled.—**Pentateuch** (*pen'tə-tūk*; Gr. *pentateuchos*, five-

volumed—*teuchos*, a tool; later, a book), the first five books of the Old Testament.—*adj.* **pentateuch'al.**—*ns.* **pentath'lete**, a competitor in the pentathlon; **pentath'lon** (Gr. *pentathlon*—*athlon*, contest), a contest in five exercises—wrestling, disk-throwing, spear-throwing, leaping, running: a five-event contest at the modern Olympic games from 1906-1924: a five-event Olympic games contest for women: (**modern pentathlon**) an Olympic games contest consisting of swimming, cross-country riding and running, fencing and revolver-shooting—also (Latin) **pentath'lum.**—*adjs.* **pentatomic** (*pent-ə-tom'ik*; Gr. *atomos*, atom), having five atoms, esp. five atoms of replaceable hydrogen: pentavalent; **pentatonic** (*pent-ə-ton'ik*; Gr. *tonos*, tone), consisting of five tones or notes—applied esp. to a scale, a major scale with the fourth and seventh omitted; **pentavalent** (*pen-tə-vā'lənt, pen-tav'-ə-lənt*), having a valency of five.—*n.* **penta-zocine** (*pen-tā'zə-sēn*), a pain-killing drug believed to be non-addictive. [Gr. *pente*, five.] **penteconter,** *pen-ti-kon'tər, n.* an ancient Greek ship with fifty oars. [Gr. *pentēkontērēs*—*pentēkonta*, fifty.] **Pentecost,** *pent'i-kost, n.* a Jewish festival held on the fiftieth day after the Passover: the festival of Whitsuntide, seven weeks after Easter.—*adj.* **Pentecost'al.**—*n.pl.* offerings formerly made to the parish priest at Whitsuntide. [Gr. *pentēkostē* (*hēmerā*), fiftieth (day).] **Pentelic, -an,** *pen-tel'ik, -ən, adjs.* of Mount *Pentel'icus* near Athens, famous for the marble found there. **penteteric,** *pen-ti-ter'ik, adj.* occurring every fourth (by the old mode of reckoning, fifth) year. [Gr. *pentetērikos—etos*, a year.] **penthemimer,** *pen-thi-mim'ər, n.* a metrical group of 2½ feet.—*adj.* **penthemim'eral.** [Gr. *pente*, five, *hēmi-*, half, *meros*, a part.] **penthia,** *pen'thi-ə, n.* according to Spenser another name for the unidentified plant Astrophel. **penthouse,** *pent'hows, n.* a shed or lean-to projecting from or adjoining a main building: a separate room or dwelling on a roof: a small, select top flat: a protection from the weather over a door or a window: anything of similar form, as an eyebrow:—*pl.* **pent'houses** (-*how-ziz*).—*v.t.* to provide or cover with, or as with, a penthouse. [For **pentice**—Fr. *appentis*—L.L. *appendicium*, an appendage.] **pentice, pentise,** *pen'tis.* Same as **penthouse.** **pentimento,** *pen-ti-men'tō, n.* something painted out of a picture which later becomes visible again:—*pl.* -**ti.** [It.—*pentirsi*, to repent.] **pentlandite,** *pent'lənd-it, n.* a native sulphide of iron and nickel. [Joseph Barclay *Pentland* (1797-1873), traveller in South America.] **pentode,** *pent'ōd, n.* a thermionic tube with five electrodes. [Gr. *pente*, five, *hodos*, way.] **pentose,** *pent'ōs, n.* a sugar (of various kinds) with five oxygen atoms.—*n.* **pent'osan** (-*san*), **pent'-osane** (-*sān*), a carbohydrate that yields pentose on hydrolysis. [Gr. *pente*, five.] **Pentothal,** *pen'tō-thal, n.* registered trademark for thiopentone, an intravenous anaesthetic, a sodium thiobarbiturate compound.—Also **pentothal sodium.** **pentroof.** See **pent** (2). **Pentstemon,** *pen(t)-stē'mən, n.* a mainly North American showy-flowered genus of Scrophulariaceae, with a sterile fifth stamen. [Gr. *pente*, five, *stēmōn*, warp, as if stamen.] **pentylene,** *pent'i-lēn, n.* an unsaturated hydrocarbon (C₅H₁₀) of the olefine series (in several isomers)—amylene.—Also **pent'ene.** [Gr. *pente*, five, *hȳlē*, matter.] **penult,** *pi-nult', also pē'nult,* **penult'ima,** *ns.* the syllable last but one.—*adj.* **penult'imate**, last but one.—*n.* the penult: the last but one. [L.

*paenultima* (*syllaba*, etc.)—*paene*, almost, *ultimus*, last.]

**penumbra**, *pen-um'brə*, *n.* a partial or lighter shadow round the perfect or darker shadow of an eclipse: the less dark border of a sun-spot or any similar spot: the part of a picture where the light and shade blend into each other.—*adj.* **penum'bral**. [L. *paene*, almost, *umbra*, shade.]

**penury**, *pen'ū-ri*, *n.* want: great poverty.—*adj.* **penū'rious**, in want (*obs.*): scanty (*obs.*): niggardly: miserly.—*adv.* **penū'riously**.—*n.* **penū'riousness**. [L. *paenūria.*]

**peon**, *pē'on*, *n.* a day-labourer, esp. formerly in Spanish-speaking America, one working off a debt by bondage: in India (*pūn*) a foot-soldier, a policeman (*hist.*), a messenger.—*ns.* **pē'onage**, **pē'onism**, agricultural servitude of the above kind. [Sp. *peón* and Port. *peão*—L.L. *pedō*, *-ōnis*, a foot-soldier—L. *pēs*, *pedis*, a foot.]

**peony, paeony**, *pē'ə-ni*, *n.* any plant of the genus Paeonia, of the buttercup family, with large showy crimson or white globular flowers: its flower.—Also (formerly) **pi'on(e)y**. [O.E. *peonie* and O.Fr. (Northern) *pione* (Fr. *pivoine*)—L. *paeōnia*—Gr. *paiōniā*—*Paiōn*, *Paiān*, physician of the gods (see **Paean**), from its use in medicine.]

**people**, *pē'pl*, *n.* a nation: a community: a body of persons held together by belief in common origin, speech, culture, political union, or other bond: a set of persons: transferred to a set of animals as if forming a nation—in these senses used as *sing.* with a *pl.* **peo'ples** (B. **peo'ple**): a body of persons linked by common leadership, headship, etc.: subjects: retainers: followers: employees: servants: congregation: attendants: near kindred: members of one's household: parents: ancestors and descendants: inhabitants of a place: transferred to animal inhabitants: the persons associated with any business: laity: the mass of the nation: general population: populace: the citizens: voters: (approaching a *pron.*) they, one, folks—in these senses used as *pl.*—*v.t.* to stock with people or inhabitants: to inhabit: to occupy as if inhabiting. [O.Fr. *poeple*—L. *pŏpulus.*]

**pep**, *pep*, (*coll.*) *n.* vigour, go, spirit.—*v.t.* to put pep into (usu. with *up*).—*adjs.* **pep'ful, pepp'y**.—**pep pill**, a pill containing a stimulant drug; **pep talk**, a strongly-worded talk designed to arouse enthusiasm for a cause or course of action. [pepper.]

**peperino**, *pep-ə-rē'nō*, *n.* a dark tuff with many crystals and rock-fragments, found in the Alban Hills. [It. *peperino*—L. *piper*, pepper.]

**peplos**, *pep'los*, *n.* an upper robe worn by women in ancient Greece.—*n.* **pep'lum** (L.), a peplos: an overskirt supposed to be like the peplos: a short skirt-like section attached to the waist-line of a dress, blouse or jacket. [Gr. *peplos.*]

**pepo**, *pē'pō*, *n.* the type of fruit found in the melon and cucumber family, a large many-seeded berry formed from an inferior ovary, usually with hard epicarp. [L. *pēpō*, *-ōnis*—Gr. (*sikyos*) *pepōn*, (a melon eaten) ripe, distinguished from a cucumber eaten unripe.]

**pepper**, *pep'ər*, *n.* a pungent aromatic condiment consisting of the dried berries of the pepper plant, entire or powdered (*black pepper*), or with the outer parts removed (*white pepper*): any plant of the genus Piper, esp. *P. nigrum*, or of the family Piperaceae: a plant of the solanaceous genus Capsicum or one of its pods (*red* or *Cayenne pepper*): extended to various similar condiments and the plants producing them.—*v.t.* to sprinkle or flavour with pepper: to sprinkle: to pelt with shot, etc.: to pelt thoroughly: to do for.—*v.i.* to pelt: to shower: to discharge shot, etc., in showers.—*ns.* **pepp'-erer**, a grocer (*obs.*): one who or that which peppers; **pepp'eriness**; **pepp'ering**.—*adj.* **pepp'-ery**, having the qualities of pepper: pungent: hot, choleric.—*adj.* **pepper-and-salt'**, mingled black and white.—**pepp'er-box**, a pepper pot: a turret or other object of similar shape; **pepp'er-cake**, a kind of spiced cake or gingerbread; **pepp'er-caster, -castor**, a pepper-pot; **pepp'er-corn**, the dried berry of the pepper plant: something of little value.—*adj.* like a peppercorn, as the small tight knots in which certain African peoples wear their hair: trivial, nominal, as **peppercorn** *rent.*—*adj.* **pepp'ercorny.**—**pepp'er-gin'gerbread** (*Shak.*), hot-spiced gingerbread; **pepp'er-grass**, any cress of the genus Lepidium: pillwort (Pilularia); **pepp'ermill**, a small hand-mill in which peppercorns are ground; **pepp'er-mint**, an aromatic and pungent species of mint (*Mentha piperita*): a liquor distilled from it: a lozenge flavoured with it; **pepp'ermint-drop**, a confection so flavoured; **pepp'er-pot**, a pot or bottle with a perforated top for sprinkling pepper: a West Indian dish of cassareep, flesh or dried fish, and vegetables, esp. green okra and chillies; **pepp'erwort**, a cress of the genus Lepidium, esp. dittander (L. *latifolium*).—**Jamaica pepper**, allspice; **long pepper**, the fruit of *Piper longum*; **Negro pepper**, the produce of Xylopia (fam. Anonaceae), also called **Ethiopian pepper**. [O.E. *pipor*—L. *piper*—Gr. *peperi*—Sans. *pippali*.]

**Pepper's ghost**, *pep'erz gōst*, *n.* a phantom produced on the stage by a sheet of glass reflecting an actor on an understage. [John H. *Pepper* (1821-1900) improver and exhibitor of H. Dircks's invention.]

**pepsin**, *pep'sin*, *n.* any of a group of closely allied proteins, digestive enzymes of the gastric juice of vertebrates: a preparation containing pepsin from a pig's or other stomach (*med.*).—*adj.* **pep'-tic**, relating to or promoting digestion: having a good digestion: of or relating to pepsin or the digestive juices.—*n.* **pepticity** (*-tis'i-ti*), eupepsia.—*n.pl.* **pep'tics** (*jocular*), the digestive organs.—*ns.* **pep'tide**, any of a number of substances formed from amino-acids in which the amino-group of one is joined to the carboxyl group of another; **peptisā'tion, -z-.**—*v.t.* **pept'ise, -ize**, to bring into colloidal solution: to form into a sol from a gel.—*ns.* **pep'tōne**, a product of the action of enzymes on albuminous matter; **peptonisā'-tion, -z-.**—*v.t.* **pep'tonise, -ize**, convert into peptones.—**peptic ulcer**, an ulcer of the stomach or duodenum, etc. [Gr. *pepsis*, digestion—*peptein*, to digest.]

**Pepysian**, *pēp'si-ən*, *adj.* pertaining to Samuel *Pepys* (1633-1703), his inimitable diary, or the collections he bequeathed to Magdalene College, Cambridge.

**per**, *pûr'*, *pər*, *prep.* for each, a: (chiefly commercial) by: in the manner or direction of (*her.*).—**as per usual** (*coll.* or *illit.*), as usual. [L. and O.Fr. *per.*]

**per**, *pûr*, *per*, (L.) through, by means of, according to.—**per annum** (**diem, mensem**) (*an'əm, -ōōm, di'əm, dē'em, men'səm, men'sem*), yearly (daily, monthly); **per ardua ad astra** (*är'dū-ə ad as'tra, är'dōō-a ad as'tra*), by steep and toilsome ways to the stars—Air Force motto; **per capita** (*kap'i-tə, kap'i-ta*), (counting) by heads: all sharing alike; **per contra** (*kon'tra, kon'trä*), on the contrary: as a set-off; **per fas et nefas** (*fas et nē'fas, fäs et ne'fäs*), through right and wrong; **per impossibile** (*im-po-si'bi-lē, im-po-si'bi-le*), by an impossibility: if it were so, which it is not; **per saltum** (*sal'təm, sal'tŏŏm*), at a single leap: all at once; **per se** (*sē, sā*), by himself, etc.: essentially: in itself; **per stirpes** (*stûr'pēz, stir'pās*), by stocks: in inheritance, the children of each descendant dividing only the share that would have been their parent's (distinguished from *per capita*).

**per,** *pûr, pər, pfx* (1) in chemistry, indicating the highest degree of combination with oxygen or other element or radical; (2) (no longer a living prefix) in words from Latin, through, beyond, or thoroughly, or indicating destruction.

**peracute,** *pûr-ə-kūt′, adj.* very sharp or violent. [L. *peracūtus*—*per-*, thoroughly, *acūtus*, sharp.]

**peradventure,** *pûr-əd-ven′chər, adv.* by adventure: by chance: perhaps.—*n.* uncertainty: question. [O.Fr. *per* (or *par*) *aventure*, by chance.]

**peraeon, peraeopod.** See **pereion.**

**perai,** *pē-rī′.* See **piranha.**

**perambulate,** *pər-am′bū-lāt, v.t.* to walk through, about, around, up and down, or over: to pass through for the purpose of surveying: to beat the bounds of: to patrol: to wheel in a perambulator.—*v.i.* to walk about.—*ns.* **perambulā′- tion,** act of perambulating: a survey or inspection by travelling through: beating the bounds: the district within which a person has the right of inspection; **peram′bulātor,** one who perambulates: a wheel for measuring distances on roads: (abbrev. **pram**) a light carriage for a child.— *adj.* **peram′bulatory.** [L. *perambulāre, -ātum*— *per,* through, *ambulāre,* to walk.]

**percale,** *per-käl′, pər-kāl′, n.* a closely woven French cambric.—*n.* **percaline** (*pûr-kə-lēn′,* or *pûr′-),* a glossy cotton cloth. [Fr.; cf. Pers. *pur-gālah,* rag.]

**percase,** *pər-kās′, (obs.) adv.* perchance: perhaps. [L. *per,* through, by, *casus,* a chance, a fall.]

**perce,** *pûrs, (Spens.)* same as **pierce.**—Also (*infin.*) **percen**—*adjs.* (*Spens.*) **perce′able,** pierceable; **perce′ant** (*Keats*), piercing.

**perceive,** *per-sēv′, v.t.* to become or be aware of through the senses: to get knowledge of by the mind: to see: to understand: to discern.—*adj.* **perceiv′able.**—*adv.* **perceiv′ably,** perceptibly.—*n.* **perceiv′er.**—*n.* and *adj.* **perceiv′ing.** [O.Fr. *percever*—L. *percipēre, perceptum*—pfx. *per-,* thoroughly, *capēre,* to take.]

**per cent** (usu. written or printed with a point after it as if an abbreviation for *per centum,* but pronounced as a complete word, *pər-sent′*), *adv.* in the hundred: for each hundred or hundred: pounds.—*n.* a percentage: (in *pl.,* in composition) securities yielding a specified percentage (as *three-percents*).—*n.* **percent′age,** rate per hundred: an allowance of so much for every hundred: a proportional part: commission (*coll.*): profit, advantage (*coll.*).—*adjs.* **percent′al, percen′tile.** —*n.* **percen′tile,** the value below which fall a specified percentage (as 25, 50, 75) of a large number of statistical units (e.g. scores in an examination): percentile rank.—**percentile rank,** grading according to percentile group. [L. *per centum.*]

**percept,** *pûr′sept, n.* an object perceived by the senses: the mental result of perceiving.—*n.* **perceptibil′ity.**—*adj.* **percep′tible,** that can be perceived: that may be known by the senses: discernible.—*adv.* **percep′tibly.**—*n.* **percep′tion,** act or power of perceiving: discernment: apprehension of any modification of consciousness: the combining of sensations into a recognition of an object: direct recognition: a percept: reception of a stimulus (*bot.*).—*adjs.* **percep′- tional; percep′tive,** able or quick to perceive: discerning: active or instrumental in perceiving. —*ns.* **percep′tiveness; perceptiv′ity.**—*adj.* **per- cep′tūal,** of the nature of, or relating to, perception. [L. *percipēre, perceptum;* see **perceive.**]

**perch,** *pûrch, n.* a spiny-finned fresh-water fish of the genus **Perca** (*pûr′ka*): extended to various fishes of the same or kindred family, or other.— *n.pl.* **Percidae** (*pûr′si-dē*), the perch family.—*adjs.* **per′ciform, per′cine** (*-sīn*), **per′coid** (*-koid*). [L. *perca* (partly through Fr. *perche*)—Gr. *perkē,* a perch, perh. conn. with *perknos,* dusky.]

**perch,** *pûrch, n.* a pole (*obs.* or *dial.* except in

special uses): a pole serving as a navigation mark: a pole joining the fore and hind gear of some vehicles: a bar or frame for stretching cloth for examination: a bar for fixing leather for softening treatment: a peg or bar for hanging things on (*obs.*): a rod for a bird to alight, sit, or roost on: anything serving the purpose for a bird, a person, or anything else: a high seat: a rod or pole, a measure of 5½ yards or (*square perch*) 30¼ square yards: a measure of stonework, 24⅔ or 25 cubic feet.—*v.i.* to alight, sit or roost on a perch: to be set on high: to be balanced on a high or narrow footing: to settle. —*v.t.* to place, as on a perch: to stretch, examine, or treat on a perch.—*adj.* **perch′ed** (*Milt.*), having perches.—*ns.* **perch′er,** a bird with feet adapted for perching; **perch′ing,** examination of cloth on a perch: a process of leather-softening.—*adj.* with feet adapted for perching: insessorial.—**perched block,** a block of rock transported by land-ice and left aloft, often in an unstable position, when the ice retires; **perching birds,** the Passeriformes. [Fr. *perche*—L. *pertica,* a rod.]

**perchance,** *pər-chäns′, adv.* by chance: as it may happen: perhaps. [A.Fr. *par chance.*]

**percheron,** *per-shə-rɔ̄, pûr′shə-ron, n.* a draught-horse of a breed originating in La *Perche* in Southern Normandy.—Also *adj.* [Fr.]

**perchloric,** *pər-klō′rik, klö′rik, adj.* containing more oxygen than chloric acid—applied to an oily explosive acid, $HClO_4$.—*n.* **perchlō′rate,** a salt of perchloric acid. [Pfx. **per-.**]

**percipient,** *pər-sip′i-ənt, adj.* perceiving: having the faculty of perception.—*n.* one who perceives or can perceive: one who receives impressions telepathically or otherwise supersensibly.—*ns.* **percip′ience,** (*rare*) **percip′iency.** [L. *percipiēns, -entis,* pr.p. of *percipēre;* cf. **perceive, percept.**]

**percoct,** *pər-kokt′, adj.* well-cooked: overdone: hackneyed. [L. *percoctus*—*percoquēre,* to cook thoroughly.]

**percoid,** *pûr′koid.* See **perch** (1).

**percolate,** *pûr′kə-lāt, v.t.* and *v.i.* to pass through pores or small openings: to filter.—*n.* a filtered liquid.—*ns.* **percolation** (*pûr-kō-lā′shən*); **per′- colātor,** an apparatus for percolating, esp. for making coffee. [L. *percōlāre, -ātum*—*per,* through, *cōlāre,* to strain.]

**percolin,** *pûr′kə-lin, n.* a small bird, a cross between a partridge and a quail.

**percurrent,** *pər-kur′ənt, adj.* running through the whole length.—*adj.* **percursory** (*kûr′*), cursory. [L. *percurrēre,* to run through, *percursor,* one who runs through.]

**percuss,** *pər-kus′, v.t.* to strike so as to shake: to tap for purposes of diagnosis.—*adj.* **percuss′ant** (*her.*), bent round and striking the side, as a lion's tail—also **percussed′.**—*n.* **percussion** (*-kush′ən*), striking: impact: tapping directly or indirectly upon the body to find the condition of an organ by the sound (*med.*): massage by tapping: the striking or sounding of a discord, etc., as distinguished from preparation and resolution (*mus.*): collectively, instruments played by striking—drum, cymbals, triangle, etc. (*mus.*): a device for making an organ-pipe speak promptly by striking the reed (*mus.*).— *adj.* **percuss′ional.**—*adj.* **percussive** (*-kus′*).— *adv.* **percuss′ively.**—*n.* **percuss′or,** a percussion hammer.—*adj.* **percutient** (*-kū′shyent*), striking or having power to strike.—*n.* that which strikes or has power to strike.—**percuss′ion-bull′et,** a bullet that explodes on striking; **percuss′ion-cap,** a metal case containing a fulminating substance which explodes when struck, formerly used for firing rifles, etc.; **percuss′ion-fuse,** a fuse in a projectile that acts on striking; **percuss′ion- hamm′er,** a small hammer for percussion in diagnosis; **percuss′ion-lock,** a gun lock in which a hammer strikes a percussion-cap; **percuss'ion-pow'der**, powder that explodes on being struck—fulminating powder.—**bulb of percussion** (see **bulb**). [L. *percussiō*, *-ōnis*—*percutĕre*, *percussum*—pfx. *per-*, thoroughly, *quatĕre*, to shake.]

**percutaneous**, *pər-kū-tā'ni-əs*, *adj.* done or applied through the skin.—*adv.* **percutā'neously.** [L. *per*, through, *cutis*, the skin.]

**percutient.** See **percuss**.

**perdendo**, *per-den'do*, (*mus.*) *adj.* and *adv.* dying away in volume of tone and in speed.—Also **perden'dosi** (*-sē*). [It.]

**perdie, perdy,** *pər-dē'*, sometimes *pûr'dē*, (*Spens., Shak.*) *adv.* assuredly.—Also **pardi(e)', pardy'.** [O.Fr. *par dé*, by God.]

**perdition,** *pər-dish'ən*, *n.* loss: ruin: utter loss or ruin: the utter loss of happiness in a future state: hell.—*adj.* **perdi'tionable.** [L. *perditiō*, *-ōnis*—*perdĕre, perditum*—pfx. *per-*, entirely, *dăre*, to give, give up.]

**perdu, perdue,** *pər-dū'*, *adj.* lost to view: concealed: in a post of extreme danger (*obs.*): on a forlorn hope or on a desperate enterprise (*obs.*): reckless.—*n.* an outlying sentinel (*Shak.*): one lying in concealment or ambush: one on a forlorn hope (*obs.*).—**lie perdu(e)** (*mil.*), to lie in ambush, concealed and on the watch. [Fr., pa.p. of *perdre*, to lose—L. *perdĕre*, to destroy; see preceding.]

**perduellion,** *pər-dū-el'yən*, *n.* treason. [L. *perduelliō, -ōnis*.]

**perdurable,** *pər-dūr'ə-bl* (*Shak. pûr'*), *adj.* very durable, long continued: everlasting.—*n.* **perdūrabil'ity.**—*adv.* **perdūr'ably** (*Shak. pûr'*), very durably: everlastingly.—*ns.* **perdūr'ance; perdūrā'tion.**—*v.i.* **perdūre'**, to endure. [L. *perdūrāre*—*per*, through, *dūrāre*, to last.]

**peregal,** *per'i-gl*, (*obs.*) *adj.* fully equal.—*n.* equal. [O.Fr. *paregal*—L. pfx. *per-*, thoroughly, *aequālis*, equal.]

**peregrine,** *per'i-grin*, *adj.* foreign: outlandish: making a pilgrimage or journey: applied to a species of falcon (*Falco peregrinus*), so named because taken not from 'he (inaccessible) nest (as an eyas is) but while in flight from it.—*n.* an alien resident: a pilgrim or traveller in a foreign land: a peregrine falcon.—*v.i.* **per'egrinate**, to travel about: to live in a foreign country: to go on pilgrimage.—*v.t.* to traverse.—*adj.* foreign-looking.—*ns.* **peregrinā'tion**, travelling about: wandering: pilgrimage: a complete and systematic course or round: a sojourn abroad; **per'egrinâtor**, one who travels about; **peregrin'ity**, foreignness: outlandishness. [L. *peregrinus*, foreign—*peregre*, abroad—*per*, through, *ager*, field.]

**pereion,** *pə-ri'on*, *n.* the thorax in Crustacea:—*pl.* **perei'a.**—*n.* **perei'opod**, a crustacean's thoracic walking-leg.—Also in corrected form, **peraeon, peraeopod.** [Faultily formed from Gr. *peraioein*, to transport, to carry across.]

**peremptory,** *pər-em(p)'-tə-ri*, or *per'əm(p)*, *adj.* precluding debate or dispute (*Rom. law*): final: admitting no refusal or denial: definitely fixed (*law*): utter (*obs.*): dogmatic: imperious: arrogantly commanding.—*adv.* **peremp'torily** (or *per'*).—*n.* **peremp'toriness** (or *per'*). [L. *peremptōrius*—*perimēre, peremptum*, to destroy, prevent—pfx. *per-*, entirely, and *emĕre*, to take, to buy.]

**perennial,** *pər-en'yəl*, *adj.* lasting through the year: perpetual: never failing: growing constantly: lasting more than two years (*bot.*): of insects, living more than one year.—*n.* a plant that lives more than two years.—*v.i.* **perenn'ate**, to live perennially: to survive from season to season, esp. through a period of inactivity.—*n.* **perennā'tion** (*per-*).—*adv.* **perenn'ially.** [L. *perennis*—*per*, through, *annus*, a year.]

**perennibranchiate,** *pər-en-i-brang'ki-it, -āt*, *adj.* re-

taining the gills throughout life.—*adj.* and *n.*

**perenn'ibranch** (*-brangk*).

**perfay,** *pər-fā'*, (*arch.*) *interj.* by my faith. [O.Fr. *par fei*.]

**perfect,** *pûr'fekt, -fikt, adj.* done thoroughly or completely: completed: mature: complete: having all organs in a functional condition: having androecium and gynaeceum in the same flower: completely skilled or versed: thoroughly known or acquired: exact: exactly conforming to definition or theory: flawless: having every moral excellence: sheer, utter: completely contented (*Shak.*): certain, convinced (*Shak.*): of the simpler kind of consonance (*mus.*): triple (*old music*; applied to time).—*n.* the perfect tense: a verb in the perfect tense.—*v.t.* **perfect** (*pər-fekt'*, or *pûr'*), to make perfect: to finish: to teach fully, to make fully skilled in anything: to print the second side of.—*ns.* **perfectā'tion** (*rare*); **perfect'er** (or *pûr'*).—*n.pl.* **perfect'i** (*-i*), a body of Cathari sts in the 12th and 13th centuries, of very strict lives.—*ns.* **perfectibil'ian**, a believer in the perfectibility of mankind; **perfect'ibilism**, the belief that man is capable of becoming perfect or of progressing indefinitely towards perfection; **perfect'ibilist; perfectibil'ity**, capability of becoming perfect: perfectibilism.—*adj.* **perfect'ible**, capable of becoming perfect.—*ns.* **perfec'tion**, state of being perfect: a quality in perfect degree: the highest state or degree: an embodiment of the perfect: loosely, a degree of excellence approaching the perfect.—*v.t.* **perfec'tionate**, to bring to perfection.—*ns.* **perfec'tionism; perfec'tionist**, one who claims to be perfect: one who aims at or calls for nothing short of perfection: one who holds some doctrine concerning perfection: one who thinks that moral perfection can be attained in this life: (*cap.*) one of the Bible Communists or Free-lovers, a small American sect founded by J. H. Noyes (1811-86), which settled at Oneida in 1848, holding that the gospel if accepted secures freedom from sin.—*adj.* **perfect'ive**, tending to make perfect.—*advs.* **perfect'ively; per'fectly**.—*ns.* **per'fectness**, state or quality of being perfect: completeness; **perfect'o** (Sp.), a large tapering cigar; **perfect'or**, one who perfects: a machine for printing both sides at once.—**perfect cadence**, one passing from the chord of the dominant (or subdominant) to that of the tonic; **perfect fifth**, the interval between two sounds whose vibration frequencies are as 2 to 3; **perfect fluid**, an ideal fluid, incompressible, of uniform density, offering no resistance to distorting forces; **perfect fourth**, the interval between sounds whose vibration frequencies are as 3 to 4; **perfect insect**, the imago or completely developed form of an insect; **perfect interval**, the fourth, fifth, or octave; **perfect metals**, noble metals; **perfect number**, a number equal to the sum of its aliquot parts, as $6 = 1+2+3$, $28 = 1+2+4+7+14$; **perfect tense**, tense signifying action completed in past (e.g. *I have said*) or at time spoken of (**past perfect, pluperfect**, e.g. *I had said*; **future perfect**, e.g. *I shall have left by then*).—**to perfection**, perfectly. [M.E. *parfit*—O.Fr. *parfit*; later assimilated to L. *perfectus*, pa.p. of *perficĕre*—pfx. *per-*, thoroughly, *facĕre*, to do.]

**perfervid,** *pər-fûr'vid*, *adj.* very fervid: ardent: eager.—*ns.* **perfervidity** (*pûr-fər-vid'i-ti*); **perfer'-vidness; perfer'vour, -or.** [L. *perfervidus*—*prae*, before, *fervidus*, fervid.]

**perfet,** *pûr'fet, adj.* an older form (used by Milton) of **perfect**.

**perficient,** *pər-fish'ənt*, *adj.* effectual: actually achieving a result. [L. *perficiēns, -entis*, pr.p. of *perficĕre*, to complete—pfx. *per-*, thoroughly, *facĕre*, to do, make.]

**perfidious,** *pər-fid'i-əs*, *adj.* faithless: unfaithful:

basely violating faith.—*adv.* **perfid'iously.**—*ns.* **perfid'iousness, perfidy** (*pûr'fid-i*). [L. *perfidiōsus—perfidia,* faithlessness—pfx. *per-,* implying destruction, *fidēs,* faith.]

**perfoliate,** *pər-fō'li-āt, adj.* (of a leaf) having the base joined around the stem, so as to appear pierced by the stem—orig. said of the stem passing through the leaf, or of the plant. [L. *per,* through, *folium,* a leaf.]

**perforate,** *pûr'fə-rāt, v.t.* to bore through or into: to pierce or to make a hole through: to penetrate: to pass through by a hole.—*adj.* pierced by a hole or holes: having an aperture: dotted with pellucid dots (*bot.*): pierced by rows of small holes for easy separation (as postage-stamps).—*adj.* **per'forable.**—*n.* **per'forans,** the long flexor muscle of the toes, or the deep flexor muscle of the fingers, whose tendons pass through those of the perforatus.—*adj.* **per'forant, perforating.**—*n.* **perforation** (*pûr-fə-rā'shən*), act of making a hole: formation of a hole or aperture: condition of being perforated: a hole through or into anything: a series, or one of a series, of small holes, as for ease in tearing paper.—*adj.* **per'forative,** having the power to pierce.—*ns.* **per'forator,** one who bores: a boring instrument or organ; **perforatus** (*pûr-fə-rā'təs*), the short flexor of the toes or the superficial flexor of the fingers. [L. *perforare, -ātum—per,* through, *forāre,* to bore.]

**perforce,** *pər-fōrs', -fôrs', adv.* by force: of necessity. [O.Fr. *par force.*]

**perform,** *pər-förm', v.t.* to do: to carry out duly: to act in fulfilment of: to carry into effect: to fulfil: to bring about: to render: to execute: to go through duly: to act: to play in due form. —*v.i.* to do what is to be done: to execute a function: to act, behave: to act a part: to play or sing: to do feats, tricks, or other acts for exhibition.—*adj.* **perform'able,** capable of being performed: practicable.—*ns.* **perform'ance,** act of performing: a carrying out of something: something done: a piece of work: manner of success in working: execution, esp. as an exhibition or entertainment: an act or action; **perform'er,** one who performs: one who does or fulfils what is required of him: an executant: one who takes part in a performance or performances: one who does feats or tricks, esp. in exhibition.—*adj.* **perfor'ming,** that performs: trained to perform tricks.—*n.* **performance.**— **performing right,** the right to give a public performance of a piece of music or play. [A.Fr. *parfourmer,* app. an altered form of *parfourner*—O.Fr. *parfournir, par*—L. *per,* through, *fournir,* to furnish.]

**perfume,** *pûr'fūm,* formerly and still sometimes *pər-fūm', n.* sweet-smelling smoke or fumes from burning: any substance made or used for the sake of its smell: fragrance.—*v.t.* **perfume** (*pər-fūm',* sometimes *pûr'fūm*), to scent.—*adjs.* **per'-fumed** (or *pər-fūmd'*); **per'fumeless** (or *-fūm'*).— *ns.* **perfu'mer,** one who fumigates: a maker or seller of perfumes; **perfu'mery,** perfumes in general: the art of preparing perfumes: the place in a shop where perfumes are sold.—*adj.* **per'fumy.** [Fr. *parfum*—L. *per,* through, *fūmus,* smoke.]

**perfunctory,** *pər-fungk'tə-ri, adj.* done merely as a duty to be got through: done for form's sake, or in mere routine: acting without zeal or interest: merely formal: hasty and superficial.—*adv.* **perfunc'torily.**—*n.* **perfunc'toriness.** [L. *perfunctōrius—perfunctus,* pa.p. of *perfungī,* to execute—pfx. *per-,* thoroughly, *fungī,* to do.]

**perfuse,** *pər-fūz', v.t.* to pour or diffuse through or over: to force, as a liquid, through an organ or tissue.—*n.* **perfusion** (*-fū'zhən*).—*adj.* **perfusive** (*-fū'siv*). [L. *perfūsus,* poured over—*per,* through, *fundĕre, fūsus,* to pour.]

**pergameneous,** *pûr-gə-mē'ni-əs, adj.* parchment-like. —*adj.* **pergamentaceous** (*-mən-tā'shəs*), parchment-like. [L. *pergamēna;* see **parchment.**]

**pergola,** *pûr'gə-lə, n.* a structure with climbing plants along a walk. [It.,—L. *pergula,* a shed.]

**pergunnah.** See **pargana.**

**perhaps,** *pər-haps', adv.* it may be: possibly: as it may happen. [From the pl. of **hap,** after the model of **peradventure, percase, perchance.**]

**peri,** *pē'ri, n.* a Persian fairy. [Pers. *pari* or *perī,* a fairy.]

**peri-,** *per'i-, pə-ri'-, pfx.* around. [Gr. *peri,* around.]

**periagua,** *per-i-ä'gwa.* See **piragua.**

**periaktos,** *per-i-ak'tos, n.* in the ancient Greek theatre, a tall revolving prism at the side of the stage, giving change of scene. [Gr., revolving.]

**perianth,** *per'i-anth,* (*bot.*) *n.* calyx and corolla together, esp. when not clearly distinguishable.— Also *adj.* [Gr. *peri,* around, *anthos,* flower.]

**periapt,** *per'i-apt,* (*Shak.*) *n.* an amulet. [Gr. *periapton,* something hung round—*peri, haptein,* to fasten.]

**periblem,** *per'i-blem,* (*bot.*) *n.* the layer of primary meristem from which the cortex is formed, covering the plerome. [Gr. *periblēma,* garment, mantle—*peri, ballein,* to throw.]

**peribolos,** *per-ib'o-los, n.* a precinct: its enclosing wall.—Also (Latinised) **perib'olus.** [Gr.,—*peri, ballein,* to throw.]

**pericardium,** *per-i-kär'di-əm,* (*anat.*) *n.* the sac round the heart.—*adjs.* **pericar'diac, pericar'dial, pericar'dian.**—*n.* **pericardi'tis,** inflammation of the pericardium. [Latinised from Gr. *perikardion—peri, kardiā,* heart.]

**pericarp,** *per'i-kärp,* (*bot.*) *n.* the wall of a fruit, derived from that of the ovary. [Gr. *perikarpion—peri, karpos,* fruit.]

**pericentral,** *per-i-sen'tral, adj.* surrounding a centre or central body.—*adj.* **pericen'tric.** [Gr. *peri, kentron,* point, centre.]

**perichaetium,** *per-i-kē'shyəm, n.* a sheath or cluster of leaves around the archegonia (or the antheridia) in mosses and liverworts.—*adj.* **perichae'tial** (*-shl*). [Gr. *peri, chaitē,* flowing hair.]

**perichondrium,** *per-i-kon'dri-əm, n.* the fibrous investment of cartilage. [Gr. *peri, chondros,* cartilage.]

**perichylous,** *per-i-ki'ləs,* (*bot.*) *adj.* having water-storing tissue outside the green tissue. [Gr. *peri, chylos,* juice.]

**periclase,** *per'i-klāz, -klās, n.* native magnesia. [Gr. pfx. *peri-,* very, *klasis,* fracture (from its perfect cleavage).]

**Periclean,** *per-i-klē'ən, adj.* of *Pericles* (d. 429 B.C.) or the golden age of art and letters at Athens.

**periclinal,** *per-i-kli'nəl, adj.* quaquaversal (*geol.*): parallel to the outer surface (*bot.*).—*n.* **per'icline,** a variety of albite feldspar of oblique appearance. [Gr. *periklinēs,* sloping on all sides—*peri, klinein,* to slope.]

**periclitate,** *pər-ik'li-tāt, v.t.* to endanger. [L. *periclitāri, -ātus.*]

**pericope,** *pər-ik'o-pē, n.* an extract, passage, esp. one selected for reading in church. [Gr. *perikopē—peri, koptein,* to cut.]

**pericranium,** *per-i-krā'ni-əm, n.* the membrane that surrounds the cranium: loosely, skull or brain.—*adj.* **pericrā'nial.**—*n.* **per'icrāny** (*obs.*), pericranium. [Latinised from Gr. *perikrānion—peri, krānion,* skull.]

**periculous,** *pər-ik'ū-ləs,* (*obs.*) *adj.* dangerous. [L. *periculum,* danger.]

**pericycle,** *per'i-sī-kl,* (*bot.*) *n.* the outermost layer or layers of the central cylinder.—*adj.* **pericy'clic.** [Gr. *perikyklos,* all round—*peri, kyklos,* a circle.]

**periderm,** *per'i-dûrm, n.* the horny cuticular covering of a hydroid colony: the cork-cambium with the cork and other tissues derived from it,

forming a protective outer covering in plants.—
*adj.* **peridrm'al**. [Gr. *peri, derma*, skin.]
**peridesmium**, *per-i-des'mi-əm, (anat.) n.* the areolar tissue round a ligament. [Gr. *peri, desmos*, a band.]
**peridinian**, *per-i-din'i-ən, n.* a dinoflagellate.—*n.* **Peridin'ium**, a genus of dinoflagellates. [Gr. *peri, dinos*, a whirl.]
**peridium**, *pər-id'i-əm, n.* the outer coat of a fungus fruit-body.—*adj.* **perid'ial**. [Latinised from Gr. *pēridion*, dim. of *pērā*, a wallet.]
**peridot**, *per'i-dot*, **peridote**, *-dōt, n.* olivine: a green olivine used in jewellery.—*adj.* **peridot'ic**.
—*n.* **peridotite** (*-dō'tīt*), a coarse-grained igneous rock mainly composed of olivine, usually with other ferro-magnesian minerals but little or no feldspar. [Fr. *péridot*; origin unknown.]
**peridrome**, *per'i-drōm, n.* the space between cell and surrounding pillars in an ancient temple. [Gr. *peridromos*, running round—*peri, dromos*, a run.]
**periegesis**, *per-i-ē-jē'sis, n.* a description in manner of a tour: a progress or journey through. [Gr. *periēgēsis—peri, hēgeesthai*, to lead.]
**perigastric**, *per-i-gas'trik, adj.* surrounding the alimentary canal.—*n.* **perigastri'tis**, inflammation of the outer surface of the stomach. [Gr. *peri, gastēr*, belly.]
**perigee**, *per'i-jē, (astron.) n.* the point of the moon's orbit at which it is nearest the earth—opp. to *apogee.*—*adjs.* **perigē'al**, **perigē'an**. [Gr. *perigeion*, neut. of *perigeios*, round or near the earth—*peri, gē*, earth.]
**perigenesis**, *per-i-jen'i-sis, n.* reproduction (according to Haeckel's theory) by transmission not only of chemical material but of vibrations of plastidules. [Gr. *peri, genesis*, generation.]
**perigone**, *per'i-gōn, (bot.) n.* an undifferentiated perianth: a covering of the seed in sedges.—*adj.* **perigō'nial**.—*n.* **perigō'nium**, a cluster of leaves round moss antheridia. [Gr. *peri, gonē*, generative organ.]
**Perigordian**, *per-i-gör'di-ən, adj.* pertaining to the Palaeolithic epoch to which the Lascaux Cave paintings and other examples of primitive art belong. [*Périgord*, region in S.W. France.]
**perigynous**, *pər-ij'i-nəs, (bot.) adj.* having the receptacle developed as a disk or open cup, with sepals, petals, and stamens borne on its margin, the carpels not embedded in it: of sepals, petals, or stamens, inserted on the receptacle in such a way—distinguished from *epigynous* and *hypogynous.*—*n.* **perig'yny**. [Gr. *peri, gynē*, woman (used for female).]
**perihelion**, *per-i-hē'li-ən, n.* the point of the orbit of a planet or a comet at which it is nearest to the sun—opp. to *aphelion*: culmination (*fig.*).—Also *adj.* [Gr. *peri, hēlios*, the sun.]
**perihepatic**, *per-i-hi-pat'ik, adj.* surrounding the liver.—*n.* **perihepatitis** (*-hep-ə-tī'tis*), inflammation of the peritoneum covering the liver. [Gr. *peri, hēpar, hēpatos*, liver.]
**peril**, *per'il, n.* danger.—*v.t.* to expose to danger:—*pr.p.* **per'illing**; *pa.t.* and *pa.p.* **per'illed**.—*adj.* **per'ilous**, dangerous.—*adv.* **per'ilously**.—*n.* **per'ilousness**. [Fr. *péril*—L. *periculum*.]
**perilymph**, *per'i-limf, n.* the fluid surrounding the membranous labyrinth of the ear. [Pfx. **peri-**, and **lymph**.]
**perimeter**, *pər-im'i-tər, n.* the circuit or boundary of any plane figure, or the sum of all its sides (*geom.*): an instrument for measuring the field of vision: the boundary of a camp or fortified position: the outer edge of any area.—*adj.* **perimetric** (*per-i-met'rik*).—*n.* **perim'etry**. [Gr. *perimetros—peri, metron*, measure.]
**perimorph**, *per'i-mörf, n.* a mineral enclosing another.—*adjs.* **perimorph'ic**, **perimorph'ous**. [Gr. *peri, morphē*, form.]
**perinaeum**, **perineum**, *per-i-nē'əm, n.* the lower part of the body between the genital organs and the anus.—*adj.* **perinae'al**, **perinē'al**. [Latinised from Gr. *perinaion*.]
**perinatal**, *per-i-nā'tl, adj.* pertaining to the period between the seventh month of pregnancy and the first week of life. [Pfx. **peri-**, and **natal**.]
**perineurium**, *per-i-nū'ri-əm, n.* the sheath of connective tissue about a bundle of nerve fibres.—*adj.* **perineu'ral**.—*n.* **perineuri'tis**, inflammation of the perineurium. [Gr. *peri, neuron*, nerve.]
**period**, *pē'ri-əd, n.* the time in which anything runs its course: an interval of time at the end of which events recur in the same order: the time required for a complete oscillation—reciprocal of the frequency: the time of a complete revolution of a heavenly body about its primary: the difference between two successive values of a variable for which a function has the same value: the recurring part of a circulating decimal: a set of figures (usu. three) in a large number marked off e.g. by commas: a series of chemical elements represented in a horizontal row of the periodic table: a stretch of time: a long stretch, an age: one of the main divisions of geological time: a stage or phase in history, in a man's life and development, in a disease, or in any course of events: a time: a division of the school day, the time of one lesson: the end of a course: a recurring time: menstrual discharge: an end: a goal: a complete sentence, esp. one of elaborate construction: in music, a division analogous to a sentence: (in pl.) rounded rolling rhetoric: a mark (.) at the end of a sentence—a full stop, the word is inserted at the end of a sentence to emphasise the finality of the statement: a rhythmical division in Greek verse.—*adj.* characteristic, representative, imitative of or dealing with, a past period (of e.g. architecture, furniture, a play).—*v.t. (Shak.)* to put an end to.—*adjs.* **periodic** (*pēr-i-od'ik*), relating to a period or periods: of revolution in an orbit: having a period: recurring regularly in the same order: loosely, occurring from time to time: characterised by or constructed in periods: pertaining to periodicals (*rare*); **period'ical**, periodic: published in numbers at more or less regular intervals: of, for, or in such publications.—*n.* a magazine or other publication that appears at stated intervals (not usually including newspapers): a recurring spree (*U.S.*).—*n.* **period'icalist**, one who writes in a periodical.—*adv.* **period'ically**, at regular intervals: in a periodic manner: in a periodical publication: loosely, from time to time.—*ns.* **periodicity** (*-dis'*), the fact or character of being periodic: frequency; **periodisation**, **-ization**, division into periods.—**periodic function** (*math.*), one whose values recur in a cycle as the variable increases; **periodic law**, that the properties of atoms are periodic functions of their atomic numbers; **periodic table**, a table of chemical elements in order of atomic number arranged in horizontal series and vertical groups, showing how similar properties recur at regular intervals; **periodic wind**, wind which blows at or for a certain period—e.g. a trade-wind, a monsoon, a land-breeze, a sea-breeze; **period piece**, an object belonging to a past age but (usu.) without charm or value: a person ludicrously behind the times: a play, etc., set in a past time.—**the period**, the current age, or age in question. [Fr. *période*—L. *periodus*—Gr. *periodos—peri, hodos*, a way.]
**periodate**, *pər-i'ō-dāt, n.* a salt of periodic acid.—**periodic acid** (*per-i-od'ik*), an acid ($H_5IO_6$) containing more oxygen than iodic acid. [Pfx. **per-**, and **iodine**.]
**periodontal**, *per-i-ō-dont'əl, adj.* (pertaining to tissues or regions) round about a tooth.—*ns.* **periodon'tia** (*-shi-ə*), **periodon'tics**, **periodontol'ogy**,

branch of dentistry concerned with periodontal diseases. [Gr. *peri, odous, odontos,* tooth.]

**Periophthalmus,** *per-i-of-thal'məs, n.* a genus of fishes, allied to gobies, with protruding mobile eyes and pectoral fins used as legs. [Latinised from Gr. *peri, ophthalmos,* eye.]

**periosteum,** *per-i-os'ti-əm, n.* a tough fibrous membrane covering the surface of bones.—Also **per'iost.**—*adjs.* **perios'teal; periostit'ic.**—*n.* **periosti'tis,** inflammation of the periosteum. [Gr. *periosteon* (neut. adj.)—*peri, osteon,* a bone.]

**periostracum,** *per-i-os'trə-kəm, n.* the horny outer layer of a mollusc's shell. [Latinised from Gr. *peri, ostrakon,* shell.]

**periotic,** *per-i-ō'tik, -ot'ik, adj.* around the inner ear.—*n.* a periotic bone. [Gr. *peri, ous, ōtos,* the ear.]

**peripatetic,** *per-i-pə-tet'ik, adj.* walking about: Aristotelian: of e.g. a teacher, itinerant.—*n.* a pedestrian: an itinerant: an Aristotelian.—*adj.* **peripatet'ical.**—*n.* **peripatet'icism** (*-i-sizm*), the philosophy of Aristotle. [Gr. *peripatētikos—peripatos,* a walk—*peri, patein,* to walk. Aristotle is said to have taught in the walks of the Lyceum at Athens.]

**Peripatus,** *pər-ip'ə-təs, n.* a genus of arthropods of the Onychophora, showing affinities with worms. [Gr. *peripatos,* a walking about; cf. **peripatetic.**]

**peripet(e)ia,** *per-i-pe-ti'ə, n.* a sudden change of fortune, esp. in drama.—Also **perip'ety.** [Gr. *peripeteia—peri,* and *pet-* the root of *piptein,* to fall.]

**periphery,** *pər-if'ə-ri, n.* bounding line or surface: the outside of anything: a surrounding region.—*adjs.* **periph'eral, peripheric** (*per-i-fer'ik*), **-al.**—**peripheral units,** in a computer system, the input (e.g. card reader), output (e.g. magnetic tape), and storage devices, which are computer-controlled; **periphery camera** (same as **all-round camera**). [Gr. *periphereia—peri, pherein,* to carry.]

**periphrasis,** *pər-if'rə-sis, n.* round-about expression:—*pl.* **periph'rases,** *-sēz.*—*n.* **periphrase** (*per'i-frāz*), **periphrasis:**—*pl.* **periphrās'es.**—*v.t.* to say with circumlocution.—*v.i.* to use circumlocution.—*adjs.* **periphrastic** (*per-i-fras'tik*), **-al.**—*adv.* **periphras'tically.** [Gr. *periphrasis—peri, phrasis,* speech.]

**periplast,** *per'i-pläst,* (*zool.*) *n.* intercellular substance: the ectoplasm of flagellates: cuticle covering the ectoplasm. [Gr. *peri, plastos,* moulded.]

**periplus,** *per'i-plus, n.* a circumnavigation: a narrative of a coasting voyage. [Gr. *periploos,* contr. *-plous—peri, ploos, plous,* a voyage.]

**periproct,** *per'i-prokt,* (*zool.*) *n.* the region about the anus, esp. in a sea-urchin. [Gr. *peri, prōktos,* anus.]

**peripteral,** *pər-ip'tə-rəl,* (*archit.*) *adj.* having one row of columns all round. [Gr. *peripteros—peri,* and *pteron,* a wing.]

**perique,** *pə-rēk', n.* a strongly-flavoured tobacco from Louisiana. [Perh. *Périque,* nickname of a grower.]

**perisarc,** *per'i-särk,* (*zool.*) *n.* in some Hydrozoans, the chitinous layer covering the polyps, etc. [Gr. *peri, sarx, sarkos,* flesh.]

**periscian,** *pər-ish'i-ən, n.* a dweller within the polar circle, whose shadow moves round in a complete circle on those days on which the sun does not set.—Also *adj.* [Gr. *peri, skiā,* a shadow.]

**periscope,** *per'i-skōp, n.* a tube with mirrors by which an observer in a trench, a submarine, etc., can see what is going on above.—*adj.* **periscopic** (*-skop'ik*). [Gr. *peri, skopeein,* to see.]

**perish,** *per'ish, v.i.* to pass away completely: to waste away: to decay: to lose life: to be destroyed: to be ruined or lost.—*v.t.* to destroy :

to ruin: to cause to decay: to distress with cold, hunger, etc.—*n.* **perishabil'ity.**—*adj.* **per'ishable,** that may perish: subject to speedy decay. —*n.* that which is perishable: (in *pl.*) food or other stuff liable to rapid deterioration.—*n.* **per'ishableness.**—*adv.* **per'ishably.**—*adj.* **per'-ished,** distressed by cold, hunger, etc. (*coll.* or *dial.*): weakened or injured by age or exposure. —*n.* **per'isher** (*slang*), a reprehensible and annoying person.—*adj.* **per'ishing** (*coll.* or *dial.*), freezingly cold: vaguely used as a pejorative.— Also *adv.*—*adv.* **per'ishingly.** [O.Fr. *perir,* p.p. *perissant*—L. *perire, perītum,* to perish—pfx. *per-, īre,* to go.]

**perisperm,** *per'i-spûrm,* (*bot.*) *n.* nutritive tissue in a seed derived from the nucellus.—*adj.* **perisper'mic.** [Gr. *peri, sperma,* seed.]

**perispomenon,** *per-i-spō'mən-on, adj.* having a circumflex accent on the last syllable.—*n.* a word so accented. [Gr., drawn round, circumflexed —*peri, spaein,* to pull, pluck.]

**perissodactyl,** *pər-is-ō-dak'til, adj.* having an odd number of toes.—*n.* an animal of the **Perissodac'tyla,** a division of ungulates with an odd number of toes on the hindfoot—horse, tapir, rhinoceros, and extinct kinds (distinguished from the *Artiodactyla*).—*adjs.* **perissodac'tylate, perissodactyl'ic, perissodac'tylous.** [Gr. *perissos,* odd, *daktylos,* a finger, toe.]

**perissology,** *per-is-ol'ə-ji, n.* verbiage: pleonasm. [Gr. *perissologiā—perissos,* excessive, *logos,* speech.]

**perissosyllabic,** *pər-is-ō-sil-ab'ik, adj.* having an additional syllable. [Gr. *perissosyllabos—perissos,* excessive, *syllabē,* syllable.]

**peristalith,** *pər-is'tə-lith, n.* a stone-circle. [Irregularly formed from Gr. *peri, histanai,* to set up, *lithos,* a stone.]

**peristaltic,** *per-i-stalt'ik, adj.* forcing onward by waves of contraction, as the alimentary canal and other organs do their contents.—*n.* **peristal'sis.**—*adj.* **peristalt'ically.** [Gr. *peristaltikos—peristellein,* to wrap round—*peri, stellein,* to place.]

**peristerite,** *pər-is'tər-it, n.* an albite feldspar with pigeon-like play of colour. [Gr. *peristerā,* pigeon.]

**peristeronic,** *pər-is-tər-on'ik, adj.* of pigeons: pigeon-fancying. [Gr. *peristerōn, -ōnos,* pigeon-house.]

**peristome,** *per'i-stōm, n.* the area, or a structure, surrounding a mouth: the fringe of teeth around the mouth of a moss-capsule: the margin of a gasteropod shell.—*adjs.* **peristōm'al, peristomat'ic, peristōm'ial.** [Gr.*peri, stoma, -atos,* mouth.]

**peristrephic,** *per-i-stref'ik, adj.* moving round, revolving, rotatory. [Irregularly—Gr. *peristrephein,* to whirl—*peri, strephein,* to turn.]

**peristyle,** *per'i-stil, n.* a range of columns round a building or round a square: a court, square, etc., with columns all round.—*adj.* **peristy'lar.** [L. *peristȳl(i)um*—Gr. *peristȳlon—peri, stȳlos,* a column.]

**perithecium,** *per-i-thē'si-əm, shi-əm, n.* a flask-shaped fruit-body in fungi:—*pl.* **-ia.**—*adj.* **perithe'cial.** [Gr. *peri, thēkē,* case.]

**peritonaeum, peritoneum,** *per-i-tən-ē'əm, n.* a serous membrane enclosing the viscera in the abdominal and pelvic cavities.—*adjs.* **peritonae'al, peritonē'al; peritonitic** (*it'ik*), of peritonitis: suffering from peritonitis.—*n.* **peritoni'tis,** inflammation of the peritonaeum. [Gr. *peritonaion—peri, teinein,* to stretch.]

**perityphlitis,** *per-i-tif-li'tis, n.* inflammation of some part near the blind-gut. [Gr. *peri, typhlos,* blind.]

**periwig,** *per'i-wig, n.* a wig.—*v.t.* to dress with, or as with, a wig:—*pr.p.* **per'iwigging;** *pa.t.* and *pa.p.* **per'iwigged.**—*adj.* **per'iwig-pā'ted,** wearing a periwig. [Earlier *perwyke, perwig, perywig*, etc.—Fr. *perruque*; see peruke, wig.]

periwinkle, *per'i-wingk-l, n.* a creeping evergreen plant, growing in woods (*Vinca minor* and *V. major*; fam. Apocynaceae). [M.E. *peruenke*—O.E. *peruince*, from L. *pervinca*.]

periwinkle, *per'i-wingk-l, n.* an edible gasteropod (*Littorina littorea*) abundant between tide-marks, or other member of the genus: extended to other kinds.—Also pennywinkle. [O.E. (pl.) *pinewinclan* (or perh. *winewinclan*)—*wincle*, a whelk.]

perjink, *pər-jingk', (Scot.) adj.* prim: finical.—Also perjink'ety.—*n.* perjink'ity, a nicety. [Origin unknown.]

perjure, *púr'jər, v.t. (refl.)* to forswear oneself: to cause to swear falsely.—*v.i.* to swear falsely.—*n.* (Shak.) a perjured person.—*adj.* per'jured, having sworn falsely: being sworn falsely, as an oath.—*n.* per'jurer.—*adjs.* perjurious (*-joo'ri-əs*), per'jurous, guilty of or involving perjury.—*n.* per'jury, false swearing: the breaking of an oath: the crime committed by one who, when giving evidence on oath or affirmation as a witness in a court of justice, gives evidence which he knows to be false (*law*). [O.Fr. *parjurer*—L. *perjūrāre*—*per-, jūrāre*, to swear.]

perk, *púrk, v.i.* to bear oneself with self-confidence or self-assertion: to cock up: to stick out: to thrust forward (also *v.t.* with *it*): to move with pert briskness: to recover spirits or energy, esp. in sickness (with *up*): to sit upright: to cock or toss or hold up the head: to prank oneself up.—*v.t.* to prank or trim: to jerk up, cock up, prop up.—*adj.* brisk: self-confident in manner.—*adv.* perk'ily.—*n.* perk'iness.—*adj.* perk'y, self-assertive: cocky: pert: in good spirits. [Origin uncertain.]

perk, *púrk,* a Northern and East Anglian form of perch.

perk, *n.* Short for perquisite.

perkin. See parkin.

perlite, *púrl'it, n.* any acid volcanic glass with perlitic structure: pearlite.—*adj.* perlitic (*-it'ik*), showing little concentric spheroidal or spiral cracks between rectilineal ones. [Fr. and Ger. *perle*, pearl.]

perlous, *púr'ləs, (Spens.) adj.* Same as perilous.

perlustrate, *pər-lus'trāt, v.t.* to traverse and inspect.—*n.* perlustrā'tion. [L. *perlustrāre, -ātum*.]

perm, *púrm, (coll.) n.* abbrev. of permutation.—*v.t.* to permute: to arrange a forecast according to some defined system of combination or permutation.

perm, *púrm, (coll.) n.* abbrev. of permanent wave.—*v.t. (coll.)* to impart a permanent wave to.

permafrost, *púr'mə-frost, n.* permanently frozen subsoil. [*permanent, frost*.]

permanent, *púr'mə-nənt, adj.* remaining, or intended to remain, indefinitely.—*ns.* per'manence, fact or state of being permanent; per'manency, permanence: a thing that is permanent.—*adv.* per'manently.—permanent magnet (see magnet); per'manent teeth, the adult teeth, which come after the milk-teeth lost in childhood; permanent wave, a long-lasting artificial wave in hair—familiarly contracted perm; permanent way, the finished road of a railway. [L. *permanēns, -entis,* pr.p. of *permanēre*—*per-,* through, *manēre,* to continue.]

permanganic, *púr-mang-gan'ik, adj.* applied to an acid ($HMnO_4$) and its anhydride ($Mn_2O_7$) containing more oxygen than manganic acid and anhydride.—*n.* permanganate (*pər-mang'gə-nāt*), a salt of permanganic acid, esp. potassium permanganate, ($KMnO_4$) which is used as an oxidising and bleaching agent and as a disinfectant. [Pfx. per-, and manganese.]

permeate, *púr'mi-āt, v.t.* to pass through the pores of: to penetrate and fill the pores of: to pervade: to saturate.—*v.i.* to diffuse.—*n.* permeabil'ity.—*adj.* per'meable.—*adv.* per'meably.—*ns.* per'meance, reciprocal of the reluctance of a magnetic circuit; permeā'tion.—*adj.* per'meative, having power to permeate.—magnetic permeability, the ratio of flux-density to magnetising force. [L. *permeāre*—*per,* through, *meāre,* to pass.]

Permian, *púr'mi-ən, (geol.) n.* the uppermost Palaeozoic system.—*adj.* of that system.—*n.* and *adj.* Permo-Carbonif'erous, Upper Carboniferous and Lower Permian. [*Perm,* in Russia, where it is widely developed.]

permis de séjour, *per-mē də sā-zhōōr, (Fr.)* permission to reside in a foreign country, given by the police of that country.

permissible, etc. See permit.

permit, *pər-mit', v.t.* to allow: (*refl.*) to indulge (in; *arch.*): to leave, refer, submit (to; *obs.*)—*v.i.* to allow:—*pr.p.* permitt'ing; *pa.t, pa.p* permitt'ed.—*n.* (*púr'*) permission, esp. in writing.—*n.* permissibil'ity.—*adj.* permiss'ible, that may be permitted: allowable.—*adv.* permiss'ibly.—*n.* permission (*-mish'ən*), act of permitting: leave.—*adj.* permiss'ive, granting permission or liberty: permitted, optional: lenient, indulgent: allowing much freedom in social conduct (as in the permissive society—from c. 1960).—*adv.* permiss'ively.—*ns.* permiss'iveness; permitt'ance (*rare*), permission; permitt'er; permittiv'ity, (*absolute permittivity*) the ratio of the electric displacement in a medium to the electric field intensity producing it: (*relative permittivity*) the ratio of the electric displacement in a medium to that which would be produced in free space by the same field. [L. *permittĕre, -missum,* to let pass through—*per, mittēre,* to send.]

permute, *pər-mūt', v.t.* to interchange: to transmute: to subject to permutation.—*n.* permūtabil'ity.—*adj.* permūt'able, interchangeable.—*v.t.* per'mūtate, to subject to permutation.—*n.* permutā'tion, barter (*obs.*): transmutation: the arrangement of a set of things in every possible order (*math.*): any one possible order of arrangement of a given number of things taken from a given number: immediate inference by obversion (*logic*): a forecast of a specified number of results from a larger number of matches based on some defined system of combination or permutation: any such system. [L. *permūtāre,* to change thoroughly—pfx. *per-, mūtāre,* to change.]

pern, *púrn, n.* a honey-buzzard (*Pernis*). [Cuvier's mistake for Gr. *pternis,* a kind of hawk.]

pernancy, *púr'nən-si, (law) n.* receiving. [A.Fr. *pernance* (O.Fr. *prenance*).]

Pernettya, *pər-net'i-ə, n.* a genus (family Ericaceae) of evergreen shrubs with bright berries. [A. J. Pernetty, explorer.]

pernicious, *pər-nish'əs, adj.* destructive: highly injurious: malevolent.—*adv.* perni'ciously.—*n.* perni'ciousness. [L. *perniciōsus*—pfx. *per-, nex, necis,* death by violence.]

pernicious, *pər-nish'əs, (Milt.) adj.* swift, ready, prompt. [L. *pernix, -icis,* nimble.]

pernickety, *pər-nik'i-ti, adj.* finical: exacting minute care.—*n.* pernick'etiness. [Scots; origin unknown.]

pernoctation, *púr-nok-tā'shən, n.* passing the night: a watch, vigil. [L. *per,* through, *nox, noctis,* night.]

perone, *per'o-nē, n.* the fibula.—*adj.* perone'al.—*n.* perone'us, one of several fibular muscles. [Gr. *peronē*.]

peroration, *per-ə-rā'shən, -ō-, -ö-, n.* the conclusion of a speech: a rhetorical performance.—*v.i.* per'orate, to make a peroration: to harangue (*coll.*). [L. *perōrātiō, -ōnis*—*per,* through, *ōrāre,* to speak—*ōs, ōris,* the mouth.]

**peroxide,** *pər-oks'id, n.* an oxide with the highest proportion of oxygen: one that yields hydrogen peroxide on treatment with an acid: colloquially, hydrogen peroxide (H₂O₂).—*v.t.* to treat or bleach with hydrogen peroxide.—*n.* peroxidā'tion (*-id-*).—*v.t.* and *v.i.* perox'idise, -ize. [Pfx. per-, and oxide.]

**perpend,** *pər-pend', v.t.* to weigh in the mind, to consider carefully. [L. *perpendĕre*—pfx. *per-*, *pendĕre*, to weigh.]

**perpend,** *pûr'pənd,* **perpent,** *-pənt.* Same as **parpen.**

**perpendicular,** *pûr-pən-dik'ū-lər, adj.* erect: vertical: upright: in the direction of gravity or at right angles to the plane of the horizon: at right angles (to a given line or surface; *geom.*): in the Perpendicular style of architecture.—*n.* an instrument for determining the vertical line: a straight line or plane perpendicular to another line or surface: verticality or erectness: in a ship, a vertical line from each end of the waterline: a meal or entertainment at which the guests do not sit (*slang*).—*n.* perpendicularity (*-lar'i-ti*), state of being perpendicular.—*adv.* perpendic'ularly.—**Perpendicular style,** a late English style of Gothic architecture (late 14th to mid-16th cent.) marked by vertical window-tracery, depressed or four-centre arch, fantracery vaulting, and panelled walls. [L. *perpendiculāris*—*perpendiculum,* a plumb-line—pfx. *per-*, *pendĕre,* to hang.]

**perpetrate,** *pûr'pi-trāt, v.t.* to execute or commit (esp. an offence).—*adj.* per'petrable.—*ns.* petrā'tion, per'petrātor. [L. *perpetrāre, -ātum* —pfx. *per-*, *patrāre,* to achieve.]

**perpetual,** *pər-pet'ū-al, adj.* never ceasing: everlasting: not temporary: incessant: unintermitting: continuously blooming: perennial.—*adv.* perpetually.—*n.* a perennial: a continuously blooming hybrid rose.—*ns.* perpet'ualism; perpet'ualist, one who advocates the perpetual continuation of anything; perpetuality (*-al'i-ti*).—*adv.* perpet'ually.—**perpetual curate,** formerly, in the Church of England, an incumbent of a parish who had no endowment of tithes—since 1868 called vicar; **perpetual motion,** a machine, or motion of a machine, that should do work indefinitely without receiving new energy from without; **perpetual-mo'tionist,** a believer in the possibility of perpetual motion; **perpetual screw,** an endless screw. [L. *perpetuālis*—*perpetuus,* continuous.]

**perpetuate,** *pər-pet'ū-āt, v.t.* to cause to last for ever or for a very long time: to preserve from extinction or oblivion: to pass on, cause to continue to be believed, known, etc.—*adj.* perpetuated.—*adj.* perpet'ūable.—*ns.* perpet'ūance, perpetuation; perpetuā'tion, continuation or preservation for ever, or for a very long time: preservation from extinction or oblivion; perpet'ūātor. [L. *perpetuāre, -ātum*—*perpetuus,* perpetual.]

**perpetuity,** *pûr-pi-tū'i-ti, n.* state of being perpetual: endless time: duration for an indefinite period: something lasting for ever: the sum paid for a perpetual annuity: the annuity itself: an arrangement whereby property is tied up, or rendered inalienable, for all time or for a very long time. [L. *perpetuitās, -ātis*—*perpetuus,* perpetual.]

**perpetuum mobile,** *pər-pet'ū-əm mō'bil-i,* *perpet'ōō-ōōm mō'bil-e,* (L.) perpetual motion (lit. movable).

**perplex,** *pər-pleks', v.t.* to embarrass or puzzle with difficulties or intricacies: to bewilder: to tease with suspense or doubt: to complicate: to interweave: to tangle.—*n.* (*obs.*) a difficulty. —*adv.* perplex'edly.—*n.* perplex'edness.—*adj.* perplex'ing.—*adv.* perplex'ingly.—*n.* perplex'ity, state of being perplexed: confusion of mind arising from doubt, etc.: embarrassment: doubt:

intricacy: tangle. [L. *perplexus,* entangled— pfx. *per-*, *plexus,* involved, pa.p. of *plectĕre.*]

**perquisite,** *pûr'kwi-zit, n.* property acquired otherwise than by inheritance (*law; obs.*): a casual profit: anything left over that a servant or other has by custom a right to keep: a tip expected upon some occasions: emoluments: something regarded as falling to one by right. —*ns.* perquisition (*-zish'ən*), a strict search: diligent inquiry; perquis'itor, the first purchaser of an estate. [L. *perquisitum,* from *perquirĕre,* to seek diligently—pfx. *per-*, *quaerĕre,* to ask.]

**perradius,** *pər-rā'di-əs, n.* any one of the primary radii of a coelenterate:—*pl.* perradii (*-i*).—*adj.* perra'dial. [Mod. L.—pfx. *per-*, *radius.*]

**perrier,** *per'i-ər,* (*obs.*) *n.* a machine or gun for discharging stones. [O.Fr.]

**perron,** *per'ən,* per-ō, *n.* a raised platform or terrace at an entrance door: an external flight of steps leading up to it. [Fr.,—L. *petra,* stone.]

**perruque, perruquier.** See **peruke.**

**perry,** *per'i, n.* a drink made from fermented pear juice. [O.Fr. *peré*—L.L. *pēra* (L. *pirum*), pear.]

**persant, persaunt** (*Spens.*). Same as **perceant.**

**perscrutation,** *pûr-skrōō-tā'shən, n.* a thorough search. [L. *per, scrūtāri,* to search carefully.]

**perse,** *pûrs, adj.* dark blue, bluish-grey.—*n.* a dark-blue colour: a cloth of such colour. [O.Fr. *pers.*]

**perse,** *pûrs,* a Spenserian form of *pierce:*—*pa.p.* and *pa.t.* **perst.**

**persecute,** *pûr'si-kūt, v.t.* to harass, afflict, hunt down, or put to death, esp. for religious or political opinions.—*n.* persecū'tion.—*adj.* per'secūtive.—*n.* per'secūtor.—*adj.* per'secūtory. [L. *persequī, persecūtus*—pfx. *per-*, *sequi,* to follow.]

**perseity,** *pər-sē'i-ti, n.* an independent existence. [L. *per sē,* in itself.]

**perseline,** *pûr'si-lēn, n.* a Spenserian form of **purslane.**

**Perseus,** *pûr'sūs, n.* a fabled Greek hero who slew the Gorgon Medusa, and rescued Andromeda from a sea-monster: a constellation in the northern sky.—*n.* Per'seid (*-si-id*), a meteor of a swarm whose radiant is in the constellation Perseus. [Gr. *Perseus.*]

**persevere,** *pûr-si-vēr',* formerly (*Shak.*) *pər-sev'ər, v.i.* to continue (*obs.*): to continue steadfastly: to keep on striving.—*n.* perseve'rance (formerly *pər-sev'ər-əns*), act or state of persevering: continued application to anything which one has begun: a going on till success is met with.—*adj.* persev'erant, steadfast.—*v.i.* persev'erate, to recur or tend to recur (*psych.*): to repeat the same actions or thoughts.—*ns.* perseveration (*pûr-sev-ər-ā'shən*), meaningless repetition of an action, utterance, thought, etc.: tendency to experience difficulty in leaving one activity for another; persev'erātor.—*adj.* perseve'ring.—*adv.* perseve'ringly.—**perseverance of saints,** the Calvinistic doctrine that those who are effectually called by God cannot fall away so as to be finally lost. [Fr. *persévérer*—L. *persevērāre*— *persevērus,* very strict—pfx. *per-*, *sevērus,* strict.]

**Persian,** *pûr'shən, -shyən, -zhən, -zhyən, adj.* of, from, or relating to *Persia,* its inhabitants, or language.—*n.* a native or citizen of Persia: the language of Persia: a male figure serving as a column (*archit.*): a Persian cat.—*v.t.* and *v.i.* Per'sianise, -ize.—*adj.* Persic (*pûr'sik*), Persian. —*n.* the Persian language.—*v.t.* and *v.i.* Per'sicise, -ize, (*-sīz*), to turn Persian: to assimilate to what is Persian.—*ns.* Per'sism, a Persian idiom; Per'sist, one who has a scholarly knowledge of Persian and things Persian.—**Persian berry,** the fruit of several buckthorns; **Persian blinds,** persiennes; **Persian carpet,** a rich, soft carpet of the kind woven in Persia; **Persian cat,** a kind of cat with long, silky hair and bushy tail; **Persian**

**powder,** an insect-powder made from Pyrethrum; **Persian wheel,** a large under-shot wheel for raising water.

**persicaria,** *pür-si-kā'ri-ə, n.* a species of knot-grass with black-blotched leaves: extended to other species of Polygonum, by some made a separate genus. [L.L. *persicāria,* peach-tree, from the similarity in leaves.]

**persico, persicot,** *pür'si-kō, n.* a cordial flavoured with kernels of peaches and apricots. [Fr. *persico* (now *persicot*)—It. *persico*—L. *persicum,* a peach.]

**persienne,** *per-si-en', n.* an Eastern cambric or muslin with coloured printed pattern: (in *pl.*) Persian blinds, outside shutters of thin movable slats in a frame. [Fr., Persian (fem.).]

**persiflage,** *pür-si-fläzh', n.* banter: flippancy.—*n.* **persifleur** (*-flür'*), a banterer. [Fr.,—*persifler,* to banter—L. *per,* through, Fr. *siffler*—L. *sibilāre,* to whistle, to hiss.]

**persimmon,** *pər-sim'ən, n.* a date-plum or date-plum tree. [From an Amer.-Indian word.]

**persist,** *pər-sist', v.i.* to continue steadfastly or obstinately, esp. against opposition (often with *in*): to persevere: to insist: to continue to be, to remain (*Milt.*): to continue to exist: to remain in the mind after the external cause is removed.—*v.t.* to assert or repeat insistently.—*ns.* **persis'tence, persis'tency,** quality of being persistent: perseverance: obstinacy: duration, esp. of an effect after the exciting cause has been removed.—*adj.* **persis'tent,** persisting: pushing on, esp. against opposition: tenacious: fixed: constant or constantly repeated: remaining after the usual time of falling off, withering, or disappearing (*zool., bot.*): continuing to grow beyond the usual time.—Also *n.*—*advs.* **persis'-tently; persis'tingly.**—*adj.* **persis'tive** (*Shak.*), persistent. [L. *persistĕre*—*per, sistĕre,* to cause to stand, to stand—*stāre,* to stand.]

**person,** *pür'sn, n.* character represented, as on the stage: a capacity in which one is acting: a living soul or self-conscious being: a personality: a human being, sometimes used slightingly or patronisingly: an individual of a compound or colonial animal: the outward appearance, etc.: bodily form: human figure (often including clothes): bodily presence or action: a personage (*obs.*): a hypostasis of the Godhead (*theol.*): a human being (*natural person*), or a corporation (*artificial person*) regarded as having rights and duties under the law: a form of inflexion or use of a word according as it, or its subject, represents the person, persons, thing, or things speaking (*first person*), spoken to (*second*), or spoken about (*third*) (*gram.*).—*n.* **persona** (*pər-sōn'ə;* L.) Jung's term for a person's system of adaptation to, or manner assumed when dealing with, the world—the outermost part of the consciousness, the expression of the personality: Roman actor's mask: character in fiction, esp. in drama: speaker in a poem: social façade or public image:—*pls.* **-ae** (*-ē, -i*), **-s.**—*adj.* **per'sonable,** having a well-formed body or person: of good appearance. —*ns.* **per'sonableness; per'sonage,** bodily frame or appearance: a person: an exalted or august person: a character in a play or story: recognised or imagined character or personality (*Spens.,* etc.). —*adj.* **per'sonal,** of the nature of a person: of or relating to a person or personality: relating, referring, or pointing to a particular person or persons: aiming offensively at a particular person or persons: belonging or peculiar to a person: own: one's own: of private concern: relating to private concerns: bodily: in bodily presence: (of telephone call) made to a particular person (timed only from the moment the named person is contacted, but subject to an initial fixed charge): by one's own action:

indicating person (*gram.*): opposed to *real,* orig. not recoverable by a *real action* (for the restitution of the specific thing), but such as compensation might be claimed for (*English law*): hence (now) passing at death not to the heir (as real property) but to the executor.—*n.pl.* **personalia** (*-ā'li-ə*), notes, anecdotes, or particulars relating to persons.—*n.* **personalisā'tion, -z-.**—*v.t.* **per'sonalise, -ize,** to personify: to apply to, or take as referring to, a definite person: to give a mark or character to (something) so that it is identifiable as belonging to a certain person (*coll.*).—*ns.* **per'sonalism,** the character of being personal: a theory or doctrine that attributes personality, or spiritual freedom and responsibility, as distinct from mere individuality, to human beings, esp. that enunciated by Emmanuel Mounier in 1936; **per'sonalist,** one who writes personal notes; **personal'ity,** fact or state of being a person or of being personal: existence as a person: individuality: distinctive or well-marked character: a person: direct reference to, or an utterance aimed at, a particular person or persons, esp, of a derogatory nature: personalty (*law; rare*): the integrated organisation of all the psychological, intellectual, emotional, and physical characteristics of an individual, especially as they are presented to other people (*psych.*).—*adv.* **per'sonally,** in a personal or direct manner: in person: individually: for my part (*coll.*).—*n.* **per'sonalty** (*law*), all the property which, when a man dies, goes to his executor or administrator, as distinguished from the realty, which goes to his heir-at-law. —*v.t.* **per'sonate,** to assume the likeness or character of: to play the part of: to mimic: to pass oneself off as: to represent in the form of a person: to symbolise.—*adj.* **feigned** (*arch.*): mask-like: of a lipped corolla, closed by an upward bulge of the lower lip (*bot.*).—*adj.* **per'sonāted,** feigned.—*ns.* **per'sonāting; personā'tion.**—*adj.* **per'sonātive,** dramatic: presenting or presented through persons.—*n.* **per'sonātor.**—*v.t.* **per'sonise, -ize,** to personify.—*n.* **personnel'** (Fr.), the persons employed in any service, as distinguished from the *matériel.*— **personal chair,** a university chair created for the period of tenure of a particular person; **personal equation** (see **equation**); **personal exception** (*Scots law*), a ground of objection which applies to an individual and prevents him from doing something which, but for his conduct or situation, he might do; **personal identity,** the continued sameness of the individual person, through all changes, as testified by consciousness; **personality cult,** excessive adulation of the individual, orig. in Communist usage; **personal rights,** rights which belong to a person as a living, reasonable being; **personal security,** security or pledge given by a person, as distinguished from the delivery of some object of value as security; **personal service,** delivery of a message or an order into a person's hands, as distinguished from delivery in any other indirect way: attention or service of the proprietor of a concern, rather than one of his employees or assistants; **personal transaction,** something done by a person's own effort, not through the agency of another.—*adj.* **person-to-person,** (of telephone call) personal: involving meeting or contact.—Also *adv.*—**in person,** in actual bodily presence: by one's own act, not by an agent or representative. [L. *persōna,* a player's mask, perh. from Etruscan *phersu,* masked figures, commonly associated (in spite of difference of quantity) with *personāre, -ātum*—*per, sonāre,* to sound; cf. **parson.**]

**persona.** See **person.**

**persona,** *pər-sōn'a,* (L.) person.—**persona grata,** *grā', grä'ta,* person who is acceptable, esp.

diplomatically acceptable to a foreign government **persona muta,** _mū′ta, mōō′ta,_ character in an opera who neither speaks nor sings.—**dramatis personae** (see drama); **in propria persona** (_L.L._), _in prō′pri-a,_ in person; **persona non grata,** opp. of **persona grata.**

**personify,** _pər-son′i-fī, v.t._ to represent as a person: to ascribe personality to: to be the embodiment of: to personate (_rare_):—_pr.p._ **person′ifying;** _pa.t._ and _pa.p._ **person′ified.**—_ns._ **personificā′tion; person′ifier.** [L. _persōna,_ a person, _facĕre,_ to make: see foregoing.]

**personnel.** See person.

**perspective,** _pər-spek′tiv,_ formerly _pûr′, n._ optics (_obs._): a telescope, microscope, or other optical instrument (also **perspective glass;** _obs._): the art or science of drawing objects on a surface, so as to give the picture the same appearance to the eye as the objects themselves: appearance, or representation of appearance, of objects in space, with effect of distance, solidity, etc.: just proportion in all the parts: a picture in perspective: a picture or model that seems confused except when viewed in the right direction, or in some other way gives a fantastic effect (_Shak._): a peep-show (_obs._): a vista: a prospect of the future: inspection (_obs._).—_adj._ optical (_obs._): pertaining or according to perspective.—_adv._ **perspec′tively.**—**perspective plane,** the surface on which the picture of the objects to be represented in perspective is drawn.—**in perspective,** according to the laws of perspective: in just proportion: in prospect (_obs._). [L. (_ars_) _perspectiva,_ perspective (art)—_perspicĕre, perspectum—per, specĕre,_ to look.]

**Perspex,** _pûr′speks, n._ a proprietary thermoplastic resin of exceptional transparency and freedom from colour, used for windscreens, etc.

**perspicacious,** _pûr-spi-kā′shəs, adj._ clear-sighted (_arch._): clear-minded.—_adv._ **perspicā′ciously.**—_n._ **perspicacity** (-_kas′i-ti_). [L. _perspicāx, -ācis;_ see perspective.]

**perspicuous,** _pər-spik′ū-əs, adj._ lucid.—_n._ **perspicū′ity.**—_adv._ **perspic′uously.**—_n._ **perspic′uousness.** [L. _perspicuus;_ see preceding.]

**perspire,** _pər-spīr′, v.i._ to exude: to sweat.—_v.t._ to exhale.—_adj._ **perspir′able,** capable of being perspired or of perspiring.—_v.i._ **perspirate** (_pûr′-spir-āt; rare_), to sweat.—_n._ **perspiration** (-_spir-ā′shən_), act of perspiring: sweat.—_adj._ **perspir′atory.** [L. _perspirāre, -ātum—per, spirāre,_ to breathe.]

**perstringe,** _pər-strinj′, v.t._ to constrain (_obs._): to touch on (_obs._): to dull (_obs._): to censure. [L. _perstringĕre_—pfx. _per-,_ thoroughly, and _stringĕre,_ to bind.]

**persuade,** _pər-swād′, v.t._ to induce by argument, advice, etc.: to bring to any particular opinion: to cause to believe: to convince: to seek to induce (_obs._): to urge (_Shak._).—_v.i._ to plead (_obs._): to prevail (_obs._): to use persuasive methods.—Also **perswade′** (_obs._).—_adj._ **persuad′able.**—_ns._ **persuad′er; persuasibility** (-_swās-i-bil′-i-ti_).—_adj._ **persuās′ible,** capable of being persuaded.—_n._ **persuasion** (-_swā′zhən_), act, process, method, art, or power of persuading: an inducement: state of being persuaded: settled opinion: a creed: a party adhering to a creed: kind (_facet._).—_adj._ **persuasive** (-_swās′_), having the power to persuade: influencing the mind or passions.—_n._ that which persuades or wins over.—_adv._ **persuā′sively.**—_n._ **persuā′siveness.**—_adj._ **persuās′ory,** persuasive. [L. _persuādēre, -suāsum_—pfx. _per-, suādēre,_ to advise.]

**persue,** _pûrs′ū,_ (_Spens._) _n._ a track of blood. [Fr. _percée,_ act of piercing, confused with pursue.]

**persue,** an obsolete spelling of pursue.

**persulphate,** _pər-sul′fāt, n._ that sulphate of a metal which contains the relatively greater quantity of oxygen or of the acid radical: a salt of **persulphuric** (-_fū′rik_) **acid** ($H_2S_2O_8$). [Pfx _per-,_ indicating excess, and sulphate.]

**perswade.** Obs. spelling of persuade.

**pert,** _pûrt, adj._ open (_obs._): unconcealed: brisk: perky (_Shak._): flourishing: adroit (_obs._): forward: saucy: impertinent: presumingly free in speech: objectionable (_obs._).—_n._ an impudent person.—_adv._ **pert′ly.**—_n._ **pert′ness.** [Aphetic for apert; see also peart.]

**pertain,** _pər-, pûr-tān′, v.i._ to belong: to relate (with _to_).—_ns._ **per′tinence, per′tinency** (_pûr′_), state of being pertinent: an appurtenance (_obs._).—_adj._ **per′tinent,** pertaining or related: to the point: fitted for the matter on hand: fitting or appropriate: suitable: apposite.—_n._ (chiefly _Scot._) anything that goes along with an estate.—_adv._ **per′tinently.** [O.Fr. _partenir_—L. _pertinēre_—pfx. _per-, tenēre,_ to hold.]

**pertake,** an old spelling (_Spens., Shak._) of partake.

**perthite,** _pûrth′īt, n._ a parallel intergrowth of orthoclase and albite.—_adj._ **perthitic** (-_it′ik_). [_Perth,_ Ontario, where it was found.]

**pertinacious,** _pûr-ti-nā′shəs, adj._ thoroughly tenacious: holding obstinately to an opinion or a purpose: obstinate: unyielding.—_adv._ **pertinā′ciously.**—_ns._ **pertinā′ciousness; pertinacity** (-_nas′i-ti_), quality of being pertinacious or unyielding: obstinacy: resoluteness. [L. _pertināx, -ācis,_ holding fast—pfx. _per-, tenāx,_ tenacious—_tenēre,_ to hold.]

**pertinent.** See pertain.

**perttaunt like,** an obscure phrase in Shakespeare (_Love's Labour's Lost,_ V, ii), possibly meaning like a _pair taunt_ or _purtaunt′,_ a double pairroyal. [pair, and Fr. _tant,_ so much, i.e. counting as much again as a pair-royal in post and pair.]

**perturb,** _pər-tûrb′, v.t._ to disturb greatly: to agitate—also **per′turbate** (_pûr′tər-bāt_).—_adj._ **pertur′bable.**—_ns._ **pertur′bance,** perturbation; **perturb′ant,** anything that perturbs.—_adj._ **perturbing.**—_n._ **perturbā′tion,** act of perturbing or state of being perturbed: disquiet of mind: irregularity: the disturbance produced in the simple elliptic motion of one heavenly body about another by the action of a third body, or by the non-sphericity of the principal body (_astron._): a perturbing agent.—_adjs._ **perturbā′tional; pertur′bative.**—_n._ **per′turbātor.**—_adj._ and _n._ **pertur′batory.**—_adj._ **perturbed′.**—_adv._ **perturb′edly.**—_n._ **pertur′ber.**—**perturbation theory** (_phys._), a mathematical method of determining the effect of small local changes on the behaviour of a system. [L. _perturbāre, -ātum_—pfx. _per-, turbāre,_ to disturb—_turba,_ a crowd.]

**pertuse,** _pər-tūs′, adj._ punched: pierced: slit.—Also **pertūs′ate** (or _pûr′_), **pertused** (-_tūst′_).—_n._ **pertusion** (-_tū′zhən_). [L. _pertundĕre, -tūsum—per, tundĕre,_ to strike.]

**pertussis,** _pər-tus′is, n._ whooping-cough.—_adj._ **pertuss′al.** [Pfx. _per-,_ indicating excess, L. _tussis,_ cough.]

**Peru,** _pə-rōō′, n._ a country of S. America.—_adj._ **Peru′vian,** of Peru.—_n._ a native, or inhabitant, of Peru.—**Peruvian bark,** cinchona bark.—**balsam of Peru, Peru balsam,** a fragrant acrid black viscid liquid, containing esters of benzoic and cinnamic acids, got from a tropical American papilionaceous tree, _Myroxylon pereirae;_ **marvel of Peru** (see marvel). [Sp. _Perú._]

**peruke,** _pər-ōōk′,_ formerly _per′, n._ a wig.—Also (Fr.) **perruque.**—_n._ **perru′quier** (per-ük-yā; Fr.), a wigmaker. [Fr. _perruque_—It. _parrucca_ (Sp. _peluca_); connection with L. _pilus,_ hair, very doubtful.]

**peruse,** _pər-ōōz′, v.t._ orig. to use up, wear out: to pass in scrutiny, one by one or piece by piece (_Shak._): to examine in detail: to revise: to read attentively or critically: loosely, to read.—_ns._ **perus′al,** the act of perusing: careful examination: scrutiny: study: reading; **per-us'er.** [L. pfx. *per-*, thoroughly, *ūtī, ūsus*, to use.]

**pervade,** *pər-vād', v.t.* to pass through (*rare*): to diffuse or extend through the whole of.—*n.* **pervasion** (-*vā'zhən*).—*adj.* **pervasive** (-*vā'siv*), tending or having power to pervade.—*adv.* **perva'sively.**—*n.* **perva'siveness.** [L. *pervādēre—per*, through, *vādēre*. to go.]

**perverse,** *pər-vurs', adj.* turned aside from right or truth: obstinate in the wrong: capricious and unreasonable in opposition: froward: wrong-headed: wayward: against the evidence or judge's direction on point of law: adverse (*Milt.*).—*adv.* **perverse'ly.**—*ns.* **perverse'ness; perversion** (-*vûr'shən*), the act of perverting: condition of being perverted: the product of the process of perverting: a diverting from the true object: a turning from right or true: a distortion: a misapplication: a pathological deviation of sexual instinct: formation of a mirror-image (*math.*): the mirror-image itself; **pervers'ity,** state or quality of being perverse.—*adj.* **pervers'ive,** tending to pervert.—*v.t.* **pervert',** to turn wrong or from the right course: to wrest from the true meaning: to corrupt: to turn from truth or virtue: to divert, turn (*Shak.*): to form a mirror-image of (*math.*).—*v.i.* to go wrong or out of the right course.—*ns.* **pervert,** (*pûr'vûrt*), one who has abandoned the doctrine assumed to be true: one whose sexual instinct is perverted; **pervert'er.**— *adj.* **pervert'ible.** [Partly through Fr.—L. *pervertēre, perversum—* pfx. *per-*, wrongly, *vertēre*, to turn.]

**pervicacious,** *pûr-vi-kā'shəs, adj.* very obstinate.— *ns.* **pervicā'ciousness, pervicacity** (-*kas'i-ti*), **pervicacy** (*pûr'vi-kə-si*; *obs.*). [L. *pervicāx, -ācis* —pfx. *per-*, *vincēre*, to prevail.]

**pervious,** *pûr'vi-əs, adj.* permeable: passable: penetrable: open.—*v.t.* **per'viate,** to make a way through.—*adv.* **per'viously.**—*n.* **per'viousness.** [L. *pervius—per*, through, *via*, a way.]

**pesade,** *pə-zäd', -säd', -zäd', n.* dressage manoeuvre in which a horse rears up on its hindlegs without forward movement. [Fr.; from It.]

**pesant, pesaunt,** old spellings of peasant.

**pesante,** *pes-an'tā, (mus.) adj.* heavy: weighty.— Also *adv.* [It.]

**peseta,** *pe-sā'ta, n.* a Spanish franc. [Sp., dim. of *pesa*, weight.]

**pesewa,** *pə-soō'a, n.* See cedi:—*pls.* **-a, -as,** etc.

**Peshito, Peshitto,** *pe-shē(t)'tō,* **Peshitta,** *-ta, n.* a Syriac translation of the Bible.—Also *adj.* [Syriac *p'shi(t)tô, -tâ*, the simple.]

**peshwa,** *pāsh'wa, n.* the chief minister of the Mahrattas, later the real sovereign.—Also **peish'-wa(h).** [Pers. *pēshwā*, chief.]

**pesky,** *pes'ki, (coll.) adj.* annoying.—*adv.* **pes'-kily.** [Perh. **pest.**]

**peso,** *pā'sō, n.* a Spanish five-peseta piece: a Mexican dollar: in S. and Central America a coin of various values. [Sp.,—L. *pēnsum*, weight.]

**pessary,** *pes'ə-ri, n.* a surgical plug, or medicated device, esp. one worn in the vagina. [Fr. *pessaire*—L.L. *pessārium*—Gr. *pessos*, a pebble, pessary.]

**pessimism,** *pes'i-mizm, n.* the worst state (*obs.*): the doctrine that the world is bad rather than good (*philos.*): a temper of mind that looks on the dark side of things: a depressing view of life: loosely, despondency, hopelessness.—*n.* **pess'imist,** one who believes that everything is tending to the worst: one who looks too much on the dark side of things—opp. to *optimist.*— *adjs.* **pessimis'tic, -al.**—*adv.* **pessimis'tically.** [L. *pessimus*, worst.]

**pest, pest,** *n.* any deadly epidemic disease: plague: anything destructive: any insect, fungus, etc., destructive of cultivated plants: troublesome

person or thing.—*adjs.* **pest'ful, pestilential; pesticid'al,** pertaining to a pesticide.—*n.* **pesticide** (*pes'ti-sid*), pest killer.—*adj.* **pestif'erous,** bringing plague or pestilence: pestilential: noxious: pestilent: annoying: plague-stricken.—*adv.* **pestif'erously.**—*n.* **pest'ilence,** any deadly epidemic disease: bubonic plague: anything that is hurtful to the morals.—*adjs.* **pest'ilent,** deadly: producing pestilence: hurtful to health and life: pernicious: mischievous: vexatious; **pestilential** (-*len'shl*), of the nature of pestilence: producing or infested with pestilence: destructive: baneful: detestable: pestering.—*advs.* **pestilen'tially, pest'ilently.**—*adj.* **pestolog'ical.**—*ns.* **pestol'ogist; pestol'ogy,** the study of agricultural pests and methods of combating them.—**pest'house,** hospital for plague or other infectious or contagious disease.—*adj.* **pest'ilence-stricken.** [Fr. *peste* and *pestilence*—L. *pestis, pestilentia*.]

**Pestalozzian,** *pes-ta-lot'sion, adj.* pertaining to Johann Heinrich *Pestalozzi* (1746-1827) or his programme of educational reform.—*n.* a follower of Pestalozzi.

**pester,** *pes'tər, v.t.* to clog (*obs.*): to huddle (*Milt.*): to infest (*arch.*): to annoy persistently. —*n.* an annoyance.—*n.* **pes'terer.**—*adv.* **pes'teringly.**—*n.* **pes'terment.**—*adj.* **pest'erous.** [App. from O.Fr. *empestrer* (Fr. *empêtrer*), to entangle —L. *in,* in, L.L. *pāstōrium*, a foot-shackle—L. *pāstus,* pa.p. of *pāscēre,* to feed; cf. **pastern;** influenced by **pest.**]

**pestle,** *pes'l,* also *pest'l, n.* an instrument for pounding: a leg, esp. as food (now *dial.*).—*v.t.* to pound.—*v.i.* to use a pestle. [O.Fr. *pestel*— L. *pistillum,* a pounder, *pinsēre, pistum,* to pound.]

**pet, pet,** *n.* a cherished tame animal: an indulged favourite: used as an endearment.—*adj.* kept as a pet: indulged: cherished: favourite.—*v.t.* to treat as a pet: to fondle: to pamper: to indulge.—*v.i.* (*coll.*) to indulge in amorous caressing:—*pr.p.* **pett'ing;** *pa.t.* and *pa.p.* **pett'ed.** —*adj.* **pett'ed.**—*ns.* **pett'er; pett'ing.**—**pet aversion,** chief object of dislike; **pet name,** a name used in familiar affection; **petting party** (*coll.*), a gathering for the purpose of caressing as an organised sport. [Origin unknown; not from Gael.]

**pet,** *pet, n.* a slighted and offended feeling: a slight, or childish, fit of aggrieved or resentful sulkiness: the sulks, huff.—*v.i.* to be peevish, to sulk.—*adj.* **pett'ed,** in a pet: apt to be in a pet.—*adv.* **pett'edly.**—*n.* **pett'edness.**—*adj.* **pett'-ish,** peevish: sulky: inclined to sulk: of the nature of or expressive of sulkiness.—*adv.* **pett'ishly.**—*n.* **pett'ishness.** [Origin unknown.]

**petal,** *pet'l, n.* a corolla leaf.—*adj.* **pet'aline** (-*in*), of or like a petal.—*n.* **pet'alism,** a method of ostracism practised in ancient Syracuse, the name being written on an olive-leaf.—*adj.* **pet'alled,** having petals: also used in composition, as *white-petalled.*—*n.* **pet'alody** (Gr. *eidos*, form), transformation, esp. of stamens, into petals.—*adj.* **pet'aloid,** having the appearance of a petal.—*n.* **petalomā'nia,** abnormal increase in number of petals. [Gr. *petalon,* a leaf.]

**pétanque,** *pā-täk', n.* a French (Provençal) game in which steel bowls are rolled or hurled towards a wooden marker ball.

**petara,** *pi-tä'rə, n.* a travelling box or basket for clothes.—Also **pita'ra(h).** [Hind. *pitārāh, petārāh*.]

**petard,** *pe-tär(d)', n.* a case containing an explosive, used for blowing in doors, etc.—(*Shak.* petar'): a moving firework.—**hoist with his own petard** (see **hoise**). [O.Fr.—*péter,* to crack or explode —L. *pēdēre,* to break wind.]

**petary,** *pē'tar-i, n.* a peat-bog. [Mediaeval L. *petāria*—root of **peat.**]

**petasus,** *pet'ə-səs, n.* a low broad hat worn by Hermes. [Latinised from Gr. *petasos*.]

petaurist, *pe-tö'rist, n.* a flying-phalanger.—*adj.* petaur'ine. [Gr. *petauristēs,* an acrobat.]
petchary, *pech'ə-ri, n.* the grey king-bird. [Imit.]
petechia, *pe-tē'ki-ə, n.* a small red or purple spot on the skin:—*pl.* pete'chiae (-ē).—*adj.* petech'ial. [Latinised from It. *petecchia.*]
peter, *pē'tər, v.i.* to dwindle away to nothing, be dissipated or exhausted (with *out*). [Origin unknown; orig. U.S. mining slang.]
peter, *pē'tər, n.* the Blue Peter (flag): call for trumps.—*v.i.* to signal for trumps (by throwing a higher card than necessary).—pe'ter-boat, kind of fishing-boat: a dredger's boat that goes equally well forward or astern; pe'ter-man, a fisherman (in allusion to the apostle); Peter-see-me', a Spanish wine (from a grape introduced by Pedro *Ximenes*).—Peter's pence (see penny).
peter, *pē'tər,* (*slang*) *n.* a safe.—pe'terman, a safe-blower.
Peter Pan, a character in J. M. Barrie's play of that name (1904), the type of the person who never grows up.—Peter Pan collar, a flat collar with rounded ends.
petersham, *pē'tər-shəm, n.* a heavy greatcoat designed by Lord *Petersham*: rough-napped cloth generally dark blue of which it was made: a heavy corded ribbon used for belts, hat-bands, etc.
pethidine, *peth'ə-dēn, n.* synthetic analgesic and hypnotic, having action similar to that of morphine. [Perh. mixture of *piperidine, ethyl.*]
petiole, *pet'i-ōl, n.* a leaf-stalk (*bot.*): a stalk-like structure, esp. that of the abdomen in wasps, etc. (*zool.*).—*adjs.* pet'iolar, of, or of the nature of, a petiole; pet'iolate, -d, pet'ioled, stalked.—*n.* pet'iolule (-*ol-ūl*), the stalk of a leaflet in a compound leaf. [L. *petiolus,* a little foot, or petiole.]
petit, formerly *pet'it,* now *pet'i, pə-tē',* or as Fr. *pə-tē, adj.* a form of petty (*q.v.*)—in sense of insignificant, *obs.* except in legal and other French phrases:—*fem.* petite (*pə-tēt'*), applied to a woman, small-made (with a suggestion of neatness): (*obs.*) a variant spelling of petit, applied to either sex.—In phrases, the earlier borrowings tend to be the more highly anglicised.—petit bourgeois (*bōōr-zhwa*), a member of the lower middle class; petite bourgeoisie (*bōōr-zhwa-zē*), the lower middle class; petit déjeuner (*dā-zhœ-nā*), breakfast; petit four (*fōr, för, fōōr*), a small very fancy biscuit; petit grain (*grän*), dried unripe bitter oranges, or an oil distilled from them or their leaves and twigs; petit maître (*me-tr'*), a fop; petit mal (*mal*), a mild form of epilepsy without convulsions; petit pain (*pē*), a breadroll; petit point (*point, pwē*), work in tent stitch. [Fr. *petit, -e.*]
petition, *pə-tish'ən, n.* a supplication: a prayer: a formal request to an authority: a written supplication signed by a number of persons: a written application to a court of law: the thing asked for: a parliamentary bill (*obs.*): an axiom or postulate (*obs.*).—*v.t.* to address a petition to: to ask for.—*adj.* peti'tionary.—*ns.* peti'-tioner, one who petitions: one of the party that petitioned Charles II in 1680 to summon Parliament—opp. to abhorrer (*hist.*); petit'ioning; peti'tionist.—*adj.* petitory (*pet'i-ta-ri*), petitioning.—Petition of Right, a parliamentary declaration, in the form of a petition of the rights of the people, assented to by Charles I in 1628. [L. *petitiō, -ōnis—petēre,* to ask.]
petitio principii, *pe-tish'i-ō prin-sip'i-ī, pe-tē'ti-ō prēn-kip'i-ē,* (*log.*) a begging of the question. [L. *petitiō principii.*]
Petrarchan, *pe-trär'kən,* Petrarchian (-*ki-ən*), *adjs.* pertaining to, imitating, the Italian poet Francesco *Petrarca* or *Petrarch* (1304-74).—*ns.* a follower or imitator of Petrarch.—*adj.*

Petrarch'al.—*ns.* Petrarch'ianism; Petrarch'-ianist.—*v.i.* Petrarchise, -ize (*pe'trärk-īz, -trärk'*), to write in Petrarch's manner, imitate Petrarch.—*ns.* Petrarchism (*pe'trärk-izm,* or *pe-trärk'izm*); Pe'trarchist (or *-trärk'*).—The older pronunciation of Petrarch, *pē'trärk,* gives alternative pronunciations for the above words.—Petrarch(i)an sonnet (see sonnet).
petrary, *pet'rə-ri, n.* an engine for hurling stones. [L.L. *petrāria*—L. *petra*—Gr. *petrā,* rock.]
petre, (*coll.*) short for saltpetre.
petrel, *pet'rəl, n.* any bird of the genus Procellaria akin to the albatrosses and fulmars, esp. the storm (popularly stormy) petrel, or Mother Carey's chicken, a dusky sea-bird, rarely landing except to lay its eggs, the smallest web-footed bird known. [L. *Petrus,* Peter, from its seeming to walk on the water; see Matt. xiv. 29.]
Petri, or petri, dish, *pā'tri dish,* a shallow glass dish with an overlapping cover used for cultures of bacteria.—Also Petri plate. [R. J. *Petri,* German bacteriologist.]
petrify, *pet'ri-fī, v.t.* to turn into stone: to fossilise by molecular replacement, preserving minute structure (*geol.*): loosely, to encrust with stony matter: to make hard like a stone: to fix in amazement, horror, etc.—*v.i.* to become stone, or hard like stone:—*pr.p.* pet'rifying; *pa.t.* and *pa.p.* pet'rified.—*n.* petrifac'tion, turning or being turned into stone: a petrified object: a fossil.—*adjs.* petrifac'tive, petrif'ic, petrifying.—*n.* petrificā'tion, petrifaction. [L. *petra*—Gr. *petrā,* rock, L. *facēre, factum,* to make.]
Petrine, *pē'trin, adj.* pertaining to, or written by, the Apostle *Peter.*—*n.* Pē'trinism (-*trin-izm*), the Tübingen theory of F. C. Baur (1792-1860) and his school, of a doctrinal trend in primitive Christianity towards Judaism, ascribed to Peter and his party in opposition to *Paulinism.* [L. *Petrīnus—Petrus,* Gr. *Petros,* Peter.]
pétrissage, *pā-trēs-äzh', n.* massage by longitudinal rubbing and lateral squeezing. [Fr.,—*pétrir,* to knead.]
petrochemical, *pet'rō-kem'i-kəl, n.* any chemical obtained from *petroleum.*—Also *adj.*
petroglyph, *pet'rō-glif, n.* a rock-carving, esp. prehistoric.—*adj.* petroglyph'ic. [Gr. *petrā,* a rock, *glyphein,* to carve.]
petrography, *pi-trog'rə-fi, n.* petrology.—*n.* petrog'-rapher.—*adjs.* petrographic (*pet-rō-graf'ik*), -al.—*adv.* petrograph'ically. [Gr. *petrā,* rock, *graphein,* to write.]
petrol, *pet'rol, -rəl, n.* formerly petroleum: now a mixture of light volatile hydrocarbons got by fractional distillation or cracking of petroleum, used for driving motor-cars, aeroplanes, etc.—*v.t.* to supply with petrol:—*pr.p.* pet'rolling; *pa.t.* and *pa.p.* pet'rolled.—*ns.* pet'rolage, treatment with petrol to stamp out mosquitoes; petrolatum (*-ā'təm*), petroleum jelly.—*adj.* petroleous (*pi-trō'li-əs*), containing, or rich in, petroleum.—*ns.* petroleum (*pi-trō'li-əm*), a mixture of hydrocarbon oils got from oil-wells; pétroleur (*pā-trol-œr; masc.*), pétroleuse (*-œz; fem.*; Fr.), an incendiary who uses petroleum, as in Paris in 1871.—*adjs.* petrolic (*pi-trol'ik*), of petrol or petroleum; petrolif'erous (*pet-*), yielding petroleum.—petroleum jelly, soft paraffin (*paraffinum molle*), a mixture of petroleum hydrocarbons used in emollients, as a lubricant, etc. (see also liquid paraffin at liquid); petrol lighter, a cigarette-lighter in which the striking of a spark ignites a petrol-soaked wick; petrol pump, a machine for transferring measured amounts of petrol to motor vehicles; petrol station, a garage which sells petrol. [L. *petra,* rock, *oleum,* oil.]
petrology, *pi-trol'ə-ji, n.* the science of the origin, chemical and mineral composition and structure, and alteration of rocks.—*adj.* petrological

(*pet-rō-loj'*).—*adv.* petrolog'ically.—*n.* petrol'-ogist. [Gr. *petrā*, rock, *logos*, discourse.]
petronel, *pet'rə-nel*, *n.* a large horse-pistol. [Fr. *petrinal*—L. *pectus, pectoris*, the chest, whence fired, or L. *petra*, stone, i.e. gun-flint.]
petronella, *pet-rən-el'ə*, *n.* a Scottish country-dance.
petrous, *pet'rəs*, *adj.* stony: petrosal.—*adj.* petrosal (*pi-trōs'əl*), relating to the stony part of the temporal bone about the ear.—Also *n.* [L. *petrōsus*—*petra*—Gr. *petrā*, rock.]
petted, pettish. See pet.
Petter engine, *pet'ər*, a kind of oil-engine. [Makers' name.]
pettichaps, petty-chaps, *pet'i-chaps*, *n.* the garden or other warbler. [N. of England; app. petty and chap (3).]
petticoat, *pet'i-kōt*, *n.* a short or small coat (*orig.*): a skirt, esp. an under-skirt, or a garment of which it forms part: any garment or drapery of similar form: a bell-shaped structure, as in telegraph insulators, etc.: a woman (*coll.*). —*adj.* feminine: female: of women.—*adj.* pett'icoated.—pett'icoat-breeches, loose short breeches worn by men in the 17th century; pett'icoat-tails', small cakes of shortbread; pett'i-coat government, domination by women. [petty, coat.]
pettifogger, *pet'i-fog-ər*, *n.* a paltry ᴄavilling lawyer.—*v.i.* pett'ifog, to play the pettifogger. —*n.* pett'ifoggery.—*n.* and *adj.* pett'ifogging. [petty; origin of second part obscure.]
pettitoes, *pet'i-tōz*, *n.pl.* pig's feet as food (for-merly app. also other parts and of other ani-mals): human feet (*Shak.*). [Origin obscure, but early associated with petty and toe.]
pettle, *pet'l*, (*Scot.*) *v.t.* to indulge, pet. [Freq. of pet.]
pettle, *pet'l*. Same as pattle.
petty, *pet'i*, *adj.* small: of less importance: minor: trifling: lower in rank, power, etc.: inconsiderable, insignificant: contemptible: small-minded.—*n.* a junior schoolboy.—*adv.* pett'ily.—*n.* pett'iness.—Petty Bag, a former office of the Court of Chancery: a clerk of that office; petty bourgeois, bourgeoisie, vari-ants of petit bourgeois, petite bourgeoisie; petty cash, miscellaneous small sums of money re-ceived or paid; petty larceny (see larceny); petty officer, a naval officer ranking with a non-commissioned officer in the army; Petty Sessions, a court in which magistrates try trivial cases and refer others to a higher court; petty whin, a low spiny papilionaceous shrub (*Genista anglica*) like a small whin. [Fr. *petit*.]
petulant, *pet'ū-lənt*, *adj.* orig. wanton, lascivious: showing peevish impatience, irritation, or caprice: forward, impudent in manner.—*ns.* pet'ulance, pet'ulancy.—*adv.* pet'ulantly. [L. *petulāns, -antis*—assumed *petulāre*, dim. of *petĕre*, to seek.]
Petunia, *pē-tū'nyə, -ni-ə*, *n.* South American genus of ornamental plants near akin to tobacco. [Tupi *petun*, tobacco.]
petuntse, *pe-toōnt'se*, *n.* a feldspathic rock used in making Chinese porcelain. Also petuntze. [Chin. *pai-tun-tse*, little white brick.]
pew, *pū*, *n.* an enclosed compartment or fixed bench in a church: formerly, a place for a preacher or reader: a box or stall in another building: a seat (*slang*).—pew'-chair, an addi-tional seat hinged to the end of a pew; pew'-fellow, occupant of the same pew: companion; pew'-holder, one who rents a pew; pew'-opener, an attendant who showed people to pews; pew'-rent, rent paid for the use of a pew. [O.Fr. *puie*, raised place, balcony—L. *podia*, pl. of *podium*—Gr. *podion*, dim. of *pous, podos*, foot.]
pewit, *pē'wit, pū'it*. Same as peewit.

pewter, *pū'tər*, *n.* an alloy of three to nine parts of tin and one of lead: now sometimes tin with a little copper and antimony: a vessel made of pewter, esp. a beer-tankard: prize-money (*slang*).—*adj.* made of pewter.—*n.* pew'terer, one who works in pewter.—pew'ter-mill, a lapidary's pewter polishing-wheel for amethyst, agate, etc. [O.Fr. *peutre*; cf. It. *peltro*, L.G. *spialter*, Eng. spelter.]
peyote, *pā-yō'tā*, *n.* a Mexican intoxicant made from cactus tops. [Nahuatl *peyotl*.]
pezant, an old spelling of peasant.
Peziza, *pe-zi'zə*, *n.* a genus of discomycete fungi with cup-like apothecia.—*adj.* pezi'zoid. [Gr. *pezis*, a puff-ball.]
pfennig, *pfen'ig, -ihh*, *n.* a German coin, the hundredth part of a mark.—Also (*obs.*) pfenn'ing.
pH (value), *pē-āch* (*val'ū*), *n.* a number used to express degrees of acidity or alkalinity in solu-tions—formerly, the logarithm to base 10 of the reciprocal of the concentration of hydrogen ions; now, related by formula to a standard solution of potassium hydrogen phthalate, which has value 4 at 15°C.
phacoid, *fak'* or *fāk'oid*, phacoidal, *fə-koi'dl*, *adjs.* lentil-shaped, lens-shaped.—*ns.* phacolite (*fak'ə-līt*), a zeolite often lenticular in shape; phac'o-lith, a small lenticular igneous intrusion, shaped by folding in an anticline. [Gr. *phakos*, a lentil, *eidos*, form, *lithos*, stone.]
Phaedra complex, *fēd'rə*, (*psych.*) the difficult relationship which can arise between a new step-parent and the (usu. teenage) son or daughter of the original marriage. [Greek story of *Phaedra* who fell in love with her stepson and committed suicide after being repulsed by him.]
phaeic, *fē'ik*, *adj.* dusky.—*n.* phae'ism, duskiness, incomplete melanism (in butterflies). [Gr. *phaios*, dusky.]
Phaelonion. See Phelonion.
phaen(ō)-, *fē-n(ō)-*. Now usu. phen(o)-.
phaenogam, *fē'nō-gam*, *n.* a spermatophyte or phanerogam.—*n.pl.* Phaenogamae (*fē-nog'ə-mē*). —*adjs.* phaenogamic (-nō-gam'ik), phaenoga-mous (-nog'ə-məs).—Also phe'nogam, etc. [Gr. *phainein*, to show, *gamos*, marriage.]
phaenology, phaenomenon, phaenotype. Same as phenology, phenomenon, phenotype.
phaeo-, *fē-ō-*, in composition, dusky, as in phaeo-melanin (*fē-ō-mel'ə-nin*), a reddish-brown pig-ment in animals, incl. birds. [Gr. *phaios*.]
Phaeophyceae, *fē-ō-fish'i-ē*, *n.pl.* the brown sea-weeds, one of the main divisions of algae, in which the chlorophyll is masked by a brown pigment. [Gr. *phaios*, dusky, *phȳkos*, seaweed.]
Phaethon, *fā'i-thon*, *n.* the son of Helios, the Greek sun-god, who came to grief in driving his father's chariot: the tropic-bird genus (as seeking to keep to the sun's course).—*adj.* Phaethon'tic. [Gr. *Phaethōn, -ontos*, lit. shining; cf. *phaos, phōs*, light.]
phaeton, *fā'(i-)tn*, *n.* an open four-wheeled carriage for one or two horses. [From the foregoing.]
phag-, -phaga. See phag(o)-.
phage. Short for bacteriophage.
-phage. See phag(o)-.
phag(o)-, *fag(-ō)-*, in composition, used to denote 'feeding', 'eating'.—phaga, in zoological names, eaters'; -phage, *-fāj, -fāzh*, eater, or destroyer; -phagous, *-fəg-əs*, feeding on; -phagus, one feeding in a particular way, or on a particular thing; -phagy, *-fə-ji*, eating of a specified nature. [Gr. *phagein*, to eat.]
phagedaena, phagedena, *faj-* or *fag-i-dē'nə*, *n.* rapidly spreading destructive ulceration, once common in hospitals—hospital gangrene.—*adj.* phagedae'nic, phagedē'nic. [Gr. *phagedaina*—*phagein*, to eat.]
phagocyte, *fag'ō-sit*, *n.* a white blood-corpuscle

that engulfs bacteria and other harmful particles.—*adjs.* phagocytic (-*sit'*), -al.—*n.* phag'ocytism (-*sit*-), the nature or function of a phagocyte.—*v.t.* phag'ocytose (-*sit*-*ōs*), to subject to phagocytic action.—*n.* phagocytō'sis, destruction by phagocytes. [Gr. *phagein*, to eat, *kytos*, a vessel.]

-phagous, -phagus, -phagy. See phag(o)-.

phalange. See phalanx.

phalanger, *fal-an'jər, n.* any one of a group of small arboreal Australasian marsupials. [Gr. *phalangion*, spider's web, from their webbed toes.]

phalanstery, *fal'ən-stə-ri, n.* the dwelling of the phalange in the ideal social system of Fourier (1772-1837), a vast structure in the midst of a square league of cultivated land.—*adj.* phalansterian (-*stē'ri-ən*).—*ns.* phalanstē'rianism; phal'ansterism; phal'ansterist. [Fr. *phalanstère*, formed from Gr. *phalanx* on the model of *monastère*, monastery.]

phalanx, *fal'angks* (or *fāl'*), *n.* a solid formation of ancient Greek heavy-armed infantry: a solid body of men, etc.: a solid body of supporters or partisans: a Fourierist community: a bone of a digit: the part of a finger or toe answering to it: a joint of an insect's leg: a bundle of stamens:—*pl.* phal'anxes or (*biol.*) phalanges (*fal-an'jēz*).—*adj.* phalangal (*fal-ang'gl*), phalangeal.—*n.* phalange (*fal'anj*), a phalanx (in biological senses): (also *fal-ăzh*), a socialistic community in Fourier's scheme, consisting of 1800 persons living in a phalanstery: Primo de Rivera's Spanish fascist party:—*pl.* phal'anges.—*adj.* phalan'geal.—*ns.* phalangid (*fal-an'jid*), a long-legged arachnid, a harvestman; phalan'gist, a Spanish fascist. [Gr. *phalanx*, -*angos*, a roller, phalanx, phalange, spider.]

phalarope, *fal'ə-rōp, n.* a wading bird (*Phalaropus*) with coot-like feet. [Gr. *phalaris*, a coot, *pous*, a foot.]

phallus, *fal'əs, n.* the penis: the symbol of generation in primitive religion: (*cap.*) the stinkhorn genus of fungi:—*pl.* phall'i.—*adj.* phall'ic.—*ns.* phall'icism (-*sizm*), phall'ism, worship of the generative power of nature; phall'in, phalloid'in, two of the poisons occurring in the fungus *Amanita phalloides.*—*adj.* phall'oid, like a phallus. [L.,—Gr. *phallos.*]

Phanariot, *fa-nar'i-ot, n.* one of the Greeks inhabiting the *Fanar* quarter of Constantinople, or of a Greek official class—in Turkish history mostly diplomatists, administrators, and bankers, also hospodars of Wallachia and Moldavia.—*adj.* Phanar'iot.—Also Fan-. [Gr. *phānarion*, lighthouse, from that on the Golden Horn.]

phanerogam, *fan'ər-ō-gam, n.* a spermatophyte.—*ns.pl.* Phanerogamae (-*og'ə-mē*), Phanerogamia (-*ō-gam'i-ə*), a division of plants comprising all spermatophytes.—*adjs.* phanerogam'ic, phanerog'amous. [Gr. *phaneros*, visible, *gamos*, marriage.]

phang, an old spelling (*Shak.*) of fang.

phantasm, *fan'tazm, n.* a vain, airy appearance: a fancied vision: an apparition: a spectre: a counterfeit: an impostor (*obs.*).—Also phantas'ma:—*pl.* phan'tasms, phantas'mata.—*n.* phan'tasim(e) (*Shak.*), a fantastic person.—*adjs.* phantas'mal; phantasmā'lian (*rare*).—*n.* phantasmal'ity.—*adv.* phantas'mally.—*adjs.* phantas'mic, -al; phantasmogenet'ic, begetting phantasms.—*adv.* phantasmogenet'ically. [Gr. *phantasma—phantazein*, to make visible—*phainein*, to bring to light—*phaein*, to shine.]

phantasmagoria, *fan-taz-mə-gō'ri-ə, -gō', n.* a fantastic series of illusive images or of real forms.—*adjs.* phantasmago'rial, pertaining to or resembling a phantasmagoria; phantasmagōr'ic, -al. [A name given to a show of optical illusions in 1802, from Fr. *phantasmagorie*—Gr. *phan-*

*tasma*, an appearance, and perh. *agorā*, an assembly.]

phantasy, phantastic, phantastry. Same as fantasy, etc.—*n.* phantā'siast, one of those Docetae who believed Christ's body to have been a mere phantom.

phantom, *fan'təm,* (*Spens.* phantosme, *fan-tōm'*), *n.* a deceitful appearance: an immaterial form: a visionary experience: a show without reality. —*adj.* illusive: unreal: spectral: imaginary: ghostly-looking: transparent and hardly visible. —*adjs.* phantomat'ic, phan'tomish, phan'tomy, relating to a phantom.—phantom circuit, (as in telecommunications) an additional circuit which does not in fact exist, the extra performance being obtained by suitable arrangements of real circuits. [O.Fr. *fantosme*—Gr. *phantasma.*]

Pharaoh, *fā'rō, n.* a title of the kings of ancient Egypt: faro (*obs.*).—*adj.* pharaonic (*fā-rā-on'ik*). —Pharaoh's serpent, the coiled ash of burning mercuric thiocyanate. [L. and Gr. *pharaō*— Heb. *par'ōh*—Egypt. *pr-'o*, great house.]

phare, *fär, n.* a lighthouse. [Fr.; see pharos.]

Pharisee, *far'i-sē, n.* one of a religious school among the Jews, marked by their strict observance of the law and of religious ordinances: any one more careful of the outward forms than of the spirit of religion, a formalist: a very self-righteous or hypocritical person.—*adjs.* pharisā'ic, -al, pertaining to, or like, the Pharisees: hypocritical.—*adv.* pharisā'ically.—*ns.* pharisā'icalness; phar'isāism (also *phar'iseeism*). [O.E. *phariseus*—L.L. *pharisaeus*—Gr. *pharisaios* —Heb. *pārūsh*, separated.]

pharmaceutic, -al, *fär-mə-sū'tik* (or -*kū'tik*), -*əl, adjs.* pertaining to the knowledge or art of preparing medicines.—*n.* pharmaceu'tical, a chemical used in medicine.—*adv.* pharmaceu'tically.— *ns.* pharmaceu'tics, the science of preparing medicines; pharmaceu'tist. [Gr. *pharmakeutikos.*]

pharmacopoeia, *fär-mə-kə-pē'-(y)ə, n.* a book or list of drugs with directions for their preparation: a collection of drugs.—*adjs.* pharmacopoe'ial, pharmacopoe'ian. [Gr. *pharmakopoiiā* —*pharmakon*, a drug, *poieein*, to make.]

pharmacy, *fär'mə-si, n.* a department of the medical art which consists in the collecting, preparing, preserving, and dispensing of medicines: the art of preparing and mixing medicines: a druggist's shop: a dispensary.—*ns.* phar'macist (-*sist*), a druggist, one skilled in pharmacy: one legally qualified to sell drugs and poisons; pharmacol'ogist; pharmacol'ogy, the science of drugs; pharmacop'olist (Gr. *pōleein*, to sell), a dealer in drugs. [Gr. *pharmakeiā*, use of drugs, *pharmakon*, a drug.]

pharos, *fā'ros, n.* a lighthouse or beacon. [From the famous lighthouse on the island of *Pharos* in the Bay of Alexandria.]

pharynx, *far'ingks, n.* the cleft or cavity forming the upper part of the gullet, lying behind the nose, mouth, and larynx:—*pl.* phar'ynges (*in-jēz*), phar'ynxes.—*adjs.* pharyngal (*fa-ring'gl*), pharyngeal (*fa-rin'ji-əl*): pharyngitic (*far-in-jit'ik*), pertaining to pharyngitis.—*n.* pharyngitis (*far-in-ji'tis*), inflammation of the mucous membrane of the pharynx.—*ns.* pharyngoscope (*fa-ring'gə-skōp*), an instrument for inspecting the pharynx; pharyngoscopy (*far-ing-gos'kə-pi*); pharyngot'omy, the operation of making an incision into the pharynx. [Gr. *pharynx*, -*ygos*, later -*yngos*.]

phase, *fāz, n.* the appearance at a given time of the illuminated surface exhibited by the moon or a planet—also phasis (*fā'sis*): aspect or appearance of anything at any stage: stage of advancement in a periodic change, measured from some standard point: a stage in growth or development (*lit.* and *fig.*): the sum of all those portions of a material system which are identical in chemical composition and physical state (*chem.*):—*pl.* **phases** (*fā'ziz, -sēz*).—*v.t.* to do by phases or stages.—*adjs.* **phased,** adjusted to be in the same phase at the same time: by stages; **phase'less,** unchanging; **phasic** (*fā'zik, -sik*).—**phase-contrast, phase-difference, microscope,** one in which the clear detail is obtained by means of a device that alters the speed of some of the rays of light, so that staining is unnecessary.—**in, out of, phase,** in the same phase together, or in different phases; **phase out,** to cease gradually to use, make, etc.; **primary phase,** crude technical raw material. [Gr. *phasis—phaein,* to shine.]

**phase.** See **feeze.**

**Phasma,** *faz'mə, n.* the spectre-insect (stick-insect, leaf-insect) genus.—*n.* **phas'mid,** a member of the **Phas'midae** or **Phasmat'idae,** the family to which the genus Phasma belongs, or of the (sub)order **Phasmato'dea.** [Gr. *phasma,* a spectre.]

**phatic,** *fat'ik, adj.* using speech for social reasons, to communicate feelings rather than ideas.—*n.* **phasis,** *fā'sis.* [Gr. *phasis,* utterance.]

**pheasant,** *fez'nt, n.* a richly-coloured gallinaceous bird (*Phasianus colchicus*), a half-wild game-bird in Britain: extended to others of the same or kindred genus (as *golden, silver, Argus, Amherst's pheasant*) and to other birds: the tufted grouse (*U.S.*): a francolin (*S.Afr.*): the lyre-bird (*Austr.*): also the coucal (*swamp pheasant*): the flesh of the bird as food:—*pl.* **pheasant(s).**—*n.* **pheas'antry,** an enclosure for rearing pheasants. —**pheas'ant's-eye,** a ranunculaceous plant (Adonis) with deep-red dark-centred flowers. [A.Fr. *fesant*—L. *phāsiānus*—Gr. *phāsiānos* (*ornis,* bird), from the river Phasis, in Colchis.]

**pheazar,** *fē'zər,* (*Shak.*) *n.* perh. one who feezes, perh. for vizier.

**pheer, pheere.** Same as **fere, mate.**

**pheeze.** Same as **feeze.**

**phellem,** *fel'əm,* (*bot.*) *n.* cork.—*ns.* **phell'oderm** (Gr. *derma,* skin), a layer of secondary cortex formed by the phellogen on its inner side; **phellogen** (*fel'ō-jen*), a layer of meristem that forms cork without, otherwise cork-cambium.— *adjs.* **phellogenetic** (*-ji-net'ik*); **phell'oid,** cork-like and formed like cork, but not, or very slightly, suberised.—*ns.* **phelloplas'tic,** a model in cork; **phelloplas'tics,** the making of models in cork. [Gr. *phellos,* cork.]

**phelonion, phaelonion,** *fi-lō'ni-on, n.* an Eastern vestment like a chasuble. [Late Gr. *phailōnion, phělōnion,* dim. of *phailonēs, phelonēs,* for *phainolēs*—L. *paenula,* a cloak.]

**phen-, pheno-, phen-,** *fēn-, fēn-ō-,* in composition, showing: visible: related to benzene (**phene**). [Gr. *phainein,* to show.]

**phenacetin,** *fin-as'i-tin, n.* an antipyretic drug, $C_{10}H_{13}NO_2$. [acetic and **phene**.]

**phenacite,** *fen'ə-sit,* pleacite, *-kit, n.* a mineral, beryllium silicate, sometimes deceptively like quartz.—*ns.* **phen'akism,** deceit; **phenakist'-oscope,** an instrument in which figures on a disk seen successively through a slit give the impression of motion. [Gr. *phenax* and *phenākistēs,* a deceiver; *skopeein,* to look at.]

**phene,** *fēn, n.* an old name for benzene.—*n.* **phēn'ate,** a phenolate.—*adj.* **phēn'ic** (or *fen'*), of benzene or of phenyl. [Gr. *phainein,* to show, because obtained in the manufacture of illuminating gas.]

**phengite,** *fen'jīt, n.* a transparent stone used by the ancients for windows, prob. selenite: sometimes applied to kinds of mica.—Also **phengites** (*fen-ji'tēz*). [Gr. *phengitēs—phengos,* light.]

**Phenician.** Same as **Phoenician.**

**pheno-.** See **phen-.**

**phenobarbitone,** *fē-nō-bär'bi-tōn, n.* a sedative and hypnotic drug.

**phenocryst,** *fē'nō-krist, n.* a larger crystal in a porphyritic rock. [Gr. *phainein,* to show, and crystal.]

**phenol,** *fē'nol, n.* carbolic acid, a weak acid, $C_6H_5OH$, got as hygroscopic needles from coal-tar, a powerful disinfectant: extended to the class of aromatic compounds with one or more hydroxyl groups directly attached to the benzene nucleus, weak acids with reactions of alcohols.— *n.* **phēn'olate,** a salt of a phenol.—*adj.* **phenol'ic.** —*n.* **phenolphthalein** (*fē-nol-fthal'i-in,* or *-thal'*), a substance ($C_{20}H_{14}O_4$) got from phenol and phthalic anhydride, brilliant red in alkalis, colourless in acids, used as an indicator.— **phenolic resins,** a group of plastics made from a phenol and an aldehyde. [See **phene; -ol** from alcohol.]

**phenology, phaenology,** *fē-nol'ə-ji, n.* the study of organisms as affected by climate, esp. dates of seasonal phenomena, as opening of flowers, arrival of migrants.—*adj.* **phenological** (*-ə-loj'*).— *n.* **phenol'ogist.** [Gr. *phainein,* to show, *logos,* discourse.]

**phenomenon,** now rarely **phaenomenon,** *fi-nom' i-non* or *-nun, n.* anything directly apprehended by the senses or one of them: an event that may be observed: the appearance which anything makes to our consciousness, as distinguished from what it is in itself: loosely, a remarkable or unusual person, thing, or appearance, a prodigy:—*pl.* **phenom'ena** (sometimes used *erron.* for *n. sing.*). —*adj.* **phenom'enal,** pertaining to a phenomenon: of the nature of a phenomenon.—*v.t.* **phenom'-enalise, -ize,** to represent as a phenomenon.—*ns.* **phenom'enalism,** the philosophical doctrine that phenomena are the only realities, or that knowledge can only comprehend phenomena—also **externalism; phenom'enalist.**—*adj.* **phenomena-list'ic.**—*n.* **phenomenality** (*-al'i-ti*), the character of being phenomenal.—*adv.* **phenom'enally.**— *v.t.* **phenom'enise, -ize,** to bring into the world of experience.—*ns.* **phenom'enism,** phenomenalism; **phenom'enist.**—*adj.* **phenomenolog'ical.**—*n.* **phenomenol'ogy,** the science, or a description, of phenomena: the philosophy of Edmund Husserl (1859-1938)—opposed to positivism, and concerned with the experiences of the self. [Gr. *phainomenon,* pl. *-a,* neut. pr.p. pass. of *phainein,* to show.]

**phenotype,** *fēn'ō-tip, n.* the observable characteristics of an organism produced by the interaction of genes and environment: a group of individuals having the same characteristics of this kind.—*adjs.* **phenotyp'ic(al)** (*-tip'*). [Gr. *phainein,* to show, and **type**.]

**phenyl,** *fē'nil, n.* an organic radical, $C_6H_5$, found in benzene, phenol, etc.—*adj.* **phenyl'ic.**—*ns.* **phenylal'anin(e),** an amino-acid present in most food proteins; **phenylbut'azone** (*-būt'ə-zōn*), an analgesic and antipyretic used in treatment of rheumatic disorders and also, illegally, in horse-doping; **phenylketonuria** (*-kē-tō-nū'ri-ə*), an inherited metabolic disorder in infants in which there is an inability to break down phenyl-alanine, commonly later resulting in mental defect, unless a phenylalanine-free diet is given. [**phene,** and Gr. *hylē,* material.]

**pheon,** *fē'on,* (*her.*) *n.* the barbed head of a dart or arrow, esp. as a heraldic bearing.

**Pherecratic,** *fer-e-krat'ik,* **Pherecrataean,** *-krā-tē'ən, adjs.* of the Greek poet *Pherecratēs.*—*n.* a metre used by him, spondee, dactyl, spondee, with variations.

**pheromone,** *fer'ə-mōn, n.* a chemical substance secreted by an animal which influences the behaviour of others of its species. e.g. queen bee substance. [Gr. *pherein,* to bear, and *horman,* to stimulate.]

**phese.** See **feeze.**

**phew,** *fū, interj.* an exclamation of petty vexation,

unexpected difficulty, impatience, relief, contempt, etc. [A half-formed whistle.]

**phi,** *fī, fē, n.* the twenty-first letter (Φ, φ) of the Greek alphabet, orig. as aspirated *p* (as in *upheave*), now pronounced as *f* and transliterated *ph*: as a Greek numeral φ' = 500, ,φ = 500,000. [Gr. *phei.*]

**phial,** *fī'əl, n.* a vessel for liquids, esp. now a small medicine-bottle.—*v.t.* to put or keep in a phial:—*pr.p.* **phi'alling;** *pa.t.* and *pa.p.* **phi'alled.**—*adj.* **phi'aliform,** saucer-shaped. [L. *phiala*—Gr. *phialē,* a broad shallow bowl.]

**Phi Beta Kappa,** *fī' or fē', bē' or bā'ta kap'a,* the oldest of the American college Greek letter societies. [Gr. Φ.B.K., the initial letters of its motto—*Philosophiā biou kybernētēs,* Philosophy is the guide of life.]

**phil-,** *fil-,* **philo-,** *fil-ō-,* in composition, used to denote loving: lover.— -**phil,** -*fil,* -**phile,** -*fīl,* lover of: loving; -**philia,** -**phily,** love of; -**philic** (also, as *n.* suffix, lover of), -**philous,** loving; -**philus,** in zoological names, lover of (usu. a specified food). [Gr. *philos,* friend—*phileein,* to love.]

**philabeg.** See **filibeg.**

**Philadelphian,** *fil-ə-del'fi-ən, adj.* of the Pergamene city of Philadelphia or Philadelpheia (Ala-shehr): of Philadelphia, Pennsylvania: of a mystic sect emphasising brotherly love, founded in London in 1652 under the influence of Boehme.—*n.* a native or inhabitant of Philadelphia: a member of the Philadelphian sect.—**Philadelphia lawyer,** a very able, shrewd, or sharp lawyer. [phil-, Gr. *adelphos,* a brother, *adelphē,* a sister.]

**philamot.** See **filemot.**

**Philander,** *fil-an'dər, n.* a conventional proper name for a lover: (without *cap.*) a lover: (without *cap.*) a dangler after women: (without *cap.*) a male flirt: (without *cap.*) a philandering.—*v.i.* to make love: to flirt or coquet.—*n.* **philan'derer.** [Gr. *philandros,* fond of men or of a husband—*anēr, andros,* a man, husband: misapplied as if meaning a loving man.]

**philanthropy,** *fil-an'thrə-pi, n.* love of mankind esp. as shown in services to general welfare.—*ns.* **philanthrope** (*fil'ən-thrōp*), **philan'thropist,** one who tries to benefit mankind.—*adjs.* **philan'thropic** (-*throp'ik*), **-al,** doing good to others, benevolent.—*adv.* **philanthrop'ically.** [Gr. *philanthrōpiā*—*anthrōpos,* a man.]

**philately,** *fil-at'i-li, n.* the study and collection of postage and revenue stamps and labels.—*adj.* **philatelic** (*fil-ə-tel'ik*).—*n.* **philat'elist.** [Fr. *philatélic,* invented in 1864—Gr. *atelēs,* tax-free *a-,* priv., *telos,* tax.]

**-phile.** See **phil-.**

**philharmonic,** *fil-är-mon'ik,* also *-här-,* -*ər-, adj.* loving music.—**philharmonic pitch,** a musical pitch slightly higher than French pitch (439 vibrations a second for A). [phil-, Gr. *harmoniā,* harmony.]

**philhellenic,** *fil-hel-ēn'ik,* or -*en'ik, adj.* loving Greece: favouring the Greeks.—*ns.* **philhellene** (-*hel'ēn*), **philhellenist** (-*hel'in-ist*), a supporter of Greece, esp. in 1821-32; **philhell'enism.** [phil-, Gr. *Hellēn,* a Greek.]

**p(h)ilhorse,** *fil'hörs,* **pil'hörs,** (*Shak.*) *n.* Same as **fillhorse** or **thillhorse.** [See **fill** (2), **thill.**]

**philibeg.** Same as **filibeg.**

**-philia.** See **phil-.**

**Philippian,** *fil-ip'i-ən, n.* a native of *Philippi* in Macedonia.—Also *adj.*

**Philippic,** *fil-ip'ik, n.* one of the three orations of Demosthenes against Philip of Macedon: any discourse full of invective.—*v.i.* **Phil'ippise, -ize,** to side with Philip: to utter an oracle inspired by Philip, or by bribery of the prevailing power. [Gr. *philippikos, philippizein*—*Philippos,* Philip.]

**philippina, philippine.** Same as **philopoena.**

**Philistine,** *fil'is-tin* (*U.S. fil-is'tīn*), *n.* one of the ancient inhabitants of south-west Palestine,

enemies of the Israelites: a name applied by German students to persons not connected with the university (also **Philis'ter;** *Ger.*): (also without *cap.*) a person of material outlook, indifferent to culture: (without *cap.*) an enemy (*slang*): (without *cap.*) a bailiff (*slang*).—*adjs.* **Philistē'an, Philis'tian** (both *Milt.*), **Phil'istine.**—*v.t.* **Phil'istinise, -ize** (-*tin-*).—*n.* **Phil'istinism.** [Gr. *Philistinos, Palaistinos*—Heb. *P'lishtim.*]

**phillipsite,** *fil'ips-it, n.* a zeolite, hydrated silicate of potassium, calcium, and aluminium, often cross-shaped by twinning. [J. W. *Phillips,* mineralogist.]

**phillumeny,** *fil-ōō'mən-i, n.* a fantastic word for collecting matchbox labels.—*n.* **phillu'menist.** [L. *lūmen, -inis,* light.]

**Phillyrea,** *fil-ir'i-ə, n.* the mock privet genus, Mediterranean shrubs akin to olive and privet. [Gr. *philyreā,* mock privet.]

**philo-.** See **phil-.**

**Philodendron,** *fil-ō-den'dron, n.* a genus of tropical American climbing plants. [Gr. *philodendros,* fond of trees.]

**philogyny,** *fil-oj'i-ni, n.* love of women.—*adj.* **philog'ynous.**—*n.* **philog'ynist.** [Gr. *philogyniā*—*gynē,* a woman.]

**philology,** *fil-ol'ə-ji, n.* the science of language: the study of etymology, grammar, rhetoric, and literary criticism: orig., the knowledge which enabled men to study and explain the languages of Greece and Rome.—*ns.* **philol'oger, philologian** (-*ə-lō'*), **philol'ogist, phil'ologue** (-*log*), one versed in philology.—*adjs.* **philologic** (-*ə-loj'ik*), **-al.**—*adv.* **philolog'ically. — comparative philology,** study of languages by comparing their history, forms, and relationships with each other. [Gr. *philologiā*—*logos,* word.]

**philomath,** *fil'ə-math, n.* a lover of learning.—*adjs.* **philomath'ic, -al.**—*n.* **philomathy** (-*om'ə-thi*), love of learning. [Gr. *philomathēs,* fond of learning—*math-,* root of *manthanein,* to learn.]

**Philomel,** *fil'ō-mel,* **Philomela,** -*mē'la, n.* the nightingale personified.—Also (*obs.*) **Phil'omene** (-*mēn*). [Gr. *Philomēla,* daughter of Pandion, changed into a nightingale or swallow.]

**philomot,** *fil'ə-mot,* (*Addison*) *n.* Same as **filemot.**

**philopoena, philippina,** *fil-ip-ē'na,* **philippine,** *fil'ip-ēn, n.* a game in which each of two persons eats a twin kernel of a nut, and one pays a forfeit to the other on certain conditions: the nut itself: the gift made as a forfeit. [Apparently from the Ger. formula of claiming the gift, *Guten Morgen, Vielliebchen,* Good morning, well-beloved, confused with Gr. *philos,* friend, *poinē,* penalty, and with Ger. *Philippchen,* little Philip.]

**philoprogenitive,** *fil-ō-prō-jen'i-tiv, adj.* having or relating to instinctive love of offspring: inclined to produce offspring.—*n.* **philoprogen'-itiveness.** [philo-, L. *progeniēs,* progeny.]

**philosopher,** *fi-los'ə-fər, n.* a lover of wisdom: one versed in or devoted to philosophy: formerly, a student of natural science or of the occult: now mainly a metaphysician: one who acts calmly and rationally in the affairs and changes of life.—*ns.* **philosophas'ter,** a superficial philosopher: one who poses as a philosopher; **phil'osophe** (-*sof, -zof,* or -*zof'*), a philosopher: a thinker of the type of the French Encyclopaedists; **philos'opheress, philos'ophess** (both *rare*).—*adjs.* **philosophic** (-*sof'* or -*zof'*), **-al,** pertaining or according to philosophy: skilled in or given to philosophy: befitting a philosopher: rational: calm. — *adv.* **philosoph'ically. — *v.i.* philos'ophise, -ize,** to reason like a philosopher: to form philosophical theories.—*ns.* **philos'-ophiser,-z-,** would-be philosopher; **philos'ophism,** would-be philosophy; **philos'ophist.**—*adjs.* **philosophist'ic, -al.**—*n.* **philos'ophy,** orig., pursuit of wisdom and knowledge: investigation of the nature of being: knowledge of the causes and laws of all things: the principles underlying any department of knowledge: reasoning: a particular philosophical system: calmness of temper.—philosopher's stone, an imaginary stone or mineral compound, long sought after by alchemists as a means of transforming other metals into gold; philosophical pitch, a pitch used in acoustical calculations based on 512 vibrations for treble C.—moral, natural, philosophy (see moral, natural). [Gr. *philosophos*—*sophiā*, wisdom.]

philtre, philter, *fil'tər*, *n.* a drink, or (rarely) a spell, to excite love. [Fr. *philtre*—L. *philtrum*—Gr. *philtron*—*phileein*, to love, *-tron*, agent-suffix.]

-phily. See phil-.

phimosis, *fī-mō'sis*, *n.* narrowing of the preputial orifice. [Gr. *phīmōsis*, muzzling—*phimos*, a muzzle.]

phinnock. Same as finnock.

phisnomy, *fiz'nə-mi*, *n.* an old form of physiognomy, the face.

phiz, *fiz*, phizog, *fiz-og'*, (*slang*) *ns.* the face. [physiognomy.]

phlebitis, *fli-bī'tis*, *n.* inflammation of a vein.—*n.* phlebolite (*fleb'ə-līt*; Gr. *lithos*, stone), a calcareous concretion found in a vein.—*v.t.* phlebot'omise, -ize (Gr. *tomē*, a cut), to bleed.—*ns.* phlebot'omist, a blood-letter; phlebot'omy, blood-letting. [Gr. *phleps*, *phlebos*, a vein.]

Phlegethontic, *fleg-i-thon'tik*, *adj.* of or like the Phlegethon, a fiery river of Hades. [Gr. *phlegethōn*, *-ontos*, pr.p. of *phlegethein*—*phlegein*, to burn.]

phlegm, *flem*, *n.* the thick, slimy matter secreted in the throat, and discharged by coughing, regarded in old physiology as one (cold and moist) of the four humours or bodily fluids: the temperament supposed to be due to its predominance, sluggish indifference: calmness: one of the principles of old chemistry, a watery distilled liquid.—Following words pron. *fleg-* unless indicated otherwise.—*adj.* phlegmagogic (-*goj'ik*, -*gog'ik*.)—*ns.* phleg'magogue (-*gog*), a medicine expelling phlegm; phlegmā'sia, inflammation, esp. *Phlegmasia alba dolens*, white-leg.—*adjs.* phlegmat'ic, -al, abounding in or generating phlegm: cold and sluggish: not easily excited.—*adv.* phlegmat'ically.—*n.* phleg'mon, purulent inflammation.—*adjs.* phlegmon'ic, phleg'monoid, phleg'-monous; phlegmy (*flem'i*). [By later return to Greek spelling, from M.E. *fleem*, *fleme*, *flemme*—O.Fr. *flemme*, *fleume*—L. *phlegma*—Gr. *phlegma*, *-atos*, flame, inflammation, phlegm (regarded as produced by heat), *phlegmasiā*, *phlegmonē*, inflammation—*phlegein*, to burn.]

Phleum, *flē'əm*, *n.* a small genus of grasses, timothy-grass. [Gr. *phleōs*, plume-grass.]

phloem, *flō'əm*, *n.* the bast or sieve-tube portion of a vascular bundle, by which elaborated food materials are transported in a plant. [Gr. *phloos*, bark.]

phlogiston, *flo-jis'ton*, *-gist'on*, or *-tən*, *n.* an imaginary element, believed in the 18th century to separate from every combustible body in burning.—*adj.* phlogis'tic, of, like, or containing phlogiston (*chem.*): combustible (*arch.*): inflammatory (*med.*): fiery.—*v.t.* phlogis'ticate, to combine with phlogiston. [Gr. neut. of vbl. adj. *phlogistos*, burnt, inflammable—*phlogizein*, to set on fire.]

phlogopite, *flog'ə-pīt*, *n.* a magnesia mica, yellow or brown. [Gr. *phlogōpos*, fiery-looking—*phlox*, flame, *ōps*, face.]

Phlox, *floks*, *n.* a Siberian and American genus of Polemoniaceae, well-known garden plants. [Gr. *phlox*, flame, wallflower—*phlegein*, to burn.]

pho, phoh. Same as foh.

phobia, *fō'bi-ə*, phobism, *fō'bizm*, *ns.* a fear, aversion, or hatred, esp. morbid and irrational.

—*adj.* pho'bic, like or pertaining to a phobia.—*n.* phō'bist. [Gr. *phobos*, fear.]

Phoca, *fō'ka*, *n.* the common seal genus: (without *cap.*) a seal: (without *cap.*) a scaly sea-monster (*Spens.*):—*pl.* pho'cas, pho'cae (-*sē*).—*n.pl.* Phocidae (*fō'si-dē*), the true seals, with backward turned hind-flippers and no external ear. [L. *phōca*—Gr. *phōkē*, a seal.]

Phocaena, *fō-sē'na*, *n.* the porpoise genus. [Gr. *phōkaina*.]

phocomelia, *fō-kō-mēl'i-ə*, -*mel'*, or -*yə*, *n.* the condition of having one or more limbs like a seal's flippers. [Gr. *phōkē*, seal, *melos*, limb.]

Phoebus, *fē'bəs*, *n.* Apollo, the Greek sun-god: the sun.—*n.* Phoebe (*fē'bē*), his sister Artemis, the moon-goddess: the moon.—*adj.* Phoebe'an. [Latinised—Gr. *Phoibos*, *Phoibē*; *phoibos*, -*ē*, bright, *phaein*, to shine.]

Phoenician, *fi-nish'ən*, -*yən*, *adj.* of Phoenicia, on the coast of Syria, its people, colonies (including Carthage), language, and arts.—*n.* one of the people of Phoenicia: their Semitic language. [Gr. *Phoinix*, -*ikos*.]

Phoenix, *fē'niks*, *n.* a fabulous Arabian bird, worshipped in ancient Egypt, the only individual of its kind, that burned itself every 500 years or so and rose rejuvenated from its ashes: hence anything that rises from its own or its predecessor's ashes: a paragon: a southern constellation. [O.E. *fenix*, later assimilated to L. *phoenix*—Gr. *phoinix*.]

Pholas, *fō'las*, *n.* the piddock genus of rock-boring molluscs:—*pl.* pholades (*fō'lə-dēz*).—*adj.* phō'las, -*ados*, (adj.) lurking in a hole, (n.) the date-shell.]

pholidosis, *fol-id-ō'sis*, *n.* arrangement of scales, as in fishes and reptiles. [Gr. *pholis*, -*idos*, scale.]

phon, *fon*, *n.* a unit of objective loudness.—In composition phon-, phono- (*fōn-*, *fō'nō-*, *fō-nō-*), sound, voice.—*adj.* phonal (*fōn'l*), vocal.—*v.i.* phōn'ate, to produce vocal sound, to utter voice.—*n.* phōnā'tion, production of vocal sound.—*adj.* phōn'atory.—*ns.* phonasthenia (*fō-nas-thē'-ni-ə*; Gr. *astheneia*, weakness), weakness of voice: difficulty in speaking: phonautograph (*fōn-ö'tə-gräf*), an instrument for recording sound vibrations.—*adj.* phonautographic (*graf'-ik*).—*adv.* phonautograph'ically.—*n.* phone (*fōn*), an elementary speech sound: a telephone receiver: (also 'phone; *coll.*) a telephone.—*v.t.*, *v.i.* (also 'phone; *coll.*) to telephone.—*adj.* phonemat'ic, phonemic.—*adv.* phonemat'ically.—*η.* phoneme (*fōn'ēm*; Gr. *phōnēma*, a sound), a group or family of speech sounds felt in any one language to be merely variants of one sound.—*adj.* phonemic (-*nēm'* or -*nem'*).—*adv.* phonēm'ically.—*n.* phonemicisā'tion, -z-.—*v.t.* phonēm'icise, -ize, to analyse into phonemes: to treat as a phoneme.—*ns.* phonēm'icist; phonēm'ics, science of phonemic groups and contrasts.—*adj.* phonetic (*fō-net'ik*), of, concerning, according to, or representing the sounds of spoken language.—Also phonet'ical.—*adv.* phonet'ically, according to pronunciation.—*n.* phonetician (*fō-ni-tish'ən*), one versed in phonetics.—*v.t.* phonet'icise, -ize, to make phonetic: to represent phonetically.—*ns.* phonet'icism, phonetic character or representation; phonet'icist, one who advocates phonetic spelling.—*n.pl.* (treated as *sing.*) phonet'ics, that branch of linguistic science that deals with pronunciation.—*ns.* pho'netism, phonetic writing; pho'netist, a phonetician: an advocate or user of phonetic spelling.—*adj.* phōn'ic (or *fon'ik*), of sound, esp. vocal sound: voiced.—*n.pl.* (treated as *sing.*) phōn'ics (or *fon'iks*), the science of sound, or of spoken sounds.—*n.* phon'meter, same as phonometer (see below).—*adj.* phonocamptic (*fō-nə-kamp'tik*; Gr. *kamptein*, to bend; *arch.*) reflecting sound, echoing: relating to echoes.—*n.* (treated as *sing.*) phonocamp'tics, the acoustics of echoes.—*ns.*

**phonogram** (*fō'nə-gram*), a character representing a sound: a phonographic record; **phonograph** (*fō'nə-gräf*; Gr. *graphein*, to write), a character used to represent a sound: Edison's instrument for recording sounds on a cylinder and reproducing them: the ordinary word for any gramophone (*U.S.*); **phonographer** (*fō-nog'rə-fər*), **phonog'raphist**, a writer of phonographic shorthand.—*adj.* **phonographic** (*fō-nə-graf'ik*), phonetic of phonography: of or by means of the phonograph.—*adv.* **phonograph'ically.**—*ns.* **phonog'raphy** (*fō-nog'rə-fi*), the art of representing each spoken sound by a distinct character: Pitman's phonetic shorthand: the use of the phonograph; **phonolite** (*fō'nə-līt*; Gr. *lithos*, a stone), clinkstone, a fine-grained intermediate igneous rock that rings under the hammer, composed of nepheline (or leucite), sanidine, and other minerals.—*adj.* **phonolitic** (*-lit'ik*).—*n.* **phonology** (*fō-nol'ə-ji*; Gr. *logos*, discourse), phonetics: now generally the study of the system of sounds in a language and of the history of their changes.—*adj.* **phonolog'ical.**—*ns.* **phonol'ogist**; **phonom'eter** (Gr. *metron*, measure), apparatus for estimating the loudness level of a sound in phons by subjective comparison; **phon'on**, quantum of thermal energy in a crystal lattice made to vibrate by sound waves or heat; **phonophore** (*fō'nə-fōr, -för*), **phonopore** (*fō'nō-pōr, -pör*; Gr. *phoros*, carrying, *poros*, passage), a sound-conducting apparatus, of various kinds: a device for telephoning and telegraphing simultaneously by the same wire; **phonotype** (*fō'nə-tip*; Gr. *typos*, impression), phonetic type.—*v.t.* to print phonetically.—*adjs.* **phonotyp'ic** (*-tip'ik*), **-al.**—*ns.* **phō'notypist** (or *-tip'ist*); **phō'notypy** (*tip-i*).—phonetic spelling, the writing of a language by means of a separate symbol for every sound: often applied to a compromise, or a departure from conventional spelling more or less adapted as a guide to pronunciation; **phonic method**, a method of teaching reading through the phonetic value of letters and groups of letters. [Gr. *phōnē*, voice, sound.]

**phonal**, **phonasthenia**, **phonate**, etc., **phonautograph**, etc.; **phone**, **phonematic**, etc., **phonemic**, etc., **phonetic**, etc. See **phon.**

**phoney**, **phony**, *fō'ni*, (*slang*), *n.* and *adj.* counterfeit: unreal.—*ns.* **phon'eyness**, **phoniness.** [Origin unknown.]

**phono-.** For words beginning thus, see **phon.**

**phony.** See **phoney.**

**-phore**, *-fōr*, *-för*, **-phor**, *-för*, in composition used to denote 'carrier', as *semaphore, chromatophore.* [Gr. *phoros*, bearing—*pherein*.]

**phorminx**, *för'mingks*, *n.* a kind of cithara. [Gr.]

**Phormium**, *för'mi-əm*, *n.* a New Zealand genus of the lily family—New Zealand flax or flax-lily. [Latinised—Gr. *phormion*, mat, faggot, kind of sage.]

**phosgene**, *fos'jēn*, *n.* a poisonous gas, carbonyl chloride ($COCl_2$) prepared from carbon monoxide and chlorine in sunlight. [Gr. *phōs*, light, and the root of *gignesthai*, to be produced.]

**phosphaturia.** See **Phosphorus.**

**phosphene**, *fos'fēn*, *n.* light seen when the eyeball is pressed: luminous pattern seen when brain is stimulated electrically. [Gr. *phōs*, light, *phainein*, to show.]

**Phosphorus**, *fos'fər-əs*, *n.* the morning-star: (without *cap.*) a non-metallic element (P; atomic number 15); a waxy, poisonous, and inflammable substance giving out light in the dark.—*n.* **phosphate** (*fos'fāt*), a salt of phosphoric acid.—*adj.* **phosphatic** (*fos-fat'ik*), of the nature of, or containing, a phosphate.—*ns.* **phosphaturia** (*fos-fat-ū'ri-ə*), excess of phosphates in the urine; **phos'phide** (*-fīd*), a compound of phosphorus and another element; **phos'phine** (*-fēn, -fīn*),

phosphuretted hydrogen gas ($PH_3$): extended to substances analogous to amines with phosphorus instead of nitrogen; **phos'phite**, a salt of phosphorous acid; **phosphōn'ium**, the radical $PH_4$, analogous to ammonium; **Phos'phor**, the morning-star: (without *cap.*) phosphorus: (without *cap.*) a phosphorescent or fluorescent substance generally.—*v.t.* **phos'phorate**, to combine or impregnate with phosphorus: to make phosphorescent.—*v.i.* **phosphoresce'**, to shine in the dark like phosphorus.—*n.* **phosphoresc'ence.**—*adj.* **phosphoresc'ent.**—*n.* **phos'phoret** (or *-et'*; *obs.*), a phosphide.—*adjs.* **phos'phoretted** (or *-et'*) (see **phosphuretted**); **phosphoric** (*fos-for'ik*), of or like phosphorus: phosphorescent: containing phosphorus in higher valency (*chem.*; **phosphoric acid**, any of the foll. acids—orthophosphoric, $H_3PO_4$, metaphosphoric, $HPO_3$, pyrophosphoric $H_4P_2O_7$; **phosphoric anhydride**, $P_2O_5$).—*v.t.* **phos'phorise**, **-ize**, to combine or impregnate with phosphorus: to make phosphorescent.—*ns.* **phos'phorism** (*obs.*), phosphorescence: poisoning by phosphorus; **phos'phorite**, impure massive apatite.—*adj.* **phos'phorous**, phosphorescent: containing phosphorus in lower valency (*chem.*; **phosphorous acid**, $H_3PO_3$; **phosphorous anhydride**, $P_2O_3$).—*ns.* **phosphor'ylase**, an enzyme playing a part in **phosphorylation**, the act or process of converting a sugar into a compound of phosphorus and of splitting the latter to yield energy for vital processes; **phosphuret** (*fos'fūr-et* or *-et'*; *obs.*), a phosphide.—*adj.* **phos'phuretted** (or *-et'*), combined with phosphorus (**phosphuretted** or **phosphoretted hydrogen**, phosphine).—**phos'phor-bronze'**, an alloy of copper, tin and phosphorus; **phoss'y-jaw**, necrosis of the jawbone with fatty degeneration of the kidney, common among matchmakers when yellow phosphorus was used. [L. *phosphorus*—Gr. *phosphoros*, light-bearer—*phōs*, light, *phoros*, bearing, from *pherein*, to bear.]

**phot**, *fōt, fot, n.* CGS unit of illumination, 1 lumen per $cm^2$.—*adj.* **photic** (*fōt'ik*), of light: lightgiving: sensitive to light: accessible to light (as e.g. uppermost layer of sea).—*n.pl.* (treated as *sing.*) **phōt'ics**, optics.—*ns.* **phōt'ism**, sensation of light accompanying another sensation or thought; **photon** (*fō'ton*), a quantum of light or other radiation. [Gr. *phōs, phōtos*, light.]

**phot-**, *fōt-*, **photo-**, *fō'tō-*, in composition, light.—*adj.* **photoac'tive**, affected physically or chemically by light or other radiation.—*n.* **pho'tocell**, a photoelectric cell.—*adj.* **photochem'ical.**—*n.* **photochem'istry**, the part of chemistry dealing with changes brought about by light, or other radiation, and with the production of radiation by chemical change. — *adj.* **photochrom'ic** (*-krōm'*), changing colour, and hence changing the amount of light transmitted when the incident light increases, or decreases.—*n.* a photochromic material.—*ns.* **photochrom'ics** (science and technology); **photochrom'ism**; **pho'tochromy**, a former process of colour photography.—*adjs.* **photoconduct'ing, -ive**, pertaining to, or showing, photoconductivity.—*n.* **photoconductivity** (*-kon-duk-tiv'i-ti*), property of varying conductivity under influence of light; **photodi'ode**, a two electrode semiconductor device; **photoelectric'ity**, electricity or a change of electric condition, produced by light or other electromagnetic radiation.—*adj.* **photoelectric** (*-i-lek'*), pertaining to photoelectricity, to photoelectrons, or to electric light (**photoelectric cell**, any device in which incidence of light of suitable frequency causes an alteration in electrical state, esp. by photo-emission).—*ns.* **photoelec'tron**, an electron ejected from a body by the incidence of ultra-violet rays or X-rays upon it; **photoelectron'ics**, the science dealing with the interactions of electricity and electromagnetic radiations, esp. those that involve free electrons; **photo-emiss'ion**, emission of electrons from the surface of a body on which light falls: **photofiss'ion**, nuclear fission induced by gamma rays; **pho'toflood (lamp)**, an incandescent tungsten lamp in which excess voltage produces very strong light, but reduces life for the lamp; **photogen** (*fō'tō-jən*; Gr. root of *gignesthai*, to be produced), a light-producing organ in animals: a light paraffin oil (also **photogene**); **pho'togene** (*-jēn*), an after-image: a sensitive emulsion: a photograph (*obs.*).—*adj.* **photogenic** (*-jen'*), producing light: produced by light: photographic (*obs.*): having the quality of photographing well: loosely, attractive, striking.—*ns.* **photogeny** (*fō-toj'i-ni*; *obs.*), photography; **photokinesis** (*-ki,-ki-nē'sis*; Gr. *kinēsis*, movement), movement occurring in response to variations in light intensity; **photolysis** (*fō-tol'i-sis*; Gr. *lysis*, loosing—*lyein*, to loose), decomposition or dissociation under the influence of radiation (*chem.*): the grouping of chloroplasts in relation to illumination (*bot.*).— *adj.* **photolytic** (*fō-tō-lit'ik*).—*ns.* **photom'eter**, instrument for measuring luminous intensity, usu. by comparing two sources of light; **photonasty** (*fō'tə-nas-ti*; Gr. *nastos*, close-pressed; *biol.*), response to the stimulus of changed intensity of light without regard to direction.—*adj.* **photonas'tic**.—*n.* **photoperiod** (*fō-tō-pē'ri-əd*), the optimum length of day, as it affects the amount of light received by a plant, for that particular plant's normal growth and development.—*adj.* **photoperiod'ic**.—*n.* **photope'riodism**, the response of a plant to the relative lengths of day and night.—*adj.* **pho'tophil** (Gr. *phileein*, to love), light-loving: turning towards the light.—*n.* an organism that seeks the light.—*adjs.* **photophil'ic, photophilous** (*-tof'*).—*ns.* **photoph'ily; photophobia** (*fō-tō-fō'bi-ə*; Gr. *phobos*, fear), a shrinking from light.—*n.* and *adj.* **phō'tophobe**.— *adj.* **photophobic** (*-fob'ik*).—*n.* **photophone** (*fō'tō-fōn*; Gr. *phōnē*, voice), an apparatus for transmitting articulate speech to a distance along a beam of light.—*adj.* **photophonic** (*-fon'ik*).—*ns.* **photophony** (*-tof'ə-ni*); **photophore** (*fō'tō-fōr, -fōr*; Gr. *phoros*, bearing; *zool.*), a luminiferous organ; **photophoresis** (*fō-tō-for-ē'sis*; Gr. *phorēsis*, transference), migration of suspended particles under the influence of light; **photōp'ia**, vision in a bright light.—*adj.* **photōp'ic**.—*n.* **photopsia, photopsy** (*fō-top'si-ə, -top'si*; Gr. *opsis*, appearance), the appearance of flashes of light, owing to irritation of the retina; **photo-recep'tor**, a nerve-ending receiving light stimuli.—*adjs.* **photo-resist'**, (of an organic material) that polymerises on exposure to ultra-violet light and in that form resists attack by acids and solvents.—*v.t.* **photosens'itise, -ize**, to make photosensitive by chemical or other means.—*n.* **photosens'itiser, -z-**.—*adj.* **photosens'itive**, affected by light, visible or invisible.— *ns.* **photo-sensitiv'ity; photosphere** (*fō'tō-sfēr*), the luminous envelope of the sun's globe, the source of light.—*adj.* **photospheric** (*-sfer'ik*).— *n.* **photosynthesis** (*fō-tō-sin'thi-sis*; *bot.*), the building up of complex compounds by the chlorophyll apparatus of plants by means of the energy of light.—*adj.* **photosynthet'ic**.—*n.* **phototaxis** (*fō-tō-taks'is*; Gr. *taxis*, arrangement; *biol.*), a change of place under stimulus of light. —*adj.* **phototac'tic**.—*ns.* **phototelegraph** (*fō-tō-tel'i-gräf*), an instrument for transmitting drawings, photographs, etc., by telegraphy; **phototeleg'raphy; phototherapy** (*fō-tō-ther'ə-pi*), **phototherapeutics** (*-pū'tiks*; Gr. *therapeuein*, to tend), treatment of disease by light.—*adj.* **phototherapeut'ic**.—*ns.* **phototropism** (*fōt-ot'rəp-izm*; Gr. *tropos*, turning), orientation in response

to the stimulus of light (*bot.*): reversible colour change on exposure to light (*chem.*); **phototrope** (*fō'tō-trōp*), a substance that changes thus.—*adj.* **phototropic** (*fō-tō-trop'ik*).—*n.* **phototrop'ropy**, change of colour due to wavelength of incident light. [Gr. *phōs, phōtos*, light.]

**photo-.** For some words beginning thus, see **phot-** (above); for others, see next entry.

**photo-**, *fō'tō-*, in composition, photographic: made by, or by the aid of, photographic means. —*n.*, *v.t.*, *adj.*, **photo**, a coll. abbrev. of **photograph(ic, -al)**.—*ns.* **pho'tocomposition** (*print.*), setting of copy by projecting images of letters successively on a sensitive material; **photocopy** (*fō'tō-ko-pi*), a photographic reproduction of written matter.—*v.t.* to make a photocopy.—*ns.* **pho'tocopying; pho'to-engraving, -etching**, any process of engraving by aid of photography, esp. from relief plates; **pho'to-finish**, a race finish in which a special type of photography is used to show the winner, etc.: a neck and neck finish of any contest; **pho'to-fit**, a method of making identification pictures, an alternative to identikit (q.v.); **photogeology** (*fō-tō-jē-ol'ə-ji*), (study of) geology by means of air photographs; **photoglyph** (*fō'tō-glif*; Gr. *glyphē*, carving), a photographic engraving: a photogravure.—*adj.* **photoglyph'ic**.—*ns.* **photoglyphy** (*fō-tog'li-fi*); **photogramm'etry**, the making of maps by using air photographs; **photogravure** (*fō-tō-grə-vūr'*; Fr. *gravure*, engraving), a method of photo-engraving in which the design etched on the metal surface is intaglio not relief: a picture produced by this method; **photolithography** (*fō-tō-li-thog'rə-fi*), a process of lithographic printing from a photograph.—*n.* and *v.t.* **photolith'ograph** (*-o-gräf*).—*n.* **photolithog'rapher**.—*adjs.* **photolithographic** (*-graf'ik*); **pho'to-mechan'ical**, pertaining to mechanical printing from a photographically prepared plate. —*adv.* **pho'to-mechan'ically**.—*ns.* **photomicrograph** (*fō-tō-mī'krō-gräf*; Gr. *mikros*, little, *graphein*, to write), an enlarged photograph of a microscopic object taken through a microscope; **photomicrographer** (*-krog'rə-fər*).— *adj.* **photomicrographic** (*-krō-graf'ik*).—*ns.* **microg'raphy; photomon'tage** (*-täzh*), (the art of making) a picture by cutting up photographs, etc., and arranging the parts so as to convey, without explicitly showing, a definite meaning; **pho'to-process**, any process by which a matrix for printing is got by photographic means; **pho'to-relief**, a plate or image in relief got by photographic means; **pho'tosetting**, photo-composition; **Photostat** (*fō'tō-stat*; Gr. *statos*, set, placed; trademark), a photographic apparatus for making facsimiles of MSS., drawings, etc., directly: a facsimile so made.—*v.t.* and *v.i.* to photograph by Photostat.—*n.* **phototype** (*fō'tō-tip*; Gr. *typos*, impression), a printing block produced photographically.—*v.t.* to reproduce by phototype.—*adj.* **phototypic** (*-tip'ik*).— *ns.* **phototypy** (*fō'tō-ti-pi* or *fō-tot'i-pi*); **photoxylography** (*fō-tō-zi-log'rə-fi*; Gr. *xylon*, wood, *graphein*, to write), wood-engraving after a photographic impression on a wood-block; **photozincography** (*fō-tō-zing-kog'rə-fi*), the process of engraving on zinc by taking an impression by photography and etching with acids; **photozinc'ograph**, a picture so produced. [**photo-graph**.]

**photography**, *fō-tog'rə-fi*, *n.* the art or process of producing permanent and visible images by the action of light, or other radiant energy, on chemically prepared surfaces.—*n.* **phot'ograph** (*fō'tō-gräf*), an image so produced.—*v.t.* to make a picture of by means of photography.— *v.i.* to take photographs: to be capable of being photographed.—*n.* **photog'rapher**.—*adjs.* **photographic** (*-graf'ik*), **-al**.—*adv.* **photograph'ically**.

—*n.* **photog'raphist.** [Gr. *phōs, phōtos,* light, *graphein,* to draw.]

**phrase,** *frāz, n.* manner of expression in language: an expression: a group of words (sometimes as in *Shak.* a single word) generally not forming a clause but felt as expressing a single idea or constituting a single element in the sentence: a pithy expression: a catchword: an empty or high-sounding expression: fussy talk about one's feelings (*Scot.*): a short group of notes felt to form a unit (*mus.*).—*v.t.* to express in words: to style: to flatter, wheedle (*Scot.*): to mark, bring out, or give effect to the phrases of (*mus.*).—*adjs.* **phrās'al,** consisting of, of the nature of, a phrase; **phrase'less,** incapable of being described.—*ns.* **phraseogram** (*frā'zi-ō-gram*), a single sign, written without lifting the pen, for a whole phrase (esp. in shorthand); **phra'seograph,** a phrase that is so written.—*adjs.* **phraseolog'ic,** **-al.**—*adv.* **phraseolog'ically.**—*ns.* **phraseol'ogist,** a maker or a collector of phrases; **phraseol'ogy,** style or manner of expression or arrangement of phrases: peculiarities of diction: a collection of phrases in a language; **phra'ser,** a mere maker or repeater of empty phrases; **phra'sing,** the wording of a speech or passage: the grouping and accentuation of the sounds in performing a melody (*mus.*).—*adj.* using phrases, esp. (*Scot.*) airing one's views or feelings or making flowery speeches.—*adj.* **phra'sy,** inclining to emptiness and verbosity of phrase.—**phrasal verb,** a phrase, consisting of a verb and one or more additional words, having the function of a verb; **phrase'-book,** a book containing or explaining phrases of a language; **phrase'man, phrase'maker** and (*disparagingly*) **phrase'monger,** a user or maker of wordy or fine-sounding phrases. [Gr. *phrāsis*—*phrazein,* to speak.]

**phratry,** *frā'tri, n.* a social division of a people, often exogamous. [Gr. *phrātriā;* cf. L. *frāter,* Eng. **brother.**]

**phreatic,** *frē-at'ik, adj.* pertaining to underground water supplying, or probably able to supply, wells or springs, or to the soil or rocks containing it, or to wells.—*n.* **phreat'ophyte,** a deep-rooted plant drawing its water from the water table or just above it.—*adj.* **phreatophyt'ic.** [Gr. *phrear,* well, *phreātia,* cistern.]

**phrenesiac,** *fri-nē'zi-ak,* (*Scott*) *adj.* hypochondriac. —*n.* **phrenesis** (*fri-nē'sis*), phrenitis: delirium: frenzy.—For *adj., n.* **phrenetic,** *adj.* **phrenetical,** *adv.* **phrenetically,** see **frenetic.**—*adjs.* **phrenic** (*fren'ik*), of or near the midriff: mental (*obs.*); **phrenit'ic,** of or affected with phrenitis.—*n.* **phreni'tis,** inflammation of the brain: brain-fever.—*adjs.* **phrenolog'ic** (*fren-*), **-al.**—*adv.* **phrenolog'ically.**—*v.t.* **phrenol'ogise, -ize,** to examine phrenologically.—*ns.* **phrenol'ogist;** **phrenol'ogy,** a would-be science of mental faculties supposed to be located in various parts of the skull and investigable by feeling the bumps on the outside of the head.—*adjs.* and *n.* **phrensical, phrensy, phrentick,** old forms of **frenzical, frenzy, frantic** (or **phrenetic**). [Gr. *phrēn, phrenos,* midriff, supposed seat of passions, mind, will.]

**phrontistery,** *fron'tis-tə-ri, n.* a thinking-place. [Gr. *phrontistērion*—*phrontistēs,* a thinker—*phroneein,* to think; applied by Aristophanes to the school of Socrates.]

**Phrygian,** *frij'i-ən, adj.* pertaining to *Phrygia* in Asia Minor, or to its people.—*n.* a native of Phrygia: a Montanist: the language of the ancient Phrygians.—**Phrygian cap,** a conical cap with the top turned forward; **Phrygian mode,** in ancient Greek music, a mode of two tetrachords with a semitone in the middle of each and a whole tone between the tetrachords (as: *d e f g; a b c d;* but reckoned downwards by the Greeks): in old Church music, an

authentic mode extending from *e* to *e,* with *e* as its final.

**phthalic,** (*f*)*thal'ik, adj.* applied to three acids, $C_6H_4(COOH)_2$, and an anhydride, derived from naphthalene.—*ns.* **phthal'ate,** a salt or ester of phthalic acid; **phthal'ein** (*-i-in*), any one of a very important class of dye-yielding materials formed by the union of phenols with phthalic anhydride; **phthal'in,** a colourless crystalline compound obtained by reducing a phthalein; **phthalocy'anin, -cyanine,** any of a group of green and blue organic colouring matters of great fastness and brilliance. [naphthalene.]

**phthiriasis,** (*f*)*thī-rī'ə-sis, n.* infestation with lice. [Gr. *phtheiriāsis*—*phtheir,* a louse.]

**phthisis,** *thī'sis,* also *fthi', ti', n.* wasting disease: tuberculosis, esp. of the lungs.—*n.* **phthisic** (*tiz'ik,* sometimes *thī'sik, fthi'sik, ti'sik*), phthisis: vaguely, a lung or throat disease.—*adjs.* **phthisical** (*tiz'*), **phthis'icky.** [Gr. *phthisis*—*phthi(n)ein,* to waste away.]

**phut,** *fut, adv.*—**to go phut,** to break, become unserviceable: to come to nothing. [Hind. *phatnā,* to split.]

**pH value.** See **pH.**

**phyco-,** *fī-kō-,* in composition, seaweed.—*ns.* **phycocyan, phycocyanin** (*-si'an, -ə-nin;* Gr. *kyanos,* dark blue), a blue pigment in algae; **phycoerythrin** (*-e-rith'rin;* Gr. *erythros,* red), a red pigment in algae.—*adj.* **phycolog'ical.**—*ns.* **phycologist** (*-kol'ə-jist*); **phycol'ogy,** the study of algae.—*n.pl.* **Phycomycetes** (*-mi-sē'tēz;* Gr. *mykētēs,* pl. of *mykēs,* a fungus), a class of fungi showing affinities with the green seaweeds. —*ns.* **phycophaein** (*-fē'in;* Gr. *phaios,* grey), a brown pigment in seaweeds; **phycoxan'thin** (Gr. *xanthos,* yellow), a yellow pigment in diatoms, brown seaweeds, etc. [Gr. *phykos,* seaweed.]

**phylactery,** *fi-lak'tə-ri, n.* a charm or amulet: among the Jews, a slip of parchment inscribed with certain passages of Scripture, worn in a box on the left arm or forehead: a reminder: ostentatious display of religious forms: a case for relics: in mediaeval art, a scroll at the mouth of a figure in a picture bearing the words he is supposed to speak.—*adjs.* **phylacteric** (*-ter'ik*), **-al.** [Gr. *phylaktērion*—*phylax,* a guard.]

**phyle,** *fī'lē, n.* a tribe or division of the people of a state in ancient Greece, at first on a kinship, later on a local, basis.—*ns.* **phylarch** (*fi'lärk*), the chief officer of a tribe: in Athens, the commander of the cavalry of a tribe; **phy'larchy,** the office of phylarch. [Gr. *phylē.*]

**phyletic,** *fī-let'ik, adj.* pertaining to a phylum: according to descent. [Gr. *phyletikos*—*phylē.*]

**phyllary,** *fil'ə-ri,* (*bot.*) *n.* an involucral bract. [Gr. *phyllarion,* dim. of *phyllon,* leaf.]

**phyllite,** *fil'it, n.* a rock intermediate between clay-slate and mica-schist. [Gr. *phyllon,* a leaf.]

**phylloclade,** *fil'ō-klād, n.* a branch with the form and functions of a leaf. [Gr. *phyllon,* leaf, *klados,* shoot.]

**phyllode,** *fil'ōd, n.* a petiole with the appearance and function of a leaf-blade.—*n.* **phyll'ody** (*-ō-di*), transformation of flower parts into leaves. —*adj.* **phyll'oid,** leaf-like. [Gr. *phyllon,* leaf, *eidos,* form.]

**phyllomania,** *fil-ō-mā'ni-ə, n.* excessive production of leaves, at the expense of flower or fruit production. [Gr. *phyllon,* leaf, *maniā,* madness.]

**phyllome,** *fil'ōm, n.* any leaf or homologue of a leaf. [Gr. *phyllōma,* foliage.]

**phyllophagous,** *fi-lof'ə-gas, adj.* leaf-eating. [Gr. *phyllon,* leaf, *phagein,* to eat.]

**phyllopod,** *fil'ō-pod, n.* a crustacean of the order **Phyllopoda** (*-op'ə-də*), entomostracans with foliaceous legs. [Gr. *phyllon,* leaf, *pous, podos,* foot.]

**phylloquinone,** *fil-ō-kwin'ōn,* or *-ōn', n.* vitamin K₁. [Gr. *phyllon,* leaf, and **quinone.**]

phyllotaxis, *fil-ō-tak'sis*, *n.* the disposition of leaves on the stem.—Also phyll'otaxy.—*adjs.* phyllotact'ic, -al. [Gr. *phyllon*, a leaf, *taxis*, arrangement.]

Phylloxera, *fil-ok-sē'ra*, *n.* a genus of insects of a family akin to green-fly, very destructive to vines. [Gr. *phyllon*, a leaf, *xēros*, dry.]

phylogeny, *fi-loj'i-ni*, *n.* evolutionary pedigree or genealogical history—also phylogenesis (*fi-lō-jen'i-sis*).—*adj.* phylogenet'ic.—*adv.* phylogenet'-ically. [Gr. *phȳlon*, race, *genesis*, origin.]

phylum, *fī'lam*, *n.* a main division of the animal or the vegetable kingdom:—*pl.* phy'la. [Mod L.—Gr. *phȳlon*, race.]

Physalia, *fi-sā'li-a*, *n.* a genus of large oceanic colonial hydrozoans with a floating bladder—Portuguese man-of-war.—*ns.* Physalis (*fis'* or *fis'a-lis*), the Cape gooseberry genus of Solanaceae, with persistent bladdery calyx; Physeter (*fi-sē'tar*), a sperm whale. [Gr. *phȳsallis*, a bladder, *phȳsētēr*, a blower, a whale, bellows—*phȳsaein*, to blow.]

physharmonica, *fis-här-mon'i-ka*, *n.* an early form of harmonium. [Gr. *phȳsa*, bellows, and harmonica.]

physic, *fiz'ik*, *n.* orig. natural philosophy, physics: the science, art, or practice of medicine: a medicine: anything healing or wholesome.—*adj.* (*obs.*) physical, natural: medicinal.—*v.t.* to give medicine to: to heal:—*pr.p.* phys'icking; *pa.t.* and *pa.p.* phys'icked.—*adj.* phys'ical, pertaining to the world of matter and energy, or its study, natural philosophy: material: materialistic (*obs.*): bodily: medical (*rare*): medicinal (*obs.*): wholesome (*Shak.*).—*n.* physical'ity, preoccupation with the bodily.—*adv.* phys'ically.—*ns.* physician (*fi-zish'n*), one skilled in the use of physic or the art of healing: one legally qualified to practise medicine: one who makes use of medicines and treatment, distinguished from a surgeon who practises manual operations: a doctor: a healer or healing influence (*fig.*); physic'iancy (*-zish'*), post or office of physician; physic'ianer (*rare*), a physician; physic'ianship; phys'icism (*-sizm*), belief in the material or physical as opposed to the spiritual; phys'icist (*-sist*), a student of nature: one versed in physics: one who believes the phenomena of life are purely physical.—*adj.* phys'icky, like medicine.—*n.* (treated as *sing.*) phys'ics, orig. natural science in general: now, the science of the properties (other than chemical) of matter and energy.—physical astronomy, the study of the physical condition and chemical composition of the heavenly bodies; physical chemistry, the study of the dependence of physical properties on chemical composition, and of the physical changes accompanying chemical reactions; physical force, force applied outwardly to the body, as distinguished from persuasion, etc.; physical geography, the study of the earth's natural features—its mountain-chains, ocean-currents, etc.; physic garden, orig. a garden of medicinal plants: a botanic garden; phys'ic-nut, the purgative seed of the tropical American *Jatropha curcas*, a tree of the spurge family. [Gr. *physikos*, natural—*physis*, nature.]

physi(o)-, *fiz-i-(ō)*, in composition, nature.—*ns.* physiocracy (*-ok'ra-si*; Gr. *krateein*, to rule), government, according to François Quesnay (1694-1774) and his followers, by a natural order inherent in society, land and its products the only true source of wealth, direct taxation of land the only proper source of revenue; phys'iocrat (*-ō-krat*), one who maintains these opinions.—*adj.* physiocrat'ic.—*ns.* physiography (*-og'ra-fi*; Gr. *graphein*, to describe), description of nature, descriptive science: physical geography; physiog'rapher.—*adjs.* physiographic (*-ō-graf'ik*), -al.—*ns.* physiolatry (*-ol'a-tri*; Gr. *latreiā*, wor-

ship), nature-worship; physiol'ater, a nature-worshipper; physiology (*-ol'a-ji*; Gr. *logos*, discourse), the science of the processes of life in animals and plants.—*adjs.* physiologic (*-a-loj'ik*), -al.—*adv.* physiolog'ically.—*ns.* physiol'ogist; physiol'ogus, a bestiary; physiotherapy (*-ō-ther'a-pi*; Gr. *therapeiā*, treatment), treatment of disease by remedies such as massage, fresh air, electricity, rather than by drugs.—Also physiotherapeutics (*-pūt'iks*).—*adj.* physiotherapeut'ic.—*ns.* physiother'apist; physitheism (*fiz'i-thē-izm*; Gr. *theos*, god), the ascription of physical form and attributes to deity: deification of powers of nature.—*adj.* physitheis'tic. [Gr. *physis*, nature.]

physiognomy, *fiz-i-on'a-mi* or *-og'na-mi*, *n.* the art of judging character from appearance, esp. from the face: the face as an index of the mind: the face (*coll.*): the general appearance of anything: character, aspect.—*adjs.* physiognomic (*-nom'*), -al.—*adv.* physiognom'ically.—*n.* physiogn'omist. [Gr. *physiognōmiā*, a shortened form of *physiognōmoniā*—*physis*, nature, *gnōmōn*, *-onos*, an interpreter.]

physique, *fiz-ēk'*, *n.* bodily type, build, or constitution. [Fr.]

phyto-, *fi-tō-*, *-to-*, in composition, plant.—*ns.* phytobenthos (*-ben'thos*; Gr. *benthos*, depth), plants living at the bottom of water collectively; phytogen'esis, phytogeny (*-toj'i-ni*), evolution of plants.—*adjs.* phytogenet'ic, -al, relating to phytogenesis; phytogenic (*-jen'ik*), of vegetable origin.—*n.* phytogeog'rapher.—*adj.* phytogeograph'ic.—*ns.* phytogeog'raphy, the geography of plant distribution; phytog'rapher, a descriptive botanist.—*adj.* phytograph'ic.—*ns.* phytog'raphy, descriptive botany; Phytolacc'a, the pokeweed genus, giving name to the family Phytolacc'eae, allied to the pinks and the goose-foots.—*adj.* phytolog'ical.—*ns.* phytol'ogist, a botanist; phytol'ogy, botany; phytonadione (*fi-tō-na-dī'ōn*), phylloquinone, vitamin K₁.—*adj.* phytopatholog'ical.—*ns.* phytopathol'ogist; phytopathology (Gr. *pathos*, suffering), the study of plant diseases.—*adjs.* phytophagic (*-faj'ik*), phytophagous (*-tof'a-gas*; Gr. *phagein*, to eat), plant-eating.—*ns.* phytoplank'ton (Gr. *plankton*, neut., wandering), vegetable plankton; phyto'sis, presence of vegetable parasites or disease caused by them; phytosterol (*-tos'ta-rol*; formed on the model of *cholesterol*), a substance very like cholesterol got from plants; phytot'omist; phytotomy (*-tot'a-mi*; Gr. *tomē*, a cut), plant anatomy; phytotron (*fi'tō-tron*), an apparatus that produces climates artificially for the study of plant growth. [Gr. *phȳton*, plant.]

pi, *pī*, *pē*, *n.* the sixteenth letter (Π, π) of the Greek alphabet, answering to the Roman P: as a numeral π' stands for 80, ,π for 80,000: a symbol for the ratio of the circumference of a circle to the diameter, approx. 3·14159 (*math.*).—pi- (or π-) meson, the source of the nuclear force holding protons and neutrons together (*phys.*).—Also called pion. [Gr. *pei*, *pi*.]

pi (*print.*). Same as pie (3).

pi, *pī*, (*slang*) *adj.* an abbreviation of pious: religious: sanctimonious.—*n.* a pious, religious, or sanctimonious person or talk.—pi'-jaw, sermonising: an admonition.

pia, *pē'a*, *n.* a tropical monocotyledonous plant (Tacca: fam. Taccaceae) with a rhizome yielding E. India or Madagascar arrowroot. [Polynesian name.]

pia, *pē'a*, *pē'a*, (L.) pious.—pia desideria (*dez-i-dēr'i-a*, *dā-sēd-er'i-a*), pious regrets; pia fraus (*frōz*, *frows*), pious fraud.

piacevole, *pya-chā'vo-lā*, (*mus.*) *adj.* pleasant, playful.

piacular, *pī-ak'ū-lar*, *adj.* expiatory: requiring expiation: atrociously bad. — *n.* piacularity

(-lar'-i-ti). [L. *piāculum*, sacrifice—*piāre*, to expiate—*pius*, pious.]

**piaffe,** *pi-af'*, *pyaf*, *v.i.* in horsemanship, to advance at a piaffer.—*n.* **piaff'er,** a gait in which the feet are lifted in the same succession as a trot, but more slowly.—Also *Spanish-walk.* [Fr. *piaffer.*]

**pia mater,** *pi'a mā'tər*, *n.* the vascular membrane investing the brain: the brain (*Shak.*). [L. *pia māter*, tender mother, a mediaeval translation of Ar. *umm raqīqah*, thin mother.]

**pianoforte,** *pya'nō-för-ti*, *pē-a'*, *pyä'*, *pē-ä'*, shortened to **piano** (*pya'*, *pē-a'*, or *-ä'*), *n.* a musical instrument with wires struck by hammers moved by keys:—*pl.* **pia'nofortes, pian'os.**—*ns.* **pianette** (*pē-ə-net'*), a small upright piano; **pianino** (*pya-nē'nō*, *pē-ə-nē'nō*), orig. an upright piano: a small upright piano; **pi'anism,** the technique of the pianoforte.—*adj.* and *adv.* **pianissimo** (*pya-nēs'si-mō*, *pē-ə-nis'i-mō*), very soft.—*n.* **pianist** (*pē'ə-nist*, *pyan'*; also *pē-an'ist*), one who plays the pianoforte, esp. expertly—also (Fr.) **pianiste** (*pē-a-nēst'*), sometimes used as *fem.*—*adj.* **pianist'ic.**—*adj.* and *adv.* **piano** (*pyä'nō*, *pē-ä'nō*), soft, softly.—*n.* a soft passage.—*n.* **Pianola** (*pyan-ō'lə*, *pē-ə-*), a pneumatic contrivance for playing the piano by means of a perforated roll (registered trademark).—**pia'no-accord'ion,** an elaborate accordion with a keyboard like a piano; **pia'no-or'gan,** a piano like a barrel-organ, played by mechanical means; **pian'o-play'er,** a mechanical contrivance for playing the piano: a pianist; **pian'o-school',** a school where piano-playing is taught: a method or book of instruction for the piano; **pian'o-stool,** a stool usually adjustable in height for a pianist; **pian'o-wire,** wire used for piano strings, and for deep-sea soundings, etc.—**player piano,** a piano with a piano-player. [It.—*piano*, soft—L. *plānus*, level, and *forte*, loud—L. *fortis*, strong.]

**piarist,** *pi'ə-rist*, *n.* one of a religious congregation for the education of the poor, founded in Rome in 1597 by Joseph Calasanza. [L. *patrēs scholārum piārum*, fathers of pious schools.]

**piassava,** *pē-əs-ä'va*, **piassaba,** *-ba*, *n.* a coarse stiff fibre used for making brooms, etc., got from Brazilian palms, Attalea (coquilla) and Leopoldinia (chiquichiqui): the tree yielding it. [Port. from Tupí.]

**piastre,** *pi-as'tər*, *n.* a silver coin of varying value, used in Turkey (100 piastres = £T1) and elsewhere: the Spanish dollar. [Fr.,—It. *piastra*, a leaf of metal; see **plaster.**]

**piazza,** *pē-ät'sa*, also *pē-ad'za*, *pē-az'a*, *n.* a place or square surrounded by buildings: erroneously, a walk under a roof supported by pillars: a veranda (*U.S.*).—*adj.* **piazz'ian.** [It.,—L. *platea*—Gr. *plateia*, a street (fem. of *platys*, broad).]

**pibroch,** *pē'brohh*, *n.* a form of bagpipe music, variations on a theme. [Gael. *piobaireachd*, pipe-music—*piobair*, a piper—*piob*, from Eng. **pipe.**]

**pica,** *pi'kə*, *n.* a size of type, 12-point, giving about 6 lines to the inch, much used in typewriters: (**small pica,** 11-point). [Possibly used for printing *pies*; see **pie** (2).]

**Pica,** *pi'kə*, *n.* the magpie genus: (without *cap.*) a craving for unsuitable food. [L. *pica*, magpie.]

**picador,** *pik-ə-dōr'*, *-dör'*, now usu. *pik'ə-dör*, *n.* a mounted bull-fighter with a lance. [Sp.,—*pica*, a pike.]

**picamar,** *pik'ə-mär*, *n.* a bitter oily liquid got from tar. [L. *pix*, *picis*, pitch, *amārus*, bitter.]

**picarian,** *pik-ā'ri-ən*, *adj.* belonging to an obsolete order (**Pica'riae**) of birds including the woodpeckers.—*n.* any member of the order. [L. *picus*, woodpecker.]

**picaroon,** *pik-ə-rōōn'*, *n.* one who lives by his wits: a cheat: a pirate.—*adj.* **picaresque** (*-resk'*).—**picaresque novels,** the tales of Spanish rogue and vagabond life, much in vogue in the 17th

century: novels of like type. [Sp. *picarón*, augmentative of *pícaro*, rogue.]

**picayune,** *pik-ə-ūn'*, *n.* a small coin worth 6¼ cents, current in United States before 1857: a five-cent piece, or other small coin: anything of little or no value.—*adj.* petty.—*adj.* **picayun'ish.** [Prov. *picaioun*, an old Piedmontese copper coin.]

**piccadill,** *pik'ə-dil*, **pikadell,** *-del*, **piccadillo,** *-dil'ō*, **piccadilly,** *-i*, (*obs.*) *n.* a cut or vandyked edging, esp. to a woman's collar: a wide high collar of the early 17th century: a stiff support for a collar or ruff: (in the form **piccadilly**) a man's standing-up collar with the points turned over, first worn about 1870. [Cf. Sp. *picadillo*, a kind of hash.]

**piccalilli,** *pik-ə-lil'i*, *n.* a pickle of various vegetable substances with mustard and spices. [Ety. dub.]

**piccaninny, pickaninny,** *pik-ə-nin'i*, *n.* a little child: a Negro child.—*adj.* very little. [Port. *pequenino*, dim. of *pequeno*, little, or possibly Sp. *pequeño niño*, little child.]

**piccolo,** *pik'ə-lō*, *n.* a small flute, an octave higher than the ordinary flute: an organ stop of similar tone:—*pl.* **picc'olos.** [It., little.]

**pice,** *pis*, *n.sing.* and *pl.* a money of account and coin, ¼ anna; (**new pice**) 1/100 rupee. [Hind. *paisā*.]

**Picea,** *pis'i-ə*, *pis'i-a*, *n.* the spruce genus of conifers. [L. *picea*, pitch-pine—*pix*, pitch.]

**piceous,** *pis'i-əs*, *pish'(i-)əs*, *adj.* like pitch: inflammable: black: reddish black.—*n.* **picene** (*pi'sēn*), a hydrocarbon (C₂₂H₁₄) got from tar. [L. *piceus*—*pix*, pitch.]

**pichiciago,** *pich-i-si-ä'gō*, or *-ä'gō*, *n.* a small burrowing South American armadillo. [Amer. Indian.]

**pichurim,** *pich'ōō-rim*, *n.* a South American tree (*Nectandra puchury*) of the laurel family: its aromatic kernel (also **pichurim bean**). [Port. *pichurim*—Tupí *puchury*.]

**picine.** See **Picus.**

**pick,** *pik*, *n.* a tool for breaking ground, rock, etc., with head pointed at one end or both, and handle fitted to the middle: a pointed hammer: an instrument of various kinds for picking: an act, opportunity, or right of choice: a portion picked: the best or choicest: dirt on a printing type: a diamond in cards, also a spade (*Northern dial.*).—*v.t.* to break up, dress, or remove with a pick: to make with a pick or by plucking: to poke or pluck at, as with a sharp instrument or the nails: to clear, to remove, or to gather, by single small acts: to detach, extract, or take separately and lift or remove: to pluck: to pull apart: to cull: to choose: to select, esp. one by one or bit by bit: to peck, bite, or nibble: to eat in small quantities or delicately: to open (as a lock) by a sharp instrument or other unapproved means: to rifle by stealth: to seek and find a pretext for (as a quarrel): to tidy up (*U.S.*).—*v.i.* to use a pick: to eat by morsels: to pilfer.—*adj.* **picked** (*pikt*), selected, hence the choicest or best: plucked, as flowers or fruit: exquisite, refined, punctilious (*Shak.*): having spines or prickles, sharp-pointed.—*ns.* **pick'edness; pick'-er,** one who picks or gathers up: a tool or machine for picking: one who removes defects from and finishes electrotype plates: a pilferer; **pick'ery** (*Scots law*), pilfering; **pick'ing,** the action of the verb to pick: the quantity picked: that which is left to be picked: dabbing in stone-working: the final finishing of woven fabrics by removing burs, etc.: removing defects from electrotype plates: (in *pl.*) odd gains or perquisites.—**pick'-cheese,** the blue or the great titmouse: the fruit of the mallow; **pick'lock,** an instrument for picking or opening locks; **pick'-me-up,** a stimulating drink: a medicinal tonic; **pick'-pocket,** one who picks or steals from other people's pockets; **pick'-purse,** one who steals the purse or from the purse of another; **pick'-thank,** one who seeks to ingratiate himself by officious favours, or by tale-bearing; **pick'-tooth,** a toothpick; **pick'-up,** an act of picking up: reception: a recovery: a thing picked up: accelerating power: a device for picking up an electric current: (also **pick-up head**) a transducer, activated by a sapphire or diamond stylus following the groove on a gramophone record, which transforms the mechanical into electrical impulses: a light motor vehicle with front part like private car and rear in form of truck: a man's chance, informal acquaintance with a woman, usu. implying a sexual relationship: the woman in such a relationship: a game, or a team, for which the captains pick their men alternately.—*adj.* for picking up: picked up.— **pick a hole in one's coat, pick holes in one,** find fault with one; **pick at,** find fault with; **pick oakum,** to make oakum by untwisting old ropes; **pick off,** to select from a number and shoot: to detach and remove; **pick on,** to single out, esp. for anything unpleasant: to nag at: to carp at; **pick one's way,** to choose carefully where to put one's feet, as on dirty ground; **pick out,** to make out, distinguish: to pluck out: to select from a number: to mark with spots of colour, etc.; **pick over,** to go over and select; **pick someone's brains,** to make use of another's brains or ideas for one's own ends; **pick to pieces,** to pull asunder: to criticise adversely in detail; **pick up,** to lift from the ground, floor etc.: to improve gradually: to gain strength bit by bit: to take into a vehicle, or into one's company: to scrape acquaintance informally with, esp. of a man with a woman: to acquire as occasion offers: to gain: to come upon, make out, distinguish (as a signal, a track, a comet, etc.). [Ety. obscure; cf. **peck, pike, pitch.**]

**pick,** *pik,* a Northern form of **pitch** (1): also of **pitch** (2), esp. *v.i.* to throw the shuttle across the loom, and *n.* a throw of the shuttle, or a weft thread: also a form of **pique.**—**pick-and-pick** (*weaving*), a term indicating alternate picks of yarns of two different colours or kinds.

**pickaback,** *pik'ə-bak, adv.* and *adj.* on the back like a pack: of a vehicle or plane, conveyed on top of another.—*n.* a ride on one's back.—Also **pick'back, pick'apack, pigg'yback.** [Connection with **pick** (pitch), **pack,** and **back** obscure.]

**pickaxe,** *pik'aks, n.* a picking tool, with a point at one end of the head and a cutting blade at the other, used in digging. [M.E. *pikois*—O.Fr. *picois,* a mattock, *piquer,* to pierce, *pic,* a pick.]

**pickeer,** *pi-kēr', v.i.* to forage (*obs.*): to skirmish: to scout: to flirt (*obs.*).—*n.* **pickeer'er.** [Ety. dub.]

**pickelhaube,** *pik-l-how'bə, pik', n.* a German spiked helmet. [Ger.]

**pickerel,** *pik'ər-əl, n.* a young pike: a pike, esp. of smaller species (*U.S.*).—**pick'erel-weed,** pondweed: Pontederia (*U.S.*). [**pike.**]

**picket,** *pik'it, n.* a pointed stake or peg driven into the ground for fortification, tethering, military punishment, surveying, or other purpose: a surveyor's mark: a small outpost, patrol, or body of men set apart for some special duty: picket-duty: a person or group set to watch and dissuade those who go to work during a strike: the old military punishment of standing on one foot on a pointed stake.—*v.t.* to tether to a stake: to strengthen or surround with pickets: to peg down: to subject to the picket: to post as a picket: to deal with as a picket or by means of pickets: to place pickets at or near.—*v.i.* to act as picket:—*pr.p.* **pick'eting;** *pa.t.* and *pa.p.* **pick'eted.**—Also **piquet, picquet.**—*n.* **pick'eter,** one who pickets in a labour dispute.—**pick'et-duty; pick'et-fence** (*U.S.*), a fence of pales;

**pick'et-guard,** a guard kept in readiness in case of alarm. [Fr. *piquet,* dim. of *pic,* a pickaxe.]

**pickle,** *pik'l, n.* a liquid, esp. brine or vinegar, in which food is preserved: an article of food preserved in such liquid: (*pl.*) preserved onions, cucumber, etc., as a condiment: acid or other liquid used for cleansing or treatment in manufacture: a plight (*coll.*): a troublesome child (*coll.*).—*v.t.* to preserve with salt, vinegar, etc.: to rub with salt or salt and vinegar, as an old naval punishment: to clean or treat with acid or other chemical.—*adj.* **pick'led,** treated with a pickle: drunk (*slang*).—*n.* **pick'ler,** one who pickles: a vessel for pickling: an article suitable, or grown, for pickling.—**pick'le-herring,** a pickled herring: a merry-andrew (*obs.*).—**have a rod in pickle,** to have a punishment ready. [M.E. *pekille, pykyl, pekkyll, pykulle;* cf. Du. *pekel;* Ger. *pökel.*]

**pickle,** *pik'l,* (*Scot.*) *n.* a small quantity: a grain of corn. [Origin unknown.]

**pickle,** *pik'l, v.t.* and *v.i.* to peck: to pick: to eat sparingly: to pilfer. [Dim. or freq. of **pick.**]

**pickmaw,** *pik'mö,* (*Scot.*) *n.* the black-headed gull. [Perh. **pick** (pitch), **maw** (mew).]

**Pickwickian,** *pik-wik'i-ən, adj.* relating to or resembling Mr *Pickwick,* the hero of Dickens's *Pickwick Papers.*—*n.* a member of the Pickwick Club.—**in a Pickwickian sense,** in a recondite or merely imaginary sense—a phrase by which a member of the Pickwick Club explained away unparliamentary language.

**picnic,** *pik'nik, n.* orig. a fashionable social entertainment, towards which each person contributed a share of the food: an open-air repast of a number of persons on a country excursion: an undertaking that is mere child's play, often ironically.—*adj.* of or for a picnic: picnicking.—*v.i.* to have a picnic—*pr.p.* **pic'nicking;** *pa.t.* and *pa.p.* **pic'nicked.**—*n.* **pic'nicker.**—*adj.* **pic'nicky.** [Fr. *pique-nique.*]

**pico-,** *pē-kō-, pi-kō-,* in composition, better term for **micromicro-.**

**picot,** *pē-kō', n.* a loop in an ornamental edging: a raised knot in embroidery.—*v.t.* to ornament with picots.—*adj.* **picoté** (*pē-kō-tā*). [Fr. *picot,* point, prick.]

**picotee,** *pik-ə-tē', n.* a florists' variety of carnation, orig. speckled, now edged with a different colour. [Fr. *picoté,* pricked.]

**picotite,** *pik'ō-tit, n.* a dark spinel containing iron, magnesium, and chromium. [From *Picot,* Baron de la Pérouse, who described it.]

**picquet.** See **picket, piquet.**

**picra,** *pik'ra, n.* short for hiera-picra.—*n.* **pic'rate,** a salt (highly explosive) of picric acid.—*adj.* **pic'ric (picric acid,** $C_6H_2(NO_2)_3$.OH, trinitrophenol, used as a yellow dye-stuff and as the basis of high explosives).—*ns.* **pic'rite,** a coarse-grained igneous rock composed mainly of olivine with ferromagnesium minerals and usually some plagioclase; **picrocar'mine,** a stain for microscope work made from carmine, ammonia, water and picric acid; **picrotox'in,** a bitter poisonous principle in the seeds of *Cocculus indicus.* [Gr. *pikros,* bitter.]

**Pict,** *pikt, n.* one of an ancient people of obscure affinities, in Britain, esp. north-eastern Scotland: in Scottish folklore, one of a dwarfish race of underground dwellers: Steele's term for a painted woman.—*adj.* **Pict'ish.**—*n.* the (enigmatical) language of the Picts.—**Picts' house,** an earth-house. [L. *Picti,* Picts: possibly the same as *picti,* pa.p. of *pingĕre,* to paint; cf. **Pecht.**]

**pictarnie,** *pik-tär'ni,* (*Scott*) *n.* a tern. [Origin unknown.]

**pictograph,** *pik'tə-gräf, n.* a picture used as a symbol in picture-writing.—*n.* **pic'togram,** a pictograph: a graphic representation.—*adj.* **pictographic** (*-graf'ik*).—*adv.* **pictograph'ically.**

—*n.* **pictography** (*pik-tog'rə-fi*), picture-writing. [L. *pictus*, painted; Gr. *graphein*, to write, *gramma*, a letter, figure.]

**pictorial**, *pik-tō'ri-əl, -tö', adj.* of a painter: of or relating to painting or drawing: of, by means of, like, or of the nature of, a picture, or pictures.—*n.* a periodical in which pictures are prominent.—*adv.* **picto'rially.**—*adj.* **pictorical** (*-tor'i-kl*).—*adv.* **pictor'ically,** in the manner of a painter. [L. *pictor, -ōris,* painter—*pingĕre, pictum,* to paint.]

**picture,** *pik'chər, n.* the art or act of painting: an imitative representation of an object on a surface: a portrait: a tableau: a visible or visual image: (an image on) a television screen: person as like another as his own portrait: an impressive or attractive sight, like a painting or worthy of being painted: a visible embodiment: a vivid verbal description: a cinema film: (in *pl.*) a cinema show, or the building in which it is given.—*v.t.* to depict, represent in a picture: to form a likeness of in the mind: to describe vividly in words.—*adj.* **pic'tural,** relating to, illustrated by, or consisting of pictures.—*n.* **pic'-tural** (*Spens.*), a picture.—**pic'ture-book,** a book of pictures; **pic'ture-card,** a court card; **pic'-ture-cord,** cord for hanging pictures; **pic'ture-frame,** a frame for surrounding a picture; **pic'-ture-gallery,** a gallery, hall, or building where pictures are exhibited; **pic'ture-goer,** one who goes much to the cinema; **pic'ture-hat,** a lady's wide-brimmed hat, such as those that appear in portraits by Gainsborough; **pic'ture-house, -palace,** a building for cinema shows; **Pic'ture-phone,** a device which allows speakers on the telephone to see each other; **pic'ture-play',** a story told in motion pictures; **pic'ture post'-card,** a postcard bearing a picture, commonly a local view; **pic'ture ratio** (see **aspect ratio**); **pic'ture-restorer,** one who cleans and restores old pictures; **pic'ture-rod, -rail, -mould'ing,** a rod, moulding, from which pictures may be hung; **pic'ture-win'dow,** a usu. large window designed to act as a frame to an attractive view; **pic'ture-wire,** wire for hanging pictures; **pic'-ture-writ'ing,** the use of pictures to express ideas or relate events.—**in the picture,** having a share of attention: adequately briefed; **put me** (etc.) **in the picture,** give me (etc.) all the relevant information. [L. *pictūra—pingĕre, pictum,* to paint.]

**picturesque,** *pik-chə-resk', adj.* like a picture: such as would make a striking picture, implying some measure of beauty with much quaintness or immediate effectiveness: of language, vivid and colourful rather than precise: having taste or feeling for the picturesque.—*adv.* **pictures-que'ly.**—*n.* **picturesque'ness.** [It. *pittoresco—pittura,* a picture—L. *pictūra.*]

**picul,** *pik'ul, n.* a Chinese weight, about 60 kg. [Malay *pikul,* a man's load.]

**Picus,** *pi'kəs, n.* an ancient Italian god, a son of Saturn, turned into a woodpecker by Circe: the woodpecker genus.—*adj.* **pi'cine** (*-sin*). [L. *Picus.*]

**piddle,** *pid'l, v.i.* to deal in trifles: to trifle: to eat with little relish: to urinate (*coll.*).—*n.* **pidd'ler,** a trifler.—*adj.* **pidd'ling,** trifling, paltry. [Origin obscure.]

**piddock,** *pid'ək, n.* the pholas. [Origin unknown.]

**pidgin,** *pij'in, n.* a Chinese corruption of **business:** affair, concern (*coll.*): any combination and distortion of two languages as a means of communication.—Also **pidg'eon, pigeon.**—**pidgin English,** a jargon, mainly English in vocabulary with Chinese arrangement, used in communication between Chinese and foreigners: any jargon consisting of English and another language.

**pi-dog, pie-dog.** See **pye-dog.**

**pie,** *pi, n.* a magpie: a chatterer. [Fr.,—L. *pica.*]

**pie, pye,** *pi, n.* a book of rules for determining the Church office for the day.—**by cock and pie** (*Shak.*), a minced oath, app. by God and the pie. [L.L. *pica,* possibly the same as L. *pica,* magpie (from the black and white appearance of the page).]

**pie, pi,** *pi, n.* type confusedly mixed: a mixed state: confusion.—*v.t.* to reduce to pie:—*pr.p.* **pie'ing, pye'ing;** *pa.t.* and *pa.p.* **pied.** [Origin obscure; perh. conn. with **pie (4),** or **pie (2).**]

**pie, pi,** *n.* a quantity of meat, fruit, or other food baked within or under a crust of prepared flour: an easy thing (*slang*): a welcome luxury, prize, or spoil (*coll.*).—*ns.* **pie'-counter,** a counter at which pies are sold: the source of patronage, bribes, spoils of office (*U.S.*); **pie chart, graph,** a circle divided into sections by radii so as to show relative numbers or quantities; **pie'crust,** the paste covering or enclosing a pie; **piecrust table,** a Chippendale table with carved raised edge; **pie'dish,** a deep dish in which pies are made.—*adj.* **pie'-eyed** (*coll.*), drunk.—**pie'man,** one who sells pies, esp. in the street; **pie'-plant** (*U.S.*), rhubarb; **pie'-shop.**—**Périgord pie,** a pie of partridge flavoured with truffles (*Périgord,* now contained in the departments of Dordogne and Lot-et-Garonne); **pie in the sky,** an improbable future good promised without guarantee (from early 20th-cent. song). [Origin unknown; possibly from the bird, as a miscellaneous collector; the Gael. *pighe* is from English.]

**pie,** *pi, n.* a small coin, withdrawn after 1957, equal to 1/3 of a pice, or 1/12 of an anna. [Marathi *pā'i,* a fourth.]

**piebald,** *pi'böld, adj.* black and white in patches: loosely, of other colours in patches: motley: heterogeneous.—*n.* a piebald horse or other animal. [**pie (1), bald.**]

**piece,** *pēs, n.* a part or portion of anything, esp. detached: a separate lump, mass, body, of any material, considered as an object (in Scots without *of* following): a distance: a span of time: a single article: a definite quantity, as of cloth or paper: a literary, dramatic, musical, or artistic composition: a production, specimen of work: an example: an exemplification or embodiment: a little bread, buttered or not, esp. as a lunch (*Scot.*): a gun: a portion (*obs.*): a wine-cup (*obs.*): a coin: a man in chess, draughts, or other game (in chess sometimes excluding pawns): a person—now usually (disrespectfully) a woman.—*v.t.* to enlarge by adding a piece: to patch: to combine.—*adj.* **piece'-less,** not made of pieces.—*adv.* **piece'meal,** in pieces: to pieces: bit by bit.—*adj.* done bit by bit: fragmentary.—*n.* a small piece: bit by bit proceeding.—*v.t.* to dismember.—*v.t.* **piec'en** (*dial.*), to join (esp. broken threads in spinning). —*ns.* **piec'ener, piec'er,** one who is employed in a spinning-factory to join broken threads.—**piece'-goods,** textile fabrics made in standard lengths; **piece'-work,** work paid for by the piece or quantity, not by time.—**all to pieces,** into a state of disintegration or collapse: through and through, thoroughly (*U.S.*); **a piece, each;** **a piece of,** an instance of: a bit of, something of (*obs.*); **a piece of one's mind,** a frank outspoken rating; **go to pieces,** to break up entirely (*lit.* and *fig.*): to lose completely ability to cope with the situation; **in pieces,** in, or to, a broken-up state; **of a piece,** as if of the same piece, same in nature: homogeneous, uniform: in keeping, consistent (with *with*); **piece of cake** (see **cake**); **piece of eight,** a Spanish dollar worth eight reals, bearing the numeral 8; **piece of goods** (*dial.*), a woman; **piece of work,** a task: a fuss, ado: person (usually with **nasty,** etc.); **piece out,** to eke out; **piece together,** to put together bit by bit; **piece up,** to patch up: perh.

to incorporate in one's own share (*Shak.*); **the piece** (*Scot.*), apiece. [O.Fr. *piece*—L.L. *pecia*, *petium*, a fragment, a piece of land—thought to be of Celtic (Brythonic) origin; cf. patch, peat, petty, and *Pit-* in place names.]
**pièce**, *pyes*, (Fr.) a piece, item.—**pièce de résistance** (*də rā-zē-stäs*), the substantial course at dinner, the joint: the best item; **pièce d'occasion** (*do-ka-zyɔ̄*), something, usu. a literary or musical work, composed, prepared, or used for a special occasion.
**pied**, *pid*, *adj.* variegated like a magpie: of various colours.—*n.* **pied′ness.** [pie (1).]
**pied-à-terre**, *pyä-da-ter*, (Fr.) temporary lodging.
**piedmont**, *pēd′mənt*, (*U.S.*) *n.* a mountain-foot region.—Also *adj.* [*Piedmont* in Italy, lit. mountain-foot.]
**piel'd**, *pēld*, (*Shak.*) *adj.* tonsured. [See peel (1).]
**piend**, *pēnd*, *n.* a salient angle. [Origin unknown.]
**piepowder**, *pi′pow-dər*, (*obs.*) *n.* a wayfarer, itinerant.—**Court of Piepowder(s)**, an ancient court held in fairs and markets to administer justice in a rough-and-ready way to all comers—also *Court of Dusty Feet.* [O.Fr. *piedpoudreux*—*pied* (L. *pēs, pedis*), foot, *poudre* (L. *pulvis*), dust.]
**pier**, *pēr*, *n.* the mass of stone-work between the openings in the wall of a building: the support of an arch, bridge, etc.: a masonry support for a telescope or the like: a buttress: a gate-pillar: a mass of stone, iron-work, or wood-work projecting into the sea or other water, as a breakwater, landing-stage, or promenade: a jetty or a wharf.—*n.* **pier′age**, toll paid for using a pier.—**pier′-glass**, orig., a mirror hung between windows: a tall mirror; **pier′-head**, the seaward end of a pier; **pier′-table**, a table fitted for the space between windows. [M.E. *pēr*, L.L. *pēra*; origin doubtful.]
**pierce**, *pērs*, *v.t.* to thrust or make a hole through: to enter, or force a way into: to touch or move deeply: to penetrate: to perforate: to make by perforating or penetrating.—*v.i.* to penetrate.—*n.* a perforation: a stab: a prick.—*adj.* **pierce′able**, capable of being pierced.—*adj.* **pier′ced**, perforated: penetrated.—*n.* **pierc′er**, one who or that which pierces: any sharp instrument used for piercing: a sting: a keen eye (*arch.*).—*adj.* **pierc′ing**, penetrating: very acute: keen.—*adv.* **pierc′ingly.**—*n.* **pierc′ingness.** [O.Fr. *percer*; of doubtful origin.]
**Pierian**, *pī-ē′ri-ən*, *adj.* of *Pieria*, in Thessaly, the country of the Muses: of the Muses.—*n.* **pierid** (*pī′ə-rid*), any butterfly of the Pieridae.—*n.pl.* **Pierides** (*pī-er′i-dēz*), the nine Muses—*sing.* **Pi′eris.**—*n.* **Pi′eris**, the cabbage butterfly genus, typical of the family **Pier′idae** (*-dē*). [Gr. *Pieriā.*]
**Pierrot**, *pē′ə-rō*, *pyer-ō*, *n.* a white-faced buffoon with loose long-sleeved garb: (without *cap*; formerly) a member of a group of entertainers in similar dress at seaside resorts, etc.: an 18th-century women's low-cut basque, with sleeves:—*fem.* **Pierrette′.** [Fr., dim of *Pierre*, Peter.]
**pierst**, Spens. for pierced (*pa.t.* and *pa.p.*).
**piert.** Same as peart. See also parsley-piert.
**piet.** Same as pyot.
**pietà**, *pyä-tä′*, *n.* a representation of the Virgin with the dead Christ across her knees. [It.,—L. *pietās, -ātis*, pity.]
**pietra-dura**, *pyä′tra-dōō′ra*, *n.* inlaid work with hard stones—jasper, agate, etc. [It., hard stone.]
**piety**, *pī′i-ti*, *n.* pity (*obs.*): the quality of being pious: dutifulness: devoutness: sense of duty towards parents, benefactors, etc.: dutiful conduct.—*ns.* **pi′etism**; **pi′etist**, one marked by strong devotional feeling: a name first applied to a sect of German religious reformers of deep devotional feeling (end of 17th century).—*adjs.* **pietist′ic, -al.** [O.Fr. *piete*—L. *pietās, -ātis.*]
**piezo-**, *pi′i-zō-*, *pī-ē′zō-*, in composition, pressure. —*adj.* **piezo**, short for piezoelectric.—*n.* **piezo-**

**chem′istry**, the chemistry of substances under high pressure.—*adj.* **piezoelec′tric.**—*n.* **piezoelectri′city**, electricity developed in certain crystals by mechanical strain, and the effect of an electric field in producing expansion and contraction along different axes.—*adj.* **piezomagnet′ic.**—*ns.* **piezomag′netism**, magnetism developed in similar way to piezoelectricity, using magnetic instead of electric field; **piezometer** (*-om′i-tər*), an instrument for measuring pressure or compressibility. [Gr. *piēzein*, to press.]
**piffero**, *pif′ə-rō*, *n.* a fife: an Italian bagpipe: a crude oboe.—*n.* **pifferaro** (*-ä′rō*), a pifferoplayer:—*pl.* **pifferari** (*-rē*). [It.,—O.H.G. *pfīfari* piper.]
**piffle**, *pif′l*, *n.* nonsense: worthless talk.—*v.t.* to trifle: to act ineffectually.—*adj.* **piff′ling**, trivial, petty.—*n.* **piff′ler.** [Origin unknown.]
**pig**, *pig*, *n.* a swine: a young swine: swine's flesh as food, esp. that of the young animal: one who is like a pig, dirty, greedy, gluttonous, or cantankerous (also used mildly in reproach): an oblong mass of unforged metal, as first extracted from the ore: the mould into which it is run, esp. one of the branches, the main channel being the *sow*: a cleaning brush, scraper, etc., for pipes or ducts: a feast (*slang*): a policeman (*slang*): segment of an orange (*slang*).—*v.i.* to bring forth pigs: to live, herd, huddle, sleep, or feed like pigs: to eat (*slang*):—*pr.p.* **pigg′ing**; *pa.t.* and *pa.p.* **pigged.**—*n.* **pigg′ery**, a place where pigs are kept: piggishness.—*adj.* **pigg′ish**, like a pig: greedy: dirty: cantankerous.—*adv.* **pigg′ishly.**—*ns.* **pigg′ishness**; **pigg′ie**, **pigg′y**, **pig′let**, **pig′ling**, a little pig.—*n.pl.* **pigg′ies**, a child's, baby's, word for toes.—*adj.* **pigg′y**, like a pig.—**pig′-bed**, a pig's sleeping place: a mould of sand in which a pig of iron is cast; **pig′boat** (*U.S. naval slang*), a submarine; **pig′-deer**, the babiroussa.—*adjs.* **pig′-eyed**, having small dull eyes with heavy lids; **pig′-faced.**—**pig′-fish** (*U.S.*), a name for various kinds of grunt (Haemulon, etc.): in Australia, a name for various wrasses; **pigg′y-bank**, a child's money-box, shaped like a pig: sometimes a child's money-box of any design.—*adj.* **pig′head′ed**, having a pig-like head: stupidly obstinate.—*adv.* **pig′head′edly**—**pig′head′edness**; **pig′-herd**; **pig′-iron**, iron in pigs or rough bars.—*v.i.* **pig′-jump** (*Austr. slang*; of a horse), to jump from all four legs without bringing them together.—**pig′-lead**, lead in pigs; **pig′-lily** (*S.Afr.*), the lily of the Nile; **pig′-nut**, the earth-nut (Conopodium); **pig′-rat**, the bandicoot rat; **pig′sconce**, a pigheaded fellow: a blockhead; **pig′skin**, the skin of a pig prepared as a strong leather: a saddle (*slang*); **pig′-sticker**; **pig′-sticking**, boar-hunting with spears; **pig′sty**, a pen for keeping pigs; **pig's′-wash**, **pig′wash**, swill; **pig's′-whis′per**, a low whisper (*dial.*): a very short space of time; **pig′tail**, the tail of a pig: the hair of the head plaited behind in a queue: a roll of twisted tobacco; **pig′weed**, goosefoot, amaranth, cow-parsnip, or other plant eaten by pigs; **pig′-woman**, a woman who roasted pigs at fairs.—**a pig in a poke** (see poke); **make a pig of oneself** (*coll.*), to overindulge in food or drink; **pig it** (*coll.*), to live in dirty surroundings; **when pigs fly** (*coll.*), never. [M.E. *pigge*; cf. Du. *bigge*, *big*.]
**pig**, *pig*, (*Scot.*) *n.* an earthenware crock, hot-water bottle, or other vessel: earthenware: a potsherd.—**pig′-man, -woman**, a dealer in pigs.—**pigs and whistles**, wrack and ruin. [Origin unknown.]
**pigeon**, *pij′ən, -in*, *n.* orig., a young dove: a dove: any bird of the dove family: extended to various other birds (e.g. the *Cape pigeon*): a girl (*obs.*): one who is fleeced (*slang*).—*v.t.* to gull.—*n.*

**pig'eonry**, a place for keeping pigeons.—**pig'eon-berry** (*U.S.*), pokeweed or its fruit.—*adj.* **pig'eon-breast'ed**, having a narrow chest with breast-bone thrown forward.—**pig'eon-flier, -flyer**, one who sends forth homing pigeons; **pig'eon-flying**.—*adj.* **pig'eon-heart'ed**, timid.—**pig'eon-hole**, a niche for a pigeon's nest: a hole of similar appearance: a compartment for storing and classifying papers, etc.: a compartment of the mind or memory: (in *pl.*) the stocks: (in *pl.*) an old outdoor game like bagatelle.—*v.t.* to furnish with or make into pigeon-holes: to put into a pigeon-hole: to classify methodically: to lay aside and treat with neglect.—**pig'eon-house**, a dovecot.—*adj.* **pig'eon-liv'ered**, mild.—**pig'eon-pair**, boy and girl twins or a boy and girl as sole children in a family; **pig'eon-pea**, dal; **pig'eon-post**, transmission of letters by pigeons; **pig'eon's-blood**, a dark red colour, ruby; **pigeon's milk**, partly digested food regurgitated by pigeons to feed their young: an imaginary liquid for which children are sent, as on 1st April.—*adj.* **pig'eon-toed**, (of birds) having all toes at one level: in-toed.—**pig'eon-wing**, a caper in dancing.—**clay pigeon** (see **clay**). [O.Fr. *pijon*—L. *pipiō, -ōnis*—*pipire*, to cheep.]

**pigeon.** Same as **pidgin**.

**piggin**, *pig'in*, *n.* a small pail or bowl of staves and hoops, one stave usually prolonged as a handle: a vessel of various other kinds. [Poss. from **pig** (2); the Celtic words seem to be from English.]

**piggy.** See **pig** (1).

**piggyback.** Variant of **pickaback**.

**pight**, *pit*, an old *pa.t.* and *pa.p.* (*Spens.*) of **pitch** (2), pitched, set: also false archaism for present tense.—*adj.* **well-knit** (*Spens.*): resolved (*Shak.*).

**pightle**, *pī'tl*, *n.* a small enclosure: a croft. [Ety. dub.]

**pigment**, *pig'mənt*, *n.* paint: any substance used for colouring: that which gives colour to animal and vegetable tissues: piment (*Scott*).—*adjs.* **pigmental** (    *᷉᷉n'tl*), **pig'mentary**.—*n.* **pigmentā'tion**, coloration or discoloration by pigments in the tissues. [L. *pigmentum*—*pingĕre*, to paint.]

**pigmy.** Same as **pygmy**.

**pignorate, pignerate**, *pig'nər-āt*, *v.t.* to give or take in pledge or pawn.—*n.* **pignorā'tion**. [L. *pignus, -eris* or *-oris*, a pledge.]

**pigsney, pigsny, pigsnie**, *pigz'ni*, *n.* a term of endearment (sometimes contempt), esp. to a woman (*arch.* or *dial.*): an eye (playfully; *obs.*). [**pig's eye**, with prosthetic *n* (from *an eye*, *mine eye*).]

**pi-jaw.** See **pi** (3).

**pika**, *pī'kə*, *n.* the tailless hare (Ochotona), a small rodent of mountain regions, akin to the rabbit. [Tungus *piika*.]

**pike**, *pik*, *n.* a sharp point: a weapon with a long shaft and a sharp head like a spear, formerly used by foot-soldiers: a spiked staff: a sharp-pointed hill or summit: a voracious freshwater fish (*Esox lucius*) with pointed snout: extended to various other fishes: a pick (*dial.*).—*v.t.* to kill or pierce with a pike: to pick (*dial.*).—*adj.* **piked** (*pikt, pik'id*), spiked: ending in a point.—*n.* **pik'er**, one who picks (*dial.*): a pilferer (*dial.*): one who bets, gambles, speculates, or does anything else in a very small way.—**pike'-head**, the head of a pike or spear; **pike'man**, a man armed with a pike: one who wields a pick; **pike'-perch**, a percoid fish with pike-like jaws; **pike'staff**, the staff or shaft of a pike: a staff with a pike at the end.—**plain as a pikestaff** (orig. **packstaff**), perfectly plain or clear. [O.E. *pīc*, pick, spike; but also partly from Fr. *pic* with the same meaning, and *pique* the weapon, and prob. partly from Scand.]

**pike**, *pik*, *v.i.* to speed.—*v.t.* to betake quickly.

[Perh. orig. *get oneself a pikestaff* (a pilgrim's spiked staff); perh. Fr. *piquer*, to spur.]

**pike**, *pik*, *n.* a turnpike: a toll: a main road (*U.S.*).—*n.* **pi'ker**, a tramp.—**pike'-keeper**, **pike'man**, a man in charge of a turnpike. [Short for **turnpike**.]

**pikelet**, *pik'lit*, (local) *n.* a kind of tea-cake, or crumpet, or muffin. [W. *bara pyglyd*, pitchy bread.]

**pikul.** Same as **picul**.

**pilaster**, *pi-las'tər*, *n.* a square column, partly built into, partly projecting from, a wall.—*adj.* **pilas'tered**. [Fr. *pilastre*—It. *pilastro*—L. *pila*, a pillar.]

**pilau**, *pi-low'*, *n.* a highly spiced Eastern dish of rice with a fowl, meat, or the like, boiled together or separately.—Also **pillau'**, **pilaw'**, **pilaff'** (or **pil'**), **pilow'**. [Pers. *pilāw*, Turk. *pilāw, pilāf*.]

**pilch**, *pilch*, *n.* a fur cloak: a coarse leather or woollen cloak: a rug for a saddle: a light saddle: a flannel cloth for wrapping a child.—*n.* **pilch'er**, a scabbard (*Shak.*). [O.E. *pyl(e)ce*—L.L. *pellicea*—L. *pellis*, skin.]

**pilchard**, *pil'chərd*, *n.* a sea-fish like the herring, but smaller, thicker, and rounder, common off Cornwall.—Earlier (*Shak.*) **pilch'er**. [Origin unknown; poss. Scand. (cf. Norw. *pilk*, artificial bait); Ir. *pilseir* is prob. from English.]

**pilcorn**, *pil'körn*, *n.* the naked oat, a variety in which the glume does not adhere to the grain. [For **pilled corn**.]

**pilcrow**, *pil'krō*, *n.* a paragraph-mark. [Origin obscure.]

**pile**, *pil*, *n.* a set of things fitted or resting one over another, or in a more or less regular figure: a heap of combustibles for cremating a dead body, or for the burnt-offering, or for burning to death: a set of weights fitting one within another: a stack of arms: a heap of shot: a set of wrought-iron bars placed together for welding and rolling into one: a series of alternate plates of two metals for generating an electric current: a set of coins placed vertically one upon another: a great supply of money, a fortune (*slang*): a large supply (*coll.*): a tall building: an atomic pile: the under iron for striking coins (*obs.*): the reverse of a coin (*obs.*).—*v.t.* to lay in a pile or heap: to collect in a mass: to heap up: to load with heaps: to accumulate.—*v.i.* to come into piles: to accumulate: to go in crowds: to get in or out (with *in* or *out*).—*n.* **pi'ler.**—**pile-up**, a collision involving several motor vehicles.—**pile arms**, to prop three muskets, orig. with fixed bayonets, so that the butts remain firm, the muzzles close together pointing obliquely—also **stack arms**; **pile on, up, the agony**, to overdo painful effects by accumulation, etc.; **pile up**, to run ashore: to form a disorderly mass or heap: to become involved in a pile-up (q.v.): to accumulate. [Fr.,—L. *pila*, a pillar.]

**pile**, *pil*, *n.* an arrow-head: a Roman javelin: a large stake or cylinder driven into the earth to support foundations: an inverted pyramidal figure (*her.*).—*v.t.* to drive piles into.—**pile'-driver**, an engine for driving in piles: in games, a very heavy stroke, kick, etc.; **pile'-dwelling**, a dwelling built on piles, esp. a lake-dwelling; **pile'work**, work or foundations made of piles; **pile'-worm**, a ship-worm. [O.E. *pīl*—L. *pilum*, a javelin.]

**pile**, *pil*, *n.* a covering of hair, esp. soft, fine, or short hair: down: human body-hair: a single hair: a raised surface on cloth—now distinguished from *nap* as made not in finishing but in weaving, either by leaving loops (which may be cut) or by weaving two cloths face to face and cutting them apart.—*adjs.* **pilif'erous**, bearing hairs: ending in a hair-like point; **pil'iform**, hair-like. [L. *pilus*, a hair.]

**pile,** *pil, n.* (usu. in *pl.*) a haemorrhoid.—*n.* **pile'-wort,** the lesser celandine (*Ranunculus ficaria*), once thought a remedy for piles. [L. *pīla,* a ball.]

**pileorhiza,** *pi-li-ō-rī'zə,* (*bot.*) *n.* a root-cap. [L. *pīleus,* -um (see next word), Gr. *rhiza,* root.]

**pileum,** *pī'li-əm, n.* the top of a bird's head:—*pl.* **pil'ea.**—*n.* **pi'leus,** a Roman felt cap: the expanded cap of a mushroom or toadstool, or other fungus:—*pl.* **pilei** (*pī'li-i*).—*adjs.* **pi'leate,** -d, cap-shaped: capped: crested. [L. *pileum, pileus,* for *pilleum, pilleus,* a felt cap; cf. Gr. *pilos,* felt, a felt cap.]

**pilfer,** *pil'fər, v.i.* and *v.t.* to steal in small quantities.—*ns.* **pil'ferage, pil'fering, pil'fery,** petty theft; **pil'ferer.**—*adv.* **pil'feringly.** [Prob. connected with **pelf.**]

**pilgarlick, peelgarlic,** *pil-, pēl-gär'lik, n.* a baldpate: a poor wretch: in whimsical self-pity, oneself.—*adj.* **pilgar'licky.** [**pill** (2), **peel,** and **garlic,** as like a pilled or peeled head of garlic.]

**pilgrim,** *pil'grim, n.* a wanderer, wayfarer (*arch.* and *poet.*): one who travels to a distance to visit a holy place: allegorically or spiritually, one journeying through life as a stranger in this world: a Pilgrim Father: an original settler: newcomer.—*adj.* of or pertaining to a pilgrim: like a pilgrim: consisting of pilgrims.—*n.* **pil'grimage,** the journeying of a pilgrim: a journey to a shrine or other holy place or place venerated for its associations: the journey of life: a lifetime.—*adj.* visited by pilgrims.—*v.i.* to go on pilgrimage: to wander.—*ns.* **pil'grimager,** contemptuously, one who goes on pilgrimage; **pil'grimer,** one who goes on pilgrimage.—*v.i.* (or *v.t.* with *it*) **pil'grimise, -ize,** to play the pilgrim. —**pil'grim-bott'le,** a flat bottle with ears at the neck for a cord; **Pilgrim Fathers,** the Puritans who sailed for America in the *Mayflower,* and founded Plymouth in 1620; **pilgrim's shell,** a scallop-shell (called a cockle) used as a sign that one had visited the shrine of St James of Compostela; **pilgrim's sign,** a badge, often a leaden brooch, obtained at the shrine and worn on the hat by a pilgrim. [Assumed O.Fr. *pelegrin* (Fr. *pèlerin*)—L. *peregrinus,* foreigner, stranger; see **peregrine.**]

**pilhorse,** *pil'hörs,* or **philhorse,** *fil'* (*Shak.*). Same as **fillhorse** or **thillhorse.**

**pili,** *pē-lē', n.* the nut (also **pili'-nut'**) of trees of the burseraceous genus Canarium. [Tagálog.]

**pill,** *pil, n.* a little ball of medicine: a ball, e.g. a cannon-ball, tennis-ball, or (*pl.*) billiards (*facet.*): anything disagreeable that must be accepted: a tiresome person: a doctor (*slang*; also in *pl.*).—*v.t.* to dose with pills: to blackball (*slang*).— **pill'-box,** a box for holding pills: a kind of one-horse carriage: a small blockhouse (*mil. slang*): a small round brimless hat; **pill'-bug,** a wood-louse that rolls itself into a ball; **pill'-worm,** a millipede that curls up; **pill'wort,** a water-fern (Pilularia) of lake-margins, with pill-like sporocarps.—**the Pill, pill,** any of various contraceptive pills (see **oral contraception**). [L. *pīla,* perh. through O.Fr. *pile,* or from a syncopated form of the dim. *pilŭla.*]

**pill,** *pil, v.t.* and *v.i.* to plunder (*arch.*): to peel (*dial.*): to make or become hairless (*obs.*).—*n.* (*Spens.*) husk, integument.—*n.* **pill'age,** act of plundering: plunder.—*v.t.* and *v.i.* to plunder.— *n.* **pill'ager.** [O.E. *pylian* and O.Fr. *peler,* both— L. *pīlāre,* to deprive of hair; cf. **peel.**]

**pillar,** *pil'ər, n.* a detached support, not necessarily cylindrical or of classical proportions (*archit.*): a structure of like form erected as a monument, ornament, object of worship, etc.: a tall upright rock: a mass of coal or rock left in a mine to support the roof: anything in the form of a column: a supporting post: the post supporting a bicycle saddle: a cylinder holding

the plates of a watch or clock in position: a pillar-box: one who, or anything that, sustains. —*ns.* **pill'arist, pill'ar-saint,** an ascetic living on the top of a pillar, a stylite.—**pill'ar-box,** a short hollow pillar for posting letters in; **pill'ar-root,** a supporting root descending from a branch.— **from pillar to post,** from one state of difficulty to another: hither and thither. [O.Fr. *piler* (Fr. *pilier*)—L.L. *pilāre*—L. *pila,* a pillar.]

**pillau.** See **pilau.**

**pillicock,** *pil'i-kok, n.* the penis (allusively in *Shak.*): a term of endearment to a boy. [Cf. Norw. dial. *pill.*]

**pillion,** *pil'yən, n.* a pad or light saddle for a woman: a cushion behind a horseman for a second rider (usu. a woman) or for a bag: the passenger-seat of a motor-cycle, or a baggage-carrier, usable as an extra seat.—*adv.* on a pillion.—*v.t.* to seat on or furnish with a pillion. —*ns.* **pill'ionist, pill'ion-rider,** one who rides pillion; **pill'ion-seat.** [Prob. Ir. *pillín,* Gael. *pillin, pillean,* a pad, a pack-saddle—*peall,* a skin or mat, L. *pellis,* skin.]

**pilliwinks,** *pil'i-wingks, n.pl.* an instrument of torture for crushing the fingers. [Origin unknown.]

**pillory,** *pil'ə-ri, n.* a wooden frame, supported by an upright pillar or post, with holes through which the head and hands were put as a punishment, abolished in England in 1837.—*v.t.* to set in the pillory: to hold up to ridicule:—*pr.p.* **pill'orying;** *pa.t.* and *pa.p.* **pill'oried.**—Also **pill'orise,** -ize. [O.Fr. *pilori;* Prov. *espilori;* of uncertain origin.]

**pillow,** *pil'ō, n.* a cushion for a sleeper's head: any object used for the purpose: a cushion for lace-making: a support for part of a structure.—*v.t.* to lay or rest for support: to serve as pillow for: to furnish or prop with pillows.—*v.i.* to rest the head.—*adjs.* **pill'owed,** supported by, or provided with, a pillow; **pill'owy,** like a pillow: round and swelling: soft.—**pill'ow-bere, -beer, -case, -slip,** a cover for a pillow; **pill'ow-cup,** a last cup before going to bed; **pill'ow-fight,** the sport of thumping one another with pillows; **pill'ow-lace,** lace worked with bobbins on a pillow; **pill'ow-lava,** lava showing pillow-structure; **pill'ow-structure,** in lavas, separation into pillow-shaped blocks. [O.E. *pyle,* also *pylu*—L. *pulvīnus.*]

**pillworm, pillwort.** See **pill** (1).

**Pilocarpus,** *pi-lō-kär'pəs, n.* a genus of S. American rutaceous shrubs, including jaborandi.—*n.* **pilo-car'pine** (*-pēn*), an alkaloid ($C_{11}H_{16}O_2N_2$) got from jaborandi leaves. [Gr. *pilos,* felt, a felt cap, *karpos,* fruit.]

**pilose,** *pi'lōs, adj.* hairy: having scattered soft or moderately stiff hairs.—*adj.* **pi'lous,** hairy.—*n.* **pilosity** (*-los'i-ti*). [L. *pilōsus*—*pilus,* hair.]

**pilot,** *pī'lət, n.* a steersman (*arch.*): one who conducts ships in and out of a harbour, along a dangerous coast, etc.: one who actually operates the flying controls of an aircraft: one who is qualified to act as pilot: a guide: a cow-catcher (*U.S.*).—*adj.* pertaining to pilot(s): acting as guide or control: trial, (esp. of model on smaller scale) serving to test the qualities of a machine, plant, etc.—*v.t.* to act as pilot to,— *n.* **pi'lotage,** piloting: a pilot's fee.—*adj.* **pi'lotless,** without a pilot: not requiring a pilot, as an automatic aeroplane.—**pi'lot-balloon',** a small balloon sent up to find how the wind blows; **pi'lot-boat,** a boat used by pilots on duty; **pi'lot-burn'er, -jet, -light** (see also below), a small gas-burner kept alight to light another; **pi'lot-cloth,** a coarse, stout cloth for overcoats; **pi'lot-en'gine,** a locomotive sent before a train to clear its way, as a pilot; **pi'lot-fish,** a carangoid fish that accompanies ships and sharks; **pi'lot-flag, -jack,** the flag hoisted at the fore by a vessel needing a pilot; **pi′lot-house,** a shelter for steering-gear and pilot—also *wheel-house*; **pi′lot-jacket,** a pea-jacket; **pi′lot-light,** a small electric light to show when current is on, or for other purpose; **pilot officer,** in the Air Force an officer ranking with an army second-lieutenant; **pi′lot-plant,** prototype machinery set up to begin a new process; **pi′lot scheme,** a scheme serving as a guide on a small scale to a full-scale scheme; **pi′lot-whale,** the ca′ing-whale. [Fr. *pilote*—It. *pilota,* app. for earlier *pedota,* which may be—Gr. *pēdon,* oar, in pl. rudder.]

**Pils(e)ner,** also without *cap., pilz′, pils′nər, n.* a light beer. [Ger. from *Pilsen,* a city in Czechoslovakia.]

**Piltdown man,** *pilt′down,* Eoanthropus (*q.v.*).

**pilule,** *pil′ūl, n.* a little pill.—Also **pil′ula.**—*adj.* **pil′ular.** [L. *pilŭla,* dim. of *pīla,* ball.]

**pilum,** *pī′ləm, n.* the heavy javelin used by Roman foot-soldiers:—*pl.* **pi′la.** [L. *pilum.*]

**pilus,** *pī′ləs, n.* a hair:—*pl.* **pi′li.** [L. *pīlus.*]

**piment,** *pi-ment′,* (*obs.*) *n.* spiced sweetened wine. —Also (*Scott*) **pigment** (*pig′mənt*).—*n.* **pimento** (*pi-ment′ō*), formerly Cayenne pepper: now allspice or Jamaica pepper, the dried unripe fruits of a W. Indian tree (*Pimenta officinalis*) of the myrtle family: the tree itself: its wood. [O.Fr. *piment,* Sp. *pimiento*—L. *pigmentum,* paint.]

**pimp,** *pimp, n.* one who procures gratifications for the lust of others: a pander.—*v.i.* to pander. [Origin obscure.]

**pimpernel,** *pim′pər-nel, n.* burnet (*obs.*): burnet-saxifrage (Pimpinella) (*obs.*): now, the poor man's weather-glass (*Anagallis arvensis*), a plant of the primrose family, with scarlet (or blue, etc.) flowers.—*n.* **Pimpinell′a,** the anise and burnet-saxifrage genus of umbelliferous plants.— **bastard pimpernel,** a small plant (*Centunculus minimus*) akin to the scarlet pimpernel; **bog pimpernel,** *Anagallis tenella;* **water pimpernel,** brookweed; **yellow pimpernel,** the wood loose-strife (*Lysimachia nemorum*). [O.Fr. *pimpernelle,* mod. Fr. *pimprenelle,* and It. *pimpinella,* burnet; origin doubtful.]

**Pimpinella.** See pimpernel.

**pimping,** *pimp′ing, adj.* petty: puny: paltry: sickly. [Origin obscure.]

**pimple,** *pim′pl, n.* a pustule: a small swelling, protuberance, or hill.—*adjs.* **pim′pled, pim′ply,** having pimples. [Origin unknown.]

**pin,** *pin, n.* a piece of wood or of metal used for fastening things together: a peg or nail: a sharp-pointed piece of wire with a rounded head for fastening clothes, etc.: an ornamental elaboration of this: a cylindrical part inserted into something, as the stem of a key, or part of a lock that a hollow-stemmed key fits: the projecting part of a dovetail joint: a peg aimed at in quoits: a peg in the centre of an archery target: the rod of a golf flag: a skittle or ninepin: a chess piece: a tuning peg in a stringed instrument: a measuring peg in a drinking-cup: a degree, stage, pitch: a leg (*coll.*): a peak: the projecting bone of the hip: a hard spot or excrescence: a cask of 4½ gallons: short for clothes-pin, rolling-pin, tirling-pin, etc.: an act of pinning or state of being pinned: anything of little value.—*v.t.* to fasten with a pin: to fix, to fasten, to enclose, to hold down (*fig.*): to make a small hole in: to insert chips of stone between the stones of:—*pr.p.* **pinn′ing;** *pa.t.* and *pa.p.* **pinned.**—*ns.* **pinn′er,** one who pins: pin-maker: a pinafore: a head-dress with lappets flying loose: one of these lappets; **pinn′ing,** a fastening: a chip of stone, etc., inserted in a joint of masonry.—**pin′ball,** a form of bagatelle: a scoring game, played on a slot-machine, in which a ball runs down a sloping board set with pins or other targets; **pin′-butt′ock** (*Shak.*), a

sharp, pointed buttock; **pin′case** (*obs.*); **pin′-cushion,** a cushion for holding pins; **pin′-dust,** brass filings, a product of pin-making.—*adj.* **pin′-eyed,** long-styled, with the stigma like a pin-head in the throat of the corolla (esp. of a *Primula*).—**pin′-feather,** a young, unexpanded feather.—*adjs.* **pin′-feathered; pin′-fire,** discharged by a pin driven into the fulminate.— **pin′fish,** a spiny fish of various kinds; **pin′head,** the head of a pin: a stupid person (*slang*); **pin′hole,** a hole for or made by a pin, or such as a pin might make; **pinhole photography,** the taking of photographs by the use of a pinhole instead of a lens; **pin′-leg′** (*Scot.*), a wooden leg; **pin′-maker; pin′-making; pin′-man,** a seller of pins: a match-stick drawing, in which the limbs and body are represented by single lines; **pin′-money,** money allotted to a wife for private expenses, ostensibly to buy pins; **pin′-point,** the point of a pin: anything very sharp or minute.—*v.t.* to place, define, very exactly.— **pin′-prick,** the prick of a pin: a petty act of irritation; **pin′-stripe,** a very narrow stripe in cloth: cloth with such stripes; **pin′table,** a pin-ball machine; **pin′tail,** a duck of the genus Dafila, with a pointed tail: a sand-grouse.—*adj.* **pin′tailed,** having a long, narrow tail.—**pin′-tuck,** a very narrow ornamental tuck.—*adj.* **pin′-up,** such as might have her portrait pinned up on a wall for admiration.—*n.* a girl of such a kind: a portrait so pinned up.—**pin′-wheel,** a wheel with pins at right angles to its plane, to lift the hammer of a striking clock: a paper toy windmill: a revolving firework.—**a merry pin** (*arch.*), a merry mood; **on pins and needles,** in agitated expectancy; **pin and web** (*Shak.*), a disease of the eye, apparently cataract, characterised by a small excrescence like a pin-head, and a film (also **web and pin**); **pin it on to (someone),** to prove, or seem to prove, that he did it; **pin one (down) to,** to keep one strictly to; **pin one's faith on,** to put entire trust in; **pin on one's sleeve** (*obs.*), to make entirely dependent on oneself, or at one's disposal; **pins and needles,** a tingling feeling in arm, hand, leg, foot, due to impeded circulation (see also above). [O.E. *pinn,* prob. —L. *pinna,* a feather, a pinnacle.]

**piña,** *pē′nya, n.* the pineapple (*obs.*): a fine cloth of pineapple leaf fibre (**piña-cloth**). [Sp., pine-cone, pineapple.]

**pinacotheca,** *pin-ə-kō-thē′kə, n.* a picture-gallery. —Also **pinakoth′ek** (Ger., from Gr.). [Latinised from Gr. *pinakothēkē—pinax, -akos,* a tablet, picture, *thēkē,* repository.]

**pinafore,** *pin′ə-fōr, -för, n.* a loose covering over a dress, esp. a child's.—*adj.* **pin′afored.**—**pinafore dress, skirt,** a skirt hung from the shoulders, or combined with a sleeveless bodice. [**pin,** afore.]

**pinakoid, pinacoid,** *pin′ə-koid, n.* a crystal face, or a crystallographic form consisting of a pair of faces, parallel to two axes.—*adj.* **pinakoid′al, pinacoid′al.** [Gr. *pinax, -ăkos,* slab, *eidos,* form.]

**pinaster,** *pi-* or *pi-nas′tər, n.* the cluster-pine. [L. *pināster—pinus,* pine.]

**pince-nez,** *pẽs′-nā, n.* a pair of eye-glasses with a spring for catching the nose:—*pl.* **pince′-nez** (*-nāz*).—*adj.* **pince′-nezed** (*-nād*). [Fr., pinch nose.]

**pincer,** *pin′sər, n.* a grasping claw or forceps-like organ: (in *pl.*) a gripping tool with jaws and handles on a pivot, used for drawing out nails, squeezing, etc.: (in *pl.*) a twofold advance that threatens to isolate part of an enemy's force (*fig.*).—*v.t.* to pinch with pincers.—**pin′cer-movement.** [(O.)Fr. *pincer,* to pinch.]

**pinch,** *pinch, pinsh, v.t.* to compress a small part of between fingers and thumb or between any two surfaces, to nip: to squeeze: to crush: to nip off: to bite (*obs.*): to bring or render by squeezing or nipping: to affect painfully or injuriously, as cold or hunger: to cause to show the effects of such pain or injury: to harass: to hamper: to restrict: to stint: to find fault with (*obs.*): to purloin (*slang*): to arrest (*slang*): to over-urge (*horse-racing*): to pluck, play pizzicato (*U.S.*): to move along with a lever.—*v.i.* to nip or squeeze: to be painfully tight: to encroach: to carp: to live sparingly: to narrow, taper off (*mining*).—*n.* an act or experience of pinching: a critical time of difficulty or hardship: an emergency: a pleat (*obs.*): an upward curl of a hat-brim (*obs.*): a place of narrowing, folding, difficulty, or steepness: a quantity taken up between the finger and thumb: an iron bar used as a lever.—*adj.* pinched, having the appearance of being tightly squeezed: hard pressed by want or cold: narrowed: straightened.—*n.* pinch′er, one who, or that which, pinches: (in *pl.*) pincers (*dial.*).—*n.* and *adj.* pinch′ing.—*adv.* pinch′ingly.—pinch′cock, a clamp that stops flow of liquid by pinching a tube; pinch′commons, a niggard of food; pinch′fist, pinch′gut, pinch′-penny, a niggard.—*v.i.* pinch′-hit (*baseball*), to bat in place of another in an emergency: also *fig.*—pinch′-hitter.—at a pinch, in a case of necessity; know where the shoe pinches, to know by direct experience what the trouble or difficulty is. [O.Fr. *pincier*; prob. Gmc.]

pinchbeck, *pinch′, pinsh′bek*, *n.* a yellow alloy of copper with much less zinc than ordinary brass, simulating gold, invented by Christopher *Pinchbeck* (*c.* 1670-1732), watchmaker.—*adj.* sham: in false taste.

pindari, pindaree, *pin-dä′rē*, *n.* a mercenary freebooter troublesome in India till 1817. [Hind. *pindāri.*]

Pindaric, *pin-dar′ik*, *adj.* after the manner or supposed manner of the Greek lyric poet *Pindar.*—*n.* a Pindaric ode: an irregular ode, according to the 17th-century conception of Pindar.—*v.t.* and *v.i.* Pin′darise, -ize (*-dar-īz*).—*ns.* Pin′darism, manner or supposed manner of Pindar: 'intoxication of style' (*Matthew Arnold*); Pin′darist. [Gr. *pindarikos—Pindaros.*]

pinder, *pin′dər*, *n.* one who impounds cattle.—Also pinn′er. [O.E. *pyndan*, to shut up—*pund*; cf. poind, pound (2).]

pine, *pin*, *n.* any tree of the north temperate coniferous genus Pinus, with pairs or bundles of needle-leaves on short shoots and scale-leaves only on long shoots, represented in Britain by the Scots pine (*P. sylvestris*; often called *Scots fir*): extended to various more or less nearly allied trees and to some plants only superficially like: the timber of the pine: a pineapple plant or its fruit.—*adj.* of pines or pine-wood.—*ns.* pin′ery, a pine-house: a pine-forest: a plantation of pine-trees: a collection of pine-trees for botanical or ornamental purposes:—*pl.* pinē′ta.—*adj.* pi′ny (wrongly pi′ney), of, like, or abounding in pine-trees.—pine′apple, a pine-cone (*obs.*): a large South American multiple fruit shaped like a pine-cone: the bromeliaceous plant (Ananas or Ananassa) bearing it: a finial shaped like a pine-cone or a pineapple: a bomb (*slang*): a hand grenade (*slang*); pine′apple-weed, the rayless mayweed (*Matricaria suaveolens*)—from its smell; pine′-barr′en, a level sandy tract growing pine-trees; pine′-beau′ty, -car′pet, kinds of moths whose larvae feed on pine-trees; pine′-beet′le, any beetle that attacks pine-trees, esp. the pine′-chā′fer (*Hylurgus piniperda*), which bores up through the leader; pine′-cone, the cone or strobilus of a pine-tree; pine′-finch, an American finch like the goldfinch: a large grosbeak of pine-forests; pine′-house, a house in which pineapples are grown; pine′-ker′nel, the edible seed of a pine-tree of various species; pine′-mar′ten, a British species of marten, *Mustela martes*, now rare, dark brown, with

yellowish throat, and partly arboreal in habit; pine′-need′le, the acicular leaf of the pine-tree; pine′-tree; pine′-wood, a wood of pine-trees: pine timber; pine′-wool, a fibrous substance prepared from the leaves of the pine.—pine-tree money, silver money coined at Boston in the 17th century, bearing the figure of a pine-tree. [O.E. *pin*—L. *pinus.*]

pine, *pin*, *n.* punishment, torture (*obs.*): suffering (*arch.*): want, starvation (*Spens.*).—*v.t.* to torment (*obs.*): to consume, cause to wear away: to starve: to grieve for (*Milt.*).—*v.i.* to waste away, esp. under pain or mental distress: to languish with longing: to long: to repine. [O.E. *pinian*, to torment—L. *poena*, punishment.]

pineal, *pin′i-əl* or *pin′*, *adj.* shaped like a pine-cone: connected with the pineal body.—pineal body, or gland, a small body at the end of an upgrowth from the optic thalami of the brain; pineal eye, a vestigial third eye in front of the pineal body, best developed in the New Zealand Sphenodon. [L. *pinea*, a pine-cone—*pinus*, pine.]

pinfold, *pin′fōld*, *n.* a pound or enclosure for cattle.—*v.t.* to impound. [O.E. *pundfald*, affected by *pyndan*; see pound, fold, pinder.]

ping, *ping*, *n.* a sharp ringing or whistling sound as of a bullet.—*v.i.* to make such a sound.—*n.* ping′er, an acoustic transmitter for the study of ocean currents: (*cap.*; trademark) a domestic clockwork device set to give a warning signal at a chosen time.—Ping′-Pong′, a trademark for table tennis. [Imit.]

pingle, *ping′(g)l*, (*Scot.* and *dial.*) *v.i.* to strive: to struggle with difficulties, exert oneself strongly: to work ineffectually: to trifle or dally, esp. with food.—*v.t.* to contend strongly with: to harass, worry: to eat with feeble appetite.—*n.* a strenuous contest or exertion.—*n.* ping′ler.—*adj.* ping′ling. [Cf. Sw. *pyngla*, to be busy in small matters, to work in a trifling way.]

pinguid, *ping′gwid*, *adj.* fat.—*v.t.* and *v.i.* ping′uefy (*-gwi-fī*), to fatten: to make or become greasy.—*ns.* Pinguic′ula, the butterwort genus; pinguid′ity, ping′uitude, fatness. [L. *pinguis*, fat.]

pinguin. Same as penguin (1).

pinguin, *ping′gwin*, *n.* a West Indian plant, *Bromelia pinguin*: its fruit.—Also peng′uin. [Perh. L. *pinguis*, fat; confused with penguin.]

pinion, *pin′yən*, *n.* a wing: the last joint of a wing: a flight feather, esp. the outermost.—*v.t.* to cut a pinion of: to confine the wings of: to confine by binding the arms. [O.Fr. *pignon*—L. *pinna* (*penna*), wing.]

pinion, *pin′yən*, *n.* a small wheel with teeth or 'leaves'. [Fr. *pignon*, pinion, in O.Fr. battlement—L. *pinna*, pinnacle.]

pink, *pingk*, *n.* a small sailing-ship, usu. with a narrow stern.—Also pink′ie, pink′y. [M.Du. *pin(c)ke*; Ger. *pinke.*]

pink, *pingk*, *v.t.* to stab or pierce: esp. with a sword or rapier: to decorate by cutting small holes or scallops: to make a serrated edge on.—*n.* a stab: an eyelet.—*adj.* pinked, pierced or worked with small holes.—pink′ing-i′ron, a tool for pinking or scalloping; pink′ing-shears, scissors with serrated cutting edges. [Cf. L.G. *pinken*, to peck.]

pink, *pingk*, *n.* any plant or flower of the caryophyllaceous genus Dianthus, including carnation and sweet-william: extended to some other plants, as sea′-pink, thrift, Carolina pink (see Carolina, pinkroot), Indian pink (see pinkroot): the colour of a wild pink, a light red: a scarlet hunting-coat or its colour: the person wearing it: one who is something of a socialist but hardly a red: the fine flower of excellence: the most perfect condition: the highest point, the extreme: an exquisite (*obs.*).—*adj.* of the colour pink: slightly socialistic: exquisite, exclusively fashionable (*U.S.*).—*v.t.* and *v.i.* to

thirty, hence, having overshot one's mark: tipsy. [Ety. dub.]

**pip,** *pip, n.* a signal sounding like the word 'pip'.

**pip,** *pip, (slang) v.t.* to blackball: to pluck, plough, reject, or fail in an examination: to foil, thwart, get the better of: to hit with a bullet or the like: to wound: to kill.—*v.i.* to die (esp. with *out*):—*pr.p.* **pipp´ing;** *pa.t.* and *pa.p.* **pipped.—pipped at the post,** defeated at the point when success seemed certain. [Perh. from pip (2).]

**pip,** *pip, v.i.* to chirp, as a young bird. [Cf. **peep** (1).]

**pipal, pipul, peepul,** *pē´pul, -pəl, n.* the bo-tree. [Hind. *pipul.*]

**pipe,** *pip, n.* a musical wind instrument, or part of an instrument, consisting of or including a tube: any tube, or tubular part or thing, natural or artificial: a pipe-like volcanic vent, mass of ore, etc.: an entrance to a decoy: a tube with a bowl at one end for smoking: a fill of tobacco: the smoking of a fill of tobacco: the note of a bird: a voice, esp. a high voice: (usu. in *pl.*) the wind-pipe: a stick of e.g. pipeclay for curling hair or a wig (*Sterne*): a boatswain's whistle: (often in *pl.*) a bagpipe.—*v.i.* to play upon a pipe: to whistle, as the wind, or a boatswain: to speak or sing, esp. in a high voice: to peep or sing, as a bird: to weep: to become pipy.—*v.t.* to play on a pipe: to lead, call, by means of a pipe: (with *in*) to accompany in with pipe music: to render, or cause to be, by playing a pipe: to propagate by piping (*hort.*): to ornament with piping: to supply with pipes: to convey by pipe. —*n.* **pip´age,** conveyance or distribution by pipe.—*adj.* **piped** (*pipt*) tubular or fistulous: transported by means of a pipe.—*n.* **pipe´ful,** enough to fill a pipe.—*adjs.* **pipe´less; pipe´like.** —*n.* **pip´er,** a player on a pipe, esp. a bagpipe: a broken-winded horse: a young pigeon or other bird: a kind of gurnard: a pipe-smoker: a decoy dog: a kind of caddis-worm.—*adj.* **pip´ing,** playing a pipe: sounding like a pipe: whistling: thin and high-pitched: characterised by pipe-playing (as opp. to martial music—*the piping times of peace*): hissing hot: very hot.— *n.* the action of the verb pipe in any sense: pipe-playing: a system of pipes: tubing: small cord used as trimming for clothes: strings and twists of sugar ornamenting a cake: a slip or cutting from a joint of a stem: hydraulicking.—*adj.* **pip´y,** pipe-like: having pipes: piping.—**pipe´-case,** a case for a tobacco-pipe; **pipe´clay,** a fine white, nearly pure, kaolin, free from iron, used for making tobacco-pipes and fine earthenware, and for whitening belts, etc.—*v.t.* to whiten with pipeclay.—**piped music, television,** etc., continuous background music, or programme, etc., piped from a central studio or station to other buildings; **pipe´-dream,** a hope or fancy as futile and unreal as an opium-smoker's dream; **pipe´-dreamer; pipe´-fish,** a fish (of several species) of the sea-horse family, a long thin fish covered with hard plates, the jaws forming a long tube; **pipe´-key,** a key with a hollow barrel; **pipe´-layer,** one who lays pipes for water, gas, etc.: a political wire-puller (*U.S.*); **pipe´-laying; pipe´less or´gan,** a musical instrument, played like an organ, in which sounds, built up from whatever harmonics may be chosen, are produced by a loud-speaker; **pipe´-light, -lighter,** a spill for lighting a pipe; **pipe´-line, pipe´line,** a long continuous line of piping to carry water from a reservoir, oil from an oil-field, etc: a line of piping to carry solid materials: a line of communication, or supply, or of progress and development (*fig.*); **pipe´-major,** chief of a band of bagpipers; **Pipe Office** (*hist.*), an office in the Court of Exchequer in which the Clerk of the Pipe made out the

Pipe Roll; **pipe´-organ,** an organ with pipes; **pipe´-rack,** a rack for tobacco-pipes; **Pipe Roll** (*hist.*), the Great Roll of the Exchequer, containing yearly accounts of sheriffs, etc. (possibly from its pipelike form); **pipe´-stem,** the tube of a tobacco-pipe; **pipe´stone,** a red argillaceous stone used by North American Indians for making tobacco-pipes; **pipe´-stopp´le, -stapp´le,** a tobacco-pipe stem (*Scot.*); anything very thin and brittle-looking; **pipe´-track,** the course of a pipe across country; **pipe´-tree** (*obs.*), mock orange (*white pipe-tree*): the lilac (*blue pipe-tree*); **pipe´work,** a vein of ore in the form of a pipe: piping or pipes collectively, as in an organ; **pipe´wort,** a rare rush-like water-plant (*Eriocaulon septangulare*) of Ireland and the Hebrides, only European representative of its family Eriocaulaceae; **pipe´-wrench,** a wrench that grips a pipe when turned one way; **pip´ing crow,** an Australian bird (Gymnorhina) called a magpie, really akin to the shrikes; **piping hare,** a pika.—**boatswain's pipe** (see whistle); **drunk as a piper,** very drunk; **in the pipeline,** waiting to be considered or dealt with: in preparation; **pay the piper,** bear the expense (and so call the tune, have control): to have to pay heavily; **pipe and tabor,** a small recorder, fingered by the left hand, and a small drum beaten by the same player with his right, formerly in use in rustic jollities; **pipe down,** to dismiss from muster, as a ship's company: to subside into silence; **pipe of peace** (see **calumet**); **pipe one's eye, tune one's pipes,** to weep; **piping hot,** hissing hot, usu. hyperbolically. [O.E. *pipe*—L. *pipāre,* to cheep; cf. Du. *pijp,* Ger. *pfeife.*]

**pipe,** *pip, n.* a cask or butt, of two hogsheads, varying according to the wine, ordinarily about 105 gallons.—**pipe´-wine** (*Shak.*), wine from the cask, not bottled. [O.F. *pipe,* cask, tube; cf. preceding.]

**pip emma,** *pip em´ə, (mil. slang) n.* the letters PM: afternoon (*post meridiem.*). [Formerly signallers' names for the letters.]

**Piper,** *pip´ər, n.* the pepper genus, giving name to a family **Piperā´ceae** of dicotyledons.—*adjs.* **piperaceous** (-ā´shəs); **piperic** (*pip-er´ik*), applied to an acid ($C_{12}H_{10}O_4$) got from piperine.—*ns.* **piper´idine,** a liquid base ($C_5H_{11}N$) got from piperine; **pip´erine,** an alkaloid ($C_{17}H_{19}O_3N$) found in pepper. [L. *piper,* pepper.]

**pipette,** *pip-et´, n.* a tube for transferring and measuring fluids. [Fr., dim. of *pipe,* pipe.]

**pipi,** *pē´pē, n.* a Brazilian Caesalpinia: its pods used in tanning. [Tupi *pipai.*]

**piping.** See under **pipe** (1).

**pipistrelle,** *pip-is-trel´, n.* a small reddish-brown bat, the commonest British bat. [Fr.,—It. *pipistrello,* a form of *vespertilio*—L. *vespertiliō,* bat—*vesper,* evening.]

**pipit,** *pip´it, n.* a lark-like genus (Anthus) of birds akin to wagtails, including the titlark. [Prob. imit.]

**pipkin,** *pip´kin, n.* a small pot, now only of earthenware: a piggin (*U.S.*). [Poss. a dim. of **pipe**.]

**pippin,** *pip´in, n.* a fruit pip (*obs.*): an apple of various varieties. [O.Fr. *pepin.*]

**pipsqueak,** *pip´skwēk, (slang) n.* something or someone insignificant, contemptible: a German shell of 1st World War: a two-stroke motor-cycle.

**pipul.** Same as **pipal.**

**pipy.** See under **pipe** (1).

**piquant,** *pē´kənt, adj.* stinging: pleasantly pungent: appetising: kindling keen interest.—*n.* **piq´uancy.**—*adv.* **piq´uantly.** [Fr., pr.p. of *piquer,* to prick.]

**pique,** *pēk, n.* animosity or ill-feeling: offence taken: a feeling of anger or vexation caused by wounded pride: resentment of a slight: dudgeon:

point or punctilio (*obs.*).—*v.t.* to wound the pride of: to nettle: to arouse, stir, provoke: (*refl.*) to pride oneself (on, upon, (*Boswell*) at). [Fr. *pique*, a pike, pique, *piquer*, to prick; cf. **pike, prick.**]

**pique**, *pēk*, *n.* in piquet, the scoring of 30 points in one hand before the other side scores at all.—*v.t.* to score a pique against.—*v.i.* to score a pique. [Fr. *pic*; see **piquet.**]

**pique**, *pēk*, (*Browning*) *n.* for **peak** (1).

**piqué**, *pē′kā*, *n.* a stiff corded cotton fabric: inlaid work of gold or silver in point or strip (sometimes with mother-of-pearl) on tortoise-shell or ivory.—Also *adj.*—**piqué work**, inlaying in piqué: needlework with raised design made by stitching. [Fr., pa.p. of *piquer*, to prick.]

**piquet.** Same as **picket.**

**piquet**, *pi-ket′*, *n.* a game for two with 32 cards, with scoring for declarations and tricks. [Fr.; origin unknown.]

**piragua**, *pi-ra′gwə*, *-rä′*, *n.* a South American dugout canoe, or a craft with a single trunk as foundation, often a schooner-rigged barge.—Also **peria′gua**, or (Fr.) **pirogue** (*pi-rōg′*). [Sp. *piragua*—Carib *piraqua.*]

**piranha**, *pē-rän′ya*, **piraya**, *pē-rä′ya*, **perai, pirai**, *pē-rī′*, *ns.* a ferocious South American river-fish (Serrasalmo or Pygocentrus) of the Characinidae. [Port. from Tupí *piranya, piraya.*]

**pirarucu**, *pē-rä-rōō-kōō′*, *n.* the arapaima.

**pirate**, *pī′rət*, *-rit*, *n.* one who, without authority, attempts to capture ships at sea: a sea-robber: a pirates' ship: one who publishes without authority of the owner of the copyright: a private bus, or its driver, plying on the recognised route of others: one who, in ordinary life, shows the predatory spirit of the sea rovers: a person who runs an unlicensed radio station.—*v.t.* to rob as a pirate: to publish without permission.—*n.* **piracy** (*pī′ra-si, pi′*), the crime of a pirate: robbery on the high seas: unauthorised publication: infringement of copyright.—*adjs.* **piratic** (*pī-rat′ik*), **-al,** pertaining to a pirate: practising piracy.—*adv.* **pirat′ically.** [L. *pīrāta* —Gr. *peirātēs—peiraein*, to attempt.]

**pirlicue, purlicue**, *pir′, pûr′li-kū*, (*Scot.*) *n.* a peroration: a résumé in conclusion.—*v.t.* and *v.i.* to summarise in conclusion. [Origin unknown.]

**pirn**, *pûrn*, (*Scot.*) *pirn, n.* a reel, bobbin, or spool. —**wind one a bonny pirn**, set a fine problem for one, involve one in difficulties. [Origin unknown.]

**pirnie**, *pir′ni*, (*Scot.*) *adj.* unevenly wrought: striped.—*n.* (*Scot.*) a striped woollen nightcap. —*adj.* **pirn′it** (*Scot.*), interwoven with different colours: striped. [App. conn. with **pirn.**]

**pirogue**, *pi-rōg′*. See **piragua.**

**pirouette**, *pir-ōō-et′*, *n.* a spinning about on tiptoe. —*v.i.* to spin round on tiptoe.—*n.* **pirouett′er.** [Fr.]

**pirrauru**, *pi-row′rōō*, *n.* among Australian aborigines a recognised supplementary husband or wife: the relation to such a person.—Also *adj.* [Native word.]

**pis aller**, *pē-zal-ā*, *pēz a′lā*, (Fr.) the last or worst shift, a makeshift.

**Pisces**, *pis′ēz*, *pīs′ēz*, *pisk′ās*, *n.pl.* the class of fishes (*zool.*): the Fishes, the twelfth sign of the zodiac, or the constellation that formerly coincided with it (*astron.*).—*ns.* **piscary** (*pisk′ə-ri*), right of fishing: a fishing pond; **pisc̆ā′tor**, an angler:—*fem.* **pisc̆ā′trix.**—*adjs.* **piscatorial** (*pis-kə-tō′ri-əl, -tō′*), **piscatory** (*pis′kə-tə-ri*), relating to fishing: fishing; **piscicolous** (*pis-ik′ə-ləs*), parasitic within fishes; **piscicul′tural.**—*ns.* **pis′-ciculture**, the rearing of fish by artificial methods; **pis′culturist; piscifau′na**, the assemblage of fishes in a region, formation, etc.—*adjs.* **pis′-ciform**, having the form of a fish; **piscine** (*pis′īn*),

of fishes: of the nature of a fish; **pisciv′orous**, feeding on fishes. [L. *piscis*, a fish; pl. *piscēs*; *piscātor*, fisher.]

**piscina**, *pis-ē′nə*, *pis-ī′nə*, *n.* a fish-pond: a swimming-pool (as in Roman baths): a basin and drain in old churches, usu. in a niche south of an altar, into which was emptied water used in washing the sacred vessels:—*pl.* **pisci′nas**, or **-ae.**—Also **piscine** (*pis′ēn*, or *-ēn′*). [L. *piscīna—piscis*, fish.]

**piscine, piscivorous.** See **Pisces.**

**piscine.** See **piscina.**

**pisé**, *pē-zā*, *n.* rammed earth or clay for walls or floors.—Also *adj.* [Fr.]

**pish**, *pish, interj.*, of impatience.—*n.* an utterance of the exclamation.—*v.t.* to pooh-pooh. [Imit.]

**pishogue**, *pi-shōg′*, (*Ir.*) *n.* sorcery. [Ir. *piseog.*]

**pisiform**, *pī′si-förm, piz′i-förm, adj.* pea-shaped.— *n.* a pea-shaped bone of the carpus. [L. *pisum*, pea, *förma*, shape.]

**pismire**, *pis′mīr*, *n.* an ant or emmet. [piss, from the strong smell of the ant-hill, M.E. *mire* (doubtful O.E. *mīre*), ant.]

**pisolite**, *pī′sō-līt, piz′ō-līt*, *n.* a coarse oolite.—*adj.* **pisolitic** (*-lit′ik*). [Gr. *pisos*, pease, *lithos*, stone.]

**piss**, *pis*, (*coll.*) *v.i.* to discharge urine.—*v.t.* to discharge as urine: to urinate on.—*n.* urine.— *adj.* **pissed** (*slang*), extremely drunk.—**piss′-a-bed** (*dial.*), the dandelion; **piss′-pot**, a chamberpot.—**piss off** (*interj.*; *vulg.*), go away. [Fr. *pisser.*]

**pissasphalt**, *pis′as-falt*, *n.* a semi-liquid bitumen. [Gr. *pissa*, pitch, *asphaltos*, asphalt.]

**pistachio**, *pis-ta′chi-ō, -shi-ō, -chyō, -shyō*, or *pis-tä′*, or *pis-tā′*, *n.* the almond-flavoured fruit-kernel of a small western Asiatic tree (*Pistacia vera*) of the same genus of the cashew family as the mastic tree:—*pl.* **pistachios.** [Sp. *pistacho* and It. *pistacchio*—L.L. *pistāquium*—Gr. *pistä-kion*—Pers. *pistah.*]

**pistareen**, *pis-tə-rēn′*, *n.* an old Spanish two-real piece formerly current in the United States. [Prob. *peseta.*]

**piste**, *pēst*, *n.* a beaten track, esp. a ski trail in the snow. [Fr.]

**pistil**, *pis′til*, (*bot.*) *n.* the ovary of a flower, with its style and stigma.—*adjs.* **pis′tillary; pis′tillate**, having a pistil but no (functional) stamens, female.—*n.* **pis′tillode**, an abortive pistil. [L. *pistillum*, a pestle.]

**pistol**, *pis′tl*, *n.* a small hand-gun, held in one hand when fired.—*v.t.* to shoot with a pistol:—*pr.p.* **pis′tolling**; *pa.t.* and *pa.p.* **pis′tolled.**— *n.* **pistoleer′**, one who carries or uses a pistol.— **pis′tol-shot.** [Through Fr. and Ger. from Czech.]

**pistole**, *pis-tōl′*, *n.* an old Spanish gold coin — about 17s. (contemporary value): an old 12-pound piece Scots = £1 English.—*n.* **pis′tolet**, a pistol: a pistole: a gold coin of various kinds worth about 6s. [O.Fr. *pistole*, earlier *pistolet.*]

**piston**, *pis′tən*, *n.* a cylindrical piece moving to and fro in a hollow cylinder, as in engines and pumps: a valve mechanism for altering the effective length of tube in brass musical instruments: a push-key for combining a number of organ stops.—**pis′ton-rod**, the rod to which the piston is fixed, and which moves up and down with it. [Fr.,—It. *pistone—pestare*, to pound—L. *pin-sěre, pistum.*]

**pit**, *pit*, *n.* a hole in the earth: a mine shaft: a mine, esp. a coal-mine: a place whence minerals are dug: a prison, esp. a castle prison entered from above (*arch.*): a cavity in the ground or in a floor for any purpose, as reception of ashes, inspection of motor-cars, a bottom-sawyer: a place beside the course where cars in a race can be refuelled and repaired: a hole for storing root-crops: a covered heap of potatoes, etc.: a grave, esp. one for many bodies: hell, or its lowest depths:

a hole used as a trap for wild beasts: an enclosure in which animals are kept (esp. bears): an enclosure for cockfights or the like: the ground-floor of a theatre, or its occupants, or the part of the ground-floor behind the stalls: part of a corn exchange floor assigned to some particular business (*U.S.*): a noisy card game mimicking a U.S. corn exchange: any hollow or depression, as the *pit of the stomach* below the breast-bone: an indentation left by smallpox: a minute depression in a surface: a hollow made by a raindrop: a thin place in a cell-wall, affording communication with another cell (*bot.*):—*v.t.* to mark with little hollows: to lay in a pit: to set to fight, as cocks in a cockpit: to match (with *against*).—*v.i.* to become marked with pits: to retain an impression for a time after pressing (*med.*):—*pr.p.* pitt'ing; *pa.t.* and *pa.p.* pitt'ed.—*adj.* pitt'ed, marked with small pits.—*ns.* pitt'ing; pitt'ite, one who frequents the pit of a theatre.—pit'-brow, the top of a shaft; pit'-coal, coal in the ordinary sense—not *charcoal*; pit'-dwelling, a primitive home made by roofing over a pit; pit'fall, a lightly covered hole as a trap: a hidden danger (*fig.*); pit'-head, the ground at the mouth of a pit, and the machinery, etc., on it; pit'man, a man who works in a coal-pit or a saw-pit, esp. at sinking, repair, and inspection of shafts and at pumping in a mine: a rod connecting a rotary with a reciprocating part (*U.S.*); pit'-pony, a pony employed for haulage in a coal-mine; pit'-prop, a, usu. timber, support in the workings of a coalmine; pit'-saw, a saw used in a saw-pit; pit'saw'yer, a bottom-sawyer; pit'-vill'age, a group of miners' houses near a pit: a cluster of pit-dwellings; pit'-vi'per, any member of an American group of snakes, including the rattlesnake, with a pit between eye and nose.—pit and gallows, a feudal baron's right to drown female and hang male felons. [O.E. *pytt*—L. *puteus*, a well.]

pit, *pit*, *n.* a fruit-stone.—*v.t.* to remove the stone from. [App. Du. *pit*.]

pit, *pit*, (*Scot.*) *v.t.* to put:—*pa.t.* pat, pät; *pa.p.* putten, *pa.t'n*, pitt'en. [See put.]

pita, *pē'ta*, *n.* the fibre of various species of Bromelia, Agave, etc.—Also pi'ta-flax', -hemp'. [Sp.,—Quechua *pita*, fine thread.]

Pitaka, *pit'a-kä*, *n.* any one of the three divisions of the Buddhist canon. [Sans., basket.]

pitapat, *pit'a-pat*, pitty-pat, *pit'i-pat*, pit-pat, *pit'pat'*, *adv.* with palpitation or pattering.—*adj.* fluttering: pattering.—*n.* a light, quick step: a succession of light taps: a patter.—*v.i.* to step or tread quickly: to patter: to palpitate. [Imit.]

pitara(h). See petara.

pitch, *pich*, *n.* the black shining residue of distillation of tar, etc.: extended to various bituminous and resinous substances, as *Burgundy pitch.*—*v.t.* to smear, cover, or caulk with pitch.—*n.* pitch'iness.—*adj.* pitch'y, like or characteristic of pitch: smeared with pitch: abounding in pitch: black.—*adj.* pitch'-black, black as pitch.—pitch'blende, a black mineral of resinous lustre, fundamentally composed of uranium oxides, a source of uranium and radium.—*adj.* pitch'-dark, utterly dark.—pitch'pine, a name for several American pines that yield pitch and timber (*Pinus palustris*, *P. rigida*, etc.); pitch'stone, a volcanic glass of resinous lustre, usu. acid; pitch'-tree, a tree yielding pitch, turpentine, or resin, esp. silver fir, spruce, kauri pine, Amboina pine. [O.E. *pic*—L. *pix*, *picis*.]

pitch, *pich*, *v.t.* to thrust or fix in the ground: to set up: to establish: to set or plant firmly: to set in position: to lay out for sale: to set, cover, stud, or face: to pave with stones set on end or on edge: to make a foundation of stones for: to set in array (*obs.*): to pit in opposition: to

determine or fix (*obs.*): to set in a key, to give this or that musical pitch, emotional tone, or degree of moral exaltation, etc., to: to fling, throw, or toss, esp. in such a manner as to fall flat or in a definite position: to loft so as not to roll much on falling (*golf*): to deliver to the batsman by an overhand or underhand throw (*baseball*).—*v.i.* to settle: to alight: to fix the choice (on): to encamp: to plunge forward: to oscillate about a transverse axis: to slope down: to descend or fall away abruptly: to interlock:—*pa.t.* and *pa.p.* pitched, *obs.* pight (q.v.).—*n.* act or manner of pitching: a throw or cast: degree, esp. of elevation or depression: highest point (*fig.*; *lit.*, *arch.*): height: a descent: slope: ground between the wickets (*cricket*): a place set apart for playing or practising a game: the point where a ball alights: a station taken by a street trader, etc.: the degree of acuteness of sound: a standard of acuteness for sounds (as concert pitch, French pitch): distance between successive points or things, as the centres of teeth in a wheel or a saw, the threads of a screw: (of a propeller) the angle between the chord of the blade and the plane of rotation: the distance a propeller would advance in one revolution.—*ns.* pitch'er, one who pitches: a paving-stone or sett: a baseball player who delivers the ball to the batsman: one who pitches a stall: a cutting or stake intended to take root; pitch'ing, the action of the verb to pitch: a facing of stone: a foundation of stone for a road surface: a cobble-stone surface of a road.—pitch-and-toss, a game in which coins are thrown at a mark, the player who throws nearest having the right of tossing all, and keeping those that come down heads up; pitch'ed battle, a deliberate battle on chosen ground between duly arranged sides; pitch'-far'thing, chuck-farthing; pitch'fork, a fork for pitching hay, etc.: a tuning-fork.—*v.t.* to lift with a pitchfork: to throw suddenly into any position.—pitch'pipe, a small pipe to pitch the voice or tune with; pitch'-wheel, a toothed wheel which operates with another of the same design.—pitch and pay (*Shak.*), pay ready-money; pitch in, to set to work briskly; pitch into, to assail vigorously; pitch (up)on, to let one's choice fall upon. [14th cent.; ety. uncertain.]

pitcher, *pich'ər*, *n.* a vessel, usu. of earthenware, for holding or pouring liquids: a cylindrical tinned milk-can (*Scot.*): jug or ewer (*U.S.*): a modified leaf or part of a leaf in the form of a pitcher, serving to catch insects.—*n.* pitch'erful.—pitch'er-plant, an insectivorous plant with pitchers, esp. Nepenthes, also Sarracenia, Darlingtonia, etc.—(little) pitchers have (long) ears, children tell tales: there may be listeners. [O.Fr. *picher*—L.L. *picārium*, a goblet—Gr. *bikos*, a wine-vessel.]

piteous, *pit'i-əs*, *adj.* compassionate (*arch.*): fitted to excite pity: paltry (*Milt.*).—*adv.* pit'eously.—*n.* pit'eousness. [O.Fr. *pitos*, *piteus*; cf. pity.]

pith, *pith*, *n.* the soft tissue within the ring of vascular bundles in the stems of dicotyledonous plants: similar material elsewhere, as the white inner skin of an orange: spinal marrow: innermost part: condensed substance, essence: mettle: vigour: significant meaning: importance.—*v.t.* to remove the pith of: to sever, pierce, or destroy the marrow or central nervous system of.—*adv.* pith'ily.—*n.* pith'iness.—*adj.* pith'ful; pith'less; pith'like; pith'y, full of pith: forcible: strong: energetic: sententious and masterful.—pith'ball, a pellet of pith; pith'-hat, a sun-helmet of sola pith; pith'-tree, a tropical African papilionaceous tree (*Herminiera elaphroxylon*) whose very pith-like wood is used for floats, canoes, etc. [O.E. *pitha*; Du. *pit*, kernel.]

Pithecanthropus, *pith-ə-kan'thro-pəs*, *pith-ē-kan-*

*thrō'pəs, n.* a fossil hominid discovered by Dr Eugene Dubois in Java in 1891-92. [Gr. *pithēkos*, ape, *anthrōpos*, man.]

**pithecoid,** *pith-ē'koid, adj.* ape-like. [Gr. *pithēkos*, ape, *eidos*, form.]

**pithos,** *pith'os, n.* a large Greek wine-jar. [Gr.]

**pit-mirk,** *pit'mirk*, (*Scot.*) *adj.* pitch-dark.

**piton,** *pē-tō, n.* iron peg or stanchion to which a rope may be attached, used in mountaineering. [Fr.]

**Pitta,** *pit'a, n.* a genus of birds, the so-called ant-thrushes of the Old World. [Telugu *pitta.*]

**pittance,** *pit'əns, n.* a special additional allowance of food or drink in a religious house, or a bequest to provide it: a dole: a very small portion or quantity: a miserable pay. [O.Fr. *pitance*—L. *pietās*, pity.]

**pitter,** *pit'ər, v.i.* to make a sound like a grasshopper.—*adv.* **pitt'er-patt'er,** with light pattering sound.—Also *n.* [Imit.]

**pittie-ward,** *pit'i-wərd, n.* an unexplained word in Shakespeare (*Merry Wives* III, i).

**Pittite,** *pit'it, n.* a follower of William Pitt (1759-1806), statesman.—*n.* **Pitt'ism.**

**pitty-pat.** See **pitapat.**

**pituita,** *pit-ū-i'tə,* **pituite,** *pit'ū-it, n.* phlegm.—*adj.* **pitū'itary.**—*n.* **pitū'itrin,** a hormone produced by the pituitary body.—**pituitary body,** a ductless gland at the base of the brain affecting growth, once thought to produce mucus. [L. *pituita.*]

**pity,** *pit'i, n.* a feeling for the sufferings and misfortunes of others: a cause or source of pity or grief: an unfortunate chance: a matter for regret.—*v.t.* to feel pity for: to feel grief at: to cause pity in (*obs.*):—*pr.p.* **pit'ying;** *pa.t.* and *pa.p.* **pit'ied.**—*adj.* **pit'iable,** to be pitied: miserable, contemptible.—*n.* **pit'iableness.**—*adv.* **pit'iably.**—*n.* **pit'ier.**—*adj.* **pit'iful,** feeling pity: compassionate: exciting pity: sad: despicable.—*advs.* **pit'iful** (*Shak.*), **pit'ifully.**—*n.* **pit'ifulness.**—*adj.* **pit'iless,** without pity: cruel.—*adv.* **pit'ilessly.**—*n.* **pit'ilessness.**—*adv.* **pit'yingly.**—it **pitieth me,** you, them, etc. (*Pr. Bk.*), it causeth pity in me, you, them, etc. [O.Fr. *pite* (Fr. *pitié*, It. *pietà*)—L. *pietās, pietātis—pius,* pious.]

**pityriasis,** *pit-i-rī'i-sis, n.* a branny scaliness of the skin.—*adj.* **pit'yroid,** bran-like. [Gr. *pityron*, bran.]

**più,** *pyōō, pē'ōō,* (It.) more.—**più mosso** (*mō'sō, mō'sō*), quicker.

**pium,** *pi-ōōm', n.* a small but very troublesome Brazilian biting fly. [Tupí.]

**pivot,** *piv'ət, n.* a pin on which anything turns: a soldier upon whom, or position on which, a body wheels: a centre-half in football: that on which anything depends or turns: a man of cardinal importance in an industry: a movement of the body as if on a pivot.—*adj.* of the nature of a pivot: cardinal: serving as a pivot.—*v.t.* to mount on a pivot.—*v.i.* to turn on or as if on a pivot.—*adj.* **piv'otal.**—*adv.* **piv'otally.**—*adj.* **piv'oted.**—*ns.* **piv'oter,** one who makes and fits pivots: a golfer who turns his body; **piv'oting,** the pivot-work in machines.—**piv'ot-bridge,** a swing-bridge moving on a vertical pivot in the middle; **piv'ot-man,** a man on whom a body of soldiers turns: a man of cardinal importance in industry, etc. [Fr. *pivot*, perh. related to It. *piva*, pipe, peg, pin.]

**pix,** *piks, n.* Same as **pyx.**

**pixy, pixie,** *pik'si,* (*dial.*; S.W. England, **pisky,** *pis'ki*) *n.* a small fairy.—*adjs.* **pix'ilated,** **pix'-illated,** bemused, bewildered: slightly crazy: intoxicated; **pix'y-led,** bewildered.—**pix'y-ring,** a fairy-ring; **pix'y-stool,** a toadstool or mushroom. [Origin obscure; cf. Sw. *pysk, pyske,* a small fairy.]

**pize,** *piz, n.* a term of imprecation, pox, pest. [Origin unknown.]

**pizza,** *pēt'sə,* (It.) an open pie of bread dough with tomatoes, cheese, etc.—**pizzeria,** *pēt-sə-rē'ə,* a bakery or restaurant where pizzas are sold and/or made.

**pizzicato,** *pit-si-kä'tō,* (*mus.*) *adj.* played by plucking the string, not with the bow—contradicted by *arco* or *col arco.*—*adv.* by plucking.—*n.* a tone so produced: a passage so played: the manner of playing by plucking. [It., twitched—*pizzicare,* to twitch.]

**pizzle,** *piz'l, n.* a penis: that of a bull used as instrument of punishment, for flogging. [L.G. *pesel* or Flem. *pezel.*]

**placable,** *plak'* or *plāk'ə-bl, adj.* that may be appeased: relenting: willing to forgive.—*ns.* **placabil'ity, plac'ableness.**—*adv.* **plac'ably.**—*v.t.* **placate** (*plə-kāt', plā-kāt', plak', plāk'āt*), to conciliate.—*n.* **placā'tion,** propitiation.—*adj.* **placatory** (*plak'* or *plāk'ə-tə-ri, plə-kā'*), conciliatory. [L. *plācāre,* to appease, akin to *placēre.*]

**placard,** *plak'ärd, n.* an official permit or proclamation with a thin seal (*obs.*): a written or printed paper stuck upon a wall or otherwise displayed as an intimation: a placcate or placket (*obs.*).—*v.t.* **placard** (*plak'ärd* or *plə-kärd'*), to publish or notify by placard: to post or set up as a placard: to put placards on or in. [O.Fr. *plackart, placard,* etc.—*plaquier,* to lay flat, plaster—M.Flem. *placken,* to plaster.]

**placate,** etc. See **placable.**

**placcate,** *plak'āt, n.* See **placket.**

**place,** *plās, n.* an open space in a town, a marketplace or square: in street names, vaguely a row or group of houses, often short, secluded, or mean: a portion of space: a portion of the earth's surface, or any surface: a position in space, or on the earth's surface, or in any system, order, or arrangement: a building, room, piece of ground, etc., assigned to some purpose (as *place of business, entertainment, worship*): a particular locality: a town, village, etc.: a dwelling or home: a mansion with its grounds: a battlefield (*obs.*): a fortress, fortified town (*obs.*): a seat or accommodation in a theatre, train, at table, etc.: space occupied: room: the position held by anybody, employment, office, a situation, esp. under government or in domestic service: due or proper position or dignity: that which is incumbent on one: precedence: position in a series: high rank: position attained in a competition or assigned by criticism: position among the first three in a race: stead: passage in a book (*obs.*): a topic, matter of discourse (*obs.*): pitch reached by a bird of prey (*obs.* except in *pride of place*).—*v.t.* to put in any place: to assign to a place: to find a place, home, job, publisher, etc., for: to lay (before; *fig.*): to induct: to identify: to invest: to arrange (loan, bet, etc.): to put (trust, etc., in): to ascribe (to; *arch.*).—*adjs.* **placed,** set in place or in a place: having a place: among the first three in a race: inducted to a charge; **place'less,** without place or office.—*ns.* **place'ment,** placing or setting: assigning to places; **plac'er.**—**place'-hunter,** one who covets and strives after a public post; **place'-kick,** in football, a kick made when the ball has been placed on the ground for that purpose; **place'man,** one who has a place or office under a government:—*pl.* **place'men; place'-monger,** one who traffics in appointments to places; **place'name,** a geographical proper name.—**give place,** to make room: to be superseded; **have place,** to have existence; **in place,** in position: opportune; **in the first place,** firstly, originally; **out of place,** out of due position: inappropriate, unseasonable; **take place,** to come to pass: to take precedence; **take someone's place,** to act as substitute for, or successor to, someone. [Partly O.E. (Northumb.) *plæce,* market-place, but mainly Fr. *place,* both from L. *platea*—Gr. *plateia* (*hodos*), broad (street).]

**placebo**, *pla-sē'bō*, *n.* vespers for the dead: a sycophant (*obs.*): a medicine given to humour or gratify a patient rather than to exercise any physically curative effect: a pharmacologically inactive substance administered as a drug either in the treatment of psychological illness or in the course of drug trials. [From the first words of the first antiphon of the office, *Placēbō Dominō*, I shall please the Lord.]

**placenta**, *pla-sen'ta*, *n.* the structure that unites the unborn mammal to the womb of its mother and establishes a nutritive connection between them: the part of the carpel that bears the ovules (*bot.*): a structure bearing sporangia: —*pl.* **placen'tae** (*-tē*).—*adj.* **placen'tal.**—*n.pl.* **Placentalia** (*plas-an-tā'li-a*), the Eutheria or placental mammals.—*n.* **placentā'tion**, the arrangement and mode of attachment of placentae or of placenta and fetus.—*adj.* **placent'iform**, cake-shaped. [L. *placenta*, a flat cake—Gr. *plakoeis* (contr. *plakous*) from *plax, plakos*, anything flat.]

**placer**, *plas'ar, plās'ar*, *n.* a superficial deposit from which gold or other mineral can be washed. [Sp. *placer*, sandbank—*plaza*, place.]

**placet**, *plā'set, pla'ket*, *n.* a vote of assent in a governing body: permission given, esp. by a sovereign, to publish and carry out an ecclesiastical order, as a papal bull or edict. [L. *plăcet*, it pleases, 3rd sing. pres. indic. of *placēre*, to please.]

**placid**, *plas'id*, *adj.* calm.—*ns.* **placid'ity, plac'idness.**—*adv.* **plac'idly.** [L. *placidus*—*placēre*, to please.]

**placitum**, *plas'i-tam, plak'i-tōōm*, *n.* a decision of a court or an assembly: a plea or pleading:—*pl.* **plac'ita.**—Also **plac'it** (wrongly **plac'et**).—*adj.* **plac'itory**, relating to pleas or pleading. [L. pa.p. neut. of *placēre*, to please.]

**plack**, *plak*, *n.* an old Scottish copper coin worth a third part of an English penny of the same period.—*adj.* **plack'less.** [Prob. Flem. *placke*, an old Flemish coin, orig. a flat disk.]

**placket**, *plak'it*, *n.* in armour, a breastplate or backplate, or a leather doublet with strips of steel (*obs.*): an apron: a petticoat: a placket-hole: a pocket, esp. in a skirt: a woman. —*Shak.* also **placc'at.**—**plack'et-hole**, a slit in a skirt. [Origin obscure; cf. *placard*.]

**placoderm**, *plak'ō-dûrm*, *adj.* covered with bony plates, as some fossil fishes.—*n.* a fish so covered. [Gr. *plax, plakos*, anything flat, *derma*, skin.]

**placoid**, *plak'oid*, *adj.* plate-like: having placoid scales, irregular plates of hard bone, not imbricated, as sharks. [Gr. *plax, plakos*, anything flat and broad, *eidos*, form.]

**plafond**, *pla-fō̃*, *n.* a ceiling, esp. decorated: a soffit: a game like contract bridge. [Fr., ceiling, score above the line in bridge—*plat*, flat, *fond*, bottom.]

**plagal**, *plā'gl*, (*mus.*) *adj.* of a Gregorian mode, having the final in the middle of the compass instead of at the bottom—opp. to *authentic.*—**plagal cadence**, one in which the subdominant chord precedes the tonic. [Gr. *plagios*, sidewise —*plagos*, a side.]

**plage**, *pläzh*, (Fr.) a fashionable beach: a bright or dark area seen on spectroheliograms, showing respectively an area of heated or cool gas on the sun's surface.

**plagiary**, *plā'ji-a-ri*, *n.* one who steals the thoughts or writings of others and gives them out as his own: the crime of plagiarism.—*adj.* (*obs.*) practising or got by literary theft.—*v.t.* **pla'giarise, -ize**, to steal from the writings or ideas of another.—*ns.* **pla'giarism**, the act or practice of plagiarising; **pla'giarist**, a plagiary. [L. *plagiārius*, a kidnapper, plagiary—*plāga*, a net.]

**plagioclase**, *plā'ji-ō-klās, -klāz*, or *plaj'*, *n.* a feld-spar whose cleavages are not at right angles—albite, anorthite, or any mixture of them. [Gr. *plagios*, oblique, *klasis*, a fracture.]

**plagiostome**, *plā'ji-ō-stōm*, *n.* a plagiostomous fish, one of the **Plagiostomata** (*-stō'ma-ta*) or **Plagiostomi** (*-os'ta-mi*), the cross-mouthed fishes, sharks and rays, having the mouth as a transverse slit on the under side of the head.—*adjs.* **plagiostom'atous, plagios'tomous.** [Gr. *plagios*, crosswise, *stoma, -atos*, mouth.]

**plagiotropism**, *plā-ji-ot'ra-pizm*, *n.* orienting at right angles to the direction of stimulus.—*adj.* **plagiotropic** (*-ō-trop'ik*).—*adv.* **plagiotrop'ically.** —*adj.* **plagiotropous** (*-ot'ra-pas*). [Gr. *plagios*, crosswise, *tropos*, a turning.]

**plagium**, *plā'ji-am*, *n.* the crime of kidnapping. [L. *plăgium*—*plăga*, a net.]

**plague**, *plāg*, *n.* a blow or wound (*obs.*): an affliction regarded as a sign of divine displeasure: a deadly epidemic or pestilence, esp. a fever caused by a bacillus (*B. pestis*) transmitted by rat-fleas from rats to man, characterised by buboes, or swellings of the lymphatic glands, by carbuncles and petechiae: murrain: any troublesome thing or person: trouble (*coll.*).—*v.t.* to infest with disease (*rare*): to pester or annoy.—*adj.* **plague'some** (*coll.*), troublesome, annoying.—*adv.* **pla'guily**, confoundedly.—*adj.* **plaguy** (*plā'gi*), of, or of the nature of, plague: vexatious: troublesome: confounded.—*adv.* (*Shak.*) confoundedly.—**plague'-pit**, a common grave for plague victims; **plague'-sore**, an ulcer due to plague; **plague'-spot**, a spot on the skin indicating plague: a place where disease is constantly present: an evil place.—*adj.* **plague'-stricken.**—**plague on**, may a curse rest on; **what the** (*Shak.* a) **plague**, what the devil. [O.Fr. *plague*—L. *plăga*, a blow; cf. Gr. *plēgē*.]

**plaice**, *plās*, *n.* a yellow-spotted flatfish of the fam. Pleuronectidae (*Pleuronectes platessa*).—**plaice'-mouth**, a mouth placed awry.—*adj.* **wry-mouthed.** [O.Fr. *plaïs* (Fr. *plie*)—L.L. *platessa*, a flatfish—perh. Gr. *platys*, flat.]

**plaid**, *plād* (by the English also *plad*), *n.* a long piece of woollen cloth, worn over the shoulder, usually in tartan as part of Highland dress, or checked as formerly worn by Lowland shepherds: cloth for it: a plaidman.—*adj.* like a plaid in pattern or colours.—*adj.* **plaid'ed**, wearing a plaid: made of plaid cloth.—*n.* **plaid'ing**, a strong woollen twilled fabric.—**plaid'man**, a Highlander; **plaid'-neuk'** (*-nük*), a pocket at the end of a plaid. [Perh. Gael. *plaide*, a blanket; but that may be from the Scots word.]

**Plaid Cymru**, *plīd kum'ri, kōōm'*, (W.) the Welsh Nationalist party.

**plain** (*arch.*), *plān*, *v.t., v.i.* to complain: to lament. —*n.* a complaint.—*n.* **plain'ant**, one who complains: a plaintiff.—*adj.* **plain'ful.**—*n.* **plain'ing** (*Shak.*), complaint. [O.Fr. *plaigner* (Fr. *plaindre*)—L. *plangĕre*, to beat the breast, lament.]

**plain**, *plān*, *adj.* flat: level: even: unobstructed: without obscurity: clear: obvious: simple: downright, utter: not ornate: unembellished: unvariegated: uncoloured: unruled: without pattern, striation, markings, etc.: without gloss: uncurled: not twilled: not elaborate: without addition: not highly seasoned: deficient in beauty: (in meiosis) ugly: without subtlety: candid: outspoken: straightforward: undistinguished: ordinary: other than a court card: other than trumps.—*n.* an extent of level land: the open country, esp. as a field of battle or as a setting for pastoral or romantic literature (*poetic*).—*adv.* clearly: distinctly.—*v.t.* (*Shak.*) to make plain.—*adj.* **plain'ish.**—*adv.* **plain'ly.**—*n.* **plain'ness.**—**plain'-chant**, plainsong.—*adj.* **plain'-clothes**, wearing ordinary clothes, not uniform, as a policeman on detective work.—*v.i.*

**plain'-cook,** to cook ordinary dishes.—*v.t.* and *v.i.* **plain'-darn,** to darn with the ordinary cross pattern.—**plain'-deal'er,** one who is candid and outspoken.—*n.* and *adj.* **plain'-deal'ing.**—*adj.* **plain'-heart'ed,** having a plain or honest heart: sincere.—**plain'-heart'edness; plain sailing** (see **plane); plains'man,** a dweller in a plain; **plain'-song,** unmeasured music sung in unison in ecclesiastical modes from early times, and still in use in R.C. and some Anglican churches: a simple melody: that to which a descant can be added.—*adj.* (*Shak.*) singing a simple theme. —**plain'-speaking,** straightforwardness or bluntness of speech.—*adj.* **plain'-spoken,** plain, rough, and sincere.—**plain'stanes** (*Scot.*), flagstones, pavement (also **plain'stones**); **plain'work,** plain needlework, as distinguished from embroidery. —**plain as a pikestaff** (see **pike** (1)). [Fr.,—L. *plānus,* plain.]

**plaint,** *plānt, n.* lamentation: complaint: a mournful song: a statement of grievance, esp. the exhibiting of an action in writing by a complainant in a court of law.—*adj.* **plaint'ful,** complaining.—*n.* **plaint'iff** (*Eng. law*), one who commences a suit against another—opp. to *defendant.*—Also *adj.* (*Spens.*).—*adj.* **plaint'ive,** mournful.—*adv.* **plaint'ively.**—*n.* **plaint'iveness.** —*adj.* **plaint'less.** [O.Fr. *pleinte* (Fr. *plainte*)— L. *plangĕre, planctum,* to beat the breast, lament.]

**plaister,** *plās'tər, n.* an obsolete or Scots form of **plaster.**

**plait,** *plat, plāt, plēt, n.* a pleat or zigzag fold (usu. **pleat,** and pron. *plēt* even when spelt **plait**): a braid in which strands are passed over one another in turn: material so braided: a braided tress or queue (in these senses usu. *plat,* and sometimes spelt **plat**).—*v.t.* to pleat (usu. *plēt*): to braid or intertwine (usu. *plat*).—*adj.* **plait'ed.** —*ns.* **plait'er; plait'ing.** [O.Fr. *pleit, ploit* (Fr. *pli*)—L. *plicāre, -ĭtum, -ātum,* to fold.]

**plan,** *plan, n.* a figure or representation of anything projected on a plane or flat surface, esp. that of a building, floor, etc., as disposed on the ground: a large-scale detailed map of a small area: a scheme for accomplishing a purpose: a purposed method: a scheme drawn up beforehand: a scheme of arrangement: in the Methodist churches, a quarterly programme of services with preachers for each church in the circuit.—*v.t.* to make a plan of: to design: to lay plans for: to devise: to purpose.—*v.i.* to make plans:—*pr.p.* **plann'ing;** *pa.t.* and *pa.p.* **planned.**—*adjs.* **planned,** intended: in accordance with, or achieved by, a careful plan made beforehand; **plan'less.**—*n.* **planner.**—**plan-position indicator** (*radar*), an apparatus in which the position of reflecting objects is shown on the screen of a cathode-ray tube, as if on a plan:—abbrev. **P.P.I.** [Fr.,—L. *plānus,* flat.]

**planarian,** *plə-nā'ri-ən, adj.* and *n.* turbellarian. [L. *plānārius,* on level ground (taken as if meaning flat)—*plānus,* flat.]

**planch,** *plansh, n.* a plank (*obs.*): a floor (*dial.*): a slab.—*v.t.* (*obs.*) to floor: to board.—*adj.* **planch'ed,** (*Shak.*) boarded.—*ns.* **planchet** (*plan'-shit*), a blank to be stamped as a coin; **planchette** (*plä-shet, plan-shet'*), a board mounted on two castors and a pencil-point, used as a medium for automatic writing and supposed spirit-messages. [Fr. *planche*—L. *planca.*]

**Planck's constant,** *plangks kon'stənt,* the constant (*h*), in the expression for the quantum of energy, equal to 6·626 × 10⁻³⁴ J s (joule second). [Max Karl Ernst Ludwig *Planck,* 1858-1947, German physicist.]

**plane,** *plān, n.* any tree of the genus Platanus (see **platane),** esp. the oriental plane (*P. orientalis*) and the North American plane or buttonwood (*P. occidentalis*), trees with palmatifid leaves shedding their bark in thin slabs: in Scotland the great maple (*Acer pseudoplatanus*).—**plane'-tree.** [Fr. *plane*—L. *platanus;* see **platane.**]

**plane,** *plān, n.* a surface on which, if any two points be taken, the straight line joining them will lie entirely on the surface (*geom.*): any flat or level material surface: one of the thin horizontal structures used as wings and tail to sustain or control aeroplanes in flight: short for aeroplane or airplane (also **'plane**): an act of planing or soaring: in mines, a main road for transport of coal or other mineral: any grade of life or of development or level of thought or existence.—*adj.* having the character of a plane: pertaining to, lying in, or confined to a plane: level: smooth.—*v.t.* to make plane or smooth (see also **plane** (3)).—*v.i.* to travel by aeroplane: to soar: to volplane.—*adj.* **planar** (*plān'ər*).—*ns.* **planation** (*plə-nā'shən*), making level; **planer** (*plān'ər*), one who levels or makes plane: a smoothing instrument (see also **plane** (3)): a wooden block beaten with a mallet to level a forme of type; **planigraph** (*plan'i-gräf*), an instrument for reducing or enlarging drawings; **planimeter** (*plan-im'i-tər*), an instrument for measuring the area of a plane figure.— *adjs.* **planimetric** (*plān-, plan-i-met'rik*), **-al.**— *ns.* **planimetry** (*plan-im'i-tri*), the mensuration of plane surfaces; **planisphere** (*plan'*), a sphere projected on a plane: map of celestial sphere, which can be adjusted so as to show the area visible at any time.—*adjs.* **planispher'ic; plā'no-con'cave,** plane on one side and concave on the other; **plā'no-con'ical,** plane on one side and conical on the other; **plā'no-con'vex,** plane on one side and convex on the other.—*ns.* **planom'-eter** (*plan-*), a plane surface used in machine-making as a gauge for plane surfaces; **Planor'bis,** a genus of pond-snails with flat spiral shell.— **planar diode,** one with plane parallel electrodes. —*adj.* **plane'-pol'arised, -ized,** (of light) consisting of vibrations in one plane only.—**plane** (or **plain) sailing,** the calculation of a ship's place in its course as if the earth were flat instead of spherical: easy work or going; **plane'-table,** an instrument used in field-mapping, with a sighting-telescope for observing objects, whose angles may be noted on a paper on the table of the instrument: an inclined table on which ore is dressed.—*v.t.* to survey with a plane-table. [L. *plānum,* a flat surface, neut. of *plānus,* flat; cf. **plain,** and next word.]

**plane,** *plān, n.* a carpenter's tool for producing a smooth surface by paring off shavings: a tool or machine for smoothing other things.—*v.t.* to smooth or remove with a plane (see also **plane** (2)).—*n.* **plā'ner,** one who uses a plane: a tool or machine for planing.—**plān'ing-machine',** a machine for planing wood or metals. [Fr. *plane* —L.L. *plāna—plānāre,* to smooth.]

**planet,** *plan'it, n.* in old astronomy, a heavenly body whose place among the fixed stars is not fixed (including sun and moon): a body (other than a comet or meteor) that revolves about the sun (including the earth) reflecting the sun's light and generating no heat or light of its own: a satellite of a planet (*secondary planet*): an astrological influence vaguely conceived.—*n.* **planetā'rium,** a machine showing the motions and orbits of the planets:—*pl.* **planetā'ria.**— *adj.* **plan'etary,** pertaining to the planets or a planet, or this planet: consisting of, or produced by, planets: under the influence of a planet: erratic: revolving in an orbit.—*n.* **planetes'imal,** in one theory of the origin of the solar system, any of many very small units absorbed into the planets as these formed.— *adjs.* **planetic** (*plan-et'ik*), **-al.**—*n.* **plan'etoid,** a minor planet: an artificial body put into orbit. — *adj.* **planetoi'dal.**—*adjs.* **plan'et-strick'en,** **plan'et-struck** (*astrol.*), affected by the influence of the planets: blasted.—**inferior planets**, those within the earth's orbit (Mercury and Venus); **minor planets**, the numerous group of very small planets between the orbits of Mars and Jupiter; **superior planets**, those outside the earth's orbit. [Fr. *planète*—Gr. *planētēs*, wanderer—*planaein*, to make to wander.]

**plangent**, *plan'jənt*, *adj.* resounding: noisy, clangorous: resounding mournfully.—*adv.* **plan'-gently.**—*n.* **plan'gency.** [L. *plangēns, -entis*, pr.p. of *plangĕre*, to beat.]

**planish**, *plan'ish*, *v.t.* to polish: to flatten.—*n.* **plan'isher**, a tool for planishing. [Obs. Fr. *planir, -issant*—*plan*, flat.]

**plank**, *plangk*, *n.* a long piece of timber, thicker than a board: a board on which fish, etc., is cooked and served (*U.S.*): one of the principles or aims that form the platform, programme of a party.—*v.t.* to cover with planks: to pay down or table (with *down*): to cook on a plank (*U.S.*). —*n.* **plank'ing**, the act of laying planks: a series of planks: work made up of planks.—**plank'-bed**, a prison bed of wood without mattress.—**walk the plank**, to walk (compulsorily) along a plank projecting over the ship's side into the sea. [L. *planca*, a board.]

**plankton**, *plangk'tən*, *n.* the drifting organisms in oceans, lakes or rivers.—*adj.* (*irreg.*) **planktonic** (*-ton'ik*). [Neut. of Gr. *planktos, -ē, -on*, wandering.]

**planoblast**, *plan'ō-bläst*, *n.* a free-swimming medusa.—*n.* **planogam'ete**, a motile gamete. [Gr. *plănos*, wandering.]

**plano-concave**, etc., **planometer, Planorbis.** See **plane** (2).

**plant**, *plänt*, *n.* a vegetable organism, or part of one, ready for planting or lately planted: a slip, cutting, or scion: an offshoot: a young person: a sapling: a cudgel: any member of the vegetable kingdom, esp. (popularly) one of the smaller kinds: growth: amount planted: the sole of the foot: mode of planting oneself, stand: something deposited beforehand for a purpose: equipment, machinery, apparatus, for an industrial activity: factory: bedded oyster (*U.S.*): thief's hoard (*slang*): spy, detective, picket or cordon of detectives, or police trap (*slang*): a deceptive trick, put-up job (*slang*).— *v.t.* to put into the ground for growth: to introduce: to insert: to fix: to place firmly: to set in position: to station, post: to found: to settle: to locate: to place or deliver (as a blow, a dart): to leave in the lurch: to bury (*slang*): to hide (*slang*): to place stolen goods, etc., in another's possession so as to incriminate him: to instil or implant: to furnish with plants: to colonise: to stock: to furnish or provide (with things disposed around): to salt (as a mine) (*slang*).—*v.i.* to plant trees, colonists, or anything else.—*n.* **plant'a**, the sole of the foot.— *adj.* **plant'able.**—*n.* **plant'age** (*Shak.*), plants in general.—*adj.* **plant'ar**, of the sole of the foot. —*ns.* **planta'tion**, a place planted, esp. with trees: a colony: an estate used for growing cotton, rubber, tea, sugar, or other product of warm countries: a large estate (*Southern U.S.*): act or process of introduction: the act of planting (*Milt.*); **plant'er**, one who plants or introduces: the owner or manager of a plantation: a pioneer colonist: a settler: an instrument for planting.—*adj.* **plant'igrade**, walking on the soles of the feet.—*n.* an animal that walks so.—*n.* **plant'ing**, the act of setting in the ground for growth: the art of forming plantations of trees: a plantation (*Scot.*).—*adj.* **plant'less.**—*ns.* **plant'-let, plant'ling**, a little plant; **plant'ule**, a plant embryo.—**plant'-associa'tion, plant'-forma'tion**, an assemblage of plants growing together under like conditions, as in a salt-marsh, a pine-wood, etc.; **plantation song**, a Negro song, such as the

workers sang on American plantations; **plant'-house**, a structure for growing plants of warmer climates; **plant'ie-cruive** (*-krōōv; Orkney* and *Shetland*), a kitchen garden, enclosure for cabbage.—*adj.* **plant'-like.**—**plant'-lore**, folk-lore of plants; **plant'-louse**, an aphis or greenfly:—*pl.* **plant'-lice.**—**plant'-pot**, a pot for growing a plant -in.—**plant out**, to transplant to open ground, from pot or frame: to dispose at intervals in planting. [O.E. *plante* (n.)—L. *planta*, shoot, slip, cutting, and O.E. *plantian* (vb.), and partly from or affected by Fr. *plante* and L. *planta*, plant, also (perh. a different word) sole.]

**plantain**, *plan'tin*, *n.* a roadside plant of genus **Plantā'gō** (e.g. waybread, ribgrass; fam. **Plantaginā'ceae**) that presses its leaves flat on the ground.—*adj.* **plantaginaceous** (*plan-taj-i-nā'-shəs*). [L. *plantāgō, -inis*—*planta*, the sole of the foot.]

**plantain**, *plan'tin*, *n.* a musaceous plant: its fruit, a coarse banana: in India, a banana.— **plan'tain-eater**, an African bird (Musophaga) of a fam. Musophagidae, a touraco. [Origin doubtful.]

**plantain**, *plan'tin*, (*obs.*) *n.* a platane or plane-tree. [Obs. Fr. *plantain*—L. *platanus.*]

**plantar, plantigrade.** See **plant.**

**planula**, *plan'ū-lə*, *n.* a free-swimming two-layered, often flattened, larva of coelenterates, etc.—*adjs.* **plan'ular; plan'uliform; plan'uloid.** [Dim. of L. *plănus*, flat.]

**planuria**, *plan-ū'ri-ə*, *n.* the discharge of urine through an abnormal passage.—Also **plan'ury.** [Gr. *plănos*, wandering, *ouron*, urine.]

**planxty**, *plangks'ti*, *n.* an Irish dance or dance-tune, like a jig but slower. [Origin unknown; not native Irish.]

**plap, plap**, *n.* a flatter sound than a plop.—*v.i.* to make, or move with, such a sound. [Imit.]

**plaque**, *pläk, plak*, *n.* a plate, tablet, or slab hung on, applied to, or inserted in, a surface as an ornament: a tablet worn as a badge of honour: a patch, such as a diseased area (*med.*): a film of saliva and bacteria formed on teeth (*dentistry*). —*n.* **plaquette'**, a small plaque. [Fr.; cf. **plack.**]

**plash**, *plash*, *v.t.* to interweave by partly cutting through, bending and twining the branches: to bend down: to break down: to make, mend, or treat, by cutting, bending, and interweaving stems and branches.—*n.* a plashed branch: a plashed place.—*n.* **plash'ing.** [O.Fr. *plassier*—L. *plectĕre*, to twist; cf. **pleach.**]

**plash**, *plash*, (*Spens.* **plesh, plesh**), *n.* a shallow pool: a puddle.—*n.* **plash'et**, a puddle.—*adj.* **plash'y.** [O.E. *plæsc.*]

**plash**, *plash*, *n.* a dash of water: a splashing sound: a sudden downpour (esp. *Scot.*).—*v.i.* to dabble in water: to splash.—*v.t.* to splash.— *adj.* **plash'y.** [Cf. M.L.G. *plaschen*, early Mod. Du. *plasschen*; perh. conn. with preceding.]

**plasm**, *plazm*, *n.* a mould or matrix: protoplasm: plasma.—*n.* **plas'ma**, plasm: a bright green chalcedony: protoplasm: the liquid part of blood, lymph, or milk: a very hot ionised gas, having approximately equal numbers of positive ions and of electrons, highly conducting.—*adjs.* **plasmat'ic, -al, plas'mic**, of, or occurring in, plasma: protoplasmic.—*n.* **plas'min**, fibrinolysin. —*ns.* **plasmodesm** (*plaz'mō-dezm; Gr. desmos*, bond), a thread of protoplasm connecting cells; **plasmo'dium**, a naked mass of protoplasm with many nuclei, as in slime-fungi:—*pl.* **plasmo'dia; plasmog'amy**, fusion of cytoplasm only.—*v.t.* **plas'molyse, -yze** (*-līz*).—*n.* **plasmolysis** (*-mol'i-sis; Gr. lysis*, loosening), removal of water from a cell by osmosis, with resultant shrinking.—*adj.* **plasmolytic** (*-mō-lit'ik*).—*n.* **plasmosō'ma, plas'mosome** (*Gr. sōma*, body), a nucleolus. [Gr. *plasma, -atos*, a thing moulded —*plassein*, to mould.]

plast, plaste, *pläst*, (*Spens.*) *pa.t.* and *pa.p.* of place.

plaster, *pläs'tər*, *n.* a fabric coated with an adhesive substance for local application as a remedy, for protection of a cut, etc.: a pasty composition that sets hard, esp. a mixture of slaked lime, sand, and sometimes hair, used for coating walls, etc.: calcium sulphate.—*adj.* made of plaster.—*v.t.* to apply plaster, or a plaster, to: to treat with plaster: to bedaub: to smear: to cover excessively, injudiciously, or meretriciously: to stick (on or over): to reduce to plaster or a sticky mass: to damage by a heavy attack: to smooth down: to smooth (over): to treat with gypsum: to attach with plaster.—*adj.* plas'tered, daubed, treated, etc., with plaster: shattered: intoxicated (*slang*).—*ns.* plas'terer, one who plasters, or one who works in plaster; plas'tering.—*adj.* plas'tery, like plaster.—*n.* plas'teriness.—plas'terboard, a building slab of plaster faced with paper or fibre: gypsum plasterboard; plaster cast, a copy got by pouring a mixture of plaster of Paris and water into a mould formed from the object; plas'terstone, gypsum; plas'ter-work.—plaster of Paris, gypsum (originally found near *Paris*) partially dehydrated by heat. [O.E. *plaster* (in medical sense) and O.Fr. *plastre* (builder's plaster) both —L.L.*plastrum*—L. *emplastrum*—Gr. *emplastron* for *emplaston*—*en*, on, *plassein*, to mould, apply as a plaster.]

plastic, *plas'*, *pläs'tik*, *adj.* having power to give form: shaping, formative: mouldable: of or pertaining to moulding or modelling: modifiable: capable of permanent deformation without giving way: capable of, or pertaining to, metabolism and growth: made of plastics.—*n.* a mouldable substance, esp. now any of a large number of polymeric substances, most of them synthetic, mouldable at some stage (see thermoplastic, thermosetting) under heat or pressure, used to make domestic articles and many engineering products: a modeller or sculptor (*obs.*): the art of modelling or of sculpture (esp. in *pl.*).—*n.* Plas'ticine (*-ti-sēn*; trademark), a substitute for modelling clay.—*n.pl.* plas'tics (used as *sing.*), plastic surgery.—*adj.* dealing with plastic materials (*as the plastics industry*).—*v.t.* plas'ticise, -ize (*-ti-sīz*), to make plastic.—*ns.* plasticis'er, -z-, substance that induces plasticity; plasticity (*-tis'i-ti*), state or quality of being plastic: quality in a picture of appearing to be three-dimensional.—plastic art, the art of shaping (in three dimensions), as sculpture, modelling: art which is, or appears to be, three-dimensional; plastic bomb, a bomb made with a certain explosive chemical that can be moulded; plastic clay, clay from which earthenware and bricks are made; plastic force, the force or power of growth in animals and plants; plastic operation, a surgical operation which restores a lost part, or repairs a deformed or disfigured part, of the body; plastic surgery, branch of surgery concerned with plastic operations. [Gr. *plastikos*—*plassein*, to mould.]

plastid, *plas'*, *pläs'tid*, *n.* a living cell (*obs.*): a differentiated granule in protoplasm.—*n.* plast'i-dule, Haeckel's hypothetical unit of living protoplasm. [Gr. *plastis*, *-idos*, modeller (fem.).]

plastilina, *pläs-ti-lē'nə*, *n.* a mixture of clay with oil, zinc oxide, wax, and sulphur for modelling. [It.]

plastogamy, *plast-og'ə-mi*, *n.* plasmogamy. [Gr. *plastos*, moulded, *gamos*, marriage.]

plastron, *plas'tron*, *n.* a breastplate worn under the hauberk: a fencer's wadded breast-shield: the under part of the shell of a tortoise or turtle, or other animal: the front of a dress-shirt: a separate ornamental front part of a woman's bodice.—*adj.* plas'tral. [Fr. *plastron*

—It. *piastrone*—*piastra*, breastplate; cf. piastre, plaister.]

plat, *plat.* Same as plait.

plat, *plat*, *n.* a plot of ground (*arch.*): a diagram or a plan (*obs.* or *U.S.*): a scheme (*obs.*).—*v.t.* (now *U.S.*) to make a plan of, plot out. [plot, infl. by plat (3).]

plat, *plat*, *n.* a flat thing (*obs.*): the flat, or flat part, or side (*obs.*): a mould-board (*dial.*): a flat place or region (esp. *U.S.*). [App. Fr. *plat.*]

platane, platan, *plat'ən*, *n.* a plane-tree, any tree of the genus Plat'anus (see plane (1)), giving name to the family Platanā'ceae, akin to the witch-hazel family.—*adj.* platanā'ceous. [L. *platanus*—Gr. *platanos*—*platys*, broad.]

platanna (frog), *pla-tan'ə*, *n.* an African frog, *Xenopus laevis*, used in research, and formerly used in tests for pregnancy. [Afrikaans,—*plathander*, flat-handed.]

platband, *plat'band*, *n.* a fascia or flat moulding projecting less than its own breadth: a lintel or flat arch: an edging of turf or flowers. [Fr. *platebande*, flat band.]

plat du jour, *pla dü zhōōr*, dish on restaurant menu specially recommended that day. [Fr.]

plate, *plāt*, *n.* a sheet, slab, or lamina of metal or other hard material, usually flat or flattish: metal in the form of sheets: a broad piece of armour: a scute or separate portion of an animal's shell: a broad thin piece of a structure or mechanism: a piece of metal, wood, etc., bearing or to bear an inscription to be affixed to anything: an engraved piece of metal for printing from: an impression printed from it, an engraving: a whole-page separately printed and inserted illustration in a book: a mould from type, etc., for printing from, as an electrotype or stereotype: part of a denture fitting the mouth and carrying the teeth: a film-coated sheet of glass or other material to photograph on: a plate-rail: a horizontal supporting timber in building: a five-sided white slab at the home-base (*baseball*): a light racing horseshoe: a thermionic valve anode (orig. flat): precious metal, esp. silver (*hist.*; Sp. *plata*, silver): a silver coin (*Shak.*): wrought gold or silver: household utensils in gold or silver: table utensils generally: plated ware: a cup or other prize for a race or other contest: a race or contest for such a prize: a shallow dish: a plateful: a portion served on a plate: a church collection.—*v.t.* to overlay with metal: to armour with metal: to cover with a thin film of another metal: to make a printing plate of.—*adj.* plā'ted, covered with plates of metal: covered with a coating of another metal, esp. gold or silver: armoured with hard scales or bone (*zool.*).—*ns.* plate'ful, as much as a plate will hold; plate'let, a minute body in blood, concerned in clotting; plā'ter, one who, or that which, plates: a moderate horse entered for a selling race; plā'ting.—*adj.* plā'ty, plate-like: separating into plates.—plate'-arm'our, protective armour of metal plates; plate'-basket, a basket for forks, spoons, etc.; plate'-fleet (*hist.*), ships that carried American silver to Spain; plate'-glass, a fine kind of glass used for mirrors and shop-windows, orig. poured in a molten state on an iron plate.—*adj.* made with, consisting of, plate-glass: of a building, having large plate-glass windows, appearing to be built entirely of plate-glass: hence, of any very modern building or institution.—plate'-layer, one who lays, fixes, and attends to the rails of a railway; plate'-leather, a chamois leather for rubbing gold and silver; plate'man, a man who has the care of silver-plate in a hotel, club, etc.; plate'-mark, a hallmark; plate'-powder, a polishing powder for silver; plate'-print'ing, the process of printing from engraved plates; plate'-proof, a proof taken from a plate; **plate'-rack**, a frame for holding plates, etc., when not in use or when draining after washing; **plate'-rail**, a flat rail with a flange; **plate'-room**, a room where silver-plated goods or printing plates are kept; **plate'-ship** (*hist*.), a ship bringing silver to Spain from America; **plate'-warmer**, an apparatus for warming plates or keeping them warm.—**half'-plate**, in photography, a size of plate measuring 4¾ by 6½ in. (4¼ by 5½ in U.S.); **quar'ter-plate**, 3¼ by 4¼ in.; **whole'-plate**, 6½ by 8½ in.; **handed to one on a plate** (*fig*.), obtained by one without the least effort; **on one's plate** (*fig*.), in front of one, waiting to be dealt with. [O.Fr. *plate*, fem. (and for the dish *plat*, masc.), flat—Gr. *platys*, broad.]

**plateasm**, *plat'i-azm*, *n*. pronunciation with a wide mouth-opening, as in Doric Greek. [Gr. *plateiasmos*—*platys*, broad.]

**plateau**, *pla'tō*, *pla-tō'*, *n*. a tableland: an ornamented tray, plate, or plaque: a lady's flat-topped hat: a temporary stable state reached in the course of upward progress: the part of a curve representing this:—*pl*. **plateaux** (-*tōz*), also **plateaus**. [Fr.,—O.Fr. *platel*, dim. of *plat*.]

**platen**, *plat'n*, *n*. the work-table of a machine-tool: a flat part that in some printing-presses pushes the paper against the forme: the roller of a typewriter. [Fr. *platine*—*plat*, flat.]

**plateresque**, *plat-ə-resk'*, (*archit*.) *adj*. applied to a style resembling silversmith's work. [Sp. *plateresco*—*platero*, silversmith—*plata*, silver.]

**platform**, *plat'förm*, *n*. a plane figure or surface (*obs*.): a ground-plan (*obs*.): a scheme, device, plan of action (*Shak*.): a scheme of church government or of administrative policy: a party programme: a site: a basis: a raised level surface: a terrace: a plateau: a flooring: a raised floor for speakers, musicians, etc.: those who have seats on the platform at a meeting: public speaking or discussion (*fig*.): a medium for discussion: a deck for temporary or special purpose: a position prepared for mounting a gun: a raised walk in a railway station giving access to trains: flooring outside an inner entrance to a bus, tram-car, or sometimes a railway carriage.—*v.t.* to furnish with a platform: to sketch, plan: to place on, or as on a platform.—*v.i.* to speak or appear on a platform. [Fr. *plateforme*, lit. flat form.]

**platforming**, *plat'förm-ing*, *n*. a process for re-forming low-grade into high-grade petrol, using a platinum catalyst. [plat(inum) and form.]

**platinum**, *plat'in-əm*, *n*. a noble metal (at. numb. 78; symbol Pt), steel-grey, very valuable, malleable and ductile, very heavy and hard to fuse—older name **plat'ina**.—*adj*. made of platinum.—*adjs*. **platinic** (*plə-tin'ik*), of quadrivalent platinum; **platinif'erous**, platinum-bearing.—*v.t.* **plat'inise**, -ize, to coat with platinum.—*ns*. **plat'-inoid**, one of the metals with which platinum is always found associated—*palladium, iridium*, etc.: an alloy of copper, zinc, nickel, and tungsten resembling platinum; **plat'inotype**, a method of photography by reducing a compound of platinum: a photograph so produced.—*adj*. **plat'inous**, of bivalent platinum.—**platinum black**, platinum in the form of a velvety black powder; **platinum blonde**, a woman with metallic silvery hair; **platinum lamp**, an electric lamp with a platinum filament. [Sp. *platina*—*plata*, silver.]

**platitude**, *plat'i-tūd*, *n*. flatness: a dull commonplace or truism: an empty remark made as if it were important.—*n*. **platitudinā'rian**, one who indulges in platitudes.—*v.i.* **plat'itudinise**, -ize. —*adj*. **platitud'inous**. [Fr.,—*plat*, flat.]

**Platonic**, *plə-ton'ik*, *adj*. pertaining to *Plato*, the Greek philosopher (about 427-347 B.C.), or to his philosophy: of love, between soul and soul,

without sensual desire (a Renaissance phrase): relating to or experiencing Platonic love.—*n*. ε Platonist: a Platonic lover: (usu. in *pl*.) Platonic love.—*adj*. **Platon'ical** (now *rare*).—*adv*. **Platon'-ically**.—*n*. **Platon'icism**, doctrine, practice, or profession of Platonic love: Platonism (*obs*.).—*v.t.* **Platonise**, **-ize**, *plā'tən-iz*, to render Platonic. —*v.i.* to follow Plato.—*ns*. **Plā'tonism**, the philosophy of Plato: Platonicism; **Plā'tonist**, a follower of Plato.—**Platonic solid**, any of the five regular polyhedrons (tetrahedron, hexahedron, octahedron, dodecahedron, and icosahedron). [Gr. *platōnikos*—*Platōn*, -*ōnos*, Plato.]

**platoon**, *pla-tōōn'*, *n*. orig. a small body of soldiers in a hollow square or such a body firing together: a subdivision of a company: a squad: a volley (*arch*.). [Fr. *peloton*, ball, knot of men—L. *pila*, ball.]

**Platt-Deutsch**, *plät'-doich*, *n*. and *adj*. Low German. [Ger.]

**platted, platting.** Same as plaited, plaiting.

**platter**, *plat'ər*, *n*. a large flat plate or dish. [A.Fr. *plater*—*plat*, a plate.]

**platy-**, *plat'i-*, in composition, flat, broad. [Gr. *platys*, broad.]

**platycephalous**, *plat-i-sef'ə-ləs*, *adj*. having the vault of the skull flattened.—Also **platycephalic** (-*si-fal'ik*). [Gr. *kephalē*, head.]

**Platyhelminthes**, *plat-i-hel-min'thēz*, *n.pl*. the flat-worms, a phylum including planarians, tapeworms, and flukes. [Gr. *helmins*, -*inthos*, intestinal worm.]

**platypus**, *plat'i-pəs*, -*pōōs*, *n*. the duck-bill:—*pl*. **plat'ypuses**. [Gr. *pous, podos*, a foot.]

**platyrrhine**, *plat'i-rin*, *adj*. broad-nosed: belonging to the division of the monkeys found in South America.—*n*. a New World monkey. [Gr. *platyrris*, -*inos*—*rhis, rhinos*, nose.]

**platysma**, *plat-iz'mə*, *n*. a broad sheet of muscle in the neck. [Gr. *platysma*, a flat piece.]

**plaudit**, *plö'dit*, *n*. (now usu. in *pl*.) an act of applause: also praise bestowed, enthusiastic approval.—*adj*. **plaud'itory**. [Shortened from L. *plaudite*, applaud, an actor's call for applause at the end of a play, pl. imper. of *plaudĕre*, *plausum*, to clap the hands.]

**plaudite**, *plö'dit-i*, *plow'dit-e*, (L.) applaud: clap your hands.

**plausible**, *plö'zi-bl*, *adj*. that may be applauded (*obs*.): acceptable (*obs*.): seemingly worthy of approval or praise: fair-showing: specious: ingratiating and fair-spoken.—*ns*. **plausibil'ity**, **plaus'ibleness**.—*adv*. **plaus'ibly**, in a plausible manner: with applause, by acclamation (*Shak*.): commendably, pleasantly (*obs*.).—*adj*. **plausive** (*plö'ziv*), plausible (*Shak*.): pleasing (*Shak*.): applauding. [L. *plaudĕre*, to clap the hands.]

**plaustral**, *plös'trəl*, *adj*. (*facet*.) of a wagon. [L. *plaustrum*, a wagon.]

**play**, *plā*, *v.i.* to operate (*obs*.): to move about irregularly, lightly, or freely: to have some freedom of movement: to flicker, flutter, shimmer, pass through rapid alternations: to move in, discharge, or direct a succession, stream, or shower (as of water, light, waves, missiles): to engage in pleasurable activity: to perform acts not part of the immediate business of life but in mimicry or rehearsal or in display: to amuse oneself: to sport: to make sport: to trifle: to behave without seriousness: to behave amorously or sexually: to take part in a game: to proceed with the game, perform one's part in turn: to send a ball or the like in the course of a game: to contend with weapons (*arch*.): to wield a weapon: to gamble: to have a holiday (*Shak*.; also *Scot*.): to be off work (*N. of England*): to perform on a musical instrument: to give forth music: to come forth as music: to act a part.—*v.t.* to perform: to ply, wield: to cause or allow to play: to set in opposition, pit: to send, let off, or discharge in succession or in a stream or shower: to give a limited freedom of movement to: hence, to manage: to allow (a fish) to tire itself by its struggles to get away: to engage in (a game or recreative mimicry): to proceed through (a game, part of a game —as a stroke, trick—or an aggregate of games— as a rubber, set): to stake or risk in play: to bring into operation in a game, as by striking (a ball), throwing on the table (a card), moving (a man): to compete against in a game: to compete on the side of (with *for*): to act (e.g. comedy, a named play): to act the part of, in a play or in real life: to act, perform, in (e.g. a circuit of theatres, halls): to make-believe in sport: to perform music on: to perform on a musical instrument: to lead, bring, send, render, or cause to be by playing: to amuse (*refl.*; *obs.* and *Scot.*):—*pr.p.* play'ing; *pa.t.* and *pa.p.* played.—*n.* activity: operation: action of wielding: light fluctuating movement or change: limited freedom of movement: scope: recreative activity: display of animals in courtship: amusement: dalliance: a game (*Shak.*): the playing of a game: manner of playing: procedure or policy in a game: holiday (*Shak.* and *Scot.*): a fair or festival (*dial.*): being off work (*N. of England*): gambling: a drama or dramatic performance: manner of dealing, as *fair-play* (*fig.*).—*adj.* play'able, capable (by nature or by the rules of the game) of being played, or of being played on.—*n.* play'er, one who plays: an actor: a trifler: an instrumental performer: a professional cricketer: a mechanism for playing a musical instrument.—*adj.* play'ful, sportive.—*adv.* play'fully.—*n.* play'fulness.—*adj.* play'some, playful.—*v.i.* play'-act.—play'-acting, performance of plays: pretence: play'-actor, -actress, (usu. in contempt) professional actor, actress; play'back, act of reproducing a recording of sound or visual material, esp. immediately after it is made: a device for doing this; play'-bill, a bill announcing a play; play'book, a printed play or book of plays; play'-box, a box for toys and other valued possessions, esp. in a boarding-school; play'boy, a boy-actor: a light-hearted irresponsible person, esp. rich and leisured:—*fem.* play'-girl; play'-day, a holiday; play'-debt, a debt incurred in gambling.—*adj.* played'-out, exhausted: used up: no longer good for anything.—play'er-pian'o (see piano); play'fellow, a playmate; play'-gōer, one who habitually attends the theatre; play'-gōing; play'ground, a place for playing in, esp. one connected with a school: a holiday region; play'house, a theatre; play'ing-card, one of a pack (e.g. of fifty-two cards, divided into four suits) used in playing games; play'ing-field, a grass-covered space set apart, marked out, and kept in order for games; play'let, a short play; play'-mare (*Scot.*), a hobby-horse, as in the old morris-dance; play'mate, a companion in play, esp. child's play; play'-off, a game to decide a tie; play'-pen, a fencing within which a young child may safely play; play'room, a room for children to play in; play'-spell, a time allowed for play; play'thing, a toy: a person or thing treated as a toy; play'time, a time for play; play'-way, the educational use of play; play'-world, an imaginary world feigned in play; play'wright, play'-writer, a dramatist.—bring, come, into play, bring, come, into exercise, operation, use; hold in play (*arch.* hold play), to keep occupied, esp. to gain time or detain; in, out of, play, in, out of, such a position that it may be played; make play, to keep things going, push on with the game; play at, engage in the game of: make a pretence of: to practise without seriousness; play ball, to co-operate; play it, one's cards, close to the chest, to be

secretive about one's actions or intentions in a particular matter; play down, to treat as less important than it is; play fast and loose, to act in a shifty, inconsistent, and reckless fashion; play fine, at billiards, to strike the object-ball near the edge—opp. to play full, to strike it nearer the middle than the edge; play for safety, to play safe; play for time, to delay action or decision in the hope or belief that conditions will become more favourable later; play hard to get, to make a show of unwillingness to co-operate with a view to strengthening one's position; play hell with, to upset, disorganise: to damage; play into the hands of, to act so as to give, usu. unintentionally, an advantage to; play it by ear, to improvise plan of action to meet the situation as it develops; play off, to manipulate so as to counteract: to play from the tee (*golf*): to toss off (*Shak.*): to bring off (as a hoax); play on, to strike the ball on to one's own wicket: to direct one's efforts to the exciting of, work upon; play out, to play to the end: to wear out, to exhaust; play safe, to take no risks; play the game, to act strictly honourably; play up, to strike up, begin the music: to redouble one's efforts, play more vigorously: to show up well in a crisis or emergency: to give (esp. undue) prominence to, or to boost: to fool; play upon, to practise upon, work upon; play upon words, a pun or other manipulation of words depending on their sound; play up to, to act so as to afford opportunities to (another actor): to flatter; play with, to play in company of, or as partner or opponent to: to dally with. [O.E. *pleg(i)an*, vb., *plega*, n.]

play'a, plä'ya, *n.* a basin which becomes a shallow lake after heavy rainfall and dries out again in hot weather. [Sp.]

plaza, plä'za, *n.* a public square or open, usu. paved, area in a city or town. [Sp.]

plea, plē, *n.* a lawsuit (*Scots law* and *hist.*): a pleading: a prisoner's or defendant's answer to a charge or claim: a claim (*Shak.*): an excuse: a pretext: urgent entreaty.—*v.t.* and *v.i.* to dispute in a law-court. [O.Fr. *plai*, *plaid*, *plait* —L.L. *placitum*, a decision—L. *placēre*, -*itum*, to please.]

pleach, plēch, *v.t.* to intertwine the branches of, as a hedge: to fold, as the arms (*Shak.*): to plash. [From form of O.Fr. *pless(i)er*—L. *plectēre*; see plash (1).]

plead, plēd, *v.i.* to carry on a plea or lawsuit: to argue in support of a cause against another: to put forward an allegation or answer in court: to implore.—*v.t.* to maintain by argument: to allege in pleading: to put forward as a plea: to offer in excuse: to sue for (*arch.*, *Scot.*):—*pa.t.*, *pa.p.* plead'ed, also (*Spens.*, *Scot.*, *U.S.*, and *dial.*) pled.—*adj.* plead'able, capable of being pleaded.—*n.* plead'er, one who pleads: an advocate.—*adj.* plead'ing, imploring.—*n.* act of putting forward or conducting a plea: (in *pl.*) the statements of the two parties in a lawsuit: entreaty.—*adv.* plead'ingly.—plead guilty, or not guilty, to admit, or refuse to admit, guilt; special pleading, unfair or one-sided argument aiming rather at victory than at truth. [O.Fr. *plaidier*; cf. plea.]

please, plēz, *v.t.* to give pleasure to: to delight: to satisfy: to choose, to will (to do).—*v.i.* to give pleasure: to like, think fit, choose (originally impersonal with dative, e.g. *it pleases* (to) *me*; later *me pleases*; then *I please*).—*n.* pleasance (*plez'ans*; *arch.* and *poet.*), pleasure: enjoyment: pleasantness: complaisance: pleasant behaviour (*obs.*): that which gives pleasure: a pleasure-ground or specialised part of a garden.—*adj.* pleas'ant, pleasing: agreeable: inoffensive: affable: good-humoured: cheerful: gay:

facetious, tipsy.—*adv.* **pleas'antly.**—*ns.* **pleas'antness; pleas'antry,** pleasantness, enjoyment (*obs.*): jocularity: a facetious utterance or trick:—*pl.* **pleas'antries.**—*adj.* **pleased** (*plēzd*), grateful: delighted.—*n.* **pleas'er.**—*adj.* and *n.* **pleas'ing.**—*adv.* **pleas'ingly.**—*n.* **pleas'ingness.**—*adj.* **pleasurable** (*plezh'ǝr-ǝ-bl*), able to give pleasure: delightful: gratifying: pleasure-seeking (*obs.*).—*n.* **pleas'urableness.**—*adv.* **pleas'urably.**—*n.* **pleasure** (*plezh'ǝr*), agreeable emotions: gratification of the senses or of the mind: sensuality: dissipation: a source of gratification: what the will prefers: purpose: command.—*v.t.* (*arch.*) to give pleasure to.—*v.i.* (*arch.*) to take pleasure (in).—*adjs.* **pleas'ureful; pleas'ureless.**—*n.* **pleas'urer,** a pleasure-seeker.—**pleaseman** (*plēz'-man, -mǝn*; *Shak.*), an officious fellow, a pickthank; **pleas'ure-boat,** a boat used for pleasure or amusement.—*adj.* **pleas'ure-giving,** affording pleasure.—**pleas'ure-ground,** ground laid out in an ornamental manner for pleasure; **pleas'urehouse,** a house to which one retires for recreation or pleasure; **pleas'ure-seeker,** one who seeks pleasure: a holiday-maker; **pleas'ure-seeking; pleas'ure-trip,** an excursion for pleasure.—**at pleasure,** when, if, or as, one pleases; **if you please,** if you like: a polite formula of request or acceptance: forsooth (*ironically*); **may it please you, so please you,** deferential or polite formulas of address or request; **please,** also **please to,** a polite formula equivalent to **if you please,** now felt as imperative, perh. orig. from the older **please it you, please it** (sometimes printed **pleaseth** in *Shak.*), **please you, may it please you; please yourself,** do as you like; **pleasure-pain principle,** principle dominating instinctual life in which activities are directed towards seeking pleasure and avoiding pain. [O.Fr. *plaisir* (Fr. *plaire*)—L. *placēre,* to please.]

**pleat,** *plēt.* Same as **plait.**

**pleb.** See **plebeian.**

**plebeian,** *pli-bē'ǝn* (in *Shak.* also **plebean,** *pleb'i-ǝn*), *adj.* of the Roman plebs: of the common people: low-born: undistinguished: vulgarlooking: vulgar.—*n.* a member of the plebs of ancient Rome: a commoner: a member of a despised social class.—*n.* **pleb** (*coll.*), a person of unpolished manners which are attributed to his low rank in society.—*adj.* **plebb'y.**—*v.t.* **plebei'anise, -ize.**—*ns.* **plebei'anism; plebificā'tion** (*plebi-*), the act of making plebeian.—*v.t.* **pleb'ify.** [L. *plēbēius*—*plēbs, plēbis.*]

**plebiscite,** *pleb'i-sit, -sīt, n.* a law enacted by the plebs assembled in the *Comitia tributa* (*Roman hist.*): a direct vote of the whole nation or of the people of a district on a special point: an ascertainment of general opinion on any matter. —*adj.* **plebisc'itary.** [Partly through Fr. *plébiscite*—L. *plēbiscitum*—*plēbs, scitum,* decree—*sciscěre,* to vote for.]

**plebs,** *plebz, n.* one of the two divisions of the Roman people, originally the less privileged politically.—See Also **plebeian.** [L. *plēbs, plēbis.*]

**Plecoptera,** *ple-kop'tǝr-ǝ, n.pl.* the stonefly order of insects, with hind-wings folded fanwise.— *adj.* **plecop'terous.** [Gr. *plekein,* plait, *pteron,* wing.]

**Plectognathi,** *plek-tog'nǝ-thī, n.* an order of bony fishes including file-fishes, globe-fishes, cofferfishes, sun-fishes.—*adjs.* **plectognathic** (*-tognath'ik*), **plectog'nathous** (*-nǝ-thǝs*). [Gr. *plektos,* plaited, *gnathos,* a jaw.]

**Plectoptera,** *plek-top'tǝ-rǝ, n.pl.* the mayfly order of insects, otherwise *Ephemeroptera.* [Gr. *plektos,* twisted, *pteron,* a wing.]

**plectrum,** *plek'trǝm, n.* the quill or other form of instrument for plucking the strings of the ancient Greek lyre or other musical instrument: a pointed device held in the fingers with which the strings of, e.g. a guitar are struck.—Also

**plec'tre** (*-tǝr*), **plec'tron:**—*pl.* **plec'tra.** [L. *plēctrum*—Gr. *plēktron*—*plēssein,* to strike.]

**pled, pled.** See **plead.**

**pledge,** *plej, n.* something given as a security: a gage: a token or assuring sign: a child, as a token of love or binding obligation: one who becomes surety for another (*obs.*): a hostage (*obs.*): a solemn promise: a friendly sentiment expressed by drinking: a state of being given, or held, as a security.—*v.t.* to give as security: to bind by solemn promise: to vow: to give assurance of: to drink a toast in response to: to drink at the invitation of another: to drink to the health of.—*ns.* **pledgee',** the person to whom a thing is pledged; **pledger, pledgor** (*plej'ǝr*).—**take,** or **sign the pledge,** to give a written promise to abstain from intoxicating liquor. [O.Fr. *plege* (Fr. *pleige*)—L.L. *plevium, plivium,* prob. Gmc.]

**pledget,** *plej'it, n.* a wad of lint, cotton, etc., as for a wound or sore: an oakum string used in caulking. [Origin unknown.]

**Pleiad,** *plī'ad, n.* any one of the seven daughters of Atlas and Pleione, changed into stars (one 'lost' or invisible): a brilliant group of seven, esp. seven Alexandrian tragic poets or (usu. as Fr., **Pléiade,** *plā-ē-äd*) the poets Ronsard, Du Bellay, Baïf, Daurat, and others variously selected.—*pl.* **Plei'ads, Pleiades** (*plī'ǝ-dēz*), a group of six naked-eye and a multitude of telescopic stars in the shoulder of the constellation Taurus. [Gr. *pleias, plēias, -ados,* pl. *-adēs.*]

**plein-air,** *plen'-er', adj.* open-air: attaching importance to painting in the open air.—*n.* **pleinair'ist,** a plein-air painter. [Fr. *en plein air,* in the open air.]

**pleio-, plio-,** *plī'ō, plī-o', * **pleo-,** *plē'ō, plē-o',* in composition, more. [Gr. *pleiōn* or *pleōn,* comp. of *polys,* many, much.]

**Pleiocene.** Same as **Pliocene.**

**pleiochasium,** *plī-ō-kā'zi-ǝm, n.* a cymose inflorescence in which each branch bears more than two lateral branches. [Gr. *chasis,* separation; but cf. **monochasium.**]

**pleiomerous,** *plī-om'ǝr-ǝs, adj.* having more than the normal number of parts.—*n.* **pleiom'ery,** the condition of having more than the normal number. [Gr. *meros,* part.]

**pleiotropic,** *plī-ō-trop'ik, adj.* (of a gene) having an effect simultaneously on more than one character in the offspring.—*n.* **pleiot'ropism.** [Gr. *tropos,* turn.]

**Pleistocene,** *plīs'tō-sēn, adj.* of the geological period following the Pliocene, having the greatest proportion of fossil molluscs of living species.—*n.* the Pleistocene system, period, or strata. [Gr. *pleistos,* most (numerous), *kainos,* recent—from the proportion of living species of molluscs.]

**plenary,** *plē'na-ri, adj.* full: entire: complete: passing through all its stages—opp. to *summary* (*law*): having full powers.—*adv.* **plē'narily.**—*n.* **plē'narty,** the state of a benefice when occupied. —**plenary indulgence,** in the Roman Catholic Church, full or complete remission of temporal penalties to a repentant sinner; **plenary inspiration,** inspiration which excludes all mixture of error; **plenary powers,** full powers to carry out some business or negotiations. [L.L. *plēnārius* —L. *plēnus,* full—*plēre,* to fill.]

**plenilune,** *plen', plēn'i-loon, -lūn, n.* the full moon: time of full moon.—*adj.* **plenilu'nar.** [L. *plēnilūnium*—*plēnus,* full, *lūna,* moon.]

**plenipotence,** *plin-ip'ō-tǝns, n.* complete power— also **plenip'otency.**—*adjs.* **plenip'otent,** having full power; **plenipotential** (*plen-i-pō-ten'shǝl*); **plenipoten'tiary** (*-shǝ-ri, -shyǝ-ri*), having full powers.—*n.* a person invested with full powers, esp. a special ambassador or envoy to some foreign court.—*Arch.*, *coll.*, shortened to **plen'i-po**. [L. *plēnus*, full, *potentia*, power.]

**plenish,** *plen'ish*, *v.t.* to supply, stock: to provide, as a house or farm, with necessary furniture, implements, stock, etc. (*Scot.*).—*n.* **plen'ishing** (*Scot.*), furniture. [O.Fr. *plenir*, *-iss-*—L. *plēnus*, full.]

**plenitude,** *plen'i-tūd*, *n.* fullness: completeness: plentifulness: repletion.—*adj.* **plenitud'inous.** [L. *plēnitūdō*, *-inis*—*plēnus*, full.]

**pleno jure,** *plē'nō jōōr'ē*, *plā'nō yōōr'e*, (L.) with full authority.

**plenty,** *plen'ti*, *n.* a full supply: all that can be needed: abundance.—*adj.* plentiful (*Shak.*): in abundance.—*adv.* (*coll.*) abundantly.—*adj.* **plenteous** (*plen'tyэs*), fully sufficient: abundant: fruitful: well provided: rich: giving plentifully.—*adv.* **plen'teously.**—*n.* **plen'teousness.**—*adj.* **plen'tiful,** copious: abundant: yielding abundance.—*adv.* **plen'tifully.**—*ns.* **plen'tifulness**; **plen'titude** (a mistake or misprint for **plenitude**).—**horn of plenty** (see **cornucopia**). [O.Fr. *plente*—L. *plēnitās*, *-ātis*—*plēnus*, full.]

**plenum,** *plē'nэm*, *n.* a space completely filled with matter—opposed to *vacuum*: a full assembly. —*n.* **plē'nist,** one who believes all space to be a plenum.—**plenum ventilation** (*archit.*), an air-conditioning system in which the air propelled into a building is maintained at a higher pressure than the atmosphere. [L. *plēnum* (*spatium*), full (space).]

**pleo-.** See **pleio-.**

**pleochroism,** *plē-ok'rō-izm*, *n.* the property in some crystals of transmitting different colours in different directions.—*adj.* **pleochroic** (*plē-ō-krō'ik*). [Gr. *chroā*, colour.]

**pleomorphic,** *plē-ō-mör'fik*, *adj.* polymorphic.— Also **pleomor'phous.**—*n.* **pleomorph'ism.**

**pleon,** *plē'on*, *n.* the abdomen of a crustacean, bearing the swimming legs.—*n.* **ple'opod,** a swimming leg. [Gr. *pleōn*, swimming, pr.p. of *plēein*.]

**pleonasm,** *plē'o-nazm*, *n.* redundancy, esp. of words: a redundant expression.—*ns.* **plē'onast,** one who is given to pleonasm; **ple'onaste** (Fr. *pléonaste*), a dark green to black magnesia-iron spinel (from its multitude of faces).—*adjs.* **pleonas'tic,** *-al.*—*adv.* **pleonas'tically.** [Gr. *pleonasmos*—*pleōn*, more.]

**pleroma,** *pli-rō'mэ*, *n.* fullness: abundance: in Gnosticism, divine being, including all aeons (*q.v.*) which emanate from it.—*adj.* **pleromatic** (*-mat'ik*). [Gr. *plērōma*—*plērēs*, full.]

**plerome,** *plē'rōm*, (*bot.*) *n.* the central part of the apical meristem. [Gr. *plērōma*, filling.]

**plerophory,** *plē-rof'э-ri*, *n.* full conviction.—Also **pleropho'ria.** [Gr. *plērŏphŏriā*.]

**plesh,** *plesh*, (*Spens.*) *n.* a plash, a pool. [plash (2).]

**plesiosaur,** *plē'si-ō-sör*, *n.* a great Mesozoic fossil Sauropterygian reptile (Plesiosaurus or kindred genus) with long neck, short tail, and four flippers.—*adj.* **plesiosaur'ian.** [Gr. *plēsios*, near, *sauros*, lizard.]

**plessor, plessimeter,** etc. See **plexor,** etc.

**plethora,** *pleth'эr-э*, sometimes *pli-thō'rэ*, *-thō'*, *n.* excessive fullness of blood: over-fullness in any way.—*adjs.* **plethoric** (*pli-thor'ik*; sometimes *pleth'эr-ik*), **plethor'ical.**—*adv.* **plethor'ically.** [Gr. *plēthōrā*, fullness—*pleos*, full.]

**pleugh,** *plōō*, *plōōhh*, *n.* Scots form of plough.— Also **pleuch.**

**pleura,** *plōō'rэ*, *n.* a delicate serous membrane that covers the lung and lines the cavity of the chest: a side-piece, esp. pleuron:—*pl.* **pleu'rae** (*-rē*). —*adj.* **pleu'ral.**—*ns.* **pleurapoph'ysis,** a lateral process of a vertebra, with the morphological character of a rib: a rib:—*pl.* **pleurapoph'yses;** **pleurisy** (*plōō'ri-si*), inflammation of the pleura; **pleu'risy-root,** an American Asclepias (*A. tuberosa*) reputed as a diaphoretic and expectorant.

—*adjs.* **pleurit'ic,** *-al,* of, affected with, or causing pleurisy.—*n.* a sufferer from pleurisy.—*ns.* **pleuri'tis,** pleurisy; **pleurodynia** (*plōō-rō-din'i-э*; Gr. *odynē*, pain), neuralgia of the chest-wall; **pleu'ron,** the side-wall of a somite, esp. of an insect's thorax:—*pl.* **pleu'ra.**—**pleuro-pneumō'nia,** pleurisy combined with pneumonia: a contagious disease of cattle, caused by a filterable virus, characterised by pleurisy and pneumonia. [Gr. *pleurā* and *pleuron*, rib, side.]

**Pleuronectes,** *plōō-rō-nek'tēz*, *n.* the plaice genus, giving name to the family **Pleuronec'tidae.** [Gr. *pleurā*, side, *nektēs*, a swimmer.]

**plexor,** *pleks'эr*, **plessor,** *ples'эr*, *ns.* a percussion hammer.—*ns.* **plexim'eter, plessim'eter,** a small plate to receive the tap in examination by percussion.—*adjs.* **pleximet'ric, plessimet'ric.**—*ns.* **plexim'etry, plessim'etry.** [Gr. *plēxis,* a stroke, *plēssein,* to strike.]

**plexus,** *pleks'эs*, *n.* a network:—*pl.* **plex'uses,** or **plex'us** (L. *plexūs*).—*n.* **plex'ure,** an interweaving. [L. *plexus*, *-ūs*, a weaving.]

**pliable,** *plī'э-bl*, *adj.* easily bent or folded: flexible: adaptable: easily persuaded: yielding to influence.—*ns.* **pliabil'ity, pli'ableness.**—*adv.* **pli'ably.** —*ns.* **pli'ancy, pli'antness.**—*adj.* **pli'ant,** bending easily: flexible: tractable: easily influenced: perh. suitable, perh. of compliant mood (*Shak.*). —*adv.* **pli'antly.** [See **ply.**]

**plica,** *plī'kэ*, *n.* a fold: plica Polonica:—*pl.* **pli'cae** (*-sē*).—*adjs.* **pli'cate** (or *-kāt*), *-d,* folded fanwise, plaited.—*v.t.* **pli'cate** (also *pli-kāt'*, *plik-āt'*), to plait.—*adv.* **pli'cately.**—*ns.* **plicā'tion, plicature** (*plik'*), act of folding: state of being folded: a fold.—**plica Polonica,** a matted condition of the hair, with an adhesive secretion, a parasitic fungus, and vermin, formerly prevalent in Poland. [L. *plīca*, a fold.]

**plied, plier, pliers, plies.** See **ply.**

**plight,** *plīt*, *n.* risk (*obs.*): pledge: engagement: promise.—*v.t.* to pledge:—*pa.p.* **plight'ed,** also **plight.**—*n.* **plight'er.**—*adj.* **plight'ful,** grievous. [O.E. *pliht*, risk; *plēon*, to risk; cf. Du. *plicht*, Ger. *pflicht*, an obligation.]

**plight,** *plīt*, *n.* a fold (*Spens.*): a plait: mode of plaiting: condition, trim: evil state: good condition (*arch.*): mood: array (*Spens.*).—*v.t.* (*obs.*) to plait, weave, fold, enfold:—*pa.p.* **plight'ed,** also (*Spens.*) **plight.**—*adj.* **plight'ed,** plaited: involved (*Shak.*). [Assimilated in spelling to the foregoing, but derived from O.Fr. *plite* —L. *plicāre*, *plicitum*; see **plait.**]

**plim,** *plim*, (*dial.*) *v.t.* and *v.i.* to swell. [Perh. conn. with **plump.**]

**plimsoll,** *plim'sэl*, *-sol,* *n.* a rubber-soled canvas shoe.—**Plimsoll line or mark,** a ship's load-line, or set of load-lines for different waters and conditions, required by the Merchant Shipping Act (1876) passed at the instance of Samuel Plimsoll (1824-98).

**plinth,** *plinth*, *n.* the square block under the base of a column: a block serving as a pedestal: a flat-faced projecting band at the bottom of a wall: a similar projecting base in furniture. [L. *plinthus*, Gr. *plinthos*, a brick, squared stone, plinth.]

**Pliocene,** *plī'ō-sēn*, (*geol.*) *adj.* of the Tertiary period following the Miocene, and having a greater proportion of molluscan species now living.—*n.* the Pliocene system, period, or strata. [Gr. *pleiōn*, greater, more numerous, *kainos*, recent.]

**Pliohippus,** *plī-ō-hip'эs*, *n.* a Miocene and Pliocene genus of fossil horses. [Gr. *hippos*, horse.]

**pliskie,** *plis'ki*, (*Scot.*) *n.* condition or plight: a mischievous trick. [Origin unknown.]

**plissé,** *plē-sā*, (Fr.) (of a fabric) chemically treated to produce a shirred effect.

**plod,** *plod*, *v.i.* to walk heavily and laboriously: to study or work on steadily and laboriously.

—*v.t.* to traverse or make by slow and heavy walking:—*pr.p.* **plodd'ing**; *pa.t.* and *pa.p.* **plodd'-ed.**—*n.* a heavy walk: a thud.—*n.* **plodd'er**, one who plods on: a dull, heavy, laborious man: one who gets on more by sheer toil than by inspiration.—*adj.* and *n.* **plodd'ing.**—*adv.* **plodd'ingly.** [Prob. imit.]

**plod**, *plod*, (*obs.*) *v.t.* to plot. [plot, by confusion with foregoing.]

**plong**, **plonge**, **plongd**, Spenserian spellings of **plunge**, **plunged**.

**plonk**, **plonker.** See **plunk**.

**plonk**, *plongk*, *n.* (orig. *Austr. slang*), wine, esp. cheap. [Ety. dub.]

**plop**, *plop*, *n.* the sound of a small object falling vertically into water: the sound of the movement of small bodies of water: the sound of a cork coming out of a bottle, or of a bursting bubble.—*adv.* with a plop: plump.—*v.i.* to make the sound of a plop: to plump into water.—*v.t.* to set with a plop:—*pr.p.* **plopp'ing**; *pa.p.* **plopped.** [Imit.]

**plosive**, *plō'siv, -ziv*, (*phon.*) *adj.*, *n.* explosive.—*n.* **plo'sion** (*phon.*), explosion.

**plot**, *plot*, *n.* a small piece of ground: a spot or small area on any surface (*obs.*): a ground-plan of a building, plan of a field, etc.: the story or scheme of connected events running through a play, novel, etc.: a secret scheme, usually in combination, to bring about something, often illegal or evil, a conspiracy: a stratagem or secret contrivance.—*v.t.* to lay out in plots, dispose: to make a plan of: to represent on or by a graph: to conspire or lay plans for.—*v.i.* to conspire:—*pr.p.* **plott'ing**; *pa.p.* **plott'ed.**—*adjs.* **plot'ful**; **plot'less.**—*n.* **plott'er.** —*n.* and *adj.* **plott'ing.**—*adv.* **plott'ingly.**—*adj.* **plot'-proof**, safe from any danger by plots.— **plott'ing-paper**, paper ruled in squares for graph-drawing. [O.E. *plot*, a patch of ground; influenced by (or partly from) Fr. *complot*, a conspiracy; cf. **plat** (2).]

**plot**, *plot, plōt*, (*Scot.*) *v.t.* to dip or steep in very hot water: to scald and pluck: to fleece.—*n.* **plott'ie**, **plott'y**, a spiced hot drink, as mulled wine. [Cf. M.Du. and Flem. *ploten*, to pluck.]

**plotter**, *plot'ər.* Same as **plouter**.

**plough**, *plow*, *n.* an instrument for turning up the soil in ridges and furrows: a joiner's plane for making grooves: agriculture(*fig.*): a plough-team: ploughed land: (*cap.*) seven stars of the Great Bear.—*v.t.* to turn up with the plough: to make furrows or ridges in: to make with a plough: to put or render with a plough: to tear, force, or cut a way through: to furrow: to wrinkle: to reject in an examination (*university slang*): to fail in (a subject; *university slang*).—*v.i.* to work with a plough: to fail (*slang*).—*adj.* **plough'able.**—*ns.* **plough'er**; **plough'ing.**—*adv.* and *adj.* **plough'wise**, as in ploughing.—**plough'boy**, a boy who drives or guides horses in ploughing; **plough'gate** (*Scots hist.*), an undetermined or variable unit of land, by later writers taken as about 50 English acres, but earlier much more: a quantity of land of the extent of 100 acres Scots; **plough'-iron**, the coulter, the share, or other iron part of a plough; **plough'-jogger** (*facet.*), a ploughman; **plough'land**, land suitable for tillage: as much land as could be tilled with one plough (with a proportionate amount of pasture)—a carucate or eight oxgangs (*hist.*); **plough'man**, a man who ploughs:—*pl.* **plough'men**; **Plough Monday**, an old ploughman's festival, the Monday after Twelfth Day, supposed to mark the resumption of work after the holidays; **plough'-share** (O.E. *scear*, ploughshare—*scieran*, to shear, cut), the detachable part of a plough that cuts the under surface of the sod from the ground: a bird's pygostyle (also **ploughshare**

bone); **plough'-staff**, a tool for clearing a plough of earth, etc.; **plough'-stilt**, a plough-handle; **plough'-tail**, the end of a plough where the handles are: farm-labour (*fig.*); **plough'-tree**, a plough-handle; **plough'wright**, one who makes and mends ploughs.—**plough a lonely furrow**, to be separated from one's former friends and associates and go one's own way; **plough back** (*fig.*), to reinvest (profits of a business) in that business; **plough in**, to cover with earth by ploughing; **plough the sands**, to work in vain or to no purpose; **put one's hand to the plough**, to begin an undertaking. [Late O.E. *plōh*, *plōg*, a ploughland; cf. O.N. *plōgr*.]

**plouter**, **plowter**, *plow'tər*, (*Scot.*) *v.i.* to dabble in liquid: to potter.—*n.* a paddling or dabbling. —Also **plott'er.** [Prob. imit.]

**plover**, *pluv'ər*, *n.* a general name for birds of the family (Charadriidae) to which the lapwing and dotterel belong: extended to some related birds: a dupe (*old slang*): a prostitute (*old slang*).—*adj.* **plov'ery**, abounding in plovers.— **plover's egg**, a lapwing's egg, or substitute. [Fr. *pluvier*—L. *pluvia*, rain; possibly from their restlessness before rain; cf. Ger. *regenpfeifer*, lit. rain-piper.]

**plow**, *plow* (chiefly American). Same as **plough**.

**ploy**, *ploi*, *n.* an employment, doings, affair, frolic, escapade, engagement for amusement: a method or procedure used to achieve a particular result: a manoeuvre in a game, conversation, etc. [Prob. *employ*.]

**pluck**, *pluk*, *v.t.* to pull off, out, or away: to pull forcibly: to snatch away: to rescue: to bring (down), humble (*arch.*): to pull: to tug: to twitch: to strip, as of feathers: to despoil, fleece: to fail, refuse a pass to, in an examination—from the custom of *plucking* (a piece of silk at the back of) *the proctor's gown*, in protest (*slang*).—*v.i.* to make a pulling or snatching movement.—*n.* a single act of plucking: the heart, liver, and lungs of an animal—hence heart, courage, spirit.—*adj.* **plucked**, subjected to plucking: having pluck.—*n.* **pluck'er.**—*adv.* **pluck'ily.**—*n.* **pluck'iness.**—*adj.* **pluck'y**, having courageous spirit and pertinacity.—**pluck off** (*Shak.*), to abate, come down the scale; **pluck up**, to pull out by the roots: to summon up, as courage: to gather strength or spirit. [O.E. *pluccian*; akin to Du. *plukken*, Ger. *pflücken*.]

**pluff**, *pluf*, (*Scot.* or *dial.*) *n.* a puff: a mild explosion: a shot: a powder-puff.—*v.t.* to puff: to shoot.—*v.i.* to go off with a puff: to rise, as a cake.—*adj.* **pluff'y**, puffed up: fluffy. [Imit.]

**plug**, *plug*, *n.* a peg stopping, or for stopping, a hole: a bung: a stopper: a mechanism releasing the flow of water in a water-closet: filling for a tooth: volcanic rock stopping a vent: a fitting for a socket for giving electrical connection: a piece of wood inserted in a wall to take nails: a fire-plug: a sparking-plug: a plug-hat (*slang*): a blow or punch: a compressed cake of tobacco: a piece of it cut for chewing: a worn-out horse: a book that will not sell: a piece of favourable publicity, esp. one incorporated in other material (*coll.*): anything worn-out or useless: a dogged plodding. —*v.t.* to stop with a plug or as a plug: to insert a plug in: to insert as a plug: to shoot (*slang*): to punch with the fist (*slang*): to force into familiarity by persistent repetition (*slang*): to din into the ears of the public.—*v.i.* (*slang*) to go on doggedly:—*pr.p.* **plugg'ing**; *pa.t.* and *pa.p.* **plugged.**—*ns.* **plugg'er**, one who plugs in any sense: that which plugs, esp. a dentist's instrument; **plugg'ing**, the act of stopping with a plug, or punching (*slang*), or promoting (*slang*): material of which a plug is made.—**plug'-hat** (*U.S.*), a top-hat; **plug'-ug'ly** (*U.S.*), a street ruffian.—**plug in**, to complete an electric circuit by inserting a plug.—*adj.* **plug′-in**. [App. Du. *plug*, a bung, a peg; cf. Sw. *plugg*, a peg, Ger. *pflock*.]

**plum**, *plum, n.* a drupe or stone-fruit, or the tree producing it (*Prunus domestica* or kindred species) of the rose family: extended to various fruits and trees more or less similar (as *sapodilla plum, coco-plum, date-plum*): a raisin as a substitute for the true plum: a sugar-plum: a big stone embedded in concrete: something choice that may be extracted (sometimes in reminiscence of Jack Horner) or attained to, as one of the best passages in a book, one of the prizes of a career, or (*U.S.*) a government office as a reward of services, etc.: (formerly) a sum of £100,000: its possessor.—*adj.* **plumm′y**, full of plums: plum-like: desirable, profitable: (of voice) too rich and resonant.—**plum′-bloss′om**; **plum′-cake**, a cake containing raisins, currants, etc.—*n.* and *adj.* **plum′-colour**, dark purple.—**plum′cot**, Luther Burbank's hybrid between *plum* and *apricot*; **plumdamas** (-dä′mᴐs; *Scot.*), a damson; **plum′-duff**, a flour-pudding boiled with raisins; **plum′-porr′idge**, an antiquated dish, of porridge with plums, raisins, etc.; **plum′-pudd′ing**, a national English dish made of flour and suet, with raisins, currants, and various spices; **plum′-stone**; **plum′-tree**. [O.E. *plūme* —L. *prūnum*; cf. Gr. *prou*(*m*)*non*.]

**plumage**, *plōō′ij, n.* a natural covering of feathers: feathers collectively.—*adj.* **plum′aged**. [Fr.,—*plume*—L. *plūma*, a feather, down.]

**plumb**, *plum, n.* a heavy mass, as of lead, hung on a string to show the vertical line, or for other purpose: verticality: a sounding lead, plummet.—*adj.* vertical: level, true (*cricket*): sheer, thorough-going, out-and-out.—*adv.* vertically: precisely: utterly (esp. *U.S.*).—*v.t.* to test by a plumb-line: to make vertical: to sound as by a plumb-line: to pierce the depth of, fathom, by eye or understanding: to weight with lead: to seal with lead: to do or furnish the plumber-work of.—*v.i.* to hang vertically: to work as a plumber.—*n.* **plumbate** (*plum′bāt*), a salt of plumbic acid.—*adj.* **plumbeous** (*plum′bi-ᴐs*), leaden: lead-coloured: lead-glazed.—*ns.* **plumber** (*plum′ᴐr*), orig. a worker in lead: now one who instals and mends pipes, cisterns, and other fittings for supply of water and gas and for household drainage; **plumb′ery**, plumber-work: a plumber's workshop.—*adjs.* **plumbic** (*plum′bik*), due to lead: of quadrivalent lead; **plumbiferous** (-*bif′*), yielding or containing lead.—*ns.* **plumbing** (*plum′ing*), the operation of making plumb: the craft of working in lead: the work of a plumber; **plum′bism** (-*bizm*), lead poisoning; **plum′bite** (-*bīt*), a salt of the weak acid lead hydroxide.—*adjs.* **plumb′less**, incapable of being sounded; **plumbous** (*plum′bᴐs*), of bivalent lead.—**plumb′-bob**, a weight at the end of a plumb-line; **plumb′er-work**; **plumbic acid**, an acid of which lead dioxide is the anhydride; **plumb′-line**, a line to which a bob is attached to show the vertical line: a vertical line: a plummet.—*adj.* **plumbosol′vent** (better **plumbisol′vent**), able to dissolve lead.—**plumb′-rule**, a board with a plumb-line and bob, for testing the verticality of walls, etc. [Fr. *plomb* and its source L. *plumbum*, lead.]

**Plumbago**, *plum-bā′gō, n.* a Mediterranean and tropical genus of ornamental plants (some cultivated) giving name to the **Plumbaginaceae** (-*baj-i-nā′si-ē*), a family of salt-steppe and seaside plants including sea-pink and sea-lavender, akin to the primrose family.—*adj.* **plumbaginaceous** (-*baj-i-nā′shᴐs*). [L. *plumbāgō*, Pliny's translation of the Greek name *molybdaina*, lead, lead ore, the plant *Plumbago* (from its blue flowers).]

**plumbago**, *plum-bā′gō, n.* graphite.—*adj.* **plum-**

**baginous** (-*baj′i-nᴐs*). [L. *plumbāgō, -inis*—*plumbum*, lead.]

**plumbate**, etc., **plumber**, etc. See under **plumb**.

**plumber-block.** See **plummer-block**.

**plume**, *plōōm, n.* a feather: a large showy feather: the vane of a feather: a bunch or tuft of feathers: a feather, or anything similar, used as an ornament, symbol, crest, etc.: a feather as a token of honour: the plumule of a seed: any feathery structure (*obs.*).—*v.t.* to preen: (*refl.*) to pride, take credit to (with *on*; *fig.*): to adorn with plumes: to set as a plume (*Milt.*): to strip of feathers.—*n.* **plumassier** (*ploo-ma-sēr′*), a worker in feathers: a feather-seller.—*adjs.* **plum′ate**, feathered: feathery; **plumed**, feathered: adorned with a plume: plucked (*obs.*).—*adj.* **plume′less.**—*ns.* **plume′let**, a plumule: a little tuft; **plum′ery**, plumes collectively.—*adjs.* **plumigerous** (-*ij′ᴐ-rᴐs*), plumaged; **plu′miped**, having feathered feet.—*n.* **plu′mist**, a feather-dresser.—*adjs.* **plu′mose**, **plu′mous**, feathery: plume-like; **plu′my**, covered or adorned with down or plume: like a plume.—**plume′-bird**, a long-tailed bird of paradise; **plume′-grass**, a tall grass (*Erianthus*) akin to sugar-cane, with great silky panicles, grown for ornament; **plume′-moth**, any moth of the families Pterophoridae and Orneodidae, with deeply cleft wings.—*adj.* **plume′-pluckt** (*Shak.*), stripped of plumes, humbled. [O.Fr.,—L. *plūma*, a small soft feather.]

**plummer-block**, *plum′ᴐr-blok, n.* a metal frame or case for holding the end of a revolving shaft. [Origin unknown.]

**plummet**, *plum′it, n.* leaden or other weight, esp. on a plumb-line, sounding-line, or fishing-line: plumb-rule.—*v.t.* to fathom, sound.—*v.i.* to plunge head-long. [O.Fr. *plomet*, dim. of *plomb*, lead; see **plumb**.]

**plump**, *plump, v.i.* to fall or drop into liquid, esp. vertically, passively, resoundingly, without much disturbance: to flop down: to rain suddenly and heavily (esp. *Scot.*): to come suddenly or with a burst: to give all one's votes without distribution: to choose, opt, decisively or abruptly (with *for*).—*v.t.* to plunge, souse: to fling down or let fall flat or heavily: to blurt: to strike or shoot (*slang*).—*n.* the sound or act of plumping: a sudden heavy fall of rain (esp. *Scot.*): a blow (*slang*).—*adj.* and *adv.* with a plump: in a direct line: downright: in plain language: without hesitation, reserve, or qualification.—*n.* **plump′er**, a plump fall or blow: an undistributed vote that could have been divided: one who gives all his votes to one candidate or option: a downright lie (*slang*): anything very big of its kind, a whacker (*slang*).—*adv.* **plump′ly**. [L.G. *plumpen* or Du. *plompen*, to plump into water; prob. influenced by **plumb** and **plump** (2).]

**plump**, *plump, adj.* pleasantly fat and rounded: well filled out.—*v.t.* and *v.i.* to make or grow plump: to swell or round.—*v.i.* (*rare*) **plump′en**.—*n.* **plump′er**, a cork ball kept in the mouth, or other device to round the cheeks.—*adj.* **plump′ish**.—*adv.* **plump′ly**.—*n.* **plump′ness**.—*adj.* **plump′y**, **plump′ie** (*Shak.*), plump. [App. the same word as Du. *plomp*, blunt, L.G. *plump*.]

**plump**, *plump, n.* a cluster: a clump, as of trees, spearmen, waterfowl. [Origin unknown.]

**plumula**, *plōōm′ū-lᴐ, n.* a plumule.—*pl.* **plum′ulae** (-*lē*).—*adjs.* **plumulā′ceous**, **plum′ular.**—*n.* **Plumulā′ria**, a genus of Hydrozoa forming feathery colonies.—*n.* and *adj.* **plumulā′rian.**—*adj.* **plum′-ulate**, downy.—*n.* **plum′ule**, a little feather or plume: a down feather: the embryo shoot in a seed: a scent-giving scale on the fore-wing of some male butterflies.—*adj.* **plum′ulose**. [L. *plūmula*, dim. of *plūma*, a feather, down-feather.]

**plunder**, *plun′dᴐr, v.t.* to carry off the goods of

by force: to pillage: to carry off as booty: to carry off booty from.—*v.i.* to pillage, carry off plunder.—*n.* pillage: booty: personal or household goods (*U.S.*).—*ns.* **plun′derage,** the stealing of goods on board ship; **plun′derer.**—*adj.* **plun′derous.** [Ger. *plündern,* to pillage—*plunder,* household stuff, now trash.]

**plunge,** *plunj, v.t.* to put or thrust with suddenness under the surface of a liquid, or into the midst of, the thick of, or the substance of, anything: to immerse.—*v.i.* to fling oneself or rush impetuously, esp. into water, downhill, or into danger or discourse: to turn suddenly and steeply downward: to fire down upon an enemy from a height: to gamble or squander recklessly: to pitch as a ship: to pitch suddenly forward and throw up the hindlegs.—*n.* act of plunging.—*n.* **plung′er,** one who plunges: part of a mechanism with a plunging movement, as the solid piston of a force-pump: a suction instrument for cleaning blockages in pipes: a cavalryman (*obs. mil. slang*): a reckless gambler or squanderer.—*adj.* and *n.* **plung′ing.**—**plunge bath,** a bath large enough to immerse the whole body; **plunging neckline,** (in woman's dress) a neckline which is cut low.—**take the plunge,** to commit oneself definitely after hesitation. [O.Fr. *plonger*—L. *plumbum,* lead.]

**plunk,** *plungk,* **plonk,** *plongk, v.t.* to twang: to put down, etc., so as to make a hollow or metallic sound.—*v.i.* to plump.—Also *n., adv., interj.* —*n.* **plunk′er, plonk′er,** a large marble. [Imit.]

**pluperfect,** *plōō-pûr′fekt, -fikt,* or *plōō′, (gram.) adj.* denoting that an action happened before some other past action referred to.—*n.* the pluperfect tense: a pluperfect verb or form. [L. *plūs quam perfectum* (*tempus*) more than perfect (tense).]

**plural,** *plōōr′l, adj.* numbering more than one: more than onefold: expressing more than one, or, where dual is recognised, more than two (*gram.*). —*n.* (*gram.*) the plural number: a plural word form.—*n.* pluralisā′tion, **-z-.**—*v.t.* **plur′alise, -ize,** to make plural.—*v.i.* to hold two or more benefices or offices simultaneously.—*ns.* **plur′alism,** plurality: the holding by one person of more than one office at once, esp. ecclesiastical livings: a system allowing this: a philosophy that recognises more than one principle of being (opp. to *monism*) or more than two (opp. to *monism* and *dualism*): a (condition of) society in which different ethnic, etc., groups preserve their own customs; **plur′alist,** one who holds more than one office at one time: a believer in pluralism.—*adj.* **pluralist′ic.**—*n.* **plurality** (*-al′i-ti*), the state or fact of being plural: numerousness: a plural number: the greater number, more than half: a majority over any other— distinguished from *majority,* which is used for an absolute majority or majority over all others combined (*U.S.*): the holding of more than one benefice at one time: a living held by a pluralist.—*adv.* **plu′rally.**—**plural society,** one in which pluralism is found; **plural vote,** power of voting in more than one constituency, or more than once in one. [L. *plūrālis*—*plūs, plūris,* more.]

**pluri-,** *plōōr′i-,* in composition, several: usu. more than two.—*adj.* **plurilit′eral** (*Heb. gram.*), containing more letters than three; **pluriloc′ular,** multilocular.—*ns.* **plurip′ara,** a multipara; **pluripres′ence,** presence in more places than one at the same time.—*adjs.* **plurise′rial, -riate,** in several rows. [L. *plūs, plūris,* more.]

**plurisie,** *plōōr′i-si,* (*Shak.*) *n.* superabundance. [L. *plūs, plūris,* more; confused with **pleurisy.**]

**plus,** *plus,* (*math.* and *coll.*) *prep.* with the addition of.—*adj.* positive: additional: having an adverse handicap.—*n.* an addition: a surplus: a positive quality or term: the sign (also **plus sign**) of addition or positivity (+); opposed to *minus* (−).—**plus′(s)age,** an extra amount.— **plus strain** (*bot.*), one of the two strains in heterothallism. [L. *plūs,* more.]

**plus-fours,** *plus′-fōrz′, -förz, n.pl.* baggy knickerbockers or knickerbocker suit. [**plus, four;** from the four additional inches of cloth required.]

**plush,** *plush, n.* a fabric with a longer and more open pile than velvet: (in *pl.*) footman's breeches.—*adj.* of plush: pretentiously luxurious (also **plushy**). [Fr. *pluche* for *peluche*—L. *pīla,* hair; cf. **pile** (3).]

**pluteus,** *plōō′ti-əs, n.* a sea-urchin or brittle-star larva, shaped like a many-legged easel.—*adj.* **plu′teal.** [L. *pluteus,* a shed, boarding, desk.]

**Pluto,** *plōōt′ō, n.* the Greek god of the underworld: a planet beyond Neptune, discovered 1930.—*adjs.* **Pluto′nian,** of Pluto: of the underworld; **Plutonic** (*-ton′ik*), of Pluto: hypogene, deep-seated, relating to, or formed under conditions of, subterranean heat (*geol.*): Plutonist. —*ns.* **Plutonism** (*plōō′tan-izm*); **Plu′tonist** (*hist. of geol.*), a Vulcanist; **plutō′nium,** the element (Pu) of atomic number 94, named as next after neptunium (93), as the planet Pluto is beyond Neptune. [L. *Plūtō, -ōnis*—Gr. *Ploutōn, -ōnos,* Pluto.]

**Plutus,** *plōō′tas, n.* the Greek god of wealth.—*ns.* **plutocracy** (*plōō-tok′rə-si*), government by the wealthy: a ruling body or class of rich men; **plutocrat** (*plōō′tō-krat*), one who is powerful because of his wealth.—*adj.* **plutocrat′ic.**—*ns.* **pluto-democ′racy,** a wealth-dominated democracy; **plutol′atry** (Gr. *latreiā,* worship), worship of wealth; **plutol′ogist, pluton′omist; plutol′ogy, pluton′omy,** political economy. [L. *Plūtus,* Gr. *Ploutos* (Gr. *ploutos,* wealth).]

**pluvial,** *plōō′vi-al, adj.* of or by rain: rainy.—*n.* (*lit.* a rain-cloak) a cope or ceremonial mantle (*hist.*).—*n.* **pluviom′eter,** a rain-gauge.—*adjs.* **pluviomet′ric, -al.**—*n.* **Pluviôse** (*plü-vē-ōz′*; Fr.), the fifth month of the French Revolutionary calendar, about 20th January to 18th February. —*adj.* **plu′vious,** rainy. [L. *pluvia,* rain.]

**ply,** *plī, n.* a fold: a layer or thickness: a layer of hard rock or of hard or soft in alternation (*min.*): a bend: a bent or set: a strand: condition, esp. good condition (*Scot.*):—*pl.* **plies.** —*v.t.* and *v.i.* to bend or fold:—*pr.p.* **ply′ing;** *pa.t.* and *pa.p.* **plied;** *3rd pers. sing.* **plies.**—*n.* **pli′er,** one who plies: (in *pl.*) small pincers for bending or cutting wire, etc.—**ply′wood,** boarding made of thin layers of wood glued together, the grain of each at right-angles to that of the next. [(O.)Fr. *pli,* a fold, *plier,* to fold—L. *plicāre.*]

**ply,** *plī, v.t.* to work at steadily: to use or wield diligently or vigorously: to keep supplying or assailing (with): to importune: to row, sail, over habitually.—*v.i.* to work steadily: to make regular journeys over a route: to be in attendance for hire: to beat against the wind: to make one's way, direct one's course:—*pr.p.* **ply′ing;** *pa.t.* and *pa.p.* **plied;** *3rd pers. sing.* **plies.**—*n.* **pli′er,** one who plies: a trader (*obs.*): a tout (*obs.*). [Aphetic, from **apply.**]

**Plymouth,** *plim′əth, n.* a port in Devon: a port named after it in Massachusetts, with the supposed landing-place of the Pilgrims (Plymouth Rock).—*ns.* **Plym′outhism; Plym′outhist; Plym′outhite, Plymouth Brother,** one of the **Plymouth Brethren,** a religious sect, originating at Plymouth *c.* 1830, out of a reaction against High Church principles and against a dead formalism associated with unevangelical doctrine; **Plymouth Rock,** an American breed of poultry: a nickname for a Plymouth Brother.

**pneuma,** *nū′ma, n.* breath: spirit, soul: a neume. —*n.* **pneumathode** (*nū′ma-thōd;* Gr. *hodos,* a way), a respiratory opening in plants.—*adjs.*

pneumatic (-*mat'ik*), relating to air or gases: containing or inflated with air: worked or driven by air: spiritual; pneumat'ical (*rare*).—*adv.* pneumat'ically.—*ns.* pneumaticity (*nū-mə-tis'i-ti*), the condition of having air-spaces; pneumat'ics (treated as *sing.*), the science of the properties of gases: pneumatology.—*adj.* pneumatolog'ical.—*ns.* pneumatol'ogist; pneumatol'ogy, the theory of spirits or spiritual beings: psychology (*arch.*): the doctrine of the Holy Spirit (*theol.*): pneumatics (*arch.*); pneumatol'ysis (Gr. *lysis*, solution), the destructive action of hot vapours of a magma of igneous rock.—*adj.* pneumatolyt'ic.—*ns.* pneumatom'eter, an instrument for measuring the quantity of air breathed or the force of breathing; pneu'matophore (or -*mat'*), an upward-growing respiratory root in swamp plants.—pneumatic trough, a vessel with a perforated shelf, for filling gas-jars over a liquid. [Gr. *pneuma, -atos*, breath—*pneein*.]

pneum(o)-, pneumon(o)-, *nū'm*(o)-, -*mon*-(o)-, in composition, lung.—pneumoconiosis (*nū-mō-kō-ni-ō'sis*; Gr. *konia*, dust), pneumokonio'sis, pneumonokonio'sis, any of various diseases caused by habitually inhaling mineral or metallic dust, as in coal-mining.—*adj.* pneumogas'tric (Gr. *gastēr*, belly), pertaining to the lungs and stomach.—*n.* vagus.—*ns.* pneumonec'tomy, surgical removal of lung tissue; pneumō'nia, inflammation of the lung.—*adj.* pneumonic (-*mon'*), pertaining to the lungs.—*n.* a medicine for lung diseases.—*n.* pneumoni'tis, pneumonia; pneu'monoultramicroscopicsil'icovolcanoconio'sis, a form of pneumoconiosis caused by very fine silicate or quartz dust.—pneumonia blouse, a low-necked blouse, once an object of dread. [Gr. *pneumōn, -onos*, lung—*pneein*, to breathe.]

Pnyx, (*p*)*niks, n.* the meeting-place of the ancient Athenian assembly. [Gr. *pnyx*, gen. *pyknos*, perh. cog. with *pyknos*, crowded.]

Poa, *pō'a, n.* a large genus of grasses, meadow-grass. [Gr. *pŏā*, grass.]

poach, *pōch, v.t.* to cook without the shell in boiling water.—*n.* poach'er, one who poaches eggs: a vessel with hollows for poaching eggs in. [App. Fr. *pocher*, to pocket—*poche*, pouch, the white forming a pocket about the yolk.]

poach, *pōch, v.i.* to intrude on another's preserves in order to pursue or kill game, or upon another's fishing to catch fish: to encroach, esp. on a partner's place or part in a game: to seek an unfair advantage: (*Shak.*, potche) to thrust: to trample in mud: to become trampled and muddy.—*v.t.* to take illegally on another's ground or in another's fishing: to seek or take game or fish illegally on: to take in unfair encroachment: to poke or thrust (*dial.*): to stir up (*dial.*): to trample into holes and mud.—*ns.* poach'er; poach'iness; poach'ing.—*adj.* poach'y, spongy and sodden. [A form of poke (3), or from O.Fr. *pocher*, to poke.]

poaka, *pō-ä'ka*, (*Maori*) a N.Z. bird, one of the stilts.

poake, a Shakespearian spelling of poke (pocket).

pocas palabras, *pō'käs pal-äb'räs*, (Sp.) few words.

pochard, pockard, poker, *pōch'*, *poch'*, *pok'ərd*, *pōk'ər, n.* a red-headed diving-duck (*Nyroca* or *Aythya ferina*), esp. the male, the female being the dunbird. [Origin obscure.]

pochay, *pō'shā*, po'chaise, -*shāz*. See post-chaise (under post).

pochette, *posh-et', n.* a small bag, esp. one carried by women: a pocket note-case or wallet. [Fr., dim. of *poche*, pocket.]

pock, *pok, n.* a small elevation of the skin containing pus, as in smallpox.—*adjs.* pocked; pock'y, marked with pustules: infected with pox: confounded (*obs.*).—pock'mark, pock'pit, the mark, pit, or scar left by a pock.—*adjs.*

pock'marked, pock'pitted. [O.E. *poc*, a pustule; Ger. *pocke*, Du. *pok*; see pox.]

pock, *pok, n.* a Scots form of poke, bag.—pockman'tie, pockmank'y, corrupt forms of portmanteau, influenced by pock; pock-pudding (*pok'-pud'n*), a bag-pudding: a Scottish contemptuous name for a mere Englishman.

pockard. See pochard.

pocket, *pok'it, n.* a little pouch or bag, esp. one attached to a garment or a billiard-table or the cover of a book: a cavity: a rock cavity filled with ore, veinstone, etc.: a portion of the atmosphere differing in pressure or other condition from its surroundings: a small isolated area or patch, as of military resistance, unemployment, etc.: the innermost compartment of a pound-net: stock of money: a bag of wool, etc., containing about ½ sack.—*adj.* for the pocket: of a small size.—*v.t.* to put in one's pocket or a pocket: to appropriate: to take stealthily: to conceal: to enclose: to hem in: to play into a pocket (*billiards*).—*v.i.* to form a pocket: to pucker (*U.S.*):—*pr.p.* pock'eting; *pa.t.* and *pa.p.* pock'eted.—*n.* pock'etful, as much as a pocket will hold:—*pl.* pock'etfuls.—*adj.* pock'etless.—pock'et-book, a notebook: a wallet for papers or money carried in the pocket: a small book for the pocket: a handbag (*U.S.*); pock'etbor'ough (see borough); pock'et-comb, a haircomb for the pocket; pock'et-glass, a small looking-glass for the pocket; pock'et-gopher, any American burrowing rodent of the family Geomyidae, with outward-opening cheek-pouches; pock'et-handk'erchief, a handkerchief for the pocket; pock'et-hole, the opening in a garment giving access to a pocket; pock'et-knife, a knife with one or more blades folding into the handle for the pocket; pock'et-money, money carried for occasional expenses: an allowance, esp. to a boy or girl; pock'et-picking, act or practice of picking the pocket; pock'et-piece, a coin carried to bring luck; pock'et-pis'tol, a pistol for the pocket: a small travelling flask for liquor.—*adj.* pock'et-sized, small enough for the pocket.—in, or out of, pocket, with, or without, money: the richer, or the poorer, by a transaction; pick a person's pocket, to steal from his pocket; pocket an insult, affront, etc., to submit to or put up with it without protest; pocket one's pride, humble oneself to accept a situation. [A.Fr. *pokete* (Fr. *pochette*, dim. of *poche*, pocket).]

poco, *pō'kō*, (It.) little.—*adj.* pococurante (-*kōō-ran'tā*, -*kū-ran'ti*; It. *curante*, pr.p. of *curare*, to care), uninterested: indifferent: nonchalant.—*n.* a habitually uninterested person.—pococurant'ism (-*kū-rant'izm*), pococurant'ist.—poco a poco, little by little.

poculiform, *pok'ū-li-förm, adj.* cup-shaped. [L. *pōculum*, cup.]

pod, *pod, n.* the fruit, or its shell, in peas, beans, and other leguminous plants—the legume: sometimes extended to the siliqua: a silk cocoon: a musk-bag: a paunch.—*v.t.* to shell or hull.—*v.i.* to form pods: to fill as pods:—*pr.p.* podd'ing; *pa.t.* and *pa.p.* podd'ed.—*adj.* podd'y, corpulent. [Origin unknown.]

pod, *pod, n.* a school, esp. of whales or seals. [Origin unknown.]

podagra, *pod-ag'ra*, also *pod', n.* gout, properly in the feet.—*adjs.* podag'ral, podag'ric, -al, pod-ag'rous, gouty. [Gr. *podagrā—pous, podos*, foot, *agrā*, a catching.]

pod(o)-, pod(ō)-, pŏd(ō)-, in composition, foot.—*adjs.* pŏ'dal, podal'ic, of the feet.—*ns.* Podargus (*pō-där'gəs*; Gr. *argos*, inactive—*a-*, neg., *ergon*, work), the typical frogmouth genus of birds; podiatry (*pod-i'ə-tri*; Gr. *iātros, iātros*, physician), treatment of disorders of the foot; podi'atrist; Podocarpus (*pod-ō-kär'pəs*; Gr. *karpos*, fruit), an eastern and southern genus of trees of the yew family; **Podogona** (*-og'ə-na*; Gr. *gonos*, reproductive organ; see **Ricinulei**), the Ricinulei.—*adj.* **podophthalmus** (*-of-thal'mas*; Gr. *ophthalmos*, eye), having eyes on stalks, as many higher crustaceans.—*ns.* **Podophyllum** (*-ō-fil'əm*, *-o'fil-əm*; Gr. *phyllon*, leaf), a genus of the barberry family; **podophyll'in**, a cathartic resin got from its rhizome; **Podostemon** (*-ō-stē'mon*; Gr. *stēmōn*, warp—as if stamen—from the stalk on which the stamens stand), the typical genus of a family of dicotyledons, **Podostemaceae** (*-mā'si-ē*), growing in tropical waterfalls, the vegetative parts more like a thallus than an ordinary flowering plant; **Podura** (*-dū'rə*; Gr. *ourā*, tail), a genus of springtails. [Gr. *pous, podos*, foot.]

**podestà**, *pod-est-tä'*, (*hist.*) *n.* a governor, chief magistrate, or judge in an Italian town. [It. *podestà*—L. *potestās, -ātis*, power.]

**podex**, *pō'deks*, *n.* the rump: the anal region. [L. *pōdex.*]

**podge**, *poj*, **pudge**, *puj, ns.* a squat, fat, and flabby person or thing.—*ns.* **podg'iness, pudg'iness**.—*adjs.* **podg'y, pudg'y**. [Origin obscure.]

**podium**, *pō'di-əm, n.* a continuous pedestal, a stylobate: a platform, dais: a foot or hand (*anat.*): a tube-foot:—*pl.* **pō'dia**.—*adj.* **pō'dial**.—*n.* **podite** (*pod'īt*), a walking leg of a crustacean. [Latinised from Gr. *pŏdion*, dim. of *pous, podos*, foot.]

**podley**, *pod'li*, (*Scot.*) *n.* a young coalfish. [pollack.]

**podo-**. See **pod(o)-**.

**Podsnappery**, *pod-snap'ər-i, n.* British Philistinism as exemplified in Mr Podsnap in Dickens's *Our Mutual Friend.*

**podsol, podzol,** *pod-zol'*, *n.* a bleached sand soil, poor in humus. [Russ.,—*pod*, under, *zola*, ash.]

**Podunk**, *pō'dungk* (*U.S.*), *n.* an imaginary typical dull, out-dated country town. [From either of two villages, near Worcester, Massachusetts, or Hartford, Connecticut.]

**poe-bird, poy-bird,** *pō'i-bûrd, n.* the New Zealand parson-bird or tui. [Captain Cook's name from Tahitian *poe*, pearl beads, taken by him to mean earrings, on account of the side-tufts of the bird's neck.]

**poem**, *pō'im, -em, n.* a composition in verse: a composition of high beauty of thought or language and artistic form, typically, but not necessarily, in verse: anything supremely harmonious and satisfying (*fig.*).—*adj.* **poemat'ic**. [Fr. *poème*—L. *poēma*—Gr. *poiēma*—*poieein*, to make.]

**poenology**. Same as **penology**.

**poesy**, *pō'i-zi, n.* poetry collectively or in the abstract: a poem (*obs.*): a motto or posy (*obs.*).—*v.i.* (*Keats*) to utter poetry. [Fr. *poésie*—L. *poēsis*—Gr. *poiēsis*—*poieein*, to make.]

**poet**, *pō'it, -et, n.* the author of a poem or (formerly) of any work of literary art: a verse-writer: one skilled in making poetry: one with a poetical imagination:—*fem.* **pō'etess**.—*ns.* **pōetas'ter**, a petty poet: a writer of contemptible verses; **pōetas'tering, pōetas't(e)ry**.—*adjs.* **poetic** (*pō-et'ik*), **-al**, of the nature or having the character of poetry: pertaining or suitable to a poet or to poetry: expressed in poetry: in the language of poetry: imaginative.—*n.* **poet'ic** (often *pl.* in form, treated as *sing.*), the branch of criticism that relates to poetry.—*adv.* **pōet'ically**.—*v.t.* and *v.i.* **poet'icise, -ize**, to make poetic: to write poetry about: to write, speak, or treat, poetically.—*n.* **poet'icism**, a word or phrase that is typically, usually tritely, poetic.—*n.* **pōet'icule**, a petty poet.—*v.i.* **pōetise, -ize**, to write as a poet or like a poet.—*v.t.* to make poetical: to record or celebrate in poetry.—*ns.* **pō'etresse** (*Spens.*), a poetess; **pō'etry**, the art

of the poet: the essential quality of a poem: poetical composition or writings collectively (rarely in *pl.*): poetical quality; **pō'etship**.— poetic justice, ideal administration of reward and punishment; poetic licence, a departing from strict fact or rule by a poet for the sake of effect; Poet Laureate (see laureate). [Fr. *poète*—L. *poēta*—Gr. *poiētēs*—*poieein*, to make.]

**po-faced**, *pō'fāst*, (*coll.*) *adj.* stupidly solemn and narrow-minded.

**poffle**, *pof'l*, (*Scot.*) *n.* a pendicle. [Origin obscure.]

**pogge**, *pog*, *n.* the armed bullhead (*Agonus cataphractus*), a bony-plated fish. [Origin unknown.]

**pogonotomy**, *pō-gō-not'ə-mi, n.* shaving. [Gr. *pōgōn, pōgōnos*, beard, *tomē*, a cutting.]

**pogo stick**, *pō'gō stik, n.* a child's toy consisting of a stick with a crossbar on a strong spring on which one stands in order to bounce along the ground. [*Pogo*, a trademark.]

**pogrom**, *pog'rom, pog-rom', n.* an organised massacre, orig. (late 19th cent.) esp. of Russian Jews. [Russ., destruction, devastation.]

**poh**, *pō, interj.* of impatient contempt. [Cf. pooh.]

**poi**, *pō'ē, n.* a Hawaiian dish, a paste of fermented taro root. [Hawaiian.]

**poignado, poinado**, *poi-nä'dō*, obsolete forms of poniard.

**poignant**, *poin'(y)ənt, adj.* stinging, pricking: sharp: acutely painful: penetrating: pungent: piquant: touching, pathetic.—*n.* **poign'ancy**.—*adv.* **poign'antly**. [O.Fr. *poignant*, pr.p. of *poindre*—L. *pungēre*, to sting.]

**poikilitic**, *poi-kil-it'ik, adj.* mottled: having small crystals of one mineral irregularly scattered in larger crystals of another (*petr.*).—*n.* **poi'kilocyte** (*-ō-sīt*), an irregular red blood corpuscle.—*adjs.* **poikilotherm'al, poikilotherm'ic**, having variable blood-temperature—'cold-blooded'.—*n.* **poikilotherm'y**, cold-bloodedness. [Gr. *poikilos*, variegated.]

**poilu**, *pwa-lü*, (Fr.) a French private soldier (nickname; meaning 'hairy').

**Poinciana**, *poin-si-ä'na, n.* a tropical genus of the Caesalpinia family—flamboyant tree, etc. [After De Poinci, a French West Indian governor.]

**poind**, *pēnd*, **pind**, (*Scot.*) *v.t.* to distrain: to impound.—*ns.* **poind'er**; **poind'ing**. [O.E. *pyndan*, to impound; cf. pound (2).]

**poinsettia**, *poin-set'i-ə, n.* a spurge, *Euphorbia pulcherrima*, with petal-like bracts, usu. scarlet, and small yellow flowers, orig. from Mexico and Central America. [From Joel Roberts Poinsett (1779-1851), American Minister to Mexico.]

**point**, *point, n.* a dot: a small mark used in Semitic alphabets to indicate a vowel, to differentiate a consonant, or for other purpose: a dot separating the integral and fractional parts of a decimal: a mark of punctuation: that which has position but no magnitude (*geom.*): a whit (as in *no point*; Shak.): a place or station, considered in relation to position only: a place in a scale, course, or cycle (as *boiling point, dead point*): a moment of time, without duration: a precise moment: a state: a juncture: a critical moment: the verge: a culmination: a conclusion: resolution (*obs.*): condition, case, plight (as in *in good point*; *obs.*): any one of nine fixed positions on a shield (*her.*): the entry, or the first notes, of a subject, as in a fugue (formerly marked by a dot; *obs.*): a short strain or phrase of music, a call on an instrument, esp. military, as in a *point of war* (*arch.*): a unit in scoring, judging, or measurement: a character taken into account in judging: a distinctive mark or characteristic: a unit of measurement of type, approximately 1/72 inch: one of thirty-two divisions of the compass, or the angle between two successive divisions (⅛ of a right angle): a

Neutral vowels in unaccented syllables: *el'ə-mənt*; for certain sounds in foreign words, see p. viii

unit in rationing by coupon: in piquet, the strongest suit held and called, or the score for holding it: a particular: a head, clause, or item: a position forming a main element in the structure of an argument or discourse: a matter in debate, under attention, or to be taken into account: that which is relevant: that upon which one insists or takes a stand: the precise matter: the essential matter: that without which a story, joke, etc., is meaningless or ineffective: a clearly defined aim, object, or reason: a particular imparted by a hint: lace made with a needle (also point'-lace): loosely, lace: a piece of point-lace (*obs.*): a sharp end: a tip, or free end: a thing, part, or mark with a sharp end: a piercing weapon or tool: an etching-needle: the sharp end of a sword: (in *pl.*) sword-fighting: a tine: a spike: a tapering piece in electrical apparatus, as the end of a lightning-conductor: a cape or headland: the tip of the chin (*boxing*): a horse's or other animal's extremity: a tagged lace formerly used for fastening clothes: a nib: a movable rail for passing vehicles from one track to another: a tapering division of a backgammon board: a fielder or his position, on the off-side straight out from and near the batsman (as if at the point of the bat) (*cricket*): the leading party of an advanced guard: a position at the head of a herd: a socket for making connection with electric wiring: pointedness: pungency: sting: act or position of pointing: the vertical rising of a hawk, indicating the position of the prey: a feat (*obs.*): pointe: 1/100 part of a carat. —*adj.* (*phon.*) articulated with the tip of the tongue.—*v.t.* to insert points in: to mark with points: to mark off in groups of syllables for singing: to sharpen: to give point to: to prick in or turn over with the point of a spade: to show the position or direction of or draw attention to (now usu. with *out*): to place in a certain direction, direct (with *at*): to indicate: to insert white hairs in (a fur): to rake out old mortar from and insert new in the joints of: to ration by points.—*v.i.* to have or take a position in a direction (with *at, to, toward*, etc.: to indicate a direction or position by extending a finger, a stick, etc.: of dogs, to indicate the position of game by an attitude: to hint: to aim.—*adj.* point'ed, having a sharp point: sharp: Gothic (*archit.*): keen: telling: epigrammatic: precise: explicit: aimed at particular persons: having marked personal application.—*adv.* point'-edly.—*ns.* point'edness; point'er, one who points, in any sense: a rod for pointing to a blackboard, map, screen, etc.: an index-hand: a hint, tip, suggestion: a tool for clearing out old mortar from joints: a breed of dogs that point on discovering game: (in *pl.*) two stars of the Great Bear nearly in a straight line with the Pole Star; point'ing.—*adj.* point'less.—*adv.* point'lessly.— *n.* point'lessness.—point'-duty, the duty of a policeman stationed at a particular point to regulate traffic; point'ing-stock, a thing to be pointed at, a laughing-stock; point'-lace (see above); point set (*math.*), an aggregate; points'-man, one on point-duty: one in charge of rail points; point'-source', a source of radiation that is, or is considered as, a mathematical point.— *adj.* point'-to-point', from one fixed point to another: across country.—*n.* a cross-country race, a steeplechase.—at (a) point, points, all points (*Shak.*, etc.), in readiness: resolved: completely: in all respects; at the point of, on the verge of; cardinal point (see cardinal); carry one's point, to gain what one contends for; dead point (see dead); from point to point, from one detail to another (*obs.*); give points to, to give odds to: to give an advantageous hint on any subject; in point, apposite; in point of, in the matter of; in point of fact, as a matter of fact;

make a point of, to treat as essential, make a special object of; not to put too fine a point on it, to speak bluntly; on a point of order, questioning whether procedural order has been followed; on the point of, close upon: very near; point for point, exactly in all particulars; point of honour (see honour); point of no return, that point on a flight from which one can only go on, for want of fuel to return:—Also *fig.*; point of order, a question raised in a deliberative society, whether proceedings are according to the rules; point of view, the position from which one looks at anything, literally or figuratively; point of the compass (see above); potatoes and point, a feigned Irish dish, potatoes alone, with a herring, etc., to point at; put upon points, to ration by points; stand upon points, to be punctilious; stretch (or strain) a point, to go further (esp. in concession) than strict rule allows; to the point, apposite; to point (*Spens., Shak.*), to the smallest detail. [Partly Fr. *point*, point, dot, stitch, lace, partly Fr. *pointe*, sharp point, pungency—L. *punctum* and L.L. *puncta*, respectively—L. *pungĕre, punctum*, to prick.]

**point**, *point*, *v.t.* to appoint, determine, fix. [Aphetic for **appoint**.]

**point d'appui**, *pwē da-pwē*, (Fr.) point of support, prop, fulcrum.

**point-blank**, *point'-blangk'*, *adj.* aimed directly at the mark without allowing for the downward curve of the trajectory: permitting such an aim: direct: straightforward: blunt.—*adv.* with point-blank aim: directly: bluntly: flat.—*n.* a point-blank shot or range: reach (of jurisdiction) (*Shak.*). [App. from **point** (vb.), and **blank** (of the target).]

**point-device, point-devise**, *point'-di-vis'*, (*obs.*) *n.* the point of perfection (in the phrase *at point device*).—*adj.* (*arch.*) fastidiously exact, esp. in dress.—*adv.* with exactitude: down to the smallest detail. [Lit. to the point arranged, or arranged to the point—O.Fr. *devis*, devised.]

**pointe**, *pwēt*, (Fr.) in ballet, the extreme tip of the toe, or the position of standing on it.

**pointel**, *poin'tl*, *n.* a sharp instrument, esp. a style: a pistil (*obs.*). [O.Fr.]

**pointillism**, *pwan'til-izm*, **pointillisme** (Fr.; *pwē-tē-yēzm*), *n.* in painting, the use of separate dots of pure colour instead of mixed pigments.—*adj.* **pointillé** (*pwē-tē-yā*), ornamented with a pattern of dots made by a pointed tool.—*n.* **poin'tillist, pointilliste** (Fr.; *-tē-yēst*). [Fr. *pointillisme—pointille*, dim. of *point*, point.]

**poise**, *poiz*, *v.t.* to weigh (*obs.*): to hold so as to get some notion of the weight: to ponder, weigh in the mind (*rare*): to weight, weigh down (*obs.*): to make stable, ballast (*obs.*): to balance: to counterbalance (*obs.*): to carry or hold in equilibrium.—*v.i.* to hang in suspense: to hover.— *n.* weight (*obs.*): balance: equilibrium: a weight, as of a clock (*obs.*): bias: momentum (*Spens.*): impact (*Shak.*): carriage or balance of body: dignity and assurance of manner: suspense.—*n.* pois'er. [O.Fr. *poiser* (Fr. *peser*)— L. *pēnsāre*, freq. of *pendĕre*, to weigh, and O.Fr. *pois*—L. *pēnsum*, weight.]

**poise**, *pwäz*, *n.* a cgs unit of viscosity (not an SI unit). [J. L. M. *Poiseuille*, French physician.]

**poison**, *poi'zn*, *n.* any substance which, taken into or formed in the body, destroys life or impairs health: any malignant influence: a substance that inhibits the activity of a catalyst (*chem.*): a material that absorbs neutrons and so interferes with the working of a nuclear reactor.—*v.t.* to administer poison to: to injure or kill with poison: to put poison on or in: to taint: to mar: to embitter: to corrupt.—*adj.* poisonous.— *adj.* poi'sonable.—*n.* poi'soner.—*adj.* poi'sonous, having the quality or effect of poison: noxious: offensive (*coll.*).—*adv.* poi'sonously.—*n.* poi'-

sonousness.—poi'son-fang, one of two large tubular teeth in the upper jaw of venomous snakes, through which poison passes from glands at their roots when the animal bites; poi'son-gas, any injurious gas used in warfare; poi'son-gland, a gland that secretes poison; poi'son-ivy, poi'son-oak, poi'son-sumac(h), names for various North American sumacs with ulcerating juice; poi'son-nut, nux vomica; poison pen, a writer of malicious anonymous letters. [O.Fr. *puison*, poison—L. *pōtiō, -ōnis*, a draught—*pōtāre*, to drink; cf. potion.]

poisson, *pwa-sɔ̃*, (Fr.) a fish.—poisson d'avril (*dav-rēl*), an April fool.

poitrel, *poi'trəl*, n. armour for a horse's breast. [O.F. *poitral*—L. *pectorāle*, a breastplate—*pectus, -oris*, the breast.]

pokal, *pō-käl'*, n. an ornamental drinking-vessel. [Ger.,—It. *boccale*—Gr. *baukālis*, a vessel for cooling wine, etc.]

poke, *pōk*, n. (now chiefly *dial.*; *Scot.* pock (2)) a bag: a pouch: a pokeful.—n. poke'ful, as much as a poke will hold.—a pig in a poke, a blind bargain, as of a pig bought without being seen. [M.E. *poke*; affinities uncertain.]

poke, *pōk*, n. a projecting brim or front of a bonnet: a poke-bonnet.—*adj.* poked.—poke'-bonnet, a bonnet with a projecting front, as worn by Salvationist women, children, and formerly by women farm workers. [Perh. from foregoing, or from following word.]

poke, *pōk*, v.t. to thrust or push the end of anything against or into: to thrust forward or endwise: to make, put, render, or achieve by thrusting or groping: to stir up, incite: to dress with a poking-stick (*obs.*): to seclude or confine in a poky place (*coll.*).—v.i. to thrust, make thrusts: to feel about, grope: to bat gently and cautiously (*cricket*): to potter: to stoop: to pry about: to live a dull or secluded life.—n. an act of poking.—n. pō'ker, one who pokes: a rod for poking or stirring a fire: an instrument for doing poker-work: a stiff person: a mace or mace-bearer (*facet.*): a poking-stick.—*adj.* pō'kerish, like a poker: stiff.—*adv.* pō'kerishly.—*adj.* pō'king, pottering: petty: confined: stuffy: shabby.—*adj.* pō'ky, poking.—pō'ker-work, work done by burning a design into wood with a heated point; pō'king-stick, a small rod formerly used for adjusting the plaits of ruffs.—by the holy poker, a facetious oath of unknown meaning, perhaps belonging to poker (1) below; poke fun at, to banter; poke one's head, to stoop, hold the head forward; poke one's nose, to pry; red-hot poker, Kniphofia or Tritoma. [M.E. *pōken*; app. of L.G. origin.]

poke, *pōk*, n. a name for various American species of Phytolacca (also poke'weed, poke'berry): American or white hellebore (Indian poke). [Of American Indian origin.]

poker, *pō'kər*, n. a bugbear.—*adj.* pō'kerish, causing terror: uncanny.—Old Poker (see old). [Cf. Dan. *pokker*, Sw. *pocker*.]

poker, *pō'kər*, n. a round game at cards, first played in America about 1835.—po'ker-face, an inscrutable face, useful to a poker-player: its possessor.—*adj.* po'ker-faced. [Ety. uncertain; poss. from German.]

Polabian, *pō-lā'bi-ən*, n. a member of a former West Slavonic people occupying the basin of the lower Elbe: their extinct language.—Also *adj.* [Slav. *po*, beside, *Labe*, the Elbe.]

polacca, *po-lak'a*, n. a three-masted Mediterranean vessel, with fore and main masts each in one piece (also polacre, *po-lä'kər*): a polonaise, or composition in the manner of a polonaise. [It. *polacca, polacra*, Polish (fem.); Fr. *polacre*: application to the vessel not explained.]

Polack, *pōl'ak*, (*Shak.*) n. a Pole.—*adj.* Polish. [Pol. *Polak*; Ger. *Polack*.]

Poland, *pō'lənd*, n. a country of Europe.—*adj.* of Poland, Polish.—n. Po'lander (*obs.*), a Pole.

polar, *pō'lər*, *adj.* of, or pertaining to, a pole (see pole (1)) or poles: belonging to the neighbourhood of a pole: referred to a pole: of the nature of, or analogous to, a pole: axial, cardinal: having polarity: directly opposed.—n. (*geom.*) the locus of the harmonic conjugate of a fixed point or pole with respect to the points in which a transversal through it cuts a circle or other conic. —n. polarim'eter, an instrument for measuring the rotation of the plane of polarisation of light. *adj.* polarimetric (*pō-lar-i-met'rik*).—ns. polarimetry (*pō-lar-im'i-tri*); Polaris (*pō-lä'ris*), the Pole Star; polarisation, -z- (*pō-lər-i-zā'shən*), act of polarising: the state of being polarised: development of poles: loosely, polarity: the effect of deposition of products of electrolysis upon electrodes, resulting in an opposing electromotive force: the restriction (according to the wave theory) of the vibrations of light to one plane; polariscope (*pō-lar'i-skōp*), an instrument for showing phenomena of polarised light.—v.t. polarise, -ize (*pō'lər-iz*), to subject to polarisation: to give polarity to: to develop new qualities or meanings in (*fig.*).—v.i. to acquire polarity.—*adj.* po'larised, -z-.—ns. po'lariser, -z-, a device for polarising light; polarity(*pō-lar'i-ti*), state of having two opposite poles: the condition of having properties different or opposite in opposite directions or at opposite ends: the tendency to develop differently in different directions along an axis, as a plant towards base and apex, some animals towards head and tail: particular relation to this or that pole or opposed property rather than the other: directedness (*fig.*): opposedness or doubleness of aspect or tendency.—*adj.* Po'laroid, a trademark applied to photographic equipment, light-polarising materials, etc.—polar bear, a large white bear found in the Arctic regions; polar circle, the Arctic or the Antarctic Circle; polar co-ordinates, co-ordinates defining a point by means of a radius vector and the angle which it makes with a fixed line through the origin; polar distance, angular distance from the pole; polar equation, an equation in terms of polar co-ordinates; polar forces, forces that act in pairs and in different directions, as in magnetism; polar lights, the aurora borealis or australis. [L. *polāris—polus*; see pole (1).]

polder, *pōl'dər*, n. piece of low-lying reclaimed land: first stage in its reclamation.—Also v.t. [Du.]

pole, *pōl*, n. the end of an axis, esp. of the earth, the celestial sphere, or any rotating sphere: of a great or small circle on a sphere, either of the two points in which its axis cuts the surface of the sphere: of a crystal face, the point where the normal from the origin cuts the sphere of projection: the end of an elongated body: a differentiated end: either of the two points of a body in which the attractive or repulsive energy is concentrated, as in a magnet: an electric terminal or electrode: a fixed point (*geom.*): a point from which a pencil of rays radiates: a fixed point defining a polar: an opposite extreme (*fig.*): the heavens (*poet.*, after Greek use).—Pole Star, Polaris, a star near the N. pole of the heavens: a guide or director.—poles apart, asunder, widely separated, very different. [L. *polus*—Gr. *polos*, pivot, axis, firmament.]

pole, *pōl*, n. a long rounded shaft, rod, or post, usu. of wood: a small tree: a single shaft to which a pair of horses may be yoked: a measuring rod of definite length: hence a measure of length, 5½ yards, of area, 30¼ square yards: position next the inner boundary-fence in a race-course: the tail of certain animals.—v.t. to propel, push, strike, or stir with a pole: to furnish with poles.

—*v.i.* to use a pole.—*n.* **pōl'ing,** supplying, propelling, or stirring with a pole or poles: poles collectively.—*adj.* **pole'-clipt** (*Shak.*), hedged in with poles.—*n.* **pole'-vault,** an athletic event in which the competitor uses a pole to achieve great height in jumping over a cross-bar.—Also *v.i.*—**under bare poles,** with all sails furled; **up the pole** (*slang*), in a predicament: drunk: crazed: in favour (*mil.*). [O.E. *pāl* (Ger. *pfahl*)—L. *pālus,* a stake.]

**Pole,** *pōl, n.* a native or citizen of Poland: a member of the people inhabiting Poland and speaking Polish.

**pole-axe, -ax,** *pōl'aks, n.* a battle-axe, originally short-handled: a long-handled axe or halbert: a sailor's short-handled axe for cutting away rigging: a butcher's axe with a hammer-faced back. [Orig. *pollax,* from **poll,** head, and **axe,** confused with **pole** (2).]

**polecat,** *pōl'kat, n.* a large relative of the weasel, which emits a stink—called also *fitchet* and *foumart* (*Mustela putorius*): a prostitute (*Shak.*): a skunk (*U.S.*). [M.E. *polcat;* poss. Fr. *poule,* hen, and **cat.**]

**polemarch,** *pol'i-märk, n.* a title of several officials in ancient Greek states, orig. a military commander. [Gr. *polemarchos—polemos,* war, *archē,* rule.]

**polemic,** *po-lem'ik, adj.* given to disputing: controversial.—*n.* a controversialist: a controversy: a controversial writing or argument: (in *pl.*) the practice or art of controversy.—*adj.* **polem'ical.**—*adv.* **polem'ically.**—*ns.* **polem'icist, pol'emist,** one who writes polemics or engages in controversy.—*v.t.* **pol'emise, -ize.** [Gr. *polemikos—polemos,* war.]

**Polemonium,** *pol-i-mō'ni-əm, n.* the Jacob's ladder genus of plants, giving name to the **Polemoniā'ceae,** the phlox family.—*adj.* **polemoniā'ceous.** [Gr. *polemōnion,* St John's wort, or other plant.]

**polenta,** *po-len'ta, n.* an Italian porridge of maize, barley, chestnut, or other meal. [It.,—L. *polenta,* peeled barley.]

**poley,** *pō'li,* (*Austr.*) *adj.* hornless. [**poll** (1).]

**polianite,** *pō'li-ən-īt, n.* a steel-grey mineral, manganese dioxide. [Gr. *poliainesthai,* to grow grey *—polios,* hoary.]

**Polianthes,** *pol-i-an'thēz, n.* the tuberose genus of the amaryllis family. [Gr. *polios,* hoary, *anthos,* a flower.]

**police,** *pol-ēs', n.* the system of regulations for the preservation of order and enforcement of law (*arch.*): the internal government of a state (*arch.*): a body of men employed to maintain order, etc.: its members collectively.—*adj.* of the police.—*v.t.* to control as police: to furnish with police: to guard or to put or keep in order.—**police burgh** (see **burgh**); **police'-con'stable,** a policeman of ordinary rank; **police'-court',** a court for trying small offences brought before it by the police; **police'-dog',** a dog trained to help the police; **police'-force',** a separately organised body of police; **police'-inspect'or,** a superior officer of police who has charge of a department, next in rank to a superintendent; **police'-judge', police'-mag'istrate,** one who presides in a police-court; **police'man,** a member of a police-force; **police'-manure'** (*Scot.*), street sweepings used as manure; **police'-off'ice, -stā'tion,** the head-quarters of the police of a district, used also as a temporary place of confinement; **police'-off'icer,** an ordinary policeman; **police'-state',** a country in which secret police are employed to detect and stamp out any opposition to the government in power; **police'-trap,** a strategic means whereby the police keep motor traffic under scrutiny and detect offenders against the law: a concealed and concerted timing arrangement to enforce a speed limit; **police'woman,** a woman member

of a police-force. [Fr.,—L. *polītīa*—Gr. *polīteiā —polītēs,* a citizen—*polis,* a city.]

**policy,** *pol'i-si, n.* a constitution (*obs.*): the art of government: statecraft: a course of action: a system of administration guided more by interest than by principle: dexterity of management: prudence: cunning: in Scotland (sometimes in *pl.*), the pleasure-grounds around a mansion. [O. Fr. *policie* (Fr. *police*)—L. *polītia*—Gr. *polīteiā* (see **police**); in Scots perh. influenced by L. *politus,* embellished.]

**policy,** *pol'i-si, n.* a writing containing a contract of insurance: a kind of gambling by betting on the numbers to be drawn in a lottery (*U.S.*).—**pol'icy-holder,** one who holds a contract of insurance; **pol'icy-shop,** a place where the game of policy is played. [Fr. *police,* policy, app.—L.L. *apodissa,* a receipt—Gr. *apodeixis,* proof.]

**polio,** *pōl'* or *pol'i-ō, n.* short for poliomyelitis: a sufferer therefrom.—Also *adj.*

**poliomyelitis,** *pōl-i-ō-mī-ə-lī'tis* (or *pol-*), *n.* inflammation of the grey matter of the spinal cord: infantile paralysis. [Gr. *polios,* grey, *myelos,* marrow.]

**Polish,** *pō'lish, adj.* of Poland, or its people or its language.—*n.* the Slavonic language of the Poles.

**polish,** *pol'ish, v.t.* to make smooth and glossy by rubbing: to bring to a finished state: to impart culture and refinement to.—*v.i.* to take a polish.—*n.* an act of polishing: gloss: refinement of manners: a substance applied to produce a polish.—*adjs.* **pol'ishable; pol'ished.**—*ns.* **pol'isher; pol'ishings,** particles removed by polishing; **pol'ishment.**—**pol'ishing-paste; pol'ishing-pow'der; polishing'-slate,** a diatomaceous slaty stone used for polishing glass, marble, and metals.—**polish off** (*slang*), to finish off: to dispose of finally. [O.Fr. *polir, polissant*—L. *polīre,* to polish.]

**Politburo, -bureau,** *po-lit'bū-rō,* or *pol', n.* in Communist countries, effectively the most powerful organ of the Communist Party's executive (in Russia from 1952 to 1966, when replaced by *Presidium*). [Russ. *politicheskoe,* political, *byuro,* bureau.]

**polite,** *po-līt', adj.* glossy, polished (*obs.*): refined: of courteous manners.—*adv.* **polite'ly.**—*ns.* **polite'ness; politesse** (*pol-ē-tes';* Fr.), superficial politeness.—**polite literature,** belles-lettres—poetry, essays, standard novels, etc., as distinguished from scientific treatises and the like. [L. *politus,* pa.p. of *polīre,* to polish.]

**politic,** *pol'i-tik, adj.* political (*rare*): constitutional (*obs.*): in accordance with good policy: acting or proceeding from motives of policy: prudent: discreet: astutely contriving or intriguing.—*adj.* **polit'ical,** pertaining to policy or government: pertaining to parties differing in their views of government: politic (*obs.*).—*adv.* **polit'ically.**—*ns.* **politicas'ter** (*Milt.*), a petty politician; **politician** (*-tish'ən*), one versed in the science of government: one engaged in political life or statesmanship: one interested in party politics: a politic person: one who makes a profession or a game of politics: an intriguer (*U.S.; obs.*).—*adj.* (*Milt.*) politic.—*v.t.* **polit'icise, -ize** (*-i-sīz*), to make political.—*v.i.* to play the politician: to discuss politics.—*n.* **pol'iticking,** engaging in political activity, as seeking votes.—*v.i.* **pol'itick.**—*adv.* **pol'iticly.**—*n.pl.* (treated as *sing.*) **pol'itics,** the art or science of government: the management of a political party: political affairs or opinions: manoeuvring and intriguing (*U.S.*).—*n.* **politique** (*pol-ē-tēk';* Fr.), in French history, one of a moderate party between Huguenots and Catholics: a religious indifferentist: a 'temporiser.'—**political economy,** the science of the production, distribution, and consumption of wealth; **political geography,** that part of geography which deals with the division

*fāte, fär; mē, hûr* (her); *mīne; mōte, ör; mūte; mōōn, fŏŏt; dhen* (then) of the earth for purposes of government, as states, colonies, counties, and the work of man, as towns, canals, etc.; **political science**, the science or study of government, as to its principles, aims, methods, etc.; **political verse**, Byzantine and modern Greek accentual verse, esp. iambic verse of fifteen syllables.—*adj.* **polit´ico-econom´ic**, of political economy. [Gr. *politikos—politēs*, a citizen.]

**politico**, *pō-lit´i-kō, n.* a politician, esp. in Spanish-speaking countries (usu. *derog.*). [It. or Sp.]

**polity**, *pol´i-ti, n.* political organisation: a body of people organised under a system of government. [Gr. *politeiā.*]

**polka**, *pōl´ka, pol´, n.* a Bohemian dance or its tune, in 2-4 time with accent on the third quaver, invented about 1830: applied to various things fashionable at the same time, esp. a woman's jacket.—*v.i.* **polk**, to dance a polka.—**pol´ka-dot**, a pattern of dots. [Perh. Czech *půlka*, half-step; or from Pol. *polka*, a Polish woman.]

**poll**, *pōl, n.* the head: the hair of the head: head and shoulders of a ling (*obs.*): the blunt end of the head of a hammer, miner's pick, etc.: a head as a unit in numbering, an individual: number of individuals (*Shak.*): a register, esp. of voters: a voting: an aggregate of votes: the taking of a vote: a taking of public opinion by means of questioning: a polled animal.—*adj.* **polled**: cut evenly (as in **deed poll**, opp. to *indenture*).—*v.t.* to cut the hair, horns, top (of a tree), edge (of a deed) from: to tax excessively, practise extortion upon (*arch.*): to receive or take the votes of: to receive, take, or cast (a vote): to receive (a stated number of votes).—*v.i.* to practise extortion (*arch.*): to vote.—*adj.* **polled**, shorn: pollarded: deprived of horns: hornless.—*ns.* **poll´er**; **poll´ster**, one who carries out, or puts his faith in, a public opinion poll.—**poll´-axe**, pole-axe (*q.v.*); **poll´ing-booth**, the place where people vote; **poll´-money**, **poll´-tax**, a tax of so much a head—i.e. on each person alike.—**at the head of the poll**, having the greatest number of votes at an election. [Cf. obs. Du. and L.G. *polle*, top of the head.]

**Poll**, poll, *pol, n.* a parrot.—**poll´-parrot.**—*v.t* and *v.i.* to parrot. [*Poll*, a common name for a parrot; see **Polly.**]

**poll**, *pol*, (*Cambridge*) *n.* the mass of students who do not seek or obtain honours: a pass-degree.—**poll´-degree´**; **poll´man**. [Said to be from Gr. *hoi polloi*, the many.]

**pollack**, *pol´ak, n.* a common fish of the cod family, with long narrow jaw and no barbel: extended to the coalfish.—Also **poll´ock**. [Ety. obscure; connection with Gael. *pollag*, doubtful.]

**pollan**, *pol´ən, n.* an Irish whitefish, esp. that (*Coregonus pollan*) found in Lough Neagh. [Perh. Ir. *poll*, lake; cf. **powan.**]

**pollard**, *pol´ərd, n.* a tree having the whole crown cut off, leaving it to send out new branches from the top of the stem: a hornless animal of horned kind: fine bran: flour or meal containing it: a base foreign coin bearing a head (*obs.*).—*adj.* pollarded: awnless: bald.—*v.t.* to make a pollard of. [**poll** (1).]

**poll-axe.** Same as **pole-axe.**

**pollen**, *pol´ən, n.* the fertilising powder formed in the anthers of flowers.—*v.t.* to cover with pollen.—*n.* **pollenos´is**, hay fever.—*v.t.* **poll´inate**, to convey pollen to.—*n.* **pollinā´tion.**—*adjs.* **pollin´ic**, of or pertaining to pollen; **pollinif´erous**, bearing, producing, pollen.—*n.* **pollin´ium**, an agglutinated mass of pollen-grains:—*pl.* **pollin´ia.**—**pollen analysis**, use of pollen grains in peat bogs, etc., as a means of determining past vegetation and climates or the age of fossil remains; **poll´en-basket**, a hollow in a bee's hindleg in which pollen is carried; **pollen**

**count**, the amount of pollen in the atmosphere, estimated from deposits on slides exposed to the air; **poll´en-grain**, a grain of pollen, the microspore in flowering plants; **poll´en-sac**, a cavity in an anther in which pollen is formed, the microsporangium of flowering plants; **poll´en-tube**, an outgrowth from a pollen-grain by which the gametes are conveyed to the ovule. [L. *pollen, -inis*, fine flour.]

**pollent**, *pol´ənt, adj.* strong. [L. *pollēns, -entis*, pr.p. of *pollēre*, to be strong.]

**pollex**, *pol´eks, n.* the thumb or its analogue:—*pl.* **pollices** (*pol´i-sēz*). [L. *pollex, -icis.*]

**pollice verso**, *pol´i-sē vûr´sō, pol´i-ke ver´, wer´sō*, (L). with the thumb turned up or outwards (now often assumed, most prob. wrongly, to mean downwards)—the signal made by the spectators for the death of a Roman gladiator.

**pollicie, pollicy** (*Spens.*). Same as **policy.**

**pollicitation**, *pol-is-i-tā´shən, n.* a promise: a promise which has not yet been accepted. [L. *pollicitātiō, -ōnis.*]

**polliwig, -wog.** See **pollywog.**

**pollock.** Same as **pollack,**

**pollusion**, *po-lōō´zhən, -lū´*, (*Love's Labour's Lost*, IV, iii) *n.* Goodman Dull's blunder for **allusion.**

**pollute**, *po-lōōt´, -lūt´, v.t.* to befoul physically: to contaminate, make (any feature of the environment) offensive or harmful to human, animal, or plant life: to make unclean morally: to defile ceremonially, profane.—*adj.* defiled.—*n.* **pollu´tant**, something that pollutes.—*adj.* **pollut´ed.**—*adv.* **pollut´edly.**—*ns.* **pollut´edness**; **pollut´er**; **pollution** (*po-lōō´shən, -lū´*). [L. *polluĕre, pollūtus—pol-*, a form of *prō* or *per*, *luĕre*, to wash.]

**Pollux**, *pol´uks, n.* the twin brother of Castor (*myth.*): a star in the constellation of the Twins. [L. for Gr. *Polydeukēs.*]

**Polly**, *pol´i, n.* a form of **Molly**: a parrot. [Cf. **Poll.**]

**polly**, *pol´i, n.* a slang abbreviation for **Apollinaris** (water).

**pollywog, polliwog**, *pol´i-wog*, **pollywig, polliwig**, *-wig, n.* a tadpole.—Also **porwigg´le.** [M.E. *pollwyggle*—**poll** (1), **wiggle.**]

**polo**, *pō´lō, n.* a game like hockey on horseback —of Oriental origin: a similar aquatic (*water polo*) or skating (*rink polo*) game.—*n.* **po´loist.**—**polo neck**, a pullover collar fitting the neck closely and doubling over, as orig. in a polo jersey. [Balti (Tibetan dial. in Kashmir) *polo*, polo ball; Tibetan *pulu*.]

**polo**, *pō´lō, n.* a Spanish gypsy dance. [Sp., an Andalusian popular song.]

**polonaise**, *pol-a-nāz, n.* a woman's bodice and skirt in one piece, showing an underskirt: a similar child's garment once worn in Scotland: a Polish national dance or promenade of slow movement in 3-4 time: a musical form in the same rhythm. [Fr., Polish (fem.).]

**Polonia**, *pol-ō´ni-a, n.* mediaeval Latin name for Poland.—*adj.* and *n.* **Polo´nian.**—*n.* **Polonisation**, *-z-* (*pō-lən-i-zā´shən*).—*v.t.* and *v.i.* to make, *-ize*, to make or become Polish.—*ns.* **po´lonism**, a Polish idiom or characteristic; **polonium** (*pol-ō´ni-əm*), a radioactive element (at. numb. 84) discovered by Mme Curie (a Pole); **polo´ny**, *-ie* (*Scot.*), a child's polonaise.

**polony**, *po-lō´ni, n.* a dry sausage of partly cooked meat. [Prob. *Bologna*, in Italy; perh. *Polonia*.]

**polt**, *pōlt, n.* a hard blow (now *dial.*): a club (*obs.*).—*v.t.* (*dial.*) to beat.—**polt´foot**, a club-foot. — *adj.* club-footed. — *adj.* **polt´-footed.** [Origin obscure.]

**poltergeist**, *pōl´, pol´-tər-gīst, n.* a mysterious invisible agency asserted to throw things about: a noisy ghost. [Ger. *poltern*, to make a racket, *geist*, ghost.]

**poltroon**, *pol-trōōn´* (*Shak.* **poul´troone**), *n.* a

dastard.—Also *adj.—n.* poltroon'ery, want of spirit. [Fr. *poltron*—It. *poltrone—poltro*, lazy.]
polverine, *pol'vər-ēn*, (*obs.*) *n.* glass-makers' potash. [It. *polverino*—L. *pulvis, pulvĕris*, dust.]
poly-, *pol'i-, pol-i'-*, in composition, many: several: much: denoting a polymer, as *polyethylene* (see below): affecting more than one part (*med.*).—*adjs.* polyacid (*-as'id*), having several replaceable hydrogen atoms: capable of replacing several hydrogen atoms of an acid; pol'yact (Gr. *aktis, -inos*, ray), polyacti'nal (or *-ukt'in-əl*), polyact'ine, many rayed.—*n pl* Polyadel'phia (Gr. *adelphos*, brother), in Linnaeus's system a class of plants with three or more bundles of stamens.—*adj.* polyadel'phous, (of stamens) united in several bundles: having the stamens so united.—*n.* polyam'ide, a polymeric amide, as nylon.—*n.pl.* Polyan'dria (Gr. *anēr, andros*, man, male), in Linnaeus's system a class of plants with many stamens inserted in the receptacle.—*adj.* polyan'drous, having or allowing several husbands or male mates (at a time): having a large and indefinite number of stamens or of antheridia (*bot.*).—*ns.* pol'yandry (or *-an'*), the condition or practice of being polyandrous: the social usage of some peoples in certain stages of civilisation in which a woman normally has several husbands; polyan'-thus (Gr. *anthos*, flower), a many-flowered supposed hybrid between cowslip and primrose:—*pl.* polyan'thuses.—*adj.* pol'yarch (*-ärk*; Gr. *archē*, origin), having many xylem strands.—*n.* pol'yarchy (*-ärk-i*; Gr. *archein*, to rule), government by many persons.—*adjs.* polyatom'ic (*chem.*), having many atoms, or replaceable atoms or groups: multivalent; polyax'ial (L. *axis*), polyax'on (Gr. *axōn*, axis), having many axes or several axis-cylinders.—*n.* a monaxonic sponge spicule.—*adjs.* polyaxon'ic; polybās'ic, capable of reacting with several equivalents of an acid: of acids, having several replaceable hydrogen atoms.—*n.* polycar'bonate, any of a range of strong thermoplastics.—*adjs.* polycarp'ic (Gr. *karpos*, fruit), fruiting many times, or year after year; polycarp'ous, polycarpic: having an apocarpous gynaeceum.—*n.pl.* Polychaeta (*-kē'tə*; Gr. *chaitē*, bristle), a class of marine Chaetopods with numerous bristles.—*ns.* polychaete, any worm of the Polychaeta; polychlor'oprene, neoprene; pol'ychrest (*-krest*; Gr. *polychrēstos—chrēstos*, useful), a thing, esp. a medicine, useful in several ways.—*adj.* polychroic (*-krō'ik*), pleochroic.—*n.* pol'ychroism.—*adj.* pol'ychrome (*-krōm*; Gr. *chrōma*, colour), many-coloured.—*n.* a work of art (esp. a statue) in several colours: varied colouring.—*adjs.* polychromat'ic, polychrom'ic.—*ns.* pol'ychromy, the art of decorating in many colours; pol'y-clinic, a general clinic or hospital.—*adjs.* polycotyle'donous, with more than two cotyledons; polycrot'ic (Gr. *krotos*, a beat), of the pulse, having several beats to each heart-beat.—*n.* polyc'rotism.—*adj.* polycyclic (*-si'klik*; Gr. *kyklos*, wheel), having many circles, rings, whorls, turns, or circuits: containing more than one ring of atoms in the molecule.—*n.* polycythaemia (*-si-thē'mi-ə*; Gr. *kytos*, a vessel, as if cell, *haima*, blood), excess of red blood-corpuscles.—*adj.* polydac'tyl, having more than the normal number of fingers or toes.—Also *n.* —*ns.* polydac'tylism, -dac'tyly.—*adj.* polydac'tylous.—*n.* polydip'sia (Gr. *dipsa*, thirst), excessive thirst.—*adjs.* polyem'bryonate; polyembryonic (*-on'ik*).—*ns.* polyembryony (*-em'bri-ən-i*), formation of more than one embryo from one ovule or from one fertilised ovum; polyes'ter, any of a range of polymerised esters, some thermoplastic, some thermosetting; polyeth'ylene, pol'ythene, a generic name for certain thermoplastics, polymers of ethylene; Polygala

(*pol-ig'ə-la*; Gr. *polygalon*, milkwort—*gala*, milk), the milkwort genus, giving name to the fam. Polygalā'ceae.—*adj.* polygalaceous (*-lā'-shəs*).—*n.pl.* Polygamia (*pol-i-gā'mi-ə*; Gr. *gamos*, marriage), in Linnaeus's classification, a class having male, female, and hermaphrodite flowers.—*adj.* polygamic (*-gam'ik*).—*n.* polygamist (*pol-ig'*).—*adj.* polyg'amous.—*ns.* polygamy (*pol-ig'ə-mi*), the rule, custom, or condition of marriage to more than one person at a time, or (now rarely) in life: sometimes used for polygyny; mating with more than one in the same breeding season (*zool.*): occurrence of male, female, and hermaphrodite flowers on the same or on different plants (*bot.*); polygen'esis, multiple origin, esp. of mankind.—*adjs.* polygenet'ic, of polygenesis: springing from several sources: of dyes, giving different colours with different mordants; polygen'ic, polygenetic: forming more than one compound with a univalent element.—*ns.* polyg'enism, belief in multiple origin, esp. of mankind; polyg'enist.—*adj.* polyg'enous, of multiple origin or composition.—*n.* polyg'eny, polygenesis.—*adj.* pol'yglot (Gr. *polyglōttos—glōtta*, tongue), in, of, speaking, or writing, many languages.—*n.* one who speaks or writes many languages: a collection of versions in different languages of the same work, esp. a Bible.—Also pol'yglott.—*adjs.* polyglott'al, polyglott'ic, polyglott'ous.—*n.* pol'ygon (*-gon, -gən*; Gr. *gōniā*, angle), a plane figure bounded by straight lines, esp. more than four: an object in the form of a polygon, esp. in the building of earthworks and fortifications.—*adj.* polyg'onal (polygonal numbers, figurate numbers).—*adv.* polyg'onally. —*ns.* Polygon'atum (Gr. *polygonăton—gony, -atos*, knee), the Solomon's seal genus of the lily family; Polyg'onum (Gr. *polygonon*), the knot-grass genus, with swollen joints and sheathing stipules, of the dock family Polygonā'ceae.—*adj.* polygonā'ceous.—*ns.* polyg'ony (*Spens.*), bistort; pol'ygraph, a copying, multiplying, or tracing apparatus: a copy.—*adj.* polygraph'ic.—*n.* polygraphy (*pol-ig'rə-fi*), voluminous writing.—*n.pl.* Polygynia (*-jin'*; Gr. *gynē*, woman, female), in various Linnaean classes of plants, an order with more than twelve styles.—*adjs.* polygyn'ian, of the Polygynia; polygynous (*-lij'* or *-lig'i-nəs*), having several wives: mating with several females: having several styles: polygynian.—*ns.* polygyny (*-lij'* or *-lig'*), the custom, practice, or condition of having a plurality of wives: the habit of mating with more than one female; polyhalite (*-hal'it*; Gr. *hals*, salt), a triclinic mineral, sulphate of magnesium, potassium, and calcium.—*adjs.* polyhedral; polyhed'ric (*-hēd', -hed*).—*ns.* polyhed'ron (Gr. *hedrā*, seat), a solid figure or body bounded by plane faces (esp. more than six); polyhis'tor (Gr. *polyistōr—histŏreein*, to inquire, learn), a person of great and varied learning; polyhistorian (*-tō'ri-ən, -tŏ'*).—*adj.* polyhistoric (*-tor'ik*).—*ns.* polyhis'tory (*-tər-i*); polyhy'brid, a cross between parents differing in several heritable characters.—*adj.* polyhy'dric, having several hydroxyl groups.—*ns.* Polyhymnia (*pol-i-him'ni-ə*), Polymnia (*pol-im'ni-ə*; Gr. *Polymnia—hymnos*, hymn, ode), the muse of the sublime lyric; polyi'soprene, a rubber-like polymer of isoprene; polymas'tia, polymast'ism, pol'ymasty (Gr. *mastos*, breast), the presence of supernumerary breasts or nipples. —*adj.* polymas'tic.—*n.* pol'ymath (Gr. *polymathēs*—the root of *manthanein*, to learn), one who knows many arts and sciences.—*adj.* polymath'ic.—*ns.* polym'athy, much and varied learning; pol'ymer (Gr. *meros*, part; *chem.*), one of a series of substances alike in percentage composition, but differing in molecular weight, especially one of those of higher molecular weight as produced by polymerisation.—*adj.* **polymeric** (*-mer'ik*), of, in a relation of, or manifesting, polymerism.—*ns.* **polym'eride,** a polymer; **polymerisā'tion.**—*v.t.* **polym'erise, -ize,** to combine to form a more complex molecule having the same empirical formula as the simpler ones combined: to render polymerous.—*v.i.* to change into a polymer.—*n.* **polym'erism.**—*adj.* **polym'erous,** having many parts: having many parts in a whorl (*bot.*).—*ns.* **polym'ery,** condition of being polymerous; **pol'ymorph** (Gr. *polymorphos,* many-formed—*morphē,* form), any one of several forms in which the same thing may occur: an organism occurring in several forms: a substance crystallising in several systems.—*adj.* **polymorph'ic.**—*n.* **polymorph'ism.**—*adjs.* **polymorph'ous; Polynē'sian** (Gr. *nēsos,* an island), of *Polynesia,* its prevailing race of brown men, or their languages (a division of the Austronesian).—*n.* a native of Polynesia: a member of the brown race of Polynesia.—*adj.* and *n.* **polynō'mial,** multinomial.—*ns.* **polynō'mialism; polyonym** (*pol'i-ō-nim*; Gr. *onyma,* a form of *onoma,* name), a name consisting of several words.—*adjs.* **polyonym'ic,** of more than two words; **polyon'ymous,** having many names.—*ns.* **polyon'ymy,** multiplicity of names for the same thing; **polyp, polype** (*pol'ip*; L. *polypus, -i,* adopted, and transformed to 2nd declension, from Gr. *polypous, -podos—pous,* foot; see **polypus**), orig. an octopus or cuttlefish (*obs.*): later extended to other animals with many arms or tentacles, esp. coelenterates and Polyzoa: an individual of a colonial animal: a polypus (*rare*):—*pl.* **pol'yps, polypes** (*pol'ips*), **polypi** (*pol'i-pī*; L.); **pol'ypary,** the common investing structure of a colony of polyps; **polypep'tide,** a peptide in which many amino-acids are linked to form a chain.—*adjs.* **polypet'alous,** with free petals; **polyphagous** (*po-lif'ə-gəs*; Gr. *phagein* (aorist), to eat), eating many different kinds of food: eating much.—*n.* **polyph'agy** (*-ji*), the character of being polyphagous.—*adjs.* **pol'y- phase,** having several alternating electric currents of equal frequency with uniformly spaced phase differences; **polyphasic** (*-fāz'ik*), going through several phases of activity followed by rest in any twenty-four hours; **Polyphē'mian, Polyphē'mic.**—*n.* **Polyphē'mus** (Gr. *Polyphēmos*), the Cyclops blinded by Odysseus.—*adjs.* **polyphloisbic** (*pol-i-flois'bik*; Gr. *polyphloisbos—phloisbos,* din), **poluphloisboiotic** (*pol- ōō-flois-boi-ot'ik*), **polyphloesboean** (*pol-i-flēs- bē'an,* the *oi* and *oe* from the genitive ending in Homer's phrase *polyphloisboio thalassēs,* of the much-roaring sea), loud-roaring; **poluphlois- boiotatot'ic** (*Thackeray*; as if from a Gr. superl. in *-otatos*).—*ns.* **pol'yphon(e)** (*-fon, -fōn*; Gr. *phōnē,* a voice), a lute-like musical instrument: a musical box playing tunes from perforated metal disks; **polyphone** (*pol'i-fōn*), a symbol with more than one phonetic value.—*adj.* **polyphonic** (*-fon'ik*), many-voiced: of polyphones: of polyphony.—*ns.* **pol'yphonist,** a contrapuntist; **polyph'ony,** composition of music in parts each with an independent melody of its own.—*adjs.* **polyphyletic** (*pol-i-fil-et'ik,* or *-ʃil-*; Gr. *phyletikos,* pertaining to a tribesman —*phylē,* a tribe), of multiple origin: descended by convergent lines from several ancestral groups; **polyphyllous** (*pol-i-fil'əs*; Gr. *phyllon,* leaf), having the perianth leaves free.—*ns.* **pol'ypide, pol'ypite,** a polyp of a colonial animal; **polyp'idom,** a polypary (Gr. *domos,* house). —*adjs.* **pol'ypine; pol'ypoid; pol'ypous.**—*n.pl.* **Polypacoph'ora** (Gr. *plax, plakos,* a plate, slab), an order of molluscs, bilaterally symmetrical, with shell composed of eight transverse dorsal plates—the chitons, etc.—*adj.* **polyploid** (*pol'i-*

*ploid*; on the analogy of *haploid, diploid*), having more than twice the normal haploid number of chromosomes.—*ns.* **pol'yploidy,** the polyploid condition; **polypod** (*pol'i-pod*), an animal with many feet: polypody; **Polypodium** (*-pō'di-əm*; Gr. *podion,* dim. of *pous,* a foot), the typical genus of **Polypodiā'ceae,** the family with stalked sporangia and vertical annulus to which most ferns belong—so named from the many-footed appearance of the rhizome; **polypody** (*pol'i- pod-i*), any fern of the genus Polypodium, esp. *P. vulgare.*—*adj.* **pol'ypoid,** like polypus.—*ns.* **Polyporus** (*po-lip'ə-rəs*; Gr. *poros,* a pore), a large genus of pore fungi (*q.v.*), often forming hoof-like and bracket-like growths on trees; **polypō'sis,** presence or development of polypi.— *adj.* **pol'ypous,** of the nature of a polyp.—*ns.* **polyprop'ylene,** a polymer of propylene, similar in properties to polyethylene; **polyprō'todont** (Gr. *prōtos,* first, *odous, odontos,* tooth), any member of the **Polyprotodont'ia,** the suborder of marsupials, including opossums, dasyures, etc., with many small incisors; **Polyp'terus** (Gr. *pteron,* a fin), an African genus of Crossopterygian river fishes, with the dorsal fin represented by detached rays; **polypus** (*pol'i-pəs*; Gr. *polypous*), a pedunculated tumour growing from mucous membrane:—*pl.* (L.) **pol'ypi; poly- saccharide** (*-sak'ə-rīd*), a sugar that hydrolyses into more than one molecule of simple sugars; **polyse'mant** (*-sē'*), **pol'yseme** (*-sēm*), a word with more than one meaning; **pol'ysemy.** —*adj.* **polysep'alous,** having the sepals separate from each other.—*ns.* **polysilox'ane,** any of a number of polymers which are the basis of silicone chemistry; **pol'ysomy,** condition in which one or more extra chromosomes, esp. sex chromosomes, are present in the cells of the body.—*adjs.* **polysty'lar, pol'ystyle** (Gr. *stylos,* column), having many columns.—*n.* **polysty'rene,** a polymer of styrene having good mechanical properties, resistant to moisture and to chemicals.—*adjs.* **polysyllabic** (*-ab'ik*), **-al.**—*adv.* **poly- syllab'ically.**—*ns.* **polysyllab'icism, polysyll'a- bism; polysyll'able,** a word of many or of more than three syllables; **polysyndeton** (*pol-i-sin'de- ton*; Gr. *syndeton,* a conjunction—*syn,* together, *deein,* to bind; *rhet.*), figurative repetition of connectives or conjunctions; **polysynthesis** (*-sin'thi-sis*).—*adjs.* **polysynthet'ic, -al,** made up of many separate elements: built up of a number of small crystals in parallel growth (*crystal.*): combining many simple words of a sentence in one, as in the native languages of America— also called *incorporating* (*philol.*).—*adv.* **poly- synthet'ically.**—*ns.* **polysynthet'icism** (*-i-sizm*), **polysyn'thetism,** the character of being polysynthetic.—*adj.* **polytechnic** (*-tek'nik*; Gr. *tech- nikos—technē,* art), of many arts or technical subjects.—*n.* a school where such subjects are taught to an advanced level.—*adj.* **polytech'nical.** —*n.* **pol'ytetrafluor(o)eth'ylene,** a plastic with non-adhesive surface properties.—*adj.* **poly- thalamous** (*-thal'ə-məs*; Gr. *thalamos,* a chamber), having several cells or chambers.—*ns.* **polytheism** (*pol'i-thē-izm*; Gr. *theos,* a god), the doctrine of a plurality of gods; **pol'ytheist.** —*adjs.* **polytheist'ic, -al.**—*adv.* **polytheist'ically.** —*n.* **pol'ythene** (see **polyethylene**).—*adjs.* **poly- tocous** (*pol-it'ə-kəs*; Gr. *tokos,* birth), producing many or several at a birth or in a clutch; **poly- ton'al.**—*ns.* **polytonal'ity,** use at the same time of two or more musical keys; **Polytrichum** (*pol-it'ri-kəm*; Gr. *thrix, trichos,* hair), a genus of tall hairy-capped mosses.—*adj.* **polytypic** (*-tip'ik*), having many types and representatives. —*n.* **polyur'ethane,** any of a range of resins, both thermoplastic and thermosetting, used in production of foamed materials.—*adj.* **poly- valent** (*pol-i-vā'lənt, pol-iv'ə-lənt*), multivalent.

—*n.* **polyvi′nyl,** a vinyl polymer.—Also *adj.* (**poly-vinyl chloride,** a vinyl plastic used as a rubber substitute for coating electric wires, cables, etc., and as a dress and furnishing fabric).—*n.* **pol′y-water,** supposed form of water, said to be a polymer, with properties different from those of ordinary water.—*n.pl.* **Polyzō′a** (Gr. *zōion,* an animal), a phylum of aquatic animals, almost all colonial, with cup-shaped body, U-shaped food-canal, and a wreath of tentacles about the mouth:—*sing.* **polyzo′on.**—*n.* and *adj.* **polyzo′an.**—*adj.* **polyzoarial** (-*ā′ri-əl*).—*ns.* **polyzoā′rium; polyzō′ary,** a polyzoan colony, or its supporting skeleton.—*adjs.* **polyzō′ic,** having many zooids: pertaining to the Polyzoa; **polyzo′nal** (Gr. *zōnē,* belt), composed of many zones or belts; **polyzō′oid,** like, or of the nature of, a Polyzoon. [Gr. *polys, poleia, poly,* much.]
**polyacid** . . . to . . . **Polynesian.** See **poly-.**
**polynia, polynya,** *pol-in′i-ə, -in′yə, n.* open water among sea ice, esp. Arctic. [Russ. *polyn′ya.*]
**polynomial** . . . to . . . **polyzooid.** See **poly-.**
**pom,** *pom,* (*coll.*) *n.* short for Pomeranian dog.
**pomace,** *pum′is, n.* crushed apples for cider-making, or the residue after pressing: any-thing crushed to pulp, esp. after oil has been expressed.—**pom′ace-fly,** a fruit-fly (Drosophila). [App. L.L. *pōmācium,* cider—L. *pōmum,* apple, etc.]
**pomade,** *pom-äd′, n.* ointment for the hair—Latinised as **pomā′tum.**—*v.t.* to anoint with pomade. [Fr. *pommade*—It. *pomada, pomata,* lip-salve—L. *pōmum,* an apple.]
**Pomak,** *pō-mäk′, n.* a Mohammedan Bulgarian.
**pomander,** *pom-* or *pōm-an′dər, n.* a ball of per-fumes, or a perforated globe or box in which it is kept or carried. [O.Fr. *pomme d′ambre,* apple of amber.]
**pomato,** *pom-ä′tō, -ā′tō, n.* a tomato grafted on a potato. [Portmanteau-word.]
**pomatum.** Same as **pomade.**
**pome,** *pōm, n.* an apple (*rare*): a fruit constructed like an apple, the enlarged fleshy receptacle en-closing a core formed from the carpels: a king′s globe or mound: a priest′s hand-warming ball of hot water.—*adj.* **pomaceous** (-*ā′shəs*), relating to, consisting of, or resembling, apples: of the apple family or the apple section of the rose family.—*n.* **pome′roy, pomroy** (*pom′, pum′roi*), an old variety of apple.—*adjs.* **pomif′erous,** bearing apples, pomes, or fruit generally; **pomolog′ical.**—*ns.* **pomol′ogist; pomol′ogy,** the study of fruit-growing.—**pome′-cit′ron,** the citron; **pome′-water,** **pom′water** (*Shak.*), a sweet juicy apple; **pom′iculture,** fruit growing: pomology. [L. *pōmum,* a fruit, an apple.]
**pomegranate,** *pom′gran-it, pom′ə-,* formerly *pom-, pum-gran′it, n.* an Oriental fruit much culti-vated in warm countries, with a thick leathery rind and numerous seeds with pulpy edible seed-coats: the tree (*Punica granatum*; fam. Punicaceae) bearing it. [O.Fr. *pome grenate*—L. *pōmum,* an apple, *grānātum,* having many grains.]
**pomelo,** *pum′,* or *pom′il-ō, n.* the shaddock: the grape-fruit—cf. **pompelmoose.** [Origin obscure.]
**Pomeranian,** *pom-i-rā′ni-ən, adj.* of *Pomerania.* —*n.* a native of Pomerania: a spitz or Pomer-anian dog, a cross from the Eskimo dog, with a sharp-pointed face and an abundant white, creamy, or black coat.
**Pomfret,** spelling representing the older pro-nunciation (*pum′frit*) of **Pontefract,** *pon′ti-frakt, n.* a town in Yorkshire.—**Pomfret-** (*pum′, pom′*), **Pon′tefract-cake,** a round flat liquorice sweet-meat made there. [A.Fr. *Pontfret,* L. *pōns, pontis,* bridge, *fractus,* broken.]
**pomfret,** *pom′frit, n.* any of several fishes, in-cluding an East Indian fish valued as food. [Earlier *pamflet*—Fr. *pample*—Port. *pampo.*]

**pommel,** *pum′l, n.* a knob (*obs.*): a ball-shaped finial: a knob on a sword-hilt: the high part of a saddle-bow: a heavy-headed ramming tool.—*v.t.* (usu. spelt **pummel,** q.v.).—*adjs.* **pomm′elled,** having a pommel—in heraldry also **pommelé** (*pom′*), **pomm′etty.** [O.Fr. *pomel* (Fr. *pommeau*)—L. *pōmum,* an apple.]
**pommy,** *pom′i,* (*Austr.*) *n.* an immigrant from the British Isles. [From **pomegranate.**]
**pomoerium,** *pō-mē′ri-əm, n.* an open space around a town, within and without the walls. [L. *pōmoerium,* app. for *postmoerium—post* and *moiros,* old form of *mūrus,* wall.]
**Pomona,** *pō-mō′na, n.* the Roman goddess of fruits. [L. *Pōmōna—pōmum,* fruit, apple.]
**pomp,** *pomp, n.* a procession: great show or dis-play: ceremony: ostentation: vain show: worldly vanity: consequential bearing.—*n.* **pom-posity** (*-os′i-ti*), solemn affectation of dignity: a ridiculously pompous action, expression, or person.—*adj.* **pomp′ous,** stately (*arch.*): solemnly consequential.—*adv.* **pomp′ously.**—*n.* **pomp′ous-ness.** [Fr. *pompe*—L. *pompa*—Gr. *pompē,* a sending, escort, procession—*pempein,* to send.]
**pompadour,** *pom′pə-dōōr, n.* a fashion of dressing women′s hair by rolling it back from the fore-head over a cushion: a corsage with low square neck: a pattern for silk, with pink, blue, and gold leaves and flowers: a pink colour.—*adj.* in, pertaining to, the style of hairdressing or dress described above, associated with Mme de Pompadour′s time. [Marquise de *Pompadour,* 1721-64.]
**pompano,** *pomp′ə-nō, n.* a general name for Car-angoid fishes, esp. American food-fishes of the genus Trachynotus. [Sp. *pámpano,* a fish of another family.]
**Pompeian,** *pom-pē′ən, adj.* pertaining to *Pompeii,* a city buried by an eruption of Mount Vesuvius in A.D. 79, excavated since 1755.—**Pompeii′an-red′,** a red colour like that on the walls of Pom-peian houses.
**pompelmoose,** *pom′pəl-mōōs, n.* the shaddock, esp. the grape-fruit.—Also **pam′pelmoose, -mouse, pom′pelmous(e), pum′ple-nose, pom′pelo, pom′-elo.** [Du. *pompelmoes*; origin obscure.]
**pompey,** *pom′pi,* (*Dickens*) *v.t.* to pamper (*q.v.*).
**Pompey,** (*slang*) Portsmouth.
**pompholyx,** *pom′fō-liks, n.* a vesicular eruption chiefly on the palms and soles: impure zinc oxide.—*adj.* **pomphol′ygous.** [Gr. *pompholyx, -ygos,* bubble, slag—*pomphos,* a blister.]
**pompier,** *pom′pi-ər,* or (Fr.) *pɔ̃-pyä, adj.* of art, conventional, traditional, uninspired. [Fr., see **pompier-ladder.**
**pompier-ladder,** *pom′pi-ər-lad′ər,* or (Fr.) *pɔ̃-pyä, n.* a fireman′s ladder, a pole with cross-bars and hook. [Fr. *pompier,* fireman—*pompe,* pump.]
**pompion,** *pump′i-ən.* See **pumpkin.**
**pompom,** *pom′pom,* (*coll.*) *n.* a machine-gun: a multi-barrelled anti-aircraft gun. [Imit.]
**pompom,** *pom′pom,* **pom′pon,** (*obs.*) **pompoon,** *pom-pōōn′, n.* a jewelled hair ornament on a pin: a fluffy or woolly ball, tuft, or tassel worn on a shoe, hat, etc. [Fr. *pompon.*]
**′pon,** *pon,* aphetic for **upon.**
**ponce,** *pons, n.* a man who lives on the immoral earnings of a woman. [Ety. dub.]
**ponceau,** *pɔ̃-sō′, n.* and *adj.* poppy colour.—*n.* a red dye:—*pl.* **ponceaux** (*-sōz′*). [Fr.]
**ponceau,** *pɔ̃-sō′, n.* a small bridge or culvert. [Fr.]
**poncho,** *pon′chō, n.* a South American cloak, a blanket with a hole for the head: a cyclist′s waterproof cape of like form: any similar gar-ment:—*pl.* **pon′chos.** [Sp. from Araucanian.]
**pond,** *pond, n.* a small, usually artificial lake: the stretch of water between locks in a canal: the Atlantic (*facet.*).—*v.t.* to make into a pond.—*v.i.* to collect into a pond.—*n.* **pond′age,** the capacity of a pond.—**pond′-life′,** animal life in

# ponder     1041     pool

ponds; **pond'-lily**, a water-lily; **pond'-master**, the man in charge of a swimming-pond; **pond'-snail**, a pond-dwelling snail, esp. Limnaea; **pond'weed**, any plant of the genus Potamogeton (**Canadian pondweed**, Anacharis). [M.E. *ponde*; cf. **pound** (2).]

**ponder**, *pon'dər*, *v.t.* to weigh, now only in the mind: to think over: to consider.—*v.i.* to think (often with *on* and *over*).—*n.* **ponderabil'ity.**—*adjs.* **pon'derable**, that may be weighed: having sensible weight; **pon'deral**, pertaining to weight: ascertained by weight.—*ns.* **pon'derance**, **pon'derancy**, weight.—*v.t.* and *v.i.* **pon'derate**, to weigh: to ponder.—*ns.* **pondera'tion**, weighing; **pon'derer.**—*adv.* **pon'deringly.**—*ns.* **pon'derment**; **ponderosity** (-*os'i-ti*).—*adj.* **pon'derous**, heavy: weighty: massive: unwieldy: lumbering: solemnly laboured.—*adv.* **pon'derously.**—*n.* **pon'derousness.** [L. *ponderāre*, and *pondus*, *ponderis*, a weight.]

**pone**, *pōn*, (*U.S.*) *n.* maize bread: a maize loaf or cake. [Algonquin *pone*.]

**pone**, *pō'ni*, *pōn*, (*cards*) *n.* the player to the right of the dealer who cuts the cards: sometimes the player to the left. [L. *pōnĕ*, imper. of *pōnĕre*, to place.]

**ponent**, *pō'nənt*, (*Milt.*) *adj.* western. [It. *ponente*, setting (of the sun)—L. *pōnēns*, -*entis*, pr.p. of *pōnĕre*, to put.]

**ponerology**, *pon-ə-rol'ə-ji*, (*theol.*) *n.* the doctrine of wickedness. [Gr. *ponēros*, bad, *logos*, discourse.]

**pong**, *pong*, (*slang*) *v.i.* to gag, to extend one's part (*theat.*).

**pong**, *pong*, *v.i.* to smell bad.—*n.* a bad smell. [Prob. Romany *pan*, to stink.]

**pongee**, *pun-*, *pon-jē'*, *n.* a soft silk, made from cocoons of a wild silkworm: a fine cotton. [Perh. Chin. *pun-chi*, own loom.]

**pongo**, *pong'gō*, *n.* an anthropoid ape, orig. prob. the gorilla, but transferred to the orang-utan: a monkey: a soldier (*Services slang*).—*adj.* and *n.* **pon'gid** (-*jid*). [Congo *mpongi*.]

**poniard**, *pon'yərd*, *n.* a small dagger.—*v.t.* to stab with a poniard. [Fr. *poignard*—*poing*—L. *pugnus*, fist.]

**pons**, *ponz*, (*anat.*) *n.* a connecting part, esp. the **pons Varolii**, a mass of fibres joining the hemispheres of the brain:—*pl.* **pon'tēs.**—*adjs.* **pon'tal**, **pon'tic**, **pon'tile**, relating to the pons of the brain. [L. *pōns*, *pontis*, a bridge.]

**pons asinorum**, *ponz as-i-nōr'əm*, -*nōr'*, *pōns as-i-nōr'ōom*, (L.) the asses' bridge (see **ass**): any severe test of a beginner.

**pontage**, *pont'ij*, *n.* a toll paid on bridges: a tax for repairing bridges. [L.L. *pontāgium*—L. *pōns*, *pontis*, a bridge.]

**Pontederia**, *pont-e-dē'ri-ə*, *n.* an American genus of monocotyledonous water- or bog-plants, called pickerel-weed, giving name to a family **Pontederiā'ceae**. [After Giulio *Pontedera* (1688-1757), Italian botanist.]

**Pontefract.** See **Pomfret** (former spelling).

**pontianac**, **pontianak**, *pont-i-ä'nak*, *n.* jelutong. [*Pontianak*, in Borneo.]

**Pontic**, *pon'tik*, *adj.* of the ancient kingdom and Roman province of *Pontus*, or of the *Pontus* Euxinus or Black Sea. [Gr. *Pontikos*—*pontos*, sea.]

**pontie.** See **punty.**

**pontifex**, *pon'ti-feks*, *n.* in ancient Rome a member of a college of priests that had control of matters of religion, their chief being *Pontifex Maximus*: a pontiff: a bridge-builder:—*pl.* **pontifices** (-*tif'i-sēz*, -*kās*).—*n.* **pon'tiff**, a pontifex: a high-priest: a bishop, esp. the pope or *sovereign pontiff* (*R.C.*): an oracular person.—*adjs.* **pontif'ic**, -**al**, of or belonging to a pontiff: splendid: pompously dogmatic.—*ns.* **pontif'ical**, an office-book for bishops; **pontifical'ity.**—*adv.*

**pontif'ically.**—*n.pl.* **pontif'icals**, the dress of a priest, bishop, or pope.—*n.* **pontif'icate**, the dignity of a pontiff or high-priest: the office and dignity or reign of a pope.—*v.i.* to perform the duties of a pontiff: to play the pontiff.—*n.* **pon'tifice** (-*fis*; *Milt.*), bridge-work, a bridge.—*v.i.* **pon'tify**, to play the pontiff.—**pontifical mass**, mass celebrated by a bishop while wearing his full vestments. [L. *pontifex*, *pontificis* (partly through Fr. *pontife*), which was supposed to be from *pōns*, *pontis*, a bridge, *facĕre*, to make, but is probably from an Oscan and Umbrian word *puntis*, propitiatory offering.]

**pontil.** See **punty.**

**pontlevis**, *pont-lev'is*, *pō-lə-vē*, *n.* a drawbridge. [Fr.]

**pontoon**, *pon-tōōn'*, *n.* a flat-bottomed boat, a ferryboat, barge, or lighter: such a boat, or a float, used to support a bridge: a bridge of boats: a low vessel carrying plant, materials, and men for work at sea or on rivers: the floating gate of a dock: a boat-like float of an aeroplane: a float.—Also **ponton** (*pon'tan*, *pon-tōōn'*).—*v.t.* to cross by pontoon.—*ns.* **pontoneer'**, **pontonier'**, **pontonnier'**, **pontoon'er**, a builder of pontoon-bridges.—**pontoon'-bridge**, a platform or roadway supported upon pontoons. [Fr. *ponton*—L. *pontō*, -*ōnis*, a punt, pontoon—*pōns*, a bridge.]

**pontoon**, *pon-tōōn'*, *n.* a card game of chance. [vingt-et-un (q.v.).]

**ponty.** See **punty.**

**pony**, formerly also **poney**, *pō'ni*, *n.* a small horse—usu. one less than 14·2 hands high: £25 (*slang*): a translation, crib or key (*U.S. slang*): a small glass, esp. of beer.—*v.t.* and *v.i.* to pay or settle (with *up*): to prepare or translate by help of a crib.—**po'ny-carr'iage**; **po'ny-en'gine**, a shunting engine; **po'ny-skin**, the skin of a foal, esp. from the Kirghiz Steppes, used as a fur; **po'ny-tail**, a woman's hair style in which the hair is gathered together at the back and hangs down like a pony's tail; **po'ny-trekking**, cross-country pony-riding in groups as a pastime.—**Jerusalem pony**, an ass. [Scots pown(e)y, **pownie**, prob.—O.Fr. *poulenet*, dim. of *poulain*—L.L. *pullānus*, a foal—L. *pullus*, a young animal.]

**pooch**, *pōōch*, (*slang*) *n.* a dog, esp. a mongrel.

**pood**, *pōōd*, *n.* a Russian weight, *c.* 36 lb. avoirdupois. [Russ. *pud*.]

**poodle**, *pōōd'l*, *n.* a breed of pet dog which has curly hair (often clipped to a standard pattern.)—**pood'le-dog**, a poodle: an assiduous follower; **pood'le-faker** (*Anglo-Indian slang*), a man who sought women's society. [Ger. *pudel*; L.G. *pudeln*, to paddle, splash.]

**poof.** See **pouf(fe).**

**pooh**, *pōō*, *pōō*, *interj.* of disdain.—*v.t.* **pooh-pooh'**, to make light of. [Imit.]

**Pooh-Bah**, *pōō'-bä'*, person who holds many offices simultaneously: one giving himself airs. [Character in Gilbert and Sullivan's *The Mikado*.]

**pooja, poojah.** Same as **puja.**

**pook, pouk**, *pōōk*, (*Scot.*) *v.t.* to pluck: to pinch:—*pa.t.* and *pa.p.* **pook'it, pouk'it.** [Origin unknown.]

**pool**, *pōōl*, *n.* a small body of still water: a temporary or casual collection of water or other liquid: a puddle: a deep part of a stream. [O.E *pōl*; Du. *poel*, Ger. *pfuhl*; relation to Ir and Gael. *poll*, W. *pwll*, undetermined.]

**pool**, *pōōl*, *n.* the stakes in certain games: the collective stakes of a number of persons who combine in a betting arrangement: an organised arrangement for betting in this way: a group of persons so combining: a game, or a set of players, at quadrille, etc.: a game or contest of various kinds in which the winner receives the pool: a game played on a billiard-table, each player trying to pocket the others' balls in

---

Neutral vowels in unaccented syllables: *el'ə-mənt*; for certain sounds in foreign words, see p. viii

rotation: a common stock or fund: a combination of interest: a combine: an arrangement for eliminating competition: a group of people who may be called upon as required, e.g., a pool of typists: (in *pl.*) football pools, betting by post on the results of a number of football games.—*v.t.* to put into a common fund or stock.—*v.i.* to form a pool.—**scoop the pool** (*coll.*; *gambling*), to win a substantial amount of money from collective stakes. [Fr. *poule*, a hen, also stakes (possibly through an intermediate sense of plunder), but associated in English with **pool** (1).]

**poon**, *pōōn*, *n.* an Indian tree, *Calophyllum inophyllum*, or other species of the genus (family Guttiferae).—**poon'-oil**, an oil expressed from its seeds; **poon'-wood**. [Sinh. *pūna*.]

**poonac**, *pōō'nak*, *n.* coconut oilcake. [Sinh. *punakku*.]

**poop**,.*pōōp*, *n.* the after part of a ship: a high deck at the stern.—*v.t.* to break over the stern of: to ship over the stern.—*adj.* **pooped**, having a poop. [Fr. *poupe*—L. *puppis*, the poop.]

**poop**, **poupe**, *pōōp*, (*obs.*) *v.t.* to befool: to cozen: to undo: to do for:—*pa.p.* in *Shak.* **poupt**. [Cf. Du. *poep*, clown.]

**poop**. Abbrev. for **nincompoop**.

**poop**, *pōōp*, *v.t.* (*slang*) to make out of breath: to exhaust.—*v.i.* (*slang*) to become winded or exhausted: (often with *out*) to cease. [Orig. unknown.]

**poor**, *pōōr*, *adj.* possessing little or nothing: without means: needy: deficient: lacking: unproductive: scanty: mere: inferior: sorry: spiritless: in sorry condition: (in modest or ironical self-depreciation) humble: unfortunate, to be pitied (esp. of the dead).—*adj.* **poor'ish.**—*adv.* **poor'ly**, in a poor manner: badly: inadequately: in a small way: meanly.—*adj.* in ill-health.—*n.* **poor'ness.**—**poor'-box**, a money-box for gifts for the poor; **poor'house** (*Scot.* poor's-house, puir's'-house, -hoose), a house established at the public expense for sheltering the poor—a workhouse; **poor-John'** (*Shak.*), salt hake; **poor'-law** (often in *pl.*), the law or laws relating to the support of the poor.—Also *adj.*—**poor'-rate**, a rate or tax for the support of the poor; **poor's'-box**, a poor-box.—*adj.* **poor'-spir'ited**, lacking in spirit.—**poor'-spir'itedness**; **poor's'-roll** (*Scots law*), the list of poor litigants allowed to sue *in formā pauperis*; **poor white**, a member of a class of poor, improvident, and incompetent white peoples in the Southern States of America, South Africa and elsewhere, called by the Negroes *poor white trash.*—**poor man of mutton** (*Scot.*), cold mutton broiled, esp. the shoulder; **poor man's weather-glass**, the pimpernel, reputed to close its flowers before rain. [O.Fr. *poure*, *povre* (Fr. *pauvre*)—L. *pauper*, poor.]

**poort**, *pōrt*, *pōōrt*, (*S.Afr.*) *n.* a mountain pass. [Du.,—L. *porta*, gate.]

**poortith**, *pōōr'tith*, (*Scot.*) *n.* poverty. [O.Fr. *pouerteit*, *poverteit*—L. *paupertās*, *-ātis*.]

**poorwill**, *pōōr'wil*, *n.* a Western North American night-jar (Phalaenoptilus), smaller than the whippoorwill. [From its note.]

**Pooter**, *pōō'tər*, *n.* a petit bourgeois, conventional and unimaginative.—*n.* **Poo'terism**. [Charles *Pooter* in *Diary of a Nobody*, by George and Weedon Grossmith.]

**pop**, *pop*, *n.* a mild explosive sound, as of drawing a cork: a shot: a pistol (*slang*): ginger-beer, champagne or other effervescing drink (*slang*): pawn, or an act of pawning (*slang*).—*v.i.* to make a pop: to shoot: to burst with a pop: to protrude: to come, go, slip, or pass, suddenly, unexpectedly, or unobtrusively: to pitch or alight: to propose marriage (*slang*).—*v.t.* to cause to make a pop or to burst with a pop: to shoot: to thrust or put suddenly: to pawn

(*slang*):—*pr.p.* **popp'ing**; *pa.t.* and *pa.p.* **popped**.—*adv.* with a pop: suddenly.—*n.* **popp'er**, one who pops: anything that makes a pop: a utensil for popping corn.—**pop'corn**, maize burst open and swelled by heating: a kind of maize suitable for this; **pop'-eye**, a prominent or protruding eye.—*adj.* **pop'-eyed**, having prominent or protruding eyes: open-eyed, agog (as from interest, excitement, etc.).—**pop'-gun**, a tube for shooting pellets by compressed air: a contemptible gun; **popp'ing-crease** (see crease); **pop'-shop** (*slang*), a pawnshop; **pop'-visit**, a visit at an odd time, casual visit; **pop'-weed**, bladderwort.—**pop off**, to make off: to die: to fall asleep; **pop the question**, to make an offer of marriage. [Imit.]

**pop**, *pop*, (*coll.*) *adj.* popular.—*n.* currently popular music (also **pop-music**).—**pop art**, art drawing deliberately on commonplace material of modern urbanised life; **pop-concert**, a concert at which pop-music is played; **pop-group**, a (usu. small) group of musicians who play pop-music; **pop-record**; **pop-singer**; **pop-song**.

**pop**. See **poppa, poppet, poppycock, popular**.

**pop(p)adum**, *pop'ə-dəm*, *n.* a thin strip or circle of dough fried in oil, etc.—Many variant spellings. [Tamil, Malayalam, *poppatam*.]

**pope**, *pōp*, (often *cap.*) *n.* the bishop of Rome, head of the R.C. Church: formerly applied also to the patriarch of Alexandria and other bishops: any spiritual head: a person wielding, assuming, or thought to assume authority like that of the pope: the ruff (fish).—*ns.* **pope'dom**, office, dignity, or jurisdiction of the pope: a pope's tenure of office; **pope'hood, pope'ship**, the condition of being pope; **pope'ling**, a little pope; **pop'ery**, a hostile term for Roman Catholicism or whatever seems to savour of it.—*adj.* **pop'ish** (*hostile*), relating to the pope or to popery.—*adv.* **pop'ishly.—Pope Joan**, a mythical female pope: an old card-game like newmarket; **pope's eye**, the gland surrounded with fat in the middle of the thigh of an ox or a sheep; **pope's head**, a long-handled brush; **pope's knights**, Roman Catholic priests, formerly called Sir; **pope's nose**, **parson's nose**, the fleshy part of a cooked bird's tail.—**Black Pope** (see black). [O.E. *pāpa*—L.L. *pāpa*—Gr. *pappas* (late Gr. *papās*), hypocoristic for father.]

**pope**, *pōp*, *n.* a parish priest in the Greek Orthodox Church. [Russ. *pop*—Late Gr. *papās*; cf. preceding.]

**poperin**. See **poppering**.

**Popian**, *pōp'i-ən*, *adj.* pertaining to Alexander *Pope*, the poet (1688-1744).

**popinjay**, *pop'in-jā*, *n.* a parrot: a figure of a parrot set up to be shot at: a fop or coxcomb. [O.Fr. *papegai*; cf. L.L. *papagallus*; Late Gr. *papagallos* (also *papagas*), a parrot; prob. Eastern; influenced by jay.]

**popjoy**, *pop'joi*, *v.i.* to amuse oneself. [Poss. connected with popinjay.]

**poplar**, *pop'lər*, *n.* a genus (Populus) of trees of the willow family, including aspen, white poplar, black poplar (with its variety Lombardy poplar), cottonwood, etc.: the tulip-tree (*U.S.*). [O.Fr. *poplier*—L. *pōpulus*, poplar-tree.]

**poplin**, *pop'lin*, *n.* a corded fabric with silk warp and worsted weft: an imitation in cotton or other material.—*n.* **poplinette'**, an imitation poplin. [Perh. Fr. *popeline*—It. *papalina*, papal, from the papal town of Avignon, where it was made.]

**popliteal**, *pop-lit'i-əl*, often *pop-lit-ē'əl*, *adj.* of the back of the knee.—Also **poplit'ic**. [L. *poples*, *-itis*.]

**poppa**, **popper**, *pop'ə(r)*, (*coll. U.S.*) *n.* papa.—Abbrev. **pop, pops**.

**poppadum**. See **popadum**.

**poppering**, *pop'ər-ing*, **poperin**, *-in*, *n.* a variety of pear.—Also **poppering pear** (*Shak.* **pop′rin**). [*Poperinghe* in Belgium.]

**poppet**, *pop′it*, *n.* a puppet: a doll (*obs.*): a darling (abbrev. **pop**): a timber support used in launching a ship: a lathe-head: a valve that lifts bodily (also **popp′et-valve**): a type of bead. [An earlier form of **puppet**.]

**popple**, *pop′l*, *v.i.* to flow tumblingly: to heave choppily: to bob up and down: to make the sound of rippling or bubbling, or of repeated shots.—*n.* a poppling movement or sound.—*adj.* **popp′ly**. [Imit.; or a freq. of **pop**.]

**poppy**, *pop′i*, *n.* a cornfield plant (of several species) or its large scarlet flowers: any other species of the genus Papaver, as the opium poppy, or of the kindred genera Glaucium (horned poppy; see **horn**), Meconopsis (see below), etc.: extended to various unrelated plants.—*adj.* **popp′ied**, covered or filled with poppies: soporific: affected by opium.—**popp′y-head**, capsule of the poppy: finial in wood, esp. at a pew end; **popp′y-oil**, a fixed oil from the seeds of the opium-poppy; **popp′y-seed**; **popp′y water**, soporific drink made from poppies.— **blue poppy**, a blue Meconopsis of the northern temperate zone; **Flanders poppy**, emblem, from 1st World War, of British fallen; **Poppy Day**, orig. Armistice Day (q.v.), later the Saturday nearest Armistice Day, or (later) Remembrance Sunday (q.v.), when artificial poppies are sold for war charity; **Welsh poppy**, *Meconopsis cambrica*, which has pale-yellow flowers. [O.E. *popig* —L. *papāver*, poppy.]

**poppycock**, *pop′i-kok*, (*slang*) *n.* balderdash.— Abbrev. **pop**. [Du. *pappekak*, lit. soft dung.]

**popsy**, *pop′si*, *n.* term of endearment for a girl.— Also **pop′sy-wop′sy**. [Prob. dim. abbrev. of **poppet**.]

**populace**, *pop′ū-ləs*, *n.* the common people: those not distinguished by rank, education, office, etc. [Fr.,—It. *popolazzo*—L. *pŏpulus*, people.]

**popular**, *pop′ū-lər*, *adj.* of the people: pleasing to, enjoying the favour of, or prevailing among, the people: liked by one's associates: suited to the understanding or the means of ordinary people: seeking the favour of the common people (*obs.*): democratic: plebeian (*obs.*): vulgar (*obs.*).—*n.* a popular or moderate-priced concert (abbrev. **pop**; cf. **pop** (2)).—*n.* **popularisā′tion, -z-**.—*v.i.* **pop′ularise, -ize**, to make popular: to democratise: to present in a manner suited to ordinary people: to spread among the people.—*ns.* **pop′ulariser, -z-**; **popularity** (*-lar′i-ti*), fact or state of being popular: seeking to gain favour with the people.—*adv.* **pop′ularly**. —*v.t.* **pop′ulate**, to people: to furnish with inhabitants: to devastate (*obs.*).—*v.i.* to multiply by propagation.—*adj.* **inhabited, peopled.**—*ns.* **populā′tion**, act of populating: number of the inhabitants: number of inhabitants of a particular class: the plants or animals in a given area: group of persons, objects, items, considered statistically.—**pop′ulism**; **pop′ulist**, in U.S. a member of the People's Party, founded in 1891, advocating public ownership of public services, graduated income-tax, etc., or of a similar party elsewhere.—*adj.* **pop′ulous**, full of people: numerously inhabited: numerous (*Shak.*): popular (*rare*).—*adv.* **pop′ulously**.— *n.* **pop′ulousness**.—**popular front**, an alliance of the more progressive or leftward political parties in the state. [L. *pŏpulus*, the people.]

**poral**, *pō′rəl*, *pö′*. See **pore** (1).

**porbeagle**, *pör′bē-gl*, *n.* a harmless North Atlantic and Mediterranean shark. [From Cornish dialect; origin unknown.]

**porcelain**, *pörs′lin*, *pörs′*, *n.* a fine earthenware, white, thin, transparent or semi-transparent, first made in China: china-ware.—*adj.* **of porcelain.**—*v.t.* **porcellanise, -ize** (*pör, pör-*

*sel′ən-īz*), **porc′elainise, -ize**, to bake into porcelain or porcellanite.—*n.* **porcell′anite**, a jasper-like shale highly indurated by contact metamorphism.—*adj.* **porcell′anous** (or *pör′, pör′*), like porcelain—also **porcellā′neous, porc′elainous**, **porcelaineous** (*pör-, pör-sə-lā′ni-əs*).—**porcelaincement**, cement for mending china; **porcelain-clay**, kaolin. [O.Fr. *porcelaine*—It. *porcellana*, cowrie.]

**porch**, *pörch, pörch*, *n.* a building forming an enclosure or protection for a doorway: a portico or colonnade: a veranda (*U.S.*): the Stoic school of philosophy, from the Painted Porch in the Agora of Athens where Zeno taught. [O.Fr. *porche*—L. *porticus*—*porta*, a gate.]

**porcine**, *pör′sīn*, *adj.* of pigs: swinish. [L. *porcinus*—*porcus*, a swine.]

**porcpisce**, *pör′pis*, (*Spens.*) *n.* Same as **porpoise**.

**porcupine**, *pör′kū-pin*, *n.* a large spiny rodent of various kinds.—**por′cupine-grass**, a coarse, hard, spiny, tussocky grass (Triodia) that covers vast areas in Australia, commonly called spinifex; **por′cupine-wood**, the wood of the coconut palm, from its spine-like markings. [O.Fr. *porc espin*—L. *porcus*, a pig, *spina*, a spine.]

**pore**, *pör, pör*, *n.* a minute passage or interstice, esp. the opening of a sweat-gland.—*adj.* **por′al**, of or pertaining to pores.—*n.* **por′iness**.—*adjs.* **poromer′ic**, permeable to water vapour, as some synthetic leather; **porose** (*-ōs′*, or *pör′ōs, pör′ōs*). —*n.* **poroscope**, *pör′*, or *pör′ō-skop*, an instrument for investigating porosity or for examining pores or fingerprints.—*adj.* **poroscopic** (*-skop′ik*).—*ns.* **poroscopy** (*os′kə-pi*); **porosity** (*os′i-ti*), the quality or state of being porous: the ratio of the volume of pores to the total volume (of, e.g. a rock): a thing or part that is porous.—*adj.* **por′ous**, having many pores: permeable by fluids, etc.—*n.* **por′ousness**.—*adj.* **por′y**.—**pore fungus**, any fungus having the spore-bearing surface within small pores or tubes; **porous alloys**, alloys obtained by taking the constituents in powder form and pressing them together; **porous plaster**, a plaster for the body, with holes to prevent wrinkling. [Fr.,—L. *porus*—Gr. *poros*, a passage.]

**pore**, *pör, pör*, *v.i.* to gaze with close and steady attention (usu. with *over* or *upon*): to ponder. —*n.* **por′er**. [Origin obscure.]

**porgy, porgie**, *pör′gi*, *n.* a name given to many fishes, chiefly American species of sea-bream. [Partly Sp. and Port. *pargo*, app.—L. *pargus*, a kind of fish; partly from American Indian names.]

**Porifera**, *por-if′ə-rə*, *n.pl.* a phylum of animals, the sponges—*sing.* **por′ifer**.—*adjs.* **porif′eral**, **porif′eran**, of the Porifera; **porif′erous**, having pores. [L. *porus*, a pore, *ferre*, to bear.]

**porism**, *pör′izm, pör′izm*, *n.* in ancient Greek geometry a corollary: also a kind of proposition intermediate between a problem and a theorem, according to some a proposition affirming the possibility of finding such conditions as will render a certain problem capable of innumerable solutions.—*adjs.* **porismat′ic** (*pör-*), **-al**; **poris′tic**, **-al**. [Gr. *porisma*, a corollary, porism—*poros*, a way.]

**pork**, *pörk, pörk*, *n.* a swine (*obs.*): swine's flesh as food: government money to be used for improvements because of their value politically (*U.S.*).—*ns.* **pork′er**, a young hog: a pig fed for pork; **pork′ling**, a young pig.—*adj.* **pork′y**, pig-like: fat.—**pork barrel** (*U.S.*), bill, policy, project, promoting or involving spending, as above; **pork′-butch′er**, one who kills pigs or sells pork; **pork′-chop′**, a slice from a pig's rib; **pork′-pie′**, a pie made of minced pork.—**pork-pie hat**, a hat somewhat like a circular pie, worn by men and women about 1850. [Fr. *porc*—L. *porcus*, a hog.]

**pornocracy**, *pör-nok′rə-si*, *n.* the influence of

courtesans—esp. over the papal court in the earlier half of the 10th century. [Gr. *pornē*, a whore, *kratos*, rule.]

**pornography**, *pör-nog'rə-fi*, *n*. description or portrayal of prostitutes and prostitution: obscene writing, painting, and the like:—*abbrev.* (*coll.*) **porn.**—*n.* **pornog'rapher.**—*adj.* **pornographic** (*pör-no-graf'ik*).—*adv.* **pornograph'ically.** [Gr. *pornē*, a whore, *graphein*, to write, draw.]

**porogamy**, *pör-* or *pör-og'ə-mi*, *n*. entry of the pollen-tube through the micropyle—opp. to *chalazogamy*.—*adj.* **porogamic** (*-ō-gam'ik*). [Gr. *poros*, a pore, *gamos*, marriage.]

**poromeric, poroscope,** etc., **porose, porous,** etc. See **pore** (1).

**porosis**, *pö-rō'sis*, *pö-*, *n*. formation of callus, the knitting together of broken bones. [Gr. *pōrōsis*—*pōros*, callus.]

**porpentine**, *pör'pən-tīn*, (*Shak.*) *n.* Same as **porcupine.**

**porpess, porpesse,** *pör'pəs*, *n.* Same as **porpoise.**

**Porphyra**, *pör'fir-ə*, *n*. a genus of seaweeds, with flat translucent red or purple fronds, purple laver. [Gr. *porphȳrā*, purple (dye).]

**porphyria**, *pör-fi'ri-ə*, *n*. an inborn error of metabolism resulting in the excretion of an abnormal pigment in the urine and characterised by great pain, abnormal skin pigmentation and photosensitivity. [Gr. *porphȳrā*, purple (dye).]

**Porphyrio**, *pör-fir'i-ō*, *n*. the purple coot genus. [Gr. *porphȳriōn*, purple coot.]

**Porphyrogenite**, *pör-fir-oj'ən-it*, *n*. a Byzantine emperor's son born in the purple or porphyry room assigned to empresses: hence, a prince born after his father's accession: one born in the purple.—*ns.* **Porphyrogenitism** (*-ō-jen'it-izm*), the Byzantine principle of the first son born after his father's accession succeeding to the throne; **Porphyrogen'iture.** [L. *porphyrogenitus* for Gr. *porphyrogennētos*—*porphyros*, purple, *gennētos*, born.]

**porphyry**, *pör'fir-i*, *n*. a very hard, variegated rock, of a purple and white colour, used in sculpture (*porfido rosso antico*), often used vaguely: loosely, an igneous rock with porphyritic texture in a fine-grained ground-mass (*geol.*).—*n.* **por'phyrite**, an old-fashioned name for an altered andesite or fine-grained diorite: porphyry.—*adjs.* **porphyritic** (*-it'ik*), like, or of the nature of, porphyry: having large crystals scattered among small or in a fine-grained or glassy ground-mass; **por'phyrous**, purple. [Gr. *porphyrītēs*—*porphyros*, purple.]

**porpoise**, *pör'pəs*, *n*. a short-snouted genus (Phocaena) of the dolphin family, 4 to 8 feet long, gregarious, affording oil and leather: extended to similar forms.—Formerly also **por'pess, porc'pisce.**—*v.i.* to move like a porpoise. [O.Fr. *porpeis*—L. *porcus*, a hog, a pig and *piscis*, a fish.]

**porporate**, *pör'por-āt*, (*Browning*) *adj.* clad in purple. [It. *porporato*—L. *purpurātus*.]

**porraceous**, *por-ā'shəs*, *adj.* leek-green. [L. *porrāceus*—*porrum*, a leek.]

**porrect**, *por-ekt'*, *v.t.* to stretch forth: to present, hold out for acceptance.—*adj.* extended forward. —*n.* **porrec'tion.** [L. *porrigĕre, porrectum*, to stretch out.]

**porridge**, *por'ij*, *n*. a kind of pudding usually made by slowly stirring oatmeal in boiling water (in Scotland often treated as a *pl.*): pottage (*obs.*). —**porr'idge-stick**, a stick for stirring porridge. [**pottage**, altered by influence of obs. or dial. *porray*, vegetable soup.—O.Fr. *porée*—L.L. *porrāta*—L. *porrum*, leek.]

**porrigo**, *por-i'gō*, *n*. scalp disease of various kinds. —*adj.* **porriginous** (*-ij'*). [L. *porrīgō, -inis*, dandruff.]

**porringer, porrenger,** *por'in-jər*, *n*. a small dish for soup, porridge, etc.: a head-dress shaped

like such a dish (*Shak.*). [See **porridge, pottage**; for inserted *n* cf. **passenger, messenger**.]

**port**, *pört*, *pört*, *n*. the larboard or left side of a ship.—*adj.* left.—*v.t.* and *v.i.* to turn left. (In helm orders, formerly, **port the helm**, meant turn the tiller to port, or the upper part of the wheel to starboard, and so the rudder, and the ship, to starboard; since 1933 **port** means turn the ship to port.) [Ety. doubtful.]

**port**, *pört*, *pört*, *n*. an instrumental tune: a bagpipe composition.—**port a beul** (*bē'əl*), mouth music. [Gael.]

**port**, *pört*, *pört*, *n*. bearing: demeanour: carriage of the body: imposing bearing: style of living: a retinue (*obs.*): the position of a ported weapon. —*v.t.* to carry or convey (*obs.*): to hold in a slanting direction upward across the body (*mil.*). —*n.* **portabil'ity.**—*adj.* **port'able**, easily or conveniently carried or moved about: endurable (*Shak.*).—*n.* a portable article.—*ns.* **port'age**, act of carrying: carriage: price of carriage: a space, track, or journey, over which goods and boats have to be carried or dragged overland: a sailor's private venture in a voyage (*Shak.*); **port'ance** (*Spens.*; *Shak.*), carriage, bearing.— *adjs.* **port'ate** (*her.*), in a position as if being carried; **port'atile**, portable; **port'ative**, easily carried.—*n.* (*obs.*) a portable organ (often *pair of portatives*).—**port(e)'-cray'on** (Fr.*porte-crayon*), a handle for holding a crayon; **porte-bonheur** (*port'-bon-ær'*, Fr.), a charm carried for luck; **porte'-monnaie** (*-mon-e'*; Fr.), a purse or pocket-book; **port'-fire**, a slow-match or matchcord. [Fr. *port, porter*—L. *portāre*, to carry.]

**port**, *pört*, *pört*, *n*. a harbour: a town with a harbour.—**port'-ad'miral**, the admiral commanding at a naval port.—*n.pl.* **port'-charges**, harbour dues.—**port of call**, a port where vessels can call for stores or repairs; **port of entry**, a port where merchandise is allowed by law to enter. [O.E. *port*—L. *portus, -ūs*, akin to *porta*, a gate.]

**port**, *pört*, *pört*, *n*. a gate or gateway (*obs.*): a town gate, or its former position (now chiefly *Scot.*): an opening in the side of a ship: a porthole or its cover: a passage-way for a ball or curling-stone: an outlet or inlet for a fluid: part of a bit curved for the tongue.—*n.* **port'age** (*Shak.*), an opening. [Fr. *porte* (perh. also O.E. *port*)—L. *porta*, gate.]

**port**, *pört*, *pört*, *n*. a fortified wine (dark-red or tawny, sometimes white) of the Douro valley, shipped from *Oporto*, Portugal.—Also **port'-wine**.—*adjs.* **port'win'y, port'y**, of the nature or colour of port.

**port**, *pört*, *pört*, (*hist.*), *n*. a town with market privileges: a borough.—**port'man** (*hist.*), a burgess, esp. one chosen to administer town affairs; **port'reeve** (O.E. *portgerēfa*; *hist.*), a mayor or principal magistrate. [Connection with **port** (4) and **port** (5) obscure.]

**porta**, *pör'*, *pör'ta*, (*zool.*) *n*. a gate-like structure, esp. the transverse fissure of the liver.—*adj.* **por'tal.**—**portal system**, the portal vein with its tributaries, etc.; **portal vein**, the vein that conveys to the liver the venous blood from intestines, spleen, and stomach. [L. *porta*, gate.]

**portage.** See **port** (3) and (5).

**Portague.** See under **Portuguese.**

**portal**, *pört'*, *pört'əl*, *n*. a gate or doorway, esp. a great or magnificent one: any entrance: the arch over a gate (*archit.*): the lesser of two gates. [O.Fr. *portal*—L.L. *portāle*—L. *porta*, a gate.]

**portal.** See **porta.**

**portamento**, *pör-ta-men'tō*, (*mus.*) *n*. a continuous glide from one tone to another: sometimes applied to an execution between staccato and legato.—Also *adj.* and *adv.* [It.]

**portance.** See **port** (3).

**portas.** See **portesse.**

**portate,** etc., **port-crayon.** See port (3).

**portcullis,** *pört-, pört-kul'is, n.* a grating that can be let down to close a gateway: a lattice (*her.*): one of the pursuivants of the English College of Heralds: an Elizabethan silver halfpenny with a portcullis on the reverse.—*v.t.* to obstruct, as with a portcullis. [O.Fr. *porte coleïce,* sliding gate.]

**Porte,** *pört, pört,* (*hist.*) *n.* the Turkish imperial government, so called from the Sublime Porte or High Gate, the chief office of the Ottoman government at Constantinople.—**porte-cochère** (*port-kosh-er';* Fr.), a house entrance admitting a carriage. [Fr. *porte*—L. *porta,* gate.]

**porte-bonheur,** etc. See port (3).

**portend,** *pör, pör-tend', v.t.* to betoken: presage. —*n.* **portent** (*pör', pör'tant*), that which portends or foreshows: foreshadowing import: an evil omen: a prodigy, marvel.—*adj.* **portentous** (*-tent'*), ominous: prodigious, extraordinary: impressive, solemn.—*adv.* **portent'ously.**—*n.* **portent'ousness.** [L. *portendĕre, portentum*—*por-,* equivalent to *prō* or *per, tendĕre,* to stretch.]

**porteous.** See portesse.

**porter,** *pört', pört'ər, n.* a doorkeeper or gatekeeper: one who waits at the door to receive messages:—*fem.* **port'eress,** port'ress.—*n.* **port'erage,** the office or duty of a porter.—**porter's lodge,** a house or an apartment near a gate for the use of the porter. [O.Fr. *portier*—L.L. *portārius*—L. *porta,* a gate.]

**porter,** *pört', pört'ər, n.* one who carries burdens for hire: a dark-brown malt liquor, prob. because a favourite drink with London porters.— *n.* **port'erage,** carriage: charge made by a porter for carrying goods.—*adv.* **port'erly,** like a porter: coarse.—**porter'-house,** a house where porter is sold: a chop-house; **port'erhouse(-steak),** a choice cut of beef-steak next to the sirloin. [O.Fr. *porteour* (Fr. *porteur*)—L. *portātor, -ōris* —*portāre,* to carry.]

**portesse,** *pört', pört'əs, -es,* (*Spens.*) *n.* a portable breviary.—Also **port'ess,** port'as, port'hors, port'-house, portous, port'hos, porteous (*pör', pör'tyəs*). —**porteous roll** (*Scots law*), a list of persons to be tried. [O.Fr. *portehors* (L.L. *porteforium*)— L. *portāre,* to carry, *foris,* out of doors.]

**portfolio,** *pört-, pört-fō'li-ō, n.* a case or pair of boards for loose papers, drawings, etc.: a collection of such papers: a list of securities held: the office of a minister of state:—*pl.* **portfo'lios.** [It. *portafogli(o)*—L. *portāre,* to carry, *folium,* a leaf.]

**porthole,** *pört', pört'hōl, n.* a hole or opening in a ship's side for light and air, or (formerly) for pointing a gun through. [port (5), hole.]

**porthos, porthouse.** See portesse.

**portico,** *pör', pör'ti-kō, n.* a range of columns along the front or side of a building (*archit.*): a colonnade: the Painted Porch (*philos.*):—*pl.* **por'ticos,** por'ticoes.—*adj.* **por'ticoed,** furnished with a portico. [It.,—L. *porticus,* a porch.]

**portière,** *por-tyer', n.* a curtain hung over the door or doorway of a room: a portress. [Fr.]

**portion,** *pör', pör'shən, n.* a part: an allotted part: an amount of food served to one person: destiny: the part of an estate descending to an heir: a dowry.—*v.t.* to divide into portions: to allot as a share: to furnish with a portion.— *adj.* **por'tioned.**—*ns.* **por'tioner** (*Scots law*), the holder of a small feu originally part of a greater: a portionist of a benefice (heir'-por'tioner, see heir); **por'tionist,** a postmaster of Merton College: one of two or more incumbents sharing a benefice.—*adj.* **por'tionless,** having no portion, dowry, or property. [O.Fr.,—L. *portiō, -ōnis.*]

**Portland,** *pört', pört'lənd, adj.* belonging to or associated with the Isle of *Portland,* a peninsula of Dorset.—*n.* **Portlandian** (*-land'i-ən*), a group of sands and limestones, the middle group of the Upper or Portland Oolite.—Also *adj.*— **Portland arrowroot, Portland sago,** a farina prepared in the Isle of Portland from wake-robin tubers; **Portland cement,** a cement made by burning a mixture of clay and chalk of the colour of Portland stone; **Portland stone,** an oolitic building-stone which is quarried in the Isle of Portland.

**portland.** See portlast.

**portlast,** *pört', pört'ləst,* (*obs. naut.*) *n.* probably the gunwale.—Also **portoise** (*pört', pört'iz*) and wrongly **port'land.**—**yards down a portlast,** with yards down on or near the deck. [Origin unknown.]

**portly,** *pört', pört'li, adj.* having a dignified port or mien (*arch.*): corpulent.—*n.* **port'liness.** [port (3).]

**portman.** See port (7).

**portmanteau,** *pört-, pört-man'tō, n.* large travelling-bag that folds back flat from the middle: a rack for hanging clothes (*rare*): Lewis Carroll's term for a word into which are packed the sense (and sound) of two words (also **port-man'teau-word**—e.g. *slithy* for *lithe* and *slimy*): —*pl.* **portman'teaus,** or **portman'teaux** (*-tōz*).— Also (*both obs.*) **portman'tle, portman'tūa.** [Fr., *—porter,* to carry, *manteau,* a cloak.]

**portoise.** See portlast.

**portolano,** *pör-tə-lä'nō, n.* in the Middle Ages a navigation manual giving sailing directions and illustrated with charts showing ports, coastal features, etc. Also **portolan, portulan chart.** [It., navigation manual, harbour-master.]

**portrait,** *pör', pör'trit, n.* the likeness of a real person: a vivid description in words: portraiture (*rare*).—*v.t.* (*obs.*) to portray.— *ns.* **por'traitist, por'trait-painter; por'traiture,** a likeness: art or act of making portraits: a collection of pictures.—*v.t.* **portray** (*pör-, pör-trā'*), to paint or draw the likeness of: to describe in words: to adorn with portraiture or representations (*obs.*).—*ns.* **portray'al,** the act of portraying: a representation; **portray'er.**—**por'trait-bust'; por'trait-gallery; por'trait-painting.** [O.Fr. *po(u)rtrait, po(u)rtraire*—L. *prōtrahĕre, -tractum;* see protract.]

**portreeve.** See port (7).

**Portuguese,** *pör-, pör-tū-gēz',* or *pör', pör', adj.* of *Portugal,* its people, and its language.—*n.* a native or citizen of Portugal: the language of Portugal:—*pl.* **Portuguese** (whence the vulgar *sing.* **Portug(u)ee'**).—*n.* **portague, portigue** (*pört', pört'ə-gū*), an old Portuguese gold coin, worth about £4.—**Portuguese man-of-war,** Physalia.

**Portulaca,** *pör-, pör-tū-lā'ka, n.* the purslane genus, giving name to the family **Portulā'ceae,** mostly succulent herbs of dry places, akin to the Caryophyllaceae. [L. *portulāca,* purslane.]

**porwiggle.** Same as pollywog.

**pos,** *poz,* (*slang*) *adj.* an abbreviation of positive.

**posada,** *pö-sä'da, n.* an inn. [Sp.,—*posar,* to lodge.]

**posaune,** *pö-zow'nə, n.* the trombone. [Ger.]

**pose,** *pōz, n.* an attitude: an assumed attitude: an affectation of a mental attitude: in dominoes, the right to begin the game: a secret hoard (*Scot.*).—*v.i.* to assume or maintain a pose: to attitudinise.—*v.t.* to put in a suitable attitude: to posit: to assert: to claim: to propound.— *ns.* **pos'er,** one who poses; **poseur** (*pōz-œr';* Fr.), an attitudiniser:—*fem.* **poseuse** (*-œz'*). [Fr. *poser,* to place—L.L. *pausāre,* to cease—L. *pausa,* pause—Gr. *pausis.* Between Fr. *poser* and L. *pōnĕre, positum,* there has been confusion, which has influenced the derivatives of both words.]

**pose,** *pōz, v.t.* to puzzle: to perplex by questions: to bring to a stand.—*ns.* **pos'er,** one who, or that which, poses: a difficult question; **pos'ing.**

Neutral vowels in unaccented syllables: *el'ə-mənt;* for certain sounds in foreign words, see p. viii

—*adv.* pos′ingly. [Aphetic, for *oppose*, or *appose*, which was confused with it.]

posé, *pō-zā′*, (*her.*) *adj.* standing still. [Fr., pa.p. of *poser*; see pose (1).]

Poseidon, *pos-i′don, -dŏn, n.* the Greek sea-god, identified with Neptune by the Romans.—*adj.* Poseidōn′ian. [Gr. *Poseidōn, -ōnos.*]

poser. See pose (1) and (2).

poseur, poseuse. See pose (1).

posh, *posh,* (*slang*) *adj.* spruced up, smart: superb. —*v.t.* and *v.i.* (usu. with *up*) to trim up, to polish. *adv.* posh′ly. *n.* posh′ness. [Pop supposed to be from ′port *outward* starboard *home*′, the most desirable position of cabins when sailing to and from the East before the days of air-conditioning, but no evidence has been found to support this.]

poshteen. See posteen.

posit, *poz′it, v.t.* to set in place, dispose: to postulate, assume as true, definitely or for argument's sake:—*pr.p.* pos′iting; *pa.t.* and *pa.p.* pos′ited. [L. *pōnĕre, positum,* to lay down.]

position, *poz-ish′ən, n.* situation: place occupied: attitude, disposition, arrangement: state of affairs: a proposition or thesis: the ground taken in argument or in a dispute: principle laid down: place in society: high standing: a post or appointment: occurrence in an open or closed syllable:- situation of the left hand in playing the violin, etc.: method of finding the value of an unknown quantity by assuming one or more values.—*adj.* of or defining position.— *v.t.* to set in place: to determine the position of, locate.—*adjs.* posi′tional; posi′tioned, placed. —position ratio, a ratio determining the position of a point in a range or of a ray in a pencil— that of the distances from two fixed points in the range, or of the sines of the angular distances from two fixed rays. [Fr.,—L. *positiō, -ōnis— pōnĕre, positum,* to place.]

positive, *poz′i-tiv, adj.* definitely, formally, or ex- plicitly laid down: express: beyond possibility of doub.. absolute: expressing a quality simply without comparison (*gram.*): downright, out-and-out: fully convinced: over-confident in opinion: matter-of-fact: concrete: material: actual: characterised by the presence of some quality, not merely absence of its opposite: of a bacteriological test, confirming the presence of the suspected organism, etc.: greater than zero, or conventionally regarded as greater than zero, indicating such a quantity (*math.*): in the direction of increase, actual or conventional: in a direction towards the source of stimulus (*biol.*): having the lights and shades not re- versed (*phot., opt.*): having a relatively high potential (*elect.*): of, having, or producing, posi- tive electricity (see below): dextrorotatory (*opt.*): having a greater index of refraction for the extraordinary than for the ordinary ray in double refraction: basic (*chem.*).—*n.* that which is positive: reality: a positive quantity: the positive degree, or an adjective or adverb in it: an image in which lights and shades or colours, or both, are unchanged: a photo- graphic plate with the lights and shades of the original: a positive organ (see below).—*adv.* pos′itively.—*ns.* pos′itiveness, state or quality of being positive: certainty: confidence; pos′itiv- ism, actual or absolute knowledge: certainty: assurance: positive philosophy (see below); pos′itivist, a believer in positivism.—*adj.* positiv- ist′ic.—*n.* positiv′ity.—positive angle, one gener- ated by a straight line moving counter-clockwise; postive electricity, such as is developed in glass by rubbing with silk, arising from deficiency of electrons; positive organ, a small supplementary church organ, originally portable and placed upon a stand; positive philosophy, the philo- sophical system originated by Comte (1798-

1857)—its foundation the doctrine that man can have no knowledge of anything but phenomena, and that the knowledge of phenomena is rela- tive, not absolute: also 20th-century develop- ments of this (logical positivism) much concerned with determining whether or not statements are meaningful; positive pole, of a magnet, that end (or pole) which turns to the north when the magnet swings freely; positive rays, canal-rays, a stream of positively electrified particles to- wards the cathode of a vacuum-tube (positive- ray analysis, the detection of gases, and deter- mination of their molecular weights, by measur- ing the parabolas produced upon a photo- graphic plate by positive rays deflected in two directions at right angles to each other by a magnetic and an electric field); positive sign, the sign (+ read *plus*) of addition. [L. *posi- tivus,* fixed by agreement—*pōnĕre, positum,* to place.]

positron, *poz′i-tron, n.* a particle differing from the electron in having a positive charge: a *posi*tive electron.—Also pos′iton.

posnet, *pos′nit, n.* a small cooking-pot with feet and handle. [O.Fr. *pocenet.*]

posology, *pos-ol′ə-ji, n.* the science of quantity: the science of dosage.—*adj.* posological (*-ə-loj′i- kl*). [Gr. *posos,* how much, and *logos,* a word, discourse.]

poss, *adj.* a slang abbreviation of possible.

posse, *pos′i, n.* power: possibility: a force or body (of constables).—in posse, in potentiality; posse comitatus (*kom-i-tā′təs, -tā′tōōs*), force of the county, men called out by the sheriff to aid in enforcing the law. [L. *posse,* to be able, *comitātūs,* of the county.]

possess, *poz-es′, v.t.* to inhabit, occupy (*obs.*): to have or hold as owner, or as if owner: to have: to seize: to obtain: to attain (*Spens.*): to main- tain: to control: to be master of: to occupy and dominate the mind of: to put in pos- session (with *of,* formerly *in*): to inform, ac- quaint: to imbue: to impress with the notion or feeling: to prepossess (*obs.*).—*adj.* possessed′, in possession: self-possessed: dominated by a spirit that has entered one, or other irresistible influence.—*n.* possession (*poz-esh′ən*), act, state, or fact of possessing or being possessed: a thing possessed: a subject foreign territory.— *adjs.* possess′ionary; possess′ionate, holding or allowed to hold possessions (opp. to *mendicant*). —*n.* a possessionate monk.—*adjs.* possess′ioned; possess′ive, pertaining to or denoting possession: genitive: showing a desire to treat as a pos- session.—*n.* (*gram.*) a possessive adjective or pronoun: the possessive case or a word in it.— *adv.* possess′ively.—*ns.* possess′iveness, extreme attachment to one's possessions: desire to domi- nate another emotionally; possess′or; possess′- orship.—*adj.* possess′ory.—what possesses him, etc.? what malign influence causes him, etc., to act so foolishly?; writ of possession, a process directing a sheriff to put a person in possession of property recovered in ejectment. [O.Fr. *possesser*—L. *possidēre, possessum.*]

posset, *pos′it, n.* a dietetic drink, milk curdled as with wine, ale, or vinegar.—*v.t.* (*Shak.*) to curdle.—*v.i.* to make a posset.—posset cup, a large cup or covered bowl for posset. [M.E. *poschote, possot;* origin unknown.]

possible, *pos′i-bl, adj.* that may be or happen: that may be done: not contrary to the nature of things: contingent: potential: practicable: such as one may tolerate, accept, or get on with. —*n.* a possibility: that which or one who is possible: the highest possible score: one's best (*Gallicism*): (in *pl.*) necessaries (*slang*).—*ns.* poss′ibilism, the policy of confining efforts to what is immediately possible or practicable; poss′ibilist; possibil′ity, state of being possible:

that which is possible: a contingency.—*adv.*
**poss'ibly.** [L. *possibilis*—*posse*, to be able.]
**possum,** 'possum, *pos'əm, n.* a colloquial aphetic form of **opossum.**—**play possum,** to feign death: to dissemble.
**post,** *pōst, n.* a stout, stiff stake or pillar of timber or other material, usually fixed in an upright position: an upright member of a frame: a winning-post, starting-post, etc.: the pin of a lock: a solid thickish stratum: a pillar of coal left in a mine as a support: a tavern doorpost, on which a score was chalked (*Shak.*).—*v.t.* to stick up on a post, hence on a board, door, wall, hoarding, etc.: to announce, advertise, or denounce by placard: to placard as having failed in an examination, or failed to be classed: to announce as overdue: to affix a bill or bills to.—*n.* post'er, a bill-sticker: a large printed bill or placard for posting.—*v.t* to stick bills on: to advertise or publish by posters.—**poster colours,** matt water-colours for designing posters and other reproduction work; **post'-mill,** a windmill pivoted on a post.—**between you and me and the** (bed-, lamp-, gate-, etc.) **post,** in confidence; **from pillar to post** (see pillar); **sheriff's post** (*hist.*), a post at a sheriff's door. [O.E. *post*—L. *postis,* a doorpost—*pōnĕre,* to place.]
**post,** *pōst, n.* a fixed place or station, esp. a place where a soldier or body of soldiers is stationed: a fixed place or stage on a road, for forwarding letters and change of horses: a body of men stationed at a post: a trading station: an office, employment, or appointment: a messenger carrying letters by stages or otherwise: a post-man (*obs.* or *dial.*): a public letter-carrier: an established system of conveying letters: a post-horse (*Shak.*): a mail-coach: a packet-boat (*obs.*): a despatch, delivery, or batch of letters: a post-office, or post-office letter-box: haste (*Shak.*): a size of writing-paper, double that of common notepaper (originally with water-mark, a post-horn): full rank as naval captain (see **post-captain** below): a bugle-call (*first* or *last*) summoning soldiers to their quarters or (*last post*) performed at a military funeral: a name often given to a newspaper: a stake in a game: a good or winning hand, as in the old card-game of **post and pair,** in which the players vied on the goodness of their hands, a pair-royal being best.—*v.t.* to station: to entrust to the post-office for transmission: to shift, transfer to another (as blame; with *over* or *off*) (*Shak.*): to transfer to another book, or enter in a book, or carry to an account (*book-k.*): to supply with necessary information: to appoint to a post: send or appoint (to a ship) as full captain: to stake.—*v.i.* to travel with posthorses or with speed: to move up and down in the saddle, in time with the horse's movements.—*adv.* with posthorses: with speed.—*n.* post'age, money paid for conveyance by post: travel with post-horses (*obs.*).—*adj.* post'al, of or pertaining to the mail-service.—*n.* (*U.S.*; in full post'al-card) a postcard issued by the post-office with printed stamp.—*n.* post'er, one who travels post (*Shak.*): a posthorse: one who posts a letter.—*n.* and *adj.* post'ing.—post'age-stamp, an embossed or printed stamp or an adhesive label to show that the postal charge has been paid; **postal order,** an order issued by the postmaster authorising the holder to receive at a post-office payment of the sum printed on it; **postal tube,** a cylinder for sending rolled-up papers by post; **postal union,** an association of the chief countries of the world for international postal purposes; **post'-bag,** a mail-bag: a term used collectively for letters received; **post'-box,** a letter-box; **post boy,** a boy that rides posthorses or who carries letters: a postilion; **post'-cap'tain,** for-

merly, a naval officer posted to the rank of captain, a full captain distinguished from a commander (called captain by courtesy); **post'-card,** a card on which a message may be sent by post: such a card not issued by the post-office (*U.S.*).—*v.t.* to send a postcard to.—**post'-chaise** (popularly po''chay, po'chay, po''chaise), a carriage, usually four-wheeled, for two or four passengers with a postilion, used in travelling with posthorses.—*v.i.* to travel by post-chaise.—**Postcode, postal code,** a short series of letters and numbers denoting a very small area used for sorting mail by machine; **post'-day,** the day on which the post or mail arrives or departs.—*adj.* and *adv.* post'-free', without charge for postage: with postage prepaid.—**post'haste'** (from the old direction on letters, *haste, post, haste*), haste in travelling like that of a post.—*adj.* speedy: immediate.—*adv.* with utmost haste or speed.—**post'-horn,** a postman's horn: a long straight brass horn blown by a coach guard; **post'horse,** a horse kept for posting; **post'house,** a house where horses are kept for posting: a post-office; **post'-letter,** a letter in the custody of the post-office; **post'man,** a post or courier: a letter-carrier; **post'mark,** the mark stamped upon a letter at a post-office defacing the postage-stamp or showing the date and place of expedition or of arrival; **post'-master,** the manager or superintendent of a post-office: one who supplies posthorses: a portioner, or scholar on the foundation of Merton College, Oxford; **Post'master-Gen'eral,** formerly, the minister at the head of the post-office department; **post'mastership; post'-mistress; post'-office,** an office for receiving and transmitting letters by post, and other business: **Post Office,** formerly, a department of the government which had charge of the conveyance of letters, converted in 1969 into a public corporation, the **Post Office Corporation.**—*adj.* post'-paid, having the postage prepaid.—**post'-road,** a road with stations for posthorses; **post'-time,** the time for the despatch or for the delivery of letters; **post'-town, post-village,** a town, village, with a post-office; **post'woman,** a female letter-carrier.—**general post,** a game in which the players change places simultaneously; **postman's knock,** a parlour kissing-game; **post-office box,** a box in the post-office into which are put the letters addressed to a particular person or firm; **post-office savings-bank,** a branch of the post-office in which money may be deposited at a fixed rate of interest. [Fr. *poste*—It. *posta* and *posto*—L. *pōnĕre, positum,* to place.]
**post-,** *pōst, pfx.* after—as *post-classical, post-primary, post-Reformation, post-war,* etc.: behind—as *post-nasal, post-ocular.*—*adj.* post'bell'um, after the war.—*n.* post-commun'ion, the part of the eucharistic office after the act of communion.—*adj.* succeeding communion.—*v.t.* post'date', to date after the real time: to mark with a date (as for payment) later than the time of signing.—*adj.* post-dilu'vial, after the Flood: after the diluvial period (*obs. geol.*).—*n.* and *adj.* post-dilu'vian.—*adj.* post'-doc'toral, pertaining to academic work carried out after obtaining a doctorate.—*n.* post'-entry, an additional entry of merchandise at a custom-house.—*adjs.* post'-exil'ian, post-exil'ic, after the time of the Babylonian captivity of the Jews.—*ns.* post'-exist'ence, existence in a subsequent life; post'fix, a suffix.—*v.t.* postfix', to add as a suffix.—*adjs.* post-glā'cial, after the glacial epoch; post-grad'uate, belonging to study pursued after graduation.— Also *n.*—*n.* **Post-Impressionism,** a movement in painting that came after Impressionism, aiming at the expression of the spiritual significance of things rather than mere representation.—*n.* and

*adj.* **Post-Impress'ionist.**—*n.* post'lude, a concluding movement or voluntary.—*adj.* post-merid'ian, coming after the sun has crossed the meridian: in the afternoon.—*n.* post-millenā'rian, a believer in post-millennialism.—*adj.* post-millenn'ial.—*n.* post-millenn'ialism, the doctrine that the Second Advent will follow the millennium.—*adj.* post'-mor'tem (L. *mortem*, acc. of *mors, mortis,* death), after death.—*n.* a post-mortem examination, autopsy: an after the event discussion, as at the end of a hand of cards.—*adjs.* post-nas'al, behind the nose; post-na'tal, after birth.—*n.pl.* post-nā'ti (see ante-nati).—*adjs.* post-Ni'cene, after the Nicene council; post-nup'tial, after marriage; post-obit (*-ob'it, -ōb'it*; L. *obitum,* acc. of *obitus, -ūs,* death), taking effect after someone's death.—*n.* a borrower's bond securing payment on the death of someone from whom he has expectations.—*adjs.* post'(-)par'tum, after parturition; post'-pran'dial (L. *prandium,* a repast), after-dinner.—*ns.* postscē'nium, the part of the stage behind the scenery; post'script (L. *scriptum,* written, *pa.p.* of *scribĕre,* to write), a part added to a letter after the signature: an addition to a book after it is finished: a talk following, e.g. a news broadcast: additional comment or information provided.—*adj.* Post-Ter'tiary, later than Tertiary—Pleistocene and Recent.—Also *n.*—*adj.* post'-war' (post-war credit, a portion of income-tax credited to an individual for repayment after World War II). [L. *post,* after, behind.]

**posteen,** *pos-tēn',* n. an Afghan greatcoat, generally of sheepskin with the fleece on.—Also (erron.) **poshteen'.** [Pers. *postī,* leather.]

**poste restante,** *pōst res-tät,* n. a department of a post-office where letters are kept till called for. [Fr., remaining post.]

**posterior,** *pos-tē'ri-ər, adj.* coming after: later: hinder: on the side next the axis (*bot.*).—*n.* (usu. *pl.*) descendants, posterity: (commonly in *pl.*) hinder parts, buttocks: (in *pl.*) latter part (*Shak.*).—*n.* posteriority (*pos-tē-ri-or'i-ti*).—*adv.* postē'riorly.—*n.* posterity (*-ter'i-ti*), those coming after: succeeding generations: a race of descendants. [L. *postērior,* comp. of *posterus,* coming after—*post,* after.]

**postern,** *pōst'ərn, n.* a back door or gate: a small private door: a sally-port.—*adj.* back: private. [O.Fr. *posterne, posterle*—L. *posterula,* a dim. from *posterus.*]

**posthorse, posthouse.** See post (2).

**posthumous,** *post'ū-məs, adj.* after death: born after the father's death: published after the author's or composer's death.—*adv.* post'humously. [L. *posthumus, postumus,* superl. of *posterus,* coming after—*post,* after; the *h* inserted from false association with *humāre,* to bury.]

**postiche,** *pos-tēsh', adj.* superfluously and inappropriately superadded to a finished work: counterfeit or false.—*n.* a superfluous and inappropriate addition: a false hairpiece, wig. [Fr.,—It. *posticio*—L. *posticus,* hinder.]

**posticous,** *pos-ti'kəs,* (*bot.*) *adj.* posterior: outward, extrorse. [L. *posticus,* hinder—*post.*]

**postil,** *pos'til, n.* a marginal note, esp. in the Bible: a commentary: a homily: a book of homilies.—*v.t.* and *v.i.* to gloss.—*v.t.* and *v.i.* pos'tillate.—*ns.* postillā'tion; pos'tillātor; pos'-tiller. [O.Fr. *postille* (It. *postilla*)—L.L. *postilla,* possibly—L. *post illa (verba),* after those (words).]

**postilion,** *pos-* or *pōs-til'yən, n.* a postboy: one who guides posthorses, or horses in any carriage, riding on one of them.—Also **postill'ion.** [Fr. *postillon*—It. *postiglione*—*posta,* post.]

**postliminary,** *pōst-lim'in-ə-ri, adj.* subsequent: sometimes used in error for **postliminiary** (see

next word).—Also **postlim'inous** (erron. post-limin'ious). [On the analogy of preliminary.]

**postliminy,** *pōst-lim'i-ni, n.* the right of a returned exile, prisoner, etc., to resume his former status: the right by which persons or things taken in war are restored to their former status. —*adj.* postlimin'iary. [L. *postlīminium,* lit. return behind the threshold—*limen, -inis,* threshold.]

**postlude.** See post-.

**postmaster.** See post (2).

**postpone,** *pōs(t)-pōn', v.t.* to put off to a future time: to defer: to delay: to subordinate.—*ns.* postpone'ment, postpōn'ence (*rare*); postpōn'er; postposition (*pōst-poz-ish'ən*), placing, or position, after: a word or particle placed after a word, usu. with the force of a preposition.—*adjs.* postposi'tional; postpositive (*-poz'*).—*advs.* postposi'tionally, postpos'itively. [L. *postpōnĕre, -positum—post,* after, *pōnĕre,* to put.]

**postscript.** See post-.

**postulate,** *pos'tū-lāt, v.t.* to claim: to take for granted, assume: to assume as a possible or legitimate operation without preliminary construction (*geom.*): to nominate, subject to sanction of ecclesiastical authority.—*v.i.* to make demands.—*n.* a stipulation: an assumption: a fundamental principle: a position assumed as self-evident: an operation whose possibility is assumed (*geom.*): an axiom (*geom.*): a necessary condition: a person nominated to a benefice by the king, pending the pope's consent (*Scot. hist.*).—*ns.* pos'tulant, a petitioner: a candidate, esp. for holy orders, or admission to a religious community; postulā'tion.—*adj.* postulā'tional.—*adv.* postulā'tionally.—*adj.* pos'tulatory, supplicatory: assuming or assumed as a postulate.—*n.* postulā'tum, a postulate. [L. *postulāre, -ātum,* to demand—*poscĕre,* to ask urgently.]

**posture,** *pos'chər, n.* relative disposition of parts, esp. of the body: carriage, attitude, pose: state of affairs: disposition of mind.—*v.t.* to place in a particular manner.—*v.i.* to assume a posture: to pose: to attitudinise.—*adj.* pos'-tural.—*ns.* pos'turer, pos'turist, an acrobat.—pos'ture-maker, pos'ture-master, one who teaches or practises artificial postures of the body: a contortionist. [Fr.,—L. *positūra—pōnĕre, positum,* to place.]

**posy,** *pō'zi, n.* a motto, as on a ring: a bunch of flowers. [poesy.]

**pot,** *pot, n.* a deep or deepish vessel for manufacturing, cooking or preserving purposes, or for growing plants, or holding jam, etc., or holding or pouring liquids: the contents, or capacity, of such a vessel: a chamber-pot (*abbreviation,* esp. as a child's expression or *facet.* **pott'y**): a pocket, or a stroke in which the object ball enters a pocket (*billiards*): earthenware: a cup or other prize (*coll.*): a large sum of money: a heavily backed horse: an important person (usu. *big pot*): a pot-shot: a simple helmet: a wicker trap for lobsters, etc.: a size of paper (also pott) about 12 in. by 15 in. (from its original watermark): cannabis, marijuana (*slang*).—*v.t.* to put up in pots for preserving: to put in pots: to cook in a pot: to plant in a pot: to drain, as sugar: to shoot for the pot, by a pot-shot, or generally, to bag, win, secure: to pocket (as a billiard-ball): to epitomise, esp. in travesty.—*v.i.* to tipple (*Shak.*): to have a pot-shot—*pr.p.* pott'ing; *pa.p* pott'ed.—*adj.* pott'ed, condensed, concentrated: abridged: (of music, etc.) recorded for reproduction.—pot'-ale, refuse from a grain distillery; pot'-bank', a pottery; pot'-bar'ley, barley whose outer husk has been removed by mill-stones.—*adj.* pot'-bellied.—pot'-bell'y, a protuberant belly; pot'-boiler, a work in art or literature produced merely to secure the necessaries of life: a producer of such works; **pot′-boiling**.—*adj.* **pot′-bound**, having roots compressed in a mass without room for growth.—**pot′-boy**, a serving boy in a public-house; **pot′-companion**, a comrade in drinking; **pot′ful**, as much as a pot will hold:—*pl.* **pot′fuls**; **pot′-gun**, a mortar: a pop-gun; **pot′-hanger**, a device for hanging a pot or a pothook on; **pot′-hat**, a bowler hat: formerly, a top-hat; **pot′-head**, a stupid person; **pot′-herb**, a vegetable (esp.) for flavouring—e.g. parsley; **pot′hole**, a hole worn in rock in a stream bed by eddying detritus: a deep hole eroded in limestone: a hole worn in a road surface; **pot′holing**, the exploration of limestone potholes; **pot′hook**, a hook for hanging a pot over a fire: a hooked stroke in writing; **pot′house**, an alehouse; **pot′-hunter**, one who hunts to get food: one who shoots for the sake of a bag or competes for the sake of prizes; **pot′-hunting**; **pot′-lid**, the cover of a pot: (*Scot.* **pat′-lid′**) a curling-stone played exactly on the tee; **pot′-liquor**, a thin broth in which meat has been boiled; **pot′-luck′**, what may happen to be in the pot for a meal, without special preparation for guests; **pot′-man**, a pot-companion: a pot-boy; **pot′-metal**, an alloy of copper and lead: scraps of old iron pots, etc.; **pot′-plant**, a plant grown in a pot; **pot′-roast**, braised meat.—*v.t.* to braise.—**pot′-shop**, a small public-house; **pot′-shot**, a shot within easy range: a casual or random shot.—*adj.* **pot′-sick**, sickly from growing in a pot.—**pot′-stick**, a stick for stirring what is being cooked in a pot; **pot′-still**, a still in which heat is applied directly to the pot containing the wash (opp. to *patent still*).—*adj.* made in a pot-still.—**pot′stone**, impure talc or steatite, a massive finely felted aggregate of talc, usually with mica and chlorite, such as has been cut into pots.—*adjs.* **pot′-val′iant**; **pot′-val′orous**, brave owing to drink.—**pot′-val′our**; **pot′-wall′oper** (see **pot-waller**).—**big pot**, important person; **go to pot, go to ruin**: go to pieces (orig. in allusion to the cooking-pot, not the melting-pot); **keep the pot (a-)boiling**, procure the necessaries of life: keep going briskly without stop. [Late O.E. *pott*; cf. Ger. *pott*; Sw. *potta*; Dan. *potte*; Fr. *pot*; origin unknown.]

**potable**, *pō′tə-bl*, *adj.* fit to drink.—*n.* (*rare*) a beverage. [L. *pōtābilis—pōtāre*, to drink.]

**potage**, *po′täzh*, *n.* thick soup. [Fr.]

**potamic**, *pot-am′ik*, *adj.* of rivers.—*adj.* **potamological** (*pot-ə-mə-loj′i-kl*).—*ns.* **potamologist** (*-mol′ə-jist*); **potamol′ogy**, the scientific study of rivers. [Gr. *potamos*, a river.]

**Potamogeton**, *pot-əm-ō-jē′ton, -gē′ton, n.* the pondweed genus of water-plants with floating and submerged leaves, giving name to a family of monocotyledons, **Potamogetonā′ceae**. [Gr. *potamogeitōn*, pondweed—*potamos*, river, *geitōn*, neighbour.]

**potash**, *pot′ash*, *n.* a powerful alkali, potassium carbonate, originally got in a crude state by lixiviating wood *ash* and evaporating in *pots*—hence **pot-ashes, pot-ash**: potassium hydroxide (*caustic potash*): sometimes the monoxide or (vaguely) other compound of potassium: potash-water.—*adj.* containing, or rich in, potassium.—*v.t.* to treat with potash.—*n.* **potass** (*pot-as′*, *pot′as*; now *rare*), potash; **potass′a** (now *rare*), potassium monoxide, or sometimes hydroxide.—*adj.* **potass′ic**, of potassium.—*n.* **potass′ium**, an alkali metal (symbol K, for *kalium*; at. numb. 19), discovered by Davy in 1807 in potash.—**pot′ash-wa′ter**, an aerated water containing potassium bicarbonate.—Also **potass′-wa′ter**.—**potassium-argon dating**, estimating the date of prehistoric mineral formation from the proportion of potassium-40 to argon-40, the latter having developed from the former by radioactive decay and being trapped in the rock. [Eng. **pot, ash**, or the corresponding Du. *pot-asschen* (mod. *potasch*).]

**potation**, *pō-tā′shən*, *n.* drinking: a draught: liquor. [L. *pōtātiō, -ōnis—pōtāre, -ātum*, to drink.]

**potato**, *pə-* or *pō-tā′tō*, *n.* originally the sweet-potato, plant or tuber (see under **sweet**): now usually a South American plant, *Solanum tuberosum*, widely grown in temperate regions, or its tuber:—*pl.* **potā′toes**.—**potā′to-app′le**, the fruit of the potato; **potā′to-bō′gle** (*Scot.*), a scarecrow.—*n.pl.* **potā′to-chips′**, long pieces of potato fried in fat.—**potā′to-disease′, -rot**, a destructive disease of the potato caused by a parasitic fungus, *Phytophthora infestans*; **potā′to-fing′er** (*Shak.*), a fat finger; **potā′to-pit**, a clamp of potatoes; **potā′to-spir′it**, alcohol made from potatoes; **potā′to-trap′** (*slang*), the mouth.—**hot potato** (*slang*), controversial issue; **small potatoes** (*U.S.*), anything of no great worth; **the (clean) potato**, the right thing. [Sp. *patata—* Haitian *batata*, sweet-potato.]

**potch, potche.** Same as **poach** (2) in sense of thrust or trample.—*n.* **potch′er**, a machine for breaking and bleaching pulp in paper-making.

**pote**, *pōt*, *v.t.* and *v.i.* to poke, thrust, esp. with the foot (*obs.* except *dial.*): to crimp with a poting-stick (*obs.*).—**pot′ing-stick**, (*obs.*) a poking-stick for ruffs, etc. [O.E. *potian*.]

**poteen, potheen**, *po-tyēn′, -chēn′, -tēn′, n.* Irish whiskey illicitly distilled. [Ir. *poitín*, dim. of *pota*, pot, from Eng. **pot** or Fr. *pot*.]

**potent**, *po′tant*, *adj.* powerful: mighty: strongly influential: cogent: formed of or terminating in crutch-heads (*her.*).—*n.* a prince, potentate (*Shak.*): a support: a crutch (*obs.*).—*n.* **pō′tence**, power: a gibbet (*obs.*): a structure shaped like a gibbet: in watchmaking, a bracket for supporting the lower pivot: a revolving ladder in a dovecot: a right-angled military formation.—*adj.* **pō′tencé** (*-sā*), in heraldry, potent.—*n.* (*her.*) a marking of the shape of T.—*ns.* **pō′tency**, power: potentiality: a wielder of power: (of a point with respect to a circle) the rectangle between the segments into which a chord of the circle is divided at the point (*geom.*); **pō′tentate**, one who possesses power: a prince.—*adj.* **pōtential** (*-ten′shl*), powerful, efficacious: latent: existing in possibility, not in reality: expressing power, possibility, liberty, or obligation (*gram.*).—*n.* anything that may be possible: a possibility: the potential mood, or a verb in it: of a point in a field of force, the work done in bringing a unit (of mass, electricity, etc.) from infinity to that point: powers or resources not yet developed.—*n.* **pōtentiality** (*pō-ten-shi-al′i-ti*).—*adv.* **pōten′tially**.—*n.* **pōtentiary** (*-ten′shi-ə-ri; rare*), a person invested with power or influence.—*v.t.* **pōten′tiate**, to give power to.—*n.* **pōtentiom′eter**, an instrument for measuring difference of electric potential: a rheostat.—*adv.* **pō′tently**.—**potential difference**, a difference in the electrical states existing at two points, which causes a current to tend to flow between them; **potential energy**, the power of doing work possessed by a body in virtue of its position. [L. *potēns, -entis*, pr.p. of *posse*, to be able—*potis*, able, *esse*, to be.]

**Potentilla**, *pō-tan-til′ə*, *n.* a genus of the rose family, including silverweed and barren strawberry, differing from Fragaria (strawberry) in having a dry receptacle. [L.L., dim. of L. *potēns*, powerful, from its once esteemed medicinal virtues.]

**potentiometer.** See **potent**.

**pothecary**, *poth′i-kə-ri, n.* an aphetic form of **apothecary**.—Also **poticary** (*pot′*).

**pother**, *podh′ər*, formerly *pudh′ər*, **pudder**, *pud′ər*, *n.* a choking smoke or dust: fuss: commotion:

turmoil.—*v.i.* to fluster, to perplex.—*v.i.* to make a pother.—*adj.* poth'ery. [Origin unknown; app. not conn. with powder.]

pothole, pothook, pothouse. See pot.

potiche, *po-tēsh'*, *n.* an Oriental vase rounded or polygonal in shape, narrowing at the neck.—*n.* potichomā'nia, a craze for imitating Oriental porcelain by lining glass vessels with paper designs, etc. [Fr. *potiche, potichomanie.*]

potin, *pot-ẽ̆*, *n.* an old compound of copper, zinc, lead, and tin. [Fr.]

potion, *pō'shon*, *n.* a draught: a dose of liquid medicine or poison. [Fr.,—L. *pōtiō, -ōnis*—*pōtāre*, to drink.]

potlatch, *pot'lach*, *n.* in north-west U.S., an Indian winter festival, or the gift-giving at that time: any feast or gift (*coll.*). [Chinook.]

potometer, *pō-tom'ə-tər*, *n.* an instrument for measuring the rate at which a plant takes in water. [Gr. *poton*, drink.]

potoroo, *pot-ō-rōō'*, *n.* the marsupial rat-kangaroo. [Native Australian name.]

pot-pourri, *pō-pōō'ri, pō'*, or *-rē'*, *n.* orig. mixed stew, olla podrida: a mixture of sweet-scented materials, chiefly dried petals: a selection of tunes strung together: a literary production composed of unconnected parts. [Fr. *pot*, pot, *pourri*, rotten.—pa.p. of *pourrir*—L. *putrēre*, to rot.]

potsherd, *pot'shûrd*, *n.* a piece of broken pottery. —pot'-shard (*obs.*), pot'-share (*Spens.*). [pot, shard (2).]

potstone, pott (paper). See pot.

pottage, *pot'ij*, *n.* vegetables boiled with or without meat (*arch.*): a thick soup: soup: oatmeal porridge (*obs.*). [Fr. *potage*—pot, jug, pot.]

potted, potting. See pot.

potter, *pot'ər*, *n.* one who makes articles of baked clay, esp. earthenware vessels.—*n.* pott'ery, articles of baked clay collectively, esp. earthenware vessels: a place where such goods are manufactured: the art of the potter. [pot.]

potter, *pot'ər*, *v.i.* to busy oneself in a desultory way: to dawdle.—*n.* pottering: diffuse talk.— *n.* pott'erer.—*n.* and *adj.* pott'ering.—*adv.* pott'eringly. [pote.]

pottingar, *pot'in-gər*, *n.* an old Scottish form of apothecary.

pottinger, *pot'in-jər*, *n.* a maker of *pottage*. [For *n.* cf. messenger, passenger, etc.]

pottle, *pot'l*, *n.* half a gallon, or thereby (*arch.*): a chip basket for strawberries.—*adjs.* pott'le-bod'ied, having a body shaped like a pottle; pott'le-deep, to the bottom of the pottle-pot. —pott'le-pot (*Shak.*), a half-gallon drinking-vessel. [O.Fr. *potel*, dim. of *pot*, pot.]

potto, *pot'ō*, *n.* a West African genus (Perodicticus) of lemurs: also applied to the kinkajou. [Said to be a West African name.]

potty, *pot'i*, (*coll.*) *adj.* trifling: petty: crazy: dotty. [Origin obscure.]

pot-waller, *pot'-wŏl'ər*, *n.* in certain English boroughs, before the Reform Bill of 1832, one who satisfied the test as a voter by boiling his pot on his own fireplace within the borough— sometimes in the open air before witnesses to establish a bogus claim.—Variously altered popularly to pot'-wabb'ler, -wobb'ler, -wall'oner, -wall'oper.—*adj.* pot'-wall'oping. [pot, and O.E. w(e)allan, to boil.]

pouch, *powch*, (*Scot. pōōch*) *n.* a poke, pocket, or bag: any pocket-like structure, as a kangaroo's marsupium, a monkey's cheek-pouch, etc.—*v.t.* to pocket: to form into a pouch: to tip.—*v.i.* to form a pouch: to be like a pouch. —*adj.* pouched, having a pouch.—*n.* pouch'ful —*pl.* pouch'fuls.—*adj.* pouch'y, baggy.—pouched mouse, a small marsupial, Phascologale: an American jumping rodent (Dipodomys) with cheek-pouches opening outwards; pouched rat,

a pocket-gopher. [O.N.Fr. *pouche* (O.Fr. *poche*); cf. poke.]

pouder, poudre, obsolete spellings of powder.

pouf, pouffe, *pōōf*, *n.* a puffed mode of hairdressing: a pad worn in the hair by women in the 18th century: in dressmaking, material gathered up into a bunch: a soft ottoman or large hassock.—*adj.* poufed. [Fr. *pouf*.]

pouf(fe), poof, puff, *pōōf*, *pōōf*, *puf*, (*slang*) *n.* a homosexual. [*pooh! poof!*]

Poujadist, *pōō-zhäd'ist*, *n.* a follower of the French politician Pierre Poujade (b. 1920), anti-parliamentarian champion of the small man and of tax reduction.—*n.* Poujadism. [Fr. *Poujadiste*.]

pouk. See pook.

pouke. See puck.

poulaine, *pōō-lān'*, *n.* a long, pointed shoe-toe [O.Fr. (*à la*) *Poulaine*, (in the fashion of) Poland.]

poulard, *pōō-lärd'*, *n.* a fattened or spayed hen. [Fr. *poularde*—poule, hen.]

poulder, pouldre, obsolete spellings of powder.

pouldron, *pōl'drən*. Same as pauldron.

poule, *pōōl*, *n.* a movement in a quadrille. [Fr.]

poulp, poulpe, *pōōlp*, *n.* the octopus. [Fr. *poulpe* —L. *pōlypus*—Doric Gr. *pōlypos = polypous*; see polyp.]

poult, *pōlt*, *n.* a chicken: the young of the common domestic fowl or of other farmyard or game bird.—*ns.* poult'er (*Shak.*), poult'erer, one who deals in dead fowls and game; poult'ry, domestic or farmyard fowls collectively.— poulters' measure, a rhymed couplet in which the first line has twelve, the second fourteen, syllables—from the varying number of eggs formerly sold by poulterers as a dozen; poult'ry-farm, -yard, a farm, yard, where poultry are confined and bred. [Fr. *poulet*, dim. of *poule*— L.L. *pulla*, hen, fem. of L. *pullus*, young animal.]

poult-foot. Same as poltfoot (see polt).

poultice, *pōl'tis*, *n.* a soft composition applied in a cloth to sores.—*v.t.* to put a poultice upon. [L. *pultēs*, pl. of *puls, pultis* (Gr. *poltos*), porridge.]

pounce, *powns*, *n.* a hawk's (or other) claw, esp. the innermost, or any but the hind-claw: a punch (now *dial.*): a puncture (*obs.*): a sudden spring or swoop with attempt to seize.—*v.t.* to emboss by blows on the other side: to puncture, pink (*obs.*): to ornament with small holes: to seize with the claws.—*v.i.* to make a pounce: to dart: to fix suddenly upon anything.—*adj.* pounced, furnished with claws. [Derived in some way from L. *punctiō, -ōnis*—*pungĕre, punctum*, to prick; cf. puncheon (1).]

pounce, *powns*, *n.* sandarach, cuttle-bone, or other fine powder for preparing a writing surface or absorbing ink: coloured powder dusted through perforations to mark a pattern.—*v.t.* to prepare with pounce: to trace, transfer, or mark with pounce: to powder or sprinkle (*obs.*).—pounce'-box, a box with a perforated lid for sprinkling pounce. [Fr. *ponce*, pumice—L. *pūmex*, *pūmicis*.]

pouncet-box, *pown'sit-boks*, *n.* a pomander (also shortened to poun'cet; *Shak.*): sometimes used for pounce-box (see above). [Prob. for *pounced-box*, i.e. perforated box; see pounce (1).]

pounching (*Spens.*). Same as punching.

pound, *pownd*, *n.* a unit of weight of varying value, long used in western and central Europe, more or less answering to the Roman *libra*, whose symbol *lb.* is used for pound: in avoirdupois weight, 16 ounces avoirdupois, 7000 grains, or 0·45359237 kilogram: formerly, in troy weight, 12 ounces troy, 5760 grains, or about 373·242 grams: a pound-weight (*Shak.*): the balance (*Spens.*): a unit of money, originally the value of a pound-weight of silver: formerly 20 shillings, later 100 new pence (the pound sterling, written

£, for *libra*): also Australian (formerly), New Zealand (formerly), and Jamaican pound (written £A, £NZ, £J); *pound scots* (at Union, 1s. 8d.); 100 piastres (the Egyptian pound, £E):—*pl.* formerly pound, now pounds (except *coll.* and in compounds and certain phrases).— *v.t.* (*slang*) to bet on as almost a certainty.— *ns.* **pound′age,** a charge or tax made on each pound: a commission, or a share in profits, of so much a pound; **pound′al,** the foot-pound-second unit of force; **pound′er,** a specimen weighing a pound: in composition, anything weighing, or worth, or carrying, or one who has, receives, or pays, so many pounds.—**pound′-cake,** a sweet cake containing proportionally about a pound of each chief ingredient; **pound′-day,** a day on which gifts of one pound weight of various goods are invited for charity.—*adj.* **pound′-fool′ish,** neglecting the care of large sums in attending to little ones.—**pound′-weight′,** as much as weighs a pound: a weight of one pound used in weighing.—**pound of flesh,** strict and literal fulfilment of a bargain (see Shak., *M. of V.* I, iii. 150, IV, i. 99 ff., etc.). [O.E. *pund*—L. (*libra*) *pondō,* (pound) by weight, *pondō,* by weight—*pendĕre,* to weigh.]

**pound,** *pownd, n.* an enclosure in which strayed animals are confined, or distrained goods kept: any confined place: a pond (now *Scot.* and *dial.*): a level part of a canal between two locks: the last compartment of a pound-net.—*v.t.* to put in a pound: to enclose, confine.—*n.* **pound′age,** a charge for pounding stray cattle.—**pound′-keeper, pound′-master; pound′-net,** an arrangement of nets for trapping fish. [O.E. *pund* (in compounds), enclosure.]

**pound,** *pownd, v.t.* to beat into fine pieces: to bruise: to bray with a pestle: to bethump: to lay on, shower (*Spens.*).—*v.i.* to beat: to thump: to beat the ground: to make one's way heavily: to struggle on.—*n.* the act or sound of pounding.—*n.* **pound′er.** [O.E. *pūnian,* to beat; *-d* excrescent, as in sound (3), bound (4).]

**poupt,** *pownd* (Shak.; *pa.p.*). See **poop** (2).

**pour,** *pōr, pōr, v.t.* to cause or allow to flow in a stream: to send forth or emit in a stream or like a stream: to send downstream (*Spens.*): to spread out (*obs.*): to drain (as cooked potatoes; *Scot.*).—*v.i.* to stream: to rain heavily: to pour out tea, coffee, etc.: to allow liquid contents to run out duly.—*n.* a pouring: an amount poured at a time.—*ns.* **pour′er; pourie** (*pōōr′i; Scot.*), a vessel with a spout: a cream-jug: an oiling-can.—*n.* and *adj.* **pour′ing.**—**it never rains but it pours,** things never happen singly; **pouring wet,** raining hard; **pour oil on troubled waters,** soothe or calm a person or situation. [M.E. *pouren;* origin obscure.]

**pourboire,** *pōōr-bwär, n.* a tip. [Fr.,—*pour,* for, *boire,* to drink.]

**pourparler,** *pōōr-pär′lā, n.* (usu. in *pl.*) an informal preliminary conference. [Fr.]

**pourpoint,** *pōōr′point, n.* a mediaeval quilted doublet. [Fr.]

**poursew, poursue, poursuit(t),** in *Spens.* for **pursue, pursuit.**

**pourtray,** an old-fashioned spelling of **portray:**—*pa.p.* in *Spens.* **pour′trahed** (3 syllables), **pourtrayd, purtraid, purtrayd.**—*n.* **pour′traict,** an obsolete spelling of **portrait.**

**pousse,** *pōōs,* (*Spens.*) *n.* pease. [pulse (2).]

**pousse-café,** *pōōs-ka-fā, n.* a cordial, liqueur, or combination of several in layers, served after coffee. [Fr., push-coffee.]

**poussette,** *pōōs-et′, n.* an act of dancing round each other in the manner of two couples in a country-dance.—*v.i.* to perform a poussette. [Fr., dim. of *pousse,* push.]

**pout,** *powt, v.i.* to push out the lips, in sullen displeasure or otherwise: to protrude.—*v.t.* to protrude.—*n.* a protrusion, esp. of the lips.—*ns.* **pout′er,** one who pouts: a variety of pigeon having its breast inflated; **pout′ing.**—*adv.* **pout′-ingly.** [M.E. *powte,* of doubtful origin.]

**pout, powt, n.** a fish, the bib—also **whit′ing-pout.** —*n.* **pout′ing,** the whiting-pout.—**eel′-pout** (see eel); **horn′-pout, horned-pout,** an American (Amiurid) catfish. [O.E. (*æle-*) *pūte,* (eel-) pout —perh. conn. with foregoing with reference to the bib's inflatable membrane on the head.]

**pout, poot,** *pōōt, n.* a Scots form of **poult.**—*v.i.* to shoot at young partridges or young grouse.

**pouther,** *pōō′dhər,* a Scots form of **powder.**

**poverty,** *pov′ər-ti, n.* the state of being poor: necessity: want: lack: deficiency: a band of pipers (*obs.*).—*adj.* **pov′erty-strick′en,** suffering from poverty. [O.Fr. *poverte* (Fr. *pauvreté*)—L. *paupertās, -ātis—pauper,* poor.]

**pow,** *pow,* (*Scot.*) *n.* head, poll: a head of hair. [poll (1).]

**pow,** *pow,* (*Scot.*) *n.* a slow-moving stream, generally found in carse lands: a small creek at the mouth of a river or in an estuary, affording a landing-place for boats, esp. on the Forth. [Scot. *poll.*]

**powan,** *pow′ən, pō′ən, n.* a species of whitefish (Coregonus) found in Loch Lomond and Loch Eck. [Scots form of **pollan.**]

**powder,** *pow′dər, n.* dust: any solid in fine particles: gunpowder: hair-powder: face-powder: a medicine in the form of powder.— *v.t.* to reduce to powder: to sprinkle, daub, or cover with powder: to salt by sprinkling: to sprinkle.—*v.i.* to crumble into powder: to use powder for the hair or face.—*adjs.* **pow′dered,** reduced to powder: sprinkled, or daubed, or dusted with powder: salted; **pow′dery,** of the nature of powder: covered with powder: dusty: friable—**pow′der-box,** box for face-, hair-powder, etc.; **powder compact** (see **compact** (1)); **pow′der-clos′et, pow′dering-clos′et,** a small room in which hair was powdered; **pow′der-down′,** a kind of down on some birds that readily disintegrates in powder; **pow′der-flask, pow′der-horn,** a flask (originally a horn) for carrying gunpowder; **pow′dering-gown,** a loose dressing-gown worn while the hair was being powdered; **pow′dering-tub,** a vessel in which meat is salted: a tub for treatment of venereal disease by sweating (*obs.*); **pow′der-mag′azine,** a place where gunpowder is stored; **pow′der-met′allurgy,** the science and art of preparing metals for use by reducing them, as a stage in the process, to powder form; **pow′der-mill,** a mill in which gunpowder is made; **pow′der-monk′ey,** boy carrying powder to the gunners on a ship-of-war; **pow′der-puff,** a soft, downy ball for dusting powder on the skin; **pow′der-room,** ship's powder-magazine: a room for powdering the hair (also **pow′dering-room**): ladies' cloakroom. [O.Fr. *poudre*—L. *pulvis, pulveris,* dust.]

**powellise,** *pow′əl-iz, v.t.* (of timber) to season and preserve by boiling in a saccharine solution. [W. *Powell,* the inventor of the process.]

**Powellism,** *pow′əl-izm, n.* the views on race problems, etc., of J. Enoch Powell, politician and scholar (b. 1912).

**powellite,** *pow′əl-it, n.* a mineral, calcium molybdate. [After John Wesley *Powell* (1834-1902), American geologist, etc.]

**power,** *pow′ər, powr, n.* ability to do anything—physical, mental, spiritual, legal, etc.: capacity for producing an effect: strength: energy: faculty of the mind: moving force of anything: right to command, authority: rule: influence: control: governing office: permission to act: a paper giving authority to act: potentiality: a wielder of authority, strong influence, or rule: that in which such authority or influence resides: a spiritual agent: a being of the sixth order of the celestial hierarchy: a state influential in international affairs: an armed force (*arch.*): a great deal or great many (now *dial.* or *coll.*): a mark of subjection (1 Corinthians xi. 10; N.E.B. 'a sign of authority'): the sound-value of a letter: rate of doing work (*mech.*): energy, or supply of energy, available for doing work: an instrument serving as means of applying energy (see **mechanical**): the product of a number of equal factors, generalised to include negative and fractional numbers (*math.*): the potency of a point with respect to a circle (*geom*): magnifying strength, or a lens possessing it (*opt.*).—*adj.* concerned with power: worked, or assisted in working, by mechanical power: involving a high degree of physical strength and skill.—*v.t.* to equip with mechanical energy.—*adjs.* **pow'-ered; pow'erful**, having great power: mighty: forcible: efficacious: intense: impressive, esp. in disagreeable way: very great (*coll.*).—*adv.* (*coll.*) exceedingly.—*adv.* **pow'erfully.**—*n.* **pow'-erfulness.**—*adj.* **pow'erless**, without power: weak: impotent: helpless.—*adv.* **pow'erlessly.**—*n.* **pow'erlessness.**—**pow'er-dive**, a usu. steep dive of an aeroplane, made faster by use of engine(s). —Also *v.i.*, *v.t.*—**pow'er-diving; pow'er-house, -station**, a place where mechanical power (esp. electric) is generated; **pow'er-lathe, -loom, -press**, a lathe, loom, press, worked by mechanical power, as water, steam, electricity; **pow'er-plant**, an industrial plant for generating power: the assemblage of parts generating motive power in a motor-car, aeroplane, etc.; **pow'er-point**, a point at which an appliance may be connected to the electrical system; **pow'er-politics**, international politics in which the course taken by states depends upon their knowledge that they can back their decisions with force or other compulsive action.—**in one's power**, at one's mercy: within the limits of what one can do; **in power**, in office: in potentiality (*Spens.*); **the powers that be**, the existing ruling authorities (from Rom. xiii. 1). [O.Fr. *poer* (Fr. *pouvoir*)—L.L. *potēre* (for L. *posse*), to be able.]

**powin, pown.** See pawn (4).

**pownd**, Spenserian spelling of **pound** (3).

**powney, pownie, powny**, *pow'ni*. See **pony.**

**powre.** Spenserian spelling of **pour.**

**powsowdy**, *pow-sow'di*, (*Scot.*) *n.* any mixture of heterogeneous kinds of food.—Also **pousow'die.** [Origin unknown.]

**powter**, *pow'tər*, (*Scot.*) *v.i.* to poke: to rummage. —*v.t.* to poke: to get by groping. [Origin obscure.]

**powwaw, pow-wö'**, (*Shak.*) *interj.* pooh.

**powwow**, *pow'wow*, **pawaw**, *pä-wö'*, *n.* an American Indian conjuror: a rite, often with feasting: a conference.—*v.i.* **powwow'**, to hold a powwow: to confer. [Algonquian *powwaw, powah.*]

**pox, poks**, *n.* (*pl.* of **pock**) pustules: an eruptive disease, esp. smallpox or syphilis (as *sing.*): sheep-pox.—*v.t.* to infect with pox.—*interj.* plague.

**poynant, poin'ənt**, (*Spens.*, etc.) *adj.* Same as **poignant.**

**poynt, poyse, poyson**, old spellings of **point, poise, poison.**

**poz, pozz, poz**, *adj.* an old slang abbreviation of positive.

**pozzolana, pot-sō-lä'na, pozzuolana, -swō-**, *n.* a volcanic dust first found at *Pozzuoli*, near Naples, which forms with mortar a cement that will set in air or water.—*adj.* **pozzola'nic.**

**praam.** Same as **pram** (1).

**prabble, prab'l**, (*Shak.*) *n.* Welsh pronunciation of **brabble.**

**practic** (old spellings **practick, practique**), *prak'tik*, *adj.* relating to or of the nature of practice or action: practising (*obs.*): in practice (*obs.*): skilled (*Spens.*): cunning (*Spens.*).—*n.* practice as

opposed to theory: (esp. in *pl.*) practices, doings: practical experience: legal usage or case-law (esp. *Scots law*): a practical man.—*n.* **practicabil'ity.**—*adj.* **prac'ticable**, that may be practised, carried out, accomplished, used, or followed: passable, as a road.—*n.* **prac'ticableness.**—*adv.* **prac'ticably.**—*adj.* **prac'tical**, in, relating to, concerned with, well adapted to, or inclining to look to, actual practice, actual conditions, results, or utility: practised: practising, actually engaged in doing something: efficient in action: workable: virtual: a piece of stage furniture, esp. electrical (lights, etc.) that can be operated on stage (*theat.*).—*n.* a practical man: a practical examination.—*ns.* **prac'ticalism**, devotion to what is practical; **prac'ticalist; practical'ity**, practicalness: a practical matter or feature, aspect, of an affair.—*adv.* **prac'tically**, in a practical way: by a practical method: to all intents and purposes: very nearly, as good as.—*ns.* **prac'ticalness; prac'tice** (*-tis*), action, performance: actual doing: proceeding: habitual action: custom: legal procedure: repeated performance as a means of acquiring skill, esp. in playing a musical instrument: form so acquired: the exercise of a profession: a professional man's business, as a field of activity or a property: negotiation (*arch.*): scheming: plotting: trickery: working upon the feelings: a compendious way of multiplying quantities involving several units, by means of aliquot parts (*arith.*); **practician** (*-tish'ən*), a practiser or practitioner: a practical man; **prac'tisant**, an agent or fellow in conspiracy.—*v.t.* **practise** (*prak'tis*, formerly *-tīz'*; *U.S.* **practice**), to put into practice: to perform: to carry out: to do habitually: to exercise, as a profession: to exercise oneself in, or on, or in the performance of, in order to acquire or maintain skill: to train by practice: to put to use: to frequent (*obs.*): to compass (*obs.*): to contrive (*Milt.*): to plot (*Shak.*).—*v.i.* to act habitually: to be in practice (esp. medical or legal): to exercise oneself in any art, esp. instrumental music: to proceed, esp. to seek to injure, by underhand means: to tamper, work (with *upon, on*): to scheme: to have dealings: to use artifices: to work by artifice (on the feelings).—*adj.* **prac'tised**, skilled through practice.—*n.* **prac'tiser.**—*adj.* **prac'tising**, actually engaged, e.g. in professional employment.—*n.* **practitioner** (*-tish'ən-ər*), irreg. from *practician*), one who is in practice, esp. in medicine: one who practises.—*adj.* **prac'tive**, practical.—**practical joke**, a joke that consists in action, not words, usually an annoying trick; **practical politics**, proposals or measures that may be carried out at once or in the near future.—**general practitioner**, one who practises medicine and surgery without specialising. [Obs. Fr. *practique*—L. *practicus*—Gr. *prāktikos*, fit for action—*prāssein*, to do.]

**prad, prad**, (*slang*) *n.* a horse. [Du. *paard*—L.L. *paraverēdus*; see **palfrey.**]

**prae-.** See **pre-.**

**praecoces, praecocial.** See under **precocious.**

**praedial, predial, prē'di-əl**, *adj.* pertaining to, connected with, or derived from, the land: landed: rural: agrarian: attached to the land.—*n.* a praedial slave. [L.L. *praediālis—praedium*, an estate.]

**praemunire, prē-mū-nī'ri, prī-, -nē'**, *n.* writ issued under statutes of Richard II, summoning a person accused of suing in a foreign court for matters cognisable by the law of England, used especially against papal claims, and later extended to various offences: an offence that could be so dealt with: the penalty for such an offence: a predicament or scrape. [From the words of the writ, *praemūnīre faciās*, cause to warn, or see that thou warn, the word *praemūnīre*, properly to fortify in front, defend, being confused with *praemonēre*, to forewarn.]

**praenomen**, *prē-nō'men, pri-nō'men, n.* the name prefixed to the family name in ancient Rome, as *Gaius* in Gaius Julius Caesar: the generic name of a plant or animal. [L. *praenōmen—nōmen,* name.]

**praeses.** Same as **preses.**

**praesidium.** See **presidial.**

**praeter-.** See **preter-.**

**praetor**, *prē'tər, -tör, pri'tor, n.* a magistrate of ancient Rome next in rank to the consuls.—*adj.* **praetorian** *(-tō',-tō').*—*n.* a former praetor or man of like rank: a member of the emperor's bodyguard.—*ns.* **praeto'rium,** a general's tent: a governor's residence: a court or headquarters; **prae'torship.**—**praetorian gate,** the gate of a Roman camp in front of the general's tent, and nearest to the enemy; **praetorian guard,** the bodyguard of the Roman Emperor. [L. *praetor,* for *praeitor—prae,* in front of, before, and *īre, itum,* to go.]

**pragmatic**, *prag-mat'ik, adj.* relating to affairs of state: relating to, or of the nature of, pragmatism: pragmatical.—*n.* an edict: a man of business: a busybody: an opinionative person. —*adj.* **pragmat'ical,** active: practical: matter of fact: interfering with the affairs of others: officious: meddlesome: self-important: opinionative: pragmatic.—*n.* **pragmatical'ity.**—*adv.* **pragmat'ically.**—*n.* **pragmat'icalness.**—*v.t.* **prag'matise, -ize,** to interpret or represent as real: to rationalise.—*ns.* **pragmatis'er, -z-; prag'matism,** pragmatical quality: matter-of-factness: a treatment of history with an eye to cause and effect and practical lessons: humanism or practicalism, a philosophy, or philosophic method, that makes practical consequences the test of truth *(phil.);* **prag'matist,** a pragmatic person: a believer in pragmatism.—**pragmatic sanction,** a special decree issued by a sovereign, such as that of the Emperor Charles VI, settling his dominions upon Maria Theresa. [Gr. *prāgma, -atos,* deed—*prāssein,* to do.]

**prahu**, *prä'(h)ōō.* Same as **prau.**

**Prairial**, *pre-ri-äl', pre-ryäl', n.* the ninth month of the French revolutionary calendar, about 20th May to 18th June. [Fr.,—*prairie,* meadow.]

**prairie**, *prā'ri, n.* a treeless plain, flat or rolling, naturally grass-covered.—*adj.* **prai'ried.**—**prai'-rie-chick'en, -hen,** an American genus (Cupidonia or Tympanuchus) of grouse: the sharp-tailed grouse (Pedioecetes) of the western United States; **prai'rie-dog,** a gregarious burrowing and barking North American marmot (Cynomys); **prai'rie-oy'ster** *(U.S.),* a raw egg with condiments; **prai'rie-schoon'er,** an emigrants' long covered wagon; **prai'rie-tur'nip,** breadroot; **prairie value,** the value of land in its natural state before it has been improved by man; **prai'rie-wolf,** the coyote. [Fr.,—L. *prātum,* a meadow.]

**praise**, *prāz, v.t.* to assign a value to, appraise *(Shak.):* to speak highly of: to commend: to extol: to glorify, as in worship.—*n.* commendation: glorifying: the musical part of worship: that for which praise is due: (in ejaculatory expressions) God *(Scot.).*—*adjs.* **praise'ful; praise'less.**—*n.* **prais'er.**—*n.* and *adj.* **prais'ing.** —*advs.* **prais'ingly; praise'worthily.**—*n.* **praise'-worthiness.**—*adj.* **praise'worthy,** worthy of praise: commendable. [O.Fr. *preiser*—L.L. *preciāre* for L. *pretiāre,* to prize—*pretium,* price.]

**Prākrit**, *prä'krit, n.* a collective name for languages or dialects in an immediate relation to Sanskrit.—*adj.* **Prākrit'ic.** [Sans. *prākṛta,* the natural—*prakṛti,* nature.]

**praline**, *prä'lēn, n.* an almond or nut kernel with a brown coating of sugar, or a similar confection made with crushed nuts.—Also **prawlin** *(prö'lin).*

[Fr. *praline,* from Marshal Duplessis-*Praslin,* whose cook invented it.]

**pralltriller**, *präl'tril-ər, n.* an inverted mordent, a grace in which the principal note is preceded in performance by itself and the note above. [Ger.]

**pram, praam,** *präm, n.* a flat-bottomed Dutch or Baltic lighter: a flat-bottomed dinghy with squared-off bow: a barge fitted as a floating battery. [Du. *praam.*]

**pram,** *pram, n.* a colloquial abbreviation of **perambulator:** a milkman's hand-cart.

**prance**, *präns, v.i.* to bound from the hind legs: to go with a capering or dancing movement: to move with exaggerated action and ostentation: to swagger: to ride a prancing horse.—*v.t.* to cause to prance.—*n.* an act of prancing: swagger.—*n.* **pranc'er.**—*adj.* and *n.* **pranc'ing.**—*adv.* **pranc'ingly.** [M.E. *praunce;* origin unknown.]

**prandial,** *pran'di-əl, (facet.) adj.* relating to dinner. [L. *prandium,* a morning or midday meal.]

**prang**, *prang, (slang) n.* a crash: a bombing-attack.—*v.t.* to crash or smash: to bomb heavily: to crash into (e.g. another car).

**prank**, *prangk, n.* an evil deed *(obs.):* a malicious or mischievous trick: a trick: a practical joke: a frolic.—*v.i.* to play pranks.—*adjs.* **prank'ful, prank'ish, prank'some, prank'y.**—*n.* **prank'ster.** [Origin unknown.]

**prank**, *prangk, v.t.* to dress or adorn showily: to bespangle: to set in adornment.—*v.i.* (also *v.t.* with *it*) to make great show.—*n.* and *adj.* **prank'ing.**—*adv.* **prank'ingly.** [Akin to Du. *pronken,* Ger. *prunken,* to show off; cf. **prink.**]

**prank**, *pranck, prancke, prangk, (obs.) v.t.* to pleat, fold: to set in order. [Origin unknown.]

**prank**, *prangk, (rare) n.* prancing.—*v.i.* (and *v.t.* with *it*) to prance.—*v.i.* **prank'le,** to prance lightly. [Poss. conn. with prance.]

**prase**, *prāz, n.* a leek-green quartz. [Gr. *prason,* leek.]

**praseodymium**, *prāz-i-ō-dim'i-əm, n.* a metal (Pr; at. numb. 59) with green salts, separated from the once-supposed element didymium. [Gr. *prasios,* leek-green—*prason,* leek, and **didymium.**]

**prat**, *prat, (slang) n.* the buttocks.—*v.t. (Shak.,* punningly) to beat.—*n.* **prat'fall,** a fall landing on the prat: a humiliating blunder or experience. [Origin unknown.]

**prate**, *prāt, v.i.* to talk foolishly: to talk boastfully or insolently: to tattle: to be loquacious.—*v.t.* to utter pratingly: to blab.—*n.* foolish or superfluous talk.—*n.* **pra'ter.**—*n.* and *adj.* **pra'ting.**—*adv.* **pra'tingly.** [Cf. L.G. *praten,* Dan. *prate,* Du. *praaten.*]

**pratie, praty,** *prā'ti, n.* an Anglo-Irish form of **potato.**

**pratincole**, *prat'ing-kōl, n.* a bird akin to the plovers, with swallow-like wings and tail. [L. *prātum,* meadow, *incola,* an inhabitant.]

**pratique**, *prat'ik, -ēk', n.* permission to hold intercourse or trade after quarantine or on showing a clean bill of health. [Fr.]

**prattle**, *prat'l, v.i.* to talk much and idly: to utter child's talk.—*v.t.* to utter in a prattling way.—*n.* empty talk.—*ns.* **pratt'lement,** prattle; **pratt'ler,** one who prattles: a child.—**pratt'lebox,** a prattler. [Dim. and freq. of **prate.**]

**prau, prahu,** *prä'ōō, prow, proa, prō'a, n.* a Malay sailing- or rowing-boat, esp. a fast sailing-vessel with both ends alike, and a flat side with an outrigger kept to leeward. [Malay *prāū.*]

**praunce,** Spenser's form of **prance.**

**pravity**, *prav'i-ti, n.* wickedness. [L. *prāvitās, -ātis.*]

**prawle,** *pröl, n.* Shakespeare's Welsh form of **brawl.**

**prawn**, *prön, n.* a small edible shrimp-like crustacean (*Palaemon serratus* or kindred species).— *v.i.* to fish for prawns. [M.E. *prayne, prane;* origin unknown.]

Neutral vowels in unaccented syllables: el'ə-mənt; for certain sounds in foreign words, see p. viii

**praxinoscope**, *praks'in-ō-skōp, n.* an optical toy giving effect of motion by reflexion of successive pictures in a rotating box. [Irregularly, from Gr. *prāxis*, doing, *skopeein*, to look.]

**praxis**, *praks'is, n.* practice: an example or a collection of examples for exercise: a model or example. [Gr. *prāxis—prāssein*, to do.]

**pray**, *prā, v.i.* to ask earnestly: to entreat: to express one's desires to, or commune with, a god or some spiritual power.—*v.t.* to ask earnestly and reverently, as in worship: to supplicate: to present as a prayer: to render, get, put, or cause to be, by praying:—*pr.p.* **pray'ing**; *pa.t.* and *pa.p.* **prayed**.—*ns.* **pray'er**, one who prays: (*prār, prā'ər*) the act of praying: entreaty: a petition to, or communing with, a god or spiritual power: the wish put forward or the words used: a form used or intended for use in praying: public or (in *pl.*) family worship: a petition to a public body, e.g. a legislature: the thing prayed for.—*adj.* **prayerful** (*prār'fŏŏl*), given to prayer: in a spirit or mental attitude of prayer.—*adv.* **prayerfully**.—*n.* **prayerfulness**.—*adj.* **prayerless**, without or not using prayer.—*adv.* **prayerlessly**.—*n.* **prayerlessness**.—*n.* and *adj.* **pray'ing**.—*adv.* **pray'ingly**.—(Position of accent on following compounds depends on whether one says *prār'* or *prā'ər*) **pray'er-bead'**, one of the beads on a rosary: a jequirity bean; **pray'er-book**, a book containing prayers or forms of devotion, esp. the Book of Common Prayer of the Church of England; **prayer'-meet'ing**, a shorter and simpler form of public religious service, in which laymen often take part; **prayer'-monger**, one who prays mechanically; **prayer'-rug**, a small carpet on which a Moslem kneels at prayer; **prayer'-wheel**, a drum wrapped with strips of paper inscribed with prayers deemed by Buddhists of Tibet to be proffered when the drum is turned; **praying insect**, the mantis.—**pray**, I pray you, I ask you; **pray in aid** (*law; Shak.*), to call in, or call for, help. [O.Fr. *preier* (Fr. *prier*), to pray, and O.Fr. *preiere*, prayer (—L.L. *precāria*)—L. *precāri—prex, precis,* a prayer.]

**pray**, Spenser's usual spelling of **prey**.

**pre-** (as living prefix), **prae-** (L. spelling more common formerly), *prē-, pri-, pfx.* (1) in front, in front of, the anterior part of, as *predentate, premandibular, presternum*; (2) before in time, beforehand, in advance, as *prehistoric, pre-war, prewarn*; (3) surpassingly, to the highest degree, as *pre-eminent, pre-potent.* [L. *prae,* in front of.]

**preace**, *prēs* (*Spens.*). Same as press.

**preach**, *prēch, v.i.* to deliver a sermon: to discourse earnestly: to give advice in an offensive, tedious, or obtrusive manner.—*v.t.* to set forth in religious discourses: to deliver, as a sermon: to proclaim or teach publicly: to render or put by preaching.—*n.* (*coll.*) a sermon.—*ns.* **preach'er**, one who discourses publicly on religious matter: a minister or clergyman: an assiduous inculcator or advocate; **preach'ership**.—*v.i.* **preach'ify**, to preach tediously: to sermonise: to weary with lengthy advice.—*adv.* **preach'ily**.—*ns.* **preach'iness**; **preach'ing**; **preach'ment**, a sermon, in contempt: a sermon-like discourse: sermonising.—*adj.* **preach'y**, given to tedious moralising: savouring of preaching.—**preach'ing-cross**, a cross in an open place at which monks, etc., preached; **preach'ing-fri'ar**, a Dominican; **preach'ing-house**, a Methodist church.—**preach down, up,** to decry, extol; **preaching with a view**, preaching as a candidate in a vacant pastoral charge; **the Preacher**, the author or spokesman

of the Book of Ecclesiastes: the book itself. [Fr. *prêcher*—L. *praedicāre, -ātum,* to proclaim.]

**pre-Adamite**, *prē-ad'ə-mīt, n.* one who lived, or a descendant of those who lived, or a believer in the existence of a human race, before *Adam.*—*adjs.* **pre-Ad'amite**; **preadamic** (*-a-dam'ik*), *-al,* existing before Adam; **preadamit'ic**, *-al.* [Pfx. **pre-** (2).]

**preadmonish**, *prē-ad-mon'ish, v.t.* to forewarn.—*n.* **preadmoni'tion.** [Pfx. **pre-** (2).]

**preamble**, *prē-am'bl, n.* preface: introduction, esp. that of an Act of Parliament, giving its reasons and purpose: (*Milt.* **praeamble**) a prelude.—Also *v.t.* and *v.i.*—*adjs.* **pream'bulary, pream'bulatory**.—*v.i.* **pream'bulate**, to go first (*obs.*): to make a preamble. [Fr. *préambule*—L. *prae, ambulāre,* to go.]

**prease, preasse** (*Spens.*). Same as press.

**preaudience**, *prē-ö'di-əns, n.* right to be heard before another: precedence at the bar among lawyers. [Pfx. **pre-** (2).]

**prebend**, *preb'ənd, n.* the share of the revenues of a cathedral or collegiate church allowed to a clergyman who officiates in it at stated times.—*adj.* **prebendal** (*pri-bend'l*).—*n.* **preb'endary**, a resident clergyman who enjoys a prebend, a canon: the honorary holder of a disendowed prebendal stall. [L.L. *praebenda,* an allowance—L. *prae-bēre,* to allow, grant.]

**Pre-Cambrian**, *prē-kam'bri-ən,* (*geol.*) *adj.* and *n.* Archaean, including all before the Cambrian. [Pfx. **pre-** (2).]

**pre-cancel**, *prē-kan'səl, v.t.* to cancel a postage stamp (e.g. by applying a postmark) before use.—Also *n.* [Pfx. **pre-** (2).]

**pre-cancerous**, *prē-kan'sər-əs, adj.* that may become cancerous. [Pfx. **pre-** (2).]

**precarious**, *pri-kā'ri-əs, adj.* depending upon the will of another: depending on chance: insecure: uncertain: dangerous, risky: supplicating (*obs.*).—*adv.* **preca'riously**.—*n.* **preca'riousness**. [L. *precārius—precāri,* to pray.]

**precast**, *prē'kåst', adj.* of concrete blocks, etc., cast before putting in position. [Pfx. **pre-** (2).]

**precatory**, *prek'ə-tə-ri, adj.* of the nature of, or expressing, a wish, request, or recommendation.—*adj.* **prec'ative**, supplicatory: expressing entreaty (*gram.*). [L. *precāri,* to pray.]

**precaution**, *pri-kö'shən, n.* a caution or care beforehand: a measure taken beforehand.—*v.t.* to forewarn.—*adjs.* **precau'tional, precau'tionary, precau'tious**. [Pfx. **pre-** (2).]

**precede**, *prē-sēd', v.t.* to go before in position, time, rank, or importance: to cause to be preceded.—*v.i.* to be before in time or place.—*ns.* **precedence** (*pres'i-dəns; prēs',* also *pri-sē'dəns*), the act of going before in time: the right of going before: priority: the state of being before in rank: the place of honour: the foremost place in ceremony—also **precedency** (*pres'i, prēs'i, pri-sē'dən-si*); **precedent** (*pres'i-dənt;* also *prēs'),* that which precedes: the original of a copy (*Shak.*): a token (*Shak.*): a model (*obs.*): a past instance that may serve as an example: a previous judicial decision or proceeding.—*adj.* (*pri-sē'dənt*) preceding. — *adjs.* **precedented** (*pres';* also *prēs'),* having a precedent: warranted by an example; **precedential** (*pres-i-den'shl*), of the nature of a precedent.—*adv.* **pre'cedently**.—*adj.* **precē'ding**, going before in time, rank, etc.: antecedent: previous: foregoing: immediately before.—**take precedence of, over,** to precede in ceremonial order. [Fr. *précéder*—L. *praecēdere, -cessum,—prae, cēdere,* to go.]

**preceese**, *pri-sēz',* a Scots form of **precise.**

**precentor**, *pri-* or *prē-sen'tər* (Scot. *pri-zen'tər*), *n.*

**preacquaint'**, *v.t.* pre- (2).    **preannounce'**, *v.t.* pre- (2).    **prearrange'ment**, *n.* pre- (2).
**preacquaint'ance**, *n.* pre- (2).    **preappoint'**, *v.t.* pre- (2).    **preassur'ance**, *n.* pre- (2).
**preadapta'tion**, *n.* pre- (2).    **prearrange'**, *v.t.* pre- (2).

*fāte, fär, mē, hûr (her); mīne; mōte, fōr; mūte, mōōn, fŏŏt; dhen (then)* the leader of the singing of a church choir or congregation: in some English cathedrals a member of the chapter who deputes this duty to a succentor:—*fem.* precen'tress, precen'trix.—*n.* precen'torship. [L.L. *praecentor, -ōris*—L. *prae, canĕre*, to sing.]

**precept**, *prē'sept, n.* a rule of action: a commandment: principle, or maxim: the written warrant of a magistrate (*law*): a mandate.—*adjs.* preceptial (*pri-sep'shl; Shak.*), consisting of precepts: precep'tive, containing or giving precepts: directing in moral conduct: didactic.—*n.* precep'tor, one who delivers precepts: a teacher: an instructor: a tutor (*U.S.*): the head of a school: the head of a preceptory of Knights Templars:—*fem.* precep'tress.—*adjs.* precepto'rial (*prē-*); precep'tory (*pri-*), giving precepts.—*n.* a community of Knights Templars (occasionally extended to a commandery of the Hospitallers): its estate or buildings. [L. *praeceptum*, pa.p. neut. of *praecipĕre*, to take beforehand—*prae, capĕre*, to take.]

**precession**, *pri-sesh'ən, n.* the act of going before: a moving forward: the precession of the equinoxes (see below) or the analogous phenomenon in spinning-tops and the like.—*adj.* precess'ional.—precession of the equinoxes, a slow westward motion of the equinoctial points along the ecliptic, caused by the greater attraction of the sun and moon on the excess of matter at the equator, such that the times at which the sun crosses the equator come at shorter intervals than they would otherwise do. [L.L. *praecessiō, -ōnis*—*praecēdĕre*; see precede.]

**précieuse**, *prā-syœz', n.* a woman affecting a fastidious over-refinement. [Fr.—from the literary women of 17th-cent. France who were extremely fastidious in their use of language.]

**precinct**, *prē'singkt, n.* a space, esp. an enclosed space, around a building or other object (also in *pl.*): a district or division within certain boundaries: a district of jurisdiction or authority: a division for police or electoral purposes (*U.S.*): (in *pl.*) environs.—shopping precinct, shopping centre, esp. if traffic-free. [L.L. *praecinctum*, pa.p. neut. of *praecingĕre*—*prae, cingĕre* to gird.]

**precious**, *presh'əs, adj.* of great price or worth: cherished: very highly esteemed: often used in irony for arrant, worthless, 'fine': affecting an over-refined choiceness.—*adv.* preciously (*Shak.*): extremely, confoundedly (*coll.*).—*n.* used as a term of endearment.—*n.* preciosity (*presh-i-os'i-ti*, or *pres-*), fastidious over-refinement.—*adv.* prec'iously.—*n.* prec'iousness.—precious metals, gold, silver (sometimes mercury, platinum, and others of high price); precious stone, a stone of value and beauty for ornamentation: a gem or jewel. [O.Fr. *precios* (Fr. *précieux*)—L. *pretiōsus*—*pretium*, price.]

**precipice**, *pres'i-pis, n.* a headlong fall (*obs.*): a high vertical or nearly vertical cliff; (*Shak.*) prec'epit.—*adj.* prec'ipiced.—*n.* precipitabil'ity (*pri-*).—*adj.* precip'itable (*chem.*), that may be precipitated.—*ns.* precip'itance, precip'itancy, quality of being precipitate: headlong fall: headlong haste or rashness: impulsively hasty action. —*adj.* precip'itant, falling headlong: rushing down with too great velocity: impulsively hasty. —*n.* anything that brings down a precipitate.— *adv.* precip'itantly.—*v.t.* precip'itate, to hurl headlong: to force into hasty action: to bring on suddenly or prematurely: to bring down from a state of solution or suspension.—*v.i.* to fall headlong (*Shak.*): to rush in haste: to come out of solution or suspension: to condense and fall, as rain, hail, etc.—*adj.* (*-āt* or *-it*) falling, hurled, or rushing headlong: sudden and hasty: with-

out deliberation: rash.—*n.* (*-āt, -it*) a substance separated from solution or suspension, usually falling to the bottom: moisture deposited as rain, snow, etc.—*adv.* precip'itately.—*n.* precipitā'tion, act of precipitating: headlong fall or rush: sheer drop (*Shak.*): impulsive action: great hurry: rash haste: impulsiveness: rain, hail, and snow (sometimes also dew): amount of rainfall, etc.: the formation or coming down of a precipitate: separation of suspended matter: a precipitate.—*adj.* precip'itātive.—*ns.* precip'itātor, one who precipitates: a precipitating agent: an apparatus or tank for precipitation; precip'-itin, an antibody which in contact with an antigen produces a precipitate in the blood.—*adj.* precip'itous, like a precipice: sheer: precipitate (*rare*).—*adv.* precip'itously.—*n.* precip'itousness. [L. *praeceps, praecipitis*, headlong, *praecipitium*, precipice, *praecipitāre, -ātum*, to precipitate— *prae, caput, -itis*, head.]

**précis**, *prā'sē, n.* an abstract:—*pl.* précis (*-sēz*). [Fr.]

**precise**, *pri-sīs', adj.* definite: exact: accurate: free from vagueness: very, identical: scrupulously exact: scrupulous in religion: puritanical: over-exact: prim: formal.—*adv.* precise'-ly.—*ns.* precise'ness; precisian (*pri-sizh'ən*), an over-precise person: a formalist: formerly, in hostility, a Puritan; precis'ianism; preci'sianist (a precisian; preci'sion, quality of being precise: exactness: minute accuracy: mental separation (partly associated with **prescission**; *Berkeley*): a precise definition (*obs.*).—*adj.* for work of minute accuracy.—*n.* precis'ionist, one who insists on precision: a purist.—*adj.* precisive (*pri-si'siv*), cutting off: pertaining to precision. [Fr. *précis, -e*—L. *praecisus*, pa.p. of *praecidĕre*—*prae, caedĕre*, to cut.]

**preclude**, *pri-klōōd', v.t.* to close beforehand: to shut out beforehand: to hinder by anticipation: to prevent.—*n.* preclusion (*pri-klōō'zhən*).—*adj.* preclusive (*-klōō'siv*), tending to preclude: hindering beforehand.—*adv.* preclu'sively. [L. *praeclūdĕre, -clūsum*—*claudĕre*, to shut.]

**precocious**, *pri-kō'shəs, adj.* early in reaching some stage of development, as flowering, fruiting, ripening, mental maturity: precocial: flowering before leaves appear: showing early development.—*n.pl.* praecoces (*prē'kō-sēz, prī'ko-kās*), praecocial birds (opp. to *altrices*).—*adj.* precocial, praecocial (*kō'shl, -shyəl*), hatched with complete covering of down, able to leave the nest at once and seek food: premature: forward.—*adv.* precō'ciously.—*ns.* precō'ciousness, precocity (*pri-kos'i-ti*), state or quality of being precocious: early development or too early ripeness of the mind. [L. *praecox, -ōcis*—*prae, coquĕre*, to cook, ripen.]

**precognition**, *prē-kog-nish'ən, n.* foreknowledge: a preliminary examination of witnesses as to whether there is ground for prosecution (*Scots law*): evidence so obtained.—*adj.* precog'nitive (*pri-*).—*v.t.* precognosce (*prē-kog-nos'*), to take a precognition of. [Pfx. pre- (2).]

**preconceive**, *prē-kən-sēv', v.t.* to conceive or form a notion of, before having actual knowledge.—*ns.* preconceit', a preconceived notion; preconcep'-tion, act of preconceiving: previous opinion formed without actual knowledge. [Pfx. pre- (2).]

**preconcert**, *prē-kən-sûrt', v.t.* to settle beforehand. —*n.* preconcert (*-kon'*), a previous arrangement. —*adv.* preconcert'edly.—*n.* preconcert'edness. [Pfx. pre- (2).]

**precondition**, *prē-kən-dish'ən, n.* a condition that must be satisfied beforehand.—*v.t.* to prepare beforehand. [Pfx. pre- (2).]

---

prechris'tian, *adj.* pre- (2).     precompose', *v.t.* pre- (2).     precondemn', *v.t.* pre- (2).
preclass'ical, *adj.* pre- (2).

Neutral vowels in unaccented syllables: *el'ə-mənt*; for certain sounds in foreign words, see p. viii

**preconise, -ize,** *prē'kən-iz, v.t.* to proclaim: to summon publicly: (of the pope) to proclaim and ratify the election of as bishop.—*n.* **preconisation** (*prē-kən-i-zā'shən,* or *-kon-i-*). [L. *praecō, -ōnis,* a crier, a herald.]

**precontract,** *prē-kən-trakt', v.t.* to contract beforehand: to betroth previously.—*n.* **precontract** (*-kon'*), a previous contract or betrothal. [Pfx. **pre-** (2).]

**precordial, praecordial,** *prē-kör'di-əl, adj.* in front of the heart. [**pre-** (1), L. *cor, cordis,* heart.]

**precurrer,** *prē-kur'ər,* (*Shak.*) *n.* a forerunner.—*n.* **precurse** (*pri-kûrs'* ; *Shak.*), a prognostication.—*adj.* **precur'sive.**—*n.* **precur'sor,** a forerunner: a predecessor: an indication of the approach of an event.—*adj.* **precur'sory.** [L. *praecurrĕre, -cursum—currĕre,* to run.]

**predacious,** (*irreg.*) **predaceous** *pri-dā'shəs, adj.* living by prey: predatory.—*n.* **predā'tion.**—*adj.* **pred'ative.**—*n.* **pred'ator.**—*adv.* **pred'atorily.**—*n.* **pred'atoriness.**—*adj.* **pred'atory,** of, relating to, or characterised by, plundering: living by plunder: deleterious (*obs.*). [L. *praeda,* booty.]

**predate,** *prē-dāt', v.t.* to date before the true date: to antedate: to be earlier than. [Pfx. **pre-** (2).]

**predecease,** *prē-di-sēs', n.* death before another's death, or before some other time.—*v.t.* to die before.—*adj.* **predeceased',** deceased at an earlier time. [Pfx. **pre-** (2).]

**predecessor,** *prē-di-ses'ər,* U.S. chiefly *pre-, n.* one who has been before another: a thing that has been supplanted or succeeded: an ancestor. [L., *praedēcessor—dēcessor,* a retiring officer—*dē,* away, *cēdĕre,* to go, depart.]

**predella,** *pri-del'ə, n.* the platform or uppermost step on which an altar stands: a retable: a painting or sculpture, on the face of either of these: a painting in a compartment along the bottom of an altarpiece or other picture. [It., prob.—O.H.G. *pret,* board.]

**predentate,** *prē-den'tāt, adj.* having teeth in the forepart of the jaw only. [Pfx. **pre-** (1).]

**predesign,** *prē-di-zin', v.t.* to design beforehand.—*v.t.* **predesignate** (*prē-dez'ig-nāt,* or *-des'*), to specify beforehand.—*adj.* designated in advance: having the quantification of the predicate distinctly expressed (*log.*; *Sir W. Hamilton*).—*n.* **predesignā'tion.**—*adj.* **predes'ignatory.** [Pfx. **pre-** (2).]

**predestine,** *prē-* or *pri-des'tin, v.t.* to destine or decree beforehand: to foreordain.—*adj.* **predestinā'rian,** believing in, or pertaining to, the doctrine of predestination.—*n.* one who holds the doctrine of predestination.—*n.* **predestinā'rianism.**—*v.t.* **predes'tinate,** to determine beforehand: to preordain by an unchangeable purpose.—*adj.* foreordained: fated.—*n.* **predestinā'tion,** act of predestinating: God's decree fixing unalterably from all eternity whatever is to happen, esp. the eternal happiness or misery of men (*theol.*): fixed fate.—*adj.* **predes'tinative.**—*ns.* **predes'tinātor,** one who predestinates or foreordains: a predestinarian (*obs.*); **predes'tiny,** irrevocably fixed fate. [Pfx. **pre-** (2).]

**predetermine,** *prē-di-tûr'min, v.t.* to determine or settle beforehand.—*adjs.* **predeter'minable; predeter'minate,** determined beforehand.—*ns.* **predeterminā'tion; predeter'minism,** determinism. [Pfx. **pre-** (2).]

**predevote,** *prē-di-vōt', adj.* foreordained. [Pfx. **pre-** (2).]

**predial.** Same as **praedial.**

**predicable,** *pred'i-kə-bl, adj.* that may be predicated or affirmed of something: attributable.—*n.* anything that can be predicated of another, or esp.

of many others: one of the five attributes—genus, species, difference, property, and accident (*log.*).—*n.* **predicabil'ity.** [L. *praedicabilis—praedicāre,* to proclaim, *-abilis,* able.]

**predicament,** *pri-dik'ə-mənt, n.* one of the classes or categories which include all predicables (*log.*): condition: an unfortunate or trying position.—*adj.* **predicamental** (*-ment'l*). [L.L. *praedicāmentum,* something predicated or asserted.]

**predicant,** *pred'i-kənt, adj.* predicating: preaching.—*n.* one who affirms anything: a preacher: a preaching-friar or Dominican: a predikant. [L. *praedicāns, -antis,* pr.p. of *praedicāre;* see next.]

**predicate,** *pred'i-kāt, v.t.* to preach (*rare*): to affirm: to assert: to state as a property or attribute of the subject (*log.*): to base on certain grounds (*U.S.*): sometimes used wrongly for **predict.**—*n.* that which is predicated of the subject (*log.*): the word or words by which something is said about something (*gram.*).—*n.* **predicā'tion.**—*adj.* **predicative** (*pri-dik'ə-tiv,* or *pred'i-kā-tiv*), expressing predication or affirmation: affirming: asserting.—*adv.* **predicatively.**—*adj.* **pred'icatory,** affirmative. [L. *praedicāre, -ātum,* to proclaim—*prae,* forth, *dicāre,* (orig.) to proclaim.]

**predict,** *pri-dikt', v.t.* to foretell.—*adj.* **predic'table.**—*ns.* **predictabil'ity, predic'tableness; prediction** (*-shən*).—*adj.* **predic'tive,** foretelling: prophetic.—*n.* **predic'tor,** that which predicts: an anti-aircraft rangefinding and radar device. [L. *praedictus,* pa.p. of *praedicĕre—dicĕre,* to say.]

**predigest,** *prē-di-jest'* or *-di-, v.t.* to digest artificially before introducing into the body.—*n.* **predigestion** (*-jest'yən*), digestion beforehand: hasty digestion (*obs.*). [Pfx. **pre-** (2).]

**predikant,** *prä-di-känt', n.* a Dutch Reformed preacher, esp. in South Africa. [Du.,—L. *praedicāns, -antis;* see **predicant, preach.**]

**predilection,** *prē-di-lek'shən, pred-i-, n.* favourable prepossession of mind: preference.—*adjs.* **predilect', -ed,** chosen: favoured: preferred. [L. *prae, diligĕre, dilectum,* to love—*di-, dis-,* apart, *legĕre,* to choose.]

**predispose,** *prē-dis-pōz', v.t.* to dispose or incline beforehand: to render favourable: to render liable.—*adj.* **predispō'sing.**—*n.* **predisposition** (*-pəz-ish'ən*).—*adj.* **predisposi'tional.** [Pfx. **pre-** (2).]

**predominate,** *pri-dom'in-āt, v.t.* to prevail over (*Shak.*).—*v.i.* to be dominant: to surpass in strength or authority: to prevail: to be most numerous or abounding: to have a commanding position.—*ns.* **predom'inance, predom'inancy.**—*adj.* **predom'inant,** ruling: having superior power: ascendant: preponderating: prevailing: commanding in position or effect.—*adv.* **predom'inantly.**—*n.* **predominā'tion.** [Pfx. **pre-** (3).]

**Pre-Dravidian,** *prē-drə-vid'i-ən, adj.* of a dark woolly-haired, broad-nosed race of man, including Sakai, Veddas, and Australian blacks.—Also *n.* [Pfx. **pre-** (2).]

**predy,** pronunciation unknown, (*obs. naut.*) *adj.* cleared for action.—*v.t.* make ready. [Origin unknown; poss. from make the ship *ready.*]

**pree,** *prē,* (*Scot.*) *v.t.* to make a trial of, esp. by tasting or by kissing. [prieve (see under **prief**).]

**pre-elect,** *prē-i-lekt', v.t.* to choose beforehand.—*n.* **pre-elec'tion,** preference (*obs.*): election in anticipation.—*adj.* before election. [Pfx. **pre-** (2).]

**pre-eminent,** *prē-em'in-ənt, adj.* eminent above others: surpassing others in good or bad qualities: outstanding: extreme.—*n.* **prē-em'inence.**—*adv.* **prē-em'inently.** [Pfx. **pre-** (3).]

---

**precon'scious,** *adj.* pre- (2).
**precon'sciousness,** *n.* pre- (2).
**preconsume',** *v.t.* pre- (2).
**pre-con'quest,** *n.* pre- (2).

**predefine',** *v.t.* pre- (2).
**predefini'tion,** *n.* pre- (2).
**predevel'op,** *v.t., v.i.* pre- (2).

**predevel'opment,** *n.* pre- (2).
**predoom',** *v.t.* pre- (2).
**pre-employ',** *v.t.* pre- (2).

---

**pre-emption**, *prē-em(p)'shən*, *n.* act or right of purchasing in preference to others: a piece of land so obtained: a belligerent's right to seize neutral contraband at a fixed price: seizure: act of attacking first to forestall hostile action.— *v.t.* **pre-empt** (*prē-empt'*, *-emt'*), to secure as first-comer: to secure by pre-emption (*U.S.*): to take possession of.—*v.i.* (*bridge*) to make a pre-emptive bid.—*adjs.* **prē-empt'ible**; **prē-empt'ive.**—*n.* **prē-empt'or.**—**prē-emptive bid** (*bridge*), an unusually high bid intended to deter others from bidding. [L. *prae*, *emptiō*, *-ōnis*, a buying —*emēre*, to buy.]

**preen**, *prēn*, *v.t.* to compose and arrange as birds do their feathers: to trim: to plume or pride (oneself).—**preen gland**, the uropygial gland that secretes oil used in preening the feathers. [App. *prune* (2) assimilated to the following word.]

**preen**, *prēn*, (*Scot.*) *n.* a pin.—*v.t.* to pin. [O.E. *prēon*, pin, brooch.]

**pre-establish**, *prē-is-tab'lish*, *v.t.* to establish beforehand.—**pre-established harmony** (see harmony). [Pfx. **pre-** (2).]

**preeve**, *prēv*, *n.* and *v.t.* obs. form of **proof** and **prove.**

**pre-exilic**, *prē-eg-zil'ik*, *adj.* before the exile—of O.T. writings prior to the Jewish exile (*c.* 586-538 B.C.).—Also **pre-exil'ian.** [Pfx. **pre-** (2).]

**pre-exist**, *prē-ig-zist'*, *v.i.* to exist beforehand, esp. in a former life.—*v.t.* to exist before.—*n.* **pre-exist'ence**, previous existence, esp. of the soul, before the generation of the body with which it is united in this world.—*adj.* **prē-exist'ent.** [Pfx. **pre-** (2).]

**prefabricate**, *prē-fab'ri-kāt*, *v.t.* to make standardised parts of beforehand, for assembling later.—*adj.* **prefab'ricated**, composed of such parts.—*ns.* **prefabricā'tion**; **prefab'ricātor**; **pre-fab'** (*coll.*), a prefabricated house. [Pfx. **pre-** (2).]

**preface**, *pref'is*, *n.* something said by way of introduction or preliminary explanation: a statement, usually explanatory, placed at the beginning of a book, not regarded as forming (like the introduction) part of the composition: the ascription of glory, etc., in the liturgy of consecration of the eucharist: anything preliminary or immediately antecedent.—*v.t.* to say by way of preface: to introduce by a preface: to precede: to front.—*v.i.* to make preliminary remarks.—*adjs.* **prefacial** (*pri-fā'shl*; *rare*); **prefatorial** (*pref-ə-tō'ri-əl*, *-tö'*), serving as a preface or introduction.—*advs.* **prefato'rially**, **prefatorily** (*pref'ə-tər-i-li*).—*adj.* **pref'atory**, pertaining to a preface: serving as an introduction: introductory. [Fr. *préface*—L.L. *prēfātia* for L. *praefātiō*—*prae*, *fāri*, *fātus*, to speak.]

**prefard**, *pri-färd'*, a Spenserian form of **preferred** (*pa.t.* and *pa.p.*).

**prefect**, **praefect**, *prē'fekt*, *n.* one placed in authority over others: a commander: a school pupil with some measure of authority over others: in France, the administrative head of a department. —*adj.* **prefectorial** (*prē-fek-tō'ri-əl*, *-tö'*).—*n.* **prē'fectship.**—*adj.* **prefect'ural** (*pri-*).—*n.* **prē'fecture**, the office, term of office, or district of a prefect: the house or office occupied by a prefect. [O.Fr. *prefect* (Fr. *préfet*) and L. *praefecius*, pa.p. of *praeficēre*—*prae*, *facēre*, to make.]

**prefer**, *pri-fûr'*, *v.t.* to set in front (*obs.*): to put forward, offer, submit, present, for acceptance or consideration (*arch.*): to promote: to advance: to hold in higher estimation: to choose or select before others: to like better (with *to*, or *rather than*; not with *than* alone):—*pr.p.* **preferring** (*pri-fûr'ing*); *pa.t.* and *pa.p.* **preferred** (*pri-fûrd'*).—*n.* **preferabil'ity** (*pref-*).—*adj.* **pref'erable** (*obs.* **preferr'able**, *pri-fûr'*), to be pre-

ferred: having priority.—*adv.* **pref'erably**, by choice: in preference.—*n.* **pref'erence**, the act of choosing, favouring, or liking one above another: estimation above another: the state of being preferred: that which is preferred: priority: an advantage given to one over another: a card game resembling auction bridge.—*adj.* **preferential** (*pref-ər-en'shl*), having, giving, or allowing, a preference.—*ns.* **preferen'tialism**; **preferen'tialist**, one who favours a preferential tariff.—*adv.* **preferen'tially.**—*ns.* **prefer'ment**, advancement: promotion: superior place, esp. in the Church; **preferr'er.**—**preference shares**, or **stock**, shares or stock on which the dividends must be paid before those on other kinds: **preferential tariff**, one by which lower customs duties are imposed on goods from certain countries than on goods from others. [Fr. *préférer*—L. *praeferre*—*ferre*, to bear.]

**prefigure**, *prē-fig'ər*, *v.t.* to imagine beforehand: to foreshadow by a type.—*adj.* **prefig'urate** (*-ū-rāt*), prefigured.—*v.t.* to prefigure.—*n.* **prefigūrā'-tion.**—*adj.* **prefig'ūrātive.**—*n.* **prefig'urement** (*-ər-mənt*). [Pfx. **pre-** (2).]

**prefix**, *prē-fiks'*, *v.t.* to put before, or at the beginning: to fix beforehand.—*ns.* **pre'fix**, a particle or word put before, and usually joined to, a word to affect its meaning: a title placed before a name, as *Mr*, *Sir*; **prefixion** (*-fik'shən*), **prefix'ture.** [L. *praefīgēre*, *-fīxum*—*fīgēre*, to fix.]

**prefloration**, *prē-flō-rā'shən*, *-flō-*, (*bot.*) *n.* aestivation. [Pfx. **pre-** (2), L. *flōs*, *flōris*, flower.]

**prefoliation**, *prē-fō-li-ā'shən*, (*bot.*) *n.* vernation. [Pfx. **pre-** (2), L. *folium*, leaf.]

**preform**, *prē-förm'*, *v.t.* to form beforehand (*Shak.*): to determine the shape of beforehand. —*ns.* **prēformā'tion**; **prēformā'tionism**; **prē-formā'tionist**, a believer in the now exploded theory that the plant or animal (and therefore all its descendants) was already preformed in the germ (the ovum according to the ovists, the sperm according to the animalculists) and had only to be unfolded without formation of any new parts.—*adj.* **prēfor'mative.** [Pfx. **pre-** (2).]

**prefrontal**, *prē-front'l*, *-frunt'l*, *adj.* in front of, or in the forepart of, the frontal bone, lobe, scale, etc.—*n.* a bone or scale so situated. [Pfx. **pre-** (1).]

**prefulgent**, *prē-ful'jənt*, *adj.* extremely bright. [Pfx. **pre-** (3).]

**pre-glacial**, *prē-glā'shl*, *adj.* earlier than the glacial period. [Pfx. **pre-** (2).]

**pregnable**, *preg'nə-bl*, *adj.* that may be taken by assault or force: vulnerable. [Fr. *prenable*—*prendre*, to take; see **impregnable.**]

**pregnant**, *preg'nənt*, *adj.* with child or young: impregnated: fertile: teeming: fruitful: fruitful in results: momentous: significant: threatening: freighted: swelling: full of thoughts, ready-witted, inventive: full of promise: disposed, ready, apt, ready to act (*Shak.*): full of meaning: pithy and to the purpose: conveying a compressed meaning beyond what the grammatical construction can strictly carry: weighty: cogent: obvious: clear.—*ns.* **preg'nance** (*obs.*), **preg'nancy.**—*adv.* **preg'nantly.** [L. *praegnāns*, *-antis*, from earlier *praegnās*, *-ātis*, app.—*prae* and the root of *gnāscī*, to be born; but in some meanings from or confused with O.Fr. *preignant*, pr.p. of *preindre*—L. *premēre*, to press.]

**pregustation**, *prē-gus-tā'shən*, *n.* a foretaste. [Pfx. **pre-** (2).]

**prehallux**, *prē-hal'uks*, *n.* a rudimentary innermost toe. [Pfx. **pre-** (2).]

**preheminence**, an obsolete spelling of **pre-eminence.**

**prehend**, *pri-hend'*, *v.t.* to seize (*rare*).—*adjs.*

**pre-engage'**, *v.t.* **pre-** (2).

**pre-engage'ment**, *n.* **pre-** (2).

**prehen′sible** (*rare*), capable of being grasped; **prehen′sile** (-*sil*), capable of grasping—also **prehen′sive, prehensō′rial** (*prē-*), **prehen′sory** (*pri-*).—*ns.* **prehensility** (*prē-hen-sil′i-ti*); **prehension** (*pri-hen′shən*); **prehen′sor**, one who seizes. [L. *praehendĕre*, -*hensum*, to seize.]

**prehistoric, -al,** *prē-his-tor′ik*, -*əl*, *adjs.* of a time before extant historical records.—*n.* **prēhistō′rian.**—*adv.* **prēhistor′ically.**—*n.* **prēhis′tory.** [Pfx. **pre-** (2).]

**prehnite,** *prān′it*, *n.* a zeolite-like mineral, an acid calcium aluminium silicate, usu. a pale green. [Named after Col. van *Prehn*, who brought it from South Africa in the 18th century.]

**prehuman,** *prē-hū′mən*, *adj.* at a stage of development before full humanity has been developed: earlier than the appearance of man. [Pfx. **pre-** (2).]

**preif, preife,** *prēf*, obs. forms of **proof.**

**pre-ignition,** *prē-ig-nish′ən*, *n.* too-early ignition of the charge in an internal combustion engine. [Pfx. **pre-** (2).]

**prejink,** *pri-jingk′*. Same as **perjink.**

**prejudge,** *prē-juj′*, *v.t.* to judge or decide upon before hearing the whole case: to condemn unheard.—*n.* **prejudg′ment** (also **prejudge′ment**).—*adj.* **prejudicant** (*prē-jōōd′i-kənt*).—*v.t.* **prejud′icāte,** to judge beforehand.—*v.i.* to form an opinion beforehand.—*n.* **prejudicā′tion.**—*adj.* **prejud′icātive.** [L. *praejūdicāre.*]

**prejudice,** *prej′ōō-dis*, *n.* a judgment or opinion formed beforehand or without due examination: a prejudgment (*obs.*): (*Spens.* **prejudize**) prognostication: prepossession in favour of or (usu.) against anything: bias: injury or hurt: disadvantage.—*v.t.* to fill with prejudice: to prepossess: to bias the mind of: to injure or hurt: to prejudge, esp. unfavourably (*obs.*).—*adjs.* **prej′udiced,** having prejudice: biased; **prejudicial** (-*dish′l*), injurious: detrimental: prejudiced (*obs.*): (*prē-jōō-*) relating to matters to be decided before a case comes into court.—*adv.* **prejudic′ially.—without prejudice,** a phrase used to require an understanding that nothing said at this stage is to detract from one's rights or to damage claims arising from future developments. [Fr. *préjudice*, wrong, and L. *praejūdicium—jūdicium*, judgment.]

**prelate,** *prel′it*, *n.* an ecclesiastic of high rank: a chief priest: a clergyman:—*fem.* **prel′atess.**—*ns.* **prelacy** (*prel′ə-si*), the office of a prelate: the order of bishops or the bishops collectively: church government by prelates: episcopacy; **prel′ateship.**—*adjs.* **prelatial** (*pri-lā′shəl*), of a prelate; **prelatic** (*pri-lat′ik*), **-al,** pertaining to prelates or prelacy: (in hostility) episcopal or episcopalian.—*adv.* **prelat′ically.**—*n.* **prelā′tion,** preferment: promotion: eminence.—*v.t.* and *v.i.* **prel′atise, -ize,** to make or to become prelatical.—*adj.* **prel′atish** (*Milt.*).—*ns.* **prel′atism,** (usu. hostile) episcopacy or episcopalianism: domination by prelates; **prel′atist,** an upholder of prelacy; **prel′ature, prel′aty** (*Milt.*), prelacy. [Fr. *prélat*—L. *praelātus—prae*, before and *lātus*, borne.]

**prelect,** *pri-lekt′*, *v.i.* to lecture.—*ns.* **prelec′tion; prelec′tor,** a public reader or lecturer. [L. *praelegĕre*, -*lectum—prae*, *legĕre*, to read.]

**prelibation,** *prē-li-bā′shən*, *n.* a foretaste: an offering of first-fruits. [L. *praelibātiō*, -*ōnis—prae*, *libāre*, to taste.]

**preliminary,** *pri-lim′in-ə-ri*, *adj.* introductory: preparatory: preceding or preparing for the main matter.—*n.* that which precedes: introduction (often in *pl.*, **prelim′inaries**): a preliminary or entrance examination (in student slang shortened to **prelim′**): (in *pl.*) preliminary pages—titles, preface, contents, introduction, etc. (in printers'

slang **prelims′**).—*adv.* **prelim′inarily.** [L. *prae, limen,* -*inis,* threshold.]

**prelingual,** *prē-ling′gwəl*, *adj.* before the use of language. [Pfx. **pre-** (2).]

**prelude,** *prel′ūd*, *n.* a preliminary performance or action: an event preceding and leading up to another of greater importance: a preliminary strain, passage, or flourish, often improvised (*mus.*): an introduction or first movement of a suite: a movement preceding a fugue: an overture: an introductory voluntary: a short independent composition such as might be the introduction to another, or developed out of the prelude in the literal sense.—*v.t.* (*prel′ūd*, formerly and still by some *pri-lūd*, -*lōōd′*) to precede as a prelude, serve as prelude to: to introduce with a prelude: to perform as a prelude.—*v.i.* to furnish a prelude: to perform a prelude: to serve as a prelude.—Also (*ns.*) **preludio** (*pre-lōō′di-ō*; It.), **praeludium** (*pri-lōō′di-ōōm*; L.), **prelu′sion** (-*zhən*).—*adjs.* **preludial** and **preludious** (*pri-lōō′*, or -*lū′*; both *rare*); **prelusive** (-*lōō′* or -*lū′siv*), of the nature of a prelude: introductory.—*advs.* **prelu′sively; prelu′sorily.**—*adj.* **prelu′sory** (-*sə-ri*), introductory. [Fr. *prélude*—L.L. *praelūdium*—L. *lūdĕre*, to play.]

**premandibular,** *prē-man-dib′ū-lər*, *adj.* in front of the lower jaw.—*n.* a bone so placed in fishes, etc. [Pfx. **pre-** (1).]

**premature,** *prem′ə-tūr*, *prēm′*, or -*tūr′*, *adj.* ripe before the time: unduly early.—*adv.* **premature′ly** (or *prem′*, *prēm′*).—*ns.* **premature′ness** (or *prem′*); **prematur′ity.** [L. *praemātūrus—prae, mātūrus*, ripe.]

**premaxilla,** *prē-maks-il′ə*, *n.* a bone in front of the maxilla.—*adj.* **premaxill′ary** (or -*maks′*).—*n.* the premaxilla. [Pfx. **pre-** (1).]

**premeditate,** *prē-med′i-tāt*, *v.t.* to meditate upon beforehand: to design previously.—*v.i.* to deliberate beforehand.—*adv.* **premed′itātedly.**—*n.* **premeditā′tion.**—*adj.* **premed′itātive.** [L. *praemeditārī*, -*ātus—prae, meditārī*, to meditate.]

**premier,** *prem′i-ər*, -*yər*, by some *prēm′i-ər*, formerly also *pri-mēr′*, *adj.* prime or first: chief: most ancient (*her.*).—*n.* the first or chief: the prime minister: the Secretary of State (*U.S.*).—*n.* **première** (*prəm-yer′*, *prem′yər*; Fr., *fem.*), a leading actress, dancer, etc.: first performance of a play or film—also *adj.*:—*v.t.* to give a first performance of.—*n.* **prem′iership.** [Fr.,—L. *primārius*, of the first rank—*primus*, first.]

**premillenarian,** *prē-mil-ən-ā′ri-ən*, *n.* a believer in the premillennial coming of Christ.—Also *adj.* —*n.* **premillena′rianism.** [Pfx. **pre-** (2).]

**premillennial,** *prē-mil-en′yəl*, *adj.* before the millennium.—*ns.* **premillenn′ialism, premillenarianism; premillenn′ialist.** [Pfx. **pre-** (2).]

**premise, premiss,** *prem′is*, *n.* a proposition stated or assumed for after-reasoning, esp. one of the two propositions in a syllogism from which the conclusion is drawn (*log.*): (in the form **premise** only, usu. in *pl.* **prem′ises**) the matter set forth at the beginning of a deed: the beginning of a deed setting forth its subject-matter: the aforesaid, hence, a building and its adjuncts, esp. a public-house: a presupposition: a condition stipulated beforehand (*Shak.*): antecedent happenings or circumstances (*Shak.*).—*v.t.* **premise** (*pri-mīz′*, also *prem′is*), to mention or state first, or by way of introduction: to prefix: to state or assume as a premise: to perform or administer beforehand (*med.*).—*adj.* **premi′sed** (*Shak.*), sent before due time. [Fr. *premisse* and L. (*sententia*, etc.) *praemissa*, (a sentence, etc.) put before—*mittĕre*, *missum*, to send.]

**premium,** *prē′mi-əm*, *n.* a reward: a prize: a bounty: payment made for insurance: a fee for admission as a pupil for a profession: ex-

---

**premar′ital,** *adj.* **pre-** (2).

*fāte, fär; mē, hûr* (her); *mīne; mōte, för; mūte; mōōn, fŏŏt; dhen* (then)

cess over original price or par—opp. to *discount*: anything offered as an incentive:—*pl.* pre'miums.—Premium Bond, a Government bond, the holder of which gains no interest, but is eligible for a money prize allotted by draw held at stated intervals.—at a premium, above par. [L. *praemium—prae*, above, *emēre*, to buy.]

premolar, *prē-mō'lər*, *adj.* in front of the true molar teeth.—*n.* a tooth between the canine and the molars (called molar or milk-molar in the milk dentition). [Pfx. pre- (1).]

premonish, *prē-mon'ish*, *v.t.* to admonish or warn beforehand.—*n.* premonition (*prē-mən-ish'ən*), a forewarning: a feeling that something is going to happen.—*adjs.* premonitive (*pri-mon'*), premon'itory, giving warning or notice beforehand.—*n.* premon'itor, one who, or that which, gives warning beforehand.—*adv.* premon'itorily. [On the model of admonish—L. *praemonēre—monēre*, to warn.]

premonstrant. See Premonstratensian.

Premonstratensian, *pri-mon-strə-ten'sh(y)ən*, *-si-ən*, *adj.* of an order of canons regular, the Norbertines or White Canons, founded by St Norbert, in 1119, at *Prémontré*, near Laon, or of a corresponding order of nuns.—*n.* a member of the order.—Also (*n.* and *adj.*) premon'strant. [L. *prātum mōnstrātum*, the meadow pointed out, or (*locus*) *praemōnstrātus*, (the place) foreshown (in a vision), i.e. *Prémontré*.]

premorse, *pri-mörs'*, *adj.* ending abruptly, as if bitten off. [L. *praemorsus*, bitten in front—*prae*, *mordēre*, *morsum*, to bite.]

premosaic, *prē-mō-zā'ik*, *adj.* before the time of *Moses*. [Pfx. pre- (2), Mosaic.]

premotion, *prē-mō'shən*, *n.* an (esp. divine) impulse determining the will.—*v.t.* premove'.—*n.* premove'ment. [Pfx. pre- (2).]

prenasal, *prē-nā'zl*, *adj.* in front of the nose.— *n.* a bone at the tip of the nose, as in pigs. [Pfx. pre- (1).]

prenatal, *prē-nā'tl*, *adj.* before birth. [Pfx. pre- (2).]

prenominate, *pri-nom'in-āt*, (*Shak.*) *adj.* forenamed.—*v.t.* to name or state beforehand. [Pfx. pre- (2).]

prenotion, *prē-nō'shən*, *n.* preconception. [Pfx. pre- (2).]

prent, *prent*, (*Scot.*). Same as print.

prentice, 'prentice, *pren'tis*, aphetic for apprentice. —*n.* pren'ticeship, 'pren'ticeship.

prenzie, app. *adj.* in *Shak.* (*Measure for Measure*, III, i. 92, 95) conjectured to mean primsie: according to others princely: or connected with prone (homily): or Fr. *prenez garde*: or a misprint.

preoccupy, *prē-ok'ū-pi*, *v.t.* to occupy, fill, or (*obs.*) wear beforehand or before others: to take or have possession of to the exclusion of others or other things: to fill the mind of: to prejudice.—*ns.* preocc'upancy, occupying before others: condition of being preoccupied; preocc'upant, a prior occupant.—*v.t.* preocc'upate, to preoccupy: to anticipate.—*n.* preoccupā'-tion.—*adj.* preocc'upied, already occupied: lost in thought, abstracted: having one's attention wholly taken up by (with *with*): of a genus or species name, not available for adoption because it has already been applied to another group. [Pfx. pre- (2).]

preoption, *prē-op'shən*, *n.* first choice. [Pfx. pre- (2).]

preoral, *prē-ō'rəl*, *-ö'*, *adj.* in front of the mouth. —*adv.* preo'rally. [Pfx. pre- (1).]

preordain, *prē-ör-dān'*, *v.t.* to ordain, appoint, or determine beforehand.—*n.* preordain'ment.— *v.t.* preor'der, arrange or ordain beforehand.— *ns.* preor'dinance, a rule previously established:

prenu'bile, *adj.* pre- (2).

that which is ordained beforehand; preordinā'-tion, preordaining. [Pfx. pre- (2).]

prep, *prep*, *adj.* (*coll.* contr. for) *prep*aratory.—*n.* school slang for *prep*aration, preparation of lessons: a preparatory school: a pupil in a preparatory school.—Also *v.t.*

prepaid. See prepay.

prepare, *pri-pār'*, *v.t.* to make ready or fit: to bring into a suitable state: to dispose: to adapt: to train, as for an examination: to get up, learn: to provide, furnish (*arch.*): to subject to a process for bringing into a required state: to make, produce: to cook and dress: to lead up to.—*v.i.* to make oneself ready: to make preparation.—*n.* preparation (*Shak.*).—*n.* preparation (*prep-ə-rā'shən*), the act of preparing: preliminary arrangement: course of being prepared: preliminary study of prescribed classwork: readiness: that which is prepared or made up, as a medicine: an anatomical or other specimen prepared for study or preservation: the day before the Sabbath or other Jewish feast-day: devotional exercises introducing an office: the previous introduction, as an integral part of a chord, of a note continued into a succeeding dissonance (*mus.*).—*adj.* preparative (*pri-par'ə-tiv*), serving to prepare: preliminary.—*n.* that which prepares the way: preparation.—*adv.* prepar'atively.—*n.* prepar'ator.—*adv.* prepar'atorily.—*adj.* prepar'atory, preparing: previous: introductory.—*adv.* preparatorily.—*adj.* prepared (*pri-pārd'*), made ready, fit, or suitable: ready.—*adv.* prepā'redly.—*ns.* prepā'redness; prepā'rer.—preparatory school, one which prepares pupils for a public or other higher school.—be prepared to, to be ready, or be willing, to (do something). [Fr. *préparer*—L. *praeparāre—prae*, *parāre*, to make ready.]

prepay, *prē'pā'*, *v.t.* to pay before or in advance. —*adj.* pre'paid'.—*adj.* prepay'able.—*n.* prepay'-ment. [Pfx. pre- (2).]

prepense, *pri-pens'*, *adj.* premeditated: intentional, chiefly in the phrase 'malice prepense' = malice aforethought or intentional.—*v.t.* (*Spens.*) to consider.—*adv.* prepense'ly.—*adj.* prepens'ive (*Fielding*). [O.Fr. *purpense*.]

prepollence, *pri-pol'əns*, *n.* predominance.—*n.* prepoll'ency.—*adj.* prepoll'ent. [L.L. *praepollentia—prae*, *pollēre*, to be strong.]

prepollex, *prē-pol'eks*, *n.* in some animals, a rudimentary innermost finger. [Pfx. pre- (1).]

preponderate, *pri-pon'dər-āt*, *v.i.* to weigh more: to turn the balance: to prevail or exceed in number, quantity, importance, influence, or force.—*v.t.* (*lit.* or *fig.*) to outweigh.—*ns.* preponderance, prepon'derancy.—*adj.* prepon'derant.—*advs.* prepon'derantly, prepon'deratingly. [L. *praeponderāre*, *-ātum—prae*, *ponderāre*, *-ātum*, to weigh—*pondus*, a weight.]

preponderate, *pri-pon'də-rāt*, (*Fielding*) *v.t.* and *v.i.* to ponder beforehand. [Pfx. pre- (2).]

preposition, *prep-ə-zish'ən*, *n.* a word placed usually before a noun or its equivalent to mark some relation: a prefix (*obs.*): (*prē*-) position in front.—*adj.* preposi'tional (*prep-*).—*adv.* preposi'tionally.—*adj.* prepositive (*pri-poz'i-tiv*), put before: prefixed.—*n.* praepostor, prepos'itor, a school prefect (for L. *praepositus*). [L. *praepositiō*, *-ōnis—praepōnēre*, *-positum—prae*, *pōnēre*, to place.]

prepossess, *prē-poz-es'*, *v.t.* to possess beforehand: to take beforehand: to fill beforehand, as the mind with some opinion or feeling: to preoccupy: to bias or prejudice, esp. favourably.—*adjs.* prepossessed', biased, prejudiced; prepossess'ing, tending to prepossess: making a favourable impression.—*adv.* prepossess'ingly.— *n.* preposession (*-esh'ən*), previous possession:

prepacked', *adj.* pre- (2).

---

preoccupation: bias, usually favourable. [Pfx. pre- (2).]

**preposterous**, *pri-pos'tə-rəs, adj.* lit. inverted, having or putting the last first (*rare*): contrary to the order of nature or reason: utterly absurd. —*adv.* **prepos'terously**.—*n.* **prepos'terousness**. [L. *praeposterus—prae*, before, *posterus*, after—*post*, after.]

**prepotent**, *prē-pō'tənt, adj.* powerful in a very high degree: prevailing over others or another in taking effect: having power to transmit to offspring more characteristics than the other parent: taking precedence in effect.—*ns.* **prepo'tence, prepo'tency**. [Pfx. pre- (3).]

**pre-print**, *prē'-print, n.* part of a publication printed in advance. [Pfx. pre- (2).]

**prepuce**, *prē'pūs, n.* the loose skin of the penis, the foreskin.—*adj.* **preputial** (*pri-pū'shyəl, -shəl*). [L. *praepūtium.*]

**prepunctual**, *prē-pungk'tū-əl, adj.* more than punctual: coming before time. [Pfx. pre- (3).]

**Pre-Raphaelite**, (or, as spelt by D. G. Rossetti) **Praeraphaelite**, *prē-raf'ā-əl-it, n.* one who seeks to return to the spirit and manner of painters before the time of *Raphael* (1483-1520): a member of a group (the Pre-Raphaelite Brotherhood, or 'P.R.B.', 1848) of painters and others (D. G. Rossetti, W. Holman Hunt, J. E. Millais, etc.) who practised or advocated a truthful, almost rigid, adherence to natural forms and effects.—Also *adj.*—*ns.* **Pre-Raph'aelism, Pre-Raph'aelitism**.—*adjs.* **Pre-Raphaelist'ic, Pre-Raphaelitist'ic; Pre-Raphaelit'ish**. [Pfx. pre- (2), *Raphael*, and suff. -ite.]

**pre-Reformation**, *prē-ref-ər-mā'shən, adj.* before the Reformation: dating from before the Reformation. [Pfx. pre- (2).]

**prerelease**, *prē-ri-lēs', n.* release of a cinematograph film before the normal date: exhibition of a film so released.—Also *adj.* [Pfx. pre- (2).]

**prerequisite**, *prē-rek'wi-zit, n.* a condition or requirement that must previously be satisfied. —*adj.* required as a condition of something else. [Pfx. pre- (2).]

**prerogative**, *pri-rog'ə-tiv, n.* a peculiar privilege shared by no other: a right arising out of one's rank, position, or nature: the right of voting first (*rare*).—*adj.* arising out of, or held by, prerogative: voting first.—*adj.* **prerog'atived**, (*Shak.*) having a prerogative.—*adv.* **prerog'atively.—Prerogative Court**, formerly a court having jurisdiction over testamentary matters. —**royal prerogative**, the rights which a sovereign has by right of office, which are different in different countries. [L. *praerogātīvus*, asked first for his vote—*prae, rogāre, -ātum*, to ask.]

**prerosion**, *prē-rō'zhən, n.* corrosion of a crystal by a solvent forming new faces (*prerosion faces*) on the corners and edges. [L. *praerōdēre*, -*rōsum*, to gnaw at the tip—*rōdēre*, to gnaw.]

**prerupt**, *prē-rupt', adj.* broken off: abrupt. [L. *praeruptus—prae, rumpēre*, to break.]

**presage**, *pres'ij*, formerly also *pri-sāj', n.* a prognostic: an omen: an indication of the future: a foreboding: a presentiment.—*v.t.* **presage** (*pri-sāj'*), to portend: to forebode: to warn of as something to come: to forecast: to point out, reveal (*Spens.*): to have a presentiment of. —*v.i.* to have or utter a presage.—*adj.* **presageful**.—*ns.* **presage'ment** (*obs.*); **presag'er**. [L. *praesāgium*, a foreboding—*prae, sāgus*, prophetic.]

**presanctify**, *prē-sangk'ti-fī, v.t.* to consecrate beforehand.—*n.* **presanctifica'tion**. [Pfx. pre- (2).]

**presbyopia**, *prez-bi-ō'pi-ə, n.* difficulty in accommodating the eye to near vision, a defect increasing with age—also **pres'byopy**.—*n.* **pres'byope**, one so affected.—*adj.* **presbyopic** (-*op'ik*). [Gr. *presbys*, old, *ōps, ōpos*, the eye.]

**presbyte**, *prez'bit, n.* eytmologically an old man but used for one who is presbyopic. [Gr. *presbȳtēs*, an old man.]

**presbyter**, *prez'bi-tər, n.* an elder: a minister or priest in rank between a bishop and a deacon: a member of a presbytery: a Presbyterian (*obs.*).—*adj.* **presbyt'eral**, of a presbyter or presbyters.—*n.* **presbyt'erate**, the office of presbyter: a body of presbyters: the order of presbyters.—*adj.* **presbyterial** (-*tē'ri-əl*), of a presbytery: of church government by elders.— *adv.* **presbytē'rially**.—*adj.* **Presbytē'rian**, pertaining to, or maintaining the system of, church government by presbyters: of a church so governed.—*n.* a member of such a church: an upholder of the Presbyterian system.—*v.t.* and *v.i.* **Presbytē'rianise, -ize**, to make or become Presbyterian: to move towards Presbyterianism. —*ns.* **Presbytē'rianism**, the form of church government by presbyters; **pres'bytership; pres'bytery**, a church court ranking next above the kirk-session, consisting of the ministers and one ruling elder from each church within a certain district: the district so represented: the Presbyterian system: part of a church reserved for the officiating priests, the eastern extremity: a priest's house (*R.C.*).—**Reformed Presbyterian Church**, the Cameronians; **United Presbyterian Church**, a religious body formed by the union of the Secession and Relief Churches in 1847, included in the United Free Church from 1900, and (except a minority) in the Church of Scotland from 1929. [Gr. *presbyteros*, comp. of *presbys*, old.]

**prescience**,*pre'sh(y)əns,-shi-əns,prē',-si-əns,n.*foreknowledge: foresight.—*adj.* **pre'scient**.—*adv.* **pre'sciently**. [L. *praesciēns, -entis*, pr.p. of *praescire—prae, scire*, to know.]

**prescientific**, *prē-sī-ən-tif'ik, adj.* before the scientific age, before knowledge was systematised. [Pfx. pre- (2).]

**prescind**, *pri-sind', v.t.* to cut off, cut short, separate: to abstract.—*v.i.* to withdraw the attention (usu. with *from*).—*adj.* **prescind'ent**.—*n.* **prescission** (*pri-sish'ən*). [L. *praescindēre*, to cut off in front.]

**prescious**, *pre', prē'shyəs, adj.* prescient. [L. *praescius—praescire*; cf. prescience.]

**prescisson**. See prescind.

**prescribe**, *pri-skrīb', v.t.* to lay down as a rule or direction: to give as an order: to appoint: to give directions for, as a remedy (*med.*): to limit, set bounds to: to claim by prescription. —*v.i.* to lay down rules: to give or make out a prescription (*med.*): to make a claim on account of long possession: to become of no force through time.—*ns.* **prescrib'er; prescript** (*prē'-skript*; formerly -*skript'*), an ordinance or rule: a remedy or treatment prescribed.—*adj.* (*prē'* or -*skript'*) prescribed.—*n.* **prescriptibil'ity** (*pri-*).—*adj.* **prescrip'tible**, subject to prescription: invalidated by lapse of time.—*n.* **prescrip'tion**, act of prescribing or directing: a written direction for the preparation of a medicine (*med.*): a recipe: custom continued until it becomes a right or has the force of law (*law*): limitation of time within which action may be taken (*law*). —*adj.* **prescrip'tive**, prescribing, laying down rules: consisting in, or acquired by, custom or long-continued use: customary.—*adv.* **prescrip'tively**.—*n.* **prescrip'tiveness**. [L. *praescrībēre, -scriptum*, to write before, lay down in advance, demur to—*prae, scrībēre*, to write.]

**prescutum**, *prē-skū'təm, n.* in insects, a tergal plate in front of the scutum. [Pfx. pre- (1).]

**preselect**, *prē-si-lekt', v.t.* to select beforehand.— *ns.* **preselec'tion; preselec'tor**, a component of a radio receiver, improving reception. [Pfx. pre- (2).]

**presence**, *prez'əns, n.* fact or state of being present

—opp. to *absence*: immediate neighbourhood: a presence-chamber or other place where a great personage is: an assembly, esp. of great persons: a present personality: impression made by one's bearing, esp. imposing bearing: something felt or imagined to be present.— **pres'ence-chamber**, the room in which a great personage receives company.—**presence of mind**, power of keeping one's wits about one: coolness and readiness in emergency, danger, or surprise; **real presence**, the true and substantial presence, according to the belief of Roman Catholics, of the body and blood of Christ in the eucharist. [O.Fr.,—L. *praesentia*; see following words.]

**presension.** See **presentient**.

**present**, *prez'ənt*, *adj.* in the place in question or implied—opp. to *absent*: at hand: ready: found or existing in the thing in question: before the mind: attentive, watchful, not absent-minded: now under view or consideration: now existing: not past or future: denoting time just now, or making a general statement (*gram.*): in or of the present tense: immediate.—*n.* that which is present: the present time: the present tense: a verb in the present tense: present business or occasion: present document or (in *pl.*) writings. —*adj.* **presential** (*pri-zen'shl*), relating to presence: having or implying actual presence: present: as if present: formed from the present tense.—*n.* **presentiality** (*-shi-al'i-ti*).—*advs.* **presen'tially; pres'ently**, at present, now (*obs.* or *Scot.* and *U.S.*): for the time being (*obs.*): at once (*obs.*): before long: directly, immediately, necessarily.—*n.* **pres'entness**.—*adj.* **pres'ent-day'**, belonging to or found in the present time, contemporary.—**at present**, at the present time, now; **for the present**, for the moment: now for the time being. [O.Fr.,—L. *praesēns, -sentis*, present.]

**present**, *prez'ənt*, *n.* a gift. [O.Fr. *present*, orig. presence, hence gift (from the phrase *mettre en present à*, put into the presence of, hence offer as a gift to).]

**present**, *pri-zent'*, *v.t.* to set before one, introduce into presence or to notice, cognisance, or acquaintance: to introduce at court: to introduce to the public, as on the stage: to put on the stage: to exhibit to view: to have as a characteristic: to put forward: to proffer: to make a gift of: to appoint to a benefice: to nominate to a foundation: to put forward or bring up for examination, trial, dedication, a degree, consideration, etc.: to deliver: to bestow something upon, endow (with *with*): to represent, depict, or symbolise: to represent the character of, act, personate (*arch.*): to point, direct, aim, turn in some direction: to apply: to offer the greetings of, 'remember' (*obs.*): to hold vertically in front of the body in salute to a superior (*mil.*): (*refl.*) to come into presence, attend, appear: (*refl.*) to offer (occur).—*v.i.* to make presentation to a living: to offer: to be directed, to be in position for coming first (*obstetrics*).— *n.* the position of a weapon in presenting arms or in aiming.—*n.* **presentabil'ity**.—*adj.* **present'-able**, capable of being presented: fit to be presented: fit to be seen: passable.—*adv.* **present'-ably**.—*n.* **presentation** (*prez-ən-tā'shən*), act of presenting: mode of presenting: right of presenting: that which is presented: immediate cognition: a setting forth, as of a truth: representation.—*adj.* that has been presented: of or for presentation.—*adj.* **presentā'tional**.— **presentā'tionism**, the doctrine of immediate cognition of objects; **presentā'tionist**.—*adj.* **presentative** (*pri-zent'ə-tiv*), subject to right of presentation: presenting to the mind (esp. that which is not imitative): pertaining to immediate cognition.—*ns.* **presentee** (*prez-ən-tē'*), one who

is presented to a benefice; **presenter** (*pri-zent'ər*). —*adj.* **present'ive**, presenting a conception to the mind, not a mere relation.—*ns.* **present'-iveness; present'ment**, act of presenting: a statement: a jury's statement to a court of matters within its knowledge: a representation: an image, delineation, picture: a presentation to consciousness.—**present arms**, to bring the weapon to a vertical position in front of the body. [O.Fr. *presenter*—L. *praesentāre*— *praesēns*, present (in place or time).]

**presentient**, *prē-sen'sh(y)ənt*, *adj.* having a presentiment.—*n.* **prēsen'sion**. [Pfx. pre- (2).]

**presentiment**, *pri-zent'i-mənt*, sometimes *-sent'*, *n.* a foreboding, esp. of evil.—*adj.* **presentimental** (*-ment'l*). [Pfx. pre- (2).]

**presentment.** See **present** (3).

**preserve**, *pri-zûrv'*, *v.t.* to keep safe from harm or loss: to keep alive: to keep in existence: to retain: to maintain, keep up: to guard against shooting or fishing by unauthorised persons: to keep sound: to keep from or guard against decay: to pickle, season, or otherwise treat for keeping.—*v.i.* to preserve game, fish, ground, or water, etc.—*n.* preserved fruit or jam (often in *pl.*): a place or water where shooting or fishing is preserved: anything regarded as closed or forbidden to outsiders: (in *pl.*) spectacles to protect the eyes from dust or strong light.—*n.* **preservabil'ity**.—*adj.* **preserv'able**.—*n.* **preservā'-tion** (*prez-*).—*adj.* **preser'vative**, serving to preserve.—*n.* a preserving agent: a safeguard: a prophylactic.—*adj.* and *n.* **preser'vatory**.—*n.* **preserv'er**. [Fr. *préserver*—L. *prae, servāre*, to keep.]

**preses, praeses**, *prē'siz*, (chiefly *Scot.*) *n.* a president or chairman. [L. *praeses, -idis*—*praesidēre*; see **preside**.]

**pre-shrink**, *prē-shringk'*, *v.t.* to shrink (cloth) before it is made up into garments, etc. [Pfx. pre- (2).]

**preside**, *pri-zīd'*, *v.i.* to be in the chair: to be at the head: to superintend: to be guardian or tutelary god: to be at the organ or piano (orig. as a kind of conductor).—*v.t.* (*rare*) to be at the head of.—*ns.* **presidency** (*prez'i-dən-si*), the office of a president, or his dignity, term of office, jurisdiction, or residence: each of three main divisions of India (*hist.*): a Mormon governing council; **pres'ident**, one who is chosen to preside over the meetings of a society, conference, etc.: the elected head of a republic: the head of a board, council, or department of government: the title of the head of certain colleges, universities, and other institutions: a colonial or state governor (*hist.*): the chairman of a company, a bank governor, or head of an organisation generally (*U.S.*).—*adj.* (*Milt.*) presiding, superintending.—*n.* **pres'identess**.—*adj.* **presidential** (*-den'shl*), presiding: of a president or presidency.—*n.* **pres'identship**.— **presiding officer**, a person in charge of a polling-place.— **Lord President**, the presiding judge of the Court of Session; **Lord President of the Council**, a member of the House of Lords who presides over the privy council. [Fr. *présider*—L. *prae-sidēre—prae, sedēre*, to sit.]

**president**, (*Spens., Shak., Milt.*) for **precedent**.

**president.** See **preside**.

**presidial**, *pri-sid'i-əl*, *adj.* pertaining to a garrison, a presidio, or a president: provincial (*Fr. hist.*).—*adj.* **presid'iary**, garrisoning: of a garrison.—*ns.* **presid'io** (*Sp. Amer.*, etc.), a military post: a penal settlement; **presid'ium**, a standing committee in the Soviet system (also **praesidium**). [L. *praesidium*, a garrison—*praesidēre*, to preside.]

**presignify**, *prē-sig'ni-fī*, *v.t.* to intimate beforehand.—*n.* **prēsignificā'tion**. [Pfx. pre- (2).]

**press**, *pres*, formerly also **preace, prease, preasse**, etc., *prēs*, *v.t.* to exert a pushing force upon: to squeeze: to compress: to clasp: to thrust onwards or downwards: to squeeze out: to imprint, stamp, print: to flatten, condense, dry, shape, or smooth by weight or other squeezing force: to put to death by application of heavy weights: to bear heavily on: to harass: to beset: to urge strongly: to invite with persistent warmth: to offer urgently or abundantly (with *upon*): to throng, crowd: to present to the mind with earnestness: to lay stress upon: to hurry on with great speed.—*v.i.* to exert pressure: to push with force: to crowd: to go forward with violence: to be urgent in application, entreaty, or effort: to strive: to strain: to strive to do too much, to the loss of ease and effectiveness (*golf*).—*n.* an act of pressing: pressure: crowd: crowding: thick of a fight: stress: urgency: a cupboard or shelved closet or recess: a bookcase: an apparatus for pressing: a printing-machine: printing: a printing organisation: often extended to a publishing house: printing activities: newspapers and periodicals collectively: the journalistic profession: a common name for a newspaper: reception by newspapers and periodicals generally.—*ns.* **press′er**; **press′ful**; **press′ing**, action of verb to press: article, articles, made from the same mould or press, esp. gramophone records.—*adj.* urgent: importunate: crowding.—*adv.* **press′ingly.**—*n.* **pression** (*presh′ən*; *rare*), pressure: impress.—**press′-agent**, one who arranges for newspaper advertising and publicity, esp. for an actor or theatre; **press′-bed**, a bed enclosed in a cupboard, or folding up into it; **press′-book**, a book printed at a private press; **press′-box**, an erection provided for the use of reporters at sports, shows, etc.; **press′-button**, a push-button.—Also *adj.*—**press conference**, a meeting of a public personage with the press for making an announcement or to answer questions; **press′-cutt′ing**, a paragraph or article cut out of a newspaper or magazine; **pressed′-day**, the third day of a three days' visit; **pressed glass**, glass given shape and pattern by pressure in a mould; **press′-fastener**, **press′-stud**, a form of button fastening in two parts, one of which can be pushed partly into the other; **press′fat** (*B.*), the vat for collecting the liquor from an olive or wine press; **press′-gall′ery**, a reporters' gallery; **press′man**, one who works a printing-press: a journalist or reporter; **press′-mark**, a mark upon a book to show its place in a library; **press′-proof**, the last proof before printing; **press′-room**, a room where printing-presses are worked: a room for the use of journalists; **press′-work**, the operation of a printing-press: journalistic work.—**at press**, **in the press**, in course of printing: about to be published; **go to press**, to begin to print or to be printed; **liberty, freedom, of the press**, right of publishing material without submitting it to a government authority for permission; **press of sail**, as much sail as can be carried; **the press**, printed matter generally, esp. newspapers: journalists as a class. [Fr. *presser*—L. *pressāre—prēmĕre*, *pressum*, to press.]

**press**, *pres*, *v.t.* to carry off and force into service, esp. in the navy: to requisition: to turn to use in an unsuitable or provisional way.—*n.* impressment: authority for impressing.—*ns.* **press′-gang**, a gang or body of sailors under an officer, empowered to impress men into the navy.—Also *v.t.*—**press′-money**, earnest-money. [prest (2).]

**pressure**, *presh′ər*, *n.* act of pressing or squeezing: the state of being pressed: impression, stamp (*Shak.*): constraining force or influence: that which presses or afflicts: urgency: strong demand: a force directed towards the thing it acts

upon, measured as so much weight upon a unit of area: difference of electric potential.—*v.t.* to apply pressure to: to compel by pressure (with *into*).—*v.t.* **pressurise, -ize,** (of an aeroplane, etc.) to fit with a device that maintains nearly normal atmospheric pressure: to subject to pressure: to force by pressure (into doing something).—**press′ure-cab′in**, a pressurised cabin in an aircraft.—*v.t.* **press′ure-cook′,** to cook in a pressure cooker.—**pressure cooker**, an autoclave, esp. one for domestic use; **pressure group**, a set putting pressure on a government for a particular purpose; **press′ure-hel′met**, an airman's helmet for use with a pressure-suit; **press′ure-suit**, an automatically inflating suit worn by airmen against pressure-cabin failure at very high altitudes; **press′ure-waist′coat**, an airman's waistcoat through which oxygen passes under pressure to the lungs to aid breathing at high altitudes. [L. *pressura—premĕre,* to press.]

**prest,** *prest,* (*Spens., Shak.*) *adj.* ready. [O.Fr. *prest*—L. *praestō,* at hand.]

**prest,** *prest,* (*obs.*) *v.t.* to lend: to pay in advance: to engage by paying earnest: to enlist: to impress for service.—*n.* a loan: payment in advance: enlistment-money.—*n.* **prestā′tion,** payment or service required by custom or promise. [O.Fr. *prester*—L. *praestāre,* to offer, discharge.]

**Prester John,** *pres′tər jon, n.* the mythical mediaeval Christian priest-king of a vast empire in Central Asia (and later in Ethiopia). [O.Fr. *prestre* (Fr. *prêtre*), priest.]

**presternum,** *prē-tûr′nəm, n.* the anterior part of the sternum. [Pfx. pre- (1).]

**prestidigitation,** *pres-ti-dij-i-tā′shən, n.* sleight-of-hand.—*n.* **prestidig′itātor.** [Fr. *prestidigitateur* —*preste,* nimble, L. *digitus,* finger.]

**prestige,** *pres-tēzh′, n.* orig. a conjuring trick, illusion: glamour: standing or ascendancy in men's minds owing to associations, station, success, etc.—*adj.* consisting in, or for the sake of, prestige.—*n.* **prestigiator** (*pres-tij′i-ā-tər*), a conjurer.—*adj.* **prestigious** (*-tij′əs*), juggling: having prestige, esteemed: deceitful. [Fr.,—L. *praestigium,* delusion—*praestringĕre,* to dazzle, blind; see **prestriction.**]

**presto,** *pres′tō, (mus.) adj.* very quick.—*n.* a presto movement or passage.—*adv.* quickly, quicker than *allegro.*—*adv.* or *interj.* (as in conjuring tricks) at once.—*adv., n.,* and *adj.* (*superl.*) **prestis′simo.** [It.,—L. *praestō,* at hand.]

**pre-stressed,** *prē′-strest′, adj.* (of concrete) strengthened with stretched wires or rods instead of large steel bars as in reinforced concrete. [Pfx. pre- (2).]

**prestriction,** *pri-strik′shən, n.* blindness: blind-folding. [L. *praestrictiō, -ōnis—praestringĕre,* to draw tight, bind, restrain, blind.]

**presume,** *pri-zūm′, -zōōm′, v.t.* to take as true without examination or proof: to take for granted: to assume provisionally: to take upon oneself, esp. with over-boldness.—*v.i.* to venture beyond what one has ground for: to act forwardly or without proper right: to rely, count (with *on, upon*), esp. unduly.—*adj.* **presūm′able,** that may be presumed or supposed to be true. —*adv.* **presūm′ably.**—*n.* **presūm′er.**—*adj.* **presūm′ing,** venturing without permission: unreasonably bold.—*adv.* **presūm′ingly.**—*n.* **presumption** (*-zum′shən, -zump′shən*), act of presuming: supposition: strong probability: that which is taken for granted: confidence grounded on something not proved: conduct going beyond proper bounds: an assumption of a fact from known facts (*law*): an assumption made failing proof to the contrary.—*adj.* **presumptive** (*-zump′, -zum′tiv*), presuming (*obs.*): grounded on probable evidence: giving grounds for presuming (see **heir** for **heir-presumptive**).—*adv.* **presump′tively.**—*adj.* **presumptuous** (*-zump′tū-əs,*

or *-zum'*), presuming.—*adv.* **presump'tuously.**—*n.* **presump'tuousness.** [L. *praesūmēre, -sūmptum—prae, sūmēre,* to take—*sub,* under, *emēre,* to buy.]
**presuppose,** *prē-sə-pōz', v.t.* to assume or take for granted: to involve as a necessary antecedent.—*n.* **presupposition** (*prē-sup-ə-zish'ən*). [Pfx. pre- (2).]
**presurmise,** *prē-sər-mīz',* (*Shak.*) *n.* a surmise previously formed. [Pfx. pre- (2).]
**pretend,** *pri-tend', v.t.* to stretch forth, or in front (*Spens.*): to offer (*obs.*): to profess, now only falsely: to feign: to claim (*obs.*): to allege (*obs.*): to allege falsely: to make believe: to purpose (*obs.*): to venture, attempt, undertake: to indicate (*obs.*).—*v.i.* to reach or go forward (*obs.*): to be a claimant (*obs.*): to aspire: to be a suitor: to make a claim: to feign: to make believe.—*n.* **pretence'** (*U.S.* pretense'), an act of pretending: something pretended: an allegation: an aim, purpose: the thing aimed at: appearance or show to hide reality: false show: a false allegation: a sham: pretentiousness: a pretext: claim.—*adj.* **pretence'less,** without a pretext.—*n.* **pretend'ant** (or **-ent**), a claimant: a suitor: a pretender.—*adj.* **preten'ded.**—*adv.* **preten'dedly.**—*ns.* **preten'der,** a claimant, esp. to a throne: a candidate: a suitor (*obs.*): one who pretends; **preten'dership.**—*adv.* **preten'dingly.**—*n.* **preten'sion,** pretence: show: pretext: claim: aspiration, esp. to marriage: pretentiousness.—*adj.* **preten'tious** (*-shəs*), over-assuming: seeming to claim much, or too much.—*adv.* **preten'tiously.**—*n.* **preten'tiousness.** [L. *praetendēre—prae, tendēre, tentum, tēnsum,* to stretch.]
**preter-,** (L. spelling occurring chiefly in obs. words) **praeter-,** *prē'tər-,* in composition, beyond.—*adjs.* **preterhu'man,** more than human; **preternat'ural,** out of the ordinary course of nature: abnormal: supernatural.—*n.* **preternat'uralism,** belief in the preternatural: preternatural character or event.—*adv.* **preternat'urally.**—*n.* **preternat'uralness.**—*adjs.* **preterperfect** (*-pûr'fekt, -fikt; old gram.*), perfect; **preterpluperfect** (*-plōō-pûr'fekt, -fikt*), pluperfect (*gram.*): beyond the more than perfect (*facet.*). [L. *praeter.*]
**preterite,** *pret'ə-rit, adj.* past.—*n.* the past tense: a word in the past tense: a form of the past tense.—*ns.* **pret'erist,** one who holds the prophecies of the Apocalypse already fulfilled; **pret'eriteness;** **preterition** (*prē-tə-rish'ən*), the act of passing over: omission of mention in a will: paraleipsis (*rhet.*): the doctrine that God passes over the non-elect in electing to eternal life.—*adjs.* **preteritive** (*pri-ter'i-tiv*), used only in the preterite; **preter'ito-pres'ent, -presen'tial, pret'erite-pres'ent,** having an original preterite still preterite in form but present in meaning. [L. *praeteritus—īre, ītum,* to go.]
**pretermit,** *prē-tər-mit', v.t.* to pass by: to omit: to leave undone: to desist from for a time:—*pr.p.* **prētermitt'ing;** *pa.t.* and *pa.p.* **prētermitt'ed.**—*n.* **pretermission** (*-mish'ən*). [L. *praetermittěre, -missum—mittěre,* to send.]
**pretext,** *prē'tekst, n.* an ostensible motive or reason, put forward as excuse or to conceal the true one. [L. *praetextus, -ūs,* pretext, outward show, *praetextum,* pretext—*praetexěre, -textum,* to weave in front, border—*texěre,* to weave.]
**pretty,** *prit'i, adj.* orig., tricky: ingenious: (esp. ironically) fine: commendable: neat: stalwart (*arch.* or *Scot.*): pleasing in a moderate way but not deeply: having some superficial attractiveness but not striking beauty: beautiful without dignity: insipidly graceful: considerable.—*n.* a pretty thing or person: a knick-knack: the fairway of a golf-course: the fluted part of a glass.—*adv.* fairly: prettily (*coll.* or

*illit.*).—*n.* **prettificā'tion.**—*v.t.* **prett'ify,** to trick out in an excessively ornamental or namby-pamby way.—*adv.* **prett'ily,** in a pretty manner: pleasingly: elegantly: neatly.—*n.* **prett'iness,** the quality of being pretty: an instance of the quality: a prettyism.—*adj.* **prett'yish,** somewhat pretty.—*ns.* **prett'yism,** trivial daintiness of style or an instance of it; **pretty-prett'iness; pretty-pretty** (*coll.*), a knick-knack.—*adj.* **namby-pamby:** insipidly pretty, over-pretty.—*adj.* **prett'y-spoken,** speaking or spoken prettily.— **a pretty penny,** a good large sum; **only pretty Fanny's way** (*T. Parnell*), only what must be expected and accepted of the person; **pretty much, very nearly; pretty well,** almost entirely; **sitting pretty,** in an advantageous position. [O.E. *prættig,* tricky—*prætt,* trickery. The origin of the word is unknown.]
**pretzel,** *pret'səl,* (Ger.) a crisp salted biscuit made in rope shape and twisted into a kind of loose knot.
**preux chevalier,** *prø shə-val-yā,* (Fr.) a valiant knight.
**prevail,** *pri-vāl', v.i.* to gain strength (*obs.*): to gain the victory: to succeed: to have the upper hand: to urge successfully (with *on* or *upon*): to be usual or most usual: to hold good, be in use, be customary.—*v.t.* (*obs.*) to avail: to persuade.—*adj.* **prevail'ing,** having great power: controlling: bringing about results: very general or common.—*adv.* **prevail'ingly.**—*ns.* **prevail'ment** (*Shak.*), power of overcoming; **prevalence** (*prev'ə-ləns*), **prev'alency,** the state of being prevalent or widespread: superior strength or influence: preponderance: effective influence.— *adj.* **prev'alent,** prevailing: having great power: victorious: widespread: most common.—*adv.* **prev'alently.** [L. *praevalēre—prae, valēre,* to be powerful.]
**prevaricate,** *pri-var'i-kāt, v.i.* to deviate (*obs.*): to shift about from side to side: to evade the truth: to quibble: to undertake a thing with the purpose of defeating or destroying it (*obs.*): to betray a client by collusion with his opponent (*law*).—*v.t.* (*obs.*) to pervert, transgress.—*ns.* **prevaricā'tion; prevar'icātor,** one who prevaricates: formerly in Cambridge University a satirical orator at Commencement. [L. *praevāricāri, -ātus,* to walk straddlingly or crookedly, to act collusively—*prae, vāricus,* straddling—*vārus,* bent.]
**prevenancy, prevene,** etc. See prevent.
**prevent,** *pri-vent', v.t.* to precede (*obs.*): to be, go, or act earlier than (*obs.*): to go faster than (*obs.*): to anticipate, forestall (*obs.*): to satisfy in advance (*obs.*): to meet or provide for in advance (*obs.*): to balk: to preclude: to stop, keep, or hinder effectually: to keep from coming to pass.—*n.* **prevenancy** (*prev'ən-ən-si; rare*), courteous anticipation of others' wishes. —*v.t.* **prevene** (*pri-vēn'*), to precede (*rare*): to anticipate (*obs.*).—*n.* **prevě'nience.**—*adj.* **prevě'nient,** antecedent: predisposing: preventive.—*n.* **preventabil'ity.**—*adj.* **preven'table** (also **-ible**).— *ns.* **preven'ter,** one who, or that which, prevents or hinders: a supplementary rope or part (*naut.*); **preven'tion,** act of preventing: anticipation or forethought: obstruction.—*adjs.* **preven'tive** (also, irregularly, **preven'tative**), tending to prevent or hinder: prophylactic: concerned with the prevention of smuggling.—*ns.* that which prevents: a prophylactic.—*adv.* **preven'tively.**—*n.* **preven'tiveness.—preventive detention,** specially prolonged imprisonment for persistent offenders of 30 or over for periods of from 5 to 14 years. [L. *praevenīre, -ventum—venīre,* to come.]
**pre-vern'al,** *prē-vûr'nl, adj.* flowering before spring: coming early into flower or leaf. [Pfx. pre- (2).]
**preview,** *prē'vū, n.* a view of a performance,

exhibition, etc., before it is open to the public.
—Also *v.t.* (*prē-vū'*). [Pfx. **pre-** (2).]
**previous,** *prē'vi-əs, adj.* going before in time:
former: premature (*facet.*).—*adv.* previously
(usu. with *to*).—*adv.* **prē'viously.**—*n.* **prē'-
viousness.**—**previous examination,** the Little-go
at Cambridge; **previous question,** in parliament,
a motion 'that the question be not now put'.
If the decision be 'ay', the debate is ended
without a vote on the main issue. In public
meetings the carrying of the 'previous question'
means that the meeting passes on to the next
business. [L. *praevius—prae, via,* a way.]
**previse,** *prē-vīz', v.t.* to foresee: to forewarn.—*n.*
**prevision** (*-vizh'ən*), foresight: foreknowledge.—
*v.t.* to endow with prevision.—*adj.* **previsional**
(*-vizh'ən-əl*). [L. *praevidēre, -visum—prae,
vidēre,* to see.]
**prewyn,** a Shakespearian form of **prune** (fruit).
**prex,** *prex, n.* in U.S. college slang the president
of a college.—Also **prex'y.**
**prey,** *prā, n.* booty, plunder: that which is
preserved from loss in battle, as one's own life
(*B.*): an animal that is, or may be, killed and
eaten by another: a victim: depredation: the
act of seizing (*Spens., Shak.*).—*v.i.* (commonly
with *on* or *upon*) to make depredations: to take
plunder: to seek, kill, and feed: to live (*on*) as a
victim: to waste, eat away, distress.—*v.t.* (*Spens.*)
to plunder.—*adj.* **prey'ful** (*Shak.*), bent upon
prey.—**beast, bird, of prey,** one that devours
other animals, esp. higher animals—applied
usually to the Carnivora and Falconiformes.
[O.Fr. *preie* (Fr. *proie*)—L. *praeda,* booty.]
**prial,** *prī'əl.* Same as **pair-royal.**
**Priapus,** *prī-ā'pəs, n.* an ancient deity personifying
male generative power, guardian of gardens.—
*adjs.* **Priapean** (*prī-ə-pē'ən*), **Priapic** (*-ap'ik*).—
*n.* **pri'apism,** persistent erection of the penis.
[Latinised from Gr. *Priāpos.*]
**pribble,** *prib'l, n.* a modification of **prabble,** usu.
coupled with it.—Also **pribb'le-prabb'le.**
**price,** *prīs* (also sometimes in Spens. **prise,** *prīs,*
*prīz*), *n.* the amount, usually in money, for which
a thing is sold or offered: that which one forgoes
or suffers for the sake of or in gaining something:
money offered for capture or killing of anybody:
(the size of) the sum, etc., by which one can
be bribed: betting odds: preciousness, worth,
value (*arch*): (also **prize**) valuation (*Spens.,
Shak.*).—*v.t.* to fix, state, or mark the price of:
to ask the price of (*coll.*): to pay the price of
(*Spens.*): to prize, value (*Shak.*).—*adjs.* **priced,**
having a price assigned: valued at such-and-such
a price; **price'less,** beyond price: invaluable: supremely and delectably absurd.—*adv.* **price'lessly.**
—*n.* **price'lessness.**—*adj.* **pric'ey** (*coll.*), expensive.—**price'-curr'ent** (often in *pl.,* **pric'es-curr'-
ent**), a list of prevailing prices at any time: a list
of prices paid for any class of goods, etc.; **price'-
cutting,** lowering of prices to secure custom;
**price level,** the average of many prices of commodities; **price'-list,** a list of prices of goods offered
for sale.—**above, beyond price,** so valuable that no
price can or would be enough; **at a price,** at a
somewhat high price; **in great price,** in high
estimation; **of price,** of great value; **price-
earnings ratio,** ratio of the market price of a
common stock share to its earnings; **price of
money,** the rate of discount in lending or
borrowing capital; **price on one's head,** a
reward for one's capture or slaughter; **what
price—?,** what about (this or that) now?: what
do you think of?; **without price,** priceless:
without anything to pay. [O.Fr. *pris* (Fr. *prix*)
—L. *pretium,* price; cf. **praise, prize** (3).]
**prick,** *prik, n.* anything sharp and piercing, as a
thorn, spine, goad: the act, experience, or
stimulus of piercing or puncturing: a puncture:
a mark or wound made by puncturing: a note

in written music (*obs.*): a graduation on a dial
(*Shak.*): a dot (*obs.*): a point of space or time:
an hour-point on a clock (*Shak.*): point, pitch
(*Spens.*): the centre of an archery target: a
mark or target: a hare's footprint: a penis
(*vulg.*).—*v.t.* to pierce slightly with a fine point:
to give a feeling as of pricking: to make by
puncturing: to urge with, or as with, a spur
or goad: to write out in musical notation (*obs.*):
to indicate with a prick or dot, to tick off, hence
select: to trace with pricks: to pin: to pick
with a point: to insert in small holes: to stick,
stick over: to erect, cock, stick up: to incite
(*fig.*): to deck out: to pain.—*v.i.* to pierce,
make punctures: to seek insensitive spots by
sticking pins in a suspected witch: to have a
sensation of puncture or prickling: to begin to
turn sour: to stand erect: to ride with spurs,
or quickly.—*ns.* **prick'er,** a piercing instrument:
a witch-finder: a light-horseman: a priming
wire; **prick'ing; prickle** (*prik'l*), a little prick:
a sharp point growing from the epidermis of a
plant or from the skin of an animal.—*v.t.* and
*v.i.* to prick slightly.—*v.i.* to have a prickly
feeling.—*n.* **prick'liness.**—*n.* and *adj.* **prick'ling.**
—*adj.* **prick'ly,** full of prickles: tingling as if
prickled: easily annoyed.—*adj.* **prick'-eared,**
having erect or noticeable ears.—**prick'le-back,**
the stickle-back; **prick'ly-ash',** the toothache-
tree (Xanthoxylum); **prick'ly-heat,** a skin disease,
inflammation of the sweat-glands with intense
irritation; **prick'ly-pear,** a cactaceous genus
(Opuntia) with clusters of prickles: its pear-
shaped fruit; **prick'-me-dain'ty** (*Scot.*), an
affected person.—*adj.* over-precise.—**prick'-song**
(*Shak.*), written music: descant; **prick'-spur,**
a spur with one point; **prick'-the-gar'ter,** fast-
and-loose; **prick'-(the-)louse** (*Scot.*), a tailor.—
**prick up one's ears,** begin to listen intently.
[O.E. *prica,* point; cf. Du. *prik.*]
**pricket,** *prik'it,* (*Shak.*) *n.* a fallow deer buck in his
second year, with straight unbranched antlers: a
spike serving as a candlestick. [**prick.**]
**pride,** *prīd, n.* state or feeling of being proud: too
great self-esteem: haughtiness: a proper sense
of what is becoming to oneself and scorn of what
is unworthy: a feeling of pleasure on account of
something worthily done or anything connected
with oneself: that of which one is proud: splendour: magnificence: beauty displayed: ostentation: a peacock's attitude of display: exuberance: prime: high spirit, mettle: sexual excitement in a female animal (*Shak.*): a company
of lions.—*v.t.* to make proud: (*refl.*) to take pride
in (with *on*).—*adj.* **pride'ful.**—*adv.* **pride'fully.**
—*n.* **pride'fulness.**—*adj.* **pride'less.**—**pride of
place,** culmination of an eagle's or hawk's
flight: distinction of holding the highest position (see **place**); **take a pride in,** make a thing
an object in which one's pride is concerned.
[O.E. *prȳde, prȳte—prūd, prūt,* proud.]
**pridian,** *prid'i-ən, adj.* pertaining to yesterday. [L.
*prīdiānus—pridiē—*stem of *prius,* before, *diēs,*
day.]
**pried, prier, pries.** See **pry.**
**prie-dieu,** *prē'dyø', n.* a praying-desk or chair for
praying on. [Fr., pray-God.]
**prief, priefe,** *prēf,* (*Spens.; Scot.*) *n.* See deriva-
tions of **proof, prove.**—*v.t.* **prieve.** See derivation
of **prove.**
**priest,** *prēst, n.* an official conductor of religious
rites: a mediator between a god and worshippers
(*fem.* **priest'ess**): a minister above a deacon and
below a bishop: a clergyman: a club or mallet
for killing fish.—*v.t.* to ordain as priest.—*v.i.* to
act as priest.—*ns.* **priest'craft,** priestly policy
directed to worldly ends; **priest'hood,** the office
or character of a priest: the priestly order.—
*adj.* **priest'ly,** pertaining to or like a priest.—*ns.*
**priest'liness; priest'ling,** a contemptible priest;

*fāte, fär; mē, hûr* (her); *mīne; mōte, för; mūte; mōōn, fŏŏt; dhen* (then)

priest'ship.—priest'-king', a king with priestly functions.—*adjs.* priest'-like; priest'-rid', -ridden, dominated by priests.—priest's hole, a secret room for a priest in time of persecution or repression.—high priest, a chief priest. [O.E. *prēost*—L. *presbyter*—Gr. *presbyteros*, an elder.]

prig, *prig, n.* a tinker (*rogues' cant; obs.*): a thief (*slang; Shak.*).—*v.t.* to filch.—*ns.* prigg'er, a thief; prigg'ing; prigg'ism. [Origin unknown.]

prig, *prig,* (*Scot.*) *v.i.* to entreat: to importune: to haggle.—prig down, to seek to beat down (a price or the seller). [Origin unknown.]

prig, *prig, n.* a coxcomb (*obs.*): a precisian: a person of precise morals without a sense of proportion.—*n.* prigg'ery.—*adj.* prigg'ish.—*adv.* prigg'ishly.—*ns.* prigg'ishness, prigg'ism. [Origin unknown.]

prim, *prim, adj.* exact and precise: stiffly formal. —*v.t.* to deck with great nicety: to form, set or purse into primness.—*v.i.* to look prim: to prim the mouth:—*pr.p.* primm'ing; *pa.t.* and *pa.p.* primmed.—*adv.* prim'ly.—*n.* prim'ness. [Late 17th-cent. cant.]

prima. See primo.

primacy, *prī'mə-si, n.* the position of first: the chief place: the office or dignity of a primate.

primaeval. Same as primeval.

prima facie, *prī'ma fāsh'ē(-ē), prē'mä fak'i-ā,* (L.) on the first view: at first sight.

primage, *prim'ij, n.* a payment, in addition to freight, made by shippers for loading, originally a gratuity to captain and crew, afterwards made to owners. [Anglo-L. *primāgium.*]

primary, *prī'mə-ri, adj.* first: original: of the first order (e.g. in a system of successive branchings): first-formed: primitive: chief: elementary: fundamental: belonging to the first stages of education, elementary: of a feather, growing on the manus: relating to primaries (*U.S.*): (*cap.*) Palaeozoic (but orig. applied to rocks supposed to be older than any fossiliferous strata; *geol.*). —*n.* that which is highest in rank or importance, a planet in relation to its satellites: a primary coil: a primary feather: a substance obtained directly, by extraction and purification, from natural, or crude technical, raw material—cf. *intermediate*: a meeting of the voters of a political party in an electoral division to nominate candidates, or to elect delegates to a nominating convention representing a larger area (*U.S. politics*): an election (also primary election) by local members of a party of candidates to be nominated for election, or of delegates to nominate them (*U.S. politics*).—*adv.* prī'marily.—*n.* prī'mariness.—primary assembly, in U.S. politics, a primary; primary battery, cell, one producing an electric current by irreversible chemical action; primary coil, one carrying an inducing current; primary colours, those from which all others can be derived—physiologically red, green, violet, or blue, for pigments red, yellow, blue: also red, orange, yellow, green, blue, indigo, and violet; primary planet, a planet distinguished from a satellite. [L. *primārius*—*primus,* first.]

primate, *prī'māt, -mit, n.* one who is first: a bishop or archbishop to whose see was formerly annexed the dignity of vicar of the holy see (*R.C. Church*): an archbishop over a province (*Ch. of Eng.*): a member of the order Primates (*zool.*).—*adj.* primā'tal.—*n.pl.* Primates (*prī-mā'tēz*), the highest order of mammals, including lemurs, monkeys, anthropoid apes, and man.—*n.* prī'mateship.—*adjs.* primā'tial (*-shl*), primatic (*-mat'ik*), -al. [L.L. *primās, -ātis*—L. *primus,* first.]

prime, *prim, adj.* first in order of time, rank, or importance: primary: chief: main: of the highest quality: original: in sexual excitement (*Shak.*): divisible by no whole number except unity and itself (*arith.*): having no common integral factor but unity.—*n.* the first of the lesser hours of the Roman breviary: the time of this office, about six in the morning, or sometimes sunrise: the time from the beginning of the artificial day to terce (about nine): the beginning: the spring: the world's youth: the new moon, or its first appearance (*obs.*): the best part: the height of perfection: full health and strength: a prime number: a first subdivision or symbol marking it (′) (*math.*): a fundamental tone: old card-game, probably the same as primero: the first guard against sword-thrusts, also the first and simplest thrust (*fencing*).—*adj.* pri'mal, first: primitive: original: chief, fundamental.—*adv.* prim'ally.- *n.* primal'ity.—*adv.* prime'ly.—*n.* prime'ness.—*adj.* prim'y (*Shak.*), in one's prime, blooming.—prime cost (see cost (1)); prime meridian, that chosen as zero for reference; prime minister, the chief minister of state; prime mover, in mediaeval astronomy, the primum mobile: a natural source of energy: a machine that transforms energy from such a source into motive power; prime number, one divisible only by itself or unity; prime vertical, a great celestial circle passing through the east and west points of the horizon, and cutting the meridian at right angles at the zenith. [L. *primus,* first; partly through O.E. *prim*—L. *prima* (*hōra*), first (hour).]

prime, *prim, v.t.* to charge, fill: to supply with powder or other means of igniting the charge (of a firearm): to lay a train to: to bring into activity or working order by a preliminary charge (as a man by giving him liquor, a pump by pouring in water, an internal-combustion engine by injecting gas or oil): to post up, coach, cram beforehand with information or instructions: to put on a primer in painting: to make up with cosmetics (*obs.*).—*v.i.* to prime a gun: (of a boiler) to send water with the steam into the cylinder: (of the tides) to recur at progressively shorter intervals.—*ns.* pri'mer, one who primes: a priming-wire: a detonator: preparatory first coat of paint, etc.: the particular type of paint used for this; pri'ming, the action of the verb in any sense: the progressive shortening of the interval between tides as spring tide approaches: a detonating charge that fires a propellant charge: a tube for priming an internal-combustion engine: a priming-wire: a first coat of paint.—pri'ming-iron, -wire, a wire passed through the touch-hole of a cannon to clear it and pierce the cartridge; pri'ming-pow'der, detonating powder: a train of powder. [Etymology obscure.]

primer, *prī'mər,* or *prim'ər, n.* a small book of hours or prayer book for laymen, used also for teaching reading: a first reading-book: an elementary introduction to any subject: (*prim'ər*) printing type of two sizes, long primer (10-point) and great primer (18-point). [L. *primārius,* primary.]

primero, *pri-mā'rō, n.* an old card-game. [Sp. *primera.*]

primeur, *prē-mœr,* (Fr.) novelty: early fruit.

primeval, primaeval, *pri-mē'vl, adj.* belonging to the first ages. [L. *primaevus*—*primus,* first, *aevum,* an age.]

primigenial, *pri-mi-jē'ni-əl, adj.* first made: original: primal.—Wrongly, also, primoge'nial. [L. *primigenius*—*primus,* first, *genus,* kind.]

primigravida, *pri-mi-grav'i-də, n.* a woman pregnant for the first time:—*pl.* primigrav'idae (*-dē*). [L. fem. adjs. *prima,* first, *gravida,* pregnant.]

primine, *pri'min, n.* the outer (rarely the inner or first formed) coat of an ovule [L. *primus,* first.]

primipara, *pri-mip'ə-rə, n.* a woman who has given birth to a child for the first time only, or is about to do so.—*adj.* primip'arous. [L. *prima* (fem.), first, *parĕre,* to bring forth.]

**primitiae**, *pri-mish'i-ē, n.pl.* first-fruits: the first year's revenue of a benefice—also **primi'tias** (*Spens.*).—*adj.* primitial (*-mish'l*), of first-fruits: (loosely) primeval, original. [L. *primitiae—primus*, first.]

**primitive**, *prim'i-tiv, adj.* belonging to the beginning, or to the first times: original: ancient: antiquated, old-fashioned: crude: not derivative: fundamental: first-formed, of early origin (*biol.*): of the earliest formation (*old geol.*).—*n.* that from which other things are derived. a root-word: a Primitive Methodist: a painter or picture of pre-Renaissance date or manner: a 19th- and 20th-century school of painting, characterised by a complete simplicity of approach to subject and technique.—*adv.* **prim'itively.**—*ns.* **prim'itiveness**; **prim'itivism**, approbation of primitive ways, primitive Christianity, primitive art, etc.: Primitive Methodism. —**Primitive Methodist**, a member of a religious body (Primitive Methodist Connection) founded in 1810, united with the Wesleyan Methodists and United Methodists in 1932. [L. *primitivus*, an extension of *primus.*]

**primo**, *prē'mō, adj.* first:—*fem.* **pri'ma.**—*n.* (*mus.*) first or principal part in duet or trio.—*adv.* **pri'mo**, in the first place.—**prima ballerina** (**assoluta**) (*bal-ə-rēn'a* (*as-so-lōō'ta*)), the leading ballerina (absolute, without rival); **prima donna** (**assoluta**) (*don'na*), the leading female singer in an opera company (without rival). [It.,—L. *primus.*]

**primogenit**, *prī-mō-jen'it*, (*obs.*) *adj.* and *n.* firstborn.—*adjs.* **primogen'ital**; **primogen'itary**; **primogen'itive.**—*n.* (*Shak.*) primogeniture.—*ns.* **primogen'itor**, earliest ancestor: forefather:—*fem.* **primogen'itrix**; **primogen'iture**, the state or fact of being first-born: inheritance by or of the first-born child or (*male primogeniture*) son; **primogen'itureship** (*rare*). [L. *primōgenitus—primō*, first (adv.), *genitus*, born, *genitor*, begetter.]

**primordial**, *prī-mör'di-əl, adj.* existing from the beginning: original: rudimentary: first-formed. —*n.* first principle or element.—*ns.* **primor'dialism**; **primordiality** (*-al'i-tti*).—*adv.* **primor'dially.**—*n.* **primor'dium**, the primitive source: the first discernible rudiment. [L. *primordium—primus*, first, *ordīrī*, to begin.]

**primp**, *primp, v.i.* to dress in a fussy or affected manner: to preen, titivate.—Also *v.t.* [Conn. **prim.**]

**primrose**, *prim'rōz, n.* a plant (*Primula vulgaris*), or its flower, common in spring in woods and meadows: extended to others of the genus Primula: formerly some other (and brighter) flower: a conventionalised flower, sometimes four-petalled (*her.*): the choicest (*Spens.*).—*adj.* pale yellow, like a primrose.—*v.i.* to go gathering primroses.—*adjs.* **prim'rosed**; **prim'rosy.**—**Primrose League**, an association for Conservative propaganda formed in 1883 in memory of Lord Beaconsfield, named from his supposed favourite flower; **primrose path**, **way** (both *Shak.*), the life of pleasure; **primrose peerless**, the two flowered daffodil.—**evening primrose** (see **evening**). [O.Fr. *primerose*, as if—L. *prima rosa*; perh. really through M.E. and O.Fr. *primerole*—L.L. *primula—primus*, first.]

**primsie**, *prim'zi*, (*Scot.*) *adj.* prim, demure. [prim.]

**Primula**, *prim'ū-lə, n.* the primrose genus, giving name to the dicotyledonous family **Primulā'ceae**, including pimpernel, water-violet, cyclamen, etc. —*adj.* **primulā'ceous.**—*n.* **prim'uline** (*-lēn*), a yellow coal-tar dye. [L.L.,—L. *primus*, first.]

**primum mobile**, *prī'məm mōb'* or *mob'i-lē, prē'mōōm mō'bi-le*, in mediaeval astronomy the outermost of the revolving spheres of the universe, carrying the others round in 24 hours: any great source of motion. [L.]

**primus**, *prī'məs, prē'mōōs, n.* presiding bishop in Scottish Episcopal Church, without metropolitan authority.—*adj.* (boys' schools) senior. [L., first.]

**Primus**, *prī'mos, n.* portable cooking stove burning vaporised oil. [Trademark.]

**primus**, *prī'məs, prē'mōōs*, (L.) first.—**primus inter pares**, (*in'tər pär'ēz, pär'ās*), first among equals.

**primy**. See under **prime** (1).

**prince**, *prins, n.* one of the highest rank: a king or queen (*obs.* or *arch.*): a sovereign (of some small countries): a male member of a royal or imperial family: a title of nobility, as formerly in Germany (*Fürst*): a chief: anybody or anything that is first in merit or demerit, or most outstanding.—*v.t.* (with *it*) to play the prince. —*ns.* **prince'dom**, a principality: the estate, jurisdiction, sovereignty, or rank of a prince; **prince'hood**, rank or quality of a prince; **prince'-kin**, a little or young prince; **prince'let**, **prince'ling**, a petty prince.—*adj.* **prince'like**, a prince: becoming a prince.—*n.* **prince'liness.**—*adj.* **prince'ly**, of a prince or princess: of the rank of prince: princelike: becoming a prince: magnificent: sumptuous: lavish.—Also *adv.*—*n.* **prin'cess** (or *-ses'*), *fem.* of **prince**: a prince's wife (of recognised rank): a size of roofing slate, 24 by 14 inches (610 by 356 mm): a woman's garment with skirt and bodice in one piece—in this sense also (*Fr.*) **princesse** (*prin'*, or *-ses'*).—*adv.* **prin'cessly**, like a princess.—*adj.* **prin'cified**, ridiculously dignified.—**prince'-bish'op**, a bishop ranking as prince or having the power of prince of his diocese; **prince'-con'sort**, a prince who is husband of a reigning queen; **prince'-impēr'ial**, the eldest son of an emperor; **prince's feather**, a tall, showy Amaranthus with spikes of rose-coloured flowers: London pride: applied also to various other plants; **prince's metal**, a gold-like alloy of copper and zinc, with more zinc than in brass, attributed to Prince Rupert; **prin'cess-roy'al**, the eldest daughter of a sovereign.—**prince of darkness, prince of this world**, Satan; **Prince of Peace**, Christ: the Messiah; **Prince of Wales**, the eldest son of the English sovereign; **Prince Rupert's drops** (see **drop**). [Fr.,—L. *princeps—primus*, first, *capĕre*, to take.]

**principal**, *prin'si-pl, adj.* taking the first place: highest in rank, character, or importance: chief: of the nature of principal or a principal.—*n.* a principal person: the head of a college or university, or sometimes of a school: one who takes a leading part: money on which interest is paid: a main beam, rafter, girder, or timber: a roof-truss: the structural framework of a roof: the person who commits a crime, or one who aids and abets him in doing it (*law*): a person for whom another becomes surety (*law*): a person who, being *sui juris*, employs another to do an act which he is competent himself to do (*law*): one who fights a duel: an organ-stop like the open diapason but an octave higher (*mus.*).—*n.* **principality** (*-pal'i-ti*), status, dignity, or power of a prince: condition of being a prince: the territory of a prince or the country that gives him title: a member of one of the orders of angels.—*adv.* **prin'cipally.**—*ns.* **prin'cipalness**, the state of being principal or chief; **prin'cipalship**, position of a principal.—**principal boy** (*theat.*), an actress (now often an actor) who plays the role of the hero in pantomime.—**the Principality**, Wales. [L. *principālis—princeps, -ipis*, chief.]

**principate**, *prin'si-pāt, n.* princehood: principality: the Roman empire in its earlier form in which something of republican theory survived. [L. *principātus*—the emperor's title *princeps* (*civitātis*), chief (of the city or state).]

**principium**, *prin-sip'i-əm, pring-kip'i-ōōm, n.* the general's quarters in a Roman camp: a beginning: a first principle: an element:—*pl.* **prin-**

cip'ia.—*adj.* princip'ial, elementary. [L. *principium.*]

principle, *prin'si-pl, n.* a beginning (*obs.*): a source, root, origin: that which is fundamental: essential nature: theoretical basis: a faculty of the mind: a source of action: a fundamental truth on which others are founded or from which they spring: a law or doctrine from which others are derived: a settled rule of action: consistent regulation of behaviour according to moral law: a component: a constituent part from which some quality is derived (*chem.*): motive power or the source of it (*Milt.*).—*v.t.* to establish in principles: to impress with a doctrine.—*adj.* prin'cipled, holding certain principles: having, or behaving in accordance with, good principles: invoking or founded on a principle.—first principles, fundamental principles, not deduced from others; in principle, so far as general character or theory is concerned without respect to details or particular application; on principle, on grounds of principle: for the sake of obeying or asserting a principle; principle of contradiction, the logical principle that a thing cannot both be and not be; principle of excluded middle (*log.*), the principle that a thing must be either one thing or its contradictory; principle of sufficient reason (see reason). [L. *principium,* beginning—*princeps.*]

princox, *prin(g)'koks* (*Shak.*), *n.* a conceited fellow: a coxcomb: a jocular, grotesque, or ironical endearment.—Also prin'cock (-*kok*). [Origin obscure.]

prink, *pringk, v.t.* and *v.i.* to deck up, smarten. [App. conn, with prank (2).]

print, *print, n.* an impression: a mould or stamp: a moulded pat of butter: exactitude of plaiting, crimping, or setting (a ruff, hair, etc.) (*arch.*): exactitude (*arch.*): printed state: printed characters or lettering: an edition: a printed copy: a printed picture: an engraving: a newspaper: a positive photograph made from a negative (or negative from positive): a printed cloth, esp. calico stamped with figures: a plaster-cast in low relief (*archit.*).—*adj.* printed (*obs.*): of printed cotton.—*v.t.* to press in: to impress: to mark by pressure: to impress on paper, etc., by means of types, plates, or blocks: to produce or reproduce by such means: to cause to be so printed: to stamp a pattern on or transfer it to: to produce as a positive picture from a negative, or as a negative from a positive (*phot.*): to write in imitation of type: to express in writing (*Shak.*): to designate in print (*Milt.*).—*v.i.* to practise the art of printing: to publish a book: to yield an impression, or give a positive, etc.—*adj.* print'able, capable of being printed: fit to print.—*ns.* print'er, one who, or that which, prints: one who is employed in printing books, etc.: a device for printing, as telegraph messages, photographs, etc.: a cotton cloth made for printing; print'ing, act, art, or business of the printer: the whole number of copies printed at one time, an impression.—*adj.* print'less, receiving or leaving no impression.—printed circuit, a wiring circuit, free of loose wiring, formed by printing the design of the wiring on copper foil bonded to a flat base and etching away the unprinted foil; printer's devil (see devil); printer's ink, printing-ink; printer's mark, an engraved device used by printers as a trademark; print'ing-house, a building where printing is carried on: a printing-office; print'ing-ink, ink used in printing—a usually thickish mixture of pigment (as carbon black) with oil and sometimes varnish; print'-ing-machine, a printing-press worked by power; print'ing-office, an establishment where books, etc., are printed; print'ing paper, a paper suitable for printing purposes; print'ing-press, a machine by which impressions are taken in ink

upon paper from types, plates, etc.; print'-seller, one who sells prints or engravings; print'-shop, a print-seller's shop; print'-works, an establishment where cloth is printed.—in print, in exact order, formally set, crimped, or plaited (*obs.*): existing in printed form: printed and still to be had (opp. to *out of print*). [M.E. print, prente, etc.—O.Fr. preinte, priente—preindre, priembre—L. preměre, to press.]

prior, *pri'ər, adj.* previous.—*adv.* previously (with *to*).—*n.* the officer next under the abbot in an abbey (*claustral prior*): the head of a priory of monks (*conventual prior*) or of a house of canons regular or of friars: in Italy formerly a magistrate:—*fem.* pri'oress.—*ns.* pri'orate, rank or term of office of a prior or prioress: a priory; priority (*prī-or'i-ti*), state of being first in time, place, or rank: preference: the privilege of preferential treatment: something that ought to be considered, dealt with, in the earliest stage of proceedings.—*adj.* having, entitling to, or allowed to those who have, priority.—*ns.* pri'orship; pri'ory, a convent of either sex subject to an abbey.—grand priory, a province of the Knights of St John, under a *grand prior*. [L. *prior, -ōris,* former.]

prisage, *pri'zij, n.* the former right of the English kings to two tuns of wine from every ship importing twenty tuns or more. [O.Fr. *prise,* taking.]

Priscianist, *prish'(y)ən-ist, n.* a grammarian.—break Priscian's head, to commit false grammar. [*Priscianus,* Latin grammarian (fl. *c.* A.D. 500).]

prise. See price, and prize (1), (2), (3) and (4).

priser. Obs. form of prizer; see prize (3), (4).

prism, *prizm, n.* a solid whose ends are similar, equal, and parallel polygons, and whose sides are parallelograms (*geom.*): an object of that shape, esp. a triangular prism of glass or the like for resolving light into separate colours: a crystal form of three or more faces parallel to an axis (*crystal.*): loosely, prismatic colours or spectrum.—*adjs.* prismat'ic, -al, resembling or pertaining to a prism: built up of prisms: separated or formed by a prism.—*adv.* prismat'ically.—*n.* pris'moid, a figure like a prism, but with similar unequal ends.—*adjs.* pris'moidal; pris'my, prismatic in colour.—prismatic colours, the seven colours into which a ray of white light is refracted by a prism—red, orange, yellow, green, blue, indigo, and violet; prismatic compass, a surveying instrument which by means of a prism enables the compass-reading to be taken as the object is sighted; prismatic powder, pebble-powder.—triangular, quadrilateral, etc., prism, one whose ends are triangles, quadrilaterals, etc. [Gr. *prisma, -atos,* a piece sawn off, sawdust, a prism—*priein,* to saw.]

prison, *priz'n, n.* a building for the confinement of criminals or others: a jail: any place of confinement: confinement.—*v.t.* to shut in prison: to enclose: to restrain.—*ns.* pris'oner, one under arrest or confined in prison: a captive, esp. in war: anyone involuntarily kept under restraint; pris'onment (*Shak.*), imprisonment, confinement.—*adj.* pris'onous (*Dickens*).—pris'on-bars (*pl.*), the bars of a prison window, door, etc.: whatever confines or restrains: prisoners'-base; pris'on-breaker, one who escapes out of prison; pris'on-breaking; pris'on-crop, hair cut very short; pris'on-door; pris'oners'- (or prisoner's-) base, a game in which those caught are held as prisoners (app. for *prison-bars*); pris'on-house, a prison or prison building; prison officer, official title of warder (still so-called unofficially) in prison; pris'on-ship; pris'on-van, a closed conveyance for carrying prisoners. [O.Fr. *prisun*—L. *prēnsiō, -ōnis,* for *praehēnsiō,* seizure —*praehendĕre, -hēnsum,* to seize.]

prissy, *pris'i, adj.* prim, prudish, fussy: effeminate. [Prob. prim and sissy.]

---

**pristine**, *pris'tin, adj.* original: former: belonging to the earliest time. [L. *pristinus*; cf. *priscus*, antique, *prior*, former.]

**prithee, prythee**, *pridh'ē, -i, interj.* for **(I) pray thee.**

**prittle-prattle**, *prit'l-prat'l, n.* empty talk. [**prattle.**]

**privacy**, *priv'ə-si,* or *priv', n.* seclusion: a place of seclusion: retreat: retirement: avoidance of notice or display: secrecy: a private matter. [**private.**]

**privado**, *pri-vä'dō, (obs.) n.* a private friend, esp. of a prince. [Sp.,—L. *privātus,* private.]

**privat dozent**, *prē-vät' dō-tsent', n.* in German universities, a recognised teacher not a member of the salaried staff. [Ger.,—L. *privātus,* private, *docēns, -entis,* teaching, *docēre,* to teach.]

**private**, *pri'vit, adj.* apart from the state: not in public office: (of member of parliament) not holding government office: (of soldier) not an officer or non-commissioned officer: peculiar to oneself: belonging to, or concerning, an individual person or company: own: relating to personal affairs: in an unofficial capacity: not public: not open to the public: not made known generally: confidential: retired from observation: alone: privy (*obs.*).—*n.* privacy: a private person (*Shak., Milt.*): (in *pl.*) private parts: a common soldier: a secret message (*Shak.*).—*adv.* **pri'vately.**—*n.* **pri'vateness** (*rare*).—**private act, bill,** one that deals with the concerns of private persons; **private company,** a company, with restrictions on the number of shareholders, whose shares may not be offered to the general public; **private enterprise,** economic system in which individual private firms operate and compete freely; **private eye,** a private detective; **private hotel,** a term of uncertain meaning popularly understood to imply that the proprietors do not bind themselves to receive chance travellers; **private judgment,** freedom to judge for oneself, untrammelled by the interpretation of the church; **private law,** that part of law which deals with the rights and duties of persons as individuals in relations with each other; **private parts,** the external sexual organs; **private school,** a school run independently by an individual or a group, especially for profit; **private wrong,** an injury done to an individual in his private capacity.—**private member's bill,** one introduced and sponsored by a private member in parliament. [L. *privātus,* pa.p. of *privāre,* to deprive, to separate.]

**privateer**, *pri-və-tēr', n.* a private vessel commissioned to seize and plunder an enemy's ships: the commander or one of the crew of a privateer. —*v.i.* to cruise in a privateer.—*ns.* **privateer'ing; privateers'man.** [**private.**]

**privation**, *pri-vā'shən, n.* state of being deprived of something, esp. of what is necessary for comfort: absence of any quality (*log.*).—*adj.* **privative** (*priv'ə-tiv*), causing privation: consisting in the absence or removal of something: expressing absence or negation (*gram.*).—*n.* that which is privative or depends on the absence of something else: a term denoting the absence of a quality (*log.*): a privative prefix, affix, or word (*gram.*). —*adv.* **priv'atively.** [L. *privātiō, -ōnis, privātivus* —*privāre,* to deprive.]

**privet**, *priv'it, n.* a half-evergreen European shrub (*Ligustrum vulgare*) of the olive family, used for hedges. [Origin unknown.]

**privilege**, *priv'i-lij, n.* an advantage granted to or enjoyed by an individual, or a few: freedom from burdens borne by others: a happy advantage: prerogative: a sacred and vital civil right: advantage yielded (*Shak.*): right of sanctuary (*Shak.*).—*v.t.* to grant a privilege to: to exempt: to authorise, license.—*adj.* **priv'ileged.**—**breach of privilege,** any interference with or slight done to the rights or privileges of a legislative body;

**privilege of parliament,** special rights or privileges enjoyed by members of parliament, as freedom of speech, and freedom from arrest except on a criminal charge; **question of privilege,** any question arising out of the rights of an assembly or of its members; **writ of privilege,** an order for the release of a privileged person from custody. [Fr. *privilège*—L. *privilēgium—privus*; private, *lēx, lēgis,* a law.]

**privy**, *priv'i, adj.* familiar, intimate (*obs.*): private: pertaining to one person: for private uses: secret: appropriate to retirement: sharing the knowledge of something secret (with *to*).—*n.* person having an interest in an action, contract, conveyance, etc. (*law*): room set apart with container in which to evacuate body waste products (esp. one in an outhouse).—*adv.* **priv'ily,** privately: secretly.—*n.* **priv'ity,** privacy (*arch.*): secrecy (*arch.*): something kept private: innermost thoughts, private counsels (*Spens.*): knowledge, shared with another, of something private or confidential: knowledge implying concurrence: any legally recognised relation between different interests.—**privy chamber,** private apartment in a royal residence; **privy council,** originally the private council of a sovereign to advise in the administration of government—its functions are now mainly formal or performed by committees, etc.; **privy councillor; privy-purse,** an allowance for the private or personal use of the sovereign; **privy seal,** the seal used by or for the sovereign in subordinate matters, or those not to pass the great seal.—**gentlemen of the privy chamber,** officials in the royal household in attendance at court. [Fr. *privé*—L. *privātus,* private.]

**prix fixe**, *prē fēks,* (Fr.) fixed price.

**prize, prise**, *priz, v.t.* to force (esp. up or open) with a lever. [Fr. *prise,* hold, grip; see **prize** (2).]

**prize** (*Spens., Shak.* **prise**), *priz, n.* seizure (*obs.*): that which is taken by force, or in war, esp. a ship.—*v.t.* to make a prize of.—**prize'-court,** a court for judging regarding prizes made on the high seas; **prize'-crew,** a crew put aboard a prize to bring her to port; **prize'-money,** share of the money or proceeds from any prizes taken from an enemy. [Fr. *prise,* capture, thing captured—L. *praehēnsa—praehendēre,* to seize.]

**prize** (*Spens., Shak.* **prise**), *priz, n.* a reward or symbol of success offered or won in competition by contest or chance, or granted in recognition of excellence: anything well worth striving for: a highly valued acquisition: privilege or advantage (*Shak.*): esteem (*Spens.*): valuation, appraisal (*Shak.*).—*adj.* awarded, or worthy of, a prize.—*v.t.* to set a price on: to value: to value highly: (*Spens.* **pryse**) to pay for.—*adjs.* **priz'able,** valuable; **prized.**—*n.* **priz'er** (*rare*), an appraiser.—**prize'-list,** a list of winners; **prize'-man,** a winner of a prize, esp. an academic prize; **prize'-winner.** [A differentiated form of price and praise—O.Fr. *pris* (n.), *prisier* (vb.) —L. *pretium,* price.]

**prize** (*Spens.* **prise**), *priz, n.* an athletic contest (*obs.*): a match.—*n.* **priz'er,** a contestant in a prize or match.—**prize'-fight,** a public boxing-match for money; **prize'-fighter,** orig. one who fights for a prize: now, a professional pugilist; **prize'-fighting; prize'-ring,** a ring for prize-fighting: the practice itself.—**play one's** (or a) **prize,** engage in a match: sustain one's part. [Possibly from the foregoing.]

**pro-**, *prō-, Gr. pfx.* before (in time or place): earlier than: in front of: the front part of: primitive: rudimentary. [Gr. prep. *prŏ,* before; cf. L. *prō,* Eng. **for, fore.**]

**pro-**, *prō-, L. pfx.* used (*a*) as an etymological element with the senses before (in place or time), forward, forth, publicly; (*b*) as a living pfx. with the sense instead of; (c) as a living pfx. (in new formations) with the sense in favour of—as pro-Boer; pro-German; pro-Negro; pro-slavery. [L. prep. prō, earlier prōd, in comp. sometimes prō-; cf. preceding.]

pro, prō, (L.) for.—pro aris et focis (ār'ēz et fōs'ēz, är'ēs et fōk'ēs), for altars and firesides: for faith and home; pro bono publico (bo'nō pub'li-kō, bō'nō pōo'bli-kō), for the public good; pro forma (för'ma, för'mä), as a matter of form: of an account, etc., made out to show the market price of specified goods; pro hac vice (hak vis'ē, wēk'e), for this turn or occasion; pro indiviso (in-di-vi'sō, -zō, in-dē-wē'sō), as undivided: applied in law to rights which two or more persons hold in common; pro memoria (ma-mōr'ē-a, -mör'-, me-mō'-ri-ä), for a memorial; pro patria (pā'trē-a, pä'tri-ä), for one's country; pro rata (rā'ta, rä'tä), in proportion; pro re nata (rē nā'ta, rä nä'tä), for a special emergency, according to the circumstances; pro tanto (tan'tō), for so much; pro tempore (tem'pa-rē, tem'pō-re), for the time being.

pro, prō, n. a coll. contraction of professional (golfer, cricketer, actor, etc.), of probationary (nurse) and of prostitute:—pl. pros (prōz).

pro, prō, n. one who favours or votes for some proposal: a reason or argument in favour:—pl. pros (prōz).—adv. pro and con (L. prō et contrā), for and against.—v.t. and v.i. to consider or discuss for and against:—pr.p. pro'ing and conn'ing, pro-and-conn'ing; pa.p. pro'd and conned, con'd, pro-and-conned'.—n.pl. pros and cons, reasons or arguments for and against. [L. prō, for.]

proa, prō'a. See prau.

proairesis, prō-ā'ri-sis, or -i', n. the act of choosing. [Gr. proairesis.]

probable, prob'a-bl, adj. that can be proved (orig., now rare): having more evidence for than against: giving ground for belief: likely: colourable, plausible.—n. probable opinion: one that has a good chance, or is likely to turn out or become the thing in question.—ns. probabil'iorism, the doctrine that in case of doubt one is bound to choose the more probable opinion; probabil'iorist; prob'abilism, the doctrine that of two opinions, both reasonable, one may follow one's own inclination, as a doubtful law cannot impose a certain obligation; prob'abilist; probabil'ity, quality of being probable: appearance of truth: that which is probable: chance or likelihood of something happening:—pl. probabil'ities.—adv. prob'ably.—probable error, a quantity assumed as the value of an error, such that the chances of the real error being greater are equal to those of its being less; probable evidence, evidence not conclusive, but admitting of some degree of force. [Fr.,—L. probābilis—probāre, -ātum, to prove.]

proball, prō'bl, (Shak.) adj. supposed to mean plausible. [Apparently a contracted form of probable.]

probang, prō'bang, n. an instrument for pushing obstructions down the oesophagus. [Called provang by its inventor, the Welsh judge, Walter Rumsey (1584-1660); origin unknown; prob. influenced by probe.]

probate, prō'bāt, -bit, n. the proof before a competent court that a written paper purporting to be the will of a person who has died is indeed his lawful act: the official copy of a will, with the certificate of its having been proved.—adj. relating to the establishment of wills and testaments.—n. probation (pra-, prō-bā'shan), testing: proof: a preliminary time or condition appointed to allow fitness or unfitness to appear: noviciate: suspension of sentence, allowing liberty under supervision on condition of good behaviour, (esp. to young, or first, offenders): time of

trial: moral trial.—adjs. probā'tional, relating to, serving purpose of, probation or trial; probā'-tionary, probational: on probation.—n. a probationer.—ns. probā'tioner, one who is on probation or trial: an offender under probation: a novice: one licensed to preach, but not ordained to a pastorate (esp. Scot.); probā'tionership.—adjs. probative (prō'ba-tiv), testing: affording proof; prōbǎtory, testing.—Probate Court, a court created in 1858 to exercise jurisdiction in matters touching the succession to personal estate in England; probate duty, a tax on property passing by will; probation officer, one appointed to advise and supervise offenders under probation. [L. probāre, -ātum, to test, prove.]

probe, prōb, n. an instrument for exploring a wound, locating a bullet, and the like: an act of probing: an exploratory bore: a prod: an investigation: any of various instruments of investigation in space research (as a multi-stage rocket), electronics, etc.: a pipelike device attached to an aircraft for making connection with a tanker aeroplane so as to refuel in flight: a device used in docking two space modules.—v.t. to examine with or as with a probe: to examine searchingly.—v.t. and v.i. to pierce.—n.pl. probe'-sciss'ors, scissors used to open wounds, the blade having a button at the end. [L. proba, proof, later examination—probāre, to prove.]

probity, prob'i-ti, or prōb', n. uprightness: moral integrity: honesty. [L. probitās, -ātis—probus, good, honest.]

problem, prob'lam, n. a matter difficult of settlement or solution: a question or puzzle propounded for solution: the question how to win in so many moves beginning with a hypothetical situation (chess): a proposition in which something is required to be constructed, not merely proved as in a theorem (geom.): a source of perplexity.—adjs. problemat'ic, -al, of the nature of a problem: questionable: doubtful.—adv. problemat'ically.—problem child, one whose character presents an exceptionally difficult problem to parents, teachers, etc.; problem novel, play, one presenting or expounding a problem, social, moral, etc. [Gr. problēma, -atos—pro, before, ballein, to throw.]

proboscis, pra-, prō-bos'is, n. a trunk or long snout: a trunk-like process, as the suctorial mouth-parts of some insects: a nose (facet.):—pl. probosc'ises, probosc'ides (-i-dēz).—n.pl. Pro-boscid'ea, the elephant order of mammals.—adj. and n. proboscid'ean.—proboscis monkey, a very long-nosed Bornean monkey (Nasalis larvatus). [L.,—Gr. proboskis, a trunk—pro, expressing motive, boskein, to feed.]

probouleutic, prō-bōō-lū'tik, adj. for preliminary deliberation. [Gr. probouleusis, preliminary deliberation.]

procacity, pra-kas'i-ti, n. petulance.—adj. procacious (-kā'shas). [L. prōcācitās, -ātis—prōcāx, forward, insolent, shameless—prŏcāre, to demand.]

procaine, prō'kān, n. a crystalline substance used as a local anaesthetic. [pro- (2b), cocaine.]

procathedral, prō-ka-thē'dral, n. a church used temporarily as a cathedral. [Pfx. pro- (2b).]

proceed, pra-, prō-sēd', v.i. to go on: to continue: to advance: to pass on: to begin and go on: to act according to a method: to go from point to point: to advance to a higher degree (as to proceed M.A.) or more developed state: to prosper: to come forth: to result: to be descended: to take measures or action: to take legal action: to prosecute: to go on, be transacted, happen (Shak.).—v.t. to say in continuation.—n. prō'-ceed (usu. in. pl.), outcome: money got from anything.—adj. procedural (-sēd'ya-ral).—ns.

**procĕ'dure**, mode of proceeding: method of conducting business, esp. in a law case or a meeting: course of action: a step taken or an act performed; **proceed'er**; **proceed'ing**, a going forward: progress: advancement: course of conduct: perh. advantage (*Shak.*): step: operation: transaction: (in *pl.*) a record of the transactions of a society. [Fr. *procéder*—L. *prōcēdĕre*—*prō*, before, and *cēdĕre*, *cessum*, to go.]

**proceleusmatic**, *pros-e-lūs-mat'ik*, *adj.* inciting, encouraging.—*n.* in ancient prosody, a foot of four short syllables. [Gr. *prokeleusmatikos*—*pro*, before, *keleuein*, to urge, order.]

**Procellaria**, *pros-e-lā'ri-a*, *n.* the petrel genus.—*adj.* **procella'rian**. [L. *procella*, a storm.]

**procephalic**, *prō-si-fal'ik*, *adj.* of the forepart of the head. [Gr. *pro*, before, *kephalē*, head.]

**procerebrum**, *prō-ser'i-brəm*, *n.* the fore-brain: the prosencephalon.—*adj.* **procer'ebral**. [L. *prō*, before, *cerebrum*, brain.]

**procerity**, *prō-ser'i-ti*, *n.* tallness. [L. *prōcēritās*, *-ātis*—*prōcērus*, tall.]

**process**, *prō'ses*, sometimes (esp. in U.S.) *pros'* (*Milt. prō-ses'*), *n.* a state of being in progress or being carried on: course: a narrative (*Shak.*): a series of actions or events: a sequence of operations or changes undergone: a photo-process (*print.*): a writ by which a person or matter is brought into court (*law*): an action, suit, or the proceedings in it as a whole: progression: proceeding: an edict (*Shak.*): a projecting part, esp. on a bone (*biol.*).—*v.t.* to serve a summons on: to sue or prosecute: to subject to a special process: to produce or print photomechanically: to prepare (e.g. agricultural product) for marketing: to arrange (documents, etc.) systematically: to examine and analyse: to test the suitability of (a person) for some purpose: (of a computer) to perform operations of adding, subtracting, etc., or other operations on (data supplied): to subject (data) to such operations.—*adj.* **prō'cessed**, produced by a special process, as synthetically, photomechanically, etc.—**pro'cess-block**, a photomechanically made block for printing a picture; **pro'cess-server** (*Shak.*), a bailiff.—**data processing**, the handling and processing of information by computers. [Fr. *procès*—L. *prōcessus*, *-ūs*, advance; cf. **proceed**.]

**procession**, *prə-*, *prō-sesh'ən*, *n.* the act of proceeding: a train of persons, or of boats, shadows, etc. moving forward together as in ceremony, display, demonstration, etc.: the movement of such a train: a litany sung in procession.—*v.i.* to go in procession.—*v.t.* to go through or around in procession: to celebrate by a procession.—*v.i.* **process** (*prō-ses'*; back-formation), to go in processions.—*adj.* **process'ional**.—*n.* a book of litanies, hymns, etc., for processions: a hymn sung in procession.—*n.* **process'ionalist**.—*adj.* **process'ionary**.—*ns.* **process'ioner** (*U.S.*), a county officer who determines boundaries; **process'ioning**, going in procession: perambulation of boundaries (*U.S.*).—**processionary moth**, a European moth (*Cnethocampa processionea*) whose caterpillars go out seeking food in great processions.—**Procession of the Holy Ghost** (*theol.*), the emanation of the Holy Spirit from the Father (*single procession*), or from the Father and Son (*double procession*). [L. *prōcessiō*, *-ōnis*; cf. **proceed**.]

**procès-verbal**, *pro-se'-ver-bäl*, (Fr.) a written statement.

**prochain** (-ein) **ami** (-y), *pro-shen-a-mē*, (Fr.) next friend (q.v.).

**prochronism**, *prō'kron-izm*, *n.* a dating of an event before the right time—opp. to *metachronism*. [Gr. *pro*, before, *chronos*, time.]

**procidence**, *pros'*, *prōs'i-dəns*, *n.* prolapse.—*adj.*

**proc'ident**. [L. *prōcidentia*—*prō*, forward, *cadĕre*, to fall.]

**procinct**, *prō-singkt'*, (*Milt.*) *n.* preparedness. [L. *prōcinctus*, *-ūs*—*prō*, beforehand, *cingĕre*, *cinctum*, to gird.]

**proclaim**, *prə-*, *prō-klām'*, *v.t.* to cry aloud: to publish abroad: to announce officially: to denounce: to announce the accession of: to place under restrictions by proclamation.—*n.* **proclaim'**, proclamation: proclaiming.—*ns.* **proclaim'ant**; **proclaim'er**; **proclamation** (*prok-lə-mā'shən*), the act of proclaiming: that which is proclaimed: official notice given to the public: proscription.—*adj.* **proclamatory** (*-klam'at-ər-i*). [Fr. *proclamer*—L. *prōclāmāre*, *prōclāmāre*—*prō*, out, *clāmāre*, to cry.]

**proclitic**, *prō-klit'ik*, *adj.* so closely attached to the following word as to have no accent.—*n.* a proclitic word. [A modern coinage on the analogy of **enclitic**—Gr. *pro*, forward, *klinein*, to lean.]

**proclivity**, *prō-kliv'i-ti*, *n.* inclination: propensity.—*adj.* **proclive** (*-kliv'*; *arch.*), inclined: prone: headlong. [L. *prōclivis*—*prō*, forward, *clivus*, a slope.]

**procoelous**, *prō-sē'ləs*, *adj.* cupped in front. [Gr. *pro*, before, *koilos*, hollow.]

**proconsul**, *prō-kon'sl*, *n.* a Roman magistrate with almost consular authority outside the city, orig. one whose consulate had expired, often governor of a province: sometimes applied to a colonial or dominion governor: (*cap.*) a genus of prehistoric African anthropoid apes.—*adj.* **procon'-sular** (*-sū-lər*).—*ns.* **procon'sulate** (*-sū-lit*, *-lāt*), **procon'sulship** (*-sl-ship*), the office, or term of office, of a proconsul. [L. *prōcōnsul*.]

**procrastinate**, *prō-kras'ti-nāt*, *v.t.* (*rare*) to put off till some future time, to defer.—*v.i.* to defer action.—*n.* **procrastinā'tion**, act or habit of putting off, dilatoriness.—*adjs.* **procras'tinātive**, **procras'tinating**, **procras'tinātory**.—*ns.* **procras'-tinativeness**; **procras'tinātor**. [L. *procrāstināre*, *-ātum*—*prō*, onward, *crāstinus*, of tomorrow—*crās*, tomorrow.]

**procreate**, *prō'kri-āt*, *v.t.* to engender: to beget: to generate.—*v.i.* to produce offspring.—*n.* **prō'-creant** (*-kri-ənt*), a generator.—*adj.* generating: connected with or useful in reproduction.—*n.* **prōcreā'tion**.—*adj.* **prō'creātive**, having the power to procreate: generative: productive.—*ns.* **prō'creātiveness**; **prō'creātor**, a parent. [L. *prōcreāre*, *-ātum*—*prō*, forth, *creāre*, to produce.]

**Procrustean**, *prō-krus'ti-ən*, *adj.* violently making conformable to a standard—from *Procrustes* (Gr. *Prōkroustēs*), a fabulous Greek robber, who stretched or cut his captives' legs to make them fit a bed. [Gr. *prokrouein*, to lengthen out.]

**procrypsis**, *prō-krip'sis*, (*biol.*) *n.* protective coloration.—*adj.* **procryp'tic**.—*adv.* **procryp'tically**. [Gr. *pro*, before, *krypsis*, hiding, *kryptein*, to hide.]

**proctal**, *prok'tl*, *adj.* anal.—*n.* **proctalgia** (*-al'ji-ə*), neuralgic pain in the rectum; **procti'tis**, inflammation of the rectum.—*adj.* **proctodae'al** (*-tō-dē'əl*).—*n.* **proctodae'um**, the posterior part of the alimentary canal, formed by invagination of ectoderm. [Gr. *prōktos*, anus, *algos*, pain, *hodaios*, on the way.]

**proctor**, *prok'tər*, *n.* a procurator or manager for another: an attorney in the spiritual courts: a representative of the clergy in Convocation: an official in the English universities whose functions include enforcement of university regulations.—*n.* **proc'torage**.—*adj.* **procto'rial** (*-tōr'*, *-tör'i-əl*).—*adv.* **procto'rially**.—*v.t.* **proc'torise**, *-ize*, to exercise the power of a proctor against.—*n.* **proc'torship**.—**king's**, **queen's**, **proctor**, an official who intervenes in divorce cases in England if collusion or fraud is suspected. [**procurator**.]

**procumbent**, *prō-kum'bənt*, *adj.* lying or leaning

forward: prone: prostrate: lying on the ground (*bot.*). [L. *prōcumbēns, -entis*, pr.p. of *prōcumbĕre—prō*, forward, *cumbĕre*, to lie down.]

**procurator**, *prok'ū-rā-tər*, *n.* a financial agent in a Roman imperial province, sometimes administrator of part of it: one who manages affairs for another: one authorised to act for another: an agent in a law court.—*adj.* **procuratorial** (*-rə-tō'ri-əl, -tör'*).—*ns.* **proc'uratorship**; **proc'uratory** (*-rə-tər-i*), authorisation to act for another.—**proc'urator-fis'cal** (see **fiscal**). [L. *prōcūrātor, -ōris*; see next word.]

**procure**, *prə-, prō-kūr'*, *v.t.* to contrive to obtain or bring about: to bring upon one: to induce: to induce to come, bring (*Shak.*): to urge earnestly (*Spens.*): to obtain for another's immoral purposes.—*v.i.* to pander, pimp.—*adj.* **procur'able**, to be had.—*ns.* **procuracy** (*prok'ū-rə-si*), office of a procurator; **procurā'tion**, management of another's affairs: the instrument giving power to do so: a sum paid by incumbents to the bishop or archdeacon on visitations: procuring; **procure'ment**, the act of procuring in any sense; **procur'er**, one who procures: a pander:—*fem.* **procur'ess**, a bawd. [Fr. *procurer*—L. *prōcūrāre*, to manage—*prō*, for, *cūrāre, -ātum*, to care for.]

**procureur**, *prō-kü-rœr*, (Fr.) a procurator.—**procureur général** (*zhān-ā-ral*), the public prosecutor-in-chief.

**Procyon**, *prō'si-on*, *n.* a first-magnitude star in the constellation of the Lesser Dog: the raccoon genus, giving name to the family **Procyon'idae** (raccoons, coatis, etc.). [Gr. *Prŏkyŏn*, the star Procyon, rising before the Dogstar—*pro*, before, *kyōn*, a dog.]

**prod**, *prod*, *v.t.* to prick: to poke, as with the end of a stick:—*pr.p.* **prodd'ing**; *pa.t.* and *pa.p.* **prodd'ed.**—*n.* an act of prodding: a sharp instrument, as a goad, an awl, a skewer. [Origin unknown; O.E. *prodbor* seems to mean auger.]

**prodigal**, *prod'i-gl*, *adj.* wasteful of one's means: squandering: lavish.—*n.* a waster: a spendthrift. —*adv.* (*Shak.*) prodigally.—*v.t.* **prod'igalise, -ize,** to spend lavishly, waste.—*n.* **prodigality** (*-gal'i-ti*), state or quality of being prodigal: extravagance: profusion: great liberality.—*adv.* **prod'igally.** [Obs. Fr.,—L. *prōdigus—prōdigĕre*, to squander—pfx. *prōd-* (early form of *prō-*), away, forth, *agĕre*, to drive.]

**prodigy**, *prod'i-ji*, *n.* a portent (*arch.*): any person or thing that causes great wonder: a wonder: a monster: a child of precocious genius or virtuosity.—*n.* **prodigios'ity.**—*adj.* **prodig'ious**, like a prodigy (*arch.*): astonishing: more than usually large in size or degree: monstrous.—*adv.* **prodig'iously.**—*n.* **prodig'iousness.** [L. *prōdigium*, a prophetic sign—pfx. *prōd-* (earlier form of *prō-*), in advance, prob. the root of *adagium* (see **adage**).]

**proditor**, *prod'i-tər*, *n.* a traitor.—*adjs.* **prodito'rious** (*-tōr, -tör'i-əs*), **prod'itory.** [L. *prōditor, -ōris—prōdĕre, -itum*, to betray—*prō*, forth, *dăre*, to give.]

**prodromus**, *prod'rom-əs*, *n.* an introductory treatise: a premonitory event: a sign of approaching disease:—*pl.* **prod'romi** (*-i*).—Also **prodrome** (*prod'rōm*).—*adjs.* **prod'romal, prodrom'ic.** [Latinised from Gr. *prodromos*, forerunner—*pro*, before, *dromos*, a run.]

**produce**, *prə-, prō-dūs'*, *v.t.* to bring forward or out: to extend: to bring into being: to bring forth: to yield: to bring about: to make: to put on the stage: to prepare for exhibition to the public.—*v.i.* to yield: to create value.—*ns.* **produce** (*prod'ūs*), that which is produced: product: proceeds: crops: yield, esp. of fields and gardens; **produce'ment** (*Milt.*), product; **produc'er**, one who produces, esp. commodities.

or a play or similar exhibition: one who exercises general control over, but does not actually make, a motion picture (cf. **director**): a furnace in which a mixed combustible gas is produced by passing air and steam through incandescent coke; **producibil'ity.**—*adj.* **produc'ible**, that may be produced: that may be generated or made: that may be exhibited.—*ns.* **product** (*prod'əkt, -ukt*), a thing produced: a result: a work: offspring: a quantity got by multiplying (*math.*): a substance obtained from another by chemical change (*chem.*); **productibil'ity** (*prə-dukt-*), capability of being produced.—*adj.* **product'ile**, capable of being drawn out in length.—*n.* **produc'tion**, act of producing: that which is produced: fruit: product: a work, esp. of art: putting upon the stage: bringing out: creation of values (*pol. econ.*): extension: in Scots law, a document produced in court.—*adjs.* **produc'tional**; **produc'tive**, having the power to produce: generative: that produces: producing richly: fertile: efficient.—*adv.* **produc'tively.**—*ns.* **produc'tiveness, productiv'ity** (*prod-, prōd-*).—**producer gas**, gas made in a producer, chiefly a mixture of hydrogen and carbon-monoxide diluted with nitrogen.—**producer(s') goods**, goods, such as raw materials and tools, used in the production of consumer(s') goods. [L. *prōdūcĕre, -ductum—prō*, forward, *dūcĕre*, to lead.]

**proem**, *prō'em*, *n.* an introduction: a prelude: a preface.—*adj.* **proemial** (*prō-ē'mi-əl*). [Fr. *proême*—L. *prooemium*—Gr. *prooimion—pro*, before, *oimē*, a song, *oimos*, a way.]

**proembryo**, *prō-em'bri-ō*, (*bot.*) *n.* a group of cells formed in the dividing zygote, from which part the embryo arises. [Pfx. **pro-** (1).]

**proenzyme**, *prō-en'zim*, *n.* an enzyme in an inactive form which can be activated—often by another enzyme. [Pfx. **pro-** (1).]

**prof**, *prof*, *n.* a familiar abbreviation of **professor.**

**proface**, *prō-fās'*, (*Shak.*) *interj.* may it profit you! —a phrase of welcome. [O.Fr. *prou*, profit, *fasse*, 3rd pers. sing. pres. subj. of *faire*, to do.]

**profane**, *prə-, prō-fān'*, *adj.* not sacred: secular: showing contempt of sacred things: uninitiated: unhallowed: ritually unclean or forbidden.—*v.t.* to treat with contempt or insult in spite of the holiness attributed: to desecrate: to violate: to put to an unworthy use.—*n.* **profanation** (*prof-ə-nā'shən*).—*adj.* **profanatory** (*prō-fan'ə-tər-i*).—*adv.* **profāne'ly.**—*ns.* **profāne'ness**; **profān'er**; **profanity** (*-fan'*), irreverence: that which is profane: profane language or conduct. [L. *profānus*, outside the temple, not sacred, unholy—*prō*, before, *fānum*, a temple.]

**profectitious**, *prō-fek-tish'əs*, *adj.* derived from a parent or ancestor. [L.L. *profecticius*—L. *prō-ficīsci, profectus*, to proceed.]

**profess**, *prə-, prō-fes'*, *v.t.* to make open declaration of: to declare in strong terms: to claim (often insincerely) to have a feeling of: to pretend to: to claim to be expert in: to be professor of: to receive into a religious order by profession (*R.C.*).—*v.i.* to enter publicly into a religious state: to pretend friendship (*Shak.*): to be a professor.—*adj.* **professed'**, openly declared: avowed: acknowledged: having made profession.—*adv.* **profess'edly.**—*adj.* **profess'ing**, avowed: pretending, soi-disant.—*n.* **profession** (*-fesh'ən*), the act of professing: open declaration: avowal: religious belief: pretence: an employment not mechanical and requiring some degree of learning: calling, habitual employment: the collective body of persons engaged in any profession: entrance into a religious order: the vow then taken.—*adj.* **profess'ional**, pertaining to a profession: engaged in a profession or in the profession in question: competing for money prizes or against those who sometimes do so: undertaken as a means of subsistence, as opp. to *amateur*: showing the skill, artistry, demeanour, or standard of conduct appropriate in a member of a profession or of a particular profession.—*n.* one who makes his living by an art, or makes it his career—opp. to *amateur, dilettante*: one who engages in sport for livelihood or gain or against those who do so (with various rules of interpretation for each sport)—opp. to *amateur*: (in full, *professional examination*) any one of the successive examinations towards a degree in medicine (in Scottish universities).—*v.t.* profess'ionalise, -ize, to give a professional character to: to give over to professionals.—*n.* profess'-ionalism, the status of professional: the competence, or the correct demeanour, of those who are highly trained and disciplined: the outlook, aim, or restriction of the mere professional: the predominance of professionals in sport.—*adv.* profess'ionally.—*ns.* professor (*prə-fes'ər*), one who professes: one who openly declares belief in certain doctrines: a teacher of the highest grade in a university or college (prefixed to the name): title assumed by charlatans, quacks, dancing-masters, etc.:—*fem.* (*rare*) profess'oress; profess'orate, professoriate.—*adj.* professorial (*prof-es-ō'ri-əl, -ō'ri-əl*).—*adv.* professo'rially.—*ns.* professo'riate, the office or chair of a professor: his period of office: body of professors; profess'orship. [L. *professus*, perf.p. of *profitērī* —*prō*, publicly, *fatērī*, to confess.]

proffer, prof'ər, *v.t.* to offer for acceptance, to tender, present: to offer to undertake:—*pr.p.* proff'ering; *pa.t.* and *pa.p.* proff'ered.—*n.* an offer, tender: an incipient act.—*n.* proff'erer. [A.Fr. *proffrir*—L. *prō*, forward, *offerre*; see offer.]

proficient, prə-, prō-fish'ənt, *adj.* competent: well-skilled: thoroughly qualified.—*n.* one who is making progress in learning (*Shak.*): an adept: an expert.—*ns.* profic'ience (now *rare* or *obs.*); profic'iency.—*adv.* profi'ciently. [L. *prōficiēns, -entis,* pr.p. of *prōficēre,* to make progress.]

profile, prō'fīl, -fēl, -fil, *n.* an outline: a head or portrait in a side-view: the side-face: the outline of any object without foreshortening: a drawing of a vertical section of country, an engineering work, etc.: a graph: a short biographical sketch in a newspaper or magazine: outline of the course of an operation.—*v.t.* to draw in profile: to make an outline of: to show in profile: to give a profile to: to shape the outline of.—*ns.* prō'filer; prō'filist, one who draws profiles. [It. *profilo*—L. *prō*, before, *filum*, a thread.]

profit, prof'it, *n.* gain: the gain resulting from the employment of capital: the excess of selling price over first cost: advantage: addition to good or value: benefit: improvement.—*v.t.* to benefit or to be of advantage to.—*v.i.* to gain advantage: to receive profit: to make progress, to improve (*Shak.*): to be of advantage.—*n.* profitabil'ity.—*adj.* prof'itable, yielding or bringing profit or gain: lucrative: productive.—*n.* prof'itableness.—*adv.* prof'itably.—*n.* profiteer', one who takes advantage of an emergency to make exorbitant profits.—*v.i.* to act as a profiteer.—*ns.* profiteer'ing; prof'iter; prof'iting.—*adj.* prof'itless, without profit.—*adv.* prof'itlessly. prof'it-o'rientated, having profit as chief aim; prof'it-sharing, a voluntary agreement under which the employee receives a share, fixed beforehand, in the profits of a business. [Fr.,—L. *prōfectus*, progress—*prōficēre, prōfectum,* to make progress.]

profiterole, prə-fit'ə-rōl, *n.* a small cake puff with filling. [Fr.; perh.—*profiter*, to profit.]

profligate, prof'li-git, -gāt, *adj.* overthrown, defeated (*obs.*): abandoned to vice: dissolute:

prodigal, rashly extravagant.—*n.* one leading a profligate life: one who is recklessly extravagant or wasteful.—*n.* prof'ligacy (*-gə-si*), state or quality of being profligate: a vicious course of life.—*adv.* prof'ligately. [L. *prōfligātus*, pa.p. of *prōfligāre*—*prō*, forward, *flīgere*, to dash.]

profluent, prō'floo-ənt, (*Milt.*) *adj.* flowing forth.—*n.* pro'fluence. [L. *prō*, forth, *fluēre*, to flow.]

profound, prə-, prō-fownd', *adj.* deep: deep-seated: far below the surface: intense: abstruse: intellectually deep: penetrating deeply into knowledge.—*n.* the sea or ocean: an abyss, great depth.—*adv.* profound'ly.—*ns.* profound'-ness, profundity (*-fund'*), state or quality of being profound: depth of place, of knowledge, etc.: that which is profound. [Fr. *profond*—L. *profundus*—*pro*, forward, *fundus*, bottom.]

profulgent, prə-, prō-ful'jent, *adj.* shining forth, radiant. [L. *prō*, forth, *fulgēns, -entis*, pr.p. of *fulgēre*, to shine.]

profuse, prə-, prō-fūs', *adj.* liberal to excess: lavish: extravagant: over-abounding.—*adv.* profūse'ly.—*ns.* profūse'ness; profuser (*-fūz'ər*; *Herrick*), a prodigal, spendthrift; profusion (*-fū'zhən*), state of being profuse: extravagance: prodigality. [L. *prōfūsus*, pa.p. of *prōfundēre*—*prō*, forth, *fundēre*, to pour.]

prog, prog, *v.t.* to pierce: to prick: to poke.—*v.i.* to poke about for anything: to forage for food: to beg.—*n.* a pointed instrument: a thrust: provisions, esp. for a journey. [Origin unknown; perh. several distinct words.]

prog, prog, *n.* university slang for proctor.—*v.t.* to proctorise.—*n.* progg'ins, a proctor.

progenitor, prō-jen'i-tər, *n.* a forefather: an ancestor: a parent: the founder of a family:—*fem.* progen'itress, progen'itrix.—*adj.* progenito'rial (*-tōr', -tör'i-əl*).—*ns.* progen'itorship; progen'i-ture, a begetting; progeny (*proj'ə-ni*), offspring: descendants: race: lineage (*Shak.*). [L. *prōgenitor, prōgeniēs*—*prōgignēre*—*prō*, before, *genēre, genitum,* to beget.]

progeria, prō-jer'i-a, *n.* a rare disease causing premature ageing in children. [Gr. *pro*, before, *gēras*, old age.]

progesterone, prō-jes'tər-ōn, *n.* a female sex hormone that prepares the uterus for the fertilised ovum and maintains pregnancy.—*ns.* proges'tin (pro- (1), *gestation, -in*), any hormone concerned with changes before pregnancy, esp. proges'-togen, any of a range of hormones of the progesterone type; several synthetic progestogens are used in oral contraceptives. [*progestin, sterol, -one.*]

proglottis, prō-glot'is, *n.* a detachable tapeworm joint:—*pl.* proglott'idēs. [Gr. *pro*, before, *glōttis, -idios*, a pipe mouthpiece.]

prognathous, prog'nə-thəs, also prog- or prōg-nā'thəs, *adj.* with projecting jaw—also prognathic (*prog-, prōg-nath'ik*).—*n.* prog'nathism (or *-nath'*, *-nāth'*). [Gr. *pro*, forward, *gnathos*, a jaw.]

Progne, prog'nē, *n.* a personification of the swallow, sometimes of the nightingale: an American genus of swallows. [Philomela's sister, (*usu.*) Procne (L. *Prognē*—Gr. *Proknē*) transformed into a swallow, or a nightingale.]

prognosis, prog-nō'sis, *n.* forecasting, or forecast, esp. of the course of a disease:—*pl.* prognos'es (*-ēz*).—*n.* prognostic (*prog-, prəg-nost'ik*), a foretelling: an indication of something to come: a presage: a symptom on which prognosis can be based.—*adj.* indicating what is to happen by signs or symptoms: of prognosis.—*v.t.* prognos'-ticate, to foretell: to indicate as to come.—*n.* prognostica'tion.—*adj.* prognos'ticative.—*n.* prognost'icātor, a predictor, esp. a weather prophet. [Gr. *prognōsis*—*pro*, before, *gignōs-kein*, to know.]

programme, (esp. *U.S.,* and often in speaking of

computer) **program,** *prō'gram, n.* a public notice (*Scot., obs.*): a paper, booklet, or the like, giving a scheme of proceedings arranged for an entertainment, conference, course of study, etc., with relevant details: the items of such a scheme collectively: a plan of things to be done: the sequence of actions to be performed by an electronic computer in dealing with data of a certain kind: course of instruction (by book or teaching machine) in which subject-matter is broken down into logical sequence of short items of information, and a student can check immediately the suitability of his responses.— *v.t.* to provide with, enter in, etc., a programme: to prepare a program(me) for (an electronic computer, etc.).—*adj.* **programmatic** (*-grə-mat'-ik*), of a programme: of, or of the nature of, programme music.—*adj.* **pro'grammed.**—*n.* **pro'-gramming.**—**programme music,** music that seeks to depict a scene or tell a story; **Programming Language 1 (PL/1),** a computer programming language which combines the best qualities of commercial- and scientific-oriented languages. [Gr. *programma,* proclamation—*pro,* forth, *gramma,* a letter.]

**progress,** *prō'gres,* sometimes (esp. in U.S.) *pro', n.* forward movement: advance: continuation: advance to something better or higher in development: gain in proficiency: course: passage from place to place: a procession: a journey of state: a circuit.—*v.i.* **progress'** (formerly, as *Shak., prō'*), to go forward: to make progress: to go on, continue: to go in progress, travel in state.—*v.t.* (*obs.*) to traverse.—*n.* **progression** (*prə-, prō-gresh'ən*), motion onward: act or state of moving onward: progress: movement by successive stages: a regular succession of chords (*mus.*): movements of the parts in harmony: change from term to term according to some law (*math.*): a series of terms so related (see **arithmetic, geometry, harmony**).—*adjs.* **progress'ional; progress'ionary.**—*ns.* **progress'ionism,** sympathy with or advocacy of progress: belief that social or other evolution is towards higher or better things; **progress'ionist,** a believer in progressionism: a progressive: one who favours progress or reform; **progress'-ism** (or *prō', pro'*), progressionism; **progress'ist** (or *prō', pro'*), one who advocates a progressive policy: progressionist.—*adj.* **progress'ive,** moving forward: making progress: of the nature of progress: advancing by successive stages: (in games, e.g. **progressive whist**) played by several sets of players, some of whom move round from table to table after each hand according to rule: advancing towards better and better or higher and higher: in favour of progress—applied to various parties in municipal and national politics more or less favouring reform: of such a party.—*n.* one who favours progress or reform: a member of a party called progressive.—*adv.* **progress'ively.**—*n.* **progress'iveness.**—**in progress,** going on: in course of publication. [Fr. *progresse* (now *progrès*)—L. *prōgressus, -ūs—prō,* forward, *gradi, gressus,* to step.]

**progymnasium,** *prō-jim-nä'zi-əm,* or (*Ger.*) *prō-gim-nä'zi-ōōm, n.* in Germany, a classical school in which the higher classes are wanting. [Ger.]

**prohibit,** *prə-, prō-hib'it, v.t.* to forbid: to prevent.—*ns.* **prohib'iter, -or;** **prohibition** (*prō-hi-bi'shən* or *prō-i-*), the act of prohibiting, forbidding, or interdicting: an interdict: the forbidding by law of the manufacture and sale of alcoholic drinks.—*adj.* **prohibi'tionary.**—*ns.* **prohibi'tionism; prohibi'tionist,** one who favours prohibition, esp. of the manufacture and sale of alcoholic drinks.—*adj.* **prohibitive** (*-hib'*), tending to make impossible or preclude.—*adv.* **prohib'-itively.**—*n.* **prohib'itiveness.**—*adj.* **prohib'itory,** that prohibits or forbids: forbidding. [L.

*prohibēre, prohibitum—prō,* before, *habēre,* to have.]

**proign, proin,** obs. form of **prune** (2); **proin, proine, proin,** obs. forms of **prune** (1), (2), and (3).

**project,** *proj'ekt, n.* a notion (*Shak.*): speculative imagination (*obs.*): a projection: a scheme of something to be done: a proposal for an undertaking: an undertaking.—*v.t.* **project** (*prə-jekt', prō-jekt'*), to throw out or forward: to speak or sing in such a way as to aim the voice at the rear of the auditorium (*theat.*): to throw, propel: to cause to jut out, stretch out: to scheme, plan, devise: to set forth, set before the mind (*Shak.*): to cast (as a light, a shadow, an image) upon a surface or into space: to throw an image of: to show outlined against a background: in geom., to derive a new figure from, so that each point corresponds to a point of the original figure according to some rule, esp. by a system of parallel, converging, or diverging rays through the original points meeting a surface: to externalise: to make objective.—*v.i.* to jut out: to throw powder of projection upon the metal to be transmuted (*alchemy*).—*adj.* **projec'tile,** caused by projection: impelling: capable of being thrown or thrust forth.—*n.* **projectile** (*proj'ik-til,* or *prə-, prō-jek'til,* in U.S. *-til*), a body projected by force: a missile, esp. one discharged by a gun.—*n.* and *adj.* **projec'-ting.**—*n.* **projec'tion** (*-shən*), an act or method of projecting: the fact or state of being projected: planning: that which is projected: a jutting out: that which juts out: the standing out of a figure: a figure got by projecting another (*geom.*): a method of representing geographical detail upon a plane: a projected image: the reading of one's own emotions and experiences into a particular situation (*psych.*): a person's unconscious attributing to other people of certain attitudes towards himself, usu. as defence against his own guilt, inferiority, etc. (*psych.*): the throwing in of a powdered philosopher's stone, to effect transmutation, hence transmutation itself in general (*alchemy*).—*adj.* **projec'tional.**—*n.* **projec'tionist,** one who projects, makes projections, esp. in map-making: an operator of a film-projector: an operator of certain television equipment.—*adj.* **projec'tive,** projecting: of projection: derivable by projection: unchanged by projection.—*ns.* **projectivity** (*proj-ək-tiv'i-ti*); **project'ment** (*rare*), design; **projec'tor,** one who projects enterprises: a promoter of speculative schemes for money-making: an apparatus for projecting, esp. an image or a beam of light: a straight line joining a point with its projection (*geom.*); **projec'ture,** a jutting out.—**projecting powder** (*alchemy*), the philosopher's stone in powder; **projective geometry,** a branch of geometry dealing with the properties of figures by two- and three-dimensional projections. [L. *prōjicēre, prōjectum—prō,* forth, *jacēre,* to throw.]

**projet de loi,** *pro-zhä də lwa,* (Fr.) a legislative bill.

**proke,** *prōk,* (*dial.*) *v.t.* and *v.i.* to poke.—*n.* **prōk'er,** a poker. [Origin obscure.]

**prolamine,** *prō'lə-mēn,* also **prolamin,** *lə-min, n.* one of a group of alcohol-soluble proteins.

**prolapse,** *prō-laps',* or *prō'laps,* (*med.*) *n.* a falling down, or out of place.—Also **prolap'sus.**—*v.i.* **prolapse',** to slip out of place. [L. *prōlābī, prō-lāpsus,* to slip forward—*prō,* forward, *lābi,* to slip.]

**prolate,** *prō'lāt, adj.* drawn out along the polar diameter, as a spheroid: widespread.—*v.t.* **pro-late'** (*obs.*), to lengthen out in utterance.—*adv.* **pro'lately.**—*ns.* **pro'lateness** (or *-lāt'*); **prolation** (*prō-lā'shən*), utterance: the time-ratio of semibreve to minim (in *great* or *perfect prolation,* three minims to a semibreve; *lesser* or *imperfect,* two) (*mediaeval mus.*).—*adj.* **prolative** (*prō-lā'tiv, prō'lə-tiv; gram.*), completing the predicate.

Neutral vowels in unaccented syllables: *el'ə-mənt;* for certain sounds in foreign words, see p. viii

[L. *prōlātus*, produced—*prō*, forward, *lātus*, used as perf.p. of *ferre*, to carry.]

**prole**, prōl, (*coll.*) *n.* and *adj.* proletarian.

**prole**, **proler**. Earlier forms of prowl, prowler.

**proleg**, prō'leg, *n.* an insect larva's abdominal leg, distinguished from a thoracic or 'true' leg. [Pfx. **pro-** (2*b*), leg.]

**prolegomena**, prō-leg-om'in-a, *n.pl.* an introduction, esp. to a treatise:—*sing.* **prolegom'enon**.—*adjs.* **prolegom'enary**, **prolegom'enous**. [Gr. *prōlegomenon*, pl. -*a*, pass. part. neut. of *prolegein* *pro*, before, *legein*, to say.]

**prolepsis**, prō-lep'sis, or -*lēp'*, *n.* anticipation: the rhetorical figure of anticipation, use of a word not literally applicable till a later time: a figure by which objections are anticipated and answered:—*pl.* **prolep'sēs**.—*adjs.* **prolep'tic**, -**al**.—*adv.* **prolep'tically**. [Gr. *prōlēpsis*—*pro*, before, *lambanein*, to take.]

**proletarian**, prō-li-tā'ri-ən, *adj.* of the poorest labouring class: having little or no property.—*n.* a member of the poorest class: a plant without reserves of food (*bot.*).—*ns.* **proletā'rianism**, the condition of the poorest classes; **proletā'riat** (-*ət*), **-ate**, the proletarian class: the wage-earning class, esp. those without capital.—*n.* and *adj.* **pro'letary** (-*ər-i*), proletarian. [L. *prōlētārius*, (in ancient Rome) a citizen of the sixth and lowest class, who served the state not with his property but with his *prōlēs*, offspring.]

**prolicide**, prō'li-sid, *n.* the killing of offspring: the killing off of the human race.—*adj.* **prolici'dal.** [L. *prōlēs*, offspring, *caedĕre*, to kill.]

**proliferate**, prō-lif'ə-rāt, *v.i.* to grow by multiplication of parts (cells, buds, shoots, etc.): to reproduce by proliferation: to reproduce abundantly: to increase in numbers greatly and rapidly.—*v.t.* to produce by proliferation.—*n.* **proliferā'tion**, growth and extension by multiplication of cells: production of vegetative shoots from a reproductive structure: repeated production of new parts: production of shoots that may become new plants: production of abnormal or supernumerary parts: a structure formed by proliferating: increase as if by proliferation (*fig.*).—*adjs.* **prolif'erative**, **prolif'erous**.—*adv.* **prolif'erously**. [L. *prōlēs*, progeny, *ferre*, to bear.]

**prolific**, prə-, prō-lif'ik, *adj.* reproductive: fertilising: fertile: producing much offspring (also *fig.* as of an author): fruitful: abounding.—*n.* **prolif'icacy** (-ə-si).—*adj.* **prolif'ical** (*rare* or *obs.*).—*adv.* **prolif'ically**.—*ns.* **prolificā'tion**, the generation of young: development of a shoot by continued growth of a flower (*bot.*); **prolificity** (-is'i-ti), **prolif'icness**. [L. *prōlēs*, offspring, *facĕre*, to make.]

**prolix**, prō'liks, or -liks', *adj.* long and wordy: long-winded: dwelling too long on particulars: long (*obs.* or *rare*).—*adj.* **prolixious** (prō-lik'shəs; Shak.), dilatory.—*n.* **prolix'ity**.—*adv.* **prolix'ly** (or prō').—*n.* **prolix'ness** (or prō'). [L. *prōlixus* —*pro*, forward, *liqui*, to flow.]

**proll**, prōl, **proler**, prōl'ər, earlier forms of prowl, prowler.

**prolocutor**, prō-lok'ū-tər, *n.* a spokesman: a chairman, esp. of the lower house of Convocation:—*fem.* **prōloc'utrix**.—*ns.* **prolocu'tion** (prō- or pro-), an introductory speech or saying; **prō-loc'utorship**. [L. *prōlocūtor*—*prōloqui*, -*locūtus*, to speak out—*loqui*, to speak.]

**prologue**, prō'log, *n.* in a Greek play, the part before the entry of the chorus: an introduction to a poem, etc.: a speech before a play: the speaker of a prologue: an introductory event or action.—*v.t.* to introduce: to preface.—*v.i.* **pro'logise**, **-ize** (-giz, -jiz), to speak a prologue —also **pro'loguise**, **-ize**. [Fr.,—L. *prologus*— Gr. *prologos*—*logos*, speech.]

**prolong**, prə-, prō-long', *v.t.* to lengthen out:

to postpone (*Spens.*, *Shak.*).—*v.i.* to lengthen out.—*adj.* **prolongable** (prō-long'ə-bl).—*v.t.* **prolongate** (prō'long-gāt), to lengthen.—*ns.* **prolongation** (-long-gā'shən), lengthening out: a piece added in continuation: continuation; **prolonger** (-long'ər). [L. *prōlongāre*—*prō*, forward, *longus*, long.]

**prolonge**, prō-lonj', *n.* a rope for a gun-carriage. [Fr.]

**prolusion**, prō-lōō'zhən, -lū', *n.* a preliminary performance, activity, or display: an essay preparatory to a more solid treatise.—*adj.* **prolu'sory** (-sə-ri). [L. *prōlūsiō*, -*ōnis*—*prō*, before, *lūdĕre*, *lūsum*, to play.]

**prom**, prom, *n.* an abbrev. of promenade: a promenade concert.

**promachos**, prom'ə-kos, Gr. -*hhos*, *n.* a champion or defender: a tutelary god. [Gr.]

**promenade**, prom-i-näd' or -*näd'*, *n.* a walk, ride, or drive for pleasure, show, or gentle exercise: a processional dance: a school or college dance (*U.S.*): a place where people walk to and fro: a paved terrace on a sea-front: an esplanade. —*v.i.* to walk, ride, or drive about: to make a promenade.—*v.t.* to lead about and exhibit: to walk, ride or drive about or through.—*n.* **promenader** (-äd'ər).—**promenade concert**, one in which part of the audience stand throughout and can move about; **promenade deck**, a deck on which passengers walk about. [Fr.,—*promener*, to lead about (*se promener*, to take a walk)—L. *prōmināre*, to drive forwards—*prō*, forward, *mināre*, to threaten.]

**prometal**, prō'met-l, *n.* a kind of cast-iron highly resistant to heat.

**Promethean**, prō-mē'thi-ən, -thyən, *adj.* pertaining to *Prometheus* (-*thūs*), who stole fire from heaven, for which Zeus chained him to a rock, to be tortured by a vulture.—*n.* a glass tube containing sulphuric acid and an inflammable mixture brought together by pressing—an early kind of match.—*n.* **prome'thium** (formerly **prome'theum**), element 61 (symbol Pm). [Gr. *Promētheus*.]

**prominent**, prom'i-nənt, *adj.* standing out: projecting: most easily seen: catching the eye of attention: in the public eye.—*ns.* **prom'inence**, state or quality of being prominent: a prominent point or thing: a projection; **prom'inency**, a prominence.—*adv.* **prom'inently**.—**solar prominence**, a reddish cloud of incandescent gas shooting out from the sun. [L. *prōminēns*, -*entis*, pr.p. of *prōminēre*, to jut forth—*prō*, forth, *minae*, projections, threats.]

**promiscuous**, prō-mis'kū-əs, *adj.* confusedly or indiscriminately mixed: collected together without order: indiscriminate (now usu. referring to one indulging in indiscriminate sexual intercourse): haphazard: belonging to a mixed set: far from choice (*old slang*): casual, accidental (*coll.*).—*n.* **promiscū'ity** (prom-), mixture without order or distinction: promiscuous sexual intercourse.—*adv.* **promis'cuously**. [L. *prōmiscuus*—*prō*, inten., *miscēre*, to mix.]

**promise**, prom'is, *n.* an engagement to do or keep from doing something: expectation, or that which raises expectation: a ground for hope of future excellence: fulfilment of what is promised (*rare*).—*v.t.* to engage by promise: to betroth: to encourage to expect: to afford reason to expect: to assure: to engage to bestow.—*v.i.* to make a promise or promises: to afford hopes or expectations: to stand sponsor (*rare*).—*n.* **promisee'**, the person to whom a promise is made.—*adjs.* **prom'iseful**; **prom'iseless**.—*n.* **prom'iser**.—*adj.* **prom'ising**, affording ground for hope or expectation: likely to turn out well.— *adv.* **prom'isingly**.—*n.* **prom'isor** (*law*).—*adj.* **promiss'ive** (prə-), conveying a promise: of the nature of a promise.—*n.* **promiss'or** (*Rom.*

*law*), the maker of a promise.—*adv.* **prom'is-sorily.**—*adj.* **prom'issory,** containing a promise of some engagement to be fulfilled.—**prom'ise-breach** (*Shak.*), violation of promise; **prom'ise-breaker** (*Shak.*).—*adj.* **prom'ise-crammed** (*Shak.*), fed to repletion with empty promises.—**prom'ise-keeping; promised land,** the land promised by God to Abraham and his seed: Canaan: heaven; **promissory note,** a written promise to pay a sum of money on some future day or on demand.—**be promised,** to have an engagement (*Shak.*); **breach of promise** (see **breach**); **the Promise,** the assurance of God to Abraham that his descendants should become the chosen people. [L. *prōmissum,* neut. pa.p. of *promittĕre,* to send forward—*prō,* forward, *mittĕre,* to send.]

**prommer,** *prom'ər,* (*coll.*) *n.* a regular attender of promenade concerts.

**promontory,** *prom'ən-tər-i, -tri, n.* a headland or high cape: a projection, ridge, or eminence (*anat.*).—*adj.* standing out like a promontory. [L.L. *prōmontōrium* (L. *prōmuntŭrium*), assimilated to *mōns,* mountain.]

**promote,** *prə-, prō-mōt', v.t.* to help forward: to further: to further the progress of: to raise to a higher grade: to take steps for the passage or formation of: to set in motion (as the office of a judge in a criminal suit): to encourage the sales of by advertising.—*ns.* **promō'ter,** one who promotes: one who takes part in the setting up of companies: a promoter: a professional informer (*obs.*): a substance that increases the efficiency of a catalyst; **promotion** (*-mō'shən*), the act of promoting: advancement in rank or in honour: encouragement: preferment: a venture, esp. in show business: advertising.—*adj.* **promō'tive.**—*n.* **promō'tor,** one who presents candidates for graduation in Scottish universities.—**be on one's promotion,** to have right or hope of promotion: to be on good behaviour with a view to promotion. [L. *prōmovēre, -mōtum—prō,* forward, *movēre,* to move.]

**prompt,** *prom(p)t, adj.* ready in action: performed at once: paid or due at once: ready for delivery: readily inclined (*Shak.*).—*adv.* promptly, punctually, to the minute.—*v.t.* to incite: to instigate: to move to action: to supply forgotten words to: to help with words or facts when one is at a loss: to suggest to the mind.—*n.* a time limit for payment: an act of prompting: words furnished by the prompter.—*ns.* **prompt'er,** one who prompts, esp. actors; **prompt'ing; prompt'itude,** promptness: readiness: quickness of decision and action.—*adv.* **prompt'ly.**—*ns.* **prompt'ness; prompt'uary,** a repository: a reference book of facts; **prompt'ure** (*Shak.*), suggestion: instigation.—**prompt'-book, -copy,** a copy of a play for the prompter's use; **prompt'-box,** a box for the prompter in a theatre; **prompt'-note,** a note of reminder of time-limit of payment; **prompt'-side,** the side of the stage where the prompter is—usually to the actor's left in Britain, to his right in U.S.A. [L. *prōmptus—prōmĕre,* to bring forward.]

**promulgate,** *prom'əl-gāt* (U.S. *prə-mul'*), *v.t.* to proclaim, publish abroad: to make widely known: to put in execution by proclamation (as a law)—(*arch.*) **promulge** (*prō-mulj'*).—*ns.* **promulgā'tion; prom'ulgātor.** [L. *prōmulgāre, -ātum.*]

**promuscis,** *prō-mus'is, n.* a proboscis, esp. of Hemiptera.—*adj.* **promusc'idate,** like or having a promuscis. [L. *promuscis, -idis,* a popular perversion of *proboscis.*]

**promycelium,** *prō-mī-sē'li-əm, n.* a short germ-tube put out by some fungal spores, producing spores of different types. [Pfx. **pro-** (1), and **mycelium.**]

**pronaos,** *prō-nā'os, n.* the vestibule in front of

a temple:—*pl.* **prona'oi.** [Gr. *prŏnāos—pro,* before, *nāos,* a temple.]

**prone,** *prōn, adj.* with the face, ventral surface, or palm of the hand downward: prostrate: directed downward: loosely, lying or laid flat: descending steeply: disposed, inclined, naturally tending: willing: ready, eager (*Shak.*): perhaps passive, or with downcast eyes, or fervent (*Shak., Meas. for Meas.*).—*v.t.* **prōn'ate,** of the hand, to turn palm downward or backward with radius and ulna crossed—opp. to *supinate.*—*ns.* **prōnā'tion,** the act of pronating; **prōnā'tor,** the muscle of the forearm that pronates the hand.—*adv.* **prone'ly.**—*n.* **prone'ness.** [L. *prōnus.*]

**prone,** *prōn,* (*obs.*) *n.* a place in a church where intimations are given out: hence, a homily.—*n.* **proneur,** *prō-nær',* a flatterer. [Fr. *prône.*]

**prong,** *prong, n.* a fork of any kind (now chiefly *dial.*): a tine, tooth, or spike of a fork or forked object: a tine, spur, or projection, as on an antler: a fork of a stream or inlet (*U.S.*).—*v.t.* to stab with a prong: to furnish with prongs.—*adj.* **pronged,** having prongs.—**prong'-buck,** the pronghorn (properly the male); **prong'-hoe,** a hoe with prongs; **prong'horn,** an American antelope-like ruminant (*Antilocapra americana*), only representative of the family *Antilocapridae,* with deciduous horns pronged in front.—*adj.* **prong'-horned.** [M.E. *prange;* origin obscure.]

**pronominal.** See **pronoun.**

**pronotum,** *prō-nō'təm, n.* the back of an insect's prothorax:—*pl.* **pronō'ta.**—*adj.* **pronō'tal.** [Pfx. **pro-** (1), Gr. *nōton,* back.]

**pronoun,** *prō'nown, n.* a word used instead of a noun, i.e. to indicate without naming.—*adj.* **pronominal** (*prə-, prō-nom'in-əl*), belonging to, or of the nature of, a pronoun.—*adv.* **pronom'inally.**

**pronounce,** *prə-, prō-nowns', v.t.* to proclaim: to utter formally: to utter rhetorically: to declare: to utter: to articulate.—*v.i.* to pass judgment: to articulate one's words.—*n.* (*Milt.*) pronouncement.—*adjs.* **pronounce'able,** capable of being pronounced; **pronounced',** marked with emphasis: marked.—*adv.* **pronoun'cedly.**—*ns.* **pronounce'ment,** a confident or authoritative assertion or declaration; **pronoun'cer.**—*n. and adj.* **pronoun'cing.**—*n.* **pronunciation** (*prō-nun-si-ā'shən*), mode of pronouncing: articulation. [Fr. *prononcer*—L. *prōnūntiāre—prō,* forth, *nūntiāre,* to announce—*nūntius,* a messenger.]

**pronto,** *pron'tō,* (*slang*) *adv.* promptly, quickly. [Sp. *pronto*—L. *prōmptus,* at hand.]

**Prontosil,** *pron'tō-sil, n.* trademark, name for some of the sulphonamide drugs.

**pronunciamento,** *prō-nun-si-ə-men'tō, n.* a manifesto: a formal proclamation. [Sp. *pronunciamiento.*]

**pronunciation.** See **pronounce.**

**proo,** pruh, *prōō,* (*Scot.*) *interj.* a call to a cow to come near.

**prooemium,** *prō-ē'mi-əm, n.* same as **proem.**—Also **prooe'mion.**

**proof,** *prōōf, n.* that which proves or establishes the truth of anything: the fact, act, or process of proving or showing to be true: demonstration: evidence that convinces the mind and goes toward determining the decision of a court: an instrument of evidence in documentary form: the taking of evidence by a judge upon an issue framed in pleading (*Scots law*): a trial before a judge without a jury (*Scots law*): a checking operation (*arith.*): a test: experience (*obs.*): issue, outcome, upshot (*obs.*): a test: testing, esp. of guns: ability to stand a test: invulnerability: impenetrability: armour of proof: a standard strength of spirit (alcohol and water of relative density 12/13 at 51°F.—i.e. 49·28 per cent. of alcohol): an impression taken for correction (*print*.): an early impression of an engraving: the first print from a negative (*phot.*):—*pl.* **proofs.**—*adj.* impervious: invulnerable: of standard strength (of alcohol).—*v.t.* to make impervious, esp. to water: to take a proof of: to test.—*n.* **proof′ing**, the process of making waterproof, gasproof, etc.: material used for the purpose.—*adj.* **proof′less**, wanting proof or evidence.—**proof′-charge**, a charge used to test the strength of a gun.—*v.t.* **proof′-correct**, to correct in proof.—**proof′-correcting**; **proof′-correction**; **proof′-house**, a house fitted up for proving firearms; **proof′-mark**, a mark stamped on a gun to show that it has stood the test; **proof′-puller**, one who pulls proofs.—*v.t.* and *v.i.* **proof′-read**, to read and correct in proof.—**proof′-reader**, one who reads printed proofs to discover and correct errors; **proof′-reading**; **proof′-sheet**, an impression taken on a slip of paper for correction before printing finally; **proof′-spirit**, a standard mixture of alcohol and water; **proof′-text**, a passage of the Bible adduced in proof of a doctrine.—**armour of proof**, armour that has been tested, or can be confidently relied upon; **artist's proof**, a first impression from an engraved plate or block; **burden of proof** (see **burden** (1)); **over, under proof**, containing in 100 volumes enough alcohol for so many volumes more, or less, than 100; **proof before letters**, one taken before the title is engraved on the plate. [O.Fr. *prove* (Fr. *preuve*); see **prove** for explanation of vowel in *obs.* forms **preeve, prief(e).**]

**prootic**, *prō-ot′ik*, *adj.* in front of the ear.—*n.* an anterior bone of the auditory capsule. [Pfx. **pro-** (1), Gr. *ous, ōtos*, ear.]

**prop**, *prop, n.* a rigid support: a supplementary support: a stay: a strut: a timber supporting a mine-roof: a supporter, upholder: a leg (*slang*): a boxer's extended arm (*slang*): an act of propping in a horse (*Austr.*).—*v.t.* to hold up by means of something placed under or against: to support or to sustain: to hit straight or knock down (*slang*).—*v.i.* (*Austr.*) to stop suddenly (of a horse):—*pr.p.* **propp′ing**; *pa.t.* and *pa.p.* **propped.**—**prop′-root**, a root growing down from a trunk or branch, serving to prop up a tree. [M.E. *proppe*; cf. Du. *proppe*, vine-prop, support.]

**prop**, *prop,* (*slang*) *n.* a tie-pin: a brooch. [Du. *prop.*]

**prop**, *prop, n.* a coll. or slang abbrev. of (aircraft) **propeller**, (theatrical) **property**, (geometrical) **proposition.**—*n.* **props**, stage properties: a property-man.

**propaedeutic**, *prō-pē-dū′tik, n.* (often in *pl.*) a preliminary study.—*adjs.* **propaedeut′ic, -al.** [Gr. *propaideuein*, to teach beforehand—*pro*, before, *paideuein*, to teach.]

**propagate**, *prop′ə-gāt, v.t.* to increase by natural process: to multiply: to pass on: to transmit: to spread from one to another: to increase (*obs.*).—*v.i.* to multiply: to breed.—*adj.* **prop′agable.**—*n.* **propagan′da**, a congregation of the Roman Catholic Church, founded 1622, charged with the spreading of Catholicism (*dē propāgāndā fidē*, 'concerning the faith to be propagated'—not a plural but ablative singular): any association, activity, plan, etc., for the spread of opinions and principles, esp. to effect change or reform: the information, etc., spread by such an association.—*v.t.* and *v.i.* **propagand′ise, -ize**—*ns.* **propagand′ism**, practice of propagating tenets or principles: zeal in spreading one's opinions: proselytism; **propagand′ist**—also *adj.*—*n.* **propagā′tion.**—*adj.* **prop′agātive.**—*n.* **prop′agātor.**—*v.t.* **propage** (*prō-pāj′*; *Congreve*), to beget, propagate.—**propaganda machine**, all the means employed in the process of spreading opinions: the process itself. [L. *prōpāgāre, -ātum*, conn. with *prōpāgō*, a layer.]

**propale**, *prō-pāl′, v.t.* to disclose.—*v.i.* (*Scott*) to make a display. [L.L. *prōpalāre*—*prōpalam*, openly—*prō*, forth, *palam*, openly.]

**propane**, *prō′pān, n.* a hydrocarbon gas ($C_3H_8$), third member of the methane series. [propionic.]

**proparoxytone**, *prō-par-ok′si-tōn, adj.* having the acute accent on the third last syllable.—*n.* a word thus accented. [Gr. *proparoxytonos*; see **paroxytone.**]

**propel**, *prə-, prō-pel′, v.t.* to drive forward:—*pr.p.* **propell′ing**; *pa.t.* and *pa.p.* **propelled′.**—*n.* **propell′ant**, that which propels: an explosive for propelling projectiles.—*adj.* **propell′ent**, driving.—*n.* a driving agent: a motive.—*ns.* **propell′er**, one who, or that which, propels: driving mechanism: a shaft with spiral blades (*screw-propeller*) for driving a ship, aeroplane, etc.: a screw-steamer: a helical blower (*air-propeller, propeller fan*): a spinning-bait; **propel′ment**, propulsion: propelling mechanism.—**propell′er-blade′; propell′er-shaft′**, the shaft of a propeller: the driving shaft between gear-box and rear axle in a motor vehicle. [L. *prōpellěre*—*prō*, forward, *pellěre*, to drive.]

**propend**, *prə-, prō-pend′*, (*Shak.*) *v.i.* to incline.—*adjs.* **propend′ent; propense** (*-pens′*), inclined: sometimes used in the sense of prepense.—*adv.* **propense′ly.**—*ns.* **propense′ness, propen′sion** (*Shak.*), **propens′ity**, inclination of mind: favourable inclination: tendency to good or evil: disposition: tendency to move in a certain direction.—*adj.* **propen′sive.** [L. *prōpendēre, -pēnsum*, to hang forward—*prō, pendēre.*]

**propene**. Same as **propylene.**

**proper**, *prop′ər, adj.* own: appropriate: peculiar: confined to one: in natural colouring (*her.*): strict: strictly applicable: strictly so-called: thorough, out-and-out (now *coll.* or *slang*): befitting: decorous, seemly: conforming strictly to convention: goodly: belonging to only one: comely: in liturgics, used only on a particular day or festival.—*n.* a service, psalm, etc., set apart for a particular day or occasion.—*adv.* (*coll.*) very, exceedingly.—*adv.* **prop′erly**, in a proper manner: strictly: entirely, extremely (*coll.*).—*n.* **prop′erness.**—**proper chant** (*obs.*), the key of C major.—*adj.* **prop′er-false′** (*Shak.*), handsome and deceitful.—**proper fraction**, a fraction that is less than 1 in value; **proper motion**, a star's apparent motion relatively to the celestial sphere, due partly to its own movement (peculiar motion), partly to that of the solar system (parallactic motion); **proper noun, name**, the name of a particular person, animal, thing, place, etc.—opp. to *common* noun. [Fr. *propre*—L. *prōprius*, own.]

**properdin**, *prō-pûr′din, n.* a natural immunising substance varyingly present in the blood, possibly with bearing on resistance to malignant disease. [L. *prō*, for, *perdēre*, to destroy.]

**properispomenon**, *prō-per-i-spōm′e-non, n.* a word with the circumflex accent on the penult.—Also *adj.* [Gr. *prōperispōmenon*, pass. part. neut. of *properispaein*, to put circumflex on the penult.]

**property**, *prop′ar-ti, n.* that which is proper to any person or thing: a quality that is always present: a characteristic: an essential detail (*Shak.*): any quality: propriety, fitness (*obs.*): that which is one's own: the condition of being one's own: a piece of land owned by somebody: right of possessing, employing, etc.: ownership: an article required on the stage: a mere tool or cat's-paw: individuality, personal identity (*Shak.*).—*v.t.* (*Shak.*) to treat as a property: to appropriate.—*adj.* of the nature of a stage property.—*adj.* **prop′ertied**, imbued with properties (*Shak.*): possessed of property.—**prop′erty-man, -mas′ter**, one who has charge of stage properties;

property qualification, a qualification (as for office, voting) depending on possession of so much property; **prop'erty-room,** the room in which stage properties are kept; **property tax,** a tax levied on property, at the rate of so much per cent. on its value. [O.Fr. *properte*; see propriety.]

**prophase,** *prō'fāz, n.* a preliminary stage of mitosis, preceding the formation of the equatorial plate. [Pfx. pro- (1).]

**prophecy,** *prof'i-si, n.* inspired or prophetic utterance: prediction: public interpretation of Scripture, or preaching (*obs.*). [O.Fr. *prophecie* — L. *prophētia* — Gr. *prophēteia* — *prophētēs,* prophet.]

**prophesy,** *prof'i-si, v.i.* to utter prophecies: to speak prophetically: to expound the Scriptures (*obs.*): to preach (*obs.*): to foretell the future. —*v.t.* to foretell:—*pa.t.* and *pa.p.* **proph'esied.**— *ns.* **proph'esier; proph'esying.** [A variant of prophecy.]

**prophet,** *prof'it, n.* a spokesman of deity: one who proclaims a divine message: an inspired teacher, preacher, or poet: the spokesman of a group, movement, or doctrine: a minister of the second order of the Catholic Apostolic Church: a foreteller, whether claiming to be inspired or not: a tipster:—*fem.* **proph'etess.**— *ns.* **proph'ethood, proph'etship.**—*adjs.* **prophetic** (*prə-fet'ik*), **-al.**—*adv.* **prophet'ically.**—*n.* **proph'- etism.**—former prophets, Joshua, Judges, Samuel, and Kings; latter prophets, the prophets properly so called; major prophets, the prophets whose books come before that of Hosea; minor prophets, the prophets from Hosea to Malachi; school of the prophets, a school among the ancient Jews for training young men as teachers of the people; the Prophet, Mahommed; the prophets, one of the three divisions into which the ancient Jews divided their Scriptures—consisting of the *former* and the *latter* prophets (see above). [Fr. *prophète*—L. *prophēta*—Gr. *prophētēs*—pro, for, *phanai,* to speak.]

**prophylactic,** *prof-i-lak'tik, adj.* guarding against disease.—*n.* a preventive of disease.—*n.* **prophylax'is** (not a Greek word), preventive treatment. [Gr. *prophylaktikos*—pro, before, *phylax,* a guard.]

**prophyll,** *prō'fil, (bot.) n.* a bracteole. [Pfx. pro- (1), Gr. *phyllon,* leaf.]

**propine,** *prə-pīn', (chiefly Scot., arch.) v.t.* to pledge in drinking: to present, offer.—*n.* a tip: a gift. [L. *propināre*—Gr. *propinein,* to drink first—pro, before, *pinein,* to drink.]

**propinquity,** *prə-ping'kwi-ti, n.* nearness. [L. *propinquitās, -ātis*—*propinquus,* near—*prope,* near.]

**propionic,** *prō-pi-on'ik,* acid, one of the fatty acids, $C_2H_5\cdot COOH$; the first of the series that yields derivatives of a fatty character. [Pfx. pro- (1), *pīōn, -on,* fat.]

**propitiate,** *prə-pish'i-āt, v.t.* to render favourable: to appease.—*adj.* **propi'tiable.**—*n.* **propitiā'tion,** act of propitiating: atonement: atoning sacrifice.—*adj.* **propi'tiātive.**—*n.* **propi'tiātor.**—*adv.* **propi'tiatorily** (-*shi-ə-tər-i-li*).—*adj.* **propi'tiatory,** propitiating: expiatory.—*n.* the Jewish mercyseat: a propitiation (*arch.*).—*adj.* **propitious** (-*pish'əs*), favourable: disposed to be gracious: of good omen.—*adv.* **propi'tiously.**—*n.* **propi'- tiousness.** [L. *propitiāre, -ātum,* to make favourable—*propitius,* well-disposed.]

**prop-jet,** *prop'-jet, (aero.) adj.* and *n.* (a jet aeroplane) having a turbine-driven propeller. [prop(eller) and jet.]

**propodeon,** *prō-pod'i-on, n.* in some Hymenoptera, the first abdominal segment, fused with the thorax and so in front of the waist.—Wrongly Latinised as **propod'eum.** [Pfx. pro- (1), Gr. *podeōn, -ōnos,* a wineskin neck.]

**propolis,** *prop'ə-lis, n.* bee-glue, a brown sticky

resinous substance gathered by bees from trees and used by them as cement and varnish. [Gr. *propolis.*]

**propone,** *prə-pōn', (now Scot.) v.t.* to put forward, propose, propound: to put before a court.—*adj.* **propōn'ent,** bringing forward, proposing: bringing an action.—*n.* a propounder or proposer: a favourer, advocate. [L. *prōpōnĕre* —*prō,* forward, *pōnĕre,* to place.]

**proportion,** *prə-pōr'shən, -pōr', n.* the relation of one thing to another in magnitude: fitness of parts to each other: due relation: relation of rhythm or of harmony: adjustment in due ratio (*Shak.*): ratio: the identity or equality of ratios (*math.*): the rule of three: equal or just share: relative share, portion, inheritance, contribution, quota, fortune: a part or portion (*coll.*): (in *pl.*) dimensions: form, figure (*obs.*). —*v.t.* to adjust or fashion in due proportion: to regulate the proportions of: to be in due proportion to (*Shak.*): to divide proportionally. —*adj.* **propor'tionable,** that may be proportioned: having a due or definite relation.—*n.* **propor'tionableness.**—*adv.* **propor'tionably.**—*adj.* **propor'- tional,** relating to proportion: in proportion: having the same or a constant ratio (*math.*): proportionate, in suitable proportion.—*n.* (*math.*) a number or quantity in a proportion.—*n.* **proportional'ity.**—*adv.* **propor'tionally.**—*adj.* **proportionate,** in fit proportion: proportional.— *v.t.* to adjust in proportion.—*adv.* **propor'tionately.**—*n.* **propor'tionateness.**—*adj.* **propor'tioned.** —*n.* **propor'tioning,** adjustment of proportions. —*adj.* **propor'tionless,** ill-proportioned.—*n.* **propor'tionment.**—**proportional representation,** a system intended to give parties in an elected body a representation as nearly as possible proportional to their voting strength: often loosely applied to the system of transferred vote. [L. *prōportiō, -ōnis*—prō, in comparison with, *portiō,* part, share.]

**propose,** *prə-pōz', v.t.* to put forward or exhibit (*obs.*): to put before one's own or another's mind: to propound: to face (*Shak.*): to imagine, suppose (*Shak.*): to offer for consideration or acceptance: to formulate as something to be exacted (*Shak.*): to proffer: to offer: to suggest or lay before one as something to be done: to purpose or intend: to move formally: to nominate: to invite the company to drink (a health): to enunciate.—*v.i.* to form or put forward an intention or design: to offer, especially marriage: to converse (*Shak.*).—*n.* a proposal (*obs.*): talk, discourse (*Shak.*).—*adj.* **propōs'able.**—*ns.* **propōs'al,** an act of proposing: an offer, esp. of marriage: a tender (*U.S.*): anything proposed: a plan; **propōs'er.** [Fr. *proposer*—pfx. *pro-, poser,* to place; see pose.]

**proposition,** *prop-ə-zish'ən, n.* an act of propounding or (more rarely) proposing: the thing propounded or proposed: an offer (*Shak.*): a question propounded (*Shak.*): a statement of a judgment: a form of statement in which a predicate is affirmed or denied of a subject (*log.*): a premise, esp. a major premise: a statement of a problem or theorem for (or with) solution or demonstration (*math.*): enunciation of a subject in a fugue (*mus.*): any situation, thing, or person considered as something to cope with, as an enterprise, job, opponent, etc. (*slang,* orig. *U.S.*).—*v.t.* to make a proposition to someone, esp. to solicit a woman for sexual relations. —*adj.* **proposi'tional.** [L. *prōpositiō, -ōnis*—prō, before; see position.]

**propound,** *prə-pownd', v.t.* to offer for consideration: to set forth as aim or reward: to purpose (*Spens.*): to produce for probate (*law*).—*n.* **pro-pound'er.** [propone.]

**propraetor,** *prō-prē'tər, -tör, prō-pri'tor, n.* a magistrate of ancient Rome, who, after acting as praetor in Rome, was appointed to the government of a province.—*adjs.* **propraetorial** (-tō´, -tö´ri-əl), **propraeto´rian**. [L. *prōpraetor*—*prō praetōre*, for the praetor.]

**proprietor**, *prō-prī´ə-tər*, *n.* an owner:—*fem.* **propri´etress**, **propri´etrix** (sham Latin).—*n.* **propri´etary**, an owner: a body of owners: ownership.—*adj.* of the nature of property: legally made only by a person or body of persons having special rights: owning property.—*adj.* **proprietorial** (-tō´, tö´ri-əl).—*adv.* **proprieto´rially.**—*n.* **propri´etorship.** [L.L. *proprietārius*—*proprius*, own; **proprietor** has been formed irregularly; it is not a Latin word.]

**propriety**, *prō-prī´ə-ti*, *n.* ownership (*obs.*): rightness, as in the use of words: appropriateness: seemliness: decency: conformity with good manners: conformity with convention in language and conduct: a character, quality, or property (*obs.*): particular nature, individuality (*Shak.*). [Fr. *propriété*—L. *proprietās*, *-ātis*—*proprius*, own.]

**proprioceptive**, *prō-pri-ō-sep´tiv*, *adj.* of, pertaining to, or made active by, stimuli arising from movement in the tissues.—*n.* **propriocep´tor**, a sensory nerve-ending receptive of such stimuli.—**proprioceptive sense**, the sense of muscular position. [L. *proprius*, own, after **receptive**.]

**proproctor**, *prō-prok´tər*, *n.* a proctor's substitute or assistant. [Pfx. **pro-** (2b).]

**proptosis**, *prop-tō´sis*, *n.* forward displacement, esp. of the eye. [Gr. *proptōsis*—*pro*, forward, *ptōsis*, fall.]

**propugnation**, *prō-pug-nā´shən*, (*Shak.*) *n.* defence. [L. *prō*, for, *pugnāre*, to fight.]

**propulsion**, *prə-pul´shən*, *n.* driving forward.—*adjs.* **propul´sive**, **propul´sory**. [L. *prōpellĕre*, *prōpulsum*, to push forward; see **propel**.]

**propyl**, *prō´pil*, *n.* the alcohol radical C₃H₇.—*ns.* **pro´pylamine**, an amine of propyl; **pro´pylene**, **propene**, a gaseous hydrocarbon (C₃H₆).—*adj.* **propyl´ic**. [**propionic** and Gr. *hylē*, matter.]

**propylaeum**, *prop-i-lē´əm*, **propylon**, *prop´i-lon*, *ns.* a gateway of architectural importance, leading into a temple, etc.:—*pl.* **propylae´a**, **prop´yla**.—*ns.* **prop´ylite**, an andesite altered by solfataric action, orig. applied to andesites of the beginning (or gateway) of the Tertiary time; **propylitisā´tion**, **-z.**—*v.t.* **prop´ylitise**, **-ize**. [Gr. *propylaion* (used in pl., *-a*) and *propylon*—*pro*, before, *pylē*, a gate.]

**prore**, *prōr*, *prör*, (*poet.*) *n.* a prow: a ship. [Obs. Fr.,—L. *prōra*, prow—Gr. *prōirā*.]

**prorector**, *prō-rek´tər*, *n.* a university or college rector's substitute or assistant. [Pfx. **pro-** (2b).]

**prorogue**, *prə-*, *prō-rōg´*, *v.t.* to prolong (*obs.*): to postpone (*Shak.*): perh., to keep from exertion (*Shak.*): to discontinue the meetings of for a time without dissolving.—*v.t.* **prō´rogāte**, to prorogue: to extend by agreement, in order to make a particular action competent (*Scots law*).—*n.* **prōrogā´tion**. [L. *prōrogāre*, *-ātum*—*prō*, forward, *rogāre*, to ask.]

**prosaic**, **-al**, *prō-zā´ik*, *-əl*, *adjs.* like prose: unpoetical: matter-of-fact: commonplace: dull: in or relating to prose (*rare*).—*adv.* **prosā´ically**.—*ns.* **prosā´icalness**; **prosā´icism** (*-sizm*), **pro´saism**; **prosā´icness**, quality of being prosaic; **prō´sāism**, a prose idiom: a prosaic phrase: prosaic character; **prō´sāist**, a writer of prose: a commonplace person. [L. *prōsa*, prose.]

**proscenium**, *prō-sē´ni-əm*, *n.* the front part of the stage: the curtain and its framework, esp. the arch that frames the more traditional type of stage (**proscenium arch**). [Latinised from Gr. *proskēnion*—*pro*, before, *skēnē*, stage.]

**proscribe**, *prō-skrīb´*, *v.t.* to put on the list of those who may be put to death: to outlaw: to ostracise: to prohibit: to denounce.—*ns.* **prō-**

**scrib´er**; **prō´script**, one who is proscribed; **prōscrip´tion**.—*adj.* **prōscrip´tive**.—*adv.* **prōscrip´tively**. [L. *prōscribĕre*—*prō-*, before, publicly, *scribĕre*, *scriptum*, to write.]

**prose**, *prōz*, *n.* ordinary spoken and written language with words in direct straightforward arrangement: all writings not in verse: a composition in prose (*obs.*, except as an exercise in Latin or Greek): a narrative (*obs.*): a piece of prosing: a familiar, gossipy, talk (*coll*; esp. formerly): (something having) prosaic character: a prosy talker.—*adj.* of or in prose: not poetical: plain: dull.—*v.i.* to write prose: to speak or write tediously.—*v.t.* to compose in prose: to turn into prose.—*n.* **prō´ser**.—*adv.* **prō´sily**.—*ns.* **prō´siness**; **prō´sing**, speaking or writing in a dull or prosy way.—*adj.* **prō´sy**, dull, tedious, humdrum: addicted to prosing.—**prose´-man** (*Pope*), **prose´man**, a writer of prose; **prose´-poem**, a prose work or passage having some of the characteristics of poetry; **prose´-writer**. [Fr.,—L. *prōsa*—*prorsus*, straightforward—*prō*, forward, *vertĕre*, *versum*, to turn.]

**prosector**, *prō-sekt´ər*, *n.* one who dissects a body for the illustration of anatomical lectures: the official anatomist of a zoological society.—*adj.* **prosecto´rial** (*-ōr´*, *-ör´i-əl*).—*n.* **prosec´torship**. [L.L. *prōsector*—*prōsecāre*, *-sectum*, to cut up—*prō-*, away, *secāre*, to cut.]

**prosecute**, *pros´i-kūt*, *v.t.* to follow onwards or pursue, in order to reach or accomplish: to engage in, practise: to follow up: to pursue, chase (*obs.*): to pursue by law: to bring before a court.—*v.i.* to carry on a legal prosecution.—*adj.* **pros´ecūtable**.—*ns.* **prosecū´tion**, the act of prosecuting in any sense: the prosecuting party in legal proceedings; **pros´ecūtor**, one who prosecutes or pursues any plan or business: one who carries on a civil or criminal suit:—*fem.* **pros´ecūtrix** (modern L.):—*pl.* **pros´ecūtrixes**, **prosecutrices** (*-kŭ-trī´sēz*, *-kŭ´tri-sēz*).—**public prosecutor**, one appointed to conduct criminal prosecutions in the public interest. [L. *prōsequī*, *-secūtus*—*prō*, onwards, *sequī*, to follow.]

**proselyte**, *pros´i-līt*, *n.* one who has come over from one religion or opinion to another: a convert, esp. from paganism to Judaism.—*v.t.* and *v.i.* (*U.S.*) to proselytise.—*v.t.* **pros´elytise**, **-ize**, to convert.—*v.i.* to make proselytes.—*ns.* **pros´elytiser**, **-izer**; **pros´elytism**, being, becoming, or making a convert: conversion.—**proselyte of the gate**, a heathen allowed to live in Palestine on making certain concessions to Judaism. [Gr. *prosēlytos*, a newcomer, resident foreigner—*pros*, to, and the stem *elyth-*, used to form aorists for *erchesthai*, to go.]

**prosencephalon**, *pros-en-sef´ə-lon*, *n.* the forebrain, comprising the cerebral hemispheres and olfactory processes.—*adj.* **prosencephalic** (*-si-fal´ik*). [Gr. *pros*, to, used as if for *pro*, before, *enkephalon*, brain—*en*, in, *kephalē*, head.]

**prosenchyma**, *pros-eng´ki-ma*, *n.* a plant-tissue of long cells with pointed ends—conducting or supporting tissue.—*adj.* **prosenchymatous** (*-kim´-ə-tas*). [Gr. *pros*, to, *enchyma*, an infusion, inpouring.]

**proseuche** (**-cha**), *pros-ū´kē* (*-ka*), *n.* a place of prayer, oratory:—*pl.* (L.) **proseu´chae** (*-kē*). [Gr. *proseuchē*, prayer, place of prayer—*pros*, to, *euchē*, prayer.]

**prosilient**, *prō-sil´i-ənt*, *adj.* outstanding.—*n.* **prosil´iency**. [L. *prōsiliēns*, *-entis*, pr.p. of *prōsilīre*, to leap forward—*prō-*, forward, *salīre*, to leap.]

**prosit**, *prō´sit*, *interj.* good luck to you, a salutation in drinking healths customary among German students. [L. *prōsit*, used as 3rd pers. sing. pres. subj. of L. *prōdesse*, to be of use—*prō(d)-*, for, *esse*, to be.]

**proslambanomenos**, *pros-lam-ban-om'e-nos*, (*anc. Gr. mus.*) *n.* an additional note at the bottom of the scale. [Gr., pr.p. pass. of *proslambanein*, to take in addition—pfx. *pros-, lambanein*, to take.]

**prosody**, *pros'ə-di, n.* the study of versification. —*adjs.* **prosodial** (*pros-, prəs-ō'di-əl*), **prcsodic** (*-od'ik*), **-al.**—*ns.* **prosō'dian, pros'odist**, one skilled in prosody.—*adv.* **prosod'ically.** [L. *prosōdia*, Gr. *prosōidiā—pros*, to, *ōidē*, a song.]

**prosopopoeia**, *pros-ō-pō-pē'ya, n.* personification. [Gr. *prosōpopoiiā—prosōpon*, face, person, *poieein*, to make.]

**prospect**, *pros'pekt, n.* outlook: direction of facing: a look-out or view-point (*Milt.*): a wide view: view, sight, field of view: a scene: a pictorial representation, view: position for being observed (*Shak.*): a survey or mental view: outlook upon the probable future: expectation: chance of success: a wide street (*Russ.* pros-pekt'): a prospect-glass (*obs.*): a probable customer (*U.S.*): a place thought likely to yield a valuable mineral (*mining*): a sample, or a test, or the yield of a test of a sample from such a place: a probable source of profit.—*v.i.* **prospect'**, to look around: (*prəs-pekt'*; *U.S.* pros') to make a search, esp. for chances of mining: to promise or yield results to the prospector.—*v.t.* (*-pekt'*) to face, view: (*-pekt'*; *pros'pekt*) to explore, search, survey, or test for profitable minerals.—*ns.* **prospect'ing** (*U.S.* pros'), searching a district for minerals with a view to further operations; **prospec'tion**, looking to the future: foresight.—*adj.* **prospec'tive**, probable or expected future: looking forward: yielding distant views: looking to the future.—*n.* prospect.—*adv.* **prospec'tively.**—*ns.* **prospec'tiveness**; **prospec'tor** (*U.S.* pros'), one who prospects for minerals; **prospec'tus**, the outline of any plan submitted for public approval, particularly of a literary work or of a joint-stock concern: an account of the organisation of a school:—*pl.* **prospec'tuses.**—**pros'pect-glass**, a telescope or field glass; **prospect'ive-glass**, a prospect-glass: a scrying crystal. [L. *prōspectus, -ūs—prōspicĕre, prōspectum—prō-*, forward, *specĕre*, to look.]

**prosper**, *pros'pər, v.i.* to thrive: to get on: to experience favourable circumstances: to flourish: to turn out well.—*v.t.* to cause to prosper.—*n.* **prosperity** (*-per'i-ti*), the state of being prosperous: success: good fortune.—*adj.* **pros'perous**, thriving: successful.—*adv.* **pros'perously.**—*n.* **pros'perousness.** [L. *prosper, prosperus.*]

**prostate**, *pros'tāt, n.* a gland in males at the neck of the bladder.—Also **prostate gland.**—*adj.* **prostatic** (*pros-tat'ik*).—*ns.* **pros'tatism** (*-tət-izm*), a morbid condition associated with enlargement of the prostate; **prostati'tis**, inflammation of the prostate gland. [Gr. *prostatēs*, one who stands in front, the prostate—*pro*, before, *sta*, root of *histanai*, to set up.]

**prosthesis**, *pros'thə-sis, n.* addition as a prefix: the fitting of artificial parts to the body.—*adj.* **prosthetic** (*-thet'ik*), pertaining to a group or radical of different nature, as a non-protein part of a protein molecule.—*n.* an artificial part of the body.—*n.* **prosthet'ics**, the surgery or dentistry involved in supplying artificial parts to the body. [Gr. *prosthesis*, adj. *prosthetikos—pros*, to, *thesis*, putting.]

**prosthodontia**, *pros-thō-don'shi-a, n.* provision of false teeth. [Gr. *prosthesis*, addition—*pros*, to, *thesis*, putting, and *odous, odontos*, tooth.]

**prostitute**, *pros'ti-tūt, v.t.* to devote to, or offer or sell for, evil or base use: to hire out for indiscriminate sexual intercourse: to devote to such intercourse as a religious act: to degrade by publicity or commonness.—*adj.* openly devoted to lewdness: given over (to evil): basely

**venal**: hackneyed, debased by commonness (*obs.*).—*n.* a common harlot or whore: a base hireling.—*ns.* **prostitū'tion**, the act or practice of prostituting: devotion to base purposes; **pros'-titūtor.** [L. *prōstituĕre, -ūtum*, to set up for sale —*prō*, before, *statuĕre*, to place.]

**prostomium**, *prō-stō'mi-əm, n.* part of a worm's head in front of the mouth.—*adj.* **prosto'mial.** [Gr. *pro*, before, *stoma*, mouth.]

**prostrate**, *pros'trāt, adj.* prone: lying or bent with face on the ground: loosely, lying at length: procumbent, trailing (*bot.*): lying at mercy: reduced to helplessness: completely exhausted. —*v.t.* **prostrate'** (or *pros'*), to throw forwards on the ground: to lay flat: to overthrow: to reduce to impotence or exhaustion: to bend in humble reverence.—*n.* **prostrā'tion.** [L. *prō-strātus*, pa.p. of *prōsternĕre—prō*, forwards, *sternĕre*, to spread.]

**prostyle**, *prō'stil*, (*Gr. archit.*) *n.* a front portico of not more than four columns, without *antae*: a building with such a portico and no other.— —*adj.* having a prostyle. [Gr. *prostylon—pro*, before, *stylos*, a column.]

**prosy.** See prose.

**prosyllogism**, *prō-sil'ə-jizm, n.* a syllogism whose conclusion becomes the major premise of another. [Gr. *pro*, before, *syllogismos*, syllogism.]

**protactinium**, *prōt-ak-tin'i-əm, n.* radioactive element (at. numb. 91) that yields actinium on disintegration. [Gr. *prōtos*, first, and **actinium.**]

**protagonist**, *prō-tag'ən-ist, n.* the chief actor, character, or combatant: loosely, a champion, advocate. [Gr. *prōtos*, first, *agōnistēs*, a combatant, actor.]

**protandry**, *prōt-an'dri, n.* in hermaphrodite organisms, ripening and shedding of the male elements before the female is ready to receive them: in flowers, opening of the anthers before the stigmas can receive pollen—opp. to *protogyny.*—*adj.* **protan'drous.** [Gr. *prōtos*, first, *anēr, andros*, man, male.]

**protanopic**, *pro-tən-op'ik, adj.* colour-blind to red. [Mod. L. *protanopia.*]

**protasis**, *prot'ə-sis, n.* the conditional clause of a conditional sentence—opp. to *apodosis*: the first part of a dramatic composition.—*adj.* **protatic** (*pra-tat'ik*). [Gr. *protasis*, proposition, premise, *protasis—pro*, before, *tasis*, a stretching, *teinein*, to stretch.]

**Protea**, *prō'ti-a, n.* a large South African genus of shrubs or small trees, of the mainly Australian family **Protea'ceae**, with big cone-shaped heads of flowers: a plant of the genus.—*adj.* **proteā'ceous.** [Proteus; from the varied character of the family.]

**Protean, protean** See Proteus.

**protect**, *pra-, prō-tekt', v.t.* to shield from danger, injury, change, capture, loss: to defend: to strengthen: to seek to foster by import duties: to act as regent for (*Shak.*): to screen off for safety (e.g. machinery).—*adjs.* **protect'ed;** **protect'ing,**—*adv.* **protect'ingly.**—*ns.* **protec'tion**, act of protecting: state of being protected: defence: that which protects: guard: a writing guaranteeing against molestation or interference: a fostering of home produce and manufactures by import duties: patronage: concubinage: control of a country's foreign relations, and sometimes internal affairs, without annexation; **protec'tionism**; **protec'tionist**, one who favours the protection of trade by duties on imports—also *adj.*—*adj.* **protec'tive**, affording protection: intended to protect: defensive: sheltering.—*n.* that which protects.—*adv.* **protec'tively.**—*ns.* **protec'tiveness; protec'tor**, one who protects from injury or oppression: a protective device: a means of protection: a guard: a guardian: a regent: the head of the state during the Commonwealth (*Lord Protector*):—*fem.* **protec'tress,**

protec′trix.—*adj.* protec′toral, of a protector or a regent.—*n.* protec′torāte, the position, office, term of office, or government of a protector: (*cap.*) the Commonwealth period (*hist.*): guardianship: authority over a vassal state: relation assumed by a state over a territory which it administers without annexation and without admitting the inhabitants to citizenship. —*adjs.* protectorial (*prō-tek-tōr′i-əl, -tōr′i-əl*); protec′torless.—*ns.* protec′torship; protec′tory, an institution for destitute or delinquent children. —protected state, a state under the protection of another state but less subject to the control of that state than a protectorate; protection money, money extorted from shopkeepers, businessmen, etc., as a bribe for leaving their property, business, etc., unharmed; protective coloration, likeness in the colour of animals to their natural surroundings tending to prevent them from being seen by their enemies; protective custody, detention of a person for his personal safety or from doubt as to his possible actions. [L. *prōtegĕre, -tēctum—prō-*, in front, *tegĕre*, to cover.]

protégé, *prō′*, or *pro′tā-zhā, n.* one under the protection or patronage of another: a pupil: a ward:—*fem.* protégée (*-zhā*). [Fr.,—pa.p. of *protéger*, to protect—L. *prōtegĕre*.]

proteiform. See Proteus.

protein, *prō′tē-in, -tēn, n.* any member of a group of complex nitrogenous substances that play an important part in the bodies of plants and animals, compounds of carbon, hydrogen, oxygen, nitrogen, usually sulphur, often phosphorus, etc., easily hydrolysed into mixtures of amino-acids.—*ns.* pro′tease (*-tē-ās, -āz*), any enzyme that splits up proteins; pro′teid (*-tē-id*), an abandoned name for protein.—*adjs.* proteinic (*prō-tēn′ik*), protein′ous.—*n.* proteolysis (*-ol′i-sis*), splitting of proteins by enzymes.—*v.t.* pro′teolyse, -yze (*-ō-līz*).—*adj.* proteolytic (*-ō-lit′ik*). [Gr. *prōteios*, primary—*prōtos*, first.]

protend, *prō-tend′, v.t.* to stretch forth: to hold out.—*ns.* protense′ (*Spens.*), extension in time; proten′sion, duration; proten′sity.—*adj.* proten′sive. [L. *prōtendĕre, -tentus (-tēnsus)—prō-*, forward, *tendĕre*, to stretch.]

proterandry, *prot-ər-an′dri*, or *prōt-, n.* protandry. —*adj.* proteran′drous. [Gr. *proteros*, earlier, *anēr, andros*, man, male.]

proterogyny, *prot-, prōt-ər-oj′i-ni*, or *-og′, n.* protogyny.—*adj.* proterog′ynous. [Gr. *proteros*, earlier, *gynē*, woman, female.]

Proterozoic, *prot-ər-ō-zō′ik*, or *prōt-, n.* and *adj.* orig., Lower Palaeozoic (Cambrian to Silurian): Pre-Cambrian: Upper Pre-Cambrian. [Gr. *proteros*, earlier, *zōē*, life.]

protervity, *prō-tûr′vi-ti, n.* peevishness: perversity: wantonness. [L. *prōtervus, prōtervus.*]

protest, *prə-, prō-test′, v.i.* to express or record dissent or objection: to make solemn affirmation, professions, or avowal.—*v.t.* to make a solemn declaration of: to declare: to note, as a bill of exchange, on account of non-acceptance or non-payment: to proclaim (*Shak.*): to vow (*Shak.*): to call to witness (*Milt.*): to make a protest against.—*ns.* prō′test, an affirmation or avowal: a declaration of objection or dissent: the noting by a notary-public of an unpaid or unaccepted bill: a written declaration, usually by the master of a ship, stating the circumstances attending loss or injury of ship or cargo, etc.; Protestant, *prot′is-tənt*, one of those who, in 1529, protested against an edict of Charles V and the Diet of Spires denouncing the Reformation: a member, adherent, or sharer of the beliefs of one of those churches founded by the Reformers (formerly by some confined to Anglicans or Lutherans, now disavowed by some Anglicans): (without *cap.*) an avowed

lover (*Herrick*): (without *cap.*; sometimes *prō-tes′tənt*) one who protests.—*adj.* Protestant (*prot′*), of, or pertaining to, Protestants, or more usually, Protestantism: (without *cap.*; *prot′is-*, or *prō-tes′tant*), protesting.—*v.t.* Prot′estantise, -ize.—*ns.* Prot′estantism, the Protestant religion: state of being a Protestant; protestation (*prō-tes-tā′shən*), an avowal: an asseveration: a declaration in pleading: a protest (*rare*); protest′er, -or, one who protests, esp. (*Scot. hist.*) a Remonstrant or opponent of the Resolutioners. —*adv.* protest′ingly. [Fr. *protester*—L. *prō-testāri, -ātus*, to bear witness in public—*prō*, before, *testāri—testis*, a witness.]

Proteus, *prō′tūs, n.* an ancient Greek sea-god who assumed many shapes to evade having to foretell the future: a European genus of cave-dwelling tailed amphibians with persistent gills. —*adjs.* Protean, protean, readily assuming different shapes: variable: inconstant; proteiform, *prō-tē′i-fôrm.* [Gr. *Prōteus.*]

Protevangelium, *prōt-ev-an-jel′i-əm, n.* the promise to Eve: a gospel attributed to James the Less: an inferred source of the canonical gospels. [Gr. *prōtos*, first, L. *evangelium*—Gr. *euangelion*, gospel.]

prothalamion, *prō-thə-lā′mi-on, n.* a poem celebrating a coming marriage. [App. coined by Spenser from Gr. *pro*, before, *thalamos*, a bride-chamber.]

prothallus, *prō-thal′əs*, prothallium, *-i-əm, ns.* the gametophyte or sexual generation in ferns and their allies, a small plate of tissue derived from a spore and bearing antheridia and archegonia: the homologous stage in gymnosperms:—*pl.* prothall′i, prothall′ia.—*adjs.* prothall′ial, prothall′oid. [Gr. *pro*, before, *thallos*, a young shoot.]

prothesis, *proth′i-sis, n.* in the Greek Church the preliminary oblation of the eucharistic elements before the liturgy: the table used: the chapel or northern apse where it stands: development of an inorganic initial sound (*gram.*).—*adj.* prothetic (*prə-, prō-thet′ik*). [Gr. *prothesis—pro*, before, and the root of *tithenai*, to place.]

prothonotary, protonotary, *prō-t(h)on′ət-ə-ri, prō-t(h)ō-nō′tə-ri, n.* a chief notary or clerk: a chief secretary of the chancery at Rome: a chief clerk or registrar of a court.—*adj.* prot(h)o-notā′rial.—*n.* prot(h)onotā′riat, the college constituted by the twelve apostolical prothonotaries in Rome. [L.L. *prōt(h)onotārius*—Gr. *prōtos*, first, L. *notārius*, a clerk.]

prothorax, *prō-thō′raks, -thôr′, n.* the anterior segment of the thorax of insects.—*adj.* prothoracic (*-ras′*). [Pfx. pro- (1).]

prothyl(e). See protyle.

Protista, *prō-tis′ta, n.pl.* a large group of unicellular organisms on the border-line between plants and animals: a proposed term for a biological kingdom including Protozoa and Protophyta:—*sing.* pro′tist.—*adj.* protist′ic.—*ns.* protistol′ogist; protistol′ogy. [Gr. *prōtistos*, very first—*prōtos*, first.]

protium, *prō′ti-əm, -shi-əm, n.* ordinary hydrogen of atomic weight 1, distinguished from deuterium and tritium. [Gr. *prōtos*, first.]

proto-, *prō′tō-*, prot-, *prōt-*, in composition, first: first of a series: first-formed: primitive: ancestral. [Gr. *prōtos*, first.]

protoactinium, *prō-tō-ak-tin′i-əm, n.* a former variant of protactinium.

Protococcus, *prō-tō-kok′əs, n.* an abandoned genus of rounded unicellular algae, one of which is named *Pleurococcus vulgaris* forms a green film common on trees, etc.—*adj.* protococc′al.—*n.pl.* Protococcales (*-ā′lēz*), the order of green algae to which *Pleurococcus vulgaris* belongs. [proto-, and Gr. *kokkos*, a berry.]

protocol, *prō′tō-kol, n.* an original note, minute, or

draft of an instrument or transaction: a draft treaty: an official or formal account or record: a record of transfer of lands (*U.S.*): an official formula: a body of diplomatic etiquette.—*v.i.* to issue, form, protocols.—*v.t.* to make a protocol of:—*pr.p.* pro'tocolling; *pa.t.* and *pa.p.* pro'tocolled.—Also prō'tocolise, -ize.—*n.* prō'tocolist, a registrar or clerk. [Fr. *protocole*—L.L. *prōtocollum*—Late Gr. *prōtokollon*, a glued-on descriptive first leaf of a MS.—Gr. *prōtos*, first, *kolla*, glue.]

protogine, *prō'tō-jin, -jēn, n.* a gneissose granite of the Alps with sericite. [Gr. *prōtos*, first, *ginesthai*, to come into being (as once thought to be the first-formed granite).]

protogyny, *prōt-oj'i-ni,* or *-og', n.* in hermaphrodite organisms, ripening of the female germ-cells before stamens.—opp. to *protandry*.—*adj.* protog'ynous. [proto-, and Gr. *gynē*, woman, female.]

proto-historic, *prō-tō-his-tor'ik, adj.* belonging to the earliest age of history, just after the prehistoric.—*n.* proto-his'tory. [proto-.]

protomartyr, *prō'tō-mär-tər, n.* the first martyr in any cause, esp. St Stephen. [Late Gr. *prōtomartyr*.]

proton, *prō'ton, n.* an elementary particle of positive charge and unit atomic mass—the atom of the lightest isotope of hydrogen without its electron.—*adj.* protonic (*-ton'ik*).—proton synchrotron (see accelerator). [Gr., neut. of *prōtos*, first.]

protonema, *prō-tə-nē'mə, n.* a branched filament produced by germination of a moss spore, giving rise to moss-plants from buds. [proto-, and Gr. *nēma*, thread.]

protonotary. Same as prothonotary.

Protophyta, *prōt-of'i-ta, n.pl.* the unicellular plants:—*sing.* protophyte (*prō'tə-fīt*).—*adj.* protophytic (*-fit'ik*). [proto-, and Gr. *phyton*, a plant.]

protoplasm, *prō'tə-plazm, n.* living matter, the physical basis of life.—*adj.* protoplasm'ic.—*n.* prō'toplast, he who, or that which, was first formed: an original: the first parent: an energid (*biol.*).—*adj.* protoplas'tic. [proto-, and Gr. *plasma*, form—*plassein*, to form.]

protospatharius, *prō-tə-spä-thā'ri-əs, n.* captain of the guards at Byzantium.—Also (*Fr.*) protospat(h)aire (*-thär', -tär'*). [Gr. *prōtos*, first, *spathārios*, a guardsman—*spathē*, a blade.]

Prototheria, *prō-tə-thē'ri-a, n.pl.* the monotremes. [proto-, and Gr. *thēr*, wild beast.]

Prototracheata, *prō-tə-trak-i-ä'ta, n.pl.* a class of primitive tracheate arthropods to which Peripatus belongs. [proto-; see trachea.]

prototype, *prō'tə-tīp, n.* the first or original type or model from which anything is copied: an exemplar: a pattern: an ancestral form.—*adjs.* pro'totypal, prototypical (*-tip'*). [Fr.,—Gr. *prōtos*, first, *typos*, a type.]

protoxide, *prō-tok'sīd, n.* that oxide of a series which has the smallest number of oxygen atoms. [proto-.]

Protozoa, *prō-tō-zō'a, n.pl.* the lowest and simplest of animals, unicellular forms or colonies multiplying by fission:—*sing.* protozō'on.—*n.* and *adj.* protozō'an.—*adjs.* protozō'ic, pertaining to the Protozoa: containing remains of the earliest life of the globe (variously applied) (*obs. geol.*); protozoolog'ical (*-zō-ə-*).—*ns.* protozool'ogist; protozool'ogy. [proto-, and Gr. *zōion*, an animal.]

protract, *prō-trakt', v.t.* to draw out or lengthen in time: to prolong: to put off in time (*obs.*): to lengthen out: to protrude: to draw to scale.—*adj.* protrac'ted, drawn out in time: prolonged: postponed (*obs.*): lengthened out: drawn to scale. —*adv.* protrac'tedly.—*adj.* protrac'tile (*-til,* in U.S. *-til*), susceptible of being thrust out.—*n.*

protrac'tion (*-shən*), act of protracting or prolonging: the delaying of the termination of a thing: the plotting or laying down of the dimensions of anything on paper: a plan drawn to' scale.—*adj.* protrac'tive, drawing out in time: prolonging: delaying.—*n.* protrac'tor, one who, or that which, protracts: an instrument for laying down angles on paper: a muscle whose contraction draws a part forward or away from the body. [L. *prōtrahĕre, -tractum*—prō, forth, *trahĕre*, to draw.]

protreptic, *prō-trep'tik, adj.* hortative.—*n.* an exhortation.—*adj.* protrep'tical. [Gr. *protreptikos* —*pro*, forward, *trepein*, to turn, direct.]

protrude, *prō-trōōd', v.t.* to thrust or push out or forward: to obtrude.—*v.i.* to stick out, project. —*adjs.* protrud'able, protru'sible (*-trōōs'i-bl*), protru'sile (*-sil,* in U.S. *-sil*), able to be protruded. —*n.* protru'sion (*-zhən*), the act of protruding: the state of being protruded: that which protrudes.—*adj.* protru'sive, thrusting or impelling forward: protruding.—*adv.* protru'sively.—*n.* protru'siveness. [L. *prōtrūdĕre, -trūsum*—prō, forward, *trūdĕre*, to thrust.]

protuberance, *prō-tūb'ər-əns, n.* a bulging out: a swelling.—*adj.* protū'berant.—*adv.* protū'berantly.—*v.i.* protū'berate, to bulge out.—*n.* protūberā'tion. [L. *prōtūberāre, -ātum*—prō, forward, *tūber*, a swelling.]

protyle, prothyle, *prō't(h)il,* prothyl, *prō'thil, n.* a hypothetical primitive matter from which the chemical elements have been thought to be formed. [Gr. *prōtos*, first, *hȳlē*, matter.]

proud, *prowd, adj.* having excessive self-esteem: arrogant: haughty: having a proper sense of self-respect: having an exulting sense of credit due to or reflected upon oneself: having a glowing feeling of gratification: giving reason for pride or boasting: manifesting pride: having an appearance of pride, vigour, boldness, and freedom: stately: mettlesome: swelling: sexually excited (esp. of some female animals).— *adj.* proud'ish, somewhat proud.—*adv.* proud'ly. —*n.* proud'ness (*rare*), pride.—proud'-flesh, a growth or excrescence of flesh in a wound.— *adjs.* proud'-heart'ed (*Shak.*), having a proud spirit: proud'-mind'ed (*Shak.*), proud in mind; proud'-pied (*Shak.*), gorgeously variegated; proud'-stom'ached, of haughty spirit, arrogant.— do one proud (*coll.*), to treat one sumptuously. [O.E. *prūd, prūt,* proud; perh. from a L.L. word connected with L. *prōdesse*, to be of advantage.]

proul, prouler. Earlier forms of prowl, prowler.

Proustian, *prōōs'ti-ən, adj.* pertaining to Marcel Proust (1871-1922), French novelist.—*n.* an admirer of Proust.

proustite, *prōōs'tit, n.* a red silver ore, sulphide of arsenic and silver. [J. L. *Proust* (1754-1826), French chemist, who distinguished it from pyrargyrite.]

provand, provend, *prov'ənd,* proviant, *prov'i-ənt, n.* an allowance of food: provender (*Shak.*): provisions: fodder.—*adj.* prov'ant, issued to soldiers, hence inferior. [M.L.G. *provande,* Du. *provande,* Ger. *proviant,* app.—L.L. *provande, proviand,* Ger. *proviant,* app.—L.L. *provenda* for L. *praebenda*—*praebēre,* to allow.]

prove, *prōōv, v.t.* to test, experience, suffer: to test the genuineness of: to ascertain: to establish or ascertain as truth by argument or otherwise: to demonstrate: to check by the opposite operation (*arith.*): to obtain probate of: to cause or allow (dough) to rise.—*v.i.* to make trial: to turn out: to be shown afterwards: to become (*arch.*): to turn out well (*obs.*): (of dough) to rise:—*pa.p.* proved.—Also (*obs.*) proven.—*Also (obs.)* preve, with *pa.p.,* prov'en, surviving as the usu. form in U.S. (*prōōv'n*) and becoming commoner in Britain; already retained specif. for *Scots law* (*prōv'n*); also *pa.p.* pree (*Scot.*).—*adj.* prov'-able (or prove').—*adv.* prov(e)'ably.—*n.* prov'er.—

**proving ground**, a place for testing scientifically: also *fig.*—**the exception proves the rule**, the making of an exception proves that the rule holds good otherwise. [O.Fr. *prover*—L. *probāre—probus*, excellent; partly perh.—O.E. *prōfian*, to assume to be L. *probāre*. O.Fr. had two forms of the verb, using respectively the vowel developed orig. in stressed, unstressed (as above), positions from L. *o*, and M.E. also has two forms, giving **preeve**, etc., as well as **prove**.

**proveditor**, *prō-ved′i-tər*, **provedor(e)**, **providor**, *prov-i-dōr′*, *-dör′*, *n.* a high official, governor, inspector, commissioner: a purveyor. [It. *provveditore*, Port. *provedor*, Sp. *provee.lor*.]

**proven**, *prōv′n*, *prōōv′n*. See **prove**.—**not proven**, a verdict declaring that guilt has been neither proved nor disproved.

**provenance**, *prov′i-nəns*, *n.* source. [Fr.,—L. *prō-*, forth, *venire*, to come.]

**Provençal**, *prov-ä-säl*, *adj.* of or pertaining to *Provence*, in France, or to its inhabitants or language.—*n.* a native or the language of Provence, *langue d'oc*. [L. *prōvinciālis—prōvincia*, province.]

**provender**, *prov′in-dər*, *-ən-dər*, *n.* food: dry food for beasts, as hay or corn: esp. a mixture of meal and cut straw or hay.—*v.t.* and *v.i.* to feed. [O.Fr. *provendre* for *provende*—L.L. *provenda*; see **provand**.]

**provenience**, *prō-vē′ni-əns*, *n.* provenance. [L. *prōvenire*; see **provenance**.]

**proverb**, *prov′ərb*, *n.* a short familiar sentence expressing a supposed truth or moral lesson: a byword: a saying that requires explanation (*B.*): (in *pl.* with *cap.*) a book of maxims in the Old Testament: (in *pl.* with *cap.*) a dramatic composition in which a proverb gives name and character to the plot.—*v.t.* to speak of proverbially: make a byword of: to provide with a proverb.—*adj.* **prover′bial** (*prə-vûr′bi-əl*), like or of the nature of a proverb: expressed or mentioned in a proverb: notorious.—*v.t.* **prover′bialise**, **-ize**, to speak in proverbs.—*ns.* **prover′bialism**, a saying in the form of, or like, a proverb; **prover′bialist**—*adv.* **prover′bially**. [Fr. *proverbe*—L. *prōverbium—prō-*, publicly, *verbum*, a word.]

**provide**, *prə-*, *prō-vīd′*, *v.t.* to make ready beforehand: to prepare for future use: to supply: to appoint or give a right to a benefice, esp. before it is actually vacant: to stipulate.—*v.i.* to procure supplies, means, or whatever may be desirable, make provision: to take measures. —*adj.* **provi′dable**.—*pa.p.* or *conj.* **provi′ded**, (often with *that*) on condition: upon these terms: with the understanding.—*n.* **provi′der.**—**provided school**, in England and Wales, a school maintained by, and under the management of, the local authority. [L. *prōvidēre—prō*, before, *vidēre*, to see.]

**providence**, *prov′i-dəns*, *n.* foresight: prudent management and thrift: timely preparation: the foresight and benevolent care of God (*theol.*): God, considered in this relation (usu. with *cap.*) (*theol.*): an ordering or intervention by God for this purpose (*theol.*): an occurrence attributed to God's ordering or intervention (*theol.*): a disaster (*U.S.*).—*adjs.* **prov′ident**, seeing beforehand, and providing for the future: prudent: thrifty: frugal; **providential** (*-den′shl*), affected by, or proceeding from, divine providence: provident (*rare*).—*advs.* **providen′tially**; **prov′idently**. [L. *prōvidēns, -entis*, pr.p. of *prōvidēre—prō*, before, *vidēre*, to see.]

**province**, *prov′ins*, *n.* a portion of an empire or a state marked off for purposes of government or in some way historically distinct: the district over which an archbishop has jurisdiction: a territorial division of the Jesuits, Templars, and other orders: a faunal or floral area: a region:

vaguely, a field of duty, activity, or knowledge: a department: (in *pl.*) all parts of the country but the capital (esp. *theat.* and *journalism*).—*adj.* **provincial** (*prə-vin′shl*), relating to a province: belonging to a province or the provinces: local: showing the habits and manners of a province: unpolished: narrow.—*n.* an inhabitant of a province or country district: the superintendent of the heads of the religious houses in a province (*R.C.*).—*v.t.* **provin′cialise**, **-ize**, to render provincial.—*ns.* **provin′cialism**, a manner, a mode of speech, or a turn of thought peculiar to a province or a country district: a local expression: state or quality of being provincial: ignorance and narrowness of interests shown by one who gives his attention entirely to local affairs; **provinciality** (*-shi-al′i-ti*).—*adv.* **provin′-cially**. [Fr.,—L. *prōvincia*, an official charge, hence a province.]

**provincial-rose**, *prə-vin′shl-rōz′*, *n.* the cabbage rose, cultivated at *Provins* in Seine-et-Marne, France: a shoe rosette (*Shak.*).

**provine**, *prə-vīn′*, *v.t.* and *v.i.* to propagate by layering. [Fr. *provigner*—O.Fr. *provain*—L. *prōpāgō, -inis*, a slip, layer.]

**provision**, *prə-vizh′ən*, *n.* act of providing: that which is provided or prepared: measures taken beforehand: a clause in a law or a deed: a stipulation: a rule for guidance: an appointment by the pope to a benefice not yet vacant: preparation: previous agreement: a store or stock: (commonly in *pl.*) store of food: (in *pl.*) food.—*v.t.* to supply with provisions or food.—*adj.* **provi′sional**, provided for the occasion: to meet necessity: (of e.g. arrangement) adopted on the understanding that it will probably be changed later: containing a provision.—*adv.* **provi′sionally**.—*adj.* **provi′sionary** (*rare*), provisional.—**provisional judgment**, a judgment given as far as the available evidence admits, but subject to correction under more light; **provisional order**, an order granted by a secretary of state, which, when confirmed by the legislature, has the force of an act of parliament; **provisional remedy**, a means of detaining in safety a person or property until a decision upon some point in which they are concerned be come to; **provision merchant**, a general dealer in articles of food. [Fr.,—L. *prōvisiō, -ōnis—prōvidēre*; see **provide**.]

**proviso**, *prə-*, *prō-vī′zō*, *n.* a provision or condition in a deed or other writing: the clause containing it: any condition:—*pl.* **provisos** (*-zōz*).—*adv.* **provi′sorily** (*-zə-ri-li*).—*adj.* **provi′sory**, containing a proviso or condition: conditional: making provision for the time: temporary. [From the L. law phrase *prōvisō quod*, it being provided that.]

**provisor**, *prə-*, *prō-vī′zər*, *n.* one who provides: a purveyor: a person to whom the pope has granted the right to the next vacancy in a benefice.—**Statute of Provisors**, an act of the English parliament passed in 1351 to prevent the pope from exercising the power of creating provisors. [L. *prōvisor, -ōris*, provider.]

**provitamin**, *prō-vīt′ə-min*, *-vit′*, *n.* a substance not a vitamin that is readily transformed into a vitamin within an organism. [L. *prō*, before, and **vitamin**.]

**provocable**, etc. See **provoke**.

**provoke**, *prə-vōk′*, *v.t.* to call forth, evoke (feelings, desires, etc.): to summon (*arch.*): to call out, challenge (*obs.*): excite or call into action, stimulate: to incite, bring about: to excite with anger or sexual desire: to annoy, exasperate.—*v.i.* (*Dryden*) to appeal.—*adj.* **provocable** (*prov′ək-ə-bl*).—*ns.* **prov′ocant**; **provocā′tion**, act of provoking: that which provokes: any cause of danger.—*adj.* **provocative** (*-vok′*), tending, or designed, to provoke or excite.—*n.* anything that provokes.—*adv.* **provoc′atively.**—

*ns.* **provoc'ativeness**; **prov'ocātor.**—*adjs.* **provoc'atory**; **provōk'able** (older spelling -vōc'-).—*ns.* **provoke'ment** (*Spens.*); **provōk'er.**—*adj.* **provōk'ing**, irritating.—*adv.* **provōk'ingly.** [L. *prōvocāre*, -*ātum*—*prō*-, forth, *vocāre*, to call.]

**provost**, *prov'əst*, *n.* the dignitary set over a cathedral or collegiate church: in certain colleges, the head: in Scotland, the chief magistrate of a burgh, answering to mayor in England: an officer who arrests and keeps in custody (*Shak.*).—*ns.* **prov'ostry**, the office or authority of a provost; **prov'ostship**, the office of a provost.—**provost-mar'shal**(*prə-*vō'; U.S.*prō'*),head of military police, an officer with special powers for enforcing discipline and securing prisoners until trial (*army*): officer (master-at-arms) having charge of prisoners (*navy*); **provost-ser'-geant** (*prə-*vō'), sergeant of military police.— **Lord Provost**, chief magistrate of Edinburgh, Glasgow, Perth, Aberdeen, or Dundee; **Lady Provost**, the wife (or other female relative) of a Lord Provost as supporting him in certain of his official duties. [O.E. *profast* (*prafost*), O.Fr. *provost* (Fr. *prévôt*)—L.L. *prōpositus*—*prō*- for *prae*, at the head, *positus*, set.]

**prow**, *prow*, formerly sometimes *prō*, *n.* the forepart of a ship: the nose of an aeroplane: a projecting front part: a ship (*poet.*). [Fr. *proue*, or Port., Span., or Genoese *proa*—L. *prōra*—Gr. *prōirā*.]

**prow**, *prow*, *adj.* (*arch.*) valiant:—*superl.* **prow'est.** —*n.* **prow'ess**, bravery: valour: daring: accomplishment.—*adj.* **prow'essed.** [O.Fr. *prou* (Fr. *preux*); conn. with L. *prōd*- in *prōdesse*.]

**prowl**, *prowl*, earlier *prōl*, *v.i.* to keep moving about as if in search of something: to rove in search of prey or plunder.—*n.* the act of prowling: a roving for prey.—*n.* **prowl'er.**—*n.* and *adj.* **prowl'ing.** —*adv.* **prowl'ingly.**—**prowl car** (chiefly *U.S.*), a police patrol car.—**on the prowl**, occupied in prowling. [M.E. *prollen*; origin unknown.]

**proximate**, *proks'i-mit*, *-māt*, *adj.* nearest or next: without anything between, as a cause and its effect: near and immediate.—*adj.* **prox'imal**, at the near, inner, or attached end (opp. to *distal*).—*advs.* **prox'imally**; **prox'imately.**—*n.* **proxim'ity**, immediate nearness in time, place, relationship, etc.—*adv.* **prox'imo**, next month— often written prox. (for L. *proximō mēnse*)— **proximate cause**, a cause which immediately precedes the effect; **proximate object**, immediate object; **proximity fuse**, a device for causing a missile to explode when it comes near the object. [L. *proximus*, next, superl. from *propior* (comp.) —*prope*, near.]

**proxy**, *prok'si*, *n.* the agency of one who acts for another: one who acts or votes for another: the writing by which he is authorised to do so: a substitute.—*adj.* **prox'y-wedd'ed** (*Tenn.*), wedded by proxy. [procuracy.]

**proyn, proyne**, *proin.* Obs. forms of **prune** (1) (2) and (3).

**prozymite**, *proz'i-mit*, *n.* one who leavened bread in the eucharist—opp. to *azymite*. [Gr. *prozȳmia*, ferments.]

**Pruce**, *prōōs*, (*obs.*) *n.* Prussia.—*adj.* **Prussian.** [A.Fr. *Prus, Pruz*, etc.]

**prude**, *prōōd*, *n.* a woman of priggish or affected modesty: one who pretends extreme propriety. —Also *adj.* (*rare*).—*n.* **pru'dery**, manners of a prude.—*adj.* **pru'dish.**—*adv.* **pru'dishly.**—*n.* **pru'-dishness.** [O.Fr. *prode*, fem. of *prou, prod*, excellent; cf. **prow** (2), **proud**.]

**prudent**, *prōō'dənt*, *adj.* cautious and wise in conduct: discreet: characterised by, behaving with, showing, having, or dictated by forethought.— *n.* **pru'dence**, quality of being prudent: wisdom applied to practice: attention to self-interest: caution.—*adj.* **prudential** (*-den'shl*), having regard to considerations of prudence: relating to

prudence: prudent: concerned with administration (*U.S.*).—*n.* (generally *pl.*) a matter or consideration of prudence: a prudent maxim.—*ns.* **pruden'tialism**, a system based on prudence alone; **pruden'tialist; prudentiality** (*-den-shi-al'i-ti*).—*advs.* **pruden'tially; pru'dently.** [L. *prūdēns, prūdentis*, contr. of *prōvidēns*, pr.p. of *prōvidēre*, to foresee.]

**prud'homme**, *prü-dom'*, (*obs.*) *n.* a discreet man: a skilled workman: in France, a member of a board for settling labour disputes. [O.Fr. *prud* or *prod* (nom. *pros*), good, *homme*, man.]

**pruh.** See proo.

**pruina**, *prōō-i'na*, (*bot.*) *n.* a powdery bloom or waxy secretion.—*adj.* **pruinose** (*prōō'i-nōs*), covered with pruina: having a frosted look. [L. *pruina*, hoar-frost.]

**pruine**, a Shakespearian spelling of **prune** (fruit).

**prune**, *prōōn*, *v.t.* to trim by lopping off superfluous parts: to divest of anything superfluous: to remove by pruning.—Formerly also **proin(e)**, **proyn(e).**—*ns.* **pru'ner; pru'ning**, the act of pruning or trimming.—**pru'ning-bill, -hook**, a hooked bill for pruning with; **pru'ning-knife**, a large knife with a slightly hooked point for pruning.—*n.pl.* **pru'ning-shears**, shears for pruning shrubs, etc. [O.Fr. *proignier*; origin unknown.]

**prune**, *prōōn*, *v.t.* to preen.—Formerly also **proin(e)**, **proyn(e), proign.** [Origin obscure.]

**prune**, *prōōn*, *n.* a plum (*obs.*): a dried plum: a plum suitable for drying (*U.S.*): the dark purple colour of prune-juice: a dud pilot (*airman's slang*).—Obs. forms **pruine, prewyn** (*Shak.*), **proin(e), proyn(e).**—*adj.* of colour of prune-juice.—**prunes and prisms**, part of a formula for setting the lips, 'serviceable in the formation of a demeanour' (Dickens, *Little Dorrit*). [Fr.,— L. *prūna*, pl. of *prūnum* (taken for a *sing.*); cf. Gr. *prou(m)non*, plum.]

**prunella**, *prōō-nel'ə*, *n.* sore throat: quinsy: (*cap.*; also **Brunella**) the self-heal genus of labiate plants, once reputed to cure prunella. [Latinised from Ger. *bräune*, quinsy (from the brownness of the tongue), or L.L. *brūnus*— general Germanic *brūn*, brown.]

**prunella**, *prōō-nel'ə*, *n.* a strong silk or woollen stuff, formerly used for academic and clerical gowns and women's shoes—also **prunelle', prunell'o.**—*adj.* of prunella. [App. Fr. *prunelle*, sloe, dim. of *prune*, plum.]

**prunello**, *prōō-nel'ō*, *n.* a little prune: a kind of dried plum:—*pl.* **prunell'os.** [Obs. It. *prunella*, dim. of *pruna* (now *prugna*), plum.]

**prunt**, *prunt*, *n.* a moulded glass ornament or glass: a tool for making it.—*adj.* **prunt'ed.** [Origin uncertain.]

**prurient**, *prōō'ri-ənt*, *adj.* itching: uneasily or morbidly interested, curious, or craving: dallying with lascivious thoughts: causing itching (*bot., rare*).—*ns.* **pru'rience, pru'riency.**—*adv.* **pru'riently.** [L. *prūriēns, -entis*, pr.p. of *prūrīre*, to itch.]

**prurigo**, *prōō-rī'gō*, *n.* an eruption on the skin, causing great itching.—*adjs.* **pruriginous** (*-rij'i-nəs*); **pruritic**, pertaining to pruritus.—*n.* **pruri'tus**, itching. [L. *prūrigō, -inis, prūritus, -ūs* —*prūrīre*, to itch.]

**Prussian**, *prush'ən*, *adj.* of or pertaining to *Prussia*. —*n.* an inhabitant, native, or citizen of Prussia. —*v.t.* and *v.i.* **Pruss'ianise, -ize**, to make or become Prussian.—*ns.* **Pruss'ianiser, -izer; Pruss'ianism**, spirit of Prussian nationality: often used for arrogant militarism; **prussiate** (*prus'* or *prush'i-āt*), a cyanide: a ferricyanide: a ferrocyanide.—*adj.* **pruss'ic** (also sometimes *prōōs'*), pertaining to Prussian blue.—*n.* **Prussification.**—*v.t.* **Pruss'ify**, to Prussianise, assimilate to the Prussian.—**Prussian** (also without *cap.*) **blue**, ferric ferrocyanide, discovered in

Berlin; **prussic acid**, hydrocyanic acid, a deadly poison, first obtained from Prussian blue.—**Old Prussian**, the extinct Baltic language of the former inhabitants of East and West Prussia.

**pry**, *prī*, *v.i.* to peer or peep into that which is private: to examine things with impertinent curiosity:—*pr.p.* **prying**; *pa.t.* and *pa.p.* **pried**; *3rd pers. sing. pr.t.* **pries**.—*n.* a prying (*rare*): one who pries—cf. *Paul Pry*, in John Poole's (1792–1879) comedy so called, first produced in 1825.— *n.* **pri′er**, one who pries—also **pry′er**.—*n.* and *adj* **pry′ing** —*adv* **pry′ingly**.—**pry out**, to investigate or find out by prying. [M.E. *prien*; origin unknown.]

**pry**, *prī*, *v.t.* a form of prize, to lever: to extract.

**prys**, **pryse**, old spellings of **price**, **prize**.

**pryse**, *priz*, (*Scott*) *n.* a horn-blast at the taking or killing of a deer. [O.Fr. *pris*, taken; cf. **prize** (2).]

**prytaneum**, *prit-an-ē′əm*, (*ant.*) *n.* the town-hall of an ancient Greek city. [Latinised from Gr. *prytaneion—prytanis*, a presiding magistrate.]

**pr′ythee**, **prythee**, *pridh′ē*. Same as **prithee**.

**Przewalski's horse**, *pzhe-val′skiz hörs*, a wild horse discovered in Central Asia by Nikolai *Przewalski* (1839-88).—Various other spellings exist.

**psalm**, *säm*, *n.* a devotional song or hymn, esp. one of those included in the Old Testament **Book of Psalms**.—*n.* **psalmist** (*säm′ist*), a composer of psalms, esp. (with *cap.*) David.—*adjs.* **psalmodic** (*sal-mod′ik*), **-al**, pertaining to psalmody.—*v.i.* **psalmodise**, **-ize** (*sal′*, *säm′*), to practise psalmody. —*ns.* **psalmodist** (*sal′*, *sä′mə-dist*), a singer of psalms; **psalmody** (*sal′*, or *säm′*; Gr. *psalmōidiā*, singing to the harp), the singing of psalms, esp. in public worship: psalms collectively.—**psalm′-book**, a book containing psalms for purposes of worship; **psalm′-tune**. [O.E. (*p*)*salm*, (*p*)*sealm*— L.L. *psalmus*—Gr. *psalmos*, music of or to a stringed instrument—*psallein*, to pluck.]

**Psalter**, *söl′tər*, *n.* the Book of Psalms, esp. when separately printed.—*adj.* **psalterian** (*sōl-tē′ri-ən*), pertaining to a psalter: like a psaltery.—*ns.* **psal′tery**, an ancient and mediaeval stringed instrument like the zither, played by plucking: (*cap.*; *rare*) the Psalter; **psal′tress**, a woman who plays upon the psaltery. [O.E. *saltere*—L. *psaltērium*—Gr. *psaltērion*, a psaltery.]

**psalterium**, *söl-tē′ri-əm*, *n.* the third division of a ruminant's stomach, the omasum or manyplies. [From the appearance of its lamellae, like a stringed instrument; see the foregoing.]

**psammite**, *sam′it*, *n.* any rock composed of sand-grains. — *adj.* **psammitic** (*-it′ik*).— *n.* **psamm′-ophil(e)**, a sand-loving plant. — *adj.* **psamm-oph′ilous**.—*n.* **psamm′ophyte** (*ō-fīt*), a plant that grows only on sand.—*adj.* **psammophytic** (*-fīt′ik*). [Gr. *psammos*, sand.]

**psellism**, (*p*)*sel′izm*, *n.* a defect in articulation— also **psellis′mus**. [Gr. *psellismos—psellos*, stammering.]

**psephism**, (*p*)*sē′fizm*, *n.* (*ant.*) a decree of the Athenian assembly (from the voting with pebbles).—*ns.* **pse′phite**, a rock composed of pebbles, a conglomerate; **psēphol′ogy**, socio-logical and statistical study of election results and trends—also **psephoanal′ysis**; **psephol′ogist**. [Gr. *psēphos*, a pebble.]

**pseud-**, (*p*)*sūd*, **pseudo-**, *sū′dō-*, in U.S. *sōō′dō*, in composition, sham, false, spurious: deceptively resembling: isomerous with: temporary, provisional.—As a separate word, *adj.* **pseu′do**, false, sham.—*n.* a pretender.—*ns.* **pseudaesthē′-sia**, imaginary feeling, as in an amputated limb; **pseudax′is**, a sympodium; **pseudepig′rapha** (*pl.*), books ascribed to Old Testament characters, but not judged genuine by scholars.—*adjs.* **pseudepig′raph′ic**, **-al**.—*ns.* **pseudepig′raphy**, the ascription to books of false names of authors; **pseud-**

**imā′go**, a subimago; **pseu′do-ac′id**, a compound, not an acid but isomeric with and transformable into an acid.—*adj.* **pseu′do-archā′ic**, sham antique: artificially archaistic: blunderingly imitative of the old.—*ns.* **pseudo-ar′chāism; pseu′dobulb**, a swollen stem internode in some orchids; **pseu′docarp**, a fruit formed from other parts in addition to the gynaeceum; **pseu′do-Christian′ity**; **pseu′doclass′icism**; **pseudocyesis** (*-si-ē′sis*; Gr. *kyēsis—kyein*, to be pregnant), a psychosomatic condition marked by many of the symptoms of pregnancy. — *adj.* and *n.* **pseu′dō-Goth′ic**, sham or would-be Gothic.—*ns.* **pseu′dograph**, a writing falsely ascribed; **pseud-og′raphy**, unsatisfactory spelling; **pseudol′ogy**, the science of lying; **pseu′domar′tyr**, a false martyr; **pseu′domem′brane**, a false membrane; **Pseudomonas** (*do-mo′nas*), a genus of schizo-mycetes comprising short rod-shaped bacteria which are found in soil and in water; **pseu′domorph**, a portion of a mineral showing the out-ward form of another which it has replaced by molecular substitution or otherwise; **pseu′-donym**, a fictitious name assumed, as by an author; **pseudonym′ity**.—*adj.* **pseudon′ymous**.— *adv.* **pseudon′ymously**.—*ns.* **pseu′dopod**, a psychic projection: a pseudopodium; **pseudopō′dium**, a temporary process sent out by the protoplasm of a unicellular organism or phagocyte, for loco-motion or feeding:—*pl.* **pseudopō′dia**; **pseu′-doscope**, a kind of stereoscope that interchanges convex and concave in appearance; **pseu′do-solu′tion**, a colloidal suspension; **pseu′do-symm′etry** (*crystal.*), a deceptively near approach to a higher degree of symmetry, as in **pseu′do-cu′bic** or **pseu′dohexag′onal** crystals, simulating cubic or hexagonal symmetry. [Gr. *pseudēs*, false.]

**pshaw**, *shö*, *pshə*, *interj.* expressing contempt or impatience.—*v.i.* to say 'pshaw'.—*v.t.* to say 'pshaw' at. [Spontaneous expression.]

**psi**, (*p*)*sī*, (*p*)*sē*, *n.* the twenty-third letter (Ψ, ψ) of the Greek alphabet, equivalent to *ps*: as a Greek numeral ψ′ = 700, ψ = 700,000.—**psi′-phenom′enon**, a phenomenon of parapsychology. [Gr. *psei*.]

**psilanthropism**, (*p*)*si-lan′thrə-pizm*, *n.* the doctrine that Christ was a mere man.—*adj.* **psilanthropic** (*-throp′*).—*ns.* **psilan′thropist**; **psilan′thropy**. [Gr. *psilos*, bare, *anthrōpos*, man.]

**psilocybin**, *si-lō-si′bin*, *n.* a hallucinogenic drug, obtained from Mexican mushrooms. [Gr. *psilos*, bare, *kybē*, head.]

**psilomelane**, (*p*)*si-lom′ə-lān*, (*p*)*si-lō-mel′ān*, *n.* an oxide of manganese, usually with barium, etc., occurring in smooth black botryoidal masses. [Gr. *psilos*, bare, *melās*, *-anos*, black.]

**Psilophyton**, (*p*)*si-lō-fi′ton*, *n.* a very simple Devonian fossil pteridophyte, giving name to the order **Psilophytales** (*-fi-tā′lēz*), early land-plants. [Gr. *psilos*, bare, *phyton*, plant.]

**psilosis** (*p*)*si-lō′sis*, *n.* loss of hair: sprue (from loss of epithelium): deaspiration (*Gr. gram.*). —*adj.* **psilot′ic**, pertaining to psilosis. [Gr. *psilōsis—psilos*, bare.]

**Psilotum**, (*p*)*si-lō′təm*, *n.* a genus of rootless pteridophytes giving name to the order **Psilotā′-ceae**. [Gr. *psilōton*, the name of some plant— *psilos*, bare (because of the almost leafless stem).]

**Psittacus**, (*p*)*sit′a-kəs*, *n.* the grey parrot genus.— *adj.* **psitt′acine** (*-sin*), of parrots.—*n.* **psittacosis** (*-kō′sis*), a contagious disease of birds, strictly of parrots, communicable to man. [Gr. *psittakos*, parrot.]

**psoas**, (*p*)*sō′as*, *n.* a muscle of the loins and pelvis: the tenderloin. [Gr. (*pl.*) *psoai*, the accus. *psoās*, being mistaken for a nom. sing.]

**Psocoptera**, (*p*)*sō-kop′tər-ə*, *n.pl.* an order of insects consisting of the book-lice and their kindred. [*Psocus*, a genus included in the order, Gr. *pteron*, wing.]

**psora** (*p*)*sō'*, *sō'rə, n.* scabies, itch.—*n.* **psori'asis**, a skin disease in which red scaly papules and patches appear.—*adjs.* **psoriat'ic**; **pso'ric**. [Gr. *psōrā, psōriāsis*, itch.]

**psyche**, *sī'kē, n.* the soul, spirit, mind: the principle of mental and emotional life, conscious and unconscious: a butterfly: a cheval-glass: (*cap.*) in late Greek mythology the personification of the soul, depicted as a young woman with butterfly wings, the beloved of Eros: (*cap.*) a genus of bombycid moths (the females wingless, sometimes legless): (*cap.*) one of the minor planets.—*v.t.* **psych, psyche** (*sik*; *slang*), to subject to psychoanalysis.—*adjs.* **psych'ic, -al**, pertaining to the psyche, soul, or mind; spiritual: spiritualistic: beyond, or apparently beyond, the physical: sensitive to or in touch with that which has not yet been explained physically.—*n.* **psych'ic**, that which is of the mind or psyche: a spiritualistic medium.—*adv.* **psych'ically.**—*ns.* **psy'chics** (treated as *sing.*), the science of psychology: psychical research; **psy'chism**, the doctrine of a universal soul; **psy'chist**, a psychologist: one interested in psychical research. —*ns.* **psych'agogue** (-*ə-gog*; Gr. *agōgos*, guide), conductor of souls to the underworld (a title of Hermes): a caller-up of spirits: one who guides the mind: a means of restoring consciousness; **psychasthē'nia** (etymologically -*the-ni'ə*; Gr. *asthēneia*, weakness), a severe functional mental disorder, characterised by fixed ideas, ruminative states, and hypochondriacal conditions; **psychedel'ia** (-*dēl'i-ə*), (production of) psychedelic experiences.—*adj.* **psychedelic** (see *psychodelic*).—*n.* **psychi'ater** (*arch.*; Gr. *iātros, iătros*, physician), psychiatrist.—*adj.* **psychiat'ric(al).**—*ns.* **psychi'atrist**, one who treats diseases of the mind; **psychi'atry.**—**psychical research**, investigation of phenomena apparently implying a connection with another world; **psychic bid** (*bridge*), bid of a suit in which one is not strong to deceive opponent, or for other reason; **psychic force**, a power not physical or mechanical, supposed to cause certain so-called spiritualistic phenomena. [Gr. *psychē*, soul, butterfly, *Psychē*, Psyche.]

**psych(o)-**, *sik-(ō-)*, *..n* composition, soul, spirit: mind, mental: psychological.—*n.* **psych'oid**, the hypothetical regulative principle directing the behaviour of a developing organism.— *adj.* **psychoac'tive**, of a drug, affecting the brain and influencing behaviour.—*v.t.* **psychoan'alyse, -yze**, to subject to psychoanalysis.—*ns.* **psychoanal'ysis**, a method of investigation and psychotherapy whereby nervous diseases or mental ailments are traced to forgotten hidden concepts in the patient's mind and treated by bringing these to light; **psychoan'alyst.**—*adjs.* **psychoanalyt'ic, -al**; **psychochem'ical.**—*n.* a substance with psychoactive effect, esp. a chemical intended as a weapon of war, specif. a psychogas.—*n.* **psychochem'istry**, the treatment of mental illness by drugs.—*adj.* **psychodel'ic** (the irregularly formed **psychedelic**, *si-kə-del'ik*, -*dēl'ik*, is commoner), pertaining to a state of relaxation and pleasure, with heightened perception and increased mental powers generally: pertaining to drugs which cause, or are believed to cause, the taker to enter such a state: pertaining to visual effects and/or sound effects whose action on the mind is a little like that of psychedelic drugs: dazzling in pattern: loosely, very up-to-date.— *n.* **psychodram'a**, a method of mental treatment in which the patient is led to objectify and understand his difficulty by spontaneously acting it out.—*adj.* **psychodynam'ic**, pertaining to mental and emotional forces, their source in past experience, and their effects.—*ns.* **psychodynam'-**

ics; **psychogas'**, a gas which makes a subject's performance deteriorate very seriously without his being aware of it; **psychogen'esis**, origin or development of the mind: origination in the mind.—*adjs.* **psychogenet'ic, -al**; **psychogen'ic**, having origin in the mind or in a mental condition.—*ns.* **psychog'ony**, origin or development of the mind or soul; **psych'ogram**, a supposed spirit-writing; **psych'ograph**, an instrument by which it is got.—*adjs.* **psychograph'ic, -al.**—*ns.* **psychog'raphy**, spirit-writing: psychological biography or delineation; **psychokinē'sis**, movement by psychic agency.—*adjs.* **psycholog'ic, -al.** —*adv.* **psycholog'ically.**—*v.i.* **psychol'ogise, -ize.** —*ns.* **psychol'ogist**; **psychol'ogism**, doctrine depending on psychological conceptions: view that philosophy, etc. should be based on psychology; **psychol'ogy**, science of mind: study of mind and behaviour: attitudes, etc., characteristic of individual, type, etc., or animating specific conduct; **psychom'eter**, one who has occult power of psychometry: instrument for measuring reaction-times, etc.—*adjs.* **psychomet'ric, -al.**—*ns.* **psychometri'cian** (-*me-trish'ən*); **psychomet'rics**, branch of psychology dealing with measurable factors; **psychom'etry**, psychometrics: occult power of divining properties of things by mere contact.—*adj.* **psy'chomōtor**, pertaining to such mental action as induces muscular contraction.—*n.* **psychoneurō'sis**, mental disease without any apparent anatomical lesion: a functional disorder of the mind in one who is legally sane and shows insight into his condition.—*n.* and *adj.* **psychoneurot'ic.** — *ns.* **psychopannychism** (-*pan'ik-izm*; Gr. *pannychos*, all night long—*pās, pāsa, pān*, all, *nychios*, nightly), (belief in the) sleep of the soul from death to resurrection; **psychopann'ychist**, one who holds this belief; **psy'chopath** (-*path*), one who shows a pathological degree of specific emotional instability without specific mental disorder: one suffering from a behavioural disorder resulting in inability to form personal relationships and in indifference to or ignorance of his obligations to society, often manifested by anti-social behaviour, as acts of violence, sexual perversion, etc.—*adj.* **psychopath'ic**, pertaining to psychopathy.—*ns.* **psychop'athist**, a psychopathologist; **psychopathol'ogist**; **psychopathol'ogy**, the branch of psychology that deals with the abnormal workings of the mind; **psychop'athy**, derangement of mental functions.—*adj.* **psychophys'ical.** —*ns.* **psychophys'icist**; **psychophys'ics**, the study of the relation or correspondence of the mental and physical; **psychophysiol'ogy**, experimental or physiological psychology; **psy'chopomp** (Gr. *pompos*, guide), a conductor of souls to the other world; **psychoprophylax'is**, a method of training for childbirth aimed at making labour painless; **psychō'sis**, mental condition: a serious mental disorder characterised by e.g. illusions, delusions, hallucinations, mental confusion and a lack of insight into his condition on the part of the patient:—*pl.* **psychō'sēs.**—*adj.* **psychosomat'ic** (Gr. *sōma*, body), of mind and body as a unit: concerned with physical diseases having emotional origin.—*n.pl.* (treated as *sing.*) **psychosomat'ics**, study of psychosomatic conditions. —*adj.* **psychosomimet'ic**, of a drug, producing symptoms like those of mental illness.—*ns.* **psychosur'gery**, brain-surgery in mental cases; **psychotherapeut'ics, -ther'apy**, treatment of disease by hypnosis, psychoanalysis and similar means; **psychother'apist.**—*adj.* **psychot'ic**, pertaining to psychosis.—*n.* one suffering from a psychosis.—*adj.* **psychotrop'ic**, affecting mental states; **psychotomimet'ic**, psychosomimetic.— **psychological moment**, properly the psychological element or factor, misunderstood by a French translator from German and applied to the moment of time when the mind could best be worked upon: hence now often the very moment, the nick of time; **psychological warfare**, the use of propaganda to influence enemy opinion or morale. [Gr. *psychē*, soul, butterfly.]

**psychrometer**, *si-krom'i-tər, n.* originally a thermometer: now a wet-and-dry-bulb hygrometer.— *adjs.* **psychrometric** (*si-krō-met'rik*), **-al.**—*n.* **psychrom'etry.** [Gr. *psychros*, cold, *metron*, a measure.]

**ptarmic**, (*p*)*tär'mik, n.* a substance that causes sneezing. [Gr. *ptarmos*, a sneeze.]

**ptarmigan**, *tär'mi-gən, n.* a mountain-dwelling grouse, white in winter: extended to other species of Lagopus, as willow-grouse. [Gael. *tàrmachan*.]

**pter(-o)-**, *ter(-o)-*, in composition, feather, wing. **— -ptera**, in zoological names, organism(s) having specified type or number of wings or wing-like parts. [Gr. *pteron*, wing.]

**Pterichthys**, (*p*)*tər-ik'this, n.* a genus of Old Red Sandstone fish-like creatures, with wing-like appendages. [Gr. *pteron*, a wing, and *ichthys*, a fish.]

**pteridophyte**, (*p*)*ter'id-ō-fīt, n.* a vascular cryptogam or a member of the **Pteridophyta** (*-of'i-ta*), one of the main divisions of the vegetable kingdom—ferns, lycopods, horsetails. [Gr. *pteris*, *-idos*, a fern, *phyton*, a plant.]

**pteridosperm**, (*p*)*ter'id-ō-spûrm, n.* a fossil plant of a group resembling ferns, but having seeds. [Gr. *pteris*, *-idos*, fern, *sperma*, seed.]

**pterin**, (*p*)*ter'in, n.* any of a group of substances occurring as pigments in butterfly wings, important in biochemistry.—**pteroic** ((*p*)*ter-ō'ik*) **acid**, the original folic acid found in spinach; **pteroylglutamic** ((*p*)*ter'ō-il-glōō-tam'ik*) **acid**, the folic acid that is therapeutically active in pernicious anaemia. [Gr. *pteron*, a wing.]

**pterion**, (*p*)*ter', or* (*p*)*tēr'i-on, n.* in craniometry, the suture where the frontal, squamosal, and parietal bones meet the wing of the sphenoid:— *pl.* **pter'ia**. [Gr. dim. of *pteron*, wing.]

**Pteris**, (*p*)*ter'is, (p)tē'ris, n.* a genus of ferns with spore-clusters continuous along the pinnule margin, usually taken to include bracken, which some separate as Pterid'ium.—*ns.* **pteridol'ogist**; **pteridol'ogy**, the science of ferns: **pteridomā'nia**, a passion for ferns; **pteridoph'ilist**, a fern-lover. [Gr. *pteris*, *-idos*, or *-eōs*, male-fern—*pteron*, a feather.]

**pterodactyl, pterodactyle**, (*p*)*ter-ə-dak'til, n.* a fossil (Jurassic and Cretaceous) flying reptile with large and bird-like skull, long jaws, and a flying-membrane attached to the long fifth finger. [Gr. *pteron*, wing, *daktylos*, finger.]

**pteropod**, (*p*)*ter'ə-pod, n.* any member of the **Pteropoda** (*-op'ə-də*), a group of gasteropods that swim by wing-like expansions of the foot.— **pteropod ooze**, a deep-sea deposit composed largely of pteropod shells. [Gr. *pteron*, wing, *pous*, *podos*, foot.]

**pterosaur**, (*p*)*ter'ə-sör, n.* a member of the Pterosaur'ia, the pterodactyls.—*n.* and *adj.* **pterosaur'ian**. [Gr. *pteron*, wing, *sauros*, lizard.]

**pterygium**, (*p*)*tər-ij'i-əm, n.* a vertebrate limb: a wing-like growth: a wing-shaped area of thickened conjunctiva which spreads over part of the cornea and sometimes over the eyeball:—*pl.* **pteryg'ia**.—*adj.* **pteryg'ial**.—*n.* a bone in a fin, [Latinised from Gr. *pterygion*, dim. of *pteryx*, *-ygos*, wing.]

**pterygoid**, (*p*)*ter'i-goid, adj.* wing-like: of or near the pterygoid.—*n.* (in full, **pterygoid bone, plate, process**) in various vertebrates, a paired bone of the upper jaw behind the palatines, known in human anatomy as the pterygoid plates of the sphenoid bone. [Gr. *pteryx*, *-ygos*, wing.]

**Pterygotus**, (*p*)*ter-i-gō'təs, n.* a genus of Eurypterids named from the broad swimming

paddles. [Latinised from Gr. *pterygōtos*, winged.]

**pteryla**, (*p*)*ter'i-lə, n.* a patch of contour feathers in birds:—*pl.* **pter'ylae** (*-lē*).—*adjs.* **pterylograph'ic, -al.** — *adv.* **pterylograph'ically.** — *ns.* **pterylog'raphy; pterylō'sis,** arrangement of pterylae. [Gr. *pteron*, feather, *hȳlē*, forest.]

**ptilosis**, *til-ō'sis, n.* plumage or mode of feathering. [Gr. *ptilōsis—ptilon*, a down feather.]

**ptisan**, *tiz'n, tiz-an', n.* a medicinal drink made from barley: a decoction.—Also **tisane**. [Gr. *ptisanē*, peeled barley, barley-gruel—*ptissein*, to winnow.]

**ptochocracy**, (*p*)*tō-kok'rə-si, n.* the rule of beggars or paupers—wholesale pauperisation. [Gr. *ptōchos*, a beggar, *kratos*, power.]

**Ptolemaic**, *tol-i-mā'ik, adj.* pertaining to the *Ptolemies*, Greek kings of Egypt (from Alexander's general to Caesar's son), or to *Ptolemy* the astronomer (fl. A.D. 150)—also **Ptolemaean** (*-mē'ən*).—*n.* **Ptolemā'ist**, a believer in the **Ptolemaic system**, Ptolemy's form of the ancient Greek planetary theory, according to which the heavenly bodies revolved about the earth in motions compounded of eccentric circles and epicycles.

**ptomaine**, *tō'mā-in, -ēn, -in* (these now rare), *tō'mān, tō-mān'* (these orig. illiterate, now established), *n.* a loosely used name for amino-compounds, some poisonous, formed from putrefying animal tissues—*putrescine, cadaverine, neurine, choline*, etc. [It. *ptomaina*—Gr. *ptōma*, a corpse.]

**ptosis**, (*p*)*tō'sis, n.* downward displacement: drooping of the upper eyelid. [Gr. *ptōsis—piptein*, to fall.]

**ptyalin**, (*p*)*ti'ə-lin, n.* a ferment in saliva that turns starch into sugar.—*adj.* **ptyalagogic** (*-ə-goj'ik, -gog'ik*).—*n.* **ptyalagogue** (*-al'ə-gog*), a sialagogue.—*v.t.* **pty'alise, -ize,** to induce ptyalism in. —*n.* **pty'alism**, excessive flow of saliva. [Gr. *ptyalon*, spittle—*ptyein*, to spit.]

**ptyxis**, (*p*)*tiks'is, n.* the folding of each individual leaf in the bud—distinguished from *vernation*, the arrangement of the whole. [Gr. *ptyxis*.]

**pub**, *pub*, (*slang*) *n.* short for public house.—**pub'-crawl**, a progression from pub to pub.—Also *v.i.*

**puberty**, *pū'bər-ti, n.* the beginning of sexual maturity.—*adjs.* **pū'beral**; **pūberulent** (*-ber'ū-lənt*), **pūber'ūlous**, feebly or minutely pubescent. —*ns.* **pū'bes** (*-bēz*), the lower part of the hypogastric region: the hair growing thereon at puberty; **pūbescence** (*-es'əns*), puberty: a soft downy covering, esp. in plants, of addressed hairs.—*adjs.* **pūbes'cent**; **pū'bic**, of the pubes or the pubis.—*n.* **pūbis** (for L. *os pūbis*, bone of the pubes), a bone of the pelvis which in man forms the anterior portion of the *os innominatum*: —*pl.* **pū'bises** (pū'bes is a blunder).—As a prefix **pū'biō-** (wrongly pū'bo-). [L. *pūber* and *pūbēs, -eris*, grown-up, downy, and *pūbēs, -is*, grown-up youth, the pubes.]

**public**, *pub'lik, adj.* of or belonging to the people: pertaining to a community or a nation: general: common to, shared in by, or open to, all: generally known: in open view, unconcealed, not private: engaged in, or concerning, the affairs of the community: devoted or directed to the general good (now *rare* except in *public spirit*): international: open to members of a university as a whole, not confined to a college: of a public house.—*n.* the people: the general body of mankind: the people, indefinitely: a part of the community regarded from a particular viewpoint, e.g. as an audience or a target for advertising: public view of a public place, society, or the open: a public house, tavern.— *ns.* **pub'lican**, the keeper of an inn or public house: a tax-farmer (*Roman hist.*): a tax-collector (*Roman hist.*); **publicā'tion**, the act of

publishing or making public: a proclamation: the act of sending out for sale, as a book: that which is published as a book, etc.—*v.t.* pub′licise, -ize (*sīz*), to give publicity to: to advertise.—*ns.* pub′licist (-*sist*), one who writes on or is skilled in public law, or on current political topics: an advertising agent; publicity (-*lis′i-ti*), state of being open to the knowledge of all: notoriety: acclaim: advertising.—*adv.* pub′licly. —*n.* pub′licness (*rare*).—public company, one whose shares can be purchased on the stock exchange by members of the public; public corporation, one owned by the government and run on business principles, being for the most part self-ruling; public enemy, someone whose behaviour is considered to be a menace to a community in general; public funds, government funded debt; public holiday, a general holiday; public house, a house open to the public (*obs.*): one chiefly used for selling alcoholic liquors to be consumed on the premises: an inn or tavern; public image, the picture in the minds of most people of what, e.g., a political party stands for; public lands, lands belonging to government, esp. such as are open to sale, grant, etc.; public law, law governing relations between public authorities, as the state, and the individual: sometimes used for international law which, however, may be either public or private; public orator, an officer of English universities who is the voice of the Senate upon all public occasions; public ownership, ownership by the state as of nationalised industry; public prosecutor, an official whose function is to prosecute persons charged with offences; public-rela′tions, the relations between a person, organisation, etc., and the public: the business of setting up and maintaining favourable relations. —Also *adj.*—public school, school under the control of a publicly elected body: an endowed classical school for providing a liberal education for such as can afford it—Eton, Harrow, Rugby, Winchester, Westminster, Shrewsbury, Charterhouse, St Paul's, Merchant Taylors', etc.—*adjs.* pub′lic-school′; pub′lic-spir′ited, having a spirit actuated by regard to the public interest: with a regard to the public interest.—*adv.* pub′lic-spir′itedly.—public trustee, an official who acts as trustee or executor if required; public utility, a service or supply provided in a town etc., for the public, as gas, electricity, water, transport: (*U.S.*) a company providing such a service, and usually having a monopoly: (in *pl.*) public utility shares; public woman (*arch.*), a prostitute.—public address system, a system that enables (large) groups of people to be addressed clearly, consisting of some or all of the following—microphones, amplifiers, loud speakers, sound projectors; public health inspector, designation in England of an official formerly known as sanitary inspector; public opinion poll, a taking of public opinion based on the answers of scientifically selected elements in the community to questioning. [L. *pūblicus*—*pop(u)lus*, the people.]
publish, pub′lish, *v.t.* to make public: to divulge: to announce: to proclaim: to send forth to the public: to put forth and offer for sale orig. any article, now books, newpapers, etc.: to put into circulation: of an author, to get published.—*v.i.* to publish a work, newspaper, etc.—*adj.* pub′lishable.—*ns.* pub′lisher, one who makes public: one who publishes books: one who attends to the issuing and distributing of a newspaper: a newspaper proprietor (*U.S.*); pub′lishment, publication, esp. (*U.S.*) of banns. [Fr. *publier*—L. *pūblicāre*, with -*ish* on the model of other verbs.]
Puccinia, *puk-sin′-i-ə*, *n.* a genus of rust-fungi, including the wheat-rust, parasitic in alternate generations on barberry and wheat or other grass.—*adj.* pucciniā′ceous. [Named after Tomaso *Puccini*, Italian anatomist.]
puccoon, *puk-ōōn′*, *n.* bloodroot: extended to species of gromwell and other American plants yielding pigments. [Virginian Indian name.]
puce, *pūs*, *n.* and *adj.* brownish-purple. [Fr. *puce* —L. *pūlex*, -*icis*, a flea.]
pucelle, *pū-sel′*, (*obs.*) *n.* a maid, virgin, esp. the Maid of Orleans, Jeanne d'Arc (1412-31): a dirty drab, a slut (also puzzle).—*n.* pū′celage, virginity. [Fr.,—L.L. *pūlicella*; origin doubtful.]
puck, *puk*, pouke, *pōōk*, *n.* a goblin or mischievous sprite: (*cap.*) Robin Goodfellow, a merry fairy in *Midsummer Night's Dream*, etc. (Puck-hairy in Ben Jonson's *Sad Shepherd*).— *adj.* puck′ish, impish: full of mischief. [O.E. *pūca*; cf. O.N. *pūki*, Ir. *puca*, W. *pwca*.]
puck, *puk*, *n.* a rubber disk used instead of a ball in ice-hockey.
pucka, pukka, pakka, *puk′ə*, (*Anglo-Ind.*) *adj.* outand-out good: thorough: complete: solidly built: settled: durable: permanent: full-weight: straight-forward: genuine: sure.—pucka sahib, a gentleman. [Hind. *pakkā*, cooked, ripe.]
pucker, *puk′ər*, *v.t.* and *v.i.* wrinkle.—*n.* a corrugation or wrinkle: a group of wrinkles, esp. irregular ones: agitation, confusion (*coll.*).— *adj.* puck′ery, astringent: tending to wrinkle. [Cf. poke, a bag.]
puckfist, *puk′fist*, -*fist*, *n.* a puff-ball: a braggart (*arch.*): a niggard (*obs.*). [App. puck, and the root of O.E. *fisting*, breaking of wind.]
pud, *pud*, (*coll.*) *n.* a paw, fist, hand.—*n.* pudd′y, a variant of *pud*. [Cf. pad (2), or Du. *poot*, paw.]
pud, *pōōd*, pudder, *pud′ər*. Same as pood, pother.
pud, *pōōd*, (*coll.*) *n.* abbrev. of pudding.
pudding, *pōōd′ing*, *n.* a skin or gut filled with seasoned minced meat and other materials (as blood, oatmeal), a kind of sausage: stuffing for a cooked carcase (*Shak.*): (usu. in *pl.*) entrails: meat, fruit, etc., cooked in a casing of flour: a soft kind of cooked dish, usually farinaceous, commonly with sugar, milk, eggs, etc.: a pad of rope, etc., used as a fender on the bow of a boat or elsewhere (also pudd′ening): material gain (*fig.*): a fat, dull, or heavy-witted person (*coll.*).—Also (now *coll.* or *dial.*) pudden (*pōōd′n*, *pud′n*).—*adj.* pudd′ingy (-*ing-i*).—pudd′ing-bag, a bag for cooking a pudding in: a piece of good fortune.—*adjs.* pudd′ing-faced, having a fat, round, smooth face; pudd′ing-head′ed (*coll.*), stupid.—pudd′ing-pie, a pudding with meat baked in it: applied to various kinds of pastry; pudd′ing-pipe, the long pulpy pod of the purging-cassia tree; pudd′ing-sleeve, a large loose sleeve gathered in near the wrist; pudd′ing-stone, conglomerate; pudd′ing-time (*obs.*), dinner-time: the right moment. [M.E. *poding*; origin unknown; relation to L.G. *pudde-wurst*, black pudding, and Fr. *boudin*, obscure.]
puddle, *pud′l*, *n.* a small muddy pool: a mixture of clay and sand: a muddle (*coll.*): a muddler (*coll.*).—*v.t.* to make muddy: to work into puddle, to stir and knead: to cover with puddle: to make watertight by means of clay: to convert from pig-iron into wrought-iron by stirring in a molten state.—*v.i.* to make a dirty stir.—*ns.* pudd′ler, pudd′ling.—*adj.* pudd′ly, full of puddles. [App. dim. of O.E. *pudd*, ditch.]
puddock, *pud′ək*, *n.* Same as paddock (1).
pudency, *pū′dəns-i*, (*Shak.*) *n.* shamefacedness, modesty.—*adjs.* pudendal (-*den′*), pertaining to the pudenda; puden′dous (*obs.*), shameful.—*n.* puden′dum, and *pl.* puden′da, the external genital organs.—*adjs.* pu′dent (*rare*), modest; pu′dibund, shamefaced: prudish.—*n.* pudibund′ity.—*adj.* pu′dic, modest (*obs.*): pudendal. —*ns.* pudicity (-*dis′i-ti*; *rare*), modesty; pu′dor

**pudge**, *(obs.)*, sense of shame. [L. *pudēre*, to make (or be) ashamed, *pudendum*, something to be ashamed of, *pudicus, pudibundus*.]

**pudge**, *puj*, **pudgy**, *puj'i*, puds(e)y, *pud'zi*. Same as **podge, podgy**.

**pueblo**, *pweb'lō*, *n.* a town or settlement (in Spanish-speaking countries): a communal habitation of the Indians of New Mexico, etc.: an Indian of the pueblos. [Sp., town—L. *populus*, a people.]

**puer**, *pūr*, *n.* and *v.t.* Same as **pure** (in tanning).

**puerile**, *pū'ər-il*, in U.S. *-il*, *adj.* pertaining to children *(rare)*: childish: trifling: silly.—*n.* **puerility** *(-il'i-ti)*, quality of being puerile: that which is puerile: a childish expression: an instance of childishness or foolish triviality. [L. *puerīlis—puer*, a boy.]

**puerperal**, *pū-ûr'pər-əl*, *adj.* relating to childbirth.—*adv.* **puer'perally.**—*n.* **puerpē'rium**, the time from onset of labour to return to normal state.—**puerperal fever**, fever occurring in connection with childbirth: now confined to morbid conditions owing to introduction of organisms into the genital tract; **puerperal mania**, mania sometimes occurring after childbirth. [L. *puerpera*, a woman in labour—*puer*, a child, *parĕre*, to bear.]

**puff**, *puf*, *v.i.* to blow in whiffs: to breathe out vehemently or pantingly: to snort scornfully *(obs.)*: to emit puffs: to issue in puffs: to make the sound of a puff: to go with puffs: to swell up.—*v.t.* to drive with a puff: to blow: to emit in puffs: to play (as a wind instrument) or smoke (as a pipe) with puffs: to inflate or swell: to elate unduly: to extol, esp. in disingenuous advertisement: to put out of breath. —*n.* a sudden, forcible breath, blast, or emission: a gust or whiff: a cloud or portion of vapour, dust, air, etc., emitted at once: a sound of puffing: a downy pad for powdering: anything light and porous, or swollen and light: a biscuit or cake of puff-paste or the like: a part of a fabric gathered up so as to be left full in the middle: a quilted bed-cover: ostentation: laudation intended as, or serving as, advertisement: a homosexual *(slang*; see **pouf**(fe)). —*adj.* **puffed**, distended: inflated: gathered up into rounded ridges, as a sleeve: out of breath.—*ns.* **puff'er**, one who puffs: a steam-engine: a steamboat: one employed to bid at an auction to incite others and run up prices; **puff'ery**, advertisement disguised as honest praise: puffs collectively.—*adv.* **puff'ily.**—*ns.* **puff'iness; puff'ing.**—*adv.* **puff'ingly.**—*adj.* **puff'y**, puffed out with air or any soft matter: tumid: bombastic: coming in puffs: puffing: short-winded.—**puff'-adder**, a thick, venomous African snake *(Bitis arietans* or kindred species) that distends its body when irritated; **puff'ball**, a gasteromycete fungus (Lycoperdon, etc.) with ball-shaped fructification filled when ripe with a snuff-like mass of spores; **puff'-bird**, any bird of a South American family akin to barbets, with the habit of puffing out the head-feathers; **puff'-box**, a box for toilet powder and puff; **puff'-paste**, a flour paste in thin layers: pastry made thereof (**puff'-pastry**); **puff'-puff**, a child's word for a railway engine or train.—**puffed out**, quite out of breath; **puffed up**, swollen with pride, presumption, or the like. [O.E. *pyffan*, or kindred form; cf. Ger. *puffen*, etc.]

**puffin**, *puf'in*, *n.* a sea-bird (Fratercula) of the auk family, with brightly coloured parrot-like beak. [Origin obscure: connection with puff is conjectured.]

**pug**, *pug*, *n.* a goblin, a puck *(obs.)*: in Ben Jonson, Pug, an inferior devil: a term of endearment: a harlot *(obs.)*: an upper servant *(arch. slang)*: a monkey: a fox: a pug-dog: a pug-nose: a pug-moth: a pug-engine.—*adjs.* **pugg'ish, pugg'y**,

like a monkey or a pug-dog: snub-nosed.—*n.* **pugg'y**, a term of endearment: a monkey *(Scot.)*: a fox.—*ns.* **pug'-dog**, a small short-haired dog with wrinkled face, upturned nose, and short curled tail; **pug'-engine**, a shunting engine.— *adj.* **pug'-faced**, monkey-faced.—**pug'-moth**, a name for the smaller moths of the geometrid fam. Larentidae; **pug'-nose**, a short, thick nose with the tip turned up.—*adj.* **pug'-nosed.** [Connection with **puck** (1) is conjectured.]

**pug**, *pug*, *n.* clay ground and worked with water. —*v.t.* to beat: to grind with water and make plastic: to pack with pugging.—*n.* **pugg'ing**, beating or punching: working of clay for making bricks, in a pug-mill: clay, sawdust, plaster, etc., put between floors to deaden sound.—**pug'-mill**, machine for mixing and tempering clay. [Origin unknown.]

**pug**, *pug*, *(Anglo-Ind.)* *n.* a beast's footprint.— *v.t.* to track. [Hind. *pag*.]

**pug.** See **pugil** (2).

**puggaree.** Same as **pagri**.

**pugging**, *pug'ing*, *(Shak.)* *adj.* thieving.—*v.t.* and *v.i.* **pug** *(dial.)*, to tug. [Origin unknown.]

**pugh**, an old spelling of **pooh**.

**pugil**, *pū'jil*, *n.* orig. a small handful, now as much as the thumb and two fingers can lift, a pinch. [L. *pugillus*.]

**pugil**, *pū'jil*, *(obs.)* *n.* a boxer.—*ns.* **pu'gilism**, the art or practice of boxing: prize-fighting; **pu'gilist** (abbrev.—*slang*, **pug**, *pug*).—*adjs.* **pugilist'ic**, **-al.**—*adv.* **pugilist'ically.** [L. *pugil*, a boxer.]

**pugnacious**, *pug-nā'shəs*, *adj.* given to fighting: combative: quarrelsome.—*adv.* **pugnā'ciously.**— *ns.* **pugnā'ciousness, pugnacity** *(-nas'i-ti)* inclination to fight: fondness for fighting: quarrelsomeness. [L. *pugnāx, -ācis—pugnāre*, to fight.]

**Pugwash**, *pug'wosh*, *n.* a conference held at intervals by scientists from many countries to discuss the dangers and difficulties into which the world is running. [Name of village in Nova Scotia.]

**puh**, a Shakespearian spelling of **pooh**.

**puir**, *pūr, pār*, *adj.* Scots form of **poor**.

**puisne** *(Shak.* **puisny**), *pū'ni*, *adj.* an obsolete form of **puny**, surviving as applied to certain judges— junior: petty, insignificant *(Shak.)*.—*n.* a puisne judge. [O.Fr. (Fr. *puiné*), from *puis*—L. *posteā*, after, *né*—L. *nātus*, born.]

**puissant, puissaunt**, *pwis'ənt*, sometimes *pū'is-, pū-is'ənt, -ōnt', -ānt', adj.* powerful.—*n.* **puissance**, **-aunce** *(-əns, -ōns', -āns')*, power: (a show-jumping competition with very high jumps showing) the power of a horse.—*adv.* **puissantly** *(-ənt-li)*. [Fr. *puissant*, app. formed as a pr.p. from a vulgar L. substitute for L. *potēns, -entis*; see **potent**.]

**puja**, *pōō'jə*, *n.* worship: reverential observance: a festival. [Sans. *pūjā*, worship.]

**puke**, *pūk*, *v.t.* and *v.i.* vomit.—*v.t.* to cause to vomit.—*n.* vomit: an emetic *(arch.)*: a despicable person *(slang)*.—*n.* **pū'ker**, an emetic. [Poss. connected with Flem. *spukken*, Ger. *spucken*.]

**puke**, *pūk*, *(obs.)* *n.* a fine woollen cloth: a colour between russet or purple and black.—*adj.* made of puke *(Shak.)*: of the colour puke. [M.Du. *puuc*, the best woollen cloth.]

**pukka.** Same as **pucka**.

**pulchritude**, *pul'kri-tūd*, *n.* beauty.—*adj.* **pulchritud'inous.** [L. *pulchritūdō, -inis—pulcher*, beautiful.]

**puldron.** Same as **pauldron**.

**pule**, *pūl*, *v.t.* and *v.i.* to pipe: to whimper or whine.—*n.* **pū'ler.**—*n.* and *adj.* **pū'ling.**—*adv.* **pū'lingly.**—*adj.* **pū'ly**, whining: sickly. [Imit.: cf. Fr. *piauler*.]

**Pulex**, *pū'leks*, *n.* the flea genus, giving name to the family Pulicidae *(-lis'i-dē)*. [L. *pūlex, -icis*.]

**pulka**, *pul'kə*, *n.* a Laplander's boat-shaped

sledge.—Also **pulk, pulk′ha.** [Finnish *pulkka*, Lappish *pulkke, bulkke.*]

**pull**, *pōol*, *v.t.* to pluck: to remove by plucking: to extract: to pick by hand: to strip, deprive of feathers, hair, etc.: to draw: to move, or try or tend to move, towards oneself or in the direction so thought of: to render, or bring to be, by pulling: to row: to transport by rowing: to stretch: to hold back (as a boxing blow, a racehorse to prevent its winning): to take as an impression or proof, orig. by pulling the bar of a hand-press: to strike to the left (right for left-handed person; *cricket, golf*): to bring down: to take a draught of: to draw or fire (a weapon): to snatch, steal (*slang*): to arrest (*slang*): to raid (*slang*).—*v.i.* to give a pull: to perform the action of pulling anything: to tear, pluck: to drag, draw: to strain at the bit: to exert oneself: to go with a pulling movement: to row: to suck: to strike the ball to the left, etc. —*n.* an act, bout, or spell of pulling: a pulling force: a row: a stiff ascent: a draught of liquor: a proof, single impression (*print.*): advantage: influence: an apparatus for pulling: the quantity pulled at one time.—*n.* **pull′er.**— **pull′-back,** a hindrance: a drawback: a device formerly used for making a skirt hang close and straight in front; **pull′-in,** a stopping-place: a transport café.—*adj.* **pull′-on,** requiring only to be pulled on, without fastening.—*n.* a pull-on garment of any kind.—**pull′over,** a jersey, a jumper, a body garment put on over the head; **pull′-through,** a cord with rag for cleaning a rifle barrel; **pull′-up′,** an act of pulling up: a sudden stoppage: a suitable place (esp. for lorry-drivers, etc.) for pulling up.—**pull a face,** to grimace; **pull a fast one on** (*slang*), to take advantage of by a sudden trick; **pull apart, to pieces,** to bring asunder by pulling: criticise harshly; **pull caps,** to scuffle; **pull devil pull baker,** do your best, both sides; **pull down,** to take down or apart: to demolish: to bring down: to reduce in health or vigour; **pull for,** to row for: to support; **pull in,** to draw in: to make tighter: to draw a motor vehicle into the side of the road and halt: to arrest: to earn: of a train, to arrive at a station; **pull off,** to carry through successfully; **pull oneself together,** to regain one's self-control: to collect oneself, preparing to think or to act; **pull one's leg** (see under leg); **pull one's punches** (see under punch); **pull one's weight,** to give full effect to one's weight in rowing: to do one's full share of work, co-operate wholeheartedly; **pull out,** to draw out: to drive a motor vehicle away from the side of the road or out of a line of traffic: of a train, to leave a station: to abandon a place or situation which has become too difficult to cope with (*coll.*); **pull round,** to bring, or come, back to good health or condition or to consciousness; **pull the long bow,** to lie or boast beyond measure; **pull through,** to bring or get to the end of something difficult or dangerous with some success; **pull up,** to pull out of the ground: to tighten the reins: to bring to a stop: to halt: to take to task: to gain ground: to arrest; **pull up stakes,** to prepare to leave a place. [O.E. *pullian,* to pluck, draw.]

**pullet,** *pōol′it,* *n.* a young hen, esp. from first laying to first moult.—**pull′et-sperm′** (*Shak.*), derisively, eggs (lit. the chalaza, once believed to be the male element in the egg). [Fr. *poulette,* dim. of *poule,* a hen—L.L. *pulla,* a hen, fem. of L. *pullus,* a young animal.]

**pulley,** *pōol′i,* *n.* a wheel turning about an axis, and receiving a rope, chain, or band on its rim, used for raising weights, changing direction of pull, transmission of power, etc.: a block: a combination of pulleys or blocks:—*pl.* **pull′eys.** [M.E. *poley, puly*—O.Fr. *polie* (Fr. *poulie*)

L.L. *polegia,* supposed to be from a dim. of Gr. *polos,* axle.]

**Pullman,** *pōol′man,* *n.* a railway saloon or sleeping-car, first made by George M. *Pullman* (1831-97) in America.—In full, **Pullman car.**

**pullulate,** *pul′ū-lāt,* *v.i.* to sprout: to sprout abundantly: to teem: to increase vegetatively. —*n.* **pullulā′tion.** [L. *pullulāre, -ātum—pullulus,* a young animal, sprout—*pullus.*]

**pulmo,** *pul′mō,* *n.* lung:—*pl.* **pulmo′nes** (*-nēz*).— *n.* **pul′mobranch** (*-brangk*), a lung-book.—*adj.* **pulmobranch′iate.**—*n.* **Pulmonaria** (*-mə-nā′ri-ə*), the lungwort genus of the borage family.—*adj.* **pul′monary** (*-mən-ər-i*), of the lungs or respiratory cavity: of the nature of lungs: having lungs: diseased or weak in the lungs.—*n.pl.* **Pulmonā′ta,** an air-breathing order of Gasteropoda.—*n.* **pul′monate,** a member of the Pulmonata.—*adj.* having lungs, lung-sacs, or lung-books, or similar organs.—*adj.* **pulmonic** (*-mon′ik*), of the lungs.—*n.* **Pul′motor,** a registered trademark for an apparatus for forcing air and/or oxygen into and out of the lungs. [L. *pulmō, -ōnis,* lung.]

**pulp,** *pulp,* *n.* any soft fleshy part of an animal, e.g. the tissue in the cavity of a tooth: the soft part of plants, esp. of fruits: any soft structureless mass: the soft mass obtained from the breaking and grinding of rags, wood, etc., before it is hardened into paper: crushed ore: nonsense (*fig.*): sentimentality (*fig.*): a cheap magazine printed on wood-pulp paper, or of a paltry and sentimental or sensational character. —*v.t.* to reduce to pulp: to make pulpy: to deprive of pulp.—*v.i.* to become pulp or like pulp.—*n.* **pulp′er,** a machine for reducing various materials to pulp.—*v.t.* **pulp′ify.**—*adv.* **pulp′ily.**—*n.* **pulp′iness.**—*adj.* **pulp′ous.**—*adj.* **pulp′y.**—**pulp′board,** cardboard made directly from a layer of pulp; **pulp′-cav′ity,** the hollow of a tooth containing pulp; **pulp′-en′gine,** a machine for making pulp for paper; **pulp′mill,** a machine or factory for pulping wood, roots, or other material; **pulp′stone,** a grindstone for pulping wood; **pulp′wood,** wood suitable for paper-making: a board of compressed wood-pulp and adhesive. [L. *pulpa,* flesh, pulp.]

**pulpit,** *pōol′pit,* *n.* a raised structure for preaching from (also *fig.*): an auctioneer's desk or the like: preachers or preaching collectively: a platform (*obs.*).—*adj.* belonging to the pulpit. —*adj.* **pul′pited.**—*ns.* **pulpiteer′, pul′piter,** one who speaks from a pulpit: a preacher; **pul′pitry,** sermonising; **pul′pitum,** a rood-loft. [L. *pulpitum,* a stage.]

**pulpitum.** See pulpit.

**pulque,** *pōol′kā, kē,* *n.* a fermented drink made in Mexico from agave sap. [Sp. Amer.]

**pulsar.** See pulsate.

**pulsate,** *pul′sāt,* or *-sāt′,* *v.i.* to beat, throb: to vibrate: to thrill with life or emotion.—*ns.* **pul′sar** (for 'pulsating star'), any of a number of interstellar sources of regularly pulsed radiation, investigated from 1967, which may be rotating neutron stars; **pulsatance** (*pul′sə-təns, pul-sā′təns*), frequency multiplied by $2\pi$.—*adj.* **pul′satile** (*-sə-til,* in U.S. *-til*), capable of pulsating: pulsatory: rhythmical: played by percussion (*mus.*).—*ns.* **Pulsatill′a,** pasque-flower (because beaten by the wind); **pulsā′tion,** a beating or throbbing: a motion of the heart or pulse: any measured beat: vibration.—*adj.* **pulsative** (*pul′sə-tiv* or *-sāt′*).—*n.* **pulsā′tor** (or *pul′sə-tər*), a machine, or part of a machine, that pulsates or imparts pulsation, as for separating diamonds from earth, for regulating the rhythmical suction of a milking machine, for pumping.—*adj.* **pulsatory** (*pul′sə-tər-i,* or *-sā′*), beating or throbbing.—**pulsating current,** an electric current that changes periodically in intensity but not direction. [L. *pulsāre*, *-ātum*, to beat, freq. of *pellĕre*, *pulsum*, to drive.]

**pulse**, *puls*, *n.* a beating or throbbing: a measured beat or throb: a vibration: a single beat or impulse: a signal of very short duration (*radio*): the beating of the heart and the arteries: a thrill (*fig.*).—*v.i.* to beat, as the heart: to throb: to pulsate.—*v.t.* to drive by pulsation: to produce, or cause to be emitted, in the form of pulses.—*adjs.* **pulsed**; **pulse´less**.—*ns.* **pulse´lessness**; **puls´idge** (Mistress Quickly in 2 *Henry IV*), **pulse**.—*adj.* **pulsif´ic**, producing a single pulse. —*ns.* **pulsim´eter**, an instrument for measuring the strength or quickness of the pulse; **pulsom´eter**, a pulsimeter: a pump that draws in water by condensation of steam in two chambers alternately.—**pulse´-rate**, the number of beats of a pulse per minute; **pulse´-wave**, the expansion of the artery, moving from point to point, like a wave, as each beat of the heart sends the blood to the extremities; **puls´ojet**, in jet propulsion, an intermittent jet.—**feel one's pulse**, to test or measure the heart-beat, usu. by holding the patient's wrist: to explore a person's feelings or inclinations in a tentative way. [L. *pulsus*— *pellĕre*, *pulsum*; partly O.Fr. *pouls*, *pous*, remodelled on Latin.]

**pulse**, *puls*, *n.* seeds of leguminous plants as food collectively—beans, pease, lentils, etc.: the plants yielding them.—*adj.* **pultā´ceous**, macerated and softened. [L. *puls*, *pultis*, porridge; cf. Gr. *poltos*, and **poultice**.]

**pultun**, **pultan**, **pulton**, **pultoon**, *pul´tun*, *-tən*, *-tōōn*, (*Ind.*) *n.* an infantry regiment. [Hind. *pultan*—Eng. **battalion**.]

**pulu**, *pōō´lōō*, *n.* a silky fibre from the Hawaiian tree-fern leaf-bases. [Hawaiian.]

**pulver**, *pul´vər*, (*obs.*) *v.t.* to reduce to powder.— *adj.* **pul´verable** (*rare*).—*ns.* **pulverā´tion** (*rare*), **pulverisation**; **pul´verine**, barilla ash.—*adj.* **pul´verisable** (or *-īz´*).—*n.* **pulverisā´tion**, *-z-*.—*v.t.* **pul´verise**, **-ize**, to reduce to dust or fine powder. —*v.i.* to fall into dust or powder.—*n.* **pul´veriser**, *-z-*, one who pulverises: a machine for pulverising or for spraying.—*adj.* **pul´verous**, dusty or powdery.—*n.* **pulverulence** (*-vûr´ū-ləns*). —*adj.* **pulver´ûlent**, consisting of fine powder: powdery: dusty-looking: readily crumbling.— **Pulver Wednesday**, pulvering day (*obs.*), Ash Wednesday. [L. *pulvis*, *pulveris*, powder.]

**pulvil**, *pul´vil*, *n.* perfumed powder: extended to snuff and other powders.—Also **pulvil´io**, **pulvill´io**, **pulville´**.—*v.t.* **pul´vil**, to powder or scent with pulvil:—*pa.p* **pul´villed**.—*adj.* **pul´vilised**, **-ized**. [It. *polviglio*—*polve*, powder—L. *pulvis*.]

**pulvinus**, *pul-vī´nəs*, *n.* a cushion-like swelling, esp. one at the base of a leaf or leaflet, by whose changes of turgidity movements are effected:—*pl.* **pulvi´ni** (*-nī*).—*adjs.* **pulvill´ar**, of a pulvillus: cushion-like; **pulvill´iform**.—*n.* **pulvill´us**, a little cushion or pad: a pad between the claws of an insect's foot:—*pl.* **pulvill´i** (*ī*).— *adj.* **pulvinar** (*-vī´nər*), cushion-like: of a pulvinus.—*n.* (*-när*) a Roman cushioned seat: a small pillow or pad: a knob on the optic thalamus.—*adjs.* **pul´vinate** (*-vin-āt*), **-d**, cushion-like: pillowy: bulging.—*n.* **pul´vinule**, the pulvinus of a leaflet. [L. *pulvīnus*, cushion, pillow; dim. *pulvillus*; *pulvinar*, a cushioned couch.]

**pulwar**, *pul´wär*, *n.* a light keelless boat used on the Ganges. [Hind. *palwār*.]

**pulza-oil**, *pōōl´zə-oil*, *n.* an oil obtained from physic-nut seeds. [Origin unknown.]

**puma**, *pū´mə*, *n.* the cougar (*Felis concolor*), a large reddish-brown American cat:—*pl.* **pu´mas**. [Peruv. *puma*.]

**pumelo.** Same as **pomelo**.

**pumice**, *pum´is*, *pū´mis*, *n.* an acid glassy lava so full of gas-cavities as to float in water: a frothy portion of any lava: a piece of such lava used for smoothing or cleaning.—*v.t.* to smooth or clean with pumice-stone—also **pumicate** (*pū´mi-kāt*; *rare*).—*adj.* **pumiceous** (*-mish´əs*).—**pum´ice-stone**; **pum´ie** (stone), **pum´y** (stone) (*Spens.*), a pebble, stone. [O.E. *pumic* (*-stān*), pumice (-stone); reintroduced—O.Fr. *pomis*; both—L. *pūmex*, *-icis*.]

**pummel**, *pum´l*, *n.* a less usual spelling of **pommel**. —*v.t.* (the usual spelling) to beat, pound, bethump, esp. with the fists:—*pr.p.* **pumm´elling**; *pa.t.* and *pa.p.* **pumm´elled**. [**pommel**.]

**pump**, *pump*, *n.* a machine for raising fluids or for compressing, rarefying, or transferring gases: a stroke of a pump: an act of pumping.—*v.t.* to raise, force, compress, exhaust, empty, remove, or inflate with a pump: to discharge by persistent effort: to move in the manner of a pump: to subject to, or elicit by, persistent questioning: to pump water on (*obs.*): to put out of breath (esp. in *pass.*; often with *out*; *coll.*).—*v.i.* to work a pump: to work like a pump: to move up and down like a pump-handle: to spurt.—*n.* **pump´er**.—**pump´-gun**, a gun whose chamber is fed by a pump-like movement; **pump´-hand´le**, the lever that works a pump; **pump´-head**, **-hood**, a frame covering the upper wheel of a chain-pump, serving to guide the water into the discharge-spout; **pump´-room**, the apartment at a mineral spring in which the waters are drunk; **pump´-water**, water from a pump; **pump´-well**, a well from which water is got by pumping: the compartment in which a pump works. [Ety. dub.]

**pump**, *pump*, *n.* a light shoe without fastening esp. for dancing.—*adj.* **pumped**, wearing pumps. [Origin unknown.]

**pumpernickel**, *pōōmp´ər-nik-l*, *n.* rye bread, much used in Westphalia. [Ger. The Ger. word means a rackety goblin, a coarse lout, rye bread (poss. from its giving forth a sound like *pump* when struck).]

**pumpkin**, *pum(p)´kin*, in U.S. often *pung´kin*, *n.* a plant (*Cucurbita pepo*) of the gourd family, or its fruit.—Also **pump´ion**. [O.Fr. *pompon*— L. *pepō*—Gr. *pepōn*, ripe; see **pepo**.]

**pumy.** See **pumice**.

**pun**, *pun*, *v.t.* to pound (*Shak.*): to ram: to consolidate by ramming:—*pr.p.* **punn´ing**; *pa.t.* and *pa.p.* **punned**.—*n.* **punn´er**, a tool for punning, a ram. [See **pound** (3).]

**pun**, *pun*, *v.i.* to play upon words alike or nearly alike in sound but different in meaning:—*pr.p.* **punn´ing**; *pa.t.* and *pa.p.* **punned**.—*n.* a play upon words.—*ns.* **punn´ing**; **pun´ster**, a maker of puns. [A late-17th-century word; origin unknown; It. *puntiglio*, fine point, has been conjectured.]

**puna**, *pōōn´ə*, *n.* bleak tableland in the Andes: cold wind there: mountain sickness. [Amer. Sp.—Quechua.]

**punalua**, *pōō-nə-lōō´ə*, *n.* a system of group-marriage, sisters (by blood or tribal reckoning) having their husbands in common, or brothers their wives, or both.—*adj.* **punalu´an**. [Hawaiian.]

**punce**, *puns*, (*Austr.*) *n.* an effeminate man.

**Punch**, *punch*, *punsh*, *n.* a hook-nosed hunchback, chief character in the street puppet-show 'Punch and Judy'; the chief illustrated English comic paper (1841). [Shortened from **Punchinello**.]

**punch**, *punch*, *punsh*, (*dial.*) *adj.* short and thick. —*n.* a thick-set short man: a short-legged, round-bodied horse, long bred in Suffolk.—*adj.* **punch´y**. [Poss. shortened from **puncheon**, or from **Punchinello**, or a variant of **bunch**.]

**punch**, *punch*, *punsh*, (*obs.* *pōōnsh*), *n.* a drink ordinarily of spirit, water, sugar, lemon-juice, and spice (with variations).—**punch´-bowl**, a large bowl for making punch in; **punch´-ladle**, a ladle for filling glasses from a punch-bowl.

[Traditionally from the five original ingredients, from Hindi *pǎc*, five—Sans. *pañca*; but the vowel presents a difficulty.]

**punch**, *punch*, *punsh*, *v.t.* to prod: to poke: to drive (cattle) (*U.S.*): to strike with a forward thrust, as of the fist: to thump: to kick (*Northern*): to stamp, pierce, perforate, indent, by a forward thrust of a tool or part of a machine: to make, obtain, or remove by such a thrust: to press in vigorously the keys or button of: to record by pressing a key.—*v.i.* to perform an act of punching: to clock (*in* or *out*).—*n.* a vigorous thrust or forward blow: striking power: effective forcefulness: a tool or machine for punching: a die: a prop for a mine-roof.—*n.* **punch′er**, one who punches: an instrument for punching: a cow-puncher, drover (*U.S.*): the driver of a team (*Austr.*).—*adj.* **punch′y**, vigorous, powerful.—**punch′-ball,** a suspended ball used for boxing practice; **punch′-card,** a card with perforations representing data, used in the operation of automatic computers.—*adj.* **punch′-drunk,** having a form of cerebral concussion from past blows in boxing, with results resembling drunkenness: dazed.—**punch line,** the last line or conclusion of a joke, in which the point lies: the last part of a story, giving it meaning or an unexpected twist; **punch′-prop,** in mines, a short piece of wood used as a prop; **punch′-up,** a fight with fists.—**pull one′s punches,** to hold back one′s blows (also *fig.*). [**pounce**; or from **puncheon** (1); possibly in some senses for **punish.**]

**puncheon**, *pun′chn*, *-shn*, *n.* a dagger (*obs.*): a tool for piercing, or for stamping: a short supporting post: a split trunk with one face smoothed for flooring, etc. [O.Fr. *poinson*—L. *pungĕre*, *punctum*, to prick.]

**puncheon**, *pun′chn*, *-shn*, *n.* a cask: a liquid measure of from 70 to 120 gallons. [O.Fr. *poinson*, a cask; origin obscure.]

**Punchinello**, *punch-*, *punsh-i-nel′ō*, *n.* a hook-nosed character in an Italian puppet-show: a buffoon, any grotesque personage. [It. *Pulcinella*, a Neapolitan buffoon, of doubtful origin.]

**punctate, -d,** *pungk′tāt*, *-id*, *adjs.* dotted: pitted.—*ns.* **puncta′tion; puncta′tor,** one who marks with dots—esp. applied to the Massoretes who invented the Hebrew vowel-points. [L. *punctum*, a point, puncture—*pungĕre*, *punctum*, to prick.]

**punctilio,** *pungk-til′i-ō*, *-yō*, *n.* a nice point in behaviour or ceremony: a point about which one is scrupulous: nicety in forms: exact observance of forms:—*pl.* **punctilios.**—*adj.* **punctil′ious,** attentive to punctilio: scrupulous and exact.—*adv.* **punctil′iously.**—*n.* **punctil′iousness.** [It. *puntiglio* and Sp. *puntillo*, dims. of *punto*—L. *punctum*, a point.]

**puncto,** *pungk′tō* (*Shak.*). Same as **punto.**

**punctual,** *pungk′tū-əl*, *adj.* of the nature of a point: pertaining to a point, or points: of punctuation: punctilious: exact in keeping time and appointments: done at the exact time: up to time.—*ns.* **punc′tualist,** an authority on or observer of punctilios; **punctuality** (*-al′i-ti*).—*adv.* **punc′tually.** [L.L. *punctuālis*—*punctum*, a point.]

**punctuate,** *pungk′tū-āt*, *v.t.* to mark with points: to mark off with the usual stops, points of interrogation, and the like: to intersperse: to emphasise.—*n.* **punctua′tion,** the act or art of dividing sentences by points or marks.—*adj.* **punc′tuative.**—*n.* **punc′tuator.** [L.L. *punctuāre*, *-ātum*, to prick.—L. *punctum*.]

**punctum,** *pungk′təm*, (*anat.*) *n.* a point, dot: a minute aperture:—*pl.* **punc′ta.**—*adjs.* **punc′tulate, -d,** minutely dotted or pitted.—*ns.* **punctū-lā′tion; punc′tūle,** a minute dot, pit, or aperture.—**punctum caecum** (*sē′kəm*; *pōōngk′tōōm kī′-kōōm*, blind spot), the point of the retina from

which the optic nerve fibres radiate. [L. *punctum*—*pungĕre*, *punctum*, to prick.]

**puncture,** *pungk′chər*, *n.* a pricking: a small hole made with a sharp point: perforation of a pneumatic tyre.—*v.t.* and *v.i.* to make or get a puncture.—*adj.* **punc′tured,** perforated: pierced: marked with little holes: consisting of little holes.—*n.* **punctūrā′tion.** [L. *punctūra*—*pungĕre*, to prick.]

**pundigrion,** *pun-dig′ri-on*, (*obs.*) *n.* a pun. [Origin unknown; It. *puntiglio* is only a conjecture.]

**pundit, pandit,** *pun′dit*, *n.* one who is learned in the language, science, laws, and religion of India: any learned man: an authority.—*n.* **pun′ditry.** [Hindi *paṇḍit*—Sans. *paṇḍita*.]

**pundonor,** *pōōn-dō-nōr′*, *-nōr′*, *n.* point of honour: —*pl.* **pundonor′es** (*-ās*). [Sp.,—*punto de honor.*]

**pungent,** *pun′jənt*, *adj.* sharp: ending in a hard sharp point (*bot.*): pricking or acrid to taste or smell: keenly touching the mind: painful: sarcastic.—*ns.* **pun′gency** (*Crabbe,* **pun′gence**).—*adv.* **pun′gently.** [L. *pungēns*, *-entis*, pr.p. of *pungĕre*, to prick.]

**Punic,** *pū′nik*, *adj.* of ancient Carthage: Carthaginian: faithless, treacherous, deceitful (as the Romans alleged the Carthaginians to be): purple (*obs.*).—*n.* the Semitic language of ancient Carthage.—*n.* **Pu′nica,** the pomegranate genus, constituting the family **Punicā′ceae** (akin to the myrtle and loosestrife families).—*adj.* **punicā′ceous.**—**Punic apple** (*obs.*), the pomegranate; **Punic faith,** treachery. [L. *Pūnicus*—*Poenī,* the Carthaginians.]

**Punica fides,** *pū′ni-ka fī′dēz, pōō′ni-ka fi′dās,* (L.) Punic faith (see above).

**punily.** See **puny.**

**punish,** *pun′ish*, *v.t.* to cause (one) to suffer for an offence: to cause one to suffer for (offence): to handle, beat, severely (*coll.*): to consume a large quantity of (*coll.*).—*v.i.* to inflict punishment.—*n.* **punishabil′ity.**—*adj.* **pun′ishable.**—*n.* **pun′isher.**—*adj.* **pun′ishing,** causing suffering or retribution: severe, testing (*coll.*).—*n.* **pun′ishment,** act or method of punishing: penalty imposed for an offence: severe handling (*coll.*). [Fr. *punir, punissant*—L. *pūnīre,* to punish—*poena,* penalty.]

**punition,** *pū-nish′ən,* *n.* punishment.—*adjs.* **pu′nitive** (*-ni-tiv*), concerned with, inflicting, or intended to inflict, punishment; **pu′nitory.** [L. *pūnīre,* to punish.]

**Punjabi, Punja(u)bee, Panjabi,** *pun-jä′bē,* *n.* a native or inhabitant of the *Punjab* in India and Pakistan: the language of the Punjab.—*adj.* of the Punjab. [Hindi *Pañjābī.*]

**punk,** *pungk,* *n.* a prostitute, strumpet (*arch.*): anything or anyone worthless: balderdash: a foolish person: a homosexual, often a boy (*slang*).—*adj.* rotten: worthless: miserable. [Origin unknown.]

**punk,** *pungk,* *n.* touchwood: tinder: a preparation of amadou used as tinder. [Poss. **spunk;** or poss. of American Indian origin.]

**punka, punkah,** *pung′ka, n.* a fan: a palm-leaf fan: a large mechanical fan for cooling a room. [Hindi *pākhā,* a fan.]

**punnet,** *pun′it, n.* a small shallow chip-basket, as for strawberries. [Origin unknown.]

**punning, punster.** See **pun.**

**punt,** *punt, n.* a flat-bottomed boat with square ends.—*v.t.* to propel by pushing a pole against the bottom: to transport by punt.—*v.i.* to go in a punt: to go shooting in a punt: to pole a punt or boat.—*n.* **punt′er.**—**punt′-fishing,** fishing from a punt; **punt′-gun,** a heavy gun of large bore used for shooting water-fowl from a punt; **punt′-pole,** a pole for propelling a punt; **punts′-man,** a sportsman who uses a punt. [O.E. *punt* —L. *pontō, -ōnis,* punt, pontoon; cf. **pontoon.**]

**punt,** *punt, v.i.* to stake against the bank: to back

a horse.—*n.* punt′er, one who punts: a professional gambler. [Fr. *ponter*.]

**punt,** *punt, n.* the act of kicking a dropped football before it touches the ground.—*v.t.* to kick in this manner: to knock. [Origin obscure.]

**puntee.** See punty.

**punto,** *pun′tō*, also **puncto,** *pungk′tō, n.* a moment (*obs.*): a point, punctilio (*obs.*): a pass or thrust in fencing (*Shak.* punc′to).—**punto dritt′o,** a direct or straight hit; **punto rever′so** (It. *riverso*), a back-handed stroke. [Sp. and It. *punto*—L. *punctum*, a point.]

**punty, puntee, pontie, ponty,** *pun′ti,* pontil, *pon′til, n.* an iron rod used in holding and manipulating glassware during the process of making. [Prob. Fr. *pontil,* app.—It. *pontello, puntello,* dim. of *punto,* point.]

**puny,** *pū′ni, adj.* puisne (*obs.*): inexperienced (*Shak.*): stunted: feeble:—*comp.* pū′nier; *superl.* pū′niest.—*adv.* pū′nily.—*n.* pū′niness. [puisne.]

**pup,** *pup, n.* a shortened form of puppy.—*v.t.* and *v.i.* to whelp:—*pr.p.* pupp′ing; *pa.t.* and *pa.p.* pupped.—**pup tent,** a small tent, easily carried.—**buy a pup,** to be swindled; **in pup,** of a bitch, pregnant; **sell a pup,** inveigle one into a specious bad bargain: to swindle.

**pupa,** *pū′pə, n.* an insect in the usually passive stage of development between larva and imago: an intermediate stage of development in some other invertebrates:—*pl.* **pupae** (*pū′pē*).—*adjs.* pū′pal, of a pupa; pūpā′rial.—*n.* pūpā′rium, the last larval skin separated but retained as a hard protective covering for the pupa: sometimes, the covering and the pupa.—*v.i.* pū′pate, to become a pupa.—*n.* pūpā′tion.—*adjs.* pūpigerous (-*pij′ə-rəs*), having a puparium; pūpip′arous, having pupae developed within the body of the mother.—**pu′pa-case,** a puparium. [L. *pūpa,* a girl, a doll.]

**pupil,** *pū′pl, -pil, n.* a boy up to the age of 14, or a girl up to 12 (*Rom.* and *Scots law*): a ward (*law*): one who is being taught: one who is being or has been taught by a particular teacher.—*adj.* under age.—*ns.* pu′pillage, state of being a pupil: the time during which one is a pupil (in *Shak.,* etc., sometimes taken as two words, **pupil age**); pupillar′ity, the state or time of being legally a pupil.—*adjs.* pu′pillary, pertaining to a pupil or ward, or one under academic discipline. (The above words are sometimes spelt with one *l.*)—**pupil teacher,** a pupil who does some teaching as part of his training for later entry into the profession. [Fr. *pupille*—L. *pūpillus, pūpilla,* dims. of *pūpus,* boy, *pūpa,* girl.]

**pupil,** *pū′pl, -pil, n.* the apple of the eye: the round opening in the eye through which the light passes: a central spot, esp. within a spot.—*n.* pupilabil′ity, an intentionally unintelligible word in *Tristram Shandy* (IV, i).—*adjs.* pu′pillary; pu′pillate (*zool.*), having a central spot of another colour. (The above words are sometimes with one *l.*) [L. *pūpilla,* pupil of the eye, orig. the same as the preceding, from the small image to be seen in the eye.]

**puppet,** *pup′it, n.* a doll or image moved by wires or hands in a show: a marionette: one who acts just as another tells him.—*adj.* behaving like a puppet: actuated by others.—*ns.* **puppeteer′,** one who manipulates puppets; **pupp′-etry,** play of, or with, puppets: puppets collectively: puppet-like action: puppet-shows: anything like or associated with puppets: dress of puppets (*obs.*).—**pupp′et-play,** a drama performed by puppets; **pupp′et-show,** an exhibition of puppets: a puppet-play; **pupp′et-valve** (see **poppet).** [Earlier **poppet;** cf. O.Fr. *poupette,* dim. from L. *pūpa.*]

**puppy,** *pup′i, n.* a puppet (*dial.*): a lap-dog, toy-dog (*obs.*): a young dog: a whelp: a young

seal: a conceited young man.—*v.t.* and *v.i.* to pup.—*ns.* **pupp′ydom;** pupp′yhood.—*adj.* pupp′y-ish.—*n.* pupp′yism, conceit in men.—**pupp′y-dog;** pupp′y-fat, temporary fatness in childhood or adolescence.—*adj.* pupp′y-head′ed (*Shak.*), having the mind of a puppy. [App. Fr. *poupée,* a doll or puppet—L. *pūpa.*]

**pupunha,** *pōō-pōōn′ya, n.* the peach-palm: its fruit. [Port. from Tupí.]

**pur.** See purr.

**pur,** *pûr,* (*obs.*) *n.* the knave in the game of post and pair.

**pur,** *pür,* (Fr.) *adj.* pure.—**pur sang** (*sã*), pure blood: thoroughbred: total.

**Purana,** *pōō-rä′nə, n.* any one of a class of sacred books in Sanskrit literature, cosmogonical, legendary, religious, etc.—*adj.* **Puranic** (-*rän′ik*). [Sans. *purāna*—*purā,* of old.]

**Purbeck,** *pûr′bek, adj.* of the Isle (really peninsula) of Purbeck, in Dorset.—*n.* and *adj.* **Purbeck′ian** (*geol.*), Jurassic of the uppermost stage.—**Purbeck marble, stone,** a freshwater shelly limestone quarried in the Isle.

**purblind,** *pûr′blīnd, adj.* orig. apparently wholly blind: nearly blind: dim-sighted, esp spiritually.—*adv.* pur′blindly.—*n.* pur′blindness. [pure (or perh. O.Fr. intens. pfx. *pur*-), and blind.]

**purchase,** *pûr′chəs, v.t.* to seek to bring about (*obs.*): to bring about (*obs.*): to acquire: to get in any way other than by inheritance (*law*): to buy: to obtain by labour, danger, etc.: to be amends for (with *out*) (*Shak.*): to raise or move by a mechanical power.—*v.i.* to strive (*Shak.*): to make purchases: to accumulate possessions (*obs.*).—*n.* act of purchasing: seizure (*obs.*): that which is purchased: acquisition: prize, booty (*arch.*): whatever one can do for oneself by shifts (*obs.*): annual rent: bargain (*obs.*): price (*obs.*): any mechanical advantage in raising or moving bodies or apparatus: advantageous hold, or means of exerting force advantageously.—*adj.* pur′chasable.—*n.* pur′chaser.—**purchase money,** the money paid, or to be paid, for anything; **purchase system,** the system by which, before 1871, commissions in the British army could be bought; **purchase tax,** a British form of sales-tax levied on specified goods and at differential rates.—**so many years′ purchase,** value, price, of a house, an estate, etc., equal to the amount of so many years′ rent or income.—**not worth a day′s,** etc., purchase, not likely to last a day, etc. [O.Fr. *porchacier* (Fr. *pourchasser*), to seek eagerly, pursue—*pur* (L. *prō*) for, *chacier, chasser,* to chase.]

**purdah,** *pûr′də, n.* a curtain, esp. for screening women′s apartments: seclusion of women. [Urdu and Pers. *pardah.*]

**purdonium,** *pûr-dō′ni-əm, n.* a kind of coal-scuttle introduced by one Purdon.

**pure,** *pūr, adj.* clean: unsoiled: unmixed: not adulterated: free from guilt or defilement: chaste: free from bad taste, meretriciousness, solecism, barbarism: modest: mere: that and that only: utter, sheer: of a study, confined to that which belongs directly to it: non-empirical, involving an exercise of mind alone, without admixture of the results of experience: excellent, fine (*obs.*): homozygous, breeding true (*biol.*): unconditional (*law*): free from ritual uncleanness.—*n.* purity: dog′s dung or similar substance used by tanners (also **puer**).—*adv.* purely: without admixture: utterly, thoroughly (*obs.*).—*v.t.* to cleanse, refine: to treat with pure (also **puer**).—*adv.* pure′ly, chastely: unmixedly: unconditionally: wholly, entirely: wonderfully, very much (*dial.*).—*n.* pure′ness.—*adjs.* pure′-blood, -ed, pure′-bred, of unmixed race.—**pure mathematics,** mathematics treated without application to observed facts of nature or to practical life; **pure reason,** reason alone, without any mixture of sensibility; **pure science**, science considered apart from practical applications. [Fr. *pur*—L. *pūrus*, pure.]

**purée**, *pū′rā*, *n*. food material reduced to pulp and passed through a sieve: a soup without solid pieces. [Fr.]

**purfle**, *pûr′fl*, *v.t.* to ornament the edge of, as with embroidery or inlay.—*n.* a decorated border: a profile (*obs*.).—*n.* **pur′fling**, a purfle, esp. around the edges of a fiddle. [O.Fr. *pourfiler*—L. *prō*, before, *filum*, a thread.]

**purfled**, *pûr′fld*, (*Scot*.) *adj.* short-winded.—*adj.* **pur′fly** (*Carlyle*).

**purge**, *pûrj*, *v.t.* to purify: to remove impurities from: to clear of undesirable elements or persons: to remove as an impurity: to clarify: to clear from accusation: to expiate: to evacuate, as the bowels.—*v.i.* to become pure by clarifying: to evacuate the bowels: to have frequent evacuations: to take a purgative.—*n.* act of purging: an expulsion or massacre of those who are not trusted: a purgative.—*n.* **purgation** (-*gā′*), a purging: a clearing away of impurities: the act of clearing from suspicion or imputation of guilt (*law*); a cleansing.—*adj.* **purgative** (*pûrg′ə-tiv*), cleansing: having the power of evacuating the intestines.—*n.* a medicine that evacuates.—*adv.* **pur′gatively.**—*adjs.* **purgato′rial, purgato′rian**, pertaining to purgatory; **pur′gatory**, purging or cleansing: expiatory.—*n.* a place or state in which souls are after death purified from venial sins (*R.C.*): any kind or state of suffering for a time: intense discomfort (*coll*.): a ravine (*U.S.*): a swamp (*U.S.*). —*n.* **purger** (*pûrj′ər*).—*n.* and *adj.* **purging** (*pûrj′*). —purging cassia, flax (see cassia, flax). [Fr. *purger*—L. *pûrgāre*, -*ātum*—earlier *pûrigāre*—*pûrus*, pure.]

**purify**, *pū′ri-fī*, *v.t.* to make pure: to cleanse from foreign or hurtful matter: to free from guilt, from ritual uncleanness or from improprieties or barbarisms in language.—*v.i.* to become pure:—*pr.p.* **pu′rifying;** *pa.t.* and *pa.p.* **pu′rified.**—*n.* **purificā′tion.**—*adj.* **pu′rificative**:— *n.* **pu′rificātor.**—*adj.* **pu′rificātory**, tending to purify or cleanse.—*n.* **pu′rifier.**—**Purification of the Blessed Virgin Mary**, a feast observed in the R.C. Church on 2nd February, in commemoration of the purification of the Virgin Mary according to the Jewish ceremonial (Lev. xii. 1-4) forty days after the birth of Christ. [Fr. *purifier*—L. *pūrificāre*—*pūrus*, pure, *facĕre*, to make.]

**purim**, *pū′rim*, *pōōr-ēm′*, *n.* the Feast of Lots held about 1st of March, in which the Jews commemorated their deliverance from the plot of Haman, as related in Esther (see esp. iii. 7). [Heb. *pūrîm* (sing. *pūr*), lots; origin unknown.]

**purin, purine**, *pū′rin*, -*ēn*, *n.* a white crystalline substance $C_5H_4N_4$, which with oxygen forms uric acid ($C_5H_4N_4O_3$), and is the nucleus of many other derivatives. [Contracted from L. *pūrum ūricum* (*acidum*), pure uric (acid).]

**purism**, *pūr′izm*, *n.* fastidious, esp. over-fastidious, insistence upon purity (esp. of language in vocabulary or idiom).—*n.* and *adj.* **pūr′ist.**—*adjs.* **pūris′tic, -al.** [L. *pūrus*, pure.]

**Puritan**, *pūr′i-tən*, *n.* one who in the time of Elizabeth and the Stuarts wished to carry the reformation of the Church of England further by purifying it of ceremony: an opponent of the Church of England on account of its retention of much of the ritual and belief of the Roman Catholics: an opponent of the Royalists in the 17th century: person of like views with, or in sympathy with, the historical Puritans: a person strictly moral in conduct: slightingly, one professing a too-strict morality: an advocate of purity in any sense.—*adj.* pertaining to the Puritans.—*adjs.* **pūritanic** (-*tan′ik*), **-al.**—

*adv.* **pūritan′ically.**—*v.t.* and *v.i.* **pūr′itanise, -ize.** —*n.* **pūr′itanism.** [L. *pūrus*, pure.]

**purity**, *pūr′i-ti*, *n.* condition of being pure: freedom from mixture of any kind, sin, defilement, or ritual uncleanness: chastity: sincerity: freedom from foreign or improper idioms or words. [L. *pūritās*, -*ātis*—*pūrus*.]

**purl**, *pûrl*, *v.i.* to flow with a murmuring sound: to flow in eddies: to curl or swirl.—*n.* a trickling rill: a movement or murmuring as of a stream among stones: an eddy or ripple (also **pirl**).— *n.* and *adj.* **purl′ing.** [Cf. Norw. *purla*, to babble, Sw. dial. *porla*, to purl, ripple.]

**purl**, *pûrl*, *v.i.* to spin round: to capsize: to go head over heels: to fall headlong or heavily.— *v.t.* to throw headlong.—*n.* a heavy or headlong fall: an upset.—*n.* **purl′er**, a headlong or heavy fall or throw. [Perh. conn. with purl (1).]

**purl**, *pûrl*, *v.t.* to embroider or edge with gold or silver thread: to fringe with a waved edging, as lace: to knit with inverted stitches.—*n.* twisted gold or silver wire: a loop or twist, esp. on an edge (also **pearl**): a succession of such loops, or a lace or braid having them: a fold, pleat, or frilling: knitting with inverted stitches (also **pearl**).—*adj.* (also **pearl**) with inverted stitches. [Origin unknown: perh. different words; cf. **pearl** (2).]

**purl**, *pûrl*, *n.* formerly, ale with wormwood: ale warmed and spiced. [Origin unknown.]

**purler**, *pûrl′ər*, (*Austr*.) *n.* something extremely good.

**purlicue.** Same as pirlicue.

**purlieu**, *pûr′lū*, *n.* orig. a tract wrongly added to a royal forest, but disafforested by a new perambulation: borders or outskirts. [A.Fr. *puralee*, land severed by perambulation—O.Fr. *pur* ( = L. *prō*), *allee*, going; infl. by Fr. *lieu*, place.]

**purlin, purline**, *pûr′lin*, *n.* a piece of timber stretching across the principal rafters to support the common or subsidiary rafters. [Origin obscure.]

**purloin**, *pər-loin′*, *pûr′*, *v.t.* to filch, steal.—*v.i.* to practise theft.—*n.* **purloin′er.** [A.Fr. *purloigner*, to remove to a distance—*pur*- (L. *prō*), for, *loin* (L. *longē*), far.]

**purpie, purpy**, *pûr′pi*, (*obs. Scot.*) *n.* purslane.— **wa′ter-pur′pie**, brooklime. [O.Fr. *parpié*—L.L. *pullī pēs*, colt's foot, purslane.]

**purple**, *pûr′pl*, *n.* crimson (*hist.*): the Tyrian crimson dye, got in ancient times from various shellfish (Murex, Purpura, Buccinum, etc.; *hist.*): the animal yielding it: a crimson cloth or garment anciently worn by kings and emperors (*hist.*): the dignity of king or emperor: cardinalate (from the red hat (former) and robes): now, any mixture of blue and red: a purple pigment: a purple-red pigment in the rods of the mammalian eye and in parts of other eyes (**visual purple**): a purple flower (see **long-purples**): (in *pl.*) purpura: (in *pl.*) swine-fever: (in *pl.*) ear-cockle.—*adj.* of the colour purple, mixed red and blue: blood-red, bloody (*hist.*). —*v.t.* to make purple.—*v.i.* to become purple. —*adjs.* **pur′plish,** **pur′ply**, somewhat purple.— **purple airway**, a reserved course for a royal flight. —*adjs.* **pur′ple-born,** porphyrogenite; **pur′ple-coloured.**—**purple emperor**, one of the largest of British butterflies and one of the most richly coloured (*Apatura iris*); **purple finch**, an American finch with red head and breast in the cock; **purple fish**, a shellfish yielding purple dye; **purple heart**, the purple-coloured wood of species of Copaifera (fam. Caesalpiniaceae) (also **purple wood**): a mauve heart-shaped tablet of a stimulant drug of amphetamine type: (*cap*.) a U.S. decoration for wounds received on active service. —*adjs.* **pur′ple-hued; pur′ple-in-grain**, fast dyed in purple.—**purple patch**, a passage of fine, or

Neutral vowels in unaccented syllables: *el′ə-mənt*; for certain sounds in foreign words, see p. viii

(often) over-ornate, writing.—**born in the purple**, born in the purple chamber (see **porphyrogenite**): hence, of exalted birth; **purple of Cassius**, a red or purple pigment discovered by Andreas Cassius (*c.* 1683), made from stannous, stannic, and gold chlorides in solution. [O.E. (Northumb.) *purpl*(*e*), purple (adj.)—*purpur* (n.)— L. *purpura*—Gr. *porphȳra*, purple-fish.]

**purport**, *pûr'pərt*, *-pōrt*, *-pôrt*, formerly also *pûr-pōrt'*, *-pôrt'*, *n.* meaning conveyed: substance, gist, tenor: outward appearance, guise, as conveying an impression (*Spens.*): purpose (*rare*).— *v.t.* **purport'** (also *pûr'*), to give out as its meaning: to convey to the mind: to seem, claim, profess (to mean, be, etc.): to purpose (*rare*). —*adv.* **purport'edly**.—*adj.* **pur'portless**. [O.Fr., from *pur* (Fr. *pour*)—L. *prō*, for, *porter*—L. *portāre*, to carry.]

**purpose**, *pûr'pəs*, *n.* idea or aim kept before the mind as the end of effort: power of seeking the end desired: act or fact of purposing: an end desired: a useful function: intention of going (*Shak.*): purport (*Shak.*): conversation, conversational speech (*Spens.*): (in *pl.*) a sort of conversational game.—*v.t.* to intend.—*v.i.* (*Spens.*) to discourse.—*adjs.* **pur'posed**, intentional: intended: purposeful; **pur'poseful**, directed towards a purpose: actuated by purpose.—*adv.* **pur'posefully**.—*n.* **pur'posefulness**.— *adj.* **pur'poseless**, without purpose: aimless: having no purpose in mind.—*adv.* **pur'poselessly**.—*n.* **pur'poselessness**.—*adj.* **pur'pose-like** (*Scot.*), efficient-looking: purposed.—*adv.* **pur'posely**, intentionally.—*adj.* **pur'posive**, directed towards an end.—*n.* **pur'posiveness**.—**on** (*arch.* **of**) **purpose**, of set purpose, with design, intentionally; **to good** (or **some**) **purpose**, with good effect; **to the purpose**, to the point, or material to the question. [O.Fr. *pourpos, propos*—L. *prōpo 'tum*, a thing intended—*prō*, forward, *pōnēre, positum*, to place; cf. **propose**.]

**purpres're**, *pûr-pres'chər, n.* encroachment upon public property. [O.Fr. *purpresture—pour*, for (L. *pro*), *prendre*—L. *praehendēre*, to take.]

**Purpura** *pûr'pū-rə, n.* a genus of marine gasteropods yielding purple dye: (without *cap.*) purples, an eruption of small purple spots, caused by extravasation of blood.—*n.* and *adj.* **pur'pure**, purple.—*adjs.* **purpū'real**, purple; **purpū'ric**, relating to purpura.—*n.* **pur'purin**, a purple colouring-matter got from madder. [L. *purpura* —Gr. *porphȳra.*]

**purr, pur,** *pûr, v.i.* to utter a low, murmuring sound, as a cat when pleased.—*v.t.* to say or utter with or by purring.—*ns.* purr; **purr'ing**.— *adv.* **purr'ingly**. [Imit.]

**purse**, *pûrs, n.* a small bag for carrying money: a sum of money in a purse: a sum given as a present or offered as a prize: funds: a live coal flying out of the fire, as an omen: a purse-like receptacle or cavity.—*v.t.* to put into a purse or one's own purse, to pocket: to contract as the mouth of a purse: to draw into folds or wrinkles. —*v.i.* to pucker: to take purses (*obs.*).—*ns.* **purse'ful**, as much as a purse can hold: enough to fill a purse; **purs'er**, formerly a naval paymaster: an officer in charge of cabins, stewards, etc.; **purs'ership**.—**purse'-bearer**, one who has charge of another's money: a treasurer: one who carries in a bag the Great Seal for the Lord Chancellor, or the royal commission for the Lord High Commissioner; **purse'-net**, a net that closes like a purse; **purse'-pride**.—*adj.* **purse'-proud**, proud of one's wealth: insolent from wealth.—**purse'-seine**, a seine that can be drawn into the shape of a bag; **purse'-snatcher**; **purse'-snatching**; **purse'-strings**, the strings fastening a purse (usu. *fig.*); **purse'-tak'ing**, robbing.—**privy purse**, an allowance for a sovereign's private expenses; **public purse**, the

nation's finances. [O.E. *purs,* app.—L.L. *bursa* —Gr. *byrsa,* a hide.]

**pursew,** Spenser's usual spelling of **pursue.**

**purslane,** *pûrs'lin, n.* a pot and salad herb (*Portulaca oleracea*) of the Portulacaceae: any member of the genus or the family.—**sea purslane,** a fleshy seaside sandwort (*Arenaria,* or *Honckenya, peploides*): orach of various species; **water purslane,** a small-flowered prostrate lythraceous plant of wet places (*Peplis portula*).—Also **purslain.** [O.Fr. *porcelaine*—L. *porcilāca, portulāca*; see **Portulaca.**]

**pursue,** *pər-sū', -sōō', v.t.* to harass, persecute, persist in opposing or seeking to injure: to prosecute or sue (*Scots law*): to follow in order to overtake and capture or kill: to chase: to hunt: to follow with haste: to follow up: to follow the course of: to be engaged in: to carry on: to seek to obtain or attain: to proceed in accordance with: to proceed with.—*v.i.* to follow: to go on or continue: to act as a prosecutor at law.—*adj.* **pursu'able**.—*ns.* **pursu'al,** (more often) **pursu'ance,** pursuit: act of carrying out or (e.g. *in pursuance of this policy*) following out.—*adj.* **pursu'ant,** pursuing: in pursuance (with *to*; approaching an *adv.*).—*adv.* **pursu'antly**.—*n.* **pursu'er,** one who pursues: a plaintiff (*Scots law*).—*n.* and *adj.* **pursu'ing**.—*adv.* **pursu'ingly**. [A.Fr. *pursuer, pursiwer*—popular L. forms *pro-, per-sequēre, -īre,* for L. *prōsequī, persequī*—*prō-, per-* (the prefixes being confused) and *sequī,* to follow.]

**pursuit,** *pər-sūt', -sōōt', n.* the act of pursuing: endeavour to attain: occupation: employment: that which is pursued. [A.Fr. *purseute,* fem. pa.p.; see **pursue**.]

**pursuivant,** *pûr's*(*w*)*i-vənt, n.* an attendant or follower: a state messenger with power to execute warrants: an officer ranking below a herald. [Fr. *poursuivant,* pr.p. of *poursuivre,* to pursue.]

**pursy,** *pûrs'i, adj.* puffy: fat and short: shortwinded.—*n.* **purs'iness**. [O.Fr. *poulsif,* brokenwinded—*poulser* (Fr. *pousser*)—L. *pulsāre,* to drive.]

**pursy,** *pûrs'i, adj.* pursed up: puckered. [**purse.**]

**purtenance,** *pûr'tən-əns, n.* that which pertains or belongs: the inwards of an animal (*B.*). [Earlier form of **pertinence.**]

**purulent,** *pū'rū-lənt, -rōō-, adj.* consisting of, of the nature of, forming, full of, characterised by, or like pus.—*ns.* **pū'rulence, pū'rulency**.—*adv.* **pū'rulently**. [L. *pūrulentus—pūs, pūris,* pus.]

**purvey,** *pûr-vā', v.t.* to provide, furnish: to supply.—*v.i.* to furnish provisions or meals as one's business.—*ns.* **purvey'ance,** the act of purveying: preparation in advance (*Spens.*): furnishings, equipment (*Spens.*): a procuring of victuals: that which is supplied: the former royal prerogative of pre-emption of necessaries; **purvey'or,** one whose business is to provide victuals or meals: an officer who formerly exacted provisions for the use of the king's household. [A.Fr. *purveier* (Fr. *pourvoir*)—L. *prōvidēre;* see **provide.**]

**purview,** *pûr'vū, n.* the body or enacting part of a statute distinguished from the preamble: enactment: scope: range: field of activity or view: competence. [A.Fr. *purveu,* provided, pa.p. of *purveier;* see **purvey.**]

**pus,** *pus, n.* a thick yellowish fluid formed by suppuration, consisting of serum, white blood cells, bacteria, and debris of tissue. [L. *pūs, pūris;* cf. Gr. *pyon.*]

**Puseyism,** *pū'zi-izm, n.* the High Church and Catholic principles of Dr E. B. *Pusey* (1800-1882), and other Oxford divines, as set forth in 'Tracts for the Times'.—*adjs.* **Pūseyist'ic, -al.**— *n.* **Pū'seyite.**

**push,** *pŏŏsh, v.t.* to thrust or press against: to

drive by pressure: to press or drive forward: to urge: to press hard: to put forth: to advance, carry to a further point: to promote, or seek to promote, vigorously and persistently: to make efforts to promote the sale of: to effect by thrusting forward: to peddle (drugs): to come near (an age or number).—*v.i.* to make a thrust: to butt (*B.*): to exert pressure: to make an effort: to press forward: to make one's way by exertion: to reach forth: to be urgent and persistent: to play a push-stroke.—*n.* a thrust: an impulse: pressure: a help to advancement: enterprising or aggressive pertinacity: an effort: an onset: an offensive: a push-stroke: a gang of convicts (*Austr. slang*): a gang of roughs: a company: dismissal (*coll.*).—**pushed**, *pa.p.* of push: in a hurry (*coll.*): short of money (*coll.*).—*n.* **push'er**, one who pushes: a machine or part that pushes: an airscrew placed behind: an aeroplane so propelled: a child's table implement, or a finger of bread, used for pushing food on to a fork: a self-assertive person: one who assiduously seeks social advancement: a dope pedlar.—*adj.* **push'ful**, energetically or aggressively enterprising.—*adv.* **push'fully.**—*n.* **push'fulness.**—*adj.* **push'ing**, pressing forward in business: enterprising: self-assertive.—*adv.* **push'ingly.**—**push'-ball**, a game in which an enormous ball is pushed; **push'-bicycle** (*coll.* -bike), -cycle, one propelled by foot; **push'-button**, a knob which when pressed puts on or cuts off an electric current, as for bells, etc. (*adj.* operated by, or using, push-button, -buttons); **push'-cart** (*U.S.*), a street vender's barrow; **push'-chair**, a folding-chair with wheels, for a child; **push'-off**, an act of pushing off a boat: a send-off; **push'-over**, an easy thing: a person or side easily overcome; **push'-pin** (*Shak.*), a children's game in which pins are pushed one across another.—*adj.* **push'-pull**, of any piece of apparatus in which two electrical or electronic devices act in opposition to each other, as, e.g., of an amplifier in which two thermionic valves so acting serve to reduce distortion.—**push'-stroke**, a push instead of an ordinary hit or stroke at a ball: in billiards one in which the cue is still or again in contact with the cue-ball when the cue-ball touches the object-ball.—**at a push**, when circumstances urgently require; **push along** (*coll.*), to depart, to go on one's way; **push around**, to bully; **push-button civilisation**, one in which the ordinary unskilled person has the benefits of technology at the pressing of a button; **push-button war**, one carried on by guided missiles, released by push-button; **push off**, of a rower or a boat, to leave the bank, shore, etc.: to depart (*coll.*); **push one's fortune**, to busy oneself in seeking a fortune; **push one's luck** (see luck); **push out**, (of person, boat) to row or be rowed out towards open water; **push the bottle**, to take one's liquor and pass the bottle round; **push up the daisies**, to be dead and buried. [Fr. *pousser*—L. *pulsāre*, freq. of *pellĕre*, *pulsum*, to beat.]

**push**, *pōōsh* (*Shak.*) *interj.* pish.—*n.* an exclamation of 'push'. [pish.]

**Pushtu, Pashtu, Pushtoo**, *push'tōō*, **Pushto, Pashto**, -*tō*, **Pakhtu**, *puhh'tōō*, **Pakhto**, -*tō*, *n.* the language of the Afghans proper. [Afghan *Pashtō, Pakhtō.*]

**pusillanimous**, *pū-si-lan'i-məs*, *adj.* wanting firmness of mind: mean-spirited: cowardly.—*adv.* **pusillan'imously.**—*n.* **pusillanim'ity.** [L. *pusillanimis*—*pusillus*, very little, *animus*, mind.]

**pusle**, an old spelling of puzzle.

**puss**, *pōōs*, *n.* a familiar name for a cat: a hare, in sportsmen's language: a playfully pejorative name for a child or a girl: a puss-moth.—*n.* **puss'y**, a dim. of **puss**: anything soft and

furry: a willow-catkin.—Also **puss'y-cat.**—**puss'-gen'tleman** (*arch.*), a dandy; **puss'-moth**, a thick-bodied hairy notodontid moth (*Dicranura*, or *Cerura, vinula*) whose caterpillar feeds on willow or poplar leaves; **Puss'yfoot**, U.S. nickname of William E. Johnson (1862-1945), from his stealthy ways as a revenue officer: (without *cap.*) hence, from his prohibitionist campaigns, a prohibitionist.—*v.i.* to go stealthily: to act timidly or cautiously.—**puss'yfooter; puss'y-will'ow**, a common American willow, *Salix discolor*, or other species with silky spring catkins.—**puss in the corner**, a children's game in which the places are continually being changed, while the player who is out tries to secure one of them. [Cf. Du. *poes*, puss; Ir. and Gael. *pus*, a cat.]

**pussel**, *pus'l*, *puz'l*, (*Shak.*) *n.* a dirty drab. [pucelle.]

**pustule**, *pus'tūl*, *n.* a pimple containing pus: pimple-like or warty spot or elevation.—*adjs.* **pus'tular, pus'tulous.**—*v.t.* and *v.i.* **pus'tulate.**—*n.* **pustulā'tion.** [L. *pustula.*]

**put**, *pōōt*, *v.t.* to push or thrust: to cast, throw, hurl (esp. by a thrusting movement of the hand from the shoulder): to drive: to impel: to convey, transport: to force, constrain: to incite: to place, or cause to be, in such and such a position, state, predicament, relation, etc.: to set: to place, lay, deposit: to apply: to append, affix: to connect: to add: to commit: to assign: to assign or suggest a course of action to (with *on*, as a diet, a study, a track; or *to*, as a task): to subject: to reduce: to convert: to render: to express: to assert, have: to propound: to submit to a vote: to impose: to impute: to call upon, oblige, stake, venture, invest: to repose (as trust, confidence).—*v.i.* to thrust (*arch.* or *Northern*): to proceed, make one's way (*naut.*): to set out, esp. hurriedly: to flow (*U.S.*):—*pr.p.* **putting** (*pōōt'*); *pa.t.* and *pa.p.* **put.**—*n.* a push or thrust: a cast, throw, esp. of a heavy stone from the shoulder: on the stock exchange, an option of selling within a certain time certain securities or commodities, at a stipulated price.—*ns.* **putter** (*pōōt'ər*), one who puts: one who pushes or hauls trams in a coal-mine; **putt'ing**, the act or sport of hurling a heavy stone or weight from the hand by a sudden thrust from the shoulder.—**put'-and-take**, a gambling game played with a top; **put'-off**, an excuse, a makeshift, evasion: a postponement; **putt'er-on** (*Shak.*), an instigator; **putt'er-out** (*obs.*), one who deposited money on going abroad, on condition of receiving a larger sum on his return, if he ever returned; **putt'ing-stone**, a heavy stone used in putting the stone.—*adj.* **put-up'**, speciously preconcerted.—**put about**, to change the course, as of a ship: to publish, circulate: to distress (*Scot.*); **put across**, to carry out successfully, bring off: to perform so as to carry the audience with one; **put an end, or a stop to**, to cause to discontinue; **put away**, to renounce: to divorce: to kill: to stow away, pack up, set aside: to imprison: to eat; **put back**, to push backward: delay: repulse: turn and sail back for port (*naut.*): reduce one's finances (*coll.*); **put by**, to set aside: parry: store up; **put case** (see case, 2); **put down**, to crush, quell: to kill: to degrade: to confute (*Shak.*): to enter, write down on paper: to reckon: to attribute: to give up (*rare*): to surpass, outshine: to preserve, put in pickle (*dial.*): of an aeroplane, to land (often with *at*); **put for**, to make an attempt to gain; **put forth**, to extend: to propose: to publish: to exert: to display: to lend at interest: to set out from port: to produce, extrude; **put forward**, to propose: to advance; **put in**, to introduce: to insert: to lodge, deposit, hand in: to make a claim or application: to enter: to enter a harbour: to interpose: to perform towards completing a total: to spend, pass, fill up with some occupation: to appoint; **put in an appearance** (see **appearance**); **put in mind**, to remind; **put it across someone**, to defeat someone by ingenuity; **put it on**, to pretend (to be ill, etc.); **put it past one**, judge it inconsistent with one's character; **put off**, to lay aside: to take off (*arch.*): to lay aside the character of: to palm off: to dismiss (*arch.*): to turn aside with evasions, excuses, or unsatisfying substitutes: to divert, turn aside from a purpose: to postpone: to idle away, spend in vain: to disconcert: to push from shore; **put on**, to don, clothe with: to assume, esp. deceptively: to superpose: to impose: to affix, attach, apply: to add (as weight, charges, etc.): to stake: to move forward: to move faster (*obs.*): to set to work: to set in operation: to incite: to turn on the supply of: to score: to stage: to impart information (with *to*): clad (as *well put on*, or *putten on*; respectably dressed, *pa.p.*; *Scot.*); **put out**, to expel: to dismiss from a game and innings: to send forth: to stretch forth: to extinguish: to place at interest: to expend: to publish: to disconcert: to put to inconvenience: to offend: to dislocate: to exert: to produce: to place with others or at a distance: to go out to sea, leave port: to remove bodily or blind (an eye); **put over**, to refer (*Shak.*): to carry through successfully: to impress an audience, spectators, the public, favourably with: to impose, pass off; **put through**, to bring to an end: to accomplish: to put in telephonic communication; **put to**, to apply: to add to: to connect with: to harness: to shut: to set to; **put to death** (see **death**); **put to it**, to press hard: to distress; **put to rights** (see **rights**); **put to sea**, to begin a voyage; **put two and two together**, to draw a conclusion from various facts; **put up**, to start from cover, as a hare: to stow away, put aside: to parcel up: to sheathe: to compound: to endure tamely (*obs.*): to accommodate with lodging: to take lodgings: to nominate or stand for election: to expose for sale: to present (as a good game, fight, or defence, a prayer): to preconcert; **put up to**, to incite to: to make conversant with, supply with useful information or tips about; **put upon**, to take undue advantage of: to impose upon; **put up with**, to endure; **stay put**, to remain passively in the position assigned. [Late O.E. *putian* (found in the verbal-noun *putung*, instigation); there were also *potian* and *pȳtan*, which may account for some of the dialect forms; cf. Dan. *putte*, Sw. *putta*.]

**put**, *put*. See **putt**.

**putamen**, *pū-tā′mən*, *n.* a fruit-stone: the membrane within an egg-shell: the lateral part of the lenticular nucleus of the cerebrum. [L. *putāmen*, clippings, waste, *putāre*, to prune.]

**putative**, *pū′tə-tiv*, *adj.* supposed: reputed: commonly supposed to be.—**putative marriage**, a marriage supposed invalid by canon law, but entered into in good faith by at least one of the parties. [L. *putātīvus*—*putāre*, -*ātum*, to suppose.]

**putchock**, **putchuk**, **pachak**, *puch-uk′*, *n.* costusroot (so-called; see **Costus**). [Hind. *pachak*; origin obscure.]

**puteal**, *pū′ti-əl*, *n.* a well-curb. [L. *pūteal*, -*ālis*—*puteus*, a well.]

**puteli**, *put′e-lē*, *n.* a flat-bottomed Ganges craft. [Hindi *paṭeli*.]

**putid**, *pū′tid*, *adj.* rotten: foul. [L. *pūtidus*.]

**putlog**, *put′log*, **putlock**, -*lok*, *n.* a cross-piece in a scaffolding, the inner end resting in a hole left in the wall. [Origin obscure; **putlock** seems to be the older form.]

**putois**, *pü-twä′*, *n.* a brush of polecat's hair, or substitute, for painting pottery. [Fr.]

**put-put**, *pŏŏt-pŏŏt*, *n.* noise of small motor. [Imit.]

**putrefy**, *pū′tri-fī*, *v.t.* to cause to rot: to corrupt. —*v.i.* to rot:—*pr.p.* pu′trefying; *pa.t.* and *pa.p.* pu′trefied.—*adj.* putrefacient (-*fā′shənt*), causing putrefaction.—*n.* putrefaction (-*fak′shən*), rotting.—*adjs.* putrefac′tive; putrefi′able.—*n.* putrescence (-*tres′əns*), incipient rottenness.—*adjs.* putresc′ent; putresc′ible.—*n.* putresc′ine (-*ēn*, -*in*), a substance, $H_2N(CH_2)_4NH_2$, formed in putrefaction of flesh.—*adj.* pu′trid, rotten: wretchedly bad (*slang*).—*adv.* pu′tridly.—*ns.* putrid′ity, pu′tridness.—**putrid fever**, typhus. [L. *putrefacĕre*, *putrēscĕre*, *putridus*—*puter*, *putris*, rotten.]

**putsch**, *pŏŏch*, *n.* a sudden revolutionary outbreak. [Swiss Ger. dialect.]

**putt**, also *put*, *put*, *v.t.* to hurl in putting (as a weight, stone; *Scot.*; see **put**): to strike in making a putt (*golf*).—*v.i.* to make a putt or putts:—*pr.p.* putting, *put′*; *pa.p.* and *pa.t.* putted, *put′*.—*n.* a throw or cast (*Scot.*; see **put**): a delicate stroke such as is made with a putter on, or sometimes near, a putting-green, with the object of rolling the ball, if possible, into the hole (*golf*).—*ns.* putter (*put′ər*), one who putts or can putt: a short stiff golf-club with upright striking-face, used in putting; putt′ing, the exercise of hurling a heavy weight (*Scot.*; see **put**): the act or art of making a putt.—putt′ing-cleek, a putter of cleek design, the blade long and narrow, running straight from the shaft; putt′ing-green, the turf, made firm and smooth for putting, round each of the holes of a golf-course: by the rules all within 20 yards of the hole, hazards excluded; putt′ing-stone (see putt). [A Scottish form of **put**.]

**putt**, **put**, *put*, *n.* an old card-game like nap. [Perh. *put*.]

**putt**, **put**, *put*, (*arch.*) *n.* a greenhorn: a bumpkin. [17th-century slang; origin unknown.]

**puttee**, **puttie**, *put′ē*, -*i*, *n.* a cloth strip wound round the leg from ankle to knee, as a legging. [Hindi. *paṭṭi*.]

**putto**, *pŏŏt′ō*, *n.* very young boy, often winged, in Renaissance art:—*pl.* putti (*pŏŏt′ē*). [It.]

**puttock**, *put′ək*, *n.* a kite: (*Shak.*): a buzzard: a kite-like person. [M.E. *puttok*, perh. conn. with O.E. *pyttel*, kite.]

**putty**, *put′i*, *n.* orig. putty-powder (*polishers′* or *jewellers′ putty*): a cement of whiting and linseed oil (*glaziers′* or *painters′ putty*): a fine cement of slaked lime and water only (*plasterers′ putty*): a yellowish grey colour.—*v.t.* to fix, coat, or fill with putty:—*pr.p.* putt′ying; *pa.t.* and *pa.p.* putt′ied.—*n.* putt′ier, a glazier.—*adjs.* putt′y-coloured; putt′y-faced, having a putty-coloured face.—putt′y-knife, a blunt, flexible tool for laying on putty; putt′y-pow′der, stannic oxide (often with lead oxide) used for polishing glass. [Fr. *potée*, potful, putty-powder—*pot*.]

**puture**, *pū′tyər*, **pulture**, *pul′*, (*hist.*) *n.* the claim of foresters, etc., to food for man, horse, and dog within the bounds of a forest. [A.Fr. *puture*, Old Northern Fr. *pulture*—L.L. *pu(l)tūra*, app.—L. *puls*, *pultis*, porridge.]

**puy**, *pwē*, *n.* a small volcanic cone, as in Auvergne. [Fr., hill—L. *podium*, a height; cf. **pew**, **podium**.]

**puzel**, **puzzel**. See **pucelle**, **pussel**, also **puzzle**.

**puzzle**, *puz′l*, *v.t.* to perplex: to bewilder: to afford difficulty of solution to: to set a problem that gives difficulty to: to entangle, complicate: to solve by systematic or assiduous thinking (with *out*).—*v.i.* to be bewildered: to labour at solution: to search about.—*n.* bewilderment: perplexity: anything that puzzles: a problem: a riddle or a toy designed to try ingenuity.—*ns.* puzz′ledom (*rare*), bewilderment; puzz′lement, the state of being puzzled; **puzz′ler.**—*adj.* **puzz′ling,** posing: perplexing.—*adv.* **puzz′lingly.** —**puzz′le-head,** one who is puzzle-headed.—*adj.* **puzz′le-head′ed,** having the head full of confused notions.—**puzz′le-head′edness; puzz′le-monkey,** monkey-puzzle; **puzz′le-peg,** a piece of wood so secured under a dog's jaw as to keep his nose from the ground. [Origin obscure.]

**puzzolana,** *pōōt-sō-lä′na.* Same as **pozzolana.**

**PVC.** See **polyvinyl chloride.**

**pyaemia,** *pī-ē′mi-a, n.* infection of the blood with bacteria from a septic focus, with abscesses in different parts of the body.—Also **pye′mia.**— *adj.* **pyae′mic.** [Gr. *pyon,* pus, *haima,* blood.]

**pycnic.** Same as **pyknic.**

**pycnidium,** *pik-nid′i-am, n.* in some fungi a receptacle like a perithecium, containing hyphae which produce conidia.—*n.* **pycnid′iospore,** a conidium produced in a pycnidium. [Gr. *pyknos,* thick, dense, dim. suff. *-idion* Latinised to *-idium.*]

**pycnite,** *pik′nit, n.* a columnar variety of topaz. [Gr. *pyknos,* dense.]

**pycno-, pykno-,** *pik′nō-, pik-no′-,* in composition, dense, close.—*ns.* **pycnoconid′ium,** a pycnidiospore; **pycnog′onid** (Gr. *gony,* knee), a seaspider.—*n.pl.* **Pycnogon′ida,** the sea-spiders, a class of marine arthropods with more leg than body.—*adj.* **pycnog′onoid.**—*ns.* **pycnom′eter, pyknom′eter,** an instrument for determining specific gravities; **pyc′non,** in Greek music, that part of the tetrachord (chromatic or enharmonic) where the smallest intervals fell: in mediaeval music, a semitone; **pyc′nospore,** a pycnidiospore.—*adj.* **pycnostyle** (Gr. *stylos,* column), with close-set columns, 1½ diameters apart.—*n.* a pycnostyle building. [Gr. *pyknos,* dense.]

**pyebald.** See **piebald.**

**pye-dog,** *pī′-dog, n.* an ownerless or pariah dog. [Hind. *pāhi,* outsider.]

**pyelitis,** *pī-a-lī′tis, n.* inflammation of the pelvis of the kidney.—*adj.* **pyelitic** (*-lit′ik*). [Gr. *pyelos,* a trough.]

**pyemia.** See **pyaemia.**

**pyengadu,** *pyeng-gä-dōō′, n.* the ironwood (Xylia; Mimosaceae) of Burma, etc. [Burmese *pyeng-kadō.*]

**pygal,** *pī′gal, adj.* belonging to the rump or posteriors of an animal.—*n.* the posterior median plate of a chelonian carapace. [Gr. *pȳgē,* rump.]

**pygarg,** *pī′gärg,* (*B.*) *n.* possibly the addax antelope.—N.E.B. says it is the 'white-rumped deer'. [Gr. *pȳgē,* rump, *argos,* white.]

**pygidium,** *pī-gid′i-am,* or *-jid′, n.* in insects, the tergum of the last abdominal somite: the tailshield of a trilobite. [Latinised from Gr. *pȳgidion,* dim. of *pȳgē,* rump.]

**pygmy, pigmy,** *pig′mi, n.* a member of the race of dwarfs said by the ancients to have warred with cranes, or of any of the actual dwarf human races, negritos, negrillos, and others: one of the ancient diminutive dwellers in underground houses, etc., in whom some scholars see the historical origins of the fairies and elves of folklore: an elf: an anthropoid ape (*obs.*): a dwarf: any person, animal or thing relatively diminutive or in some way insignificant.—*adj.* dwarfish: diminutive: of the pygmies.—*adjs.* **pygmaean; pyg-, pigmean** (*-mē′an*); **pyg′moid.** [Gr. *pygmaios,* measuring a *pygmē* (13½ inches, distance from elbow to knuckles).]

**pygostyle,** *pī′gō-stil, n.* the bone of a bird's tail. [Gr. *pȳgē,* rump, *stylos,* a column.]

**pyjamas,** *pa-, pi-,* or *pi-jä′maz, n.pl.* loose trousers tied round the waist, worn by Indians: (in European use) a sleeping-suit.—Also **paja′-mas.**—*adj.* **pyja′ma′d, pyja′maed,** wearing pyjamas.—**pyja′ma-jacket, -trousers.** [Pers. and Hind. *pāējāmah—pāē,* leg, *jāmah,* clothing.]

**pyknic,** *pik′nik, adj.* characterised by short squat

stature, small hands and feet, relatively short limbs, domed abdomen, short neck, round face. [Gr. *pyknos,* thick.]

**pyknometer.** Same as **pycnometer.**

**pylon,** *pī′lon, n.* a gateway, gate-tower, gatehouse, or mass of building through which an entrance passes, esp. the gateway of an Egyptian temple (*archit.*): a guiding mark at an aerodrome: a structure for support of power-cables:—*pl.* **py′lons.** [Gr. *pylōn, -ōnos—pylē,* a gate.]

**pylorus,** *pī-, pi-lō′ras, -lō′, n.* the opening from the stomach to the intestines.—*adj.* **pylor′ic** (*-lor′*). [L.,—Gr. *pylōros,* gate-keeper, pylorus— *pylē,* an entrance, *ōra,* care; cf. *ouros,* a guardian.]

**pyne.** Same as **pine** (2).

**pyogenic,** *pī-a-jen′ik, adj.* pus-forming.—*adj.* **py′oid,** purulent.—*n.* **pyorrhoea** (*-rē′a;* Gr. *rhoiā,* flow), discharge of pus: now, suppuration in the sockets of teeth. [Gr. *pyon,* pus.]

**pyoning.** See **pioneer.**

**pyorrhoea.** See **pyogenic.**

**pyot, pyat, pyet, piet,** *pī′at, (Scot.) n.* a magpie. —*adj.* **pied.**—*adj.* **pi′oted.** [pie (1).]

**pyracanth,** *pī′ra-kanth,* **pyracantha,** *-kan′tha, n.* a thorny evergreen shrub near akin to hawthorn. [Gr. *pȳrakantha—pȳr,* fire, *akanthos,* thorn.]

**pyralis,** *pir′a-lis, n.* an insect feigned to live or breed in fire (*obs.*): (*cap.*) a genus of moths, giving name to a heterogeneous family, the **Pyralidae** (*pir-al′i-dē*).—*n.* **pyr′alid,** a member of the family. [Gr. *pȳrălis—pȳr,* fire.]

**pyramid,** *pir′a-mid, n.* a solid figure on a triangular, square, or polygonal base, with triangular sides meeting in a point: any object or structure of that or similar form, esp. a great Egyptian monument: a crystal form of three or more faces each cutting three axes (*crystal.*): (in *pl.*) a game played on a billiard-table in which the balls are arranged in pyramid shape:—*pl.* usu. **pyr′amids,** also **pyramides** (*pir-am′i-dēz*), and sometimes (*poet.*) **pyram′id(e)s.**—*adjs.* **pyram′idal, pyramid′ic, -al,** having the form of a pyramid.—*advs.* **pyram′idally,** **pyramid′ically.**—*ns.* **pyramid′ion,** the small pyramidal apex of an obelisk; **pyram′-idist,** one who studies the Egyptian Pyramids; **pyr′amis** (*Shak.,* etc.), a pyramid:—*pl.* **pyram′-ides, pyr′amises; pyram′idon,** an organ-stop with pipes like inverted pyramids. [Gr. *pyramis, -idos.*]

**pyrargyrite,** *pir-,* or *pir-är′jir-it, n.* ruby-silver ore, sulphide of silver and antimony. [Gr. *pȳr,* fire, *argyros,* silver.]

**pyre,** *pir, n.* a pile of combustibles for burning a dead body.—*adj.* **pyr′al.** [L. *pyra*—Gr. *pȳrā—pȳr,* fire.]

**pyrene,** *pī′rēn, n.* a fruit-stone.—*ns.* **pyrē′nocarp** (Gr. *karpos,* fruit), a perithecium; **pyrē′noid,** a small round albuminous body concerned in starch-formation, found in the chloroplasts of some algae, etc.—*n.pl.* **Pyrēnomyce′tēs** (Gr. *mykēs,* fungus), a group of Ascomycetes whose characteristic fructification is the perithecium.— *adj.* **pyrenomyce′tous.** [Gr. *pȳrēn, -ēnos,* fruit-stone.]

**pyrene,** *pī′rēn, n.* a hydrocarbon ($C_{16}H_{10}$) got by dry distillation of coal. [Gr. *pȳr,* fire.]

**Pyrenean, Pyrenaean,** *pir-a-nē′an, adj.* of the *Pyrenees,* the mountains between France and Spain.—*n.* a native of the Pyrenees: (in *pl.*) the Pyrenees (*obs.*).—*n.* **pyrenē′ite,** a black garnet. —**Pyrenean mountain dog,** a large dog with a dense white coat, bred in the Pyrenees to guard flocks. [L. *Pȳrēnaeus—*Gr. *Pȳrēnaios.*]

**Pyrethrum,** *pi-rēth′ram, pi-reth′ram, pir-eth′ram, n.* a former genus of composite plants now merged in Chrysanthemum, including feverfew: (without *cap.*) still applied to various garden flowers, esp. varieties of *Chrysanthemum coccineum*: (without *cap.*) insect-powder of flower-heads of various species of pyrethrum:

(without *cap.*) in pharmacy, the root of pellitory of Spain. [L.,—Gr. *pȳrĕthron*, pellitory of Spain.]

**pyretic**, *pī-ret'ik*, *pir-et'ik*, *adj.* of, of the nature of, for the cure of, fever.—*ns.* **pyretol'ogy**, study of fevers; **pyretother'apy**, treatment by inducing high body temperature; **pyrex'ia**, fever. [Gr. *pȳretikos*, feverish—*pȳretos*, fever; and *pȳressein*, to be feverish—*pȳr*, fire.]

**Pyrex**, *pī'reks*, *n.* a registered trademark applied to glassware resistant to heat. [Gr. *pȳr*, fire, and L. *rēx*, king.]

**pyrexia.** See **pyretic**.

**pyrheliometer**, *pir-*, *pir-hē-li-om'i-tər*, *n.* an instrument for measuring the heating effect of the sun's rays.—*adj.* **pyrheliometric** (*-ō-met'rik*). [Gr. *pȳr*, fire, *hēlios*, sun, *metron*, measure.]

**pyridine**, *pir'*, or *pir'i-dēn*, *-din*, *n.* a strong-smelling, colourless, strongly basic liquid, $C_5H_5N$, got in distillation of bone-oil, coal-tar, etc.—*n.* **pyridox'-in(e)**, a pyridine derivative, a member of the vitamin B complex. [Gr. *pȳr*, fire.]

**pyriform**, *pir'i-förm*, *adj.* pear-shaped. [L. *pirum*, a pear, *förma*, form.]

**pyrimethamine**, *pi-ri-meth'ə-mēn*, or *pī-*, *n.* a powerful anti-malaria drug. [Gr. *pȳr*, fire, *methyl*, and **amine**.]

**pyrites**, *pir-*, *pir-ī'tēz*, *n.* a brassy yellow mineral, iron disulphide, crystallising in the cubic system, occurring in octahedra, pyritohedra, etc. (also called **pyrite**, *pī'rīt*, **iron pyri'tes**): extended to a large class of mineral sulphides and arsenides.—*adjs.* **pyritic** (*pir-*, *pir-it'ik*), **-al**; **pyritif'erous**.—*v.t.* **pyr'itise**, **-ize**, to convert into, or replace by, pyrites.—*adj.* **pyritohē'dral**.—*n.* **pyritohē'-dron**, a pentagonal dodecahedron:—*pl.* **pyritohē'-dra**.—*adj.* **pyr'itous**.—**arsenical pyrites**, mispickel; **cockscomb pyrites**, **spear pyrites**, twinned forms of marcasite; **copper pyrites**, sulphide of copper and iron, chalcopyrite, a mineral much resembling iron pyrites; **magnetic pyrites**, pyrrhotite. [Gr. *pȳrītēs*, striking fire—*pȳr*, fire.]

**pyrithiamine**, *pi-ri-thī'ə-mēn*, *n.* an anti-vitamin causing thiamine (vitamin $B_1$) deficiency. [Gr. *pȳr*, fire, and **thiamine**.]

**pyro-**, *pī'rō-*, in composition, fire, heat, fever: obtained by heating or as if by heating, or by removing (theoretically) a molecule of water (*chem.*).—*adjs.* **pyro-acet'ic**, **pyrophosphor'ic**, **pyrosulphu'ric**, **pyrotartar'ic**, etc., related in this way to acetic, phosphoric, etc., acid.—*ns.* **pyrophos'phate**, **pyrotar'trate**, etc., a salt of such an acid.—*n.* **pyrolysis** (*pi-rol'is-is*; Gr. *lysis*, loosing), decomposition of a substance by heat. [Gr. *pȳr*, in compounds *pȳr-*, fire.]

**pyro**, *pī-rō*, (*photog.*) *n.* a familiar abbreviation of **pyrogallol**.

**pyroballogy**, *pi-rō-bal'ə-ji*, (*Sterne*) *n.* the science of artillery. [Gr. *pȳr*, fire, *ballein*, to throw, *logos*, discourse.]

**pyroclastic**, *pi-rō-klas'tik*, *adj.* formed of fragments by igneous agency. [Gr. *pȳr*, fire, *klastos*, broken.]

**pyro-electric**, *pi-rō-i-lek'trik*, *adj.* becoming positively and negatively electrified at opposite poles on heating or cooling: of pyro-electricity.—*n.* **pyro-electricity** (*-el-ik-tris'i-ti*), the property of being pyro-electric: the study of the phenomena shown by pyro-electric crystals. [Gr. *pȳr*, fire, and **electric**.]

**pyrogallol**, *pi-rō-gal'ol*, *n.* a phenol got by heating *gallic* acid—also called **pyrogall'ic acid**.

**pyrogenic**, *pi-rō-jen'ik*, **pyrogenetic**, *-jin-et'ik*, *adjs.* produced by, or producing, heat or fever. [Gr. *pȳr*, fire, root of *gignesthai*, to become.]

**pyrognostic**, *pi-rog-nos'tik*, *adj.* pertaining to testing of minerals by flame. [Gr. *pȳr*, fire, *gnōstikos*, discriminating.]

**pyrography**, *pi-rog'rə-fi*, *n.* poker work.—*n.* **pyrogravure'**. [Gr. *pȳr*, fire, *graphein*, to write.]

**Pyrola**, *pir'ə-lə*, *n.* the wintergreen genus, giving name to the family **Pyrolā'ceae**, akin to the heaths. [Dim. of *pyrus*, a misspelling of L. *pirus*, a pear-tree.]

**pyrolatry**, *pī-rol'ə-tri*, *n.* fire-worship.—*n.* **pyrol'-ater**, a fire-worshipper. [Gr. *pȳr*, fire, *latreiā*, worship.]

**pyroligneous**, *pi-rō-lig'ni-əs*, *adj.* got by distillation of wood.—**pyroligneous acid**, wood-vinegar, a mixture of acetic acid, methyl alcohol, etc.; **pyroligneous alcohol**, wood-spirit, methyl alcohol. [Gr. *pȳr*, and L. *ligneus—lignum*, wood.]

**pyrolusite**, *pi-rō-lū'sit*, *-loō'*, *n.* native manganese dioxide. [Gr. *pȳr*, *lousis*, washing, from its use in decolorising molten glass.]

**pyromancy**, *pī'rō-man-si*, *n.* divination by fire.—*adj.* **pyromant'ic**. [Gr. *pȳr*, fire, *manteiā*, divination.]

**pyromania**, *pi-rō-mā'ni-ə*, *n.* an incendiary mania.—*n.* and *adj.* **pyromā'niac**.—*adj.* **pyromaniacal** (*-mə-nī'ə-kl*). [Gr. *pȳr*, fire, and **mania**.]

**pyromeride**, *pi-rom'ər-id*, *n.* a nodular rhyolite. [Gr. *pȳr*, fire, *meros*, part, as if meaning only partly fusible.]

**pyrometer**, *pī-rom'i-tər*, *n.* an instrument for measuring high temperatures.—*adjs.* **pyrometric** (*pī-rō-met'rik*), **-al**.—*n.* **pyrom'etry**. [Gr. *pȳr*, fire, *metron*, measure.]

**pyromorphite**, *pi-rō-mör'fit*, *n.* an ore (chloride and phosphate) of lead, so called because the blowpipe bead crystallises on cooling. [Gr. *pȳr*, fire, *morphē*, form.]

**pyrope**, *pī'rōp*, *n.* a fiery red gemstone (also *poet.* **pyrō'pus**): a red magnesia-alumina garnet, used in jewellery (*min.*). [Gr. *pyrōpos*, fiery-eyed—*ōps*, *ōpos*, eye, face.]

**pyrophone**, *pi'rō-fōn*, *n.* an organ producing interference-tones by pairs of flames in tubes, invented by Eugène Kastner (1852-82). [Gr. *pȳr*, fire, *phōnē*, sound, voice.]

**pyrophorus**, *pi-rof'ə-rəs*, *n.* anything that takes fire on exposure to air: (*cap.*) a genus of tropical American fireflies (elaterid beetles).—*adjs.* **pyrophoric** (*-rō-for'ik*), **pyroph'orous**. [Gr. *pȳrophoros*, fire-bearer—*pȳr*, fire and *pherein*, to carry.]

**pyrophotograph**, *pi-rō-fō'tə-gräf*, *n.* a burnt-in photograph, as on glass or porcelain.—*adj.* **pyrophotograph'ic**.—*n.* **pyrophotog'raphy**. [Gr. *pȳr*, fire, and **photograph**.]

**pyrophyllite**, *pi-rō-fil'it*, *n.* a clay mineral that exfoliates before the blowpipe. [Gr. *pȳr*, fire, *phyllon*, leaf.]

**pyroscope**, *pi'rō-skōp*, *n.* an instrument for measuring the intensity of radiant heat. [Gr. *pȳr*, fire, *skopeein*, to view.]

**pyrosis**, *pi-rō'sis*, *n.* water-brash. [Gr. *pȳrōsis*—*pȳr*, fire.]

**Pyrosoma**, *pi-rō-sō'mə*, *n.* a genus of compound tunicates, with brilliant phosphorescence.—*n.* **py'rosome**. [Gr. *sōma*, body.]

**pyrotechnics**, *pi-rō-tek'niks*, *n.* the art of making fireworks: display of fireworks: showy display in talk, music, etc.—*adjs.* **pyrotech'nic**, **-al**.—*adv.* **pyrotech'nically**.—*ns.* **pyrotech'nist**, a maker of fireworks: one skilled in, or given to, pyrotechnics; **py'rotechny**, pyrotechnics. [Gr. *pȳr*, fire, *technikos*, skilled—*technē*, art.]

**pyroxene**, *pi'rok-sēn*, a general name for a group of minerals distinguished from amphiboles by a cleavage angle about 87°, metasilicates of calcium, magnesium, aluminium, and other metals, usually green or black, very common in igneous rocks—augite, diopside, enstatite, etc.—*adj.* **pyroxenic** (*-sen'ik*).—*n.* **pyrox'enite** (*-ən-it*, or *-ēn'it*), a rock compound essentially of pyroxene. [Gr. *pȳr*, fire, *xenos*, stranger (because Haüy thought that pyroxene crystals in lava had only been accidentally caught up).]

**pyroxylic**, *pi-rok-sil'ik*, (*obs.*) *adj.* pyroligneous.—

*ns.* **pyroxyle** (*-rok'sil*), **pyrox′ylin**, **-e**, nitrated cotton. [Gr. *pŷr*, fire, *xylon*, wood.]

**pyrrhic**, *pir′ik*, *n.* an ancient Greek war-dance: a foot of two short syllables.—*adj.* pertaining to the dance or to the foot.—*n.* **pyrrhicist** (*pir′i-sist*), a pyrrhic dancer. [Gr. *pyrrichē* (*orchēsis*), pyrrhic dance, said to be from *Pyrrichos*, the inventor.]

**Pyrrhic**, *pir′ik*, *adj.* of or pertaining to *Pyrrhus*, king of Epirus (318-272 B.C.).—**Pyrrhic victory**, a victory gained at too great a cost, in allusion to Pyrrhus's exclamation after his defeat of the Romans at Heraclea on the Siris (280), 'Another such victory and we are lost'.

**Pyrrhonism**, *pir′ən-izm*, *n.* the complete scepticism of *Pyrrhō* (Gr. *Pyrrōn*) of Elis (3rd cent. B.C.).—*adj.* and *n.* **Pyrrhonian** (*pir-ō′ni-ən*).—*adj.* **Pyrrhonic** (*-on′ik*).—*n.* **Pyrrh′onist**.

**pyrrhotite**, *pir′ō-tīt*, *n.* magnetic pyrites, an iron sulphide, often with nickel.—Also **pyrrh′otine** (*-tēn*). [Gr. *pyrrotēs*, redness—*pŷr*, fire.]

**pyrrhous**, *pir′əs*, *adj.* reddish. [Gr. *pyrros*, flame-coloured—*pŷr*, fire.]

**Pyrus**, *pī′ras*, *n.* pear and apple genus of the rose family. [Misspelling of L. *pirus*, pear-tree.]

**Pythagorean**, *pī-* or *pī-thag-ər-ē′ən*, *adj.* pertaining to *Pythagoras* (of Samos; 6th cent. B.C.), the Greek philosopher, or to his philosophy: transformed, as if by transmigration of the soul (taught by Pythagoras): vegetarian.—*n.* a follower of Pythagoras.—*ns.* **Pythagorē′anism**, **Pythag′orism**, his doctrines.—**Pythagorean letter**, or **Samian letter**, the Greek letter Υ which was, for Pythagoras, a symbol of the parting of the ways for vice and virtue; **Pythagorean theorem**, that the square on the hypotenuse of a right-angled triangle is equal to the sum of the squares on the other two sides.

**Pythia**, *pith′i-ə*, *n.* the priestess who delivered the oracles of Pythian Apollo at Delphi.—*adj.* **Pyth′ian**, of Delphi, the oracle there, the priestess, or the games held near.—*n.* a native or inhabitant of Delphi: the priestess of Apollo there: Apollo.—*adj.* **Pyth′ic**, Pythian: ecstatic.—**Pythian games**, one of the four national festivals of ancient Greece, in honour of Apollo, held every four years at Delphi; **Pythian verse**, the dactylic hexameter. [Gr. *Pŷthō*, old name of Delphi; see python.]

**Pythium**, *pith′i-əm*, *n.* a genus of fungi, cause of damping-off of seedlings. [Gr. *pŷthein*, to cause to rot.]

**pythogenic**, *pī-thō-jen′ik*, *adj.* produced by filth. [Gr. *pŷthein*, to rot, root of *gignesthai*, to become.]

**Python**, *pī′thən*, *n.* the great snake killed by Apollo at Pŷthō (Delphi), according to legend from *pŷthein*, to rot, because it rotted: (without *cap.*) a familiar or possessing spirit: (without *cap.*) one possessed by a spirit: (without *cap.*) an utterer of oracles: (without *cap.*) a large snake that crushes its victims, esp. and properly one of the Old World genus *Python*, akin to the boas.—*n.* **Py′thoness**, the priestess of the oracle of Apollo at Delphi: (without *cap.*) a witch.—*adj.* **pythonic** (*-thon′ik*).

**pyx**, *piks*, *n.* a box: a vessel in which the host is kept after consecration, now usu. that in which it is carried to the sick (*R.C.*): a box at the Mint in which sample coins are kept for testing.—*v.t.* to test the weight and fineness of, as the coin deposited in the pyx.—*ns.* **pyxid′ium** (*bot.*), a capsule that opens by a transverse circular split:—*pl.* **pyxid′ia**; **pyx′is**, a little box or casket as for jewels, drugs, toilet materials, etc.—**trial of the pyx**, trial by weight and assay of gold and silver coins by a jury of goldsmiths. [L. *pyxis*, a box—Gr. *pyxis*, *-idos*, dim. *pyxidion* —*pyxos*, box-tree.]

Neutral vowels in unaccented syllables: *el′ə-mənt*; for certain sounds in foreign words, see p. viii

# Q

**Q, q,** *kū, n.* the seventeenth letter of our alphabet, derived from the abandoned Greek letter koppa (q.v.), and representing in English the same sound as *K*; always in English followed by *u* (*qu* being sounded as *kw*, except in words from or modelled on French, Spanish, etc.), except sometimes in transliteration of the related Semitic letter qōph (pron. *kōf*), as in *qadi* (more usu. *cadi* or *kadi*): Old English used *cw* instead of *qu*, and mediaeval Scots had *quh* for *hw* (*wh*): as a mediaeval Roman numeral Q = 500, Q̄ = 500,000.—**Q'-boat,** a naval vessel disguised as a merchant ship or fishing-boat, to deceive and destroy submarines; **Q-Celt, Q-Kelt** (see Celt). [L. *cū.*]

**qa-, qe-, qi-, qo-, qu-.** Arabic and Hebrew words spelt thus are in most cases given at **k-** or **c-**.

**Qoran.** Same as **Koran.**

**qua,** *kwā, kwä, adv.* in the capacity of. [L. *quā,* adverbial abl. fem. of *quī,* who.]

**quack,** *kwak, n.* the cry of a duck.—*v.i.* to make the sound of a quack.—*v.i.* **quack'le,** to quack. [Imit.]

**quack,** *kwak, n.* a shortened form of **quacksalver:** a charlatan.—Also *adj.*—*v.i.* to play the quack. —*v.t.* to puff, vend, or treat in the manner of a quack.—*n.* **quack'ery,** the pretensions or practice of a quack, esp. in medicine.—**quack'salver,** a boastful pretender to knowledge and skill (esp. in medicine) that he does not possess.—*adj.* **quack'salving.** [Du. *quacksalver* (now *kwak-zalver*), perh. one who quacks about his salves.]

**quad,** *kwod, n.* an abbreviation of **quadrangle, quadrat, quadruped** (i.e. horse), **quadruplet.**—*adj.* abbreviation for **quadruple.**—*v.t.* to fill with quadrats.

**quad.** Same as **quod** (2).

**quadragenarian,** *kwod-rə-ji-nā'ri-ən, n.* one who is forty years old.—Also *adj.* [L. *quādrāgēnārius—quadrāgēnī,* forty each.]

**Quadragesima,** *kwod-rə-jes'i-mə, n.* the forty days of Lent (*obs.*): the first Sunday in Lent.—*adj.* **quadrages'imal,** of the number forty: of Lent. [L. *quadrāgēsimus, -a, -um,* fortieth—*quadrāgintā,* forty—*quattuor,* four.]

**quadrangle,** *kwod-rang'gl,* also *kwod', n.* a plane figure with four angles (and therefore four sides): an object or space of that form: a court or open space, usually rectangular, enclosed by a building (as a college): sometimes the enclosing building.—*adj.* **quadrang'ular** (*-gū-lər*).—*adv.* **quadrang'ularly.—complete quadrangle,** a figure composed of four points joined by six straight lines or sides. [Fr.,—L. *quadrangulum—quattuor,* four, *angulus,* an angle.]

**quadrans,** *kwod'ranz, kwad'räns, n.* a Roman copper coin, the fourth part of the as:—*pl.* **quadran'tēs.**—*n.* **quadrant** (*kwod'rənt*), the fourth part of a circle or its circumference, a sector or an arc of 90°: an area, object, street, of that form: an instrument with an arc of 90° for taking altitudes.—*adj.* **quadrantal** (*-rant'l*). [L. *quadrāns, -antis,* a fourth part—*quattuor,* four.]

**quadrat,** *kwod'rat, n.* a piece of type-metal lower than the letters, used in spacing between words and filling out blank lines (commonly **quad**) —distinguished as *en* ( ▌ ), *em* ( ▐ ), *two-em* ( ▐▐ ), and *three-em* ( ▐▐▐ ).—*adj.* **quad'-rate** (*-rāt, -rit*), square: rectangular: squarish: squared: square, as a power or root: balanced (*fig.*): conformable.—*n.* a square or quadrate figure or object: the quadrate bone, suspending the lower jaw in vertebrates other than mammals: quartile (*obs.*).—*v.t.* and *v.i.* to square: to conform.—*adj.* **quadratic** (*-rat'ik*), of or like a quadrate: involving the square but no higher power (*alg.*): tetragonal (*crystal.*).—*n.* a quadratic equation.—*adj.* **quadrat'ical.**—*ns.* **quadrā'-trix,** a curve by which a curved figure (as the circle) may be squared; **quad'rature** (*-rə-chər*), squareness: a square space (*Milt.*): squaring: the finding of a square equal to a given figure: an angular distance of 90°: the position of a heavenly body at such an angular distance, or the time of its being there; **quadrā'tus,** the name of several quadrangular muscles.—**B quadrā'tum,** quadrate B (see **B**); **quadrature of the circle** (see **square**). [L. *quadrātus,* pa.p. of *quadrāre,* to square—*quattuor,* four.]

**quadrennium,** etc. See **quadr(i)-.**

**quadr(i)-,** *kwod-r(i),* in composition, four: square.—*adjs.* **quad'ric,** of the second degree; **quadricentennial** (*kwod-ri-sen-ten'i-əl*; modelled on **centennial**), lasting four hundred years: once in four hundred years.—*n.* **quadriceps** (*kwod'ri-seps*; L. *caput, -itis,* head), the great thigh muscle that extends the leg (from its four insertions).—*adj.* **quadricipital** (*-sip'i-tl*).—*ns.* **quadricone** (*kwod'ri-kōn*), a quadric cone, or cone having a conic as base; **quadriennium** (*kwod-ri-en'i-əm*; L. *annus,* year), four years:—*pl.* **quadrienn'ia.**—*adj.* **quadrienn'ial,** lasting four years: once in four years.—*n.* a quadriennial event.—*adv.* **quadrienn'ially.**—The forms **quadrenn'ium,** etc., are etymologically incorrect but now usual.—*adjs.* **quadrifarious** (*kwod-ri-fā'ri-əs*; L. poss. from *fāri,* to speak), fourfold: in four rows; **quadrifid** (*kwod'ri-fid;* L. from the root of *findēre,* to cleave), four-cleft; **quadrifoliate** (*kwod-ri-fō'li-āt;* L. *folium,* a leaf); four-leaved; **quadriform** (*kwod'ri-förm;* L. *förma,* form), fourfold: having four forms or aspects.—*n.* **quadriga** (*kwod-rī'gə;* *kwad-rē'ga;* L., a later singular from *quadrigae,* a team of four, for *quadrijugae—jugum,* yoke), in Greek and Roman times a two-wheeled car drawn by four horses abreast:—*pl.* **quadri'gae** (*-jē, -gī*).—*adjs.* **quadrigeminal** (*kwod-ri-jem'i-nl;* L. *gemini,* twins), having four similar parts.—Also **quadrigem'-inate, quadrigem'inous; quadrilateral** (*kwod-ri-lat'ər-l;* L. *latus, lateris,* a side), four-sided.—*n.* a plane figure bounded by four straight lines (*geom.*): a group of four fortresses, esp. Mantua, Verona, Peschiera, and Legnaga.—*adj.* **quadriliteral** (*kwod-ri-lit'ər-l;* L. *litera,* a letter), of four letters.—*n.* a word or a root of four letters.—*n.* **quadrillion** (*kwod-, kwad-ril'yən*; modelled on **million**), a million raised to the fourth power, represented by a unit and 24 ciphers: in U.S., a thousand to the fifth power, a unit with 15 ciphers.—*n.* and *adj.* **quadrill'ionth.**—*adj.* **quadrilocular** (*kwod-ri-lok'ū-lər;* L. *loculus,* dim. of *locus,* place), having four compartments.—*n.* **quadringenary** (*kwod-rin-jē'nər-i;* L. *quadringenārius,* of four hundred each), a four-hundredth anniversary or its celebration.—*adjs.* **quadrinomial** (*kwod-ri-nō'mi-əl;* irregularly from L. *nōmen, -inis,* a name; *alg.*), of four terms.—*n.* an expression of four terms.—*adj.* **quadripartite** (*kwod-ri-pär'tīt;* L. *partīrī, -ītum,* to divide), in four parts: having four parties: deeply cleft into four parts, as a leaf (*bot.*): divided, as a vault, into four compartments (*archit*.).—*n*. **quadriparti'tion**.—*n*. **quadriplegia** (*kwod-ri-plēj'(i)ə, plēj'yə*; Gr. *plēgē*, a blow), paralysis of both arms and both legs.—*n*. and *adj*. **quadripleg'ic**.—*ns*. **quadrireme** (*kwod'ri-rēm*; L. *rēmus*, an oar), an ancient ship with four sets of oars; **quadrisection** (*kwod-ri-sek'-shən*; L. *sectiō, -ōnis*, cutting), division into four equal parts; **quadrisyllable** (*kwod-ri-sil'ə-bl*), a tetrasyllable.—*adj*. **quadrisyllab'ic**.—*adj*. **quadrivalent** (*kwod-riv'ə-lənt*, or *-vǎ'lənt*), having a valency of four.—*ns*. **quadriv'alence** (or *-vǎ'*); **quadrivium** (*kwod-riv'i-əm*; L., the place where four roads meet—*via*, a way), in mediaeval education, the four branches of mathematics (arithmetic, geometry, astronomy, music).— *adj*. **quadriv'ial**.—complete **quadrilateral**, a figure consisting of four straight lines intersecting in six points or vertices. [L. *quadri*—*quattuor*, four.]

**quadriliteral . . . quadrivium.** See **quadr(i)-**.

**quadrille**, *kwə-dril'* or *kə-*, *n*. one of four groups of horsemen (or others): a square dance for four couples or more, in five movements: music for such a dance.—*v.i.* to dance quadrilles.—*n*. **quadrill'er**. [Fr.,—Sp. *cuadrilla*, a troop, app.—*cuadra*—L. *quadra*, a square.]

**quadrille**, *kwə-dril'* or *kə-*, *n*. a four-handed game with 40 cards, not unlike ombre.—*v.i.* to play quadrille. [Fr., perh.—Sp. *cuatrillo*, the game of quadrille, or *cuartillo*, fourth part.]

**quadroon**, *kwod-rōōn'*, *n*. the offspring of a mulatto and a white: extended to any analogous cross.—Also **quarteroon'**. [Sp. *cuarterón*—*cuarto*, a fourth.]

**quadru-**, *kwod-rōō*, a variant of **quadr(i)-**.—*adj*. **quadrumanous** (*kwod-rōō'mən-əs*; L. *manus*, a hand), four-handed: of the obsolete order **Quadru'mana**, the Primates other than man:—*sing*. **quadru'man**, **-mane** (*-man, -mǎn*).—*ns*. **quadrumvir** (*kwod-rum'vər*; L. *vir*, a man), a member of a **quadrum'virate**, a group of four men acting together in some capacity; **quadruped** (*kwod'rōō-ped*; L. *pēs, pedis*, a foot), a four-footed animal, usu. a mammal, esp. a horse.— *adj*. **four-footed**.—*adj*. **quadrupedal** (*-rōō'pi-dəl*).

**quadruple**, *kwod'rōō-pl*, also (esp. in Scotland) *-rōō'*, *adj*. **fourfold**: having four parts, members, or divisions.—*n*. four times as much: a coin worth four pistoles.—*v.t.* to increase fourfold: to equal four times.—*v.i.* to become four times as much.—*n*. **quad'ruplet** (or *-rōō'*), any combination of four things: a group of four notes performed in the time of three: a cycle for four riders: one of four born at a birth.—*adv*. **quad'ruply** (*-pli*, or *-rōō'pli*), in a fourfold manner.—**Quadruple Alliance**, a league formed in 1718 by Britain, France, Austria, and Holland against Spain. [Fr.,—L. *quadruplus*, from the root of *plēre*, to fill.]

**quadruplex**, *kwod'rōō-pleks*, *adj*. **fourfold**: of a telegraphic system, capable of sending four messages at once, two each way, over one wire.— *n*. an instrument of this kind.—*v.t.* to make quadruplex.—*adj*. **quadru'plicate**, fourfold.—*n*. one of four corresponding things: fourfoldness. —*v.t.* to make fourfold.—*ns*. **quadruplicā'tion**; **quadruplicity** (*-plis'i-ti*); **quad'ruply** (*-pli*; Scots *law*), a reply to a triply. [L. *quadruplex, -icis*, fourfold—*plicāre, -ātum* to fold.]

**quaere**, *kwē'rē, kwī're*, (L. imper. of *quaerĕre, quaesītum*, to inquire) inquire (suggesting doubt, or desirability of investigation).—See also **query**.—**quaeritur** (*kwē-rī'tər, kwī'ri-tōōr*), the question is asked; **quaesitum** (*kwē-sī'təm, kwi-sē'tōōm*), something sought for: the true value.

**quaestor**, *kwēs'tör, -tər, kwis'tor*, *n*. an ancient Roman magistrate, in early times an investigator, prosecutor, or judge in murder cases, later a treasurer with various other functions: in the Middle Ages an officer (usu. **ques'tor**) who

granted indulgences: a treasurer.—*n*. **quaes'-tionary** (*-tyən-ə-ri*; *Scott*), a pardoner.—*adj*. **quaestorial** (*-tō'ri-əl, tö'*). — *n*. **quaes'torship**. — *adj*. **quaes'tuary**, money-making: gain-seeking.— *n*. a gain-seeker: a pardoner. [L. *quaestor, -ōris*—*quaerĕre, quaesītum*, to seek.]

**quae vide.** See **quod** (1).

**quaff**, *kwäf, kwof*, *v.t.* to drink or drain in large draughts.—*v.i.* to drink largely.—*n*. a draught.— *n*. **quaff'er**. [Origin obscure.]

**quaff**, *kwäf*, a variant of **quaich**.

**quag**, *kwag, kwog, n.* a boggy place, esp. one that quakes underfoot.—*n*. **quagg'iness**.—*adj*. **quagg'y**. [Cf. **quake**.]

**quagga**, *kwag'ə, n.* an extinct S. African wild ass (*Equus quagga*), less fully striped than the zebras, to which it was related. [Perh. Hottentot *quacha*.]

**quagmire**, *kwag'mir*, or *kwog'*, *n*. wet, boggy ground that yields or quakes under the feet.— *v.t.* to entangle, as in a quagmire.—*adj*. **quag'-miry**. [App. **quag**, **mire**.]

**quahog, quahaug**, *kwō'hog, -hög, kwə-hog', -hög'*, *n*. an edible Venus mollusc (*Venus mercenaria*) of the N. American Atlantic coast—also known as round clam: also *Cyprina islandica* (*black quahog*).—Also **cohog**. [Narraganset Ind. *poquauhock*.]

**quaich, quaigh**, *kwähh*, (*Scot*.) *n*. a drinking-cup, usually of staves and hoops. [Gael. *cuach*, a cup.]

**Quai d'Orsay**, *kā dör-sā*, the French Foreign Office. [Name of a quay on the Seine faced by the French Ministry of Foreign Affairs.]

**quail**, *kwāl*, *v.i.* to languish, decline (*arch*.): flinch: fail in spirit: to slacken (*Shak*.).—*v.t.* (*obs*.) to subdue: to daunt.—*n*. **quail'ing** (*Shak*.). [M.E. *quayle*; origin obscure.]

**quail**, *kwāl, n.* a genus (*Coturnix*) of small birds of the partridge family: in America extended to various similar small game-birds, as the California quail (*Lophortyx*) and the bobwhite: a whore (*Shak*.).—**quail'-pipe**, a whistle for alluring quails into a net (also **quail'-call**): the throat (*obs*.). [O.Fr. *quaille*; prob. Gmc.]

**quaint**, *kwānt, adj*. skilful, esp. in use of language (*Shak*.): cunning (*obs*.): ingenious (*obs*.): fine (*Spens., Milt*.): affectedly fanciful or elaborate (*obs*.): affectedly nice or prim (*Spens*.): pleasantly odd: whimsical.—*adv*. **quaint'ly**.—*n*. **quaint'ness**. [O.Fr. *cointe*—L. *cognitus*, known; perh. confused with *comptus*, neat.]

**quair**, *kwār*, obs. form of **quire** (1).

**quake**, *kwāk, v.i.* to quiver or vibrate, as the earth or a quagmire: to tremble, esp. with cold or fear.—*v.t.* to cause to tremble (*Shak*.): to shake by earthquake.—*n*. a tremor: an earthquake: a shudder.—*ns*. **quā'kiness**; **quā'king**.—*adv*. **quā'-kingly**.—*adj*. **quā'ky**, shaky.—**quā'king-grass**, a moorland grass of the genus *Briza*, with pendulous, panicled tremulous spikelets. [O.E. *cwacian*; perh. allied to **quick**.]

**Quaker**, *kwā'kər, n.* one of the Society of Friends, founded by George Fox (1624-91): a dummy cannon.—*adj*. of Quakers: (*U.S.*) of Philadelphia ('the Quaker city', because founded by William Penn, Quaker).—*ns*. **Qua'kerdom**; **Qua'keress**; **Quā'kerism**.—*adjs*. **Quā'kerish, Quā'kerly**, like a Quaker.—**Quā'ker-bird**, the sooty albatross; **Quā'ker-butt'ons**, the round seeds of nux vomica; **Quā'ker-colour**, drab. [Nickname (not adopted by themselves, and earlier applied to another sect) given them by Justice Bennet at Derby, because Fox bade him and others *quake* at the word of the Lord.]

**qualify**, *kwol'i-fi, v.t.* to ascribe a quality to: to characterise: to add a quality to the connotation of: to render capable or suitable: to furnish with legal power: to limit by modifications: to moderate: to mitigate: to appease: to abate: to reduce the strength of: to vary: to prove, confirm (*Scots law*).—*v.i.* to take the necessary steps to fit oneself for a certain position, activity, or practice:—*pr.p.* qual'ifying; *pa.p.* and *pa.t.* qual'ified.—*adj.* qual'ifiable (*-fi-ə-bl*).—*n.* qualification (*-fi-kā'shən*), qualifying: distinctive quality: modification: restriction: that which qualifies: a quality that fits a person for a place, etc.: an accomplishment (*obs.*): a necessary condition: the attaching of quality, or the distinction of affirmative and negative, to a term (*log.*).—*adj.* and *n.* qual'ificative.—*n.* qual'ificator (*R.C.*), one who prepares ecclesiastical causes for trial.—*adj.* qual'ificatory.—*adj.* qual'ified (*fid*), fitted: competent: having the necessary qualification: modified: limited.—*adv.* qual'ifiedly (*-fid-li*).—*n.* qual'ifier (*-fi-ər*).—*n.* and *adj.* qual'ifying. [Fr. *qualifier* or L.L. *quālificāre*—L. *quālis*, of what sort, *facĕre*, to make.]

qualis ab incepto, kwa'lis ab in-sep'tō, kwä'lis ab in-kep'tō, (L.) as from the beginning.

quality, kwol'i-ti, n. that which makes a thing what it is: nature: character: kind: property: attribute: social status: high social status: persons of the upper class collectively: grade of goodness: excellence: profession, esp. (*Shak.*) the actor's profession: manner (*Shak.*): skill, accomplishment: timbre, that character of a sound that depends on the overtones present, distinguished from loudness and pitch: the character of a proposition as affirmative or negative (*log.*).—*adj.* of high grade of excellence.—*adj.* qual'itative, relating to, or concerned with, quality, esp. opp. to *quantitative.*—*adv.* qual'itatively.—*adj.* qual'itied, endowed with a quality or qualities.—quality newspaper, one seeking to provide material that will interest educated readers. [O.Fr. *qualité*—L. *quālitās*, -*tātis*—*quālis*, of what kind.]

qualm, kwäm, also kwŏm, n. an access of faintness or sickness: a sickly feeling: an uneasiness, as of conscience.—*adjs.* qualm'ing; qualm'ish.—*adv.* qualm'ishly.—*n.* qualm'ishness.—*adjs.* qualm'less; qualm'y. [Perh. O.E. *cwealm*, death, murder, torment, pain.]

quamash, kwom'ash, kwə-mash'. Same as camass.

quandary, kwon'də-ri, also kwon-dā'ri, n. a state of perplexity: dilemma: a hard plight (*obs.*). [Origin obscure.]

quand même, kā mem, (Fr.) nevertheless, whatever the consequences may be.

quandong, kwan' or kwon'dong, n. a small Australian tree (*Fusanus acuminatus*) of the sandalwood family: its edible drupe (*native peach*) or edible kernel (quan'dong-nut).—Also quan'dang, quan'tong.

quannet, kwon'it, n. a file mounted like a plane. [Origin unknown.]

quant, kwant, kwont, (Kent, E.Angl.) n. a punting or jumping pole, with a flat cap.—*v.t.* to punt. [Cf. kent; poss. conn. with L. *contus*, Gr. *kontos*.]

quantic, kwon'tik, (math.) n. a rational integral homogeneous function of two or more variables.—*adj.* quan'tical. [L. *quantus*, how great.]

quantify, kwon'ti-fi, v.t. to qualify (a term in a proposition) by stating the quantity (*log.*): to fix or express the quantity of: to express as a quantity.—*ns.* quantification (*-fi-kā'shən*); quan'tifier.—quantification of the predicate (*log.*), the attachment of a sign of quantity to the predicate. [L. *quantus*, how great, *facĕre*, to make.]

quantise, -ize. See quantum.

quantity, kwon'ti-ti, n. the amount of anything: bulk: size: a sum: a determinate amount: an amount, portion: a considerable amount: a fragment, scrap (*Shak.*): a large portion: length or shortness of duration of a sound or syllable: extension (*log.*): the character of a proposition as universal or particular: anything which can be increased, divided, or measured: proportion (*Shak.*).—*adj.* quan'titative (less justifiably quan'titive), relating to, or concerned with, quantity, esp. opp. to *qualitative.*—*adv.* quan'titatively.—quantity surveyor, one who estimates quantities required, obtains materials, evaluates work done, etc.—unknown quantity, a quantity whose mathematical value is not known: a factor, person or thing whose importance or influence cannot be foreseen (*fig.*). [O.Fr. *quantité*—L. *quantitās*, -*tātis*—*quantus*, how much.]

quantivalence, kwon-tiv'ə-ləns, or -ti-vā'ləns, n. valency.—*adj.* quantiv'alent (or -vā'). [L. *quantus*, how much—*valēns*, -*entis*, pr.p. of *valēre*, to be worth.]

quantometer, kwon-tom'i-tər, n. an instrument that shows by spectrographical analysis the percentages of the various elements present in a metallic sample. [L. *quantus*, how much, meter.]

quantum, kwon'təm, n. quantity: amount: a naturally fixed minimum amount of some entity which is such that all other amounts of that entity occurring in physical processes in nature are integral multiples thereof (*phys.*):—*pl.* quan'ta.—*v.t.* quan'tise, -ize, to express in terms of quanta or in accordance with the quantum theory.—quantum number, any of a set of integers or half-integers which together describe the state of a particle or system of particles; the principal quantum number, for instance, specifies the shell an electron occupies; quantum theory, Planck's theory of the emission and absorption of energy not continuously but in finite steps. [L. *quantum*, neut. of *quantus*, how much.]

quantum meruit, kwon'təm mer'ū-it, kwan'tōōm mer'ōō-it, (L.; as much as he deserved) a fair reward for services rendered where there is no agreed rate of payment.

quantum sufficit, kwon'təm suf'is-it, kwan'tōōm sōō'fik-it, (L.) a sufficient quantity.

quaquaversal, kwä-kwə-vûr'sl, kwä-kwä-, adj. dipping outward in all directions from a centre (*geol.*): facing or bending all ways.—*adv.* quaquaver'sally. [L. *quāquā*, whithersoever, *vertēre*, to turn.]

quarantine, kwor'ən-tēn, n. forty days: a time (orig. for a ship forty days) of compulsory isolation or detention to prevent spread of contagion or infection: isolation or detention for such a purpose: the place where the time is spent.—*v.t.* to subject to quarantine.—quarantine flag, a yellow flag displayed by a ship in quarantine, with a black spot if there be contagious disease on board. [It. *quarantina*—*quaranta*, forty—L. *quadrāgintā*.]

quare impedit, kwä'rē im'pə-dit, kwä'rā im-ped'it, (L.; why does he hinder?) a writ issued in cases of disputed presentation to a benefice, requiring the defendant to state his reasons for hindering the presentation.

quark, kwörk, kwärk, n. any of a triplet of particles, not yet found, suggested as the units out of which all other subatomic particles are formed. [From word coined by James Joyce in *Finnegans Wake*.]

quarrel, kwor'l, n. a square-headed arrow as for a cross-bow (*Spens*). quar'le): a diamond pane of glass: a square tile.—quarr'el-pane. [O.Fr. *quarrel* (Fr. *carreau*)—L.L. *quadrellus*—*quadrus*, a square.]

quarrel, kwor'l, n. a complaint, charge (*obs.*): an objection (*obs.*): action at law (*obs.*): ground of complaint or action: a cause contended for: an unfriendly contention or dispute: a breach of friendship: quarrelsomeness (*Shak.*): a quarreller (*Shak.*).—*v.i.* to cavil, find fault: to dispute violently: to fall out: to disagree violently.—*v.t.* to call in question (*obs.*): to object to (*obs.*): to chide (now *Scot.*): to bring, render, by quarrelling:—*pr.p.* **quarr′elling**; *pa.t.* and *pa.p.* **quarr′-elled.**—*n.* **quarr′eller.**—*n.* and *adj.* **quarr′elling.**—*adjs.* **quarr′ellous** (*Shak.*), quarrelsome; **quarr′-elsome**, disposed to quarrel.—*adv.* **quarr′el-somely.**—*n.* **quarr′elsomeness.**—**quarrel with one's bread and butter**, to act in a way prejudicial to one's means of subsistence; **take up a quarrel** (*Shak.*), to settle a dispute. [O.Fr. *querele*—L. *querēla*—*querī*, *questus*, to complain.]

**quarrender, quarender,** *kwor′ən-dər*, **quarantine, quarenden, quarrington,** *-ən-tin*, *-dən*, *-ing-tən*, (*S.W.England*) *n.* a kind of red apple. [Origin unknown.]

**quarry,** *kwor′i*, *n.* an open excavation for building-stone, slate, etc.: any source of building-stone, etc.: a great mass of stone or rock (*obs.*): a source from which information can be extracted.—*v.t.* to dig from, or as from, a quarry: to cut into or cut away:—*pr.p.* **quarr′ying**; *pa.t.* and *pa.p.* **quarr′ied.**—*adj.* **quarr′iable.**—*n.* **quarr′ier**, a quarryman.—**quarr′yman**, one who works in a quarry; **quarr′ymaster**, the owner of a quarry; **quarr′y-sap, quarr′y-water**, the water in the pores of unquarried or newly quarried stone. [L.L. *quareia*, for *quadrāria*—L. *quadrāre*, to square.]

**quarry,** *kwor′i*, *n.* a deer's entrails given on a hide, to the dogs (*obs.*): a hawk's reward for a kill: a bird flown at by a hawk: a hunted animal: prey: a victim: a hunter's heap of dead game: a heap of corpses (*Shak.*): (*Shak., Macbeth*, I, ii) according to some, slaughter, or spoil; others would read quarrel. [O.Fr. *cuiree, curee*, said to be from *cuir*—L. *corium*, nide.]

**quarry,** *kwor′i*, *n.* a quarrel of glass: a square paving-tile or slab. [A form of **quarrel** (1); or perh. from O.Fr. *quarré*—L. *quadrātus*, squared.]

**quart, quarte,** *kärt*, *n.* a sequence of four cards: a position in fencing.—**quart and tierce**, practice between fencers: [Fr. *quarte*.]

**quart,** *kwört*, *n.* the fourth part of a gallon, or two pints (1·14 litres): a vessel containing two pints: as much as will fill it: a quarter, region (*Spens.*): a fourth (*mus.*).—*n.* **quartā′tion**, the mixing of gold with three parts of silver as a stage towards purification.—**quart′-pot.** [Fr. *quart, -e*—L. *quārtus, -a, -um*, fourth—*quattuor*, four.]

**quartan,** *kwör′tən*, *adj.* occurring every third (by inclusive reckoning fourth) day, as a fever.—*n.* **quartan malaria.** [L. *quārtānus*, of the fourth.]

**quarter,** *kwör′tər*, *n.* a fourth part: the fourth part of a cwt.=28 (*U.S.* 25) lb. avoirdupois: 8 bushels (perh. orig. a fourth of a ton of corn): the fourth part of an hour—of the year—of the moon's period (or the moon's position at the end of it)—of the world, etc.: 25-cent piece: a limb with adjacent parts of the trunk, esp. of the dismembered body of one who has been executed, or of a beast's carcass: a haunch: one of the four parts of a quartered shield (*her.*): an ordinary occupying one-fourth of the field (*her.*): a quartering: a cardinal point, or any point, of the compass: the region about any point of the compass: hence a region generally, and also figuratively: a town district inhabited by a particular class: a part of an army, camp, etc. (*Shak.*): lodging, as for soldiers, esp. in *pl.*: an assigned station: terms, relations, treatment, esp. favourable (*Shak.*): mercy granted to an antagonist (perh. from sending to quarters): the part of a ship's side abaft the beam: a quarter-mile race.—*v.t.* to divide into four equal parts: to divide into parts or compartments: to station, lodge, or impose in quarters: to bear, place, or divide quarterly (*her.*): to beat or range as for game.—*v.i.* to be stationed: to lodge: to range for game: to drive with wheels between the ruts, or horse astride of a rut:

hence, to drive to the side of the road, or from side to side.—In composition, **quar′ter-**, *adjectivally*, one-fourth part (of); *adverbially*, to the extent of one-fourth.—*n.* **quar′terage**, a quarterly payment: quarters, lodging.—*adjs.* **quar′tered**; **quar′tering**, sailing nearly before the wind: striking on the quarter of a ship, as a wind.—*n.* assignment of quarters: a series of small upright posts for forming partitions, lathed and plastered only, or boarded also (*archit.*): the division of a coat by horizontal and vertical lines (*her.*): one of the divisions so formed: the marshalling of coats in these divisions, indicating family alliances: any one of the coats so marshalled.—*adj.* **quar′terly**, relating to a quarter, esp. of a year: recurring, or published, once a quarter: divided into or marshalled in quarters (*her.*).—*adv.* once a quarter: in quarters or quarterings (*her.*).—*n.* a quarterly periodical.—**quar′ter-blood**, offspring of a white and a half-breed.—*adj.* **quar′ter-bound**, having leather or cloth on the back only, not the corners.—**quar′ter-boy, quar′ter-jack**, an automaton that strikes the quarter-hours.—*adj.* **quar′ter-bred**, having only one-fourth pure blood, as horses, cattle, etc.—**quar′ter-day**, the first or last day of a quarter, on which rent or interest is paid; **quar′ter-deck**, part of the deck of a ship abaft the mainmast—used by cabin passengers and by superior officers (and saluted on warships); **quar′ter-decker** (*coll.*), a stickler for naval etiquette; **quar′ter-evil, -ill**, black-quarter; **quar′ter-gallery**, a projecting balcony on a ship's quarter; **quar′ter-guard**, a guard of a battalion in camp; **quar′ter-gunner** (*U.S.*), a naval petty-officer, under the gunner; **quar′ter-horse** (*U.S.*), a horse that can run a quarter of a mile or so at great speed; **quar′ter-jack**, a quarter-boy: a quarter-master (*slang*); **quar′termaster**, an officer who finds quarters for soldiers, and attends to supplies: a petty officer who attends to the helm, signals, etc. (*naut.*):—*fem.* **quar′termistress** (or **quartermaster**); **quar′termaster-gen′eral**, a staff-officer who deals with questions of transport, marches, quarters, fuel, clothing, etc.; **quar′termaster-ser′geant**, a non-commissioned officer who assists the quartermaster; **quar′ter-note**, a crotchet: a quarter-tone; **quar′ter-plate** (see plate); **quar′ter-road**, a road divided into four strips by ruts and horse-track; **quar′ter-round**, a moulding whose section is about a quadrant, an ovolo; **quar′ter-seal**, the seal kept by the director of the Chancery of Scotland—known also as the 'testimonial of the Great Seal'; **quar′ter-sessions**, a court held quarterly by justices of the peace (superseded in 1972 by crown courts); **quar′ter-staff**, a long wooden pole, an old weapon of defence: play with this weapon; **quar′ter-tone**, half a semitone; **quar′ter-wind**, a wind blowing on a ship's quarter.—**at close quarters**, in very near proximity: hand-to-hand; **keep a (bad) quarter** (*obs.*), to make a disturbance; **keep good quarter** (*Shak.*), keep good watch or good order. [O.Fr. *quarter*—L. *quārtārius*, a fourth part—*quārtus*, fourth.]

**quartern,** *kwör′tə(r)n*, *n.* a quarter, esp. of a peck, a stone, a pound (weight), a pint, or a hundred.—**quar′tern-loaf**, a four-pound loaf, as is made from a quarter of a stone of flour. [A.Fr. *quartrun*, O.Fr. *quarteron*—*quart(e)*, fourth part.]

**quarteroon.** Same as **quadroon.**

**quartet, quartette, quartett,** *kwör-tet′*, *n.* a set of four: a composition for four voices or instruments: a set of performers or instruments for such compositions.—Also (*It.*) **quartett′o.** [It. *quartetto*, dim. of *quarto*—L. *quārtus*, fourth.]

**quartic,** *kwör′tik*, (*math.*) *adj.* of the fourth degree.—*n.* a function, curve, or surface of the fourth degree. [L. *quārtus*, fourth.]

**quartier,** *kär-tē-ā*, (Fr.) a particular district in a

French town or city.—**quartier latin** (*la-tē*), the 'Latin quarter' of Paris, on the left bank of the Seine, inhabited by writers, artists and students.

**quartile,** *kwör'til, n.* an aspect of planets when their longitudes differ by 90° (*astrol.*): in frequency-distribution, a value such that a fourth, a half, or three-quarters of the numbers under consideration fall below it.—Also *adj.*—**quartile deviation,** the distance between the values below which the last fourth and above which the highest fourth fall. [L. *quārtus,* fourth.]

**quarto,** *kwör'tō, adj.* having the sheet folded into four leaves or eight pages (often written 4to).— *n.* a book of sheets so folded, or of such a size:— *pl.* **quar'tos** (demy quarto, 8¾ × 11¼ in.; medium quarto, 9 × 11½ in.; royal quarto, 10 × 12½ in.). —**small quarto,** a square octavo: a book having eight leaves to a sheet but the shape of a quarto. [L. (*in*) *quārtō,* (in) one-fourth.]

**quartodeciman,** *kwör-tō-des'i-mən, n.* one who celebrated Easter on the 14th of Nisan without regard to the day of the week.—Also *adj.* [L.L. *quartodecimānus*—L. *quārtus decimus,* fourteenth.]

**quartz,** *kwörts, n.* the commonest rock-forming mineral, composed of silica, occurring in hexagonal crystals (clear and colourless when pure) or crypto-crystalline.—*adj.* of quartz.—*adj.* **quartzif'erous,** quartz-bearing.—*n.* **quartz'ite,** a metamorphosed sandstone with the grains welded together.—*adjs.* **quartzitic** (*-it'ik*), of or like quartzite; **quartz'ose,** of, like, or rich in quartz; **quartz'y.**—**quartz**(-crystal) **clock,** a clock depending, not on the swing of a pendulum, but on the more rapid vibrations of a ring of quartz; **quartz glass,** fused quartz; **quartz'-halo'gen lamp** (commonly **quartz'-i'odine lamp,** using iodine), a compact source of light used for high-intensity flooding of large areas, car (fog-) lamps, cine-projectors, etc.; **quartz'-mill,** a mill or machine for crushing auriferous quartz: **quartz-por'phyry,** an igneous rock with crystals of quartz and feldspar in a compact or finely crystalline ground-mass of the same; **quartz'-rock',** quartzite; **quartz'-schist',** a schistose quartzite with mica. [Ger. *quarz.*]

**quasar,** *kwā'sər, n.* a *quasi-star,* a point (star-like) source of radiation (usu. light) outside our galaxy, claimed by some to be merely an optical effect.

**quash,** *kwosh, v.t.* to crush: to subdue or extinguish suddenly and completely: to annul. [O.Fr. *quasser* (Fr. *casser*)—L. *quassāre,* intens. of *quatēre,* to shake.]

**Quashee, Quashie,** *kwosh'i, n.* a West African Negro personal name: (without *cap.*) a Negro, esp. in the West Indies. [Ashanti name given to one born on Sunday.]

**quasi,** *kwā'sī, kwā'zē, adv.* as if, as it were.—In composition, **quasi-,** in a certain manner, sense, or degree: in appearance only, as **quasi-historical.** [L.]

**Quasimodo,** *kwas-i-mō'dō, n.* the first Sunday after Easter, Low Sunday. [From the first words of the introit for the day, 1 Peter, ii. 2; L. *quasi modo geniti infantes,* as new-born babes, etc.]

**quassia,** *kwosh'(y)a, n.* a South American tree (*Quassia amara;* fam. Simarubaceae), whose bitter wood and bark are used as a tonic: now generally a West Indian tree of the same family (*Picraena excelsa*). [Named by Linnaeus from a Negro *Quassi,* who discovered its value against fever.]

**quat,** *kwot, n.* a pimple: an insignificant person (*Shak.*). [Origin unknown.]

**quatch.** See quich.

**quatch-buttock,** *kwoch'-but'ək,* (*Shak.*) *n.* appar. a flat or squat buttock.

**quatercentenary,** *kwot-, kwat-ər-sen-tēn'ər-i, -sin-,* -ten'ər-i, -sen'-tin-, *n.* a quadringenary or 400th anniversary, or its celebration. [L. *quater,* four times.]

**quaternary,** *kwo-tûr'nər-i, adj.* consisting of four: by fours: in fours: of the fourth order: based on four: with four variables: (*cap.;* geol.) Post-Tertiary.—*n.* the number four: a set of four: (*cap.;* geol.) the Post-Tertiary era or group of strata (Pleistocene and Recent).—*adj.* **quater'nate,** in sets of four.—*n.* **quater'nion,** a set or group of four: in mathematics, the operation of changing one vector into another, or the quotient of two vectors, depending on four geometrical elements and expressible by an algebraical quadrinomial: (in *pl.*) a calculus concerned with this, invented by Sir William Rowan Hamilton (1805-65).—*adj.* **quater'nion'd** (*Milt.*), divided into groups of four.—*ns.* **quater'nionist,** a student of quaternions; **quatern'ity,** fourfoldness: a set of four: a fourfold godhead. [L. *quaterni,* four by four.]

**quatorze,** *kə-törz', n.* the four aces, kings, queens, knaves, or tens in piquet, counting 14.—*n.* **quatorzain** (*kat'ər-zān, kät-ör'zān*), a stanza or poem of fourteen lines. [Fr. *quatorze, quatorzaine.*]

**quatrain,** *kwot'rān, n.* a stanza of four lines usually rhyming alternately. [Fr.]

**quatrefoil,** *kat'ər-foil,* or *kat'rə-foil, n.* a four-petalled flower or leaf of four leaflets: an open-work design or ornament divided by cusps into four lobes (*archit.*).—Also **quat'refeuille** (*fœ-ē, -fīl*). [O.Fr. *quatre,* four, *foil* (Fr. *feuille*), leaf.]

**quattrocento,** *kwät-rō-chen'tō, n.* the 15th century in Italian art and literature.—*ns.* **quattrocent'ism; quattrocen'tist.** [It., four hundred.]

**quaver,** *kwā'vər, v.i.* to tremble, quiver: to speak or sing with tremulous uncertainty: to trill.— *v.t.* utter or sing tremulously.—*n.* a trembling, esp. of the voice: half a crotchet (*mus.*).—*n.* **quā'verer.**—*n.* and *adj.* **quā'vering.**—*adv.* **quā'veringly.**—*adj.* **quā'very.** [Freq. from obs. or dial. *quave,* M.E. *cwavien,* to shake; akin to **quake, quiver.**]

**quay,** *kē, n.* a landing-place: a wharf for the loading or unloading of vessels.—*n.* **quay'age,** provision of quays: space for, or system of, quays: payment for use of a quay.—*n.* and *adj.* **quay'side.**—Earlier forms **kay** (*kā*), **key.** [O.Fr. *kay, cay,* perh. Celtic; partly assimilated to mod. Fr. spelling *quai.*]

**quayd,** *kwād,* (*Spens.*) *adj.* or *pa.p.* daunted. [Perh. for **quelled.**]

**queach,** *kwēch,* (*obs.*) *n.* a thicket.—*adj.* **queach'y, queech'y,** forming a thicket: boggy: sickly. [Origin obscure.]

**quean,** *kwēn, n.* a saucy girl: a woman of worthless character: a girl (*Scot.*).—in N.E. Scotland **queyn, quine** (*kwin*), dim. **queyn'ie, quinie,** the ordinary words for a girl. [O.E. *cwene,* woman; cf. **queen** (O.E. *cwēn*).]

**queasy, queazy,** *kwē'zi, adj.* unsettled: hazardous: uneasy: causing nausea: sick, squeamish: inclined to vomit: fastidious: nice.—*adv.* **quea'sily.**—*n.* **quea'siness.** [Poss. O.Fr. *coisier,* to hurt; poss. O.N. *kveisa,* a boil.]

**quebracho,** *kā-brä'chō, n.* name of several S. American trees yielding very hard wood (*white quebracho,* Aspidosperma—fam. Apocynaceae; *red quebracho,* Schinopsis—fam. Anacardiaceae): their wood or bark. [Sp.,—*quebrar,* to break, *hacha,* axe.]

**Quechua,** *kech'wa,* **Quichua,** *kēch'wa, n.* a Peruvian Indian of the race that was dominant in the Inca empire: the language of the Quechua. —Also *adj.*—*adj.* **Quech'uan, Quich'uan.**—Also *n.* [Sp. *Quechua, Quichua.*]

**queechy.** See queach.

**queen,** *kwēn, n.* the consort or wife of a king: a female monarch: a presiding goddess: a woman or (*fig.*) anything that is pre-eminent in excellence, beauty, etc.: a sexually functional female social insect: female cat: male homosexual adopting female role (*slang*): a playing-card bearing the figure of a queen, in value next below a king: in chess, a piece that can be moved any distance in any straight line: a size of roofing-slate, 3 feet by 2.—*v.t.* to make a queen of: to substitute a queen (or other piece) for: to rule as queen: to supply with a queen: to play the queen (with *it*).—*ns.* queen'craft, craft or policy on the part of a queen; queen'dom, queenhood: the realm of a queen; queen'hood, the state of being a queen; queen'ing, an apple, of various varieties; queen'-ite, a queen's partisan; queen'let, a petty queen.—*adjs.* queen'less; queen'-like, like a queen.—*n.* queen'liness.—*adj.*queen'ly, becoming or suitable to a queen: like a queen.—*adv.* in the manner of a queen.—*n.* queen'ship, the state, condition or dignity of a queen.—queen'-bee, a fertile female bee: a woman who dominates her associates: a woman in an important business position: a senior female secretary; queen'-con'sort, the wife of a reigning king; queen'-dow'ager, a king's widow; queen'-moth'er, a queen-dowager that is mother of the reigning king or queen: a queen or queen-bee that is a mother; queen'-of-the-mead'ow(s), the meadow-sweet; queen'-post, one of two upright posts in a trussed roof, resting upon the tie-beam, and supporting the principal rafters; queen'-rē'gent, a queen who reigns as regent; queen'-reg'nant, a queen reigning as monarch; queen's'-arm, a musket; queen'-stitch, an embroidery pattern of square within square; queen's ware, cream-coloured Wedgwood ware; queen's yellow, basic mercuric sulphate.—Queen Anne's Bounty, a fund for augmenting poorer livings of the Church of England, formed (1703) out of first-fruits and tenths; Queen Anne's dead, that is old news; Queen Anne style (*archit.*), the simplified Renaissance manner of the early 18th century, or an imitation of it, plain and simple, with classic cornices and details; queen-bee substance, a substance secreted by a queen-bee which attracts drones and affects workers; Queen of Heaven, Ashtoreth: the Virgin Mary (*R.C.*); Queen of the May, May Queen; Queen's tobacco pipe, a kiln at London Docks for burning contraband goods (till 1891).—For Queen's Bench, Counsel, etc., see King's. [O.E. *cwēn*; Goth. *qēns*; O.N. *kvæn, kvān*; Gr. *gynē*; cf. quean.]

queene-apple, *kwēn'-ap'l*, (*Spens.*) *n.* app. a quince. [See quince.]

Queensberry Rules, *kwēnz'bər-i rōōlz*, rules applied to boxing, originally drawn up in 1867 and named after the Marquess of *Queensberry*, who took a keen interest in sport.

Queensland-nut, *kwēnz'land-nut'*, *n.* a proteaceous tree of *Queensland* and New South Wales: its edible nut.

queer, *kwēr*, *adj.* odd, singular, quaint: open to suspicion: counterfeit: slightly mad: having a sensation of coming sickness: sick, ill (*dial.*): homosexual (*slang*).—*v.t.* (*slang*), to quiz: to cheat: to spoil.—*n.* (*slang*) a homosexual.—*adj.* queer'ish.—*n.* queer'ity.—*adv.* queer'ly.—*queer'-ness.*—Queer Street, the feigned abode of persons in debt or other difficulties.—queer the pitch, to make the place of performance unavailable (*showman's slang*): to spoil one's chances; shove the queer (*slang*), to pass bad money. [Perh. Ger. *quer*, across; cf. thwart.]

queest, *kwēst*, Same as cushat.—Also quest, quoist, quist.

queez-maddam, *kwēz'-mad'əm*, (*Scott*) *n.* a French jargonelle pear. [Fr. *cuisse-madame*.]

queint, *kwānt*, (*Spens.*) *adj.* Same as quaint.

queint, *kwānt*, (*Spens.*) *pa.p.* of quench.

quelch, *kwel(t)sh*, *v.i.* and *v.t.* to squelch. [Imit.]

Quelea, *kwē'li-ə*, *n.* a genus of African weaver-birds, very destructive to crops. [From African name.]

quell, *kwel*, *v.t.* to kill (*obs.*): to extinguish: to crush: subdue: to disconcert, to abash (*Spens.*).—*v.i.* to die, perish (*Spens.*): to subside, abate (*Spens.*).—*ns.* quell, slaying (*Shak.*): power of quelling (*Keats*); quell'er, one who quells or crushes: a slayer. [O.E. *cwellan*, to kill, causal of *cwelan*, to die; cf. quail (vb.).]

queme, *kwēm*, (*Spens.*) *v.t.* to please, suit, fit. [O.E. *cwēman*; Ger. *bequem*, fit.]

quench, *kwen(t)sh*, *v.t.* to put out: to put out the flame, light, or sight of: to stop (a discharge of electrically charged particles): to cool with liquid: to slake: to damp down: to put an end to: to put to silence: to destroy: to extinguish hope, etc., in (*obs.*).—*v.i.* to be extinguished: to die down: to lose zeal: to subside in passion, grow cold (*Shak.*).—*n.* quenching.—*adj.* quench'-able.—*n.* quench'er, one who, or that which, quenches: a draught or drink.—*n.* and *adj.* quench'ing.—*adj.* quench'less, not to be extinguished.—*adv.* quench'lessly.—quenched spark, an oscillatory spark discharge extinguished after the first few oscillations. [O.E. *cwencan*, found only in the compound *ācwencan*, to quench, causative of *cwincan* (*ācwincan*); cf. Old Fris. *kwinka*, to go out.]

quenelle, *ka-nel'*, *n.* a forcemeat ball of chicken, veal, or the like. [Fr.]

quep, *kwep*, (*Scott*) *interj.* erroneously for gup (1).

Quercus, *kwûr'kəs*, *n.* the oak genus of the beech family.—*ns.* quercetum (*kwûr-sē'tam*), a collection of oak-trees; quer'citron (*si-trən*), a North American oak, the dyer's oak or yellow-barked oak: its inner bark, yielding a yellow dye (from citron). [L. *quercus*, oak.]

querimony, *kwer'i-man-i*, *n.* complaint.—*adj.* querimonious (*-mō'ni-əs*).—*adv.* querimō'niously. [L. *querimōnia*—*queri*, to complain.]

querist. See query.

quern, *kwûrn*, *n.* a stone handmill.—quern'stone. [O.E. *cweorn*; O.N. *kvern*, Goth. (*asilu*-) *qairnus*, (ass-)mill.]

querpo. See cuerpo.

quersprung, *kver'shprōōng*, *n.* in skiing, a jump-turn at right angles. [Ger.]

querulous, *kwer'ū-ləs*, also *-ōō-, -ə-*, *adj.* complaining: peevish.—*adv.* quer'ulously.—*n.* quer'ulousness. [L.L. *querulōsus*—*queri*, to complain.]

query, formerly often quaere, *kwē'ri*, *n.* an inquiry: doubt: interrogation mark (?).—*v.t.* to inquire into: to question: to doubt: to mark with a query.—*n.* que'rist, an inquirer.—*v.i.* to question:—*pa.t.* and *pa.p.* que'ried.—*n.* and *adj.* que'rying.—*adv.* que'ryingly. [L. *quaere*, imper. of *quaerĕre, quaesitum*, to inquire.]

quest, *kwest*, *n.* the act of seeking: search: pursuit: an adventure, expedition, or undertaking with the purpose of achieving or finding some definite object: a searching party: a jury of inquest: inquiry, investigation: a collection of alms or donations (*R.C.*): a searching for game by dogs, or their outcry on finding it.—*v.i.* to go in search: to go begging: to give tongue.—*v.t.* to go in quest of or after.—*ns.* quest'ant (*Shak.*), quest'er, quest'rist (*Shak.*), one who goes on a quest.—*n.* and *adj.* quest'ing. [O.Fr. *queste* (Fr. *quête*)—L. (*rēs*) *quaesita*, (a thing) sought—*quaerĕre, quaesitum*, to seek.]

quest. See quested.

question, *kwes'chən*, *n.* an inquiry: an interrogation: the putting of a problem: a demand for an answer: an interrogative sentence or other form of words in which it is put: a unit task in an examination: a problem: a subject of doubt or controversy: discussion, conversation (*Shak.*): a subject of discussion, esp. the particular point actually before the house, meeting, or company:

Neutral vowels in unaccented syllables: *el'ə-mənt*; for certain sounds in foreign words, see p. viii

subjection to examination: examination by torture (*hist.*): objection, demur: doubt: the measure to be voted upon: vaguely, a relevant matter.—*v.t.* to put questions to: to call to account: to examine by questions: to inquire: to inquire concerning: to throw doubt upon: to regard as doubtful: to challenge, take exception to.—*v.i.* to ask questions: to inquire: to discuss, converse (*Shak.*).—*adj.* quest′ionable, that may be questioned: doubtful: uncertain: open to suspicion: possibly dishonest, improper, immoral, etc.: such as questions may be put to, not unwilling to be conversed with (*Shak.*).—*n.* quest′ionableness.— *adv.* quest′ionably. — *adj.* quest′ionary, asking questions: in the form of questions.—*n.* an asker of questions: a questionnaire: a quaestionary (see quaestor).—*n.* quest′ioner.—*n.* and *adj.* quest′ioning.—*adv.* quest′ioningly.—*n.* quest′ionist, a questioner, a doubter: formerly, an undergraduate in his last term before proceeding to a degree.—*adj.* quest′ionless, unquestioning: beyond question or doubt.—*adv.* certainly.—*n.* questionnaire (*kwes-chən-ār′, kes-tē-on-er′*), a series of questions: a prepared set of written questions, for purposes of compilation or comparison.—ques′tion-begg′ing, begging the question (see beg).— Also *adj.*—ques′tion-mark, a point of interrogation; ques′tion-mas′ter, one who presides at a gathering whose purpose is the putting and answering of questions.—at question, questionable, open to question; in question, under consideration: in dispute, open to question; make question, demur; out of question, doubtless; out of the question, not to be thought of. [O.Fr.,—L. *quaestiō, -ōnis—quaerĕre, quaesitum,* to ask.]

questor. See quaestor.

quetch. See quich.

quetsch, *kwech, kvech, n.* a variety of plum, or brandy distilled from it. [Ger. *quetsch(e),* wild plum.]

quetzal, *ket-säl′, k(w)et′səl, n.* a golden green Central American bird (the *resplendent trogon*) with very long tail-feathers: the Gautemalan currency unit, or dollar. [Aztec *quetzalli.*]

queue, *kū, n.* a pendent braid of hair at the back of the head, a pigtail: a file of persons, etc., awaiting their turn: the tail of a beast (*her.*).— *v.t.* to place or arrange in a queue: to track, dog. —*v.i.* to form, or take one's place in, a queue (usu. with *up*).—*adj.* queued (*kūd*), tailed: in a queue.—*n.* queu′ing, queue′ing. [Fr.,—L. *cauda,* a tail.]

quey, *kwā, (Scot.) n.* a heifer: a young cow that has not yet had a calf. [O.N. *kvíga*; Dan. *kvie.*]

quh-, hw-, older Scots spelling for wh-. [O.E. *hw-.*]

quibble, *kwib′l, n.* an evasive turning away from the point in question into matters irrelevant, merely verbal, or insignificant: a pun: a petty conceit.—*v.i.* to evade a question by a play upon words: to cavil: to trifle in argument: to pun. —*ns.* quibb′ler; quib′lin (*obs.*), a quibble.—*n.* and *adj.* quibb′ling.—*adv.* quibb′lingly. [Perh. dim. of obs. *quib,* quibble, which may be—L. *quibus,* dat. or abl. pl. of *quī,* who, a word frequent in legal use; or a variant of quip.]

quich, *kwich,* (*Spens.*) *v.i.* to stir, to move.—Also (*obs.* or *dial.*) quatch, quetch, quitch. [O.E. *cweccan,* to shake, causative of *cwacian,* to quake.]

quiche, *kēsh, n.* a shell of unsweetened pastry filled with egg custard and cheese, etc. [Fr.,— Ger. dial. *küche,* dim. of *kuche,* cake.]

Quichua, *kēch′wa.* Same as Quechua.

quick, *kwik, adj.* living (*arch.*): alive (*arch.*): lively: swift: speedy: nimble: fresh: ready: sensitive: readily responsive: ready-witted: prompt in perception or learning: hasty: pregnant (*arch.*): at the stage of quickening:

quickset: active: mobile: piercing.—*adv.* without delay: rapidly: soon.—*n.* the living (*arch.*): a living thing (*Spens.*): a living plant, esp. hawthorn in a hedge (also collectively): the life (*arch.*): the living flesh (*arch.*): the sensitive parts, esp. under the nails: the tenderest feelings. —*v.t.* quick′en, to give life to: to stimulate: to impart energy or liveliness to: to invigorate: to revive: to accelerate.—*v.i.* to become alive or lively: to revive: to be stimulated: to reach the stage in pregnancy when the mother becomes conscious of the movement of the child: to move faster.—*n.* quick′ener.—*n.* and *adj.* quick′ening.—*n.* quick′ie (*coll.*), something that takes, or is to be done in, a short time, e.g. a film, quiz question, crossword, etc.—*adv.* quick′ly.—*n.* quick′ness.—*adjs.* quick′-an′swered (*Shak.*), quick at answering; quick′-born, born alive; quick′-change, quick in making a change, esp. (of a performer) in appearance; quick′-conceiv′ing, quick at understanding; quick′-eyed, having acute sight or lively eyes; quick′-fire, -firing, designed to allow a quick succession of shots.—quick′-firer; quick′-freeze, very rapid freezing of food so that its natural qualities are unimpaired.—Also *v.*—*adj.* quick′-frozen.— quick′-hedge, a hedge of living plants; quick′-lime, unslaked lime (CaO); quick′-lunch, a snack served promptly.—Also *adj.*—quick′-match, cotton thread impregnated with an inflammable mixture; quick′sand, a loose watery sand ready to swallow those who walk on it, boats, etc.: anything similarly treacherous. —*adjs.* quick′-sandy; quick′-scent′ed, quick′-scent′ing, having a keen scent; quick′-selling; quick′set, formed of living plants.—*n.* a living plant, slip, or cutting, esp. of hawthorn, or a series of them, set to grow for a hedge: a quickset hedge.—*adj.* quick′-sighted, having quick sight or discernment.—quick′-sight′ed-ness; quick′silver, mercury.—*adj.* of mercury.— *v.t.* to overlay or to treat with quicksilver or amalgam.—*adj.* quick′silvered.—quick′silvering, the mercury on the back of a mirror.—*adjs.* quick′silverish, quick′silvery.—quick′step, a march step or tune in fast time: a fast fox-trot.—*adv.* quick′-stick, -s, without delay.—*adj.* quick′-tem′pered, irascible.—quick′thorn, hawthorn; quick′-trick, a card that should win a trick in the first or second round of the suit; quick′-water, a solution of nitrate of mercury.— *adj.* quick′-witted, having ready wit.—quick′-witt′edness.—a quick one, a quick drink; quick on the draw, swift to draw a gun from its holster: prompt in response or action. [O.E. *cwic*; O.N. *kvikr,* living.]

quick, *kwik, n.* couch-grass or its rootstocks.— Also quick′en, quick′-grass. [Northern form of quitch.]

quicken, *kwik′ən,* (*Northern*) *n.* the rowan.—Also quick′beam (*Southern*), quick′en-tree, wick′en, wick′y. [O.E. *cwicbēam, cwictrēow,* aspen.]

quicken. See quick (1 and 2).

quid, *kwid, n.* that which a thing is, substance. [L., what.]

quid, *kwid, n.* something chewed or kept in the mouth, esp. a piece of tobacco. [cud.]

quid, *kwid,* (*slang*) *n.* a pound (£1): formerly, a guinea:—*pl.* quid: or in sense of ready money (*obs. slang*) quids. [Origin obscure.]

quidam, *kwi′dam, kwē′, n.* somebody: a certain person:—*pl.* quidam. [L. *quidam.*]

quiddany, *kwid′ə-ni,* a confection of quince-juice and sugar. [L. *cotōnea,* quince—*cydōnia*; see quince.]

quiddity, *kwid′i-ti, n.* the whatness or essence of anything: any trifling nicety: a cavil: a captious question: quibble.—Also (contracted) quidd′it.—*adj.* quidd′itative. [Schoolman's L. *quidditās, -tātis.*]

**quiddle**, *kwid'l*, (*dial.*) *v.i.* to trifle.—*ns.* **quidd'le**, a fastidious person; **quidd'ler**.

**quidnunc**, *kwid'nungk*, *n.* a newsmonger. [L. *quid nunc?*, what now?]

**quid pro quo**, *kwid prō kwō*, (L.) something for something: something given or taken as equivalent to another, often as retaliation: action or fact of giving or receiving thus.

**quiesce**, *kwi-es'*, *v.i.* to quiet down: to become silent (as a Hebrew consonant).—*ns.* **quiesc'-ence**, **quiesc'ency**, rest: inactivity: silence of a consonant.—*adj.* **quiesc'ent**, resting: not sounded: inactive: still.—*adv.* **quiesc'ently**. [L. *quiēscĕre*, to rest.]

**quiet**, *kwī'ət*, *adj.* at rest: calm: undisturbed: unaccompanied by disturbance: without loudness, gaudiness, ostentation, formality, or obtrusiveness of any kind: still: without bustle or restlessness: without much activity: peaceable: gentle: inoffensive.—*n.* rest: repose: calm: stillness: peace: freedom from noise or disturbance.—*v.t.* and *v.i.* to make or become quiet.—*v.t.* and *v.i.* **qui'eten**, to quiet.—*n.* and *adj.* **qui'etening**.—*n.* **qui'eter**.—*n.* and *adj.* **qui'eting**.—*ns.* **qui'etism**, mental tranquillity: the doctrine that religious perfection on earth consists in passive and uninterrupted contemplation of the Deity; **qui'etist**.—*adj.* **quietist'ic**.—*n.* and *adj.* **qui'etive**, sedative.—*adv.* **qui'etly**.—*n.* **qui'etness**.—*adj.* **qui'etsome** (*Spens.*), undisturbed.—*n.* **qui'etude**, quietness.—**on the quiet** (or **Q.T.**; *slang*), clandestinely: unobtrusively. [L. *quiētus*, quiet, calm.]

**quietus**, *kwī-ē'təs*, *kwi-ā'tōōs*, *n.* an acquittance: discharge from office: discharge from life: extinction: silencing. [L. *quiētus est*, he is quiet.]

**quiff**, *kwif*, *n.* a lock of hair oiled and brushed down on the forehead or turned up and back from it. [Poss. **coif**.]

**quight**, *kwīt*, (*Spens.*). See **quit**, **quite**.

**qui-hi**, **-hye**, *kwī'-hī'*, *n.* an Englishman in India, esp. in Bengal, in colonial days. [Hind. *koī hai*, the call for a servant, Is anyone there?—*koi*, anyone, *hai*, is.]

**quill**, *kwil*, *n.* a reed, hollow stalk or internode, or the like (*obs.*): a small tube (*obs.*): the hollow basal part of a feather: a large feather: a porcupine's spine: a goose or other feather used as a pen: hence a pen generally, or the profession of letters: a thing made from a quill feather, as a toothpick, an angler's float, a plectrum: a weaver's bobbin of reed or other material: a hollow shaft (*mach.*): a musical pipe made from a reed or the like: hence (Shak., *M.N.D.*, III, i. 134) throat, or perh. voice: a roll of curled bark, as cinnamon: a cylindrical plait (*obs.*).—*v.t.* to goffer: to wind on a bobbin.—*adj.* **quilled**, furnished with, or formed into quills: tubular.—*n.* **quill'ing**, a ribbon or strip gathered into flutings.—**quill'-driver** (*used derogatorily*), a clerk: an assiduous writer; **quill'-driving**; **quill'-feather**, a large stiff wing or tail feather; **quill'man**, a clerk; **quill'-nib**, a quill-pen shortened for use with a holder; **quill'-pen**; **quill'wort**, any plant of the genus Isoëtes (from the quill-like leaves). [Origin obscure; cf. L.G. *quiele*, Ger. *kiel*.]

**quill**, *kwil*, (*Shak.*) *n.* a combination (in the phrase **in the quill**, in a body, in concert). [Fr. *cueille*.]

**quillet**, *kwil'it*, *n.* a subtlety in argument: a quibble. [Perh. L. *quidlibet*, what you will.]

**quillon**, *kē-yō*, *n.* either arm of the cross-guard of a sword-handle. [Fr.]

**quilt**, *kwilt*, *n.* a bed-cover of two thicknesses with padding sewn in compartments: any material or piece of material so treated, esp. when worn under or instead of armour: a thick coverlet: a thick covering placed over beehive frames.—*v.t.* to pad, cover, or line with a quilt: to form into a quilt:

to stitch in: to seam like a quilt: to cover with interlaced cord: to thrash.—*adj.* **quilt'ed**.—*ns.* **quilt'er**, a person or machine that makes quilting; **quilt'ing**, the act of making a quilt: that which is quilted: a cloth for making quilts: a cloth with a pattern like a quilt: a covering of rope-yarn: a thrashing with a rope's end.—**quilt'ing-bee**, a gathering of women to help one in quilting a counterpane, combined with social amusement; **quilt'ing-cott'on**, cotton wadding; **quilt'ing-frame**, an adjustable frame for holding a fabric for quilting. [O.Fr. *cuilte* (Fr. *couette*)—L. *culcita*, a cushion.]

**quin**, *kwin*, *n.* short for **quintuplet**.

**quina**, **kina**, **china**, *kē'nə*, *n.* cinchona bark: any tree yielding it: quinine.—Also **quinaquina**, **kinakina**, **chinachina** (*kē-nä-kē'nə*), **quinquina** (*kin*- or *king-kē'nə*, *kwing-kwi'nə*).—*adj.* **quinic** (*kwin'ik*).—**quinic acid**, an acid got from cinchona bark. [Sp. *quina*, *quinaquina*—Quechua *kina*, *kina-kina*, *kinkina*, bark.]

**quinary**, *kwī'nər-i*, *adj.* fivefold: by fives: in fives: of the fifth order: based on five: with five variables.—*adj.* **qui'nate**, in sets of five: with five leaflets arising at one point. [L. *quīnī*, five bv five.]

**quince**, *kwins*, *n.* a golden, globose or pear-shaped, fragrant, acid fruit, good for jellies, marmalade, etc., or the tree or shrub (*Cydonia oblonga*), akin to pear and apple, that bears it: extended to the near-allied *Japanese quince* (see **japonica**) and to the unrelated *Bengal quince*, the bael-fruit. [Orig. pl. of *quine*—O.Fr. *coin* (Fr. *coing*)—L. *cotōneum*—Gr. *kydōnion*—*Kydōniā*, in Crete.]

**quincentenary**, *kwin-sin-tēn'ər-i*, *-sin-ten'ər-i*, or *-sen'tin-ər-i*, *n.* and *adj.* quingentenary. [Irreg. formed—L. *quinque*, five, and **centenary**.]

**quinche**, *kwinsh* (*Spens.*), *v.i.* stir, move. [Ety. dub.]

**quincunx**, *kwin'kungks*, *n.* an arrangement of five things at the corners and centre of a square, or of a great number of things (esp. trees) spaced in the same way.—*adj.* **quincuncial** (*-kun'shl*), of or in a quincunx: of aestivation, having two leaves overlapping at each edge, two underlapping at each edge, and one overlapping and underlapping (*bot.*).—*adv.* **quincun'cially**. [L. *quincunx*—*quinque*, five, *uncia*, a twelfth part.]

**quine**, **quinie**. See **quean**.

**quingentenary**, *kwin-jen-tē'nər-i*, *-ten'ər-i*, or *-jen'-tən-ər-i*, *n.* a five-hundredth anniversary or its celebration.—Also *adj.* [L. *quingentī*, five hundred.]

**quinine**, *kwin-ēn'*, *kwin'ēn*, in U.S. *kwī'nīn*, *n.* a colourless, inodorous, very bitter alkaloid ($C_{20}H_{24}O_2N_2{\cdot}3H_2O$), got from cinchona bark, or one of its salts, used against malaria and fevers. [See **quina**.]

**quinnat**, *kwin'ət*, *n.* the king-salmon. [From an Amer. Ind. name.]

**quinoa**, *kē'nō-ə*, *n.* a South American goosefoot, used like rice (seeds) or spinach (leaves). [Sp. *quínoa*—Quechua *kinua*.]

**quinol**, *kwin'ol*,' *n.* a reducing agent and photographic developer, $C_6H_4(OH)_2$, got by reduction of quinone.—*ns.* **quin'oline** (*-ō-lēn*), a pungent, colourless liquid ($C_9H_7N$), first got from quinine; **quinone** (*kwin'ōn*, *kwin-ōn'*), a golden-yellow crystalline compound ($C_6H_4O_2$) usually prepared by oxidising aniline: a reddish or colourless isomer of this: a general name for a benzene derivative in which two oxygen atoms replace two hydrogen.—Also **kinone** (*kē'nōn*). [**quina**.]

**quinqu-**, **quinque-**, *kwin-kw(i)-*, in composition, five.—*n.* **quinquagenarian** (*kwin-kwə-ji-nā'ri-ən*; L. *quīnquāgēnārius*—*quinquāgēnī*, fifty each), one who is fifty years old.—Also *adj.*—*adjs.* **quinquecostate** (*kwin-kwi-kos'tāt*; L. *costa*, rib), five-ribbed; **quinquefarious** (*kwin-kwi-fā'ri-əs*; L. poss. from *fārī*, to speak), fivefold: in five rows; **quinquefoliate** (kwin-kwi-fo'li-āt; L. folium, leaf), with five leaflets.—n. **quinquennium** (kwin-kwen'i-əm; L. annus, year), a period of five years:—pl. **quinquenn'ia.**—Also (irreg.) **quinquenn'iad.**—adj. **quinquenn'ial,** occurring once in five years: lasting five years.—n. a fifth anniversary or its celebration.—adv. **quinquenn'ially.**—n. **quinquereme** (kwin'kwi-rēm; L. rēmus, an oar), an ancient ship with five sets of oars.—adj. **quinquevalent** (kwin-kwev'ə-lənt or -kwi-vā°), having a valency of five.—n. **quinquev'alence** (or -vā'). [L. quinque, five.]

**Quinquagesima,** kwin-kwə-jes'i-mə, n. Shrove Sunday (also **Quinquagesima Sunday**)—apparently as fifty days before Easter Sunday (both counted).—adj. **quinquages'imal,** of the number fifty: of fifty days. [L quinquāgēsimus, -a, -um, fiftieth; cf. **quadragesima, sexagesima, septuagesima.**]

**quinque-, quinquennium,** etc. See **quinqu-.**

**quinquina.** See **quina.**

**quinsy,** kwin'zi, n. suppurative tonsillitis.— **quin'sy-berry,** the blackcurrant; **quins'y-wort,** squinancy-wort. [L.L.quinancia—Gr. kynanchē; see **cynanche.**]

**quint,** kwint, n. a fifth (mus.): an organ-stop a fifth above the foundation stops: the E string of a violin: (kint; old-fashioned kent) a sequence of five cards in piquet.—**quint'-ma'jor,** ace to ten; **quint'-mi'nor,** knave to seven. [Fr. quinte —L. quintus, -a, -um, fifth.]

**quint-, kwint-,** in composition, fifth. [L. quintus, fifth.]

**quinta,** kin'tə, n. a country house. [Sp. and Port.]

**quintain,** kwin'tin, -tən, n. a post for tilting at, often with a turning cross-piece to strike the unskilful tilter. [O.Fr.quintaine, thought to be— L. quintāna via, the road adjoining the fifth maniple in a camp.]

**quintal,** kwin'tl, n. formerly, a hundredweight: now, 100 kilograms. [Fr. and Sp. quintal—Ar. qintār—L. centum, a hundred.]

**quintan,** kwin'tən, adj. occurring every fourth (by inclusive reckoning fifth) day. [L. quintānus, of the fifth.]

**quintessence,** kwin-tes'əns, or kwin', n. orig. a fifth entity, in addition to the four elements: the pure concentrated essence of anything: the most essential part, form, or embodiment of anything. —adj. **quintessential** (-ti-sen'shl).—v.t. **quintessen'tialise, -ize.** [Fr.,—L. quinta essentia, fifth essence.]

**quintet, quintette, quintett,** kwin-tet', n. a composition for five voices or instruments: a set of performers or instruments for such compositions: a group of five people or things.—Also (It.) **quintet'to.** [It. quintetto, dim. of quinto— L. quintus, fifth.]

**quintic,** kwin'tik, adj. of the fifth degree.

**quintillion,** kwin-til'yən, n. the fifth power of a million, represented by a unit and thirty ciphers: in U.S., the sixth power of one thousand—a unit with eighteen ciphers.—n. and adj. **quintill'ionth.** [Modelled on **million.**]

**quintroon,** kwin-trōōn', n. the offspring of a person of European descent and an octoroon: one who is fifth (inclusive) in descent from a Negro. [Sp. quinterón—L. quintus, fifth.]

**quintuple,** kwin'tū-pl, adj. fivefold: having five parts, members, or divisions.—n. five times as much.—v.t. and v.i. to increase fivefold.—n. **quin'tūplet** (also -tū'), a set of five things: a group of five notes played in the time of four: one of five born at a birth. [L. quintus, fifth, on the model of **quadruple.**]

**quintuplicate,** kwin-tū'pli-kāt, adj. fivefold.—n. one of five corresponding things: fivefoldness.— v.t. to make fivefold.—n. **quintuplicā'tion.** [L. quintuplex, -icis—quintus, fifth, plicāre, to fold.]

**quinze,** kwinz, n. a card game, like vingt-et-un, the

object being to count as nearly to fifteen as possible without going above it. [Fr., fifteen.]

**quip,** kwip, n. a short, clever remark, a repartee: a gibe: a quibble: a fanciful jest or action: a knick-knack.—v.i. to utter quips.—v.t. to assail with quips.—adj. **quipp'ish.** [Perh. from obs. quippy, which may be—L. quippe, forsooth.]

**quipu,** kē'pōō, n. a mnemonic contrivance of knotted cords used by the ancient Peruvians— depending on order, colour, and kind.—Also **quip'o.** [Quechua quipu, knot.]

**quire,** kwir, n. formerly, four sheets of paper or parchment folded together in eight leaves; later, the twentieth part of a ream, twenty-four sheets, each having a single fold: a (quire-filling) book or poem (obs.; also **quair,** kwār).— v.t. to fold in quires. [O.Fr. quaier (Fr. cahier), prob. from L.L. quaternum, a set of four sheets— L. quattuor, four.]

**quire,** kwir, n. obs. spelling of **choir.**—n. **quirister** (kwir'), chorister.

**Quirinus,** kwi-rī'nəs, L. kwi-rē'nōōs, n. an Italic god of war, etc., afterwards identified with the deified Romulus—n. **Quirinal** (kwir'in-əl), one of the hills of Rome: the Italian government, as opposed to the Vatican (from the palace on the hill).—n.pl. **Quirinalia** (kwir-i-nā'li-ə), a festival held in honour of Quirinus, on 17th February. [L. Quirinus.]

**Quirites,** kwi-rī'tēz, kwi-rē'tās, n.pl. the citizens of ancient Rome in their civil capacity. [L. Quiritēs, orig. the Samnite people of Cures (united with the Romans).]

**quirk,** kwûrk, n. a trick or peculiarity of action or behaviour: a sudden turn, twist, jerk, or flourish: an artful evasion: a quibble: a quip: a trick, knack, way (Shak.): an acute sharp-edged groove alongside a moulding (archit.).— v.i. to turn sharply: to utter or execute quips: to move jerkily.—v.t. to assail with a quirk: to furnish with a quirk.—n. **quirk'iness.**—adjs. **quirk'ish; quirk'y.** [Origin unknown.]

**quirt,** kwûrt, n. a Spanish-American braided hide riding-whip.—v.t. to strike with a quirt. [Mexican-Sp. cuarta.]

**quisling,** kwiz'ling, n. one who aids the enemy: a native puppet prime minister set up by an occupying foreign power. [Vidkun Quisling, who played that part in Norway during German occupation (1940-45).]

**quist,** kwist. See **queest.**

**quit,** kwit, (arch.) **quite** (Spens. quight, quyte), kwit, v.t. to pay: to repay: to absolve: to requite: to release from obligation: to clear off: to discharge: to remit: to free: to clear of blame, etc.: to acquit: to depart from: to cease to occupy: to rid (obs. except reflex.): to let go: to leave off: to behave, acquit (reflex.): to be worth.—v.i. to leave off: to depart:— pr.p. **quitt'ing** (arch. **quit'ing**); pa.p. **quitt'ed** (quit'ed, quit).—adj. **quit,** set free: clear: quits: acquitted: released from obligation.—adj. **quits,** even: neither owing nor owed.—ns. **quitt'al** (Shak.), requital; **quitt'ance,** release: discharge: acquittance: requital.—v.t. (obs.) to repay.—n. **quitt'er,** a shirker: one who gives up easily.—**quit'-claim,** a deed of release.—v.t. to relinquish claim or title to: to release, discharge.—**quit'-rent,** a rent in money or kind in lieu of services.—**cry quits** (formerly **quittance**), to declare oneself even with another, and so satisfied; **double or quits,** the alternative, left to chance, of doubling or cancelling payment; **quit scores,** to balance accounts. [O.Fr. quitter (Fr. quitter)—L.L. quiētāre, to pay—L. quiētāre, to make quiet—quiētus, quiet.]

**qui tam,** kwī tam, kwē tam, n. an action by an informer partly on his own behalf, partly on the state's. [From the first words, L. qui tam, who as much (for the king as for himself).]

quitch, *kwich, n.* couch-grass.—Also quitch'-grass. [O.E. *cwice*; cf. couch-grass, quick (2).]

quitch. Same as quich.

quite. See quit.

quite (*Spens.* quight), *kwīt, adv.* completely, wholly, entirely: enough fully to justify the use of the word or phrase qualified: exactly, indeed, yes (*coll.*; often quite so). [quit.]

quitter, quittor, *kwit'ǝr, n.* pus: a fistulous sore on a horse's hoof. [Poss. O.Fr. *quiture*, cooking—L. *coctūra*.]

quiver, *kwiv'ǝr,* (*Shak.*) *adj.* nimble, active. [M.E. *cwiver*—O.E. *cwifer*, found in the adverbial form *cwiferlice*, zealously.]

quiver, *kwiv'ǝr, n.* a case for arrows.—*adv.* quiv'-ered, furnished with a quiver: sheathed, as in a quiver.—*n.* quiv'erful (*fig.*), a large family (Psalms cxxvii. 5). [O.Fr. *cuivre*; prob. Gmc. in origin; cf. O.H.G. *kohhar* (Ger. *kocher*), O.E. *cocer.*]

quiver, *kwiv'ǝr, v.i.* to shake with slight and tremulous motion: to tremble: to shiver.—*ns.* quiv'er, quiv'ering.—*adv.* quiv'eringly.—*adj.* quiv'-erish. [Perh. conn. quiver (1).]

qui vive, *kē vēv, n.* alert. [From the French sentry's challenge, lit. (long) live who?—*qui*, who, *vive*, 3rd pers. sing. pres. subj. of *vivre*, to live—L. *vīvĕre.*]

quixotic, *kwiks-ot'ik, adj.* like Don *Quixote*, the knight-errant in the great romance of Cervantes (1547-1616), extravagantly romantic in ideals or chivalrous in action: (of ideals, actions) absurdly generous and unselfish.—*adv.* quixot'-ically.—*ns.* quix'otism; quix'otry.

quiz, *kwiz, n.* an odd-looking person or (*Jane Austen*) thing: a monocle, often with a handle: a piece of banter or quiet mockery: a mocking look: a hoax: one who practises any of these: an oral examination (*U.S.*): a sportive catechism or general-knowledge test: a bandalore (*q.v.*; *obs.*):—*pl.* quizz'es.—*v.t.* poke fun at: to eye, often with an air of mockery: to catechise, interrogate.—*v.i.* to practise derisive joking:—*pr.p.* quizz'ing; *pa.t.* and *pa.p.* quizzed.—*ns.* quizz'er; quizz'ery.—*adj.* quizz'ical.—*adv.* quizz'ically.—*n.* quizzifica'tion; quizzing.—*v.t.* quizz'ify, to turn into a quiz.—*ns.* quizz'iness, oddness; quizz'ing.—quiz'-mas'ter, question-master; quizz'ing-glass, a monocle. [Origin obscure.]

quo', *kǝ, ko, v.t.* A Scots form of quoth.—quod, an obsolete form of quoth, used esp. at the end of a poem, followed by the poet's name.

quoad, *kwō'ad,* (L. *quō*, whither, *ad*, to) as far as: to this extent.—quoad hoc (*hōk, hok*), as far as this; quoad omnia (*om'ni-ǝ, -a*), in respect of all things; quoad sacra (*sā'krǝ, sa'kra*), as far as concerns sacred matters (of a parish disjoined for ecclesiastical purposes only).

quod, *kwod,* neut. of L. *qui*, which.—quod erat demonstrandum (*er'at dem-ǝn-stran'dǝm, er-at' dēm-ōn-stran'doŏm*), (abbrev. Q.E.D.) which was to be proved or demonstrated; quod erat faciendum (*fā-shē-en'dǝm, fa-ki-en'doŏm*), (ab-brev. Q.E.F.) which was to be done; quod (*pl.* quae, *kwē, kwī*) vide (*vi'dē, vi', wi'de*), which see.

quod, *kwod,* (*slang*) *n.* prison.—*v.t.* to imprison. [Origin unknown.]

quodlibet, *kwod'li-bet, n.* a scholastic argument: a humorous medley of tunes.—*n.* quodlibetā'-rian, one given to quodlibets.—*adjs.* quodlibet'ic, -al. [L., what you please—*quod*, what, *libet*, it pleases.]

quodlin, *kwod'lin,* an obsolete form of codlin.

quoif, *koif.* Same as coif.

quoin, *koin, n.* a wedge, esp. for locking type in a forme, or for raising a gun: a salient angle, esp. of a building: a corner-stone, esp. a dressed corner-stone: a keystone: a voussoir.—*v.t.* to

wedge: to secure, or raise by wedging. [See coin.]

quoist, *kwoist.* See queest.

quoit, *koit, kwoit, n.* a heavy flat ring for throwing as near as possible to a hob or pin: a dolmen cover: a dolmen: (in *pl.*, treated as *sing.*) the game played with quoits.—*v.i.* to play at quoits.—*v.t.* to throw like a quoit.—*n.* quoit'er. [Origin obscure.]

quo jure?, *kwō jōō'rē, yōō're,* (L.) by what right?

quondam, *kwon'dam, adj.* former. [L., formerly.]

Quonset hut, *kwon'set,* the U.S. equivalent of the Nissen hut. [Trademark.]

quooke, *kwoŏk* (*Spens.*), *pa.t.* of quake.

quop, *kwop,* (*obs.* or *dial.*) *v.i.* to throb. [M.E. *quappe*, quap.]

quorum, *kwō', kwö'rǝm, n.* orig. a number of specially named justices of the peace of whom some must be present before any business could be done: loosely, the whole body of justices: a minimum number of persons necessary for transaction of business in any body. [L. *quōrum*, of whom, from the wording of the commission, of whom we will that you, so-and-so, be one (two, etc.).]

quota, *kwō'tǝ, n.* a proportional share, a part assigned: a regulated quantity of goods allowed by a government to be manufactured, exported, imported, etc.:—*pl.* quo'tas.—quota immigrant, an immigrant to the U.S.A.) admitted as one of the yearly quota allowed to his country of origin, as opposed to a non-quota immigrant (as child, wife, or resident citizen). [L. *quota* (*pars*), the how-manieth (part)—*quotus*, of what number—*quot*, how many.]

quote, *kwōt,* old-fashioned *kōt* (*Shak.* čoat, coate, cote), *v.t.* orig. to divide into chapters, verses, etc., number the chapters of, or mark with refer-ences: to refer to: to cite: to adduce as author-ity, illustration, or example: to give the actual words of: to examine as if looking up a reference (*Shak.*): to record: to note, set down, mention, in writing or mentally: to set down in the prompter's book as due to be called (*theat.*): to give the current price of: to enclose within quotation-marks.—*v.i.* to make quotations: word used to indicate that what follows im-mediately is a quotation.—*n.* a quotation: a quotation-mark.—*adj.* quō'table, lending itself (or himself) to quotation: fit to quote.—*ns.* quō'tableness, quōtabil'ity.—*adv.* quō'tably.—*n.* quōtā'tion, act of quoting: that which is quoted: a price quoted: a quadrat for filling blanks in type (orig. those between marginal re-ferences).—*adjs.* quōtā'tious, quō'tative, given to quoting.—*n.* quō'ter.—*adj.* quōte'worthy.—quōtā'tion-mark, one of the marks (*print.* quotes) used to note the beginning and end of a quotation. [L.L. *quotāre*, to divide into chapters and verses —L. *quotus*, of what number—*quot*, how many.]

quoth, *kwōth, v.t.* (1st and 3rd pers. sing., past tense, of the otherwise obs. vb. queathe) said (followed by its subject).—*interj.* quōtha, for-sooth, indeed (lit. quoth he; see a, *pron.*). [O.E. *cwæth*, pret. of *cwethan*, to say; cf. bequeath.]

quotidian, *kwot-id'i-ǝn, adj.* daily: everyday, commonplace: of any activity of a living creature or a living part, that follows a regular recurrent pattern.—*n.* a fever or ague that recurs daily. [L. *quotidiānus—quotidiē*, daily—*quot*, how many, *diēs*, day.]

quotient, *kwō'shǝnt,* (*math.*) *n.* the number of times one quantity is contained in another: a ratio, usu. multiplied by 100, used in giving a numerical value to ability, etc. (see achievement, intelligence, quotient). [L. *quotiēns, quotiēs,* how often—*quot*, how many (with *t* from false appearance of being a participle).]

Neutral vowels in unaccented syllables: *el'ǝ-mǝnt*; for certain sounds in foreign words, see p. viii

**quotition,** *kwō-tish'ən, n.* division regarded as repeated subtraction or measuring. [From L. *quot.*]

**quotum,** *kwō'təm, n.* quota. [L. neut. of *quotus*; see **quota.**]

**quo warranto,** *kwō wo-ran'tō, n.* a writ calling upon one to show by what warrant he holds or claims a franchise or office. [L.L. *quō warrantō* (abl.), by what warrant.]

**Qurân,** *koō-rän', n.* Same as **Koran.**

# R

**R, r,** *är, n.* the eighteenth letter in our alphabet —the 'dog letter', from the trilling (evanescent in Southern England) of the tip of the tongue: as a mediaeval numeral, R = 80; R̄ = 80,000: r is the abbrev. for röntgen unit.—**R months,** the time when oysters are in season (from the spelling of the names of the months from September to April); **the three R's,** reading, writing, and arithmetic. [L. *er.*]

**Ra, rä,** *n.* the Egyptian sun-god.

**rabanna,** *rə-ban′ə, n.* a Madagascan raffia fabric. [Malagasy.]

**rabat, rabatte,** *rə-bat′, (geom.) v.t.* to rotate into coincidence with another plane.—*ns.* **rabatt′ing; rabat′ment, rabatte′ment.** [Fr. *rabattre,* to lower.]

**rabato,** *rə-bä′tō.* Same as **rebato.**—*n.* **rabatine** (*rab′ə-tēn; Scott*), a low collar.

**rabbet,** *rab′it, n.* a groove cut to receive an edge. —*v.t.* to groove: to join by a rabbet:—*pr.p.* **rabb′eting;** *pa.t.* and *pa.p.* **rabb′eted.**—**rabb′et-ing machine′, -plane, -saw; rabb′et-joint.** [Fr. *rabat—rabattre,* to beat back.]

**rabbi,** *rab′ī, (cap.* when prefixed), *rab′ī,* **rabbin,** *rab′in, n.* a Jewish expounder or doctor of the law: —*pl.* **rabb′is, rabb′ins.**—*n.* **rabb′inate,** the dignity or tenure of office of a rabbi: a body of rabbis. —*adjs.* **rabbin′ic, -al,** pertaining to the rabbis or to their opinions, learning, and language.—*n.* **Rabbin′ic,** late Hebrew.—*adv.* **rabbin′ically.**— *ns.* **rabb′inism,** the doctrine or teaching of the rabbis: a rabbinical peculiarity of expression: the late Jewish belief which esteemed the oral equally with the written law; **rabb′inist, rabb′in-ite,** one who adheres to the Talmud and traditions of the rabbis; **rabboni** (*rab-ō′ni, -ni*), my great master. [Heb. *rabbi,* my great one—*rabh,* great, master.]

**rabbit,** *rab′it, n.* the cony, a small burrowing animal of the hare family: its flesh (as food): its fur: a persistent but incurably inferior player at lawn-tennis or other game.—*v.i.* to hunt rabbits.—*ns.* **rabb′iter,** one who hunts rabbits; **rabb′itry,** a place where rabbits are kept: the play of a rabbit in games.—*adj.* **rabb′ity.**—**rabb′it-fish,** the king of the herrings (*Chimaera*) or other fish fancied to resemble a rabbit; **rabb′it-hole,** a rabbit's burrow; **rabb′it-hutch,** a box for housing rabbits; **rabb′it-punch,** a blow on the back of the neck; **rabb′it-squirrel,** a chincha; **rabb′it-sucker** (*Shak.*), a sucking rabbit; **rabb′it-warren.**—**Welsh rabbit,** melted cheese with or without ale, etc., poured over hot toast—sometimes written 'Welsh rarebit' by wiseacres. [M.E. *rabet*; poss. from O.N.Fr.]

**rabbit,** *rab′it, v.t.* confound (often in *od rabbit, d′rabbit,* or *drabbit,* for *God rabbit*). [Perh. a facetious substitution for **rat.**]

**rabble,** *rab′l, n.* a disorderly assemblage or crowd: a mob: the lowest class of people: a confused stream of words.—*adj.* of or like a rabble.—*v.t.* and *v.i.* to gabble.—*v.t.* to mob.—*ns.* **rabb′lement,** a rabble: tumult; **rabb′ling,** esp. (*Scot. hist.*) the mobbing and ousting of the Episcopal 'curates' at the Revolution.—**rabble rout** (*obs.*), the mob, rabble. [Cf. Du. *rabbelen,* to gabble, L.G. *rabbeln.*]

**rabble,** *rab′l, n.* a puddling-iron.—*v.t.* to stir with a rabble.—*n.* **rabb′ler.** [Fr. *râble*—L. *rutābulum,* a poker.]

**Rabelaisian,** *rab-ə-lā′zi-ən, n.* a follower, admirer,

or student of François *Rabelais* (d. 1553 or 1554). —*adj.* of or like Rabelais: extravagantly humorous: robustly outspoken: (loosely) coarsely indecent.—*n.* **Rabelais′ianism.**

**rabi,** *rub′ē, n.* the spring grain harvest in India. [Ar. *rabi′,* spring.]

**rabid,** *rab′id, adj.* raging: fanatical: affected with rabies.—*adj.* **rab′ic,** of rabies.—*adv.* **rab′idly.**—*ns.* **rabid′ity, rab′idness; rabies** (*ra′bēz, -bi-ēz,* or *ra′*), the disease called hydrophobia, caused by a virus transmitted by the bite of an infected animal. [L. *rabidus* (adj.), *rabiēs* (n.)— *rabĕre,* to rave.]

**raca,** *rä′ka, (B.) adj.* worthless. [Chaldee *rēkā* (a term of reproach).]

**rac(c)ahout,** *rak′ə-hōōt, n.* acorn meal. [Fr.,— Ar. *rāqaut.*]

**raccoon, racoon,** *rə-kōōn′, n.* an American animal (*Procyon lotor,* or other species) related to the bears: its fur.—**raccoon′-berry,** *Podophyllum*; **raccoon′-dog,** a raccoon-like wild dog (*Nycte-reutes*) of Eastern Asia. [From an Amer. Ind. name.]

**race,** *rās, n.* the descendants of a common ancestor: esp. those who inherit a common set of characteristics: such a set of descendants, narrower than a species: a breed: a stud or herd (*obs.*): ancestry, lineage, stock: the condition of belonging by descent to a particular group: inherited disposition: a class or group, defined otherwise than by descent: a sex (*obs.*): peculiar flavour, as of wine, by which its origin may be recognised: raciness, piquancy.—*adj.* **racial** (*rā′shl, -shyəl, -shi-əl*), of, relating to, race.—*ns.* **ra′cialism,** race hatred, rivalry, or feeling: belief in inherent superiority of some races over others, usu. with implication of a right to rule: discriminative treatment based on such belief; **ra′cialist; racia′tion,** formation locally of new distinct biological groups smaller than species.—*adv.* **racily** (*rās′i-li*).—*ns.* **ra′ciness,** quality of being racy; **rac′ism, racialism** (*q.v.*); **rac′ist.**—*adj.* **ra′cy,** having a distinctive flavour imparted by the soil, as wine: exciting to the mind by strongly characteristic thought or language: spirited: pungent: zestful: risqué. —**race′-ha′tred,** animosity accompanying difference of race; **race′-su′icide,** voluntary cessation of reproduction, leading to the extinction of the race. [Fr.,—It. *razza,* of doubtful origin.]

**race,** *rās, n.* a run or onward rush (*arch.* and *Scot.*): a fixed course, track, or path, over which anything runs: a channel bringing water to or from a wheel: a groove in which anything runs (as ball-bearings, a rope): a regular running over a fixed course, as of the sun: a rapid current: a competitive trial of speed in progression: (in *pl.*) a meeting for horse-racing: a competition in getting ahead of others figuratively: a running or racing place (*rare*).—*v.i.* to run swiftly: to contend in speed: to run wildly (as an engine, a propeller) when resistance is removed.—*v.t.* to cause to race: to rush: to contend in a race with.—*ns.* **ra′cer,** one who or that which races; **ra′cing.**—*adj.* **ra′cy.**—**race′-ball,** a ball in connection with a race-meeting; **race′-card,** a programme for a race-meeting; **race′course, -path, -track,** a course for running races over; **race′-cup,** a piece of plate forming a prize at a race; **race′goer,** an attender at race-meetings; **race′going; race′horse,** horse bred for racing; **race'-meet'ing** (see **meeting**); **race'-way**, a mill-race; **ra'cing-bit**, light jointed ring-bit. [O.N. *rās*; O.E. *ræs*.]

**race**, *rās*, (*Shak.*) *n.* a rootstock of ginger. [O.Fr *rais*—L. *rādīx, -icis*, a root.]

**race**, *rās*, also **ratch**, *rach, n.* a white streak down a beast's face. [Origin unknown.]

**race**, *rās, v.t.* to scratch: to raze (*Spens.*): to erase (*Spens.*): to slash (*Shak.*).—*n.* a cut, slit, scratch. [An otherwise obs. form of **raze** or **rase**.]

**race**, *rās,* (*Spens.*) *v.t.* to tear away or off, pluck, snatch.—Also **rase** (*Shak.*). [O.Fr. *arrachier*.]

**raceme**, *ra-, rə-, rā-sēm', ras'ēm, n.* an indefinite inflorescence in which stalked flowers are borne in acropetal succession on an unbranched main stalk: a similar group of sporangia.—*n.* **racema'tion** (*ras-i-mā'shən*), a gleaning or gathering of grapes: a residue: a cluster or bunch of grapes or of anything else.—*adjs.* **racemed'** (or *ras', rās'*), in or having racemes; **racemic** (*ra-sē'mik, -sem'ik*), applied to an acid obtained from a certain kind of grape, an optically inactive form of tartaric acid: hence applied to similar compounds of dextrorotatory and laevorotatory enantiomorphs.—*n.* **racemisa'tion, -z-,** a changing into a racemic form.—*v.t.* and *v.i.* **rac'emise, -ize.**—*n.* **rac'emism**, the quality of being racemic.—*adj.* **racemose** (*ras'i-mōs*), of the nature of or like a raceme: of, in, or having racemes: like a bunch of grapes. [L. *racēmus*, a bunch of grapes.]

**rache**, also **rach, ratch,** *rach, n.* a dog that hunts by scent. [O.E *racc*, setter; O.N. *rakki*.]

**rachis**, sometimes **rhachis**, *rā'kis, n.* the spine: an axis, as of a feather, an inflorescence, a pinnate leaf.—*adjs.* **ra'chial**; less correctly **rachidial** (*rə-kid'*), **rachid'ian.**—*n.* **rachilla** (*rə-kil'ə*), the axis of a grass spikelet. [Gr. *rhachis, -ios,* or *-eōs,* spine.]

**rachitis**, *ra-, rə-ki'tis, n.* rickets.—*adj.* **rachitic** (*-kit'ik*). [Gr. *rhachitis*, inflammation of the spine: adopted by Dr Gleeson in 1650 in the belief that it was the etymon of **rickets**.]

**Rachmanism**, *rak'man-izm, n.* conduct of a landlord who charges extortionate rents for property in which very bad slum conditions prevail. [From the name of one such landlord exposed in 1963.]

**racial**, etc., **raciness, racism,** etc. See **race** (1).

**rack**, *rak, n.* an instrument for stretching, esp. an instrument of torture: hence an extreme pain, anxiety, or doubt (*fig.*): stress, esp. of weather: a framework, grating, shelf, or the like, on or in which articles are disposed or set aside: a grating from which beasts may pull down fodder: a bar or framework as for chaining a prisoner (*Spens.*): a bar with teeth to work into those of a wheel, pinion, or endless screw.—*v.t.* to stretch forcibly or excessively: to strain: to wrest, overstrain, distort: to torture: to practise rapacity upon: to extort (*Spens.*): to put in a rack: to move or adjust by rack and pinion.—*n.* **rack'er.**—*n.* and *adj.* **rack'ing.**—**rack'-rail**, a cogged rail; **rack'-rail'-way**, a mountain railway with a rack in which a cog-wheel on the locomotive works; **rack'-rent**, a rent stretched to the utmost annual value of the things rented, exorbitant rent.— *v.t.* to subject to such rents.—**rack'-rent'er**, one who exacts or pays rack-rent; **rack'work**, mechanism with a rack.—**(live at) rack and manger**, (to live in) wasteful abundance: waste and destruction (perh. from confusion with *rack and ruin*); **rack and pinion**, a means of turning rotatory into linear or linear into rotatory motion by a toothed wheel engaging in a rack; **rack one's brains**, strain one's memory, ingenuity, etc. [Prob. M.Du. *recke* (Du. *rek, rak*) or L.G. *reck, recke, rack*; cf. O.N. *rakkr,*

straight, Ger. *rack*, rail, *recken*, to stretch; Eng. **reach**.]

**rack**, *rak, n.* same as **wrack**, destruction: a crash (*Milt.*).—**rack and ruin**, a state of neglect and collapse. [**wrack** (1), or O.N. *rek*, wreckage.]

**rack**, *rak, n.* flying cloud (*Shak.*): driving mist: a track: a shallow ford (*Scot.*).—*v.i.* (*Shak.*) to drift, to drive. [App. O.N. *rek*, drifting wreckage, or some kindred form; cf. **wrack, wreck, wreak**; O.E. *wrecan*, to drive.]

**rack**, *rak, v.t.* to draw off from the lees. [Prov. *arracar*—*raca*, husks, dregs.]

**rack**, *rak, n.* the neck and spine of a forequarter of a carcass (*dial.*): a vertebra (*obs.*): a horse's bones.—*n.* **rack'abones** (*U.S.*), a very thin horse, man, etc. [Perh. O.E. *hracca*, occiput.]

**rack**, *rak,* (now *U.S.*) *n.* a horse's gait at which the legs at the same side move nearly together. —*v.i.* to go in that gait.—*n.* **rack'er.** [Origin obscure.]

**rack**, *rak, n.* aphetic for **arrack**.—**rack'-punch.**

**rack**, *rak, n.* a young rabbit's skin. [Origin unknown.]

**racket**, *rak'it, n.* a bat with usu. roughly elliptical head, of wood or metal strung with catgut or nylon, for playing tennis, badminton, etc.: a snowshoe of like design: (in *pl.*) a simplified derivative of the old game of tennis, played against an end-wall.—*v.t.* to strike with a racket. —**rack'et-court, -ground**; **rack'et-press**, a press for keeping a racket in shape; **rack'et-tail**, a humming-bird with two long racket-shaped feathers.—*adj.* **rack'et-tailed.** [Fr. *raquette*, poss.—Ar. *rāhat*, coll. form of *rāha*, the palm of the hand.]

**racket**, *rak'it, n.* din: clamour: hubbub: hurly-burly: fuss: noisy or hustling gaiety: dissipation: a noisy merry-making: a dodge: fraudulent, violent, or otherwise unscrupulous money-making activities: strain of excitement: responsibility: liability for expenses.—*v.i.* to make or engage in racket.—*v.t.* to disturb, stir, affect by racket:—*pr.p.* **rack'eting**; *pa.t.* and *pa.p.* **rack'-eted.**—*n.* **racketeer'**, one who extorts money or other advantage by threats or illegal interference. —*v.i.* to act as a racketeer.—*ns.* **racketeer'ing**; **rack'eter**, a noisy or gay person; **rack'etry.**— *adj.* **rack'ety**, noisy: energetically gay.—**stand the racket**, endure the strain: take the consequences or responsibility: pay expenses. [Prob. imit.]

**racket(t)**, *rak'it, n.* an old instrument like the bassoon. [Origin uncertain.]

**racloir**, *rä-klwär, n.* a scraper. [Fr.]

**raconteur**, *ra-kon-tûr', rä-kɔ̃-tœr, n.* a teller of anecdotes:—*fem.* **raconteuse** (*-tœz*). [Fr.]

**racoon**. See **raccoon.**

**Racovian**, *rə-kō'vi-ən, n.* a 17th-century Polish Socinian—their seminary being at *Raków*.—Also *adj.*

**racquet.** Same as **racket** (1).

**racy.** See **race** (1) and (2).

**rad**, *rad* (*Spens.*), *pa.t.* and *pa.p.* of **read**, and *pa.t.* of **ride**.

**rad**, *rad,* (*Scot.*) *adj.* afraid. [O.N. *hræddr.*]

**rad**, *rad, n.* short for **radical** (in politics).

**rad**, *rad, n.* a unit of dosage of any radiation, equal to 100 ergs of energy for one gram of mass of the material irradiated. [**rad**(iation).]

**radar**, *rā'där, n.* the use of high-powered radio pulses, reflected or regenerated, for locating objects or determining one's own position.— **radar altimeter**, a high altitude radio altimeter. [American codeword, from *radio detection and ranging*, appropriately a palindrome word.]

**raddle**, *rad'l, n.* a flexible rod or strip of wood used to make hurdles, fences, or (with plaster) walls, by weaving between uprights: a hurdle, door, fence, or the like so made: a hedge formed by interweaving the branches of trees:

a wooden bar used in weaving.—*v.t.* to interweave: to thrash (*Northern*). [A.Fr. *reidele*, rail.]

**raddle**, *rad'l*, *n.* reddle or ruddle (red ochre). —*v.t.* to colour or mark with red ochre: to rouge coarsely.—*adj.* **radd'led**.—**radd'leman**. [See **ruddle**.]

**raddocke**, *rad'ək* (*Shak.*). Same as **ruddock**.

**rade**, *rād*. Northern form of **rode**. [See **ride**.]

**radial**, *rā'di-əl*, *adj.* pertaining to a ray or radius: along, in the direction of, a radius or radii: having rays, spokes, or parts diverging from a centre: arranged like spokes or radii: near the radius of the arm.—*n.* a radiating part: a radial artery, nerve, engine, plate, etc.—*ns.* **radiale** (*-ā'li*; L. *ra-di-ā'le*), a wrist-bone in line with the radius:—*pl.* **radia'lia**; **radialisation** (*-z-*; *răd-yəl-i-zā'shən*).—*v.t.* **ra'dialise**, **-ize**, to arrange radially.—*n.* **rādiality** (*-al'*), radial symmetry.—*adv.* **rā'dially**, in the manner of radii or of rays.—**radial artery**, the smaller branch of the brachial artery at the elbow; **radial engine**, one with its cylinders radially arranged; **radial symmetry**, symmetry about several planes intersecting in a common axis; **radial velocity**, the component of velocity along the observer's line of sight.—**radial-ply tyre**, tyre in which layers or plies of fabric in the carcass are wrapped in a direction radial to the centre of the wheel. [L.L. *radiālis*—L. *radius*.]

**radian**, *rā'di-ən*, *n.* a unit of circular measure, the angle subtended at the centre of a circle by an arc equal to the radius, nearly 57·3°. [L. *radius*.]

**radiant**, *rā'di-ənt*, *rā'dyənt*, *adj.* emitting rays: issuing in rays: glowing: shining: beaming with happy emotion.—*n.* that which emits radiations: a point from which rays emanate: the centre from which meteoric showers seem to proceed: a straight line from a point about which it is conceived to revolve (*geom.*).—*ns.* **rā'diance**, **rā'diancy**.—*adv.* **rā'diantly**. [L. *radiāns*, *-antis*, pr.p. of *radiāre*, to radiate— *radius*.]

**radiate**, *rā'di-āt*, *v.i.* to emit rays: to shine: to issue in rays: to diverge from a point or points: to transmit wirelessly.—*v.t.* to send out in or by means of rays: to communicate by wireless: to broadcast.—*adj.* (*-it*, *-ət*, *-āt*) having rays: having ray-florets: spreading like a ray or rays: radial: radially arranged: of the Radiata.—*n.* an animal of the Radiata.—*n.pl.* **Rādiā'ta**, in Cuvier's obsolete classification, the lowest subkingdom of animals, radially symmetrical— echinoderms, coelenterates, polyzoans, etc.— *adj.* **rā'diated**.—*adv.* **rā'diately**.—*n.* **rādiā'tion**, act of radiating: the emission and diffusion of rays: that which is radiated: energy transmitted in electromagnetic waves: radial arrangement.—*adj.* **rā'diātive**.—*n.* **rā'diātor**, that which radiates: apparatus for radiating heat, as for warming a room, or cooling an engine: a wireless transmitting aerial.—**radiation sickness**, an illness due to excessive absorption of radiation in the body, marked by internal bleeding, decrease in blood cells, loss of teeth and hair, reduction of sperm in the male, etc. [L. *radiāre*, to shine, *radiātus*, rayed—*radius*.]

**radical**, *rad'i-kl*, *adj.* pertaining to, constituting, proceeding from, or going to the root: fundamental: original: intrinsic: inherent: thorough: primary: primitive: implanted by nature: not derived: proceeding from near the root (*bot.*): favouring thorough-going but constitutional social and political reform, advanced Liberal (*politics*; usu. with *cap.*).—*n.* a root, in any sense: a group of atoms behaving like a single atom and passing unchanged from one compound to another—now usually confined to electrically neutral entities as distinguished from

charged ions (*chem.*; sometimes **rad'icle**): (*cap.*) an advocate of radical reform or member of the Radical party.—*v.t.* and *v.i.* **rad'icalise**, **-ize**, to make or become radical.—*ns.* **Rad'icalism**, the principles or spirit of a Radical; **radicality** (*-kal'i-ti*).—*adv.* **rad'ically**.—*n.* **rad'icalness**.— *adjs.* **rad'icant**, rooting from the stem; **rad'icāte**, rooted: deeply rooted: firmly established: fixed.—*v.t.* to root: to plant or fix deeply and firmly.—*adj.* **rad'icāted**, rooted, established.— *ns.* **radicā'tion**, rooting: implanting: rootedness: general character of the root-system; **rad'icel** (*-sel*), a rootlet.—*adjs.* **rad'icellose**; **radicicolous** (*-sik'ə-ləs*), inhabiting, or parasitic on, roots; **radiciform** (*rə-dis'*), like a root; **radiciv'orous**, root-eating.—*n.* **rad'icle**, a little root: the part of a seed that becomes the root: a rhizoid: a radical (*chem.*).—*adj.* **radic'ūlar**, pertaining to a radicle, a rootlet, or the root of a tooth, nerve, etc.—*n.* **rad'icūle**.—*adj.* **radic'ulose**, having many rootlets or rhizoids.—**radical axis**, the locus of a point of equal potency with respect to two circles. [L. *rādix*, *-īcis*, a root.]

**radio-**, *rā-di-ō-*, in composition (most terms can be spelt as one word, a hyphenated word, or two words), rays, radiation, radium, radius: radio, wireless: (of product or isotope) radioactive, as **rādio-actin'ium**, **rādio-tho'rium**, both isotopes of thorium, **rādio-el'ement** (*chem.*).—*n.* **rā'dio**, wireless communication: a wireless receiving or transmitting set: a wireless message or broadcast.—*adj.* of, for, transmitted or transmitting by, wireless.—*v.t.* and *v.i.* to communicate by wireless.—*adj.* **rādioact'ive**.—*ns.* **rādioactiv'ity**, spontaneous disintegration, first observed in certain naturally occurring heavy elements (radium, actinium, uranium, thorium) with emission of α-rays, β-rays, and γ-rays: disintegration effected by high-energy bombardment; **radio altimeter** (see **altimeter**); **radio amateur**, a person licensed to send and receive wireless messages privately on certain shortwave bands.—Also **radio ham** (*slang*); **radioastronomy**, astronomical study by means of radar: study of radio waves generated in space; **rādioaut'ograph**, deprecated term for **autoradiograph**; **radio-beacon**, apparatus that transmits signals for direction-finding; **radiobiol'ogy**, the study of the effects of radiation on living tissue; **radiocar'bon**, a radioactive isotope of carbon, *specif.* carbon-14; **rādiochem'istry**, the chemistry of radioactivity; **radio-communication**, wireless telegraphy or telephony; **radio-compass**, a wireless direction-finding instrument; **rādioel'ement**, a radio-isotope; **radio frequency**, a frequency suitable for radio transmission.—*adj.* **rādiogenic** (*-jen'ik*), produced by radioactive disintegration: suitable for broadcasting.—*ns.* **rādiogoniom'eter**, a wireless direction-finder; **rā'diogram**, an X-ray photograph: a wireless telegram: (for **rādio-gram'ophone**) a combined wireless receiver and gramophone; **rā'diograph** (*-gräf*), an instrument for recording radiation: an X-ray, etc., photograph: (formerly) the wireless telegraph.—*adj.* **rādiographic** (*-graf'ik*).—*ns.* **radiography** (*og'rə-fi*), photography of interior of body or specimen by radiations other than light, as X-rays, etc.: (formerly) radiotelegraphy: study of radioactivity; **radio-isotope**, a radioactive isotope of a stable element; **radiolocā'tion**, position-finding by radio signals: radar. —*adj.* **rādiolog'ical**.—*ns.* **rādiol'ogist**; **rādiol'ogy**, the study of radioactivity and radiation or their application to medicine; **rādiom'eter**, an instrument that measures radiant energy by the rotation of a vane with bright and black sides.— *adj.* **rādiomet'ric**.—*n.* **rā'diophōne**, an instrument for producing sound by radiant energy: a wireless telephone.—*adj.* **rādiophonic** (*-fon'ik*). —*ns.* **rādiophon'ics**, **rādiophony** (*-of'ə-ni*); **radio**

pill, a capsule which may be swallowed containing a tiny radio transmitter that will send out information about bodily processes; **radios'-copy**, examination by X-rays, etc.—*v.t.* **radiosen'sitise, -ize**, to make (e.g. cancer cells) more radiosensitive.—*adj.* **radiosen'sitive**, quickly injured or changed by radiation.—*ns.* **radio sonde** (Fr. *sonde*, plummet, probe), apparatus for ascertaining atmospheric conditions at great heights, consisting of a hydrogen-filled balloon, radio transmitter(s), etc.; **radio star**, a discrete source of radio waves in outer space, generally corresponding with no visual object and known only by radio-astronomy; **radio-strontium**, a radioactive isotope of strontium, esp. strontium-90; **rā'diotel'egram, rā'diotel'egraph, -teleg'-raphy, rā'diotel'ephone, -teleph'ony**, wireless telegraph, telephone, etc.; **radio telescope**, an apparatus for the reception in radio-astronomy of radio waves from outer space; **rādiothera-peut'ics, -ther'apy**, treatment of disease by radiation, as by X-rays, etc.; **radio wave**, an electromagnetic wave of radio frequency. [L. *rădius*, a rod, spoke, radius, ray.]

**Radiolaria**, *rā-di-ō-lā'ri-a*, *n.pl.* an order of marine Protozoa with fine radial pseudopodia. —*adj.* **radiola'rian**.—Also *n.*—**radiolarian ooze**, a deep-sea deposit in which the siliceous skeletons of Radiolaria predominate. [L.L. *radiolus*, dim. of L. *rădius*, radius.]

**radish**, *rad'ish*, *n.* a cruciferous plant, *Raphanus sativus* or other member of the genus: its pungent root, eaten as a salad. [Fr. *radis*—Prov. *raditz* or It. *radice*—L. *rādix, -icis*, a root.]

**radium**, *rā'di-əm*, *n.* a radioactive metallic element (Ra; at. numb. 88) discovered by the Curies in 1898, found in pitchblende and other minerals, remarkable for its active spontaneous disintegration.—**radium A, B**, etc., successive products in the disintegration of radon; **radium bomb**, an apparatus containing radium, emitting gamma rays for medical treatment (better **tele-radium unit**); **radium emanation, radon**. [L. *rădius*, a ray.]

**radius**, *rā'di-əs*, *n.* a straight line from the centre to the circumference of a circle or surface of a sphere (*geom.*): a radiating line: anything placed like a radius, as the spoke of a wheel, the movable arm of a sextant: a radial plane of symmetry in a coelenterate: a line from a fixed point (e.g. the focus of a conic) to a point on a curve: the outer bone (in supine position) of the forearm in man, or its homologue in other animals: a barbule of a feather: the third vein of an insect's wing: a ray-flower or the ray-flowers of a head collectively (*rare*): a distance from a centre, conceived as limiting an area or range:—*pl.* **radii** (*rā'di-ī*; L. *ra'di-ē*).—*adj.* **ra'dial** (q.v.).—**radius vector** (*pl.* **radii vectō'res**), a straight line joining a fixed point and a variable point. [L. *rădius*, a rod, spoke, ray.]

**radix**, *rā'diks, rä'dēks, n.* a root, root-number, root-word (*obs.*): a source: a basis: the quantity on which a system of numeration, or of logarithms, etc., is based:—*pl.* **radices** (*rā'di-sez, rä-dē'käs*). [L. *rādix, -icis*, root.]

**radome**, *rā'dōm*, *n.* a protective covering for micro-wave antennae. [*radar dome*.]

**radon**, *rā'don*, *n.* a gaseous radioactive element (Rn; at. numb. 86), the first disintegration product of radium—radium emanation, formerly called niton. [**radium**, and **-on**, as in *argon*, *xenon*, etc.]

**radula**, *rad'ū-lə*, *n.* a mollusc's tongue or rasping ribbon.—*adjs.* **rad'ular; rad'ūlate; rad'ūliform**, rasp-like. [L. *rādula*, a scraper—*rādēre*.]

**Raetian**. See Rhaetian.

**Raf**, *raf*, (*coll.*) *n.* the R.A.F. (Royal Air Force).

**rafale**, *rä-fäl'*, *n.* a burst of artillery in quick rounds. [Fr., gust of wind.]

**raff**, *raf*, *n.* riff-raff: one of the riff-raff: a rakish, flashy, or blackguardly fellow.—*adj.* **raffish**.—*adj.* **raff'ish**, rakish: flashy.—*adv.* **raff'ishly**.—*n.* **raff'ishness**. [Cf. **riff-raff**.]

**raffia**, *raf'i-ə*, *n.* the Raphia palm or its leaf-bast. [**Raphia**.]

**raffinose**, *raf'i-nōs*, *n.* a trisaccharide sugar.—*n.* **raff'inate**, liquid left after a desired solute has been extracted. [Fr. *raffiner*, to refine.]

**raffle**, *raf'l*, *n.* an old dicing game, the stakes going to the thrower of a pair-royal: a lottery for an article.—*v.t.* to dispose of by raffle.—*v.i.* to engage in a raffle.—*n.* **raff'ler**. [Fr. *rafle*, a pair-royal.]

**raffle**, *raf'l*, *n.* a rabble: riff-raff: lumber: rubbish: a jumble: a tangle. [Cf. **raff**.]

**raffle**, *raf'l*, *v.t.* to notch: to crumple. [Ety. dub.]

**Rafflesia**, *raf-lē'zi-a*, *n.* a genus (giving name to the family **Rafflesia'ceae**, akin to the birthwort family) of parasitic plants in Sumatra, Java, etc., one species having the largest known flowers, a yard across, carrion-scented, the rest of the plant reduced to threads within the tissues of its host-plant. [Named after Sir T. Stamford *Raffles* (1781-1826), British governor in Sumatra (1818), who sent it to Brown, the botanist.]

**raft**, *räft*, (*U.S.*) *n.* a crowd: a miscellaneous lot. [**raff**.]

**raft**, *räft*, *n.* a flat floating mass of logs or other material (ice, vegetation, etc.): a flat structure of logs, etc., for support or for conveyance on water: a dense mass of floating water-fowl (*U.S.*): a wide layer of concrete to support a building on soft ground.—*v.t.* to transport on a raft: to form into a raft: to transverse by raft.—*v.i.* to manage a raft: to travel by raft: to form into a raft: to pile up by overriding, as ice.—*n.* **raft'er**, a raftsman.—**raft'-bridge**, a raft used as a bridge: a bridge supported on rafts; **raft'man**, a raftsman; **raft'-port**, in ships, a large port for timber; **raft'-rope**, a rope for towing blubber; **rafts'man**, one who works on a raft. [O.N. *raptr*, rafter.]

**raft**, *räft*, obs. *pa.t.* and *pa.p.* of **reave**: in Keats *pa.p.* of **rive**.

**rafter**, *räf'tər*, *n.* an inclined beam supporting a roof.—*v.t.* to furnish with rafters: to plough so that a strip is overturned upon unploughed ground.—*adj.* **raft'ered**, having (esp. visible) rafters.—*n.* **raft'ering**.—**raft'er-bird**, the spotted flycatcher. [O.E. *ræfter*, a beam.]

**rag**, *rag*, *n.* a worn, torn, or waste scrap of cloth: a tatter: a shred, scrap, or smallest portion: a farthing (*old slang*): a jagged projection: contemptuously or playfully, a flag, sail, theatre curtain, garment, newspaper, or paper money: the pithy part of an orange, lemon, etc.: a worthless or beggarly person: a person in a state of exhaustion: (in *pl.*) tattered clothing: ragtime, or a piece of ragtime music.—*adj.* of, for, or dealing in rags.—*v.t.* to tear to rags: to make ragged: to perform in ragtime.—*v.i.* to become ragged, to fray: to dress (with *out* or *up*; *U.S.* arch. slang).—*adj.* **ragg'ed**, shaggy: rough-edged: jagged: uneven in execution: raguly (*her.*): torn or worn into rags: wearing ragged clothes.—*adv.* **ragg'edly**.—*n.* **ragg'edness**. —*adj.* **ragg'edy**, ragged-looking.—*n.* **ragg'ery**, rags or the ragged collectively: clothes, esp. women's (*slang*): raggedness.—*adj.* **ragg'y**, rough: ragged: of the nature of a rag.—**rag-and-bone'-man**, one who collects or traffics in rags, bones, or other rubbish; **rag-ba'by**, a rag-doll; **rag'-bag**, a bag for rags and abandoned garments: a slattern; **rag'bolt**, a bolt with barbs to prevent withdrawal; **rag'-book**, a child's book mounted on cloth; **rag'-bush**, a bush to which shreds of cloth are tied as offerings to the local spirit, esp. by a well; **rag'-doll'**, a doll made of rags: a slattern; **rag'-dust**, finely divided rags, used for making flock-paper; **rag'-fair'**, an old-clothes market: a kit inspection (*mil. slang*); **ragg'ed-la'dy**, *Nigella damascena*; **ragg'ed-Rob'in**, a campion (*Lychnis flos-cuculi*) with deep-cleft petals; **ragged school**, a voluntary school for destitute children (*hist.*); **ragged staff** (*her.*), a stick with branch stubs; **rag'man**, a man who collects or deals in rags: the devil; **rag'-mon'ey** (*slang*), paper money; **rag'-paper**, paper made from rags; **rag'-picker**, one who collects rags from bins, heaps, etc.; **rag'-tag**, the rabble (also **ragg'le-tagg'le**); **rag'time**, a form of music of American Negro origin, highly syncopated in the melody: tune, song, or dance in ragtime; **rag'timer**; **rag trade**, the trade concerned with designing, making and selling clothes; **rag'weed**, ragwort: any species of the composite genus *Ambrosia* (*U.S.*); **rag'wheel**, a toothed wheel: a polishing-wheel made of cloth disks clamped together; **rag'-woman**; **rag'-wool**, shoddy; **rag'worm**, a pearly white burrowing marine worm (*Nephthys caeca*), used as bait by fisherman; **rag'wort**, a common coarse yellow-headed composite weed (*Senecio jacobaea*) of pastures: any similar species of the genus with long rays (from the cut leaves).—**rag-tag and bobtail**, riff-raff. [O.E. *ragg*, inferred from the adj. *raggig*, shaggy; O.N. *rögg*, shagginess, tuft.]

**rag**, ragg, *rag*, *n.* a rough hard stone of various kinds, esp. one breaking in slabs: a large rough slate (3 ft. by 2).—**rag'stone**; **rag'work**, undressed masonry in slabs. [Poss. from foregoing.]

**rag**, *rag*, *v.t.* to rate: to banter: to assail or beset with questions, chaff, horseplay.—*v.i.* to wrangle: to indulge in a rag:—*pa.t.* and *pa.p.* **ragged**, *ragd.*—*n.* an outburst of organised horseplay, usually in defiance of authority: riotous festivity, esp. and orig. of undergraduates—now, in British universities, associated with the raising of money for charity.—*n.* **ragg'ing.**—*adj.* **ragg'y** (*slang*), irritated.—**lose one's rag** (*coll.*), to lose one's temper. [Perh. shortened from **bullyrag**; perh. from **rag** (1), as in **red rag**.]

**raga**, *rä'ga*, *n.* a traditional Hindu musical form or mode. [Sans. *rāga*, colour, tone (in music).]

**ragamuffin**, *rag'ə-muf-in*, *-muf'*, *n.* a ragged, disreputable boy or man: (*cap.*; *obs.*) the name of a devil. [Poss. **rag** (1).]

**rag'd**, ragde, *ragd*, (*Shak.*) for **ragged**, shaggy, jagged: perh. unruly: poss. also (*rājd*) for **raged**, irritated (as if *pa.p.* of *v.t.*).

**rage**, *rāj*, *n.* madness: overmastering passion of any kind, as desire or (esp.) anger: inspired frenzy: ardour: a fit of any of these: a mania or craze (for something): vogue: a thing in vogue: violence, stormy or furious activity: a flood (*Shak.*).—*v.i.* to behave or speak with passion, esp. with furious anger: to be violent: to storm: to be prevalent and violent: to scold (with *at* or *on*; *Scot.*): to be violently bent on (*Milt.*).—*v.t.* (see **rag'd**).—*adj.* **rage'ful.**—*n.* **rä'ger.**—*adj.* **rä'ging.**—*adv.* **rä'gingly.**—**all the rage**, quite the fashion. [Fr.,—L. *rabiēs*—*rabĕre*, to rave.]

**ragg**, ragged, raggee. See **rag** (2), **rag** (1), **ragi**.

**raggle**, *rag'l*, (*Scot.*) *n.* a groove in masonry, esp. to receive the edge of a roof.—*v.t.* to make a raggle in. [Origin obscure.]

**ragi**, raggee, raggy, *rä'gē*, *rag'i*, *n.* a millet (*Eleusine coracana*) much grown in India, Africa, etc. [Hind. (and Sans.) *rāgī*.]

**raglan**, *rag'lən*, *n.* an overcoat with sleeve in one piece with the shoulder.—*adj.* of a sleeve, in one piece with the shoulder. [From Lord Raglan (1788-1855), commander in the Crimea.]

**ragman**, *rag'mən*, ragment, *rag'mənt*, *n.* a cata-logue (*obs.*): a document with pendent seals (*obs.*): a rigmarole (*obs. Scot.*).—**Ragman Rolls**, a collection of instruments by which the Scottish nobles, etc., subscribed allegiance to Edward I. [Origin obscure.]

**ragman.** See **rag** (1).

**ragmatical**, *rag-mat'i-kl*, (*Fielding*, *Smollett*) *adj.* app. riotous, disorderly. [Perh. from **rag** (1) after **pragmatical**.]

**Ragnarök**, *rag'na-rək*, (*Scand. myth.*) *n.* the coming mutual destruction of the gods and the powers of evil, and the end of this world, to be superseded by a better. [O.N. *ragna rök*, history or judgment of the gods (—*rögn*, *régin*, gods—*rök*, reason, judgment), sophisticated into *ragna rökr*, twilight of the gods (—*rökr*, darkness).]

**ragout**, *ra-gōō'*, *n.* a highly seasoned stew of meat and vegetables.—*v.t.* to make ragout of. [Fr. *ragoût*—*ragoûter*, to restore the appetite.]

**ragstone.** See **rag** (2).

**ragtime**, ragweed, ragwort. See **rag** (1).

**raguly**, *rag'ū-li*, (*her.*) *adj.* with projections like oblique stubs of branches.—Also **rag'ūled.** [Origin obscure.]

**rah**, 'rah, *rä*, *rö*, *interj.*, *n.*, *v.i.*, abbrev. for **hurrah.**

**Rahu**, *rä'hōō*, (*Hindu myth.*) *n.* the demon that swallows the sun and moon at eclipses.

**raid**, *rād*, *n.* a sudden swift inroad, orig. by horsemen, for assault or seizure: an air attack: an invasion unauthorised by government: an incursion of police: an onset or onslaught for the purpose of obtaining or suppressing something.—*v.t.* to make a raid on.—*v.i.* to go on a raid.—*n.* **raid'er**, one who raids: a raiding aeroplane.—**raid the market**, to derange prices artificially for future gain. [Scots form of **road** (revived by Scott)—O.E. *rād*, riding.]

**raik**, *rāk*, *n.* course, journey: range: pasture.—*v.i.* to go: to range. [O.N. *reik* (n.), *reika* (vb.) walk; coalescing later with **rake** (4).]

**rail**, *rāl*, *n.* a bar extending horizontally or at a slope between supports or on the ground, often to form a support, a fence, a guard, a track for wheels: the railway as a means of travel or transport: a horizontal member in framing or panelling (as in a door): the capping part of bulwarks: (in *pl.*) a racecourse barrier: (in *pl.*) railway shares.—*v.t.* to enclose or separate with rails: to furnish with rails: to send by railway.—*v.i.* to travel by railway.—*n.* **rail'ing**, fencing: fencing materials: (often in *pl.*) a barrier or ornamental structure, usu. of upright iron rods secured by horizontal connections.—*adj.* **rail'-less.**—**rail'bus**, a light-weight railway coach powered by a bus-type diesel engine.—*adj.* **rail'-borne**, carried by railway.—**rail'-car** (*U.S.*), a railway carriage: a self-propelled railway carriage; **rail'-fence** (*U.S.*), a fence of wooden posts and rails; **rail'head**, the furthest point reached by a railway under construction: the end of railway transport; **rail'man**, a railway employee; **rail'-mo'tor**, a self-propelled railway carriage; **rail'road** (chiefly *U.S.* and *Canada*), a railway.—*v.t.* to push forward unduly (*U.S.*): to get rid of, esp. by sending to prison on a false charge.—**railroad car** (*U.S.*), a railway carriage or a railway van or truck.—**rail'roader** (*U.S.*), a railway worker or official; **rail'-splitter** (*U.S.*), one who splits logs for fence-rails; **rail'way**, a track laid with rails for wheels to run on, esp. for locomotives with passengers and goods wagons: a system of such tracks with equipment and organisation.—Also **rail'-way-carr'iage**, a railway vehicle for passengers; **rail'way-cross'ing**, an intersection of railway lines or of road and railway, esp. without a bridge; **rail'way-stitch**, a name for various quickly worked stitches. [O.Fr. *reille*—L. *rēgula*, a ruler.]

**rail**, *rāl*, *v.i.* to scoff: to use vigorously or mockingly reproachful language: to banter: to revile.—*v.t.* to bring or render by raillery.—*n.* (*Spens.* rayle) reviling.—*n.* rail′er.—*adj.* and *n.* rail′ing.—*adv.* rail′ingly.—*n.* raillery (*räl′ər-i;* old-fashioned (*ral′*), railing or mockery: banter: playful satire. [Fr. *railler.*]

rail, *räl, n.* any bird of the genus *Rallus,* esp. the water-rail, or other member of the family Rallidae, esp. the corncrake or land-rail. [O.Fr. *rasle* (Fr. *râle*).]

rail (*Spens.* rayle, raile), *räl,* (*arch.*) *v.i.* to flow, gush. [Origin obscure.]

rail, *räl,* (*obs.* except in night-rail) *n.* a garment: a cloak: a neckerchief.—*n.* raill′y (*Scott*), a jacket. [O.E. *hrægl.*]

raiment, *rä′mənt, n.* clothing. [arrayment.]

rain, *rān, n.* water from the clouds in drops: a shower: a fall of anything in the manner of rain: (in *pl.*) the rainy season.—*v.i.* to fall as or like rain: to send down rain.—*v.t.* to shower. —*n.* rain′iness.—*adjs.* rain′less; rain′y.—rain′-band, a dark band in the solar spectrum, due to water vapour in the earth's atmosphere; rain′-bird, a bird, as the green woodpecker and various kinds of cuckoo, supposed to foretell rain.—*adj.* rain′-bound, detained by rain.—rain′-bow, the coloured bow caused by refraction and internal reflexion of light in raindrops: any similar array of colours: a much discoloured bruise (*slang*): a rainbow-trout: a S. American humming-bird, the cock with rainbow-coloured head.—*adj.* of, or coloured like, the rainbow.—rain′bow-chaser, a visionary, one who tries to reach the end of the rainbow.—*adj.* rain′bow-coloured.—rainbow dressing, a gaudy display of flags on a ship.—*adjs.* rain′bowed, rain′bow-tint′ed.—rain′bow-trout, a finely marked and coloured Californian trout (*Salmo irideus*).—*adj.* rain′bowy.—rain′-chamber, a compartment for condensing noxious fumes by spray; rain′-check (*U.S.*), a ticket for future use given to spectators when a game or a sports meeting is cancelled or stopped because of bad weather: a request or promise to accept an invitation at a later date; rain′-cloud, nimbus, a dense dark sheet of cloud that may shed rain or snow; rain′coat, a light overcoat proof against moderate rain; rain′-doctor, a rain-maker; rain′drop, a drop of rain; rain′fall, a shower of rain: the amount (by depth of water) of rain that falls; rain′-forest, tropical forest with very heavy rainfall; rain′-gauge, an instrument for measuring rainfall; rain′-maker, one who professes to bring rain; rain′-plover, the golden plover; rain′-print, a little pit made by a raindrop in clay, etc., sometimes preserved in rocks.—*adj.* rain′proof, more or less impervious to rain.—*v.t.* to make rainproof.—*n.* a rainproof overcoat.—rain′-shadow, an area sheltered by hills from the prevailing winds and having a lighter rainfall than the windward side of the hills; rain′-stone, a stone used in magic rites aimed at bringing rain; rain′storm.—*adj.* rain′tight, rainproof.—rain′-tree, a S. American tree (*Pithecolobium saman*) of the mimosa family, under which there is a constant rain of juice ejected by cicadas; rain′-wash, the washing away of earthy matters by rain: downward creep of superficial deposits soaked in rain: matter so transported; rain′-water, water that falls or has lately fallen as rain.—a rainy day (*fig.*), a possible future time of need; right as rain, perfectly in order. [O.E. *regn;* Du. and Ger. *regen,* O.N. *regn.*]

rain, raine (*Spens.*). Same as reign.

raise, *rāz, v.t.* to cause to rise: to make higher or greater: to lift: to exalt: to advance: to elevate: to set up or upright: to rouse: to stir up: to elate: to rear, grow, or breed: to produce: to give rise to: to build, erect: to bring into being: to bring to life: to utter: to

establish: to institute: to bring forward into consideration or notice: to bring into relief: to intensify: to call up: to cause to rise in view by approaching (*naut.*): to levy, get together, collect: to cause to swell: to extol: to remove, take off: to produce a nap on.—*n.* a rising road: an increase in wages or salary (*coll.*).—*adj.* rais′able.—*ns.* rais′er, one who, or that which, raises a building, etc.: the riser of a step; rais′ing.—raised beach (*geol.*), an old sea-margin above the present water-level; raised pastry, pie, pastry, pie without support of a dish at the sides; rais′ing-bee (*U.S.*), a gathering of neighbours to help in raising the frame of a house, etc.—raise a siege, to abandon, or put an end to, a siege; raise money on, to get money by pawning; raise one's hat, to take one's hat off in salutation; raise the market (upon), to bring about a rise in prices (to the disadvantage of); raise the roof, to make a prodigious din; raise the wind, to get together the necessary money by any shift. [M.E. *reisen* —O.N. *reisa,* causative of *rīsa,* to rise; cf. rise, rear.]

raise, *rāz,* (*N. of England*) *n.* a cairn. [O.N. *hreysi.*]

raisin, *rā′zn, n.* a dried grape. [Fr., grape—L. *racēmus,* a bunch of grapes.]

raison d'être, *rā-zō detr′,* (Fr.) reason for existence (purpose or cause).

raisonné, *rā-zon-ā, adj.* (Fr.) logically set out, systematically arranged, and (usu.) provided with notes. [Fr.]

rait. Same as ret.

raiyat, raiyatwari. Same as ryot, ryotwari.

raj, *räj, n.* rule, sovereignty: government.—*n.* ra′ja(h), an Indian prince or king: a Malay chief.—*ns.* ra′ja(h)ship; raj′pramukh (*-mook*), head of a state or states union in the Democratic Republic of India; Rajput, -poot (*räj′pōōt*), a member of a race or class claiming descent from the original Hindu military and ruling caste. [Hind. *rāj, rājā, Rājpūt*—Sans. *rājan,* a king (cog. with L. *rēx*), *putra,* son.]

rake, *rāk, n.* a toothed bar on a handle, for scraping, gathering together, smoothing, etc.: a tool for various purposes, toothed, notched, or bladed and with long handle (e.g. croupier's implement for drawing in money): a wheeled field implement with long teeth for gathering hay, scraping up weeds, etc.: an extremely thin person or horse.—*v.t.* to scrape, smooth, clear, break up, draw, gather, remove, cover, uncover, search, ransack, with a rake or as if with a rake: to cover with ashes so as to keep smouldering: to pass over violently and swiftly: to enfilade: to afford or take a view all over or quite through. —*v.i.* to work with or as if with a rake: to search minutely.—*n.* rā′ker, one who rakes: a scavenger: a raking implement: in games, a long, fast, low-flying shot (perh. partly from rake (4)).—*n.* and *adj.* rā′king.—rake′-off, pecuniary share, esp. unearned or illicit; rake′shame (*Milt.*), a base, dissolute wretch.—rake up, to revive from oblivion (usu. something scandalous). [O.E. *raca;* Ger. *rechen,* rake; O.N. *reka,* shovel.]

rake, *rāk, n.* a debauched or dissolute person, esp. a man of fashion.—*v.i.* to lead a rake's life: to make a practice of lechery.—*n.* rā′kery, dissoluteness.—*adj.* rā′kish.—*adv.* rā′kishly.—*n.* rā′kishness. [rakehell.]

rake, *rāk, n.* inclination from the vertical or horizontal.—*v.i.* to incline.—*v.t.* to slope: to cut aslant.—*n.* rā′ker, a sloping shore, support. —*adj.* rā′kish, with raking masts: swift-looking: pirate-like: dashing: jaunty.—*adv.* rā′kishly. [Ety. dub.]

rake, *rāk,* (now *dial.*) *v.i.* to proceed, esp. swiftly: to roam, range about: of a hawk, to fly wide:

of a dog, to follow the scent wanderingly along the ground.—*n.* rā′ker, a very fast pace: a plunge in betting.—*adj.* rā′king, advancing swiftly. [O.E. *racian*, to go forward, hasten.]

rake, *rāk*, (*Northern*) *n.* a track, esp. up a hill or in a gully or a pasture: a pasture: a journey, esp. in fetching things: the amount carried at one journey, load, gang: an irregular, usu. vertical, vein of ore: a string, as of wagons.—*v.i.* to form into single file, as sheep. [O.N. *rāk*, stripe: partly coalescing with raik.]

rakehell, *rāk′hel, n.* an utterly debauched person.—*adjs.* rake′hell, -y.—See also rake (2). [Prob. rake (1) and hell: such as might be found by raking out hell.]

raki, *rāk′ē, n.* a spirituous liquor used in the Levant and Greece.—Also rak′ee. [Turk. *rāqi.*]

rakshas, rakshasa, *rāk′shäs, -a,* (*Hindu myth.*) *n.* an evil spirit. [Sans. *rākṣasa.*]

râle, *räl,* (*path.*) *n.* a sound from a diseased lung. [Fr.]

rallentando, *ral-ən-tan′dō,* (*mus.*) *adj.* and *adv.* becoming slower.—*n.* a slowing. [It., pr.p. of *rallentare,* to slacken.]

Rallus, *ral′əs, n.* the water-rail genus of birds, giving name to the family Rall′idae.—*adj.* rall′ine (-*in*). [Latinised from Fr. *râle.*]

rally, *ral′i, v.t.* to reassemble: to gather to one's support: to bring together for united effort: to muster by an effort (as the faculties): to pull together, revive.—*v.i.* to come together, esp. from dispersal, or for renewed effort, or in support of a leader, friend, or cause: to recover: to recover in some degree lost health, power, vigour, value, etc.:—*pr.p.* rall′ying; *pa.p.* and *pa.t.* rall′ied.—*n.* a reassembly for renewed effort: a gathering for a common purpose: a mass-meeting: a competition to test skill in driving, and ability to follow an unknown route (U.S. also **rallye**), or to test quality of motor vehicles: a pantomime mêlée: a temporary or partial recovery: a quick exchange of blows in boxing: a series of to and fro strokes in deciding a point, as in tennis.—*n.* rall′ier.— rall′ying-cry, a slogan to attract support for a cause, etc.; rall′ying-point. [O.Fr. *rallier*—pfx. *re-* and *allier*; see ally.]

rally, *ral′i, v.t* and *v.i.* to banter:—*pr.p.* rall′ying; *pa.t.* and *pa.p.* rall′ied.—*n.* rall′ier.—*adv.* rall′yingly. [Fr. *railler*; cf. rail (2).]

Ralph, *ralf, rāf, n.* the imp of mischief in a printing-house. [Personal name—O.E. *Rædwulf.*]

ram, *ram, n.* a male sheep, a tup: Aries (*astron.*): a battering-ram: a ship's beak for striking an enemy ship: a warship with such a beak: a water-ram or hydraulic ram (see hydraulic): the monkey of a pile-driver: the striking head of a steam-hammer: a piston applying pressure: a machine with such a piston: a rammer: an act of ramming.—*v.t.* to thrust roughly, cram (also *fig.*): to block up: to beat hard: to drive hard down: to strike, batter, pierce with a ram: to strike, dash into, violently:—*pr.p.* ramm′ing; *pa.t.* and *pa.p.* rammed.—*n.* ramm′er, one who or that which rams: esp. a paviour's tool.—*adj.* ramm′ish, rank in smell or taste: strongly sexual.—ram′cat, a he-cat; ram′-jet (**engine**), a simple form of aero-engine, consisting of forward air intake, combustion chamber, and rear expansion nozzle, in which thrust is generated by compression due solely to forward motion; ram′rod, a rod for ramming down a charge or for cleaning a gun-barrel: a stern, inflexible person: a strict disciplinarian.—*adj.* rigid, inflexible: stern; ram′s′-horn, the horn of a ram: a trumpet, snuff-box, or other thing like or made of it.—Also *adj.* [O.E. *ram, rom*; Ger. *ramm.*]

Rāma, *rä′ma, n.* an incarnation of Vishnu.—*n.*

Rāmāyana, *rä-mä′yä-na,* the Sanskrit epic of *Rāma.*

Ramadan, Ramadhan, *ram-ə-dän′, n.* the Mohammedan month of fasting by day. [Ar. *Ramadān.*]

ramakin. See ramekin.

ramal, ramate, etc. See ramus.

Rāmāyana. See Rāma.

ramble, *ram′bl, v.i.* to go as fancy leads: to wander: to walk for pleasure: to wander in mind or discourse: to be desultory, incoherent, or delirious: to straggle or trail, as a plant.—*n.* a roving about: an irregular excursion: rambling.—*n.* ram′bler, one who rambles: a trailing climbing plant, esp. a rose with small clustered flowers.—*n.* and *adj.* ram′bling.—*adv.* ram′blingly. [M.E. *romblen*; app. conn. with roam.]

rambunctious, *ram-bungk′shəs, adj.* difficult to control, boisterous, exuberant.—*adv.* rambunc′-tiously.—*n.* rambunc′tiousness. [Perh. rumbustious.]

rambutan, *ram-bōō′tən, n.* a lofty Malayan tree (*Nephelium lappaceum*), akin to the longan: its hairy edible fruit. [Malay *rambūtan*—*rambut,* hair.]

rameal, rameous. See ramus.

ramekin, ramequin, ramakin, *ram′ə-kin, n.* a mixture of cheese, eggs, etc., baked in small moulds, or served on toast: a baking dish for one person. [Fr. *ramequin*—obs. Flem. *rammeken.*]

ramentum, *ra-ment′əm, n.* a chaffy scale, as on ferns:—*pl.* rament′a. [L. *rāmentum,* a scraping —*rādēre,* to scrape.]

ramequin. See ramekin.

ramfeezle, *ram-fē′zl,* (*Scot.*) *v.t.* to weary out.

ramgunshoch, *ram-gun′shohh,* (*Scot.*) *adj.* rough.

rami, ramie, ramee, *ram′ē, n.* rhea or China grass (*Boehmeria nivea*), a plant of the nettle family, long cultivated in China: its fibre, used for cloth, bank-note paper, gas mantles, etc.: a garment thereof. [Malay *rami.*]

ramify, etc. See under ramus.

Ramil(l)ie(s), *ram′i-li(z), n.* a name for several articles and modes of dress in fashion after Marlborough's victory at *Ramillies* (1706)—esp. a form of cocked hat, and a wig with a long plaited tail.—Also *adj.*

Ramism, *rā′mizm, n.* the system of logic of Peter *Ramus* (1515-72).—*ns.* and *adjs.* Rā′mean, Rā′mist.

rammer, rammish. See ram.

rammy, *ram′i, n.* a row, free-for-all fight. [Perh. from Scots *rammle,* an uproar, noisy drinking spree.]

ramose, ramous. See under ramus.

ramp, *ramp, v.i.* to climb: to grow rankly: to rear as if climbing: to slope from one level to another: to rage: to range about wildly.—*v.t.* to provide with a ramp: to bend into a ramp: to snatch: to rob: to hustle into paying a fictitious debt: to swindle.—*n.* a romp, tomboy: a disorderly or loose woman: an act of ramping: an inclined plane: the slope of a wall-top or the like between two levels: an upwardly concave bend in a handrail: a swindle: a stunt worked for private profit: a worked-up excitement or craze, esp. for some gain: an exploitation of a special situation to increase prices or the like.—*adj.* rampā′cious (*Dickens*), rampageous.—*n.* rampāge′ (*U.S.* also *ram′*; *Scot.* rampauge, -*pöj′*), turbulently or aggressively excited behaviour or rushing about.—*v.i.* to storm: to rush about wildly.—*adj.* rampā′geous.—*ns.* rampā′geousness; rampall′ian (*Shak.*), a term of abuse; ramp′ancy.—*adj.* ramp′ant, rearing: standing in profile, on the left hindleg (*her.*): high-spirited: fierce: unrestrained: unchecked in growth or prevalence: (of an arch) having springers on different levels.—*adv.* ramp′antly. —*n.* ramp′er, one who ramps: esp. one who makes a disturbance to cover the activities of others: a rampsman.—**ramps′man** (*slang*), one who ramps bookmakers. [Fr. *ramper*, to creep, to clamber.]

**rampart**, *ram′pärt*. *-pərt*, *n.* a flat-topped defensive mound: that which defends.—*v.t.* to fortify or surround with ramparts. [Fr. *rempart*—O.Fr. *rempar*—*remparer*, to defend—L. pfx. *re-*, *ante*, *parāre*, to prepare.]

**rampick**, *ram′pik*, **rampike**, *-pīk*, (*arch.* and *U.S.*) *n.* a dead tree, or one decayed at the top, broken off, or partly burned.—*adjs.* **ram′pick**, *-ed.* [Origin obscure.]

**rampion**, *ramp′yən*, *-i-ən*, *n.* a bell-flower (*Campanula rapunculus*) whose root is eaten as a salad: any species of the kindred genus Phyteuma. [Cf. It. *raponzolo*, Ger. *rapunzel*, Fr. *raiponce*.]

**rampire**, *ram′pīr*, *n.* arch. for **rampart**.—*adj.* **ram′pired**.

**ramrod**. See ram.

**ramshackle**, *ram′shak-l*, *adj.* tumbledown. [Ety. uncertain.]

**ramson**, *ram′zən*, *n.* (orig. pl. of the now *dial.* **rams**; usu. in double pl. form **ramsons**) wild or broad-leaved garlic. [O.E. *hramsa*, *hramse*, *hramsan* (pl.).]

**ramstam**, *ram′stam′*, (*Scot.*) *adj.* and *adv.* headlong. [Poss. **ram**.]

**ramus**, *rā′məs*, *n.* a branch of anything, esp. a nerve: a process of a bone: the mandible, or its ascending part: a feather barb:—*pl.* **rā′mi**.—*adjs.* **rā′mal**, **rā′meal**, **rā′meous**, **rā′mous**, of a branch; **rā′mate**, **rā′mous**, **ramose** (*rə-mōs′*, *rā′mōs*), branched.—*n.* **ramification** (*ram-i-fi-kā′shən*), branching: arrangement of branches: a single branch or part of a complex arrangement, or of a situation or problem, esp., when used *fig.*, a consequence that must be taken into account. —*v.t.* and *v.i.* **ram′ify**, to divide into branches: —*pr.p.* **ram′ifying**; *pa.t.* and *pa.p.* **rami′fied**. —*adjs.* **ram′ular**, of a branch; **ram′ulose**, **ram′ulous**, having ramuli.—*n.* **ram′ulus**, a little branch: —*pl.* **ram′uli**. [L. *rāmus*, a branch.]

**ran**, *pa.t.* of run.

**Rana**, *rā′na*, *n.* the typical genus of frogs, giving name to the family **Ranidae** (*ran′i-dē*).—*adj.* **ranarian** (*rə-nā′ri-ən*).—*n.* **ranā′rium**, a place where frogs are reared.—*adjs.* **raniform** (*ran′*), frog-like; **ranine** (*rā′nin*), of the under side of the tongue (seat of ranula); **ranivorous** (*rə-niv′ər-əs*), frog-eating.—*n.* **ranula** (*ran′ū-lä*), a cyst in the gland under the tongue (poss. from a fancied resemblance to a little frog). [L. *rāna*, dim. *rānula*, a frog, ranula.]

**rana**, *rā′nä*, *n.* a Rajput prince. [Hind.]

**rance**, *rans*, (chiefly *Scot.*) *n.* a prop, shore: a bar.—*v.t.* to prop: to bar. [Fr. *ranche*.]

**rancel**. See ranzel.

**ranch**, *rän(t)sh*, *ran(t)sh*, *n.* a stock-farm, as in western N. America, with its buildings and persons employed.—*v.i.* to manage or work upon a ranch.—*ns.* **ranch′er**, **rancho** (*ran-chā′rō*, Sp. *rän-che′rō*), **ranch′man**, one employed in ranching; **rancheria** (*ran-chā-rē′a*, Sp. *rän-che-*), a herdsmen's hut or village: a settlement of Indians; **ranch′ing**; **rancho** (*ran′chō*, Sp. *rän′*), a rude hut, or group of huts, esp. for travellers, a ranch:—*pl.* **ran′chos**. [From Amer. Sp.—Sp. *rancho*, mess, mess-room.]

**ranch**, *rän(t)sh*, *ran(t)sh*, (*Dryden*) *v.t.* to tear. [Cf. **race** (5).]

**rancid**, *ran′sid*, *adj.* rank in smell or taste, as butter or oil that is going bad.—*ns.* **rancid′ity**, **ran′cidness**. [L. *rancidus*.]

**rancour**, *rang′kər*, *n.* harboured bitterness: deep-seated enmity: spite: virulence: sourness (*Shak.*).—*adj.* **ran′corous**.—*adv.* **ran′corously**. [O.Fr.,—L. *rancor*, *-ōris*, an old grudge—*rancēre*, to be rancid.]

**rand**, *rand*, *n.* a border, margin: a strip, esp. of flesh or of leather: a ridge overlooking a valley (*S.Afr. ront*, *rand*): the basic unit of the South African decimal coinage, introduced 1961 as equivalent to ten shillings.—*pl.* **rand(s)**.—the Rand, the Witwatersrand goldfield. [O.E. and Du. *rand*, border.]

**rand**, *rand*, *v.i.* an old form of rant.

**randan**, *ran-dan′*, *n.* a din, uproar: riotous conduct: spree. [Origin obscure.]

**randan**, *ran-dan′*, *n.* a boat rowed by three, the second with two oars.—Also **randan gig**. [Origin obscure.]

**randem**, *ran′dəm*, *n.*, *adj.*, and *adv.* tandem with three horses.

**randle-balk**, *ran′dl-bök*, *-perch*, *-pûrch*, *-tree*, *-trē* (*Scot.* and *N.England*) *ns.* a bar in a chimney for hanging pots; **randle-tree** (*Scott*), applied to a tall, raw-boned woman.—Also **rann′el(l)-**, **rann′le-**, **ran′tle-**. [Cf. Norw. *randa-tre*—*rand*, space above a fireplace.]

**random**, *ran′dəm*, also formerly (*Spens.*, *Shak.*) **randon**, *-dən*, *n.* a rush, full speed (*obs.*): uncontrolled or unguarded state, freedom (*Spens.*): haphazard: elevation of a gun (*obs.*): irregular masonry.—*adj.* haphazard, chance: fired at an elevation: uncontrolled: irregular.—*advs.* **ran′domly**, **ran′domwise**.—**random access** (*computer*), access to any data in a large store of information without affecting other data. [O.Fr. *randon*—*randir*, to gallop.]

**randy**, **randie**, *ran′di*, *adj.* boisterous (*dial.*): aggressively or coarsely loud-spoken (*Scot.*): lustful.—*n.* a violent beggar, esp. a woman: a coarse virago: a romping girl. [Poss. **rand** (2).]

**ranee**. See rani.

**rang**, *rang*, *pa.t.* of **ring**.

**range**, *rānj*, *v.t.* to set in a row or rows: to assign a place among others to (esp., *refl.*, to take sides): to classify: to arrange: to straighten, level: to traverse freely or in all directions: to sail along: to bring to bear.—*v.i.* to lie in a direction: to extend: to take or have a position in a line, or alongside: to take sides: to lie evenly: to move, have freedom of movement, occur, or vary, within limits: to rove at large: to beat about, as for game: to be inconstant: to have a range. —*n.* a row or rank: a system of points in a straight line: anything extending in line, as a chain of mountains, a row of connected buildings: a mountain (*Austr.*): a stretch of open country, esp. one used for grazing: a north and south strip of townships six miles wide (*U.S.*): line of fire: an act of ranging: scope, compass: movement, freedom of movement, or variation between limits: space or distance between limits: area, or distance within which anything moves, can move, occurs, is possible, acts efficiently, or varies: a place for practice in shooting: firing elevation of a gun, etc.: an enclosed kitchen fireplace fitted with appliances of various kinds.—*ns.* **ran′ger**, a rover: a dog that beats the ground: a forest or park officer: a member of a body of troops, usu. mounted and employed in policing an area: a soldier specially trained for raiding combat: a member of a senior branch of the Girl Guide organisation: (in *pl.*) a name sometimes taken by football clubs; **rang′ership**; **rang′iness**.—*adj.* **ran′gy**, disposed or well able to roam: roomy: long-legged and thin: mountainous (*Austr.*).—**range′finder**, an instrument for finding the distance of an object. —**free range** (see free); **to range oneself**, to side (with), to take sides: (as a Gallicism) to settle down to reputable ways, esp. on marrying. [Fr. *ranger*, to range—*rang*, a rank.]

**rani**, **ranee**, *rän′ē*, *n. fem.* of **raja**. [Hind. *rānī*— Sans. *rājñī*, queen, fem. of *rājan*.]

**Ranidae**, etc. See Rana.

**rank**, *rangk*, *n.* a row: a row of soldiers standing side by side (opp. to *file*): any row thought of as as so placed (e.g. of squares along the player's side of a chessboard): (in *pl.*) soldiers, esp. private soldiers—often (with *the*) private soldiers collectively: (in *pl.*) persons of ordinary grade: a row of cabs awaiting hire: a cabstand: a set of organ pipes: arrangement in line: order, grade, or degree: station: high standing.—*v.t.* to place in a line: to assign to a particular class or grade: to place on the list of claims against a bankrupt: to take rank over (*U.S.*).—*v.i.* to have a place in a rank, grade, scale, or class: to move in rank: to be admitted as a claim against the property of a bankrupt.—*adj.* ranked (*Shak.*), app. bordered with rows.—*n.* rank′er, one who serves or has served as a private soldier: an officer who has risen from the ranks.—rank and file, common soldiers: ordinary people: those in an organisation, etc. not involved in its management; take rank of, to take precedence of. [O.Fr. renc (Fr. rang), perh.—O.H.G. *hring, hrinc*, ring.]

rank, *rangk, adj.* strong, lusty, vigorous (*obs.*): violent (*obs.*): growing high and luxuriantly: coarsely overgrown: swollen (*Shak.*): excessive (*taw*): abounding (*Spens.*): dense (*Spens.*): out-and-out, arrant, utter: over-productive: offensively strong-scented or strong-tasted: gross: foul: lustful, in heat (*Shak.*): grossly obvious: deep-cutting.—*adv.* (*Spens.*) violently: utterly.—*adv.* rank′ly.—*n.* rank′ness.—rank′-ri′der, a hard rider: a moss-trooper: a highwayman.—*adj.* rank′-ri′ding. [O.E. *ranc,* proud, strong.]

ranke, *rangk,* (Shak., *As You Like It,* III, ii. 103) *n.* app. a jog-trot (perh. a misprint for rack (6)): passage otherwise explained as meaning a repetition of the same rhyme like a file (rank) of so many butterwomen.

Rankine, *rang′kin, adj.* pertaining to an absolute scale of temperature on which the units are the same as those on the Fahrenheit scale. [After William J. M. *Rankine* (1820-72) Scottish engineer and scientist.]

rankle, *rangk′l, v.i.* to fester: to cause festering: to go on vexing, irritating, or embittering.—*v.t.* to cause to fester: to envenom: to embitter.—*n.* a rankling. [O.Fr. *rancler, raoncler—draoncler,* app.—L.L. dra(cu)nculus, an ulcer, dim. of L. *dracō*—Gr. *drakōn,* dragon.]

rannel(l)-, rannle-, etc. See randle-.

ransack, *ran′sak* (or -sak′), *v.t.* to search thoroughly: to plunder: to pillage.—*n.* eager search.—*n.* ran′sacker. [O.N. *rannsaka—rann,* house, *sækja,* to seek.]

ransel. See ranzel.

ransha(c)kle, *ran-shak′l,* (*Scott*) *v.t.* to search, ransack. [Dial. Eng. ransackle, ram-—ransack.]

ransom, *ran′səm, n.* redemption from captivity: price of redemption or reclamation: expiation: an extortionate price.—*v.t.* to pay, demand, or accept ransom for: to redeem: to expiate.—*adj.* ran′somable.—*n.* ran′somer.—*adj.* ran′somless.—hold to ransom, to retain until a ransom shall be paid: to hold up to gain a concession; put to ransom, to offer to release for ransom. [Fr. rançon—L. redemptiō, -ōnis, redemption.]

rant, *rant, v.i.* to declaim bombastically: to storm, scold: to sing, play, or make merry, noisily.—*v.t.* to utter declamatorily.—*n.* empty declamation: bombast: a tirade: a noisy frolic (*Scot.*): a lively tune.—*ns.* ran′ter, one who rants: an extravagant preacher: a member of a Commonwealth antinomian sect: (as a byname) a Primitive Methodist: a roisterer: a noisy musician (*Scot.*); ran′terism.—*adv.* rant′ingly. [Obs. Du. *ranten,* to rave; L.G. *randen,* Ger. *ranzen.*]

rantipole, *rant′i-pōl, n.* a wild reckless person.—Also *adj.* [Perh. rant.]

rantle-. See randle-.

ranula. See Rana.

Ranunculus, *rə-nung′kū-ləs, n.* the buttercup genus:—*pl.* ranun′culi, ranun′culuses.—*adj.* ranunculā′ceous, of the buttercup family (Ranunculā′-ceae). [L. *rānunculus,* dim. of *rāna,* a frog.]

ranz-des-vaches, *rä(s)-dä-väsh, n.* a French Swiss herdsman's song or alpenhorn melody. [Swiss Fr.; *ranz,* of uncertain meaning, Fr. *des vaches,* of the cows.]

ranzel, *ran′zl,* rancel, -sel, -sl, *n.* formerly in Orkney and Shetland a search for stolen goods.—ran′zelman, etc. (Ran′zellaar, *Scott*), an official who did this. [O.Scot. *ransell;* O.N. *rannsaka;* ranshackle.]

rap, *rap, n.* a sharp blow: the sound of a knock.—*v.t.* and *v.i.* to strike or knock sharply: to swear or testify, esp. falsely (*obs. slang*): to communicate by raps.—*v.t.* to censure, reprove: to utter sharply.—*v.i.* to rattle, patter:—*pr.p.* rapp′ing; *pa.t.* and *pa.p.* rapped.—*n.* rapp′er, one who raps: a door-knocker: a great lie or oath: a spirit-rapper.—take the rap (*slang*), to take the blame or punishment, esp. in place of another. [Imit.]

rap, *rap, v.t.* to snatch: to grab: to carry away in spirit or with joy (*Shak.*):—*pr.p.* rapp′ing; *pa.p.* rapped or rapt. [Perh. partly akin to M.L.G. *rappen,* Sw. *rappa,* to snatch; mainly a back-formation from rapt.]

rap, *rap, n.* an 18th-century Irish counterfeit halfpenny: as a type of worthlessness, a whit. [Origin obscure.]

rapacious, *rə-pā′shəs, adj.* grasping: greedy of gain: living by prey.—*adv.* rapā′ciously.—*ns.* rapā′ciousness; rapacity (-*pas′*). [L. *rapāx, -ācis—rapĕre,* to seize and carry off.]

rape, *rāp, n.* rapine, plunder, seizure (*obs.*): sexual intercourse with a woman without her legal consent.—*v.t.* to seize and carry off (*obs.*): to commit rape upon: to ravish or transport, as with delight (*obs.*).—*ns.* rā′per; rā′pist.—*adj.* rā′ping, tearing prey (*her.*): ravishing, delighting (*obs.*). [Prob. L. *rapĕre,* to snatch, confused with rap (2).]

rape, *rāp, n.* a division of Sussex. [Origin obscure.]

rape, *rāp, n.* a plant (*Brassica napus*) near akin to the turnip, cultivated for its herbage and oil-producing seeds: applied to various closely allied species or varieties.—rape′-cake, refuse of rape-seed after the oil has been expressed; rape′-oil; rape′-seed. [L. *rāpa, rāpum,* a turnip.]

rape, *rāp, n.* the refuse left after wine-making. [Fr. *râpe.*]

Raphanus, *raf′ə-nəs, n.* the radish genus.—*n.* raphania (*rə-fā′ni-ə*), ergotism (attributed by Linnaeus to wild radish seeds). [Gr. *rhaphanis.*]

raphe, *rā′fē, n.* a seam-like junction: the ridge on the side of an anatropous ovule continuing the funicle to the chalaza. [Gr. *rhāphē,* a seam.]

Raphia, *rā′fi-ə, raf′i-ə, n.* a genus of handsome pinnately-leaved palms: (without *cap.*) raffia. [Malagasy.]

raphis, raphides, *rā′fis,* raphide, rhaphide, *rā′fīd, n.* a needle-like crystal, usu. of calcium oxalate, occurring in plant cells:—*pl.* r(h)aphides (*raf′i-dēz,* ra′fīdz). [Gr. *rhāphis, -idos,* a needle—*rhaptein,* to sew.]

rapid, *rap′id, adj.* swift: quickly accomplished: steeply-sloping: requiring short exposure (*phot.*).—*n.* a very swift-flowing part of a river with steep descent and often broken water but no actual drop (usu. in *pl.*).—*n.* rapidity (*rə-pid′i-ti*).—*adv.* rap′idly.—*n.* rap′idness.—rapid eye movement (abbrev. REM), an observed manifestation of a phase of sleep during which dreams are particularly vivid: hence, of, pertaining to, this phase. [L. *rapidus—rapĕre,* to seize.]

rapier, *rā′pi-ər, n.* a long slender sword, suitable for thrusting. [Fr. *rapière.*]

**rapine**, *rap'īn*, *in*, *n.* plundering: prey: ravishment, transport (*Milt.*). [L. *rapina*—*rapĕre*, to seize.]

**raploch**, *rap'lohh*, (*Scot.*) *n.* and *adj.* homespun. [Origin unknown.]

**rapparee**, *rap-ər-ē'*, *n.* a wild Irish plunderer. [Ir. *rapaire*, half-pike, robber.]

**rappee**, *ra-pē'*, *n.* a coarse, strong-flavoured snuff. [Fr. *râpé*, rasped, grated—*râper*, to rasp.]

**rappel**, *rä-*, *rə-pel'*, *n.* call to arms by beat of drum. [Fr.]

**rapper, rapping.** See rap.

**Rappist**, *rap'ist*, **Rappite**, *-īt*, *ns.* a Harmonist, follower of George *Rapp.*

**rapport**, *ra-pōr'*, *n.* relation: connection: sympathy: emotional bond: spiritualistic touch. [Fr.]

**rapporteur**, *ra-pōr-tœr*, *n.* one whose task it is to carry out an investigation and/or draw up a report (for a committee, etc.). [Fr.—*rapporter*, to bring back.]

**rapprochement**, *ra-prosh'mä*, *n.* a drawing together: establishment or renewal of cordial relations. [Fr.]

**rapscallion**, *rap-skal'yən*, *n.* See rascal.

**rapt**, *rapt*, *adj.* snatched or carried away: abducted: carried out of this world: transported, enraptured, entranced: wholly engrossed. [L. *raptus*, pa.p. of *rapĕre*, to seize and carry off; but partly also pa.p. of rap (2).]

**raptor**, *rap'tər*, *n.* a ravisher: a plunderer: a bird of prey, member of the abandoned order **Raptores** (*-tō'rēz*).—*adjs.* **raptatō'rial, raptō'rial,** predatory: adapted to predatory life. [L. *raptor*, -*ōris*, a plunderer—*rapĕre*, to seize.]

**rapture**, *rap'chər*, *n.* a seizing and carrying away: extreme delight: transport: ecstasy: a paroxysm.—*v.t.* to enrapture.—*adj.* **rap'tured.**—*adj.* **rap'tureless.**—*v.i.* **rap'turise,** *-ize,* to go into raptures.—*n.* **rap'turist.**—*adj.* **rap'turous.**—*adv.* **rap'turously.**—**rapture of the deep,** nitrogen narcosis. [rapt.]

**rara avis**, *rä'rə ä'vis*, *rä'ra ä'wis.* See *Quotations from Latin, etc.* in Appendices.

**rare**, *rār*, *adj.* thin: not dense: sparse: seldom met with: uncommon: excellent: especially good: extraordinary: used as a mere intensive, esp. in **rare** and (*coll.*).—*n.* **rarefac'tion** (*rār-i-, rar-i-*), rarefying.—*adjs.* **rarefac'tive, rar'efiable.** —*v.t., v.i.* **rar'efy,** make, become less dense, refine:—*pr.p.* **rar'efying;** *pa.t.* and *pa.p.* **rar'efied.**—*adv.* **rāre'ly,** seldom: choicely: remarkably well.—*ns.* **rāre'ness;** **rarity** (*rār'* or *rar'i-ti*), state of being rare: thinness: something valued for its scarcity: uncommonness.—**rare'bit,** a would-be correction of (*Welsh*) **rabbit;** **rare earth,** an oxide of a rare-earth element, any of a group of metallic elements (some of them rare) closely similar in chemical properties and very difficult to separate: now more usu. a rare-earth element itself. [Fr.,—L. *rārus.*]

**rare**, *rār*, *adj.* of eggs, lightly cooked (*obs.* or *dial.*): of meat, underdone. [rear (3) influenced by rare (1).]

**rare**, *rār*, **rear**, *rēr*, (*obs.*) *adj.* and *adv.* early.—*adv.* **rare'ly.**—*adj.* **rare'-ripe,** early ripe. [rathe.]

**raree-show**, *rär'ē-shō*, *n.* a show carried about in a box: a spectacle. [App. a Savoyard showman's pron. of **rare show.**]

**raring**, *rā'ring*, *adj.* eager (for), full of enthusiasm and sense of urgency (with *infin.*). [rear (2).]

**ras**, *räs*, *n.* a headland: an Abyssinian prince. [Ar. *ras*, *ra's*, head.]

**rascaille**, *räs-kä'i*, *n.* and *adj.* an old form of **rascal,** rabble (*Scott*, etc.).

**rascal**, *räs'kl*, *n.* the rabble (*obs.*): one of the rabble (*obs.*): a knave, rogue, scamp: (playfully) a fellow: a deer out of condition (*Shak.*). —*adj.* of the rabble: knavish: wretched: out of condition.—*ns.* **ras'caldom,** the world or conduct of rascals; **ras'calism; rascality** (*-kal'*), the rabble: character or conduct of rascals; **rascallion** (*-kal'yən*), **rapscall'ion,** a rascal: a low, mean wretch.—*adjs.* **ras'cal-like, ras'cally** (*superl., Shak., ras'calliest*). [O.Fr. *rascaille* (Fr. *racaille*), scum of the people.]

**rase**, *rāz.* Same as raze. See also **race** (5 and 6), and **rise.**

**rash**, *rash*, *adj.* over-hasty: wanting in caution: operating suddenly (*Shak.*): calling for haste (*Shak.*).—*adv.* **rashly.**—*adv.* **rash'ly.**—*n.* **rash'ness.** [Cf. Dan. and Sw. *rask;* Du. and Ger. *rasch,* rapid.]

**rash**, *rash*, *n.* an eruption on the skin: a large number of instances at the same time or in the same place. [Perh. O.Fr. *rasche* (Fr. *rache*).]

**rash**, *rash*, (*obs.*) *v.t.* to tear, drag. [O.Fr. *arrachier,* to uproot; cf. **race** (6).]

**rash**, *rash*, (*Spens.*) *v.t.* to slash. [Variant of **raze, rase, race.**]

**rash**, *rash*, *v.i.* to dash, rush (*obs.*).—*v.t.* (*Shak.*) to stick, thrust forcibly. [Origin obscure.]

**rash**, *rash*, *n.* a Scots form of **rush** (plant).

**rasher**, *rash'ər*, *n.* a thin slice of bacon. [Poss. from **rash** (4).]

**Raskolnik**, *ras-kol'nik*, *n.* in Russia, a dissenter from the Orthodox Church. [Russ.]

**rasorial**, *ra-*, *rə-sō'-,sō'ri-əl*, *adj.* scraping the ground for food.—*n.pl.* **Rasō'res** (*-rēz*), an obsolete order, gallinaceous birds with or without the pigeons. [L. *rāsor, -ōris,* scraper.]

**rasp**, *räsp*, *n.* a coarse file: any similar surface: a mollusc's tongue: an insect's stridulating apparatus: a risp at a door: a grating sound or feeling.—*v.t.* to grate as with a rasp: to grate upon: to risp: to utter gratingly.—*v.i.* to have a grating effect: to scrape, as on a fiddle.—*ns.* **rasp'atory,** a surgeon's rasp; **rasp'er,** one who, or that which, rasps: a difficult fence (*coll.*); **rasp'ing,** a filing.—*adj.* grating, harsh.—*adv.* **rasp'ingly.** — *adj.* **rasp'y,** rough. — **rasp'-house** (Du. *rasphuis*), a house of correction, where dye-wood was rasped. [O.Fr. *raspe* (Fr. *râpe*): perh. Gmc.]

**rasp**, *räsp*, (now *coll.* and *Scot.*) *n.* a raspberry.—*n.* **raspberry** (*räz'bar-i*), the fruit of *Rubus idaeus:* the plant producing it: extended to some kindred species: a sign of disapproval, esp. a noise produced by blowing hard with the tongue between the lips (*slang*).—*adj.* of, made with, or like raspberry.—**rasp'berry-bush; raspberry jam tree,** an Australian acacia (from the smell of its wood). [Earlier *raspis;* origin unknown.]

**rasse**, *ras'(ə)*, *n.* a small civet. [Jav. *rase.*]

**rast**, *räst* or *räst*, a Spenserian pa.p. of **race** = **raze.**

**raster**, *ras'tər*, (*television*) *n.* a complete set of scanning lines appearing at the receiver as a rectangular patch of light on which the image is reproduced. [Perh.—L. *rāstrum,* as next word.]

**rastrum**, *ras'trəm*, *n.* a music-pen. [L. *rāstrum,* rake.]

**rasure, razure**, *rā'zhər*, *n.* the act of scraping or shaving: erasure: obliteration. [L. *rāsūra.*]

**rat**, *rat*, *n.* any of the larger animals of the genus Mus (distinguished from *mouse*): extended to various kindred or superficially similar animals: a renegade, turn-coat (from the rat's alleged desertion of a doomed ship): a strike-breaker: one who works for less than recognised wages: a miserable or ill-looking specimen.—*v.i.* to hunt or catch rats: to desert or change sides for unworthy motives: (of a workman) to work as a rat:—*pr.p.* **ratt'ing;** *pa.t.* and *pa.p.* **ratt'ed.**—*adj.* **rat'proof.**—*interj.* **rats** (*slang*), expressing contemptuous incredulity.—*ns.* **ratt'er,** a killer of rats, esp. a dog: one who rats; **ratt'ery,** apostasy: a place where rats are kept or abound; **ratt'ing,** apostasy: rat-hunting.—Also *adj.*—*adjs.* **ratt′ish**, rat-like: rat-infested; **ratty**, rat-like: rat-infested: wretched: angry, irritable (*slang*).—**rat′-catcher**, a professional killer of rats: unconventional hunting garb; **rat′-catching**; **rat′-flea**, a flea that infests rats; **rat′-guard**, a metal disk put on a hawser to prevent rats from boarding a ship in port; **rat′-hole**; **rat′-hunting**; **rat′-kangaroo′**, the potoroo, a marsupial of various species about the size of a rabbit, akin to the kangaroo; **rat′-pit**, an enclosure where rats are worried by dogs; **rat′-poison**, any poison for rats; **rat race**, the scramble to get on in the world by fair means or foul; **rats′bane**, poison for rats, esp. white arsenic: a name for many poisonous plants; **rat′s′-tail**, **rat′-tail**, the tail of a rat: anything like a rat's tail: a thin coherent dangling lock of hair: an excrescence on a horse's leg.—*adj.* **rat′s′-tail**, **rat′-tail**, **rat′-tailed**, having a tail like a rat: like a rat's tail: of a spoon, ridged along the back of the bowl. —**rat′-trap**, a trap for catching rats: a toothed bicycle pedal.—Also *adj.*—**rat on**, to inform against; **smell a rat**, to have a suspicion that something is afoot. [O.E. *ræt*; cf. Ger. *ratte*.]

**rat**, *rat*, *v.t.* (in imprecations) used for **rot**. [Cf. **drat**.]

**rata**, *rä′ta*, *n.* a myrtaceous New Zealand tree (*Metrosideros*) with hard wood. [Maori.]

**ratable**, **rateable**, *rä′tə-bl*, *adj.* See **rate** (1).

**ratafia**, *rat-ə-fē′ə*, *n.* a flavouring essence made with the essential oil of almonds: a cordial or liqueur flavoured with fruit-kernels: an almond biscuit or cake. [Fr.; ety. dub.; cf. **tafia**.]

**ratan**, *ra-tan′*, *n.* Same as **rattan**.

**rataplan**, *rat-ə-plan′*, *n.* a drumming sound. [Fr.]

**rat-a-tat**, *rat-ə-tat′*. Same as **rat-tat**.

**ratch**, *rach*, *n.* a ratchet: a ratchet-wheel.—*n.* **ratch′et**, a pawl and/or ratchet-wheel.—**ratch′et-wheel**, a wheel with inclined teeth with which a pawl engages. [Cf. Ger. *ratsche*, Fr. *rochet*.]

**ratch.** Same as **rache**.

**ratch.** Same as **race** (4).

**rate**, *rät*, *n.* estimated amount or value (*Shak.*): estimation (*Shak.*): a fixed quantity (*obs.*): price or cost: amount corresponding to: ratio: esp. time-ratio, speed: amount determined according to a rule or basis: a standard: a class or rank, esp. of ships or of seamen: manner, mode: extent, degree: (often *pl.*) an amount levied by a local authority according to the assessed value of property: a clock's gain or loss in unit time.—*v.t.* to allot (*Shak.*): to calculate (*Shak.*): to estimate: to value: to settle the relative rank, scale, or position of: to esteem, regard as: to deserve, be worthy of: to value for purpose of rate-paying.—*v.i.* to be placed in a certain class.—*n.* **rāt(e)abil′ity**.—*adj.* **rāt(e)′able**.—*adv.* **rāt(e)′ably**.—*ns.* **rāt′er**, one who makes an estimate: (in composition) a ship, etc., of a given rate (as *second-rater*); **rāt′ing**, a fixing of rates: classification according to grade: the class of any member of a crew: a sailor of such a class: the tonnage-class of a racing yacht.—**rāte′-cutting**, a lowering of charges to obtain traffic; **rāte′payer**, one who pays a local rate. [O.Fr.,—L.L. (*pro*) *ratā* (*parte*), according to a calculated part—*rērī*, *rātus*, to think, judge.]

**rate**, *rät*, *v.t.* to scold: to chide: to reprove: to drive by scolding.—*v.i.* to scold.—*n.* a reproof to a dog. [M.E. *raten*; origin obscure.]

**rate.** Same as **ret**.

**Ratel**, *rä′təl*, *rä′təl*, *n.* a badger-like genus (*Mellivora*) of Africa and India, akin to the gluttons. [Afrikaans; origin uncertain.]

**rath**, *räth*, **rathe**, *rādh*, (*arch.*) *adj.* quick: eager: early:—*comp.* **rather** (*rädh′ər*; *Spens.*), earlier; *superl.* **rath′est** (*obs.* or *dial.*), earliest.—*adv.* **rathe** (*rādh*; *Milt.*), early:—*comp.* **rather** (see below); *superl.* (*obs.*) **rath′est**. [O.E. *hræd* (rarely

*hræth*), quick, *hræthe*, *hrathe*, quickly; O.N. *hrathr.*]

**rath**, *räth*, *n.* a prehistoric hill-fort. [Ir.]

**rather**, *rä′dhər*, *adv.* sooner, more quickly (*Shak.*): more readily: more willingly: in preference: more than otherwise: more properly: somewhat, in some degree:—*irreg. superl.* **ra′therest** (*Shak.*).—*interj.* **ra′ther** (sometimes affectedly *rä-dhúr′*), I should think so: yes, indeed.—*adv.* (*coll.*) **ra′therish**.—**the rather**, all the more. [Comp. of **rath** (1); O.E. *hrathor*.]

**ratheripe**, *rādh′rip*, **rathripe**, *räth′rip*, (*arch.* and *dial.*) *adj.* early ripe.—*n.* an early-ripening variety. [**rath**(e), **ripe**.]

**ratify**, *rat′i-fī*, *v.t.* to approve and sanction, esp. by signature: to give validity or legality to: to confirm the correctness of (*obs.*):—*pr.p.* **rat′ifying**; *pa.t.* and *pa.p.* **rat′ified**.—*ns.* **ratificā′tion**; **rat′ifier**. [Fr. *ratifier*—L. *rātus*, pa.p. of *rērī* (see **rate** (1)), *facĕre*, to make.]

**ratine**, **ratteen**, *rat-ēn′*, *n.* a rough, open dress-fabric. [Fr. *ratine*.]

**ratio**, *rä′shi-ō*, *räsh′-yō*, *n.* the relation of one thing to another of which the quotient is the measure: quotient: proportion: a portion, allowance (*rare*).—**compound, inverse, ratio** (see **compound, inverse**). [L. *rătiō*, -*ōnis*, reason—*rērī*, *rātus*, to think.]

**ratiocinate**, *rat-* or *rash-i-os′i-nāt*, *v.i.* to reason.—*n.* **ratiocinā′tion**.—*adjs.* **ratioc′inative**, **ratioc′inatory**. [L. *ratiōcinārī*, -*ātus*.]

**ration**, *ra′shən*, sometimes *rä′*, *n.* a fixed allowance or portion: (in *pl.*) food (*coll.*).—*v.t.* to put on an allowance: to supply with rations: to restrict the supply of to so much for each.—**ra′tion-book, -card**, a book, card, of coupons or vouchers for rationed commodities; **ra′tion-money**, money in lieu of rations. [Fr.,—L. *rătiō*, -*ōnis*.]

**rational**, *rash′ən-əl*, *adj.* of the reason: endowed with reason: agreeable to reason: sane: intelligent: judicious: commensurable with natural numbers.—*n.* a rational being or quantity: (in *pl.*) rational dress, i.e. knickerbockers instead of skirts for women (*hist.*).—*ns.* **rationale** (*rash-i-ō-nä′li*, -*yə-nä′li*), underlying principle: a rational account: a theoretical explanation or solution; **rationalisation, -z-**, (*rash-nəl-i-zä′shən*).—*v.t.* **rat′ionalise, -ize**, to make rational: to free from irrational quantities: to conform to reason: to reorganise scientifically: to interpret rationalistically: to substitute conscious reasoning for unconscious motivation in explaining: to organise (an industry) so as to achieve greater efficiency and economy.—*v.i.* to think, or argue, rationally or rationalistically: to employ reason, rationalism, or rationalisation.—*ns.* **rat′ionalism**, a system of belief regulated by reason, not emotion: a disposition to apply to religious doctrines the same critical methods as to science and history, and to attribute all phenomena to natural rather than miraculous causes; **rat′ionalist**.—*adj.* **rationalist′ic**.—*adv.* **rationalist′ically**.—*n.* **rationality** (*rash-ən-al′i-ti*), quality of being rational: the possession or due exercise of reason: reasonableness.—*adv.* **rat′ionally**.—**rational horizon** (see **horizon**); **rational number**, a number expressed as the ratio of two integers. [L. *ratiōnālis*, -*e*—*ratiō*.]

**rational**, *rash′ən-əl*, *n.* the Jewish high-priest's breastplate: a bishop's vestment like the pallium. [L. *ratiōnāle*, Vulgate translation of Gr. *logion*, oracle.]

**ratite**, *rat′īt*, *adj.* having a keel-less breastbone: of the **Ratitae** (*rä-ti′tē*), flightless birds—ostrich, rhea, emu, kiwi, etc. [L. *ratis*, raft.]

**ratlin**, **rattlin**, **-line**, **-ling**, *rat′lin*, *n.* one of the small lines forming steps of the rigging of ships. [Origin obscure.]

**ratoon**, *rat-*, *rət-ōōn′*, *n.* a new shoot from the

ground after cropping, esp. of sugar-cane or cotton.—*v.i.* to send up ratoons.—*v.t.* to cut down so as to obtain ratoons.—*n.* ratoon′er, a plant that ratoons. [Sp. *retoño*, shoot.]

rat-rhyme, *rat′rim*, (*Scot.*) *n.* a bit of doggerel: a screed.

rattan, ratan, *ra-tan′*, *n.* a climbing palm (*Calamus* or other) with very long thin stem: a cane made of it. [Malay *rōtan*.]

rattan, *rə-tan′*, *n.* the continuous beat of a drum.

rat-tat, *rat′-tat′*, *n.* a knocking sound. [Imit.]

ratteen. Same as ratine.

ratten, *rat′n*, *v.t.* to practise sabotage against (workman, employer).—*n.* ratt′ening (found earlier than verb). [Origin uncertain.]

ratter, ratting, etc. See rat (1).

rattle, *rat′l*, *v.i.* to make a quick succession or alternation of short hard sounds: to move along rapidly with a rattle: to chatter briskly and emptily.—*v.t.* to cause to rattle: to assail with rattling (*Shak.*): to utter glibly, as by rote: to perform or push through to completion in a rapid, perfunctory, or noisy manner: to scold loudly (*obs.*): to fluster, disconcert, irritate (*slang*).—*n.* an instrument or toy for rattling: an instrument for making a whirring noise, formerly used by watchmen: a similar device used at merrymaking or other gatherings: a dice-box (*old slang*): a plant whose seeds rattle in the capsule—applied to two scrophulaceous plants, *yellow-rattle* or cock's-comb (*Rhinanthus crista-galli*) and *red-rattle* or marsh lousewort (*Pedicularis palustris*): the rings of a rattle-snake's tail: a vivacious prattler: the sound of rattling: the crackling of paper: a sound in the throat of a dying person: racket.—*ns.* ratt′ler, a rattle: a coach (*old slang*): a rattlesnake (*coll.*): a telling blow (*coll.*): an excellent specimen of the kind (*coll.*); ratt′ling.—*adj.* making a rattle: smart, lively: strikingly good (*coll.*).—Also *adv.*—ratt′lebag, a rattle or rattling apparatus: one who causes commotion (*Scot.*); ratt′le-brain, -head, -pate, a shallow, voluble, volatile person.—*adjs.* ratt′le-brained, -headed, -pated.—ratt′lesnake, a venomous American pit-viper (Crotalus) with rattling horny rings on the tail; ratt′le-trap, a contemptuous name for any apparatus, equipment, finery, bric-à-brac: a rickety vehicle: the mouth (*slang*). [M.E. *ratelen*; cf. Ger. *rasseln*, Du. *ratelen*, to rattle; connection with O.E. plant names *hratele*, *hrætelwyrt* is questioned.]

rattlin, rattling. Same as ratlin.

ratton, *rat′n*, (now *Northern*) *n.* a rat. [Fr. *raton*.]

ratty. See rat (1).

raucle, *rök′l*, (*Scot.*) *adj.* rough: vigorous: hale.

raucous, *rö′kəs*, *adj.* hoarse, harsh.—*adv.* rau′-cously.—*n.* rau′cousness.—*adj.* raucid (*rö′sid*; *Lamb*), raucous. [L. *raucus*, hoarse.]

raught, *röt*, obs. *pa.t.* and *pa.p.* of reach (1 and 2) and reck.

raun (*Scott*). Same as rawn.

raunch, *rönsh*, (*Spens.*) *v.t.* Same as race (6).

raunge, *rönj*, an obs. form of range.

Rauwolfia, *rö-wol′fi-ə*, *n.* a tropical genus of apocynaceous trees and shrubs, of which *R. serpentina* and other species yield valuable drugs. [After the German botanist Leonhard *Rauwolf* (died *c.* 1600).]

ravage, *rav′ij*, *v.t.* and *v.i.* to lay waste: to destroy: to pillage.—*n.* devastation: ruin.—*n.* rav′ager. [Fr. *ravager*—*ravir*, to carry off by force—L. *rapēre*.]

rave, *rāv*, *v.i.* to rage: to talk as if mad, delirious, or enraptured.—*v.t.* to utter wildly.—*n.* in-fatuation (*slang*): extravagant praise (*slang*).—*adj.* (*slang*) extravagantly enthusiastic: crazy.—*n.* rā′ver.—*n.* and *adj.* rā′ving.—*adv.* rā′-vingly. [Perh. O.Fr. *raver*, which may be—L. *rabēre*, to rave.]

rave, *rāv*, *n.* a side piece of a wagon. [Ety. obscure.]

rave, *rāv*, (*Scot.*) *pa.t.* of rive.

ravel, *rav′l*, *v.t.* to entangle: to disentangle, un-twist, unweave, unravel (usu. with *out*).—*v.i.* to become entangled: to be untwisted or unwoven: to search (with *into*; *obs.*):—*pr.p.* rav′elling; *pa.t.* and *pa.p.* rav′elled.—*n.* a tangle: a broken thread.—*ns.* rav′elling, a ravelled out thread; rav′elment. [App. Du. *ravelen*.]

ravel bread, *rav′l bred*, (*obs.* or *dial.*) *n.* whole-meal bread, intermediate between white and brown.—Also ravelled bread. [Orig. unknown.]

ravelin, *rav′lin*, *n.* a detached work with two em-bankments raised before the counterscarp. [Fr.]

raven, *rā′vn*, *n.* a large glossy black species of crow.—*adj.* black as a raven.—rā′ven('s)-bone, the gristle on the spoon of the brisket, the raven's perquisite in the chase; rā′ven('s)-duck, fine hempen sail-cloth. [O.E. *hræfn*; O.N. *hrafn*.]

raven, *rav′n*, *n.* (same as ravin, *n.*).—*v.t.* to take away by force (*obs.*): to devour hungrily or greedily.—*v.i.* to prey rapaciously: to be intensely hungry: to hunger intensely (*for*): to roam about hungrily after prey.—*adj.* rav′enous, plundering: rapacious: voracious: intensely hungry.—*adv.* rav′enously.—*n.* rav′enousness. [O.Fr. *ravine*, plunder—L. *rapina*, plunder.]

raven. See ravin.

ravin, also raven, ravine, *rav′in*, *n.* rapine: prey-ing: prey (*Spens.*, *Milt.*).—*adj.* (*Shak.*) ravening.—*v.t.* and *v.i.* same as raven, *vb.*—*adj.* rav′in'd (*Shak.*), prob. sated, gorged. [Same as fore-going.]

ravine, *rə-vēn′*, *n.* a deep, narrow gorge.—*adj.* ravined′, scored with ravines: trenched. [Fr.,—L. *rapina*, rapine, violence.]

ravine. See ravin.

ravioli, *rav-i-ōl′ē*, *n.* little edible paste cases with savoury filling. [It., *pl.* of *raviòlo*.]

ravish, *rav′ish*, *v.t.* to seize or carry away by violence: to abduct: to snatch away from sight or from the world: to rape: to enrapture.—*n.* rav′isher.—*adj.* rav′ishing, delighting to rapture: transporting.—*adv.* rav′ishingly.—*n.* rav′ish-ment. [Fr. *ravir*, *ravissant*—L. *rapēre*, to seize and carry off.]

raw, *rö*, *adj.* not altered from its natural state: not cooked or dressed: unwrought: not pre-pared or manufactured: not refined: not corrected: not mixed: having the skin abraded or removed (also *fig.*): showing through the skin (*Spens.*): crude: hard, harsh, cruel: un-trained: out of condition (*Spens.*): red and in-flamed: immature: inexperienced: chilly and damp: naked.—*n.* a skinned, sore, or sensitive place: the raw state: that which is raw.—*adj.* raw′ish.—*adv.* raw′ly.—*n.* raw′ness.—*adjs.* raw′-bone (*Spens.*), raw′boned, with little flesh on the bones: gaunt.—raw′head (-and-bloody-bones), a bugbear or pair of bugbears to frighten children.—*adj.* raw′hide, of untanned leather.—*n.* a rope or whip of untanned leather.—raw material, material (often in its natural state) that serves as the starting-point of a manufacturing or tech-nical process: that out of which something is made, or makable, or may develop (*fig.*).—a raw deal, harsh, inequitable treatment. [O.E. *hrēaw*; Du. *rauw*, O.N. *hrār*, Ger. *roh*.]

rawn, raun, *rön*, (*Scot.*) *n.* fish-roe: a female fish. [Cf. Dan. *ravn*, roe.]

rax, raks, (*Scot.*) *v.t.* to stretch: to strain: to reach: to reach out, hand.—*v.i.* to stretch: to reach out.—*n.* a stretch: a strain. [O.E. *raxan*.]

ray, *rā*, *n.* array (*obs.*).—*v.t.* to array (*obs.*): to dress (*obs.*): to defile, dirty (*Shak.*). [array.]

ray, *rā*, *n.* a line along which light or other energy, or a stream of particles, is propagated: a narrow beam: a gleam of intellectual light: a look or glance: a radiating line or part: the radially extended fringing outer part of an inflorescence: a supporting spine in a fin.—*v.t.* to radiate: to furnish with rays.—*v.i.* to radiate.—*adjs.* rayed; **ray'less.**—ray'-fungus, a bacterium (*Actinomyces*) that forms radiating threads, some species pathogenic. [O.Fr. *rais* (accus. *rai*)—L. *radius*, a rod.]

**ray,** *rā, n.* a skate, thornback, torpedo, or kindred flat-bodied elasmobranch fish. [Fr. *raie*—L. *raia.*]

**ray.** Same as re (1).

**rayah,** *ri'a, n.* a non-Mohammedan subject of Turkey. [Ar. *ra'iyah*—*ra'ā*, to pasture.]

**rayle, rayne,** old spellings of rail, rain, reign.

**rayon,** *rā'ən, n.* a ray (*Spens.*): artificial silk (see silk). [Fr. *rayon*, ray.]

**raze,** *rāz,* (*Shak.*) *n.* Same as race (3).

**raze,** *rāz, v.t.* to graze: to scrap: to erase: to slash, cut into ornamental devices: to lay level with the ground.—*adj.* razed. [Fr. *raser*—L. *rādēre, rāsum,* to scrape.]

**razee,** *rā-zē', n.* a ship cut down by reducing the number of decks. [Fr. *rasé,* cut down.]

**razor,** *rā'zər, n.* a keen-edged implement for shaving.—*adj.* rā'zorable (*Shak.*), fit to be shaved.—rā'zor-back, a sharp ridge: a rorqual: a sharp-backed pig.—*adj.* sharply ridged.— rā'zor-bill, a species of auk, with compressed bill; rā'zor-blade; rā'zor-edge, a very fine sharp edge, as that on which a balance swings: a critically balanced situation; rā'zor-fish, -clam, a lamellibranch mollusc (*Solen*), with shell like a razor handle; rā'zor-shell, its shell, or the animal itself; rā'zor-strop.—Occam's razor (see Occamism). [O.Fr. *rasour*; see raze (2).]

**razure.** Same as rasure.

**razz,** *raz, n.* raspberry in slang sense.—*v.t.* and *v.i.* to jeer (at).

**razzia,** *raz'ya, n.* a pillaging incursion. [Fr.,— Algerian Ar. *ghāziah.*]

**razzle-dazzle,** *raz'l-daz'l,* (*slang*) *n.* a rowdy frolic or spree.—Also razz'le. [App. from dazzle.]

**raz(z)mataz(z),** *raz-mə-taz', n.* to-do, hullabaloo.

**re,** *rā,* (*mus.*) *n.* the second note of the scale in solfa notation—also anglicised in spelling as ray. [See Aretinian.]

**re,** *rē,* (*commercial jargon*) *prep.* concerning. [L. *in rē* (abl. of *rēs,* thing), in the matter.]

**re,** *rē, n.* See ruff (2).

**re-,** *rē-, pfx.* again: again and in a different way —used so freely, esp. with verbs, that it is impossible to give a full list. [L.]

**reach,** *rēch, v.t.* to stretch forth, hold out: to hand, pass: to deal, strike: to succeed in touching or getting: to arrive at: to extend to: to attain to: to get at: to take, snatch, seize (*obs.*): to stretch, lengthen out (*obs.*).—*v.i.* to stretch out the hand: to extend: to amount: to attain: to succeed in going or coming:—*pa.t.* and *pa.p.* reached, (*obs.*) raught (*röt*).—*n.* act or power of reaching: extent of stretch: range, scope: artifice (*obs.*): a stretch or portion between defined limits, as of a stream between bends: the distance traversed between tacks (*naut.*): a bay (*obs.*).—*adj.* reach'able.—*n.* reach'er.—*p.adj.* reach'ing.—*adis.* reach'less, unattainable. [O.E. *ræcan* (pa.t. *ræhte, rāhte;* pa.p. *geræht*); Ger. *reichen,* to reach.]

**reach.** Same as retch.

**react,** *rē'akt', v.t.* to act a second, etc., time.

**react,** *ri-akt', v.i.* to return an impulse in the opposite direction: to act in return: to act with mutual effect: to act in resistance: to swing

back in the opposite direction: to respond to a stimulus: to undergo chemical change produced by a reagent: loosely, to act, behave.—*ns.* reac'tance (*elect.*), the component of impedance due to inductance or capacitance; reac'tant (*chem.*), a substance taking part in a reaction; reac'tion, action resisting other action: mutual action: an action or change in an opposite direction: backward tendency from revolution, reform, or progress: response to stimulus: the chemical action of a reagent: a transformation within the nucleus of an atom: acidity or alkalinity: loosely, feeling or thought aroused by, in response to, a statement, situation, person, etc.; reac'tionarism; reac'tionarist.—*adj.* reac'tionary, of or favouring reaction.—*n.* one who attempts to revert to past political conditions. —*n.* and *adj.* reac'tionist, reactionary.—*v.t.* reac'tivate, to restore to an activated state.—*n.* reactivā'tion.—*adj.* reac'tive, of, pertaining to, reaction: readily acted upon or responsive to stimulus: produced by emotional stress.—*adv.* reac'tively.—*ns.* reac'tiveness, reactivity (*rē-ak-tiv'i-ti*); reactor (*ri-ak'tər*), one who or that which undergoes a reaction: a device which introduces reactance into an electric circuit: a container in which a chemical reaction takes place: a nuclear reactor (see nucleus).—reaction-time, the interval between stimulus and reaction. [L.L. *reagĕre, -actum*—*agĕre,* to do.]

**read,** *rēd, v.t.* to advise (*arch.;* see rede): to make out: to interpret: to expound: to make known (*Spens.*): to declare: to name (*Spens.*): to solve: to understand as by interpretation of signs: to collect the meaning of: to go over progressively with silent understanding of symbols or with utterance aloud of words or performance of notes: to accept or offer as that which the writer intended: to learn from written or printed matter: to find recorded: to observe the indication of: to register, indicate: to teach, lecture on: to study: to impute by inference (as to read a meaning into).—*v.i.* to perform the act of reading: to practise much reading: to study: to find mention: to give the reader an impression: to endure the test of reading: to deliver lectures: to have a certain wording: —*pa.t.* and *pa.p.* read (*red*).—*n.* read (*red*), a spell of reading: an opportunity of reading (*Scot.*): counsel, a saying, an interpretation (*Spens.*).—*adj.* read (*red*), versed in books: learned.—*ns.* readabil'ity (*rēd-*), read'ableness. —*adj.* read'able, legible: easy to read: interesting without being of highest quality.—*adv.* read'ably.—*ns.* read'er, one who reads or reads much: one who reads prayers in church: a lecturer, esp. a higher grade of university lecturer: a proof-corrector: one who reads and reports on MSS. for a publisher: a reading-book: a pocket-book (*thieves' cant*); read'ership.—*adj.* read'ing, addicted to reading.—*n.* the action of the verb *read:* perusal: study of books: public or formal recital, esp. of a bill before Parliament: the actual word or words that may be read in a passage of a text: the indication that can be read off from an instrument: matter for reading: lettering: an interpretation: a performer's conception of the meaning, rendering—read'ing-book, a book of exercises in reading; read'ing-boy (*print.; obs.*), a reader's assistant; read'ing-desk, a desk for holding a book or paper while it is read: a lectern; read'ing-lamp, a lamp for reading by; read'ing-room, a room for consultation, study, or investigation of books in a library: a room

| rĕabsorb', *v.t.* | rĕaddress', *v.t.* | rĕadmiss'ion, *n.* |
| rĕabsorp'tion, *n.* | rĕadjust', *v.t.* | rĕadmit', *v.t.* |
| rĕaccus'tom, *v.t.* | rĕadjust'ment, *n.* | rĕadmitt'ance, *n.* |
| rĕacquire', *v.t.* | | |

Neutral vowels in unaccented syllables: el'ə-mənt; for certain sounds in foreign words, see p. viii

with papers, periodicals, etc., resorted to for reading: a proof-readers' room; **read'-out**, output unit of a computer: data from it, printed, or registered on magnetic tape or punched paper tape: data from a radio transmitter.—**first, second,** and **third reading**, the three successive formal readings of a bill before parliament; **read between the lines**, to detect a meaning not expressed; **read off**, to take as a reading from an instrument; **read (oneself) in** (Church of England), to enter into possession of a benefice by reading the Thirty-nine Articles; **read up**, to amass knowledge of by reading. [O.E. *rǣdan*, to discern, read—*rǣd*, counsel.]

**read,** *rĕd, n.* a ruminant's fourth stomach, the abomasum. [O.E. *rēad.*]

**ready,** *red'i, adj.* prepared: dressed, attired (*obs.*): willing: inclined: liable: dexterous: prompt: quick: handy: at hand: immediately available: direct.—*adv.* readily (now only in *compar.* and *superl.*, **read'ier, read'iest**).—*n.* (usu. with *the*) the position of a firearm ready to be fired: **ready money** (*slang*): time of, or for, making ready (*coll.*).—*v.t.* to make (*usu.* oneself) ready.—*adv.* **read'ily.**—*n.* **read'iness.**—*adj.* **read'y-made,** made before sale, not made to order.—*n.* a ready-made article, esp. a garment.—**ready money,** money ready at hand: cash.—*adjs.* **read'y-money,** paying, or for payment, in money on the spot: **read'y-moneyed, -monied,** having, or of the nature of, ready money.—**ready reckoner,** a book of tables giving the value of so many things at so much each, and interest on any sum of money from a day upwards.—*adjs.* **read'y-to-eat'; read'y-to-wear'; read'y-witted.**—**make ready,** to dress, put on one's clothes (*obs.*): to prepare (esp. a forme for printing). [O.E. (*ge*)-*rǣde*; cf. Ger. *bereit.*]

**reaedify.** Same as re-edify.

**reagent,** *rē-ā'jənt, n.* a substance with characteristic reactions, used as a chemical test.—*n.* **reā'gency.** [See react.]

**reak, reik,** *rēk,* (*obs.*) *n.* a prank—usu. in *pl.*

**reaks, rex** (*reks*), sometimes with an allusion to L. *rēx*, king. [Origin obscure.]

**real,** *rē'əl, ri', adj.* actually existing: not counterfeit or assumed: true: genuine: sincere: authentic: pertaining to things fixed, as lands or houses (*law*).—*adv.* (*coll., U.S., Scot.*) really, quite, veritably.—*n.* a real thing: that which is real: a realist.—*adj.* **reali'sable, -z-** (or *rē'*).—*n.* **realisā'tion, -z-** (or *-li-*).—*v.t.* **rē'alise, -ize,** to make real, or as if real: to bring into being or act: to accomplish: to convert into real property or money: to obtain, as a possession: to feel strongly: to comprehend completely: to bring home to one's own experience: to provide a detailed artistic version of music where the composer has (as he often did in the 17th and 18th centuries) left much to be filled in by the performer: to provide the drawings for an animated cartoon.—*n.* **rē'aliser, -z-.**—*adj.* **rē'-alising, -z-.**—*ns.* **rē'alism,** the mediaeval doctrine that general terms stand for real existences—opp. to *nominalism*: the doctrine that in external perception the objects immediately known are real existences: the tendency to look to, to accept, or to represent things as they really are (often in their most ignoble aspect): literalness and precision of detail, with the effect of reality: the taking a practical view in human problems; **rē'alist.**—*adj.* **realist'ic,** pertaining to the realists

or to realism: life-like.—*adv.* **rēalist'ically.**—*n.* **reality** (*ri-al'i-ti,* or *rē-*), the state or fact of being real: that which is real and not imaginary: truth: verity: the fixed permanent nature of real property (*law*).—*adv.* **rē'ally,** in reality: actually: in truth.—*ns.* **rē'alness; rē'altie** (*Milt.*), sincerity, honesty; **rē'altor** (*U.S.*; irregularly formed), an agent for the buying and selling of landed property; **rē'alty** (*law*), land, with houses, trees, minerals, etc., thereon: the ownership of, or property in, lands—also **real estate.**—*adj.* **re'al-estate',** concerned with or dealing in property in land.—**real image** (see image); **real number,** any rational or irrational number; **real presence** (see presence); **real school** (Ger. *realschule, rā-äl'shoō'lə*), a German school teaching modern languages, science, and technical subjects, not classics—highest grade being the **real gymnasium** (Ger. *realgymnasium, rā-äl'gim-nä'zi-ōōm*), opp. to the *gymnasium* proper, or classical school.—**for real** (*slang*), in reality: intended to be carried out or put into effect; **the real Mackay, McCoy,** the genuine article, esp. good whisky (the expression has been variously explained). [L.L. *reālis*—L. *rēs*, a thing.]

**real,** *rē'əl,* (*obs.*) *adj.* royal.—*n.* **re'alty** (*obs.*), royalty.—**real tennis,** royal tennis, or tennis properly so called, not lawn-tennis. [O.Fr.,—L. *rēgālis*, royal.]

**real,** *rā-äl', rē'əl, n.* a quarter of a peseta: a former Spanish coin, one-eighth of a dollar. See also **reis.** [Sp.,—L. *rēgālis*, royal.]

**realgar,** *ri-al'gär, -gər, n.* a bright red monoclinic mineral, arsenic monosulphide. [Mediaeval L.—Ar. *rahj-al-ghār*, powder of the mine or cave.]

**realign,** *rē-ə-līn', v.t.* to align afresh: to group or divide on a new basis.—*n.* **realign'ment.** [Pfx. re-.]

**really,** *rē-ə-li'*, (*obs.*) *v.t.* to rally: (*Spens.* **reallie**) to form anew. [Obs. Fr. *realier = rallier;* see rally.]

**realm,** *relm,* earlier **reame,** *rēm, n.* a kingdom: a domain, province, region.—*adj.* **realm'less.** [O.Fr. *realme*—hypothetical L.L. *rēgālimen*—L. *rēgālis,* royal.]

**realpolitik,** *rā-äl'po-lē-tēk',* (Ger.) practical politics.

**ream,** *rēm, n.* 20 quires: (in *pl.*) a large quantity (*coll.*).—**printer's ream,** 516 sheets of paper. [Ar. *rizmah,* a bundle.]

**ream,** *rēm,* (*Scot.*) *n.* cream: froth.—*v.i.* to cream: to froth: to overflow.—*v.t.* to skim.—*adjs.* **ream'ing** (*Scot.*), foaming: brimming; **ream'y** (*Scot.*). [O.E. *rēam.*]

**ream,** *rēm, v.t.* to enlarge the bore of.—*n.* **ream'er,** a rotating instrument for enlarging, shaping, or finishing a bore.—**ream'ing-bit.** [Apparently O.E. *rȳman,* to open up, to make room—*rūm,* room.]

**reame,** *rēm,* (*Spens.*, etc.) *n.* See realm.

**reanimate,** *rē-an'i-māt, v.t.* to restore to life: to infuse new life or spirit into.—*v.i.* to revive.—*n.* **reanimā'tion.** [Pfx. re-.]

**reanswer,** *rē-än'sər,* (*Shak.*) *v.t.* to be equivalent to. [Pfx. re-.]

**reap,** *rēp, v.t.* to cut down, as grain: to clear by cutting a crop: to derive as an advantage or reward.—*n.* **reap'er,** one who reaps: a reaping-machine.—**reap'ing-hook,** a sickle; **reap'ing-machine,** a machine for cutting grain; **reap'-**

| | | |
|---|---|---|
| **rĕadopt'**, *v.t.* | **rĕaffor'est**, *v.t.* | **rĕ-ally'**, *v.t. and v.i.* |
| **rĕadop'tion**, *n.* | **rĕafforestā'tion**, *n.* | **rĕ-al'ter**, *v.t.* |
| **rĕadvance'**, *n., v.t., v.i.* | **rĕall'ocate**, *v.t.* | **rĕamend'**, *v.t.* |
| **rĕadvise'**, *v.t.i., v.i.* | **rĕallocā'tion**, *n.* | **rĕamend'ment**, *n.* |
| **rĕaffirm'**, *v.t.* | **rĕallot'**, *v.t.* | **rĕannex'**, *v.t.* |
| **rĕaffirmā'tion**, *n.* | **rĕallot'ment**, *n.* | **rĕannexā'tion**, *n.* |

silver, money paid in commutation for service in reaping. [O.E. *rīpan* or *ripan*.]

**rear**, *rēr*, *n*. the back or hindmost part or position, especially of an army or fleet: a position behind: a latrine (*slang*).—*adj*. placed behind: hinder.—*v.t.* (*Bunyan*) to attack in the rear.—*adjs.* **rear'-most**, last of all; **rear'ward**, **rere'ward**, in or toward the rear.—*adv.* backward: at the back.—*n.* (*arch.*) rear: rear-guard (partly from A.Fr. *rerewarde*).—**rear-ad'miral**, an officer next below a vice-admiral—orig. one in command of the rear; **rear'-arch**, **-dorse**, **-dos**, **-dorter** (see rere-); **rear'-guard** (O.Fr. *rereguarde*), the rear of an army: a body of troops protecting it; **rear'-lamp**, **-light**, a light carried at the back of a vehicle; **rear'-rank**; **rear'view-mirror**, a mirror that shows what is behind a vehicle.—**bring up the rear**, to come last (in a procession, etc.). [Aphetic for **arrear**; also partly from O.Fr. *rere* (Fr. *arrière*).]

**rear**, *rēr*, *v.t.* to raise, cause or help to rise: to set up: to originate, to bring into being (*Spens.*): to erect: to build up: to lift up or off: to hold up: to take up: to take away (*Spens.*): to bring up: to breed and foster: to rouse: to stir up: to dislodge from covert.—*v.i.* to rise on the hind-legs.—*n.* **rear'er.**—**rear'horse**, a praying insect (from its attitude). [O.E. *rǣran*, to raise, causative of *rīsan*, to rise.]

**rear**, *rēr*, *adj.* (now *obs.* or *dial.*; see rare (2)) lightly cooked—orig. applied to eggs.—*adjs.* **rear'-boiled**; **rear'-roast'ed.** [O.E. *hrēr*.]

**rear.** Same as rare (3).

**rearmouse.** Same as reremouse.

**reason**, *rē'zn*, *n*. ground, support, or justification of an act or belief: a premise, esp. when placed after its conclusion: a motive or inducement: an underlying explanatory principle: a cause: the mind's power of drawing conclusions and determining right and truth: the exercise of this power: sanity: conformity to what is fairly to be expected or called for: moderation: fair treatment, e.g. satisfaction by a duel, or doing one's fair share in drinking: a remark, a sententious saying (*Shak.*): proportion (*Spens.*).—*v.i.* to exercise the faculty of reason: to deduce inferences from premises: to argue: to debate: to converse (*Shak.*).—*v.t.* to examine or discuss: to debate: to think out: to set forth logically: to bring by reasoning.—*adj.* **rea'sonable**, endowed with reason: rational: acting according to reason: agreeable to reason: just: not excessive: moderate—*adv.* (now *illit.*) reasonably.—*n.* **rea'sonableness.**—*adv.* **rea'sonably.**—*adj.* **rea'soned**, argued out.—*ns.* **rea'soner**; **rea'soning.**—*adj.* **rea'sonless**—**by reason of**, on account of: in consequence of; **do one reason** (*obs.*), to give one the satisfaction of a duel: to drink without shirking; **no reason but** (*Shak.*), no reason for it being otherwise, hence, no possible alternative; **principle of sufficient reason**, that nothing happens without a sufficient reason why it should be as it is and not otherwise; **pure reason**, reason absolutely independent of

experience. [Fr. *raison*—L. *ratiō*, *-ōnis*—*rēri*, *rătus*, to think.]

**reassure**, *rē-ə-shōōr'*, *v.t.* to assure anew: to re-insure: to give confidence to: to confirm.—*ns.* **reassur'ance**; **reassur'er.**—*adj.* **reassur'ing.**—*adv.* **reassur'ingly.** [Pfx. re-.]

**reast, reest, reist,** *rēst*, *v.i.* to become rancid (esp. of bacon).—*n.* **reast'iness**, etc.—*adj.* **reast'y**, etc. [ME. *rest*, *reest*, rancid.]

**reast.** Same as reest (2).

**reata, riata**, *rē-ä'tä*, *n*. a lariat. [Sp.]

**reate**, *rēt*, *n*. water-crowfoot. [Origin obscure.]

**Réaumur**, *rā-ō-mür*, *adj.* of a thermometer or thermometer scale, having the freezing-point of water marked 0° and boiling-point 80°. [From the French physicist, R. A. F. de *Réaumur* (1683-1757), who introduced the scale.]

**reave**, also (orig. *Scot.*) **reive**, *v.t.* and *v.i.* to plunder: to rob:—*pa.t.* and *pa.p.* **reft** (*obs.* raft).—*n.* **reav'er, reiv'er.** [O.E. *rēafian*, to rob; cf. Ger. *rauben*, to rob.]

**reback**, *rē-bak'*, *v.t.* to put a new back on. [Pfx. re-.]

**rebarbative**, *ri-bärb'ə-tiv*, *adj.* repellent. [Fr. *rébarbatif*—*barbe*, beard.]

**rebate**, *ri-bāt'*, *v.t.* to reduce: to abate: to dull: to blunt: to diminish by removal of a projection (*her.*).—*n.* (or *rē'*) discount: repayment or drawback—*n.* **rebate'ment**, abatement: reduction: discount: a narrowing (*B.*). [Fr. *rabattre*, to beat back—pfx. re- and *abattre*, to abate.]

**rebate**, *rab'it*. Same as rabbet.

**rebato**, *rə-bä'tō*, (*Shak.*) *n*. a stiff collar or support for a ruff.—Also **reba'ter, raba'to.** [Fr. *rabat*.]

**Rebecca**, *ri-bek'ə*, *n*. a leader of those who demolished toll-gates in the **Rebecca** riots in Wales from 1843.—*ns.* **Rebecc'aism**; **Rebecc'aite.** [In allusion to Gen. xxiv. 60.]

**rebecca-eureka**, *ri-bek'ə-ū-rē'kə*, *n*. a secondary-radar system in which the interrogating installation is in an aircraft and the fixed beacon responder on the ground.

**rebeck, rebec**, *rē'bek*, *n*. a mediaeval instrument of the viol class shaped like a mandoline. [O.Fr. *rebec*—Ar. *rebāb*, *rabāb* (change of ending unexplained); other forms occur in European languages, including, in M.E., *ribibe*, *ribible*.]

**rebel**, *reb'(ə)l*, *n*. one who rebels: one who resents and resists authority or grievous conditions.—*adj.* rebellious.—*v.i.* (*ri-bel'*) to renounce the authority of the laws and government, or to take up arms and openly oppose them: to oppose any authority: to revolt: to offer opposition: to feel repugnance:—*pr.p.* **rebell'ing**; *pa.t.* and *pa.p.* **rebelled'.**—*pr.p.* **reb'eldom**; **rebell'er** (now *rare*)—*adv.* **reb'el-like** (*Shak.*).—*n.* **rebell'ion** (*-yən*), act of rebelling: revolt.—*adj.* **rebell'ious**, engaged in rebellion: characteristic of a rebel or rebellion: inclined to rebel: refractory.—*adv.* **rebell'iously.**—*n.* **rebell'iousness.** [Fr. *rebelle*—L. *rebellis*, insurgent—pfx. re-, *bellum*, war.]

**rebellow**, *rē-bel'ō*, (*Spens.*) *v.i.* to bellow in return: to echo back a loud noise. [Pfx. re-].

---

---

Neutral vowels in unaccented syllables: *el'ə-mənt*; for certain sounds in foreign words, see p. viii

**rebid**, *rē-bid'*, *v.t.* and *v.i.* to bid again, esp. (*bridge*) on the same suit as a previous bid.—*n.* a renewed bid, esp. on one's former suit. [Pfx. re-.]

**rebirth**, *rē-bûrth'*, *n.* reincarnation: revival of, e.g. an interest: spiritual renewal. [Pfx. re-.]

**rebite**, *rē-bīt'*, *v.t.* to freshen (a plate) by a new application of acid. [Pfx. re-.]

**reboant**, *reb'ō-ənt*, *adj.* rebellowing: loudly resounding.—*n.* **reboā'tion**. [L. *reboāns*, *-antis*, pr.p. of *reboāre*—*re*, again, *boāre*, to cry aloud.]

**rebore**, *rē'bōr'*, *-bōr'*, *v.t.* to bore again (the cylinder of a car engine) so as to clear it.—Also *n.* [Pfx. re-.]

**reborn**, *rē-börn'*, *p.adj.* born again (*q.v.*).

**rebound**, *rē'bownd'*, *p.adj.* given a new binding. [Pfx. re-, bound (1).]

**rebound**, *ri-bownd'*, *v.i.* to bound back from collision: to spring back (*lit.* and *fig.*): to re-echo: to recover quickly after a setback.—*v.t.* to throw back: to re-echo.—*n.* (*rē'*) act of rebounding.—**on the rebound**, after bouncing: while reacting against a setback, disappointment, etc. [Fr. *rebondir*; see bound (3).]

**rebuff**, *ri-buf'*, *n.* a blowing back (*Milt.*): a sudden check: unexpected refusal: snub.—*v.t.* to blow back: to check: to repulse: to snub. [O.Fr. *rebuffe*—It. *ribuffo*, a reproof—It. *ri-* (=L. *re-*), back, *buffo*, puff.]

**rebuke**, *ri-būk'*, *v.t.* to check, restrain, beat back (*obs.*): to put to shame (*arch.*): to reprove sternly.—*n.* a check (*obs.*): a putting to shame (*obs.*): a reproach: stern reproof, reprimand.—*adjs.* **rebūk'able**; **rebūke'ful.**—*adv.* **rebūke'fully.**—*n.* **rebūk'er.**—*adv.* **rebūk'ingly.** [A.Fr. *rebuker* (O.Fr. *rebucher*)—pfx. re-, *bucher*, to strike.]

**rebus**, *rē'bəs*, *n.* an enigmatical representation of a name by pictures punningly representing parts of the word, as in a puzzle or a coat of arms:—*pl.* **re'buses.** [L. *rēbus*, by things, abl. pl. of *rēs*, thing.]

**rebut**, *ri-but'*, *v.t.* to drive back: to repel: to meet in argument or proof: to refute.—*v.i.* to recoil (*Spens.*): to return an answer (*law*):—*pr.p.* **rebutt'ing**; *pa.t.* and *pa.p.* **rebutt'ed.**—*adj.* **rebutt'able.**—*ns.* **rebutt'al**; **rebutt'er.** [O. Fr. *reboter*, *rebouter*, *rebuter*, to repulse; see butt.]

**recalcitrate**, *ri-kal'si-trāt*, *v.t.* and *v.i.* to kick back. —*v.i.* to have repugnance: to be refractory.—*n.* **recal'citrance**, repugnance or opposition: refractoriness.—*adj.* **recal'citrant**, refractory: obstinate in opposition.—*n.* a recalcitrant person. —*n.* **recalcitrā'tion.** [L. *recalcitrāre*, to kick back—*calx*, *calcis*, the heel.]

**recalesce**, *rē-kal-es'*, *v.t.* to show anew a state of glowing heat.—*n.* **recales'cence** (*phys.*), the renewed glowing of iron at a certain stage of cooling from white-heat. [L. *re-*, again, *calēscēre*, to grow hot.]

**recall** (rarely recal), *ri-köl'*, *v.t.* to call back: to command to return: to bring back as by a summons: to remove from office: to revoke: to call back to mind.—*n.* act, power, or possibility of recalling or of revoking: a signal or order to return: the calling back of a performer to the stage or platform by applause: a right of electors to dismiss an official by a vote: remembrance of things learned or experienced, esp. in the phrase **total recall**, (power of) remembering accurately in full detail.—*adj.* **recall'able**, capable of being recalled.—*n.* **recal(l)'ment.** [Pfx. re-.]

**recant**, *ri-kant'*, *v.t.* to retract.—*v.i.* to revoke a former declaration: to unsay what has been said, esp. to declare one's renunciation of one's former religious belief.—*ns.* **recantā'tion** (*rē-*);

**recant'er** (*ri-*). [L. *recantāre*, to revoke—*cantāre*, to sing, to charm.]

**recap**, *rē-kap'*. Short for **recapitulate** and **recapitulation.**

**recapitulate**, *rē-kə-pit'ū-lāt*, *v.t.* to go over again the chief points of: to go through again each life-history the stages of.—*n.* **recapitulā'tion**, act of recapitulating: summing up: the final repetition of the subjects in sonata form after development.—*adjs.* **recapit'ūlātive**; **recapit'ūlatory**, repeating again: of the nature of a recapitulation. [L. *recapitulāre*, *-atum*—*re-*, again, *capitulum*, heading, chapter—*caput*, head.]

**recaption**, *rē-kap'shən*, *n.* reprisal: taking back by peaceable means of goods, wife, or children from one who has no right to detain them (*law*). [Pfx. re-.]

**recapture**, *rē-kap'chər*, *v.t.* to capture back, as a prize from a captor: to recover by effort.—*n.* act of retaking: recovery: a thing recaptured. —*ns.* **recap'tor**; **recap'turer.** [Pfx. re-.]

**recast**, *rē-käst'*, *v.t.* to cast or mould anew: to reconstruct: to compute anew:—*pa.t.* and *pa.p.* **recast'.**—*n.* (*rē'käst*, *rē-käst'*) shaping anew: that which has been shaped anew. [Pfx. re-.]

**recce**, *rek'i*, (*mil.*) *n.* reconnaissance.

**recede**, *ri-sēd'*, *v.i.* to go back, go farther off, become more distant (*lit.* and *fig.*): to go, draw, back (from; *lit.* and *fig.*): to differ (from; *arch.*): to grow less, decline: to bend or slope backward: to give up a claim, renounce a promise, etc.—*adj.* **reced'ing.** [L. *recēdēre*, *recēssum*—*re-*, back, *cēdēre*, to go, yield.]

**re-cede**, **recede**, *rē'sēd'*, *v.t.* to cede again or back. [Pfx. re-.]

**receipt**, *ri-sēt'*, *n.* receiving: place of receiving: capacity (*obs.*): a written acknowledgment of anything received: that which is received: a recipe, esp. in cookery: anything prepared after a recipe (*obs.*).—*v.t.* to mark as paid. [O.Fr. *receite*, *recete* (Fr. *recette*)—L. *recepta*, fem. pa.p. of *recipĕre*, to receive, with *p* restored after L.]

**receive**, *ri-sēv'*, *v.t.* to take, get, or catch, usu. more or less passively: to have given or delivered to one: to experience: to take in or on: to admit: to accept: to meet or welcome on entrance: to harbour: to await in resistance: to experience, or learn of, and react towards: to accept as authority or as truth: to take into the body: to reset: to be acted upon by, and transform, electrical signals.—*v.i.* to be a recipient: to participate in communion: to receive signals: to hold a reception of visitors.—*ns.* **receivabil'ity**, **receiv'ableness.**—*adj.* **receiv'able.** —*n.* **receiv'al** (*rare*).—*adj.* **received'**, generally accepted.—*ns.* **receiv'er**, one who receives: an officer who receives taxes: a person appointed by a court to manage property under litigation, receive money, etc.: one who receives stolen goods: a vessel for receiving the products of distillation, or for containing gases (*chem.*): the glass vessel of an air-pump in which the vacuum is formed: an instrument by which electrical signals are transformed into audible or visual form, as a telephone receiver: a receiving-set; **receiv'ership.**—*n.* and *adj.* **receiv'ing.**—**Received (Standard) English**, the English of the public schools and of those in what is called society; **Received Pronunciation**, pronunciation of this; **receiv'er-gen'eral**, an officer who receives revenues; **receiv'ing-house**, a depot: a house where letters, etc., are left for transmission; **receiv'ing-office**, a branch post-office for receipt of letters, etc.; **receiv'ing-order**, an order putting a receiver in temporary possession of a debtor's

---

estate, pending bankruptcy proceedings; **receiv'-ing-room**, a room where patients, inmates, etc., are received; **receiv'ing-set**, apparatus for receiving wireless communications; **receiv'ing-ship'**, a stationary ship for naval recruits. [A.Fr. *receivre* (Fr. *recevoir*)—L. *recipĕre*, *receptum*—*re-*, back, *capĕre*, to take.]

**recense**, *ri-sens'*, *v.t.* to revise critically.—*n.* **recen'sion**, a critical revision of a text: a text established by critical revision: a review. [L. *recēnsiō, -ōnis—re-*, again, and *cēnsēre*, to value, to assess.]

**recent**, *rē'sənt*, *adj.* of late origin or occurrence: fresh: modern: (*cap.*) of the present geological period—Post-Glacial.—*n.* **rē'cency.**—*adv.* **rē'-cently.**—*n.* **rē'centness.** [L. *recēns, recentis.*]

**recept**, *rē'sept*, *n.* an image or idea formed by repeated similar perceptions.—*n.* **receptacle** (*ri-sep'tə-kl*; also, as *Shak.*, *res'ip-tə-kl*), that in which anything is or may be received or stored: the enlarged end of an axis bearing the parts of a flower or the crowded flowers of an inflorescence: in flowerless plants a structure bearing reproductive organs, spores, or gemmae.—*adj.* **receptacular** (*res-ip-tak'ū-lər*).—*n.* **receptac'ulum**, a receptacle:—*pl.* **receptac'ula.**—*n.* **receptibil'ity** (*ri-*).—*adj.* **recept'ible**, capable of receiving.—*ns.* **reception** (*ri-sep'shən*), the act, fact, or manner of receiving or of being received: taking in: act or manner of taking up signals: a formal receiving, as of guests: treatment on coming: capacity for receiving (*Milt.*); **recep'tionist**, one employed to receive callers, hotel-guests, patients, customers, or the like, and make arrangements.—*adj.* **recep'tive**, capable of receiving: quick to receive or take in resp. (*fig.*) ideas: pertaining to reception or receptors.—*ns.* **recep'tiveness, receptivity** (*res-ep-tiv'i-ti*); **recep'tor**, a receiver: an organ adapted for reception of stimuli.—**recep'tion-order**, an order for the reception and detention of a person in a mental hospital; **recep'tion-room**, a room for formal receptions: any public room in a house. [L. *recipĕre, receptum*, to receive.]

**recess**, *rē-ses'*, *n.* a going back or withdrawing: retirement: seclusion: remission of business: part of a room formed by a receding of the wall: a niche or alcove: an indentation: a retired spot: a nook: a sinus or depression.—*v.t.* to make a recess in: to put into a recess.—*v.i.* to adjourn.—*adj.* **recessed'.**—*ns.* **recession** (*ri-sesh'-ən*), act of receding: withdrawal: the state of being set back: a slight temporary decline in trade; **recessional** (*ri-sesh'ən-əl*), hymn sung during recession or retirement of clergy and choir after a service.—*adjs.* **recess'ional; recessive** (*-ses'*), tending to recede: of an ancestral character, apparently suppressed in cross-bred offspring in favour of the alternative character in the other parent, though it may be transmitted to later generations (*Mendelīsm*): of accent, tending to move toward the beginning of the word.—*adv.* **recess'ively.**—*n.* **recess'iveness.**—**recessed arch**, one arch within another. [See **recede.**]

**recession**, *rē'sesh'ən*, *n.* a ceding again or back. [Pfx. **re-.**]

**Rechabite**, *rek'ə-bīt*, *n.* a descendant of Jonadab, son of *Rechab*, who did not drink wine or dwell in houses (Jer. xxxv. 6-7): a total abstainer from intoxicating drinks, esp. a member of the order so named: a tent-dweller.—*n.* **Rech'abitism.**

**réchauffé**, *rā-shō'fā*, *n.* a warmed-up dish: a fresh concoction of old material. [Fr.]

**recheat**, *ri-chēt'*, **rechate**, *ri-chāt'*, (*Shak.*) *n.* a horn-call to assemble hounds.—*v.i.* to sound the recheat. [O.Fr. *racheter, rachater*, to re-assemble.]

**recherché**, *rə-sher'shā*, *adj.* carefully chosen: particularly choice: rare or exotic. [Fr.]

**rechlesse**, *rech'lis*, (*Spens.*) *adj.* Same as **reckless.**

**recidivism**, *ri-sid'i-vizm*, *n.* the habit of relapsing into crime.—*n.* **recid'ivist.** [Fr. *récidivisme*—L. *recidivus*, falling back.]

**recipe**, *res'i-pi*, *n.* directions for making something, esp. a food or drink: a prescription: a method laid down for achieving a desired end:—*pl.* **rec'ipes.** [L. *recipe*, take, imper. of *recipĕre*.]

**recipient**, *ri-sip'i-ənt*, *adj.* receiving: receptive.—*n.* one who or that which receives.—*ns.* **recip'-ience, recip'iency**, a reception: receptivity. [L. *recipiēns, -entis*, pr.p. of *recipĕre*, to receive.]

**reciprocal**, *ri-sip'rō-kl*, *adj.* acting in return: mutual: complementary: inverse: alternating: interchangeable: giving and receiving or given and received: expressing mutuality (*gram.*): reflexive.—*n.* that which is reciprocal: the multiplier that gives unity (*math.*).—*n.* **reciprocality** (*-kal'i-ti*).—*adv.* **recip'rocally.**—*n.* **recip'rocant**, a differential invariant.—*v.t.* **recip'rocāte**, to give and receive mutually: to requite: to interchange: to alternate.—*v.i.* to move backward and forward: to make a return or interchange (*coll.*).—*n.* **reciproca'tion.**—*adj.* **recip'rocātive**, characterised by or inclined to reciprocation.—*ns.* **recip'rocātor**, one who or that which reciprocates: a double-acting steam-engine; **reciprocity** (*res-i-pros'i-ti*), mutual relation: concession of mutual privileges or advantages, esp. mutual tariff concessions.—**recip'rocating-en'gine**, an engine in which the piston moves to and fro in a straight line. [L. *reciprocus.*]

**recision**, *ri-sizh'ən*, *n.* cutting back (*obs.*): rescinding. [L. *recisiō, -ōnis—recidĕre*, to cut off.]

**recite**, *ri-sīt'*, *v.t.* to repeat from memory: to declaim: to read aloud (*rare*): to narrate: to give (the details of): to repeat to a teacher, be heard a lesson in (*U.S.*).—*v.i.* to give a recitation: to repeat, or be heard, a lesson (*U.S.*).—*ns.* **reci'tal**, act of reciting: setting forth: enumeration: narration: a public performance of music, usu. by one performer, or one composer, or of some particular character: that part of a deed which recites the circumstances (*law*); **recitation** (*res-i-tā'shən*), act of reciting: a piece for declaiming: the repeating or hearing of a prepared lesson (*U.S.*): hence a lesson generally (*U.S.*); **recitā'tionist**, a declaimer; **recitative** (*-tə-tēv'*) or (*It.*) **recitativo** (*re-sit-ä-tē'vō* or *rä-chē-tä-tē'vō*), a style of song resembling speech in its succession of tones and freedom from melodic form: a passage to be sung in this manner.—*adj.* in the style of recitative.—*n.* **reciter** (*ri-sīt'ər*).—**recitā'-tion-room** (*U.S.*), a classroom; **recit'ing-note**, the note on which, in a Gregorian chant, the greater part of a verse is sung. [L. *recitāre—citāre, -ātum*, to call.]

**reck**, *rek*, (usu. with a negative) *v.t.* to care, desire (with *infin.*; *arch.*): to care about, heed: (used *impers.*) to concern.—*v.i.* (usu. with *of*) to care, concern oneself: (used *impers.*) to matter: —*pa.t.* and *pa.p.* **recked**, *obs.* or *arch.* **raught, röt.**—*n.* care: heed.—*adj.* **reck'less**, careless: heedless of consequences: rash.—*adv.* **reck'lessly.**—*n.* **reck'lessness.**—**what reck?** (*Scot.*), what does it matter? [O.E. *reccan, rēcan*; cf. O.H.G. *ruoh*, care, Ger. *ruchlos*, regardless.]

**reckan**, *rek'ən*, (*Scott*, ostensibly Cumberland dial.) *adj.* or *pa.p.* perh. **racked** or **ricked.**

**reckling**, *rek'ling*, *n.* the weakest, smallest, or youngest of a litter or family.—*adj.* puny. [Origin obscure.]

**reckon**, *rek'n*, *-ən*, *v.t.* to enumerate (*arch.*): to count: to calculate (often with *up*): to include (in an account): to place or class: to estimate, judge to be: to think, believe, suppose, or expect: to attribute (to; *arch.*).—*v.i.* to calculate: to judge: to go over or settle accounts (with): to concern oneself (with): to count or rely (on, upon).—*ns.* reck'oner; reck'oning, counting: calculation, esp. of a ship's position: a tavern bill: settlement of accounts: judgment. [O.E. *gerecenian*, to explain; Ger. *rechnen*.]

**reclaim**, ri-klām', *v.t.* orig. to call back (as a hawk): to win back: to win from evil, wildness, waste, submersion: (*rē-klām'*) to claim back.— *v.i.* (*ri-klām'*) to exclaim in protest: to appeal (*Scots law*).—*n.* recall: possibility of reform.— *adj.* reclaim'able.—*adv.* reclaim'ably. [O.Fr. *reclamer*—L. *reclāmāre*.]

**reclamation**, rek-lə-mā'shən, *n.* act of reclaiming: state of being reclaimed. [L. *reclāmātiō*, *-ōnis*—*reclāmāre*—*clāmāre*, to cry out.]

**réclame**, rā-kläm', *n.* art or practice by which publicity or notoriety is secured: publicity. [Fr.]

**recline**, ri-klīn', *v.t.* to lay on the back: to incline or bend (properly backwards).—*v.i.* to lean in a recumbent position, on back or side: (of the plane of a sundial) to make an angle with the vertical: to rely (on, upon).—*adj.* or *adv.* (*Milt.*) recumbent.—*adj.* **reclinate** (*rek'li-nāt*), bent down or back.—*n.* reclinā'tion (*rek-li-*), reclining: bending back: angle of a dial with the vertical. —*adj.* reclined', recumbent: reclinate.—*n.* recli'ner.—*adj.* recli'ning. [L. *reclīnāre*, *-ātum*—*clīnāre*, to bend.]

**recluse**, ri-klōōs', *adj.* enclosed, as an anchorite: secluded: retired: solitary.—*n.* a religious devotee who lives shut up in a cell: one who lives retired from the world.—*adv.* recluse'ly.—*ns.* recluse'ness, seclusion from society: retirement; **reclusion** (*-klōō'zhən*), religious seclusion: the life of a recluse: seclusion in prison.—*adj.* reclu'sive (*-siv*), of seclusion.—*n.* reclu'sory, a recluse's cell. [L. *reclūsus*, pa.p. of *reclūdĕre*, to open, in later Latin, shut away—*re-*, back, away, *claudĕre*.]

**recognise**, **-ize**, rek'əg-nīz, *v.t.* to know again: to identify as known or experienced before: to show sign of knowing (a person): to see, acknowledge, the fact of: to acknowledge (that): to acknowledge the validity of (a claim): to acknowledge the status or legality of (e.g. a government): to reward (meritorious conduct).— *adj.* recognis'able, **-z-** (or *rek'*).—*adv.* recognis'ably, **-z-** (or *rek'*).—*ns.* recognisance, **-z-** (*ri-kog'ni-zəns*), a recognition: acknowledgment: a token (*arch.*): (*ri-kon'i-zəns*) a legal obligation entered into before a magistrate to do, or not to do, some particular act: money pledged for the performance of such an obligation; recogniser, **-z-** (*rek'əg-nīz-ər*, or *-nīz'ər*); recognition (*rek-əg-nish'ən*), act of recognising: state of being recognised: acknowledgment: acknowledgment of status: a sign, token, or indication of recognising: a return of the feu to the superior (*Scots law*).—*adjs.* recognitive (*ri-kog'*), recog'-nitory. [L. *recognōscĕre* and O.Fr. *reconoistre*, *reconoiss-*; see cognosce, cognition.]

**recoil**, ri-koil' (*Spens.* recoyle, recule, recuile), *v.t.* (*obs.*) to force back.—*v.i.* to retreat, fall back (*arch.*): to revert (*obs.*): to start back: to stagger back: to shrink in horror, etc.: to rebound: to kick, as a gun: to degenerate (*Shak.*).—*n.* retreat (*arch.*): a starting or springing back:

rebound: the kick of a gun: change in motion of a particle caused by ejection of another particle, or (*sometimes*) by a collision (*nucleonics*).—*n.* recoil'er.—**recoil escapement** (same as **anchor escapement**). [Fr. *reculer*—*cul*—L. *cūlus*, the hinder parts.]

**recollect**, rek-əl-ekt', *v.t.* to recall to memory: to remember, esp. by an effort: to absorb in mystical contemplation: to recall to the matter in hand, or to composure or resolution (usu. *refl.*).—*n.* (*rek'*) a Franciscan friar of a reformed branch, aiming at detachment from creatures and recollection in God.—Also (Fr.) **récollet** (*rā-kol-ā*).—*adj.* recollect'ed.—*adv.* recollect'edly. —*ns.* recollect'edness; recollec'tion (*rek-*), act or power of recollecting: a memory, reminiscence: a thing remembered: mystical contemplation.—*adj.* recollec'tive.—**recollected terms** (*Shak.*), variously explained as known by heart, picked, studied, wanting spontaneity. [L. *recolligĕre*, to gather again or gather up—*colligĕre*; see **collect**.]

**recollect**, **re-collect**, rē'kol-ekt', *v.t.* to collect (*obs.*): to gather together again: to summon up: to bring back again (*Milt.*). [Partly recollect (1); partly pfx. re- and collect.]

**recomfort**, ri-kum'fərt, (*arch.*) *v.t.* to comfort: to console: to reinvigorate: to refresh.—*adj.* recom'fortless (*Spens.*), comfortless.—*n.* recom'-forture (*Shak.*), consolation. [Pfx. re-.]

**recommend**, rek-ə-mend', *v.t.* to commend, commit, or consign: to commend or introduce as suitable for acceptance, favour, appointment, or choice: to make acceptable: to advise: to inform (*Shak.*).—*adj.* recommend'able.—*adv.* recommend'ably.—*n.* recommendā'tion.— *adj.* recommend'atory.—*n.* recommend'er. [Pfx. re-.]

**recompense**, rek'əm-pens, *v.t.* to return an equivalent to or for: to repay.—*n.* (formerly recompence) return of an equivalent: that which is so returned: requital. [O.Fr. *recompenser*—L. *compēnsāre*, to compensate.]

**reconcile**, rek'ən-sil, *v.t.* to restore or bring back to friendship or union: to bring to agreement or contentment: to pacify: to make, or to prove consistent: to admit or restore to membership of a church: to adjust or compose: to regain, conciliate (*Spens.*): to reconsecrate (a desecrated holy place).—*n.* rec'oncilability (or *-sil'*).—*adj.* rec'oncilable (or *-sil'*).—*n.* rec'oncilableness (or *-sil'*).—*adv.* rec'oncilably (or *-sil'*).—*ns.* rec'on-cilement (or *-sil'*); rec'onciler; reconcilia'tion (*-sil'*).—*adj.* reconciliatory (*-sil'-ə-tər-i*). [L. *reconciliāre*, *-ātum*—*conciliāre*, to call together.]

**recondite**, ri-kon'dīt, rek'ən-dīt, *adj.* hidden: obscure: abstruse: profound. [L. *recondĕre*, *-itum*, to put away—*re-*, again, *condĕre*, to establish, store.]

**recondition**, rē-kən-dish'ən, *v.t.* to repair and refit: to restore to original or sound condition. [Pfx. re-.]

**reconnaissance**, ri-kon'i-səns, *n.* reconnoitring: a preliminary survey.—**reconnaissance in force**, an attack by a large body to discover the enemy's position and strength. [Fr.]

**reconnoitre**, in U.S. usu. **reconnoiter**, rek-ə-noi'tər, *v.t.* to examine with a view to military operations or other purpose: to remember (*obs.*).—*v.i.* to make preliminary examination.—*n.* a reconnaissance.—*n.* reconnoi'trer. [Fr. *reconnoitre*

| | | |
|---|---|---|
| rēclose', *v.t.* | rēcommiss'ion, *n.*, *v.t.* and *v.i.* | rēconfirm', *v.t.* |
| rēclothe', *v.t.* | rēcommit', *v.t.* | rēcon'quer, *v.t.* |
| rēcoin'age, *n.* | rēcommit'ment, *n.* | rēcon'quest, *n.* |
| rēcolonisā'tion, -z-, *n.* | rēcommitt'al, *n.* | rēcon'secrate, *v.t.* |
| rēcol'onise, -ize, *v.t.* | rēcompact', *v.t.* | rēconsecrā'tion, *n.* |
| rēcombina'tion, *n.* | rēcompose', *v.t.*, *v.t.* | rēconsid'er, *v.t.* |
| rēcombine', *v.t.* and *v.i.* | rēcomposi'tion, *n.* | rēconsiderā'tion, *n.* |
| rēcommence', *v.t.* and *v.i.* | rēcondensā'tion, *n.* | rēconsol'idate, *v.t.*, *v.i.* |
| rēcommence'ment, *n.* | rēcondense', *v.t.* and *v.i.* | rēconsolidā'tion, *n.* |

(now *reconnaitre*)—L. *recognōscĕre*, to recognise.]

**reconstitute**, *rē-kon'sti-tūt*, *v.t.* to constitute anew: to restore the constitution of (esp. dried foods). —*adj.* **reconstit'uent** (*-kən-*).—*n.* **reconstitū'tion**, constituting afresh: refounding: restoration to original condition: theoretical reconstruction on the spot of the details of a crime. [Pfx. **re-**.]

**reconstruct**, *rē-kən-strukt'*, *v.t.* to construct again: to rebuild: to remodel: to restore in imagination or theory.—*n.* **reconstruc'tion**, the act of reconstructing: a thing reconstructed: reorganisation: a model representing a series of sections: a theoretical representation or view of something unknown: the upbuilding of moral and material public well-being after a great upheaval: the process of restoring the Seceding States to the rights and privileges of the Union after the Civil War (*U.S.*).—*adjs.* **reconstruc'-tional; reconstruc'tionary.**—*n.* **reconstruc'tionist.** —*adj.* **reconstruc'tive.**—*n.* **reconstruc'tor.** [Pfx. **re-**.]

**reconvalescence**, *ri-kon-vəl-es'əns*, *n.* recovery from illness. [Pfx. **re-**.]

**reconvert**, *rē-kən-vûrt'*, *v.t.* to convert again to a former state, religion, etc.—*n.* **reconver'sion.** [Pfx. **re-**.]

**reconvey**, *rē-kən-vā'*, *v.t.* to transfer again to a former owner, as an estate.—*n.* **reconvey'ance.** [Pfx. **re-**.]

**record**, *ri-körd'*, *v.t.* to get by heart (*obs.*): to go over in one's mind (*Spens.*): to repeat from memory (*Spens.*): to narrate, set forth (*arch.*): to sing in an undertone, practise quietly (esp. of birds): to call to mind (*arch.*): to set down in writing or other permanent form: to trace a curve or other representation of: to perform before a recording instrument: to make a recording of (music, etc., person speaking, etc.): to mark, indicate: to bear witness to: to register (as a vote or verdict): to celebrate.—*v.i.* to sing, warble, esp. in quiet rehearsal: to make a record.—*n.* **record** (*rek'örd*, formerly *ri-körd'*), a register: a formal writing of any fact or proceeding: a book of such writings: past history: a witness, a memorial: memory, remembrance: anything entered in the rolls of a court, esp. the formal statements or pleadings of parties in a litigation: a curve or other representation of phenomena made by an instrument upon a surface: a disk or cylinder on which sound is registered for reproduction by an instrument such as a gramophone: a performance or occurrence not recorded to have been surpassed. —*adj.* not surpassed.—*adj.* **record'able** (*ri-*), able to be recorded: worthy of record.—*ns.* **recordā'-tion** (in *Shak.*, *rek'*), remembrance: commemoration: recording; **record'er** (*ri-*), one who records or registers, esp. the rolls, etc., of a city: a judge of a city or borough court of quarter-sessions: one who performs before a recording instrument: a recording apparatus: a fipple-flute, once called the 'English flute', much used in the 16th to 18th centuries and again in the 20th century; **record'ership**, the office of recorder, or the time of holding it; **record'ing**, a record of sound or images made, for later reproduction, e.g. on magnetic tape, film, or gramophone disk. —Also *adj.*—*n.* **record'ist**—**recording angel**, an angel supposed to keep a book in which every misdeed is recorded against the doer; **Record Office**, a place where public records are kept; **record player**, a small, portable instrument for playing gramophone records, run on batteries or mains electricity, not spring-driven.—**beat**, or **break, the record**, to outdo the highest achievement yet recorded; **close the record**, an act of a Scottish judge after each party has said all he wishes to say by way of statement and answer; **off the record**, not for publication in the press,

etc.; **on record**, recorded in a document, etc.: publicly known; **public records**, contemporary officially authenticated statements of acts and proceedings in public affairs, preserved in the public interest; **trial by record**, a common law mode of trial when a former decision of the court is disputed and the matter is settled by producing the record. [O.Fr. *recorder*—L. *recordāri*, to call to mind, get by heart—*cor*, *cordis*, the heart.]

**recount**, *ri-kownt'*, *v.t.* to narrate the particulars of: to detail.—*ns.* **recount'al** (*ri-*); **recount'ment** (*Shak.*), relation in detail, recital. [O.Fr. *reconter*—*conter*, to tell.]

**recount**, **re-count**, *rē-kownt'*, to count over again. —*n.* a second or new counting (as of votes). [Pfx. **re-**.]

**recoup**, *ri-kōōp'*, *v.t.* to deduct or keep back (from what is claimed by a counterclaim; *law*): to make good: to indemnify.—*n.* **recoup'ment.** [Fr. *recouper*, to cut back—*couper*, to cut.]

**recoure, recower**, *ri-kowr'*, (*Spens.*) *v.t.* a variant of *recover*. See also *recure*.

**recourse**, *ri-kōrs'*, *-körs'*, *n.* flowing back: withdrawal: recurrence: flow (*Shak.*): return: freedom to return: access: resort: resort for aid or protection: right to payment, esp. by the drawer or endorser of a bill of exchange not met by the acceptor.—*v.i.* (*Spens.*) to return, go back, revert. in the mind.—**without recourse**, a qualified endorsement of a bill or promissory note indicating that the endorser takes no responsibility for non-payment (law, commerce). [Fr. *recours*—L. *recursus*—*re-*, back, *currĕre*, *cursum*, to run.]

**re-cover, recover**, *rē-kuv'ər*, *v.t.* to cover again. [Pfx. **re-**.]

**recover**, *ri-kuv'ər*, *v.t.* to get or find again: to regain: to reclaim: to bring back: to retrieve: to cure: to revive: to restore: to rescue: to succeed in reaching: to attain: to obtain as compensation: to obtain for injury or debt.— *v.i.* to regain health or any former state: to get back into position: to obtain a judgment (*law*). —*n.* **recovery** (*obs.*): possibility of recovery (*obs.*): return to a former position, as in rowing or exercise with a weapon: the position so resumed.—*n.* **recoverabil'ity**.—*adj.* **recov'erable.**—*ns.* **recov'erableness; recoveree'**, one against whom a judgment is obtained in common recovery; **recov'erer**, one who recovers; **recov'eror**, one who recovers a judgment in common recovery; **recov'ery**, the act, fact, process, possibility, or power of recovering, or state of having recovered, in any sense: a verdict giving right to the recovery of debts or costs (*law*).—**common recovery**, a former method of transferring an entailed estate by a legal fiction; **recover the wind of** (*Shak.*), to get to windward of (so as to drive a hare into a toil, or take the wind out of one's sails): to gain an advantage over. [O.Fr. *recovrer*—L. *recuperāre*; see **recuperate**.]

**recower.** See **recoure.**

**recreant**, *rek'ri-ənt*, *adj.* surrendering: craven: false: apostate.—*n.* one who yields in combat: a craven: a mean-spirited wretch: an apostate: a renegade.—*n.* **rec'reance, rec'reancy.**—*adv.* **rec'reantly.** [O.Fr., pr.p. of *recroire*, to yield in combat—L.L. *recrēdĕre*, to surrender—L. *crēdĕre*, to entrust.]

**recreate**, *rē-krē-āt'*, *v.t.* to create again: (in the following senses *rek'ri-āt*), to reinvigorate: to refresh: to indulge, gratify, or amuse by sport or pastime.—*v.i.* to take recreation.—*n.* **recrea-tion** (*rē-krē-ā'shən*) the act of creating anew: a new creation: (in the following senses *rek-ri-ā'-shən*), refreshment after toil, sorrow, etc.: pleasurable occupation of leisure time: an amusement or sport: a source of amusement.—

*adjs.* recrea'tional (*rek*-), rĕcrea'tive (and *rek'ri-ā-tiv*). [Pfx. re-.]

recrement, *rek'ri-mənt*, *n.* waste, dross: a secretion that is reabsorbed.—*adjs.* recre:ental (*-ment'l*), recrementitial (*-mən-tish'l*), recrementi'tious. [L. *recrēmentum*, dross—*cernĕre*, to sift.]

recriminate, *ri-krim'in-āt, v.i.* to charge an accuser.—*n.* recrimina'ti ، act of accusing in return: counter-charge.—*adj.* recrim'inative.—*n.* recrim'inator.—*adj.* recrim'inatory. [L. *criminārī*, to accuse.]

recrudesce, *rē-krōō-des', v.i.* to break out afresh.—*ns.* recrudesc'ence, recrudesc'ency.—*adj.* recrudesc'ent. [L. *recrūdēscēre—crūdus*, raw.]

recruit, *ri-krōōt'*, *n.* a reinforcement (*obs.*): a new supply (of men, money, health, etc.): renewal: restoration: a soldier or other newly enlisted.—*v.i.* to obtain fresh supplies: to recover in health, pocket, etc.: to enlist new soldiers.—*v.t.* to reinforce: to replenish: to restore: to reinvigorate: to enlist or raise.—*ns.* recruit'al, renewed supply: restoration; recruit'er.—*adj.* recruit'ing.—*n.* recruit'ment, recruiting.—recruit'ing-ground, a place where recruits may be obtained. [Obs. Fr. *recrute*, reinforcement, prov. pa.p. fem. of *recroître*—L. *recrēscēre*, to grow again.]

recta, rectal, etc. See rectum.

rectangle, *rek'tang-gl*, or *-tang'*, *n.* a four-sided plane figure with all its angles right angles.—*adjs.* rec'tangled, having a right angle; rectang'-ūlar, of the form of a rectangle: at right angles: right-angled.—*n.* rectangūlar'ity.—*adv.* rectang'-ūlarly.—rectangular hyperbola, one whose asymptotes are at right angles; rectangular solid, one whose axis is perpendicular to its base. [L.L. *rēct(i)angulum*—L. *angulus*, an angle.]

rect(i)-, *rekt(i)*-, in composition, right: straight.—*adjs.* rectilineal (*rek-ti-lin'i-əl*), rectilinear (*rek-ti-lin'i-ər*; L. *līnea*, a line), in a straight line or lines: straight: bounded by straight lines.—*n.* rectilinearity (*-ar'i-ti*).—*adv.* rectilin'early.—*ns.* rectipetality (*rek-ti-pi-tal'i-ti*), rectipetaly (*-pet'-əl-i*; L. *petĕre*, to seek; *bot.*), tendency to grow in a straight line.—*adjs.* rectirostral (*rek-ti-ros'tral*; L. *rōstrum*, a beak), straight-billed; rectiserial (*rek-ti-sēr'i-əl*; L. *seriēs*, a row), in straight rows. [L. *rēctus*, straight, right.]

rectify, *rek'ti-fī, v.t.* to set right: to correct: to redress: to adjust: to purify by distillation (*chem.*): to determine the length of (an arc): to change to direct (an alternating current):—*pr.p.* rec'tifying; *pa.t.* and *pa.p.* rec'tified.—*adj.* rec'tifiable.—*ns.* rectificā'tion (*-fi*); rec'tifier, one who rectifies (esp. alcohol): apparatus for rectifying (esp. spirit, an alternating current, or electromagnetic waves). [Fr. *rectifier*—L.L. *rēctificāre—facĕre*, to make.]

rectilineal, etc. See rect(i)-.

rection, *rek'shən*, (*gram.*) *n.* syntactical government. [L. *rēctiō, -ōnis*, government.]

rectipetality . . . to . . . rectiserial. See rect(i)-.

rectitis. See rectum.

rectitude, *rek'ti-tūd*, *n.* straightness (*obs.*): rightness: uprightness: integrity. [Fr.,—L.L. *rēctitūdō*—L. *rēctus*, straight.]

recto, *rek'tō*, *n.* the right-hand page of an open book, the front page of a leaf—opp. to verso. [L. *rēctō (foliō)*, on the right (leaf).]

recto-. See rectum.

rector, *rek'tər*, *n.* a ruler, governor, or controller (*obs.*): in the Church of England, a clergyman of a parish where the tithes are not impropriate: an Episcopal clergyman with charge of a congregation in the United States or (since 1890) Scotland: the head-master of certain schools in Scotland, esp. those called academies: the chief elective officer of many Scottish (*Lord Rector*) and foreign universities: a college head (as at Lincoln and Exeter Colleges, Oxford; Science and Technology, London): an ecclesiastic in charge of a congregation, an important mission, a college, or a religious house, esp. the head of a Jesuit seminary (*R.C.*).—*adj.* rec'toral, of God as a ruler.—*ns.* rec'torate, a rector's office or term of office; rec'toress, rec'tress, a female rector: a rector's wife (*coll.*).—*adj.* rectorial (*-tō'ri-əl*), of a rector.—*n.* an election of a Lord Rector.—*ns.* rec'torship; rec'tory, the province or residence of a rector.—Rector Magnificus, the head of a German university.—lay rector, a layman who enjoys the great tithes of a parish. [L. *rēctor, -ōris—regĕre, rēctum*, to rule.]

rectrix, *rek'triks*, *n.* a female governor: a long tail-feather, used in steering:—*pl.* rectrices (*rek-trī'sēz*).—*adj.* rectricial (*-trish'l*). [L. *rēctrix, -īcis*, fem. of *rēctor*.]

rectum, *rek'təm*, *n.* the terminal part of the large intestine:—*pl.* rec'ta.—*adj.* rec'tal.—*adv.* rec'-tally.—*n.* rectitis (*rek-ti'tis*), inflammation of the rectum.—*adj.* rectitic (*-tit'ik*).—In composition, rec'to-. [L. neut. of *rēctus*, straight.]

rectus, *rek'təs*, *n.* a straight muscle:—*pl.* rec'ti. [L.]

recuile, recule, *ri-kūl'* (*Spens.*). Same as recoil.

recumbent, *ri-kum'bənt, adj.* reclining.—*ns.* recum'bence, recum'bency.—*adv.* recum'bently. [L. *recumbĕre—cubāre*, to lie down.]

recuperate, *ri-kū'pər-āt, v.t.* and *v.i.* to recover.—*adj.* recu'perable, recoverable.—*n.* recuperā'tion.—*adj.* recu'perative (*-ə-tiv*).—*n.* recu'perātor, an arrangement by which something lost is regained, as the heat of waste gases in a furnace.—*adj.* recu'peratory. [L. *recuperāre*, to recover.]

recur, *ri-kûr', v.i.* to revert: to have recourse: to come up or come round again, or at intervals: recurr'ing (or *-kur'*); *pa.t.* and *pa.p.* recurred' (*-kûrd*).—*ns.* recurr'ence, recurr'ency (*-kur'*).—*adj.* recurr'ent (*-kur'*), returning at intervals: running back in the opposite direction or toward the place of origin.—*adv.* recurr'ently.—*n.* recur'sion (*-kûr'; rare*), a going back, return.—*adj.* (*math.* ; of a formula) enabling a term in a sequence to be computed from one or more of the preceding terms.—*adj.* recur'sive (*math.* ; of a definition), consisting of rules which allow values or meaning to be determined with certainty.—recurring decimal, a fraction in which after a certain point one figure (*repeating decimal*) or a group of figures (*circulating*) is repeated to infinity. [L. *recurrĕre—currĕre*, to run.]

recure, *ri-kūr', v.t.* to cure, remedy, heal, bring back to a better state (*Spens., Shak., Milt.*): to recover, get back (*Spens.*).—*v.i.* (*obs.*) to recover, get well.—*n.* (*obs.*) cure: recovery.—*adj.* recure'less (*obs.*), incurable. [Partly L. *recūrāre*, to cure, partly for recoure (q.v.).]

recurve, *ri-kûrv', v.t.* and *v.i.* to bend back.—*adj.* recurved'.—*adj.* recurviros'tral, with up-bent bill. [L. *recurvāre*; *rōstrum*, beak.]

recuse, *ri-kūz', v.t.* to reject, object to (e.g. a judge).—*ns.* recusance (*rek'ū-zəns* or *ri-kū'zəns*; *rare*), recusancy (*-i*); recusant (*rek'* or *ri-kū'*), one (esp. a Roman Catholic) who refused to attend the Church of England when it was legally compulsory: a dissenter: one who refuses, esp. to submit to authority.—Also *adj.*—*n.* recusā'tion (*law*), an objection or appeal. [L. *recūsāre—causa*, a cause.]

recycle, *rē-sī'kl, v.t.* to pass again through a series of changes or treatment: to cause (material) to be broken down by bacteria and then reconstitute it: to direct into a different channel. [Pfx. re-.]

red, red, *adj.* (*comp.* redd'er; *superl.* redd'est) of

a colour like blood: extended traditionally to mean golden, and by custom to other colours more or less near red: revolutionary, or supposedly revolutionary.—*n*. the colour of blood: a red pigment: red clothes: a revolutionary or one who favours sweeping changes, variously applied to radical, republican, anarchist, socialist, communist, etc.: a former squadron of the British fleet: a cent.—*v.t.* redd′en, to make red.—*v.i.* to grow red: to blush.—*adj.* redd′ish. —*n.* redd′ishness.—*adj.* redd′y.—*adv.* red′ly.—*n.* red′ness.—**red admiral**, a common butterfly (*Vanessa atalanta*) with reddish-banded wings; **red algae**, one of the great divisions of seaweeds, the Rhodophyceae or Florideae; **red′-belly**, char, or other red-bellied fish: the slider, a terrapin; **red bidd′y**, a drink made of red wine and methylated spirit.—*adj.* **red′-blood′ed**, having red blood: abounding in vitality, and usually in crudity.—**red′-book**, a book bound in red, esp. a court-guide, peerage, directory of persons in the service of the state, official regulations, or the like; **red′-box**, a minister's red-covered box for official papers; **red′breast**, the robin; **red brick**, a brick, made from clay containing iron compounds which are converted into ferric oxide.—*adj.* **red′brick** (**redbrick university**, a general name given to a later English type of university, contrasted with Oxford and Cambridge).—**red′-bud**, the Judas-tree; **red cabbage**, a purplish cabbage used for pickling; **red′-cap**, a goldfinch: a Scottish castle goblin (also **red′-cowl**): military policeman (*slang*): railway porter (*U.S.*); **red carpet**, a strip of carpet put out for the highly favoured to walk on (as *adj.* **red′-car′pet**); **red cedar**, a name for various species of *Cedrela* and of juniper; **red cent**, a cent (formerly made of copper): a whit; **red clay**, a clayey deposit of oceanic abysses, stained reddish or brown by manganese and iron oxides: cave-earth; **red′coat**, a British soldier; **red cock**, a figurative name for an incendiary fire; **Red Crag**, a middle division of the English Pliocene; **Red Cross**, a red cross on a white ground, the old national flag of England (in Spenser's **Redcross Knight**, representing holiness and the Church of England): the Swiss flag with colours reversed, the copyrighted symbol of an organisation (known as the **Red Cross**) for tending sick, wounded in war, etc., enjoying privileges under the Convention of Geneva (1864); **redcurr′ant**, the small red berry of a shrub of the gooseberry genus.—*adj.* **red′-currant**.—**red′-deer**, the common stag or hind, reddish-brown in summer; **Red Devils**, the Parachute Regiment; **red′-dog**, the lowest grade of flour in high milling; **Red Ensign** (*slang* **Red Duster**), red flag with Union Jack in canton, till 1864 flag of Red Squadron, now flown by British merchant ships; **red′eye**, the rudd; **red face**, a blushing from discomfiture.—*adj.* **red′-fig′ured**, (of Greek vases) having red (unpainted) figures on a blackglazed ground.—**red flag**, a flag used as a signal of danger, defiance, no quarter, or an auction sale: the banner of socialism or of revolution: a socialist's song; **red giant, dwarf**, a red star of high, low, luminosity; **red′-gum**, an eruption of the skin in teething infants: a Eucalyptus (of various kinds) with red gum.—*adj.* **red′-haired**.—**red′-hand**, the bloody hand (see **hand**).—*adj.* and *adv.* **red′-hand′ed**, in the very act, or immediately after, as if with bloody hands.—**red′-hat**, a cardinal: a cardinal's hat (award of this to cardina's was discontinued 1969): a staff officer (*army slang*); **red′-head**, a person with red hair.—*adj.* **red′-head′ed**, having a red head or red hair: angrily excited (*slang*).—**red′-heat**, the temperature at which a thing is red-hot.—*adj.* **red′-heeled′**.—**red herring**, a herring cured and

dried, of reddish appearance: a subject introduced to divert discussion as a herring drawn across a track would throw hounds out.—*adj.* **red′-hot**, heated to redness: extreme (*fig.*): (**red-hot poker**, the plant Kniphofia or Tritoma).— **Red Indian**, an American Indian.—*adj.* **red′-latt′ice** (*Shak.*), savouring of the alehouse (whose lattice was conventionally painted red). —**red lead**, an oxide of lead ($Pb_3O_4$) of a fine red colour, used in paint-making.—*adjs.* **red′-legged; red′-letter**, marked with red letters, as holidays or saints' days in the old calendars: deserving to be so marked.—**red light**, a rear-light: a danger-signal: a brothel (*coll.*).—*adjs.* **red′-light** (*coll.*), disreputable; **red′-looked** (*Shak.*), having a red look; **red′-mad** (*Scot.*), stark mad.—**red′-man, red man**, a redskin, an American Indian: prob. red mercuric sulphide (*alchemy*); **red pepper** (see **pepper**); **red′-plague**, -murrain (*Shak.*), bubonic plague; **red′poll**, a name for two birds (*lesser* and *mealy redpoll*) akin to the linnet: a beast of a red breed of polled cattle.—*adj.* **red′-polled**, having a red poll: red and polled.—**red rag**, the tongue (*slang*): a cause of infuriation (as red is said to be to a bull); **red ratt′le**, lousewort; **red ribbon, riband**, the ribbon of the Order of the Bath; **red′-root**, a genus (*Ceanothus*) of the buckthorn family— *New Jersey tea*; **red rot**, a disease of oaks, etc., caused by Polyporus, the wood becoming brown and dry; **red′-san′ders**, a papilionaceous tree (*Pterocarpus santalinus*) of tropical Asia, with heavy dark-red heartwood, used as a dye, etc. (see also **sandalwood**); **red seaweed**, any of the red algae, esp. one of the genus *Polysiphonia*; **red′-seed**, the food of mackerel, small floating crustaceans, etc.; **red′-shank**, a sandpiper with red legs: (in derision) a Highlander or an Irishman; **red shift**, a shift of lines in the spectrum towards the red, usu. considered to occur because the source of light is receding (see under **dopplerite**); **red′-shirt**, a follower of Garibaldi (1807-82), from his garb: a revolutionary or anarchist; **red′skin**, a Red Indian; **red snow**, snow coloured by a microscopic red alga; **red spider**, a spinning mite that infests leaves; **red′-start** (O.E. *steort*, tail), a bird (Ruticilla or Phoenicurus) with a conspicuous chestnut-coloured tail: an American warbler, superficially similar; **red′streak**, an apple with streaked skin; **red tape**, the tape used in government offices: rigid formality of intricate official routine.—*adj.* **red′-tape′**.—**red-tap′ism**, **red-tap′ist**; **red′top** (*U.S.*), a kind of bent grass (*Agrostis stolonifera*); **red′-water**, a cattle disease due to a protozoan parasite in the blood, transmitted by ticks; **red wine**, wine coloured by (red) grape skins during fermentation (cf. **rosé**); **red′wing**, a thrush with reddish sides below the wings; **red′-wood**, a species of Sequoia with reddish wood much used commercially: any wood or tree yielding a red dye.—*adj.* **red-wood′, -wud′** (*Scot.*), stark mad.—**in the red**, overdrawn at the bank, in debt; **red out**, to experience a red hazy field of vision, etc., as a result of aerobatics; **Royal Red Cross**, a decoration for nurses. instituted 1883; **see red**, to grow furious: *t̀o* thirst for blood. [O.E. *rēad*; cf.' Ger. *rot*, L. *ruber*, *rūfus*, Gr. *erythros*, Gael. *ruadh*.]

**red.** Same as **redd** (1 and 2).

**redact**, *ri-dakt′*, *v.t.* to edit, work into shape: to frame.—*ns.* redac′tion; redac′tor.—*adj.* redactō′rial (*re-*, *rē-*). [L. *redigĕre*, *redactum*, to bring back—pfx. *red-*, *agĕre*, to drive.]

**redan**, *ri-dan′*, (*fort.*) *n.* a fieldwork of two faces forming a salient. [O.Fr. *redan*—L. *re-*, *dēns*, *dentis*, a tooth.]

**redargue**, *ri-där′gū*, (*obs.* or *Scot.*) *v.t.* to refute: to confute. [L. *redarguĕre*—*red-*, *arguĕre*, argue.]

**redd, red,** *red,* (chiefly *Scot.*) *v.t.* to put in order, make tidy: to clear up: to disentangle: to comb: to separate in fighting.—*v.i.* to set things in order, tidy up (usu. with *up*):—*pr.p.* **redd´ing;** *pa.t.* and *pa.p.* **redd, red.**—*n.* an act of redding: refuse, rubbish.—*adj.* (*Scots law*) vacated.—*ns.* **redd´er; redd´ing.**—redd´ing-up´, setting in order, tidying up; **redd´ing-comb, -kame,** a hair-comb; **redd´ing-straik,** a stroke received in trying to separate fighters. [Partly O.E. *hreddan,* to free, rescue (cf. Ger. *retten,* to rescue); prob. partly from or influenced by O.E. *rǣdan* (see **rede, read**); cf. also **rid.**]

**redd, red,** *red, pa.t.* and *pa.p.* of **read** (*Spens.*): same as **rede** (*pres. tense*; *Scot.*).

**redd,** *red,* (*Scot.*) *n.* fish or frog spawn: a spawning-place. [Origin obscure.]

**reddendum,** *ri-den´dəm,* (*law*) *n.* a reserving clause in a lease:—*pl.* **redden´da.**—*n.* **redden´do** (*Scots law*), service to be rendered or money to be paid by a vassal, or the clause in a charter specifying it. [L., to be rendered, gerundive of *reddĕre.*]

**reddle, reddleman.** See **ruddle.**

**rede,** *rēd, v.t.* an old spelling of **read,** retained as an archaism in the senses of 'to counsel or advise, expound, relate'.—*n.* (*arch.*) advice: resolution: saying, tale: interpretation (*Browning*).—*n.* **rede´craft** (*arch.*), logic.—*adj.* **rede´less** (*arch.*), without counsel or wisdom.

**redeem,** *ri-dēm´, v.t.* to buy back: to compound for: to recover or free by payment: to free oneself from, by fulfilment: to ransom: to rescue, deliver, free: to get back: to reclaim: to pay the penalty of: to atone for: to compensate for: to put (time) to the best advantage.—*n.* **redeemabil´ity.**—*adj.* **redeem´able.**—*n.* **redeem´ableness.**—*adv.* **redeem´ably.**—*n.* **redeem´er.**—*adjs.* **redeem´ing; redeem´less,** not to be redeemed.—**the Redeemer,** the Saviour, Jesus Christ. [L. *redimēre* (perh. through Fr. *rédimer*)—*red-,* back, *emĕre,* to buy.]

**redeliver,** *rē-di-liv´ər, v.t.* to restore: to free again: to report the words of (*Shak.*).—*ns.* **redeliv´erance; redeliv´erer; redeliv´ery.** [Pfx. **re-.**]

**redemption,** *ri-dem(p)´shən, n.* act of redeeming: atonement.—*ns.* **redemp´tioner,** an emigrant who bound himself to service until his fare was made up; **Redemp´tionist,** a Trinitarian friar.—*adj.* **redemp´tive.**—*n.* **Redemp´torist,** a missionary priest of a congregation founded by Alfonso Liguori in 1732 for work among the people.—*adj.* **redemp´tory.** [L. *redimĕre, redemptum*; cf. **redeem.**]

**redeploy,** *rē-di-ploi´, v.t.* to transfer (e.g. military forces, supplies, industrial workers) from one area to another.—Also *v.i.*—*n.* **redeploy´ment.** [Pfx. **re-.**]

**redia,** *rē´di-a, n.* a form in the life-cycle of the trematodes:—*pl.* **rē´diae** (*-ē*). [Named after Francesco *Redi* (d. prob. 1698), Italian naturalist.]

**redingote,** *red´ing-gōt, n.* a long double-breasted (orig. man's, later woman's) overcoat. [Fr.,—Eng. **riding-coat.**]

**redintegrate,** *red-in´ti-grāt, v.t.* to restore to wholeness: to re-establish.—*adj.* restored: renewed.—*n.* **redintegrā´tion.** [L. *redintegrāre, -ātum*—*red-,* again, *integrāre,* to make whole—*integer.*]

**redisburse,** *rē-dis-bûrs´,* (*Spens.*) *v.t.* to refund. [Pfx. **re-.**]

**redivivus,** *red-i-vī´vəs, re-di-wē´wŏŏs, adj.* resusci-

tated: come to life again. [L.,—*red-,* again, *vivus,* alive—*vivĕre,* to be alive.]

**redolent,** *red´o-lənt, adj.* fragrant: smelling (of, or with): suggestive (of), imbued (with).—*ns.* **red´olence, red´olency.**—*adv.* **red´olently.** [L. *redolēns, -entis*—*red-,* again, *olēre,* to emit smell.]

**redouble,** *ri-dub´l, v.t.* and *v.i.* to double: to repeat: to re-echo: to increase: (*rē´dub´l*) to double after previous doubling.—*n.* (*rē´dub´l*) an act or fact of redoubling, as in bridge.—*n.* **redoub´lement** (*ri-*). [Pfx. **re-.**]

**redoubt,** *ri-dowt´,* (*fort.*) *n.* a field-work enclosed on all sides, its ditch not flanked from the parapet: an inner last retreat. [Fr. *redoute*—It. *ridotto*—L. *reductus,* retired—*redūcĕre*; the *b* from confusion with next word.]

**redoubt,** *ri-dowt´, v.t.* to fear (*arch.*).—*adjs.* **redoubt´able,** formidable: valiant; **redoubt´ed,** redoubtable (*arch.*). [O.Fr. *redouter,* to fear greatly—L. *re-,* back, *dubitāre,* to doubt.]

**redound,** *ri-downd´, v.i.* to overflow (*Spens.*): to be in excess (*Milt.*): to surge (*Spens.*): to be filled (*Spens.*): to flow back: to return: to rebound, be reflected or echoed: to turn, recoil, be reflected, as a consequence (to one's credit, discredit, advantage, etc.): to conduce: to rise one above another in receding series (*Spens.*).—*v.t.* (*fig.*) to cast, reflect.—*n.* the coming back, as an effect or consequence, return.—*n.* and *adj.* **redound´ing.** [Fr. *rédonder*—L. *redundāre*—*red-,* back, *undāre,* to surge—*unda,* a wave.]

**redowa,** *red´ō-va, n.* a Bohemian dance: music for it, usually in quick triple time. [Ger. or Fr.,—Czech *reydovák.*]

**redraft,** *rē-dräft´, n.* a revised draft or copy: a new bill of exchange which the holder of a protested bill draws on the drawer or endorsers, for the amount of the bill, with costs and charges.—*v.t.* to make a revised draft of. [Pfx. **re-.**]

**redress,** *ri-dres´, v.t.* to set right: to readjust: to restore (*Spens.*): to remedy: to compensate.—*n.* relief: reparation.—*n.* **redress´er** (*ri-*), one who redresses abuses or injuries.—*adj.* **redress´ive** (*Thomson*), affording redress. [Fr. *redresser* (see **dress**); partly from pfx. **re-** and **dress.**]

**re-dress,** *rē´dres´, v.t.* and *v.i.* to dress again: to dress in different clothes. [Pfx. **re-.**]

**redruthite,** *red´rŏŏth-īt, n.* copper-glance, a mineral found at *Redruth* in Cornwall.

**redshort,** *red´shört, adj.* brittle at red-heat.—Also **red´sear, -share, -shire.** [Sw. *rödskör—röd,* red, *skör,* brittle.]

**reduce,** *ri-dūs´, v.t.* to bring back (*arch.*): to restore to an old state: to bring into a new state: to put back into a normal condition or place, as a dislocation or fracture (*surg.*): to change to another form: to express in other terms: to range in order or classification: to adapt, adjust: to translate: to put into (writing, practice; with *to*): to bring into a lower state: to lessen: to diminish in weight or girth: to weaken: to degrade (*mil.*): to impoverish: to subdue: to subject to necessity: to drive into (a condition; with *to*): to break up, separate, disintegrate: to disband (*mil., obs.*): to bring to the metallic state: to remove oxygen from, or combine with hydrogen, or lessen the positive valency of (an atom or ion) by adding electrons:

*fāte, fär; mē, hûr* (her); *mīne; mōte, för; mūte; mōōn, fŏŏt; dhen* (then)

to annul (*Scots law*).—*v.i.* to resolve itself: to slim, or lessen weight or girth.—*p.adj.* **reduced'**, in a state of reduction: weakened: impoverished: diminished: simplified in structure.—*ns.* **reduc'er**, one who reduces: a means of reducing: a joint-piece for connecting pipes of varying diameter; **reducibil'ity.**—*adj.* **reduc'ible**, that may be reduced.—*n.* **reduc'ibleness.**—*adj.* **reduc'ing.**—*ns.* **reduc'tant**, a reducing agent; **reduction** (-*duk'shən*), act of reducing or state of being reduced: diminution: lowering of price: subjugation: changing of numbers or quantities from one denomination to another (*arith.*); **reduc'tionism**, the belief that complex data and phenomena can be explained in terms of something simpler.—*n.* and *adj.* **reduc'tionist.**—*adj.* **reduc'tive**, bringing back (*arch.*): reducing.—*adv.* **reduc'tively.**—**reducing agent**, a substance with a strong affinity for oxygen, or the like, serving to remove it from others; **reducing flame**, a non luminous blowpipe flame in which substances can be reduced; **reduction division** (*biol.*), meiosis; **reduction works**, smelting works. —**reduce to the ranks**, to degrade, for misconduct, to the condition of a private soldier. [L. *redūcĕre, reductum—re-*, back, *dūcĕre*, to lead.]

**reductio ad absurdum**, *ri-duk'shi-ō ad ab-sûr'dəm, re-doōk'ti-ō ad ab-soōr'doōm*, reduction to absurdity: the proof of a proposition by proving the falsity of its contradictory. [L.]

**reduit**, *rā-dwē, n.* an inner fortified retreat for a garrison. [Fr. *réduit*.]

**redundant**, *ri-dun'dənt, adj.* surging (*Milt.*): overflowing (*obs.*): copious: over-copious: superfluous: of workers, no longer needed and therefore dismissed.—*ns.* **redun'dance, redun'dancy.**—*adv.* **redun'dantly.** [L. *redundāns, -antis*, pr.p. of *redundāre*, to overflow.]

**reduplicate**, *ri-dū'pli-kāt, v.t.* to double: to repeat. —*v.i.*to double: to exhibit reduplication (*gram.*). —*adj.* doubled: showing reduplication (*gram.*): in aestivation, valvate with edges turned outwards (*bot.*).—*n.* **reduplica'tion**, a folding or doubling: the doubling of the initial part, in inflection and word-formation, as in L. *fefelli*, perf. of *fallō*, Gr. *tetypha*, perf. of *typtō* (*gram.*): the combination of two rhyming words (the second sometimes a coinage for the purpose) to form one, as in *hurry-skurry, popsy-wopsy*. —*adj.* **redū'plicātive.** [L. *reduplicāre, -ātum— duplicāre*, to double.]

**ree**, *rē*, see **ruff** (2).

**reebok**, *rā'bok, n.* a South African antelope. [Du.]

**reech**, *rēch.* Same as **reek.**—*adj.* **reech'y** (*Shak.* rechie, reechie), smoky, grimy.

**re-echo**, *rē-ek'ō, v.t.* to echo back: to repeat as if an echo.—*v.i.* to give back echoes: to resound. —*n.* a re-echoing. [Pfx. re-.]

**reed**, reede (*Spens.*). Same as **rede.**

**reed**, *rēd, n.* a tall stiff hard-culmed marsh or water grass of various kinds, esp. *Phragmites communis*: a thing made, or formerly made, of a reed or reeds—a pen, an arrow, a measuring rod, a music pipe, the vibrating tongue of an organ-pipe or woodwind instrument (with or without the parts to which it is attached), a weaver's appliance for separating the warp threads and beating up the weft: thatching: a small reedlike moulding: a reed-instrument.—*adj.* (*Shak.*) reedlike.—*v.t.* to thatch.—*adjs.* **reed'ed**, covered with reeds: having reed(s); **reed'en**, of reed.— *ns.* **reed'er**, a thatcher; **reed'iness**; **reed'ing**, the milling on the edge of a coin: a reed moulding; **reed'ling**, the bearded titmouse.—*adj.* **reed'y**,

abounding with reeds: resembling a reed: sounding as a reed instrument.—**reed'-band**, a band of reed-instruments; **reed'-bed**; **reed'-bird**, the bobolink; **reed'-bunt'ing**, the blackheaded bunting; **reed'-drawing**, the combing out of rough straw by means of a frame; **reed'-grass**, a reedlike grass of various kinds (as Phalaris, Arundo); **reed'-instrument**, a woodwind with reed—as clarinet, oboe, bassoon; **reed'-knife**, a tool for organ-tuning; **reed'-mace**, cat's tail (*Typha*); **reed'-or'gan**, a keyboard instrument with free reeds, as the harmonium, the American organ; **reed'-pheas'ant**, the bearded titmouse; **reed'-pipe**, an organ-pipe whose tone is produced by the vibration of a reed, the pipe acting as resonator; **reed'-rand, -rond** (*East Anglia*), a reed thicket; **reed'-sparr'ow**, the reed-bunting: the sedge-warbler; **reed'-stop**, a set of reed-pipes controlled by a single stop-knob; **reed'-war'bler**, a warbler that frequents marshy places and builds its nest on reeds—also called **reed'-wren**, the **reed'-thrush** being a larger species (**greater reed-warbler**).— **broken reed** (*fig.*), a person who is too weak or unreliable to be depended upon; **free reed**, a reed vibrating in an opening without touching the sides. [O.E. *hrēod*; cf. Du. and Ger. *riet*.]

**re-edify**, *rē-ed'i-fi, v.t.* to rebuild.—(*Spens.*) **reæd'ifye.**—*ns.* **re-edifica'tion; re-ed'ifier.** [L. *aedificāre*, to build.]

**reef**, *rēf, n.* a chain of rocks at or near the surface of water: a shoal or bank: a gold-bearing lode or vein (orig. *Austr.*): the encasing rock of a diamond-mine, all ground in the mine other than diamondiferous (*S.Afr.*).—**reef'-builder**, a coral-animal that forms reefs. [Du. *rif*—O.N. *rif*.]

**reef**, *rēf, n.* a portion of a sail that may be rolled or folded up.—*v.t.* to reduce the exposed surface of, as a sail: to gather up in a similar way.—*ns.* **reef'er**, one who reefs: a midshipman (*slang*): a reefing-jacket: a cigarette containing marijuana (*coll.*); **reef'ing.**—**reef'-band**, a strengthening strip across a sail; **reef'ing-jack'et**, a short thick double-breasted jacket; **reef'-knot**, a flat knot used in tying reef-points, consisting of two loops passing symmetrically through each other; **reef'-point**, a short rope on a reef-band to secure a reefed sail. [O.N. *rif*.]

**reek**, *rēk, n.* smoke: vapour: fume.—*v.i.* to emit smoke, fumes, or (esp. evil) smell: to exhale.— *v.t.* to expose to smoke: to exhale.—*adj.* **reek'ing.**—*adj.* **reek'y** (*Scot.* **reek'ie**), smoky: smoked: reeking: foul (*Shak.*).—**Auld Reekie**, Edinburgh. [O.E. *rēc*; O.N. *reykr*, Ger. *rauch*, Du. *rook*, smoke; a Northern form; cf. **reech.**]

**reel**, *rēl, n.* a cylinder, drum, spool, bobbin, or frame on which thread, fishing-line, wire, cables, photographic film, or the like may be wound: a length of material so wound: a loud rattling, a din (*Scot.*): a whirl, a stagger: a lively dance, esp. Highland or Irish: a tune for it, usu. in 4-4, sometimes in 6-8 time: (in *pl.*) revelry (*Shak.*).—*v.t.* to wind on a reel: to take off by or from a reel: to draw by means of a reel: to cause to whirl or roll (*Spens.*): to stagger along (*Shak.*).—*v.i.* to whirl: to seem to swirl or sway: to totter: to stagger: (of e.g. line or battle) to waver: to rattle (*Scot.*): to dance a reel.—*n.* **reel'er**, one who reels: the grasshopper-warbler.—*n.* and *adj.* **reel'ing.**—*adv.* **reel'ingly.**— **(right) off the reel**, in uninterrupted course or succession: without stop or hesitation; **reel off**, to utter rapidly and fluently; **Virginia reel**, an American country-dance. [O.E. *hrēol*, but

rē-ed'it, *v.t.*  rē-elect', *v.t.*  rē-eleva'tion, *n.*
rē-ed'ucate, *v.t.*  rē-elec'tion, *n.*  rē-eligibil'ity, *n.*
rē-educa'tion, *n.*  rē-el'evate, *v.t.*  rē-el'igible, *adj.*

Neutral vowels in unaccented syllables: *el'ə-mənt*; for certain sounds in foreign words, see p. viii

possibly partly of other origin; Gael. *righil* (the dance) may be from English.]

**re-enforce**, *rē-in-fōrs'*, *-fōrs*, *v.t.* to enforce again: to reinforce (*rare*): to reassemble, rally (*Shak.*).—*n.* **re-enforce'ment**, reinforcement. [Pfx. **re-.**]

**re-enter**, *rē-en'tər*, *v.t.* and *v.i.* to enter again or anew: in engraving, to cut deeper.—*p.adj.* **re-en'tering**, entering again: pointing inwards: **reflex** (*math.*).—*n.* **re-en'trance**, act or achievement of entering again: fact of being re-entrant (in this sense also **re-en'trancy**).—*adj.* **re-en'trant**, re-entering (opp. to *salient*): reflex (*math.*): returning upon itself at the ends (*elect.*).—*n.* a re-entering angle: a valley, depression, etc., running into a main feature: the concavity between two salients.—*n.* **re-en'try**, entering again: resumption of possession: a card allowing a hand to take the lead again. [Pfx. **re-.**]

**reest, reasty**. See **reast** (1).

**reest, reist, reast**, *rēst*, (*Scot.*) *v.t.* to dry, cure, with smoke.—*v.i.* to be smoke-dried. [Origin obscure.]

**reest, reist**, *rēst*, (*Scot.*) *v.i.* of a horse, suddenly to refuse to move, to baulk.—*n.* a sudden fit of stubbornness.—*adj.* **reest'y**. [Perh. **rest**, or **arrest**.]

**reeve**, *rēv*, (*hist.*) *n.* a high official, chief magistrate of a district: a bailiff or steward. [O.E. *gerēfa*; cf. **grieve** (*Scot.*).]

**reeve**, *rēv*, *v.t.* to pass the end of a rope through: to pass through any hole: to thread one's way through: to fasten by reeving:—*pa.t.* and *pa.p.* **reeved, rove**. [Origin obscure.]

**reeve**, *rēv*, see **ruff** (2).

**refection**, *ri-fek'shən*, *n.* refreshment or relief (*lit.* and *fig.*): a meal.—*v.t.* **refect** (*-fekt'*; back-formation), to refresh.—*v.i.* to take a repast.—*ns.* **refec'tioner, refectorian** (*rē-fek-tō', tō'ri-ən*), the officer in charge of the refectory and its arrangements; **refectory** (*ri-fek'tər-i*; sometimes *ref'ik-*), a dining-hall, esp. monastic.—**refectory table**, a long narrow dining-table supported on two shaped pillars each set in a base; **Refection Sunday**, Refreshment Sunday. [L. *reficĕre, refectum—facĕre*, to make.]

**refel**, *ri-fel'*, (*obs.*) *v.t.* to refute: to disprove: to confute: to repulse:—*pr.p.* **refell'ing**; *pa.t.* and *pa.p.* **refelled'**. [L. *refellĕre—fallĕre*, to deceive.]

**refer**, *ri-fûr'*, *v.t.* to reproduce, represent (*obs.*): to assign: to impute: to attribute: to bring into relation: to deliver, commit, or submit: to hand over for consideration: to direct for information, confirmation, testimonials, or whatever is required: to direct the attention of: to postpone (*obs.*): to recount (*arch.*): to direct to sit an examination again, fail.—*v.i.* (with *to* in all cases) to have relation or application, to relate: to direct the attention: to turn for information, confirmation, etc.: to turn, apply, or have recourse: to make mention or allusion:—*pr.p.* **referr'ing**; *pa.t.* and *pa.p.* **referred'**.—*adj.* **referable** (*ref'ər-ə-bl*; sometimes **referrible**, *ri-fer'i-bl*), that may be referred or assigned.—*n.* **referee** (*ref-ə-rē'*), one to whom anything is referred: an arbitrator, umpire, or judge.—*v.t.* to act as referee for.—*v.i.* to act as referee.—*ns.* **ref'erence**, the act of referring: a submitting for information or decision: the act of submitting a dispute for investigation or decision (*law*): relation: allusion: loosely, one who is referred to: loosely, a testimonial: a direction to a book or passage; **referendary** (*-end'ə-ri*), a referee: formerly a court official who was the medium of communication with the pope, emperor, etc.; **referen'dum**, the principle or practice of submitting a question directly to the vote of the entire electorate (*pl.* **-da, -dums**); **ref'erent**, the object of reference or discussion: the first term in a proposition.—*adj.* **referential** (*-en'shl*), containing a reference: having reference (to): used for reference.—*adv.* **referen'tially**.—*n.* **referr'al**, act or instance of referring or being referred; esp. to another person or organisation for, e.g. consideration, treatment, etc.—**reference book**, a book to be consulted on occasion, not for consecutive reading: a pass book (*S.Afr.*); **ref'erence-mark**, a character, as *, †, or a cock-up figure, used to refer to notes.—**terms of reference**, a guiding statement defining the scope of an investigation or similar piece of work: loosely, the scope itself. [L. *referre*, to carry back—*ferre*, to carry.]

**refigure**, *rē-fig'ər*, *v.t.* to represent anew, reproduce (*Shak.*): to restore to form: to calculate anew. [Pfx. **re-.**]

**refill**, *rē-fil'*, *v.t.* to fill again.—*n.* (*rē'* or *-fil'*) a fresh fill: a duplicate for refilling purposes. [Pfx. **re-.**]

**refine**, *ri-fīn'*, *v.t.* to purify: to clarify: to free from coarseness, vulgarity, crudity: to make more cultured.—*v.i.* to become more fine, pure, subtle, or cultured: to apply or affect subtlety or nicety: to improve by adding refinement or subtlety (with *on* or *upon*).—*adj.* **refined'**.—*adv.* **refin'edly**, in a refined manner with affected elegance.—*ns.* **refin'edness**; **refine'ment**, act or practice of refining: state of being refined: culture in feelings, taste, and manners: an improvement: a subtlety: an excessive nicety; **refin'er**; **refin'ery**, a place for refining; **refin'ing**. [L. *re-*, denoting change of state, and **fine**.]

**refit**, *rē-fit'*, *v.t.* to fit out afresh and repair.—*v.i.* to undergo refitting.—*ns.* **refit'**, **refit'ment**, **refitt'-ing**. [Pfx. **re-** and **fit** (1).]

**reflation**, *rē-flā'shən*, *n.* inflation, increase in the amount of currency, after deflation.—*v.t.* (back-formation from *n.*) **reflate'**.—*adj.* **reflā'tionary**. [Pfx. **re-**, and in**flation**.]

**reflect**, *ri-flekt'*, *v.t.* to bend or send back or aside: to throw back after striking: to give an image of in the manner of a mirror: to express, reproduce (*fig.*): to cast, shed (e.g. credit, discredit) (*fig.*): to consider meditatively (that, how, etc.).—*v.i.* to bend or turn back or aside: to be mirrored: to cast a light (*Shak.*): to meditate: to cast reproach or censure (on, upon): to bring harmful results.—*n.* **reflect'ance**, ratio of reflected radiation to incident radiation.—*adj.* **reflect'ed**, cast or thrown back: turned or folded back: mirrored.—*n.* **reflect'er** (*Swift*), one who casts reflections.—*adj.* **reflect'ing**.—*adv.* **reflect'ingly**, meditatively: with implication of censure.—*n.* **reflection**, also (now chiefly in scientific use) **reflexion** (*ri-flek'shən*), a turning, bending, or folding aside, back, or downwards: folding upon itself: rebound: change of direc-

| | | |
|---|---|---|
| **rē-embark'**, *v.t.* and *v.i.* | **rē-engage'**, *v.t.* and *v.i.* | **rē-exist'**, *v.i.* |
| **rē-embarkā'tion**, *n.* | **rē-engage'ment**, *n.* | **rē-exist'ence**, *n.* |
| **rē-embod'iment**, *n.* | **rē-enlist'**, *v.t.* and *v.i.* | **rē-expand'**, *v.t.* and *v.i.* |
| **rē-embod'y**, *v.t.* | **rē-enlist'er**, *n.* | **rē-expan'sion**, *n.* |
| **rē-emerge'**, *v.i.* | **rē-enlist'ment**, *n.* | **rē-export'**, *v.t.* |
| **rē-emer'gence**, *n.* | **rē-erect'**, *v.t.* | **rē-ex'port**, *n.* |
| **rē-enact'**, *v.t.* | **rē-erec'tion**, *n.* | **rē-exportā'tion**, *n.* |
| **rē-enact'ment**, *n.* | **rē-estab'lish**, *v.t.* | **rēface'**, *v.t.* |
| **rē-encour'age**, *v.t.* | **rē-estab'lishment**, *n.* | **rēfash'ion**, *v.t.* |
| **rē-endow'**, *v.t.* | **rē-examinā'tion**, *n.* | **rēfash'ionment**, *n.* |
| **rē-endow'ment**, *n.* | **rē-exam'ine**, *v.t.* | |

tion when an electromagnetic wave or sound-wave strikes on a surface and is thrown back: reflected light, colour, heat, etc.: an image in a mirror: (production of) a mirror image of a line or figure (by reflecting it in an axis of symmetry): the action of the mind by which it is conscious of its own operations: attentive consideration: contemplation: a thought or utterance resulting from contemplation: censure or reproach.—*adjs.* reflec'tionless; reflect'ive, reflecting: reflected: meditative.—*adv.* reflect'ively.—*ns.* reflect'iveness; reflectiv'ity, ability to reflect rays: reflectance; reflect'or, a reflecting surface, instrument, or body: a reflecting telescope; reflet (*rə-fle'*, *-flā'*; Fr.), an irridescent or metallic lustre.—*adj.* reflex (*re'fleks*, formerly *ri-fleks'*), bent or turned back: reflected: reciprocal: of an angle, more than 180°: turned back upon itself: involuntary, produced by or concerned with response from a nerve-centre to a stimulus from without: illuminated by light from another part of the same picture (*paint.*): using the same valve or valves for high- and low-frequency amplification (*radio*).—*n.* reflection: reflected light: a reflected image: an expression, manifestation, outward representation: a reflex action: a reflex radio receiving set.—*v.t.* (*-fleks'*) to bend back: to project, direct (*Shak.*).—*adj.* reflexed' (*bot.*), bent abruptly backward or downward.—*n.* reflexibil'ity.—*adjs.* reflex'ible; reflex'ive (*gram.*), indicating that the action turns back upon the subject.—*advs.* reflex'ively; reflex'ly (or *rē'*).—reflecting microscope, one using a system of mirrors instead of lenses; reflecting telescope, one (as, e.g. the Gregorian or Newtonian) which has a concave mirror instead of an object glass (lens or lenses); reflex light, a lens with a reflecting back, returning a beam of red light when the headlight, e.g. of a motor-car, shines on it. [L. *reflectĕre*, *reflexum* —*flectĕre*, to bend.]

reflow, *rē-flō'*, *v.i.* to ebb: to flow again.—*ns.* reflow', reflow'ing, ebb: reflux. [Pfx. re-.]

refluent, *ref'lōō-ənt*, *adj.* flowing back: ebbing: tidal.—*ns.* ref'luence, reflux (*rē'fluks*), flowing back: ebb. [L. *refluēns*, *-entis*, pr.p. of *refluĕre* —*fluĕre*, *fluxum*, to flow; *fluxus*, *-ūs*, a flow.]

refocillate, *ri-fos'il-āt*, (*obs.*) *v.t.* to refresh, cherish.—*n.* refocillā'tion. [L. *refocillāre*, *-ātum*, to cherish—*focus*, a hearth.]

re-form, also reform, *rē'förm'*, *v.t.* and *v.i.* to form again or anew.—*n.* rē(-)formā'tion.—*adj.* rē(-)formed'. [Pfx. re-.]

reform, *ri-förm'*, *v.t.* to transform: to restore, rebuild (*Milt.*): to amend: to make better: to remove defects from: to redress: to bring to a better way of life: to chastise (*Spens.*): to prune (*Milt.*): to break up in reorganisation, hence to disband, dismiss (*mil. hist.*).—*v.i.* to abandon evil ways.—*n.* amendment or transformation, esp. of a system or institution: a stricter offshoot or branch of a religious order: an extension or better distribution of parliamentary representation.—*adj.* reform'able (*ri-*).—*ns.* reformabil'ity; reformation (*ref-ər-mā'shən*), the act of reforming: amendment: improvement: (*rap.*) the great religious revolution of the 16th century, which gave rise to the various evangelical or Protestant organisations of Christendom; re-formā'tionist.—*adjs.* reformative (*ri-förm'ə-tiv*), tending to produce reform; reform'atory, re-forming: tending to produce reform.—*n.* (in U.K., formerly) an institution for reclaiming young delinquents, or women.—*adj.* reformed', changed: amended: improved: (*cap.*) Protestant, esp. Calvinistic, in doctrine or polity.—*ns.*

reform'er, one who reforms: one who advocates political reform: (*cap.*) one of those who took part in the Reformation of the 16th century; reform'ism; reform'ist, a reformer: an advocate of reform, or of not very thorough-going reform. —Reformed Presbyterian, Cameronian; reform school, reformatory. [L. *refōrmāre*, *-ātum*—*fōrmāre*, to shape—*fōrma*, form.]

reformado, *ref-ör-mā'dō*, *-mä'dō*, (*hist.*) *n.* a disbanded or dismissed soldier: an officer whose company has been disbanded or who is for other reason without a command: a volunteer serving as an officer: a reformed person: a reformer:— *pl.* -do(e)s.—Also reformāde' (*Bunyan*).—Also *adj.* [Sp. *reformado*, reformed.]

refract, *ri-frakt'*, *v.t.* (of a medium) to deflect (rays of light, sound, etc., passing into it from another medium): to produce by refraction (*rare*).—*adj.* (*rare*) refracted.—*adjs.* refract'able, refrangible; refrac'ted, deflected on passage into another medium: bent sharply back from the base (*bot.*); refract'ing.—*n.* refrac'tion.—*adj.* refrac'tive, refracting: of refraction.—*ns.* refractivity (*rē-frak-tiv'i-ti*); rēfractom'eter, an instrument for measuring refractive indices; refrac'tor (*ri-*), anything that refracts: a refracting telescope.— refracting telescope, one in which the principal means of focusing the light is an object glass; —refractive index, the ratio of the sine of the angle of incidence to that of the angle of refraction when a ray passes from one medium to another.—angle of refraction, the angle between a refracted ray and the normal to the bounding surface; double refraction, the separation of an incident ray of light into two refracted rays, polarised in perpendicular planes. [L. *refringĕre*, *refrāctum*—*frangĕre*, to break.]

refractory (formerly refractary), *ri-frak'tər-i*, *adj.* unruly: unmanageable: obstinate: perverse: resistant to ordinary treatment, stimulus, disease, etc.: esp. difficult of fusion: fire-resisting.—*n.* a substance that is able to resist high temperatures, etc., used in lining furnaces, etc.— *adv.* refrac'torily.—*n.* refrac'toriness. [L. *refrāctārius*, stubborn.]

refrain, *ri-frān'*, *n.* a burden, a line or phrase recurring, esp. at the end of a stanza: the music of such a burden. [O.Fr. *refrain*—*refraindre*— L. *refringĕre*—*frangĕre*, to break.]

refrain, *ri-frān'*, *v.t.* to curb (*arch.*): to restrain (*arch.*): to abstain from (*Shak.*): to keep away from (*obs.*).—*v.i.* to keep oneself from action, forbear: to abstain (from; *obs.* with *to*). [O.Fr. *refrener*—L.L. *refrēnāre*—*re-*, back, *frēnum*, a bridle.]

refrangible, *ri-fran'ji-bl*, *adj.* that may be refracted. —*n.* refrangibil'ity. [See refract.]

refresh, *ri-fresh'*, *v.t.* to make fresh again: to freshen up: to give new vigour, life, liveliness, spirit, brightness, fresh appearance, coolness, moistness, etc., to.—*v.i.* to become fresh again: to take refreshment, esp. drink (*coll.*).—*v.t.* refresh'en, to make fresh again.—*ns.* refresh'ener; refresh'er, one who, or that which, refreshes: a cool drink (*coll.*): a fee paid to counsel for continuing his attention to a case, esp. when adjourned: a douceur to encourage further exertions (*coll.*): a subsequent course of training or instruction to maintain or reattain the old standard (also *adj.*).—*adj.* refresh'ful, full of power to refresh: refreshing.—*adv.* refresh'fully. —*adj.* refresh'ing, pleasantly cooling, inspiriting, reviving, invigorating.—*adv.* refresh'ingly.—*ns.* refresh'ment, the act of refreshing: state of being refreshed: renewed strength or spirit: that which refreshes, as food or rest: (in *pl.*) drink or

refoot', *v.t.*
reform'ulate, *v.t.*
refortificā'tion, *n.*

refort'ify, *v.t.*
refound', *v.t.*
refoundā'tion, *n.*

refound'er, *n.*
refrac'ture, *n.*
reframe', *v.t.*

a light meal.—refresh'ment-room; Refreshment, or Refection, Sunday, the fourth Sunday in Lent, when the story of the loaves and fishes is read in English and R.C. churches. [O.Fr. refrescher— re-, freis (fem. fresche), fresh.]

refrigerant, ri-frij'ə-rənt, adj. cooling: giving a feeling of coolness: refreshing.—n. a freezing or cooling agent: that which gives a cool feeling.— v.t. refrig'erāte, to freeze: to make cold: to make to feel cool: to expose to great cold (as food for preservation).—v.i. to become cold.—n. refrigerā'tion.—adj. refrig'erative (-rə-tiv), cooling.—n. refrig'erator (-rā-tər), an apparatus or chamber for producing and maintaining a low temperature.—adj. refrig'eratory (-rə-tər-i), cooling: refrigerative.—n. a refrigerator: a chamber in which ice is formed: a water-filled vessel for condensing in distillation. [L. refrigerāre, -ātum —re-, denoting change of state, frigerāre—frigus, cold.]

refringe, ri-frinj', (obs.) v.t. to refract.—n. refring'ency, refractivity.—adj. refring'ent. [L. refringēre; see refract.]

reft, reft, pa.t. and pa.p. of reave.

refuge, ref'ūj, n. shelter or protection from danger or trouble: an asylum or retreat: a street island for pedestrians: recourse in difficulty.—v.t. and v.i. to shelter.—n. refugee', one who flees for refuge to another country, esp. from religious or political persecution: a fugitive.—house of refuge, a shelter for the destitute. [Fr.,—L. refugium—fugēre, to flee.]

refulgent, ri-ful'jənt, adj. casting a flood of light: radiant: beaming.—ns. reful'gence, reful'gency. [L. refulgēns, -entis, pr.p. of refulgēre—re-, inten., fulgēre, to shine.]

refund, ri- or rē-fund', v.t. to pour back (now rare): to repay.—v.i. to restore what was taken.—ns. refund (rē'fund or ri-fund'); refund'er; refund'ment (ri-). [L. refundēre—fundēre, to pour.]

refund, rē-fund', v.t. to fund anew: to replace (an old issue) by a new: to borrow so as to pay off an old loan. [Pfx. re-.]

refuse, ri-fūz', v.t. to decline to take or accept: to renounce: to decline to give or grant: of a horse, to decline to jump over: to fail to follow suit to (cards): to decline to meet in battle: to hold back from the regular alignment in action (mil.).—v.i. to make refusal.—v.t. re-fuse (rē-fūz'), to fuse again.—adj. refus'able (ri-).—ns. refus'al, the act of refusing: the option of taking or refusing: a thing refused; refus'er. [Fr. refuser—L. refūsum, pa.p. of refundēre—fundēre, to pour; cf. refund.]

refuse, ref'ūs, adj. rejected as worthless.—n. that which is rejected or left as worthless. [Fr. refus; see foregoing.]

refute, ri-fūt', v.t. to disprove.—adj. refutable (ref'ūt-ə-bl, or ri-fūt').—adv. ref'utably (or ri-fūt').—ns. refu'tal, refutā'tion (ref-), act of refuting: that which disproves; refu'ter. [L. refūtāre, to drive back.]

regain, ri- or rē-gān', v.t. to gain back: to get back to.—n. recovery.—adj. regain'able.—ns. regain'er; regain'ment. [Fr. regaigner (now regagner).]

regal, rē'gl, adj. royal: kingly.—adj. regalian (rigā'li-ən), regal.—ns. regalism (rē'gal-izm), royal supremacy, esp. in Church matters; re'galist; regality (ri-gal'i-ti), state of being regal: royalty: sovereignty: a territorial jurisdiction formerly conferred by the king (Scot.).—adv. re'gally. [L. rēgālis—rēx, a king—regēre, to rule.]

regal, rē'gl, n. a small portable organ. [Fr. régale.]

regale, ri-gāl', v.t. to feast: to give pleasure to. —v.i. to feast.—n. a feast: a choice dish.—n.

regale'ment. [Fr. régaler—It. regalare, perh.— gala, a piece of finery.]

regalia, ri-gā'li-ə, rā-gä'li-a, n.pl. royal privileges or powers, as (hist.) that of enjoying the revenues of vacant sees, etc. (sing. rega'le): the insignia of royalty—crown, sceptre, etc.: loosely, insignia or special garb generally, as of the Freemasons. [L. rēgālis, royal, neut. sing. -e, pl. -ia.]

regalia, ri-gā'li-ə, n. a big cigar. [Sp., royal right.]

regar. See regur.

regard, ri-gärd', v.t. to look at: to observe: to heed: to look to: to esteem or consider: to esteem highly: to have kindly feelings for: to respect: to take into account: to have respect or relation to.—v.i. to look: to give heed.—n. orig., look: a thing seen (Shak.): intention (Shak.): attention with interest: observation: estimation: esteem: kindly, affectionate, and respectful feeling: care: consideration: a thing to be considered: repute: respect: relation: reference: (in pl.) in messages of greeting, respectful good will.—adjs. regard'able, worthy of consideration; regard'ant, attentive: looking backward (her.).—n. regard'er.—adj. regard'ful, heedful: respectful. — adv. regard'fully. — n. regard'fulness.—prep. regard'ing, concerning. —adj. regard'less, heedless: inconsiderate.— adj. and adv. (coll.) without regard to expense.— adv. regard'lessly.—n. regard'lessness.—as regards, with regard to; in regard of, to (arch.), in comparison with: out of consideration for (Shak.); in this regard, in this respect; with regard to, concerning: so far as relates to. [Fr. regarder—garder, to keep, watch.]

regatta, ri-gat'ə, n. a yacht or boat race-meeting. [It. (Venetian) regata.]

regelation, rē-ji-lā'shən, n. freezing together again (as of ice melted by pressure when the pressure is released).—v.t. and v.i. rē'gelāte. [Pfx. re- and L. gelāre, to freeze.]

regency, rē'jən-si, n. the office, term of office, jurisdiction, or dominion of a regent: a body entrusted with vicarious government: specif., in French history, the minority of Louis XV, 1715-1723, when Philip of Orleans was regent: in English history, the years 1810-20, when the Prince of Wales (George IV) was Prince Regent. —adj. of, or in the style prevailing during, the French (or English) regency.—n. rē'gence (obs.), government.—adj. regent, ruling: invested with interim or vicarious sovereign authority.—n. a ruler: one invested with interim authority on behalf of another: formerly in Scotland and elsewhere, a professor: a master or doctor who takes part in the regular duties of instruction and government in some universities.—n. rē'gentship.—rē'gent-bird, a bower-bird (Sericulus) named in honour of the Prince Regent. [L. regēns, -entis, pr.p. of regēre, to rule.]

regenerate, ri-jen'ər-āt, v.t. to produce anew: to renew spiritually (theol.): to put new life or energy into: to reform completely: to reproduce (a part of the body): to produce again in the original form (chem., nucleonics, etc.).—v.i. to undergo regeneration: to be regenerated.—adj. (-it, -āt) regenerated, renewed: changed from a natural to a spiritual state.—adj. regen'erable.— ns. regen'eracy (-ə-si); regenerā'tion, renewal of lost parts: spiritual rebirth: reformation: recovery of waste heat or other energy that would have been lost.—adj. regen'erative.—adv. regen'eratively.—n. regen'erātor, one who, or that which, regenerates: a chamber in which waste heat is, by reversal of draught, alternately stored up and given out to the gas and air entering.—adj. regen'eratory (-ə-tər-i). [L. regenerāre,

rēfū'el, v.t.
rēfur'bish, v.t.

rēfur'nish, v.t. and v.i.

rēfū'sion, n.

*-ātum*, to bring forth again—*re-*, again, *generāre*, to generate.]

**regent.** See **regency.**

**regest,** *ri-jest'*, (*Milt.*) *n.* a register. [See **register.**]

**Reggae,** *reg'ā, rā'gā, n.* gay, aggressive rock music of the West Indies, imported into Britain by immigrants in the mid-1960s.

**regicide,** *rej'i-sid, n.* the killing or killer of a king.—*adj.* **regici'dal.** [L. *rēx, rēgis,* a king, on the analogy of **homicide, parricide,** etc.]

**régie,** *rā-zhē, n.* a system of government monopoly, esp. in tobacco: the department concerned: tobacco sold by it. [Fr.]

**régime,** *rā-zhēm', n.* regimen: administration.—Also **regime.** [Fr.,—L. *regimen.*]

**regimen,** *rej'i-men, n.* government: system of government: course of treatment, as diet (*med.*): grammatical government: prevailing system or set of conditions.—*adj.* **regim'inal.** [L. *regimen, -inis—regēre,* to rule.]

**regiment,** *rej'mənt, rej'i-mənt, n.* government: control: rule: regimen: a region under government: (often *rej'mənt*) a body of soldiers constituting the largest permanent unit, commanded by a colonel.—*v.t.* (*rej'i-ment, -ment'*) to form into a regiment or regiments: to systematise, classify: to organise: to subject to excessive control.—*adj.* **regimental** (*-i-ment'l*), of a regiment.—*n.* (in *pl.*) the uniform of a regiment.—*n.* **regimentation** (*-i-men-tā'shən*). [L.L. *regimentum*—L. *regēre,* to rule.]

**regina,** *ri-jī'nə, n.* queen: title of a reigning queen, abbrev. to R in signature.—*adj.* **reginal** (*-jī'nl*), of a queen: siding with a queen. [L. *rēgīna.*]

**region,** *rē'jən, n.* a tract of country: any area or district, esp. one characterised in some way: a realm: a portion or division, as of the body: a portion of space: the atmosphere, or a division of it, esp. the upper air (*Shak., Milt.*): the heavens (*obs.*).—*adj.* (*Shak.*) of the air.—*adj.* **re'gional.**—*ns.* **re'gionalism,** regional patriotism or particularism; **re'gionalist.**—*adv.* **re'gionally.**—*adj.* **re'gionary**—**in the region of,** near: about, approximately. [A.Fr. *regiun*—L. *rēgiō, -ōnis—regēre,* to rule.]

**régisseur,** *rā-zhē-sœr,* (Fr.) manager: stage manager.

**register,** *rej'is-tər, n.* a written record or official list regularly kept: the book containing such a record: an entry in it: a recording or indicating apparatus: a registrar (now *rare* or *U.S.*): apparatus for regulating a draught: a register-plate: an organ stop or stop-knob: the set of pipes controlled by an organ stop, or a set of strings in a harpsichord: part of the compass of any instrument having a distinct quality of tone (also *fig.*): the compass of an instrument or voice: the range of tones of a voice produced in a particular manner: exact adjustment of position, as of colours in a picture, or letterpress on opposite sides of a leaf (*print.*): registration: an entry in a register: a certificate of registration.—*v.t.* to enter or cause to be entered in a register: to record: to indicate: to put on record: to express: to represent by bodily expression: to adjust in register.—*v.i.* to enter one's name (esp. as a hotel guest): to correspond in register: to make an impression, reach the consciousness (*coll.*).—*adj.* **reg'istered,** recorded, entered, or enrolled (as a voter, a letter requiring special precautions for security, etc.): made with a register-plate; **reg'istrable.**—*ns.* **reg'istrant,** one who registers, or has registered (a trademark, etc.); **reg'istrar** (*-trär,* or *-trär'*), one who keeps a register or official record: one who makes an official record of births, deaths, and marriages registered locally: a hospital doctor in one of the intermediate grades (**medical, surgical,**

**registrar**); **reg'istrarship,** office of a registrar; **reg'istrary,** Cambridge University registrar; **registrā'tion,** the act or fact of registering: something registered: the act or art of combining stops in organ-playing; **reg'istry,** registration: an office or place where a register is kept: a register: an entry in a register.—**Register House,** the building in Edinburgh where Scottish records are kept; **register office,** a record-office: an employment office; **reg'-ister-plate,** in rope-making, a disk with holes to give each yarn its position: a chimney damper; **Reg'istrar-Gen'eral,** an officer having the superintendence of the registration of all births, deaths, and marriages; **registry office,** an office for putting domestic servants in touch with employers: a registrar's office, where births, etc., are recorded and civil marriages are celebrated.—**gross,** or **net, register (tonnage),** gross or net, tonnage; **Lord Clerk-Register,** an officer of the General Register House with duties concerned with the election of Scottish representative peers, formerly custodian of records and registers; **parish register,** a book in which births, deaths, and marriages are inscribed; **ship's register,** a document showing the ownership of a vessel. [O.Fr. *registre* or L.L. *registrum,* for L. pl. *regesta,* things recorded—*re-,* back, *gerēre,* to carry.]

**regius,** *rē'ji-əs, rā'gi-ōōs, adj.* royal, as **regius professor,** one whose chair was founded by Henry VIII, or, in Scotland, by the Crown; **rē'gium dō'num,** a former annual grant of public money to nonconformist ministers in England, Scotland, and esp. Ireland. [L. *rēgius—rēx,* king.]

**reglet,** *reg'lit, n.* a flat, narrow moulding: a fillet: a strip for spacing between lines (*print.*). [Fr. *réglet,* dim. of *règle*—L. *rēgula,* a rule.]

**regma,** *reg'mə,* (bot.) *n.* a fruit that splits into dehiscent parts—*pl.* **reg'mata.** [Gr. *rhēgma, -atos,* a breaking.]

**regnal,** *reg'nl, adj.* of a reign.—*adj.* **reg'nant,** reigning (often after the noun, as **queen regnant** a reigning queen, not a *queen consort*): prevalent. [L. *rēgnālis—rēgnum,* a kingdom, *rēgnāns, -antis,* pr.p. of *rēgnāre,* to reign.]

**regnant.** See **regnal.**

**regolith,** *reg'ə-lith, n.* mantle-rock. [Gr. *rhēgos,* a blanket, *lithos,* a stone.]

**regorge,** *ri-, rē-görj', v.t.* to disgorge, regurgitate: to swallow again: to gorge to repletion (*Milt.*).—*v.i.* to gush back. [Pfx. **re-,** and **gorge;** or Fr. *regorger,* to overflow, abound.]

**regrate,** *ri-grāt', (hist.) v.t.* to buy and sell again in or near the same market, thus raising the price—once a criminal offence in England.—*ns.* **regrā'ter, -tor,** one who regrates (*hist.*): a middleman (*S.W.England*); **regrā'ting.** [O.Fr. *regrater;* of doubtful origin.]

**regrede,** *ri-grēd', v.i.* to retrograde (*rare*).—*n.* **regrē'dience** (*Herrick*). [L. *regredi—re-, gradī,* to go.]

**regreet,** *ri-grēt', v.t.* to greet in return: to greet again (*Shak.*): to greet (*Shak.*).—*v.i.* to exchange greetings.—*n.* a greeting, esp. in return: (in *pl.*) greetings, salutation (*Shak.*). [Pfx. **re-.**]

**regress,** *rē'gres, n.* passage back: return: reversion: backward movement or extension: right or power of returning: re-entry.—*v.i.* (*ri-gres'*) to go back: to recede: to return to a former place or state: to revert: to move from east to west (*astron.*).—*n.* **regression** (*ri-gresh'ən*), act of regressing: reversion: return towards the mean: return to an earlier stage of development.—*adj.* **regressive** (*ri-gres'iv*), going back: returning.—*adv.* **regress'ively,** in a regressive manner: by return.—*ns.* **regress'iveness** (*ri-*);

---

**rēgive',** *v.t.*                                      **rēgrant',** *n.* and *v.t.*

regressiv'ity (rē-). [L. *regressus—regredī*; see regrede.]

regret, ri-gret', *v.t.* to remember with sense of loss or feeling of having done amiss: to wish otherwise:—*pr.p.* regrett'ing; *pa.t.* and *pa.p.* regrett'ed.—*n.* sorrowful wish that something had been otherwise: sorrowful feeling of loss: compunction: an intimation of regret or refusal. —*adj.* regret'ful, feeling regret.—*adv.* regret'-fully.—*adj.* regrett'able, to be regretted.—*adv.* regrett'ably. [O.Fr. *regreter, regrater*; poss. conn. with greet (2).]

reguerdon, ri-gûr'dən, (*Shak.*) *n.* reward.—*v.t.* to reward. [O.Fr. *reguerdon.*]

regula, reg'ū-la, *n.* the rule of a religious order: a fillet, esp. under the Doric taenia, below each triglyph (*archit.*):—*pl.* reg'ulae (-lē).—*adj.* reg'ular (-lər), subject to a monastic rule (opp. to *secular*): governed by or according to rule, law, order, habit, custom, established practice, mode prescribed, or the ordinary course of things: of a marriage, celebrated by a minister of religion after proclamation of banns: normal: habitual: constant: steady: uniform: periodical: duly qualified: inflected in the usual way, esp. of weak verbs (*gram.*): symmetrical, esp. (*bot.*) radially symmetrical or actinomorphic: having all the sides and angles equal or all faces equal, equilateral, and equiangular, the same number meeting at every corner (*geom.*): also (of a pyramid) having a regular polygon for base and the other faces similar and equal isosceles triangles: permanent, professional, or standing (*mil.*; opp. to *militia, volunteer,* and *territorial*): thorough, out-and-out, esp. (*U.S.*) in party politics (*coll.*): of the same way of thinking as the speaker, hence ready to help or abet him, loyal, swell (*slang*): veritable (*coll.*).—*n.* a member of a religious order who has taken the three ordinary vows: a soldier of the regular army: a regular customer. —*n.* regularisā'tion, -z-.—*v.t.* reg'ularise, -ize, to make regular.—*n.* regularity (-lar'i-ti), state, character, or fact of being regular.—*adv.* reg'ularly.—*v.t.* reg'ulate, to control: to adapt or adjust continuously: to adjust by rule.—*v.i.* to make regulations.—*n.* regulā'tion, act of regulating: state of being regulated: a rule or order prescribed.—*adj.* prescribed by regulation.—*adj.* reg'ulātive, tending to regulate.—*n.* reg'ulātor, one who, or that which, regulates: a controlling device, esp. for the speed of a clock or watch.— *adj.* reg'ulatory (-lə-tər-i). [L. *rēgula,* a rule— *regēre,* to rule.]

regulus, reg'ū-ləs, *n.* an impure metal, an intermediate product in smelting of ores: antimony: (*cap.*) a first-magnitude star in Leo: the goldcrest genus of birds.—*adj.* reg'uline.—*v.t.* reg'ulise, -ize, to reduce to regulus. [L. *rēgulus,* dim. of *rēx,* a king.]

regur, regar, rā', rē'gər, *n.* the rich black cotton soil of India, full of organic matter. [Hind. *regar.*]

regurgitate, ri-, rē-gûr'ji-tāt, *v.t.* to cast out again: to pour back: to bring back into the mouth after swallowing.—*v.i.* to gush back.—*adj.* re-gur'gitant.—*n.* regurgitā'tion. [L.L. *regurgitāre,* -*ātum*—*re,* back, *gurges, gurgitis,* a gulf.]

reh, rā, *n.* an efflorescence of sodium salts on the soil in India. [Hindustani.]

rehabilitate, rē-(h)ə-bil'i-tāt, *v.t.* to reinstate, restore to former ⎰privileges, rights, rank, etc.: to clear the charter of: to bring back into good condition, working order, prosperity: to make fit, after disablement or illness, for earning a

living or playing a part in the world.—*n.* rehabilitā'tion. [L.L. *rehabilitāre,* -*ātum*; see habilitate.]

rehash, rē-hash', *n.* something made up of materials formerly used, esp. a restatement in different words of ideas already expressed by oneself or someone else.—Also *v.t.* [Pfx. re-, hash, n.]

rehear, rē-hēr', *v.t.* to hear again: to try over again, as a lawsuit.—*n.* rehear'ing. [Pfx. re-.]

rehearse, ri-hûrs', *v.t.* to repeat, say over, or read aloud: to enumerate: to recount, narrate in order: to perform privately for practice or trial: to practise beforehand: to train by rehearsal.—*v.i.* to take part in rehearsal.—*ns.* rehears'al, the act of rehearsing: repetition: enumeration: narration: a performance for trial or practice; rehears'er; rehears'ing. [O.Fr. *rehercer, reherser*—*re-,* again, *hercer,* to harrow—*herce* (Fr. *herse*)—L. *hirpex, -icis,* a rake, a harrow.]

reheat, rē-hēt', *v.t.* to heat again.—*n.* (the use of) a device to inject fuel into the hot exhaust gases of a turbojet in order to obtain increased thrust.—*n.* reheat'er, a person who reheats: an apparatus for reheating. [Pfx. re-.]

rehoboam, rē-(h)ō-bō'əm, *n.* a large liquor measure or vessel, two jeroboams. [*Rehoboam,* king of Israel.]

rehouse, rē-howz', *v.t.* to provide with a new house or houses.—*n.* rehous'ing. [Pfx. re-.]

Reich, rihh, *n.* the German state: Germany as an empire (**First Reich,** Holy Roman Empire, 962-1806; **Second Reich,** under Hohenzollern emperors, 1871-1918), and as a dictatorship (**Third Reich,** under Nazi régime, 1933-45).— *ns.* **Reichsbank** (rīhhs'bängk), the German state bank; **Reichsland** (-länt), imperial territory, i.e. Alsace-Lorraine, 1871-1919; **reichsmark** (-märk), the German monetary unit 1924-48 (see **mark,** 2); **Reichsrat,** earlier -**rath** (-rät), upper house of the parliament of the former Austrian Empire: a deliberative Council of the Weimar Republic in Germany (1919-33), representing the States; **Reichstag** (-tähh), the lower house of the parliament of Germany during the Second Reich and the Weimar Republic. [Ger., O.E. *rice,* kingdom: cf. **bishopric.**]

reif, rēf, (*Scot.*) *n.* spoliation. [O.E. *rēaf;* cf. reave.]

reify, rē'i-fī, *v.t.* to think of as a material thing: to convert into a material thing, to materialise.— *n.* reification (-fi-kā'shən). [L. *rēs,* a thing.]

reign, rān, *n.* kingdom (*obs.*): realm (*obs.*): domain (*obs.*): rule, actual or nominal, of a monarch: predominance: predominating influence: time of reigning.—*v.i.* to be a monarch: to be predominant: to prevail. [O.Fr. *regne*— L. *rēgnum—regēre,* to rule.]

reik. Same as reak.

reimbattell'd, rē-im-bat'ld, (*Milt.*) *pa.p.* drawn up again in battle array. [Pfx. re-.]

reimburse, rē-im-bûrs', *v.t.* to repay: to pay an equivalent to for loss or expense.—*n.* reimburse'-ment. [L.L. *imbursāre—in,* in, *bursa,* purse.]

reim-kennar, rim'ken-ər, *n.* an enchanter, enchantress. [App. invented by Scott—Ger. *reim,* rhyme, *kenner,* knower.]

rein, rān, *n.* the strap of a bridle or either half of it: any means of curbing or governing (*fig.*).— *v.t.* to fasten or tie by the rein (*Shak.*): to furnish with reins: to govern with the rein: to restrain or control: to stop or check (with *in* or *up*).— *v.i.* to answer (*Shak.*): to stop or slow up.—*adj.* rein'less, without rein or restraint.—rein'-arm, rein'-hand, normally the left (opp. to *whip-hand*);

---

rēgrind', *v.t.*
rēgroup', *v.t.*
rēgrowth', *n.*
rēhand'le, *v.t.*

rēhand'ling, *n.*
rēheel', *v.t.*
rē-ignite', *v.t.*
rēillume', *v.t.*

rēillum'ine, *v.t.*
rēimpose', *v.t.*
rēimposi'tion, *n.*

**reins′man**, a skilful driver.—**draw rein**, to pull up, stop riding; **give rein** (or **the reins**) **to**, to allow free play to, apply no check to; **take the reins**, to take control. [O.Fr. *rein, resne, rene* (Fr. *rêne*), perh. through (hypothetical) L.L. *retina*, from L. *retinēre*, to hold back.]

**rein.** See **reindeer, reins.**

**reincarnate**, *rē-in-kär′nāt*, *v.t.* to cause to be born again in another body or form: to embody again in flesh.—*adj.* reborn.—*ns.* **rēincarnā′tion**; **rēincarnā′tionism**, belief in reincarnation of the soul; **rēincarnā′tionist**. [Pfx. re-.]

**reindeer**, *rān′dēr*, *n.* a large heavy deer (Rangifer), wild and domesticated, of northern regions, antlered in both sexes, the American variety (or species) called the caribou.—Also (*rare*) **rein.**—**Reindeer Age** (*archaeol.*), the Magdalenian; **reindeer moss**, a lichen (*Cladonia rangiferina*), the winter food of the reindeer. [O.N. *hreinndȳri*, or O.N. *hreinn* (O.E. *hrän*) and **deer**.]

**reinette**, *rā-net′.* Same as **rennet** (apple).

**re infecta**, *rē, rā in-fek′ta, -tä*, (L.) without finishing the business.

**reinforce**, *rē-in-fōrs′, förs′*, *v.t.* to enforce again (*rare*): to strengthen with new force or support: to strengthen: to increase by addition.—*v.i.* (*Shak.*) to get reinforcements.—*n.* something that reinforces: a reinforced part near the rear of a gun.—*n.* **reinforce′ment**, act of reinforcing: additional force or assistance, esp. of troops (commonly in *pl.*).—**reinforced concrete**, concrete strengthened by embedded steel bars or mesh. [Alt., by 17th cent., of **renforce**.]

**reinform**, *rē-in-förm′*, *v.t.* to inform anew: to give form to again: to reanimate [Pfx. re-.]

**reinfund**, *rē-in-fund′*, (*Swift*) *v.i.* to flow in again. [Pfx. re-, L. *infundēre—fundēre*, to pour.]

**reins**, *rānz*, *n.pl.* (*rare* or *obs.* in *sing.*) the kidneys, esp. as formerly supposed seat of emotion: the loins. [O.Fr. *reins*—L. *rēn*, pl. *rēnēs.*]

**reinstall**, *rē-in-stöl′*, *v.t.* to install again.—*n.* **reinstal′ment.** [Pfx. re-.]

**reinstate**, *rē-in-stāt′*, *v.t.* to insure again: to restore to or re-establish in a former station or condition.—*ns.* **reinstāte′ment: reinstā′tion** (*rare*). [Pfx. re-.]

**reinsure**, *rē-in-shōōr′*, *v.t.* to insure against the risk undertaken by underwriting an insurance.—*ns.* **reinsur′ance; reinsur′er.** [Pfx. re-.]

**reintegrate**, *rē-in′ti-grāt*, *v.t.* to integrate again: to redintegrate.—*n.* **reintegrā′tion.**

**reinvest**, *rē-in-vest′*, *v.t.* to clothe again: to endow again: to invest again.—*n.* **reinvest′ment.** [Pfx. re-.]

**reinvigorate**, *rē-in-vig′ər-āt*, *v.t.* to put new vigour into.—*n.* **reinvigorā′tion.** [Pfx. re-.]

**reird**, *rērd*, **raird**, *rārd*, (*Scot.*) *n.* an uproar, clamour, din. [O.E. *reord.*]

**reis**, *ris.* Same as **rice** (2).

**reis**, *rās, n.pl.* (*sing.* **real**, *rā-äl′*) an obsolete Portuguese and Brazilian money of account, 1000 reis making a *milreis.* [Port.]

**reist.** Same as **reast** (1), or as **reest** (2 or 3).

**reiter**, *rī′tər*, *n.* a German cavalry soldier. [Ger.]

**reiterate**, *rē-it′ər-āt*, *v.t.* to repeat: to repeat again and again.—*n.* **reit′erance.**—*adjs.* **reit′erant**, reiterating; **reit′erate, -d.**—*adv.* **reit′erately.**—*n.* **reiterā′tion**, act of reiterating: the printing of the second side of a sheet.—*adj.* **reit′erative.**—*n.* a word expressing reiteration of utterance or act: a word formed by re-

duplication, the second element usu. differing from the first (e.g. *helter-skelter*). [Pfx. re-.]

**reive, reiver.** Same as **reave, reaver.**

**reject**, *ri-jekt′*, *v.t.* to throw away: to discard: to refuse to accept, admit, or accede to: to refuse: to renounce.—*n.* (usu. *rē′*) one who or that which is rejected.—*adjs.* **rejec′table** or **-ible.**—*n.pl.* **rejectamen′ta**, refuse: excrement.—*ns.* **rejec′tion; reject′or** (also **-er**). [L. *rejicĕre, rejectum—re-*, back, *jacĕre*, to throw.]

**rejig**, *rē-jig′*, **rejigger**, *-jig′ər*, *v.t.* to change or rearrange in a new or unexpected way that is sometimes regarded as unethical (*commerce*).—*n.* **re′jig.**

**rejoice**, *ri-jois′*, *v.t.* to make joyful: to gladden: to be joyful because of (*Shak.*).—*v.i.* to feel joy: to exult: to make merry.—*adj.* **rejoice′ful.**—*ns.* **rejoice′ment**, rejoicing; **rejoic′er; rejoic′ing**, act of being joyful: expression, subject, or experience of joy: (in *pl.*) festivities, celebrations, merry-makings.—*adv.* **rejoic′ingly.**—**rejoice in**, to be happy because of: (*facet.*), to have. [O.Fr. *resjoir, resjoiss-* (Fr. *réjouir*)—L. *re-, ex, gaudēre*, to rejoice.]

**rejoin**, *ri-join′*, (*law*) *v.i.* to reply to a charge or pleading, esp. to a plaintiff's replication.—*v.t.* to say in reply, retort.—*n.* **rejoin′der** (*ri-*) the defendant's answer to a plaintiff's replication (*law*): an answer to a reply: an answer. [O.Fr. *rejoindre.*]

**rejoin**, *ri-, rē-join′*, *v.t.* and *v.i.* to join again.—*n.* **rejoin′dure (reioyn′dure,** *Shak.*), a joining again. [Pfx. re-.]

**rejourn**, *ri-jûrn′*, (*Shak.*) *v.t.* to postpone, defer. [Cf. **adjourn.**]

**rejuvenate**, *ri-jōō′vi-nāt*, *v.t.* to make young again: to restore to youthful condition or to activity: to restore (by uplift) to earlier condition of active erosion (*geol.*).—*v.i.* to rejuvenesce.—*ns.* **rejuvenā′tion; reju′venator.** — *v.i.* **rejuvenesce** (*-es′*), to grow young again: to recover youthful character: to undergo change in cell-contents to a different, usu. more active, character (*biol.*): to resume growth.—*v.t.* to rejuvenate.—*n.* **rejuvenesc′ence.**—*adj.* **rejuvenesc′ent.**—*v.t.* **reju′venise, -ize**, to rejuvenate. [Pfx. re-, L. *juvenis*, young, *juvenēscĕre*, to become young.]

**reke**, *rēk*, (*Spens.*) *v.i.* to reck. [O.E. *rēcan.*]

**relâche**, *rə-läsh*, (Fr.) *n.* relaxation: rest: no performance.

**relapse**, *ri-laps′*, *v.i.* to slide, sink, or fall back, esp. into evil: to return to a former state or practice: to backslide: to fall away.—*n.* a falling back into a former bad state: the return of a disease after partial recovery (*med.*).—*adj.* **relapsed′**, having relapsed.—*n.* **relap′ser.**—*adj.* **relap′sing.**—**relapsing fever**, an infectious disease characterised by recurrent attacks of fever with enlargement of the spleen, caused by a spirochaete transmitted by ticks and lice. [L. *relābī, relāpsus—lābī*, to slide.]

**relate**, *re-lāt′*, *v.t.* to recount, narrate, tell: to give an account of (*Milt.*): to bring back (*Spens.*): to refer, bring into connection or relation.—*v.i.* to date back in application (*law*): to have reference or relation: to connect: to discourse (*Shak.*).—*adj.* **relā′ted**, narrated: referred (to; *rare*): connected: allied by kindred or marriage.—*ns.* **relā′tedness; relā′ter**, one who relates; **relā′tion**, act of relating: state or mode of being related: narrative or recital: statement:

---

**rēincrease′**, *v.t.*      **rēinspir′it**, *v.t.*      **rēintroduce′**, *v.t.*
**rēinfuse′**, *v.t.*      **rēinter′**, *v.t.*      **rēintroduc′tion**, *n.*
**rēinhab′it**, *v.t.*      **rēinter′ment**, *n.*      **rēinvig′orate**, *v.t.*
**rēinsert′**, *v.t.*      **rēinter′pret**, *v.t.*      **rēiss′uable**, *adj.*
**rēinser′tion**, *n.*      **rēinterpretā′tion**, *n.*      **rēiss′ue**, *v.t.* and *n.*
**rēinspect′**, *v.t.*      **rēinterr′ogate**, *v.t.*      **rēkin′dle**, *v.t.* and *v.i.*
**rēinspec′tion**, *n.*      **rēinterrogā′tion**, *n.*
**rēinspire′**, *v.t.*

Neutral vowels in unaccented syllables: *el′ə-mənt*; for certain sounds in foreign words, see p. viii

an information (law): way in which one thing is connected with another: a quality that can be predicated, not of a single thing, but only of two or more together (philos.): respect, reference: a relative by birth or marriage: (in pl.) mutual dealings.—adj. relā′tional, pertaining to, expressing, or of the nature of, relation.—adv. relā′tionally.—ns. relā′tionism (philos.), the doctrine that relations have an objective existence: the doctrine of relativity of knowledge; relā′tionist.—adj. relā′tionless, kinless: unrelated.—n. relā′tionship, state or mode of being related: relations.—adjs. relatival (rel-ə-tī′vl), pertaining to relation, esp. grammatical relation; rel′ative (-ə-tiv), in or having relation: correlative: corresponding: having the same key-signature (mus.): relevant: comparative: not absolute or independent: relating, having reference: referring to an antecedent (gram.).—n. that which is relative: a relative word, esp. a relative pronoun: one who is related by blood or marriage.—adv. rel′atively. —ns. rel′ativeness; rel′ativism, relationism: a doctrine of relativity: the view that accepted standards of right and good vary with environment and from person to person; rel′ativist.— adj. relativis′tic, pertaining to relativity, or to relativism.—ns. relativ′itist, one who studies or accepts relativity; relativ′ity, state or fact of being relative: a principle which asserts that only relative, not absolute, motion can be detected in the universe (Einstein's Special Theory of Relativity, 1905, starts from two fundamental postulates: a. that all motion is relative, b. that the velocity of light is always constant relative to an observer; his General Theory of Relativity, 1916, which embraces the Special Theory deals with varying velocities, or accelerations— whereas the Special Theory dealt with constant relative velocity, or zero acceleration—and it is much concerned with gravitation; in each case Einstein derived important equations and made predictions); relator (ri-lā′tər), one who relates: a narrator: one who lays an information before the Attorney-General, enabling him to take action (law).—relative density, specific gravity (q.v.); relative humidity, the ratio of the amount of water vapour in the air to the amount that would saturate it at the same temperature.—relativity of knowledge, the doctrine that the nature and extent of our knowledge is determined not merely by the qualities of the objects known but necessarily by the conditions of our cognitive powers. [L. relātus, -a, -um, used as pa.p. of referre, to bring back—re, ferre.]

relative, etc. See relate.

relax, ri-laks′, v.t. and v.i. to loosen: to slacken: to make or become less close, tense, rigid, strict, or severe.—n. a relaxing.—adj. and n. relax′ant, laxative: (a substance) having the effect of relaxing.—n. relaxā′tion (re-, rē-), act of relaxing: state of being relaxed: partial remission (law): release from outlawry (Scots law): recreation.—adjs. relax′ative; relax′ing, enervating. [L. relaxāre, -ātum—laxus, loose.]

relay, ri-lā′, also rē′lā, rē′lā′, n. a fresh set of dogs in hunting: a supply of horses, etc., to relieve others on a journey: a station for either of these: a relieving shift of men: a supplementary store of anything: a relay-race, one of its stages: any device by which a weak electric current or other small power is used to control a strong one: a relayed programme, or act or fact of relaying it.—v.t. to place in, relieve, control, supply, or transmit by relay: to broadcast anew (programme received from another station or source).—v.i. to obtain a relay: to

operate a relay:—pa.t. and pa.p. relayed.— re′lay-race′, a race between teams, each man running part of the total distance. [O.Fr. relais, relay of horses or dogs; origin obscure.]

relay, rē-lā′, v.t. to lay again:—pa.t. and pa.p. rēlaid′. [Pfx. re-.]

release, rē-lēs′, v.t. to grant a new lease of. [Pfx. re-.]

release, ri-lēs′, v.t. to let loose: to set free: to let go: to relieve: to slacken: to undo: to remit: to relinquish: to surrender, convey, give up a right to (law): to make available, authorise sale, publication, exhibition, etc., of.—n. a setting free: liberation: discharge or acquittance: remission: mode of releasing: the giving up of a claim, conveyance: a catch for holding and releasing: authorisation to make available on a certain date: a thing so made available. —adj. releas′able.—ns. releasee′, one to whom an estate is released; release′ment, release; releas′er; releas′or (law). [O.Fr. relaissier— L. relaxāre, to relax.]

relegate, rel′i-gāt, v.t. to banish: to consign (to a, usu. unimportant, place or position): to remove to a lower class (football): to assign (to a class): to refer (to another, others) for decision or action: to refer (a person, for something, to another; arch.).—adj. rel′egable.—n. relegā′tion. [L. relēgāre, -ātum—re-, away, lēgāre, to send.]

relent, ri-lent′, v.i. to melt (obs.): to soften, become less severe: to give way (Spens., Milt.): to abate, slacken (Spens.): to slacken pace (Spens.).—v.t. to melt (obs.): to soften, cause to relent (Spens., Burns): to relax, moderate (Spens.): to slow down (Spens.): to regret, repent (Spens.).—n. relenting: slowing (Spens.). —n. and adj. relent′ing.—adj. relent′less, unrelenting: inexorable: merciless, stern.—adv. relent′lessly.—ns. relent′lessness; relent′ment (rare). [L. re-, back, lentus, sticky, sluggish, pliant.]

relevant, rel′i-vənt, adj. bearing upon, or applying to, the matter in hand, pertinent: related, proportional (to): sufficient legally.—ns. rel′evance, rel′evancy. — adv. rel′evantly. [L. relevāns, -antis, pr.p. of relevāre, to raise up, relieve; from the notion of helping; cf. relieve.]

reliable, etc. See rely.

relic, rel′ik, n. that which is left after loss or decay of the rest: a corpse (usu. in pl.): any personal memorial of a saint, held in reverence as an incentive to faith and piety (R.C.): a souvenir: a memorial of antiquity or object of historic interest: (of, e.g. a custom) a survival from the past.—Also (obs.) rel′ique.—rel′ic-monger, one who traffics in or collects relics. [Fr. relique—L. reliquiae; see reliquiae.]

relict, rel′ikt, n. a relic (obs.): a survivor or surviving trace (arch.): a widow (arch.).—adj. (ri-likt′) left behind: surviving: formed by removal of surrounding materials (geol.). [L. relictus, -a, -um, left, pa.p. of relinquĕre, to leave.]

relide, ri-līd′, (Spens.) pa.p. for relied, in the sense of 'rejoined'.

relief, ri-lēf′, n. the lightening or removal of any burden, discomfort, evil, pressure, or stress: release from a post or duty: one who releases another by taking his place: that which relieves or mitigates: aid in danger, esp. deliverance from siege: assistance to the poor: fresh supply of provisions: feeding or seeking food (hunting; obs.): a certain fine paid to the overlord by a feudal tenant's heir on coming into possession: release from obligation, or right to reimbursement of expenses thereby incurred (Scots law): anything that gives diversity: projection or standing out from the general surface, ground,

rēlet′, v.t.

or level: a sculpture or other work of art executed in relief: appearance of standing out solidly: distinctness by contrast, esp. in outline. —*adj.* providing relief in cases of overloading, distress, danger, difficulty.—*adj.* **relief'less.**— **Relief Church,** body that left the Church of Scotland because of oppressive exercise of patronage, organised in 1761, united with the United Secession Church in 1847 to form the United Presbyterian Church; **relief map,** a map in which the form of the country is shown by elevations and depressions of the material used, or by the illusion of such elevations and depressions, or (loosely) by other means. [O.Fr. *relef*— *relever*; see **relieve,** also **rilievo.**]

**relieve,** *ri-lēv′, v.t.* to lift up (*Shak.*): to bring, give, or afford relief to: to release: to release from duty by taking the place of: to ease (e.g. a burden): (*refl.*) to urinate or to defecate: to mitigate: to raise the siege of: to set off by contrast: to break the sameness of: to bring into relief: to feed (*obs.*).—*adj.* **reliev′able.**—*n.* **reliev′er.**—*adj.* **reliev′ing.**—**relieving arch,** an arch in a wall to relieve the part below it from a superincumbent weight; **relieving officer,** an official formerly appointed to superintend the relief of the poor.—**relieve one of,** to take from one's possession, with or without one's approval: to steal from one: to free one from (a necessity, restriction, etc.). [O.Fr. *relever*—L. *relevāre,* to lift, relieve—*levāre,* to raise—*levis,* light.]

**relievo,** *ri-lē′vō,* also (*It.*) **rilievo,** *rē-lyä′vō,* (*art*) *n.* relief: a work in relief: appearance of relief. [It. *rilievo.*]

**religieux,** *rə-lē-zhyø,* (Fr.) *n.* a monk or friar:— *fem.* **-gieuse** (*-zhyœz*), a nun.

**religio loci,** *ri-lij′i-ō lō′sī, re-lig′i-ō lok′ē.* See Quotations from Latin, etc., in Appendices.

**religion,** *ri-lij′ən, n.* belief in, recognition of, or an awakened sense of, a higher unseen controlling power or powers, with the emotion and morality connected therewith: rites or worship: any system of such belief or worship: devoted fidelity: monastic life: a monastic order:— Protestantism (*obs.*).—*adj.* **relig′ionary** (*rare*), religious.—*n.* a member of a religious order: a Protestant (*obs.*).—*n.* **relig′ioner,** a member of an order: a Protestant (*obs.*).—*v.t.* **relig′ionise, -ize,** to imbue with religion.—*v.i.* to make profession of being religious.—*ns.* **relig′ionism, religiosity:** bigotry; **relig′ionist,** one attached to a religion: a bigot: one professionally engaged in religion, e.g. an evangelist (*U.S.*).— *adjs.* **relig′ionless; religiose** (*-lij′i-ōs,* or *-ōs′*), morbidly or sentimentally religious.—*n.* **religiosity** (*-i-os′it-i*), spurious or sentimental religion: religious feeling.—*adj.* **relig′ious** (*-əs*), of, concerned with, devoted to, or imbued with, religion: scrupulous: bound to a monastic life (*R.C.*): strict, very exact.—*n.* one bound by monastic vows.—*adv.* **relig′iously.**—*n.* **relig′iousness.** [L. *religiō, -ōnis, n., religiōsus,* adj., perh. conn. with *religāre,* to bind.]

**religiose,** etc. See **religion.**

**religioso,** *rə-lij-i-i-ō′sō,* (It.) *adj.* and *adv.* in a devotional manner (*mus.*).

**reline,** *rē-lin′, v.t.* to mark with new lines: to renew the lining of. [Pfx. re-.]

**relinquish,** *ri-ling′kwish, v.t.* to give up: to let go. —*n.* **relin′quishment.** [O.Fr. *relinquir, relinquiss-* —L. *relinquĕre, relictum*—re-, *linquĕre,* to leave.]

**relique,** *rel′ik, ri-lēk′, n.* an old form of **relic.**— *ns.* **reliquaire** (*rel-i-kwār′*), **rel′iquary** (*-kwar-i*), a receptacle for relics.—*adj.* **rel′iquary,** of relics: residual. [Fr.]

**reliquiae,** *ri-lik′wi-ē, re-lik′wi-ī, n.pl.* remains. [L.,—*relinquĕre,* to leave.]

**relish,** *rel′ish, n.* a flavour: characteristic flavour:

enough to give a flavour: appetising flavour: zest-giving quality or power: an appetiser, condiment: zestful enjoyment: gusto: pleasureful inclination.—*v.t.* to like the taste of: to be pleased with: to enjoy: to appreciate discriminatingly: to give a relish to: to taste, experience (*obs.*).—*v.i.* to savour, smack: to have an agreeable taste: to give pleasure.—*adj.* **rel′ishable.** [O.Fr. *reles, relais,* remainder— *relaisser,* to leave behind.]

**relish, rellish,** *rel′ish, n.* a musical ornament.— *v.t.* (*Shak.*) to warble. [Origin obscure.]

**relive,** *rē-liv′, v.t.* and *v.i.* to live again: (*rē-liv′*) to revive (*Spens.*).

**reliver,** *ri-liv′ər,* (*Shak.*) *v.t.* to deliver back. [O.Fr. *relivrer;* also pfx. re-, *liver,* to deliver, *obs.* and *dial.*]

**relucent,** *ri-lū′-, -lōō′sənt, adj.* reflecting: shining. [L. *relūcēns, -entis,* pr.p. of *relūcēre,* to shine back.]

**reluct,** *ri-lukt′, v.i.* to be unwilling (with *at*): to hold back.—*ns.* **reluc′tance,** opposition, resistance (*Milt.*): unwillingness: magnetomotive force applied to whole or part of a magnetic circuit divided by the flux in it; **reluc′tancy.**—*adj.* **reluc′tant,** struggling (*Milt.*): unwilling: resisting.—*adv.* **reluc′tantly.**—*v.i.* **reluct′āte,** to be reluctant.—*n.* **reluctā′tion** (*rel-*), repugnance. [L. *reluctāri*—re-, against, *luctāri,* to struggle.]

**relume,** *ri-lūm′, -lōōm′, v.t.* to light anew: to rekindle: to light up again.—*v.t.* **relu′mine** (*-in*), to relume. [L. *relūmināre—lūmen, -inis,* light.]

**rely,** *ri-li′, v.i.* to rally (*obs.*): to rest as on a support (*obs.*): to depend confidently:—*pr.p.* **rely′ing;** *pa.t.* and *pa.p.* **relied′.**—*n.* **reliabil′ity.** —*adj.* **reli′able,** to be relied on, trustworthy.—*n.* **reli′ableness.**—*adv.* **reli′ably.** (These four words are sometimes condemned as formed neither from a trans. verb nor from a noun.)—*n.* **reli′ance,** trust: that in which one trusts.—*adj.* **reli′ant.**—*n.* **reli′er** (*Shak.*).—**reliability test,** **trial,** a public test of the qualities of motor vehicles (now known as a **rally**). [O.Fr. *relier* —L. *religāre,* to bind back.]

**rem,** *rem, n.* a unit of radiation dosage, the amount which has the same effect as one rad of X-radiation. [röntgen equivalent *man* or mammal.]

**remain,** *ri-mān′, v.i.* to stay or be left behind: to continue in the same place: to dwell, abide (*Shak.*): to be left after or out of a greater number: to continue in one's possession, mind: to continue unchanged: to continue to be: to be still to be dealt with (often without subject *it*): to await (*Spens., Milt.*).—*n.* stay, abode (*Shak.*): a surviving part (*arch.*): in most uses, **remains′** (*pl.* in form, but occasionally with sing. verb), as follows:—what is left: relics: a corpse: the literary productions of one dead.—*n.* **remain′der,** that which remains or is left behind after the removal of a part or after division: the residue, rest: balance of an account (*Shak.*): an interest in an estate to come into effect after a certain other event happens: right of next succession to a post or title: residue of an edition when the sale of a book has fallen off. —*adj.* (*Shak.*) left over.—*v.t.* to sell (book) as a remainder.—**remain′der-man,** to one whom a legal remainder is devised. [O.Fr. *remaindre*— L. *remanēre*—re-, back, *manēre,* to stay.]

**remake,** *rē-māk′, v.t.* to make anew.—*adj.* **remade′.**—*ns.* **remade′, rēmake′,** a thing (as a gutta golf-ball) made over again from the original materials. [Pfx. re-.]

**remand,** *ri-mänd′, v.t.* to send back (esp. a prisoner into custody to await further evidence). —*n.* act of remanding: recommittal.—**remand home,** a place of detention for children and young persons on remand or awaiting trial; also for some undergoing punishment. [O.Fr. *remander*, or L.L. *remandāre—mandāre*, to order.]

**remanent**, *rem'ən-ənt, adj.* remaining.—*n.* a remainder: a remnant.—*ns.* **rem'anence, -ency**; **rem'anet**, a remainder: a postponed case or parliamentary bill. [L. *remanēns, -entis*, pr.p., and *remanet*, 3rd pers. sing. pres. indic. of *remanēre*.]

**remanié**, *rə-mä-nyā, (geol.) n.* a fossil or other relic of an older rock preserved as a fragment in a later deposit. [Fr. pa.p. of *remanier*, to rehandle.]

**remark**, *ri-märk', v.t.* to mark out (*Milt.*): to notice: to comment (that), or say incidentally (that).—*v.i.* (*ri-*) to comment, make an observation.—*n.* noteworthiness: observation: comment: (also as Fr., **remarque'**) a marginal drawing or other distinguishing mark on an engraving or etching indicating an early state of the plate: also a print or proof bearing this special remark.—*adj.* **remark'able**, noteworthy: unusual, singular, strange, distinguished.—*n.* a remarkable thing.—*n.* **remark'ableness**.—*adv.* **remark'ably**.—*adj.* **remarked'**, conspicuous: (also **remarqued'**) bearing a remark, as an etching.—*n.* **remark'er**. [O.Fr. *remarquer—re-*, inten., *marquer*, to mark.]

**remark**, **re-mark**, *rē-märk', v.t.* to mark again. [Pfx. re-.]

**remblai**, *rä-ble, n.* earth used to form a rampart, embankment, etc.: stowage in a mine. [Fr.]

**remble**, *rem'(b)l, (N.E. England) v.t.* to remove, clear. [Origin obscure.]

**Rembrandtesque**, *rem-bran-tesk', or -brən-, adj.* like the work of *Rembrandt* (1606-69), esp. in his contrast of high lights and deep shadows.—*adj.* **Rem'brandtish**.—*n.* **Rem'brandtism**.

**remeasure**, *rē-mezh'ər, v.t.* to measure anew: to retrace (*Spens.*).—*n.* **remeas'urement**. [Pfx. re-.]

**remedy**, *rem'i-di, obs.* and *Scot.* **remede, remeid, remead** (*ri-mēd'), n.* any means of curing a disease, redressing, counteracting, or repairing any evil or loss: reparation: redress: range of tolerated variation in the weight of a coin.—*v.t.* to cure (a person, diseased part) (*arch.*): to put right, repair, counteract:—*pr.p.* **rem'edying**; *pa.t.* and *pa.p.* **rem'edied**.—*adj.* **remē'diable**.—*adv.* **remē'diably**.—*adj.* **remē'dial**, tending or intended to remedy.—*adv.* **remē'dially**.—*adjs.* **remē'diat(e)**, remedial (*Shak.*): **rem'ediless** (formerly *-med'*), without remedy: incurable.—*adv.* **rem'edilessly** (or *-med'*).—*n.* **rem'edilessness** (or *-med'*).—**no remedy** (*Shak.*), of necessity; **what remedy?**, how can it be helped or avoided? (*obs.*). [A.Fr. *remedie*, O.Fr. *remede*—L. *remedium*.]

**remember**, *ri-mem'bər, v.t.* to keep in or recall to memory or mind: to mention, record (*obs.*): to commemorate (*obs.*): to bear in mind as something to be mentioned (*Shak.*): to bear in mind as one deserving of honour or gratitude, or as one to be rewarded, tipped, or prayed for: to remind (*arch.* or dial.): to bethink (*reflex.*; *Shak.*): to occur to (*impers.*; *arch.*): to recall to the memory of another (often as a greeting).—*v.i.* to have the power or perform the act of memory: to have memory (with *of*; *Shak.*, *Milt.*; now *Scot.* and *U.S.*).—*adj.* **remem'berable**.—*adv.* **remem'berably**.—*ns.* **remem'berer**; **remem'brance**, memory: that which serves to bring to or keep in mind: a reminder: a souvenir: a memorandum: a memorial: the reach of memory: (in *pl.*) a message of friendly greeting; **remem'brancer**, one who or that which reminds: a recorder: an officer of exchequer (**King's Remembrancer**).—**Remembrance**

**Sunday**, the Sunday nearest to 11th November commemorating the fallen of the two World Wars (see **Armistice Day**).—**remember your courtesy** (*obs.*), remember to put your hat on, which you have taken off in courtesy. [O.Fr. *remembrer*—L. *re-*, again, *memor*, mindful.]

**remercy**, *ri-mûr'si, (obs.) v.t.* to thank:—*pa.t.* (*Spens.*) **remer'cied**. [(O.) Fr. *remercier*.]

**remerge**, *rē-mûrj', v.t.* to merge again. [Pfx. re-.]

**remex**, *rē'meks, n.* one of the large feathers of a bird's wing—primary or secondary:—*pl.* **remiges** (*rem'i-jēz*).—*v.i.* **remigate** (*rem'i-gāt*), to row.—*n.* **remigā'tion**. [L. *rēmex, -igis*, a rower.]

**remigrate**, *rem'i-grāt, v.i.* to change back: (also *rē-mī'*) to migrate again or back.—*n.* **remigrā'tion** (*rem-i-* or *rē-mī-*). [Pfx. re-.]

**remind**, *ri-mīnd', v.t.* to put in mind (of), to cause to remember.—*n.* **remind'er**, that which reminds.—*adj.* **remind'ful**, mindful: reminiscent, exciting memories. [Pfx. re- and mind, *v.t.*]

**reminiscence**, *rem-i-nis'əns, n.* recollection: an account of something remembered: the recurrence to the mind of the past.—*v.i.* **reminisce** (*-nis'*; back-formation), to recount reminiscences.—*adj.* **reminisc'ent**, suggestive, remindful: addicted to reminiscences: pertaining to reminiscence.—Also *n.*—*adj.* **reminiscen'tial** (*-sen'shl*), of, or of the nature of, reminiscence.—*adv.* **reminisc'ently**. [L. *reminiscēns, -entis*, pr.p. of *reminisci*, to remember.]

**remise**, *ri-miz', n.* surrender of a claim (*law*): (*rə-mēz'*) an effective second thrust after the first has missed (*fencing*): a coach-house: a livery-carriage.—*v.t.* (*ri-miz'*) to surrender. [Fr. *remis*, *remise—remettre*—L. *remittĕre*, to send back, remit, relax.]

**remiss**, *ri-mis', adj.* negligent: slack: lax: wanting in vigour.—*n.* **remissibil'ity**.—*adj.* **remiss'ible**, that may be remitted.—*n.* **remission** (*ri-mish'ən*), act of remitting: slackening: abatement: relinquishment of a claim: pardon: forgiveness.—*adj.* **remiss'ive**, remitting: forgiving.—*adv.* **remiss'ly**.—*n.* **remiss'ness**.—*adj.* **remiss'ory**, of remission. [L. *remittĕre, remissum*; see remit.]

**remit**, *ri-mit', v.t.* to relax: to pardon: to refrain from exacting or inflicting: to give up: to desist from: to transfer: to transmit, as money, etc.: to put again in custody: to refer to another court, authority, etc.: to refer for information: to send or put back.—*v.i.* to abate: to relax: to desist:—*pr.p.* **remitt'ing**; *pa.t.* and *pa.p.* **remitt'ed**.—*n.* (*law*) reference of a case or matter to another.—*ns.* **remit'ment**, remission: remitting: remittance; **remitt'al**, remission: reference to another court, etc.; **remitt'ance**, the sending of money, etc., to a distance: the sum or thing sent: **remittē̄'**, the person to whom a remittance is sent.—*adj.* **remitt'ent**, remitting at intervals.—*adv.* **remitt'ently**.—*n.* **remitt'er**, one who makes a remittance.—**remitt'ance-man**, one dependent upon remittances from home; **remittent fever**, a severe type of malaria in which the temperature falls slightly from time to time. [L. *remittĕre, remissum—re-*, back, *mittĕre*, to send.]

**remnant**, *rem'nənt, n.* a fragment or a small number surviving or remaining after destruction, defection, removal, sale, etc., of the greater part: esp. a remaining piece of cloth: a tag or quotation: a surviving trace: trace of a fact (*Scott*).—*adj.* remanent, remainder. [remanent.]

**remonstrance**, *ri-mon'strəns, n.* a strong or formal protest, expostulation.—*adj.* **remon'strant**, remonstrating: (*cap.*) Dutch Arminian.—*n.* one who remonstrates: (*cap.*) a Protester (*Scot. hist.*): (*cap.*) a member of the Dutch Arminian party whose divergence from Calvinism was

---

**rĕmarr'iage**, *n.*  **rĕmod'el**, *v.t.*  **rĕmon'etise, -ize**, *v.t.*
**rĕmarr'y**, *v.t.* and *v.i.*  **rĕmonetisā'tion, -z-**, *n.*

*fāte, fär; mē, hûr (her); mīne; mōte, fŏr; mūte; mō̄n, fō̄t; dhen (then)* expressed in five articles in the Remonstrance of 1610.—*adv.* remon'strantly.—*v.i.* remon'-strāte (sometimes *rem'*), to make a remonstrance. —*v.t.* to say or (*obs.*) state in remonstrance: to demonstrate (*obs.*).—*adv.* remon'stratingly.— *n.* remonstrā'tion (*rem-ən-*).—*adjs.* remon'strative, remon'stratory (-*strə-tar-i*), expostulatory. —*n.* remon'strator.—Grand Remonstrance, a statement of abuses presented to Charles I by the House of Commons in 1641. [L. *re-*, again, *mōnstrāre*, to point out.]

remontant, ri-mon'tənt, *adj.* blooming more than once in the same season.—*n.* a remontant plant, esp. a rose. [Fr.]

remora, rem'o-rə, *n.* the sucking-fish, formerly believed to stop ships by attaching its sucker: an obstacle. [L. *rēmŏra*, delay, hindrance—*mora*, delay.]

remorse, ri-mörs', *n.* the gnawing pain of conscience: compunction: pity, compassionate feeling (*Spens.*, *Shak.*, *Milt.*): mitigation (*Shak.*): probably, matter of conscience (*Shak.*): bite (*Spens.*).—*adj.* remorse'ful, penitent: compassionate (*obs.*).—*adv.* remorse'fully.—*n.* remorse'fulness.—*adj.* remorse'less, without remorse: cruel.—*adv.* remorse'lessly.—*n.* remorse'-lessness. [O.Fr. *remors* (Fr. *remords*)—L.L. *remorsus*—L. *remordēre*, *remorsum*, to bite again—*re-*, again, *mordēre*, to bite.]

remote, ri-mōt', *adj.* far removed in place, time, chain of causation or relation, resemblance or relevance: widely separated: very indirect.—*adv.* remote'ly.—*ns.* remote'ness; remō'tion, removal (*Shak.*): remoteness (*rare*).—remote control, control of a device from a distance by the making or breaking of an electric circuit or by means of radio waves. [L. *remōtus*, pa.p. of *removēre*; see remove.]

remoud, ri-mōōd', *pa.t.* (*Spens.*) for removed.

remould, rē'mōld', *n.* a used tyre which has had a new tread vulcanised to the casing and the walls coated with rubber.—Also *v.t.* [Pfx. re-.]

remount, rē-mount', *v.t.* and *v.i.* to mount again.— *n.* a fresh horse, or supply of horses. [Pfx. re-.]

remove, ri-mōōv', *v.t.* to put or take away: to transfer: to withdraw: to displace: to make away with: (in *pass.*; *Thackeray*) of a dish on the table, to be succeeded (by).—*v.i.* to go away: to change abode.—*n.* removal: the raising of a siege (*Shak.*): absence (*Shak.*): step or degree of remoteness or indirectness: in some schools, an intermediate class: promotion: a dish removed to make way for another, or taking the place of one so removed.—*n.* removabil'ity.— *adj.* remov'able.—*adv.* remov'ably.—*n.* remov'al, the act of taking away: displacing: change of place: transference: going away: change of abode: a euphemism for murder.—*adj.* re-moved', remote: distant by degrees, as in descent.—*ns.* remov'edness; remov'er, one who or that which removes: one who conveys furniture from house to house.—removal terms (*Scot.*), 28th May and 28th November, called Whitsunday and Martinmas. [O.Fr. *remouvoir*—L. *removēre*, *remōtum*—*re-*, away, *movēre*, to move.]

remuda, ri-mū'də, rā-mōō'dhä, *n.* a supply of remounts. [Sp., exchange.]

remunerate, ri-mū'nə-rāt, *v.t.* to recompense: to pay for service rendered.—*adj.* remū'nerable.— *n.* remūnerā'tion, recompense: reward: pay.— *adj.* remū'nerative, profitable.—*ns.* remū'nerativeness; remū'nerātor.—*adj.* remū'neratory (-ə-tər-i), giving a recompense. [L. *remunerāri* (late *-āre*), *-ātus*—*mūnus*, *-ĕris*, a gift.]

remurmur, ri-mûr'mər, *v.t.* and *v.i.* to echo, repeat, or resound in murmurs. [Pfx. re-.]

renaissance, ri-nā'səns, ren'i-säns, *-säns'*, *n.* a new birth: (*cap.*) the revival of arts and letters, the

transition from the Middle Ages to the modern world.—*adj.* of the Renaissance. [Fr.; cf. renascence.]

renal, rē'nl, *adj.* of the kidneys. [L. *rēnālis*—*rēnēs* (sing. *rēn*, is rare), the kidneys.]

renascent, ri-nas'ənt, also *-nās'*, *adj.* coming into renewed life or vitality.—*n.* renasc'ence, being born anew: (*cap.*) Renaissance. [L. *renāscēns*, *-entis*, pr.p. of *renāscī*—*nāscī*, to be born.]

renay, reney, ri-nā', reny, ri-ni', (*obs.*) *v.t.* to renounce, abjure, forswear: to deny:—*pr.p.* renay'ing, reny'ing; *pa.p.* renayed', renied'. [O.Fr. renaier, renier—L. renegāre.]

rencounter, ren-kownt'ər, rencontre, rä-kõ-tr', (Fr.), *n.* a chance meeting: an encounter: a casual combat: a collision.—*v.t.* to meet: to encounter. [Fr. rencontre.]

rend, rend, *v.t.* to tear asunder with force: to split: to tear away.—*v.i.* to become torn:—*pa.t.* and *pa.p.* rent. [O.E. *rendan*, to tear.]

render, ren'dər, *v.t.* to give up: to give back, return, give in return: to make up: to deliver: to hand over: to give: to surrender: to yield: to tender or submit: to show forth: to represent or reproduce, esp. artistically: to perform: to translate: to perform or pay as a duty or service: to present or betake (with *at*; *refl.*): to cause to be: to melt: to extract, treat, or clarify by melting: to plaster with a first coat.—*n.* an act of rendering: that which is rendered.—*adj.* ren'derable.—*ns.* ren'derer; ren'dering; rendi'tion, surrender: rendering. [O.Fr. *rendre*—L.L. *rendēre*, app. formed by influence of *prendēre*, to take—L. *reddēre*—*re-*, back, *dăre*, to give.]

rendezvous, rä'dā-vōō, ron'di-, *n.* appointed meeting-place: a meeting by appointment: a general resort:—*pl.* rendezvous (*-vōōz*), (*obs.*) rendez-vous'es.—*v.i.* to assemble at any appointed place. [Fr. *rendez-vous*, render yourselves—*rendre*, to render.]

renegade, ren'i-gād, renegate, -gāt, *n.* one faithless to principle or party: an apostate: a turncoat: esp. a Christian turned Mohammedan—also renegā'do.—*v.i.* ren'egade, to turn renegade. —*adjs.* ren'egade, -ate, apostate.—*n.* renegā'-tion.—*v.t.* renegue, renege (ri-nēg'), to renounce: to apostatise from.—*v.i.* to deny: to refuse: to revoke at cards.—Also renig (-nig'), renague (-nāg'; *Ir.*).—*n.* reneg'(u)er. [L.L. *renegātus*— L. *re-*, inten., *negāre*, *-ātum*, to deny; partly through Sp. *renegado*.]

renew, ri-nū', *v.t.* to renovate: to transform to new life, revive: to begin again: to repeat: to make again: to invigorate: to substitute new for: to restore: to renovate: to regenerate.— *v.i.* to be made new: to begin again.—*adj.* renew'able.—*ns.* renew'al, renewing; renew'ed-ness; renew'er; renew'ing. [Pfx. re-, and new, *adj.*]

renfierst, ren-fērst', (*Spens.*) *pa.p.* made fierce. [App. modelled on the next.]

renforce, ren-fōrs', *-förs*, (*obs.*) *v.t.* to reinforce: to force again.—*v.i.* to renew efforts:—(in *Spens.* *pa.t.* re'nforst', *pa.p.* renforst'). [(O.)Fr. renforcer.]

renga. Same as linked verse. See link.

reniform, ren'i-förm, *adj.* kidney-shaped. [L. *rēnēs* (sing. *rēn*), the kidneys, and *förma*, form: see renal.]

renig. See renegue (under renegade).

renitent, ri-ni'tənt, ren'i-tənt, *adj.* resistant: reluctant: recalcitrant.—*n.* reni'tency (or *ren'*). [L. *renitēns*, *-entis*, pr.p. of *renitī*, to resist.]

renne, ren, (*Spens.*) *v.i.* to run.—Also *pa.p.*—*n.* renn'ing. [See run.]

rennet, ren'it, *n.* any means of curdling milk, esp. a preparation of calf's stomach.—renn'et-bag,

rēname', *v.t.*

the fourth stomach of a ruminant. [O.E. *rinnan*, to run; cf. **earn** (2), **yearn** (3).]

**rennet**, *ren'it*, *n.* apple of certain old varieties. [Fr. *reinette*, *rainette*; origin uncertain.]

**renounce**, *ri-nowns'*, *v.t.* to disclaim: to disown: to reject publicly and finally: to recant: to abjure.—*v.i.* to fail to follow suit at cards.—*n.* a failure to follow suit.—*ns.* **renounce'ment**; **renoun'cer**. [O.Fr. *renuncer*—L. *renuntiāre*—*re-*, away, *nuntiāre*, -*ātum*, to announce.]

**renovate**, *ren'ō-vāt*, *v.t.* to renew or make new again: to make as if new: to regenerate.—*ns.* **renovā'tion**; **ren'ovātor**. [L. *re-*, again, *novāre*, -*ātum*, to make new—*novus*, new.]

**renown**, *ri-nown'*, *n.* fame.—*v.t.* to make famous: to celebrate.—*adj.* **renowned'**, famous.—*n.* **renown'er**, one who gives renown. [O.Fr. *renoun* (Fr. *renom*)—L. *re-*, again, *nōmen*, a name.]

**rent**, *rent*, *n.* an opening made by rending: a fissure.—*v.t.* and *v.i.* (*obs.* or *dial.*) to rend.— Also *pa.t.* and *pa.p.* of **rend**. [**rend**.]

**rent**, *rent*, *n.* periodical payment for use of another's property, esp. houses and lands: revenue.—*v.t.* to hold or occupy by paying rent: to let or hire out for a rent: to charge with rent.—*v.i.* to be let at a rent.—*adj.* **rent'able**.—*ns.* **rent'al**, a rent-roll: rent: annual value: something rented or hired (*U.S.*): a kindly (*q.v.*) tenant's lease (*Scot.*); **rent'aller** (*Scot.*), a kindly tenant; **rent'er**, a tenant who pays rent: one who lets out property: a farmer of tolls or taxes: a theatre shareholder.—**rental library** (*U.S.*), a lending-library which takes fees for books borrowed; **rent'-charge**, a periodical payment charged upon rent; **rent'-collector**; **rent'-day**.—*adj.* and *adv.* **rent'-free**, without payment of rent.—**rent'-restric'tion**, restriction of landlord's right to raise rent; **rent'-roll**, a list of tenements and rents: total income from property.—**for rent** (orig. *U.S.*), to let. [Fr. *rente* —L. *reddita* (*pecūnia*), money paid—*reddĕre*, to pay; cf. **render**.]

**rente**, *rät*, annual income: (in *pl.*) French or other government securities or income from them.—*n.* **rentier**, *rä-tyā*, a fund-holder: one who has, or who lives on, an income from investments. [Fr.]

**renunciation**, *ri-nun-si-ā'shən*, *n.* act of renouncing: self-resignation.—*adjs.* **renun'ciative** (-*shə-tiv*, -*syə-tiv*, -*si-ā-tiv*), **renun'ciatory** (-*shə-tər-i*, -*si-ə-tər-i*). [L. *renūntiāre*, proclaim; see **nuncio**.]

**renverse**, *ren-vûrs'*, *v.t.* to reverse: to upset:— *pa.t.* and *pa.p.* **renversed'**, **renverst'** (*Spens.*). [Fr. *renverser*—pfx. *re-*, *enverser*, to overturn.]

**renvoi**, (esp. formerly) **renvoy**, *ren-voi'*, Fr. *rä-vwä*, sending back by a government of an alien to his own country: a referring or relegation. [Fr.]

**reny**. See **renay**.

**reorient**, *rē-ō'*, -*ō'ri-ənt*, *adj.* rising again.—*v.t.* (-*ent*) to orient again.—*v.t.* **reō'rientate**, reorient. —*n.* **reōrientā'tion**. [Pfx. **re-**.]

**rep, repp**, *rep*, *n.* a corded cloth.—Also **reps** (*reps*). —*adj.* **repped** (*rept*), transversely corded. [Fr. *reps*, perh.—Eng. **ribs**.]

**rep**, *rep*, *n.* a colloquial or slang abbreviation of **repertory** (*theatrical*), **repetition** (*school*), **reputation** (early 18th cent. and *U.S.*), **representative**, and **reprobate**.

**rep**, *rep*, *n.* unit of radiation dosage, now superseded by **rad**. [*r*öntgen *e*quivalent *p*hysical.]

**repaid**, *pa.t.* and *pa.p.* of **repay**.

**repaint**, *rē-pānt'*, *v.t.* to paint anew.—*n.* a repainted golf-ball.—*n.* **repaint'ing**. [Pfx. **re-**.]

**repair**, *ri-pār'*, *v.i.* to betake oneself: to go: to resort: to return (*Shak.*).—*v.t.* (*Spens.*) to re-

store to its position: to withdraw.—*n.* resort: place of resort: concourse. [O.Fr. *repairer*, to return to a haunt—L.L. *repatriāre*, to return to one's country—L. *re-*, back, *patria*, native country.]

**repair**, *ri-pār'*, *v.t.* to mend: to make amends for: to make good: to restore, refresh, revivify (*Shak.*).—*n.* restoration after injury or decay: supply of loss: sound condition: condition in respect of soundness.—*adj.* **repair'able**, capable of being mended (esp. of material things): falling to be repaired.—*ns.* **repair'er**; **reparability** (*rep-ər-ə-bil'i-ti*).—*adj.* **reparable** (*rep'ar-ə-bl*), capable of being made good or (*rare*) being mended: falling to be repaired.—*adv.* **rep'arably**. —*n.* **reparā'tion**, repair: supply of what is wasted: amends: compensation.—*adjs.* **reparative** (*ri-par'ə-tiv*); **repar'atory**.—**repair'man**, one who does repairs, esp. on something mechanical; **repair'-shop**. [O.Fr. *reparer*—L. *reparāre*— *parāre*, to prepare.]

**repand**, *ri-pand'*, *adj.* slightly wavy. [L. *repandus* —*re-*, back, *pandus*, bent.]

**reparable**, etc. See **repair** (2).

**repartee**, *rep-är-tē'*, *n.* a ready and witty retort: skill in making such retorts.—*v.t.* and *v.i.* to retort with ready wit. [O.Fr. *repartie*—*repartir* —*partir*, to set out—L. *partīri*, to divide.]

**repartition**, *rep-ar-tish'ən*, *n.* distribution: (*rē-pär-*), a second partition: a division into smaller parts.—*v.t.* (*rē-pär-*) to partition anew. [Pfx. **re-**.]

**repass**, *rē-päs'*, *v.t.* and *v.i.* to pass again: to pass in the opposite direction.—*n.* **repassage** (*rē-pas'ij*). [Pfx. **re-**.]

**repast**, *ri-päst'*, *n.* a meal: refreshment of sleep (*Spens.*).—*v.t.* and *v.i.* (*Shak.*) to feed.—*n.* **repas'ture** (*Shak.*), food. [O.Fr. *repast* (Fr. *repas*) —L.L. *repastus*—L. *pascĕre*, *pastum*, to feed.]

**repatriate**, *rē-* or *ri-pāt'ri-āt*, or -*pat'*, *v.t.* to restore or send back to one's country.—*n.* a repatriated person.—*n.* **repatriā'tion**. [L.L. *repatriāre*, -*ātum*, to return to one's country— *patria*.]

**repay**, *rē-pā'*, *ri-pā'*, *v.t.* to pay back: to make return for: to recompense: to pay or give in return.—*v.i.* to make repayment:—*pr.p.* **repay'-ing**; *pa.t.* and *pa.p.* **repaid'**.—*adj.* **repay'able**, that is to be repaid: due.—*n.* **repay'ment**. [Pfx. **re-**.]

**repeal**, *ri-pēl'*, *v.t.* to revoke: to annul: to quash, repress, set aside (*Spens.*, *Milt.*): to recall from banishment (*obs.*): to try to have restored to favour (*Shak.*).—*n.* abrogation: (*cap.*) dissolution of the Union between Great Britain and Ireland called for by O'Connell.—*adj.* **repeal'able**.—*n.* **repeal'er**, one who repeals: (*cap.*) an advocate of Repeal. [O.Fr. *rapeler*—pfx. *re-*, *apeler*, to appeal.]

**repeat**, *ri-pēt'*, *v.t.* to say, do, perform, go over, again: to iterate: to quote from memory: to say off: to recount: to celebrate (*Milt.*): to say or do after another: to tell to others, divulge: to cause to recur: to reproduce: to repeat the words or actions of (*refl.*): to seek again (*obs.*): to ask back (*obs.*).—*v.i.* to recur: to make repetition: to strike the last hour, quarter, etc., when required: to fire several shots without reloading: to rise so as to be tasted after swallowing: to vote (illegally) more than once (*U.S.*).—*n.* a repetition: a retracing of one's course: a passage repeated or marked for repetition (*mus.*): dots or other mark directing repetition: a unit of a repeated pattern: an order for more goods of the same kind.— *adj.* done or occurring as a repetition.—*adjs.*

**rēnum'ber**, *v.t.*
**rēoccupā'tion**, *n.*
**rēocc'upy**, *v.t.*

**rēo'pen**, *v.t.* and *v.i.*
**rēordain'**, *v.t.*
**rēordinā'tion**, *n.*

**rēorganisā'tion**, -z-, *n.*
**rēor'ganise**, -ize, *v.t.*
**rēpā'per**, *v.t.*

repeat'able, able to be done again: fit to be told to others; repeat'ed, done again: reiterated.— *adv.* repeat'edly, many times repeated: again and again.—*n.* repeat'er, one who, or that which, repeats, or does a thing that he or it has done before: a decimal fraction in which the same figure (or sometimes figures) is repeated to infinity: a watch or clock, or a firearm, that repeats: a ship that repeats an admiral's signals: an instrument for automatically retransmitting a message (*teleg.*): a thermionic amplifier inserted in a telephone circuit (also repeating coil). —*n.* and *adj.* repeat'ing.—repeat oneself, to say again what one has said already. [Fr. *répéter*— L. *repetĕre*, *repetītum*—*re*-, again, *petĕre*, to seek.]

repechage, *rep'ə-shäzh*, Fr. *rə-pesh-äzh*, (rowing, etc.) *adj.* pertaining to a supplementary race in which second-bests in earlier eliminating races get a second chance to go on to the final race. [Fr. *repêchage*, a fishing out again.]

repel, *ri-pel'*, *v.t.* to drive off or back: to repulse: to reject: to hold off: to provoke aversion in: to repudiate:—*pr.p.* repell'ing; *pa.t.* and *pa.p.* repelled'.—*ns.* repell'ence, repell'ency.—Also repell'ance, repell'ancy.—*adj.* repell'ent, driving back: able or tending to repel: distasteful.—*n.* that which repels.—*adv.* repell'ently.—Also repell'ant; repell'antly.—*n.* repell'er.—*adj.* repell'ing.—*adv.* repell'ingly. [L. *repellĕre*—*pellĕre*, to drive.]

repent, *ri-pent'*, *v.i.* to regret, sorrow for, or wish to have been otherwise, what one has done or left undone (with *of*): to change from past evil: to feel contrition: to sorrow (*Spens.*).—*v.t.* (*refl.* or *impers.*) to affect with contrition or with regret (*arch.*): to regret, or feel contrition for (an action).—*n.* (*Spens.*) repentance.—*n.* repent'-ance, act of repenting: penitent state of mind.— *adj.* repent'ant, experiencing or expressing repentance.—*n.* (*rare*) a penitent.—*adv.* repent'antly.— *n.* repent'er.—*adv.* repent'ingly. [O.Fr. *repentir* —L. *paenitēre*, to cause to repent.]

repent, *rē'pənt*, (*bot.*) *adj.* lying on the ground and rooting. [L. *repēns*, *-entis*, pr.p. of *repĕre*, to creep.]

repercuss, *rē-pər-kus'*, *v.t.* (*obs.*, or now *coll.*) to drive back, reflect, reverberate, or have consequences.—*n.* repercussion (-*kush'ən*), driving back: reverberation: echo: reflection: a return stroke, reaction, or consequence.—*adj.* repercussive (-*kus'iv*), driving back: reverberating: echoing: repeated. [L. *repercutĕre*, *-cussum*— *re*-, *per*, *quatĕre*, to strike.]

repertory, *rep'ər-tər-i*, *n.* a storehouse, repository: a stock of pieces that a person or company is prepared to perform.—Also *adj.*—*n.* repertoire (*rep'ər-twär*; Fr. *répertoire*), performer's or company's repertory.—repertory theatre, a theatre with a repertoire of plays and a stock or permanent company of actors, called a repertory company. [L.L. *repertōrium*—L. *reperīre*, to find again—*parĕre*, to bring forth.]

répétiteur, *rā-pā-tē-tœr*, *n.* a coach, tutor: one who rehearses opera singers, etc. [Fr.; cf. repeat.]

repetition, *rep-i-tish'ən*, *n.* act of repeating: recital from memory: a thing repeated: power of repeating a note promptly.—*n.* rep'etend (-*tend*, or *-tend'*), the recurring part of a decimal fraction: a recurring note, word, refrain, etc.—*adj.* (*rep'*) to be repeated.—*adjs.* repeti'tional, repeti'-tionary, repetitious (-*tish'əs*), of the nature of, or characterised by, repetition; repetitive (*ri-pet'-i-tiv*), iterative: overmuch given to repetition. —*advs.* repeti'tiously, repet'itively.—*ns.* repeti'-

tiousness, repet'itiveness. [L. *repetĕre*; see repeat.]

repine, *ri-pīn'*, *v.i.* to fret (with *at* or *against*): to feel discontent: to murmur.—*v.t.* (*obs.*) to lament: to grudge.—*n.* (*Shak.*) a repining.—*ns.* repine'ment; repin'er.—*n.* and *adj.* repin'ing.— *adv.* repin'ingly. [App. from pine (2).]

repique, *ri-pēk'*, *n.* at piquet, the winning of thirty points or more from combinations in one's own hand, before play begins.—*v.t.* to score a repique against.—*v.i.* to score a repique. [Fr. *repic*.]

replace, *ri-* or *rē-plās'*, *v.t.* to put back: to provide a substitute for: to take the place of, supplant.—*adj.* replace'able.—*ns.* replace'ment, act of replacing: a person or thing that takes the place of another: the occurrence of a face or faces in the position where the principal figure would have a corner or edge (*crystal.*); replac'er, a substitute.—replaceable hydrogen, hydrogen atoms that can be replaced in an acid by metals to form salts. [Pfx. re-.]

replenish, *ri-plen'ish*, *v.t.* to fill again: to fill completely: to stock abundantly: to people. —*adj.* replen'ished (*Shak.*), complete, consummate.—*ns.* replen'isher, one who replenishes: an apparatus for maintaining an electric charge; replen'ishment. [O.Fr. *replenir*, *-iss-*, from *re-plein*, full—L. re-, again, *plēnus*, full.]

replete, *ri-plēt'*, *adj.* full: completely filled: filled to satiety: abounding (with *with*).—*v.t.* to fill to repletion.—*ns.* replete'ness, replē'tion, superabundant fullness: surfeit: fullness of blood (*med.*): plethora. [L. *replētus*, pa.p. of *replēre* —*plēre*, to fill.]

replevy, *ri-plev'i*, *v.t.* to bail (*arch.*): to recover, or restore to the owner (goods distrained) upon pledge to try the right at law.—*n.* replevin.— *adjs.* replev'iable, replev'isable (-*i-səb-l*).—*n.* re-plev'in, replevying: a writ or action in such a case.—*v.t.* to recover by replevin (*Swift*, etc.). [O.Fr. *replevir*—*plevir*, to pledge.]

replica, *rep'li-kə*, *n.* a duplicate, properly one by the original artist: a facsimile: a repeat (*mus.*). [It.,—L. *replicāre*, to repeat.]

replicate, *rep'li-kāt*, *v.t.* to fold back: to repeat: to make a replica of: to reply.—*v.i.* of molecules of living material, to reproduce molecules identical with themselves.—*n.* (*mus.*) a tone one or more octaves from a given tone.—*adj.* folded back.—*n.* replicā'tion, a reply: the plaintiff's answer to the defendant's plea: doubling back: copy, reproduction: reverberation, echo (*Shak.*). [L. *replicāre*, *-ātum*, to fold back— *plicāre*, to fold.]

replum, *rep'ləm*, *rē'pləm*, *n.* a partition in a fruit formed by ingrowth of the placentas, as in Cruciferae:—*pl.* rep'la. [L. *replum*, the upright in the frame of a folding door.]

reply, *ri-plī'*, *v.t.* to say in answer.—*v.i.* to answer: to respond in action, as by returning gun-fire: to echo: to answer a defendant's plea:—*pr.p.* reply'ing; *pa.t.* and *pa.p.* replied'.—*n.* an answer, response: a replication (*Scots law*): the answer in a fugue (*mus.*).—*n.* repli'er. [O.Fr. *replier*—L. *replicāre*; see replicate.]

répondez s'il vous plaît, *rā-pō-dā sēl vōō ple*, or R.S.V.P., (Fr.) please answer (this invitation).

repone, *ri-pōn'*, (*Scots law*) *v.t.* to restore to office or status: to rehabilitate. [L. *repōnĕre*, to put back—*pōnĕre*, to put.]

report, *ri-pōrt'*, *-pört'*, *v.t.* to convey (*Spens.*): to bring back, as an answer, news, or account of anything: to give an account of, esp. a formal, official, or requested account: to state in such an account: to relate: to circulate publicly:

| | | |
|---|---|---|
| rēpeo'ple, *v.t.* | rēplant', *v.t.* | rēplay', *v.t.* |
| rēperus'al, *n.* | rēplantā'tion, *n.* | rē'play, *n.* |
| rēperuse', *v.t.* | | |

to transmit as having been said, done, or observed: to write down or take notes of, esp. for a newspaper: to lay a charge against: to echo back: (*refl.*) to make personal announcement of the presence and readiness of.—*v.i.* to make a statement: to write an account of occurrences: to make a formal report: to report oneself: to act as a reporter.—*n.* a statement of facts: a formal or official statement, as of results of an investigation or matter referred: a statement on a school pupil's work and behaviour or the like: an account of a matter of news, esp. the words of a speech: reporting, testimony (*Shak*): general talk: rumour: hearsay: repute (*B.*): explosive noise.—*adj.* report'able.—*ns.* report'-age, journalistic reporting, style, or manner: gossip; report'er, one who reports, esp. for a newspaper.—*n.* and *adj.* report'ing.—*adv.* report'ingly (*Shak.*), by common report.—*adj.* reportō'rial (*rep-ər-*, *-ör-*).—reported speech, indirect speech; reported verses (Fr. *vers rapportés*), verses that combine a number of parallel sentences by collocation of corresponding parts, as Sidney's 'Virtue, beauty, and speech did strike, wound, charm, My heart, eyes, ears, with wonder, love, delight'; report stage, the stage at which a parliamentary bill as amended in committee is reported to the House, before the third reading. [O.Fr. *reporter*—L. *reportāre*—*re-*, back, *portāre*, to carry.]

repose, *ri-pōz'*, *v.t.* to lay at rest: to rest (oneself) in confidence (on; *arch.*): to give rest to, refresh by rest: to place, set (as confidence): to place in trust.—*v.i.* to rest: to be still: to rely, place one's trust (with *on*, *upon*; *arch.*).—*n.* rest: quiet: stillness: calm: ease of manner: serenity: restful feeling or effect: a place of rest (*Milt.*).—*n.* repōs'al (*Shak.* repos'all, another reading repōs'ure), reposing.—*adj.* repōsed', calm: settled.—*adv.* repō'sedly.—*n.* repōs'edness.—*adj.* repōse'ful.—*adv.* repōse'fully. [Fr. *reposer*—L.L. *repausāre*; confused with the following.]

reposit, *ri-poz'it*, *v.t.* to lay away, deposit.—*ns.* reposition (*rep-o-zish'ən*), replacing: reinstatement (*Scot.*): laying up; repos'itor, an instrument for replacing a displaced organ; repos'i-tory, a place or receptacle in which anything is laid up: a collection or museum: a mart, esp. for horses: an abode of souls: a storehouse, magazine, as of information: a place of accumulation: a confidant. [L. *repōnĕre*, *repositum*, to put back, lay aside—*pōnĕre*, to put; confused with foregoing.]

re-position, reposition, *rē-poz-ish'ən*, *v.t.* to put in a different position. [Pfx. re-.]

repossess, *rē-poz-es'*, *v.t.* to regain possession of: to take back because payment has not been made: to put again in possession.—*n.* repossession (*-esh'ən*). [Pfx. re-.]

repost. Same as riposte.

repoussé, *rə-pōō-sā*, or *-pōō'*, *adj.* raised in relief by hammering from behind or within.—*n.* repoussé work.—*n.* repoussage (*-säzh'*). [Fr.]

repp. Same as rep (1).

reprehend, *rep-ri-hend'*, *v.t.* to find fault with: to reprove.—*n.* reprehend'er.—*adj.* reprehen'sible, blameworthy.—*adv.* reprehen'sibly.—*n.* reprehen'sion, reproof: censure.—*adj.* reprehen'sive, containing reproof: given in reproof.—*adv.* reprehensively.—*adj.* reprehen'sory. [L. *repraehendĕre*, *-hēnsum*—*re-*, intens., *praehendĕre*, to lay hold of.]

represent, *rep-ri-zent'*, *v.t.* to exhibit the image of: to use, or serve, as a symbol for: to stand for: to exhibit, depict, personate, show an image of, by imitative art: to act: to be a substitute, agent, deputy, member of parliament, or the like, for: to correspond or be in some way

equivalent or analogous to: to serve as a sample of: to present earnestly to mind: to give out, make to appear, allege (that).—*adj.* represent'-able (*rep-ri-*).—*ns.* representā'men (*psych.*), the product of representation; represent'ant, a representative; representation (*-zən-tā'shən*), act, state, or fact of representing or being represented: that which represents: an image: picture: dramatic performance: a mental image: a presentation of a view of facts or arguments: a petition, remonstrance, expostulation: assumption of succession by an heir: a body of representatives.—*adj.* representā'tional (*rep-ri-zən-*).—*ns.* representā'tionism, the doctrine that in the perception of the external world the immediate object represents another object beyond the sphere of consciousness; representā'tionist.—*adj.* representative (*rep-ri-zent'ə-tiv*), representing: exhibiting a likeness: typical: pertaining to representation.—*n.* a sample: a typical example or embodiment: one who represents another or others, as a deputy, delegate, ambassador, member of parliament, agent, successor, heir: the head of a family (*Jane Austen*): a representative legislative body (*obs.*).—*adv.* represent'atively.—*ns.* represent'ativeness; represent'er; represent'ment.—representative peers, Scottish and Irish peers chosen by their fellows to sit in the House of Lords.—House of Representatives, the lower branch of the United States Congress, consisting of members chosen biennially by the people: also of various State and other legislatures. [L. *repraesentāre*, *-ātum*—*praesentāre*, to place before.]

re-present, *rē'-pri-zent'*, *v.t.* to present again.—*ns.* re'(-)presentā'tion, rē'(-)present'ment. [Pfx. re-.]

repress, *ri-pres'*, *v.t.* to restrain: to keep under: to put down: to banish to the unconscious.—*adj.* repress'ible.—*adv.* repress'ibly.—*n.* repression (*-presh'ən*).—*adj.* repress'ive.—*adv.* repress'ively.—*n.* repress'or. [L. *reprimĕre*, *repressum*—*premĕre*, to press.]

re-press, *rē'-pres'*, *v.t.* to press again. [Pfx. re-.]

repriefe, *ri-prēf'*, (*Spens.*) *n.* reproach, insult, shame, reproof.—*v.t.* reprieve (*-prēv'*), to reprove. [Same root as reproof; for vowel, see prove.]

reprieve, *ri-prēv'* (*Shak.* repreeve'; *Spens.* reprive, repryve, *-priv'*), *v.t.* to delay the execution of: to give a respite to: to rescue, redeem.—*n.* a suspension of a criminal sentence: interval of ease or relief.—*n.* repriev'al. [Supposed to be from A.Fr. *repris*, pa.p. of *reprendre*, to take back (see reprise); the *v* app. by confusion, perh. with reprieve, reprove.]

reprimand, *rep'ri-mänd*, *-mand*, *n.* a severe reproof.—*v.t.* (also *-mänd'*, *-mand'*) to reprove severely, esp. publicly or officially. [Fr. *réprimande*—L. *reprimĕre*, *repressum*, to press back—*premĕre*, to press.]

reprime, *ri-prīm'*, (*rare*) *v.t.* to repress. [See repress.]

reprint, *rē-print'*, *v.t.* to print again: to print a new impression of, esp. with little or no change.—*n.* rē'print, a later impression: printed matter used as copy.

reprise (*Spens.* reprize), *ri-prīz'*, *v.t.* to gain anew (*obs.*): to recapture (*obs.*).—*n.* a yearly charge or deduction: reprisal (*Dryden*): a renewed or alternating spell of action: (*-prēz'*) resumption of the first subject (*mus.*).—*n.* repris'al, seizure in retaliation: a prize (*Shak.*): an act of retaliation: recapture: compensation. [Fr. *reprise*—*reprendre*—L. *repraehendĕre*.]

reproach, *ri-prōch'*, *v.t.* to cast (something) in one's teeth (with *to*, *against*, also *on*; *Dryden*, etc.): to upbraid: to blame (oneself, etc., for, with): to reprove gently: to bring into discredit.—*n.*

upbraiding: reproof: censure: disgrace: a source or matter of disgrace or shame.—*adj.* **reproach′able.**—*n.* **reproach′er.**—*adj.* **reproach′ful,** reproving: deserving of reproach, disgraceful (*obs.*).—*adv.* **reproach′fully.**—*n.* **reproach′fulness.**—*adj.* **reproach′less,** irreproachable.—**the Reproaches,** antiphons chanted in R.C. churches on Good Friday, in which Christ reproaches the Jewish people. [Fr. *reprocher*, perh. from L. *prope*, near; cf. **approach**; or from *reprobāre*; see **reprobate.**]

**reprobate,** *rep′rō-bāt, adj.* failing to pass a test (esp. of silver) (*arch.*): base: rejected by God: given over to sin: depraved: unprincipled: condemnatory.—*n.* one rejected by God: an abandoned or profligate person: one lost to shame: (often playfully) a scamp.—*v.t.* to reject: to disapprove of: to censure: to disown (*obs.*).—*ns.* **rep′robacy** (*-ba-si*), state of being a reprobate; **rep′robance** (*Shak.*), reprobation; **rep′robātor; reprobā′tion,** the act of reprobating: rejection: foreordination to eternal perdition: utter abandonment: severe censure or condemnation.—*adjs.* **rep′robātive, rep′robatory,** condemnatory.—*n.* **rep′robātor** (*Scots law*), an action to prove a witness perjured or biased. [L. *reprobāre*, *-ātum*, to reprove, contrary of *approbāre*—*probāre*, to prove.]

**reproduce,** *rē-prō-dūs′, v.t.* to produce a copy of: to form anew: to propagate: to reconstruct in imagination.—*v.i.* to produce offspring: to prove suitable for copying in some way: to turn out (well, badly, etc.) when copied.—*n.* **reprodū′cer.**—*adj.* **reprodū′cible.**—*n.* **reproduction** (*-duk′shon*), the act of reproducing: the act of producing new organisms—the whole process whereby life is continued from generation to generation: regeneration: a copy, facsimile: a representation.—*adj.* **reproduc′tive.**—*adv.* **reproduc′tively.**—*ns.* **reproduc′tiveness, reproductiv′ity.** [Pfx. **re-.**]

**reproof,** *ri-prōōf′, n.* a reproving: rebuke: censure: reprehension: shame, disgrace (*Shak.*): disproof (*obs.*): (*rē-*) a second or new proof.—*v.t.* (*rē-*) to make waterproof again.—*n.* **reproval** (*ri-prōō′vl*), reproof.—*v.t.* **reprove′,** to rebuke: to censure, condemn: to disprove or refute (*obs.*): to accuse or convict (of; *B.*, A.V.).—*ns.* **repro′ver; repro′ving.**—*adv.* **repro′vingly.** [O.Fr. *reprover* (Fr. *réprouver*)—L. *reprobāre*; see **reprobate.**]

**repryve.** See **reprieve.**

**reps,** *reps.* See **rep** (1).

**reptation,** *rep-tā′shon, n.* squirming along, or up, a smooth-walled narrow passage. [L. *reptāre*, to creep.]

**reptile,** *rep′til, adj.* creeping: like a reptile in nature.—*n.* any animal of the class **Reptilia** (*-til′i-a*), vertebrates with scaly integument, cold blood, right and left aortic arch, partially divided heart, single occipital condyle, pulmonary respiration, and pentadactyl limbs (sometimes wanting): a creeping thing: a base, malignant, abject, or treacherous person.—*adjs.* **reptilian** (*-til′i-ən*); **reptilif′erous,** bearing fossil reptiles; **reptil′ious,** like a reptile. [L.L. *reptilis, -e*—*repēre,* to creep.]

**republic,** *ri-pub′lik, n.* the state (*arch.*): a form of government without a monarch, in which the supreme power is vested in the people and their elected representatives: a state or country so governed.—*adj.* **repub′lican,** of or favouring a republic: (*cap.*) of the Republican party.—*n.* one who advocates a republican form of government: (*cap.*) in U.S., orig. an Anti-Federal—now a member of the political party opposed to the *Democrats,* and favouring an extension

of the powers of the national government.—*v.t.* **repub′licanise, -ize.**—*n.* **repub′licanism.**—**Republican era,** the era adopted by the French after the downfall of the monarchy, beginning with 22nd September 1792.—**republic of letters,** the world of books and authors. [L. *rēspublica,* commonwealth—*rēs,* affair, *publica* (fem.), public.]

**repudiate,** *ri-pū′di-āt, v.t.* (of a husband) to divorce: to cast off, disown: to refuse, or cease, to acknowledge (debt, authority, claim): to deny as unfounded (a charge, etc.).—*adj.* **repū′diable.**—*ns.* **repūdiā′tion; repūdi′ātionist,** one who favours repudiation of public debt.—*adj.* **repū′diative.**—*n.* **repū′diātor.** [L. *repudiāre, -ātum*—*repudium,* divorce—*re-,* away, and the root of *pudēre,* to be ashamed.]

**repugn,** *ri-pūn′, v.t.* to fight against, to oppose (*Shak.*): to be repugnant to.—*v.i.* to be repugnant.—*ns.* **repugnance** (*-ri-pug′*), inconsistency: aversion; **repug′nancy,** repugnance: opposition (*Shak.*).—*adj.* **repug′nant,** inconsistent with (with *to*): (of things) incompatible: distasteful: disgusting: resisting, unwilling (*arch.*). [L. *repugnāre*—*re-,* against, *pugnāre,* to fight.]

**repulse,** *ri-puls′, v.t.* to drive back: to beat off: to rebuff.—*n.* a driving back: a beating off: a check: a refusal: a rebuff.—*n.* **repulsion** (*-pul′shon*), driving off: a repelling force, action, or influence.—*adj.* **repul′sive,** that repulses or drives off: repelling: cold, reserved, forbidding: causing aversion and disgust.—*adv.* **repul′sively.**—*n.* **repul′siveness.** [L. *repulsus,* pa.p. of *repellēre*—*re-,* back, *pellēre,* to drive.]

**repure,** *ri-pūr′, v.t.* to purify again: to refine thoroughly. [Pfx. **re-.**]

**repute,** *ri-pūt′, v.t.* to account, deem.—Also (*arch.*) *v.i.* with *of.*—*n.* general opinion or impression: attributed character: widespread or high estimation: fame.—*adj.* **reputable** (*rep′ūt-ə-bl*), in good repute: respectable: honourable: consistent with reputation.—*adv.* **rep′ūtably.**—*n.* **repūtā′tion** (*rep-*), repute: estimation: character generally ascribed: good report: fame: good name.—*adj.* **rep′ūtātive,** reputed: putative.—*adv.* **rep′ū-tātively,** by repute.—*adj.* **reputed** (*ri-pūt′id*), supposed, reckoned to be such: of repute.—*adv.* **reput′edly,** in common repute or estimation.—*adj.* **repute′less** (*Shak.*), without good repute.—*n.* **reput′ing** (*Shak.*), pluming oneself.—**reputed owner,** a person who has to all appearance the title to the property; **reputed pint,** what is commonly called a pint though not necessarily of legal standard. [L. *reputāre, -ātum*—*putāre,* to reckon.]

**requere,** *ri-kwēr′,* (*Spens.*) *v.t.* to require.

**request,** *ri-kwest′, n.* the asking of a favour: a petition: a favour asked for: the state of being sought after.—*v.t.* to ask as a favour: to ask politely: to ask for.—*n.* **request′er.**—**request note,** an application for a permit to remove excisable goods.—**Court of Requests,** a former English court of equity, abolished 1641: a local small debt court, superseded by the County Court—called also *Court of Conscience.* [O.Fr. *requeste* (Fr. *requête*)—L. *requisitum,* pa.p. of *requirēre*—*re-,* away, *quaerēre,* to seek.]

**requicken,** *rē-kwik′n,* (*Shak.*) *v.t.* to give new life to. [Pfx. **re-.**]

**requiem,** *rek′wi-əm, rē′kwi-əm, n.* a mass for the rest of the soul of the dead: music for it: any music of similar character: rest (*obs.*). [L., accus. of *requiēs* (*re-,* inten., *quiēs,* rest); first word of the introit.]

**requiescat,** *n.* a prayer for the rest of the soul of the dead.—**requiescat in pace,** *re-kwi-es′kät in pä′chä, pä′sē, pä′ke,* abbrev. R.I.P., may he (or

**repub′lish,** *v.t.* **repub′lisher,** *n.* **repur′chase,** *v.t.* and *n.*
**republica′tion,** *n.* **repulp′,** *v.t.*

Neutral vowels in unaccented syllables: *el′ə-mənt*; for certain sounds in foreign words, see p. viii

she) rest in peace. [L., third pers. sing. subj. of *requiescĕre*.]

**requight**, a Spenserian spelling of **requite**.

**require**, ri-kwīr′, v.t. to ask (one) a question (*obs.*): to ask for (*obs.*): to demand, exact: to direct (a person to do something): to request (*arch.*): to call for, necessitate.—*v.i.* to ask.—*adj.* **requir′able**.—*adj.* **required′**, compulsory as part of a curriculum.—*ns.* **require′ment**, a need: a thing needed: a necessary condition: a demand; **requir′er**; **requir′ing**. [L. *requīrĕre*; partly through O.Fr. *requerre*, later assimilated to L.]

**requisite**, rek′wi-zit, adj. required: needful: indispensable.—*n.* that which is required, necessary, or indispensable.—*ns.* **req′uisiteness**; **requisi′tion**, the act of requiring: a formal demand or request: a formal call for the doing of something that is due: a demand for the supply of anything for military purposes: a written order for the supply of materials: the state of being in use or service.—*v.t.* to demand a requisition from: to demand or take by requisition: to seize: to call in: to press into service.—*adj.* **requisi′tionary**.—*ns.* **requisi′tionist**, **requis′itor**, one who makes a requisition.—*adj.* **requis′itory**. [L. *requīsītus*, pa.p. of *requīrĕre*; see require.]

**requite**, ri-kwīt′, v.t. to repay (an action): to avenge: to repay (a person, for): to retaliate on: to counterbalance, compensate for (*obs.*):—*pa.t.* **requit′ed** (*Spens.* **requit′**); *pa.p.* **requit′ed** (*Shak.* **requit′**, **requitt′ed**).—Also (*Spens.*) **requight** (-*kwīt*′).—*n.* **requite′**, requital.—*v.t.* requit (-*kwīt*′; *obs.*), to requite (*pa.p.*, *Shak.*, **requitt′ed**).—*n.* (*Burns*) **requital**.—*adj.* **requi′table**.—*n.* requi′tal, the act of requiting: payment in return: recompense: reward.—*adjs.* **requite′ful**; **requite′less**, without requital, free.—*ns.* **requite′ment**; **requi′ter**. [Pfx. re-, and quit.]

**requoyle**, a Shakespearian spelling of **recoil**.

**rerail**, rē-rāl′, v.t. to replace on the rails. [Pfx. re-.]

**rere-**, rēr-, in composition the same as rear (1).—*ns.* **rere′-arch**, **rear′-arch**, an arch supporting the inner part of a wall's thickness, as in a splayed window; **rere′brace** (-brās; Fr. *bras*, arm), armour for the arm from shoulder to elbow; **rere′dorse**, **-dosse**, **-dos** (L. *dorsum*, Fr. *dos*, back), a screen or panelling behind an altar or seat: a choir-screen: the back of a fireplace; **rere′dorter**, a privy behind a monastic dormitory; **rere′-supper**, a late meal, after supper; **rere′ward**, rearward.

**reread**, rē′rēd′, v.t. to read again:—*pa.t.* and *pa.p.* **re′read′** (-red). [Pfx. re-.]

**reremouse**, **rearmouse**, rēr′mows, n. a bat:—*pl.* **rere′-**, **rear′mice**. [O.E. *hrēremūs*, app.—*hrēran*, to move, *mūs*, a mouse.]

**re-scale**, **rescale**, rē-skāl′, v.t. to plan, form, on a new (usu. reduced) scale. [Pfx. re-.]

**rescind**, ri-sind′, v.t. to cut away: to annul, abrogate.—*n.* **rescission** (-sizh′an), abrogation: cutting off (*obs.*).—*adj.* **rescissory** (-*sis′ər-i*), annulling. [L. *rescindĕre*, *rescissum—re-*, back, *scindĕre*, to cut.]

**rescript**, rē′skript, n. the official answer of a pope or an emperor to any legal question: an edict or decree: a rewriting. [L. *rescriptum—re-*, *scrībĕre*, *scriptum*, to write.]

**rescue**, res′kū, v.t. to free from danger, captivity, or evil plight: to deliver forcibly from legal custody: to recover by force:—*pr.p.* **res′cuing**; *pa.t.* and *pa.p.* **res′cued**.—*n.* the act of rescuing: deliverance from danger or evil: forcible recovery: forcible release from arrest or imprisonment: relief of a besieged place: a beach-rescue: a rescuer or rescuing party (*arch.*): a person or

thing rescued: a bid (**rescue bid**) to bring one's partner out of a dangerous situation (*bridge*).—*adj.* **res′cuable**.—*n.* **res′cuer**. [O.Fr. *rescourre*—L. *re-*, *excutĕre—ex*, out, *quatĕre*, to shake.]

**rescue-grass**, res′kū-gräs, n. a S. American bromegrass. [Origin unknown.]

**research**, ri-sûrch′, n. a careful search: investigation: systematic investigation towards increasing the sum of knowledge.—*v.i.* to make researches: **re-search** (rē′), to search again.—*n.* **research′er**.—*adj.* **research′ful**. [Obs. Fr. *recerche* (mod. Fr. *recherche*); see **search**.]

**réseau**, rā-zō′, n. a fine meshed ground for lacework: a network of lines for reference in star-photographs. [Fr., network.]

**resect**, ri-sekt′, v.t. to cut away part of, esp. the end of a bone.—*n.* **resection** (-sek′shən), cutting away, esp. bone (*surg.*): a positional fix of a point by sighting it from two or more known stations (*surveying*). [L. *resecāre*, *-sectum*, to cut off—*secāre*, to cut.]

**Reseda**, re′si-da, ri-sē′da, n. the mignonette genus, giving name to the family **Reseda′ceae**: (without *cap.*; *re′*), a pale green colour (often as Fr. **réséda**, rā-zā-dä).—Also *adj.* [L. *resēda*, said to be from *resēdā morbīs*, assuage diseases, first words of a charm used in applying it as a poultice.]

**reseize**, rē-sēz′, (*Spens.*) v.t. to reinstate. [Pfx. re- and seise.]

**resemble**, ri-zem′bl, v.t. to be like: to compare (*arch.*): to depict (*obs.*).—*v.i.* to be like each other: to be like (with *to*; *arch.*).—*n.* **resem′blance**, likeness: appearance: an image.—*adj.* **resem′blant**.—*n.* **resem′bler**.—*adj.* **resem′bling**. [O.Fr. *resembler* (Fr. *ressembler*)—*re-*, again, *sembler*, to seem—L. *simulāre*, to make like—*similis*, like.]

**resent**, ri-zent′, v.t. to take ill, consider as an injury or affront: to feel joy or sorrow because of (*obs.*): to receive (a person), well or ill (*obs.*).—*v.i.* (*obs.*) to savour (of).—*n.* **resent′er**.—*adj.* **resent′ful**.—*advs.* **resent′fully**; **resent′ingly**.—*adj.* **resent′ive**.—*n.* **resent′ment**. [O.Fr. *ressentir*—L. *re-*, in return, *sentīre*, to feel.]

**reserpine**, ri-zûr′pin, -pēn, n. a drug got from *Rauwolfia serpentina* used against high bloodpressure, and as a tranquilliser.

**reserve**, ri-zûrv′, v.t. to hold back: to save up, esp. for a future occasion or special purpose: to keep, retain: to preserve: to spare: to set apart: to book, engage.—*n.* the keeping of something reserved: state of being reserved: that which is reserved: a reservation: a reserved store or stock: a tract of land reserved for a special purpose: a substitute kept in readiness (*sport*): (esp. in *pl.*) a military force kept out of action until occasion serves: (esp. in *pl.*) a force not usually serving but liable to be called up when required: (often *pl.*) resources of physical or spiritual nature available in abnormal circumstances: part of assets kept readily available for ordinary demands: artistic restraint: restrained manner: reticence: aloofness: a secret information withheld (*arch.*): limitation, restriction: a mental reservation.—*adj.* kept in reserve: of the reserves.—*adj.* **reserv′able**.—*ns.* **reservā′tion** (rez-), the act of reserving or keeping back, or keeping for oneself: an expressed, or tacit, proviso, limiting condition, or exception: something withheld: a tract of public land reserved for some special purpose, as for Indians, schools, game, etc.: the pope's retention to himself of the right to nominate to a benefice: a limitation: the booking of a seat, room, passage, etc.: a booked

---

**rēreg′ister**, v.t. and v.i.
**rē′revise**, v.t. and n.
**rē′sale′**, n.

**rēsalute′**, v.t.
**rēseat′**, v.t.
**rēsell′**, v.t.:—*pa.t.* and *pa.p.* **rēsōld′**.

seat, room, etc.; **reservatory** (*ri-zûrv′ə-tər-i*; *obs.*), a receptacle: a reservoir.—*adj.* **reserved′**, reticent: uncommunicative: aloof in manner: booked: having the original colour of the surface or background (*ceramics*).—*adv.* **reserv′edly**. —*ns.* **reservedness** (*ri-zûrvd′nis*); **reserv′ist**, a member of a reserve force.—**reserve currency**, one ranking with gold in world banking transactions; **reserved occupation**, employment of national importance that exempts from service in the armed forces; **reserve price**, the minimum price acceptable to the vendor of an article for sale or auction.—**judgment reserved** (see **judgment**); **mental reservation**, a reservation made mentally but not openly expressed; **reservation of the sacrament**, the practice of reserving part of the consecrated bread of the eucharist for the communion of the sick; **without reserve**, frankly, not holding back any information: fully, without reservation: without restrictions or stipulations regarding sale: without a reserve price. [O.Fr. *reserver*—L. *reservāre*—*re-*, back, *servāre*, to save.]

**reservoir**, *rez′ər-vwär*, *-vwör*, *n.* a receptacle: a store: a receptacle for fluids, esp. a large basin, artificial lake, or tank for storing water.—*v.t.* to store. [Fr.]

**reset**, *ri-set′*, (*Scot.*) *v.t.* to harbour (*arch.*): to receive, knowing to be stolen.—Also *v.i.*—*n.* (*rē′*) harbouring of a proscribed person (*arch.*): receiving of stolen goods.—*n.* **resett′er**. [O.Fr. *recet(t)er*—L. *receptāre*—*recipēre*, to receive.]

**res gestae**, *rēz jes′tē*, *rās ges′tī*, (L.) exploits: facts relevant to the case and admissible in evidence (*law*).

**resiant**, *rez′i-ənt*, *-ant*, (*obs.* or *arch.*) *adj.* and *n.* resident.—*n.* **res′iance**. [O.Fr. *reseant*, pr.p. of *reseoir*—L. *residēre*.]

**reside**, *ri-zid′*, *v.i.* to dwell permanently: to be in residence: to abide: to be vested: to inhere. —*ns.* **residence** (*rez′i-dəns*), act of dwelling in a place: the act of living in the place required by regulations or performance of functions: a stay in a place: a dwelling-place: a dwelling-house, esp. one of some pretensions: that in which anything permanently inheres or has its seat; **res′idency**, a residence: the official abode of a resident or governor of a protected state: an administrative district under a resident.—*adj.* **res′ident**, dwelling in a place for some time: residing on one's own estate, or the place of one's duties, or the place required by certain conditions: not migratory: not moving (*obs.*): inherent.—*n.* one who resides: an animal that does not migrate: a doctor who works in, and usu. resides at, a hospital to gain experience in a particular field: a representative at a foreign court of lower rank than an ambassador (*hist.*): a representative of a governor in a protected state: the governor of a residency or administrative district (esp. in the former Dutch East Indies).—*n.* **res′identer** (*Scot.* -*dent′*), an inhabitant.—*adjs.* **residential** (-*den′shl*), of, for, or connected with, residence: suitable for or occupied by houses, esp. of a better kind; **residentiary** (-*den′shə-ri*), resident: officially bound to reside: pertaining to or involving official residence.—*n.* an inhabitant: one bound to reside, as a canon.—*ns.* **residen′tiaryship**; **res′identship**; **resi′der**. [L. *residēre*—*re-*, back, *sedēre*, to sit.]

**residue**, *rez′i-dū*, in U.S. also -*dōō*, *n.* that which is left, remainder: what is left of an estate after payment of debts, charges, and legacies.—*adj.* **resid′ual**, remaining as residue or difference.—*n.* that which remains as a residue or as a differ-

ence.—*adjs.* **resid′uary**, of, or of the nature of, a residue, esp. of an estate; **resid′uous** (*rare*), residual.—*n.* **residuum**, *rə-zij′ōō-əm*, *-wəm*, *rez-id′ū-əm*, a residue:—*pl.* -**ua**. [L. *residuum*—*residēre*, to remain behind.]

**resign**, *ri-zin′*, *v.t.* to yield up: to submit calmly: to relinquish: to entrust.—*v.t.* to give up office, employment, etc.: to submit (*rare*).—*n.* **resignation** (*rez-ig-nā′shən*), act of giving up: state of being resigned or quietly submissive: the form by which a vassal returns the feu into the hands of a superior (*Scots law*).—*adj.* **resigned** (*ri-zind′*), calmly submissive.—*adv.* **resignedly** (*ri-zin′id-li*).—*ns.* **resign′edness**; **resign′er**; **resign′ment**. [O.Fr. *resigner*—L. *resignāre*, *-ātum*, to unseal, annul—*signāre*, to seal—*signum*, a mark.]

**re-sign**, *rē-sin′*, *v.t.* to sign again. [Pfx. **re-**.]

**resile**, *ri-zil′*, *v.i.* to recoil: to rebound: to recover form and position elastically: to draw back from a statement, agreement, course: to back out (esp. *Scot.*).—*ns.* **resilience** (*ri-zil′i-əns*), **resiliency**: elasticity, physical or mental; **resil′iency**. —*adj.* **resil′ient**, elastic, physically or in spirits. [L. *resilīre*, to leap back—*salīre*, to leap.]

**resin**, *rez′in*, *n.* any of a number of substances, products obtained from the sap of certain plants and trees (*natural resins*), used in plastics, etc.: any of a large number of substances made by polymerisation or condensation (*synthetic resins*) which, though not related chemically to natural resins, have some of their physical properties, very important in the plastics industry, etc.—*v.t.* to treat with resin: to remove resin from: to rosin.—*ns.* **res′ināte**, a salt of any of the acids occurring in natural resins; **res′iner**, a resin gatherer.—*adj.* **resinif′erous**, yielding resin.—*n.* **resinifica′tion**.—*v.t.* and *v.i.* **res′inify**, to make or become a resin or resinous.—*v.t.* **res′inise**, -**ize**, to treat with resin.—*n.* **resinō′sis**, abnormal flow of resin.—*adj.* **res′inous**, of, like, containing, of the nature of, resin: of the lustre of resin: negative (as produced by rubbing a resin; *elect.*, *obs.*).—*adv.* **res′inously**. [Fr. *résine* —L. *rēsina*.]

**resinata**, *rez-i-nä′tä*, *n.* Greek white wine with resinous flavour. [L. *rēsināta* (fem.), resined.]

**resipiscence**, *res-i-pis′əns*, *n.* change to a better frame of mind.—Also **resipisc′ency**.—*adj.* **resipisc′ent**. [L. *resipīscentia*—*resipīscēre*—*re-*, again, *sapēre*, to be wise.]

**resist**, *ri-zist′*, *v.t.* to strive against, oppose: to withstand: to hinder the action of: to be distasteful to: to be distasteful to (*Shak.*).—*v.i.* to make opposition.—*n.* a protective coating, esp. one on parts of a textile to protect the blank areas of the design that is being printed, or an acid-proof coating on parts of a metal plate.—Also *adj.*—*ns.* **resis′tance**, act or power of resisting: opposition: the opposition of a body to the motion of another: that property of a substance in virtue of which the passage of an electric current through it is accompanied with a dissipation of energy: an electrical resistor; **resis′tant**, one who, or that which, resists.—*adj.* **resis′tant** (less usu. **resis′tent**), making resistance: withstanding adverse conditions, as parasites, germs, antibiotics.—*ns.* **resis′tor**; **resistibil′ity**.—*adj.* **resis′tible**.—*advs.* **resis′tibly**; **resis′tingly**.—*adj.* **resis′tive**.—*adv.* **resis′tively**.—*n.* **resistiv′ity** (*rez-*), capacity for resisting: (also **specific resistance**) a property of a conducting material expressed as resistance × cross-sectional area over length.—*adj.* **resist′less**, irresistible: unable to resist.—*adv.* **resist′lessly**.—*ns.* **resist′lessness**; **resist′or**, a piece

---

**rēset′**, *v.t.*        **rēshape′**, *v.t.*        **rēship′ment**, *n.*
**rēsett′le**, *v.t.* and *v.i.*        **rēship′**, *v.t.* and *v.i.*        **rēshuff′le**, *v.t.* and *n.*
**rēsett′lement**, *n.*

Neutral vowels in unaccented syllables: *el′ə-mənt*; for certain sounds in foreign words, see p. viii

of apparatus used to offer electric resistance.—
**resis´tance-box**, a box containing resistors; **re-sis´tance-coil**, a coil of wire used to offer resistance to the passage of electricity; **resistance (movement)**, a party continuing opposition to a foreign occupying power after the country has nominally capitulated; **resistance pyrometer, thermometer**, a device for measuring high temperatures by means of the variation in the electrical resistance of a wire as the temperature changes; **resistance thermometry**, temperature measurement of this kind; **resis´tance-welding** (see weld).—**line of least resistance**, the easiest course of action. [L. *resistĕre*—*re-*, against, *sistĕre*, to make to stand.]
**resit**, *rē-sit´*, *v.i.* to sit an examination again after failing.—*n.* (*rē´*) an opportunity or act of resitting. [Pfx. re-.]
**res judicata**, *rēz jōō-di-kä´ta, räs yōō-di-kä´ta*, (L.) a case or suit already decided.
**reskew, reskue** (*Spens.*). Same as rescue.
**resoluble**, *rez´əl-ū-bl, adj.* that may be resolved, dissolved, analysed.—*adj.* **resolute** (*rez´al-ōōt,-ūt*), having a fixed purpose: constant in pursuing a purpose: determined.—*n.* (*Shak.*) a determined person. — *adv.* **res´olutely.** — *ns.* **res´oluteness; resolution** (*rez-əl-ōō´shən, -ū´shən*), act of resolving: analysis: separation of components: melting: solution: the separation of an optically inactive mixture or compound into its optically active components (*chem.*): the definition of a picture in TV or facsimile (measured by the number of lines used to scan the image of the picture): the smallest measurable difference, or separation, or time interval (*phys., electronics, nucleonics*): state of being resolved: fixed determination: that which is resolved: removal of or freedom from doubt: progression from discord to concord (*mus.*): a formal proposal put before a meeting, or its formal determination thereon: substitution of two short syllables for a long: the making visible of detail: the disappearance or dispersion of a tumour or inflammation; **re-solu´tion** (*rē-sol-*), renewed or repeated solution; **resolu´tioner** (*rez-əl-*), one who joins in or accepts a resolution: **Resolutioner** (*Scot. hist.*), one who approved of the resolutions of 1650 admitting to civil and military office all persons except those excommunicate and hostile to the Covenant—opposed to *Protester*.—*adj.* **res´olutive.**—*n.* **resolvabil´ity.**—*adj.* **resolvable** (*ri-zolv´*).—*v.t.* **resolve´**, to separate into components: to make visible the details of: to analyse: to break up: to melt: to transform: to relax: to solve: to dissipate: to free from doubt or difficulty: to convince (of; *obs.*): to assure (*obs.*): to inform (*obs.*): to answer (a question; *obs.*): to dispel (fears: *Shak.*): to pass as a resolution: to determine: to disperse, as a tumour: to make (a discord) pass into a concord (*mus.*).—*v.i.* to undergo resolution: to come to a determination (often with *on* to indicate the course chosen): to decide to go to a place (with *on*; *Shak.*): to take counsel (*Spens.*): to lapse (*law*).—In some *obs.* senses also used reflexively.—*n.* resolution: fixed purpose: firmness of purpose: solution (*obs.*).—*adj.* **resolved´**, fixed in purpose. —*adv.* **resolvedly** (*ri-zol´vid-li*), resolutely.—*n.* **resol´vedness.**—*adj.* **resol´vent**, having power to resolve.—*n.* that which causes or helps solution or resolution.—*n.* **resol´ver.** [L. *resolvĕre, resolūtum*—*re-*, inten., *solvĕre*, to loose.]
**resolve.** See resoluble.
**resonance**, *rez´ən-əns, n.* resounding: sonority: the sound heard in auscultation: sympathetic vibration: (the state of a system in which) a large vibration (is) produced by a small stimulus

of approx. the same frequency as that of the system (*phys., elect.*): increased probability of a nuclear reaction when the energy of an incident particle or photon is around a certain value appropriate to the energy level of the compound nucleus: a property of certain compounds, in which the most stable state of the molecule is a combination of theoretically possible bond arrangements or distributions of electrons (*chem.*): the complex of bodily responses to an emotional state, or of emotional responses to a situation.—*adj.* **res´onant**, resounding, ringing: giving its characteristic vibration in sympathy with another body's vibration.—*adv.* **res´onantly.**—*v.i.* **res´onate**, to resound: to vibrate sympathetically.—*n.* **resona´tor**, a resonating body or device, as for increasing sonority or for analysing sound.—**res´onance-box**, a chamber in a musical instrument for increasing its sonority by vibration in sympathy with the strings. [L. *resonāre, -ātum*—*re-*, back, *sonāre*, to sound.]
**resorb**, *ri-sörb´, v.t.* to absorb back.—*adj.* **resorb´ent.** [L. *resorbēre*, to suck back.]
**resorcin**, *ri-zör´sin, n.* a colourless phenol, $C_6H_4(OH)_2$, used in dyeing, photography, and medicine.—Also **resor´cinol.** [resin and orcin.]
**resorption**, *ri-sörp´shən, n.* resorbing, esp. of a mineral by rock magma.—*adj.* **resorp´tive.** [See resorb.]
**resort**, *ri-zört´, v.i.* to revert (*obs.*): to go: to betake oneself: to have recourse: to apply: to go or be habitually.—*n.* act of resorting: a place much frequented: a haunt: that which one has or may have recourse to: concourse: thronging: repair.—*n.* **resort´er**, a frequenter.—**in the last resort**, orig. (a Gallicism, *en dernier ressort*), without appeal: hence, as a last expedient. [O.Fr. *resortir* (Fr. *ressortir*), to rebound, retire—*sortir*, to go out; origin obscure.]
**resound**, *ri-zownd´, v.t.* to echo: to sound with reverberation: to sound or spread (the praises of a person or thing).—*v.i.* to echo: to re-echo, reverberate: to sound sonorously.—*adj.* **resound´ing**, echoing: thorough, decisive (*resounding victory*).—*adv.* **resound´ingly.** [Pfx. re-.]
**resource**, *ri-sörs´, -sörs, -z-, n.* source or possibility of help: an expedient: (*pl.*) money or means of raising money: means of support: means of occupying or amusing oneself: resourcefulness. —*adj.* **resource´ful**, fertile in expedients: rich in resources.—*n.* **resource´fulness.**—*adj.* **resource´less.** [O.Fr. *ressource*—*resourdre*—L. *resurgĕre*, to rise again.]
**respeak**, *rē-spēk´*, (*Shak.*) *v.t.* to echo. [Pfx. re-.]
**respect**, *ri-spekt´, v.t.* to look to, regard, consider, take into account: to heed: to refer to, relate to, have reference to: to treat with consideration, refrain from violating: to feel or show esteem, deference, or honour to: to value (a thing; *Shak.*): to face, look at (*obs.* and *her.*). —Also *v.i.*—*n.* heed (*Spens.*): an aspect (*obs.*): a particular: a relation: reference: regard: consideration: partiality or favour towards (with *of*): deferential esteem: (often in *pl.*) a greeting or message of esteem.—*n.* **respectabil´ity.** —*adj.* **respec´table**, worthy of respect: considerable: passable: mediocre: of good social standing (*obs.*): fairly well-to-do: decent and well-behaved: reputable: seemly: presentable: timidly or priggishly conventional.—*n.* **respec´tableness.**—*adv.* **respec´tably.**—*adj.* **respec´tant**, facing each other (*her.*): looking back.—*n.* **respec´ter**, one who respects, esp. in *respecter of persons*, one who, something that, singles out individual(s) for unduly favourable treatment (usu. in *neg.*).—*adj.* **respect´ful**, showing or feeling respect.—*adv.* **respect´fully.**—*n.* **respect´fulness.**—*prep.* **respect´ing**, concerning: consider-

**re-site´**, *v.t.*

ing.—*adj.* **respec′tive,** having respect: regardful, considerate (*Shak.*): heedful: discriminating: respectful (*obs.*): worthy of respect (*Shak.*): relative: particular or several, relating to each distributively.—*adv.* **respec′tively.**—*adj.* **respect′-less,** regardless.—**respect of persons,** undue favour, as for wealth, etc.; **in respect of,** in the matter of: because of (*obs.*): in comparison with (*obs.*); **with respect to, with regard to.** [L. *respicĕre, respectum*—*re-,* back, *specĕre,* to look.]
**respire,** *ri-spīr′, v.i.* to breathe: to take breath. —*v.t.* to breathe: to exhale.—*adj.* **respirable** (*res′par-a-bl, ri-spīr′a-bl*), fit for breathing.—*ns.* **respiration** (*res-par-ā′shan*), breathing: the taking in of oxygen and giving out of carbon dioxide, with associated physiological processes: a breath: a breathing-space; **res′pirātor,** an appliance worn on the mouth or nose to filter and warm the air breathed: a gas-mask.—*adj.* **respiratory** (*res′par-a-tar-i, ri-spī′ra-tar-i*), of or for, pertaining to, or serving for, respiration. [L. *respirāre, -ātum*—*spīrāre,* to breathe.]
**respite,** *res′pit, -pit, n.* temporary cessation of something that is tiring or painful: postponement requested or granted: temporary suspension of the execution of a criminal (*law*): delay in action (*obs.*): leisure (*obs.*).—*v.t.* to grant a respite to: to relieve by a pause (*obs.*): to delay, put off: to grant postponement to: to prolong (*Shak.*): to give up, cease from (*obs.*).—*v.i.* to rest (from) (*obs.*). [M.E. *respit*—O.Fr. (Fr. *répit*)— L. *respectus, respicĕre;* see **respect.**]
**resplend,** *ri-splend′, v.i.* to shine brilliantly.—*ns.* **resplend′ence, resplend′ency**—*adj.* **resplend′ent,** shining, brilliant, and splendid.—*adv.* **resplend′-ently.** [L. *resplendēre*—*re-,* inten., and *splendēre,* to shine.]
**respond,** *ri-spond′, v.i.* to answer: to utter liturgical responses: to act in answer: to react.—*n.* a response to a versicle in liturgy: a half-pillar or half-pier attached to a wall to support an arch (answering to one at the other end of an arcade, etc.).—*ns.* **respond′ence, response** (*Spens.*): correspondence, agreement; **respond′-ency,** correspondence.—*adj.* **respond′ent,** answering: corresponding: responsive.—*n.* one who answers: one who refutes objections: a defendant, esp. in a divorce suit.—*ns.* **respondentia** (*res-pon-den′sha*), a loan on a ship's cargo, payable only on safe arrival; **respond′er** (*ris-*), one who, or that which, responds: the part of a transponder which replies automatically to the correct interrogation signal; **response′,** an answer: an oracular answer: an answer made by the congregation to the priest during divine service: a responsory: a reaction, esp. sympathetic.—*adj.* **response′less.**—*n.* **responsibil′ity,** state of being responsible: a trust or charge for which one is responsible.—*adj.* **respon′sible,** liable to be called to account as being in charge or control: answerable (*to* person, etc., *for* something): deserving the blame or credit of (with *for*): governed by a sense of responsibility: being a free moral agent: morally accountable for one's actions: trustworthy: able to pay: respectable-looking: involving responsibility: correspondent (*obs.*).—*adv.* **respon′sibly.** —*n.pl.* **respon′sions** (*-shanz*), the first of three examinations for the B.A. degree at Oxford, 'smalls'.—*adj.* **respon′sive,** ready to respond: answering: correspondent: with responses.—*adv.* **respon′sively.**—*n.* **respon′siveness.**—*adj.* **responsorial** (*ri-, rē-spon-sō′ri-al, -sō′ri-al*), responsive.—*n.* an office-book containing the responsories. —*adj.* **respon′sory,** making answer.—*n.* an anthem sung after a lesson: a liturgical response. [L.

*respondēre, respōnsum*—*re-,* back, *spondēre,* to promise.]
**ressaldar.** Same as **risaldar.**
**rest,** *rest, n.* repose, refreshing inactivity: intermission of, or freedom from, motion or disturbance: tranquillity: repose of death: invigoration by resting (*Shak.*): a place for resting: a prop or support (e.g. for a musket, a billiard cue, a violinist's chin): motionlessness: a pause in speaking or reading: an interval of silence in music, or a mark indicating it.—*v.i.* to repose: to be at ease: to be still: to be supported (on): to lean (on): to put trust in (with *on*): to have foundation in (with *on*): to settle, alight: to remain: to be unemployed (*slang,* esp. *theatrical*).—*v.t.* to give rest to: to place or hold in support (on): to lean (on): to base (on): (*refl.*) to give (oneself) rest, or (*obs.*) to rely (upon).—*n.* **rest′er.**—*adj.* **rest′ful,** at rest: rest-giving: tranquil.—*adv.* **rest′fully.** —*n.* **rest′fulness.**—*n.* and *adj.* **rest′ing.**—*adj.* **rest′less,** unresting, not resting, sleeping, or relaxing: never still: uneasily active: impatient (of; *Pope*): impatient of inactivity or of remaining still: never-ceasing: unrestf..l, giving or allowing no rest.—*adv.* **rest′lessly.**—*n.* **rest′lessness.**—**rest′-centre,** a place of shelter for numbers of people driven from their homes by an emergency; **rest′-cure,** treatment consisting of inactivity and quiet; **rest′-day,** a day of rest: the first day of a three days' visit; **rest′-home,** an establishment for those who need special care and attention, e.g. invalids, old people, etc.; **rest′-house,** a house of rest for travellers; **rest′ing-place,** a place of rest: a stair-landing: (one's last resting-place, one's grave); **rest′ing-spore,** a spore that can germinate after a period of dormancy; **rest′ing-stage,** a state of suspended activity; **rest′-room,** a room in a building other than a private house with lavatory (lavatories), etc., adjoining.—**at rest,** stationary: in repose: free from disquiet. [O.E. *rest, ræst;* Ger. *rast,* Du. *rust;* converging and merging in meaning with the following words.]
**rest,** *rest, n.* remainder: all others: reserve fund: a rapid continuous series of returns (*tennis,* etc.): a stake whose loss ends the game (*primero*).— *v.i.* to remain (see also preceding word).—**for the rest,** as regards other matters; **set up one's rest** (*arch.*), to make one's final stake: hence, to take a resolution: to take up abode. [Fr. *reste*—L. *restāre,* to remain—*re-,* back, *stāre,* to stand.]
**rest,** *rest, n.* a contrivance on a breastplate to prevent the spear from being driven back.—*v.t.* (*Shak.*) to arrest. [Aphetic for **arrest.**]
**restaurant,** *rest′(a-)-rā, -rong, -ront, -rant, n.* a place where meals may be had.—*n.* **restaurateur** (*res-tar-a-tūr′, -tær′*), the keeper of a restaurant.— **res′taurant-car,** a dining-car. [Fr.,—*restaurer,* to restore.]
**restem,** *rē-stem′,* (*Shak.*) *v.t.* to force (a way) back against the current. [Pfx. **re-.**]
**rest-harrow,** *rest′-har-ō, n.* a papilionaceous plant (Ononis) with long, tough, woody roots. [**rest** (3), and **harrow** (1).]
**restiff,** *res′tif,* an obsolete form of **restive.**
**restiform,** *res′ti-förm, adj.* cord-like. [L. *restis,* a cord, *förma,* form.]
**restitute,** *res′ti-tūt, v.t.* to restore.—*v.i.* to make restitution.—*ns.* **restitū′tion, restitū′tionism,** restorationism; **restitū′tionist.**—*adj.* **restitūtive** (*ri-stit′,* or *res′tit-*).—*n.* **res′titūtor.**—*adj.* **restit′ū-tory.** [L. *restituĕre, -ūtum*—*re-,* back, *statuĕre,* to make to stand.]
**restive,** *res′tiv, adj.* inert (*obs.*): unwilling to go

forward: obstinate, refractory: uneasy, as if ready to break from control.—*adv.* res'tively.
—*n.* res'tiveness. [O.Fr. *restif*—L. *restāre*, to rest.]

**restore**, ri-stōr', -stör, *v.t.* to repair: to bring, put, or give back: to make good: to reinstate: to bring back to a (supposed) former state, or to a normal state: to reconstruct mentally, by inference or conjecture.—*n.* (*Spens.*) restitution.— *adj.* restor'able.—*ns.* restor'ableness; restoration (*res-tō-rā'shən*, or -tö-, -tə-, -to-), act or process of restoring: a reinstatement of or in kingship (as the Restoration of the Stuarts, the Bourbons): renovations and reconstruction (sometimes little differing from destruction) of a building, painting, etc.: a reconstructed thing or representation.—*adj.* (with *cap.*) of the time of the Restoration of Charles II.—*ns.* restorā'tionism (*theol.*), receiving of a sinner to divine favour: the final recovery of all men; restorā'tionist, one who holds the belief that after a purgation all wicked men and angels will be restored to the favour of God, a universalist.—*adj.* restorative (*ris-tor'ə-tiv*, -*tör'*), tending to restore, esp. to strength and vigour.—*n.* a medicine that restores.—*adv.* restor'atively.—*n.* restor'er. [O.Fr. *restorer*—L. *restaurāre*, -*ātum.*]

**restrain**, ri-strān', *v.t.* to hold back: to control: to subject to forcible repression: to tighten (*Shak.*): to forbid (*Milt.*).—*v.i.* (*rare*) to refrain. —*adjs.* restrain'able; restrained', controlled: self-controlled: showing restraint: forbidden (*Shak.*).—*adv.* restrain'edly.—*ns.* restrain'edness; restrain'er.—*n.* and *adj.* restrain'ing.—*ns.* **restraint'**, act of restraining: state of being restrained: a restraining influence: restriction: forcible control: artistic control or reticence: want of liberty: reserve.—restraint of princes, embargo; restraint of trade, interference with free play of economic forces, as by monopolies. [O.Fr. *restraindre*, *restrai(g)n*- —L. *restringĕre*, *restrictum*—re-, back, *stringĕre*, to draw tightly.]

**restrict**, ri-strikt', *v.t.* to limit.—*adj.* restrict'ed. —*adv.* restrict'edly.—*ns.* restric'tion; restric'tionist, one who favours restriction.—Also *adj.* —*adj.* restric'tive, restricting: tending to restrict: expressing restriction.—*adv.* restric'tively.—*v.t.* **restringe** (*ri-strinj'*), to restrict.—*n.* and *adj.* **restrin'gent**, astringent.—restricted area, one from which certain classes of people are excluded: one within which there is a speed limit; restrictive practice, a trade practice that is against the public interest, as e.g. an agreement to sell only to certain buyers, or to keep up resale prices: used also of certain trade union practices, as the closed shop, demarcation, working to rule. [L. *restringĕre*, *restrictum.*]

**restringe.** See restrict.

**resty**, *rest'i*, *adj.* restive: sluggish (*Shak.*): inoperative, ineffectual (*Spens.*). [restive, or partly **rest** (1).]

**result**, ri-zult', *v.i.* to issue (with *in*): to follow as a consequence: to rebound (*obs.*): to be the outcome: to revert (*law*).—*n.* consequence: outcome: outcome aimed at: quantity obtained by calculation: decision, resolution, as of a council (*obs.* and *U.S.*).—*adj.* result'ant, resulting: resulting from combination (as of tones sounded together).—*n.* a force compounded of two or more forces: a sum of vector quantities: a resultant tone: a result of combination.— *adjs.* result'ative, expressing result; result'ful; result'ing; result'less.—*n.* result'lessness. [L. *resultāre*, to leap back—*saltāre*, to leap.]

**resume**, ri-zūm', -zōōm', *v.t.* to take back: to assume again: to take up again: to begin again. —*v.i.* to take possession again: to begin again in continuation.—*adj.* resum'able.—*ns.* résumé

(*rā-zü-mā*, *rez'ū-mā*; Fr. *pa.p.*), a summary; resumption (*ri-zump'shən*, or *zum'*), act of resuming.—*adj.* resumptive (-*zump'*, -*zum'*).—*adv.* resump'tively. [L. *resūmĕre*, -*sūmptum*—re-, *sūmĕre*, to take.]

**resupinate**, ri-sōō'pin-āt, -*sū'*, *adj.* upside down by twisting (*bot.*).—*n.* resupinā'tion.—*adj.* resupine (*rē-sū-pin'*, or -*sōō*-), lying on the back. [L. *resupināre*, -*ātum*, and *resupinus*—re-, back, *supinus*, bent backward.]

**resurge**, ri-sûrj', *v.i.* to rise again.—*n.* resur'gence. —*adj.* resur'gent.—*v.t.* **resurrect** (*rez-ər-ekt'*; back-formation), to restore to life: to revive: to disinter.—*v.i.* to come to life again.—*n.* resurrection (-*ek'shən*), a rising from the dead: resuscitation: revival: a thing resurrected: body-snatching.—*adjs.* resurrec'tional; resurrec'tionary.—*v.t.* resurrec'tionise, -ize.—*ns.* resurrec'tionism; resurrec'tionist, resurrec'tionman, one who stole bodies from the grave for dissection.—*adj.* resurrect'ive.—*n.* resurrect'or. —resurrec'tion-pie, a dish compounded of remnants of former meals; resurrec'tion-plant, a plant that curls in a ball in drought and spreads again in moisture, as rose of Jericho, some selaginellas. [L. *resurgĕre*, *resurrēctum*—re-, *surgĕre*, to rise.]

**resuscitate**, ri-sus'i-tāt, *v.t.* and *v.i.* to revive.— *adjs.* resusc'itable; resusc'itant.—*n.* one who, or that which, resuscitates.—*n.* resuscitā'tion. —*adj.* resusc'itātive, tending to resuscitate: reviving: revivifying: reanimating.—*n.* resusc'itātor, one who, or that which, resuscitates: an oxygen-administering apparatus used to induce breathing after asphyxiation. [L. *resuscitāre*, -*ātum*—re-, *sus*-, *sub*-, from beneath, *citāre*, to put into quick motion—*ciēre*, to make to go.]

**ret**, *ret*, *rate*, *rait*, *rāt*, *v.t.* to expose to moisture. —*v.t.* and *v.i.* to soak: to soften, spoil, or rot by soaking or exposure to moisture: to rot:— *pr.p.* rett'ing, rāt'ing, rait'ing; *pa.t.* and *pa.p.* rett'ed, rāt'ed, rait'ed.—*n.* rett'ery, a place where flax is retted. [App. akin to rot.]

**retable**, ri-tā'bl, *n.* a shelf behind an altar. [Fr. *rétable*—L.L. *retrōtabulum.*]

**retail**, *rē'tāl*, formerly (still by some) ri-, *rē-tāl'*, *n.* sale to consumer, or in small quantities.— *adj.* in, of, engaged in, concerned with, such sale.—*adv.* by retail.—*v.t.* (*ri*-, *rē-tāl'*) to sell by retail: to repeat in detail: to put about, hand on my report.—*ns.* retail'er; retail'ment. [O.Fr. *retail*, piece cut off—*tailler*, to cut.]

**retain**, ri-tān', *v.t.* to keep: to hold back: to continue to hold: to keep up: to employ or keep engaged, as by a fee paid: to keep in mind. —*adj.* retain'able.—*ns.* retain'er, one who or that which retains: a dependent of a person of rank, owing some service to him (*hist.*): a family servant of long standing: an authorisation: a retaining fee (general, to secure a priority of claim on a counsel's services; special, for a particular case); retain'ership; retain'ment.—retaining fee, the advance fee paid to a lawyer to defend a cause; retaining wall, a wall to hold back solid material, as earth, or (loosely) water. [Fr. *retenir*—L. *retinēre*—re-, back, *tenēre*, to hold.]

**retake**, *rē-tāk'*, *v.t.* to take again: to take back, recapture:—*pa.t.* retook'; *pa.p.* retā'ken.—*n.* (*rē'*) a second or repeated photographing or photograph, esp. for a motion picture.—*ns.* retāk'er; retāk'ing. [Pfx. re-.]

**retaliate**, ri-tal'i-āt, *v.t.* to repay in kind (now usu. an injury): sometimes *upon* a person).—*v.i.* to return like for like (esp. in hostility).—*ns.* retaliā'tion, return of like for like: imposition of a tariff against countries that impose a tariff;

---

retaliā'tionist.—*adj.* retal'iātive.—*n.* retal'iātor. *adj.* retal'iatory (-*āt-ər-i*, -*ət-ər-i*). [L. *retāliāre*, -*ātum*—re-, *tāliō*, -*ōnis*, like for like—*tālis*, such.]

retama, re-tä'mə, *n.* a name for various desert switch-plants—papilionaceous and caesalpiniaceous—including Spanish broom. [Sp.,—Ar. *retām* (pl.).]

retard, ri-tärd', *v.t.* to slow: to keep back development or progress of: delay: to postpone (*rare*): to delay the timing of (an ignition spark).—*v.i.* to slow down: to delay.—*n.* delay: lag.—*adj.* retar'dant, serving to delay or slow down a chemical reaction, as rusting.—Also *n.*—*n.* retardā'tion (rē-), slowing: delay: lag.— *adjs.* retardative (ri-tärd'ə-tiv); retar'datory; retar'ded, delayed or slowed down: slow in development, esp. mental, or having made less than normal progress in learning.—*ns.* retar'der, retardant: a substance that delays or prevents setting of cement; retard'ment. [L. *retardāre*, -*ātum*—re-, *tardāre*, to slow.]

retch, rēch, also *rech*, *v.i.* to strain as if to vomit.— *n.* an act of retching. [O.E. *hrǣcan*—*hrāca*, a hawking.]

retch, rech, rech'less, etc. Obs. forms of reck, etc.

rete, rē'tē, *n.* a network, as of blood-vessels or nerves.—*adj.* retial (rē'shi-əl). [L. *rēte*, net.]

retene, rē'tēn, ret'ēn, *n.* a hydrocarbon (C₁₈H₁₈) got from tar.—*ns.* retinalite (ret', or ri-tin'), a resinous-lustred serpentine; retinis'pora, retinos'-pora, a cypress or kindred conifer in a perpetuated juvenile form, once placed in a separate genus; ret'inite, pitchstone (*obs.*): a fossil resin; ret'inol, an oil distilled from resin. [Gr. *rhētinē*, pine resin.]

retention, ri-ten'shən, *n.* act or power of retaining: memory: custody: inability to void (*med.*).— *adj.* reten'tive, retaining: tenacious: retaining moisture.—*adv.* reten'tively.—*ns.* reten'tiveness, retentiv'ity (rē-). [L. *retentiō*, -*ōnis*; O.Fr. *re-tentif*; see retain.]

retexture, rē-teks'chər, *n.* weaving anew. [L. *retexĕre*, to weave anew, earlier to unweave.]

retexture, rē-teks'chər, *v.t.* to treat (a material) so as to restore firmness lost through the action of spirit in process of dry-cleaning. [Pfx. re-, texture, to give a texture to.]

rethink, rē-thingk', *v.t.* to consider again and come to a different decision about.—Also *n.* [Pfx. re-.]

retiarius, rē-shi-ā'ri-əs, rā-ti-ä'ri-ōōs, *n.* a gladiator armed with a net.—*adj.* retiary (rē'shi-ər-i), of nets: using a net as a weapon, as a gladiator or a spider. [L. *rētiārius*—*rēte*, net.]

reticent, ret'i-sənt, *adj.* reserved or sparing in communication.—*ns.* ret'icence, ret'icency. [L. *reticēns*, -*entis*, pr.p. of *reticēre*—re-, *tacēre*, to be silent.]

reticle, ret'i-kl, *n.* an attachment to an optical instrument consisting of a network of lines of reference.—*adj.* reticular (ri-tik'ū-lər), netted: netlike: reticulated: of the reticulum.—*adv.* retic'ularly.—*adj.* retic'ulary.—*v.t.* retic'ulate, to form into or mark with a network: to distribute (e.g. water, electricity) by a network.—*v.i.* to form a network.—*adj.* netted: marked with network: net-veined.—*adj.* retic'ulated, reticulate: (of masonry) of lozenge-shaped stones, or of squares placed diamond-wise: of rusticated work with ridges of uniform width between irregular sinkings.—*adv.* retic'ulately.—*ns.* reticulā'tion, network: netlike structure; reticule (ret'i-kūl), a reticle: a small bag, orig. and properly of network, carried by ladies; retic'-ulum, a network: the second stomach of a ruminant: (with *cap.*) a southern constellation, also called the Net, between Hydrus and Dorado. [L. *rēticulum*, dim. of *rēte*, net.]

retiform, rē'ti-förm, *adj.* having the form of a net. [L. *rēte*, net, *förma*, form.]

retina, ret'i-nə, *n.* the sensitive layer of the eye:— *pl.* ret'inas, ret'inae (-nē).—*adj.* ret'inal.—*ns.* retini'tis, inflammation of the retina; retinos'-copist; retinos'copy, examination of the eye by observing a shadow on the retina; retinula (ri-tin'ū-lə), a cell playing the part of retina to an ommatidium:—*pl.* retin'ulae (-lē).—*adj.* retin'ular.—retina camera, an instrument that photographs the minute blood-vessels at the back of the eye in full colour. [L.L. *rētina*, app. —L. *rēte*, net.]

retinaculum, ret-i-nak'ū-ləm, *n.* a connecting band: a means of retention: the apparatus that holds an insect's forewing and hindwing together: the sticky attachment of a pollen-mass, as in orchids:—*pl.* retinac'ula.—*adj.* retinac'ūlar. [L. *retināculum*, a holdfast—*retinēre*; see retain, retention.]

retinite, retinol, etc. See under retene.

retinue, ret'i-nū, formerly ri-tin'ū, *n.* a body of retainers: a suite or train. [Fr. *retenue*, fem. pa.p. of *retenir*; see retain.]

retire, ri-tīr', *v.i.* to withdraw: to retreat: to recede: to withdraw from society, office, public or active life, business, profession, etc.: to go into seclusion or to bed: to return (*obs.*).—*v.t.* to withdraw: to draw back: to withdraw from currency: to cause to retire.—*n.* (now *rare*) retirement: retreat (*obs.*): a place of retirement (*obs.*): return (*obs.*): a signal to retreat.—*ns.* reti'racy (*U.S.*), seclusion: enough to retire on; reti'ral, giving up of office, business, etc.: withdrawal.—*adj.* retired', withdrawn: reserved in manner: secluded, sequestered: withdrawn from business or profession: recondite (*obs.*).— *adv.* retired'ly (or ri-tī'rid-li).—*ns.* retired'ness (or ri-tī'rid-nis); retire'ment, act of retiring: state of being or having retired: solitude: privacy: a time or place of seclusion.—*adj.* retir'ing, reserved: unobtrusive: retreating: modest: given to one who retires from a public office or service.—*adv.* reti'ringly.—*n.* reti'ringness.—retired list, a list of officers who are relieved from active service but receive a certain amount of pay (retired pay). [Fr. *retirer*—re-, back, *tirer*, to draw.]

retort, ri-tört', *v.t.* to throw back: to return upon an assailant or opponent: to answer in retaliation: to answer sharply or wittily: to reject (*Shak.*): to purify or treat in a retort.—*v.i.* to make a sharp reply.—*n.* retaliation: a ready and sharp or witty answer: the art or act of retorting: a vessel in which substances are placed for distillation, typically a flask with long bent-back neck.—*adj.* retor'ted, bent back: thrown back: turned back.—*ns.* retor'ter; retortion (-tör'shən; also retor'sion), retorting: bending, turning, or casting back: retaliation.—*adj.* retor'tive. [L. *retorquēre*, *retortum*—re-, back, *torquēre*, to twist.]

retouch, rē-tuch', *v.t.* to touch again: to touch up, seek to improve by new touches.—*n.* an act of touching up, esp. of a photograph by pencilwork on the negative.—*n.* retouch'er. [Pfx. re-.]

retour, ri-tōōr', *n.* a return: an extract from chancery of the service of an heir to his ancestor (Scots law).—*v.t.* to return as heir: to return to chancery. [O.Fr. *retour*, return.]

retrace, ri-, or rē-trās', *v.t.* to trace back: to go back upon: to run over with the eye or in the memory: (rē-) to renew the outline of.—*adj.* retrace'able (ri-). [Fr. *retracer*.]

retract, ri-trakt', *v.t.* to draw back: to withdraw: to revoke: to unsay: to undo (the previous move; *chess*): to pronounce with tongue drawn back.—*v.i.* to take back, or draw back

---

rētell', *v.t.*:—pa.p. rētold'.  rētell'er, *n.*  rētie', *v.t.*

Neutral vowels in unaccented syllables: *el'ə-mənt*; for certain sounds in foreign words, see p. viii

from, what has been said or granted.—*adj.*
**retrac'table**, able to be retracted: that can be
drawn up into the body or wings (*aero.*): that
can be drawn up towards the body of a vehicle.
—*n.* **retractā'tion** (*rē-*), revoking: recantation.—
*adj.* **retrac'ted**, drawn in: turned back: cancelled: revoked: pronounced with tongue
drawn in.—*adj.* **retrac'tile** (*-til*), that may be
drawn back.—*ns.* **retractility** (*rē-trak-til'i-ti*);
**retraction** (*ri-trak'shən*), drawing back: retrac-
tation.—*adj.* **retrac'tive**, tending to retract: involving the reversal of the previous move (*chess*).
—*adv.* **retrac'tively.**—*n.* **retrac'tor**, a device or
instrument for holding parts back, esp. a surgical
instrument for this purpose: a muscle that pulls
in a part: a chess-problem that involves the
reversal of the previous move. [Mainly from L.
*retrahēre, retractum*; partly from *retractāre,
retractātum*—*re-*, back, *trahēre*, to draw.]
**retraict, retrait, retraite,** *ri-trāt'*, obs. forms of
**retreat** (*n.* and *v.i.*).
**retraitt.** See **retrate** (2).
**retranslate,** *rē-trans-lāt'*, *-trəns-*, *-trans-*, *-z-*, *v.t.*
to translate anew: to translate back into the
original language: to transfer back.—*n.* **retrans-
lā'tion.** [Pfx. **re-.**]
**retransmit,** *rē-trāns-mit'*, *v.t.* to transmit again:
to transmit back: to transmit a stage further.—
*n.* **retransmiss'ion.** [Pfx. **re-.**]
**retrate,** *ri-trāt'*, (*Spens.*) *n.* and *v.i.* Same as
**retreat.**
**retrate, retraitt,** *ri-trāt'*, (*Spens.*) *n.* a portrait,
portraiture. [It. *ritratto*.]
**retread,** *rē-tred'*, *v.t.* to tread again:—*pa.t.* **retrod'**;
*pa.p.* **retrodd'en:** to repair the tread of (a tyre):—
*pa.t.* and *pa.p.* **retread'ed.**—*n.* a used tyre which
has been given a new tread: a soldier who
fought in the first and second World Wars
(*Austr.* and *U.S.*). [Pfx. **re-.**]
**retreat,** *ri-trēt'*, *n.* a withdrawal: an orderly withdrawal before an enemy, or from a position of
danger or difficulty: a signal (by bugle or drum)
for withdrawal or for retirement to quarters:
recall of pursuers (*Shak.*): retirement: seclusion: retirement for a time for religious meditation: a time of such retirement: place of
privacy, seclusion, refuge, or quiet: an institution for treatment of the insane, drunkards,
or others.—*v.i.* to draw back: to relinquish a
position: to retire: to recede.—*v.t.* (*rare*) to
withdraw. [O.Fr. *retret, -e*, pa.p. of *retraire*—L.
*retrahēre*, to draw back.]
**retree,** *ri-trē'*, *n.* slightly damaged paper. [Perh.
Fr. *retret, retrait*; see preceding.]
**retrench,** *ri-trench'*, *-trensh'*, *v.t.* to cut off, out, or
down: to protect by a retrenchment.—*v.i.* to cut
down expenses.—*n.* **retrench'ment**, an act or
instance of retrenching: economy: a work within another for prolonging defence (*fort.*). [O.Fr.
*retrencher* (Fr. *retrancher*)—*re-*, off, *trencher*;
see **trench.**]
**retribute,** *ri-trib'ūt*, *ret'ri-būt*, *v.t.* to give in
return: to give in return for.—*v.i.* to make
requital.—*n.* **retribution** (*ret-ri-bū'shən*), requital
(now esp. of evil).—*adj.* **retrib'ūtive** (*ri-*), repaying: rewarding or punishing suitably.—*n.*
**retrib'ūtor.**—*adj.* **retrib'ūtory.** [L. *retribuēre,
-ūtum*, to give back—*re-*, back, *tribuēre*, to give.]
**retrieve,** *ri-trēv'*, *v.t.* to search for and fetch, as a
dog does game: to recover, repossess: to rescue
(from, out of): to save (time): to restore
(honour, fortune): to make good (loss, error).—
*v.i.* to find and fetch in game.—*n.* retrieving.—
*adj.* **retriev'able.**—*n.* **retriev'ableness.**—*adv.* **re-
triev'ably.**—*ns.* **retriev'al**, retrieving; **retrieve'-
ment** (*rare*); **retriev'er**, a dog (of a breed that can
be) trained to find and fetch game that has been

shot: one who retrieves.—*n.* and *adj.* **retriev'ing.**
[O.Fr. *retroev-, retreuv-*, stressed stem of
*retrover* (Fr. *retrouver*)—*re-*, again, *trouver*, to
find.]
**retro-,** *ret-rō-*, *rē-trō-*, *pfx.* backwards: behind.
[L. *retrō*.]
**retroact,** *rē-trō-akt'*, or *ret'rō-*, *v.i.* to act backward, or apply to the past (*law*): to react.—
*n.* **retroac'tion.**—*adj.* **retroac'tive**, applying to,
affecting, things past: operating backward.—
*adv.* **retroac'tively.**—*n.* **retroactiv'ity.** [L. *retro-
agēre, -actum*—*agēre*, to do.]
**retrobulbar,** *rē-trō-bul'bər*, or *ret-rō-*, *adj.* behind
the eyeball. [**retro-**, and L. *bulbus*, onion.]
**retrocede,** *ret-rō-*, *rē-trō-sēd'*, *v.i.* to move back or
(*med.*) inwards.—*v.t.* to cede back, grant back.—
*adj.* **retrocē'dent.**—*n.* **retrocession** (*-sesh'ən*).—
*adj.* **retrocess'ive.** [L. *retrōcēdēre, -cēssum*—
*cēdēre*, to go, yield; partly from **retro-** and **cede**,
or Fr. *céder*.]
**retrochoir,** *rē'trō-kwīr*, or *ret'rō-*, (*archit.*) *n.* an
extension of a church behind the position of the
high altar. [Pfx. **retro-.**]
**retrocognition,** *ret'rō-kog-ni'shən*, *n.* extrasensory
knowledge of past events. [Pfx. **retro-.**]
**retroflex,** *ret'rō-fleks*, or *rē'trō-*, *adj.* bent back.—
Also **retroflect'ed, ret'roflexed.**—*n.* **retroflexion**
(*-flek'shən*). [L.L. *retroflexus*—L. *retro-*, back—
L. *flectēre, flexum*, to bend.]
**retrograde,** *ret'rō-grād* (or *rē'trō-*), *adj.* moving or
directed backward or (*astron.*) from east to west,
relatively to the fixed stars: inverse: habitually
walking or swimming backwards: degenerating:
reverting: contrary (*Shak.*).—*n.* one who goes
back or degenerates: backward movement.—
*v.i.* to go back or backwards: to have a retrograde movement (*astron.*).—*v.t.* to cause to go
back.—*ns.* **retrogradation** (*-grə-dā'shən*), retrogression (esp. *astron.*); **ret'rogress** (*-gres*), backward movement: degeneration.—*v.i.* **retrogress'**,
to retrograde.—*n.* **retrogression** (*-gresh'ən*), a
going backward: a decline in quality or merit:
retrograde movement (*astron.*).—*adjs.* **retrogress'ional, retrogress'ive.**—*adv.* **retrogress'ively.**
[L. *retrōgradus*, going backward, *retrōgressus*,
retrogression—*retrō-*, backward, *gradī, gressus*,
to go.]
**retromingent,** *ret-rō-*, *rē-trō-min'jənt*, *adj.* urinating backward.—*n.* a retromingent animal.—*n.*
**retromin'gency.** [Pfx. **retro-**, and L. *mingēre*, to
urinate.]
**retro-operative,** *ret-rō-*, *rē-trō-op'ər-ə-tiv*, *adj.*
retrospective in effect. [Pfx. **retro-.**]
**retropulsion,** *ret-rō-*, *rē-trō-pul'shən*, *n.* pushing
backwards: a tendency in the paralysed to walk
backwards.—*adj.* **retropul'sive.** [Pfx. **retro-**,
*pulsion* (*rare*)—L. *pulsiō, -ōnis*.]
**retro-rocket,** *ret'rō-rok'it*, *rēt'*, *n.* a rocket whose
function is to slow down, fired in a direction
opposite to that in which a body, e.g. a spacecraft, an artificial satellite, is travelling. [Pfx.
**retro-.**]
**retrorse,** *ri-trörs'*, *adj.* turned back or downward.—
*adv.* **retrorse'ly.** [L. *retrōrsus*—*retrōversus*.]
**retrospect,** *ret'rō-spekt* (or *rē'trō-*), *n.* reference,
regard: a backward view: a view or a looking
back: a contemplation of the past.—*v.i.* to look
back.—*v.t.* to look back on.—*n.* **retrospec'tion.**—
*adj.* **retrospec'tive**, looking back: retroactive.—
*adv.* **retrospec'tively.** [L. *retrōspicēre*—L. *specēre*,
*spectum*, to look.]
**retroussé,** *rə-trōōs'ā*, *rə-trōōs'ā*, *adj.* turned up
(esp. of the nose).—*n.* **retroussage** (*-äzh'*), wiping
aside of ink on an engraved plate to soften tones.
[Fr. *retrousser* (pa.p. *retroussé*), to turn up.]
**retrovert,** *ret-rō-*, *rē-trō-vûrt'*, *rē'trō-vûrt*, *v.t.* to
turn back.—*n.* **retrover'sion**, a turning or falling

back: backward displacement. [L. *retrōvertĕre,* -*versum*—*vertĕre,* to turn.]

**retry,** *rē-trī',* *v.t.* to try again (judicially):—*pr.p.* **retry'ing;** *pa.t.* and *pa.p.* **retried'.**—*n.* **rētri'al.** [Pfx. re-.]

**retsina,** *ret-sēn'ə, n.* a Greek resin-flavoured wine. [Gr.]

**retted, rettery, retting.** See ret.

**retund,** *ri-tund',* *v.t.* to blunt. [L. *retundĕre,* to beat back.]

**return,** *ri-tûrn',* *v.i.* to come or go back: to revert: to recur: to turn away (*B.*): to continue with change of direction (*archit.*).—*v.t.* to turn round (*Shak.*): to make a turn at an angle (*archit.*): to turn back (*Spens.*): to give, put, cast, bring, or send back: to answer: to retort: to report officially: to report as appointed or elected: hence, to elect to parliament: to give in return: (in games) to lead back or hit back: to requite: to repay: to respond to with the like: to render: to yield: to come back over (*Shak.*). —*n.* the act of returning: a recurrence: reversion: continuation, or a continuing stretch, at an angle, esp. a right angle (*archit.,* etc.): that which comes in exchange: proceeds, profit, yield: recompense: requital: an answer: an answering performance: a thing returned, esp. an unsold newspaper: (in *pl.*) a light-coloured mild tobacco (orig. refuse): the rendering back of a writ by the sheriff, with his report (*law*): an official report: hence, election to parliament: a return ticket.—*adj.* returning: for return: in return: at right angles.—*adjs.* return'able; return'less.—return crease (see crease (1)); returning officer, the officer who presides at an election; return match, a second match played by the same (sets of) players; return shock, an electric shock due to induction sometimes felt after a lightning-flash; return ticket, a ticket entitling a passenger to travel to a place and back to his starting-point.—by return (of post), by the next post leaving in the opposite direction. [Fr. *retourner*—*re*-, back, *tourner,* to turn.]

**re-turn,** *rē'-tûrn',* *v.t.* and *v.i.* to turn again or back. [Pfx. re-.]

**retuse,** *ri-tūs',* *adj.* with the tip blunt and broadly notched. [L. *retūsus*—*retundĕre,* to blunt.]

**reunion,** *rē-ūn'yən, n.* a union, or a meeting, after separation: a social gathering of friends or persons with something in common.—*ns.* **reun'ionism; reun'ionist,** one who wishes to have the Anglican and Roman Catholic Churches reunited.—Also *adj.*—*adj.* **reunionis'tic.** [Fr. *réunion*—*re*-, again, *union,* union.]

**reunite,** *rē-ū-nīt',* *v.t.* and *v.i.* to join after separation. [Pfx. re-.]

**rev,** *rev, n.* a revolution in an internal-combustion engine.—*v.t.* to increase the speed of revolution in (often with *up*).—*v.i.* to revolve: to increase in speed of revolution:—*pr.p.* **revv'ing;** *pa.t.* and *pa.p.* **revved.** [revolution.]

**revalenta,** *rev-ə-len'tə, n.* lentil-meal.—Earlier **ervalen'ta.** [*Ervum Lens,* Linnaean name of the lentil—L. *ervum,* bitter vetch, *lēns, lentis,* lentil.]

**revalorise, -ize,** *rē-val'ər-īz, v.t.* to give a new value to, esp. to restore the value of (currency).— *ns.* **rēvalorisā'tion, -z-; rēvalūā'tion.**—*v.t.* **rēval'ue,** to make a new valuation of: to give a new value to. [Pfx. re-.]

**revamp,** *rē-vamp', v.t.* to renovate, revise, give a new appearance to.—Also *n.* [Pfx. re-.]

**revanche,** *ri-vänch', n.* revenge: policy directed towards recovery of territory lost to an enemy.— *ns.* **revanch'ism, revanch'ist.**—Also *adj.* [Fr.; conn. with revenge (q.v.).]

**reveal,** *ri-vēl', v.t.* to make known, as by divine agency or inspiration: to disclose: to divulge: to make visible: to allow to be seen.—*adj.* **reveal'able.**—*n.* **reveal'er.**—*n.* and *adj.* **reveal'ing.** —*n.* **reveal'ment,** revelation. [O.Fr. *reveler* (Fr. *révéler*)—L. *revēlāre*—*re*-, back, *vēlāre,* to veil— *vēlum,* a veil.]

**reveal,** *ri-vēl', n.* the side surface of a recess, or of the opening for a doorway or window between the frame and the outer surface of the wall. [O.Fr. *revaler,* to lower.]

**reveille,** *ri-val'i, ri-vel'i, ri-vāl'yi,* (*U.S.*) *rev'ə-lē, n.* the sound of the drum or bugle at daybreak to awaken soldiers: a summons to awake, get up, or begin. [Fr. *réveillez,* awake, imper. of *réveiller*—L. *re*-, *vigilāre,* to watch.]

**revel,** *rev'l, v.i.* to feast or make merry in a riotous or noisy manner: to take intense delight, to luxuriate (with *in*).—*v.t.* to spend in revelry:— *pr.p.* **rev'elling;** *pa.t.* and *pa.p.* **rev'elled.**—*n.* a riotous feast: merrymaking: a festival or (often in *pl.*) occasion of merrymaking, dancing, masking, etc.—*ns.* **rev'eller; rev'elling; rev'elry,** revelling.—**rev'el-rout',** boisterous revelry: a crowd of revellers.—**Master of the Revels,** an official organiser of entertainments, esp. at court or in the Inns of Court. [O.Fr. *reveler*— L. *rebellāre,* to rebel.]

**revelation,** *rev-i-lā'shən, n.* the act or experience of revealing: that which is revealed: a disclosure: an enlightening experience: divine or supernatural communication: **Revelation (of St John),** or, popularly, **Revelations,** the Apocalypse or last book of the New Testament.—*adj.* **revelā'tional.**—*n.* **revelā'tionist,** a believer in divine revelation: one who makes a revelation: the author of the Apocalypse or an apocalyptic book.—*adj.* **rev'elātive.**—*n.* **rev'elātor.**—*adj.* **rev'elatory.** [L. *revēlāre, -ātum;* see reveal.]

**revenant,** *rəv-nã, rev'ə-nənt, n.* one who returns after a long absence, esp. from the dead: a ghost. [Fr., pr.p. of *revenir,* to come back.]

**revendicate,** *rē-vend'i-kāt, v.t.* to make formal claim to, or recover by such claim (e.g. lost territory): to endeavour to have unpaid-for and undamaged goods restored when buyer is bankrupt.—*n.* **revendicā'tion.** [Variant, through Fr., of vindicate.]

**revenge,** *ri-venj', v.t.* to inflict injury in retribution for: (esp. *refl.*) to avenge.—*v.i.* to take vengeance. —*n.* (act of inflicting) a malicious injury in return for injury received: the desire for retaliation of evil (also in *pl.; Shak.*): avenging (*Shak.*): in games, opportunity of retaliation in a return game: punishment (*obs.*).—*adj.* **revenge'ful,** ready to seek revenge.—*adv.* **revenge'fully.**—*n.* **revenge'fulness.**—*adj.* **revenge'-less.**—*ns.* **revenge'ment** (now *rare*); **reveng'er.**—*n.* and *adj.* **reveng'ing.**—*adv.* **reveng'ingly.**—*adj.* **reveng'ive** (*Shak.*). [O.Fr. *revenger, revencher* (Fr. *revancher*)—L. *re*-, *vindicāre,* to lay claim to.]

**revenue,** *rev'in-ū* (formerly also *ri-ven'ū*), *n.* receipts or return from any source: income: the income of a state: a government department concerned with it.—*adj.* **rev'enued**—**rev'enue-cutt'er,** an armed vessel employed in preventing smuggling.—**Inland Revenue,** revenue from excise, income-tax, etc. [Fr. *revenue,* pa.p. (fem.) of *revenir,* to return—L. *revenire*—*re*-, back, *venire,* to come.]

**reverberate,** *ri-vûr'bər-āt, v.t.* to beat or send back: to reflect: to echo: to heat in a reverberatory furnace.—*v.i.* to recoil, rebound: to be reflected: to re-echo: to resound.—*adj.* **reverberated:** reverberating (*Shak.*).—*v.t.* **reverb'** (after *Shak.*).

---

**rēturf',** *v.t.*
**rēurge',** *v.t.*
**rēuse'** (*-ūz'*), *v.t.*

**rēuse'** (*-ūs'*), *n.*
**rēutt'er,** *v.t.*
**rēvac'cinate,** *v.t.*

**rēvaccinā'tion,** *n.*
**rēval'idate,** *v.t.*
**rē-val'idate,** *v.t.*

—*adj.* rever′berant, reverberating.—*n.* reverberā′-
tion.—*adj.* rever′berātive.—*n.* rever′berātor.—
*adj.* rever′beratory (-ət-ər-i, or -āt-).—reverberatory furnace, a furnace in which the flame is
turned back over the substance to be heated. [L.
*reverberāre, -ātum—re-,* back, *verberāre,* to beat
—*verber,* a lash.]
revere, ri-vēr′, *v.t.* to regard with high respect: to
venerate.—*adj.* revēr′able.—*n.* reverence (rev′ər-
əns), high respect: respectful awe: veneration:
state of being held in high respect: a gesture or
observance of respect.—*v.t.* to venerate.—*n.*
rev′erencer.—*adj.* rev′erend, worthy of reverence: clerical: (*cap.*; usu. written Rev.), a title
prefixed to a clergyman's name.—*n.* a clergyman.
—*adjs.* rev′erent, feeling or showing reverence;
reverential (-en′shl), proceeding from reverence:
respectful: submissive.—*advs.* reveren′tially,
rev′erently.—*n.* reverer (ri-vēr′ər).—His, Your,
Reverence, (now Ir. or playful) a mode of
referring to or addressing a clergyman; Most
Reverend is used of an archbishop, Right
Reverend, a bishop, or Moderator of the Church
of Scotland, Very Reverend, a dean, a former
Moderator, or (if a clergyman) a Scottish
University principal; Reverend Mother, a Mother
Superior of a convent; save or saving (your)
reverence (*obs.* contr. to sir-reverence), with all
due respect to you—an apology for introducing
an unseemly word or subject. [O.Fr. *reverer*
(Fr. *révérer*)—L. *reverēri—re-,* inten., *verēri,* feel
awe.]
reverie, revery, rev′ə-ri, *n.* an undirected train of
thoughts or fancies in meditation: a fanciful
notion (*arch.*): mental abstraction: a piece of
music expressing such a state of mind.—*n.*
rev′erist. [Fr. *rêverie—rêver,* to dream.]
revers, ri-vēr′, U.S. -vûr′, rə-ver′, *n.* any part of a
garment that is turned back, as a lapel:—*pl.*
revers (as *sing.,* or -vērz, -vûrz). [Fr.,—L.
*reversus.*]
reverse, ri-vûrs′, *v.t.* to bring back (*Spens.*): to
turn aside (*Spens.*): to turn the other way about,
as upside down, outside in, etc.: to invert: to
set moving backwards: to annul.—*v.i.* to move
in the opposite direction: to set an engine
moving backwards: to return (*Spens.*).—*n.* the
contrary, opposite: the back, esp. of a coin or
medal (opp. to *obverse*): a set-back, misfortune,
defeat: a back-handed sword-stroke: an act
of reversing.—*adj.* contrary, opposite: turned
about: acting in the contrary direction: reversing: back-handed (*obs.*): of the rear (*mil.*).—*n.*
rever′sal, act of reversing.—*adj.* reversed′.—*adv.*
rever′sedly.—*adj.* reverse′less, unalterable.—*adv.*
reverse′ly.—*ns.* rever′ser, one who, or that which,
reverses: a reversing device: a borrower on
wadset (*Scots law*); rever′si (-sē), a game in
which a captured man is not removed from the
board but turned upside down to show the
captor's colour: reversis; reversibil′ity.—*adj.*
rever′sible.—*n.* a fabric having both sides well
finished.—*n.* and *adj.* rever′sing.—*n.* rever′sion
(-shən), the act or fact of reverting or of returning: that which reverts or returns: the return, or
the future possession, of any property after some
particular event: the right to succeed to possession or office: a sum payable upon death: that
which is left over, remains: return to ancestral
type (*biol.*).—*adj.* rever′sional.—*adv.* rever′-
sionally.—*adj.* rever′sionary, relating to reversion: of reversion: of the nature of a reversion.
—*n.* one who has a reversion.—*ns.* rever′sioner,
a reversionary; rever′sis, an old card-game in
which the taker of fewest tricks wins; rever′so,
a verso: a back-handed sword-stroke.—re-

versing layer, a layer of the sun's chromosphere
that reverses bright lines of the spectrum to dark
absorption lines.—reverse the charges, charge a
telephone call to the one who receives it instead
of to the caller. [L. *reversāre,* to turn round;
partly through Fr.]
revert, ri-vûrt′, *v.t.* to turn back: to reverse.—
*v.i.* to return: to fall back to a former state: to
recur to a former subject: to return to the original owner or his heirs.—*adj.* rever′ted, reversed:
turned backwards.—*adjs.* rever′tible; revert′ive
(*Thomson*). [L. *re-, vertĕre,* to turn.]
rêveur, re-vœr, fem. rêveuse, re-vœz, (Fr.) a day-
dreamer.
revest, ri-vest′, *v.t.* to clothe again (*Spens.*): to
vest again.—*v.i.* to vest again.—*ns.* revest′iary,
revest′ry, a vestry. [O.Fr. *revestir,* or *re-, vestir*
—L. *revestire, vestire,* to clothe again, to clothe.]
revet, ri-vet′, *v.t.* to face with masonry, etc:—
*pr.p.* revett′ing; *pa.t.* and *pa.p.* revett′ed.—*n.*
revet′ment, a retaining wall, facing. [Fr. *revêtir,*
to reclothe.]
revie, rē-vī′, *v.t.* to stake more than an opponent
has proposed on (e.g. the taking of a trick): to
bandy (words) in emulation (*obs.*).—*v.i.* to stake
higher (*obs.*):—*pr.p.* rēvy′ing; *pa.t.* and *pa.p.* rē-
vied′.—Also *n.* (*obs.*). [Fr. *renvier*—L. *re-, invitāre,* to invite.]
review, ri-vū′, *n.* a viewing again (also re-view, rē′-
vū′): a looking back, retrospect: a reconsideration: a survey: a revision: a critical examination: a critique: a periodical with critiques of
books, etc.: a display and inspection of troops
or ships: the judicial revision of a higher court
(*law*).—*v.t.* to see, view, or examine again (also
rē-view′): to look back on or over: to survey:
to examine critically: to write a critique on: to
inspect, as troops: to revise.—*v.i.* to write
reviews.—*adj.* review′able, capable of being
reviewed.—*ns.* review′al, a review of a book:
reviewing; review′er, a writer of critiques: a
writer in a review.—review′-copy, a copy of a
book sent by the publisher to a periodical for
review. [Partly pfx. re- and view; partly Fr.
*revue,* pa.p. (fem.) of *revoir*—L. *revidēre—
vidēre,* to see.]
revile, ri-vīl′, *v.t.* to assail with bitter abuse.—*v.i.*
to rail, use abusive language.—*n.* revilement
(*obs.*).—*ns.* revile′ment, the act of reviling: a
reviling speech; revil′er.—*n.* and *adj.* revil′ing.—
*adv.* revil′ingly. [O.Fr. *reviler*—L. *re-, vilis,*
worthless.]
revindicate, ri-vin′di-kāt, *v.t.* to claim and get back:
to vindicate anew.—*n.* revindica′tion. [Pfx. re-.]
revise, ri-vīz′, *v.t.* to examine and correct: to
make a new, improved version of: to study
anew: to look at again (*obs.*).—Also *v.i.*—*n.*
act of revising or being revised: review: a
further proof-sheet in which previous corrections
have been given effect to.—*adj.* revis′able, liable
to revision.—*ns.* revi′sal, revision; revi′ser (also
-or); revision (-vizh′ən), act or product of revising.—*adjs.* revi′sional, revi′sionary, pertaining
to revision.—*ns.* revi′sionism; revi′sionist, an
advocate of revision (e.g. of a treaty): a Communist favouring modification of stricter orthodox Communism and evolution, rather than
revolution, as a means of achieving world
domination: a reviser of the Bible.—*adj.* revi′-
sory.—Revised Version, an English translation
of the Bible issued 1881-85 (Apocrypha 1895);
revising barrister, till 1918, a barrister appointed
to revise the parliamentary voters' roll. [Fr.
*reviser* and L. *revisĕre—re-,* back, *visĕre,* inten.
of *vidēre,* to see.]
revive, ri-vīv′, *v.t.* and *v.i.* to bring back or come

revictual (rē-vit′l), *v.t.* and *v.i.:—pr.p.* revict′ual-
ling; *pa.t.* and *pa.p.* revict′ualled.
rēvis′it, *v.t.* and *n.*

rêvis′itant, *n.*
rêvisitā′tion, *n.*
rêvit′alise, -ize, *v.t.*

back to life, vigour, being, activity, consciousness, memory, good spirits, freshness, vogue, notice, currency, use, the stage, or natural metallic form.—*n.* revivabil'ity.—*adj.* revi'vable. —*adv.* revi'vably.—*ns.* revi'val, act or fact of reviving: state of being revived: recovery from languor, neglect, depression, etc.: renewed performance, as of a play: renewed interest or attention: a time of extraordinary religious awakening or sometimes worked-up excitement: a series of meetings to encourage this: quickening: renewal: awakening; revi'valism; revi'valist, one who promotes religious, architectural, or other revival: an itinerant preacher.— *adj.* revivalist'ic.—*ns.* revive'ment (*rare*); revi'ver, one who, or that which, revives: a renovating preparation: a stimulant (*slang*).—*n.* and *adj.* revi'ving.—*adv.* revi'vingly.—*n.* revi'vor (*law*), the revival of a suit which was abated by the death of a party or other cause.—**Gothic Revival**, the resuscitation of Gothic architecture in (and before) the 19th century; **Romantic Revival** (see **romantic**); **Revival of Learning**, the Renaissance. [L. *revivĕre*, to live again—*vivĕre*, to live.]

**revivify**, ri-viv'i-fī, *v.t.* to restore to life: to put new life into: to reactivate.—*v.t.* and *v.i.* (*chem.*) to revive, restore (e.g. metal) to its uncombined state:—*pr.p.* reviv'ifying; *pa.t.* and *pa.p.* reviv'ified.—*n.* revivifica'tion. [L.L. *revivificāre*—re-, *vivus*, alive, *facĕre*, to make.]

**reviviscent**, rev-i-vis'ənt, revivescent, -ves'ənt, *adj.* reviving.—*ns.* revivisc'ence, revivisc'ency (also -esc-). [L. *reviviscĕre*, -ēscĕre.]

**revoke**, ri-vōk', *v.t.* to recall, call back (now *rare*): to withdraw (*Spens.*): to check (*Spens.*): to annul: to retract.—*v.i.* to make revocations: to neglect to follow suit at cards.—*n.* revocation, recall: act of revoking at cards.—*adj.* revocable (rev'ō-ka-bl).—*ns.* rev'ocableness, revocabil'ity. —*adv.* rev'ocably.—*n.* revoca'tion, recall: act of revoking.—*adj.* rev'ocatory.—*n.* revoke'ment (*Shak.*), revocation. [L. *revocāre*—*vocāre*, to call.]

**revolt**, ri-vōlt', *v.i.* to renounce allegiance: to rise in opposition: to turn or rise in disgust, loathing, or repugnance.—*v.t.* to turn back (*Spens.*): to cause to rise in revolt (*obs.*): to inspire revulsion or repugnance in.—*n.* a rebellion: insurrection: secession: revulsion (*Shak.*): a rebel (*Shak.*).—*adj.* revolt'ed, insurgent: shocked, outraged.—*n.* revol'ter.—*adj.* revol'ting.—*adv.* revol'tingly. [Fr. *révolter*—L. *re-*, *volūtāre*, freq. of *volvĕre*, *volūtum*, to turn.]

**revolution**, rev-əl-ōō'shən, or -ū', *n.* act or condition of revolving: movement in an orbit, as distinguished from rotation: less commonly, rotation: a complete turn by an object or figure, through four right angles, about an axis: a cycle of phenomena or of time: recurrence in cycles: turning over in the mind (*arch.*): mutation (*Shak.*): a great upheaval: a complete change, e.g. in outlook, social habits or circumstances: a radical change in government: a time of intensified change in the earth's features (*geol.*). —*adjs.* revolu'tional, of revolution in movement; revolu'tionary, of, favouring, or of the nature of, revolution, esp. in government or conditions.— *n.* one who takes part in, or favours, a revolution. —*n.* revolu'tioner (*hist.*), a supporter of a revolution, esp. that of 1688.—*v.t.* revolu'tionise, -ize, to cause radical change in.—*ns.* revolu'tionism; revolu'tionist, one who favours revolution.— **Revolutionary Calendar**, calendar used in France from 1793 to 1805 (see **Vendémiaire**, **Brumaire**, **Frimaire**, **Nivôse**, **Pluviôse**, **Ventôse**, **Germinal**, **Floréal**, **Prairial**, **Messidor**, **Thermidor**, **Fructi-**

dor).—**the American Revolution**, the change from the condition of British colonies to national independence effected by the thirteen states of the American Union in 1776; **the French Revolution**, the overthrow of the old French monarchy and absolutism (1789); **the Revolution**, the expulsion of James II from the British throne (1688-89), and the establishment of a really constitutional government under William III and Mary. [L.L. *revolūtiō, -ōnis.*]

**revolve**, ri-volv', *v.t.* and *v.i.* to roll back, return (*obs.*): to ponder: to move about a centre: to rotate.—*n.* turning, revolution: (*theatre*) a part of the stage which can be revolved by electrical means, providing one method of scene-changing. —*adj.* revolute (rev'əl-ūt, -ōōt), rolled backward. —*ns.* revol'vency, revolution: tendency to revolve; revol'ver, a revolving device of various kinds: a pistol with a rotating magazine.—*n.* and *adj.* revol'ving. [L. *revolvĕre*, *revolūtum*—*volvĕre*, to roll.]

**revue**, ri-vū', *n.* a loosely constructed theatrical show, more or less topical and musical. [Fr., review.]

**revulsion**, ri-vul'shən, *n.* diversion to another part, esp. by counter-irritation (*med.*): withdrawal: disgust: a sudden change or reversal, esp. of feeling.—*adjs.* revul'sionary; revul'sive (-siv). [L. *revellĕre*, *revulsum*, to pluck back—*vellĕre*, to pluck.]

**rew**, rōō (*Spens.*). Same as **rue** (1 and 2) and **row** (1).

**reward**, ri-wörd', *n.* that which is given in return for good (sometimes evil), or in recognition of merit, or for performance of a service.—*v.t.* to give or be a reward to or for: to give as a reward (*B.*).—*adj.* reward'able, capable or worthy of being rewarded.—*ns.* reward'ableness; reward'er.—*adjs.* reward'ful, yielding reward; reward'ing, profitable: yielding a result well worth while; reward'less, unrewarded. [O.Fr. *rewarder*, *regarder*—re-, again, *warder*, *garder*, to guard; see **regard**, **guard**, **ward**.]

**reword**, rē-würd', *v.t.* to repeat, re-echo (*Shak.*): to put into different words. [Pfx. re-.]

**rewth**, rōōth (*Spens.*). Same as **ruth**.

**rex**. See **reak**.

**Rex**, reks, *n.* king: title used by reigning king, abbrev. to R in signature.—**Rex** (cat), a type of cat (of two varieties, Devon Rex and Cornish Rex) with curly but thin coat.—**Rex** (rabbit), a type of domestic rabbit in which the hair that would normally form the outer coat is shorter than that of the under coat, one variety of Rex (*Astrex*; *Ast-* from Astrakhan) having curly or wavy fur.

**Reynard**, **reynard**, rān' or ren'ärd, -ərd, *n.* a fox, from the name given to the fox in the famous beast epic of L.Ger. origin, *Reynard the Fox.*— in Spens. **Reyn'old**. [M.Du. *Reynaerd*—O.H.G. *Reginhart*, lit. strong in counsel.]

**rhabdus**, rab'dəs, *n.* a rodlike sponge spicule.— *adj.* rhab'doid, rodlike.—*n.* a rodlike body.—*ns.* rhab'dolith (Gr. *lithos*, stone), a calcareous rod in some Protozoa; rhab'dom (Gr. *rhabdōma*, bundle of rods), a fourfold rod in the compound eye of an arthropod; rhab'domancy (Gr. *manteiā*, divination), divination by rod; rhab'domantist; rhabdomyō'ma, a tumour of striped muscle.—*n.pl.* **Rhabdoph'ora**, the graptolites.—*n.* rhab'dosphere, an aggregation of rhabdoliths in oceanic ooze. [Latinised from Gr. *rhabdos*, rod.]

**rhachis**, **rhachitis**. Same as **rachis**, **rachitis**.

**Rhadamanthine**, rad-ə-man'thin, *adj.* rigorously just and severe, like *Rhadamanthus* (Gr. · *əs*), a judge of the lower world.

**Rhaetia**, **Raetia**, rē'sh(y)ə, *n.* a province of the

rewind', *v.t.*:—*pa.t.* and *pa.p.* rewound'.
rewire', *v.t.*

rework', *v.t.*
rewrite', *v.t.*:—*pa.t.* rewrote'; *pa.p.* rewritt'en.

Neutral vowels in unaccented syllables: *el'ə-mənt*; for certain sounds in foreign words, see p. viii

Roman Empire, roughly Grisons and Tirol, to which Vindelicia was added.—*adj.* and *n.* **R(h)ae′tian.**—*adj.* Rhaetic (*rē′tik*; *geol.*), uppermost Trias (also **Keuper**) or (acc. to others) lowest Jurassic.—Also *n.*—**Rhae′to-Roman′ic,** a general name for a group of Romance dialects spoken from south-eastern Switzerland to Friuli (Romansch, Ladino, Friulian).—Also *adj.*

**Rhamnus,** *ram′nəs, n.* the buckthorn genus, giving name to the family **Rhamnā′ceae.**—*adj.* **rhamnā′ceous.** [Latinised from Gr. *rhamnos.*]
**rhamphoid,** *ram′joid, adj.* hook-beak-shaped.—*ns.* **Rhamphast′os,** the typical genus of toucans; **Rhamphorhynchus** (*ram-fō-ring′kəs;* Gr. *rhynchos,* snout), a genus of pterodactyls; **rhamphothē′ca** (Gr. *thēkē,* case), the horny sheath of a bird's bill. [Gr. *rhamphos,* a hooked beak.]
**rhaphe, rhaphis.** Same as **raphe, raphis.**
**rhapontic,** *ra-pon′tik, n.* ordinary kitchen-garden rhubarb. [L.L. *rhā ponticum,* Pontic rhubarb; see **rhubarb.**]
**rhapsody,** *raps′ə-di, n.* an epic or instalment of an epic recited at one sitting (*Gr. hist.*): a patching or stringing together of poems (*obs.*): an orderless, unconnected composition, or collection of things said, beliefs, etc. (*obs.*): an ecstatic utterance of feeling: an irregular emotional piece of music.—*n.* **rhapsode** (*raps′ōd*), a reciter of Homeric or other epics.—*adjs.* **rhapsodic** (*-od′ik*), of rhapsodes or rhapsodies: of the nature of rhapsody; **rhapsod′ical,** rhapsodic: unrestrainedly enthusiastic, rapt.—*adv.* **rhapsod′ically.**—*v.t.* **rhaps′odise, -ize** (*-ə-dīz*), to piece together (*obs.*): to recite in rhapsodies.—*v.i.* to write or utter rhapsodies.—*n.* **rhaps′odist,** a rhapsode: one who rhapsodises. [Gr. *rhapsōidiā,* an epic, a rigmarole—*rhaptein,* to sew, *ōidē,* a song.]
**rhatany,** *rat′ə-ni, n.* a South American caesalpiniaceous plant (species of *Krameria*): its astringent root. [Sp. *ratania*—Quechua *rataña.*]
**rhea,** *rē′a, n.* ramie. [Assamese *rihā.*]
**Rhea,** *rē′a, n.* the daughter of Uranus and Ge, wife and sister of Kronos: the fifth satellite of Saturn: (without *cap.*) the South American ostrich (*Rhea*). [Gr. *Rhĕā.*]
**rhematic,** *rē-mat′ik, adj.* of words or verbs: word-making. [Gr. *rhēma, -atos,* word, verb.]
**Rhemish,** *rē′mish, adj.* of Rheims (Reims) in north-eastern France.—**Rhemish version,** the English translation of the New Testament by Roman Catholics of the English college there (1582).—*n.* **Rhē′mist,** a translator of the Rhemish version.
**Rhenish,** *ren′ish, adj.* of the river Rhine.—*n.* Rhine wine.—*n.* **rhenium** (*rē′ni-əm*), a chemical element (Re; at. numb. 75) discovered by X-ray spectroscopy in Germany in 1925. [L. *Rhēnus,* the Rhine.]
**rheo-,** *rē′ō-, rē-o′-,* in composition, current, flow.—*n.* **rhe′ochord, rhe′ocord,** a wire rheostat.—*adjs.* **rheolog′ic, -al.**—*ns.* **rheol′ogist; rheol′ogy,** the science of the deformation and flow of matter; **rheom′eter,** an instrument for measuring a current of fluid: a galvanometer (*obs.*); **rhe′ostat,** an instrument for varying an electric resistance; **rheotax′is,** rheotropism; **rhe′otome** (*elect.*), an interrupter; **rhe′otrope,** a commutator for reversing an electric current.—*adj.* **rheotrop′ic.**—*n.* **rheot′ropism** (*biol.*), response to the stimulus of flowing water. [Gr. *rheos,* flow.]
**rhesus,** *rē′səs, n.* a macaque, the bandar (*Macacus rhesus,* or *Macaca mulatta*), an Indian monkey.—Also **rhesus monkey.**—**Rhesus factor, Rh (-factor),** any of a group of weakly antigenic agglutinogens usu. found in human red blood cells and in those of rhesus monkeys, inherited according to Mendelian laws, **Rh-positive** persons being those who have the factor and **Rh-negative** those (a very much smaller number) who do not—a difference important in blood

transfusion and as explaining haemolytic disease of the newborn. [Gr. *Rhēsos,* a king of Thrace, arbitrarily applied.]
**rhetor,** *rē′tör, n.* (*Gr. hist.*) a teacher of rhetoric or professional orator.—*n.* **rhetoric** (*ret′ər-ik*), the theory and practice of eloquence, whether spoken or written, the whole art of using language so as to persuade others: the art of literary expression, esp. in prose: false, showy, artificial, or declamatory expression.—*adjs.* **rhetoric** (*ri-tor′ik*); **rhetor′ical, pertaining to rhetoric:** oratorical: inflated, over-decorated, or insincere in style.—*adv.* **rhetor′ically.**—*n.* **rhetorician** (*ret-ər-ish′ən*), one who teaches the art of rhetoric: an orator: a user of rhetorical language.—*v.i.* **rhetorise, -ize** (*rē′*), to play the orator.—*v.t.* to address rhetorically.—**rhetorical question,** a question in form, for rhetorical effect, not calling for an answer. [Gr. *rhētōr.*]
**rheum,** *rōōm, n.* a mucous discharge, esp. from the nose: tears (*poet.*): cold in the head (*obs.*): rheumatic pains (in *pl.*; *rare*): ill humour (*obs.*).—*adj.* **rheumatic** (*rōō-mat′ik;* Shak. *rōō′*), of the nature of, pertaining to, apt to cause, or affected with, rheumatism or (*obs.*) rheum.—*n.* one who suffers from rheumatism: (in *pl.*) rheumatic pains (*coll.*).—*adj.* **rheumat′ical.**—*adv.* **rheumat′ically.**—*adj.* **rheumat′icky.**—*n.* **rheumatism** (*rōō′mə-tizm*), condition characterised by pain and stiffness in muscles and joints (*dial.* **rheu′matiz, -tize, -tise, -teese**).—*adjs.* **rheumatis′mal; rheum′atoid,** resembling rheumatism; **rheumatolog′ical.**—*ns.* **rheumatol′ogist; rheumatol′ogy,** the study of rheumatism.—*adjs.* **rheumed; rheum′y.**—**rheumatic fever,** an acute disease characterised by fever, multiple arthritis, and liability of the heart to be inflamed and which is caused by a streptococcal infection; **rheumatoid arthritis,** a disease or diseases characterised by inflammation and swelling of joints, often leading to their complete stiffening. [Gr. *rheuma, -atos,* flow—*rheein,* to flow.]
**Rheum,** *rē′əm, n.* the rhubarb genus. [Latinised from Gr. *rhēon.*]
**rhexis,** *reks′is, n.* rupture, esp. of a blood-vessel. [Gr. *rhēxis,* breach.]
**Rh(-factor).** See **rhesus.**
**rhime,** an obs. spelling of **rhyme, rime** (1).
**rhin-,** *rin-,* **rhino-,** *rin-ō-,* in composition, nose.—*adj.* **rhi′nal,** of the nose.—*n.* **rhinencephalon** (*rin-en-sef′ə-lon;* Gr. *enkephalon,* brain), the olfactory lobe of the brain.—*adj.* **rhinencephalic** (*-al′ik*).—*ns.* **rhini′tis,** inflammation of the mucous membrane of the nose; **rhinolalia** (*-lā′li-ə;* Gr. *laliā,* talk), nasal speech; **rhi′nolith** (Gr. *lithos,* stone), a concretion in the nose.—*adj.* **rhinolog′ical.**—*ns.* **rhinol′ogist,** a nose specialist; **rhinol′ogy,** study of the nose: nasal pathology; **rhinopharyngitis** (*ri-nō-far-in-ji′tis*), inflammation of the nose and pharynx; **rhinophy′ma** (Gr. *phȳma,* growth, tumour), overgrowth of skin and subcutaneous tissue of the nose.—*adj.* **rhinoplas′tic.**—*ns.* **rhi′noplasty,** plastic surgery of the nose; **rhinorrhagia** (*ri-nō-rā′jyə;* Gr. *rhēgnynai,* to break), excessive nose-bleeding; **rhinorrhoea** (*-rē′ə;* Gr. *rhoiā,* flow), excessive mucous discharge from the nose.—*adj.* **rhinorrhoe′al.**—*ns.* **rhinoscleroma** (*-sklē-rō′mə*), a disease with hard swelling in the nose, etc.; **rhi′noscope,** an instrument for examining the nose.—*adj.* **rhinoscop′ic.**—*ns.* **rhinos′copy;** **rhinothē′ca** (Gr. *thēkē,* case), the sheath of a bird's upper mandible. [Gr. *rhis, rhinos,* nose.]
**Rhine,** *rin, n.* a river of Europe.—**Rhine′berry, Rhein′berry,** the buckthorn berry: the buckthorn; **Rhine′grave,** a count with possessions on the Rhine:—*fem.* **Rhine′gravine** (*-ēn;* Du. *Rijngrave,* now *-graaf*; fem. *Rijngravin*); **Rhine′stone** (also without *cap.*), a rock-crystal: a paste diamond; **Rhine′-wine,** wine made from

grapes grown in the Rhine valley. [Ger. *Rhein*; Du. *Rijn*.]

**rhine**, *rēn*, (Somerset, etc.) *n.* a ditch or watercourse. Also spelt **reen, rean,** etc.

**rhinencephalic, rhinencephalon.** See **rhin-**.

**Rhineodon,** *rī-nē′ō-don,* **Rhinodon,** *ri′nō-don, n.* a gigantic shark of the Indian Ocean. [Gr. *rhinē*, a file, a shagreen shark, *odous, odontos,* tooth.]

**rhinitis.** See **rhin-**.

**rhino.** Abbreviation for **rhinoceros.**

**rhino,** *ri′nō,* (*slang*) *n.* money.—*adj.* **rhinocerical** (*-ser′i-kl;* old slang), rich. [Connection with **rhino, rhinoceros** obscure.]

**rhinoceros,** *rī-nos′ər-əs, ri-,* (*obs.*) **rhinoc′erot,** *-ot, -ote, -ōt, ns.* a large ungulate of several species in Africa and southern Asia, constituting a family (**Rhinocerot′idae**), characterised by one or two horns on the nose:—*pl.* **rhinoc′eroses,** *obs.* **rhinocerotes** (*-ō′tēz*).—*adj.* **rhinocerot′ic.**—**rhinoceros-beetle,** a very large beetle (of various genera) with a large up-curved horn on the head; **rhinoceros-bird,** a beefeater that alights on the rhinoceros: a hornbill. [Gr. *rhinokerōs, rhis, rhinos,* nose, *keras,* horn.]

**Rhinodon.** See **Rhineodon.**

**rhinolalia** . . . **rhinotheca.** See **rhin-**.

**rhipidate,** *rip′i-dāt, adj.* fan-shaped.—*ns.* **rhipid′ion,** in the Greek Church, the eucharistic fan or flabellum; **rhipid′ium,** a fan-shaped cymose inflorescence.—*ns.pl.* **Rhipip′tera, Rhipidop′tera,** the Strepsiptera. [Gr. *rhipis, rhipidos,* a fan.]

**rhiz-,** *riz-,* **rhizo-,** *ri-zō-,* in composition, root.—*adjs.* **rhizan′thous,** seeming to flower from the root; **rhi′zic,** of the root of an equation.—*ns.* **rhi′zine** (*-zin*), a lichen rhizoid; **rhi′zocarp** (Gr. *karpos,* fruit), a water-fern or heterosporous fern: a plant with sporangia on rootlike processes: a perennial herb: a plant fruiting underground.—*adjs.* **rhizocar′pic, rhizocar′pous.** —*n.* **rhi′zocaul** (Gr. *kaulos,* stalk), the rootlike stalk of a hydrozoan colony.—*n.pl.* **Rhizoceph′-ala** (Gr. *kephalē,* head), an order of Cirripedes parasitic on crabs.—*adjs.* **rhizogen′ic, rhizogenet′ic,** producing roots.—*n.* **rhi′zoid,** a short hairlike organ in the lower plants, serving as a root.—*adjs.* **rhizoi′dal; rhizō′matous.**—*ns.* **rhi′zome** (Gr. *rhizōma,* a root-mass), a root-stock, an underground stem producing roots and leafy shoots; **rhi′zomorph** (Gr. *morphē,* form), a rootlike mass of fungal hyphae.—*adjs.* **rhizoph′agous,** root-eating; **rhizoph′ilous,** growing on roots.—*ns.* **Rhizoph′ora,** the mangrove genus, with great development of aerial roots, giving name to the family **Rhizophorā′ceae; rhi′zophore,** a rootbearing structure, esp. in *Selaginella;* **rhi′zopod,** any member of the **Rhizop′oda,** Protozoa with rootlike pseudopodia; **Rhi′zopus,** a genus of moulds. [Gr. *rhiza,* root.]

**Rh-negative.** See **rhesus.**

**rho,** *rō, n.* the seventeenth letter (P, ρ) of the Greek alphabet, answering to R: as a numeral ρ′ = 100, ͵ρ = 100,000. [Gr. *rhō.*]

**rhod-,** *rōd-,* **rhodo-,** *rō-dō-,* in composition, rose: rose-coloured.—*ns.* **rhō′damine** (*-mēn;* see *amine*), a dye-stuff, usually red, akin to fluorescein; **rhō′danate,** in dyeing, a thiocyanate.—*adj.* **rhōdan′ic,** thiocyanic.—*v.t.* **rhō′danise, -ize,** to electroplate with rhodium.—*adj.* **rhō′dic,** of rhodium in higher valency.—*ns.* **Rhodites** (*rō-dī′tēz*), a gall-fly that forms bedeguars on the wild-rose; **rhō′dium,** a metallic element (Rh; at. numb. 45) of the platinum group, forming rose-coloured salts; **rhōdochro′site** (*-krō′sīt;* Gr. *rhodochrōs,* rose-coloured), manganese spar, a pink rhombohedral mineral, manganese carbonate; **rhōdodaph′ne** (or *rod-;* Spens.; Gr. *daphnē,* laurel), oleander; **Rhōdoden′dron** (or *rod-;* Gr. *dendron,* tree), a genus of trees and shrubs of the heath family, with leathery leaves

and large showy slightly zygomorphic flowers, some species being called Alpine rose: (without *cap.*) a member of the genus; **rhō′dolite,** a pink or purple garnet, gemstone; **rhō′donite,** a rosered anorthic pyroxene, manganese silicate; **rhō′dophane** (Gr. *phainein,* to show), a red pigment in the retinal cones of birds, etc:—*n.pl.* **Rhōdophyceae** (*-fish′i-ē;* Gr. *phỹkos,* seaweed), the red seaweeds (including some forms that are neither red nor found in the sea), one of the main divisions of the algae, in which the chlorophyll is usually masked by a red pigment.—*n.* **rhōdop′sin** (Gr. *opsis,* sight), visual purple.—*adj.* **rhō′dous,** of rhodium in lower valency.—*n.* **Rhodymenia** (*rō-di-mē′ni-a;* Gr. *hymēn,* a membrane), the dulse genus of red seaweeds.—**rhō′dium-wood,** the scented wood of Canary Island convolvulus, yielding **oil of rhodium.** [Gr. *rhodon,* rose.]

**Rhode Island,** *rōd i′lənd, n.* an island of the United States, named from a supposed resemblance to the island of *Rhodes:* the state of which it forms part.—**Rhode Island red,** an American breed of domestic fowl.

**Rhodes,** *rōdz, n.* an island and ancient city-state of the Aegean.—*n.* and *adj.* **Rhō′dian.**—**Rhodian laws,** the earliest system of marine law; **Rhodian school,** a school of Hellenistic sculpture, of which the Laocoön is the greatest product. [Gr. *Rhodos.*]

**Rhodesia,** *rō-dē′zhyə, -zhi-ə, -zi-ə, n.* a region of southern Africa named after Cecil John *Rhodes.* —*adj.* and *n.* **Rhode′sian.**—**Rhodesian man,** an extinct type of man represented by a skull found at Broken Hill, in northern Rhodesia (now Zambia), in 1921; **Rhodesian ridgeback** (*rij′bak*), a hunting dog with a ridge of hair along the back.

**rhodium** . . . **rhododendron.** See **rhod-**.

**rhodomontade.** Same as **rodomontade.**

**rhodonite** . . . **rhodopsin.** See **rhod-**.

**rhodora,** *rō-dō′ra, -dō′, n.* a handsome N. American species of Rhododendron, or separate kindred genus. [L. *rhodōra,* meadow-sweet, said to be a Gallic plant-name.]

**rhodous.** See **rhod-**.

**Rhoeadales,** *rē-ə-dā′lēz, n.pl.* an order of dicotyledons including poppies, Cruciferae, etc.—*n.* **rhoe′adine** (*-dēn*), an alkaloid found in poppies. [Gr. *rhoias, -ados,* corn-poppy.]

**rhomb,** *rom*(*b*), *n.* an equilateral parallelogram (usu. excluding the square): a lozenge-shaped object: anything that whirls, as (*Milt.*) the wheel of day and night (*obs.*): a magic wheel: a rhombohedron (*crystal.*).—*ns.* **rhombencephalon** (*rom-bən-sef′ə-lon;* Gr. *enkephalon,* brain), the hind-brain; **rhombenporphyr** (*rom-bən-pōr′fēr;* Ger.), **rhomb′(en)por′phyry,** an intermediate, moderately fine-grained igneous rock with feldspar phenocrysts rhombic in section.—*adjs.* **rhombic** (*rom′bik*), shaped like a rhombus: orthorhombic (*crystal.*); **rhombohē′dral,** of a rhombohedron: trigonal (*crystal.*).—*n.* **rhombohē′dron,** a crystal form of six rhombi, in the trigonal or hexagonal system, a hemihedral form of the hexagonal pyramid:—*pl.* **rhombohē′-dra** (Gr. *hedra,* seat).—*adj.* **rhom′boid,** like a rhombus: nearly square, with petiole at one of the acute angles (*bot.*).—*n.* a figure approaching a rhombus, a parallelogram, usu. one that is not a rhombus nor a rectangle.—*adj.* **rhomboid′al,** more or less like a rhomboid.—*ns.* **rhomboi′dēs,** a rhomboid; **rhom′bos,** a bull-roarer:—*pl.* **rhom′boi; rhom′bus,** a rhomb (*geom.*): an object shaped like a rhomb:—*pl.* **rhom′bi.** [Gr. *rhombos,* bull-roarer, magic wheel, rhombus.]

**rhonchus,** *rong′kəs, n.* a bronchial sound, heard in auscultation.—*adjs.* **rhonch′al, rhonch′ial,** of snoring. [Latinised from Gr. *rhonchos,* wheezing.]

**rhone.** Same as **rone.**

**rhopalic,** *rō-pal'ik, adj.* of a verse, having each word a syllable longer than the one before.—*n.* **rho'palism.** [Gr. *rhopalikos,* club-like, *rhopalon,* a club.]

**Rhopalocera,** *rō-pəl-os'ə-ra, n.pl.* butterflies, distinguished from moths.—*adjs.* **rhopaloc'eral, rhopaloc'erous.** [Gr. *rhopalon,* a club, *keras,* a horn.]

**rhotacise, -ize,** *rō'tə-siz, v.t.* and *v.i.* to change to an *r*-sound (esp. from *z*).—*n.* **rho'tacism,** excessive, exceptional, or exceptionable sounding of *r*: burring: change or tendency to change to *r.* [Gr. *rhōtakizein—rhō,* the Greek R.]

**Rh-positive.** See **rhesus.**

**rhubarb,** *rōō'bärb, -bərb, n.* any species of the genus *Rheum,* of the dock family: the rootstock, or a cathartic got from it (chiefly from *R. officinale*): the leaf-stalks (chiefly of *R. rhaponticum*) cooked and used as if fruit: a squabble, row, rumpus (*slang*): word muttered repeatedly to give the impression of conversation inaudible to the audience (*theat.*): nonsense.—*adj.* **rhu'barby.**—monk's **rhubarb,** patience dock. [O.Fr. *reubarbe*—L.L. *rheubarbarum,* for *rhābarbarum*—Gr. *rhā,* rhubarb—*Rhā,* the Volga, and L. *barbarum* (neut.)—Gr. *barbaron,* foreign; influenced by *rhēum,* Gr. *rhēon.*]

**rhumb,** *rum, n.* a loxodromic curve: any point of the compass.—**rhumb'-line, -course, -sailing.** [Fr. *rumb,* or Sp. or Port. *rumbo*—L. *rhombus;* see **rhomb.**]

**rhumba.** Same as **rumba.**

**Rhus,** *rus, n.* the sumach genus of the cashew-nut family. [L.,—Gr. *rhous.*]

**rhy,** (*Spens.*) for **rye.**

**rhyme, rime,** *rim, n.* in two (or more) words, identity of sound from the last stressed vowel to the end, the consonant or consonant group preceding not being the same in both (all) cases: extended to other correspondences in sound, as head-rhyme or alliteration, to inexact correspondences, as eye-rhyme, and to variations such as French, rich rhyme, or *rime riche* (where the consonants immediately preceding the stressed vowel are alike), identical rhyme (where likesounding words of different meaning are used): a word or group of words agreeing in this way with another: versification, verses, a poem or a short piece of verse, in which this correspondence occurs at the ends of lines (or within the lines, in internal rhyme): a jingle.—*v.i.* to be in rhyme: to correspond in sound: to make or find a rhyme or rhymes: to harmonise: to chime: to make rhymes or verses.—*v.t.* to put into rhyme: to compose in rhyme: to use or treat as a rhyme. *adjs.* **rhymed, rimed** (*rimd*), in rhyme; **rhyme'less.** —*ns.* **rhy'mer,** a user of rhyme: a poet: an inferior poet: a minstrel; **rhyme'ster,** a poetaster: a would-be-poet; **rhym'ist,** a versifier.—**rhyme'-letter,** the alliterating letter; **rhyme'-roy'al** (app. a commendatory name), a seven-line stanza borrowed by Chaucer from the French—its formula, *a b a b b c c;* **rhyme'-word,** a word used as a rhyme.—**identical rhyme,** rich rhyme (see **rhyme,** above): **without rhyme or reason,** without reasonable or sensible purpose or explanation: **rhyme to death,** to kill by incantations (as rats were supposed to be killed in Ireland): to pester with rhymes. [O.Fr. *rime*—L. *rhythmus*—Gr. *rhythmos;* see **rhythm;** associated and confused with O.E. *rim,* number.]

**rhynch-,** *ringk-,* **rhyncho-,** *ringk-ō,* in composition, snout.—*ns.pl.* **Rhynchobdell'ida** (Gr. *bdella,* leech), an order of leeches with proboscis but no jaw; **Rhynchocephalia** (*-si-fā'li-a;* Gr. *kephalē,* head), a primitive order of reptiles extinct except for the New Zealand tuatara.—*n.* **rhynch'ocoel** (*-sēl;* Gr. *koilos,* hollow), the

cavity in which the proboscis of a nemertine lies.—*adj.* **rhynch'odont** (Gr. *odous, odontos,* tooth), with toothed beak.—*n.* **Rhynchonell'a,** a genus of hinged brachiopods with prominent beak.—*n.pl.* **Rhynchoph'ora** (Gr. *pherein,* to bear), a group of beetles with snouts—the weevils.—*adj.* **rhynchoph'orous,** of the Rhynchophora: snouted.—*n.pl.* **Rhyncho'ta,** the Hemiptera. [Gr. *rynchos,* a snout.]

**Rhyniaceae,** *ri-ni-ā'si-ē, n.pl.* a family of very simple land plants (Psilophytales) found as Old Red Sandstone fossils at *Rhynie* in Aberdeenshire.

**rhyolite,** *ri'ō-lit, n.* an acid igneous rock with a glassy or cryptocrystalline groundmass and generally phenocrysts of quartz and alkalifeldspar—called also *liparite.*—*adj.* **rhyolitic** (*-lit'ik*). [Irregularly—Gr. *rhyax, -ākos,* a (lava) stream, *lithos,* a stone.]

**rhyparography,** *rip-ə-rog'rə-fi, n.* genre or still-life pictures, esp. of sordid subjects.—*n.* **rhyparog'rapher.**—*adj.* **rhyparographic** (*-graf'ik*). [Gr. *rhyparos,* dirty, *graphein,* to write.]

**rhythm,** *rim,* an obs. spelling of **rhyme.**

**rhythm,** *ridhm,* or *rithm, n.* regular recurrence, esp. of stresses or of long and short sounds: a pattern of recurrence.—*adjs.* **rhyth'mal; rhythmed** (*ridhmd, rithmd*), **rhyth'mic, -al.**—*n.* **rhyth'mic** (also in *pl.*), the science or theory of rhythm. —*adv.* **rhyth'mically.**—*v.t.* **rhyth'mise, -ize,** to subject to rhythm.—*v.i.* to act in or observe rhythm.—*n.* **rhyth'mist,** one skilled in rhythm. —*adj.* **rhythm'less.**—*ns.* **rhythmom'eter,** a kind of metronome; **rhythmopoeia** (*-ō-pē'ə;* Gr. *poieein,* to make), the art of composing rhythmically; **rhyth'mus,** rhythm.—**rhythm method,** a method of birth control requiring the avoidance of sexual intercourse during the period in which conception is most likely to occur. [L. *rhythmus* —Gr. *rhythmos—rheein,* to flow; cf. **rhyme.**]

**Rhytina,** *ri-ti'na, n.* a recently extinct genus of Sirenia—Steller's sea-cow. [Gr. *rhytis,* a wrinkle.]

**Rhytisma,** *rit-iz'ma, n.* a genus of fungi that cause black spots on maple leaves. [Gr. *rhytisma,* a patch or darn.]

**rhyton,** *ri'ton, n.* drinking-cup or pottery horn (Greek, etc.) with a hole in the point to drink by: —*pl.* **rhy'ta.** [Gr. *rhyton,* neut. of *rhytos,* flowing.]

**ria,** *rē'ə,* (*geol.*) *n.* a normal drowned valley. [Sp. *ria,* river-mouth.]

**rial.** Same as **ryal.**

**Rialto,** *rē-al'tō, n.* a district and island of Venice, with a famous bridge over the Grand Canal. [It., contracted from *rialzato,* raised.]

**riant,** *ri'ənt, adj.* laughing: gay.—*n.* **ri'ancy.** [Fr., pr.p. of *rire*—L. *ridēre,* to laugh.]

**riata.** See **reata.**

**rib,** *rib, n.* one of the bones that curve round and forward from the backbone: a wife (from Gen. ii. 21-23; *facet.*): a piece of meat containing one or more ribs: a curved member of the side of a ship running from keel to deck: a strengthening bar: a rodlike structure supporting or strengthening a membrane, as one of the greater veins of a leaf, a nervure in an insect's wing, a member supporting the fabric of an aeroplane wing or of an umbrella: a bar of a grate (*Scot.*): the shaft of a feather: one of the parallel supports of a bridge: the side of a guitar, violin, etc.: a framing timber: a purlin: a raised band: a prominence running in a line: a ridge: a ridge raised in weaving or knitting: a moulding or projecting band on a ceiling.—*v.t.* to furnish, form, cover, or enclose with ribs: to plough with spaces between the furrows (rib'-plough):—*pr.p.* **ribb'ing;** *pa.t.* and *pa.p.* **ribbed.**—*adj.* **ribbed,** having ribs: ridged.—*n.* **ribb'ing,** an arrangement of ribs.—*adjs.* **rib'less; rib'like—rib'-**

bone, a rib; rib'-grass, the ribwort plantain.—
*v.t.* rib'-roast, to beat soundly (*obs.*).—rib'-
roaster (*arch.*), a severe blow on the ribs; rib-
roast'ing (*arch.*); rib'-vaulting; rib'work; rib'-
wort (or ribwort plantain), a common weed
(*Plantago lanceolata*) with narrow strongly
ribbed leaves and short brown heads.—false
rib, one joined indirectly to the breast-bone or
(floating rib) not at all; true rib, one joined
directly by its cartilage. [O.E. *ribb*, rib, *ribbe*,
ribwort; Ger. *rippe*, rib.]
rib, *rib*, (*slang*) *v.t.* to tease, ridicule, make fun of.
[Perh. rib (1)—the tickling of one's ribs causing
laughter.]
ribald, *rib'əld*, *n.* a menial of the lowest grade
(*obs.*): a loose, low character (*obs.*): an obscene
speaker or writer.—*adj.* low, base, mean:
licentious: foul-mouthed or coarse: sometimes
loosely, jeering, floutingly derisive.—Also rib'-
aud, ryb'auld (*Spens.*).—*n.* rib'aldry, obscenity:
coarse jesting.—Also rib'audry (*obs.*).—*adj.*
rib'audred (Shak., *Ant. and Cleop.*), an obscure
word, perh. for *ribaud-rid*, ridden by a ribald, or
for *ribaldried*, composed of ribaldry. [O.Fr.
*ribald*, *ribaut* (Fr. *ribaud*); origin uncertain.]
riband, ribband, *rib'ən(d)*, spellings of ribbon,
used also in heraldic and sporting use.
ribaud, ribaudred. See ribald.
ribattuta, *rē-bät-tōō'tä*, (*mus.*) *n.* the slow beginning of a trill. [It.]
ribband. Same as riband, ribbon.
ribble-rabble, *rib'l-rab'l*, *n.* a mob: gabble.
[rabble.]
ribbon, *rib'ən*, *n.* material woven in narrow bands
or strips: a strip of such or other material: anything resembling such a strip, as a road, a stripe
of colour: a torn strip, tatter, shred: a watch-
spring: an endless saw: a mollusc's radula: a
strip of inking cloth, as for a typewriter: a
diminutive of the bend, one-eighth of its width
(*her.*): (in *pl.*) driving reins.—*adj.* made of ribbon: like a ribbon: having bands of different
colours.—*v.t.* to adorn with ribbons: to stripe:
to streak.—*n.* Ribb'onism, an Irish secret society
movement, at its height about 1835-55, opp. to
the Orangemen, named from its badge, a green
ribbon.—*adj.* ribb'ony.—*n.* ribb'onry, ribbons
collectively.—ribb'on-building, -development, unplanned building, growth of towns, in long
strips along the main roads; ribb'on-fish, a
long, slender, laterally compressed fish of the
family Trachypteridae, esp. the oarfish; ribb'on-
grass, gardener's garters, a striped canary-grass;
Ribb'on-man, a member of the Ribbonism movement; ribb'on-seal, a banded North Pacific seal;
ribb'on-weed, sugar-wrack; ribb'on-worm, a
nemertine. [O.Fr. *riban*; origin obscure.]
Ribes, *rī'bēz*, *n.* the black and red currant genus of
the saxifrage family (generally including gooseberry), in some classifications giving name to a
separate family Ribēsiā'ceae. [L.L. *ribes*—Ar.
*ribās*, sorrel.]
ribibe, *rib'ib*, *rib-ib'*, (*obs.*) *n.* a rebeck: an old
crone.—*n.* ribible (*ri-bib'l*, *ri-bi'bl*), a rebeck.
[See rebeck.]
ribose, *rī'bōs*, *n.* a pentose, $C_5H_{10}O_5$.—*ns.* riboflavin (*rī-bō-flā'vin*; L. *flāvus*, yellow), member
of vitamin B complex, in yellowish-brown
crystals, promoting growth in children; ribo-
nuclease (*rī-bō-nū'kli-ās*, *-āz*), enzyme in the
pancreas, etc., first enzyme to be synthesised
(1969); ribosome (*rī'bō-sōm*), one of numerous
particles in a cell on which proteins are assembled.—ribonucleic acids (*rī'bō-nū-klē'ik*), nucleic acids containing ribose, present in living cells,
where they play an important part in the development of proteins.—abbrev. RNA. [From
arabinose, by transposition of letters.]
ribston(e), *rib'stən*, *n.* (in full Ribston pippin) a

variety of winter apple brought from Normandy
to *Ribston Hall* in Yorkshire.
Ricardian, *ri-kär'di-ən*, *adj.* pertaining to David
*Ricardo* (1772-1823), or his economic teaching.
—*n.* a follower of Ricardo.
Riccia, *rik'si-a*, *n.* a genus of liverworts. [From
the Italian botanist P. Francisco *Ricci*.]
rice, *ris*, *n.* a grass (*Oryza sativa*) grown in warm
climates: its grain, a valuable food.—*adj.*
rice'y, ri'cy.—rice'-beer, a fermented drink
made from rice; rice'-bird, the bobolink (as a
feeder on true rice or so-called wild rice): the
paddy bird or Java sparrow; rice'-bis'cuit, a
sweet biscuit made of flour mixed with rice; rice'-
field; rice'-flour; rice'-glue, a cement made by
boiling rice-flour in soft water; rice'-grain,
a marking like a grain of rice on the sun's
photosphere: a decoration in pottery made by
pressing rice or other seeds into the clay before
firing; rice'-grass, cord-grass; rice'-milk, milk
boiled and thickened with rice; rice'-paper,
sliced and flattened pith of an Asiatic tree of the
Araliaceae: a similar material made from other
plants, or from linen trimmings; rice'-pol'ishings, the parts rubbed off in milling rice; rice'-
pudd'ing; rice'-soup; rice'-wa'ter, an invalid's
drink of water in which rice has been boiled: a
cholera patient's evacuation, of similar appearance.—Canada, Indian, water, or wild rice,
Zizania. [O.Fr. *ris*—L. *oryza*—Gr. *oryza*, a
word of Eastern origin.]
rice, *ris*, (*obs.* except *dial.*) *n.* twigs or small
branches collectively, brushwood: a twig or
small branch.—Also reis. [O.E. *hris*; Ger.
*reis*.]
ricercar, *rē-chər-kär'*, ricercare, *-kä'rā*, ricercata,
*kä'tä*, (*mus.*) *n.* a contrapuntal forerunner of the
fugue; later, a very elaborate form of fugue.
[It.,—*ricercare*, to seek again with effort.]
rich, *rich*, *adj.* abounding in possessions: wealthy:
fortunate in having any good thing: abundantly
furnished: having any ingredient or quality in
great abundance: productive: fertile: deep in
colour: full-toned: full-flavoured: abounding
in fat, sugar, fruit, or seasonings: full: splendid
and costly: sumptuous: elaborately decorated:
ample: pregnant with matter for laughter.—*v.t.*
(*Shak.*) to enrich.—*v.i.* (*obs.*) to grow rich.—*v.t.*
and *v.i.* rich'en, to make or become richer.—*adv.*
rich'ly.—*n.* rich'ness.—*adj.* rich'-left (*Shak.*), left
heir to much wealth. [O.E. *rice*, great, powerful;
Ger. *reich*, Du. *rijk*, Goth. *reiks*; perh. reinforced by Fr. *riche*, rich.]
Richardia, *ri-chär'di-a*, *n.* an older name for
*Zantedeschia*. [From the French botanists
L. C. M. *Richard* (1754-1821) and his son.]
riches, *rich'iz*, *n.* (now usu. treated as *pl.*) wealth—
(*Spens.*) rich'esse. [O.Fr. *richesse*—*riche*, rich.]
richt, *rihht*, Scots form of right.
Richter Scale, *rihht'ər skāl*, *n.* a seismological
scale of measurement. [From its inventor, Dr
Charles F. *Richter*.]
Ricinulei, *ris-i-nū'li-ī*, *n.pl.* the Podogona, a rare
order of blind arachnids with male organs on the
third leg. [L. *ricinus*, a tick.]
Ricinus, *ris'i-nəs*, *n.* a genus of one species
(*Ricinus communis*, castor-oil plant) of the
spurge family.—*adj.* ricinolē'ic (or *-ō'lē-ik*), pertaining to castor-oil, as ricinoleic acid ($C_{18}H_{34}O_3$),
an oily acid got from castor-oil. [L. *ricinus*, the
castor-oil plant.]
rick, *rik*, *n.* a stack: a heap.—*v.t.* to stack.—*n.*
rick'er, an implement for shocking hay.—rick'-
barton, a stack-yard; rick'-burner, an incendiary
who fired stacks; rick'-lifter; rick'stand, a
flooring of a stack; rick'stick, a toothed stick
for combing thatch on a stack; rick'yard. [O.E.
*hrēac*; O.N. *hraukr*.]
rick, *rik*, *v.t.* to sprain or strain.—*n.* a sprain or
strain. [App. a variant of wrick.]

**ricker,** *rik'ər, n.* a spar or young tree-trunk. [Perh. Ger. *rick,* pole.]

**rickets,** *rik'its, n.sing.* a disease of children, characterised by softness of the bones caused by deficiency of vitamin D.—*adv.* **rick'etily,** shakily.—*n.* **rick'etiness,** unsteadiness.—*adj.* **rick'ety** (formerly, and still by some, **rick'etty**), affected with rickets: feeble, unstable: tottery, threatening to collapse. [First recorded in S.W. England in the 17th cent., perh. M.E. *wrikken,* to twist; or Gr. *rhachitis* (see *rachitis*).]

**Rickettsia,** *rik-et'si-a, n.* a genus of micro-organisms found in lice and ticks and, when transferred to man by a bite, causing typhus and other serious diseases:—*pl.* **Rickett'siae** (*-ē*).— Also **Rickettsia body.**—*Fam.* **Rickettsia'ceae** (*-ā'si-ē*); order **Rickettsia'les** (*-ā'lēz*).—*adj.* **rickett'sial.** [After Howard Taylor *Ricketts* (1871-1910), American pathologist.]

**rickle,** *rik'l,* (*Scot.*) *n.* a loose heap: a rickety or ramshackle structure or collection.—*adj.* **rick'ly.** [Poss. Scand.; connection with rick (1) very doubtful.]

**ricksha, rickshaw,** *rik'shä, -shō, n.* a small two-wheeled, hooded carriage drawn by a man or men, or powered by a man on a bicycle or motor-bicycle.—Also **jinrick'sha, jinrick'shaw, jinrik'isha.** [Jap. *jin,* man, *riki,* power, *sha,* carriage.]

**rick-rack,** *ric-rac, rik'rak, n.* a decorative braid in even zigzag form, or openwork made with it. [rack (1).]

**ricochet,** *rik-ō-shā', -shet',* or *rik', n.* a glancing rebound or skip, as of a projectile flying low.— *v.i.* to glance: to skip along the ground:—*pr.p.* **ricocheting** (*-shā'ing*), **ricochetting** (*-shet'ing*); *pa.t.* and *pa.p.* **ricocheted** (*-shād'*), **richochetted** (*-shet'id*). [Fr.]

**rictus,** *rik'təs, n.* the gape, esp. of a bird: the chink or aperture of a lipped corolla: unnatural gaping of the mouth, e.g. in horror.—*adj.* **ric'tal,** of the gape: at the corners of the mouth. [L. *rictus, -ūs.*]

**rid,** *rid, v.t.* to free: to deliver: to clear: to disencumber: to expel: to remove, as by banishment, or by murder, make away with (*obs.*):—*pr.p.* **ridd'ing;** *pa.t.* and *pa.p.* **rid** or **ridd'ed.**—*n.* **ridd'ance,** clearance: removal: disencumberment: deliverance: a thing that one is well rid of.—**a good riddance,** a welcome relief; **get rid of,** to disencumber oneself of; **rid way** (*Shak.*), to cover ground, make progress. [O.N. *rythja,* to clear; with senses converging upon **redd** (1).]

**rid, ridden.** See **ride.**

**riddle,** *rid'l, n.* an obscure description of something which the hearer is asked to name: a puzzling question: anything puzzling.—*v.t.* to solve: to puzzle.—*v.i.* to make riddles: to speak obscurely.—*ns.* **ridd'ler; ridd'ling,** propounding of riddles: speaking in riddles.—*adj.* enigmatic, obscure, puzzling: speaking in riddles: explaining riddles.—*adv.* **ridd'lingly.**— *adj.* and *adv.* **riddl'e-like** (*Shak.*).—**ridd'le-me-ree',** a fanciful modification of *riddle me a riddle,* or *riddle my riddle,* hence, *n.* a rigmarole. [O.E. *rǣdelse—rǣdan,* to guess; to read—*rǣd,* counsel; cog. with Du. *raad,* Ger. *rath.*]

**riddle,** *rid'l, n.* a large coarse sieve.—*v.t.* to separate with a riddle: to make full of holes like a riddle, as with shot.—*v.i.* to use a riddle: to sift.—*ns.* **ridd'ler; ridd'ling.**—*n.pl.* **ridd'lings,** the less desirable part, whether finer or coarser, separated by riddling and usu. rejected: refuse. [O.E. *hriddel,* earlier *hridder.*]

**ride,** *rid, v.i.* to travel or be borne on the back of an animal, on a bicycle, or in a public vehicle, sometimes, and commonly in U.S., in any vehicle or (*U.S.*) boat, also on a broomstick, the waves, the whirlwind, etc.: to float or seem to float buoyantly: to go on horseback on a raid,

in procession, across a ford: to serve as a cavalryman: to lie at anchor: to sit or move as if on horseback: to turn, rest, or grate upon something: to work up out of position: to admit of riding: to weigh when mounted.—*v.t.* to traverse, trace, ford, or perform on horseback, on a bicycle, etc.: to sit on: to bestride: to sit on and control: to travel on: to control at will, or oppressively: to oppress, domineer over, badger, annoy: to improvise on (a theme; *jazz*): to rest or turn on: to overlap: to mount upon: to sustain, come through, esp. while riding at anchor (usu. with *out*): to give a ride to, or cause to ride: to convey by vehicle (*U.S.*): —*pa.t.* **rōde,** *arch.* **rid,** *Scot.* **raid, rade;** *pa.p.* **ridd'en,** *arch.* **rid, rode.**—*n.* a journey on horseback, on a bicycle, or in a vehicle: a spell of riding: a road for horse-riding, esp. one through a wood: an excise officer's district.—*n.* **rid-abil'ity,** fitness for riding or driving, or for riding or driving along or across.—*adj.* **ri'dable, ride'able.**——**-ridden,** in composition, oppressed by the dominance or prevalence of (e.g. **hag-ridden, cliché-ridden**).—*n.* **ri'der,** one who rides or can ride: a commercial traveller (*obs.*): a mosstrooper: an object that rests on or astride of another, as a piece of wire on a balance for fine weighing: an added clause or corollary: a proposition that a pupil or candidate is asked to deduce from another: a gold coin bearing a mounted figure (Du. and Flem. *rijder*).—*adjs.* **ri'dered; ri'derless.**—*n.* **ri'ding,** the action of the verb ride: a track, esp. a woodland track, for riding on: an excise-officer's district: anchorage. —Also *adj.*—**ri'ding-boot,** a high boot worn in riding.—*n.pl.* **ri'ding-breeches,** breeches for riding, with loose-fitting thighs and tight-fitting legs.—**ri'ding-cloak; ri'ding-clothes; ri'ding-coat,** a coat of a style worn by riders; **ri'ding-committ'ee,** a committee of ministers sent by the General Assembly to carry out an ordination or induction, where the local presbytery refused to act, under the 18th-cent. Moderate domination in Scotland; **ri'ding-crop; ri'ding-glove; ri'ding-habit,** a woman's dress for riding, esp. one with a long skirt for riding side-saddle; **ri'ding-hood,** a hood formerly worn by women when riding; **ri'ding-horse; ri'ding-in'terest** (*Scots law*), an interest depending on other interests; **ri'ding-light,** a light hung out in the rigging at night when a vessel is riding at anchor; **ri'ding-master,** a teacher of riding; **ri'ding-rhyme,** the heroic couplet, perh. from Chaucer's use of it in the *Canterbury Tales;* **ri'ding-robe,** a riding-habit; **ri'ding-rod,** a light cane for equestrians; **ri'ding-school; ri'ding-skirt; ri'ding-suit; ri'ding-whip.** —**let it ride,** let it alone, do not try to stop it; **ride a hobby** (see **hobby**); **ride and tie,** to ride and go on foot alternately, each tying up the horse, or leaving the bicycle by the roadside, and walking on—also *n., adv., v.i.* **ride'-and-tie';** **ride down,** to overtake by riding: to charge and overthrow or trample; **ride for a fall,** to court disaster; **ride out,** to keep afloat throughout (a storm): to cut out from a herd by riding; **ride to hounds,** to take part in fox-hunting; **ride up,** to work up out of position; **riding the fair,** the ceremony of opening a fair by a procession; **take for a ride,** to give (someone) a lift in a car with the object of murdering him in some remote place: play a trick on, dupe. [O.E. *rīdan;* Du. *rijden,* Ger. *reiten.*]

**rident,** *rī'dənt, adj.* laughing or beamingly smiling. [L. *ridēns, -entis,* pr.p. of *rīdēre,* to laugh.]

**ridge,** *rij, n.* the back (*obs.*): the earth thrown up by the plough between the furrows: a strip of arable land, usu. between furrows: a rib on a stocking, etc.: a long narrow top or crest: the horizontal line of a roof of two slopes: a narrow elevation: a hill-range.—*v.t.* and *v.i.* to form into ridges: to wrinkle.—*adj* ridged, having ridges.—*n*. ridg′ing, the forming of ridges: covering with ridge-tiles.—*adj*. ridg′y, having ridges.— ridge′back, Rhodesian ridgeback (*q.v.*); ridge′-bone, the spine; ridge′-piece, ridge′-pole, the timber forming the ridge of a roof; ridge′-rope, the central rope of an awning; ridge′-tile, a tile that bestrides the ridge of a roof; ridge′way, a track along a hill-crest. [O.E. *hrycg*; O.N. *hryggr*, Ger. *rücken*, back.]

ridgel, ridgil, *rij′əl*, *n*. a male animal with but one testicle in position or remaining.—Also ridgling (*rij′ling*), rig (*rig*).—Northern forms rigg′ald, rig′ling, rig′lin (*rig′*). [App. from preceding, from the undescended testicle near the back.]

ridicule, *rid′i-kūl*, *n*. absurdity (*rare*): derision: mockery.—*v.t.* to laugh at: to expose to merriment: to deride: to mock.—*n*. rid′iculer.—*adj*. ridic′ulous, deserving or exciting ridicule: absurd.—*adv*. ridic′ulously.—*n*. ridic′ulousness. [L. *ridiculus*—*ridēre*, to laugh.]

ridicule, *rid′i-kūl*, *n*. for reticule.

Riding, *ri′ding*, *n*. one of the three divisions of Yorkshire: extended to divisions elsewhere. [For *thriding*—O.N. *thrithi*, third.]

riding. See ride.

ridotto, *ri-dot′ō*, *n*. a public dancing-party. [It.]

riebeckite, *rē′bek-it*, *n*. a monoclinic amphibole, silicate of sodium and iron. [Named after the German traveller Emil *Riebeck* (1853-85).]

riem, *rēm*, *n*. a raw-hide thong. [Du.]

Riemannian, *rē-man′i-ən*, *adj*. pertaining to the German mathematician Georg Friedrich Bernhard *Riemann* (1826-66), or to his work or concepts, especially to Riemannian geometry, the geometry of Riemannian space. (With certain nouns the adjective used is Riemann, as Riemann surface, Riemann integral.)

Riesling, *rēz′ling*, *n*. a dry white table wine, named from a type of grape. [Ger.]

rieve, riever. Same as reave, reaver.

rifacimento, *rē-fä-chi-men′tō*, *n*. a recasting of a literary or musical work:—*pl*. -ti (-*tē*). [It.]

rife, *rif*, *adj*. prevalent: abounding: current.—Also *adv*.—*adv*. rife′ly.—*n*. rife′ness. [O.E. *rȳfe*, *rīfe*; Du. *rijf*. O.N. *rifr*.]

riff, *rif*, (*jazz*) *n*. a phrase or figure played repeatedly. [Perh. refrain.]

riffle, *rif′l*, *n*. shallow section in a river where the water flows swiftly (*U.S.*).—*v.t.* to form a riffle: to turn or stir lightly and rapidly (as the pages of a book), often in cursory search for something: to treat thus the pages of (a book; with *through*): to shuffle by allowing the corner of a card from one part of the pack to fall alternately with that of a card in the other.—Also *v.i.* [Cf. ripple (1).]

riffle, *rif′l*, *n*. (gold washing) groove or slat in a sluice to catch free particles of ore. [Cf. rifle (2).]

riffler, *rif′lər*, *n*. a small file with curved ends used by sculptors, wood- or metal-workers, etc., for intricate work. [Fr. *rifloir*, from *rifler*, to scrape, file.]

riff-raff, *rif′-raf*, *n*. the scum of the people: rubbish.—*adj*. rubbishy. [M.E. *rif and raf*—O.Fr. *rif et raf*.]

rifle, *ri′fl*, *v.t.* to plunder: to ransack: to disarray: (of a hawk) to seize only the feathers of: to injure.—*n*. ri′fler. [O.Fr. *rifler*.]

rifle, *ri′fl*, *v.t.* to groove spirally (also *v.i.*) to shoot with a rifle.—*n*. a firearm with spirally grooved barrel.—*n*. ri′fling, the spiral grooving of a gun-bore.—ri′fle-bird, ri′fleman-bird, an Australian bird of paradise: a New Zealand bushwren; ri′fle-corps, a body of soldiers armed with rifles; ri′fle-green, a dark green, the colour of a rifleman's uniform (also *adj*.); ri′fle-grenade′, a grenade or bomb fired from a rifle; ri′fleman, a soldier armed with a rifle: a rifle-bird; ri′fle-pit, a pit to shelter riflemen; ri′fle-

range, the range of a rifle: a place for rifle practice; ri′fle-shot. [O.Fr. *rifler*, to scratch; cf. Ger. *riefeln*, and preceding word.]

rift, *rift*, *n*. a cleft: a fissure: a chink: a riven fragment (*Spens.*).—*v.t.* and *v.i.* to cleave, split.—rift valley, a valley formed by subsidence of a portion of the earth's crust between two faults. [Cf. Dan. and Norw. *rift*, a cleft.]

rifte, *rift*, (*Spens.*) *pa.p.* of rive.

rig, *rig*, *v.t.* to fit with sails and tackling (*naut.*): to fit up or fit out: to equip: to set up, set in working order: to dress, clothe (now *coll.*):—*pr.p.* rigg′ing; *pa.t.* and *pa.p.* rigged.—*n*. form and arrangement of masts, sails, and tackling: an outfit: garb: general appearance: a driving turnout (*U.S.*): a well-boring plant.—*n*. rigg′er, one who rigs ships: one who puts together and attends to the rigging of aircraft: one who puts up and looks after the scaffolding, lifting apparatus, etc., that is used for building operations: outrigger: in machinery, a narrow drum.— -rigger, in composition, ship rigged in manner indicated.—*n*. rigg′ing, tackle: the system of cordage which supports a ship's masts and extends the sails: the system of wires and cords in an aircraft.—rigg′ing-loft, a long workshop where rigging is fitted: the place in a theatre from which the scenery is manipulated; rig′-out, an outfit.—rig out, to furnish with complete dress, etc; rig up, to dress or equip: to put up quickly from available, rather inadequate, materials. [Origin obscure; perh. conn. with Norw. *rigga*, to bind.]

rig, *rig*, *n*. the Northern form of ridge.—*ns*. rigg′-ing, the roof; rigg′ing-tree, a roof-tree.

rig, *rig*, *n*. a frolic, prank, trick.—*v.t.* to manipulate unscrupulously.—*n*. rigg′ing, manipulating, as in price-rigging.—run a rig, to play a prank. [Origin obscure.]

rig, *rig*, *n*. a wanton.—*v.i.* to wanton: to romp.—*adj*. rigg′ish (*Shak.*), wanton. [Origin obscure.]

rig, riggald, rigling. See ridgel.

rigadoon, *rig-ə-dōōn′*, *n*. a lively jig-like dance for one couple, or its music. [Fr. *rigaudon*.]

Rigel, *ri′gəl*, *-jəl*, *n*. a first-magnitude star in the foot of Orion. [Ar. *rijl*, foot.]

right, *rit*, *adj*. straight: direct: perpendicular: forming one-fourth of a revolution: with axis perpendicular to base: true: genuine: veritable: characteristic: truly judged or judging: appropriate: in accordance, or identical, with what is true and fitting: not mistaken: accurate: fit: sound: intended to be exposed (as a side, e.g. of cloth): morally justifiable or incumbent: just: in accordance with what should be: equitable: justly to be preferred or commended: at or towards that side at which in a majority of people is the better-developed hand (of a river, as referred to one going downstream: on the stage, from the point of view of an actor looking at the audience): sitting at the president's right hand (in Continental assemblies): hence, conservative or inclined towards conservatism.—*adv*. straight: straightway: quite: just, exactly: in a right manner: justly: correctly: very (*arch*. and *dial*. or in special phrases): to or on the right side.—*n*. that which is right or correct: rightness: fair treatment: equity: truth: justice: just or legal claim: what one has a just claim to: due: (in *pl*.) a stag's brow, bez, and trez antlers (*arch*.): territory (*Spens.*): the right hand: the right side: a glove, shoe, etc., for the right hand, foot, etc.: the region on the right side: the right wing: the conservatives.—*v.t.* to set right: to set in order: to rectify: to redress: to vindicate: to do justice to: to avenge: to set right side up or erect.—*v.i.* to recover an erect position.—*interj*. expressing agreement, acquiescence, or readiness.—*adj*. right′able, capable of being righted.—*v.t.* right′en, to set right.—*n*. right′er, one who sets right or redresses wrong.—*adj.* right'ful, having a just claim: according to justice: belonging by right.—*adv.* right'fully.—*ns.* right'-fulness, righteousness: justice; right'ing; right'-ist, an adherent of the political right (conservatives).—Also *adj.* right'ing; right'ist.—*adv.* right'ly.—*n.* right'ness.—*interj.* righto', right-oh' (*coll.*), expressing acquiescence.—*n., adj.,* and *adv.* right'ward.—*adv.* right'wards.—right'-about', the directly opposite quarter (in drill or dismissal; also right-about face).—*adv.* to the right-about (face).—*v.i.* to turn right-about (face).—*adj.* right'-and-left', having a right and a left side, part, etc.: bilaterally symmetrical: on both sides: from both barrels.—*n.* a shot or a blow from each barrel or hand.—*adv.* on both sides: on all hands: towards one side, then the other: in all directions.—*adjs.* right-ang'led, having a right angle, one equal to a fourth of a revolution; right ascension (see ascension); right'-bank, on the right bank.—*adj.* and *adv.* right'-down, out-and-out.—*adjs.* right'-drawn (*Shak.*), drawn in a just cause; right'-hand. at the right side: with thread or strands turning to the right: chiefly relied on (as *one's* right-hand *man*); right'-hand'ed, using the right hand more easily than the left: with or for the right hand: with rotation towards the right, or clockwise.—*adv.* towards the right.—right'-hand'edness; right'-hand'er, a blow with the right hand: a right-handed person.—*n.* and *adj.* Right Honourable, a title of distinction given to peers below the rank of marquis, to privy councillors, to present and past cabinet ministers, to certain Lord Mayors and Lord Provosts, etc.—*adjs.* right'-lined, rectilinear; right'-mind'ed, having a mind disposed towards what is right, just, or according to good sense: sane.—right'-mind'edness; right-of-way, a track over which there is a right of way (see below): the strip of land occupied by a railway track, a road, etc. (*U.S.*).—*n.* and *adj.* Right Reverend (see reverend).—*adj.* right'-think'ing, of approved opinions.—right'-whale, a whale of the typical genus Balaena, esp. the Greenland whale.—*adj.* right'-wing, of or on the right wing: pertaining to the extreme political right.—right'-wing'er, a player on the right wing: a member of the right wing of a party.—all right (see all); bill of rights (often *caps.*), an accepted statement of the rights and privileges of the people or of individuals, which the government or state must not infringe (e.g. that embodied in the Bill of Rights, 1689, or in the U.S. Constitution); by rights (formerly right), rightfully: if all were right; civil rights (see civil): do one right, to do one justice: keep pace with one in drinking: drink one's health; have a right, no right, to be entitled or not entitled: to be under a moral obligation, no obligation (*illit.* or *dial.*); have right (*arch.*), to be right; in one's own right, by absolute and personal right, not through another; in one's right mind, quite sane; in right of, by virtue of: by title vested in; in the right, right: maintaining a justifiable position; put, set, to rights, to set in order; right as a trivet, as rain (see trivet, rain); right away (chiefly *U.S.*), straightway: without delay; right down, plainly; right off, without delay; right out (*Shak.*), outright; right of entry, a legal right to enter a place; right of way, the right of the public to pass over a piece of ground; right the helm, to put it amidships, in a line with the keel; send, etc., to the right-about (*coll.*), to dismiss summarily, or force to retreat. [O.E. *riht* (n. and adj.), *rihte* (adv.), *rihten* (vb.); cf. Ger. *recht* and L. *rēctus*, straight, right.]

right, (*Shak., Milt.*) for rite.

righteous, ri'chəs, *adj.* just, upright.—*adv.* right'eously.—*n.* right'eousness, rectitude: a

righteous act. [O.E. *rihtwis—riht*, right, *wis*, wise, prudent, or *wise*, wise, manner.]

rigid, rij'id, *adj.* stiff: unbending: unyielding: rigorous: strict: of an airship, having a rigid structure to maintain shape.—*n.* a rigid person or airship.—*n.* rigid'ity.—*adv.* rig'idly.—*n.* rig'idness. [L. *rigidus—rigēre*, to be stiff.]

Rigil, rij'il, *n.* a first-magnitude double star in the foot of the Centaur. [Cf. Rigel.]

rigmarole, rig'mə-rōl, *n.* a long rambling discourse.—*adj.* prolix and incoherent. [ragman roll.]

rigol, rigoll, rig'əl, *n.* a gutter or water-channel: a groove, esp. an encircling groove: a circlet (*Shak.*). [Fr. *rigole*, gutter, groove.]

rigor, ri'gör, rig'ör, *n.* a sense of chilliness with contraction of the skin, a preliminary symptom of many diseases (*med.*): failure to react to stimulus, under unfavourable conditions (*bot.*): a rigid irresponsive state caused by a sudden shock, as when an animal is said to sham dead (*zool.*): (*rig'ər*) another, chiefly American, spelling of rigour.—*ns.* rigorism (*rig'ər-izm*), extreme strictness: the doctrine that in doubtful cases the strict course should be followed; rig'orist.—*adj.* rig'orous, rigidly strict or scrupulous: exact: unsparing: severe: harsh, violent (*Spens.*).—*adv.* rig'orously.—*ns.* rig'-orousness; rigour (*rig'ər*), stiffness: hardness: rigor: severity: unswerving enforcement of law, rule, or principle: strict exactitude: austerity: extreme strictness: severity of weather or climate.—rigor mortis (L.), stiffening of the body after death. [L. *rigor—rigēre*, to be stiff.]

Rigsdag, rigz'dag, rēgz'däg, *n.* the parliament of Denmark. [Dan.,—*rige*, a kingdom, and *dag*, a day.]

Rigveda, rig-vā'da, *n.* the first of the four Vedas. [Sans. *ric*, a hymn, *veda*, knowledge.]

rigwiddie, rigwoodie, rig-wid'i, -wûd'i, -wud'i, or rig', (*Scot.*) *n.* a cart-horse's back-band.—*adj.* lean and tough: stubborn: a vague word of reproach, with a suggestion of the *widdy*, or halter. [rig, widdy=with.]

rile, ril, riley, ril'i, forms of roil, roily.

rilievo, rēl-yā'vō, (*sculp., archit.*) *n.* relief. [It.]

rill, ril, *n.* a very small brook: a runnel: a small trench: a narrow furrow on the moon or Mars (also rille from Ger. *rille*).—*v.i.* to flow in a rill cr rills.—*n.* rill'et, a little rill.—rill'mark (*geol.*), a marking produced by water trickling down a beach or bank. [Cf. Du. *ril*, Ger. (orig. L.G.) *rille*, channel, furrow.]

rim, rim, *n.* the outermost circular part of a wheel, not including the tire: an edge, border, brim, or margin, esp. when raised or more or less circular: an encircling band, mark, or line. *v.t.* to form or furnish a rim to:—*pr.p.* rimm'ing; *pa.t.* and *pa.p.* rimmed.—*adjs.* rim'less; rimmed.—rim'-brake, a brake acting on the rim of a wheel. [O.E. *rima* (found in compounds).]

rim, rim, *n.* a membrane: the peritoneum. [O.E. *rēoma*; cf. riem.]

rima, ri'ma, rē'ma, *n.* a chink: esp. the gap between vocal cords and arytaenoid cartilages:—*pl.* rimae (ri'mē, rē'mi).—*n.* rime (rim; obs.), chink, fissure.—*adjs.* ri'mose (or -mōs'), ri'mous, full of chinks: covered with cracks. [L. *rima*.]

rime, rim, *n.* hoar-frost or frozen dew: ice deposited by freezing of supercooled fog (*meteor.*).—*v.t.* to cover with rime.—*adj.* ri'my. [O.E. *hrim*; Du. *rijm*, Ger. *reif*.]

rime, rimer, etc. Same as ream (3), reamer, rhyme, rhymer, etc.

rime riche, rēm rēsh, (Fr.) lit. rich rhyme (q.v. at rhyme); rime suffisante (sü-fē-zät), lit. sufficient rhyme, corresponding to ordinary rhyme in English.

rin, rin, a Scots form of run.

rind, rind, *n.* bark: peel: crust: outside.—*v.t.* to

bark.—*adjs.* rind'ed; rind'less; rind'y. [O.E. rinde; Du. and Ger. *rinde*.]

**rind, rynd,** *rīnd, n.* a fitting that supports an upper millstone, cross-shaped with expanded ends. [Cf. M.Du. *rijn*, M.L.G. *rin*.]

**rinderpest,** *rin'dər-pest, n.* a malignant and contagious disease of cattle. [Ger., cattle-plague.]

**rine, rin,** (*Spens.*, etc.) *n.* Same as **rind.**

**rinforzando,** *rin-för-tsan'dō,* (*mus.*) *adj.* with sudden accent. [It., reinforcing.]

**ring,** *ring, n.* a circlet or small hoop, esp. one of metal, worn on the finger, in the ear, nose, or elsewhere: any object, mark, arrangement, group, or course of like form: an encircling band: a rim: a short cylinder for holding a table-napkin: a link of chain-mail: an encircling cut in bark: a zone of wood added in a season's growth, as seen in sections: a mark of fungus growth in turf (**fairy ring**): a flat crowd of very small satellites encircling Saturn: an annulus: a segment of a worm, caterpillar, etc.: a closed chain of atoms: a system of elements in which addition is associative and commutative and multiplication is associative and distributive with respect to addition (*math.*): a circular ripple: a circular earthwork or rampart: an arena: a space set apart for boxing, wrestling, circus performance, riding display of animals, or the like: an enclosure for bookmakers: pugilism: prize-fighters or bookmakers with their associates collectively: a combination or clique, esp. organised to control the market or for other self-seeking purpose: a system operated by some antique dealers who refrain from bidding against each other at an auction, so that one of their number may buy cheaply, and then share the profit made by subsequent resale.—*v.t.* to encircle: to put a ring on or in: to put on in the manner of a ring: to cut a ring in the bark of: to cut into rings: to go in rings round: to excel, be the quickest sheep-shearer in (*Austr.*).—*v.i.* to move in rings: to gather or be in a ring:—*pa.t.* and *pa.p.* ringed; formerly sometimes, and still in sheep-shearing competitions, rung.—*adj.* **ringed,** surrounded by, or marked with, a ring or rings: ring-shaped: composed of rings: of a car, put together from parts of other cars (*slang*).—*n.* **ringer** (*ring'ər*), one who rings: a throw of a quoit that encircles the pin: a quoit so thrown: person or thing of the highest excellence: quickest, most expert of a group of shearers (*Austr.*).—*n.* and *adj.* **ring'ing.**—*adj.* **ring'less.**—*n.* **ring'let,** a little ring: a fairy ring: a fairy dance in a ring: a long curl of hair.—*adj.* **ring'leted.**—*n.* **ring'ster,** a member of a ring, esp. in a political or price-fixing sense.—*adv.* **ring'wise.**—*ring'-ar'mature,** one with a ring-shaped core.—*v.t.* **ring'-bark,** to strip a ring of bark from.—**ring'bit,** a horse's bit with rings at the ends; **ring'-bolt,** a bolt with a ring through a hole at one end; **ring'bone,** a bony callus on a horse's pastern-bone: the condition caused by this; **ring'-canal,** a circular canal within the rim of a jellyfish: a circular vessel of the water-vascular system of echinoderms; **ring'-carrier** (*Shak.*), a go-between; **ring'-compound,** a chemical compound with a closed chain; **ring'-cross,** a circle with crossed diameters; **ring'-dance,** a round dance; **ring'-dial,** a portable sundial; **ring'-dott'erel,** the ringed plover; **ring'-dove,** the wood-pigeon, from the broken white ring or line on its neck; **ring'-dropping,** a sharper's trick of pretending to find a dropped ring and selling it; **ring'-dyke** (*geol.*), a dyke with more or less circular outcrop; **ring'-fence,** a fence continuously encircling an estate: a complete barrier.—*v.t.* to shut off completely.—**ring'-finger,** the third finger, esp. of the left hand, on which the wedding-ring is worn; **ring'-gauge,** a gauge in the form of a ring: either a

collection of graded rings or a graduated stick for measuring ring- or finger-size; **ring'leader,** one who takes the lead in mischief; **ring'man,** the third finger of the hand (*obs.* or *dial.*): a bookmaker; **ring'-master,** one who has charge of performances in a circus-ring; **ring'-money,** money in the form of rings.—*adj.* **ring'-necked** (*-nekt*), having the neck marked with a ring.—**ring'-ou'zel, -ou'sel** (see **ouzel**): **ring'-plov'er,** a ring-necked plover of various kinds.—*adj.* **ring'-porous,** having annual rings marked by large pores.—**ring'-road,** a road or boulevard encircling a town or its inner part; **ring'-shake,** a defect in timber, separation along the annual rings; **ring'side,** the side of the prize-ring; **ring'-sider,** one who attends prize-fights.—*adj.* **ring'-small,** small enough to pass though a ring of standard size.—*n.* **stones** of such a size.—**ring'-snake,** a common English snake, the grass-snake (also **ringed snake**): a harmless American snake with yellow collar; **ring'stand,** a stand for chemical vessels, with rings clamped to a vertical rod: a stand for finger-rings; **ring'-stopper,** a rope for securing an anchor-ring to the cat-head.—*adjs.* **ring'-straked** (*B.*), **-streaked,** streaked in rings.—**ring'-tail,** a studding-sail set upon the gaff of a fore-and-aft sail (*naut.*): a light sail set abaft and beyond the spanker (*naut.*): the female or young male of the hen-harrier, from a rust-coloured ring on the tail-feathers: (without *hyphen*) a ring-tailed cat (see **cacomistle**).—*adjs.* **ring'-tail, -tailed** (*-tāld*), having the tail marked with bars or rings of colour, as a lemur: having a tail curled at the end.—**ring'-taw,** a game of marbles, with rings marked on the ground; **ring'-time** (*Shak.*), time for giving rings; **ring'-walk,** an encircling walk; **ring'-wall,** an enclosing wall; **ring'-winding,** winding that threads a ring.—**ring'work,** work executed in rings; **ring'worm,** a skin disease characterised by ring-shaped patches, caused by fungi.—**a ringside seat, view** (*fig.*), (a position which allows one to have) a very clear view; **hold, keep, the ring,** to watch a fight and keep others from interfering; **ride, or tilt, at the ring,** to practise the sport of riding rapidly and catching a hanging ring on a spear; **ring the shed** (*Austr.*), to win a sheep-shearing competition; **make, run, rings round,** to be markedly superior to. [O.E. *hring*; O.N. *hringr*; Ger., Dan., and Sw. *ring*.]

**ring,** *ring, v.i.* to give a metallic or bell-like sound: to sound aloud and clearly: to give a characteristic or particular sound: to resound, re-echo: to be filled with sound, or a sensation like sound, or report, or renown: to cause a bell or bells to sound, esp. as a summons or signal.—*v.t.* to cause to give a metallic or bell-like sound: to sound in the manner of a bell: to summon, usher, announce by a bell or bells: to call on the telephone: to re-echo, resound, proclaim:—*pa.t.* **rang,** now rarely **rung,** *obs.* **rong;** *pa.p.* **rung.**—*n.* a sounding of a bell: the characteristic sound or tone, as of a bell or a metal, or of a voice: a ringing sound: a set of bells.—*n.* **ring'er,** one who, or that which, rings: a horse raced under the name of another horse.—*n.* and *adj.* **ring'ing.**—*adv.* **ring'ingly.**—**ring a bell,** to begin to arouse a memory; **ring down, or up (the curtain),** to give the signal for lowering or raising; **ring in,** to ring more rapidly before stopping, as a final intimation to lingering church-goers; **ring in, out,** to usher in, out (esp. the year) with bell-ringing: **ring off,** to signal the ending of a telephone conversation; **ring out,** to sound loudly, clearly, and suddenly; **ring the bell,** to achieve a great success (from the bell of a shooting-gallery bull's-eye); **ring the bells backward,** to reverse the order of chimes; **ring the changes,** to proceed through all the permutations in ringing a chime of bells: to do a limited number of things repeatedly in varying order; **ring true,** to sound genuine (like a tested coin); **ring up,** to summon by bell, esp. to the telephone. [O.E. *hringan*; O.N. *hringja*; Ger. *ringen*; Dan. *ringe.*]

**ring,** *ring, n.* and *v.i.* an obs. Scots form of **reign:** —*pa.t.* **rang.**

**Ringelmann chart,** *ring'l-man,* a chart giving a scale of shades of grey against which density of smoke may be gauged. [After the deviser.]

**ringent,** *rin'jənt, adj.* gaping. [L. *ringēns, -entis,* pr.p. of *ringi.*]

**rink,** *ringk, n.* a course for tilting or racing: a portion of a bowling-green, curling-pond, etc., allotted to one set of players: a division of a side playing on such a portion: a piece of ice prepared for skating: a building or floor for roller-skating or ice-skating.—*v.i.* to skate on a rink. [Orig. Scots; origin obscure.]

**rinse,** *rins,v.t.* to wash lightly by pouring, shaking, or dipping: to wash in clean water to remove soap traces.—*n.* an act of rinsing: liquid used for rinsing: a solution used in hair-dressing, esp. one to tint the hair slightly and impermanently. —*ns.* **rins'er; rins'ing.**—*n.pl.* **rins'ings,** liquid in which something has been rinsed. [O.Fr. *rinser* (Fr. *rincer*).]

**rintheroot,** *rin'dhə-rōōt, (Scot.) n.* and *adj.* vagrant: vagabond. [**run thereout.**]

**riot,** *ri'ət, n.* wild revelry: debauchery: loose living: unrestrained squandering or indulgence: tumult: a great, usu. boisterous, success: a disturbance of the peace by a crowd (legally three or more): of colour, a striking display.—*v.i.* to take part or indulge in riot: to revel.—*ns.* **ri'oter; ri'oting; ri'otise, -ize (-*iz; Spens.*),** riot, extravagance.—*adj.* **ri'otous.**—*adv.* **ri'otously.**—*ns.* **ri'otousness; ri'otry.**—**Riot Act,** a statute designed to prevent riotous assemblies: a form of words read as a warning to rioters to disperse.—**read the riot act** (*fig.*), to give vehement warning that something must cease; **run riot,** to act or grow without restraint. [O.Fr. *riot, riotte.*]

**rip,** *rip, v.t.* to slash or tear open, apart, off, or ‧out: to make by such an action: to reopen (with *up*): to cleave or saw with the grain: to strip (as a roof): to utter explosively (with *out*). —*v.i.* to part in rents: to break out violently: to rush, go forward unrestrainedly:—*pr.p.* **ripp'ing;** *pa.t.* and *pa.p.* **ripped,** or **ript.**—*n.* a rent: an unchecked rush.—**ripp'er,** one who rips: a tool for ripping: a person or thing especially admirable (*slang*).—*adj.* **ripp'ing** (*slang*), excellent.— Also *adv.*—*adv.* **ripp'ingly.**—**rip'-cord,** a cord for opening a balloon's gas-bag or enabling a parachute to open; **ripp'ing-saw, rip'-saw,** a saw for cutting along the grain.—*adj.* **rip'-roaring,** wild and noisy.—**rip'snorter** (*slang*), a fast and furious affair, or person: a gale.—*adj.* **rip'-snorting.**—**let rip,** to express oneself, or to act, violently or with abandon: to increase speed in greatly; (**let it rip**), to refrain from trying to check an action or process. [Uncertain; cf. Fris. *rippe*, Flem. *rippen*, Norw. *rippa.*]

**rip,** *rip, (dial.) n.* a wicker basket: a coop.— *n.* **ripp'er, ripp'ier,** (*obs.*) one who carries fish inland to sell. [O.N. *hrip*, basket.]

**rip,** *rip, n.* an inferior horse: a disreputable person. [Poss. **rep.** (2).]

**rip,** *rip, n.* stretch of broken water: disturbed state of the sea.—*n.* **rip'tide,** tidal rip. [Perh. **rip** (1).]

**rip, ripp,** *rip, (Scot.) n.* a handful, esp. a plucked handful, of grass or corn. [Poss. **rip** (1); connection with **reap** involves difficulty.]

**riparian,** *ri-pā'ri-ən, adj.* of or inhabiting a river-bank.—*n.* an owner of land bordering a river.— *adj.* **ripā'rial.** [L. *riparius—ripa,* a river-bank.]

**ripe,** *rip, adj.* ready for harvest: arrived at perfection: fit for use: fully developed: finished: ready: resembling ripe fruit: mature.—*v.t.* and

*v.i.* to ripen.—*adv.* **ripe'ly.**—*v.t.* and *v.i.* **ri'pen,** to make or grow ripe or riper.—*n.* **ripe'ness.** [O.E. *ripe*, ripe, *ripian*, to ripen; conn. with *rip*, harvest, and perh. **reap;** cf. Du. *rijp*, Ger. *reif.*]

**ripe,** *rip, (Scot.) v.t.* and *v.i.* to grope, search, ransack.—*n.* **rip'er.** [O.E. *rȳpan*, to rob.]

**ripidolite,** *rip-id'ō-līt,* or *rip-,* clinochlore. [Gr. *rhipis, -idos,* fan.]

**ripieno,** *ri-pyā'nō, (mus.) adj.* supplementary.—*n.* a supplementary instrument or performer:—*pl.* **ripie'ni** ( *nē).*—*n.* **ripie'nist,** a supplementary instrumentalist. [It.]

**riposte,** *ri-post', -pōst', n.* a quick return thrust after a parry: a repartee.—*v.t.* and *v.i.* to answer with a riposte. [Fr.,—It. *risposta,* reply.]

**ripp, ripper, rippier, ripping.** See **rip** (various).

**ripple,** *rip'l, n.* light fretting of the surface of a liquid: a little wave: a similar appearance in anything: a sound as of rippling water.—*v.t.* to ruffle the surface of: to mark with ripples.—*v.i.* to move or run in ripples: to sound like ripples. —*n.* **ripp'let,** a small ripple.—*n.* and *adj.* **ripp'-ling.**—*adv.* **ripp'lingly.**—*adj.* **ripp'ly.**—**ripp'le-mark,** an undulatory ridging produced in sediments by waves, currents, and wind, often preserved in sedimentary rocks.—*adj.* **ripp'le-marked.** [Origin obscure.]

**ripple,** *rip'l, n.* a toothed implement for removing seeds, etc., from flax or hemp.—*v.t.* to clear of seeds by drawing through a ripple: to remove by a ripple.—*n.* **ripp'ler.** [Cf. L.G. and Du. *repel,* a ripple, hoe, Ger. *riffel.*]

**Rippon,** *rip'ən, (obs.;* in full **Rippon spur**) *n.* a spur made at *Rippon,* once famous for the manufacture.

**rip-rap, riprap,** *rip'-rap, n.* loose broken stones, or a foundation formed of them on soft ground or under water. [From an obs. word imit. of the sound of repeated blows.]

**Ripstone pippin,** (*Dickens*) for **Ribstone pippin.**

**ript.** Same as **ripped** (see **rip,** 1).

**Ripuarian,** *rip-ū-ā'ri-ən, adj.* applied to the Franks on the lower Rhine and their laws.—*n.* a Ripuarian Frank. [Generally said to be from L. *ripa,* a river-bank.]

**Rip Van Winkle,** *rip van wing'kl,* one very much behind the times, as was a character of that name in a story by Washington Irving; according to the story he returned home after having slept in the mountains for twenty years.

**risaldar,** *ris-äl-där', n.* the commander of a troop of Indian cavalry. [Hind. *risāldār.*]

**rise,** *riz, v.i.* to get up: to become erect, stand up: to come back to life: to become hostile: to revolt: to close a session: to break up camp: to raise a siege: to move upward: to come up to the surface: to fly up from the ground: to come above the horizon: to grow upward: to advance in rank, fortune, etc.: to swell: to increase: to increase in price: to become more acute in pitch: to be excited: to be cheered: to come into view, notice, or consciousness: to spring up: to take origin: to have source: to come into being: to extend upward: to tower: to slope up: to come to hand, chance to come: to respond as to provocation, or to a situation calling forth one's powers: to excavate upward.—*v.t.* to cause to rise: to surmount (*U.S.*): to raise, view better by nearing (*naut.*): —*pa.t.* **rose,** *rōz,* Scot. **raise, rase,** *rāz,* U.S. coll. **riz;** *pa.p.* **risen,** *riz'n,* U.S. coll. **riz.**—*n.* **rising:** ascent: a coming up to the surface, as of a fish: the sport of making a butt of one by deception: increase in height: vertical difference or amount of elevation or rising: increase of salary, price, etc.: an upward slope: a sharpening of pitch: origin: occasion: time of rising: a shaft excavated from below.—*ns.* **ris'er,** one who rises, esp. from bed: that which rises: the upright portion of a step; **ris'ing,** the action or process of the verb in any sense: a revolt: a prominence: a swelling: a hill.—*adj.* and *pr.p.* ascending: increasing: coming above the horizon: advancing: growing up: approaching the age of: quite as much as (*U.S.*).—**give rise to,** to cause, bring about; **on the rise,** in process of rising, esp. in price; **rise from the ranks,** to work one's way up from private soldier to commissioned officer: to become a self-made man; **rise to it** (*fig.*, from fishing), to take the lure; **rise to the occasion,** to prove equal to an emergency; **take a rise out of,** to lure into reacting to provocation, or loosely, to make sport of; **take rise,** to originate; **the rise of** (*U.S.*), more than. [O.E. *risan*; O.N. *risa*, Goth. *reisan*, Ger. *reisen*.]

**rishi,** *rish'i, n.* a sage or poet. [Sans.]

**risible,** *riz'i-bl, adj.* able or inclined to laugh: of laughter: ludicrous.—*n.* **risibil'ity,** laughter: inclination to laugh: faculty of laughter. [L. *risibilis*—*ridēre, risum,* to laugh.]

**risk,** also (*obs.*) **risque,** *risk, n.* hazard, danger, chance of loss or injury: degree of probability of loss: person, thing, or factor likely to cause loss or danger.—*v.t.* to expose to hazard: to incur the chance of unfortunate consequences by (doing something).—*n.* **risk'er.**—*adj.* **risk'ful.**—*adv.* **risk'ily.**—*n.* **risk'iness.**—*adjs.* **risk'y,** dangerous, liable to mischance: **risqué** (a' Gallicism); **risqué** (*rēs-kā*; Fr. *pa.p.*), audaciously bordering on the unseemly.—**risk'-money,** allowance to a cashier to compensate for ordinary errors.—**at risk,** in a situation or circumstances where loss, injury, etc., are possible; **run a risk,** to be in, get into, a risky situation; **run a, the, risk of,** to risk (failing, etc.). [Fr. *risque*—It. *risco*; origin uncertain.]

**risoluto,** *rē-zō-lōō'tō, adj.* and *adv.* with resolution. [It.]

**risorgimento,** *ri-sör-ji-men'tō, n.* a revival, rebirth: (with *cap.*), the Renaissance: the liberation and unification of Italy in the 19th century. [It.,—L. *resurgēre.*]

**risotto,** *ri-zot'tō, n.* a dish of rice cooked with onions and cheese, or with gravy, etc. [It.,—*riso*, rice.]

**risp,** *risp,* (*Scot.*) *v.t.* to rasp: to grate.—*v.i.* to make a grating sound: to tirl.—*n.* a rasp or coarse file: a baker's grater: a roughened bar, on which a ring is grated, used instead of a knocker or door-bell: a grating sound.—*n.pl.* **risp'ings,** portions risped off. [O.N. *rispa,* to scratch.]

**risque, risqué.** See **risk.**

**Riss,** *ris, n.* the third stage of glaciation in the Alps.—*adjs.* **Riss, Riss'ian.** [From a tributary of the Danube in Württemberg.]

**rissole,** *ris'ōl, rēs-ōl', n.* a fried ball or cake of minced food. [Fr.]

**risus,** *ri'sas, rē'soōs, n.* a laugh: a grin.—**risus sardonicus** (*sär-don'ik-as, -ōōs*), a sardonic grin, or drawing back of the corners of the mouth by spasm of the muscles, as in tetanus. [L. *risus, -ūs,* laugh.]

**rit, ritt,** *rit,* (*Scot.*) *v.t.* to score: to scratch: to slit.—*n.* a scratch: a slit. [M.E. *ritten;* cf. Ger. *ritzen.*]

**ritardando,** *rē-tär-dan'dō, adj.* and *adv.* with diminishing speed.—*n.* a ritardando passage: a slowing down. [It.]

**rite,** *rit, n.* a ceremonial form or observance, esp. religious: a liturgy.—*adj.* **rite'less.** [L. *ritus.*]

**ritenuto,** *rit-a-nū'to,* (*mus.*) *adj.* restrained—indicating a sudden slowing-down of tempo. [It., *pa.p.* of *ritenere,* to restrain, hold back.]

**ritornello,** *rit-ör-nel'ō, n.* a short instrumental passage in a vocal work, e.g. a prelude or refrain:—*pl.* **ritornelli** (*-ē*).—Also **ritornel', -nell', -nelle', ritournelle'.** [It.]

**ritter,** *rit'ar, n.* a knight.—*n.* **ritt'-mas'ter,** a captain of cavalry. [Ger. *ritter, rittmeister.*]

**ritual,** *rit'ū-al, adj.* relating to, or of the nature of, rites.—*n.* manner of performing divine service, or a book containing it: a body or code of ceremonies: an often repeated series of actions: performance of rites: ceremonial.—*n.* **ritualisā'-tion, -z-.**—*v.i.* **rit'ualise, -ize,** to practise or turn to ritualism.—*v.t.* to make ritualistic.—*ns.* **rit'ūalism,** attachment of importance to ritual, esp. with the implication of undue importance; **rit'ūalist,** one skilled in or devoted to a ritual: one of the High Church party in the Church of England.—*adj.* **ritūalist'ic.**—*adv.* **ritūalist'ically.** —*adv.* **rit'ūally.**—**ritual choir,** part of a church used as a choir; **ritual murder,** killing of a human being as part of a tribal religious ceremony. [L. *ritualis*—*ritus;* see **rite.**]

**ritzy,** *rit'zi,* (*slang*) *adj.* stylish, elegant, ostentatiously rich. [The *Ritz* hotels.]

**riva,** *riv'a, rēv'a,* (*Shetland*) *n.* a cleft in rock. [O.N. *rifa.*]

**rivage,** *riv'ij, riv'ij,* (*poet.*) *n.* a bank, shore. [Fr., —L. *ripa,* a bank.]

**rival,** *ri'vl, n.* one pursuing an object in competition with another: one who strives to equal or excel another: one for whom, or that for which, a claim to equality might be made: a partner, fellow (*Shak.*).—*adj.* standing in competition: of like pretensions or comparable claims.—*v.t.* to stand in competition with: to try to gain the same object against: to try to equal or excel: to be worthy of comparison with:—*pr.p.* **ri'valling;** *pa.t.* and *pa.p.* **ri'valled.** —*n.* **ri'valess,** a female rival.—*v.i.* **ri'valise, -ize,** to enter into rivalry.—*n.* **rivality** (*-val'i-ti*), rivalry: equality (*Shak.*).—*adj.* **ri'valless.**—*ns.* **ri'valry,** state of being a rival: competition: emulation: feeling of a rival; **ri'valship,** emulation.—*adj.* **ri'val-hating** (*Shak.*). [L. *rivalis,* said to be from *rivus,* river, as one who draws water from the same river.]

**rive,** *riv, v.t.* to tear asunder: to tear: to rend: to split: to discharge as if with rending (*Shak.*): to pierce (*obs.*): to plough up (*Scot.*).—*v.i.* to tug, tear: to split:—*pa.t.* **rived**—*Scot.* **rave** (*rāv*): *pa.p.* **riven** (*riv'n*), **rived** (*rivd*)—*Spens.* **rive** (*riv*) —*Keats* **rafe.** [O.N. *rifa.*]

**rivel,** *riv'l, v.t.* and *v.i.* to wrinkle.—*adj.* **riv'elled.** [O.E. *rifelede,* rivelled.]

**river,** *riv'ar, n.* a large stream of water flowing over the land: sometimes extended to a strait or inlet: a place for hawking (*arch.*): a stream in general.—*adj.* of a river or rivers: dwelling or found in or near a river or rivers.—*adj.* **riv'-erain** (*-ān*), of a river or its neighbourhood.—*n.* riverside dweller.—*adj.* **riv'ered,** watered by rivers.—*n.* **riv'eret** (*arch.*), a small river.—*adjs.* **riv'erine** (*-in, -ēn*), of, on, or dwelling in or near a river: well rivered.—**riv'er-bank; riv'er-basin,** the whole region drained by a river with its affluents; **riv'er-bed,** the channel in which a river flows; **river blindness,** a West African disease carried by a fly; **riv'er-bottom** (*U.S.*), alluvial land along the margin of a river; **riv'er-craft,** small vessels that ply on rivers; **riv'er-dragon,** Pharaoh (*Milt.,* with ref. to Ezek. xxix. 3): a crocodile; **riv'er-drift,** old alluvia of rivers; **ri'ver-driver** (*U.S.*), one who conducts logs downstream; **riv'er-flat,** a piece of alluvial land by a river; **riv'er-front,** land, quays, buildings, etc., facing a river; **riv'er-god,** the tutelary deity of a river; **riv'er-head,** the source of a river; **riv'er-hog,** the capybara: an African wild pig; **riv'er-horse,** the hippopotamus: the kelpie: a pole bestridden in a primitive method of crossing rivers (*S.Afr.*); **riv'er-jack** (or **river-jack viper**), a West African viper; **riv'er-man,** one who makes his livelihood on or along a river; **riv'er-mouth; riv'er-mussel,** a freshwater mussel; **river novel** (see **roman fleuve**) riv´er-rat, a thief who prowls about a river; riv´er-sand, sand from a river-bed; riv´erscape, a picture of river scenery; riv´erside, the bank or neighbourhood of a river.—*adj.* beside a river.— riv´er-terr´ace, a terrace formed when a river eats away its old alluvium deposited when its flood-level was higher; riv´er-tide, the current of a river: the tide from the sea rising or ebbing in a river; riv´er-wall, a wall confining a river within bounds; riv´er-wa´ter; riv´erway, a river as a waterway; riv´erwood, Podostemon. [O.Fr. *rivere* (Fr. *rivière*)—L. *ripārius*, adj.—*ripa*, bank; cf. It. *riviera*.]

rivet, riv´it, *n.* bearded wheat. [Origin obscure.]

rivet, riv´it, *n.* a bolt fastened by hammering the end.—*v.t.* to fasten with rivets: to fix immovably: to clinch or hammer out the end of:—*pr.p.* riv´eting; *pa.t.* and *pa.p.* riv´eted (formerly often riv´etting, riv´etted).—*ns.* riv´eter, one who rivets: a machine for riveting; riv´eting.— riv´et-head; riv´et-hearth, a forge for heating rivets; riv´et-hole, a hole to receive a rivet. [O.Fr. *rivet*—*river*, to clinch; origin obscure.]

riviera, riv-i-ā´rə, *n.* a warm coastal district reminiscent of the Riviera in France and Italy on the Mediterranean Sea.

rivière, rē-vyer, *n.* a necklace of diamonds or other precious stones, usu. in several strings. [Fr., river.]

rivo, rē´vō, ri´vō, (*Shak.*) *interj.* a drinking-cry.

rivulet, riv´ū-lit, *n.* a small river. [L. *rivulus*, dim. of *rivus*, a stream, perh. through It. *rivoletto*—*rivolo*—*rivo*.]

rix-dollar, riks´-dol-ər, *n.* a silver coin, once current in various countries. [Obs. Du. *rijcksdaler* (Du. *rijksdaalder*)—Du. *rijk*, kingdom (cf. O.E. *rice*), *daler*, dollar.]

riz, riz, (*U.S. dial.*) *pa.t.* and *pa.p.* of rise.

rizzer, rizzar, rizzor, riz´ər, (*Scot.*) *v.t.* to dry, esp. in the sun.—*n.* a rizzered haddock. [Cf. obs. Fr. *ressorer*, to dry.]

rizzer, rizzar, rizard, rizzart, riz´ər(d), -ərt, (*Scot.*) *n.* a red currant. [Earlier *razour*; origin unknown.]

roach, rōch, *n.* a silvery fresh-water fish of the carp family: applied to various American fishes.—as sound as a roach, perfectly sound. [O.Fr. *roche*.]

roach, rōch, *n.* a concave curve in the foot of a square sail.—*v.t.* to arch: to cut short (as a horse's mane): to cut, or cut the hair or mane of, in an upright ridge. [Origin uncertain.]

road (*Shak.*, *Spens.*, etc., rode), rōd, *n.* a ride, horseback journey (*Shak.*): a raid, incursion (*Shak.*, *Spens.*): a track suitable for wheeled traffic, esp. for through communication (often in street-names): a highway: a roadway: a way of approach: course: a mine-passage: (often in *pl.*) a roadstead: a railway (*U.S.*): journeying: wayfaring, tour: dismissal (*coll.*): a prostitute (*Shak.*).—*n.* road´ster, a horse, cycle or car, suitable for ordinary use on the road: a coach-driver or other traveller by road.—road´-agent (*U.S.*), a highwayman; road´-bed, the foundation of a railway track: the material laid down to form a road; road´block, an obstruction set up across a road; road´-book, a guide-book to the roads of a district.—*adj.* road´-borne, carried by road.—road´-bridge, a bridge carrying a road; road´-craft, knowledge and skill useful to wayfarers and drivers; road´-end´, the place where a road branches off from another; road´-hog, a swinishly selfish or boorishly reckless motorist or other user of the road.— Also *v.i.*—*adj.* road´-hoggish.—road´house, a roadside public-house, refreshment-room, or inn, catering for motorists, cyclists, etc.; road´-maker; road´-making; road´man, one who keeps a road in repair: one who uses the roads, an itinerant; road´-mender; road´-mending; road´-metal, broken stones for roads; road´-

metalling; road´-roller, a heavy roller used on roads; road´-runner, the chaparral cock; road´-scraper, an implement for clearing roads of loose material; road´-sense, aptitude for doing the right thing in driving; road´side, the border of a road: wayside.—*adj.* by the side of a road.— roads´man, a driver: a roadman; road´stead, a place near a shore where ships may ride at anchor; road´-survey´or, one who supervises roads; road´way, the way or part of a road used by horses and vehicles; road´-worthiness.—*adj.* road´worthy, fit for the road. —in, out of, the (or one's) road (chiefly *Scot.*), in, out of, the way; on the road, travelling, esp. as a commercial traveller or a tramp: on the way to some place; road up, road surface being repaired; rule of the road (see rule); take the road, to set off, depart; take to the road, to become a highwayman (*arch.*), or a tramp. [O.E. *rād*, a riding, raid, cf. raid, ride.]

roading. See rode (3).

roadster, roadstead. See road.

roam, rōm, *v.i.* to rove about: to ramble.—*v.t.* to wander over: to range.—*n.* a wandering: a ramble.—*n.* roam´er. [M.E. *romen*; origin obscure.]

roan, rōn, *adj.* bay or dark, with spots of grey and white: of a mixed colour, with a decided shade of red.—*n.* a roan colour: a roan animal, esp. a horse. [O.Fr. *roan* (Fr. *rouan*).]

roan, rōn, *n.* grained sheepskin leather.—*adj.* of roan. [Poss. *Roan*, early form of *Rouen*.]

roan. Same as rone.

roar, rōr, rör, *v.i.* to make a full, loud, hoarse, low-pitched sound, as a lion, fire, wind, the sea, cannon: to bellow: to bawl: to guffaw: to take in breath with a loud noise, as a diseased horse: to behave in a riotous, bullying, noisy manner (*obs.*): to rush forward with loud noise from the engine.—*v.t.* to utter vociferously. —*n.* a sound of roaring.—*ns.* roar´er, one who roars: a horse that roars as a result of disease: a roaring boy (*obs.*); roar´ing, the action of the verb in any sense: a disease of horses marked by roaring.—*adj.* uttering or emitting roars: riotous: proceeding with very great activity or success.— *adv.* roar´ingly.—*adj.* roary, -ie (*Scot.*), noisy: garish, too bright.—roaring boy (*obs.*), a boister-ous bullying reveller, swaggerer, or brawler; roaring forties (see forty); the roaring game, curling. [O.E. *rārian*; but partly from M.Du. *roer*, stir, disturbance.]

roast, rōst, *v.t.* to cook before a fire: to bake: to parch by heat: to heat strongly: to dissipate the volatile parts of (esp. sulphur) by heat: to criticise excessively, even sarcastically: to banter (*slang*).—*v.i.* to undergo roasting.—*adj.* roasted.—*n.* a joint, esp. of beef, roasted or to be roasted: an operation of roasting: banter (*slang*).—*n.* roas´ter, apparatus for roasting: a pig, etc., suitable for roasting: a very hot day. —*n.* and *adj.* roast´ing.—roast´-beef; roas´ting-jack, an apparatus for turning a joint in roasting; roast´-meat.—cry roast-meat, to publish one's good luck foolishly; roast-beef plant, the fetid iris (from its smell); rule the roast (mistakenly roost), to lord it, predominate. [O.Fr. *rostir* (Fr. *rôtir*); of Gmc. origin.]

roate, an old spelling (*Shak.*) of rote (1).

rob, rob, *v.t.* to deprive wrongfully and forcibly: to steal from: to plunder: to deprive: to take as plunder: to carry off.—*v.i.* to commit robbery:—*pr.p.* robb´ing; *pa.t.* and *pa.p.* robbed.—*ns.* robb´er, one who robs; robb´ery, theft from the person, aggravated by violence or intimidation: plundering.—robb´er-crab, a large coconut-eating land-crab of the Indian Ocean: a hermit-crab; robb´er-fly, any fly of the Asilidae, large, bristly, insect-eating flies.—daylight robbery, glaring extortion; Robber Council or

**Synod,** a council held at Ephesus in 449, afterwards repudiated, which reinstated Eutyches (from the violence of its proceedings); **rob Peter to pay Paul,** to satisfy one by depriving another. [O.Fr. *rober,* of Gmc. origin; cf. **reave,** O.H.G. *roubōn,* Ger. *rauben.*]

**rob,** *rob, n.* a fruit syrup. [Ar. *robb.*]

**robalo,** *rob'ə-lō, n.* an American pike-like fish (Centropomus), of a family akin to the seaperches. [Sp. *róbalo,* bass.]

**robe,** *rōb, n.* a gown or loose outer garment: a gown or dress of office, dignity, or state: a rich dress: a woman's dress: a dressing-gown: (in *pl.*) clothes garb: a dressed bison hide, or the like.—*v.t.* to dress: to invest in robes.—*v.i.* to assume official vestments.—*n.* **rob'ing,** the putting on of robes or clothes: apparel: a trimming on a robe.—**robe-de-chambre** (*rob-də-shã-br'*; Fr.), a dressing-gown; **robe'-maker,** a maker of official robes; **rob'ing-room,** room in which official robes may be put on.—**Mistress of the robes,** the head of a department in a queen's household; **the robe,** or **the long robe,** the legal profession. [Fr. *robe,* orig. booty; cf. **rob, reave,** O.H.G. *raup* (Ger. *raub*), booty.]

**robersdman,** *rob'ərdz-man,* (*obs.*) *n.* a stout robber. —Also **rob'ertsman.** [App. from *Robert;* allusion unknown.]

**robin,** *rob'in, n.* the redbreast or **rob'in-red'breast** (*Erithacus rubecula*), a widely-spread singing bird with reddish-orange breast: extended to other birds, as a red-breasted thrush of N. America (**American robin**).—**Rob'in Good'fellow,** a tricky English domestic spirit or brownie—Puck; **Rob'in-run-(in-)the-hedge,** cleavers or goosegrass: ground-ivy: also various other hedgeside plants. [A form of *Robert;* cf. *Jack*daw, *Mag*pie.]

**robin,** *rō'bin,* (*obs.*) *n.* trimming on a gown. [robing.]

**Robinia,** *ro-bin'i-a, n.* the locust or false acacia genus of Papilionaceae. [From its introducer to cultivation, the Paris gardener Jean *Robin* (1550-1629.]

**roble,** *rō'blä, n.* a name for various species of oak, *Nothofagus,* and other trees. [Sp.,—L. *rōbur,* oak.]

**roborant,** *rob'ər-ənt, n.* strengthening drug or tonic.—Also *adj.* [L. *rōborāns, -antis,* pr.p. of *rōborāre,* to strengthen, invigorate.]

**robot,** *rō'bot, n.* a mechanical man: a more than humanly efficient automaton: an automatic traffic signal. [Czech *robota,* statute labour; from Karel Čapek's play *R.U.R.* (1920).]

**roburite,** *rō'bər-it, n.* a flameless explosive, chlorinated dinitro-benzene with ammonium nitrate. [L. *rōbur,* strength.]

**robust,** *rō-bust', adj.* stout, strong, and sturdy: constitutionally healthy: vigorous: thick-set: overhearty.—*adj.* **robust'ious** (*-yəs*), robust: violent (*Shak.*): strong or rough (*Milt.*).—*adv.* **robust'iously.**—*n.* **robust'iousness.**—*adv.* **robust'ly.**—*n.* **robust'ness.** [L. *rōbustus*—*rōbur,* strength, oak.]

**roc,** *rok, n.* a fabulous bird, able to carry off an elephant—also **rok, ruc, rukh** (*rōōk*). [Pers. *rukh.*]

**rocaille,** *rō-kä'ē, n.* artificial rockwork or similar ornament: scroll ornament: rococo. [Fr.]

**rocambole,** *rok'əm-bōl, n.* a plant close akin to garlic. [Fr.]

**Roccella,** *rok-sel'a, n.* a genus of lichens, yielding archil and litmus. [It. *orcella,* remodelled on *rocca,* rock; see archil.]

**Rochelle,** *rō-shel',* properly **La Rochelle,** a town of France.—**Rochelle'-pow'der,** seidlitz powder; **Rochelle'-salt,** sodium potassium tartrate, discovered in 1672 by Seignette, a *Rochelle* apothecary.

**roche moutonnée,** *rosh mōō-to-nā, n.* a smooth, rounded hummocky rock-surface due to glacia-

tion:—*pl.* **roches moutonnées** (same pron.). [Fr. *roche,* a rock, *moutonnée,* a kind of wig; applied by De Saussure.]

**rochet,** *roch'it, n.* a mantle (*obs.*): a close-fitting surplice-like vestment proper to bishops and abbots. [O.Fr., of Gmc. origin; cf. Ger. *rock,* O.E. *rocc.*]

**rock,** *rok, n.* a large outstanding natural mass of stone: a natural mass of one or more minerals consolidated or loose (*geol.*): any variety or species of such an aggregate: a diamond or other precious stone (*slang*): a stone, pebble, lump of rock (*U.S.*): a hard sweetmeat made in sticks: a sure foundation or support, anything immovable, a danger or obstacle (*fig.*): for rock-fish, rock-pigeon, Plymouth Rock fowl: a coin (*U.S. slang*).—*adj.* of rock: found on, in, or among rocks.—*v.t.* to stone (*U.S. slang*): to clear of calcareous deposit.—*ns.* **rock'er, rock'ier,** the rock-dove; **rock'ery,** a heap of rock fragments in a garden, for growing rock-plants; **rock'iness; rock'ling,** a small fish of the cod family with barbels on both jaws.—*adj.* **rock'y,** full of rocks: like rocks.—**rock'-al'um,** alum prepared from alunite; **rock'-badger,** the Cape hyrax; **rock'-basin,** a lacustrine hollow in rock, excavated by glacier-ice; **rock'-bird,** a puffin or other bird that nests or lives on rocks; **rock'-borer,** any mollusc or other animal that bores into rocks; **rock'-bottom,** bedrock: the very bottom, esp. of poverty or despair.—*adj.* the lowest possible.—*adj.* **rock'-bound,** hemmed in by rock.—**rock'-brake,** parsley-fern; **rock'-breaker,** a machine for breaking stones; **rock'-butt'er,** a butter-like exudation from rocks, containing alum; **rock'-cake,** a small hard bun with irregular top; **rock'-cod,** a cod found on rocky sea-bottoms: a name for various Australian and other fishes, mostly of the sea-bass family; **rock'-cook,** the small-mouthed wrasse; **rock'-cork,** mountain-cork; **rock'cress,** a cruciferous plant, Arabis; **rock'-crys'tal,** colourless quartz, esp. when well crystallised; **rock'-dove,** a pigeon that nests on rocks, source of the domestic varieties; **rock'-drill,** a tool for boring rock; **rock'-fall,** a fall of rock: a mass of fallen rock; **rock'-fish,** any fish that haunts rocks or rocky bottoms: applied as a name to several such fishes, as wrasse, striped bass, black goby; **rock'-flour,** finely divided rock material, such as is found under glaciers.—*adj.* **rock'-forming,** occurring as a dominant constituent of rocks.— **rock'-garden,** a garden of rockery, for rockplants; **rock'-gua'no,** a rock phosphatised by percolations from guano.—*adj.* **rock'-hewn,** hewn out of rock.—**rock'-hopper,** a crested penguin; **rock'-lark,** the rock-pipit; **rock'-leather,** mountain-leather; **rock'-oil,** petroleum; **rock'-perch,** a scorpion-fish; **rock'-pigeon,** the rock-dove; **rock'-pipit,** a pipit inhabiting rocky coasts; **rock'-plant,** a plant adapted to growing on or among rocks; **rock'-rabb'it,** a hyrax.—*adj.* **rock'-ribbed** (*U.S.*), unyielding.—**rock'-rose,** a plant of either of the genera *Cistus* and *Helianthemum* of the family Cistaceae; **rock'-salm'on,** rock'-tur'bot, wolf-fish disguised for the market; **rock'-salt,** salt as a mineral, halite; **rock'-scor'pion,** a person born in Gibraltar (also **rock'-liz'ard**); **rock'-snake,** a python: a krait; **rock'-sparrow,** a genus (*Petronia*) akin to the true sparrow; **rock'-tar',** petroleum; **rock'-temple,** temple hewn out of the solid rock; **rock'-tripe,** an edible arctic lichen of various kinds; **rock'-vi'olet,** a violet-scented alga growing on mountain rocks; **rock'water,** water issuing from a rock; **rock'weed,** bladderwrack or kindred seaweed growing on rocks; **rock'-wood',** a woodlike asbestos; **rock wool,** mineral wool; **rock'-work,** masonry in imitation of rock (*archit.*): rockery: rock-climbing.—**on the rocks,** penniless:

(of whisky, etc.) on ice; **Rock English,** the Gibraltar dialect; **Rock fever,** undulant fever (from Gibraltar): **Rocky Mountain goat,** a white N. American animal intermediate between goat and antelope; the **Rock,** Gibraltar; **the Rockies,** the Rocky Mountains. [O.Fr. *roke*—L.L. *rocca*.]

**rock,** *rok, n.* a distaff.—*n.* **rock'ing,** (*Scot.*) an evening party, orig. for spinning. [M.E. *roc*; cf. M.Du. *rocke*; O.N. *rokkr*; Ger. *rocken*.]

**rock,** *rok, v.t. and v.i.* to sway to and fro, tilt from side to side: to startle, stagger (*coll.*).—*n.* a rocking movement.—*n.* **rock'er,** one who rocks: apparatus that rocks: a curved support on which anything rocks: a rocking-horse: a rocking-chair: (*cap.*) a member of a teenage faction of the 1960s who wore leather jackets, rode motor bicycles, and were at enmity with the Mods: a mining cradle: a skate with curved blade: a mezzotint engraver's tool for preparing a surface.—*adv.* **rock'ily.**—*n.* **rock'-iness.**—*n.* and *adj.* **rock'ing.**—*adj.* **rock'y,** disposed to rock: shaky: tipsy: unpleasant, unsatisfactory (*slang*).—**rocker switch,** a dolly switch; **rock'abilly,** a hillbilly song; **rock'ing-chair,** a chair mounted on rockers; **rock'ing-horse,** the figure of a horse mounted on rockers; **rock'ing-stone,** a logan, or finely poised boulder that can be made to rock; **rock'ing-tool,** an engraver's tool for roughing a plate; **rock'-shaft,** in engines, a shaft that oscillates instead of revolving.—**off one's rocker,** out of one's right mind; **rock 'n' (or and) roll** (now usu. **rock**), a simple form of jazz music, two-beat, strongly accented: dancing thereto; **rock the boat,** to make thing difficult for one's colleagues. [O.E. *roccian.*]

**rockaway,** *rok'ə-wä, n.* an American four-wheeled pleasure carriage, formerly made at *Rockaway,* New Jersey.

**rocket,** *rok'it, n.* a simple device, a cylinder full of inflammable material, projected through the air for signalling, carrying a line to a ship in distress, or for firework display: a missile projected by a rocket system: a system, or a vehicle, obtaining its thrust from a backward jet of hot gases, all the material for producing which is carried within the rocket: a severe reprimand (*slang*).—*v.i.* to move like a rocket: to fly straight up rapidly when flushed: of e.g. prices, to become higher very rapidly (*fig.*): to come to an important position with remarkable speed (*fig.*).—*ns.* **rocketeer',** a rocket technician or pilot of rockets: a specialist in rocketry, especially a designer of rockets; **rock'eter,** a game bird which rockets; **rock'etry,** the scientific study of rockets.—**rock'et-motor,** a jet motor which uses an internally stored oxidiser instead of atmospheric oxygen, for combustion; **rock'et-plane,** an aeroplane driven by rocket-motor; **rock'et-range,** a place for experimentation with rocket projectiles. [It. *rocchetta,* of Gmc. origin.]

**rocket,** *rok'it, n.* a cruciferous salad plant (*Eruca sativa*) of Mediterranean countries: extended to dame's violet (*Hesperis*) and other plants of the same family (**sea'-rocket,** Cakile; **wall'-rocket,** Diplotaxis; **yell'ow-rocket,** winter-cress, Barbarea) or of other families (**blue'-rocket,** monk's hood: larkspur; **dy'er's-rocket,** weld). [O.Fr. *roquette*—L. *ērūca.*]

**rococo,** *rō-kō'kō, rō-kō-kō', n.* a debased style of architecture, decoration, and furniture-making prevailing in Louis XV's time, marked by endless multiplication of ornamental details unrelated to structure with rockwork, shells, scrolls, and un-symmetrical and broken curves, a lighter, freer, frivolous development of the baroque: any art showing the same spirit.—*adj.* in the style of rococo: florid and tasteless: grotesque: old-

fashioned and odd (*obs.*). [Fr., prob.—*rocaille* rockwork.]

**rocquet,** *rok'it, n.* a rochet. [O.Fr., a Northern form of *rochet.*]

**rod,** *rod, n.* a long straight shoot: a slender stick: a slender bar of metal or other matter: a sceptre or similar emblem of authority: a stick or bunch of twigs as emblem or instrument of punishment: a stick or wand for magic, divination: a riding-crop: a slender pole or structure carrying a fishing-line: a measuring stick: a pole or perch (5½ yards, or 16½ feet): a square pole (272¼ sq. ft): (of brickwork) 272 sq. ft of standard thickness of 1½ bricks or 306 cubic ft: race or tribe (*B.*): a rod-shaped body of the retina sensitive to light: a revolver, a pistol (*U.S. slang*).—*adjs.* **rod'less; rod'like.**—*n.* **rod'ster,** an angler.—**rod'fisher; rod'fishing; rod'man, rods'-man,** one who holds, carries or uses a rod, esp. an angler.—**a rod in pickle,** punishment in reserve; **kiss the rod,** accept punishment with submission; **Napier's rods** (see **Napierian**). [O.E. *rodd;* cf. O.N. *rudda,* club.]

**rode,** *rōd, pa.t.* of **ride.**

**rode,** *rōd,* (*Spens., Shak.*) *n.* an old spelling of **road.**—*n.* (*Shak.*) **rode'way.**

**rode,** *rōd, v.i.* to perform a regular evening flight, esp. of woodcock.—*n.* **rōd'ing, road'ing,** a woodcock's evening flight. [Origin obscure.]

**rodent,** *rō'dənt, adj.* gnawing: of the Rodentia.—*n.* a member of the Rodentia.—*n.pl.* **Rodentia** (*-den'sha,-shya*), an order of mammals with prominent incisor teeth and no canines, as squirrels, beavers, rats, rabbits.—*n.* **roden'ticide,** a substance that kills rodents.—**rodent officer,** an official rat-catcher. [L. *rōdēns, -entis,* pr.p. of *rōdēre,* to gnaw.]

**rodeo,** *rō'di-ō, rō-dā'ō, n.* a place where cattle are assembled: a round-up of cattle: an exhibition of cowboy skill: a contest suggestive of a cowboy rodeo involving, e.g. motor-bicycles. [Sp.,—*rodear,* to go round—L. *rotāre,* to wheel.]

**rodomontade,** *rod-ō-mon-tād', n.* extravagant boasting, like that of *Rodomonte* in Ariosto's *Orlando Furioso.*—*v.i.* to bluster or brag.—*n.* **rodomontā'-der.**

**roe,** *rō, n.* a mass of fish-eggs (also *hard roe*): sometimes milt (*soft roe*).—*adj.* **roed,** containing roe.—*n.* **roe'stone,** oolite. [M.E. *rowe;* cf. O.N. *hrogn,* M.H.G. *roge,* Ger. *rogen.*]

**roe,** *rō, n.* a small species of deer: sometimes applied to the female red deer.—**roe'buck,** the male roe; **roe'buck-berry, roe'-blackberry,** the stone-bramble; **roe'-deer,** a roe. [O.E. *rā, rāha;* Ger. *reh,* Du. *ree.*]

**Roe (Richard).** See **Doe (John).**

**roentgen.** See **röntgen.**

**rogation,** *rō-gā'shən, n.* an asking: supplication.—*adj.* **rogatory** (*rog'ə-tə-ri*).—**letters rogatory** (see **letter**); **Rogation Days,** the three days before Ascension Day, when supplications were recited in procession; **Rogation flower,** the milkwort, which was carried in Rogation Day processions; **Rogation Sunday,** that before Ascension Day; **Rogation Week,** the week in which the Rogation Days occur. [L. *rogātiō, -ōnis—rogāre,* to ask.]

**Roger,** *roj'ər, n.* a man's personal name: a goose (*cant*): a word used in signalling and radio-communication for R, in the sense of received (and understood).—**Jolly Roger,** the pirates' skull-and-cross-bones flag; **(Sir) Roger de Coverley** (*da-kuv'ər-li*), an English country-dance (whence the name of the *Spectator* character). [Fr., of Gmc. origin, equivalent to O.E. *Hrōthgār.*]

**rogue,** *rōg, n.* a vagrant: a rascal: a wag: a mischievous person (often playfully or affectionately): a plant that falls short of a standard, or is of a different type from the rest of the crop: a sport, or variation from type: a horse that shirks: a savage elephant or other animal cast out or withdrawn from its herd.—*v.i.* to play the rogue.—*v.t.* to cheat: to eliminate rogues from.—*ns.* **roguery** (*rōg'ər-i*), rascally tricks: fraud: mischievousness: waggery; **rogue'ship.**—*adjs.* **roguing** (*rōg'ing*), roaming, or behaving like a rogue; **roguish** (*rōg'ish*), rascally: mischievous: waggish: villainous: confounded. —*adv.* **rog'uishly.**—*n.* **rog'uishness.**—*adj.* **rog'uy** (*obs.*).—**rogue'-el'ephant**; **rogue'-money,** a former assessment in Scotland for the expense of catching, prosecuting and maintaining rogues; **rogues' gallery,** a police collection of photographs of criminals; **rogues' Latin,** cant; **rogues' march,** derisive music played at a drumming-out. [Cant; origin unknown.]

**roi fainéant,** *rwä fā-nā-ä,* (Fr.) a king without royal power (see **fainéant**).

**roil, roil** (also **rile, ril**), *v.t.* to make turbid: to annoy, irritate (now usu. **rile**).—*adj.* **roil'y,** turbid. [Origin doubtful.]

**roin, roinish.** Same as **royne, roynish.**

**roister, royster,** *rois'tər, n.* a blusterer: a noisy reveller.—*v.i.* to bluster, swagger: to revel noisily.—*v.i.* **roist, royst** (back-formation from the n.), to roister.—*n.* **rois'terer, roys'terer.**—*adj.* **rois'terous, roys'terous.**—*adj.* **rois'ting, roys'ting,** blustering, boisterous: rousingly defiant (*Shak.*). [O.Fr. *rustre*, a rough, rude fellow—O.Fr. *ruste*—L. *rusticus*, rustic.]

**rok.** Same as **roc.**

**roke, rōk,** *n.* vapour: steam: mist: small rain: smoke.—*v.t.* and *v.i.* to steam: to smoke.—*adj.* **rōk'y.** [Perh. Scand.]

**rokelay, rocklay,** *rok'(ə)-lā,* (*Scot.*) *n.* a woman's short cloak, worn in the 18th century. [Fr. *roquelaire*; see **roquelaure.**]

**roker,** *rōk'ər, n.* any ray other than skate, esp. the thornback. [Perh. Dan. *rokke,* Sw. *rocka,* ray.]

**Roland,** *rō'lənd, n.* a hero of the Charlemagne legend: hence a hero: a worthy match (with allusion to a drawn contest between Roland and his comrade-in-arms, Oliver).—**a Roland for an Oliver,** tit for tat: as good as one got.

**rôle, role,** *rōl, n.* a part played by an actor: function, part played in life or in any event. [Fr.]

**roll,** *rol, n.* a scroll: a sheet of paper, parchment, cloth, or other material bent spirally upon itself into a nearly cylindrical form: a document in such form: a register: a list, esp. of names: a spirally wound cake, or one of dough turned over to enclose other material: a small loaf: a revolving cylinder: a roller: a more or less cylindrical package, mass, or pad: a cylindrical moulding: a volute: a bookbinder's tool with a small wheel for impressing designs: a part turned over in a curve: an act of rolling: a swaying about an axis in the direction of motion: a continuous reverberatory or trilling sound: an undulation: a wavelike flow.—*v.i.* to move like a ball, a wheel, a wheeled vehicle, or a passenger in one: to perform revolutions: to sway on an axis in the direction of motion: to turn over or from side to side: to swagger: to wallow: to go with a roll: to move in, on, or like waves: to flow: to undulate: to wander: to sound with a roll: to use a roller: to curl. —*v.t.* to cause to roll: to turn on an axis: to move with a circular sweep (as the eyes): to wrap round on itself: to enwrap: to curl: to wind: to drive forward: to move upon wheels: to press, flatten, spread out, thin, or smooth with a roller or between rollers: to round by attrition: to beat rapidly, as a drum: to rumble: to peal: to trill: to pour in waves: (of a clock) to wind (*Scot.*).—*adj.* **rolled.**—*ns.* **roll'er,** one who or that which rolls: a revolving or rolling cylinder: a contrivance including a heavy cylinder or cylinders for flattening roads or turf: a long, coiled-up bandage (**roll'er-band'-**

age); a long heavy wave: a small solid wheel: a cylinder on which hair is wound to curl it: a kind of tumbler pigeon: a bird (Coracias) of a family akin to the kingfishers, with a habit of flight like a tumbler pigeon (Ger. *roller*): a kind of canary with a soft trilling song.—*n.* and *adj.* **roll'ing.**—*adj.* **roll'-about',** podgy.—**roll'-call,** the calling of a list of names, to ascertain attendance; **roll'collar,** a collar of a garment turned back in a curve; **rolled gold,** metal coated with gold rolled very thin; **roll'ercoast'er,** a circular switchback railway ridden in open coasting cars for amusement; **roll'erskate,** a skate with wheels instead of a blade.— Also *v.i.*—**roll'er-skat'er**; **roll'er-skat'ing**; **roll'er-tow'el,** an endless towel on a roller; **rolling adjustment,** (*U.S.*) a period of slackening business, distinct from a recession as being confined to certain industries only; **roll'ing-mill,** factory or machine for rolling metal into various shapes between rolls; **roll'ing-pin,** a cylinder for rolling dough; **roll'ing-stock,** the stock or store of engines and vehicles that run upon a railway; **roll'-on,** a corset that fits on by stretching.—*adj.* **roll-on'-roll-off',** (of a ferry-boat or ferry service) designed to allow goods vehicles to embark and disembark without unloading.—**roll'-out,** bringing out a prototype of an aeroplane to show it to the public.—*adjs.* **roll'-top,** having a flexible cover of slats that rolls up; **roll'-up,** suitable for rolling up.—*n.* an accumulator bet: assembling in large numbers, a meeting (*Austr.*).—**a rolling stone gathers no moss,** a rover does not grow rich; **be rolling in,** to have large amounts of (e.g. money); **Master of the Rolls,** head of the Record Office; **heads will roll,** severe punishments will be meted out, esp. loss of status or office; **roll along,** to arrive by chance, or with a casual air; **roll in,** to arrive in quantity; **roll on!,** may (a specified event) come quickly!; **roll up** (*coll.*), to assemble, arrive. [O.Fr. *rolle* (n.), *roller* (vb.)—L. *rotula,* dim. of *rota,* a wheel.]

**rollick,** *rol'ik, v.i.* to behave in a careless, swaggering, frolicsome manner.—*adj.* **roll'icking.** [Origin unknown.]

**rollock.** See **rowlock.**

**roly-poly,** *rōl'i-pōl'i, n.* a pudding made of a sheet of dough, covered with jam or fruit, rolled up, and baked or steamed: a round, podgy person: an old game in which balls are bowled into holes or thrown into hats placed on the ground.—*adj.* round, podgy. [Prob. **roll.**]

**rom, rom,** *n.* a gypsy man. [Romany, man, husband.]

**romage,** *rum'ij,* (*Shak.*) *n.* tumult. [**rummage.**]

**Romaic,** *rō-mā'ik, n.* and *adj.* modern Greek.—*n.* **romā'ika,** a modern Greek dance. [Mod. Gr. *Rhōmaikos,* Roman (i.e. of the Eastern Roman Empire)—*Rhōmē,* Rome.]

**romal,** *rō-mäl', rumal, rōō-mäl', n.* a handkerchief: a head-cloth. [Pers. *rūmāl.*]

**Roman,** *rō'mən, adj.* pertaining to Rome, esp. ancient Rome, its people, or the empire founded by them: pertaining to the Roman Catholic religion, papal: (of type) of the ordinary upright kind (indicated in proofs by **rom.**), as opp. to *italics*: (of numerals) written in letters (as IV, iv), opp. to *Arabic*: (of handwriting) round and bold: (of a nose) high-bridged.—*n.* a native or citizen of Rome: a Roman Catholic: Roman letter or type.—*adj.* **Romanic** (*rō-man'ik*), of Roman or Latin origin: Romance.—*n.* the Romance language or languages collectively.—*n.* **Romanisation, -z-** (*rō-mə-nī-zā'shən*).—*v.t.* **Ro'manise, -ize,** to make Roman or Roman Catholic: to bring under Roman or Roman Catholic influence: to represent by the Roman alphabet. —*v.i.* to accept Roman or Roman Catholic ways, laws, doctrines, etc.: to become Roman Catholic.—*n.* **Romani'ser, -z-.**—*adj.* **Ro'manish,**

(in hostility) Roman Catholic: savouring of Roman Catholicism.—*ns.* Ro'manism, Roman Catholicism; Ro'manist, a Roman Catholic: one versed in Romance philology or Roman law or antiquities.—*adj.* Roman Catholic.—*adj.* Romanist'ic.—in composition, Romano- (*rō-mā'-nō*), Roman: Romanised: Roman and (as Roma'no-Brit'ish).—Roman candle, a firework discharging a succession of white or coloured stars: a bad landing by aeroplane: a landing by parachute when the parachute fails to open.—*v.i.* to make such a landing.—*adj.* Roman Catholic, recognising the spiritual supremacy of the Pope or Bishop of Rome.—*n.* a member of the Roman Catholic Church.—Roman Catholicism, the doctrines and polity of the Roman Catholic Church collectively; Roman cement, a hydraulic cement made from calcareous nodules from the London Clay; Roman Empire, the ancient empire of Rome, divided in the 4th century into the Eastern and Western Empires (see also Holy); Roman law, the system of law developed by the ancient Romans—civil law; Roman nettle, a nettle, rare in Britain, with female flowers in heads, traditionally introduced by the Romans; Roman snail, the edible snail (*Helix pomatia*), much valued by the Romans. [L. *Rōmānus—Rōma*, Rome.]

roman, *ro-mä*, *n.* a mediaeval romance, tale of chivalry: a novel.—roman à clef (*nä klä*), a *key novel*), a novel about real people under disguised names; roman à thèse (*nä tez*), a novel that sets out to demonstrate a thesis or proposition; roman fleuve (*flœv*; *lit. river novel*), a novel in a series of self-contained narratives telling the story of a family or other social group over successive generations.—Also saga novel. [Fr.]

Romance, *rō-mans'*, *n.* a general name for the vernaculars that developed out of popular Latin—French, Provençal, Italian, Spanish, Portuguese, Rumanian, Romansch, with their various dialects.—Also *adj.*—*n.* romance', a tale of chivalry, orig. one in verse, written in one of these vernaculars: any fictitious and wonderful tale: a fictitious narrative in prose or verse which passes beyond the limits of ordinary life: a Spanish historical ballad: romantic fiction as a literary genre: a romantic occurrence or series of occurrences: a love affair, (journalistically) esp. any affair involving a marriage between different social classes: romantic atmosphere or feeling: a leaning towards the romantic: an imaginative lie: romanticism: a composition of romantic character (*mus.*).—*v.i.* to write or tell romances: to talk extravagantly or with an infusion of fiction: to lie: to build castles in the air.—*n.* roman'cer.—*adj.* roman'cical (*Lamb*), dealing with romance.—*n.* and *adj.* roman'cing. [O.Fr. *romanz*—(hypothetical) L.L. *rōmānicē* (*adv.*), in (popular) Roman language.]

Romanesque, *rō-man-esk'*, *adj.* of the transition from Roman to Gothic architecture, characterised by round arches and vaults.—*n.* the Romanesque style, art, or architecture. [Fr.]

Romansch, Romansh, R(o)umansch, Rumonsch, *rō-*, *rōō-mansh'*, *-mänsh'*, *-monsh'*, *n.* and *adj.* Rhaeto-Romanic: sometimes confined to the Upper Rhine dialects. [Romansch.]

romantic, *rō-man'tik*, *adj.* pertaining to, of the nature of, inclining towards, or savouring of, romance: fictitious: extravagant, wild: fantastic.—*adj.* roman'tical.—*n.* romantical'ity.—*adv.* roman'tically.—*n.* romanticisā'tion, *-z-.*—*v.t.* roman'ticise, *-ize* (*-ti-siz*), to make seem romantic.—*v.i.* to have or express romantic ideas.—*ns.* roman'ticism (*-sizm*), romantic quality, feeling, tendency, principles, or spirit; roman'ticist.—Romantic Revival, the late 18th-century and early 19th-century revolt against classicism or

neo-classicism to a more picturesque, original, free, and imaginative style in literature and art. [Fr. *romantique*—O.Fr. *romant*, romance.]

Romany, Rommany, *rom'ə-ni*, *n.* a gypsy (also Rom'anes, *-nes*): the Indic language of the gypsies (in pure form not now common in Britain).—*adj.* gypsy.—Romany rye (*rī*), a gentleman who affects the society of gypsies. [Gypsy *rom*, man.]

romaunt, *rō-mönt'*, (*arch.*) *n.* a romance. [O.Fr. *romunt*; see romance.]

Rome, *rōm*, formerly *rōōm*, *n.* the capital of the Roman Empire, now of Italy: often used for the Roman Catholic Church or Roman Catholicism.—*adj.* and *adv.* Rome'ward.—*adv.* Rome'wards.—*n.* Rōm'ic, a phonetic notation devised by Henry Sweet, based upon the original Roman values of the letters.—*adj.* Rōm'ish, Roman Catholic (hostile): Roman (*obs.*).—Rome'-penny, -scot (*obs.*), Peter's penny; Rome'-runner (*obs.*), a self-seeking cleric who had much resort to Rome. [L. *Rōma*.]

Romeo, *rō'mi-ō*, *n.* a young man very much in love: a Don Juan in the making. [Shakespearean character.]

romp, *romp*, *v.i.* to frolic actively: to move along easily and quickly, esp. in winning a race.—*n.* one, esp. a girl, who romps: a tomboy: a vigorous frolic: a swift easy run.—*n.* romp'er, one who romps: (usu. in *pl.*) a child's garb for play (also romp'er-suit', and later bus'ter-suit').—*adv.* romp'ingly.—*adj.* romp'ish.—*adv.* romp'ishly.—*n.* romp'ishness. [ramp.]

roncador, *rong-ka-dōr'*, *-dör'*, *n.* a name for various American fishes, esp. of the maigre family, from the sounds they emit. [Sp., snorer.]

rondache, *ron-dash'*, *-däsh*, *n.* a buckler. [Fr.]

rondavel, *ron-dav'əl*, *ron'*, *n.* in S. Africa, a round hut, usu. with grass roof: a more sophisticated building of similar shape, used e.g. as guest house. [Afrik. *rondawel.*]

ronde, *rond*, *n.* a script printing-type. [Fr., round (*fem.*).]

rondeau, *ron'dō*, *rō-dō*, *n.* a form of poem characterised by closely-knit rhymes and a refrain, and, as defined in the 17th century, consisting of thirteen lines, divided into three unequal strophes, not including the burden (repeating the first few words) after the eighth and thirteenth lines—brought into vogue by Swinburne: a rondo (*mus.*):—*pl.* ron'deaux (*-dōz*).—*ns.* ron'del, a verse-form of thirteen or fourteen lines on two rhymes, the seventh and thirteenth being identical with the first, and the eighth and (if present) the fourteenth with the second: a circular part or ornament in jewellery: a circular badge; rondino (*-dē'nō*; It. dim.), a short rondo:—*pl.* rondi'nos; ron'do (It., from Fr.), a musical composition whose principal subject recurs in the same key in alternation with other subjects, often the last movement of a sonata:—*pl.* ron'dos; rondolet'to, a short rondo. [Fr. *rondeau*, earlier *rondel*—*rond*, round.]

rondure, *rond'yər*, a Shakespearian form of round-ure.

rone, roan, rhone, *rōn*, (*Scot.*) *n.* a roof-gutter. [Origin unknown.]

Roneo, *rō'ni-ō*, *n.* a duplicating machine.—*v.t.* ro'neo, to produce copies of by duplicating machine. [Trademark.]

rong, *rong* (*Spens.*), *pa.t.* of ring.

ronne, ronning (*Spens.*). Same as run (*infin.* and *pa.p.*), running.

ront, ronte (*Spens.*). Same as runt.

röntgen, roentgen, *rænt'gən*, *rent'*, *ront'*, *runt'*, also *-gen*, (sometimes *cap.*), *adj.* of the German physicist Konrad von *Röntgen* (1845-1923), discoverer of the röntgen rays, or X-rays (see X).—*n.* the international unit of dose of X-rays or gamma rays, defined in terms of the ionisation

*fāte, fär; mē, hûr (her); mīne; mōte, för; mūte; mōōn, fōōt; dhen (then)*

it produces in air under stated conditions.—
*v.t.* **rönt′genise, -ize,** to treat by röntgen rays.—
*ns.* **rönt′genogram,** a photograph made with
these rays; **röntgenog′raphy,** photography by
these rays; **röntgenol′ogy,** the study of the rays;
**röntgenos′copy,** observation by means of them;
**röntgenother′apy,** treatment of disease by means
of them.

**ronyon, runnion,** *run′yən,* (*Shak.*) *n.* a term of reproach to a woman. [Some connect with Fr.
*rogne,* mange.]

**rood,** *rōōd, n.* Christ's cross: a cross or crucifix,
esp. at the entrance to a church chancel: a
rod, pole, or perch, linear or square (with
variations in value; *locally*): the fourth part of
an acre, or forty square poles.—**rood′-beam,** a
beam for supporting the rood; **Rood Day (Holy-
rood Day, Rood′mas Day),** the feast of the
Exaltation (14th September) or of the Invention
(3rd May) of the Cross; **rood′-loft,** a gallery
over the rood-screen; **rood′-screen,** an ornamental partition separating choir from nave;
**rood′-steeple, -tower,** that over the crossing of a
church; **rood′-tree** (*obs.*), Christ's cross. [O.E.
*rōd,* gallows, cross.]

**roof,** *rōōf, n.* the top covering of a building or
vehicle: a ceiling: the overhead surface, structure, or stratum of a vault, arch, cave, excavation,
etc.: the upper covering of the mouth (the
palate) or of any cavity: a dwelling: a culmination: a high or highest plateau (as *the roof of
the world,* the Pamir): an upper limit: an
aeroplane's ceiling or limiting height:—*pl.*
**roofs.**—*v.t.* to cover with a roof: to shelter.—
*adj.* **roofed.**—*ns.* **roof′er,** one who makes or
mends roofs: a roof-board: a letter of thanks
for hospitality (*coll.*); **roof′ing,** covering with
a roof: materials for a roof: the roof itself:
shelter.—*adj.* for roofing.—*adjs.* **roof′less; roof′-
like; roof′y,** having a roof or roofs.—**roof′board,**
a board lying under slates or tiles; **roof′-garden,**
a garden on a flat roof; **roof′-guard,** a device to
prevent snow from sliding off a roof; **roof′-plate,**
a wall-plate that receives the lower ends of the
rafters of a roof; **roof′-tree,** the ridge-pole: the
roof. [O.E. *hrōf;* Du. *roef.*]

**rooinek,** *rō′i-nek, n.* an Afrikaans nickname for an
Englishman. [Afrikaans, red neck—Du. *rood,
nek,* from his complexion.]

**rook,** *rōōk, n.* a gregarious species of crow: a
sharper: a simpleton (*obs.*).—*v.t.* to fleece.—*n.*
**rook′ery,** a breeding-place of rooks in a group of
trees: a breeding-place of penguins or seals, etc.:
a crowded cluster of mean tenements: an evil
resort: a disturbance (*slang* or *dial.*).—*adjs.*
**rook′ish; rook′y** (*Shak.*), abounding in rooks:
or poss. black, murky (see **roky**). [O.E. *hrōc.*]

**rook,** *rōōk, n.* a castle in chess. [O.Fr. *roc*—Pers.
*rukh.*]

**rook,** *rōōk* (*Shak.*). Same as **ruck** (2).

**rookie, rooky,** *rōōk′i,* (*slang*) *n.* a raw beginner: a
callow recruit. [App. from **recruit.**]

**room,** *rōōm, rōōm, n.* space: necessary or available
space: space unoccupied: opportunity, scope,
or occasion: stead: a particular place: an
assigned place, as in a theatre (*obs.*): a seat (*B.*):
appointment, office: a holding of land (*obs.*): a
compartment: a chamber: a cottage sitting-
room: company in a room.—*v.t.* and *v.i.*
(chiefly *U.S.*) to lodge: to share a room or
rooms (with *with*).—*adj.* **roomed,** having rooms.
—*ns.* **room′er** (*U.S.*), a lodger, usu. taking meals
elsewhere; **room′ful,** as much or as many as a
room will hold:—*pl.* **room′fuls.**—*adv.* **room′ily.**
—*n.* **room′iness.**—*adjs.* **room′some,** roomy;
**room′y,** having ample room: wide: spacious.—
**room′-fellow,** one who shares a room; **room′ing-
house** (*U.S.*), a house with furnished rooms to
let; **room′-mate,** a fellow-lodger (*U.S.*): one
who shares a room.—*adj.* **room′-ridden,** confined

to one's room. [O.E. *rūm;* Ger. *raum,* Du.
*ruim*].

**roon,** *rōōn,* **rund,** *run(d),* *rōōn(d),* (*Scot.*) *n.* a list or
selvage: a strip or thread of cloth.—Also (*Galt*)
**royne** (*roin*). [Origin obscure.]

**roop,** *rōōp, v.i.* (*Scot.*) to make a hoarse sound.—*n.*
a hoarse sound: hoarseness.—*adjs.* **roop′it,
roop′y,** (*Scot.*) hoarse. [Variant of **roup.**]

**roose,** *rōōz,* (*Scot.*) *rūz, (dial.) v.t.* to praise. [M.E.
*rosen*—O.N. *hrōsa,* to praise.]

**roost,** *rōōst, n.* a perch or place for a sleeping bird:
a henhouse: a sleeping-place: bed: a set of
fowls resting together: a loft or garret or its roof
(*Scot.*).—*v.i.* to settle or sleep on a roost or
perch: to perch: to go to rest for the night.—
*n.* **roost′er,** a domestic cock.—**come home to
roost,** to recoil upon oneself: to return to a place
(usu. after travel) in order to settle down; **rule
the roost** (see **roast**). [O.E. *hrōst;* Du. *roest.*]

**roost,** *rōōst,* (*Orkney and Shetland*) *n.* a tidal race.
[O.N. *rōst.*]

**root,** *rōōt, n.* ordinarily and popularly, the underground part of a plant, esp. when edible: that
part of a higher plant which never bears leaves or
reproductive organs, ordinarily underground
and descending, and serving to absorb salts in
solution, but often above-ground, often arising
from other parts, often serving other functions,
though morphologically comparable (*bot.*): the
source, cause, basis, foundation, occasion of
anything, as an ancestor, an element from which
words are derived: an embedded or basal part,
as of a tooth, a hair, a dam: a growing plant
with its root: the factor of a quantity which,
taken so many times, produces that quantity
(*math.*): any value of the unknown quantity for
which an equation is true (*math.*): the fundamental note on which a chord is built (*mus.*).—
*v.i.* to fix the root: to be firmly established: to
develop a root.—*v.t.* to plant in the earth: to implant deeply: to fix by the root: to uproot (usu.
with *up*): to remove entirely by uprooting, clear
away, eradicate, extirpate (usu. with *out*).—*n.*
**root′age,** the act of striking root: state of being
rooted: roothold; root-system.—*adj.* **root′ed,**
having roots: fixed by roots or as by roots:
firmly established.—*adv.* **root′edly.**—*ns.* **root′-
edness;** **root′er.**—*adj.* **root′less.**—*n.* **root′let.**—
*adj.* **root′y,** abounding in, consisting of, or like
roots: rank.—*adj.* and *adv.* **root′-and-branch′,**
without leaving any part.—**root′-beer,** a drink
made from roots of dandelion, sassafras, etc.—
*adj.* **root′-bound,** rooted to the ground (*Milt.*):
potbound.—**root′-cap,** a sheath of cells at the tip
of a root; **root′-cause,** fundamental cause; **root′-
climber,** a plant that climbs by means of roots,
as ivy; **root′-crop,** a crop of esculent roots;
**root′-eater.**—*adjs.* **root′-fallen,** fallen, by roots
giving way; **root′-fast,** firmly rooted.—**root′-
hair,** a fine tubular outgrowth from a cell by
which a young root absorbs water; **root′hold,**
maintenance of position by roots: a footing;
**root′-house,** a summer-house built of roots: a
storehouse for potatoes, etc.; **root′-knot,** an
enlargement of a root caused by a nematode;
**root′-par′asite,** a plant parasitic on a root;
**root′-pressure,** an upward forcing of sap,
shown by the bleeding of plants.—*v.t.* **root′-
prune,** to prune the roots of.—**root′-pruning;**
**root′-rubb′er,** rubber got from the roots of
certain African apocynaceous plants; **root′-
sheath,** the sheath of the root of an orchid,
a hair, a feather, etc.; **root′stock,** rhizome,
esp. if short, thick, and more or less erect (*bot.*):
a source, ancestral form; **root′-sys′tem;** **root′-
tu′bercle,** a swelling on a root, inhabited by
symbiotic bacteria.—**strike, take root,** to root,
to become established. [Late O.E. *rōt*—O.N.
*rōt;* Dan. *rod;* Goth. *waurts,* O.E. *wyrt.*]

**root,** earlier **wroot,** *rōōt, v.t.* to turn up with the

# root 1174 rose

snout.—*v.i.* to grub: poke about.—*n.* root′er.—
*n.* and *adj.* root′ing.—*v.t.* and *v.i.* root′le, to
grub. [O.E. *wrōtan*—*wrōt*, a snout; see also
rout (3).]
root, *rōōt*, (*U.S.*) *v.i.* to shout, to applaud, encourage a contestant.—*n.* root′er. [Prob. from
rout (4).]
rooty, *rōōt′i*, (*mil. slang*) *n.* bread. [Urdu *roti*,
loaf.]
rope, *rōp*, *n.* a stout twist of fibre, wire, etc., technically over 1 in. round: a string of pearls,
onions, etc.: a glutinous stringy formation: a
local lineal measure, 20 feet: a climbing party
roped together.—*v.t.* to fasten, bind, enclose,
mark off, or (*U.S.* and *Austr.*) catch with a rope:
to hold back to avoid winning (*horse-racing*).—
*v.i.* to form into a rope.—*adjs.* rop(e)′able
(*Austr.*), of cattle or horses, wild, unmanageable:
very angry; roped (*rōpt*).—*ns.* rō′per, a ropemaker: one who ropes a horse: a decoy (also
rō′per-in′); rōp′ery, ropework: knavery.—*adv.*
rōp′ily.—*n.* rōp′iness.—*n.* and *adj.* rōp′ing.—
*adj.* rō′py, stringy: glutinous: wrinkled like
loops of rope: bad of its kind (*slang*).—rope′-
dance, a tight-rope performance; rope′-danc′er;
rope′-drilling, boring by a drill worked by a rope;
rope′-house, a storehouse for ropes: a house
where salt is crystallised from brine trickling
along ropes; rope′-ladder, a ladder of ropes;
rope′-machine; rope′-maker; rope′-making.—
*adj.* rope′-ripe, deserving to be hanged.—*v.t.*
rope′s-end, to beat with a rope's end.—*adj.*
rope′-soled, having a sole of rope.—rope′-stitch,
work in stitches laid diagonally side by side;
rope′-trick, a disappearing trick with a rope:
poss. a rhetorical figure, or, acc. to some, a trick
deserving the gallows (*Shak.*); rope′-walk, a long
narrow shed or alley for rope-spinning; rope′-
walker, a tight-rope performer; rope′way, a
means of transmission by ropes; rope′work, a
rope-walk or rope factory: a system of ropes;
rope′-yarn, yarn for making ropes, or got by untwisting ropes; rop′ing-down′, abseiling.—give
one rope (to hang oneself), to allow a person
full scope to defeat his own ends; know the
ropes (see know); on the high ropes, elated:
arrogant; rope in, bring in, enlist (esp. one who
has some reluctance); rope's end, the end of a
rope used for flogging; ropes of sand, a bond
with no cohesion. [O.E. *rāp*; O.N. *reip*, Ger.
*reif*.]
Roquefort, *rok′för*, *n.* a cheese orig. made (of ewe's
milk) at *Roquefort* in France.
roquelaure, *rok′ə-lōr*, *-lōr*, *n.* a man's short cloak
worn in the 18th and early 19th century. [Fr.,
after the Duc de *Roquelaure* (1656-1738).]
roquet, *rō′kā*, *n.* in croquet, a stroke by which the
player's ball strikes an opponent's.—*v.t.* to strike
by a roquet.—*v.i.* to play a roquet.—*n.* roque
(*rōk*), an American game, a modification of
croquet. [Prob. formed from croquet.]
rore, *rōr*, *rör*, an obs. spelling (*Shak.*) of roar
(tumult).
roric, *rō′rik*, *rö′*, rorid, *rō′rid*, *rö′*, roral, *rō′rəl*, *rö′*,
*adjs.* dewy. [L. *rōs*, *rōris*, dew.]
rorqual, *rör′kwəl*, *n.* any whale of the genus
Balaenoptera (finback). [Fr.,—Norw. *röyrkval*,
lit. red whale.]
Rorschach test, *rör′shak test*, a test, designed to
show intelligence, personality, and mental state,
in which the subject interprets ink-blots of
standard type. [Hermann *Rorschach*, Swiss
psychiatrist.]
rorty, *rör′ti*, (*slang*) *adj.* gay: rowdy.—*ns.* rort
(*Austr.*), a racket; ror′ter (*Austr.*), a spiv.
[Ety. dub.]
rory, rorie. Same as roary.
Rosa, *rōz′a*, *roz′a*, *n.* the rose genus, giving name
to the family Rosā′ceae.—*n.* rosace (*rō-zās′*, *-zäs′*;
Fr.; *archit.*), a rosette: a rose-window.—*adj.*

rosaceous (*rō-zā′shəs*), of the rose family: roselike.—*ns.* rosā′rian, a rose-fancier; rosā′rium, a
rose-garden; rosary (*rō′zər-i*), a rose-garden or
rose-bed (also ro′sery): a chaplet (*obs.*): a series
of prayers: a string of beads used by Roman
Catholics as a guide to devotions. [L. *rōsa*,
rose; *rosārium*, rose-garden; *rosāceus*, *roseus*,
rosy.]
rosaker, *ros-ā′kər*, resalgar, *res-al′gər*, obs.
variants of realgar.
rosalia, *rō-zä′lyä*, (*mus.*) *n.* a series of repetitions
of the same passage, each a tone higher. [Said to
be from an Italian folksong, *Rosalia cara mia*.]
rosaniline, *rō-zan′i-lin*, *-lēn*, *-lin*, *n.* a base derived
from aniline, with red salts used in dyeing. [rose,
aniline.]
rosary. See Rosa, rose.
rosa-solis, *rō-zä-sō′lis*, (*obs.*) *n.* the sundew: a
cordial, orig. flavoured with sundew juice, afterwards with various spices. [Orig. L. *rōs sōlis*,
dew of the sun, altered to *rōsa*, rose.]
roscid, *ros′id*, *adj.* dewy. [L. *rōscidus*—*rōs*, dew.]
Roscius, *rosh′i-əs*, *rōs′ki-ōos*, *n.* a famous Roman
actor (d. 62 B.C.): hence, a great actor.—*adj.*
Rosc′ian. [L. *Rōscius*.]
rose, *pa.t.* of rise.
rose, *rōz*, *n.* the flower of any species of the genus
Rosa—national emblem of England: shrub
bearing it, mostly prickly, with white, yellow,
pink, orange, or red flowers, numerous stamens
and carpels, achenes enclosed in the receptacle:
extended to various flowers or plants, some
little like the true rose (see, e.g., under Christmas,
guelder-rose, rock): a paragon: a rosette, esp.
on a shoe: a rose-cut stone: a rose-window: a
perforated nozzle: the typical colour of the
rose—pink or light crimson: the pink glow of
the cheeks in health: erysipelas.—*adj.* of, for,
or like the rose or roses: rose-coloured.—*v.t.* to
make like a rose, in colour or scent.—*adjs.*
roseal (*rō′zi-əl*), roselike; rō′seate (*-zi-it*, *-zi-āt*),
rosy: rose-scented: of roses: unduly favour-
able or sanguine; rosed, flushed (*Shak.*):
having a rose or roses; rose′less; rose′like.—*ns.*
rō′sery, a rose-garden (cf. rosary); rosier
(*rō′zhər*; *Spens.* rosiere, *rō-zi-är′*, *-ēr′*; Fr.
*rosier*), a rose tree or bush.—*adv.* rō′sily.—*n.*
rōsiness.—*adj.* rō′sy, of or abounding in roses:
roselike: rose-red: blooming: blushing:
bright: hopeful: promising.—*n.* (*old slang*)
wine.—*v.t.* and *v.i.* to redden.—rose′-apple, an
E. Indian tree of the clove genus: its edible
fruit; rose′-bay, the oleander (rose-bay laurel,
rose-laurel): any rhododendron: a willow-herb
(rose-bay willow-herb) common where woods
have been felled or land cleared by fire (also
fire-weed, *q.v.*); rose′-beetle, the rose-chafer:
the rose-bug; rose′-bowl, an ornamental bowl
for cut flowers; rose′-bud; rose′-bug, an
American beetle that eats roses; rose′-bush;
rose′-camp′ion, a garden species of campion
(*Lychnis coronaria*); rose′-chafer, a beetle
(*Cetonia aurata*) that eats roses.—*adj.* rose′-
cheeked.—rose′-colour, pink.—*adj.* rose′-col′-
oured, pink: seeing or representing things in
too favourable a light.—rose′-comb, a fowl's
low tubercled comb.—*adj.* rose′-combed.—
rose′-cross, a cross within a circle: a Rosicrucian.
—*adj.* rose′-cut, cut in nearly hemispherical form,
with flat base and many small facets rising to a
low point above.—rose′-di′amond, a rose-cut
diamond; rose′-drop, a rose-flavoured sweet: a
red eruption on the nose; rose′-el′der, the
guelder-rose; rose′-en′gine, an apparatus for
engine-turning; rose′-fish, the bergylt; rose′-
garden; rose′-hip, the fruit of the rose.—*adj.*
rose′-hued.—rose′-knot, a rosette of ribbon or
the like; rose′-lau′rel, oleander; rose′-leaf, the
leaf of a rose: usu. a rose-petal.—*adj.* rose′-
lipped, having red lips.—rose′-mall′ow, holly-

*fāte, fär; mē, hûr (her); mīne; mōte, för; mūte; mōōn, fōōt; dhen (then)* hock: hibiscus; **rose'-no'ble,** an old English gold coin with the figure of a rose.—*adj.* **rose'-pink,** rose-coloured: sentimental.—*n.* a pink colour: a pink pigment.—**rose'-quartz,** a rose-coloured quartz; **rose'-rash,** roseola.—*adj.* **rose'-red,** red as a rose.—**rose'-root,** a stonecrop (*Sedum rosea*) with rose-scented root; **rose'-to'paz,** a topaz coloured pink by heat; **rose'-tree,** a standard rose; **rose'-wa'ter,** water distilled from rose-leaves.—*adj.* sentimental: superfine.—**rose'-win'dow,** round window with tracery of radiating compartments; **rose'wood,** valuable heavy dark-coloured wood of many trees, notably Brazilian and Indian species of Dalbergia (Papilionaceae), said to smell of roses when fresh-cut; **rose'wood-oil,** oil of rhodium.—*adjs.* **ro'sy-bos'omed; ro'sy-cheeked; ro'sy-col'oured.**—**rosy cross,** the emblem of the Rosicrucians; **ro'sy-drop,** rose-drop. — *adjs.* **ro'sy-fing'ered,** Homer's favourite epithet (*rhodo-daktylos*) of the dawn; **ro'sy-foot'ed.**—**rose of Jericho,** a cruciferous plant (*Anastatica hiero-chuntica*) of N. Africa and Syria, that curls in a ball in drought; **rose of Sharon,** (*Song of Solomon*) probably a narcissus: now applied to a species of hibiscus; **under the rose,** in confidence; **Wars of the Roses,** a disastrous dynastic struggle in England (1455-85), between the Houses of Lancaster and York, from their emblems, the red and the white rose. [O.E. *rōse*—L. *rosa,* prob.—Gr. *rhŏdeā,* a rose-bush, *rhodon,* rose.]

**rosé,** *ro'zā, n.* a pinkish table wine in making which grape skins are removed early in fermentation. (Cf. **red wine.**) [Fr. lit., pink.]

**roseate,** etc. See **rose.**

**rosella,** *rō-zel'ə, n.* a handsome Australian para-keet, first observed at Rose Hill near Sydney. [For *rosehiller.*]

**roselle, rozelle,** *rō-zel', n.* an East Indian hibiscus.

**rosemary,** *rōz'mə-ri, n.* a small fragrant pungent Mediterranean labiate shrub (Rosmarinus). [*rōs marinus,* sea dew.]

**roseola,** *rō-zē'ə-lə, n.* rose-coloured rash: German measles. [Dim. from L. *roseus,* rosy.]

**rosery.** See **Rosa, rose.**

**roset, rosit, rozet, rozit,** *roz'it,* (*Scot.*) *n.* rosin.—*v.t.* to rosin.—*adj.* **ros'ety** (sometimes **ros'etty**), etc. [**rosin.**]

**Rosetta stone,** *rō-zet'ə stōn,* a tablet, found near Rosetta in Egypt in 1799, which carried the same inscription in hieroglyphics and demotic script and also in Greek and thus enabled a beginning to be made in deciphering hieroglyphics: any comparable first clue.

**rosette,** *rō-zet', n.* a knot of radiating loops of ribbon or the like in concentric arrangement: a close radiating group of leaves, usu. pressed to the ground: a rose-shaped ornament (*archit.*): any structure, arrangement, or figure of similar shape: a curve whose polar equation is $r = a \sin m\theta$: a disk, esp. of copper, formed by throwing water on molten metal: any of several diseases of plants (also **rosette disease**).—*adj.* **rosett'ed.** [Fr., dim. of **rose.**]

**Rosicrucian,** *roz'* or *rōz'i-krōō'sh(y)ən, n.* a member of an alleged secret society whose members made great pretensions to knowledge of the secrets of Nature, transmutation of metals, elemental spirits, magical signatures, etc.—affirmed to have been founded (1459) by Christian *Rosenkreuz:* a member of one or other of various modern fraternities.—Also *adj.* —*n.* **Rosicru'cianism.** [Prob. a Latinisation of *Rosenkreuz,* rose cross, L. *rōsa,* rose, *crux,* cross.]

**rosin,** *roz'in, n.* a resin obtained, e.g. when turpentine is prepared from dead pine wood—also called *colophony.*—*v.t.* to rub with rosin: to add rosin to.—*adj.* **ros'ined.**—*ns.* **ros'inate,** a resinate; **ros'in-oil,** an oil distilled from rosin:

**ros'in-plant, -weed,** *Silphium.*—*adj.* **ros'iny.** [**resin.**]

**Rosinante, Rozinante,** *roz-in-an'ti, n.* Don Quixote's horse: a sorry nag. [Sp. *Rocinante,* explained as *rocin antes,* formerly a rouncy.]

**rosmarine,** *roz'mə-rin,* (*Spens.*) *n.* a walrus, or a sea-monster supposed to lick dew off the rocks. [Dan. *rosmar,* walrus; influenced by the following word.]

**rosmarine,** *roz'mə-rin, -rēn, n.* rosemary (*Spens.*): sea dew (*Jonson*). [See **rosemary.**]

**Rosminian,** *ros-min'i-ən, adj.* of Antonio Rosmini-Serbati (1797-1855), his philosophy, or the Institute of Charity founded by him.—Also *n.*—*n.* **Rosmin'ianism.**

**rosolio, rosoglio,** *rō-zō'lyō, n.* a sweet cordial made with raisins (formerly, it is said, with sundew). [It. *rosolio*—L. *rōs sōlis,* dew of the sun.]

**rosser.** Variant spelling of **rozzer.**

**rost,** an old spelling of **roast.**

**rostellum,** *ros-tel'əm, n.* a little beak: a beaklike outgrowth from an orchid column: the forepart of a tapeworm's head. [L. *rōstellum,* dim. of *rōstrum,* beak.]

**roster,** *rōs'ter* (or *ros'*), *n.* a list showing order of rotation, as for army duties: any roll of names (*coll.*).—*v.t.* to put in a roster. [Du. *rooster,* orig. gridiron (from the ruled lines)—*roosten,* to roast.]

**rostrum,** *ros'trəm, rōs'trōōm, n.* a beak: (properly in *pl.,* *ros'tra*) a platform for public speaking (from the *Rostra* in the Roman forum, adorned with the beaks of captured ships).—*adjs.* **ros'tral,** of or like a rostrum; **ros'trate, -d,** beaked; **rostrocarinate** (*ros-trō-kar'in-āt;* L. *carina,* keel), beaked and keeled.—*n.* a supposed flint implement with beak and keel. [L. *rōstrum,* beak—*rōdĕre, rōsum,* to gnaw.]

**rosula,** *roz'ū-lə, n.* a leaf-rosette.—*adj.* **ros'ūlate,** in a rosette. [L.L. dim. of L. *rōsa,* rose.]

**rosy.** See **rose.**

**rot,** *rot, v.i.* to putrefy: to decay: to become corrupt: to suffer from wasting disease, esp. in prison, or sheep-rot: to talk nonsense, to chaff (*slang*).—*v.t.* to cause to rot: to chaff (*slang*):—*pr.p.* **rott'ing;** *pa.t.* and *pa.p.* **rott'ed.**—*n.* decay: putrefaction: corruption: collapse: applied to various diseases of sheep, timber, etc.: worthless or rotten stuff (*slang*): bosh (*slang*).—*interj.* expressing contemptuous disagreement.—*n.* **rott'er,** a thoroughly depraved or worthless person.—**rot'grass,** soft grass, butterwort, pennywort, or other plant reputed to cause sheep-rot; **rot'-gut,** bad liquor; **rot'-stone,** rottenstone. [O.E. *rotian,* pa.p. *rotod;* cf. **rotten.**]

**rota,** *rō'ta, n.* a roster: a course, round, routine, cycle, of duty, etc.: the Roman Catholic supreme ecclesiastical tribunal: a round, a canon, a rondo, or other composition with much repetition.—*adj.* **rō'tal.**—*ns.* **rō'taplane,** rotor-plane; **Rōtarian** (*-tā'ri-ən*), a member of a Rotary Club.—Also *adj.*—*n.* **Rōtā'rianism.**—*adj.* **rotary** (*rō'tər-i*), turning like a wheel: of the nature of rotation: working by rotation of a part: (*cap.*) of an international system of clubs with a wheel as a badge, each member being of a different occupation.—*n.* **rotary,** a rotary apparatus: (*cap.*) a Rotary Club: (*cap.*) Rotarianism: a traffic roundabout.—*adj.* **rōtāt'able.**—*v.t.* and *v.i.* **rōtāte',** to turn like a wheel: to put, take, go, or succeed in rotation.—*adj.* **rō'tate,** wheel-shaped—with united petals in a plane with almost no tube.—*n.* **rotā'tion,** a turning round like a wheel: succession in definite order, as of crops: recurrent order.—*adjs.* **rotā'tional; rota-tive** (*rō'tə-tiv*).—*n.* **rotā'tor.**—*adj.* **rotatory** (*rō'tə-tər-i; rō-tāt'ər-i*), rotary. [L. *rŏta,* a wheel, *rotāre, -ātum,* to turn.]

**rotch, rotche, roch,** *roch, n.* the little auk.—Also

rotch'ie. [Cf. Du. *rotje*, petrel; Fris. *rotgies*, pl. of *rotgoes*, brent-goose.]

rote, *rōt*, *n.* mechanical memory, repetition, or performance without regard to the meaning.—*v.t.* (*Shak*. roate) to fix by rote (according to others, to root): to discourse by rote. [Origin obscure; L. *rŏta*, a wheel, and O.Fr. *rote*, road, have been conjectured.]

rote, *rōt*, *n.* a mediaeval stringed instrument. [O.Fr. *rote*, a fiddle, prob. through Gmc. from Cclt.; W. *crwth*, Gael. *cruit*.]

rote, *rōt*, (now *U.S.*) *n.* the roar of surf. [Ety. obscure.]

rotenone, *rō'ti-nōn*, *n.* an insecticide prepared from derris and other plants. [Origin unknown.]

rother, *rodh'ər*, (*Shak.*, *emendation*) *n.* an ox, cow. —roth'er-beast. [O.E. *hrȳther*, an ox, a cow; cf. Ger. pl. *rinder*, horned cattle.]

rotifer, *rōt'if-ər*, *n.* a wheel-animalcule, or member of the Rotif'era, minute aquatic animals whose rings of waving cilia suggest a rotating wheel. [L. *rŏta*, a wheel, *ferre*, to carry.]

rôtisserie, rotisserie, *rō'tis-ri*, *rō-tēs-rē*, *n.* a cooking apparatus incorporating a spit: a shop or restaurant in which meats are cooked by direct heat. [Fr., cookshop—*rôtir*, to roast.]

rotl, *rot'l*, *n.* a variable Levantine weight. [Ar. *ratl*.]

rotograph, *rō'tə-gräf*, *n.* a photograph as of a manuscript, made directly by throwing a reversed image on a roll of sensitive paper.—*v.t.* to photograph by this method. [L. *rŏta*, a wheel, Gr. *graphein*, to write.]

rotogravure, *rō-tō-grə-vūr'*, *n.* a photogravure process using a rotary press: a print so produced. [L. *rŏta*, a wheel, Fr. *gravure*, engraving.]

rotolo, *rō'tō-lō*, an Italian form of rotl.

rotor, *rō'tər*, *n.* a rotating part, esp. of a dynamo, motor, or turbine: a revolving cylinder for propulsion of a ship: a revolving aerofoil.—ro'tor-plane, a helicopter or autogyro; ro'tor-ship; ro'tor-station, an aerodrome designed specially for helicopters. [For rotator.]

rotten, *rot'n*, *adj.* putrefied: decaying: affected by rot: corrupt: unsound: disintegrating: deplorably bad (*slang*): miserably out of sorts (*slang*).—*adv.* rott'enly.—*n.* rott'enness.—rotten borough, a borough that still (till 1832) sent members to parliament though it had few or no inhabitants; rott'enstone, a decomposed silicious limestone that has lost most of its calcareous matter, used for polishing metals.—*v.t.* to polish with rottenstone. [O.N. *rotinn*; cf. rot.]

rotten, rottan, *rot'n.* Same as ratton.

rotter, rotting, etc. See rot.

Rottweiler, *rot'vil-ər*, *n.* a large black German dog with smooth coat, used by drovers. [*Rottweil*, in S.W. Germany.]

rotula, *rot'ū-lə*, *n.* the knee-pan: a radial piece of Aristotle's lantern in sea-urchins. [L. *rotula*, dim. of *rota*, a wheel.]

rotund, *rō-tund'*, *adj.* round: rounded: nearly spherical: convexly protuberant.—*v.t.* to round. —*n.* rotund'a, a round (esp. domed) building or hall.—*adj.* rotund'ate, rounded off: orbicular. —*n.* rotund'ity, roundness: a round mass.—*adv.* rotund'ly. [L. *rotundus*—*rota*, a wheel.]

roturier, *ro-tü-ryā*, *n.* a plebeian. [Fr., prob.— L.L. *ruptūra*, ground broken by the plough—L. *rumpĕre*, *ruptum*, to break.]

rouble. Same as ruble.

roucou, *rōō-kōō'*, *n.* annatto. [Fr.,—Tupi *urucú*.]

roué, *rōō'ā*, *n.* a profligate, rake, debauchee. [A name given by Philippe, Duke of Orléans, Regent of France 1715-23, to his dissolute companions—Fr. *roué*, broken on the wheel— pa.p. of *rouer*—*roue*—L. *rota*, a wheel.]

Rouen cross, *rōō-ā kros*, a cross in fretwork as a brooch or pendant. [*Rouen* in France.]

rouge, *rōōzh*, *n.* a mixture of safflower and talc, or other powder used to redden the face: a polishing powder of hydrated ferric oxide.—*v.t.* to colour with rouge.—*v.i.* to use rouge: to blush. —Rouge Croix (*krwä*), Rouge Dragon, two of the pursuivants of the Heralds' College; rouge-et-noir (*rōōzh-ā-nwär*), a gambling card-game played on a table with two red and two black diamond marks on which stakes are laid.—Also trente-et-quarante. [Fr. *rouge*—L. *rubeus*, red.]

rouge, *rōōj*, (*Eton*) *n.* a scrimmage: a touchdown in football. [Origin unknown.]

rough, *ruf*, *adj.* uneven: rugged; unshorn: unshaven: unpolished: harsh: crude: unelaborated: without attention to minute correctness: unbroken (as a horse): coarse: rude: unrefined: ungentle: turbulent: aspirate: astringent.—*adv.* roughly: with roughness or risk of discomfort. —*n.* rough state: that which is rough: rough ground, esp. uncut grass, etc., beside a golf fairway: a piece inserted in a horse's shoe to keep him from slipping: a hooligan, a rowdy: a crude preliminary sketch, etc.—*v.t.* to make rough: to ruffle: to roughen the shoes of: to shape roughly: to treat roughly.—*n.* rough'age, refuse of grain or crops: bran, fibre, etc., in food: coarse food that promotes intestinal movement. —*v.t.* rough'en, to make rough.—*v.i.* to become rough.—*ns.* rough'er, one who performs preliminary operations; rough'ie (*Scott*), a dry bough, esp. one used as a torch.—*adj.* rough'ish. —*adv.* rough'ly.—*ns.* rough'ness, the quality of being rough: a rough place: roughage (*U.S.*); rough'y (same as roughie).—*adjs.* rough'-and-read'y, ready to hand or easily improvised, and serving the purpose well enough: willing and moderately efficient; rough'-and-tum'ble, haphazard and scrambling.—Also *adv.*—*n.* a scuffle: haphazard struggling.—*v.t.* rough'cast, to shape roughly: to cover with roughcast.—*n.* plaster mixed with small stones, used to coat walls.— *adj.* coated with roughcast.—*adj.* rough'-coat'ed. —*vs.t.* rough'-draft, -draw, to draft roughly; rough'-dry, to dry without smoothing.—*adjs.* rough'-foot'ed, with feathered feet; rough'-grained, coarse-grained.—*vs.t.* rough'-grind', to grind roughly; rough'-hew (*Shak.*), to hew to the first appearance of form.—rough'-hew'er.— *adj.* rough'-hewn.—rough'-hound, a small species of dogfish; rough'-house, (*U.S.*; also rough house) a disturbance: a brawl.—*v.i.* to brawl: to make a disturbance.—*v.t.* to maltreat.— rough justice, approximate justice, hastily assessed and carried out.—*adj.* rough'-legged, with feathered or hairy legs.—rough'-neck (*U.S. slang*), an unmannerly lout: a hooligan or tough. —*adj.* rough'-per'fect, nearly perfect in the memorising of a part.—rough'-rider, a rider of untrained horses: a horse-breaker: an army riding-master's assistant: an irregular cavalryman.—*adj.* rough'-shod, provided with roughened horse-shoes.—rough shooting, shooting over moorland (mainly grouse).—*adj.* rough'-spoken, rough in speech.—rough'-string, an intermediate support for the steps of a wooden stairway: rough'-stuff, coarse paint laid on after the priming, and before the finish: violent behaviour. —*adj.* rough'-wrought, shaped out or done roughly, or in a preliminary way.—cut up rough (see cut); ride rough-shod over, to set at nought, domineer over without consideration; rough in, to sketch in roughly; rough it, to take whatever hardships come; rough on, hard luck for: pressing hard upon; rough out, to shape out roughly; sleep rough, to sleep out-of-doors. [O.E. *rūh*, rough; Ger. *raunch*, *rauh*, Du. *ruig*.]

rought, *rōt*, an obs. pa.t. of reck.

roul, roule, obs. forms of roll.

roulade, *rōō-läd*, (*mus.*) *n.* melodic embellishment: a run, turn, etc., sung to one syllable. [Fr.]

rouleau, *rōō-lō'*, *n.* a roll or coil: a cylindrical pile

or column of coins, blood corpuscles, or other disks:—*pl.* **rouleaus, rouleaux** (-*lōz'*). [Fr.]

**roulette**, *rōōl-et'*, *n.* a little roller: a game of chance in which a ball rolls from a rotating disk into one or other of a set of compartments answering to those on which the players place their stakes: a tool with a toothed disk for engraving rows of dots, for perforating paper, etc.: a cylinder for curling hair or wigs: the locus of a point carried by a curve rolling upon a fixed curve (*geom.*). [Fr.]

**roum**, *rōōm*, an old spelling of room.—*n.* **roum'ing** (see **souming and rouming**, under **soum**).

**Roumanian.** Same as **Rumanian.**

**Roumansch.** Same as **Romansch.**

**rounce**, *rowns*, *n.* in a hand printing-press, the apparatus, or its handle, for moving the carriage. [Du. *ronse*.]

**rounceval**, *rown'si-vl*, *n.* a giant (*obs.*): a great bouncing woman (*obs.*): a marrow-fat pea.—*adj.* **gigantic.** [Poss. *Roncesvalles*, in the Pyrenees.]

**rouncy**, *rown'si*, (*arch.*) *n.* a riding-horse: a nag. [O.Fr. *ronci*.]

**round**, *rownd*, (*arch.*) *v.t.* to whisper: to whisper to.—*v.i.* to whisper. [O.E. *rūnian*, to whisper; cf. **rune.**]

**round**, *rownd*, *adj.* having a curved outline or surface: approaching a circular, globular, or cylindrical form: in a course returning upon itself: enveloping: with horizontal swing: plump: pronounced with lips contracted to a circle: smooth and full-sounding: sonorous: well finished-off: periodic, as a sentence: approximate, without regarding minor denominations: full: not inconsiderable in amount: plain-spoken: candid: honest: unsparing: without mincing: vigorous: unqualified.—*adv.* about: on all sides: every way: in a ring: in a curve: in rotation: from one to another successively: indirectly: circuitously: towards the opposite quarter: roundly (*Shak.*): in the neighbourhood.—*prep.* about: around: on every side of: all over: to every side of in succession: past, beyond.—*n.* a round thing or part: a ring, circumference, circle, or globe, esp. the earth or the sky: a ladder rung or similar rounded connecting part: a slice of toast: a cut of beef across the thigh-bone: a brewer's vessel for beer during fermentation: a projecting corner-turret (not necessarily round in shape): a carving in the round: a coil: a bend: a circuit: a course returning upon itself: a dance in a ring, or its tune: a canon sung in unison: a cycle or recurring series of events or doings: a complete revolution or rotation: an accustomed walk: a prescribed circuit: a complete series of holes in golf: scope: routine: a volley, as of firearms or applause: ammunition of one shot: a successive or simultaneous action of each member of a company or player in a game: a portion dealt around to each: a bout, as in boxing: a defined stage in a competition: roundness: the condition of being visible from all sides, not merely in relief (*sculp.*).—*v.t.* to make round: to surround: to go round: to turn round: to finish off: to give finish to.—*v.i.* to become round: to go round: to go the rounds.—*adj.* **round'ed**, (of a sound) round: finished, complete, developed to perfection.—*ns.* **round'edness; round'er**, one who or that which rounds: a thing that is round (see also **roundure**): one who goes the round: a complete circuit in rounders: (in *pl.*) a bat-and-ball game in which players run from station to station.—*n.* and *adj.* **round'ing.**—*adj.* **round'ish.**—*adv.* **round'ly.**—*n.* **round'ness.**—*adj.* **round'about,** circuitous: indirect: cut evenly, without tails or train: plump.—*n.* a merry-go-round: a place where traffic circulates in one direction: a devious way: a round earthwork: a round dance: a short jacket (*U.S.*).—*v.i.* to go

round and round.—(*facet.*) **roundaboutā'tion, roundaboutil'ity.**—*advs.* **roundabout'edly, round'-aboutly.** — **round'aboutness.** — *adjs.* **round'arch, -ed,** having semicircular arches; **round'-arm,** with nearly horizontal swing of the arm; **round'-backed.**—**round dance,** a dance in a ring: a dance in which couples revolve about each other.—*adjs.* **round'-eared; round'-eyed; round'-faced.**—**round'-fish,** any fish other than a flat fish: the carp: an American whitefish; **round game,** a game, esp. a card-game, in which each plays for his own hand; **round'hand,** a style of penmanship in which the letters are well rounded and free; **Round'head,** a Puritan (from the close-cut hair).—*adj.* **round'-head'ed,** puritanical: having a round head, top or end: brachycephalic.—**round'-house,** a lock-up (*obs.*): a cabin on the after part of the quarter-deck: an engine-house with a turntable (*U.S.*).—*adj.* **round'-leaved.**—**round'-mouth,** a cyclostome.—*adjs.* **round'-mouthed; round'-nosed.**—**round robin (Robin),** a paper with signatures in a circle, that no one may seem to be a ringleader.—*adj.* **round'-shoul'dered,** with shoulders bending forward from the back.—**rounds'man,** one who goes round, esp. one sent by a shopkeeper to take orders and deliver goods: a policeman who acts as inspector (*U.S.*).—*adj.* **round'-ta'ble,** meeting on equal terms, like the inner circle of King Arthur's knights, who sat at a round table.—**round tower,** a tall tapering tower of circular section, of early Christian origin, common in Ireland; **round'-trip,** a trip to a place and back again.—*adj.* (*U.S.*) return.—**round'-top,** a mast-head platform; **round'-up,** a driving together, as of all the cattle on a ranch, a set of persons wanted by the police, etc.—*adj.* **round'-winged.**—**round'-worm,** a threadworm or nematode, a member of the Nematoda, unsegmented animals with long rounded body, mostly parasitic.—**bring, come, round** (see **bring, come**); **get round to,** to have the time or inclination to do (something) after delay; **in round numbers,** roughly, approximately; **in the round,** capable of being viewed from all sides, not merely in relief: taking everything into consideration: with all features, etc., fully displayed; **round about,** an emphatic form of round: the other way about: about; **round off,** to finish off neatly; **round on,** to turn on, assail in speech; **round out,** to fill out to roundness; **round the bend** (see **bend**); **round the clock,** for twenty-four hours on end; **round to,** to turn the head of a ship to the wind; **round up,** to ride round and collect: to gather in (wanted persons). [O.Fr. *rund* (Fr. *rond*)—L. *rotundus*—*rōta,* a wheel.]

**roundel**, *rown'dl*, *n.* anything circular: a circle: a disk: a ladder rung: a ring-dance, a rondel: a round turret.—*ns.* **roun'delay,** a song with a refrain: a dance in a ring; **roun'dle,** a roundel; **round'let** (-*lit*), a little circle or disk; **rown'dell** (*Spens.*), a bubble. [O.Fr. *rondel, -le, rondelet,* dims. of *rond,* round.]

**roundure**, *rownd'yar* (*Shak.* **round'er, rond'ure**), *n.* roundness: a round form or space: a circle, circuit: a globe. [Fr. *rondeur*—*rond,* round.]

**roup**, *rowp*, (*Scot.*) *n.* sale by auction.—*v.t.* to sell by auction.—**rouping'-wife,** a woman who conducts or buys at auctions. [Scand.]

**roup**, *rōōp*, *n.* an infectious disease of the respiratory passages of poultry: hoarseness (*Scot.*).—*adjs.* **roup'it** (*Scot.*); **roup'y.** [Perh. imit.]

**rouse**, *rowz*, *v.t.* to shake the feathers of (orig. *refl.*; *obs.*): to ruffle, set up (*obs.*): to start, as from cover or lair: to stir up: to awaken: to disturb (*rare*): to excite: to put in action: to haul in (as a cable).—*v.i.* to shake oneself (*obs.*): to rise from cover (*rare*): to stand erect (of hair; *Shak.*): to awake: to be excited to action.—*n.* a shake of the feathers, body, etc.

(*obs.*): reveille.—*adj.* rous′ant (*her.*), rising as a bird.—*ns.* rouse′about (*Austr.*), an odd man on a station; rouse′ment (*U.S.*), religious excitement; rous′er, one who, or that which, rouses: anything astonishing.—*adj.* rous′ing, awakening: stirring: vigorously active: great: violent.— *adv.* rous′ingly.—*v.t.* roust, to stir up: to rout out.—*v.i.* to move energetically.—*ns.* roust′-about, a wharf labourer (*U.S.*): one who does odd jobs (*U.S.*): a rouseabout (*U.S.* and *Austr.*); roust′er, a roustabout. rouse on (*Austr.*), to reprove. [Origin obscure.]

rouse, rowz, (*arch.*) *n.* a carousal: a bumper. [Prob. from carouse; poss. Scand. *rus*, drunkenness.]

roussette, rōō-set′, *n.* a fruit-bat: a dogfish. [Fr.]

roust, roustabout, rouster. See rouse (1).

rout, rowt, *n.* a tumultuous crowd: a rabble: a pack, herd, or flock: a large party: a fashionable evening assembly: a defeated body: an utter defeat: disorderly flight: disturbance: brawl: riot: clamour: a fuss.—*v.i.* to behave riotously. —*v.t.* to defeat utterly: to put to disorderly flight.—*n.* rout′ing, going to receptions.—*adj.* rout′ous.—*adv.* rout′ously.—rout′-cake, a rich sweet cake for receptions (*Thackeray*); rout′-seat, a bench hired out for routs. [O.Fr. *route*, from the pa.p. of L. *rumpĕre*, *ruptum*, to break.]

rout, rowt, *v.i.* to snore. [O.E. *hrūtan*.]

rout, rowt, *v.t.* to grub up, as a pig: to scoop out: to turn up: to turn out, fetch out: to rummage out: to bring to light.—*v.i.* to grub: to poke about.—*n.* rout′er. [An irreg. variant of root (2).]

rout, rowt, (*dial.*) *v.i.* and *v.t.* to roar. [O.N. *rauta*.]

route, rōōt (formerly, and still in the army, rowt), *n.* a way, course that is or may be traversed: marching orders.—*v.t.* to fix the route of: to send by a particular route.—route′-march, a long march of troops in training; route′-step, an order of march in which soldiers are not required to keep step.—route-proving flight, a flight of aeroplanes sent out to test the possibilities and advantages of variants of a new service. [Fr.,—L. *rupta* (*via*), broken (way); see rout (1).]

routh, rowth, rowth, (*Scot.*) *n.* abundance.—*adj.* plentiful.—*adj.* routh′ie. [Origin obscure.]

routine, rōō-tēn′, *n.* regular, unvarying, or mechanical course of action or round: the set series of movements gone through in a dancing, skating, or other performance.—*adj.* keeping an unvarying round: forming part of a routine.—*ns.* routineer′; routi′nism; routi′nist. [Fr.]

roux, rōō, *n.* a thickening made of equal quantities of butter and flour cooked together. [Fr. (*beurre*) *roux*, brown (butter).]

rove, rōv, *v.t.* to wander over or through: to discharge at random.—*v.i.* to practise piracy: to aim, as in archery, at some casual mark: to wander about: to ramble: to change about inconstantly: to troll with live bait.—*n.* wandering: a mode of incomplete ploughing.—*n.* rō′ver, a pirate: a robber: a random or distant mark: an arrow for shooting at rovers: a wanderer: an inconstant person: a croquet ball or player ready to peg out: (formerly) member of a senior branch of (Boy) Scout organisation (also rover scout).—*n.* and *adj.* rō′ving.—*adv.* rō′vingly.—rove′-over, (of a kind of verse in sprung rhythm) having an extra syllable at the end of one line, which forms a foot with the beginning of the next line.—at rovers, at a distant mark: at random: conjecturally. [Partly at least from Du. *rooven*, to rob, *roofer*, robber—*roof*, plunder; perh. partly from a Midland form of obs. Northern English *rave*, to wander.]

rove, rōv, *v.t.* to twist slightly in preparation for spinning.—*n.* a roved sliver.—*ns.* rō′ver, a

machine for roving: one who attends it; rō′ving, the process of giving the first twist to yarn: rove. [Origin obscure.]

rove-beetle, rōv′-bē′tl, *n.* the devil's coach-horse, or other beetle of the family Staphylinidae. [Cf. Du. *roof-kever*, lit. reif chafer—*roof*, robbery.]

row, rō, *n.* a line or rank of persons or things, as seats, houses, turnips: a series in line, or in ordered succession: often in street-names, of a single or double line of houses.—*v.t.* (*rare*) to set in or with a row or rows.—a hard row to hoe, a destiny fraught with hardship; in a row, in unbroken sequence; twelve-tone, -note, row (see twelve, serial). [O.E. *rāw*; Ger. *reihe*, Du. *rij*.]

row, rō, *v.t.* to propel with an oar: to transport by rowing: to achieve, render, perform, effect, compete in, by use of oars; to use, as an oar.—*v.i.* to work with the oar: to be moved by oars.—*n.* an act or spell of rowing: a journey in a rowing-boat.—*adj.* row′able, capable of being rowed or rowed on.—*n.* row′er.—row′-barge; row′boat (*U.S.*); row′ing-boat; row′-port, a small square hole for an oar in a vessel's side. [O.E. *rōwan.*]

row, row, *n.* a noisy squabble: a brawl: a din, hubbub: a chiding or rating.—*v.t.* (*obs.*) to rag: to rate.—*v.i.* to make a disturbance. [A late 18th-century word, poss. a back-formation from rouse (2).]

row, row, *n.* and *vb.* a Scots form of roll.

row, row, an obs. or dial. form of rough.

rowan, row′an, also rō′an, *n.* the mountain-ash (*Sorbus*, or *Pyrus*, *aucuparia*), a tree of the rose family with pinnate leaves: its small red berry-like fruit.—row′an-berry; row′an-tree. [Cf. Norw. *raun*, Sw. *rönn*.]

row-dow(-dow), row′-dow′(-dow′), *n.* the sound of a drum.—*n.* rowdedow′, rowdydow′, hubbub. —*adj.* row′dy-dow′dy, uproarious. [Echoic.]

rowdy, row′di, *n.* orig. a lawless American backwoodsman: a noisy, turbulent person.—Also *adj.*—*adv.* row′dily.—*n.* row′diness.—*adj.* row′dyish.—*n.* row′dyism. [Origin unknown.]

rowdy, row′di, *n.* (*obs.* slang) *n.* money.

rowel, row′al, *n.* a little spiked wheel on a spur: the rowel-head: a knob, ring, or disk on a horse's bit: a disk used as a seton for animals.— *v.t.* to prick with the rowel:—*pr.p.* row′elling; *pa.t.* and *pa.p.* row′elled.—row′el-head, the axis of a rowel; row′el-spur, a spur with a rowel. [Fr. *rouelle*—L.L. *rotella*, dim. of L. *rŏta*, a wheel.]

rowen, row′an, *n.* aftermath.—Also row′an, row′-ing, raw′ing, rawn (rön). [From a Northern form of O.Fr. *regain*.]

rowlock, rol′ak, rul′, rōl,′ *n.* a contrivance serving as fulcrum for an oar.—Also roll′ock, rull′ock. [Prob. for oarlock—O.E. *ārloc*.]

rowme, rowm, (*Spens.*) *n.* room: station. [room.]

rownd, an obs. spelling of round (1 and 2).

rowt. Same as rout (3).

rowth. Same as routh.

Roxburghe, roks′bar-a, *n.* a style of binding for books, with cloth or paper sides, plain leather back, gilt top, other edges untrimmed, named from the Duke of *Roxburghe* (1740-1804), book-collector.

royal, roi′al, *adj.* of a king or queen: kingly: being a king or queen: of a reigning family: founded, chartered, or patronised by a king or queen: magnificent: of more than common size or excellence: of writing-paper, 19 by 24 in., of printing-paper, 20 by 25 (royal octavo, a book size 6¼ by 10 in.).—*n.* a royal person: a gold coin of various kinds: a sail immediately above the topgallant sail: formerly a stag's second tine, now the third: a stag of twelve points.—*n.* roy′alet, a petty king.—*v.t.* roy′alise, -ize, (*Shak.*)

to make royal or (*Milt.*) royalist: to fill with royal presence.—*v.i.* to play the king.—*ns.* roy'alism, attachment to monarchy; roy'alist, an adherent of royalism: a cavalier during the English civil war: in American history, an adherent of the British government: in French history, a supporter of the Bourbons.—Also *adj.* —*adv.* roy'ally.—*n.* roy'alty, kingship: the character, state, or office of a king: kingliness: the person of the sovereign: members of royal families collectively or (*coll.*) one such member: a queen-bee, queen-termite, etc.: kingdom: royal authority: a right or prerogative granted by a king or queen, esp. a right over minerals: payment to an author, composer, etc., for every copy sold or every public performance: the area of a royal domain: a royal burgh.— **Royal Academy**, an academy of fine arts in London, founded in 1768, to which members and associates are elected (in very limited number): a teaching, degree-giving academy of music in London; **royal blue**, a bright, deep-coloured blue; **royal commission**, a body of persons nominated by the Crown to inquire into and report on some matter; **royal fern** (*Osmunda regalis*), the most striking of British ferns; **royal fish**, a 'fish' that is the king's perquisite when cast ashore or caught near the land (whale, sturgeon, porpoise); **royal jelly**, the food of a developing queen-bee; **royal marriage**, in bezique, king and queen of trumps; **royal mast**, the fourth and highest part of the mast, commonly made in one piece with the top-gallant mast; **royal palm**, a palm (*Oreodoxa regalis*) of the cabbage-palm genus; **Royal Peculiar**, an ecclesiastical peculiar whose superior is the sovereign; **royal road**, a short and easy way of circumventing difficulties; **royal tennis**, the old game of tennis, distinguished from lawn tennis. —**the Royals**, formerly the first regiment of foot in the British Army (the Royal Scots). [Fr.,— L. *rēgālis*, regal.]

**royne, roin** (*Spens.*) *v.i.* to mutter, growl, roar. [Prob. conn. with groin (2).]

**royne.** See roon.

**roynish, roin'ish,** (*Shak.*) *adj.* scurvy, mangy: mean. [O.Fr. *roigne*, mange.]

**royster,** etc. Same as roister, etc.

**rozelle.** Same as roselle.

**rozet, rozit.** See roset.

**rozzer, roz'ər,** (*slang*) *n.* a policeman. [Orig. obscure.]

**rub, rub,** *v.t.* to apply friction to: to move something with pressure along the surface of: to move with pressure along the surface of something: to clean, polish, or smooth by friction: to remove, erase, or obliterate by friction (usu. with *away, off, out*): to grind, sharpen, chafe, treat, by friction: to cause to pass by friction (with *in, through,* etc.): to impede (*Shak.*): to irritate, fret: to take a rubbing of.—*v.i.* to apply, or move with, friction: to meet an impediment (esp. of a bowl): to chafe: to grate: to fret: to make shift to get along somehow: to admit of being rubbed: —*pr.p.* rubb'ing; *pa.t.* and *pa.p.* rubbed.—*n.* process or act of rubbing: an impediment, or a meeting with an impediment (*bowls*): an inequality or uneven place: a difficulty: a hitch: an irritating experience.—*n.* rubb'er, one who, or that which, rubs or massages: an eraser: a thing for rubbing with, as a hard brush, a file, a whetstone, emery-cloth, a coarse towel, a polishing-pad: a rubbing part of a machine: a soft brick that can be cut and smoothed: an uneven place: a rub or impediment in bowls: a rebuff or irritating experience: caoutchouc, india-rubber, or a substitute: a piece of india-rubber, esp. for erasing, or as part of a brake: (*pl.*) plimsolls: india-rubber overshoe (*U.S.*): rubber-neck (*U.S.*): condom (*U.S.*): (*pl.*) sheep disease

with heat, itchiness.—*adj.* of, yielding, or concerned with, india-rubber.—*v.t.* to coat, cover, or furnish with rubber.—*v.i.* (*U.S.*) to rubber-neck.—*v.t.* rubb'erise, -ize, to treat or coat with rubber.—*adj.* rubb'ery, resembling rubber in some quality.—*n.* rubb'ing, application of friction: experience of rubs (*Shak.*): an impression of an inscribed surface produced by rubbing heel-ball or plumbago upon paper laid over it.—*adj.* rubb'er-cored, of a golf-ball, having a tightly wound band of rubber enclosed in a gutta-percha cover.—rubb'er-ne:k, (*U.S.*) one who cranes or twists his neck in curiosity.—*v.i.* (*U.S.*) to behave as a rubber-neck.—rubb'er-solu'tion, a solution of rubber in naphtha or carbon disulphide, for repairing pneumatic tires; rubb'er-stamp, stamp of rubber for making inked impressions: one unquestioningly devoted to routine or officialdom.—*v.t.* to imprint with a rubber-stamp: approve without exercise of judgment.—Also *adj.*—rubb'ing-post, one for cattle to rub against; rubb'ing-stone, a stone for smoothing; rub'down, an act or experience of rubbing down; rub'stone, a whetstone.—rub down, to rub from head to foot: to search by passing the hands over the body; rub in, to force into the pores by friction: to be unpleasantly insistent in emphasising; rub on (or of) the green (*golf*), a chance outside interference with the ball:—also *fig.*; rub out, to erase: to murder (*slang*); rub shoulders, to come into social contact; rub the wrong way, to irritate by tactless handling; rub up, to polish: to freshen one's memory of. [Cf. L.G. *rubben*.]

**rub.** See rubber (2).

**rub, rub,** a Scots form of rob:—*pa.t.* rubb'it, rubb'et.

**rub-a-dub(-dub), rub'ə-dub(-dub'),** *n.* the sound of a drum. [Echoic.]

**rubato, rōō-bä'tō,** (*mus.*) *adj.* and *adv.* in modified or distorted rhythm. [It., pa.p. of *rubare*, to steal.]

**rubber, rubberise,** etc. See under rub (1).

**rubber, rub'ər,** *n.* formerly in bowls (also rubbers, *sing.* or *pl.*), now chiefly in bridge and whist, the winning of, or play for, the best of three games (sometimes five): vaguely, a spell of card-playing: in bowls also a rub (see rub, 1).—Also rub. [Origin obscure.]

**rubbish, rub'ish,** *n.* fragments of ruinous buildings: waste matter: litter: trash: trumpery: nonsense.—*adjs.* rubb'ishing; rubb'ishly (*rare*); rubb'ishy, worthless: paltry: trashy.—rubb'ish-heap. [Origin obscure; app. conn. with rubble.]

**rubble, rub'l,** *n.* loose fragments of rock or ruined buildings: undressed irregular stones used in rough masonry and in filling in: masonry of such a kind.—*adj.* of rubble.—*adj.* rubb'ly.—rubb'le-stone; rubb'le-work, coarse masonry. [Origin obscure; cf. rubbish.]

**rube, rōōb,** (*U.S.*) *n.* a country bumpkin: an uncouth, unsophisticated person. [*Reuben.*]

**rubefy, rōō'bi-fī,** *v.t.* to redden.—*adj.* rubefacient (-fā'shənt), reddening.—*n.* an external application that reddens the skin.—*n.* rubefaction (-fak'shən), reddening. [L. *rubefacĕre—rubeus*, red, *facĕre*, to make.]

**rubella, rōō-bel'a,** *n.* German measles, an infectious disease with pink rash, like measles but milder.—*ns.* rubell'an (or rōō'), an altered biotite; rubell'ite, a red tourmaline; rubeola (-bē'o-la), measles: German measles. [Dims. from L. *rubeus*, red.]

**Rubia, rōō'bi-a,** *n.* the madder genus, giving name to the **Rubia'ceae**, a family of sympetalous dicotyledons akin to the Caprifoliaceae.—*adj.* rubia'ceous. [L. *rubia*, madder—*rubeus*, reddish.]

**rubicelle, rōō'bi-sel,** *n.* an orange-coloured spinel. [Fr., prob.—*rubis*, ruby.]

Rubicon, rōōb'i-kon, -kən, n. a stream of Central Italy (perhaps the Fiumicino), separating Caesar's province of Gallia Cisalpina from Italia proper—its crossing by Caesar (49 B.C.) being thus a virtual declaration of war against the republic: (without *cap*.) in piquet, the winning of a game before one's opponent scores 100.—*v.t.* to defeat in this way.—cross the Rubicon, take a decisive, irrevocable step. [L. *Rubicō*, *-ōnis*.]

rubicund, rōō'bi-kund, -kənd, *adj.* ruddy.—*n.* rubicund'ity. [L. *rubicundus*—*rubēre*, to be red.]

rubidium, rōō-bid'i-əm, n. a soft silvery-white metallic element (Rb; at. numb. 37). [L. *rubidus*, red (so called from two red lines in its spectrum).]

rubify, a less commendable spelling of rubefy.

rubiginous, rōō-bij'i-nəs, *adj.* rusty-coloured.— Also rubig'inose (-nōs). [L. *rūbigō* or *rōbigō*, *-inis*, rust.]

rubin, etc. See ruby.

ruble, rouble, rōō'bl, n. the Russian monetary unit, 100 kopecks. [Russ. *rubl'*, perh.—*rubit'*, to cut; or Pers. *rūpiya*, a rupee.]

rubric, rōō'brik, (*arch.*) n. red ochre: a heading, guiding rule, entry, liturgical direction, orig. one in red: a flourish after a signature: a thing definitely settled.—*adj.* in red: ruddy: inscribed with book titles (*obs.*).—*adj.* ru'brical.—*adv.* ru'brically.—*v.t.* ru'bricate, to mark with red: to write or print in red: to make a red-letter saint: to furnish with rubrics: to regulate by rubric.—*ns.* rubricā'tion; rubricā'tor; rubrician (-*brish'ən*), one who follows, or is versed in, liturgical rubrics. [L. *rubrica*, red ochre—*ruber*, red.]

Rubus, rōō'bəs, n. the raspberry and bramble genus of the rose family. [L. *rubus*, a bramble-bush.]

ruby, rōō'bi, n. a highly-prized stone, a pure transparent red corundum: extended to other stones, as varieties of spinel and garnet: redness: applied to various red things (lip, pimple, wine, glass, blood): a type smaller than non-pareil and larger than pearl (5½ points; *print.*).—*adj.* red as a ruby.—*v.t.* to redden:—*pr.p.* ru'bying; *pa.t.* and *pa.p.* ru'bied.—*adj.* ru'bied, red as a ruby.—*n.* ru'bin, ru'bine (-*bin*; *Spens.*), a ruby.—*adjs.* rubin'eous; ru'bious, ruby, red, ruddy.—*adjs.* ru'by-coloured; ru'by-red'.—ru'by-sil'ver, proustite: pyrargyrite; ru'by-spinel', a ruby-red spinel (also *spinel-ruby*); ru'by-tail, a gold-wasp, or cuckoo-fly; ru'by-throat, a humming-bird with a ruby gorget.—*adj.* ru'by-throated. [O.Fr. *rubi* and *rubin*—L. *rubeus*—*ruber*, red.]

ruc. Same as roc.

ruche, rōōsh, n. a plaited frilling.—*v.t.* to trim with ruche.—*n.* ruch'ing. [Fr.; prob. Celt.]

ruck, *ruk*, n. a wrinkle, fold, or crease.—*v.t.* and *v.i.* to wrinkle.—*n.* ruck'le, a pucker, crease.—*v.t.* and *v.i.* to pucker, crease. [O.N. *hrukka*, a wrinkle.]

ruck, *ruk*, *v.i.* to squat: to crouch down: to cower: to huddle.—*v.t.* (*Shak.* rook, rōōk, *refl.*) to set squatting. [Prob. Scand.; cf. Norw. dial. *ruka*, to crouch.]

ruck, *ruk*, n. a heap, stack, or rick, as of fuel, hay, etc.: a multitude: the common run.—*v.t.* to heap. [Prob. Scand.]

ruckle, *ruk'l*, (*Scot.*) n. a rattle in the throat: a gurgle.—*v.i.* to rattle: to gurgle. [Cf. Norw. dial. *rukl*.]

rucksack, rōōk', *ruk'sak*, -*zak*, n. a bag carried on the back by tourists. [Ger. dial. *ruck* (Ger. *rücken*), back, and Ger. *sack*, bag.]

ruckus, *ruk'əs*, (*U.S.*) n. a disturbance. [Perh. a combination of ruction and rumpus.]

ructation, *ruk-tā'shən*, (*obs.*) n. eructation. [L. *ructāre*, to belch.]

ruction, *ruk'shən*, (*slang*) n. a disturbance: a rumpus. [Poss. for insurrection.]

rud, *rud*, n. redness: flush: complexion: ruddle (*dial.*).—*v.t.* (*Spens.*) to redden:—*pa.p.* rudd'ed. [O.E. *rudu*, redness, *rēodan*, to redden.]

rudas, rōō'dəs, (*Scot.*) n. a foul-mouthed old woman: a randy, a hag.—*adj.* coarse. [Origin obscure.]

Rudbeckia, *rud-* or *rōōd-bek'i-a*, n. a N. American genus of composites, of the sunflower sub-family. [Named by Linnaeus in honour of Swedish botanist(s) *Rudbeck*, father and/or son.]

rudd, *rud*, n. the red-eye, a fish close akin to the roach. [Prob. O.E. *rudu*, redness.]

rudder, *rud'ər*, n. a steering apparatus: a flat structure hinged to the stern of a ship or boat for steering: a vertical control surface for steering an aeroplane to right or left: (*fig.*) something, as a principle, that guides a person in life.—*adj.* rudd'erless.—rudd'er-fish, the pilot-fish, or other fish that accompanies ships. [O.E. *rōthor*, oar; Ger. *ruder*, oar.]

ruddle, *rud'l*, n. red ochre.—*v.t.* to mark with ruddle: to rouge coarsely.—Also radd'le, redd'le.—rudd'leman, one who digs or deals in ruddle.—Also radd'leman, redd'leman. [Cf. rud.]

ruddock, *rud'ək*, n. the redbreast: a gold coin: a kind of apple. [O.E. *rudduc*; cf. rud.]

ruddy, *rud'i*, *adj.* red: reddish: of the colour of the skin in high health: rosy, glowing, bright: (euphemistically) bloody:—*comp.* rudd'ier, *superl.* rudd'iest.—*v.t.* to make red:—*pr.p.* rudd'ying; *pa.t.* and *pa.p.* rudd'ied.—*adv.* rudd'ily.—*n.* rudd'iness. [O.E. *rudig*; cf. rud, red.]

rude, rōōd, *adj.* uncultured: unskilled: discourteously unmannerly: ungentle: harsh: crude: undeveloped: unwrought: coarse: rugged: rough: roughly or unskilfully fashioned: violent: robust.—*adv.* (*rare*) rudely.—*adv.* rude'ly.—*ns.* rude'ness; rudesby (rōōdz'bi; *Shak.*), an uncivil fellow.—*adj.* rud'ish. [L. *rudis*, rough.]

ruderal, rōō'dər-əl, (*bot.*) *adj.* growing in waste places or among rubbish. [L. *rūdus*, *-eris*, rubbish.]

Rüdesheimer, Rudesheimer, *rü'*, rōō'dəs-hī-mər, n. a white Rhine wine—named from *Rüdesheim*, opposite Bingen.

rudiment, rōōd'i-mənt, n. (usu. in *pl.*) a first principle or element: anything in a rude or first state: an organ in the first discernible stage: often applied to an organ that never develops beyond an early stage.—*adj.* rudimental (-*ment'l*), rudimentary.—*adv.* rudimen'tarily.—*n.* rudimen'tariness.—*adj.* rudimen'tary, of rudiments: elementary: in an early or arrested stage of development. [L. *rudimentum*—*rudis*, rough, raw.]

rue, rōō, n. a strong-smelling shrubby Mediterranean plant (*Ruta graveolens*), with pinnately divided leaves and greenish-yellow flowers, punningly (see next word) symbolic of repentance, compunction, or compassion: any other member of its genus: extended with qualification to other plants (see goat's-rue, meadow-rue, wall-rue).—*adj.* rue'-leaved. [Fr. *rue*—L. *rūta*—Peloponnesian Gr. *rhytē*.]

rue, rōō, n. repentance: regret: sorrow: pity.—*v.t.* to affect with regret, grieve (*arch.*): to be sorry for: to repent of: to wish not to have been or happened: to compassionate.—*v.i.* to feel remorse or regret: to take pity: to change one's mind, contemplate backing out:—*pr.p.* rue'ing, ru'ing; *pa.t.* and *pa.p.* rued.—*adj.* rue'ful, sorrowful: piteous: deplorable: mournful: melancholy.—*adv.* rue'fully.—*ns.* rue'fulness; ru(e)'ing, repentance.—rue'-bargain, a forfeit for withdrawing from a bargain.—take the rue (*Scot.*), to change one's mind, esp. about an intended marriage. [O.E. *hrēow*, n., *hrēowan*, vb.; cf. Ger. *reue*, O.H.G. *hriuwa*, mourning.]

**ruelle**, *rü-el'*, *n.* the space between a bed and the wall: a bed-chamber where great French ladies held receptions in the morning in the 17th and 18th centuries: a morning reception: a narrow lane. [Fr., dim. of *rue*, street.]

**Ruellia**, *rōō-el'i-a*, *n.* a genus of the acanthus family. [Named after the French botanist Jean *Ruel* (1479-1537).]

**rufescent**, *rōō-fes'ənt*, *adj.* inclining to redness. [L. *rufescens, -entis*, pr.p. of *rŭfēscĕre*, to turn reddish—*rūfus, reddish*.]

**ruff**, *ruf*, *n.* a frill, usu. starched and plaited, worn round the neck, esp. in the reigns of Elizabeth and James; a beast's or bird's collar of long hair or feathers: a ruffed breed of domestic pigeons.—*v.t.* to furnish with a ruff: to ruffle (*Spens.*): to strike without securing (*falconry*).—*adj.* **ruffed** (*ruft*), having a ruff. [Cf. **ruffle**.]

**ruff**, *ruf*, *n.* a kind of sandpiper, the male with an erectile ruff during the breeding season:—*fem.* **reeve, ree**. [Poss. ruff (1), but the fem. is a difficulty.]

**ruff**, *ruf*, *n.* an old card-game, slam, trump (also called **ruff and honours**): an act of trumping.—*v.t.* and *v.i.* to trump. [Perh. conn. with O.Fr. *roffle*, It. *ronfa*, a card-game.]

**ruff**, *ruf*, *n.* a low vibrating beat of a drum: applause, esp. with the feet (*Scot.*).—*v.t.* and *v.i.* to beat or be beaten with a ruff: to applaud (*Scot.*).—*ns.* **ruff'-a-duff'**, drumming; **ruff'le**, a ruff of drums.—*v.i.* to ruff. [Prob. imit.]

**ruff**, *ruf*, a variant of rough.

**ruff, ruffe**, *ruf*, *n.* the pope, a small fresh-water fish of the perch family, with one dorsal fin. —*n.* **ruff'in**, (*Spens.*) the ruff. [Perh. rough.]

**ruff, ruffe**, *ruf*, (*obs.*) *n.* pitch or height of exaltation: elation: excitement. [Cf. Sw. *ruff*, spirit.]

**ruffian**, *ruf'i-ən, -yən*, *n.* a brutal, violent person: a bully.—*adj.* brutal: ruffianly: violent.—*v.i.* to play the ruffian.—*adj.* **ruff'ianish**.—*n.* **ruff'ianism**.—*adj.* **ruff'ianly**.—*adj.* **ruff'ian-like**. [O.Fr. *ruffian* (Fr. *rufien*); source obscure.]

**ruffle**, *ruf'l*, *v.t.* to make uneven, disturb the smoothness of: to set up (as feathers): to wrinkle: to disorder: to agitate: to turn the leaves of hastily: to disturb the equanimity of, to irritate, discompose.—*v.i.* to wrinkle: to grow rough: to flutter.—*n.* a frill, esp. at the wrist or neck: a ruff: a rippled condition: annoyance: a quarrel: agitation.—*adj.* **ruff'led**, having a ruffle.—*n.* **ruff'ler**, an apparatus for making ruffles.—*n.* and *adj.* **ruff'ling**. [Cf. L.G. *ruffelen*.]

**ruffle**, *ruf'l*, *v.i.* to struggle: to bluster: to swagger.—*v.t.* to handle roughly or offensively: to snatch (*Shak.*).—*n.* an encounter, a tumult: bustle (*Shak.*).—*n.* **ruff'ler**, a beggar posing as a maimed soldier (*obs.*): a swaggerer. [Origin obscure.]

**ruffle.** See ruff (4).

**ruffler.** See ruffle (1) and (2).

**rufous**, *rōō'fəs*, *adj.* reddish or brownish-red. [L. *rūfus*, akin to *ruber*, red.]

**rug**, *rug*, *n.* a coarse, rough woollen fabric (*obs.*): a thick, heavy floor-mat, esp. for the hearth: a thick covering or wrap, as for travelling.—*adj.* made of rug.—*n.* **rugg'ing**.—**rug'-gown**, a gown of rug: a watchman (*obs.*).—*adj.* **rug'-head'ed**, (*Shak.*) shock-headed. [Cf. Norw. *rugga, rogga*, coarse coverlet, Sw. *rugg*, coarse hair.]

**rug**, *rug*, (*Scot.*) *v.t.* to pull roughly.—*n.* a tug: a haul, share.—*n.* **rugg'ing**. [Prob. Scand.]

**rug**, *rug*, (old slang) *adj.* secure: snug.

**Rugby, rugby**, *rug'bi*, *n.* a form of football using an oval ball which (unlike *Association*) permits carrying the ball:—(*coll.*) **rugg'er**.—**Rugby (Union) football**, the original form of the game, with 15 players; **Rugby League football**, a modified form of the game subject to professional rules, with 13 players. [From *Rugby* school.]

**rugged**, *rug'id*, *adj.* rough: uneven: uncouth: toilsome: sturdy and rough: massively irregular: robust, vigorous: stormy (now *U.S.*).—*adv.* **rugg'edly**.—*n.* **rugg'edness**.—*adj.* **rugg'y**, rough: uneven. [Prob. related to rug (1).]

**rugose**, *rōō'gōs, -gōs'*, *adj.* wrinkled: covered with sunken lines.—Also **ru'gous**.—*adv.* **ru'gosely** (or *-gōs'*).—*n.* **rugosity** (*-gos'i-ti*).—*adj.* **ru'gulose**, finely rugose. [L. *rūgōsus—rūga*, a wrinkle.]

**ruin**, *rōō'in, rōō'in*, *n.* downfall: collapse: overthrow: complete destruction: wreck: loss of fortune or means: bankruptcy: undoing: seduction or departure from chastity of life: downfallen, collapsed, wrecked, or irretrievably damaged state (often in *pl.*): cause of ruin: broken-down remains, esp. of a building (often in *pl.*): devastation: bad gin (as *blue ruin*; *slang*).—*v.t.* to reduce or bring to ruin.—*v.i.* to fall headlong: to go to ruin.—*adj.* **ru'inable**. —*v.t.* **ru'inate**, (*Shak.*) to ruin, to destroy: to demolish: to reduce to poverty: to fling headlong (*Spens.*; *refl.*).—*adj.* (*arch.*) in ruins: ruined.—*n.* **ruinā'tion**, act of ruining: state of being ruined.—*adj.* **ru'ined**.—*n.* **ru'iner**.—*n.* and *adj.* **ru'ining**.—*adj.* **ru'inous**, fallen to ruins: decayed: bringing ruin: as of crashing (*Milt.*).—*adv.* **ru'inously**.—*n.* **ru'inousness**, the state or quality of being ruinous: mischievousness.—**ruin agate, marble**, one with markings like ruins. [L. *ruīna* —*ruĕre*, to tumble down.]

**rukh.** Same as roc.

**rule**, *rōōl*, *n.* a straight-edged strip used as a guide in drawing straight lines or as a measuring-rod, or means of mechanical calculation: a type-high strip of metal for printing straight lines: a straight line printed or drawn on paper, etc.: a dash: a straight-edge used for securing a flat surface in plaster or cements: a straight shaft of light (*Milt.*): government: control: prevalence: that which is normal or usual: conformity to good or established usage: well-regulated condition: conduct (*obs.*): misrule (*obs.*): a principle: a standard: a code of regulations, as of a religious order: a regulation, whether imposed by authority or voluntarily adopted: an order of a court: a guiding principle: a method or process of achieving a result: a regulation that must not be transgressed: a maxim or formula that it is generally best, but not compulsory, to follow: (in *pl.*) an area around a prison in which privileged prisoners were allowed to live: the privilege of living there: (in *pl.*) Australian football (see **Australian rules**).—*v.t.* to draw with a ruler: to mark with (esp. parallel) straight lines: to govern: to control: to manage: to prevail upon: to determine or declare authoritatively to be: to determine, decree.—*v.i.* to exercise power (with *over*): to decide: to be prevalent: to stand or range in price.—*adjs.* **ru'lable**, governable: allowable (*U.S.*); **rule'less** (*Spens.* **ru'lesse**), unruly, lawless: without rules.—*n.* **ru'ler**, a strip or roller for ruling lines: one who rules.—*v.t.* to strike with a ruler.—*n.* **ru'lership**.—*adj.* **ru'ling**, predominant: prevailing: reigning.—*n.* a determination by a judge, esp. an oral decision: the act of making ruled lines.—*adj.* **ru'ly**, orderly in behaviour.—*adj.* **rule-of-thumb'**, according to rule of thumb (see below).—**as a rule**, usually; **be ruled**, take advice; **rule of faith**, in polemical theology, the authoritative sources of the doctrines of the faith; **rule of the road**, the regulations to be observed in traffic by land, water, or air—thus in Britain drivers, riders, and cyclists take the left side in meeting, and the right in overtaking; **rule of three**, the method of finding the fourth term of a proportion when three are given; **rule of thumb**, any rough-and-ready practical method; **rule out**, to exclude as a choice or possibility. [O.Fr. *reule* (Fr. *règle*)— L. *rēgula*—*regĕre* to rule.]

**rullion**, *rul'yən*, (*Scot.*) *n.* a raw-hide shoe. [O.E. *rifeling*.]

**rullock.** See rowlock.

**rum**, *rum*, *n.* a spirit distilled from fermented sugar-cane juice or from molasses: intoxicating liquor generally (*U.S.*).—*n.* **rum'bo**, rum-punch. —*adj.* **rumm'y.**—**rum'-bloss'om**, -bud, a pimple on the nose; **rum'-butt'er**, a mixture of butter and sugar with rum, etc.; **rum'-punch'**, punch made with rum; **rum'-runn'er**, one who smuggles rum; **rum'-runn'ing**; **rum'-shop**; **rum'-shrub**, a liqueur of rum, sugar, lime or lemon juice, etc.—**rum baba**, baba au rhum (see baba). [Perh. from rumbullion, or kindred form.]

**rum**, *rum*, *adj.* good (*obs. slang*): queer, droll, odd (*slang*).—*n.* a queer person.—*advs.* **rum'ly**; **rumm'ily.**—*n.* **rumm'iness.**—*adjs.* **rumm'ish**; **rumm'y.** [Cant.]

**rumal.** See romal.

**Rumanian, Roumanian,** *rōō-mā'ni-ən*, **Ruman Rouman,** *rōō'man, adjs.* pertaining to *Rumania* or its language.—*n.* a native or citizen of Rumania, or member of the same people: the (Romance) language of Rumania. [Rumanian *Românîa*—L. *Rōmānus*, Roman.]

**rumba, rhumba,** *rōōm'ba, rum'ba, n.* a violent Cuban Negro dance or a modification of it. [Sp.]

**rumbelow,** *rum'bi-lō, n.* a meaningless word, occurring as burden in old sea-songs.

**rumble,** *rum'bl, v.i.* to make a low heavy grumbling or rolling noise: to move with such a noise.— *v.t.* to give forth, or to agitate or move, with such a sound: to inform against, betray to the police (*slang*).—*n.* a sound of rumbling: a seat for servants behind a carriage, or for extra passengers in a two-seater car: a quarrel, disturbance, gang fight.—*n.* and *adj.* **rum'bler.**—*adj.* **rum'bling.**—*adv.* **rum'blingly.**—**rum'ble-tum'ble,** a rumble-seat: a lumbering vehicle: a tumbling motion. [Cf. Du. *rommelen*, Ger. *rummeln*.]

**rumble,** *rum'bl, (slang) v.t.* grasp: see through. [Obscure.]

**rumbullion,** *rum-bul'yən, (obs.) n.* rum. [Obscure.]

**rumbustical,** *rum-bust'i-kl,* **rumbustious,** -*yəs,* (*coll.*) *adjs.* boisterous. [Prob. robust.]

**rume,** a Shakespearian spelling of **rheum.**

**rumen,** *rōō'men, n.* the paunch or first stomach of a ruminant:—*pl.* **ru'mina.** [L. *rūmen, -inis,* gullet.]

**Rumex,** *rōō'meks, n.* the dock and sorrel genus of Polygonaceae. [L. *rŭmex, -icis,* a kind of dart, also sorrel (from its hastate leaves).]

**rumfustian,** *rum-fus'chən, n.* a hot drink, a kind of negus. [rum (1), fustian.]

**rumgumption,** *rum-gum(p)'shən, (Scot.) n.* common sense.—Also **rum(m)el-, rum(m)le-, rumble-gump'tion** (*rum'l-*).

**ruminant,** *rōō'min-ənt, n.* an animal that chews the cud.—*adj.* cud-chewing: meditative.—*n.pl.* **Ruminantia** (-*an'shya,* -*sha*), the cud-chewing division of the even-toed ungulates.—*adv.* **ru'minantly.**—*v.i.* **ru'mināte,** to chew the cud: to regurgitate for chewing: to meditate.—*v.t.* to chew over again: to muse on.—*adj.* (*bot.*) mottled as if chewed.—*adv.* **ru'minātingly.**—*n.* **ruminā'tion.**—*adj.* **ru'minative.**—*adv.* **ru'minatively.**—*n.* **ru'minātor.** [L. *rūmināre, -ātum*—*rūmen, -inis,* the gullet.]

**rumkin,** *rum'kin, (obs.) n.* a kind of drinking-vessel.

**rumkin,** *rum'kin, n.* a tailless fowl. [App. **rump.**]

**rummage,** *rum'ij, n.* orig. stowage of casks, etc., in a ship's hold: a thorough search, as by customs officers: an overhauling search: (*Shak.* **romage**) commotion, upheaval.—*v.t.* to arrange, esp. orig. in a ship's hold: to ransack:

to overhaul: to search: to stir.—*v.i.* to make a search.—*n.* **rumm'ager.**—**rummage sale,** a sale at which buyers are allowed to rummage among the goods: also a sale of odds and ends or undesired goods. [Fr. *arrumage* (now *arrimage*), stowage.]

**rummer,** *rum'ər, n.* a large drinking-glass. [Du. *roemer*; Ger. *römer*.]

**rummy.** See rum (1 and 2).

**rummy,** *rum'i, n.* a card-game in which cards are drawn from the stock and sequences, triplets, etc., are laid on the table.

**Rumonsch.** See Romansch.

**rumour,** *rōō'mər, n.* clamour: general talk, repute: hearsay: flying report: a current story.—*v.t.* to put about by report.—*adj.* **ru'morous,** resounding: full of rumours: of the nature of rumours: vaguely heard.—*n.* **ru'mourer.** [O.Fr.—L. *rūmor, -ōris,* a noise.]

**rump,** *rump, n.* the hinder part of an animal's body, the root of the tail with parts adjoining: in birds, the uropygium: contemptuously, a remnant.—*v.t.* to turn one's back upon: to clean out of money (*Scot.*).—**Rump'er,** a member or supporter of the Rump Parliament; **rum'ple** (*Scot.*), a rump.—*adj.* **rump'less.**—**rump'bone',** the coccyx; **rump'-end.**—*adj.* **rump'-fed** (*Shak.*), prob. with well-nourished rump.—**rump'le-bane',** rump-bone; **rump'-post,** the share bone or pygostyle of a bird; **rump'-steak,** steak cut from the thigh near the rump. —**the Rump,** the remnant of the long Parliament, after Pride's expulsion (1648), of about a hundred Presbyterian royalist members. [Scand.; cf. Dan. *rumpe,* Sw. and Norw. *rumpa,* O.N. *rumpr,* Ger. *rumpf,* Du. *romp.*]

**rumple,** *rum'pl, n.* a fold or wrinkle.—*v.t.* to crush out of shape: to make uneven. [Du. *rompel*; cf. O.E. *hrimpan,* to wrinkle.]

**rumpus,** *rum'pəs, n.* an uproar: a disturbance.

**rumti-iddity, rumpti-iddity,** *rum(p)-ti-id'i-ti, interj.* a meaningless refrain.

**run,** *run,* formerly also **ren,** *ren*; *Scot.* **rin,** *rin, v.i.* to proceed by lifting one foot before the other is down: to go swiftly, at more than a walking pace: to hasten: to proceed quickly: to betake oneself: to flee: to progress, esp. smoothly and quickly: to go about freely: to ride at a running pace: to roll: to revolve: to go with a gliding motion: to slip: to go on wheels: to travel, cover a distance: to make a short journey: to swim in shoals: to ascend a river for spawning: to ply: to have a definite sequence, as of notes, words: to proceed through a sequence of operations, work, or go, as a machine: to follow a course: to keep the stage without interruption: to flow: to spread, diffuse: to emit or transmit a flow: to melt: to fuse: to curdle (now *dial.*): to have a course, stretch, or extent: to range: to average: to elapse: to tend: to come to be, become, pass: to be current: to be valid: to recur repeatedly or remain persistently (in the mind): to come undone, as by the dropping or breaking of a stitch: to compete in a race: to be a candidate (*U.S.*).—*v.t.* to cause to run: to chase, hunt: to drive forward: to thrust: to pierce: to drive: to pass quickly: to range, run about or throughout: to hurry through: to enter, promote, put forward (as a horse, candidate, or protégé): to render, by running or otherwise: to conduct, manage: to follow: to traverse: to cause to extend, form in a line: to sew slightly: to shoot along or down: to perform, achieve, or score by running, or as if by running: to flee or desert from: to incur: to risk and pass the hazard of: to smuggle: to have or keep current or running: to compete with in a race: to press or put to it, in competition or difficulty: to coagulate: to fuse: to emit, dis-

# run 1183 rung

**run**, charge, flow with:—*pr.p.* **runn'ing**; *pa.t.* **ran**; *pa.p.* **run**.—*n.* an act, spell, or manner of running: a journey, trip: distance, time or quantity run: a continuous stretch, spell, series, or period: a shoal, migration, or migrating body: a roulade: a spell of being in general demand: a rush for payment, as upon a bank: a unit of scoring in cricket: a batsman's passage from one popping-crease to the other: a circuit in baseball: flow or discharge: course: prevalence: the ordinary or average kind, the generality: a track: a path made by animals: a small stream (*U.S.*): a range of feeding-ground: an enclosure for chickens, etc.: freedom of access to all parts: the playing of a salmon: general direction: a ladder in knitting or knitted fabrics, esp. stockings.—*adj.* having been poured, smuggled, coagulated: having run.—*n.* **run'let**, a runnel.—*adj.* **runn'able**, of a stag, fit for hunting.—*n.* **runn'er**, one who, or that which, runs or can run: a fugitive: a racer: a messenger: an agent: a tout: an intelligencer: a rooting stem that runs along the ground: a rope to increase the power of a tackle: a smuggler: a Bow Street officer (*hist.*): a ring, loop, or the like, through which anything slides or runs: the part on which a sledge, a skate, or a drawer slides: the passage by which metal is poured into a mould: a strip of cloth as a table ornament: a revolving millstone: a slice across a carcase of beef below the breast (*Scot.*): a climbing plant of the kidney-bean genus (*Phaseolus multiflorus*; **runner-bean, scarlet-runner**): a breed of domestic duck (**runner duck**): a vessel for conveying fish, oysters, etc.—*adj.* **runn'ing**, racing: habitually going at a run: current: successive: continuous: flowing: discharging: easy: cursive: itinerant: done at or with a run: hasty.—*n.* action of the verb: the pace.—*adv.* **runn'ingly.**—*adj.* **runn'y**, inclined to run or liquefy.—**run'about**, a gadabout: a vagabond: a small light vehicle or aeroplane; **run'away**, a fugitive: a horse that bolts: a flight.—*adj.* fleeing: done by or in flight.—*adj.* **run'-down**, in weakened health.—*n.* (usu. without *hyphen*), a reduction in numbers: a statement bringing together all the main items.—**runn'er-up'**, a competitor (orig. a dog) that holds out to the last heat: the competitor next after the winner; **runn'ing-banq'uet**, a slight or hasty collation; **runn'ing-board**, a footboard along the side of a motor-car or (*U.S.*) locomotive; **running commentary**, a commentary accompanying a text: a broadcast description of a game or other event in progress; **running fight**, a fight between pursuer and pursued; **running fire** (*mil.*), a rapid succession of firing; **running footman**, a servant who ran before or alongside a horseman or carriage; **runn'ing-gear**, the wheels and axles of a vehicle; **runn'ing-hand**, a style of rapid writing without lifting the pen; **runn'ing-knot**, a knot that will form a noose on pulling; **running lights**, the lights shown by vessels between sunset and sunrise; **running mate**, a runner who makes the pace for another: a horse teamed with another, or making the pace for another: in U.S., the candidate for the less important of two associated offices, esp. the candidate for the vice-presidency considered in relation to the presidential candidate; **running ornament**, an ornament in which the design is continuous; **running rigging**, all the rigging except the shrouds, stays and lower mast-head pendants; **running title**, the title of a book, etc., continued from page to page on the upper margin; **run'-off**, a race to decide a dead heat: urination.—*adj.* **run-of-the-mill**, constituting an ordinary fair sample, not selected: mediocre.—**run-on'**, in verse, carrying the sense on beyond the end of the line; **run'way**, a trail, track, or passageway: a path for aircraft to take

off from.—**give the runaround**, to give a vague, indecisive, or deceptive reply to a question or meet a request with evasion; **get the runaround**, to be treated thus; **in the long run**, in the end or final result; **in, out of, the running**, competing with, without, a fair chance of success; **make, take up, the running**, to take the lead: to set the pace; **run across**, to come upon by accident; **run down**, to pursue to exhaustion or capture: to collide with and knock over or sink: to disparage: to become unwound or exhausted; **run hard**, to press hard behind; **run in**, to go in: to arrest and take to a lock-up: to insert a word, etc., without making a break or new paragraph (*print.*): to bring (new machinery, car) into good condition by preliminary working; **run in the blood, family**, to be a hereditary character; **run into debt**, to get into debt; **run it fine**, to allow very little margin, as of time; **run off**, to cause to flow out: to take impressions of, to print: to repeat, recount; **run on**, to talk on and on: to continue in the same line, and not in a new paragraph (*print.*); **run one's eyes over**, to look at cursorily; **run out**, to run short: to terminate, expire, determine: to leak, let out liquid: to put out (a batsman running between the wickets and not yet in his ground): dismissed thus; **run over**, to overflow: to overthrow: to go over cursorily: of a road vehicle, to knock down a person or animal; **run short**, to come to be short, lacking, or exhausted; **run through**, to exhaust: to transfix: to read or perform quickly or cursorily but completely; **run to**, to be sufficient for; **run together**, to mingle or blend; **run to seed**, to shoot up too rapidly in preparation for seeding, instead of producing the vegetative growth desired by the grower: to become exhausted: to go to waste; **run up**, to make or mend hastily: to build hurriedly: to string up, hang: to send the ball rolling or flying low towards the hole (*golf*): to incur increasingly. [O.E. *rinnan, irnan, iernan*, to run; causative *rennan*, to curdle; see also **earn** (2).]

**runagate**, *run'ə-gāt*, *n.* a vagabond: a renegade: an apostate: a fugitive.—Also *adj.* [renegade, influenced by **run, agate** (*adv.*).]

**runch**, *runsh*, (*Scot.*) *n.* charlock: wild radish. [Origin obscure.]

**runcible**, *run'si-bl*, *adj.* app. a nonsense-word of Edward Lear's, whose phrase *runcible spoon* has been applied to a sharp-edged, broad-pronged pickle-fork.

**runcinate**, *runs'in-āt*, (*bot.*) *adj.* with backward-pointing lobes. [L. *runcina*, a plane, formerly misunderstood as a saw.]

**rund**, *run*(*d*), *ran*(*d*). Same as **roon**.

**rundale**, *run'dāl*, *n.* a system of holding land in single holdings made up of detached pieces: land or a share of it so held.—Also *adj.* [run, and the Northern form of **dole** (1).]

**rundle**, *run'dl*, *n.* a round, a ladder-rung: a ring, circle, disk, or ball.—*adj.* **run'dled**. [roundel.]

**rundlet**, *rund'lit*, **runlet**, *run'lit*, *n.* a small barrel. [Fr. *rondelet*.]

**rune**, *roōn*, *n.* a letter of the futhork or ancient Germanic alphabet: a secret, a mystic symbol, sentence, spell, or song: a song or canto.—*adjs.* **runed**; **ru'nic**, of, pertaining to, written in, inscribed with runes: Scandinavian: Northern: (wrongly) in the manner of ancient Northumbrian and Celtic interlacing ornament.—**rune'-craft**, knowledge of runes; **rune'-stave** (O.E. *rūnstæf*), a runic letter. [O.E. and O.N. *rūn*, mystery, rune; Goth. and O.H.G. *rūna*.]

**rung**, *rung*, *n.* a spoke: a cross-bar or rail: a ladder round or step: a ship's floor-timber: a cudgel (*Scot.*). [O.E. *hrung*; Ger. *runge*.]

**rung**, *rung*. See **ring** (2).

Neutral vowels in unaccented syllables: *el'ə-mənt*; for certain sounds in foreign words, see p. viii

rung, *rung*, *adj.* having a ring through the nose. [ring (1).]

runkle, *rung'kl*, *n.* a wrinkle, crease.—*v.t.* and *v.i.* to wrinkle: to crease. [Prob. Scand.; cf. ruck, ruckle.]

runlet. See run, rundlet.

runnel, *run'l*, *n.* a little brook. [O.E. *rynel*, dim. of *ryne*, a stream—*rinnan*, to run.]

runner, running. See run.

runnet Dial, variant of rennet (1).

runnion. See ronyon.

runrig, *run'rig*, (*Scot.*) *n.* a form of land-tenure, the same as rundale.—Also *adj.* and *adv.* [run, rig.]

runt, *runt*, *n.* a small, stunted, or old ox or cow: a small pig, esp. the smallest of a litter: anything undersized: a large breed of domestic pigeon: a dead tree-stump or trunk: a cabbage-stem: a vague term of reproach, esp. to the old or boorish.—*adjs.* runt'ed; runt'ish; runt'y. [Origin uncertain.]

Runyonesque, *run-yən-esk'*, *adj.* in the style of the American writer A. Damon *Runyon* (1884-1946), portrayer of gangsters in their milder moments.

rupee, *roō-pē'*, *n.* monetary unit and nickel (orig. silver) coin of India, Pakistan, and Ceylon containing respectively 100 new pice, 100 pice, 100 cents. [Urdu *rūpiyah*—Sans. *rūpya*, wrought silver.]

Rupert's drop, *roō'pərts-drop'*, *n.* a tailed bulb formed by dropping molten glass in water, bursting when the tail is broken—probably discovered by Prince *Rupert* (1619-82).

rupestrian, *roō-pes'tri-ən*, *adj.* composed of rock: inscribed on rock. [L. *rūpēs*, rock.]

rupia, *roō'pi-a*, *n.* a skin ulcer covered by crusts of dried secretion and dead tissue. [Gr. *rhypos*, filth.]

rupicoline, *roō-pik'ō-lin*, rupicolous, *-ləs*, *adjs.* rock-dwelling. [L. *rūpēs*, a rock, *colěre*, to inhabit.]

rupture, *rup'chər*, *n.* a breach, breaking, or bursting: the state of being broken: breach of harmony, relations, or negotiations: hernia, esp. abdominal.—*v.t.* and *v.i.* to break or burst.—rup'turewort, a caryophyllaceous plant (Herniaria), once thought to cure hernia. [L.L. *ruptūra*—L. *rumpěre*, *ruptum*, to break.]

rural, *roō'rl*, *adj.* of the country.—*n.* (*obs.*) a country-dweller.—*n.* ruralisā'tion, *-z-*.—*v.t.* ru'-ralise, -ize, render rural.—*v.i.* to become rural: to rusticate.—*ns.* ru'ralism; ru'ralist; rurality (*-al'i-ti*).—*adv.* ru'rally.—*n.* ru'ralness.—*adj.* ruri-decanal (*roō-ri-di-kā'nl*; sometimes *-dek'ən-l*), of a rural dean(ery).—rural dean (see dean). [L. *rūrālis*—*rūs*, *rūris*, the country.]

Ruritania, *roōr-i-tān'yə*, *n.* a fictitious land of historical romance (in S.E. Europe) discovered by Anthony Hope.—*n.* and *adj.* Rurităn'ian.

Rusa, *roō'sa*, *n.* the sambur genus of deer.—*adj.* ru'sine (*-sīn*). [Malay *rūsa*.]

rusa, roosa, *roō'sa*, *n.* an Indian grass (rusa grass) from which an aromatic oil (rusa oil) is distilled. [Hind. *rūsā*.]

rusalka, *roō-sal'ka*, *n.* a Russian water-nymph. [Russ.]

Ruscus, *rus'kəs*, *n.* a small genus of European evergreen shrubs (family Liliaceae): any plant of the genus. [L. *rūscum*, butcher's-broom.]

ruse, *roōz*, *n.* a trick, stratagem, artifice.—*adj.* rusé (*rü-zā*; Fr.), artful, deceitful, cunning.—ruse contre ruse (*rüz kõtr' rüz*; Fr.), cunning against cunning: ruse de guerre (*də ger*; Fr.), a stratagem of war. [O.Fr. *ruse*—*ruser*, *reüser*, to get out of the way, double on one's tracks; see rush (1).]

rush, *rush*, *v.i.* to move forward with haste, impetuosity, or rashness.—*v.t.* to force out of place: to hasten or hustle forward, or into

any action: to move, transport, drive, push, in great haste: to capture, secure, surmount, pass, by a rush: to defraud (*coll.*): to overcharge (*coll.*).—*n.* a swift impetuous forward movement: a sudden simultaneous or general movement (as a gold rush): an onset: a stampede: a migratory movement or body: a run upon anything: an unedited print of a motion picture scene or series of scenes for immediate viewing by the film makers: rapidly increased activity: bustling activity: a sound of rushing.—*n.* rush'er.—rush hours, day's time of maximum activity or traffic; rush one's fences, to act precipitately. [A.Fr. *russcher*, O.Fr. *reusser*, *reüser*, *ruser* (Fr. *ruser*); see ruse.]

rush, *rush*, *n.* any plant of the grass-like marsh-growing genus Juncus: a stalk or round stalk-like leaf of such a plant: extended to various more or less similar plants (see bulrush, club-rush, Dutch or scouring rush, wood-rush): a rushlight, a rush wick: a type of something of no value or importance: a rush-ring (*Shak.*).—*adj.* of rush or rushes.—*v.t.* to make or strew with rushes.—*v.i.* to gather rushes.—*adj.* rush'en, made of rushes.—*n.* rush'iness.—*adjs.* rush'-like; rush'y, rush-like: abounding in or made of rushes.—rush'-bearing, a country observance of carrying rushes to strew the church: the day of the festival.—*adj.* rush'-bottomed, having a seat made with rushes.—rush'-candle, rush'light, a candle or night-light having a wick of rush-pith: a small, feeble light.—*adj.* rush'-grown.—rush'-holder, a stand for a rushlight; rush'-ring, a ring of plaited rush, sometimes formerly as an improvised wedding-ring.—*adj.* rush'y-fringed. [O.E. *risce*; Ger. *risch*.]

rusk, *rusk*, *n.* a small cake like a piece of very hard toast. [Sp. *rosca*, a roll; origin unknown.]

rusma, *ruz'ma*, *n.* a depilatory of lime and orpiment. [App. Turk. *khirisma*—Gr. *chrisma*, ointment.]

russel, *rus'l*, *n.* a ribbed cotton and woollen material.—russ'el-cord, a kind of rep made of cotton and wool. [Poss. Flem. *Rijssel*, Lille.]

Russellite, *rus'əl-īt*, *n.* a member of the International Bible Students' Association, or Jehovah's Witnesses, a millennialist sect founded by the American Pastor C. T. *Russell* (1852-1916).—Also *adj.*

russet, *rus'it*, *n.* a coarse homespun cloth or dress: a reddish-brown colour: a reddish-brown variety of apple.—*adj.* made of russet: homespun, homely, rustic: reddish-brown: of brown leather.—*v.t.* and *v.i.* to make or become russet in colour.—*n.* russ'eting, a russet apple.—*adj.* russ'ety. [O.Fr. *rousset*—L. *russus*, red.]

Russian, *rush'(y)ən*, *adj.* of *Russia* or its people.—*n.* a native or citizen of Russia: the Slavonic language of most Russians.—*n.* and *adj.* Russ (*rus*), Russian.—*adj.* Russia (*rush'ə*, *-yə*), Russian.—*ns.* russia, russia leather; Russianisā'-tion,*-z-*.—*v.t.* Russ'ianise, -ize, to give Russian characteristics to: to make Russian.—*ns.* Russ'ianism; Russ'ianist; Russification (*rus-i-fi-kā'shən*).—*v.t.* Russ'ify, to Russianise.—*ns.* Russ'ophil(e), one who favours Russian policy (also *adj.*); Russoph'ilism; Russoph'ilist; Russ'o-phobe, one who dreads or hates the Russians (also *adj.*); Russoph'obist; Russophō'bia, the dread of Russian policy.—russia (or Russia) leather, a fine brownish-red leather with a characteristic odour; Russian roulette, an act of bravado, *specif.* that of loading a revolver with one bullet, spinning the cylinder, and firing at one's own head.—*adj.* Russo-Byzan'tine, Byzantine as developed in Russia.

Russniak, *rus'ni-ak*, *n.* and *adj.* Ruthenian: Ukrainian or Little Russian. [Ruthenian *Rusnjak*.]

rust, *rust*, *n.* the reddish-brown coating on iron

exposed to moisture: any similar coating or appearance: a plant disease characterised by a rusty appearance, caused by various fungi of the Uredineae: a fungus causing such disease, notably *Puccinia graminis*, which attacks wheat: corrosion: injurious influence or consequence, esp. of mental inactivity or idleness: the colour of rust.—*v.i.* to become rusty: to affect with rust: to become dull or inefficient by inaction.—*v.t.* to make rusty: to impair by time and inactivity.—*adj.* rust′ed.—*adv.* rust′ily.—*n.* rust′iness.—*n.* and *adj.* rust′ing.—*adjs.* rust′less, free from rust: proof against rust; rust′y, covered with rust: impaired by inactivity, out of practice: dull: affected with rust-disease: rust-coloured: of a rusty black: time-worn: rough: raucous: obstinate: discoloured.—*adj.* rust′-coloured.—rust′-fungus.—*adjs.* rust′-proof; rust′-resistant.—rust′y-back, the scale-fern.—*adj.* rust′y-coloured. [O.E. *rūst*; Ger. *rost*.]

rustic, rus′tik, *adj.* of, or characteristic of, the country or country-dwellers: country-dwelling: like countryfolk or their works: simple and plain: awkward: uncouth: unrefined: roughly made: made of rough branches: of masonry, with sunken or chamfered joints, sometimes with roughened face.—*n.* a peasant: a clown: a rough-surfaced brick or stone: rustic masonry.—*adj.* and (*rare*) *n.* rus′tical.—*adv.* rus′tically.—*v.t.* rust′icate, to send into the country: to banish for a time from town or college: to build in rustic masonry.—*v.i.* to live in the country: to become rustic.—*n.* rustica′tion.—*adj.* rusticial (-*tish′l; Scott*, as a false archaism).—*v.t.* and *v.i.* rus′ticise, -ize (-*ti-siz*).—*n.* rusticity (-*tis′i-ti*), rustic manner: simplicity: rudeness.—rus′tic-ware, a terra-cotta of a light brown paste, having a brown glaze; rus′tic-work, rusticated masonry: summer-houses, etc., of rough branches. [L. *rūsticus*—*rūs*, the country.]

rustle, rus′l, *v.i.* to make a soft, whispering sound, as of dry leaves: to go about with such a sound: to stir about, hustle (*U.S.*): to steal cattle (*U.S.*).—*v.t.* to cause to rustle: to get by rustling (*U.S.*).—*n.* a quick succession of small sounds, as that of dry leaves: a rustling: bustle (*U.S.*).—*n.* rus′tler.—*n.* and *adj.* rus′tling.—*adv.* rus′tlingly.—rustle up, to arrange, gather together. [Imit.; cf. Flem. *ruysselen*.]

rustre, rus′tər, (*her.*) *n.* a lozenge pierced with a circular opening.—*adj.* rus′tred. [Fr.]

rusty. See rust.—Also a variant of reasty and of reesty.

rut, *rut*, *n.* a furrow made by wheels: a fixed course difficult to depart from.—*v.t.* to furrow with ruts:—*pr.p.* rutt′ing; *pa.t.* and *pa.p.* rutt′ed.—*adj.* rutt′y. [Origin obscure; prob. not Fr. *route*.]

rut, *rut*, *n.* sexual excitement in male deer: also in other animals.—*v.i.* to be in heat.—*v.t.* (*rare*) to copulate with.—*n.* and *adj.* rutt′ing.—*adj.* rutt′ish, lustful.—rut′-time. [O.Fr. *ruit, rut*—L. *rugitus*—*rugire*, to roar.]

Ruta, rōō′ta, *n.* the rue genus of dicotyledons, giving name to the family Rutā′ceae, which is usually made to include the orange, etc.—*adj.* rutā′ceous. [L. *rūta*; see rue (1).]

rutabaga, rōō-ta-bā′gə, *n.* the Swedish turnip. [Sw. dial. *rotabagge*.]

ruth, rōōth, *n.* pity: remorse: sorrow: matter for pity: misfortune, calamity (*obs.*).—*adj.* ruth′-ful, pitiful, sorrowful: piteous, causing pity.—*adv.* ruth′fully.—*adj.* ruth′less, pitiless: unsparing.—*adv.* ruth′lessly.—*n.* ruth′lessness. [M.E. *ruthe, reuth*; see rue (2); ending influenced by Scand., as O.N. *hryggth*.]

Ruthene, rōō-thēn′, *n.* a member of a branch of the Little Russian division of the Slavs on both sides of the Carpathians: the language of the Ruthenes.—*n.* and *adj.* Ruthēn′ian, Ruthene.

ruthenium, rōō-thē′ni-əm, *n.* a metallic element (Ru; at. numb. 44) of the platinum group, found in the Ural Mountains. [L.L. *Ruthenia*, Russia.]

rutherford, rudh′ər-fərd, *n.* a unit of radioactive disintegration, equal to a million disintegrations a second—abbrev. rd. [After the physicist Baron *Rutherford* (1871-1937).]

rutilant, rōō′ti-lənt, *adj.* shining: glowing ruddily. [L. *rutilāns, -antis*, pr.p. of *rutilāre*, to be reddish.]

rutile, rōō′til, *n.* a reddish-brown mineral of the tetragonal system, titanium oxide.—*adj.* rutilated (*rōō′til-āt-id*), enclosing needles of rutile. [L. *rutilus*, reddish.]

rutin, rōō′tin, *n.* a drug used against the fragility of small blood-vessels. [Formed from Ruta.]

rutter, rut′ər, (*obs.*) *n.* a mercenary horse-soldier. [M.Du. *rutter*—O.Fr. *routier*.]

ry-, in many words an old spelling of ri-.

ryal, rial, rī′əl, (*obs.*) *adj.* and *n.* royal.—esp. *n.* a coin of various kinds—an old English gold coin worth about ten shillings, a Spanish real, and others. [O.Fr. *rial*, royal.]

rybat, rib′ət, *n.* a dressed stone at the side of a door, window, etc. [Prob. conn. with rebate (2).]

rybaudrye, rib′öd-ri, (*Spens.*) *n.* Same as ribaldry.

rye, rī, *n.* a grass (Secale, esp. *S. cereale*) allied to wheat and barley: its grain, used for making bread: rye-grass: rye-whisky.—*adj.* of rye.—rye′-bread; rye′-coffee, a coffee-substitute made from rye; rye′-corn (*Austr.*), rye; rye′-flour; rye′-grass, a pasture and fodder grass (species of Lolium), with flat spikelets appressed edgewise in a two-rowed spike; rye′-roll′, a dark treacly cookie, understood not to be of rye.—*n.* and *adj.* rye′-straw.—rye′-whis′ky, spirituous beverage made chiefly from rye; rye′-wolf (Ger. *Roggenwolf*), an evil creature of German folklore lurking in the rye-fields. [O.E. *ryge*; O.N. *rugr*, Ger. *roggen* (also *rocken*).]

rye, rī, *n.* a gypsy word for gentleman. [Romany *rei, rai*, lord.]

ryepeck, rypeck, ripeck, rī′pek, (*dial.*) *n.* a pole used for mooring a punt. [Origin obscure.]

ryfe, rif, (*Spens.*) *adj.* Same as rife.

ryke, rik, a Scots form of reach.

rymme, an old spelling of rim (1 and 2).

rynd. Same as rind (2).

ryot, raiyat, rī′ət, *n.* an Indian peasant.—*n.* ry′otwari, raiyatwari (-*wä-rē*), a system of land-tenure by which each peasant holds directly of the state. [Hind. *raiyat, raiyatwārī*—Ar. *ra′iyah*, a subject.]

rype, rü′pə, *n.* a ptarmigan:—*pl.* ry′per. [Dan.]

rythme, rim, an old spelling of rhyme.

ryve, an old spelling of rive.

Neutral vowels in unaccented syllables: *el′ə-mənt*; for certain sounds in foreign words, see p. viii

# S

**S, s,** *es, n.* the nineteenth letter in our alphabet, seventeenth in the Roman, a consonant, its usual sound a voiceless alveolar fricative (sibilant), but often voiced, and sometimes a voiceless palato-alveolar fricative (represented usually by *sh*), or voiced (as in *pleasure*): any mark or object of the form of the letter: as a mediaeval Roman numeral, S = 7 or 70; S̄ = 70,000.—**collar of SS** (see **ess**).

**'s,** *z,* a shortened form of **God's, has, is,** or (*Scot.*) **as, sal** (1).—Also shortened form of **us** (pron. *s*; e.g. *let's go*), **his** (e.g., *obs.*, *in's hand*).

**sa', sä,** *v.t.* an obs. contraction of **save.**

**sab,** *sab,* (*Scot.*) *n.* a form of **sob.**

**Saba,** *sä'bä, n.* Sheba, an ancient people of Yemen.—*n.* and *adj.* **Sabaean, Sabean** (-*bē'ən*).—Also applied by confusion to adherents of Sabaism and of Sabianism. [Gr. *Saba*—Ar. *Saba'*; Heb. *Shebā.*]

**sabadilla,** *sab-ə-dil'ə, n.* seeds of a liliaceous plant, Schoenocaulon, yielding veratrine.—Also **cebadill'a, cevadill'a.** [Sp. *cebadilla*, dim. of *cebada*, barley.]

**Sabaism,** *sä'bā-izm, n.* the worship of the host of heaven. [Heb. *tsābā*, host.]

**Sabal,** *sä'bal, n.* an American genus of palms, the palmettos. [Origin unknown.]

**Sabaoth,** *sa-bā'oth, n.pl.* armies, used only in the Bible phrase, 'Lord of Sabaoth': (*sab'əth*) erroneously for Sabbath (*Spens.*). [Heb. *tsebāōth* (transliterated *sabaōth* in Gr.), pl. of *tsabā*, an army.]

**sabaton,** *sab'ə-ton, n.* armour for the foot, not necessarily broad-toed. [Prov. *sabató*; cf. **sabot,** Sp. *zapata*.]

**Sabbath,** *sab'əth, n.* among the Jews, Saturday, set apart for rest from work: among most Christians, Sunday: a sabbatical year of the Jews: a time of rest: (also **sabb'at**) a witches' midnight meeting.—*adj.* of or appropriate to the Sabbath.—*n.* **Sabbatā'rian,** one who observes Saturday as Sabbath: one who believes in or practises observance, or strict observance, of the Sabbath (Saturday or Sunday).—Also *adj.*—*n.* **Sabbatā'rianism.**—*adjs.* **Sabb'athless; sabbatic** (*sab-at'ik*), **-al,** pertaining to, or resembling, the Sabbath: enjoying or bringing rest; **sabb'atine,** pertaining to Saturday.—*v.t.* **sabb'atise, -ize,** to observe as a Sabbath.—*v.i.* to keep a Sabbath.—*n.* **sabb'atism,** sabbatical rest: observance of the Sabbath.—**Sabbath'-breach; Sabb'ath-breaker; Sabb'ath-breaking** (also *adj.*); **Sabb'ath-day** (also *adj.*); **Sabbath-day's journey,** 2000 cubits, or about one kilometre, which a Jew was permitted to walk on the Sabbath (Josh. iii. 4).—**Sabbath school,** a Sunday school; **sabbat'ical year,** every seventh year, in which the Israelites allowed their fields and vineyards to lie fallow: a year off, for study, travel, etc. [Heb. *Shabbāth.*]

**Sabella,** *sə-bel'ə, n.* a genus of tube-building sea-worms. [L. *sabulum*, sand.]

**Sabellian,** *sə-bel'i-ən, n.* and *adj.* orig. Sabine: now generally used in a wide sense to include kindred peoples and languages. [L. *Sabellus*, poet. dim. of *Sabīnus*.]

**Sabellian,** *sə-bel'i-ən, n.* a follower of *Sabellius* (3rd century).—Also *adj.*—*n.* **Sabell'ianism,** the teaching of Sabellius, that Father, Son, and Holy Ghost are one and the same person in different aspects.

**saber,** American spelling of **sabre.**

**Sabian,** *sä'bi-ən,* **Zabian,** *zä', n.* **Tsabian,** *tsä', n.* an adherent of a religion or a group of religions mentioned in the Koran as entitled to toleration, prob. akin to the Mandaeans: Mandaean: by confusion sometimes a Sabaean, sometimes an adherent of Sabaism.—Also *adj.*—*n.* **Sä'bianism.** [Ar. *Sābi'.*]

**Sabine,** *sab'in, n.* one of an ancient people of central Italy, afterwards united with the Romans.—Also *adj.* [L. *Sabīnus.*]

**Sabin vaccine,** *sā'bin,* a live-virus poliomyelitis vaccine taken by the mouth. [Albert Bruce *Sabin,* American physician (born 1906).]

**sable,** *sā'bl, n.* an arctic and subarctic marten: its lustrous dark brown fur: a paintbrush of its hair.—*adj.* of sable. [O.Fr.; prob. from Slav.]

**sable,** *sā'bl, n.* and *adj.* black (orig. *her.*, now chiefly *poet.*): dark.—*n.* a sable antelope: (in *pl.*) mourning garments.—*v.t.* to darken.—**sable antelope,** a large South African antelope (*Hippotragus niger*), black above, white below.—*adj.* **sa'ble-coloured.** [Fr. *sable*; poss. the same as the foregoing.]

**sabot,** *sab'ō, n.* a wooden shoe, as worn by the French peasantry: an attachment to guide a projectile through the bore.—*n.* **sabotage** (-*täzh'*, now usu. *sab'*, also -*tij*), malicious destruction: action taken to prevent the achievement of any aim.—Also *v.t.* and *v.i.*—*ns.* **saboteur** (-*tœr'*), one who sabotages; **sabotier** (-*tyā'*), a wearer of wooden shoes: a Waldensian. [Fr. *sabot.*]

**sabra,** *sä'brə, n.* a native-born Israeli, not an immigrant. [Mod. Hebrew *sābrāh*, type of cactus.]

**sabre,** in U.S. **saber,** *sā'bər, n.* a curved, cutting, cavalry sword: a soldier armed with a sabre.—*v.t.* to wound or kill with a sabre.—**sä'bre-cut.** *v.i.* **sä'bre-ratt'le.**—**sä'bre-rattling,** military bluster; **sä'bre-tooth** (in full **sabre-toothed tiger**), a Tertiary fossil carnivore (Machaerodus) with extremely long upper canine teeth; **sä'bre-wing,** a humming-bird of a group with bent outer primaries in the male. [Fr. *sabre*—Ger. *sabel* (now *säbel*); origin unknown.]

**sabretache,** *sab'ər-tash, n.* a flat bag slung from a cavalry officer's sword-belt. [Fr. *sabretache*—Ger. *säbeltasche*—*säbel*, sabre, *tasche*, pocket.]

**sabulous,** *sab'ū-ləs, adj.* sandy: gritty. [L. *sabulum*, sand.]

**saburra,** *sə-bur'ə, n.* a granular deposit, as in the stomach.—*adj.* **saburr'al.**—*n.* **saburrā'tion** (*med.*), application of hot sand. [L. *saburra*, sand.]

**sac,** *sak,* (*biol.*) *n.* a pouch.—*adjs.* **sacc'ate,** pouched: pouch-like: gibbous: enclosed in a sac; **sacciform** (*sak'si-förm*), **sacc'ūlar,** sac-like; **sacc'ūlated,** formed in a series of sac-like expansions: enclosed.—*ns.* **sacculā'tion; sacc'ūle, sacc'ūlus,** a small sac:—*pl.* **sacc'ules, sacc'uli,** [L. *saccus,* a bag; see **sack** (1).]

**sac,** *sak,* (*law*) *n.* the privilege of a lord of manor of holding courts.—*adj.* **sac'less** (*Scott*), unchallengeable, not to be molested (see **sack'less,** *s.v.*). See also **soc.** [O.E. *sacu,* strife.]

**Saccharum,** *sak'ə-rəm, n.* the sugar-cane genus of grasses.—*n.* **sacch'arate,** a salt of saccharic acid.—*adjs.* **sacch'arated,** sugared, sweetened; **saccharic** (*sak-ar'ik*), of sugar (**saccharic acid,** an acid, $H_2C_6H_8O_8$, got by oxidation of sugar).—*n.* **sacch'aride,** a carbohydrate: a compound with sugar.—*adj.* **saccharif'erous,** sugar-yielding.—*v.t.* **sacchar'ify** (or *sak'*), to convert into sugar.

—*ns.* **saccharim′eter,** a polarimeter or other instrument for testing concentration of sugar solutions; **saccharim′etry; sacch′arin, -ine** (*-in, -en*), an intensely sweet, white crystalline solid ($C_6H_4COSO_2NH$) prepared from toluene: sickly sweetness (*fig.*).—*adj.* **sacch′arine** (*-in, -en*), of the nature of sugar: of, containing, or yielding sugar: sugary: of sickly sweetness.— *n.* **saccharinity** (*-in′i-ti*).—*adjs.* **sacch′aroid, -oid′al,** like loaf-sugar in texture.—*ns.* **saccharom′eter,** a hydrometer or other instrument for measuring concentration of sugar solutions; **Saccharomyces** (*-ō-mī′sēz*; Gr. *mykēs,* fungus), the yeast genus of ascomycete fungi; **sacch′arose** (*-ōs*), any carbohydrate, esp. cane sugar. [L. *saccharum*—Gr. *sakcharon,* sugar, a word of Eastern origin; cf. jaggery, sugar.]

**saccos.** Same as sakkos.

**sacellum,** *sə-sel′əm, n.* a god's unroofed sanctuary: a little chapel: a tomb or monument in the form of a chapel within a church:—*pl.* **sacell′a.** [L. dim. of *sacrum,* a holy place— *sacer,* consecrated.]

**sacerdotal,** *sas-ər-dō′tl, adj.* priestly: sacerdotalist. —*v.t.* **sacerdō′talise, -ize,** to render sacerdotal. —*ns.* **sacerdō′talism,** the spirit of the priesthood: devotion to priestly interests: priestcraft: the belief that the presbyter is a priest in the sense of offering a sacrifice in the eucharist: claim for, or attribution to, a priesthood, of special or supernatural powers; **sacerdō′talist.**—*adv.* **sacerdō′tally.** [L. *sacerdōs, -ōtis,* a priest— *sacer,* sacred, *dăre,* to give.]

**sachem,** *sā′chəm, n.* a North American Indian chief: a Tammany leader.—*ns.* **sā′chemdom, sā′chemship.** [Algonquian.]

**sachet,** *sa′shā, n.* a bag of perfume, or a bag for holding handkerchiefs, etc. [Fr.]

**sack,** *sak, n.* a large bag of coarse material: a sackful: a varying measure of capacity: a woman's gown, loose at the back: a train hung from the shoulders of such a gown: a loose coat, hanging at the back: a woman's loose-fitting waistless dress: (with **the**) dismissal (*slang*): (with **the**) the punishment of death by sewing in a sack and drowning.—*v.t.* to put into a sack: to dismiss (*slang*).—*ns.* **sack′ful,** as much as a sack will hold:—*pl.* **sack′fuls; sack′ing,** sackcloth.—**sack′cloth,** cloth for sacks: coarse cloth, formerly worn in mourning or penance; **sack′-coat,** a man's short loose coat. —*adj.* **sack-doudling** (*-dōōd′lin*; *Scott*), bagpiping (cf. doodle and Ger. *dudelsack*).—**sack′-race,** one in which each runner's legs are encased in a sack; **sack′-tree,** the upas (from the use of its inner bark to make sacks).—**sad sack,** one who seems to attract mishap and disaster. [O.E. *sacc*—L. *saccus*—Gr. *sakkos*; prob. Phoenician.]

**sack,** *sak, n.* the plundering or devastation of a town: pillage.—*v.t.* to plunder: to ravage.— *ns.* **sack′age, sack′ing,** sack. [Fr. *sac*; according to some the same as the foregoing (putting in a bag).]

**sack,** *sak, n.* the old name of a Spanish wine, the favourite drink of Falstaff.—**sack′-poss′et,** posset made with sack.—**burnt sack,** mulled sack. [Fr. *sec*—L. *siccus,* dry.]

**sackbut,** *sak′but, n.* an old instrument with a slide like the trombone: a mistranslation of Aramaic *sabbekā,* the sambuca (*B.*). [Fr. *saquebute,* perh. O.Fr. *saquier,* to draw out, and *bouter,* to push.]

**sackless,** *sak′lis,* (*arch.* and *Scot.*) *adj.* innocent: guileless: feeble: dispirited (see also under sac). [O.E *saclēas*—*sacu*; sac, sake.]

**sacque,** a sham-French spelling of **sack** (garment).

**sacra, sacral.** See sacrum.

**sacrament,** *sak′rə-mənt, n.* a religious rite variously regarded as a channel or as a sign of grace— amongst Protestants generally *Baptism* and the *Lord's Supper*—amongst Roman Catholics, also *Confirmation, Penance, Holy Orders, Matrimony,* and *Extreme Unction:* the Lord's Supper specially: a symbol of something spiritual or secret: a sign, token, or pledge of a covenant: a religious mystery: a Roman soldier's oath on enlistment: a pledge deposited by each party to a suit (*Rom. law*): a solemn oath: an oath of purgation: materials used in a sacrament.— *v.t.* to bind by an oath.—*adj.* **sacramental** (*-ment′l*).—*n.* (*R.C.*) an act or object which may transmit or receive grace.—*ns.* **sacramen′talism; sacramen′talist,** one who attaches importance to the spiritual nature of the sacraments. —*adv.* **sacramen′tally.**—*n.* **sacramentā′rian,** one who holds a high or extreme view of the efficacy of the sacraments: a denier of the real presence in the sacrament of the Lord's Supper (*obs.*).— Also *adj.*—*n.* **sacramentā′rianism.**—*adj.* **sacramen′tary,** pertaining to the sacrament or sacraments: sacramentarian.—*n.* a book containing all the prayers and ceremonies used at the celebration of the R.C. sacraments: one who denies the doctrine of the real presence.— **sac′rament-house,** an ambry for reservation of the sacrament.—**take the sacrament upon** or **to,** to take communion in confirmation of (an oath). [L. *sacrāmentum,* an oath, pledge—*sacrāre,* to consecrate—*sacer,* sacred.]

**sacrarium,** *sā-krā′ri-əm,* L. *sa-krä′ri-ōōm, n.* a place where the Penates or other holy things were kept (*Rom. Ant.*): the presbytery of a church. [L. *sacrārium*—*sacer,* holy.]

**sacred,** *sā′krid, adj.* consecrated: devoted: set apart or dedicated, esp. to God: holy: proceeding from God: religious: entitled to veneration: not to be violated: accursed.— *adv.* **sa′credly.**—*n.* **sa′credness.—sacred ape,** the hanuman of India; **sacred beetle,** an Egyptian scarab; **sacred cat,** the house cat of Egypt, sacred to Pasht; **sacred college,** the body of cardinals; **sacred cow,** an institution, custom, etc., so venerated that it is above criticism; **sacred fish,** oxyrhyncus; **Sacred Heart** (*R.C.*), the physical heart of Christ, adored with special devotion since the 18th century. [Pa.p. of obs. *sacre*—O.Fr. *sacrer*—L. *sacrāre*—*sacer,* sacred.]

**sacrifice,** *sak′ri-fis,* in the poets sometimes *-fīz, n.* the offering of a slaughtered animal on an altar to a god: any offering to a god: Christ's offering of himself (*theol.*): the Mass (*R.C.*): destruction, surrender, or foregoing of anything valued for the sake of anything else, esp. a higher consideration: loss by selling cheap: a victim offered in sacrifice.—*v.t.* to offer up in sacrifice: to make a sacrifice of: to give up for a higher good or for mere advantage: to make a victim of: to allow to come to destruction or evil.— *v.i.* to offer sacrifice.—*n.* **sac′rificer.**—*adj.* **sacrificial** (*-fish′l*).—*adv.* **sacrifi′cially.**—*v.t.* and *v.i.* **sac′rify** (*obs.*), to sacrifice:—*pa.p.* (*Spens.*) **sac′rifide.—sacrifice hit,** in baseball, a hit to enable another player to score or to gain a base. [L. *sacrificium*—*sacer,* sacred, *facĕre,* to make.]

**sacrilege,** *sak′ri-lij, n.* a profanation of anything holy: the breaking into a place of worship and stealing therefrom.—*adj.* **sacrilegious** (*-lij′əs*).— *adv.* **sacrile′giously.**—*ns.* **sacrile′giousness; sacri-le′gist.** [Fr. *sacrilège*—L. *sacrilegium*—*sacer,* sacred, *legĕre,* to gather.]

**sacring,** *sā′kring,* (*arch.*) *n.* consecration.— **sa′cring bell,** in R.C. churches, a small bell! rung to call attention to the more solemn parts of the service of the Mass. [See sacred.]

**sacrist,** *sak′rist, sā′krist, n.* a sacristan: a person in a cathedral who copies out music for the choir and takes care of the books.—*ns.* **sacristan** (*sak′*), an officer in a church who has care of the sacred vessels and other movables: a sexton; **sacristy** (*sak′*), an apartment in a church where the sacred utensils, vestments, etc., are kept: vestry. [L.L. *sacrista, sacristānus,* a sacristan, *sacristia,* a vestry—L. *sacer.*]

**sacro-.** See **sacrum.**

**sacrosanct,** *sak'rō-sang(k)t, adj.* inviolable.—*n.* **sacrosanc'tity.** [L. *sacrōsanctus—sacer,* sacred, *sanctus,* pa.p. of *sancire,* to hallow.]

**sacrum,** *sā'krəm, n.* a triangular bone composed of fused vertebrae wedged between two innominate bones, so as to form the keystone of the pelvic arch:—*pl.* **sā'cra.**—*adj.* **sā'cral.**—**sā'crō-,** in composition, sacrum, e.g. *adjs.* **sācrocos'tal,** connected with the sacrum and having the character of a rib (also *n.*); **sācrŏil'iac,** pertaining to the sacrum and ilium. [L. (*os*) *sacrum,* holy (bone): so called for unknown reason.]

**sad,** *sad,* (*comp.* **sadd'er,** *superl.* **sadd'est**) *adj.* sated (*orig.*): steadfast, constant (*Spens., Milt.*): staid: sedate: serious: earnest: grave: sober-minded: sorrowful: deplorable (often playfully): heavy, stiff: doughy: sober, dark-coloured.—*v.t.* **sadd'en,** to make sad.—*v.i.* to grow sad.—*adj.* **sadd'ish.**—*adv.* **sad'ly.**—*n.* **sad'-ness.**—*adjs.* **sad'-coloured; sad'-eyed, -faced, -hearted** (all *Shak.*).—**sad'-iron,** a flat-iron.— **sad sack** (see **sack**); **in sober sadness,** in serious earnest. [O.E. *sæd,* sated; cf. Du. *zat,* Ger. *satt;* L. *sat, satis.*]

**saddhu.** See **sadhu.**

**saddle,** *sad'l, n.* a seat for a rider: a pad for the back of a draught animal: anything of like shape: a col: that part of the back on which the saddle is placed: a mark on that part: a butcher's cut including a part of the backbone with the ribs: the hinder part of a cock's back: a worm's clitellum: in a structure, e.g. a bridge, a support having a groove shaped to fit another part.—*v.t.* to put a saddle on: to encumber: to impose as a burden of encumbrance.—*adj.* **sadd'leless.**—*ns.* **sadd'ler,** a maker or seller of saddles: a soldier who has charge of cavalry saddles (also **sadd'ler-cor'poral, -ser'geant**): the harp-seal: a saddle-horse (*U.S.*); **sadd'lery,** occupation of a saddler: his shop or stock-in-trade: a saddle-room.—**sadd'leback,** a saddle-shaped hill, coping, animal, or object: the great black-backed gull: the hooded crow: the male harp-seal: a breed of goose: a breed of pig: a saddle-roof.—*adj.* (also **sadd'lebacked**) saddle-shaped: with a depression in the middle of the back: marked on the back: of a coping, sloping from the middle to each side.—**sadd'le-bag,** a bag carried at, or attached to, the saddle. —*adj.* upholstered in cloth in imitation of camels' saddle-bags.—**sadd'le-bar,** a bar for sustaining stained glass in a window; **sadd'le-blanket,** a folded blanket used as a saddle-cloth; **sadd'le-bow** (-*bō*), the arched front of a saddle; **sadd'le-cloth,** a housing cloth placed under a saddle.—*adj.* **sadd'le-fast,** firmly seated in the saddle.—**sadd'le-feather, -hackle,** one of the long, slender feathers drooping from a cock's saddle; **sadd'le-girth,** a band that holds the saddle in its place; **sadd'le-horse,** a riding horse; **sadd'le-lap,** the skirt of a saddle.—*adj.* **sadd'le-nosed,** with nose sunken at the bridge.—**sadd'le-pillar, -pin,** the support of a cycle saddle, which fits a socket in the frame; **sadd'le-roof,** a tower roof with two gables; **sadd'le-room,** a room where saddles and harness are kept.—*adjs.* **sadd'le-shaped,** arched: concave and convex in sections at right angles to each other; **sadd'le-sick, -sore,** chafed with riding.—**sadd'le-spring,** a spring supporting a cycle-saddle; **sadd'le-tree,** the frame of a saddle.—**in the saddle,** in control; **put the saddle on the right horse,** to impute blame where it is deserved; **saddle up,** to saddle a horse: to mount (*S.Afr.*). [O.E. *sadol, sadel;* cf. Du. *zadel,* Ger. *sattel.*]

**Sadducee,** *sad'ū-sē, n.* one of a Jewish sceptical

school or party of aristocratic traditionists in New Testament times.—*adjs.* **Sadducae'an, Sadducean** (-*sē'ən*).—*ns.* **Sadd'uceeism, Sadd'ucism,** scepticism. [Gr. *Saddoukaios*—Heb. *Tsadūqim.*]

**sadhu, saddhu,** *sä'dōō, n.* a Hindu holy man, ascetic and mendicant. [Sans. *sādhu,*—*adj.,* straight, pious.]

**sadism,** *säd'izm, n.* sexual perversion with passion for cruelty: love of cruelty.—*n.* **sad'ist.**—*adj.* **sadistic** (*sə-dis'*).—*ns.* **sado-mas'ochism,** obtaining pleasure by inflicting pain on oneself or another; **sado-masochist.**—*adj.* **sado-masochist'ic.** [Comte (called Marquis) de *Sade* (1740-1814), who died insane, notoriously depicted this perversion in his novels.]

**sae, sā,** *adv.* Scottish form of **so.**

**saeculum, seculum,** *sek'ūl-əm, n.* an astronomical or geological age. [L., a generation.]

**saeter,** *set'ər, sāt', n.* in Norway, an upland meadow which provides summer pasture for cattle, and where butter and cheese are made: a hut on a saeter providing shelter for those looking after the animals. [Norw.]

**saeva indignatio,** *sē'və in-dig-nä'shi-ō, sī'wa, sī'va in-dig-nä'ti-ō,* (L.) fierce indignation (see **ubi** in appendix of quotations).

**safari,** *sə-fä'rē, n.* an expedition or caravan, especially for hunting: a long expedition involving difficulty or danger and/or requiring planning.—*v.i.* to go on safari.—**safari suit,** a suit for men, boys, or women, typically of cotton and consisting of long square-cut jacket and long or short trousers. [Swahili.]

**safe,** *sāf, adj.* unharmed: free from danger: secure: sound: certain: sure: reliable: cautious.—*n.* a chest or closet, safe against fire, thieves, etc.: a ventilated box or cupboard for meat, etc.—*v.t.* to make safe (*obs.*): to bring safely (*Shak.*).—*prep.* (*Spens.*)save.—*adv.* **safe'ly.** —*ns.* **safe'ness; safe'ty** (in Spens. often *sāf'i-ti*), state or fact of being safe: close custody (*obs.*): a safeguard: a safety-bicycle.—**safe'-blow'ing,** forcing of safes, using explosives; **safe'-break'-ing,** illegal opening of safes; **safe'-con'duct,** a permission to pass or travel with guarantee of freedom from molestation: a convoy.—*v.t.* (-*kon',* or -*dukt'*) to convoy.—**safe'-deposit,** a safe storage for valuables; **safe'guard,** keeping safe, protection: safety: a guard: a contrivance, condition, or provision to secure safety: a safe-conduct: an overskirt for riding (*obs.*). —*v.t.* to protect.—**safe'guarding,** protection, especially by import duties; **safe'-keeping,** keeping in safety: safe custody; **safe period,** that part of the menstrual cycle during which conception is most unlikely; **safe seat,** a seat that the specified political party will certainly win in an election; **safe'ty-arch,** an arch in the body of a wall to relieve the pressure; **safe'ty-belt,** a belt for fastening a workman, etc., to a fixed object while he carries out a dangerous operation: one fastening a passenger to his seat as a precaution against injury in a crash; **safety bicycle,** a common low-wheeled bicycle; **safety bolt,** the safety lock of a firearm; **safe'ty-cage,** a mine-cage with a catch to prevent a fall; **safe'ty-catch,** any catch to secure safety, as in a miners' cage or a gun; **safety curtain,** a fireproof theatre curtain; **safety fuse,** a slow-burning fuse that can be lighted at a safe distance: a fuse inserted for safety in an electric circuit; **safety glass,** a sandwich of plastic between sheets of glass: glass reinforced with wire, or toughened; **safety lamp,** a miners' lamp that will not ignite inflammable gases; **safety light,** a warning light: a light that will not readily cause a fire; **safety lock,** a lock that cannot be picked by ordinary means: in firearms, a device for preventing accidental discharge; **safe'ty-match,** a match that can be ignited only on a prepared surface; **safety paper**, paper difficult to imitate or tamper with without detection, as for bank-notes; **safe'ty-pin**, a pin in the form of a clasp with a guard covering its point: a pin for locking a piece of machinery, a grenade, a mine, etc.; **safe'ty-plug**, a plug that melts when the temperature rises too high; **safety razor**, a razor with protected blade; **safe'ty-rein**, a rein for preventing a horse from running away; **safe'ty-stop**, a contrivance for preventing accidents in machinery; **safe'ty-valve**, a valve that opens when the pressure becomes too great: any outlet that gives relief (*fig.*).—**err on the safe side**, to choose the safer alternative; **safe and sound**, secure and uninjured. [O.Fr. *sauf*—L. *salvus*.]

**saffian**, *saf'i-ən*, *n.* leather tanned with sumach and dyed in bright colours. [Russ. *saf'yan.*]

**safflower**, *saf'lowr*, *n.* a thistle-like composite (*Carthamus tinctorius*) cultivated in India: its dried petals, used for making a red dye and rouge. [Cf. Du. *saffloer*, O.Fr. *saffleur*.]

**saffron**, *saf'rən*, *n.* a species of crocus: its dried stigmas, used as a dye and flavouring: its colour, orange-yellow.—*adj.* **saff'roned**, coloured or flavoured with saffron.—*adj.* **saff'rony**, coloured somewhat like saffron.—*n.* **saf'ranin(e)**, a coal-tar dye, giving various colours.—**saff'ron-cake**, a cake flavoured with saffron.—**bastard saffron**, safflower; **meadow saffron**, Colchicum. [O.Fr. *safran*—Ar. *za'farān*.]

**sag**, *sag*, *v.i.* to bend, sink, or hang down, esp. in the middle: to yield or give way as from weight or pressure: to hang heavy: to droop: to drag oneself heavily along: to make leeway: —*pr.p.* **sagg'ing**; *pa.p.* and *pa.t.* **sagged**.—*n.* a droop.—*adj.* **sagging**.—*n.* and *adj.* **sagg'ing**. [Cf. Sw. *sacka*, to sink down; L.G. *sacken*, to sink.]

**saga**, *sä'gə*, *n.* a prose tale in the old literature of Iceland: a body of legend about some subject: a long, detailed story (*coll.*).—**sa'gaman**, a narrator of sagas; **saga novel** (see roman fleuve). [O.N. *saga*; cf. saw (3).]

**sagacious**, *sə-gā'shəs*, *adj.* keen in perception or thought: discerning and judicious: wise.—*adv.* **sagā'ciously**.—*ns.* sagā'ciousness, sagacity (*-gas'i-ti*). [L. *sagāx, -ācis.*]

**sagamore**, *sag'ə-mōr*, *n.* an American Indian chief. [Penobscot *sagamo*; cf. sachem.]

**sagapenum**, *sag-ə-pē'nəm*, *n.* a fetid gum-resin, from *Ferula persica.* [Gr. *sagapēnon*.]

**sagathy**, *sag'ə-thi*, *n.* a woollen stuff. [Origin unknown; cf. Fr. *sagatis*, Sp. *sagati*.]

**sage**, *sāj*, *n.* a garden labiate plant (*Salvia officinalis*) used for stuffing for goose, etc.: any plant of the genus, as (*Salvia*): extended to wood germander (*wood-sage*).—**sage'-apple**, an edible gall formed on Mediterranean sage; **sage'brush**, a plant-formation of shrubby Artemisias, on dry American plains: any of the Artemisias forming it; **sage'-cheese**, a cheese flavoured and mottled with sage leaves; **sage'-cock**, **-grouse**, a large North American grouse that feeds on sagebrush; **sage'-green**, greyish green, as in sage leaves; **sage'-rabbit**, a small hare of the sagebrush; **sage'-tea**, an infusion of sage leaves, a domestic tonic; **sage'-thrash'er**, the mountain mocking-bird. [O.Fr. *sauge* (It. *salvia*)—L. *salvia*—*salvus*, safe.]

**sage**, *sāj*, *adj.* wise.—*n.* a man of great wisdom. —*adv.* **sage'ly**.—*n.* **sage'ness**.—**seven sages** (see seven). [Fr. *sage*—L. *sapĕre*, to be wise.]

**sagene**, *sə-jēn'*, *n.* a net.—*n.* **sagenite** (*saj'ən-it*, *sə-jē'nit*), rutile in the form of a network of needles.—*adj.* **sagenitic** (*saj-ən-it'ik*). [Gr. *sagēnē*, drag-net.]

**saggar, saggard, sagger, seggar, sag', seg'ər(d)**, *n.* a clay box in which pottery is packed for baking. [Perh. safeguard.]

**sagged, sagging.** See sag.

**saginate**, *saj'i-nāt*, *v.t.* to fatten.—*n.* **sagina'tion**. [L. *saginăre*, to fatten.]

**sagitta**, *sə-jit'ə*, *n.* a keystone: a versed sine: the middle stroke of the letter epsilon: the Arrow, a northern constellation.—*adj.* **sagittal** (*saj'it-l*), arrow-shaped: like a sagitta: pertaining or parallel to the sagittal suture.—*adv.* **sag'ittally**. —*ns.* **Sagitta'ria**, the arrow-head genus; **Sagittā'rius**, the Archer, a constellation and a sign of the zodiac; **sag'ittary**, a centaur: an archer. —*adj.* **sag'ittate**, shaped like an arrow-head with the barbs pointing backwards.—**sagittal suture**, that between the two parietal bones of the skull. [L. *sagitta*, an arrow.]

**sago**, *sā'gō*, *n.* a nutritive farinaceous substance produced from the pith of Metroxylon and other palms (Arenga, Caryota, Oreodoxa), and Cycads (Cycas).—**sa'go-palm**. [Malay *sāgū*.]

**saguaro**, *sä-(g)wä'rō*, *n.* the giant cactus. [From an American Indian language.]

**saguin, sagoin, sagouin**, *sag'win*, *sag-oin'*, *n.* a titi monkey. [Fr. *sago*(*u*)*in*—Port. *saguim*— Tupi *saguin*.]

**sagum**, *sā'gəm*, (L. *sag'ōōm*) *n.* a Roman military cloak:—*pl.* **sa'ga**. [L. *sāgum*; prob. Gaulish.]

**sahib**, *sä'ib*, *n.* a term of respect given in India to persons of rank and to Europeans: Sir or Mr: a European: a gentleman:—*fem.* sahiba(h). [Ar. *sāhib*, orig. friend.]

**sai**, *sä'i*, *n.* the capuchin monkey. [Tupí, monkey.]

**saibling**, *zip'ling*, *n.* the char. [Ger. dial.]

**saic**, **sack**, **saique**, *sä-ēk'*, *sā'ik*, *n.* a Levantine vessel like a ketch. [Fr. *saique*—Turk. *shāiqā*.]

**saice**. Same as syce.

**said**, *sed*, *pa.t.* and *pa.p.* of say.—*adj.* beforementioned.

**saiga**, *sī'gə*, *n.* a west Asian antelope. [Russ.]

**saikless**, *sāk'lis*, *adj.* a Scots form of sackless.

**sail**, *sāl*, *n.* a sheet of canvas, framework of slats, or other structure, spread to catch the wind, so as to propel a ship, drive a windmill, etc.: a wing, esp. a hawk's: any sail-like organ or object: sails collectively: a ship or ships: a trip in a vessel: an act or distance of sailing: a number sailing or flying together: a condition of having sails set or filled.—*v.i.* to progress or travel by sail: to go by water: to set out on a voyage: to make excursions in sailing-craft: to glide or float smoothly along.—*v.t.* to navigate: to cause to sail, as a toy boat: to pass over or along in a ship: to fly through.—*adjs.* **sail'-able**, navigable; **sailed**, having sails.—*ns.* **sail'er**, a boat or ship that can sail; **sail'ing**, travelling or journey by sails or on water: a ship's departure from port: act or mode of directing a ship's course.—Also *adj.*—*adj.* **sail'less**.—*ns.* **sail'or**, one who is employed in the management of a ship, esp. one who is not an officer: a mariner: a seaman: a navigator: one who is tolerant of the motion of a ship: a sailor-hat (*coll.*); **sail'oring**, occupation as a sailor.— *adjs.* **sail'orless**; **sail'or-like**, **sail'orly**, **sail'y**.— **sail arm**, one of the arms of a windmill; **sail'-boat** (*U.S.*), a sailing-boat.—*adjs.* **sail'-borne**; **sail'-broad** (*Milt.*), broad or spreading like a sail.—**sail'-cloth**, a strong cloth for sails; **sail'-fish**, a fish that shows a large dorsal fin, esp. the basking shark or a kind of swordfish (Histiophorus); **sail'-fluke**, the whiff (from exposing its tail); **sail'-flying**, flying in a sailplane; **sail'ing-boat**, a boat moved by sails; **sail'ing-master**, an officer in charge of navigation, esp. of a yacht (formerly in U.S. navy a warrant officer); **sailing orders**, instructions to the captain of a ship at setting forth on a voyage; **sail'ing-ship**, a ship driven by sails; **sail'-loft**, a loft where sails are made; **sail'-maker**; **sail'or-hat'**, a lady's hat like a man's straw hat: a hat with a wide, upcurved brim; **sail'or-man**, a seaman;

sail'plane, a glider that can rise with an upward current; sail'-room, a room in a vessel where sails are stowed; sail'-yard, the yard on which sails are extended.—full sail, with sails filled with the wind: with all sails set; make sail, to spread more canvas; sail close to (or near) the wind (see wind); set sail, to spread the sails: to set forth on a voyage; shorten sail, to reduce its extent; strike sail, to lower the sail or sails: to abate one's pretensions (Shak.); under sail, having the sails spread: moved by sails. [O.E. segel; cf. Du. zeil, Ger. segel.]

sail, sāl, v.i. to project.—n. projection. [O.Fr. saillir, to jut—L. salīre, to leap.]

saimiri, si-mē'rē, n. a squirrel-monkey. [Tupí sai, monkey, miri, little.]

sain, sān, (arch.) v.t. to make the sign of the cross over: (by association with L. sānāre) to heal. [O.E. segnian—L. signāre—signum, mark.]

saine, sān, a Spenserian form of the infin. and the pres. indic. pl. of say: an editor's reading for faine (Love's Lab. Lost III, i. 88) taken as a pa.p. of say (Shak.).

sainfoin, sān'foin, n. a leguminous fodder-plant (Onobrychis viciaefolia).—Also saint'foin. [Fr. sainfoin, prob.—sain, wholesome, foin, hay—L. sānum fēnum.]

saint, sānt, when prefixed to a name sint, sn(t), adj. (or n. in apposition) holy.—n. a holy person: one eminent for virtue: an Israelite, a Christian, or one of the blessed dead (B.): one canonised: an angel: a member of various religious bodies, esp. Puritans, as used of themselves or as a nick-name: a sanctimonious person.—v.i. (or v.t. with it) to play the saint.—v.t. to make a saint of: to hail as saint.—n. saint'dom.—adj. saint'ed, made a saint, holy: sacred: gone to heaven: canonised. — ns. saint'ess; saint'hood. — adj. saint'ish, saintlike.—n. saint'ism, the character or quality of a saint: sanctimoniousness.—adj. saint'like. — ns. saint'liness; saint'ling. — adj. saint'ly, of, like, characteristic of, or befitting a saint.—n. saint'ship.—saint's day, a day set apart for the commemoration of a particular saint; St Agnes's Eve, 20th January; St Agnes's flower, the snowflake; St Andrew's cross, a cross in the form of the letter X: a white saltire on a blue field, as borne on the banner of Scotland; St Andrew's Day, 30th November; St Anthony pig, St Anthony's cross, fire, nut (see Anthony); St Barbara's cress, yellow rocket; St Barnaby's thistle, a knapweed flowering about the saint's day (11th June); St Bernard's dog or (great) St Bernard, a breed of very large dogs, named after the hospice of the Great St Bernard, used, especially formerly, to rescue travellers lost in the snow; St Crispin's Day, a shoemakers' festival, 25th October; St Cuthbert's beads (see Cuthbert); St Dabeoc's heath, a rare Irish heath; St David's Day, 1st March; St Elmo's fire, a corposant; St George's cross, a red cross on a white field; St George's Day, 23rd April; St Hubert's disease, hydrophobia; St Ignatius's bean, the poisonous seed of a plant (Strychnos ignatii) akin to nux vomica; St James's, the British court; St John's bread, the carob bean; St John's Day, 27th December; St Johnston's ribbon, or tippet, the hangman's rope (St Johnsto(u)n = Perth, associated in the 18th cent. with hangings); St John's wort, any Hyperi-cum; St Julien, an esteemed red Bordeaux wine from the Médoc region; St Leger, a horse-race run since 1776 at Doncaster, so called since 1778 from Col. St Leger; St Luke's summer, a spell of pleasant weather about the middle of October; St Martin's evil, drunkenness; St Martin's summer, a spell of mild, damp weather in late autumn; St Nicholas's clerks, thieves; St Patrick's cabbage, London pride; St Patrick's Day, 17th March; St Peter's fish, the dory

St Peter's wort, square-stalked St John's wort: extended to several plants; St Stephen's, Houses of Parliament; St Swithin's Day, 15th July; (St) Tib(b)'s Eve, never; St Valentine's Day, 14th February (see valentine); St Vitus's dance, chorea. [Fr.,—L. sanctus, holy.]

Saintpaulia, sānt-pö'li-ə, n. genus to which the African violet (q.v.) belongs. [Baron Walter von Saint Paul, who discovered it.]

Saint-Simonism, sən(t)-, sin(t)-si'mən-izm, n. the socialistic system of the Comte de Saint-Simon (1760-1825).—ns. Saint-Simō'nian (also adj.); Saint-Simō'nianism; Saint-Si'monist.

sair, sār, Scots form of sore, savour, serve.

saist (Spens., Milt.). Same as sayest (see say).

saith, seth, (arch.) 3rd pers. sing. pres. indic. of say.

saith, saithe, sāth, (Scot.) n. the coalfish. [O.N. seithr.]

Saiva, Shaiva, s(h)ī'va, n. a votary of Siva.—n. S(h)ai'vism.

sajou, sä-zhöö', -jöö', n. a capuchin monkey. [Fr.,—Tupí sai, monkey and augmentative -uassu.]

Sakai, sä'kī, n. a group of forest tribes of Malaya: an individual of this group: their language, of the Mon-Khmer group:—pl. Sakai.—Also adj.

sake, sä'ki, sä'kē, n. Japanese rice-beer: alcoholic liquor generally.—Also saké, saki. [Jap.]

sake, sāk, n. cause: account: regard: advantage: behalf: purpose: aim, object.—for any sake, by all means: I beseech you; for old sake's sake, for the sake of old times, for auld lang syne. [O.E. sacu, strife, a lawsuit; Du. zaak, Ger. sache; O.E. sacan, to strive, Goth. sakan; cf. sac, sackless, seek.]

saker, sä'kər, n. a species of falcon (Falco sacer) used in hawking, esp. the female: an obsolete small cannon.—n. sa'keret, the male saker. [Fr. sacre, prob.—Ar. saqr, confounded with L. sacer sacred.]

saki, sä'ki, -kē, n. a South American monkey of the genus Pithecia, with long bushy non-prehensile tail. [Fr., for Tupí sai, or saguin; cf. sai, saguin.]

saki. See sake (1).

sakieh, sakiyeh, sakia, sä'ki-(y)ə, n. an Eastern water-wheel. [Ar. sāqiyah.]

sakkos, sak'os, n. an Eastern bishop's vestment like an alb or a dalmatic. [Gr. sakkos, a bag.]

saksaul. Same as saxaul.

Sakti, Shakti, s(h)äk', shuk'tē, (Hinduism) n. the female principle, esp. as personified in the wife of Siva or other god.—ns. S(h)ak'ta, a wor-shipper of the Sakti; S(h)ak'tism. [Sans. śakti, divine energy.]

sal, sāl, a Northern form of shall.

sal. See sial.

sal, sāl, n. a large gregarious tree (Shorea robusta; fam. Dipterocarpaceae) of north India with teaklike wood. [Hind. sāl.]

sal, sal, (chem. and pharmacy) n. a salt.—sal alem'broth (an alchemists' word of unknown origin), mercury ammonium chloride—also salt of wisdom; sal ammoniac, ammonium chloride; sal prunella, prunelle, saltpetre cast in cakes; sal volatile (vol-at'i-li), ammonium carbonate, or a solution of it in alcohol and/or ammonia in water: smelling salts. [L. sāl.]

sal Atticum, säl at'i-kəm, säl at'i-kōōm, (L.) Attic salt (see Attic).

salaam, sä-läm', n. a word and gesture of saluta-tion in the East, chiefly among Moslems: obeisance: greeting.—v.i. to perform the salaam. [Ar. salām, peace; Heb. shālōm.]

salable, salableness, salably. See sale.

salacious, sə-lā'shəs, adj. lustful: lecherous.—adv. salā'ciously.—ns. salā'ciousness, salacity (-las'i-ti). [L. salāx, -ācis—salīre, to leap.]

salad, sal'əd, also (arch.) sallad, sallet (sal'it), n.

a cold dish of vegetables or herbs (either raw or pre-cooked), generally mixed, with or without oil and vinegar or other dressing, sometimes including slices of egg, lobster, etc.: a plant grown for or used in salads: something savoury (*fig.*; *Shak.*): a confused mixture.—*n.* sal′ading, herbs and vegetables for salads.—salad bowl; salad burnet, the common burnet; salad cream, a type of bottled mayonnaise; salad days (*Shak.*), the time when one is 'green in judgement, cold in blood' (*Ant. and Cleo.* I, v. 74); salad dressing, oil, sauce, olive-oil used in dressing salads; salad herb, plant; salad plate.—fruit′-salad (see fruit); word salad, copious but incoherent utterance, sometimes a symptom of schizophrenia. [Fr. *salade*—L. *sāl*, salt.]

salade. Same as sallet (1).

sallal, sallal, *sal′al, n.* a N.W. American ericaceous shrub (*Gaultheria shallon*).—sal(l)′al-berry, its edible fruit. [Chinook jargon.]

salamander, *sal′ə-man-dər*, or *-man′, n.* a genus (Salamandra) of tailed amphibians, nearly related to the newts, harmless, but long dreaded as poisonous, once supposed able to live in fire or to put out fire: an elemental spirit believed by Paracelsists to live in fire: one who braves exposure to fire unscathed (physical, military, or amatory): a poker used red-hot for kindling fires: a hot metal plate for browning meat, etc. —*adjs.* salaman′der-like (also *adv.*); salaman′-drian; salaman′drine; salaman′droid (also *n.*). [Fr. *salamandre*—L. *salamandra*—Gr. *salamandrā*; prob. of Eastern origin.]

salami, *sə-lä′mi*, sə-lä′mē, (*pl.* of salame, -mä; treated as *sing.*), *n.* a highly seasoned Italian sausage. [It.]

salamon. See salmon (2).

salangane, *sal′ang-gān, n.* a swiftlet (Collocalia) that builds edible nests. [Tagálog *salangan*.]

salary, *sal′ə-ri, n.* a periodical payment (usually at longer intervals than a week) for services other than mechanical.—*v.t.* to pay a salary to.—*n.* salariat (*sə-lä′ri-ət*), the salary-drawing class or body.—*adj.* sal′aried. [O.Fr. *salarie* (Fr. *salaire*)—L. *salārium*, salt-money, *sāl*, salt.]

salband, *säl′band*, zäl′bänt, (*geol.*) *n.* the crust of a dyke or vein. [Ger. *salband*, selvage—*selb*, self, *ende*, end.]

sale, *sāl, n.* act of selling: the exchange of anything for money: power or opportunity of selling: demand: public offer of goods to be sold, esp. at reduced prices or by auction: the state of being offered to buyers.—*adj.* intended for selling: vendible.—*n.* salabil′ity (also saleabil′ity).—*adj.* sal(e)′able, that may be sold: in good demand.—*n.* sal(e)′ableness.—*adv.* sal(e)′ably.—sale′-cat′alogue; sale′-price, price asked at a special sale; sale′-room, an auction-room; sales′-clerk (*U.S.*), one who sells in a store or shop; sales′man, a man who sells goods, esp. in a shop: a commercial traveller or canvasser (*U.S.*):—*fem.* sales′woman; sales′man-ship, the art of selling: skill in presenting wares in the most attractive light or in persuading purchasers to buy; sales resistance, unwillingness to buy; sales′-talk, boosting talk to effect a sale; sales′-tax, a tax on the sale of goods and services, esp. one general in character and flat in rate (cf. purchase-tax); sale′work, work or things (made) for sale: work carelessly done. —forced sale, a sale compelled by a creditor; sale of work, a sale of things made by members of a church congregation or association so as to raise money. [Late O.E. *sala*, perh.—O.N. *sala*.]

sale, *sāl, n.* sallow: wicker (*Spens.*). [Also seal; form of sallow (1).]

salep, *sal′əp, n.* dried Orchis tubers: a food or drug prepared from them. [Turk. *sālep*, from Ar.]

saleratus, *sal-ə-rā′təs*, (*U.S.*) *n.* potassium or sodium bicarbonate, used in baking-powders. [L. *sāl aerātus*, aerated salt.]

Salesian, *səl-ē′shən, adj.* of St Francis of *Sales* or his order, the Visitants.—*n.* a follower of St Francis: a member of his order.

salewd, (*Spens.*) *pa.t.* of salue.

salfern, *sal′fərn, n.* gromwell (*Lithospermum arvense*).

Salian, *sā′li-ən, adj.* pertaining to a tribe of Franks on the lower Rhine.—*n.* one of this tribe.—*adj.* Salic, Salique (*sal′ik*).—Salic law, a law among the Salian Franks limiting the succession of certain lands to males—held later to apply to the succession to the crown of France. [L. *Salii*, Salians.]

Salian, *sā′li-ən, adj.* pertaining to the *Salii*, or priests of Mars in ancient Rome.

Salicaceae, *sal-i-kā′si-ē, n.pl.* a family of Archichlamydeae, willows and poplars.—*adj.* salicā′-ceous (-shəs).—*ns.* sal′icet (-set), salicional (*sal-ish′ə-nəl*), an organ stop with a tone like that of willow pipes; salicetum (*-sē′təm*), a thicket or plantation of willows:—*pl.* salice′tums, salicē′ta; sal′icin (-sin), a bitter crystalline glucoside (C₁₈H₁₈O₇) got from willow-bark, etc.; salicylate (*sə-lis′i-lāt*), a salt of salicylic acid.—*v.t.* to treat with salicylic acid.—*adj.* salicylic (*sal-i-sil′ik*; Gr. *hȳlē*, matter, material).—salicylic acid, an acid (C₇H₆O₃) originally prepared from salicin. [L. *salix*, *salicis*, a willow.]

Salicornia, *sal-i-kör′ni-ə, n.* the glasswort or marsh-samphire genus of the goosefoot family, small cactus-like salt-marsh plants. [Perh. L. *sāl*, salt, *cornū*, a horn.]

salient, *sā′li-ənt, adj.* leaping or springing: projecting outwards, as an angle: outstanding: prominent: striking.—*n.* an outward-pointing angle, esp. of a fortification or line of defences. —*ns.* sā′lience, the quality or condition of being salient: projection: (*Spens.*) saliaunce) onset; sā′liency.—*n.pl.* Salientia (*-en′shyə*), the frog and toad order of Amphibia.—*adv.* sā′liently.—salient point, first rudiment, esp. (formerly) of the heart. [L. *saliēns*, *-entis*, pr.p. of *salīre*, to leap.]

saliferous, *sə-lif′ər-əs, adj.* salt-bearing. [L. *sāl*, *salis*, salt, *ferre*, to bear.]

salify, *sal′i-fī, v.t.* to combine or impregnate with or form into a salt:—*pr.p.* sal′ifying; *pa.t.* and *pa.p.* sal′ified.—*adj.* sal′ifiable.—*n.* salificā′tion. [Fr. *salifier*—L. *sāl*, *salis*, salt, *facēre*, to make.]

saligot, *sal′i-got, n.* the water-chestnut. [Fr.]

salina, *sə-lē′nə*, or -lī′, *n.* a salt lagoon, lake, marsh, or spring: a salt-pan: a salt-work. [Sp., —L. *salīna* (in pl. only)—*sāl*, salt.]

saline, *sā′līn, sa′, sə-lin′, adj.* salt: salty: of the nature of a salt: abounding in salt: of the salts of alkali metals and magnesium: adapted to an environment with salt.—*n.* (*sə-lin′*, also *sā′lin*) a salina: a salt: crude potash: an effervescent aperient powder: a salt solution used in investigation or treatment of a physiological condition. —*ns.* salinity (*sə-lin′i-ti*), saltness; salinometer (*sal-i-nom′i-tər*), a hydrometer for measuring saltness of water. [L. *salīnus*, cf. salina.]

Salique. Same as Salic (see Salian).

saliva, *sə-lī′və, n.* spittle, a liquid secreted in the mouth to soften food and begin the process of digestion.—*adjs.* sali′val (*rare*); salivary (*sal′i-vər-i*), pertaining to, secreting, or conveying, saliva.—*v.i.* sal′ivate, to produce or discharge saliva, esp. in excess.—*v.t.* to cause to secrete excess of saliva.—*n.* salivā′tion, flow of saliva, esp. in excess. [L. *saliva*.]

Salix, *sal′iks, sā′liks, n.* the willow genus. [L. *sălix*, *-icis*.]

Salk vaccine, *sö(l)k*, a vaccine developed by the American Dr Jonas E. *Salk* and others, used against poliomyelitis.

Neutral vowels in unaccented syllables: *el′ə-mənt*; for certain sounds in foreign words, see p. viii

sallal. See salal.

salle, *sal*, (Fr.) hall.

sallee, *sal'ē* (*Austr.*) *n.* Acacia of various kinds: a species of Eucalyptus. [From a native word, or sally = sallow.]

sallee-man, *sal'ē-man*, *n.* a Moorish pirate: a hydrozoan with sail-like crest.—Also sall'y-man.—sall'ee-rover. [*Sallee*, on the coast of Morocco.]

sallenders, *sal'ən-dərz*, *n.* a skin disease affecting the hocks of horses. [Cf. Fr. *solandre*.]

sallet, *sal'it*, *n.* a light helmet (esp. 15th century) with neck-guard.—Also salade (*sä-läd'*). [Fr. *salade*; cf. It. *celata*; perh.—L. *galea caelāta*, engraved helmet.]

sallet. See salad.

sallow, *sal'ō*, *n.* a willow, esp. the broader-leaved kinds with comparatively brittle twigs—(*Scot.*) sauch, saugh (*sōhh*).—*adj.* sall'owy, abounding in sallows.—sall'ow-kitten, a small puss-moth whose larva feeds on sallow; sall'ow-thorn, sea-buckthorn. [O.E. (Anglian) *salh*, late stem *salg-* (W.S. *sealh*, *sēales*); cf. Ger. *sal*(*weide*), L. *salix*.]

sallow, *sal'ō*, *adj.* of a pale yellowish colour.—*v.t.* to make sallow.—*adj.* sall'owish, somewhat sallow.—*n.* sall'owness.—*adj.* sall'owy. [O.E. *salo*, *salu*; cf. O.H.G. *salo*.]

sally, *sal'i*, *n.* a leap: a swaying: an outrush: a sudden rushing forth of troops to attack besiegers: a going forth, excursion: outburst of fancy, wit, etc.: a projection: a running from side to side.—*v.i.* to rush out suddenly: to set forth, issue.—*v.t.* to sway by running from side to side (of a ship):—*pr.p.* sall'ying; *pa.t.* and *pa.p.* sall'ied—sall'yport, a gateway for making a sally from a fortified place: a large port for the escape of the crew from a fire-ship. [Fr. *saillie*—*saillir* (It. *salire*)—L. *salire*, to leap.]

sally, *sal'i*, *n.* the raising of a bell by pull of the rope: the woolly grip of a bell rope.—*v.t.* to bring into position of sally. [Perh. from preceding.]

sally, *sal'i*, a variant of sallee and of sallow (willow).

Sally Lunn, *sal'i lun'*, *n.* a sweet tea-cake, usu. served hot with butter. [From a girl who sold them in the streets of Bath, *c.* 1797.]

salmagundi, *sal-mə-gun'di*, *n.* a dish of minced meat with eggs, anchovies, vinegar, pepper, etc.: a medley, miscellany.—Also salmagun'dy. [Fr. *salmigondis*; origin obscure.]

salmi, *sal'mē*, *n.* a ragout, esp. of game. [Fr.; perh. from preceding, or from It. *salame*, sausage.]

Salmo, *sal'mō*, *n.* the salmon and trout genus of fishes, giving name to the family Salmonidae (*sal-mon'i-dē*).—*n.* sal'monid.—*n.* and *adj.* sal'-monoid. [L. *salmō*, *-ōnis*, salmon.]

salmon, *sam'ən*, *n.* a large, highly esteemed fish (*Salmo salar*), with silvery sides, that ascends rivers to spawn: extended to many closely allied fishes, and to some that resemble it superficially in some respects: the flesh of any of these as food: the colour of salmon flesh, a pinkish orange:—*pl.* salmon; or salmons, of kinds of salmon.—*adj.* salmon-coloured.—*n.* salm'onet, a samlet.—salm'on-berry, a salmon-coloured American raspberry; sal'mon-coble, a salmon-fisher's boat; salm'on-colour, an orange-pink. —*adj.* salm'on-coloured.—salm'on-disease, a bacterial disease of salmon formerly attributed to a fungus (Saprolegnia); salm'on-fisher, -fishery, -fishing; salm'on-fly, any artificial fly for taking salmon; salm'on-fry'; salm'on-ladder, a series of steps to permit a salmon to pass upstream; salm'on-leap, a waterfall ascended by salmon at a leap; salm'on-leister, -spear, an instrument for spearing salmon; salm'on-tackle, rod,

line, and fly for taking salmon; salm'on-trout', a fish (*Salmo trutta*) like the salmon, but smaller and thicker in proportion: in America applied to various kinds of trout.—Burnett salmon, the Australian lungfish (from the Burnett River). [O.Fr. *saumon*—L. *salmō*, *-ōnis*, from *salīre*, to leap.]

salmon, *sam'ən*, salamon, *sal'ə-mən*, (*obs.*) *n.* supposed to mean the mass, as in the vagrants' inviolable oath *by* (*the*) *salmon.* [Origin obscure.]

Salmonella, *sal-mə-nel'ə*, *n.* a large genus of bacteria many of which are associated with poisoning by contaminated food.—*n.* salmonellos'is, a disease caused by Salmonella. [Daniel E. *Salmon*, veterinarian.]

Salomonic. Same as Solomonic.

salon, *sal-ō*, *-on*, *n.* a drawing-room: a reception-room: a periodic gathering of notable persons in the house of a society queen: a somewhat elegant shop or business establishment (e.g. *beauty salon*): (*cap.*) a great annual exhibition of works by living artists in Paris. [Fr.]

saloon, *sə-lōōn'*, *n.* a spacious hall for receptions, for works of art, etc.: a large public room (for billiards, for dancing, for hairdressing, etc.): a large public cabin or dining-room for passengers: a saloon-carriage: a saloon-car: a drinking-bar (*U.S.*).—*n.* saloon'ist.—saloon'-bar', a quieter and more comfortably furnished part of a public house than the public bar, usu. separated from it; saloon'-car', a motor-car with enclosed body; saloon'-carr'iage, a railway carriage with interior open from end to end; saloon'-deck, an upper deck reserved for saloon or first-class passengers; saloon'-keeper (*U.S.*), a publican; saloon'-passenger, a passenger entitled to use the principal cabin: a first-class passenger on board a ship; saloon'-pistol, saloon'-rifle, one for use in a shooting gallery. [Fr. *salon*.]

saloop, *sə-lōōp'*, *n.* salep: a drink made from salep, later from sassafras. [salep.]

salop. Same as salep.—*adj.* salop'ian (*Lamb*)

Salop, *sal'əp*, *n.* Shropshire.—*adj.* Salopian (*-ō'pi-ən*), of Shropshire: of Shrewsbury School.—*n.* a native or inhabitant of Shropshire: one educated at Shrewsbury School. [A.Fr. *Sloppesberie* —O.E. *Scrobbesbyrig.*]

salp, *salp*, *n.* a free-swimming tunicate (Salpa). —*n.* and *adj.* salp'ian. [L. *salpa*—Gr. *salpē*, a kind of fish.]

salpinx, *sal'pingks*, *n.* an ancient Greek trumpet: the Eustachian tube: the Fallopian tube.— *n.* salpingectomy (*-pin-jek'tə-mi*), surgical removal of a Fallopian tube.—*adj.* salpingian (*-pin'ji-ən*), of the salpinx; salpingit'ic, of, of the nature of, salpingitis.—*n.* salpingitis (*-ji'tis*), inflammation of a Fallopian tube. [Gr. *salpinx*, *-ingos*, a trumpet.]

salse, *sals*, *n.* a mud volcano. [*Salsa*, name of one near Modena.]

salsify, salsafy, *sal'si-fi*, *n.* a purple-flowered species of goat's-beard, cultivated for its root, tasting like asparagus.—black salsify, scorzonera. [Fr. *salsifis*, prob.—It. *sassefrica*.]

Salsola, *sal'sō-lə*, *n.* the saltwort genus of the goosefoot family.—*adj.* salsolā'ceous. [Obs. It. dim. of *salso*—L. *salsus*, salt (*adj.*).]

salsuginous, *sal-sōō'ji-nəs*, *adj.* salty: growing in salty soil. [L. *salsūgō*, *-inis*, saltness.]

salt, *sölt*, *n.* chloride of sodium, occurring naturally as a mineral (rock-salt) and in solution in sea-water, brine-springs, etc.: smack, savour: piquancy: wit and good sense: saving or preserving quality: a salt-marsh or salting: an influx of salt water: a sailor, esp. an old sailor: a salt-cellar: a compound in which metal atoms or electropositive radicals replace one or more of the replaceable hydrogen atoms of an acid

—generalised to include the acid itself: (in (*pl.* smelling-salts: Epsom salt or other salt or mixture of salts used in medicine, esp. as a purgative: money collected at Montem.—*adj.* containing salt: tasting of salt: seasoned or cured with salt: overflowed with salt water: growing in salt soil: inhabiting salt water: pungent: excessively costly (*coll.*).—*v.t.* to sprinkle, season, cure, impregnate with salt: to immunise (as by inoculation): to season: to acclimatise: to assign an excessive value to or in (*slang*): to add gold, ore, etc., to, in order to give a false appearance of riches (*mining slang*).—*adj.* salt′ed.—*ns.* salt′er, one who salts, or who makes or deals in salt: a drysalter; salt′iness; salt′ing, the act of preserving, seasoning, etc., with salt: the celebration of the Eton Montem: a meadow flooded by the tides (suff. *-ing*, indicating a meadow in place-names).—*adj.* salt′ish.—*adv.* salt′ishly.—*n.* salt′ishness.—*adj.* salt′less.—*adv.* salt′ly.—*n.* salt′ness.—*adj.* salt′y, saltish: piquant, racy, witty.—salt′-box, a box for holding salt, esp. one with a clapper lid, once used as in burlesque music along with the marrowbones, tongs, etc.; salt′-bush, any Australian shrubby plant of the goosefoot family.—*adj.* salt′-butt′er (*Shak.*), fed on nothing better than salt butter, gross.—salt′-cake, crude sodium sulphate; salt′-cat, a salt mixture given as a digestive to pigeons; salt′-cellar (O.Fr. *saliere*—L. *salārium*—*sāl*, salt), a table vessel for holding salt: a depression behind the collar-bone; salt′-cote (*obs.*), a building where salt is made; salt′-fat (erron. salt′-foot), a large salt-cellar marking the class boundary at table: a pickling-tub; salt′-glaze, a glaze produced on pottery by volatilisation of common salt in the kiln; salt′-horse (*slang*), salt beef; salt′-junk (*sailors' slang*), salt beef; salt′-lick, a place to which animals resort for salt; salt′-marsh, land liable to be flooded with salt water; salt′-mine, a mine of rock-salt; salt′-money, an allowance for salt: money collected at Montem; salt′-pan, a large basin for obtaining salt by evaporation: a salt-work: a natural depression in which salt accumulates or has accumulated by evaporation; salt′-pit, a pit for obtaining salt by evaporation; salt′-rheum (also without *hyphen*), a discharge of mucus from the nose (*Shak.*): eczema (*U.S.*); salt′-spoon, a small spoon for taking salt at table; salt′-spring, a brine spring.—*adj.* salt′-water, of salt water.—salt′-work(s), a place where salt is made; salt′-wort, a fleshy, prickly plant (*Salsola kali*) of sandy seashores, of the goosefoot family, or other plant of the genus: sometimes applied to the glasswort (Salicornia). —above, below, the salt, among those of high, or low, social class, the salt-cellar marking the boundary when all dined together; lay, put, cast salt on one's tail, find or catch one, from the jocularly recommended method of catching a bird; salt away, to store away: to hoard; salt down, to preserve with salt: hence, to lay by, store up; salt of sorrel, acid potassium oxalate, a solvent for ink-stains; salt of tartar, a commercial name for purified potassium carbonate; salt of the earth, the choice few of the highest excellence (Matt. v. 13); salt of vitriol, sulphate of zinc; salt of wisdom, sal alembroth; salt of wormwood, potassium carbonate; salt out, to obtain as a precipitate by adding a salt; take with a grain of salt, to believe with some reserve; worth one's salt, good for anything at all—worth the value of the salt one consumes. [O.E. (Anglian) *salt* (W.S. *sealt*); cf. Ger. *salz*, also L. *sāl*, Gr. *hals.*]

salt, sŏlt, *n.* sexual desire, esp. in bitches.—*adj.* in heat: salacious (*Shak.*). [L. *saltus, -ūs*, leap.]

saltando, *sāl-tän′dō*, saltato, *-tä′tō*, *adv.* and *adj.*

arco saltando. [Gerund. and pa.p. respectively of It. *saltare*, to jump, skip.]

saltant, *sal′tant*, *sŏl′tənt*, *adj.* leaping: dancing: salient (*her.*).—*n.* (*biol.*) a changed form developed suddenly.—*v.i.* sal′tate.—*n.* saltā′tion, a leaping or jumping: spurting, pulsation: an abrupt variation (*biol.*).—*adjs.* saltato′rial, saltato′rious; sal′tatory, leaping: dancing: having the power of, or used in, leaping or dancing: changing abruptly. [L. *saltāre, -ātum*, inten. of *salīre*, to leap.]

saltarello, *sal-tə-rel′ō*, *n.* a lively dance with skips, for two dancers: its music, in triple time. [It. *saltarello*, Sp. *saltarelo*—L. *saltāre*, to dance.]

saltato. Same as saltando.

saltern, *sŏlt′ərn*, *n.* a salt-works. [O.E. *s(e)altern*—*s(e)alt*, salt, *ærn*, house.]

saltier. See saltire, satyr.

saltigrade, *sal′ti-grād*, *adj.* going by leaps.—*n.* a jumping spider. [L. *saltus, -ūs*, a leap, *gradī*, to go.]

saltimbanco, *sal-tim-bangk′ō*, (*obs.*) *n.* a mountebank, a quack. [It.]

saltire, saltier, *sal′*, *sŏl′tīr*, (*her.*) *n.* an ordinary in the form of a St Andrew's cross.—*adj.* sal′tierwise. [O.Fr. *saultoir, sautoir*—L.L. *saltātōrium*, a stirrup—L. *saltāre*, to leap.]

saltpetre (in U.S. saltpeter), *sŏlt-pē′tər*, *n.* potassium nitrate.—saltpē′treman (*hist.*), one authorised to search for saltpetre: one who prepares saltpetre; saltpe′tre-paper, touch-paper.—Chile or cubic saltpetre, sodium nitrate; Norway saltpetre, calcium nitrate. [O.Fr. *salpetre*—L.L. *salpetra*, prob. for L. *sāl petrae*, salt of stone.]

saltus, *sal′təs*, *n.* a breach of continuity: a jump to conclusion. [L., a leap, pl. *saltūs.*]

salubrious, *sə-lōō′bri-əs*, *-lū′*, *adj.* healthful, health-giving.—*adv.* salu′briously.—*ns.* salu′briousness, salu′brity. [L. *salūbris*—*salūs, salūtis*, health.]

salue, *sal-ōō′*, or *-ū′*, or *sal′*, (*obs.*) *v.t.* to salute: —*pa.t.* (*Spens.*) salewd′ (also sal′ued, which may be for salve′d, hailed with *salve*, the Latin greeting). [Fr. *saluer*—L. *salutāre.*]

saluki, *sə-lōō′kē*, *-gē*, *n.* a silky-haired Persian or Arabian greyhound. [Ar. *seluqi.*]

salutary, *sal′ū-tər-i*, *adj.* promoting health or safety: wholesome.—*adv.* sal′utarily.—*n.* sal′ūtariness. [L. *salūtāris*—*salūs*, health.]

salute, *sə-lōōt′*, *-ūt′*, *v.t.* to greet with words or (now esp.) with a gesture or with a kiss: to greet: to hail: to honour formally by a discharge of cannon, striking of colours, etc.: to affect, act upon (*Shak.*).—*v.i.* to perform the act of saluting, esp. in the military manner.—*n.* act or position of saluting: greeting: a kiss: a complimentary discharge of cannon, dipping colours, presenting arms, etc.—*n.* salutation (*sal-ū-tā′shən*), act or words of greeting: a visit of ceremony: a quickening (of the blood), excitement (*Shak.*): the Angelic Salutation (see ave). —*adj.* salūtā′tional.—*n.* salutatorian (*sə-lōō-tə-tō′ri-ən, -tō′*), in American colleges, the graduand who pronounces the address of welcome.— *adv.* salu′tatorily.—*adj.* salu′tatory.—*n.* an audience chamber: an address of welcome, esp. in American colleges.—*n.* salu′ter, one who salutes: in Spain, one who professed to work miracles in the name of St Catherine (Sp. *saludador; hist.*). [L. *salūtāre, -ātum* (vb.), and *salūs, salūtis* (n.), partly through Fr. *salut.*]

salutiferous, *sal-ū-tif′ər-əs*, *adj.* conducive to health or well-being. [L. *salūtifer*—*salūs, salūtis*, health, *ferre*, to bring.]

salvable, etc. See salve (1).

salvage, *sal′vij*, (*Spens., Shak.*, etc.) *n.* and *adj.* Same as savage.

salvage, *sal′vij*, *n.* compensation made by the owner to persons, other than the ship's company, for preserving ship or cargo from danger of loss: rescue of property from fire or other peril: the raising of sunken or wrecked ships: saving of waste material for utilisation: anything saved in any of these ways.—*v.t.* to save from danger of loss or destruction: to recover or save as salvage.—**sal′vage-corps**, a body of men employed in salvage work. [L.L. *salvāgium*—*salvāre*, to save.]

**salvarsan**, *sal′vər-san, sal′vär′san, n.* a compound of arsenic, first used by Paul Ehrlich (1854-1915) as a remedy for syphilis (since superseded by antibiotics). [L. *salvus*, safe, whole, Ger. *arsen*, arsenic.]

**salve**, *salv, v.t.* to explain by hypothesis (*obs.*): to explain, clear up, harmonise (*obs.*): to save (an opinion) from objection (*obs.*): to vindicate (*obs.*): to preserve unhurt (*obs.*): to salvage.—*n.* **salvabil′ity**—*adj.* **salv′able.**—*ns.* **salvā′tion**, act of saving: means of preservation from any serious evil: the saving of man from the power and penalty of sin, the conferring of eternal happiness (*theol.*); **Salvā′tionism**; **Salvā′tionist**, a member of the Salvation Army; **sal′vatory**, a repository.—*adj.* **saving.**—*adjs.* **salvif′ic(al)**, having the purpose or intention of saving.—*adv.* **salvif′ically.**—**Salvation Army**, an organisation for the spread of religion among the masses, founded by Wm. Booth in 1865. [L.L. *salvāre*, to save; partly back-formation from salvage.]

**salve**, *säv, also salv, n.* an ointment: a remedy: anything to soothe the feelings or conscience.—*v.t.* to anoint: to smear: to heal: to soothe.—*n. and adj.* **salv′ing.** [O.E. *s(e)alf*, ointment; Ger. *salbe*, Du. *zalf*.]

**salve**, *sal′vi, interj.* hail.—*n.* a greeting: an antiphon beginning *Salve Regina* (*R.C.*). [L. *salvē*, imper. of *salvēre*, to be well.]

**salver**, *sal′vər, n.* a tray on which anything is presented.—*adj.* **sal′ver-shaped**, of a corolla, having a long tube with limbs spread out flat. [Sp. *salva*, the precautionary tasting of food, as by a prince's taster, hence the tray on which it was presented to the prince—*salvar*, to save—L.L. *salvāre*.]

**Salvia**, *sal′vi-ə, n.* the sage genus. [L. *salvia*, sage.]

**salvific**, etc. See salve (1).

**Salvinia**, *sal-vin′i-ə, n.* a genus of water-ferns, giving name to a family **Salviniā′ceae.**—*adj.* **salvinia′ceous.** [Named after Antonio Maria *Salvini* (1653-1729), Italian Greek scholar.]

**salvo**, *sal′vō, n.* a saving clause: a reservation (*obs.*): a pretext (*obs.*): an expedient for saving appearances, avoiding offence, etc. [L. *salvō*, ablative of *salvus*, safe: (one's right, honour, etc.) being saved.]

**salvo**, *sal′vō, n.* a simultaneous discharge of artillery in salute or otherwise: a simultaneous discharge of bombs, etc.: a round of applause: —*pl.* **salvo(e)s.** [It. *salva*, salute—L. *salvē*, hail.]

**salvo jure**, *sal′vō jōō′rē, sal′vō, ′wō, yōō′re,* (L.) saving the right (the right being saved).

**sal volatile.** See sal (4).

**salvor**, *sal′vər, n.* one who salvages.

**sam**, *sam,* (*Spens.*) *adv.* together. [O.E. *samen*.]

**samara**, *sam′ə-ra, sə-mä′ra, n.* a dry indehiscent, usually one-seeded fruit, with a wing. [L. *samara, samera*, elm seed.]

**Samaritan**, *sə-mar′i-tən, adj.* of *Samaria*, in Palestine.—*n.* a native of Samaria, an adherent of the religion of Samaria, slightly differing from Judaism: the Aramaic dialect of Samaria: one who charitably gives help in need (*good Samaritan;* Luke x. 30-37).—*n.* **Samar′itanism.**
—**Samaritan Pentateuch**, a recension of the Hebrew Pentateuch accepted by the Samaritans as alone canonical. [L. *Samāritānus.*]

**samarium**, *sə-mā′ri-əm, n.* a metallic element (Sm: at. numb. 62) observed spectroscopically in samarskite.—*n.* **samarskite** (*sə-mär′skit*), a mineral containing uranium. [Named in honour of Col. *Samarski.*]

**Samaveda**, *sä-mä-vä′dä, n.* the name of one of the four Vedas. [Sans. *Sāmaveda.*]

**samba**, *sam′ba, n.* a Brazilian Negro dance in duple time with syncopation: a ballroom development thereof: a tune for it.

**sambar, sambur**, *sam′bər, n.* a large Indian deer. [Hindi *sâbar*.]

**sambo**, *sam′bō, n.* offspring of an American Indian or mulatto and a Negro: (*cap.*) colloquially used as a proper name for a Negro. [Sp. *zambo*, said to be from L. *scambus*—Gr. *skambos*, bow-legged; perh. partly Fulah *sambo*, uncle.]

**Sam Browne**, *sam-brown′, n.* a military officer's belt with shoulder strap. [Invented by General Sir Samuel James *Browne* (1824-1901).]

**sambuca**, *sam-bū′ka, n.* an ancient musical instrument like a harp. [L. *sambūca*—Gr. *sambȳkē*, prob. an Asiatic word; cf. Aramaic *sabbekā.*]

**sambur.** Same as sambar.

**same**, *sām, adj.* identical (commonly with *as*, also with *with* or a relative): not different: unchanged: unvaried: mentioned before.—*pron.* (*coll.*) the aforesaid, it, them, they, etc.—*n.* (*rare*) an identical thing.—*adj.* **same′ly**, unvaried.—*n.* **same′ness**, the being the same: tedious monotony.—**all the same**, for all that; **at the same time**, still, nevertheless; **the same**, the same thing or person: the aforesaid: in the same way. [O.E. *same* (only in phrase *swā same*, likewise); Goth. *sama*; L. *similis*, like, Gr. *homos*.]

**samel**, *sam′l, adj.* underburnt (as a brick). [App. O.E. pfx. *sam-*, half, *æled*, burned.]

**samen**, *sām′ən, an* obs. Scots form of same.

**Samian**, *sā′mi-ən, adj.* of the Greek island of *Samos.*—*n.* (also **Sā′miot, Sā′miote**) a native of Samos.—**Samian earth**, an argillaceous astringent earth; **Samian letter**, the Pythagorean letter; **Samian stone**, a goldsmiths' polishing stone; **Samian ware**, brick-red or black pottery, with lustrous glaze: a later imitation made in Roman Gaul, etc.

**samiel**, *sā′mi-əl, n.* the simoom. [Ar. *samm*, poison, Turk. *yel*, wind.]

**samisen**, *sam′i-sen, shamisen, sham′, n.* a Japanese guitar. [Jap.]

**samite**, *sam′it, n.* a kind of heavy silk stuff. [O.Fr *samit*—L.L. *examitum*—Gr. *hexamiton*—*hex*, six, *mitos*, thread.]

**samlet**, *sam′lit, n.* a young salmon. [salmon, suff. -let.]

**Sammy**, *sam′i, n.* a noodle (*slang*): an American expeditionary soldier (*mil. slang*; from *Uncle Sam*). [Samuel.]

**Samnite**, *sam′nit, n.* a member of an ancient Sabine people of central Italy: their language: a Roman gladiator armed like a Samnite.— Also *adj.* [L. *Samnis, -itis.*]

**samnitis**, *sam-nī′tis,* (*Spens.*) *n.* an unknown poisonous plant.

**samovar**, *sam′ō-vär, -vär′, n.* a Russian tea-urn heated by charcoal in a tube that passes through it. [Russ. *samovar*, lit. self-boiler.]

**Samoyed(e)**, *sam-ō-yed′, or sam′, n.* one of a Ugrian people of north-west Siberia: their Ural-Altaic language: (*sa-moi′ed*) a dog of a breed used by them.—Also *adj.* (*Milt.* **Sam′oed**). —*adj.* **Samoyed′ic.** [Russ. *Samoyed.*]

**samp**, *samp, n.* a coarsely ground maize: porridge made from it. [From an American Indian word.]

**sampan**, *sam′pan, n.* a Chinese boat.—Also **san′-pan.** [Chin. *san*, three, *pan*, board.]

**samphire**, *sam′fir, samphire, -pir, n.* an umbelliferous plant (*Crithmum maritimum*) of sea-cliffs, whose fleshy leaves are used in pickles: extended to other plants used in the same way—to *Inula crithmoides*, a plant related to elecampane (*golden samphire*), to glasswort (*marsh samphire*), to saltwort (*prickly samphire*). [Fr. (*herbe de*) *Saint Pierre*, Saint Peter('s herb).]

**sampi**, *sam'pi*, *-pē*, *n*. supposed name of a Greek numerical character, τ, ϙ, or ⋌, representing 900 and perhaps originally the same as the letter san. [Gr. *sampi*.]

**sample**, *säm'pl*, *n*. a specimen, a small portion to show the quality of the whole: an example for imitation (*Spens.*, *Shak.*) or (*obs.*) warning.— *adj*. serving as a sample.—*v.t*. to match (*obs.*): to take, try, or offer a sample or samples of. —*ns*. **sam'pler**; **sam'pling**. [M.E. *essample*; see example.]

**sampler**, *säm'plər*, *n*. an exemplar, type, pattern (*obs.*): a test-piece of embroidery formerly expected from a girl, commonly including an alphabet, with figures, often names, etc.—*n*. **sam'plery**.—**sam'pler-work**. [O.Fr. *essemplaire* —L. *exemplar*; see exemplar.]

**samshoo, samshu**, *sam'shoō*, *n*. Chinese rice spirit. [Pidgin; origin doubtful.]

**Samson**, *sam'sn*, *n*. an abnormally strong man (from the Hebrew champion of Judges xiii-xvi). —**Samson('s) post**, a kind of mousetrap (*obs.*): a strong post in a ship.

**samurai**, *sam'oō-ri*, *-ū-ri*, (*Jap. hist.*) *n*. a military retainer of a daimio: a member of the military caste:—*pl*. **samurai**. [Jap.]

**san**, *san*, *n*. a discarded letter of the Greek alphabet, C, perh. originally the same as sampi. [Doric Gr. *san*, sigma.]

**sanative**, *san'ə-tiv*, *adj*. healing.—*n*. **sanatō'rium** (imitation Latin), a hospital, esp. for consumptives or convalescents: a health station:—*pl*. **-toriums, -toria**.—*adj*. **san'atory**, healing: of healing. [L. *sānāre*, *-ātum*, to heal.]

**sanbenito**, *san-be-nē'tō*, *n*. a garment worn by Inquisition victims at public recantation or execution:—*pl*. **-'tos**. [Sp. *San Benito*, St Benedict, from its resemblance to St Benedict's scapular.]

**sancho, sanko**, *sang'kō*, *n*. a West African guitar. [Ashanti *osanku*.]

**sancho-pedro**, *sang'kō-pē'drō*, *n*. a card game— the nine of trumps called sancho, the five pedro.

**sanctify**, *sang(k)'ti-fī*, *v.t*. to make, declare, regard as, or show to be sacred or holy: to set apart to sacred use: to free from sin or evil: to consecrate: to invest with a sacred character: to make efficient as the means of holiness: to sanction:—*pr.p*. **sanc'tifying**; *pa.t*. and *pa.p*. **sanc'tified**.—*n*. **sanctifica'tion**.—*adj*. **sanc'tified**, made holy: sanctimonious.—*adv*. **sanc'tifiedly** (*-fi-id-li*), sanctimoniously.—*n*. **sanc'tifier** (*-fi-ər*), one who sanctifies: the Holy Spirit.—*n*. and *adj*. **sanc'tifying**.—*adv*. **sanc'tifyingly**. [Fr. *sanctifier*—L. *sanctificāre*—*sanctus*, holy, *facĕre*, to make.]

**sanctimony**, *sang(k)'ti-mən-i*, *n*. holiness (*obs.*): outward, affected, or simulated holiness.—*adj*. **sanctimonious** (*-mō'ni-əs*), holy (*obs.*): simulating holiness.—*adv*. **sanctimō'niously**.—*n*. **sanctimō'niousness**. [L. *sanctimōnia*—*sanctus*.]

**sanction**, *sang(k)'shən*, *n*. motive for obedience to any moral or religious law (*ethics*): penalty or reward expressly attached to non-observance or observance of a law or treaty (*law*): act of ratifying, or giving authority: confirmation: support: permission, countenance.—*v.t*. to give validity to: to authorise: to countenance. [L. *sanctiō*, *-ōnis*—*sancīre*, *sanctum*, to ratify.]

**sanctitude**, *sang(k)'ti-tūd*, *n*. saintliness. [L. *sanctitūdō*, *-inis*.]

**sanctity**, *sang(k)'ti-ti*, *n*. quality of being sacred or holy: purity: godliness: inviolability: saintship: (in *pl*.) holy feelings, obligations, or objects. [L. *sanctitās*, *-ātis*, sanctity.]

**sanctuary**, *sang(k)'tū-ər-i*, *n*. a holy place: a place of worship: the most holy part of a temple, church, etc.: the sacrarium: the chancel: a place affording immunity from arrest: the privilege of refuge therein: a place of refuge: a private retreat: a nature, animal, or plant reserve.—*v.t*. **sanc'tuarise, -ize**, to afford sanctuary to. [L. *sanctuārium*.]

**Sanctus**, *sang(k)'təs*, *n*. the hymn *Holy, holy, holy*, from Isa. vi: music for it.—*n*. **sanc'tum**, a sacred place: a private room.—**sanc'tum sancto'-rum**, the Holy of Holies: any specially reserved retreat or room; **sanc'tus bell**, a bell rung at the Sanctus: the sacring bell. [L. *sanctus*, *-a*, *-um*, holy.]

**sand**, *sand*, *n*. a mass of rounded grains of rock, esp. quartz: (in *pl*.) a tract covered with this, as on a sea-beach or desert: a sand-grain (*rare*): (in *pl*.) sandstones: (in *pl*.) moments of time, from use in the hour-glass (*fig.*): firmness of character (*U.S. slang*).—*adj*. of sand.—*v.t*. to sprinkle, cover, mix, or polish with sand.—*adj*. **sand'ed**, yellow (*Shak.*): sprinkled, covered, or mixed with sand.—*ns*. **sand'iness**, sandy quality, esp. in colour; **sand'ing**; **sand'ling**, the launce.— *adjs*. **sand'y**, consisting of, covered with, containing, like, or (*Shak.*) measured by sand: loose: coloured like sand; **sand'yish**.—**sand'-bag**, a bag of sand or earth: an engraver's leather cushion.—*v.t*. to furnish with sandbags: to assail with a sandbag:—*pa.p*. **sand'bagged**.— **sand'bagger**; **sand'-bank**, a bank of sand; **sand'-bar**, a long sand-bank in a river or sea; **sand'-bath**, a bath in sand: a vessel for heating without direct exposure to the source of heat; **sand'-bed**, a layer of sand, esp. one used in founding or moulding: a toper (*fig*, *Scot.*); **sand'-binder**, a plant whose roots or rootstocks fix shifting sands; **sand'-blast**, a sand-laden wind: sand driven by a blast of air or steam for glass-engraving, finishing metal surfaces, cleaning stone and metal surfaces, etc.—Also *v.t*.—**sand'-blasting**; **sand'-box**, a box for sand for sprinkling, for golf-tees, or other purpose: the explosive capsule of a tropical American tree (Hura) of the spurge family, formerly used to sprinkle sand on wet ink; **sand'-boy**, a young sand-hawker, proverbial for jollity; **sand'-break**, sandy ground diversifying the country; **sand'-bunker**, a model of a castle made by children at play on the sands; **sand'-cherry**, an American dwarf cherry; **sand'-crack**, a crack in a hoof; **sand'-dance**, a dance performed on a sanded surface; **sand'-dart**, a British noctuid moth; **sand'-devil**, a small whirlwind; **sand'-dollar**, a flat sea-urchin; **sand'-dune**, a ridge of loose sand drifted by the wind; **sand'-eel**, the launce; **sand'-flag**, a fissile sandstone; **sand'-flea**, the chigoe or jigger: a sand-hopper; **sand'-fly**, a small biting midge (Simulium): a small moth-like midge (Phlebotomus) that transmits **sand-fly fever**, a fever due to a viral infection; **sand'-glass**, a glass instrument for measuring time by the running out of sand; **sand'-grain**; **sand'-grass**, any grass that grows on sand; **sand'groper**, a West Australian (orig. a pioneer); **sand'-grouse**, any bird of the genera Pterocles and Syrrhaptes, with long pointed wings, once mistaken for grouse because of their feathered legs but now reckoned as a sub-order (Pterocletes) akin to pigeons; **sand'-heap**; **sand'-hill**, a hill of sand; **sand'-hog** (*U.S. slang*), one who works in compressed air; **sand'-hole**; **sand'-hopper**, an amphipod crustacean (Talitrus, Orchestia, etc.) of the seashore (and also inland regions) that jumps by suddenly straightening its bent body; **sand'-lark**, a name applied to various smaller shore birds: a sandpiper; **sand'-launce**, the launce; **sand'-lizard**, an oviparous lizard (*Lacerta agilis*) of Europe and S. England:

sand'man, a fairy who supposedly throws sand into children's eyes towards bedtime; sand'-martin, a martin that nests in sandy banks; sand'-mason, a tube-worm that makes its tube of sand; sand'-mole, the Cape mole-rat; sand'-paper, paper or cloth coated with sand.—v.t. to smooth or polish with sandpaper.—sand'-peep (U.S.), any small sand-piper; sand'-pipe, a tubular hollow in chalk, usually filled with clay, sand, etc., from above; sand'piper, the summer snipe or other bird of a group intermediate between plovers and snipe, haunting sandy shores and river banks and uttering a clear piping note; sand'-pit, a place from which sand is dug: a pit filled with sand for children's play; sand'-pride, a small river lamprey; sand'-pump, a pump for raising wet sand or mud; sand'-saucer, an egg-mass of certain sea-snails; sand'-screw, a burrowing amphipod (from its wriggling movements); sand'-shoe, a shoe for walking or playing on the sands, usually with canvas upper and rubber sole; sand'-skipper, a sand-hopper; sand'-snake, a short-tailed, boa-like genus (Eryx) of Old World snakes; sand'-spout, a moving pillar of sand; sand'-star, an ophiurid, esp. of the short-armed kind, as Ophiura; sand'stone, a rock formed of compacted and more or less indurated sand (Old Red Sandstone; see old); sand'-storm, a storm of wind carrying along clouds of sand; sand'-sucker, the rough dab; sand'-table, a tray for moulding sand on or for demonstration of military tactics: an inclined trough for separating heavier particles from a flow of liquid, as in ore-dressing, paper-making (also sand'-trap); sand'-thrower, a tool for throwing sand on newly sized or painted surfaces; sand'-trap, a bunker: a sand-table; sand'-wasp, a solitary burrowing insect of several families akin to the true wasps; sand'-worm, the lugworm or other worm that lives on the sand; sand'wort, any species of Arenaria; sand'wort-spurr'ey, Spergularia; sand'-yacht, sand'-yachting (see yacht); sand'y-lav'erock (Scot.), a sand-lark. [O.E. sand; Du. zand, Ger. sand, O.N. sandr.]

sandal, san'dl, n. a sole bound to the foot by straps: an ornate shoe or slipper: a slipper-strap: a slight rubber overshoe.—adj. san'dalled, wearing or fastened with sandals.—sandal shoon (arch.), sandals. [L. sandalium—Gr. sandalion, dim. of sandalon.]

sandal, san'dal, n. a long narrow N. African boat. [Turk., Pers., and Ar.]

sandal, san'dl, sandalwood, -wŏŏd, ns. a compact and fine-grained very fragrant East Indian wood: the parasitic tree yielding it, Santalum album (white sandalwood), or other species: extended to other woods, as red-sanders, Barbados pride (Adenanthera), both called red sandalwood. [L.L. santalum—Gr. sandanon.]

sandarach, sandarac, san'dər-ak, n. realgar: the resin (in full gum sandarach, sandarac resin) of the Moroccan sandarach tree (Collitris quadrivalvis; Coniferae) powdered to form pounce and used in making varnish. [L. sandaraca—Gr. sandărăkē, -chē.]

sand-blind, sand'blind, adj. half-blind. [Prob. O.E. pfx. sam-, half, and blind, affected by sand.]

Sandemanian, san-di-mā'ni-ən, n. a Glassite, or follower of Robert Sandeman (1718-71).—Also adj. [Ger.]

sander, zander, san', zan'dər, n. a pike-perch. [Ger.]

sanderling, san'dər-ling, n. a sandpiper without a hind toe. [App. from sand.]

sanders, san', sän'dərz, sanderswood, -wŏŏd, ns. sandalwood, esp. red sandalwood (red-sanders; see red). [O.Fr. sandre, variant of sandal, santal, sandalwood.]

sandhi, sän'dē, n. modification of the sound of a word or affix caused by the context in which it is uttered. [Sans. saṁdhi, placing together.]

sandiver, san'di-vər, n. glass-gall. [O.Fr. suin de verre, lit. exudation of glass.]

sandwich, san(d)'wich, -wij, n. any sort of food between two slices of bread, said to be named from the fourth Earl of Sandwich (1718-92), who ate a snack of this kind in order not to have to leave the gaming-table: anything in like arrangement.—v.t. to lay or place between two layers: to fit tight between two others of two of another kind: to intercalate.—sand'wich-board; sand'-wich-man, a man who perambulates the streets carrying two advertising boards hung over his shoulders, so that one is in front, the other behind.

Sandy, san'di, (coll.) n. a Scot. [From Alexander.]

sane, sān, adj. sound, healthy (rare): sound in mind: rational.—adv. sane'ly.—n. sane'ness. [L. sānus.]

Sanforise, -ize, san'fər-īz, v.t. to make (cotton or linen fabrics) proof against shrinking by mechanically compressing the fibres. [After Sanford L. Cluett, American inventor of the process.]

sang, sang, pa.t. of sing.—n. a Scots form of song.

sang, sang, n. blood (Scot. in oaths; her. sā.): anthrax (sāng; vet.).—sang-de-boeuf (sä-də-bœf'), a deep red colour (lit. ox-blood); sang-froid (-frwä'), coolness, self-possession (lit. cold blood). [Fr., blood.]

sang, säng, n. a Chinese organ played by mouth. [Chin. shêng.]

sangar, sungar, sung'gər, n. a stone breastwork. [Pushtu sangar.]

sangaree, sang-gə-rē', n. a West Indian drink of wine, diluted, sweetened, spiced, etc.—Also sangria (sang-grē'a). [Sp. sangría.]

sangfroid. See sang (2).

sanglier, sang'li-ər, (obs. and her.) n. a wild boar. [Fr.,—L. singulāris, solitary.]

Sangraal, Sangrail, Sangreal, san(g)-grāl', san(g)'-grāl, n. the holy grail (see grail (3)). [saint, grail.]

Sangrado, san(g)-grä'dō, n. a bloodletter, from Dr Sangrado in Gil Blas. [Sp. sangrador, one who lets blood.]

sangria. See sangaree.

sangui-, sang-gwi-, in compounds, blood.—adj. sanguiferous (-gwif'ər-əs; L. ferre, to bear), blood-carrying.—n. sanguifica'tion, blood-making.—v.i. sang'uify (-fi), to make blood.—v.t. to turn into blood.—n. Sanguinaria (-gwi-nā'ri-a), blood-root.—adv. sang'uinarily (-gwin-ə-ri-'i).—n. sang'-uinariness.—adjs. sang'uinary, b.oody; san-guine (sang'gwin), of blood (rare): blood-red: bloody: of the complexion or temperament in which blood was supposed to predominate over the other humours: hence ardent, confident and inclined to hopefulness: abounding in blood: ruddy: florid: of a full habit.—n. a blood-red colour: a red chalk: a drawing in red chalks.—v.t. to colour blood-red: to stain with blood.—adv. sang'uinely.—n. sang'uineness.—adj. sanguin'eous, of or having blood: blood-red: bloody: sanguine: full-blooded.—n. sanguin'ity, sanguineness.—adj. sanguin'olent, bloody.—n. Sanguisorb'a, burnet (L. sorbēre, to absorb, from its supposed styptic property).—adj. sangu(in)-iv'orous, feeding on blood (L. vorāre, to devour). [L. sanguis, -inis, blood; adjs. sanguineus, sanguinārius, sanguinolentus; partly through Fr. sanguin.]

Sanhedrim, Sanhedrin, san'i-drim, -drin, n. a Jewish council or court, esp. the supreme council and court at Jerusalem (hist.): any similar assembly, a parliament.—n. San'hedrist, a member of the Sanhedrin. [Heb. sanhedrīn—Gr. synedrion—syn, together, hedrā, a seat.]

sanicle, san'ik-l, n. a woodland umbelliferous plant (in full wood'-san'icle; Sanicula europaea) with glossy leaves, head-like umbels, and hooked fruits: any plant of the genus: extended to various other plants. [O.Fr., perh. L. *sānāre*, to heal, from once-supposed power.]

**sanidine**, *san'i-dēn, n.* a clear glassy variety of potash feldspar, usually tabular. [Gr. *sanis, sanidos*, a board.]

**sanies**, *sā'ni-ēz, n.* a thin discharge from wounds or sores.—*adj.* **sa'nious**. [L. *saniēs*.]

**sanify**, *san'i-fī, v.t.* to make healthy. [L. *sānus*, sound, *facēre*, to make.]

**sanitary**, *san'i-tər-i, adj.* pertaining to, or concerned with the promotion of health, esp. connected with drainage and sewage disposal: conducive to health.—*n.* **sanitā'rian**, one who favours or studies sanitary measures.—Also *adj.*—*n.* **sanitā'rianism**.—*adv.* **san'itarily**.—*ns.* **san'itarist**; **sanitā'rium** (sham Latin), a sanatorium:—*pl.* **-ia, -iums**.—*v.t.* **san'itate** (back-formation), to make sanitary: to furnish with sanitary appliances or ware.—*ns.* **sanitā'tion**, measures for the promotion of health, esp. drainage and sewage disposal; **sanitā'tionist**—**sanitary engineer; sanitary engineering**, branch of civil engineering dealing with provision of pure water supply, disposal of waste, etc.; **sanitary inspector** (see **public health inspector**); **sanitary towel**, an absorbent cotton pad for use in menstruation; **sanitary ware**, coarse-glazed earthenware for sewerpipes. [Fr. *sanitaire*—L. *sānitās*, health.]

**sanity**, *san'i-ti, n.* health (*arch.*): soundness of mind. [L. *sānitās*—*sānus*, healthy.]

**sanjak**, *san'jak, n.* formerly, a subdivision of a Turkish vilayet or eyalet. [Turk. *sancak*, flag, sanjak.]

**sank**, *sangk, pa.t.* of **sink**.

**Sankhya**, *säng'kya, n.* one of the six great systems of orthodox Hindu philosophy. [Sans. *sāṁkhya*.]

**sannup**, *san'əp, n.* the husband of a squaw: a brave. [Amer. Ind. word.]

**sans**, *sä* (*Shak. sanz*), (Fr.) without.—**sans-appel** (*säz-a-pel*), one against whose decision there is no appeal; **sansculotte** (*sä-kü-lot*; Fr. *culotte*, knee-breeches), in the French Revolution, the court party's nickname for a democrat (apparently as wearing long trousers instead of knee-breeches): hence generally (usu. in hostility) a strong republican, democrat, or revolutionary: one whose breeches are wanting or defective.— **sansculotterie** (*-rē* or *-ə-rē*).—*adj.* **sansculott'ic**.— **sansculott'ism**; **sansculott'ist**; **sanserif** (*sanser'if*; *print.*), a type without serifs.—Also *adj.* —**sans cérémonie** (*sä-rā-mon-ē*), without ceremony; **sans gêne** (*zhen*), at ease, without constraint or consideration of politeness; **sans nombre** (*nɔbr'*; *her.*), repeated often, and covering the field; **sans phrase** (*fräz*), without phrases (of courtesy), without more ado; **sans souci** (*sōō-sē*), without care, worry.

**sansa**, *san'sa.* Same as **zanze**.

**Sansevieria**, *san-sev-i-ēr'i-ə, n.* the bowstringhemp genus of the lily family. [Named after the Neapolitan inventor Raimondo di Sangro, Prince of *San Severo* (1710-71).]

**Sanskrit**, or (old-fashioned) **Sanscrit**, *sans'krit, n.* the ancient Indo-Germanic literary language of India.—Also *adj.*—*n.* **San'kritist**, one skilled in Sanskrit. [Sans. *saṁskṛta*, put together, perfected—*sam*, together, *karoti*, he makes, cog. with L. *creāre*, to create.]

**Santa Claus**, *san'ta klöz', n.* a fat rosy old fellow who brings children Christmas presents: an improbable source of improbable benefits. [U.S. modification of Du. dial. *Sante Klaas*, St Nicholas.]

**santal**, *san'təl, n.* sandalwood.—*n.pl.* **Santalā'ceae** (*-ā'si-ē*), the sandalwood family.—*adj.* **santalā'ceous**.—*ns.* **san'talin**, the colouring matter of red sandalwood; **San'talum**, the sandalwood genus. [Gr. *santalon*.]

**santir**, *san-tēr'*, **santur**, **santour**, *-tōōr', n.* an Eastern dulcimer. [Ar. *santir*, Pers. and Turk. *sāntūr*.]

**santon**, *san'ton, n.* an Eastern dervish or saint. [Sp. *santón*—*santo*, holy—L. *sanctus*, holy.]

**santonica**, *san-ton'i-kə, n.* the dried unexpanded flower-heads of a species of wormwood.—*n.* **san'tonin** (*-tən-*), an anthelmintic extracted from it. [Gr. *santonikon*, as found in the country of the *Santones* in Gaul.]

**saouari**. Same as **souari**.

**sap**, *sap, n.* vital juice: juice generally: sapwood: a saphead: a plodding student: food (*slang*).— *v.i.* to play the part of a ninny: to be studious.— *v.t.* to drain or withdraw the sap from.—*adjs.* **sap'ful**, full of sap; **sap'less**.—*ns.* **sap'lessness**; **sap'ling**, a young tree (*also adj.*): a young greyhound; **sapp'iness**.—*adj.* **sapp'y**.—**sap'-green**, a green paint made from the juice of buckthorn berries: its colour (also *adj.*); **sap'head**, a silly fellow.—*adj.* **sap'headed**.—**sap'ling-cup**, a wooden ale-cup of staves and hoops; **sap'-rot**, dry-rot; **sap'-wood**, alburnum. [O.E. *sæp*; L.G. *sap*, juice, Ger. *saft*.]

**sap**, *sap, n.* sapping: a trench (usually covered or zigzag) by which approach is made towards a hostile position.—*v.t.* to undermine.—*v.i.* to make a sap: to proceed insidiously:—*pr.p.* **sapp'ing**; *pa.p.* and *pa.t.* **sapped**.—*n.* **sapp'er**, one who saps: a private in the Royal Engineers (formerly Royal Sappers and Miners).—**sap'-head**, the furthest point reached by a sap. [It. *zappa* and Fr. *sappe* (now *sape*); cf. L.L. *sappa*, a pick.]

**sapajou**, *sap'ə-jōō, n.* a capuchin monkey: a spider monkey (*obs.*). [Fr. from a Tupi name.]

**sapan**. Same as **sappan**.

**sapego**. See **serpigo**.

**sapele**, *sa-pē'lē, n.* a wood resembling mahogany, used for furniture: a tree of the genus *Entandrophragma* giving such wood, esp. *E. cylindricum*. [W. African name.]

**saphead**. See **sap** (1) and (2).

**sapid**, *sap'id, adj.* perceptible by taste: having a decided taste: well-tasted: savoury: grateful, relishing, exhilarating.—*n.* **sapid'ity**.—*adj.* **sap'idless** (*Lamb*), insipid. [L. *sapidus*—*sapēre*, to taste.]

**sapience**, *sā'pi-əns, n.* discernment: wisdom (often ironical): judgment.—*adjs.* **sā'pient**; **sāpiential** (*-en'shl*).—*adv.* **sā'piently**. [L. *sapientia*—*sapēre*, to be wise.]

**Sapindus**, *sə-pin'dəs, n.* the soapberry genus, giving name to the **Sapindā'ceae**, a family akin to the maples and horse-chestnuts.—*adj.* **sapindā'ceous**. [L. *sāpō Indicus*, Indian soap.]

**sapi-outan**. See **sapi-utan**.

**Sapium**, *sā'pi-əm, n.* the tallow-tree genus of the spurge family.

**sapi-utan**, *sä-pi-ōō'tän, n.* the wild ox of Celebes.— Also **sapi-ou'tan**. [Malay *sāpi*, cow, *ūtan*, wild, wood.]

**sapling**. See **sap** (1).

**sapodilla**, *sap-ō-dil'a, n.* a large evergreen sapotaceous tree of W. Indies, etc., *Achras sapota* (naseberry): its edible fruit (**sapodilla plum**): its durable timber. [Sp. *zapotilla*, dim. of *zapota* (see **Sapota**).]

**saponaceous**, *sap-ō-, or sap-ə-nā'shəs, adj.* soapy: soap-like.—*n.* **Sapona'ria**, the soapwort genus.— *adj.* **saponifiable** (*sap-on'i-fī'ə-bl*).—*n.* **saponificā'tion**, turning into or forming of soap: hydrolysis of esters.—*v.t.* **sapon'ify**, to convert into soap.—*v.i.* to become soap:—*pr.p.* **sapon'-ifying**; *pa.t.* and *pa.p.* **sapon'ified**.—*ns.* **saponin** (*sap'ə-nin*), a glucoside from soapwort, etc., that gives a soapy froth; **sap'onite**, a soapy amorphous silicate of magnesium and aluminium found in cavities in serpentine. [L. *sāpō, -ōnis*, soap, prob. from Gmc.]

Neutral vowels in unaccented syllables: *el'ə-mənt*; for certain sounds in foreign words, see p. viii

**sapor**, sā'pŏr, n. taste.—adj. **sā'porous** (-pər-əs). [L. sapor, -ōris.]

**Sapota**, sə-pō'tə, n. a genus (by some included in Achras) giving name to the **Sapotaceae** (sap-ō-tā'si-ē), a tropical family mostly of trees, often abounding in milky juice (gutta-percha).—adj. **sapotā'ceous** (-shəs). [Sp. zapote—Nahuatl tzapotl.]

**sappan**, **sapan**, sap'an, -ən, n. brazilwood (Caesalpinia sappan)—usu. **sap(p)'an-wood**. [Malay sapang.]

**sapped**, **sapper**, **sapping**. See sap (2).

**sapperment**, sap-ər-ment', interj. a German oath. [Ger. sakrament, sacrament.]

**sapphire**, saf'īr, n. a brilliant precious variety of corundum, generally of a beautiful blue: the blue colour of a sapphire.—adj. of sapphire: deep pure blue.—adj. **sapph'ired**, coloured with sapphire blue.—adj. **sapph'irine** (-ir-īn), of, or like, sapphire.—n. a blue mineral, aluminium-magnesium silicate.—**sapph'ire-quartz**, a blue quartz; **sapph'ire-wing**, a blue-winged hummingbird. [O.Fr. safir—L. sapphirus—Gr. sappheiros, lapis lazuli.]

**Sappho**, saf'ō, n. a great Greek lyric poetess (c. 600 B.C.) of Lesbos: a kind of humming-bird.—adj. **Sapph'ic**.—n. usu. in pl. (also without cap.) verses in a form said to have been invented by Sappho in stanzas of four lines each, three Lesser Sapphics thus: –∪ | –∪̄ | –∪∪ | –∪ | –∪̄, followed by an adonic, viz. –∪∪ | –∪.—n. **Sapph'ism** (also without cap.) lesbianism, of which she was accused. [Gr. Sapphō.]

**sapples**, sap'lz, (Scot.) n.pl. soap-suds.

**sapr(o)-**, sap-r(ō)-, in composition, rotten, decayed.—n. **sapraemia** (sap-rē'mi-ə; Gr. haima, blood), presence of products of putrefactive bacteria in the blood.—adj. **saprae'mic**.—n. **saprobe** (sap'rōb; Gr. bios, life), an organism living in foul water.—adjs. **saprobiotic** (sap-rō-, sap-rə-bī-ot'ik), feeding on dead or decaying plants or animals; **saprogenic**, **saprogenous** (sap-rō-jen'ik or -rə-, sə-proj'i-nəs; Gr. root of gignesthai, to produce), growing on decaying matter: causing or caused by putrefaction.—ns. **Saprolegnia** (sap-rō-leg'ni-ə or -rə-; Gr. legnon, border), a genus of fungi, one species of which grows on diseased salmon and was formerly thought to be the cause of the disease; **sapropel** (sap-rə-pel; Gr. pēlos, clay, mud), slimy sediment laid down in water, largely organic in origin.—adj. **sapropel'ic**, pertaining to, living in, or derived from, sapropel.—n. **sapropel'ite**, coal formed from sapropel.—adj. **saprophagous** (sap-rof'ə-gəs; Gr. phagein (aor.), to eat), feeding on decaying organic matter.—n. **saprophyte** (sap'rō-fīt or -rə-; Gr. phyton, a plant), a plant that feeds upon decaying organic matter.—adj. **saprophytic** (-fit'ik).—adv. **saprophyt'ically**.—n. **sap'rophytism**. [Gr. sapros, rotten.]

**sapsago**, sap-sā'gō, sap'sə-gō, n. a hard green cheese made from skim milk and melilot. [Ger. schabziger.]

**sapucaia**, sap-ōō-kä'yə, n. a Brazilian tree (Lecythis) whose urn-shaped fruit (monkey-pot) contains a number of finely-flavoured oval seeds or nuts.—**sapuca'ia-nut**. [Tupí.]

**sar**, sär. See Sargus.

**sar**, **sa'r**, sär, a Scots form of **savour** (both n. and vb.).

**saraband**, sar'ə-band, n. a slow Spanish dance, or dance-tune: a suite-movement in its rhythm, in 3-4 time strongly accented on the second beat (a dotted crotchet or minim). [Sp. zarabanda.]

**Saracen**, sar'ə-sən, n. a Syrian or Arab nomad: a Mohammedan: an opponent of the Crusaders: a Moor or Berber: a non-Christian (obs.).—Also adj.—adjs. **Saracenic** (-sen'ik), **-al**.—n. **Sar'acenism**.—Saracenic architecture, a general name for Mohammedan architecture. [O.E.

**Saracene** (pl.)—L. Saracēnus—late Gr. Sarakēnos.]

**sarafan**, sar-ə-fan', or sar', n. a Russian peasant woman's cloak. [Russ.]

**sarangi**, sä'rung-gē, n. an Indian fiddle. [Hind.]

**Sarapis**. See Serapis.

**Saratoga**, sar-ə-tō'ga, n. (in full **Saratoga trunk**; U.S.) a large travelling trunk. [Saratoga Springs, resort in New York State.]

**sarbacane**, sär'ba-kān, n. a blow-gun. [Fr.]

**sarcasm**, sär'kazm, n. a bitter sneer: a satirical remark in scorn or contempt, often but not necessarily ironical: a jibe: the quality of such sayings.—adjs. **sarcas'tic**, **-al**, containing or inclined to sarcasm:—abbrev. **sarky**.—adv. **sarcas'tically**. [L. sarcasmus—Gr. sarkasmos—sarkazein, to tear flesh like dogs, to speak bitterly—sarx, sarkos, flesh.]

**sarcenchyme**, sär-seng'kim, n. a soft tissue of sponges with close-packed cells and reduced gelatinous matrix.—adj. **sarcenchymatous** (-kim'-ə-təs). [Gr. sarx, sarkos, flesh, enchyma, an infusion.]

**sarcenet**. See sarsenet.

**sarco-**, sär'kō, -ko'-, in composition, flesh.—ns. **sarcocarp** (sär'kō-kärp; Gr. karpos, fruit; bot.), the fleshy pericarp of a stone fruit; **sarcocystis** (sär-kō-sis'tis; Gr. kystis, a bladder), a genus of Sporozoa parasitic in muscles of mammals; **sarcolemma** (sär-kō-lem'ə; Gr. lemma, husk), the sheath of muscle fibre; **sarcol'ogy** (Gr. logos, discourse), the anatomy of the fleshy parts; **Sarcoptes** (sär-kop'tēz; irreg., from Gr. koptein, to cut), the itch-mite genus.—adjs. **sarcop'tic**; **sarcous** (sär'kas), of flesh or muscle. [Gr. sarx, sarkos, flesh.]

**sarcocolla**, sär-kō-kol'ə, n. a Persian gum from Astragalus or other plants, reputed to heal wounds. [Gr. sarkokolla—kolla, glue.]

**sarcode**, sär'kōd, n. protoplasm, esp. of Protozoa.—n. **Sarcodes**, sär-kōd'ēz, the Californian snow-plant.—adj. **sarcodic** (-kod'ik), protoplasmic: flesh-like.—n.pl. **Sarcodina** (-kō-dī'nə), a class of Protozoa with pseudopodia.—adj. **sar'coid**, flesh-like. [Gr. sarkōdēs, sarkoeides—eidos, form.]

**sarcoma**, sär-kō'mə, n. a tumour derived from connective tissue: any fleshy excrescence: a fleshy disk (bot.):—pl. **sarco'mata**.—adj. **sarcō'matous**. [Gr. sarkōma—sarx, flesh.]

**Sarcophaga**, sär-kof'ə-gə, n. a genus of flesh-flies.—adjs. **sarcoph'agal**, flesh-eating: pertaining to sarcophagi; **sarcoph'agous**, feeding on flesh.—ns. **sarcoph'agus**, a limestone used by the Greeks for coffins, thought to consume the flesh of corpses: a stone coffin, esp. one with carvings: a tomb or cenotaph of similar form:—pl. **sarcoph'agi** (-jī, -gī), **sarcoph'aguses**; **sarcoph'agy** (-ji), flesh-eating. [Latinised from Gr. sarkophagos—phagein (aor.), to eat.]

**sard**, särd, n. a deep-red chalcedony.—Also **sard'ius**. [L. sarda, sardius, and Gr. sardion, also sardios (lithos), the Sardian (stone)—Sardeis, Sardis, in Lydia.]

**Sard**, särd, n. and adj. Sardinian. [L. Sardus.]

**sardel**, sär-del', **sardelle**, -del'(ə), n. a small fish related to the sardine.

**sardine**, sär'dēn, sär-dēn', a young pilchard, commonly tinned in oil: applied at various times and places to other fishes.—**packed like sardines**, crowded closely together. [Fr. sardine—It. sardina—L. sardina; Gr. sardīnos, or -ē.]

**sardine**, sär'dīn, -din, n. sard (stone).—Also adj. (Rev. iv. 3).—Also **sar'dius**. [Gr. sardīnos (lithos)—sardios.]

**Sardinian**, sär-din'i-ən, -yən, adj. of the island or former kingdom of Sardinia or of the inhabitants.—n. a native, citizen, or member of the people of Sardinia: their language or dialect of Italian.

**sardonic**, sär-don'ik, adj. scornful, heartless, or

bitter, said of a forced unmirthful laugh: sneering.—*adjs.* **sardō'nian** (*obs.*); **sardon'ical.**—*adv.* **sardon'ically.** [Fr. *sardonique*—L. *sardonius*—late Gr. *sardonios*, doubtfully referred to *sardonion*, a plant of Sardinia (Gr. *Sardō*) which was said to screw up the face of the eater.]

**sardonyx**, *sär'də-niks*, *n.* an onyx with layers of cornelian or sard. [Gr. *sardonyx—Sardios*, Sardian, *onyx*, a nail.]

**saree.** See sari.

**sargasso**, *sär-gas'ō*, *n.* gulf-weed (Sargassum): a floating mass or expanse of it, as the **Sargasso Sea** in the North Atlantic. [Port. *sargaço*.]

**sarge.** Coll. abbrev. for sergeant.

**Sargus**, *sär'gəs*, *n.* a genus of sea-breams, known also as sar, **sar'go** (Sp.). [Gr. *sargos*.]

**sari**, *sär'ē*, *n.* a Hindu woman's chief garment, a long cloth wrapped round the waist and passed over the shoulder and head.—Also **sar'ee.** [Hind. *sārī*.]

**sark**, *särk*, **serk**, *serk*, (*Scot.*) *n.* a shirt or chemise: a surplice.—*ns.* **sark'ful**; **sark'ing**, a lining for a roof: material for shirts.—**sark'-tail'**, the tail, skirt, of a shirt or chemise. [O.E. *serc*; O.N. *serkr*.]

**sarky.** See sarcasm.

**Sarmatia**, *sär-mā'shyə*, *-shi-ə*, *n.* anciently a region reaching from the Vistula and Danube to the Volga and Caucasus: Poland (*poet.*).—*n.* and *adj.* **Sarmā'tian.**—*adj.* **Sarmatic** (*-mat'ik*).

**sarment**, *sär'mənt*, *n.* a cut twig or cutting (*obs.*): a sarmentum: a long weak twig.—*adjs.* **sarmentaceous** (*-ā'shəs*), **sar'mentose** (or *-ōs'*), **sarmentous** (*-ment'əs*), having sarmenta or runners: creeping.—*n.* **sarmentum** (*-ment'əm*), a runner:—*pl.* **sarment'a.** [L. *sarmentum*, a twig—*sarpĕre*, to prune.]

**sarong**, *sä'rong*, *sə-rong'*, *n.* Malay skirt-like garment for man or woman: a cloth for making it. [Malay *sārung*.]

**saros**, *sā'ros*, *sä'ros*, *n.* a Babylonian cycle of 3600 years: now (from a misunderstanding) an astronomical cycle of 6585days and 8 hours, after which relative positions of the sun and moon recur.—*adj.* **saronic** (*sə-ron'ik*). [Gr. *saros*—Babylonian *shāru*, 3600.]

**Sarracenia**, *sär-ə-sē'ni-ə*, *n.* the side-saddle flower, an American genus of insectivorous plants, with pitchers, giving name to the family **Sarraceniā'ceae**, akin to the sundew family. [After Dr *Sarrazin*, who sent them to Europe from Quebec.]

**sarrasin, sarrazin**, *sär'ə-zin*, *n.* buckwheat. [Fr. (*blé*) *sarrasin*, Saracen (corn).]

**sarrusophone**, *sə-rus'ō-fōn*, *n.* a reed instrument of brass, devised by a French bandmaster, *Sarrus*. [Gr. *phōnē*, voice.]

**sarsaparilla**, *sär-sə-pə-ril'ə*, *n.* any tropical American Smilax: its dried root: a soft drink flavoured with this (*U.S.*): a medicinal preparation from it: extended to various plants or roots of like use.—Shortened to **sar'sa**, **sar'za.** [Sp. *zarzaparilla—zarza*, bramble (from Basque), and a dim. of *parra*, vine.]

**sarsen**, *sär'sn*, *n.* a grey-wether.—Also **sars'den**, **sar'sen-stone**, **Sar'acen's-stone.** [App. forms of Saracen.]

**sarsenet, sarcenet, sarsnet**, *särs'nit*, *-net*, *n.* a thin tissue of fine silk.—*adj.* of sarsenet: mild (*Shak.*). [A.Fr. *sarzinett*, probably *Sarzin*, Saracen.]

**sartor**, *sär'tör*, (*facet.*) *n.* a tailor.—*adj.* **sartorial** (*-tō'ri-əl*, *-tö'*).—*adv.* **sarto'rially.**—*adj.* (*rare*) **sarto'rian.**—*n.* **sarto'rius** (L. *adj.*), a thigh muscle that crosses the leg, as when a tailor sits. [L. *sartor*, a patcher.]

**Sartrian**, *sär'tri-ən*, *adj.* pertaining to the French philosopher, dramatist and novelist Jean-Paul *Sartre* (*b.* 1905).—*n.* a follower or admirer of Sartre.

**sarus**, *sä'rəs*, *sā'rəs*, *n.* an Indian crane.—Also **sarus crane.** [Hind. *sāras*.]

**sa sa**, *sä sä'*, *interj.* of incitement: a fencer's exclamation on thrusting. [Fr. *ça ça*, there, there.]

**sasarara.** Same as siserary.

**sash**, *sash*, *n.* (orig. shash, *shash*) a turban cloth: a band or scarf, worn round the waist or over the shoulder.—*v.t.* to dress or adorn with a sash. [Ar. *shāsh*.]

**sash**, *sash*, *n.* a frame, esp. a sliding frame, for window panes.—*v.t.* to furnish with sashes.—**sash'-door**, a door having panes of glass; **sash'-frame**, the frame in which the sash of a window is suspended; **sash'-tool**, a glazier's brush for removing oil: a house-painter's small brush; **sash'-window**, a window with sash or sashes, opp. to casement window. [Fr. *châssis*.]

**sasin**, *sas'in*, *n.* the common Indian antelope. [Nepalese.]

**sasine**, *sā'sin*, (Scots *law*) *n.* the act of giving legal possession of feudal property, infeftment. [A variant of seisin, Law L. *sasina*.]

**saskatoon**, *sas-kə-tōōn'*, *n.* the shad-bush: its fruit. [Cree *misáskwatomin*.]

**sass**, *sas*, **sassy**, *sas'i*. Same as sauce, saucy.

**sassaby**, *sə-sä'bi*, *n.* the bastard hartebeest, a large S. African antelope. [Tswana *tsessébe*.]

**sassafras**, *sas'ə-fras*, *n.* a tree (*Sassafras officinale*) of the laurel family common in N. America: the bark, esp. of its root, a powerful stimulant: an infusion of it: extended to various plants with similar properties.—**sassafras nut**, the pichurim bean; **sassafras oil**, a volatile aromatic oil distilled from sassafras. [Sp. *sasafrás*.]

**Sassanid**, *sas'ə-nid*, *n.* one of the *Sassanidae*, the dynasty that ruled Persia from A.D. 226 to 641.—*adj.* **Sassā'nian.**

**sassarara.** Same as siserary.

**sasse**, *sas*, (*obs.*) *n.* a sluice or lock. [Du. *sas*.]

**Sassenach**, *sas'ə-nahh*, *n.* a Saxon: an Englishman: (Scott, etc.) a Lowlander. [Gael. *Sasunnach*.]

**sassolite**, *sas'ə-lit*, *n.* native boric acid—first found near *Sasso* (province of Pisa).—Also **sass'olin.**

**sastruga.** Seè zastruga.

**sat**, *sat*, *pa.t.* and *pa.p.* of sit.

**Satan**, *sā'tən* (old-fashioned *sat'ən*), *n.* the chief fallen angel: chief evil spirit, adversary of God and tempter of men, the Devil: a devil.—Also **Satanas** (*sat'ən-as*), **Sathan** (*sā'thən*), **Sathanas** (*sath'*).—*adjs.* **satanic** (*sə-tan'ik*), **-al.**—*adv.* **satan'ically.**—*ns.* **satan'icalness**; **sā'tanism**, devilish disposition: Satan-worship: the characteristics of the Satanic school.—*n.* and *adj.* **Sā'tanist.**—*ns.* **satanity** (*sə-tan'*), devilishness; **sātanol'ogy**; **sātanoph'any** (Gr. *phainein*, to show), an appearance of Satan; **sātanophō'bia** (Gr. *phobos*, fear), fear of the Devil.—**Satanic school**, Southey's name for Byron, Shelley, and other unorthodox revolutionaries; **Satan monkey**, the black saki. [Gr. and L. *Satān, Satanās*—Heb. *sātān*, enemy—*sātan*, to be adverse.]

**satara**, *sä-tä'rə*, *sat'ə-rə*, *n.* a ribbed, hot-pressed and lustred woollen cloth. [*Sátára* in India.]

**satchel**, *sach'l*, *n.* a small bag, as for school-books.—*adj.* **satch'elled.** [O.Fr. *sachel*—L. *saccellus*, dim. of *saccus*; see sack, sac.]

**sate**, *sāt*, *v.t.* to satisfy fully: to glut.—*adjs.* **sāt'ed**; **sate'less**, insatiable.—*n.* **sat'edness.** [Blend of M.E. *sade* (cf. sad) and L. *sat*, enough, or satiate, shortened.]

**sate**, *sat*, also (in rhyme) *sāt*, an archaism for sat.

**sateen**, *sa-tēn'*, *n.* a glossy cotton or woollen fabric resembling satin.

**satellite**, *sat'ə-lit*, *n.* an attendant: an obsequious follower: a body revolving about a planet: a smaller companion to anything.—Also *adj.*—*n.* **satelles** (*sat-el'ēz*; *obs.*), a satellite:—*pl.*

satell'ites (-i-tēz;  Pope).—adj. satellitic (-lit'ik).
—satellite state, country, one which relies on and obeys the dictates of a larger, more powerful state;  satellite town, a garden city, limited in size, built near a great town to check overgrowth.
—artificial, earth, satellite, any man-made body, including spacecraft, launched by rocket into space and put into orbit round the earth. [L. satelles, satellitis, an attendant.]

satem languages, sä'tɔm, the group of Indo-Germanic languages in which an original palatal consonant developed as a sibilant (as in Avestic satem, hundred); cf. centum languages.

sati. Same as suttee.

satiate, sä'shi-āt, v.t. to gratify fully: to glut.—adj. glutted.—n. sātiabil'ity.—adj. sā'tiable.—ns. sātiā'tion; satiety (sə-ti'ə-ti), state of being satiated: surfeit. [L. satiāre, -ātum—satis, enough.]

satin, sat'in, n. a closely woven silk with a lustrous and unbroken surface showing much of the warp.—adj. of, like, or (obs.) clad in satin.—v.t. to make satiny.—n. satinet', satinette (Scott, satinett'a), a thin satin: a modification of satin with a slightly different weave: a cloth with a cotton warp and a woollen weft.—adj. sat'iny, like satin.—sat'in-bird, or satin bower-bird, a satiny blue and black bower-bird;  sat'in-fin'ish, a satiny polish;  sat'in-paper, a fine, glossy writing-paper;  sat'in-sheet'ing, a twilled cotton and silk fabric with a satin surface;  sat'in-spar, a satiny fibrous calcite, or aragonite, or gypsum;  sat'in-stitch, an embroidery stitch, repeated in parallel lines, giving a satiny appearance;  sat'in-stone, a fibrous gypsum;  sat'inwood, a beautiful, smooth, satiny ornamental wood from India: the rutaceous tree (Chloroxylon swietenia) yielding it: extended to several more or less similar woods and trees. [Fr. satin, app.—L.L. sēta, silk (L. saeta, bristle).]

satinet, satinette, satinetta. See satin.

satire, sat'īr, n. a literary composition, orig. in verse, essentially a criticism of folly or vice, which it holds up to ridicule or scorn—its chief instruments, irony, sarcasm, invective, wit, and humour: satirical writing as a genre: its spirit: the use of, or inclination to use, its methods: satirical denunciation or ridicule: (from confusion with satyr) a satirist (obs.).—adjs. satiric (sə-tir'ik), -al, pertaining to, or conveying, satire: sarcastic: abusive.—adv. satir'ically.—n. satir'icalness, the state or quality of being satirical.—v.t. satirise, -ize (sat'ər-iz), to make the object of satire: to censure severely.—v.i. to write satire.—n. sat'irist, a writer of satire. [L. satira, satura (lanx), full (dish), a medley.]

satisfy, sat'is-fī, v.t. to pay in full: to compensate or atone for: to give enough to: to be enough for: to supply fully: to fulfil the conditions of: to meet the requirements of: to content: to free from doubt: to convince.—v.i. to give content: to make payment or atonement:—pr.p. sat'isfying;  pa.t. and pa.p. sat'isfied.—n. satisfaction (-fak'shən), act of satisfying: state of being satisfied, content: payment: quittance: gratification: comfort: that which satisfies: amends: atonement: reparation: satisfying of honour, as by a duel: conviction.—adv. satisfac'torily.—n. satisfac'toriness.—adjs. satisfac'tory, satisfying: giving contentment: such as might be wished: making amends or payment: atoning: convincing;  sat'isfiable;  sat'isfied.—n. sat'isfier.—adj. sat'isfying.—adv. sat'isfyingly.—satisfaction theory (of the Atonement), the ordinary theory of Catholic orthodoxy that Christ made satisfaction to Divine justice for the guilt of human sin by suffering as the human representative, and that thus Divine forgiveness was made possible. [O.Fr. satisfier—L. satisfacĕre, satis, enough, facĕre, to make.]

satis verborum, sä'tis vûr-bō'rəm, -bö', sat'is ver-, wer-bō'rōōm, (L.) enough of words.
sative, sä'tiv, (obs.) adj. cultivated. [L. sativus.]
satori, sa-tō'rē, -tö', n. sudden enlightenment—sought in Zen Buddhism. [Jap.]
satrap, sat'rap, -rəp, sä'trap, n. a viceroy or governor of an ancient Persian province: a provincial governor, esp. if powerful or ostentatiously rich: a tyrannical person.—adjs. sat'rapal, satrap'ic, -al.—n. sat'rapy, a satrap's province, office, or time of office. [Gr. satrapēs, from Old Pers. khshathrapāvan-, country-protector.]
sat sapienti, sap-i-en'ti, -tē, (L.) enough for the wise, a nod to the wise.
Satsuma, sat'sōō-ma, n. a province of S.W. Japan.—satsuma (orange), a thin-skinned seedless type of mandarin orange, or its tree;  Satsuma ware, a yellowish pottery with gilding and enamel made in Satsuma from end of 16th century.
saturate, sat'ū-rāt, sa'chə-rāt, v.t. to interfuse: to soak: to imbue: to charge to the fullest extent possible: to satisfy all the valencies of: to cover (a target area) completely with bombs dropped simultaneously.—adj. saturated: deep in colour, free from white.—n. a saturated compound (chem.).—adjs. sat'urable;  sat'urant, which saturates.—n. a saturating substance.—adj. sat'urated.—n. saturā'tion.—Also used as adj., meaning of very great, or greatest possible, intensity (e.g. saturation bombing).—n. sat'urātor;  saturation diving, diving to the deepest level possible using special apparatus, e.g. bathyscaphe;  saturation point, the point at which saturation is reached: dewpoint: the limit in numbers that can be taken in, provided with a living, used, sold, etc.: the limit of emotional response, endurance, etc. [L. saturāre, -ātum—satur, full, akin to satis, enough.]
Saturday, sat'ər-di, n. the seventh day of the week, dedicated by the Romans to Saturn, the Jewish Sabbath. [O.E. Sæter-, Sætern(es)dæg, Saturn's day.]
Saturn, sat'ərn, n. the ancient Roman god of agriculture: commonly used for the Greek Kronos, with whom he came to be identified: the second in size and sixth in distance from the sun of the major planets, believed by the astrologers to induce a cold, melancholy, gloomy temperament: the metal lead (alch.).—n.pl. Saturnā'lia, the festival of Saturn in mid-December, when slaves and masters exchanged garb and parts: hence (often as sing. without capital) an orgy.—adj. saturnā'lian, of the Saturnalia: riotously merry.—n. Satur'nia (sat-, sət-), a genus of very large moths.—adj. Satur'nian, pertaining to Saturn, whose fabulous reign was called the golden age: happy: pure: simple: in the metre in which the oldest Latin poems were written: of the planet Saturn: of the genus Saturnia.—n. one born under Saturn, or of saturnine temperament: the son of Saturn (Jupiter or Zeus): a fancied inhabitant of Saturn.—adjs. satur'nic, affected with lead-poisoning;  sat'urnine, grave: gloomy: phlegmatic: caused or poisoned by lead.—ns. sat'urnism, lead-poisoning;  sat'urnist (obs.), a gloomy person.—Saturn's tree, an arborescent deposit of lead from a solution of a lead salt. [L. Sāturnus—serĕre, sătum, to sow.]
satyagraha, sut'ya-gru-hə, or -grä', n. orig. Mahatma Gandhi's policy of passive resistance to British rule in India, now any non-violent campaign for reform. [Sans., reliance on truth.]
satyr, sat'ər, n. a Greek wood-god, with tail and long ears, represented by the Romans as part goat: a desert demon (B.): a very lecherous person: an orang-utan: any butterfly of the Satyridae: (formerly, by confusion) a satire or satirist.—Shakespeare's saltiers (Wint. Tale IV,

vi. 353) is perh. meant to mark a rustic confusion of satyr and saultier (jumper):—*fem.* **sat'yra**, **sat'yress**.—*n.* **sat'yral** (*her.*), a monster compounded of man, lion, and antelope.—*adj.* **satyresque'**.—*n.* **satyri'asis**, morbid, overpowering, sexual desire in men, corresponding to nymphomania in women.—*adjs.* **satyric** (*sə-tir'ik*), **-al**, of satyrs: having a chorus of satyrs.—*n.pl.* **Satyridae** (*-tir'i-dē*), a family of butterflies (otherwise **Satyri'nae**, a sub-family of Nymphalidae) including meadow-browns, heaths, marbled whites, etc.—*n.* **sat'yrisk**, a little satyr. [L. *satyrus*—Gr. *satyros*.]

**sauba**, *sä-ōō'bə*, *sö'bə*, *n.* a S. American leaf-carrying ant.—Also **sau'ba-ant**. [Tupí.]

**sauce**, *sös*, *n.* a dressing poured over food: anything that gives relish (*fig.*): vegetables eaten with meat (*U.S.*): stewed fruit (*U.S.*): a solution of salt, etc., used in individual processes: a pert or impudent person (*obs.*): pert or impertinent language (*coll.*).—*v.t.* to add or give sauce to: to make piquant or pleasant: to rebuke (*Shak.*): to make to pay dear (*Shak.*): to belabour (*obs.*).—*adv.* **sauc'ily**.—*n.* **sauc'iness**.—*adj.* **sauc'y** (*comp.* **sauc'ier**; *superl.* **sauc'iest**), tasting of sauce: pert: piquantly audacious: smart and trim (as of a ship): disdainful: lascivious (*Shak.*).—**sauce'-alone'**, garlic-mustard; **sauce boat**, a vessel for sauce; **sauce'-box**, a saucy person; **sauce-crayon** (*sōs krā-yɔ̃*; Fr.), a soft black pastel used for backgrounds; **sauce'man** (*U.S.*), a vegetable seller; **sauce'pan**, a handled and usu. lidded metal pan for boiling, stewing, etc.—orig. for sauces; **sauce'pan-fish**, the king-crab. [Fr. *sauce*—L. *salsa*—*sallēre*, *salsum*, to salt—*sāl*, salt.]

**saucer**, *sö'sər*, *n.* orig., a dish for salt or sauce: a shallow dish, esp. one placed under a tea or coffee cup: anything of like shape.—*n.* **sau'cerful**:—*pl.* **sau'cerfuls**.—**sau'cer-eye**, a large round eye.—*adj.* **sau'cer-eyed**.—**flying saucer** (see fly). [O.Fr. *saussiere*—L.L. *salsārium*—L. *salsa*, sauce.]

**sauch**, **saugh**, *söhh*, Scots form of **sallow** (willow).

**saucisse**, *sö-sēs'*, **saucisson**, *-ɔ̃*, *ns.* a tube of powder for firing a mine. [Fr., sausage.]

**sauerkraut**, *sow'*, *zow'ər-krowt*, *n.* a German dish of cabbage allowed to ferment with salt, etc. [Ger., sour cabbage.]

**saufgard**, *söf-gärd'*, (*Spens.*) *n.* Same as **safe-guard**.

**sauger**, *sö'gər*, *n.* a small American pike-perch.

**saul**, a Scots form of **soul**.

**saulge**, *söj*, (*Spens.*) *n.* Same as **sage** (plant).

**saulie**, *sö'li*, (*Scot.*) *n.* a hired mourner. [Origin obscure.]

**sault**, *sölt*, *n.* a leap (also **salt**) (*obs.*): in N. America (*sōō*) a waterfall or rapid. [Fr. *saut*, 17th-cent. *sault*—L. *saltus*, *-ūs*, leap.]

**sauna**, *sö'na*, *sow'na*, *n.* (a building or room equipped for) a Finnish form of steam bath. [Finn.]

**saunt**, *sönt*, a Scots form of **saint**.

**saunter**, *sön'tər*, *v.i.* to wander about idly: to loiter: to lounge: to stroll: to dawdle (*obs.*).—*n.* a sauntering: a sauntering gait: a leisurely stroll.—*ns.* **saun'terer**; **saun'tering**.—*adv.* **saun'teringly**. [Origin obscure.]

**saurel**, *sö-rel'*, *sör'əl*, *n.* the horse-mackerel, scad. [Fr.]

**Sauria**, *sö'ri-ə*, *n.pl.* in old classifications an order of reptiles, the lizards with (at first) the crocodiles.—*adj.* **sau'rian**.—*n.* a member of the Sauria: a lizard-like fossil reptile.—*adjs.* **saurog'-nathous**, having a lizard-like arrangement of the palate-bones (as woodpeckers, **Saurog'nathae**; Gr. *gnathos*, jaw); **saur'oid**, lizard-like.—*n.pl.* **Saurop'oda** (Gr. *pous*, *podos*, foot), a suborder of gigantic herbivorous dinosaurs.—*adj.* **saurop'odous**.—*n.pl.* **Saurop'sida** (Gr. *opsis*, *-eōs*,

appearance), a main division of the Vertebrata—birds and reptiles.—*n.* and *adj.* **saurop'sidan**.—*n.pl.* **Sauropterygia** (*sö-rop-tər-ij'i-ə*; Gr. *pterygion*, a fin), an order of fossil reptiles, aquatic or amphibious, including Plesiosaurus.—*adj.* **sauropteryg'ian**.—*n.pl.* **Saururae** (*-rōō'rē*; Gr. *ourā*, tail), extinct (Jurassic) subclass of birds, with teeth and jointed tail—Archaeopteryx, etc. [Gr. *saurā*, *sauros*, a lizard.]

**saury**, *sö'ri*, *n.* sharp-beaked fish (*Scombresox saurus*) akin to the garfish. [Perh. Gr. *sauros*, lizard.]

**sausage**, *sos'ij*, *n.* chopped meat seasoned and stuffed into a tube of gut or the like or formed into the shape of a tube: anything of like shape, e.g. an observation balloon.—**saus'age-bassoon'**, the rackett; **saus'age-meat'**, meat prepared for making sausages; **saus'age-poi'soning**, botulism; **saus'age-roll'**, minced meat cooked in a roll of pastry: a curl of hair of similar shape; **sau'sage-tree'**, tropical tree (*Kigelia africana*) with bell-shaped flowers and sausage-shaped fruits. [Fr. *saucisse*—L.L. *salsicia*—L. *salsus*, salted.]

**saussurite**, *sö-sū'rit*, *n.* a dull opaque mass of zoisite, albite, etc., formed by the alteration of feldspar.—*adjs.* **saussuritic** (*-it'ik*); **saussu'ritised**, **-ized**. [After the Swiss geologist H. B. de Saussure (1740-99).]

**saut**, *söt*, a Scottish form of **salt**.

**sauté**, *sö'tā*, *adj.* fried lightly and quickly.—Also *v.t.* [Fr.]

**Sauterne(s)**, *sö-tûrn'*, *-tern'*, *n.* esteemed white wine produced at *Sauternes* in the Gironde, France.

**savage**, *sav'ij*, also (*arch.*) **salvage**, *sal'vij*, *adj.* in a state of nature: wild: uncivilised: ferocious: furious.—*n.* a wild beast (now *rare*): an enraged horse or other animal: a human being in a wild state: a brutal, fierce, or cruel person.—*v.t.* to make savage: to assail savagely, esp. with teeth.—*v.i.* to play the savage.—*n.* **sav'agedom**, a savage state: savages collectively.—*adv.* **sav'-agely**.—*ns.* **sav'ageness**; **sav'agery** (*-ri*, also *-ər-i*), fierceness: ferocity: uncivilised condition: wildness: wild growth of plants; **sav'-agism**. [O.Fr. *salvage*—L. *silvāticus*, pertaining to the woods—*silva*, a wood.]

**savanna**, **savannah**, *sə-van'ə*, *n.* a tract of level land, covered with low vegetation, treeless, or dotted with trees or patches of wood.—**savanna flower**, a West Indian apocynaceous plant (Echiles); **savann'a-forest**, parklands; **savann'a-sparr'ow**, a N. American sparrow (Passerculus); **savann'a-watt'le**, fiddlewood. [Sp. *zavana* (now *sabana*), said to be from Carib: not from *sábana*, sheet.]

**savant**, *sa'vä*, *sä-vä'*, *n.* a learned man. [Fr. obs. pr.p. of *savoir*, to know.]

**savate**, *sä-vät*, *n.* boxing with the use of the feet. [Fr.]

**save**, *sāv*, *v.t.* to bring safe out of evil: to rescue: to bring or keep out of danger: to protect: to prevent or avoid the loss, expenditure, or performance of, or the gain of by an opponent: to reserve: to spare: to deliver from the power of sin and from its consequences: to husband: to hoard: to be in time for: to obviate, to prevent.—*v.i.* to act as a saviour: to be economical.—*prep.* except.—*conj.* were it not that (*Shak.*): unless.—*n.* an act of saving, esp. in games.—*adj.* **sav'able**.—*n.* **sav'ableness**.—*adj.* **saved**.—*n.* **sa'ver**.—*adj.* **sa'ving**, protecting: preserving: redeeming: securing salvation (*theol.*): frugal: making a reservation: directed towards the avoidance of loss rather than the making of profit.—*prep.* excepting.—*n.* the action of saving: that which is saved: (*pl.*) earnings.—*adv.* **sa'vingly**.—*n.* **sa'vingness**.—**save'-all**, a contrivance intended to save anything from being wasted or damaged: a miser.—*adj.* stingy.—*v.t.*

**save′gard** (*Spens.*), to guard, protect.—**saving clause**, a legal clause, or a statement, in which a reservation or condition is made; **saving game**, a policy or procedure aimed rather at avoiding loss than at making a profit; **saving grace** (see grace); **savings bank**, a bank established to encourage thrift by taking small amounts, investing under regulations for safety, and giving compound interest; **savings certificate**, a certificate of having invested a small sum in government funds.—**save appearances**, to make hypothesis accord with observation (*astron., Milt.*): to keep up an appearance of wealth, comfort, consistency, harmony, propriety, etc; **save one's bacon, face, save the mark** (see bacon, face, mark); **save up**, to accumulate or hold for some purpose by refraining from spending or using; **save you** (*arch.*), a greeting = God keep you. [Fr. *sauver* —L. *salvāre*—*salvus*, safe.]

**saveloy**, *sav′ə-loi*, *n.* a highly seasoned sausage, orig. of brains. [Fr. *cervelat, cervelas*, a saveloy —It. *cervellata*—*cervello*, brain—L. *cerebellum*, dim. of *cerebrum*, the brain.]

**savin, savine**, *sav′in*, *n.* a species of juniper (*Juniperus sabina*) with very small imbricated leaves: its tops yielding an irritant volatile oil, anthelmintic and abortifacient: extended to Virginian juniper ('red cedar') and other plants. [O.Fr. *sabine*—L. *sabina* (*herba*), Sabine (herb).]

**saviour**, *sā′vyər*, *n.* one who saves from evil: **Saviour**, a title applied by Christians to Jesus Christ.

**savoir-faire**, *sav-wär-fer′*, *n.* the faculty of knowing just what to do and how to do it: tact. [Fr.]

**savoir-vivre**, *sav-wär-vē′vr′*, *n.* good breeding: knowledge of polite usages. [Fr.]

**savory**, *sā′vər-i*, *n.* a labiate flavouring herb (Satureia, esp. *S. hortensis*, summer savory, or *S. montana*, winter savory). [App.—L. *satureia.*]

**savour**, also (*U.S.*) **savor**, *sā′vər*, *n.* taste: odour: flavour: relish: repute (*B.*).—*v.i.* to taste or smell in a particular way: to have a flavour (*lit.* or *fig.*): to smack.—*v.t.* to flavour, season: to taste, smell: to be conscious of: to relish: to perceive critically: to taste with conscious direction of the attention.—*adjs.* **sā′vorous**, pleasant to the taste; **sā′voured**, having a savour.—*adv.* **sā′vourily.**—*n.* **sā′vouriness.**—*adj.* **sā′vourless.**— *adv.* **sā′vourly** (*obs.*), relishingly: feelingly: understandingly.—*adj.* **sā′voury**, of good savour or relish: fragrant: having savour or relish: appetising: salty or spiced (opp. to *sweet*): savouring of edification or holiness (*arch.*).—*n.* a savoury course or dish. [O.Fr. *sav(o)ur* (Fr. *saveur*)—L. *sapor*—*sapĕre*, to taste.]

**Savoy**, *sə-voi′*, *n.* a district, formerly of the kingdom of Sardinia, now of S.E. France, giving name to a former palace and sanctuary and to a theatre in London: (without *cap.*) a winter cabbage with a large close head and wrinkled leaves—originally from *Savoy.*—*n.* **Savoyard** (*sav′oi-ärd*), a native or inhabitant of Savoy, or of the Savoy precinct in London: a performer in the Gilbert and Sullivan operas produced at the Savoy theatre.—Also *adj.* [Fr. *Savoie, Savoyard.*]

**savvy, savvey, savey**, *sav′i*, (*slang*) *v.t.* and *v.i.* to know: to understand.—*n.* general ability: common sense. [Sp. *sabe*—*saber*, to know—L. *sapĕre*, to be wise.]

**saw**, *sö*, *pa.t.* of see.

**saw**, *sö*, *n.* a toothed cutting instrument.—*v.t.* to cut with, or as with, or as, a saw: to play harshly or crudely (as a fiddler).—*v.i.* to use a saw: to make to and fro movements, as if with a saw:— *pa.t.* sawed; *pa.p.* sawed or (usu.) sawn.—*adj.* **sawed.**—*n.* and *adj.* **saw′ing.**—*adj.* **sawn.**—*ns.* **saw′er** (*rare*); **saw′yer**, one who saws timber, esp. at a sawpit: a stranded tree that bobs in a river (*U.S.*).—**saw′-bill**, a merganser: a motmot;

**saw′-blade; saw′-bones** (*slang*), a surgeon; **saw′-dust**, dust or small particles of wood, etc., detached in sawing.—*v.t.* to sprinkle with sawdust.—*adj.* **saw′dusty.**—**saw′-edge.**—*adj.* **saw′-edged**, serrated.—**saw′-fish**, a ray (Pristis) or (sometimes) a shark (Pristiophorus); **saw′-shark**) with a flattened bony beak toothed on the edges; **saw′-fly**, a hymenopterous insect of various kinds with saw-like ovipositor; **saw′-frame**, the frame in which a saw is set; **saw′-gate, -kerf**, the gap made by a saw; **saw′-horse**, a trestle for supporting wood that is being sawn; **saw′-mill**, a mill for sawing timber.—*adj.* **sawn′-off** (or **sawed off**) shortened by cutting with a saw: short in stature (*slang*).—**saw′pit**, a pit in which one sawyer stands while another stands above; **saw′-set**, an instrument for turning saw-teeth to right and left; **saw′-tones**, harsh notes; **saw′-tooth.**—Also *adj.*—*adj.* **saw′-toothed.**—**saw′-wort**, a name for various composites with serrate leaves (Serratula, Saussurea, etc.). [O.E. *saga*; Ger. *säge.*]

**saw**, *sö*, *n.* a saying: a proverb: a decree (*Spens.*). [O.E. *sagu*, from the root of *secgan*, to say, tell.]

**saw**, *sö*, a Scots form of sow (*vb.*) and of **salve** (ointment).

**sawder**, *sö′dər*, *v.t.* to flatter, blarney.—*n.* (in phrase *soft sawder*) flattery. [Prob. **solder.**]

**sawn**, *sön*, *pa.p.* of saw; also (*Northern*) of sow (*Shak.*) perh. of sow, perh. of see.

**Sawney, Sawny**, *sö′ni*, *n.* an old nickname for a Scotsman. [For *Sandy*, from *Alexander.*]

**sawney**, *sö′ni*, (*slang*) *n.* a fool. [Poss. from prec.: poss. from **zany.**]

**sax**, *saks*, *n.* a chopper for trimming slates. [O.E. *sæx* (W.S. *seax*), a knife.]

**sax**, a Scottish form of six.

**saxatile**, *sak′sə-til*, *-til*, *adj.* rock-dwelling. [L. *saxātilis*—*saxum*, a rock.]

**saxaul, saksaul**, *sak′söl*, *n.* a low, thick, grotesquely contorted tree (Haloxylon) of the goose-foot family, found on the salt steppes of Asia.

**Saxe**, *saks*, *adj.* made in, or characteristic of, Saxony (of china, etc): of a deep shade of light blue (*Saxe blue*, also *Saxon* or *Saxony blue*).—*n.* Saxon blue, a dye colour: an albuminised paper (*phot.*). [Fr. *Saxe*, Saxony.]

**saxhorn**, *saks′hörn*, *n.* a brass wind-instrument having a long winding tube with bell opening, invented by Antoine or Adolphe Sax (1814-94).

**saxicavous**, *sak-sik′ə-vəs*, *adj.* rock-boring.—*n.* **Saxic′ava**, a genus of rock-boring lamellibranchs. [L. *saxum*, a rock, *cavāre*, to hollow.]

**saxicolous**, *sak-sik′ə-ləs*, *adj.* living or growing among rocks.—*n.* **Saxic′ola**, the wheatear genus. —*adj.* **saxic′oline.** [L. *saxum*, a rock, *colĕre*, to inhabit.]

**saxifrage**, *sak′si-frij, -fräj*, *n.* any species of the genus Saxifraga: extended to other plants (see burnet saxifrage, golden saxifrage).—*n.* **Saxifraga** (*-sif′rə-gə*), the London pride genus, giving name to the family **Saxifragā′ceae**, near akin to the rose family.—*adj.* **saxifragā′ceous.** [L. *saxifraga*—*saxum*, a stone, *frangĕre*, to break (from growing in clefts of rock, or, according to Pliny, from supposed efficacy in breaking up a calculus in the bladder).]

**Saxon**, *saks′ən*, *n.* one of a N. German people that conquered most of Britain in the 5th and 6th centuries (including or excluding the Angles and Jutes): the language of that people on the Continent (Old Saxon) or in Britain (Anglo-Saxon, Old English): an Englishman or Lowland Scotsman: one whose native language is English: the English language: a native, inhabitant, or citizen of Saxony in the later German sense (now in S. Germany).—*adj.* pertaining to the Saxons in any sense, their language, country, or architecture.—*n.* **Sax′ondom**, the Anglo-Saxon or English-speaking world.—*adj.*

**Saxonic** (-*on'ik*).—*v.t.* and *v.i.* Sax'onise, -ize, to make or become Saxon.—*ns.* Sax'onism, a Saxon or English idiom: a preference for native English words, institutions, etc.; Sax'onist, a scholar in Old English; sax'onite, a hypersthene peridotite; sax'ony, a soft woollen yarn or cloth.—**Saxon architecture,** a style of building in England before the Norman Conquest, marked by the peculiar 'long and short' work of the quoins, the projecting fillets running up the face of the walls and interlacing like woodwork, and the baluster-like shafts between the openings of the upper windows resembling the turned woodwork of the period; **Saxon Shore** (L. *Litus Saxonicum*), in Roman times, the coast districts from Brighton to the Wash, peculiarly exposed to the attacks of the Saxons, or perh. already partly settled by them, and therefore placed under the authority of a special officer, the 'Count of the Saxon Shore'. [L. *Saxōnēs* (pl.); of Ger. origin; cf. O.E. *Seaxe*: Ger. *Sachsen*; perh. conn. O.E. *sæx* (W.S. *seax*), O.H.G. *sahs*, knife, short sword.]

**saxophone,** *sak'sō-fōn, n.* a military and dance band instrument with reed, (properly) metal tube, and about twenty finger-keys.—*n.* saxophonist (-*sof'ən-ist*). [*Sax,* the inventor (see **saxhorn**), Gr. *phōnē,* the voice.]

**say,** *sā, v.t.* to utter or set forth, as words or in words: to speak: to assert, affirm, state, declare: to tell: to go through in recitation or repetition.—*v.i.* to make a statement: to speak: to declare, set forth in answer to a question:—*2nd sing. pr. ind.* sayst (*sāst*), sayest (*sā'ist*); *3rd sing.* says (*sez, səz*), archaic saith (*seth*); *pr.p.* say'ing; *pa.p.* and *pa.t.* said (*sed*); *2nd sing.* saidst (*sedst*), also said'est.—*n.* something said: a remark: a speech: a saw (*obs.*): what one wants to say: opportunity of speech: a voice, part, or influence in a decision.—*adj.* say'able.—*ns.* say'er; say'ing, something said: an expression: a maxim.—say'-so, a dictum: authority: a rumour: hearsay.—**I say,** an exclamation calling attention or expressing surprise, protest, sudden joy, etc.; **it is said,** or **they say,** it is commonly reputed; **it says (that),** the text runs thus (*coll.*); **nothing to say for oneself,** no defence of oneself to offer: no small-talk; **nothing to say to,** no dealings with; **not to say,** indeed one might go further and say; **say, for example:** suppose: I say (*U.S.*): in 18th-cent. verse a common introduction to a rhetorical question; **says I, says you,** (in *illit.* or jocular use) ungrammatical substitutes for said I, you; **says you,** *interj.* expressing incredulity; **sooth to say,** in truth: if the truth must be told; **that is to say,** in other words; **to say nothing of,** not to mention; **what do you say to?,** how about?: are you inclined towards? [O.E. *secgan* (*sægde, gesægd*); O.N. *segja,* Ger. *sagen.*]

**say,** *sā,* (*obs.*; *Spens., Shak.*) *n., v.t.,* and *v.i.* an aphetic form of **assay.**—*n.* say'er.—say'-master; say'-piece.

**say,** *sā, n.* a woollen stuff like serge.—*adj.* (*Shak.*) of say.—*n.* say'on, a mediaeval peasant's sleeveless jacket. [O.Fr. *saie*—L. *saga,* pl. of *sagum,* military cloak.]

**sayne,** *sān,* (*Spens.*) *inf.* and *pl.* of *pr.t.* of say (1).

**sayonara,** *sä-yo-nä'ra,* (Jap.) good-bye.

**sayyid, sayid, said,** *sī'* or *sā'(y)id, säd, n.* a descendant of Mohammed's daughter Fatima. [Ar. *Sayyid.*]

**sazhen,** *sä-zhen', n.* a Russian measure, about 2 metres. [Russ.]

**sbirro,** *zbir'rō, n.* an Italian police officer:—*pl.* **sbirri** (-*rē*). [It.]

**'sblood,** *zblud,* **'sbodikins,** *zbod'i-kinz,* **'sbuddikins,** *zbud',* **'zbud,** *zbud, interjs.* obsolete oaths. [God's blood, body.]

**scab,** *skab, n.* vaguely, a skin disease, esp. with

scales or pustules, and esp. one caused by mites (as in *sheep scab*): a fungous disease of various kinds in potatoes, apples, etc.: a crust formed over a sore, or in any of these diseases: a scoundrel: a black-leg.—*v.i.* to develop a scab: to play the scab.—*adj.* scabbed (*skabd, skab'id*), affected or covered with scabs: diseased with scab: vile, worthless.—*ns.* scabb'edness; scabb'iness.—*adj.* scabb'y. [App. from an O.N. equivalent of O.E. *scæb, sceabb* (see **shabby**), influenced by association with L. *scabiēs.*]

**scabbard,** *skab'ərd, n.* a sheath, esp. for a sword.—*v.t.* to sheathe.—*adj.* scabb'ardless.—scabb'ard-fish, a long narrow fish (Lepidopus) of the hairtail family. [M.E. *scauberc,* app.—A.Fr. *escaubers* (pl.), prob. Gmc.]

**scabble,** *skab'l.* Same as **scapple.**

**scabies,** *skā'bi-ēz, n.* the itch. [L. *scăbiēs*—*scabĕre,* to scratch.]

**scabious,** *skā'bi-əs, n.* any plant of the genus Scabio'sa of the teasel family, as the *Devil's-bit scabious,* long thought efficacious in scaly eruptions: a plant (*Jasione montana*): *sheep's,* or *sheep's-bit scabious*) of the bell-flower family, of similar appearance. [L. *scăbiōsus*—*scăbiēs,* the itch.]

**scabrous,** *skā'brəs, adj.* rough: rough with projecting points: scurfy: harsh: beset with difficulties: bordering on the indecent.—*adjs.* scaberulous (*skə-ber'ū-ləs*), scā'brid, somewhat scabrous.—*ns.* scabridity (*skə-brid'i-ti*), scā'-brousness. [L. *scăbrōsus, scăbridus*—*scăber,* rough.]

**scad,** *skad, n.* a carangoid fish (*Caranx,* or *Trachurus, trachurus*) with armoured and keeled lateral line, superficially like a coarse mackerel, also called *horse-mackerel.* [App. Cornish dial.; perh. **shad.**]

**scaff,** *skaf, n.* food (*Scot.*): riff-raff (also scaff'-raff'). [Perh. Du. or Ger. *schaffen,* to procure food; cf. **scoff** (2).]

**scaffie,** *skaf'i,* (*Scot. coll.*) *n.* short for **scavenger.**

**scaffold,** *skaf'əld, n.* a temporary erection for men at work on a building, and their tools and materials: a raised platform, as for performers, spectators, or executions: a raised framework, as for hunters, or among some primitive peoples for disposal of the dead: a framework: capital punishment (*fig.*).—*v.t.* to furnish with a scaffold: to put on a scaffold: to sustain.—*ns.* scaff'oldage (*Shak.* scaff'olage), a scaffolding: the gallery of a theatre; scaff'older; scaff'olding, a framework for painters, builders, etc., at work: materials for scaffolds: a frame, framework (*fig.*): the action of the verb. [O.Fr. *escadafault* (Fr. *échafaud*), of obscure origin; cf. It. *catafalco.*]

**scaglia,** *skal'yə, n.* an Italian limestone, usu. reddish.—*n.* scagliō'la, an imitation stone of cement and chips.—Also *adj.* [It. *scaglia,* scale, dim. *scagliuola.*]

**scail,** *skāl.* Same as **skail.**

**scaith.** See **scathe.**

**scala,** *skā'lə, skä'lə, n.* a ladder-like structure, as any of the canals of the cochlea:—*pl.* scalae (-*lē, -li*).—*adj.* scā'lable, that can be climbed.—*ns.* scalade (*skə-lād'*), scalado (-*lä'dō, -lä'dō*; It. *scalada*), an escalade.—*adj.* scalar (*skā'lər*), ladder-like: numerical: represented by a point in a scale: having magnitude only, not direction.—*n.* a scalar quantity.—*n.* Scalaria (*skə-lā'ri-ə*), the wentletrap genus.—*adj.* scalariform (*skə-lar'i-förm*), ladder-like. [L. *scāla,* a ladder.]

**scal(l)awag.** Same as **scallywag.**

**scald,** *sköld, v.t.* to injure with hot liquid: to cook or heat short of boiling: to treat with very hot water: to burn, scorch (now *dial.*).—*v.i.* to be scalded: to be hot enough to scald.—*n.* a burn caused by hot liquid.—*n.* scald'er.—*n.* and *adj.* scald'ing.—scaldings, a cry of warning to get out of the way, as if of hot water. [O.Fr. *escalder*

(Fr. *échauder*)—L.L. *excaldāre*, to bathe in warm water—*ex*, from, *calidus*, warm, hot.]

**scald, scaldic.** Same as skald, skaldic.

**scald,** *sköld, adj.* scabby: scurfy: paltry.—*n.* scurf on the head: a scurvy fellow.—**scald'-berry,** the blackberry (from a belief that it causes scald-head); **scald'-crow** (*Ir.*), the hooded crow; **scald'fish,** the smooth sole; **scald'-head,** a diseased scalp: scalp disease of various kinds. [For scalled.]

**scaldino,** *skal-, skäl-dē'nō, n.* an Italian earthenware brazier:—*pl.* scaldi'ni (-*nē*). [It. *scaldare*, to warm.]

**scale,** *skāl.* Same as skail.

**scale,** *skāl, n.* a ladder (*obs.*): a scaling-ladder (*Milt.*): a flight of steps (*obs.*): a graduated series or order: a graduated measure: a system of definite tones used in music: a succession of 'these performed in ascending or descending order of pitch through one octave or more: compass or range of a voice or instrument: a numeral system: a system or scheme of relative values or correspondences: ratio of representation to object: relative extent.—*v.t.* to mount, as by a ladder: to climb: to change according to scale (often with *up* or *down*).—*v.i.* to mount.—*ns.* **scal'er,** an instrument incorporating more than one **scaling circuit** (a device that counts very rapid pulses, by recording at the end of each group of specified numbers instead of after individual pulses): a scaling circuit; **scal'ing,** climbing: adjustment to or in a scale.—**scale'-stair'(case)** (*Scot.*), stairs in straight flights; **scal'ing-ladder,** a ladder for escalade: a fireman's ladder.—**full-scale** (see full); **on a large, small, scale, in a great, small, way; on the scale of,** in the ratio of; **scale and platt** (*Scot.*), stairs with straight flights and landings; **to scale,** in proportion to actual dimensions. [L. *scāla,* a ladder—*scandĕre,* to mount.]

**scale,** *skāl, n.* a thin plate on a fish, reptile, etc.: a readily detached flake: a lamina: an overlapping plate in armour: a small, flat, detachable piece of cuticle: a reduced leaf or leaf-base, often membranous, or hard and woody: a small flat structure clothing a butterfly's or moth's wing: the waxy shield secreted by a scale-insect: an encrustation: a film, as on iron under the hammer: a side piece of a razor or clasp-knife handle.—*v.t.* to clear of scales: to peel off in thin layers.—*v.i.* to come off in thin layers or flakes.—*adjs.* **scaled,** having scales: cleared of scales; **scale'less; scale'like.**—*ns.* **scal'er,** one who scales fish, boilers, etc.: an instrument for scaling, as for removing tartar from the teeth; **scal'iness; scal'ing,** formation, peeling off, shedding, removal, or arrangement of scales or scale: a scaled-off piece.—Also *adj.*—*adj.* **scal'y,** covered with scales: like scales: shabby: formed of scales: inclined to scale.—**scale'-arm'our,** armour of overlapping scales; **scale'-board,** a very thin slip of wood; **scale'-fern,** a fern (*Ceterach officinarum*) whose back is densely covered with rusty-coloured scales; **scale'-fish,** a dry-cured fish, as haddock, hake, pollack: a fish with scales; **scale'-insect,** any insect of the homopterous family Coccidae, in which the sedentary female fixes on a plant and secretes a waxy shield; **scale'-leaf,** a scale that is homologically a leaf; **scale'-moss,** a liver-wort with small leaflike structures, as Jungermannia; **scale'-work,** imbricated ornament; **scal'y-bark,** hickory: hickory-nut; **scal'y-leg,** a disease of legs and feet in poultry, caused by a mite. [M.E. *scāle*—O.Fr. *escale*, husk, chip of stone, of Gmc. origin; cf. scale (4), shale, shell.]

**scale,** *skāl, n.* a balance pan: (usu. in *pl.*; by Shak. treated as *sing.*) a balance: (in *pl.*) Libra, a constellation and a sign of the zodiac.—*v.t.* to weigh: to weigh up.—*v.i.* to be weighed, as a

jockey (often *scale in*).—**scale'-beam,** the beam of a balance. [A Northern form from O.N. *skál,* bowl, pan of balance; cf. O.E. *scealu,* shell, cup, Du. *schaal,* Ger. *schale,* and preceding word.]

**scale,** *skāl,* (Shak., *Cor.* I, i. 97) *v.t.* variously explained as, to spread, disseminate (see skail), to lay bare, make clear (see scale (3)), or as a misprint for stale.

**scalene,** *skāl'ēn, skal-ēn', adj.* (of a triangle) with three unequal sides: (of a cone or cylinder) with axis oblique to the base: (of a muscle) obliquely situated and unequal-sided, connecting ribs with neck.—**scalēnohē'dron** (*crystal.*), a hemihedral form bounded in the hexagonal system by twelve, in the tetragonal by eight, faces, each a scalene triangle. [Gr. *skalēnos,* uneven, *hedrā,* seat.]

**scall,** *sköl, n.* (*B.*) scabbiness, esp. of the scalp.—*adj.* (Shak.) scurvy: mean.—*adj.* **scalled** (see scald (3)). [O.N. *skalli,* bald head.]

**scallion,** *skal'yən, n.* the shallot (*dial.*): the leek: an onion with defective bulb. [O.N. Fr. *escalogne*—L. *Ascalōnia* (*cēpa*), Ascalon (onion).]

**scallop,** *skol'əp, skal'əp, n.* a bivalve (Pecten) having a sub-circular shell with sinuous radiating ridges and eared hinge-line: a valve of its shell: a dish or other object of like form: a shallow dish in which oysters, etc., are cooked, baked, and browned: hence, the cooked oysters, etc., themselves: a potato slice cooked in batter: one of a series of curves in the edge of anything: a scallop-shell as pilgrim badge: a slice of veal, etc., cut thin and often beaten out still thinner.—*v.t.* to cut into scallops or curves: to cook in a scallop with sauce and usu. breadcrumbs.—*adj.* **scall'oped,** having the edge or border cut into scallops or curves.—**scall'op-shell,** the shell of a scallop, esp. that of a Mediterranean species, the badge of a pilgrim to the shrine of St James of Compostela.—Also **scollop.** [O.Fr. *escalope*; of Gmc. origin; cf. Du. *schelp,* shell; Ger. *schelfe,* husk.]

**scallywag, scallawag, scalawag,** *skal'i-wag, -ə-wag, n.* an undersized animal of little value: a good-for-nothing: a Southerner who co-operated with the Republicans in the Reconstruction period (*U.S. hist.*). [Origin obscure; association with *Scalloway* in Shetland, in allusion to its small cattle or ponies, is regarded as a joke.]

**scalp,** *skalp* (*Scot.* scaup, *sköp*), *n.* the skull (*obs.*): the outer covering of the skull: the top or hairy part of the head: the skin on which the hair of the head grows: a piece of that skin torn off as a token of victory by the North American Indians: a bare rock or mountain-top: a bed of oysters or mussels.—*v.t.* to cut the scalp from: to buy cheap in order to sell below ordinary price: of theatre, travel, or other tickets, to buy up and sell at other than official prices (*U.S.*): to destroy the political influence of (*U.S.*).—*n.* **scalp'er.**—*adj.* **scalp'less.**—**scalp'ing-knife,** a knife for scalping enemies; **scalp'ing-tuft,** a scalp-lock; **scalp'-lock,** a long tuft of hair left unshaven as a challenge. [M.E. *scalp;* perh. Scand.; cf. O.N. *skälpr,* sheath; cf. scallop.]

**scalp,** *skalp,* (*rare*) *v.t.* and *v.i.* to scrape: to cut: to engrave.—*n.* **scalp'el,** a small knife for dissecting or operating.—*adj.* **scalpell'iform,** shaped like a scalpel.—*n.* **scalp'er,** a scalprum: an engraver's scauper.—*adj.* **scalp'riform,** chisel-shaped.—*n.* **scalp'rum,** a surgeon's rasping instrument. [L. *scalpĕre,* to scrape, cut, *scalper, scalprum,* dim. *scalpellum,* a knife.]

**scamble,** *skam'bl, v.i.* to scramble (for e.g. something scattered; *Shak.*): to get along somehow (*obs.*): to shamble (*dial.*): to sprawl (*dial.*).—*v.t.* to get together with effort (now *dial.*): to remove piecemeal: to scatter as for a scramble (*dial.*): to squander (*dial.*).—*ns.* **scam'bler** (*Scot.*), a mealtime sponger; **scam'bling** (*obs.*), scrambling: a haphazard meal—also *adj.*—*adv.* **scam'-blingly, strugglingly.**—*n.pl.* **scam'bling-days** (*obs.*), days of makeshift meals in Lent. [Origin obscure; app. related to **shamble** and **scramble.**]

**scamel,** *skam'l,* (*Shak.*) *n.* alleged to be a Norfolk name for the bar-tailed godwit: or a misprint for **staniel, stannel,** or for **sea-mell,** an alleged variant of **sea-mew.**

**scammony,** *skam'ən-i, n.* an Anatolian convolvulus: its dried root: a cathartic gum-resin obtained from its root or that of a substitute. [Gr. *skammōniā.*]

**scamp,** *skamp, v.i.* to go about idly (*dial.*): to take to the highway (as a robber; *obs.*).—*n.* a highwayman (*obs.*): a rascal: a lively, tricky fellow. —*v.i.* **scamp'er,** to decamp (*obs.*): to run or skip about briskly.—*n.* an act of scampering.—*adj.* **scamp'ish.**—*adv.* **scamp'ishly.**—*n.* **scamp'ishness.** [O.Fr. *escamper* or It. *scampare,* to decamp.]

**scamp,** *skamp, v.t.* to do, execute, perfunctorily or without thoroughness.—*ns.* **scamp'er; scamp'-ing.**—**scamp'-work.** [Poss. O.N. *skemma* to shorten; cf. **skimp, scant.**]

**scampo,** *skam'pō, n.* a Norway lobster.—*pl.* **scam'pi, -pē,** an Italian dish of cooked Norway lobsters or prawns. [It.]

**scan,** *skan, v.t.* to analyse metrically: to utter so as to bring out the metrical structure: to examine critically: to judge (*obs.*): to interpret, read (*Shak.*): to make out: to examine closely: to scrutinise: to examine all parts of in systematic order: (in television) to pass a beam over every part of in turn: to make pictorial records of (part of) the body by various techniques, e.g. ultrasonics (*med.*): loosely, to cast an eye negligently over: (*Spens.,* in *pa.p.* **scand**) to climb, scale: to search out by swinging the beam (*radar*).—*v.i.* to agree with the rules of metre:— *pr.p.* **scann'ing;** *pa.t.* and *pa.p.* **scanned** (*Spens.* **scand**).—*n.* a scanning.—*n.* **scann'er,** one who scans or can scan: a perforated disk (also **scann'ing-disk**) used in television: the rotating aerial by which the beam is made to scan (*radar*).—*n.* and *adj.* **scann'ing.**—*n.* **scan'sion,** act, art, or mode of scanning verse: scanning in television. [L. *scandĕre, scānsum,* to climb.]

**scand.** See **scan.**

**scandal,** *skan'dl, n.* a stumbling-block to faith: anything that brings discredit upon religion: injury to reputation: something said which is injurious to reputation: a false imputation: malicious gossip: slander: opprobrious censure: a disgraceful fact, thing, or person: a shocked feeling.—*v.t.* to defame: to disgrace (*obs.*): to shock (*obs.*).—*n.* **scandalisā'tion, -z-.**—*v.t.* **scan'-dalise, -ize,** to give scandal or offence to: to shock: to disgrace: to slander.—*v.t.* to talk scandal.—*adj.* **scan'dalled,** disgraceful: slandered; **scan'dalous,** giving scandal or offence: calling forth condemnation: openly vile: defamatory.—*adv.* **scan'dalously.**—*n.* **scan'dalousness.**—**scan'dal-bearer,** a propagator of malicious gossip; **scan'dal-monger,** one who deals in defamatory reports; **scan'dal-mongering, -mong-ing.**—**scan'dalum magnā'tum,** slandering high personages, abbrev. *scan. mag.* [L. *scandalum*— Gr. *skandalon,* a stumbling-block.]

**scandent,** *skan'dənt, adj.* climbing. [L. *scandēns, -entis.*]

**Scandinavian,** *skan-di-nā'vi-ən, adj.* of, or characteristic of, *Scandinavia,* the peninsula divided into Norway and Sweden, but, in a historical sense, applying also to Denmark and Iceland: North Germanic (*philol.*).—*n.* a native of Scandinavia: a member of the dominant Nordic race of Scandinavia.—*n.* and *adj.* **Scan'dian.**—*adj.* **Scan'dic.** —*n.* **scan'dium,** a metallic element (Sc; at. numb. 21) discovered in 1879 in the Scandinavian mineral euxenite. [L. *Scandinăvia* (from Gmc. word which did not have *n* before *d*),

applied to the southern part of the peninsula, and its shortened form *Scandia.*]

**Scandix,** *skan'diks, n.* the Venus's comb genus of umbelliferous plants. [Gr.]

**scansion.** See **scan.**

**Scansores,** *skan-sō'rēz, -sō', n.pl.* in old classifications, an order of birds, climbers, with two toes before and two behind.—*adj.* **scansō'rial,** climbing: adapted for climbing. [L. *scandĕre, scānsum,* to climb.]

**scant,** *skant, adj.* not full or plentiful: scarcely sufficient: deficient: short, poorly supplied: sparing.—*n.* scarcity.—*adv.* barely: scantily.— *v.t.* to stint: to restrict: to reduce: to dispense sparingly: to slight.—*adv.* **scant'ily.**—*ns.* **scant'iness; scant'ity** (*rare*).—*adv.* **scant'ly.**—*n.* **scant'ness.**—*adj.* **scant'y,** meagre: deficient: skimped: wanting in fulness: parsimonious.— **scant'-o'-grace** (*Scot.*), a good for nothing. [O.N. *skamt,* neut. of *skammr,* short.]

**scantle,** *skan'tl, v.t.* (*obs.*): to stint: to make scant: to shorten (sail).—*v.i.* (*obs.*) to become scant.—*n.* (*Shak.*; various reading for **cantle**) a portion.—*n.* **scant'ling,** a small portion.—*adj.* petty. [Prob. **scant,** with senses merging in the following word.]

**scantling,** *skant'ling, n.* a measured size: a measurement: an allotted portion (*arch.*): dimensions of a cross-section: a sample or pattern: a gauge (*obs.*): a narrow piece of timber.—*n.* **scan'tle,** a gauge for slates.—*v.t.* to adjust to measure. [O.Fr. *escantillon, eschantillon,* of uncertain etymology; with senses merging in foregoing word.]

**scapa.** Same as **scarper.**

**scape,** *skāp, n.* an escape: an escapade: a transgression: a slip.—*v.t.* and *v.i.* (also **'scape**) to escape.—*adj.* **scape'less,** not to be escaped.—*n.* **scape'ment,** escapement.—**scape'gallows,** one who deserves hanging; **scape'grace,** a graceless, hare-brained fellow; **scape'-wheel,** escapewheel. [**escape.**]

**scape,** *skāp, n.* a peduncle rising from the ground, without foliage leaves (*bot.*): the basal part of an antenna (*entom.*): the shaft or stem of a feather: the shaft of a column (*archit.*).—*adjs.* **scape'less; scapigerous** (*ska-pij'ər-əs*), having a scape. [L. *scāpus,* a shaft.]

**scape,** *skāp, n.* the cry of the snipe when flushed: the snipe itself. [Prob. imit.]

**scape,** *skāp, n.* a landscape or other picture of scenery (often in compounds). [**landscape.**]

**scapegoat,** *skāp'gōt, n.* a goat on which, once a year, the Jewish high-priest laid symbolically the sins of the people, and which was then allowed to escape into the wilderness (Levit. xvi): any animal used in like manner: one who is made to bear the misdeeds of another. [**escape** and **goat.**]

**scaphocephalus,** *skaf-ō-sef'ə-las, -kef', n.* boat-shaped head.—*adjs.* **scaphocephalic** (*-si-fal'ik*), **scaphocephalous** (*-sef'ə-ləs*).—*n.* **scaphoceph'aly.** [Gr. *skaphē,* a boat, *kephalē,* a head.]

**scaphoid,** *skaf'oid, adj.* boat-shaped. [Gr. *skaphē,* a boat, *eidos,* form.]

**Scaphopoda,** *skaf-op'ə-də, n.pl.* the tusk-shell class of molluscs, in which the foot is trilobed or has a terminal disk and the mantle forms a tube enclosed by the tubular univalve shell.—*n.* and *adj.* **scaph'opod.** [Gr. *skaphos,* a spade, *pous, podos,* a foot.]

**scapolite,** *skap'ō-līt, n.* a silicate of aluminium, calcium, and sodium with some chlorine, crystallising in the tetragonal system. [Gr. *skāpos,* a rod, *lithos,* a stone.]

**scapple,** *skap'l,* **scabble,** *skab'l, v.t.* to work without finishing, as stone before leaving the quarry. [O.Fr. *escapeler,* to dress timber.]

**scapula,** *skap'ū-lə, n.* the shoulder-blade.—*adj.* **scap'ular,** of the shoulder-blade or shoulder.—*n.* originally an ordinary working garb, now the mark of the monastic orders, a long strip of cloth with an opening for the head, worn hanging before and behind over the habit: two pieces of cloth tied together over the shoulders, worn by members of certain lay confraternities of the Roman Catholic Church: a supporting bandage worn over the shoulder: a shoulder feather.—*adj.* and *n.* **scap′ūlary,** scapular.—*adj.* **scap′ū-lated,** with noticeable scapular feathers.—*n.* **scap′ūlimancy** (Gr. *manteiā,* divination), divination by means of shoulder-blades.—*adj.* **scapū-liman′tic.** [L. *scapulae,* the shoulder-blades.]

**scapus,** skā′pəs (L. skä′poōs). Same as scape (2): —*pl.* **scapi** (*-pī*; L. *-pē*). [L.]

**scar,** skär, *n.* the mark left by a wound or sore: any mark or blemish: any mark, trace, or result of injury, material or moral (*fig.*): a mark at a place of former attachment, as of a leaf or a muscle.—*v.t.* to mark with a scar.—*v.i.* to become scarred:—*pr.p.* **scarr′ing;** *pa.t.* and *pa.p.* **scarred.**—*adjs.* **scar′less,** without scars: unwounded; **scarred.**—*n.* and *adj.* **scarr′ing.**—*adj.* **scarr′y.** [O.Fr. *escare*—L. *eschara*—Gr. *escharā,* a hearth, brazier, burn, scar.]

**scar,** skär, **scaur,** skör, *n.* a precipitous bare place on a hill-face: a cliff: a reef in the sea.—*adj.* **scarr′y.** [App. O.N. *sker, skera,* to cut.]

**scar,** skär, **scar′fish,** *ns.* a parrot-wrasse.—*n.* **Scarus** (skā′rəs), the parrot-wrasse genus, giving name to the family **Scaridae** (skar′i-dē). [L. *scārus*—Gr. *skăros.*]

**scar, scarre,** skär, (*Shak., Milt., Scot.*) a form of **scare:**—*pa.t.* and *pa.p.* **scarred, scarr′d.**

**scarab,** skar′əb, *n.* a dung-beetle, esp. the sacred beetle of the ancient Egyptians (*Scarabaeus,* or *Ateuchus, sacer,* or kindred species): a gem cut in the form of a beetle: a term of abuse (*obs.*).—*ns.* **scarabaeid** (skar-ə-bē′id), any beetle of the *Scarabaeidae;* **scarabae′ist,** one who studies dung-beetles; **scarabae′oid,** a gem more remotely resembling a beetle; **Scarabae′us,** the scarab genus, giving name to the **Scarabae′idae,** a large family of lamellicorn beetles, some of them of great size (chafers, dung-beetles): a scarab; **scar′abee,** a scarab; **scar′aboid,** a scarabaeoid. —*adj.* like a scarab. [L. *scarabaeus;* cf. Gr. *kărabos.*]

**scaramouch,** skar′ə-mowch, *n.* a bragging, cowardly buffoon. [Fr. *Scaramouche*—It. *Scaramuccia,* a stock character in Italian comedy.]

**scarce,** skärs, *adj.* by no means plentiful: not often found: hard to get: short in supply: short (with *of*): sparing (*obs.*).—*adv.* scarcely: with difficulty (*Milt.*): hardly ever.—*adv.* **scarce′ly,** only just: not quite: scantily (*obs.*).—*ns.* **scarce′ness; scarc′ity,** state or fact of being scarce: shortness of supply, esp. of necessaries: dearth: want: deficiency: niggardliness.—**make oneself scarce,** to leave quickly, unobtrusively, for reasons of prudence, tact, etc. [O.N.Fr. *escars* (Fr. *échars*), niggardly, from a L.L. substitute for L. *excerptus,* pa.p. of *excerpēre* —*ex,* out, *carpēre,* to pick.]

**scarcement,** skärs′mənt, (*Scot.*) *n.* a ledge formed by the setting back of a wall, buttress, or bank. [Poss. from **scarce.**]

**scare,** skär, *v.t.* to startle, to affright: to drive or keep off by frightening.—*n.* a fright: a panic: a baseless public alarm.—*adj.* **frightened.**—*n.* **scar′er.**—*adj.* **scar′y,** frightening: timorous: fluttered.—**scare′crow,** anything set up to scare birds: a vain cause of terror: a person meanly clad; **scare′-head, -heading, -line,** a newspaper heading designed to raise a scare; **scare′-monger,** an alarmist, one who causes panic by initiating or encouraging rumours of trouble; **scare′mongering.**—**scare up,** to beat up (game; U.S. and *dial.*): to hunt out: to produce quickly. [M.E. *skerre*—O.N. *skirra,* to avoid—*skiarr,* shy; vowel history obscure.]

**scarf,** skärf, *n.* a light, usually decorative piece of dress thrown loosely on the shoulders about the neck, or over the head, etc.: a military or official sash: a band worn about the neck with ends hanging in front, formerly the mark of a clergyman of some degree of dignity, esp. a nobleman's chaplain: hence, a chaplaincy: a crape streamer: a veil: a necktie: a muffler: a cravat: a sling:—*pl.* **scarfs, scarves.**—*v.t.* to cover, as if with a scarf: to wrap as a scarf.—*adj.* **scarfed,** decorated with pendants.—*adv.* **scarf′-wise.**—**scarf′-pin,** an ornamental pin worn in a scarf: a tie-pin; **scarf′-ring,** an ornamental ring through which the ends of a scarf are drawn. [Perh. O.N.Fr. *escarpe* (Fr. *écharpe*), sash, sling.]

**scarf,** skärf, *n.* a joint between pieces placed end to end, cut so as to fit with overlapping like a continuous piece: an end so prepared: a longitudinal cut in a whale's carcase.—*v.t.* to join with a scarf-joint: to make a scarf in.—*n.* **scarf′ing.**—**scarf′-joint.** [Perh. Scand.]

**scarfskin,** skärf′skin, *n.* the surface skin. [Origin doubtful; perh. *scarf* (1); perh. related to **scurf.**]

**scarify,** skar′i-fī, *v.t.* to make a number of scratches or slight cuts in: to break up the surface of: to lacerate: to criticise severely:—*pr.p.* **scar′ifying;** *pa.t.* and *pa.p.* **scar′ified.**—*ns.* **scarification** (-fi-kā′shən); **scar′ificātor,** a surgical instrument for scarifying: a scarifier; **scar′ifier,** one who scarifies: an implement for breaking the surface of the soil or of a road. [L.L. *scarificāre, -ātum,* for L. *scarifāre*—Gr. *skariphaesthai*—*skariphos,* an etching tool.]

**scarious,** skā′ri-əs, *adj.* thin, dry, stiff, and membranous (*bot.*): scaly, scurfy (*zool.*). [Origin unknown.]

**scarlatina,** skär-lə-tē′na, *n.* scarlet fever, esp. in a mild form. [It. *scarlattina.*]

**scarlet,** skär′lit, *n.* orig. a fine cloth, not always red: a brilliant red: a brilliant red cloth, garment, or garb, or its wearer.—*adj.* of the colour called scarlet: dressed in scarlet.—*v.t.* to redden.—**scar′let-bean,** the scarlet-runner; **scar′let fever,** an infectious fever, usually marked by a sore throat and a scarlet rash; **scarlet geranium,** a scarlet-flowered pelargonium; **scar′let-hat,** a cardinal's (former) hat; **scar′let-runn′er,** scarlet-flowered climber (*Phaseolus multiflorus*) of the kidney-bean genus, with edible beans; **scarlet woman,** the woman referred to in Rev. xvii.— variously taken as pagan Rome, Papal Rome, or the world in its anti-Christian sense: a whore. [O.Fr. *escarlate* (Fr. *écarlate*), thought to be from Pers. *saqalāt,* scarlet cloth.]

**scarmoge,** skär′maj, (*Spens.*) *n.* same as skirmish.

**scarp,** skärp, (*her.*) *n.* a diminutive of the bend sinister, half its width. [O.Fr. *escarpe;* cf. **scarf** (1).]

**scarp,** skärp, *n.* an escarp: an escarpment.—*v.t.* cut into a scarp.—*adj.* **scarped.**—*n.* **scarp′ing.** [It. *scarpa.*]

**scarper,** skär′pər, (*slang*) *v.i.* to run away, escape, leave without notice. [It. *scappare.*]

**scarpines,** skär′pinz, *n.pl.* an instrument of torture for the feet.—*n.* **scarpet′to,** a hemp-soled shoe or climbing-boot:—*pl.* **scarpet′ti** (*-tē*). [It. *scarpino, scarpetto,* dims. of *scarpa,* shoe.]

**scarre,** (*Shak.*) *n.* a word of unknown meaning in *All's Well* (IV, ii. 38), probably a misprint, but never satisfactorily explained.

**scarred, scarring, scarry.** See scar (1 and 2).

**scart,** skärt, (*Scot.*) *v.t.* to scratch: to scrape.—*n.* a scratch: a dash or stroke of a pen.—*adj.* **scart′-free** (*Scot.*). [See scat.]

**scart, scarth; Scarus; scarves; scary.** See skart; scar (3); scarf; scare.

**scat, scatt,** skat, (*hist.*) *n.* tribute: a tax: esp. udaller's land-tax. [O.N. *skattr;* cf. O.E. *sceatt,* money, Du. *schat,* Ger. *schatz.*]

**scat**, *skat, interj.* be off!—*v.t.* to scare away.

**scat**, *skat, (Western) n.* a blow: a spell: a sudden shower.—*adv.* in collapse: to bankruptcy.

**scat**, *skat, skat, n.* an animal dropping.—*adj.* **scatolog'ical (sk-)**.—*n.* **scatol'ogy (sk-)**, study of excrement, esp. in order to assess diet: obscene literature: interest in the obscene.—*adj.* **scatoph'agous** (Gr. *phagein* (2nd aorist), to eat), dung-eating.—*n.* **scatoph'agy.** [Gr. *skōr, skatos,* dung.]

**scat**, *skat, n.* singing a melody to nonsense syllables.—Also *v.t.* and *v.i.* [Perh. imit.]

**scatch**, *skach, n.* a stilt. [O.N.Fr. *escache* (Fr. *échasse*); cf. **skate** (1).]

**scathe**, *skādh (Spens.* also **scath, skath**; *Scot.* **skaith, scaith,** *skāth), n.* hurt: injury: damage.—*v.t.* to injure: to blast, scorch, wither: to scorch with invective.—*adj.* **scathe'ful,** hurtful.—*n.* **scathe'fulness.**—*adjs.* **scathe'less** (*Scot.* **skaith'less, scaith'less),** without injury; **scath'ing.**—*adv.* **scath'ingly.** [O.N. *skathe*; cf. O.E. *sceatha,* an injurer; Ger. *schade,* injury.]

**scatole.** Same as **skatole.**

**scatter**, *skat'ər, v.t.* to disperse: throw loosely about: strew: sprinkle: dispel: to reflect or disperse irregularly (waves or particles).—*v.i.* to disperse: throw shot loosely.—*n.* scattering: a sprinkling: dispersion: extent of scattering.—*adj.* **scatt'ered,** dispersed irregularly, widely, in all directions, or here and there: thrown about: casually dropped (*Spens., Shak.*): distracted.—*adv.* **scatt'eredly (-ərd-li).**—*ns.* **scatt'-erer; scatt'ering,** dispersion: radiation afresh of wave-energy when a ray is incident on an obstacle or when it enters an irregularly ionised region: that which is scattered: a small proportion occurring sporadically: the deflection of photons or particles as a result of collisions with other particles.—*adj.* dispersing: sporadic: diversified.—*adv.* **scatt'eringly.**—*n.* **scatt'erling** (*Spens.*), a vagrant.—*adj.* **scatt'ery,** dispersed: sparse: giving an effect of scattering.—**scatt'er-brain,** one incapable of sustained attention or thought.—*adj.* **scatter'-brained.**—**scatt'ergood,** a spendthrift; **scatt'er-gun,** a shot-gun. [Origin obscure; *scatered* occurs in the *O.E. Chronicle* (anno 1137); cf. **shatter.**]

**scattermouch**, *skat'ər-mowch, (sailors' slang) n.* any Latin or Levantine. [**scaramouch** influenced by **scatter.**]

**scatty**, *skat'i, (coll.) adj.* slightly crazy and unpredictable in conduct.—*n.* **scatt'iness.** [Poss. *scatter*brain.]

**scaturient**, *skat-ū'ri-ənt, adj.* gushing. [L. *scatūriēns, -entis—scatūrire,* to gush out.]

**scaud**, *sköd,* a Scots form of **scald.**

**scaup**, *sköp, (Scot.) n.* a scalp: a scaup-duck.—**scaup'-duck** (*Scot.*), a pochard that feeds on mussel-scaups. [**scalp** (1).]

**scauper**, *skö'pər, n.* a tool with semicircular face, used by engravers. [**scalper.**]

**scaur**, *skör,* a Scots form of **scare.**

**scaur.** Same as **scar** (2).

**scaury**, *skō'ri, skö', (Orkney* and *Shetland) n.* a young gull.—Also (*Scott*) **scou'rie, scow'rie.** [O.N. *skāri.*]

**scavage**, *skav'ij, n.* a toll formerly levied in boroughs on goods offered for sale by outsiders: street refuse (*obs.*).—*n.* **scav'ager,** the officer who collected the toll, later charged with keeping the streets clean.—*v.t.* **scav'enge (-inj, -inzh;** back-formation), to cleanse.—*v.i.* to act as scavenger.—*n.* the sweeping out of waste gases from an internal-combustion engine.—*n.* **scav'-enger (-jər),** one who cleans the streets: a person or apparatus that removes waste: an animal that feeds on garbage: one who deals or delights in filth.—*v.i.* to act as scavenger.—*ns.* **scav'-engering; scav'engery,** street-cleaning; **scav'-enging,** street-cleansing: scavenge. [A.Fr.

**scawage**, inspection; prob. of Gmc. origin; cf. O.E. *scēawian,* to inspect; see **show.**]

**scavenger**, *skav'in-jər, n.* a perversion of the name of *Skevington,* Lieutenant of the Tower under Henry VIII, inventor of an instrument of torture known as the **scavenger's** or **Skevington's,** daughter.

**scaw.** Same as **skaw.**

**scazon**, *skā'zon, n.* a choliamb.—*n.* and *adj.* **scazontic (skə-zon'tik).** [Gr. *skazōn,* limping.]

**sceat, sceatt,** *shat, (hist.) n.* a small silver (or gold) coin of Old English times:—*pl.* **sceatt'as.** [O.E.]

**scedule.** See **schedule.**

**scelerate,** *sel'ər-āt, -it, (obs.) adj.* wicked.—*n.* (also **scelerat,** after Fr. *scélérat*) a villain. L.] *scelerātus—scelus,* crime.]

**scena,** *shā'na, n.* an operatic scene: an elaborate dramatic recitative followed by an aria:—*pl.* **scene** (*shā'nä*).—*n.* scenario (*si-, se-, shä-nä'ri-ō*), a skeleton of a dramatic work, film, etc., scene by scene: an outline of future development, or of a plan to be followed, which shows the operation of causes and where points of decision or difficulty occur.—*n.* **scenarisā'tion, -z-.**—*v.t.* **scena-rise, -ize (si-nä'riz, -nä')** to make a scenario of.—*ns.* **scena'rist; scenary (sē'nər-i; obs.),** disposition of scenes: scenery. [It.,—L. *scēna.*]

**scenario.** See **scena.**

**scend, 'scend.** See **send** (*n.*).

**scene,** *sēn, n.* the stage (*orig.*): a stage performance (*obs.*): the place of action in a play (hence in a story, an actual occurrence, etc.): its representation on the stage: a painted slide, hanging, or other object, used for this purpose: a curtain, veil, or screen: a division of a play marked off by the fall of the curtain, by a change of place, or (in Latin, French, and some English plays) by the entry or exit of any important character: an episode: a dramatic or stagy incident, esp. an uncomfortable, untimely, or unseemly display of hot feelings: a landscape, picture of a place or action: a view, spectacle.—*v.t.* to set in a scene.—*n.* **scēn'ery,** dramatic action (*obs.*): theatrical slides, hangings, etc., collectively: prospects of beautiful, picturesque, or impressive country.—*adjs.* **scenic (sē'nik, sen'ik),** pertaining to scenery: dramatic: theatrical; **scen'ical.**—*adv.* **scen'ically.**—*adjs.* **scēno-graph'ic, -al.**—*adv.* **scēnograph'ically.**—*n.* **scēno-og'raphy,** perspective drawing: scene-painting.—**scene'-dock,** the space where scenery is stored; **scene'-man,** a scene-shifter; **scene'-painter,** one who paints scenery for theatres; **scene'-shifter,** one who sets and removes the scenery in a theatre; **scenic railway,** a railway on a small scale, running through artificial representations of picturesque scenery.—**behind the scenes,** at the back of the visible stage: away from the public view (*lit.* and *fig.*): in a position to know what goes on: in private. [L. *scēna*—Gr. *skēnē,* a tent, stage building.]

**scent,** earlier sent, *sent, v.t.* to track, find, or discern by smell, or as if by smell: to perfume.—*v.i.* to give forth a smell: to smell: to smell.—*n.* odour: sense of smell: a substance used for the sake of its smell: trail by smell: paper strewn by the pursued in hare and hounds.—*adjs.* **scent'ed,** having a smell, fragrant: impregnated or sprinkled with perfumery: endowed with a sense of smell; **scent'ful,** odoriferous: quick of scent.—*n.* and *adj.* **scent'ing.**—*adj.* **scent'less,** having no smell: affording, retaining, or carrying no scent.—**scent'-bag,** a scent-gland: a sachet: a bag of strong smelling stuff dragged over the ground for a drag-hunt; **scent'-bottle,** a small bottle for holding perfume; **scent'-box; scent'-gland,** a gland that secretes a substance of distinctive smell, for recognition, attraction, or defence; **scent'-organ,** a scent-gland: a smelling organ; **scent'-scale,** on male butterflies' wings, a scale that gives off a scent. [Fr. *sentir*—L. *sentīre*, to perceive.]

**scepsis, skepsis,** *skep'sis*, *n.* philosophic doubt. [Gr.; see next.]

**sceptic,** sometimes (and in U.S.) **skeptic,** *skep'tik*, *adj.* pertaining to the philosophical school of Pyrrho and his successors, who asserted nothing positively and doubted the possibility of knowledge: sceptical (*rarely*).—*n.* a sceptic philosopher: one who withholds from prevailing doctrines, esp. In religion. one who inclines to disbelieve: an inquirer who has not arrived at a conviction.—*adj.* **scep'tical,** of or inclined to scepticism: (now often) doubtful, or inclined towards incredulity.—*adv.* **scep'tically.**—*v.i.* **scep'-ticise, -ize,** to act the sceptic.—*n.* **scep'ticism,** that condition in which the mind is before it has arrived at conclusive opinions: doubt: the doctrine that no facts can be certainly known: agnosticism: sceptical attitude towards Christianity: general disposition to doubt. [L. *scepticus*—Gr. *skeptikos*, thoughtful, *skeptesthai*, to consider.]

**sceptre,** *sep'tǝr*, *n.* a staff or baton borne as an emblem of kingship.—*adjs.* **scep'tral,** regal; **scep'tred,** bearing a sceptre: regal; **scep'treless; scep'try** (*Keats*), sceptred. [L. *scēptrum*—Gr. *skēptron*, a staff—*skēptein*, to prop, stay.]

**scerne,** *sûrn*, (*Spens.*) *v.t.* to discern. [**discern,** or It. *scernere*.]

**sceuophylax,** *s(k)ū-of'i-laks,* (*Greek Church*) *n.* a sacristan.—*n.* **sceuophylacium** (*-lă'si-ǝm*), a sacristy. [Gr. *skeuos*, a vessel, *phylax*, a watcher.]

**schadenfreude,** *shä'dǝn-froi-dǝ,* *n.* pleasure in others' misfortunes. [Ger.,—*schade,* hurt, *freude,* joy.]

**schalstein,** *shäl'shtin,* *n.* a slaty diabase tuff. [Ger., —*schale,* shell, scale, *stein,* stone.]

**schappe,** *shap'ǝ,* *n.* silk with gum, etc., partly removed by fermentation.—*v.t.* to subject to this process. [Swiss Ger.]

**schedule,** *shed'ūl* (in U.S. *sked'ūl*), formerly (as *Shak.*) **scedule,** *sed'ūl,* *n.* a slip or scroll with writing: a list, inventory, or table: a supplementary, explanatory, or appended document: an appendix to a bill or act of parliament: a form for filling in particulars, or such a form filled in: a timetable, plan, programme, or scheme.—*v.t.* to set as in a schedule: to plan, appoint, arrange.—*adj.* **sched'uled,** entered in a schedule (**scheduled castes,** the former untouchables): planned, appointed, arranged (to happen at a specified time). [O.Fr. *cedule* (Fr. *cédule*)—L.L. *sc(h)edula,* dim. of *scheda,* a strip of papyrus—Gr. *schedē.*]

**scheelite,** *shē'līt,* *n.* native calcium tungstate.—**Scheele's** (*shā'laz*) **green,** a poisonous yellowish green pigment, copper hydrogen arsenite. [From the Swedish chemist K. W. *Scheele* (1742-86), who investigated them.]

**schellum,** Same as **skellum.**

**schelm,** older form of **skelm.**

**schema,** *skē'ma,* *n.* a scheme, plan: a diagrammatic outline or synopsis: the image of the thing with which the imagination aids the understanding in its procedure: the monastic habit (*Greek Church*):—*pl.* **schē'mata.**—*adjs.* **schematic** (*ski-mat'ik*), **-al.**—*adv.* **schemat'ically.** —*n.* **schematisā'tion, -z-.**—*v.t.* **schē'matise, -ize,** to reduce to or represent by a scheme.—*ns.* **schē'matism,** form or outline of a thing: arrangement, disposition in a scheme: **schē'matist,** one who frames a scheme: a projector (*obs.*). [Gr. *schēma, -atos,* form, from the reduced grade of the root of *echein,* to have (as in the fut. *schēsein*).]

**scheme,** *skēm,* *n.* a rhetorical figure (*obs.*): a diagram of positions, esp. (*astrol.*) of planets: a diagram: a table: a system: a plan of purposed action for achieving an end: a plan for building operations of various kinds, or the buildings, etc.,

constructed, or the area covered (e.g. *housing scheme, irrigation scheme*): a plan pursued secretly, insidiously, by intrigue, or for private ends: a project: a programme of action: an escapade (*obs.*).—*v.t.* to plan: to reduce to a system: to lay schemes for.—*v.i.* to form a plan: to lay schemes: to indulge in an escapade.—*n.* **schē'mer.**—*n.* and *adj.* **schē'ming.** [schema.]

**schemozzle.** See **shemozzle.**

**scherzo,** *sker'tsō, skūr', n.* a lively busy movement in triple time, usually with a trio, now generally taking the place of the minuet in a sonata or a symphony.—*adj.* and *adv.* **scherzan'do,** with playfulness.—*n.* a scherzando passage or movement. [It.,—Gmc.; cf. Ger. *scherz,* jest.]

**schiavone,** *skyä-vō'nǎ, n.* a 17th-century basket-hilted broadsword used by the Doge's bodyguard of Slavs. [It. *Schiavoni,* Slavs.]

**schiedam,** *skē'dam,* or *-dam', n.* Holland gin, chiefly made at Schiedam (*s'hhē-däm'*), near Rotterdam.

**schiller,** *shil'ǝr, n.* a peculiar bronze-like lustre in certain minerals, as hypersthene, due to diffraction caused by minute plates of haematite, etc., developed in separation planes.—*n.* **schillerisā'-tion,** the development of such plates.—*v.t.* **schill'erise, -ize,** to impart a schiller to.— **schill'er-spar,** schillerised enstatite (bronzite). [Ger.]

**schilling,** *shil'ing, n.* an Austrian coin (in use after 1925) equal to one hundred groschen, the unit of the Austrian monetary system. [Ger.; cf. **shilling.**]

**schimmel,** *shim'l, n.* a roan horse. [Ger., white horse; also Du.]

**schindylesis,** *skin-di-lē'sis, n.* an articulation formed by the fitting of one bone into a groove in another.—*adj.* **schindyletic** (*-let'ik*). [Gr. *schindylēsis,* cleaving.]

**schipperke,** *skip'ǝr-kǝ, -ki,* also *ship',* or (Du.) *s'hhip', n.* a small tailless breed of dogs, orig. watchdogs on barges. [Du., little boatman.]

**schism,** *sizm, skizm, n.* a breach, esp. in the unity of a church: promotion of such a breach: a body so formed.—*ns.* **schisma** (*skiz'ma*), half the difference between twelve perfect fifths and seven octaves; **schismatic** (*siz-mat'ik*), one who favours a schism or belongs to a schismatic body: a Catholic who avoided penalties by occasional conformity (*R.C.*).—*adjs.* **schismat'ic, -al,** tending to, favouring, or of the nature of, a schism.—*adv.* **schismat'ically.**—*n.* **schismat'-icalness.**—*v.i.* **schis'matise, -ize,** to practise schism: to make a schism.—**schism'-house, -shop,** contemptuous Anglican terms for a non-conformist church.—**great Eastern,** or **Greek, schism,** the separation of the Greek church from the Latin, finally completed in 1054; (**great**) **Western schism,** the division in the Western church from 1378 to 1417, when there were antipopes under French influence at Avignon. [Gr. *schisma,* a split, rent, cleft, partly through O.Fr. (*s*)*eisme.*]

**schist,** *shist, n.* any crystalline foliated metamorphic rock not coarse and feldspathic enough to be called gneiss, as mica-schist, hornblende-schist: sometimes extended (as in French) to shaly rocks.—*adj.* **schist'ose.**—*n.* **schistosity** (*-os'-i-ti*).—*adj.* **schist'ous.** [Fr. *schiste*—Gr. *schistos,* split; pron. due to German influence.]

**Schistosoma,** *shis-tǝ-sō'ma, skis-, n.* the Bilharzia genus.—*ns.* **schistosome,** a member of the genus; **schistosomi'asis,** the disease bilharzia. [Gr. *schistos,* split.]

**schiz-,** *skiz-, skiz-,* **schizo-,** *skiz'ō, ski-zo'* (now usu. *skit'sō-, skid'zō,* in commoner words), in composition, cleave, cloven.—*n.* **Schizaea** (*-zē'ǝ*), a tropical genus of ferns giving name to the fam. **Schizaeā'ceae,** with sporangia splitting longitudinally by an apical annulus.—*adj.*

schizaeā'ceous.—*ns.* Schizanthus (-*an'thəs*; Gr. *anthos*, flower), a showy Chilean genus of Solanaceae; schi'zocarp (-*kärp*; Gr. *karpos*, fruit), a dry fruit that splits into several indehiscent one-seeded portions.—*adj.* schizocar'-pous.—*n.* schizogenesis (-*jen'i-sis*; Gr. *genesis*, *gonē*, generation), reproduction by fission.—*adjs.* schizogen'ic, schizogenetic (-*ji-net'ik*), schizogenous (-*oj'i-nəs*), reproducing, reproduced, or formed by fission or splitting; schizogonous (-*og'ən-əs*).—*n.* schizog'ony.—*adjs.* schizognathous (-*og'nə-thəs*; Gr. *gnathos*, jaw), of some birds, having the bones of the palate separate; schizoid (*skit'soid*, *skid'zoid*; Gr. *eidos*, form), showing qualities of a schizophrenic personality, such as asocial behaviour, introversion, tendency to phantasy, but without definite mental disorder.—*n.* a schizoid person. —*adj.* schizoid'al.—*n.pl.* Schizomycetes (-*mi-sē'tēz*; Gr. *mȳkēs*, pl. *mȳkētēs*, a fungus), the bacteria:—*sing.* schizomycete (-*sēt'*).—*ns.* schiz'-ophrene (-*frēn*; Gr. *phrēn*, mind), one who suffers from schizophrenia; schizophrenia (-*frē'ni-ə*), a psychosis marked by introversion, dissociation, inability to distinguish reality from unreality, delusions, etc; schizophrenic (-*fren'ik*), a schizophrene.—Also *adj.*—*adjs.* schizophrenet'-ic(al).—*adv.* schizophrenet'ically.—*n.pl.* Schizophyta (-*of'i-tə*; Gr. *phyton*, plant), plants that multiply only by fission—bacteria and blue-green algae.—*adj.* schi'zopod (-*pod*; Gr. *pous*, *podos*, foot), having each leg divided into exopodite and endopodite.—*n.* a member of the Schizopoda (-*op'*), an order (according to some) of Malacostraca.—*adjs.* schizop'odal, schizop'-odous.—*n.* schizothymia (-*thī'mi-ə*; Gr. *thymos*, mind, temper), manifestation of schizoid traits within normal limits. [Gr. *schizein*, to cleave.]

schläger, *shlä'gər*, *n.* a German student's duelling-sword. [Ger.,—*schlagen*, to beat.]

schlemiel, *shlemihl*, *shlə-mēl'*, (*slang*) *n.* a clumsy person. [Yiddish.]

schlep, *shlep*, (*U.S. slang*) *v.t.* to pull, drag. [Yiddish.]

schlich, *shlihh*, *n.* the finer portions of crushed ore, separated by water. [Ger.]

schlieren, *shlē'rən*, *n.pl.* streaks of different colour, structure, or composition in igneous rocks. [Ger.]

schlimazel, shlimazel, *shli-mä'zl*, (*U.S. slang*) *n.* a persistently unlucky person. [Yiddish; see shemozzle.]

schlock, *shlok'*, (*U.S. slang*) *adj.* of inferior quality.—*n.* a thing or things of inferior quality. [Yiddish.]

schloss, *shlos*, (Ger.) a castle, palace, manor house.

schmaltz, *shmölts*, *shmälts*, (*U.S. slang*) *n.* mush: a production in music or other art that is very sentimental, or showy: sentimentality.—*adj.* schmaltz'y, old-fashioned, old-style, outmoded: sentimental. [Yiddish—Ger. *schmalz*, cooking fat, grease.]

schmelz, *shmelts*, *n.* glass used in decorative work. [Ger. *schmelz*, enamel.]

schmo, *shmō*, (*U.S. slang*) *n.* a stupid or a boring person:—*pl.* schmoes. [Yiddish.]

schmock. See schmuck.

schmoe. Same as schmo.

schmooze, shmoose, *shmōōz*, -s, (*U.S. slang*) *v.i.* to gossip. [Yiddish.]

schmuck, *shmuk*, schmock, *shmok*, schnook, *shnōōk*,(*U.S. slang*)*n.* a stupid person. [Yiddish.]

schnapper, *shnap'ər*. Same as snapper (Australian fish). [Germanised.]

schnapps, schnaps, *shnaps*, *n.* Holland gin, Hollands. [Ger. *schnapps*, a dram.]

schnauzer, *shnowt'sər*, *n.* a very old German breed of terrier. [Ger. *schnauze*, snout.]

Schneiderian, *shni-dē'ri-ən*, *adj.* pertaining to the German anatomist Konrad Victor *Schneider*

(1614-1680).—Schneiderian membrane, the olfactory mucous membrane, studied by him.

schnell, *shnel*, (Ger.) quick; quickly.

schnitzel, *shnit'sl*, *n.* a veal cutlet. [Ger.]

schnook. See schmuck.

schnorkel, *shnör'kl*, *n.* a retractable tube or tubes containing pipes for discharging gases from, or for taking air into, a submerged submarine: a tube for bringing air to a submerged swimmer.—Anglicised as snor'kel, snort. [Ger., *schnörkel*, a spiral ornament.]

schnorrer, *shnö'*, *shnö'*, *shno'rər*, (*U.S. slang*) *n.* a beggar. [Yiddish.]

scholar, *skol'ər*, *n.* a pupil: a disciple: a student: (in times of less widespread education) one who could read and write, or an educated person: one whose learning (formerly esp. in Latin and Greek) is extensive and exact, or whose approach to learning is scrupulous and critical: generally a holder of a scholarship.—*adj.* schol'ar-like, like or befitting a scholar.—*n.* schol'arliness.—*adj.* schol'arly, of, natural to a scholar: having the learning of a scholar.—*adv.* (*Shak.*) as becomes a scholar.—*n.* schol'arship, scholarly learning: a foundation or grant for the maintenance of a pupil or student: the status and emoluments of such a pupil or student. [O.E. *scōlere*, and (in part) O.Fr. *escoler*, both from L.L. *scholāris—schola*; see school (1).]

scholarch, *skō'lärk*, *n.* the head of a school, esp. of philosophy. [Gr. *scholarchēs*.]

scholastic, *skol-*, *skəl-as'tik*, *adj.* pertaining to schools, universities, or to their staffs or teaching, or to schoolmen: subtle: pedantic.—*n.* a schoolman, one who adheres to the method or subtleties of the Mediaeval schools: a Jesuit who has taken first vows only: a university teacher (esp. with implication of pedantry).—*adj.* (*arch.*) scholas'tical.—*adv.* scholas'tically.—*n.* scholas'ticism (-*sizm*), the aims, methods, and products of thought which constituted the main endeavour of the intellectual life of the Middle Ages: the method or subtleties of the schools of philosophy: the collected body of doctrines of the schoolmen. [Gr. *scholastikos—scholē*; see school (1).]

scholion, *skō'li-on*, scholium, -*əm*, *n.* an explanatory note, such as certain ancient grammarians wrote on passages in manuscripts: an observation or note added to a mathematical proposition: often in *pl.* (Gr. and L.) scho'lia.—*n.* scho'liast, a writer of scholia: an annotator: a commentator.—*adj.* scholias'tic. [Gr. *scholion*, *scholiastēs—scholē*; see school (1).]

school, *skōōl*, *n.* a place for instruction: an institution for education, esp. primary or secondary, or for teaching of special subjects: a division of such an institution: a building or room used for that purpose: the work of a school: the time given to it: the body of pupils of a school: the disciples of a particular teacher: those who hold a common doctrine or follow a common tradition: a method of instruction: an instruction book (now usu. in music): the body of instructors and students in a university, college, faculty, or department: a group of studies in which honours may be taken: (in *pl.*) academic institutions: (in *pl.*) an academic disputation: (in Oxford, in *pl.*) the B.A. examinations: a university building, now (Oxford) the examination hall.—*adj.* of school, schools, or the schools. —*v.t.* to educate in a school: to train: to instruct: to coach in a part to be played: to teach overbearingly: to admonish (*obs.*): to discipline.—*adj.* schooled, trained: experienced. —*ns.* school'ery (*Spens.*), something taught, precepts; school'ing, instruction or maintenance at school: tuition: training: discipline: school fees: reproof: reprimand.—*adj.* and *adv.* school'ward.—*adv.* school'wards.—school'bag, a bag for carrying school-books; **school'-bell**, a bell to announce time for school; **school'-board**, formerly, an elected board of school managers for a parish, town, or district; **school'-book**, a book used in school; **school'boy**, a boy attending school.—Also *adj.*—*adjs.* **school'boy'ish**; **school'-bred'**.—**school'-child**; **school'craft**, learning; **school'-dame**, mistress of a dame's school; **school'-day**, a day on which schools are open: (in *pl.*,) time of being a school pupil; **school'-divine'**; **school'-divin'ity**, scholastic or seminary theology; **school'-doc'tor**, a schoolman: a school-teacher (*obs.*): a physician appointed to examine or attend the pupils of a school or schools; **school'fellow**, one taught at the same school at the same time; **school'-friend**, one who is or has been a friend at school; **school'-friend'ship**; **school'girl**, a girl attending school.—*adj.* **school'girlish**.—*n.* and *adj.* **school'-going**.—**school'house**, a building used as a school: a house provided for a school-teacher (**school house**, a headmaster's or headmistress's boarding-house: its boarders); **school'-inspec'-tor**, an official appointed to examine schools; **school'-leav'er**, one who is leaving school because he has reached the statutory age, or the stage, for doing so.—*n.* and *adj.* **school'-leav'-ing**.—**school'-ma'am**, a schoolmistress (*U.S.*): a prim pedantic woman (*coll.*); **school'maid**, a schoolgirl; **school'man**, a philosopher or theologian of mediaeval scholasticism: a teacher (*U.S.*); **school'master**, the master or one of the masters of a school: a tutor (*Shak.*).—Also *v.t.* and *v.i.*—*n.* and *adj.* **school'mastering**.—*adjs.* **school'masterish**; **school'masterly**.—**school'mastership**; **school'-mate**, a school-friend: a schoolfellow; **school'-miss**, a raw or affected schoolgirl; **school'mistress**; **school'-point**, a point for scholastic disputation; **school'-room**, a school classroom: in a house, a room for receiving or preparing lessons in; **school'-ship**, a training-ship.—*adj.* **school'-taught**, taught at school or in the schools.—**school'-teach'er**, one who teaches in a school; **school'-teach'ing**; **school'-term**, a word or term in use in the schools or among schoolmen: a division of the school year; **school'-tide**, school-days; **school'-time**, the time at which a school opens, or during which it remains open: school-days.—*adj.* **school'-trained**, trained at school.—**school'-work**.—**the schoolmaster is abroad**, a phrase of Brougham's implying that education and intelligence are now widely spread. [O.E. *scōl*—L. *schŏla*—Gr. *schŏlē*, leisure, a lecture, a school.]

**school**, *skōōl*, *n.* a shoal of fish, whales, or other swimming animals: a flock, troop, assemblage, esp. of birds.—*v.i.* to gather or go in schools.—*adj.* (or in composition) going in schools.—*n.* and *adj.* **school'ing**.—**school'master**, the leader of a school, esp. of whales. [Du. *school*; cf. **shoal** (1).]

**schoole** (*Shak.*, *Macb.* I, vii. 6). Same as **shoal** (2).

**schooner**, *skōōn'ər*, *n.* a sharp-built, swift-sailing vessel, generally two-masted, fore-and-aft rigged, or with top and topgallant sails on the foremast: a covered emigrant-wagon (**prairie schooner**): a large beer glass: also a large sherry glass.—*adj.* **schoon'er-rigged.** [Early 18th-century (Massachusetts) *skooner*, *scooner*, said to be from a dial. Eng. word *scoon*, to skim.]

**schorl**, *shörl*, *n.* black tourmaline.—*adj.* **schorlā'-ceous**.—**schorl'-rock'**, a rock compound of schorl and quartz. [Ger. *schörl*.]

**schottische**, *sho-tēsh'*, *shot'ish*, *n.* a dance, or dance-tune, similar to the polka. [Ger. (*der*) *schottische* (*tanz*), (the) Scottish (dance); pronunciation sham French.]

**schout**, *skowt*, *n.* a municipal officer. [Du.]

**schrecklich**, *shrek'lihh*, *adj.* frightful.—*n.* **schreck-lichkeit** (*-kīt*), frightfulness. [Ger.]

**schuit**, **schuyt**, *skoit*, *n.* a Dutch flat-bottomed river-boat. [Du.]

**schul.** Same as **shul.**

**schuss**, *shōōs*, *n.* in skiing, a straight slope on which it is possible to make a fast run: such a run.—*v.i.* to make such a run. [Ger.]

**schutzstaffel** (abbrev. **S.S.**), *shōōts'shtä-fəl*, (Ger.) Hitler's bodyguard.

**schwa**, *shvä*, *shwä*, *n.* an indistinct vowel sound shown in Hebrew by two dots (:)—transliterated *ĕ*, etc.: in phonetics, a neutral vowel (ə).—Cf. **sheva**. [Ger.,—Heb. *schĕwa*.]

**schwärmerei**, *shver'mər-ī*, *n.* sentimental enthusiasm, as of a schoolgirl. [Ger., swarming.]

**Schwenkfelder**, *shvengk'fel-dər*, *n.* a member of a religious sect, founded by Kaspar von *Schwenckfeld* (1490-1561).—Also **Schwenkfeld'ian.**

**scia-.** For various words see under **skia-.**

**Sciaena**, *si-ē'nə*, *n.* the maigre genus of fishes, giving name to the fam. **Sciae'nidae.**—*adj.* **sciae'noid.** [Gr. *skiaina*, a kind of fish.]

**sciarid**, *si-ar'id*, *n.* a minute, dark-coloured, two-winged fly of the family **Sciar'idae.**—Also *adj.* [Gr. *skiaros*, shady, dark-coloured—*skia*, shadow.]

**sciatic**, *si-at'ik*, *adj.* of, or in the region of, the hip.—Also **sciat'ical.**—*n.* **sciat'ica**, neuritis of the great sciatic nerve which passes down the back of the thigh. [L.L. *sciaticus*, fem. *-a*—Gr. *ischion*, hip-joint.]

**science**, *si'əns*, *n.* knowledge: knowledge ascertained by observation and experiment, critically tested, systematised and brought under general principles: a department or branch of such knowledge or study: a skilled craft (*obs.*): trained skill, esp. in boxing (now usu. *joc.*).—*adjs.* **sci'enced**, versed, learned; **sci'ent**, having science; **sciential** (*-en'shl*), of, having, or producing, science: scientific; **scientif'ic** (L. *facĕre*, to make), orig. (of a syllogism) demonstrative, producing knowledge: hence of, relating to, based on, devoted to, according to, used in, or versed in, science.—Also (*rare*) **scientif'ical.**—*adv.* **scientif'ically.**—*ns.* **sci'entism**, the methods or mental attitudes of men of science: a belief that the methods used in studying natural sciences should be employed also in investigating all aspects of human behaviour and condition, e.g. in philosophy and social sciences: scientific or pseudo-scientific language; **sci'entist**, a man of science, esp. natural science.—*adj.* **scientis'tic.**—*n.* **Scientol'-ogy**, a cult claimed by its promoters to bring about improved conditions of mental and physical life for any individual who follows a course of study laid down by them.—**science fiction**, fiction dealing with life on the earth in future, with space travel, and with life on other planets, or the like.—**the (noble) science**, the art of boxing. [L. *scientia*—*sciēns*, *-entis*, pr.p. of *scire*, to know.]

**scilicet**, *si'li-set*, *skē'li-ket*, *adv.* to wit, namely. [L. *scilicet*—*scire licet*, it is permitted to know.]

**Scilla**, *sil'ə*, *n.* the squill genus of the lily family, including some bright blue spring flowers. [L.,—Gr. *skilla*, the officinal squill.]

**Scillonian**, *si-lō'ni-ən*, *adj.* of, belonging to, concerning, the *Scilly* Isles, off the south-west coast of Britain.—*n.* an inhabitant of these islands.

**scimitar**, *sim'i-tər*, *n.* a short, single-edged, curved sword, broadest at the point end, used by the Turks and Persians. [Poss. through Fr. *cimeterre* or It. *scimitarra*—Pers. *shamshir*; but doubtful.]

**scincoid**, *singk'oid*, *adj.* like a skink. [Gr. *skinkos*, a skink, *eidos*, form.]

**scintilla**, *sin-til'ə*, *n.* a spark.—*adj.* **scin'tillant** sparkling.—*v.i.* **scin'tillate**, to sparkle: to talk wittily.—*v.t.* to emit in sparks: to sparkle with.—*ns.* **scintilla´tion**, a flash of light produced in a phosphor by an ionising particle, e.g. an alpha particle, or a photon; **scin´tillātor**, an instrument for detecting radioactivity; **scintillo´meter**, an instrument for detecting and measuring radioactivity; **scintill´oscope**, an instrument which shows scintillations on a screen.—**scintillation counter**, a scintillometer. [L., a spark.]

**scio-.** For various words see **skia-**.

**sciolism**, *sī´ə-lizm*, *n.* superficial pretensions to knowledge.—*n.* **sci´olist**, a pretender to science.—*adjs.* **sciolis´tic**; **sci´olous**. [L. *sciolus*, dim. of *scius*, knowing—*scīre*, to know.]

**sciolto**, *shol´tō*, (*mus.*) *adj.* and *adv.* free. [It.]

**scion**, *sī´ən*, *n.* a detached piece of a plant capable of propagating, esp. by grafting: a young member of a family: a descendant, offshoot. [O.Fr. *sion*, *cion*; origin obscure.]

**sciosophy**, *sī-os´ō-fi*, *n.* a system of what claims to be knowledge but is without basis in ascertained scientific fact, as astrology. [Gr. *skiā*, a shadow, *sophiā*, wisdom.]

**scire facias**, *sī´ri fā´shi-as*, *skē´re fa´ki-äs*, *n.* a writ requiring a person to appear and show cause why a record should not be enforced or annulled. [L. *scīre faciās*, make him to know.]

**scirocco.** See sirocco.

**Scirpus**, *sûr´pəs*, *n.* the club-rush genus of the sedge family. [L., a rush.]

**scirrhus**, *skir´əs*, *sir´əs*, (*med.*) *n.* a hard swelling: a hard cancer.—*adj.* **scirr´hous.** [Latinised from Gr. *skirros*, *skiros*, a tumour.]

**scissel**, *sis´l*, *n.* metal clippings: scrap left when blanks have been cut out.—Also **sciss´il.** [O.Fr. *cisaille—ciseler—cisel*, a chisel; for the spelling cf. **scissors**.]

**scissile**, *sis´il*, *adj.* capable of being cut: readily splitting.—*ns.* **scission** (*sish´ən*, *sizh´ən*), cutting: division: splitting: schism; **scissiparity** (*sis-i-par´i-ti*; L. *parĕre*, to bring forth), reproduction by fission; **scissure** (*sish´ər*), a cleft: a fissure: a rupture: a division: cutting. [L. *scissilis*, *scissiō̆*, *-ōnis*, *scissūra—scindĕre*, *scissum*, to cut, to split, cleave.]

**scissors**, *siz´ərz*, *n.pl.* (rarely treated as *sing.*) a cutting instrument with two blades pivoted to close together and overlap—usu. smaller than shears: a position or movement like that of scissors: movement of the legs suggesting opening and closing of scissors (*gymnastics*): locking the legs round body or head of an opponent (*wrestling*): a style of high jump in which the leg nearest the bar leads throughout.—*v.t.* **sciss´or**, to cut with scissors.—*n.* **sciss´orer**, a scissors-and-paste compiler.—*adv.* **sciss´orwise.**—**sciss´or-bill**, a skimmer; **sciss´or-blade**; **sciss´-or-case**; **sciss´or-cut**; **sciss´or-leg**, the deformity of crossed legs; **sciss´ors-and-paste´**, literary or journalistic matter collected from various sources with little or no original writing.—Also *adj.* **sciss´or-tail**, an American fly-catcher; **sciss´or-tooth**, a carnassial tooth. [O.Fr. *cisoires*—L.L. *cisŏrium*, a cutting instrument—*caedĕre*, *caesum*, to cut; the spelling *sc-* is due to erroneous association with *scindĕre*, *scissum*; cf. foregoing.]

**Scitamineae**, *sit-ə-min´i-ē*, *n.pl.* an order of monocotyledons including the banana, ginger, Indian shot, and arrowroot families.—*adj.* **scitamin´eous.**—Also **Musales.** [App.—L. *scitāmenta*, delicacies.]

**Sciurus**, *sī-ū´rəs*, *n.* the squirrel genus, giving name to the fam. **Sciu´ridae.**—*adjs.* **sciurine** (*si-ūr´in*, or *sī´*); **sciuroid** (*-ū´*).—*n.* **Sciuro´pterus** (Gr. *pteron* wing), a genus of flying squirrels. [L. *sciūrus*—Gr. *skiouros*—*skiā*, shadow, *ourā*, tail.]

**sclaff**, *sklaf*, *skläf*, *n.* a light slap or its sound (*Scot.*): a stroke in which the sole of the club scrapes the ground before striking the ball (*golf*).—*v.t.* and *v.i.* to strike or play with a sclaff. [Imit.]

**sclate**, *sklāt*, a Scots form of **slate.**—**sclate´stane´**, a piece of slate (such as money got from the Devil turned into).

**sclaunder**, **sclave**, **Sclave**, **Sclavonian**, etc., *sklön´dər*, etc., obs. forms of **slander**, **slave**, **Slav**, **Slavonian**, etc.

**sclera**, *sklēr´ə*, *n.* the sclerotic.—*adj.* **sclē´ral.**—*ns.* **sclere** (*sklēr*), a skeletal element: a sponge spicule; **sclereid**, **-eide** (*sklēr´i-id*; *bot.*), a thick-walled cell; **sclerema** (*sklər-ē´mə*), hardening of (esp. subcutaneous) tissues; **sclerenchyma** (*sklər-eng´ki-mə*; Gr. *enchyma*, in-filling), plant tissue with thick, lignified cell-walls: hard skeletal tissue, as in corals.—*adj.* **sclerenchymatous** (*skler-eng-kim´ə-təs*).—*ns.* **scleri´asis**, hardening of tissue: a hard tumour: an induration; **sclē´rite**, a hard skeletal plate or spicule; **scleritis** (*sklər-ī´tis*), sclerotitis.—*adj.* **sclerocaulous** (*sklēr-ō-kö´ləs*).—*ns.* **sclē´rocauly** (Gr. *kaulos*, stem), possession of a hard, dry stem; **scleroderm** (*skler´*, *sklēr´*), a hard integument.—*adj.* **scleroder´matous.**—*n.* **scleroder´m(i)a**, hardness and rigidity of skin by substitution of fibrous tissue for subcutaneous fat.—*adjs.* **scleroder´mic**, **scleroder´mous**, hard-skinned: pertaining to a scleroderm or to sclerodermia.—*ns.* **scleroder´mite**, the integument of a segment in arthropods; **scleroma** (*sklar-ō´mə*), hardening: morbid hardening: formation of nodules in the nose, etc.; **sclerom´eter**, an instrument for measuring the hardness of minerals; **sclerophyll** (*skler´ō-fil*), a hard, stiff leaf.—*adj.* **sclerophyll´ous.**—*ns.* **scleroph´ylly**, possession of sclerophylls; **scleropro´tein**, insoluble protein forming the skeletal parts of tissues.—*v.t.* **sclerose** (*sklər-ōs´*), to harden: to affect with sclerosis.—*v.i.* to become sclerosed.—*n.* **sclerosis** (*sklər-ō´sis*), hardening: morbid hardening, as of arteries (*med.*): hardening of tissue by thickening or lignification (*bot.*).—*adj.* **sclerō´tal**, sclerotic.—*n.* a bony plate in the sclerotic of some animals.—*adj.* **sclerŏt´ic**, hard, firm, applied esp. to the outer membrane of the eyeball: of sclerosis: sclerosed.—*n.* the outermost membrane of the eye-ball.—*ns.* **scleroti´tis** (*skler-*, *sklēr-*), inflammation of the sclerotic; **sclerotium** (*sklər-ō´shi-əm*), a hard, tuber-like body, the resting stage of many fungi—*pl.* **sclero´tia.**—*adj.* **sclē´rous**, hard or indurated: ossified or bony.—**disseminated (or multiple) sclerosis** see **disseminate**. [Gr. *sklēros*, hard.]

**sclim**, **sklim**, *sklim*, a Scots form of **climb.**

**scoff**, *skof*, *n.* mockery: a jibe, jeer: an object of derision.—*v.i.* to jeer (with *at*).—*v.t.* (*Shak.*) to jeer at.—*n.* **scoff´er.**—*n.* and *adj.* **scoff´ing.**—*adv.* **scoff´ingly.** [Cf. obs. Dan. *skof*, jest, mockery, O.Fris. *schof.*]

**scoff**, **skoff**, *skof*, (*dial.* and *slang*) *v.t.* to devour: to plunder.—*v.i.* to feed quickly or greedily.—*n.* food: a meal. [App. **scaff**, reinforced from S. Africa by Du. *schoft*, a meal.]

**scog.** See **skug** (1).

**Scoggin**, **Scogan**, *skog´ən*, *n.* a supposed fool of Edward IV, on whom the contents of a 16th-century jest-book were fathered: hence a buffoon.

**scoinson**, *skoin´sən.* Same as **scuncheon.**

**scold**, *skōld*, *n.* a rude clamorous woman or other: a scolding.—*v.i.* to brawl: to vituperate: to find fault vehemently or at some length.—*v.t.* to chide: to rebuke.—*n.* **scold´er.**—*n.* and *adj.* **scold´ing.** [App. O.N. *skäld*, poet (through an intermediate sense, lampooner).]

**scolex**, *skō´leks*, *n.* a tapeworm head.—*pl.* **scoleces**, *skō-lē´sēz*; erroneously **sco´lices**.—*adjs.* **scō´lecid** (*-lə-sid*), **scōleciform** (*-les´i-fö̆rm*), like a scolex.—*n.pl.* **Scōleciform´ia**, the lugworm order.—*n.* **scō´lecite** (*-sit*), a lime zeolite that curls before the blowpipe.—*adj.* **scōlecoid**

(-lē′koid), like a scolex. [Gr. *skolēx, -ēkos*, a worm.]

**scoliosis**, *skol-i-ō′sis*, *n.* lateral spinal curvature.— *adj.* **scoliotic** (*-ot′ik*). [Gr. *skoliōsis*, obliquity.]

**scollop.** Same as **scallop**.

**Scolopax**, *skol′ə-paks*, *n.* the woodcock genus, giving name to the fam. **Scolopacidae** (*-pas′i-dē*). —*adj.* **scolopaceous** (*-pā′shəs*). [Gr. *scolopax, -ākos*, a woodcock.]

**Scolopendra**, *skol-ə-pen′drə*, *n.* a genus of centipedes, some a foot long: (without cap., *Spens.*) a fabulous fish that voided the hook.—*adjs.* **scolopen′driform, scolopen′drine.**—*n.* **Scolopen′drium,** the hart's-tongue fern genus (from the appearance of the sori). [Gr. *skolopendra, skolopendrion*.]

**Scolytus**, *skol′i-təs*, *n.* typical genus of Scolytidae (*-it′i-dē*), a family of bark-beetles.—*adj.* **scol′ytoid.** [Gr. *skolyptein*, to strip.]

**Scomber**, *skom′bər*, *n.* the mackerel genus, giving name to the fam. **Scom′bridae** (*-bri-dē*).—*n.* **Scom′bresox** (L. *esox*, pike), the skipper genus, giving name to the **Scombresocidae** (*-sos′i-dē*).— *adj.* **scom′broid,** of or like the mackerel family. [L. *scomber*—Gr. *skombros*, a mackerel.]

**scomfish,** *skum′fish*, (*Scot.*) *v.t.* to stifle: to disgust. [From *discomfish*, a by-form of **discomfit**, from the stem appearing in the Fr. pr.p.]

**sconce,** *skons*, *n.* a small fort or earthwork: a shelter: a chimney-seat: a slab of floating ice.— *v.t.* to entrench: to screen—**build a sconce,** to run up a debt (e.g. in a tavern) and have to keep away. [Du. *schans*.]

**sconce,** *skons*, *n.* the head: the crown of the head: brains, wits. [Origin obscure.]

**sconce,** *skons*, (*Oxford*) *n.* a fine (paid in ale or otherwise): a two-handled mug used for the purpose (holding about a quart): a forfeit.—*v.t.* to fine. [Origin obscure.]

**sconce,** *skons*, *n.* a candlestick or lantern with a handle: a bracket candlestick: a street wall-lamp. [O.Fr. *esconse*—L.L. *absconsa*, a dark lantern—*abscondĕre*, to hide.]

**sconcheon.** Same as **scuncheon**.

**scone,** *skon*, in the South of England often pronounced *skōn*, (*Scot.*) *n.* a flattish, usually round or quadrant-shaped plain cake of dough without much butter, with or without currants, baked on a girdle or in an oven. [Perh. from Du. *schoon* (*brot*), fine (bread).]

**scontion.** Same as **scuncheon**.

**scoog.** See **skug** (1).

**scoop,** *skōōp*, *n.* a bailing-vessel: a concave shovel or lipped vessel for skimming or shovelling up loose material: an instrument for gouging out apple-cores, samples of cheese, etc.: anything of like shape: an act of scooping: a sweeping stroke: a scooped-out place: anything got by or as by scooping, a haul: the forestalling of other newspapers in obtaining a piece of news: an item of news so secured.— *v.t.* to bail out: to lift, obtain, remove, hollow, or make with, or as if with, a scoop: to secure in advance of or to the exclusion of others.— *adjs.* **scooped.**—*ns.* **scoop′er,** one who scoops: an engraver's tool: the avocet; **scoop′ful:**— *pl.* **scoop′fuls; scoop′ing.**—*adj.* **scooped′-out.**— **scoop′-net,** a long-handled dipping net: a net for scooping along the bottom.—**scoop the pool** (see **pool** (2)). [Prob. partly M.L.G. or M.Du. *schôpe*, bailing-vessel, partly M.Du. *schoppe*, shovel.]

**scoot,** *skōōt*, *v.t.* and *v.i.* (*Scot.*) to squirt.—*v.i.* to slip suddenly (*Scot.*): to make off with celerity (*coll.*).—*n.* a squirt (*Scot.*): an act of scooting.—*n.* **scoot′er,** one who scoots: a child's toy, a wheeled footboard with steering handle, propelled by kicking the ground: a development thereof driven by a motor (also *motor-scooter, auto-scooter*): a boat for sailing on ice and

water: a swift motor-boat: a simple form of plough (*U.S.*). [Prob. from O.N., akin to **shoot**.]

**scoot,** *skōōt*, (*Scot.*) *n.* an insignificant person.

**scopa,** *skō′pə*, *n.* a bee's pollen-brush:—*pl.* **sco′pae** (*-pē*).—*adj.* **scō′pate,** tufted.—*n.* **scopula** (*skop′ū-lə*), a little tuft of hairs. [L. *scōpae*, twigs, a broom.]

**scope,** *skōp*, *n.* point aimed at: aim: range: field or opportunity of activity: room for action: spaciousness: length of cable at which a vessel rides at liberty. [It. *scopo*—Gr. *skopos*, watcher, point watched, (*fig.*) aim—*skopeein*, to view.]

**scope,** *skōp*, *n.* short for **microscope, telescope, horoscope,** etc.

**Scopelus,** *skop′ə-ləs*, *n.* a genus of deep-water fishes with luminous spots, giving name to the fam. **Scopelidae** (*-el′i-dē*). [Gr. *skopelos*, a rock, thought by Cuvier to mean a kind of fish.]

**scopolamine,** *sko-pol′ə-mēn*, *n.* an alkaloid got from the genus Scopolia and other plants of the Solanaceae (see **hyoscine**). [Named after *Scopoli* (1723-88), Italian naturalist; **amine**.]

**scopophilia,** *skop-ō-fil′i-ə*, *n.* act of obtaining sexual pleasure from things seen, as e.g. naked bodies.—*n.* **scopophil′iac.**—*adj.* **scopophilic.** [Gr. *skopos*, watcher (*skopeein*, to view), *philia*, loving.]

**Scops,** *skops*, *n.* a genus of owls. [Gr. *skōps*.]

**scoptophilia,** etc. Same as **scopophilia,** etc.

**scorbutic, -al,** *skör-bū′tik*, *adjs.* of, like, of the nature of, or affected with, scurvy. [L.L. *scorbūticus*, poss. from M.L.G. *schorbuk*.]

**scorch,** *skörch*, *v.t.* to burn slightly or superficially: to parch: to dry up, wither, or affect painfully or injuriously by heat or as if by heat: to wither with scorn, censure, etc.—*v.i.* to be burned on the surface: to be dried up: to cycle or drive furiously.—*n.* an act of scorching: an injury by scorching.—*adj.* **scorched.**—*n.* **scorch′er,** one who, that which, scorches: a day of scorching heat: anything stinging.—*n.*, *adj.*, and *adv.* **scorch′ing.**—*adv.* **scorch′ingly.**—*n.* **scorch′ingness.**—**scorched earth,** country devastated before evacuation so as to be useless to an advancing enemy. [Perh. M.E. *skorken*; cf. O.N. *skorpna*, to shrivel; poss. affected by O.Fr. *escorcher*, to flay.]

**scorch,** *skörch*, (*Shak.*; *Scott*) *v.t.* to slash (in *Macbeth* Theobald conjecturally read *scotch'd* for *scorch'd*). [Perh. **score,** influenced by **scratch**.]

**scordato,** *skör-dä′tō*, (*mus.*) *adj.* put out of tune.— *n.* **scordatura** (*-tōō′ra*), a temporary departure from normal tuning. [It.]

**score,** *skōr, skör, n.* a notch, gash, or scratch: an incised line: a boldly drawn line, as one marking a deletion: a line marking a boundary, starting-place, or defined position: an arrangement of music on a number of staves (perh. orig. with the bar divisions running continuously through all): a composition so distributed: a notch in a tally: an account of charges incurred (as in a tavern) by tallies or (later) chalk marks or the like: a debt incurred: a reckoning, account, ground: total number, tale (*Spens.*): the total or record of points made in a game: an addition made thereto: a set of twenty (sometimes verging upon numeral *adj.*): applied also to an indefinitely large number: twenty or twenty-one pounds: twenty paces (*Shak.*): a fixed number (20 to 26) of tubs of coal.—*v.t.* to mark with or by scores: to record in or with a score: to make a score through as a mark of deletion (with *out*): to write in score: to distribute among the instruments of the orchestra: to make as a score: to add to a score: to achieve: to enumerate: to record: to rebuke (*U.S.*).—*v.i.* to keep or run up a score (*obs.*): to make a point: to achieve a success.—*ns.* **scor′er,** one who, or that which, scores: one who keeps the marks in a game; **scor'ing.**—**score'-board, scor'ing-board,** a board on which the score is exhibited, as at cricket; **scor'ing-card,** a card for recording the score in a game.—**go off at score,** to make a spirited start; **know the score,** to know the hard facts of the situation; **pay off, settle, old scores,** to repay old grudges; **run up a score,** to run up a debt; **score off,** achieve a success against, get the better of. [Late O.E. *scoru*—O.N. *skor, skora*; cf. O.E. *sceran* (pa.p. *scoren*), to shear.]

**scoria,** *skō´, skō´ri-ə, n.* dross or slag from metal-smelting: a piece of lava with steam-holes:—*pl.* **scō´riae** (*-ē*).—*adjs.* **scō´riac, scōriaceous** (*-ri-ā´-shəs*).—*n.* **scōrifica´tion,** reduction to scoria: assaying by fusing with lead and borax; **scō´rifier,** a dish used in assaying.— *v.t.* **scō´rify,** to reduce to scoria.—*adj.* **scō´rious.** [L.,—Gr. *skōriā—skōr,* dung.]

**scorn,** *skörn, n.* hot or extreme contempt, usu. less self-conscious than disdain: an expression of contempt: the object of contempt.—*v.t.* to feel or express scorn for: to refuse with scorn: to make a mock of (*obs.*).—*v.i.* (*obs.*) to scoff.—*n.* **scorn'er.**—*adj.* **scorn'ful.**—*adv.* **scorn'fully.**—*ns.* **scorn'fulness; scorn'ing.**—**think scorn of,** to disdain or think beneath one. [O.Fr. *escarn,* mockery; of Gmc. origin; cf. O.H.G. *skern,* mockery.]

**scorodite,** *skor'ō-dīt, n.* hydrous ferric arsenate. [Gr. *skorodon,* garlic, from the smell under the blowpipe.]

**Scorpaena,** *skör-pē´nə, n.* a genus of large-headed, spiny fishes giving name to the fam. **Scorpae´-nidae,** the scorpion-fishes or sea-scorpions. [Gr. *skorpaina,* a kind of fish.]

**scorper,** *skör´pər, n.* a gouging chisel. [For scauper.]

**scorpioid,** *skör´pi-oid, adj.* like a scorpion, or a scorpion's curled tail.—**scorpioid cyme,** a uniparous cymose inflorescence in which the plane of each daughter axis is at right angles, to right and left alternately, with its parent axis, that of the whole coiled in bud—a cincinnus or cicinnus. [Gr. *skorpios,* scorpion, *eidos,* form.]

**scorpion,** *skör´pi-ən, n.* any member of the Scorpionid´ea, or Scorpionida (*-on´i-də*), an order of Arachnida with head and thorax united, pincers, four pairs of legs, and a segmented abdomen including a tail with a sting: a form of scourge (*B*): an old engine for hurling missiles: any person of virulent hatred or animosity: a rock-scorpion (*mil. slang;* see rock): (*cap.*) the constellation or the sign Scorpio (*astron.*).—*n.* **Scor'pio** (*-ō*), a genus of scorpions: a constellation and a sign of the zodiac.—*adj.* **scorpion´ic.**—**scor'pion-fish,** any of the Scorpaenidae; **scor'pion-fly,** an insect of the Mecoptera (from the male's upturned abdomen); **scor'pion-grass,** forget-me-not; **scorp'ion-spider,** a whip-scorpion. [L. *scorpiō, -ōnis*—Gr. *skorpios.*]

**scorse,** *skōrs, skörs, (Spens.) v.t.* to chase. [It. *scorsa,* a run—*scorrere*—L. *excurrĕre.*]

**scorse,** *skōrs, skörs, (Spens.) n.* exchange.—*v.t.* and *v.i.* to exchange.—*n.* (*obs.*) one who barters. [Poss. from *horse-scorser* for **horse-courser.**]

**scorzonera,** *skör-zō-nē´rə, n.* a plant like dandelion, with edible root—*black salsify.* [It.]

**scot,** *skot, n.* a payment, esp. a customary tax: a share of a reckoning (also **shot**).—*adj.* **scot'-free',** free from scot: untaxed: entirely free from expense, injury, etc.—**scot and lot,** an old legal phrase embracing all parochial assessments for the poor, the church, lighting, cleansing, and watching. [O.E. *scot, sceot;* but prob. partly from O.N. *skot,* and O.Fr. *esco;* see **shot, escot.**]

**Scot,** *skot, n.* one of a Gaelic-speaking people of Ireland, afterwards also in Argyllshire (*hist.*): (now) a Scotsman or Scotswoman of any race

or language.—*n.* **Scotland** (*skot'lənd*), Ireland (*hist.*): now, the country forming the northern member of the United Kingdom.—*adv.* **Scot(t)ice** (*skot'i-sē*), in Scots.—*v.t.* **Scott'icise, -ize,** to render Scottish or into Scots.—*n.* **Scott'icism** (*obs.* **Scot'icism**), a Scottish idiom: Scottish feeling.—*v.t.* **Scot(t)ify,** to make Scottish:—*pr.p.* **Scot(t)'ifying;** *pa.t.* and *pa.p.* **Scot(t)'ified.**—*n.* **Scot(t)ificā'tion.**—*adj.* **Scottish** (*obs.* **Scotish;** *skot'ish*); O.E. *Scottisc,* earlier *Scyttisc*), of Scotland, its people, or its English dialect.—*n.* Scots (see separate entry): (as *pl., rare*) the Scots.—*v.t.* to translate into Scots.—*ns.* **Scott'ishman; Scott'ishness; Scott'y,** a nickname for a Scotsman: a Scotch terrier (*coll.*)—**Scotland Yard,** earliest or (New Scotland Yard) two more recent headquarters (1890 and 1967) of the Metropolitan Police (said to be from a palace of the kings of Scotland on the orig. site): hence the London Criminal Investigation Department.—**Irish Scot** (*obs.*), a Highlander. [O.E. *Scottas* (pl.)—L.L. *Scottus;* see also **Scotch, Scotia, Scots.**]

**Scotch,** *skoch, adj.* a form of **Scottish** or **Scots,** in common use even among Scottish dialect speakers, though disliked or resented by many Scotsmen: applied esp. to products or supposed products of Scotland: having the character popularly attributed to a Scotsman—an excessive leaning towards defence of oneself and one's property.—*n.* Scotch whisky, or a glass of it: the Scottish (Northern English) dialect: (as *pl.*) the Scots.—*ns.* **Scotch'ness; Scotch'y,** a nickname for a Scotsman.—*adj.* having Scottish characteristics.—**Scotch attorney,** (*W. Indies*) a climber (Clusia) that strangles trees; **Scotch barley,** pot or hulled barley; **Scotch bluebell,** the harebell; **Scotch bonnet,** a round flat blue woollen cap with a tuft on the top: the fairy-ring mushroom; **Scotch broth,** broth made with pot-barley and plenty of various vegetables chopped small; **Scotch cart** (*S. Afr.; arch.*), a strong, springless, two-wheeled uncovered farm cart with one shaft; **Scotch catch or snap,** a short accented note followed by a longer—not peculiar to Scottish music; **Scotch collops,** minced beef (sometimes called **scotched collops**); **Scotch cuddy** (cuddy = donkey), a Scotch draper; **Scotch curlies,** a variety of kale; **Scotch draper,** an itinerant dealer differing from a pedlar in not carrying his goods about with him: a credit itinerant draper (also **Scotch cuddy**); **Scotch egg,** a hard-boiled egg (often cut in two) enclosed in sausage-meat; **Scotch elm,** the wych elm (*Ulmus montana*): sometimes the common English elm (*U. campestris*); **Scotch fiddle,** the itch (from the movements of the fingers it excited); **Scotch fir,** Scots pine; **Scotch hand,** a wooden bat for manipulating butter.—*adj.* and *n.pl.* (*U.S.*) **Scotch-Irish,** Irish of Scottish descent.—**Scotch kale,** a variety of kale; **Scotch'-man,** a Scotsman: a florin (from a tradition of a Scotsman who benefited from its resemblance to a half-crown; *S. Afr.; obs.*); **Scotch mist,** a fine rain; **Scotch pebble,** an agate or similar stone; **Scotch rose,** the burnet rose (*Rosa spinosissima*); **Scotch snap,** a Scotch catch (see above); **Scotch tape,** a transparent tape, adhering to paper, etc., when pressure is applied; **Scotch terrier,** a rough-haired, prick-eared, stronglybuilt little dog; **Scotch thistle,** the cotton thistle, national emblem of Scotland (not native); **Scotch verdict,** not proven; **Scotch'woman; Scotch woodcock,** egg and anchovies on toast.—**Scotch and English,** prisoners' base (q.v.). [From **Scottish.**]

**scotch,** *skoch, v.t.* to gash: to score: (from Theobald's conjecture in *Macbeth;* see **scorch,** 2) to maim, cripple for the time without killing: to frustrate: to quash.—*n.* a gash (*Shak.*): a score on the ground (as for hop-scotch). [Origin unknown.]

**scotch**, *skoch, n.* a strut, wedge, block etc., to prevent turning or slipping, as of a wheel, gate, ladder.—*v.t.* to stop or block: to frustrate. [Perh. a form of **scratch**.]

**scoter**, *skō'tər, n.* a genus (Oedemia) of northern sea-ducks, usu. black or nearly.—Also **scoter duck**. [Origin obscure.]

**scotia**, *skō'ti-ə, -shi-ə, n.* a hollow moulding, esp. at the base of a column. [Gr. *skōtiā—skotos,* darkness.]

**Scotia**, *skō'sh(y)a, n.* (*poet.*) Scotland.—*adjs.* **Sco'tian** (*rare*); **Scotic** (*skot'ik*), of the ancient Scots of Ireland; **Scot'ican** (*eccles.*), of Scotland. —For **Scotice, Scoticism, Scotish**, see **Scot**. [L.L. *Scōtia, Scōticus.*]

**Scotism**, *skō'tizm, n.* the metaphysical system of Johannes Duns *Scotus* (*c.* 1265-1308), a native of Maxton in Roxburghshire (not Duns, Berwickshire, Dunstane, Northumberland, or Down, north Ireland), the great assailant of the method of Aquinas in seeking in speculation instead of in practice the foundation of Christian theology— his theological descendants were the Franciscans, in opposition to the Dominicans, who followed Aquinas.—*n.* **Scō'tist**, a follower of Duns Scotus.—*adj.* **Scotist'ic**.

**scoto-**, *skot-ō-*, in composition, dark.—*ns.* **scotodinia** (*-din'i-ə*; Gr. *dīnos,* whirling), dizziness with headache and impairment of vision; **scotoma** (*-ōm'ə*; Gr. *skotōma,* dizziness), a blind spot due to disease of the retina or optic nerve:— *pl.* **scoto'maṭa**.—*ns.* **scot'omy** (*obs.*); **scotōp'ia**, vision in a dim light.—*adj.* **scotop'ic** (*-op'*). [Gr. *skotos,* darkness.]

**Scots**, *skots, adj.* Scottish (almost always used of money, measures, law, and preferably of language).—*n.* the dialect of Lowland Scotland, Northern English.—**Scots Greys**, a famous regiment of dragoons, established in 1683, amalgamated with the 3rd Carabiniers in 1971; **Scots Guards**, a Scottish force which served the kings of France from 1418 to 1759, nominally to 1830: a well-known regiment of Guards in the British army, formerly Scots Fusilier Guards; **Scots'man; Scots pine**, the only native British pine, *Pinus sylvestris;* **Scots'woman;** see also **mile, pint, pound.** [Shortened form of Scots *Scottis,* Scottish.]

**Scottish**, etc. See **Scot**.

**scoug**. Same as **skug**.

**scoundrel**, *skown'drəl, n.* a low mean blackguard: a man without principle.—*ns.* **scoun'dreldom**, the world of scoundrels; **scoun'drelism**.—*adj.* **scoun'drelly**. [Origin unknown.]

**scoup, scowp**, *skowp,* (*Scot.*) *v.i.* to bound: to caper: to scamper. [Origin unknown.]

**scour**, *skowr, v.t.* to clean, polish, remove, or form by hard rubbing: to scrub: to cleanse: to free from grease, dirt, or gum: to flush or cleanse by a current: to purge, esp. drastically: to clear out: to rake with fire: to punish (*fig.*).—*v.i.* to scrub or polish: to be scoured: (of cattle) to have diarrhoea.—*n.* the action, place, or means of scouring: diarrhoea in cattle: a swig of liquor (*Scot.*).—*ns.* **scour'er**, one who scours: an instrument or container for scouring: a cathartic; **scour'ing**, scrubbing: vigorous cleansing: clearing: erosion: purging: (often in *pl.*) matter removed or accumulated by scouring: off- scouring.—Also *adj.* **scour'ing-rush** (*U.S.*), Dutch rush; **scour'ing-stick**, a rod for scouring a gun. [Prob. M.Du. or M.L.G. *schüren*— O.Fr. *escurer*—L. *ex cūrāre,* take care of.]

**scour**, *skowr, v.i.* to rush or scurry along: to range about, esp. in quest or pursuit: to make off.—*v.t.* to range over or traverse swiftly, vigorously, riotously, or in pursuit: to search thoroughly: to molest as a scourer.—*n.* **scour'er**

(*obs.* **scowr'er;** *hist.*), a member of a roistering band that scoured the streets, maltreating watchmen and others. [Poss. O.N. *skūr,* storm, shower; cf. **shower**.]

**scourer**, *skowr'ər, n.* a scout. [Aphetic; see **discoverer**.]

**scourer**. See **scour** (1) and (2).

**scourie**. See **scaury**.

**scourge**, *skûrj, n.* a whip: an instrument of divine punishment: a cause of widespread affliction. —*v.t.* to whip severely: to afflict.—*n.* **scourg'er**. [A.Fr. *escorge*—L. *excoriāre,* to flay—*corium,* leather (perh. as made of a strip of leather, perh. as a flaying instrument).]

**scourse**. See **scorse** (2).

**scouse**, *skows,* (*coll.*) *n.* a native of Liverpool: the northern English dialect spoken in and around Liverpool. [Short for **lobscouse**.]

**scout**, *skowt, n.* watch, spying: one (or *obs.,* a party) sent out to bring in information: a spy: a member of the Scouts Association: a patrolman on the roads: one who watches or attends at a little distance: a fielder, as in cricket: a person (usually term of approbation; *slang*): a ship for reconnoitring: a small light aeroplane orig. intended for reconnaissance: a light armoured car for reconnaissance: a college servant at Oxford (perh. a different word; cf. Cambridge *gyp,* and Dublin *skip*).—*v.t.* to watch closely: to reconnoitre (often with *about* or *around*).—*v.i.* to act the scout.—*ns.* **scout'er**, an adult working with instructors, etc., in the Scouts; **scout'ing—scout'craft**, the knowledge and skill proper to a scout; **scout'-law**, the code of rules of the (Boy) Scouts; **scout'-master**, the leader of a band of scouts: formerly, an adult in charge of a troop of Boy Scouts. [O.Fr. *escoute*—*escouter*—L. *auscultāre,* to listen.]

**scout**, *skowt, v.t.* to mock, flout: to dismiss or reject with disdain. [Cf. O.N. *skūta,* a taunt.]

**scout**. Same as **scoot** (2).

**scouth, scowth**, *skṓōth, skowth,* (*Scot.*) *n.* free range: scope: plenty.

**scouther, scowder**, *skow'd(h)ər,* (*Scot.*) *v.t.* to scorch, singe: to overheat: to toast slightly: to blight.—*v.i.* to drizzle: to threaten to rain or snow.—*n.* a scorch or burn: a slight or flying shower.—*adj.* **scou'thering, scow'dering**, scorching, blighting.—*n.* a scorching, blighting: a sprinkle of snow.—*adj.* **scou'thery**. [Conn. with **scald**.]

**scow**, *skow, n.* a flat-bottomed boat. [Du. *schouw.*]

**scowl**, *skowl, v.i.* to contract the brows in a look of baleful malevolence: to look gloomy and threatening.—*v.t.* (*Milt.*) to give forth with a scowl.— *n.* a scowling look.—*adj.* **scow'ling.**—*adv.* **scow'lingly**. [Cf. Dan. *skule,* to cast down the eyes, look sidelong.]

**scowp, scowther**. See **scoup, scouther**.

**scowrie**. See **scaury**.

**scrab**, *skrab, v.t.* to scratch.—*v.t.* and *v.i.* **scrabb'le**, to scratch: to scrape: to scrawl.—*v.i.* to scramble.—*n.* a scrawl: (with *cap.*) a word-building game (*trademark*). [Du. *schrabben,* to scratch, freq. *schrabbelen;* cf. **scrape**.]

**scrae**, *skrā,* (*Scott*) *n.* Same as **scree**.

**scrag**, *skrag, n.* a sheep's or (*slang*) human neck: the bony part of the neck: a lean person or animal.—*v.t.* to hang: to throttle: to wring the neck of: to tackle by the neck.—*adj.* **scragg'ed** (or *skragd*), scraggy.—*n.* **scragg'edness.**—*adv.* **scragg'ily.**—*n.* **scragg'iness.**—*adj.* **scragg'y**, lean, skinny, and gaunt.—**scrag'-end'**, the scrag of a neck. [Prob. **crag** (2).]

**scrag**, *skrag, n.* a stump: a rough projection.— *adjs.* **scragged, scragg'ling, scragg'ly, scragg'y,** irregular, straggling.—*adv.* **scragg'ily.**—*n.* **scragg'- iness.**—**scrag'-whale**, a whale with knobbed back. [Cf. **scrog.**]

**scraich, scraigh**, *skrāhh,* (*Scot.*) *v.i.* to screech: to make a scratchy sound.—*n.* a screech: a scratchy sound. [Cf. **scraugh, skreigh**.]

**scram**, *skram*, (*slang*) *v.i.* (usu. in the *imper.*) to be off. [Perh. **scramble**.]

**scram**, *skram*, (*S.W. England*) *adj.* puny: withered. —*v.t.* to benumb: to paralyse. [Cf. **scrimp**.]

**scramble**, *skram'bl*, *v.i.* to make one's way with disorderly struggling haste: to get along somehow: to clamber: to wriggle irregularly: to sprawl: to dash or struggle for what one can get before others.—*v.t.* to throw down to be scrambled for: to put, make, get together, scramblingly: to jumble up (a message) so that it can be read only after decoding: (of eggs) to beat up and heat to thickness with milk, butter, etc.: (of radiotelephone conversation) to make unintelligible by a device that alters frequencies. —*n.* act of scrambling: a disorderly performance: a dash or struggle for what can be had: a form of motor or motor-cycle trial.—*ns.* **scram'bler**, one who, or that which, scrambles, esp. a telephone device.—*adj.* **scram'bling**, confused and irregular. —*adv.* **scram'blingly**. [Cf. the dialect word *scramb*, to rake together with the hands.]

**scran**, *skran*, *n.* provisions: broken victuals.—**bad scran to you** (*Ir.*), bad fare to you. [Ety. dub.]

**scranch**, *skranch, skransh*, *v.t.* to crunch. [Prob. imit.; cf. Du. *schransen*, to eat heartily.]

**scrannel**, *skran'l*, *adj.* thin: meagre: squeaking: grating, scratchy (*Milt.*).—*adj.* **scrann'y**, lean: meagre.

**scrap**, *skrap*, *n.* a small fragment: a piece of leftover food: a remnant: a punched-out picture, cutting, or the like, intended or suited for preservation in a scrap-book: residue after extraction of oil from blubber, fish, etc.: metal clippings or other waste: anything discarded as worn-out, out of date, or useless.—*adj.* consisting of scrap.—*v.t.* to consign to the scrapheap: to discard:—*pr.p.* **scrapp'ing**; *pa.p.* and *pa.t.* **scrapped**.—*adv.* **scrapp'ily**.—*n.* **scrapp'iness**. —*adj.* **scrapp'y**, fragmentary: disconnected: made up of scraps.—**scrap'-book**, a blank book for pasting in scraps, cuttings, etc.; **scrap'-heap**, a place where old iron is collected: rubbish-heap; **scrap'-iron, scrap'-metal**, scraps of iron or other metal, of use only for remelting; **scrap'-man**, scrap-merchant, one who deals in scrap-metal.—**not a scrap**, not in the least; **throw on the scrap'-heap**, to reject as useless. [O.N. *skrap*, scraps; cf. **scrape**.]

**scrap**, *skrap*, (*slang*) *n.* a fight: scrimmage.—Also *v.i.*

**scrape**, *skrāp*, *v.t.* to press a sharp edge over: to move gratingly over: to smooth, clean, clear, reduce in thickness, abrade, remove, form, collect, bring, render, by such an action: to get together, collect by laborious effort (often *scrape together*, *scrape up*): to erase: contemptuously, to fiddle.—*v.i.* to graze: to scratch: to scratch the ground: to grate: to make a grating sound (as with the feet, in disapprobation): to fiddle: to draw back the foot in making obeisance: to fiddle: to save penuriously: to get with difficulty (with *through, along, home*, etc.).—*n.* an act, process, or spell of scraping: a shave: a stroke of the bow: a grating sound: a stroke (of a pen): a scraped place in the ground: an abrasion: a mass of earth scraped up, as by a rabbit: a backward movement of one foot accompanying a bow: a scraping or thin layer: thin-spread butter: a predicament that threatens disgrace or friction with authority.—*ns.* **scrap'er**, one who scrapes: a fiddler: a barber: a scraping instrument or machine, esp. for shoe-soles, hides, roads: an engraver's tool: a scratching bird; **scrap'ing**, the action of the verb: its sound: a piece scraped off.—**scrape'-good**, a miser; **scrape'-gut**, a fiddler; **scrape'-penny**, a miser; **scrap'er-board**, a clay-surface board on which drawings

can be made by scraping tints off as well a applying them: such a drawing: this method.— **bow and scrape**, to be over-obsequious; **scrape acquaintance with**, to contrive somehow to get on terms of acquaintance; **scrape the bottom of the barrel**, utilise the very last of one's resources. [O.E. *scrapian* or O.N. *skrapa*.].

**scrat**, *skrat*, (*obs.* or *dial.*) *v.t.* and *v.i.* to scratch. [M.E. *scratte*; origin doubtful.]

**scratch**, *skrach*, *v.t.* to draw a sharp point over the surface of: to hurt, mark, render, seek to allay discomfort in, by so doing: to dig or scrape with the claws: to write hurriedly: to erase or delete (usu. with *out*): to strike along a rough surface: to withdraw from a competition.—*v.i.* to use the nails or claws: to scrape: to make a grating or screechy noise: to retire from a contest or engagement: to get (along or through) somehow.—*n.* an act, mark, or sound of scratching: a slight wound: a scrawl: the line up to which boxers are led—hence test, trial, as in ' to come up to (the) scratch ': the starting-point for a competitor without handicap: one who starts from scratch: a fluke, esp. in billiards: a scratchwig: (in *pl.*) a disease in horses with the appearance of scratches on the pastern.—*adj.* improvised: casual: hastily or casually got together: without handicap.—*n.* **scratch'er**.—*adv.* **scratch'ily**.—*n.* **scratch'iness**.—*n.* and *adj.* **scratch'ing**.—*adv.* **scratch'ingly**.—*adjs.* **scratch'less; scratch'y**, like scratches: uneven: ready or likely to scratch: grating or screechy: itchy.—**scratch'-back**, a back-scratcher: a toy that makes a sound of tearing cloth; **scratch'-brush**, a wire brush; **scratch'-coat**, a first coat of plaster; **scratch'-wig**, a wig that covers only part of the head; **scratch'-work**, sgraffito in plaster.—**come up to scratch** (*fig.*), to reach an expected standard: to fulfil an obligation; **start from scratch** (*fig.*), to start at the beginning: to embark on (a task, career etc.) without any advantages or without any preparatory work having been done. [Poss. M.E. *cracchen*, to scratch, modified by **scrat**.]

**Scratch**, *skrach*, *n.* the Devil (see **Old Scratch**). [Cf. O.N. *skratte*, goblin, monster.]

**scrattle**, *skrat'l*, (*W. of England*) *v.i.* to keep scratching: to scuttle. [Freq. of **scrat**.]

**scraugh**, *skrauch*, *skröhh*, (*Scot.*) *n.* a raucous squawk.—*v.i.* to make a scraugh. [Imit.]

**scraw**, *skrö*, *n.* a thin sod. [Ir. *sgrath*.]

**scrawl**, *skröl*, *v.t.* and *v.i.* to make or write irregularly or hastily: to scribble.—*n.* irregular, hasty, or bad writing: a letter, etc., written thus: a small crab (*Lincolnshire*; *Tennyson*).—*n.* **scrawl'er**.—*n.* and *adj.* **scrawl'ing**.—*adv.* **scrawl'ingly**.—*adj.* **scrawl'y**. [Perh. conn. with **crawl** or **sprawl**.]

**scrawm**, *skröm*, (*dial.*) *v.t.* to scratch. [Prob. Du. *schrammen*, to graze.]

**scrawny**, *skröni*, (*orig. U.S.*). Same as **scranny** (see **scrannel**).

**scray**, **scraye**, *skrā*, *n.* the tern. [Cf. W. *ysgraell*.]

**screak**, *skrēk*, *v.t.* to screech: to creak.—*n.* a screech: a creak. [Cf. O.N. *skrækja*.]

**scream**, *skrēm*, *v.t.* and *v.i.* to cry out in a loud shrill voice, as in fear or pain: to laugh shrilly and uncontrolledly: to shriek.—*v.i.* (*coll.*; of colours) to be acutely inharmonious.—*n.* a shrill, sudden cry, as in fear or pain: a shriek: a loud whistling sound: anything or anyone supposed to make one scream with laughter (*coll.*).—*n.* **scream'er**, one who screams: a large spur-winged S. American bird (Palamedea, *horned screamer*; Chauna, *crested screamer*) with loud harsh cry: a different S. American bird, the seriema (also called *crested screamer*): anything likely or intended to thrill with emotion, as a sensational headline (*slang*): an exclamation mark (*slang*). —*adj.* **scream'ing**.—*adv.* **scream'ingly**.—**screaming farce**, one highly ludicrous; **screaming**

meemies (U.S. nickname for German shells in World War I), hysterical fear or wild attack of nerves. [Late O.E. *scræmen.*]

scree, *skrē, n.* sloping mass of débris at the base of a cliff. [O.N. *skritha,* a landslip—*skritha,* to slide.]

screech, *skrēch, v.i.* to give forth a harsh, shrill, and sudden cry or noise.—*v.t.* to utter in such tones.—*n.* a harsh, shrill, and sudden cry: a strident creak: a screeching or screaming bird (as barn-owl, swift, missel-thrush).—*n.* screech′er, one who screeches: the swift or other screeching bird.—*adj.* screech′y, shrill and harsh, like a screech.—screech′-hawk, the nightjar; screech′-martin, the swift; screech′-owl, the barn-owl: a bringer of bad news; screech′-thrush, the missel-thrush: the fieldfare. [M.E. *scrichen;* cf. scritch.]

screed, *skrēd, n.* a shred: a strip: a border: a long effusion, spoken or written: a drinking bout (*obs.*): a band of plaster laid on the surface of a wall as a guide to the thickness of a coat of plaster to be applied subsequently (*building*): a layer of mortar finishing off the surface of a floor: a strip of wood or metal temporarily inserted in a road surface to form a guide for the template for forming the final surface of the road (*civil engineering*): a rent, a tear (*Scot.*).—*v.t.* to repeat glibly.—*v.i.* to rend. [O.E. *scrēade,* shred.]

screen, *skrēn, n.* a shield against danger, observation, wind, heat, light, or other outside influence: a piece of room furniture in the form of a folding framework or of a panel on a stand: a clotheshorse (*Scot.*): a protection against wind on a vehicle: a large scarf: a sheltering row of trees: a body of troops or formation of ships intended as a cover: a wall masking a building: a partial partition cutting off part of a room, a church choir, or side chapel: a coarse sifting apparatus: a net-ruled plate for half-tone photography: a mosaic of primary colours for colour photography: a white sheet or the like on which images may be projected: hence, the cinematograph: a white erection against which the batsman sees the bowler (*cricket*).—*v.t.* to shelter or conceal: to sift coarsely: to sort out by, or subject to, tests of ability, desirability, etc.: to protect from stray electrical interference: to prevent from causing outside electrical interference: to project or exhibit on a screen or on the screen: to make a motion-picture of.—*v.i.* to show up on, or be suitable for, the screen.—*ns.* screen′er; screen′ing.—*n.pl.* screen′ings, material eliminated by sifting.—screen′play, the written text for a film, with dialogue, stage-directions, and descriptions of characters and setting; screen printing (see silk-screen printing); screen test, one to determine whether an actor or actress is suitable for cinema work; screen′-wiper, a contrivance for wiping the windscreen of a car in rain; screen′-writer, a writer of screenplays. [App. related in some way to O.Fr. *escran* (Fr. *écran*), which may be—O.H.G. *skirm, skerm* (Ger. *schirm*).]

screeve, *skrēv,* (*slang*) *v.t.* and *v.i.* to write, esp. begging letters: to draw on the pavement.—*n.* piece of writing: begging letter.—*ns.* screev′er; screev′ing. [Prob. It. *scrivere*—L. *scribĕre,* to write.]

screich, screigh. See skreigh.

screw, *skrōō, n.* a cylinder with a helical groove or (the *thread*) ridge, used as a fastening driven into wood, etc. by rotation (a *male screw;* for *female screw,* see female), as a mechanical power, and otherwise: anything of similar form: a screw-propeller or ship driven by one: a thumbscrew: a corkscrew: a twisted cone of paper, or portion of a commodity contained in it: a turn of the screw: pressure (*fig.*): a twist: a spin imparted to a ball: a stingy fellow, an extortioner, a skinflint (*slang*): a prison officer (*slang*): a broken-winded horse: salary, wages (*coll.*).—*v.t.* to fasten, tighten, compress, force, adjust, extort by a screw, a screwing motion, or as if by a screw: to apply a screw to: to twist: to turn in the manner of a screw: to pucker: to summon up (courage, etc.; with *up*): to have sexual intercourse with (a woman; *vulg.*): to practise extortion upon: to cheat (*slang*): to enter by means of a skeleton key (*slang*),—*v.i.* to admit of screwing: to wind: to worm.—*adj.* screwed (*slang*), tipsy.—*n.* screw′er.—*n.* and *adj.* screw′ing.—*adv.* screw′-wise.—*adj.* screwy, exacting: close: worthless: tipsy: eccentric, slightly mad: fishy, not quite normal or honest.—screw′ball (*U.S.*) a ball in baseball that breaks contrary to its swerve: a crazy person, an eccentric.—Also *adj.*—screw′-bolt, a bolt with a screw-thread.—*adj.* screw′-down, closed by screwing.—screw′driver, an instrument for turning and driving screws; screw′-nail, a nail made in the form of a screw; screw′-pile, a pile ending in a screw; screw′-pine, a plant of the genus Pandanus or its family—from the screw-like arrangement of the leaves; screw′-plate, a plate of steel with holes for cutting screw-threads; screw′-press, a press worked by a screw; screw′-propell′er, a propeller with helical blades; screw′-steam′er, a steamer driven by screw; screw′-thread, the ridge of a screw; screw′top, a bottle with a stopper that screws in, esp. a beer-bottle of the kind with its contents; screw′-wrench, a tool for gripping screw-heads;—a screw loose, something defective (esp. mentally); put on, turn, the screw, to apply pressure progressively: to exact payment; put the screws on, to coerce. [Earlier scrue; app. O.Fr. *escroue,* of obscure origin; prob. conn. with L.G. *schrûve,* Ger. *schraube.*]

scribble, *skrib′l, v.t.* to scrawl: to write badly, carelessly, or worthlessly (in handwriting or substance).—*n.* careless writing: a scrawl.—*ns.* scribb′lement; scribb′ler, a petty author; scribb′ling.—*adv.* scribb′lingly.—*adj.* scribb′ly.—scribb′ling-book, -paper. [A freq. of scribe, or L.L. *scribillāre*—L. *scribĕre,* to write.]

scribble, *skrib′l, v.t.* to card roughly.—*ns.* scribb′ler, a carding machine: one who tends it; scribb′ling. [Prob. from L.G.]

scribe, *skrib, n.* an expounder and teacher of the Mosaic and traditional law (*B.*): a writer: a public or official writer: a clerk, amanuensis, secretary: a copyist: a penman: a pointed instrument to mark lines on wood, etc.—*v.t.* to mark, score: to fit by so marking: to incise: to write.—*v.i.* to play the scribe.—*adjs.* scri′bable, capable of being written upon; scribā′cious, given to writing.—*n.* scribā′ciousness.—*adj.* scri′bal.—*n.* scri′ber, a scribing tool; scri′bing; scri′bism. [L. *scriba,* a scribe, and *scribĕre,* to write.]

scriech. See skreigh.

scriene (*Spens.*). See screen.

scrieve, *skrēv,* (*Scot.*) *v.i.* to glide swiftly along. [Prob. O.N. *skrefa*—*skref,* stride.]

scriggle, *skrig′l, v.i.* to writhe: to wriggle.—*n.* a wriggling.—*adj.* scrigg′ly. [Cf. struggle.]

scrike, *skrik,* (*Spens.*) *v.i.* to shriek.—*n.* (*obs.*) a shriek. [Prob. Scand.]

scrim, *skrim, n.* open fabric used in upholstery, bookbinding, for curtains, etc. [Ety. obscure.]

scrimmage, *skrim′ij,* scrummage, *skrum′ij, n.* a tussle: a scrum.—*v.i.* to take part in a scrimmage.—*n.* scrimm′ager, scrumm′ager. [See skirmish.]

scrimp, *skrimp, adj.* scanty: stinted.—*adv.* (*obs.*) barely.—*v.t.* to stint: to keep short.—*v.i.* to be sparing or niggardly.—*adj.* scrimped, pinched.—*adv.* scrimp′ily.—*n.* scrimp′iness.—*adv.* scrimp′ly, sparingly: scarcely.—*n.* scrimp′ness.—*adj.*

**scrimp′y**, scanty. [Cf. Sw. and Dan. *skrumpen*, shrivelled, O.E. *scrimman*, to shrink.]

**scrimshank.** Same as **skrimshank.**

**scrimshaw**, *skrim′shö*, *n*. a sailor's spare-time handicraft, as engraving fanciful designs on shells, whales' teeth, etc.: anything so executed. —Also **scrim′shander, scrim′shandy.**—*v.t.* and *v.i.* to work or decorate in this way.—*n.* **scrim′-shoner**, one who does scrimshaw. [Origin obscure.]

**scrimure**, *skrim′yər*, (*Shak.*) *n.* a fencer. [Fr. *escrimeur*.]

**scrine, scryne**, *skrin*, (*Spens.*) *n.* a chest for records: a shrine. [O.Fr. *escrin*—L. *scrinium*, a chest; cf. **shrine.**]

**scrip**, *skrip*, *n.* a writing: a scrap of paper or of writing: (for *subscription*) a preliminary certificate, as for shares allotted: share certificates, or shares or stock collectively: paper money less than a dollar (*U.S.*): a dollar bill, money (*U.S slang*).—**scrip issue**, a bonus issue. [script, subscription; partly perh. **scrap.**]

**scrip**, *skrip*, *n.* a small bag: a satchel: a pilgrim's pouch.—*n.* **scripp′age** (*Shak.*), contents of a scrip. [Cf. O.N. *skreppa*, a bag, and O.Fr. *escrep*(*p*)*e*.]

**script**, *skript*, *n.* a writing: an original document (*law*): a list of actors and their parts (*Shak.*): a text for broadcasting: handwriting, system or style of handwriting: scenario (*cinema*): handwriting in imitation of type: type in imitation of handwriting: (also 'script) short for *manuscript* or *typescript*: a set of characters used in writing a language (as *Cyrillic script*).—*v.t.* to write a script for, or make a script from, esp. for broadcasting or the theatre or cinema.—**script′writer.** [L. *scriptum*—*scrībēre*, to write.]

**scriptorium**, *skrip-tō′ri-əm*, *-tō′ri-əm*, *n.* a writing-room, esp. in a monastery:—*pl.* **scripto′ria.**— *adjs.* **scripto′rial; scrip′tory** (*-tar-i*), by, in, or relating to writing. [L. *scriptōrium*—*scrībēre*.]

**scripture**, *skrip′chər*, *n.* handwriting: something written: (in *sing.* or *pl.*) sacred writings of a religion, esp. (*cap.*) the Bible: a biblical text (*rare*).—Also *adj.*—*adj.* **scrip′tural**, of, in, warranted by Scripture: of writing.—*ns.* **scrip′-turalism**, literal adherence to the Scriptures; **scrip′turalist**, a literalist in obedience to the letter of Scripture: a student of Scripture (*obs.*).—*adv.* **scrip′turally.**—*ns.* **scrip′turism; scrip′turist**, one versed in Scripture: one who bases his belief on the Bible and the Bible alone.—**scrip′ture-read′er**, one who read the Bible in cottages, barracks, etc., to those who could not read for themselves. [L. *scriptūra*—*scrībēre*, to write.]

**scritch**, *skrich*, *n.* a screech.—*v.t.* and *v.i.* to screech.—**scritch′-owl.** [See **screech.**]

**scrive**, *skrīv*, *v.t.* to describe: to scribe.—**scrive′-board, scrieve′-board**, a shipbuilder's drawing-board.

**scrivener**, *skriv′nər*, (*obs.*) *n.* a scribe: a copyist: one who draws up contracts, etc.: one who lays out money at interest for others.—*ns.* **scriv′-enership; scriv′ening**, writing.—**scrivener's palsy**, writer's cramp. [O.Fr. *escrivain* (Fr. *écrivain*)— L.L. *scribānus*—L. *scriba*, a scribe.]

**scrobe**, *skrōb*, *n.* a grove.—*adj.* **scrobic′ulate** (*skrob-*), pitted. [L. *scrobis*, a ditch.]

**scroddled**, *skrod′ld*, *adj.* (of pottery) made of clay scraps of different colours. [Cf. L.G. *schrodel*, scrap.]

**scrofula**, *skrof′ū-lə*, *n.* tuberculosis, esp of the lymphatic glands, called also king's evil.—*adj.* **scrof′ulous.** [L. *scrōfulae*—*scrōfa*, a sow (supposed to be liable to it).]

**scrog**, *skrog*, (*Scot.*) *n.* a stunted bush or small tree: a crab-apple, fruit or tree: a bushy place: scrubby wood: a broken branch: a branch (*her.*).—*adj.* **scrogg′ie, scrogg′y**, covered with scrogs: stunted.—**scrog′-apple; scrog′-bush (-buss).** [Origin obscure.]

**scroll**, *skrōl*, *n.* a roll of paper, parchment, etc.: a ribbon-like strip, partly coiled or curved, often bearing a motto: a writing in the form of a roll: a rough draft: a schedule: a spiral ornament or part: a flourish to a signature representing a seal (*U.S.*).—*v.t.* to set in a scroll: to draft.—*v.i.* to curl.—*adj.* **scrolled**, formed into a scroll: ornamented with scrolls.—*ns.* **scroll′ery, scroll′work**, ornament in scrolls.—*adv.* **scroll′wise.**—**scroll′-saw**, a saw for cutting scrolls. [Earlier **scrowl(e)**, formed (perh. as dim.) from **scrow.**]

**scrooge.** See **scrouge.**

**Scrooge**, *skrōōj*, *n.* a miser. [From Ebenezer Scrooge in Dickens's *Christmas Carol.*]

**scroop**, *skrōōp*, *n.* a scraping noise.—*v.i.* to make a scroop. [Imit.]

**Scrophularia**, *skrof-ū-lā′ri-ə*, *n.* the figwort genus, giving name to the **Scrophulariaceae** (*-lar-i-ā′si-ē*), a family of sympetalous dicotyledons with zygomorphic flowers, including foxglove, mullein, speedwell, eyebright.—*adj.* **scro‚hulariā′ceous.** [L. *scrōfulae*, as reputedly cure for scrofula (*q.v.*)]

**scrotum**, *skrō′təm*, *n.* the bag that contains the testicles.—*adj.* **scrō′tal.** [L. *scrōtum.*]

**scrouge**, *skrowdge, skrowj*, **scrooge**, *skrōōj*, *v.t.* and *v.i.* to squeeze: to crowd.—*n.* **scroug′er** (*U.S.*), a whopper: something large. [Cf. **scruze.**]

**scrounge**, *skrownj*, (orig. *mil. slang*) *v.t.* to purloin: to cadge.—*v.i.* to hunt around: to sponge.—*ns.* **scroung′er; scroung′ing.** [Origin doubtful.]

**scrow**, *skrō*, *n.* a scroll: a writing: a hide clipping. [A.Fr. *escrowe*; see **escroll, escrow, scroll.**]

**scrowl, scrowle**, *skrōl*, old spellings of **scroll.**

**scrowdge.** See **scrouge.**

**scroyle**, *skroil*, (*Shak.*) *n.* a wretch. [Origin doubtful.]

**scrub**, *skrub*, *v.t.* to rub hard: to wash by hard rubbing with a stiff brush: to purify (*gasmaking*): to cancel (*slang*).—*v.i.* to use a scrubbing-brush: to drudge: to make a rapid to-and-fro movement as if with a scrubbing-brush:— *pr.p.* **scrubb′ing;** *pa.t.* and *pa.p.* **scrubbed.**—*n.* an act of scrubbing: a worn or short-bristled brush or broom: a drudge.—*ns.* **scrubb′er**, one who scrubs: apparatus for freeing gas from tar, ammonia, and sulphuretted hydrogen: an unattractive woman (*slang*); **scrubb′ing.**— **scrubb′ing-board**, a washing-board; **scrubb′ing-brush**, a brush with short stiff bristles for scrubbing floors, etc.—**scrub round** (*slang*), to cancel: to ignore. [Perh. obs. Du. *schrubben*, or a corresponding lost O.E. word.]

**scrub**, *skrub*, *n.* a stunted tree: stunted trees and shrubs collectively: brushwood: country covered with bushes or low trees, esp. the Australian evergreen xerophytic dwarf forest or bush of Eucalyptus, Acacia, etc.: an undersized or inferior animal, esp. one of indefinite breed: a player in a second or inferior team: a team of inferior players, or one with too few players: an insignificant or mean person: anything small or mean.—*adj.* **mean:** insignificant: undersized: (of a team) improvised, hastily got together for the occasion: (of a player) in a second or inferior team.—*adj.* **scrubb′ed** (*Shak.*), stunted.—*n.* **scrubb′er** (*Austr.*), an animal that has run wild.—*adj.* **scrubb′y**, stunted: covered with scrub: mean.—**scrub′-bird**, an Australian bird (Atrichomis) akin to the lyre-bird; **scrub′-rider**, one who looks for cattle that stray into the scrub; **scrub′-turkey**, a mound-bird; **scrub′-ty‚phus**, a typhus-like disease transmitted by a mite. [A variant of **shrub.**]

**scruff**, *skruf*, *n.* the nape of the neck. [See **scuft.**]

**scruff**, *skruf*, *n.* scurf: an untidy, dirty person (*coll.*).—*n.* **scruff′iness.**—*adj.* **scruff′y**, scurvy: untidy, dirty (*coll.*). [scurf.]

**scrum**, *skrum*, *n.* a scrimmage: a closing-in of rival forwards round the ball on the ground, or in readiness for its being inserted (by the scrum-half) between the two compact pushing masses (*Rugby*).—*v.i.* to form a scrum.—**scrum'-half** (*Rugby*), a half-back whose duty it is to put the ball into the scrum and secure it as soon as it emerges therefrom. [Abbreviation of **scrummage**; see **scrimmage, skirmish**.]

**scrump, skrump, skrimp,** *skrump, skrimp,* (*dial.*) *v.t.* to shrivel up: to gather windfalls, hence to raid orchards.—*n.* anything shrivelled, small or undersized, esp. an apple: an undersized person.—*n.* **scrump'y,** cider made from small, sweet apples. [Origin obscure.]

**scrumptious,** *skrump'shəs,* (*slang*) *adj.* delightful: delicious.—Also **scrumm'y.**—*adv.* **scrump'tiously.** [Origin uncertain.]

**scrunch, skrunch, skrunsh,** variant of **crunch.**—*adj.* **scrunch'y.**

**scrunt, skrunt,** (*Scot.*) *n.* anything stunted (as an apple, a tree) or worn: a niggard.—*adj.* **scrunt'y.**

**scruple,** *skrōō'pl, n.* a small weight—in apothecaries' weight, 20 grains: a sexagesimal division, as a minute of time or arc (*obs.*): a very small quantity: a difficulty or consideration, usu. moral, obstructing action, esp. one turning on a fine point or one that is baseless: a doubt, disbelief, or difficulty: protest, demur: scrupulousness.—*v.i.* to hesitate from a scruple.—*v.t.* to cause to feel scruples (*obs.*): to question, doubt (*arch.*): to have scruples about (*arch.* when followed by noun, but current followed by infinitive).—*ns.* **scru'pler; scrupulosity** (*-pū-los'i-ti*).—*adj.* **scru'pulous,** directed by scruples: having scruples, doubts, or objections: conscientious: cautious: exact: captious.—*adv.* **scru'pulously.**—*n.* **scru'pulousness.**—make no **scruple(s), make scruples, about** (formerly **to, at**), to offer (no) moral objections to. [L. *scrūpulus,* dim. of *scrūpus,* a sharp stone, anxiety.]

**scrutiny,** *skrōō'ti-ni, n.* a vote by poll: close, careful, or minute investigation or examination: a searching look: official examination of votes: examination of the catechumens (*hist.*).—*adj.* **scru'table,** accessible to scrutiny.—*ns.* **scrutā'tor,** a close examiner: a scrutineer; **scrutineer',** one who makes a scrutiny, esp. of votes.—*v.t.* and *v.i.* **scru'tinise, -ize,** to examine closely.—*n.* **scru'tiniser, -z-.**—*adj.* **scru'tinising.**—*adv.* **scru'tinisingly.**—*adj.* **scru'tinous.**—*adv.* **scru'tinously.**—**scrutin-de-liste** (*skrü-tē-də-lēst*; Fr.), a method of voting for the French Chamber of Deputies, in which the voter casts his ballot for any combination of the whole number of candidates for the department—opp. to **scrutin d'arrondissement** (*dar-ɔ̃-dēs-mã*), in which method he votes only for his local candidates. [L. *scrūtinium,* and *scrūtāri,* to search even to the rags—*scrūta,* rags, trash.]

**scruto,** *skrōō'tō, n.* a kind of stage trap-door. [Origin obscure.]

**scrutoire,** *skrōō-twär', -tōr', -tör', n.* Same as **escritoire.**

**scruze, skrōōz,** (*Spens.;* now *dial.*) *v.t.* to squeeze. [Perh. screw combined with **squeeze**.]

**scry, skrī,** *v.t.* to descry (*arch.* and *dial.*).—*v.i.* to practise crystal-gazing:—*pr.p.* **scry'ing;** *pa.t.* and *pa.p.* **scried,** (*Spens.*) **scryde.**—*ns.* **scry'er; scry'ing.** [Aphetic for **descry**.]

**scryne** (*Spens.*). Same as **scrine.**

**scuba,** *skōō'bə, skū', n.* a device used by skin-divers.—Also *adj.* [self-contained underwater breathing apparatus.]

**scuchin, scuchion,** Spenserian forms of **scutcheon.**

**scud,** *skud, v.i.* to sweep along easily and swiftly: to drive before the wind.—*v.t.* to traverse swiftly:—*pr.p.* **scudd'ing;** *pa.t.* and *pa.p.* **scudd'ed.**—*n.* act of scudding: driving cloud, shower or spray: a gust: a swift runner (*school slang*).—*n.* **scudd'er.**—*v.t.* **scudd'le,** to scuttle. [Perh. Du. or L.G.]

**scud,** *skud,* (*Scot.*) *v.t.* to slap, spank.—*n.* a slap: (in *pl.*) a spanking.

**scuddaler, scudler.** Same as **skudler.**

**scudo,** *skōō'dō, n.* an old Italian silver coin:—*pl.* **scu'di** (*-dē*). [It.,—L. *scūtum,* a shield.]

**scuff,** *skuf, n.* a form of **scruff** or **scuft.**

**scuff,** *skuf, v.t.* and *v.i.* to shuffle: to brush, graze, touch lightly: to abrade: to make or become shabby by wear.—*v.t.* to cuff.—*n.* (*Scot.*) a glancing touch or blow or its sound.—*adv.* with a scuff.—*v.i.* **scuff'le,** to struggle confusedly: to shuffle.—*v.t.* to hoe, scarify: to shuffle.—*n.* a confused struggle: a thrust-hoe: an agricultural scuffler.—*n.* **scuff'ler,** one who scuffles: an implement for scarifying the soil.—*adj.* **scuff'y** (*Scot.*), shabby: rubbed, abraded: with the sound of a light rubbing. [Cf. Sw. *skuffa,* to shove; Du. *schoffelen;* **shove, shovel, shuffle**.]

**scuft,** *skuft,* (*dial.*) *n.* the nape of the neck.—Also **scuff, scruff.** [Poss. O.N. *skopt, skoft,* the hair.]

**scug.** See **skug** (1).

**scul, scull, sculle,** *skul,* (*Shak., Milt.*) *n. obs.* spellings of **school** (of fish).

**sculdudd(e)ry, skulduddery,** *skul-dud'(ə-)ri,* (*Scot., facet.*) *n.* breach of chastity: bawdy talk or writing.—*adj.* **bawdy.**—*n.* **skulduggery** (*-dug'*), (perh. a different word) underhand malpractices. [Origin obscure.]

**sculk, scull,** obs. spellings of **skulk, skull.**

**scull,** *skul, n.* a short, light spoon-bladed oar for one hand: an oar used over the stern: a sculling-boat (*obs.*): a sculler (*obs.*): an act or spell of sculling.—*v.t.* to propel with sculls, or with one oar worked like a screw over the stern.—*v.i.* to use sculls.—*ns.* **scull'er,** one who sculls: a small boat pulled by one man with a pair of sculls; **scull'ing;—scull'ing-boat.** [Origin obscure.]

**scull, skull,** *skul, n.* a shallow basket for fish, etc. [Poss. O.N. *skjöla,* pail.]

**scull(e).** See **scul.**

**scullery,** *skul'ər-i, n.* a room for rough kitchen work, as cleaning of utensils.—**scull'ery-maid.** [O.Fr. *escuelerie*—L. *scutella,* a tray.]

**scullion,** *skul'yən, n.* a servant for drudgery.—*adj.* base. [Poss. O.Fr. *escouillon,* a dish-clout—L. *scōpa,* a broom; or from Fr. *souillon,* scullion, influenced by **scullery**.]

**sculp, skulp,** *v.t.* and *v.i.* to carve: to engrave: to sculpture. [L. *sculpěre;* not a back-formation from **sculptor, sculpture**.]

**sculpin,** *skul'pin, n.* the dragonet: a marine Cottus or other large-headed, spiny, useless fish (*U.S.*): a good-for-nothing person or animal (*slang*). [Poss. **scorpaena**.]

**sculpsit,** *skulp'sit, skōōlp'sit, v.* (he) sculptured (this). [L.]

**sculpt, skulpt,** *v.t.* and *v.i.* to sculpture: to carve. [Fr. *sculpter*—L. *sculpěre,* to carve; not, as commonly thought, a back-formation from **sculptor, sculpture**.]

**sculptor,** *skulp'tər, n.* an artist in carving: a statuary:—*fem.* **sculp'tress.**—*adj.* **sculp'tural** (*-chər-əl*).—*adv.* **sculp'turally.**—*n.* **sculp'ture,** the act of carving, esp. in stone: extended to clay-modelling or moulding for casting: work, or a piece of work, in this kind: engraving (*obs.*): shaping in relief: spines, ridges, etc., standing out from the surface (*biol.*).—*v.t.* to carve: to represent in sculpture: to shape in relief: to mark with sculpturings: to mould, or form, so as to have the appearance, or (*fig.*) other quality, of sculpture: to modify the form of (the earth's surface).—*adjs.* **sculp'tured,** carved: engraved: (of features) fine and regular: having elevations on the surface (*bot., zool.*); **sculpturesque',** statue-like.—*n.* **sculp'turing.** [L. *sculptor, -ōris, sculptūra*—*sculpěre, sculptum,* to carve.]

**scum, skum,** *n.* foam or froth: matter coming to or floating on the surface: offscourings or refuse population (*fig.*).—*v.t.* to skim.—*v.i.* to form, throw up a scum:—*pr.p.* scumm′ing; *pa.t.* and *pa.p.* scummed.—*n.* scumm′er, a skimming instrument.—*n.pl.* scumm′ings, skimmings.—*adj.* scumm′y. [Cf. Dan. *skum*, Ger. *schaum*, foam.]

scumber, *skum′bər*, *v.t.* and *v.i.* to defecate (of dog or fox).—*n.* dung.—Also skumm′er. [Prob. O.Fr. *descumbrer*, to disencumber.]

scumble, *skum′bl*, *v.t.* to soften the effect of by a very thin coat of opaque or semi-opaque colour, or by light rubbing.—*n.* colour so laid: the effect so produced.—*n.* scum′bling. [Freq. of scum.]

scumfish. Same as scomfish.

scuncheon, sconcheon, scontion, *skun′*, *skon′shən*, *n.* the inner part of a jamb. [O.Fr. *escoinson*.]

scunner, *skun′ər*, (*Scot.*) *v.i.* to take a loathing.—*v.t.* to excite a loathing in: to disgust, nauseate.—*n.* a loathing: an object, or a manifestation, of loathing. [Perh. M.E. *scurn*, to shrink; origin unknown.]

scup, *skup*, scuppaug, *skup′ŏg*, or *-ŏg′*, *ns.* the porgy. [Narraganset *mishcuppauog*.]

scupper, *skup′ər*, *n.* a hole to drain a ship's deck. [Origin disputed.]

scupper, *skup′ər*, (*slang*) *v.t.* to slaughter: to do for: to ruin. [Perh. conn. with above.]

scuppernong, *skup′ər-nong*, *n.* a grape from the *Scuppernong* river, N. Carolina: wine from it.

scur, *skŭr*. Same as skirr.

scurf, *skûrf*, *n.* small flakes or scales of dead skin, esp. on the scalp: a crust of branny scales: an incrustation.—*n.* scurf′iness.—*adj.* scurf′y. [O.E. *scurf*, *sceorf*.]

scurril(e), *skur′il*, (*arch.*) *adj.* like or worthy of a vulgar buffoon: indecently opprobrious or jocular.—*n.* scurril′ity.—*adj.* scurr′ilous, scurril.—*adv.* scurr′ilously.—*n.* scurr′ilousness. [L. *scurrilis*—*scurra*, a buffoon.]

scurriour, scurrier, *skur′i-ər*, (*obs.*) *n.* a scout. [See discoverer.]

scurry, skurry, *skur′i*, *v.i.* to hurry briskly or flutteringly: to scuttle.—*n.* flurried haste: a flurry. [From hurry-skurry, reduplication of hurry; or back-formation of scurrier; or from scour.]

scurvy, *skûr′vi*, *adj.* scurfy: shabby: vile, contemptible.—*n.* a disease marked by bleeding and sponginess of the gums, due to lack of fresh vegetables and consequently of vitamin C.—*adv.* scur′vily, in a scurvy manner: meanly, basely.—*n.* scur′viness—scur′vy-grass, a cruciferous plant (*Cochlearia officinalis*) used by sailors as an anti-scorbutic: ale medicated with it. [scurf; the application to the disease helped by similarity of sound; see scorbutic.]

scuse, ’scuse, *skūs*, *n.* and *skūz*, *v.t.* aphetic for excuse.

scut, *skut*, *n.* a short erect tail like a hare's: a hare. [Origin obscure.]

scutage, *skū′tij*, *n.* a tax on a knight's fee, esp. one in lieu of personal service. [L.L. *scūtāgium*—L. *scūtum*, shield.]

scutch, *skuch*, *v.t.* to dress (e.g. flax) by beating: to switch.—*n.* a swingle: a bricklayer's cutting tool.—*ns.* scutch′er, a person, tool, or part of a machine that scutches: the striking part of a threshing-mill; scutch′ing. [Prob. O.Fr. *escousser*, to shake off.]

scutcheon, *skuch′ən*, *n.* an aphetic form of escutcheon.

scute, *skūt*, *n.* a scutum: an écu: a dermal plate.—*adjs.* scūt′al; scūt′ate, protected by scutes: buckler-shaped; scūt′iform.—*ns.* scūt′iger (*jocular*), a squire; scūt′um, the oblong shield of Roman heavy-armed infantry (*hist.*): a scute: the second tergal plate of a segment of an insect's thorax:—*pl.* scūt′a. [L. *scūtum*, a shield.]

scutellum, *skūt-el′əm*, *n.* a scale of a bird's foot: the third tergal plate of a segment of an insect's thorax: a structure, supposed to be the cotyledon,

by which a grass embryo absorbs the endosperm:—*pl.* scūtell′a.—*adjs.* scūtell′ar, of a scutellum; scūt′ellate.—*n.* scūtellā′tion, scale arrangement. [L. *scutella*, a tray, dim. of *scutra*, a platter, confused in scientific use with *scūtulum*, dim. of *scūtum*, a shield.]

scutter, *skut′ər*, *v.i.* to run hastily: to scurry.—*n.* a hasty run. [A variant of scuttle (3).]

scuttle, *skut′l*, *n.* a shallow basket: a vessel for holding coal.—*n.* scutt′leful. [O.E. *scutel*—L. *scutella*, a tray.]

scuttle, *skut′l*, *n.* an opening in a ship's deck or side: its lid: a shuttered hole in a wall, roof, etc.: its shutter or trap-door.—*v.t.* to make a hole in, esp. in order to sink: to destroy, ruin. scutt′le-butt (in U.S. scutt′lebutt), a cask with a hole cut in it for drinking-water (also scuttlecask): a drinking fountain on a ship (*U.S.*): rumour, gossip (*U.S.*). [O.Fr. *escoutille*, hatchway.]

scuttle, *skut′l*, *v.i.* to dash with haste.—*n.* an act of scuttling.—*n.* scutt′ler. [scuddle.]

scybalum, *sib′ə-ləm*, *n.* a hard fecal mass in the intestine:—*pl.* scyb′ala.—*adj.* scyb′alous. [Latinised from Gr. *skybalon*, dung.]

scye, *sī*, *n.* an opening for insertion of a sleeve. [Origin obscure.]

Scylla, *sil′ə*, *n.* a six-headed monster who sat over a dangerous rock opposite Charybdis. [Gr. *Skylla*.]

scyphus, *sīf′əs*, *n.* a large Greek drinking-cup (*ant.*): a cup-shaped structure:—*pl.* scyph′i.—*n.* scyphis′toma, the segmenting polyp stage of a jellyfish (Gr. *stoma*, mouth).—*ns.pl.* Scyphomedū′sae, Scyphozō′a, the jellyfishes as a class. [Gr. *skyphos*, cup.]

scytale, *sit′ə-lē*, *n.* a Spartan secret writing on a strip wound about a stick, unreadable without a stick of like thickness. [Gr. *skytalē*, a staff.]

scythe, *sīdh*, *n.* an instrument with a large curved blade for mowing: a blade attached to a war-chariot wheel.—*v.t.* and *v.i.* to mow with a scythe.—*adj.* scythed, armed or cut with scythes.—*n.* scyth′er, one who uses a scythe.—scythe′-man, scyther; scythe′-stone, a whet for scythes. [O.E. *sīthe*; cf. O.N. *sigthr*, Ger. *sense*.]

Scythian, *sith′i-ən*, *adj.* of Scythia, an ancient country N. and E. of the Black Sea, of its nomadic people or of their language.—*n.* a member of the people: the language of Scythia.—Scythian lamb, barometz.

’sdeath, *zdeth*, (*obs.*) *interj.* an exclamation of impatience—for *God's death*.

sdeigne, sdein, sdaine, sdayn, *zdān*, (*Spens.*, *Milt.*) *v.t.* and *v.i.* to disdain.—*adj.* sdeign′full.—*adv.* sdeign′fully. [It. *sdegnare*, aphetic for *disdegnare*; or Eng. disdain.]

sdrucciola, *zdrōōt′chō-la*, *adj.* (of rhyme) triple. [It., slippery.]

sea, *sē*, *n.* the great mass of salt water covering the greater part of the earth's surface: the ocean: any great expanse of water: a great (esp. salt) lake—mainly in proper names: swell or roughness: a great wave: the tide: a wide expanse.—*adj.* marine.—*adj.* sea′-like, like the sea.—*adv.* in the manner of the sea.—*adj.*, *adv.* sea′ward, towards the (open) sea.—*n.* seaward side, direction or position.—*adj.*, *adv.* sea′wardly.—*adv.* sea′wards.—sea′-ā′corn, an acorn-shell; sea′-add′er, a pipefish: a marine stickleback; sea′-air′, the air at sea or by the sea; sea′-an′chor, a floating anchor used in a gale; sea′-anem′one, a solitary soft-bodied polyp of the Zoantharia; sea′-ape, the sea-otter: the thresher shark: a manatee; sea′-bank, the sea-shore: an embankment to keep out the sea; sea′-bass (*-bas*), a perch-like marine fish of various kinds, especially of the Serranidae and the Sciaenidae; sea′-bat, a name for various fishes with long or outspread fins; sea′-bā′ther;

sea'-bā'thing; sea'-beach, a strip of sand, gravel, etc., bordering the sea; sea'-bean', the cacoon (Entada) or other foreign seed cast up by the sea: a mollusc's operculum, worn as an amulet; sea'-bear, the polar bear: the fur-seal; sea'-beast.—*adjs.* sea'-beat, -en, lashed by the waves.
—sea'-beet, wild beet; sea'berry, Halorhagis; sea'-bird, any marine bird; sea'-bis'cuit, ship-biscuit; sea'-blite, a salt-marsh plant (*Suaeda maritima*) of the goosefoot family; sea'-blubb'er, a jellyfish —*adj.* sea'-blue, blue like the sea.—sea'board, the country bordering the sea. —Also *adj.*—sea'-boat, a craft considered with reference to her behaviour in bad weather.—*adjs.* sea'-born, produced by the sea; sea'borne, carried on the sea.—sea'-bottle, a translucent inflated seaweed (Valonia): bladderwrack; sea'-bott'om, the floor of the sea; sea'-boy (*Shak.*), a sailor-boy; sea'-breach, an inroad of the sea; sea'-bream, any fish of the Sparidae, a family of spiny-finned fishes, with teeth of the character of incisors and molars: any fish of the Bramidae, a family akin to the mackerels; sea'-breeze, a breeze from the sea, esp. owing to convection in the daytime; sea'-buck'thorn, a willow-like seaside shrub (*Hippophae rhamnoides*) of the family Eleagnaceae; sea'-bun, a heart-urchin; sea'-bur'dock, clotbur (Xanthium); sea'-butt'er-fly, a pteropod; sea'-calf, the common seal; sea'-canā'ry, the white whale; sea'-cap (*Shak.*), a cap worn on shipboard; sea'-captain, the captain of a merchant ship; sea'-card, a compass card: a sea-chart; sea'-cat, a catfish: a weaver-fish: also other sea creatures; sea'-change, a change effected by the sea (*Shak.*): a transformation; sea'-chart, a chart of the sea, its coasts, etc.; sea'-chest, a seaman's trunk; sea'-cliff, a cliff fronting or formed by the sea; sea'-coal (*arch.*), coal in the ordinary sense, not charcoal (possibly as first worked where exposed by the sea).—Also *adj.*—sea'coast, the land adjacent to the sea; sea'-cob, a seagull; sea'-cock, a gurnard: a valve communicating with the sea through a vessel's hull: a bold mariner or sea rover; sea'-cole'wort, sea-kale: wild cabbage; sea'-cook, a ship's cook (by sailors supposed to disgrace his son); sea'-cow, the walrus: rhytina (Steller's sea-cow) or other sirenian: the hippopotamus (*S.Afr.*; Du. *zeekoe*); sea'craft, skill in navigation: seamanship: seagoing craft; sea'-craw'fish, -cray'fish, a spiny lobster; sea'-crow, a name of many birds, as skua, chough, cormorant; sea'-cū'cumber, a holothurian (as trepang, bêche-de-mer); sea'-dace, the bass; sea'-dev'il, a devil dwelling in the sea: a devilfish; sea'-dog, the seal: a dogfish: an old sailor: a pirate: a beast like a talbot with dorsal fin and beaver's tail (*her.*); sea'-dott'erel, the turnstone; sea'-dove, the little auk; sea'-drag'on, the dragonet: the fish Pegasus: an Australian leafy-seahorse; sea'drome, a floating aerodrome; sea'-duck, any duck of the pochard group; sea'-dust, dust from distant land falling at sea; sea'-ea'gle, erne or other Haliaetus: the eagle-ray; sea'-ear, an earshell (Haliotis); sea'-eel, a conger; sea'-egg, a sea-urchin; sea'-el'ephant, the elephant-seal; sea'-fan, an alcyonarian coral with fan-like skeleton; sea'farer, a traveller by sea, usu. a sailor; sea'fāring.—Also *adj.*—sea'-feath'er, a feathery alcyonarian, sea-pen; sea'-fight, a battle between ships at sea; sea'-fir, a sertularian colony; sea'-fire, phosphorescence at sea; sea'-fish, any saltwater or marine fish; sea'-fish'er; sea'-fish'ing; sea'-floor, the bottom of the sea; sea'-foam, the froth of the sea; sea'-fog, a fog coming from the sea; sea'-folk, seafaring people; sea'food, food got from the sea, esp. shellfish; sea'fowl, a sea-bird; sea'-fox, the thresher, or fox-shark; sea'-fret, fog coming in off the sea; sea'front, the side of the land, of a town, or of a building that looks towards the sea: a promenade with its buildings fronting the sea; sea'-froth, the foam of the sea; sea'-fur'below, a brown seaweed (Saccorhiza) with a bulb of tentacular outgrowths above the primary holdfast; sea'-gate, a seaward gate of a tidal basin, etc.: an outlet to the sea; sea'-gill'iflower, thrift; sea'-gin'ger, millepore coral; sea'-gir'dle, tangle, esp. *Laminaria digitata.*—*adj.* sea'-girt, surrounded by sea —sea'-god, -godd'ess, a god, goddess, ruling over or dwelling in the sea.—*adj.* sea'-going, sailing on the deep sea: suitable for deep-sea voyage.—sea'-goose'berry, a common ctenophore like a gooseberry in shape; sea'-gown (*Shak.*), a short-sleeved garment worn at sea; sea'-grape, any plant of the genus Ephedra, or its fruit: seaside-grape: glasswort: gulf-weed: (in *pl.*) cuttlefish eggs in masses; sea'-grass, a grass or grasslike plant growing by or in the sea—Enteromorpha, thrift, grasswrack, etc.; sea'-green, green like the sea. —Also *adj.*—Also sea'-water-green (*Shak.*).—sea'gull, a gull: a dock-labourer not yet admitted to a union (*N.Z.*); sea'-haar, a haar (*q.v.*); sea'-hare, a tectibranch gasteropod (Aplysia) with ear-like tentacles; sea'-hawk, a skua; sea'-heath', a wiry heath-like pink-flowered plant (Frankenia) of salt-marshes and chalk-cliffs; sea'-hedge'hog, a sea-urchin: a globe-fish; sea'-hog, a porpoise; sea'-holl'y, eryngo; sea'horse, the fabulous hippocampus: Hippocampus or kindred fish: the walrus: the hippopotamus (*obs.*); sea'-hound, dogfish; sea'-ice'.—*adj.* sea'-island, (of cotton) of the kind grown on the islands off the coast of South Carolina.—sea'-jell'y, a jellyfish; sea'-kale, a fleshy glaucous cruciferous seaside plant (*Crambe maritima*) cultivated for its blanched sprouts; sea'-king, a king of the merfolk: Poseidon or Neptune: a viking chief; sea'-lane, a navigable passage between islands, ships, icefloes, etc.; sea'-lark, a name for various shore-birds, as sandpipers: the rock-pipit; sea'-lav'ender, a plumbaginaceous genus (Statice) of salt-marsh plants; sea'-law, maritime law, esp. mediaeval customary law; sea'-law'yer, a captious sailor: a sha⁻rk; sea'-legs, ability to walk on a ship's deck when it is pitching: resistance to seasickness; sea'-lem'on, shell-less mollusc (fam. Dorididae) with smooth yellow body; sea'-len'til, gulf-weed; sea'-leop'ard, a spotted seal of the southern seas: wolf-fish skin; sea'-lett'er, -brief, a document of description that used to be given to a ship at the port where she was fitted out; sea'-lett'uce, a seaweed (Ulva) with flat translucent green fronds—green laver; sea'-lev'el, the mean level of the surface of the sea.—sea'-lil'y, a crinoid; sea'-line, a coastline: a sea-horizon: a line for sounding or fishing in deep water; sea'-lion, a seal with external ears and with hind flippers turned forward (usu. excluding the sea-bears or fur-seals): a lion with the tail of a fish (*her.*); sea'-loach, a rockling; sea'-loch (*Scot.*), a lakelike arm of the sea; sea'-long'-worm, a long nemertean (Lineus); sea'-lord, a naval member of the Board of Admiralty; sea'-lungs, a ctenophoran; sea'-maid, a mermaid (*Shak.*): a sea-nymph; sea'man, a sailor: a man other than an officer or apprentice, employed aboard ship: a merman.—*adjs.* sea'man-like, showing good seamanship; sea'manly, characteristic of a seaman.—sea'manship, the art of handling ships at sea; sea'-marge, the margin of the sea; sea'mark, a mark of tidal limit: any object serving as a guide to those at sea: a signal of danger; sea'-mat, hornwrack (Flustra), a common polyzoan like a flat horny seaweed; sea'-maw (now *Scot.*), a sea-mew; sea'-mew, any gull; sea'-mile, a geographical

or nautical mile; sea'-milk'wort, Glaux; sea'-mon'ster, any huge marine animal, esp. fabulous; sea'-moss, carrageen: seaweed: a polyzoan; sea'-mount, sea'mount, a mountain under the sea; sea'-mouse, an elliptical polychaet (Aphrodite) covered with iridescent silky hairs; sea'-nett'le, a jellyfish; sea'-nymph, a minor sea-goddess; sea'-on'ion, the officinal squill; sea'-or'ach(e), any seaside species of orach; sea'-or'ange, a large globose orange-coloured holothurian; sea'-ott'er, a N. Pacific animal (Enhydris) akin to the true otters: its silvery brown fur, now very rare; sea'-owl', the lumpsucker; sea'-parr'ot, a puffin; sea'-pass, a neutral ship's passport in wartime; sea'-pass'age, a journey by sea; sea'-path' (Milt.), a way that a fish may take; sea'-pay', pay for actual service on a ship in commission; sea'-pen', a feather-like alcyonarium (Pennatula or kindred form): a squid's internal shell; sea'-perch, a bass or other fish of the Serranidae; sea'-pie, a sailor's dish made of salt meat, vegetables, and dumplings baked: the oyster-catcher; sea'-piece, a picture representing a scene at sea; sea'-pig', a porpoise: a dolphin: a dugong; sea'-pike', a pike-like marine fish of various kinds—robalo, belone, hake, etc.; sea'-pink, thrift; sea'plane, an aeroplane with floats instead of landing-wheels; sea'plane-carr'ier, a ship that carries seaplanes; sea'-poach'er, the pogge; sea'-por'cupine, the globe-fish (Diodon); sea'port, a port or harbour on the sea: a place with such a harbour; sea'-power, a nation strong at sea: naval strength; sea'-purse, a mermaid's purse; sea'-purs'lane (see purslane) sea'quake, a seismic disturbance at sea; seaqua'rium (see oceanarium); sea'-răn'ger, in the Girl Guide organisation a ranger who trains specially in seamanship and the like; sea'rat, a pirate; sea'-reed, marram-grass; sea'-risk, hazard of injury or loss by sea; sea'-road, a route followed by ships; sea'-robb'er, a pirate; sea'-rob'in, an American fish (esp. Prionotus) of the gurnard family, with red or brown colouring; sea'-rock'et, fleshy cruciferous seaside plant (Cakile); sea'-room, space to manoeuvre a ship safely; sea'-rose'mary (U.S.), sea-lavender; sea'-rō'ver, a pirate; sea'-rō'ving, piracy; sea'-salm'on, inaptly, coalfish, pollack; sea'-salt', salt got from sea-water.—adj. salt as the sea.—sea'-sand', sands of the seashore; sea'satyre (Spens.), a sea-monster of some kind; sea'scape, a sea-piece; sea'-scor'pion, scorpion-fish: a father-lasher (Cottus scorpius); Sea'-Scout, a member of a marine branch of the (Boy) Scouts; sea'-scout'ing; sea'-serp'ent, an enormous marine animal of serpent-like form, frequently seen and described by credulous sailors, imaginative landsmen, and common liars: a sea-snake; sea'-ser'vice, service on board ship; sea'shell, a marine shell; sea'shore', the land immediately adjacent to the sea: the foreshore (law).—adj. sea'-should'ring (Spens.), having shoulders that displace the seas.—sea'-shrub', a sea-fan.—adj. sea'sick', sick owing to the rolling of a vessel at sea: travel-worn (Shak.).—seasick'ness; sea'-side, the neighbourhood of the sea.—Also adj. —sea'side-grape', the grape-tree (Coccoloba) or its fruit; sea'-sleeve', a cuttlefish; sea'-slug, a nudibranch: a holothurian; sea'-snail, any snail-like marine gasteropod: an unctuous fish (Liparis) akin to the lumpsucker; sea'-snake, a snake that lives in the sea, esp. of the very venomous family Hydrophidae of the Indian and Pacific oceans: the sea-serpent; sea'-snipe, a sandpiper: the snipe-fish; sea'-sol'dier, a marine; sea'-sorr'ow (Shak.), afflictions at sea; sea'-spi'der, a pycnogonid; sea'-squirt, an ascidian; sea'-star', a starfish; sea'-stick, a herring cured at sea; sea'-stock, fresh provisions for use at sea; sea'-storm'; sea'-strand'; sea'-sur'geon, a tropical genus (Acanthurus) of spiny-finned fishes with a lancet-like spine ensheathed on each side of the tail; sea'-swall'ow, a tern: the storm petrel: a flying-fish.—adj. (Shak.) sea'-swall'ow'd.—sea'-swine, a porpoise: the ballan-wrasse; sea'-tang, -tan'gle, tangle; sea'-term, a nautical word.—adj. sea(s)'-tost (Shak.). —sea'-trout, the salmon-trout (Salmo trutta), or its variety the bull-trout (var. eriox): extended to various other fishes in U.S. and Australia; sea'-turn, a gale from the sea; sea'-tur'tle, a marine turtle: a black guillemot; sea'-ū'nicorn, the narwhal; sea'-ur'chin, one of the Echinoidea, a class of Echinoderms with globular, ovoid, or heart-shaped, sometimes flattened body and shell of calcareous plates, without arms; sea'-view', a view of the sea: a seascape; sea'-wall', a wall to keep out the sea.—adj. sea'-walled, walled against or by the sea.—sea'-ware, seaweed; sea'-wa'ter, water of or from the sea; sea'-wave; sea'-way (often sea'way), a way by sea: progress through the waves: a heavy sea: a regular route taken by ocean traffic: an inland waterway on which ocean-going vessels can sail; sea'weed, marine algae collectively: any marine alga; sea'-whis'tle, a seaweed (Ascophyllum nodosum) whose bladders can be made into whistles; sea'-wife, a kind of wrasse; sea'-wind', a wind from the sea; sea'-wing, a sail; sea'-wolf, the wolf-fish: the bass: the sea-elephant (obs.): a viking: a pirate; sea'-woman, a mermaid; sea'-worm, any marine worm.—adj. sea'-worn, worn by the sea or by seafaring.—sea'-worthiness.—adj. sea'worthy, fit for sea: able to endure stormy weather.—sea'-wrack, coarse seaweeds of any kind: grasswrack.—all at sea, out of one's reckoning: completely at a loss; at full sea, at full tide; at sea, away from land: on the ocean: astray; go to sea, to become a sailor; heavy sea, a sea in which the waves run high; molten sea, the great brazen laver of 1 Kings vii. 23-26; sea-green incorruptible, one honestly and unshakably devoted to an ideal or purpose, esp. in public life (orig. used by Carlyle of Robespierre); short sea, a sea in which the waves are choppy, irregular, and interrupted; the four seas, those bounding Great Britain; Seven Seas (see seven). [O.E. sǣ; Du. zee, Ger. see, O.N. sǣr, Dan. sö.]

Seabee, sē'bē, n. a member of a U.S. Navy construction battalion.

seacunny, sē'kun-i, n. a lascar steersman or quartermaster. [App. Pers. sukkāni—Ar. sukkān, rudder, confused with sea and con.]

seal, sēl, n. a piece of wax, lead or other material, stamped with a device and attached as a means of authentication or attestation: a wafer, circular mark, or other substitute: a piece of wax, etc., stamped or not, used as a means of keeping closed a letter, door, etc.: the design stamped: an engraved stone or other stamp for impressing a device, or a trinket of like form: a confirming token: that which closes: an obligation to secrecy: an impression: a device to prevent passage of a gas: water in a gas-trap: an otter's (or other) footprint.—v.t. to set a seal to: to stamp: to fasten with a seal: to confirm: to ratify: to close up: to enclose: to settle irrevocably: to set apart.—v.i. to set one's seal to something.—n. seal'ant, something that seals a place where there is a leak.—adj. sealed.—ns. seal'er; seal'ing.—seal'-cyl'inder, a cylinder-seal; sealed book, something beyond one's knowledge or understanding; seal'-engrav'ing, the art of engraving seals; seal'ing-day (Shak.), a day for sealing; seal'ing-wax, formerly beeswax, now usually a composition of shellac, turpentine, vermilion or other colouring matter, etc., for sealing—also (obs.) seal'-wax; seal'-pipe a dip-pipe; **seal'-ring,** a signet-ring.—**Great Seal,** the state seal of the United Kingdom; **Privy Seal,** the seal appended to grants, and in Scotland authenticating royal grants of personal rights; **seal off,** to make it impossible for any thing, person, to leave or enter (e.g. an area); **set one's seal to,** to give one's authority or assent to; **the seals,** symbolically the office of Lord Chancellor or of Secretary of State; **under seal,** authenticated; **under sealed orders,** under orders only to be opened at sea. [O.Fr. seel—L. sigillum, dim. of signum, a mark.]

**seal,** sēl, n. a member of the Pinnipedia, usually excluding the walrus and often excluding the otaries: sealskin.—adj. of seal or sealskin.—v.i. to hunt seals.—ns. **seal'er,** a seal-fisher; **seal'ery,** seal-fishery; **seal'ing.—seal'-fish'er,** a hunter of seals: a sealing ship; **seal'-fish'ing; seal'-rook'ery,** a seals' breeding-place; **seal'skin,** the prepared fur of the fur-seal, or an imitation (as of rabbit-skin, or of mohair): a garment made of this.—Also adj. [O.E. seolh (gen. sēoles); O.N. selr.]

**seal.** Same as seel (1).

**seal,** sēl, v.t. to tie up.—n. a rope or chain for tying up an animal. [O.E. sǣlan—sāl, rope.]

**seal.** See sale (2).

**sealgh, sealch,** selhh, (Scot.) n. a seal. [seal (2).]

**sealyham,** sēl'i-əm, n. (in full sealyham terrier) a long-bodied, short-legged, hard-coated terrier, first bred at Sealyham in Pembrokeshire.

**seam, seame,** sēm, n. grease (Shak.): hog's lard (Scot. saim, sām).—v.t. to grease. [O.Fr. saim, O.E. seime; cf. L. sagīna, stuffing, feasting.]

**seam,** sēm, n. a line of junction between edges sewn together, or between other edges generally: the turned-up edges of such a line on the wrong side of the cloth: ornamentation of such a junction: a suture: a crack: the mark of a cut: a wrinkle: a stratum, esp. if thin or valuable: a piece of sewing-work.—v.t. to join, furnish, or mark with seams: to pick out the seams of.—ns. **seam'er,** one who, or that which, seams: a ball delivered by seam bowling (cricket); **seam'iness.—adj. seam'less.—ns. seamster** (sem'), seam'stress (see sempster); **seam'-stressy** (Sterne), sewing.—adj. **seamy** (sēm'i), having a seam or seams: showing the disreputable side.—**seam bowler, seam bowling** (cricket), bowling in which the seam of the ball is used in delivery to make the ball swerve in flight or first to swerve and then to break in the opposite direction on pitching; **seam'ing-lace,** a lace, braid, etc., to insert in or cover seams.—adj. **seam'-rent,** rent along a seam.—**seam'-set,** a tool for flattening seams in metal, etc.; **seam welding,** resistance welding of overlapping sheets of metal using wheels or rollers as electrodes: welding two pieces of sheet plastic along a line by dielectric heating; **seam'y-side** (Shak.), the wrong side of a garment: hence the disreputable side or aspect. [O.E. sēam—sīwian, to sew; Du. zoom, Ger. saum.]

**seam,** sēm, (obs. except dial.) n. a pack-horse load (e.g. 8 bushels of grain, 9 pecks of apples, 120 lb. of glass): a cartload. [O.E. sēam, a burden—L.L. sauma—Gr. sagma, a pack-saddle.]

**sean,** sēn. Same as seine.

**Seanad,** shan'ədh, n. the upper house of the legislature of the Republic of Ireland. [Ir., senate.]

**séance,** sā'äs, n. a sitting, esp. of psychical researchers or Spiritualists. [Fr.,—L. sedēre, to sit.]

**seannachie,** sen'ə-hhē, n. Highland or Irish genealogist and transmitter of family lore.—Also **seann'achy, senn'achie.** [Gael. seanachaidh.]

**sear,** sēr, n. the catch that holds a gun at cock or half-cock.—**tickle(d) a th' sere** (Shak.), ready to go off. [Cf. O.Fr. serre—L. sera, a bar.]

**sear,** sēr, adj. (usu. **sere**) dry and withered: (Spens. **seare**) burning.—v.i. (rarely **sere**) to become sere.—v.t. to make sere: to dry up: to scorch: to brand: to cauterise: to render callous or insensible.—n. a mark of searing.—adj. **seared.**—n. **seared'ness.**—n. and adj. **sear'ing.**—ns. **sear'ness, sere'ness.**—**sear'ing-iron.**—**the sere, the** (so Shak.; not and) **yellow leaf,** the autumn of life. [O.E. sēar, dry, sēarian, to dry up; L.G. soor, Du. zoor.]

**searce, sûrs, search,** sûrch, v.t. to sift.—n. a sieve. [O.Fr. saas; r unexplained.]

**search,** sûrch, v.t. to explore all over with a view to finding something: to examine closely: to examine for hidden articles by feeling all over: to ransack: to scrutinise: to probe: to penetrate all parts of: to put to the test: to seek out (usu. with out).—v.i. to make a search.—n. the act or power of searching: thorough examination: quest: a search-party (Shak.).—adj. **search'able.**—n. **search'er,** one who searches: one appointed to search, as a custom-house officer: an inspector of various kinds: a probe.—adj. **search'ing,** penetrating: thorough-going.—adv. **search'ingly.**—n. **search'ingness.**—adj. **search'less,** unsearchable.—**search'light,** a lamp and reflector throwing a strong beam of light for picking out objects by night: the light so projected; **search'-par'ty,** a party sent out in search of somebody or something; **search'-warr'ant,** a warrant authorising the searching of a house, etc.—**right of search,** the right of a belligerent to search neutral ships for contraband of war; **search me** (slang), I don't know. [O.Fr. cerchier (Fr. chercher)—L. circāre, to go about—circus, a circle.]

**sease, seasd.** See under seize.

**season,** sē'zn, n. one of the four divisions of the year: the usual, natural, legal, or appropriate time, or time of year, for anything: any particular time: time, esp. of some continuance, but not long: a season ticket (coll.): seasoning (obs.).—v.t. to mature: to temper: to bring into suitable condition: to inure: to render savoury: to flavour: to imbue: to preserve from decay (Shak.): to mature, confirm, imbue with the flavour of (Shak.).—v.i. to become seasoned.—adj. **sea'sonable,** in due season: timely.—n. **sea'sonableness.**—adv. **sea'sonably.**—adj. **sea'sonal,** according to season.—adv. **sea'sonally.**—adj. **sea'soned.**—ns. **sea'soner; sea'soning,** the process or act by which anything is seasoned: the process of acclimatisation: that which is added to food to give relish: in diamond-cutting, the charging of the laps or wheels with diamond-dust and oil: the coating of dyed leather with liquid albumen.—adj. **sea'sonless,** without difference of seasons.—**sea'soning-tub,** a trough in which dough is set to rise; **season ticket,** a ticket valid any number of times within a specified period.—**close season** (see close); **in season,** ripe, fit and ready for use: allowed to be killed: fit to be eaten; **in season and out of season,** at all times; **out of season,** inopportune: not in season. [O.Fr. seson (Fr. saison)—L. satiō, -ōnis, a sowing.]

**seasure.** See under seize.

**seat,** sēt, n. anything used or intended for sitting on: a chair, bench, saddle, etc.: part of a chair on which the body rests: a sitting: a mode of sitting: a place where one may sit, as in a theatre, church, etc.: a right to sit: a constituency: membership: that part of the body or of a garment on which one sits: that on which anything rests: site, situation: a place where anything is located, settled, or established: post of authority: a throne: a capital city: station: abode: mansion: sitting-room.—v.t. to place on a seat: to cause to sit down: to place in any situation, site, etc.: to establish: to fix: to assign a seat to: to furnish with a seat or seats: to fit accurately: to make baggy by sitting.— *v.i.* (*Spens.*) to sit or lie down: to become baggy by sitting.—*adj.* seat′ed.—*ns.* -sea′ter (in composition) a vehicle seated for so many; seat′ing, the taking, provision, or arrangement of seats: a supporting surface: material for seats.—*adj.* seat′less.—seat′-belt, a belt which can be fastened to hold a person in his seat in car or aircraft; seat′-rent, payment for a church sitting; seat′-stick, a walking-stick that can be made to serve as a seat.—lord of seat, a lord of Session; take a seat, to sit down. [O.N. *sæti*, seat; cf. O.E. *sæt*, ambush.]

se-baptist, *sē-bap′tist, n.* one who baptises himself. [L. *sē*, himself.]

Sebat. See Shebat.

sebesten, *si-bes′tən, n.* an Oriental boraginaceous tree (Cordia): its edible plum-like fruit. [Ar. *sabastān.*]

sebum, *sē′bəm, n.* the fatty secretion that lubricates the hair and skin.—*adjs.* sebaceous (*si-bā′shəs*), tallowy: of, like, of the nature of, or secreting sebum; sebacic (*si-bas′ik*), applied to an acid, $(CH_2)_8(COOH)_2$, got from fats.—*n.* sebate (*sē′bāt*), a salt of sebacic acid.—*adjs.* sebif′erous (*si-*), bearing fatty matter; sebif′ic, producing fatty matter.—*n.* seborrhoea (*seb-ə-rē′ə*), excessive discharge from the sebaceous glands.—*adj.* seborrhoe′ic. [L. *sēbum*, suet.]

sebundy, *si-bun′di, n.* Indian irregular soldiery or soldier. [Urdu *sibandi.*]

sec, *sek, adj.* dry, of wines. [Fr.]

secant, *sē′kənt, sek′ənt, adj.* cutting.—*n.* a cutting line: orig., a straight line from the centre of a circle through one end of an arc to the tangent from the other end (*trig.*): now, as a function of an angle, the ratio of the hypotenuse to the base of a right-angled triangle formed by dropping a perpendicular from a point on one side of the angle to the other (negative if the base is the side produced)—in trigonometrical notation written sec. [L. *secāns, -antis,* pr.p. of *secāre,* to cut.]

sécateur, *sek′ə-tûr, n.* (usu. in *pl.* and without accent) pruning-shears. [Fr.]

secco, *sek′kō, adj.* (*mus.*) unaccompanied: plain. —*n.* painting on dry plaster. [It., dry—L. *siccus.*]

secede, *si-sēd′, v.i.* to withdraw, esp. from a party, religious body, federation, or the like.— *ns.* sece′der, one who secedes: one of a body of Presbyterians (Secession Church; see presbyterian) who seceded from the Church of Scotland about 1733; secession (*-sesh′ən*), the act of seceding: a body of seceders.—Also *adj.*—*ns.* secess′ionism (*U.S. slang* also secesh′, secesh′er), one who favours or joins in secession. —Also *adjs.*—War of Secession, the American Civil War. [L. *sēcēdĕre, sēcessum, sē-,* apart, *cēdĕre,* to go.]

secern, *si-sûrn′, v.t.* to separate: to discriminate: to secrete.—*n.* and *adj.* secern′ent.—*n.* secern′-ment. [L. *sēcernĕre, sēcrētum,* to separate.]

seckel, *sek′l, n.* a variety of pear. [Owner's name.]

seclude, *si-klōōd′, v.i.* to shut off, esp. from association or influence.—*adj.* seclud′ed, retired: withdrawn from observation or society.—*adv.* seclud′edly.—*ns.* seclusion (*si-klōō′zhən*), the act of secluding: the state of being secluded: retirement: privacy: solitude; seclu′sionist.—*adj.* seclu′sive (*-siv*), tending to or favouring seclusion. [L. *sēclūdĕre, -clūsum,—sē-,* apart, *claudĕre,* to shut.]

secodont, *sek′ə-dont, adj.* with cutting back teeth. —Also *n.* [L. *secāre,* to cut, Gr. *odous, odontos,* tooth.]

Seconal, *sek′ə-nəl, n.* a proprietary name of a hypnotic and soporific barbiturate.

second, *sek′ənd, adj.* next after or below the first:

other, alternate: additional: supplementary: another, as it were: inferior: referring to the person or persons addressed (*gram.*): helpful, favouring (*Shak.*).—*adv.* next after the first: in the second place.—*n.* one who, or that which, is second or of the second class: a place in the second class: second gear: one who attends another in a duel or a prize fight: a supporter: the 60th part of a minute of time, or of angular measurement: a time interval variously measured (see under atom, Ephemera, universe): the second person (*gram.*): the interval between successive tones of the diatonic scale (*mus.*): (in *pl.*) goods of a second quality.—*v.t.* to follow: to act as second to: to back: to further: to assist: to encourage: to support after the mover of a nomination or resolution: to sing second to (*mus.*): to follow up with another: to transfer temporarily to some special employment (*si-kond′, -gōōnd′*; esp. *mil.*).—*adv.* sec′-ondarily.—*n.* sec′ondariness.—*adj.* sec′ondary, subordinate: subsidiary: of a second order: of a second stage: derivative: induced: of education, between primary and higher: of a feather, growing in the second joint of the wing: (*cap.*; *geol.*) Mesozoic.—*n.* a subordinate: a delegate or deputy: a satellite: that which is secondary, as a feather, coil, etc.—*n.* sec′onder, one who seconds a motion, etc.: a supporter: a member of a second group.—*adv.* sec′ondly, in the second place.—*n.* second′ment, temporary transfer to another position.—Second Advent, Coming, a second coming of Christ; Sec′ond-ad′ventist, one who expects a second coming of Christ; secondary alcohol, one containing the group CH·OH; secondary battery, cell, one on which the chemical action is reversible; secondary coil, one carrying an induced current; secondary electron, an electron in a beam of secondary emission; secondary emission, emission of electrons from a surface or particle by bombardment with electrons, etc., from another source; secondary radar, radar in which a responder is triggered by received pulses so that it retransmits a signal; second ballot, a system of election whereby a second vote is taken, the candidate or candidates who received fewest votes in the first ballot being eliminated.—*n.* and *adj.* sec′ond-best, next to the best (come off second-best, to get the worst of a contest).—second chamber, in a legislature of two houses, the house with fewer powers, usu. acting as a check on the other; second childhood, mental weakness in extreme old age.—*n.* and *adj.* sec′ond-class, of the class next to the first.—second cousin, one who has the same pair of great-grandparents, but different grandparents: loosely, a first cousin's child, or a parent's first cousin (properly first cousin once removed); sec′ond-day′, Monday.—*n.* and *adj.* sec′ond-floor (see floor).—*adj.* sec′ond-hand′, derived from another: not original: already used by a previous owner: dealing in second-hand goods.—*n.* (*sek′*) a hand on a watch or clock that indicates seconds.—*adv.* indirectly, at second hand: after use by a previous owner.— sec′ond-in-command′, the next under the commanding officer; sec′ond-lieuten′ant, an army officer of lowest commissioned rank—formerly ensign or cornet; second man, a man assisting the driver of a train (formerly, in steam trains, the fireman); sec′ond-mark, the character ″, used for seconds of arc or time or for inches; second nature, a deeply ingrained habit.—*adj.* sec′ond-rate, inferior: mediocre.—second-rāt′er; second self, a person with whom one has the closest possible ties, sharing beliefs, attitudes, feelings, ways of behaving; sec′onds-hand, a hand that marks seconds; sec′ond-sight′, a gift of prophetic vision attributed to certain persons,

Neutral vowels in unaccented syllables: el′ə-mənt; for certain sounds in foreign words, see p. viii

esp. Highlanders; sec'onds-pen'dulum, a pendulum that makes one swing a second; second storey, the first floor; second thoughts, reconsideration; second wind, recovery of breath in prolonged exertion.—at second hand, through an intermediate source, indirectly: by hearsay; second-class citizen, a member of a group in the community not given the full rights and privileges enjoyed by the community as a whole; second-class mail, mail sent at a cheaper rate either because of its character or because the sender is prepared to accept slower delivery. [Fr.,—L. *secundus*—*sequi*, *secūtus*, to follow.]

seconde, si-kond', sə-gɔ̄d, (Fr.) (*fencing*) a position in parrying.

secondo, si-kon'dō, (It.) the lowei part in a duet.

secret, sē'krit, *adj.* kept back from knowledge of others: guarded against discovery or observation: unrevealed: hidden: secluded: recondite, occult: preserving secrecy: admitted to confidence, privy.—*adv.* (*poet.*) secretly.—*n.* a fact, purpose, method, etc., that is kept undivulged: participation in knowledge of such a fact: a nostrum (*obs.*): anything unrevealed or unknown: secrecy: a secret or private place (*obs.*): a piece of armour hidden by clothes: the key or principle that explains or enables: an inaudible prayer, esp. in the Mass: (in *pl.*) external sex organs (*obs.*).—*n.* secrecy (sē'kri-si), the state or fact of being secret: concealment: seclusion: confidence: power or habit of keeping secrets: the keeping of secrets: a secret.— *n.pl.* secreta (si-krē'tə), products of secretion.— —*n.* sē'cretage, treatment of furs with mercury before pelting.—*v.t.* secrete (si-krēt'), to hide: to appropriate secretly: to form and separate by the activity of living matter.—*ns.* secrē'tin, a hormone that stimulates the pancreas; secrē'tion, the act of secreting: that which is secreted: a mass of mineral matter formed by inward growth in a cavity.—*adjs.* secrē'tional; sē'cretive (also si-krē'tiv), given to secrecy: very reticent: indicative of secrecy. — *adv.* secretively.— *n.* secretiveness.—*adv.* sē'cretly, in secret: in concealment: inaudibly (of prayers).—*n.* sē'cretness.—*adj.* secrē'tory, secreting.—secret agent, one employed in secret service; Secret Service, a department of government service whose operations are not disclosed: its activities: espionage.—in secret, with precautions against being known: in confidence, as a secret: secretly; in the secret, admitted to, participating in, knowledge of the secret; of secret (*Shak.*), of a secret character; open secret (see open); secret of, secret de (sə-krä də), Polichinelle (po-lē-shē-nel'; Fr. name and character equivalent to Punchinello), something known to everyone. [L. *sēcernēre*, *sēcrētum*—*sē*-, apart, *cernēre*, to separate.]

secretary, sek'ri-tə-ri, *n.* one employed to write or transact business for another or for a society, company, etc.: the minister at the head of certain departments of state: an ambassador's or minister's assistant: a secretaire: secretary hand: secretary type.—*n.* secretaire (sek'ri-tār, sək-rə-ter; Fr.) a secret repository: a writing desk, escritoire.—*adj.* secretarial (-tār'i-əl).— *ns.* secretā'riat(e) (-ət), secretaryship: a secretary's office: a body of secretaries; sec'retaryship, the office, duties, or art of a secretary. —sec'retary-bird, a long-legged snake-eating African bird of prey (Serpentarius), said to be named from the tufts of feathers at the back of its head like pens stuck behind the ear; sec're tary hand, an old legal style of handwriting; sec'retary type, a type in imitation of secretary hand.—Secretary of State, a cabinet minister holding one of the more important folios: in U.S, the foreign secretary. [M.E. *secretarie*— L.L. *sēcrētārius*—L. *sēcrētum*; see secret.]

sect, *sekt*, *n.* a body of followers: a school of opinion, esp. in religion or philosophy: a subdivision of one of the main religious divisions of mankind: an organised denomination, used esp. by members of the greater churches to express their disapprobation of the lesser: a dissenting body: a party: a class of people: a sex (now *illit.*).—*adjs.* sectā'rial, distinguishing a sect (esp. in India); sectā'rian, of a sect or sectary: narrow, exclusive: denominational.— *n.* an Independent (*hist.*): one of a sect: one strongly imbued with the characteristics of a sect.—*v.t.* sectā'rianise, -ize.—*ns.* sectā'rianism; sectary (sekt'ər-i), a follower, a votary: one of a sect: a dissenter; sectā'tor (*rare*), an adherent of a school or party. [L. *secta*, a school or following—*sequi*, *secūtus*, to follow, influenced by *secāre*, to cut.]

sect, sekt, (*Shak.*) *n.* a cutting.—*adj.* sectile (sek'til), capable of being cut with a knife without breaking.—*ns.* sectility (-til'i-ti); sec'tion (-shən), act of cutting: a division: a portion: one of the parts into which anything may be considered as divided or of which it may be built up: the line of intersection of two surfaces: the surface formed when a solid is cut by a plane: an exposure of rock in which the strata are cut across (*geol.*): a plan of anything represented as if cut by a plane or other surface: a thin slice for microscopic examination: a one-mile square of American public lands: a subdivision of a company, platoon, battery, etc.: a number of men detailed for a special service: a district or region (*U.S.*): a frame for a honeycomb: a section-mark.—*v.t.* to divide into sections: to make a section of.—*adj.* sec'tional, of a section: in section: built up of sections.—*n.* sec'tionalism, class spirit.—*adv.* sec'tionally.— *v.t.* sec'tionise, -ize, to section.—*n.* sec'tor (-tər), a plane figure bounded by two radii and an arc: an object of like shape: an instrument of like shape for measuring angular distance (*astron.*): a length or section of a fortified line or army front: a mathematical instrument consisting of two graduated rules hinged together, originally with a graduated arc: a telescope turning about the centre of a graduated arc: a division, section, of (usu.) a nation's economic operations.—*v.t.* to divide into sectors.— *adjs.* sec'toral, of a sector; sectorial (-tō'ri-əl, -tō'); sectorial: adapted for cutting.—*n.* a carnassial tooth.—sec'tion-cutter, an instrument for making sections for microscopic work; sec'tion-mark, the sign §, used to mark the beginning of a section of a book or as a reference mark. [L. *secāre*, *sectum*, to cut.]

secular, sek'ū-lər, *adj.* pertaining to or coming or observed once in a lifetime, generation, century, age (*Rom. hist.* about 100 to 120 years): appreciable only in the course of ages: age-long: age-old: pertaining to the present world, or to things not spiritual: civil, not ecclesiastical: lay: not concerned with religion: not bound by monastic rules (opp. to *regular*): of the secular clergy.—*n.* a layman: an ecclesiastic (as a parish priest) not bound by monastic rules: a Negro song other than a spiritual (*U.S.*).—*n.* secūlarisā'tion, -z-.—*v.t.* sec'ularise, -ize, to make secular.—*ns.* sec'ularism, the belief that the state, morals, education, etc., should be independent of religion: G. J. Holyoake's (1817-1906) system of social ethics.—*n.* and *adj.* sec'ularist. — *adj.* secularist'ic.— *n.* secularity (-lar').—*adv.* sec'ularly.—secular arm, the civil power; secular games (*Rom. hist.*), games held at long intervals; secular hymn, a hymn for the secular games. [L. *saeculāris*—*saeculum*, a lifetime, generation.]

seculum. See saeculum.

secund, sē'kund, also sek'und, si-kund', *adj.* (*bot.*)

all turned to the same side.—*ns.* sec'undine (-*in*, -*in*), the afterbirth: the inner (rarely outer and second formed) coat of an ovule; secundogeniture (-*jen'*), inheritance of or by a second child or son. [L. *secundus*, following, second.]

secundum, *si-kun'dum, se-kōōn'dōōm*, (L.) following, according to.—secundum artem (*är'tem*), skilfully: professionally; secundem ordinem (*ör'di-nem*) in order; secundem quid (*kwid*), in some respects only.

secure, *si-kūr'*, *adj.* without care or anxiety: confident: over-confident: free from danger: safe: assured: affording safety: stable: firmly fixed or held.—*adv.* (*poet.*) in security.—*v.t.* to make secure, safe, or certain: to make secure the possession of: to establish in security: to prevent (*obs.*): to seize and guard: to get hold of: to contrive to get: to plight or pledge (*obs.*): to guarantee: to fasten.—*v.i.* to make sure.—*adj.* secūr'able.—*n.* secūr'ance (*rare*).—*adv.* secure'ly.—*ns.* secure'ment; secure'ness; secūr'er; secūr'itan (*obs.*), one who dwells in fancied security; secūr'ity, state, feeling, or means of being secure: protection from espionage: certainty: carelessness (*arch.*): a pledge: a surety: a guarantee: a right conferred on a creditor to make him sure of recovery: (usu. in *pl.*) bonds or certificates in evidence of debt or property.—*adj.* for securing security.—Security Council, a body of the United Nations consisting of five permanent members (China, France, U.K., U.S.A., U.S.S.R.—each with the right of veto) and six elected two-yearly members, charged with the maintenance of international peace and security; security risk, a person considered from his political affiliations or leanings to be unsafe for state service. [L. *sēcūrus—sē-*, without, *cūra*, care.]

securiform, *si-kū'ri-förm*, *adj.* axe-shaped. [L. *secūris*, axe—*secāre*, to cut, *förma*, form.]

sed, se'd, Miltonic spellings of said (*pa.t.* and *pa.p.*).

sedan, *si-dan'*, *n.* a covered chair for one, carried on two poles (also sedan'-chair): a litter: a palanquin: a large closed motor-car (*U.S.*), a saloon-car. [App. not conn. with *Sedan* in France; poss. It. *sedere*, to sit.]

sedate, *si-dāt'*, *adj.* composed: staid.—*adv.* sedāte'ly.—*ns.* sedāte'ness; sedā'tion, act of calming, or state of being calmed, by means of sedatives.—*adj.* sedative (*sed'ə-tiv*), calming: composing: allaying excitement or pain.—*n.* a sedative medicine or agent. [L. *sēdātus*, pa.p. of *sēdāre*, to still.]

se defendendo, *sē di-fend-end'ō, sā de-fend-end'ō*, (L.) in self-defence.

sedent, *sē'dənt*, *adj.* seated.—*adv.* sedentarily (*sed'ən-tər-i-li*).—*n.* sed'entariness.—*adj.* sed'entary, sitting much: requiring much sitting: inactive: stationary: not migratory: lying in wait, as a spider: attached to a substratum (*zool.*).—sedentary soil, soil remaining where it was formed. [L. *sedēns*, *-entis* (pr.p.), and *sedentārius—sedēre*, to sit.]

sederunt, *si-dē'runt, si-dā'rənt, sä-dā'rōōnt*, *n.* in Scotland a sitting, as of a court: a list of persons present.—Acts of Sederunt, ordinances of the Court of Session. [L. *sēdērunt*, there sat—*sedēre*, to sit.]

sedes, *sē'dēz, sed'ās*, (L.) seat.—sedes impedita (*im-pə-di'ta, im-ped'i-ta*), a papal or episcopal see where there is a partial cessation by the incumbent of his episcopal duties; sedes vacans (*vā'kənz, va', wa'känz*), also sede vacante (*sē'dē və-kan'ti, sed'e va-, wa-kan'te*; *ablative*), a term of canon law to designate a papal or episcopal see when vacant.

sedge, *sej*, *n.* any species of Carex or other plant of the Cyperaceae, a family distinguished from grasses by its solid triangular stems and leaf-

sheaths without a slit: extended to iris and other plants: (also sedge fly) any of several mayflies or caddis flies common along rivers: an artificial fly resembling a sedge fly.—*adjs.* sedged, of sedge: bordered with sedge; sedg'y, of, like, abounding with sedge.—sedge'-bird, sedge'-war'bler, sedge'-wren, a common British warbler of watery places. [O.E. *secg*; cf. L.G. *segge*.]

sedge, *sej*, *n.* See siege.

sedigitated, *sē-dij'i-tā-tid*, *adj.* six-fingered. [L. *sēdigitus—sex*, six, *digitus*, finger.]

sedilia, *si-dil'i-ə*, *n.pl.* seats (usu three, often in niches) for the officiating clergy, on the south side of the chancel—*sing.* sedile (*si-di'li*, L. *se-dē'le*). [L. *sedile*, pl. *sedilia*, seat.]

sediment, *sed'i-mənt*, *n.* what settles at the bottom of a liquid: dregs: a deposit.—*v.t.* to deposit as sediment: to cause or allow to deposit sediment.—*adj.* sedimentary (*-men'tər-i*).—*n.* sedimentā'tion, deposition of sediment.—sedimentary rocks, those formed by accumulation and deposition of fragmentary materials or organic remains. [L. *sedimentum—sedēre*, to sit.]

sedition, *si-dish'ən*, *n.* insurrection: public tumult: vaguely, any offence against the state short of treason.—*n.* sedi'tionary, an inciter to sedition: inducement to attempt, otherwise than by lawful means, alteration in church or state.—*adj.* sedi'tious.—*adv.* sedi'tiously.—*n.* sedi'tiousness. [O.Fr.,—L. *sēditiō, -ōnis—sēd-*, away, *īre, ītum*, to go.]

seduce, *si-dūs'*, *v.t.* to draw aside from party, belief, allegiance, service, duty, etc.: to lead astray: to entice: to corrupt: to induce to have sexual intercourse.—*ns.* sedūce'ment, act of seducing or drawing aside: allurement; sedū'cer.—*n.* and *adj.* sedū'cing.—*adv.* sedū'cingly.—*n.* seduction (*si-duk'shən*), act of seducing: allurement.—*adj.* seduc'tive, alluring.—*adv.* seduc'tively.—*ns.* seduc'tiveness; seduc'tor (*obs.*), one who leads astray; seduc'tress. [L. *sēdūcere, sēductum—sē-*, aside, *dūcēre*, to lead.]

sedulous, *sed'ū-ləs*, *adj.* assiduous.—*ns.* sedulity (*si-dū'li-ti*); sed'ulousness.—*adv.* sed'ulously. [L. *sēdulus—sē dolō*, without deception, hence in earnest.]

Sedum, *sē'dəm*, *n.* the stonecrop genus of Crassulaceae. [L. *sēdum*, house-leek.]

see, *sē*, *n.* a seat, esp. of dignity or authority (*obs.*): a throne, esp. a bishop's (*arch.*): the office of bishop of a particular diocese: (wrongly according to some) a cathedral city, also a diocese.—Holy See, the papal court. [O.Fr. *se, sied*—L. *sēdēs, -is—sedēre*, to sit.]

see, *sē*, *v.t.* to perceive by the sense seated in the eye: to perceive mentally: to apprehend: to recognise: to understand: to learn: to be aware by reading: to look at: to judge, to deem: to refer to: to ascertain: to make sure: to make sure of having: to wait upon, escort: to call on: to receive as a visitor: to meet: to consult: to experience: to meet and accept by staking a similar sum: to spend on seeing (Shak.; with *away*).—*v.i.* to have power of vision: to see things well enough: to look or inquire: to be attentive: to consider:—*pa.t.* saw (illit. see, seed, seen); *pa.p.* seen.—*imper.*, passing into *interj.*, see, look: behold.—*n.* (*rare*) an act of seeing.—*adj.* see'able.—*n.* see'ing, sight: vision: clear-sightedness: atmospheric conditions for good observation.—*adj.* having sight, or insight: observant: discerning.—*conj.* (also seeing that) since: in view of the fact.—*n.* seer, (*sē'ər*) one who sees: (*sēr*) one who sees into the future.—see'ing stone, a scrying crystal.—have seen better days, one's best days, to be now on the decline; let me see, a phrase employed to express reflection; see about, to consider: do whatever is to be done about: attend to; **see off**, to accompany at one's departure: to reprimand (*slang*); **see out**, to conduct to the door: to see to the end: to outlast; **see over**, to be conducted all through; **see things** (*coll.*), to have hallucinations; **see through**, to participate in to the end: to back up till difficulties end: to understand the hidden nature of; **see to**, to look after: to make sure about; **see what I can do**, do what I can; **well (ill) seen**, well (ill) versed. [O.E. *sēon*; Ger. *sehen*, Du. *zien*.]

**see**, *sē*, *n.* the third letter of the alphabet (C, c).

**seecatchie**, *sē′kach-i*, *n.pl.* male Aleutian fur-seals:—*sing.* **see′catch**. [Russ. *sekach*, prob. from Aleutian Indian.]

**seed**, *sēd*, *n.* that which is sown: a multicellular structure by which flowering plants reproduce, consisting of embryo, stored food, and seed-coat, derived from the fertilised ovule (*bot.*): a small hard fruit or part in a fruit, a pip: a seed-like object or aggregate: semen: spawn: condition of having or proceeding to form seed: sown land: grass and clover grown from seed: first principle: germ: a crystal introduced to start crystallisation: offspring, descendants, race: a small bubble in glass: a tournament player who has been seeded (*slang*).—*v.i.* to produce seed: to run to seed.—*v.t.* to sow: to sprinkle, powder, dust: to remove seeds from: in lawn-tennis tournaments, etc., to arrange (the draw) so that the best players do not meet in the early rounds: to deal with (good players) in this way: to disperse freezing fog by scattering small pellets of dry ice above it.—*adj.* **seed′ed**, cleaned of seeds: having seeds: bearing seed: full-grown: sown: showing seeds or carpels (*her.*): of a tournament player, who has been seeded.—*n.* **seed′er**, a seed-drill: an apparatus for removing seeds from fruit: a seed-fish.—*adv.* **seed′ily**.—*n.* **seed′iness**.—*n.* and *adj.* **seed′ing**.—*adjs.* **seed′less**; **seed′-like**.—*n.* **seed′ling**, a plant reared from the seed: a young plant ready for planting out from a seedbed.—*also adj.*—*n.* **seed′ness** (*Shak.*), sowing.—*adj.* **seed′y**, abounding with seed: having the flavour of seeds: not cleared of seeds: run to seed: worn out: out of sorts: shabby.—**seed′bed**, a piece of ground for receiving seed; **seed′box**, a plant capsule; **seed′cake**, a cake with caraway seeds; **seed′-coat**, the covering derived from the ovule's integuments; **seed′-coral**, coral in small irregular pieces; **seed′-corn**, grain for sowing; **seed′-drill**, a machine for sowing seeds in rows; **seed′-field**, a field in which seed is sown; **seed′-fish**, a fish about to spawn; **seed′-lac**, granular residues of lac after trituration; **seed′-leaf**, a cotyledon, leaf contained in a seed; **seed′lip**, a sower's basket (O.E. *sǣdlēap—lēap*, basket); **seed′-lobe**, a cotyledon; **seed′-oil**, oil expressed from seeds; **seed′-oyster**, a very young oyster; **seed′-pearl**, a very small pearl; **seed′-plant**, a spermatophyte or flowering plant: a plant grown from or for seed; **seed′-plot**, a piece of nursery ground, a hot-bed; **seed′-potato**, a potato tuber for planting; **seed′-shop**, seeds′man, a dealer in seeds: a sower; **seed′-stalk**, the funicle; **seed′-time**, the season for sowing seeds; **seed′-vessel**, a dry fruit: the ovary of a flower; **seed′y-toe**, a disease of the horse's foot.—**run to seed** (see run). [O.E. *sǣd*; cf. *sāwan*, to sow; O.N. *sāth*; Ger. *saat*.]

**seek**, *sēk*, *v.t.* to look for: to try to find, get, or achieve: to ask for: to aim at: to resort to, betake oneself to: to advance against: to try: to search, examine.—*v.i.* to make search: to resort (*Milt.*):—*pa.t.* and *pa.p.* **sought** (*söt*).—*ns.* **seek′er**, one who seeks: an inquirer: a dissector's probing instrument: a telescopic finder: (*cap.*) a member of a 17th-century sect who sought for the true church.—**seek-no-**

**furth′er**, a reddish winter apple.—**seek after**, to go in quest of; **seek for**, to look for; **seek out**, to look for and find: to bring out from a hidden place; **sought after**, in demand; **to seek**, not to be found: wanting: at a loss to know (*arch.*; e.g. *What real good is, I am to seek*): defective (in; *arch.*). [O.E. *sēcan* (pa.t. *sōhte*, pa.p. *gesōht*); cf. Ger. *suchen*.]

**seel**, *sēl*, *v.t.* to sew up the eyelids of, as a hawk: to blindfold: to blind, hoodwink. [O.Fr. *siller*, *ciller—cil—*L. *cilium*, eyelid, eyelash.]

**seel**, **sele**, **seal** (Scot. seil), *sēl*, (*dial.*) *n.* happiness: good fortune: opportune time: season: time of day.—*adj.* **seel′y**, fortunate, happy, good (*obs.*): simple, innocent (*Spens.*): pitiful, wretched, trifling: to be pitied, poor (*obs.*): foolish (see silly).—**pass the seel of the day**, to greet in passing. [O.E. *sǣl*, time, due time, happiness; see silly.]

**seel**, *sēl*, (*naut.*; *obs.*) *v.i.* to heel over suddenly. —*n.* a sudden heeling. [Origin obscure.]

**seeld**, *sēld*, **seel′ing**, Spenserian forms of **seld**, **ceiling**.

**seely**. See seel (2).

**seem**, *sēm*, *v.i.* to appear: to appear to oneself: to appear to be: to be befitting (*Spens.*).—*v.t.* (*arch.*) to beseem, befit.—*ns.* **seem′er**; **seem′ing**, appearance: semblance: a false appearance: way of thinking.—*adj.* apparent: ostensible.—*adv.* apparently: in appearance only (esp. in composition, as **seem′ing-sim′ple**, **seem′ing-vir′tuous**).—*adv.* **seem′ingly**, apparently: as it would appear.—*n.* **seem′ingness**.—*adj.* **seem(e)′-less(e)** (*Spens.*), unseemly: indecorous.—*ns.* **seem′lihe(a)d** (*Spens.* **seem′lyhed**), seemliness; **seem′liness**.—*adj.* **seem′ly** (*comp.* **seem′lier**, *superl.* **seem′liest**), becoming: suitable: decent: handsome.—Also *adv.*—**it seems**, it appears: it would seem; **it would seem**, it turns out: I have been told; **meseems, meseemed, himseemed**, etc., it seems, seemed, to me, etc. (*arch.*). [O.N. *sæma*, to beseem.]

**seen, seer**. See see (2).

**seep**, *sēp*, *v.i.* to ooze, percolate.—*n.* **seep′age**.—*adj.* **seep′y**. [Cf. sipe.]

**seer**, *sēr*, *n.* an Indian weight of widely ranging amount, officially about 2 lb. [Pers. *sīr*.]

**seersucker**, *sēr′suk-ər*, *n.* a thin crinkly Indian linen (or cotton) striped or checked fabric. [Pers. *shīr o shakkar*, lit. milk and sugar.]

**seesaw**, *sē′sö′*, *sē′sö*, *n.* alternate up-and-down motion: repeated alternation, as a cross-ruff at cards, sing-song speech: a plank balanced so that its ends may move up and down alternately: the sport of rising and sinking on it.—*adj.* going like a seesaw.—*adv.* in the manner of a seesaw. —*v.i.* to play at seesaw: to move or go like a seesaw.—*v.t.* to make to go up and down. [Prob. a redup. of *saw*, from a sawyer's jingle —See saw sack a down.]

**seethe**, *sēdh*, *v.t.* to boil: to soak to a condition as if boiled.—*v.i.* to boil: to surge (*lit.* or *fig.*): to be agitated (by anger, excitement, etc.).—*pa.t.* **seethed**, (*arch.*) **sod**; *pa.p.* **seethed**, (*arch.*) **sodd**:—*n.* surge.—*n.* **seeth′er**.—*n.* and *adj.* **seeth′ing**. [O.E. *sēothan* (pa.t. *sēath*, pl. *sudon*; pa.p. *soden*) Ger. *sjötha*, Ger. *sieden*.]

**seewing**, a Spenserian spelling of **suing** (see sue).

**seg**, *seg*, (*obs.* or *dial.*) *n.* Same as **sedge**.

**seggar**. Same as **saggar**.

**seg(h)ol**, *se-göl′*, *n.* a vowel-point in Hebrew with sound of *e* in *pen*, placed under a consonant, thus (⸱⸱).—*n.* **seg(h)′olate**, a disyllabic noun form with tone-long vowel in the first and a short seghol in the second syllable. [Heb.]

**segment**, *seg′mənt*, *n.* a part cut off: a portion: part of a circle, ellipse, etc., cut off by a straight line, or of a sphere, ellipsoid, etc., by a plane: a section: one of a linear series of similar portions, as of a vibrating string between nodes, a somite or metamere of a jointed animal, or a joint of an appendage: a lobe of a leaf-blade not separate enough to be a leaflet.—*v.t.* and *v.i.* (also *-ment'*) to divide into segments.—*adj.* segmental (*-ment'l*), of a segment: by segments: forming or formed of a segment, segments, arc, or arcs.—*adv.* segmen'tally.—*adjs.* seg'mentary, seg'mentate.—*n.* segmentā'tion.—*adj.* segment'ed (or *seg'*).—segmental arch, an arch forming an arc of a circle whose centre is below the springing. [L. *segmentum*—*secāre*, to cut.]

segno, sā'nyō, (*mus.*) *n.* a sign to mark the beginning or end of repetitions—*𝄋* . [It.,—L. *signum*, a mark.]

sego, sē'gō, *n.* a showy liliaceous plant (Calochortus) of western U.S. [Ute Indian name.]

segreant, *seg'ri-ənt,* (*her.*) *adj.* gener. understood to mean with raised wings. [Earlier sergreant, origin unknown.]

segregate, *seg'ri-gāt, v.t.* to set apart: to seclude: to isolate: to group apart.—*v.i.* to separate out in a group or groups or mass.—*adj.* set apart.— *n.* that which is segregated.—*adj.* seg'regable.— *n.* segregā'tion, act of segregating: state of being segregated: dispersal (*Shak.*): separation of dominants and recessives in the second generation of a cross (*Mendelism*): a segregated mass or group: separation of one particular class of persons from another, as on grounds of race; segregā'tionist, a believer in racial or other segregation.—*adj.* seg'regative. [L. *sēgregāre, -ātum—sē-,* apart, *grex, gregis,* a flock.]

segue, sā'gwā, (It.) follows.

seguidilla, *seg-i-dēl'yä, n.* a Spanish dance: a tune for it, in triple time. [Sp.,—L. *sequī,* to follow.]

seiche, *sāsh, sesh, n.* a tide-like fluctuation in lakes. [Swiss Fr.]

Seidlitz, *sed'lits,* adj. applied to an aperient powder (or rather pair of powders), Rochelle salt and sodium bicarbonate mixed together, and tartaric acid—totally different from the mineral water of *Sedlitz* in Bohemia.

seignior, *sā', sē'nyər,* seigneur, *sen-yœr, n.* a title of address: a feudal lord, lord of a manor.— *ns.* seign'iorage, seign'orage, lordship: an overlord's royalty on minerals: a percentage on minted bullion; sei'gnioralty, seignory.—*adjs.* seignio'rial, seigneu'rial, seignoral (*sān', sen'*), signo'rial (*sin-*), manorial.—*ns.* seign'iorship; seign'(i)ory, feudal lordship: the council of an Italian city-state (*hist.*); (also seigneurie, *sen'yə-rē*) a domain.—grand seigneur, a great lord: a man of aristocratic dignity and authority; Grand Seignior, the Sultan of Turkey. [Fr. *seigneur*— L. *senior, -ōris,* comp. of *senex.* old. In L.L. *senior* is sometimes equivalent to *dominus,* lord.]

seil. Same as sile.

seine, *sān,* or *sēn, n.* a large vertical fishing-net whose ends are brought together and hauled. —*v.t.* and *v.i.* to catch or fish with a seine.— *ns.* sein'er; sein'ing.—seine'-boat; seine'-fishing; seine'-net; seine'-shooting. [O.E. *segne*—L. *sagēna*—Gr. *sagēnē,* a fishing-net.]

seise, *sēz, v.t.* an old spelling of seize, still used legally in the sense of to put in possession:— *pa.p.* seis'ed (*Spens.*), reached, attained.—*n.* seis'in, possession (now, as freehold): an object handed over as a token of possession: sasine (*Scots law*).

seism, *sīzm, n.* an earthquake.—*adjs.* seis'mal, seis'mic.—*ns.* seismicity (*-mis'i-ti*), liability to or frequency of earthquakes; seis'mism, earthquake phenomena; seis'mogram, a seismograph record; seis'mograph, an instrument for registering earthquakes; seismog'rapher.—*adjs.* seismograph'ic, *-al.*—*n.* seismog'raphy, the study of earthquakes.—*adjs.* seismolog'ic, *-al.*—*ns.* seismol'ogist; seismol'ogy, the science of earth-

quakes; seismom'eter, an instrument for measuring earth-movements. — *adjs.* seismomet'ric, *-al.*—*n.* seismom'etry.—*adj.* seismonas'-tic.—*ns.* seismonas'ty (Gr. *nastos,* pressed; *bot.*), response to mechanical shock; seis'moscope, an instrument for detecting earthquakes.—*adj.* seismoscop'ic.—seismic prospecting, investigating the depth and character of subsurface rock formations by noting the travel times of reflected and refracted artificial shock waves. [Gr. *seismos,* a shaking—*seiein,* to shake.]

seity, *sē'i-ti, n.* a self: selfhood, personal identity. [L. *sē,* oneself.]

seize, form., and still in legal sense, seise (*Spens., Shak., Milt.,* sease, seaze, ceaze, etc.), *sēz, v.t.* to put in legal possession: to fix: to take possession of: to grasp suddenly, eagerly, or forcibly: to take by force: to take prisoner: to apprehend: to lash or make fast: to reach, attain (*naut.* and *Spens.*).—*v.i.* to lay hold: to clutch: to penetrate (*Spens.*): to jam or weld partially for want of lubrication.—*adj.* seiz'able. —*ns.* seiz'er; seiz'in, seisin (see seise); seiz'ing, the action of the verb: a cord to seize ropes with; seizure (*sē'zhər*), act of seizing: capture: grasp: thing seized: a sudden fit or attack of illness.—seize, seise, of, to put in possession of; seized, seised, of, in (legal) possession of: aware of: in process of considering; seize up, to jam, seize. [O.Fr. *seisir, saisir*—L.L. *sacīre,* prob. Gmc.; cf. O.H.G. *sazzan,* to set, Ger. *setzen,* Eng. *set.*]

sejant, *sē'jənt,* (*her.*) *adj.* sitting. [O.Fr. *seiant,* Fr. *séant,* pr.p. of *seoir*—L. *sedēre,* to sit.]

sekos, *sē'kos, n.* a sacred enclosure. [Gr. *sēkos.*]

sel, sel, (Scot.) *n.* self.

selachian, *si-lā'ki-ən, n.* any fish of the shark class.—Also adj. [Gr. *selachos.*]

seladang, *se-lä'dang,* sladang, slä'dang, *n.* the gaur. [Malay *seladang, saladang.*]

Selaginella, *si-laj-i-nel'ə, n.* a genus of heterosporous club-mosses constituting the family Selaginellā'ceae. [Dim. of L. *selāgō, -inis,* a plant mentioned by Pliny.]

selah, *sē'lä, n.* in the psalms, a Hebrew word probably meaning pause.

Selbornian, *sel-bör'ni-ən,* adj. of Selborne in Hampshire, or of Gilbert White (1720-93), author of *The Natural History and Antiquities of Selborne*: of Gault and Upper Greensand (*geol.*).—*n.* an admirer of Gilbert White: the Gault and Upper Greensand.

selcouth, *sel'kōōth,* (*Spens.*) *adj.* strange. [O.E. *sel(d)cūth—seldan,* seldom, *cūth,* known— *cunnan,* to know.]

seld, seld, adj. (*Spens.*) rare, uncommon.—*adv.* (*obs.*) seldom, rarely.—*adjs.* seld'seen, rarely seen; seld'shown (*Shak.*), rarely shown. [See seldom.]

seldom, *sel'dəm, adv.* rarely.—*adj.* infrequent.— *n.* sel'domness.—*adv.* sel'dom-times. [O.E. *seldum,* altered (on the analogy of *hwīlum,* whilom) from *seldan*; Ger. *selten.*]

sele. Same as seel (2).

select, *si-lekt', v.t.* to pick out from a number by preference: to free-select (*Austr.*).—*adj.* picked out: choice: exclusive.—*adj.* selec'ted.—*n.* selec'tion, act of selecting: thing or collection of things selected: a pot-pourri (*mus.*): a horse selected as likely to win a race: free-selection. —*adj.* selec'tive, having or exercising power of selection: able to discriminate, e.g. between different frequencies.—*adv.* selec'tively.—*ns.* selectiv'ity (*sel-*), ability to discriminate; select'-ness; select'or.—*adj.* selecto'rial.—select committee, a number of members of parliament chosen to report and advise on some matter; selective weedkiller, a weedkiller that does not destroy garden plants; select'-man, in New England towns, one of a board of officers chosen to manage local business. [L. *sēlĭgĕre*, *sēlectum*—*sē-*, aside, *legĕre*, to choose.]

**Selene**, *se-lē'nē*, *n.* the Greek moon-goddess—Artemis, Phoebe.—*n.* **selenate** (*sel'i-nāt*), a salt of selenic acid.—*adj.* **selenic** (*si-lē'nik*, *-len'ik*), of the moon: of selenium in higher valency (**selenic acid**, $H_2SeO_4$).—*n.* **selenide** (*sel'i-nid*), a compound of selenium with an element or radical.—*adj.* **selē'nious**, of selenium in lower valency (**selenious acid**, $H_2SeO_3$). *n.* **selenite** (*sel'i-nit*), a moon-dweller: gypsum, esp. in transparent crystals (anciently supposed to wax and wane with the moon): a salt of selenious acid.—*adj.* **selenitic** (*sel-i-nit'ik*).—*n.* **selenium** (*si-lē'*), a non-metallic element (Se; at. numb. 34) discovered by Berzelius in 1817 and named from its resemblance to tellurium.—*adj.* **selē'nodont** (Gr. *odous, odontos*, tooth), having crescentic ridges on the crowns of the molar teeth.—*ns.* **selē'nograph**, a delineation of the moon; **selenographer** (*sel-in-og'rə-fər*), a student of selenography.—*adjs.* **selenographic** (*si-lē-nə-graf'ik*), *-al.*—*n.* **selenography** (*sel-in-og'rə-fi*), delineation or description of the moon: study of the moon's physical features.—*adj.* **selēnolog'ical.**—*ns.* **selenol'ogist**, a selenographer; **selenol'ogy**, scientific study of the moon.—**selenium cell**, a photoelectric cell depending on the fact that light increases the electric conductivity of selenium. [Gr. *selēnē*, moon.]

**Seleucid**, *se-lū'sid*, *n.* a member of the dynasty (**Seleu'cidae**) that ruled Syria from 312 to 65 B.C., beginning with Alexander's general, *Seleucus I* (Nicator).—Also *adj.*—*adj.* **Seleu'cidan.**

**self**, *self*, *pron.* (*obs.*, *commercial*, or *illit.*) oneself, myself, himself, etc.—*n.* an identical person, personality, ego: a side of one's personality: identity: personality: what one is: self-interest: a self-coloured plant or animal: a thing (esp. a bow) made in one piece—*pl.* **selves** (*selvz*); of things in one colour or one piece, **selfs.**—*adj.* very, same, identical (*arch.*): own (*arch.*): uniform in colour: made in one piece.—*v.t.* to fertilise by the same individual (self-fertilise), or by the same strain (inbreed).—*n.* **self'hood**, personal identity: existence as a person: personality: selfishness.—*adj.* **self'ish**, chiefly or wholly regarding one's own self: void of regard to others.—*adv.* **self'ishly.**—*ns.* **self'ishness;** **self'ism**, concentration upon self: the selfish theory of morals—that man acts from the consideration of what will give him the most pleasure; **self'ist.**—*adj.* **self'less**, having no regard to self.—*ns.* **self'lessness;** **self'ness**, egotism: personality.—**one self** (*Shak.*), one and the same, one only; **one's self** (see oneself). [O.E. *self*; Du. *zelf*; Ger. *selbe*, Goth. *silba*.]

**self-**, *self-*, in composition, acting upon the agent: by, of, in, in relation to, etc., oneself or itself: automatic.—*ns.* **self'-aban'donment**, disregard of self; **self'-abase'ment**; **self'-abnega'-tion**, renunciation of one's own interest: self-denial.—*adj.* **self'-absorbed'**, wrapped up in one's own thoughts or affairs.—*ns.* **self'-absorp'tion**, state of being self-absorbed: self-shielding (*phys.*); **self'-abuse'**, self-deception (*Shak.*): revilement of oneself: masturbation; **self'-abus'er;** **self'-accusā'tion.**—*adjs.* **self'-accus'atory;** **self'-act'ing**, automatic.—*ns.* **self'-ac'tion**, spontaneous or independent action; **self'-activ'ity**, an inherent power of acting.—*adj.* **self'-adjust'ing**, requiring no external adjustment.—*ns.* **self'-admiss'ion** (*Shak.*), admission of self-will alone as motive; **self'-advert'isement;** **self'-advertis'er.**—*n.pl.* **self'-affairs'** (*Shak.*), one's own affairs.—*adj.* **self'-affec'ted** (*Shak.*), affected well towards oneself.—*n.* **self'-affirma'tion**, assertion of the existence of the self.—*adj.* **self'-affright'ed** (*Shak.*), frightened at oneself.—*n.*

**self'-applause'.** — *adjs.* **self'-appoint'ed;** **self'-approv'ing;** **self'-assert'ing**, **self'-assert'ive**, given to asserting one's opinion or to putting oneself forward.—*n.* **self'-asser'tion.**—*adj.* **self'-assumed'**, assumed by one's own act.—*ns.* **self'-assump'tion**, conceit; **self'-assū'rance**, assured self-confidence.—*adjs.* **self'-assured'; self'-bal'anced**, balanced without outward help: stable; **self'-begot'**, **self'-begott'en**, being its own parent, as the phoenix.—*n.* **self'-bind'er**, a reaping-machine with automatic binding apparatus: a portfolio that grips loose sheets.—*adjs.* **self'-blind'ed; self'-born'**, born of itself, as the phoenix; **self'-borne'** (*Shak.*), perh. carried by and against itself, perh. native-born.—*ns.* **self'-boun'ty** (*Shak.*), native goodness; **self'-breath'** (*Shak.*), one's own utterances; **self'-capac'itance**, capacitance (see **capacity**).—*adj.* **self'-cen'tred**, fixed independently: centred in self.—*n.* **self'-char'ity** (*Shak.*), love of oneself.—*adj.* **self'-clōs'ing**, shutting automatically.—*n.* **self'-cock'er**, a firearm in which the hammer is raised by pulling the trigger.—*adjs.* **self'-cock'ing; self'-collect'ed**, self-possessed.—*n.* **self'-colour**, uniform colour: natural colour.—*adj.* **self'-coloured.**—*ns.* **self'-command'**, self-control; **self'-commun'ion**, communing with oneself, introspective meditation; **self'-compar'ison** (*Shak.*), something to compare with oneself; **self'-complā'cence**, satisfaction with oneself, or with one's own performances.—*adj.* **self'-complā'cent.**—*n.* **self'-conceit'**, an over-high opinion of oneself, one's own abilities, etc.: vanity.—*adj.* **self'-conceit'ed.**—*ns.* **self'-conceit'edness; self'-concentrā'tion**, concentration of one's thoughts upon oneself; **self'-condemna'tion.**—*adjs.* **self'-condemned'**, condemned by one's own actions or out of one's own mouth; **self'-condemn'ing.**—*n.* **self'-con'fidence**, confidence in, or reliance on, one's own powers: self-reliance.—*adj.* **self'-con'fident.**—*adv.* **self'-con'fidently.**—*adj.* **self'-confid'ing**, relying on one's own powers.—*n.* **self'-congratulā'tion.**—*adjs.* **self'-con'jugate**, conjugate to itself; **self'-con'scious**, conscious of one's own mind and its acts and states: conscious of being observed by others.—*ns.* **self'-con'sciousness; self'-con'sequence**, self-importance.—*adjs.* **self'-con'sequent; self'-consid'ering**, considering in one's own mind, deliberating.—*n.* **self'-consist'ency**, consistency of each part with the rest: consistency with one's principles.—*adjs.* **self'-consis'tent, self'-con'stituted**, constituted by oneself; **self'-consūmed'; self'-consūm'ing**, consuming oneself, or itself; **self'-contained'**, wrapped up in oneself, reserved: of a house, not approached by an entrance common to others: complete in itself.—*ns.* **self'-contempt'; self'-content'**, self-complacency; **self'-contradic'tion**, the act or fact of contradicting oneself: a statement whose terms are mutually contradictory.—*adj.* **self'-contradic'tory.**—*n.* **self'-control'**, power of controlling oneself.—*adj.* **self'-convict'ed**, convicted by one's own acts or words, —*n.* **self'-convic'tion.**—*adj.* **self'-cov'ered** (*Shak.*), perh. disguised by oneself, perh. clothed in one's native semblance.—*ns.* **self'-crit'icism**, critical examination and judgment of one's own works and thoughts; **self'-cult'ure**, development and education of one's personality by one's own efforts; **self'-dān'ger** (*Shak.*), danger to oneself; **self'-deceit'**, self-deception.—*adjs.* **self'-deceit'-ful; self'-deceived'.**—*ns.* **self'-deceiv'er; self'-decep'tion**, deceiving oneself.—*n.* **self'-defeat'ing**, that defeats its own purpose.—*ns.* **self'-defence'**, defending one's own person, rights, etc. (**art of self-defence**, boxing); **self'-delight'**, delight in one's own being or thoughts; **self'-delu'sion**, the delusion of oneself by oneself; **self'-deni'al**, forbearing to gratify one's own appetites or desires.—*adj.* **self'-deny'ing.**—*adv.*

**self'-deny'ingly.**—*adj.* **self'-depraved'**, depraved by one's own act.—*ns.* **self'-despair'**, a despairing view of one's own nature, prospects, etc.; **selfe'-despight'** (*Spens.*), injury to oneself; **self'-destruc'tion**, the destruction of anything by itself: suicide.—*adj.* **self'-destruc'tive.**—*n.* **self'-determinā'tion**, determination without extraneous impulse: direction of the attention or will to an object: the power of a population to decide its own government and political relations or of an individual to live his own life.—*adjs.* **self'-deter'mined; self'-deter'mining; self'-devō'ted.** —*n.* **self'-devō'tion**, self-sacrifice.—*adjs.* **self'-direct'ed; self'-direct'ing.**—*ns.* **self'-direc'tion; self'-direct'or; self'-dis'cipline.**—*adj.* **self'-disliked'** (*Spens.* **selfe'-dislik'ed**).—*n.* **self'-dispar'agement.**—*adj.* **self'-displeased'.**—*ns.* **self'-dispraise'; self'-distrust'; self'-doubt'; self'-dramatisā'tion, -izā'tion**, presentation of oneself as if a character in a play: seeing in oneself an exaggerated dignity and intensity.—*adjs.* **self'-draw'ing** (*Shak.*), of one's, its, own drawing, or drawn from itself; **self'-drive'**, of a motor vehicle, to be driven by the hirer; **self'-driv'en**, driven by its own power; **self'-ed'ucated**, educated by one's own efforts.—*n.* **self'-efface'ment**, keeping oneself in the background out of sight: withdrawing from notice or rights.—*adjs.* **self'-effac'ing; self'-elect'ed**, elected by oneself or itself; **self'-elect'ive**, having the right to elect oneself or itself, as by co-option of new members.—*n.* **self'-elec'tion.**—*adj.* **self'-employed'**, working independently in one's own business. —*ns.* **self'-employ'ment; self-end'** (*obs.*), a private or selfish end.—*adj.* **self'-endeared'**, **-indeared'**, self-loving.—*ns.* **self'-enjoy'ment**, internal satisfaction; **self'-esteem'**, good opinion of oneself: self-respect; **self'-ev'idence.**—*adj.* **self'-ev'ident**, evident without proof.—*ns.* **self'-examinā'tion**, a scrutiny into one's own state, conduct, etc.; **self'-exam'ple**, one's own example.—*adj.* **self'-excit'ing**, itself supplying the exciting current. —*n.* **self'-exist'ence.**—*adjs.* **self'-exist'ent**, existing of or by oneself or itself, independent of any other cause; **self'-explan'atory**, obvious, bearing its meaning in its own face.—*ns.* **self'-explicā'tion**, the power of explaining oneself; **self'-express'ion**, the giving of expression to one's personality, as in art.—*adjs.* **self'-faced'**, undressed or unhewn. esp. of a stone showing a natural cleavage; **self'-fed'**, fed by itself or automatically: fed upon itself.—*n.* **self'-feed'er.**—*adj.* **self'-feed'ing.**—*n.* **self'-feel'ing**, one's own experience.—*adj.* **self'-fer'tile**, fertile by its own pollen or sperm.—*ns.* **self'-fertilisā'tion, -izā'tion; self'-fertil'ity.**—*adj.* **self'-fig'ured**, of one's own devising.—*n.* **self'-fill'er**, a fountain-pen that can be filled without a dropping-tube.—*adj.* **self'-forget'ful**, unselfishly forgetful of self.—*adv.* **self'-forget'fully.**—*adjs.* **self'-glazed'**, glazed in one tint; **self'-glō'rious**, boastful; **self'-gov'erning.** —*n.* **self'-gov'ernment**, self-control: autonomy: government without outside interference: democracy.—*adjs.* **self'-gra'cious**, gracious towards oneself or spontaneously gracious; **self'-harm'ing.**—*ns.* **self-heal'**, prunella; **self'-heal'ing**, spontaneous healing: healing oneself.—Also *adj.*—*n.* **self'-help'**, doing things for oneself without help of others.—*adj.* **self'-het'erodyne**, autodyne.—*ns.* **self'-humiliā'tion; self'-iden'tity**, identity of a thing with itself; **self'-immolā'tion**, offering oneself up in sacrifice: suttee; **self'-import'ance**, an absurdly high sense of one's own importance: pomposity.—*adjs.* **self'-import'ant; self'-imposed'**, taken voluntarily on oneself.—*n.* **self'-impregnā'tion**, impregnation of a hermaphrodite by its own sperm.—*adj.* **self'-incompat'ible**, having reproductive organs that cannot function together.—*ns.* **self'-induc'tance**, the property of an electric circuit whereby self-

induction occurs; **self'-induc'tion**, the property of an electric circuit by which it resists any change in the current flowing in it; **self'-indul'gence**, undue gratification of one's appetites or desires.—*adj.* **self'-indul'gent.**—*n.* **self'-infec'tion**, infection of the entire organism from a local lesion.—*adj.* **self'-inflict'ed**, inflicted by oneself on oneself.—*ns.* **self'-insū'rance**, laying aside a fund to cover losses; **self'-in'terest**, private interest: regard to oneself.—*adjs.* **self'-in'terested; self'-invi'ted**, invited by nobody but oneself; **self'-involved'**, wrapped up in oneself or one's own thoughts: inwoven into itself; **self'-killed'.**—*n.* **self'-kill'er.**—*adj.* **self'-know'ing.** —*n.* **self'-knowl'edge**, knowledge of one's own nature.—*adj.* **self'-left'**, left to oneself.—*n.* **self'-life'**, self-existence: life only for oneself.—*adjs.* **self'-light'ing**, igniting automatically; **self'-like**, exactly similar; **self'-lim'ited** (*path.*), running a definite course; **self'-lock'ing**, locking automatically; **self-lost'**, lost by one's own act.— *n.* **self-love'**, the love of oneself: tendency to seek one's own welfare or advantage: desire of happiness.—*adjs.* **self'-lov'ing; self'-lum'inous**, emitting a light of its own; **self'-made'**, made by oneself: risen to a high position from poverty or obscurity by one's own exertions.—*ns.* **self'-mas'tery**, self-command: self-control; **self'-mett'le** (*Shak.*), natural spirit.—*adj.* **self'-misused'**, spoken ill of by oneself.—*n.* **self'-mo'tion**, spontaneous motion.—*adj.* **self'-moved'**, moved spontaneously from within.—*ns.* **self'-mur'der**, suicide; **self'-mur'derer.**—*adj.* **self'-mur'dering.** —*ns.* **self'-neglect'**, **-ing** (*Shak.*), neglect of oneself; **self'-offence'**, one's own offence: failure in what is due to oneself.—*adj.* **self-o'pened**, opened of its own accord.—*n.* **self'-opin'ion**, high, or unduly high opinion of oneself or of one's own opinion.—*adjs.* **self'-opin'ionated, -opin'ionātive, -opin'ioned**, obstinately adhering to one's own opinion; **self'-pi'ous**, hypocritical. —*n.* **self'-pit'y**, pity for oneself.—*adjs.* **self'-plant'ed**, planted without man's agency; **self'-pleas'ing; self'-poised'**, balanced without outside help.—*ns.* **self'-pollinā'tion**, transfer of pollen to the stigma of the same flower (or sometimes the same plant or clone); **self'-pollu'tion**, masturbation; **self'-por'trait**, a portrait of oneself painted by oneself; **self'-por'traiture.**— *adj.* **self'-possessed'**, having self-possession.—*ns.* **self'-possess'ion**, collectedness of mind: calmness; **self'-praise'**, the praise of oneself by oneself; **self'-preservā'tion**, care, action, or instinct for the preservation of one's own life.—*adjs.* **self'-preser'vative, self'-preser'ving.** — *ns.* **self-pride'**, self-esteem; **self'-prof'it**, private interest. —*adjs.* **self'-prop'agating**, propagating itself when left to itself; **self'-propell'ing**, carrying its own means of propulsion.—*ns.* **self'-protec'tion**, self-defence; **self'-prun'ing**, natural shedding of twigs.—*adjs.* **self-raised'**, raised by oneself: grown without cultivation; **self'-rais'ing**, (of flour) already mixed with something that causes it to rise (also **self'-ris'ing**).—*n.* **self'-realisā'tion**, **-z-**, attainment of such development as one's mental and moral nature is capable of.—*adj.* **self'-record'ing**, recording its own readings.—*n.* **self'-regard'ing**, self-interest: self-respect.—*adjs.* **self'-regard'ing; self'-reg'istering**, self-recording; **self'-reg'ulating**, regulating itself.—*n.* **self'-reli'ance**, healthy confidence in one's own abilities.—*adjs.* **self'-reli'ant; self'-rely'ing.**—*ns.* **self'-renunciā'tion**, self-abnegation; **self'-repress'ion**, restraint of expression of the self; **self'-reproach'**, prickings of conscience; **self'-reproof'**, self-reprov'ing, reproof of conscience; **self'-repug'nance.**—*adj.* **self'-repug'nant**, self-contradictory: inconsistent.—*ns.* **self'-resem'blance** (*Spens.*), appearance of being what one really is; **self'-respect'**, respect for oneself or

one's own character.—*adjs.* self'-respect'ful;
self'-respect'ing; self'-restrained', restrained by
one's own will.—*ns.* self'-restraint', a refraining
from excess: self-control; self'-rev'erence,
great self-respect.—*adjs.* self'-rev'erent; self'-
right'eous, righteous in one's own estimation:
pharisaical.—*n.* self'-right'eousness.—*adjs.* self'-
right'ing, righting itself when capsized; self'-
rig'orous, rigorous towards oneself; self'-
rolled *(Milt.* self'-rowld'), coiled on itself.—*n*
self'-rule'.—*adj.* self'-rul'ing.—*n.* self'-sac'rifice,
forgoing one's own good for the sake of others.
—*adjs.* self'-sac'rificing; self'-same, the very
same.—*ns.* self'-same'ness, identity; self'-
satisfac'tion, satisfaction with oneself.—*adjs.*
self'-sat'isfied; self'-sat'isfying, giving satisfaction to oneself.—*n.* self'-seek'er, one who looks
mainly to his own interests.—*n.* and *adj.* self'-
seek'ing.—*n.* self'-ser'vice, helping oneself, as
in restaurant, etc.—*adj.* self'-severe'
*(Milt.).*—*n.* self'-shield'ing *(phys.),* in large
radioactive sources, the absorption in one part,
of the radiation arising in another part.—*adj.*
self'-slain'.—*n.* self'-slaugh'ter, suicide.—*adj.*
self'-slaugh'tered.—*ns.* self'-slay'er; self'-sov'ereignty, sovereignty over, or inherent in, oneself.
—*adj.* self'-sown', sown naturally without man's
agency.—*n.* self'-star'ter, an automatic contrivance for starting a motor: a car fitted with
one.—*adj.* self'-ster'ile, unable to fertilise itself.
—*n.* self'-steril'ity.—*adjs.* self'-styled', called by
oneself: pretended; self'-subdued' *(Shak.),* subdued by one's own power; self'-substan'tial
*(Shak.),* composed of one's own substance.—*n.*
self'-suffi'ciency.—*adjs.* self'-suffi'cient, requiring
nothing from without: excessively confident
in oneself; self'-suffic'ing.—*ns.* self'-sugges'tion,
autosuggestion; self'-support', support or maintenance without outside help: paying one's
way.—*adjs.* self'-support'ed; self'-support'ing.—
*n.* self'-surren'der, a yielding up of oneself or
one's will.—*adjs.* self'-surviv'ing, remaining as a
mere ruin of itself; self'-sustained', sustained
by one's own power; self'-sustain'ing.—*ns.*
self'-sustain'ment; self'-sus'tenance, self'-sus-
tentā'tion.—*adjs.* self'-taught; self'-tempt'ed;
self'-think'ing, thinking for oneself; self'-
torment'ing.—*n.* self'-torment'or.—*adj.* self'-
tor'turable *(Shak.).*—*ns.* self'-tor'ture; self'-
trust', self-reliance: confidence in one's own
faithfulness to oneself *(Shak.).*—*adj.* self'-
unā'ble *(Shak.),* insufficient of one's own ability.
—*ns.* self'-vi'olence, suicide; self-will', obstinacy.
—*adjs.* self-willed'; self'-wind'ing, (of a watch)
wound by the wearer's spontaneous movements,
or by opening and shutting the case: automatically wound by electricity.—*n.* self'-wrong'
*(Shak.),* wrong done to a person by himself.—
second self (see second). [O.E. *self;* Du. *zelf,*
Ger. *selbe,* Goth. *silba.*]
-self, *self, pl.* -selves, *selvz,* a suff. forming reflexive and emphatic pronouns.—be oneself, himself, etc., to be in full possession of one's
powers: to be (once more) at one's best: to be
alone *(Scot.);* by oneself, etc., alone.
selictar, *se-lik'tär, n.* a sword-bearer. [Turk.
*silihdār*—Pers. *silahdār*—Ar. *silh,* weapon.]
Seljuk, *sel-jōōk', n.* a member of any of the
Turkish dynasties (11th-13th cent.) descended
from *Seljūq* (grandfather of Togrul Beg): a
Turk subject to the Seljuks.—*adjs.* Seljuk',
Seljuk'ian.
sell, selle, *sel, n.* a seat *(arch.):* a saddle *(Spens.).*
[O.Fr. *selle*—L. *sella*—*sedēre,* to sit.]
sell, *sel, v.t.* to give or give up for money or
other equivalent: to betray: to impose upon,
trick: to promote the sale of: to cry up *(obs.):*
to make acceptable: to cause someone to accept
(e.g. an idea, plan): to convince of the value of
something.—*v.i.* to make sales: to be sold, to

be in demand for sale:—*pa.t., pa.p.* sold.—*n,*
*(slang)* a deception: let-down.—*adj.* sell'able,
that can be sold.—*n.* sell'er, one who sells:
that which has a sale.—sellers' market, one in
which sellers control the price, demand exceeding supply; sell'ing-price, the price at which a
thing is sold; selling race, plate, a race of which
the winning horse must be put up for auction
at a price previously fixed (cf. claiming race);
sell'-out, a betrayal: a show for which all seats
are sold.—sell a bargain (see bargain); sell
down the river, to play false, betray; sell off, to
sell cheaply in order to dispose of; sell one's
life dearly, to do great injury to the enemy
before one is killed; sell out, to dispose entirely
of: to sell one's commission: to betray; sell
short, to belittle, disparage; sell the pass, to
betray a trust; sell up, to sell the goods of,
for debt; to sell, for sale. [O.E. *sellan,* to give,
hand over; O.N. *selja,* Goth. *saljan.*]
sell, *sel, n.* a Scots form of self:—*pl.* sells.
seltzer, *selt'sər, n.* a mineral water from Nieder-
*Selters* in Prussia, or an imitation.—*n.* selt'zo-
gene, a gazogene.
selva, *sel'va, n.* (usu. in *pl.* selvas) wet forest in
the Amazon basin. [Sp., Port.—L. *silva,* wood.]
selvage, selvedge, *sel'vij, n.* a differently finished
edging of cloth: a border.—*v.t.* to border.
[self, edge.]
selves, *selvz, pl.* of self.
semantic, *si-man'tik, adj.* relating to meaning,
esp. of words.—*n.* (usu. *pl.* treated as *sing.*) the
science of the development of the meaning of
words.—*n.* seman'teme, a unit of meaning, a
word or the base of a word, that conveys a
definite idea.—*adv.* seman'tically.—*n.* seman'ticist. [Gr. *sēmantikos,* significant.]
semantron, *sem-an'tron, n.* a wooden or metal bar
used instead of a bell in Orthodox churches and
in mosques:—*pl.* seman'tra. [Gr. *sēmantron,*
sign, signal.]
semaphore, *sem'ə-fōr, -för, n.* a signalling apparatus, an upright with arms that can be
turned up or down—often the signaller's own
body and arms with flags.—*v.t.* and *v.i.* to signal
thus.—*adj.* semaphor'ically. [Fr. *sémaphore*—
Gr. *sēma,* sign, signal, *-phoros,* bearing, bearer.]
semasiology, *si-mā-zi-ol'ə-ji,* or *-si-, n.* semantics.
[Gr. *sēmāsia,* meaning.]
sematic, *si-mat'ik, (biol.) adj.* serving for recognition, attraction, or warning. [Gr. *sēma,* sign.]
semble, *sem'bl, (obs.) v.i.* to seem: to be like (to).
—*(obs.) v.t.* to pretend: to picture, image:
to make a picture, image, of.—*adj.* sem'blable
*(Shak.)* resembling, similar, like.—*n. (Shak.)*
like, fellow.—*adv.* sem'blably *(Shak.),* in like
manner.—*n.* sem'blance, likeness: appearance:
outward show: apparition: image.—*adj.* sem'-
blant, resembling: seeming.—*n. (Spens.)* semblance: cheer, countenance, entertainment:
demeanour.—*adj.* sem'blative *(Shak.),* resembling or seeming: simulative. [Fr. *sembler,* to
seem, to resemble—L. *simulāre*—*similis,* like.]
semble, *sem'bl, v.t.* to bring together, collect,
esp. as some female moths do males by scent.
—sem'bling-box, a collector's box enclosing a
captive female. [Aphetic from assemble.]
semé, semée, *sem'ā, (her.) adj.* strewn or scattered
over with small bearings, powdered. [Fr., pa.p.
of *semer*—L. *sēmināre,* to sow.]
semeiology, *sem-i-, sēm-i-ol'ə-ji, n.* the study of
symptoms: the study of signs and symbols.—*n.*
semeion *(sē-mī'on),* in ancient prosody, the unit
of time: one of the two divisions of a foot: a
mark of metrical or other division:—*pl.* semei'a.
—*adj.* semeiot'ic, pertaining to symptoms.—
*n.pl.* (treated as *sing.*) semeiot'ics, semeiology.
[Gr. *sēmeion,* sign.]
semen, *sē'men, n.* the liquid that carries spermatozoa.—See seminal. [L. *sēmen, -inis,* seed.]

semester, *si-mes'tər*, *n*. a university half-year course (German, etc.).—*adjs*. semes'tral, semes'-trial, half-yearly. [L. *sēmēstris—sex*, six, *mēnsis*, a month.]

semi-, *sem'i-*, *pfx*. half: loosely, nearly, partly, incompletely.—*ns*. sem'i, sem'ie, a semi-bajan; sem'iangle, a half-angle.—*adj*. sem'i-ann'ual, (chiefly *U.S.*) half-yearly.—*adv*. sem'i-ann'ually. —*adj*. sem'i-ann'ular, half-ring-shaped.—*n*. and *adj*. sem'i-Ā'rian, homoiousian.—*n*. sem'i-Ā'rianism.—*adjs*. sem'i-attached', partially bound; sem'i-automat'ic, partly automatic but requiring some tending by hand.—*ns*. sem'i-ax'is, a half-axis; sem'i-bā'jan (*hist., Scot. univ.*), a second-year student.—*n*. and *adj*. sem'i-barbā'rian.—*ns*. sem'i-bar'barism; sem'ibrēve, half a breve (2 minims or 4 crochets); sem'ibull, a pope's bull issued between election and coronation; semicar'bazide, a base ($H_2N \cdot CO \cdot NH \cdot NH_2$) reacting with aldehydes and ketones to form semicar'bazones.—*adj*. sem'i-centenn'ial, occurring at the completion of fifty years.—*n*. (*U.S.*) a jubilee.—*ns*. sem'ichōr'us, half a chorus: a passage sung by it; sem'icircle, half a circle, bounded by the diameter and half the circumference.—*adjs*. sem'icircled; semicir'cular (semicircular canals, the curved tubes of the inner ear concerned with equilibrium).—*adv*. semicir'cularly.—*ns*. sem'icirque, a semicircular hollow: a semicircle; sem'icolon, the point (;) marking a division greater than the comma; semicō'ma, a condition approaching coma.—*adj*. semico'matose.—*ns*. semiconductiv'ity; semiconduct'or, formerly, any substance with electrical conductivity between that of metals and of non-conductors: now, any solid, non-conducting at low temperatures or in pure state, which is a conductor at higher temperatures or when very slightly impure.—*adj*. sem'icon'scious.—*ns*. semicyl'inder, a longitudinal half-cylinder; sem'idem'isem'iquaver, half a demisemiquaver.—*adj*. semidepō'nent, passive in form in the perfect tenses only.—Also *n*.—*adj*. sem'i-detached', partly separated: joined by a party wall to one other house only.—*n*. sem'i-diam'eter, half the diameter, esp. the angular diameter.—*adjs*. semi-diur'nal, accomplished in twelve hours: pertaining to half the time or half the arc traversed between rising and setting; semi-divine', half-divine': of, of the nature of, a demigod.—*ns*. semidocument'ary, a cinematograph film with an actual background but an invented plot; sem'i-dome', half a dome, esp. as formed by a vertical section.—*adjs*. semidomes'ticated, partially domesticated: half-tame; sem'i-doub'le, having only the outermost stamens converted into petals.—*n*. a festival less solemn than a double.—*adj*. sem'i-dry'ing, of oils, thickening without completely drying on exposure.—*n*. sem'i-ellipse', half of an ellipse, bounded by a diameter, esp. the major axis.—*adjs*. sem'i-ellip'tical; semifi'nal, immediately before the final.—*n*. a last round but one.—*n*. semifi'nalist, a competitor in a semifinal.—*adj*. semiflu'id, nearly solid but able to flow to some extent.—Also *n*.—*adj*. semiglob'ular.—*n*. semigrand, a square piano with curtailed keyboard. —Also *adj*.—*n*. and *adj*. semi-im'becile.—*adj*. sem'i-independ'ent, not fully independent.—*ns*. semi-ju'bilee, the twenty-fifth anniversary; sem'i-lat'us rec'tum, half the latus rectum, terminated at the focus.—*adjs*. sem'i-liq'uid, half-liquid; sem'ilog(arithm), of graph paper, graph, etc., having one scale logarithmic, the other arithmetical; semilu'cent, half-transparent; sem'i-lu'nar, -lu'nate, half-moon shaped.—*n*. sem'ilune (*-lōōn*), a half-moon-shaped object, body, or structure.—*adj*. sem'imen'strual, half-monthly. —*n*. sem'i-met'al (*obs.*), a metal that is not malleable.—*adj*. sem'i-month'ly (chiefly *U.S.*),

half-monthly.—*n*. a half-monthly periodical.— *adj*. sem'i-mute', with speech impaired by loss of hearing.—Also *n*.—*adjs*. sem'i-nūde', half-naked; semi-occā'sional (*U.S.*), occurring now and then.—*adv*. semi-occā'sionally.—*adj*. sem'i-offic'ial, partly official.—*adv*. sem'i-offic'ially. —*n*. sem'i-ō'pal, a dull variety of opal.—*adjs*. sem'i-opaque', partly opaque; sem'iovip'arous, producing imperfectly developed young; semi-pal'mate, half-webbed: half web-footed.—*ns*. semipalmā'tion; semipar'asite, a partial parasite, feeding partly independently.—*adj*. sem'i-parasit'ic.—*n*. sem'iped, in verse, a half-foot. —*n*. and *adj*. Sem'i-Pelā'gian.—*n*. Sem'i-Pelā'gianism, the middle course between Augustinian predestination and Pelagian free-will.— *adj*. sem'ipellu'cid, imperfectly transparent.—*n*. semiperim'eter, half the perimeter.—*adj*. sem'i-per'meable, permeable by a solvent but not by the dissolved substance.—*ns*. sem'iplume, a feather with ordinary shaft but downy web; semipor'celain, a coarse ware resembling porcelain.—*adj*. semi-prec'ious, valuable, but not valuable enough to be reckoned a gemstone.— *n*. sem'iquāver, half a quaver.—*adj*. sem'i-rig'id, of an airship, having a flexible gasbag and stiffened keel.—*n*. sem'i-ring, a half-ring.—*adj*. sem'i-sag'ittate, shaped like half an arrowhead. —*n*. and *adj*. Sem'i-Sax'on (*obs.*), Early Middle English (*c*. 1150-1250).—*adjs*. sem'i-skilled'; semiterete', half-cylindrical.—*n*. sem'itone, half a tone—one of the lesser intervals of the musical scale as from B to C.—*adj*. semiton'ic.—*n*. semitranspā'rency.—*adjs*. semitranspā'rent, imperfectly transparent; semi-trop'ical, subtropical; semi-tū'bular, like half of a tube divided longitudinally; sem'i-un'cial, intermediate between uncial and minuscule.—*n*. a semi-uncial letter.—*n*. sem'ivowel, a sound partaking of the nature of both a vowel and a consonant: a letter representing it.—*adj*. sem'i-week'ly, issued or happening twice a week.— Also *n*. and *adv*. [L. *sēmi-*, half-; cf. Gr. *hēmi-*, O.E. *sam-*.]

seminal, *sem'in-l*, *adj*. pertaining to, or of the nature of, seed or of semen: generative: notably creative or influential in future development(*fig.*).—*n*. seminal'ity, germinating principle: germ.—*adv*. sem'inally.—*v.t*. sem'ināte, to sow: to propagate.—*n*. seminā'tion, sowing: seed-dispersal: seeding.—*adj*. seminif'erous, seed-bearing: producing or conveying semen. [L. *sēmen, -inis*, seed.]

seminar, *sem'i-när*, *n*. (orig. *Ger*.) a group of advanced students working in a specific subject of study under a teacher: a class at which a group of students and a tutor discuss a particular topic.—*adjs*. seminarial (*-ā'ri-əl*); seminā'rian, of a seminary.—*n*. a student in a seminary, esp. of R.C. theology.—*ns*. sem'inarist (*-ər-ist*), a student in a seminary or in a seminar: a Roman Catholic priest educated in a foreign seminary: a teacher in a seminary; sem'inary (*-ə-ri*), a seed-plot: a breeding-place: a place of origin and fostering, nursery: formerly, a pretentious name for a school (esp. for young ladies): a college, esp. for R.C. (in *U.S.* also other) theology: a seminary priest.—*adj*. seminal: of a seminary: of a seminar. [L. *sēminārium*, a seed-plot—*sēmen*, seed.]

Seminole, *sem'i-nōl*, *n*. an American Indian of an offshoot of the Creeks, originally in Florida, now mostly in Oklahoma. [Creek *Simánole*, lit. runaway.]

semiology, semiotic(s). Same as semeiology, semeiotic(s).

semis, *sē'mis*, *sā'mis*, *n*. a bronze coin of the ancient Roman republic, half an as. [L. *sēmis*, *sēmissis*.]

semitar, semitaur, old spellings of scimitar

**Semite**, *sem'* or *sēm'it, n.* a member of any of the peoples said (Gen. x) to be descended from Shem, or speaking a Semitic language.—*adj.* **Semitic** (*sem-, sim-, sǝm-it'ik*).—*n.* any Semitic language: (in *pl.*) Semitic studies.—*n.* **Semitisā'tion, -z-.**—*v.t.* Sem'itise, -ize, to render Semitic in language, religion, or otherwise.—*ns.* **Sem'itism**, a Semitic idiom or characteristic: Semitic ways of thought: the cause of the Semites, esp. the Jews; **Sem'itist**, a Semitic scholar.—**Semitic languages**, Assyrian, Aramaic, Hebrew, Phoenician, Arabic, Ethiopic, etc. [Gr. *Sēm*, Shem.]

**semmit**, *sem'it, (Scot.) n.* an undershirt.

**Semnopithecus**, *sem-nō-pith-ē'kǝs, n.* the hanuman genus. [Gr. *semnos*, honoured, *pithēkos*, an ape.]

**semolina**, *sem-ǝ-lē'nǝ, -li'nǝ, n.* the particles of fine, hard wheat that do not pass into flour in milling. [It. *semolino*, dim. of *semola*, bran—L. *simila*, fine flour.]

**semper**, *sem'pǝr, -per,* (L.) always.—**semper idem** (*i'dem, id'em, ē'dem*), always the same; **semper paratus** (*pǝ-rä'tǝs, pa-rä'tōōs*), always ready.

**sempiternal**, *sem-pi-tûr'nl, adj.* everlasting.—Also **semp'itern**.—*ns.* **sempiter'nity; sempiter'num,** (*obs.*) a durable woollen cloth. [L. *sempiternus* —*semper*, ever.]

**semple**, *sem'pl, adj.* a Scottish form of simple, esp. meaning not of gentle birth.

**semplice**, *sem'plē-che,* (*mus.*) *adj.* simple, without embellishments. [It.]

**sempre**, *sem'pre,* (*mus.*) *adv.* always, throughout. [It.]—L. *semper*, always.]

**sempster, seamster**, *sem'stǝr, n.* one who sews— orig. *fem.*, now only *masc.*:—*fem.* **semp'stress, seam'stress**.—*ns.* **semp'stering, semp'stressing, semp'stress-ship**. [O.E. *sēamestre*; see seam.]

**semsem**, *sem'sem, n.* sesame. [Ar. *simsim.*]

**semuncia**, *si-mun'sh(y)ǝ, n.* a Roman half-ounce: a bronze coin, an as in its ultimate value.—*adj.* **semun'cial**. [L. *sēmuncia—sēmi-*, half, *uncia*, a twelfth.]

**sen**, *sen, n.* a Japanese copper coin, the hundredth part of a yen:—*pl.* sen. [Jap.]

**senary**, *sēn', sen'ǝr-i, adj.* of, involving, based on, six.—*n.* a set of six: a senarius.—*n.* **senarius** (*se-nä'ri-ǝs*), a verse of six iambs or equivalents. [L. *sēnārius—sēnī*, six each—*sex*, six.]

**senate**, *sen'it, n.* the governing body of ancient Rome: a legislative or deliberative body, esp. the upper house of a national or state legislature: a body of venerable or distinguished persons: the governing body of certain British universities (in Scotland, **Senā'tus Academ'icus**).—*n.* **senator** (*sen'ǝ-tǝr*), a member of a senate (Senator of the College of Justice, a Lord of Session).—*adj.* **senatorial** (*sen-ǝ-tō'ri-ǝl, -tō'ri-ǝl*).—*adv.* **senatō'rially**, with senatorial dignity.—*n.* **sen'atorship**.—*n.* **sen'ate-house**, the meeting-place of a senate.—**senā'tus consult'** (L. *senātūs consultum*), a decree of the senate. [L. *senātus—senex, senis*, an old man.]

**senatus populusque Romanus**, *sǝ-nä'tǝs pop'ūl-ǝs-kwē rōm-an'ǝs, sen-ä'tōōs pop-ōōl-ōōs'kwe rō-mä'nōōs,* (L.) the Roman senate and people:— abbrev. S.P.Q.R.

**send**, *send, v.t.* to cause, direct, or tell to go: to propel: to cause to be conveyed: to dispatch: to forward: to grant: orig. of jazz, to rouse (someone) to ecstasy.—*v.i.* to dispatch a message or messenger: to pitch into the trough of the sea (*naut.*; sometimes **scend**, **'scend**):—*pa.t.* and *pa.p.* **sent**; *naut.* **send'ed**.—*n.* a messenger (*Scot.*): one or more sent to fetch a bride (*Scot.*): a message: an impetus or impulse: a plunge.— *ns.* **send'er**, one who sends: a transmitting instrument; **send'ing**, dispatching: pitching: transmission: that which is sent (esp. by a wizard).—**send'-off**, a demonstration at starting or at departing; **send-up**, a process of making

fun of someone or something.—**send down**, to rusticate or expel; **send for**, to require by message to come or be brought; **send on**, to send in advance: to re-address and re-post (a letter or package); **send up**, to make fun of (*slang*): to sentence to imprisonment; **send word**, to send an intimation. [O.E. *sendan*; O.N. *senda*, Goth. *sandjan*, Ger. *senden*.]

**sendal**, *sen'dǝl, n.* a thin silk or linen. [O.Fr. *cendal*, prob.—Gr. *sindōn*; see sindon.]

**Seneca**, *sen'i-ka, n.* an Iroquois Indian of a tribe in New York state, etc.—*adj.* **Sen'ecan**.—**Seneca oil**, crude petroleum, used by them.

**Senecan**, *sen'i-kan, adj.* of, in the manner of, Lucius Annaeus *Seneca*, Stoic philosopher and writer of declamatory tragedies (*c.* 4 B.C.-A.D. 65).

**Senecio**, *se-nē's(h)i-ō, n.* the groundsel and ragwort genus of composite plants. [L. *senex*, an old man, from the hoary pappus.]

**senega**, *sen'i-gǝ, n.* an American milkwort (*Polygala senega*; **senega snakeroot**): its dried root, reputed by the *Seneca* Indians good for snakebites.

**senescent**, *si-nes'ǝnt, adj.* verging on old age: ageing.—*n.* **senesc'ence**. [L. *senēscēns, -entis,* pr.p. *of senēscěre*, to grow old—*senex*, old.]

**seneschal**, *sen'i-shl, n.* a steward: a major-domo. —*n.* **sen'eschalship**. [O.Fr. (Fr. *sénéchal*), of Gmc. origin, lit. old servant; cf. Goth. *sineigs,* old, *skalks*, O.E. *scealc*, servant.]

**sengreen**, *sen'grēn, n.* the house-leek. [O.E. *singrēne*, evergreen, house-leek, periwinkle—*pfx. sin-*, one, always (cf. L. *semel*, once), *grēne,* green; cf. Ger. *sin(n)grüne*, periwinkle.]

**Senhor**, *se-nyōr', -nyōr', Senhora, -a, Senhorita, -ē'ta, ns.* the Portuguese forms corresponding to the Spanish Señor, Señora, Señorita.

**senile**, *sē'nil, adj.* characteristic of or attendant on old age: showing the decay or imbecility of old age.—*n.* **senility** (*si-nil'i-ti*), old age: the imbecility of old age. [L. *senīlis—senex, senis,* old.]

**senior**, *sēn'yǝr, adj.* elder: older or higher in standing: more advanced: first.—*n.* one who is senior: a fourth-year student (*U.S.*).—*ns.* **seniority** (*sē-ni-or'i-ti*), state or fact of being senior: priority by age, time of service, or standing: a body of seniors or senior fellows.— **senior optime** (see optime); **senior service**, the navy. [L. *senior, -ōris,* comp. of *senex*, old.]

**senna**, *sen'ǝ, n.* a shrub (Cassia, of various species): its purgative dried leaflets.—**senna tea**, an infusion of senna.—**bladder senna**, a papilionaceous shrub (Colutea) with similar properties. [Ar. *sanā*.]

**sennachie**. Same as **seannachie**.

**ser.net**, *sen'it,* (*Shak.*) *n.* a trumpet or woodwind announcement of a stage entrance (or exit) in state. [App. a form of **signet**.]

**sennight**, *sen'it,* (*arch.*) *n.* a week. [**seven, night**.]

**sennit**, *sen'it,* **sinnet**, *sin'it, n.* a flat braid of rope yarn. [Origin uncertain.]

**Senonian**, *si-nō'ni-ǝn,* (*geol.*) *n.* a Cretaceous stage answering to the English Upper Chalk.—Also *adj.* [L. *Senonēs,* a tribe of central Gaul.]

**Señor**, *se-nyōr', -nyōr', n.* a gentleman: in address, sir: prefixed to a name, Mr:—*fem.* **Señora** (*se-nyō'ra, -nyō'*), a lady: madam: as a title, Mrs. —*n.* **Señorita** (*sen-yō-rē'ta, -yō-*), a young lady: Miss. [Sp.,—L. *senior*, older.]

**Senoussi**. See **Senussi**.

**sens**, *sens, adv.* (*Spens.*) since.

**sense**, *sens, n.* faculty of receiving sensation, general or particular: immediate consciousness: inward feeling: impression: opinion: mental attitude: discernment: understanding: appreciation: feeling for what is appropriate: discerning feeling for things of some particular kind: (usu. in *pl.*) one's right wits: soundness of judgment: reasonableness: sensible or reasonable discourse: that which is reasonable:

plain matter of fact: the realm of sensation and sensual appetite: a sense-organ (*Shak.*): meaning: interpretation: purport: gist: direction (esp. in *geom.*, after Fr. *sens*).—*adj.* pertaining to a sense or senses.—*v.t.* to have a sensation, feeling, or appreciation of: to appreciate, grasp, comprehend: to become aware (that): of computers, to detect (e.g. a hole, constituting a symbol, in punched card or tape).—*n.* **sensation** (*sen-sā'shən*), awareness of a physical experience, without any element derived from previous experiences: awareness by the senses generally: an effect on the senses: power of sensing: an emotion or general feeling: a thrill: a state, or matter, of general excited interest in the public, audience, etc.: melodramatic quality or method: enough to taste, as of liquor (*slang*).—*adj.* **sensā'tional.**—*ns.* **sensā'tionalism,** the doctrine that our ideas originate solely in sensation: a striving after wild excitement and melodramatic effects; **sensā'tionalist.**—*adj.* **sensātionalist'ic.**—*adv.* **sensā'tionally.**—*ns.* **sensā'tionism; sensā'-tionist, sensā'tion-monger,** a dealer in the sensational.—*adjs.* **sensed,** endued with meaning; **sense'ful,** significant: full of good sense: **sense'-less,** unconscious: deficient in good sense: meaningless.—*adv.* **sense'lessly.**—*ns.* **sense'lessness; sensibil'ity,** sensitiveness, sensitivity: capacity of feeling or emotion: readiness and delicacy of emotional response: sentimentality: (often in *pl.*) feelings that can be hurt.—*adj.* **sen'sible,** perceptible by sense: perceptible: easily perceived: appreciable: having power of sensation: conscious: sensitive: having sensibility (*obs.*): easily affected: delicate: cognisant: aware: emotionally conscious: having or marked by good sense, judicious.—*n.* an object of sense: that which is sensible.—*n.* **sen'sibleness.**—*adv.* **sen'-sibly,** in a sensible manner: to a sensible or perceptible degree: so far as the senses show.—*adj.* **sensile** (*sen'sil*), sentient: capable of affecting the senses.—*n.* and *adj.* **sen'sing.**—*ns.* **sen'sism,** sensationalism in philosophy; **sen'sist; sensitisā'-tion, -z-.**—*v.t.* **sen'sitise, -ize,** render sensitive, or more sensitive, or sensitive in a high degree.—*adj.* **sen'sitised.**—*n.* **sen'sitiser.**—*adj.* **sen'sitive,** having power of sensation: feeling readily, acutely, or painfully: capable of receiving stimuli: reacting to outside influence: ready and delicate in reaction: sensitised: susceptible to the action of light (*phot.*): pertaining to, or depending on, sensation.—*n.* one who or that which is sensitive, or abnormally or excessively sensitive.—*adv.* **sen'sitively.**—*ns.* **sen'sitiveness, sensitiv'ity,** response to stimulation of the senses: heightened awareness of oneself and others within the context of personal and social relationships: abnormal responsiveness as to an allergen: degree of responsiveness to electric current, or radio waves, or to light: (of an instrument) readiness and delicacy in recording changes; **sensitom'eter,** an instrument for measuring sensitivity, as of photographic films; **sen'sor,** a device that detects a change in a physical stimulus and turns it into a signal which can be measured or recorded, or which operates a control.—*adj.* **senso'rial,** sensory.—*ns.* **senso'rium,** the seat of sensation in the brain: the brain: the mind: the nervous system; **sen'sory,** the sensorium.—*adj.* of the sensorium: of sensation.—*adj.* **sen'sual** (*-sū-əl, -shoo-əl*), of the senses, as distinct from the mind: not intellectual or spiritual: carnal: worldly: connected with gratification, esp. undue gratification of bodily sense: voluptuous: lewd. —*n.* **sensualisā'tion, -z-.**—*v.t.* **sen'sualise, -ize,** to make sensual: to debase by carnal gratification. —*ns.* **sen'sualism,** sensual indulgence: the doctrine that all our knowledge is derived originally from sensation: the regarding of the gratification of the senses as the highest end;

**sen'sualist,** one given to sensualism or sensual indulgence: a debauchee: a believer in the doctrine of sensualism.—*adj.* **sensualist'ic.**—*n.* **sensual'ity** (*Milt.* **sen'sualty**), indulgence in sensual pleasures: lewdness.—*adv.* **sen'sually.**—*ns.* **sen'sualness; sen'suism** (*philos.*), sensationalism; **sen'suist; sen'sum,** sense-datum.—*adj.* **sen'suous,** pertaining to sense (without implication of lasciviousness or grossness): connected with sensible objects: easily affected by the medium of the senses.—*adv.* **sen'suously.**—*n.* **sen'suousness.**— sensa'tion-monger (see sensationist above); **sensation novel,** one dealing in violent effects and strained emotion; **sense'-datum,** what is received immediately through the stimulation of a sense-organ; **sense'-organ,** a structure specially adapted for the reception of stimuli, as eye, ear, nose; **sense'-percep'tion,** perception by the sense; **sensible horizon,** the visible horizon; **sensible note,** leading note; **sensitive flame,** a flame that rises or falls in response to sound; **sensitive plant,** a plant, esp. *Mimosa pudica,* that shows more than usual irritability when touched or shaken, by movements of leaves, etc.—**five senses,** sight, hearing, smell, taste, and touch; **bring one to his senses,** to make one recognise the facts: let one understand one must mend one's behaviour; **common sense** (see **common**); **in a sense,** in a sense other than the obvious one: in a way: after a fashion; **in, out of, one's senses,** in or out of one's right wits, normal rational condition; **make sense,** to be understandable or sensible, rational; **make sense of,** to understand: to see the purpose in, or explanation of; **sixth sense,** an ability to perceive what lies beyond the powers of the five senses. [L. *sēnsus—sentire,* to feel.]

**sent,** an earlier spelling (*Spens., Shak., Milt.*) of **scent,** *n., v.t.,* and *v.i.,* smell: sense.

**sent,** *sent, pa.t.* and *pa.p.* of **send.**

**sentence,** *sen'təns, n.* opinion: a judgment, decision: determination of punishment pronounced by a court or a judge: a maxim: a number of words making a complete grammatical structure, generally begun with a capital letter and ended with a full-stop or its equivalent: an assertion in logic or mathematics: sense, meaning, matter (*obs.*).—*v.t.* to pronounce judgment on: to condemn.—*n.* **sen'tencer.**—*adj.* **sentential** (*-ten'shl*).—*adv.* **senten'tially.**—*adj.* **senten'tious,** full of meaning: aphoristic, abounding (often superabounding) in maxims.—*adv.* **senten'tiously.**—*n.* **senten'tiousness.**—**Master of the Sentences,** Peter Lombard (12th cent.), from his collection of opinions from Augustine, etc.; **open sentence,** a sentence which, having an undefined variable is, as it stands, neither true nor false (*math.*) [Fr.,—L. *sententia—sentire,* to feel.]

**sentient,** *sen'sh(y)ənt, adj.* conscious: capable of sensation: aware: responsive to stimulus.—*n.* that which is sentient: a sentient being or mind. —*ns.* **sen'tience, sen'tiency.** [L. *sentiēns, -entis,* pr.p. of *sentire,* to feel.]

**sentiment,** *sen'ti-mənt, n.* a thought or body of thought tinged with emotion: opinion: judgment: a thought expressed in words: a maxim: a thought or wish propounded to be ratified by drinking: emotion: feeling bound up with some object or ideal: regard to ideal considerations: sensibility, refined feelings: consciously worked-up or partly insincere feeling: sentimentality. —*adj.* **sentimental** (*-men'tl*), pertaining to, given to, characterised by, expressive of, sentiment: given to, indulging in, expressive of, sentimentality. —*v.i.* **sentimen'talise, -ize,** to behave sentimentally: to indulge in sentimentality.—*v.t.* to make sentimental: to treat sentimentally.—*ns.* **sentimen'-talism, sentimentality** (*-man-tal'i-ti*), disposition to wallow in sentiment: self-conscious working up of feeling: affectation of fine feeling: sloppiness; **sentimen'talist,** one who affects, seeks to work up, or luxuriates in sentiment or fine feeling: one guided by mere sentiment: one who regards sentiment as more important than reason.—*adv.* **sentimen'tally.** [L.L. *sentimentum*—L. *sentire,* to feel.]

**sentinel,** *sen'ti-nl, n.* one posted on guard, a sentry: guard.—*adj.* acting as a sentinel.—*v.t.* to watch over: to post as a sentinel: to furnish with sentinels.—*v i* to keep guard, aentinel **crab,** a crab of the Indian Ocean with long eye-stalks. [Fr. *sentinelle*—It. *sentinella,* watch, sentinel.]

**sentry,** *sen'tri, n.* a sentinel: a soldier on guard: watch, guard.—**sen'try-box,** a box to shelter a sentry; **sen'try-go,** a sentry's beat or duty: a watch-tower (*obs.*). [Etymology obscure.]

**Senussi,** *sen-ōōs'ē, n.* a member of a Moslem sect or confraternity, chiefly in N.E. Africa, founded by Sidi Mohammed ben Ali es-Senussi (d. 1860; named from the *Senus* Mountains):—*pl.* **Senussi.**—Also **Senoussi.**

**senvy,** *sen'vi,* (*obs.*) *n.* mustard (plant or seed). [O.Fr. *senevé*—L. *sināpi*—Gr. *sināpi,* mustard.]

**senza,** *sen'tsä,* (*mus.*) *prep.* without. [It.]

**sepad,** *sə-päd', v.t.* to suppose: to warrant. [A ghost-word; from J. M. Barrie's mishearing of **I'se** ( =I sal) **uphaud,** I shall uphold.]

**sepal,** *sep'l,* also *sēp'l, n.* a member of a flower calyx.—*adjs.* **sep'aline** (*-in*), **sep'aloid, sep'alous.** —*n.* **sep'alōdy** (Gr. *eidos,* form), transformation of other members into sepals. [Fr. *sépale,* invented by N. J. de Necker (1790) from Gr. *skepē,* cover.]

**separate,** *sep'ə-rāt, v.t.* to divide: to part: to sunder: to sever: to disconnect: to disunite: to remove: to isolate: to keep apart: to seclude: to set apart for a purpose: to shut off from cohabitation, esp. by judicial decree: to remove cream from by a separator.—*v.i.* to part: to withdraw: to secede: to come out of combination or contact: to become disunited.—*adj.* (*sep'ə-rit, -rāt, sep'rit*) separated: divided: apart from another: distinct.—*n.* an off-print: (in *pl.*) two items of dress, e.g. blouse and skirt, worn together as an outfit.—*n.* **separability** (*-ə-bil'i-ti*).—*adj.* **sep'arable,** that may be separated or disjoined.—*n.* **sep'arableness.**—*advs.* **sep'arably; sep'arately.**—*ns.* **sep'arateness; separā'tion,** act of separating or disjoining: state of being separate: disunion: chemical analysis: cessation of cohabitation by agreement or judicial decree, without a formal dissolution of the marriage tie; **separā'tionist,** one who favours separation, esp. political or ecclesiastical; **sep'aratism** (*-ə-tizm*); **sep'aratist,** one who withdraws or advocates separation from an established church, federation, organisation, etc.: a dissenter: an Independent (*hist.*): (by Unionists) a Home Ruler: a believer in separate authorship of parts, esp. of the Homeric poems.—*adj.* **sep'arative** (*-ə-tiv*), tending to separate.—*ns.* **sep'arātor,** one who, or that which, separates: a machine for separating cream from milk by whirling; **separatory** (*sep'ər-ə-tər-i*), an instrument for separating.—*adj.* having the function of separating.—*ns.* **sep'arātrix,** a separating line; **separā'tum,** a separate off-print.—**separate development,** segregation of different racial groups, each supposed to progress in its own way; **separate maintenance,** a provision made by a husband for his separated wife; **separation allowance,** government allowance to a serviceman's wife and dependents. [L. *sēparāre, -ātum*—*sē-,* aside, *parāre,* to put.]

**Sephardim,** *se-fär'dēm, n.pl.* the Spanish and Portuguese Jews.—*adj.* **Sephar'dic.** [Heb.]

**sephen,** *sef'en, n.* a sting-ray. [Ar. *safan,* shagreen.]

**sepia,** *sē'pi-ə, n.* a cuttlefish, esp. of Sepia or

kindred genus: cuttlefish ink: a pigment made from it, or an artificial imitation: its colour, a fine brown: a sepia drawing.—*adj.* of the colour of sepia: done in sepia.—*ns.* **sē'piolite** (Gr. *lithos,* stone), meerschaum; **sē'piost, sēpiostaire'** (Fr. *sépiostaire*—Gr. *osteon,* bone), **sē'pium,** cuttlebone. [L.,—Gr. *sēpiā,* cuttlefish, *sēpion,* cuttlebone.]

**sepiment,** *sep'i-mənt, n.* a hedge, a fence. [L. *saepimentum,* a hedge.]

**sepoy,** *sē'pol, n.* an Indian soldier in European service (*hist.*): a soldier: a policeman. [Urdu and Pers. *sipāhi,* horseman.]

**seppuku,** *sep-ōō'kōō, n.* hara-kiri. [Jap.]

**seps,** *seps, n.* a very venomous snake known to the Greeks: (*cap.*) a genus of almost legless skinks. [Gr. *sēps.*]

**sepsis,** *sep'sis, n.* putrefaction: invasion by pathogenic bacteria. [Gr. *sēpsis,* putrefaction.]

**sept,** *sept, n.* orig. in Ireland, a division of a tribe. —*adj.* **sept'al.** [Prob. for sect, influenced by L. *saeptum*; see next.]

**sept,** *sept, n.* an enclosure: a fence.—*n.pl.* **sept'a** (see **septum** below).—*adjs.* **sept'al,** partitional: growing in hedges; **septā'rian.**—*n.* **septā'rium,** a nodule with a network of mineral-filled cracks:—*pl.* **septā'ria.**—*adj.* **sept'ate,** partitioned.—*n.* **septā'tion,** division by partitions.—*adjs.* **septici'dal** (L. *caedēre,* to cut), with splitting of septa, as when a fruit dehisces by separation of the carpels; **septif'erous,** having partitions; **sept'iform,** in the form of a partition; **septif'ragal** (root of L. *frangēre,* to break), with separation of the outer walls of the carpels from the septa.—*n.* **sept'um** (*biol.*), a partition:—*pl.* **sept'a.** [L. *saeptum* (used in pl.), a fence, enclosure—*saepire,* to fence.]

**sept-, septi-, septem-,** in composition, seven.—*adj.* **septemfid** (*sep'təm-fid;* root of L. *findēre,* to cleave), seven-cleft.—*n.* **septemvir** (*sep-tem'vir;* L. *vir,* man), one of a board of seven:—*pl.* **septem'viri, -virs.**—*n.* **septem'virate,** the office of a septemvir: a board of septemviri: a group of seven men.—*adj.* **septilateral** (*sep-ti-lat'ər-əl;* L. *latus, lateris,* a side), seven-sided.—*n.* **septillion** (*sep-til'yən;* modelled on **million**), the seventh power of a million: the eighth power of a thousand (*U.S.*). [L. *septem.*]

**September,** *sap-, sep-tem'bər, n.* ninth, earlier seventh, month of the year.—*adj.* **Septem'berish.** —*ns.* **Septembriser** (*sep'təm-bri-zər*), a Septembrist: a partridge-shooter; **Septem'brist,** a participator in the September massacres in Paris, 2nd to 7th Sept. 1792. [L. *September, -bris.*]

**septenarius,** *sep-ti-nā'ri-əs, n.* a seven-foot verse, esp. a trochaic tetrameter catalectic.—*adj.* **septenary** (*sep-tē'nə-ri,* or *sep'tə-nə-ri*), numbering or based on seven.—*n.* a seven, set of seven (esp. years): a septenarius. [L. *septēnārius,* of seven.]

**septennium,** *sep-ten'i-əm, n.* seven years:—*pl.* **septenn'ia.**—*n.* **septenn'ate,** a period of seven years.—*adj.* **septenn'ial.**—*adv.* **septenn'ially.**— **Septennial Act,** a statute of 1716, in force till 1911, limiting the duration of a parliament to seven years. [L. *septennis*—*annus,* a year.]

**septentrion,** *sep-ten'tri-ən,* (*Shak.*) *n.* the north:— *pl.* **septen'trions, septentriō'nēs,** the seven stars of the Plough: the Great Bear.—*adjs.* **septen'trion** (*Milt.*), **-al,** northern.—*adv.* **septen'trionally.** [L. *septentriōnēs,* i.e. *septem triōnēs,* the seven plough-oxen.]

**septet, septette, septett,** *sep-tet', n.* a composition for seven performers: a set of seven (esp. musicians). [Ger. *septett*—L. *septem.*]

**sept-foil,** *set'foil, n.* tormentil: a figure divided by seven cusps. [Fr. *sept,* seven, O.Fr. *foil*—L. *folium,* a leaf.]

**septic,** *sep'tik, adj.* putrefactive.—*n.* **septicaemia** (*sep-ti-sē'mi-ə;* Gr. *haima,* blood), presence of pathogenic bacteria in the blood.—*adv.* **sep'-**

tically.—*n*. septicity (*-tis'i-ti*).—septic tank, a tank in which sewage is decomposed by anaerobic bacteria. [Gr. *sēptikos—sēpein*, to putrefy.]
septimal, *sep'ti-ml*, *adj*. relating to, based on, seven.—*ns*. septime (*sep'tēm*), the seventh position in fencing; sep'timole (*-mōl*), a group of seven notes to be played in the time of four or six. [L. *septimus*, seventh—*septem*, seven.]
septleva, *set'lə-vä*, *n*. in basset, seven times as much added to the first stake. [Fr. *sept-et-le-va*, seven and the first stake.]
septuagenarian, *sep-tū-ə-ji-nā'ri-ən*, *n*. a person seventy years old, or between seventy and eighty.—*adj*. of that age.—*adj*. septuagenary (*-ə-jē'nər-i*, *-aj'in-ər-i*), consisting of or relating to seventy.—*n*. one seventy years old. [L. *septuāgēnārius—septuāgēni*, seventy each.]
Septuagesima, *sep-tū-ə-jes'i-mə*, *n*. the third Sunday before Lent (also Septuagesima Sunday) —apparently in continuation of the sequence Quadragesima, Quinquagesima, etc. [L. *septuāgēsimus, -a, -um*, seventieth.]
Septuagint, *sep'tū-ə-jint*, *n*. the Greek Old Testament, traditionally attributed to 72 translators at Alexandria in the 3rd century B.C.—usually expressed by LXX.—*adj*. Septuagin'tal. [L. *septuāgintā—septem*, seven.]
septum. See sept (2).
septuor, *sep'tū-ör*, *n*. a septette. [Fr.,—L. *septem*, after *quatuor*.]
septuple, *sep'tū-pl*, also *-tū'*, *-tōō*, *-tōō'*, *adj*. sevenfold.—*v.t.* to multiply sevenfold.—*n*. sep'tuplet, a septimole: one of seven at a birth. [L.L. *septuplus*—L. *septem*, seven; cf. quadruple.]
sepulchre, *sep'əl-kər*, *n*. a tomb: a recess, usually in the north chancel wall, or a structure placed in it, to receive the reserved sacrament and the crucifix from Maundy Thursday or Good Friday till Easter (Easter sepulchre): burial.—*v.t.* (formerly sometimes *si-pul'kər*) to entomb: to enclose as a tomb.—*adjs*. sepulchral (*si-pul'krəl*), of, of the nature of, a sepulchre: funeral: as if of or from a sepulchre: funereal, gloomy, dismal: hollow-toned; sepul'chrous (*rare*), sepul'tural.—*n*. sep'ulture, burial: a tomb or burial-place.—*v.t.* to entomb.—whited sepulchre (see white). [L. *sepulcrum*, *sepultūra—sepelīre*, *sepultum*, to bury.]
sequacious, *si-kwā'shəs*, *adj*. ready to follow a leader or authority: compliant: pliant: observing logical sequence or consistence: in long-drawn-out sequence or train.—*ns*. sequā'ciousness, sequacity (*si-kwas'i-ti*). [L. *sequāx, sequācis—sequi*, to follow.]
sequel, *sē'kwəl*, *n*. that which follows: followers (*obs*.): successors (*obs*.): consequences: upshot: a resumption of a story already complete in itself: sequence (*Shak*.).—*n*. sequela (*si-kwē'lə*), morbid affection following a disease: often in *pl*. sequē'lae (*-lē*). [L. *sequēla—sequi*, to follow.]
sequence, *sē'kwəns*, *n*. a state or fact of being sequent or consequent: succession: order of succession: a series of things following in order: a set of three or more cards consecutive in value: that which follows: consequence: successive repetition in higher or lower parts of the scale or in higher or lower keys (*mus*.): in cinematography, a division of a film: in liturgics, a hymn in rhythmical prose, sung after the gradual and before the gospel.—*adj*. sē'quent, following: consequent: successive: consecutive.—*n*. a follower (*Shak*.): that which follows.—*adj*. sequential (*si-kwen'shl*).—*n*. sequentiality (*-shi-al'i-ti*).—*adv*. sequen'tially.—sequence of tenses, the relation of tense in subordinate clauses to that in the principal. [L. *sequēns, -entis*, pr.p. of *sequi*, to follow.]
sequester, *si-kwes'tər*, *v.t.* to set aside: to seclude:

to set apart: to confiscate: to remove from one's possession until a dispute can be settled, creditors satisfied, or the like: to hold the income of for the benefit of the next incumbent: to sequester the estate or benefice of: to remove or render ineffective (a metal ion) by adding a reagent that forms a complex with it (e.g. as a means of preventing or getting rid of precipitation in water). —*v.i.* (*obs*.) to seclude oneself.—*n*. (*sek'wes-tər*; *Shak*.) seclusion.—*adj*. seques'tered, retired, secluded.—*v.t.* sequestrate (*sek'*, *sēk'*, or *si-kwes'*), to sequester: to make bankrupt.—*ns*. sequestrā'tion (*sek-*, *sēk-*), act of sequestering: bankruptcy (*Scots law*); seq'uestrator. [L.L. sequesträre, -ätum—L. *sequester*, a depositary—*secus*, apart.]
sequin, *sē'kwin*, *n*. an old Italian gold coin worth about 46p.: a spangle. [Fr.,—It. *zecchino—zecca*, the mint; of Ar. origin.]
Sequoia, *si-kwoi'ə*, *n*. a genus of gigantic conifers, the Californian big tree or mammoth tree and the redwood—sometimes called Wellingtonia. [After then Cherokee Indian scholar *Sequoiah*.]
sérac, *sā-rak'*, *sā'rak*, *n*. one of the cuboidal or pillar-like masses into which a glacier breaks in a steep incline. [Swiss Fr., originally a kind of cheese.]
seraglio, *sə-*, *se-rä'li-ō*, *-lyō*, *n*. women's quarters in a Mohammedan house or palace: a harem: a collection of wives or concubines: an enclosure: a Turkish palace, esp. that of the sultans at Constantinople. [It. *serraglio*—L. *sera*, a door-bar, confused with Turk. *saray*, *serāi*, a palace.]
serai, *se-rä'i*, *n*. a khan, caravanserai: erron., a seraglio, harem. [Turk. (orig. Pers.) *saray*, *serai*.]
serail, *se-räl'*, *n*. seraglio. [Fr. *sérail*.]
serang, *se-rang'*, *n*. a lascar boatswain. [Pers. *sarhang*, a commander.]
serape, *se-rä'pä*, *n*. a Mexican riding-blanket. [Sp. *sarape*.]
seraph, *ser'əf*, *n*. a six-winged celestial being (Isa. vi): an angel of the highest of the nine orders: a person of angelic character or mien:—*pl*. ser'aphs, ser'aphim, formerly also ser'aphin, ser'aphins, ser'aphims, the plurals in -im and -in also occurring as *obs. sing.*—*adjs*. seraphic (*-af'*), -al.—*adv*. seraph'ically.—*n*. ser'aphine (*-ēn*), a keyboard reed instrument, precursor of the harmonium.—Seraphic Doctor, St Bonaventura: St Teresa; Seraphic Father, St Francis; Seraphic Order, the Franciscans. [Heb. *Serāphim* (pl.).]
Serapis, Sarapis, *sə-*, *se-rä'pis*, *n*. a god of the Greeks of Egypt, identified with Apis and Osiris. —*n*. Serapeum (*ser-ə-pē'əm*), a temple of Serapis.—*adj*. Ser-, Sarapic (*-ap'ik*). [Gr. *Sarāpis*, later (also L.) *Serāpis*.]
seraskier, *ser-as-kēr'*, *n*. a Turkish commander-in-chief or war minister.—*n*. seraskier'ate, the office of seraskier. [Turk. pron. of Pers. *ser'asker—ser*, head, Ar. '*asker*, army.]
Serb, *sûrb*, Serbian, *sûr'bi-ən*, *ns*. a native or citizen of Serbia (formerly a kingdom, now a republic of Yugoslavia): a member of the people principally inhabiting Serbia: the South Slav language of Serbia.—*adj*. of Serbia, its people, or their language.—*ns*. and *adjs*. Serbo-Cro'at, Serbo-Croa'tian. [Serb. *Srb*.]
Serbonian, *sər-bō'ni-ən*, *adj*. like *Sirbōnis*, *Serbōnis*, a now dry lake in the N.E. corner of Egypt, 'Where armies whole have sunk' (*Paradise Lost*, II, 594).
serdab, *sər-däb'*, *n*. an underground chamber: a secret chamber in an Egyptian tomb. [Pers. *sard*, cold, *āb*, water.]
sere. See sear (1 and 2), cere.
sere, *sēr*, (*obs*.) *n*. a claw. [O.Fr. *serre—serrer*, to hold.]
sere, *sēr*, *n*. a series of plant communities following each other.—*adj*. sēr'al.—seral community, a

plant community which is not stabilised but represents a stage in a succession. [L. *seriēs*, series.]

**serein**, *sə-rē'*, *n.* fine rain from a cloudless sky. [Fr.,—L. *sērum*, evening, *sērus*, late.]

**serenade**, *ser-i-nād'*, *n.* a composition like a symphony, usually slighter and in more movements: a performance in the open air by night, esp. at a lady's window: a piece suitable for such performance.—*v.t.* to entertain with a serenade. —*v.i.* to perform a serenade.—*ns.* serenā'der; serenata (*-i-nä'tä*), a (symphonic) serenade: a pastoral cantata; ser'enate (*Milt.*), a serenade. [Fr. *sérénade*, and It. *serenata*—L. *serēnus*, bright clear sky; meaning influenced by L. *sērus*, late.]

**serendipity**, *ser-ən-dip'i-ti*, *n.* the faculty of making happy chance finds. [*Serendip*, a former name for Ceylon. Horace Walpole coined the word (1754) from the title of the fairy-tale 'The Three Princes of Serendip', whose heroes 'were always making discoveries, by accidents and sagacity, of things they were not in quest of'.]

**serene**, *sə-rēn'*, *adj.* calm: unclouded: unruffled: an adjunct to the titles of some princes (translating Ger. *Durchlaucht*).—*n.* calm brightness: serenity: serene sky or sea: pure air.—*v.t.* to tranquillise: to clear.—*adv.* serēne'ly, calmly, coolly.—*ns.* serēne'ness; serenity (*-ren'i-ti*).—**all serene** (*slang*), everything as it should be: all right; **drop serene** (*Milt.*), amaurosis. [L. *serēnus*, clear.]

**serene**, *ser'ēn*, *sə-rēn'*, (*obs.*) *n.* a supposedly unwholesome night-dew: serein. [serein.]

**serf**, *sûrf*, *n.* a person in modified slavery, esp. one attached to the soil: a villein:—*pl.* serfs.—*ns.* serf'age, serf'dom, serf'hood, serf'ship.—*adj.* serf'ish. [Fr.,—L. *servus*, a slave.]

**serge**, *sûrj*, *n.* a strong twilled fabric, now usually of worsted.—*adj.* of serge. [Fr.,—L. *sērica*, silk; see Seric.]

**sergeant, serjeant**, *sär'jənt*, *n.* orig. a servant: an officer who made arrests (*obs.*): (usu. with *g*) a non-commissioned officer next above a corporal: (with *g*) an officer of police: (usu. with *g*) alone or as a prefix, designating certain officials: (with *j*) formerly, a barrister of highest rank (in full serjeant-at-law).—*ns.* ser'gean(t)cy, ser'jean(t)cy, office or rank of sergeant, serjeant; ser'geantship, ser'jeantship; ser'jeantry, serjeanty; ser'jeanty, a condition of tenure by service in person to the king (**grand serjeanty**) or rendering some small object (**petty serjeanty**).—**ser'geant-** (or **ser'jeant-) at-arms**, an officer of a legislative body or the Court of Chancery, for making arrests, etc.; ser'geant-drumm'er, drum-major; ser'geant-fish, a fish with stripes, esp. the cobia (Rhachicentron) of S.E. U.S., akin to the mackerels; ser'geant-mā'jor, formerly, an officer of rank varying from major to major-general: now, the highest non-commissioned officer (**regimental sergeant-major**, a warrant officer on the staff of a battalion, regiment, etc.).—**Common Serjeant**, in London, an assistant to the Recorder. [Fr. *sergent*—L. *serviēns*, *-entis*, pr.p. of *servīre*, to serve.]

**serial.** See series.
**seriate.** See series.
**seriatim.** See series.

**Seric**, *ser'ik*, *adj.* Chinese: (without *cap.*) silken. —*adj.* **sericeous** (*sə-rish'əs*), silky: covered with soft silky appressed hairs: with silky sheen.—*ns.* **sericin** (*ser'i-sin*), the gelatinous substance of silk; **ser'icite**, a silky soapy potash mica.—*adj.* **sericitic** (*-sit'ik*).—*ns.* **sericitisā'tion**, **izā'tion**, conversion (esp. of orthoclase) into sericite; **ser'iculture**, silkworm breeding—also **sericiculture** (*ser'i-si-kul-chər*); **ser(ic)icul'turist**.—*ns.* **ser'igraph**, a print made by silk-screen process; **serig'rapher**.—*adj.* **serigraph'ic**.—*n.* **serig'raphy.**

[Gr. *sērikos*—*Sēr*, a Chinese, a silkworm (pl. *Sērĕs*).]

**sericon**, *ser'i-kon*, *n.* conjectured to be a red (or black) tincture in alchemy.

**seriema**, *ser-i-ē'mə*, *-ā'mə*, *n.* the crested screamer. [Tupi.]

**series**, *sē'rēz*, *-iz*, rarely *sē'ri-ēz*, *n.* a set of things in line or in succession, or so thought of: a set of things having something in common, esp. of books in similar form issued by the same house: a set of things differing progressively: a succession of quantities each derivable from its predecessor according to a law: a taxonomic group (of various rank): a geological formation: succession: sequence: linear or end-to-end arrangement: in music, a set of notes in a particular order, taken, instead of a traditional scale, as the basis of a composition—the twelve note row of twelve tone music is an example:—*pl.* sē'ries.—*adj.* sē'rial, forming a series: in series: in a row: in instalments: of publication in instalments: using series as the basis of composition (*mus.*): of supernumerary buds, one above another.—*n.* a publication, esp. a story, in instalments: a motion picture, television or radio play appearing in instalments.—*v.t.* sē'rialise, -ize, to arrange in series: to publish serially.—*ns.* serialisā'tion, publication in instalments: the use of notes and/or other elements of music in regular patterns; sē'rialism, serial technique, or use of it (*mus.*); sē'rialist, a writer of serials, or of serial music; seriality (*-al'i-ti*).—*adv.* sē'rially.—*adj.* sē'riate, in rows.—*advs.* sē'riately; seriā'tim, one after another.—**serial technique**, the technique of music based on series; **serial time**, time regarded as an infinite regression of successive times each needed for the descripton of its predecessor (J. W. Dunne, 1875-1949).—**arithmetical series**, a series progressing by constant difference; **geometrical series**, a series progressing by constant ratio. [L. *seriēs*—*serĕre*, *sertum*, to join.]

**serif**, *ser'if*, *n.* the short cross-line at the end of a stroke in a letter.—Also **seriph** and **ceriph**. [Origin obscure; poss. Du. *schreef*, stroke.]

**serigraph, serigrapher**, etc. See under Seric.

**serin**, *ser'in*, *n.* a smaller species of canary.—*n.* **serinette'**, a small barrel-organ for training songbirds. [Fr., canary.]

**seringa**, *sə-ring'gə*, *n.* a Brazilian rubber-tree (Hevea): mock-orange (Philadelphus). [Port.; see syringa.]

**serious**, *sē'ri-əs*, *adj.* grave: staid: earnest: disinclined to lightness: in earnest: not to be taken lightly: approaching the critical or dangerous: concerned with weighty matters: professedly religious.—*adjs.* se'riocom'ic, -al, partly serious and partly comic.—*adv.* se'riously. —*n.* se'riousness. [L.L. *sēriōsus*—L. *sērius*.]

**seriph.** See serif.
**serjeant.** See sergeant.
**serk.** See sark.

**serkali**, *ser-käl'ē*, *n.* the Government: white rulers. [Swahili.]

**sermon**, *sûr'mən*, *n.* a discourse, esp. one delivered, or intended to be delivered, from the pulpit, on a Biblical text: a harangue.—*v.t.* and *v.i.* to preach: to discourse.—*ns.* **sermoneer'**, **ser'moner** (both *rare*), a preacher: a sermoniser; **sermonet(te)'**, a little sermon.—*adjs.* **sermonic** (*-mon'ik*), **-al**.—*n.* **ser'moning**.—*v.i.* **ser'monise**, **-ize**, to compose sermons: to preach.—*v.t.* to preach to.—*n.* **sermonis'er**.—*adj.* **ser'monish**. [L. *sermō*, *sermōnis*—*serĕre*, to join.]

**sero-**, *sē'rō-*, in composition, serum.

**serologist**, etc. See serum.

**seron, seroon**, *si-rōn'*, *-ron'*, *-rōōn'*, *n.* a crate or hamper: a bale wrapped in hide. [Sp. *serón*.]

**serosa**, *si-rō'zə*, (*zool.*) *n.* the chorion: the serous membrane (see serum):—*pl.* serō'sas, -sae (*-zē*).

[Modern L.; fem. of *serōsus—serum* (see serum).]

**serotine**, *ser'ō-tin*, *-tin*, *n.* a small reddish bat.—*adj.* late, in occurrence, development, flowering, etc.—*adj.* **serotinous** (*si-rot'i-nəs*). [L. *serōtinus*—*sērus*, late.]

**serous**, etc. See serum.

**serow**, *ser'ō*, *n.* a Himalayan goat-antelope. [Lepcha (Tibeto-Burman language) *sa-ro*.]

**serpent**, *sûr'pənt*, *n.* formerly, any reptile or creeping thing, esp. if venomous: now, a snake: a person treacherous or malicious: an obsolete crooked bass wind instrument of wood covered with leather: a twisting firework: (*cap.*) a northern constellation.—*adj.* serpentlike: serpent's.—*v.i.* to wind.—*adjs.* serpentiform (*-pent'*), snake-shaped; ser'pentine (*-tin*), snakelike: winding: tortuous.—*n.* a winding track: an old kind of cannon: a soft, usually green mineral, a hydrated magnesium silicate, occurring in winding veins and in masses, formed by alteration of olivine, etc.: a rock (in full ser'pentine-rock), commonly an altered peridotite, composed mainly of the mineral serpentine.—*v.t.* and *v.i.* to wind: to insinuate.—*adv.* ser'pentinely.—*adj.* serpentinic (*-tin'ik*).—*n.* and *adj.* ser'pentining.—*adv.* serpenti'ningly.—*n.* serpentinisā'tion, *-z-* (*-tin-iz*).—*v.t.* ser'pentinise, -ize, to convert into serpentine.—*v.i.* to wind.—*adj.* serpenti'nous, of serpentine: winding.—*v.i.* ser'pentise, -ize, to wind.—*v.t.* to make to wind.—*adj.* and *adv.* ser'pentlike.—*n.* ser'pentry, serpents collectively.—ser'pent-eater, the secretary-bird: the markhor; ser'pent-god, -goddess, a deity in the form of a snake: a deified snake; serpentine verse, a line that begins and ends with the same word (from the figure of a snake with its tail in its mouth, common as a symbol of eternity); ser'pent-liz'ard, the lizard Seps; ser'pent-star, a brittle star; ser'pent-stone, an ammonite: a snake-stone; ser'pent-wor'ship.—the old serpent, Satan. [L. *serpēns, -entis*, pr.p. of *serpĕre*, to creep; cf. Gr. *herpein*.]

**serpigo**, *sər-pī'gō*, *n.* (*Shak*. sapego, or suppeago) any spreading skin disease.—*adj.* serpiginous (*-pij'*). [L.L. *serpigō*—L. *serpĕre*, to creep.]

**serpula**, *sûr'pū-lə*, *n.* a polychaete worm (Serpula or kindred genus) with twisted calcareous tube:—*pl.* ser'pulae (*-lē*).—*n.* ser'pulite, a fossil resembling a worm-tube. [L., a snake—*serpĕre*, to creep.]

**serr, serre.** See serried.

**serra**, *ser'ə*, *n.* a saw: anything sawlike (L.): a mountain-range (*Port.*):—*pl.* serr'ae (*-ē*; L.); serr'as (*Port.*).—*ns.* serradill'a, serradell'a (*Port.*), bird's-foot (Ornithopus); serr'an, a fish of the genus Serranus, or its family; Serranus (*sə-rā'nəs*), the typical genus of Serranidae (*-ran'i-dē*), the sea-perch family, akin to the perches.—*ns.* and *adjs.* serranid (*ser'ən-id*); serr'anoid.—*n.* Serrasal'mo (L. *salmō*, salmon), the piranha genus of fishes.—*adjs.* serr'āte, serrā'ted, notched like a saw: with sharp forward-pointing teeth (*bot.*).—*v.t.* to notch.—*n.* serrā'tion, saw-edged condition: (usu. in *pl.*) a sawlike tooth.—*adjs.* serratiros'tral (L. *rōstrum*, beak), saw-billed; serratulate (*sər-at'ū-lāt*), minutely serrate.—*ns.* serrature (*ser'ə-chər*), serration; serrā'tus, one of several muscles of the thorax.—*adjs.* serricorn (*ser'*; L. *cornū*, horn), having serrate antennae; serr'ulate, -d, finely serrate.—*n.* serrulā'tion. [L. and Port. (from L.) *serra*, a saw.]

**serrate(d)**, etc., serricorn. See serra.

**serried**, *ser'id*, *adj.* close-set.—*v.t.* serr, serre (*sûr*), to press close: to close the ranks of.—*n.* serrefile, serafile (*ser'ə-fil*; see file), a file of officers or men detailed to ride in rear of the rear rank of a squadron when in line: a soldier so detailed.—*v.t.* and *v.i.* serr'y, to close together.

[Fr. *serrer* or its pa.p. *serré*—L. *sera*, bar, lock.]

**serrulate**, etc. See serra.

**Sertularia**, *sûr-tū-lā'ri-ə*, *n.* a common genus of hydroids with double row of sessile hydrothecae.—*n.* and *adj.* sertulā'rian. [L. *serta*, garlands.]

**seruewe** (i.e. servewe), Spenserian spelling of surview.

**serum**, *sē'rəm*, *n.* a watery liquid, esp. that which separates from coagulating blood: blood serum containing antibodies, taken from an animal that has been inoculated with bacteria or their toxins, used to immunise persons or animals: watery part of a plant fluid:—*pl.* sēr'ums, sēr'a.—*adj.* serolog'ical.—*adv.* serolog'ically.—*ns.* serol'ogist; serol'ogy, the study of serums and their properties; seros'ity; sērother'apy, treatment or prevention of disease by injecting blood-serum containing the appropriate antibodies.—*adj.* sē'rous, pertaining to, like, of the nature of, serum.—serous membrane, a thin membrane, moist with serum, lining a cavity and enveloping the viscera within, e.g. the pericardium, the peritoneum; sēr'um-ther'apy, serotherapy. [L. *sĕrum*, whey.]

**serval**, *sûr'vl*, *n.* a large, long-legged, short-tailed African cat or tiger-cat. [Port. (*lobo*) *cerval*, lit. deer-wolf, transferred from another animal.]

**servant**, *sûr'vənt*, *n.* one who is hired to perform service, especially personal or domestic service of a menial kind, or farm labour, for another or others: one who is in the service of the state, the public, a company, or other body: one who serves: a ministrant: formerly, a man conventionally accepted by a lady (called his *mistress*) as binding himself to devoted attendance: in formal epistolary use, formerly in greeting and leave-taking, now sometimes in colloquial jocularity, applied in seeming humility to oneself: a slave: (in *pl.*) formerly a designation conceded by a great personage to a company of actors, to evade legal difficulties.—*v.t.* to subject.—*adj.* ser'vantless.—*ns.* ser'vantry, servants collectively; ser'vantship, position or relation of a servant.—ser'vant-girl, ser'vant-lass, ser'vant-maid, a female domestic servant; ser'vant-man, a male servant; servants' hall, a servants' dining-and sitting-room.—civil servant, one in the civil service (see civil). [Fr., pr.p. of *servir*—L. *servīre*, to serve.]

**serve**, *sûrv*, *v.t.* to be a servant to: to be in the service of: to worship (*obs.*): to work for: to render service to: to perform service for or under: to perform the duties or do the work connected with: of a male animal, to cover: to attend as assistant: to be of use to or for: to avail: to suffice for: to satisfy: to further: to minister to: to attend to the requirements of: to supply: to furnish with materials: to help to food, etc.: to send or bring to table: to deal: to put into action, bring to bear (*Spens.*): to put into play by striking (*tennis*, etc.): to treat, behave towards: to be opportune to: to conform one's conduct to: to undergo, work out, go through: to bind (rope, etc.) with cord, etc.: to deliver or present formally, or give effect to (*law*): to declare (heir; *Scots law*).—*v.i.* to be a servant: to be in service or servitude: to render service: to be a member, or take part in the activities, of an armed force: to perform functions: to wait at table: to attend to customers: to act as server: to answer a purpose, be of use, do: to be opportune or favourable: to suffice.—*n.* service of a ball.—*ns.* ser'ver, one who serves, esp. at meals, mass, or tennis: a salver: a fork, spoon, or other instrument for distributing or helping at table; serv'ery, a room or rooms adjoining a diningroom, from which meals and liquors are served and in which utensils are kept.—*n.* and *adj.* serv'ing.—serv'ing-mall'et, a mallet with grooved head used in

serving ropes; serv'ing-man (*arch*.), a man-servant.—serve as, to act as: to take the place of; serve one a trick, to play a trick on one; serve one right, to be no more than one deserves; serve one's time, to pass through an apprenticeship or a term of office; serve out, to deal or distribute: to punish: to retaliate on; serve the (or one's) turn, to suffice for one's immediate purpose or need; serve time, to undergo a term of imprisonment, etc.; serve up, to bring to table. [Fr. *servir*—L. *servire*, to serve.]
Servian (*obs*.). Same as Serbian.
Servian, *sûr'vi-ən, adj*. of *Servius* Tullius, legendary king of Rome.
service, *sûr'vis, n*. condition or occupation of a servant or of one who serves: work: act or mode of serving: employ: employment as a soldier, sailor, or airman, or in any public organisation or department: the personnel so employed: the force, organisation, or body employing it (in *pl*. usu. the fighting forces): that which is required of its members: that which is required of a feudal tenant: performance of a duty or function: actual participation in warfare: a warlike operation: a performance of religious worship: a liturgical form or office or a musical setting of it: a good turn, good offices, benefit to another: duty or homage ceremonially offered, as in health-drinking, correspondence, or greeting: use: hard usage: availability: disposal: supply, as of water, railway-trains: expediting: waiting at table: that which is served, a course: order of dishes: a set, as of dishes for a particular meal: supplementary activities for the advantage of customers: cost of interest and sinking-fund charges: cord or other material for serving a rope.—*adj.* of the army, navy, or air force: (sometimes in *pl*.) of the army, navy and air force collectively: for the use of servants: of industry, etc., providing services rather than manufactured products.—*v.t.* to provide or perform service for (e.g. motor-cars).—*ns.* serviceabil'ity, ser'viceableness.—*adj.* ser'viceable, able or willing to serve: advantageous: useful: capable of rendering long service, durable.—*adv.* ser'viceably.—*adj.* ser'viceless.—ser'vice-book, a book of forms of religious service: a prayer-book; ser'vice-court, in lawn-tennis, the area outside of which a served ball must not fall; ser'vice-flat, a flat in which domestic service is provided, its cost being included in rent; service hatch, one connecting dining room to kitchen, etc., through which dishes, etc., may be passed; ser'vice-line, the boundary of the service-court, 21 feet from the net; ser'viceman, a member of a fighting service; ser'vice-pipe, -wire, a branch from a main to a building; ser'vice-res'ervoir, a reservoir for supplying water to a particular area; service road, a minor road parallel to a main road and serving local traffic without obstructing the main road; ser'vice-room, a room in a club or hotel where visitors' requirements are attended to; service station, an establishment providing general services for motorists.—active service, service of a soldier, etc., in the field (widely interpreted by the authorities); at your service, at your disposal: also a mere phrase of civility; civil service (see civil); have seen service, to have fought in war: to have been put to long or hard use. [Fr.,—L. *servitium*.]
service, *sûr'vis, n*. a tree (*Pyrus domestica*) very like the rowan.—ser'vice-berry, its pear-shaped fruit: shadbush or its fruit (*U.S.*); ser'vice-tree.—wild service, a tree of the same genus (*P. torminalis*) with sharp-lobed leaves. [O.E. *syrfe*—L. *sorbus*.]
servient, *sûr'vi-ənt, adj*. subordinate: subject to a servitude or easement. [L. *serviēns, -entis*, pr.p. of *servire*, to serve.]

serviette, *sûr-vi-et'*, (in older Scottish use and now general, but not the preferred term) *n.* a table-napkin. [Fr.]
servile, *sûr'vil, adj.* pertaining to slaves or servants: slavish: meanly submissive: cringing: controlled, subject: slavishly or unintelligently imitative: expressing mere grammatical relations.—*n.* a servile person.—*adv.* ser'vilely.—*ns.* ser'vilism (*-vil-izm*), systematic or habitual servility: servile spirit: a system based on slavery or advocacy of it; servility (*-vil'i-ti*), servitude: slavishness of manner or spirit: slavish deference. [L. *servīlis*—*servus*, a slave.]
Servite, *sûr'vit, n.* a member of the mendicant order of Servants of the Virgin, founded at Florence in 1233.
servitor, *sûr'vi-tar, n.* one who serves: a servant: a man-servant: one who serves in war (*obs*.): an assistant, apprentice, lawyer's clerk, assistant schoolmaster, or the like (*Scot., obs*.): a follower or adherent: formerly, in Oxford, an undergraduate partly supported by the college, his duty to wait on the fellows and gentlemen commoners at table: in Edinburgh, a classroom janitor:—*fem.* ser'vitress.—*adj.* servito'rial.—*n.* ser'vitorship. [L.L. *servitor, -ōris*—L. *servire*, to serve.]
servitude, *sûr'vi-tūd, n.* a state of being a slave or (now *rare*) servant: slavery: subjection: compulsory labour: subjection to irksome conditions: a burden on property obliging the owner to allow another person or thing an easement. [L. *servitūdō*.]
servo, *sûr'vō, adj.* of a system in which the main mechanism is set in operation by a subsidiary mechanism and is able to develop a force greater than the force communicated to it. —ser'vo-control', a reinforcing mechanism for the pilot's effort, usu. small auxiliary aerofoil; ser'vo-mech'anism, a closed-cycle control system in which a small input power controls a larger output power in a strictly proportionate manner; ser'vo-mo'tor, a motor using a servo-mechanism. [L. *servus*, a servant, slave.]
servus servorum Dei, *sûr'vəs sûr-vō'rəm, -vö'rəm, dē'i, ser'vŏŏs, 'wŏŏs, ser-vō'rōōm, -wō', de'ē,* (L.) a servant of the servants of God (a title adopted by the popes).
sesame, *ses'ə-mi, n.* a plant (*Sesamum indicum*) of the Pedaliaceae, yielding gingili-oil.—*adj.* ses'amoid, shaped like a sesame seed.—*n.* a small rounded bone in the substance of a tendon.—ses'ame-grass, zama grass.—open sesame (see open). [Gr. *sēsamē*, a dish of sesame (Gr. *sēsamon*).]
Seseli, *ses'ə-li, n.* a genus of the Umbelliferae. [Gr. *seseli*, a name for several umbellifers of this and other genera.]
sesqui-, *ses'kwi*, in composition, in the ratio of one and a half to one, or one and an *n*th to one.—*adj.* sesquialter (*-al'tar*; L. *alter*, second), as three to two.—*ns.* sesquial'tera (*mus*.), a perfect fifth: three notes against two: an organ stop reinforcing harmonics; sesquicentenn'ial, a hundred and fiftieth anniversary.—Also *adj*.—*n.* sesquiox'ide, an oxide with three atoms of oxygen to two of the other constituent.—*adjs.* sesquip'edal, sesquipedā'lian (L. *sēsquipedālis—pēs, pedis*, foot; of objects or words), a foot and a half long—of words (after Horace, *Ars Poetica*, line 97), very long and pedantic.—*ns.* sesquipedā'lianism, sesquipedality (*-pi-dal'i-ti*).—*adj.* sesquip'licate (L. *sēsquiplex, -plicis*), of, or as, the square roots of the cubes.—*ns.* sesquisul'-phide, a compound with three atoms of sulphur to two; sesquiter'tia, a perfect fourth: four notes against three. [L. *sēsqui—sēmisque—sēmis* (for *sēmi-as*), half a unit, *que*, and.]
sess, *ses, n.* Same as cess.
sessa, *ses'a*, sesey, *ses'ē*, (Shak.) *interj.* or *interjs.*

of disputed meaning.—Other readings are
caese, cease; ceas, sese. [Poss. reduplication of
sa; poss. Sp. cesa, or Fr. cessez, cease.]
sessile, ses'il, -il, adj. stalkless: sedentary.—adj.
sess'ile-eyed. [L. sessilis, low, squat—sedēre,
sessum, to sit.]
session, sesh'ən, n. an act of sitting: a seated
position: the enthronement of Christ at God's
right hand: a sitting, series of sittings, or time of
sitting, as of a court or public body: the time
between the meeting and prorogation of Parliament: a school year (sometimes a school day):
in Scotland, etc., a division of the academic year
(winter session of two terms, summer session of
one): the kirk-session: formerly, the Court
of Session: (in pl.) quarter-sessions: a period
of time spent engaged in any one activity (coll.).
—adj. sess'ional.—adv. sess'ionally.—sess'ion-
clerk', the official who records the transactions
of a kirk-session; sess'ion-house, a building
where sessions are held (also sess'ions-house):
the room where a kirk-session meets.—Court of
Session, the supreme civil court of Scotland.
[Fr.,—L. sessiō, sessiōnis—sedēre, sessum, to sit.]
sesspool. Same as cesspool.
sesterce, ses'tərs, n. a Roman coin, the sestertius,
worth 2½ asses, later 4 asses.—n. sester'tium
(-shi-əm), a money of account equal to 1000
sesterces:—pl. sester'tia. [L. sestertius, two and
a half—sēmis, half, tertius, third; sestertium,
prob. orig. gen. plur. for mille sestertium, a
thousand sesterces.]
sestet, sestett, sestette, ses-tet', n. a group of six:
the last six lines of a sonnet: a composition for
six performers (also sestet'to). [It. sestetto—
sesto—L. sextus, sixth.]
sestina, ses-tē'nə, n. an old verse-form of six
six-lined stanzas having the same end-words in
different orders, and a triplet introducing all of
them.—Also sestine (-tēn'). [It.,—L. sextus,
sixth.]
set, set, v.t. to seat: to place: to put: to fix: to
put, place, or fix in position or required condition: to apply: to cause to be: to plant: to
stake: to put on eggs: to put under a hen: to
dispose, array, arrange: to put to catch the
wind: to spread, lay, cover, as a table: to compose, as type: to put in type: to embed: to
frame: to mount: to beset or bestow about: to
stud, dot, sprinkle, variegate: to form or represent, as in jewels: to imprint (Shak.): to make
to become solid, coagulated, rigid, fixed, or
motionless: to begin to form (as fruit or seed):
to regulate: to appoint: to ordain: to assign:
to prescribe: to propound: to present for
imitation: to put upon a course, start off: to
incite, direct: to escort (Northern): to put in
opposition: to posit: to rate, value: to pitch,
as a tune: to compose or fit music to: to
sharpen, as a razor: to indicate by crouching:
to lease or let to a tenant (Scot. and local): to
become, befit (chiefly Scot.): conversely, to
appear to advantage in: to arrange (hair) in
waves or curls: to defeat (a bridge contract),
usu. by (so many tricks).—v.i. to sit (now arch.
or dial.): to hang in position: to be in session:
to go down towards or below the horizon, to
decline: to offer a stake: to become rigid, fixed,
hard, solid, or permanent: to coagulate: of a
bone, to knit: to settle down: to begin to
develop, as fruit: to have or take a course or
direction: to begin to go: to dance in a facing
position: to acquire a set or bend: of dogs, to
point out game: to apply or betake oneself:
—pr.p. sett'ing; pa.t. and pa.p. set.—adj. in
any of the senses of the participle: prescribed:
deliberate, intentional: prearranged: formal:
settled: fixed: rigid: determined: regular:
established: ready: of mature habit of body.—
n. a group of persons or things, esp. such as

associate, occur, or are used together or have
something in common: a clique: a coterie: a
complete series, collection, or complement: a
company performing a dance: a series of dance
movements or figures: a complete apparatus,
esp. for wireless receiving: an act, process, mode,
or time of setting: a setting: an inclination:
direction of flow: a dog's indication of game:
bodily build (now dial.): permanent effect of
strain: hang of a garment: a young plant-slip
for planting: a set scene: any collection of
objects, called 'elements', defined by specifying
the elements (math.): habitual or temporary
form, posture, carriage, position, or tendency:
(for the following senses, set or sett) the number
of a weaver's reed, determining the number of
threads to the inch: the texture resulting: a
square or a pattern of tartan: a paving-block of
stone or wood: a lease or letting (Scots.): a
mining lease or area worked (Cornwall, etc.): a
place with fixed fishing-nets: a tool for setting in
various senses: a badger's burrow: a group of
games in which the winning side wins six, with
such additional games as may be required in the
case of deuce (tennis): the constitution of a
burgh.—ns. set'ness; sett'er, one who or that
which sets: a dog that sets: a dog of a breed
derived from the spaniel and (probably) pointer:
one who finds victims for thieves, etc.: a spy;
sett'ing, act of one who sets: direction of
current: fixation: surroundings: environment:
mounting of jewellery: the period of time in
which a play, novel, etc., is set: adaptation to
music: music composed for a song, etc.—set'-
back, a check, reverse, or relapse; set'-down', an
unexpected rebuff: a snub: a rating; set'-off', a
claim set against another: a counterbalance: an
ornament: a setting forth: an offset (archit.,
print.); set'-out', an outfit: preparations: a
display of dishes, dress, etc.: a company,
clique; set piece, a piece of theatrical scenery
with a supporting framework, distinguished
from a side-scene or drop-scene: a picture in
fireworks: an elaborately prepared performance;
set-screw, a screw used to prevent relative motion
by exerting pressure with its point; set speech, a
studied oration; set square, a right-angled
triangular drawing instrument.— adj. set'-
stitch'd (Sterne), perh. embroidered.—set terms,
deliberately picked, usually outspoken, language;
sett'er-forth'; sett'er-off'; sett'er-on'; sett'er-
out'; sett'er-up'; set'-to', a bout: a hot contest:
—pl. set'-tos', set'-to's'; set-up', bodily carriage
and physique: configuration, arrangement,
structure, situation.—dead set (see dead-set); set
about, to begin, take in hand: to attack: to
spread, as a rumour; set against, to assail; set
(a)going, to put in motion; set alight, set light to,
set fire to, set on fire, to cause to break into flame
and burn; set apart, to put aside, or out of consideration; set aside, to put away: to reject: to
annul: to lay by; set at naught (see naught);
set back, to check, reverse: cost (in money;
slang); set by, to lay up: to put aside: to value
or esteem, to care (arch.); set down, to lay on
the ground: to put in writing: to appoint (Shak.,
a time for): to judge, esteem: to snub: to pitch,
encamp (Shak.): to attribute, charge: to lay
down authoritatively; set eyes on, to see, catch
sight of; set fair, steadily fair; set fire to, to
ignite; set forth, to exhibit, display: to expound,
declare: to praise, recommend: to publish: to
start on a journey; set free, to release, put at
liberty; set hand to, to set to work on; set in, to
begin: to become prevalent: to run landwards;
set in hand, to undertake: to set someone about
doing; set little, much, etc., by, to regard, esteem
little, much, etc.; set off, to mark off, lay off: to
start off: to send off: to show in relief or to
advantage: to counterbalance: to make an

offset, mark an opposite page; **set on**, to move on: to incite to attack: to instigate: bent upon; **set one's face against** (see **face**); **set one's hand to**, to sign; **set one's heart on** (see **heart**); **set oneself**, to bend one's energies; **set oneself against**, to discountenance, oppose; **set one's teeth**, to clench the teeth, as in a strong resolution; **set on fire**, to ignite; **set on foot**, to set agoing, to start; **set out**, to mark off: to equip and send forth: to start, go forth: to begin with an intention: to adorn: to expound: to display; **set sail** (see **sail**); **set to**, to affix: to apply oneself: to set, as a bone (*Shak.*); **set up**, to erect: to put up: to exalt (jeeringly in Scots, **set you, him**, etc., **up**): to begin: to enable to begin: to place in view: to put in type: to begin a career: to make pretensions; **set upon**, (to) set on. [O.E. *settan*; cog. with Ger. *setzen*, O.N. *setja*, Goth, *satjan*; *settan* is the weak causative of *sittan*, to sit; the noun is from the verb, but may be partly from O.E *set*, seat, partly from O.Fr. *sette*—L. *secta*, sect.]

**seta**, *sē'tä*, *n.* a bristle: a bristle-like structure: the stalk of a moss capsule:—*pl.* **se'tae** (*-tē*).— *adjs.* **setaceous** (*si-tā'shäs*), **setose** (*sē'tōs*, *-tōs'*). [L. *saeta* (*sēta*), bristle.]

**seton**, *sē'tn*, *n.* a thread or the like passed through the skin as a counter-irritant and means of promoting drainage: an issue so obtained. [L.L. *sētō*, *-ōnis*, app.—L. *sēta*, *saeta*, bristle.]

**sett.** See **set.**

**settee**, *se-tē'*, *n.* a long seat with a back. [Prob. **settle.**]

**settee**, *se-tē'*, *n.* a single-decked Mediterranean vessel with long prow and lateen sails. [Prob. It. *saettia*.]

**setter, setting.** See under **set.**

**setter**, *set'ər*, (chiefly *Northern*) *v.t.* to treat with a seton of setterwort root.—*n.* an issue so produced in cattle.—**sett'erwort**, stinking hellebore. [Perh. from M.L.G.]

**settle**, *set'l*, *n.* a long high-backed bench: a ledge (*B.*).—*v.t.* to dispose in stability, rest, or comfort: to adjust: to lower: to compact, cause to subside: to regulate: to fix: to establish, set up, or install (e.g. in residence, business, marriage, a parish): to colonise: to make clear: to determine: to decide: to put beyond doubt or dispute: to restore to good order: to quiet: to compose: to secure by gift or legal act: to create successive interests in, use or income going to one person while the corpus of the property remains another's: to make final payment of: to dispose of, put out of action, stun, kill.—*v.i.* to alight: to come to rest: to subside: to sink to the bottom (or form a scum): to dispose oneself: to take up permanent abode: to become settle: to fix one's habits (often with *down*): to grow calm or clear: to come to a decision or agreement: to adjust differences: to settle accounts (often with *up*).—*adj.* **sett'led.**— *ns.* **sett'ledness; sett'lement**, act of settling: state of being settled: payment: arrangement: placing of a minister: a subsidence or sinking: a settled colony: a local community: an establishment of social workers aiming at benefit to the surrounding population: a settling of property, an instrument by which it is settled, or the property settled, esp. a marriage-settlement: residence in a parish or other claim for poor-relief in case of becoming destitute; **sett'ler**, one who settles: a colonist: a decisive blow, argument, etc.; **sett'ling.**—**sett'le-bed**, a settle adaptable as a bed; **sett'ling-day**, a date fixed by the stock exchange for completion of transactions.— **settle for**, to agree to accept (usu. as a compromise); **settle in**, to prepare to remain indoors for the night: to adapt to a new environment; **settle with**, to come to an agreement with: to deal with. [O.E. *setl*, seat, *setlan*, to place; the vb.

may be partly from, or influenced by, late O.E. *sehtlian*, to reconcile.]

**setwall**, *set'wol*, *n.* orig. zedoary: now, valerian —Also **setuale** (*-ū-āl*; *Spens.*), **cet'ywall**, etc. [O.Fr. *citoual*—L.L. *zedoāria*—Ar. *zzdwār*.]

**seven**, *sev'n*, *n.* the cardinal number next above six: a symbol representing it (7, vii, etc.): a set of that number of persons or things: a shoe or other article of a size denoted by that number: a card with seven pips: a score of seven points, tricks, etc.: the seventh hour after midday or midnight.—*adj.* of the number seven.—*adj.* **sev'enth**, last of seven: next after the sixth: equal to one of seven equal parts.—*n.* a seventh part: a tone or semitone less than an octave: a note at that interval.—*adv.* **sev'enthly**, in the seventh place.—**sev'en-a-side**, a speedy form of Rugby football played by seven men on each side instead of fifteen (also **sev'ens**).—*adj.* **sev'en-day**, for seven days.—*adj.* and *adv.* **sev'enfold**, in seven divisions: seven times as much.—*adj.* **sev'en-league**, taking seven leagues at a stride, as the ogre's boots acquired by Hop-o'-my-Thumb. —**sev'enpence**, the value of seven pennies.—*adj.* **sev'enpenny**, costing or worth sevenpence.—*n.* a sevenpenny book.—*n.* and *adj.* **sev'en-score.**— **sev'enth-day**, Saturday.—*adj.* observing Saturday as Sabbath.—**Seven against Thebes**, the war of seven heroes to reinstate Polynices in Thebes against Eteocles; **Seven Champions of Christendom**, St George for England, St Andrew for Scotland, St Patrick for Ireland, St David for Wales, St Denis for France, St James for Spain, St Anthony for Italy; **seven deadly sins**, pride, covetousness, lust, anger, gluttony, envy, and sloth; **Seven Sages**, Solon of Athens, Thales of Miletus, Pittacus of Mitylene, Bias of Priene in Caria, Chilon of Sparta, Cleobulus tyrant of Lindus in Rhodes, and Periander tyrant of Corinth: an Eastern cycle of tales in which seven wise men contend in story-telling against a woman for the life of a belied prince; **Seven Seas**, the Arctic, Antarctic, North and South Atlantic, North and South Pacific, and Indian Oceans; **Seven Sleepers**, seven Christian youths at Ephesus said to have slept walled up in a cave *c.* A.D. 250 to 447; **Seven Stars**, the planets known to the ancients: the Plough: the Pleiades; **Seventh-day Adventists**, a sect that expect the second coming of Christ and observe Saturday as the Sabbath; **seventh heaven** (see **heaven**); **Seven Wonders of the World**, the Pyramids, the Hanging Gardens of Babylon, the Temple of Artemis at Ephesus, Phidias's statue of Zeus at Olympia, the Mausoleum at Halicarnassus, the Colossus of Rhodes, and the Pharos of Alexandria; **Seven Years' War**, the struggle for Silesia between Frederick the Great and the Empress Maria Theresa (1756-63). [O.E. *seofon*; Du. *zeven*, Ger. *sieben*, Goth. *sibun*, Gr. *hepta*, L. *septem.*]

**seventeen**, *sev-n-tēn'*, or *sev'*, *n.* and *adj.* seven and ten.—*adj.* **sev'enteen-hund'er** (*Burns*), woven with a reed of 1700 divisions, i.e. fine linen.— *adj.* and *n.* **sev'enteenth** (or *-tēnth'*).—*adv.* **seventeenth'ly.** [O.E. *seofontiene—seofon, tien,* ten.]

**seventy**, *sev'n-ti*, *n.* and *adj.* seven times ten:— *pl.* **sev'enties**, the numbers seventy to seventy-nine: the years so numbered in a life or any century.—*adj.* **sev'entieth**, last of seventy: equal to one of seventy equal parts.—*n.* a seventieth part.—**sev'enty-eight**, a seventy-eight revolutions per minute gramophone record, standard before the introduction of long-playing microgroove records—usu. written 78.—**the Seventy**, the Jewish Sanhedrin: the disciples sent out in Luke x: the Septuagint translators—often LXX. [O.E. *(hund)seofontig.*]

**sever**, *sev'ər*, *v.t.* and *v.i.* to separate: to divide:

to cleave.—*adj.* sev'erable.—*n.* sev'erance.—severance pay, an allowance granted to an employee on the termination of his employment. [Fr. *sevrer*, to wean—L. *sēparāre*, to separate.]

several, *sev'ər-l, adj.* separate: private: belonging or pertaining distributively, not jointly: particular: distinct: different: various: sundry: more than one (usu. more than three), but not very many.—*n.* privately owned land, esp. enclosed pasture: private property: a detail, particular (*Shak.*): an individual person (*Shak.*): a few.—*adj., adv.* sev'eralfold.—*adv.* sev'erally, separately.—*n.* sev'eralty, separateness: individual ownership.—in several, separately, individually. [O.Fr.,—L. *sēparāre*, to separate.]

severe, *si-vēr', adj.* rigorous: very strict: unsparing: pressing hard: hard to endure: austerely restrained or simple.—*adv.* severe'ly.—*ns.* severe'ness; severity (*si-ver'i-ti*). [L. *sevērus.*]

severy, *sev'ə-ri, n.* a compartment of vaulting. [O.Fr. *civoire*—L. *cibōrium*; see ciborium.]

Sèvres, *sev'r', adj.* made at *Sèvres*, near Paris.—*n.* Sèvres porcelain.

sew, *sō, v.t.* to join, attach, enclose, or work upon with a needle and thread or with wire.—*v.i.* to ply the needle:—*pa.t.* sewed (*sōd*); *pa.p.* sewn (*sōn*) or sewed.—*ns.* sew'er; sew'ing, the act of sewing: that which is being sewn.—sew'ing-machine.—sew up, to enclose or close up by sewing: to complete satisfactorily (*slang*): to tire out, bring to a standstill, nonplus, or make drunk (*slang*). [O.E. *siwian, sēowian*; O.H.G. *siuwen*, Goth. *siujan.*]

sew (*Spens.*). Same as sue.

sew, *sū, v.t.* (*dial.*) to drain:—*v.i.* to ooze (*dial.*): to be aground (*naut.*).—*ns.* sew'age, refuse carried off by sewers; sewer (*sōō'ər, sū'ar*, old-fashioned *shōr, shör*), a channel for receiving the discharge from house-drains and streets.—*v.t.* to provide with sewers.—*ns.* sew'erage, system or provision of sewers: sewage; sew'ering.—sew'age-farm, a place where sewage is treated so as to be used as manure: also a farm on which sewage is used as fertiliser; sew'er-gas, the contaminated air of sewers; sew'er-rat, the brown rat. [O.Fr. *essever*, to drain off—L. *ex*, out, *aqua*, water.]

sewel. See shewel.

sewellel, *si-wel'əl, n.* an American rodent linking beavers and squirrels. [Chinook *shewallal*, a robe of its skin.]

sewer, *sū'ər, n.* an officer who superintends the service at table. [O.Fr. *asseour*—*asseoir*, to set down—L. *ad*, to, *sedēre*, to sit. Skeat makes it from M.E. *sew*, to set, serve, *sew*, pottage—O.E. *sēaw*, juice.]

sewerage. See sew (3).

sewin, sewen, *sū'in, n.* a Welsh sea-trout grilse. [Origin unknown.]

sex, *seks, n.* that by which an animal or plant is male or female: the quality of being male or female: either of the divisions according to this, or its members collectively: the whole domain connected with this distinction: sexual intercourse: (by confusion) sect.—Also *adj.*—*v.t.* to ascertain the sex of.—*adj.* sexed (*sekst*), having sex: being male or female: having sexual characteristics, feelings or desires to a specified degree (as in over-, under-, highly-, etc., sexed).—*n.* sex'iness.—*adj.* sex'less, of neither sex: without sex: without sexual feelings.—*n.* sex'lessness.—*adj.* sex'ual, of, by, having, characteristic of, sex, one sex or other, or organs of sex.—*v.t.* sex'ualise, -ize, to attribute sex to.—*ns.* sex'ūalism, emphasis on sex; sex'ūalist; sexual'ity.—*adv.* sex'ually.—*adj.* sex'y, over-concerned with sex: of a person, very attractive to the opposite sex: stimulating sexual instincts.—sex'-appeal', power of attract-

ing, esp. of exciting desire in, the other sex; sex'-cell, an egg-cell or sperm; sex'-chro'mosome, a chromosome that determines sex; sex'-determinā'tion, the settling of what the sex of a new organism is to be.—sex'-in'tergrade, an intersex; sex'-kitten, a young woman (mischievously) playing up her sex-attraction.—*adjs.* sex'-lim'ited, developed only in one sex; sex'-linked', inherited along with sex, that is, by a factor located in the sex-chromosome.—sexpot (*slang*), a person of very great or obvious physical attraction; sex'-rever'sal, change from male to female or female to male in the life of the individual; sexual selection, that province of natural selection in which preference for mates having certain characters comes into play; sexual system, the Linnaean system of plant classification according to sexual organisation.—the sex (*arch.*), the female sex, women. [L. *sexus, -ūs.*]

sex-, seks-, se:xi-, -i-, in composition, six.—*adj.* sex'fid, six-cleft.—*n.* sex'foil, a window, design, etc., with six lobes or leaves.—*adjs.* sex(i)vā'lent (or -*iv'ə-lənt*), of valency six; sexloc'ūlar, with six compartments; sexpart'ite, parted in six. [L. *sex*, six.]

sexagenarian, *sek-sə-ji-nā'ri-ən, n.* a person sixty years old, or between sixty and seventy.—*adj.* of that age.—*adj.* sexagenary (*sek-sə-jē'nər-i, -saj'in-ər-i*), of, containing, based on, sixty: sexagenarian.—*n.* a sexagesimal fraction: a sexagenarian. [L. *sexāgēnārius*, pertaining to sixty—*sexāgintā*, sixty.]

Sexagesima, *sek-sə-jes'i-mə, n.* the second Sunday before Lent (also Sexagesima Sunday)—apparently so named on the false analogy of Quadragesima, etc.—*adj.* sexages'imal, pertaining to, based on, sixty.—*n.* a sexagesimal fraction.—*adv.* sexages'imally, by sixtieths. [L. *sexāgēsimus, -a, -um*, sixtieth.]

sexcentenary, *seks-sin-tēn'ər-i, -sin-ten'*, or -*sen'tin-ər-i, n.* a 600th anniversary.—Also *adj.*

sexennial, *sek-sen'yəl, adj.* lasting six years: recurring every six years.—*adv.* sexenn'ially. [L. *sex*, six, *annus*, year.]

sext, *sekst, n.* the office of the sixth hour, said at midday, afterwards earlier (*eccles.*): a sixth (*mus.*): an organ stop giving the twelfth and the tierce (a sixth apart).—*adj.* sex'tan, recurring every fifth day (sixth by old reckoning). [L. *sextus*, sixth—*sex*, six.]

sextans, *seks'tanz, n.* a Roman bronze coin worth a sixth of an *as*.—*n.* sex'tant (-*tənt*), an instrument with an arc of a sixth of a circle, for measuring angular distances.—*adj.* sextantal (-*tant'l*). [L. *sextāns, -antis*, a sixth.]

sextet, sextett, sextette, *seks-tet', n.* altered forms (partly through Ger.) of sestet.

sextile, *seks'til, -til, (astrol.) n.* a position 60° apart (also sextile aspect). [L. *sextilis*, sixth.]

sextillion, *seks-til'yən, n.* the sixth power of a million: the seventh power of 1000 (*U.S.*). [For *sexillion*, after billion, etc.]

sextodecimo, *seks-tō-des'i-mō, n.* a book or a size of book made by folding each sheet into sixteen leaves:—*pl.* sextodec'imos.—Also *adj.* [L. (*in*) *sextō decimō* (in) one-sixteenth.]

sextolet, *seks'tə-let, n.* a group of six notes performed in the time of four. [Ger. *sextole*—L. *sex.*]

sexton, *seks'tən, n.* an officer who rings a church bell, attends the clergyman, digs graves, etc.: a burying-beetle (also sex'ton-bee'tle).—*ns.* sex'-toness; sex'tonship. [sacristan.]

sextuor, *seks'tū-ör, n.* a sextet. [Fr.,—L. *sex*, after *quatuor*, four.]

sextuple, *seks'tū-pl, adj.* sixfold.—*n.* six times as much.—*v.t.* and *v.i.* to increase or multiply sixfold.—*n.* sex'tūplet, a sextolet (*mus.*): one of six born at a birth. [L.L. *sextuplus.*]

**sey**, *sī*, (*Scot.*) *n.* part of a carcase of beef including the sirloin. [Origin obscure.]

**seyen, seysure**, Shakespearean spellings of **scion**, **seizure**.

**sez**, slang spelling of **says**.

**'sfoot**, *sfōōt*, (*Shak.*) *interj.* for God's foot.

**sforzando**, *sför-tsän'dō*, **sforzato**, *sför-tsä'tō*, (*mus.*) *adjs.* and *advs.* forced, with sudden emphasis. *Abbrev. sf.* and *sfz.*, or marked >, ∧.—*Also ns* —Also **forzando, forzato**. [It., pr.p. and pa.p. of *sforzare*, to force—L. *ex*, out, ̄̄̄̄, *fortia*, force.]

**sgraffito**, *zgräf-fē'tō*, *n.* decorative work in which different colours are got by removal of parts of outer layers of material laid on: pottery with such decoration:—*pl.* **sgraffi'ti** (*-tē*). [It.,—L. *ex-*, and It. *graffito*, q.v.]

**sh**, *sh*, *interj.* hush.

**shabble**, *shab'l*, (*Scot.*) *n.* an old rusty sword. [Cf. It. *sciabola*, Pol. *szabla*, and **sabre**.]

**shabby**, *shab'i*, *adj.* dingy, threadbare, or worn, as clothes: having a look of poverty: mean in look or conduct: low: paltry.—*adv.* **shabb'ily**. —*n.* **shabb'iness**.—*adj.* **shabb'y-genteel'**, keeping up or affecting an appearance of gentility, though really very shabby. [Obs. or dial. *shab*, scab—O.E. *sceabb.*]

**shabrack**, *shab'rak*, *n.* a trooper's housing or saddle-cloth. [Ger. *schabracke*, prob.—Turk. *çāprāq.*]

**shack**, *shak*, *n.* a roughly built hut.—**shack up** (**with**), (*slang*) to live with someone, esp. though unmarried. [Amer.; origin obscure.]

**shackle**, *shak'l*, *n.* a prisoner's or slave's ankle-ring or wrist-ring, or the chain connecting a pair: a hobble: a staple-like link, closed with a pin: the curved movable part of a padlock: a coupling of various kinds: (in *pl.*) fetters, manacles: a hindrance.—*v.t.* to fetter: to couple: to hamper.—**shack'le-bolt**, the pin of a shackle; **shack'le-bone** (*Scot.*), the wrist. [O.E. *sceacul.*]

**shad**, *shad*, *n.* an anadromous fish akin to the herring: extended to various other fishes.—*adj.* **shad'-bell'ied**, flat-bellied—opp. to *pot-bellied*—of a coat, sloping away gradually in front.—**shad'bush**, the June-berry (Amelanchier), flowering at shad spawning-time. [O.E. *sceadd.*]

**shaddock**, *shad'ǝk*, *n.* an Oriental citrus fruit like a very large orange, esp. the larger pear-shaped variety, distinguished from the finer grapefruit: the tree that bears it. [Introduced to the W. Indies *c.* 1700 by Captain *Shaddock.*]

**shade**, *shād*, *n.* partial or relative darkness: interception of light: obscurity: a shadow: a momentary expression of face: a shady place: (in *pl.*) the abode of the dead, Hades: shelter from light or heat: that which casts a shadow: a screen: a window-blind (*U.S.*): a cover to modify or direct light of a lamp: an inverted glass vessel formerly put over a clock or ornament: a projecting cover to protect the eyes from glare: an awning for a shop-window: a lace head-covering (*obs.*): a variety or degree of colour: a hue mixed with black: the dark part of a picture: a very minute difference: the disembodied soul: a ghost.—*v.t.* to screen: to overshadow: to mark with gradations of colour or shadow: to soften down: to darken: to shadow forth (*Spens.*): to lower very slightly, as a price (*U.S.*).—*v.i.* to pass imperceptibly (*away, into,* etc.).—*adjs.* **shā'ded; shade'less.**— *adv.* **shā'dily.**—*ns.* **shā'diness; shā'ding**, making a shade: the marking of shadows or shadow-like appearance: the effect of light and shade: fine gradations: nuances: toning down: modification of sound by anything put on top of an organ-pipe: slight lowering of prices.—*adj.* **shā'dy**, having, or in, shade: sheltered from light or heat: not fit to bear the light, disreput-

able (*coll.*).—**shade'-plant,** a plant adapted to light of low intensity; **shade'-tree,** a tree planted to give shade.—**in the shade,** sheltered from strong light: overlooked, forgotten, in relative obscurity; **on the shady side of,** over (a specified age); **put in the shade,** to outdo completely; **shades of** (a specified person or thing)! exclamation greeting something which reminds one in some way of the person or thing. [O.E. *sceadu*; see **shadow**.]

**shade**, *shād*, (*Scot.*) *v.t.* to part (the hair). [Northern form of **shed**, 2.]

**shadoof, shaduf**, *shä-dōōf'*, *n.* a contrivance for raising water by a bucket on a counterpoised pivoted rod. [Egyptian Ar. *shādūf.*]

**shadow**, *shad'ō*, *n.* shade cast by interception of light by an object: the dark figure so projected on a surface, mimicking the object: the dark part of a picture: a reflected image: a mere appearance: a ghost, spirit: an unreal thing: a representation: a person or thing wasted away almost to nothing: an inseparable companion: a spy or detective who follows one: shade: protective shade: darkness: gloom: affliction.—*adj.* unreal: feigned: existing only in skeleton: inactive but ready for the time when opportunity or need arises.—*v.t.* to shade: to cloud or darken: to represent as by a shadow: to typify: to hide: to attend like a shadow, follow and watch: to shadowcast.—*v.i.* to cast a shadow: to darken. —*ns.* **shad'ower; shad'owiness; shad'owing.**— *adjs.* **shad'owless; shad'owy, shady**: like a shadow: symbolic: secluded: unsubstantial.— **shad'ow-box'ing,** sparring practice with an imaginary opponent: making a show of opposition or other action, as a cover for taking no effective steps; **shad'ow cab'inet,** a body of opposition leaders meeting from time to time and ready to take office.—*v.t.* **shad'owcast,** in microscopy, to cast shadows of projecting parts of (a specimen) by exposing to a stream of vapour of a heavy metal.—**shad'owcasting; shad'ow-fight,** a fight between or with shadows or imaginary foes; **shad'ow-fig'ure,** a silhouette; **shad'ow-mark,** trace of an archaeological site revealed by observation from the air; **shad'ow-pan'tomime, -play,** one in which the spectators see only shadows on a screen.—**shadow of death,** the darkness of death: threatening approach of death. [O.E. *sceadwe*, gen., dat., and accus. of *sceadu* (**shade** representing the nom.); cf. O.H.G. *scato*, Gr. *skotos*, darkness.]

**Shafiite**, *shaf'i-it*, *n.* a member of one of the four principal sects of the Sunnites, or orthodox Muslims. [Ar. *Shāfi'i*, the name of the founder.]

**shaft**, *shäft*, *n.* anything long and straight: a stem: an arrow: a missile (esp. *fig.*): the main, upright, straight, or cylindrical part of anything: the part of a cross below the arms: the part of a column between the base and the capital: the rachis of a feather: the thill of a carriage on either side of the horse: a straight handle: a pole: a ray or beam of light: a rotating rod that transmits motion: a well-like excavation or passage.—*adj.* **shaft'ed.**—*ns.* **shaft'er, shaft'-horse,** a horse harnessed between shafts; **shaft'-ing,** system of shafts.—*adj.* **shaft'less.**—**make a shaft or a bolt of it** (*Shak.* **on't**), to venture and take what comes of it—the shaft and the bolt being the arrows of the long-bow and the cross-bow respectively. [O.E. *sceaft*; perh. partly Ger. *schacht*, pit-shaft.]

**shag**, *shag*, *n.* a ragged mass of hair, or the like: a long coarse nap: a kind of tobacco cut into shreds: the green cormorant (app. from its crest), or other species.—*adj.* shaggy: shaggy-haired.—*v.t.* to make shaggy.—*v.i.* (*Spens.*) to hang in shaggy clusters.—*adj.* **shagged** (*shag'id, shagd*), shaggy, rough: tired out (*coll.*).—*n.* **shagg'edness.**—*adv.* **shagg'ily.**—*n.* **shagg'iness.**—

*adj.* **shagg'y,** long, rough, and coarse: having long, rough, coarse hair, wool, vegetation, etc.: unkempt: rugged.—**shag'-bark,** a kind of hickory tree.—*adjs.* **shag'eared** (*Shak.* **shagge-ear'd**); **shag'-haired.**—**shaggy dog story** (from the shaggy dog featured in many), a whimsically extravagant story humorous from its length and the inconsequence of its ending. [O.E. *sceacga;* cf. O.N. *skegg,* a beard.]

**shagreen,** *shə-grēn',* *n.* a granular leather made from horse's or ass's skin: the skin of shark, ray, etc., covered with small nodules—formerly **chagrin'.**—*adj.* **shagreen(ed)',** of, or covered with, shagreen. [Fr. *chagrin*—Turk. *sagri,* horse's rump, shagreen.]

**shagroon,** *shə-grōōn',* *n.* an original settler in New Zealand of other than English origin. [Perh. Ir. *seachrān,* wandering.]

**shah,** *shä,* *n.* the king of Persia; also formerly of certain other Eastern countries. [Pers. *shāh.*]

**shairn.** Same as **sharn.**

**Shaitan,** *shī-tän',* *n.* Satan: (without *cap.*) an evil spirit: a devilish person: a dust storm. [Ar. *shaitān*—Heb. (see **Satan**).]

**shake,** *shāk,* *v.t.* to move with quick, short, to-and-fro movements: to brandish: to make to tremble or to totter: to disturb the stability of: to cause to waver: to disturb: to put, send, render, cause to be, by shaking: to scatter or send down by shaking: to split: to get rid of, give up.—*v.i.* to be agitated: to tremble: to shiver: to shake hands: to trill:—*pa.t.* **shook,** *obs.* **shāked, shākt;** *pa.p.* **shāk'en,** *obs.* **shāked, shākt, shook.**—*n.* a shaking: tremulous motion: damaging or weakening blow: shaken-up drink: a trillo, rapid alternation of two notes a tone or semitone apart, commonly ending with a turn: fissure: a moment (*coll.*).—*adjs.* **shak(e)-able; shāk'en,**—*ns.* **shāk'er,** one who shakes: a contrivance for shaking (e.g. drinks): (*cap.*) a name applied to members of various religious bodies, as the Quakers, the Believers in Christ's Second Appearing (founded in Manchester about 1750), the Children of God (founded about 1864); **shāk'erism.**—*adv.* **shāk'ily.**—*n.* **shāk'iness.**—*n.* and *adj.* **shāk'ing.**—*adj.* **shāk'y,** shaking or inclined to shake: loose: tremulous: precarious: uncertain: wavering: unsteady: full of cracks or clefts.—**shake'-bag,** fighting-cock turned out of a bag: large fighting-cock; **shake'-down,** temporary bed (orig. made by shaking down straw): any action of the phrasal verb 'shake down'; **shake'-rag** (*obs.*), disreputable ragged fellow.—**(no) great shakes,** of (no) great account; **shake down** (*slang*), to cheat of one's money at one stroke: to extort protection money from: to go to bed (esp. in a temporary bed): to settle down; **shake hands,** to salute by grasping the hand and moving it up and down; **shake, shiver, in one's shoes,** to be extremely afraid, shiver with fear; **shake off,** to get rid of, often by shaking: also *fig.*; **shake (off) the dust (of) from one's feet,** used *lit.* and symbolically in Matthew x. 14, (*B.*): (*fig.*) to leave hurriedly or gladly; **shake one's sides,** to laugh uproariously; **shake the head,** to turn the head from side to side in token of reluctance, disapproval, etc.; **shake up,** to rouse, mix, disturb, loosen by shaking: to upbraid (*Shak.*). [O.E. *sc(e)acan.*]

**Shakespearian, Shaksperian, Shakesperean,** *shāk-spē'ri-ən,* *adj.* of or relating to *Shak(e)-spe(a)re,* or his works.—*n.* a student of Shakespeare.—*n.* **Shak(e)spe(a)riana** (-*i-ä'nə*), items or lore relating to Shakespeare.

**shako,** *shak'ō,* *n.* a nearly cylindrical military cap. [Hung. *csákó.*]

**shale,** *shāl,* *n.* clay rock splitting readily into thin laminae along the bedding-planes.—*adj.* **shā'ly.** —**shale'-mine;** -**miner; shale'-oil',** oil distilled from oil-shale. [Ger. *schale,* lamina; or from the following word.]

**shale,** *shāl,* (*Shak.*) *n.* a shell or husk.—*v.t.* to shell. [O.E. *sc(e)alu;* cf. **scale.**]

**shall,** *shal, shəl, v.t.* originally expressing debt or moral obligation, now used with the infinitive of a verb (without *to*) to form (in sense) a future tense, expressing in the first person mere futurity (as **will** in the second and third), in the second and th:rd implying also promise, command, decree, or control on the part of the speaker (rules for use of *shall, will,* are often ignored): must, will have to, is to, etc. (2nd and 3rd persons, and interrogatively 1st): may be expected to, may chance to, may well (all persons): may in future contingency, may come to (all persons):—*inf.* obsolete; no *participles*; *2nd pers. sing.* (*arch.*) **shalt;** *3rd,* **shall;** *pa.t.* **should** (*shŏŏd, shəd*); *2nd pers.* (*arch.*) **shouldest, shouldst.** [O.E. *sculan,* pr.t. *sceal, scealt, sceal;* pa.t. *sceolde;* cf. Ger. *soll,* Goth. *skal,* O.N. *skal.*]

**shallon,** *shal'ən, n.* **salal.**

**shalloon,** *shə-lōōn', n.* a light woollen stuff for coat-linings, etc. [Perhaps made at *Châlons-sur-Marne.*]

**shallop,** *shal'əp, n.* formerly, a heavy fore-and-aft-rigged boat: a dinghy: a small or light boat. [Fr. *chaloupe;* cf. **sloop.**]

**shallot, shalot,** *shə-lot',* **eschalot,** *esh-ə-lot',* or *esh',* *n.* a garlic-flavoured species (*Allium ascalonicum*) of onion. [O.Fr. *eschalote,* variant of *escalogne;* see **scallion.**]

**shallow,** *shal'ō, adj.* of no great depth, concavity, profundity, penetration: superficial.—*adv.* at or to no great depth.—*n.* a shallow place: (used in plural with the) the shallow part.—*v.t.* to make shallow.—*v.i.* to grow shallow.—*n.* and *adj.* **shall'owing.**—*adv.* **shall'owly** (*Shak.*), simply, foolishly.—*n.* **shall'owness.** [M.E. *schalowe,* perh. related to **shoal.**]

**shalm,** *shäm.* Same as **shawm.**

**shalt,** *shalt,* 2nd *pers. sing.* of **shall.**

**sham,** *sham, n.* a hoax (*obs.*): a counterfeit.—*adj.* pretended: false.—*v.t.* to pretend: to feign: to impose upon (*obs.*).—*v.i.* to make false pretences: to pretend to be (as *to sham dead, sick*):—*pr.p.* **shamm'ing;** *pa.t.* and *pa.p.* **shammed.**—*n.* **shamm'er.—sham Abraham** (see **Abrahamman**). [First found as slang, late 17th cent.]

**shama,** *shä'ma, n.* an Indian songbird of the thrush family. [Hindi *šāmā.*]

**shaman,** *shäm'an, -ən, n.* a doctor-priest working by magic, primarily of N. Asia:—*pl.* **sham'ans.** —Also *adj.*—*adj.* **shamanic** (-*an'*).—*ns.* **Sham'an-ism,** the religion of N. Asia, based essentially on magic and sorcery; **sham'anist.**—*adj.* **shaman-ist'ic.** [Russ.,—Tungus.]

**shamateur,** *sham'ə-tər, -tūr, n.* one rated as an amateur in sport who yet makes gains from playing or competing.—Also *fig.* [**sham,** amateur.]

**shamble,** *sham'bl, v.i.* to walk with an awkward, unsteady gait.—*n.* a shambling gait.—*n.* and *adj.* **sham'bling.** [Poss. from next word, in allusion to trestle-like legs.]

**shamble,** *sham'bl, n.* a butcher's market stall: in *pl.* (sometimes treated as *sing.*), a flesh-market, hence, a slaughterhouse: a place of carnage (*fig.*): mess, muddle (*slang*).—*adj.* **shambol'ic** (*slang*); ill-formed, chaotic. [O.E. *scamel* (Ger. *schemel*), stool—L.L. *scamellum,* dim. of *scamnum,* a bench.]

**shame,** *shām, n.* the humiliating feeling of having appeared to disadvantage in one's own eyes, or those of others, as by shortcoming, offence, or unseemly exposure, or a like feeling on behalf of anything one associates with oneself: susceptibility to such feeling: fear or scorn of incurring disgrace or dishonour: modesty:

bashfulness: disgrace, ignominy: disgraceful wrong: cause or source of disgrace: a thing to be ashamed of: an instance, a case of hard, bad, luck (*coll.*): those parts of the body that it is felt to be immodest to expose (*arch.*).—*v.t.* to make ashamed: to cover with reproach: to disgrace: to put to shame by greater excellence: to drive or compel by shame.—*v.i.* to be ashamed. —*adjs.* shamed, ashamed; shame'ful, disgraceful —*adv.* shame'fully.—*n.* shame'fulness.—*adj.* shame'less, immodest: done without shame. *adv.* shame'lessly.—*ns.* shame'lessness; shā'mer, one who or that which makes ashamed.—*adj.* shame'faced (orig. shame'fast, O.E. *scamfæst*), very modest or bashful: abashed.—*adv.* shame'-facedly.—shame'-facedness, shame'fastness, modesty.—*adjs.* shame'-proof (*Shak.*), insensible to shame; shame'worthy.—for shame, an interjectional phrase, you should be ashamed; put to shame, to disgrace, esp. by excelling; tell the truth and shame the devil, put the devil to disgraceful defeat by boldly telling the truth; think shame, to be ashamed. [O.E. *sc(e)amu*; Ger. *scham*.]
shamiana(h), shä-mē-ä'na, *n.* a large tent or canopy. [Hindi *shāmiyāna*; from Pers.]
shamisen. See samisen.
shammy, sham'i, *n.* (in full shamm'y-leath'er) a soft leather, originally made from chamois-skin, now usually from sheepskin, by working in oil: a piece of it.—Also *adj.*—*v.t.* sham'oy (or -moi'), to prepare thus. [chamois.]
shampoo, sham-pōō', *v.t.* to massage: to wash and rub (the scalp and hair): to clean (carpet, etc.) by rubbing with a special preparation:— *pa.t.* and *pa.p.* shampooed', shampoo'd.—*n.* an act or process of shampooing: a preparation for the purpose:—*pl.* shampoos'.—*n.* shampoo'er. [Hindi *cāpnā*, to squeeze.]
shamrock, sham'rok, *n.* the national emblem of Ireland, a trifoliate leaf or plant: in living popular tradition the lesser yellow trefoil: in the English poets often wood-sorrel: according to some, white clover, hop-trefoil, black medick, or some other (or any) leaf or plant with three leaflets. [Ir. *seamróg*, Gael. *seamrag*, dim. of *seamar*, trefoil.]
Shan, shän, *n.* a member of a people akin to the Thais, in China, Thailand, Burma, and Assam: their language.—Also *adj.*
shanachie, shan'a-hhē. Same as seannachie.
shand, shan, shan(d), (*cant*) *n.* base coin.
Shandean, shan'di-an, shan-dē'an, *adj.* characteristic of Tristram *Shandy* or the Shandy family, or their creator Laurence Sterne.—*n.* a person of Shandean character.
shandry, shan'dri, (*N. England*) *n.* a light cart on springs.—*n.* shan'drydan, a shandry: an oldfashioned chaise: a rickety vehicle. [Origin unknown.]
shandy, shan'di, *n.* a mixture of beer and gingerbeer or lemonade.—Also shan'dygaff. [Origin unknown.]
shanghai, shang-hi', *v.t.* to drug or make drunk and ship as a sailor: to trick into performing an unpleasant task:—*pr.p.* shanghai'ing; *pa.t.* and *pa.p.* shanghaied', shanghai'd.—*n.* shanghai'er. [*Shanghai* in China.]
Shangri-la, shang'gri-lä, *n.* an imaginary pass in the Himalayas, an earthly paradise, described in James Hilton's *Lost Horizon* (1933).
shank, shangk, *n.* the leg from knee to foot: the lower part of the foreleg: a shaft, stem, straight or long part: the part of a shoe connecting sole with heel: the leg of a stocking: a longhandled ladle for molten metal: an act of shanking a golf-ball: the end, latter part (*dial.*). —*v.i.* to be affected with disease of the footstalk: to take to one's legs (also *v.t.* with *it*).— *v.t.* to dispatch unceremoniously (*Scot.*): to

strike with junction of the shaft (*golf*).—*adj.* shanked, having a shank: affected with disease of the shank or footstalk.—shank'-bone.—on Shanks's mare, nag, pony, etc., on foot. [O.E. *sc(e)anca*, leg; Du. *schonk*, L.G. *schanke*.]
shanny, shan'i, *n.* the smooth blenny. [Origin obscure.]
shan't (sometimes sha'n't), shänt, (*coll.*) a contraction of shall not.
shantung, shan-tung', -tōōng', *n.* a plain rough cloth of wild silk. [*Shantung* province in China.]
shanty, shant'i, *n.* a roughly built hut: a ram shackle dwelling: a low public-house.—shanty'-man, one, esp. a logger, who lives in a shanty; shanty town, a town, or an area of one, where housing is makeshift and ramshackle. [Perh. Fr. *chantier*, a timber-yard (in Canada a woodcutters' headquarters); perh. Ir. *sean tig*, old house.]
shanty, shan'ti, *n.* a song with chorus, sung by sailors while heaving at the capstan, or the like —also chanty, chantie, chantey (shan'ti).—*n.* shant'yman, the solo-singer in shanties. [Said to be from Fr. *chantez* (imper.), sing.]
shape, shāp, *v.t.* to form: to fashion: to give form to: to body forth: to embody: to devise: to purpose (*obs.*): to direct: to determine.— *v.i.* to take shape: to develop: to give promising signs: to conduce (*Shak.*): to become fit:—*pa.t.* shaped, *Spens.* shope, shōp; *pa.p.* shāped, *arch.* shāp'en.—*n.* form: figure: disposition in space: guise: form or condition: that which has form or figure: an apparition: a pattern: a mould (*cook.*): a jelly, pudding, etc., turned out of a mould.—*adjs.* shāp'able, shape'able; shaped, having a shape, or a definite, determinate, or adapted shape; shape'less, of ill-defined or unsatisfactory shape: purposeless (*Shak.*).— *ns.* shape'lessness; shape'liness.—*adjs.* shape'ly, well-proportioned; shap'en, fashioned: definitely shaped.—*n.* shap'er.—*n.* and *adj.* shap'ing. —in any shape or form, (often merely) at all; in shape, in good condition; in the shape of, in the guise of: of the nature of; shape one's course, direct one's way; shape up, to assume a shape: to develop, to be promising; take shape, to assume a definite form or plan: to be embodied or worked out in practice. [O.E. *sciéppan*, *pa.t.* *scōp*, *pa.p.* *scapen*, to create, form, with new present developed from the pa.p., influenced by the n. *gesceap*, creation, form; cf. O.N. *skapa*, Ger. *schaffen*, *schöpfen*.]
shaps, shaps, *n.pl.* short for chaparejos.
shard, shärd, (*Shak.*) *n.* a piece of cow-dung.— *adj.* shard'ed (*Shak.*), sheltered under dung.— shard'-beetle, a dor-beetle, laying its eggs under cow-dung.—*adj.* shard'-borne (see separate article). [Cf. sharn.]
shard, shärd, sherd, shûrd, *n.* a gap (now *dial.*): a boundary ridge or mark (*Spens.*): a scrap, broken piece, esp. of pottery. [O.E. *sceard*, cleft, potsherd; cf. *sceran*, to cut; Ger. *scharte*, notch.]
shard, shärd. Same as chard.
shard, shärd, *n.* a beetle's wing-case. [From a misunderstanding of Shakespeare's shard-borne.]
shard, shar'd, shärd, (*Spens.*) *pa.t.* and *pa.p.* share (1 and 2).
shard-borne, shärd'börn, -börn, (*Shak.*) *adj.* born in dung: later used as meaning borne on elytra. [shard (1); cf. shard (4).]
share, shär, *n.* a part allotted, contributed, owned, taken, or (*Spens.*) cut off: a division, section, portion: a fixed and indivisible section of the capital of a company.—*v.t.* to divide into shares: to apportion: to give or take a share of: to participate in: to have in common.—*v.i.* to have, receive, or give a share.—*ns.* shar'er; shar'ing.—share bone, pubis; share'-cap'ital, money derived from the sale of shares in a business, and used for carrying it on; share'-

**cropper,** a tenant farmer who himself supplies only his labour, receiving seed, tools, etc., from his landlord and, with adjustment to allow for what he has already received, a share of the crop.—*v.i.* share'crop.—share'holder, one who owns a share, esp. in a company; share'man, shares'-man, a fisherman who shares profits with the owners; share'-out, a distribution in shares; share'-pusher, one who seeks to sell shares otherwise than through recognised channels.— go shares, to divide; lion's share (see lion); share and share alike, in equal shares. [O.E. *scearu*; cf. shear.]

**share,** *shār, n.* ploughshare or corresponding part of another implement.—*v.t.* to cut, cleave:— *pa.t.* and *pa.p.* shared; (*Spens.*) shard (*shärd*). [O.E. *scear*; cf. foregoing word, and shear.]

**shark,** *shärk, n.* a general name for elasmobranchs other than skates, rays, and chimaeras— voracious fishes, with fusiform body, lateral gill-slits, and mouth on the under side: sometimes confined to the larger kinds, excluding the dogfishes: an extortioner: a swindler: a sharper: a sponging parasite: a person dangerous to sailors.—*v.i.* to play the shark: to sponge.— *v.t.* to get by sharking: to get together hastily, to pick up (with *up*).—*ns.* shark'er; shark'ing. —shark'-oil, oil from shark's liver, used like cod-liver oil; shark'skin, a woollen or worsted suiting in twill weave: a heavy rayon material with dull finish. [Origin doubtful; Ger. *schurke*, scoundrel, Austrian Ger. *schirk*, sturgeon, Fr. dial. *cherquier*, to seek, L. *carcharus*, dogfish—Gr. *karcharos*, jagged, have been suggested.]

**sharn,** *shärn,* (dial.) *n.* cow-dung.—*adj.* sharn'y.— sharny peat, a cake of cow-dung mixed with coal. [O.E. *scearn*; cf O.N. *skarn*.]

**sharp,** *shärp, adj.* cutting: piercing: penetrating: acute: having a thin edge or fine point: affecting the senses as if pointed or cutting: severe: harsh: keen: eager: hungry (*Shak.*): alive to one's own interests: barely honest: of keen or quick perception: alert: pungent, sarcastic: brisk: abrupt: sudden in onset: clear-cut: unblurred: well-defined: stylish (*slang*): too dressy (*slang*): high in pitch, or too high: raised a semitone: voiceless (*obs. phon.*).—*adv.* high or too high in pitch: punctually, precisely: sharply.—*n.* a note raised a semitone: the symbol for it: the key producing it: sharpness (*Milt.*): a long slender needle: a small sword or duelling-sword: (in *pl.*) hard parts of wheat, middlings: (in *pl.*) sword-fighting in earnest.— *v.t.* and *v.i.* (*obs.* or *dial.*) to sharpen: to shark. —*v.t.* and *v.i.* sharp'en, to make or become sharp in any sense.—*ns.* sharp'ener; sharp'er, a cheat.—*n.* and *adj.* sharp'ing, cheating.—*adj.* sharp'ish.—*adv.* sharp'ly.—*n.* sharp'ness.—*adjs.* sharp'-cut, well-defined: clear-cut; sharp'-edged; sharp'-eyed; sharp'-ground, ground to a sharp edge; sharp'-looking (*Shak.*), hungry-looking; sharp'-nosed, having a pointed nose: keen of scent; sharp'-pointed.—sharp practice, unscrupulous dealing, verging on dishonesty.— *adjs.* sharp'-set, hungry: keen in appetite for anything, esp. food or sexual indulgence; sharp'-shod, (of a horse) having spikes in the shoes to prevent slipping.—sharp'shooter, a good marksman: a soldier set apart for work as a marksman; sharp'shooting.—*adjs.* sharp'-sight'ed, having acute sight: shrewd; sharp'-toothed; sharp'-vis'aged, thin-faced; sharp'-witt'ed.—look sharp, be quick: hurry up; sharp's the word, be brisk; sharp-tailed grouse, a grouse of western Canada and U.S. whose middle tail-feathers are longer than the rest. [O.E. *scearp*; O.N. *skarpr*, Ger. *scharf*.]

**shaster,** *shas'tər,* **shastra,** *shäs'trä, n.* a holy writing. [Sans. *śāstra—śās.* to teach.]

**shatter,** *shat'ər, v.t.* to scatter (*Milt.*): to dash to pieces: to wreck.—*v.i.* to break into fragments. —*n.* a fragment: impaired state.—*adj.* shatt'ery, brittle.—shatt'er-brain, a scatter-brain.—*adjs.* shatt'er-brained; shatt'er-proof, proof against shattering. [Perh. L.G.; cf. scatter.]

**shauchle,** *shöhh'l,* (*Scot.*) *v.i.* to shuffle.—*v.t.* to put out of shape or down-at-heel.—*n.* a shuffling gait: a down-at-heel shoe.—*adj.* shauchly. [Origin obscure.]

**shave,** *shāv, v.t.* to scrape or pare off a superficial slice, hair (esp. of the face), or other surface material from: to tonsure: to remove by scraping or paring: to pare closely: to graze the surface of: to plunder, fleece.—*v.i.* to remove hair by a razor: to pass or escape with little margin:—*pa.p.* shāved, or *arch.* shāv'en.— *n.* the act or process of shaving: a paring: a narrow miss or escape (esp. *close shave*): a paring or slicing tool.—*n.* shave'ling, a tonsured cleric.—*adj.* shā'ven, shaved: tonsured: close-cut: smoothed.—*ns.* shā'ver, one who shaves: a barber: a sharp or extortionate dealer: a chap, a youngster (*coll.*); shā'vie (*Scot.*), a trick; shā'ving, the act of scraping or using a razor: a thin slice, esp. a curled piece of wood planed off.—shave'-grass, Dutch rush; shā'ving-brush, a brush for lathering the face; shā'ving-soap, soap for lathering in preparation for shaving; shā'ving-stick, a cylindrical piece of shaving-soap. [O.E. *sc(e)afan*; Du. *schaven*, Ger. *schaben*.]

**Shavian,** *shā'vi-ən, adj.* pertaining to the dramatist George Bernard Shaw (1856-1950).—*n.* a follower or admirer of Shaw.

**shaw,** *shö, n.* a small wood. [O.E. *sc(e)aga*; O.N. *skögr*, Dan. *skov*.]

**shaw,** *shö, v.t.* and *v.i.* Scots form of show.—*n.* show, appearance: the above-ground parts of a potato plant, turnip, etc.

**shawl,** *shöl, n.* a loose covering for the shoulders, etc.—*v.t.* to wrap in a shawl.—*n.* shawl'ing.— *adj.* shawl'less.—shawl'-patt'ern, a pattern like that of an Eastern shawl such as those woven in Kashmir; shawl'-waist'coat, a waistcoat with a large staring pattern like that of a shawl.— Paisley shawl (see paisley). [Pers. *shāl.*]

**shawm,** *shöm,* **shalm,** *shäm, n.* a musical instrument of the oboe class, having a double reed and a flat circular piece against which the lips are rested. [O.Fr. *chalemie, -mel*—L. *calamus*, reed.]

**Shawnee,** *shö-nē', n.* an Indian of an Algonquin tribe now mostly in Oklahoma.—shawnee'-wood, a species of Catalpa. [Shawnee *Shawunogi.*]

**shay,** *n.* See chaise.

**shaya,** *n.* See chay (2).

**shchi, shtchi,** *shchē, n.* cabbage soup. [Russ.]

**she,** *shē* (or when unemphatic *shi*), *nom.* (irregularly or ungrammatically *accus.* or *dat.*) *fem. pron. of the 3rd pers.* the female (or thing spoken of as female) named before, indicated, or understood (*pl.* they).—*n.* (*nom., accus.,* and *dat.*) a female (*pl.* shes).—*adj.* female (esp. in composition, as she'-ass', she'-bear', she'-dev'il). [Prob. O.E. *sēo,* fem. of the def. art., which in the 12th cent. came to be used instead of the pron. *hēo.*]

**shea,** *shē, shē'a, n.* an African tree (shea'-tree, Butyrospermum), whose seeds (shea'-nuts) yield shea'-butt'er. [Mungo Park's spelling of Mandingo (W.Afr. language) *si.*]

**sheading,** *shē'ding. n.* one of the six divisions or districts of the Isle of Man. [shedding.]

**sheaf,** *shēf, n.* a bundle of things bound side by side, esp. stalks of corn: a bundle of (usually 24) arrows:—*pl.* sheaves (*shēvz*).—*vs.t.* sheaf, sheave, to bind in sheaves.—*vs.i.* to make sheaves. —*adj.* sheaf'y.—*adj.* sheaved, in sheaves: flared:

perh., made of straw (*Shak.*). [O.E. *scēaf*; cf. Ger. *schaub*, Du. *schoof*.]

**sheal, sheel, shiel,** *shēl*, **shill,** *shil*, (*Shak.*) *v.t.* to shell or husk.—**sheal'ing-** (**sheel'ing-,** etc.) hill, a hill where grain is winnowed by the wind. [Related to **shell, shale, scale.**]

**sheal, shealing.** Same as **shiel, shieling.**

**shear,** *shēr*, *v.t.* to cut, or clip, esp. with shears: to cut superfluous nap from: to achieve or make by cutting: to tonsure: to reap with a sickle (*Scot.*): to subject to a shear.—*v.i.* to separate: to cut: to penetrate: to reap with a sickle:—*pa.t.* **sheared,** *arch.* and *poet.* **shore;** *pa.p.* **shorn,** also, less commonly in ordinary senses, but always of deformation and usually of metal-cutting, **sheared.**—*n.* a shearing or clipping: a strain, stress, or deformation in which parallel planes remain parallel, but move parallel to themselves.—*ns.* **shear'er,** one who shears sheep: a reaper (*Scot.*); **shear'ing; shear'ling,** a shear-hog.—*n.pl.* **shears,** orig. scissors (also *Scot.*): now usu. a larger instrument of similar kind, with pivot or spring: applied by Spenser to wings (**winged sheares**) as instruments for cutting the air: a hoisting apparatus (see **sheers**).—**shear'-hog,** a sheep between first and second shearings; **shear'-hulk, -leg** (see **sheer,** 2); **shear'man,** one who shears superfluous nap from cloth; **shear'-steel,** steel suitable for making shears, etc.; **shear'water,** a genus (*Puffinus*; not the puffins, but akin to the petrels) of oceanic birds that skim the water. [O.E. *sceran*; O.N. *skera,* to clip, Ger. *scheren,* to shave.]

**'sheart,** *särt,* (*obs.*) *interj.* for God's heart.

**sheat-fish,** *shēt'-fish,* **sheath-fish,** *shēth',* *n.* a gigantic fish (*Silurus glanis*) of European rivers: any kindred fish. [Ger. *scheidfisch.*]

**sheath,** *shēth,* *n.* a case for a sword or blade: a close-fitting (esp. tubular or long) covering: a clasping leaf-base: an insect's wing-case: a contraceptive device for men:—*pl.* **sheaths** (*shēdhz*).—*v.t.* **sheathe** (*shēdh*), to put into or cover with a sheath or casing.—*adj.* **sheathed** (*shēdhd*), having or enclosed in a sheath.—*n.* **sheath'ing** (-*dh*-), that which sheathes: casing: covering of a ship's bottom.—*adjs.* **sheath'less; sheath'y** (-*th*- or -*dh*-), sheath-like.— **sheath'-knife,** a knife encased in a sheath.—*adj.* **sheath'-winged,** coleopterous.—**sheathe the sword,** to end war. [O.E. *scēath, scǣth;* Ger. *scheide,* O.N. *skeithir.*]

**sheave,** *shēv,* *n.* a shive, slice, slab: a grooved wheel, pulley-wheel: a fragment: a speck, particle of impurity, as in paper. [Related to **shive.**]

**sheave, sheaves,** etc. See **sheaf.**

**Sheba,** *shē'bə.* See **Saba.**

**shebang,** *shē-bang',* *n.* a room, house, shop, hut, etc.: a vehicle: affair, matter, etc. [U.S. slang.]

**Shebat,** *shē'bät,* *n.* the fifth (ecclesiastically eleventh) Jewish month, parts of January and February.—Also **Se'bat.** [Heb. *Sh'bāt.*]

**shebeen,** *shi-bēn',* *n.* an illicit liquor-shop.—*v.i.* to keep a shebeen.—*ns.* **shebeen'er; shebeen'ing.** [Anglo-Ir.]

**Shechinah,** *shi-kī'nə, n.* Same as **Shekinah.**

**shecklaton.** See **checklaton.**

**shed,** *shed,* *v.t.* to part, separate: to cast off: to drop: to emit: to pour forth: to cast, throw (as light): to impart: to cause effusion of: to spill (*dial.*): to besprinkle (*Spens.*).—*v.i.* to fall off: to dispense (*Spens.*):—*pr.p.* **shedd'ing;** *pa.t.* and *pa.p.* **shed.**—*n.* (*obs.* or *dial.*) a parting.—*adj.* cast: spilt, emitted.—*ns.* **shedd'er,** one who sheds: a female salmon or the like after spawning; **shedd'ing.** [O.E. *scādan, scēadan* (strong vb.), to separate; Ger. *scheiden.*]

**shed,** *shed,* *n.* a structure, often open-fronted, for storing or shelter: an outhouse. [App. a variant of **shade.**]

**sheel, sheeling.** See under **sheal,** 1, **shieling.**

**sheen,** *shēn, adj.* (*poet.*) beautiful: bright: shining.—*n.* shine: lustre: radiance: glistening attire.—*v.i.* (*obs.* except *Scot.*) to shine: to gleam: to have a lustre.—*adj.* **sheen'y,** lustrous: glistening. [O.E. *scēne* (W.S. *sciene, scȳne*), beautiful; Du. *schoon,* Ger. *schön;* influenced by **shine.**]

**sheeny,** *shēn'i,* (*slang*) *offensive*) *n.* a Jew.—*adj.* Jewish. [Origin unknown.]

**sheep,** *shēp, n.* a beardless woolly wild or domestic animal (*Ovis*) of the goat family: sheepskin: a sheepish person: one who is like a sheep, as in being a member of a flock (or congregation), in following an example, in being at the mercy of the wolf or the shearer, in tameness of spirit, etc.:—*pl.* **sheep.**—*adj.* **sheep'ish,** like a sheep: embarrassed through having done something foolish or wrong.—*adv.* **sheep'ishly.**—*n.* **sheep'ishness.**—*adj.* **sheep'y** (*rare*), sheeplike.—**sheep'-biter,** a dog that bites or worries sheep: prob. an oppressive supervisor (*Shak.*).—*adj.* **sheep'-biting,** given to biting sheep: (*fig. arch.*) sneaking, thieving.—Also *n.*—**sheep'-cote,** an enclosure for sheep; **sheep'-dip,** a disinfectant vermin-killing preparation used in washing sheep; **sheep'dog,** a dog trained to watch sheep, or of a breed used for that purpose: a chaperon (*slang*).—*adj.* **sheep'-faced,** sheepish, bashful.— **sheep'-farmer; sheep'fold; sheep'-hook,** a shepherd's crook; **sheep'-ked,** a wingless fly (*Melophagus*) that sucks sheep's blood; **sheep'-louse,** a louse (*Trichodectes*) that infests sheep: loosely, a sheep-ked:—*pl.* **sheep'-lice; sheep'-master,** owner of sheep; **sheep'-pen; sheep'-plant,** vegetable sheep; **sheep'-pox,** a contagious eruptive disease of sheep, resembling smallpox; **sheep'-rot,** liver rot; **sheep'-run,** a tract of grazing country for sheep; **sheep's'-bit** (or **sheep's scabious**), a campanulaceous plant (*Jasione*) with blue heads resembling scabious; **sheep'-scab,** a mange in sheep transmitted by mites; **sheep'-scor'ing,** the counting of sheep (**sheep-scoring numerals,** numerals of Old Welsh origin, used by shepherds, knitters, and in counting-out rhymes by children); **sheep's'-eye,** a wishful amorous look; **sheep's'-foot,** a printer's claw-hammer; **sheep'-shank,** a sheep's leg: something of slender importance (*Scot.*): a nautical knot for shortening a rope; **sheep's'-head,** the head of a sheep, esp. as food (also *adj.*): a dolt: an American fish allied to the porgie; **sheep'-shearer; sheep'-shearing; sheep'-silver,** money paid in commutation of some right connected with sheep; **sheep'skin,** the skin of a sheep: leather or parchment prepared from it.—Also *adj.*—**sheep'-stealer; sheep'-stealing; sheep'-tick,** strictly, a tick (*Ixodes*) that infests sheep: commonly, a sheep-ked; **sheep'-track; sheep'walk,** a range of pasture for sheep; **sheep'-wash,** sheep-dip.—*adj.* **sheep'-whis'tling** (*Shak.*), tending sheep.—**black sheep,** the disreputable member of a family or group. [O.E. *scēap;* Ger. *schaf.*]

**sheer,** *shēr, adj.* bright, clear (*arch.*): thin: pure: unmingled: mere, downright: plumb: unbroken: vertical or very nearly.—*adv.* clear: quite: plumb: vertically.—*n.* a very thin fabric.—*adv.* **sheer'ly.** [M.E. *schēre,* perh. from a lost O.E. equivalent of O.N. *skærr,* bright.]

**sheer,** *shēr, v.i.* to deviate: to swerve.—*v.t.* to cause to deviate.—*n.* deviation: oblique position: fore-and-aft upward curve of a ship's deck or sides.—*n.pl.* **sheers, shears,** an apparatus for hoisting heavy weights, having legs or spars spread apart at their lower ends, and hoisting tackle at their joined tops.—**sheer'-hulk,** an old dismantled ship with a pair of sheers mounted on it: popularly, a mere hulk, as if from **sheer** (1); **sheer'-leg, shear'-leg,** one of the spars of sheers.—**sheer off,** to move aside: to take oneself off. [Partly at least another spelling of **shear**; perh. partly from the L.G. or Du. equivalent, *scheren*, to cut, withdraw.]

**sheet**, *shēt*, *n.* a large wide expanse or thin piece: a large broad piece of cloth, esp. for a bed, a penitent, or a corpse: a large broad piece of paper: a section of a book printed upon one piece of paper, a signature: as much copy as will' fill a sheet: a pamphlet, brcadside, or newspaper: a sail (*poet.*): a sill (**intrusive sheet**; *geol.*): sheet-rubber: one of the separate pieces or planes that make up a surface: air-craft structural material under 0·25 in. (6·35 mm.) thick, thinner than 'plate'.—*adj.* in the form of a sheet: printed on a sheet.—*v.t.* to wrap or cover with, or as with, a sheet: to furnish with sheets: to form into sheets.—*v.i.* to form or run in a sheet.—*adj.* **sheet′ed**, wrapped or covered with a sheet, esp. a winding-sheet: with a white band or belt, as a cow: spread as a sheet.—*n.* **sheet′ing**, cloth for sheets: protective boarding or metal covering: formation into sheets.—*adj.* **sheet′y**.—**sheet′-copper, -iron, -lead, -metal, -rubber, -tin**, etc., copper, iron, etc., in thin sheets; **sheet′-glass**, a kind of crown-glass made in a cylinder and flattened out; **sheet′-light′ning**, diffused appearance of distant lightning. [O.E. *scēte* (W.S. *sciete*), *scēat*; cf. next word.]

**sheet**, *shēt*, *n.* a rope attached to the lower corner of a sail: (in *pl.*) the part of a boat between the thwarts and the stern or bow.—**a sheet**, or **three sheets, in the wind**, half-drunk, or drunk. [O.E. *scēata*, corner; akin to foregoing.]

**sheet-anchor**,' *shēt′angk′ər*, *n.* an anchor for an emergency: chief support: last refuge. [Formerly *shut-, shot-, shoot-anchor*; origin doubtful.]

**sheikh, sheik**, *shāk, shēk, n.* an Arab chief: a girl's young man or ideal film hero (*slang*): a Hindu convert to Islam. [Ar. *shaikh—shākha*, to be old.]

**sheila**, *shē′la*, *n.* a young girl (*Austr.*): a white Teddy girl (*S.Afr.*). [From proper name.]

**sheiling**. Same as **shieling**.

**shekel**, *shek′l*, *n.* a Jewish weight (about 14 grams) and coin of this weight: (in *pl.*) money (*slang*). [Heb. *sheqel—shāqal*, to weigh.]

**Shekinah, Shechinah**, *shi-kī′na*, *n.* the divine presence. [Heb. *shekīnāh—shākan*, to dwell.]

**sheldrake**, *shel′drāk*, *n.* a large duck (Tadorna) with free hind-toe.—Also **shell′drake, shiel′-drake**—*fem.* **sheld′duck, shel′duck, shell′duck, shiel′duck**. [Prob. dial. *sheld* (cf. Du. *schillede*), variegation, and **drake**.]

**shelf**, *shelf*, *n.* a board fixed on a wall, in a book-case, etc., for laying things on: a shelf-ful: a terrace: a ledge: a shoal: a sandbank:—*pl.* **shelves** (*shelvz*).—*v.t.* to shelve.—*n.* **shelf′-ful**, enough to fill a shelf:—*pl.* **shelf′-fuls**.—*adj.* **shelf′y**.—**shelf′-cat′alogue**, a library catalogue arranged by shelves; **shelf′-mark**, indication on a book of its place in a library; **shelf′room**, space or accommodation on shelves.—**on the shelf**, shelved: laid aside from employment or prospect of marriage. [O.E. *scylf*, shelf, ledge, pinnacle, or L.G. *schelf*; perh. partly from some other source.]

**shell**, *shel*, *n.* a hard outer covering, esp. of a shellfish, a tortoise, an egg, or a nut: a husk, pod, or rind: a shelled mollusc: an outer framework: a crust: a hollow sphere or the like: a mere outside, empty case, or lifeless relic: any frail structure: a frail boat: a light coffin: a conch trumpet: a lyre of tortoise-shell: an explosive projectile shot from a cannon: a piece of quicklime: in some schools, an intermediate class (from one that met in an apse at Westminster).—*adj.* of, with, or like shell or shells.—*v.t.* to separate from the shell: to case: to throw shells at.—*v.i.* to peel, scale:

to separate from the shell.—*n.* **shellac, shell-lac** (*shel-ak′*; also *shel′ak*), lac in thin plates, got by melting seed-lac, straining, and dropping.—*v.t.* to coat with shellac: (*shel-ak′*) to beat (*U.S.*): to trounce (*U.S.*):—*pr.p.* **shellack′ing**; *pa.t.* and *pa.p.* **shellacked′**.—*n.* **shellack′ing**.—*adj.* **shelled**, having a shell: separated from the shell.—*ns.* **shell′er; shell′ful; shell′iness; shell′-ing**.—*adjs.* **shell′-less; shell′y**, of or like shell or shells: abounding in shells: having a shell: testaceous.—**shell′back**, an old sailor; **shell′bark**, a hickory with peeling bark.—*adj.* **shell′bound**, unable to escape from the shell.—**shell′-crater**, a hole in the ground made by a bursting shell; **shell′-egg**, one in the shell, in its natural state; **shell′fire**, bombardment with shells; **shell′fish**, a shelled aquatic invertebrate, esp. a mollusc or crustacean, or such animals collectively; **shell′-heap**, a heap of shells: a kitchen midden; **shell′-hole**, a shell-crater; **shell′-ice**, ice no longer supported by water; **shell′-jack′et**, tight, short undress military jacket.—*adj.* **shell′-like**.—**shell′-lime**, lime made from seashells; **shell′-lime′stone**, a limestone mainly consisting of shells; **shell′-marl**, a white, earthy lacustrine deposit; **shell′-mon′ey**, wampum; **shell′-mound**, a shell-heap; **shell′-or′nament**, decoration in which a shell-form is prominent; **shell′-parakeet, -parrot**, the budgerigar.—*adj.* **shell′proof**, able to resist shells or bombs.—**shell′-sand**, sand consisting in great part of calcareous organic remains; **shell′shock**, former name for mental disturbance due to war experiences, once thought to be caused by bursting of shells.—*adj.* **shell′-shocked**.—**shell′work**, work composed of or adorned with shells; **shell′ycoat** (*Scot.*), a water goblin dressed in shells: a sheriff's messenger.—**come out of one's shell**, to cease to be shy and reticent; **electron shell** (see **electron**); **shell out** (*slang*), to pay up: to disburse. [O.E. *scell* (W.S. *sciell*); Du. *schil*, O.N. *skel.*]

**Shelta**, *shel′ta*, *n.* an Irish vagrants secret jargon. [*Shelrū*, poss. a perversion of O.Irish *béulra*, language.]

**shelter**, *shel′tər*, *n.* a shielding or screening structure, esp. against weather: a place of refuge, retreat, or temporary lodging in distress: asylum: screening: protection. — *v.t.* to screen: to shield: to afford asylum or lodging to: to harbour.—*v.i.* to take shelter.—*adj.* **shel′tered**.—*n.* **shel′terer**. *n.* and *adj.* **shel′tering**.—*adjs.* **shel′terless; shel′tery**, affording shelter. [Origin obscure.]

**sheltie, shelty**, *shel′ti*, *n.* a Shetland pony. [Perh. O.N. *Hjalti*, Shetlander.]

**shelve**, *shelv*, *v.t.* to furnish with shelves: to place on a shelf: to put aside.—*v.i.* to slope, incline.—*n.* a ledge: a shelf.—*n.pl.* **shelves**, *pl.* of **shelf** and of **shelve**.—*n.* **shelv′ing**, provision of, or material for, shelves: shelves collectively: the act of putting upon a shelf or setting aside: a slope.—*adj.* **shallowing**: sloping.—*adj.* **shel′vy**, having sandbanks: overhanging. [See **shelf**.]

**Shema**, *she-mä′*, *n.* a Jewish prayer with a long history, recited at morning and evening. [Heb., hear.]

**Shemite**, etc. Earlier forms of **Semite**, etc.

**shemozzle**, *shi-moz′l*, (*slang*) *n.* a mess: a scrape: a rumpus.—Also **shimozz′le, shlemozz′le, she-mozz′le**.—*v.i.* to make off. [Yiddish,—Ger. *schlimm*, bad, Heb. *mazzāl*, luck; cf. **schlimazel**.]

**shenanigan**, *shi-nan′i-gən*, (*slang*) *n.* trickery: humbug. [Origin unknown.]

**shend**, *shend*, (*obs.* or *poet.*) *v.t.* to put to shame: to disgrace: to reproach: to punish: to discomfit:—*pa.t.* and *pa.p.* **shent**. [O.E. *scendan*, to disgrace.]

**she-oak**, *shē′-ōk*, (*Austr.*) *n.* a casuarina tree. [**she**, denoting inferior, and **oak**, from its grain.]

**She'ol**, *shē'ōl*, *n.* the place of departed spirits. [Heb. *she'ōl.*]

**shepherd**, *shep'∂rd*, *n.* one who tends sheep (*fem.* **shep'herdess**): a swain: a pastor.—*v.t.* to tend or guide as a shepherd: to watch over, protect the interests of, or one's own interests in.—*v.i.* to tend sheep.—*adj.* **shep'herdless.**—*n.* **shep'herdling**, a little shepherd.—**Shepherd kings**, the Hyksos; **shepherd('s) check, plaid, tartan**, (cloth with) small black-and-white check: **shepherd's club**, great mullein; **shepherd's cress**, a small cruciferous plant, Teesdalia; **shepherd's glass**, scarlet pimpernel; **shepherd's myrtle**, butcher's broom; **shepherd's needle**, Venus's comb; **shepherd's pie**, a dish of meat cooked with potatoes on the top; **shepherd's purse**, a cosmopolitan cruciferous weed with flat obcordate pods (*Capsella bursa-pastoris*); **shepherd's rod**, the small teasel.—**the Good Shepherd**, Jesus Christ (John x. 11). [O.E. *scēaphirde*; see **sheep, herd.**]

**sherardise, -ize**, *sher'∂rd-īz*, *v.t.* to coat with zinc by heating with zinc-dust in absence of air. [From *Sherard* Cowper-Coles, the inventor of the process.]

**Sheraton**, *sher'∂-t∂n*, *n.* a kind or style of furniture designed by Thomas *Sheraton* (1751-1806).

**sherbet**, *shûr'b∂t*, *n.* a fruit-juice drink: an effervescent drink, or powder for making it: a kind of water-ice. [Turk. and Pers. *sherbet*, from Ar.; cf. **shrub** (2), **syrup.**]

**sherd**, *shûrd*, *n.* See **shard.**

**shere**, a Spenserian spelling of **sheer** (bright).

**sheriat**, *sher-ē'at*, *n.* the body of Islamic religious law. [Turk. *sheri'at*, law.]

**sherif, shereef**, *sh∂-rēf'*, *n.* a descendant of Mohammed through his daughter Fatima: a prince, esp. the Sultan of Morocco: the chief magistrate of Mecca.—*adj.* **sherif'ian, shereef'ian.** [Ar. *sharif*, noble, lofty.]

**sheriff**, *sher'if*, *n.* the king's representative in a shire, with wide powers judicial and executive (*hist.*): now in England, the chief officer of the crown in the shire, county, with duties chiefly ministerial rather than judicial: in Scotland, the chief judge of the county: in the United States, the chief executive officer of the county, his principal duties to maintain peace and order, attend courts, guard prisoners, serve processes and execute judgments.—*ns.* **sher'iffalty**, **shrievalty**; **sher'iffdom**, the office, term of office, or territory under the jurisdiction of a sheriff; **sher'iffship**, the office of sheriff.—**sher'iff-clerk'**, in Scotland, the registrar of the sheriff's court, who has charge of the records of the court:—*pl.* **sher'iff-clerks'**; **sher'iff-court'**, the sheriff's court; **sher'iff-dep'ute**, in Scotland, till the abolition of the heritable jurisdictions in 1748, a lawyer who acted as deputy for the sheriff: thereafter sometimes the sheriff himself:—*pl.* **sher'iff-dep'utes**; **sher'iff-prin'cipal**, in Scotland, a sheriff properly so-called; **sher'iff-off'icer**, in Scotland, an officer connected with the sheriff-court, charged with arrests, serving of processes, etc.; **sher'iff's-post** (*hist.*), painted post at sheriff's door for affixing proclamations; **sher'iff-sub'stitute**, a Scottish acting-sheriff, appointed by the crown, in most cases resident in his judicial district:—*pl.* **sher'iffs-sub'stitute.**—**high sheriff**, an English sheriff proper: the chief executive officer of a district (*U.S.*); **honorary sheriff-substitute**, one who may act in the absence of the sheriff-substitute; **under sheriff**, an English sheriff's deputy who performs the execution of writs. [O.E. *scīrgerēfa*—*scīr*, shire, *gerēfa*, reeve; cf. **reeve, grieve** (2), Ger. *graf*, **count.**]

**Sherlock (Holmes)**, *shûr'lok* (*hōmz*), *n.* one who shows highly developed powers of observation and deduction, as did the detective, Sherlock Holmes, in the stories of Conan Doyle (1859-1930)—often used ironically.

**Sherpa**, *shûr'p∂*, *n. sing.* and *pl.* one or more of an eastern Tibetan people living high on the south side of the Himalayas. [Tibetan *shar*, east, *pa*, inhabitant.]

**sherris**, *sher'is*, (*Shak.*) *n.* Same as **sherry.**—**sherr'is-sack'**, sack imported from *Xeres.*

**sherry**, *sher'i*, *n.* a fortified wine grown in the neighbourhood of Jerez de la Frontera in Spain: a wine of like type.—**sherry-cobb'ler**, a drink composed of sherry, lemon, sugar, ice, etc.; **sherry party**, a gathering at which sherry is drunk. [*Xeres*, earlier form of Jerez.]

**shet**, *shet*, *obs.* or *dial.* form of **shut.**

**shetland**, *shet'l∂nd*, (usu. with *cap.*) *adj.* pertaining to the Shetland Islands off the N. coast of Scotland.—**Shetland pony**, a small, hardy pony with a thick coat, originating in the Shetland Islands: **Shetland sheep**, a breed of sheep of Shetland and formerly Aberdeenshire; **Shetland sheepdog**, a breed of dog resembling and presumably bred from, the collie, though smaller in size and with a thicker coat.

**sheuch, sheugh**, *shōōhh*,' (*Scot.*) *n.* a ditch, drain. —*v.t.* to plant temporarily. [**sough** (2).]

**sheva**, *shē'a-vä'*, *n.* Hebrew point or sign (simple, or in compound forms) indicating absence of vowel or a neutral vowel.—Also **schwa.** [Heb. *shewā.*]

**shew**, *shō*, formerly (as *Milt.*) *shōō.* Same as **show**:—*pa.p.* **shewn** (*shōn*).—**shew'bread**, the twelve loaves offered weekly in the sanctuary by the Jews.

**shewel**, *shōō'∂l*, *n.* a scarecrow or mark to scare deer. [Connected with **shy.**]

**Shiah**, *shē'a*, *n.* a Mohammedan sect, or a member of it, recognising Ali, Mohammed's son-in-law, as his successor.—**Shiite** (*shē'īt*), a member of this sect. [Ar. *shi'a*, sect.]

**shibboleth**, *shib'∂-leth*, *n.* the Gileadite test-word for an Ephraimite, who could not pronounce *sh* (Judges xii. 5-6; *B.*): any such test: a peculiarity of speech: the criterion or catchword of a group: a cant phrase. [Heb. *shibbō'-leth*, an ear of corn, or a stream.]

**shicker**, *shik'∂r*, *n.* strong drink.—*adj.* **shick'ered**, drunk. [Yiddish.]

**shicksa.** Same as **shiksa.**

**shidder**, *shid'∂r*, (*Spens.*) *n.* a female animal. [she, deer; cf. **hidder.**]

**shied, shier, shies, shiest.** See **shy** (1 and 2).

**shiel.** Same as **sheal.**

**shiel, sheal**, *shēl*, (*Scot.*) *n.* a hut: a shelter.—*n.* **shiel'ing, sheal'ing**, a shepherd's summer hut: a summer grazing. [Prob. from a lost O.E. equivalent of O.N. *skǎli*, hut.]

**shield**, *shēld*, *n.* a broad plate carried to ward off weapons, esp. one with a straight top and tapering curved sides: a protective plate, screen, pad, or other guard: a protection: a tubular structure pushed forward in tunnelling: a shield-shaped escutcheon used for displaying arms: a shield-shaped piece of plate as a prize: any shield-shaped design or object: the area of Archaean rocks in the earth's crust: a policeman's badge (*U.S.*).—*v.t.* to protect by shelter: to ward off: to forfend (*Shak.*).—*n.* **shiel'der.**—*adj.* **shield'less.**—*n.* **shield'ling**, a protected person.—**shield'-bearer**; **shield'-bug**, a heteropterous insect with much developed scutellum (fam. Pentatomidae); **shield'-fern**, Aspidium; **shield'-hand**, the left hand; **shield'-maid, -maiden, -may**, an Amazon: a Valkyrie.—*adj.* **shield'-shaped**, usu., shaped like the conventional shield: sometimes, buckler-shaped: peltate.— **shield'wall**, a defence of interlocked shields.— **shield of brawn**, the thick skin of a pig's side, esp. when stuffed with meat. [O.E. *sceld* (W.S. *scield*); Ger. *schild*, O.N. *skjöldr*, protection.]

**shift**, *shift*, *v.i.* to manage, get on, do as one can:

to change: to change position: to fluctuate: to change one's clothes (*arch.* or *dial.*): to resort to expedients: to move: to go away: to move quickly (*coll.*): to undergo phonetic change.—*v.t.* to change: to change the clothes of (*dial.*): to change the position of: to remove: to dislodge: to transfer: to evade (*obs.*): to rid: to quit: to swallow (*slang*): to put off.—*n.* an expedient: an artifice: provision of clothes or (*arch.*) other things for use in rotation or substitution: hence, (*arch.*) a smock: a chemise: a shirt (*dial.*): a loose dress roughly triangular or oblong: a set of persons taking turns with another set: time of working of such a set: a change: change of position: a general or bodily displacement of a series (as of lines in the spectrum, consonant or vowel sounds, faulted strata): in violin-playing, any position of the left hand except that nearest the nut: a removal.—*adj.* **shift′ed.**—*ns.* **shift′er,** one who shifts, esp. a scene-shifter: one who resorts to shifts, tricks, evasions, or sophistry; **shift′iness;** **shift′ing.**—*adj.* unstable: shifty.—*adj.* **shift′less,** without a smock: without resource or expedient: inefficient: feckless.—*adv.* **shift′lessly.**—*n.* **shift′-lessness.**—*adj.* **shift′y,** full of, or ready with, shifts or expedients: evasive, tricky, suggesting trickery.—**shif′ting-boards,** partitioning to prevent shifting of cargo; **shift′-key,** a typewriter key used to bring a different set of letters (as capitals) into play.—**make (a) shift,** contrive to do somehow; **shift about,** to vacillate: to turn quite round to the opposite point; **shift for oneself,** to depend on one's own resources; **shift one's ground** (usu. *fig.*), to change the position one has taken, e.g. in a discussion. [O.E. *sciftan,* to divide, allot; O.N. *skipta.*]

**shih tzu,** *shēd-zōō, n.* a small dog of Tibetan and Chinese breed.

**Shiite.** See **Shiah.**

**shikar,** *shi-kär′, n.* hunting, sport.—*ns.* **shikar′ee, shikar′i,** a hunter. [Urdu, from Pers. *shikār.*]

**shiksa,** *shik′sa, n.* a non-Jewish woman. [Yiddish.]

**shill, shilling.** See **sheal.**

**shillela(g)h,** *shi-lā′li, ′lə, n.* conventional Irishman's oak or blackthorn cudgel. [*Shillelagh,* an oakwood in County Wicklow, or *sail,* willow, *éille* (*gen.*) thong.]

**shilling,** *shil′ing, n.* a coin or its value, 12 pence, 5 new pence or (**East Africa shilling,** Kenya, etc.) 100 cents.—*adj.* costing or offered for a shilling: also in compounds, as **two′-shilling, three′-shilling,** etc.—*adj.* **shill′ingless.**—*n.* **shill′ingsworth.**—**shilling shocker,** a sensational story, orig. one published at a shilling.—**take the (king's, queen's) shilling,** to enlist as a soldier by accepting recruiting officer's shilling—discontinued 1879. [O.E. *scilling;* Ger. *schilling.*]

**shilly-shally,** *shil′i-shal′i, adv.* in silly hesitation. —*n.* vacillation: one who vacillates.—*v.i.* to vacillate.—**shill′y-shall′ier.** [A redup. of **shall I?**]

**shilpit,** *shil′pit,* (*Scot.*) *adj.* sickly-looking: washy. [Ety. dub.]

**shim,** *shim, n.* a slip of metal, wood, etc., used to fill in space or to adjust parts. [Ety. dub.]

**shimmer,** *shim′ər, v.i.* to gleam tremulously, to glisten.—*ns.* **shimm′er, shimm′ering,** a tremulous gleam.—*adj.* **shimm′ery.** [O.E. *scimerian*—*scimian,* to shine; Ger. *schimmern.*]

**shimmy,** *shim′i, n.* a shivering dance (also **shimm′y-shake**): vibration in a motor-car or an aeroplane. —*v.i.* to dance the shimmy: to vibrate. [App. from **chemise.**]

**shimozzle.** See **shemozzle.**

**shin,** *shin, n.* the forepart of the leg below the knee: the lower part of a leg of beef.—*v.i.* to swarm, climb by gripping between the legs: to use one's legs, hasten along.—*v.t.* to climb by

swarming (usu. with **up**): to kick on the shins. —**shin′-barker,** a cur that barks at one's shins; **shin′-bone,** the tibia; **shin′-plas′ter** (*U.S.*), a brown-paper patch for a sore on the shin: paper money of small value. [O.E. *scinu,* the shin; Du. *scheen;* Ger. *schiene,* a thin plate.]

**shindig,** *shin′dig,* (*slang*) *n.* a lively celebration or party: a row. [Cf. **shindy.**]

**shindy,** *shin′di,* (*slang*) *n.* a row, rumpus.—**kick up a shindy,** make a disturbance. [Perh. **shinty.**]

**shine,** *shin, v.i.* to give or reflect light: to beam with steady radiance: to glow: to be bright: to appear pre-eminent.—*v.t.* to cause to shine: —*pa.t.* and *pa.p.* **shone,** *shon; B.,* and in sense of polished, **shined.**—*adj.* (*Spens.*) **sheen.**—*n.* brightness: lustre: sunshine: a dash, brilliant appearance: an act or process of polishing; a tea-party or the like (*slang*): a shindy (*slang*). —*adj.* **shine′less.**—*n.* **shin′er,** one who or that which shines: a coin, esp. a sovereign (*slang*): a small glittering fish of various kinds: a black eye (*slang*).—*adj.* **shin′ing.**—*adv.* **shin′ingly.**— *n.* **shin′ingness.**—*adj.* **shin′y,** clear, unclouded: glossy.—Also *adv.* (*Spens.*).—**take a shine to** (*slang*), to fancy, take a liking to; **shine at,** to be very good at; **take the shine out of,** (*slang*) to outshine, eclipse: to take the brilliance or pleasure-giving quality out of. [O.E. *scinan;* Ger. *scheinen;* in some senses perh. a different word; cf. **shindy.**]

**shingle,** *shing′gl, n.* a wooden slab (or substitute) used as is a roofing-slate (also collectively): a board: a small signboard or plate (*U.S.*): a mode of hair-cutting showing the form of the head at the back (from the overlap of the hairs). —*v.t.* to cover with shingles: to cut in the manner of a shingle.—*adj.* **shing′led.**—*ns.* **shing′ler;** **shing′ling.**—*adj.* **shing′le-roofed.** [L.L. *scindula,* a wooden tile—L. *scindĕre,* to split.]

**shingle,** *shing′gl, n.* coarse gravel: a large pebble: a bank or bed of large rounded stones.—*adj.* **shing′ly.** [Origin obscure.]

**shingles,** *shing′glz, n.pl.* the disease *Herpes zoster,* an eruption usually running along an intercostal nerve. [L. *cingulum,* a belt—*cingĕre,* to gird.]

**shinne,** *shin,* (*Shak.*) *n.* a form of **chin.**

**shinny.** Same as **shinty.**

**Shinto,** *shin′tō, n.* the Japanese nature and hero cult.—*ns.* **Shin′tōism; Shin′tōist.** [Jap.,—Chin. *shin tao*—*shin,* god, *tao,* way, doctrine.]

**shinty,** *shin′ti,* **shinny,** *shin′i, n.* a game like hockey: the stick (also **shin′ty-stick**), or ball (or substitute) used therein. [Origin obscure.]

**ship,** *ship, n.* a large vessel, esp. a three-masted square-rigged sailing vessel: a racing-boat: sometimes any floating craft: an aircraft.—*v.t.* to put, receive, or take on board: to send or convey by ship: to send by land or air: to dispatch, send (off): to engage for service on board: to fix in position.—*v.i.* to embark: to engage for service on shipboard:—*pr.p.* **shipp′-ing;** *pa.t.* and *pa.p.* **shipped.**—*n.* **ship′ful.**—*adj.* **ship′less.**—*n.* **ship′ment,** putting on board: a consignment by ship.—*adj.* **shipped,** furnished with a ship or ships (*Shak.*): embarked.—*ns.* **shipp′er,** one who sends goods by ship; **shipp′ing,** ships collectively: accommodation on board ship: putting aboard ship: transport by ship: a voyage (*Shak.*).—**ship′-bis′cuit,** hard biscuit for use on shipboard; **ship′board,** a ship's side, hence a ship; **ship′-boy,** a boy that serves on a ship; **ship′-breaker,** one who breaks up old ships; **ship′-broker,** a broker for sale, insurance, etc., of ships; **ship′builder; ship′building; ship′-canal′,** a canal large enough for ships; **ship′-cap′tain,** one who commands a ship; **ship('s)′-car′penter,** a carpenter employed on board ship or in a shipyard; **ship′-chand′ler,** a dealer in supplies for ships; **ship′-chand′lery; ship′-fē′ver,**

typhus; **ship'-hold'er**, a remora; **ship'lap**, arrangement of boards or plates in which the lower edge of one overlaps the upper edge of the next below it.—Also *v.t.* and *v.i.*—**ship'-lett'er**, a letter sent by a vessel which does not carry mails; **ship'-load**, the actual or possible load of a ship; **ship'man** (*arch.*), a sailor: a skipper: a pilot:—*pl.* **ship'men**; **ship'-master**, the captain of a ship; **ship'mate**, a fellow-sailor; **ship'-money**, a tyrannical tax imposed by the king on seaports, revived without authorisation of parliament by Charles I in 1634-37; **ship'-of-the-line'**, before steam navigation, a man-of-war large enough to take a place in a line of battle; **ship'-owner**, the owner of, or owner of a share in, a ship or ships; **shipp'ing-art'icles**, articles of agreement between the captain and his crew; **ship'pound**, in the Baltic ports, twenty lispounds; **ship'-rail'way**, a railway for carrying ships overland.—*adjs.* **ship'-rigged**, having three masts with square sails and spreading yards; **ship'shape**, in a seaman-like condition: trim, neat, proper.—**ship's hus-band** (see **husband**); **ship's papers**, documents that a ship is required to carry; **ship'-tire** (*Shak.*), a shiplike head-dress; **ship'-way**, a sliding-way for launching ships: a support for ships under examination or repair: a ship-canal; **ship'-worm**, a wormlike lamellibranch mollusc (Teredo, etc.) that makes shell-lined tunnels in wood; **ship'wreck**, the wreck or destruction (esp. by accident) of a ship: destruction, ruin, disaster: wreckage (*rare*).—*v.t.* to wreck: to make to suffer wreck.—*v.i.* to suffer wreck.—**ship'wright**, a wright or carpenter employed in shipbuilding; **ship'yard**, a yard where ships are built or repaired.—**on shipboard**, upon or within a ship; **ship a sea**, **water**, to have a wave come aboard; **ship of the desert**, the camel; **ship it green**, to ship waves, not mere spray; **ship the oars**, to put the oars in the rowlocks: to bring the oars into the boat; **ship water** (see **ship a sea**); **take ship**, or **shipping**, to embark; **when one's ship comes home**, when one becomes rich. [O.E. *scip*; Goth. *skip*, O.N. *skip*, Ger. *schiff*.]

**shippen**, **shippon**, *ship'n*, (*dial.*) *n.* cowhouse, cattle-shed. [O.E. *scypen*; cf. **shop**.]

**shippo**, *ship-ō'*, *n.* Japanese cloisonné ware. [Jap. *shippô*, seven precious things.]

**shire**, *shīr* (in composition *-shir*, *-shər*), *n.* a county: applied also to certain smaller districts as Richmondshire and Hallamshire.—**shire'-horse**, a large, strong draught-horse, once bred chiefly in the Midland shires; **shire'man**, a sheriff; **shire'-moot** (O.E. *scīrgemōt*; *hist.*), the court of the shire; **shire'-reeve** (see **sheriff**).—**the Shires** (often *shērz*), those English counties whose names end in -shire, esp. (for hunting) Leicestershire, Rutlandshire (later Rutland), Northamptonshire, and part of Lincolnshire. [O.E. *scir*, office, authority.]

**shirk**, *shûrk*, *v.t.* to evade: to slink out of facing or shouldering.—*v.i.* to go or act evasively.—*n.* one who shirks.—*n.* **shirk'er**. [Cf. **shark**.]

**Shirley poppy**, *shûr'li pop'i*, *n.* a variety of common poppy produced at *Shirley*, Croydon.

**shirr**, **shir**, *shûr*, *n.* a puckering or gathering.—*v.t.* to pucker, make gathers in: to bake (eggs broken into a dish).—*adj.* **shirred**.—*n.* **shirr'ing**. [Origin unknown.]

**shirra**, *shir'ə*, *n.* a Scots form of **sheriff**.

**shirt**, *shûrt*, *n.* a man's loose sleeved garment typically with fitted collar and cuffs: a woman's blouse of similar form: an undershirt: a nightshirt: a close covering.—*v.t.* to put a shirt on.—*n.* **shirt'ing**, cloth for shirts.—*adjs.* **shirt'less**; **shirt'y** (*slang*), ruffled in temper.—**shirt'-band**, the neckband of a shirt; **shirt'-butt'on**; **shirt dress**, a straight dress with a shirt-

type collar, resembling an elongated shirt: a shirtwaister (*U.S.*); **shirt'-frill'**, a frill on the breast of the shirt; **shirt'-front'**, the breast of a shirt: a dickey; **shirt'-pin**, an ornamental pin fastening a shirt at the neck; **shirt'-sleeve**; **shirt'-stud**; **shirt'-tail'**, the flap at the back of a shirt; **shirt'waist** (*U.S.*), a woman's blouse; **shirt'waister**, a tailored dress with shirtwaist top.—**Black Shirt**, a fascist; **boiled shirt**, a white shirt (with starched front); **Brown Shirt**, a Nazi; **in one's shirt**, wearing nothing but a shirt, or nothing over the shirt; **in one's shirt sleeves**, with coat off; **keep one's shirt on**, keep calm; **lose one's shirt**, to lose all one has; **put one's shirt on**, bet all one has on; **Red Shirt**, a follower of Garibaldi. [O.E. *scyrte*; cf. **short**.]

**shish kebab**. See **kabob**.

**shit**, **shite**, *shit*, *shīt*, (*vulg.*) *n.* excrement: a contemptuous term for a person.—*v.i.* to evacuate the bowels.—*v.t.*(*fig.*).—*interj.* expressing annoyance, disappointment, etc.—**bull'shit** (see **bull** (1)). [O.E. *scitan*.]

**shittim**, *shit'im*, *n.* in full **shitt'im wood** (*B.*), the wood of the **shitt'ah tree**, believed to be an acacia: applied also to various other trees. [Heb. *shittāh*, pl. *shittīm*.]

**shiv**. See **chiv**.

**shivaree**, *shiv-ə-rē'*, *n.* a U.S. form of **charivari**.—*v.t.* (*U.S.*) to give a mock serenade to.

**shive**, *shiv*, *n.* a slice, as of bread (*Scot.*): a thin wide cork or bung. [M.E. *schive*; cf. O.N. *skífa*; Du. *schijf*, Ger. *scheibe*.]

**shiver**, *shiv'ər*, *n.* a splinter: a chip: a small fragment.—*v.t.* and *v.i.* to shatter.—*adj.* **shiv'ery**, brittle.—**shiver my timbers**, a stage sailor's oath. [Early M.E. *scifre*; cf. **shive**, **sheave**; Ger. *schiefer*.]

**shiver**, *shiv'ər*, *v.i.* to quiver: to make an involuntary muscular movement as with cold.—*v.t.* to cause to quiver.—*n.* a shivering movement or feeling.—*n.* and *adj.* **shiv'ering**.—*adv.* **shiv'eringly**.—*adj.* **shiv'ery**, inclined to shiver or to cause shivers.—**shiver in one's shoes** (see **shake**); **the shivers** (*coll.*), a shivering fit: the ague: a thrill of horror or fear. [M.E. *chivere*.]

**shlemozzle**. See **shemozzle**.

**shoal**, *shōl*, *n.* a multitude of fishes, etc., swimming together: a flock, swarm, great assemblage.—*v.i.* to gather or go in shoals, swarm.—*adv.* **shoal'wise**, in shoals. [O.E. *scolu*, troop; cf. **school** (2).]

**shoal**, *shōl*, *adj.* shallow.—*n.* a shallow.—*v.i.* to grow shallow: to come to shallow water.—*v.t.* to find to be shallowing: to make shallow.—*ns.* **shoal'ing**; **shoal'ness**.—*adj.* **shoal'y**, full of shallows.—**shoal'-mark**, an indication of shoal-water; **shoal'-water**. [O.E. *sceald*, shallow.]

**shoat**, **shote**, *shōt(t)*, *shōt*, *n.* a young hog. [From M.E.; conn. Flem. *shote*.]

**shock**, *shok*, *n.* a violent impact, orig. of charging warriors: a dashing together: a shaking or unsettling blow: a sudden shaking or jarring as if by a blow: a blow to the emotions or its cause: outrage at something regarded as improper: a convulsive excitation of nerves, as by electricity: prostration of voluntary and involuntary functions caused by trauma, a surgical operation, or excessive sudden emotional disturbance: a stroke of paralysis (*coll.*).—*v.t.* to meet or assail with a shock: to shake or impair by a shock: to give a shock to: to harrow or outrage the feelings of: to affect with abashed and horrified indignation.—*v.i.* to collide with violence.—*adj.* **shocked**.—*n.* **shock'er** (*coll.*), a very sensational tale.—*adj.* **shock'ing**, giving a shock: revolting to the feelings, esp. to oversensitive modesty: execrable: deplorably bad.—*adv.* (*coll.*) deplorably.—*adv.* **shock'ingly**.—*n.* **shock'ingness**.—**shock'-absorber**, a contrivance for damping shock, as in an aeroplane alighting or a car on a bad road.—*adj.* shock'-proof, protected in some way from giving, or suffering effects of, shock: unlikely to be upset, or to feel moral outrage; shock stall (*aero.*), loss of lift at high speed caused by the formation of shock waves; shock tactics, orig. tactics of cavalry attacking in masses and depending for their effect on the force of impact: any action that seeks to achieve its object by means of suddenness and force (*fig.*); shock therapy, treatment, use of electric shocks in treatment of mental disorders: use of violent measures to change one's way of thinking (*fig.*); shock'-troops, troops trained or selected for attacks demanding exceptional physique and bravery; shock wave, a wave of the same nature as a sound wave but of very great intensity, caused, e.g. by an atomic explosion, or by a body moving with supersonic velocity. [App. Fr. *choc* (n.), *choquer* (vb.), or perh. directly from a Gmc. source; cf. Du. *schok*.]

shock, *shok*, *n.* a stook, or propped-up group of sheaves, commonly twelve: three score.—*v.t.* to set up in shocks.—*n.* shock'er. [M.E. *schokke*; the corresponding word in some Gmc. languages has come to mean sixty.]

shock, *shok*, *n.* a dog with long, shaggy hair: a mass of shaggy hair.—Also *adj.*—shock'-dog; shock'-head.—*adjs.* shock'-head, -ed. [Cf. shough.]

shod. See shoe.

shoddy, *shod'i*, *n.* wool from shredded rags: cloth made of it, alone or mixed: anything inferior seeking to pass for better than it is.—*adj.* of shoddy: inferior and pretentious: cheap and nasty: sham.—*adv.* shodd'ily.—*n.* shodd'iness. [Origin unknown.]

shoder, *shōd'ər*, *n.* a set of skins in which goldleaf is beaten the second time (see cutch). [From obs. Fr. *chaucher*, to press; ult. from L. *calx*, heel.]

shoe, *shōō*, *n.* a stiff outer covering for the foot, not coming above the ankle (or in U.S. not much above): a rim of iron nailed to a hoof: anything in form, position, or use like a shoe, as in a metal tip or ferrule, a piece attached where there is friction, a drag for a wheel, the touching part of a brake, the block by which an electric tractor collects current:—*pl.* shoes, *shōōz*; also, *arch.* and *dial.*, shoon, *shōōn*, Scot. *shiin*, *shin.*—*v.t.* to put shoes or a shoe on:—*pr.p.* shoe'ing; *pa.t.* and *pa.p.* shod (rarely shoed).—*adj.* shod (*shod*).—*n.* shoe'ing.—*adj.* shoe'less.—*n.* shoer (*shōō'ər*), a horse-shoer.—shoe'-bill, the whale-head, a large African bird (Balaeniceps) with heavy bill; shoe'black, one who blacks shoes; shoe'-brush, shoe'-buckle; a buckle for the front of a shoe, as fastening or ornament; shoe'horn, shoe'ing-horn, an instrument for helping the heel into the shoe: any means of drawing on; shoe'ing-smith; shoe'-lace, a string passed through eyelet holes to fasten a shoe; shoe'-latchet, a thong for fastening a shoe, sandal, etc.; shoe'-leather, leather for shoes: shoes or shoeing generally; shoe'maker, one who makes (now more often only sells or mends) shoes and boots; shoe'making; shoe'-nail, a nail for fastening a horseshoe: a nail for a shoe sole; shoe'-peg, a peg for fastening parts of a shoe together; shoe'-rose, a rosette on a shoe; shoe'-shop; shoe'string, a shoe-lace (*U.S.*): anything paltry (*U.S.*): a minimum of capital.—Also *adj.*—shoestring fungus, any fungus forming long rhizomorphs, esp. one that destroys trees; shoe'-tie, a shoe-lace, esp. an ornate one; shoe'-tree, a support, usually of wood or metal, inserted in a shoe when it is not being worn in order to preserve its shape.—another pair of shoes (*coll.*), quite a different matter;

be in, step into, one's, or a dead man's, shoes, to be in, or succeed to, one's place; die in one's shoes, to die by violence, esp. by hanging; on a shoestring, with an extremely small amount of capital. [O.E. *scōh* (pl. *scōs*); Goth. *shōhs*, Ger. *schuh*.]

shog, *shog*, *v.i.* to shake: to sway: to jog: to move on, be gone.—*v.t.* to shake:—*pr.p.* shogg'-ing:—*pa.t.* and *pa.p.* shogged.—*n.* a jog, shock. [M.E. *shogge*, perh. related to shock and O.H.G. *scoc*, a swing.]

shogun, *shō'gōon*, *-gōōn*, *n.* the commander-in-chief and real ruler of feudal Japan.—*adj.* shō'gunal.—*n.* shō'gunate. [Jap. *shōgun*.]

shoji, *shō'jē*, *n.* a screen of paper covering a wooden framework, forming a wall or sliding partition in Japanese homes. [Jap.]

shola, *shō'la*, (*India*) *n.* thicket. [Tamil *çolai*.]

shola. See sola.

Shona, *shō'nə*, *n.* a group of African peoples living south of the Zambesi: any member of the group: any language spoken by the group: (Union Shona) a literary language designed for use by the whole group.

shone, *shon*, *pa.t.* and *pa.p.* of shine.

shoo, *shōō*, *interj.* used to scare away fowls, etc. —*v.i.* to cry 'Shoo!'—*v.t.* to drive away by calling 'Shoo!' [Instinctive; cf. Ger. *schu*, Gr. *sou*.]

shook, *shook*, *pa.t.* of shake.

shook, *shook*, *n.* a bundle of sheaves, shock, stook: a set of cask staves and heads, or of parts for making a box, etc. [Orig. unknown.]

shool, *shōōl*, *v.i.* to saunter about, skulk: to beg: to sponge. [Perh. Ir.]

shool, *shōōl*, *shōl*, Scot. *shül*, *shil*, *n.* and *v.* a dialect form of shovel.

shoon, *shōōn*, an old *pl.* of shoe.

shoot, *shōōt*, *v.t.* to dart: to let fly with force: to discharge: to precipitate, launch forth: to tip out, dump: to cast: to send down a shoot: to kick or hit at goal (*games*): to score, for a hole or the round (*golf*): to thrust forward: to slide along: to slide the bolt of: to put forth in growth: to crystallise: to pass rapidly through, under, or over: to hit, wound, or kill with a shot: to photograph, esp. for motion pictures: to variegate: to produce play of colour in (usu. in *pa.p.*).—*v.i.* to dart forth or forward: of a cricket ball, to start forward rapidly near the ground: to send darting pains: to sprout: to elongate rapidly: to jut out far or suddenly: to begin, esp. to speak one's mind or to tell what one knows (*coll.*; usu. in *imper.*): to tower: to send forth a missile, etc.: to discharge a shot or weapon: to use a bow or gun in practice, competition, hunting, etc.: to crystallise:—*pa.t.* and *pa.p.* shot; see also shotten.—*n.* a shot (*Shak.*): a shooting: a shooting match, party, expedition: a shooting pain: a movement of the shuttle: a weft thread: the shooting of a film: new growth: a sprout: the stem and leaf parts of a plant: a dump: a chute (see chute).—*adj.* shoot'able, that may be shot, or shot over.—*ns.* shoot'er; shoot'ing, action of the verb in any sense: a twinge of quick pain: killing of game with firearms over a certain area: the right to do so: the district so limited: the planing of edges that are to be joined.—Also *adj.*—shoot'ing-board, a board for steadying a piece of wood for shooting; shoot'ing-box, -lodge, a small house in the country for use in the shooting season; shoot'ing-brake, a motor-car for the carriage both of passengers and of burden; shoot'ing-gall'ery, a long room used for practice or amusement with firearms; shoot'ing-iron (*slang*), a revolver; shoot'ing-jack'et, a short coat for shooting in; shoot'ing-range, a place for shooting at targets; shoot'ing-star, a meteor;

**shoot′ing-stick**, a printer's tool for driving quoins: a walking-stick with a head that opens out into a seat; **shooting war**, actual war as distinct from cold war.—**get shot of** (*slang*), to get rid of; **have shot one's bolt** (see **bolt**); **shoot a line** (*slang*), to brag, exaggerate (*n.* **line′-shooter**); **shoot down**, to kill, or to bring down (an aeroplane) by shooting: to rout in argument; **shoot down in flames** (*slang*), to reprimand severely; **shoot home**, to hit the target (also *fig.*); **shoot it out**, to settle by military action (also *fig.*); **shoot off**, to discharge a gun: to begin: to rush away; **shoot the sun**, to take the sun's altitude; **shoot the works** (*slang*), at games of chance, to risk (one's all) on one play: hence, to make one's maximum effort; **shoot up**, to kill or injure by shooting: to grow very quickly; **the whole shoot** (*coll.*), the whole lot. [O.E. *scēotan*; Du. *schieten*, Ger. *schiessen*; in some senses merging with Fr. *chute*, fall.]

**shoot.** Same as **shoat.**

**shop**, *shop*, *n.* a building or room in which goods are sold: a place where mechanics work, or where any kind of industry is pursued: a place of employment or activity, esp. a theatre: prison (*slang*): talk about one's own business. —*v.i.* to visit shops, esp. for the purpose of buying.—*v.t.* to imprison, or cause to be imprisoned (*slang*): to betray (someone), e.g. to inform against (him) to the police (*slang*; *n.* **shopp′er**): to give employment to:—*pr.p.* **shopp′ing**; *pa.p.* **shopped.**—*ns.* **shop′ful**; **shopp′er**; **shopp′ing**, visiting shops to buy or see goods.— *adj.* for shopping.—*adj.* **shopp′y**, commercial: abounding in shops: given to talking shop: concerning one's own pursuit.—**shop′-assist′ant**, one who sells goods in a shop; **shop′-bell**, a bell that rings at the opening of a shop-door; **shop′board**, a counter: a bench on which tailors work; **shop′-boy**, **-girl**, a boy or girl employed in a shop; **shop′breaker**, one who breaks into a shop; **shop′breaking**; **shop′-door**; **shop′-front**; **shop′keeper**, one who keeps a shop of his own; **shop′keeping**; **shop′-lift′er**; **shop′-lift′ing**, stealing from a shop; **shop′man**, one who serves in a shop: a shopkeeper (*rare*): a workshop man (*U.S.*); **shopping centre**, a place where there is a concentration of shops of different kinds; **shopping precinct** (see **precinct**); **shop′-sign**, indication of trade and occupier's name over a shop.—*adj.* **shop′-soiled**, somewhat tarnished by shop exposure.—**shop′-stew′ard**, a representative of factory or workshop hands elected from their own number; **shop′-walker**, one who walks about in a shop to see customers attended to; **shop′-window**, a window of a shop in which wares are displayed (also *fig.*); **shop′woman.**—*adj.* **shop′worn.**—**all over the shop**, dispersed all around; **on the shop floor**, among the workers in a factory or workshop (*adj.* **shop′floor**); **set up shop**, to open a trading establishment: to begin operations generally; **shop around**, to compare prices and quality of goods at various shops before making a purchase; **talk shop**, to talk about one's own work or business; **the Shop**, former Royal Military Academy at Woolwich; **the wrong shop**, the wrong place to look for, e.g. sympathy or help. [O.E. *sceoppa*, a treasury.]

**shope**, *shōp*, *obs. pa.t.* (*Spens.*) of **shape.**

**shore**, *shōr*, *shōr*, *n.* the land bordering on the sea or a great sheet of water: the foreshore.—*v.t.* to set on shore.—*adj.* **shore′less**, having no shore, unlimited.—*adj.* and *adv.* **shore′ward.**—*adv.* **shore′wards.**—**shore′-boat**, a boat plying near or to the shore; **shore′-crab**, a crab (*Carcinus maenas*) very common between tidemarks; **shore′-due** (*Scot.*), a harbour-due.—*adj.* **shore′going**, going, or for going, ashore: land-dwelling.—**shore′-leave**, leave of absence to go ashore;

**shore′line**, the line of meeting of land and water: a rope connecting a net with the land; **shore′man**, a dweller on the shore: a landsman: (*U.S.* also **shores′man**) one who has a shore-going job connected with fishery; **shore′-side**, the neighbourhood of the shore.—Also *adj.*— **shore′-weed**, a plant (*Litorella lacustris*) of lake-margins of the plantain family.—**on shore**, on the land: ashore. [M.E. *schore*; cf. Du. *schoor*, *schor.*]

**shore**, *shōr*, *shōr*, *n.* a prop.—*v.t.* to prop (often with *up*).—*ns.* **shor′er**; **shor′ing**, propping: a set of props. [Cf. Du. *schoor*, O.N. *skortha.*]

**shore**, *shōr*, *shōr*, (*Scot.*) *v.t.* to warn, threaten: to offer.—*n.* threatening. [Origin obscure.]

**shore**, *shōr*, *shōr*, (*arch.* and *coll.*) *n.* a sewer—usu. (as *Shak.*) **common-shore.** [Perh. **sewer**; perh. **shore** (1).]

**shore**, *shōr*, *shōr*, *pa.t.*, **shorn**, *shōrn*, *pa.p.* See **shear.**

**short**, *shōrt*, *adj.* of little length, tallness, extent, or duration: in the early future (as *short day, date*): concise: curt: abrupt: snappish: crisp yet readily crumbling: brittle: on the hither side: failing to go far enough or reach the standard: deficient: lacking: scanty, in inadequate supply: in want, ill supplied: in default: unable to meet engagements: pertaining to the sale of what one cannot supply: in accentual verse, loosely, unaccented (*pros.*): undiluted with water, neat (*coll.*): short-woolled. —*adv.* briefly: abruptly: without leaving a stump: on this or the near side: (see **sell short**): at a disadvantage (e.g. *taken short*).—*n.* that which is short: shortness, abbreviation, summary: a short-circuit: (in *pl.*, formerly) small-clothes (now) short trousers (as for football): (in *pl.*) the bran and coarse part of meal, in mixture: a short film subordinate to a main film in a programme: a short alcoholic drink (*coll.*).—*v.t.* to shortchange.—*v.t.* and *v.i.* to shorten (*obs.*): to short-circuit: to fall short of, or perh. make to fail (*Shak.*).—*n.* **short′age**, deficiency.—*v.t.* **short′en**, to make shorter: to make to seem short or to fall short: to draw in or back: to check: to make friable: to put in short-clothes.—*v.i.* to become shorter.—*ns.* **short′ener**; **short′ening**, making or becoming shorter: fat for making pastry short.—*adj.* **short′ish.**—*adv.* **short′ly**, soon: briefly: curtly: for a short time (*rare*): a little: with shortness in that which is indicated.—*n.* **short′ness.**— **short′bread**, a brittle crumbling cake of flour and butter; **short′cake**, shortbread or other friable cake: a light cake, prepared in layers with fruit between, served with cream (*U.S.*).— *v.t.* **short′change′**, to give less than the correct change to: to deal dishonestly with (a person).— *adj.* **short′-change**, pertaining to cheating.— **shortchanger**; **short′-cir′cuit**, a new path of comparatively low resistance between two points of a circuit (*elect.*): a deviation of current by a path of low resistance.—*v.t.* to establish a short-circuit in: to interconnect where there was obstruction between (*surg.*): to provide with a short-cut (*fig.*).—*v.i.* to cut off current by a short-circuit: to save a roundabout passage.— **short′-clothes**, **short′-coats**, the shortened skirts of a child when the first long clothes are left off.—*v.t.* **short′-coat**, to put into short-coats.— **short′coming**, act of coming or falling short: neglect of, or failure in, duty: defect; **short commons**, minimum rations.—*adj.* **short′-cut**, cut short instead of in long shreds.—*n.* tobacco so cut: a shorter way than the usual.—*adj.* **short′-dāt′ed**, having little time to run from its date, as a bill.—**short′-divi′sion**, division without writing down the working out; **short′fall**, fact or amount of falling short; **short′gown** (*Scot.*), a woman's loose jacket; **short′hand**, a method of swift writing to keep pace with speaking: writing of such a kind.—Also *adj.*—*adj.* **short'-hand'ed**, short of workers: with short hands.— **short'-horn**, one of a breed of cattle having very short horns—*Durham* or *Teeswater*; **short'-leg** (*cricket*), the fielder or the field near the batsman on the leg side behind the wicket; **short list** (see also **leet**), a selected list of candidates for an office.—*v.t.* **short'-list**, to include (someone) in a short list.—*adj.* **short'-lived** (or *-livd*), living or lasting only for a short time.—**short measure**, less than the amount promised or paid for; **short odds**, in betting, favourable odds; **short oil** (see **oil length**); **short'-rib**, a floating rib; **short sheep**, short-woolled sheep.—*adj.* **short'-sight'ed**, having clear sight only of near objects: lacking foresight. — *adv.* **short'-sight'edly.** — **short'-sight'edness**; **short'-slip** (*cricket*), the fielder, or the field, near the batsman on the off side behind the wicket.—*adjs.* **short'-sp5'ken**, curt in speech; **short'-stä'ple**, having the fibre short.—**short'-stop**, the player at baseball between the second and third base; **short'-sword**, a sword with a short blade.—*adjs.* **short'-tem'pered**, easily put into a rage; **short'-term**, extending over a short time: of a policy, concerned with the immediate present as distinct from time ahead; **short-wave**, of, or using wavelengths 50 metres or less; **short'-wind'ed**, soon becoming breathless.—**at short sight**, payable soon after being presented; **by a short head**, by a distance less than the length of a horse's head: narrowly, barely (*fig.*); **cut short** (see **cut**); **fall short** (see **fall**); **for short**, as an abbreviation; **in short**, in a few words; **in short supply**, not available in desired quantity, scarce; **make short work of**, to settle or dispose of promptly; **run short** (see **run**); **short of**, less than: without going so far as: (also **short on**; *coll.*): having insufficient supplies of; **stop short**, come to a sudden standstill; **take (up) short**, to take by surprise or at a disadvantage: to interrupt curtly; **the short and the long (of it**; *Shak.*), same as **the long and the short**. [O.E. *sc(e)ort*; cf. O.H.G. *scurz*.]

**shot**, *shot*, *pa.t.* and *pa.p.* of **shoot**.—*adj.* hit or killed by shooting: elongated by rapid growth: advanced (in years; *Spens.*): with warp and weft of different colours: showing play of colours: rid (*local*).—*n.* a rejected animal.

**shot**, *shot*, *n.* act of shooting: a blast: an explosive charge: a photographic exposure, esp. for motion pictures: a unit in film-production: a stroke or the like in a game: an attempt: a spell: a turn: a guess: the casting of a net: a set of nets or length of net cast: an aggressive remark: an injection (*coll.*): a dram (*coll.*): a marksman: a projectile, esp. one that is solid and spherical, without bursting charge: a cannon-ball: a weight for putting: a bullet: a small pellet of which several are shot together: such pellets collectively: flight of a missile, or its distance: range, reach: a plot of land: (also **scot**) a payment, esp. of a tavern reckoning: a contribution.—*v.t.* to load with shot:— *pr.p.* **shott'ing**; *pa.t.* and *pa.p.* **shott'ed**.—*adj.* **shott'ed**—**shot'-clog** (*arch.*), one who is good for nothing but paying the bill.—*adj.* **shot'-free**, scot-free: safe from shot.—**shot'gun**, a smooth-bore gun for small shot, a fowling-piece.—*adj.* pertaining to a shotgun: involving coercion (e.g. *a shotgun merger, marriage*): covering a wide field in random, haphazard fashion with a resultant hit-or-miss effect.—**shot'-hole**, a hole made by a shot, or in timber by a boring insect, or in a leaf by a fungus: a hole in a wall for shooting from: a hole bored for a blast.—*adj.* **shot'proof**, proof against shot.—**shot'-tower**, a tower where small shot is made by dropping molten lead into water; **shot'-window** (*obs.*),

app. a window with a hinged shutter or a projecting window.—**a shot in the arm**, an injection in the arm (*med.*): a revivifying injection, as of money, new effort, fresh talent (*fig.*); **a shot in the dark**, a random guess; **a shot in the locker**, something yet in reserve; **big shot** (*coll.*), person of importance; **like a shot**, instantly, quickly: eagerly, willingly; **stand shot**, to pay the bill. [O.E. *sc(e)ot*, *gesc(e)ot*; cf. **shoot**.]

**shote**, **shot(t).** Same as **shoat.**

**shotten**, *shot'n*, (*obs.*) *pa.p.* of **shoot**.—*adj.* having ejected the spawn (*Shak.*): in composition, dislocated, also shooting out.

**shough** (*Shak.* **showghe**), *shog*, *shok*, *shuf*, *n.* a shaggy kind of lapdog. [Perh. **shock** (3).]

**should**, *shōōd*, *pa.t.* of **shall**. [O.E. *sceolde*.]

**shoulder**, *shōl'dər*, *n.* the part about the junction of the body with the fore-limb: the upper joint of a foreleg cut for the table: part of a garment covering the shoulder: a coat-hanger: a bulge, protuberance, offshoot like the human shoulder: a curve like that between the shoulder and the neck or side: either edge of a road.—*v.t.* to thrust with the shoulder: to take upon the shoulder or in a position of rest against the shoulder: to undertake: to take responsibility for: to set shoulder to shoulder: to fashion with a shoulder or abutment.—*v.i.* to jostle. —*adj.* **shoul'dered**, having a shoulder or shoulders (**shouldered arch**, a lintel on corbels). —*n.* and *adj.* **shoul'dering.**—**shoul'der-belt**, a belt that passes across the shoulder; **shoul'der-blade**, the broad, flat, blade-like bone (*scapula*) of the shoulder; **shoul'der-bone**, shoulder-blade; **shoul'der-clapp'er** (*Shak.*), a bailiff; **shoul'der-gir'dle**, the pectoral girdle.—*adv.* **shoul'der-height**, as high as the shoulder.—*adj.* and *adv.* **should'er-high'**, as high as the shoulder.— **shoul'der-joint**; **shoul'der-knot**, a knot worn as an ornament on the shoulder; **shoul'der-mark** (*U.S.*), a badge of naval rank worn on the shoulder; **shoul'der-note**, a note at the upper outside corner of a page.—*adj.* **shoul'der-shott'en** (*Shak.*), with dislocated or sprained shoulder.—**shoul'der-slip**, a sprain of the shoulder.—*adj.* **shoul'der-slipped**.—**should'er-strap**, a strap worn on or over the shoulder esp. one suspending a garment, etc.: a narrow strap of cloth edged with gold lace worn on the shoulder with uniform to indicate rank (*U.S.*).—**cold shoulder** (see **cold**); **put one's shoulder to the wheel**, set to work in earnest, as if to get a coach out of the mire; **shoulder-of-mutton sail**, a triangular sail; **shoulder to shoulder**, side by side: in unity. [O.E. *sculdor*; Ger. *schulter*, Du. *schouder*.]

**shout**, *showt*, *n.* a loud cry: a call: a call for a round of drinks (*slang*).—*v.i.* to utter a shout: to stand drinks all round (*slang*).—*v.t.* to utter with a shout.—*n.* **shout'er**.—*n.* and *adj.* **shout'ing**.—*adv.* **shout'ingly**.—**shout down**, to make another's speech inaudible by shouting or talking loudly. [Ety. unknown.]

**shouther**, *shōō'dhar*, Scots form of **shoulder**.

**shove**, *shuv*, *v.t.* and *v.i.* to thrust: to push: to jostle.—*n.* a push, thrust.—*n.* **shov'er**, one who shoves: punningly, a chauffeur.—**shove'-groat**, **shovel-board** (also *adj.* as in **shove'-groat shilling**, a smooth-worn shilling suitable for playing shovel-board); **shove'-half'penny**, a similar game.—**shove off**, to push (a boat) from the shore: go away (*coll.*). [O.E. *scúfan*; Du. *schuiven*, Ger. *schieben*.]

**shovel**, *shuv'l*, *n.* a broad spade-like tool: a scoop: a shovelful: a shovel-hat.—*v.t.* to move with, or as if with, a shovel: to gather in large quantities.—*v.i.* to use a shovel:—*pr.p.* **shov'elling**; *pa.t.* and *pa.p.* **shov'elled**.—*ns.* **shov'elful**, as much as a shovel will hold:—*pl.* **shov'elfuls**; **shov'eller**, one who shovels: a duck (Spatula) with expanded bill.—shov'el-hat, a hat with a broad brim, turned up at the sides, and projecting in front—affected by Anglican clergy; shov'el-head, a Mississippi sturgeon. [O.E. *scofl*, from *scūfan*, to shove.]

shovel-board, *shuv'l-bōrd*, *-bōrd*, shuffle-board, *shuf'*, *n.* an old game in which a coin or other disk was driven along a table by the hand: a modern development played in America: a deck game played with wooden disks and cues: a table for the game: a shove-groat shilling (*Shak.*). [App. shove and board, confused with shovel and shuffle.]

show (now rarely shew), *shō*, *v.t.* to present to view: to exhibit: to display: to set forth: to cause or allow to be seen or known: to prove: to manifest: to indicate: to usher or conduct (with *in*, *out*, *over*, *round*, *up*, etc.).—*v.i.* to appear: to come into sight: to be visible:—*pa.t.* showed, rarely shewed, *shōd*; *pa.p.* shown, shewn, *shōn*, or showed, shewed.—*n.* act of showing: display: exhibition: a sight or spectacle: an entertainment: parade: a demonstration: appearance: plausibility: pretence: a sign, indication: performance.—*adj.* of the nature of, or connected with, a show: for show.—*n.* shower (*shō'ər*).——*adv.* show'ily.—*ns.* show'iness; show'ing, act of displaying, pointing out, etc.: appearance: a setting forth, representation.—*adj.* show'y, cutting a dash: making a show: ostentatious: gaudy: flashy.—show'-bill, a bill announcing a show; show'-boat, a steamer serving as a travelling theatre; show'-box, a showman's box out of which he takes his materials; show'bread (see shewbread); show business, the entertainment business, esp. the branch of the theatrical profession concerned with variety entertainments.—also (*coll.*) show'biz, show biz; show'-card, a shopkeeper's advertising card: a card of patterns; show'-case, a glass case for a museum, shop, etc.; show'-down, putting one's cards face-up on the table: a game like poker: an open disclosure of plans, means, etc.: an open clash; show'girl, a girl whose part in variety entertainments is mainly decorative; show'ground, ground where a show is held; show'jumping, competition in which riders have to jump a succession of obstacles; show'man, one who exhibits, or owns, a show: one who is skilled in publicly showing off things (e.g. his own merits); show'manship, skilful display, or a talent for it; show'-off, one who behaves in an ostentatious manner in an effort to win admiration; show'-place, a place visited or shown as a sight: a place where shows are exhibited; show'room, a room where goods or samples are displayed; show'-yard, a yard for cattle-shows.—give the show away, to let out a secret; good, bad, show, well, not well, done: fortunate, unfortunate, occurrence or circumstances; show a leg (*coll.*), to get out of bed; show fight, to show a readiness to resist; show forth, to manifest, proclaim; show off, to display or behave ostentatiously; show of hands, a vote indicated by raising hands; show up, to expose: to appear to advantage or disadvantage: to show clearly by contrast: to be present: to lodge, hand in, as a school exercise. [O.E. *scēawian*, to look; Du. *schouwen*, Ger. *schauen*, to behold.]

shower, *show'(ə)r*, *n.* a short fall, as of rain: a fall of drops of liquid: a fall, flight, or accession of many things together, as meteors, arrows, blows, volcanic dust or (esp. *U.S.*) wedding gifts: a party at which gifts are presented (*U.S.*): a shower-bath: an attack, a pang (*obs.*): fast particles in number arising from a high-energy particle.—*v.t.* and *v.i.* to drop in a shower or showers: to sprinkle: to water.—*v.i.* to take a shower-bath.—The position of the accent in the

following words depends on whether one says *show'ər* or showr.—*adj.* shower'ful.—*n.* shower'-iness.—*n.*, *adj.* shower'ing.—*adjs.* shower'less; shower'y, marked by showers: raining by fits and starts.—shower'-bath, a bath of water showered from above: the apparatus for the purpose.—*adj.* shower'proof, impervious to showers.—*v.t.* to render showerproof. [O.E. *scūr*; O.N. *skūr*, Ger. *schauer*.]

shrank, *shrangk*, *pa.t.* of shrink.

shrapnel, *shrap'nl*, *n.* a shell filled with musketballs with a bursting-charge, invented by General *Shrapnel* (1761-1842): pieces scattered by the bursting of a shrapnel or other shell: any later improved version of the orig. shell.

shred, *shred*, *n.* a scrap, fragment: a paring, esp. a curled paring: a ragged strip.—*v.t.* to prune (*obs.*): to cut, cut off: to cut, tear or scrape into shreds.—*v.i.* to be reduced to shreds:—*pr.p.* shredd'ing; *pa.t.* and *pa.p.* shredd'ed, shred.—*adj.* shredd'ed.—*ns.* shredd'er, a device or machine for shredding, e.g. vegetables, waste paper; shredd'ing.—*adjs.* shredd'y; shred'less.—shred'-pie, mince-pie. [O.E. *scrēade*; cf. screed; Ger. *schrot*.]

shrew, *shrōō*, *n.* a small mouselike animal of the Insectivora, formerly thought venomous: an evil being (*obs.*): a brawling, troublesome person, now only a woman, a scold.—*v.t.* (*Shak.*) to beshrew.—*adj.* shrewd, evil, hurtful, ill-natured, ill-conditioned, mischievous (*Shak.*, *Milt.*): severe, hard: formidable: uncomfortably near the mark: biting, keen: shrewish, vixenish (*Shak.*): (now usually) of keen practical judgment.—*adv.* (*Shak.*) keenly.—*adv.* shrewd'ly.—*n.* shrewd'ness.—*adj.* shrew'ish, of the nature of a shrew or scold: ill-natured.—*adv.* shrew'ishly.—*n.* shrew'ishness.—shrew'-mouse, a shrew (the beast):—*pl.* shrew'mice.—*adjs.* shrew'-run, -struck, blasted by a shrew.—a shrewd turn, an ill turn, disservice. [O.E. *scrēawa*, a shrewmouse.]

Shri. See Sri.

shriek, *shrēk*, *v.i.* to utter a shriek.—*v.t.* to utter shriekingly.—*n.* a shrill outcry: a wild piercing scream: an exclamation mark (*slang*).—Also shreek (*Shak.*, *Spens.*), shreik (*Milt.*), shriech (*Spens.*).—*n.* shriek'er.—*n.* and *adj.* shriek'ing.—*adv.* shriek'ingly.—shriek'-owl, also (*Spens.*) shriech-, scriche-, etc., schreech- (*Shak.*), same as screech-owl. [Cf. screak, screech.]

shrieval, *shrē'vl*, *adj.* pertaining to a sheriff.—*n.* shriev'alty, office, term of office, or area of jurisdiction, of a sheriff. [shrieve, obs. form of sheriff.]

shrieve, *shrēv*. Same as shrive.

shrift, *shrift*, *n.* orig. a prescribed penance: absolution: confession: a confessional (*Shak.*).—short shrift, short time for confession before execution: summary treatment of a person or a matter. [O.E. *scrift*—*scrīfan*, to shrive.]

shright, *shrīt*, (*Spens.*) *n.* a shriek. See also shritch. [Perh. a misreading of Chaucer, *Troilus* IV, 1147.]

shrike, *shrīk*, *n.* a butcher-bird, a passerine bird, of which some kinds impale small animals on thorns. [App. O.E. *scric*, perh. thrush.]

shrike, *shrīk*, *v.i.* to shriek (*Spens.*, *Shak.*): to pipe as a bird.—*n.* (*Spens.*, *Shak.*) a shriek. [Cf. scrike, shriek.]

shrill, *shril*, *adj.* high-pitched and piercing: keen: pungent.—*adv.* shrilly: often in compounds, as shrill-shriek'ing (*Shak.*).—*n.* a piercing sound.—*v.t.* and *v.i.* to sound or cry shrill'y.—*n.* and *adj.* shrill'ing.—*n.* shrill'ness.—*adj.* shrill'y, somewhat shrill.—*adv.* shrill'ly.—*adjs.* shrill'-gorged (*Shak.*), shrill in throat; shrill'-tongued; shrill'-voiced. [Cf. L.G. *schrell*, whence prob. Ger. *schrill*.]

shrimp, *shrimp*, *n.* a little wizened or dwarfish

person: a small edible crustacean, esp. a decapod of Crangon or kindred genus: the colour of a shrimp, a bright pink: a very small person (coll.).—v.i. to fish for shrimps.—n. shrimp'er.—n. and adj. shrimp'ing.—shrimp'-girl, a girl who sells shrimps; shrimp'-net. [Cf. scrimp, and O.E. scrimman, to shrink.]

shrine, shrīn, n. orig. a chest or cabinet: a casket for relics or an erection over it: a place hallowed by its associations: app. an image (Shak.).—v.t. to enshrine.—adj. shrin'al. [O.E. scrīn—L. scrīnium, a case for papers—scrībĕre, to write.]

shrink, shringk, v.i. to contract: to shrivel: to give way: to draw back: to withdraw: to feel repugnance: to recoil.—v.t. to cause to contract: to withdraw: to fix by allowing to contract:—pa.t. shrank, old-fashioned shrunk; pa.p. shrunk.—n. act of shrinking: contraction: withdrawal or recoil.—adj. shrink'able.—ns. shrink'-age, a contraction into a less compass: extent of such diminution; shrink'er.—adv. shrink'ingly.—adjs. shrunk, shrunk'en, contracted, reduced, shrivelled.—adjs. shrink'-proof, -resis'tant, that will not shrink on washing.—shrink'-resis'tance. [O.E. scrincan, scranc, gescruncen.]

shritch, shrich, (obs. or dial.) v.i. to shriek, screech (pa.t., Spens. shright, shrit).—n. (Spens. shriech) a shriek.—shritch'-owl, screech-owl. [Cf. scritch.]

shrive, shrīv, also (after Spenser) shrieve, shrēv, v.t. to hear a confession from and give absolution to: to confess: to disburden by confession or otherwise.—v.i. to receive or make confession:—pa.t. shrōve, shrived, shrieved (shrēvd); pa.p. shriven (shriv'ən), shrived, shrieved.—ns. shri'ver, one who shrives: a confessor; shri'ving (Spens.), shrift.—shri'ving-time (Shak.), time for confession. [O.E. scrīfan, to write, to prescribe penance—L. scrībĕre.]

shrivel, shriv'l, v.i. and v.t. to contract into wrinkles:—pr.p. shriv'elling; pa.t. and pa.p. shriv'elled. [Cf. Sw. dial. skryvla, to wrinkle.]

shroff, shrof, n. in the East, a banker, money-changer, or money-lender: an expert in detection of bad coin.—v.i. to examine with that view.—v.i. to practise money-changing.—n. shroff'age, commission for such examination. [Ar. sarrāf.]

shroud, shrowd, n. a garment, clothes (obs.): a winding-sheet: a covering, screen, shelter, or shade: (in pl.) a set of ropes from the masthead to a ship's sides to support the mast.—v.t. to enclose in a shroud: to cover: to hide: to shelter.—v.i. to take shelter.—adj. shroud'ed.—n. and adj. shroud'ing.—adjs. shroud'less, without a shroud; shroud'y, giving shelter.—shroud'-line, any one of the cords of a parachute by which the load is suspended from the canopy. [O.E. scrūd; O.N. skrúth, clothing.]

shroud, shrowd, (dial.) n. a branch: loppings.—v.t. to lop. [Prob. same as preceding, with sense from the root meaning of cut.]

Shrove, shrōv, n. (obs.) Shrovetide.—v.i. (obs.) shrove, to celebrate Shrovetide (to go a-shroving, to go round singing for money at Shrovetide).—Shrove'tide, the days preceding Ash Wednesday; Shrove Tuesday, the day before Ash Wednesday. [Related to O.E. scrīfan, to shrive.]

shrow, shrō, shrowd, shrōd, old forms (Shak.) of shrew, shrewd.

shrub, shrub, n. a low woody plant, a bush, esp. one with little or no trunk: a scrub (obs.).—v.t. to lop: to cudgel (obs.).—adj. shrubb'eried.—ns. shrubb'ery, a plantation of shrubs; shrubb'iness.—adjs. shrubb'y, of, like, having the character of, a shrub: covered with shrubs; shrub'less. [O.E. scrybb, scrub.]

shrub, shrub, n. a drink of lemon or other juice with spirits, esp. rum, or (U.S.) of fruit juice (as raspberry) and vinegar. [Ar. sharāb, for shurb, drink.]

shrug, shrug, v.i. to shudder, shiver: to hitch: to draw up the shoulders.—v.t. to shrink: to raise in a shrug:—pr.p. shrug'ging; pa.t. and pa.p. shrugged.—n. a jerk: an expressive drawing up of the shoulders.—shrug off, to shake off: to show indifference to or unwillingness to tackle (e.g. responsibility, a difficulty, fig.). [Origin obscure.]

shrunk, shrunken. See shrink.

shuck, shuk, (U.S.) n. a husk, shell, or pod.—v.t. to remove the shuck from: to strip off.—ns. shuck'er; shuck'ing.—interj. shucks (slang), expressive of contempt or disappointment. [Origin unknown.]

shudder, shud'ər, v.i. to shiver as from cold or horror.—n. a tremor as from cold or horror.—n. and adj. shudd'ering.—adv. shudd'eringly.—adjs. shudd'ersome; shudd'ery. [Cf. Ger. (orig. L.G.) schaudern.]

shuffle, shuf'l, v.t. to mix at random, as playing-cards: to jumble: to put (out, in, off, etc.) surreptitiously, evasively, scramblingly, or in confusion: to manipulate unfairly: to patch up: to shove (the feet) along without lifting clear: to perform with such motions.—v.i. to mix cards in a pack: to scramble: to behave shiftily: to shift ground: to evade fair questions: to move by shoving the feet along: to shamble: to hitch about.—n. act of shuffling: a shuffling gait or dance: an evasion or artifice.—n. shuff'ler.—n. and adj. shuff'ling.—adv. shuff'lingly.—shuff'le-cap, a game in which money is shaken in a cap.—to shuffle off, to thrust aside, put off, wriggle out of. [Early modern; cf. scuffle, shove, shovel; L.G. schüffeln.]

shuffle-board. See shovel-board.

shul, shool, shōōl, n. a synagogue. [Yiddish—M.H.G. schuol, school.]

shun, shun, v.t. to avoid:—pr.p. shunn'ing; pa.t. and pa.p. shunned.—adj. shun'less (Shak.), not to be shunned.—upon the shun, bent on evading notice. [O.E. scunian.]

shunamitism, shōō'na-mit-izm, n. rejuvenation of an old man by means of a young woman. [Abishag the Shunammite (I Kings i. 3).]

shunt, shunt, v.t. and v.i. to turn or move aside: to move to another track, esp. a side-track.—v.t. to by-pass: to side-track: to shelve: to get rid of.—v.i. (coll.) to be off.—n. an act of shunting: a conductor diverting part of an electric current: a switch: an accident, mishap (racing motorist's slang).—n. shunt'er.—n. and adj. shunt'ing. [Perh. conn. with shun.]

shush, shush, v.t., v.i., interj. hush.

shut, shut, v.t. to shoot, as a bolt (obs.): to lock: to fasten: to bar: to stop or cover the opening of: to place so as to stop an opening: to forbid entrance into: to bring together the parts or outer parts of: to confine: to catch or pinch in a fastening.—v.i. to become closed: to admit of closing: to close in:—pr.p. shutt'ing; pa.t. and pa.p. shut.—adj. made fast: closed: rid (coll.).—n. (Mill.) time of shutting.—n. shutt'er, one who, or that which, shuts: a close cover for a window: a device for regulating the opening of an aperture, as in photography, cinematography: a removable cover, gate, or piece of shuttering.—v.t. to close or fit with a shutter or shutters.—adj. shutt'ered.—n. shutt'ering, closing and fitting with a shutter: material used as shutters: temporary support for concrete work.—shut'-down, a temporary closing, as of a factory.—adj. shut-in' (or shut'), enclosed.—n. (-in'; U.S.) an invalid or cripple confined to his house.—adj. shut'-out, intended to exclude, as (bridge) a bid to deter opponents from bidding.—shut away, to keep hidden or repressed: to isolate: to confine; shut down, to close down, often temporarily; shut in, to enclose: to confine: to settle down, or fall (said, e.g., of evening); shut off, to exclude:

to switch off; **shut out**, to prevent from entering; **shut up**, to close finally or completely: to confine: to cease speaking (*coll.*): to reduce to silence. [O.E. *scyttan*, to bar; cf. *scēotan*, to shoot.]

**shuttle**, *shut'l*, *n.* an instrument used for shooting the thread of the woof between the threads of the warp in weaving or through the loop of thread in a sewing-machine: anything that makes similar movements: a shuttlecock.—*v.t.* and *v.i.* to move shuttlewise.—*adv.* **shutt'lewise**, to and fro like a shuttle.—**shutt'lecock**, a cork stuck with feathers to be driven to and fro with battledores or badminton rackets: the game played with battledores.—*v.t.* and *v.i.* to shuttle.—**shuttle service**, a train or other transport service moving constantly between two points. [O.E. *scytel*, dart; *scēotan*, to shoot; Dan. and Sw. *skyttel*.]

**shuttle**, *shut'l*, **shottle**, *shot'l*, (esp. *Scot.*) *n.* a small drawer, esp. in a cabinet or chest. [Perh. *shut*; perh. O.E. *scyttel*, bolt, bar.]

**shy**, *shī*, *adj.* shrinking from notice or approach: bashful: chary: disposed to avoidance: secluded: warily reluctant: unproductive: scanty: lacking: of doubtful repute: (esp. in poker) short in payment:—*comp.* **shy'er**, or **shi'er**; *superl.* **shy'est**, **shi'est**.—*v.i.* to recoil, to boggle: to start aside, as a horse from fear.—*v.t.* to snun:—*3rd pers. sing.* **shies**; *pr.p.* **shy'ing**; *pa.t.* and *pa.p.* **shied**, *shid*.—*n.* a sudden swerving aside:—*pl.* **shies**.—*n.* **shi'er**, **shy'er**, a shying horse.—*adj.* **shy'ish**.—*adv.* **shy'ly**, **shi'ly**.—*n.* **shy'ness** (*obs.* **shi'ness**).—**shy'-cock**, one not easily caught.—**fight shy of**, to shrink from. [O.E. *scēoh*, timid; cf. skeigh, M.H.G. *schiech*.]

**shy**, *shī*, *v.t.* and *v.i.* to fling, toss:—*3rd pers. sing.* **shies**; *pr.p.* **shy'ing**; *pa.t.* and *pa.p.* **shied**.—*n.* a throw: a fling: a gibe: an attempt, shot: a point in the wall game: a thing to shy at:—*pl.* **shies**.—*n.* **shi'er**, **shy'er**. [Origin obscure.]

**Shylock**, *shī'lok*, *n.* a ruthless creditor, or a very grasping person. [From Shylock in *The Merchant of Venice*.]

**shyster**, *shī'stər*, (*slang*) *n.* an unscrupulous or disreputable lawyer: an unscrupulous practitioner in any profession or business. [App. from **shy** (1) in sense of 'of doubtful repute'.]

**SI (units)**, the modern scientific system of units, using the fundamental units listed at absolute units (q.v.). [Système International (d'Unités).]

**si**, *sē*, *n.* the seventh note of the scale, a later addition to the six Aretinian syllables. [Perhaps from the initial letters of *Sancte Ioannes*, the last line of the hymn which gave the Aretinian (q.v.) syllables.]

**sial**, *sī'al*, *-əl*, *n.* the lighter partial outer shell of the earth, rich in *si*lica and *al*umina.—Also **sal** (*sal*). —*adj.* **sial'ic**.

**siala-**, *sī'əl-ə-*, *sī-al'ə-*, **sialo-**, *sī-al'ō-*, *-o'-*, in composition, saliva.—*adjs.* **sial'ic**, of, relating to, saliva; **si'aloid**, resembling saliva.—*n.* **sialagogue** (faultily **sialogogue**; *si-al'ə-gog*; Gr. *agōgos*, leading), anything that stimulates flow of saliva.—Also *adj.*—*adj.* **sialagog'ic**.—*ns.* **sial'-ogram**, a röntgenogram of the salivary tract; **sialog'raphy**; **sial'olith** (Gr. *lithos*, a stone), a calculus of a salivary gland; **sialorrhoe'a** (Gr. *rhoiā*, flow), excessive secretion of saliva. [Gr. *sialon*, saliva.]

**sialic**. See **sial** and **siala-**.

**siamang**, *sē'ə-mang*, *syä'mang*, *n.* the largest of the gibbons, found in Sumatra and Malacca. [Malay.]

**Siamese**, *sī-əm-ēz'*, *adj.* of Siam (Thailand).—*n.* a native, or citizen, or the language of Siam: a Siamese cat.—*v.t.* **siamese**, **-eze**, to join (e.g. pipes) in a way suggestive of the union of Siamese twins.—**Siamese cat**, a domestic fawn-coloured cat, with blue eyes and small head, prob. descended from the jungle cat of India, Africa, etc.; **Siamese twins**, Chinese twins (1811-74),

born in Siam, joined from birth by a fleshy ligature: any similar monstrosity: inseparables (*fig.*).

**sib** (*Spens.* **sybbe**, *Scott* **sibb**), *sib*, *n.* kinship (*rare*): kindred (*rare*): a kinsman or kinswoman: a blood relation: a brother or sister: a group descended from one ancestor (*gen.*).—*adj.* akin, related by common descent (*Scot.*): of canaries, inbred.—*n.* **sib'ling**, one who has a parent or an ancestor in common with another: one who has both parents in common with another but is not of the same birth. also *adj*—*n.* **sib'ship**, a group of sibs: blood-relationship: clan-relationship. [O.E. *sibb*, relationship, *gesibb*, related; Ger. *sippe*.]

**sibilate**, *sib'i-lāt*, *v.t.* and *v.i.* to hiss.—*ns.* **sib'-ilance**, **sib'ilancy**.—*adj.* **sib'ilant**, hissing.—*n.* a hissing consonant sound, as of *s* and *z*.—*n.* **sibilā'tion**.—*adjs.* **sib'ilatory** (*-ə-tər-i*), **sib'ilous**. [L. *sibilāre*, *-ātum*, to hiss.]

**Sibyl**, *sib'il*, *n.* one of several ancient prophetesses (*myth.*): (without *cap.*) a prophetess, sorceress, or witch: an old crone.—*adj.* **Sib'ylline** (*-in*).—*n.* **Sib'yllist**, a believer in the Sibylline prophecies.—**Sibylline Books**, prophetic books offered to Tarquinius Superbus by the Cumaean Sibyl, of which he ultimately bought three for the price he had refused to give for nine: a later set got together after their destruction. [Gr. *Sibylla*.]

**sic**, *sik*, *adj.* a Scots form of **such**.—*adjs.* **sicc'an** (for *sic kin*, such kind), such: in exclamation, what; **sic'like**, suchlike.—*adv.* in like manner.

**sic**, *sik*, (L.) so, thus—printed within brackets in quoted matter to show that the original is being faithfully reproduced even though incorrect or apparently so.—**sic passim** (*pas'im*), so throughout.

**sic.** Same as **sick** (2).

**Sican**, *sik'ən*, *n.* one of an aboriginal people in Sicily.—*n.* and *adj.* **Sicanian** (*-ā'ni-ən*). [L. *Sicānus*, *Sicānus*—Gr. *Sikānos*.]

**siccar.** Same as **sicker**.

**siccative**, *sik'ə-tiv*, *adj.* drying.—*n.* a drying agent. —*n.* **siccity** (*sik'si-ti*), dryness. [L. *siccus*, dry.]

**sice**, *sīs*, **size**, *sīz*, *n.* the number six at dice. [O.Fr. *sis*.]

**sice.** Same as **syce**.

**Sicel**, *sis'əl*, *sik'əl*, **Siceliot**, *si-sel'i-ot*, *-kel'.* Same as **Sikel**.

**sich**, *sich*, (*Spens.*) *adj.* a form of **such**.

**Sicilian**, *si-sil'yən*, *adj.* of Sicily: a cloth of cotton and mohair.—*ns.* **siciliana** (*sē-chēl-yä'nä*; It.), **-no** (*-nō*), a Sicilian pastoral dance, dance-tune, or movement, in 6-8 or 12-8 time; **sicilienne** (*si-si-li-en'*; Fr. *sē-sēl-yen*), a ribbed silk fabric: a siciliano.—**Sicilian Vespers**, the massacre of the French in Sicily in 1282—beginning, according to a late tradition, at the first stroke of the vesper-bell.

**sick**, *sik*, *adj.* unwell, ill: diseased: vomiting or inclined to vomit: pining: mortified: thoroughly wearied: out of condition: sickly: of or for the sick: (of humour, joke, comedy), gruesome, macabre: disappointed (*coll.*).—*v.i.* (*Shak.*) to grow sick.—*v.t.* **sick'en**, to make sick: to disgust: to make weary of anything.—*v.i.* to become sick: to be disgusted: to become disgusting or tedious: to become weakened.—*n.* **sick'ener**.—*n.* and *adj.* **sick'ening**.—*adv.* **sick'-eningly**.—*adj.* **sick'ish**.—*adv.* **sick'ishly**.—*n.* **sick'-ishness**.—*adj.* **sick'lied**.—*adv.* **sick'lily**.—*n.* **sick'-liness**.—*adj.* **sick'ly**, inclined to be ailing: feeble: languid: pallid: suggestive of sickness: slightly or insipidly sickening: mawkish: of sickness or the sick.—*adv.* in a sick manner: feebly.—*v.t.* (*obs.*) to make sickly-looking.—*n.* **sick'ness**.—**sick'-bay**, a compartment for sick and wounded on a ship (also **sick'-berth**): an infirmary at a boarding-school; **sick'-bed**, a bed on which one lies sick; **sick'-ben'efit**, a benefit paid to one who is out of work by illness.—*adjs.* **sick'-fallen**, struck with sickness; **sick'-feath'ered**, with immature feathers at moulting.—**sick'-flag**, a quarantine flag; **sick'-head'ache**, headache with nausea; **sick'-house**, a hospital; **sick'-leave**, leave of absence owing to sickness; **sick'-list**, a list of sick.—*adjs.* **sick'-list'ed**, entered on the sick-list; **sick'-mak'ing** (*coll.*), sickening.—**sick'-man** (*Shak.*), one who is ill; **sick'nurse**, a nurse who attends the sick; **sick'nurs'ing**; **sick'room** (also **sick'-cham'ber**), a room to which one is confined by sickness; **sick'-ser'vice** (*Shak.*), tending in sickness.—*adjs.* **sick'-thought'ed** (*Shak.*), lovesick; **sick'-tired'** (*coll.*), wearied to the point of disgust.—**sicken for**, show early symptoms of; **the Sick Man**, the Ottoman Empire, or Sultan; **sick of**, tired of. [O.E. *sēoc*; Ger. *siech*, Du. *ziek.*]

**sick**, *sik*, *v.t.* to set upon, chase: to incite (e.g. dog) to make an attack (on). [A variant of **seek**.]

**sicker**, *siccar*, *sik'ər*, *adj.* (*arch.* and *Scot.*) sure, certain, firm.—*adv.* (*Spens.*) surely, certainly.—*adv.* **sick'erly** (*Scot.*).—*n.* **sick'erness** (*Scot.*). [O.E. *sicor*—L. *sēcūrus*; Ger. *sicher*.]

**sickle**, *sik'l*, *n.* a reaping-hook, an implement with a curved blade and a short handle: a sicklefeather.—*adj.* **sick'led**, bearing a sickle.—**sick'lebill**, a bird of paradise, humming-bird, etc., with sickle-shaped bill; **sick'le-feath'er**, a cock's tail feather; **sick'leman**, a reaper:—*adj.* **sick'leshaped.**—**sickle-cell(ed)** anaemia, a severe anaemia in which sickle-shaped red blood-cells appear in the blood. [O.E. *sicol*, *sicel*, perh.—L. *secula*—*secāre*, to cut.]

**sickle**, *sik'l*, (*Shak.*) *n.* a shekel. [O.Fr. *sicle*—Heb. *sheqel*.]

**Siculian**, *si-kū'li-ən*, *adj.* of the *Sīcŭli* (L.), or **Sikels**, an ancient people that colonised Sicily from Italy.—Also *n.*

**Sida**, *si'də*, *n.* the Queensland hemp genus of the mallow family, tropical fibre-yielding herbs. [Gr. *sidē*, a plant name.]

**side**, *sīd*, *n.* a line or surface forming part of a boundary, esp. that which is longer: the part near such a boundary: a surface or part turned in some direction, esp. one more or less upright, or one regarded as right or left, not front or back, top or bottom: the part of the body between armpit and hip: half of a carcase divided along the medial plane: either of the extended surfaces of anything in the form of a sheet: a page: a portion of space lying in this or that direction from a boundary or a point: the father's or mother's part of a genealogy: a department or division, as of a school, a prison: an aspect: a direction: a region: a neighbouring region: a border or bank: the slope of a hill: the wall of a vessel or cavity: any party, team, interest, or opinion opp. to another: part (as on *my side*, for my part): the womb (*Milt.*): a spin given to a billiard ball causing it to swerve and regulating its angle of rebound: a pretentious air (*slang*): a speech in a play.—*adj.* at or toward the side: sidewise: subsidiary.—*v.i.* to take sides.—*v.t.* to cut into sides: thrust or set aside: adjudge or assign to one side or other (*Shak.*): assign in this way to (*Shak.*): be on the side next (*Spens.*).—*adj.* **sid'ed**, having sides: flattened on one or more sides.—*adj.* and *adv.* **side'ling**, sidewise: with a slope.—*adj.* **side'long**, oblique: sloping: tilted: sideways. —*adv.* in the direction of the side: obliquely: on the side.—*n.* **sid'er**, one who takes a side.— *adj.* and *adv.* **side'ward**.—*adv.* **side'wards**.—*adjs.*, *advs.* **side'way(s)**, **side'wise**, toward or on one side.—*n.* **sid'ing**, a short track for shunting or lying by.—*n.* and *adj.* taking sides.—*v.i.* **si'dle** (prob. back-formation from sideling), to go or edge along sideways: to move furtively or cringingly.—*v.t.* to turn sideways.—**side'arms**,

weapons worn at the side; **side'-band** (*wireless*), a band of frequencies not much above or below the carrier frequency; **side'board**, a side table (*arch.*): a piece of dining-room furniture for holding plate, etc., often with drawers and cupboards: a board at the side, as of a cart: (in *pl.*) side-whiskers.—*n.pl.* **side'-bones**, ossifications of the lateral cartilages of a horse's hoof.— **side'-box**, a box at the side of a theatre; **side'-burns**, short side-whiskers; **side'car**, a jaunting-car: small car attached to the side of a motorcycle: kind of cocktail; **side'-chain**, a chain of atoms forming a branch attached to a ring; **side'-comb**, a small comb in the hair at the side; **side'-cutt'ing**, an excavation along the side of a railway or canal to get material for an embankment; **side'-dish**, a supplementary dish; **side'-door**, a door at the side of a building or of a main door; **side'-drum**, a small double-headed drum with snares, slung from the drummer's side or from a stand; **side'-effect, side effect**, a subsidiary effect: an effect, often undesirable, additional to the effect sought; **side'-face**, profile; **side'-glance**, a side-long glance: a passing allusion; **side'-issue, side issue**, something subordinate, incidental, not important in comparison with main issue; **side'-kick** (*slang*), partner, deputy: a special friend; **side'light**, light coming from the side: any incidental illustration: a window, as opposed to a skylight: a window above or at the side of a door: a light carried on the side of a vessel or vehicle; **side'-line**, a line attached to the side of anything: a branch route or track: a subsidiary trade or activity; **side'lock**, a lock of hair at the side of the head; **side'-note**, a marginal note.—*adj.* and *adv.* **side'-on**, with side presented.—**side'-path**, a by-path: a way for foot-passengers alongside a roadway; **side'-post**, a doorpost: a post supporting a roof at the side; **side'-road**, by-road; **side'-saddle**, saddle for riding with both feet on one side (also *adv.*); **side'-saddle-flower**, Sarracenia; **side'-show**, an exhibition subordinate to a larger one: any subordinate or incidental doings; **side'-slip**, an oblique offshoot: a bastard: a skid: a lateral movement of an aircraft: a side-on downward slide (*skiing*).—*v.i.* to slip sideways.—**sides'man**, a deputy churchwarden: a partisan (*Milt.*).— *adj.* **side'-splitting**, extremely funny, making one laugh till one's sides ache.—**side'-step**, a step taken to one side: a step attached to the side. —*v.i.* to step aside.—*v.t.* to avoid, as by a step aside.—**side'-stroke**, a stroke given sideways: a stroke performed by a swimmer lying on his side; **side'-table**, a table used as a sideboard, or placed against the wall, or to the side of the main table; **side'-track**, a siding.—*v.t.* to divert or turn aside: to shelve.—**side'view**, a view on or from one side: **side'walk** (*U.S.*), pavement or foot-walk.—*adj.* **side'-wheel**, with paddle wheels. —**side'-whisker** (see **whisker**); **side-wind**, lateral wind: indirect means.—**choose sides**, to pick teams; **on the side**, in addition to ordinary occupation; **on the short, long, tight, etc., side**, rather too short, long, etc., than the contrary; **put on one side**, to shelve; **put on side**, to assume pretentious airs; **right, wrong side, the side** intended to be turned outward or inward; **side by side**, close together: abreast; **take sides**, to range oneself with one party or other; **this side (of)**, between here and ...: short of. [O.E. *sīde*; Ger. *seite*, Du. *zijde*.]

**side**, *sīd*, (now *dial.*; *Shak.*) *adj.* long.—*adj.* and *adv.* **side'long** (*Spens.*). [O.E. *sīd*, ample.]

**sidereal**, *si-dē'ri-əl*, *adj.* of, like, or relative to the stars.—*adj.* **sideral** (*sid'ər-əl*), sent from the stars.—*ns.* **siderā'tion**, a blast, blight, or stroke: paralysis: erysipelas; **sid'erostat**, a mirror, or telescope with a mirror, for reflecting the rays of a star in a constant direction, on the principle of the coelostat.—**sidereal day, time, year** (see **day, time, year**). [L. *sīdus, sideris*, a star, constellation.]

**siderite**, *sid'ər-it, n.* a meteorite mainly of iron: chalybite.—*adj.* **sideritic** (*-it'ik*).—*ns.* **sid'erolite** (Gr. *lithos*, stone), a meteorite, partly stony, partly of iron; **sideropēn'ia**, deficiency of iron; **sideros'is**, lung disease caused by breathing in iron or other metal fragments. [Gr. *sidēros*, iron.]

**sidesman, siding, sidle.** See side (1).

**siege**, *sēj, n.* a seat, esp. of dignity (*arch.*): rank or class (*obs.*): a privy (*obs.*): dung (*Shak.*): a work-bench: investment or beleaguering of a town or fortress: a company of herons (also sedge).—*v.t.* to besiege.—*n.* sieg'er, a besieger.—**siege'-artill'ery**, **siege'-gun**; **siege'-bas'ket**, a gabion; **siege'craft**, the art of the besieger; **siege'-piece**, a coin, generally of imperfect workmanship, issued in a besieged place: a siege-gun; **siege'-train**, a train of artillery for besieging a place; **siege'-works**, a besieger's engineering works.—**state of siege**, a condition of suspension of civil law or its subordination to military law. [O.Fr. *sege* (Fr. *siège*), seat—L. *sēdēs*, seat.]

**sield**, *sēld*, a Spenserian spelling of ceiled.

**siemens**, *sē'mənz, n.* unit of conductance equal to 1 mho, a supplementary SI unit.

**sien** (*Shak.*). See scion.

**Sien(n)ese**, *sē-e-nēz', adj.* of Siena or its school of painting.—*n.* a native of Siena.—*n.* **sienna** (*sē-en'ə*), a fine pigment made from ferruginous ochreous earth—browny-yellow when *raw*, warm reddish-brown when *burnt* (i.e. roasted): its colour.

**sient**, *si'ant*, (*Spens.*) *n.* Same as scion.

**sierra**, *si-er'ə, n.* a mountain range.—*adj.* sierr'an. [Sp.,—L. *serra*, saw.]

**siesta**, *si-es'tə, n.* a midday or afternoon nap. [Sp., —L. *sexta* (*hōra*), sixth (hour).]

**sieth**, a Shakespearean spelling of scythe.

**sieve**, *siv, n.* a vessel with meshed or perforated bottom for sifting—generally finer than a riddle: a refuse-basket (*Shak.*).—*v.t.* and *v.i.* to sift.—**sieve'-plate**, a perforated area by which a sieve-tube connects with another; **sieve'-tube**, a conducting element in phloem.—**sieve of Eratosthenes** (*er-ə-tos'then-ēz*), a method of finding prime numbers, namely, starting with the odd numbers in order and crossing out every third number above 3, every fifth above 5, etc; **to have a head like a sieve**, to be very forgetful. [O.E. *sife*; Ger. *sieb*.]

**siffle**, *sif'l, v.i.* to whistle, hiss. [Fr. *siffler*—L. *sibilāre*.]

**sift**, *sift, v.t.* to separate as by passing through a sieve: to sprinkle as from a sieve: to examine closely and discriminatingly.—*v.i.* to use a sieve: to find passage as through a sieve.—*ns.* sift'er; **sift'ing**, putting through a sieve: separating or sprinkling by a sieve: (in *pl.*) material separated by a sieve and rejected.—*adj.* sift'ing.—*adv.* sift'ingly. [O.E. *siftan*—*sife*, a sieve.]

**sigh**, *si, v.i.* to heave a sigh: to make a whispering sound.—*v.t.* to utter, regret, while away, bring, or render, with sighs.—*n.* a long, deep, audible respiration expressive of yearning, dejection, relief, etc.—*n.* sigh'er.—*adjs.* sigh'ful; sigh'ing.—*adv.* sigh'ingly.—**sigh for**, to yearn for. [Prob. a back-formation from the weak pa.t. of M.E. *siche*—O.E. (strong) *sican*; Sw. *sucka*.]

**sight**, *sit, n.* act, opportunity, or faculty of seeing: view: estimation: a beginning or coming to see: an instrumental observation: visual range: that which is seen: a spectacle: an object of especial interest: an unsightly, odd or ridiculous object: a visor (*Shak.*): a guide to the eye on a gun or optical or other instrument: a sight-hole: a great many or a great deal (*slang*).—*v.t.* to

catch sight of: to view: to take a sight of: to adjust the sights of.—*v.i.* to take a sight.—*adj.* **sight'ed**, having sight or a sight.—*n.* sight'er, a sighting-shot.—*adj.* sight'less, blind: invisible (*Shak.*): unsightly (*Shak.*).—*adv.* sight'lessly. —*ns.* sight'lessness; sight'liness.—*adjs.* sight'ly, pleasing to look at: comely; sight'worthy, worth looking at.—**sight'-hole**, an aperture for looking through; **sight'-player, -reader, -singer**, one who can read or perform music at first sight of the notes; **sight'-playing, -reading, -singing**; **sight'-screen**, a screen placed behind the bowler at cricket; **sight'seeing**, going around to see objects of interest; **sight'seer** (*-sē-ər*).—**at sight**, without previous view or study: as soon as seen: on presentation: payable as soon as presented; **at so many days' sight**, (of draft, etc.) payable so many days after it is presented; **catch sight of**, to get a glimpse of, begin to see; **keep sight of, keep in sight**, to keep within seeing distance of: to remain in touch with; **lose sight of**, to cease to see: to get out of touch with; **on sight**, as soon as seen, at sight; **out of sight**, not in a position to be seen or to see: out of range of vision: beyond comparison (*coll.*); **put out of sight**, to remove from view: to eat or drink up (*slang*); **sight for sore eyes**, a most welcome sight. [O.E. *sihth, gesiht*; Ger. *sicht*.]

**sight**, *sit*, an old *pa.t.* of sigh.

**sigil**, *sij'il, n.* a seal: a magical mark.—*n.* **Sigillā'ria**, a chiefly carboniferous genus of fossil lycopod trees, forming the family **Sigillāria'ceae**, with parallel rows of seal-like leaf-scars.—*n.* and *adj.* **sigillā'rian**.—*adjs.* **sig'illary** (*-ə-ri*), pertaining to a seal; **sig'illate**, sealed: with seal-like impressions.—*n.* **sigillā'tion**. [L. *sigillum*, dim. of *signum*, sign.]

**sigisbeo.** Same as cicisbeo. [It.]

**sigla**, *sig'lə, n.pl.* abbreviations and signs, as in MSS., seals, etc. [L.]

**sigma**, *sig'mə, n.* the eighteenth letter (Σ, early form C; σ, or when final ς) of the Greek alphabet, answering to S: as a numeral σ´ = 200, ͵σ = 200,000.—*adj.* **sig'mate** (*-māt*), shaped like Σ, C, or S.—*v.t.* to add σ or ς to.—*adj.* **sigmatic** (*-mat'ik*), characterised by σ.—*ns.* **sigmā'tion** (*-shən*), the adding of σ or ς at the end of a syllable; **sig'matism**, repetition of the *s*-sound; **sig'matron**, a machine consisting of two accelerators (cyclotron and betatron), for the generation of very high-energy X-rays.—*adjs.* **sig'moid, -al**, C-shaped: S-shaped.—*adv.* **sigmoid'ally**.—**sigma particles**, three hyperons of medium mass, having respectively positive, neutral and negative charge. [Gr. *sigma*.]

**sign**, *sin, n.* a gesture expressing a meaning: a signal: a mark with a meaning: a symbol: an emblem: a token: a portent: a miraculous token: an ensign, banner (in *pl.* insignia; *Spens.*): an indication of positive or negative value, or that indicated: a device marking an inn, etc., formerly also a house, instead of a street number: a board or panel giving a shopkeeper's name or trade, etc.: an effigy (*obs.*): a mere semblance (*obs.*): an indication: an outward evidence of disease: a trail or track (*U.S.*): a trace: a twelfth part (30°) of the zodiac, bearing the name of, but not now coincident with, a constellation.—*v.t.* to indicate, convey, communicate, direct, mark, by a sign or signs: to mark: to cross, make the sign of the cross over: to make the sign of: to attach a signature to: to write as a signature: to designate by signature: to engage by signature.—*v.i.* to make a sign: to bode: to sign one's name.— *ns.* **signary** (*sig'nə-ri*), a system of symbols, as an alphabet or syllabary; **sign'er; signet** (*sig'-nit*), a small seal: the impression of such a seal: a signet-ring: one of the royal seals for authenticating grants (for **Writer to the Signet** see under **write**).—*adjs.* **sig′neted**, stamped with a signet; **sign′less**.—**sign′board**, a board bearing a notice or serving as a shop or inn sign; **sig′net-ring**, a ring with a signet; **sign′-man′ual**, a signature, esp. a king's; **sign′-painter**, one who paints signs for shops, etc.; **sign′post**, a post for an inn sign: a finger-post.—*v.t.* to furnish with a signpost: point out as a signpost does.—**sign′-writer**, an expert in lettering for shop-signs, etc.; **sign′-writing**.—**sign away**, to transfer by signing; **sign off**, to record departure from work: to stop work, etc.: to discharge from employment: to leave off broadcasting: to signal that one does not intend to bid further (*bridge*); **sign of the cross**, a gesture of tracing the form of a cross; **sign in**, **out**, to sign one's name on coming in, going out; **sign on**, to engage (*v.t.* or *v.i.*) by signature: to record arrival at work. [Fr. *signe*—L. *signum*.]

**signal**, *sig′nl*, *n.* a token: an intimation, e.g. of warning, conveyed to a distance: a transmitted effect conveying a message: apparatus used for the purpose: play intended to give information to one's partner (*cards*): an intimation of, or event taken as marking, the moment for action: an initial impulse.—*v.t.* to intimate, convey, or direct by signals: to signalise.—*v.i.* to make signals:—*pr.p.* **sig′nalling**; *pa.t.* and *pa.p.* **sig′nalled**.—*adj.* remarkable: notable.—*v.t.* **sig′nalise, -ize,** to mark or distinguish signally.—*ns.* **sig′naller**; **sig′nalling**.—*adv.* **sig′nally.**—**sig′nalbox**, a railway signalman's cabin; **sig′nalman**, one who transmits signals: one who works railway signals. [Fr. *signal*—L. *signum*.]

**signature**, *sig′nə-chər*, *n.* a signing: a stamp: a signed name: an indication of key, also of time, at the beginning of a line of music, or where a change occurs: a letter or numeral at the foot of a page to indicate sequence of sheets: a sheet so marked: a symbolic indication once believed to show what a plant, etc., was good for, e.g. a kidney-shaped leaf to mark a cure for kidney diseases: a signature-tune.—*n.* **sig′natory**, one who has signed.—Also *adj.*—**sig′nature-tune′**, a tune heralding the broadcast or appearance of some particular person or group. [L.L. *signātūra* —L. *signāre, -ātum,* to sign.]

**signet.** See **sign.**

**signeur**, a Shakespearean spelling of **senior.**—*ns.* **sign′eurie** (*Shak.*), seniority; **sign′ieur** (*Shak.*), seigneur.

**signify**, *sig′ni-fī*, *v.t.* to be a sign for: to mean: to denote: to betoken: to indicate or declare.—*v.i.* to be of consequence:—*pr.p.* **sig′nifying**; *pa.t.* and *pa.p.* **sig′nified.**—*adj.* **sig′nifiable.**—*n.* **signif′icance** (-*i-kəns*), meaning: import—also **signif′icancy.**—*adj.* **signif′icant**, having a meaning: full of meaning: important, worthy of consideration: indicative.—*n.* that which carries a meaning: a sign.—*adv.* **signif′icantly.**—*ns.* **signif′icate**, a thing signified; **significā′tion**, meaning: that which is signified: importance.—*adj.* **signif′icative** (-*kə-tiv*), indicative: significant.—*adv.* **signif′icatively.**—*n.* **signif′icātor** (*astrol.*), a planet ruling a house.—*adj.* **signif′icatory** (-*kə-tər-i*).—*n.pl.* (treated as *sing.*) **signif′ics**, the science of meaning.—**significant figures** (*arith.*), the figures 1 to 9, or ciphers occurring medially (the following numbers are expressed to three significant figures—3·15, 0·0127, 1·01). [L. *significāre, -ātum—signum,* a sign, *facĕre,* to make.]

**Signor**, anglicised as **Signior**, *sē′nyör*, **Signore**, *-nyō′rā*, *-nyō′*, *n.* an Italian word of address equivalent to Mr or sir: (without *cap.*) a gentleman.—*ns.* **Signora** (*sē-nyō′rā*, *-nyō′*), feminine of *Signor*, Mrs, madam: (without *cap.*) a lady; **Signorina** (*sē-nyō-rē′nä*), Miss: (without *cap.*) an unmarried lady; **signoria** (*-rē′ä*; *hist.*), the governing body of an Italian city-state; **si′gnory**, seignory: **signoria.**—

**Grand Signior** (*hist.*), the Sultan of Turkey. [It. *signor, signore.*]

**sika**, *sē′kə*, *n.* a Japanese deer, small, spotted white in summer. [Jap. *shika.*]

**sike, syke**, *sīk*, (*Scot.*) *n.* a rill or small ditch. [Northern,—O.E. *sīc.*]

**sike**, Spenserian spelling of **sic** (such).

**Sikel**, *sik′əl*, *n.* and *adj.* Siculian.—*adj.* **Sikelian** (*-el′*).—*n.* **Sikel′iot**, an ancient Greek colonist in Sicily.—Also **Sicel, Sicelian,** etc. [Gr. *Sikelos, Sikeliōtēs.*]

**Sikh**, *sēk, sik, n.* one of a North Indian monotheistic sect, founded by Nának (1469-1538), later a military confederacy: a Sikh soldier in the Indian army.—Also *adj.*—*n.* **Sikh′ism.** [Hind., disciple.]

**silage**, *sī′lij, n.* fodder preserved by ensilage in a silo.—*v.t.* to put in silo. [ensilage, after **silo.**]

**sild**, *sild, n.* a young herring. [Norw.]

**sile, seil**, *sīl*, (*Scot.*) *v.t.* to strain.—*n.* a strainer (also **sil′er**). [Scand.; cf. Sw. and Norw. *sila*, to strain.]

**silence**, *sī′ləns, n.* absence of sound: abstention from sounding, speech, mention, or communication: a time of such absence or abstention: taciturnity: of spirits, flavourlessness.—*v.t.* to cause to be silent.—*interj.* be silent.—*adj.* **si′lenced**, put to silence: forbidden to preach.—*n.* **si′lencer**, one who or that which puts to silence: a device for reducing the sound of escaping gases by gradual expansion, used, e.g. for small-arms and internal combustion engines.—*adj.* **si′lent**, noiseless: without sound: unaccompanied by sound: refraining from speech, mention, or divulging: taciturn: not pronounced: of distilled spirit, without flavour or odour: inoperative: of the new moon, not yet visible (*Milt.*).—*n.* (*Shak.*) a time of silence.—*n.* **silentiary** (-*len′shi-ər-i*), one who observes or calls for silence.—*adv.* **si′lently.**—*n.* **si′lentness.** [L. *sīlēre,* to be silent.]

**Silene**, *sī-lē′ni, n.* a large genus (fam. Caryophyllaceae) with variously coloured showy flowers. [Prob. L. *Silēnus*; see **silenus.**]

**silentium altum.** See **altum.**

**silenus**, *sī-lē′nəs, n.* a wood-god or old satyr: **Silenus**, their chief, foster-father of Bacchus, pot-bellied, bald, snub-nosed: the lion-tailed macaque.—Also **si′len** (*-lin*). [L. *Silēnus*—Gr. *Seilēnos.*]

**silex**, *sī′leks, n.* silica. [L. *sīlex, silicis,* flint.]

**silhouette**, *sil-ōō-et′, n.* a shadow-outline filled in with black.—*v.t.* to represent or show in silhouette. [Étienne de *Silhouette* (1709-67), French minister of finance in 1759—reason disputed.]

**silica**, *sil′i-kə, n.* silicon dioxide or silicic anhydride, occurring in nature as quartz, chalcedony, etc., and (amorphous and hydrated) as opal.—*adj.* composed of silica.—*ns.* **sil′icane**, a gas, silicon hydride, SiH$_4$; **sil′icate**, a salt of silicic acid.—*v.t.* to combine, coat, or impregnate with silica or silicates.—*adjs.* **siliceous, -ious** (-*ish′əs*), of, containing, silica; **silicic** (-*is′ik*), pertaining to, or obtained from, silica (**silicic acid**, a general name for a group of acids, as **orthosilicic**, H$_4$SiO$_4$; **metasilicic**, H$_2$SiO$_3$).—*n.* **sil′icide** (-*sīd*), a compound of silicon and another element.—*adjs.* **silicicolous** (-*sik′*; L. *colĕre,* to cultivate, inhabit), growing on siliceous soil; **silicif′erous**, containing silica.—*n.* **silicification** (*si-lis-i-fi-kā′shən*).—*adj.* **silicified** (-*lis′*).—*v.t.* **silic′ify**, to render siliceous: to impregnate or cement with or replace by silica.—*v.i.* to become siliceous.—*ns.* **sil′icon** (-*kon, -kən*), a non-metallic element (Si; at. numb. 14), most abundant of all except oxygen, forming grey crystals or brown amorphous powder—originally called **silicium** (-*lis′*, -*lish′*); **sil′icone**, any of a number of extremely stable organic derivatives of silicon, used in rubbers, lubricants, polishes, etc.; **silicosis**

(-kō'sis), disease caused by inhaling silica dust.— *n.* and *adj.* silicot'ic. [L. *silex, silicis,* flint.]

siliqua, *sil'i-kwə, n.* a long pod of two carpels with a replum, characteristic of the Cruciferae.—Also silique (-ēk').—*n.* silicula (-*ik'ū-la*), a short pod of the same kind.—Also sil'icle, sil'icule.—*adjs.* silic'ulose; sil'iquose. [L. *siliqua,* pod, dim. *silicula.*]

silk, *silk, n.* a fibre produced by the larva of a silk-worm moth, mainly of fibroin coated with sericin, formed by the hardening of a liquid emitted from spinning-glands: a similar fibre from another insect or a spider: an imitation (**artificial silk**) made by forcing a viscous solution of modified cellulose through small holes: a thread, cloth, garment, or attire made from such fibres: the silk gown, or the rank, of a king's or queen's counsel: the styles of maize: silky lustre in the ruby, etc.—*adj.* of or pertaining to silk: silky (*Shak.*).—*v.t.* to cover or clothe with silk.—*adj.* silk'en, of, like, clad in, silk: glossy: soft and smooth: ingratiating: luxurious.—*v.t.* to make silken.—*adv.* silk'ily.—*n.* silk'iness.—*adj.* silk'y. —silk'-cott'on, the silky seed-covering of *Eriodendron anfractuosum* and other trees of the family Bombacaceae; silk'-gland, a gland (at a silkworm's mouth, on a spider's abdomen) from which silk is spun; silk'-grass, a name for various plants with fibrous leaves—Karatus (Bromeliaceae), Yucca, Agave: silk'grower, a breeder of silkworms for silk; silk'-hat', a top-hat; silk'-man (*Shak.*), a dealer in silks; silk'-screen, a stencil process in which the colour applied is forced through silk or other fine-mesh cloth; silk'tail, the waxwing; silk'-thrower, -throwster, one who makes raw silk into thread; silk'worm, the moth (*Bombyx mori* or other) whose larva produces silk: opprobriously, a wearer of silk (*obs.*): one who haunts draper's shops without buying (*obs.*); silk'worm-gut, the drawn-out glands of the silkworm.—take silk, to become a K.C. or Q.C. [O.E. *seolc*—L. *sēricum;* see Seric.]

sill, *sil, n.* the timber, stone, etc., at the foot of an opening, as for a door, window, embrasure, port, dock-entrance, or the like: the bottom (of a title-page, a plough, a ledge): a bed of rock (*mining*): a sheet of intrusive rock more or less parallel to the bedding (*geol.*). [O.E. *syll;* O.N. *syll;* Ger. *schwelle.*]

sillabub, syllabub, *sil'ə-bub, n.* a dish of cream curdled (as with wine), flavoured, and frothed up: anything frothy or unsubstantial. [Origin obscure.]

silladar, *sil'ə-där, n.* an irregular cavalryman. [Urdu and Pers. *silāhdār.*]

siller, *sil'ər, n.* a Scots form of silver: money.— Also *adj.*

Sillery, *sil'ə-ri, n.* champagne from *Sillery,* near Rheims.

sillimanite, *sil'i-mən-it, n.* fibrolite. [After Benjamin Silliman (1779-1864), American man of science.]

sillock, *sil'ək,* (*N.Scot.*) *n.* a young coalfish. [Cf. O.N. *silungr,* a small salmon.]

silly, *sil'i, adj.* (of e.g. sheep) harmless: simple, humble (*arch.*): witless: foolish: to be pitied (*arch.*): defenceless (*arch.*): feeble: feeble-minded: senseless: close-in (*cricket;* e.g. *silly mid-off*).—*n.* a silly person.—*adv.* sill'ily.—*n.* sill'iness.—sill'y-how (O.E. *hūfe,* head-dress), a caul; silly season, (esp. formerly) a season, usu. late summer, when newspapers fill up with trivial matter for want of more newsworthy material. [O.E. *sælig;* see seely.]

silo, *si'lō, n.* a pit or airtight chamber for storing grain, or for ensilage, or for storing other loose materials: a storage tower above ground, typically tall and cylindrical: an underground chamber housing a guided missile ready to be fired:—*pl.* si'los.—*v.t.* to put, keep, in a silo:— *pa.p.* si'lo'd, si'loed. [Sp.,—L. *sīrus*—Gr. *siros, siros, seiros,* a pit.]

silphium, *sil'fi-əm, n.* a plant (perh. the umbelliferous *Ferula tingitana*) imported from Cyrenaica by the Greeks for food and medicine (*hist.*): (*cap.*) a genus of American composites, compass-plants. [L.,—Gr. *silphion.*]

silt, *silt, n.* fine sediment.—*v.t.* to choke, block, cover, with silt.—*v.i.* to become silted up.—*adj.* silt'y. [M.E. *sylt;* cf. Dan. and Norw. *sylt,* salt-marsh.]

Silurian, *sil-ōō'ri-ən, -ū', adj.* of the *Sil'ūrēs,* a British tribe of S. Wales, etc.: applied by Murchison in 1835 to the geological system preceding the Devonian.—Also *n.*—*n.* sil'urist, a Silurian, applied to the poet Henry Vaughan (1621 or 22-95).

Silurus, *sil-ōō'rəs, -ū', n.* the sheat-fish genus, giving name to the family Silu'ridae.—*n.* and *adj.* silu'roid. [Gr. *silouros.*]

silva, *sil'və, n.* the assemblage of trees in a region —*adj.* sil'van, of woods: woodland: wooded.— *n.* a wood-god: a forest-dweller.—*adjs.* silvat'ic, silves'trian, of the woods: woodland: rustic.— *n.* silvicul'ture, forestry.—All these words are often found spelt with *y.* [L. *silva* (sometimes *sylva*), a wood.]

silver, *sil'vər, n.* a white precious metal (Ag, for L. *argentum;* at. numb. 47): silver money: silver ware.—*adj.* of or like silver: silver-coloured: clear and ringing in tone.—*v.t.* to cover with silver: to make silvery.—*v.i.* to become silvery.—*ns.* sil'veriness; sil'vering, coating with, or of, silver or quicksilver.—*v.t.* silverise, -ize, to coat or treat with silver.—*n.* sil'verling (*B.*), a small silver coin.—*adv.* sil'verly, with the appearance or sound of silver.—*adjs.* sil'vern, made of silver: silvery; sil'very, like silver: silver-coloured: light in tone.—Silver Age, the reign of Zeus, less innocent than the Golden Age of Kronos: in Latin literature the time of Martial, Tacitus and Juvenal; sil'ver-bath (*phot.*), a solution of a silver salt, or a vessel for it, for sensitising plates; sil'ver-beater, one who beats silver into foil; sil'ver-bell', snowdrop-tree (Halesia); sil'ver-fir', a fir with two white lines on the under-side of the needle; sil'ver-fish, Lepisma, a springtail: a whitish goldfish, or other white fish; sil'ver-foil', silver-leaf.— *adj.* sil'ver-foot'ed.—sil'ver-fox', an American fox with white-tipped black fur; silver gate (see gate); sil'ver-gilt', gilded silver. —Also *adj.*—sil'ver-glance', argentite; sil'ver-grain', medullary rays in longitudinal section; sil'ver-leaf, silver beaten into thin leaves: a disease of plum-trees.—*adj.* sil'ver-mount'ed.— sil'ver-pap'er, fine white tissue-paper: silver-foil: (usu.) tinfoil; silver pheasant, a white-tailed Chinese pheasant, reared in Europe, etc.; sil'ver-plate', utensils of silver: electroplate.— *adj.* sil'ver-plā'ted.—sil'ver-point, the process or product of drawing with a silver-tipped pencil; silver salmon, the cohoe; silver screen, the cinema screen.—*adjs.* sil'ver-shaft'ed, carrying silver arrows, as Diana; sil'ver-shedding (*Shak.*), scattering silver.—sil'verside, the top of a round of beef; sil'verskin, the fine skin of a coffee bean; sil'versmith, a worker in silver; sil'ver-stick, a palace officer—from his silvered wand.—*adj.* sil'ver-tongued, plausible, eloquent. —sil'ver-tree, a silvery-leaved S. African proteaceous tree (*Leucadendron argenteum*).—*adj.* sil'ver-voiced.—silver wedding, the twenty-fifth anniversary; sil'verweed, a roadside plant (*Potentilla anserina*) with leaves silky underneath.—*adj.* sil'ver-white.—born with a silver spoon in one's mouth, born to affluence; tree of silver (see tree). [O.E. *silfer, seolfor;* O.N. *silfr,* Ger. *silber.*]

**sima**, *sī'mə, n.* the part of the earth's crust underlying the sial. [From *si*licon and *ma*gnesium.]

**simar, simarre**, *si-mär'.* Same as **cymar, chimer.**

**Simaruba**, *sim-ə-roo'bə, n.* a genus of tropical American trees, giving name to the family **Simarubā'ceae**, akin to the Rutaceae. [Carib name.]

**Simeonite**, *sim'i-ən-it, n.* a low-churchman—often **sim.** [Charles *Simeon* (1759-1836).]

**simian**, *sim'i-ən, adj.* of the apes: apelike.—Also (*rare*) **sim'ial, sim'ious.** [L. *sīmia*, ape.]

**similar**, *sim'i-lər, adj.* like: resembling: exactly corresponding in shape, without regard to size (*geom.*).—*n.* **similarity** (*-lar'i-ti*).—*adv.* **sim'ilarly.** [Fr. *similaire*—L. *similis*, like.]

**simile**, *sim'i-li,* (*rhet.*) *n.* an explicit likening of one thing to another:—*pl.* **sim'iles.**—*adj.* **sim'ilātive**, expressing similarity.—*v.t.* **sim'ilise, -ize**, to liken.—*v.i.* to use simile.—*n.* **simil'itude**, likeness: semblance: comparison: parable. [L. neut. of *similis*, like.]

**similor**, *sim'i-lör, n.* a yellow alloy used for cheap jewellery. [Fr.,—L. *similis*, like, *aurum*, gold.]

**simitar.** Same as **scimitar.**

**sim(p)kin**, *sim'kin, n.* an Urdu corruption of **champagne.**

**Simmental**, *zim'ən-täl, n.* a breed of cattle, orig. native to Switzerland, used in many parts of Europe for meat and milk.—Also **Simmenthal, -thaler** (*-täl-ər*). [From the *Simmental* or Simme valley.]

**simmer**, *sim'ər, v.i.* to boil gently: to be near boiling or breaking out.—*n.* a simmering state.— **simmer down**, to calm down. [Earlier *simper*; origin unknown.]

**'simmon**, *sim'ən, n.* short for **persimmon.**

**simnel**, *sim'nl, n.* a sweet cake for Christmas, Easter, or Mothering Sunday.—Also **sim'nel-bread', -cake'.** [O.Fr. *simenel*—L. *simila*, fine flour.]

**Simon Pure**, *sī'mən-pūr', n.* the real person (or thing). [From a character in Mrs Centlivre's comedy, *A Bold Stroke for a Wife*.]

**simony**, *sī'mən-i, sim'ən-i, n.* the buying or selling of a benefice.—*n.* **simō'niac**, one guilty of simony.—*adjs.* **simoni'acal, simō'nious** (*obs.*).—*adv.* **simoni'acally.**—*n.* **si'monist**, one who practises or defends simony. [*Simon* Magus (Acts viii).]

**simoom**, *si-mōōm', n.* a hot suffocating desert wind.—Also **simoon'.** [Ar. *samûm*—*samm*, to poison.]

**simpai**, *sim'pī, n.* the black-crested langur of Sumatra. [Malay.]

**simpatico**, *sim-pat'i-kō, adj.* sympathetic in the sense of congenial. [It.]

**simper**, *sim'pər, v.i.* to smile in a silly, affected manner.—*n.* a silly or affected smile.—*n.* **sim'-perer.**—*adj.* **simp'ering.**—*adv.* **simp'eringly.** [Cf. Norw. *semper*, smart.]

**simple**, *sim'pl, adj.* consisting of one thing or element: not complex or compound: not divided into leaflets (*bot.*): easy: plain: unornate: unpretentious: mean, sorry: mere, sheer: ordinary: unlearned, or unskilled: of humble rank or origin: unaffected: artless: guileless: unsuspecting: credulous: weak in intellect: silly.—*n.* a simple person (also collectively) or thing: a medicine of one constituent: hence a medicinal herb.—*v.i.* to gather medicinal plants.—*ns.* **sim'pleness; sim'-pler**, a gatherer of simples: **sim'plesse** (*Spens.*), simplicity; **sim'pleton**, a weak or foolish person: one easily imposed on (*abbrev.* **simp**).—*adv.* **simpliciter** (*-plis', -plik'*), simply, not relatively: naturally: unconditionally. — *ns.* **simplicity** (*-plis'*); **simplificā'tion**, making simple.—*adj.* **sim'plificātive.**—*ns.* **sim'plificātor, simplifi'er**, one who simplifies.—*v.t.* **sim'plify**, to make simple, simpler, or less difficult:—*pr.p.* **sim'plifying;**

*pa.t.* and *pa.p.* **sim'plified.**—*ns.* **sim'pling**, simple-gathering; **sim'plism**, affected simplicity: oversimplification of a problem or situation; **sim'-plist**, one skilled in simples.—*adj.* **simplis'tic.**—*adv.* **sim'ply**, in a simple manner: considered by itself: alone: merely: without qualification: veritably: absolutely: really (*coll.*).—*adjs.* **sim'ple-heart'ed, sim'ple-mind'ed.**—**sim'ple-mind'edness; simple sentence**, a sentence with one predicate. [Fr. *simple*, and L. *simplus, simplex*.]

**simplex**, *sim'pleks, n.* a figure with the minimum number of vertices for space of a particular number of dimensions (e.g. a triangle in 2-dimensional space):—*pl.* **simplices** (*-pli-sēz*) one-way transmission and reception over a channel (*teleg.*). [L.]

**simplicity, etc.** See **simple.**

**simulacrum**, *sim-ū-lā'krəm, n.* an image: a semblance (*pl.* **simula'cra**).—Also **sim'ulācre.** [L. *simulācrum*.]

**simulate**, *sim'ū-lāt, v.t.* to feign: to have or assume a false appearance of: to mimic.—*adj.* **feigned.** —*adj.* **sim'ulant**, simulating: mimicking (*biol.*). —*n.* a simulator.—*adj.* **sim'ular**, counterfeit: feigned.—*n.* a simulator.—*n.* **simulā'tion**, feigning: mimicry: making working replicas or representations of machines for demonstration or for analysis of problems.—*adj.* **sim'ulātive.**—*n.* **sim'ulātor**, one who or that which simulates: a device used in simulation.—*adj.* **sim'ulatory.**— **simulated pearl**, a bead resembling a pearl. [L. *simulāre, -ātum*; cf. **similar, simultaneous**.]

**simultaneous**, *sim-əl-tā'nyəs,* (*U.S.*) *sīm'ul-, adj.* being or happening at the same time: satisfied by the same roots (of equations) (*math.*).—*ns.* **simultaneity** (*-tə-nē'i-ti*), **simultā'neousness.**—*adv.* **simultā'neously.**—**simultaneous translation,** at a meeting of people of different nationality, translation of a speaker's words into other languages at the same time as he is speaking. [L. *simul*, at the same time.]

**simurg(h)**, *si-moorg', -mûrg', simorg, -mörg', n.* a monstrous bird of Persian fable. [Pers. *simurgh*.]

**sin, sin'**, *sin, prep., conj.,* and *adv.* (*arch.* or *Scot.*) **since—long sin,** (*Spens.*) for a long time in the past. [Shortened from **sithen**.]

**sin**, *sin, n.* moral offence or shortcoming, esp. from the point of view of religion: condition of so offending: an offence generally: a shame, pity. —*v.i.* to commit sin.—*v.t.* to commit: to burden with sin (as *sin one's soul*): to bring, drive, or render by sin (hence *sin one's mercies*, to be ungrateful):—*pr.p.* **sinn'ing;** *pa.t.* and *pa.p.* **sinned.**—*adj.* **sin'ful**, tainted with sin: wicked: involving sin: morally wrong.—*n.* **sin'fulness.**— *adj.* **sin'less.**—*adv.* **sin'lessly.**—*ns.* **sin'lessness; sinn'er.**—*v.t.* (with *it*; *Pope*) to act as a sinner.— **sin'-eat'er**, one who by eating bread and salt at a funeral takes upon himself the dead man's sins. —*adj.* **sin'-eat'ing.**—**sin'-off'ering**, a sacrifice in expiation of sin.—**live in sin**, to cohabit in an unmarried state; **original sin** (see **origin**). [O.E. *synn*; O.N. *synth*; Ger. *sünde*; perh. L. *sōns, sontis*, guilty.]

**Sinaean**, *sin-ē'ən* (*Milt.*), **Sinic**, *sin'ik, adjs.* Chinese.—*v.t.* and *v.i.* **sin'icise, -ize** (*-siz*), to make or become Chinese or of Chinese character. —*n.* **Sin'icism** (*-sizm*), a Chinese custom, idiom, etc. [L.L. *Sinae*, Gr. *Sinai*, Chinese (pl.).]

**Sinaitic**, *sī-nā-it'ik, adj.* of Mount Sinai.

**Sinanthropus**, *sin-* or *sin-an'thrō-pəs* or *-thrō', n.* Peking (fossil) man. [Gr. *Sinai*, (the) Chinese, *anthrōpos*, man.]

**sinapism**, *sin'ə-pizm, n.* a mustard plaster. [Gr. *sināpi*.]

**since**, *sins, adv.* from that time on: after that time: past: ago.—*prep.* after: from the time of.—*conj.* from the time that: seeing that: because. [M.E. *sins, sithens*; see under **sith**.]

**sincere**, *sin-sēr'*, *adj.* pure, unmixed: unadulterated: unfeigned: 'genuine: free from pretence: the same in reality as in appearance.—*adv.* sincēre'ly.—*ns.* sincēre'ness, sincerity (-ser').  [Fr. *sincère*—L. *sincērus*, clean.]

**sinciput**, *sin'si-put*, *n.* the forepart of the head or skull.—*adj.* sincip'ital.  [L.,—*sēmi-*, half, *caput*, head.]

**sind.** See synd.

**sindon**, *sin'dən*, (*arch.*) *n.* a fine cloth or anything made of it.  [Gr. *sindōn*.]

**sine**, *sīn*, (*math.*) *n.* orig. the perpendicular from one end of an arc to the diameter through the other: now (as a function of an angle) the ratio of the side opposite it (or its supplement) in a right-angled triangle to the hypotenuse.—*abbrev.* sin.—*adj.* sinical (*sin'i-kl*).  [L. *sinus*, a bay.]

**sine.** See syne.

**sine**, *sī'nē*, *sī'ne*, (L.) without.—**sine die** (*dī'ē*, *di'ā*), without a day (appointed)—of a meeting or a matter indefinitely adjourned; **sine dubio** (*dū'bi-ō*, *dōōb'i-ō*), without doubt; **sine prole** (*prō'lē*, *prō'le*), without issue; **sine qua non** (*kwā non*, *kwä nōn*), an indispensable condition.

**sinecure**, *sī'ni-kūr*, or *sin'*, *n.* a benefice without cure of souls: an office without work.—Also *adj.*—*ns.* sin'ecurism; sin'ecurist.  [L. *sine*, without, *cūra*, care.]

**sinew**, *sin'ū*, *n.* that which joins a muscle to a bone, a tendon: strength or that which it depends on (*fig.*).—*v.t.* to bind as by sinews: to strengthen.—*adjs.* sin'ewed; sin'ewless; sin'ewy.—**sinews of war**, money.  [O.E. *sinu*, gen. *sinwe*.]

**sinfonia**, *sin-fō-nē'ə*, *n.* symphony.—**sinfonia concertante** (*kon-chər-tan'ti*), an orchestral work with parts for more than one solo instrument.  [It.]

**sing**, *sing*, *v.i.* to utter melodious sounds in musical succession in articulating words: to emit more or less songlike sounds: to compose poetry: to give a cantabile or lyrical effect: to ring (as the ears): to be capable of being sung.—*v.t.* to utter, perform by voice, musically: to chant: to celebrate: to proclaim, relate, in song or verse or in comparable manner: to bring, drive, render, pass, etc., by singing:—*pa.t.* sang; or (now rarely) sung; *pa.p.* sung.—*adj.* sing'able.—*ns.* sing'ableness; sing'er; sing'ing.—*adv.* sing'ingly.—sing'ing-bird, a songbird; singing flame, a flame that gives a musical note in a tube; sing'-ing-gall'ery, a gallery occupied by singers; sing'ing-hinn'y (*Northern*), a currant cake that hisses on the girdle; sing'ing-man (*Shak.*), one employed to sing, as in a church choir; sing'ing-master, a teacher of singing; singing sand, musical sand; sing'song, a ballad: jingly verse: monotonous up-and-down intonation: an informal concert where the company sing: a meeting for community singing.—*adj.* of the nature of singsong.—*v.t.* and *v.i.* to sing, speak, utter, in a singsong way.—sing another song or tune, to change to a humbler tone; sing out, to call out distinctly, to shout: to inform, peach; sing small, to assume a humble tone.  [O.E. *singan*; Ger. *singen*, Goth. *siggwan*.]

**singe**, *sinj*, *v.t.* to burn on the surface: to scorch: to remove by scorching—*v.i.* to become scorched:—*pr.p.* singe'ing; *pa.t.* and *pa.p.* singed.—*n.* a burning on the surface: a slight burn.—singed cat, a person who is better than he looks.  [O.E. *sen(c)gan*.]

**Singhalese.** Same as Sinhalese.

**single**, *sing'gl*, *adj.* consisting of one only or one part: unique: one-fold: uncombined: unmarried: for one: man to man: slight, poor (*Shak*): of ale, weak, small: undivided: unbroken: of a flower, without development of stamens into petals or of ligulate instead of tubular florets: sincere.—*adv.* singly.—*n.* any-

thing single: a game played by one against one: a hit for one run: a talon of a hawk: a gramophone record with one tune, or other short recording on each side.—*v.t.* to separate: to pick (out): to pick out challengingly (*Milt.*): to take aside: to thin.—*v.i.* (*Spens.*) to come forth alone.—*ns.* sing'leness (*-gl-nis*); sing'let (*-glit*), a thing that is single: an undershirt; sing'leton (*-gl-tən*), a single card of its suit in a hand: anything single: sing'ling (*-gling*).—*adv.* sing'ly (*-gli*), one by one: alone: by oneself.—*adjs.* sing'le-act'ing, acting effectively in one direction only; sing'le-breast'ed, with one thickness over the breast and one row of buttons; sing'le-chamb'er, having one legislative house.—sing'le-deck'er, a vessel or vehicle with one deck; single'-en(d) (*Scot.*), a one-roomed dwelling; sing'le-en'try, a system of bookkeeping in which each entry appears only once on one side or other of an account.—*adj.* sing'le-eyed, one-eyed: devoted, unselfish.—sing'le-foot, a rack or amble.—*adjs.* sing'le-hand'ed, by oneself: unassisted: with or for one hand; sing'le-heart'ed, sincere: without duplicity.—*adv.* sing'le-heart'-edly.—single house (*Scot.*), a house one room deep.—*adj.* sing'le-mind'ed, ingenuous: bent upon one sole purpose.—sing'le-mind'edness.—*adj.* sing'le-phase, of an alternating electric current, requiring one outward and one return conductor for transmission.—sing'le-seat'er, a car, aeroplane, etc., seated for one; single soldier (*Scott*), a private.—*adj.* sing'le-soled, having one thickness of sole.—sing'lestick (*-gl-stik*), a fighting stick for one hand: a fight or game with singlesticks; single tax, a tax on ground-rent or land-values to supersede all other taxes; single ten (*Shak.*), the ten of a card suit; sing'le-wicket, cricket with one wicket, and with one batsman at a time.  [O.Fr.,—L. *singulī*, one by one.]

**singletree**, *sing'gl-trē*, *n.* Same as swingletree.

**singsong.** See sing.

**singspiel**, *sing'spēl*, Ger. *zing'shpēl*, *n.* a semi-dramatic representation in dialogue and song.  [Ger.,—*singen*, to sing, *spiel*, play.]

**singular**, *sing'gū-lar*, *adj.* single: unique: proper: private: denoting or referring to one: pre-eminent: pre-eminently good or efficacious: extraordinary: peculiar: strange: odd.—*adv.* singularly.—*n.* an individual person or thing: the singular number or a word in the singular number.—*n.* singularisā'tion, -z-.—*v.t.* sing'-ularise, -ize, to make singular: to signalise.—*ns.* sing'ularism, a philosophy that recognises but one principle, opp. to *pluralism*; sing'ularist, one who affects singularity: an upholder of singularism; singularity (*-lar'i-ti*), fact or state of being singular: peculiarity: individuality: oddity: oneness: anything curious or remarkable.—*adv.* sing'ularly, in a singular manner: peculiarly: strangely: singly: pre-eminently (*arch.*).  [L. *singulāris*.]

**singult**, *sing'gult*, (*arch.*) *n.* a sob.—*n.* singult'us (*med.*), hiccuping.  [L. *singultus*, a sob.]

**sinh**, *shin*, *n.* a conventional abbreviation of hyperbolic *sine*.

**Sinhalese**, *sin'hə-lēz*, *-lēz'*, **Singhalese**, **Cingalese**, *sing'gə-lēz*, *-lēz'*, also **Sinhala**, *adj.* of Ceylon: of the most numerous of its peoples: of or in their language, akin to Pali.—*n.* a native or citizen of Ceylon: a member of the Sinhalese people: their language.  [Sans. *Siṁhala*, Ceylon.]

**Sinic**, etc. See Sinaean.

**sinical**, *sin'i-kl*. See sine.

**sinister**, *sin'is-tər*, formerly also *-is'*, *adj.* left: on the left side (in *her.* from the point of view of the bearer of the shield, not the beholder, and similarly sometimes in description of an illustration, etc.): misleading (*obs.*): underhand: inauspicious: suggestive of threatened evil: unlucky: malign.—*n.* sinisterity (*-ter′*), left-handedness (*rare*): sinister quality.—*advs.* sin′isterly; sin′isterwise.—*adj.* sin′istral, turning to the left: of flatfish, lying left side up: of a shell, coiled contrary to the normal way.—*n.* sinistral′ity.—*adv.* sin′istrally.—*adj.* sinistrous (*sin-is′* or *sin′is-*), inauspicious: sinister (*obs.*).—*adv.* sinistrously. [L.]

sinistrorse, sin-is-trörs′, or *sin′*, (*biol.*) *adj.* rising spirally and turning to the right, i.e. crossing an outside observer's field of view from right to left upwards (like an ordinary spiral stair): formerly used in the contrary sense (dextrorse).—Also sinistrors′al.—*adv.* sinistrors′ally. [L. *sinistrōrsus*, *sinistrōversus*, towards the left side—*sinister*, left, *vertēre*, *versum*, to turn.]

sink, *singk*, *v.i.* to become submerged, wholly or partly: to subside: to fall slowly: to go down passively: to pass to a lower level or state: to penetrate: to be absorbed: to slope away, dip: to diminish: to collapse: to be withdrawn in-wards.—*v.t.* to cause or allow to sink: in games, to cause to run into the hole (*coll.*): to suppress: to degrade: to conceal: to appropriate surrep-titiously: to excavate: to let in, insert: to abandon: to abolish: to merge: to pay: to lose under the horizon: to invest, esp. unprofit-ably or beyond easy recovery: to damn or ruin (esp. in imprecation):—*pa.t.* sank, now rarely sunk; *pa.p.* sunk, also sunk′en, *obs.* exc. as *adj.*—*n.* a receptacle or drain for filth or dirty water: a cesspool: a kitchen or scullery trough or basin with a drain: a place where things are engulfed or where foul things gather: a depression in a surface: an area without surface drainage: a swallow-hole (*geol.*): a shaft.—*ns.* sink′age, act or process of sinking: amount of sinking: a sunk area, depression: shrinkage; sink′er, one who sinks: a weight for sinking anything, as a fishing-line: a doughnut (*U.S. slang*): a mistle-toe root.—*n.* and *adj.* sink′ing.—*adj.* sink′y, yielding underfoot.—sink′-hole, a hole for filth: a swallow-hole (*U.S.*); sink′ing-fund, a fund formed by setting aside income to accumulate at interest to pay off debt.—*adj.* sink′ing-ripe (*Shak.*), ready to sink.—sink in, to be absorbed: to be understood; sink unit, a fitting con-sisting of sink, draining board, with cupboards, etc., underneath. [O.E. *sincan* (intrans.); Ger. *sinken*, Du. *zinken*.]

sink(e)-a-pace. See cinque-pace.

sinner. See under sin (2).

sinnet, *sin′it.* Same as sennit.

Sinn Fein, *shin fān*, *n.* a political movement and party in Ireland championing a republic and later opposing partition.—*ns.* Sinn Fein′er; Sinn Fein′ism. [Ir., ourselves.]

Sinningia, *sin-in′ji-ə*, *n.* a Brazilian genus of Gesneriaceae, grown in greenhouses under the name of Gloxinia. [W. *Sinning*, German gardener.]

Sino-, *sin′ō*, *si′nō*, *pfx.* Chinese.—*n.* Sinologue (*sin′ə-log*, or *sin′*), one versed in Chinese.—*adj.* Sinolog′ical (*-loj′*).—*ns.* Sinologist (*-ol′ə-jist*); Sinol′ogy.—*n.* and *adj.* Sin′ophil(e) (*-fil*, *-fīl*), (one who is) friendly to the Chinese or attracted by Chinese culture.—*ns.* Sinoph′ily, -ophilism.—Sino-American, etc., (pertaining to) Chinese and American, etc. [Gr. *Sinai*, Chinese (pl.).]

sino-, *sin′ō*, *si′nō*, *pfx.* sinus.

sinopia, *sin-ō′pi-ə*, *n.* a reddish-brown pigment used for one of the preparatory drawings of a fresco, obtained from sin′opite, an iron ore: the drawing.—Also sinō′pis. [L. *sinopis*, sinopite.]

sinsyne, *sin-sin′*, (*Scot.*) *adv.* since that time. [sin (1), syne.]

sinter, *sin′tər*, *n.* a deposit from hot springs.—*v.t.* to heat a mixture of powdered metals to the melting-point of the metal in the mixture which has the lowest melting-point, the melted metal

binding together the harder particles.—*v.i.* to coalesce under heat without liquefaction.—*adj.* sin′tery. [Ger. *sinter*; cf. cinder.]

sinus, *si′nəs*, *n.* an indentation: a notch: a cavity a narrow cavity through which pus is discharged: —*pl.* sinuses.—*adjs.* sinuate (*sin′ū-āt*), -d (*-id*) wavy-edged: winding.—*adv.* sin′uately.—*ns.* sinuā′tion, winding; sinuitis (*-i′tis*), sinusi′tis (*sin-* or *sin-əs-*), inflammation of a sinus of the skull communicating with the nose.—*adj.* sinuose (*sin′ū-ōs*), sinuous.—*n.* sinuos′ity.—*adj.* sin′uous, wavy: winding: bending in a supple manner.—*adv.* sin′uously.—*n.* sin′uousness.—*adjs.* sinupall′ial, -pall′iate, with indented pallial line.—*n.* sinusoid (*si′nəs-oid*), the curve of sines (*y = a* sin *x*): a blood-space in tissue.—*adj.* sinusoid′al.—*adv.* sinusoid′ally. [L. *sinus*, *-ūs*, a bend, fold, bay.]

Sioux, *sōō*, *n.* an American Indian of a tribe now living in the Dakotas, Minnesota, and Montana (*pl.* Sioux, *sōō*, *sōōz*).—Also *adj.*—*adj.* Siou′an, of a larger group to which the Sioux belong. [Fr. from a native word.]

sip, *sip*, *v.t.* and *v.i.* to drink, or drink from, in small quantities by action of the lips:—*pr.p.* sipp′ing; *pa.t.* and *pa.p.* sipped.—*n.* the act of sipping: the quantity sipped at once.—*n.* sipp′er. [Cf. sup; O.E. *sypian*; L.G. *sippen.*]

sipe, *sip*, (*dial.*) *v.i.* to soak through.—Also seep. [O.E. *sipian*, to soak.]

siphon, *si′fən*, *n.* a bent tube or channel by which a liquid may be drawn off by atmospheric pressure: a tubular organ for intake and output of water, as in lamellibranchs: an aerated-water bottle that discharges by a siphon.—*v.t.* to con-vey by means of a siphon.—*n.* si′phonage.—*adj.* si′phonal.—*n.pl.* Siphonap′tera, the flea order of insects.—*adj.* si′phonate, having a siphon.—*n.* si′phonet, a greenfly's honeydew tube.—*adj.* siphonic (*-fon′*).—*ns.* siphon′ogam, a seed-plant; siphonog′amy, fertilisation by pollen-tube.—*n.pl.* Siphonoph′ora, an order of colonial Hydrozoa.—*ns.* siphonostele (*-stē′lē*, or *-stēl′*) a hollow cylinder of vascular tissue; si′phuncle, a tube connecting the chambers of a nautilus: a si-phonet. [Gr. *siphōn*, *siphōn*, siphon.]

Siporex, *sip′ər-eks*, *n.* a material used by builders, and also by artists, a form of aerated concrete, which can be sawn, etc. [Trademark.]

sippet, *sip′it*, *n.* a morsel, esp. of bread with soup. —*v.t.* and *v.i.* sipp′le, to sip at leisure. [Cf. sip, sup.]

Sipunculacea, -loidea, *si-pungk-ū-lā′si-ə*, *-loi′di-ə*, *ns.* a group of marine worms.—*ns.* and *adjs.* sipunc′ulid, -uloid, (pertaining to) a worm of this group. [Mod. L.—L. *siphunculus*, a little pipe.]

si quis, *sī*, *sē kwis*, *n.* a public intimation. [L. *si quis*, if anybody (wants, knows, has found, etc.).]

sir, *sûr*, *n.* a word of respect (or disapprobation) used in addressing a man: a gentleman: pre-fixed to the Christian name of a knight or baronet (hence, a knight or baronet) and for-merly used of a priest (hence, Sir John, a priest): word of address to a man in a formal letter: formerly used as a translation of L. *dominus*, bachelor of arts (as distinguished from *magister*, master of arts): in *pl.* used in *Scot.* in addressing persons of either sex, passing into an *interj.* of surprise.—*v.t.* to address as 'sir'. [O.Fr. *sire*, from L. *senior*, an elder.]

sircar, sirkar, circar, *sər-kär′*, *sûr′*, *n.* government: the authorities: a province or district: an Indian clerk or factotum. [Urdu *sarkār*, a superintendent,—Pers. *sar*, head, *kār*, agent.]

sirdar, *sər-där′*, *sûr′*, *n.* a military head: a com-mander-in-chief. [Urdu *sardār*—Pers. *sar*, head, *dār*, holding.]

sire, *sīr*, *n.* a senior, elder: a master, lord (*rare*): a term of address to a king (*arch*): a father, esp.

of a horse or other beast: an ancestor.—*v.t.* to beget, esp. of beasts. [sir.]

**Siren,** *sī'rən, n.* one of certain sea-nymphs, part woman, part bird, whose songs lured sailors to death (*Gr. myth.*): (without *cap.*) a fascinating woman, insidious and deceptive: a bewitching singer: a mermaid: an instrument for counting sound vibrations: (formerly **sirene,** still *illit. si-rēn'*; without *cap.*) a signalling or warning instrument that produces sound by the escape of air or steam through a rotating perforated plate: (*cap.*) an American genus of eel-like amphibians without hind legs.—Also *adj.—n.pl.* **Sirē′nia,** an order of aquatic mammals now represented by the dugong and the manatee.—*n.* and *adj.* **sirē′nian.**—*adj.* **sirenic** (-*ren'*).—**siren suit,** a close-fitting trousered overall orig. for use in air-raids. [Gr. *Seirēn.*]

**sirgang,** *sûr'gang, n.* a green Asiatic jay-like bird. [Prob. from native name.]

**sirih, siri,** *sē'ri, n.* betel. [Malay *sīrih.*]

**Sirius,** *sir'i-əs, n.* the Dogstar.—*adj.* **Sir′ian.**—*n.* **siri′asis,** sunstroke. [L. *Sīrius*—Gr. *Seirios.*]

**sirkar.** Same as **sircar.**

**sirloin, surloin,** *sûr'loin, n.* the loin or upper part of a loin of beef. [From a by-form of Fr. *surlonge*—*sur,* over, and *longe* (cf. **loin**).]

**sirname.** Same as **surname.**

**sirocco,** *si-rok'ō,* **scirocco,** *shi-, n.* in Southern Italy, a hot, dry, dusty and gusty wind from North Africa, becoming moist further north: any oppressive south or south-east wind: a wind from the desert: a drying machine.—Also **s(c)iroc** (*si-rok', sī'rok*). [It. *s(c)irocco*—Ar. *sharq,* east.]

**sirrah,** *sir'ə, n.* sir, used in anger or contempt.—**sirree′** (*sûr-ē'; U.S.*), sir, sirrah. [An extension of **sir.**]

**sir-reverence,** *sə-rev'ə-rəns,* (*obs.*) the phrase *save reverence,* used apologetically when anything disgusting has to be mentioned: hence *n.* a piece of excrement.

**sirup.** See **syrup.**

**sirvente,** *sēr-vät, n.* a troubadour's lay. [Fr.]

**sis, siss,** *sis,* (*U.S.*) *n.* an abbreviation of **sister** (used in addressing a girl).—*n.* and *adj.* **siss′y** (orig. chiefly *U.S.*), cissy.

**-sis, -sis,** *n. suff.* signifying action, process: condition caused by:—*pl.* **-ses** (-*sēz*). [Gr.]

**sisal,** *si'səl, sī'zəl, n.* (in full **sis′al-hemp′,** or -grass'), agave fibre. [First exported from *Sisal,* in Yucatan.]

**siserary, sisserary,** *sis-ər-ā'ri,* **sas(s)arara,** *sas-ər-ā'rə, n.* orig. a corruption of *certiorari:* a scolding: a blow.—**with a siserary,** suddenly: on the spot.

**siskin,** *sis'kin, n.* a yellowish-green finch. [Ger. dial. *sisschen;* app. Slav.]

**sissoo,** *sis'ōō, n.* a papilionaceous Indian timber tree (Dalbergia) or its wood. [Hind. *sīsū.*]

**sissy.** See **sis.**

**sist,** *sist,* (Scots *law*) *v.t.* to stop, stay: to cite, summon.—*n.* a stay. [L. *sistĕre,* to make to stand.]

**sister,** *sis'tər, n.* a daughter of the same parents: a half-sister: formerly, a sister-in-law: a female fellow: a member of a sisterhood: a nun: a senior nurse, esp. one in charge of a ward.—*adj.* of the same origin: a fellow: built on the same model.—*v.t.* to be a sister to: to call sister.—*adjs.* **sis′tering** (*Shak.*), neighbouring; **sis′terless; sis′terly,** like or becoming a sister: kind: affectionate.—*ns.* **sis′terliness; sis′terhood,** act or state of being a sister: the relationship of sister: a society, esp. a religious community, of women: a set or class of women.—**sis′ter-hook,** one of a pair of hooks that close each other; **sis′ter-in-law,** a husband's or wife's sister, or a brother's wife.—*adj.* **sis′ter-like.** [App O.N *systir;* O.E. *sweostor;* Du. *zuster,* Ger. *schwester.*]

**Sistine,** *sis'tīn, -tēn, -tin, adj.* of Pope *Sixtus,* esp. Sixtus IV (1471-84) or V (1585-90)—also **Six′tine.**—**Sistine Chapel,** the Pope's chapel in the Vatican, built by Sixtus IV; **Sistine Madonna,** a picture by Raphael of the Madonna with Sixtus II (257-8).

**sistrum,** *sis'trəm, n.* an ancient Egyptian wire rattle used in Isis-worship:—*pl.* **sis′tra.** [L. *sistrum*—Gr. *seistron.*]

**Sisyphean,** *sis-i-fē'ən, adj.* relating to *Sisyphus,* king of Corinth, condemned in Tartarus to roll a huge stone ceaselessly up a hill.

**sit,** *sit, v.i.* to rest on the haunches or (*obs.*) knees: to perch, as birds: to brood: to have a seat, as in parliament: to be in session: to reside: to be a tenant: to be located, have station or (as the wind) direction: to pose, be a model: to undergo an examination, be a candidate: to weigh, bear, press: to be disposed in adjustment, hang, fit: to befit.—*v.t.* to seat: to have a seat on, ride: to undergo or be examined in:—*pr.p.* **sitt′ing;** *pa.t.* and *pa.p.* **sat.**—*n.* mode or spell of sitting—*ns.* **sitt′er,** one who sits: one who sits to an artist or with a medium: a baby-sitter: a sitting bird: an easy shot: an easy dupe (*slang*): anything difficult to fail in: a sitting-room (*slang*); **sitt′ing,** state of being seated or act of taking a seat: brooding on eggs: a clutch: a continuous meeting of a body: a spell of posing to an artist, etc.: a spell: seat: a church seat.—*adj.* seated: brooding: in the course of a parliamentary session: befitting.—**sit′down,** a spell of sitting.—*adj.* that one sits down to: (of a strike) in which workers down tools but remain in occupation of the plant, workshop, etc.—**sit′fast,** a lump in a horse's skin under the saddle; **sitt′er-in,** a baby-sitter; **sitt′ing-room,** a room in which members of a family commonly sit: a space for sitting.—**sit at,** to live at the rate of expense of; **sit back,** to give up taking any active part; **sit down,** to take a seat: to pause, rest: to begin a siege; **sit down under,** to accept, to submit to; **sit in,** to act as a baby-sitter: to be present as a visitor, and (usu.) take part, as at a conference; **sit on,** or **upon,** to hold an official inquiry regarding: to repress, check (*slang*); **sit out,** to sit apart without participating: to sit to the end of: to outstay; **sit tight,** to maintain one's seat: to keep one's position quietly and unobtrusively; **sitting pretty** (see **pretty**); **sit under,** to be in the habit of hearing the preaching of; **sit up,** to rise from a recumbent to a sitting position, or from a relaxed to an erect seat: to become alert or startled: to remain up instead of going to bed: to keep watch during the night. [O.E. *sittan;* Ger. *sitzen,* L. *sedēre.*]

**sit(t)ar,** *si-tär', n.* a Hindu plucked-string instrument with a long neck. [Hind. *sitār.*]

**site,** *sīt, n.* situation, esp. of a building: ground occupied or set apart for a building, etc.: posture (*obs.*).—*v.t.* to locate. [L. *situs,* set—*sinēre.*]

**sith,** *sith,* (Shak.) *adv., prep.,* and *conj.* since—*obs.* **sith′en,** (Spens., Shak.) **sith′ence, sith′ens.** [O.E siththan, for sīth than (instrumental), after that; cf. since, syne.]

**sith, sithe, sythe,** *sidh,* (Spens.) *n.* time:—*pl.* **sith, sithes.** [O.E. sīth, time.]

**sithe,** *sidh,* (Spens., Shak., Milt.) *n.* and *v.t.* Same as **scythe.**

**sithe,** *sidh, n.* and *v.i.* an obs. or dial. form of **sigh.**

**Sitka spruce,** *sit'kə,* a spruce tree with sharp blue-green needles. [*Sitka* in Alaska.]

**sitology,** *sī-tol'ə-ji,* **sitiology,** *sit-i-, n.* dietetics.—*n.* **sit(i)ophō′bia,** morbid aversion to food. [Gr. *sitos,* dim. *sition,* grain, food.]

**Sitta,** *sit'ə, n.* the nuthatch genus.—*adj.* **sitt′ine.** [Gr. *sittē.*]

**sitter, sitting,** etc. See **sit.**

**sittlichkeit**, *zit'lihh-kit*, (Ger.) morals, morality: that which is becoming or suitable.

**situate**, *sit'ū-it*, *adj.* (now *rare*) situated.—*v.t.* (-*āt*) to set, place, locate: to circumstance.—*adj.* **sit'uated**, set, located: circumstanced.—*n.* **situā'tion**, location: place: position: momentary state: condition: a set of circumstances, a juncture: a critical point in the action of a play or the development ǒf the plot of a novel: office, employment.—*adj.* **situā'tional**.—**situation comedy**, a comedy set in a particular situation and depending on that situation; **situation ethics**. (see **ethic**). [L.L. *situātus*—L. *situĕre*, to place.]

**situla**, *sit'ū-lə*, (*ant.*) *n.* a bucket. [L.]

**sitz-bath**, *sits'-bäth*, *n.* a hip-bath. [Ger. *sitzbad*.]

**sitzkrieg**, *sits'krēg*, *zits'krēhh*, (Ger.) the period (September 1939 to May 1940) of comparative military quiet at the opening of World War II. [Ger. *sitz*, sedentary, *krieg*, war; cf. **blitzkrieg**.]

**Sium**, *sī'əm*, *n.* the water-parsnip genus. [Gr. *sion*.]

**Siva**, *s(h)ē'va*, *n.* the third god of the Hindu triad, destroyer and reproducer.—*n.* **Si'vaism**.—*adj.* **Sivaist'ic**.—*ns.* **Si'vaite**; **Sivapithē'cus** (or -*pith'*), an Indian Miocene fossil anthropoid; **Sivathē'rium**, a gigantic giraffe-like Indian Pliocene fossil animal. [Sans. *śiva*, happy.]

**Sivan**, *sē-vän'*, *n.* the ninth month of the Jewish civil, third of the ecclesiastical, year, part of May and June. [Heb. *siwān*.]

**siver**. See **syver**.

**siwash**, *sī'wosh*, *n.* a N.W. American Indian.—Also *adj.* [Chinook,—Fr. *sauvage*, wild.]

**six**, *siks*, *n.* the cardinal numeral next above five: a symbol representing it (6, vi, etc.): a set of that number: an article of tare denoted by it: a card with six pips: a score of six points, tricks, etc.: the sixth hour after midnight or after midday: a six-cylinder engine or car: a six-syllable line.—*adj.* of the number six.—*n.* **six'er**, anything counting for six (as a hit at cricket) or indicated by six.—*adj.* and *adv.* **six'fold**, in six divisions: six times as much.—*adj.* **sixth**, last of six: next after the fifth: equal to one of six equal parts.—*n.* a sixth part: an interval of five (conventionally called six) diatonic degrees (*mus.*): a combination of two tones that distance apart (*mus.*).—*adv.* **sixth'ly**, in the sixth place.—*adjs.* **six'-day**, for six days (i.e. usu. excluding Sunday); **six'-foot**, measuring six feet.—**six'-foot'er**, a person six feet high; **six'-gun**, a six-shooter; **six'pence**, a coin worth six old pence: its value.—*adj.* **six'penny**, costing or worth sixpence: cheap: worthless.—*n.* a sixpenny book.—*n.* and *adj.* **six'score**.—**six'-shooter**, a six-chambered revolver.—**at sixes and sevens**, in disorder; **hit, knock for six**, to overcome completely: to take by surprise; **long, short, sixes**, candles weighing six to the pound, about 8 or 4 inches long respectively; **six of one and half a dozen of the other**, equal, attributable to both parties equally. [O.E. *siex*; Ger. *sechs*; Gael. *sé*; L. *sex*, Gr. *hex*, Sans. *ṣaṣ*.]

**sixaine**, *siks-ān'*, *n.* a stanza of six lines.—*n.* **sixte** (*sikst*), a parry with hand on guard opposite the right breast, sword point a little raised to the right. [Fr.]

**sixteen**, *siks-tēn'*, or *siks'*, *n.* and *adj.* six and ten.—*n.* **sixteen'er**, a verse of sixteen syllables.—*n.*, *adj.* **sixteen'mo**, sextodecimo.—*adj.* **sixteenth'** (or *siks'*), last of sixteen: equal to one of sixteen equal parts.—*n.* a sixteenth part. [O.E. *siextēne* (-*tiene*); see **six, ten**.]

**sixty**, *siks'ti*, *adj.* and *n.* six times ten:—*pl.* **six'ties**, the numbers sixty to sixty-nine: the years so numbered in a life or century.—*adj.* **six'tieth**, last of sixty: equal to one of sixty equal parts.—*n.* a sixtieth part.—**sixty-four dollar question** (from a U.S. quiz game), the final and most difficult question one has to answer to win sixty-four

dollars, having first won one dollar and placed this on oneself to win double on the second question, and so on until sixty-four dollars are at stake: hence, a hard question to answer, the supreme or crucial question.—Also **sixty-four thousand dollar question**. [O.E. *siextig*.]

**size**, *sīz*, *n.* an assize (*obs.*): a portion of food and drink (*obs.*): an allowance (*obs.*): bigness: magnitude.—*v.t.* to arrange according to size: at Cambridge, to buy or score, as rations: to measure.—*v.i.* to draw a size: to assume size.—*adj.* **si'zable** (or **size'able**), of a fair size.—*ns.* **si'zar** (also **si'zer**), at Cambridge and Dublin, a student receiving an allowance from his college towards his expenses; **si'zarship**.—*adj.* **sized**, having this or that size.—*ns.* **si'zer**, a measurer: a gauge: a thing of considerable or great size (*slang*); **si'zing**, sorting by size: order for extra food from a college buttery.—**size up**, to take mental measure of. [assize.]

**size**, *sīz*, *n.* weak glue or gluey material.—*v.t.* to cover or treat with size.—*adj.* **sized**.—*ns.* **siz'er**; **siz'iness**; **siz'ing**, application of size, or material for the purpose.—*adj.* **siz'y**. [Origin obscure.]

**size**, *sīz*. Same as **sice** (1).

**sizel**. See **scissel**.

**sizzle**, *siz'l*, *v.i.* to make a hissing sound of frying.—*v.t.* and *v.i.* to fry, scorch, sear.—*n.* a hissing sound: extreme heat.—*ns.* **sizz'ler**, a sizzling heat or day: a thing strikingly fierce or effective; **sizz'ling**, a hissing.—*adj.* very hot: very striking. [Imit.]

**sjambok**, *sham'bok*, *n.* a whip of dried hide.—*v.t.* to flog. [Cape Du.,—Malay *samboq*—Urdu *chābuk*.]

**skail**, **scail**, **skale**, *skāl*, (*Scot.*) *v.t.* and *v.i.* to disperse: to scatter: to spill. [Ety. dub.]

**skaines mate**, *skānz'māt*, (*Shak.*) *n.* perh. a companion, a scapegrace.

**skaith**. See **scathe**.

**skald**, **scald**, *sköld*, *n.* a poet: a Scandinavian bard.—*adj.* **skald'ic**, **scald'ic**. [O.N. *skáld*.]

**skart**, **scart**, **skärt**, **scarth**, **skarth**, **skärth**, (*Scot.*) *n.* a cormorant. [O.N. *skarfr*.]

**skat**, *skät*, *n.* a three-handed card-game. [O.Fr. *escart*, laying aside.]

**skate**, *skät*, *n.* a sole or sandal mounted on a blade (for moving on ice) or on rollers: a spell of skating.—*v.i.* to go on skates.—*ns.* **skā'ter**; **skā'ting**—**skā'ting-rink**.—**skate on thin ice**, to deal with a potentially difficult or dangerous situation; **skate over** (*fig.*), to hurry over lightly. [Du. *schaats*—O.N.Fr. *escache*, stilt—L.G. *schake*, shank.]

**skate**, *skät*, *n.* a kind of ray (*Raia batis*, or kindred species). [O.N. *skata*.]

**skatole**, *skat'öl*, *skä'töl*, *n.* a compound ($C_9H_9N$) found in faeces. [Gr. *skōr*, *skatos*, dung.]

**skaw**, **scaw**, *skö*, *n.* a low cape, ness (in place-names). [O.N. *skagi*.]

**skean**. See **skene**: also an old spelling of **skein**.

**skedaddle**, *ski-dad'l*, (*coll.*) *v.i.* to scamper off.—*n.* a scurrying off. [Ety. unknown.]

**skeely**, *skē'li*, (*Scot.*) *adj.* skilful. [skill.]

**skeer**, **skear**, **skeery**, **skeary**, dial. forms of **scare**, **scary**.

**skeesicks**, *skē'ziks*, (*U.S.*) *n.* a rascal.

**skeet**, *skēt*, *n.* a form of clay-pigeon shooting.

**skeeter**, *skēt'ər*, (*U.S.*) *n.* short for **mosquito**.

**Skeffington's daughter**. See **scavenger**.

**skegger**, *skeg'ər*, *n.* a young salmon. [Origin obscure.]

**skeigh**, *skēhh*, (*Scot.*) *adj.* shy: coy: aloof: skittish. [Cf. O.E. *sceoh*, shy.]

**skein**, *skān*, *n.* a loosely tied coil or standard length of thread or yarn: a tangle: a web: the nuclear network (*biol.*): a flock of wild geese in flight. [O.Fr. *escaigne*.]

**skelder**, *skel'dər*, *v.i.* to beg: to swindle. [Cant; of obscure origin.]

---

Neutral vowels in unaccented syllables: *el'ə-mənt*; for certain sounds in foreign words, see p. viii

skeleton, *skel'i-tn, n.* the hard parts of an animal: the bones: the veins of a leaf: a framework or outline of anything: a scheme reduced to its essential or indispensable elements: a set of persons reduced to its lowest strength: an emaciated person or animal.—Also *adj.*—*adjs.* skel'etal; skeletogenous (-*toj'*), skeleton-forming. —*v.t.* skel'etonise, -ize, to reduce to a skeleton. —skeleton key, a key for picking locks, without the inner bits; skel'eton-shrimp', a ghostly-looking amphipod (Caprella, etc.), skeleton suit, an early 19th-cent. boy's suit with trousers buttoning over the coat.—skeleton in the cupboard, closet, house, etc., a hidden domestic sorrow or shame. [Gr. *skeleton* (*sōma*), dried (body)—*skellein*, to dry.]

skelloch, *skel'əhh,* (*Scot.*) *v.i.* to yell.—*n.* a yell. skellum, *skel'əm,* (*Scot.*) *n.* a ne'er-do-well: a scamp. [Du. *schelm,* a rogue; cf. skelm.]

skelly, *skel'i* (*Scot.*) *n.,* *adj.,* and *v.i.* squint. [Prob. O.N.; cf. O.E. *sceolh,* squint.]

skelm, *skelm,* (*S.Afr.*) *n.* a rascal. [Du. and Ger. *schelm.*]

skelp, *skelp,* (*Scot.*) *v.t.* to slap.—*v.i.* to move briskly along: to bound along.—*n.* a slap.—*adj.* skelp'ing, very big or full: smacking: lusty.—*n.* a smacking. [Ety. unknown.]

skelter, *skel'tar, v.i.* to scurry.—*n.* a scurry.

skene, skean, *skēn, n.* an Irish or Highland dagger, knife, or short sword.—skene'-dhu, skean'-dhu (-*dōō'*), a dirk, dagger, stuck in the stocking; skene'-occle (-*ok'l*), one carried in the sleeve. [Ir. and Gael. *sgian,* knife, *dhu,* black, *achlais,* armpit.]

skeo. Same as skio.

skep, *skep, n.* a basket: a beehive.—*v.t.* to hive.—*n.* skep'ful. [O.N. *skeppa.*]

skeptic, skepsis. Same as sceptic, scepsis.

sker. Same as skirr.

skerry, *sker'i, n.* a reef of rock. [O.N. *sker.*]

sketch, *skech, n.* a drawing, slight, rough, or without detail, esp. as a study towards a more finished work: an outline or short account: a short and slightly constructed play, dramatic scene, musical entertainment, etc.: a short descriptive essay.—*v.t.* to make or give a sketch of: to outline, or give the principal points of. —*v.i.* to practise sketching.—*n.* sketchabil'ity. —*adj.* sketch'able, worth sketching.—*n.* sketch'er. — *adv.* sketch'ily. — *n.* sketch'iness. — *adj.* sketch'y, like a sketch: incomplete, slight: imperfect, inadequate.—sketch'-book, a book of or for sketches (in drawing, literature or music). [Du. *schets,* prob.—It. *schizzo*—L. *schedium,* an extempore—Gr. *schedios,* offhand.]

Skevington's daughter. See scavenger.

skew, *skū, adj.* oblique.—*adv.* awry.—*n.* obliquity. —*v.t.* and *v.i.* to set, go, or look obliquely.—*adj.* skewed, distorted.—skew'-back (*archit.*), the part, or inclined surface on which a segmented arch abuts; skew'-bridge, a bridge having its arch or arches set obliquely on its abutments.— *adj.* and *adv.* skew-whiff', crooked, awry. [App. O.N.Fr. *eskiu*(*w*)*er*—O.Fr. *eschuer*; see eschew; or M.Du. *schuwe,* to shun; cf. shy.]

skew, *skū, n.* the coping or a coping-stone of a gable.—skew'-corbel, -put, -table, the corner-stone supporting the coping of a gable. [O.Fr. *escu*—L. *scūtum,* a shield.]

skewbald, *skū'böld, adj.* marked in white and another colour (not black).—*n.* a skewbald horse. [Origin obscure.]

skewer, *skū'ər, n.* a long pin of wood or metal, esp. for meat.—*v.t.* to fasten or pierce with a skewer: to transfix. [skiver.]

ski, *skē,* (formerly also *shē*) *n.* a long narrow runner orig. of wood, now also of metal, etc., fastened to the foot to enable the wearer to slide across snow, etc.—*pl.* ski or skis.—*v.i.* to travel on skis:—*pr.p.* ski'ing; *pa.t.* and *pa.p.* skied,

ski'd.—*adj.* ski'able, (of surface) in condition for skiing on.—*ns.* ski'er; ski'ing.—ski'-bob, a low bicycle on small skis instead of wheels; ski'-bobbing, ski'-bobs; ski(-)joring (-*jör'*, -*jör'*), Norw. skikjöring (*shihh-yûr'ing*), the sport of being towed on skis by a horse or motor vehicle; ski'-jump'ing; ski'-kiting, water-skiing holding on to a bar on a kite-like device; ski'-lift, -tow, devices for taking skiers uphill; ski-runn'ing; ski'-school; ski'-slope.—bird-, dry-, water-skiing (see bird, dry, water). [Norw.,—O.N. *skīth,* snow-shoe, piece of split wood; O.E. *scīd.*]

skia-, *ski'ə-,* -*a'-,* in composition, shadow.—Also scia- (*si-*), skio-, scio-.—*ns.* ski'agram, ski'a-graph, an X-ray photograph; skiamachy (-*am'ə-ki;* Gr. *machē,* a fight), a sham fight: a fight with shadows; skias'copy, retinoscopy; ski'atron, a dark trace tube. [Gr. *skiā,* a shadow.]

skid, *skid, n.* a support on which something rests, is brought to the desired level, or slides: a ship's wooden fender: a shoe or other device to check a wheel on a down-slope: an aeroplane runner: a skidding: a sideslip.—*v.i.* to slide along without revolving: to slip, esp. sideways.—*v.t.* to check with a skid: to make to skid.—skid'-lid (*slang*), a crash helmet; skid pad, pan, a piece of slippery ground on which motorists can learn to control a skidding car; skid'pan (*slang*), a drag for a wheel (also *fig.*); skid road, row, a squalid quarter where vagrants, chronic drunks, etc., live.—the skids (*fig.*; *coll.*) a downward path. [Prob. related to ski.]

skier, skies, skiey. See ski, sky, skyey.

skiff, *skif, n.* a small light boat. [Akin to ship.]

skiff, *skif,* (*Scot.*) *v.i.* and *v.t.* to skim.—*n.* a skimming or grazing movement or blow: a slight touch: a sketch: a puff.

skiffle, *skif'l, n.* strongly accented jazz type of folk-music played by guitars, drums, and often unconventional instruments, etc., popular about 1957. [Origin obscure.]

skijoring. See ski.

skill, *skil, n.* reason (*Shak.*): discrimination (*obs.*): expertness: expert knowledge (*arch.*): a craft or accomplishment.—*v.t.* and *v.i.* (*arch.*) to matter: to make (a difference): to signify.—*adj.* skil'ful. —*adv.* skil'fully.—*n.* skil'fulness.—*adjs.* skilled, expert—(*Scot.*) skill'y, skee'ly; skill'-less, skil'-less. [O.N. *skil,* distinction, *skilja,* to separate.]

skillet, *skil'it, n.* a small, long-handled pan. [Origin doubtful.]

skilling, *skil'ing,* an obsolete coin of Scandinavian countries, of small value. [Dan.]

skilly, *skil'i, n.* thin gruel.—Also skilligalee', skilligolee'. [Ety. dub.]

skim, *skim, v.t.* to remove floating matter from the surface of: to take off by skimming: to glide lightly over: to read superficially and skippingly. —*v.i.* to pass over lightly: to glide along near the surface: to become coated over:—*pr.p.* skimm'ing; *pa.t.* and *pa.p.* skimmed.—*n.* the act of skimming: skim-milk.—*ns.* skimm'er, one who skims: a utensil for skimming milk: a sea-bird (Rhyncops) that skims the water; skimm'ing. —*adv.* skimm'ingly.—skim'-milk, milk from which the cream has been skimmed. [App. related to scum.]

skimble-skamble, *skim'bl-skam'bl, adj.* wild, rambling, incoherent. [A reduplication of scamble.]

Skimmia, *skim'i-ə, n.* an Asiatic genus of rutaceous shrubs, cultivated for its holly-like leaves and drupes. [Jap. *skimmi.*]

skimmington, *skim'ing-tən, n.* a burlesque procession in ridicule of husband or wife in case of infidelity or other ill-treatment. [Ety. unknown.]

skimp, *skimp, v.t.* and *v.i.* to scrimp: to stint.— *adj.* scanty, spare.—*adv.* skimp'ily.—*adj.* skimp'ing.—*adv.* skimp'ingly.—*adj.* skimp'y. [Poss. scamp combined with scrimp.]

skin, *skin, n.* the natural outer covering of an

animal: a hide: a thin outer layer or covering: an integument: a membrane: a wine vessel made of an animal's skin.—*adj.* of skin.—*v.t.* to cover with a skin: to strip the skin from: to fleece.—*v.i.* to become covered with skin: to slip through or away:—*pr.p.* **skinn′ing**; *pa.t.* and *pa.p.* **skinned**.—*n.* **skin′ful**, as much liquor as one can hold.—*adj.* **skin′less**.—*ns.* **skinn′er**, one who prepares hides; **skinn′iness**.—*adj.* **skinn′y**, of or like skin: emaciated.—*adj.* **skin′-deep**, superficial.—**skin′-diver; skin′-diving**, diving and swimming under water, with simple equipment, not wearing the traditional diver's helmet and suit, and not connected with a boat; **skin effect**, the tendency, increasing with frequency, for an alternating current to be greater in the surface layer of a conductor; **skin′flint**, a very niggardly person; **skin′-game**, a swindling trick; **skin′-head**, a member of certain gangs of young people (1969) wearing simple, severe, clothes, the boys having closely cropped hair.—*adj.* **skin′-tight**, fitting close to the skin.—*n.* (in *pl.*) tights.—**skin′-wool**, wool from a dead sheep.—**by** or **with the skin of one's teeth**, very narrowly; **get under one's skin**, to annoy one, or to interest one seriously; **save one's skin**, to save one's life. [O.N. *skinn*; late O.E. *scinn*.]

**skink**, *skingk*, *v.i.* and *v.t.* to pour out.—*n.* (*Scot.*) liquor.—*n.* **skink′er**.—*adj.* **skink′ing** (*Scot.*), thin, watery. [Perh. L.G. *schenken*; cf. O.E. *scencan*; Ger. *schenken*.]

**skink**, *skingk*, *n.* an African lizard (Scincus) or kindred kind. [L. *scincus*—Gr. *skinkos*.]

**skink**, *skingk*, *n.* (*Scot.*) shin-bone soup. [L.G. *schinke*.]

**skint**, *skint*, (*slang*) *adj.* without money, hard up. [skinned.]

**skio, skeo,** *skyō*, (*Orkney* and *Shetland*) *n.* a hut: a shed. [Norw. *skjaa*.]

**skio-**. See **skia-**.

**skip**, *skip*, *v.i.* to spring or hop lightly: to make jumps over a twirling rope: to pass discontinuously.—*v.t.* to overleap: to omit:—*pr.p.* **skipp′ing**; *pa.t.* and *pa.p.* **skipped**.—*n.* an act of skipping: a belt of inaudibility in wireless transmission: a college servant.—*n.* **skipp′er**, one who skips: a dancer: a young and thoughtless person (*Shak.*): a butterfly of the Hesperiidae, with short jerky flight: the saury.—*adj.* **skipp′ing**, flighty, giddy.—*adv.* **skipp′ingly**.—**skip′jack**, a pert fop: a jumping fish (bluefish, saurel, etc.): a click-beetle: a jumping toy made of a fowl's merrythought; **skip′-kennel** (*obs.*), a lackey; **skipp′ing-rope**.—**skip it!** never mind, forget it! [Cf. O.N. *skopa*, to run.]

**skip**, *skip*, *n.* a box or truck for raising minerals from a mine: a large container for transporting building, etc., materials or refuse. [skep.]

**skip**, *skip*, *n.* captain of a rink in bowls or curling. —*v.t.* and *v.i.* to act as a skip. [skipper.]

**skipper**, *skip′ər*, *n.* a ship captain.—**skipper's daughters**, white-topped waves. [Du. *schipper*.]

**skippet**, *skip′it*, *n.* a flat box for protecting a seal (as of a document). [Origin unknown.]

**skirl**, *skirl*, *skûrl*, (*Scot.*) *v.t.* and *v.i.* to shriek or sing shrilly.—*n.* a shrill cry.—*n.* **skirl′ing**, a shrill sound.—**skirl′-in-the-pan′**, the noise of frying: a fried dish. [Scand.]

**skirmish**, *skûr′mish*, *n.* an irregular fight between small parties.—*v.i.* to fight slightly or irregularly. —*ns.* **skir′misher; skir′mishing**. [O.Fr. *escarmouche*.]

**skirr, sker, scur, squirr**, *skûr*, *v.t.* to scour, search, range over (*Scot.*): to send skimming.—*v.i.* (*Shak.*) to scurry. [Origin doubtful.]

**skirret**, *skir′it*, *n.* a water-parsnip with edible roots. [M.E. *skirwhit*, as if *skire white*, pure white, but perh. altered from O.Fr. *eschervis*.]

**skirt**, *skûrt*, *n.* a garment, or part of a garment, generally a woman's, that hangs from the waist:

the lower part of a gown, coat, or other garment: a saddle-flap: a midriff (of meat): a rim, border, margin: a part of, or attachment to, an object that suggests a skirt: a woman (*slang*).— *v.t.* to border: to pass along the edge of: to scour the outskirts of.—*v.i.* to be on or pass along the border: to leave the pack.—*adj.* **skirt′ed**, wearing or having a skirt.—*ns.* **skir′ter**, a huntsman who dodges his jumps by going round about; **skir′ting**, material for skirts: skirting-board: (in *pl.*) dirty wool from the skirts of a fleece.—Also *adj.*—*adj.* **skirt′less**.— **skirt′-danc′ing**, dancing with waving of flowing skirts; **skir′ting-board**, the narrow board next the floor round the walls of a room.—**divided skirt**, trousers made to look like a skirt. [O.N. *skyrta*, a shirt, kirtle; cf. **shirt**.]

**skit**, *skit*, *n.* a piece of banter or burlesque, esp. in dramatic or literary form: a humorous hit: a hoax: a sudden slight shower of rain or snow, etc. (*dial.*).—*v.i.* **skite, skyte** (*skīt*; *Scot.*), to dart or glide obliquely.—*n.* a glancing blow: a spree: a trick: a queer person. [Perh. related to O.N. *skjōta*, to shoot.]

**skite**, *skīt*, (*Austr. slang*) *v.i.* to boast.—*n.* a boaster. [blatherskite.]

**skitter**, *skit′ər*, *v.i.* to skim over the surface of water: to fish by drawing the bait over the surface. [Perh. from **skite** (see **skit**).]

**skittish**, *skit′ish*, *adj.* unsteady: light-headed: frivolous: frisky: lively: volatile: changeable: wanton: coy.—*adv.* **skitt′ishly**.—*n.* **skitt′ishness**. [Perh. conn. with **skit**.]

**skittle**, *skit′l*, *n.* a pin for the game of **skittles**, a form of ninepins in which a flattened ball or cheese-shaped missile is used.—*v.t.* to knock down.—**skitt′le-alley, -ball, -ground**. [Origin doubtful.]

**skive**, *skīv*, *v.t.* to pare, split.—*ns.* **ski′ver**, split sheepskin leather; **ski′ving**. [O.N. *skifa*; cf. **shive**.]

**skive**, *skīv*, (*slang*) *v.t.* and *v.i.* to evade (a duty). —*adj.* **ski′vy**. [Origin uncertain.]

**skiver**, *skiv′ər*, (*dial.*) *n.* and *v.t.* Same as **skewer**. [Origin unknown.]

**skivie**, *ski′vi*, (*obs. Scot.*) *adj.* deranged: askew. [Cf. O.N. *skeifr*.]

**skivvy**, *skiv′i*, (*slang*) *n.* a disrespectful word for a maidservant. [Origin uncertain.]

**sklate**, *sklāt*, **sklent**, *sklent*, Scottish form of **slate**, **slant**.

**skoal**, *skōl*, *interj.* hail!: a friendly exclamation in salutation before drinking, etc. [O.N. *skāl*; Norw. *skaal*, a bowl, Sw. *skål*; cf. **scale** (3 and 4).]

**skoff**. See **scoff** (2).

**skolion**, *skō′li-on*, *n.* a short drinking-song in ancient Greece, taken up by the guests in irregular succession:—*pl.* **skō′lia**. [Gr. *skólion*.]

**skran**. Same as **scran**.

**skreen** (*Spens.* **skreene**). Same as **screen** (esp. partition of wood or stone).

**skreigh, skriech, skriegh, scraich, screich, screigh, scriech**, *skrēhh*, *skrähh*, *skrehh*, (*Scot.*) *n.* and *v.* screech, shriek.—**skreigh of day**, cock-crow, daybreak. [Imit. improvement upon **screak**.]

**skrimmage**. See **scrimmage**.

**skrimp, skrump**. See **scrump**.

**skrimshank, scrimshank**, *skrim′shangk*, (*mil. slang*) *v.i.* to evade work or duty.—*n.* evasion of work.—*n.* **skrim′shanker**. [Origin obscure.]

**skry, skryer**. Same as **scry, scryer**.

**skua**, *skū′ə*, *n.* a genus (Stercorarius) of large predatory gulls.—**skū′a-gull**. [O.N. *skūfr*.]

**skudler, scuddaler, scudler**, *skud′lər*, (*Shetland*) *n.* the leader of a band of guisers: the conductor of a festival. [Origin obscure.]

**skug, scug, skug** (*Scot.* **scoug, scoog**, *skoōg*, **scog, skog**), *n.* orig. shadow: shelter.—*v.t.* and *v.i.* to shelter. [O.N. *skuggi*, shadow.]

skug, *skug*, (*dial.*) *n.* a squirrel.

skulduddery, skulduggery. See sculdudd(e)ry.

skulk, *skulk*, *v.i.* to sneak out of the way: to lurk: to malinger.—*ns.* skulk, skulk′er, one who skulks.—*n.* and *adj.* skulk′ing.—*adv.* skulk′ingly. —skulk′ing-place. [Scand., as Dan. *skulke*.]

skull, *skul*, *n.* the bony case that encloses the brain: the sconce, noddle: a skullcap, esp. of metal: a crust of solidified metal on a ladle, etc. —skullcap, a close-fitting cap: a protective cap of metal for the top of the head: the top of the skull: a labiate plant (Scutellaria) with helmet-like calyx.—skull and crossbones (see cross). [M.E. *scolle*; perh. Scand.]

skull. Same as scull (2).

skulpin. Same as sculpin.

skunk, *skungk*, *n.* a small American musteline animal that emits an offensive fluid: its fur: a low fellow.—*v.t.* (*U.S.*) to defeat without allowing to score.—skunk′-bird, -black′bird, the bobolink (from his colouring); skunk′-cabb′age, an ill-smelling plant (Symplocarpus) of the arum family. [Algonkian *segonku*.]

Skupshtina, *skōōp′shti-na*, *n.* the Yugoslav (*hist.* Serbian and Montenegrin) national assembly. [Serb.]

skurry, skuttle. See scurry, scuttle.

skutterudite, *skŏŏt′ər-ōō-dīt*, a cubic mineral, cobalt arsenide. [*Skutterud* in Norway, a source.]

sky, *skī*, *n.* the apparent canopy over our heads: the heavens: the weather: the upper rows of pictures in a gallery: sky-blue.—*v.t.* to raise aloft: to hit high into the air: to hang above the line of sight.—*adjs.* sky′ey (or ski′ey), of the weather: of or like the sky; sky′ish (*Shak.*), like or approaching the sky, lofty.—*adj.* and *adv.* sky′ward.—*adv.* sky′wards.—*adj.* sky′-aspiring (*Shak.*).—*n.* and *adj.* sky′-blue, light blue like the sky.—*adjs.* sky′born, of heavenly birth; sky′-bred; sky′clad, naked.—sky′-col′our.—*adj.* sky′-col′oured.—sky-diving, -jumping, jumping by parachute as a sport, using a special steerable parachute, and delaying opening it for a specified time.—*adj.* sky′-high′, very high.—Also *adv.*—sky′lark, the common lark.—*v.i.* to frolic boisterously.—*v.t.* to trick.—sky′larking, running about the rigging of a ship in sport: frolicking; sky′light, a window in a roof or ceiling: light from or in the sky: light through the bottom of an empty glass; sky′line, the horizon: a silhouette or outline against the sky; sky′man, a paratrooper; sky′-par′lour, a lofty attic; sky′-pi′lot, a clergyman, chaplain.—*adj.* sky′-plant′ed, placed in the sky.—sky′-rock′et, a firework that bursts high in the sky.—*v.i.* to shoot up high: to rise high and fast.—skysail (*skī′sl*), a sail above the royal; sky′scape, a view or a picture of the sky; sky′scraper, a very lofty building: a triangular skysail: anything very high; sky′-sign, an elevated advertising sign, as of lights on a high building.—*adj.* sky′-tinc′tured, of the colour of the sky.—sky′-troops, paratroopers: airborne troops; sky wave, radio wave reflected from the ionosphere; sky′way, a route for aircraft; sky′-writing, tracing of words by smoke from an aircraft.—the sky is the limit (*coll.*), there are no restrictions on amount or extent (of something); to the skies (*coll.*), in a lavish or enthusiastic manner. [O.N. *skȳ*, cloud.]

Skye, *skī*, *n.* (in full, Skye terrier) a small long-haired Scotch terrier. [From the island of *Skye*.]

skyr, *shür*, *skēr*, *n.* curds. [Norw., Sw., and Icel., —O.N.]

skyre, *skīr*, (*Scot.*) *v.i.* to shine, be gaudy, flaunt. [Origin obscure.]

skyte. Same as skite (see skit).

slab, *slab*, *n.* a plane-sided plate: a large thick slice of cake, etc.: outer plank sawn from a log: a thin flat piece of stone, etc.—*v.t.* to cut slabs

from: to form into slabs: to cover with slabs.— *adjs.* slabbed; slab′-sid′ed, flat-sided (*U.S.*): tall and lank.—slab′stone, flagstone. [Origin obscure.]

slab, *slab*, *adj.* semi-liquid, viscous.—*n.* mud.—*n.* slabb′iness.—*adj.* slabb′y, muddy. [Scand.; cf. Norw., Sw. *slabb*, wet filth.]

slabber, *slab′ər*, *v.i.* to slaver, to drivel.—*v.t.* to beslaver, beslobber, or beslubber: to gobble sloppily and grossly.—*n.* slabb′erer.—*adj.* slabb′-ery. [Cf. L.G. and Du. *slabberen* and slobber.]

slack, *slak*, *adj.* lax or loose: not firmly extended or drawn out: not holding fast: remiss: not strict: not eager or diligent, inattentive: not busy: not violent or rapid, slow: pronounced with wide, not tense, tongue (*phon.*).—*adv.* in a slack manner: partially: insufficiently.—*n.* the slack part of a rope, belt, etc.: a time, occasion, or place of relaxed movement or activity: a slack-water haul of a net: (in *pl.*) long, loose trousers.—*vs.i.* slack, slack′en, to become loose or less tight: to be remiss: to abate: to become slower: to fail or flag: to be inactive or lax.— *vs.t.* to make slack or less tight: to loosen: to slow, retard: to be remiss or dilatory in: to relax: to slake.—*n.* and *adj.* slack′ening.—*n.* slack′er, an idler: one who is reprehensibly inactive: a shirker.—*adv.* slack′ly.—*n.* slack′ness. —*v.t.* slack′-bake, to half-bake.—*adj.* slack′-hand′ed, remiss.—slack′-jaw (*slang*), impudent talk; slack′-rope, a loosely stretched rope for a funambulist; slack′-water, turn of the tide: a stretch of still or slow-moving water.—*adj.* pertaining to slack-water.—slack away, to ease off freely; slack in stays, slow in going about, of a ship; slack off, to ease off; slack up, to ease off: to slow. [O.E. *slæc* (*sleac*); cf. Sw. *slak*, O.N. *slakr*.]

slack, *slak*, *n.* coal-dross. [Cf. Ger. *schlacke*.]

slack, *slak*, (*Scot.*) *n.* a cleft between hills: a boggy place. [O.N. *slakki*, dell.]

sladang. Same as seladang.

slade, *slād*, *n.* a little valley or dell: a piece of low, moist ground. [O.E. *slæd*, dell.]

slade, slaid, *slād*, Scots *pa.t.* of slide.

slae, *slā*, a Scots form of sloe.

slag, *slag*, *n.* solid scum on melted metal: vitrified cinders: scoriaceous lava: a piece of slag.—*v.t.* and *v.i.* to form into slag.—*adj.* slagg′y.—slag′-wool, fibre made from molten slag. [M.L.G. *slagge*; cf. Ger. *schlacke*, dross.]

slain, *slān*, *pa.p.* of slay.

slàinte, *slän′chə*, (Gael.) good health!

slaister, *slās′tər*, (*Scot.*) *n.* a slobbery mess: wet slovenly work.—*v.t.* to bedaub.—*v.i.* to do anything in a wet, dirty, slobbery way.—*adj.* slais′-tery.—*n.* slops: drudgery. [Origin obscure.]

slake, *slāk*, *v.t.* to quench: to extinguish: to deaden: to abate, mitigate, allay, reduce, moderate: to moisten: to hydrate (as lime): to refresh with moisture: to slacken.—*v.i.* to become slaked: to subside: to abate: to die down.—*adj.* slake′less, that cannot be slaked.— [O.E. *slacian*, *sleacian*, to grow slack—*slæc*, *sleac*, slack.]

slake, *slāk*, (*Scot.*) *v.t.* and *v.i.* to lick, smear, daub. —*n.* a slabbery daub: a smear. [O.N. *sleikja*, to lick; Ger. *schlecken*, to lick.]

slake, *slāk*, (*Northern*) *n.* mud: slime: a mud-flat.

slalom, *slä′lom*, *n.* a race in which tactical skill is required, esp. a downhill or zigzag ski-run among posts or trees or an obstacle race in canoes. [Norw.]

slam, *slam*, *v.t.* or *v.i.* to shut or strike with violence and noise: to bang: to censure, criticise (*coll.*):—*pr.p.* slamm′ing; *pa.t.* and *pa.p.* slammed.—*n.* the act or sound of slamming: a harsh criticism (*coll.*).—*adv.* with a slam. [Cf. Norw. *slemna*.]

slam, *slam*, *n.* an old card-game, also called ruff

**or trump**: the winning of every trick (*whist*; in bridge called *grand slam*; of all but one, *little slam*).—*v.t.* to inflict a slam upon. [Origin unknown.]

**slammakin, slammerkin,** *slam'ə(r)-kin,* (*obs.*) *n.* a loose gown: a slovenly-dressed woman: a slattern.—*adj.* slovenly. [Origin obscure.]

**slander,** *slän', slan'dər, n.* a false or malicious report: injurious defamation by spoken words or by looks, signs, or gestures (distinct from *libel*; *Eng. law*): defamation whether spoken or written (*Scots law*): calumny.—*v.t.* to defame: to calumniate.—*n.* **slan'derer.**—*adj.* **slan'derous.** —*adv.* **slan'derously.**—*n.* **slan'derousness.** [O.Fr. *esclandre*—L. *scandalum*—Gr. *skandalon,* snare, scandal.]

**slane,** *slän, n.* a turf-cutting spade. [Ir. *sleaghan*.]

**slang,** *slang, n.* a jargon of thieves and disreputable persons: the jargon of any class, profession, or set: colloquial language with words and usages not accepted for dignified use.—Also *adj.*— *v.t.* to scold, vituperate.—*adv.* **slang'ily.**—*ns.* **slang'iness; slang'ing,** a scolding.—Also *adj.*— *adv.* **slang'ingly.**—*adjs.* **slang'ish; slang'ular** (*Dickens*); **slang'y.**—*v.t.* and *v.i.* **slang'-whang,** to rail, to rant.—**slang'-whanger.**—**slanging match,** a bitter verbal quarrel, usu. involving an exchange of insults.—**back slang** (see **back**). [Of cant origin; connection with **sling** very doubtful.]

**slang,** *slang,* (*slang*) *n.* a counterfeit weight or measure: a travelling show, or performance: a hawker's licence. [Cant; origin obscure.]

**slang,** *slang, n.* a watch-chain: (in *pl.*) leg-irons. [Perh. Du. *slang,* snake.]

**slant,** *slänt, slant, v.t.* and *v.i.* to slope: to turn, strike, fall, obliquely.—*v.t.* to incline in a certain direction in presentation.—*n.* a slope: obliquity: a sloping surface, line, ray, or movement: a divergence from a direct line: a glance (*U.S.*): a jibe: a point of view, way of looking at a thing: a chance (*slang*).—*adj.* sloping: oblique: inclined from a direct line.—*adjs.* **slant'ed,** biased, prejudiced; **slantendic'ular, slantin(g)- dic'ular,** oblique (*jocular*; founded on *perpendicular*).—*adj.* **slant'ing.**—*advs.* **slan'tingly, slant'- ingways, slant'ly, slant'ways, slant'wise.** [M.E. *slent*; cf. Norw. *slenta,* Sw. *slinta,* to slope, slip.]

**slant,** *slänt, slant, n.* a transitory breeze. [Earlier *slent*; Scand.; cf. Norw. *slett*.]

**slap,** *slap, n.* a blow with the hand or anything flat: a snub, rebuke.—*v.t.* to give a slap to: to bring or send with a slap: to rebuke (also with *down*):— *pr.p.* **slapp'ing;** *pa.t.* and *pa.p.* **slapped.**—*adv.* with a slap: suddenly, violently: directly, straight.—*n.* **slapp'er,** one who or that which slaps: a whopper, a thing very big of its kind (*slang*).—*adj.* **slapp'ing** (*slang*), whopping.—*adv.* **slap'-bang,** violently, all at once.—*adj.* dashing, violent.—*n.* a cheap eating-house: a simple firework that makes a noise when thrown down. —*adv.* **slap'-dash,** in a bold, careless way.—*adj.* off-hand, rash.—*n.* roughcast: careless work. —*v.t.* to do in a hasty, imperfect manner: to roughcast.—*adj.* **slap'-happy** (*slang*), recklessly or boisterously happy: slap-dash, happy-go-lucky: punch-drunk.—**slap'jack** (*U.S.*), a flapjack, griddle-cake; **slap'stick,** a harlequin's double lath that makes a noise like a slap: (also **slapstick comedy**) knockabout low comedy or farce.—*adj.* **slap'-up** (*slang*), superlatively fine. [Allied to L.G. *slapp,* Ger. *schlappe*; imit.]

**slap,** *slap,* (*Scot.*) *n.* a gap in a fence, wall, hedge, etc.: a hill pass: a passage in a salmon cruive: hence the weekly close time when the passage is open.—*v.t.* to breach: to pierce. [Du. or L.G. *slop.*]

**slash,** *slash, v.t.* to cut by striking with violence and at random: to make long cuts in: to slit so as to show lining or material underneath: to lash:

to criticise very harshly: to crack as a whip: to cut down, reduce drastically or suddenly (*coll.*): to clear by felling trees (*U.S.*).—*v.i.* to strike violently and at random with an edged instrument: to strike right and left.—*n.* a long cut: cut at random: a cut in cloth to show colours underneath: a stripe on a non-commissioned officer's sleeve: débris of trees (*U.S.*): a forest clearing, esp. cumbered with débris (*U.S.*).—*adj.* **slashed,** cut with slashes: gashed.—*ns.* **slash'er; slash'ing,** a slash or slashes: the felling of trees as a military obstacle: felled trees: a clearing.— *adj.* cutting mercilessly, unsparing: dashing: very big, slapping. [Perh. O.Fr. *esclachier,* to break; or conn. with **lash.**]

**slat,** *slat, v.t.* and *v.i.* to strike, beat: to flap.—*n.* a sudden sharp blow. [Poss. O.N. *sletta,* to slap, splash.]

**slat,** *slat, n.* a slate or roofing slab (*dial.*): a thin strip of wood, etc.—*adj.* **slatt'ed,** having, or composed of, slats. [O.Fr. *esclat.*]

**slate,** *slāt, n.* a fine-grained argillaceous rock which by regional metamorphism has developed a cleavage along close-spaced planes independent of the bedding, usu. a dull blue, grey, purple, or green: a slab of this material (or a substitute) for roofing, or for writing upon: a preliminary list of candidates: slate-colour.—*adj.* of slate: slate-coloured, dull dark blue.—*v.t.* to cover with slate: to enter on a slate: to clear of fine hair with a slater: to note down for nomination or appointment (*U.S.*).—*adj.* **slat'ed,** covered with slates.—*ns.* **slat'er,** one who covers roofs with slates: a tool with slate blade for removing fine hair from hides: a wood-louse (*dial.*); **slat'iness; slat'ing,** covering with slates: a covering of slates: materials for slating.—*adj.* **slat'y,** of or like slate.—**slate'-axe,** a slater's sax; **slate'-club,** a society whose members make weekly contributions towards benefits against misfortune or towards getting Christmas cheer.—*adjs.* **slate'- coloured,** dull bluish grey approaching black; **slate'-gray, -grey,** of a light slate colour.—**slate'- pencil,** a cut or turned stick of soft slate, compressed slate-powder, or pyrophyllite, for writing on slate; **slate'-writer; slate'-writing,** mysterious production of writing on a covered slate; **slaty cleavage,** fissility like that of slate along planes independent of bedding.—**a slate loose,** a slight mental derangement; **clean slate** (see **clean**). [O.Fr. *esclate*; cf. **slat (2).**]

**slate,** *slāt, v.t.* to abuse: to review unsparingly: to bait with dogs (*dial.*): to set on (*dial.*).—*n.* **slā'ting.** [From the O.N. word answering to O.E. *slǣtan,* to bait.]

**slather,** *sladh'ər,* (*U.S. slang*) *n.* a large quantity.

**slattern,** *slat'ərn, n.* a slut, a dirty untidy woman. —*v.i.* **slatt'er** (*dial.*), to be untidy or slovenly.— *v.t.* (*dial.*) to spill, splash, slop about.—*n.* **slatt'ernliness.**—*adj.* **slatt'ernly,** sluttish.—Also *adv.*—*adj.* **slatt'ery** (*dial.*), sloppy: slovenly. [App. **slat** (1).]

**slaughter,** *slö'tər, n.* killing of animals, esp. for food: killing of great numbers: wanton or inexcusable killing, esp. of the helpless: carnage: butchery: bodies of the slain.—*v.t.* to make slaughter of.—*n.* **slaugh'terer.**—*adj.* **slaugh'- terous,** given to slaughter: destructive: murderous.—*adv.* **slaugh'terously.**—*n.* **slaugh'tery** (*rare*), slaughter: a slaughterhouse.—**slaugh'ter- house,** a place where beasts are killed for the market; **slaugh'terman,** a man employed in killing or butchering animals. [O.N. *slātr,* butchers' meat, whence *slātra,* to slaughter (cattle).]

**Slav,** *släv, n.* one whose language is Slavonic, i.e. belongs to that division of the Indo-Germanic tongues that includes Russian, Polish, Wendish, Czech, Slovak, Serbian, Slovenian, and Bulgarian.—*adjs.* **Slav, Slav'ic.**—*n.* **Slav'dom,** the

Neutral vowels in unaccented syllables: *el'ə-mənt*; for certain sounds in foreign words, see p. viii

Slavs collectively, the Slavonic world.—*v.t.* **Slav'ify**, to assimilate to the Slavs.—*n.* **Slavonia** (*slə-, slä-vō'ni-ə*), a region bounded by the Danube, Sava, and Drava.—*adj.* **Slavo'nian**, of Slavonia: Slav.—Also *n.*—*adj.* **Slavonic** (*-von'-ik*), of the group of languages indicated above, or the peoples speaking them.—*n.* the parent language of the Slavs or any of its descendants.—*v.t.* **Slavon'icise, -ize, Slavonise, -ize** (*slav'ən-īz*), to make Slavonic.—*adj.* **Slav'ophil(e)**, favourable or friendly to Slavs.—Also *n.*—*adj.* **Slav'ophobe**, hostile to Slavs. [Mediaeval L. *Sclavus*—Late Gr. *Sklabos*, from the stem of Slav *slovo*, word, *sloviti*, to speak; cf. **Slovene**.]

**slave**, *slāv*, *n.* a person held as property: an abject: one who is submissive under domination: one who is submissively devoted: one whose will has lost power of resistance: one who works like a slave, a drudge: a mechanism controlled by another mechanism: a master-slave manipulator.—*v.i.* to work like a slave: to drudge.—*v.t.* to enslave: to treat as a slave: perh. make subservient to his own views (*Shak.*; *King Lear* IV, i. 69).—*ns.* **slav'er**, a slave-trader: a ship employed in the slave-trade; **slav'ery**, the state of being a slave: the institution of ownership of slaves: drudgery; **slav'ey** (*slang*), a domestic drudge, a maid of all work.—*adj.* **slav'ish**, of or belonging to slaves: befitting a slave: servile: abject: servilely following or conforming: laborious.—*adv.* **slav'ishly**.—*ns.* **slav'ishness**; **slavoc'racy**, slave-owners collectively: their power, interests, etc.; **slav'ocrat**.—**slave'-ant**, an ant kept as a worker in a community of another species.—*adj.* **slave'-born**, born in slavery.— **slave'-driver**, one who superintends slaves at their work: a hard taskmaster; **slave'-fork**, a long and heavy forked branch fixed on a slave's neck to prevent escape.—*adj.* **slave'-grown**, grown by slave-labour.—**slave'-holder**, an owner of slaves; **slave'-holding**; **slave'-hunt**, a hunt after runaway slaves or after persons to enslave; **slave'-labour**; **slave'-owner; -owning; slave'-ship**, a ship used for transporting slaves.—*n.pl.* **slave'-states**, those states of the American Union which maintained domestic slavery before the Civil War—Delaware, Maryland, Virginia, North and South Carolina, Georgia, Florida, Alabama, Mississippi, Louisiana, Texas, Arkansas, Missouri, Kentucky, and Tennessee. —**slave'-trade, -traff'ic**, the buying and selling of slaves; **slave'-trader, -traff'icker**. [O.Fr. (Fr.) *esclave*, orig. a Slav.]

**slaver**, *slav'ər* (*Scot. slāv'ər*), *n.* spittle running from the mouth.—*v.i.* to let spittle run out of the mouth: to drivel: to fawn.—*v.t.* to beslobber. —*n.* **slav'erer**.—*adj.* **slav'ering**.—*adv.* **slav'eringly**. —*adj.* **slav'ery**, slabbery. [Akin to **slabber**.]

**Slavonian.** See **Slav**.

**slaw**, *slö*, *n.* cabbage salad. [Du. *sla*—*salade*.]

**slay**, *slā*, *v.t.* to kill:—*pa.t.* **slew** (*slōō*); *pa.p.* **slain** (*slān*).—*n.* **slay'er**. [O.E. *slēan*, to strike, to kill; O.N. *slā*, Goth. *slahan*, Ger. *schlagen*, to strike.]

**sleave**, *slēv*, *n.* (*Shak.*) a fine filament that can be separated from a silk fibre.—*v.t.* (*dial.*) to separate, as threads.—*adj.* **sleaved**, used in term **sleaved silk**, floss silk. [O.E. *slæfan*, to divide.]

**sleazy**, *slē'zi*, *adj.* flimsy: slatternly (*coll.*): squalid (*coll.*).—*n.* **slea'ziness**. [Origin doubtful.]

**sled**, *sled*, *n.* a sledge, esp. a small sledge: a drag or wheelless structure for conveying goods, formerly for taking the condemned to execution. —*v.t.* to convey by sled.—*v.i.* to go on a sled:— *pr.p.* **sledd'ing**; *pa.t.* and *pa.p.* **sledd'ed**.—*adj.* **sledd'ed** (*Shak.*), having sleds.—*n.* **sledd'ing**. [M.Du. or M.L.G. *sledde*; Ger. *schlitte*, O.N. *slethi*; cf. **sledge, sleigh, slide**.]

**sleded.** See **sleided**.

**sledge**, *slej*, *n.* carriage with runners for sliding on

snow: framework without wheels for dragging goods along: iron- or flint-studded board for threshing corn.—*v.t.*, *v.i.* to convey, or to travel, by sledge.—*ns.* **sledg'er**; **sledg'ing**.—**sledge'-chair**, chair on runners for ice. [M.Du. *sleedse*; cf. **sled**.]

**sledge**, *slej*, *n.* a large heavy hammer.—Also **sledge'-hammer**. [O.E. *slecg*—*slēan*, to strike, slay.]

**slee**, *slē*, Scots form of **sly**.

**sleech**, *slēch*, *n.* slimy mud: a mud-flat.—*adj.* **sleech'y**. [Origin uncertain.]

**sleek**, *slēk*, *adj.* smooth: glossy: having an oily, plastered-down look: insinuating, plausible: slick.—*v.t.* to make smooth or glossy: to calm or soothe.—*v.i.* to glide.—*adv.* smoothly, oilily.— *v.t.* **sleek'en**, to sleek.—*ns.* **sleek'er**, a slicker; **sleek'ing**.—*adj.* **sleek'it** (*Scot.*), smooth: sly, cunning, fair-spoken.—*adv.* **sleek'ly**.—*n.* **sleek'ness**.—*adj.* **sleek'y**, smooth: sly, untrustworthy. —*adj.* **sleek'-headed**.—*n.* **sleek'stone**, a polishing stone. [A later form of **slick**.]

**sleep**, *slēp*, *v.i.* to take rest by relaxation of consciousness: to slumber: to be motionless, inactive, or dormant: to appear still or restful: to take or have the nocturnal position (*bot.*): to be dead: to rest in the grave: to be numb: (of a top) to spin steadily without movement of the axis.—*v.t.* to be in the state of (with *sleep*, etc., as cognate object): to render, make, put, by sleep: to outsleep: to afford sleeping accommodation for:—*pa.t.* and *pa.p.* **slept** (*slept*).—*n.* the state of being asleep: a spell of sleeping: dormancy: vertical disposition of leaves at night (*bot.*).—*n.* **sleep'er**, one who sleeps: a horizontal beam supporting and spreading a weight: a support for railway rails: a sleeping-car: a compartment or berth in a sleeping-coach: a Communist (or other) agent who spends a long time (often years) establishing himself as an inoffensive citizen preparing for the moment when he will be required to pass on a particular vital piece of information.—*adj.* (*Scot.*) **sleep'(e)ry**, sleepy.— *adv.* **sleep'ily**.—*ns.* **sleep'iness**; **sleep'ing**, sleep: abeyance.—*adj.* in a state of, occupied with, or for, sleeping: dormant.—*adj.* **sleep'less**, without sleep: unable to sleep.—*adv.* **sleep'lessly**.—*n.* **sleep'lessness**.—*adj.* **sleep'y**, inclined to sleep: drowsy: inducing or suggesting sleep: partially decayed internally, esp. of a pear, soft and lacking juice.—**sleep'ing-bag**, a bag for sleeping in, used by travellers, campers, etc.; **sleep'ing-car, -carr'iage, -coach**, a railway-carriage with berths for sleeping in; **sleep'ing-draught**, a drink to induce sleep; **sleep'ing-part'ner**, one who has money invested in a business but takes no part in management; **sleep'ing-pill**, one containing a sleep-inducing drug; **sleep'ing-sick'ness**, a deadly disease of tropical Africa, characterised by headache, great drowsiness, and exhaustion, caused by a trypanosome introduced by the bite of a tsetse-fly: sometimes erroneously applied to sleepy-sickness; **sleep'-learn'ing** (see **hypnopaedia**); **sleep'-walk'er**, a somnambulist; **sleep'-walk'ing; sleep'y-head**, a lazy, or sleepy-looking person; **Sleepy Hollow**, a very quiet place, from *A Legend of Sleepy Hollow*, by Washington Irving; **sleep'y-sick'ness**, encephalitis lethargica: formerly applied to sleeping-sickness.—**on sleep** (*B.*), asleep; **sleep around**, to be sexually promiscuous; **sleep in** (*Scot.*), to oversleep; **sleep off**, to recover from by sleeping; **sleep on**, to consider overnight, postpone a decision; **sleep with**, to have sexual relations with. [O.E. *slǣpan* (vb.), *slǣp* (n.); Ger. *schlaf*, Goth. *slēps*.]

**sleet**, *slēt*, *n.* rain mingled with snow or hail.—*v.i.* to hail or snow with rain mingled.—*n.* **sleet'iness**. —*adj.* **sleet'y**. [Prob. an unrecorded O.E. (Anglian) *slēt*; Ger. *schlosse*, hail.]

**sleeve**, *slēv*, *n.* a covering for the arm: a tube into which a rod or other tube is inserted: a thin covering, container for a gramophone record: a wind-sock: a drogue.—*v.t.* to furnish with sleeves.—*adjs.* **sleeved,** with sleeves; **sleeveless,** without sleeves: futile, vain (see **errand**).— **sleeve'-board,** a board for ironing sleeves; **sleeve'-button,** a button or stud for the wristband or cuff; **sleeve'-dog,** a little dog that could be carried in the sleeve; **sleeve'-fish,** the squid; **sleeve'hand** (*Shak.*), a wristband; **sleeve'-link,** two buttons joined by a link for fastening a shirt-cuff; **sleeve'-nut,** a double-nut for attaching the joint-ends of rods or tubes; **sleeve(d) waistcoat,** a waistcoat with long sleeves, worn by porters, boots, etc.—**hang, pin,** (oneself, belief, etc.) **on a person's sleeve,** to rely, or make depend, entirely upon him, her: to attribute to him, her (*Milt.*): see also **pin; laugh in one's sleeve,** to laugh privately or unperceived; **up one's sleeve,** in secret reserve; **wear one's heart on one's sleeve** (see **heart**). [O.E. (Anglian) *slēfe* (W.S. *sliefe*).]

**sleezy.** Same as **sleazy.**

**sleided, sleded,** *slēd'id,* (*Shak.*) *adj.* app. irregular forms of **sleaved.**

**sleigh,** *slā, n.* (esp. in *U.S.* and *Canada*) a sledge.— *v.i.* to travel by sleigh.—*n.* **sleigh'ing.**—**sleigh'- bell,** a small bell attached to a sleigh or its harness. [Du. *slee.*]

**sleight** (*obs.* **slight**), *slīt, n.* cunning: dexterity: an artful trick: a juggling trick: trickery: a design, device, pattern (*Spens.*).—**sleight'-of- hand',** legerdemain.—Also *adj.* [O.N. *slœgth,* cunning, *slœgr,* sly.]

**slender,** *slen'dər, adj.* thin or narrow: slim: slight.—*adv.* **slen'derly.**—*n.* **slen'derness.** [Origin obscure.]

**slept,** *slept, pa.t.* and *pa.p.* of **sleep.**

**sleuth,** *slōōth, n.* a track or trail: a bloodhound: a relentless tracker, a detective.—*v.t.* and *v.i.* to track.—**sleuth'-hound,** a bloodhound: a detective. [O.N. *slōth,* track.]

**slew,** *slōō, pa.t.* of **slay.**

**slew, slue,** *slōō, v.t.* and *v.i.* to turn about the axis: to swing round.—*n.* a turn, twist, swing round: a position so taken.—*adj.* **slewed, slued,** tipsy. [First recorded as a sailor's word: origin unknown.]

**sley,** *slā, n.* a weaver's reed. [O.E. *slege*—*slēan,* to strike.]

**slice,** *slīs, n.* a thin broad piece: a flat or broad-bladed instrument of various kinds, esp. a broad knife for serving fish: a slash: a sliced stroke (*golf*): a share (*coll.*): a representative section. —*v.t.* to cut into slices: to cut a slice from: to cut as a slice: in golf, to strike or play so as to send the ball curving to the right (left in left-hand play).—*v.i.* to slash: to cut in the manner of slicing: (of a boat) to move through the water in such a manner: to slice a stroke.—*n.* **sli'cer.**—*n.* and *adj.* **sli'cing.** [O.Fr. *esclice*— O.H.G. *slīzan,* to split.]

**slick,** *slik, adj.* sleek: smooth: smooth-tongued: glib: adroit: trim.—*adv.* smoothly: glibly: deftly: quickly: altogether.—*n.* a smooth place or surface: a slicker: a film of spilt oil: a glossy magazine.—*v.t.* to polish, make glossy: to tidy up.—*v.t.* **slick'en,** to smooth, polish.—*ns.* **slick'er,** a smoothing tool: a waterproof, esp. oilskin (*U.S.*): a swindler: shifty person: a sophisticated city-dweller; **slick'ing.**—*adv.* **slick'ly.**—*n.* **slick'ness.**—**slick'enside** (*geol.*), a smooth, polished or striated surface produced by friction.—*adj.* **slick'ensided.**—**slick'stone,** a sleek-stone. [M.E. *sliken*—O.E. *slīcian,* (in composition) to smooth.]

**slid, slidden.** See **slide.**

**'slid, slid,** (*arch.*) *interj.* for **god's lid** (eyelid).

**slidder,** *slid'ər, v.i.* to slip, slide.—*n.* a steep path or trench down a hillside.—*adj.* **slidd'ery,**

slippery. [O.E. *slidor,* slippery, *sliderian,* to slip.]

**slide,** *slīd, v.i.* to slip or glide: to pass along smoothly: to glide in a standing position (without skates or snow-shoes) over ice or other slippery surface: to lapse: to pass quietly, smoothly, or gradually: to take its own course: to decamp (*coll.*).—*v.t.* to thrust along glidingly: to slip:—*pa.t.* **slid,** *obs.* **slid'ed,** *Scot.* **slade;** *pa.p.* **slid,** *obs.* **slid'ed,** *rare* **slidd'en.**—*n.* a slip: a polished slippery track (on ice): a chute or shoot: a bed, groove, rail, etc., on or in which a thing slides: a sliding part, e.g. of a trombone: a sliding clasp: a slip for mounting objects for the microscope: a case (*dark slide*) for photographic plates or its sliding cover: a picture for projection on a screen: a sliding lid: a sledge: a runner: a sliding seat: a landslip: a gliding from one note to another (*mus.*).—*ns.* **slid'er,** one who, or that which, slides: a sliding part: ice-cream between wafers (*Scot.*): a red-bellied terrapin.—*n.* and *adj.* **slid'ing.**—*adv.* **slid'ingly.**— **slide'-rest,** an apparatus for carrying the cutting-tool of a lathe, etc.; **slide'-rule,** a mechanical calculating device consisting of two logarithmic graduated scales sliding one against the other (also **slid'ing-rule**); **slide'-valve,** a valve in which openings are covered and uncovered by a sliding part; **slid'ing-keel,** a centreboard; **sliding scale,** a scale, e.g. of duties, varying according to variation in something else, e.g. prices: a slide-rule; **sliding seat,** a racing-boat seat, moving with the swing of the rower's body.—**let slide,** to take no action over. [O.E. *slīdan,* to slide.]

**'slife, slif, 'slight, slīt,** (*arch.*) *interjs.* for **God's life, light.**

**slight,** *slīt, adj.* smooth (*obs.*): flimsy: lacking solidity, massiveness, weight, significance: slim: slender: trifling: small: slighting (*obs.*).—*adv.* slightly: slightingly, meanly.—*v.t.* to smooth (*obs.*): to raze, level to the ground (*arch.*): to ignore or overlook disrespectfully: to insult: to toss contemptuously (*Shak.*).—*n.* contemptuous indifference: discourteous disregard: an affront by showing neglect or want of respect.—*adv.* **slight'ingly.**—*adj.* **slight'ish.**—*adv.* **slight'ly.**—*n.* **slight'ness.**—**slight off** (*Shak.*), to put off, set aside, with contempt; **slight over,** to ignore. [Cf. O.E. *eorthslihtes,* close to the ground; O.N. *slēttr,* O.L.G. *slicht,* plain, Du. *slecht,* bad, Ger. *schlecht,* bad.]

**slight,** old spelling of **sleight.**

**slily, sli'li,** *adv.* See under **sly.**

**slim, slim,** *adj.* very thin: slender: slight: crafty: —*comp.* **slimm'er,** *superl.* **slimm'est.**—*v.t.* to make thin.—*v.i.* to use means to become more slender:—*pr.p.* **slimm'ing;** *pa.t.* and *pa.p.* **slimmed.** — *adv.* **slim'ly.** — *n.* **slimm'ing.** — *adj.* **slimm'ish.**—*n.* **slim'ness.**—*adj.* **slim'sy** (*U.S.*), frail, flimsy. [Du., L.G., Fris. *slim,* crafty; Dan. *slem,* worthless, Ger. *schlimm,* bad; reintroduced from Cape Du.]

**slime, slīm, n.** ooze: very fine, thin, slippery, or gluey mud: bitumen: any viscous organic secretion, as mucus: matter, esp. as forming the human body: moral filth: obsequiousness: (in *pl.*) finely crushed ore in mud form.—*v.t.* to smear or cover with slime: to grind to slime: to clear of slime.—*v.i.* to go slimily.—*adv.* **slim'ily.** —*n.* **slim'iness.**—*adj.* **slim'y,** viscous: covered with slime: disgusting: obsequiously servile.— **slime'-fungus,** a myxomycete; **slime'-pit,** a hole where bitumen is got: a pit for receiving metallic slimes. [O.E. *slim;* Ger. *schleim.*]

**sling, sling, n.** a strap or pocket with a string attached to each end, for hurling a stone: a catapult: a ballista: a loop for hoisting, lowering, or carrying a weight: a hanging support for an injured arm or foot: an attached strap for carrying: a throw: a sweep or swing.—*v.t.* to throw with a sling: to hang loosely: to move or swing by means of a rope: to hurl, toss, fling (*coll.*): to utter, to pass (*slang*).—*v.i.* to discharge stones from a sling: to bound along with swinging steps:—*pa.t.* and *pa.p.* slung.—*n.* sling′er.—sling′-fruit, a fruit that ejects its seeds by elastic tissue; sling′shot (*U.S.*), a catapult; sling′stone, a stone to be thrown from a sling.— sling-back, -back(ed) shoe, one from which the back is absent except for a strap representing the top edge; sling ink, to write for the press; sling one's hook (*slang*), to go away, remove oneself. [Prob. from several sources; cf. O.N. *slyngva*, to fling, O.E. *slingan*, to wind, twist, L.G. *sling*, noose.]

sling, *sling*, *n.* an American drink, spirits and water sweetened and flavoured. [Perh. foregoing in sense of toss off; poss. Ger. *schlingen*, to swallow.]

slink, *slingk*, *v.i.* to go sneakingly: to miscarry.— *v.t.* to slip: to droop: to cast prematurely:— *pa.t.* and *pa.p.* slunk.—*n.* a prematurely born calf or other animal: its flesh or hide: a bastard child: a slinking gait.—*adj.* prematurely born: lean, starved: mean.—*n.* slink′er.—*adj.* slink′y, slinking: lean: sinuous: close-fitting.—slink′butch′er, a dealer in slink and diseased meat; slink′skin, the skin of a slink, or leather made from it; slink′weed, rose-bay willow herb or other plant believed to cause cows to slink. [O.E. *slincan*; L.G. *slinken*; Ger. *schlinken*.]

slip, *slip*, *v.i.* to escape: to pass quietly, easily, unobtrusively, or stealthily: to glide: to get out of position accidentally: to slide, esp. accidentally: to lose one's former skill, grip, or control of the situation (*coll.*): to lose one's footing: to make a slight mistake from inadvertence rather than ignorance: to lapse morally.—*v.t.* to cause or allow to slide: to put with a sliding motion: to convey quietly or secretly: to let pass: to let slip: to cast: to disengage: to let loose: to escape from: to elude: to cast prematurely, slink: to dislocate:—*pr.p.* slipp′ing; *pa.t.* and *pa.p.* slipped, sometimes slipt.—*n.* act of slipping: a mistake from inadvertence: a slight error or transgression: an escape: an inclined plane, sloping down to the water: a slight dislocation: a landslip: a pillow-case: a garment easily slipped on, esp. one worn under a dress: a leash: the difference between the pitch of a propeller and the distance actually travelled: a fielder or (often in *pl.*) position on the off side somewhat behind the batsman (*cricket*): a sledge-runner: (in *pl.*) the place at the side of the stage for slipping scenery from: the side of a theatre gallery.—*adj.* slipp′er (*Spens.*, *Shak.*), slippery.—*n.* a loose shoe easily slipped on: a skid for a wheel: a sledge-runner: one who slips (e.g. greyhounds).—*v.t.* to furnish with slippers: to beat with a slipper.—*adj.* slipp′ered.—*adv.* slipp′erily.—*ns.* slipp′eriness, slipp′iness.—*adjs.* slipp′ery, slipp′y, so smooth or slimy as to allow or cause slipping: elusive: evasive: apt to slip: unstable: uncertain.—slip angle, attitude angle; slip′-board, a board sliding in grooves; slip′carriage, -coach, a railway carriage that can be left behind without stopping the train; slip′dock, a dock with a slipway; slip form (*building*), a form that can be moved slowly as work progresses (*adj.* slip′form); slipform paver, a machine for laying continuously a concrete road surface; slip′-knot, a knot that slips along a rope: a knot untied by pulling.—*adjs.* slip′-on, slip′-over, slipped on or over: slipped over the head without unbuttoning.—*ns.* a garment easily slipped on: one slipped over the head.— slipped disk (see disk); slipper animalcule, paramecium; slipper limpet, an American mollusc (Crepidula) with somewhat slipper-like shell; slipper satin, fine satin with a dull finish; slipp′er-

wort, calceolaria; slippery elm, a N. American elm: its mucilaginous bark used as a demulcent; slip′rail (*Austr.*), a movable rail serving as a gate: a gap so closed; slip road, a local bypass.—*adj.* slip′shod, shod with slippers, or with shoes down at the heel: slovenly.—slip′-shoe (*obs.*), a slipper; slip stream, slip′stream, the stream of air driven back by an aircraft propeller; slip′-string, a crack-halter.—Also *adj.*—slip′-up, an error or failure; slip′way, a pier in a dock or shipyard that slopes down into the water.—give one the slip, to escape stealthily from him, let slip, to reveal accidentally: slip off, to fall off: to take off quickly: go away quietly; slip on, to put on loosely or in haste; slip one's ways (*Scot.*), to make one's way quietly; slip the cable, to let it go overboard instead of waiting to weigh the anchor: to die; slip up, to make a mistake, to fail (*slang*): to deceive, disappoint (*Austr.*). [Perh. L.G. or Du. *slippen*; but O.E. has *slipor*, slippery, *slȳpescōh*, slipper.]

slip, *slip*, (*obs.*) *n.* a counterfeit coin. [Perh. slip (1).]

slip, *slip*, *n.* a scion, cutting: a scion, descendant: a young or slender person: a young pig (*dial.*, *Austr.*): a small sole (fish): a strip: nything slender or narrow: a small piece of paper, etc., for a memorandum, or for indexing, etc.: a galley-proof.—*v.t.* to take cuttings from: to tear obliquely (*her.*). [Perh. M.Du. or M.L.G. *slippe*, strip.]

slip, *slip*, *n.* a creamy paste for coating and decorating pottery. [O.E. *slipa*, *slypa*, slime, paste.]

slipe, *slip*, *n.* in mining, a skip or sledge: a runner. [App. L.G. *slipe*.]

slipslop, *slip′slop*, *n.* sloppy stuff: twaddle: a malapropism (from Mrs *Slipslop* in Fielding's *Joseph Andrews*): one who commits malapropisms: a loose sandal.—*adj.* slip′sloppy.

slish, *slish*, (*Shak.*) *n.* a cut. [slash.]

slit, *slit*, *v.t.* to cut lengthwise: to split: to cut into strips:—*pr.p.* slitt′ing; *pa.t.* and *pa.p.* slit.— *n.* a long cut: a narrow opening.—*adj.* cut lengthwise: cut open: having a slit.—*n.* slitt′er.— slit′-pockèt, an overcoat pocket with a slit to give access to a pocket within; slit′-trench (*mil.*), a narrow trench for one or more people. [M.E. *slitten*, app. related to O.E. *slītan*; Ger. *schlitzen*.]

slither, *slidh′ər*, *v.i.* to slide, esp. interruptedly. —*adj.* slippery.—*n.* a scree.—*adj.* slith′ery, slippery. [slidder.]

slive, *sliv*, (*dial.*) *v.t.* and *v.i.* to slip:—*pa.t.* slove, slived; *pa.p.* slived, sliven (*sliv′ən*). [Cf. O.E. *slēfan*, to slip (on).]

sliver, *sliv′ər*, or *sli′vər*, *v.t.* to split, to tear off lengthwise, to slice.—*n.* a piece cut or rent off, a slice, splinter: a continuous strand of loose untwisted wool or other fibre. [O.E. (*tō-*)*slifan*, to cleave.]

slivovitz, *sliv′ə-vitz*, *n.* a dry plum brandy.—Also slivovic(a), slivowitz. [Serbo-Croatian *sljivovica* —*sl(j)iva*, plum.]

sloan, *slōn*, (*Scot.*) *n.* a snub: a reproof. [Ety. dub.]

slob, *slob*, *n.* mud: ooze: mud-flat: a sloven: a boor (*slang*): a person of wealth but no refinement (*slang*).—*adj.* slobb′y.—slob′land, a mud flat: reclaimed alluvial land. [Ir. *slab*.]

slobber, *slob′ər*, *v.t.* and *v.i.* to slabber.—*adj.* slobb′ery. [Cf. Du. *slobberen*, to eat or work in a slovenly way; cf. slabber, slubber.]

slockdolager, -iger, -oger. See sockdologer.

slocken, sloken, *slok′n*, *slōk′n*, (*Scot.*) *v.t.* to quench: to slake: to moisten: to extinguish. [O.N. *slokna*, to go out.]

sloe, *slō*, *n.* the blackthorn fruit or bush.—*adj.* of blackthorn wood: made with sloes: black.— sloe′bush, sloe′-gin, a liqueur made from sloes;

**sloe'thorn, sloe'tree.** [O.E. *slā*, *slāg*, *slāh*; Du. *slee*.]

**slog,** *slog*, *v.t.* and *v.i.* to hit hard.—*v.i.* to work or walk doggedly.—*n.* a hard blow (generally with little regard to direction): a strenuous spell of work.—*n.* **slogg'er.**

**slogan,** *slō'gən*, *n.* a clan war-cry: a party catchword: an advertising catch-phrase. [Earlier **slog(h)orne, sloggorne;** said to be from Gael. *sluagh*, army, *gairm*, cry; see **slughorn(e).**]

**sloid.** See **sloyd.**

**sloom,** *slōōm*, (*Northern*) *n.* slumber.—*v.i.* to slumber.—*adj.* **sloom'y.** [O.E. *slūma*.]

**sloop,** *slōōp*, *n.* a light boat: a one-masted cutter-rigged vessel, differing from a cutter in having a fixed bowsprit and proportionally smaller sails: (also **sloop'-of-war**) formerly a vessel, of whatever rig, between a corvette and a gun vessel, under a commander, carrying from ten to eighteen guns. [Du. *sloep*; cf. **shallop.**]

**slop,** *slop*, *n.* slush: spilled liquid: a puddle: (in *pl.*) liquid refuse: (in *pl.*) weak or insipid liquor or semi-liquid food: (in *pl.*) gush, wishy-washy sentiment.—*v.t.* and *v.i.* to spill: to splash with slops: to slobber.—*v.t.* to wash away.—*v.i.* to walk in slush:—*pr.p.* **slopp'ing;** *pa.t.* and *pa.p.* **slopped.**—*adv.* **slopp'ily.**—*n.* **slopp'iness.**—*adj.* **slopp'y,** wet: muddy: wishy-washy, watery: slipshod (of work or language): sentimental: maudlin.—**slop'-basin, -bowl,** a basin for slops at table; **slop'-pail,** a pail for removing bedroom slops. [O.E. (*cū-*)*sloppe*, (cow-)droppings (cowslip)—*slūpan*, to slip.]

**slop,** *slop*, *n.* a loose garment—gown, cassock, smock-frock, etc.: (in *pl.*) wide baggy trousers or breeches: the wide part of these: (in *pl.*) ready-made clothing: (in *pl.*) clothes and bedding issued to seamen.—*adj.* **slop'-built,** jerry-built.—**slop'-clothing; slop'-pouch; Sloppy Joe** (*slang*), a large, loose sweater; **slop'-seller; slop'-shop,** a shop for ready-made clothes; **slop'work,** the making of slop-clothing: cheap inferior work. [Cf. O.E. *oferslop*, loose outer garment; M.Du. *slop*; O.N. *sloppr*.]

**slop,** *slop*, *n.* a policeman. [Back-slang.]

**slope,** *slōp*, *n.* an incline: an inclined surface: an inclined position: an inclination, upward or downward slant.—*adj.* slanting (*poet.*): moving aslope (*Milt.*).—*adv.* aslant.—*v.t.* to form with a slope, or obliquely: to put in a sloping position: to turn downwards, bow.—*v.i.* to have or take a sloping position or direction: to move down a slope: to decamp, disappear (*slang*).—*adv.* **slope'wise,** obliquely.—*adj.* **slop'ing.**—*adv.* **slop'ingly.**—*adj.* **slop'y,** sloping.—**at the slope,** (of a rifle) on the shoulder with the barrel sloping back and up; **slope arms,** to place or hold in this position; **slope off** (*slang*), to go away, esp. suddenly or furtively. [Aphetic from **aslope.**]

**slops.** See **slop** (1 and 2).

**slosh,** *slosh*, *n.* slush: a watery mess: a heavy blow (*slang*).—*v.i.* to flounder or splash in slush: to loaf around (*U.S.*): to hit (*slang*).—*v.t.* to splash: to smite, beat (*slang*).—*adjs.* **sloshed** (*coll.*), intoxicated; **slosh'y.** [**slush.**]

**slot,** *slot*, *n.* a bar or bolt: a cross-piece that holds other parts together. [L.G. or Du. *slot*, lock.]

**slot,** *slot*, *n.* the hollow down the middle of the breast, cleavage (now *Scot.*): a long narrow depression or opening, as one to receive a coin, an armature winding, or part of a mechanism, or opening into the conduit of an electric or cable tramway or railway: a slit: a (usu. regular) place or position in e.g. a radio or television programme: a niche in an organisation.—*v.t.* to make a slot in, furnish with a slot: to pass through a slot: to put into a slot.—**slot'-machine', -me'ter,** one operated by inserting a coin in a slot; **slott'ing-machine',** machine for cutting slots.—**slot-car racing,** racing on a track by tiny model cars powered and controlled electrically. [O.Fr. *esclot*.]

**slot,** *slot*, *n.* track, esp. a deer's footprints.—*v.t.* to track. [O.Fr. *esclot*—O.N. *slōth*; cf. **sleuth.**]

**sloth,** *slōth*, or *sloth*, *n.* laziness, sluggishness: a sluggish arboreal tropical American edentate.—*v.t.* and *v.i.* to pass, spend (time) in sloth.—*adj.* **sloth'ful,** given to sloth: inactive: lazy.—*adv.* **sloth'fully.** — *n.* **sloth'fulness.** — **sloth'-bear,** a black Indian bear, with prolonged snout and lips. [M.E. *slawthe*, altered from O.E. *slǣwth*—*slāw*, slow.]

**slouch,** *slowch*, *n.* an awkward lubberly clown: an inefficient person (*U.S.* slang): a slouch-hat: a droop: a stoop: a loose, ungainly stooping gait.—*adj.* drooping.—*v.i.* to go or bear oneself slouchingly: to droop.—*v.t.* to turn down the brim of.—*n.* **slouch'er.**—*adjs.* **slouch'ing; slouch'y.** —**slouch'-hat,** a soft, broad-brimmed hat.—*adj.* **slouch'-hatt'ed.** [Cf. O.N. *slōka*, a slouching fellow.]

**slough,** *slow*, *n.* a hollow filled with mud: a marsh: (*slōō*) a backwater, a marshland creek (*U.S.*).—*adj.* sloughed (*slowd*), bogged, swallowed in a slough.—*adj.* **slough'y.** [O.E. *slōh*.]

**slough,** *sluf*, *n.* a cast skin: a coating: dead tissue in a sore.—*v.i.* to come away as a slough (with *off*): to cast the skin: to develop a slough.—*v.t.* to cast off, as a slough.—*adj.* **slough'y.** [M.E. *sloh*; origin uncertain.]

**Slovak,** *slō'vak*, *slō-vak'*, *n.* a member of a Slavonic people living E. of the Czechs: their language.—Also *adj.*—*adjs.* **Slovakian** (*-vak'*, *-vāk'*), **Slovak'ish.** [Slovak *Slovák*.]

**sloven,** *sluv'n*, *n.* a person, esp. a man, carelessly or dirtily dressed or slipshod in work.—Also *adj.* —*adj.* **slov'enlike.**—*n.* **slov'enliness.**—*adj.* and *adv.* **slov'enly.**—*n.* **slov'enry** (*Shak.*), slovenliness. [Cf. *n.*Du. *slof, sloef*, L.G. *sluf*, slow, indolent.]

**Slovene,** *slō-vēn'*, *n.* a member of a branch of the Southern Slavs found chiefly in Styria, Carinthia, Carniola, and Istria.—Also *adj.*—*n.* and *adj.* **Slove'nian.** [O.Slav. *Slovēne*.]

**slow,** *slō*, *adj.* not swift: late: behind in time: not hasty: not ready: not progressive: dull.—*n.* anything that is slow.—*adv.* slowly (also in compounds).—*v.t.* to delay, retard, slacken the speed of.—*v.i.* to slacken in speed.—*adj.* **slow'ish.** —*n.* **slow'ing,** a lessening of speed.—*adv.* **slow'ly.** —*n.* **slow'ness.**—**slow'back,** a lazy lubber; **slow'coach,** a laggard: a sluggish person.—*adjs.* **slow'-foot, -ed,** slow of pace; **slow'-gait'ed** (*Shak.*), accustomed to walk slowly.—**slow'-match,** a slowly burning rope for firing explosives. —*adj.* **slow'-mo'tion,** much slower than normal or (*cinematograph*) actual motion.—*adjs.* **slow'-mov'ing; slow'-paced.**—**slow'poke,** an irritatingly slow person.—*adjs.* **slow'-sight'ed; slow'-winged.**—**go slow, go-slow, go slow with** (see **go**); **slow down,** to slow (*n.* **slow'-down**). [O.E. *slāw*; Du. *slee*, O.N. *sljōr*.]

**slow-hound,** *slō'hownd*, *n.* app. a form of **sleuth-hound,** assimilated to **slow.**

**slow-worm,** *slō'wûrm*, *n.* the blindworm, a harmless snakelike legless lizard. [O.E. *slāwyrm*, prob. from root of *slēan*, to strike, *wyrm*, worm, assimilated to **slow.**]

**sloyd, sloid, sloid,** *n.* a Swedish system of manual training by woodwork. [Sw. *slöjd*, dexterity; cf. **sleight.**]

**slub, slubb,** *slub*, *v.t.* to twist after carding to prepare for spinning.—*n.* a roving.—*ns.* **slubb'er;** **slubb'ing.**

**slub,** *slub*, *n.* a lump in yarn.—*adj.* lumpy.—*adj.* **slubbed.** [Origin obscure.]

**slubber,** *slub'ər*, *v.t.* to smear, soil, daub: to perform hurriedly and carelessly, slur over: to gobble.—*v.i.* to wallow.—*n.* **slubberdegull'ion,** a sloven.—*n.* and *adj.* **slubb'ering.**—*adv.* **slubb'eringly.** [Du. *slobberen*, to lap, L.G. *slubbern*.]

**sludge**, *sluj*, *n*. soft mud or mire: half-melted snow: a slimy precipitate, as from sewage.—*adj.* **sludg′y**, miry: muddy. [Cf. **slush**.]

**slue**. Same as **slew**.

**slug**, *slug*, *n.* a heavy, lazy fellow: a land-mollusc with shell rudimentary or absent: a sea-slug: anything slow-moving.—*v.i.* to be inert: to go sluggishly: to hunt for slugs.—*v.t.* to make sluggish.—*n.* **slugg′ard**, one habitually inactive. —Also *adj.*—*v.t.* **slugg′ardise, -ize,** (*Shak.*) to make lazy.—*adj.* **slugg′ish,** habitually lazy: slothful: slow: inert.—*adv.* **slugg′ishly.**—*n.* **slugg′ishness.**—**slug′-a-bed, slugg′abed** (*Shak.*), one who lies long abed. [Cf. Norw. dial. *slugg,* a heavy body, *sluggje,* a slow heavy person, Sw. dial. *slogga,* to be sluggish.]

**slug**, *slug*, *n.* a lump of crude ore (*mining*): a lump of metal, esp. one for firing from a gun: a bullet: a solid line of type cast by a composing machine (*print.*): the gravitational unit of mass, approx. 32·174 pounds (=14·5939 kg.) in the slug-foot-second system (47·88 kg. in slug-metre-second reckoning): a quantity of liquor that can be swallowed in one gulp. [Perh. conn. with foregoing or following.]

**slug**, *slug*, *v.t.* and *v.i.* to slog: to fling heavily.— Also *n.*—**slug′fest** (Ger. *fest,* festival, celebration), a match, struggle, characterised by heavy blows. [Cf. **slog**.]

**slughorn(e)**, *slug′hörn*, *n.* an old form of **slogan**: by Chatterton (followed by Browning) imagined to be a musical instrument not unlike a hautboy, or a kind of clarion.

**sluice**, *slōōs*, *n.* a structure with a gate for stopping or regulating flow of water: a floodgate or water-gate: a regulated outlet or inlet: a drain, channel: a trough for washing gold from sand, etc.: a sluicing.—*v.t.* to let out or drain by a sluice: to wet or drench copiously: to wash in or by a sluice: to flush or swill by flinging water: to dash.—*adj.* **sluic′y,** streaming as from a sluice: sluice-like: soaking.—**sluice′-gate.** [O.Fr. *escluse* (Fr. *écluse*)—L.L. *exclūsa* (*aqua*), a sluice, i.e. (water) shut out, pa.p. of L. *exclūdĕre,* to shut out.]

**sluit**, *slü′it, slōot,* (*S.Afr.*) *n.* a narrow water-channel.—Also **sloot**. [Du. *sloot,* ditch.]

**slum**, *slum,* *n.* an overcrowded squalid neighbourhood.—*v.i.* to visit slums, esp. for pleasure.—*ns.* **slumm′er; slum′ming.**—*adj.* **slumm′y.** [Cant.]

**slum**, *slum,* *n.* the non-lubricating part of crude oil.

**slumber**, *slum′bər,* *v.i.* to sleep, esp. lightly: to be negligent or inactive.—*v.t.* to pass in slumber.— *n.* light sleep: repose.—*n.* **slum′berer.**—*adj.* **slum′berful.** — *n.* and *adj.* **slum′bering.** — *adv.* **slum′beringly.**—*adjs.* **slum′berless; slum′b(e)rous,** inviting or causing slumber: sleepy.—*adv.* **slum′b(e)rously.**—*adjs.* **slum′bersome; slum′b(e)ry,** sleepy, drowsy.—**slum′berland,** the state of slumber. [M.E. *slūmeren*—O.E. *slūma,* slumber.]

**slump**, *slump,* *v.i.* to fall or sink suddenly into water or mud: to fail or fall through helplessly: (of prices, trade, etc.) to fall suddenly or heavily: to flop, clump: to plump.—*n.* a boggy place: a sinking into slush, etc.: the sound so made: a sudden or serious fall of prices, business, etc.— opp. to **boom**.—*adj.* **slump′y,** marshy. [Cf. Norw. *slumpe,* to slump, plump, L.G. *schlump,* marshy place.]

**slump**, *slump,* (*Scot.*) *v.t.* to throw into a lump or mass, to lump.—*v.i.* to flow lumpily.—*n.* a gross amount, a lump.—**slump sum,** a lump sum. [Cf. L.G. *slump,* Du. *slomp,* mass.]

**slung**, *pa.t.* and *pa.p.* of **sling**.—**slung′-shot,** a weight attached to a cord, used as a weapon.

**slunk**, *pa.t.* and *pa.p.* of **slink**.

**slur**, *slûr,* *n.* thin mud (*dial.*): an aspersion, stain, imputation of blame: disparagement: discredit

to one's reputation: a slight: a gliding movement in dancing (*obs.*): a gliding throw in cheating with dice (*obs.*): a blur: a running together resulting in indistinctness in writing or speech: a smooth or legato effect (*mus.*): a curved line indicating that notes are to be sung to one syllable, played with one bow, or with a smooth gliding effect.—*v.t.* to smear, besmirch (*dial.*): to disparage, asperse: to slip glidingly out of the dice-box (*obs.*): to cheat (*obs.*): to glide over slyly so as to mask or to avert attention: to blur: to sound indistinctly: to sing or play legato: to go through perfunctorily:—*pr.p.* **slurr′ing;** *pa.t.* and *pa.p.* **slurred.**—*adj.* **slurred.**— *n.* **slurr′y** (*slur′i*), thin paste, semi-fluid mixture. [Origin obscure, perh. different words that have run together.]

**slurb**, *slûrb,* *n.* an area combining the appearance and qualities of a slum and a suburb. [**slum**, **suburb**.]

**sluse**, a Miltonic spelling of **sluice**.

**slush**, *slush,* *n.* liquid mud: melting snow: a protective coating for metal: worthless sentimental drivel or gush.—*v.t.* to splash or cover with slush: to sluice, wash by throwing water: to fill the joints of with mortar (with *up*).—*v.i.* to splash in slush.—*adj.* **slush′y.** [Cf. **slosh**.]

**slut**, *slut,* *n.* a dirty, untidy woman: a wench, a jade: a bitch, female dog: a greased rag used as a candle.—*adj.* **slutt′ish.**—*adv.* **slutt′ishly.**—*ns.* **slutt′ishness, slutt′ery.** [Cf. Ger. dial. *schlutt(e)*.]

**sly**, *slī,* *adj.* expert (*obs.* or *dial.*): cunningly made (*obs.*): skilful in doing anything so as to be unobserved: cunning: wily: secretive: surreptitious: done with artful dexterity: with hidden meaning: illicit (*Austr.*):—*compar.* **sly′er;** *superl.* **sly′est.**—*adj.* **sly′ish.**—*adv.* **sly′ly** (or **sli′ly**).—*n.* **sly′ness.**—**sly′boots,** a sly or cunning person or animal.—**on the sly,** surreptitiously. [O.N. *slægr;* cf. **sleight**; cf. Ger. *schlau*.]

**slype**, *slip,* *n.* a passage between walls: esp. a covered passage from a cloister between transept and chapterhouse. [Perh. **slip**.]

**smack**, *smak,* *n.* taste: a distinctive or distinguishable flavour: a trace, tinge: a mere tasting: enough to taste.—*v.i.* to have a taste: to savour. [O.E. *smæc*.]

**smack**, *smak,* *n.* a small decked or half-decked coaster or fishing-vessel, usu. rigged as cutter, sloop, or yawl. [Du. *smak;* Ger. *schmacke*.]

**smack**, *smak,* *v.t.* to strike smartly, to slap loudly: to kiss roughly and noisily: to make a sharp noise with, as the lips by separation: to taste with relish or with smacking sound.—*v.i.* to make such a sound.—*n.* a sharp sound: a crack: a slap: a hearty kiss.—*adv.* sharply, straight.—*n.* **smack′er** (*slang*), a £1 note: a kiss.—*n.* and *adj.* **smack′ing.** [Prob. imit.; Du. or L.G. *smakken,* to smite, Ger. *schmatzen,* to smack.]

**smaik**, *smāk,* (*Scot.*) *n.* a contemptible fellow, rascal.

**small**, *smöl,* *adj.* slender: narrow: fine in grain, texture, gauge, etc.: slight: little in size, extent, quantity, value, power, importance, or degree: unimposing, humble: ungenerous, petty: dilute: short of full standard: operating on no great scale: soft or gentle in sound: minor.—*n.* a small thing, portion or piece: the narrow part (as of the back, the leg): small-coal: (in *pl.*) small-clothes: (in *pl.*) underclothes: (in *pl.*) at Oxford, the examination called Responsions (answering to Little-go at Cambridge: a size of roofing slate, 12 × 8 inches (305 × 203 mm.).— *adv.* in a low tone: gently: in small pieces: on a small scale: but slightly (*Shak.*).—*v.t.* and *v.i.* to make or become small.—*adj.* **small′ish.**—*n.* **small′ness.**—**small ads,** classified advertisements; **small′-ale,** ale with little malt and unhopped; **small′-and-earl′y** (*coll.; Dickens,* etc.), informal evening party; **small′-arm** (commonly in *pl.*), a weapon that can be carried by a man; **small beer** (see **beer**); **small capitals** (*coll.* **small caps**), capital letters of the height of lower case.—*n.pl.* **small'-clothes**, knee-breeches, esp. those of the close-fitting 18th-century form.—**small'-coal**, coal in small pieces; **small'-craft**, small vessels generally.—*n.pl.* **small'-debts**, in Scotland debts up to £20, recoverable in the Sheriff Court.—**small'-hand**, writing such as is ordinarily used in correspondence; **small'holder**; **small'holding**, a holding of land smaller than an ordinary farm: esp. one provided by a local authority: the working of such.—*n.pl.* **small'-hours**, hours immediately after midnight.—**small lady**, a size of roofing slate, 14 × 12 inches (356 × 305 mm.).—*adj.* **small'-mind'ed**, petty.—*n.pl.* **small'-pipes**, the Northumberland bagpipe.—**small'pox**, (orig. *pl.*) a contagious, febrile disease, characterised by pock eruptions; **small screen**, television (*adj.* **small'-screen**); **small'-sword**, a light thrusting sword for fencing or duelling: **small'-talk**, light or trifling conversation.—*adj.* **small'-time** (*slang*), unimportant.—*n.pl.* **small'-wares**, small articles such as tape, braid, buttons, hooks: trifles—**by small and small** (*Shak.*), little by little; **feel small**, to feel insignificant; **in a small way**, with little capital or stock: unostentatiously; **in small**, on a small scale; **in the smallest** (*Shak.*), in the least; **look small**, to look silly: be snubbed; **small-tooth comb**, comb with row of fine teeth on each side: arrangement for minute investigation (*fig.*); **the small print**, (place where) important information (is) given inconspicuously. [O.E. *smæl*; Ger. *schmal*.]

**smallage.** *smöl'ij*, *n.* wild celery. [**small**, Fr. *ache*—L. *apium*, parsley.]

**smalm.** See **smarm**.

**smalt.** *smölt*, *n.* glass coloured with cobalt oxide: its powder, used as a pigment: its deep blue colour: smalto.—*adj.* deep blue.—*ns.* **smalt'ite**, a cubic mineral, cobalt arsenide; **smalto** (*smöl'tō*; It. *zmäl'tō*), coloured glass or enamel for mosaic work: a cube of it. [It. *smalto*—O.H.G. *smalzjan* (Ger. *schmelzen*), to melt.]

**smaragd,** *smar'agd*, *n.* the emerald.—*adj.* **smarag'-dine** (-*din*,-*dēn*,-*din*), emerald green.—*n.* **smarag'-dite**, a green amphibole. [L. *smaragdus*—Gr. *smaragdos*.]

**smarm,** *smärm*, **smalm,** *smäm*, *v.t.* and *v.i.* to smear, daub, plaster: to sleek.—*v.i.* to fawn ingratiatingly and fulsomely: to be unctuous.—*adv.* **smarm'ily**, **smalm'ily**—*adj.* **smarm'y**, **smalm'y**. [Origin obscure.]

**smart,** *smärt*, *v.i.* to feel a smart: to be punished.—*v.t.* to cause to smart.—*n.* quick, stinging pain: smart-money: a dandy.—*adj.* sharp and stinging: brisk: acute, witty: pert, vivacious: trim, spruce, fine: fashionable: keen, quick, and efficient in business: considerable (esp. *U.S.*).—*adv.* smartly.—*v.t.* **smart'en**, to make smart, to brighten (with *up*.).—*adv.* **smart'ly**.—*ns.* **smart'-ness**; **smart'y**, a would-be smart fellow.—**smart-Al'ick, -Al'eck**, a would-be clever person.—Also *adj.*—**smart'-money**, money paid by a recruit for his release before being sworn in: money paid for escape from any unpleasant situation or engagement: excessive damages: money allowed to soldiers and sailors for wounds; **smart'-tick'et**, a certificate granted to one entitled to smart-money; **smart'-weed**, waterpepper, from its acridity. [O.E. *smeortan*; Du. *smarten*.]

**smash,** *smash*, *v.t.* to shatter violently: to ruin: to strike overhand with great force (*lawn-tennis*): to dash violently.—*v.i.* to fly into pieces: to be ruined, to fail: to dash violently: to smash a tennis ball.—*n.* an act or occasion of smashing, destruction, ruin, bankruptcy: bad money (*slang*).—*ns.* **smash'er**, one who smashes: one who passes bad money (*slang*): anything great or extraordinary (*slang*): person of dazzling

charm (*slang*); **smash'ing**.—*adj.* crushing: dashing: strikingly good (*slang*).—*adj.* **smash-and-grab'**, effected by smashing a shop-window and grabbing goods.—**smash'-hit'** (*slang*), overwhelming success; **smash'-up**, a serious smash. [Imit; cf. Sw. dial. *smaske*, to smack.]

**smatch,** *smach*, *n.* smack, taste: tincture (*Shak.*): touch: smattering.—*v.i.* to smack, have a flavour.—*v.t.* to smack of. [**smack**.]

**smatter,** *smat'ər*, *v.i.* to talk superficially: to have a superficial knowledge: to dabble.—*v.t.* to talk or utter smatteringly: to dabble in.—*n.* a smattering.—*ns.* **smatt'erer**; **smatt'ering**, a scrappy, superficial knowledge.—*adv.* **smatt'-eringly**. [M.E. *smateren*, to rattle, to chatter; connections doubtful.]

**smear,** *smēr*, *n.* grease (*obs.*): a rub with, mark or patch of, anything sticky or oily: the matter so applied, esp. to a slide for microscopic study: a fine glaze for pottery: a slur.—*v.t.* to anoint: overspread with anything sticky or oily: apply as a smear: rub smearily: defame.—*adv.* **smear'ily**.—*n.* **smear'iness**.—*adj.* **smear'y**, sticky: greasy: ready to smear: showing smears.—**smear'-dab** (see **lemon** (2)); **smear tcst** (see **cytodiagnosis**). [O.E. *smeru*, fat, grease; Ger. *schmer*, grease; O.N. *smjör*, butter.]

**smeddum,** *smed'əm*, *n.* fine powder: spirit, mettle (*Scot.*). [O.E. *smed(e)ma*, *smeodoma*, fine flour.]

**smee,** *smē*, **smeath,** **smeeth,** *smēth*, *ns.* names for various ducks—smew, pochard, widgeon, pintail.

**smeech,** *smēch* (*S.W. dial.*), **smeek,** *smēk* (*Scots.*) forms of smoke, *n.*, *v.t.*, *v.i.*

**smegma,** *smeg'mə*, *n.* a sebaceous secretion, esp. that under the prepuce. [Gr. *smēgma*, -*atos*, soap.]

**smell,** *smel*, *n.* the sense by which gases, vapours, substances very finely divided, are perceived, located in the higher animals in the mucous membrane of the nose: the specific sensation excited by such a substance: a pleasant scent or (often) an unpleasant one: the property of exciting it: an act or instance of exercising the sense: a smack, savour, property of suggesting, intimation (*fig.*).—*v.i.* to affect the sense of smell: to have odour (esp. unpleasant), or an odour (of): to have or use the sense of smell: to have a savour, give suggestion (of something; *fig.*).—*v.t.* to perceive, detect, find, by smell: to take a smell at: to impart a smell to: to emit a smell of:—*pa.t.* and *pa.p.* **smelled** or **smelt**.—*ns.* **smell'er**; **smell'iness**.—*n.* and *adj.* **smell'ing**.—*adjs.* **smell'less**; **smell'y**, having a bad smell.—**smell'-feast**, a sponger; **smell'ing-bottle**, a bottle of smelling-salts or the like; **smell'ing-salts**, a preparation of ammonium carbonate with lavender, etc., used as a stimulant in faintness, etc.; **smell'-trap**, a drain-trap.—**smell a rat** (see **rat**); **smell at** (formerly **to**, **of**), to sniff at, take a smell at; **smell of**, to have the smell of: to savour of; **smell out**, to find out by prying: to detect by witchcraft (*S.Afr.*). [Very early M.E. *smel*, prob. O.E. but not recorded.]

**smelt,** *smelt*, *n.* a fish of or akin to the salmon family, with cucumber-like smell. [O.E. *smelt*.]

**smelt,** *smelt*, *v.t.* to melt in order to separate metal from ore.—*ns.* **smel'ter**; **smel'tery**, a place for smelting; **smelt'ing-fur'nace**, **-house**, **-works**. [Prob. M.L.G. or M.Du. *smelten*; cf. Norw. *smelta*, Sw. *smälta*.]

**smelt,** *smelt*, (*obs. slang*; *Scott*) *n.* a half-guinea. [Origin obscure.]

**smew,** *smū*, *n.* a small species of merganser. [Origin uncertain.]

**smicker,** *smik'ər*, (*obs.*) *adj.* beautiful: smirking, wanton.—*v.i.* to look amorously.—*n.* **smick'-ering**, an amorous inclination.—*adv.* **smick'ly**, amorously. [O.E. *smicer*, beautiful.]

**smicket**, *smik'it*, *n.* a smock. [Prob. dim.]

**smiddy**, *smid'i*, Scots form of **smithy**.

**smifligate**, *smif'li-gāt*. See **spiflicate**.

**smight**, a Spenserian spelling of **smite**.

**Smilax**, *smī'laks*, *n.* a genus of the lily family, mostly climbers with net-veined leaves, some yielding sarsaparilla. [Gr. *smilax*.]

**smile**, *smil* (*Shak.*, etc., also **smoile**, **smoyle**, *smoil*), *v.i.* to express amusement, slight contempt, favour, pleasure, etc., by a slight drawing up of the corners of the lips: to look joyous: to be favourable: to drink, esp. whisky (*slang*).—*v.t.* to render, drive, express, by smiling: to smile at (*Shak.*): also with cognate object.—*n.* act of smiling: the expression of the features in smiling: favour: a drink, a treat (*slang*).—*adjs.* **smile'ful**; **smile'less**.—*ns.* **smil'er**; **smil'et** (*Shak.*), a little smile.—*n.* and *adj.* **smil'ing**.—*adv.* **smil'ingly**.—*n.* **smil'ingness**, the state of being smiling.—**smile at**, to show amusement at, disregard of; **smile on**, to show favour to, be propitious to. [M.E. *smilen*; poss. from L.G.]

**snir, smirr.** See **smur**.

**smirch**, *smûrch*, *v.t.* to besmear, dirty: to sully.—*n.* a stain. [Earlier *smorch*, supposed to be from O.Fr. *esmorcher*, to hurt, influenced by **smear**.]

**smirk**, *smûrk*, *v.i.* to smile affectedly, smugly, or foolishly: to look affectedly soft.—*n.* an affected, smug, or foolish smile.—*adjs.* **smirk**, trim, spruce; **smirk'y**, simpering. [O.E. *smercian*.]

**smit**, *smit*, (*obs.* or *poet.*) *pa.t.* and *pa.p.* of **smite**.

**smit**, *smit*, *v.t.* (*Northern dial.*) to stain, taint, mark with ruddle, infect.—*n.* a stain (*obs.*): ruddle, a mark on sheep, infection (*Northern dial.*).—*adj.* (*Northern*) **smitt'le**, infectious. [O.E. *smittian*, to befoul, infect, intens. of *smitan*, to smear; **smitte**, spot.]

**smite**, *smit*, *v.t.* to strike: to beat: to kill: to overthrow in battle: to affect with feeling: to afflict.—*v.i.* to strike: to meet forcibly:—*pa.t.* **smōte** (*arch.* or *poet.* **smit**); *pa.p.* **smitt'en** (**smit**).—*n.* **smi'ter.**—**smite off,** to cut off. [O.E. *smitan*, to smear.]

**smith**, *smith*, *n.* one who forges with the hammer: a worker in metals: one who makes anything.—*v.t.* to forge: to fashion.—*v.t.* to do smith's work.—*ns.* **smith'ery**, a smithy: smith's work, smithing; **smithy** (*smidh'i*), a smith's workshop.—*v.t.* and *v.i.* to smith.—**smith'craft.** [O.E. *smith*; Ger. *schmied*.]

**smithers**, *smidh'ərz*, *n.pl.* shivers, small fragments.—*n.* **smithereens'** (with Irish dim. suffix). [Origin obscure.]

**Smithsonian**, *smith-sō'ni-ən*, *adj.* pertaining to James Macie *Smithson* (1765-1829), an Englishman, founder of a great scientific and cultural institution at Washington.—*n.* **smith'sonite** (*-sən-it*), calamine: also electric calamine.

**smitten**, *smit'n*, *pa.p.* of **smite**.

**smittle.** See **smit** (2).

**smock**, *smok*, *n.* a woman's shift, chemise (*arch.*): a smock-frock: a loose, protective garment, usu. of coarse cloth, worn by artists, etc.: a wench (*obs.*).—*v.t.* to clothe in a smock or smock-frock.—*n.* **smock'ing**, honeycombing, as on the yoke and cuffs of a smock.—*adj.* **smock'-faced**, pale-faced.—**smock'-frock**, an outer garment of coarse white linen formerly worn by farm-workers in the south of England; **smock'-race**, a race for the prize of a smock. [O.E. *smoc*.]

**smog**, *smog*, *n.* smoky fog.

**smoile, smoyle**, *smoil*, old forms of **smile**.

**smoke**, *smōk*, *n.* the gases, vapours, and fine particles that come off from a burning body: solid particles suspended in a gas: fumes: vapour: fog: a cloud or column of smoke: that which may be smoked—tobacco, a cigarette, or cigar (*coll.*): a spell of smoking: S. African brandy (**Cape smoke**): tear gas (*coll.*).—*v.i.* to exhale or emit smoke, vapour, dust, etc.: to reek: to send smoke in a wrong direction: to move like smoke: to dash along in a cloud of smoke, vapour, spray, or dust: to suffer (orig. at the stake), smart: to take into the mouth and puff out the smoke of tobacco or the like: to lend itself to, admit of, smoking.—*v.t.* to dry, scent, preserve, fumigate, suffocate, blacken, taint, drive, render by smoke: to take in and emit the smoke from: to scent out, suspect, have an inkling of (*arch.*): to observe (*arch.*): to quiz, ridicule (*arch.*): to thrash (*arch.*).—*adjs.* **smok'able**, fit to be smoked; **smoked**; **smoke'less**, emitting no smoke: containing little or no smoke.—*adv.* **smoke'lessly**.—*ns.* **smoke'lessness**; **smok'er**, apparatus for emitting smoke: one who smokes tobacco: a smoking-carriage or compartment: one who smoke-dries meat: a smoking-concert.—*adv.* **smok'ily**.—*n.* **smok'iness**.—*n.* and *adj.* **smok'ing**.—*n.* **smok'o**, **smoke-ho**.—*adj.* **smok'y**, giving out smoke: like smoke: coloured like or by smoke: filled, or subject to be filled, with smoke: tarnished or noisome with smoke: suspicious (*arch.*).—*n.* (*Scot.*) a smoked haddock.—**smoke abatement,** (measures directed to) reducing amount of smoke in the atmosphere of towns; **smoke'-ball**, a shell emitting smoke as a screen or to drive out an enemy; **smoke'-black**, lampblack; **smoke'-board**, a board suspended before the upper part of a fireplace to prevent the smoke coming out into the room; **smoke'-bomb**, a bomb that emits smoke on bursting; **smoke'-box**, part of a steam-boiler where the smoke is collected before passing out at the chimney; **smoke'-bush, -tree**, a sumach with light feathery or cloudlike panicles; **smoke'-consumer**, an apparatus for burning all the smoke from a fire.—*adj.* **smoke'-dried**.—*v.t.* **smoke'-dry**, to cure or dry by means of smoke.—**smoke'-helmet**, a head-covering for firemen or others who work in dense smoke; **smoke'-ho'** (*Austr.*), a break for a smoke during the working day; **smoke'-hole**, a fumarole: a hole for escape of smoke; **smoke'-house**, a building where meat or fish is cured by smoking, or where smoked meats are stored; **smoke'-jack**, a contrivance for turning a spit by means of an ascending current of air: a muddled brain; **smokeless fuel**, one authorised for use in a smoke control area; **smokeless zone** (*coll.*), a smoke control area.—*adj.* **smoke'proof**, impervious to smoke.—**smoke'-room; smoke'-sail**, a small sail hoisted to drive off the smoke from the galley; **smoke'-screen**, a cloud of smoke raised to conceal movements; **smoke'-stack**, a ship's funnel: a chimney.—*adj.* **smoke'tight**, impervious to smoke.—**smoke tunnel**, a wind tunnel into which smoke is put at certain points in order to make wind effects visible; **smoking cap, jacket**, a light ornamental cap or jacket formerly worn by smokers; **smoking carriage, compartment, room**, a railway-carriage, compartment, room, set apart for smokers; **smoking'-con'cert**, a concert at which smoking (euphemistically) is allowed; **smoky quartz**, Cairngorm stone.—**end, go up, in smoke**, (of e.g. hopes) to vanish: (of e.g. plan) to come to nothing; **like smoke**, very quickly; **sell smoke** (L. *fūmum venděre*, make empty promises), to swindle; **smoke control area**, one in which the emission of smoke from chimneys is prohibited; **smoke out**, to discover: to drive out of a hidng place by smoke or fire; **smoke-room story**, one unsuitable for telling elsewhere. [O.E. *smoca* (n.), *smocian* (vb.); Ger. *schmauch*.]

**smolder.** American spelling of **smoulder**.

**smolt**, *smōlt*, *n.* a young river salmon when it is bluish along the upper half of the body and silvery along the sides. [Orig. Scot.; see **smout**.]

**smooch**, *smōōch*, (*coll.*), *v.i.* to kiss, pet. [Origin uncertain.]

**smoor.** See smore.

**smoot,** *smōot,* (*slang*) *n.* a compositor who does odd jobs in various houses.—*v.i.* to work in this way. [Origin obscure.]

**smooth,** *smōodh, adj.* having an even surface: without roughness: evenly spread: glossy: hairless: of even consistency: slippery: gently flowing: easy: bland: fair-spoken.—*adv.* smoothly.—*v.t.* **smooth,** rarely **smoothe,** to make smooth: to free from obstruction, difficulty, harshness: to reduce from diphthong to simple vowel: to remove by smoothing: to calm, soothe: to blandish: to gloze over (often with *over*).—*v.i.* to become smooth: to flatter, blandish, behave ingratiatingly (also *v.t.* with *it, Shak.*).—*n.* a smooth place or part: an act of smoothing.—*v.t.* **smooth'en,** to make smooth.—*ns.* **smooth'er,** one who, or that which, smooths: a smoothing tool: a flattener (*obs.*); **smooth'ie** (*slang*), a plausible person.—*n.* and *adj.* **smooth'ing.**—*adj.* **smooth'ish.** —*adv.* **smooth'ly.**—*n.* **smooth'ness.**—*adj.* **smooth'-bore,** not rifled.—*n.* a gun with a smooth-bored barrel.—*adjs.* **smooth'-browed,** with unwrinkled brow; **smooth'-chinned,** beardless; **smooth'-coated,** not shaggy-haired.—**smooth dab** (see lemon (2)).—*adjs.* **smooth'-ditt'ied** (*Milt.*), set to words that smoothly fit the tune: or, poss., having a smooth ditty, or set of words; **smooth'-faced,** having a smooth face or surface: pleasant-looking: beardless: unwrinkled: plausible.— **smoothing iron,** a flatiron; **smoothing plane,** a small fine plane used for finishing.—*adjs.* **smooth'-leaved;** **smooth'-paced,** having a regular easy pace.—**smooth'pate.**—*adjs.* **smooth'-shod,** having shoes without spikes; **smooth'-spoken,** **smooth'-tongued,** conciliatory, plausible, flattering, or soft in speech. [O.E. *smōth* (usu. *smēthe*).]

**smörbröd, smørrebrød,** *smör'brōō, smær'brō, smær'ə-bræth, smör'ə-bröd,* (*Norw.* and *Dan.*) lit., bread and butter: hors d'œuvres served on slices of buttered bread. [Sw.]

**smore,** *smōr, smör, smoor, smōōr,* (*Scot.*) *v.t.* and *v.i.* to smother, suffocate: to put out (a fire, light).—*n.* smoor, smoke. [O.E. *smorian.*]

**smörgåsbord,** *smör'gas-börd,* Sw. *smær'gōs-bōörd, n.* a Swedish-style table assortment of hors d'œuvres and many other dishes to which one helps oneself. [Sw.]

**smorzando,** *smört-san'dō* (It. *zmort-sän'dō*), **smorzato, -sä'tō,** *adjs.* and *advs.* with a gradual fading away: growing slower and softer. [It.; ger. and pa.p. of *smorzare,* to tone down, extinguish.]

**smote,** *smōt, pa.t.* of smite.

**smother,** *smudh'ər, v.t.* to suffocate by excluding the air, esp. by a thick covering: to stifle: to envelop closely: to cover up thickly: to suppress: to conceal.—*v.i.* to be suffocated or suppressed: to smoulder.—*n.* smoke: thick floating dust: a smouldering fire or condition: a welter: suffocation.—*adj.* **smoth'ered.**—*ns.* **smoth'erer;** **smoth'eriness.**—*n.* and *adj.* **smoth'ering.**—*adv.* **smoth'eringly.**—*adj.* **smoth'ery,** tending to smother: stifling.—**smothered mate** (*chess*), checkmate by a knight, the king having been prevented from moving by the positions of his own forces; **smother'-fly,** an aphis. [M.E. *smorther*—O.E. *smorian,* to smother; cf. smore.]

**smouch,** *smowch,* (*dial.*) *n.* a smack, a hearty kiss. —*v.t.* to kiss, to buss. [Cf. Ger. *schmutz.*]

**smouch,** *smowch,* smous(**e**), *smowz, n.* a Jew (*obs. slang*): a pedlar (*S.Afr.*).—*v.i.* (*S.Afr.*) to trade as a pedlar.—*n.* smous'er (*S.Afr.*), a pedlar. [Afrik. *smous,* perh. from Heb. *sh'mū'ōth,* news.]

**smouch,** *smowch, v.t.* to filch.—*v.i.* to cheat.

**smouch,** *smowch, n.* a form of smutch, smudge.

**smoulder,** *smōl'dər, v.t.* to smother.—*v.i.* to burn slowly or without flame: to linger on in a suppressed or hidden state.—*n.* smother: smoulder-ing fire.—*n.* and *adj.* **smoul'dering.**—*adj.* **smoul'-dry** (*Spens.*). [M.E. *smolder;* origin obscure.]

**smout,** *smowt.* Same as smoot.

**smout, smowt,** *smowt, n.* Scots form of smolt: a small person or child.

**smoyle,** an old form of smile.

**smudge,** *smuj, n.* a smear: a blur: a rubbed blot. —*v.t.* to smear: to blur: to soil: to daub.—*n.* **smudg'er.**—*adv.* **smudg'ily.**—*n.* **smudg'iness.**— *adj.* **smudg'y.** [Cf. smutch.]

**smudge,** *smuj, n.* a choking smoke: fuel for obtaining smoke.—*v.t.* to fumigate with smoke. —*adj.* **smud'gy,** smoky. [Origin obscure.]

**smug,** *smug, adj.* neat, prim, spruce: smooth: sleek: affectedly smart: offensively self-complacent.—*n.* a smug person: an industrious student who does not take part in social activities (*university slang*).—*v.t.* to make trim.—*adv.* **smug'ly.** — *n.* **smug'ness.** — *adj.* **smug'-faced.** [Connection with L.G. *smuk,* trim, presents difficulty.]

**smug,** *smug,* (*slang*) *v.t.* to seize without ceremony: to steal: to hush up. [Origin obscure.]

**smuggle,** *smug'l, v.t.* to import or export illegally or without paying duty: to convey secretly.— *adj.* **smugg'led.**—*n.* **smugg'ler,** one who smuggles: a vessel used in smuggling.—*n.* and *adj.* **smugg'-ling.** [L.G. *smuggeln;* Ger. *schmuggeln.*]

**smuggle,** *smug'l, v.t.* to fondle, cuddle. [Origin obscure.]

**smur,** *smūr, smir(r), smir,* (*Scot.*) *n.* fine misty rain, —*v.i.* to drizzle, rain very finely.—*adj.* **smurr'y,** smirr'y.

**smut,** *smut, n.* soot: worthless or bad coal: a flake or spot of dirt, soot, etc.: a black spot: a disease of plants, esp. cereals, giving an appearance of soot: the fungus causing it: obscene discourse.—*v.t.* to soil, spot, or affect with smut: to become smutty.—*adj.* **smutt'ed.**— *adv.* **smutt'ily**—*n.* **smutt'iness.**—*adj.* **smutt'y,** stained with smut: affected with smut: obscene, filthy.—**smut'-fungus,** any member of the Ustilaginales, an order of Basidiomycetes, parasitic on plants, causing smut and bunt. [Cf. L.G. *schmutt;* Ger. *schmutz,* dirt.]

**smutch,** *smutch, v.t.* to smut: to sully.—*n.* a dirty mark: soot: grime: a stain. [Cf. smudge.]

**smytrie,** *smit'ri,* (*Scot.*) *n.* a collection of small things. [Cf. Flem. *smite.*]

**snab.** See snob.

**snack,** *snak, n.* a snap, bite (*dial.*): a share: a mere taste: a light repast.—*v.i.* to snap (*Scot.*): to share (*obs.*): to take a snack.—**snack'-bar, snack'-counter,** a place where light meals can be bought. [Cf. M.Du. *snacken,* to snap; snatch.]

**snaffle,** *snaf'l, n.* a jointed bit (less severe than the curb).—*v.t.* to put a snaffle on: to control by the snaffle: (the following meanings *slang;* also **snabb'le**) to arrest: to capture: to purloin: to get possession of.—**snaff'le-bit; snaff'le-bridle; snaff'le-rein; snaff'ling-lay,** the trade of highwayman. [Ety. dub.; cf. Du. *snavel,* Ger. *schnabel,* beak, mouth.]

**snafu,** *sna-fōō',* (*U.S. slang*) *n.* chaos.—*adj.* chaotic. [*situation normal—all fouled* (euphemism) *up.*]

**snag,** *snag, n.* a stump, as of a branch or tooth: a jag: a short tine: an embedded tree, dangerous for boats: hence a catch, a hidden obstacle or drawback: a caught thread in a stocking.—*v.t.* to catch on a snag: to tear on a snag: to hack so as to form snags: to clear of snags.—*adjs.* **snagged, snagg'y.** [Cf. O.N. *snagi,* peg.]

**snail,** *snāl, n.* any terrestrial or air-breathing gasteropod mollusc with well-developed coiled shell: extended to other shelled gasteropods and (*dial.*) to slugs: a sluggish person or animal: a snail-wheel: medick of various kinds (from its coiled pods).—*v.i.* to crawl, go very slowly (also *v.t.* with *it*).—*n.* **snail'ery,** a place where edible snails are bred.—*adj.* and *adv.* snail'-like.—*adj.* snail'y.—snail'-fish, the fish called sea-snail; snail'-flower, any flower pollinated by snails.—*adj.* snail'-paced.—snail'-shell.—*adj.* snail'-slow'. — snail'-wheel, a cam that controls the striking of a clock.—giant African snail, a 10-inch snail, a serious plant pest except in its place of origin, East Africa. [O.E. *snegl, snægl, snǣl.*]

'snails, *snālz*, (*obs.*) *interj.* for God's nails.

snake, *snāk*, *n.* a serpent, or member of the Ophidia, a class of elongated limbless (or all but limbless) scaly carnivorous reptiles, often venomous, with forked tongue, no eyelids or external ears, teeth fused to the bones that bear them: an ungrateful or treacherous person (in allusion to Aesop): a wretch, drudge: anything snakelike in form or movement: apparatus for blasting a passage through a mine-field.—*v.i.* to wind: to creep.—*v.t.* to drag.—*adj.* snake'like.—*advs.* snake'wise, in the manner of a snake; snāk'ily.—*n.* snāk'iness.—*adj.* snāk'ish. —*n.* snāk'ishness.—*adj.* snāk'y.—snake'bird, the darter: the wryneck; snake'bite, the bite of a venomous snake; snake'-charmer, one who handles snakes and sets them to perform rhythmical movements; snake'-cult, serpent-worship; snake'-dance, a religious dance of the Hopi Indians in which snakes are handled; snake'-eel, an eel without tail-fin; snake'-fence (*U.S.*), a worm-fence; snake'-fly, a neuropterous insect (Raphidia) with neck-like prothorax; snake'-oil, any substance or mixture without medicinal value but sold as medicine; snake'-pit (*fig.*), a mental hospital: a place, or circumstances, characterised by disordered emotions and relationships; snake'root, bistort, milkwort, Aristolochia, or other plant whose root has been thought good for snakebites; snake's'-head, fritillary; snake'stone, a fossil ammonite: a stone thought to cure snakebite; snake'weed, bistort; snake'wood, letterwood.—snake in the grass (*fig.*), one who injures furtively: a lurking danger. [O.E. *snaca.*]

snap, *snap*, *v.i.* to make a bite (often with *at*): to speak tartly in sudden irritation: to grasp (with *at*): to shut suddenly, as by a spring: to make a sharp noise: to go with a sharp noise: to break suddenly.—*v.t.* to bite suddenly: to seize, secure promptly (usu. with *up*): to answer or interrupt sharply (often with *up*): to shut with a sharp sound: to cause to make a sharp sound: to send or put with a sharp sound: to utter snappishly: to break suddenly: to take an instantaneous photograph of, esp. with a hand-camera:—*pr.p.* snapp'ing; *pa.t.* and *pa.p.* snapped.—*n.* an act, instance, or noise of snapping: a small catch or lock: an earring (*rare*): (in *pl.*) a kind of handcuffs: a share: a scrap: a whit: a snack: a crack: a gingerbread biscuit: a quick, crisp, incisive, epigrammatic quality in style: lively energy: a brief theatrical engagement (*slang*): an easy and profitable place or task: a sharper, a cheat: a riveter's or glass-moulder's tool: a snapshot: a sudden cold spell: a card game.— *adj.* sudden, unexpected: offhand: (of decision, judgment) taking, made, on the spot without deep consideration of all possibilities: snapping shut.—*adv.* with a snap.—*interj.* used in claiming cards from an opponent in the game of snap.—*n.* snapp'er, an animal that snaps: one who snaps or snaps up: the end of a whiplash (*U.S.*): (also schnapper) any fish of the family Lutianidae, akin to the basses: a highly esteemed food-fish of Australian and New Zealand waters, Pagrosomus, one of the sea-bream family.—*adv.* snapp'ily.—*n.* and *adj.* snapp'ing.—*adv.* snapp'ingly.—*adj.* snapp'ish, inclined to snap: quick and tart.—*adv.* snapp'ishly.—*n.* snapp'ishness.— *adj.* snapp'y, snappish: snapping: having the quality of snap: instantaneous.—*adj.* snap'-brim, having a brim that turns down springily.—

snap'dragon, plant (Antirrhinum) of the figwort family whose flower when pinched and released snaps like a dragon: Christmas game of snatching raisins out of burning brandy; snap'-link, link with a side opening closed by a spring; snapp'er-up' (*Shak.*), one who snaps up; snapp'-ing-tur'tle, a large American fiercely snapping fresh-water tortoise; snap'shooter; snap'-shooting; snap'shot, a hasty shot: an instantaneous photograph.—look snappy (*coll.*), to hurry; Scotch snap (see Scotch); snap into it, get going quickly; snap one's head, nose, off, to answer irritably and rudely; snap out of it, of a mood, habit, etc., to give it up at once. [Prob. Du. *snappen*, to snap; Ger. *schnappen.*]

snapha(u)nce, *snap'hāns*, *-hōns*, snaphaunch, *-hōnsh*, (*obs.*) *n.* a freebooter: a flintlock or a weapon with one: a spring catch or trap. [Cf. Du. *snapshaan*—*snappen*, to snap, *haan*, a cock.]

snapper, *snap'ar*, (*Scot.*) *n.* a stumble: a slip in conduct: a scrape.—*v.i.* to stumble. [Cf. Ger. dial. *schnappen*, to stumble.]

snapper. See snap.

snar, *snär*, (*Spens.*) *v.i.* to snarl. [Cf. Du. and L.G. *snarren.*]

snare, *snār*, *n.* a running noose for trapping: a trap: an allurement, temptation, entanglement, moral danger: a loop for removing tumours, etc.: a string stretched across the lower head of a side-drum.—*v.t.* to catch, entangle, entrap, in a snare: to remove with a snare.—*ns.* snar'er; snar'ing. —*adj.* snar'y.—snare'-drum, a side-drum. [O.E. *sneare* or O.N. *snara*; prob. partly from Du. *snaar* or L.G. *snare.*]

snark, *snärk*, *n.* an imaginary animal created by Lewis Carroll (1876).

snarl, *snärl*, *v.i.* to make a surly resentful noise with show of teeth: to speak in a surly manner.—*v.t.* to utter snarlingly.—*n.* an ill-natured growling sound: a snarling.—*n.* snar'ler.—*n.* and *adj.* snarl'ing.—*adj.* snarl'y. [snar.]

snarl, *snärl*, *n.* a knot: a tangle: a knot in wood.— *v.t.* to ensnare (*dial.*): to tangle: to raise with a snarling-iron.—*v.i.* to tangle.—*adj.* snarled.—*ns.* snar'ler; snar'ling.—snarl'ing-iron, -tool, a curved tool for raised work in hollow metal-ware. [snare.]

snash, *snash*, (*Scot.*) *n.* insolence, abusive language. —*v.i.* to talk impudently. [Prob. imit.]

snaste, *snāst*, (now *dial.*) *n.* a wick: a candle-snuff. [Origin obscure.]

snatch, *snach*, *v.t.* to seize suddenly: to pluck away quickly: to grab: to take as opportunity occurs.—*v.i.* to make a snap or seizure.—*n.* a snap (*Shak.*): a seizure or attempt to seize: a grab: a short spell: a fragment, as of song, verse: a snack: a catch (of the voice) (*Shak.*): a quibble (*Shak.*).—*n.* snatch'er.—*advs.* snatch'ily, snatch'ingly.—*adj.* snatch'y, irregular.— snatch'-block, a block with a side opening for the bight of a rope; snatch'-purse, -thief, a thief who snatches. [M.E. *snacchen*; poss. related to snack.]

snath, *snath*, snathe, *snādh*, snead, *snēd*, sneath, *snēth*, sned, *sned*, *n.* the curved handle or shaft of a scythe. [O.E. *snǣd*, a scythe handle, a slice.]

snazzy, *snaz'i*, (*slang*) *adj.* very attractive or fashionable: flashy. [Origin obscure.]

snead. See snath.

sneak, *snēk*, *v.i.* to go furtively or meanly, slink, skulk: to cringe: to behave meanly: to tell tales.—*v.t.* to pass furtively: to steal (*slang*).—*n.* a sneaking fellow: one who sneaks away: a sneaking thief: a tell-tale: a ball bowled along the ground (*cricket*).—*n.* sneak'er, one who, or that which, sneaks: a soft-soled shoe: a sand-shoe.—*adv.* sneak'ily.—*n.* sneak'iness.—*adj.* sneak'ing, mean, crouching: secret, underhand, not openly avowed: lurking under other feelings.—*adv.* sneak′ingly.—*adj.* sneak′ish, befitting a sneak.—*adv.* sneak′ishly.—*ns.* sneak′-ishness; sneaks′by, a sneak.—*adj.* sneak′y, sneaking.—sneak′-cup, in some editions of Shakespeare (1 *Hen. IV* III, iii. 99), probably a misreading of a blurred sneakeup (see sneak-up) in the first quartos, but by some taken to be a correction and explained as one who balks his cup, or a stealer of cups; sneak′-raid, a bombing or other raid made under conditions of concealment; sneak′-thief, a thief who steals through open doors or windows without breaking in; sneak′-up, a sneak, shirker, skulker. [Connection with O.E. *snican*, to crawl, is obscure.]

sneap, *snēp*, *v.t.* to nip, pinch: to put down, repress, snub.—*n.* a snub, check.—*adj.* sneap′ing (*Shak.*). [Earlier *snape*—O.N. *sneypa*.]

sneath. See snath.

sneb, snebbe. old forms of snib, snub.

sneck, *snek*, (*Scot.*) *n.* a latch: a door-catch.—*v.t.* to fasten with a sneck.—sneck′-drawer, one who lifts the latch: an insinuating or crafty person. —Also sneck′-draw—sneck′-drawing.—Also *adj.* [Cf. snack, snatch.]

sneck. See snick (1). sneck-up. See snick-up.

sned, *sned*, *v.t.* to cut: to lop: to prune. [O.E. *snǣdan*.]

sned. See snath.

sneer, *snēr*, *v.i.* to show cynical contempt by the expression of the face, as by drawing up the lip: to express such contempt in other ways: to grin (*obs.*).—*v.t.* to utter sneeringly: to sneer at (*obs.*): to render, drive, by sneering.—*n.* a sneering expression: an act of sneering.—*n.* sneer′er.—*n.* and *adj.* sneer′ing.—*adv.* sneer′ingly.—*adj.* sneer′y. [Perh. related to Fris. *sneere*, to scorn.]

sneesh, *snēsh*, (*Scot.*) *n.* a pinch of snuff: snuff. —*ns.* sneesh′in(g), sneesh′an, snuff: a pinch of snuff.—snee′shin-mull, a snuffbox. [Poss. sneeze, sneezing; or imit.; cf. snush.]

sneeze, *snēz*, *v.i.* to make a sudden, involuntary and audible expiration through the nose, due to irritation of the inner nasal membrane.—*n.* an act of sneezing.—*ns.* sneez′er; sneez′ing.—*adj.* sneez′y.—sneeze′-box (*slang*), a snuffbox; sneeze′weed, an American composite (Helenium); sneeze′wood, a S. African meliaceous timber tree (Ptaeroxylon), or its wood, whose sawdust causes sneezing; sneeze′wort, a species of yarrow (*Achillaea ptarmica*) once used as a substitute for snuff: white hellebore.—not to be sneezed at, not to be despised. [M.E. *snesen*, *fnesen*—O.E. *fnēsan*, to sneeze; Du. *niezen*.]

snell, *snel*, (*Scot.*) *adj.* keen, sharp, severe.—*adv.* snell′ly. [O.E. *snell*, active; Ger. *schnell*, swift.]

snell, *snel*, *n.* a short piece of hair, gut, etc., attaching a hook to a line.—*v.t.* to attach (a hook) to a line. [Origin obscure.]

snib, *snib*, (*Spens.*; *Scot.*) *n.* and *v.t.* Same as snub.

snib, *snib*, (*Scot.*) *n.* a small bolt: a catch for a window-sash.—*v.t.* to fasten with a snib. [Cf. L.G. *snibbe*, beak.]

snick, *snik* (Scott sneck, *snek*), *v.t.* to cut out, snip, nick: to deflect slightly by a touch of the bat (*cricket*).—*n.* a small cut: a glancing stroke in cricket. [Origin doubtful.]

snick, *snik*, *n.*, *v.t.*, and *v.i.* click. [Imit.]

snicker, *snik′ər*, *v.i.* to snigger: to nicker, neigh.— *v.t.* to say gigglingly.—*n.* a giggle. [Imit.; cf. nicker (1), snigger.]

snickersnee, *snik′ər-snē*, *n.* a large knife for fighting: fighting with knives (*obs.*).—*v.i.* (*obs.*) to fight with knives.—Also earlier snick-a-snee, snick and snee, snick (earlier stick) or snee. [App. Du. *steken*, to thrust, *snijen*, to cut.]

snick-up, snick up, *snik-up′*, (*Shak.*) *v.i.* used in imper., go hang.—Also sneck up.

snide, *snīd*, *adj.* sham: counterfeit: base: mean:

dishonest: derogatory in an insinuating way: showing malice.—Also *n.* [Ety. dub.]

sniff, *snif*, *v.t.* to draw in with the breath through the nose: to smell: to suspect or detect by smell or as if by smell.—*v.i.* to draw in air sharply and audibly through the nose: to draw up mucus or tears escaping into the nose: to smell tentatively: to express disapprobation with reticence by a slight sound in the nose: to snuffle.—*n.* an act or a sound of sniffing: a smell: a small quantity inhaled by the nose.—*n.* sniff′er.—*adv.* sniff′ily. —*n.* sniff′iness.—*n.* and *adj.* sniff′ing.—*adv.* sniff′ingly.—*v.i.* sniff′le, to snuffle slightly, to sniff.—*n.* sniff′ler, one who sniffles: a slight breeze.—*adj.* sniff′y, inclined to be disdainful.— *vs.i.* snift, to sniff, snivel: to blow out steam, etc.; snift′er, to snift.—*n.* a snift: (in *pl.*) stoppage of the nasal passages in catarrh: a dram (*slang*): a strong breeze.—*adj.* snift′y (*slang*), having a tempting smell: inclined to sniff in disdain.— snift′ing-valve, an air-valve of a cylinder, etc. [Imit.; cf. snuff.]

snig, *snig*, (*dial.*) *n.* a river-eel, esp. an immature (olive and yellow) eel.—*v.t.* to drag a load with chains or ropes.—*v.t.* snigg′er, to catch (salmon) with a weighted hook.—*v.i.* snigg′le, to fish for eels by thrusting the bait into their hiding places: to fish for salmon, etc., by striking with a hook.—*v.t.* to catch thus.—*n.* a baited hook.—*ns.* snigg′ler; snigg′ling. [Origin obscure.]

snigger, *snig′ər*, *v.i.* to laugh in a half-suppressed way, often offensively.—*v.t.* to say with a snigger.—*n.* a half-suppressed laugh.—*n.* snigg′erer. —*n.*, *adj.* snigg′ering.—*adv.* snigg′eringly. [Imit.]

snigger. See snig.

snip, *snip*, *v.t.* to cut as with scissors: to snatch, snap (*obs.*):—*pr.p.* snipp′ing; *pa.t.* and *pa.p.* snipped.—*n.* a small cut, as with scissors: a small shred: a slip, small slender or despicable person: a small piece: a notch, slit, or slash: the sound of a stroke of scissors: a white or light patch or stripe on a horse, esp. on the nose: a share: a tailor: a certainty: a bargain.—*ns.* snipp′er; snipp′et, a little piece snipped off: a scrap, as of literature, news; snipp′etiness.—*adj.* snipp′ety, trivial, fragmentary.—*n.* snipp′ing, a clipping.—*adj.* snipp′y, fragmentary: stingy: snappish.—*n.pl.* snips, hand-shears for sheet-metal.—snip′-snap′, the action or sound of scissors: quick snappy dialogue.—Also *adj.*, *adv.*, *interj.*, *v.i.*; snipp′er-snapper, a whipper-snapper. —snipt taffeta fellow (*Shak.*), one who goes about in slashed silk. [L.G. or Du. *snippen*; Ger. dial. *schnippen*.]

snipe, *snip*, *n.* a bird akin to the woodcock, with a long straight flexible bill, or other of its genus (Gallinago or Capella) or family (Scolopacidae): a fool or contemptible person (*Shak.*): a cigar or cigarette end (*U.S.*): a sniping shot:—*pl.* usu. snipe, of the bird, snipes, of species of the bird, and in other senses.—*v.i.* to shoot snipe, go snipe-shooting: to shoot at single men from cover.—*v.t.* to pick off by rifle-fire from (usu. distant) cover.—*ns.* snip′er; snip′ing.—*adj.* snip′y, snipe-like: snipe-beaked: frequented by snipe.—snipe′-fish, the trumpet-fish. [Prob. Scand.; the O.E. word is *snite*.]

snip-snap-snorum, *snip-snap-snō′rəm*, *-snō′*, *n.* a childish game of turning up cards. [L.G. *snipp-snapp-snorum*.]

snirt, *snirt*, *snûrt*, (*Scot.*) *n.* a smothered laugh.— *v.i.* snirt′le, to snicker. [Imit.]

snitch, *snich*, (*slang*) *n.* the nose: a fillip on the nose: an informer.—*v.i.* to inform, peach.—*v.t.* (*coll.*) to pilfer.—*n.* snitch′er, an informer: a handcuff.

snivel, *sniv′l*, *n.* mucus of the nose: a sniff: a hypocritical snuffle: cant.—*v.i.* to run at the nose: to sniff: to snuffle: to whimper: to cry, as a child.—*v.t.* to utter with snivelling:—*pr.p.*

sniv'elling; *pa.t.* and *pa.p.* sniv'elled.—*n.* sniv'eller.—*adjs.* sniv'elling; sniv'elly. [O.E. *snofl*,
mucus.]
snob, *snob*, *n.* a shoemaker, shoemaker's apprentice, cobbler (*coll.*; *Scot.* snab): a townsman
(*Cambridge slang*): a person of ordinary or low
rank (*obs.*): an ostentatious vulgarian (*obs.*): a
blackleg (*obs.*): one who makes himself ridiculous or odious by the value he sets on social
standing or rank, by his fear of being ranked too
low, and by his different behaviour towards
different classes.—*n.* snobb'ery, snobbishness:
snobbish behaviour.— *adj.* snobb'ish.— *adv.*
snobb'ishly.—*ns.* snobb'ishness; snobb'ism.—
*adj.* snobb'y.—*ns.* snob'ling, a little snob;
snoboc'racy, snobs as a powerful class; snobog'-
rapher; snobog'raphy, the description of snobs
and snobbery. [Orig. slang.]
snod, *snod*, (*Scot.*) *adj.* smooth, neat, trim, snug.—
*v.t.* to trim, set in order (with *up*):—*pa.t.* and
*pa.p.* snodd'ed, snodd'it. [Poss. conn. with O.N.
*snothinn*, bald.]
snoek. See snook (2).
snog, *snog* (*slang*), *v.i.* to embrace, kiss, indulge in
love-making.—Also *n.* [Origin obscure.]
snood, *snood*, *n.* a fillet for the hair, once in
Scotland the badge of virginity: revived in the
sense of a conspicuous net supporting the back-
hair: the hair-line, gut, etc., by which a fish-
hook is fixed to the line.—*v.t.* to bind, dress,
fasten, with a snood.—*adj.* snood'ed. [O.E.
*snōd*.]
snook, *snook*, snoke, *snōk*, (*Scot.*) snowk, *snowk*,
*v.i.* to snuff or smell about: to lurk, prowl about.
[Prob. Scand.]
snook, *snook*, *n.* one of several fishes—the cobia,
a robalo, a garfish, or (in S. Africa and now
elsewhere also snoek, *snoek*) the barracouta
(*Thyrsites atun*). [Du. *snoek*, pike.]
snook, *snook*, *snook*, *n.* the gesture of putting the
thumb to the nose, to express derision, defiance,
etc.—Also snooks.—to cock a snook, to make that
gesture. [Origin obscure.]
snooker, *snook'ər*, *n.* a variety of the game of
pool.—*v.t.* to render a direct stroke impossible
for: to get the better of, to vanquish: to upset.
[Origin obscure.]
snool, *snool*, (*Scot.*) *n.* one who submits tamely to
wrong or oppression.—*v.t.* to keep in subjection:
to snub.—*v.i.* to be tamely submissive. [Ety.
dub.]
snoop, *snoop*, (*slang*) *v.i.* to go about sneakingly,
to pry.—Also *n.*—*n.* snoop'er. [Du. *snoepen*, to
eat (*slily*).]
snoot, *snoot*, *n.* snout (*illit.*): the face (*U.S.*): an
expression of contempt.—*v.t.* to regard contemptuously.—Also *v.i.*—*n.* snoot'ful, enough
alcohol to make one drunk.—*adj.* snoot'y,
haughtily supercilious. [Cf. Du. *snuit*, snout,
face.]
snooze, *snooz*, *v.i.* to doze.—*n.* a nap.—*n.* snooz'er.
[Origin obscure; perh. orig. slang.]
snoozle, *snoo'zl*, *v.i.* to nuzzle.—*v.t.* to thrust
nuzzlingly. [Cf. snooze, nuzzle.]
snore, *snōr*, *snōr*, *v.i.* to breathe roughly and
hoarsely in sleep with vibration of uvula and
soft palate or of the vocal chords: to snort.—
*v.t.* to pass in snoring: to render by snoring.—
*n.* a noisy breathing of this kind.—*ns.* snōr'er;
snōr'ing. [Imit.: cf. snort.]
snorkel, *snōr'kl*. See schnorkel.
snort, *snōrt*, *v.i.* to force the air with violence and
noise through the nostrils, as horses: to snore
(*Shak.*).—*v.t.* to express by or utter with a snort:
to force out, as by a snort.—*n.* an act or sound of
snorting: a quick drink (*slang*): a submarine
that can stay long submerged.—*n.* snort'er, one
who snorts: anything characterised by extreme
force, esp. a gale (*coll.*).—*n.* and *adj.* snort'ing.
—*adv.* snort'ingly.—*adj.* snort'y, snorting:

inclined to snort (*coll.*): contemptuous and
ready to take offence.—snort'-mast, a ventilator
raised to allow a submarine to stay long under
water. [Imit.]
snot, *snot*, *n.* mucus of the nose: a mean fellow.—
*v.t.* to blow (the nose).—*v.i.* snott'er, to breathe
through an obstruction in the nostrils: to sob,
snuffle, blubber.—*n.* the wattles of a turkey-cock:
snot (*Scot.*).—*n.* snott'ery, snot, filthiness.—
snott'ily.—*n.* snott'iness.—*adj.* snott'y, like, or
foul with snot: superciliously stand-offish, with
nose in air: mean, of no importance.—*n.*
(*naval slang*) a midshipman.—*adj.* snott'y-
nosed. [O.E. *gesnot*; *snȳtan*, to blow the nose;
cf. Du. *snot*; allied to snout.]
snotter, *snot'ər*, *n.* the lower support of the sprit.
[Origin obscure.]
snout, *snowt*, *n.* the projecting nose of a beast, as
of a swine: any similar projection: a cigar or
cigarette (*slang*).—*v.t.* to furnish with a snout.—
*adjs.* snout'ed; snout'y, like a snout: snouted:
haughtily supercilious (see snooty). [M.E.
*snūte*, prob. from unrecorded O.E.; cf. Sw.
*snut*; Ger. *schnauze*, Du. *snuit*; also snot.]
snow, *snō*, *n.* atmospheric vapour frozen in crystalline form, whether in single crystals or aggregated
in flakes: a snowfall: any similar substance, as
carbonic acid snow (frozen carbon dioxide):
snowlike specks on the screen caused by electrical
interference (*TV*): a mass or expanse of snow:
a winter: anything white, as hair (*fig.*): a
white-fleshed variety of apple: linen, esp.
drying or bleaching (*slang*): cocaine, morphine,
heroin (*slang*).—*adj.* of snow.—*v.i.* to shower
snow: to fall as snow or like snow.—*v.t.* to
shower like snow: to strew as with snow:
to whiten, whiten the hair of (*fig.*): (with *up*,
*under*) to bury, block, shut in, overwhelm, with
snow or as if with snow.—*adv.* snow'ily.—*n.*
snow'iness.—*adjs.* snow'ish, resembling snow;
snow'less; snow'like; snow'y, abounding or
covered with snow: white, like snow: pure.—
snow'ball, a ball made of snow pressed hard
together: the guelder-rose: a round white pudding, cake, or sweetmeat: (ironically) a Negro,
chimney-sweep, etc.: something that grows like
a snowball rolled in snow, esp. a distribution of
begging letters, each recipient being asked to send
out so many copies.—*v.t.* to throw snowballs
at.—*v.i.* to throw snowballs: to grow greater
ever more quickly.—snow'-berry, white berry of
American shrub (*Symphoricarpos*) of the honeysuckle family: the shrub itself; snow'-bird, any
finch of the N. American genus Junco, white
underneath, familiar in winter: applied to
various other birds that appear in winter.—*adj.*
snow'-blind.—snow'-blind'ness, amblyopia caused
by the reflection of light from snow; snow'-
blink, a reflection from fields of snow, like ice-
blink; snow'-boot, a boot or overshoe for
walking in snow.—*adj.* snow'-bound, shut in,
prevented from travelling, by snow.—snow'-box,
a theatrical apparatus for representing a snowfall;
snow'-break, a melting of snow; snow'-broth,
melted or melting snow; snow'-bunt'ing, a
black-and-white (in summer partly tawny)
bunting of the Arctic regions, a winter visitor in
Britain; snow'cap, a cap of snow as on the
polar regions or a mountain-top.—*adjs.* snow'-
capped, -capt; snow'-cold, as cold as snow.—
snow'drift, a bank of snow drifted together by
the wind; snow'drop, a drooping white flower of
early spring, or the plant (*Galanthus nivalis*;
fam. Amaryllidaceae) that bears it: a military
policeman, from the white helmet worn (*U.S.*);
snow'-dropper (*slang*), a linen thief; snow'drop-
tree, fringe-tree: silver-bell or calico-wood
(*Halesia*), an American tree of the Styrax
family, with white bell-shaped flowers.—*n.pl.*
snow'-eyes, an Eskimo contrivance to prevent

snow-blindness—a piece of wood with slits.—
snow'fall, a quiet fall of snow: the amount
falling in a given time.—*adj.* snow'-fed, begun or
increased by melted snow, as a stream.—snow'-
field, a wide range of snow, esp. where permanent; snow'-finch, an Alpine bird like the snow-
bunting; snow'flake, a feathery clump of snow
crystals: a garden-plant (Leucojum) or its
flower like a big snowdrop: (also snow'fleck,
-flick) the snow-bunting; snow'-flea, a springtail; snow'-fly, a stone-fly or other insect found
on snow.—*n.pl.* snow'-goggles, goggles to guard
against snow-blindness: snow-eyes.—snow'-
goose, a white Arctic American goose; snow'-
guard, a board to keep snow from sliding off a
roof; snow'-ice, ice formed from freezing slush
or compacted snow; snow-in-summ'er, a white-
flowered garden mouse-ear chickweed; snow'-
leop'ard, the ounce; snow'line, the limit of
perpetual snow; snow'man', a great snowball
made in human form: abominable snowman (see
abominate); snow'mobile, a motorised sleigh;
snow'-plant, a red Californian saprophyte of the
wintergreen family (Sarcodes) appearing among
snow: the organism of red snow (see red);
snow'-plough, an implement for clearing snow
from roads and railways; snow'scape, a snowy
landscape; snow'-shoe, a long broad framework
strapped to the foot for walking on snow: a
ski (*obs.*).—*v.i.* to travel on snow-shoes.—*n.pl.*
snow'-spec'tacles, spectacles worn as a protection
against the glare of snow.—snow'storm; snow'-
water, water from melted snow.—*adj.* snow'-
white, as white as snow.—snow'-wreath, a
snowdrift; snowy owl, a great white owl of
northern regions.—snowed under with, overwhelmed with rapid accumulation of; snow-shoe
rabbit, a hare of Canada and U.S., white in
winter, brownish with white feet in summer;
snowed up, blocked or isolated by snow. [O.E.
*snāw;* Ger. *schnee,* L. *nix, nivis.*]
snow, *snō, n.* a vessel like a brig, with a trysail-mast.
[Du. *snaauw.*]
snub, *snub, v.t.* to rebuke: to take up, cut short,
rebuff, in a humiliating or mortifying manner: to
check: to bring to a sudden stop: to cut or break
short: to make snub:—*pr.p.* snubb'ing; *pa.t.*
and *pa.p.* snubbed.—*n.* an act of snubbing:
a check: a snub nose: (*Spens.* snubbe) a stub,
snag, knob.—*adj.* flat, broad, and turned up.—*n.*
snubb'er, one who snubs: a device for stopping
a rope: a shock-absorber.—*n.* and *adj.* snubb'ing.
—*adv.* snubb'ingly.—*adjs.* snubb'ish, snubb'y,
inclined to snub or check: somewhat snub.—
snubb'ing-post, a post for passing a rope round,
as to stop a boat or horse; snub nose, a short
turned-up nose.—*adj.* snub'-nosed. [O.N.
*snubba,* to chide, snub.]
snudge, *snuj,* (*obs.*) *v.i.* to be snug and quiet.
[Origin obscure.]
snudge, *snuj, v.i.* to save in a miserly way.—*n.* a
mean stingy fellow. [Origin unknown.]
snuff, *snuf, v.i.* to draw in air violently and noisily
through the nose: to sniff: to smell at anything
doubtfully: to take snuff.—*v.t.* to draw into the
nose: to smell, to examine, suspect, or detect by
smelling.—*n.* a powdered preparation of tobacco
or other substance for snuffing: a pinch of snuff
or act of snuffing: a sniff: resentment, huff.—*ns.*
snuff'er, one who snuffs; snuff'iness.—*n.* and *adj.*
snuff'ing.—*adj.* snuff'y, like, smelling of, soiled
with or showing traces of, snuff: touchy, huffy.—
snuff'box, a box for snuff (snuffbox bean, the
cacoon); snuff'-colour, -brown, a dark brown.—
*adj.* snuff'-coloured.—snuff'-dipper; snuff'-dipp-
ing, the Southern U.S. habit of rubbing the
gums and teeth with a wet stick dipped in snuff;
snuff'-mill, a factory or a hand-mill for grinding
tobacco into snuff: a snuff-mull; snuff'-mull, a
snuffbox (see mill); snuff'-paper (Scott; con-

*temptuous*), bank-notes; snuff'-spoon, a spoon
for taking snuff from a snuffbox; snuff'-taker;
snuff'-taking.—take it in snuff (*Shak.*), to take
offence; up to snuff, knowing, not likely to be
taken in. [M.Du. *snuffen;* Ger. *schnaufen,* to
snuff.]
snuff, *snuf, n.* a sooty ill-smelling knob on a wick:
a worthless or offensive residue: a heeltap.—*v.t.*
to remove the snuff from: to make brighter: to
put out as with snuffers (with *out*).—*n.* snuff'er
(in later use snuffers, or pair of snuffers), an
instrument like a pair of scissors for removing
snuffs from the wicks of candles, or of oil-lamps:
one with a cap-shaped part for extinguishing
candles: an attendant, esp. in a theatre, who
snuffed candles.—snuff'-dish, a dish or tray for
candle snuffs.—snuff it, snuff out (*slang*), to die.
[M.E. *snoffe;* connection with foregoing and with
L.G. *snuppen,* Ger. *schnappen,* is obscure.]
snuffle, *snuf'l, v.i.* to breathe hard or in an obstructed manner through the nose: to sniff: to
speak through the nose.—*v.t.* to sniff: to say or
utter nasally.—*n.* an act or sound of snuffling:
a snuffling tone: cant: (in *pl.*) an obstructed
condition of the nose.—*n.* snuff'ler.—*n.* and *adj.*
snuffling (*snuf'ling, snuf'l-ing*). [Freq. of snuff;
cf. snivel, and Du. *snuffelen,* Ger. *schnüffeln.*]
snug, *snug, adj.* lying close and warm: comfortable: sheltered: not exposed to view or notice:
in good order: compact: fitting close.—*n.* a
snuggery.—*v.i.* to lie close.—*v.t.* to make snug:
to stow aways nugly:—*pr.p.* snugg'ing; *pa.t.*
and *pa.p.* snugged.—*n.* snugg'ery, a snug
room or place, esp. a bar-parlour.—*v.i.* snugg'le,
to nestle.—*v.t.* to hug close: to wrap close.—
*adv.* snug'ly.—*n.* snug'ness. [Origin obscure.]
snush, *snush,* (*obs.*) *n.* snuff.—*v.t.* and *v.i.* (*obs.*) to
snuff. [Poss. imit.; cf. sneesh, Dan. and Sw.
*snus.*]
snuzzle, *snuz'l,* (*dial.*) *v.i.* to grub or root: to rub
or poke and sniff: to nuzzle. [Cf. nuzzle,
snoozle.]
so, *sō, adv.* merging in *conj.* or *interj.* in this, that,
or such manner, degree, or condition: to such an
extent: likewise: accordingly: well: therefore:
in due course, thereupon, thereafter: as: soever:
thus: for like reason: in a high degree: as has
been stated: provided: in case: in order (*coll.*):
be it: that will do: very good.—so'-and-so,
this or that person or thing: such-and-such a
person or thing: used to replace a descriptive
oath (*slang*): also *adj.*).—*adj.* so'-called, styled
thus—usu. implying doubt or denial.—so many,
such-and-such a number of; so much, such-and
such an amount: in such a degree: to such an
extent: such an amount (of): that amount of:
an equal amount.—and so forth, and so on, and
more of the same or the like: and the rest of it;
or so, or thereabouts; quite so, just as you have
said, exactly; so as, in such a manner as or that:
in order (with *to*) (*coll.*): if only, on condition
that; so far, to that, or to such an, extent,
degree, or point; so long!, so long as (see
long); so much as, as much as: even; so
much for, that disposes of: that is the end of:
no more of; so so (see so-so); so that, with the
purpose that: with the result that: if only; so
then, thus then it is, therefore; so to say, or
speak, if one may use that expression; so what
(see what). [O.E. *swā;* O.N. *svā,* Goth, *swa,*
Ger. *so.*]
so, soh, *sō.* See sol (2).
soak, *sōk, v.t.* to steep in a liquid: to drench: to
saturate: to draw through the pores: to bathe
thoroughly (*U.S.*): to beat, pummel, give it hot
(*slang*): to overcharge (*slang*).—*v.i.* to be steeped
in a liquid: to pass through pores: to drink to
excess, to guzzle: to soften by heating:—*pa.p.*
soaked, rarely soak'en.—*n.* process or act of
soaking: a drenching: a marshy place: a hard

drinker, a carouse.—*ns.* **soak'age**, soaking: liquid that has percolated; **soak'er**.—*n.* and *adj.* **soak'ing**.—*adv.* **soak'ingly**.—**soak'away**, a depression into which water percolates. [M.E. *soke*—O.E. *socian*, a weak vb. related to *sūcan*, to suck.]

**soap**, *sōp, n.* an alkaline salt of a higher fatty acid: esp. such a compound of sodium (*hard soap*) or potassium (*soft soap*), used in washing: smooth words, flattery (*slang*): money, esp. used for bribery and other secret political purposes (*U.S. slang*).—*v.t.* to rub with soap: to flatter.—*adv.* **soap'ily**.—*n.* **soap'iness**.—*adjs.* **soap'less; soap'y.** —**soap'-ball**, soap made into a ball, often with starch, as an emollient; **soap'-bark**, a S. American rosaceous tree (*Quillaja saponaria*), or its bark, used as soap; **soap'berry**, the fruit of *Sapindus saponaria*, or other species, used as soap, or the S. American tree yielding it: **soap'-boiler**, a maker of soap; **soap'-boiling; soap'box**, a box for packing soap: a wayside orator's improvised platform; **soap'-bubb'le**, a globe of air enclosed in a film of soap-suds; **soap'-dish; soap opera**, a broadcast serial chiefly concerned with the emotional involvement of the characters, orig. American and often sponsored by soap manufacturers; **soap'-root**, species of Gypsophila, Saponaria, and other plants whose roots can be used as soap; **soap'stone**, steatite, or French chalk, a compact kind of talc with soapy feel.— *n.pl.* **soap'-suds**, soapy water, esp. when frothy. —**soap'-test**, a test for determining hardness of water by amount of standard soap solution required to make a lather; **soap'-tree**, the soap-bark tree, the soapberry tree, or other yielding saponin; **soap'-work(s); soap'wort**, a tall herb (*Saponaria officinalis*, or other species) of the pink family, whose roots and leaves contain saponin. [O.E. *sāpe*; Du. *zeep*, Ger. *seife*.]

**soar**, *sōr, sör, v.i.* to mount high in the air: to fly aloft: to rise to a great height: to glide or skim high in the air: to glide in a rising current. —*v.t.* to reach, traverse, or accomplish in upward flight.—*n.* and *adj.* **soar'ing**.—*adv.* **soar'ingly**. [Fr. *essorer*, to expose to air, raise into air—L. *ex*, out, *aura*, air.]

**soar(e)**. See sore (2).

**sob**, *sob, v.i.* to catch the breath convulsively in distress or other emotion: to make a similar sound.—*v.t.* to utter with sobs: to bring by sobbing:—*pr.p.* **sobb'ing**; *pa.t.* and *pa.p.* **sobbed**.—*n.* a convulsive catch of the breath: any similar sound.—*n.* and *adj.* **sobb'ing**.—*adv.* **sobb'ingly**.—**sob'-sister** (*slang*), a woman (rarely, a man) who seeks to draw tears by writing, acting, etc.: a journalist who answers questions in a woman's magazine; **sob'-story**, a pitiful tale told to arouse sympathy; **sob'-stuff**, cheap and extravagant pathos, to stir tears: maudlin films or scenes. [Imit.]

**sobeit**, *sō-bē'it, conj.* provided. [so be it.]

**sober**, *sō'bər, adj.* not drunk: temperate, esp. in use of intoxicants: moderate: restrained: without excess or extravagance: serious: sedate: quiet in colour: sombre: sane, rational (*obs.*): poor, feeble (*Scot.*).—*v.t.* to make sober.—*v.i.* to become sober.—*v.t.* **so'berise, -ize,** to make sober. —*adv.* **so'berly**.—*ns.* **so'berness; sobriety** (*sō- or sə-brī'i-ti*), state or habit of being sober: calmness: gravity.—*adjs.* **so'ber-blood'ed**, staid; **so'ber-mind'ed**.—*ns.* **so'ber-mind'edness**, the state of being sober-minded: freedom from inordinate passion: calmness; **so'bersides**, a sedate and solemn person.—*adj.* **so'ber-suit'ed**, dressed in sad-coloured clothes. [Fr. *sobre*—L. *sōbrius*— *sē-*, apart, not, *ēbrius*, drunk.]

**sobole**, *sō'bōl,* **soboles**, *sob'ō-lēz,* (*bot.*) *n.* a creeping underground stem producing roots and buds.—*adj.* **sobolif'erous**, having soboles. [L.

*sobolēs, subolēs,* a shoot—*sub,* under, and the root of *alĕre,* to nourish, sustain.]

**Sobranje,** *sō-brän'ye, n.* the national assembly of Bulgaria.—Also **Sobran'ye**. [Bulg.]

**sobriquet,** *sō'brē-kā, n.* a nickname.—Also **soubriquet** (*sōō'*). [Fr. *sobriquet,* earlier *soubriquet.*]

**soc,** *sok,* (*law*) *n.* the right of holding a local court. —*ns.* **soc'age, socc'age,** tenure of lands by service fixed and determinate in quality; **soc'ager, soc'man, sōke'man,** a tenant by socage; **soke** (*sōk*), **soc:** a district under a particular jurisdiction; **soke'manry,** tenure by socage; **sōk'en,** a district under a particular jurisdiction. [O.E. *sōcn,* inquiry, jurisdiction.]

**so-called,** *sō'-köld, adj.* See under so.

**soccer,** *sok'ər,* (*coll.*) *n.* association football.

**socdolager, -iger, -oger.** See **sockdologer.**

**sociable,** *sō'shə-bl, adj.* inclined to society: companionable: favourable to social intercourse.— *n.* a four-wheeled open carriage with seats facing: a seat, tricycle, aeroplane, etc., for two persons side by side: a social (*U.S.*).—*ns.* **sociabil'ity, so'ciableness.**—*adv.* **so'ciably.**—*adj.* **social** (*sō'shl*), pertaining to life in an organised community: pertaining to welfare in such: growing or living in communities: pertaining to, or characterised by, friendly association: convivial: gregarious, sociable: pertaining to fashionable circles: sympathetic (*obs.*).—*n.* an informal party or gathering of club, church, etc.—*n.* **socialisā'tion, -z-,** act or process of socialising: process by which infants and young children become aware of society and their relationships with others.—*v.t.* **so'cialise, -ize,** to render social: to put on a socialistic footing.—*v.i.* (*coll.*) to behave in a sociable manner.—*ns.* **so'cialism,** theory, principle, or scheme of social organisation which places means of production and distribution in the hands of the community; **so'cialist,** an adherent of socialism.—Also *adj.*—*adj.* **socialist'ic.**—*adv.* **socialist'ically,** in a socialistic manner.—*ns.* **so'cialite** (*coll.*), one who has a place in fashionable society; **sociality** (*sō-shi-al'i-ti*), the quality or fact of being social: social relations, association, or intercourse: sociability: a social function or formality.—*adv.* **so'cially.**—*ns.* **so'cialness; so'cialty** (*-shi-āt; arch.*), an associate.—Also *adj.*—*adjs.* **so'ciātive,** expressing association; **soci'etal** (*-sī'*), pertaining to society, social; **societarian** (*sə-sī-i-tā'ri-ən*), of or pertaining to society or fashionable society: Fourieristic: socialist.—Also *n.*—*adj.* **soci'etary** (*-tər-i*).—*n.* **soci'ety,** fellowship, companionship: company: association: a community: the body of mankind, the fashionable world generally: a corporate body: any organised association.—*adj.* of fashionable society.—**social contract,** the voluntary agreement between individuals upon which an organised society, its rights, functions, and the relationships within it are founded; **social credit,** a movement stressing the element of unearned increment in the returns of industry and advocating the achievement of social wellbeing by the stable adjustment of production and consumption through monetary reform: (with *cap.*) a theory that the government should distribute national dividends in order to spread purchasing power and thus increase consumption (regarded as a benefit); **social evil,** any evil, such as intemperance, that affects society, esp. prostitution; **social insurance,** state insurance by compulsory contributions against sickness, unemployment, and old age; **social science,** sociology; **social security,** security against sickness, unemployment, old age; **social service,** welfare work; **Social War,** the war (90-88 B.C.) of Rome's Italian allies (*Socii*) against Rome for admission to Roman citizenship; **social whale,** the ca'ing whale;

society verse, vers de société.—socialism of the chair, professorial socialism, the doctrines of a school of political economists (c. 1872) in Germany whose aim was mainly to better the condition of the working-classes by factory-acts, savings-banks, insurance against sickness and old age, etc.; the alternative society, a better, more humane, form of society as envisaged by those who refuse to follow the ways of society as it is today; the Societies, the Cameronians organised from 1681 for maintenance of Presbyterianism. [L. socius, a companion.]

société anonyme, so-syā-tā a-no-nĕm, (Fr.) lit. anonymous society: joint-stock company.

Socinian, sō-sin'i-ən, adj. pertaining to or following, Laelius (1525-62) and Faustus (1539-1604) Socinus, uncle and nephew, Italian Unitarians.—Also n.—v.t. and v.i. Socin'ianise, -ize.—n. Socin'ianism.

socio-, sō'si-ō-, sō'shi-ō-, -si-o'-, -shi-o'-, in composition, (generally in hybrids) social.—n. so'ciogram (-gram), a chart representing personal interrelationships within a social group.—adjs. sociolog'ic, -al, pertaining to sociology: dealing solely with environmental factors in considering a human problem: social.—ns. sociol'ogism, a concept or explanation taking into consideration social factors only, disregarding others; sociol'ogist.—adj. sociologis'tic.—n. sociol'ogy, the study of the structure and functioning of human society.—adj. sociomet'ric.—ns. sociom'etry, the measurement of social phenomena: the study of personal interrelationships within a social group; so'ciopath.—adj. sociopath'ic.—n. sociop'athy, any of several personality disorders resulting in asocial or antisocial behaviour. [L. socius, a companion.]

sock, sok, n. a light shoe, worn by Roman actors of comedy (obs. except hist. and allusively) now, a short stocking.—sock'-suspender, a strap to support a sock.—pull up one's socks, to brace oneself for doing better. [O.E. socc—L. soccus.]

sock, sok, n. a ploughshare. [O.Fr. soc—Celt., Bret. souc'h, Gael. soc.]

sock-, sok, (dial. and slang) v.t. to thrust hard: to strike hard: to drub: (with it) to give a drubbing, or a blow (to a person).—n. a violent blow, esp. with the fist.—n.pl. socks, a beating. [Origin obscure.]

sockdologer, sok-dol'ə-jər, also soc-, sog-, slock-, -dolager, -doliger, (Amer. slang) n. a conclusive argument: a hard or decisive blow: anything very big, a whopper. [Cf. foregoing; perh. reminiscent of doxology as the closing act of a service.]

socker. Same as soccer.

socket, sok'it, n. a hollow into which something is inserted, as the receptacle of the eye, of a bone, a tooth, the shaft of an iron golf-club: the hollow of a candlestick: a stroke with the socket of a golf-club.—v.t. to provide with or place in a socket: to strike with the socket:—pr.p. sock'eting; pa.t. and pa.p. sock'eted.—adj. sock'eted. [O.Fr. soket, dim. of soc; see sock (2).]

sockeye, sok'i, n. the blueback salmon. [Amer. Ind. sukai, the fish of fishes, the native name on the Fraser River.]

socle, sō'kl, sok'l, (archit.) n. a plain face or plinth at the foot of a wall, column, etc. [Fr.,—It. zoccolo—L. socculus, dim. of soccus, a shoe.]

Socratic, -al, sō-krat'ik, -i-kl, adjs. pertaining to Socrates, the celebrated Greek philosopher (d. 399 B.C.), to his philosophy, or to his method of teaching, by a series of simple questions revealing to his interlocutors their own ignorance.—n. Socrat'ic, a follower of Socrates.—adv. Socrat'ically.—v.i. Socratise, -ize (sok', sōk'rə-tīz), to practise the Socratic method.

sod, sod, n. a turf, usu. one cut in rectangular shape: sward.—adj. of sod.—v.t. to cover with

sod.—adj. sodd'y, covered with sod: turfy. [M.L.G. sode; Ger. sode.]

sod, sod. See seethe.

sod, sod, (vulg.) n. abbrev. for sodomite—a term of abuse, affection, etc.

soda, sō'də, n. sodium oxide (Na₂O): sodium hydroxide (caustic soda): sodium carbonate, the soda of commerce (in powder form, anhydrous, soda-ash; in crystals, with water of crystallisation, washing-soda): sodium bicarbonate (baking-soda): soda-water (coll.): a drink made of soda-water with flavouring, ice-cream, etc. (U.S.).—adj. so'da, or of containing soda or sodium.—adj. sodaic (sō-dā'ik), containing, pertaining to, soda.—ns. so'dalite, a cubic mineral consisting of sodium aluminium silicate with chlorine; so'damide (-mid), a compound (NaNH₂) formed when ammonia gas is passed over hot sodium.—adj. so'dic.—n. so'dium, a bluish-white alkaline metal (Na; at. numb. 11), the base of soda.—so'da-fountain, apparatus for supplying, counter for serving, sodas, ice-cream, etc.; soda jerk(er) (U.S.), one who serves at a soda-fountain; so'da-lake', a lake containing and depositing much sodium salt; so'da-lime, a mixture of caustic soda and quicklime; so'da-scone', a scone made with baking-soda; so'da-wa'ter, water (now commonly without sodium bicarbonate) charged with carbon dioxide; sodium amytal, a salt (C₁₁H₁₇O₂N₂Na) used as a sedative and hypnotic; sodium lamp, a street lamp using sodium vapour and giving yellow light. [It. and L.L. soda; origin doubtful.]

sodain, sodaine, old spellings of sudden.

sodality, sō-dal'i-ti, n. a fellowship or fraternity. [L. sodālitās—sodālis, a comrade.]

sodden, sod'n, pa.p. of seethe.—adj. boiled (rare): soaked thoroughly: boggy: doughy, not well baked: bloated, saturated with drink.—v.t. and v.i. to make or become sodden: to soak.—n. sodd'enness.—adj. sodd'en-witt'ed (Shak.), heavy, stupid.

sodger. See soldier.

sodium. See soda.

Sodom, sod'əm, n. one of the 'cities of the plain' (see Gen. xviii, xix): any place of utter depravity (fig.).—n. Sodomite (-it), an inhabitant of Sodom: (without cap.) one who practises sodomy.—adjs. sodomitic (-it'ik), -al.—adv. sodomit'ically.—n. sod'omy, male homosexuality or copulation with an animal, imputed to the inhabitants of Sodom.—apple of Sodom (see apple).

soever, sō-ev'ər, adv. generally used to extend or render indefinite the sense of who, what, where, how, etc.

sofa, sō'fə, n. in the East, a raised portion of the floor forming a bench: a long upholstered seat with back and arms—formerly sō'pha.—sō'fa-bed, a piece of furniture serving as a sofa by day, a bed at night; so'fa-ta'ble, a narrow table with a flap at each end, used as a writing-table from c. 1790. [Ar. suffah.]

soffioni, sof-yō'nē, n.pl. volcanic steam-holes. [It.]

soffit, sof'it, n. a ceiling, now generally restricted to the ornamented underside of a stair, entablature, archway, etc. [It. soffitto—L. suffixus, pa.p. of suffigēre, to fasten beneath—sub, under, figēre, to fix.]

Sofi, Sofism. See Sufi, Sufism.

soft, soft, sŏft, adj. easily yielding to pressure: easily cut: easily scratched (min.): malleable: yielding: not rigorous enough: not loud: not glaring: diffused: weak in muscle or mind: out of training: of low penetrating power (of rays): smooth: pleasing or soothing to the senses: tender: mild: sympathetic: gentle: effeminate: gently moving: easy: free from calcium and magnesium salts, as water: bituminous, of coal:

unsized, of paper: rainy (*Scot.*): pronounced with a somewhat sibilant sound, not guttural or explosive: voiced or sonant: of silk, freed from natural gum: of drinks, non-alcoholic: apt to fall in price: of drug, not habit-forming in an obvious degree: of radiation, not highly penetrating.—*n.* a softy, a fool.—*adv.* softly: gently: quietly.—*v.t.* (*Spens.*) to soften.—*interj.* (also **soft** you) hold: not so fast.—*v.t.* **soften** (*sof'n*), to make soft or softer: to mitigate: to tone down, make less glaring or smoother.—*v.i.* to grow soft or softer.—*ns.* **softener** (*sof'nər*); **softening** (*sof'ning*).—*adj.* **soft'ish,** rather soft.— *n.* **soft'ling,** a weakling: an effeminate person: a soft object.—*adv.* **soft'ly.**—*adj.* (*Spens.*) soft: slack in enterprise.—*ns.* **soft'ness; soft'ty,** a silly person, a weak fool.—**soft'ball,** an American game similar to baseball, played on a smaller diamond with a soft ball.—*adjs.* **soft'billed; soft'-bod'ied.**—*v.t.* **soft'-boil'.**—*adjs.* **soft'-boiled,** boiled not long enough to be quite solid; **soft'-con'scienc'd** (*Shak.*), having a not very rigorous conscience.—**soft currency,** one unstable in value in the international money-market through fluctuation in its gold backing.—*adjs.* **soft'-finned,** without fin-spines; **soft'-foot'ed,** softly treading.—**soft'-goods** (*pl.*), cloth, and cloth articles, as opp. to *hardware,* etc.; **soft'-grass,** a worthless grass (*Holcus mollis* or other species) akin to oats; **soft'head,** a simpleton.—*adjs.* **soft'-head'ed; soft'-heart'ed,** tender-hearted; **soft'ly-spright'ed** (*Shak.*), tame-spirited.—**soft mark** (see mark); **soft meat,** regurgitated food given by pigeons to their young.—*adj.* **soft'-nosed,** of a bullet, with a tip that expands on striking.—**soft option,** an alternative that is easy to carry out, undergo, etc.; **soft palate,** the back part of the palate.—*adj.* **soft'-paste,** of porcelain, made of a paste of various kinds requiring less heat in firing than china-clay.—**soft pedal,** a pedal for reducing tone in the piano, esp. by causing the hammer to strike only one string (*una corda*).—*v.t.* and *v.i.* **soft'-ped'al,** to play with the soft pedal down: to subdue, tone down (*slang*).—**soft'-saw'der** (*U.S.*), flattery.—*v.t.* to flatter, blarney.—**soft sell,** selling or sale by preliminary softening up or other indirect method.—*adjs.* **soft'shell, -ed,** having a soft shell: moderate in policy or principles.—**soft'-shell,** a soft-shell crab, clam, or river-turtle: a moderate.—*adjs.* **soft'-shoe,** characteristic of or pertaining to a form of tap-dancing done in soft-soled shoes; **soft'-slow** (*Shak.*), soft and slow.—**soft soap,** potash soap: flattery: blarney. —*v.t.* **soft'-soap,** to rub or cover with soft soap: to flatter for some end.—*adj.* **soft'-spo'ken,** having a mild or gentle voice: affable: suave: plausible in speech.—**soft spot** (see spot); **soft thing,** an easy task: a snug job; **soft underbelly,** the vulnerable part; **software,** computer programmes, esp. general ones for routine operations: material recorded in microform; **soft'-wood,** timber of a conifer (also *adj.*).—**softening of the brain,** softening of brain tissues: marked deterioration of mental faculties (*coll.*); **soften up,** to lessen resistance in (*coll.*): to wear down by continuous shelling and bombing. [O.E. *softe, sēfte;* Du. *zacht,* Ger. *sanft.*]

**softa,** *sof'tə, n.* a Moslem theological student, attached to a mosque. [Turk. *sōfta.*]

**sog,** *sog, n.* a soft wet place.—*v.t.* and *v.i.* to soak.—*adj.* **sogged.**—*adv.* **sogg'ily.**—*n.* **sogg'-iness.**—*n.* and *adj.* **sogg'ing.**—*adj.* **sogg'y,** soaked: boggy: soppy: sultry: spiritless. [Ety. dub.]

**sogdolager, -iger, -oger.** See sockdologer.

**soger.** See soldier.

**sogged, soggy,** etc. See sog.

**soh.** See sol (1).

**so-ho,** *sō-hō', (Shak.) interj.* a form of call from a distance, a sportsman's halloo. [A.Fr.]

**soi-disant,** *swä-dē-zä, adj.* self-styled, pretended: would-be. [Fr.]

**soigné,** *fem.* **soignée,** *swa-nyä, adj.* well groomed. [Fr.]

**soil,** *soil, n.* the ground: the mould in which plants grow: the earth which nourishes plants: country.—*adj.* having soil.—*adj.* **soil'-bound,** attached to the soil.—**soil mechanics,** a branch of civil engineering concerned with the ability of different soils to withstand the use to which they are put; **soil science,** the study of the composition and uses of soil. [O.Fr. *soel, suel, sueil*—L. *solum,* ground.]

**soil,** *soil, n.* a wallowing-place (*obs.*): a watery place where a hunted animal takes refuge: dirt: dung: filth: sewage: a spot or stain.—*v.t.* to make dirty: to stain: to manure.—*v.i.* to take a soil: to tarnish.—*adj.* **soiled.**—*n.* **soil'iness** (*rare*), stain: foulness.—*n.* and *adj.* **soil'ing.**—*adj.* **soil'less,** destitute of soil.—*n.* **soil'ure,** stain: pollution.—*adj.* **soil'y.**—**soil'-pipe,** an upright discharge-pipe which receives the general refuse from water-closets, etc., in a building. [O.Fr. *soil, souil* (Fr. *souille*), wallowing-place.]

**soil,** *soil, v.t.* to feed on fresh-cut green food: to purge by so doing: to fatten.—*adj.* **soiled** (*Shak.* **soyled**). [O.Fr. *saouler—saol, saoul*—L. *satullus* —*satur,* full; or from **soil** (2).]

**soirée,** *swär'ā, swör'ā, n.* an evening party: an evening social meeting with tea, etc. [Fr.,—*soir,* evening—L. *sērus,* late.]

**soja.** See soy.

**sojourn,** *sō', so', su'jərn,* sometimes *-jûrn', v.t.* to stay for a day: to dwell for a time.—*n.* a temporary residence.—*ns.* **so'journer; so'journing, so'journment.** [O.Fr. *sojourner*—L. *sub,* under, *diurnus,* of a day—*diēs,* a day.]

**Sōka Gakkai,** *sō-kə gak'i,* Japanese Buddhist sect and political party, characterised by militant nationalism. [*Jap.,* value creating society.]

**soke, sokeman, socage.** See under soc.

**Sokol,** *sō'kol, n.* a Czech gymnastic club. [Czech, falcon, from their badge.]

**Sol,** *sol, n.* the sun personified, Helios or Phoebus: gold (*alch.*): the tincture or (*her.*): (without *cap.*; *sōl*), the Peruvian monetary unit (one-tenth of a libra), and formerly a coin bearing a sun with rays—*pl.* **soles** (*sō'läs*), **sols** (*sōlz*).—*adj.* **solar,** etc. (see below). [L. *sōl,* sun.]

**sol,** *sol, n.* the fifth nōte of the scale in sol-fa notation.—Also **so, soh** (*sō*). [See Aretinian.]

**sol,** *sol, n.* a colloidal suspension in a liquid: a solution of a difficulty (see ob).—*n.* **solā'tion,** liquefaction of a gel. [For solution.]

**sol,** *sol, n.* an old French coin, one-twentieth of a livre. [O.Fr. *sol* (now *sou*)—L. *solidus,* solid.]

**sola,** *sō-lä', interj.* a cry to a person at a distance.

**sola,** *sō'lə, n.* the hat-plant or spongewood, an Indian papilionaceous plant (Aeschynomene): its pithlike stems.—*adj.* of sola.—**sola** (often **solar**) **hat, helmet,** a topi of sola.—Also **sō'lah,** (*corr.*) **sōl'ar.** [Hindi *śolā.*]

**sola.** See solus.

**solace,** *sol'is, -əs, n.* consolation, comfort in distress: pleasure, amusement: a source of comfort or pleasure.—*v.t.* to comfort in distress: to console: to allay.—*v.i.* to take comfort.—*n.* **sol'acement.**—*adj.* **solacious** (*-ā'shəs; arch.*), giving solace. [O.Fr. *solas*—L. *sōlātium*—*sōlāri, -ātus,* to comfort in distress.]

**solan,** *sō'lan, n.* the gannet.—Also **soland, solan goose.** [O.N. *sûla.*]

**solander,** *sō-lan'dər, n.* a box in the form of a book, invented by the Swedish botanist Daniel *Solander* (1736-82).

**solano,** *sō-lä'nō, n.* a hot south-east wind in Spain. [Sp.,—L. *sōlānus* (*ventus*), the east wind—*sōl,* the sun.]

**Solanum,** *sō-lā'nəm, n.* the potato and night-shade genus, giving name to the family **Solana-**

ceae (-lə-nā′si-ē).—adj. solanā′ceous.—n. solanine (sol′-, sōl′ə-nēn), a glucoside got from potato sprouts, etc. [L. sōlānum, nightshade.]

**solar**, sō′lər, adj. of, from, like, or pertaining to the sun: measured by the sun: influenced by the sun: powered by energy from the sun's rays: with branches radiating like the sun's rays.— n. (also sō′ler, sollar, soller, sol′ər; O.E. solor, or O.Fr. soler; arch.) an upper room: a garret: a landing between ladders in a mine.—n. sōlarisā′tion, -izā′tion, the act, process, or effect of solarising: reversal of image by over-exposure (phot.): interruption of photosynthesis by long exposure to bright light (bot.).—v.t. sō′larise, -ize, to expose to sunlight or affect by such exposure, esp. excessive or injurious exposure.— v.i. to be so affected.—ns. sō′larism, excessive use of solar myths in the explanation of mythology; sō′larist, one addicted to solarism; solā′rium, a sundial: a place for sunning or sunbathing.—solar battery, a battery of solar cells; solar cell, a photoelectric cell converting the energy of sunlight into electric power; solar day, time, year (see day, time, year); solar flare, a short-lived bright outburst in the sun's chromosphere, generally associated with sun spots and often the cause of radio and magnetic disturbances on earth; solar microscope, an apparatus for projecting an enlarged image; solar myth, a sun-myth, or a myth allegorising the course of the sun; solar noise, a hissing background noise heard in radio communication, due to radiation from the sun and its atmosphere; solar plexus (anat.), a network of nerves behind the stomach (so called from its radiating nerves); solar prominences, large prominent or protruding parts of the great volumes of heated gas surrounding the sun; solar salt, salt got by evaporation of sea-water by the sun; solar system, the sun with its attendant bodies—major and minor planets, meteors, comets, satellites; solar wind, protons from the sun travelling at about one and a half million kilometres an hour. [L. sōlāris, solar, sōlārium, a sundial—sōl, the sun.]

**solar**, sō′lər. See sola (2).

**solatium**, sō-lā′shi-əm, sō-lä′ti-ōōm, n. compensation for disappointment, inconvenience, wounded feelings. [L. sōlātium.]

**sold**, sōld, pa.t. and pa.p. of sell.—sold on, enthusiastic about.

**sold**, sold, n. (Spens.) pay, remuneration.—Also **solde** (Meredith). [Fr. solde—L. solidus, a piece of money.]

**soldado**, sōl-dä′dō, n. a soldier. [Sp.]

**soldan**, sol′dən, (arch.) n. a sultan, esp. of Egypt. [Fr.; see sultan.]

**soldatesque**, sol-də-tesk′, adj. soldierlike. [Fr.,—soldat, a soldier.]

**solde**. See sold (2).

**solder**, sod′ər, also sol′, sö′, sō′, sōl′, n. a fusible alloy for uniting metals.—v.t. to make fast with solder: to join: to mend, patch up.—v.i. to adhere.—ns. sol′derer; sol′dering.—sol′dering-bolt, -iron, a tool with pointed or wedge-shaped copper bit for use in soldering. [O.Fr. soudre, souldure—souder, soulder, to consolidate—L. solidāre, to make solid.]

**soldier**, sōl′jər, sōld′yər, formerly sō′jər, soger (dial.), sō′jər, sodger (dial.), soj′, n. man engaged in military service: a private: a man of military skill: shirker (naut.): an ant, or white ant, of a specialised fighting caste: a scarlet, pugnacious, or armoured animal of various kinds (beetle, fish, etc.): a red herring (slang): the ribwort plantain (used by children for a game of soldiers): a brick set upright in a wall.—v.i. to serve as a soldier: to shirk.—n. sol′diering.—adj. sol′dierlike, having the appearance of a soldier: soldierly. —adv. in the manner of a soldier.—n. sol′dierli-ness.—adj. sol′dierly, befitting a soldier: having the qualities of or befitting a soldier.—ns. sol′-diership, state or quality of being a soldier: military qualities: martial skill; sol′diery, soldiers collectively: a military body or class: soldiership.—sol′dier-crab, a hermit crab.— old soldier (see old); soldier of fortune, one ready to serve anywhere for pay or his own advancement; soldier on, to continue doggedly in face of difficulty or discouragement; soldier's heart, heart symptoms (in various diseases) attributable to soldiering or detected in soldiers. [O.Fr. soldier—L. solidus, a piece of money, the pay of a soldier.]

**soldo**, sol′dō, n. a former Italian coin, one-twentieth of a lira:—pl. sol′di (-dē). [It.,—L. solidus.]

**sole**, sōl, n. the underside of the foot: the bottom of a boot or shoe: the under-surface of a golf-club head: the floor of an oven or furnace: a sill (now dial.): the bottom, under-structure, floor, or under-surface of various things: a thrust-plane (geol.).—v.t. to put a sole on. [O.E. and O.Fr. sole—L. solea, sole, sandal—solum, bottom.]

**sole**, sōl, n. an elliptical flat-fish (Solea) with small twisted mouth and teeth on the underside only. —n. solenette (sōl-net′, sōl-ə-net′), a small species of sole.—lemon sole (see lemon (2)). [Fr. sole—L. solea.]

**sole**, sōl, adj. alone: only: without husband or wife: without another: solitary: consisting of one person: exclusive: uniform.—advs. sole; sole′ly, alone: only: singly.—n. sole′ness. [Fr., —L. sōlus, alone.]

**sole**, sōl (Shak.), dial. sowl, sowle, soole, sowl, sōl, sōōl, v.t. to pull (by the ears). [Origin obscure.]

**solecism**, sol′i-sizm, n. a breach of syntax: absurdity, impropriety, or incongruity.—v.i. sol′-ecise, -ize, to commit solecisms.—n. sol′ecist.— adjs. solecist′ic, -al.—adv. solecist′ically. [Gr. soloikismos, said to come from the corruption of the Attic dialect among the Athenian colonists (oikizein, to colonise) of Soloi in Cilicia.]

**solein**, an old form (Spens.) of sullen.

**solemn**, sol′əm, adj. attended with or marked by special (esp. religious) ceremonies, pomp, or gravity: attended with an appeal to God, as an oath: grave: in serious earnestness: with formal dignity: awed: awe-inspiring: stately: pompous: glum: sombre.—n. solemnisation (sol-əm-ni-zā′shən).—v.t. sol′emnise, -ize (-nīz), to perform religiously or solemnly: to celebrate with rites: to make solemn.—ns. sol′emniser; solemnity (-lem′ni-ti), a solemn ceremony: high seriousness: affected gravity; solemnize′ (Spens.), solemnisation.—adv. sol′emnly.—n. sol′emn-ness (also sol′emness).—solemn mass, high mass. [O.Fr. solempne, solemne (Fr. solennel)—L. sollemnis, sōlennis, doubtfully referred to sollus, all, every, annus, a year.]

**Solen**, sō′lən, n. the razor-fish genus of lamellibranch molluscs.—n. sō′lenoid, a cylindrical coil of wire, acting as a magnet when an electric current passes through it.—adj. solenoid′al.—adv. solenoid′ally. [Gr. sōlēn, a pipe.]

**soler**. See solar (n.).

**soleus**, sō′li-əs, n. the flat muscle of the leg beneath the gastrocnemius. [Mod. L.,—L. soles, sole.]

**sol-fa**, sol′fä′, (mus.) n. a system of syllables (do or ut, re, mi, fa, sol or so, la, si or ti) representing and sung to the notes of the scale.—adj. belonging to the system.—v.t. and v.i. to sing to sol-fa syllables:—pr.p. sol-faing (-fä′ing); pa.t. and pa.p. sol-faed, -fa'd (-fäd′).—ns. sol-fa′ism, singing by syllables: solmisation; sol-fa′ist, a teacher, practiser, or advocate of solmisation; solfeggio (-fed′jō; It.), an exercise in sol-fa syllables:—*pl.* **solfeggi** (*-fed'jē*).—tonic **sol-fa** (see tonic). [sol (2); 1a.]

**solfatara,** *sol-fä-tä'rǝ, n.* a volcanic vent emitting only gases, esp. one emitting acid gases (hydrochloric acid and sulphur dioxide):—*pl.* **solfata'-ras.**—*adj.* **solfata'ric.** [From the *Solfatara* (lit. sulphur-mine, sulphur-hole) near Naples—It. *solfo,* sulphur.]

**solfeggio.** See **sol-fa.**

**solferino,** *sol-fǝ-rē'no, n.* the colour of rosaniline—discovered soon after the battle of *Solferino* in Italy (1859).

**solicit,** *sō-lis'it, v.t.* to disquiet: to incite: to allure: to urge: to petition: to importune: to seek after: to call for, require: to invite to immorality: to extract gently (*obs.*): to conduct, manage.—*v.i.* to petition: to act as solicitor: (of prostitutes) to make advances: (of beggars) to importune for alms.—*n.* (*Shak.*) solicitation (another reading **solic'ity**).—*ns.* **solic'itant,** one who solicits (also *adj.*); **solicitā'tion,** a soliciting: earnest request: invitation; **solic'iting** (*Shak.*), solicitation (also *adj.*); **solic'itor,** one who asks earnestly: one who is legally qualified to act for another in a court of law (esp. formerly a court of equity): a lawyer who prepares deeds, manages cases, instructs counsel in the superior courts, and acts as an advocate in the inferior courts: a canvasser (*U.S.*); **solic'itorship.**—*adj.* **solic'itous,** soliciting or earnestly asking or desiring: very desirous: anxious: careful.—*adv.* **solic'itously.**—*ns.* **solic'itousness, solic'itude,** state of being solicitous: anxiety or uneasiness of mind: trouble.—**Solic'itor-Gen'eral,** in England, the law-officer of the crown next in rank to the Attorney-General—in Scotland, to the Lord-Advocate. [L. *sōlicitāre, sollicitāre—sō-, sollici-tus—sollus,* whole, *citus,* aroused—*ciēre,* to cite.]

**solid,** *sol'id, adj.* resisting change of shape, having the particles firmly cohering (opp. to *fluid*; distinguished from *liquid* and *gaseous*): hard: compact: full of matter: not hollow: strong: having or pertaining to three dimensions: substantial: worthy of credit: weighty: of uniform undivided substance: financially sound, wealthy: unanimous: unbroken: unvaried.—*n.* a substance, body, or figure that is solid: a solid mass or part.—*ns.* **solidare** (*sol'i-där; Shak.*), a small coin; **sol'idarism** (*-dǝ-rizm*), **sol'idarist,** an advocate of solidarity; **solidarity** (*-dar'i-ti*), oneness of interests, aims, etc.—*adj.* **sol'idary** (*dǝr-i*), marked by solidarity: jointly responsible: joint and several.—*v.t.* **sol'idate** (*rare*), to consolidate.—*adj.* **solidifiable** (*sǝ-lid'i-fī-ǝ-bl*).—*n.* **solidificā'tion.**—*v.t.* **solid'ify,** to make solid or compact.—*v.i.* to grow solid:—*pr.p.* **solid'i-fying;** *pa.t.* and *pa.p.* **solid'ified.**—*adj.* **sol'idish.** —*ns.* **sol'idism,** the doctrine that refers all diseases to alterations of the solid parts of the body; **sol'idist,** a believer in solidism; **solid'ity,** the state of being solid: fulness of matter: strength or firmness, moral or physical: soundness: volume: a solid thing (*Shak.*).—*adv.* **sol'idly.**—*ns.* **sol'idness; sol'idum,** the die of a pedestal (*archit.*): a complete sum (*Scots law*); **sol'idus,** a Roman gold coin introduced by Constantine, later called the *bezant:* in the Middle Ages, a silver coin of 12 denarii: a sign (/) denoting former English shilling, representing old lengthened form of *s* (£ s. d. = *librae, solidi, denarii,* pounds, shillings, pence), used also for other purposes, as in writing fractions:—*pl.* **solidi** (*-dī*).—**solid colour,** a colour covering the whole of an object: a uniform colour.—*adj.* **sol'id-hoofed,** with uncloven hoofs.—**solid matter** (*print.*), matter set without leads between the lines. —**solid of revolution,** a solid figure regarded as formed by a plane figure turning round on an axis; **solid-state light,** light produced by means of a semiconductor device; **solid-state physics,**

branch of physics which covers all properties of solid materials, now esp. electrical conduction in crystals of semiconductors, and superconductivity and photoconductivity; **solid with,** packed tight with: on a firm footing of understanding with: supporting fully; **the Solid South** (*U.S.*), the southern states traditionally voting for the Democratic party. [L. *solidus, -a, -um,* solid.]

**solidum.** See **solid.**

**solidungulate,** *sol-id-ung'gū-lǝt, adj.* with uncloven hoofs.—Also **solidung'ulous** [L. *solidus,* solid, *ungula,* a hoof.]

**solidus.** See **solid.**

**solifidian,** *sō-li-fid'i-ǝn, n.* one who holds that faith alone is necessary for justification.—Also *adj.*—*n.* **solifid'ianism.** [L. *sōlus,* only, *fidēs,* faith.]

**solifluxion, solifluction,** *sol-i-fluk'shǝn, n.* creep of soil down a slope. [L. *solum,* soil, *fluxiō, -ōnis,* flow.]

**Solifugae,** *sol-i-fū'jē, n.pl.* an order of spider-like arachnids, with head and three-jointed thorax distinct. [See **Solpuga**; modified by popular association with L. *sōl,* the sun, *fugēre,* to flee.]

**soliloquy,** *so-, sō-, sǝ-lil'ǝ-kwi, n.* a talking to oneself: a speech of this nature made by a character in a play, etc.—*v.i.* **solil'oquise, -ize,** to speak to oneself: to utter a soliloquy in a play, etc. [L. *sōliloquium—sōlus* alone, *loquī,* to speak.]

**soliped,** *sol'i-ped, n.* an animal with uncloven hoofs. —*adjs.* **sol'iped, solip'edous.** [L. *sōlus,* alone, *pēs, pedis,* a foot.]

**solipsism,** *sol'ip-sizm, n.* the theory that self-existence is the only certainty, absolute egoism—the extreme form of subjective idealism.—*n.* and *adj.* **sol'ipsist.**—*adj.* **solipsis'tic.** [L. *sōlus,* alone, *ipse,* self.]

**solitaire,** *sol-i-tār', n.* a recluse: a game played by one person with a board and balls: patience (card game) (*U.S.*): a diamond, etc., set by itself: (18th cent.) a large loose silk necktie: a gigantic flightless pigeon (*Pezophaps solitarius*) of Rodriguez, extinct since the 18th cent.: an American or West Indian fly-catching thrush.—**solitaire'-board,** a board with cups for playing solitaire. [Fr., see next.]

**solitary,** *sol'i-tǝr-i, adj.* alone: single, separate: living alone, not social or gregarious: without company: remote from society: retired, secluded: lonely: growing single (*bot.*).—*n.* one who lives alone: a hermit.—*n.* **solitarian** (*-tā'ri-ǝn*), a hermit.—*adv.* **sol'itarily.**—*n.* **sol'i-tariness.** [L. *sōlitārius—sōlus,* alone.]

**solito,** *sol'i-tō,* (*mus.*) *adv.* in the usual manner. [It.]

**solitude,** *sol'i-tūd, n.* solitariness: absence of company: a lonely place or desert.—*n.* **solitūdinā'-rian.**—*adj.* **solitūd'inous.** [L. *sōlitūdō—sōlus,* alone.]

**solivagant,** *sō-liv'ǝ-gǝnt, adj.* wandering alone.— Also *n.* [L. *sōlus,* alone, *vagāns, -antis,* wandering.]

**solive,** *so-lēv', n.* a joist or beam of secondary importance. [Fr.,—L. *sublevāre,* to support.]

**sollar, soller.** See **solar** (1).

**solleret,** *sol'ǝr-et, n.* a jointed steel shoe. [O.Fr., dim. of *soler,* slipper.]

**solmisation, -ization,** *sol-mi-zā'shǝn, n.* sol-faing: a recital of the notes of the gamut. [sol (2), mi.]

**solo,** *sō'lō, n.* a piece or passage for one voice or instrument, accompanied or unaccompanied: any performance in which no other person or instrument participates: a motor-bicycle without side-car: a card game (**solo whist**) based on whist, in which various declarations are made and the declarer may or may not have a partner:—*pl.* **sō'los, soli,** *sō'lē.*—*adj.* performed, or for performances, as a solo: performing a solo: for one.—*adv.*—*v.i.* to fly solo.—*n.* **sō'loist.** [It.,—L. *sōlus,* alone.]

**Solomon,** *sol'ǝ-mǝn, n.* a person of unusual wisdom, from *Solomon,* king of Israel (see 1 Kings

iii. 5-15).—*adjs.* **Solomonian** (-mō′ni-ən), **Solomonic** (-mon′ik).—**Sol′omon's-seal,** any species of Polygonatum, a genus of the lily family, with small dangling greenish flowers (perh. from the scars on the rootstock): a symbol formed of two triangles interlaced or superposed, forming a six-pointed star.

**Solon,** sō′lon, *n.* a famous lawgiver of Athens (594 B.C.), one of the Seven Sages: a sage: a wiseacre: a Congressman (*U.S.*).—*adj.* **Solō′nian.**

**so-long, so long,** sō-long′, (*coll.* or *slang*) *interj.* good-bye. [Prob. so and long; poss. **salaam.**]

**Solpuga,** sol-pū′gə, *n.* a genus of very venomous Solifugae. [L. *solpūga, salpūga, solipūga, solipugna,* a venomous animal supposed to be the same, a word derived from Spain.]

**solstice,** sol′stis, *n.* the time when the sun reaches its maximum distance from the equator (*summer solstice* when it touches the tropic of Cancer, about 21st June; the *winter solstice* when it touches that of Capricorn, about 21st December): the turning-point then reached.—*adj.* **solstitial** (-stish′l), pertaining to, or happening at, a solstice, esp. at the summer solstice. [Fr.,—L. *sōlstitium*—sōl, the sun, *sistĕre, stătum,* to make to stand—*stāre.*]

**soluble,** sol′ū-bl, *adj.* capable of being solved, dissolved, or resolved.—*n.* **solubilisā′tion,** -z-.—*v.t.* **sol′ubilise, -ize,** to render soluble: to make more soluble.—*ns.* **solūbil′ity; sol′ūte,** a dissolved substance.—*adj.* (*sol′* or -ūt′) loose: free: not adhering: dissolved.—*n.* **solution** (*sэl-, sol-ōō′shэn, -ū′shэn*), act of solving or dissolving: condition of being dissolved: the preparation resulting therefrom: the separating of parts: abnormal separation: explanation: removal of a doubt: solving of a problem: the crisis of a disease: breach (as of continuity): a solution of rubber.—*v.t.* to mend or cement with rubber solution.—*adj.* **solutional** (-ōō′ or -ū′).—*n.* **solu′tionist,** a solver (as of puzzles).—*adj.* **sol′ūtive,** tending to dissolve: laxative.—**solution of triangles** (*trig.*), finding the values of the remaining sides and angles, some being given. [L. *solvĕre, solūtum,* to loosen.]

**solum,** sō′lэm, *n.* ground, soil: a piece of ground. [L. *sōlum,* the ground.]

**solus,** sō′lэs, *adj.* alone, in dramatic directions—fem. form, **sō′la.** [L. *sōlus,* alone.]

**Solutrean, Solutrian,** sol-ōōt′ri-эn, -ūt′, or -trē′, *adj.* belonging to an upper Palaeolithic culture which succeeded the Aurignacian and preceded the Magdalenian. [*Solutré,* in Saône-et-Loire, where objects of this culture have been found.]

**solve,** solv, *v.t.* to unbind: to dissolve: to settle: to clear up or explain: to find an answer to or a way out of.—*n.* **solvabil′ity.**—*adj.* **solv′able,** capable of being solved: capable of being paid, dissolved, or resolved (*rare* or *obs.*): solvent (*obs.*).—*ns.* **sol′vate,** a definite combination of solute and solvent; **solvā′tion,** association of the molecules of a solvent with solute ions or molecules; **sol′vency.**—*adj.* **sol′vent,** able to solve or dissolve: able to pay all debts.—*n.* anything that dissolves another.—*n.* **sol′ver,** one who solves. [L. *solvĕre,* to loosen, prob. from *sē-, sĕ-,* aside, *luĕre,* to loosen.]

**soma, Soma,** sō′mэ, *n.* a plant (perhaps an asclepiad, Sarcostemma), or its intoxicating juice, used in ancient Indian religious ceremonies, and personified as a god. [Sans. *soma* (Avestan *haoma,* juice).]

**soma,** sō′mэ, *n.* an imaginary perfect drug described by Aldous Huxley in *Brave New World:* (*cap.*) trademark for a drug which relieves pain and is a muscle-relaxant. [soma (1).]

**soma,** sō′mэ, *n.* the body: the body of an animal or plant excluding the germ-cells.—*n.* **somascope** (sō′mэ-skōp; Gr. *skopeein,* to view), an instrument using ultrasonic waves converted into a television image to show the character of diseased internal tissues of the body.—*adj.* **somatic** (-mat′ik).—*adv.* **somat′ically.**—*ns.* **so′matism** (-mэ-tizm), materialism; **so′matist** (also *adj.*).—*adjs.* **somatogenic** (sō-mэ-tō-jen′ik), originating in somatic cells; **somatolog′ic, -al.**—*ns.* **somatol′ogy,** the science of the properties of matter: the science of the human body; **so′matoplasm,** protoplasm of the somatic cells; **so′matopleure** (-plōor; Gr. *pleurä,* side), the outer body-wall or the layer that gives rise to it; **somatoton′ia,** a pattern of temperament and body type in which alertness and aggression are combined with mesomorphic build.—*adj.* **somatoton′ic** (-ton′).—**somat′otype,** a type consisting of a physical build paired with a particular temperament.—*v.t.* to place with regard to somatotype.—*n.* **so′mite,** a body-segment.—*adjs.* **somital** (sō′mi-tl), **somit′ic.** [Gr. *sōma,* body.]

**sombre,** som′bэr, *adj.* dark and gloomy.—*v.t.* and *v.i.* to make or become sombre.—*adv.* **som′brely.**—*n.* **som′breness.**—*adj.* **som′brous,** sombre. [Fr. *sombre* (cf. Sp. *sombra,* shade)—perh. L. *sub,* under, *umbra,* a shade.]

**sombrerite,** som-brā′rit, *n.* rock-guano. [*Sombrero* in the West Indies.]

**sombrero,** som-brā′rō, *n.* a broad-brimmed hat. [Sp., hat—*sombra,* shade.]

**some,** sum, *indef. pron.* one, one or other (*obs.*): an indefinite part of the whole number or quantity: certain (undetermined) ones: a great deal (*U.S.*): a good deal more (*U.S.*).—*adj.* one or other: in an indefinite number or quantity: a little: not a little: considerable: a certain: certain unspecified: several: a few: in approximate number, length, etc., more or less: remarkable, outstanding, of note (*coll.,* esp. U.S.; also *ironical*).—*adv.* somewhat, in some degree, rather, a little (*local*): very much (*U.S.*): sometimes (*Shak.*).—*n.* (or *pron.*) **some′body,** some person: a person of importance:—*pl.* **some′bodies.**—*advs.* **some′day,** at an unspecified time in the future; **some′deal** (*arch.*), some dele (*Spens.*), in some degree, somewhat; **some′gate** (*Scot.*), somewhere, somehow; **some′how,** in some way or other.—*ns.* (or *prons.*) **some′one** (also **some one**), somebody; **some′thing,** a thing undefined: a thing of some account: a portion.—*adv.* in some degree.—*adj.* (*Shak.*) that is something.—Also used as substitute for any word (*n., adj., vb.*) or component of any word forgotten or avoided.—*adv.* **some′time,** at a time not fixed: at one time or other: formerly.—*adj.* former: late.—*adv.* **some′times,** at times: now and then: sometime (*obs.*).—*adj.* (*Shak.*) sometime.—*advs.* **some′way, -ways, -wise,** in some way: somehow.—*n.* **some′what,** an unfixed quantity or degree: something.—*adv.* in some degree.—*advs.* (all *rare* except somewhere) **some′when,** some time or other; **some′whence;** **some′where,** in or to some place; **some′while, -s,** sometimes; **some′whither;** **some′why.**—**some one else,** some other person; **some one else's,** some other person's. [O.E. *sum;* Goth. *sums,* O.N. *sumr.*]

**-some, -sum, -sэm,** *suff.* forming adjectives with the meaning full of, e.g. gladsome, wholesome. [O.E. *-sum;* Ger. *-sam;* cf. **same.**]

**somersault,** sum′эr-sölt, *n.* a leap or other movement in which one turns heels over head.—*v.i.* to turn a somersault.—Also **som′erset.** [O.Fr. *sombre saut* (Fr. *soubresaut*)—L. *suprā,* over, *saltus, -ūs,* a leap—*salīre,* to leap.]

**somite.** See under **soma** (3).

**sommelier,** som′(ə-)lyā, *n.* a butler: a wine waiter. [Fr.]

**Somnus,** som′nэs, *n.* the god of sleep (L.; Gr. *Hypnos*).—*n.* **somnambulance** (som-nam′bū-lэns) L. *ambulāre,* to walk), sleep-walking.—*adj.* and *n.* **somnam′bulant.**—*adjs.* **somnam′bular, -y.**—

*v.i.* **somnam′būlate**, to walk in one's sleep.—*ns.*
**somnambūlā′tion**; **somnam′būlātor**, **somnam′-
būle**, a sleep-walker.—*adj.* **somnam′būlic.**—*ns.*
**somnam′būlism**, walking in sleep: a hysterical
state of automatism in which acts are performed
that are not remembered afterwards; **somnam′-
būlist.**—*adjs.* **somnambūlis′tic**; **som′nial**, pertaining to dreams; **somnic′ūlous**, drowsy; **som-
nif′erous** (L. *ferre*, to bring), **somnif′ic** (L. *facĕre*,
to make), sleep-bringing.—*ns.* **somnil′oquence,
somnil′oquism, somnil′oquy** (L. *loqui*, to talk),
talking in sleep.—*v.i.* **somnil′oquise, -ize.**—*ns.*
**somnil′oquist**; **somniv′olent** (L. *velle*, to wish),
one who wishes to sleep; **som′nolence, -ency,**
sleepiness.—*adj.* **som′nolent.**—*adv.* **som′nolently.**
—*adj.* **somnolesc′ent**, half-asleep. [L. *somnus*,
sleep, *somnium*, a dream.]
**son**, *sun*, *n.* a male child or offspring: formerly
extended to a son-in-law: a descendant, or one
so regarded or treated: a disciple: a native or
inhabitant: the produce of anything.—*adj.* **son′-
less.**—*ns.* **sonn′y**, a little son: a familiar mode
of address to a boy; **son′ship**, state or character
of a son.—**son′-in-law**, a daughter's husband:
formerly, a stepson:—*pl.* **sons′-in-law.**—**son of
man**, a man: applied to Jesus Christ or the
Messiah; **son of the manse**, a minister's son;
**The Son**, the second person in the Trinity. [O.E.
*sunu*; Du. *zoon*, Ger. *sohn*.]
**sonant**, *sō′nant*, *adj.* voiced.—*n.* a voiced sound.—
*ns.* **so′nance** (*Shak.* **son′uance**, prob. a misprint),
a sounding; **so′nancy**, sonant character. [L.
*sonāns*, *-antis*, pr.p. of *sonāre*, to sound.]
**Sonar**, *sō′nər*, *n.* the American equivalent of
Asdic: (without *cap.*) natural equipment that
provides echo location in bats and some marine
animals.—**sonar buoy** (same as **sonobuoy**).
[*sound navigation and ranging*.]
**sonata**, *sō-, sə-, so-nä′tä*, *n.* orig., an instrumental
composition: a composition usually of three or
more movements designed chiefly for a solo
instrument.—*n.* **sonatina** (*son-ə-tē′na*), a short
sonata.—**sonata form**, the form usual in the first
movement of a sonata or symphony. [It., fem.
pa.p. of *sonare*—L. *sonāre*, to sound.]
**sondage**, *sɔ̄-däzh*, *n.* a trial bore or excavation.
[Fr.]
**sonde**, *sond*, *n.* any device for obtaining information about atmospheric and weather conditions
at high altitudes. [Fr.]
**sondeli**, *son′de-li*, *n.* the Indian musk-shrew.
[Kanarese *sundili*.]
**sone**, *sōn*, *n.* a unit of loudness related to the
hearing of an individual listener. [L. *sonus*,
sound.]
**soneri**, *son′, sōn′ə-rē*, *n.* cloth of gold. [Hind.
*sonā*, gold.]
**son et lumière**, *son ä lüm′yer*, a dramatic spectacle
presented after dark, involving lighting effects
on natural features of the country or on a
chosen building and an appropriate theme illustrated by spoken words and by music. [Fr.]
**song**, *song*, *n.* that which is sung: a short poem
or ballad suitable for singing or set to music:
the melody to which it is sung: an instrumental
composition of like form and character: singing: the melodious outburst of a bird: any
characteristic sound: a poem, or poetry in
general: a theme of song: habitual utterance,
manner, or attitude towards anything: a fuss:
a mere trifle.—*adj.* **song′ful**, abounding in song:
melodious: songlike: like singing: ready to
break into song.—*adv.* **song′fully.**—*n.* **song′ful-
ness.**—*adjs.* **song′less**, without song or power of
song; **song′-like.**—*n.* **song′ster**, a singer:—*fem.*
**song′stress.**—**song′bird**, a bird that sings: any
one of the Oscines; **song′book**, a service-book
(*obs.*): a book of songs; **song′craft**, the art of
making songs; **song′-cycle**, a sequence of songs
connected in subject; **song form**, the form of

composition usual in songs; **song′-hit**, a song
that has made a hit, or caught on; **song′man**
(*Shak.*), a singer: a choir singer; **song′-school**;
**song′smith**, a composer; **song′-sparrow**, an
American songbird (Melospiza); **song′-thrush**,
the mavis or throstle.—**make a song (and dance)
about**, to make overmuch of: to make an unnecessary fuss about; **Song of Songs**, or of
Solomon, Canticles, a book of the O.T. long
attributed to Solomon. [O.E. *sang*—*singan*, to
sing; Goth. *saggws*, O.N. *söngr*.]
**song**, (*Spens.*) *pa.t.* of **sing**.
**sonic**, *son′ik*, *adj.* pertaining to or using sound-
waves: travelling at about the speed of sound.
—*n.* (in *pl.*, treated as *sing.*) the study of the
technological application of sounds, esp. supersonic waves.—**sonic bang, boom** (*aero.*), a loud
double report caused by shock-waves projected
outward and backward from the leading and
trailing edges of an aircraft travelling at supersonic speed; **sonic barrier**, sound barrier; **sonic
mine**, an acoustic mine. [L. *sonus*, sound.]
**sonne**, an old spelling of **son**, **sun**.
**sonnet**, *son′it*, *n.* formerly, a short (esp. lyrical)
poem: now, always one of fourteen lines of ten
or eleven syllables, rhymed according to one or
other of certain definite schemes, forming an
octave and a sestet, properly expressing two
successive phases of one thought.—*v.i.* to write
sonnets.—*v.t.* to celebrate in sonnets.—*adj.*
**sonn′etary.**—*n.* **sonneteer′**, a sonnet-writer: a
poetaster (*obs.*).—*vs.i.* **sonneteer′**, **sonn′etise, -ize**,
to compose sonnets.—*vs.t.* to celebrate in sonnets.
—*n.* and *adj.* **sonneteer′ing.**—*ns.* **sonn′eting**;
**sonn′etist**, a sonneteer; **sonn′etry.**—**sonn′et-
se′quence**, a connected series of sonnets.—
**Petrarch(i)an sonnet**, one rhymed *abbaabba cdc-
dcd*; **Miltonic**, *abbaabba cdecde*; **Shakespearian**,
*ababcdcd efefgg*. [It. *sonetto*, dim. of *suono*—
L. *sonus*, a sound.]
**sono-**, in composition, sound.—*n.* **sonobuoy** (*son′ō-
boi*, *U.S.* also *-bōō-ē*), equipment dropped to
float on the sea and pick up underwater noise,
e.g. from a submarine, and to transmit bearings
of the source to aircraft.
**sonofabitch**, son of a bitch, opprobrious term of
address or of description, or vulgar exclamation.
**sonorous**, *so-, sə-nō′rəs, so′nə-rəs*, *adj.* sounding:
full-sounding: sounding or ringing when struck.
—*n.* **sonority** (*sō-, sə-nor′i-ti*), sonorousness.—
*adv.* **sono′rously.**—*n.* **sono′rousness**, sonorous
quality or character—**sonorous figures**, patterns
made in sand by vibrating a metal plate on which
it is spread. [L. *sonōrus*—*sonor*, *-ōris*, a sound
—*sonāre*, to sound.]
**sonse**, **sonce**, *sons*, (*Scot.*) *n.* good luck: abundance.—*adj.* **sons′y**, **sons′ie** (*Scot.*), luck-bringing:
comely: comfortable-looking: good-natured:
plump, buxom. [Gael. *sonas*, good fortune.]
**sontag**, *son′tag*, *zōn′tähh*, *n.* a woman's knitted
cape, tied down round the waist. [From the
famous German singer Henriette *Sontag* (1806-
1854).]
**sonties**, *son′tiz*, (*Shak.*, in an oath) *n.pl.* prob. for
**sanctities**.
**sook**. Same as **souk**.
**soole**. See **sole** (4).
**soom**, *sōōm*, a Scots form of **swim**.
**soon**, *sōōn*, *adv.* immediately or in a short time:
without delay: early: readily: willingly.—*adj.*
early (*rare*): speedy (*Shak.*).—**soon at** (*Shak.*),
about. [O.E. *sōna*.]
**soop**, *sōōp*, (*Scot.*) *v.t.* to sweep.—*n.* **soop′ing**
(*Scot.*).—*adv.* **soop′stake** (*Shak.*), with a sweep
of the stakes (another reading **swoop′-stake-**
like). [O.N. *sōpa*; cf. **sweep**, **swoop**.]
**soot**, *sōōt*, *n.* a black deposit from imperfect
combustion of carbonaceous matter: a smut.—
*v.t.* to cover, smear, dirty, clog, or treat with
soot.—*n.* **soot′erkin**, a fabulous afterbirth in-

duced by Dutch women sitting huddled over their stoves: a Dutchman: a Negro: a chimney-sweep: anything supplementary, fruitless, or abortive.—*adv.* **soot'ily.**—*n.* **soot'iness.**—*adjs.* **soot'less; soot'y,** of, foul with. or like, soot.—**soot'flake,** a smut of soot. [O.E. *sōt;* Dan. *sod.*]
**soot, soote,** *sōōt, adj.* and *n.* (*obs.*) sweet.—*adv.* (*Spens.*) sweetly. [See **sweet.**]
**sooterkin.** See **soot** (1).
**sooth,** *sōōth, n.* truth, reality: blandishment (*Shak.*): augury, foretokening (*obs.;* *Spens.* **soothe**).—*adj.* true: truthful: smooth, soft (*Keats*).—*adv.* in truth: indeed.—*adj.* **sooth'ful,** truthful: faithful.—*advs.* **sooth'lv, sooth'lich** (*Spens.*), truly, indeed.—*adj.* **sooth'fast,** truthful, honest, faithful.—*adv.* **sooth'fastly.**—*n.* **sooth'-fastness.**—*v.i.* **sooth'say,** to foretell, to divine.— *n.* prediction: (*Spens.* **soothsay'**) omen.—**sooth'-sayer** (*Spens. -sā'*), one who foretells, a diviner or prognosticator: a truth-teller (*obs.*); **sooth'-saving.** [O.E. *sōth,* truth, true: O.N. *sannr.*]
**soothe,** *sōōdh, v.t.* to prove or declare true (*obs.*): to confirm, support, back up (*obs.*): to blandish, cajole, flatter: to gloss over (*obs.*): to calm, comfort, compose, tranquillise: to appease: to allay, soften.—*v.i.* to have a tranquillising effect. —*n.* **sooth'er.**—*v.t.* (*Ir.*) to flatter, blandish.—*n.* and *adj.* **sooth'ing.**—*adv.* **sooth'ingly.** [O.E. (*ge*)*sōthian,* to confirm as true—*sōth,* true.]
**sop,** *sop, n.* bread or other food dipped or soaked in liquid: a puddle: a soaking: a propitiatory gift or concession (from the drugged sop the Sibyl gave to Cerberus to gain passage for Aeneas to Hades, *Aen.* vi. 420).—*v.t.* to steep in liquor: to take up by absorption (with *up*): to soak.—*v.i.* to soak in, percolate: to be soaked:—*pr.p.* **sopp'ing;** *pa.t.* and *pa.p.* **sopped.** —*adv.* **sopp'ily.**—*n.* **sopp'iness.**—*n., adj.,* and *adv.* **sopp'ing.**—*adj.* **sopp'y,** drenched: thoroughly wet: sloppily sentimental.—**sops'-in-wine',** the clove pink (*obs.*): a variety of apple. [O.E. *sopp* (n.), *soppian* (vb.); prob. conn. with *sūpan,* to sup.]
**soph,** *sof, n.* an abbreviation of **sophister** and of **sophomore.**
**sopherim,** *sō'fə-rim, n.pl.* the scribes, the ex-pounders of the Jewish oral law.—*adj.* **sopheric** (*-fer'ik*). [Heb. *sōferim.*]
**Sophi.** Same as **Sophy.**
**sophia,** *sof'i-ə, n.* wisdom: divine wisdom (often personified **Sophia, Hagia Sophia, Saint Sophia**). —*adjs.* **soph'ic, -al.**—*adv.* **soph'ically.**—*ns.* **soph'ism,** a specious fallacy: **soph'ist,** one of a class of public teachers of rhetoric, philosophy, etc., in ancient Greece: a captious or inten-tionally fallacious reasoner: **soph'ister,** a sophist (*Shak.*): a student in his second or third year (*Cambridge: hist.*), in his third or fourth (*Dublin*).—*adj.* **sophis'tic,** pertaining to, or of the nature of, a sophist or sophistry: fallaciously subtle.—*n.* (also in *pl.*) the art of sophistry.— *adj.* **sophist'ical.**—*adv.* **sophis'tically.**—*v.t.* **sophis'-ticāte,** to adulterate: to falsify: to make soph-istic(al): to give fashionable air of worldly wisdom to: to make (e.g., machine) highly complex and efficient.—*v.i.* to practise sophistry. —*adjs.* **sophis'ticāte, sophis'ticāted,** adulterated: falsified: worldly-wise and disillusioned: very refined and subtle: with qualities produced by special knowledge and skill: with the most up-to-date devices.—*ns.* **sophis'ticāte,** a sophisti-cated person: **sophisticā'tion: sophis'ticātor:** soph'istry, specious but fallacious reasoning. [Gr. *sophiā,* wisdom, *sophisma,* skill.]
**Sophoclean,** *sof-ō-klē'ən, adj.* pertaining to *Sopho-cles,* Athenian tragic poet (*c.* 496 -*c.* 406 B.C.).
**sophomore,** *sof'ə-mōr, -mōr,* (now *U.S.*) *n.* a second-year student.—Also *adj.*—*adjs.* **sopho-moric** (*-mor'*), **-al,** of a sophomore: bombastic.

[Prob. from *sophom* (obs. form of *sophism*) and *-or,* as if from *sophos,* wise, *mōros,* foolish.]
**Sophy,** *sō'fi,* (*obs.*) *n.* the shah of Persia. [From the *Çafi* or Safawi dynasty (1502-1736) descended from Çafi-ud-dīn.]
**sopite,** *sō-pīt', v.t.* to dull, lull, put to sleep: to put an end to. [L. *sōpitus,* pa.p. of *sōpire,* to put to sleep, calm, settle.]
**sopor,** *sō'pŏr,* (*path.*) *n.* unnaturally deep sleep. —*adj.* **soporiferous** (*sop-, sōp-ər-if'ər-əs*), induc-ing sleep.—*adv.* **soporif'erously.**—*n.* **soporif'er-ousness.**—*adj.* **soporif'ic,** inducing sleep.—*n.* a sleep-bringing agent.—*adjs.* **sop'orōse, sop'orous,** sleepy. [L. *sopor, -ōris,* deep sleep—*ferre,* to bring, *facēre,* to make.]
**sopped, sopping, soppy.** See **sop.**
**sopra,** *sō'prä,* (*mus.*) *adv.* above. [It.,—L. *suprā,* above.]
**soprano,** *sō-. sə-prä'nō, n.* the highest variety of voice. treble: a singer with such a voice: a part for such a voice:—*pl.* **sopra'nos, sopra'ni** (*nē*).—*adj.* of, or possessing, a treble voice or a part for it: in a group of instruments of the same type but of different sizes, that with the range close to the range of a soprano voice.— *adj.* **sopranino** (*sō-prə-nē'nō*). (of an instrument) higher than the corresponding soprano.—Also *n.*—*n.* **sopra'nist,** a soprano singer. [It., from *sopra*—L. *suprā* or *super,* above.]
**sora,** *sō'ra, sō', n.* a N. American short-billed rail.—Also **so'ree.** [Indian name.]
**sorage.** See **sore** (2).
**soral.** See **sorus.**
**sorb,** *sōrb, n.* the service-tree, the wild service-tree, or (sometimes) the rowan-tree: its fruit. —**sorb'-app'le; sorbic acid,** an acid obtained from the rowan-berry, used in food preserva-tion. [L. *sorbus* (the tree), *sorbum* (the fruit).]
**Sorb,** *sōrb, n.* a Wend.—*ns.* and *adjs.* **Sor'bian, Sor'bish,** Wendish. [Ger. *Sorbe:* cf. **Serb.**]
**sorb,** *sōrb, v.t.* to absorb or adsorb.—*adj.* **sorbe-facient** (*-i-fā'shənt*), promoting absorption.— Also *n.*—*n.* and *adj.* **sor'bent.** [L. *sorbēre,* to suck in, *faciens, -entis,* pr.p. of *facēre,* to make.]
**sorbet,** *sōr'bət, sōr'bā, n.* sherbet: water-ice. [Fr.,—It. *sorbetto;* cf. **sherbet.**]
**sorbic acid.** See **sorb** (1).
**Sorbonne,** *sōr-bon', n.* a theological college of the mediaeval university of Paris, founded in 1253 bv Robert of *Sorbon,* long dominant in matters of doctrine, suppressed 1792, revived 1808, seat of the faculties of science and letters (arts).— *adj.* **Sorbon'ical, Sorbonn'ical.**—*n.* **Sor'bonist,** **Sor'bonnist,** a doctor or student of the Sorbonne.
**sorcery,** *sōr'sə-ri, n.* divination by the assistance of evil spirits: enchantment: magic: witch-craft.—*n.* **sor'cerer:**—*fem.* **sor'ceress.**—*adj.* **sor'-cerous.** [O.Fr. *sorcerie*—L. *sors, sortis,* lot.]
**sord,** *sōrd, sōrd,* (*Milt.*) *n.* a form of **sward.**
**sord,** *sōrd, sōrd, n.* a flock of mallard. [O.Fr. *sordre*—L. *surgēre,* to rise.]
**sordamente.** See **sordo.**
**sordes,** *sōr'dēz, n. sing.* or *pl.* filth: refuse: a foul accumulation: a crust on the teeth in fevers.— *adj.* **sor'did,** dirty: squalid: mean: meanly avaricious: mercenary: of low or unworthy ideals: dirt-coloured.—*adv.* **sor'didly.**—*ns.* **sor'-didness; sor'dor,** dirt: sordidness. [L. *sordēs* (pl.: sing. defective), dirt, *sordidus,* dirty.]
**sordid,** etc. See **sordes.**
**sordo,** *sōr'dō, adj.* muted, damped:—*fem.* **sor'da.** —*adv.* **sordamente** (*-dä-men'tā*), gently, softly. —*n.* **sordino** (*-dē'nō*), a mute or damper to soften or deaden the sound of an instrument:— *pl.* **sordini** (*-nē*).—Also **sordine** (*-dēn'*; Fr. *sourdine*)—**con sordino,** with mute: **senza sordino,** without mute. [It.,—L. *surdus,* deaf, noiseless.]
**sore,** *sōr, sōr, n.* a painful or tender injured or diseased spot: an ulcer or boil: grief: an

affliction.—*adj.* wounded: tender: readily sensitive to pain: irritable: touchy: painful: afflicted: vexed: irritated: causing pain: painful to contemplate: grievous: aching (*Scot.*): bringing sorrow or regret: aggrieved (*coll.*).—*adv.* painfully: grievously: severely: distressingly: in distress: hard: eagerly: very much.—*v.t.* to make sore: to wound.—*adv.* sore′ly.—*n.* sore′ness.—sore′head (*U.S.*), one discontented with his reward for political services.—*adj.* sore′head′ed.—sore point, a subject provoking bitter argument.—a sore thumb, something obtrusive, too painful or too awkward to be ignored. [O.E. *sār*; Ger. *sehr*, very, O.N. *sārr*, sore.]

sore, soar, soare, *sōr*, *sör*, *adj.* (*obs.*) sorrel, reddish-brown: of hawks, etc., in reddish-brown plumage of the first year.—*n.* a hawk of the first year (*obs.*): buck of fourth year (*Shak.*). —*n.* sor′age, the first year of a hawk: a sore-hawk.—sore′-, soar′-ea′gle (*Milt.*), -fal′con, -hawk′. [A.Fr. and O.Fr. *sor* (Fr. *saur*, *saure*), sorrel, reddish; cf. sorrel (2).]

soredium, *sō-rē′di-əm*, *sö-*, *n.* a small vegetative reproductive body in lichens, consisting of a few algal cells enclosed in fungal hyphae:—*pl.* sore′dia.—*adjs.* sore′dial, sore′diate. [Gr. *sōros*, a heap.]

sorehon, *sör′hon*, *sör′*, *n.* an ancient Irish exaction of free accommodation by a lord from a freeholder or tenant. [See sorn.]

sorel. See sorrel (2).

Sorex, *sō′reks*, *sö′*, *n.* the common shrew genus, giving name to the family Soricidae (*sō-ris′i-dē*, *sö-*).—*adjs.* soric′ident (L. *dēns*, *dentis*, tooth), having teeth like the shrew; soricine (*sor′i-sin*, *-sin*), of the shrew: shrewlike; sor′icoid (*-koid*), shrewlike. [L. *sōrex*, *-icis*, shrew; cf. Gr. *hȳrax*.]

Sorghum, *sör′gəm*, *n.* a tropical Old World genus of grasses near akin to sugar-cane, including durra and Kaffir corn: (without *cap.*) molasses made from its juice (*U.S.*).—*n.* sor′go, sor′gho, a variety of durra from which sugar is prepared (sweet sorghum, or Chinese sugar-cane). [It. *sorgo*, prob. from an East Ind. word.]

Soricidae, etc. See Sorex.

s'orienter, *so-rē-ā-tā*, (Fr.) to take one's bearings.

sorites, *sō-rī′tēz*, *sö-*, *n.* a string of propositions in which the predicate of one is the subject of the next (or the same in reverse order): a sophistical puzzle on the model of 'How many grains make a heap?' [Gr. *sōreitēs*—*sōros*, a heap.]

sorn, *sörn*, (*Scot.*) *v.i.* to obtrude oneself as an uninvited guest.—*ns.* sor′ner; sorn′ing. [Obs. Ir. *sorthan*, free quarters.]

soroban, *sör′ə-bän*, *n.* a Japanese abacus. [From Jap.—Chin. words meaning 'calculating board'.]

soroche, *so-rō′chä*, *n.* mountain sickness. [Sp.—Quechua *suruchi*, antimony (present in the Andes and formerly believed to cause the sickness).]

Soroptimist, *sor-opt′i-mist*, *adj.* of an international organisation of women's clubs.—*n.* a member of one of these clubs. [L. *soror*, sister, and optimist.]

sororal, *sor-ō′rəl*, *-ö′*, sororial, *-ri-əl*, *adjs.* sisterly: of, of the nature of, a sister.—*n.* soro′rate (or *sor′ər-āt*), a custom that allows or requires marriage with a wife's sister.—*adv.* soro′rially. —*n.* sororicide (*-or′i-sīd*; L. *caedĕre*, to kill), killing or killer of a sister.—*v.i.* sororise, -ize (*sor′ər-īz*), to associate in a sisterly way.—*n.* sorority (*sor-or′i-ti*), a sisterhood: a women's academic society (*U.S.*). [L. *soror*, sister.]

sorosis, *so-*, *sö-*, *sə-*, *sō-rō′sis*, *n.* a fleshy fruit formed from a crowd of flowers, as the pine-apple: a women's club (*U.S.*). [Gr. *sōros*, a heap.]

sorrel, *sor′l*, *n.* any of the acid-tasting species of the dock genus, Rumex (common sorrel, *R.*

acetosa; sheep's sorrel, *R. acetosella*; French or Roman sorrel, *R. scutatus*) or the kindred Oxyria digyna (mountain sorrel): applied also to other plants as roselle and wood-sorrel.—salts of sorrel, a very poisonous combination of potassium acid oxalate and oxalic acid. [O.Fr. *sorele*, *surele* (Fr. *surelle*)—*sur*, sour—O.H.G. *sûr* (Ger. *sauer*), sour.]

sorrel, *sor′l*, *adj.* reddish-brown or light chestnut. —*n.* a reddish-brown colour: a sorrel horse: (also sorel, sorell, *sōr′el*, *sör′*; *Shak.*) a third-year buck. [O.Fr. *sorel* *sor* (Fr. *saur*, *saure*), sorrel; poss. L.G.; cf. sore (2).]

sorrow, *sor′ō*, *n.* pain of mind: affliction: lamentation: one sorrowed for: devil (in imprecations, as an emphatic negative, and applied as a term of abuse; Irish sorra).—*v.t.* and *v.i.* to grieve.—*adj.* sorr′owed (*Shak.*), accompanied with sorrow.—*n.* sorr′ower.—*adj.* sorr′owful, full of sorrow: causing, showing, or expressing sorrow: sad: dejected.—*adv.* sorr′owfully.—*n.* sorr′owfulness.—*n.* and *adj.* sorr′owing.—*n.* sorr′owless, free from sorrow. [O.E. *sorg*, *sorh*; Ger. *sorge*, O.N. *sorg*.]

sorry, *sor′i*, *adj.* regretful: often merely formally apologetic: distressing: poor, miserable, wretchedly bad, contemptible, worthless:—*compar.* sorr′ier; *superl.* sorr′iest.—*interj.* of slight apology.—*adv.* sorr′ily.—*n.* sorr′iness.—*adj.* sorr′yish. [O.E. *sārig*, wounded—*sār*, pain; Du. *zeerig*; influenced in meaning by sorrow, but not connected in origin.]

sort, *sört*, *n.* a lot (in sortilege) (*Shak.*): a company, group, collection, parcel (*obs.*): a class, kind, or species: quality or rank: one, a specimen or instance, of a kind (often ungrammatically in the singular with these or those, to denote examples of this or that kind): something of the nature but not quite worthy of the name: a letter, stop, or other character in a fount of type: manner.—*v.t.* to allot, assign (*Shak.*): to dispose (*Shak.*): to befit (*rare*): to separate into lots or classes: to group, classify: to pick out: to select: to provide (*Scot.*): to procure (*Scot.*): to set in accord: to adjust, put to rights, attend to (*Scot.*): to geld: to deal effectively with (esp. in a vague threat) (*coll.*). —*v.i.* to come about, turn out (*obs.*): to fit, accord: to agree (*Scot.*): to consort (*dial.*).—*adj.* sort′able, capable of being sorted: assorted: suitable, befitting (*rare*).—*ns.* sort′ance (*Shak.*), suitableness, agreement; sorta′tion, sorting out; sort′er, one who separates and arranges, as letters.—*n.pl.* sort′es (*-ēz*; L. *-ās*), divination by chance opening of the Bible, Homer, Virgil, etc.—*ns.* sort′ilege (*-i-lij*; L. sortilegus, a diviner), divination; sortil′eger; sortil′egy.—*n.* and *adj.* sort′ing.—*ns.* sorti′tion, the casting of lots; sort′ment, a sorting out: an assortment. —a good sort, a decent fellow; in a sort, in a manner; in some sort, in a way: as it were; in sort, in a body (*Shak.*): inasmuch (*Spens.*); of a sort, of sorts, inferior: out of sorts, out of order, slightly unwell: with some sorts of type in the fount exhausted (*print.*); sort of (*coll.*, used adverbially and parenthetically), as it were: rather; that's your sort, that's right: well done: go on. [L. *sors*, *sortis*, a lot, *sortīrī*, to draw lots; partly through O.Fr.]

sortie, *sör′tē*, *n.* a sally of besieged to attack the besiegers: a raiding excursion.—*v.i.* to sally. [Fr.,—*sortir*, to go out, to issue; origin doubtful.]

sortilege, etc. See sort.

sorus, *sō′rəs*, *sö′*, *n.* a cluster of sporangia or soredia:—*pl.* so′ri.—*adj.* so′ral. [Gr. *sōros*, a heap.]

S O S, *es-ō-es′*, *n.* an appeal for help or rescue. —*v.i.* to make such an appeal. [Arbitrary code signal.]

**so-so** (or **so so**), *sō'sō, adj.* neither very good nor very bad: tolerable: indifferent.—Also *adv.* [so.]

**soss**, *sos, n.* a mess: a dish of sloppy food: a puddle: a heavy fall: a plump.—*v.t.* to dirty: to slobber up: to throw carelessly about.—*v.i.* to plump down: to splash about.—*adv.* plump. —*n.* **soss'ing.** [Imit.]

**sostenuto**, *sos-te-nōō'tō, -nū', (mus.) adj.* sustained. —*adv.* with full time allowed for each note. [It.]

**sot**, *sot, n.* a fool *(obs.)*: one stupefied by drinking: a habitual drunkard.—*v.i.* to play the sot. —*adj.* **sott'ed**, besotted.—*n.* **sott'ing.**—*adj.* **sott'- ish**, like a sot: foolish: stupid with drink.— *adv.* **sott'ishly.**—*n.* **sott'ishness.** [O.Fr. *sot.*]

**Sotadic**, *sō-tad'ik,* **Sotadean**, *sō-* or *so-tə-dē'ən, adjs.* pertaining to *Sōtadēs,* a lascivious and scurrilous Greek poet (fl. 276 B.C.), or his writings, or in his metre: coarse and scurrilous: palindromic.—*n.* a satire in his manner: a catalectic tetrameter of ionics *a majore* (see **Ionic**).

**soterial**, *sō-tē'ri-əl, adj.* pertaining to salvation. —*adj.* **sōtēriolog'ical.**—*n.* **sōtēriol'ogy,** the doctrine of salvation. [Gr. *sōtēriā,* salvation— *sōtēr,* a saviour.]

**Sothic**, *sō'thik, adj.* of or pertaining to Sirius.— **Sothic cycle,** or **period,** a period of 1460 years, after which the beginning of the Egyptian year of 365 days again coincides with the beginning of the Sothic year, which was reckoned from the heliacal rising of Sirius. [Egyptian name of Sirius, given in Gr. as *Sōthis.*]

**sotho.** See **Basuto.**

**sottisier**, *so-tēz-yā, n.* a collection of jokes, etc. [Fr.—*sottise,* folly.]

**sotto voce**, *sot'tō vō'che, adv.* in an undertone, aside. [It., below the voice.]

**sou**, *sōō, n.* a French five-centime piece. [Fr.,— L. *solidus;* cf. **sold, soldier, soldo.**]

**souari, saouari**, *sow-ä'ri, n.* a tree (Caryocar) of Guiana yielding a durable timber and edible butternuts.—**s(a)oua'ri-nut.** [Fr. *saouari,* from Galibi.]

**soubise**, *sōō-bēz', n.* an 18th-cent. cravat: an onion sauce (**soubise sauce**). [Fr., after the French Marshal Prince de *Soubise* (1715-87).]

**soubrette**, *sōō-bret', n.* a pert, coquettish, intriguing maid-servant in comedy: a singer of light songs of similar character: a maid-servant, lady's maid. [Fr.,—Prov. *soubreto* (fem.), coy.]

**soubriquet.** See **sobriquet.**

**souce, souct,** old spellings *(Spens., Shak.)* of **souse, soused.**

**souchong**, *sōō-shong', -chong', n.* a fine sort of black tea. [Chin. *siao,* small, *chung,* sort.]

**Soudan(ese).** See **Sudan.**

**souffle**, *sōō'fl, n.* a murmuring in auscultation. [Fr.]

**soufflé**, *sōō'flā, n.* a light dish, properly one with white of egg whisked into a froth.—*adj.* prepared thus. [Fr., pa.p. of *souffler*—L. *sufflāre,* to blow.]

**sough**, *sow, suf,* or *(Scot.) sōōhh, v.i.* to sigh, as the wind.—*v.t.* to whine out: to sigh out: to hum.—*n.* a sighing of the wind: a deep sigh: a vague rumour: a whining tone of voice.— **keep a calm sough,** to keep quiet. [O.E. *swōgan,* to rustle.]

**sough**, *suf, n.* a drain, sewer, mine-adit.—**sough'- ing-tile,** a drain-tile. [Cf. Flem. dial. *zoeg,* a small ditch.]

**sought**, *söt, pa.t.* and *pa.p.* of **seek.**

**souk**, *sōōk, n.* among Eastern Muslim people, a market-place. [Ar. *sūq.*]

**soul**, *sōl, n.* life *(obs.)*: that which thinks, feels, desires, etc.: the ego: a spirit, embodied or disembodied: innermost being or nature: that which one identifies with oneself: moral and emotional nature, power, or sensibility: nobleness of spirit or its sincere expression: a complete embodiment or exemplification: an element: essence: the essential part: an indwelling or animating principle: the moving spirit, inspirer, leader: a person: the lungs of a goose, etc.: a violin sound-post.—*interj.* by my soul.— *adjs.* **souled,** having a soul, esp., in compounds, of this or that kind; **soul'ful,** having or expressive of deep or elevated feeling, sincere or affected.—*adv.* **soul'fully.**—*n.* **soul'fulness.**—*adj.* **soul'less,** without a soul: lacking animation or nobleness of mind: mean, without spirit.—*adv.* **soul'lessly,** in a soulless manner.—*n.* **soul'- lessness.**—**soul'-bell,** a passing bell.—*adj.* **soul'- confirming** *(Shak.),* ratifying the devoting of the soul.—**soul'-cūr'er** *(Shak.),* a parson.—*adjs.* **soul'-fear'ing** *(Shak.),* terrifying the soul; **soul'- killing** *(Shak.).*—**soul'-search'ing,** a critical examination of one's actions, motives, etc.— Also *adj.*—**soul'-shot, -scot, -scat,** a payment to the church on behalf of a dead person, a funeral payment.—*adj.* **soul'-sick,** morally diseased.— **soul'-sleeper,** a psychopannychist.—*adj.* **soul'- stirring.** [O.E. *sāwol;* Ger. *seele.*]

**souldan,** an old form of **soldan.**

**souldier,** an old spelling of **soldier.**

**soum, sowm,** *sōōm, (Scot.) n.* the proportion of sheep or cattle suitable for any pasture: pasture for one cow or its equivalent in sheep, etc.— *v.t.* and *v.i.* to determine in terms of soums.— *n.* **soum'ing.**—**souming and rouming,** the determination of the number of soums appropriate to a common pasture, and their apportionment (according to ability to fodder through winter) to the various roums or holdings. [A form of **sum.**]

**sound,** *sownd, adj.* safe: whole: uninjured, unimpaired: in good condition: healthy: wholesome: deep (as sleep): solid: thorough (as a beating): well-founded: well-grounded: trustworthy: of the right way of thinking: orthodox. —*adv.* soundly, completely fast, as in sleep.— *adv.* **sound'ly.**—*n.* **sound'ness.** [O.E. *gesund;* Ger. *gesund.*]

**sound,** *sownd, n.* a strait: a fish's swimming bladder. [O.E. *sund,* swimming.]

**sound,** *sownd, n.* sensation of hearing: transmitted disturbance perceived or perceptible by the ear: esp. a tone produced by regular vibrations (opp. to *noise*): mere noise, without meaning or sense or distinguished from sense: report, rumour: hearing-distance.—*v.i.* to give out a sound: to resound: to be audible: to be sounded: to be famed: to give an impression on hearing: to tend *(obs.)*: to call, as by trumpet.—*v.t.* to cause to make a sound: to produce, utter, make, the sound of: to utter audibly: to pronounce: to announce, publish, proclaim, celebrate, signal, direct, by sound: to mean *(obs.)*: to examine by percussion and listening. —*ns.* **sound'er; sound'ing,** emission of sound: a signal by trumpet, bell or the like, as for the rise of the curtain: examination by percussion. —*adj.* making a sound: sonorous: resounding: having a magnificent sound.—*adv.* **sound'ingly.** —*adj.* **sound'less.**—*adv.* **sound'lessly.**—**sound'- bar,** a bass-bar; **sound barrier** *(aero.),* difficulty met about the speed of sound when power required to increase speed rises steeply; **sound'- board,** a thin resonating plate of wood or metal in a musical instrument: in an organ, the apparatus that conveys the air from the wind-chest to the appropriate pipes: a sounding-board; **sound'-boarding,** boards between joists carrying pugging to make a floor soundproof; **sound'-body,** a resonance-box; **sound'-box,** a resonance-box: part of a gramophone supporting the diaphragm; **sound broadcasting,** broadcasting by radio as opposed to television; **sound effects,** sounds other than dialogue or music used in films, radio and television; **sound'-film**, a cinematograph film with sychronised sound-track; **sound'-hole**, an *f*-shaped hole in the belly of a violin, etc; **sound'ing-board**, a structure for carrying a speaker's voice towards the audience: a sound-board; **sound mixer**, the person who controls the tone and volume of sound to be recorded for a motion picture; **sound'-post**, a short post connecting the belly and back of a violin, etc., under the bridge.—*adj.* **sound'proof**, impenetrable by sound.—*v.t.* to render soundproof.—**sound'proofing**; **sound'-shadow**, a region of silence behind a barrier to sound; **sound'-shift**, a series of regular changes in stop-consonants differentiating Germanic from other Indo-Germanic languages, or (*second shift*) High German from other Germanic; **sound spectrogram**, a record produced by a **sound spectrograph**, an electronic instrument which makes a graphic representation of qualities of a sound, as frequency, intensity, etc.; **sound spectrography**; **sound'-track**, on a cinematograph film, the magnetic tape on which sounds are recorded; **sound'-wave**, a longitudinal disturbance propagated through air or other medium.—**sound off** (about, on), to speak loudly and freely, esp. in complaint: to boast. [M.E. *soun*—A.Fr.—L. *sonus*; for *d cf. pound (3).]

**sound**, *sownd*, *v.t.* to measure the depth of: to probe: to try to discover the inclinations, thoughts, etc., of.—*v.i.* to take soundings: to dive deep, as a whale.—*n.* a probe for examining the bladder, etc.—*ns.* **sound'er**, one who sounds: apparatus for taking soundings; **sound'ing**, the action of that which or one who sounds: an ascertained depth: (in *pl.*) waters in which an ordinary sounding-line will reach the bottom. —**sound'ing-lead**, the weight at the end of a sounding-line; **sound'ing-line**, a line with a plummet at the end for soundings; **sounding rocket**, a rocket devised to gather high-altitude meteorological data and to radio it back to earth; **sound'ing-rod**, a rod for measuring water in a ship's hold. [O.E. *sund-* (in compounds), cf. **sound** (2); or perh. O.Fr. *sonder*, to sound, which may be from Gmc.]

**sound**, *sownd*, (*obs.*) *n.* and *v.i.* Same as **swound.** See **swoon.**

**sounder**, *sown'dər*, *n.* a herd of swine: a young boar. [O.Fr. *sundre*; of Gmc. origin; cf. O.E. *sunor.*]

**soup**, *sōōp*, *n.* the nutritious liquid obtained by boiling meat or vegetables in stock: a photographic developer (*slang*): stolen plate melted down (*slang*): various slang senses, as nitroglycerine, dope for a horse.—*ns.* **soup'er**, in Ireland, one who dispenses soup as a means of proselytising: one really or supposedly so converted.—*adj.* **soup'y.**—*adj.* **soup'ed-up** (*slang*), of e.g. an engine, having had the power increased. —**soup'-kitchen**, a place for supplying soup to the poor; **soup'-mai'gre** (or **mea'gre**), a thin fish or vegetable soup, originally for fast-days; **soup'-plate**, a large deep plate; **soup'spoon**; **soup'-ticket**, a ticket entitling one to soup at a soup-kitchen; **soup'-tureen.**—**in the soup**, in difficulties or trouble; **soup up** (*slang*), to increase the power of; **the ticket for soup** (*slang*), the ticket (q.v.). [O.Fr. *soupe*; cf. **sop.**]

**soupçon**, *sōōp-sɔ̃*, *n.* a hardly perceptible quantity. [Fr., suspicion.]

**souple**, *sōōp'l*, *adj.* a form of **supple** (*dial.*): of silk, lightly scoured: clever (*Scot.*).—*v.t.* to make supple or souple.

**souple**, *sōōp'l*, *n.* a Scots form of **swipple**: a cudgel (*Scott*).

**sour**, *sowr*, *adj.* having an acid taste or smell: turned, rancid, or fermented: rank: of beasts, heavy, strong: cold and wet: embittered, crabbed,

or peevish: disagreeable: inharmonious (*lit., fig.*): bad, unsuccessful: containing sulphur compounds.—*v.t.* to make sour: to treat with dilute acid.—*v.i.* to become sour.—*n.* an acid drink, as a gin or whisky cocktail that contains lemon or lime-juice.—*n.* **sour'ing**, turning or becoming sour: vinegar: the crab-apple: treatment with dilute acid in bleaching.—*adj.* **sour'ish.**—*advs.* **sour'ishly**; **sour'ly.**—*n.* **sour'ness.**—*adj.* **sour'-cold** (*Shak.*).—**sour'-crout** (see **sauerkraut**); **sour'-dough**, leaven: a piece of dough reserved to leaven a new batch: in Canada and Alaska, an old-timer.—*adj.* **sour'-eyed**, morose-looking.— **sour'-gourd**, the cream-of-tartar tree: a tropical grass akin to millet: sorrel; **sour'puss** (*slang*), a sour-tempered person; **sour'-sop**, a tropical American fruit: the tree (of the custard-apple genus) that bears it. [O.E. *sūr*; Ger. *sauer*, O.N. *sūrr.*]

**source**, *sōrs, sörs*, *n.* a spring: the head of a stream: origin: rise: (*Spens.* **sourse**) perh. surging: originating cause: that from which anything rises or originates: a book or document serving as authority for history, or furnishing matter or inspiration for an author.— **source'-book**, a book of original documents for historic study. [O.Fr. *sorse* (Fr. *source*), from *sourdre*—L. *surgĕre*, to rise.]

**sourdeline**, *sōōr'də-lēn*, *n.* a small bagpipe. [Fr.]

**sourdine**, *sōōr-dēn'*, (*mus.*) *n.* a mute or sordino. [Fr.; cf. **sordino.**]

**sourock**, *sōō'rək*, (*Scot.*) *n.* sorrel. [**sour.**]

**souse**, *sows, sows*, (*obs.*) *n.* Same as **sou**:—*pl.* **souse, sous'es.**

**souse**, *sows*, *n.* pickled meat, esp. pig's feet or ears: an ear (*dial.* or *facet.*): pickling liquid: a plunge in pickling or other liquid: a ducking: a drenching: a wash: a sluicing with water: a getting drunk (*slang*): a drunkard (*U.S.*): a heavy blow or fall: a thump: an impact: a rising from the ground, taking wing (in the falconer's phrase *at souse, at the souse*, when the hawk gets a chance of striking): hence the downward swoop of a bird of prey.—*adv.* with a plunge: with a heavy impact: plump: suddenly.—*v.t.* to pickle: to plunge, immerse, duck: to drench, soak: to make drunk: to dash: to fling down: to smite: to swoop down upon.—*v.i.* to fall with a plunge: to be drenched: to wash thoroughly: to get drunk: to strike: to impinge: to fall heavily: to swoop as a hawk.—*adj.* **soused**, pickled: very wet: drunk (*slang*).—*n.* and *adj.* **sous'ing.**— **souse'-tub**; **souse'wife.**—Also **sauce, sowce, sows(s)e** in old writers. [Partly O.Fr. *sous, souce* —O.H.G. *sulza*, from the root of **salt**; partly imit. (cf. German *saus*); partly **source** in its old sense of rising.]

**souslik.** Same as **suslik.**

**sout** (*Spens.*). Same as **soot.**

**soutache**, *sōō-täsh'*, *n.* a narrow braid. [Fr.]

**soutane**, *sōō-tän'*, *n.* a cassock. [Fr.,—It. *sottana* —L. *subtus*, beneath.]

**soutar.** See **souter.**

**souteneur**, *sōōt'nœr*, *n.* a prostitute's bully or exploiter. [Fr., supporter, protector; cf. **sustain.**]

**souter**, *sōō'tər*, (*Scot.*) *n.* a shoemaker, a cobbler. — Also **sow'ter**, **sou'tar** — *adj.* **sou'terly.**— **souter's clod** (*Scott*), a brown wheaten roll. [O.E. *sūtere* (O.N. *sūtari*)—L. *sūtor—suĕre*, to sew.]

**souterrain**, *sōō-te-rẽ, sōō'tə-rān*, *n.* an underground chamber. [Fr.]

**south**, *sowth*, *adv.* in the direction contrary to north.—*n.* the point of the horizon, the region, or the part, in that direction: the south wind: (*cap*; with *the*) Southern States of U.S.—*adj.* lying towards the south: forming the part, or that one of two, that is towards the south: blowing from the south: (of a pole of a magnet, usu.)

south-seeking.—*v.i.* (*sowdh*) to move or veer towards the south: to cross the meridian.—*n.* souther (*sowdh'ər*), a south wind or gale.—*v.i.* (*sudh'ər*) to move or veer towards the south.—*adj.* southering (*sudh'*).—*n.* southerliness (*sudh'*). —*adj.* and *adv.* southerly (*sudh'*), towards or (of wind) from the south.—*adj.* southern (*sudh'*), of the south: in the south or in the direction toward it: (of wind) from the south: (*cap.*) of, from or pertaining to the South.—*n.* a southerner. —*n.* southerner (*sudh'*), a native or inhabitant of the south: (*cap.*) an inhabitant of the U.S. South.—*v.t.* southernise, -ize (*sudh'*), to render southern in character.—*n.* southernism (*sudh'*), a form of expression peculiar to the south, esp. the Southern States of America.—*adj.* southernly (*sudh'*), southerly. — *adv.* towards the south.—*adjs.* (*superl.*) southermost (*rare*), southernmost (*sudh'*).—*n.* southing (*sowdh'*), distance, deviation, tendency or motion to the south: meridian passage.—*adj.* (*superl.*) south'-most. — *adj.* southron, Southron, Southroun (*sudh'rən*; *Scot.*), southern, esp. English as distinguished from Scots.—*n.* a southerner: an Englishman: the English of England.—*adj.*, *adv.*, and *n.* southward (*sowth'wərd*; *naut.* *sudh'ərd*).—*adj.* and *adv.* south'wardly.—*adv.* south'wards.—*adjs.* south-bound (*sowth'*), bound for the south; south'-country.—*adj.* and *adv.* south-east' (or *sowth'*), midway between south and east.—*n.* the direction midway: the region lying in, the wind blowing from, that direction. —south-east'er, a strong wind from the southeast.—*adj.* and *adv.* south-east'erly, towards or (of wind) from the south-east.—*adj.* south-east'ern, belonging to, or being in, the southeast, or in that direction.—*adj.* and *adv.* south-east'ward, toward the south-east.—*n.* the region to the south-east.—*adj.* and *adv.* south-east'-wardly.—*adj.* south-east'wards.—Southern Cross, a conspicuous southern constellation with four bright stars placed crosswise; southernwood (*sudh'*), an aromatic plant of southern Europe, of the wormwood genus (Artemisia); southland (*sowth'*), the south (also *adj.*); south'lander.— *adj.* south'paw, left-handed.—*n.* a left-handed person, esp. in sport.—*adj.* south'-pō'lar.— south pole, the end of the earth's axis in Antarctica: its projection on the celestial sphere: (usually) the south-seeking pole of a magnet (logically the north-seeking); South Sea, the Pacific ocean.—*adj.* south-seeking (*sowth'*), turning towards the earth's magnetic south pole.— *ns.*, *adjs.* and *advs.* south-south-east', south-south-west', in a direction midway between south and south-east or south-west.—*adj.* and *adv.* south-west (*sowth'* or *sow'*, or -*west'*), midway between south and west.—*n.* the direction between south and west: the region lying that way: the wind blowing from that direction.—south-, sou'-west'er, a gale from the south-west: a waterproof hat with flap at the back of the neck.— *adjs.* south'-west'erly, toward or (of wind) from the south-west; south'-west'ern, belonging to, or lying in, the south-west or in that direction. —*adj.*, *adv.*, and *n.* south-west'ward.—*adj.* and *adv.* south-west'wardly.—*adv.* south-west'wards. [O.E. *sūth*; Ger. *süd*, O.N. *suthr.*]

Southcottian, *sowth-kot'i-ən*, *n.* a follower of Joanna Southcott (1750-1814), who was expected to give birth to a Shiloh or Prince of Peace.— Also *adj.*

Southdown, *sowth'down*, *adj.* pertaining to the *South Downs* in Hampshire and Sussex, the famous breed of sheep so named, or their mutton. —*n.* a sheep of this breed, or its mutton.

southsay, southsayer. Same as soothsay, etc.

souvenir, *sōō'və-nēr*, *n.* a memento: a keepsake. —*n.* sov'ena(u)nce (*Spens.*), remembrance, memory. [Fr. *souvenir*—L. *subvenīre*, to come

up, to come to mind—*sub*, under, *venīre*, to come.]

sovereign, or (after *Milt.*) sovran, *sov'rin*, -*rən*, *n.* a supreme ruler or head: a monarch: an Irish mayor (*obs.*): a gold coin from Henry VII to Charles I worth 22s. 6d. to 10s., from 1817 a pound (*coll.* sov, sov).—*adj.* supreme: excelling all others: having supreme power residing in itself or himself: of sovereignty: (of contempt) utmost: highly efficacious.—*adv.* sov'ereignly, supremely: as a sovereign.—*n.* sov'ereignty, (*poet.*) sov'ranty, pre-eminence: supreme and independent power: the territory of a sovereign or of a sovereign state. [O.Fr. *sovrain* and It. *sovrano*—L. *super*, above.]

soviet, *sō'vi-et*, *so'*, *n.* a council, esp. one of those forming since 1917 the machinery of local and national government in Russia (the Union of Soviet Socialist Republics)—the local councils elected by workers, peasants, and soldiers, the higher councils consisting of deputies from the lower.—*adj.* (*cap.*) of the U.S.S.R.—*adj.* soviet'ic.—*v.t.* so'vietise, -ize, to transform to the soviet model.—*n.* so'vietism, the principles and practices of a soviet government, specif. communism: a characteristic mannerism indicative of soviet ideology.—*adj.* Sovietolog'ical. —*n.* Sovietol'ogist, one who has made a special study of the theory and practice of government in the U.S.S.R. and of current affairs there.— the Soviet, the U.S.S.R. [Russ. *sovet*, council.]

sow, sow, *n.* a female pig: a female badger, etc.: a term of reproach for a fat, lazy, greedy, or sluttish person, esp. a woman: a main channel for molten iron, leading to *pigs*: metal solidified there: a movable shed for protecting besiegers (*hist.*).—sow'-bread, a cyclamen, esp. *C. europaeum*, whose tubers are eaten by swine; sow'-bug, a wood-louse.—*adj.* sow'-drunk (*coll.*), beastly drunk.—sow'-gelder, one who spays sows.—*n.* and *adj.* sow'-skin.—sow'-thistle, a thistle-like genus of plants (Sonchus) with milky juice and yellow flowers. [O.E. *sū*, *sugu*; Ger. *sau*, O.N. *syr*; L. *sūs*, Gr. *hȳs*.]

sow, *sō*, *v.t.* to scatter or put in the ground, as seed: to plant by strewing: to scatter seed over: to spread, strew, disseminate.—*v.i.* to scatter seed for growth:—*pa.t.* sowed (*sōd*); *pa.p.* sown (*sōn*), or sowed.—*ns.* sow'er; sow'ing.— sow'ing-machine, a machine for sowing seed. [O.E. *sāwan*; Ger. *säen*, O.N. *sā*, Goth. *saian.*]

sowar, *sō-wär*, *n.* an Indian trooper, mounted policeman, or attendant.—*n.* sowarr'y, sowarr'ee, a mounted retinue, cavalcade. [Urdu *sawār*, horseman.]

sowce. See souse.

sowens, sowans, *sō'ənz*, (*Scot.*) *n.pl.* a dish made from the farina remaining among the husks of oats, flummery. [Supposed to be from Gael. *sùghan*, the liquid of sowens—*sùgh*, juice.]

sowf(f). See sowth.

sowl, sowle. See sole (4).

sowm. See soum.

sownd, sownd, (*Spens.*) *v.t.* app., to wield.

sownd, sownd, (*Spens.*) *n.* Same as swound, swoon.

sowne, sown, (*Spens.*) *n.* Same as sound (3).

sowp, sowp, (*Scot.*) *n.* a spoonful, sip, small drink. [O.N. *saup*; cf. sop, sup.]

sowse, sowsse, sows, (*Spens.*; *Shak.*) *vb.* and *n.* Same as souse.

sowter. See souter.

sowth, sowth, sowf, sowff, *sowf*, (*Scot.*) *v.i.* and *v.t.* to whistle or hum over softly. [Scots forms of obs. *solf*—Fr. *solfier*, to sol-fa.]

sox, soks, *n.pl.* a slang spelling of socks.

soy, soi, soya, *sō'ya*, *soi'a*, soja, *sō'ya*, *sō'ja*, *n.* a thick, piquant sauce made from the soy-bean (also soy, soya, soja sauce): the soy bean, rich in oil and protein: the eastern Asiatic papilionaceous plant (*Glycine soja*, *G. hispida* or *max*) producing it.—**soy bean; soya bean, soja bean; soy, soya, soja flour.** [Jap. *shō-yu*, coll. *soy*, Du. *soya*, *soja*—Chin. *shi-yu*, salt bean oil.]

**soyle**, *soil*, (*Spens.*) *n*. app., body, prey. [Unexplained.]

**sozzle**, *soz'l*, *v.t.* (*U.S.* and *dial.*) to splash: to make sloppy: to intoxicate: to perform sluttishly.—*n.* (*U.S.* and *dial.*) slops: sluttishness: a slattern.—*adjs.* **sozz'led** (*coll.*), drunk; **sozz'ly** (*U.S.* and *dial.*), sloppy. [Cf. **soss.**]

**spa**, *spä*, formerly *spō*, *n*. a mineral spring: a mineral water resort.—*n.* **spa'-well.** [*Spa* in Belgium.]

**space**, *späs*, *n*. that in which material bodies have extension: a portion of extension: room: intervening distance: interval: an open or empty place: regions remote from the earth: an interval between lines or words: a type used for making such an interval: an interval between the lines of the stave: a portion, extent, or interval of time: a short time: opportunity, leisure.—*v.t.* to make, arrange, or increase intervals between.—*v.i.* (*Spens.*) to walk about.—*adjs.* **spaced; space'less.**—*ns.* **spac'er,** one who, or that which, spaces: an instrument for reversing a telegraphic current: a space-bar; **spacing** (*späs'ing*).—*adjs.* **spacial** (*spā'shl*; see spatial); **spacious** (*spā'shəs*), extensive: ample: roomy: wide.—*adv.* **spa'ciously.**—*n.* **spa'ciousness.**—**space age,** the present time when exploration of, and ability to travel in, space up to the limit of, and beyond the earth's atmosphere are increasing; **space'-band,** a wedge for justifying the line in mechanical type-setting; **space'-bar,** a bar for making spaces in typewriting; **space'-craft,** a vehicle, manned or unmanned, designed for putting into space, orbiting the earth, or reaching other planets; **space'-heater,** an electrical device which puffs out hot air to warm a room; **space'-heat'ing; space'-lattice,** an arrangement of points in three-dimensional space at the intersections of equally spaced parallel lines—such as the arrangement of atoms in a crystal disclosed by X-ray spectroscopy; **space'-man, -woman,** a traveller in space; **space medicine,** branch of medicine concerned with effects of conditions in space on the human body; **space'-platform, space'-station,** a platform in space planned as an observatory and/or a landing-stage in space travel; **space probe,** a spacecraft designed to obtain, and usu. transmit, information about the environment into which it is sent; **space'ship,** a spacecraft; **space'-suit,** a suit devised for use in space-travel; **space'-time',** normal three-dimensional space plus dimension of time, modified by gravity in relativity theory; **space'-travel; space'-traveller; space'-travelling; space vehicle** (see vehicle); **space'-writ'er,** one paid by space filled; **spacious times,** days of expansion (in knowledge, trade, etc.) and scope (for discovery, adventure, and the like), as in the reign of Queen Elizabeth I.—**space out,** to set wide apart or wider apart. [Fr. *espace*—L. *spatium*; Gr. *spaein*, to draw.]

**spadassin,** *spad'ə-sin*, *n*. a swordsman, a bravo. [Fr.,—It. *spadaccino*—*spada*, a sword.]

**spade,** *spād*, *n*. a broad-bladed digging tool: a whaler's knife: a spade's depth, spit.—*v.t.* to dig or remove with a spade.—*n.* **spade'ful,** as much as a spade will hold:—*pl.* **spade'fuls.**—**spade'-beard,** a spade-shaped beard; **spade'-bone,** the scapula; **spade'-foot,** a toad with digging foot; **spade'-guin'ea,** a guinea with spade-shaped shield, coined 1787-99; **spade'-hus'bandry,** cultivation by digging instead of ploughing; **spade(s)'man,** a worker with the spade; **spade'work,** preparatory drudgery.—**call a spade a spade,** to speak out plainly without euphemism.

[O.E. *spadu*, *spædu*; akin to Gr. *spathē* (see next word).]

**spade,** *spād*, *n*. a playing-card with black leaf-shaped (on Spanish cards sword-shaped) pips: (not polite) a Negro or other coloured person. [Sp. *espada*, sword—L. *spatha*—Gr. *spathē*, a broad blade.]

**spade.** See **spado.**

**spadille,** *spə-dil'*, *n*. the ace of spades in the games of ombre and quadrille.—Also **spadill'o, spadill'io.** [Fr., Sp. *espadilla*, dim. of *espada*; see **spade** (2).]

**spadix,** *spā'diks*, (*bot.*) *n*. a fleshy spike of flowers:—*pl.* **spādices** (-*di'sēz*).—*adjs.* **spadiceous** (*spə-dish'əs*), having, like, of the nature of, a spadix: coloured like a date: shaped like a palm-branch; **spadicifloral** (*spā-di-si-flō'rəl, -flō'*), having flowers in a spathe, as arum, palms, and some other monocotyledons. [Gr. *spādix, -ikos*, a torn-off (palm) branch, in L. date-coloured, bay.]

**spado,** *spā'dō*, *spä'*, *n*. a castrated or impotent person or animal:—*pl.* **spadones** (*spä-dō'nēz, -näs*), **spä'do(e)s.**—Also (*rare*) **spade.** [L. *spādō, -ōnis*—Gr. *spädōn, -ōnos*—*spaein*, to pull, tear.]

**spadroon,** *spə-drōōn'*, (*hist.*) *n*. a cut-and-thrust sword: swordplay with it. [Fr. (Genevan dialect) *espadron*.]

**spae,** *spā*, (*Scot.*) *v.t.* and *v.i.* to foretell, divine.—*n.* **spä'er.**—**spae'man; spae'wife.** [O.N. *spä.*]

**spaghetti,** *spä-, spə-get'ti*, *n*. an edible, cord-like paste intermediate between macaroni and vermicelli.—**spaghetti (alla) bolognese,** spaghetti served with a meat and tomato sauce. [It., pl. of *spaghetto*, dim. of *spago*, a cord.]

**spagyric, -al,** *spə-jir'ik, -əl, adjs.* alchemical.—*ns.* **spagyr'ic, spagyrist** (*spaj'ər-ist*), an alchemist.—Also **spagir'ic, spager'ic,** etc. [Prob. coined by Paracelsus.]

**spahi,** *spä'hē*, *n*. formerly a Turkish, now a French Algerian cavalryman.—Also **spa'hee.** [Turk. (from Pers.) *sipāhi*; cf. **sepoy.**]

**spain.** Same as **spane.**

**spairge.** See **sparge.**

**spake,** *spāk*. See **speak.**

**spald, spall, spalle.** See **spauld.**

**spale,** *spāl*, (*Scot.*) *n*. a splinter: a chip. [Cf. next.]

**spall,** *spöl*, *v.t.* and *v.i.* to split, splinter, to chip.—*n.* a chip or splinter, esp. of stone.—*v.t.* and *v.i.* **spalt,** to splinter.—*adj.* brittle.—*n.* **spallā'tion,** a nuclear reaction in which bombardment by high-energy particles produces a large number of disintegration particles not entirely identifiable. [Cf. M.E. *spalden*, to split; Ger. *spalten.*]

**spalpeen,** *spal-pēn'*, *n*. a rascal, a mischievous fellow: a boy. [Ir. *spailpín*, a (migratory) labourer.]

**span,** *span*, *n*. the space from the end of the thumb to the end of the little finger when the fingers are extended: nine inches: distance from wing-tip to wing-tip in an aeroplane: distance between abutments, piers, supports, etc., or the portion of a structure (e.g. a bridge) between: total spread or stretch: a stretch of time, esp. of life.—*v.t.* to measure by spans: to measure: to arch over, bridge: to stretch over: to bridge: to encompass:—*pr.p.* **spann'ing;** *pa.t.* and *pa.p.* **spanned.**—*adj.* **span'less,** that cannot be spanned or measured.—**span'-counter, span'-farthing,** a game in which one tries to throw a counter or coin within a span of his opponent's.—*adj.* **span'-long,** of the length of a span.—**span'-roof,** a roof with equal slopes. [O.E. *spann*; cf. Ger. *spanne.*]

**span,** *span*, *n*. a pair of horses: a team of oxen.—*v.t.* to yoke: to wind up (*obs.*). [Du. and L.G. *span.*]

**span,** *span*, *adj.* fresh, short for **span'-new'**, quite new, new as a fresh-cut chip.—**spick and span** (see **spick**). [O.N. *spān-nȳr*—*spān*, chip (cf. **spoon**), *nȳr*, new.]

**span**, *span*. See **spin**.

**spanaemia**, *span-ē'mi-ə*, *n.* deficiency of red corpuscles in the blood.—*adj.* **spanae'mic.** [Gr. *spanos*, lacking, *haima*, blood.]

**spancel**, *span'sl*, *n.* a hobble, esp. for a cow.—*v.t.* to hobble.—*adj.* **span'celled.** [Du. or L.G. *spansel*.]

**spandrel, spandril**, *span'drəl*, *n.* the space between the curve of an arch and the enclosing mouldings, string-course, or the like. [Poss. conn. with **expand**.]

**spane, spain, spean**, *spān*, (*Scot*.) *v.t.* to wean. [M.Du. or M.L.G. *spanen*, or O.Fr. *espanir*; cf. Ger. *spänen*.]

**spang**, *spang*, *n.* a glittering ornament (*obs*.): a clasp (*arch*.).—*v.t.* (*obs*.) to sprinkle with spangs. —*n.* **spangle** (*spang'gl*), a small, thin, glittering plate of metal: a sparkling speck, flake, or spot. —*v.t.* to adorn with spangles.—*v.i.* to glitter. — *adj.* **spang'led.** — *ns.* **spang'ler; spang'let** (*Shelley*).—*n.* and *adj.* **spang'ling.**—*adj.* **spang'ly.** [O.E. *spang*, clasp; cf. Du. *spang*, Ger. *spange*, *spängel*.]

**spang**, *spang*, (chiefly *Scot*.) *n.* a bound: a sudden movement or blow.—*v.i.* to bound.—*v.t.* to dash.—**spang'-cockle**, the flicking of a marble, etc., from the forefinger with the thumb-nail. [Origin obscure.]

**spangle**, etc. See **spang** (1).

**Spaniard**, *span'yərd*, *n.* a native or citizen of *Spain*: a Spanish ship (*arch*.). [M.E. *Spaignarde* —O.Fr. *Espaignart*.]

**spaniel**, *span'yəl*, *n.* a kind of dog, usu. liver-and-white, or black-and-white, with large pendent ears: one who fawns.—*adj.* like a spaniel: fawning, mean.—*v.t.* (*Shak*.) to follow or fawn on like a spaniel.—*v.i.* (or *v.t.* with *it*) to play the spaniel.—*adj.* and *adv.* **span'iel-like.**— **Blenheim spaniel**, red-and-white (see **Blenheim**); **clumber spaniel**, lemon-and-white (see **clumber**); **field-** or **land-spaniel**, hunting breeds (e.g. *cockers, springers*); (**Irish**) **water spaniel**, a (liver-coloured) spaniel for retrieving waterfowl; **King Charles spaniel**, black-and-tan, brought into notice by *Charles* II; **Sussex spaniel**, golden-liver or brown; **toy spaniel**, a lapdog (see *Blenheim, King Charles*). [O.Fr. *espaigneul* (Fr. *épagneul*)—Sp. *Español*, Spanish.]

**spaniolate**, *span'yō-lāt*, **spaniolise, -ize, -liz**, *vs.t.* to hispanicise. [O.Fr. *Espaignol*, a Spaniard.]

**Spanish**, *span'ish*, *adj.* of or pertaining to *Spain*. —*n.* the language of Spain.—**Spanish bayonet**, a yucca with straight sword-shaped leaves; **Spanish broom**, a broom-like Mediterranean shrub (*Spartium junceum*) with showy yellow fragrant flowers; **Spanish chalk**, soapstone, French chalk; **Spanish chestnut**, the true chestnut; **Spanish cress**, a species of pepperwort; **Spanish dagger**, *Yucca gloriosa*; **Spanish fly**, a cantharid: a preparation of cantharides formerly used medicinally; **Spanish fowl**, a breed of domestic hen—also *white-faced black Spanish*; **Spanish grass**, esparto; **Spanish influenza**, a severe form of influenza, which, first noted in Spain, spread all over the world in 1918; **Spanish juice**, extract of liquorice-root; **Spanish Main** (i.e. mainland), the mainland coast of the Caribbean Sea: often popularly the Caribbean Sea itself; **Spanish needles**, an American weed of the bur-marigold genus with hooked fruits; **Spanish onion**, a large mild kind of onion; **Spanish sheep**, a merino; **Spanish soap**, Castile soap; **Spanish walk**, the piaffer.—**ride the Spanish mare** (*hist*.), to bestride the boom as a punishment; **walk Spanish**, to compel or be compelled to walk on tiptoe, lifted by the collar and the seat of the trousers—hence to proceed

or act under force. [*Spain*, with vowel-shortening.]

**spank**, *spangk*, *v.t.* and *v.i.* to move or drive with speed or spirit.—*n.* **spank'er**, one who walks with long vigorous strides: a fast-going horse: any person or thing particularly striking or dashing: a gold coin (*obs. slang*): a fore-and-aft sail on the aftermost mast.—*adj.* **spank'ing**, spirited, going freely: striking, beyond expectation: very large.—*adv.* **spank'ingly.** [Poss. back formation from **spanking**.]

**spank**, *spangk*, *v.t.* to strike with the flat of the hand, to smack.—*n.* a loud slap, esp. on the buttocks.—*n.* **spank'ing.** [Prob. imit.]

**spanner**, *span'ər*, *n.* an instrument for winding up a spring (*obs*.): a wrench for nuts, screws, etc. —**throw a spanner in the works**, to cause confusion or difficulty, upset plans. [Ger. *spanner*— *spannen*, to stretch; cf. **span** (2).]

**spar**, *spär*, *n.* a rafter: a pole: a bar or rail (chiefly *Scot*.; *Spens*. **sparre**): an undressed tree stem of medium girth: a general term for masts, yards, booms, gaffs, etc.—*v.t.* to fasten with a spar (*Spens*. **sperre**): to fasten: to shut: to fit with spars.—**spar deck**, a light upper deck. [O.E. *gesparrian*, to bar; Du. *spar* (n.), *sperren* (vb.); O.N. *sparri*; Ger. *sperren* (vb.).]

**spar**, *spär*, *n.* any bright non-metallic mineral, with a good cleavage (esp. in compounds, as *calc-spar, fluorspar, feldspar*; also *Iceland spar*): a crystal or fragment thereof: an ornament made of it.—*adj.* **sparry** (*spär'i*), of or like spar. [M.L.G. *spar*, related to O.E. *spærstān*, gypsum.]

**spar**, *spär*, *v.i.* to fight with spurs: to box, or make the actions of boxing: to dispute:—*pr.p.* **sparr'ing**; *pa.t.* and *pa.p.* **sparred.**—*n.* a boxing-match or demonstration: a cock-fight: a dispute.—*ns.* **sparr'er; sparr'ing.**—**sparring partner**, one with whom a boxer practises: a friend with whom one enjoys lively arguments. [Perh. O.Fr. *esparer* (Fr. *éparer*), to kick out; prob. Gmc.]

**sparable**, *spar'ə-bl*, *n.* a small headless nail used by shoemakers. [**sparrow-bill**.]

**spard**, *spärd*, *Spens*. for **spared**.

**spare**, *spär*, *v.t.* to use frugally: to do without: to part with voluntarily: to afford: to allow oneself, concede to oneself (*Milt*.): to abstain from using: to refrain from: to forbear to hurt, injure, punish, kill, end: to treat mercifully: to relieve or save from: to avoid: to avoid incurring: to save, hoard (*obs*.).—*v.i.* to be frugal: to forbear: to be merciful.—*adj.* sparing: frugal: scanty: lean: not in actual use: not required: kept or available for others or for such purposes as may occur.—*adv.* sparely.—*n.* spareness (*Milt*.): sparing: a spare room: a spare man: a spare part: a duplicate kept or carried for emergencies: in skittles, overturning all the pins with the first two balls —i.e. with a ball to spare (a *double spare*, with first ball only): the score for so doing.— *adj.* **spare'less**, unmerciful.—*adv.* **spare'ly.**—*ns.* **spare'ness; spar'er.**—*adj.* **spar'ing.**—*adv.* **spar'-ingly.**—**spare part**, a part for a machine ready to replace an identical part if it becomes faulty; **spare rib**, a piece of pork consisting of ribs with a little meat adhering to them; **spare room**, a bedroom for visitors: a parlour (*U.S.*); **spare time**, leisure time.—**to spare**, over and above what is required. [O.E. *sparian*, to spare, *spær*, sparing; Ger. *sparen*.]

**spare**, *spär*, (now *Scot*.) *n.* the slit at the top of a skirt. [Origin obscure.]

**Sparganium**, *spär-gā'ni-əm*, *n.* the bur-reed genus, constituting a family **Sparganiā'ceae**, akin to the reed-maces. [Gr. *sparganion*.]

**sparge**, *spärj*, *v.t.* to sprinkle—(*Scot*.) **spairge**, *spärj*.—*n.* **spar'ger**, a sprinkler. [L. *spargĕre*, to sprinkle.]

**spar-hawk**, *spär'-hök*, *n.* same as **sparrow-hawk**.

**Sparidae,** *spar'i-dē, n.pl.* the sea-bream family.—
*adj.* **spar'oid.** [Gr. *sparos,* the fish sargus.]
**spark,** *spärk, n.* a glowing or glittering particle:
anything of like appearance or character, as
easily extinguished, ready to cause explosion,
burning hot: a flash: an electric discharge
across a gap: anything active or vivid: a gay
sprightly person: a lover, a beau: (in *pl.*) a
ship's wireless operator (*naut. slang*).—*v.i.* to
emit sparks: to sparkle: to play the gallant
or lover.—*v.t.* to send forth as sparks: to send
sparks through.—*adj.* **spark'ish,** gay, jaunty,
showy.—*adv.* **spark'ishly.**—*adj.* **spark'less.**—*adv.*
**spark'lessly.**—*n.* **spark'let,** a small spark.—
**spark'-coil,** an induction coil: a connection of
high-resistance used to prevent sparking in
electrical apparatus; **spark'-gap,** the space between electrodes across which electric sparks
pass: apparatus with such a space; **spark'ing-
plug** (*U.S.* **spark'-plug**), in an internal-combustion
engine, a plug carrying wires between which an
electric spark passes to fire the explosive mixture
of gases.—**spark (off),** to cause to begin, kindle,
animate. [O.E. *spærca, spearca;* Du. *spark.*]
**sparke,** *spärk,* (*Spens.*) *n.* a weapon of some kind,
perh. an error for **sparthe.**
**sparkle,** *spärk'l, n.* a little spark: glitter: scintillation: emission of sparks: appearance of effer-
vescence (as of carbon dioxide in wine): vivacity: spirited animation: coruscation of wit.—
*v.i.* to emit sparks: to glitter: to effervesce with
glittering bubbles: to be bright, animated,
vivacious, or witty.—*v.t.* to cause to sparkle:
to throw out as, in, or like sparks.—*n.* **spark'ler,**
that which sparkles: a diamond or other gem
(*slang*): a small firework which can be held in
the hand.—*n.* and *adj.* **spark'ling.**—*adv.* **spark'-
lingly.** [Dim. and freq. of **spark.**]
**sparling,** *spär'ling,* **spirling,** *spûr', spir'ling,* (now
*Scot.*) *n.* the smelt. [Partly O.Fr. *esperlinge* (of
Gmc. origin), partly M.L.G. *spirling* or M.Du.
*spierling.*]
**sparrow,** *spar'ō, n.* a plain brown bird of the finch
family (*Passer domesticus,* house-sparrow, *P.
montanus,* tree-sparrow, or other of the genus):
extended to many other, usually brown, birds,
as the hedge-sparrow.—**sparr'ow-bill** (see **sparable**).—*adj.* **sparr'ow-blasted,** (in contempt)
dumbfounded.—**sparr'ow-hawk,** a genus (Accipiter) of long-legged, short-winged falcons, like
the goshawks, but smaller. [O.E. *spearwa;*
Goth. *sporwa,* O.N. *spörr,* Ger. *sperling.*]
**sparrow-grass,** *spar'ō-gräs, n.* a corruption of
**asparagus.**
**sparse,** *spärs, adj.* thinly scattered: scanty.—Also
*adv.*—*advs.* **spars'edly** (now *rare*); **sparse'ly.**—
*ns.* **sparse'ness; spars'ity.** [L. *sparsus,* pa.p. of
*spargĕre,* to scatter; Gr. *speirein,* to sow.]
**spart,** *spärt, n.* esparto: Spanish broom (*obs.*).—
*n.* **sparterie** (*-ə-rē;* Fr.), articles of esparto.
[L. *spartum,* Spanish broom, esparto, and Sp.
*esparto.*]
**Sparta,** *spär'tə, n.* a city of Greece, capital of
ancient Laconia.—*n.* **Spar'tan,** a citizen or native
of Sparta or Laconia: one displaying Spartan
qualities.—*adj.* of Sparta: Laconian: characteristic of Sparta—simple, hardy, rigorous, frugal,
laconic, militaristic, despising culture: of a
breed of bloodhounds.—*adv.* **Spar'tanly.** [Gr.
*Spartē* (Doric *Spartā*).]
**Spartacist,** *spär'tə-sist, n.* a follower of *Spartacus,*
leader of the revolted slaves in the Third Slave
War against Rome (73-71 B.C.): a German
communist of extreme type in the revolution of
1918.
**sparth(e),** *spärth,* (*arch.*) *n.* a long **battle-axe.**
[O.N. *spartha.*]
**spasm,** *spazm, n.* a violent involuntary muscular
contraction: a sudden convulsive action, movement, or emotion: a section of a performance,

e.g. a verse (*slang*).—*adjs.* **spasmat'ic, -al** (*rare*);
**spasm'ic; spasmod'ic, -al,** relating to, or consisting in, spasms: convulsive: intermittent.—
*adv.* **spasmod'ically.**—*n.* **spas'modist,** one whose
work is spasmodic.—*adj.* **spas'tic,** of the nature
of spasm: characterised or affected by spasms:
spasmodic.—*n.* one affected with spastic para-
lysis.—*adv.* **spas'tically.**—*n.* **spasticity** (*-tis'i-ti*),
tendency to spasm.—**Spasmodic School,** a group
of English poets, P. J. Bailey, Sydney Dobell,
Alexander Smith, etc., marked by over-strained
and unnatural sentiment and expression; **spastic
paralysis,** permanent muscle constriction or involuntary jerky muscle movement caused by
injury to the muscle-controlling part of the
brain. [Gr. *spasma, -atos,* and *spasmos, -ou,*
convulsion; adjs. *spasmōdēs, spastikos—spaein,*
to draw, convulse.]
**spat,** *spat, pa.t.* and *pa.p.* of **spit** (2).
**spat,** *spat, n.* the spawn of shellfish.—*v.i.* and *v.t.*
to spawn. [Perh. from root of **spit** (2).]
**spat,** *spat, n.* a slap: a large drop, as of rain:
a splash, spattering: a petty quarrel.—*v.t.* to
slap, to strike lightly.—*v.i.* to engage in a petty
quarrel. [Prob. imit.; cf. Du. *spat,* spot, stain,
spatter.]
**spat,** *spat, n.* a gaiter: a fairing covering an aircraft wheel. [**spatterdash.**]
**Spatangus,** *spa-, spə-tang'gəs, n.* the typical genus
of heart-urchins.—*adj.* and *n.* **spatang'oid.**—*n.pl.*
**Spatangoid'ea,** the heart-urchins, an order of
sea-urchins, more or less heart-shaped, without
Aristotle's lantern, with eccentric anus. [Gr.
*spatangēs,* a kind of sea-urchin.]
**spatchcock,** *spach'kok, n.* a fowl killed and
cooked at once.—*v.t.* to treat in this way: to
interpolate. [Prob. **dispatch** and **cock.**]
**spate,** **speat,** *spāt,* (orig. *Scot.*) *n.* a flood. [Origin
doubtful.]
**spathe,** *spādh,* (*bot.*) *n.* a sheathing bract, usu.
a conspicuous one enclosing a spadix.—*adjs.*
**spathaceous** (*spa-thā'shəs*), **spathed** (*spädhd*),
having a spathe. [Gr. *spathē,* a broad blade.]
**spathic,** *spath'ik, adj.* of the nature of, or like,
spar: lamellar.—*adj.* **spath'ose** (or *-ōs'*), spathic.
—**spathic iron,** chalybite. [Ger. *spat(h),* spar.]
**spathulate,** *spath'ū-lāt.* Same as **spatulate.**
**spatial,** *spā'shl, adj.* relating to space.—*n.* **spati-
ality** (*spā-shi-al'i-ti*).—*adv.* **spa'tially.**—*adj.* **spa-
tiotemp'oral,** of space-time or space and time
together. [L. *spatium,* space.]
**spattee,** *spat-ē', n.* a protective outer stocking or
long gaiter. [**spat** and **puttee.**]
**spatter,** *spat'ər, v.t.* to throw out or scatter
upon: to scatter about: to sprinkle, esp. with
mud or liquid.—*v.i.* to fly or fall in drops: to
let drops fall or fly about.—*n.* a spattering:
what is spattered.—**spatt'erdash,** a long gaiter
or legging; **spatt'er-dock** (*U.S.*), the yellow
water-lily; **spatt'er-work,** reproduction of designs by covering the surface with the pattern
and spattering colour on the parts exposed.
[Cf. Du. and L.G. *spatten.*]
**spatula,** *spat'ū-lə, n.* a broad blunt blade or
flattened spoon: (*cap.*) a genus of ducks,
the shovellers.—*adjs.* **spat'ular; spat'ulate,**
shaped like a spatula: broad and rounded at
the tip and tapering at the base.—*n.* **spat'ule,** a
spatula. [L. *spatula, spathula,* dim. of *spatha*—
Gr. *spathē,* a broad blade.]
**spauld,** *spöld,* (now *Scot.*) *n.* the shoulder: a
limb.—Also **spald, spall, spaul,** and (*Spens.*)
**spalle.**—**spauld'-bone,** shoulder-blade; **spauld'-
ill,** quarter-evil. [O.Fr. *espalde* (Fr. *épaule*)—L.
*spatula* (see foregoing).]
**spavin,** *spav'in, n.* see **bone-spavin.**—*Scot.* **spavie**
(*spā'vē*).—*adj.* **spav'ined,** affected with spavin.—
**bog'-spavin** (see **bog**). [O.Fr. *espa(r)vain* (Fr.
*éparvin*); connection with **sparrow** obscure.]
**spaw,** *spö,* **spaw-well,** etc., obs. forms of **spa,** etc.

spawl, *spöl, n.* spittle, slaver.—*v.i.* to emit spawl.

spawn, *spön, n.* a mass of eggs laid in water: fry: brood: contemptuously, offspring: mushroom mycelium.—*v.t.* to produce as spawn: contemptuously, to generate, esp. in mass.—*v.i.* to produce or deposit spawn: to teem: to come forth as or like spawn.—*n.* spawn′er, one who spawns: a female fish, esp. at spawning-time. —*n.* and *adj.* spawn′ing.—spawn′-brick, -cake, a consolidated cake of horse-dung with mushroom spawn; spawn′ing-bed, -ground, a bed or place in the bottom of a stream on which fish deposit their spawn. [O.Fr. *espandre*, to shed—L. *expandĕre*, to spread out.]

spay, *spā, v.t.* to remove or destroy the ovaries of. [A.Fr. *espeier—espee* (Fr. *épée*), sword.]

spayad, *spā′ad*, spayd, spade, *spād*, spay, *spā*, (*obs.*) *n.* a hart in his third year. [Origin obscure.]

speak, *spēk, v.i.* to utter words: to talk: to discourse: to make a speech: to sound: to give tongue: to give expression, information, or intimation by any means.—*v.t.* to pronounce: to utter: to express: to declare: to mention: to describe (*arch.*): to hail or communicate with: to use as a language, talk in: to bring or render by speaking:—*pa.t.* spōke, or (*arch.*) spāke; *pa.p.* spō′ken, or (*arch.*) spōke.—*adj.* speak′able, able or fit to be spoken or expressed in speech: able to speak (*Milt.*).—*ns.* speak′er, one who speaks: the president (orig. the mouthpiece) of a legislative body, as the House of Commons: a loudspeaker; speak′ership, the office of speaker; speak′ing, the act of expressing ideas in words: discourse.—*adj.* uttering or transmitting speech: seeming to speak, lifelike.—*adv.* speak′ingly.—speak′-eas′y (*U.S.*), an illicit dramshop, shebeen; speaking terms (see terms); speak′-ing-trum′pet, an instrument for making the voice heard at a distance; speak′ing-tube, a tube for speaking through to another room; speak′-ing-voice, the kind of voice used in speaking.—so to speak, as one might put it, as it were; speak a ship, to hail and speak to some one on board her; speak fair (*arch.*), to address one in conciliatory terms; speak for, to speak on behalf of or in favour of: to be a proof of: to witness to: to bespeak, engage; speak out, to speak boldly, freely, unreservedly, or so as to be easily heard; speak the same language (see language); speak to, to reprove: to attest, testify to: to discuss; speak up, to speak so as to be easily heard; to speak of, worth mentioning; to speak to, so as to have conversation with. [Late O.E. *specan* (for *sprecan*); Ger. *sprechen*.]

speal-bone, *spēl′-bōn, n.* See spule.

spean. See spane.

spear, *spēr, n.* a long weapon made of a pole with a pointed head: a barbed fork for catching fish: anything sharp or piercing: a spearman: a spire: a spiky shoot or blade: a reed.—*v.t.* to pierce with a spear.—*adjs.* speared, armed with the spear; spear′y.—spear′fish, a kind of swordfish (*Tetrapturus*); spear′-grass, a name for many spearlike grasses; spear′head, the head of a spear: the front of an attack.—Also *v.t.*—spear′man, a man armed with a spear; spear′-mint, the common garden-mint; spear′-point; spear′-running, a tourney; spear′-shaft; spear′-side, the male side or line of descent (opp. to *spindle-side*, or *distaff-side*); spear′-this′tle, a common thistle (*Cnicus lanceolatus* or *Cirsium lanceolatum*); spear′-thrower, a throwing-stick; spear′-wood, an Acacia or a Eucalyptus (both Australian) whose wood is good for spearshafts; spear′wort, a Ranunculus with lanceshaped leaves (*R. lingua*, greater, *R. flammula*, lesser spearwort). [O.E. *spere*; Ger. *speer*; with some senses from spire.]

speat. See spate.

spec, *spek, n.* a colloquial abbrev. of speculation.—on spec, as a gamble, on the chance of achieving something.

special, *spesh′l, adj.* particular: peculiar: distinctive: exceptional: additional to ordinary: detailed: intimate: designed for a particular purpose: confined or mainly applied to a particular subject.—*n.* any special or particular person or thing: any person or thing set apart for a particular duty—a constable, a railwaytrain, etc.: a newspaper extra, a dispatch from a special correspondent.—*n.* specialisā′tion, -izā′tion.—*v.t.* spec′ialise, -ize, to make special or specific: to differentiate: to adapt to conditions: to specify: to narrow and intensify: to become or be a specialist in (with *in*).—*v.i.* to become or be a specialist: to become differentiated: to be adapted to special conditions.—*ns.* specialis′er, -iz′er; spec′ialism, devotion to some particular study or pursuit; spec′ialist, one who devotes himself to a special subject.—*adj.* specialist′ic.—*n.* speciality (*spesh-i-al′i-ti*), the particular characteristic of a person or thing: a special occupation or object of attention.—*adv.* specially (*spesh′ə-li*).—*n.* spec′ialty, something special or distinctive: any special product, article of sale or of manufacture: any special pursuit, department of study, etc.: a special contract for the payment of money: a deed under seal (*law*).—special area, an earlier name for development area; special constable (see constable); special correspondent, a person employed to send reports to a particular newspaper, agency, etc.; special licence, pleading, verdict (see licence, etc.).—in special (*arch.*), in particular: especially. [L. *speciālis—speciēs*, species.]

spécialité de la maison, *spās-yal-ē-tā də la mez-õ*, the dish regarded by a restaurant as its best and most distinctive. [Fr., speciality of the house.]

speciate, -ation. See species.

species, *spē′shēz, -shiz, -shi-ēz, n.* outward appearance, visible form (*obs.* except *theol.*): a eucharistic element: a visual image (*obs.*): a group of individuals having common characteristics, specialised from others of the same *genus* (*log.*): a group (sometimes rather arbitrarily defined) of closely allied mutually fertile individuals showing constant differences from allied groups, placed under a genus (*biol.*): a kind, sort:—*pl.* spe′cies.—*n.* speciā′tion, formation of new biological species incl. formation of polyploids.—*v.t.* spe′ciate.—*n.* specie (*spē′shē, -shi-ē*; orig. the L. abl. as in the phrase *in speciē*, in kind), formerly, payment or requital in the same kind: commodities, kind (*obs.*): now, coined money.—spe′cies-monger, a hair-splitter in classification. [L. *speciēs*, pl. *-ēs*, appearance, kind, species—*specĕre*, to look at.]

specify, *spes′i-fī, v.t.* to mention particularly: to make specific: to set down as requisite:—*pr.p.* spec′ifying; *pa.t.* and *pa.p.* spec′ified.—*adjs.* spec′ifiable (or *fī′*); specific (*spi-sif′ik*), constituting or determining a species: pertaining to a species: peculiar to a species: of special application or origin: specifying: precise: of a parasite, restricted to one particular host: of a stain, colouring certain structures or tissues only: of a physical constant, being the ratio per unit volume, area, (or especially) mass, etc.—*n.* a remedy or medicine for a particular disease or part of the body: anything that is specific.—*adj.* specif′ical.—*adv.* specif′ically.—*v.t.* specif′icate, to specify.—*ns.* specificā′tion (*spes-*), making, becoming, or being specific: the act of specifying: any point or particular specified: the description of his invention presented by an applicant for a patent; specificity (*spes-i-fis′i-ti*).—*adj.* spec′ified.—specific gravity, the weight of any given substance as compared with the weight of an equal bulk or volume of water or other standard substance at the same, or at standard, temperature and pressure; **specific heat**, the number of heat-units necessary to raise the unit of mass of a given substance one degree in temperature; **specific impulse**, a measure of the efficiency of a rocket engine, the ratio of the thrust obtained to the fuel consumed, usu. per second; **specific name**, in biological nomenclature, the name of the species, i.e. the second name, the first being the generic name. [O.Fr. *specifier*—L.L. *specificāre*—L. *speciēs*, kind, *facĕre*, to make.]

**specimen**, *spes'i-min*, *n.* an object or portion serving as a sample, esp. for purposes of study or collection: a remarkable type: derogatorily, a person (*coll.*). [L. *specimen*—*specĕre*, to see.]

**specious**, *spē'shəs*, *adj.* beautiful (*obs.*): showy: looking well at first sight: fair-showing: plausibly deceptive.—*ns.* **speciosity** (*-shi-os'i-ti*), **spe'ciousness.**—*adv.* **spe'ciously.** [L. *speciōsus*, showy—*speciēs*, form—*specĕre*, to look at.]

**speck**, *spek*, *n.* a small spot: a particle: a small American fish, a darter.—*v.t.* to spot.—*adjs.* **speck'less; speck'y.** [O.E. *specca.*]

**speck**, *spek*, *n.* fat: bacon: blubber.—*n.* **specktioneer** (*spek-shən-ēr'*), the chief harpooner in whale-fishing. [Ger. *speck*, Du. *spek*, fat; cf. O.E. *spic*, fat bacon.]

**speckle**, *spek'l*, *n.* a little spot, esp. of colour.—*v.t.* to mark with speckles.—*adj.* **speck'led.**—*n.* **speck'ledness.** [speck (1).]

**specs**, also **specks**, *speks*, *n.pl.* a colloquial abbrev. of spectacles.

**spectacle**, *spek'tə-kl*, *n.* a sight: a show, pageant, exhibition: (in *pl.*) a pair of lenses mounted in frames with side-pieces to grip the temples: (in *pl.*) a marking resembling spectacles, as in the cobra.—*adjs.* **spec'tacled; spectacular** (*-tak'ū-lər*), of the nature of, or marked by, display: sensational, very impressive.—*n.* a theatrical show, esp. on television, or any display, that is large-scale and elaborate.—*n.* **spectacularity** (*-lar'i-ti*).—*adv.* **spectac'ularly.**—**pair of spectacles** (*cricket*), a duck in both innings. [L. *spectāculum*—*spectāre*, *-ātum*, intens. of *specĕre*, to look at.]

**spectator**, *spek-tā'tər*, *n.* one who looks on:—*fem.* **spectā'tress, spectā'trix.**—*adj.* **spectatorial** (*-tə-tō'ri-əl*, *-tō'*).—*n.* **spectā'torship**, the action, office, or quality of a spectator. [L. *spectātor*—*spectāre*, to look.]

**spectre**, in U.S. **specter**, *spek'tər*, *n.* an apparition: a phantom: a ghost: any insect of the Phasmidae (stick-insects, leaf-insects).—*adj.* **spec'tral**, relating to, or like, a spectre.—*n.* **spectral'ity**, the state of being spectral, a spectral object.—*adv.* **spec'trally.**—*adj.* **spectrolog'ical.**—*adv.* **spectrolog'ically.**—*n.* **spectrol'ogy**, the study of ghosts.— **spec'tre-bat**, a leaf-nosed bat; **spec'tre-crab'**, a glass-crab; **spec'tre-in'sect**, a phasmid; **spec'tre-lē'mur**, the tarsier; **spec'tre-shrimp'**, a skeleton-shrimp. [Fr. *spectre*—L. *spectrum*—*specĕre*, to look at.]

**spectro-**, *spek'trō*, *-tro'*, in composition. See spectrum.

**spectrum**, *spek'trəm*, *n.* an after-image: the range of colour produced by a prism or diffraction-grating: any analogous range of radiations in order of wavelength: range of frequencies of sound or a sound: range of opinions, activities, etc. (*fig.*):—*pl.* **spec'tra.**—*adj.* **spec'tral**, relating to, or like, a spectrum.—*ns.* **spectral'ity; spec'trogram**, a photograph of a spectrum: a sound spectrogram (q.v.); **spec'trograph**, a spectroscope designed for use over a wide range of frequencies (well beyond visible spectrum) and recording the spectrum photographically.—*adjs.* **spectrograph'ic, -al.**—*ns.* **spectrog'raphy; spec-**

**trohē'liogram**, a photograph of the sun by monochromatic light; **spectrohē'liograph**, an instrument for taking it.—*adj.* **spectrolog'ical.**—*adv.* **spectrolog'ically.**—*ns.* **spectrol'ogy**, the science of the spectrum or spectrum analysis; **spectrom'eter**, an instrument for measuring refractive indices: one used for measurement of wavelength or energy distribution in a heterogeneous beam of radiation.—*adj.* **spectromet'ric.**—*ns.* **spectrom'etry; spectrophotom'eter**, an instrument for measuring intensity of each colour or wavelength present in an optical spectrum; **spec'troscope**, a general term for an instrument (*spectrograph, spectrometer*, etc.) used in spectroscopy, the basic features of which are a slit and collimator for producing a parallel beam of radiation, a prism or grating for 'dispersing' different wavelengths through differing angles of deviation, and a telescope, camera or counter tube for observing the dispersed radiation.—*adjs.* **spectroscop'ic, -al.**—*adv.* **spectroscop'ically.**—*ns.* **spectroscopist** (*spek-tros'kə-pist*, or *spek'trə-skop-ist*); **spectros'copy** (or *spek'*), the study of spectra.—**spectrum analysis**, determination of chemical composition by observing the spectrum of light or X-rays coming from or through the substance. [L. *spectrum*, an appearance—*specĕre*, to look at.]

**specular**, *spek'ū-lər*, *adj.* mirror-like: having a speculum: by reflection: visual: giving a wide view.—**specular iron**, a brilliant steely crystallised haematite; **specular stone**, a transparent or semitransparent mineral, as mica, selenite, talc. [L. *speculāris*—*speculum*, a mirror, and *specula*, a watch-tower.]

**speculate**, *spek'ū-lāt*, *v.t.* to look at or into, view, examine (*lit.* or *fig.*; *arch.*): to observe (*arch.*): to view in a mirror (*obs.*): to make conjectures about (*obs.*).—*v.i.* to reflect: to theorise: to make conjectures or guesses: to take risk in hope of gain, esp. in buying and selling.—*ns.* **speculā'tion**, act of speculating or its result: vision (*obs.*): viewing (*obs.*): reflection: theorising: conjecture: mere guesswork: a more or less risky investment of money for the sake of unusually large profits: a card game in which trumps are bought and sold: an observer (*Shak.*); **spec'ulātist**, a speculative philosopher: a speculator.—*adj.* **spec'ulātive**, of the nature of, based on, given to, speculation or theory.—*adv.* **spec'ulātively.**—*ns.* **spec'ulātiveness; spec'ulātor**, one who speculates in any sense: a watchman, lookout (*arch.*).—*adj.* **spec'ulatory**, exercising speculation: adapted for spying or viewing (*arch.*).—*n.* **spec'ulātrix**, a female speculator. [L. *speculātus*, pa.p. of *speculāri*—*specula*, a lookout—*specĕre*, to look at.]

**speculum**, *spek'ū-ləm*, *n.* a mirror: a reflector, usu. of polished metal: an instrument for viewing cavities of the body (*med.*): a bright patch on a wing, esp. a duck's:—*pl.* **spec'ula.**— **speculum metal**, an alloy of copper and tin, with or without other ingredients. [L. *speculum*, a mirror—*specĕre*, to look at.]

**sped**, *sped*, *pa.t.* and *pa.p.* of speed.

**speech**, *spēch*, *n.* that which is spoken: language: the power of speaking: manner of speaking: a continuous spoken utterance: a discourse, oration: talk: colloquy: mention: a rumour (*obs.*): a saying (*obs.*): the sounding of a musical instrument.—*v.t.* and *v.i.* (*rare* or *dial.*) to harangue.—*adj.* **speech'ful**, loquacious: expressive.—*ns.* **speech'fulness; speechificā'tion** (*coll.*); **speech'ifier.**—*v.i.* **speech'ify**, to make speeches, harangue (implying contempt).—*adj.* **speech'less**, destitute or deprived of the power of speech.—*adv.* **speech'lessly.**—*n.* **speech'lessness.**—**speech'craft**, philology: rhetoric; **speech'cri'er** (*hist.*), a hawker of broadsides giving hanged criminals' dying speeches; **speech day,**

the public day at the close of a school year; **speech'-maker**, one accustomed to speak in public; **speech'-making**; **speech'-reading**, lip-reading; **speech therapy**, treatment of speech defects; **speech'-train'ing**, training in clear speech. [Late O.E. *spēc*, *spǣc*, O.E. *sprēc*, *sprǣc*; Ger. *sprache*.]

**speed**, *spēd*, *n.* success, good fortune (*arch.*): a help to success (*arch.*): quickness, swiftness, dispatch: the rate at which a distance is covered: amphetamine (*slang*).—*v.i.* to succeed, fare (*arch.*): to move quickly: to hurry: to drive at high, or at dangerously, unduly, or illegally high, speed.—*v.t.* to give or bring success to (*arch.*): to further: to send forth with good wishes: to bring to an end or finished state (*arch.*): to bring to a sorry plight, to do for (in *passive*; *arch.*): to send swiftly: to push forward: to haste: to betake with speed: to urge to high speed: to set or regulate the speed of:—*pa.t.* and *pa.p.* **sped** (also **speed'ed**).—*n.* **speed'er**, one who, or that which, speeds or promotes speed.—*adj.* **speed'ful.**—*advs.* **speed'fully**; **speed'ily.**—*ns.* **speed'iness**, quickness; **speed'ing**, success: promotion, furtherance: progressive increase of speed (often with *up*): motoring at excessive speed.—Also *adj.*—*adj.* **speed'less.**—*ns.* **speedom'eter**, a device indicating the speed at which a vehicle is travelling (abbrev. **speed'ō**); **speed'ster**, a speedboat: one who speeds.—*adj.* **speed'y**, swift: prompt: soon achieved.—**speed'-ball** (*slang*), a mixture of cocaine and other opiates, esp. heroin or morphine; **speed'-boat**, a very swift motor-boat; **speed'boating**; **speed'-cop** (*slang*), a policeman who watches out for motorists who are exceeding a speed-limit; **speed'-limit**, the maximum speed at which motor vehicles may be driven legally on certain roads; **speed merchant**, one who drives a motor vehicle exceedingly fast; **speed'-up**, an acceleration, esp. in work; **speed'way**, a road for fast traffic: a motor-cycle racing track; **speed'well**, any species of the scrophulariaceous genus *Veronica*, typically blue-flowered, posterior petals united, posterior sepal wanting; **speedy cut, cutting**, injury to a horse's foreleg by the opposite shoe.—**speed up**, to quicken the rate of working. [O.E. *spēd*; Du. *spoed*.]

**speel**, *spēl*, (*Scot.*) *v.t.* and *v.i.* to climb.—*n.* a climb.—**speel'er**, an acrobat (*obs.*): a climber: a climbing-iron. [Poss. L.G. *speler*, a performer.]

**speir, speer**, *spēr*, (*Scot.*) *v.t.* and *v.i.* to ask, inquire.—*n.* **speir'ings, speer'ings**, news. [O.E. *spyrian*, to inquire after, *spor*, a trace.]

**speisade.** See lance speisade, under lance prisado.

**speiss**, *spīs*, *n.* a mass of arsenides and commonly antimonides, a first product in smelting certain ores.—**speiss-cob'alt**, smaltite. [Ger. *speise*.]

**spekboom**, *spek'bōm*, *n.* a S. African succulent shrub of the purslane family. [Du., bacon tree.]

**spelaean**, also (esp. in U.S.) **spelean**, *spi-lē'ən*, *adj.* cave-dwelling.—*adj.* **spelaeological** (in U.S. **speleo-**; *spel-i-ō-loj'i-kl*).—*ns.* **spelaeologist** (in U.S. **speleo-**; *-ol'ə-jist*); **spelaeol'ogy** (in U.S. **speleo-**), the scientific study of caves: exploration of caves. [Gr. *spēlaion*, cave.]

**speld, speld, spelder**, *spel'dər*, (*Scot.*) *vs.t.* to spread open or sprawlingly: to slit and lay open. —*ns.* **speld'in(g), speld'rin(g)**, a haddock (or other fish) split open and dried. [Cf. M.E. *spalden*, to split; Ger. *spalten*.]

**spelean**, etc. See spelaean, etc.

**spell**, *spel*, *n.* speech, discourse, talk, a sermon (*obs.*): a magic formula: a magic influence: enchantment: entrancement.—*v.t.* to utter (*obs.*): to say a spell over: to bind with a spell: to enchant.—*v.i.* (*obs.*) to discourse.—*adj.* **spell'ful**, magical.—*v.t.* **spell'bind** (*back-formation*).—**spell'binder** (*U.S.*), an orator, usu. political or

evangelical, who holds his audience spellbound. —*adjs.* **spell'bound**, bound by a spell: entranced; **spell'-stopt**, brought to a standstill by a spell. [O.E. *spell*, narrative, *spellian*, to speak, announce; cf. Goth. *spill*, O.N. *spjall*, tale.]

**spell**, *spel*, *v.t.* to read laboriously, letter by letter: to make out, unriddle, come to understand: to scan: to name or set down in order the letters of: to constitute or represent orthographically: to import, amount to (*fig.*).—*v.i.* to spell words, esp. correctly: to contemplate (*poet.*): to express or hint a desire:—*pa.t.* and *pa.p.* **spelled, spelt**.—*n.* a mode of spelling.—*adj.* **spell'able.**—*ns.* **spell'er**; **spell'ing.**—*adv.* **spell'ingly**, letter by letter.—**spell'down** (*U.S.*), a spelling competition; **spell'ing-bee**, a spelling competition; **spell'ing-book**, a book for teaching to spell.—**spell backward**, to spell in reverse order: perversely to misrepresent or misconstrue the qualities of; **spell baker**, to do something difficult, prob. because *baker* was one of the first disyllables in old spelling-books; **spell (it) out**, to be extremely specific in explaining something. [O.Fr. *espeller* (Fr. *épeler*), of Gmc. origin; cf. foregoing.]

**spell**, *spel*, *v.t.* to take the place of at work: to relieve, give a rest to: to take a turn at.—*v.i.* to take turns: to rest:—*pr.p.* **spell'ing**; *pa.t.* and *pa.p.* **spelled.**—*n.* a shift: a turn at work: a bout, turn: a short time: a stretch of time: a rest: a fit of irritation, illness, etc. [O.E. *spelian*, to act for another: cf. Du. *spelen*, Ger. *spielen*, to play.]

**spell**, *spel*, (*dial.*) *n.* a splinter: a rung: a trap for throwing up the knur in knur and spell. [Perh. **speld**; but cf. Ger. *spellen*, to split.]

**spelt**, *spelt*, *n.* an inferior species of wheat (*Triticum spelta*), grown in the mountainous parts of Europe. [O.E. *spelt*.]

**spelter**, *spel'tər*, *n.* zinc, esp. impure zinc. [Cf. L.G. *spialter*.]

**spence**, *spens*, *n.* a larder (*dial.*): a pantry (*dial.*): an inner room, parlour (*U.S.*). [O.Fr. *despense*, a buttery—*despendre*—L. *dispendēre*.]

**spencer**, *spens'ər*, *n.* a kind of wig: a short double-breasted overcoat: a woman's short undergarment, formerly over-jacket. [After various persons of the name.]

**spencer**, *spens'ər*, *n.* in ships and barques, a fore-and-aft sail abaft the fore and main masts. [Perh. the name Spencer, as foregoing.]

**Spencerian**, *spen-sē'ri-ən*, *adj.* pertaining to the synthetic philosophy or evolutionary cosmology of Herbert Spencer (1820–1903).—*n.* a follower of Spencer.—*n.* **Spence'rianism.**

**spend**, *spend*, *v.t.* to expend: to pay out: to give, bestow, employ, for any purpose: to shed: to consume: to use up: to exhaust: to waste: to pass, as time.—*v.i.* to make expense:—*pa.t.* and *pa.p.* **spent.**—*adj.* **spen'dable.**—*ns.* **spen'der**; **spen'ding.**—*adj.* **spent**, used up: exhausted: of fish, exhausted by spawning.—**spend'all**, a spendthrift; **spending money**, pocket money; **spend'thrift**, one who spends the savings of thrift: a prodigal.—*adj.* excessively lavish. [O.E. *spendan*—L. *expendēre* or *dispendēre*, to weigh out.]

**Spenserian**, *spen-sē'ri-ən*, *adj.* pertaining to Edmund Spenser (1552–99) or esp. his stanza in *The Faerie Queene*, of eight decasyllabic lines and an Alexandrine, rhymed *a b a b b c b c c.*

**spent, spent.** See spend.

**speos**, *spē'os*, *n.* grotto-temple or tomb. [Gr., cave.]

**Spergula**, *spûr'gū-lə*, *n.* the spurrey genus, akin to chickweed.—*n.* **Spergulā'ria**, the allied sandwort-spurrey genus. [L.L.]

**sperling**, *spûr'ling*, Same as sparling.

**sperm**, *spûrm*, *n.* seed or semen: generative substance: a male gamete or germ-cell: eggs, spawn, brood, offspring (*obs.*): the chalaza of a hen's egg (formerly believed to be contributed by the cock) (*obs.*): a sperm-whale: sperm-oil: a sperm-candle: spermaceti.—For some compounds beginning sperma-, spermo-, see spermato- (*spûr'mɔ-tō-*).—*ns.* sper'maduct, sper'miduct, a duct conveying spermatozoa; spermā'- rium:—*pl.* spermā'ria; sper'mary, the male germ-gland; sperma(to)thē'ca (Gr. *thēkē*, receptacle), in female insects, etc., a receptacle in which sperms received are stored. *adjs.* spermathē'cal; spermat'ic, -al, of, pertaining to, conveying sperm: generative.—*ns.* spermat'ic, a spermatic vessel; sper'matid, a cell that develops directly into a spermatozoon; sper'- matist, a believer in the doctrine that the sperm contains all future generations in germ; spermatium (*-mā'shɔm*), a non-motile male gamete in red seaweeds: a spore-like structure, possibly sexual, in some fungi:—*pl.* spermā'tia; sper'- matoblast (Gr. *blastos*, a shoot), a spermatid.— *adj.* spermatoblas'tic.—*ns.* sper'matocele (Gr. *kēlē*, tumour), tumour of the testicle; sper'mato- cyte (Gr. *kytos*, vessel), a sperm mother-cell or its predecessor; spermatogenesis (*-jen'*), sperma- togeny (*-ɔ-toj'i-ni*), sperm-formation.—*adjs.* sper- matogenet'ic, spermatogen'ic, spermatog'enous. —*ns.* spermatogonium (*-gō'ni-ɔm*), one of the cells that by repeated division form the spermato- cytes; sper'matophore, a case enclosing the spermatozoa.—*n.pl.* Spermatoph'yta (also Sper- maph'yta, Spermoph'yta; Gr. *phyton*, plant), the flowering plants as one of the four phyla of the vegetable kingdom.—*n.* spermat'ophyte (sperm'aphyte, etc.).—*adj.* spermatophytic (*-fit'ik*); also sperma-, spermo-).—*ns.* spermatorrhoe'a (Gr. *rhoiā*, flow), involuntary seminal discharge; spermatozō'id, spermatozō'on (Gr. *zōion*, animal; *pl.* -zō'a), a male germ-cell.—For some compounds in spermo-, see spermato-.—*ns.* sper'- mogone, spermogō'nium (*pl.* -ia), a flask-shaped structure in which spermatia are produced.— sperm'-candle, a candle of spermaceti; sperm'- cell, a male gamete; sperm'-oil, oil from the sperm-whale; sperm'-whale, the cachalot, a whale from which spermaceti is obtained. [Gr. *sperma*, *-atos*, seed, semen—*speirein*, to sow.]

spermaceti, *spûr-mɔ-set'i*, *n.* a waxy matter obtained mixed with oil from the head of the sperm-whale and others.—Also *adj.* [L. *sperma cēti* (gen. of *cētus*, a whale—Gr. *kētos*), whale's sperm, from a wrong notion of its origin.]

spermophile, *spûr'mō-fīl*, *-fil*, *n.* a ground-squirrel (Spermophilus), a rodent akin to the true squirrels. [Gr. *sperma*, seed, *phileein*, to love.]

sperre, *spûr*, (*Spens.*) *v.t.* to bolt, bar.—In Shak., *Troilus and Cressida*, Prol. 19, stirre is probably a misprint for sperre. [spar.]

sperrylite, *sper'i-līt*, *n.* an arsenide of platinum, found at Sudbury, Ontario. [After F. L. *Sperry*, with Gr. *lithos*, stone.]

sperse, *spûrs*, (*arch.*) *v.t.* and *v.i.* aphetic form of disperse:—*pa.t.* and *pa.p.* (*Spens.*) sperst; also spersed.

sperthe. Same as sparth.

spessartite, *spes'ärt-īt*, *n.* a manganese-alumina garnet found at *Spessart* in Bavaria.

spet, *spet*, (*Milt.*) *v.t.* and *v.i.* a form of spit (2).

spetch, *spech*, *n.* a piece of skin used in making glue. [speck.]

spew, spue, *spū*, *v.t.* to vomit.—*v.i.* to vomit: to ooze, run.—*n.* vomited matter: a marshy spot (*dial.*).—*ns.* spew'er; spew'iness.—*adj.* spew'y (*dial.*), boggy. [O.E. *spiwan*, *spiowan*, to spit; Du. *spuwen*, Ger. *speien*; also L. *spuĕre*, Gr. *ptyein*.]

sphacelus, *sfas'ɔ-lɔs*, *n.* necrosis.—*adjs.* sphac'- elate, -d, necrosed: dark and shrunken (*bot.*).— *n.* sphacelā'tion. [Gr. *sphakelos*.]

sphaer(e). Same as sphere.

sphaeridium, *sfē-rid'i-ɔm*, *n.* a minute spheroidal body on the surface of a sea-urchin, perh. a sense-organ:—*pl.* sphaerid'ia.—*ns.* sphae'rite, a hydrous aluminium phosphate; sphaeroco'- baltite, cobalt carbonate, occurring in rounded masses; sphaerocrys'tal, a rounded crystalline mass; sphaerosid'erite, concretionary clay- ironstone. [Gr. *sphairā*, a ball.]

Sphagnum, *sfag'nɔm*, *n.* a genus of mosses—peat or bog-moss, constituting the family Sphagna- ceae (*ɔfag nā'si-ē*), peat-formers, formerly useful as wound-dressings.—*adj.* sphagnic'olous (L. *colēre*, to inhabit), living in peat-moss.—*ns.* sphagnol'ogist; sphagnol'ogy, the study of the peat-mosses.—*adj.* sphag'nous. [Gr. *sphagnos*, a name for various plants.]

sphalerite, *sfal'ɔr-īt*, *n.* zinc-blende. [Gr. *spha- leros*, deceptive, from its resemblance to galena.]

sphendone, *sfen'do-nē*, *n.* an ancient Greek women's head-band: an elliptical or semi- elliptical auditorium. [Gr. *sphendonē*, a sling.]

sphene, *sfēn*, *n.* titanite.—*adj.* sphē'nic, wedge-like. —*n.pl.* Sphenisciformes (*sfē-nis-i-för'mēz*), the penguin order of birds.—*ns.* Sphenis'cus (*-kɔs*), the jackass-penguin genus; Sphē'nodon (Gr. *odous*, *odontos*, a tooth); genus, also known as Hatteria, to which the tuatara (*q.v.*) belongs; sphē'nogram, a cuneiform character—*adj.* sphē'noid, wedge-shaped, applied to a set of bones at the base of the skull.—*n.* a sphenoid bone: a wedge-shaped crystal form of four triangular faces.—*adj.* sphenoid'al. [Gr. *sphēn*, *sphēnos*, a wedge.]

sphere (*Shak.*, *Milt.*, sphear, spheare), *sfēr*, *n.* a solid figure bounded by a surface of which all points are equidistant from a centre: its bounding surface: the apparent sphere of the heavens: upon which the stars are seen in projection: any one of the concentric spherical shells which were once supposed to carry the planets in their revolutions: a circle of society, orig. of the higher ranks (as if a planetary sphere): domain, scope, range: a field of activity: condition of life: a world, mode of being: a ball: a spherical object, esp. a planet: an orbit (*Spens.*).—*v.t.* to round: to place in a sphere: to encompass: to send about.—*adjs.* sphēr'al; sphered; sphere'- less; spheric (*sfer'ik*), -al, of a sphere or spheres: having the form of a sphere.—*n.* spherical'ity.— *adv.* spher'ically.—*ns.* spher'icalness, sphericity (*-is'i-ti*), state or quality of being spherical; spher'ics, the geometry and trigonometry of the sphere; spheristē'rion (Gr. *sphairistērion*), a room or court for ball-games; sphē'roid, a body or figure nearly spherical, but not quite so—a species of ellipsoid (*prolate spheroid*, a slightly lengthened sphere; *oblate spheroid*, a slightly flattened sphere).—*adj.* sphēroi'dal.—*ns.* sphē- roidi'city; sphēroidisa'tion, -z-.—*v.t.* sphēr'oidise, -ize, to develop spherulitic or granular structure in.—*n.* sphērom'eter, an instrument for measuring curvature of surfaces.—*adj.* spherūlar (*sfer'*). —*ns.* spher'ūle, a little sphere; spher'ūlite, a radiating spherical group of minute crystalline fibres in rocks.—*adjs.* spherūlitic (*-lit'ik*); sphē'ry, spherical, round: belonging to the celestial spheres.—*adjs.* sphere'-born; sphere'- like.—spherical triangle, a three-sided figure on the surface of a sphere, bounded by arcs of great circles.—music of the spheres, the music, inaudible to mortal ears, produced according to Pythagoras by the motions of the celestial spheres in accordance with the laws of harmony. [Gr. *sphairā*.]

sphincter, *sfingk'tɔr*, (*anat.*) *n.* a muscle whose contraction narrows or shuts an orifice.—*adjs.* sphinc'teral, sphincterial (*-tē'ri-ɔl*), sphincteric (*-ter'ik*). [Gr. *sphinktēr*—*sphingein*, to bind tight.]

Sphinx, sphinx, *sfingks*, *n.* a monster of Greek

mythology, with the head of a woman and the body of a lioness, that proposed riddles to travellers, and strangled those who could not solve them: any similar monster or representation of one: an enigmatic or inscrutable person: a hawk-moth: the Guinea baboon.—*n.* and *adj.* **sphingid** (*sfin'jid*).—*n.pl.* **Sphin'gidae,** the hawk-moth family.—**sphinx'-moth.** [Gr.,—*sphingein,* to draw tight.]

**sphragistic,** *sfrə-jist'ik, adj.* pertaining to seals and signets.—*n.pl.* **sphragist'ics,** the study of seals. [Gr. *sphrăgistikos*—*sphrăgis,* a seal.]

**sphygmus,** *sfig'məs, n.* the pulse.—*adj.* **sphyg'mic.** —*ns.* **sphyg'mogram,** a sphygmograph record; **sphyg'mograph,** an instrument for recording pulse-beat.—*adj.* **sphygmograph'ic.**—*n.* **sphygmog'raphy.**—*adj.* **sphyg'moid,** pulse-like.—*ns.* **sphygmol'ogy,** the science of the pulse; **sphygmōmanom'eter, sphygmom'eter,** an instrument for measuring arterial blood-pressure; **sphyg'mophōne,** an instrument by means of which a pulse-beat makes a sound; **sphyg'moscope,** an instrument for making arterial pulsations visible. [Latinised from Gr. *sphygmos,* pulse.]

**spial,** *spi'əl* (*obs.*) *n.* espial: a spy, a scout.

**Spica,** *spi'kə, n.* a first-magnitude star in Virgo: (without *cap.*) a spiral bandage with reversed turns suggesting an ear of barley: (without *cap.*) in birds, a spur.—*adjs.* **spi'cate, -d,** in, having, or forming a spike: spikelike.—*ns.* **spicilege** (*spi'si-lij*; L. *spicilegium*—*legĕre,* to gather), a gleaning: an anthology; **spicula** (*spik'ū-lə*), a spicule, prickle, or splinter.—*adjs.* **spic'ular,** of the nature of or like a spicule; **spic'ūlate,** having spicules.—*ns.* **spic'ūle,** a minute needle-like body, crystal, splinter, or process; **spic'ūlum** (L.), a little spine: a spicula: a snail's dart:—*pl.* **spic'ūla.** [L. *spica,* an ear of corn.]

**spiccato,** *spik-kä'tō, adj.* and *adv.* half staccato.— *n.* spiccato playing or passage. [It.]

**spice,** *spis, n.* an aromatic and pungent vegetable substance used as a condiment and for seasoning food—pepper, cayenne pepper, pimento, nutmeg, mace, vanilla, ginger, cinnamon, cassia, etc.: such substances collectively or generally: a characteristic smack, flavour: anything that adds piquancy or interest: an aromatic odour: sweetmeats (*dial.*): a touch, tincture (*fig.*).—*v.t.* to season with spice: to tincture, vary, or diversify.—*adj.* **spiced,** impregnated with a spicy odour: seasoned with spice: over-scrupulous (*obs.*).—*ns.* **spic'er** (*obs.*), a dealer in spices or drugs; **spic'ery,** spices in general: a repository of spices: spiciness.—*adv.* **spic'ily.**—*n.* **spic'iness.**—*adj.* **spic'y,** producing or abounding with spices: fragrant: pungent: piquant, pointed: racy: risqué: showy.—**spice'-box,** a box, often ornamental, for keeping spices; **spice'-bush,** an aromatic American shrub (Lindera) of the laurel family; **spice'-cake,** a spiced cake. [O.Fr. *espice* (Fr. *épice*)—L.L. *species,* kinds of goods, spices—L. *speciēs,* a kind.]

**spicilege.** See under **Spica.**

**spick,** *spik, n.* a nail, a spike.—*adj.* tidy, fresh.— **spick and span,** trim and speckless, like a spike new cut and a chip new split; **spick and span new,** brand-new. [spike.]

**spicknel.** See **spignel.**

**spicule.** See under **Spica.**

**spide,** obs. spelling of **spied** (see **spy**).

**spider,** *spi'dər, n.* an arachnid of the order Araneida, the body divided into two distinct parts— an unsegmented cephalothorax with four pairs of legs, and a soft unsegmented abdomen with spinnerets: formerly, a light high-wheeled vehicle: a frying-pan, properly one with feet: any of various spider-like radiating structures.—*adj.* **spi'dery,** spider-like: abounding in spiders.— **spi'der-crab,** a crab with long thin legs; **spi'der-leg,** a long thin leg.—*adjs.* **spi'der-legged;**

**spi'der-like.**—**spi'der-line,** a thread of silk spun by a spider: any fine thread in an optical instrument, for measurement, position-marking, etc.; **spi'der-man,** an erector of steel building structures; **spi'der-monkey,** an American monkey (Ateles) with long slender legs and tail; **spi'der-stitch,** a stitch in lace or netting in which threads, are carried diagonally and parallel to each other; **spi'der-web,** the snare spun by a spider; **spi'der-wheel,** in embroidery, a circular pattern with radiating lines; **spi'der-work,** lace worked by spider-stitch; **spi'der-wort,** any plant of the American commelinaceous genus Tradescantia, esp. *T. virginica,* with deep-blue or reddish-violet flowers. [O.E. *spithra*—*spinnan,* to spin; cf. Dan. *spinder,* Ger. *spinne.*]

**spie** (*Spens., Milt.,* etc. spelling of **spy**), **spied,** **spies.** See **spy.**

**spiegeleisen,** *spē'gl-ī-zn, n.* a white cast-iron containing manganese, largely used in the manufacture of steel by the Bessemer process. [Ger.,— *spiegel*—L. *speculum,* a mirror, Ger. *eisen,* iron.]

**spiel,** *spēl, shpēl, n.* talk, story.—*v.i.* to talk glibly, tell the tale.—Also *v.t.*—*n.* **spieler,** a person with a glib, persuasive line of talk: a swindler: a card sharper: a gambling den. [Ger. *spielen,* to play.]

**spiff,** *spif, adj.* (*dial.*) smart, spruce.—Also **spiff'y.** —*adj.* **spiff'ing** (*coll.*), excellent. [Origin obscure.]

**spifflicate, spifflicate,** *spif'li-kāt,* (*slang*) *v.t.* to do for: to quell: to confound: to handle roughly. —*n.* **spif(f)lica'tion.**

**Spigelia,** *spī-jē'li-ə, n.* the pink-root genus of Loganiaceae.—*adj.* **Spigē'lian,** of van der Spiegel or of Spigelia: applied to the *lobulus Spigelii,* one of the lobes of the liver. [From the Belgian Adrian van der *Spiegel* (1578-1625).]

**spight,** *spit, vb.* and *n.* (*Spens., Shak.*). Same as **spite.**

**spignel,** *spig'nl, n.* baldmoney (Meum).—Also (*obs.*) **spick'nel.** [Origin obscure.]

**spigot,** *spig'ət, n.* a vent-peg or peg controlling a faucet. [Prov. *espigot*—L. *spiculum.*]

**spike,** *spik, n.* an ear of corn: an inflorescence in which sessile flowers or spikelets are arranged on a long axis (*bot.*): a kind of lavender (**spike'-lav'ender**).—*v.i.* to develop a spike.—*n.* **spike'let,** in grasses, etc., a small crowded spike, itself forming part of a greater inflorescence.—**spike'-grass,** Uniola or other American grass with conspicuous spikelets; **spike'-oil,** the oil of spike-lavender; **spike'-rush,** a sedge (Heleocharis) with a solitary spike. [L. *spica,* an ear of corn.]

**spike,** *spik, n.* a hard thin pointed object: a large nail: (in *pl.*) spiked shoes, worn to prevent slipping.—*v.t.* to fasten, set, or pierce with a spike or spikes: to make useless (as a gun), orig. by driving a spike into the vent.— *adj.* **spiked.**—*adv.* **spik'ily.**—*n.* **spik'iness.**—*adj.* **spik'y,** having, furnished with, spikes: having a sharp point.—**spike'-fish,** a kind of sail-fish; **spike heel,** a very narrow metal heel on a woman's shoe; **spike'-nail,** a large small-headed nail. [O.E. *spicing,* a spike-nail; poss. from L. *spica,* an ear of corn.]

**spikenard,** *spik'närd, n.* an aromatic oil or balsam yielded by an Indian valeriaceous plant (Nardostachys) or a substitute: the plant itself. [L. *spica nardi.*]

**spile,** *spil, n.* a plug: a spigot: a pile for a foundation.—*v.t.* to pierce and provide with a spile.—*n.* **spil'ing.** [Cf. L.G. *spile,* Du. *spijl,* Ger. *speil.*]

**spilite,** *spi'lit, n.* a very fine-grained basic igneous rock.—*adj.* **spilitic** (*-it'ik*).—*n.* **spi'losite,** a spotted slate, formed by contact metamorphism. [Gr. *spilos,* a spot.]

**spill,** *spil, v.t.* to kill (*obs.*): to destroy (*obs.*): to allow to run out of a vessel: to shed: to waste: to throw from a vehicle or the saddle (*coll.*): to

Neutral vowels in unaccented syllables: *el'ə-mənt;* for certain sounds in foreign words, see p. viii

empty from the belly of a sail or empty of wind for reefing: to overlay as if by spilling (*Spens.*). —*v.i.* to come to grief or ruin (*obs.*): to overflow: to be shed: to be allowed to fall, be lost, or wasted:—*pa.t.* and *pa.p.* spilled, spilt.—*n.* a fall, a throw: a spilling.—*ns.* spill'age, the act of spilling: that which is spilt; spill'er; spilth, spilling: anything spilt or poured out lavishly: excess.—spill'ing-line, a rope for spilling the wind out of a square sail; spill'-stream, an overflow channel: a bayou; spill'way, a passage for overflow-water.—spill the beans, to cause embarrassment by letting out a secret. [O.E. *spillan*; Du. *spillen*, O.N. *spilla*, to destroy.]

spill, *spil*, *n.* a spile: a thin strip of wood or paper for lighting a candle, a pipe, etc.—*n.* spill'ikin, a small slip of wood, ivory, etc., to be picked out from a heap without disturbing the others in the game of spillikins.—Also spilikin, spel(l)ikin. [Connection with spile or with spell (4) doubtful.]

spilt, *spilt.* See spill (1).—Also *adj.*

spin, *spin*, *v.t.* to draw out and twist into threads: to draw out a thread as spiders do: to form by spinning: to draw out: to make to last (usu. with *out*): to send hurtling: to twirl, set revolving rapidly: to fish with a swivel or spoon-bait: to reject at an examination (*slang*). —*v.i.* to practise the art or trade or perform the act of spinning: to rotate rapidly: to whirl: to hurtle: to go swiftly, esp. on wheels: to spirt: to stream vigorously: to lengthen out, last (usu. with *out*): to fish with rotating bait:—*pr.p.* spinn'ing; *pa.t.* spun, *arch.* span; *pa.p.* spun.— *n.* act or result of spinning: a rotatory motion: a cycle ride: a short trip in a motor-car: a spurt at high speed: a spiral descent (*lit.* and *fig.*): of a subatomic particle, quantised angular momentum in the absence of orbital motion: of a nucleus, quantised angular momentum including contributions from the orbital motion of nucleons: confused excitement.—*ns.* spinn'er, one who spins: a spider (*Shak.*): a spinneret: a spinning-machine: a ball with imparted spin, causing it to swerve or break: an artificial fly that revolves in the water; spinn'eret, a spinning organ in spiders, etc.: a plate with holes from which filaments of plastic material are expressed (also spinnerette); spinn'erule (-*ə-rōōl*, -*rŭl*), one of the tubules of a spinneret; spinn'ery, a spinning-mill.—*n.* and *adj.* spinn'ing.—spin'-dri'er, a device that dries washed clothes without wringing, to a point ready for ironing, by forcing the water out of them under pressure of centrifugal force in a rapidly revolving drum.—*v.t.* spin'-dry'. —spinn'ing-house (*hist.*), a place of correction where lewd and incorrigible women were made to spin; spinn'ing-jenn'y, a machine by which a number of threads can be spun at once: a crane-fly (*dial.*); spinn'ing-mill, a factory where thread is spun; spinn'ing-wheel, a machine for spinning yarn, consisting of a wheel driven by the hand or by a treadle, which drives one or two spindles; spin'-off, a process of transference of business on the U.S. stock-market: a by-product that proves profitable on its own account.—Also *adj.*— flat spin, a state of panic; spin a yarn, to tell a story; spin out, to prolong, protract. [O.E. *spinnan*; Ger. *spinnen.*]

spina, spinal. See spine.

spinach, spinage, *spin'ij*, *n.* a plant (*Spinacia oleracea*) of the goosefoot family: its young leaves used as a vegetable: extended to various other plants.—*adj.* spinaceous (*spin-ā'shəs*).— spin'ach-beet, a kind of beet used like spinach. [O.Fr. *espinage*, *espinache*; of doubtful origin, poss.—L. *spīna*, poss. Ar. *isfināj.*]

spindle, *spin'dl*, *n.* the pin by which thread is twisted: a pin on which anything turns: the fusee of a watch: anything very slender: a spindle-shaped structure formed in mitosis

(*biol.*).—*v.i.* to grow long and slender.—*n.* spin'dling, a person or thing too long and slender: a slender shoot.—*adj.* long and slender.—*adj.* spin'dly, disproportionally long and slender.— *adjs.* spin'dle-legged, -shanked, having long slender legs, like spindles.—*ns.pl.* spin'dle-legs, -shanks, long slim legs: hence (as a *sing.*) an overlong and slender person.—spin'dle-oil, very light and fluid lubricating oil.—*adj.* spin'dle-shaped, shaped like a spindle, thickest in the middle and tapering to both ends.—spin'dle-shell, a gasteropod (Fusus) with spindle-shaped shell; spin'dle-side, the female side or line of descent, distaff-side (opp. to *spear-side*); spin'dle-tree, a shrub (*Euonymus europaeus*) of the Celastraceae, whose hard-grained wood was used for making spindles; spin'dle-whorl, a heavy ring giving momentum to the spindle. [O.E. *spinel*—*spinnan*, to spin; Ger. *spindel.*]

spindrift, *spin'drift*, *n.* the spray blown from the crests of waves. [See spoon (1).]

spine, *spin*, *n.* a thorn, esp. one formed by a modified branch or leaf: a long sharp process of a leaf: a thin, pointed spike, esp. in fishes: the spinal column: any ridge extending lengthways: heartwood: the back of a book.—*n.* spi'na, the spinal column: a quill of a spinet: a lengthwise barrier in the Roman circus (*ant.*).—*adjs.* spi'nal, of the backbone; spi'nate, spined, having a spine or spines; spine'less, having no spine: weak: vacillating: lacking courage, esp. moral courage. —*adv.* spine'lessly.—*ns.* spinelessness; spinesc'ence.—*adjs.* spinesc'ent, growing into a spine: somewhat spiny; spinif'erous, thorn-bearing; spi'niform, like a thorn; spinig'erous, bearing spines; spi'nigrade, moving by means of spines, as an echinoderm.—*n.* spi'niness.—*adjs.* spi'nose (or -*nōs'*), spi'nous, full of spines: thorny.—*ns.* spinos'ity, thorniness; spinule (*spin'* or *spin'*), a minute spine.—*adjs.* spin'ulate, spinulesc'ent, spinulif'erous, spin'ulose, spin'ulous; spi'ny, full of spines: thorny: troublesome: perplexed.—spina bifida (*bi'fi-da, bif'*), condition in which (a) vertebra(e) fail to unite perfectly at the embryo stage, exposing spinal cord; spinal anaesthesia, injection of an anaesthetic into the spinal canal, producing loss of sensation but not unconsciousness; spinal canal, a passage running through the spinal column, containing the spinal cord; spinal column, in vertebrates, the articulated series of vertebrae extending from the skull to the tip of the tail, forming the axis of the skeleton and enclosing the spinal cord; spinal c(h)ord, the main neural axis in vertebrates; spine'-chiller, a frightening story, thought, happening.—*adj.* spine'-chilling. [L. *spina*, a thorn.]

spinel, *spi-nel'* (or *spin'əl*), *n.* a mineral, magnesium aluminate or other member of a group of aluminates, ferrates, and chromates, crystallising in octahedra.—spinel ruby, ruby-spinel, a precious variety of typical spinel formerly confounded with ruby. [It. *spinella.*]

spinet(te), *spin'it*, or *spi-net'*, *n.* an instrument like a small harpsichord.—Also spinnet. [It. *spinetta*, poss. from maker G. *Spinetti* (fl. 1500).]

Spinifex, *spin'*, *spin'i-feks*, *n.* properly, a genus of grasses (Australian, etc.) whose spiny heads blow about and disseminate seed: popularly applied in Australia to porcupine-grass. [L. *spina*, spine, and the root of *facĕre*, to make.]

spink, *spingk*, (now *dial.*) *n.* a finch, esp. the chaffinch. [Perh. imit.]

spink, *spingk*, *n.* the lady's-smock. [Ety. dub.]

spinnaker, *spin'ə-kər*, *n.* triangular sail carried on side opposite mainsail by vessels sailing before the wind: large sail carried by racing yachts. [Prob. spin, not *Sphinx* (yacht that carried a spinnaker).]

spinner, spinneret, etc. See spin.

**spinney, spinny,** *spin'i, n.* a small clump of trees or copse:—*pl.* **spinn'eys, spinn'ies.** [O.Fr. *espinei*—L. *spinētum,* a thorn-hedge, thicket—*spina,* thorn.]

**spino-,** *spi-nō-,* in composition, spine.

**spinode,** *spi'nōd, (geom.) n.* a cusp or stationary point of a curve. [L. *spina,* thorn, *nōdus,* knot.]

**Spinozism,** *spi-nōz'izm, n.* the pantheistic monism of Benedict *Spinoza* (1632-77).—*n.* **Spinō'zist,** a follower of Spinoza.—*adj.* **Spinōzis'tic.**

**spinster,** *spin'stər, n.* a spinner (*obs.*; *Shak.*): an unmarried woman: an old maid: a woman fit for the spinning-house (*obs.*).—*ns.* **spin'sterdom,** the world of old maids collectively; **spin'sterhood.**—*adjs.* **spinsterial** (*-stē'ri-əl*), **spinstē'rian, spin'sterish, spin'sterly.**—*ns.* **spin'stership; spin'stress,** a woman who spins: a spinster. [spin, and suffix **-ster.**]

**spintext,** *spin'tekst, n.* a long-winded preacher. [spin and text.]

**spinthariscope,** *spin-thär'i-skōp, n.* an instrument for counting alpha particles by observing the sparks produced by their impact on a fluorescent screen. [Gr. *spintharis,* a spark, *skopeein,* to observe.]

**spinule, spiny,** etc. See under **spine.**

**spiracle,** *spir'ə-kl, n.* a breathing-hole: a vent, orifice, passage.—*adjs.* **spiracular** (*-ak'ū-lər*); **spirac'ulate.**—*n.* **spirac'ulum:**—*pl.* **spirac'ula.** [L. *spirāculum*—*spirāre,* to breathe.]

**Spiraea,** *spi-rē'ə, n.* the meadow-sweet genus of the rose family. [Gr. *speiraiā,* meadow-sweet, or privet—*speira,* a coil (from its coiled fruits).]

**spiral.** See **spire** (1 and 2).

**spirant,** *spi'rənt, (phon.) adj.* fricative, open, produced by narrowing without stopping the air-passage.—*n.* a spirant consonant (including or excluding nasals, liquids, and semi-vowels).—*n.* **spirā'tion,** breathing: the procession of the Holy Ghost (*theol.*). [L. *spirāre,* to breathe.]

**spire,** *spir, n.* a shoot, sprout: a stalk: a long slender stalk: a tapering or conical body, esp. a tree-top: a flower-spike: a reed or reedlike plant (also collectively): a deer's tine: a spike: a cone: a summit, peak: a tall slender architectural structure tapering to a point.—*v.i.* to sprout: to shoot up.—*v.t.* to furnish with, or form into, a spire: to put forth as a shoot or fruit (*Spens.*).—*adjs.* **spir'al,** towering and tapering (see also next article); **spired,** having a spire: tapering, conical: peaked: spiked: sprouted; **spire'less.**—*adv.* **spire'wise.**—*adj.* **spir'y,** shooting into spires: spire-like: tapering: abounding in spires (see also next article).—*n.* **spire'-steeple,** a steeple with a spire. [O.E. *spir,* shoot, sprout.]

**spire,** *spir, n.* a coil: a spiral: the spiral part of a shell, excluding the body-whorl.—*v.i.* to wind, mount, or proceed in spirals.—*adj.* **spir'al,** winding like the thread of a screw: with parts arranged in spirals (*bot.*).—*n.* a spiral line, course, or object: a curve (usu. plane), the locus of a point whose distance from a fixed point varies according to some rule as the radius vector revolves (*math.*): a helix (see also previous article): a gradual but continuous rise or fall, as of prices.—*v.i.* to go in a spiral.—*v.t.* to make spiral.—*n.* **spirality** (*-al'i-ti*).—*adv.* **spir'ally.**—*n.* **spiras'ter** (Gr. *astēr,* star), a coiled sponge-spicule with radiating spines.—*adj.* **spir'āted,** spirally twisted.—*n.* **spir'ēme,** in mitosis, the coiled thread formed by nuclear chromatin.—*adj.* **spir'ic,** like a tore or anchor-ring.—*n.* a curve, the plane section of a tore.—*n.* **Spir'ifer** (L. *ferre,* to bear), a genus (chiefly Silurian to Carboniferous) of brachiopods, with coiled arm-supports.—*adj.* **spirill'ar.**—*ns.* **spirillō'sis,** infection with a spirillum; **spirill'um,** a spirally bent bacterium:—*pl.* **spirill'a;** **spir'ochaete** (*-kēt;* Gr. *chaitē,* hair, mane), a spirally coiled bacterium (genus **Spirochae'ta,** or **-tē,** or kindred), cause of

syphilis and other diseases; **spirochaetō'sis,** infection with a spirochaete, as in syphilis, relapsing fever, etc.; **Spirogyra** (*spi-rō-jī'rə,* or *-gi'*; Gr. *gyros,* a ring), a genus of freshwater algae with chlorophyll in spiral bands.—*adj.* **spir'y,** spirally coiled (see also previous article). [Gr. *speira,* a coil, a tore.]

**spirit,** *spir'it, n.* vital principle: the principle of thought: the soul: a disembodied soul: a ghost: an incorporeal being: a kidnapper (*obs.*): enthusiasm: actuating emotion, disposition, frame of mind: a leading, independent, or lively person: animation: verve: courage: mettle: real meaning: essence, chief quality: a breath of wind: a breath (*obs.*): a breathing (*Gr. gram.*): (usu. in *pl.*) a formerly supposed subtle substance in the body: a distilled liquid: an aqueous solution of ethyl alcohol: (usu. in *pl.*) spirituous liquor: a solution in alcohol: (in *pl.*) cheerful or exuberant vivacity: (in *pl.*) mental powers, mind.—*v.t.* to give spirit to: to inspirit, encourage, cheer: to convey away secretly, to kidnap. —*adj.* **spir'ited,** full of spirit, life, or fire: animated: possessed by a spirit.—*adv.* **spir'itedly.**—*n.* **spir'itedness.**—*adj.* **spir'itful.**—*ns.* **spir'iting,** the action of one who spirits in any sense: the offices of a spirit or sprite; **spir'itism,** spiritualism: animism; **spir'itist.**—*adjs.* **spiritist'ic;** **spir'itless,** without spirit, cheerfulness, or courage: dejected: dead.—*adv.* **spir'itlessly.**—*n.* **spir'itlessness.**—*adj.* and *adv.* **spiritoso** (*-ō'sō;* It.), with spirit.—*adj.* **spir'itous,** of the nature of spirit, pure: ardent, spirituous.—*n.* **spir'itousness.**—*adj.* **spir'itūal,** of, of the nature of, relating to, spirit, a spirit, spirits, the mind, the higher faculties, the soul: highly refined in thought and feeling, habitually or naturally looking to things of the spirit: incorporeal: ecclesiastical: as a Gallicism, witty, clever: spirituous (*obs.* or *rare*).—*n.* that which is spiritual: an American Negro religious song.—*n.* **spiritualisā'tion, -z-.** —*v.t.* **spir'itualise, -ize,** to make spiritual: to imbue with spirituality: to refine: to free from sensuality: to give a spiritual meaning to.—*ns.* **spir'ituaiser, -z-; spir'itualism,** a being spiritual: the philosophical doctrine that nothing is real but soul or spirit: the doctrine that spirit has a real existence apart from matter: the interpretation of a varied series of abnormal phenomena as for the most part caused by spiritual beings acting upon specially sensitive persons or mediums (also **spiritism**); **spir'itualist,** one who has a regard only to spiritual things: (with *cap.*) one who holds doctrine of spiritualism or spiritism.—*adj.* **spiritualist'ic.**—*n.* **spirituality** (*-al'i-ti*), state of being spiritual: that which is spiritual: property held or revenue received in return for spiritual service (*hist.*): the clergy (*hist.*).—*adv.* **spir'itually.**—*ns.* **spir'itualness,** the state or quality of being spiritual; **spir'itualty** (*obs.* or *hist.*), spirituality.—*adj.* **spirituel,** also *fem.* (indiscriminately used) **spirituelle** (Fr. *spē-rē-tü-el;* coll. *spir-it-ū-el'*), showing refined and witty grace and delicacy.—*n.* **spirituos'ity,** spirituous character: immateriality.—*adj.* **spir'ituous,** sprightly (*obs.*): spiritual (*obs.*): containing, or of the nature of, a volatile principle (*arch.*): alcoholic.—*ns.* **spir'ituousness; spiritus** (*spir', spir'i-tas;* L. *spē'ri-toōs*), spirit: a breathing (*Gr. gram.*); **spiritus asper,** the rough, **lenis,** the smooth, breathing).—*adj.* **spir'ity** (*dial.* or *coll.*), spirited: spirituous.—**spir'it-blue,** aniline blue; **spir'it-duck,** the bufflehead, from its rapid diving; **spir'it-gum,** a preparation used by actors for attaching false beards; **spir'it-lamp,** lamp burning methylated or other spirit to give heat; **spir'it-leaf,** Ruellia; **spir'it-level,** a glass tube nearly filled with alcohol, showing perfect levelness when the bubble is central; **spirit photography,** the taking of photographs of persons in which other shadowy figures appear; **spir'it-rapper,** one who claims to receive messages from disembodied spirits by raps or knocks; **spir'it-rapping.**—*adj.* spir'it-stirring, rousing the spirit. —**spir'itual-mind'edness; spir'it-varnish,** shellac or other resin in a volatile solvent, usu. alcohol; **spir'it-world,** the world of disembodied spirits.— **animal spirits,** a subtle form of matter formerly believed to be sent along the nerves from the brain: hence constitutional liveliness; **(Holy) Spirit** (see holy); **in spirits,** cheerfully vivacious; **out of spirits,** depressed; **spirit(s) of salt,** hydrochloric acid; **spirit(s) of wine,** alcohol. [L. *spīritus,* a breath—*spīrāre,* to breathe.]

**spirling.** See sparling.

**spiro-.** For some words see spire (2).

**spirograph,** *spī'rō-gräf, n.* an instrument for recording breathing movements.—*n.* spirom'eter, an instrument for measuring lung capacity.—*adj.* spiromet'ric.—*ns.* spirom'etry; spi'rophore (Gr. *phoros,* a bringing), an apparatus for inducing artificial respiration by means of an airtight case for the body and an air-pump. [L. *spīrāre,* to breathe.]

**spirt,** *spûrt, v.i.* to shoot out forcibly, or in a fine strong jet.—*v.t.* to squirt in a fine strong jet.—*n.* a sudden fine jet. [Origin uncertain; cf. Ger. dial. *spirzen,* to spit; **spurt.]**

**spirt,** *spûrt,* (*Shak.*) *v.i.* to sprout, shoot up. [O.E. *spryttan*; cf. **sprout.]**

**spirtle.** Same as spurtle.

**spiry.** See under spire (1 and 2).

**spissitude,** *spis'i-tūd, n.* density. [L. *spissitūdō—spissus,* thick.]

**spit,** *spit, n.* a broach for roasting meat: jocularly, a sword: a long narrow tongue of land or sand running into the sea: a wire or spindle holding a spool in a shuttle.—*v.t.* to transfix: to string on a rod or wire:—*pr.p.* spitt'ing; *pa.t.* and *pa.p.* spitt'ed.—*adj.* spitt'ed.—*ns.* spitt'er, a young deer with unbranched antlers; spitt'ing, piercing. [O.E. *spitu*; Du. *spit,* Ger. *spiess.*]

**spit,** *spit, v.t.* to throw out from the mouth: to eject with violence: to utter with hate, scorn or violence: to spawn.—*v.i.* to throw out saliva from the mouth: to rain in scattered drops: to make a spitting sound: to sputter:—*pr.p.* spitt'-ing; *pa.t.* and *pa.p.* spat, *arch.* spit, *obs. pa.p.* spitt'en, spitt'ed (*B.*).—*n.* saliva, spume: a light fall of rain or snow: an exact replica (*slang*; usu. *dead* or *very spit,* from the phrase *as like him as if he had spit him out of his mouth*).—*ns.* spitt'er; spitt'ing, the act of ejecting saliva: the ejection of oxygen, with drops of molten metal, when silver or platinum heated in air cools slowly: the resulting surface-appearance.—Also *adj.*—*ns.* spitt'le, spit, saliva; spittoon', a vessel for spitting in.—*adjs.* spit'-box, a spittoon; spit'-curl (*coll.*), a curl pressed flat on the temple; spit'-fire, that which emits fire, e.g. a volcano, cannon: a type of fighting aeroplane: a hot-tempered person; spitting image (form of *dial. spitten image*—for *spit and image*), the exact likeness of (see above).—spit and polish, cleaning up of uniform and equipment, esp. to excess; spit (it) out, to speak out, tell (it). [Northern O.E. *spittan,* O.N. *spýta,* Ger. dial, *spitzen, spützen.*]

**spit,** *spit, v.t.*and *v.i.* to dig: to plant with a spade. —*n.* a spade's depth: a spadeful. [O.E. *spittan,* or (M.)Du. and (M.)L.G. *spit.*]

**spital.** Same as spittle (see spit (2)).

**spitch-cock,** *spich'-kok, n.* an eel split and broiled. —*v.t.* to split and broil, as an eel. [Cf. spatch-cock.]

**spitcher,** *spit'cha,* (*naval slang*) *adj.* done for. [Maltese *spićća,* pron. *spitch'a,* finished, ended.]

**spite,** *spit, n.* grudge: lasting ill-will: hatred: a cause of vexation.—*v.i.* to vex: to thwart: to hate.—*adj.* spite'ful, full of spite: desirous to vex or injure: malignant.—*adv.* spite'fully.—*n.*

spite'fulness.—**in spite of,** in opposition to all efforts of, in defiance of, in contempt of: notwithstanding; spite (of), despite. [despite.]

**spittle.** See under spit (2).

**spittle,** also spital, *spit'l,* (*arch.*) *n.* a hospital, esp. for foul diseases, a lazar-house.—spitt'le-house. [hospital.]

**spitz,** *spits, n.* a Pomeranian dog: a group of breeds of dog generally having long hair, pointed ears and a tightly curled tail, incl. husky, samoyed, Pomeranian, etc. [Ger.]

**spiv,** *spiv,* (*slang*) *n.* a flashy black-market hawker: one who makes money by dubious means: an idler.—*n.* spivv'ery, the world or the practices of spivs. [Perh. conn. with spiff.]

**splanchnic,** *splangk'nik, adj.* visceral, intestinal.— *n.* splanch'nocele (*-sēl*; Gr. *koilos,* hollow), a visceral cavity: the posterior part of the coelom. [Gr. *splanchnon,* pl. *splanchna,* entrails.]

**splash,** *splash, v.t.* to spatter, as with water or mud: to throw about brokenly, as liquid: to dash liquid on or over: to effect by or with splashing: to variegate as if by splashing: to display, print very prominently.—*v.i.* to dabble: to dash liquid about: to move, go, with throwing about of broken liquid: to fly about dispersedly: of bullets, to throw about fragments or molten metal on striking.—*n.* the dispersion of liquid suddenly disturbed, as by throwing something into it or by throwing it about: liquid thrown on anything: a spot formed by or as if by throwing liquid: a little soda-water: lead thrown about by a bullet on striking: ostentation, publicity, display: a sensation, excitement, dash.—*n.* splash'er, one who, or that which, splashes: a guard against splashing: a board attached to the foot for walking on mud.—*adv.* splash'ily.—*n.* and *adj.* splash'ing.—*adj.* splash'y, splashing: with splashing: wet and muddy: full of puddles. —splash'-board, a mudguard: a dashboard; splash'down, (moment of) the landing of a manned spacecraft on the sea.—*adj.* splash'-proof.—splash down, of spacecraft, to land on the sea on completion of mission. [plash.]

**splat,** *splat, n.* a thin strip forming the upright middle part of a chair-back. [plat (3).]

**splatch,** *splach,* (*Scot.* and *U.S.*) *n.* a splash or clot of dirt or colour: a splotch.—*v.t.* to splotch. [Cf. splotch.]

**splatter,** *splat'ər, v.t.* and *v.i.* to spatter: to splash: to sputter.—*n.* a spatter: a spattering. [Cf. spatter.]

**splay,** *splā, v.t.* and *v.i.* to display (*obs.*): to slope, slant, or bevel (*archit.*): to spread out.—*n.* a slant or bevel, as of the side of a doorway, window, or the like.—*adj.* and *adv.* with a splay. —splay foot, a flat foot turned outward.—*adjs.* splay'-foot, -ed; splay'-mouthed, wide-mouthed. [display.]

**spleen,** *splēn, n.* a soft, pulpy, blood-modifying organ close to the stomach, once thought the seat of anger and melancholy: hence various meanings, mostly in Shak. and more or less obs.—spite: boredom: ill-humour: melancholy: mirth: caprice: impulse: high spirit.— *adjs.* spleen'ful; spleen'ish; spleen'less; spleen'y (*Shak.*), spleenish.—*n.* splenec'tomy (*splin-*; Gr. *ek,* out, *tomē,* a cutting), excision of the spleen. —*adj.* splenetic (*splin-et'ik*; formerly *splēn'i-tik*), of the spleen: affected with spleen: peevish: melancholy.—*n.* a splenetic person.—*adj.* splenet'i-cal.—*adv.* splenet'ically.—*adj.* splenic (*splen'ik*), of the spleen.—*ns.* splēnisā'tion, -izā'tion, conversion (of the lung) into spleen-like substance; spleni'tis (*splin-*), inflammation of the spleen; splēnomeg'aly (Gr. *megas, megalē, mega,* big), enlargement of the spleen.—spleen'-stone (*obs.*), jade; spleen'-wort, any fern of the genus Asplenium; splenic fever, anthrax. [L. *splēn*—Gr. *splēn.*]

**splendent,** *splen'dənt, adj.* brightly shining.—*adjs.* **splen'did,** brilliant, resplendent: magnificent: excellent (*coll.*); **splendid'ious** (*obs.*).—*adv.* **splen'didly.**—*n.* **splen'didness.**—*adjs.* **splen'didous** (*obs.*); **splendif'erous** (now only *coll.*); **splen'-dorous.**—*n.* **splen'dour** (*-dər*), brilliance: magnificence. [L. *splendēre,* to shine, *splendidus, splendor.*]

**splenetic,** etc. See **spleen.**

**splenial,** *splē'ni-əl, adj.* splint-like: of the splenium or the splenius.—*ns.* **splē'nium,** the round pad-like posterior border of the *corpus callosum*; **splē'nius,** a large thick muscle on the back of the neck. [Gr. *splēnion,* pad, compress.]

**splent.** See **splint.**

**spleuchan,** *splōōhh'ən,* (*Scot.*) *n.* a tobacco-pouch: a purse. [Gael. *spliuc(h)an.*]

**splice,** *splīs, v.t.* to unite by interweaving the strands: to join together by overlapping: to unite, esp. (*slang*; also *v.i.*) in matrimony.—*n.* act of splicing: joint made by splicing: the part of the handle of a cricket-bat or the like that fits into the blade.—**sit on the splice** (*cricket slang*), to play a defensive game; **splice the mainbrace** (*nautical slang*), to serve out an allowance of spirits: to fall to drinking. [Du. (now dial.) *splissen.*]

**spline,** *splin, n.* a key to make wheel and shaft revolve together: a thin strip or slat. [Orig. E. Anglian.]

**splint,** *splint,* also **splent,** *splent, n.* an overlapping strip in armour: a strip, slip of wood, lath: a splinter: a contrivance for holding a broken bone, or the like, in position: a bony enlargement on a horse's leg between knee and fetlock: **splint-coal.**—*v.t.* to put in splints.—*n.* **splint'er,** a piece of wood, etc., split off, esp. a needle-like piece: a slender strip of wood, esp. one used as a torch: a splint (*obs.*).—*v.t.* and *v.i.* to split into splinters.—*v.t.* (*Shak.*) to put in splints, hence join, piece.—*adj.* **splint'ery,** made of, or like, splinters: apt to splinter.—**splint'-arm'our,** armour of narrow overlapping plates; **splint'-bone,** a small bone alongside the cannon bone in the horse, etc., the second or the fourth metacarpal or metatarsal; **splint'-coal,** a hard coal of uneven fracture that does not cake; **splint'er-bar,** the cross-bar of a coach, supporting the springs; **splint'er-bone,** the fibula; **splinter party, group,** a party or group formed by a breakaway from a larger body.—*adj.* **splint'er-proof,** proof against the splinters of bursting shells or bombs, or against splintering.—**splintery fracture** (*min.*), the property of breaking with a surface like broken wood; **splint'wood,** sapwood. [M.Du. *splinte* (Du. *splint*) or (M.)L.G. *splinte, splente*; Du. and L.G. *splinter,* Ger. *splenter.*]

**split,** *split, v.t.* to break in pieces, wreck: to rend: to cleave lengthwise: to divide: to disunite: to divulge (*coll.*).—*v.i.* to be dashed to pieces: to suffer shipwreck: to divide or part asunder: to divulge secrets (*coll.*): to divide one's votes instead of plumping: to burst with laughter: to go at full speed: to break off relations (with) (*slang*).—*pr.p.* **splitt'ing;** *pa.t.* and *pa.p.* **split** (*Shak.,* etc., **splitt'ed**).—*n.* a crack or rent lengthwise: a schism: a half-bottle of aerated water, a half-glass of spirits: (in *pl.*) the acrobatic feat of going down to the floor with the legs spread out laterally.—*n.* **splitt'er,** one who, or that which, splits: one who splits hairs in argument, classification, etc.: a splitting headache (*coll.*).—*adj.* **splitt'ing,** rending: cleaving: ear-splitting: of a headache, very severe: very rapid.—**split infinitive,** an infinitive with an adverb between 'to' and the verb; **split mind,** schizophrenia.—*adj.* **split'-new** (*Scot.*), brand-new.—**split pea,** a dried pea deprived of its seed-coat and thus broken across at the embryo; **split personality,** a tendency towards schizo-

phrenia; **split ring,** a ring formed as if split spirally, as for keeping keys together; **split second,** a fraction of a second.—*adj.* **split'-second,** timed to a fraction of a second.—**split hairs** (see **hair**); **split investment trust** (see **trust**); **split-level house,** one-storey house with rooms on more than one level; **split on a rock,** to meet some unforeseen and disastrous difficulty, to go to ruin; **split one's sides,** to laugh immoderately; **split-seconds hand,** a double seconds hand in a chronograph, of which first one and then the other member can be stopped by pressing a button; **split the difference,** to divide equally the sum of matter in dispute, to take the mean. [Du. *splitten,* related to *splijten,* Ger. *spleissen.*]

**splore,** *splōr, splör,* (*Scot.*) *n.* a frolic: a spree: an escapade: a row: a scrape. [Origin obscure.]

**splotch,** *sploch,* **splodge,** *sploj, ns.* a big or heavy splash, spot, or stain.—*vs.t.* to mark with splotches or splodges.—*v.i.* to trudge flounderingly or splashily.—*adjs.* **splotch'y, splodg'y.** [Perh. conn. with O.E. *splott,* spot.]

**splurge,** *splûrj, n.* any boisterous display.—*v.i.* to make such a display.—*adj.* **splur'gy.** [Imit.]

**splutter,** *splut'ər, v.i.* to eject drops: to scatter ink upon a paper, as a bad pen: to scatter liquid with spitting noises: to articulate confusedly as in rage.—*v.t.* to utter splutteringly.—*n.* an act or noise of spluttering.—*n.* **splutt'erer.**—*n.* and *adj.* **splutt'ering.**—*adv.* **splutt'eringly.**—*adj.* **splutt'ery.** [Prob. imit.; cf. **sputter.**]

**Spode,** *spōd, n.* a porcelain made with addition of bone-ash by Josiah *Spode* (1754-1827) at Stoke. —Also *adj.*

**spode,** *spōd,* **spodium,** *spō'di-əm, ns.* powder got by calcination: bone-black.—*n.* **spodomancy** (*spod'ə-man-si*), divination by means of ashes.— *adj.* **spodoman'tic.**—*n.* **spod'ūmene,** a monoclinic pyroxene, silicate of aluminium and lithium. [Gr. *spodos,* dim. *spodion,* ashes; *spodoumenos* (contracted participle), burnt to ashes, from its appearance under the blowpipe.]

**spoffish,** *spof'ish, adj.* fussy, officious—also **spoff'y.** [Origin obscure.]

**spoil,** *spoil, n.* (often in *pl.*) plunder, booty: acquisitions, prizes: spoliation: pillage: a cast or stripped-off skin: remains of an animal body: material cast out in excavation: damage, impairment (*rare*): a thing spoiled in making (*rare*).—*v.t.* to take by force: to plunder: to despoil: to strip: to deprive: to destroy, end (*Shak.*): to corrupt: to mar: to impair: to make useless: to treat over-indulgently: to harm the character so.—*v.i.* to practise spoliation: go bad: deteriorate:—*pa.t.* and *pa.p.* **spoiled** or (only in sense of damage) **spoilt.**—*n.* **spoil'age,** waste by spoiling.—*adj.* **spoiled.**—*n.* **spoil'er.**—*adj.* **spoil'ful** (*Spens.* **spoylefull**), plundering.—**spoil'-bark, -heap,** a deposit of spoil; **spoil'-five,** a card game drawn or *spoiled* if no player wins three out of five tricks; **spoils'-man,** one who looks for profit out of politics; **spoil'-sport,** one who stops or interferes with sport or other people's pleasure: a meddler; **spoils system,** the system of supplanting civil servants on a change of government, on the principle that 'to the victor belong the spoils'. —**spoiling for,** (a fight, etc.) more than ripe or ready for: intent on. [O.Fr. *espoille*—L. *spolium,* spoil.]

**spoke,** *spōk, pa.t.* of **speak.**

**spoke,** *spōk, n.* one of the radiating bars of a wheel.—*adv.* **spoke'wise.**—**spoke'shave,** a two-handled planing tool for curved work.—**put a spoke in one's wheel,** to thwart one. [O.E. *spāca;* Du. *speek,* Ger. *speiche.*]

**spoken,** *spōk'n, pa.p.* of **speak.**—In composition, of speech, speaking, as **fair'-spoken, plain'-spoken.**

**spokesman,** *spōks'mən, n.* one who speaks for

another, or for others:—*pl.* spokes'men:—*fem.* spokes'woman. [speak, man.]

spolia opima, *spō'li-ə ōp'i-mə, spo'li-a op-ē'ma*, (L.) the richest booty—spoil taken in battle by a leader from a leader.

spoliate, *spō'li-āt, v.t.* and *v.i.* to despoil, to plunder.—*n.* spōliā'tion.—*adj.* spō'liātive, serving to take away or diminish.—*n.* spō'liātor.—*adj.* spō'liatory (-ə-tər-i). [L. *spoliāre, -ātum—spolium*, spoil.]

spondee, *spon'dē, n.* a foot of two long syllables. *adj.* spondaic (-dā'ik). [L. *spondēus (pēs)*—Gr. *spondeios (pous)*, (a foot) used in the slow solemn hymns sung at a *spondē* or drink-offering —*spendein*, to pour out, make a libation.]

spondulicks, *spon-doo'liks, (U.S. slang) n.pl.* money. [Origin unknown.]

spondyl, *spon'dil, n.* a vertebra: a thorny oyster (Spondylus).—*n.* spondyli'tis, inflammation of a vertebra.—*adj.* spon'dylous. [Gr. *sp(h)ondylos*, a vertebra.]

sponge, *spunj, n.* any member of the phylum Porifera, sessile aquatic animals with a single cavity in the body, with numerous pores: the fibrous skeleton of such an animal, remarkable for its power of sucking up water: a piece of such a skeleton, or a substitute, used for washing, obliterating, absorbing, etc.: a swab for a cannon: any sponge-like substance, as leavened dough, a pudding, swampy ground: a bedeguar: a hanger-on or parasite: a drunkard: an application of a sponge: the life or behaviour of a sponger upon others.—*v.t.* to wipe, wipe out, soak up, remove, with a sponge: to drain, as if by squeezing a sponge: to gain by the art of the parasite.—*v.i.* to suck in, as a sponge: to fish for sponges: to live on others parasitically. —*adj.* spongeous (*spun'jəs*), spongy.—*n.* spong'er, one who uses a sponge: a sponge-fisher: a sponge-fishing boat: an apparatus for sponging cloth: a sponge or parasite.—*adjs.* spongicolous (*spun-, spon-jik'ə-ləs*; L. *colēre*, to inhabit), living in association with, usually within, a sponge; spon'giform, like or akin to a sponge.— *adv.* spon'gily, in a spongy way, or manner.— *ns.* spongin (*spun'jin*), a horny substance in the skeletons of various sponges: spon'giness.— *adjs.* spongiose (*spun'*, or *-ōs'*), spongious (*spun'-jəs*), spongoid (*spong'goid*).—*ns.* spongologist (*spong-gol'ə-jist*); spongol'ogy, the science of sponges.—*adj.* spongy (*spun'ji*), absorptive: porous: wet and soft: drunken.—sponge'-bag, a waterproof bag for carrying a sponge: (in *pl.*) checked or striped trousers.—*adj.* checked.— sponge'-bath, an application of water to the body by or from a sponge: sponge'-cake, a very light sweet cake of flour, eggs, and sugar; sponge'-cloth, a cotton cloth of open texture; sponge'-fing'er, a finger-shaped sponge-cake; sponge'-fisher; sponge'-fishing; sponge'-rubber, rubber processed into sponge-like form; sponge'wood, sola; spon'ging-house, spun'ging-house, a bailiff's lodging-house for debtors in his custody before their committal to prison; spongy parenchyma (*bot.*), a loose tissue in leaves with much inter-cellular space; spongy platinum, platinum sponge, platinum in a finely divided state.—set a sponge, to leaven a small mass of dough for use in leavening a large quantity; throw up the sponge, to acknowledge defeat by throwing into the air the sponge with which a boxer is rubbed down between rounds: to give up any struggle. [O.E. *sponge, spunge*, and O.Fr. *esponge*—L. *spongia*— Gr. *spongiā*.]

sponsal, *spon'sl, adj.* spousal.—*n.pl.* sponsā'lia, espousals.—*n.* spon'sion, the act of becoming surety for another.—*adj.* spon'sional.—*n.* spon'-sor, one who promises solemnly for another: a surety: a godfather or godmother: a promoter: one who pays for radio or television broad-cast introducing advertisement.—Also *v.t.*— *adj.* sponso'rial.—*n.* spon'sorship. [L. *spondēre*, *spōnsum*, promise.]

sponsible, *spon'si-bl*, (now *dial.*) *adj.* aphetic for responsible, respectable.

sponsing. See sponson.

sponson, *spon'sn, n.* outward expansion from ship's deck: short projecting length of plane: wing-section giving extra lift: an air-filled tank on the side of a canoe to give buoyancy: a structure to give a seaplane steadiness on the water.—Also spon'sing. [Ety. dub.]

sponsor. See sponsal.

spontaneous, *spon-tā'nyəs, -ni-əs, adj.* of one's free will: acting by its own impulse or natural law: produced of itself: impulsive: unpre-meditated.—*ns.* spontaneity (-tə-nē'i-ti), spontā'-neousness. — *adv.* spontā'neously. — spontaneous combustion, catching fire by causes at work with-in, esp. slow oxidation of a mass of matter; spontaneous generation, production of living organisms from dead matter. [L. *spontāneus— sponte*, of one's own accord.]

sponte sua, *spon'te soo'a*, (L.) of one's own accord.

spontoon, *spon-toon', n.* a small-headed halberd formerly carried by some officers. [Fr. *sponton* —It. *spontone—punto—*L. *punctum*, a point.]

spoof, *spoof, (slang) n.* a hoaxing game invented and named by Arthur Roberts (1852–1933), comedian: a card game.—*adj.* bogus.—*v.t.* and *v.i.* to hoax.—*ns.* spoof'er; spoof'ery.

spook, *spook, n.* a ghost.—*v.i.* to play the spook. *adj.* ghostly.—*n.* spook'ery.—*adv.* spook'ily.—*n.* spook'iness.—*adjs.* spook'ish, spook'y. [App. L.G.; cf. Ger. *spuk*, Du. *spook*.]

spool, *spool, n.* a cylinder, bobbin, or reel for winding yarn, etc., upon.—*v.t.* and *v.i.* to wind on spools.—*n.* spool'er. [L.G. *spōle*; Du. *spoel*, or O.N.Fr. *espole*; Ger. *spule*.]

spoon, *spoon, v.i.* to scud before the wind.—Also spoom.—*adj.* spoom'ing (*Keats*), foaming.—*n.* spoon'drift, light spray borne on a gale.—Also (orig. *Northern*) spin'drift. [Origin unknown.]

spoon, *spoon, n.* an instrument with a shallow bowl and a handle: anything of like shape, as an oar: a wooden-headed golf-club with face slightly hollowed: a spoon-bait: the wooden spoon (*Cambridge*; see under wood): a simple-ton: a maudlin love-maker: mawkish love-making.—*v.t.* to transfer with, or as if with, a spoon: to shove, scoop, or hit softly up into the air, instead of striking cleanly and definitely: to dally sentimentally with: to catch with a spoon-bait: to pack together like spoons.—*v.i.* to make love sentimentally: to fish with a spoon-bait.—*n.* spoon'ful, as much as fills a spoon: a small quantity:—*pl.* spoon'fuls.—*advs.* spoon'ily; spoon'ways, -wise, like spoons packed closely together.—*adj.* spoon'y, spoon'ey, silly: foolishly and demonstratively fond.—*n.* one who is spoony.—spoon'-bait, -hook, a lure on a swivel, used in trolling for fish; spoon'bill, any bird of a family (Plataleidae) akin to the ibises, with long, flat, broad bill, spoon-shaped at the tip.—*adj.* spoon'-fed, fed with a spoon: artificially fostered (*fig.*): taught by doled-out doses of cut-and-dried information.—*v.t.* spoon'-feed.— spoon'-food; spoon'meat, food taken or given with a spoon.—spoons on, silly in manifestation of love for. [O.E. *spōn*, sliver, chip, shaving, Ger. *span*, chip, O.N. *spǎnn, spōnn*, chip, spoon.]

Spoonerism, *spoo'nər-izm, n.* a transposition of initial sounds of spoken words—e.g. 'shoving leopard' for 'loving shepherd'. [Rev. W. A. Spooner (1844–1930), a noted perpetrator of transpositions of this kind.]

spoor, *spoor, n.* track, esp. of a hunted animal.— *v.t.* and *v.i.* to track.—*n.* spoor'er. [Du. *spoor*, a track; cf. O.E. and O.N. *spor*, Ger. *spur*; also speir.]

**sporadic,** *spor-ad'ik*, *adj.* scattered: occurring here and there or now and then: occurring casually.—Also (*rare*) **sporad'ical.**—*adv.* **sporad'-ically.** [Gr. *sporadikos—sporas, sporados,* scattered—*speirein,* to sow.]

**spore,** *spōr, spör, n.* a unicellular asexual reproductive body: sometimes extended to other reproductive bodies.—*adj.* **sporangial** (*spor-an'ji-əl*).—*ns.* **sporan'giole, sporan'giolum** (or -*ji'*; *pl.* -a), a sporangium containing one or few spores; **sporan'giophore,** the part that bears sporangia; **sporan'giospore,** a spore developed in a sporangium; **sporan'gium** (*pl.* **sporan'gia**), a spore-case, sac in which spores are produced.—Also **spore'-case; spor'idesm** (Gr. *desmos,* a bond; *bot.*), a multicellular body or group of spores, of which every cell is capable of germinating.—*adj.* **sporid'ial.**—*ns.* **sporid'ium** (*pl.* -a), a spore borne on a promycelium; **spor'ocarp** (Gr. *karpos,* fruit), a structure containing the sori and sporangia in water-ferns; a multicellular structure in which spores are formed; **spor'ocyst,** the cyst developed in the process of sporulation.—*adj.* **sporocyst'ic.**—*n.* **sporogen'esis,** production of spores.—Also **sporogeny** (-*oj'*).—*adj.* **sporog'-enous,** spore-bearing.—*ns.* **sporogonium** (-*gō'*), the capsule or asexual generation in mosses; **spor'ophore,** a spore-bearing stalk or structure. *adjs.* **sporophor'ic, sporoph'orous.**—*ns.* **spor'-ophyll** (Gr. *phyllon,* leaf), a leaf that bears sporangia; **spor'ophyte** (Gr. *phyton,* plant), the spore-bearing or asexual generation in the life-cycle of a plant.—*adj.* **sporophytic** (-*fit'ik*).—*n.pl.* **Sporozo'a,** a parasitic group of Protozoa reproducing by spores, including the causal organisms of malaria and pébrine.—*n.* **sporozō'ite** (Gr. *zōion,* an animal), in Protozoa, an infective stage developed within a spore.—*adj.* **spor'ūlar.**—*v.i.* **spor'ūlate,** to produce spores.—*ns.* **sporūlā'tion,** formation of spores: breaking up into spores; **spor'ule,** a spore. [Gr. *sporā,* a seed—*speirein,* to sow.]

**sporran,** *spor'ən, n.* an ornamental pouch worn in front of the kilt by the Highlanders of Scotland. [Gael. *sporan.*]

**sport,** *spōrt, spört, v.i.* to play: to frolic (also *v.t.* with *it*): to make merry: to practise field diversions: to trifle: to deviate from the normal.—*v.t.* to amuse (*obs.*): to wear, use, exhibit, set up, publicly or ostentatiously: to wager: to squander (*rare*).—*n.* to shut (see **oak**): to force open (*obs.*).—*n.* recreation: pastime: dalliance, amorous behaviour: play: a game, esp. one involving bodily exercise: mirth: jest: contemptuous mirth: a plaything (esp. *fig.*): a laughing-stock: field diversion: success or gratification in shooting, fishing, or the like: a sportsman: a person of sportsmanlike character, a good fellow: an animal or plant that varies singularly and spontaneously from the normal type: (in *pl.*) a meeting for races and the like.—*adj.* **sports,** suitable for sport.—Also (esp. *U.S.*) **sport.**—*n.* **sportabil'ity,** sportiveness.—*adj.* **sport'able.**—*ns.* **sport'ance** (*rare*), play; **sport'er,** one who sports: a sportsman.—*adj.* **sport'ful,** full of sport: merry: full of jesting.—*adv.* **sport'fully.**—*n.* **sport'fulness.**—*adj.* **sport'ily.**—*n.* **sport'iness.**—*adj.* **sport'ing,** relating to, engaging in, or fond of sports.—*adv.* **sport'ingly.**—*adj.* **sport'ive,** inclined to sport: playful: merry: amorous, wanton.—*adv.* **sport'ively.**—*n.* **sport'iveness.**—*adjs.* **sport'less,** without sport or mirth: sad; **sport'y** (*coll.*), sportsmanlike.—**sporting chance,** as good a chance of winning or being successful as of losing or failing; **sports car,** a low car, usu. for two, capable of attaining high speed; **sports jacket,** a man's jacket, usu. tweed, for casual wear; **sports'man,** one who practises, or is skilled in, sport: one who shows a good spirit in sport.—*adj.* **sports'manlike.**—**sports**-manship; **sports'wear; sports'woman.**—**sport one's oak** (see **oak**). [Aphetic for **disport.**]

**sposh,** *sposh,* (*U.S.*) *n.* slush.—*adj.* **sposh'y.** [Imit.]

**spot,** *spot, n.* a mark made by a drop of wet matter: a blot: a small discoloured or differently coloured place: a locality, place of limited area, precise place: one of the marked points on a billiard-table, from which balls are played: a relatively dark place on the sun: a small quantity of anything: a spotlight: a white pigeon with a spot on the forehead: a name for various American fishes: a job, piece (of work) (*obs.*): perhaps, a pattern, or piece, of needle-work (*Shak.* **spotte**): a place on e.g. a television or radio programme: a turn, performance, esp. a short one: (in *pl.*) a leopard (*coll.*).—*v.t.* to mark with spots: tarnish, as reputation: reprehend (*Spens.*): pick out, detect, locate, identify (*coll.*): free from spots (often with *out*): place on a spot.—*v.i.* become spotted:—*pr.p.* **spott'ing;** *pa.t.* and *pa.p.* **spott'ed.**—*adj.* **spot'less,** without a spot: untainted: pure.—*adv.* **spot'lessly.**—*n.* **spot'lessness.**—*adj.* **spott'ed.**—*ns.* **spott'edness;** **spott'er,** one who spots or detects.—*adv.* **spott'-ily.**—*n.* **spott'iness.**—*adj.* **spott'y.**—**spot advertising,** advertising by means of brief items, usu. in dramatised form, on television or radio.—*adj.* **spot'-barred,** under the condition that the spot-stroke may not be played more than twice consecutively.—**spot cash,** money down; **spot'-check,** a check on the spot without warning: a check of random samples to serve in place of a general check; **spot dance,** a dance after which a prize is given to the couple spotlighted when the music stopped; **spot'light,** (apparatus for projecting) circle of light on actor or small part of stage: also *fig.*: adjustable, focused-beam car lamp additional to fixed lights—*v.t.* to turn the spotlight on.—*adj.* **spot-on'** (*coll.*), on the target: accurate.—**spot'-stroke,** a stroke in billiards by which the player pockets the red ball from the spot, leaving his own ball in position to repeat the stroke; **spotted dog,** a Dalmatian dog: a pudding or loaf with currants.—**in a spot,** in a difficult situation; **knock (the) spots off,** to surpass easily; **on the spot,** at the very place: there and then: straightway: alert, equal to the occasion: in difficulty or danger (e.g. *put on the spot,* orig. to doom to be murdered).—As *adj.* **on-the-spot'.**—**soft spot** (*coll.*), affectionate feeling. [Cf. obs. Du., L.G., *spot,* O.N *spotti.*]

**spouse,** *spowz, n.* a husband or wife.—*v.t.* to betroth (*Spens.*): to marry (*Milt.*).—*n.* **spous'age,** marriage.—*adj.* **spous'al,** nuptial: matrimonial.—*n.* usually in *pl.* nuptials: marriage.—*adj.* **spouse'less.** [O.Fr. *spus, -e, espous, -e* (Fr. *époux,* fem. *épouse*)—L. *spōnsus,* pa.p. of *spondēre,* to promise.]

**spout,** *spowt, v.t.* to throw out in a jet: to declaim: to pawn (*slang*).—*v.i.* to issue in a jet: to blow as a whale: to declaim.—*n.* a projecting lip or tube for discharging liquid from a vessel, a roof, etc.: a gush, discharge, or jet: an undivided waterfall: a waterspout: the blowing, or the blow-hole, of a whale: a shoot: a lift in a pawnshop: hence, a pawnshop.—*ns.* **spout'er,** one who, or that which, spouts: a declaimer: a spouting oil-well: a spouting whale: a whaling ship.—*adjs.* **spout'less; spout'y,** spirting water when trodden on.—**spout'-hole,** a blow-hole.—**up the spout** (*slang*), pawned. [M.E. *spouten;* cf. Du. *spuiten,* to spout, O.N. *spȳta,* to spit.]

**sprack,** *sprak,* (*W. Midland* and *S.W.*) *adj.* vigorous, sprightly, alert.—Also (after the pron. of Sir Hugh Evans, *Merry Wives* IV, i. 85) **sprag.** [Origin obscure.]

**sprackle, sprak'l, spraickle,** *sprāk'l,* (*Scot.*) *v.i.* to clamber. [Origin obscure.]

**sprad,** *sprad,* (*Spens.*) *pa.p.* of **spread.**

**sprag,** *sprag, n.* a mine prop: a bar inserted to

stop a wheel: a device to prevent a vehicle from running backwards.—*v.t.* to prop, or to stop, by a sprag:—*pr.p.* spragg'ing; *pa.t.* and *pa.p.* spragged. [Origin obscure.]

sprag. See sprack.

sprain, *sprān*, *v.t.* to overstrain the muscles of.— *n.* a wrenching of a joint with tearing or stretching of ligaments. [Connection with O.Fr. *espreindre*, to squeeze out, is disputed.]

spraint, *sprănt*, *n.* otter's dung. [O.Fr. *espraintes*, lit. pressed out.]

sprang, *pa.t.* of spring.

sprangle, *sprang'l*, (now *U.S.* and *dial.*) *v.i.* to sprawl: to straggle: to ramify: to struggle.—*n.* a straggle. [M.E. *spranglen.*]

sprat, *sprat*, *n.* a fish like the herring, but much smaller: a term of contempt (*Shak.*).—sprat'-weath'er, the dark days of November and December. [O.E. *sprot*; Du. *sprot*, Ger. *sprotte.*]

sprattle, *sprat'l*, (*Scot.*) *v.i.* to scramble. [Cf. Sw. *sprattla.*]

sprauchle, *spröhh'l*, (*Scot.*) a later form of sprackle.

sprawl, *spröl*, *v.i.* to toss or kick about the limbs (*arch.*): to lie or crawl with limbs flung about: to straggle.—*v.t.* to spread stragglingly.—*n.* a sprawling posture, movement, or mass.—*n.* sprawl'er.—*adjs.* sprawl'ing, sprawl'y. [O.E. *sprēawlian*, to move convulsively.]

spray, *sprā*, *n.* a cloud of small flying drops: an application or dispersion of such a cloud: an apparatus or a preparation for so dispersing.— *v.t.* to sprinkle in or with fine mist-like jets.— *n.* spray'er.—*adj.* spray'ey.—spray'-gun, a device for applying paint, etc., by spraying. [M.Du. *sprayen.*]

spray, *sprā*, *n.* a shoot or twig, esp. one spreading out in branches or flowers: an ornament, casting, etc., of similar form.—*v.i.* to spread or branch in a spray.—*adj.* spray'ey, branching. [Poss. conn. with sprig or with O.E. *spræc*, twig.]

spray, *sprā*, spreathe, spreethe, *sprēdh*, spreaze, spreeze, *sprēz*, (*S.W. dial.*) *v.t.* and *v.i.* to chap, roughen—usu. in *pa.p.* sprayed, spraid, etc. [Origin obscure.]

spread, *spred*, *v.t.* to cause to extend more widely or more thinly: to scatter abroad or in all directions: to stretch: to extend, esp. over a surface: to open out so as to cover a wider surface: to overlay: to set with provisions, as a table.—*v.i.* to extend or expand: to be extended or stretched: to open out: to go further apart: to unfold: to admit of spreading: to be propagated or circulated:—*pa.t.* and *pa.p.* spread.—*n.* extent: compass: reach: expanse: an expanded surface: act or degree of spreading: an expansion: that which is spread out, a feast: anything for spreading on bread: a cover, esp. a bedcover.— *adj.* extended: flat and shallow (as a gem).—*n.* spread'er.—*n.* and *adj.* spread'ing.—*adv.* spread'-ingly.—spread'-ea'gle, a heraldic eagle with the wings and legs stretched out: a fowl split and spread out for cooking: a man tied for punishment (*naut.*): a skating figure.—*adj.* bombastic, boastful, and frothy, esp. in American patriotism.—*v.t.* to tie up with outstretched limbs: to spread out: to outrun.—*v.i.* to cut spread-eagles: to lie, fall, etc., with outstretched limbs: to talk in spread-eagle strain.—spread-ea'gleism. —*adv.* spread-eagle'wise.—spread'-over, an act of spreading out: an elastic distribution of working hours. [O.E. *sprǣdan*; Du. *spreiden*, Ger. *spreiten.*]

spreagh, *sprăhh*, sprehh, *n.* a prey: a foray.—*n.* spreagh'ery, sprech'ery, cattle-lifting: petty possessions, esp. plunder. [Gael. *spréidh*, cattle.]

spreathe, spreaze. See spray (3).

spreckled, *sprek'ld*, (now *dial.*) *adj.* speckled. [Cf. obs. Ger. *gespreckelt.*]

spred, spredd, spredde, obs. spellings of spread (*pres.*, *pa.t.*, *pa.p.*).—Also *inf.* spredd'en.

spree, *sprē*, *n.* a merry frolic: a drunken bout.— *v.i.* to carouse. [Orig. slang.]

spreethe, spreeze, See spray (3).

sprent, *sprent*, (*arch.*) *adj.* sprinkled. [Pa.p. of obs. *sprenge*—O.E. *sprengen, sprengan*, causative of *springan*, to spring.]

sprig, *sprig*, *n.* a small shoot or twig: a scion, a young person: an ornament like a spray: a headless or almost headless nail: a sprig-like object, ornament, or design, esp. embroidered or applied.—*v.t.* to embroider with representations of twigs: to nail with sprigs:—*pr.p.* sprig'ing; *pa.t.* and *pa.p.* sprigged.—*adjs.* sprigged; sprig'gy, full of or like sprigs. [Origin obscure.]

spright, *sprit*, *n.* (*Spens., Shak.*) an unhistorical spelling of sprite, obs. except perhaps in the sense of impish person.—*v.t.* (*Shak.*) to haunt.— *adj.* spright'ful (*Shak.*), spirited.—*adv.* spright'-fully (*Shak.*).—*n.* spright'fulness.—*adj.* spright'-less (*obs.*), spiritless.—*n.* spright'liness.—*adj.* spright'ly, vivacious: animated: lively: brisk: ghostly (*Shak.*).

spring, *spring*, *v.i.* to move suddenly, as by elastic force: to bound: to start up suddenly: to break forth: to appear: to issue: to come into being: to take origin: to sprout: to dawn (*B.*): to branch off: to begin to arch: to give way, split, burst, explode, warp, or start.—*v.t.* to cause to spring up: to start: to release the elastic force of: to let off, allow to spring: to cause to explode: to make known suddenly (with *on* or *upon*): to open, as a leak: to crack, as a mast: to bend by force, strain: to start from an abutment, etc. (*archit.*): to leap over: to set together with bevel-joints: to attach or fit with springs: to procure escape of (a prisoner) from jail (*slang*):—*pa.t.* sprang, now rarely sprung, *Spens.* sprong:—*pa.p.* sprung, *Spens.* sprong.—*n.* a leap: a sudden movement: a recoil or rebound: elasticity: an elastic contrivance usu. for setting in motion or for reducing shocks: a source of action or life: rise: beginning: cause or origin: a source: an outflow of water from the earth: the time of beginning (*Shak.*): the dawn (*B.*): (often with *cap.*) the season when plants spring up and grow—in North temperate regions roughly February or March to April or May, astronomically from the spring equinox to the summer solstice: a shoot (*obs.*): a youth (*Spens.*): copse (*obs.*): undergrowth (*Spens.*): high water: spring tide: a lively dance-tune (now *Scot.*): a Norwegian dance or dance-tune: a flock of teal: the springing of an arch: a crack in a mast.—*adj.* of the season of spring: sown, appearing, or used in spring: having or worked by a spring.—*ns.* spring'al, spring'ald, an active springy young man, a youth; spring'er, one who or that which springs: a kind of spaniel, useful in copses: the bottom stone of an arch.—*adv.* spring'ily.—*ns.* spring'iness; spring'ing, the act of leaping, sprouting, starting, rising, or issuing: the beginning of curvature of an arch: a place of branching: providing with springs.—*adj.* leaping: arising: dawning: sprouting: with the freshness of youth: resilient: starting: beginning to curve.—*adj.* spring'less.—*n.* spring'let, a little spring.—*adjs.* spring'like; spring'y, elastic: resilient: abounding with springs.—See also sprung.—spring'-bal'ance, an instrument for weighing by the elasticity of a spiral spring; spring'-beau'ty, the plant *Claytonia virginica*; spring'-bed, a spring-mattress; spring'-bee'tle, a click-beetle.—*adj.* spring'-blad'ed, of a knife, having a blade that springs out on pressure of a button.—spring'board, a springy board for jumping or diving from; spring'bok (Du.), a beautiful S. African antelope, larger than a roebuck (also spring'buck): (with *cap.*) S.A. international sportsman (from emblems of sporting teams, orig. 1906 rugby team; abbrev., **Bok**): hence also a South African, esp. when overseas; **spring'-box**, a box or barrel in which a spring is coiled: the frame of a sofa, etc., in which the springs are set; **spring'-carr'iage**; **spring'-cart**, one mounted upon springs.—*v.t.* and *n.* **spring'-clean'**.—**spring'-clean'er**; **spring'-clean'ing**, a thorough house-cleaning, usu. in spring; **spring fever** (*facet.*), spring lassitude; **spring'-gun**, a gun set to go off like a trap; **spring'-haas** (Du.), **spring'-hare**, the jumping hare; **spring'-halt**, a jerking lameness in which a horse suddenly twitches up his leg or legs; **spring'head**, a fountain-head, source: a head or end-piece for a carriage-spring.—*adjs.* **spring'-head'ed** (*Spens.*), having heads spring afresh; **spring'-heeled**, having springs on one's heels, as **spring-heeled Jack**, supposed to do great leaps and play pranks or commit robberies.—**spring'-house** (*U.S.*), a larder, dairy, etc., built over a spring or brook; **spring'-keeper**, a salamander; **spring'-lig'ament**, a ligament of the sole of the foot.—*adj.* **spring'-load'ed**, having or operated by a spring.—**spring'-lock**, a lock that fastens by a spring: one that opens when a spring is touched; **spring'-matt'ress**, a mattress of spiral springs in a frame; **spring'tail**, any member of the Collembola; **spring'tide**, springtime; **spring'-tide'**, **spring tide**, a tide of maximum amplitude after new and full moon, when sun and moon pull together; **spring'time**, the season of spring; **spring'-wa'ter**, water of or from a spring; **spring'-wheat**, wheat sown in the spring, rather than autumn or winter; **spring'wood**, secondary wood with larger and thinner-walled elements formed in spring and early summer; **spring'-wort**, a magical root, perh. mandrake.—**spring a leak**, begin to leak; **spring a mine**, cause it to explode. [O.E. *springan*; Ger. *springen*.]

**springe**, *sprinj*, *n.* a snare with noose and spring or gin.—Also **spring** (*spring*).—*v.t.* to catch in a springe:—*pr.p.* **spring'ing**; *pa.t.* and *pa.p.* **springed** (*sprinjd*).—*n.* **springle** (*spring'gl*), a snare. [Earlier *sprenge*, from a probable O.E. *sprencg*; cf. **sprent, spring**.]

**springe**, *sprinj*, (*George Eliot*) *adj.* active, nimble. [Ety. unknown.]

**sprinkle**, *spring'kl*, *v.t.* to scatter in small drops or particles: to scatter on: to baptise with a few drops of water: to strew, dot, diversify.—*v.i.* to scatter in drops.—*n.* an aspersorium or utensil for sprinkling.—*ns.* **sprin'kle, sprin'kling**, the act of one who sprinkles: a small quantity sprinkled: in bookbinding, mottling of edges by scattering a few drops of colour; **sprin'kler**. [Freq. from O.E. *sprengan*, the causative of *springan*, to spring; cf. Ger. *sprenkeln*.]

**sprint**, *sprint*, *n.* a short run, row, or race at full speed.—*v.i.* to run at full speed.—*ns.* **sprin'ter**; **sprin'ting**. [Cf. O.N. *spretta*, Sw. *spritta*.]

**sprit**, *sprit*, (*naut.*) *n.* a spar set diagonally to extend a fore-and-aft sail.—**spritsail** (*sprit'sl*), a sail extended by a sprit. [O.E. *sprēot*, pole; Du. and Ger. *spriet*, sprit.]

**sprite**, *sprit*, *n.* spirit—*obs.* except in the senses of goblin, elf, imp, impish or implike person.—*adjs.* **sprite'ful, sprite'ly**, etc. (see **sprightful**, etc.). [O.Fr. *esprit*; cf. **spirit, spright**.]

**sprocket**, *sprok'it*, *n.* a tooth on the rim of a wheel or capstan for engaging the chain: a toothed cylinder for driving a cinematograph film: a sprocket-wheel.—**sprock'et-wheel**, a wheel with sprockets. [Origin unknown.]

**sprod**, *sprod*, (*Northern*) *n.* a second-year salmon. [Origin obscure.]

**sprong**, *sprong*, (*Spens.*) *pa.t.* and *pa.p.* of **spring**.

**sprout**, *sprowt*, *n.* a new growth: a young shoot: a side bud, as in **Brussels sprouts** (see **Brussels**): a scion, descendant: sprouting condition.—*v.i.*

to shoot: to push out new shoots.—*v.t.* to put forth as a sprout or bud: to cause to sprout: to remove sprouts from (*dial.*).—*adj.* **sprout'ed**.—*n.* and *adj.* **sprout'ing**. [O.E. *sprūtan* (found in compounds), *Du. spruiten*, Ger. *spriessen*.]

**spruce**, *sprōōs*, *adj.* smart: neat, dapper: overfastidious, finical.—*adv.* sprucely.—*v.t.* to smarten.—*v.i.* to become spruce or smart (often with *up*).—*adv.* **spruce'ly**.—*n.* **spruce'ness**. [Prob. from next word, from the vogue of 'spruce leather' (obtained from Pruce or Prussia) in the 16th century.]

**Spruce**, *sprōōs*, *n.* Prussia (*obs.*): (without *cap.*) spruce-fir or its wood: (without *cap.*) spruce-beer.—*adj.* brought from Prussia: (without *cap.*) of spruce or its wood.—**spruce'-beer'**, a drink made from a solution of sugar or treacle and green tops of spruce; **spruce'-fir'**, any conifer of the genus Picea, with long shoots only, four-angled needles, and pendulous cones: extended to some other trees. [For **Pruce**.]

**sprue**, *sprōō*, *n.* a passage by which molten metal runs into a mould: the metal that solidifies in it —**deadhead**. [Origin obscure.]

**sprue**, *sprōō*, *n.* infantile thrush (*obs.*): a tropical disease affecting mouth, throat, and digestion. [Du. *spruw*.]

**sprue**, *sprōō*, (*London*) *n.* inferior asparagus.

**sprug**, *sprug*, (*Scot.*) *n.* a sparrow.

**spruit**, *sprāt, sprü'it, sprit*, (*S.Afr.*) *n.* a small, deepish watercourse, dry except during and after rains. [Du., sprout.]

**sprung**, *pa.t.* and *pa.p.* of **spring**.—*adj.* strained: split: loosed: furnished with springs: tipsy (*coll.*).—**sprung rhythm**, a poetic rhythm close to the natural rhythm of speech, with mixed feet, and frequent single stressed syllables.

**sprush**, *sprōōsh, sprush, adj., adv.*, and *v.t.* a Scots form of **spruce** (2).

**spry**, *spri, adj.* nimble: agile:—*comp.* **spry'er**; *superl.* **spry'est**.—*adv.* **spry'ly**.—*n.* **spry'ness**. [Origin doubtful.]

**spud**, *spud*, *n.* a small narrow digging tool: a stumpy person or thing: a potato (*slang*).—*v.t.* and *v.i.* to dig with a spud.—*adj.* **spudd'y**, podgy. —**spud'-bashing** (*slang*), peeling potatoes. [Origin obscure.]

**spue**, an old-fashioned spelling of **spew**.

**spule**, *spūl, spül*, (*Scot.*) *n.* the shoulder.—Also **speal** (*spēl*).—**spule'bane (-bone), -blade**. [Relation to **spauld** obscure.]

**spulzie, spuilzie, spulye, spulyie**, *spūl'(y)i*, (*Scot.*) *n.* spoliation.—*v.t.* and *v.i.* to plunder. [See **spoil**.]

**spume**, *spūm*, *n.* foam: scum.—*v.i.* to foam.—*v.t.* to throw up or off as foam or scum.—*n.* **spūmesc'ence**.—*adjs.* **spūmesc'ent**, foamy, frothing; **spū'mous, spū'my**. [L. *spūma—spuĕre*, to spew.]

**spun**, *pa.t.* and *pa.p.* of **spin**, and *adj.*—*adj.* **spun'-out**, unduly lengthened.—**spun sugar**, sugar spun into fine fluffy threads, as in candy floss; **spun'-yarn**, rope-yarn twisted into a cord.

**spunge**, *spunj*, obs. spelling of **sponge**.—**spung'ing-house** (see **sponge**).

**spunk**, *spungk*, *n.* a spark (*dial.*, esp. *Scot.*): a spirited, usu. small or weak, person (*dial.*): spirit, mettle, courage: touchwood, tinder (*obs.*): a fungus from which tinder is made (*dial.*): a match (*dial.*).—*v.i.* to take fire, flame up: to fire up: to show spirit (*U.S.*): to come to light (*Scot.*, with *out*).—*n.* **spunk'ie** (*Scot.*), a Will-o'-the-wisp: a fiery or mettlesome person: whisky (*Burns*).—*adj.* **spunk'y**, spirited: fiery-tempered. [Cf. Ir. *sponc*, tinder, sponge—L. *spongia*, a sponge—Gr. *spongiā*.]

**spur**, *spūr*, *n.* a goading instrument on a rider's heel: incitement, stimulus: a hard sharp projection: a claw-like projection at the back of a cock's or other bird's leg: an artificial substitute for this on a game-cock: a short, usu. flowering or fruit-bearing, branch: a great lateral root: ergot: a tubular pouch at the base of a petal: an expansion of a leaf-base: a lateral branch, as of a hill range: a strut: a structure to deflect the current from a bank.—*v.t.* to apply the spur to: to urge on: to provide with a spur or spurs: to prune into spurs.—*v.i.* to press forward with the spur: to hasten: to kick out:—*pr.p.* spurr′ing; *pa.t.* and *pa.p.* spurred.—*adjs.* spur′less; spurred, having or wearing spurs or a spur: in the form of a spur: urged: affected with ergot, as rye.— *ns.* spurr′er, one who, or that which, spurs; spurr′ier, a maker of spurs.—*n.* and *adj.* spurr′ing. —*adj.* spurr′y, like, of the nature of, having, a spur.—*v.t.* spur′-gall (*Shak.*), to gall or wound with a spur.—spur′-gear, -gear′ing, a system of spur-wheels.—*adj.* spur′-heeled, having a long straight hind-claw.—spur′-leather, a strap for fastening a spur; spur′-row′el, the rowel of a spur; spur′-roy′al, -ry′al, ri′al, a former English fifteen-shilling piece of gold, bearing a star like a spur-rowel; spur′-way (*dial.*), a bridle-road; spur′-whang (*Scot.*), a spur-leather; spur′-wheel, a cog-wheel.—*adj.* spur′-winged, with a horny spur on the pinion of the wing.—gilt spurs, a mark of knighthood; on the spur of the moment, without premeditation; set spurs to, to apply the spur and ride off quickly; win one's spurs, to earn knighthood: to gain distinction by achievement. [O.E. *spura, spora*; O.N. *spori*, Ger. *sporn*.]

spurge, *spûrj, n.* any species of Euphorbia, a genus of very varied habit, with milky, generally poisonous, juice, and an inflorescence (cyathium) of flowers so reduced as to simulate a single flower.—spurge′-lau′rel, a European evergreen shrub (*Daphne laureola*) with yellowish-green flowers, thick leaves, and poisonous berries. [O.Fr. *espurge* (Fr. *épurge*)—L. *expurgāre*, to purge—*ex*, off, *purgāre*, to clear.]

spurious, *spūr′i-əs, adj.* bastard: illegitimate: not genuine: false: sham: forged: simulating but essentially different.—*n.pl.* spūr′iae (-*i-ē*), feathers of the bastard-wing.—*n.* spurios′ity.—*adv.* spūr′iously.—*n.* spūr′iousness. [L. *spurius*, false.]

spurling, *spûr′ling.* Same as sparling.

spurn, *spûrn, v.t.* to kick: to tread, esp. in contempt: to reject with contempt.—*v.i.* (*obs.*) to trip: to kick (often with *at, against*).—*n.* a kick: kicking: disdainful rejection.—*n.* spurn′er.—*n.* and *adj.* spurn′ing. [O.E. *spornan, spurnan*, related to spur.]

spurne, *spûrn,* (*Spens.*) *v.t.* to spur.

spurrey, sometimes spurry, *spûr′i, n.* any plant of the genus Spergula: applied to kindred plants, Spergularia (*sandwort-spurrey*) and Sagina (knotted pearlwort or *knotted spurrey*). [Du. *spurrie*.]

spurt, *spûrt, v.t.* to spout, or send out in a sudden stream or jet.—*v.i.* to gush out suddenly in a small stream: to flow out forcibly or at intervals: to make a sudden short intense effort.—*n.* a sudden or violent gush: a jet: a short spell, esp. of intensified effort, speed, etc. [Variant of spirt.]

spurtle, *spûr′tl,* (*Scot.*) *n.* a porridge-stick: a sword (also spur′tle-blade). [Origin doubtful.]

sputnik, *spoot′nik, n.* a man-made earth satellite. [After the Russian *Sputnik* ('travelling companion') 1, the first such satellite, put in orbit in 1957.]

sputter, *sput′ər, v.i.* to spit or throw out moisture in scattered drops: to speak rapidly and indistinctly, to jabber: to make a noise of sputtering. —*v.t.* to spit out or throw out in or with small drops: to utter hastily and indistinctly: to deposit (a thin layer of metal) on glass, plastic, another metal, etc., in a vacuum tube from a cathode made of the metal to be sputtered (*n.* sputt′ering).—*n.* sputtering: matter sputtered

out.—*n.* sputt′erer.—*n.* and *adj.* sputt′ering.— *adv.* sputt′eringly.—*adj.* sputt′ery. [Imit.; cf. Du. *sputteren*, and spit.]

sputum, *spū′təm, n.* matter spat out:—*pl.* spū′ta. [L. *spūtum*—*spuĕre*, to spit.]

spy, *spī, n.* a secret agent employed to watch others or to collect information, esp. of a military nature: a spying: a look: an eye (*fig.*):—*pl.* spies.—*v.t.* to watch, observe, investigate, or ascertain secretly: to descry, make out: to discover.—*v.i.* to play the spy: *pr.p.* spy′ing; *pa.t.* and *pa.p.* spied; *3rd pers. pres. indic.* spies. —*n.* spy′al (*Spens.*), a spy (see spial).—*n.* and *adj.* spy′ing.—spy′glass, a small hand-telescope; spy′-hole, a peep-hole; spy′-money, money paid for secret intelligence. [O.Fr. *espie* (n.), *espier* (vb.); see espy.]

spyre, obs. spelling (*Spens.*) of spire (1).

squab, *skwob, adj.* fat, clumsy: unfledged, newly hatched: shy, coy: curt, abrupt (*obs.*).—*n.* a young pigeon or rook: a fledgling: a short stumpy person: a soft thick cushion: a padded sofa or ottoman: a carriage cushion: the back part of a motor-car seat.—*adj.* having a squab.— *v.t.* to upholster or stuff thickly and sew through in places.—*v.i.* to fall heavily.—*adv.* plump and squashily.—*adjs.* squabb′ish, thick, heavy; squabb′y, squat.—squab′-pie, a pie made of mutton or pork, onions, and apples. [Poss. Scand.; cf. Sw. dial. *sqvabb*, loose flesh, *sqvabbig*, flabby.]

squabash, *skwə-bash′, v.t.* to crush, smash.—*n.* a crushing.—*n.* squabash′er. [Prob. squash and bash.]

squabble, *skwob′l, v.i.* to dispute in a noisy manner: to wrangle.—*n.* a noisy, petty quarrel: a brawl.—*n.* squabb′ler. [Cf. Sw. dial. *sqvabbel*.]

squacco, *skwak′ō, n.* a small crested heron. [It. dial. *sguacco*.]

squad, *skwod, n.* a small group of soldiers drilled or working together: any working party: a set or group.—awkward squad, a body of recruits not yet competent in drill, etc. [Fr. *escouade*; cf. Sp. *escuadra*, It. *squadra*.]

squadron, *skwod′rən, n.* a body of soldiers drawn up in a square (*obs.*): a detachment, body, group: a division of a cavalry regiment under a major or captain: a section of a fleet under a flag-officer: a group of aeroplanes forming a unit under one command.—*v.t.* to form into squadrons.—*adjs.* squad′ronal; squad′roned.— squad′ron-leader, an air-force officer answering in rank to a lieutenant-commander or major; squadrone volante (*skwa-drō′nă vō-län′tä*; It., flying squadron), an early 18th-cent. Scottish political party opposed to the Argathelians. [It. *squadrone*—*squadra*, square.]

squail, *skwāl, v.i.* to throw sticks (as at birds or fruit).—*v.t.* to pelt with sticks: to hit by throwing a stick.—*n.* a stick for throwing: a counter for playing squails: (in *pl.*) ninepins: (in *pl.*) a parlour-game in which small disks are snapped from the edge of the table to a centre mark.—*ns.* squail′er, a throwing-stick; squail′ing. [Cf. kail (obs. *skail, skayle*), a ninepin.]

squalid, *skwol′id, adj.* filthy, foul: neglected, uncared-for, unkempt: sordid and dingy: poverty-stricken.—*n.* squalid′ity.—*adv.* squal′idly.—*ns.* squal′idness; squal′or, state of being squalid: dirtiness: filthiness. [L. *squālidus*, stiff, rough, dirty, *squālor*, -*ōris*.]

squall, *skwöl, v.i.* to cry out violently: to yell: to sing loudly and unmusically.—*v.t.* to sing or utter loudly and unmusically.—*n.* a loud cry or yell: a short violent wind.—*n.* squall′er.—*n.* and *adj.* squall′ing.—*adj.* squall′y, abounding or disturbed with squalls or gusts of wind: gusty, blustering: threatening a squall.—white squall, a tropical whirlwind, coming on without warning other than a small white cloud. [Prob. imit.]

squama, *skwā'mə, skwä'ma, n.* a scale: a scale-like structure: the expodite of an antenna in Crustacea:—*pl.* squā'mae (*-mē, -mi*).—*n.pl.* Squamā'ta (*skwə-*), an order of reptiles—snakes and lizards.—*adj.* squā'mate, scaly.—*ns.* squamā'-tion (*skwə-*), scaliness: mode of arrangement of scales; squame (*skwām*), a scale or squama; squamell'a (*skwə-*), a little scale.—*adj.* squā'mi-form, like a scale.—*n.* squamosal (*skwə-mō'sl*), a paired membrane bone of the vertebrate skull, the squamous portion of the temporal bone.— Also *adj.*—*adjs.* squā'mose, squā'mous, scaly.— *ns.* squāmos'ity; squamula (*skwam'ū-la,* or *skwām'*), squam'ule, a little scale.—*adj.* squam'-ūlose. [L. *squāma,* a scale.]

squander, *skwon'dər, v.t.* to scatter, disperse: to spend lavishly or wastefully.—*v.i.* to wander, roam, straggle: to scatter.—*n.* a squandering.— *adj.* squan'dered.—*n.* squan'derer.—*n.* and *adj.* squan'dering.—*adv.* squan'deringly.—*n.* squan-dermā'nia (*slang*), a spirit of reckless expendi-ture (in a government). [Origin obscure.]

square, *skwār, n.* an equilateral rectangle: an ob-ject, piece, space, figure, of approximately that shape, as a window-pane, paving-stone, space on a chessboard: an open space, commonly but not necessarily of that shape, in a town, along with its surrounding buildings: a rectangular block of buildings (*U.S.*): a body of troops drawn up in that form: the product of a quantity multi-plied by itself: the yoke of a garment (*Shak.*): a unit of flooring, 100 square feet: an instru-ment for drawing or testing right angles: a carpenter's measure: a canon, criterion, rule: squareness: quartile aspect (*old astron.*): due proportion: order: honesty, equity, fairness: quarrel, dissension (*obs.*): possibly part, com-partment (Shak., *King Lear* I, i): person of square tastes in the arts and square outlook (*slang*). —*adj.* having or approaching the form of a square: relatively broad, thick-set: right-angled: equal to a quantity multiplied by itself: measur-ing an area in two dimensions: exact, suitable, fitting: true, equitable, fair, honest: even, leav-ing no balance, equal in score: directly opposed: complete, unequivocal: solid, full, satisfying: (of taste in music, etc.), traditional and orthodox (*slang*): bourgeois in attitude (*slang*).—*v.t.* to make square or rectangular, esp. in cross-section: to make nearly cubical: to form into squares: to construct or determine a square equal to: to multiply by itself: to reduce to any given measure or standard, to adjust, regulate: to bring into accord, reconcile: to place at right angles with the mast or keel (*naut.*): to make equal: to pay: to bribe.—*v.i.* to suit, fit: to accord or agree: to take an attitude of offence and defence, as a boxer: to swagger (*obs.*): to make the score or account even.—*adv.* at right angles: solidly: directly: evenly: fairly, honestly.—*adj.* squared.—*adv.* square'ly.—*ns.* square'ness; squar'er, one who or that which squares: a fighting, quarrelsome person, or perh. a swaggerer (*Shak.*).—*adv.* square'wise.— *n.* and *adj.* squar'ing.—*adj.* squar'ish.—square'-bashing, parade-ground drill (*mil. slang*).— *adj.* square'-built, of a form suggesting square-ness: broad in proportion to height.—square'-dance, a folk-dance done by a group of couples in a square formation; square'-danc'ing; square'-face (*S.Afr.*), gin (from the shape of the bottle); square foot, inch, mile, an area equal to that of a square whose side measures a foot, etc.; square'-head, a free immigrant (*old Austr. slang*): a Scandinavian or German (*slang*); square knot, a reef-knot; square'-leg (*cricket*), a fielder to the left of, and in line with, the batsman; square'-meas'ure, a system of measures for sur-faces, its unit the square of the lineal unit.— *adjs.* square'-pierced (*her.*), having a square

opening so as to show the field; square'-rigged, having the chief sails square, and ex-tended by yards suspended by the middle at right angles to the masts—opp. to *fore-and-aft.* —square'-root, that quantity which being multi-plied into itself produces the quantity in ques-tion; square'-sail (*-sl*), a four-sided sail ex-tended by yards suspended by the middle at right angles to the mast.—*adjs.* square'-shoul'-dered, with broad, straight shoulders; square'-toed, ending square at the toes.—square'-toes, (*pl.*) square-toed shoes: (*sing.*) an old-fashioned, punctilious person.—back to square one, back to the original position with the problem, etc., unchanged; how squares go (*obs.*), what is doing: how things are going; on the square, honestly; square up to, face up to and tackle; squaring the circle (quadrature of the circle), finding a square of the same area as a circle—for hundreds of years this was attempted by Euclidian means (i.e. with straight-edge and compass) until in 1882 it was proved impossible: any impossible task. [O.Fr. *esquarre* (Fr. *équerre*)—L. *ex* and *quadra,* a square.]

squarrose, *skwar'ōs, skwor'ōs, -ōs', adj.* rough with projecting or deflexed scales, bracts, etc.: standing out straight or deflexed. [L. *squarrōsus,* scurfy.]

squarson, *skwär'sn, n.* a clergyman who is also a squire or landowner in his parish.—*n.* squar'-sonage, his residence. [squ(ire) and (p)arson.]

squash, *skwosh, v.t.* to press into pulp: to crush flat: to squeeze: to put down, suppress: to snub.—*v.i.* to form a soft mass as from a fall: to crowd: to squelch: to become crushed or pulpy.—*n.* an unripe peascod (*Shak.*): anything soft and unripe or easily crushed: a crushed mass: a drink made from fruit juice: a crushed condition: a close crowd: a squeezing: a soft rubber ball for playing squash racquets: squash racquets.—*adv.* with a squash.—*n.* squash'er.— *adv.* squash'ily.—*n.* squash'iness.—*adj.* squash'y, pulpy: squelching: sopping.—squash rackets, racquets, a game like rackets played one-a-side on a smaller court with larger and hollow ball. [O.Fr. *esquacer* (Fr. *écacher*), to crush—L. *ex, quassāre*; see quash.]

squash, *skwosh, n.* the gourd of several species of Cucurbita: the plant bearing it. [Narragansett *askutasquash.*]

squat, *skwot, v.i.* to sit down upon the hams or heels: to sit close, as an animal: to settle on land or in unoccupied buildings without title or (*Austr.*) with a view to acquiring a title.—*v.t.* to cause to squat:—*pr.p.* squatt'ing; *pa.t.* and *pa.p.* squatt'ed.—*adj.* crouching: short and thick, dumpy.—*n.* the act of squatting.—*ns.* squat'ness; squatt'er, one who squats: a large landowner (*Austr.*); squatt'iness.—*v.t.* and *v.i.* squatt'le, to squat down.—*n.* squattoc'racy (*Austr.*), the powerful squatter class.—*adj.* squatt'y, short and thick. [O.Fr. *esquatir,* to crush—L. *ex, coactus,* pa.p. of *cōgĕre,* to drive together.]

squatter, *skwot'ər, v.i.* to splash along.—*n.* a fluttering: a splashing, spattering. [Prob. imit.]

squaw, *skwö, n.* an American Indian woman, esp. a wife.—squaw'man, a white man with an Indian wife. [Massachusett *squa.*]

squawk, *skwök, n.* a croaky call or cry: a com-plaint, protest (*slang*).—*v.i.* to utter a squawk. —*v.t.* to utter with a squawk.—*n.* squawk'er.— *n.* and *adj.* squawk'ing.—*adj.* squawk'y. [Imit.]

squeak, *skwēk, v.i.* to give forth a high-pitched nasal-sounding note or cry: to inform, peach, or confess (*slang*).—*v.t.* to utter, sing, render, squeakily.—*n.* a squeaky sound: a narrow escape or bare chance: a feeble newspaper (*slang*).—*ns.* squeak'er, one who squeaks: a

young bird: an informer: a squeaking toy consisting of a bladder and a tube; squeak'ery.—
adv. squeak'ily.—n. squeak'iness.—n. and adj.
squeak'ing.—adv. squeak'ingly.—adj. squeak'y.
—a narrow squeak, a narrow escape. [Imit.; cf.
Sw. sqväka, to croak, Ger. quieken, to squeak.]
squeal, skwēl, v.i. to utter a high-pitched cry of
some duration: to cry out in pain: to complain: to turn informer.—v.t. to utter, sing,
render, express, with squealing.—n. a high sustained cry.—n. squeal'er, one who squeals, esp.
a bird of various kinds, a young pigeon: an
informer.—n. and adj. squeal'ing. [Imit.; cf.
Sw. dial. sqväla, to cry out.]
squeamish, skwēm'ish, adj. sick: easily nauseated:
qualmish: easily shocked, disgusted, or offended:
fastidious: coy: reluctant from scruples or compunction.—adv. squeam'ishly.—n. squeam'ishness. [M.E. scoymous—A.Fr. escoymous; ety.
dub.]
squeedge, skwēj, an illit. form of squeeze.
squeegee, skwē'jē, -jē', also squilgee, skwil'jē, ns.
an implement with edge of rubber, leather, etc.,
for clearing water or mud from decks, floors,
windows, etc.: a photographer's roller or brush
for squeezing out moisture.—v.t. to clear, press,
or smooth with a squeegee. [App. squeeze.]
squeeze, skwēz, v.t. to crush, press hard, compress:
to grasp tightly: to embrace: to force by pressing: to effect, render, or put by pressing: to
crush the juice or liquid from: to force to discard winning cards: to fleece, extort from: to
take a rubbing of.—v.i. to press: to crowd: to
crush: to force a way: to yield to pressure.—n.
act of squeezing: pressure: a restriction or
time of restriction (usually financial or commercial): a crowded assembly: an embrace: a
close grasp: a portion withheld and appropriated as by an Oriental official: a rubbing: a
few drops got by squeezing.—n. squeezabil'ity.
—adj. squeez'able.—n. squeez'er, one who
squeezes: an instrument, machine, or part, for
squeezing: a playing-card marked in the corner
with suit and value.—n. and adj. squeez'ing.—
adj. squeez'y, confined, cramped, contracted.—
squeeze-box (slang), a concertina. [Origin obscure.]
squelch, skwelch, skwelsh, n. the gurgling and
sucking sound of walking in wet mud: a heavy
blow on, or fall of, a soft body: its sound: a
pulpy mass: a disconcerting or quashing retort
or rebuff.—v.i. to make, or walk with, the sound
of a squelch.—v.t. to crush under heel: to put
down, suppress, snub, crush.—n. squelch'er, one
who squelches: an overwhelming blow, retort,
etc.—n. and adj. squelch'ing.—adj. squelch'y.
[Imit.; cf. quelch.]
squeteague, skwi-tēg', n. an Atlantic American
spiny-finned food-fish (Cynoscion), misnamed
salmon or trout. [Narragansett pesukwiteauq,
they make glue.]
squib, skwib, n. a paper tube filled with combustibles, thrown up into the air burning and
exploding: a petty lampoon: a paltry fellow
(Spens.).—v.t. aim squibs at: lampoon.—v.i.
write lampoons: use squibs: sound or skip
about like a squib.—n. and adj. squibb'ing.
[Perh. imit.]
squid, skwid, n. any ten-armed cephalopod, esp.
Loligo: a bait or lure of, or in imitation of, a
squid: an anti-submarine mortar.—v.i. to fish
with a squid. [Origin obscure.]
squier. See squire (2).
squiffer, skwif'ər, (slang) n. a concertina.
squiff(y), skwif'('i), (coll.) adj. tipsy.
squiggle, skwig'l, v.i. to squirm, wriggle: to make
wriggly lines.—n. a twist, wriggle, wriggly line.
—adj. squigg'ly. [Imit.]
squilgee. See squeegee.
squill, skwil, n. any plant of the liliaceous genus

Scilla: the sea-onion (Urginea), formerly included in that genus: (usu. in pl.) its dried bulbs
used as a diuretic and expectorant: the mantis
shrimp (Squilla). [L. squilla, scilla, sea-onion,
shrimp—Gr. skilla, sea-onion.]
squinancy, skwin'an-si, (obs.) n. quinsy.—n.
squin'ancy-wort, a species of woodruff once
thought good for quinsy. [L.L. squinanchia, a
combination of Gr. synanchē, sore throat, and
kynanchē (see cynanche).]
squinch, skwinch, skwinsh, n. an arch or other
support across a re-entrant or interior angle.
[scuncheon.]
squinny, swkin'i, squiny, skwī'ni, (Shak.) v.i. to
squint, peer.
squint, skwint, adv. asquint, obliquely.—adj. looking obliquely: looking askance: squinting:
strabismic: oblique: indirect.—v.i. to look
obliquely: to be strabismic: to have a side
reference or allusion: to hint disapprobation:
to glance aside or casually: to glance.—v.t. to
cause to squint: to direct or divert obliquely.—
n. act or habit of squinting: strabismus: an
oblique look: a glance: a peep: an oblique
reference, hint, tendency, or aim: an oblique
opening in a wall, as a hagioscope.—n. squint'er.
—n. and adj. squint'ing.—adv. squint'ingly.—
squint'-eye(s), one who squints.—adj. squint'-
eyed. [Aphetic for asquint.]
squire, skwīr, n. an esquire, an aspirant to knighthood attending a knight: one who escorts or
attends a lady: an English or Irish landed
gentleman, esp. of old family: one who has
been a justice of the peace, etc. (U.S.).—v.t. to
escort or attend.—ns. squir(e)'age, squiral'ity,
squir'alty, landed gentry collectively; squir(e)'-
arch.—adj. squir(e)arch'al.—ns. squir(e)'archy,
the rule of squires: the body of squires: squire'-
dom; squireen' (Ir. dim. suff. -in; Anglo-Ir.),
a petty squire; squire'hood.—adjs. and advs.
squire'-like, squire'ly.—ns. squire'ling, a squire
of small possessions; squire'ship; squir'ess, a
squire's wife.—squire of dames, one who devotes
himself to the ladies, from a character in Spenser
(Faerie Queene III, vii. 53). [esquire.]
squire, squier, skwīr, (Spens., Shak.) n. a carpenter's square or rule: a canon, rule.—by the
squire, precisely. [See square.]
squirm, skwûrm, v.i. to writhe, go writhing.—n.
a wriggle.—adj. squirm'y. [Prob. imit.]
squirr. Same as skirr.
squirrel, skwir'əl, n. a nimble, bushy-tailed
arboreal rodent (Sciurus or kindred genus): the
pelt of such an animal.—adj. made of the pelt
of a squirrel.—squirr'el-cage, a cage with a
treadmill for a squirrel: in an induction motor,
a rotor whose winding suggests this; squirr'el-
monkey, a small golden-haired South American
monkey; squirr'el-shrew, a tree-shrew; squirr'el-
tail, a grass of the barley genus with long hairlike awns: a broad-tailed lobworm (Walton):
a cap of squirrel-skins, with a tail hanging down
behind. [O.Fr. escurel—L.L. scurellus, dim. of
L. sciūrus—Gr. skiouros—skiā—shade, ourā,
tail.]
squirt, skwûrt, v.t. to throw out in a jet.—v.i. to
spirt.—n. an instrument for squirting: a jet: an
unimportant and irritatingly pretentious person
(slang).—n. squirt'er.—n. and adj. squirt'ing.—
squirting cucumber, a cucurbitaceous plant
(Ecballium elaterium) that squirts out its ripe
seeds. [Cf. L.G. swirtjen, swürtjen.]
squish, skwish, v.i. to make a squelching or squirting sound.—n. the sound of squishing: bosh
(slang): marmalade (slang).—adj. squish'y.
squit, skwit, (slang) n. a contemptible person:
nonsense. [Cf. squirt.]
squitch, skwich, n. quitch-grass.
sraddha, shraddha, s(h)rä'dä, n. an offering to the
manes of an ancestor. [Sans. śräddha.]

Sri, Shri, *shrē*, in India a title of respect given to a man, chiefly in writing. [Sans. *śri*, majesty, holiness.]

st, 'st, *st, interj.* hush.

'st, *st*, a shortened form of hast.

stab, *stab, v.t.* to wound or pierce by driving in a pointed weapon: to give a sharp pain (also *fig.*): to roughen with a pick so as to hold plaster: to pierce near the back edges, for the passage of thread or wire (*bookbinding*).—*v.i.* to thrust or pierce with a pointed weapon:—*pr.p.* stabb'ing; *pa.t.* and *pa.p.* stabbed.—*n.* an act of stabbing: a wound with a pointed weapon: an attempt, a go (*slang*).—*n.* stabb'er.—*n.* and *adj.* stabb'ing.—*adv.* stabb'ingly.—stab in the back (*lit.* and *fig.*), to injure in a treacherous manner. [Cf. stob.]

Stabat Mater, *stä'bat mä'tər, stä'bat mä'ter, n.* a Latin hymn on the seven dolours of the Virgin: a musical setting of it. [Its opening words, the mother stood.]

stabile. See stable (1).

stable, *stā'bl, adj.* standing firm: firmly established: durable: firm in purpose or character: constant: not ready to change: not radioactive. —*adj.* stā'bile (-*bil*, -*bil*), stable (*rare*): not moving: not fluctuating: not decomposing readily, e.g. under moderate heat.—*n.* an abstract art construction of metal, wire, wood, differing from a mobile in having no movement.—*ns.* stabilisation, -z- (*stab-*, *stäb-i-li-zä'shən*, or -*li-*); sta'bilisātor, -z-.—*v.t.* stabilise, -ize (*stab'*, *stäb'*), to render stable or steady: to fix: to fix the value of: to establish, maintain, or regulate the equilibrium of.—*ns.* stab'iliser, -z-, anything that stabilises: an additional plane or other device for giving stability to an aircraft: a gyroscope or other means of steadying a ship: a substance that retards chemical action; stability (*stə-bil'i-ti*), state of being stable: steadiness: fixity: power of recovering equilibrium: fixing by vow of a monk or nun to one convent for life; stā'bleness.—*adv.* stā'bly.—stable equilibrium, the condition in which a body will return to its old position after a slight displacement. [Fr., —L. *stabilis*—*stāre*, to stand.]

stable, *stā'bl, n.* a building for horses, or sometimes other animals: a set of horses kept together: a horse-keeping establishment, organisation, or staff (as a horse-keeping establishment often *pl.* in form but treated as *sing.*): a number of skilled trained persons, esp. young men, who work together under one head or one manager: (in *pl.*) a cavalry soldier's duty in the stable, or the call summoning to it.—*v.t.* to put or keep in a stable.—*v.i.* to dwell in a stable or as in a stable.—*ns.* sta'bler (*Scot., arch.*), a stable-keeper, an inn-keeper; sta'bling, act of putting into a stable: accommodation for horses, cattle, cycles, etc.—sta'ble-boy, -man, one who works at a stable; stable companion, one who lodges in the same place or is a member of the same club, etc. (*coll.*); sta'ble-room, accommodation in a stable.—out of the same stable, having the same social background, esp. a privileged one. [O.Fr. estable (Fr. étable)—L. *stabulum*—*stāre*, to stand.]

stablish, *stab'lish*, (*B., Shak., Milt., arch.*) *v.t.* an old form of establish: to set up: to make stable: to confirm.—*n.* stab'lishment, establishment: confirmed possession (*Shak.*).

staccato, *stə-kä'tō, stäk-kä'tō, (mus.) adj.* and *adv.* with each note detached.—*n.* a staccato performance, manner, or passage.—*adj.* and *adv.* (*superl.*) staccatis'simo. [It., pa.p. of *staccare*, for *distaccare*, to separate.]

stack, *stak, n.* a large built-up pile of hay, corn, wood, etc.: a group or cluster of chimneys or flues: the chimney or funnel of a steamer, steam-engine, etc.: an isolated pillar of rock,

often rising from the sea: a set of compactly arranged bookcases for storing books not on the open shelves of a library: a pyramid of three rifles, etc.: a pile: a standard quantity of gambler's chips bought at one time: aircraft waiting to land and circling at definite heights according to intructions: a large amount (*slang*). —*v.t.* to pile into a stack: to shuffle (cards) for cheating: arrange (aircraft waiting to land) in a stack (see above).—*n.* stack'ing.—stack'-room, in a library, a room where books are stored in stacks; stack'yard, a yard for stacks.—stack against, in favour of, to arrange (circumstances) to the disadvantage, advantage, of; stack up, to pile or load high. [O.N. *stakkr*, a stack of hay.]

stacket, *stak'it, (obs. Scot.) n.* a palisade. [Du. *staket*.]

stacte, *stak'tē, n.* a Jewish spice, liquid myrrh.— *n.* stactom'eter, a pipette for counting drops. [Gr. *staktos*, -*ē*, -*on*, dropping.]

stadda, *stad'ə, n.* a comb-maker's double-bladed hand-saw. [Origin unknown.]

staddle, *stad'l, n.* a support, esp. for a stack: the bottom of a stack: a small tree left unfelled: a stump left for coppice. [O.E. *stathol*, foundation; Ger. *stadel*.]

stadia, *stā'di-ə, n.* a graduated rod used in measuring distances at one observation, by the angle subtended by the distance between two hairs in the telescope (also sta'dia-rod'): the telescope so used (*U.S.*). [Origin obscure.]

stadium, *stā'di-əm, n.* a Greek measure of length, 600 Greek, or 606¾ English feet: a race-course, sports-ground: a stage in development:—*pl.* stā'dia.—*n.* stade (*stād*), a stadium. [Latinised from Gr. *stadion*.]

stadtholder, stadholder, *stat', stät', stad', städ'hōl-dər, n.* a Dutch viceroy or provincial governor: the head of the Dutch republic (*hist.*). [Du. *stadhouder*, lit. stead-holder (Ger. *statthalter*, Fr. *lieutenant*)—*stad*, place (now only town), *houder*, holder; spelling influenced by Ger. *stadt*, town.]

staff, *stäf, n.* a stick carried in the hand: a prop: a long piece of wood: a pole: a flagstaff: a long handle: a stick or ensign of authority: a token authorising an engine-driver to proceed: a set of lines and spaces on which music is written or printed: a stanza: in a watch or clock, the spindle of a balance-wheel (these have *pl.* staffs or staves, *stāvz*; see also stave): a body of officers who help a commanding officer, or perform special duties: a body of persons employed in an establishment (these two meanings have *pl.* staffs, *stäfs*).—*adj.* (or in composition) belonging or attached to the staff: applied also to officers of a higher grade.—*v.t.* to provide with a staff.—staff'-coll'ege, a college that trains officers for staff appointments; staff'-corps, a body of officers and men assisting a commanding officer and his staff: formerly a body that supplied officers to the Indian army; staff'-duty, the occupation of an officer who serves on a staff, having been detached from his regiment; staff'-notation, musical notation in which a staff is used, as opposed to the tonic sol-fa system; staff'-off'icer, an officer serving on a staff; staff'room, a room for the use of the staff, as of a school; staff'-ser'geant, a non-commissioned officer serving on a regimental staff; staff'-sur'geon, a navy surgeon of senior grade: an army surgeon on the staff of a hospital, not with his regiment; staff'-sys'tem, a block-system that uses a staff; staff'-tree, an American shrub (Celastrus) akin to spindle-tree.—staff of life, staple food, esp. bread. [O.E. *stæf*, O.N. *stafr*, Ger. *stab*.]

staffage, *sta'fäzh', n.* accessories in a picture. [Sham Fr.,—Ger. *staffieren*, to garnish.]

stag, *stag, n.* a male deer, esp. a hart or red deer over four years old: a male of various kinds (cock, turkey-cock, etc.): a man who goes to dances, etc., unaccompanied by a woman: a stag-party (*U.S.*): (*Scot.* staig, *stāg*) a colt or stallion: (*Scot.* staig) an animal castrated in maturity: one who applies for shares in order to sell at once at a profit: an informer (*obs. slang*).—*adj.* male: of males.—*v.t.* to follow, dog, shadow.—*v.i.* to deal as a stag (also *v.t.* with *it* or *the market*): to go as a stag.—*n.* stagg'ard, a hart in its fourth year.—stag'-beet'le, any beetle of the family Lucanidae, from the large antler-like mandibles of the males; stag'-dance, one of men only; stag'-head, dying back of a tree giving antler-like appearance.—*adj.* stag-head'ed.—stag'horn, stag's antler as a material (staghorn-fern, Platycerium, a fern with antler-like leaves; staghorn moss, common club-moss); stag'hound, the buck-hound: the Scottish deer-hound; stag'-hunt; stag'-par'ty, a party of men only. [O.E. *stagga*, stag; cf. O.N. *steggr*, cock-bird, gander, in mod. Ice. he-cat.]

stage, *stāj*, *n.* a tier, shelf, floor, storey: a tiered structure for plants: a scaffold: an elevated platform, esp. for acting on: the theatre: theatrical representation: the theatrical calling: any field of action, scene: a place of rest on a journey or road: the portion of a journey between two such places: in a microscope, etc., the support for an object to be examined: a subdivision of a geological series or formation: a point reached in, or a section of, life, development, or any process: a stagecoach: one of the sections in a step-rocket: one of the elements in a complex piece of electronic equipment.—*adj.* pertaining to the stage: as conventionally represented on the stage (e.g. *a stage rustic*).—*v.t.* to represent or put on the stage: to contrive dramatically, organise and bring off.—*v.i.* (or *v.t.* with *it*) to travel by stages or by stagecoach.—*adj.* staged, in storeys or tiers: put on the stage.—*ns.* sta'ger, one who has had much experience in anything, an old hand (*old stager*): a stage-horse: an actor (*arch.*); sta'gery, theatrical contrivances. — *adv.* sta'gily. — *ns.* stag'iness; sta'ging, scaffolding: stagecoaching: putting on the stage.—*adj.* sta'gy (also sta'gey), savouring of the stage: artificially histrionic.—stage'-box', a box over the proscenium; stage'-coach, a coach that runs regularly with passengers from stage to stage; stage'coaching; stage'-coachman; stage'-craft, skill in the technicalities of the theatre; stage'-direc'tion, in a copy of a play, an instruction to the actor to do this or that; stage'-door, the actors' entrance to a theatre; stage'-driver, one who drives a stage; stage'-effect', theatrical effect; stage'-fe'ver, a passion to go on the stage; stage'-flower, a flower exhibited on a tiered stand; stage'-fright, nervousness before an audience, esp. for the first time; stage'-hand, a workman employed about the stage; stage'-horse, a stagecoach horse.—*v.t.* stage'-man'age (back-formation), used *lit.*: also *fig.* to arrange (an event) effectively as if it were a stage scene.—stage'-man'ager, one who superintends the production of plays, with general charge behind the curtain; stage'-name, a name assumed professionally by an actor or actress; stage'-play, a play played or intended to be played on a stage; stage'-play'er.—*adj.* stage'-struck, sorely smitten with stage-fever.—stage'-wag'on, a wagon for conveying goods and passengers at fixed times; stage'-whis'per, an audible utterance conventionally understood by the audience to represent a whisper: a loud whisper meant to be heard by people other than the person addressed; sta'ging-area, a point for the assembly of troops en route for an operation; sta'ging-post, a regular point of call on an air-route. [O.Fr. *estage* (Fr. *étage*),

a storey of a house—inferred L.L. *staticus*—L. *stāre*, to stand.]

stagger, *stag'ər*, *v.i.* to reel: to go reeling or tottering: to waver.—*v.t.* to cause to reel: to give a shock to: to cause to waver: to nonplus, confound: to dispose alternately or variously: to arrange so that one thing or part is ahead of another.—*n.* a staggering: a wavering: a staggered arrangement (*positive* where the upper plane of a biplane is advanced, *negative* where the lower)· (in *pl*, often treated as *sing.*) giddiness, also a disease of various kinds causing horses, etc., to stagger (grass, or stomach, staggers, an acute indigestion; mad, or sleepy, staggers, an inflammation of the brain).—*adj.* stagg'ered.—*n.* stagg'erer.—*n.* and *adj.* stagg'ering.—*adv.* stagg'eringly. [Earlier stacker—O.N. *stakra*, freq. of *staka*, to push.]

Stagirite (misspelt Stagyrite), *staj'i-rīt*, *n.* a native or inhabitant of *Stagira* (Gr. *Stagiros*) in Macedonia, esp. Aristotle (384–322 B.C.).

stagnant, *stag'nant*, *adj.* still, standing, without current: foul, unwholesome, or dull from stillness: inert.—*n.* stag'nancy.—*adv.* stag'nantly.—*v.i.* stag'nate, to be stagnant.—*n.* stagnā'tion.—stagnation point, the point at or near the nose of a body in motion in a fluid, where the flow divides. [L. *stagnāre, -ātum—stagnum*, pond.]

Stagyrite. See Stagirite.

Stahlhelm, *shtäl'helm*, *n.* a German old soldiers' conservative nationalist and militaristic organisation after the 1st World War.—*ns.* Stahl'helmer, Stahl'helmist. [Ger., steel helmet.]

Stahlian, *stäl'i-ən*, *adj.* pertaining to Georg Ernst *Stahl*, German physician (1660–1734), or his animism.—*ns.* Stahl'ianism, Stahl'ism.

staid, *stād*, *adj.* steady: sober: grave: sedate.—*adv.* staid'ly.—*n.* staid'ness. [For stayed—stay.]

staig, *stāg*, *n.* a Scots form of stag.

stain, *stān*, *v.t.* to deprive of colour (*obs.*): to pale by comparison (*obs.*): to impart a new colour to: to tinge: to dye: to sully: to tarnish: to impregnate with a substance that colours some parts so as to show composition and structure: to bring reproach on.—*v.i.* to take or impart a stain.—*n.* a dye or colouring-matter: discoloration: a spot: taint of guilt: pollution: cause of reproach: shame.—*adj.* stained.—*n.* stain'er.—*n.* and *adj.* stain'ing.—*adj.* stain'less, free from stain: not liable to stain, rust, or tarnish.—*adv.* stain'lessly.—*n.* stain'lessness.—stained glass, glass painted with certain pigments fused into its surface; stainless steel, a steel that will not rust, containing 8 to 25 per cent. of chromium. [distain.]

stair, *stār*, *n.* a series of steps (in Scotland, the whole series from floor to floor, elsewhere, usu. in *pl.*, a flight from landing to landing): one such step.—*adj.* staired, having, or arranged like, stairs.—*adv.* stair'wise, by steps: in the manner of a stair.—stair'-car'pet, a long carpet for stairs; stair'case, the structure enclosing a stair: stairs with banisters, etc.; stair'foot, the level place at the foot of stairs; stair'head, the level place at the top of stairs; stair'-rod, a rod for holding a stair-carpet in place; stair'-tower, -turret, one enclosing a winding stair; stair'way, a staircase: a passage by stairs; stair'-well, the well of a staircase; stair'-work, backstairs intriguing.—below stairs, in the basement: among the servants. [O.E. *stæger—stīgan*, to ascend; Ger. *steigen*, to climb, Norw. *steg*, step.]

staith(e), *stāth*, (*N. England*) *n.* a wharf: a structure for shipping coal: an embankment. [O.E. *stæth*, bank, and O.N. *stöth*, landing-stage.]

stake, *stāk*, *n.* a stick or pole pointed at one end: a post: a post to which one condemned to be burned was tied: hence, death or martyrdom by burning: a tinsmith's anvil.—*v.t.* to fasten to or with, to protect, shut, support, furnish, pierce, with a stake or stakes: to mark the bounds of with stakes (often with *off* or *out*).— **stake'-net**, a net hung on stakes.—**stake a claim (for, to)**, to intimate one's right to or desire to possess. [O.E. *staca*, stake.]

**stake**, *stāk*, *v.t.* to deposit as a wager: to risk, hazard: to furnish, supply, fit out (*U.S.*).—*n.* anything pledged as a wager: a prize: anything to gain or lose: an interest, concern: the condition of being at hazard: a grubstake: (in *pl.*) a race for money staked or contributed.—**at stake** (*Shak.* also **at the stake**), hazarded: in danger: at issue. [Perh. M.Du. *staken*, to place.]

**stakhanovite**, *stə-kan'ō-vīt*, *n.* a worker who has received recognition for his part in increasing the rate of production in the factory, etc., where he works. [*Stakhanov*, a Russian worker.]

**stalactite**, *stal'ək-tīt* (also *sta-lak'tīt*), *n.* an icicle-like pendant of calcium carbonate, formed by evaporation of water percolating through limestone, as on a cave roof: the material it is composed of: anything of similar form.—*adjs.* **stalac'tic, -al, stalac'tiform, stalacti'tal, stal'actited** (also *-ak'*), **stalactitic** (*tit'ik*; the usual *adj.*), **-al, stalactitiform** (*-tit'*), **stalactitious** (*-tish'əs*).—*adv.* **stalactit'ically.**—*ns.* **stalag'ma, stalagmite; stal'agmite** (also *-ag'*), an upward-growing conical formation on the floor, formed by the drip from the roof or from a stalactite.—*adjs.* **stalagmitic** (*-mit'ik*), **-al.**—*adv.* **stalagmit'ically.**—*ns.* **stalagmom'eter,** an instrument for determining surface tension by drops; **stalagmom'etry.** [Gr. *stalaktos, stalagma, stalagmos,* a dropping—*stalassein,* to drip.]

**stalag**, *stä'läg, shtä'lähh, n.* a German camp for prisoners of war (non-commissioned officers and men). [Ger. *stamm,* base, *lager,* camp.]

**stalagma, stalagmite.** See under stalactite.

**stal'd**, *stōld,* (*Spens.*) *pa.p.* See stall.

**stale**, *stāl, adj.* altered (usu. for the worse) by age: of liquor, old, clear, and strong (*obs.*): no longer fresh: past the best: out of condition by over-training or overstudy: impaired by lapse of time: tainted: vapid or tasteless from age.—*v.t.* and *v.i.* to make or become stale, over-familiar, or insipid.—*adv.* **stale'ly.**—*n.* **stale'ness.** [Perh. from the root *sta-*, as in stand.]

**stale**, *stāl, n.* a decoy-bird: a thief's decoy (*obs.*): a lure: a low prostitute employed as a decoy, or generally (*Shak.*): a stalking-horse, cover to a real purpose (*Shak.*): a pretext: a lover made a butt of by or for one preferred. [Cf. A.Fr. *estal, -e,* pigeon used to entice a hawk, O.E. *stælhrān,* decoy-reindeer, Ger. *stellvogel,* decoy-bird; prob. from root of O.E. *stellan,* to place.]

**stale**, *stāl, n.* urine, now esp. of horses.—*v.i.* to urinate. [Cf. Du. *stalle,* Ger. *stall,* O.Fr. vb. *estaler.*]

**stale**, *stāl,* (*dial.*) *n.* a handle, shaft: a stalk. [O.E. *stalu,* app. part of a harp.]

**stale**, *stāl,* (now *rare* or *obs.*) *n.* and *v.t.* stalemate.—**stale'mate,** an unsatisfactory draw resulting when a player not actually in check has no possible legal move (*chess*): an inglorious deadlock.—*v.t.* to subject to a stalemate. [Cf. A.Fr. *estale,* perh.—Eng. stall.]

**stale.** See steal (1).

**Stalinism**, *stä'lin-izm, n.* the rigorous rule of the Russian Communist dictator Josef *Stalin* (1879-1953), esp. in its concentration of all power and authority in the Communist world in Russia.

**stalk**, *stök, n.* the stem of a plant: a slender connecting part: a shaft: a tall chimney.—*v.t.* to remove the stalk from.—*adjs.* **stalked,** having a stalk; **stalk'less,** running to stalk: like a stalk.—*adj.* **stalk'-eyed,** having the eyes on

stalks. [Dim. from the root of O.E. *stæla, stalu,* stalk.]

**stalk**, *stök, v.i.* to stride stiffly or haughtily: to go after game keeping under cover.—*v.t.* to approach under cover: to stalk over or through.—*n.* an act of stalking: a stalking gait.—*n.* **stalk'er.**—*n.* and *adj.* **stalk'ing.**—**stalk'ing-horse,** a horse or substitute behind which a sportsman hides while stalking game: anything put forward to mask plans or efforts. [O.E. (*bi*)*stealcian,* freq. of steal.]

**stalko**, *stö'kō, (Anglo-Ir.) n.* a gentleman without fortune or occupation. [Perh. Ir. *stócach,* idler.]

**stall**, *stöl, n.* a standing-place: a stable, cowshed, or the like: a compartment for one animal: a bench, table, booth, or stand for display or sale of goods, or used as a working-place: a church-seat with arms, usu. one of those lining the choir or chancel on both sides, reserved for cathedral clergy, for choir, for monks, or for knights of an order: an office entitling one to such a seat: a doorless pew: an individual armed seat in a theatre, etc., esp. an orchestra stall: a working place in a mine: a covering for a finger (as in *finger-stall*): an instance of stalling in aircraft or engine: a standstill: (*Scot.* staw) a surfeit.—*v.t.* to put or keep in a stall: to induct, install: to bring to a standstill: to cause (an aeroplane) to fly in such a way that the angle between the aerofoils and the direction of motion is greater than that at which there is maximum lift and so lose control: to stop (an engine) by sudden braking, over-loading, etc.: to mire: to snow up (*U.S.*): (esp. in Scots form staw) to surfeit: (*Spens.* in *pa.p.* stal'd, *stöld*) to release on payment by instalments.—*v.i.* to dwell (*obs.*): to inhabit a stall: to share a dwelling (*obs.*): to come to a standstill: of aircraft or engine, to be stalled.—*n.* **stallage** (*stöl'ij*), rent for liberty of erecting a stall in a fair or market.—*adjs.* **stalled,** kept or fed in a stall: fatted: having a stall or stalls: stuck: sated (*Scot.* stawed).—*ns.* **stall'ing, stabling; stall'inger, stallenger** (*-in-jər; hist.*), a keeper of a stall: one who paid for the privilege of trading in a burgh of which he was not a freeman.—*adj.* **stall'-fed,** fed and fattened in a stall.—*v.t.* **stall'-feed.**—**stall'ing-keen'** (*obs. cant*), a house for receiving stolen goods; **stall'man,** a keeper of a stall, esp. a bookstall; **stall'-master** (Ger. *stallmeister*), a master of horse; **stall'-plate,** a plate with a knight's arms affixed to his stall; **stall'-reader,** one who stands and reads at a bookstall.—**stall starting gate, starting stall, gate,** a group of stalls into which horses are shut for the start of a race. [O.E. *stall, steall,* O.N. *stallr,* Ger. *stall.*]

**stall**, *stöl, n.* a ruse, trick: a decoy, esp. one who diverts attention from a criminal action.—*v.t.* to delay or obstruct: to stave off (with *off*).—*v.i.* to hang back, play for time: to be obstructive, evasive or deceptive. [stale (2).]

**stallion**, *stal'yən, n.* an uncastrated male horse, esp. one kept for breeding. [O.Fr. *estalon* (Fr. *étalon*)—O.H.G. *stal,* stall.]

**stallion**, *stal'yən,* (*obs.*) *n.* a courtesan (*Hamlet,* another reading, *scullion*). [Fr. *estalon;* cf. stale (2).]

**stallion** (*Shak.*). Same as staniel.

**stalwart**, *stöl'wərt, adj.* stout, strong, sturdy: determined in partisanship.—*n.* a resolute person.—(*arch.*) **stal'worth** (*-wərth*).—*adv.* **stal'wartly.**—*n.* **stal'wartness.** [Orig. Scots form (popularised by Scott) of stalworth—O.E. *stælwierthe,* serviceable—*stæl,* place (—*stathol,* foundation), *wierthe,* worth.]

**stamen**, *stā'mən, n.* the pollen-producing part of a flower, consisting of anther and filament:—*pl.* **stā'mens.**—*adj.* **stā'mened,** having stamens.—*n.pl.* (sometimes treated as *sing.*) **stamina**

Neutral vowels in unaccented syllables: *el'ə-mənt*; for certain sounds in foreign words, see p. viii

(*stam'*), germinal elements, rudiments: native or constitutional strength: staying power: mainstay: stamens (*rare*).—*adjs.* stam'inal, of stamens or stamina; stam'inate, having stamens but no carpels; stamineal (*stə-* or *stā-min'i-əl*), stamin'eous (both *rare*); staminif'erous (*stam-* or *stām-*), having stamens.—*ns.* stam'inode, staminō'dium, a sterile stamen; stam'inody, metamorphosis of other parts into stamens.—*adj.* stam'inoid, like, or metamorphosed into, a stamen. [L. *stāmen* (pl. *stāmina*), a warp thread (upright in an old loom)—*stāre*, to stand.]
stamina, etc. See stamen.
stammel, *stam'l*, (*hist.*) *n.* a kind of woollen cloth, usu. dyed red: red colour.—*adj.* of stammel: red. [Fr. *estamel*, or independently formed M.E. *stamin*—O.Fr. *estamin*, both—L. *stāmina*, warp threads.]
stammer, *stam'ər*, *v.i.* to falter in speaking: to stutter.—*v.t.* to utter falteringly or with a stutter.—*n.* hesitation in speech: a stammering mode of utterance.—*n.* stamm'erer.—*n.* and *adj.* stamm'ering.—*adv.* stamm'eringly. [O.E. *stamerian*; Du. *stemeren*.]
stamnos, *stam'nos*, *n.* an ancient Greek shortnecked jar. [Gr.]
stamp, *stamp*, *v.t.* to bray, pound, crush: to bring the foot forcibly down upon: to trample: to strike flatwise with the sole (or other part) of: to impress, imprint, or cut with a downward blow, as with a die or cutter: to mint, make, shape by such a blow: to fix or mark deeply: to impress with a mark attesting official approval, ratification, payment, etc.: to affix an adhesive stamp to: to attest, declare, prove to be: to characterise.—*v.i.* to bring the foot down forcibly and noisily: to walk with a heavy tread: to be furiously angry (*U.S.*).—*n.* the act of stamping: an impression: a stamped device, mark, imprint: an adhesive paper used as a substitute for stamping: attestation: authorisation: a coin (*Shak.*): pounded maize (*S.Afr.*): cast, form, character: distinguishing mark, imprint, sign, evidence: an instrument or machine for stamping.—*n.* stamp'er.—*n.* and *adj.* stamp'ing.—Stamp Act, an act of parliament imposing or regulating stamp-duties, esp. that of 1765 imposing them on the American colonies; stamp'-album, a book for keeping a collection of postage-stamps in; stamp'-collector, a receiver of stamp-duties: one who makes a hobby of collecting postage-stamps; stamp'-duty, a tax imposed on the paper on which legal documents are written; stamp'ing-ground, an animal's usual resort: a person's habitual place of resort; stamp'ing-machine', a machine used for stamping coins, in the stamping of brass-work, or in crushing metallic ores; stamp'-, stamp'ing-mill, a crushing-mill for ores; stamp'-note, a certificate from a custom-house officer for goods to be loaded as freight of a ship; stamp'-office, an office where stamp-duties are received and stamps issued; stamp'-paper, paper bearing a government revenue stamp.—stamp out, to put out by tramping: to extirpate: to make by stamping from a sheet with a cutter. [M.E. *stampen*, from an inferred O.E. *stampian* from the same root as *stempan*; Ger. *stampfen*.]
stampede, *stam-pēd'*, *n.* a sudden rush of a panic-stricken herd: any impulsive action of a multitude.—*v.i.* to rush in a stampede.—*v.t.* to send rushing in a stampede.—Also *n.* and *v.t.* (*obs.*)
stampē'do. [Sp. *estampida*, crash—*estampar*, to stamp.]
stance, *stans*, *n.* a station, standing-place (*Scot.*): a building-site (*Scot.*): a mode of standing, as in golf: a stanza (*obs.*). [Fr. *stance* (now meaning 'stanza')—It. *stanza*, a stopping-place, station—L. *stāre*, to stand.]
stanch, staunch, *stänch, stänsh, stönch, stönsh, v.t.*

to stop the flowing of, as blood: to quench, allay.—*v.i.* (*B.*) to cease to flow.—*n.* a styptic: a floodgate.—*ns.* stanch'er; stanch'ing.—*adj.* stanch'less, that cannot be quenched or stopped. [O.Fr. *estancher* (Fr. *étancher*)—L.L. *stancāre*, to stanch—L. *stagnāre*, to be or make stagnant —*stagnum*, a pond.]
stanch (*adj.*), etc. See staunch.
stanchel, -er. See stanchion.
stanchion, *stän'shən, stan'shən* (*Scot.* stanchel, *stän', stān', stan'cher*), *n.* an upright iron bar of a window or screen: an upright beam used as a support (*naut.*).—*v.t.* to fasten by means of or to a stanchion.—*adj.* stan'chioned. [O.Fr. *estançon*—*estance*, prop—L. *stāre*, to stand.]
stanck, *stangk*, (*Spens.*) *adj.* faint. [It. *stanco*.]
stand, *stand*, *v.i.* to be, become, or remain upright, erect, rigid, or still: to be on, or rise to, one's feet: to be steadfast: to have or take a position: to be or remain: to be set or situated: to be set down: to have a direction: to hold good: to endure, continue to exist: to scruple, demur: to insist punctiliously: to be a representative, representation, or symbol: to be a candidate: to cost.—*v.t.* to withstand: to tolerate: to endure: to sustain: to suffer: to abide by: to be at the expense of, offer and pay for: to station, cause to stand: to set erect or in position (*pa.t.* and *pa.p.* stood, *Scot.* stood'en, studd'en; *infin., Spens.,* standen).—*n.* an act, manner, or place of standing: a taking up of a position for resistance: resistance: a standing position: a standstill: a stoppage: a loss, a nonplus: a post, station: a place under cover for awaiting game: a place for vehicles awaiting hire: an erection for spectators: a stop on tour to give one or more performances, or the place where it is made (*theat.*): a platform: a witness-box (*U.S.*): a base or structure for setting things on: a piece of furniture for hanging things from: a company of plovers: a complete set, esp. (*Scot.*) a suit of clothes or armour: a standing growth or crop: a young tree left standing: a tub or vat.—*n.* stan'der.—*adj.* stand'ing, established: settled: permanent: fixed: stagnant: erect: having a base: done as one stands: from a standing position, without preliminary movement (e.g. *standing jump, start*).—*n.* the action of one who or that which stands: duration: continuance: place to stand in: position or grade in a profession, university, in society: a right or capacity to sue or maintain an action. —stand'ish (*arch.*; poss. for *stand-dish*), an inkstand.—stand'-by', that which, or one whom, one relies on or readily resorts to; stand'er-by' (*Shak.*), a bystander:—*pl.* stand'ers-by'; stand'in', a substitute; stand'ing-bed, a high bedstead, not a truckle-bed; stand'ing-bowl, -cup, one with a foot; stand'ing-ground, a place, basis, or principle to stand on; standing orders, permanent rules for conduct of proceedings; stand'ing-place, a place that one may or does stand on; stand'ing-rig'ging, the fixed ropes in a ship; stand'ing-room, room for standing, without a seat; stand'ing-stone (*archaeol.*), a great stone set erect in the ground; standing wave (*phys.*), the pattern of maxima and minima when two sets of oppositely travelling waves of the same frequency interfere with each other; stand'-off, a Rugby half-back who stands away from the scrum as a link between scrum-half and the three-quarters.—*adj.* stand-offish.—*adj.* stand-off'ish, inclined to hold aloof, keep others at arm's-length. — stand'-off'ishness; stand-patt'er, (*U.S.*) one who stands pat: a political die-hard; stand-patt'ism; stand'-pipe, a vertical pipe into which water is pumped to give it a head: one used to obtain water for an attached hose; stand'point, a viewpoint; stand'still, a complete stop.—*adj.* stationary: unmoving: for-

bidding or refraining from movement.—stand'-to, a precautionary parade or taking of posts. —*adj.* stand'-up, erect: done or taken in a standing position: of a fight, in earnest: delivering, or consisting of, a comic monologue without feed or other support.—all standing, everything remaining as it stands: without unrigging: fully clad; make a stand, to halt and offer resistance; stand against, to resist; stand by, to support: to adhere to, abide by: to be at hand: to hold oneself in readiness: to prepare to work at; stand down, to leave the witness box: to go off duty: to withdraw from a contest or from a controlling position (*v.i.* and *v.t.*): —*pa.p.* stood down; stand fast, to be unmoved; stand fire, to remain steady under the fire of an enemy—also *fig.*; stand for, to be a candidate for: to direct the course towards (*naut.*): to be a sponsor for: to represent, symbolise: to champion: to put up with, endure (*coll.*); stand from, to direct the course from; stand in, to cost: to become a party: to have an understanding, be in league: to deputise; stand in with, to support, act together with; stand low (*print.*), to fall short of the standard height; stand off, to keep at a distance: to direct the course from: to forbear compliance or intimacy (*Shak.*): to suspend temporarily from employment:—*pa.p.* stood off; stand off and on, to sail away from shore and then towards it; stand on, to continue on the same tack or course: to insist on: to set store by (see ceremony): to behove: to found upon; stand one's ground, to maintain one's position; stand one's hand, stand shot, stand treat, to treat, esp. to drinks; stand on one's own feet, to manage one's own affairs without help; stand out, to project, to be prominent: not to comply, to refuse to yield; stand pat (*U.S.*), to play one's hand in poker as it was dealt, without drawing any cards: to adhere to an established political principle, resisting all compromise (*fig.*); stand to, to fall to, set to work: to back up: to uphold: to be likely to: to take up position in readiness for orders; stand up, to get to one's feet: to take position for a dance: to be clad (with *in*): to fail to keep an appointment with; stand up for, to support or attempt to defend; stand upon, to stand on: to attack (*B.*); stand up to, to meet face to face, to fulfil manfully; stand well, to be in favour; stand with, to be consistent. [O.E. *standan*; Goth. *standan*; cf. Ger. *stehen*, Gr. *histanai*, to place, L. *stāre*, to stand.]

standard, *stand'ərd, n.* a flag or military symbolic figure on a pole, marking a rallying-point: a rallying-point (also *fig.*): a long tapering flag notched and rounded at the end, bearing heraldic symbols and fixed in the ground (*her.*): a flag generally: a cavalry regimental flag: a standard-bearer: the uppermost petal of a papilionaceous flower: a streaming wing-feather: that which stands or is fixed: an upright post, pillar, stick: a standing shrub or tree not trained on an espalier or a wall: a tree left growing amidst coppice: a structure erected at a conduit (*obs.*): an exemplar or substance chosen to be or afford a unit: a basis of measurement: a criterion: an established or accepted model: an accepted authoritative statement of a church's creed: in schools (formerly) a grade of classification: a definite level of excellence or adequacy required, aimed at, or possible: fineness of gold or silver. —*adj.* serving as or conforming to a standard: of enduring value: growing as a standard: standing upright.—*n.* stand'ardisātion, -z-.—*v.t.* stand'ardise, -ize, to make, or keep, of uniform size, shape, etc.—*n.* stand'ardiser, -z-.—standard atmosphere, 101,325 newtons per sq. metre, or 1,013,250 dynes per sq. centimetre: a standard of measurement of atmospheric conditions used

in comparing the performance of aircraft (*aero.*, etc.); stand'ard-bearer, one who carries a standard or banner: an outstanding leader; standard bread, bread made with flour containing 80 per cent. of the whole-wheat including germ and semolina; standard deviation, the root of the average of the squares of the differences from their mean of a number of observations; standard English, the form of English used (with minor variations) by the majority of cultured English-speakers; standard error, standard deviation: standard deviation divided by the root of the number of observations; standard lamp, a lamp on a tall support; standard solution, a solution of known concentration, used for purposes of comparison, commonly containing the equivalent, in grammes, of the solute to a litre of solution (*normal solution*) or some simple fraction (as *decinormal*, one-tenth normal); stand'ard-wing, a bird of paradise of the Moluccas with a pair of erectile white feathers at the bend of the wing.—(international) standard book number, a number allotted to a book by agreement of (international) publishers which shows area, publisher and individual title. [O.Fr. *estandart*; prob. conn. either with extend or stand, and in any case influenced by or partly from stander.]

stane, *stān,* Scots form of stone.

stang, *stang, n.* a stake, pole.—riding the stang, punishment by carrying astride of a stang. [O.N. *stöng*; cf. O.E. *stæng,* Du. *stang.*]

stang, *stang, stöng,* (*Scot.*) *v.i.* to sting.—*n.* a sting. [O.N. *stanga,* to prick.]

stanhope, *stan'əp, -hōp, n.* a light open one-seated carriage first made for Fitzroy Stanhope (1787-1864).—Stanhope press, a printing-press invented by the third Earl Stanhope (1753-1816).

staniel, stanyel, *stan'yəl,* stannel, *stan'l* (*Shak.* stallion, *stal'yən*), *n.* the kestrel. [O.E. *stāngella,* lit. stone yeller.]

Stanislavski method, system, *stan-i-släv'ski, -släf',* method acting (q.v.). [K. *Stanislavski* (1863-1938), Russian actor and director.]

stank, *stangk, pa.t.* of stink.

stank, *stangk,* (chiefly *Scot.*) *n.* a ditch, a pool: a dam. [O.Fr. *estanc,* a pond—L. *stagnum,* a pond.]

stann-, *stan-,* in composition, tin.—*n.* stann'ary (*-ə-ri*), a tin-mining district (esp. the Stannaries in Cornwall and Devon).—Also *adj.*—*n.* stann'-ate, a salt of stannic acid.—*adjs.* stann'ic, of quadrivalent tin; stannif'erous, tin-bearing.—*ns.* stann'ite, a mineral composed of tin, copper, iron, and sulphur (*min.*): a salt of stannous hydroxide, $Sn(OH)_2$, acting as a weak acid (*chem.*); stann'otype, a photo-mechanical process in which an exposed and developed bichromated film is coated with tinfoil and used directly for pressure printing.—*adj.* stann'ous, of bivalent tin.—stannary courts, courts (abolished 1896) for the tinners of the Stannaries; stannic acid, $H_2SnO_3$. [L. *stannum,* tin.]

stannel. See staniel.

stanza, *stan'zə* (*Shak.* stanze, stan'zo), *n.* a group of lines of verse forming a definite pattern: a pattern so composed.—*adj.* stanzā'ic. [It. *stanza* —L. *stāre,* to stand.]

stap, *stap, v.t.* an obsolete affectation for stop: also (*stap,* stäp) a Scots form, in the senses of stuff, thrust, cram.

stapedial, -ius. See stapes.

Stapelia, *stə-pē'li-ə, n.* the carrion-flower genus. [After the Dutch botanist J. B. van *Stapel* (d. 1636).]

stapes, *stā'pēz, n.* the stirrup-shaped innermost ossicle of the ear.—*adj.* stapedial (*stə-pē'di-əl*). —*n.* stape'dius, the muscle of the stapes. [L.L. *stapēs, -edis,* a stirrup.]

staphyle, *staf'i-lē, n.* the uvula.—*n.* Staphyle'a,

the bladder-nut genus of shrubs, giving name to the family **Staphyleā′ceae**, akin to Sapindaceae. —*adj.* **staph′yline**, like a bunch of grapes.—*n.pl.* **Staphylin′idae**, the rove-beetle family. — *ns.* **staphyli′tis**, inflammation of the uvula; **Staphylococc′us** (Gr. *kokkos*, a grain), a pus-causing bacterium found in clustered masses; **staphylō′ma**, protrusion of the sclerotic or of the cornea; **staphylorr′aphy** (Gr. *rhaphē*, stitching), the operation of uniting a cleft palate. [Gr. *staphylē*, a bunch of grapes, a swollen uvula.]

**staple**, *stā′pl, n.* a settled mart or market: a leading commodity: main element (as of diet, reading, conversation): unmanufactured wool or other raw material: textile fibre, or its length and quality.—*adj.* constituting a staple: leading, main.—*v.t.* to grade according to staple.—*n.* **sta′pler**, a merchant of a staple: one who grades and deals in wool.—**merchant of the staple**, a member of a mediaeval association of merchants privileged to trade in a staple commodity, esp. wool, at the **staple town** (or towns) appointed by the king. [O.Fr. *estaple*—L.G. *stapel*, heap, mart.]

**staple**, *stā′pl, n.* a bent rod or wire for driving into a wall, post, etc., as a fastening: the part that passes through the slot of a hasp, receives a bolt, etc.: the metallic tube to which the reed is fastened in the oboe, etc.—*v.t.* to fasten with a staple. — *n.* **sta′pler.** — **sta′pling-machine,** a machine that stitches paper with wire. [O.E. *stapol*, post, support; cf. foregoing.]

**stapple, staple,** *stap′l,* (*Scot.*) *n.* See **stopple** (2).

**star,** *stär, n.* any of the heavenly bodies, esp. of those visible by night whose places in the firmament are relatively fixed (**fixed stars**), but sometimes including planets, comets, and meteors, less commonly the sun and moon, or even the earth: a planet as a supposed influence, hence (usu. in *pl.*) one's luck: an object or figure with pointed rays, most commonly five: an asterisk: a starfish: a radial meeting of ways: a star-shaped badge of rank or honour: a white mark on a beast's forehead: a pre-eminent or exceptionally brilliant person: a leading performer, or one supposed to draw the public.— *adj.* of stars: marked by a star: leading, pre-eminent, brilliant.—*v.t.* to make a star of: to have (a specified person) as a star performer: to mark with a star: to shatter or crack in a radiating form: to set with stars: to bespangle. —*v.i.* to shine, as a star: to attract attention: to appear as a star performer:—*pr.p.* **starr′ing;** *pa.t.* and *pa.p.* **starred.**—*n.* **star′dom,** state of being, status of, a star performer esp. of stage or screen.—*adj.* **star′less.**—*n.* **star′let,** kind of starfish (*Asterina*): a little star: a young film actress, esp. one hailed as a future star.—*adj.* and *adv.* **star′like.**—*adj.* **starred,** adorned or studded with stars: influenced by or having a star: decorated or marked with a star: turned into a star: star-shaped: radially cracked, fissured.—*adv.* **starr′ily.** —*n.* **starr′iness.**—*n., adj.* **starr′ing.**—*adj.* **starr′y,** abounding or adorned with stars: consisting of, or proceeding from, the stars: like, or shining like, the stars.—**star′-anise,** a Chinese evergreen tree (*Illicium*) of the magnolia family, with aromatic oil; **star′-apple,** the fruit of the West Indian sapotaceous tree *Chrysophyllum cainito*; **star′-blast′ing,** the noxious influence of the stars.—*adj.* **star′-bright,** bright as a star or with stars.—**star′-cat′alogue,** a list of stars, with their places, magnitudes, etc.—*adj.* **star′-crossed, -crost,** thwarted by the stars.—**star′-drift,** a common proper motion of a number of fixed stars in the same region; **star′-dust,** cosmic dust, meteoric matter in fine particles: distant stars seen like dust-grains; **star′fish,** any member of the Asteroidea, a class of echinoderms

with five arms merging in a disk, and tube-feet on the under surface: sometimes extended to the ophiuroids.—*v.i.* **star′gaze.**—**star′-gazer,** an astrologer: an astronomer: one who gazes at the sky, or in abstraction: a dreamer or wool-gatherer: a fish with upward-looking eyes (Uranoscopus or other); **star′-gazing; star′-grass,** a name for many grasslike plants with star-shaped flowers or leaf-arrangement; **star′-jell′y,** Nostoc, once thought to be a fallen star. —*adj.* **star′-led,** guided by a star.—**star′light,** light from the stars: an unknown plant, otherwise called astrophel or penthia (*Spens.*).—*adj.* of or with starlight: lighted by the stars: bright as a star.—*adj.* **star′lit,** lighted by the stars. —**star′-man,** an astrologer: a first-offender, wearing a star; **star′-map,** a map showing the positions of stars; **star′monger,** an astrologer; **star′-nose** (or **star-nosed mole**), a North American mole with star-shaped nose-tip.—*adjs.* **star′-pav′d** (*Milt.*), paved with stars; **star′-proof** (*Milt.*), impervious to starlight.—**star′-read′** (*Spens.*), astronomy.—*adj.* **starr′y-eyed,** out of touch with reality: innocently idealistic: radiantly happy.—**star sapphire,** an asteriated sapphire.—*adj.* **star′-shaped,** shaped like a conventional star, with pointed rays.—**star′-shell,** a shell that explodes high in the air, lighting up the scene; **star′shine,** starlight.—*adj.* **star′-spang′led,** spangled or studded with stars (**Star-spangled Banner,** the Stars and Stripes: an American national hymn).—**star′-stone,** a sapphire, ruby, or other stone showing asterism; **star′-this′tle,** a species of Centaurea with radiating spiny bracts; **star′-trap,** a stage trap of several wedge-shaped pieces meeting in a centre; **star′-turn,** the chief item in an entertainment: a pre-eminent performer; **star′-wheel,** a spur-wheel with V-shaped teeth; **star′wort,** any plant of the genus Aster (not the China aster): stitchwort: a water-plant (**water-starwort,** Callitriche).—*adj.* **star-ypointing** (*stär′-i-point′ing*), *Milt.;* incorrectly formed), pointing to the stars.—**see stars** (*coll.*), to see spots of light, as result e.g. of blow on the head: be in a dazed condition; **star-of-Bethlehem,** a plant (Ornithogalum) of the lily family with starlike flowers; **Star of David,** the Jewish religious symbol—Solomon's-seal (see second meaning of this); **star-of-the-earth,** buck's-horn plantain; **star-of-the-night,** Clusia; **Stars and Stripes,** the flag of the United States of America, with thirteen stripes alternately red and white, and a blue field containing as many stars as there are states. [O.E. *steorra;* cf. **stern** (3), Ger. *stern,* L. *stēlla* (for *sterula*), Gr. *astēr.*]

**star, starr,** *stär, n.* Ammophila or other coarse seaside grass, sedge, or rush.—Also **star(r)′-grass.** [O.N. *störr.*]

**staragen,** *star′ə-gən,* (*obs.*) *n.* the tarragon plant. [Cf. Sp. *estragón,* Fr. *estragon, tarragon.*]

**starboard,** *stär′bə(r)d, -bōrd, -börd, n.* the right-hand side of a ship.—*adj.* and *adv.* of, to, towards, or on, the right.—*v.t.* to turn to the right (see note at **port** (1))—opp. to *port.* [O.E. *stēorbord* —*stēor,* steering, *bord,* board, side of a ship (ancient Gmc. ships being steered by a paddle at the right side).]

**starch,** *stärch, n.* the principal reserve food-material stored in plants, chemically a carbohydrate, $(C_6H_{10}O_5)x$, used in the laundry as a stiffener: stiffness, formality.—*adj.* of starch: stiff, rigid, formal.—*v.t.* to stiffen or stick with starch.—*adj.* **starched.**—*adv.* **starchedly** (*stärcht,* **stärch′id-**).—*ns.* **starched′ness** (or *-id-*); **starch′er.** —*adv.* **starch′ily.**—*n.* **starch′iness.**—*adj.* **starch′y,** of or like starch: stiff: precise.—**starch′-grain,** in plants, a layered cell-inclusion of starch; **starch′-hy′acinth,** grape-hyacinth, from its smell; **starch′-paper,** a test-paper for iodine, coated with starch and potassium iodide. [O.E. *stercan*, to stiffen, inferred from *stercedferhth*, stiff-spirited; cf. Ger. *stärke*, starch, and **stark**.]

**Star Chamber**, *stär' chäm'bər*, *n.* a tribunal (abolished 1641) with a civil and criminal jurisdiction, which met in the old council chamber at Westminster. [Prob. named from the gilt *stars* on the ceiling, not from the Jewish bonds (*starrs*, Heb. *sh'tār*) kept in it.]

**stare**, *stär*, *v.i.* to look with a fixed gaze: to glare: to be insistently or obtrusively conspicuous (with indirect obj. as *to stare one in the face*): to look (as *as like as he can stare*; formerly *coll.*): to stand on end.—*v.t.* to render by staring.—*n.* a fixed look.—*n.* **star'er**, one who stares: (in *pl.*) a lorgnette.—*n., adj.,* and *adv.* **star'ing**.—*adv.* **star'ingly**. [O.E. *starian*, from ˙ᵒoot seen in Ger. *starr*, rigid; also in Eng. ˙ᵗᵉrn.]

**stare**, *stär*, *n.* a starling. [O.E. *stær.*]

**stark**, *stärk*, *adj.* stiff: strong: stern: harsh: unyielding: sheer: out-and-out (see also **stark-naked**).—*adv.* stoutly: utterly.—*v.t.* and *v.i.* to stiffen.—*v.t.* and *v.i.* **stark'en**, to make or become stark.—*adv.* **stark'ly**.—*n.* **stark'ness**. [O.E. *stearc*, hard, strong; O.N. *sterkr*, Ger. *stark*.]

**stark-naked**, *stärk'-nā'kid*, *adj.* utterly naked: quite bare—sometimes shortened to **stark**.— Earlier (now *dial.*) **start'-nak'ed**. [M.E. *stertnaked*—O.E. *steort*, tail, *nacod*, naked; influenced by foregoing.]

**starling**, *stär'ling*, *n.* a black, brown-spotted bird with purple or green reflections, a good mimic: any other member of its genus, Sturnus. [O.E. *stærling*, dim. of *stær* (see **stare** (2)).]

**starling**, *stär'ling*, *n.* piling protecting a bridge pier. [Prob. for *staddling*.]

**starn**. Same as **stern** (3); also (*naut.* or *dial.*) for **stern** (2).

**starosta**, *stär'os-tə*, (*hist.*) *n.* a Russian village headman: a Polish noble holding a **star'osty** or domain by grant of life-estate from the crown. [Russ. and Pol. *starosta*, elder.]

**starr**. See under **Star Chamber**; see also **star** (2).

**start**, *stärt*, *v.i.* to shoot, dart, move suddenly forth, or out: to spring up or forward: to strain forward: to break away: to make a sudden involuntary movement as of surprise or becoming aware: to spring open, out of place, or loose: to begin to move: to set forth on a journey, race, career.—*v.t.* to begin: to set going: to set on foot: to set up: to drive from lair or hiding-place: to cause or undergo displacement or loosening of: to startle (*obs.*): to pour out or shoot.—*n.* a sudden movement: a sudden involuntary motion of the body: a startled feeling: a spurt: an outburst or fit: a beginning of movement, esp. of a journey, race, or career: a beginning: a setting in motion: a help in or opportunity of beginning: an advantage in being early or ahead: the extent of such an advantage in time or distance.—*n.* **start'er**, one who starts, esp. in a race: one who gives the signal for starting: a dog that starts game: apparatus for starting a machine: anything used to begin a process, as a bacterial culture in making butter or cheese.—*adj.* **start'ful**, apt to start.—*n.* and *adj.* **start'ingly** (*Shak.*), by starts.—*adj.* **start'ish**, apt to start, skittish.—**starting block**, a device for helping a sprinter make a quick start to a race, consisting of a framework with blocks of wood or metal attached, on which the sprinter braces his foot; **starting gate**, **stall** (see **stall** (1)); **start'ing-hole**, a hiding place: an evasive trick; **start'ing-point**, the point from which anything starts, or from which motion begins; **start'ing-post**, the post or barrier from which the competitors start in a race; **start'ing-price**, odds on a horse when

the race begins; **start'-up**, an upstart (*Shak.*): a rustic half-boot or short legging (*obs.*).—Also *adj.*—**start in**, to begin; **start out**, to begin: to begin a journey; **start up**, to rise suddenly: to come suddenly into notice or being: to set in motion. [M.E. *sterten*; closely akin to Du.˙ *storten*, to plunge, Ger. *stürzen*.]

**startle**, *stärt'l*, *v.i.* to start: to undergo a start: to feel sudden alarm.—*v.t.* to surprise as with fright: to cause to undergo a start: to take aback: to awake, excite.—*n.* sudden alarm or surprise.—*adj.* **start'led**.—*n.* **start'ler**.—*n.* and *adj.* **start'ling**.—*adv.* **start'lingly**.—*adjs.* **start'lish**, **start'ly**, apt to start. [M.E. *stertle*—O.E. *steartlian*, to stumble, struggle, kick, or formed afresh from **start**.]

**starve**, *stärv*, *v.i.* to die, now only of hunger or (chiefly *Scot.* and *Northern*) cold: to suffer extreme hunger (or cold): to be in want: to deteriorate (*obs.*).—*v.t.* to cause to starve: to afflict with hunger (or cold): to deprive of food: to force, subdue, cure, by want of food: to deprive of anything needful.—*n.* **starvā'tion** (attributed to Lord Melville, 1775).—*adj.* **starved**.—*n.* **starve'ling**, a lean, hungry, weak, or pining person, animal, or plant.—Also *adj.*—*n.* and *adj.* **starv'ing**. [O.E. *steorfan*, to die; Du. *sterven*, Ger. *sterben*, to die.]

**stash**, *stash*, *v.t.* to stow in hiding. [Origin obscure.]

**stasis**, *stā'sis*, *stas'is*, *n.* stoppage, esp. of growth, of blood-circulation, or of the contents of the bowels.—*ns.* **stasid'ion** (Mod. Gr. *dim.*), a stall in a Greek church; **stas'imon** (Gr., stationary), in Greek tragedy, an ode sung after the chorus had taken their places, or without interruption by dialogue:—*pl.* **stas'ima**; **stas'imorphy**, structural modification by arrested development. [Gr. *stasis*, stoppage.]

**statant**, *stā'tənt*, (*her.*) *adj.* standing on four feet. [L. *stāre*, to stand.]

**state**, *stāt*, *n.* condition: a perturbed condition of mind (*coll.*): mode of existence: circumstances at any time: a phase or stage: an impression taken at a stage of progress in engraving or etching or in printing a book: status: station in life: high station: grave import (*Shak.*): pomp, display, ceremonial dignity: a seat of dignity (*Shak.*): a canopy (*Milt.*): an estate, order, or class in society or the body politic: hence (in *pl.*) the legislature (*hist.*): an exalted personage (*Milt.*): public welfare: constitution: a republic (*obs.*): the civil power: the organisation of the body politic, or of one of the constituent members of a federation: the territory of such a state: high politics: an interest in property (*Spens.*): property, estate (*Shak.*): a body of men united by profession: a statement, report (now chiefly *mil.*).—*adj.* of, belonging to, relating to, the state or a federal state: public: ceremonial: pompous: affectedly solemn and mysterious: magnificent.—*adv.* or *adj.* (*Spens.*) explained in old gloss as stoutly (perh. pompous).—*v.t.* to set forth: to express the details of: to set down fully and formally: to assert, affirm: to install, establish, endow, place in a condition (esp. favourable; *arch.*): to set in state: to specify: perh., to determine the value of (*Milt.*): to settle.—*adjs.* **stāt'able**, capable of being stated; **stāt'al**, of a federal state; **stāt'ed**, settled: established: declared: regular: circumstanced (*obs.*):—*adv.* **stāt'edly**.—*n.* **state'hood**, the status of a state.—*adj.* **state'less**, without nationality: unworthy to be accounted a state: without pomp.—*n.* **state'lessness**.—*adv.* **state'lily**.—*n.* **state'liness**.—*adj.* **state'ly**, showing state or dignity: majestic, grandly impressive.— *adv.* majestically: loftily.—*ns.* **state'ment**, the act of stating: that which is stated: a formal account, declaration of facts, etc.: a financial

record; stat'er.—*adj.* state'wide.—*n.* stat'ism (*stāt'izm*), state control of the general affairs of the citizen.—*adj.* state'-aid'ed, receiving contributions from the state.—state'-cabin, a stateroom on a ship; state'craft, the art of managing state affairs; State Department, the U.S. equivalent of the Foreign Office; state'-house, the building in which a state legislature sits; stately home, a large, fine old house in private ownership but usu. open to the public; state'-monger, one who would be thought a politician; state' paper, an official paper or document relating to affairs of state; state'-pris'on; state'-pris'oner, a prisoner confined for offence against the state; state'-relig'ion, a religion recognised by the state as the national religion; state'room, a room of state: a private cabin or railway compartment; States'-Gen'eral, the representative body of the three orders (nobility, clergy, burghers) of the French kingdom (*hist.*): the Dutch parliament; states'man, one skilled in government: one who takes an important part in governing the state, esp. with wisdom and broad-mindedness: one who farms his own estate, a small landholder (*N. of England*):— *fem.* states'woman.—*adjs.* states'manlike, states'-manly, befitting a statesman.—*ns.* states'man-ship; state'-tri'al, a trial for an offence against the state.—lie in state, of a corpse, to be laid out in a place of honour before being buried; States of the Church (*hist.*), an area of central Italy ruled by the popes as a temporal domain.— Also Papal States. [L. *status*, *-ūs*—*stāre*, *statum*, to stand; partly through O.Fr. (see estate).]
stater, stā'tər, *n.* an ancient Greek standard coin of various kinds—gold daric, silver tetradrachm, etc. [Gr. *statēr*, orig. a pound weight—*histanai*, to set, establish, weigh.]
static, -al, stat'ik, -əl, *adjs.* pertaining to statics: pertaining to bodies, forces, charges, etc., in equilibrium: stationary: stable: resting: acting by mere weight: pertaining to sense of bodily equilibrium.—*n.* (static) atmospheric disturbances in wireless reception: white specks or flashes on a television picture: crackling on a long-playing plastic record.—*adv.* stat'ically. —*n.* Statice (*stat'i-sē*), the sea-lavender genus (from its astringency).—*n.* (*pl.* in form treated as *sing.*) stat'ics, the science of forces in equilibrium.—static line, a cord joining a parachute pack to the aircraft so that, when the wearer of the pack jumps, the parachute is automatically opened. [Gr. *statikē* (fem. of adj.), bringing to a standstill—root of *histanai*, to cause to stand.]
station, stā'shən, *n.* a standing still: a mode of standing: position: a chosen fixed point: a standing-place: a fixed stopping-place, esp. one on a railway with associated buildings and structures: a place set apart and equipped for some particular purpose: a local office, head-quarters, or depot: a branch post office (*U.S.*): a habitat: an actual spot where a species has been found: an assigned place or post: an assigned region for naval duty: a place in India where officials and officers reside: an Australian stock-farm: position in life (esp. a high position) or in the scale of nature: a holy place visited as one of a series, esp. one of (usu. fourteen) representations of stages in Christ's way to Calvary, disposed around a church interior or elsewhere (*R.C.*).—*adj.* of a station.—*v.t.* to assign a station to: to set: to appoint to a post, place, or office.—*adj.* sta'tional.—*n.* sta'-tionariness.—*adj.* sta'tionary, still: unmoving: fixed: settled: permanently located: continuously resident.—Also *n.*—*n.* sta'tioner (L. *statiōnārius*, a shopkeeper, in the Middle Ages a university bookseller, distinguished from an itinerant), a bookseller or publisher (*obs.*): a dealer in writing-materials and the like.—*adj.*

sta'tionery, belonging to a stationer.—*n.* the goods sold by a stationer.—Stationers' Hall, hall in London of the Company of Stationers, who until the passing of the Copyright Act in 1842 enjoyed an absolute control over printing and publishing; Stationery Office, an office for providing books, stationery, etc., to government offices and for arranging the printing of public papers; sta'tion-hand (*Austr.*), a man employed on a station; sta'tion-house, a lock-up at a police station: a police station (*U.S.*): a small railway station; sta'tion-master, -manager, one in charge of railway station; sta'tion-wagon, a motor vehicle usable by adjustment for either passengers or light hauling. [L. *statiō*, *-ōnis*— *stāre*, to stand.]
statism. See state.
statist, stā'tist, *n.* a statesman: a politician: a statistician.—*adj.* statistic (*stə-tist'ik*), statistical: political (*obs.*): relating to status.—*n.* a statistician: (in *pl.*) tabulated numerical facts, orig. those relating to a state: (in *pl.* form, treated as *sing.*) the classification, tabulation, and study of such facts.—*adj.* statist'ical, of, concerned with, of the nature of, statistics.—*adv.* statist'i-cally.—*n.* statistician (*stat-is-tish'ən*), one skilled in statistics: a compiler or student of statistics. [It. *statista* and Ger. *statistik*—L. *status*, state.]
stative, stā'tiv, *adj.* permanent, fixed (now only of a Roman camp): indicating a physical state or reflex action (of certain Hebrew verbs). [L. *stativus*—*stāre*, to stand.]
stato-, stat'ō-, in composition, standing.—*ns.* statocyst (*stat'ō-sist*; Gr. *kystis*, bladder), an organ of equilibrial sense, containing statoliths: a cell with starch-grains by which a plant is supposed to be sensitive to gravity; stat'olith (Gr. *lithos*, stone), a starch grain or other free solid body in a statocyst; stat'oscope, a sensitive barometer for detecting minute differences. [Gr. *statos*, set, placed.]
stator, stā'tər, *n.* a stationary part within which a part rotates. [L. *stātor*, stander.]
statue, stat'ū, *n.* a representation (usu. near or above life-size) of human or animal form in the round.—Also (*obs.*) stat'ua.—*adj.* stat'uary, of or suitable for sculpture: sculptured: statu-esque.—*n.* sculpture: a sculptor.—*adjs.* stat'ued, furnished with statues: sculptured; statuesque (*-esk'*), like a 'statue.—*adv.* statuesque'ly.—*ns.* statuesque'ness; statuette', a small statue, figurine. [L. *statua*—*statuĕre*, to cause to stand —*stāre*.]
stature, stā'chər, stat'yər, *n.* body height.—*adj.* stat'ured, having a stature. [L. *statūra*.]
status, stā'təs, *n.* state: condition: standing: position, rank, importance, in society or in any group:—*pl.* (*rare*) status (*-tūs*).—status symbol, a possession or a privilege considered to mark a person out as having a high position in his social group. [L. *status*.]
status quo, stā'təs, stat'ōōs, kwō, (L.) the state in which: the existing condition.
statute, stat'ūt, *n.* a law expressly enacted by the legislature (as distinguished from a customary law or law of use and wont): a written law: the act of a corporation or its founder, intended as a permanent rule or law: a bond or other proceeding based on a statute: a hiring-fair.—*adj.* stat'utable, prescribed, permitted, recognised by, or according to statute.—*advs.* stat'utably; stat'utorily.—*adj.* stat'utory, enacted by statute: depending on statute for its authority.—stat'ute-book, a record of statutes or enacted laws; stat'ute-cap (*Shak.*), a kind of cap enjoined by statute (1571) to be worn on Sundays by all below a certain rank; stat'ute-labour, compulsory labour on roads, etc.; stat'ute-law, law in the form of statutes.—Statute of Westminster, an act (1931) of the United Kingdom parliament

# staunch

conferring independent sovereign status on the self-governing dominions. [L. *statūtum*, that which is set up—*statuĕre*.]

**staunch, stanch,** *stönch, stönsh, stänch, stänsh, adj.* watertight: stout and firm: firm in principle, pursuit, or support: trusty, hearty, constant, zealous.—*adv.* **sta(u)nch′iy.**—*n.* **sta(u)nch′ness.** [O.Fr. *estanche*; see stanch.]

**staunch** (*v.t.*). See stanch.

**staurolite,** *stör′ə-līt, n.* a silicate of aluminium with ferrous oxide, magnesia, and water, common as twinned cruciform crystals.—*adj.* **staurolitic** (*-lit′ik*). [Gr. *stauros*, cross, *lithos*, stone.]

**stave,** *stāv, n.* one of the pieces of which a cask or tub is made: a staff, rod, bar, shaft: a staff (*mus.*): a stanza, verse of a song.—*v.t.* to break a stave or the staves of: to break: to burst inward (often with *in*): to drive off, as with a staff: to delay (e.g. the evil day; with *off*): to ward (off), keep back: to put together, or repair, with staves: to sprain (*Scot.*).—*v.i.* to thrust onward (*Scot.*): to break up:—*pa.t.* and *pa.p.* **stāved** or **stöve.—stave and tail,** in bear-baiting, to intervene with staves and by grasping the dogs' tails. [By-form of staff.]

**stave-church,** *stāv′-chûrch, n.* an ancient Norwegian wooden church supported on masts, with gabled roofs rising one above another. [Norw. *stav-kirke—stav,* staff, stave, *kirke,* church.]

**staves,** *stāvz,* plural of staff and of stave.

**stavesacre,** *stāvz′ā-kər, n.* a tall larkspur whose seeds were formerly used against lice. [O.Fr. *stavesaigre*—L.L. *staphisagria*—Gr. *staphis,* raisins, *agrios,* wild.]

**staw,** *stö,* a Scots form of stall (*n.* and *vb.*, *pr.t.*) and stole (*pa.t.* of steal).

**stay,** *stā, n.* a rope supporting a mast: a guy: a support: a prop: a connecting piece or brace to resist tension: (in *pl.*) a stiff corset (often **pair of stays**): a stopping, bringing or coming to a standstill: a suspension of legal proceeding: delay: an obstacle (*obs.*): a sojourn: duration: staying-power: a permanent state (*obs.*).—*v.t.* to support or incline with a stay or stays: to put in stays or on the other tack: to support: to prop: to sustain: to abide: to endure: to endure to the end: to stop: to detain: to hold, restrain, check the action of: to bring to rest: to discontinue: to allay: to hold back: to await (*arch.*): to remain to participate in, be present at or endure (*old-fashioned*): to stop for, be stopped by (*Spens.*).—*v.i.* to turn to windward in tacking: to rely, to found (*Shak.*): to stop: to remain: to tarry: to wait: to be kept waiting: to sojourn: to dwell (*Scot.*): to hold out, last, endure: to wait, attend as a servant (*Shak.*):—*pa.t.* and *pa.p.* **stayed** (now rarely **staid**).—*adj.* **stayed,** wearing stays: staid (*Spens.*).—*n.* **stay′er,** one who, or that which, remains, stops, holds, or supports: a person or animal of good lasting or staying qualities for a race.—*n.* and *adj.* **stay′ing.**—*adj.* **stay′less,** not to be stopped: without stop: without stays: unsupported: impermanent.—*adj.* **stay′-at-home,** keeping much at home: untravelled.—*n.* a stay-at-home person.—**stay′-bolt,** a bolt or rod binding together opposite plates.—*adjs.* **stay′-down,** of a mining strike, without leaving the working place; **stay′-in′,** without leaving the working-place (as a strike).—**stay′ing-power,** ability to go on long without flagging; **stay′-lace,** a lace for fastening a corset; **stay′-maker,** a maker of corsets; **staysail** (*stā′sl*), a sail extended on a stay; **stay′-tackle,** hoisting-tackle hung from a ship's mainstay; **stay′-tape,** a stay-lace: tape for binding edges.—**come to stay,** become permanent or established; **in stays,** head to windward in tacking; **miss stays** (see miss); **stay out,** to outstay: to stay to the end of; **stay put,** to

remain where one, or as it, is put; **stay the course,** to endure to the end of the race (*lit.* and *fig.*); **stay the stomach, the pangs of hunger,** to allay cravings of hunger for the time. [Partly O.E. *stæg,* stay (rope); partly O.Fr. *estayer,* to prop, from the same Gmc. root; partly O.Fr. *ester*—L. *stāre,* to stand.]

**stayne, stayre,** old spellings (*Spens.* etc.) of stain, stair.

**stead,** *sted, n.* a place (now chiefly in compounds and idiomatic phrases): esp. the place which another had or might have: a farm: a site: a bedstead: a space of time (*Spens.*): circumstances, case, condition (*Spens.*): service, avail, advantage.—*v.t.* to set (*obs.*): to set in a plight: to avail, help, serve (*arch.*): to fulfil in substitution (*Shak.* **steed up**):—*pa.t.* and *pa.p.* **stead′ed, stead** (*sted*).—*adj.* **stead′fast,** firmly fixed or established: firm: constant: resolute: steady.—*adv.* **stead′fastly.**—*n.* **stead′fastness.**—*adv.* **stead′ily.**—*ns.* **stead′iness; stead′ing,** farmbuildings with or without the farmhouse.—*adj.* **stead′y** (*comp.* **stead′ier,** *superl.* **stead′iest**), firm in standing or in place: fixed: stable: constant: resolute: consistent: regular: uniform: sober, industrious.—*v.t.* to make steady: to make or keep firm:—*pr.p.* **stead′ying;** *pa.t.* and *pa.p.* **stead′ied.**—*n.* a rest or support, as for the hand, a tool, or a piece of work: a regular boy friend or girl friend (*coll.*).—*adj.* **stead′y-going,** of steady habits or action.—**steady state** (*astron.;* see continuous creation).—**go steady** (*coll.*), to go about regularly and exclusively with one person of the opposite sex; **stand one in good stead,** prove of good service to one. [O.E. *stede,* place; cf. Ger. *stadt,* town, *statt,* place, Du. *stad,* town; O.E. *stedefæst,* steadfast.]

**steak,** *stāk, n.* a slice of meat (esp. hindquarter of beef) or fish. [O.N. *steik; steikja,* to roast on a spit.]

**steal,** *stēl, v.t.* to take by theft, esp. secretly: to take, gain or win by address, by contrivance, unexpectedly, insidiously, gradually, or furtively: to snatch: in golf, to hole (a long putt) by a delicate stroke—the opposite of *gobble:* to put surreptitiously, smuggle.—*v.i.* to practise theft: to take feloniously: to pass quietly, unobtrusively, gradually, or surreptitiously:—*pa.t.* **stōle** (*obs.* **stāle;** *Scot.* **staw, stealed, stealt**); *pa.p.* **stōl′en** (*arch.* **stōle;** *Milt.* **stōln;** *Scot.* **stown, stealed, stealt**).—*n.* **steal′er.**—*n.* and *adj.* **steal′ing.**—*adv.* **steal′ingly.—steal a march on** (see **march**); **steal a marriage,** to marry secretly; **steal one's thunder,** to make use of another's invention against him (as when John Dennis's stage thunder was used in a rival's play): to rob someone of the opportunity of achieving a sensational effect by forestalling him. [O.E. *stelan;* Ger. *stehlen,* Du. *stelen.*]

**steal, steale, steel, stele, steil,** *stēl,* (*dial.* and *Spens.*) *n.* a handle, shank, shaft. [O.E. *stela,* stalk; conn. stale (3, 4).]

**stealed, stealt.** See steal (1).

**stealth,** *stelth, n.* a theft (*Spens., Shak.*): a thing stolen (*Milt.*): secret or unobtrusive going or passage (*Shak.*): secret procedure or manner: furtiveness.—*adv.* **stealth′ily.**—*n.* **stealth′iness.** —*adj.* **stealth′y,** acted or acting with stealth: furtive. [steal (1).]

**steam,** *stēm, n.* water in the form of gas or vapour or of a mist or film of liquid drops: a steamed dish: steam-power: a spell of travel by steam-power: energy, force, spirit (*fig.*).—*adj.* of, for, using, worked by, steam.—*v.i.* to rise or pass off in steam or vapour: to emit or generate steam, vapour, or smell: to become dimmed with condensed vapour (often with *up*): to move by means of steam power.—*v.t.* to exhale: to expose to steam: to cook by means of steam: to dim with vapour.—*adj.* **steamed.**—*n.* **steamer,**

one who steams: apparatus for steaming: a steamship: a motor-car, a road-locomotive, fire-engine, etc., worked by steam.—*adv.* steam'ily.—*n.* steam'iness.—*n., adj.,* and *adv.* steam'ing.—*adj.* steam'y, of, like, full of, covered with, as if covered with, emitting, steam or vapour.—steam'boat, steam'ship, steam'-vessel, a vessel driven by steam; steam'-boiler, a boiler for generating steam; steam'-car, -carriage, steam-driven road vehicle; steam'-chest, -dome, a chamber above a steam-boiler serving as a reservoir for steam; steam'-coal, coal suitable for raising steam; steam'-crane; steam'-digger.—*adj.* steam'-driv'en.—steam'-engine, any engine worked by steam; steam'-gauge, a pressure gauge for steam; steam'-gov'ernor, the governor of a steam-engine; steam'-hamm'er, a vertical hammer worked by steam; steam iron, an electric iron having a compartment in which water is heated to provide steam to damp material; steam'-jack'et, a hollow casing supplied with steam; steam'-launch, a large steam-driven boat; steam'-naviga'tion, the propulsion of vessels by steam; steam'-navvy, -shovel, an excavator driven by steam; steam'-pack'et, a steam-vessel plying between certain ports; steam'-pipe, a pipe for conveying steam; steam'-plough, a plough or gang of ploughs worked by a steam-engine; steam'-port, an opening for the passage of steam; steam'-power, the force or agency of steam when applied to machinery; steam radio, sound radio; steam'-roll'er, a steam-engine with a heavy roller for wheels, used in road-mending, etc.: any weighty crushing force (*fig.*).—*adj.* steam'tight, impervious to steam.—steam'-trap, a contrivance for allowing the passage of water but not of steam; steam'-tug, a small steam-vessel used in towing ships; steam'-tur'bine, an engine in which expanding steam acts on blades attached to a drum; steam'-whis'tle, a whistle sounded by passage of steam; steam'-yacht.—full steam ahead, forward at the greatest speed possible: with maximum effort; get up steam, to build up steam pressure: to collect one's forces: to become excited; let off steam, to release steam into the atmosphere: to work off energy: to give vent to anger or annoyance; steamed up (*slang*), indignant; steam open, to open by softening gum by exposure to steam; under one's own steam, by one's own unaided efforts. [O.E. *stēam*; Du. *stoom*.]

stean, steen, *stēn*, (*dial.*; *Spens.* steane) *n.* a stone or earthenware vessel. [O.E. *stæne*.]

stear, steare, steard, stearage, stearsman, stearsmate, old spellings (*Spens., Milt.*) of steer, steered, etc.

stear-, steat-, in composition, suet, fat.—*n.* stearate (*stē'ər-āt*), a salt of stearic acid.—*adj.* stearic (*stē-ar'ik*), of stearin (stearic acid, a fatty acid C₁₇H₃₅COOH).—*n.* ste'arin, glyceryl ester of stearic acid: a mixture of stearic and palmitic acids (also ste'arine): the solid part of a fat.—*adj.* ste'arine, made of stearin(e), as candles.—*n.* steatite (*stē'ə-tīt*), soapstone.—*adj.* steatitic (*-tit'ik*).—*ns.* steat'ocele (Gr. *kēlē*, tumour), a fatty tumour in the scrotum; steatō'ma, a fatty encysted tumour.—*adj.* steatom'atous.—*n.* steatopygia (*stē-ə-tō-pī'ji-ə, -pij'i-ə*; Gr. *pȳgē*, buttock), an accumulation of fat on the buttocks.—*adj.* steatopygous (*-tō-pī'gəs, -top'i-gəs*), fat-buttocked.—*n.* steatō'sis, fatty degeneration. [Gr. *stĕăr, stĕătos*, suet.]

steare, *stēr*, (*Spens.*) *n.* a steer or ox.

steat-. See stear-.

sted, stedd, stedde, stede (*Spens.*), steed (*Shak.*), forms of stead (*n.* and *v.t.*); stedfast, an obsolescent spelling (*Shak., Milt.*, etc.) of steadfast; steddy, steedy, old spellings of steady.

steed, *stēd*, *n.* a horse, esp. a spirited horse. [O.E.

stēda, stud-horse, stallion; cf. O.E. *stōd*, stud; Ger. *stute*, stud-mare, *gestüte*, stud.]

steed, steedy. See sted.

steek, *stēk*, (*Scot.*) *n.* a stitch.—*v.t.* and *v.i.* to stitch.—*v.t.* to pierce: to fasten: to shut:—*pa.t.* and *pa.p.* steek'it. [Partly at least O.E. *stice*, stitch, puncture; perh. partly confused with stick.]

steel, *stēl*, *n.* iron containing a little carbon with or without other things: a cutting tool or weapon, an instrument, object, or part made of steel, as a steel knife-sharpener, a skate: a piece of steel, as for stiffening a corset, striking fire from a flint: a steel-engraving: extreme hardness, staying power, trustworthiness (*fig.*): any chalybeate medicine.—*adj.* of or like steel.—*v.t.* to cover or edge with steel: to harden: to nerve: to make obdurate.—*adj.* steeled, made of, covered, protected, provided or edged with, steel: hardened: nerved.—*ns.* steel'iness; steel'ing.—*adj.* steel'y, of or like steel.—steel band, a West Indian band, with instruments made from old petrol drums, etc.—*n.* and *adj.* steel'-blue', blue like a reflection from steel.—*adj.* steel'-clad, clad in armour.—steel'-engrav'-ing, engraving on steel plates: an impression or print so got; steel erector, a spider man.—*n.* and *adj.* steel'-grey', -gray', bluish-grey like steel.—*adj.* steel'-head'ed.—steel'-pen, a nib of steel; steel'-plate, a plate of steel: one on which a design is engraved: a print from it.—*adj.* steel'-plat'ed, plated with steel.—steel'-trap', one with steel jaws and spring; steel'-ware, articles of steel collectively; steel'-wool', steel shavings used for cleaning and polishing; steel'-work, work executed in steel: (often in *pl.* form) a factory where steel is made; steel'-worker. [O.E. *style*; Ger. *stahl*.]

steelbow, *stēl'bō*, (*Scots law*) *n.* stock and goods received from a landlord with obligation to return a like amount and value when the lease expires: a contract or tenure on these terms. Also adj. [steel, in the sense of rigidly fixed, and obs. *bow*—O.N. *bū*, stock of cattle.]

steeld. See stell.

steelyard, *stēl'yärd*, *n.* a weighing machine consisting of a lever with a short arm for the thing weighed and a long graduated arm on which a single weight moves. [Prob. steel and yard, but suggested or fixed in use by the *Steelyard* or *Stålhof* (L.G.; prop. sample yard, mistranslated steel yard), the Hanse headquarters in London.]

steem, *stēm*, (*Spens.*) *v.t.* Same as esteem; also same as steam.

steen, *stēn*, *v.t.* to line (a well) with stone.—*n.* such a lining.—Also steen'ing. [O.E. *stænan*.]

steen. See stean.

steenbok, *stän'*, *stēn'bok*, *n.* a small S. African antelope. [Du.,—*steen*, stone, *bok*, buck.]

steenkirk, *stēn'kûrk*, *n.* a lace cravat loosely worn. [From the battle of *Steenkerke*, 3rd August 1692.]

steep, *stēp*, *adj.* lofty (*obs.*): rising or descending with great inclination: precipitous: headlong: difficult: excessive, exorbitant.—*n.* a precipitous place.—*v.t.* (*S.W. England*) to cause to stoop, slope.—*v.i.* to rise or fall precipitou̇sly.—*v.t.* and *v.i.* steep'en, to make or become steeper.—*n.* steep'iness (*obs.*).—*adj.* steep'ish.—*adv.* steep'ly.—*n.* steep'ness.—*adj.* steep'y₍ (*poet.*), steep.—*adjs.* steep(e)'-down(en), (*Shak.*) precipitous; steep'-to' (*naut.*), going down precipitously into the water; steep(e)'-up, (*Shak.*) precipitous. [O.E. *stēap*; cf. stoop.]

steep, *stēp*, *v.t.* to soak: to wet thoroughly: to saturate: to imbue.—*v.i.* to undergo soaking or thorough wetting.—*n.* a soaking process: a liquid for steeping anything in: rennet.—*n.* steep'er, one who steeps: a vessel for steeping in. [M.E. *stepen*; perh. conn. with stoup.]

steeple, *stēp'l*, *n.* a church or other tower with

or without, including or excluding, a spire: a structure surmounted by a spire: the spire alone. —*adj.* **steep'led**, having a steeple or steeples or appearance of steeples.—**steep'le-bush**, hardhack; **steep'lechase**, orig. an impromptu horse-race with some visible church-steeple as goal: a horse-race across-country: one over a course with obstacles to be jumped: a foot-race of like kind.—*v.i.* to ride or run in a steeplechase.— **steep'lechaser**; **steep'lechasing**; **steep'le-crown**, a high conical hat.—Also *adj.*—*adj.* **steep'le-crowned**.—**steep'le-fair** (*obs.*), a market in church-livings; **steep'le-hat**; **steep'le-house** (*obs.*), a church-building; **steep'lejack**, one who repairs steeples and chimney-stalks. [O.E. *stēpel*, *stȳpel*, *stipel*, from root of **steep**.]

**steer**, *stēr*, *n.* a young ox, esp. a castrated one from two to four years old.—*n.* **steer'ling**, a little or young steer. [O.E. *stēor*; Ger. *stier*.]

**steer**, *stēr*, *v.t.* to direct with, or as with, the helm: to guide: to govern.—*v.i.* to direct a ship, cycle, etc., in its course: to be directed, take or follow a course in answer to the helm.—*ns.* **steer'age**, act or practice of steering: the effect of a rudder on the ship: course: government: apparatus for steering: part (in front of the great cabin) from which a ship used to be steered: part of a passenger ship with lowest fares (also *adj.*); **steer'er**; **steer'ing**.—**steer'age-way**, sufficient movement of a vessel to enable it to be controlled by the helm; **steering committee** (*U.S.*), a group who decide what measures shall be brought forward and when; **steer'ing-gear**, the mechanism that transmits motion from the steering-wheel; **steer'ing-wheel**, the wheel whereby a ship's rudder is turned, or a motor-car, etc., guided; **steers'man**, **steers'mate** (*obs.*; *Milt.*), **stears'-mate**), one who steers.—**steer clear of**, to avoid. [O.E. *stēoran*, *stȳran*, to steer.]

**steer**, *stēr*, *n.*, *v.t.*, and *v.i.* a Scots form of **stir**.— *n.* **steer'y** (*Scott*), commotion.

**steeve**, *stēv*, *n.* angular elevation, esp. of a bowsprit.—*v.t.* and *v.i.* to incline to the horizon. [Origin unknown.]

**steeve, stieve,** *stēv*, (*Scot.*) *adj.* stiff, firm: sturdy. —Also *adv.*—*adv.* **steeve'ly, stieve'ly**. [M.E. *stef*; ety. doubtful.]

**steeve**, *stēv*, *v.t.* to stuff, pack close.—*n.* **steev'ing**. [Perh. Fr. *estiver*—L. *stipāre*, to stuff.]

**stegano-, stego-**, in composition, covered, roofed, hidden, watertight.—*ns.* **steganogram** (*steg'ən-ə-gram*), **-graph**, a cryptogram; **steganographer** (*-og'*), one who works with ciphers.—*adj.* **steganograph'ic**.—*ns.* **steganog'raphist**; **steganog'raphy**; **steg'anopod** (Gr. *pous*, *podos*, foot), any bird of the Steganop'odēs, the pelican order of birds, with all four toes webbed together.—*adj.* **steganop'odous**.—*n.* **stegno'sis**, constriction of the pores and vessels: constipation.—*adjs.* **stegnot'ic**; **stegocarp'ous** (Gr. *karpos*, fruit), with lidded capsule.—*n.pl.* **Stegocephalia** (*-se-fā'li-ə*; Gr. *kephalē*, head), an extinct order of tailed amphibians (Labyrinthodon, etc.).—*adj.* and *n.* **stegocephā'lian**.—*adj.* **stegocephalous** (*-sef'ə-ləs*). —*ns.* **Stegomyia** (*-mī'yə*; Gr. *myia*, fly), the yellow-fever mosquito or other of its genus; **stegoph'ilist** (Gr. *stegos*, roof, *phileein*, to love), one who climbs buildings for sport; **steg'osaur** (Gr. *sauros*, lizard), a gigantic Jurassic dinosaur (Stegosaur'us), with heavy armour of bony plates.—*adj.* **stegosaur'ian**. [Gr. *steganos*, covered, watertight, *stegein*, to cover, hold water, protect, hide, *stegnoein*, to make costive.]

**stein**, *stēn*, *stīn*, *shtīn*, *n.* a large beer mug, often earthenware and frequently with a hinged lid. [Ger.]

**Steinberger**, *stīn'bûr-gər*, *shtīn'ber-hhər*, *n.* an esteemed Rhenish white wine, from *Steinberg*, near Wiesbaden.

**steinbock**, *stīn'bok*, *n.* the Alpine ibex: also used for **steenbok**. [Ger. *stein*, stone, *bock*, buck.]

**stele**, *stē'lē*, *n.* an upright stone slab or tablet (also **stē'la**): (*stē'lē, stēl*) the central cylinder (vascular bundles with pith and pericycle) in stems and roots of the higher plants (*bot.*):—*pl.* (L.) **stē'lae**.—*adjs.* **ste'lar, ste'lene**. [Gr. *stēlē*—root of *histanai*, to set, stand.]

**stell**, *stel*, *v.t.* to set, post (*Scot.*): to delineate (*arch.*; *Shak.*), *pa.p.* **steeld, steld**).—*n.* (*Scot.*) an enclosure (usu. a ringwall) for sheltering sheep, etc.—*adj.* **stelled**, fixed (see also under **stellar**). [O.E. *stellan*, to fix, put.]

**stellar**, *stel'ər*, *adj.* of the stars: of the nature of a star: starry.—*n.* **Stellā'ria**, the chickweed genus of the pink family.—*adjs.* **stell'ate**, star-shaped: with branches radiating from a point: with sides that intersect one another, giving a starlike effect, as in the pentagram; **stell'āted**, stellate: starred. —*adv.* **stell'ately**.—*adjs.* **stelled**, starred (*Shak.*; see **stell** above); **stellif'erous**, having or bearing stars or starlike marks or forms; **stell'ified**; **stell'iform**, star-shaped.—*v.t.* **stell'ify**, to turn into a star: to set among the stars: to set with stars (*obs.*).—*n.* **stell'ifying**.—*adjs.* **stell'ūlar**, **stell'ūlate**, like a little star. [L. *stēlla*, a star.]

**Stellenbosch**, *stel'ən-bosh*, (*mil. slang*) *v.t.* to relegate to a post where incompetence matters less: to supersede. [From *Stellenbosch*, Cape of Good Hope, such a dumping-ground.]

**stelliferous**, etc. See **stellar**.

**stellion**, *stel'yən*, or **stellio lizard**, *stel'i-ō liz'ərd*, *n.* a Levantine lizard (*Agama stellio*) with starry spots.—*n.* **stell'ionate**, a fraud that does not come under any specific head (*law*). [L. *stēlliō*, *-ōnis*, a star-spotted lizard, a knave—*stēlla*, star.]

**stem**, *stem*, *n.* the leaf-bearing axis of a plant: a stalk: anything stalk-like, as the slender upright part of a note, of a wine-glass, the winding shaft of a watch: an upright stroke of a letter: the main line (or sometimes a branch) of a family: a race or family: the base of a word, to which inflectional suffixes are added (*philol.*): a curved timber at the prow of a ship: the forepart of a ship.—*v.t.* to provide with a stem: to deprive of stalk or stem: to oppose the stem to: hence, to make way against, breast: to ram.—*v.i.* to grow a stem: to spring, take rise.—*adjs.* **stem'less**; **stemmed**.—*n.* **stem'son**, a timber behind the apron of a ship.—**stem'-form**, ancestral form; **stem stitch**, an overlapping stitch used in embroidery; **stem'winder** (*U.S.*), a keyless watch.—**from stem to stern**, from one end of a vessel to the other: completely, throughout. [O.E. *stefn*, *stemn*; Ger. *stamm*; perh. conn. with **stand**.]

**stem**, *stem*, *v.t.* to stop, check: to dam: to tamp: to staunch: in skiing, to slow down by pushing the heels apart:—*pr.p.* **stemm'ing**; *pa.t.* and *pa.p.* **stemmed**.—*n.* in skiing, the act of stemming. [O.N. *stemma*.]

**stembuck**, *stem'buk*, **stembok**, *-bok*, for **steenbok**.

**steme**, *stēm*, (*Spens.*) *v.t.* for **steam**, i.e. evaporate.

**stemma**, *stem'ə*, *n.* a garland: a scroll: a pedigree: an ocellus:—*pl.* **stemm'ata**.—*adj.* **stemm'atous**. —*v.t.* **stemme** (*stem*; *Spens.*), to encircle. [Gr. *stemma*, usu. in pl. *stemmata*.]

**stempel, stemple**, *stem'pl*, *n.* a cross-timber in a shaft, as support or step. [Cf. Ger. *stempel*.]

**stemson**. See **stem** (1).

**sten.** See **stend** and **sten gun**.

**stench**, *stench*, *-sh*, *n.* stink.—*v.t.* to cause to stink.—*adj.* **stench'y**.—**stench'-trap**, a device to prevent rise of gases in drains. [O.E. *stenc*, smell (good or bad); cf. **stink**; Ger. *stank*.]

**stencil**, *sten'sl*(*i*)*l*, *v.t.* and *v.i.* to paint by brushing over a perforated plate: to make a stencil for

producing copies of typewriting or writing:—
*pr.p.* **sten′cilling**; *pa.t.* and *pa.p.* **sten′cilled.**—*n.*
the plate or the colouring-matter so used: the
design or lettering so produced: a piece of
waxed paper, etc., on which letters are cut by
typewriter or stylus so that ink will pass through.
—*adj.* **sten′cilled.**—*ns.* **sten′ciller; sten′cilling.**—
**sten′cil-plate.** [O.Fr. *estinceller*, to spangle—
*estincelle*—L. *scintilla*, a spark.]
**stend**, *stend*, (*Scot.*) *v.i.* to bound, stride vigorously.
—*n.* a bound or great stride: a dart of pain.—
Also **sten.** [Poss. L. *extendĕre.*]
**stengah**, *steng′ga*, **stinger**, *sting′ər*, (*Anglo-Indian*)
*n.* a peg of whisky and soda. [Malay *sa tenah*,
one half.]
**Sten, sten gun**, *sten gun*, *n.* a small automatic gun.
[*ST* (designers′ initials) and *En*field, as in bren
gun.]
**stenlock**, *sten′lək*, (*Scot.*) *n.* a coalfish: an overgrown coalfish. [Origin doubtful.]
**steno-**, *sten-ō-*, *-ə-*, in composition, contracted.—
*ns.* **sten′ochrome** (*-krōm*; Gr. *chrōma*, colour), a
print by stenochromy; **sten′ochromy** (or *-ok′ro-
mi*), printing in several colours at one printing;
**sten′ograph**, a shorthand character or report.—
*v.t.* to write in shorthand.—*n.* **stenog′rapher.**—
*adjs.* **stenograph′ic, -al.**—*adv.* **stenograph′ically.**
—*ns.* **stenog′raphist; stenog′raphy**, the art, or
any method, of writing very quickly: shorthand.—*adjs.* **stenopaeic** (*-pē′ik*; Gr. *opaios*,
holed—*opē*, an opening), with a narrow opening
(also **stenopā′ic**); **stenosed** (*sti-nōst′*), morbidly
contracted.—*n.* **stenō′sis**, constriction, narrowing
of a tube or passage: constipation.—*adj.* **stenotic**
(*sti-not′ik*).—*ns.* **sten′otype**, a phonetic typewriter or its use; **sten′otyper, sten′otypist;**
**sten′otypy.** [Gr. *stenos*, narrow.]
**stent**, *stent*, *n.*, *v.t.*, and *v.i.* Same as **stint** (1),
with meanings shading off into those of next
word.
**stent**, *stent*, (*Scot.*) *n.* assessment: valuation: tax.
—*v.t.* to assess: to tax: to levy.—*ns.* **stent′or,
stent′our, stentmaster.**—**stent′master**, one who
determines amount of tax to be paid. [extent, or
O.Fr. *estente*; see also **stent** (1) and **stint** (1).]
**Stentor**, *stent′ör*, *n.* a very loud-voiced Greek at
Troy (*Iliad*), hence a loud-voiced person: a
genus of ciliate protozoans.—*adjs.* **stento′rian;
stentorophon′ic** (Gr. *phōnē*, voice).—*n.* **stent′-
orphone**, apparatus for intensifying the voice.
[Gr. *Stentōr.*]
**step**, *step*, *n.* a pace: a movement of the leg in
walking, running, or dancing: the distance so
covered: a footstep: a footfall: a footprint:
gait: a small space: a short journey: a degree
of a scale: a stage upward or downward: one
tread of a stair: round of a ladder: a doorstep:
something to put the foot on in mounting or dismounting: a stage in discontinuous or stairwise
rise or fall: a move towards an end or in a course
of proceeding: coincidence in speed and phase:
a support for the end of a mast, pivot, or the like:
(in *pl.*) walk, direction taken in walking: a self-
supporting hinged ladder (often *pair of steps*): a
stair.—*v.i.* to advance, retire, mount, or descend
by taking a step or steps: to pace: to walk:
to walk slowly or gravely: to walk a short
distance.—*v.t.* to perform by stepping: to
measure by pacing: to arrange or shape stepwise:
to set, as a foot (now *U.S.*): to fix, as a mast:
—*pr.p.* **stepp′ing;** *pa.t.* and *pa.p.* **stepped** (also
**stept**).—*n.* **stepp′er.**—*adv.* **step′wise**, in the
manner of steps.—**step′-dance**, a dance involving
an effective display of steps by an individual
dancer; **step′-dancer; step′-dancing; step′-
fault′** (*geol.*), one of a series of parallel faults
throwing in the same direction; **step′-in**, a
garment that needs no fastening; **step′-ladder**,
a ladder with flat treads and a hinged prop;
**stepp′ing-stone**, a stone rising above water or

mud to afford a passage: a means to gradual
progress (*fig.*); **step′-rock′et**, one made in
sections operating successively and then discarded; **step′-stone**, a door-step.—*adj.* **step′-up′**,
increasing or changing by steps: raising voltage.
—**break step**, to change the sequence of right and
left foot, so as to get out of step; **keep step**, to
continue in step; **in step**, with simultaneous
putting forward of the right (or left) feet in
marching, etc.: (*fig.*) in conformity or agreement
(with others); **out of step**, not in step; **step
in**, to enter easily or unexpectedly (also **step
into**): to intervene; **step on it** (*slang*; see **gas,
juice**), to hurry; **step out**, to go out a little way:
to increase the length of the step and so the
speed: to have a gay social life; **step out of line**,
to depart from the usual, or accepted, course of
action; **step short**, to shorten the length of one′s
step; **step up**, to come forward: to build up
into steps: to raise by a step or steps: to increase
the voltage of: to increase the rate of, as production; **take steps**, to take action. [O.E.
(Mercian) *steppe* (W.S. *stæpe*); Du. *step*, Ger.
*stapfe.*]
**step-**, *step-*, *pfx.* indicating affinity by another
marriage or mating.—*ns.* **step′bairn** (*Scot.*),
**-child, -daughter, -son**, a wife′s or husband′s
but not one′s own child, daughter, son; **step′-
dame** (*arch.*), **step′mother**, a father′s wife not
one′s own mother: a bird that hatches another′s
eggs: a cruel, niggardly, or negligent guardian
(*fig.*).—*adj.* **step′motherly.**—*ns.* **step′father**, a
mother′s husband not one′s own father; **step′-
parent; step′brother, -sister**, the son, daughter,
of a stepfather or stepmother. [O.E. *stēop-*
(as in *stēopmōdor*), orig. meaning orphan;
Ger. *stief-.*]
**stephane**, *stef′ə-nē*, *n.* an ancient Greek head-dress
like a diadem. [Gr. *stephanē*—*stephein*, to
encircle.]
**stephanite**, *stef′ə-nīt*, *n.* brittle silver ore, composed of silver, sulphur, and antimony. [After
Archduke *Stephan* (1817-67).]
**Stephanotis**, *stef-ə-nō′tis*, *n.* a genus of asclepiads
of Madagascar, etc., cultivated for their scented
flowers. [Gr. *stephanōtis*, fit for a wreath—
*stephanos*, a crown, wreath.]
**stepney**, *step′ni*, *n.* a spare wheel, often *fig.*: a
mistress, esp. a white slaver′s. [Said to be from
the name of a street where the wheels were made.]
**steppe**, *step*, *n.* a dry, grassy, generally treeless and
uncultivated and sometimes salt plain, as in the
south-east of Europe and in Asia. [Russ. *step′.*]
**steradian**, *sti-rā′di-ən*, *n.* a unit of measurement for
solid angles, the angle subtended at the centre of
a sphere by an area on its surface numerically
equal to the square of the radius. [Gr. *stereos*,
solid, and **radian.**]
**stercoraceous**, *stûrk-ə-rā′shəs*, *adj.* of, of the nature
of, dung.—*adj.* **sterc′oral**, stercoraceous.—*ns.*
**sterc′oranism**, the belief that the sacramental
bread was digested and evacuated like other
food; **sterc′oranist.**—*adjs.* **stercorā′rious, sterc′-
orary.**—*v.t.* **sterc′orate**, to manure. [L. *stercus,
-oris*, dung.]
**Sterculia**, *stər-kū′li-ə*, *n.* the gum tragacanth genus
giving name to the **Sterculiā′ceae**, a family of
large trees and shrubs akin to the mallows,
including kola and cacao. [L. *Sterculius*, god of
manuring—*stercus*, dung, from the stinking
flowers.]
**stere**, *stēr*, *n.* a timber measure, a cubic metre—
about 35·315 cubic feet.—Also in compounds, as
**decastere** (*dek′ə-*), 10 steres, **decistere** (*des′i-*), a
tenth of a stere.—Gr. *stereos*, solid.]
**stereo-**, *stēr′i-ō-*, *ster′i-ō-*, in composition, solid,
hard, three-dimensional.—*n.* **ster′eo**, stereophonic reproduction of sound.—*adj.* **stereophonic.**—*n.*, *adj.*, *v.t.*, and *v.i.* a contr. of
**stereotype, stereoscope, stereoscopic.**—*n.* **ster′-**

eobate (root of Gr. *bainein*, to go, walk), a substructure, foundation.—*adj.* stereobatic (*-bat'-ik*).—*ns.* stereochem'istry, the study of the spatial arrangement of atoms in molecules; ster'eochrome (Gr. *chrōma*, colour); ster'-eochrōmy, mural painting fixed with water-glass; stereoflu'oroscope, a fluoroscope giving a three-dimensional view; ster'eogram, a picture or diagram suggestive of solidity: a stereographic double picture; a radiogram for reproducing stereophonic records; ster'eograph, a stereogram (in picture senses).—*adjs.* stereograph'ic, -al.—*ns.* stereog'raphy; stereoi'somer, an isomer differing only in spatial arrangement of atoms.—*adj.* stereoisomer'ic.—*ns.* stereoisom'-erism; ster'eome, mechanical tissue in plants; stereom'eter, an instrument for measuring specific gravity or for measuring solids.—*adjs.* stereomet'ric, -al.—*adv.* stereomet'rically.—*n.* stereom'etry.—*adj.* stereophon'ic, giving the effect of sound from different directions in three-dimensional space.—*adv.* stereophon'ically, by stereophony.—*ns.* stereoph'ony, stereophonic reproduction of sound; stereops'is (Gr. *opsis*, vision), binocular stereoscopic vision; stereopt'icon, a double projecting lantern, by means of which the one picture dissolves into another; stereop'tics, the optics of stereoscopy; ster'eoscope, an instrument by which the images of two pictures differing slightly in point of view are seen one by each eye and so give an effect of solidity.—*adjs.* stereoscop'ic, -al.—*adv.* stereoscop'ically.—*ns.* stereos'copist; stereos'copy.—*adj.* stereoson'ic, stereophonic.—*ns.* stereot'omy (Gr. *tomē*, a cut), section-cutting of solids: stone-cutting; ster'eotype, a solid metallic plate for printing, cast from a plastic mould of movable types: the art, method, or process of making such plates: a fixed conventionalised representation.—*adj.* pertaining to, or done with, stereotypes.—*v.t.* to make a stereotype of: to print with stereotypes.—*adj.* ster'eotyped, transferred as letterpress from set-up movable type to a mould, and thence to a metal plate: fixed, unchangeable, as opinions: conventionalised.—*n.* ster'eotyper.—*adj.* stereotyp'-ic.—*ns.* ster'eotyping; ster'eotypy.—*adj.* steric (*ster'ik*), relating to spatial arrangement of atoms. [Gr. *stereos*, solid.]

steric. See stereo-.

sterigma, *ster-ig'mə*, *n.* the stalk of a spore:—*pl.* sterig'mata. [Gr. *stērigma*, support.]

sterile, *ster'il* (*U.S.* -il), *adj.* unfruitful: barren: not producing, or unable to produce, offspring, fruit, seeds, or spores: of a flower, without pistils: of a glume, not subtending a flower: sterilised: destitute of ideas or results.—*n.* sterilisation, -z- (*ster-i-li-zā'shən*).—*v.t.* ster'ilise, -ize, to cause to be fruitless: to deprive of power of reproduction: to destroy micro-organisms in.—*ns.* ster'iliser, one who, or that which sterilises: apparatus for destroying germs; steril'ity, quality of being sterile: unfruitfulness, barrenness, in regard to reproduction. [L. *sterilis*, barren.]

sterlet, *stûr'lit*, *n.* a small sturgeon. [Russ. *sterlyad*.]

sterling, *stûr'ling*, (*obs.*) *n.* an old English silver penny: English, Scottish, or British money of standard value.—*adj.* of sterling or standard English money: genuine: of authority: of thoroughly good character: (of silver) of standard quality.—sterling area, a group of countries with currencies tied to sterling and freely settling transactions among themselves through London. [Prob. a coin with a star— O.E. *steorra*, star—some early Norman pennies being so marked.]

Sterling, *stûr'ling*, *n.* a submachine-gun that fires bursts or single shots, and does not jam. [From the makers' name.]

sterling, *stûr'ling*. Same as starling (2).

stern, *stûrn*, *adj.* severe: austere: rigorous: unrelenting.—Also *adv.* (*Milt.*).—*adv.* stern'ly.—*n.* stern'ness. [O.E. *styrne*.]

stern, *stûrn*, *n.* the hind-part of a vessel: the rump or tail: steering-gear, helm, the steersman's place (*obs.*; *Shak.*).—*v.t.* to back, to row backward.—*n.* stern'age (*Shak.*), sterns collectively.— *adjs.* sterned, having a stern (in compounds); stern'most, farthest astern.—*advs.* stern'ward (also *adj.*), -s.—stern'board, backward motion of a ship: loss of way in tacking; stern'-chase, a chase in which one ship follows directly in the wake of another; stern'-chaser, a cannon in the stern of a ship; stern'-fast, a rope or chain for making fast a ship's stern to a wharf, etc.—*adv.* stern'-fore'most.—stern'-frame, the framework of a ship's stern; stern'port, a port or opening in the stern of a ship; stern'-post, the aftermost timber of a ship, supporting the rudder; stern'-sheet, (usu. in *pl.*) the part of a boat between the stern and the rowers; stern'son, the hinder extremity of a ship's keelson, to which the sternpost is bolted; stern'way, the backward motion of a vessel; stern'-wheel'er (*U.S.*), a small vessel with one large paddle-wheel at the stern.—*n.pl.* stern'works, hinder parts. [O.N. *stjōrn*, a steering, or lost O.E. equivalent.]

stern, *stûrn*, stern, starn, stärn, (*obs.* and *Scot.*) *n.* a star.—*n.* (*dim.*) starn'ie. [O.N. *stjarna*.]

sternum, *stûr'nəm*, *n.* the breast-bone: the under part of a somite in arthropods.—*adj.* ster'nal.— *ns.* ster'nebra (modelled on *vertebra*), a segment of the breast-bone; ster'nite, the ventral plate of a segment in arthropods.—*adjs.* sternit'ic; ster'notribe (Gr. *tribē*, a rub), pollinated by touching an insect's under surface. [Latinised from Gr. *sternon*, chest.]

sternutation, *stûr-nū-tā'shən*, *n.* sneezing.—*adjs.* sternū'tative, sternū'tatory, that causes sneezing. —*n.* a substance that causes sneezing.—Also ster'nūtător. [L. *sternūtāre*, intens. of *sternuēre*, to sneeze.]

sterol, *ster'ol*, *n.* a solid higher alcohol such as cholesterol, ergosterol.—*n.* ster'oid, any of a class of compounds including the sterols, bile acids, adrenal hormones, etc. [See cholesterol.]

stertorous, *stûr'tər-əs*, *adj.* with snoring sound.— *adv.* ster'torously.—*n.* ster'torousness. [L. *stertēre*, to snore.]

sterve, *stûrv*, *v.t.* and *v.i.* an old form (*Spens.*) of starve, to starve, to die.

stet, *stet*, *v.t.* to restore after marking for deletion: —*pr.p.* stett'ing; *pa.t.* and *pa.p.* stett'ed. [L., let it stand, 3rd sing. pres. subj. of *stāre*, to stand; written on a proof-sheet with dots under the words to be retained.]

stethoscope, *steth'ə-skōp*, *n.* an instrument for auscultation.—*adjs.* stethoscopic (*-skop'ik*), -al.— *adv.* stethoscop'ically.—*ns.* stethoscopist (*-os'kə-pist*); stethos'copy. [Gr. *stēthos*, chest, *skopeein*, to look at, examine.]

Stetson, *stet'sn*, *n.* a broad-brimmed felt hat. [Maker's name.]

stevedore, *stēv'ə-dōr, -dör, n.* one who loads and unloads shipping vessels. [Sp. *estivador*, packer—*estivar*, to stow—L. *stipāre*, to press.]

steven, *stev'n, n.* a voice (now *dial.*): an outcry (*Spens.*). [O.E. *stefn*, voice.]

Stevengraph, *stēv'n-gräf, n.* a silk picture woven in colours. [T. *Stevens*, ribbon weaver.]

stew, *stū, n.* a boiling pot (*Spens., Shak.*): a room for hot-air baths: a hot bath: an overheated or sweaty state: mental agitation: worry: (usu. in *pl.* form with sing. or collective sense) a brothel, or prostitutes' quarter: a prostitute (*obs.*): one who studies hard, esp. unintelligently (*slang*): a dish of stewed food, esp. meat with vegetables. —*v.t.* to bathe in hot air or water: to bathe in sweat: to keep in a swelter or narrow confinement: to simmer or boil slowly with some moisture: to over-infuse.—*v.i.* to swelter: to undergo stewing: to be in a state of worry or agitation: to study hard (*slang*).—*adj.* **stewed**, having been stewed: drunk (*coll.*).—*n.* **stew′er**. —*n.* and *adj.* **stew′ing**.—*adj.* **stew′y**, like a stew: sweltering.—**stew′-can** (*naval slang*), a destroyer; **stew′pan, stew′pot**, one used for stewing.—**let one stew in one's own juice**, leave him alone and await developments, let him reap the consequences of his own actions. [O.Fr. *estuve* (Fr. *étuve*), stove; prob. conn. with **stove**.]

**stew**, *stū*, *n.* a fish-pond: a fish-tank: an artificial oyster-bed.—**stew′pond**. [O.Fr. *estui* (Fr. *étui*).]

**steward**, *stū′ərd*, *n.* one who manages the domestic concerns of a family or institution: one who superintends another's affairs, esp. an estate or farm: the manager of the provision department or attendant on passengers in a ship, aircraft, etc.: a college caterer: one who helps in arrangements, marshalling, etc., at races, a dance, a wedding, an entertainment: an overseer: a foreman: the treasurer of a congregation, guild, society, etc.:—*fem.* **stew′ardess**.—*ns.* **stew′ardship, stew′ardry**, office of a steward: management: the individual's function in the practical work of the Christian church involving obligation to give a share of his time and goods to others; **stew′artry** (*Scot.*), a stewardship, or the extent of a stewardship—still applied nominally to the county of Kirkcudbright.—**Lord High Steward**, one of the great officers of state, and anciently the first officer of the crown in England. [O.E. *stig-weard*—*stig*, hall ('sty'), *weard*, ward, keeper.]

**stey**, *stui, stī*, (*Scot.*) *adj.* steep. [Cf. **stile, stirrup**.]

**sthenic**, *sthen′ik*, *adj.* strong, robust: morbidly active. [Gr. *sthenos*, strength.]

**stibble**, *stib′l*, *n.* a Scots form of **stubble**.—*n.* **stibb′ler**, a horse turned out to feed on stubble: one who cuts the handfuls left by the reaper: a probationer (*Scott*).

**stibium**, *stib′i-əm*, *n.* antimony.—*adj.* **stib′ial**.—*ns.* **stib′ialism**, antimony poisoning; **stib′ine** (-*ēn*, -*īn*), antimony hydride, a poisonous gas; **stib′nite**, native antimony trisulphide. [L.,—Gr. *stibi*, *stimmi*—Egypt. *stm* (Copt. *stēm*).]

**sticcado**, *stik-ä′dō*, **sticcato**, -*tō*, *n.* a kind of xylophone. [Perh. It. *steccato*, palisade.]

**stich**, *stik*, *n.* a line of verse or section of prose of comparable length.—*ns.* **stichar′ion** (Gr. *stichārion*), a Greek vestment like the Western alb; **stichē′ron**, a short hymn.—*adj.* **stich′ic**, of or pertaining to stichs.—*ns.* **stichid′ium**, a branch producing tetraspores, in red seaweeds:—*pl.* **stichid′ia**; **stichol′ogy**, metrical theory.—*adjs.* **stichomet′ric, -al**.—*adv.* **stichomet′rically**.—*ns.* **stichom′etry**, measurement by lines: division into lines: a statement of such measurements; **stichomythia** (-*mith′*; Gr. *stichomȳthiā*), dialogue in alternate lines.—*adj.* **stichomyth′ic**.—*n.* **stich′os**, a line of ordinary length in measuring a manuscript: (*Gr. Ch.*) a verse or versicle:—*pl.* **stich′oi**. [Gr. *stichos*, a row—*steichein*, to march.]

**stick**, *stik*, *v.t.* to pierce, transfix: to stab: to spear: to thrust: to fasten by piercing: to insert: to set in position: to set or cover with things fastened on: to cause to adhere: to endure (esp. with *it*; *coll.*): to bring to a standstill or nonplus.—*v.i.* to be fixed by insertion: to jut, protrude: to adhere: to become or remain fixed: to remain: to be detained by an impediment: to jam: to fail to proceed or advance: to scruple: to hold fast, keep resolutely (with *to*):—*pa.t.* **stuck**, *Scot.* **stack**; *pa.p.* **stuck**, *Scot.* **stick′it**.—*n.* a stoppage: a difficulty: a hitch: adhesiveness.—*n.* **stick′er**, one who kills pigs, etc.: one who or that which sticks: a piercing weapon: a person or thing difficult to

get rid of: one who is constant or persistent: a gummed label or poster: a poser: a piano jack: an upright rod that transmits motion from an organ key.—*adv.* **stick′ily**, in a gluey, muggy, etc., way.—*n.* **stick′iness**.—*n.* and *adj.* **stick′ing**.— *adj.* **stick′y**, adhesive: tenacious: gluey: muggy: difficult (*coll.*): unpleasant (*coll.*).—*v.t.* to make sticky.—**stick′ing-place, -point**, the point at which a thing sticks or stays; **stick′ing-plaster**, an adhesive plaster for closing wounds; **stick′-in-the-mud**, an old fogy.—Also *adj.*—**stickit minister** (*Scot.*), a licentiate who never gets a pastoral charge; **stick′jaw**, a claggy pudding or sweetmeat; **stick′up**, a stand-up collar: a holdup; **stick′y-back**, a gummed photograph; **sticky end**, an unpleasant end, disaster; **sticky wicket**, a difficult situation to cope with.—**stuck′-up′**, self-importantly aloof.—**beat to sticks**, to defeat and surpass utterly; **stick around** (*coll.*), to remain in the vicinity; **stick at**, to hesitate or scruple at (often with *nothing*): to persist at; **stick by**, to be firm in supporting, to adhere closely to; **stick 'em up**, hold up your hands (or be shot); **stick in** (*Scot.*), to persevere assiduously: also (of a dressing, etc.) to adhere to a wound; **stick in one's throat**, to be difficult, or against one's conscience, for one to countenance; **stick it into**, to overcharge systematically; **stick one's neck, chin, cut** (see under **neck**); **stick out**, to project: to be obvious: to continue to resist; **stick out for**, insist upon; **stick to**, to persevere in holding to; **stick together**, to be allies: to support each other; **stick up**, to stand up: to waylay and plunder, as a mailcoach by bushrangers; **stick up for**, to speak or act in defence of; **stick with**, to remain with: to force (a person) to cope with (something unpleasant)—often in passive, i.e. **be stuck with**; **stuck on**, enamoured of. [O.E. *stician*; cf. **stick** (2), **stitch**.]

**stick**, *stik*, *n.* a rod of wood, esp. for walking with or for beating: a twig: a timber tree or trunk: a piece of firewood: a tally: an instrument for beating a percussion instrument: an instrument for playing hockey or other game: a bow for a fiddle, or the wooden part of it: a person of stiff manner: one lacking enterprise: a rod: a control-rod of an aeroplane: a group of bombs, or of paratroops, released at one time from an aeroplane: a piece of furniture (usu. in *pl.*): a ray of a fan: a support for a candle: (in *pl.*) hurdles in steeple-chasing: a printer's composing-stick: a stickful.—*adj.* in the form of a stick: made of sticks.—*v.t.* to furnish or set with sticks: arrange in composing-stick:—*pa.t., pa.p.* **sticked**. —*n.* **stick′ful**, as much as composing-stick holds. —**stick′-in-sect**, twig-like phasmid insect; **stick′-lac**, twigs with attached lac, insects, ova.—**big stick**, force, coercion; **in a cleft stick**, in a dilemma; **right** or **wrong end of the stick**, a true or mistaken understanding of the situation; **the sticks**, rural areas, the backwoods. [O.E. *sticca*; O.N. *stika*.]

**stickle**, *stik′l*, *v.i.* to regulate a contest (*obs.*): to mediate (*obs.*): to interpose (*obs.*): to contend, stand up (with *for*): to be scrupulous or obstinately punctilious.—*v.t.* to compose (*obs.*): to stop contention between (*obs.*): to contend (*obs.*): to scruple.—*n.* **stick′ler**, a regulator or umpire, a mediator (*obs.* exc. *dial.*): a second (*obs.*): a backer (*obs.*): a punctilious and pertinacious insister or contender, esp. for something trifling.—*adj.* or *adv.* **stick′ler-like** (*Shak.*). [Prob. M.E. *stightle*—O.E. *stihtan*, to set in order.]

**stickle**, *stik′l*, (*S.W. dial.*) *adj.* steep: rapid.— *n.* a rapid. [O.E. *sticol*, steep.]

**stickleback**, *stik′l-bak*, *n.* a small spiny-backed river-fish. [O.E. *sticel*, sting, prick, and **back**.]

**stiddie**, *stid′i*. Same as **stithy**.

stie, an old spelling of sty (2 and 3).—stied, sties. See sty (1, 2 and 3).

stieve. Same as steeve (2).

stiff, *stif, adj*. not easily bent: rigid: wanting in suppleness: moved or moving with difficulty or friction: dead: approaching solidity: dense, difficult to mould or cut: resistant: difficult: toilsome: pertinacious: stubborn: formidable: strong: firm, high, or inclining to rise (in price, etc.): excessive: not natural and easy: constrained: formal: keeping upright (*naut.*): certain (not to run, to win, to lose; *slang*): excessively bored (with a pun on *board*). —*adv*. stiffly: stark: very, extremely (*coll.*).—*n*. (*slang*) one who, that which, is stiff: a corpse: a good-for-nothing: negotiable paper: forged paper.—*v.t*. and *v.i*. to make or become stiff or stiffer.—*n*. stiff′ener, one who, or that which stiffens: a strong alcoholic drink (*coll.*): a cigarette-card or the like, used to stiffen a package.—*n*. and *adj*. stiff′ening.—*adj*. stiff′ish. —*adv*. stiff′ly.—*n*. stiff′ness.—stiff′-bit, a jointless bit.—*adj*. stiff′-hearted (*B*.), obstinate, stubborn.—stiff′-neck, a drawing down of the head towards the shoulder, often due to cold or draught: torticollis.—*adj*. stiff′-necked, obstinate: haughty: formal and unnatural.—stiff′-necked′ness.—*adj*. stiff′-rumped, -rumpt (*arch.*), proud, unbending.—stiff upper lip (see lip). [O.E. *stif*, stiff; Du. *stijf*, Ger. *steif*.]

stifle, *sti′fl, v.t*. to stop the breath of by foul air or other means: to make breathing difficult for: to suffocate, smother: to choke down: to suppress: to repress: to make stifling.—*v.i*. to suffocate.— *n*. a stifling atmosphere, smell, or condition.— *adj*. sti′fled.—*n*. sti′fler, one who stifles: the gallows.—*n*. and *adj*. sti′fling (-*fling*).—*adv*. sti′flingly. [Origin obscure.]

stifle, *sti′fl, n*. the joint of a horse, dog, etc., answering to the human knee.—sti′fle-bone, the knee-cap; sti′fle-joint. [Connection with stiff doubtful.]

stigma, *stig′mə, n*. a brand: a mark of infamy: a disgrace or reproach attached to any one: any special mark: a spot: a bleeding spot: a scar: a spot sensitive to light: the part of a carpel that receives pollen (*bot.*): a spiracle: a pore: (in *pl.*) the marks of Christ's wounds or marks resembling them, claimed to have been impressed on the bodies of certain persons, as Francis of Assisi in 1224:—*pl*. stig′mata; also (esp. *bot*. or *fig*. stig′mas.—*n*. Stigmā′ria, the pitted underground part of Sigillaria or other fossil tree.— *adjs*. stigmā′rian (also *n*.); stigmatic (-*mat′ik*), of, pertaining to, of the nature of, a stigma: marked or branded with a stigma: giving infamy or reproach: anastigmatic, or not astigmatic.— *n*. one who has received the stigmata: one who is branded (*Shak. stig′*, with deformity).— *adj*. stigmat′ical.—*adv*. stigmat′ically.—*adj*. stigmatif′erous (*bot.*), stigma-bearing.—*n*. stigmatisā′tion, -z-, act of stigmatising: production of stigmata or bleeding spots upon the body, as by hypnotism.—*v.t*. stig′matise, -ize, to mark with a stigma or the stigmata: to brand, denounce, describe condemnatorily (with *as*).—*ns*. stig′-matism, impression of the stigmata: anastigmatism; stig′matist, one impressed with the stigmata. —*adj*. stig′matose.—*n*. stig′mē, (Gr. *palaeog*.) a dot used as a punctuation mark. [Gr. *stigma*, -*atos*, tattoo-mark, brand, *stigmē*, a point.]

stilb, *stilb, n*. the CGS unit of intrinsic brightness, one candela/cm². [Gr. *stilbein*, to shine.]

stilbite, *stil′bit, n*. a pearly zeolite. [Gr. *stilbein*, to shine.]

stilboestrol, *stil-bēs′trəl, n*. a synthetic oestrogen. [Gk. *stilbos*, glistening and oestrus.]

stile, *stil, n*. a step, or set of steps, for climbing over a wall or fence. [O.E. *stigel*; cf. O.E. *stigan*, Ger. *steigen*, to mount.]

stile, *stil, n*. an upright member in framing or panelling. [Perh. Du. *stijl*, pillar, doorpost.]

stile, an older spelling of style.

stilet. See stylet (under style).

stiletto, *sti-let′ō, n*. a dagger with a narrow blade: a pointed instrument for making eyelet-holes: a stiletto heel:—*pl*. stilett′os.—*v.t*. to stab with a stiletto:—*pr.p*. stilett′oing; *pa.t*. and *pa.p*. stilett′oed.—stiletto heel, a high, thin heel on a woman's shoe.—*adj*. stilett′o-heeled. [It., dim. of *stilo*, a dagger—L. *stilus*, a style.]

still, *stil, adj*. motionless: inactive: silent: calm: quiet: not sparkling or effervescing: continual, constant (*Shak.*).—*v.t*. to quiet: to silence: to appease: to restrain.—*v.i*. to become still.—*adv*. motionlessly: inactively: quietly: always, constantly (*arch.*; so also in many obvious compounds): up to the present time or time in question: as before: yet, even (usu. with a comparative): even so, even then: nevertheless, for all that.—*n*. calm: quiet: an ordinary photograph, not a cinematographic one.—*n*. still′er, one who, or that which, stills or quiets, or prevents splashing over.—*n*. and *adj*. still′ing.—*n*. still′ness.—*adj*. still′y, still: quiet: calm.—*adv*. stil′ly, silently: gently.—still′-birth, birth of the already dead or very nearly dead, as in suspended animation: publication not followed by sales: anything born without life.—*adj*. still′-born, dead, or in suspended animation, when born.— still′-hunt, -hunting (*U.S.*), stalking.—*v.t*. and *v.i*. still′-hunt (*U.S.*).—still′-hunter (*U.S.*).— —still′-life, the class of pictures representing inanimate objects:—*pl*. still-lifes.—Also *adj*.— *adj*. still′-peer′ing (*Shak.*), perh. a misprint for still-piecing (i.e. repairing) or still-piercing.— still′-stand, a standstill (*Shak.*): an armistice (*obs.*).—still and anon (*Shak.*), still and end (*Shak.*), from time to time; still and on (*Scot.*), still and all (*coll.*), nevertheless. [O.E. *stille*, quiet, calm, stable: Du. *stil*, Ger. *still*.]

still, *stil, v.t*. to exude or cause to fall by drops: to distil.—*v.i*. to fall in drops.—*n*. an apparatus for distillation.—*n*. still′er, a distiller.—still′-head, the head of a still; still′-house (*U.S.*), a distillery; still′-room, an apartment where liquors, preserves, and the like are kept, and where tea, etc., is prepared for the table: a housekeeper's pantry; still′-room-maid. [Aphetic for distil.]

stillage, *stil′ij, n*. a frame, stand, or stool for keeping things off the floor: a cask-stand.—*ns*. still′ing, still′ion, a cask-stand. [Prob. Du. *stellage, stelling—stellen*, to place.]

stillatory, *stil′ə-tər-i, n*. a still: a distillery. [L.L. *stillātōrium*—L. *stillāre*, to drip, *stilla*, a drop.]

stillicide, *stil′i-sid, n*. a drip: eavesdrop: an urban servitude allowing one's eavesdrop to fall on a neighbour's ground (otherwise forbidden; *Roman law*). [L. *stillicidium—stilla*, drop, *cadēre*, to fall.]

stilpnosiderite, *stilp-nō-sid′ər-it, n*. limonite. [Gr. *stilpnos*, shining, *sidēros*, iron.]

stilt, *stilt, n*. a thin wooden prop with a foot-rest enabling one to walk above the ground: a tall support: a plough-handle (now *dial.*): a very long-legged wading bird (*Himantopus candidus* or other species) akin to the avocets (also stilt′-bird, -plov′er).—*v.t*. to raise on stilts or as if on stilts. —*adj*. stilt′ed, elevated as if on stilts: stiff and pompous.—*adv*. stilt′edly.—*ns*. stilt′edness; stilt′er; stilt′iness; stilt′ing.—*adjs*. stilt′ish, stilt′y.—stilted arch, an arch that springs from above the capital; stilt′-walker. [M.E. *stilte*; cf. Du. *stelt*, Ger. *stelze*, Sw. *stylta*.]

Stilton, *stil′tən, n*. a rich white, often blue-veined, cheese first sold chiefly at Stilton in Huntingdonshire.

stime, stimie. Same as styme, stymie.

stimulus, *stim′ū-ləs, n*. a sting or stinging hair: an action, influence, or agency that produces a response in a living organism: anything that rouses to action or increased action:—*pl.* **stim'uli**.—*adj.* **stim'ulable**, responsive to stimulus. —*n.* **stim'ulancy**.—*adj.* **stim'ulant**, stimulating: increasing or exciting vital action.—*n.* anything that stimulates or excites: a stimulating drug: alcoholic liquor.—*v.t.* **stim'ulate**, to incite: to instigate: to excite: to produce increased action in (*physiol.*).—*adj.* **stim'ulating**.—*n.* **stimulā'tion**.— *adj.* **stim'ulātive**, tending to stimulate.—*n.* that which stimulates or excites.—*n.* **stim'ulātor**, one who stimulates: an instrument for applying a stimulus. [L. *stimulus*, a goad.]

**sting**, *sting*, *n.* in some plants and animals a weapon (hair, modified ovipositor, fin-ray, tooth, etc.) that pierces and injects poison: the act of inserting a sting: the pain or the wound caused: any sharp, tingling, or irritating pain or its cause (also *fig.*): the point of an epigram: stinging power: pungency: a goad: an incitement.—*v.t.* to pierce, wound, pain, or incite with or as if with a sting: to cause or allow anything to sting: to rob, cheat, or involve in expense (*slang*).—*v.i.* to have or use a power of stinging: to have a stinging feeling:—*pa.t.* and *pa.p.* **stung**.—*adj.* **stinged**, having a sting.—*n.* **sting'er**, one who, or that which, stings: anything stinging or pungent.—*n.* and *adj.* **sting'ing**.—*adv.* **sting'ingly**.—*adj.* **sting'less**.—**sting-bull, -fish**, the weever; **sting'-ray** (*U.S.* and *Austr.* **stingaree,** *sting'gə-rē, -ə-rē,* or *-rē'*), a ray (Trygon, etc.) with a formidable barbed dorsal spine on its tail. [O.E. *sting*, puncture, *stingan*, to pierce.]

**sting**, *sting*, (*Scot.*) *n.* a pole.—**sting and ling**, with a rope slung from a pole: by force (*fig.*). [O.E. *steng*.]

**stingaree.** See sting (1).

**stinger.** Same as stengah.

**stingo**, *sting'gō*, *n.* strong malt liquor: vigour, punch. [sting.]

**stingy**, *stin'ji*, *adj.* niggardly: ill-tempered (*dial.*). —*adv.* **stin'gily**.—*n.* **stin'giness**. [Prob. sting.]

**stink**, *stingk*, *v.i.* to give out a strong, offensive smell: to be offensive, have a bad reputation, suggest or imply evil or dishonesty (*fig.*).— *v.t.* to impart a bad smell to: to drive by an ill smell:—*pa.t.* **stank, stunk**; *pa.p.* **stunk**.— *n.* an offensive smell: (in *pl.*) chemistry or science, a science master (*slang*).—*ns.* **stink'ard**, one who stinks: a base fellow: the stinking badger of Java; **stink'er**, one who, or that which, stinks: a disagreeable person or thing (*coll.*): a stinkard: a petrel of offensive smell.— *adj.* **stink'ing**, which stinks: very, extremely (*coll.*).—Also *n.*—*adv.* **stink'ingly**.—**stink'-ball, -pot,** a ball or jar filled with a stinking, combustible mixture, used in boarding an enemy's vessel; **stink'-bird**, the hoatzin; **stink'-bomb,** a usually small bomb which releases ill-smelling gases when exploded; **stink'-brand**, bunt; **stink'horn,** a stinking gasteromycete fungus, *Phallus impudicus*; **stink'stone,** a limestone that gives a fetid urinous smell when rubbed; **stink'-trap,** a stench-trap; **stink'-wood,** the ill-smelling wood of various trees, esp. the lauraceous *Ocotea bullata* of S. Africa.—**raise a stink**, to complain: to cause trouble, esp. disagreeable publicity. [O.E. *stincan*, to smell (well or ill).]

**stint**, *stint*, *v.t.* to stop (*obs.*): to restrain (*arch.* or *dial.*): to check: to limit: to apportion (esp. pasturage): to allot: to set as a task or as a day's work: to restrict (*obs.*): to keep short: to be niggardly with or towards: to allot stingily: to spare: to serve successfully, get with foal, lamb, etc.—*v.i.* to cease, stop (*obs.*): to be sparing, go short (*dial.*).—*n.* cessation (*obs.*): limit (*obs.*): restraint, restriction: proportion alloted, fixed amount: allowance: a set task: a (conventional) day's work.—*adj.* **stint'ed**.—*adv.* **stint'edly**.—*ns.* **stint'edness**; **stint'er**.—*n.* and

*adj.* **stint'ing**.—*adv.* **stint'ingly**.—*adj.* **stint'less**; **stint'y**. [O.E. *styntan*, to dull—*stunt*, stupid; cf. **stent, stunt**.]

**stint**, *stint*, *n.* the dunlin or other small sandpiper. [Origin obscure.]

**Stipa**, *stī'pə*, *n.* the feather-grass genus. , [L. *stipa*, tow.]

**stipe**, *stīp*, *n.* a stalk, esp. of a fungal fruit-body, a fern-leaf, a pappus, or an ovary.—Also **stipes** (*stī'pēz*; L. *stē'pes*; *pl.* **stipites**, *stip'i-tēz*; L. *stē'pi-tās*).—*adj.* **stipitate** (*stip'*). [L. *stipes, -itis*, post, stock.]

**stipel**, *stī'pl*, *n.* a stipule-like appendage at the base of a leaflet.—*adj.* **stipellate** (*stī'pəl-āt, stip-el'āt*), having stipels. [Dim. from **stipule**.]

**stipend**, *stī'pand*, *n.* a soldier's pay: a salary, esp. a Scottish parish minister's (*Scot. stēp'ənd*): a periodical allowance.—*adj.* **stipendiary** (*stī-, sti-pen'di-ə-ri*), receiving stipend.—*n.* one who performs services for a salary, esp. a paid magistrate.—*v.t.* **stipen'diate**, to provide with a salary. [L. *stipendium*—*stips*, payment, dole, *pendēre*, to weigh.]

**stipple**, *stip'l*, *v.t.* to engrave, paint, draw, etc., in dots or separate touches.—*n.* painting, engraving, etc., in this way: the effect so produced: a brush for stippling.—*adj.* **stipp'led**.—*ns.* **stipp'ler; stipp'ling**. [Du. *stippelen*, dim. of *stippen*, to dot.]

**stipulate**, *stip'ū-lāt*, *v.t.* to set or require as a condition or essential part of an agreement: to guarantee (*rare*).—*v.i.* to make stipulations: to become surety (*obs.*).—*ns.* **stipulā'tion**, act of stipulating: a contract: a condition of agreement: a requiring of such a condition; **stip'-ulator**.—*adj.* **stip'ulatory** (*-ə-tər-i*). [L. *stipulāri, -ātus*, prob.—Old L. *stipulus*, firm, conn. *stipāre*, press firm.]

**stipule**, *stip'ūl*, *n.* a paired, usu. leafy, appendage at a leaf-base.—*adjs.* **stipulā'ceous, stip'ular, -y; stip'ulāte, stip'uled**. [L. *stipula*, straw, stalk, dim. of *stipes*; new meaning assigned by Linnaeus.]

**stir**, *stûr* (*Scot.* **steer, stēr**, *Spens.* **stire, styre, stir**), *v.t.* to set in motion: to move around: to disturb: to rouse: to move to activity: to excite: to moot.—*v.i.* to make a movement: to begin to move: to go about: to be active or excited: (esp. in *pr.p.*) to be out of bed: to go forth:— *pr.p.* **stirr'ing**; *pa.t.* and *pa.p.* **stirred**.—*n.* movement: slight movement: activity: commotion: sensation: an act of stirring.—*adjs.* **stir'less**, without stir; **stirred**.—*n.* **stirr'er**.—*n.* and *adj.* **stirr'ing**.—*adv.* **stirr'ingly**.—**stir'about** (*Anglo-Ir.*) porridge: a bustling or stirring person.—*adj.* busy, active.—**stir abroad, forth, out,** to go out of doors; **stir up**, to excite: to incite: to arouse: to mix by stirring. [O.E. *styrian*; Du. *storen*, Ger. *stören*, to disturb.]

**stir**, *stûr*, **stirra(h)**, *stir'ə* (*Scot.*), *ns.* app. corruptions of **sir, sirrah**, applied to both sexes.

**stir**, *stûr*, (*slang*) *n.* prison. [Perh. O.E. *stēor*, *stŷr*, punishment.]

**stire**, *stir*, a Spens. form of **steer** and **stir**.

**stirk**, *stûrk*, *n.* a yearling or young ox or cow. [O.E. *stirc*, calf.]

**Stirling engine**, a closed-cycle external-combustion engine using heated air (devised by Dr Robert *Stirling*, d. 1878), or a more sophisticated 20th-cent. version using, e.g. helium under pressure.

**stirps**, *stûrps*, *n.* family, race: a permanent variety: pedigree:—*pl.* **stirpes** (*stûr'pēz*; L. *stir'pās*).—Also **stirp**:—*pl.* **stirps**.—*n.* **stirp'i-culture**, selective breeding. [L. *stirps, stirpis*.]

**stirre.** See **sperre**.

**stirrup**, *stir'əp*, *n.* a support for a rider's foot: a foot-rest, clamp, support, of more or less similar shape: the stirrup-bone: a rope secured to a yard, having a thimble in its lower end for reeving a foot-rope.—**stirr'up-bone**, the stapes; **stirr'up-cup**, a cup (not paid for) taken on horseback on departing, or arriving (also **stirr′up-dram**): a vessel in the form of a fox's head from which a stirrup-cup was drunk (*rare*); **stirr′up-iron**, the metal part of a stirrup, usu. reckoned the stirrup itself; **stirr′up-leath′er, -strap**, the strap of a stirrup; **stirr′up-pump**, a portable pump held in position by the foot in a rest. [O.E. *stigrāp*—*stigan*, to mount, *rāp*, rope.]

**stitch**, *stich, n.* a sharp pricking pain, now esp. in the intercostal muscles: a complete movement of the needle in sewing, knitting, surgery, or the like: a loop or portion of thread, etc., so used: a mode of stitching: a fastening with thread or wire through all sections (*bookbinding*): the least scrap of clothing, sails, etc.: a ridge of land (*dial.*): a shock of corn (*dial.*).—*v.t.* to join, adorn, or enclose, with stitches.—*v.t.* to sew.—*adj.* **stitched.**—*ns.* **stitch′er; stitch′ery** (*Shak.*), needlework; **stitch′ing.**—**stitch′craft**, the art of needlework; **stitch′wort**, any plant of the chickweed genus (Stellaria), once thought good for stitches in the side.—**in stitches**, in pained helplessness with laughter. [O.E. *stice*, prick; cf. **stick.**]

**stithy**, *stidh′i*, **stiddie**, *stid′i, ns.* an anvil: a smithy.—*v.t.* to forge on an anvil. [O.N. *stethi*; Sw. *städ*, an anvil.]

**stive**, *stiv*, (*dial.*) *v.t.* and *v.i.* to stifle.—*adjs.* **stived, stived′-up**, without fresh air; **stiv′y**, stuffy. [Cf. **stew.**]

**stiver**, *sti′vər, n.* a Dutch penny: a very small coin or sum. [Du. *stuiver.*]

**stoa**, *stō′ə, n.* a portico or covered colonnade: esp. the Painted Porch (see **porch**):—*pl.* **sto′as, sto′ai** (*-i*). [Gr. *stoā.*]

**stoat**, *stōt, n.* a larger weasel, with black-tipped tail, called ermine in its northern winter coat. [M.E. *stote.*]

**stob**, *stob*, (*Scot.*) *n.* a stake, stump, or stub: an awl. [Variant of **stub.**]

**stoccado**, *stok-ä′dō*, **stoccata**, *-ta, n.* a thrust in fencing. [It. *stoccata*, thrust—*stocco*, rapier—Ger. *stock*, stick.]

**stochastic**, *stə-kas′tik, adj.* conjectural (*obs.*): random. [Gr. *stochastikos*, skilful in aiming.]

**stock**, *stok, n.* a trunk or main stem: the perennial part of a herbaceous plant: the rooted trunk that receives a graft: a log: a post: a block: a stump: an upright beam: anything fixed, solid and senseless: a stupid person: a part, usually massive, to which others are attached: an intrusive boss (*geol.*): the wooden part of a gun: a handle: stock-gillyflower (see below; **Virginia stock**, a Mediterranean, not Virginian, cruciferous garden plant, Malcolmia): a stocking (also **neth′erstock**; the **upp′er-stock** being the upper part of a hose when separate): a stiff band worn as a cravat, often fastened with a buckle at the back: a fireside ledge (*dial.*): (in *pl.*) a device for holding a delinquent by the ankles, and often wrists: (in *pl.*) a framework on which a ship is built: a box or trough: cross-piece of an anchor: the original progenitor: source: race: kindred: family: a fund: capital of a company, divisible into shares: repute, estimation (*fig.*): shares of a public debt: (in *pl.*) public funds: a tally for money paid to the exchequer (*obs.*): supply, store, equipment: the animals kept on a farm: supply of goods for sale: the undealt part of a pack of cards or set of dominoes: raw material, as foundation for soap, etc.: liquor from simmered meat, bones, etc.—*v.t.* to store: to keep for sale: to put in the stocks: to fit with a stock: to supply or furnish with stock (e.g. a river with fish): to keep unmilked before selling: to root up: to stunt.—*adj.* concerned with stock or stocks: kept in stock: conventionally used, standard: hence banal, trite: used for breeding purposes.—*adv.* **stock′ily.**—*n.* **stock′iness.**—*adj.* **stock′ish**,

resembling a stock, stupid.—*ns.* **stock′ishness**; **stock′ist**, one who keeps a commodity in stock. —*adjs.* **stock′less**; **stock′y**, thickset, strong-stemmed.—**stock′-breeder**, one who raises livestock; **stock′-breeding**; **stock′broker**, a stock exchange member who buys and sells stocks or shares for clients; **stock′broking; stock company**, a permanent repertory company attached to a theatre; **stock′-dove**, a dove like a small wood-pigeon—from nesting in stumps or rabbit-holes, or from representing (as wrongly supposed) the ancestor of the domestic breeds; **stock exchange**, a building for the buying and selling of stocks and shares: an association of persons transacting such business; **stock′-farmer**, a farmer who rears livestock; **stock′-feeder**, one who fattens livestock; **stock′-gill′yflower**, now usu. **stock**, a favourite cruciferous garden plant (*Matthiola incana*; from its half-shrubby character); **stock′holder**, one who holds stocks in the public funds, or in a company; **stock′-in-trade**, all the goods a shopkeeper has for sale: standard equipment or devices necessary for a particular trade or profession: a person's basic intellectual and emotional resources (often implying inadequacy or triteness); **stock′-jobber**, a stock exchange member who deals only with other members (in some special group of securities): a stockbroker (*U.S.*): an unscrupulous speculator; **stock′-jobbery, -jobbing; stock′-list**, a list of stocks and current prices regularly issued; **stock′-lock**, a lock with wooden case; **stock′man** (esp. *Austr.*), man in charge of farm-stock; **stock′-market**, a stock exchange: stock exchange business; **stock′pile**, heap of road-metal, ore, etc.: reserve supply.—Also *v.t.*—**stock′piling**, accumulating reserves, as of raw materials; **stock′-pot**, the pot in which the stock for soup is kept.—*adj.* **stock′-pun′isht** (*Shak.*), put in the stocks.—**stock′-raising**, breeding of stock; **stock′-rider** (*Austr.*), a mounted herdsman; **stock′-room**, a store-room: a room in a hotel for display of commercial travellers' wares; **stock′-saddle**, a cowboy's saddle.—*adj.* and *adv.* **stock′-still**, still as a post or stock.—**stock′taking**, inventorying and valuation of stock; **stock′-whip**, a herdsman's whip with short handle and long lash; **stock′yard**, a large yard with pens, stables, etc., where cattle are kept for slaughter, market, etc.—**on the stocks**, in preparation; **stockbrokers′ Tudor** (*archit.*), imitation Tudor; **stock-car racing**, motor racing in which ordinary cars are used, not cars built as racers; **stocks and stones**, inanimate idols; **take stock (of)**, to make an inventory of goods on hand: to make an estimate of; **take stock in**, to trust to, attach importance to. [O.E. *stocc*, a stick; Ger. *stock*.]

**stock**, *stok*, (*Shak.*) *n.* a stoccado. [It. *stocco*, rapier.]

**stockade**, *stok-ād′, n.* a barrier of stakes.—*v.t.* to defend with a stockade. [Fr. *estacade*—Sp. *estacada*; cf. **stake.**]

**stock-and-horn**, *stok′-ənd-hörn, n.* an old Scottish musical instrument made of a cow's horn, a sheep's thigh bone or elder pipe with stops, and an oaten reed. [O.E. (Northumbrian) *stocc*, trumpet.]

**stockfish**, *stok′fish, n.* unsalted dried hake, cod, etc., commonly beaten with a stick before cooking. [Prob. Du. *stokvisch*.]

**stocking**, *stok′ing n.* a close covering for the foot and lower leg: distinctive colouring or feathering of an animal's leg: a hoard of savings.—*n.* **stockinet′, -ette′, stockingette′**, an elastic knitted fabric for undergarments, etc.—*adj.* **stock′-inged**, wearing stockings (but usu. not shoes).—*n.* **stock′inger** (*-ing-ər*), a maker of stockings.—*adj.* **stock′ingless.**—*ns.* **stock′ing-foot**, the foot of a stocking; **stock′ing-frame**, a knitting-machine;

Neutral vowels in unaccented syllables: *el′ə-mənt*; for certain sounds in foreign words, see p. viii

stock′ing-sole′.—in one's stocking-feet, -soles, with stockings but no shoes. [stock, in sense of **netherstock**.]

**stockwork**, *stok′wərk*, *n.* a mass of veins, impregnations, etc., that can be worked as one deposit. [Anglicised from Ger. *stockwerk*.]

**stodge**, *stoj*, *v.t.* to stuff, cram, gorge: to sate: to bog.—*v.i.* to trudge: to plod.—*n.* claggy stuff: heavy, often uninteresting, meal.—*n.* **stodg′er**, a heavy, dull, spiritless, or unenterprising person. *adv.* **stodg′ily.**—*n.* **stodg′iness.**—*adj.* **stodg′y**, heavy and claggy: solemnly dull. [Perh. imit.]

**stoep**, *stōōp*, *(S.Afr.)* *n.* a platform along the front, and sometimes the sides, of a house: a verandah. [Du.; cf. **step**.]

**Stoic**, *stō′ik*, *n.* a disciple of the philosopher Zeno (d. *c.* 261 B.C.), who taught in the *Stoa Poikilē* (Painted Porch) at Athens.—*adjs.* **Stō′ic, -al**, pertaining to the Stoics, or to their opinions: (without *cap.*) indifferent to pleasure or pain. —*adv.* **stō′ically.**—*ns.* **stō′icalness**; **stō′icism** (*-sizm*), the philosophy of the Stoics: indifference to pleasure or pain: limitation of wants: austere impassivity. [Gr. *Stōikos—stōä*, a porch.]

**stoich(e)iometry**, *stoi-ki-om′i-tri*, *n.* the branch of chemistry that deals with the numerical proportions in which substances react. [Gr. *stoicheion*, an element, *metron*, measure.]

**stoit**, *stoit*, *(Scot.)* *v.i.* to stumble, lurch.—*v.i.* **stoit′er** *(Scot.)*, to stagger. [Perh. Du. *stuiten*, to bounce.]

**stoke**, *stōk*, *v.t.* to feed with fuel.—*v.i.* to act as stoker.—*n.* **stok′er**, one who, or that which, feeds a furnace with fuel.—**stoke′hold**, a ship's furnace chamber: a stoke-hole; **stoke′-hole**, the space about the mouth of a furnace: the space allotted to the stokers: a hole in a reverberatory furnace for introducing a stirring-tool.—**stoke up**, to make a good meal. [Du. *stoker*, stoker—*stoken*, to stoke.]

**stokes**, *stōks*, *n.* the CGS unit of kinematic viscosity.—Also (esp. *U.S.*) **stoke**. [Sir G. **Stokes** (1819-1903), British physicist.]

**stole**, *stōl*, *pa.t.* and obs. *pa.p.* of **steal**.

**stole**, *stōl*, *n.* a long robe: a narrow vestment worn on the shoulders, hanging down in front: a woman's outer garment of similar form: loosely, a gown, a surplice.—Also (L.) **stō′la** (L. *stol′a*).— *adj.* **stoled** (*stōld*), wearing a stole. [O.E. *stole*— L. *stŏla*, a Roman matron's long robe—Gr. *stolē*, equipment, garment—*stellein*, to array.]

**stole**. See **stolon, stool**.

**stolen**, *stōl′ən*, *pa.p.* of **steal**.—Also *adj.*—*adv.* **stol′enwise**, by stealth.

**stolid**, *stol′id*, *adj.* impassive: blockish: unemotional.—*ns.* **stolid′ity, stol′idness**.—*adv.* **stol′-idly**. [L. *stolidus*.]

**stolon**, *stō′lən*, *n.* a shoot from the base of a plant, rooting and budding at the nodes (also **stole**): a stemlike structure or budding outgrowth from a colony (*zool.*).—*adj.* **stōlonif′erous**, producing stolons. [L. *stolō, -ōnis*, twig, sucker.]

**stoma**, *stō′mə*, *n.* a mouthlike opening, esp. one (including its guard-cells or not) by which gases pass through the epidermis of green parts of a plant:—*pl.* **stō′mata**.—*adjs.* **stomatal** (*stōm′*, *stom′ə-tl*), **stomat′ic**.—*ns.* **stomati′tis**, inflammation of the mucous membrane of the mouth; **stomatodaeum** (*-dē′əm*), **stomodae′um** (Gr. *hodaios*, on the way), in embryology, the invagination that forms the anterior part of the digestive tract.—*adj.* **stomatogas′tric**, of, pertaining to, the mouth and stomach, or the upper alimentary tract.—*ns.* **stomatol′ogy**, study of the mouth; **stom′atopod**, a crustacean of the order **Stomatop′oda**, the mantis shrimps, with legs mostly near the mouth. [Gr. *stŏma, -atos*, mouth.]

**stomach**, *stum′ək*, *n.* the strong muscular bag into which food passes when swallowed, and where it is principally digested: the cavity in any animal for the digestion of its food: loosely or euphemistically, the belly: appetite, relish for food, inclination generally: disposition, spirit, courage, pride, spleen.—*v.t.* to brook or put up with: to digest: to turn the stomach of (*arch*): to resent (*arch.*): to find offensive (*arch.*).—*adj.* of the stomach.—*adjs.* **stom′achal**; **stom′ached**. —*ns.* **stom′acher** (*-char, -kər*), a covering or ornament for the chest, esp. one worn under the lacing of a bodice; **stom′achful**, as much as the stomach will hold (*pl.* **stom′achfuls**).—*adj.* spirited: haughty: obstinate: resentful: angry. —*n.* **stom′achfulness**.—*adj.* **stomachic** (*stəmak′ik*), of the stomach: good for the stomach.— *n.* a stomachic medicine.—*adjs.* **stomach′ical**; **stom′achless; stom′achous** (*Spens.*), resentful: haughty: spirited: courageous; **stom′achy**, haughty: easily offended: spirited: paunchy.— **stom′ach-ache**; **stom′ach-pump**, a syringe with a flexible tube for withdrawing fluids from the stomach, or injecting them into it. [O.Fr. *estomac*, L. *stomachus*, Gr. *stomachos*, throat, later stomach—*stoma*, a mouth.]

**stomp**, *stomp*, *v.i.* to stamp (*coll.*): to dance (*coll.*).—*n.* an early jazz composition with heavily accented rhythm: a lively dance with foot stamping: a stamp (*coll.*). [Variant of **stamp**.]

**-stomy**, *-stəm-i*, in composition, used in naming a surgical operation to form a new opening into an organ. [Gr. *stoma*, a mouth.]

**stond**, *stond*, *n.* a Spens. form of **stand**.

**stone**, *stōn*, *n.* a detached piece of rock, usu. small: the matter of which rocks consist: a gem: a mirror (*Shak.*): a tombstone: a printer's table for imposing: a concretion: a diseased state characterised by formation of a concretion in the body: (now *slang*) a testicle: a hard fruit kernel: a hailstone: (with *pl.* **stone**) a standard weight of 14 lb. avoirdupois (other stones have been in use, as that of 24 lb. for wool, 22 lb. for hay, 16 lb. for cheese, etc.).—*adj.* of stone: of stoneware: of the Stone Age: not castrated.— *v.t.* to pelt with stones: to free from stones: to lay or wall with stones: to rub or sharpen with a stone: to turn to stone (*Shak.*).—*v.i.* to form a stone.—*adjs.* **stoned**, having, containing, or freed from, a stone or stones: very drunk, or very high on drugs (*slang*); **stone′less**; **ston′en**, **ston′ern** (*obs.* or *dial.*), of stone.—*n.* **ston′er**, one who stones: one who weighs, or a horse that carries, so many stone.—*adv.* **ston′ily.**—*n.* **ston′iness.**—*adj.* **ston′y**, of or like stone: abounding with stones: hard: pitiless: obdurate: rigid: petrifying: stony-broke.—**Stone Age**, a stage of culture before the general use of metal, divided into the Old Stone Age (Palaeolithic) and the New (Neolithic); **stone axe**, one made of stone: (with hyphen) two-edged axe for cutting stone.—*adj.* **stone′-blind**, completely blind.—**stone boat** (*U.S.*), low sled for carrying rocks or other heavy objects; **stone′-boiling**, boiling water by putting hot stones in it; **stone′-borer**, **-eater**, any boring mollusc; **stone′-bow**, a cross-bow or catapult for shooting stones; **stone′-bramble**, a bramble (*Rubus saxatilis*) of rocky places; **stone′-brash**, a soil of finely-broken rock; **stone′-break**, saxifrage; **stone′-breaker**, one who, or that which, breaks stones: a stone-crushing machine; **stone′-bruise**, a bruise caused by a stone, esp. on the sole of the foot; **stone′-canal**, a calcified vertical tube in the water-vascular system of echinoderms; **stone′-cast** (or **stone′s cast**), a stone-throw; **stone′-cell** (*bot.*), a cell not much longer than broad with thick lignified walls; **stone′chat**, a little black, ruddy and white bird of furzy places, with a note like the clicking of two stones (also stone'-chatter); stone circle, a circle of standing-stones; stone'-coal, mineral coal, as opp. to charcoal: any hard coal: anthracite.—*adj.* stone'-cold', cold as a stone.—*n.* and *adj.* stone'-colour, grey.—*adj.* stone'-coloured.—stone'crop, any plant of the wall-pepper genus (Sedum); stone'-cur'lew, a large plover, the thick-knee; stone'-cutter, one who hews stone; stone'-cutting.—*adjs.* stone'-dead, stone'-deaf, dead, deaf, as a stone.—stone'-dresser, one who prepares stones for building; stone'-fal'con, -hawk, the merlin; stone'-fly, a plecopterous insect (Perla) whose larvae live under stones in streams; stone'-fruit, a fruit with a stone; stone'-hammer, a hammer for breaking stones: (without *hyphen*) a hammer with a stone head. —*adj.* stone'-hard (*Shak.*), as hard as a stone. —stone'horse, a stallion; stone'-lil'y, an encrinite; stone'-mar'ten, a white-breasted marten, the beech-marten; stone'-ma'son, a mason who works with stone; stone'-mill, a machine for breaking stone; stone'-oil, petroleum; stone'-pine, a Mediterranean nut-pine; stone'-pit, a quarry; stone'-plov'er, the stone-curlew; stone'-rag, -raw (O.E. *ragu*, lichen), a lichen *Parmelia saxatilis*, yielding a dye; stone'shot, a stone-throw: stones or a stone used as shot; stone'-snipe, an American plover; stone'(s)'-throw, the distance a stone may be thrown.—*adv.* and *adj.* stone'-still (*Shak.*), as still as a stone.—stone'wall, parliamentary obstruction (*Austr.*): defensive play in cricket.—*v.i.* to obstruct: to block: to offer wall-like resistance. —stone'wall'er; stonewall'ing; stone'ware, a coarse kind of potter's ware baked hard and glazed: a high-fired, vitrified, non-porous ceramic material or objects made of it; stone'-work, work in stone; stone'wort, any plant of the Characeae (from the limy crust): an umbelliferous plant (*Sison amomum*) akin to parsley.—*adjs.* ston'y-broke' (*slang*), penniless, or nearly so (also ston'y, stone'-broke'); ston'y-heart'ed, hard-hearted.—leave no stone unturned, to do everything that can be done in order to secure the effect desired; mark with a white stone, to mark as particularly fortunate. [O.E. *stān*; Ger. *stein*, Du. *steen*.]

stong, stonn(e), old forms of stung, stains.

stonker, *stong'kər* (*slang*), *v.t.* to kill, destroy, overthrow, thwart.—*n.* stonk (*stongk*; *mil. slang*), back-formation), intense bombardment. [Ety. dub.]

stony, *ston'i*, (*obs.*) *v.t.* aphetic for astony (see astonish); *pa.p.*, *Spens.*, ston'ied).

stony. See stone.

stood, *stood*, *pa.t.* and *pa.p.* of stand.

stooge, *stōōj*, (*slang*) *n.* a performer speaking from the auditorium: an actor's feeder: a stage butt: a subordinate or drudge: a scapegoat.—Also *v.i.*—stooge around, to wander about leisurely, purposelessly, or idly. [Origin unknown.]

stook, *stook*, *n.* a shock of sheaves, set up in the field.—*v.t.* to set up in stooks.—*n.* stook'er. [Cf. L.G. *stuke*, bundle.]

stool, *stool*, *n.* a chair, seat of authority or dignity, throne (*obs.*): a seat without a back: a low support for the feet or knees: a seat used in evacuating the bowels: defecation: faeces: a stand: a stump from which sprouts shoot up: a growth of shoots: the wicket in stoolball: a piece of wood to which a bird is fastened as a decoy.—*v.i.* to evacuate the bowels: to put forth shoots.—stool'ball, an old game resembling cricket; stool'-pigeon, a decoy-pigeon: a decoy: an informer.—fall between two stools, to lose both possibilities by hesitating between them, or trying for both; groom of the stole (an old form of stool), formerly an officer over the lords of the bedchamber; stool of repentance, a place in church where delinquents, esp. fornicators,

were exposed. [O.E. *stōl*; Ger. *stuhl*; cf. Ger. *stellen*, to place.]

stoop, *stōōp*, *v.i.* to bend the body forward: to lean forward: to submit: to descend from rank or dignity: to condescend: to lower oneself by unworthy behaviour: to swoop down, as a bird of prey.—*v.t.* to bend, incline, lower, or direct downward.—*n.* a bending of the body: inclination forward: descent: condescension: a swoop. —*adj.* stooped, having a stoop, bent.—*n.* stoop'er.—*adj.* stoop'ing.—*adv.* stoop'ingly.—stoop'-gallant (*obs.*), that which humbles gallants, orig. the sweating-sickness.—Also *adj.* (*Spens.* stoope-gallaunt). [O.E. *stūpian*; O.N. *stūpa*; the vowel preserved by the following *p.*]

stoop, stoope. See stoup.

stoop. American spelling of stoep.

stoop, stoup, *stōōp*, *n.* a post (*dial.*): a prop, supporter, patron (*Scot.*): a massive supporting pillar of coal in a mine (*dial.*).—stoop and roop, stoup and roup (*Scot.*), stump and rump, completely. [O.N. *stolpi*, post.]

stoor, stour, *stōōr*, sture, *stūr*, stowre, *stowr*, (*obs.*) *adj.* great, formidable: stiff, harsh, austere. [Partly M.E. *stūr*, harsh (cf. M.L.G. *stūr*), partly O.E. *stōr*, great.]

stoor, *stōōr*. See stour (2).

stop, *stop*, *v.t.* to snuff, block, plug, choke, close up: to thrust, cram (*obs.* except as Scots stap): to obstruct: to render impassable: to hinder or prevent the passage of: to bring to a standstill: to bring down, hit with a shot: to cause to cease: to counter: to restrain: to withhold: to hinder: to prevent: to cease from, leave off, discontinue: to limit the vibrating length of, esp. by pressure of a finger (*mus.*): to pinch off (*hort.*): to punctuate: to place a pause in, esp. at the end of a line or couplet (*pros.*): to adjust the aperture of, with a diaphragm: to make fast by lashing (*naut.*).—*v.i.* to come to a standstill, halt: to cease: to desist: to come to an end: to stay, tarry, sojourn (*coll.*):—*pr.p.* stopp'ing; *pa.t.* and *pa.p.* stopped.—*n.* act of stopping: state of being stopped: cessation: a halt: a pause: a halting-place: hindrance: obstacle: interruption: a contrivance that limits motion: a card that interrupts the run of play: a diaphragm: the stopping of an instrument or string: a fret on a lute or guitar: a finger-hole, a key for covering it, or other means of altering pitch or tone: a set of organ pipes of uniform tone quality: a knob operating a lever for bringing them into use: mechanism on a harpsichord for bringing particular strings into play: a sound requiring complete closure of the breath passage, a mute (*phon.*): a punctuation mark.—*adj.* stop'less.—*n.* stopp'age, act of stopping: state of being stopped: obstruction: an amount stopped off pay.—*adj.* stopped.—*n.* stopp'er, one who stops: that which stops: a plug: a plug (usu. glass) for a bottle: a short rope for making something fast (*naut.*).—*v.t.* to close or secure with a stopper.—*ns.* stopp'ing, the action of one who or that which stops in any sense (double stopping, simultaneous stopping of and playing on two strings): stuffing or filling material, esp. for teeth.—stop-cock, a short pipe opened and stopped by turning a key or handle: loosely, the key or handle; stop'-gap, a temporary expedient or substitute.—*adj.* stop'-go', (of policy) alternately discouraging and encouraging forward movement.—stop'-off, stop'-o'ver, a break of journey; stopp'ing-out, use in places of a protective covering against acids in etching, against light in photography; stopp'ing-place; stop'-press, late news inserted in a newspaper after printing has begun: a space for it.—Also *adj.*—stop'-watch, an accurate watch readily started and stopped, used in timing a race, etc.—pull out all the stops, to express with as much emotion as possible: to act with great energy; **pull out a** (specified) **stop,** to emphasise a (specified) emotional element in a situation; **stop off, stop over,** to break one's journey; **stop thief,** a cry for help to catch a thief. [O.E. *stoppian,* found in the compound *forstoppian,* to stop up—L. *stuppa,* tow—Gr. *styppē.*]

**stope,** *stōp, n.* a step-like excavation in mining.— *v.t.* to excavate, or extract in this way.—*n.* **stop'ing.** [Perh. conn. with **step.**]

**stopple,** *stop'l, n.* a stopper: a plug.—*v.t.* to stopper, plug. [**stop.**]

**stopple,** *stop'l, n.* a tobacco-pipe stem—*Scot.* **stapp'le.** [M.Du. *stapel,* stem.]

**storax,** *stō'raks, stō', n.* the resin of *Styrax officinalis,* once used in medicine: now that of *Liquidambar orientale* (*liquid storax*). [L. *storax*—Gr. *stÿrax.*]

**store,** *stōr, stör, n.* a hoard: a stock laid up: sufficiency or abundance: keeping: a store-house: a shop: a co-operative shop or one with many departments or branches: an animal fattening for the market: value, esteem: a computer memory unit, in which programme and data are stored: (in *pl.*) supplies of provisions, ammunition, etc., for an army, ship, etc.—*adj.* and *adv.* (*arch.*) in abundance.—*adj.* of a store: sold in a shop, ready-made.—*v.t.* to stock, furnish, supply: to lay up, keep in reserve: to deposit in a repository: to give storage to: to put (data) into a computer memory.—*adj.* **stor'able.**—*ns.* **stor'age,** placing, accommodation, reservation, or safe-keeping, in store: reservation in the form of potential energy: charge for keeping goods in store; **stör'er.**—**storage battery,** an accumulator; **store'-cattle,** cattle kept for fattening; **store'-farm** (*Scot.*), a stock-farm, a cattle-farm; **store'-farmer; store'house,** a house for storing goods of any kind: a repository: a treasury; **store'-keeper,** a man in charge of stores: a shopkeeper (chiefly *U.S.*): an unsaleable article (*U.S.*); **store'room,** a room in which stores are kept: space for storing; **store'-ship,** a vessel used for carrying naval stores; **store teeth** (*U.S.*), false teeth.—**in store,** in hoard for future use, ready for supply: in reserve, awaiting; **set store by,** to value greatly. [O.Fr. *estor, estoire*—L. *instaurāre,* to provide.]

**storey** (also now less frequently **story**), *stō'ri, stö', n.* all that part of a building on the same floor: a tier:—*pl.* **storeys.**—*adj.* **sto'reyed** (**stor'ied**), having storeys.—**first storey,** the ground floor; **second storey,** the first floor, etc. [Prob. same word orig. as **story.**]

**storge,** *stör'gē, -jē, n.* parental affection. [Gr.]

**storied.** See under **story** and **storey.**

**stork,** *störk, n.* a large white and black wading bird (*Ciconia alba*) with a great red bill and red legs: any member of its genus or of its family (akin to the ibises).—**stork's'-bill,** a genus (Erodium) of the geranium family, with beaked fruit: also applied to Pelargonium. [O.E. *storc;* Ger. *storch.*]

**storm,** *störm, n.* a violent commotion of the atmosphere: a tempest: a wind just short of a hurricane: any intense meteorological phenomenon: a fall of snow, long frost (*Scot.*): a violent commotion or outbreak of any kind: a paroxysm: a violent assault (*mil.*): calamity (*fig.*).—*v.i.* to be stormy: to rage: to rush violently or in attack: to upbraid passionately. —*v.t.* to take or try to take by assault: to disturb by a storm.—*adj.* **storm'ful,** stormy.— *adv.* **storm'fully.**—*n.* **storm'fulness.**—*adv.* **storm'- ily.**—*n.* **storm'iness.**—*n.* and *adj.* **storm'ing.**— *adjs.* **storm'less; storm'y,** having many storms: agitated with furious winds: boisterous: violent: passionate.—*adjs.* **storm'-beat, -beat'en,** beaten by storms.—**storm'-belt,** a belt of maxi-

mum storm frequency; **storm'-bird,** a petrel.— *adj.* **storm'bound,** delayed, cut off, confined to port by storms.—**storm'-centre,** the position of lowest pressure in a cyclonic storm: any focus of controversy or strife; **storm'-cock,** the missel-thrush; **storm'-cone, -drum,** a cone, drum, hoisted as a storm-signal; **storm'-glass,** a tube containing a solution supposed to change appearance with the weather; **storm'ing-par'ty,** the party sent to lead in storming a fortress; **storm'-lantern,** a lantern with flame protected from wind and weather; **storm'-pet'rel,** or (popularly) **storm'y-pet'rel** (see **petrel**).—*adj.* **storm'proof,** proof against storms or storming.—**storm'-sail** (*-sl, -sāl*), a small very strong sail for stormy weather; **storm'-shutter,** an outside window-shutter; **storm'-signal,** a signal hoisted in warning of the approach of a storm; **storm'-stay,** a stay on which a storm-sail is set.—*adjs.* **storm'-stayed,** hindered from proceeding by storms; **storm'-tossed,** tossed about by storms: much agitated by conflicting passions.— **storm'-track,** the path of a storm-centre; **storm'-trooper.**—*n.pl.* **storm'-troops,** shock-troops: a body formed in Germany by Adolf Hitler, disbanded 1934.—**storm'-warning; storm'-water,** surface drainage in excess of the normal in a storm; **storm'-wind,** a stormy wind; **storm'-window,** a window raised above the roof, slated above and at the sides: an additional outer casement.—**a storm in a teacup** (or other small vessel), a great commotion in a narrow sphere, or about a trifle; **take by storm,** to take by assault: to captivate totally and instantly (*fig.*). [O.E. *storm;* O.N. *stormr;* from root of **stir.**]

**stornello,** *stör-nel'ō, n.* a short (usually three-lined) popular Italian verse-form:—*pl.* **stornell'i** (*-ē*). [It.]

**Storthing,** *stōr'ting, stör', n.* the legislative assembly of Norway. [Norw. *stor,* great, *ting* (O.N. *thing*), assembly.]

**story,** *stō'ri, stö', n.* history (*obs.*): legend: a narrative of incidents in their sequence: a fictitious narrative: a tale: an anecdote: the plot of a novel or drama: a theme: an account, report, statement, allegation: a news article: a lie, a fib.—*v.t.* to tell or describe historically, to relate: to adorn with scenes from history.— *v.i.* to relate.—*adjs.* **sto'riated,** decorated with elaborate ornamental designs; **sto'ried,** told or celebrated in a story: having a history: interesting from the stories belonging to it: adorned with scenes from history.—*ns.* **storiette',** story-ette',** a short tale; **storiol'ogist; storiol'ogy,** the scientific study of folk-tales.—*n.* and *adj.* **sto'rying.**—**sto'ry-book,** a book of tales true or fictitious.—*adj.* rather luckier or happier than in real life.—**story line,** the main plot; **sto'ry-teller,** one who relates tales: a liar; **sto'ry-telling.** [A.Fr. *estorie*—L. *historia.*]

**story.** See **storey.**

**stot,** *stot, n.* a young ox, steer. [O.E. *stot,* horse.]

**stot,** *stot,* (*Scot.*) *v.i.* to rebound, bounce.—*v.t.* to cause to bounce.—*n.* a rebound.—Also **stott'er.** [Origin obscure.]

**stoun,** *stoon,* (*Spens.*) *v.t.:—pa.t.* and *pa.p.* **stound.** Same as **stun.**

**stound, stownd,** *stownd, stōond,* (*Spens.* and *Scot.*) *n.* a time, moment: a time of trouble: a pang: an assault, stroke: a shock: a din.—*v.i.* to shoot like a pang: to experience a pang. [O.E. *stund.*]

**stound, stownd,** *stōond,* (*Spens.*) *v.t.* to stun, astound.—*n.* a stunned or astounded condition. [**stoun** or **astound.**]

**stoup, stoop,** *stōōp* (*Shak.* **stoope; stoope,** *stōp*), *n.* a bucket (*obs.*): a drinking vessel (*arch.*); a holy-water vessel. [Cf. O.N. *staup* and Du. *stoop;* O.E. *stēap.*]

**stour.** See **stoor** (1).

**stour, stowre, stoor, stowr, stōōr,** n. battle, assault: tumult: turmoil: dust (Scot.).—adj. **stour'y,** (Scot.) dusty. [O.Fr. estour, tumult.]

**stout, stowt,** adj. fierce (B., Spens.): proud (obs.): arrogant (obs.): unyielding (obs. or dial.): stubborn (obs.): resolute: dauntless: vigorous: enduring: robust: strong: thick: fat.—adv. stoutly.—n. extra strong porter.—v.t. and v.i. **stout'en,** to make, or grow, stout(er).—adj. **stout'ish.**—adv. **stout'ly.**—n. **stout'ness.**—adj. **stout'-heart'ed.**—adv. **stout'-heart'edly.**—stout'-heart'edness. [O.Fr. estout, bold—Du. stout; Ger. stolz, proud.]

**stouth, stōōth,** (obs. Scot.) n. theft.—ns. **stouth'rie, stouth'erie,** theft: stolen goods: provision, furniture; **stouth'rief** (Scots law), theft with violence (later only in a dwelling-house).— **stouth and routh,** plenty, abundance (cf. **stoop and roop**). [O.N. stuldr, theft.]

**stovaine, stō-vā'in,** or stō', or -vän', n. a local anaesthetic, a substitute for cocaine, used for spinal analgesia. [stove, Eng. trans. of the name of Prof. Furneau, who first prepared it.]

**stove, stōv,** n. a hot-air bath: a heated room or chamber: a hothouse: a closed heating or cooking apparatus: a fire-grate: a kiln or oven for various manufacturing operations: a drying room.—v.t. to put, keep, heat, or dry in a stove: to stew (Scot.).—n.pl. (Scot.) **stov'ies,** stewed potatoes, Irish stew.—n. **stov'ing,** drying a specially prepared paint quickly by application of heat.—**stove'pipe,** a metal pipe for carrying smoke and gases from a stove: a tall silk hat (U.S.; in full **stovepipe hat); stove'-plant,** a hothouse plant. [O.E. stofa; Ger. stube.]

**stove, stōv,** pa.t. and pa.p. of **stave.**—Also used as pr.t.

**stover, stō'vər,** (Shak.) n. fodder. [Aphetic for **estover.**]

**stow, stō,** v.t. to place, put, lodge: to put away: to store: to put under hatches: to put down one's throat (jocularly): to desist from (stow it, stop it; slang): to pack: to have room for: to arrange.—v.i. (with away) to hide as a stowaway.—ns. **stow'age,** act or manner of stowing: state of being laid up: room for stowing: a place for stowing things: money paid for stowing goods: things stowed; **stow'er; stow'ing.**— **stow'away,** one who hides in a ship, etc., to get a passage; **stow'down,** the process of stowing down in a ship's hold. [O.E. stōw, place.]

**stow, stōō,** (Scot.) v.t. to crop. [O.N. stūfr, stump.]

**stown, stown,** a Scots form of **stolen.**—adv. **stow(n)'lins** (Scot.), by stealth.

**stownd.** See **stound** (1).

**stowre.** See **stoor** (1) and **stour** (2).

**strabism, strā'bizm, strabismus, strə-biz'məs,** ns. squint.—adjs. **strabis'mal, strabis'mic, -al.**—ns. **strabismom'eter** (strab-iz-), **strabom'eter,** an instrument for measuring strabismus; **strabot'omy** (Gr. tomē, a cut), the surgical operation for the cure of squinting. [Gr. strābos and strabismos, squinting; cf. strephein, to twist.]

**stracchino, strä-kē'nō,** n. a North Italian soft cheese. [It.,—stracco, weak.]

**strad.** See **Stradivarius.**

**straddle, strad'l,** v.i. to part the legs wide: to sit, stand, or walk with legs far apart: to seem favourable to both sides, to trim.—v.t. to bestride: to set far apart: to overshoot and then shoot short of, in order to get the range, to bracket: to cover the area of with bombs.— n. act of straddling: an attempt to fill a non-committal position: a stock transaction in which the buyer obtains the privilege of either a put or a call: a vertical mine-timber supporting a set: combination of a shot beyond the mark and one short of it.—adv. astride.—adv. **stradd'le-back,** stridelegs.—**straddle carrier,** a high self-propelled vehicle which can straddle a

container and lift, carry, and deposit where required.—adj. **stradd'le-legged,** having the legs wide apart. [Freq. of **stride.**]

**stradiot, strad'i-ot,** (hist.) n. a Venetian light horseman from Albania or Greece. [It. stradiotto—Gr. stratiōtēs, soldier.]

**Stradivarius, strad-i-vä'ri-əs,** or -vā', **Stradivari,** -vä'rē, (coll.) **strad,** ns. an instrument, usu. a violin, made by Antonio Stradivari (1644-1737) of Cremona.—Also **Stradūa'rius.**

**strae, strä,** n. Scots form of **straw.**—**strae death,** natural death in bed.

**strafe, straff, strāf** (in U.S. strāf), (originally war slang of 1914) v.t. to punish: to bombard: to assail: to rake with machine-gun fire from low-flying aeroplanes.—n. an attack. [Ger. strafen, to punish, used in the phrase Gott strafe England, God punish England, a German slogan of World War I.]

**straggle, strag'l,** v.i. to wander from one's company or course: to be absent without leave but not long enough to be counted a deserter: to stretch dispersedly or sprawlingly: to grow irregularly and untidily.—n. a straggling line or group.—ns. **strag** (dial.), a straggler: a stray: a vagrant; **stragg'ler.**—n. and adj. **stragg'ling.**— adv. **stragg'lingly.**—adj. **stragg'ly,** straggling: irregularly spread out. [Origin obscure.]

**straight, strāt,** adj. uncurved: in a right line: direct: upright: flat, horizontal: in good order: frank and honourable: respectably conducted: balanced, even, square: settled: downright: normal: in sequence (poker): in succession (tennis): undiluted, neat: consistent in support of one party or policy.—n. a straight condition: good behaviour: a straight line, part, course, flight, esp. the last part of a racecourse.—adv. in a straight line: directly: all the way: immediately: upright: outspokenly: honestly.—v.t. to straighten. —v.t. and v.i. **straight'en,** to make or become straight.—n. **straight'ener.**—adv. **straight'forth,** directly forward: straightway.—adj. **straight'ish.** —adv. **straight'ly,** in a straight line or manner: straightway.—n. **straight'ness.**—adv. **straight'way,** directly: immediately: without loss of time.—Also **straight'ways.**—**straight angle,** a right angle (obs.): now, two right angles.—adjs. **straight'away,** straight forward; **straight'-cut,** cut lengthwise of the leaf, of tobacco.—**straight'-edge,** a strip or stick for testing straightness or drawing straight lines; **straight fight,** esp. in politics, a contest in which only two persons or sides take part.—adj. **straightfor'ward,** going forward in a straight course: without digression: without evasion: honest: frank.—adv. **straightforwardly.**—adv. **straightfor'wardly.**—straight-for'wardness.—adjs. **straight'-jet,** (of aircraft or engine) driven or driving by jet directly, without a propeller; **straight'-out** (U.S., esp. in party politics), out-and-out—**straight part** (theat.), one portraying the normal without emphasis on eccentricities of manner, etc.—adj. **straight'-pight** (Shak.), straight, erect.—**straight play,** one without music; **straight talk,** a candid outspoken talk; **straight ticket** (see **ticket**); **straight tip,** a racing tip that comes straight from the owner: inside information that can be relied on.— **straight away, off,** immediately; **go straight,** to give up criminal activities; **keep a straight face,** to refrain from smiling. [O.E. streht, pa.p. of streccan; see **stretch.**]

**straight.** See **straucht.**

**straik, strāk,** n. and vb. a Scots form of **stroke.**— n. (Scott) proportion of malt in brewing.

**strain, strān,** v.t. to stretch: to draw tight: to draw with force: to exert to the utmost: to injure by overtasking: to force unnaturally, unduly, or amiss: to exalt emotionally: to change in form or bulk by subjecting to a stress: to constrain: to urge, insist upon, press for

(*Shak.*): to press to oneself, embrace: to squeeze, press: to grip, grasp tightly: to compress: to restrain: to squeeze out, express: to sing or play: to filter (esp. coarsely).—*v.i.* to make violent efforts: to tug: to retch: to have difficulty in swallowing or accepting (with *at*): to make efforts at evacuation: to percolate, filter.—*n.* the act of straining: a violent effort: an injury by straining, esp. a wrenching of the muscles: any change of form or bulk under stress: pitch, height: a section of a melody: a melody: an outpouring or flow of language: emotional tone, key, manner.—*adj.* **strained**, having been strained: forced or unnatural.—*adv.* **strain′edly** (or *strānd′li*).—*n.* **strain′er**, one who, or that which, strains: a sieve, colander, etc.—*n.* and *adj.* **strain′ing.**—**strain′ing-beam**, a tie-beam uniting the tops of queen-posts.—**strain a point**, to waive a scruple; **strain at**, in Matt. xxiii. 24, to remove by straining, strain in the event of finding (not as often understood, to be unable to swallow); **strain courtesy**, (*Shak.*, *Rom.* and *Jul.*) to treat with scant courtesy, or (*Venus and Adonis*) to be over-punctilious in courtesy. [O.Fr. *estraindre*—L. *stringĕre*, to stretch tight.]

**strain,** *strān, n.* offspring (*arch.*): breed, race, stock, line of descent: natural, esp. inherited, tendency or element in one's character: kind. [App. O.E. (*ge*)*strēon*, gain, getting, begetting (see **strene**), with altered vowel by confusion with foregoing.]

**straint,** *strānt*, (*Spens.*) *n.* pressure. [strain, on the model of **constraint**, etc.]

**strait** (formerly also, and still erroneously, **straight;** *Spens.*, *Milt.* streight), *strāt*, *adj.* (*obs.* or *rare*) tight (*Shak.*): close: narrow: strict: rigorous: hard-pressed, needy: sparing in giving.—*n.* a narrow part, place, or passage, esp. (often in *pl.*) by water: (usu. in *pl.*) difficulty, distress, hardship.—*adv.* (*obs.* or *rare*) tightly: closely: narrowly: strictly: rigorously: with hardship.—*v.t.* (*obs.* or *rare*) to tighten: to narrow: to put in a difficulty: to reduce to hardship.—*v.t.* **strait′en**, to tighten (*obs.*): to narrow: to confine (*arch.*): to distress: to put into difficulties: to run short.—*v.i.* to narrow.—*adj.* **strait′ened.**—*adv.* **strait′ly** (*obs.* or *arch.*), tightly: narrowly: closely: strictly.—*n.* **strait′-ness** (*rare*).—*v.t.* and *v.i.* **strait′-lace.**—*adj.* **strait′-laced**, tight-laced: narrow in principles of behaviour: prudish.—**strait′-lacer**; **strait′-lac-ing**; **strait′-waistcoat, strait′-jack′et**, a garment for restraint of the violently insane: anything which inhibits freedom of movement or initiative. [O.Fr. *estreit* (Fr. *étroit*)—L. *strictus*, pa.p. of *stringĕre*, to draw tight.]

**strake,** *strāk*, obs. *pa.t.* of **strike.**

**strake, straik,** *strāk, n.* a stripe (*Spens.*): a strip: one breadth of plank or plate in a ship, from stem to stern: a section of a cart-wheel rim: a trough for washing ore. [Akin to **stretch**, coalescing with **streak.**]

**stramash,** *stra-mash′*, (*Scot.*) *n.* a tumult, disturb-ance: a broil: wreck.—*v.t.* to wreck, smash. [Perh. an elaboration of **smash**.]

**stramazon, stramaçon,** *stram′a-zon, -son*, (*obs.*) *n.* a downward cut in fencing. [It. *stramazzone*, and Fr. *estramaçon*.]

**stramineous,** *stra-min′i-as, adj.* strawy: light, worthless: straw-coloured. [L. *strāmineus*—*strāmen*, straw.]

**strammel,** *stram′l.* See **strummel.**

**stramonium,** *stra-mō′ni-am, n.* the thorn-apple: a drug like belladonna got from its seeds and leaves. [Mod. L., poss. from a Tatar word.]

**stramp,** *stramp*, (*Scot.*) *v.t.* and *v.i.* to tread, stamp, or trample.—*n.* a stamp of the foot.

**strand,** *strand, n.* a sea or lake margin: a landing-place (*Milt.*).—*v.t.* and *v.i.* to run aground.—

*adj.* **strand′ed**, driven on shore: left helpless with-out further resource. [O.E. *strand*; Ger. *strand*, O.N. *strönd*, border.]

**strand,** *strand*, (*Scot.*) *n.* a rivulet: a gutter.—**strand′-scouring**, searching of gutters. [Origin obscure.]

**strand,** *strand, n.* a yarn, thread, fibre, or wire twisted or plaited with others to form a rope, cord, or the like: a thread, filament: a tress.—*v.t.* to break a strand of: to insert a strand in: to form of strands. [Origin obscure.]

**strange,** *strānj, adj.* foreign (*Shak.*): alien: from elsewhere: not of one's own place, family, or circle: not one's own: not formerly known or experienced: unfamiliar: interestingly unusual: odd: estranged: like a stranger: distant or reserved: unacquainted, unversed: exceedingly great, exceptional (*obs.*).—*adv.* **strange′ly.**—*ns.* **strange′ness**, the quality of being strange: a quantum number which represents unexplained delay in strong interactions between certain elementary particles; **strān′ger**, a foreigner: one whose home is elsewhere: one unknown or little known: one who is outside of one's familiar circle or kindred: a visitor: a new-born child: a non-member: an outsider: a person not con-cerned: one without knowledge, experience, or familiarity (with *to*): a thing believed or feigned to foretell the coming of a visitor, as a tea-leaf floating in a cup, a flake of soot in a fireplace.—*v.t.* (*Shak.*) to make a stranger.—**strange particles**, K-mesons and hyperons, which have a non-zero strangeness (*q.v.*) number: **strange woman**, a whore.—**make it strange** (*Shak.*), to make difficulties, show reluctance. [O.Fr. *estrange* (Fr. *étrange*)—L. *extrāneus*—*extrā*, beyond.]

**strangle,** *strang′gl, v.t.* to kill by compressing the throat: to choke: to kill (*obs.*): to constrict: to choke back, suppress, stifle: to involve and impede.—*ns.* **strang′lement**; **strang′ler.**—*n.pl.* **strang′les**, a contagious disease of horses.—**strang′lehold**, a choking hold in wrestling: a strong repressive influence; **strang′le-weed**, dodder: broomrape. [O.Fr. *estrangler* (Fr. *étrangler*)—L. *strangulāre*; see next word.]

**strangulate,** *strang′gū-lāt, v.t.* to strangle: to com-press so as to suppress or suspend function.—*adj.* **strang′ulated**, strangled: constricted, much narrowed.—*n.* **strangulā′tion**. [L. *strangulāre*, *-ātum*—Gr. *strangalaein*, to strangle, *strangos*, twisted.]

**strangury,** *strang′gū-ri, n.* painful retention of, or difficulty in discharging, urine. [L. *strangūria*—Gr. *strangouriā*—*stranx*, a drop, trickle, *ouron*, urine.]

**strap,** *strap, n.* a narrow strip, usu. of leather: a thong: a strop (*obs.* or *dial.*): a metal band or plate for holding things in position: a narrow flat projection, as on a strap-hinge: a looped band: a string or long cluster: anything strap-shaped: an application of the strap or tawse in punishment: a barber (*slang*, after Hugh *Strap* in Smollett's *Roderick Random*): a term of abuse to a woman (*Anglo-Ir.*): credit, esp. for liquor (*slang*).—*v.t.* to beat or bind with a strap: to strop: to hang (*Scot.*).—*v.i.* to work vigorously: to admit of or suffer strapping:—*pr.p.* **strapp′ing**; *pa.t.* and *pa.p.* **strapped**.—*adj.* **strap′less**, without a strap or straps, esp. (of woman's dress) without shoulder-straps.—*ns.* **strapp′er**, one who works with straps, esp. a groom: a vigorous worker: a tall robust person: a whopping lie; **strapp′ing**, fastening with a strap: materials for straps: strengthening bands: a thrashing.—*adj.* tall and robust. — **strap′-game**, prick-the-garter. — *v.i.* **strap′-hang.**—**strap′-hanger**, standing passenger who holds on to a strap for safety; **strap′-hinge**, hinge fastened by a long leaf or flap; **strap′-oil**, a thrashing. — *adj.* **strap′-shaped.** — **strap′-work** (*archit.*), ornamentation of crossed and interlaced fillets; **strap'wort**, a seaside caryophyllaceous plant (*Corrigiola littoralis*) of S.W. England, etc., with strap-shaped leaves. [Northern form of **strop**.]

**strappado**, *strap-ä'dō, -ä'dō, n.* torture by hoisting to a height and letting fall to the length of the rope (*Shak.*): later, a strapping (*erron.*).—*v.t.* to torture or punish by the strappado. [Sham Spanish, from It. *strappata—strappare*, to pull.]

**strass**, *stras, n.* paste for making false gems. [Josef *Strasser*, its inventor.]

**strata**, *strā'tə, strä', pl.* of **stratum.**

**stratagem**, *strat'ə-jəm, n.* a plan for deceiving an enemy or gaining an advantage: any artifice generally. [Fr. *stratagème*—L.—Gr. *stratēgēma*, a piece of generalship, trick; see next word.]

**strategy**, *strat'i-ji, n.* generalship, or the art of conducting a campaign and manoeuvring an army: artifice or finesse generally.—*adjs.* **strategetic** (*-jet'ik*) (both *rare*), **strategic** (*strət-ēj'ik, -ej'ik*), **-al**, pertaining to, dictated by, of value for, strategy.—*n.* (usu. in *pl.* form) **strateg'ic.**—*adv.* **strateg'ically.**—*n.* **strat'egist**, one skilled in strategy.—**strategic materials**, materials necessary for carrying on a war; **strategic position**, a position that gives its holder a decisive advantage. [Gr. *stratēgia—stratēgos*, a general—*stratos*, an army, *agein*, to lead.]

**strath**, *strath, n.* in the Highlands of Scotland, a broad valley. [Gael. *srath*, a valley—L. *strāta*, a street.]

**strathspey**, *strath-spā', n.* a Scottish dance, allied to and danced alternately with the reel: a tune for it, differing from the reel in being slower, and abounding in the jerky motion of dotted notes and semiquavers. [*Strathspey*, the valley of the *Spey*.]

**stratify**, etc. See under **stratum.**

**Stratiotes**, *strat-i-ō'tēz, n.* the water-soldier genus. [Gr. *stratiōtēs*, a soldier.]

**stratocracy**, *strat-, strət-ok'rə-si, n.* military despotism.—*n.* **stratocrat** (*strat'ō-krat*).—*adjs.* **stratocrat'ic; stratonic** (*-on'ik*), of an army. [Gr. *stratos*, an army.]

**stratum**, *strā'təm, strä', n.* layer: bed of sedimentary rock: a layer of cells in living tissue: a region determined by height or depth: a level of society:—*pl.* **stra'ta.**—*n.* **stratificā'tion** (*strat-*).—*adjs.* **strat'ified; strat'iform**, forming a layer.—*v.t.* **strat'ify**, to deposit or form in layers:—*pr.p.* **strat'ifying**; *pa.t.* and *pa.p.* **strat'ified.**—*ns.* **stratig'rapher, stratig'raphist.**—*adjs.* **stratigraph'ic, -al.**—*adv.* **stratigraph'ically.**—*n.* **stratig'raphy**, the geological study of strata and their succession: stratigraphical features.—*adj.* **stra'tose**, in layers.—*n.* **stratosphere** (*strat'* or *strāt'ō-sfēr*), a region of the atmosphere beginning about 4½ to 10 miles up, in which temperature does not fall as altitude increases.—*adjs.* **stratospheric** (*-sfer'ik*); **stra'tous**, of stratus.—*n.* **strā'tus**, a wide-extended horizontal sheet of low cloud.—**strato-cruiser** (*strat', strāt'*; *proprietary name*), an aeroplane for the stratosphere; **stra'to-cū'mulus**, a cloud in large globular or rolled masses, not rain-bringing. [L. *strātum, -ī, strātus, -ūs*, something spread, a bedcover, horse-cloth—*sternĕre, strātum*, to spread.]

**straucht, straught**, *ströhht, (Scot.) v.t.* a form of stretch: esp. to lay out (a corpse).—*adj.* and *adv.* a form of straight.—Also (*adj.* and *adv.*) **straicht, straight** (*strehht*).

**straunge**, *strönj, (Spens.) adj.* Same as **strange**: foreign, borrowed.

**stravaig**, *strə-vāg', (Scot.) v.i.* to wander about idly.—*n.* **stravaig'er**. [Cf. **stray, extravagant**.]

**straw**, *strö, n.* the stalk of corn: dried stalks, etc., of corn, or of peas or buckwheat, etc. (*collec.*): a tube for sucking up a beverage: a straw hat: a trifle, a whit.—*adj.* of straw.—*adjs.* **straw'en** (*Spens.*), of straw; **straw'less; straw'y**, of or

like straw.—**straw'board**, a thick cardboard, made of straw; **straw'-breadth**, the breadth of a straw.—*n.* and *adj.* **straw'-colour**, delicate yellow.—*adj.* **straw'-coloured.**—**straw'-cutter**, an instrument for chopping straw; **straw'-hat'**; **straw'-plait**, plaited straw for hats; **straw poll**, an unofficial vote taken to get some idea of the general trend of opinion; **straw'-rope**, a rope of twisted straw; **straw'-stem**, the fine stem of a wine-glass pulled out from the material of the bowl, instead of being attached separately: a wine-glass having such a stem; **straw'-worm**, a caddis-worm; **straw'-yard**, a yard strewn with straw for animals.—**last straw** (see **last**, 4); **man of straw** (see **man**); **straw in the wind**, a sign of possible future developments. [O.E. *strēaw*; Ger. *stroh*; cf. **strae, strew**.]

**straw**, *strö, v.t.* an archaic form of **strew**:—*pa.t.* **strawed**; *pa.p.* **strawed, strawn.**

**strawberry**, *strö'bə-ri, -bri, n.* the fruit (botanically the enlarged receptacle) of any species of the rosaceous genus Fragaria, close akin to Potentilla: the plant bearing it.—**strawberry blonde**, a woman with reddish-yellow hair; **straw'berry-leaf'**, the leaf of the strawberry plant: symbolically (esp. in *pl.*) the rank of duke or duchess, from the ornaments like strawberry leaves on a duke's (also a marquess's or earl's) coronet; **straw'berry-mark**, a reddish birthmark; **straw'berry-shrub**, Calycanthus; **strawberry roan**, a reddish roan; **straw'berry-toma'to**, the Cape gooseberry; **straw'berry-tree**, *Arbutus unedo*, a small tree (wild at Killarney) of the heath family, with red berries.—**barren strawberry**, a Potentilla distinguished from the wild strawberry by its dry fruit. [O.E. *strēawberige*, possibly from the chaffy appearance of the achenes.]

**stray**, *strā, v.i.* to wander: to wander away, esp. from control, or from the right way: to get lost. *v.t.* (*Shak.*) to set astray.—*n.* a domestic animal that has strayed or is lost: a straggler: a waif: anything occurring casually, isolatedly, out of place: body of strays (*Shak.*): a common: (in *pl.*) atmospherics: a straying (*Shak.*).—*adj.* gone astray: casual: isolated.—*adj.* **strayed**, wandering, gone astray.—*n.* **stray'er.**—*n.* and *adj.* **stray'ing.**—*n.* **stray'ling**, a stray. [O.Fr. *estraier*, to wander—L. *extrā*, beyond, *vagāri*, to wander.]

**streak**, *strēk, n.* an irregular stripe: the colour of a mineral in powder, seen in a scratch: a scratch: a strain, vein, interfused or pervading character: the line or course as of a flash of lightning: a rush, swift dash: a course, succession, as of luck.—*v.t.* to mark with streaks.—*v.i.* to become streaked: to rush past (cf. **streek**).—*adj.* **streaked**, streaky, striped: confused (*U.S.*).—*adv.* **streak'-ily.**—*ns.* **streak'iness; streak'ing.**—*adj.* **streak'y**, marked with streaks, striped: fat and lean in alternate layers: uneven in quality.—**like a streak**, like (a flash of) lightning. [O.E. *strica*, a stroke, line, mark; Ger. *strich*; cf. **strike**.]

**streak**. See **strake, streek.**

**stream**, *strēm, n.* a running water: a river or brook, esp. a rivulet: a flow or moving succession of anything: a large number or quantity coming continuously: a division of pupils on the roll of a school consisting of those of roughly equal ability or similar bent, or those following a particular course of study: a current: a drift: a tendency.—*v.i.* to flow, issue, or stretch, in a stream: to pour out abundantly: to float out, trail: to wash for ore.—*v.t.* to discharge in a stream: to wave, fly: to wash for ore: to divide (pupils) into streams.—*n.* **stream'er**, a pennon, ribbon, plume, or the like streaming or flowing in the wind: a luminous beam or band of light, as of the aurora: one who washes detritus for gold or tin: a headline: a narrow roll of coloured paper.—*adj.* **stream'ered.**—*n.* **stream'iness.**

—*n*. and *adj*. **stream'ing**.—*adv*. **stream'ingly**. —*adj*. **stream'less**, not watered by streams: waterless: without a current.—*ns*. **stream'let**, **stream'ling**, a little stream.—*adj*. **stream'y**, abounding in streams: flowing in a stream.— **stream'-anch'or**, a small anchor used in warping or for stemming an easy current; **stream'-gold**, placer-gold; **stream'-ice**, pieces of drift ice swept down in a current; **stream'line**, a line followed by a streaming fluid: natural course of air-streams.—*v.t.* to make streamlined.—*adj*. **stream'lined**, having boundaries following streamlines so as to offer minimum resistance: a term of commendation with a variety of meanings, as efficient, without waste of effort, up-to-the-minute, of superior type, graceful, etc. (*slang*).—**stream'-tin**, tin-ore found in alluvial ground.—**stream of consciousness**, the continuous succession of thoughts, emotions, and feelings, both vague and well-defined, that forms an individual's conscious experience. [O.E. *strēam*; Ger. *strom*, O.N. *straumr*.]

**streek, streak**, *strēk*, *v.t.* and *v.i.* a Northern form of **stretch**, not confined to Northern use: esp. (*v.t. Scot.*) to lay out for burial: (*v.i.*) to go at full speed.

**streel**, *strēl*, (*Ir.*) *v.i.* to trail: to stream: to wander. [Cf. Ir. *straoillim*, to trail.]

**street**, *strēt*, *n*. a paved road, esp. Roman (*ant*.): a road lined with houses, broader than a lane, including or excluding the houses and the footways: those who live in a street or are on the street: a passage or gap through or among anything: brokers as a body: (often in *pl*.) prostitution.—*n*. **street'age** (*U.S.*), a toll for street facilities.—*adj*. **street'ed**, having streets.—*n*. **street'ful**:—*pl*. **street'fuls**.—*adv*. and *adj*. **street'-ward** (-*wərd*), towards or facing the street.—*adv*. **street'wards**.—*adj*. **street'y**, savouring or characteristic of the streets.—**street'-Ar'ab** (see **Arab**); **street'-boy**, a boy who lives mainly on the street; **street'-car** (*U.S.*), a tram-car; **street'-door**, the door that opens on the street; **street'-keeper**, an officer formerly employed to keep order in a street or streets; **street'-or'derly**, a scavenger; **street'-rail'road**, **-rail'way**, a town tramway.— *adj*. **street'-raking** (*Scott*), ranging the streets.— **street'-room**, space enough in the street; **street'-sweep'er**, one who, or that which, sweeps the streets clean; **street'-walker**, any one who walks in the streets, esp. a whore.—*n*. and *adj*. **street'-walking**.—**street'-ward** (-*wörd*), an officer who formerly took care of the streets; **streetway**, the roadway.—**not in the same street as**, much inferior to; **on the street** (*slang*), homeless, destitute; **on the streets** (*slang*), practising prostitution; **streets ahead of**, far superior to; **up one's street** (*fig*.), in the region in which one's tastes, knowledge, abilities, lie. [O.E. *strǣt* (Du. *straat*, Ger. *strasse*, It. *strada*)—L. *strāta* (*via*), a paved (way), from *sternĕre*, *strātum*, to spread.]

**streight**, *strit*, a Spenserian form of **strait**, **straight**.

**streigne**, an old spelling of **strain**.

**strelitz**, *strel'its*, *n*. a soldier of the Muscovite guards, abolished by Peter the Great:—*pl*. **strel'itzes**, **strel'tzi**. [Russ. *strelets*, bowman.]

**Strelitzia**, *strel-it'si-ə*, *n*. a S. African genus of the banana family, with large showy flowers. [From Queen Charlotte, wife of George III, of the house of Mecklenburg-*Strelitz*.]

**strene**, *strēn*, (*Spens*.) *n*. a form of **strain**, race.

**strength**, *strength*, *n*. quality, condition, or degree of being strong: power of action or resistance: force: vigour: a strong place, stronghold: numbers: a military force: number on the muster-roll, or normal number.—*v.t.* **strength'en**, to make strong or stronger: to confirm.—*v.i.* to become stronger.—*n*. **strength'ener**.—*n*. and *adj*. **strength'ening**.—*adjs*. **strength'ful**; **strength'less**, without strength.—**go from strength to strength**,

to move successfully forward, through frequent triumphs or achievements; **on the strength**, on the muster-roll; **on**, or **upon**, **the strength of**, in reliance upon: founding upon. [O.E. *strengthu* —*strang*, strong.]

**strenuous**, *stren'ū-əs*, *adj*. active: vigorous: urgent: zealous: necessitating exertion.—*ns*. **strenuity** (*stri-nū'i-ti*); **strenuosity** (*stren-ū-os'i-ti*), strenuousness: a straining after effect.—*adv*. **stren'uously**.—*n*. **stren'uousness**. [L. *strēnuus*.]

**strepent**, *strep'ənt*, (*rare*) *adj*. noisy.—*adjs*. **strep'-erous**, loud: harsh-sounding; **strep'itant**, loud: noisy: clamorous.—*n*. **strepitā'tion**.—*adj*. **strepitoso** (*-i-tō'sō*; *mus*.; It.), noisy, boisterous.— Also *adv*.—*adj*. **strep'itous**. [L. *strepĕre*, to make a noise; freq. *strepitāre*.]

**Strephon**, *stref'on*, *-ən*, *n*. a love-sick shepherd in Sir Philip Sidney's *Arcadia*: a love-sick swain.

**Strepsiptera**, *streps-ip'tə-rə*, *n.pl*. an order of insects (or group of Coleoptera) parasitic in other insects, the females wormlike, the males with twisted fore-wings.—*adj*. **strepsip'terous**. [Gr. *strepsis*, a twist, *pteron*, a wing.]

**strepto-**, *strep'tō-*, in composition, bent, flexible, twisted.—*adjs*. **streptococcal** (*-kok'l*), **streptococcic** (*-kok'sik*).—*ns*. **Streptococc'us** (Gr. *kokkos*, a grain), a genus of bacteria forming bent chains:—*pl*. **streptococ'ci** (*-sī*); **streptomycin** (*-mī'sin*; Gr. *mykēs*, fungus), an antibiotic got from fission-fungi.—*n.pl*. **Streptoneu'ra** (Gr. *neuron*, nerve), a subclass of gasteropods with twisted visceral nerve-loop—limpets, whelks, etc. [Gr. *streptos*, twisted, flexible.]

**Strepyan**, *strep'i-ən*, *adj*. of the oldest known Palaeolithic culture. [*Strépy*, a village near Charleroi, where stone implements of this stage occur.]

**stress**, *stres*, *n*. hardship, straits (*obs*.): strain: constraining influence: pressure: force: system of forces applied to a body: insistent assigning of weight or importance: emphasis: relative force of utterance: distraint (*law*).—*v.t.* to apply stress to: to lay stress on: to emphasise.—*adjs*. **stressed**; **stress'ful**; **stress'less**. [Aphetic for **distress**; prob. partly also from O.Fr. *estrece*— L. *strictus*—*stringĕre*, to draw tight.]

**stretch**, *strech*, *v.t.* to extend: to draw out: to expand, make longer or wider by tension: to spread out: to reach out: to exaggerate, strain, or carry further than is right: to lay at full length: to lay out: to place so as to reach from point to point or across a space: to hang (*slang*). —*v.i.* to be drawn out: to reach: to be extensible without breaking: to straighten and extend fully one's body and limbs: to exaggerate: to go swiftly.—*n*. act of stretching: state of being stretched: reach: extension: utmost extent: strain: undue straining: exaggeration: extensibility: a single spell: a continuous journey: a straight part of a course: a term of imprisonment (*slang*).—*adj*. capable of being stretched.— *adj*. **stretched**.—*n*. **stretch'er**, one who stretches: anything used for stretching, as gloves, hats, etc.: a frame for stretching a painter's canvas: a frame for carrying the sick or wounded: a rower's footboard: a cross-bar or horizontal member: a brick, stone, sod, sandbag, etc., placed with its length in the direction of the wall: an exaggeration or lie.—*adjs*. **stretch'less**, no longer liable to stretch; **stretch'y**, able, apt, or inclined to stretch.—**stretch'er-bearer**, one who carries injured from the field; **stretch'er-bond**, **stretch'ing-bond**, a method of building with stretchers only, the joints of one course falling between those above and below; **stretch'ing-course**, a course entirely of stretchers; **stretch'-ing-frame**, a machine for stretching cotton rovings: a frame on which starched fabrics are dried; **stretch'ing-iron**, a currier's tool for dressing leather.—*adj*. **stretch'-mouth'd** (*Shak*.)

wide-mouthed.—at a stretch, continuously, without interruption; stretch a point (see point); stretch one's legs, to take a walk, esp. for exercise. [O.E. *streccan*.]

stretto, *stret'ō, n.* part of a fugue in which subject and answer are brought closely together: (also strett'a) a passage, esp. a coda, in quicker time. [It., contracted.]

strew, *strōō* (or *strō*), arch. strow, *strō* (or *strōō*), straw, *strō, v.t.* to scatter loosely: to bestrew, cover dispersedly: to spread (*rare*): to level (*poet.*):—*pa.t.* strewed, strawed; *pa.p.* strewed, strewn, arch. strowed, strown, strawed, strawn.—*n.* an assemblage of things strewn.—*ns.* strew'age; strew'er, strow'er; strew'ing, strow'ing; strew'ment (*Shak.*), strewings. [O.E. *strewian, streowian*.]

'strewth, *strōōth, interj.* an vulg. minced oath (for *God's truth*).

stria, *strī'ə, strē'a, n.* a fine streak, furrow, or thread-like line, usu. parallel to others: one of the fillets between the flutes of columns, etc. (*archit.*):—*pl.* stri'ae (*strī'ē, strē'ī*).—*v.t.* stri'ate, to mark with striae.—*adjs.* stri'ate, -d.—*ns.* striā'tion; striā'tum, the *corpus striatum*, the great ganglion of the fore-brain; stri'ature, mode of striation. [L. *stria*, a furrow, flute of a column.]

strich, *strich,* (*Spens.*) *n.* the screech-owl. [L. *strix*, prob. modified by scritch.]

stricken, *strik'n, pa.p.* of strike, and *adj.*, struck, now chiefly poet. in U.K. or in special senses and phrases: wounded in the chase: afflicted: advanced (*stricken in years*, from the sense of go, make one's way): expunged.—stricken field, a pitched battle, or the scene of it; stricken hour, an hour as marked by the clock.

strickle, *strik'l, n.* an instrument for levelling the top of a measure of grain or shaping the surface of a mould: a template: a tool for sharpening scythes.—*v.t.* to level a measure of grain or shape the surface of a mould with a strickle. [O.E. *stricel*.]

strict, *strikt, adj.* tight (*Shak.*): narrow (*arch.*): stiff and straight (*bot.*): close, intimate (*obs.*): restricted: exact: rigorous: allowing no laxity: austere: observing exact rules, regular: severe: exactly observed: thoroughgoing.—*adj.* strict'ish.—*adv.* strict'ly.—*ns.* strict'ness; strict'ure, binding: closure: tightness: abnormal narrowing of a passage (*med.*): strictness (*Shak.*): a (now only adverse) remark or criticism.—*adj.* strict'ured, morbidly narrowed. [L. *strictus,* pa.p. of *stringĕre*, to draw tight.]

strid, stridden. See stride.

stride, *strīd, v.i.* to walk with long steps: to take a long step: to straddle.—*v.t.* to stride over: to bestride:—*pa.t.* strōde, *obs.* strid; *pa.p.* stridd'en, (*strid'n*).—*n.* a long step: a striding gait: the length of a long step.—*n.* strid (*strid*), a place where a river can be stridden over (from that on the Wharfe).—*v.i.* striddle (*strid'l*), to straddle (back-formation from *stridling*).—*advs.* stride'-ways, stridling (*strid'*; *dial.*), astride.—*advs.* stride'legs, stride'legged (*Scot.*), astride.—make great strides, to make rapid progress; take in one's stride, to accomplish without undue effort or difficulty. [O.E. *stridan,* to stride.]

stridence, *strī'dəns,* -cy, *-dən-si, ns.* harshness of tone.—*adj.* stri'dent, loud and grating.—*adv.* stri'dently.—*n.* stri'dor, a harsh shrill sound: a harsh whistling sound of obstructed breathing (*med.*).—*adj.* stridūlant (*strid'*), stridulating.—*v.i.* strid'ūlate, to make a chirping or scraping sound, like a grasshopper.—*ns.* stridūlā'tion, the act of stridulating; strid'ūlātor, an insect that makes a sound by scraping: the organ it uses.—*adjs.* strid'ūlatory; strid'ūlous. [L. *strīdēre* and *strīdĕre,* to creak.]

strife, *strīf, n.* contention: contest: variance:

striving.—*adjs.* strife'ful (*Spens.* stryf'ull, etc.); strife'less.—*n.* strift (*strift*; arch.), struggle. [O.Fr. *estrif*; see strive.]

strig, *strig,* (*Southern*) *n.* a stalk.—*v.t.* to remove the stalk from:—*pr.p.* strigg'ing. [Origin obscure.]

striga, *strī'gə,* L. *strig'a, n.* a stria: a bristle, usu. an appressed bristle:—*pl.* strigae (*strī'jē,* L. strig'ī).—*adjs.* stri'gate, stri'gose. [L. *strīga,* a swath, a furrow, a flute of a column.]

Striges, *strī'jēz,* L. *strig'ās;* also Strigiformes, *strij-i-för'mēz, n.pl.* in some classifications, the order comprising the owls.—*adjs.* strig'iform; stri'gine, owl-like: of the owls. [L. *strix, strigis,* an owl.]

strigil, *strij'il, n.* a flesh-scraper: in bees, a mechanism for cleaning the antennae. [L. *strigilis.*]

Strigops, *strī'gops,* Stringops, *string'gops, n.* the kakapo or owl-parrot genus. [Gr. *strinx,* or *strix, stringos,* owl, *ōps,* face.]

strike, *strīk, v.t.* to smooth (*dial.*): to strickle (*dial.*): to draw, describe, give direction to (as a line, path): to delete, cancel: to constitute (orig. by cutting down a list): to mark off: to lower (as a sail, flag, tent): to take down the tents of (*strike camp*): to remove: to leave off or refuse to continue: to deal, deliver, or inflict: to give a blow to or with: to hit, smite: to come into forcible contact with: to impinge on: to bring forcibly into contact: to impel: to put, send, move, render, or produce by a blow or stroke: to render as if by a blow: to sound by percussion or otherwise: to announce by a bell: to dash: to pierce: to stamp: to coin: to print: to impress: to impress favourably: to thrust in or down, cause to penetrate: to broach (*Shak.*): to fight (a battle) (*Shak.*): to blast, bewitch: to visit, afflict: to assail, affect: to affect strongly or suddenly: to arrive at, estimate, compute, fix, settle (as a balance, an average, prices): to make (a compact or agreement), to ratify: to come upon: to reach: to achieve: to occur to: to assume: to hook by a quick turn of the wrist: to make a sudden demand of (as for a loan or subscription; *slang*): to cause to strike.—*v.i.* to make one's way: to set out: to take a direction or course: to dart, shoot, pass quickly: to penetrate: to put forth roots: to chance, alight, come by chance: to interpose: to deal or aim a blow, perform a stroke: to sound or be sounded or announced by a bell: to hit out: to seize the bait: to strike something, as a rock, sail, flag: to touch: to run aground: to surrender: to admit of striking: to do menial work (for an officer; *U.S. army*): to go on strike: to blast, blight (*Shak.*):—*pa.t.* struck, *obs.* strake, stroke, strook, strooke; *Scot.* strak, strack; *pa.p.* struck, arch. strick'en, q.v.; *obs.* strook, strooke, strook'en, strok'en, struck'en.—*n.* a strickle: proportion of malt (cf. straik): a stroke, striking: an attack, esp. by aircraft: the direction of a horizontal line at right angles to the dip of a bed (*geol.*): a find (as of oil), stroke of luck: a cessation of work, or other obstructive refusal to act normally, as a means of putting pressure on employers, etc.: the part that receives the bolt of a lock: blackmail, esp. by introducing a bill in the hope of being bought off (*U.S. slang*).—*ns.* strik'er, one who, that which, strikes: a footpad (*Shak.*): a batsman (*baseball*): the batsman facing the bowling (*cricket*): the player who receives the service (*tennis*; also strik'er-out); strik'ing.—*adj.* that strikes or can strike: impressive, arresting, noticeable.—*adv.* strik'ingly.—*n.* strik'ingness.—strike'-breaker, one who works during a strike, esp. one brought in with a view to defeating it; strike'-breaking; strike'-fault (*geol.*), a fault parallel to the strike;

strike'-pay, an allowance paid by a trade-union to men on strike.—**on strike**, taking part in a strike; **strike a match**, to light it by friction or a grazing stroke; **strike at**, to attempt to strike, aim a blow at; **strike back**, to return a blow: to backfire, burn within the burner; **strike bottom**, **soundings**, to reach the bottom with the lead; **strike hands**, to join or slap together hands in confirmation of agreement; **strike home**, to strike right to the point aimed at; **strike in**, to enter suddenly: to interpose: to agree, fit (*obs.*); **strike into**, to enter upon suddenly, to break into; **strike off**, to erase from an account, to deduct: to print: to separate by a blow; **strike oil**, to find petroleum when boring for it: to make a lucky hit; **strike out**, to efface: to bring into light: to direct one's course boldly outwards: to swim away: to strike from the shoulder: to form by sudden effort; **strike root** (see root); **strike up**, to begin to beat, sing, or play: to begin (as an acquaintance); **struck in years** (*Shak.*; same as **stricken in years**); **struck on**, inclined to be enamoured of. [O.E. *strican*, to stroke, go, move.]

**Strine,** *strin*, *n.* Australian speech. [Alleged pron. of *Australian*.]

**string,** *string*, *n.* small cord or a piece of it: cord of any size: a hangman's rope: a piece of anything for tying: anything of like character, as a tendon, nerve, fibre: a leash: a shoelace (*U.S.*): a stretched piece of catgut, silk, wire, or other material in a musical instrument: (in *pl.*) the stringed instruments played by a bow in an orchestra or other combination: (in *pl.*) their players: the cord of an archery bow: the thread of a necklace or the like: anything on which things are threaded: a filing cord: a set of things threaded together or arranged as if threaded: a train, succession, file, or series: a drove of horses, camels, etc.: a long bunch: in billiards, the buttons strung on a wire by which the score is kept: hence the score itself: a sloping joist supporting the steps in wooden stairs: a string-course: a hoax (*slang*): (in *pl.*) awkward conditions or limitations.—*adj.* of or for string or strings.—*v.t.* to fit or furnish with a string or strings: to put in tune (*poet.*): to make tense or firm: to tie up: to hang: to extend like a string: to put on or in a string: to take the strings off: to hoax, humbug (*slang*).—*v.i.* to stretch out into a long line: to form into strings: to be hanged (*Scot.*): in billiards, to drive the ball against the end of the table and back, to decide who is to begin:—*pa.t.* and *pa.p.* **strung.**—*adj.* **stringed** (*stringd*), having strings: of stringed instruments.—*n.* **stringer** (*string'ər*), one who, or that which, strings: a horizontal member in a framework: an inside horizontal plank, supporting beam-ends of a ship (*naut.*): a narrow mineral vein.—*adv.* **string'ily**, in a stringy fashion.—*ns.* **string'iness**; **string'ing.**—*adjs.* **string'less**; **string'y**, consisting of, or abounding in, strings or small threads: fibrous: capable of being drawn into strings: like string or a stringed instrument.—**string'-bag**, a bag made of, or for holding, string; **string'-band**, a band of stringed instruments: the strings of an orchestra; **string'-bean** (*U.S.*), the French bean; **string'-board**, a board facing the well-hole of a staircase, and receiving or covering the ends of the steps; **string'-course**, a projecting horizontal course or line of mouldings running quite along the face of a building; **string figure**, structure of string looped around the fingers in a symmetrical pattern that can be altered by manipulation, as cat's-cradle; **string'-pea**, a pea with edible pods; **string'-piece**, a long, heavy, usu. horizontal timber: the string of a staircase; **string'-tie**, a narrow necktie of uniform width; **string'y-bark**, one of a class of Australian gum-trees with

very fibrous bark.—**no strings (attached)**, with no conditions or limitations; **on a string**, under complete control: kept in suspense; **pull (the) strings**, use influence behind the scenes, as if working puppets (*n.* string'-pulling); **string along** (*v.t.*), to string, fool: to give someone false expectations; (*v.i.*) to go along together, co-operate; **string up**, hang; **strung up**, nervously tensed; **two strings to one's bow** (see **bow**, 2). [O.E. *streng*; cf. Du. *streng*, Ger. *strang*, O.N. *strengr*.]

**stringent,** *strin'jənt*, *adj.* tight: binding: rigorous: convincing: astringent: characterised by difficulty in finding money.—*n.* strin'gency.—*adj.* and *adv.* **stringendo** (*-jen'dō*; It.; *mus.*), hastening the time.—*adv.* **strin'gently.**—*n.* **strin'gentness.** [L. *stringēns*, *-entis*, pr.p. of *stringĕre*, to draw together.]

**stringhalt,** *string'hölt*, *n.* a catching up of a horse's legs, usu. of one or both hind-legs.—Also **spring'halt.** [App. string (sinew) and **halt**.]

**strinkle,** *string'kl*, (*Scot.*) *v.t.* to sprinkle.—*n.* **strink'ling.** [Cf. **sprinkle**.]

**strip,** *strip*, *v.t.* to pull, peel, or tear off: to doff: to divest: to undress: to deprive of livery and dismiss: to reduce to the ranks: to deprive of a covering: to skin, to peel, to husk: to lay bare: to expose: to deprive: to clear, empty: to dismantle: to clear of fruit, leaves, stems, midribs, or any other part: to tear off or wear off the screw-thread from: to press out the last milk from, or obtain in this way: to press out the roe or milt from: to handle as if milking a cow: to cut in strips: to put strips on: to outstrip, press (*obs.*).—*v.i.* to undress: to lose the thread, as a screw: to come off: to go swiftly (*obs.*):—*pr.p.* **stripp'ing**; *pa.t.* and *pa.p.* **stripped.**—*n.* a long narrow piece: a long thin piece of rolled metal, as steel strip: a narrow space in a newspaper in which a story is told in pictures (**strip cartoon**): light garb for running, football, etc.—*n.* **stripp'er**, one who or that which strips: a strip-tease artist.—*n.pl.* **stripp'ings**, last milk drawn at a milking.—**strip club**, one which regularly features strip-tease artists; **strip'-leaf**, tobacco stripped of stalks; **strip lighting**, lighting by means of long fluorescent tubes; **strip map**, a map showing a long narrow strip of country, used esp. by airmen; **strip'-mine**, an opencast mine; **stripped atom**, an ionised atom from which one or more electrons have been removed; **strip'-tease**, an act of undressing slowly and seductively in a place of entertainment. [O.E. *strȳpan*; Ger. *streifen*; perh. partly from other sources.]

**stripe,** *strip*, *n.* a blow, esp. with a lash: a band of colour: a chevron on a sleeve, indicating non-commissioned rank or good behaviour: a striped cloth or pattern: a strain: kind, particular sort (*U.S.*): magnetic sound track(s) on cinematograph film for sound-film reproduction.—*v.t.* to make stripes upon: to mark with stripes: to lash.—*adjs.* **striped**, having stripes of different colours; **stripe'less.**—*ns.* **stripes** (*coll.*), a tiger; **strip'iness**; **strip'ing.**—*adj.* **strip'y**, stripe-like. [Perh. different words; cf. Du. *streep* (earlier *strijpe*), Ger. *streif*, stripe, O.N. *strip*, striped fabric, Du. *strippen*, to whip.]

**stripling,** *strip'ling*, *n.* a youth: one yet growing. [Dim. of **strip**.]

**strive,** *striv*, *v.i.* to contend: to be in conflict: to struggle: to endeavour earnestly: to make one's way with effort:—*pa.t.* **strove** (*strōv*), Shak. **strived**; *pa.p.* **striven** (*striv'n*), Shak. **strove**, B. **strived.**—*n.* **striv'er.**—*n.* and *adj.* **striv'ing.**—*adv.* **striv'ingly.** [O.Fr. *estriver*; poss. Gmc., from the root of **stride**, or that of Ger. *streben*, to strive.]

**stroam,** *strōm*, (*dial.*) *v.i.* to wander idly about: to stride. [Perh. **stroll** and **roam**.]

strobic, *strob'ik*, *adj*. like a spinning-top: spinning or seeming to spin.—*n.* strobe (*strōb*), process of viewing vibrations with a stroboscope: a stroboscope.—*n.* stroboscope (*strob'*, *strōb'ə-skōp*), an optical toy giving an illusion of motion from a series of pictures seen momentarily in succession: an instrument for studying rotating machinery or other periodic phenomena by means of a flashing lamp which can be synchronised with the frequency of the periodic phenomena so that they appear to be stationary.—*adj.* stroboscopic (*strob-*, *strōb-ə-skop'ik*). [Gr. *strobos*, a whirling—*strephein*, to twist.]

strobila, *stro-bī'lə*, *n.* in the life-cycle of jellyfishes, a chain of segments, cone within cone, that separate to become medusoids: a chain of segments forming the body of a tapeworm:—*pl.* strobi'lae (*-lē*).—*adj.* strobilaceous (*strob-i-lā'-shəs*), of or like a strobile: bearing strobiles.—*v.i.* strob'ilate, to undergo strobilation.—*adj.* of the nature of a strobilus.—*ns.* strobilā'tion, strobilisā'tion, -izā'tion, production or reproduction by strobilae; strobile (*strob'* or *strōb'il, -il*), a strobila: a strobilus.—*adjs.* strobiliform (*-il'*), strob'iline, strob'iloid.—*n.* strobi'lus, a close group of sporophylls with their sporangia, a cone: a scaly spike of female flowers, as in the hop:—*pl.* strobi'li (*-lī*). [Gr. *strobīlē*, a conical plug of lint, *strobilos*, a spinning-top, whirl, pine-cone—*strobos* (see foregoing).]

strode, *strōd*, *pa.t.* of stride.

strodle, stroddle, *strod'l* (*obs.* or *dial.*). Same as straddle.

stroke, *strōk*, *n.* an act or mode of striking: a hit or attempt at hitting: a blow: a striking by lightning: a reverse: an attack of apoplexy or of paralysis: the striking of a clock or its sound: a dash or line: a touch of pen, pencil, brush, etc.: a trait (*obs.*): a beat, pulse: a single complete movement in a repeated series, as in swimming, rowing, pumping, action of an engine: a stroke-oar: a single action towards an end: an effective action, feat, achievement.—*v.t.* to put a stroke through or on: to cross (commonly with *out*): to row stroke in or for: to row at the rate of.—*v.i.* to row stroke.—stroke'-oar, the aftmost oar in a boat: its rower (also stroke, strokes'man), whose stroke leads the rest. [O.E. (inferred) *strāc*; cf. Ger. *streich*.]

stroke, *strōk*, *v.t.* to rub gently in one direction: to rub gently in kindness: to put by such a movement: to soothe, or flatter (*obs.*): to milk, strip: to tool in small flutings: to whet: to set in close gathers.—*n.* an act of stroking.—*ns.* stroke'er; strok'ing. [O.E. *strācian*—*strāc*, stroke (n.); cf. Ger. *streichen*, to rub.]

stroke, *strōk*, stroken, *strōk'n*, obs. forms (*Spens., Shak.*) of struck. See strike.

stroll, *strōl*, *v.i.* to wander as a vagrant or itinerant: to walk leisurely: to saunter.—*n.* a leisurely walk: a stroller (now *U.S.*).—*n.* stroll'er, one who strolls: a wanderer: a saunterer: a vagrant: an itinerant.—*n.* and *adj.* stroll'ing—strolling player, an itinerant actor. [Perh. Ger. *strolchen* (obs. *strollen*)—*strolch*, vagrant.]

stroma, *strō'mə*, *n.* a supporting framework of connective tissue (*zool.*): a dense mass of hyphae in which a fungus fructification may develop (*bot.*): the denser part of a blood-corpuscle, chloroplast, etc.:—*pl.* strōm'ata.—*adjs.* strōmatic, (*-mat'ik*), strō'matous. [Gr. *strōma*, a bed, mattress.]

stromb, *strom(b)*, *n.* a very large gasteropod akin to the whelk: its shell with short spire and expanded lip.—*adjs.* strombūlif'erous, bearing spirally coiled organs or parts; strombū'liform, top-shaped: spirally twisted.—*n.* Strom'bus, the stromb, or wing-shell, genus: (without *cap.*) a spirally coiled pod. [Gr. *strombos*, a spinning-top, snail, whirlwind.]

strond, *strond*, (*Spens., Shak.*) *n.* Same as strand.

strong, *strong*, *adj.* powerful: forcible: forceful: vigorous: hale: robust: of great staying power: firm: resistant: difficult to overcome: steadfast: excelling: efficient: of great tenacity of will and effective in execution: able: well-skilled or versed: competent: rich in resources or means to power: well provided: numerous: numbering so many: of vigorous growth: stiff, coarse, and abundant, indicating strength: without ambiguity, obscurity, or understatement: intemperate, offensive and unseemly: gross: violent: grievous: having great effect: intense: ardent and convinced: performed with strength: powerfully, or unpleasantly powerfully, affecting the senses: rank: vivid: marked: bold in definition: in high concentration: showing the characteristic properties in high degree: (of prices, markets) steady or tending to rise: of Germanic verbs, showing ablaut variation in conjugation (*gram.*): of Germanic nouns and adjectives, having a stem originally in a vowel or a consonant other than *n*: (*compar.* stronger, *strong'gər*; *superl.* strong'est, *-gist*).—*adv.* strongly (*rare*): very (*obs.*).—*adj.* strongish (*strong'ish*).—*adv.* strong'ly.—strong'arm, one who uses violence.—*adj.* by, having, or using, physical force.—strong'-box, a safe or strongly made coffer for valuables; strong drink, waters, alcoholic liquors; strong flour, wheat, one rich in gluten, giving bread that rises well; strong head, power to withstand alcohol or any dizzying influence; strong'hold, a fastness or fortified refuge: a fortress: a place where anything is in great strength; strong interaction, one produced by short-range forces, involving baryons or mesons, and completed in about $10^{-23}$ seconds.—*adj.* strong'-knit, firmly jointed or compacted.—strong language, swearing: plain, emphatic language; strong meat, solid food, not milk (Heb. v. 12, 14).—*adj.* strong'-mind'ed, having a vigorous mind—formerly applied by disapprovers to emancipated women.—strong'-mind'edness; strong'point (*mil.*), a favourably situated and well-fortified defensive position; strong point, that in which one excels, one's forte; strong'-room, a room constructed for safe-keeping of valuables or prisoners.—come it strong (see come); going strong (see going). [O.E. *strang*, strong; O.N. *strangr*, Ger. *streng*, tight.]

strongyle, *stron'jil*, *n.* a blunt rhabdus: a parasitic thread-worm (Strongylus or kindred).—*adj.* and *n.* stron'gyloid.—*n.* strongylō'sis, infestation with strongyles. [Gr. *strongylos*, round.]

strontium, *stron'sh(i-)əm*, *stron'ti-əm*, *n.* a yellow metal (Sr; at. numb. 38) found in celestine.—*ns.* stron'tia, its oxide; stron'tianite, its carbonate, an orthorhombic mineral (first found in 1790 near Strontian (*stron-tē'ən*) in Argyllshire).—strontium-90, a radioactive isotope of strontium, an important element in nuclear fall-out.

strook, strooke, *strŏŏk*, obs. *pa.t.* and *pa.p.* (*Spens., Shak., Milt.,* etc.) and strook'en, obs. *pa.p.* of strike.—*n.* strooke (*strōk*; *Spens.*), stroke.

strop, *strop*, *n.* a strip of leather, etc., for sharpening razors.—*v.t.* to sharpen on a strop:—*pr.p.* stropp'ing; *pa.t.* and *pa.p.* stropped. [Older form of strap—O.E. *strop*, prob.—L. *struppus*, a thong.]

Strophanthus, *strof-*, *strōf-an'thəs*, *n.* an African and Asiatic genus of the periwinkle family, yielding arrow-poison: its dried seeds used in medicine.—*n.* strophan'thin, a very poisonous glucoside in its seeds. [Gr. *strophos*, twisted band, *anthos*, flower, from the ribbonlike prolongation of the petals, twisted in bud.]

strophe, *strof'i*, *strōf'i*, *n.* in a Greek play, the song sung by the chorus as it moved towards one side, answered by an exact counterpart, the *anti-strophe*, as it returned: part of any ode thus answered: loosely, a stanza.—*adj.* **stroph'ic.** [Gr. *strŏphē*, a turn.]

**strophiole,** *strof'i-ōl, (bot.) n.* a caruncle.—*adjs.* **stroph'iolate, -d.** [Gr. *strophiolon,* a fringe—*strophos,* a twisted band.]

**stroppy,** *strop'i, (slang) adj.* quarrelsome, bad-tempered: rowdy, obstreperous. [Perh. **obstropalous.**]

**strossers,** *stros'ərz, (Shak.) n.* trousers. [Cf. **trousers.**]

**stroud,** *strowd, n.* a blanket made for trading with American Indians.—*n.* **stroud'ing,** its material. [Prob. made at Stroud, Gloucestershire.]

**stroup,** *strōōp, (Scot.) n.* a spout, nozzle. [Cf. Sw. *strupe,* throat.]

**strout,** *strowt, v.i.* to bulge, swell: to stand out, protrude: to flaunt: to strut.—*v.t.* to cause to protrude. [O.E. *strūtian,* to protrude.]

**strove,** *strōv, pa.t.* of **strive.**

**strow,** *strō, strōō.* Same as **strew:**—*pa.t.* **strowed;** *pa.p.* **strown.**

**stroy,** *stroi, v.t. (Shak.)* to destroy.—*n. (Bunyan)* destruction. [**destroy.**]

**struck, strucken.** See **strike.**

**structure,** *struk'chər, n.* manner or *(obs.)* act of putting together: construction: arrangement of parts: manner of organisation: a thing constructed: an organic form.—*v.t.* to organise, build up: to construct a framework for: to allot to (a linguistic element) its function or syntactical relationship.—*adj.* **struc'tural.**—*n.* **struc'turalism,** belief in and study of unconscious, underlying patterns in thought, behaviour, social organisation, etc.—*adv.* **struc'turally.**—*adjs.* **struc'tured,** having a certain structure: having a definite structure or organisation; **struc'tureless.** [L. *structūra—struĕre, structum* to build.]

**strudel,** *s(h)trōō'dl, n.* very thin pastry enclosing fruit, or cheese, etc. [Ger., eddy, whirlpool.]

**struggle,** *strug'l, v.i.* to strive vigorously in resistance, contention, or coping with difficulties: to make great efforts or exertions: to contend strenuously: to make way with difficulty: to move convulsively.—*n.* a bout or course of struggling: strife: a hard contest with difficulties: a convulsive movement.—*n.* **strugg'ler.**—*n.* and *adj.* **strugg'ling.**—*adv.* **strugg'lingly.** [M.E. *strogelen*; origin unknown.]

**Struldbrug,** *struld'brug, n.* one of a class among the Luggnaggians in Swift's *Gulliver's Travels,* endowed with immortality, but doomed to decrepitude after eighty, and most wretched. [A capricious coinage.]

**strum,** *strum, v.t.* and *v.i.* to play in a haphazard unskilful way:—*pr.p.* **strumm'ing;** *pa.t.* and *pa.p.* **strummed.**—*n.* a strumming. [Cf. **thrum.**]

**struma,** *strōō'mə, n.* scrofula: a scrofulous tumour: goitre: a cushion-like swelling *(bot.):*—*pl.* **stru'mae** *(-mē, -mī)*.—*adjs.* **strumatic** *(strōō-mat'ik),* **strumose** *(strōō'mōs),* **stru'mous.**—*n.* **strumi'tis,** inflammation of the thyroid gland. [L. *strūma,* a scrofulous tumour.]

**strummel,** *strum'l,* **strammel,** *stram'l, (obs. slang) n.* straw: hence, hair. [Cf. L. *strāmen,* straw.]

**strumpet,** *strum'pit, n.* a whore.—*adj.* like a strumpet: inconstant: false.—*v.t.* to make a strumpet of: to call a strumpet. [Origin obscure.]

**strung, strung,** *pa.t.* and *pa.p.* of **string.**

**strunt,** *strunt, (Scot.) v.i.* to strut. [Cf. Norw. *strunta.*]

**strunt,** *strunt, (Scot.) n.* spirituous liquor. [Origin obscure.]

**strunt,** *strunt, (Scot.;* often in *pl.) n.* the huff, the sulks. [Origin unknown.]

**strut,** *strut, v.i.* to bulge, protrude *(obs.):* to flaunt, glory *(obs.):* to stand stiffly upright *(obs.):* to walk stiffly in vanity or self-importance:—*pr.p.* **strutt'ing;** *pa.t.* and *pa.p.* **strutt'ed.** —*n.* a strutting gait.—*n.* **strutt'er.**—*n.* and *adj.*

**strutt'ing.**—*adv.* **strutt'ingly.** [O.E. *strūtian* or some kindred form; see **strout.**]

**strut,** *strut, n.* a rod or member that resists pressure: a prop.—*v.t.* to support as, or with, a strut or struts. [Cf. L.G. *strutt,* rigid, and foregoing.]

**Struthio,** *strōō'thi-ō, n.* the African ostrich genus. —*n.pl.* **Struthio'nes** *(-nēz),* an order of birds including ostriches, rheas, kiwis, emus, and cassowaries.—*adjs.* **stru'thioid, stru'thious.** [L., —Gr. *strouthiōn,* an ostrich.]

**strychnine,** *strik'nēn, n.* a very poisonous alkaloid $(C_{21}H_{22}N_2O_2)$ got from nux vomica seeds.—*v.t.* to poison with strychnine.—*n.* **strych'nia** (now *rare*), **strychnine.**—*adj.* **strych'nic.**—*ns.* **strych'-ninism, strych'nism,** strychnine poisoning. [Gr. *strychnos,* nightshade (of various kinds).]

**stub,** *stub, n.* a stump: (also **stub'-nail**) a short thick nail or worn horse-shoe nail, esp. in *pl.,* old nails used as scrap: a counterfoil: a short piece left after the larger part has been used (as a cigarette, pencil, etc.): something blunt and stunted.—*v.t.* to grub up: to remove stubs from: to wear or cut to a stub: to wound with a stub: to strike as against a stub: to extinguish by pressing the end on something (often with *out):—pr.p.* **stubb'ing;** *pa.t., pa.p.* **stubbed.**—*adj.* **stubbed,** cut or worn to a stub: cleared of stubs: stumpy: blunt.—*n.* **stubb'iness.**—*adj.* **stubb'y,** abounding with stubs: short, thick, and strong. [O.E. *stubb, stybb.*]

**stubble,** *stub'l, n.* a stump of reaped corn: such stumps collectively: straw: a reaped field: an ill-shaven beard.—*adjs.* **stubb'led,** stubbly; **stubb'ly,** like or covered with stubble.—*adj.* **stubb'le-fed,** fed on the natural grass growing among stubble.—**stubb'le-field; stubb'le-goose,** a goose fed on stubble; **stubb'le-rake,** a rake with long teeth for raking stubble. [O.Fr. *estuble—*L.L. *stupula—*from L. *stipula;* see **stipule.**]

**stubborn,** *stub'ərn, adj.* obstinate: unreasonably or troublesomely obstinate: pertinacious: refractory: hard to work or treat: rigid.—*v.t. (Keats)* to make stubborn.—*adv.* **stubb'ornly.** —*n.* **stubb'ornness.** [Connection with **stub** is obscure.]

**stubby,** See **stub.**

**stucco,** *stuk'ō, n.* a plaster used for coating walls, making casts, etc.: work done in stucco *(pl.* **stucc'ōs**).—*v.t.* to face or overlay with stucco: to form in stucco:—*pa.t.* and *pa.p.* **stucc'oed, stucc'ō'd.**—*n.* **stucc'ōer,** a worker or dealer in stucco. [It. *stucco;* from O.H.G. *stucchi,* crust, coating.]

**stuck, stuck-up.** See **stick.**

**stuck,** *stuk, (Shak.) n.* a thrust. [**stock,** 2.]

**stud,** *stud, n.* a horse-breeding establishment: the animals kept there: a collection of horses or other animals, or of cars, belonging to the same owner: short for **stud-horse.**—*adj.* kept for breeding: of a stud.—**stud'-book,** a record of horses' (or other animals') pedigrees; **stud'-farm,** a horse-breeding farm; **stud'-groom,** a groom at a stud, esp. the head-groom; **stud'-horse,** a stallion kept for breeding; **stud poker,** a variety of the game of poker. [O.E. *stōd;* cf. **steed;** Ger. *stute,* mare, *gestüt,* stud.]

**stud,** *stud, n.* a wooden post *(obs.):* a tree-trunk *(Spens.):* a spur, stump, or short branch: an upright scantling as in a timber framework or partition: a cross-piece strengthening a link in a chain: a projecting boss, knob, or pin: a large-headed nail: a stud-bolt: a double-headed button: the height of a room *(U.S.).*—*v.t.* to adorn, set, or secure with studs: to set at intervals:—*pr.p.* **studd'ing;** *pa.t.* and *pa.p.* **studd'ed.**—*adj.* **studd'ed.**—*n.* **studd'ing.**—**stud'-bolt,** a bolt with a thread on each end, screwed into a fixed part at one end, receiving a nut upon the other;

**stud'work**, brickwork walls between studs: studded leather. [O.E. *studu*, post.]

**studden.** See **stand.**

**studding-sail**, *stun'sl*, *n.* a narrow sail set at the outer edges of a square sail when wind is light. —Also **stunsail.** [Origin unknown.]

**studdle**, *stud'l*, *n.* a post: a prop. [O.E. *stodla*.]

**student**, *stū'dənt*, *n.* one who studies: one devoted to books or to any study: one who is enrolled for a course of instruction in a college or university: an undergraduate: a member of the foundation of Christ Church, Oxford, answering to a fellow elsewhere: the holder of a studentship.—*ns.* **stu'dentry**, students collectively; **stu'dentship**, an endowment for a student in a college: in Christ Church, Oxford, the equivalent of a fellowship: the condition or time of being a student.—*adj.* **studied** (*stud'id*), well considered: deliberately contrived, designed: overelaborated with loss of spontaneity: well prepared by study: deep read: versed.—*adv.* **stud'iedly.**—*ns.* **stud'iedness; stud'ier; studio** (*stū'di-ō*), an artist's workroom (*It.*): a workshop for photography, cinematography, radio or television broadcasting, making of gramophone records, etc.:—*pl.* **stu'dios.**—*adj.* **studious** (*stū'di-əs*), devoted to or assiduous in study: heedful: intent: solicitous: studied: deliberate.—*adv.* **stu'diously.**—*n.* **stu'diousness.**—*v.t.* **study** (*stud'i*), to apply the mind to in order to acquire knowledge or skill: to make one's object, seek to achieve: to be solicitous about: to consider: to scrutinise: to look contemplatively at: to take into consideration: to consider the wishes, advantage, feelings of: to devise: to elaborate with self-consciousness: to think out: to instruct (*Shak.*).—*v.i.* to apply the mind closely to books, nature, acquisition of learning or of skill: to take an educational course: to rack one's mind: to muse, meditate, reflect:—*pr.p.* **stud'ying;** *pa.t.* and *pa.p.* **stud'ied.**—*n.* inclination: interest: zeal: an object of endeavour, solicitude, or mental application: a state of doubtful consideration: attentive and detailed examination: a scrutiny: a reverie: application of the mind to the acquisition of knowledge or skill: a department of knowledge: a preliminary essay towards a work of art: an exercise in art: a musical composition affording an exercise in technique: a presentation in literature or art of the results of study: committing to memory, hence a memoriser (*theat.*): a room devoted to study, actually or ostensibly.—**studio couch**, a couch, usu. without a back, that can be converted into a bed; **study group**, a group of people studying a specific subject, who meet informally at regular intervals to discuss their work. [L. *studēre* (pr.p. *studēns*, *-entis*), to be zealous, *studium* (O.Fr. *estudie*; It. *studio*), zeal, study.]

**studio, study, etc.** See **student.**

**stuff**, *stuf*, *n.* stuffing, filling (*obs.*): matter: substance: essence: material: a preparation used or commodity dealt in in some particular industry or trade: garden produce: cloth, esp. woollen: a medicinal mixture: goods: luggage: provision: furniture: money: literary or journalistic copy: liquor (**good stuff**, often whisky): rubbish: nonsense: indecent matter (*obs.*).—*adj.* woollen—*v.t.* to garrison (*obs.*): to store, furnish (*Shak.*): to provision (*obs.*): to line: to be a filling for: to fill very full: to thrust in: to crowd: to cram: to obstruct, clog: to cause to bulge out by filling: to fill with seasoning, as a fowl: to fill the skin of, so as to reproduce the living form: to hoax (*slang*): to have sexual intercourse with (*vulg.*).—*v.i.* to feed gluttonously: to practise taxidermy.—*adj.* **stuffed**, provisioned: well stored: filled: filled out with stuffing: clogged in nose or throat, etc. —*n.* **stuff'er.**—*adv.* **stuff'ily.**—*ns.* **stuff'iness;**

**stuff'ing**, that which is used to stuff or fill anything—straw, sawdust, feathers, hair, etc.: savoury ingredients put into meat, poultry, etc., in cooking.—*adj.* **stuff'y**, badly ventilated, musty: stifling: stout, sturdy (*Scot.*): stodgy (*slang*): strait-laced: sulky (*U.S.*).—**stuffed shirt**, a pompous, unbendingly correct person, esp. if of little real importance; **stuff'-gown**, a gown of stuff, not silk, esp. that of a junior barrister; **stuff'ing-box**, a cavity filled with packing to make a pressure-tight joint.—**and stuff**, and that sort of thing or rubbish; **do one's stuff**, to do what is expected of one; **knock the stuffing out of**, to reduce (an opponent) to helplessness; **know one's stuff**, to have a thorough knowledge of the field in which one is concerned; **that's the stuff!** excellent! [O.Fr. *estoffe*, stuff—L. *stuppa*—Gr. *styppē*, tow.]

**stuggy**, *stug'i*, (*dial.*) *adj.* thick-set, stout.

**stull**, *stul*, (*dial.*) *n.* a horizontal prop in a mine.— *n.* **stulm** (*stulm*), an adit: a small draining-shaft. [Cf. Ger. *stollen.*]

**stultify**, *stul'ti-fi*, *v.t.* to allege or prove to be of unsound mind (*law*): to dull the mind: to cause to appear foolish or ridiculous: to destroy the force of, as by self-contradiction:—*pr.p.* **stul'tifying;** *pa.t.* and *pa.p.* **stul'tified.**—*ns.* **stultifica'tion; stul'tifier; stultil'oquence** (L. *loqui*, to talk), **stultil'oquy**, foolish talk or discourse, babbling. —*adj.* **stultil'oquent.** [L. *stultus*, foolish.]

**stum**, *stum*, *n.* must, grape-juice unfermented: new wine used to revive dead or vapid wine: a mixture used to impart artificial strength, etc., to weak beer or wine: wine revived by the addition of stum or by a second fermentation.—*v.t.* to renew or doctor with stum: to fume, as a cask of liquor, with burning sulphur:—*pr.p.* **stumm'-ing;** *pa.t.* and *pa.p.* **stummed.** [Du. *stom*, must —*stom*, mute; Ger. *stumm*, dumb.]

**stumble**, *stum'bl*, *v.i.* to take a false step, come near to falling in walking: to walk unsteadily: to lapse into wrongdoing: to flounder: to light by chance or error (with *across* or *on*): to boggle.—*v.t.* to disconcert.—*n.* a trip: a false step: a lapse: a blunder.—*n.* **stum'bler.**—*adv.* **stum'blingly.**—*adj.* **stum'bly**, apt to stumble or to cause stumbling.—**stum'bling-block, -stone**, an obstacle: a cause of perplexity or error. [M.E. *stomble*, *stumble*; cf. Norw. *stumla*, and **stammer.**]

**stumer**, *stū'mər*, (*slang*) *n.* a counterfeit coin or note: a forged or worthless cheque: a sham: a dud: a failure, bankruptcy: a horse sure to lose: a stupid mistake, clanger. [Origin obscure.]

**stummel**, *stum'l*, *n.* the bowl and adjacent part of a pipe. [Ger.]

**stump**, *stump*, *n.* the part of a felled or fallen tree left in the ground: a tree-stump used as a platform: hence, a campaign of stump-oratory: a short thick remaining basal part, esp. of anything that projects: a short thick branch: a leg (*facet.*): a wooden leg: anything stumpy: a stumping walk or its sound: a pencil of soft material for softening hard lines, blending, etc.: one of the three sticks forming (with the bails) a wicket (*cricket*): a challenge to perform a feat (*U.S.*).—*adj.* reduced to a stump: stumpy.—*v.t.* to reduce to a stump: to remove stumps from: (of the wicket-keeper; sometimes with *out*) to dismiss by breaking the wicket when the striker is out of his ground (*cricket*): to clear out of money (*slang*): to nonplus, foil, defeat: to soften or tone with a stump: to walk over or strike heavily and stiffly: to traverse making stump-speeches: to dare, challenge (*U.S.*).—*v.i.* to walk stiffly and heavily, as if on wooden legs: to make stump-speeches.—*n.* **stump'er.**—*adv.* **stump'-ily.** —*n.* **stump'iness.**—*adj.* **stump'y**, short and thick: full of stumps (*U.S.*).—*n.* (*slang*) cash.—**stump'-orator**, one who speaks from an improvised platform, usu. with an implication of rant: in U.S. a political public speaker in general; **stump'-oratory; stump'-speech; stump'-work**, elaborate raised embroidery of the 15th-17th cents. using various materials and raised by stumps of wood or pads of wool.—**draw stumps** (*cricket*), to end play; **stir one's stumps,** to move, be active; **stump up,** to pay up, fork out. [Cf. Du. *stomp*, M.L.G. *stump*, O.N. *stumpr*, Ger. *stumpf*.]

**stun,** *stun, v.t.* to render unconscious as by a blow: to stupefy, daze, as with din or sudden emotion: to abrade, bruise:—*pr.p.* **stunn'ing;** *pa.t.* and *pa.p.* **stunned.**—*n.* a shock, stupefying blow: stunned condition.—*ns.* **stunn'er** (*slang*), a person or thing supremely excellent: a very attractive person; **stunn'ing,** stupefaction.—*adj.* stupefying, dazing: supremely excellent (*slang*): very attractive (*slang*).—*adv.* **stunn'ingly.** [O.Fr. *estoner* (Fr. *étonner*), to astonish; cf. O.E. *stunian*, to make a din—*stun,* a din.]

**Stundist,** *stoon'dist, n.* a member of a Russian Protestant sect.—*n.* **Stun'dism.** [Ger. *stunde*, hour, lesson, from their Bible-reading meetings.]

**stung,** *stung, pa.t.* and *pa.p.* of sting.

**stunk,** *stungk, pa.t.* and *pa.p.* of stink.

**stunkard,** *stungk'ərd*, (*Scot.*) *adj.* sulky: sullen. [Origin obscure.]

**stunsail,** *stun'sl.* See studding-sail.

**stunt,** *stunt, adj.* dwarfed: stumpy.—*v.t.* to hinder from growth, to dwarf, check.—*n.* a check in growth: a stunted animal.—*adj.* **stunt'ed,** dwarfed.—*n.* **stunt'edness.** [O.E. *stunt*, dull, stupid: O.N. *stuttr*, short.]

**stunt,** *stunt, n.* a difficult, often showy, performance, enterprise, or turn (*orig. U.S. college slang*): a newspaper craze or campaign.—Also *adj.*—*v.i.* to perform stunts.—**stunt'man,** one paid to perform dangerous and showy feats (esp. a stand-in for a film actor). [Perh. a variant of stint (1), stent (1); cf. stunt (1); or perh. Ger. *stunde*, hour, lesson.]

**stupa,** *stoo'pə, n.* a tope or Buddhist dome-shaped memorial shrine. [Sans. *stūpa*.]

**stupe,** *stūp, n.* a medicated piece of tow or cloth used in fomentation.—*v.t.* to treat with a stupe. [L. *stūpa* for *stuppa*—Gr. *styppē*, tow.]

**stupefy,** *stū'pi-fī, v.t.* to make stupid or senseless: to stun with amazement, fear, etc.—*v.i.* to become stupid or dull:—*pr.p.* **stū'pefying;** *pa.t.* and *pa.p.* **stū'pefied.**—*adj.* **stupefacient** (*-fā'shənt*), stupefying.—*n.* **stupefaction** (*-fak'shən*), the act of stupefying: the state of being stupefied: extreme astonishment.—*adjs.* **stupefac'tive,** stupefying; **stu'pefied.**—*n.* **stu'pefier.**—*adj.* **stu'pefying.** [L. *stupēre*, to be struck senseless, *facēre*, to make.]

**stupendous,** *stū-pen'dəs* (formerly, as *Milt.*, **stupendious,** *-i-əs*), *adj.* astounding: astoundingly huge: often used as a coll. term of approbation or admiration.—*adv.* **stupen'dously.**—*n.* **stupen'dousness.**—*adj.* **stu'pent,** astounded: dumbfounded. [L. *stupendus*, gerundive, and *stupēns, -entis*, pres. part. of *stupēre*, to be stunned.]

**stupid,** *stū'pid, adj.* stupefied: senseless: insensible: deficient or dull in understanding: showing lack of reason or judgment: foolish: dull: boring.—*n.* (*coll.*) a stupid person (also *coll.* **stupe**).—*ns.* **stupid'ity, stu'pidness.**—*adv.* **stu'pidly.** [L. *stupidus*.]

**stupor,** *stū'pər, n.* torpor: lethargy: stupefaction: wonder.—*adj.* **stu'porous.** [L. *stupor, -ōris*—*stupēre*.]

**stuprate,** *stū'prāt, v.t.* to ravish, violate.—*n.* **stuprā'tion.** [L. *stuprāre, -ātum*.]

**sturdy,** *stûr'di, adj.* orig., giddy: impetuous, violent, rough (*obs.*): refractory: obstinate: resolute: robust: stout.—*n.* gid, a disease of sheep characterised by staggering, due to a bladderworm in the brain: a sturdy person.—

*adj.* **stur'died,** affected with sturdy.—*adv.* **stur'dily.**—*n.* **stur'diness.** [O.Fr. *estourdi* (Fr. *étourdi*), stunned, giddy.]

**sture.** See stoor (1).

**sturgeon,** *stûr'jən, n.* any member of a genus (Acipenser) of large fishes of the Chondrostei, with cartilaginous skull, long snout, heterocercal tail, and rows of bony shields on the skin. [A.Fr. *sturgeon*, of Gmc. origin (O.H.G. *sturjo*).]

**sturmabteilung,** *shtoorm'ap-tī-loong, n.* storm troops (*q.v.*), Brownshirts. [Ger. *sturm*, storm, *abteilung*, division.]

**Sturnus,** *stûr'nəs, n.* the starling genus, giving name to the family **Stur'nidae** (*-ni-dē*).—*adjs.* **stur'nine, stur'noid.** [L. *sturnus*, starling.]

**sturt,** *stûrt*, (chiefly *Scot.*) *n.* contention: disturbance.—*v.t.* to trouble.—*v.i.* to start with fear. [strut.]

**stutter,** *stut'ər, v.i.* and *v.t.* to speak, say, or pronounce with spasmodic repetition of initial sounds, stammer.—*n.* a stammer.—*n.* **stutt'erer.**—*n.* and *adj.* **stutt'ering.**—*adv.* **stutt'eringly.** [A freq. of obs. *stut*, to stutter, M.E. *stutten*; cf. O.N. *stauta*; Ger. *stossen*.]

**sty,** *stye, stī, n.* a small inflamed tumour on the eyelid. [Obs. or dial. *stian, styan*—O.E. *stigend*, from *stīgan*, to rise.]

**sty** (*Spens.*, **stye, stie**), *stī,* (*obs.*) *v.i.* to mount, rise, climb.—*n.* a path (*obs.*): a ladder (*dial.*). [O.E. *stīgan*, to mount, *stig*, path, and O.N. *stige*, path, O.E. *stīge*, ascent or descent.]

**sty,** rarely **stye,** *stī, n.* a pen for swine: any place extremely filthy: any place of gross debauchery: —*pl.* **sties, styes.**—*v.t.* and *v.i.* to lodge in a sty:—*pr.p.* **sty'ing;** *pa.t.* and *pa.p.* **stied, styed;** *3rd sing. pres. ind.* **sties.** [O.E. *stig*, pen, hall; Ger. *steige*.]

**Stygian,** *stij'i-ən, -yən, adj.* of the *Styx*, one of the rivers of Hades, across which Charon ferries the shades of the departed: hellish, infernal: black as the Styx.—**Stygian oath,** an inviolable oath, like that of the gods, by the Styx. [Gr. *Styx*; cf. *stygeein*, to hate.]

**style,** *stil, n.* a pointed instrument for writing on wax tablets: a similar instrument or tool of various kinds, as a graver, a blunt probe, a tracing or cutting point: a slender process of various kinds (*biol.*): the slender part of the gynaeceum, bearing the stigma (*bot.*): the gnomon of a dial: a hand, pointer, index: a literary composition (*obs.*): manner of writing, mode of expressing thought in language or of expression, execution, action or bearing generally: the distinctive manner peculiar to an author or other: particular custom or form observed, as by a printing-house in optional matters (*style of the house*), or by lawyers in drawing up deeds: designation: manner: form: fashion: an air of fashion or consequence: kind, type: method in calico-printing: mode of reckoning dates—*Old Style*, according to the Julian calendar, as in Britain till 1752, Russia till 1917; *New Style*, according to the Gregorian calendar, adopted in Britain by omitting eleven days, 3rd to 13th September 1752.—*v.t.* to designate: to arrange, dictate, the fashion or style of.—*adjs.* **sty'lar;** style, having a style, or a persistent style; **style'less.**—*n.* **sty'let,** **sti'let,** a probe: a wire in a catheter: a bristle-like process: a graving tool: a writing instrument.—*adjs.* **stylif'erous,** bearing a style; **sty'liform,** like a style or a bristle.—*n.* **stylisā'tion.**—*v.t.* **sty'lise, -ize,** to conventionalise.—*adj.* **sty'lish,** displaying style: fashionable: showy: imposingly smart: pretending to style.—*adv.* **sty'lishly.**—*ns.* **sty'lishness;** **sty'list,** one with a distinctive and fine literary style: one who arranges a style, esp. in hairdressing.—*adj.* **stylist'ic.**—Also *n.*—*adv.* **stylist'ically.**—*n.* **sty-**

lis'tics, the science of the variations in language, including the effective values of different words, forms, and sounds, that constitute style in the literary and also the wider sense.—*adj.* sty'loid, like a style or bristle: forming a slender process. —*n.* a spiny process of the temporal bone.—*n.* sty'lus, a style: the cutter used in making gramophone records: a gramophone needle.—style'-book, a book of forms for deeds, etc.—in style, in a grand manner. [L. *stilus*, a writing instrument, literary composition or style, confused with Gr. *stylos*, a column; in some senses perh. from the Gr. word.]

stylite, *sti'lit*, *n.* an anchorite living on the top of a pillar. [Gr. *stylitēs*—*stylos*, a pillar.]

stylobate, *sti'lō-bāt*, *n.* the substructure of a row of columns. [Gr. *stylobatēs*—*stylos*, a column, *batēs*, one who treads, from the root of *bainein*, to go.]

stylography, *sti-log'rə-fi*, *n.* a mode of writing with a style.—*n.* styl'ograph (*sti'lə-gräf*; *abbrev.* sty'lō):—*pl.* sty'lōs), a stylographic pen, a pencil-like pen from which ink is liberated by pressure on a needle-point.—*adj.* stylographic (*-graf'ik*). —*adv.* stylograph'ically. [Gr. *stylos*, a style, *graphein*, to write.]

stylopised, -ized, *sti'lop-izd*, *adj.* infested (as bees) with a strepsipterous parasite of Stylops or kindred genus.

stylopodium, *sti-lō-pō'di-əm*, *n.* the disk from which the styles rise in Umbelliferae. [Gr. *stylos*, pillar (as if style), *podion*, dim. of *pous*, *podos*, foot.]

stylus. See style.

styme, stime, *stim*, (*Scot.*) *n.* a glimmer: a glimpse: a minimum of vision (or of other things).—*v.i.* to peer.—*n.* stymie, stimie, stimy (*sti'mi*), a purblind person (*Scot.*): a situation on the putting-green in which an opponent's ball blocks the way to the hole (*golf*).—Also *fig.*—*v.t.* to put in such a situation (also lay one a stymie). [Origin obscure.]

styptic, *stip'tik*, *adj.* drawing together: astringent: checking bleeding.—*n.* a styptic agent.—*adj.* styp'tical.—*n.* stypticity (*-tis'i-ti*).—styptic pencil, healing agent for minor cuts. [Gr. *styptikos*—*styphein*, to contract.]

Styrax, *sti'raks*, *n.* a genus of plants abounding in resinous and aromatic substances, as benzoin, giving name to the family Styracā'ceae, akin to the ebony family.—*n.* sty'rene, an unsaturated hydrocarbon obtained from essential oils (as the balsam storax) and coal-tar, forming thermoplastics on polymerisation. [Gr. *styrax*; cf. storax.]

styre. See stir (1).

Styx, *stiks*. See Stygian.

suable, *sū'* or *sōō'ə-bl*, *adj.* that may be sued.—*n.* suabil'ity.

suasion, *swā'zhən*, *n.* persuasion.—*adjs.* sua'sible (*-si-bl*); sua'sive (*-siv*).—*adv.* sua'sively.—*n.* sua'siveness.—*adj.* sua'sory. [L. *suāsiō, -ōnis*—*suādēre*, to advise.]

suave, *swäv* (formerly *swāv*), *adj.* smooth, bland.—*adv.* suave'ly.—*n.* suavity (*swav'i-ti*). [Fr.,—L. *suāvis*, sweet.]

suaveolent, *swə-vē'ə-lənt*, *adj.* fragrant. [L. *suāveolēns, -entis*—*suāvē*, sweetly, *olēns*, smelling.]

sub-, *sub-*, *səb-*, *pfx.* (1) under, below; (2) subordinate, subsidiary; (3) part of, a subdivision of; (4) almost, nearly, slightly, imperfectly, bordering on; (5) secretly; (6) (*chem.*) in smaller proportion.—*n.* sub (*coll. abbrev.*), a subordinate: a subaltern: a subeditor: a sublieutenant: subsidiary: subway: a subscription: a subscriber: a substitute: a submarine: subsistence money.—*v.i.* to act as a sub: to work as a substitute: to work as a newspaper subeditor.—*v.t.* to subedit:—*pr.p.* subb'ing; *pa.t.* and *pa.p.* subbed.—*n.* subb'ing, advancing of part of the wages while the work is going on. [L. *sub*, under, near; in composition also in some degree, secretly.]

subact, *sub-akt'*, *v.t.* to work up: to subdue.—*n.* subac'tion (*-shən*). [L. *subactus*, pa.p. of *subigĕre*—*sub*, under, *agĕre*, to drive, do.]

subacute, *sub-ə-kūt'*, *adj.* slightly or moderately acute: between acute and chronic (*med.*). [Pfx. sub- (4).]

subadar. See subah.

subaerial, *sub-ā-ē'ri-əl*, *adj.* in the open air: on the land surface.—*adv.* subāē'rially. [Pfx. sub- (1).]

subah, *sōō'bä*, *n.* a province of the Mogul empire: a subahdar.—*ns.* suba(h)dar', governor of a subah: an Indian captain; subahdar'y, su'bah-ship, office of subahdar. [Urdu.]

subalpine, *sub-al'pin*, *adj.* bordering on the alpine: at the foot of the Alps. [Pfx. sub- (4), (1).]

subaltern, *sub'əl-tərn* (*U.S.* except in logic usu. *sub-öl'tərn*), *adj.* ranked successively: subordinate: holding or held of a vassal: (of officers) under the rank of captain: particular (*log.*): being at once genus and species of a higher genus (*log.*).—*n.* a subordinate: a subaltern officer: a proposition differing from another in quantity alone (both being affirmative or both negative, but one universal the other particular; *log.*).—*ns.* subalter'nant (*log.*), a universal in relation to the subaltern particular; subalter'-nate, a particular proposition in relation to the subaltern universal.—*adj.* subservient: alternate with tendency to become opposite (*bot.*).—*ns.* subalternation (*sub-öl-tər-nā'shən*), relation between universal and particular of the same quality; subalter'nity, subordinate position. [L. *subalternus*—sub, under, *alter*, another.]

subapostolic, *sub-ap-os-tol'ik*, *adj.* of the time just after the apostles. [Pfx. sub- (4).]

subaquatic, *sub-ə-kwat'ik*, *adj.* under water (also subā'queous): partially aquatic (*zool.* and *bot.*). [Pfx. sub- (1), (4).]

subarcuate, *sub-är'kū-āt*, *adj.* somewhat arched: with two or more arches under a main arch.—*n.* subarcuā'tion. [Pfx. sub- (4), (1).]

subarr(h)ation, *sub-ə-rā'shən*, *n.* an ancient mode of betrothal by bestowal of a ring or gift. [L. *subarr(h)ātiō, -ōnis*—sub, under, *arr(h)a*, earnest-money.]

subastral, *sub-as'trəl*, *adj.* beneath the stars. terrestrial. [Pfx. sub- (1).]

subatom, *sub-at'əm*, *n.* a constituent part of an atom.—*adj.* subatom'ic, relating to particles constituting the atom and changes within the atom.—*n.* (*pl.* in form, treated as *sing.*) subatom'ics, the study of these particles and changes. [Pfx. sub- (3).]

subaudition, *sub-ö-dish'ən*, *n.* a sense understood, not expressed. [Pfx. sub- (5).]

subbasal, *sub'bās'əl*, *adj.* near or below the base. —*n.* the lowest part of a base (*archit.*): a division of a military base. [Pfx. sub- (1), (3).]

subchanter, *sub'chänt'ər*, *n.* a precentor's deputy. [sub- (2).]

---

suba'cid, *adj.* sub- (4).
subacid'ity, *n.* sub- (4).
subacid'ulous, *adj.* sub- (4).
subac'rid, *adj.* sub- (4).
subā'gency, *n.* sub- (2).
subā'gent, *n.* sub- (2).
subang'ular, *adj.* sub- (4).

subappear'ance, *n.* sub- (2).
subarach'noid, *adj.* sub- (1).
subboresc'ent, *adj.* sub- (4).
subarc'tic, *adj.* sub- (4).
subar'id, *adj.* sub- (4).
subax'illary (or *-il'*), *adj.* sub- (1).

subcan'tor, *n.* sub- (2).
subcat'egory, *n.* sub- (3).
subcau'dal, *adj.* sub- (1).
subcelest'ial, *adj.* sub- (1).
subcent'ral, *adj.* sub- (1), (4).
sub'class, *n.* sub- (3).

**subclavian,** *sub-klā'vi-ən,* **subclavicular,** *-klə-vik'-* *-ū-lər, adjs.* under the clavicle. [Pfx. **sub-** (1), clavicle.]

**subclinical,** *sub-klin'i-kəl, adj.* of a slightness not detectable by usual clinical methods. [Pfx. **sub-** (1).]

**subconscious,** *sub-kon'shəs, adj.* dimly conscious: away from the focus of attention: not conscious but of the nature to the conscious.—*n.* the subconscious mind or activities.—*adv.* **subcon'sciously.**—*n.* **subcon'sciousness.** [Pfx. sub- (4).]

**subcontinent,** *sub-kon'ti-nənt, n.* a great portion of a continent with a character of its own (term formerly applied to South Africa, later to India): a land-mass hardly great enough to be called a continent.—*adj.* **subcontinent'al,** almost continental: underlying a continent.—**Indian subcontinent,** the area covered by India and Pakistan. [Pfx. sub- (2), (4), (1).]

**subcontract,** *sub-kon'trakt, n.* a contract subordinate to another contract, as for the subletting of work.—*v.i.* **subcontract'**, to make a subcontract.—*v.t.* to make a subcontract for: to betroth when already married (as if subleased by the actual husband to another; *Shak.*).—*n.* **subcontract'or.** [Pfx. sub- (2).]

**subcontrary,** *sub-kon'trə-ri, adj.* contrary in an inferior degree: (of a particular proposition in relation to another differing only in quality) such that at least one must be true (*log.*).—*n. a* subcontrary proposition.—*n.* **subcontrari'ety.** [Pfx. sub- (4).]

**subcosta,** *sub-kost'ə, n.* the nervure next the costa in an insect's wing.—*adj.* **subcost'al,** near or under a rib or the ribs: behind or near the costa.—*n.* the subcostal nervure. [Pfx. sub- (1).]

**subcritical,** *sub-krit'i-kl, adj.* of insufficient mass to sustain a chain reaction (*phys*): below the critical temperature for hardening metals. [Pfx. sub- (1).]

**subculture,** *sub'kul'chər, n.* a culture (as of bacteria) derived from a previous one: a social, ethnic or economic group with a particular character of its own within a culture or society. [Pfx. sub- (2), (3).]

**subdeacon,** *sub-dē'kən, n.* a member of the order (major in the R.C., minor in the Eastern churches) of the ministry next below that of deacon, preparing the vessels, etc., at the eucharist.—*ns.* **subdea'conry; subdea'conship.** [Pfx. sub- (2).]

**subdew.** See subdue.

**subdivide,** *sub'di-vīd', v.t.* and *v.i.* to divide into smaller divisions: to divide again.—*n.* **subdivid'er.**—*adj.* **subdivisible** (*-viz'*).—*n.* **subdivision** (*-vizh'ən*).—*adjs.* **subdivis'ional; subdivi'sive.** [Pfx. sub- (3).]

**sub divo,** *sub dī'vō, sōōb dē'vō, -wō, adv.* under the sky: in the open air. Also **sub Jove** (*jō'vē, yō've, -we*), under Jupiter (the sky-god). [L.]

**subdolous,** *sub'dō-ləs, (rare) adj.* crafty. [L. pfx. *sub-,* in sense of somewhat, *dolus,* a wile.]

**subdominant,** *sub'dom'i-nənt, n.* (*mus.*) the tone next below the dominant.—*adj.* not quite ranking as dominant: partially dominant. [Pfx. sub- (1), (4).]

**subduce,** *sub-dūs', (obs.) v.t.* to withdraw.—*v.t.* **subduct** (*-dukt'*), to withdraw: to abstract secretly: to lift up.—*v.i.* to take something away.

—*n.* **subduc'tion.** [L. *sub,* and *dūcĕre, ductum,* to lead, take.]

**subdue** (*Spens.,* **subdew**), *sub-dū', v.t.* to overcome: to overpower: to subject: to make submissive: to bring into cultivation: to allay: to reduce: to tone down: to achieve (*Spens.*).—*adj.* **subdu'able.**—*n.* **subdu'al,** subjugation: overcoming.—*adj.* **subdued',** toned down.—*adv.* **subdued'ly** (or *-dū'id-li*).—*ns.* **subdued'ness; subdue'ment; subdu'er.** [O.Fr. *souduire*—L. *subdūcĕre;* see foregoing.]

**subduple,** *sub-dū'pl, sub'dū-pl, adj.* in the ratio of one to two.—*adj.* **subdū'plicate,** (of a ratio) expressed as the ratio of square roots. [L.L. *subduplus.*]

**subedar.** Same as subahdar.

**subedit,** *sub-ed'it, v.t.* to select and dispose matter for (a newspaper); also, to assist in editing.—*n.* **subed'itor.**—*adj.* **subeditorial** (*-tōr', tör'*).—*n.* **subed'itorship.** [Pfx. sub- (2).]

**subentire,** *sub-en-tīr' (bot.), adj.* with very faintly indented margin. [Pfx. sub- (4).]

**suber,** *sū'bər, (bot.) n.* cork.—*n.* **su'berate,** a salt of suberic acid.—*adjs.* **subē'reous, suberic** (*-ber'ik*), of cork (suberic acid, an acid, $HOOC \cdot (CH_2)_6 \cdot$ COOH, got by action of nitric acid on cork).—*ns.* **su'berin,** the chemical basis of cork; **suberisā'-tion, -z-.**—*v.t.* **su'berise, -ize,** to convert into cork. —*adjs.* **su'berose, su'berous,** corky. [L. *sūber, -eris,* the cork oak.]

**subfamily,** *sub'fam'i-li, n.* a primary division of a family, of one or more genera. [Pfx. sub- (3).]

**subfeu,** *sub'fū, n.* a feu granted to a vassal.—*v.t.* **subfeu'**, to make subinfeudation of.—*n.* **subfeudā'tion,** subinfeudation.—*adj.* **subfeud'atory.** [Pfx. sub- (2).]

**subfusc, subfusk,** *sub-fusk', adj.* dusky: sombre.— Also **subfusc'ous.** [L. *subfuscus*—sub, *fuscus,* dusky.]

**subgenus,** *sub-jē'nəs, n.* a primary division of a genus.—*adj.* **subgener'ic.**—*adv.* **subgener'ically.** [Pfx. sub- (3).]

**subhastation,** *sub-has-tā'shən, n.* sale by public auction. [L. *sub,* under, *hasta,* a lance (set up as a sign by the Romans).]

**subhuman,** *sub-hū'mən, adj.* below the human: below but near the human. [Pfx. sub- (4).]

**subimago,** *sub-im-ā'gō, n.* a stage in the life of a mayfly, already winged before the last moult. [Pfx. sub- (4).]

**subincision,** *sub-in-sizh'ən, n.* the formation of an opening into the urethra by incision of the underside of the penis—practised by some savage tribes.—*v.t.* **subincise'**, to perform subincision upon. [Pfx. sub- (1).]

**subindicate,** *sub-in'di-kāt, v.t.* to hint.—*n.* **subindicā'tion.**—*adj.* **subindic'ative.** [Pfx. sub- (4).]

**subinfeudation,** *sub-in-fū-dā'shən, n.* the granting of land by a vassal to be held of him by his vassal.—*v.t.* **sub'infeudate.**—*adj.* and *n.* **subinfeud'atory.** [Pfx. sub- (2).]

**subintellection,** *sub-in-ti-lek'shən, n.* an understood implication.—Also **subintelligence** (*sub-in-tel'i-jəns*), **subintelligitur** (*sub-in-tel-i'ji-tər*; L. *sōōb-in-tel-i'gi-tŏŏr, lit.* it is more or less understood).— *adj.* **subintelligen'tial.** [Pfx. sub- (5).]

**subintelligitur.** See subintellection.

**subintrant,** *sub-in'trənt, adj.* with paroxysms succeeding close upon one another. [Pfx. sub- (4).]

**subintroduce,** *sub-in-trō-dūs', v.t.* to bring in surreptitiously or subtly. [Pfx. sub- (5).]

---

| | | |
|---|---|---|
| **subcommitt'ee,** *n.* sub- (2), (3). | **sub'dean'ery,** *n.* sub- (2). | **subglobose'**, *adj.* sub- (4). |
| **subcontig'uous,** *adj.* sub- (4). | **subdia'conal,** *adj.* sub- (2). | **subglob'ular,** *adj.* sub- (4). |
| **subcontin'uous,** *adj.* sub- (4). | **subdia'conate,** *n.* sub- (2). | **sub'group,** *n.* sub- (3). |
| **subcor'date,** *adj.* sub- (4). | **subdis'trict,** *adj.* sub- (3). | **sub-head'**, **-head'ing,** *ns.* sub- (3). |
| **subcort'ical,** *adj.* sub- (1). | **subē'qual,** *adj.* sub- (4). | **subinsinuā'tion,** *n.* sub- (4), (5). |
| **subcūtā'neous,** *adj.* sub- (4). | **suberect'**, *adj.* sub- (4). | **subinspec'tor,** *n.* sub- (2). |
| **subcūtā'neously,** *adv.* sub- (1). | **subglā'cial,** *adj.* sub- (1). | **subinspec'torship,** *n.* sub- (2). |
| **sub'dean'**, *n.* sub- (2). | | |

**subirrigation,** *sub-ir-i-gā'shən,* (*U.S.*) *n.* irrigation by underground pipes. [Pfx. **sub-** (1).]

**subitaneous,** *sub-i-tā'ni-əs, adj.* sudden: hasty: hastily made. [L. *subitāneus—subitus,* sudden.]

**subjacent,** *sub-jā'sənt, adj.* underlying. [L. *subjacēns, -entis—sub, jacēre,* to lie.]

**subject,** *sub'jikt, adj.* (often with *to*) under rule, government, jurisdiction, or control: owing allegiance: under obligation: subordinate: subservient: dependent: liable: exposed: prone, disposed: cognisable: dependent upon condition or contingency: underlying, spread out below (*Spens.*).—*adv.* conditionally (with *to*).—*n.* one who is subject: one who is under, or owes allegiance to, a sovereign, a state, a feudal superior, etc.: a citizen: a body of such persons (*Shak.*): a thing over which a legal right is exercised: a piece of property (*Scot.*): substance (*obs.*): that in which attributes inhere: a thing existing independently: the mind regarded as the thinking power (opp. to the *object* about which it thinks): that of which something is predicated, or the term denoting it (*log.*): that part of a sentence or clause denoting that of which something is said (*gram.*): topic: matter of discourse, thought, or study: a department of study: a theme: that on which any operation is performed: that which is treated or handled: matter for any action or operation: ground: a sufferer from disease, a patient: a dead body for dissection (*anat.*): a person peculiarly sensitive to hypnotic influence: that which it is the object of the artist to express: a picture representing action and incident: a theme or phrase upon which a movement of music is built.—*v.t.* **subject** (*səbjekt'*), to make subject: to make liable: to subordinate: to submit: to subdue: to lay open.—*adj.* **subject'ed,** made subject; **subjacent** (*Milt.*).—*v.t.* **subject'ify,** to make subjective.—*n.* **subjec'tion.**—*adj.* **subject'ive** (also *sub'*), relating to the subject: derived from, expressive of, existing in, one's own consciousness: introspective.—*adv.* **subject'ively.**—*n.* **subject'iveness.**—*v.t.* **subject'ivise, -ize.**—*ns.* **subject'ivism,** a philosophical doctrine which refers all knowledge to, and founds it upon, subjective states; **subject'ivist.**—*adj.* **subjectivist'ic.**—*adv.* **subjectivist'ically.**—*ns.* **subjectiv'ity; sub'jectship,** the state of being subject.—**sub'ject-cat'alogue,** a catalogue of books arranged according to subjects dealt with; **sub'ject-heading; sub'ject-matter,** subject, theme, topic; **sub'ject-ob'ject,** the immediate object of cognition, or the thought itself. [L. *subjectus,* thrown under—*sub,* under, *jacēre,* to throw.]

**subjoin,** *sub-join', v.t.* to add at the end or afterwards.—*n.* **subjoin'der** (*Lamb*), a remark following on another. [Pfx. **sub-,** in addition, **join.**]

**sub judice,** *sub jōō'di-sē, ū'di-ke,* under consideration. [L.]

**subjugate,** *sub'jōō-gāt, v.t.* to bring under the yoke: to bring under power or domination: to conquer.—*ns.* **subjugā'tion; sub'jugator.** [L. *subjugāre, -ātum—sub, jugum,* a yoke.]

**subjunctive,** *səb-jungk'tiv, adj.* subjoined: added to something: expressing condition, hypothesis, or contingency (*gram.*).—*n.* the subjunctive mood: a subjunctive form: a verb in the subjunctive mood.—*adv.* **subjunct'ively.** [L. *subjunctivus—sub, jungēre,* to join.]

**subkingdom,** *sub'king-dəm, n.* a subordinate kingdom: a phylum (*biol.*). [Pfx. **sub-** (2).]

**Sublapsarian,** *sub-lap-sā'ri-ən, n.* a believer in Sublapsarianism.—Also *adj.*—*n.* **Sublapsā'rianism,** a doctrine of moderate Calvinists, that God permitted the fall of Adam without preordaining it. [L. *sub, lāpsus,* fall.]

**sublate,** *sub-lāt', v.t.* to remove (*obs.*): to deny

(*log.*): to resolve in a higher unity (*phil.*).—*n.* **sublā'tion.** [L. *sublātum,* used as supine of *tollēre,* to take away—*sub* in sense of away, *lātum.*]

**sublease,** *sub'lēs, n.* an underlease or lease by a tenant to another.—*v.t.* and *v.i.* **sublease'.**—*ns.* **sublessee',** the holder of a sublease: **subless'or,** one who grants a sublease. [Pfx. **sub-** (2).]

**sublet,** *sub-let', v.t.* to underlet or lease as by one himself a tenant to another:—*pa.t.* and *pa.p.* **sublet'.**—*n.* a subletting.—*ns.* **sublett'er; sublett'ing.** [Pfx. **sub-** (2).]

**sublieutenant,** *sub-lə-ten'ənt, n.* in the navy formerly *mate,* or *passed midshipman,* an officer ranking with an army lieutenant: (**acting-**), an officer entrant to the navy since the discontinuance of midshipmen in 1957: (**-lef-**), a former rank in the army, now second lieutenant. [Pfx. **sub-** (2).]

**sublime,** *səb-līm', adj.* set aloft (passing into *adv.*): lifted on high: exalted: lofty: majestic: elate: blindly supercilious: supreme: of the highest or noblest nature: awakening feelings of awe and veneration: just under the skin (*anat.*).—*n.* that which is sublime: the lofty or grand in thought or style: the supreme degree.—*v.t.* to raise aloft: to exalt: to transmute into something higher: to subject to, or obtain by, sublimation: to deposit as a sublimate: to purify as by sublimation.—*v.i.* to undergo sublimation.—*adj.* **sublim'able.**—*v.t.* **sublimate** (*sub'lim-āt*), to elevate: to sublime: to purify by sublimation: to transmute into something higher: to direct unconsciously the sexual impulse into some nonsexual activity: to direct into a higher channel.—*n.* a product of sublimation, esp. corrosive sublimate.—*adj.* **sublimed** or **sublimated.**—*adj.* **sub'limated.**—*n.* **sublimā'tion,** change from solid to vapour without passing through the liquid state—usu. with subsequent change back to solid: a sublimate: purification by this process: elevation: ecstasy: the acme, height: transmutation into something higher: the unconscious diversion towards higher aims of the energy attaching to an instinct (often sexual instinct).—*adj.* **sublimed** (*sab-limd'*).—*adv.* **sublime'ly.**—*n.* **sublime'ness.**—*n.* and *adj.* **sublim'ing.**—*v.t.* **sublimise, -ize** (*sub'lim-*), to exalt: to purify: to refine: to make sublime.—*n.* **sublimity** (*səb-lim'*) loftiness: elevation: grandeur: nobleness of nature, thought, execution: the emotion of awe and veneration: that which evokes it: the summit, height, acme. [L. *sublimis,* in a high position, exalted—*sublimāre, -ātum,* to exalt; origin unknown.]

**subliminal,** *sub-lim'in-əl, adj.* beneath the threshold of consciousness, subconscious.—**subliminal advertising,** advertising in the cinema, etc., directed to the subconscious, shown too rapidly and briefly to make a conscious impression. [L. *sub,* under, *limen, -inis,* threshold.]

**sublinear,** *sub-lin'i-ər, adj.* under the line: nearly linear (*bot.*).—*n.* **sublineā'tion,** underlining. [Pfx. **sub-** (1), (2).]

**sublittoral,** *sub-lit'o-rəl, adj.* growing, living, occurring, near but not on the shore, whether on land or at sea. [Pfx. **sub-** (4).]

**sublunar,** *sub-lōōn'ər, adj.* under the moon: earthly: of this world: directly under the moon, as a point on the earth's surface where the moon is vertically overhead.—*n.* being or thing of the earth or of this world.—Also *n.* and *adj.* **sublunary.**—*adj.* **sublu'nate,** approaching the form of a crescent. [Pfx. **sub-** (1), (4).]

**submachine-gun,** *sub-mə-shēn'-gun, n.* a light machine-gun, usu. one fired from the shoulder. [Pfx. **sub-** (4).]

---

**sublan'ceolate,** *adj.* sub- (4).     **sublibrā'rian,** *n.* sub- (2).     **subluxā'tion,** *n.* sub-( 4).
**sublē'thal,** *adj.* sub- (4).     **subling'ual,** *adj.* sub- (1).

**subman,** *sub'man, n.* an animal not quite a man: a man of lowest type. [Pfx. **sub-** (4).]

**submarginal,** *sub-mär'ji-nəl, adj.* near the margin. [Pfx. **sub-** (4).]

**submarine,** *sub'mə-rēn, adj.* under the sea: under the surface of the sea.—*n.* a submersible vessel, esp. for warfare: a submarine organism or dweller.—*v.t.* to attack by submarine.—*n.* submarin'er (or *-mar'in-*), a member of the crew of a submarine. [Pfx. **sub-** (1).]

**submaxillary,** *sub-maks'i-lə-ri,* or *-il'ə-, adj.* of or under the lower jaw. [Pfx. **sub-** (1).]

**submediant,** *sub-mē'di-ənt, (mus.) n.* the sixth above the tonic. [Pfx. **sub-** (1).]

**submental,** *sub-ment'əl, adj.* below the chin: of the submentum.—*n.* **subment'um,** the basal part of the lower lip in insects. [L. *sub,* under, *mentum,* chin.]

**submerge,** *səb-mûrj', v.t.* to put under the surface of liquid: to sink: to cover over with liquid.—*v.i.* to sink under the surface of liquid.—*adj.* **submerged',** sunk: entirely under the surface of liquid: growing under water, submersed: sunk hopelessly in poverty and misery (*fig.*).—*ns.* **submerge'ment** (*rare*), **submerg'ence,** submersion.—*adj.* **submerg'ible,** submersible.—*n.* **submergibil'ity.**—*v.t.* **submerse** (*-mûrs'*), to submerge.—*adj.* **submersed'** (*bot.*), growing quite under water.—*n.* **submers'ibility.**—*adj.* **submers'ible,** capable of being submerged at will.—*n.* a submersible boat.—*n.* **submer'sion** (*-shən*), act of submerging: state or fact of being submerged. [L. *submergēre, -mersum—sub, mergēre,* to plunge.]

**submicron,** *sub-mī'kron, n.* a particle visible to ultramicroscope but not by the ordinary microscope (50-2000 Å). [Pfx. **sub-** (1).]

**submit,** *sub-mit', v.t.* to yield, resign: to subordinate: to subject: to refer for decision, consideration, sanction, arbitration, etc.: to put forward in respectful contention: to lodge: to lower, lay down (*obs.*).—*v.i.* to yield: to surrender: to be resigned: to consent:—*pr.p.* **submitt'-ing;** *pa.t.* and *pa.p.* **submitt'ed.**—*adjs.* **submiss'** (*arch.*), submissive: subdued, low-toned; **submiss'ible.**—*n.* **submission** (*-mish'ən*), act of submitting: reference, or agreement to refer, to arbitration: a view submitted: resignedness: submissiveness: surrender: confession (*Shak.*).—*adj.* **submiss'ive,** willing or ready to submit: yielding.—*adv.* **submiss'ively.**—*n.* **submiss'iveness.**—*adv.* **submiss'ly** (*arch.*).—*n.* **submiss'ness** (*arch.*).—*adj.* **submitt'ed.**—*n.* **submitt'er.**—*n.* and *adj.* **submitt'ing.** [L. *sub,* beneath, and *mittĕre, missum,* to send.]

**submontane,** *sub-mon'tān, adj.* under or at the foot of a mountain range. [Pfx. **sub-** (1).]

**submultiple,** *sub-mul'ti-pl, n.* an aliquot part. [L.L. *submulliplus.*]

**subnascent,** *sub-nas'ənt, -nās', adj.* growing beneath (*obs.*): growing up from beneath. [L. *subnāscēns, -entis.*]

**subneural,** *sub-nūr'əl, adj.* beneath a main neural axis or nervous cord. [Pfx. **sub-** (1).]

**subniveal,** *sub-niv'i-əl, adj.* under snow.—Also **subniv'ean.** [Pfx. **sub-** (1), L. *nix, nivis,* snow.]

**subnormal,** *sub-nör'məl, adj.* less than normal, esp. medically, of a person with a low range of intelligence.—*n.* (*geom.*) the projection of the normal on the axis.—*n.* **subnormal'ity.** [Pfx. **sub-** (4), (1).]

**suboccipital,** *sub-ok-sip'it-əl, adj.* below or behind the occiput, or the occipital lobe. [Pfx. **sub-** (1).]

**suboctave,** *sub-ok'tāv, n.* the octave below: (also

**suboctave coupler)** an organ coupler that gives an octave below. [Pfx. **sub-** (1).]

**suboctuple,** *sub-ok-tū'pl, sub-ok'tū-pl, adj.* in the ratio of one to eight. [L.L. *suboctuplus.*]

**suboperculum,** *sub-o-pûr'kū-ləm, n.* in fishes, a bone of the gill-cover below and partly behind the operculum.—*adj.* **suboper'cular.** [Pfx. **sub-** (1).]

**suborbital,** *sub-ör'bi-təl, adj.* below the orbit of the eye. [Pfx. **sub-** (1).]

**subordinary,** *sub-ör'di-nə-ri,* (*her.*) *n.* a less honourable armorial charge. [Pfx. **sub-** (2).]

**subordinate,** *sub-ör'di-nāt, adj.* lower in order, rank, nature, power, etc.: dependent: under orders of another: submissive (*obs.*): lower in a series of successive divisions: underlying.—*n.* a person or thing that is subordinate or ranked lower: one who works under another.—*v.t.* to place in a lower order: to consider of less value: to subject.—*n.* **subor'dinacy,** subordination.—*adv.* **subor'dinately.**—*ns.* **subor'dinateness;** **subordinā'tion,** arrangement in a series of successive orders: disposition of successive recessed arches in an archway: act of subordinating or placing in a lower order: state of being subordinate: inferiority of rank or position: submission and obedience to authority; **subordinā'tionism,** the doctrine of the inferiority of the second and third Persons of the Trinity to the first.—*adj.* **subor'dinātive,** tending to, or expressing, subordination. [L.L. *subordinātus—sub-, ordināre,* to ordain.]

**suborn,** *səb-örn', v.t.* to bribe or procure to commit perjury or other unlawful or wrongful act: to prepare, provide, or achieve by stealthy means. —*ns.* **suborna'tion** (*sub-ör-*); **suborn'er** (*səb-*). [L. *sub,* in sense of secret, *ornāre,* to equip.]

**subpanation,** *sub-pan-ā'shən, n.* the doctrine that the body and blood of Christ are locally and materially present in the eucharist under the form of bread and wine. [L. *sub,* under, *pānis,* bread.]

**subplot,** *sub'plot, n.* a subordinate plot, as in a play. [Pfx. **sub-** (2).]

**sub poena,** *sub pē'nə,* under a penalty.—*n.* **subpoena** (*sub-* or *sə-pē'nə*), a writ commanding attendance in court under a penalty.—*v.t.* to serve with such a writ:—*pa.t.* and *pa.p.* **subpoe'na'd.** [L.]

**subreference,** *sub-ref'ə-rəns, n.* an incomplete or surreptitious reference: an appeal by a veiled understanding. [Pfx. **sub-** (5).]

**subreption,** *sub-rep'shən, n.* procuring an advantage (esp., Scots law, a gift of escheat) by concealing the truth (distinguished from *obreption*): false inference from such a concealment.—*adjs.* **subreptitious** (*-tish'əs*), obtained by subreption: surreptitious; **subrep'tive,** surreptitious: arising out of obscure and unconscious suggestions of experience (*phil.*). [L. *subreptiō, -ōnis—sub-,* secretly, *rapĕre,* to snatch; cf. **surreptitious.**]

**subrogate,** *sub'rō-gāt,* or *-rə-, v.t.* to substitute: (*legal*) to put in place of another, as successor to his rights.—*n.* **subrogā'tion.** [See **surrogate.**]

**sub rosa,** *sub, sōōb, rō'zə, ro'zä,* (L.) under the rose: privately.

**subroutine,** *sub'rōō-tēn', n.* part of a computer program, complete in itself, which performs a specific task, e.g. calculation of a square root, and which can be called into use at any time throughout the running of the main program. [Pfx. **sub** (2).]

**subsacral,** *sub-sāk'rəl, adj.* below (in man in front of) the sacrum. [Pfx. **sub-** (1).]

---

**subnat'ural,** *adj.* sub- (4).
**suboc'ular,** *adj.* sub- (1).
**subor'der,** *n.* sub- (3).
**subor'dinal,** *adj.* sub- (4).
**subō'vate,** *adj.* sub- (4).

**subprē'fect,** *n.* sub- (2).
**subprē'fecture,** *n.* sub- (2).
**sub'prior** (*fem.* **subpri'oress**), *n.* sub- (2).
**subrē'gion,** *n.* sub- (3).
**subrē'gional,** *adj.* sub- (3).

**subscapular**, *sub-skap'ū-lər*, *adj.* below (in man in front of) the shoulder-blade.—*n.* a subscapular vessel or nerve. [Pfx. sub- (1).]

**subscribe**, *səb-skrīb'*, *v.t.* to write beneath: to sign (orig. and esp. at the bottom): to set down, declare, in writing (*Shak.*): to profess to be (by signing): to declare assent to: to make a signed promise of payment for: to contribute: to give up by signing (*Shak.*).—*v.i.* to sign one's name: to assent: to submit (*Shak.*): to make acknowledgment: to undertake to answer: to contribute money: to put one's name down as a purchaser or donor: to make periodical payments by arrangement.—*adjs.* **subscrib'able; subscribed'.** —*n.* **subscrib'er.**—*n.* and *adj.* **subscrib'ing.**—*adj.* **subscript** (*sub'skript*), written beneath, esp. the iota under a Greek long vowel, in ᾳ, ῃ, ῳ.—*n.* **subscrip'tion**, an act of subscribing: that which is subscribed: a signature: assent: submission (*Shak.*): a raising of money from subscribers: a method of sale to subscribers: a contribution to a fund, society, etc.: a membership fee.—*adj.* **subscrip'tive.—subscriber trunk dialling**, a dialling system in which subscribers in W. European and N. American exchanges can dial each other directly:—abbrev. **S.T.D.** [L. *subscribĕre—sub, scribĕre*, to write.]

**subsecive**, *sub'si-siv*, *adj.* remaining over: spare. [L. *subsecivus—sub, secāre*, to cut.]

**subsellium**, *sub-sel'i-əm*, *n.* a misericord:—*pl.* **subsell'ia.** [L., a low bench—*sub, sella*, seat.]

**subsensible**, *sub-sen'si-bl*, *adj.* below the range of sense. [Pfx. sub- (1).]

**subsequent**, *sub'si-kwənt*, *adj.* following or coming after: of a stream, flowing approximately at right angles to the original slope of the land—distinguished from *consequent* and *obsequent.*—Also *adv.* (with *to*) after.—*n.* **sub'sequence.**—*adj.* **subsequential** (-kwen'shl), subsequent.—*adv.* **sub'sequently.** [L. *subsequēns, -entis*, pr.p. of *subsequi—sub*, under, after, *sequī*, to follow.]

**subserve**, *sub-sûrv'*, *v.t.* to help forward.—*v.i.* to help in a subordinate way: to be subordinate (*Milt.*).—*ns.* **subser'vience, subser'viency.**—*adj.* **subser'vient**, subserving: serving to promote: subject: slavish: obsequious.—*n.* a subservient person or thing.—*adv.* **subser'viently.** [L. *subservīre—sub*, under, *servīre*, to serve.]

**subshrub**, *sub'shrub*, *n.* an undershrub.—*adj.* **subshrubb'y.** [Pfx. sub- (1).]

**subside**, *səb-sīd'*, *v.i.* to settle, sink down: to fall into a state of quiet.—*ns.* **subsidence** (*sub'si-dəns*, often *səb-sī'dəns*), rarely **sub'sidency** (or *-sī'*), process of subsiding, settling, or sinking. [L. *subsidĕre—sub*, down, *sidĕre*, to settle.]

**subsidy**, *sub'si-di*, *n.* assistance (*obs.*): aid in money: a special parliamentary grant of money to the king (*hist.*): a payment exacted by a king or feudal lord: a grant of public money in aid of some enterprise, industry, etc., or to keep down the price of a commodity, or from one state to another.—*adv.* **subsid'iarily.**—*adj.* **subsid'iary**, furnishing a subsidy, help, or additional supplies: aiding: subordinate: relating to or depending on subsidies.—*n.* one who, or that which, aids or supplies: an assistant: a subordinate.—*v.t.* **sub'sidise, -ize**, to furnish with a subsidy, grant, or regular allowance: to purchase the aid of, to buy over: to pay for as mercenaries.—**subsidiary company**, one of which another company holds most of the shares; **subsidiary troops**, mercenaries. [L. *subsidium*, orig. troops stationed behind in reserve, aid—*sub*, under, *sidĕre*, to settle.]

**subsist**, *səb-sist'*, *v.i.* to have existence: to remain, continue: to hold out, stand fast (*Milt.*): to

inhere: to have the means of living.—*n.* **subsist'ence**, state of being subsistent: real being: means of supporting life: livelihood.—*adj.* (used e.g. of allowance, wage) providing the bare necessities of living.—*adjs.* **subsist'ent**, subsisting: having real being: inherent; **subsistential** (*sub-sis-ten'shl*).—**subsistence level**, the level of income which will purchase bare necessities only; **subsistence money**, part of wages paid in advance for immediate needs—colloquially known as **sub**: a special allowance for exceptional circumstances. [L. *subsistĕre*, to stand still—*sub*, under, *sistĕre*, to stand.]

**subsizar**, *sub-sīz'ər*, *n.* a Cambridge undergraduate ranking below a sizar. [Pfx. sub- (1).]

**subsoil**, *sub'soil*, *n.* broken-up rock underlying the soil.—*v.t.* to turn up or loosen the subsoil of.—*ns.* **sub'soiler**, one who subsoils: a plough for subsoiling; **sub'soiling**, ploughing the subsoil: unseen activities (*fig.*). [Pfx. sub- (1).]

**subsolar**, *sub-sōl'ər*, *adj.* directly under the sun, as a point on the earth's surface where the sun is vertically overhead. [Pfx. sub- (1).]

**subsonic**, *sub-son'ik*, *adj.* of speed, less than that of sound. [Pfx. sub- (1).]

**sub specie**, *sub spē'shi-ē, soōb spek'i-ā*, (L.) under the appearance, or aspect (of).—**sub specie aeternitatis** (*ē-tûr-ni-tāt'is, i-ter-ni-tät'is*), (seen) under the aspect of eternity, and hence as it essentially is—Spinoza.

**substage**, *sub'stāj*, *n.* apparatus under the stage of a microscope: a division of a stage (esp. *geol.*). —Also *adj.* [Pfx. sub- (1), (3).]

**substance**, *sub'stəns*, *n.* that in which qualities or attributes exist, the existence to which qualities belong: that which constitutes anything what it is: the principal part: gist: subject-matter: body: matter: kind of matter, esp. one of definite chemical nature: amount (*Shak.*): wealth, property: solidity, body: solid worth: foundation, ground.—*adj.* **substantial** (*səb-stan'shl*), of or having substance: being a substance: essential: in essentials: actually existing: real: corporeal, material: solid and ample: massy and stable: solidly based: durable: enduring: firm, stout, strong: considerable in amount: well-to-do: of sound worth.—*v.t.* **substan'tialise, -ize**, to give reality to.—*ns.* **substan'tialism**, the theory that there is a real existence or substratum underlying phenomena; **substantiality** (*-shi-al'i-ti*).—*adv.* **substan'tially.** —*n.* **substan'tialness.**—*n.pl.* **substan'tials**, essential parts.—*v.t.* **substan'tiate** (*-shi-āt, -si-āt*), to make substantial: to embody: to prove or confirm.—*n.* **substantiā'tion.**—*adj.* **substantival** (*sub-stən-tī'vl*), of, of the nature of, a substantive.—*adv.* **substantiv'ally.**—*adj.* **sub'stantive** (*-tiv*), relating to substance: expressing existence: real: of real, independent importance: substantival: of (dyes) taking effect without a mordant: definite and permanent: considerable in amount.—*n.* (*gram.*) a noun.—*adv.* **sub'stantively.**—*n.* **sub'stantiveness.**—*v.t.* **sub'stantivise, -ize** (or *-stan'*), to turn into a noun.—*n.* **substantiv'ity**, substantiality: affinity for a dyestuff. [L. *substantia*, substance, essence, property—*sub*, under, *stāre*, to stand.]

**substellar**, *sub-stel'ər*, *adj.* directly under a star, as a point on the earth's surface where the star is vertically overhead. [Pfx. sub- (1).]

**substitute**, *sub'sti-tūt*, *n.* a deputy: a proxy (*Shak.*): one nominated in remainder: one put in place of another: a thing used instead of another.—*v.t.* to put in place of another: to appoint as deputy: to nominate in remainder: to put in place of another: to use instead of

---

**sub'sec'tion**, *n.* sub- (3).
**sub'sess'ile**, *adj.* sub- (4).
**subspē'cies**, *n.* sub- (3).
**subspecif'ic**, *adj.* sub- (3).
**subspecif'ically**, *adv.* sub- (3).
**subspi'nous**, *adj.* sub- (4).
**substan'dard**, *adj.* sub- (1).
**sub'station**, *n.* sub- (2).
**subster'nal**, *adj.* sub- (1).

something else: to replace, be a substitute for (*erron.*).—*v.i.* (orig. *U.S.*) to act as substitute.— *n.* **substit'uent**, something that may be, is, substituted, esp. an atom or group replacing another in a molecule.—*adj.* **sub'stituted**.—*n.* **substitū'- tion** (*Shak.*), delegation: act of substituting: condition of being a substitute: the substituting of one atom or radical for another without breaking up the molecule (*chem.*).—*adjs.* **substitū'tional**, **substitū'tionary**.—*adv.* **substitū'tion- ally**.—*adj.* **sub'stitūtive**.—**substitution product**, a substance got by substitution of so many equivalents for certain atoms or groups. [L. *substi- tuĕre*, *-ūtum*—*sub*, under, *statuĕre*, to set.]

**substract**, *səb-strakt'*, *v.t.* (now illiterate) to subtract.—*ns.* **substrac'tion** (now illiterate); **substrac'tor** (*Shak.*), a detractor. [L.L. *substrahĕre*, *substractum*, for L. *subtrahĕre*, after the model of **abstract**.]

**substratosphere**, *sub-strat'ō-sfēr*, *n.* the region of the atmosphere below the stratosphere and over 3½ miles above the earth. [Pfx. **sub-** (4).]

**substratum**, *sub-strā'təm*, *-strä'*, *n.* the substance in which qualities inhere: a basis, foundation, ground: the material in which a plant grows or on which an animal moves or rests: an underlying layer:—*pl.* **substra'ta**.—*adj.* **substrā'tal**.—*n.* **sub'strate**, a substratum: a base: the substance on which an enzyme acts: the substances used by a plant in respiration (*bot.*). [L. *substernĕre*, *-strātum*—*sub*, *sternĕre*, to spread.]

**substruct**, *sub-strukt'*, *v.t.* to build beneath, lay as a foundation.—*n.* **substruc'tion**.—*adj.* **substruc'tural**.—*n.* **sub'structure**, an understructure: a foundation. [Pfx. **sub-** (1).]

**substyle**, *sub'stil*, *n.* the straight line on which the style of a dial is erected.—*adj.* **sub'stylar** (or *-sti'*). [Pfx. **sub-** (1).]

**subsultive**, *sub-sult'iv*, **subsultory**, *-ər-i*, *adjs.* moving by starts: twitching.—*adv.* **subsult'orily**. —*n.* **subsult'us**, a convulsive movement. [L. *subsultāre*, to jump, hop—*sub*, up, *salīre*, to leap.]

**subsume**, *sub-sūm'*, *v.t.* to state as minor premiss: to take in under a more general term or proposition: to include in something larger: to take over (*officialese*).—*n.* **subsumption** (*səb-sump'- shən*).—*adj.* **subsump'tive**. [L. *sub*, under, *sūmĕre*, to take.]

**subtack**, *sub'tak'*, *n.* an underlease in Scotland.— *n.* **sub'tack'sman**, a holder by subtack. [Pfx. **sub-** (2).]

**subtangent**, *sub'tan'jənt*, (*geom.*) *n.* the projection of the tangent on the axis. [Pfx. **sub-** (1).]

**subtemperate**, *sub'tem'pər-it*, *-āt*, *adj.* slightly colder than temperate, cold-temperate. [Pfx. **sub-** (4).]

**subtend**, *səb-tend'*, *v.t.* to be opposite to (*geom.*): to have in the axil (*bot.*).—*n.* **subtense'**, a subtending line.—*adj.* placed so as to subtend an angle, as a rod used as base in tacheometry. [L. *sub*, under, *tendĕre*, *tentum* or *tēnsum*, to stretch.]

**subter-**, *sub'tər-*, in composition, under.—*n.* **subterfuge** (*sub'tər-fūj*; L. *fugĕre*, to take flight), an evasive device, esp. in discussion: a refuge (*obs.*).—*adjs.* **subterhū'man**, less than human: below man; **subterjā'cent**, subjacent; **subternat'ural**, below nature, less than natural.—*n.* **subterposi'tion**, position or placing underneath. —*adj.* **subtersen'suous**, below the level of sense. [L. *subter*, under.]

**subterranean**, *sub-tə-rā'ni-ən*, *adj.* underground: operating underground: hidden, working, etc, in secret.—*n.* a dweller underground: an underground chamber or dwelling.—*adj.* **subterrā'- neous**, underground.—*adv.* **subterrā'neously**.— *adj.* **subterrene'**, underground.—*n.* an under-

ground dwelling: the underworld.—*adj.* **subterres'trial**. [L. *sub*, under, *terra*, the earth.]

**subthreshold**, *sub-thresh'ōld*, *adj.* subliminal. [Pfx. **sub-** (1).]

**subtil**, **subtile**, *sut'l*. Same as **subtle**.

**subtitle**, *sub'tī-tl*, *n.* an additional or second title, as to a book: a half-title: a repetition of the title at the head of the text: descriptive reading matter in a cinematograph film, esp. a printed translation at the foot of the screen of dialogue that is in a language foreign to the viewers. [Pfx. **sub-** (2).]

**subtle**, also (slightly *arch.*, and used chiefly in physical senses) **subtil**, **subtile**, *sut'l*, (*Milt.*) **suttle**, *sut'l*, *adj.* fine, delicate, thin: tenuous: rarefied: impalpable: elusive: showing or calling for fine discrimination: nice: over-refined or overrefining: abstruse: cunning: ingenious: crafty: insidious: penetrating: ticklish, tricky (*Shak.*).—*n.* **subtilisā'tion**, **-z-** (*sut-*).— *v.t.* **subtilise, -ize** (*sut'*), to rarefy, refine: to make subtle.—*v.i.* to refine, use subtlety.—*ns.* **subt'le- ness**, also **subt'il(e)ness**, **subtlety**, also **subtil(e)ty** (*sut'l-ti*; *Milt.* **suttletie**), **subtility** (*sub-til'i-ti*), state or quality of being subtle: a subtle trick or refinement: an ornamental device in sugar (*cook.*, *obs.*); **subt'list**, **-ilist**, one who practises subtleties. —*adv.* **subt'ly**, also **subt'il(e)ly**.—*adj.* **subt'ile- witt'ed** (*Shak.*). [O.Fr. *soutil* and its source L. *subtilis*—*sub*, under, *tēla*, a web.]

**subtonic**, *sub-ton'ik*, (*mus.*) *n.* the note next below the tonic, the leading note. [Pfx. **sub-** (1).]

**subtopia**, *sub-tō'pi-ə*, (*derog.*) *n.* a region where the city has sprawled into the country. [L. *sub*, under, Gr. *topos*, a place; modelled on **utopia**.]

**subtract**, *səb-trakt'*, *v.t.* to withdraw, remove: to withhold: to take from another quantity so as to find the difference (*math.*).—*n.* **subtrac'tion**, withdrawal, removal: withholding, esp. in violation of a right: the operation of finding the difference between two quantities by taking one from the other (*math.*).—*adj.* **subtract'ive**, indicating, tending towards, of the nature of, subtraction: negative.—*ns.* **subtract'or**, a light-filter to eliminate a particular colour; **subtrahend** (*sub'trə- hend*), that which is to be subtracted. [L. *sub-*, in sense of away, *trahĕre*, *tractum*, to draw, gerundive *trahendus*, requiring to be drawn.]

**subtriplicate**, *sub-trip'li-kit*, *-kāt*, *adj.* expressed by the cube root. [L.L. *subtriplus*, in the ratio of one to three.]

**subtrist**, *sub-trist'*, *adj.* somewhat sad. [L. *subtristis*—*sub*, *tristis*, sad.]

**subtrude**, *sub-trōōd'*, *v.i.* to push in stealthily. [L. *sub*, in sense of secretly, *trūdĕre*, to thrust.]

**subucula**, *sub-ū'kū-lə* (L. *sŏŏb-ōō'kŏŏ-la*), *n.* a Roman man's undergarment or shirt: in the early English Church, a kind of cassock worn under the alb. [L. *subūcula*—*sub*, and the root of *induĕre*, to put on, *exuĕre*, to take off.]

**subulate**, *sū'bū-lāt*, *adj.* awl-shaped. [L. *sūbula*, an awl.]

**subumbrella**, *sub-um-brel'ə*, *n.* the under-surface of a jellyfish's umbrella.—*adj.* **subumbrell'ar**. [Pfx. **sub-** (1).]

**subungual**, *sub-ung'gwəl*, *adj.* under a nail or hoof. —*n.pl.* **Subungulā'ta**, animals by some included in the Ungulata though not typical hoofed animals, by others placed near the Ungulata— elephants and hyraxes.—*adj.* and *n.* **subung'- ulate**. [Pfx. **sub-** (1), (4).]

**suburb**, *sub'ərb*, *n.* a district adjoining a town: (in *pl.*) the outskirts of a town, esp. formerly as the prostitutes' quarters: confines, outskirts generally.—*adj.* **suburban**: characteristic of the suburbs.—*adj.* **suburban** (*səb-ûr'bən*), situated or

---

| | | |
|---|---|---|
| **sub'sur'face**, *adj.* **sub-** (1). | **sub'treas'urer**, *n.* **sub-** (2). | **subtrop'ic, -al**, *adjs.* **sub-** (4). |
| **sub'ten'ancy**, *n.* **sub-** (2). | **subtriang'ular**, *adj.* **sub-** (4). | **subtrop'ics**, *n.pl.* **sub-** (4). |
| **sub'ten'ant**, *n.* **sub-** (2). | **sub'tribe**, *n.* **sub-** (3). | **subur'sine**, *adj.* **sub-** (4). |

living in the suburbs: typical of the suburbs: without the good qualities either of town or country: smug, comfortable, half-cultured, narrow in outlook.—*n.* one living in a suburb.— *n.* **suburbanisā′tion,** -z-.—*v.t.* **subur′banise, -ize,** to make suburban.—*ns.* **subur′banism,** the state of being suburban; **subur′banite,** one who lives in the suburbs; **suburbanity** (*sub-ər-ban′i-ti*), suburban quality: suburbanism: a suburban place; **subur′bia,** the suburban world.—*adj.* **suburbicā′- rian,** being near the city, esp. of the dioceses and churches of the cardinal bishops in the suburbs of Rome. [L. *suburbium*—*sub,* under, near, *urbs,* a city.]

**subvention,** *səb-ven′shən, n.* a grant of money in aid. [L. *subventiō, -ōnis,* a coming to help—*sub, venīre, ventum,* to come.]

**subvert,** *səb-vûrt′, v.t.* to overthrow: to overturn: to pervert.—*n.* **subver′sal.**—*v.t.* **subverse′** (*obs.*; *pa.p.* and *adj.* in *Spens.* **subverst′**),—*n.* **subver′- sion,** overthrow: ruin.—*adjs.* **subver′sionary, subver′sive,** tending to overthrow.—*n.* a subver- sive person.—*n.* **subvert′er.** [L. *sub,* under, *vertĕre, versum,* to turn.]

**sub voce,** *sub vō′sē, sōōb vō′ke, wō′,* (L.) under that heading.

**subway,** *sub′wā, n.* a tunnel for foot-passengers: an underground passage for water-pipes, gas-pipes, sewers, etc.: (esp. *U.S.*) an underground railway. [Pfx. **sub-** (1).]

**succade,** *suk-ād′, n.* fruit or vegetable candied or in syrup. [A.F. *sukade,* perh.—L. *succus,* juice.]

**succedaneum,** *suk-si-dā′ni-əm, n.* a substitute.— *adj.* **succedā′neous,** serving as a substitute. [L., neut. of *succēdāneus*—*succēdĕre,* to come after.]

**succeed,** *sək-sēd′, v.t.* to come after: to follow up or in order: to follow: to take the place of, esp. in office, title, or possession: to inherit (*Shak.*): to cause to succeed (*obs.*).—*v.i.* to follow in order: to take the place of another (often with *to*): to devolve, pass in succession (*Shak.*): to turn out: to turn out well: to prosper: to obtain one's wish or accomplish what is attemp- ted: to avail, be successful (with *in*): to ap- proach (*Spens.*).—*ns.* **succeed′er,** one who is successful: a successor.—*adj.* **succeed′ing.**—*n.* **success** (*sək-ses′*), fortune (good or bad): up- shot: prosperous progress, achievement, or termination: prosperity: attainment of wealth, influence or acclaim: a successful person, book, affair, etc.: sequence (*obs.*): succession (*obs.*).— *adv.* **success′antly** (*Shak.*), in succession.—*adj.* **success′ful,** resulting in success: achieving, having achieved, or having, the desired effect or termination: prosperous.—*adv.* **success′fully,** with success: with promise of success (*Shak.*).— *ns.* **success′fulness; succession** (-*sesh′ən*), a coming after or following: a coming into an- other's place: a sequence in time or place: law, recognised mode, right, order, or turn, of suc- ceeding one to another: in Roman and Scots law, the taking of property by one person in place of another: rotation of crops: heirs collectively: posterity.—*adj.* **success′ional.**— *adv.* **success′ionally.**—*n.* **success′ionist,** a believer in the necessity of Apostolic succession.—*adjs.* **success′ionless; successive** (*sək-ses′iv; Shak.* *suk′*), coming in succession or in order: heredi- tary (*obs.*).—*adv.* **success′ively.**—*n.* **success′ive- ness.**—*adj.* **success′less.**—*adv.* **success′lessly.** —*ns.* **success′lessness; success′or** (*Shak. suk′*), one who, or that which, succeeds or comes after: sometimes, one appointed to succeed; **success′orship.**—**succession duty,** a tax imposed on succession to property, varying with the degree of relationship; **succession house,** a

forcing-house in a graded series, in which plants are moved on from one to the next; **succession states,** states resulting from the break-up of Austria and Hungary.—**plant succession,** a series of vegetation types following one another in the same region. [L. *succēdĕre, -cēssum*—*sub-,* in sense of near, next after, *cēdĕre,* to go.]

**succentor,** *sək-sent′ər, n.* a subcantor: the bass soloist in a choir. [L. *succentor*—*succinĕre*— *sub,* under, *canĕre,* to sing.]

**succès,** *sük-se,* (Fr.) success.—**succès d'estime** (*des-tēm*), a success of esteem or approval (if not of profit); **succès fou** (*fōō*), success with wild enthusiasm; **succès de scandale** (*də skä-dal*), success of a book, dramatic entertainment, due not to merit but to its connection with or refer- ence to a topical scandal.

**succinct,** *sək-, suk-singkt′, adj.* girded up (*arch.* and *poet.*): close-fitting (*arch.* and *poet.*): con- cise.—*adv.* **succinct′ly.**—*ns.* **succinct′ness; suc- cincto′rium, succinct′ory,** a band embroidered with an Agnus Dei, worn hanging from the girdle by the pope on some occasions. [L. *succinctus*—*sub,* up, *cingĕre,* to gird.]

**succinum,** *suk′sin-əm, n.* amber.—*n.* **suc′cinate,** a salt of succinic acid.—*adj.* **succin′ic,** of, relating to, or got from, amber.—*n.* **suc′cinite,** amber, esp. a variety from which succinic acid was first got.—**succinic acid,** an acid, $C_4H_6O_4$, got from resins, etc. [L. *succinum,* amber.]

**succory,** *suk′ər-i, n.* a variant of **chicory.**

**succose.** See **succus.**

**succotash,** *suk′ō-tash, n.* a stew of green Indian corn and beans and sometimes pork. [Narra- gansett *msiquatash.*]

**succour,** *suk′ər, v.t.* to aid in distress: to relieve.— *n.* aid: relief.—*adj.* **succ′ourable.**—*n.* **succ′ourer.** —*adj.* **succ′ourless.** [A.Fr. *socorre*—L. *succur- rĕre,* to run to help—*sub,* up, *currĕre,* to run.]

**succous.** See **succus.**

**succubus,** *suk′ū-bəs,* **succuba,** -*bə, ns.* a devil supposed to assume a female body and consort with men in their sleep: a strumpet:—*pl.* **succ′- ubuses, succ′ubas, succ′ubi, succ′ubae** (-*bē*).— *adjs.* **succ′ubine,** of a succuba; **succ′ubous** (*bot.*), having the lower leaf-margin overlapping the leaf below. [L. *succuba,* a whore—*sub,* under, *cubāre,* to lie.]

**succulent,** *suk′ū-lənt, adj.* juicy: sappy: juicy and fleshy, or (loosely) merely fleshy (*bot.*).—*n.* a succulent plant.—*ns.* **succ′ulence, succ′ulency.** —*adv.* **succ′ulently.**—**succ′ulent-house′,** a house for succulent plants. [L. *sūculentus*—*sūcus,* juice.]

**succumb,** *sə-kum′, v.i.* to lie down under or sink under pressure, difficulty, temptation, etc. (often with *to*): to die. [L. *sub,* under, *cumbĕre,* to lie down.]

**succursal,** *suk-ûr′sl, adj.* subsidiary: branch.—*n.* a branch of an institution (often as Fr. fem. **succursale,** *sü-kür-sal*). [Fr.,—L. *succurrĕre,* to succour.]

**succus,** *suk′əs, n.* juice: fluid secretion of a gland: expressed juice:—*pl.* **succi** (*suk′sī*).—*adjs.* **succ′- ose, succ′ous.** [L. *sūcus,* juice.]

**succuss,** *suk-us′, v.t.* to shake up.—*ns.* **succussā′- sion,** a shaking up: a horse's trot (*obs.*); **succus- sion** (-*ush′ən*), a shaking: a shock: a shaking of the thorax to detect pleural effusion.—*adj.* **suc- cuss′ive.** [L. *succutĕre, succussum,* to toss up— *sub, quatĕre,* to shake.]

**such,** *such, adj.* of that kind, the like kind, or the same kind (often followed by *as* or by a clause beginning with *that*): so characterised: of what kind: what (exclamatory): so great: before- mentioned: some particular but unspecified.—

---

**subvari′ety,** *n.* sub- (3).      **subver′tical,** *adj.* sub- (4).      **subzōn′al,** *adj.* sub- (1).

**sub′vassal,** *n.* sub- (2).      **subvit′reous,** *adj.* sub- (4).      **sub′zone,** *n.* sub- (3).

**subver′tebral,** *adj.* sub- (1).      **sub′war′den,** *n.* sub- (2).

Neutral vowels in unaccented syllables: *el′ə-mənt;* for certain sounds in foreign words, see p. viii

*adv.* so (preceding the indefinite article if any).—*pron.* such a person, persons, thing, or things: the before-mentioned: that.—*adj.* such'like, of such a kind.—*pron.* suchlike persons or things (or person or thing).—*n.* such'ness, quality.—*adv.* such'wise, in such a manner.—*adj.* such'-and-such, this or that, some, some or other (before the indefinite article if any).—*pron.* such-and-such a person.—such as, for example; such as it is, being what it is (and no better). [O.E. *swilc*; cog. with Goth. *swaleiks*; cf. so, like.]

suck, *suk*, *v.t.* to draw in with the mouth: to draw something (esp. milk) from with the mouth: to apply to or hold in the mouth and perform the movements of sucking: to draw by suction: to render by suction: to absorb: to draw in: to extract: to imbibe: to drain.—*v.i.* to draw with the mouth: to draw the breast: to draw by suction: to make a noise of sucking: to draw in air as a dry pump: to draw in: to engulf.—*n.* act or spell of sucking: milk drawn from the breast: suction: a short drink, esp. a dram of spirits (*slang*).—*adj.* sucked.—*n.* suck'er, one who, or that which, sucks, a sucking-pig, new-born whale, or other unweaned animal: a sucking-fish: an American fish akin to the carps, that feeds by sucking up small animals from the bottom: an adhesive organ: a device that adheres, draws water, etc., by suction, as a pump piston: a toy consisting of a leather disk and a string, for lifting stones, etc.: a haustorium or other sucking organ: a sweet for sucking (*local*): a shoot rising from underground and developing into a new plant: a new shoot: a parasite, toady, sponge: a hard drinker: a gullible person, one taken advantage of (*coll.*): a native of Illinois (*U.S.*).—*v.t.* to strip off superfluous shoots from.—*v.i.* to develop suckers.—*adj.* suck'ered, having suckers.—*n.* and *adj.* suck'ing.—suck-in' (*slang*), a disconcerting disappointment; suck'ing-bottle, a milk bottle for infants; suck'ing-fish, remora or other fish with an adhesive disk, e.g. a lumpsucker; suck'ing-pig, a young milk-fed pig.—sucks (to you)! a derisive expression; suck up to (*slang*), to toady to. [O.E. *sūcan*, *sūgan*; Ger. *saugen*; cf. L. *sūgĕre*.]

sucken, *suk'n*, (Scots law) *n.* the district or population thirled to a mill: thirlage: an area of jurisdiction or field of operation.—*n.* suck'ener, a tenant so bound. [soken (see soc).]

sucket, *suk'it*, an obs. form of succade.—sucket spoon, fork, an old table implement, spoon at one end, fork at the other.

suckle, *suk'l*, *v.t.* to give suck to, as a mammal feeding its young: to put out to suck.—*n.* suck'ler, an animal that suckles: a suckling.—*n.pl.* suck'lers, heads of clover.—*n.* suck'ling, an unweaned child or animal: the act of giving suck: clover, also honeysuckle (*dial.*).—*adj.* giving suck: putting to suck: sucking. [suck.]

sucre, *sōō'krä*, *n.* the monetary unit of Ecuador. [Named after Antonio José de *Sucre* (1795-1830).]

sucrose, *sōō'*, *sū'krōs*, *n.* cane-sugar ($C_{12}H_{22}O_{11}$) from any source. [Fr. *sucre*, sugar.]

suction, *suk'shən*, *n.* act or power of sucking or of drawing or adhesion by reducing pressure of air.—*n.pl.* Suctoria (*suk-tō'ri-ə*), a subclass of Ciliata.—*adj.* suctō'rial, adapted for sucking.—suction(al) stop, a stop consonant in which the contact of the articulating organs is followed by an inrush of air (*phon.*). [L. *sūgĕre*, *sūctum*; related to suck.]

sucurujú, *sōō-kōō-rōō-zhōō'*, *n.* a S. American Indian name for the anaconda.

sudamina, *sōō-*, *sū-dam'i-nə*, *n.pl.* whitish vesicles due to retention of sweat in the sweat-glands:—*sing.* sudamen (*-dā'mən*).—*adj.* sudam'inal. [L. *sūdāmen*, pl. *sūdāmina*—*sūdāre*, to sweat.]

Sudan, *sōō-dan'*, *n.* a region of Africa, south of the Sahara and Libyan deserts.—*n.* Sudanese (*-ēz'* or *sōō'*), a native or inhabitant of the Sudan:—*pl.* Sudanese.—*adj.* of or pertaining to the Sudan or its inhabitants.—Sudan grass, a Sorghum, *Sorghum vulgare sudanensis*, grown for hay and fodder.—Also Soudan(ese).

sudate, *sū'dāt*, *sōō'*, (*rare*) *v.i.* to sweat.—*ns.* sudā'rium, su'dary (*-də-ri*), a cloth for wiping sweat: a handkerchief: a veronica; sudā'tion, sweating: sweat: a watery exudation from plants; sudatorium (*-də-tō'ri-əm*, *-tö'*), a sweating-room; su'datory (*-tə-ri*), a sudatorium.—*adj.* of sweat: inducing sweating. [L. *sūdāre*, *-ātum*, to sweat.]

sudd, *sud*, *n.* a mass of floating vegetable matter obstructing the White Nile: a temporary dam. [Ar. *sudd*, obstruction.]

sudden, *sud'n*, *adj.* without warning or apparent preparation: unexpected: hasty: abrupt: prompt: swift in action or production: glancing quickly: improvised.—*adv.* suddenly.—*adv.* sudd'enly.—*ns.* sudd'enness, (*Scot.*) sudd'enty.—sudden death (*sport*), an extended period to settle a tied contest, play terminating the moment one of the contestants scores.—(all) on a sudden, of a (or the) sudden, all at once. [A.Fr. *sodain*—L. *subitāneus*, sudden—*subitus*, coming stealthily—*subīre*, *-ītum*, to go stealthily—*sub*, *ire*.]

sudder, *sud'ər*, (in India) *adj.* chief.—*n.* a supreme court. [Ar. *çadr*, chief.]

sudor, *sū'dör*, *sōō'*, *-dər*, (*med.*) *n.* sweat.—*adjs.* sudorif'erous, provoking or secreting sweat; sudorif'ic, causing sweat.—*n.* a diaphoretic.—*adjs.* sudorip'arous, secreting sweat; su'dorous, sweaty. [L. *sūdor*, *-ōris*, sweat.]

Sudra, *sōō'dra*, *n.* a member of the fourth and lowest of the Hindu castes. [Sans. *śūdra*.]

suds, *sudz*, *n.pl.* froth of soapy water (rarely in *sing.* sud). [Prob. conn. with seethe.]

sue, *sū*, *sōō*, (*obs.*; *Spens.* sew), *v.t.* to follow: to prosecute at law: to petition for, apply for: to court (*arch.*).—*v.i.* to make legal claim: to make application: to entreat: to be a wooer (*Shak.*): to do service (*Spens.*):—*pr.p.* su'ing; *pa.t.* and *pa.p.* sued.—*n.* sueabil'ity (*see* suability).—*adj.* sue'able (see suable).—*n.* and *adj.* su'ing.—sue out, to petition for and take out. [O.Fr. *suir* (Fr. *suivre*)—L. *sequi*, *secūtus*, to follow.]

suède, *swād* (Fr. *süed*), *n.* undressed kid: its colour.—Also *adj.*—*v.t.* to give a suède finish to (leather or cloth). [Fr. (*gants de*) *Suède*, (gloves of) Sweden.]

suet, *sū'it*, *sōō'*, *n.* a solid fatty tissue, accumulating about the kidneys and omentum of the ox, sheep, etc.—*adj.* su'ety (also su'etty).—suet pudding, a boiled pudding made with suet. [O.Fr. *seu* (Fr. *suif*)—L. *sēbum*, fat.]

suffer, *suf'ər*, *v.t.* to undergo: to endure: to be affected by: to permit: to inflict pain on (*Shak.*).—*v.i.* to feel pain or punishment: to sustain loss: to be injured: to die: to be executed or martyred: to be the object of an action.—*adj.* suff'erable.—*n.* suff'erableness.—*adv.* suff'erably.—*ns.* suff'erance, suffering: endurance: forbearance: tacit assent: permission: toleration; suff'erer.—*n.* and *adj.* suff'ering.—on sufferance, tolerated, but not encouraged. [L. *sufferre*—*sub*, under, *ferre* to bear.]

suffete, *suf'ēt*, *n.* one of the chief administrative officials of ancient Carthage. [L. *sūfes*, *-etis*, from a Punic word.]

suffice, *sə-fīs'*, *v.i.* to be enough: to be competent or adequate.—*v.t.* to satisfy.—*ns.* sufficience (*sə-fish'əns*; *rare*), -cy, state of being sufficient: competence: ability: capacity: a sufficient quantity: means enough for a comfortable living, a competency: conceit.—*adj.* suffic'ient, sufficing: competent: adequate: effective: well-to-do: (not a satisfactory word for *enough* in quantity).—*n.* (*coll.*) a sufficient quantity, enough.—*adv.* **suffic'iently.**—*adj.* **suffic'ing.**—*ns.* **suffic'ingness; suffisance** (*suf'i-zəns*; *obs.*), sufficiency: satisfaction: enjoyment.—**suffice it,** be it enough. [Through Fr.—L. *sufficĕre*, to suffice—*sub*, *facĕre*, to make.]

**suffigance,** *suf'i-gans*, (Shak., *Much Ado*) *n.* Dogberry's blunder for **suffisance**.

**suffix,** *suf'iks*, *n.* a syllable or other addition at the end of a word: an index placed after and below a symbol, as *n* in *x*$_n$ (*math.*).—*v.t.* **suffix'**, to add as a suffix: to subjoin. [L. *suffixus*—*sub*, under, *figĕre*, to fix.]

**suffocate,** *suf'ə-kāt*, *v.t.* and *v.i.* to choke by stopping of the breath: to stifle (also *fig.*).—*adj.* (*Shak.*) **suffocated.**—*n.* and *adj.* **suff'ocāting.**—*adv.* **suff'ocātingly.**—*n.* **suffocā'tion.**—*adj.* **suff'-ocātive,** tending to suffocate. [L. *suffōcāre*—*sub*, under, *faucēs*, the throat.]

**suffragan,** *suf'rə-gən*, *n.* an assistant, a coadjutor-bishop: any bishop in relation to his metro-politan.—Also *adj.*—*n.* **suff'raganship.** [L.L. *suffrāgāneus,* assistant, supporting.—L. *suffrā-gium,* a vote.]

**suffrage,** *suf'rij*, *n.* a prayer, esp. for the dead, or in a litany: a vote: a voting paper, pebble, or the like: sanction: supporting opinion: power of voting.—*ns.* **suffragette** (*suf'rə-jet'*); an im-properly formed word), a woman seeking by violent methods (or sometimes otherwise) to obtain votes for women; **suff'ragist,** a believer in the right (e.g. of women) to vote. [L. *suffrāgium*, a vote.]

**suffruticose,** *sə-frōōt'i-kōs*, *adj.* herbaceous with woody persistent stem-base. [L. *sub*, under, *frutex, -icis,* a shrub.]

**suffumigate,** *sə-fū'mi-gāt*, *v.t.* to fumigate from below.—*n.* **suffumigā'tion.** [L. *sub, fūmigāre.*]

**suffuse,** *sə-fūz'*, *v.t.* to pour over: to overspread or cover, as with a liquid, a tint.—*adj.* (*sə-fūs'*; *bot.*) spread out on the substratum.—*n.* **suffū'-sion** (*-zhən*). [L. *sub*, underneath, *fundĕre*, *fūsum*, to pour.]

**Sufi,** *sōō'fē*, *n.* a pantheistic Mohammedan mystic: —*pl.* **Su'fis.**—*n.* **Su'fi(i)ism.**—*adjs.* **Su'fic, Suf(i)-ist'ic.** [Ar. *çūfī*, lit. man of wool—*çuf*, wool.]

**sugar,** *shŏŏg'ər, n.* a sweet substance (*sucrose, cane-sugar,* $C_{12}H_{22}O_{11}$), obtained chiefly from cane and beet: extended to any member of the same class of carbohydrates: money (*slang*): a term of endearment (*coll.*): flattery (*slang*).—*adj.* (*Shak.*) sweet: of sugar.—*v.t.* to sprinkle, coat, or mix with sugar.—*adj.* **sug'ared,** sweetened or coated with sugar: sugary.—*ns.* **sug'ariness;** **sug'aring,** sweetening with sugar: coating trees with sugar as a method of collecting insects: formation of sugar from maple sap (*sugaring off*; *U.S.*).—*adjs.* **sug'arless; sug'ary,** like sugar in taste or appearance: abounding in sugar: offensively or cloyingly sweet.—**sug'ar-ally** (*-al'i*; *Scot.*), liquorice; **sug'ar-apple,** the sweet-sop; **sug'ar-baker** (*obs.*), a sugar-refiner: also a confectioner; **sugar basin, bowl,** a small basin for holding sugar at table; **sug'ar-bean,** the Lima bean; **sug'ar-beet,** any variety of common beet, esp. variety *Rapa,* grown for sugar; **sug'ar-can'dy,** sugar in large crystals; **sug'ar-cane,** a woody grass (*Saccharum officinarum*) from which sugar is chiefly obtained.—*adj.* **sug'ar-coat'ed,** coated with sugar.—**sug'ar-daddy,** an elderly man lavishing money on a young woman or young women; **sug'ar-grass,** sweet sorghum; **sug'ar-gum,** a eucalyptus with sweetish foliage; **sug'ar-house,** a sugar factory; **sug'ar-loaf,** a loaf or mass of sugar, usu. more or less cigar-shaped: a hill, hat, or other object of like form; **sug'ar-ma'ple,** a N. American maple (*Acer saccharum* or kindred species) from whose sap sugar is made; **sug'ar-mill,** a machine for pressing out the juice of the sugar-cane; **sug'ar-mite,** a mite infesting unrefined sugar; **sug'ar-palm,** a palm (of many kinds) yielding sugar; **sug'ar-pine,** a Western American pine (*Pinus lambertiana*) with sugary heartwood; **sug'ar-plum,** a small round boiled sweet: a compliment or other gratification (*fig.*); **sug'ar-refi'ner;** **sug'ar-refi'nery;** **sug'ar-refi'-ning;** sugar soap, an alkaline cleansing or stripping preparation for paint surfaces; **sugar tongs,** small tongs for lifting lumps of sugar at table; **sug'ar-wrack,** a kind of tangle (*Laminaria saccharina*) from which mannite is got.—**heavy sugar** (*slang*), big money; **sugar of lead,** lead acetate, sweet and poisonous, used as a mordant for dyeing and printing textiles, and as a drier for paints and varnishes. [O.Fr. (Fr.) *sucre*—Ar. *sukkar*; the *g* unexplained; cf. **Saccharum.**]

**suggest,** *sə-jest'*, old-fashioned *sug-*, *v.t.* to intro-duce indirectly to the thoughts: to call up in the mind: to put forward, as a plan, hypothesis, thought, etc.: to give an impression of: to tempt (*Shak.*): to insinuate (*Shak.*): to in-fluence hypnotically.—*v.i.* to make suggestions.—*ns.* **suggest'er; suggestibil'ity.**—*adj.* **suggest'ible,** capable of being suggested, or of being influenced by suggestion, esp. hypnotic.—*ns.* **suggest'ion** (*-yən*), process or act of suggesting: hint: pro-posal: indecent proposal: incitement, tempta-tion: information without oath, not being pleadable (*law*): a false or underhand represen-tation (*obs.*): communication of belief or impulse to a hypnotised person; **suggestionisā'-tion, -z-.**—*v.t.* **suggest'ionise, -ize,** to subject to suggestion.—*ns.* **suggest'ionism,** treatment by suggestion: the theory that hypnotic effects are entirely due to the action of suggestion; **sug-gest'ionist.**—*adj.* **suggest'ive,** containing a hint: fitted to suggest: awaking the mind: stimula-ting: pertaining to hypnotic suggestion: tending to awake indecent imaginations (*coll. euphemism*). —*adv.* **suggest'ively.**—*n.* **suggest'iveness.** [L. *suggerĕre, -gestum, sub,* under, *gerĕre,* to carry.]

**sui,** *sōō'ī, sōō'ē, sōō'ē,* (L.) of himself, herself, itself.—**sui generis** (*jen'ər-is, ge'ne-ris*), of its own kind, the only one of its kind.—**sui juris** (*jŏŏr'is, ūr'*), having full legal capacity to act: (in Roman law) having the rights of a freeman.

**suicide,** *sū'i-sīd, sōō',* *n.* one who kills himself in-tentionally: self-murder: a self-inflicted disas-ter.—*adj.* **suici'dal.**—*adv.* **suici'dally.** [L. *sui,* of himself, *caedĕre,* to kill.]

**Suidae,** *sū'i-dē, sōō',* *n.pl.* the pig family. [L. *sūs, suis,* pig.]

**suint,** *swint, n.* dried perspiration in wool. [Fr.]

**suit,** *sūt, sōōt, n.* pursuit (*Spens.*): process or act of suing: an action at law: courtship: a petition: a series: a suite (*obs.*): a sequence: a set: a set of cards of the same denomination, in the pack or in one hand: a number of things of the same kind or made to be used together, as clothes or armour.—*v.t.* to attire (*obs.*): to provide, fur-nish: to fall in with the requirements of: to fit: to become: to please.—*v.i.* to agree: to corres-pond.—*n.* **suitabil'ity.**—*adj.* **suit'able,** that suits: fitting: accordant: adequate.—*n.* **suit'ableness.** —*adv.* **suit'ably.**—*adj.* **suit'ed** (*Shak.*), dressed, clothed.—*ns.* **suit'ing** (usu. in *pl.*), cloth suitable for making suits; **suit'or,** one who sues: a peti-tioner: a wooer: (*fem.* **suit'ress**).—*v.i.* to play the suitor.—**suit'-case,** an easily portable oblong travelling-bag for carrying suits or clothes.— **follow suit,** to play a card of the suit led: to do the same; **strong suit,** one's forte. [Fr. *suite*; cf. **sue, suite.**]

**suite,** *swēt, n.* a train of followers or attendants: a set, as of furniture or rooms: a sequence of instrumental movements, usu. dance-tunes, in related keys: a sequel. [Fr.,—a L.L. form of L. *secūta,* fem. pa.p. of *sequi,* to follow.]

**suivez,** *swē-vā,* (Fr.) follow (the solo part, in accompanying).

**sukiyaki,** *s(ōō)kē'(y)ä-kē,* *n.* beef, vegetables,

sauce, etc., cooked together, often at table. [Jap.]

**sulcus,** *sul'kəs, n.* a groove, furrow, fissure: a fissure between two convolutions of the brain:— *pl.* **sul'ci** (-*sī*).—*adj.* **sul'cal** (-*kl*), of a sulcus: grooved: furrowed: pronounced with sulcal tongue.—*v.t.* **sul'calise, -ize,** to furrow.—*adjs.* **sul'cate, -d,** furrowed, grooved: with parallel longitudinal furrows.—*n.* **sulcā'tion.** [L. *sulcus,* a furrow.]

**sulfate, sulfur,** etc. U.S. spellings of **sulphate, sulphur,** etc.; adopted by International Union of Pure and Applied Chemistry.

**sulk,** *sulk, v.i.* to be sullen.—*n.* one who sulks: (usu. in *pl.*) a fit of sulking.—*adv.* **sulk'ily.**—*n.* **sulk'iness.**—*adj.* **sulk'y,** sullen: inclined to sulk. —*n.* a light two-wheeled, sometimes bodiless, vehicle for one person. [Prob. from the root seen in O.E. *āseolcan,* to slack, be slow, pa.p. *āsolcen.*]

**sullage,** *sul'ij, n.* filth: refuse: scum: scoria: silt. [Perh. conn. with **sully.**]

**sullen,** *sul'ən, adj.* gloomily angry and silent: malignant, baleful: dark: dull.—*adv.* **sullenly.**— *n.* (usu. in *pl.*) a fit of sullenness, the sulks.—*adv.* **sull'enly.**—*n.* **sull'enness.** [App. through an O.Fr. deriv. from L. *sōlus,* alone.]

**sully,** *sul'i, v.t.* to soil: to spot: to tarnish.—*v.i.* to be soiled:—*pr.p.* **sull'ying;** *pa.t.* and *pa.p.* **sull'ied.**—*n.* spot: tarnish. [O.E. *sylian,* to defile—*sol,* mud; or from O.Fr. *souiller,* to soil.]

**sulphur,** *sul'fər, sulfur* (q.v.), *n.* brimstone, a yellow non-metallic element (S; at. numb. 16) and mineral, very brittle, fusible, and inflammable: an impression from a plate spread with molten sulphur.—*adj.* of sulphur.—*v.t.* to treat or fumigate with sulphur.—*adj.* **sul'pha,** of a class of synthetic antibacterial drugs, the sulphonamides.—*ns.* **sulphaguan'idine,** a sulphonamide used against dysentery, etc.; **sul'phanil'amide,** a sulphonamide ($C_6H_8N_2O_2S$) used against bacteria; **sulphapy'ridine,** one of the sulphonamides known as M & B formerly much used in the treatment of pneumonia, meningitis, etc.; **sul'phate,** a salt of sulphuric acid.— *v.t.* to form a deposit of lead sulphate on: to treat or impregnate with sulphur or a sulphate.—*v.i.* to become sulphated.—*n.* **sulphathi'azole,** a sulphonamide used against staphylococci.—*adj.* **sulphatic** (-*at'ik*).—*ns.* **sul'phide,** a compound of an element or radical with sulphur: a salt of hydrosulphuric acid; **sul'phite,** a salt of sulphurous acid. — *pfx.* **sul'pho-,** sulphur: obs. for **thio-.**—*n.* **sulphon'amide,** an amide of a sulphonic acid, any of a group of drugs with antibacterial action.—*v.t.* **sul'phonate,** to treat (esp. an aliphatic or aromatic compound) with sulphuric acid and so convert it into a sulphonic acid or other substance.—*n.* **sul'phone,** any of a class of substances consisting of two organic radicals combined with $SO_2$.—*adj.* **sulphon'ic,** containing the group $SO_2 \cdot OH$.—*v.t.* **sul'phūrate,** to combine with, or subject to the action of, sulphur.—*ns.* **sulphūrā'tion; sulphūrā'tor.**—*adj.* **sulphū'reous,** sulphury: sulphur-yellow.—*adv.* **sulphū'reously.**—*ns.* **sulphū'reousness; sul'phūret** (*obs.*), a sulphide.—*adjs.* **sul'phūretted,** combined with sulphur; **sulphū'ric,** containing sulphur in higher valency—opp. to *sulphurous*; **sul'phurous** (-*fūr-,* or -*fər-*), pertaining to, resembling, or containing sulphur: hellish: thundery: containing sulphur in lower valency (*chem.*; -*fūr'*); **sulphury** (*sul'fər-i*), like sulphur.— **sulphite pulp,** in paper-making, wood chips treated with calcium or magnesium acid sulphite; **sul'phur-bacte'ria,** bacteria that liberate sulphur from sulphuretted hydrogen, etc., and ultimately form sulphuric acid; **sul'phur-bottom,** the blue whale (from the yellowish spots underneath); **sulphur dioxide,** $SO_2$, a suffocating

gas discharged into the atmosphere in waste from industrial processes, used in manufacture of sulphuric acid, and in bleaching, preserving, etc.; **sulphuretted hydrogen,** hydrogen sulphide, $H_2S$; **sulphuric acid,** oil of vitriol, $H_2SO_4$; **sulphuric anhydride,** sulphur trioxide, $SO_3$; **sulphurous acid,** $H_2SO_3$; **sulphurous anhydride,** sulphur dioxide, $SO_2$; **sul'phur-root, sul'phurwort,** an umbelliferous plant (Peucedanum, various species) akin to parsnip, with yellow flower and juice.—*n.* and *adj.* **sul'phuryell'ow,** pale yellow. [L. *sulphur, sulfur, sulpur, -uris.*]

**sultan,** *sul'tən, n.* a Mohammedan ruler, esp. the Ottoman emperor: the purple coot: a small white (orig. Turkish) variety of hen.—*ns.* **sultana** (*sul-* or *səl-tä'nə*), a lady of a sultan's harem: a king's mistress: a magnificent courtesan: a concubine: a fiddle strung with wires in pairs: a small, pale, seedless raisin; **sul'tanate;** **sul'taness.**—*adj.* **sultanic** (*sul-tan'ik*).—*n.* **sul'tanship.**—**sweet sultan, yellow sultan,** species of Centaurea. [Ar. *sultān.*]

**sultry,** *sul'tri, adj.* sweltering: close and oppressive: hot with anger: passionate, voluptuous: (of language) lurid, verging on the indecent.— *adv.* **sul'trily.**—*n.* **sul'triness.** [**swelter.**]

**sum,** *sum, n.* total: whole: aggregate: result of addition: amount: a quantity of money: a problem in addition, hence in arithmetic generally: chief points: substance or result: summary: height, culmination, completion.— *v.t.* to add: to make up the total of: to be an epitome of, exemplify in little: to summarise: to reckon up, form an estimate of: to complete the development of, bring to perfection (*Milt.*).— *v.i.* to amount, turn out on adding: to do sums: —*pr.p.* **summ'ing;** *pa.t.* and *pa.p.* **summed.**—*n.* **sum'mand** (or -*and'*), an addend: part of a sum. —*adjs.* **sum'less,** not to be summed or counted: incalculable; **summed.**—*n.* **summ'er,** one who sums.—*n.* and *adj.* **summ'ing.**—**summ'ing-up,** a recapitulation or review of the leading points, a judge's summary survey of the evidence given to a jury before it withdraws to consider its verdict; **sum total,** complete or final sum.—**in sum,** in short: to sum up; **sum and substance,** the gist: the essence; **sum of things,** the public weal: the universe. [O.Fr. *summe*—L. *summa—summus,* highest.]

**sumac, sumach,** *sōō'*, *shōō'*, *sū'mak, n.* any tree or shrub of the genus Rhus, esp. *R. coriaria*: the leaves and shoots used in dyeing. [Fr. *sumac* or L.L. *sumach*—Ar. *summāq.*]

**sumatra,** *sōō-mä'trə, n.* a short, violent squall about the Straits of Malacca, coming from *Sumatra.*

**summa,** *sum'ə, n.* a treatise giving a summary of a whole subject.—*adj.* **summar** (*sum'ər; Scot.*), summary (**Summar Roll,** a list of cases requiring dispatch).—*adv.* **summ'arily.**—*n.* **summ'ariness.** —*v.t.* **summ'arise, -ize,** to present in a summary or briefly.—*ns.* **summ'arist,** one who summarises.— *adj.* **summ'ary,** summed up or condensed: short: brief: compendious: done by a short method: without unnecessary formalities or delay, without further application to the court.—*n.* an abstract, abridgment, or compendium.—*n.* **summā'tion,** process of finding the sum: addition: accumulation: an aggregate.—*adjs.* **summā'tional; summ'ative,** additive.—*n.* **summ'ist,** a writer of a summa: an epitomist. [L. *summa,* sum, *summārium* a summary.]

**summa cum laude,** *sum'ə kum lō'dē, sōōm'ä kōōm low'de,* (L.) with greatest distinction (*laus, laudis,* praise).

**summand.** See **sum.**

**summat,** *sum'ət,* a dial. form of **something,** somewhat.

**summation,** etc. See **summa.**

**summer,** *sum'ər, n.* the warmest season of the year: a spell of warm weather (see **Indian, St Luke's, St Martin's, summer**): a year of age or time.—*adj.* of, for, occurring in, summer.—*v.i.* to pass the summer.—*v.t.* to keep through the summer.—*n.* **summ'ering.**—*adjs.* **summ'erlike; summ'erly,** warm and bright like summer; **summ'ery,** like summer: suitable for summer.— **summ'er-house,** a structure in a garden for sitting in: a summer residence.—*adj.* **summ'er-seeming** (*Shak.*), perh. hot and passing, like summer.— **summ'ertide,** the summer season; **summ'ertime,** the summer season: **summer time,** time adopted (from 1916; but see **British Standard Time**) for daylight-saving purposes—one hour (**double summer time,** two hours) in advance of Greenwich time. [O.E. *sumer, sumor*; Du. *zomer,* Ger. *sommer.*]

**summer,** *sum'ər, n.* a pack-horse, a sumpter-horse (*obs.*): a great horizontal beam or lintel (also **summ'er-tree**). [See **sumpter.**]

**summerset.** Same as **somersault.**

**summit,** *sum'it, n.* the highest point or degree: the top.—*adj.* **summ'itless.**—*n.* **summ'itry,** the practice or technique of holding summit conferences. —**summit conference,** a conference between heads of states; sometimes extended to mean a conference between heads of lesser organisations; **summ'it-level,** the highest level. [O.Fr. *sommette, somet* (Fr. *sommet*), dim. of *som*—L. *summum,* highest.]

**summon,** *sum'ən, v.t.* to call up, forth, or together: to call upon to appear or to do something: to rouse to exertion.—*adj.* **summ'onable.**—*ns.* **summ'oner,** one who summons: an officer who serves summonses: an apparitor; **summ'ons,** a summoning or an authoritative call: a call to appear, esp. in court: a call to surrender.—*v.t.* to serve with a summons. [O.Fr. *somoner*—L. *summonēre—sub-,* secretly, *monēre,* to warn: sense partly from O.E. *somnian,* to assemble.]

**summum bonum,** *sum'əm bō'nəm, sŏŏm'ŏŏm bo'nŏŏm,* (L.) the chief good.

**sumo,** *sŏŏ'mō, n.* a traditional Japanese sport, a form of wrestling. [Jap. *sumō.*]

**sump,** *sump, n.* a bog, pool, puddle (now *dial.*): a hole or depression that receives liquid, as for molten metal, for sea-water at a salt-work, drainage-water in a mine, oil in an engine. [Du. *somp*; Ger. *sumpf.*]

**sumph,** *sumf,* (*Scot.*) *n.* a soft sheepish fellow.— *adj.* **sumph'ish.**—*n.* **sumph'ishness.** [Origin unknown.]

**sumpit,** *sum'pit, sumpitan, -an, ns.* a Malay blow-pipe. [Malay.]

**sumpsimus,** *sump'si-məs, n.* a correct expression displacing an incorrect but common one. [L. *sūmpsimus*; see **mumpsimus.**]

**sumpter,** *sum(p)'tər, n.* a pack-horse. [O.Fr. *sommetier,* a pack-horse driver—Gr. *sagma,* a pack-saddle, *sattein,* to pack.]

**sumptuary,** *sum(p)'tū-ər-i, adj.* pertaining to or regulating expense.—*n.* **sumptūos'ity,** sumptuousness.—*adj.* **sump'tūous,** costly: magnificently luxurious.—*adv.* **sump'tūously.**—*n.* **sump'-tūousness.** [L. *sūmptus,* cost—*sūmĕre, sūmptum,* to take.]

**sun,** *sun, n.* the body which is the gravitational centre and source of light and heat to our planetary system: the central body of a system: a great luminary: a climate: sunshine: a year: a day: sunrise: sunset.—*v.t.* to expose to the sun's rays.—*v.i.* to bask:—*pr.p.* **sunn'ing;** *pa.t.* and *pa.p.* **sunned.**—*adj.* **sun'less.**—*n.* **sun'lessness.** —*adjs.* **sun'like; sunned,** exposed to the sun.— *adv.* **sunn'ily.**—*n.* **sunn'iness.**—*adj.* **sunn'y,** of, from, like or lighted, coloured or warmed by the sun: genial: cheerful.—*adj.* and *adv.* **sun'ward,** towards the sun.—*advs.* **sun'wards; sun'wise,** in the direction of the sun's apparent revolution.—

*adj.* **sun'-and-plan'et,** geared so that one wheel moves round another.—**sun'-animal'cule,** a heliozoan; **sun'-bath,** exposure of the body to the sun's rays.—*v.i.* **sun'bathe.**—**sun'bather** (*-bādh*); **sun'bathing.**—*adj.* **sun'-baked.**—**sun'beam,** a shaft of sunlight.—*adjs.* **sun'beamed, -beamy.**—**sun'-bear,** the Malayan bear: sometimes the Himalayan bear.—*adjs.* **sun'-beat, -en,** continually exposed to the sun.—**sun'-bird,** any of the Nectariniidae, a family of small tropical birds akin to honey-eaters, superficially like humming-birds; **sun'bittern,** a S. American bird (*Eurypyga helias*) with brilliant many-coloured markings; **sun'-blind,** an outside shade or awning for a window.—*adj.* blinded by the sun.—**sun'-blink** (*Scot.*), a gleam of sunshine; **sun'-bonnet,** a light bonnet projecting beyond the face to protect from the sun; **sun'bow,** an iris formed by the sun, esp. in the spray of a cataract.—*adj.* **sun'-bright,** bright as the sun.—**sun'burn,** reddening (often excessive) or browning of the skin by the sun.—*v.t.* to brown or tan by exposure to the sun.—*v.i.* to become so browned.—*adjs.* **sun'-burned, sun'burnt.**—**sun'burst,** a strong outburst of sunlight: a jewel or ornament resembling the rayed sun.—*adj.* **sun'-clad,** clothed in radiant light.—**sun'-crack,** a crack formed in clayey ground as it dries in the sun, often preserved in rocks; **sun'-cult,** worship of a sun-god or of the sun.—*adj.* **sun'-cured,** cured in the sun.—**sun'-dawn,** the light of the rising sun; **sun'-dew,** an insectivorous bog-plant (Drosera); **sun'dial,** a device for telling the time by a shadow cast by the sun; **sun'-disk,** the visible disk of the sun: a winged disk, symbol of the sun-god; **sun'-dog,** a mock sun or parhelion; **sun'down,** sunset: a woman's broad-brimmed hat (*U.S.*); **sun'-downer,** in Australia, a loafer who arrives at a station in time for a meal and lodging, but too late for work: a government official who practises a profession after hours (*U.S.*): in India and Africa, a drink after sunset.—*adj.* **sun'-dried,** dried in the sun.—**sun'-drops,** an American evening primrose.—*adj.* **sun'-expelling** (*Shak.*), keeping off the sun.—**sun'-fish,** a fish of nearly circular profile, as the opah, or any member of the family Molidae: the basking-shark; **sun'flower,** a composite plant (Helianthus) or its large head with yellow rays, fabled to turn toward the sun: applied to various more or less similar kinds; **sun'glasses,** dark-lensed spectacles used against strong light; **sun'god,** a god personifying or concerned with the sun; **sun'hat,** a hat with shady brim; **sun'-lamp,** a lamp that gives out ultraviolet rays curatively or to induce artificial sunburn; **sun'light,** the light of the sun.—*adj.* **sun'lit,** lighted up by the sun.— **sun'-myth,** a solar myth; **sunny side,** a pleasant or cheerful part or point of view: an age less than one specified; **sun'-parlour,** a room with glass walls or large windows for getting advantage of the sun's rays; **sun'-picture, -print,** a photograph.—*adj.* **sun'proof.**—**sun'-ray; sun'-rise, sun'rising,** the rising or first appearance of the sun above the horizon: the time or colour-effects of this rising: the east; **sun'set, sun'-setting,** the setting or going down of the sun: the time or phenomenon of going down: the west; **sun'-shade,** a parasol: an awning; **sun'shine,** bright sunlight: brightness: prosperity: geniality.—*adjs.* **sun'shine,** sunshiny: fair-weather; **sun'shiny,** bright with sunshine: pleasant: bright like the sun: genial.—**sun'shine-recorder,** an instrument for recording duration of sunshine; **sun'shine-roof,** a car-roof that can be pushed open; **sun'spot,** a relatively dark patch on the surface of the sun; **sun'-spurge,** a spurge (*Euphorbia helioscopia*) supposed to turn with the sun, a common weed; **sun'stone,** aventurine feldspar; **sun'stroke,** a nervous disease caused

Neutral vowels in unaccented syllables: *el'ə-mənt*; for certain sounds in foreign words, see p. viii

by great heat.—*adj.* **sun'struck,** affected with sunstroke.—**sun'tan,** a browning of the skin as a result of exposure to the sun.—*adj.* **sun'-tanned.** —**sun'-up,** sunrise; **sun'-worship,** adoration of the sun; **sun'-worshipper.**—**a place in the sun,** a place or opportunity for good living or attaining prosperity; **between** (*Shak.* **'twixt**) **sun and sun,** **from sun to sun,** between sunrise and sunset; **have been in the sunshine, have the sun in one's eyes,** to be drunk; **take the sun,** to ascertain the sun's meridian altitude: to walk or laze in the sun; **under the sun,** on earth. [O.E. *sunne*; O.N. *sunna*, O.H.G. *sunnô.*]

**sundae,** *sun'dā, -di, n.* an ice with syrup or crushed fruit: a mixed nougat or confection. [Perh. **Sunday.**]

**sundari,** *sun'dɔ-rē, n.* an East Indian sterculiaceous timber-tree (Heritiera).—Also **sun'dra, sun'dri, sun'der.** [Sans. *sundari.*]

**Sunday,** *sun'di, n.* the first day of the week, anciently dedicated to the sun, now regarded as the Sabbath by most Christians.—*adj.* of, for, occurring on, Sunday.—**Sunday best,** one's best clothes.—*adj.* **Sun'day-go-to-the-meeting,** appropriated to Sunday and church-going.—**Sunday painters,** people who paint seriously but in their spare time; **Sunday saint,** one whose religion or morality is confined to Sundays; **Sunday school,** a school for religious (orig. general) instruction on Sunday.—**a month of Sundays,** a long time; **the Sundays,** the Sunday newspapers. [O.E. *sunnan dæg*; Ger. *sonntag.*]

**sunder,** *sun'dɔr, v.t.* and *v.i.* to separate: to part. —*n.* **sun'derance.**—*adj.* **sun'dered.**—*n.* **sun'derer.** —*n.* and *adj.* **sun'dering.**—*n.* **sun'derment.**—**in sunder** (*B.*), asunder. [O.E. *syndrian*, to separate, *sundor*, separate; O.N. *sundr*, asunder.]

**sunder, sundra, sundri.** See **sundari.**

**sundry,** *sun'dri, adj.* separate: more than one or two: several: divers: varied (*Shak.*).—*n.pl.* **sun'dries,** sundry things: different small things. —**all and sundry,** all collectively and individually. [O.E. *syndrig*; cf. **sunder.**]

**sung** *sung.* See **sing.**

**Sung,** *soong, n.* a Chinese dynasty (960-1279).— *adj.* of the dynasty, or its culture, including its pottery.

**sunk,** *sungk,* **sunken,** *sungk'n.* See **sink.**

**sunk,** *sungk,* (*Scot.*) *n.* a turf seat: a pad: a bank. —*n.* **sunk'ie,** a stool. [Origin unknown.]

**sunket,** *sung'kit,* (*Scot.*) *n.* a dainty. [From *sum-quhat,* Scots form of **somewhat.**]

**sunn,** *sun, n.* an Indian Crotalaria grown for fibre. —Also **sunn'-hemp'.** [Hind. *san.*]

**Sunna,** *soon'ɔ, sun'ɔ, n.* Mahommedan traditional teaching.—*n.* **Sunn'i** (*-ē*), an orthodox Muslim. —Also **Sonn'ite, Sunn'ite.**

**Suomi,** *swō'mē, n.* the Finnish language.—*n.pl.* the Finns.—*adjs.* **Suo'mic, Suo'mish.**

**suovetaurilia,** *sū-ov-i-tö-ril'i-a,* L. *sōō-o-we-tow-rē'li-a*), *n.pl.* a Roman sacrifice of a sheep, a pig, and an ox. [L. *sūs,* pig, *ovis,* sheep, *taurus,* ox.]

**sup,** *sup, v.t.* to take into the mouth, as a liquid: to eat with a spoon (*Scot.*): to furnish supper for (*Shak.*).—*v.i.* to eat the evening meal: to sip (*B.*):—*pr.p.* **supp'ing**; *pa.t.* and *pa.p.* **supped.**—*n.* a small mouthful, as of a liquid. [O.E. *sūpan*; O.N. *sūpa,* Ger. *saufen,* to drink; partly from O.Fr. *soper, souper* (Fr. *souper*), to take supper.]

**supawn.** See **suppawn.**

**super-,** *sōō', sū'pɔr,* in composition, above, beyond, in addition, in excess.—*n.* **su'per,** a colloquial abbrev. of **supernumerary** (esp. a supernumerary actor, further abbreviated **supe**), and of **superintendent.**—*adj.* coll. abbrev. of **superfine**: very good or very delightful.—*v.i.* to act as super.—*v.i.* **superabound',** to be more, very, or excessively abundant.—*n.* **superabun'dance.**— *adj.* **superabund'ant.**—*adv.* **superabund'antly.**— *adj.* **superacute',** abnormally or excessively acute.

—*v.t.* **superadd',** to add over and above.—*ns.* **superaddi'tion; superall'oy,** an alloy that has good stability at 600°C to 1000°C; **superalt'ar,** a slab of stone used as a portable altar to be laid on the top of an unconsecrated altar: a structure over an altar.—*v.t.* **supercal'ender,** to give a high polish to by calendering.—*adj.* **supercal'endered.** —*n.* **supercar'go,** a person in a ship placed in charge of the cargo and superintending all commercial transactions of the voyage:—*pl.* **supercar'goes.**—*n.* **supercar'goship.**—*adj.* **supercelest'-ial,** above the heavens: more than heavenly. —*v.t.* **supercharge',** to fill to excess: to charge above the normal: to add pressure to: to charge exorbitantly, overcharge: to place as an overcharge (*her.*).—*ns.* **su'percharge,** an excessive, exorbitant, or greater than normal charge: a charge borne upon an ordinary or other charge (*her.*); **su'percharger,** a device for increasing the pressure in an internal combustion engine; **superconductiv'ity,** complete loss of electrical resistivity shown by certain pure metals at temperatures approaching absolute zero. —*adjs.* **superconduc'ting; superconduc'tive.**—*n.* **superconduc'tor.**—*v.t.* **supercool',** to cool below normal freezing-point without freezing.—*adjs.* **supercrit'ical,** capable of sustaining a chain reaction such that the rate of reaction increases; **superdaint'y** (*Shak.*), over-dainty.—*ns.* **superdom'inant** (*mus.*), the submediant; **super-Dread'nought,** a warship excelling the original Dreadnought class.—*adj.* **su'per-du'per,** superlatively fine or great.—*ns.* **super-ego** (*psych.*), the strong unconscious inhibitory mechanism which criticises the ego and causes it pain and distress when it accepts unworthy impulses from the id; **superelevā'tion,** excess in height; **superem'inence,** eminence in a superior degree: excellence beyond others.—*adj.* **superem'inent.**—*adv.* **superem'inently.**—*adj.* **superessen'tial,** transcending mere being and essence.—*v.t.* **superexalt',** to exalt to a superior degree.—*ns.* **superexaltā'tion; superexc'ellence,** excellence above others, or in an uncommon degree.—*adj.* **superexc'ellent.**— *n.* **su'perfamily,** a group between a suborder and a family.—*adj.* **superfatt'ed,** (of soap) having an excess of fat, so that there is no free alkali; **su'perfine,** of specially fine size or quality (abbrev. **super**): over-nice.—*ns.* **su'perfineness; super-fluid'ity,** a phenomenon observed in a form of helium (*helium* II), obtained below 2·19 K, in which internal friction is negligible; **super-front'al,** a covering hanging over the upper edge of an altar frontal.—*v.t.* **superfuse',** to pour over something else: to supercool.—*n.* **superfu'sion.** —*v.t.* **superheat',** to heat to excess: to heat (steam, etc.) above the temperature of saturation: to heat above normal boiling-point without vaporisation.—*n.* state of being superheated: amount of superheating.—*n.* **superheat'er.**—*adj.* **superhet'erodyne,** heterodyne with beats above audible frequency (*coll.* **superhet'**).—*n.* a super-heterodyne receiver.—*ns.* **superhigh'way** (*U.S.*), a wide road for fast motor-traffic; **su'perhive,** a detachable upper compartment of a beehive.— *adj.* **superhū'man,** above man: above the capacity of man: more or higher than human.—*v.t.* **superhū'manise, -ize.**—*n.* **superhūman'ity.**—*adv.* **superhū'manly.**—*n.* **superhū'meral,** any vestment worn on the shoulders.—*v.t.* **superimpose',** to set on the top of something else: to place one over another: to establish in superaddition.—*adj.* **superimposed'.**—*ns.* **superimposi'tion; super-incum'bence.**—*adj.* **superincum'bent,** resting on the top: overlying: overhanging.—*v.t.* **super-induce',** to bring in over and above, or in supersession of, something else: to superadd.—*ns.* **superinduce'ment, superinduc'tion.**—*v.t.* **super-intend',** to have or exercise oversight or charge of: to control, manage.—*v.i.* to exercise supervision.—*ns.* **superinter.'dence**, oversight: direction: management; **superinten'dency**, office or district of a superintendent.—*adj.* **superinten'dent**, superintending.—*n.* one who superintends: an overseer: the head of a Sunday school: in some Protestant churches a clergyman having the oversight of the clergy of a district: a police officer above an inspector: the administrator of a local school system (*U.S.*).—*n.* **superinten'dentship**.—*adjs.* **superlu'nar, superlu'nary**, above the moon: not of this world.—*ns.* **su'perman**, a being of higher type than man: ideal man: a dominating man; **su'permarket** (orig. *U.S.*), a large, mainly self-service, retail store selling food and other domestic goods.—*adjs.* **supermun'-dane**, above the world; **supernat'ional**, transcending the national.—*n.* **supernat'ionalism**.—*adj.* **supernat'ural**, above or beyond nature: not according to the course of nature: miraculous: spiritual.—*n.* that which is supernatural: a supernatural being.—*v.t.* **supernat'uralise, -ize**, to bring into the supernatural sphere.—*ns.* **supernat'uralism**, the belief in the influence of the supernatural in the world; **supernat'uralist**, a believer in the supernatural.—*adj.* of or pertaining to the supernatural.—*adj.* **supernaturalist'ic**.—*adv.* **supernat'urally**.—*ns.* **supernat'uralness**; **su'pernature**, the supernatural.—*adj.* **supernor'-mal**, beyond what is normal: in greater number, amount, concentration, etc., than the normal.—*n.* **su'peroctave**, an organ-coupler giving an octave higher: an organ-stop two octaves above the principal; **superord'er**, a category between an order and a subclass or sometimes class (*biol.*).—*adjs.* **superord'inal**, pertaining to a superorder; **superord'inary**, above or beyond the ordinary; **superord'inate**, superior in rank: in the relation of superordination.—*n.* a superior in rank.—*v.t.* to make superordinate.—*n.* **superordinā'tion** (*log.*), the relation of a universal proposition to a particular proposition in the same terms.—*adj.* **superorgan'ic**, above or beyond the organic, psychical: pertaining to a higher organisation, social.—*ns.* **superovulā'tion**, the production of a larger number of ova than usual, e.g. under stimulus of injected hormones; **superphos'phate**, an acid phosphate: now usu. a mixture of calcium sulphate and calcium acid phosphate used as a manure.—*adj.* **superphys'-ical**, beyond, or of higher order than, the physical.—*n.* **su'perplus** (*obs.*), surplus.—*adj.* **super-pos'able**.—*v.t.* **superpose'**, to bring, or suppose to to brought, into coincidence: to place vertically over or on something else.—*adj.* **superposed'**.—*n.* **superposi'tion**, act or superposing: state of being superposed: that which is above anything.—*v.t.* **superpraise'** (*Shak.*), to praise excessively.—*ns.* **superre'alism**, surrealism; **superre'alist**.—*adj.* **super-roy'al**, of paper-size larger than royal.—*n.* **su'persalt**, an acid salt.—*v.t.* **supersat'urate**, to saturate beyond the normal point.—*n.* **supersaturā'tion**.—*adj.* **supersens'ible**, above the range, or outside the realm, of the senses.—*adv.* **supersen'sibly**.—*adj.* **supersen'sitive**, excessively sensitive. — *n.* **supersen'sitiveness**.—*adjs.* **supersen'-sory**, beyond the ordinarily recognised senses; **supersen'sual**, beyond the senses: extremely sensual; **superser'viceable** (*Shak.*), officious.—*ns.* **su'persound**, sound vibrations too rapid to be audible; **su'per-state**, a greater organisation transcending the state; **superstrā'tum** (or *-strä'*), overlying stratum.—*v.t.* **superstruct'**, to build on something else as a foundation.—*n.* **superstruc'-tion**.—*adjs.* **superstruct'ive**; **superstruct'ural**.—*n.* **su'perstructure**, an upper structure or part of a structure.—*adjs.* **supersubstan'tial**, transcending substance, esp. material substance; **supersubt'le**, **-subt'ile** (*Shak.*), over-subtle: extremely subtle. —*ns.* **su'pertanker**, a very large tanker; **su'per-tax**, an extra or additional tax on large incomes.

—*adj.* **superterres'trial**, supermundane.—*n.* **superton'ic**, the tone next above the tonic.—*adj.* **su'pervolute** (*bot.*), convolute. [L. *super*, above; cf. over, Gr. *hyper*.]

**superannuate**, *sōō-*, *sū-pər-an'ū-āt*, *v.t.* to antiquate: to set aside or cause to retire on account of age: to pension off.—*adj.* superannuated.—*n.* a superannuated person.—*adj.* **superann'ūated**.—*n.* **superannūā'tion**. [L. *super*, above; *annus*, year.]

**superate**, *sōō'*, *sū'pər-āt*, (*obs.*) *v.t.* to overcome, outdo, or top.—*adj.* **su'perable**.—*adv.* **su'perably**. —*n.* **superā'tion**. [L. *superāre*, to go over, surmount.]

**superb**, *sōō-*, *sū-pûrb'*, *adj.* proud, haughty (*obs.*): magnificent: gorgeous: triumphantly effective: supremely excellent (*coll.*).—*n.* **superb'ity**.—*adv.* **superb'ly**.—*n.* **superb'ness**. [L. *superbus*, proud.]

**supercalender** ... to ... **supercharger**. See **super-**.

**supercherie**, *sü-per-sha-rē*, *n.* a taking at disadvantage: fraud. [Fr.]

**superciliary**, *sōō'*, *sū'pər-sil'i-ər-i*, *adj.* of, on, or near the eyebrow: marked above the eye.—*n.* a superciliary ridge or mark.—*adj.* **supercil'ious**, disdainfully superior in manner: overbearing (*obs.*): superciliary (*rare*).—*adv.* **supercil'iously**. —*n.* **supercil'iousness**. [L. *supercilium*, eyebrow, superciliousness—*super*, above, *cilium*, eyelid.]

**superconductivity** ... to ... **supereminently**. See **super-**.

**supererogation**, *sōō-*, *sū-pər-er-ō-gā'shən*, *n.* doing more than is required.—*v.i.* **superer'ogate**.—*adj.* **supererogatory** (*-ə-rog'ə-tər-i*).—Also (*rare*) **super-erer'ogant, supererog'ative**.—**works of supererogation** (*R.C.*), works which, not absolutely required of each individual for salvation, may be done for the sake of greater perfection—affording the church a store of surplus merit, to eke out the deficient merit of others. [L. *super*, above, *ērogāre*, *-ātum*, to pay out.]

**superessential** ... to ... **superfatted**. See **super-**.

**superfetation**, *sōō-*, *sū-pər-fē-tā'shən*, *n.* fertilisation of an ovum in one already for some time pregnant: superabundant production or accumulation.—*v.i.* **superfē'tate**. [L. *superfētāre*—pfx. *super-*, over, *fētus*, a fetus.]

**superficies**, *sōō-*, *sū-pər-fish'i-ēz*, *n.* a surface, that which has length and breadth but no thickness (*geom.*): a bounding or outer surface: a surface layer: a surface area: external features, appearance:—*pl.* **superfic'ies**.—*adj.* **superficial** (*-fish'l*), of, on, or near the surface: not going much deeper than the surface.—*n.* that which is, or those who are, superficial: surface characters.— *v.t.* **superfic'ialise, -ize**, to make superficial.—*v.i.* to deal superficially.—*n.* **superficiality** (*-fish-i-al'i-ti*).—*adv.* **superfic'ially**.—*n.* **superfic'ialness**. [L. *superficiēs*—*super*, *faciēs*, face.]

**superfine** ... to ... **superfluidity**. See **super-**.

**superfluous**, *sōō-*, *sū-pûr'flōō-əs*, *adj.* above what is enough: redundant: unnecessary.—*n.* **super-fluity** (*-flōō'*), state of being superfluous: a thing that is superfluous: superabundance. — *adv.* **super'fluously**.—*ns.* **super'fluousness**, **superfluity**; **su'perflux** (*Shak.*), superfluity. [L. *superfluus*, overflowing—*super*, *fluĕre*, to flow.]

**superfoetation**. Same as superfetation.

**superfrontal** ... to ... **superintendentship**. See **super-**.

**superior**, *sōō-*, *sū-pē'ri-ər*, *adj.* upper: higher in nature, place, rank, or excellence: better (with *to*): surpassing others: beyond the influence, rising above (with *to*): supercilious or uppish: (often patronisingly) very worthy and highly respectable: of wider application, generic: set above the level of the line (*print.*): of an ovary, inserted on the receptacle above the other parts (*bot.*): of other parts, seeming to take rise above the ovary.—*n.* one superior to others: the head of a religious house, order, etc.: the feudal lord of a vassal: one to whom feu-duty is paid (*Scots law*):—*fem.* supe′rioress, the head of a nunnery. —*n.* superiority (-*or′i-ti*), quality or state of being superior: pre-eminence: advantage: the right which the superior enjoys in the land held by the vassal (*Scots law*).—*adv.* supe′riorly, in a superior manner or position.—*n.* supe′riorship.—superiority complex (*psych.*), over-valuation of one's worth, often affected to cover a sense of inferiority; superior planets, those more distant from the sun than is the earth. [L., comp. of *superus*, on high—*super*, above.]

superjacent, *sōō-*, *sū-pər-jā′sənt*, *adj.* lying above. [L. *super*, *jacēns*, *-entis*, pr.p. of *jacēre*, to lie.]

superlative, *sōō-*, *sū-pûr′lə-tiv*, *adj.* raised above others or to the highest degree: superior to all others: most eminent: expressing the highest degree (*gram.*).—*n.* the superlative or highest degree (*gram.*): an adjective or adverb in the superlative degree: any word or phrase of exaggeration.—*adv.* super′latively.—*n.* super′lativeness. [L. *superlātivus*—*super*, *lātus*, carried.]

superlunar ... to ... supermundane. See super-.

supernaculum, *sōō′*, *sū′pər-nak′ū-ləm*, *adv.* to the last drop.—*n.* liquor of the best kind, too good to leave heeltaps: a bumper.—*adj.* supernac′ular. [Sham L. *super naculum*, on the nail—L. *super*, Ger. *nagel*, nail; from the custom of turning the glass up to show that no more is left than will stand on the thumbnail.]

supernal, *sōō-*, *sū-pûr′nl*, *adj.* on high: celestial: of a higher world: exalted: topmost.—*adv.* super′nally. [L. *supernus*—*super*.]

supernatant, *sōō-*, *sū-pər-nā′tənt*, *adj.* floating or swimming above, esp. of an upper layer of liquid. [L. *supernatāns*, *-antis*—*super*, *natāre*, swim, float.]

supernatural ... to ... supernormal. See super-.

supernova, *sōō-*, *sū-pər-nō′və*, *n.* very brilliant nova resulting from an explosion which blows the star's material into space, leaving an expanding cloud of gas. [L. *super-*, above, and nova.]

supernumerary, *sōō-*, *sū-pər-nū′mər-ər-i*, *adj.* over and above the stated, usual, normal, or necessary number.—*n.* a supernumerary person or thing: an actor without speaking parts. [L.L. *supernumerārius*—L. *super*, *numerus*, number.]

superoctave ... to ... supersaturation. See super-.

superscribe, *sōō-*, *sū-pər-skrīb′*, *v.t.* to write or engrave above, on the top or on the outside of something: to address (as a letter): to sign at the top.—*adj.* su′perscript (-*skript*), written above.—*n.* (*Shak.*) the superscription, address.— *n.* superscrip′tion, act of superscribing: that which is superscribed. [L. *super*, above, *scrībere*, *scriptum*, to write.]

supersede, *sōō-*, *sū-pər-sēd′*, *v.t.* to desist or refrain from (*obs.*): to override (*obs.*): to set aside: to set aside in favour of another: to come or put in the room of, to replace.—*v.i.* (*obs.*) to refrain, desist.—*ns.* superse′deas, (*-di-as*), a writ to stay proceedings, or to suspend the powers of an officer (from the use of the L. word, *2nd pers. sing. pres. subj.*, you are to desist); superse′dence; superse′der; supersedere (*-si-dē′ri*, *sōō-per-se-dā′re*, *infin.*), a private agreement among creditors, under a trust-deed, to supersede or sist diligence for a certain period (*Scots law*): an order of court granting protection to a debtor; superse′dure; supersession (*-sesh′ən*). [L. *supersedēre*, to sit above, refrain from—*super*, above, *sedēre*, *sessum*, to sit.]

supersensible ... to ... superserviceable. See super-.

supersonic, *sōō-*, *sū-pər-son′ik*, *adj.* above the audible limit: too high-pitched for human hearing (ultrasonic): also, above the speed of sound.—*n.* a supersonic wave: (in *pl.*) the study of such waves.—*n.* su′persound (see super-). [L. *super*, above, *sonus*, sound.]

superstate. See super-.

superstition, *sōō-*, *sū-pər-stish′ən*, *n.* false worship or religion: an ignorant and irrational belief in supernatural agency, omens, divination, sorcery, etc.: a deep-rooted but unfounded general belief: a rite or practice proceeding from superstitious belief or fear (*obs.*).—*adj.* superstit′ious.—*adv.* superstit′iously.—*n.* superstit′iousness. [L. *superstitiō*, *-ōnis*.]

superstratum ... to ... supertonic. See super-.

supervene, *sōō-*, *sū-pər-vēn′*, *v.i.* to come in addition, or closely after.—*n.* supervēn′ience.—*adj.* supervēn′ient, supervening. — *n.* supervention (-*ven′shən*). [L. *super*, above, *venīre*, *ventum*, to come.]

supervise, *sōō′*, *sū′pər-vīz*, or -*vīz′*, *v.i.* to read over (*Shak.*): to superintend.—*n.* (*Shak.*) reading over.—*ns.* supervi′sal, supervision (-*vizh′ən*), act of supervising: inspection: control; supervisor (*vī′zər*; also *sōō′*, *sū′*), one who supervises: an overseer: an inspector: a spectator (*Shak.*); supervi′sorship.—*adj.* supervi′sory, pertaining to, or having, supervision. [L. *super*, over, *vidēre*, *visum*, to see.]

supervolute. See super-.

supine, *sōō′*, *sū′pin*, or *pin′*, *adj.* lying on the back: leaning backward, inclined, sloping: negligently inert: indolent: passive.—*n.* a Latin verbal noun in -*tum* (*first supine*, an old accusative) or -*tū* (*second supine*, an old locative), possibly as formed from the stem of the passive participle: the English infinitive with *to*.—*v.t.* su′pinate (-*pin-āt*), to bring palm upward or forward.—*ns.* supina′tion, the placing or holding of the palm of the hand upward or forward; su′pinator, a muscle that supinates the hand.—*adv.* supine′ly.—*n.* supine′ness. [L. *supīnus*, supine; related to *sub*, under, *super*, over.]

suppawn, supawn, *sə-pön′*, *n.* maize porridge. [Natick *saupáun*, softened.]

suppeago, *sə-pē′gō*. See serpigo.

supper, *sup′ər*, *n.* a meal taken at the close of the day.—*v.t.* to furnish with supper.—*adj.* supp′erless.—supper cloth, a table-cloth, larger than a tea-cloth, on which supper is served; supp′ertime, the time at which supper is usually taken. [O.Fr. *soper* (Fr. *souper*).]

supping. See sup.

supplant, *sə-plänt′*, *v.t.* to overthrow, to lay low (*Milt.*): to oust: to supersede: to dispossess and take the place of: to uproot (*Shak.*).—*ns.* supplantation (*sup-lən-tā′shən*); supplant′er. [L. *supplantāre*, to trip up—*sub*, under, *planta*, the sole.]

supple, *sup′l*, *adj.* pliant: lithe: yielding to the humour of others: fawning.—*v.t.* to make supple: to make soft or compliant.—*v.i.* to become supple.—*n.* supp′leness.—*adv.* supp′ly.— supple jack, a woody liane of many kinds: a pliant cane. [Fr. *souple*—L. *supplex*, bending the knees—*sub*, under, *plicāre*, to fold.]

supple, *sōōp′l*, a Scots form of swipple. See also souple (2).

supplement, *sup′li-mənt*, *n.* that which supplies a deficiency or fills a need: that which completes or brings closer to completion: any addition by which defects are made good: a special part of a periodical publication accompanying an ordinary part: the quantity by which an angle or an arc falls short of 180° or a semicircle.—*v.t.* supplement (-*ment′*; also *sup′li-mənt*), to supply or fill up: to add to.—*adjs.* supplement′al, supplement′ary, added to supply what is wanting: additional.—Also *ns.*—*advs.* supplement′ally, supplement′arily.—*ns.* supplementā′tion; supplement′er.—*adjs.* supp′letive, supp′letory, supplemental. [L. *supplēmentum*, a filling up, *supplēre*, to fill up.]

supplial, suppliance (1), suppliant (1). See under supply.

**suppliant**, *sup'li-ənt*, *adj.* supplicating: asking earnestly: entreating.—*n.* a humble petitioner.—*n.* **supp'liance**, supplication.—*adv.* **supp'liantly**. [Fr. *suppliant*, pr.p. of *supplier*—L. *supplicāre*; see next.]
**supplicant**, *sup'li-kənt*, *adj.* supplicating: asking submissively.—*n.* one who supplicates or entreats earnestly.—*n.* **supp'licat**, in the English universities, a petition.—*v.t.* and *v.i.* **supp'licate**, to entreat earnestly: to petition: to pray.—*adj.* **supp'licating**.—*adv.* **supp'licatingly**.—*n.* **supplicā'-tion**, act of supplicating: an earnest or humble petition: in ancient Rome, a solemn service or day decreed for giving formal thanks to the gods for victory, etc.: earnest prayer or entreaty, esp. in liturgies, a litany petition for some special blessing.—*adj.* **supp'licatory**, containing supplication or entreaty: humble.—*n.* **supplicā'vit**, formerly a writ issued by the King's Bench or Chancery for taking the surety of the peace against a person. [L. *supplicāre*, *-ātum*—*supplex*; see **supple**.]
**supply**, *sə-plī'*, *v.t.* to fill up a deficiency in (*obs.*): to supplement (*obs.*): to reinforce, to help (*obs.*): to make good: to satisfy: to provide, furnish: to fill, occupy (as a substitute): to serve instead of: —*pr.p.* **supply'ing**; *pa.t.* and *pa.p.* **supplied'**.—*n.* act of supplying: that which is supplied or which supplies a want: amount provided or in hand: available amount of a commodity: amount of food or money provided (used generally in *pl.*): a parliamentary grant for expenses of government: a person who takes another's duty temporarily, a substitute, esp. a clergyman.—*ns.* **suppli'al**, the act of supplying; **suppli'ance** (*Shak.*), supplying, something to fill up time, pastime, gratification.—*adj.* **suppli'ant** (*Shak.*), supplementary, reinforcing.—*ns.* **suppli'er**, one who supplies; **supply'ment** (*Shak.*), replenishment, supplementing.—**Commissioners of Supply**, a former administrative and rating authority in Scotland, superseded by the County Council. [O.Fr. *suppleier*, *supplier* (Fr. *suppléer*)—L. *supplēre*, to fill up.]
**support**, *sə-pōrt'*, *-pört'*, *v.t.* to bear the weight of: to hold up: to endure: to sustain: to maintain: to keep going: to corroborate: to make good: to uphold: to back up: to second: to contend for: to represent in acting: to supply with means of living: to nourish: to strengthen.—*n.* act or fact of supporting or upholding: that which, or one who, supports, sustains, or maintains: maintenance: backing: a prop: an actor playing a subordinate part with a star.—*adj.* **support'able**, capable of being held up, borne, sustained, or maintained.—*n.* **support'ableness**.—*adv.* **support'ably**.—*ns.* **support'ance** (*Shak.*), support; **support'er**, one who, or that which, supports: an adherent: a defender: one who attends matches and watches with interest the fortunes of a team: a figure on each side of the escutcheon (*her.*).—*n.* and *adj.* **support'ing**.—*adjs.* **support'ive** (*rare*); **support'less**.—*ns.* (all *rare*) **support'ment**; **support'ress**; **support'ure**. [L. *supportāre*—*sub*, up, *portāre*, to bear.]
**suppose**, *sə-pōz'*, *v.t.* to place underneath (*obs.*): to believe (*Shak.*): to incline to believe: to conceive, imagine, guess: to assume provisionally or for argument's sake: to imply, presuppose: to pretend: to expect (*Milt.*): (esp. in *pass.*) to expect in accordance with rules or conventions: to substitute fraudulently (*obs.*).—*n.* a supposition: an instance of supposing or saying 'suppose': (*Shak.*) expectation.—*adj.* **suppo's-able**.—*adv.* **suppo'sably**.—*n.* **suppo'sal**, supposition: notion (*Shak.*): proposal (*obs.*).—*adj.* **supposed'**, believed to be: assumed: conjectured: feigned (*Shak.*): supposititious (*obs.*): placed below, or having a note below, the fundamental of the chord (*mus.*).—*adv.* **suppo'sedly**,

according to supposition.—*ns.* **suppo'ser**; **suppo'sing.**—**suppose** (*Scot.*), even if; supposing (*coll.*), what if, how about. [Fr. *supposer*—pfx. *sup-* (*sub-*), *poser*; see **pose**, and cf. **compose**, **dispose**, etc.]
**supposes**, *sə-pōz'iz*, (*Shak.*, *Taming of the Shrew*, V, i. 120) *n.pl.* perh. substitutes, or substitutions, or suppositions. See repeated play on the word in Shakespeare's source, Gascoigne's *Supposes* (and its original, Ariosto's *I Suppositi*).
**supposition**, *sup-ə-zi'shən*, *n.* an act of supposing: that which is supposed: assumption: presumption, opinion.—*adj.* **supposi'tional**, hypothetical: conjectural: supposed.—*adv.* **supposi'tionally**.—*adjs.* **supposi'tionary**, suppositional; **supposi'tious** (*-zi'shəs*; *rare*), suppositional: usu. a blunder for supposititious; **suppositi'tious** (*sə-poz-i-tish'əs*), put by trick in the place of another: spurious: suppositional.—*adv.* **suppositi'tiously**.—*n.* **suppositi'tiousness**.—*adj.* **suppos'itive** (*-i-tiv*), suppositional.—*n.* **suppos'itory**, a medicated plug for administration by the rectum or other canal. [L. *suppōnĕre*, *-positum*, to set under, substitute—*sub*, *pōnĕre*, to put.]
**suppress**, *sə-pres'*, *v.t.* to crush, put down: to subdue: to hold or press down (*Spens.*): to ravish (*Spens.*): to hold back, esp. from publication, circulation, divulgation, expression, development: to check, stop, restrain: to hold in: to moderate: to leave out.—*adj.* **suppressed'**.—*adv.* **suppress'edly**.—*adj.* **suppress'ible**.—*n.* **suppression** (*-presh'*), act of suppressing: stoppage: concealment.—*adj.* **suppress'ive**, tending to suppress: subduing.—*n.* **suppress'or**, one who suppresses anything: a device for suppressing anything, e.g. the echo of one's own voice on a telephone, electrical interference with television reception.—**suppressor grid**, a grid between the anode and screen of a pentode valve to repel secondary electrons back to the anode. [L. *supprimĕre*, *suppressum*—*sub*, under, *premĕre*, to press.]
**suppurate**, *sup'ū-rāt*, *v.i.* to gather pus or matter.—*n.* **suppurā'tion**.—*adj.* **supp'urative**, promoting or attended by suppuration.—*n.* a suppurative agent. [L. *sub*, under, *pūs*, *pūris*, pus.]
**supra-**, *sōō'pra-*, *sū'pra-*, in composition, above.—*adjs.* **supra-ax'illary**, arising above an axil; **supraciliary** (*-sil'*), above the eyebrow; **supra-cost'al**, above or on a rib.—*n.* **Supralapsarian** (*-laps-ā'ri-ən*; L. *lāpsus*, fall), one of a class of Calvinists who make the decree of election and predestination to precede the Creation and the Fall—opp. to *Sublapsarian*.—Also *adj.*—*n.* **Supralapsā'rianism**.—*adjs.* **supralu'nar**, beyond the moon: very lofty; **supramun'dane**, above the world; **supranat'ional**, overriding national sovereignty; **supra-or'bital**, above the orbit of the eye; **suprarē'nal**, above the kidneys (**suprarenal capsules**, the adrenal glands; **suprarenal extract**, an extract from these used in haemorrhage, Addison's disease, etc.); **suprasens'ible**, above the reach of the senses; **supratemp'oral**, transcending time: of the upper part of the temples or temporal region. [L. *suprā*, above.]
**supreme**, *sū-*, *sōō-prēm'*, poet. also *sū'*, *sōō'*, *adj.* highest: greatest: most excellent.—*n.* the highest point: the highest authority.—*ns.* **supremacy** (*-prem'ə-si*), state of being supreme: supreme position or power; **suprematism** (*sōō-prem'ə-tizm*), an extreme form of cubism using very simple geometrical shapes.—*n.* and *adj.* **suprem'atist**.—*adv.* **supremely** (*-prēm'*).—*ns.* **supreme'ness**, **supremity** (*-prem'*). —**supreme sacrifice**, giving up of one's life; **Supreme Soviet**, the legislature of the U.S.S.R., consisting of two bodies, the Council of the Union, in which each deputy represents so many of the population, and the Council of Nationalities, in which each deputy represents one of the

Republics or other distinct regions within the U.S.S.R. [L. *suprēmus*, superl. of *superus*, high —*super*, above.]
**supremo**, *sū-*, *soō-prā'mō*, *n.* a supreme head. [Sp.,—L. *suprēmus*, highest.]
**sur-**, *sür-*, *pfx.* over. [Fr.,—L. *super*.]
**sur**, *sür*, (Fr.) on, above.—**sur le tapis** (*lə ta-pē*), on the carpet (table-cover): under discussion, subject of talk; **sur place** (*plas*), on the spot.
**sura, surah**, *soō'ra*, *n.* a chapter of the Koran. [Ar. *sūra*, *sūrah*, step.]
**sura**, *soō'ra*, *n.* fermented palm-sap. [Sans. *surā*.]
**suraddition**, *sür-ə-dish'ən*, (*Shak.*) *n.* an additional title or designation. [Pfx. **sur-**.]
**surah**, *sū'*, *soō'ra*, *n.* a soft twilled silk or artificial fabric.—Also *adj.* [Poss. from *Surat*.]
**sural**, *sū'rl*, *adj.* pertaining to the calf of the leg. [L. *sūra*, the calf.]
**surance**, *shoōr'əns*, (*Shak.*) *n.* assurance.
**surat**, *soō-rat'*, or *soō'*, *n.* coarse uncoloured cotton. [*Surat*, in India.]
**surbase**, *sür'bās*, *n.* a cornice or series of mouldings above the base of a pedestal, etc.—*adj.* **surbased** (-*bāst'*), of an arch, lower than half the span.—*n.* **surbase'ment**. [Pfx. **sur-**.]
**surbate**, *sür-bāt'*, *v.t.* (*Spens. sür'*) to bruise with walking, make footsore:—*pa.p.* **surbat'ed**, (*Spens.*) **surbet'**. [O.Fr. *surbatu*, excessively beaten, but with the meaning of Fr. *solbatu*.]
**surbed**, *sür-bed'*, (*obs.*) *v.t.* to set on edge, as a stone with reference to the grain. [Pfx. **sur-**.]
**surcease**, *sür-sēs'*, *v.i.* to cease.—*v.t.* to desist or refrain from: to end, put a stop to.—*n.* cessation. [O.Fr. *sursis*, pa.p. of *surseoir*—L. *supersedēre*, to refrain from; cf. **supersede**; spelling influenced by **cease**.]
**surcharge**, *sür-chärj'*, *v.t.* to overcharge: to overload: to overburden: to overstock: to saturate: to charge with overwhelming force (*Spens.*): to print over the original printing: to disallow: to exact a surcharge from.—*n.* **sur'charge** (or -*chärj'*), an overcharge: an extra charge: an excessive load: an overloaded condition: an amount not passed by an auditor, which must be refunded: a new valuation or cancel-mark printed on or over a stamp: the earth supported by a retaining wall above the level of its top.—*adj.* **surcharged'**.—*ns.* **surcharge'ment**; **sur-charg'er**. [Pfx. **sur-**.]
**surcingle**, *sür'sing-gl*, *n.* a girth or strap for holding a saddle on an animal's back: the girdle of a cassock.—*v.t.* to gird, fasten, or thrash with a surcingle. [O.Fr. *surcengle*—L. *super*, *cingulum*, a belt.]
**surcoat**, *sür'kōt*, *n.* a mediaeval outer garment, usu. sleeveless, often with heraldic devices, worn by men and women over armour or ordinary dress. [O.Fr. *surcote*, *surcot*—*sur*, over, *cote*, garment.]
**surculus**, *sür'kū-ləs*, (*bot.*) *n.* a sucker. [L. *sürculus*.]
**surd**, *sürd*, *adj.* deaf (*obs.*): senseless (*obs.*): that cannot be expressed in rational numbers (*math.*): voiceless (*phon.*).—*n.* an irrational quantity (*math.*): a voiceless consonant.—*n.* **surd'ity**, deafness. [L. *surdus*, deaf.]
**sure**, *shoōr*, *adj.* secure: safe: fit to be depended on: unerring: stable: bound in alliance (esp. by betrothal or marriage; *obs.*): certain: assured: confident beyond doubt: without other possibility.—*interj.* (*coll.*) certainly, undoubtedly, yes.—*advs.* **sure** (now chiefly *Ir.* or *U.S.*, except in comp. and in conventional phrases), **surely**, firmly: confidently: safely: certainly: assuredly: as it would seem (often ironically).—*ns.* **sure'ness**; **sure'ty**, certainty: safeguard: legal security against loss: one who becomes bound for another: a sponsor.—*v.t.* (*Shak.*) to be security for.—*n.* **sure'tyship**.—*adjs.* **sure'-enough'** (*U.S.*), genuine, real; **sure'-fire**, in-

fallible; **sure'footed**, not liable to stumble.— *adv.* **surefoot'edly**.—*ns.* **surefoot'edness**; **sure thing**, a certainty, certain success: beyond doubt.—**be sure**, do not omit; **for sure**, certainly: of a certainty; **make sure** (see **make**); **sure enough**, no doubt: in very fact: accordingly: there's no denying; **to be sure**, certainly: I admit. [O.Fr. *sur*, *seur* (Fr. *sür*)—L. *sēcūrus*; see **secure**.]
**sure**, an old spelling of **sewer**.
**Sûreté**, *sür-tā*, (Fr.) the French criminal investigation department.
**surety**. See **sure** (1).
**surf**, *sürf*, *n.* surging water or waves rushing up a sloping beach: sea-foam.—*v.i.* to bathe in or ride on surf.—*ns.* **surf'er**; **surf'ing**, riding breaking waves on a surf-board or in a surf-canoe.— *adj.* **surf'y**.—**surf'-bathing**, bathing in surf; **surf'-bather**; **surf'-bird**, an American Pacific shorebird (Aphriza) akin to sandpipers; **surf'-board**, **surf'ing-board**, a board on which a bather allows himself to be carried inshore by the surf; **surf'-boarding**; **surf'-boat**, a boat for use in surf; **surf'-canoe**, a slalom canoe or a kayak used for surfing; **surf'-duck**, the scoter; **surf'-fish**, any fish of a Western American viviparous perch-like family, Embiotocidae; **surf'man**, one skilful in handling boats in surf; **surf'-riding**, riding on a surf-board. [Origin obscure.]
**surface**, *sür'fis*, *n.* the outer boundary or face of anything: the outside or upper layer: that which has length and breadth but no thickness (*gecm.*): area: outer appearance, character or texture: an aerofoil.—*adj.* of, on, or near a surface.— *v.t.* to put a surface, or some kind of surface or finish, upon.—*v.i.* to rise to the surface: to regain consciousness (*coll.*): to get out of bed (*coll.*).—*adj.* **sur'faced**, having this or that kind of surface.—*ns.* **sur'facer**, one who, or that which, smooths or levels a surface; **sur'facing**, giving a surface to anything: material for a surface layer: washing surface deposits for gold. —**sur'face-craft**, a floating, not submersible, craft; **sur'face-mail**, mail sent otherwise than by air; **sur'faceman**, one who keeps a railway-bed in repair; **surface tension**, that property in virtue of which a liquid surface behaves like a stretched elastic membrane.—*adj.* **sur'face-to-air'**, of a missile, etc., travelling from a base on the ground to a target in the air.—Also *adv.* —*adj.* and *adv.* **sur'face-to-sur'face**.—**sur'face-vessel**; **sur'face-water**, drainage-water. [Fr., from *sur*—L. *super*, and *face*—L. *faciēs*, face.]
**surfactant**, *sar-fak'tənt*, *n.* a substance, e.g. a detergent, which has the effect of altering the interfacial tension of water and other liquids or solids. [*surface-active agent*.]
**surfeit**, *sür'fit*, *n.* overfulness: gorging: gluttony: excess: an excessive meal: sickness or satiety caused by overeating or overdrinking.—*v.t.* to feed or fill to satiety or disgust.—*v.i.* to indulge to excess, esp. in food and drink: to suffer from excess.—*adj.* **sur'feited**.—*n.* **sur'feiter**.—*n.* and *adj.* **sur'feiting**. [O.Fr. *surfait*, excess—L. *super*, above, *facēre*, to make.]
**surficial**, *sür-fish'l*, (*geol.*) *adj.* superficial, subaerial. [*surface*, altered in analogy with *superficial*.]
**surge**, an old spelling (*Shak.*) of **serge**.
**surge**, *sürj*, *n.* an uprush, boiling or tumultuous movement of liquid: a great wave: a swell: a sudden oscillation: a jerk on a rope: of space-craft, movement in the direction of travel.—*v.i.* to well up: to heave tumultuously: to slip back: to jerk.—*v.t.* to send in surges: to slack suddenly. —*adjs.* **surge'ful**; **surge'less**; **sur'gent**.—*n.* and *adj.* **sur'ging**.—*adj.-sur'gy*. [L. *surgēre*, to rise.]
**surgeon**, *sür'jən*, *n.* one who treats injuries or diseases by manual operations: an army or naval doctor: a ship's doctor: a surgeon-fish.

*fāte, fär; mē, hûr* (her); *mīne; mōte, för; mūte; moōn, foōt; dhen* (then)

—*ns.* sur'geoncy, sur'geonship, the office or employment of a surgeon in the army or navy; sur'gery, the art and practice of a surgeon: a doctor's or dentist's consulting-room.— *adj.* sur'gical, pertaining to surgery.—*adv.* sur'gically.
—sur'geon-fish, a sea-surgeon; surgeon's knot, a knot like a reef-knot but with a double turn in the first part (used in ligaturing a cut artery); surgical boot, shoe, a boot, shoe designed to correct deformities of the foot; surgical spirit, methylated spirit with small amounts of castor oil and oil of wintergreen. [A.Fr. *surgien*; see chirurgeon.]

suricate, *sōō'ri-kāt, n.* a S. African animal of the civet family. [Origin unknown.]

Surinam, *sū-, sōō-ri-nam', sū', sōō', n.* part of the Kingdom of the Netherlands in northern S. America.—Surinam poison, fish poison got from a S. American papilionaceous plant, Tephrosia; Surinam toad, a S. American amphibian that hatches its eggs in pits in its back.

surloin. Same as sirloin.

surly (*Spens.* syrlye), *sûr'li, adj.* haughty (*Shak.*): morose: gruff and grumpy: rough and gloomy: refractory.—*adv.* (*Shak.*) surlily.—*adv.* sur'lily.— *n.* sur'liness. [From sir and like; cf. lordly.]

surmaster, *sûr'mäs-tǝr, n.* a second master in a school. [Pfx. sur-.]

surmise, *sǝr-mīz', n.* allegation (*obs.*): suspicion: conjecture.—*v.t.* to imagine: to suspect: to conjecture, guess.—*adj.* surmis'able.—*ns.* surmis'al; surmis'er.—*n.* and *adj.* surmis'ing. [O.Fr.,— *surmettre,* to accuse—L. *super,* upon, *mittĕre,* to send.]

surmount, *sǝr-mownt', v.t.* to mount above: to be on or go to the top of: to surpass: to get the better of.—*adjs.* surmount'able; surmount'ed, surpassed: overcome: higher than half the span (*archit.*): having another figure laid over (*her.*).—*n.* surmount'er.—*n.* and *adj.* surmount'ing. [O.Fr. *surmunter* (Fr. *surmonter*)—L.L. *supermontāre*; see mount.]

surmullet, *sǝr-mul'it, n.* a species of red mullet, admired by the Romans for its colour-changes as it died. [Fr. *surmulet.*]

surname, *sûr'nām, n.* an additional name: a family name.—*v.t.* to name by a surname.—*adj.* surnom'inal. [On the analogy of Fr. *surnom,* from Eng. name and L. *nōmen, -inis.*]

surpass, *sǝr-päs', v.t.* to go or be beyond: to exceed: to excel.—*adjs.* surpass'able; surpass'ing, passing beyond others: excellent in a high degree.—Also (*obs.* or *poet.*) *adv.*—*adv.* surpass'- ingly.—*n.* surpass'ingness. [Fr. *surpasser*—*sur-,* *passer,* to pass.]

surplice, *sûr'plis, n.* a white linen vestment worn over the cassock.—*adj.* sur'pliced, wearing a surplice. [Fr. *surplis*—L.L. *superpellicium,* an over-garment—*pellis,* skin.]

surplus, *sûr'plǝs, n.* that which is left over: remainder: excess over what is required: excess of revenue over expenditure.—Also *adj.*—*n.* sur'- plusage, surplus: superfluity. [Fr.,—L.L. *super- plūs*—*super, plūs,* more.]

surprise, *sǝr-prīz', n.* a taking unawares: a sudden capture owing to unpreparedness: the emotion caused by anything sudden or contrary to expectation: loosely, astonishment: anything that causes or is intended to cause this emotion.— Also *adj.*—*v.t.* to come upon suddenly or unawares: to capture by an unexpected assault: to seize (*obs.*): to lead or bring unawares, to betray (with *into*): to strike with wonder or astonishment: to confuse.—*n.* surpris'al, act of surprising.—*adj.* surprised'.—*adv.* surpris'edly.— *n.* surpris'er.—*n.* and *adj.* surpris'ing.—*adv.* surpris'ingly.—*n.* surpris'ingness. [O.Fr. (Fr.) fem. pa.p. of *surprendre*—L. *super, prehendĕre,* to catch.]

surquedry, *sûr'kwi-dri,* (*Spens.*) *n.* arrogance.—

Also (*Scott*) sur'quedy. [O.Fr. *surcuiderie*— *surcuidier*—L. *super,* above, and *cōgitāre, -ātum,* to think.]

surra, *sōō'rǝ, n.* a trypanosome disease of horses, etc., in Eastern Asia. [Marathi *sūra,* wheezing.]

surrealism, *sǝr-ē'ǝ-lizm, n.* a movement in French art and literature, from about 1919 on, that aimed at drawing upon the subconscious and escaping the control of reason or any preconceptions.—*adj.* surre'al.—*adj.* and *n.* surre'alist. —*adj.* surrealist'ic.—*adv.* surrealist'ically. [Fr. *surréalisme*—*sur,* above, and *réalisme,* realism.]

surrebut, *sur-i-but', v.i.* to reply to a defendant's rebutter.—*ns.* surrebutt'al, a plaintiff's evidence or presentation of evidence, in response to a defendant's rebuttal; surrebutt'er, the plaintiff's reply, in common law pleading, to a defendant's rebutter. [Pfx. sur-.]

surreined, *sûr'ānd, adj.* (*Shak.* sur-reyn'd) over-ridden. [App. *sur-* and rein.]

surrejoin, *sur-i-join', v.t.* and *v.i.* to reply to a defendant's rejoinder.—*n.* surrejoind'er, a plaintiff's reply to a defendant's rejoinder. [Pfx. sur-.]

surrender, *sǝ-ren'dǝr, v.t.* to deliver over: to relinquish: to yield up: to resign.—*v.i.* to yield oneself up: to yield.—*n.* act of surrendering.— *ns.* surrenderee', one to whom a legal surrender is made; surren'derer; surren'deror (*law*), one who makes a surrender; surren'dry (*obs.*), a surrender.—surrender value, the amount to be paid to an insured person who surrenders his policy. [A.Fr. *surrender,* O.Fr. *surrendre*—*sur-,* *rendre*; see render.]

surreptitious, *sur-ǝp-tish'ǝs, adj.* done by stealth or fraud: stealthy.—*adv.* surrepti'tiously. [See subreption.]

surrey, *sur'i,* (*U.S.*) *n.* a light four-wheeled vehicle for four, usu. with two seats. [Developed from a vehicle used in *Surrey.*]

sur-reyn'd. See surreined.

surrogate, *sur'ō-gāt, n.* a substitute: a deputy, esp. of an ecclesiastical judge: one who grants marriage licences: a judge of probate (*U.S.*): a person or thing standing, e.g. in a dream, for another person or thing, or a person who fills the role of another in one's emotional life (as *a mother, a father,* surrogate).—*ns.* surr'ogateship; surroga'tion, subrogation; surroga'tum, a substitute. [L. *surrogāre, -ātum*—*sub,* in the place of, *rogāre,* to ask.]

surround, *sǝ-rownd', v.t.* to overflow (*obs.*): to go or extend all around: to encompass, environ: to invest: to make a circuit of.—*n.* an act of surrounding (esp. hunted animals): a border, esp. the floor or floor-covering around a carpet.—*adj.* surround'ing, encompassing: neighbouring.—*n.* an encompassing: (in *pl.*) environment, things round about. [O.Fr. *suronder*—L. *superundāre,* to overflow—*super, unda,* wave; confused with round.]

surroyal, *sǝ-roi'ǝl, n.* any tine of a stag's horn above the royal. [Pfx. sur-.]

surtarbrand. See surturbrand.

surtax, *sûr'taks, n.* an additional tax.—*v.t.* to tax additionally. [Pfx. sur-.]

surtout, *sǝr-tōō', -tōōt', n.* an overcoat (*obs.*): a lady's hood (*obs.*): (19th cent.) a close-bodied frock-coat: a raised portion of the parapet of a work at the angles, to protect from enfilade fire (*fort.*). [Fr.,—L.L. *supertōtus,* an outer garment—L. *super, tōtus,* all.]

surturbrand, surtarbrand, *sûr'tar-brand, n.* lignite found interbedded with lavas in Iceland. [Ice. *surtarbrandr*—*Surtar,* gen. of *Surtr,* name of a fire-giant, *brandr,* brand.]

surucucu, *sōō-rōō-kōō-kōō', n.* a S. American Indian name for the bushmaster.

surveillance, *sǝr-vā'lǝns,* or *-lyǝns, n.* vigilant supervision: spy-like watching: superintendence.

—*n.* **surveill'ant.** [Fr.,—*surveiller—sur, veiller,* to watch—L. *vigilāre.*]

**survew.** See **survew.**

**survey,** *sər-vā', v.t.* to view comprehensively and extensively: to examine in detail: to obtain by measurements data for mapping: to perceive, spy (*Shak.*).—*ns.* **sur'vey** (also *-vā'*), a general view, or a statement of its results: an inspection: collection of data for mapping: an organisation or body of men for that purpose: superintendence; **survey'al; survey'ance; survey'or,** an overseer: a measurer of land: an inspector (of roads, of weights and measures, of customs duties, etc.); **survey'orship.** [O.Fr. *surveoir—* L. *super,* over, *vidēre,* to see.]

**surview,** *sər-vū', Spens.* **survew,** *v.t.* to survey, look over: to command a view of. [Pfx. **sur-.**]

**survive,** *sər-vīv', v.t.* to live beyond: to outlive. —*v.i.* to remain alive.—*n.* **survi'val,** a surviving or living after: anything that continues to exist after others of its kind have disappeared, or after the time to which it naturally belongs.— *adj.* (esp. of standard equipment) designed to help one to survive exposure or other dangerous condition.—*n.* **survi'vance,** survival: succession or right to succeed on surviving the present holder.—*adj.* **survi'ving.**—*ns.* **survi'vor; survi'vorship.**—survival of the fittest, the longer average life of the fit in the struggle for existence, and the consequent transmission of favourable variations in greater proportion to later generations. [Fr. *survivre—*L. *super,* beyond, *vīvēre,* to live.]

**Surya,** *sōōr'ya, n.* the Hindu sun-god. [Sans.]

**susceptible,** *sə-sep'ti-bl, adj.* capable, admitting: capable of receiving: impressionable: easily affected by emotion (esp. amatory).—*ns.* **susceptibil'ity, suscep'tibleness.**—*adv.* **suscep'tibly.** —*adj.* **suscep'tive,** capable of receiving or admitting: readily admitting.—*ns.* **suscep'tiveness; susceptiv'ity** (*sus-*); **suscep'tor** (*obs.*), a sponsor; **suscip'ient,** a recipient, esp. of a sacrament.— *adj.* receiving. [L. *suscipēre, susceptum,* to take up—*sus-* (*subs-*), up, *capēre,* to take.]

**suscitate,** *sus'i-tāt, v.t.* to excite, rouse.—*n.* **suscitā'tion.** [L. *suscitāre, -ātum—sus-* (*subs-*), under, *citāre,* to arouse.]

**suslik,** *sus'lik, sōōs'lik, n.* a spermophile, zizel, or ground-squirrel. [Russ.]

**suspect,** *səs-pekt', v.t.* to mistrust: to imagine to be guilty: to doubt: to be ready to believe, but without sufficient evidence: to incline to believe the existence, presence, or agency of: to have an inkling of: to conjecture.—*v.i.* to imagine guilt, to be suspicious.—*n.* **suspicion:** (*sus'pekt*) a person suspected.—*adj.* suspected.—*adjs.* **suspect'able; suspect'ed.**—*adv.* **suspect'edly.**—*n.* **suspect'edness.**—*adjs.* **suspect'ful,** suspicious; **suspect'less,** unsuspicious: unsuspected. [L. *suspicēre, suspectum,* to look at secretly or askance—*sus-* (*sub-*), *specēre,* to look.]

**suspend,** *səs-pend', v.t.* to hang: to make to depend: to sustain from falling: to put or hold in a state of suspense or suspension: to make to stop for a time: to defer: to debar from any privilege, office, emolument, etc., for a time: to sustain into a following chord, producing discord (*mus.*): to hold in an indeterminate state. —*adj.* **suspen'ded.**—*ns.* **suspend'er,** one who, or that which, suspends: a strap to support a sock or stocking: (in *pl.*) braces (*U.S.*); **suspense',** intermission: cessation: deferring, as of judgment: uneasy uncertainty: indecision.— *adj.* in suspense: (*Milt.* **suspens', suspence'**) suspended, held back.—*adj.* **suspense'ful.**—*n.* **suspensibil'ity.**—*adj.* **suspen'sible.**—*ns.* **suspen'sion** (*-shən*), act of suspending: interruption: delay: temporary privation of office or privilege: a conditional withholding: holding a note from a chord into the next chord (*mus.*): a discord

so produced (*mus.*): a mixture of a fluid with dense particles which are prevented from settling by viscosity and impact of molecules (*chem.*): in a motor vehicle or railway carriage, the system of springs, etc., supporting the chassis on the axles.—*adj.* **suspen'sive.**—*adv.* **suspen'sively.**—*ns.* **suspen'soid** (*chem.*), a colloid dispersed with difficulty, yielding an unstable solution that cannot be reformed after coagulation; **suspen'sor,** a chain of cells to which a plant-embryo is fixed (*bot.*): a suspensory bandage.—*adj.* **suspensorial** (*sus-pen-sō'ri-əl, -sō'*).— *n.* **suspenso'rium,** that which holds up a part, esp. the arrangement joining the lower jaw to the cranium in vertebrates below mammals.— *adj.* **suspen'sory,** suspending: having the power or effect of delaying or staying: of the suspensorium.—*n.* a suspensorium.—**suspended animation,** temporary cessation of the outward signs and of some of the functions of life; **suspen'der-belt,** a woman's undergarment with stocking suspenders; **suspense account,** an account in which items are entered which cannot at once be placed in an ordinary account; **suspen'sion-bridge,** a bridge with roadway supported by chains passing over elevated piers; **suspension building,** building round a concrete core and from the top downward.—**suspend payment,** publicly to stop paying debts from insolvency. [L. *suspendēre, -pēnsum*—pfx. *sus-* (*subs-*), *pendēre,* to hang.]

**supercollate,** *sus-pər-kol'āt,* (*facet.*) *v.t.* to hang. [*Sus. per coll.,* abbrev. for L. *suspendātur per collum,* let him be hanged by the neck.]

**suspicion,** *səs-pish'ən, n.* act of suspecting: state of being suspected: the imagining of something without evidence or on slender evidence: inkling: mistrust: a slight quantity, as of spirits (*coll.*): ground for suspicion (*Shak.*).—*v.t.* (*dial.* and *U.S.*) to suspect.—*adjs.* **suspi'cionless; suspi'cious,** full of suspicion: showing suspicion: inclined to suspect: giving ground for suspicion: liable to suspicion, doubtful.—*adv.* **suspi'ciously.** —*n.* **suspi'ciousness.** [L. *suspiciō, -ōnis;* see **suspect.**]

**suspire,** *səs-pīr', v.i.* to sigh: to breathe.—*v.t.* to breathe forth.—*n.* **suspiration** (*sus-pə-rā'shən*), sighing.—*adj.* **suspirious** (*səs-pir'i-əs*), breathing labouredly: sighing. [L. *suspīrāre—su-* (*sub-*), *spīrāre,* to breathe.]

**sussarara.** Same as **siserary.**

**sustain,** *səs-tān', v.t.* to hold up: to bear: to support: to provide for: to maintain: to sanction: to keep going: to keep up: to support the life of: to prolong.—*n.* (*Milt.*) means of sustenance. —*adjs.* **sustain'able; sustained'.**—*adv.* **sustain'-edly.**—*n.* **sustain'er,** one who, or that which, sustains: the main motor in a rocket, continuing with it throughout its flight—cf. **booster.**— *n.* and *adj.* **sustain'ing.**—*ns.* **sustain'ment,** act of sustaining: sustenance; sustenance (*sus'ti-nəns*), that which sustains: maintenance: nourishment.—*adj.* **sustentac'ular,** supporting.—*n.* **sustentac'ulum,** a supporting part.—*v.t.* **sus'tentāte,** to sustain.—*n.* **sustentā'tion.**—*adj.* **sustentative** (*sus'tən-tā-tiv, səs-ten'tə-tiv*), sustaining.—*ns.* **sus'tentātor,** a sustaining part or structure; **susten'tion,** the act of sustaining.—*adjs.* **susten'tive; sus'tinent,** sustaining. [L. *sustinēre*—pfx. *sus-* (*subs-*), *tenēre,* to hold; partly through O.Fr. *sustenir* (Fr. *soutenir*).]

**sustenance.** See **sustain.**

**susurrus,** *sū-, sōō-sur'əs, n.* a murmuring: a whisper: a rustling.—*adj.* **susurr'ant.**—*n.* **susur-rā'tion.** [L. *susurrus.*]

**sutile,** *sū', sōō'til, -til, adj.* done by stitching. [L. *sūtilis—suēre,* to sew.]

**sutler,** *sut'lər, n.* one who sells liquor or provisions to soldiers in camp or garrison: a camp-hawker. —*n.* **sut'lery,** a sutler's work or stall.—*v.i.* **sutt'le,**

to trade as a sutler. [Du. *zoetelaar* (earlier *soeteler*).]

**sutor**, *sū'*, *sōō'tor*, *-tər*, *n.* a cobbler.—*adjs.* **suto'rial**, **suto'rian**, relating to cobbling or to sewing. [souter; or directly from L. *sūtor*, *-ōris*, cobbler.]

**sutra**, *sōōt'rə*, *n.* in Sanskrit literature, an aphoristic rule or book of aphorisms on ritual, grammar, metre, philosophy, etc. [Sans. *sūtra*, thread.]

**suttee**, **sati**, *sut'ē*, *sut-ē'*, *n.* an Indian widow who burned herself on her husband's pyre: the custom of so doing.—*n.* **suttee'ism**. [Sans. *satī*, a true wife.]

**suttle**, *sut'l*, *adj.* light (esp. of weight when tare is subtracted; *obs.*): subtle (*Milt.*). [subtle.]

**suttle**. See sutler.

**suture**, *sū'*, *sōō'char*, *-tūr*, *n.* a seam: a stitching: the stitching of a wound: a stitch: a junction or meeting of margins, esp. of bones or of carpels: a line of dehiscence: a line of union.—*v.t.* to stitch up.—*adj.* **su'tural**.—*adv.* **su'turally**. —*adj.* **su'tured**.—*n.* **sutura'tion**. [L. *sūtūra*, a *seam*—*suēre*, to sew.]

**suum cuique**, *sōō'əm kwi'* or *ki'kwi*, *sōō'ōōm kōō-ē'kwe*, (L.) to each his own.

**suversed**, *sū-vûrst'*, (*trig.*) *adj.* versed of the supplement. [From the contraction *sup. versed.*]

**suzerain**, *sōō'zə-rān*, or *sū'*, *n.* a feudal lord: supreme or paramount ruler: a state having supremacy over another.—*adj.* paramount.—*n.* **su'zerainty**, position or power of a suzerain. [Fr., formed in imitation of *souverain* from *sus-*, over—L. *sūsum* (for *sūrsum*, *subvorsum*).]

**svarabhakti**, *svä-räb-häk'tē*, *n.* development of a vowel between consonants. [Sans. *svara*, vowel, *bhakti*, separation.]

**Svarga**. Same as Swarga.

**svastika**, *svas'tik-ə*, *n.* Same as swastika.

**svelte**, *svelt*, *adj.* lissom, lithe: in art, free, easy, light and bold. [Fr.]

**swab**, *swob*, *n.* a mop for cleaning or drying floors or decks: a brush for wetting foundry moulds: a sponge or the like for cleaning the bore of a fire-arm: a bit of cotton-wool or the like for mopping up blood or discharges, applying antiseptics, cleaning a patient's mouth, or taking a specimen of morbid secretion for examination: a specimen so taken: a naval officer's epaulet (*slang*): a lubber or clumsy fellow (*slang*): in an old form of whist a card entitling its holder to a share of the stakes.—*v.t.* to mop with a swab:—*pr.p.* **swabb'ing**; *pa.t.* and *pa.p.* **swabbed**. —*n.* **swabb'er**, one who uses a swab: a mop for cleaning ovens: a swab in whist as formerly played: (in *pl.*) whist so played (also **whisk** and **swabbers**). [Du. *zwabber*, swabber.]

**swack**, *swak*, *swäk*, (*Scot.*) *adj.* pliant: nimble. [Cf. L.G. *swak*, Du. *zwak*; Ger. *schwach*, weak.]

**swad**, *swod*, *n.* a country lout: a soldier.—*n.* **swadd'y**, a soldier, esp. a militiaman. [Perh. Scand.]

**swaddle**, *swod'l*, *v.t.* to swathe: to bandage: to bind tight with clothes, as an infant: to thrash (*cbs.*).—*n.* swaddling-clothes: a bandage.—*n.* **swadd'ler** (*Anglo-Ir.*), a Methodist or Protestant in general.—**swadd'ling-band**, **swadd'ling-cloth**, a cloth for swaddling an infant:—*pl.* **swadd'ling-clothes** (*B.*). [O.E. *swæthel*, *swethel*, bandage; cf. swathe.]

**Swadeshi**, *swä-dā'shē*, *n.* a pre-Independence Indian nationalist movement, favouring home industries and boycott of foreign goods: a product made in India.—Also *adj.*—*n.* **Swade'shism**. [Bengali, own country.]

**swag**, *swag*, *v.i.* to sway: to sag:—*pr.p.* **swagg'-ing**; *pa.t.* and *pa.p.* **swagged**.—*n.* a swagging: a festoon: a subsidence, as of ground over a mine: a depression: a bundle, esp. a tramp's bundle:

baggage, esp. in the Australian bush: plunder (*slang*).—*v.i.* **swagg'er**, to walk with a blustering or overweening air of superiority and self-confidence: to brag noisily or ostentatiously: to bully.—*v.t.* to do, bring, render, by swaggering.—*n.* a swaggering gait, manner, mien, or behaviour: one who carries a swag.—*adj.* (*slang*) ostentatiously fashionable: smart.—*n.* **swagg'erer**.—*n.* and *adj.* **swagg'ering**.—*adv.* **swagg'eringly**.—*adj.* swag'-bellied, having a pendulous belly.—**swag'-belly**, a pendulous belly: one whose belly swags; **swagg'er-cane**, **swagg'er-stick**, a short military cane; **swagg'er-coat**, a coat which hangs loosely from the shoulder; **swag'man**, one who carries his swag about with him in his search for work; **swag'shop** (*slang*), a place where cheap and trashy goods are sold; **swags'man**, a swagman: a burglar's accomplice who carries the plunder (*slang*). [Related to sway; prob. Scand.]

**swage**, *swāj*, *n.* a grooved or moulded border (*obs.*): any of several tools including a tool in two grooved parts, for shaping metal.—*v.t.* to shape with a swage: to reduce the cross-section of a rod or tube, e.g. by forcing it through a tapered aperture between two grooved dies. [O.Fr. *souage*.]

**swage**, *swāj*, (*Milt.*) *v.t.* to assuage. [A.Fr. *suagier*—L. *suāvis*, mild, or aphetic for assuage.]

**swagshop**, **swagsman**. See swag.

**Swahili**, *swä-hē'li*, *n.* the people of Zanzibar and the opposite coast: one of them: loosely, their language (*Kiswahili*), a Bantu tongue modified by Arabic. [Ar. *sawāhil*, pl. *sāhil*, coast, with suffix.]

**swain**, *swān*, (*arch.*, *poet.*, often *ironical*) *n.* a young man: a peasant: rustic: a lover.—*n.* **swain'ing**, love-making.—*adj.* **swain'ish**, boorish. —*n.* **swain'ishness**, boorishness. [O.N. *sveinn*, young man, servant; O.E. *swān*.]

**swale**, *swāl*, *n.* a shady spot: shade: a sunken or marshy place.—*adj.* **swāl'y**. [Cf. O.N. *svalr*, cool.]

**swale**, *swāl*, *v.i.* to sway.

**swale**. See sweal.

**swallow**, *swol'ō*, *n.* a long-winged migratory bird (*Hirundo rustica*) that catches insects on the wing: any bird of its genus or family: extended to various unrelated birds of similar form or habits.—**swall'ow-dive**, a dive during which one's arms are outstretched to the sides—Also *v.i.*—**swall'ow-tail**, a forked tail: a long-tailed dress coat: a butterfly (Papilio) with prolongations of the hind wings: a barbed arrow: a pennon: a swallow-tailed bird (humming-bird, kite).—*adj.* **swall'ow-tailed**, with forked and pointed tail.—**swall'ow-wort**, an asclepiad (Cynanchum or Vincetoxicum), from the swallow-tailed appearance of its paired pods: hence any asclepiad: greater celandine (q.v.). [O.E. *swalwe*, *swealwe*; Ger. *schwalbe*.]

**swallow**, *swol'ō*, *v.t.* to receive through the gullet into the stomach: to engulf: to take in: to accept, sit down under (as an affront): to believe credulously.—*v.i.* to perform the action of swallowing something.—*n.* an abyss: a swallow-hole: a throat: an act of swallowing: a gulp: a quantity swallowed at once: capacity for swallowing: the aperture in a block, between the sheave and frame, through which the rope runs (*naut.*).—*ns.* **swall'et**, a swallow-hole; **swall'ower**.—**swall'ow-hole**, a funnel or fissure through which water passes underground, esp. in limestone. [O.E. *swelgan* (vb.) *geswelg* (n.); cf. Ger. *schwelgen*.]

**swam**, *swam*, *pa.t.* (and *Shak.*, etc., *pa.p.*) of swim.

**swami**, *swä'mē*, *n.* a Hindu idol: a Hindu religious instructor. [Hindi *svāmī*, lord, master.]

**swamp**, *swomp*, *n.* a tract of wet, spongy (in U·S.

generally tree-clad) land: low ground filled with water.—*v.t.* to sink or involve in, or as in, a swamp: to cause to fill with water, as a boat: to overwhelm, inundate.—*v.i.* to become swamped.—*adj.* of, of the nature of, swamp: living or growing in swamps.—*adj.* swamp′y,—swamp cypress, Taxodium, a deciduous conifer of swamps in Southern U.S.; swamp oak, Casuarina. [Perh. from L.G.; prob. akin to O.E. *swamm*, mushroom, Ger. *schwamm*, sponge, fungus.]

swan, *swon*, *n.* any species of Cygnus, a genus of large, graceful, stately, long-necked birds of the duck family.—*adj.* swan′like.—*n.* swann′ery, a place where swans are kept or bred.—*adj.* swann′y, swanlike.—swan′-goose, the China goose; swan′herd, one who tends swans; swan′-hopping (see swan-upping); swan′-maid′en, in Germanic folklore, a maiden who can become a swan by putting on her feather-garment; swan′-mark, the notch made on the swan's upper mandible; swan′-mussel, a large fresh-water mussel; swan′-neck, an S-shaped bend or piece; swans′-down, swans′down, the under-plumage of a swan: a soft woollen or mixed cloth: a thick cotton with a soft nap on one side; swan′-shot, a shot of large size, like buck-shot; swan′-skin, the unplucked skin of a swan: a soft, nappy, fine-twilled fabric; swan′-song, the fabled song of a swan just before its death: a writer's or musician's last work: last work of any kind: final appearance; swan′-upp′ing, an annual expedition up the Thames for the marking of young swans belonging to the crown and to the Dyers' and Vintners' Companies (see up, verb).—swan around (*slang*), to move about aimlessly. [O.E. *swan*; Ger. *schwan*, Du. *zwaan*.]

swang, *swang*, (*Wordsworth*) a rare *pa.t.* of swing.

swank, *swangk*, *adj.* (*Scot.*) slender, pliant: agile.—*n.* (*slang*) ostentation: pretentiousness.—*v.i.* (*slang*) to show off: to swot.—*n.* swank′er.—*adj.* swank′ing, strapping: showing off (*slang*): showy (*slang*).—*n.* swank′y (*Scot.*), an active fellow: poor thin beer or any sloppy drink, even sweetened water and vinegar.—Also swank′ey.—*adj.* (*slang*) ostentatiously smart. [Cf. O.E. *swancor*, pliant.]

swap, swop, *swop*, *v.t.* to strike: to reap close: to slam, plump, slap down: to strike (as a bargain): to give in exchange: to barter.—*v.i.* to smite: to flop: to barter:—*pr.p.* swapp′ing, swopp′ing; *pa.t.* and *pa.p.* swapped, swopped, swapt, swopt.—*n.* a stroke: an exchange.—*adv.* suddenly.—*n.* swapp′er, swopp′er, one who swaps: a very big thing, whopper.—*n.* and *adj.* swapp′ing, swopp′ing. [M.E. *swappen*; perh. imit.; or conn. with sweep, swoop.]

swaraj, *swä-räj′*, (*Ind.*) *n.* self-government, independence, home-rule.—*n.* swaraj′ist, formerly, an advocate of Indian political independence. [Sans. *svarājya—sva*, own, *rājya*, rule.]

sward, *swörd*, *n.* the grassy surface of land: green turf.—Also swarth.—*v.t.* to cover with sward.—*adjs.* sward′ed, sward′y, covered with sward. [O.E. *sweard*, skin, rind; Du. *zwoord*, Ger. *schwarte*.]

sware, *swär*, *arch. pa.t.* of swear.

swarf, *swörf*, swerf, *swûrf*, swerve, *swûrv* (*Scot.*) *v.i.* to faint.—*n.* swarf, swerf, a swoon.

swarf, *swörf*, *n.* grit from an axle, etc.: stone or metal grindings, filings, turnings. [O.N. *svarf*, file-dust.]

Swarga, Svarga, *swär′gä*, *swur′*, *n.* heaven: Indra's paradise—(*Southey*) Swer′ga. [Sans. *Svarga*.]

swarm, *swörm*, *n.* a body of bees going off to found a new community: a colony, offshoot: a throng of insects or other small animals: a throng.—*v.i.* to go off in a swarm: to occur or

come in swarms: to abound, teem.—*v.t.* to cause to swarm: to throng (chiefly *U.S.* except in *pass.*).—*n.* swarm′er.—*n.* and *adj.* swarm′ing.—swarm′-spore, a free-swimming generally cili-ated asexual reproductive body (*bot.*): an active germ produced by sporulation in Protozoa (*zool.*). [O.E. *swearm*; Ger. *schwarm*.]

swarm, *swörm*, *v.t.* and *v.i.* to climb by clasping with arms and legs. [Origin unknown.]

swart, *swört*, swarth, *swörth*, *adj.* black: dusky: blackening, hence, malignant, baleful.—*n.* swarthiness (*swör′dhi-nis*).—*adj.* swarthy (*swör′-dhi*), blackish: dark-skinned.—*n.* swart′ness.—*adj.* swart′y.—swart′-back (O.N. *svartbakr*), the great black-backed gull; swart star (*Milt.*), app. the Dog-star, because at the time of its appearance the complexion darkens. [O.E. *sweart*; O.N. *svartr*, Ger. *schwarz*, black.]

swarth, *swörth*. Same as sward, swart, or (*Shak.*) swath.

swarve. See swerve.

swash, *swosh*, *n.* slush: pig-wash: a splash: a wash of liquid: a dash: a heavy blow: a clash-ing or dashing sound: a swashbuckler: swag-gering.—*v.t.* and *v.i.* to dash: to splash: to clash.—*n.* swash′er (*Shak.*), a blusterer.—*n.* and *adj.* swash′ing, slashing, crushing: blustering.—*adj.* swash′y, slushy.—swash′buckler, one who clashes a sword on a buckler, hence a bully, a blusterer. [Imit.]

swash, *swosh*, *n.* a piece of turner's work with mouldings oblique to the axis: a flourish on a letter.—Also *adj.*—swash letters, Italic capitals with top and bottom flourishes, swash plate, a disk set obliquely on a revolving axis; swash′-work, turner's work cut obliquely. [Origin un-known.]

swastika, *swos′ti-kə*, swas′, svastika, *svas′*, *n.* an ancient and worldwide symbol, a cross with arms bent at a right angle, esp. clockwise (see also fylfot), emblematic of the sun, good luck, anti-semitism, or Nazism. [Sans. *svastika—svasti*, well-being—*su*, good, *asti*, he is.]

swat, *swot*, *v.t.* to hit smartly or heavily.—*n.* a sharp or heavy blow.—*n.* swatt′er, a flexible fly-killer. [squat.]

swat, *swot*, *swöt*, (*Scot.* and *Spens.*) *pa.t.* of sweat.

swat. See swot.

swatch, *swoch*, (*Scot.*) *n.* a sample, esp. of cloth. [Origin unknown.]

swath, *swöth*, swoth, *n.* a band of mown ground or of grass or corn cut by the scythe or mowing-machine or ready for these: a broad band: the sweep of a scythe or mowing-machine.—Also swathe (*swädh*).—*v.t.* swathe (*Canada*), to cut grain and leave it lying in swathes to ripen on the ground.—*adj.* swathy (*swöth′i*, *swädh′i*). [O.E. *swæth* and *swathu*, track; Du. *zwade*.]

swath, *swoth*, (*Shak.*) *n.* Same as swathe.

swathe, *swädh*, *v.t.* to bind round, envelop: to bandage.—*n.* a bandage: a wrapping.—*n.pl.* swath′ing-clothes (*Shak.*; another reading, swath′ling-, swoth′ling-), -clouts, swaddling-clothes. [O.E. *swathian*.]

swats, *swots*, (*Scot.*) *n.* new ale. [O.E. *swatan* (pl.), beer.]

swatter, *swot′ər*, swat′ər, (*dial.*) *v.i.* to squatter: to splash or spill about. [Cf. squatter.]

sway, *swä*, *v.t.* to incline about or from side to side: to cause to incline: to divert: to influence by power or moral force: to wield: to govern: to control: to have a preponderating influence upon: to hoist (*naut.*).—*v.i.* to swing: to oscil-late: to swerve: to proceed, bend one's course (*Shak.*): to advance in hostility (*Spens.*): to incline to one side: to rule: to have preponder-ating weight or influence.—*n.* rotation (*Shak.*): a sweep: a swing: a swerve: directing force or influence: preponderance: rule.—*adjs.* swayed, sway′-back, bent down in the back, as a horse

—*n.* sway′er.—*n.* and *adj.* sway′ing.—*n.* sway′-
back, a nervous disease of lambs causing difficulty in walking or standing. [Perh. from a
lost O.E. word, or the corresponding O.N.
*sveigja,* to bend, swing; prob. partly from L.G.
*swâjen* (Ger. *schweien*), to swing.]
swayl. See sweal.
sweal, sweel, *swēl,* swale, swayl, *swāl, v.t.* to
scorch: to singe: to roast in the skin: to burn
off, as heather and gorse, soot in a chimney:
to cause to gutter: to waste away.—*v.i.* to be
burning hot: to gutter as a candle.—*n.* and *adj.*
sweal′ing, swal′ing, swayl′ing. [O.E. *swǣlan*
(trans.), *swelan* (intrans.), to burn.]
swear, *swār, v.i.* to take or utter an oath: to
utter imprecations: to utter defiant noises (as
a cat): to give evidence on oath (*rare*).—*v.t.* to
assert, promise, agree to, confirm, or value, on
oath: to assert loudly or boldly: to invoke
(*Shak.*): to administer an oath to: to put on
oath: to bind by oath: to admit to office by
an oath: to bring, put, render, by swearing:—
*pa.t.* swōre, *arch.* swāre; *pa.p.* swōrn, *arch.* and
*illit.* swōre.—*n.* an oath: an expression that is
formally an oath or a curse, or bad language
generally.—*n.* swear′er.—*n.* and *adj.* swear′ing.
—*adj.* sworn, attested: bound by oath: having
taken an oath: devoted, inveterate, confirmed,
as if by oath.—swear′-word, a word that is considered bad language.—swear at, to hurl oaths
and curses at: to be very incongruous with,
esp. in colour; swear by, to invoke as witness
to an oath: to put complete confidence in;
swear in, to inaugurate by oath; swear off, to
renounce, promise to give up; swear to, to
affirm or identify on oath. [O.E. *swerian;* Du.
*zweren,* Ger. *schwören.*]
sweard, *swērd,* (*Spens.*) *n.* Same as sword.
sweat, *swet, n.* the moisture excreted by the skin:
moisture exuding or seeming to exude from anything: a state, fit, or process of exuding sweat:
exercise or treatment inducing sweat: sweating
sickness: labour: drudgery: fidgety anxiety:
a soldier (*slang*).—*v.i.* to give out sweat or
moisture: to toil, drudge for poor wages: to
suffer penalty, smart: exude: become coated
with moisture.—*v.t.* to give forth as, or like,
sweat: wet or soil with sweat: cause to sweat:
squeeze money or extortionate interest from:
exact the utmost from: to wring evidence or
confession from (*U.S.*): to extract undue gains
from, e.g. by removing gold from a coin: to compel to hard work for mean wages: to unite by partial fusion of metal surfaces:—*pa.t.* and *pa.p.*
sweat′ed (or sweat).·—*adj.* sweat′ed.—*ns.* sweat′er,
one who sweats: a cause of sweating: a diaphoretic: a heavy jersey, orig. one for reducing
weight by sweating, now for intervals in exercise,
leisure wear, etc.: one who sweats coins or
workers: a London street ruffian in Queen
Anne's time who prodded passers-by with his
sword; sweat′iness.—*n.* and *adj.* sweat′ing.—
*adj.* sweat′y.—sweat band, the leather or similar
band inside a man's hat: an absorbent wristlet
worn by e.g. tennis players to prevent sweat
running down to their hands; sweater-girl (*coll.*),
a woman with a well-developed bust, usually
wearing a tight-fitting sweater; sweating sickness,
an epidemic disorder (usu. fatal) which ravaged
Europe and esp. England in the 15th and 16th
centuries—a violent inflammatory fever, with a
fetid perspiration over the whole body; sweating
system, the practice of working poor people at
starvation wages, for long hours, at home or in
unhealthy rooms; sweat′-shirt, a short-sleeved
sweater; sweat shop, a factory or shop where the
sweating system operates.—in a cold sweat (*fig.*),
in a state of terror or anxiety. [O.E. *swǣtan* to
sweat; cf. Ger. *schweissen;* the O.E. n. was
*swāt.*]

sweath-band, *swēth′-band,* (*Spens.*) *n.* a swaddling-
band. [swathe.]
Swede, *swēd, n.* a native or citizen of *Sweden:* a
Swedish turnip—a buff-flowered, glaucous-
leaved kind.—*adj.* Swēd′ish.—*n.* the Scandinavian language of Sweden.
Swedenborgian, *swē-dn-bör′ji-ən, n.* a follower of
Emanuel *Swedenborg,* a Swedish religious
teacher (1688-1772), founder of the New
Jerusalem Church.—*n.* Swedenbor′gianism.
swee, *swē,* (*Scot.*) *n.* a sway: a swing.—*v.t.* and
*v.i.* to sway: to swing. [sway.]
sweel. See sweal.
sweeny, *swē′ni, n.* atrophy of the shoulder muscles
of a horse. [O.E. *swindan,* to pine away, disappear.]
sweep, *swēp, v.i.* to pass swiftly or forcibly, esp.
with a swinging movement or in a curve: to
move with trailing or flowing drapery, hence
with pomp, indignation, etc.: to extend in a
long curve: to row with sweeps: to range
systematically or searchingly.—*v.t.* to pass something brushingly over: to elicit by so doing
(*poet.*): to pass brushingly: to wipe, clean,
move, or remove with a broom: to carry along
or off with a long brushing stroke or force: to
wipe out or remove at a stroke: to perform
with a sweeping movement: to trail with a
curving movement: to drag as with a net or
rope: to describe, generate, or swing through,
as a curve, angle, or area: to row with sweeps:
—*pa.t.* and *pa.p.* swept.—*n.* act of sweeping: a
swinging movement, swing: onrush: impetus:
a clearance: range, compass: a curved stair: a
curved carriageway before a building: sweepings: a sweepstake: a pump-handle: a long
oạr: a wire drag used in searching for shoals,
mines, etc.: a chimney-sweeper: a blackguard
(*slang*).—*ns.* sweep′er; sweep′ing, the action of
the verb in any sense: (usu. in *pl.*) things collected by sweeping, rubbish.—*adj.* performing
the action of sweeping in any sense: of wide
scope, wholesale, indiscriminate.—*adv.* sweep′-
ingly.—*n.* sweep′ingness.—*adj.* sweep′y, swaying,
sweeping, curving.—sweep′back, the angle at
which an aeroplane wing is set back relatively
to the axis.—*adj.* swept′-back.—sweep′-net, a
long net paid out in a curve and dragged ashore:
an insect net with a handle; sweep′-saw, a
turning-saw; sweep′stake(s), a method of
gambling by which participators' stakes are
pooled, numbers, horses. etc., assigned by lot,
and prize(s) awarded accordingly on decision
of event: such a prize, race, etc. (for *adv.* see
soopstake); sweep′-wash′er, one who recovers
gold or silver from the sweepings of refineries.
—sweep the board (see board). [Prob. from a
lost O.E. word related to *swāpan,* to sweep,
*geswǣpe,* sweepings; cf. soop, swoop.]
sweer, sweir, *swēr,* (*Scot.*) *adj.* slothful: loth.—
Also sweered, sweert, sweirt.—*n.* sweir′ness.
[O.E. *swǣr, swǣre,* heavy, grievous, sluggish; cf.
Ger. *schwer.*]
sweet, *swēt, adj.* having one of the fundamental
varieties of taste, that of sugar, honey, ripe
fruits (distinguished from *salt, acid* or *sour,* and
*bitter*): sugary: cloying: sickly in taste, smell,
etc.: grateful to the taste, senses, or feelings:
taking: fragrant: clear and tuneful: smoothly
running: easy, free from harshness, benign:
fresh, not salt: fresh, not tainted: wholesome:
gracious: amiable: mild, soft, gentle: delightful, charming (*coll.*): dear, beloved: ingratiating, often insipidly: more or less enamoured
(with *on,* or *upon; coll.*).—*adv.* sweetly.—*n.* that
which is sweet: a sweet dish (pudding, fruit,
etc.) as a course: a sweetmeat, confection: (in
*pl.*) wines and cordials sweetened with syrup:
a beloved person.—*v.t.* (now *rare*) to sweeten.—
*v.t.* sweet′en, to make sweet.—*ns.* sweet′ener,

one who or that which sweetens: a bribe (*slang*); **sweet'ening**; **sweet'ing**, a sweet apple: a darling (*Shak.*).—*adj.* **sweet'ish**.—*n.* **sweet'ishness**.—*adv.* **sweet'ly**.—*ns.* **sweet'ness**; **sweet'y**, **sweet'ie**, a sweetmeat, confection: a sweetheart (*coll.*).—*adjs.* **sweet'-and-sour'**, cooked with sugar and vinegar or lemon juice: in Oriental cookery, having a seasoning of sugar, vinegar, soy sauce, etc.; **sweet'-and-twen'ty**, at once fair and young—after Shakespeare, who perhaps meant only sweet indeed (see **twenty** for intensive use).—**sweet'-bay**, the laurel (*Laurus nobilis*): a kind of magnolia (*U.S.*); **sweet'bread**, the pancreas, or sometimes the thymus, esp. as food; **sweet'-brier**, **-briar**, a wild rose with fragrant foliage (*Rosa rubiginosa*); **sweet'-Cic'ely**, an aromatic umbelliferous plant, *Myrrhis odorata*; **sweet'-corn**, a sweet variety of maize; **sweet'-flag**, an aromatic araceous pond-plant, *Acorus calamus*; **sweet'-gale**, bog-myrtle, a low-growing aromatic shrub found in bogs; **sweet'heart**, a lover or beloved.—*v.t.* and *v.i.* to court.—**sweet'-meat**, a confection made wholly or chiefly of sugar: any sweet food (*obs.*); **sweet'-oil**, olive-oil: rape-oil: any oil of mild pleasant taste; **sweet'pea'**, a S. European papilionaceous garden plant (*Lathyrus odoratus*) with bright-coloured fragrant flowers; **sweet'-potä'to**, batata, a tropical and sub-tropical twining plant (*Ipomoea batatas*) of the convolvulus family, with large sweetish edible tubers.—*adjs.* **sweet'-sa'voured**; **sweet'-scent'ed**, having a sweet smell.—**sweet'-sop**, a tropical American evergreen (*Anona squamosa*): its pulpy fruit; **sweet'-stuff**, confectionery.—*adjs.* **sweet'-tem'pered**, having a mild, amiable disposition; **sweet'-toothed'**, fond of sweet things; **sweet'-water**, freshwater.—*n.* a very sweet white grape.—**sweet'-will'iam**, *Dianthus barbatus*, a garden pink with bearded petals; **sweet'-will'ow**, one of various trees, e.g. bay-leaved sweet-willow, *Salix pentandra*: sweet-gale; **sweet'wood**, a name for various S. American and West Indian lauraceous trees; **sweet'-wort**, wort before addition of hops. [O.E. *swēte*; Ger. *süsz*, Gr. *hēdys*, L. *suāvis*, Sans. *svādu*, sweet.]

**sweir**. See **sweer**.

**swelchie**, *swelhh'i*, (*Orkney*) *n.* a whirlpool: a tidal race. [O.N. *svelgr*; cf. **swallow**.]

**swell**, *swel*, *v.i.* to expand: to increase in volume: to be inflated: to bulge out: to grow louder: to rise into waves: to heave: to well up: to rise and fall in loudness: to be bombastic: to be elated or dilated with emotion: to give a feeling of expansion or welling up.—*v.t.* to augment: to expand: to dilate: to fill full: to louden: to elate:—*pa.t.* **swelled**; *pa.p.* **swelled**, **swollen**, *swōln*, *swōl'an*, sometimes **swōln**.—*n.* act, power, habit, or condition of swelling: distension: a heaving: a bulge: an enlargement: a loudening: a device in an organ for increasing tone: a crescendo followed by a diminuendo: a rising ground: a dandy, a fashionable or finely dressed person, a member of the governing class, a bigwig, an adept (*slang*).—*adj.* (*slang*) of, of the nature of, befitting a swell, a vague word of commendation.—*n.* **swell'dom** (*slang*), the fashionable world.—*adj.* **swelled**.—*n.* **swell'er**.—*adj.* and *n.* **swell'ing**.—*adv.* **swell'ingly**.—*adj.* **swell'ish** (*slang*), foppish, dandified.—**swelled head**, self-conceit, esp. in one carried away by success.—*adj.* **swelled'-head'ed**, also **swell'-head'ed**, conceited.—**swell'-mob**, well-dressed pickpockets collectively; **swell'-mobs'man**. [O.E. *swellan*; Ger. *schwellen*.]

**swelt**, *swelt*, *v.i.* to die (*obs.* or *dial.*): to faint (*Spens., Scot.*): to swelter: to pass like a fever (*Spens.*):—*pa.t.* **swelt'ed**, (*Spens.*) **swelt**.—*v.i.* **swelt'er**, to endure great heat: to sweat copiously: to exude.—*v.t.* to overpower, as with heat: to

exude.—*n.* a sweltering: a sweating: sweltered venom.—*adj.* **swelt'ered**.—*n.* and *adj.* **swelt'ering**.—*adv.* **swelt'ry**, sultry: oppressive or oppressed with heat. [O.E. *sweltan*, to die.]

**swept**, *swept*, *pa.t.* and *pa.p.* of **sweep**.

**swerf**. See **swarf**.

**Swerga**. See **Swarga**.

**swerve**, *swûrv*, *v.i.* to turn aside: to deviate: to give way, shrink (*Milt.*): to swarm, scramble (*Dryden*).—*v.t.* to deflect: to cause a ball to swerve in the air.—*n.* a turning aside: a deviation: a deflection: a ball that swerves in the air (*cricket*): the act or trick of making it do so (*cricket*).—*adj.* **swerve'less**, unswerving.—*n.* **swerv'er**.—*n.* and *adj.* **swerv'ing**. [M.E.; the O.E. *sweorfan*, to rub, file, scour, is not known to have had this sense.]

**swerve**. See **swarf**.

**sweven**, *swev'n*, (*obs.*) *n.* a dream. [O.E. *swefn*.]

**swift**, *swift*, *adj.* fleet: rapid: speedy: prompt.—*adv.* swiftly.—*n.* a bird (*Apus*, or *Cypselus*, *apus*) superficially like a swallow but structurally nearer the humming-birds and goatsuckers: any bird of its genus or family: the common newt: a reel for winding yarn: the main cylinder of a carding-machine: a rapid.—*n.* **swift'let**, a bird (*Collocalia*) akin to the swift, the builder of edible nests.—*adv.* **swift'ly**.—*n.* **swift'ness**. *adjs.* **swift'-foot**, **-ed**; **swift'-winged**. [O.E. *swift*, from same root as **swoop**.]

**swift**, *swift*, *v.t.* to tighten with a rope.—*n.* **swift'er**, a rope used to tighten or keep a thing in its place. [Prob. Scand. or L.G.]

**swig**, *swig*, *n.* a pulley with ropes not parallel.—*v.t.* to tighten by hauling at right angles: to castrate by ligature. [Prob. conn. with **swag**.]

**swig**, *swig*, *n.* a draught: toast and ale: a wassail (*Oxford*).—*v.t.* to take a swig or swigs of or from.—*v.i.* to drink, take swigs. [Origin unknown.]

**swill**, *swil*, *v.t.* or *v.i.* to rinse: to dash water over: to wash: to drink greedily or largely.—*n.* a large draught of liquor: hog-wash.—*n.* **swill'er**.—*n.* and *adj.* **swill'ing**.—**swill'-tub**, a tub for hog-wash. [O.E. *swilian*, to wash.]

**swim**, *swim*, *v.i.* to propel oneself in water (or other liquid): to float: to come to the surface: to travel or be conveyed by water: to be suffused: to be immersed or steeped: to glide smoothly: to be dizzy.—*v.t.* to pass by swimming: to make to swim or float: to test for witchcraft by immersion:—*pr.p.* **swimm'ing**; *pa.t.* **swam**, *swam*, old-fashioned **swum**; *pa.p.* **swum** (*Shak.*, etc., **swam**).—*n.* an act, performance, or spell of swimming: any motion like swimming: a crossing-place for swimmers: a place where many fishes swim: the general movement or current of affairs: air-bladder of a fish.—*adj.* **swimm'able**, capable of being swum.—*ns.* **swimm'er**; **swimm'eret**, a crustacean's abdominal appendage used in swimming.—*n.* and *adj.* **swimm'ing**.—*adv.* **swimm'ingly**, in a gliding manner as if swimming: smoothly, successfully.—*n.* **swimm'ingness**, the state of swimming: a melting look, tearfulness.—*adj.* **swimm'y**, inclined to dizziness.—**swim'-bladder**, a fish's air-bladder; **swimm'ing-bath**; **swimm'ing-bell**, a medusoid modified as a swimming organ; **swimm'ing-pond**, **-pool**; **swim'suit**, a garment for bathing in.—**in the swim**, in the main current (of affairs, business, etc.). [O.E. *swimman*; Ger. *schwimmen*.]

**swindge** (*Milt.*; *Shak.*—also in **swindge-buckler**). Same as **swinge** (1) and **swinge-buckler**.

**swindle**, *swin'dl*, *v.t.* and *v.i.* to cheat.—*n.* a fraud: anything not really what it appears to be.—*n.* **swin'dler**, a cheat.—*n.* and *adj.* **swin'dling**. [Ger. *schwindler*, a giddy-minded person, swindler—*schwindeln*, to be giddy.]

**swine**, *swīn*, *n.* a pig: a sensual person: a term

of strong abuse:—*pl.* **swine.**—*ns.* **swine′hood,** the status of a swine; **swin′ery,** a place where pigs are kept: swinishness: swine collectively. —*adj.* **swin′ish,** of or like swine: sensual: filthy: voracious: beastly.—*adv.* **swin′ishly.**—*n.* **swin′-ishness.**—*adj.* **swine′-drunk** (*Shak.*), bestially drunk.—**swine′-fe′ver,** hog-cholera, a highly contagious disease of swine due to a virus; **swine′-fish,** the wolf-fish; **swine′herd,** one who herds swine; **swine′-keeping;** **swine′-pox,** chicken-pox: a skin disease of swine; **swine′s′-cress,** a cruciferous weed of waste places (Senebiera or Coronopus): applied to various other plants; **swine′s′-succ′ory,** a small plant (Arnoseris) akin to chicory; **swine′stone,** stinkstone; **swine′-sty,** a pig-sty. [O.E. *swin,* a pig; Ger. *schwein,* L. (adj.) *suinus*—*sūs,* Gr. *hŷs.*]

**swing,** *swing, v.i.* to sway or wave to and fro, as a body hanging freely: to amuse oneself on a swing: to oscillate: to hang: to be hanged: to sweep, wheel, sway: to swerve: to move forward with swaying gait: to turn round as a ship (e.g. to test the compass): to attract, excite, be perfectly appropriate to place or mood (*slang*): of a person, to be thoroughly responsive (to jazz, any of the arts, any aspect of living; *slang*): to be gay or up-to-date (*slang*).—*v.t.* to cause to swing: to set swinging: to control: to sway: to hurl, whirl: to brandish: to transport in suspension: to move in a sweep: to sound or send forth by swinging: to indicate by an oscillation: to impart swing to: to perform as swing-music: to fix up so as to hang freely: to influence the result of (e.g. a doubtful election) in favour of an individual or party:—*pa.t.* **swung,** *rarely* **swang;** *pa.p.* **swung.**—*n.* act, manner, or spell of swinging: oscillating, waving, sweeping: motion to and fro: the sweep or compass of a swinging body: the sweep of a golf-club, bat, or the like: sway: scope, free indulgence: impetus: vigorous sweeping rhythm: jazz music with impromptu complications: a suspended seat or carriage for the amusement of swinging: a reversal of fortune.—*ns.* **swing′er** (*swing′ər*), a person or thing that swings: either of the middle pair in a team of six horses: a Hindu votary who swings from hooks in his flesh: a ball bowled so as to swerve in the air (*cricket*): an ill-centred gramophone record; **swinging** (*swing′ing*), the act of moving to and fro in suspension, esp. as a pastime: hanging (*coll.*): hanging by hooks, as by a Hindu devotee.—*adj.* swaying: turning: with a swing: having a free easy motion: with it, fully alive to, and appreciative of, the most recent trends and fashions in living (*coll.*): up-to-date (*coll.*): gay (*coll.*): daring (*coll.*).—*adv.* **swing′ingly.**— **swing′-back,** a reaction: a camera back that can be tilted; **swing′boat,** a boat-shaped swinging carriage for fairs, etc.; **swing′-bridge,** a bridge that may be opened by swinging it to one side; **swing′-door′,** a door (usu. one of a pair) that opens either way and swings to of itself; **swing′-han′dle,** a pivoted (esp. arched) handle.— **swing′ing-boom,** the spar that stretches the foot of a lower studding-sail; **swing′ing-post,** the post to which a gate is hung; **swing′-music,** big-band jazz with strong rhythm and improvisations; **swing′-plough,** a plough without a fore-wheel under the beam; **swing′-shelf,** a hanging shelf; **swing′-stock,** an upright timber, with a blunt upper edge for swingling flax on—also **swing′ing-block;** **swing′-swang,** a complete (to and fro) oscillation; **swing′tree,** a whippletree; **swing′-wheel,** the wheel that drives a clock pendulum; **swing′-wing** (aircraft), variable-geometry aircraft.—**in full swing,** in mid-career: in fully active operation; **swingtail cargo aircraft,** an aircraft with tail that swings aside to give access to the full cross-section of the fuselage for rapid

loading and unloading of cargo; **swing the lead** (see **lead**). [O.E. *swingan;* Ger. *schwingen.*]

**Swing,** *swing, n.* a fictitious captain in whose name rick-burners sent threatening letters to users of threshing-mills about 1830-33: the movement, operations, or methods of the rick-burners.— Also *adj.*—*n.* **swing′ism.**

**swinge,** *swinj, v.t.* to beat: to chastise: to lash, sway, flourish:—*pr.p.* **swinge′ing.**—*n.* **swinge′-buckler,** a swashbuckler.—*adj.* **swinge′ing,** great, huge, thumping.—*adv.* **swinge′ingly.**—*n.* **swinger** (*swinj′ər*), any person or thing great or astonishing: a bold lie, a whopper. [M.E. *swenge*— O.E. *swengan,* to shake, causative of *swingan,* to swing.]

**swinge,** *swinj,* (*Spens.*) *v.t.* Same as **singe.**

**swingle,** *swing′gl, n.* a scutching tool: the swipple of a flail.—*v.t.* to scutch.—*n.* **swing′ling.**— **swing′le-bar, swing′letree,** a whippletree: a swing-stock; **swing′le-hand,** a scutching tool; **swing′ling-stock,** a swing-stock. [Cf. O.E. *swingell,* stroke, scourge, rod, and M.Du. *swinghel.*]

**swink,** *swingk,* (*arch.*) *v.i.* to toil.—*n.* toil.—*adj.* **swinked** (*Milt.* **swink′t**), toil-worn, fatigued. [O.E.*swinc* (n.), *swincan* (vb.).]

**swipe,** *swip, n.* a sweeping stroke: a swath.—*v.t.* to strike with a swipe: to gulp: to purloin.— *v.i.* to make a swipe: to sweep for old anchors. —*ns.* **swip′er;** swipes, bad or spoilt beer: small-beer.—*adj.* **swip′ey,** fuddled with malt liquor. [O.E. *swipian,* to beat.]

**swipple,** *swip′l, n.* a swingle or striking part of a flail. [Cf. **swipe,** **sweep.**]

**swire,** *swir, n.* a neck (*obs.*): a hollow between two hills. [O.E. *swēora* (Northern *swira*), neck.]

**swirl,** *swûrl, n.* an eddy: a whirl: a curl.—*v.t.* to whirl: to wind.—*v.i.* to eddy: to whirl: to spin.—*adj.* **swirl′y.** [Orig. Scot.; cf. Norw. dial. *svirla.*]

**swish,** *swish, n.* the sound of twigs sweeping through the air: dashing spray: a cane or birch.—*v.t.* to whisk with a swish: to flog, thrash.—*v.i.* to go with a swish.—*adv.* with a swish.—*n.* **swish′er.**—*n.* and *adj.* **swish′ing.**—*adj.* **swish′y.** [Imit.]

**swish,** *swish,* (*slang*) *adj.* smart. [Origin unknown.]

**Swiss,** *swis, adj.* of Switzerland.—*n.* a native or citizen of Switzerland: the High German dialect spoken by most of the Swiss:—*pl.* **Swiss** (formerly **Swiss′es**).—*n.·* **Swit′zer,** a Swiss: a Swiss (or other) mercenary or member of a bodyguard.—**Swiss chard** (see **chard**); **Swiss Guards,** a body of Swiss mercenaries in the French guards from 1616, wiped out in the Revolution: the Pope's bodyguard; **Swiss roll,** a thin cake rolled up with jam: a flexible floating pier.

**swissing,** *swis′ing, n.* ordinary calendering. [Origin unknown.]

**switch,** *swich* (*Shak.* **swits,** *swits*), *n.* a long flexible twig: a tapering riding-whip: a rod, cane: an application of a switch: a brushing blow: a whisk, jerk: a tool for beating eggs or cream: a tress, usu. false: a movable rail for shunting: a changeover (esp. in cards to another suit, led or called): a device for making, breaking, or changing an electric circuit: a switchboard: a turn of a switch.—*v.t.* to strike with a switch: to drive, as with a switch: to brush against: to whisk, jerk, lash: to beat up, whip (as an egg, cream): to prune: to shunt: to divert: to turn (off, on, or to another circuit): to race (a horse) under the name of another horse.—*v.i.* to use a switch: to turn aside: to change over: to whisk.—*n.* **switch′ing.**—*adj.* **switch′y.**—**switch′-back,** orig. a zigzag mountain railway on which the train shunted back at each stage: an up-and-down track on which cars rise by the momentum gained in coming down: an up-and-down

Neutral vowels in unaccented syllables: *el′ə-mənt;* for certain sounds in foreign words, see p. viii

road; **switch'board**, a board or frame bearing apparatus for making or breaking an electric current or circuit: a board for connecting telephones; **switch'man**, a pointsman; **switch'-over**, action of the verb: a changeover; **switch'-plant**, a plant with long slim green shoots, the leaves reduced or wanting; **switch selling**, the practice of arousing the interest of a prospective buyer by offering him a low-priced article, then telling him the shortcomings of the cheap article and trying to sell him a more expensive one.—**switched on**, aware of and responsive to all that is most up to date; under the influence of drugs (*coll.*). [Earlier *swits* (Shak.), *switz*; prob. from Du. or L.G.]

**switchel**, *swich'l*, *n.* treacle-beer, molasses and water, etc. [Origin unknown.]

**swith**, *swith*, (*obs.*) *adv.* quickly: at once.—*interj.* away. [O.E. *swithe*, very.]

**swither**, *swidh'ər*, (*Scot.*) *v.i.* to be undecided.— *n.* indecision: flurry. [Poss. O.E. *swethrian*, to subside.]

**swivel**, *swiv'l*, *n.* a ring or link that turns round on a pin or neck: a swivel-gun.—*v.t.* and *v.i.* to turn on a pin or pivot.—**swiv'el-eye**, a squinteye; **swiv'el-gun**, a gun that turns on a pivot; **swiv'el-hook**, a hook secured to anything by means of a swivel. [O.E. *swifan*, to move quickly, to turn round.]

**swiz**, *swiz*, **swizzle**, *swiz'l*, (*slang*) *ns.* fraud: great disappointment. [Poss. **swindle**.]

**swizzle**, *swiz'l*, *v.i.* to drink to excess.—*n.* a mixed or compounded drink containing rum or other spirit.—**swizzle'-stick**, a stick or whisk used to mix a swizzle. [Origin unknown.]

**swob, swobbers**, etc. See **swab**.

**swollen**, *swōl'ən*, *swōln*, *pa.p.* of **swell**, and *adj.*

**swoon**, *swōōn*, also (*arch.* and *poet.*) **sound**, *sownd*, **swoun**, *swown*, **swound**, *swownd*, *swownd* (Spens. **swone**), *n.* a fainting fit: a sleep (Spens.).—*v.i.* to faint: to be languorous, give a feeling of fainting (*poet.*): to subside (*poet.*).—*adj.* **swooned**, in a swoon.—*n.* and *adj.* **swoon'ing.**— *adv.* **swoon'ingly**. [Prob. from M.E. *iswowen*— O.E. *geswōgen* (pa.p.; other parts unknown), in a swoon, wrongly analysed as *in swoon*.]

**swoop**, *swōōp*, *v.i.* to sweep along (*obs.*): to come down with a sweeping rush: to rush suddenly. —*v.t.* (*obs.*) to pounce on, to snatch with a sweep, esp. on the wing.—*n.* an act of swooping: a sudden onslaught.—*adv.* **swoop'stake-like** (see under **soop**).—**at one fell swoop** (Shak., Macb. IV, iii. 219) by one terrible blow: (also **in, with**), by one complete decisive action: suddenly. [App. O.E. *swāpan*, to sweep; perh. influenced by **soop**.]

**swop.** See **swap**.

**sword**, *sörd*, *sōrd*, *n.* a weapon with a long blade, sharp upon one or both edges, for cutting or thrusting: a blade or flat rod resembling a sword: a swordfish's snout: destruction or death by the sword or by war: war: military force: the emblem of vengeance or justice, or of authority and power.—*v.i.* to wield a sword. —*n.* **sword'er**, a gladiator: an assassin, a cutthroat: a swordsman.—*adjs.* **sword'less**; **sword'like**.—*adj.* **sword'-and-buck'ler**, fought or armed with sword and buckler.—**sword'-arm, -hand**, the arm, hand, that wields the sword; **sword'-bay'onet**, a bayonet shaped somewhat like a sword, and used as one; **sword'-bean**, an Indian papilionaceous plant (Canavalia) with long sword-shaped edible pods: its seed; **sword'-bearer**, a public officer who carries the sword of state; **sword'-belt**, a belt from which the sword is hung; **sword'-bill**, a S. American humming-bird with a bill longer than its body; **sword'-blade**, the blade of a sword; **sword'-break'er**, an old weapon for grasping and breaking an adversary's sword; **sword'-cane, -stick**, a

cane or stick containing a sword; **sword'craft**, swordsmanship: military power; **sword'-cut**, a cut with the edge of a sword: a wound or scar so produced; **sword'-dance**, a dance performed sword in hand or among or over swords; **sword'-doll'ar**, a Scottish silver coin of James VI, worth 30s. Scots (2s. 6d. English), with a sword on the reverse; **sword'fish**, a large fish (Xiphias or other genus of the family Xiphiidae) with upper jaw compressed and prolonged as a stabbing weapon; **sword'-grass**, a name for many plants with sword-shaped leaves; **sword'-guard**, the part of a sword-hilt that protects the bearer's hand; **sword'-knot**, a ribbon tied to the hilt of a sword; **sword'-law**, government by the sword; **sword'man**, a swordsman: a fighting man; **sword'play**, fencing; **sword'player**.—*adj.* **sword'-proof**, capable of resisting the blow or thrust of a sword.—**sword'-rack**, a rack for holding swords.—*adj.* **sword'-shaped**.—**swords'man**, a man skilled in the use of a sword; **swords'manship**; **sword'-swallower**, a performer who seems to swallow swords; **sword'-tail**, a small Central American freshwater Cyprinodont fish with swordlike tail-lobe. [O.E. *sweord*; Ger. *schwert*.]

**swore, sworn.** See **swear**.

**swot, swat**, *swot*, (*slang*) *v.t.* and *v.i.* to study hard.—*n.* hard study: one who swots.—*ns.* **swott'er**; **swott'ing**. [sweat.]

**swothling.** See **swathe**.

**swound, swownd.** See **swoon**.—**swoune, swownd, swowne** also in Spens.

**swum, swum**, *pa.p.* and old-fashioned *pa.t.* of **swim**.

**swung, swung**, *pa.t.* and *pa.p.* of **swing**.

**Sybarite**, *sib'ə-rit*, *n.* an inhabitant of *Sybaris*, a Greek city in Italy, on the Gulf of Tarentum, noted for luxury: one devoted to luxury.—Also *adj.*—*adjs.* **Sybaritic** (*-rit'ik*), **-al**, **Sybarit'ish**.—*n.* **Sy'baritism**.

**sybo(w), syboe**, *si'bō, -bā*, (*Scot.*) *n.* a cibol: a young onion:—*pl.* **sy'boes, sybows.** [cibol.]

**sybotic**, *si-bot'ik*, *adj.* pertaining to a swineherd. —*n.* **sybotism** (*sib'ə-tizm*). [Gr. *sybōtēs*, swineherd—*sỹs*, swine, *boskein*, to feed, tend.]

**sycamine**, *sik'ə-min*, (B.) *n.* the mulberry-tree. [Gr. *sỹkaminos*, of Semitic origin, influenced by *sỹkon*, a fig.]

**sycamore**, *sik'ə-mōr, -mōr*, *n.* a kind of fig-tree (now often **sycomore**, or **sycomore fig**): in England, the great maple (*Acer pseudo-platanus*) called in Scotland the plane (formerly **sycomore**): in U.S., any true plane (Platanus). [Gr. *sỹkomoros*—*sỹkon*, a fig, *moron*, black mulberry.]

**syce, sice, saice**, *sis*, (*India*) *n.* a groom, mounted attendant. [Ar. *sā'is*.]

**sycee**, *si-sē'*, *n.* silver ingots used as Chinese money. [Chin. *si sz'*.]

**sycomore.** See **sycamore**.

**syconium**, *si-kō'ni-əm*, *n.* a multiple fruit in which the true fruits (the pips) are enclosed in a hollow fleshy receptacle—the fig. [Gr. *sỹkon*, a fig.]

**sycophant**, *sik'ō-fənt*, *n.* a common informer (Gr. *hist.*): a servile flatterer.—*n.* **syc'ophancy**, the behaviour of a sycophant: mean talebearing: obsequious flattery: servility.—*adjs.* **sycophantic** (*-fant'ik*), **-al**.—*adv.* **sycophant'ically**. —*v.i.* **syc'ophantise, -ize**, to play the sycophant. —*adj.* **syc'ophantish** (or *-fant'*).—*adv.* **syc'ophantishly**.—*n.* **syc'ophantry**, the arts of the sycophant. [Gr. *sỹkophantēs*, an informer, swindler, confidential agent—*sỹkon*, a fig, *phainein*, to show; variously but unsatisfactorily explained.]

**sycosis**, *si-kō'sis*, *n.* inflammation of the hair follicles, esp. of the beard. [Gr. *sỹkōsis*, a figshaped ulcer—*sỹkon*, a fig.]

**sye**, *si*, (now *dial.*) *v.t.* to strain.—*n.* a sieve: a milk-strainer. [O.E. *sion, sēon*, to strain.]

**syen,** a Shakespearian spelling of **scion.**

**syenite,** *sī'ən-īt, n.* a coarse-grained plutonic rock composed of orthoclase and a ferromagnesian mineral, usu. hornblende.—*adj.* **syenitic** (*-it'ik*), relating to *Syene* in Egypt: pertaining to syenite. [L. *syēnītēs* (*lapis*), a hornblende granite (not syenite) found at Assuan (Gr. *Syēnē*).]

**syker,** *sik'ər,* (*Spens.*) *adv.* surely. [**sicker.**]

**syllable,** *sil'ə-bl, n.* a word or part of a word uttered by a single effort of the voice.—*v.t.* to express by syllables, to utter articulately.—*n.* **syll'abary,** a set of characters representing syllables.—Also **syllabā'rium.**—*adjs.* **syllabic** (*sil-ab'ik*), **-al,** of or constituting a syllable or syllables: syllable by syllable.—*adv.* **syllab'ically.**—*ns.* **syllabicā'tion,** syllabification; **syllab'ics,** verse patterned not by stresses but by syllables; **syllabificā'tion,** pronunciation as a syllable: division into syllables.—*v.t.* **syll'abise, -ize,** to form or divide into syllables: to sing to syllables.—*n.* **syll'abism,** use of a syllabary: division into syllables.—*adj.* **syll'abled,** having (in compounds, so-many) syllables.—**syllable verse,** syllabics. [L. *syllaba*—Gr. *syllabē*—*syn*, with, *lab-,* root of *lambanein,* to take; *-le* as in principle, participle.]

**syllabub,** *sil'ə-bub, n.* Same as **sillabub.**

**syllabus,** *sil'ə-bəs, n.* an abstract or programme, as of a series of lectures or a course of studies: a catalogue of positions condemned by the R.C. Church (1864, 1907):—*pl.* **syll'abuses, syll'abi** (*bī*). [L.,—Gr. *sillybē,* a book-label.]

**syllepsis,** *sil-ep'sis, n.* a figure in rhetoric by which a word does duty in a sentence in the same syntactical relation to two or more words but has a different sense in relation to each:—*pl.* **syllep'ses** (*-sēz*).—*adjs.* **syllep'tic, -al.**—*adv.* **syllep'tically.** [Gr. *syllēpsis,* a taking together—*syn,* together, and the root of *lambanein,* to take.]

**syllogism,** *sil'ō-jizm, -ə-jizm, n.* a logical argument in three propositions, two premises and a conclusion that follows necessarily from them.—*n.* **syllogisation, -z-** (*-ji-zā'shən*).—*v.i.* **syll'ogise, -ize,** to reason by syllogisms.—*v.t.* to deduce syllogistically.—*n.* **syll'ogiser, -z-.**—*adjs.* **syllogistic** (*-jist'ik*), **-al.**—*adv.* **syllogist'ically.** [Gr. *syllogismos*—*syllogizesthai*—*syn,* together, *logizesthai,* to reckon—*logos,* speech, reason.]

**sylph,** *silf, n.* a spirit of the air: a sylph-like being: a slim person: a kind of humming-bird.—*n.* **sylph'id, sylph'ide,** a little sylph.—Also *adj.*—*adjs.* **sylph'idine, sylph'ine, sylph'ish.** [Coined by Paracelsus.]

**sylva, sylvan, sylviculture.** See **silva.**

**sylvanite,** *sil'vən-īt, n.* a mineral, telluride of gold and silver. [*Transylvania,* where it is found.]

**Sylvia,** *sil'vi-ə, n.* the warbler genus, giving name to a family **Sylvi'idae** or subfamily **Sylvii'nae** of the thrush family.—*adj.* **syl'viine.** [L. *silva,* a wood.]

**Sylvian,** *sil'vi-ən, adj.* of *Sylvius,* i.e. either the French anatomist Jacques Dubois (1478-1555), or Franz de la Boë (1614-72), the Dutch-German iatrochemist.—**Sylvian fissure,** a deep lateral fissure in the cerebrum, discovered apparently by the latter.

**sylvine,** *sil'vēn,* **sylvite,** *sil'vīt, ns.* native potassium chloride, a source of potash.—*n.* **syl'vinite** (*-vin-īt*), a rock composed of sylvine and rock salt. [Formerly called digestive salt of *Sylvius.*]

**symar.** See **cymar.**

**symbiosis,** *sim-bi-ō'sis, n.* a mutually beneficial partnership between organisms of different kinds: esp. such an association where one lives within the other.—*ns.* **sym'bion, sym'biont** (*-bi-ont*), an organism living in symbiosis.—*adj.* **symbiotic** (*-bi-ot'ik*).—*adv.* **symbiot'ically.** [Gr. *syn,* together, *bios,* livelihood.]

**symbol,** *sim'b(ə)l, n.* an emblem: that which by custom or convention represents something else: a type: a creed, compendium of doctrine, or a typical religious rite, as the eucharist (*theol.*).—*v.t.* to symbolise.—*adjs.* **symbolic** (*-bol'ik*), **-al.**—*adv.* **symbol'ically.**—*ns.* **symbol'icalness; symbol'ics,** study of creeds; **symbolisā'tion, -z-.**—*v.t.* **sym'bolise, -ize,** to be symbolical of: to represent by symbols: to combine (*obs.*): to formulate in a creed.—*v.i.* (*obs.*) to agree.—*ns.* **sym'boliser; sym'bolism,** representation by symbols or signs: a system of symbols: use of symbols: use of symbols in literature or art: a movement (*c.* 1880) chiefly in French poetry that treated the actual as an expression of something underlying: symbolics.—*n.* and *adj.* **sym'bolist.**—*adjs.* **symbolist'ic, -al; sym'bolled,** symbolised: bearing symbols.—*ns.* **symbolog'raphy,** symbolic writing or representation; **symbol'ogy** (for **symbol'ogy**), the study or use of symbols; **symbolol'atry** (Gr. *latreiā,* worship), undue veneration for symbols. [Gr. *symbolon,* a token—*syn,* together, *ballein,* to throw.]

**symbole,** an old spelling of **cymbal.**

**symitar(e),** old spellings of **scimitar.**

**symmetry,** *sim'i-tri, n.* exact correspondence of parts on either side of a straight line or plane, or about a centre or axis: balance or due proportion: beauty of form: disposition of parts.—*adj.* **symm'etral,** of symmetry.—*n.* **symmetrian** (*si-met'ri-ən*), one who studies or theorises on the due proportions of things.—*adjs.* **symmet'ric, -al,** having symmetry.—*adv.* **symmet'rically.**—*ns.* **symmet'ricalness; symmetrisā'tion, -z-.**—*v.t.* **symm'etrise, -ize,** to make symmetrical.—*n.* **symmetrophō'bia** (Gr. *phŏbos,* fear), fear or dislike of symmetry. [Gr. *symmetriā*—*syn,* together, *metron,* a measure.]

**sympathectomy,** *sim-pəth-ek'tə-mi, n.* excision of part of a sympathetic nerve. [From **sympathetic,** and Gr. *ektomē,* excision.]

**sympathy,** *sim'pə-thi, n.* community of feeling: power of entering into another's feelings or mind: harmonious understanding: compassion, pity: affinity or correlation whereby one thing responds to the action of another or to action upon another: agreement.—*adjs.* **sympathet'ic, -al,** feeling, inclined to, expressing sympathy: in sympathy: acting or done in sympathy: induced by sympathy (as sounds in a resonating body): congenial: compassionate: of the sympathetic nervous system (see below): (a Gallicism) able to awake sympathy.—*adv.* **sympathet'ically.**—*v.i.* **sym'pathise, -ize,** to be in sympathy: to feel with or for another: to be compassionate: to be in accord, correspond.—*v.t.* (*Shak.*) to be in sympathy, accord, or harmony with: to compound harmoniously: to represent or understand sympathetically: perh., to affect all alike.—*n.* **sym'pathiser.**—**sympathetic ink** (see **ink**); **sympathetic magic,** magic depending upon a supposed sympathy, e.g. between a person and his name or portrait, between rainfall and libations; **sympathetic nervous system,** a system of nerves supplying the involuntary muscles and glands, esp. those originating from the cervical, thoracic, and lumbar regions of the spinal cord; sometimes also including those from the brain and the sacral region (the **para-sympathetic nervous system**). [Gr. *sympatheia*—*syn,* with, *pathos,* suffering.]

**sympetalous,** *sim-pet'ə-ləs, adj.* having the petals united.—*n.pl.* **Sympet'alae** (*-lē*), a main division of dicotyledons, typically having united petals. [Gr. *syn,* together, *petalon,* leaf.]

**symphile,** *sim'fīl, n.* an animal of another kind kept as a guest or domestic animal in an ants' or termites' nest.—*ns.* **sym'philism** (*fil-izm*), **sym'-phily.**—*adj.* **sym'philous.** [Gr. *symphiliā,* mutual friendship—*syn,* *philos,* a friend.]

symphony, *sim'fə-ni, n.* an obs. name for various musical instruments—bagpipe, drum, hurdy-gurdy, virginal: harmony, esp. of sound: an orchestral composition on a great scale in sonata form (*mus.*): an instrumental portion of a work primarily vocal (*arch.*).—*adj.* symphonic (*sim-fon'ik*).—*n.* symphō'nion, a combination of piano and harmonium.—*adj.* symphonious (*-fō'ni-əs*), agreeing or harmonising in sound: accordant: harmonious.—*n.* sym'phonist, a composer or performer of symphonies. symphonie poem, a large orchestral composition in programme music with the movements run together. [Gr. *symphōniā*, harmony, orchestra—*syn*, together, *phōnē*, a sound.]

Symphyla, *sim'fi-lə, n.* a class or order of arthropods linking the bristle-tails with the centipedes.—*adj.* sym'phylous. [Gr. *symphȳlos*, of the same race—*syn*, with, *phȳlē, phȳlon*, a race, clan.]

symphysis, *sim'fi-sis, n.* the union or growing together of parts, concrescence: union of bones by fusion, cartilage, or ligament: a place of junction of parts.—*adj.* symphyseal, -ial (*sim-fiz'i-əl*).—*n.* symphyseot'omy, -iot'omy (Gr. *tomē*, a cut), the operation of cutting through the pubic symphysis.—*adj.* symphytic (*-fit'ik*), by fusion.—*n.* Sym'phytum, the comfrey genus of the borage family, perh. from its supposed virtue of closing wounds. [Gr. *symphysis*—*syn*, with, *phyein*, to grow.]

sympiesometer, *sim-pi-i-zom'i-tər, n.* a barometer with a gas instead of a vacuum: an instrument for measuring the pressure of a current. [Gr. *sympiesis*, a pressing together—*syn*, with, *piezein*, to press, *metron*, a measure.]

symploce, *sim'plō-sē,* (*rhet.*) *n.* the repetition of a word at the beginning and another at the end of successive clauses. [Gr. *symplokē*, an interweaving—*syn*, with, *plekein*, to weave.]

sympodium, *sim-pō'di-əm,* (*bot.*) *n.* a stem composed of a succession of branches each supplanting and seeming to continue its parent branch.—*adj.* sympo'dial.—*adv.* sympo'dially. [Gr. *syn*, together, *pous, podos*, foot.]

symposium, *sim-pō'zi-əm, n.* a drinking party (*hist.*): a meeting for philosophic conversation: a conference: a collection of views on one topic:—*pl.* sympō'sia.—*adjs.* sympō'siac, sympō'sial.—*ns.* sympō'siarch (*-ärk*; Gr. *archos*, leader), the master of the feast or conference; sympō'siast, one who takes part in a symposium. [Latinised from Gr. *symposion*—*syn*, together, *posis*, drinking.]

symptom, *sim(p)'təm, n.* a characteristic sign or indication of the existence of a state, esp. a disease.—*adjs.* symptomat'ic, -al.—*adv.* symptomat'ically.—*v.t.* symp'tomatise, -ize, to be a symptom of.—*ns.* symptomatol'ogy, the study of symptoms: the symptoms of a patient or a disease taken as a whole; sympto'sis, wasting: emaciation.—*adj.* symptotic (*-tot'ik*). [Gr. *symptōma, symptōsis*—*syn*, with, and root of *piptein*, to fall.]

syn-, sy-, syl-, sym-, *pfxs.* together, with. [Gr. *syn*, with.]

synadelphite, *sin-ə-del'fit, n.* a manganese aluminium arsenate. [Gr. *syn*, with, *adelphos*, brother, as found along with kindred minerals.]

synaeresis, *sin-ē'rə-sis, n.* the running together of two vowels into one or into a diphthong: the spontaneous expulsion of liquid from a gel. [Gr. *syn*, together, *hairesis*, taking—*haireein*, to take.]

synaesthesia, *sin-ēs-thē'zi-ə, -zhyə, n.* sensation produced at a point different from the point of stimulation: a sensation of another kind suggested by one experienced (e.g. in colour-hearing).—*adj.* synaesthet'ic. [Gr. *syn*, together, *aisthēsis*, sensation.]

synagogue, *sin'ə-gog, n.* an assembly of Jews for worship: a Jewish place of worship.—*adjs.* syn'-

agogal (*-gō-gl*), synagog'ical (*-gog'*, *-goj'i-kl*). [Gr. *synagōgē*—*syn*, together, *agōgē*, a bringing—*agein*, to lead.]

synallagmatic, *sin-a-lag-mat'ik, adj.* mutually or reciprocally obligatory. [Gr. *synallagmatikos*—*synallagma*, a covenant—*syn*, together, *allagma*, exchange.]

synaloepha, *sin-ə-lē'fə, n.* the melting of a final vowel or diphthong into the initial vowel or diphthong of the next word. [Latinised from Gr. *synaloiphē*—*synaleiphein*, to coalesce, smear together—*syn*, together, *aleiphein*, to anoint.]

synandrium, *sin-an'dri-əm, n.* a mass of united stamens.—*adj.* synan'drous, having united stamens. [Gr. *syn*, together, *anēr*, a man (male).]

synangium, *sin-an'ji-əm, n.* an arterial trunk: a group of united sporangia (found in Marattiaceae). [Gr. *syn*, together, *angeion*, a vessel.]

synantherous, *sin-an'thər-əs, adj.* syngenesious. [Gr. *syn*, and anther.]

synanthesis, *sin-an-thē'sis,* (*bot.*) *n.* simultaneous ripening of stamens and stigmas.—*adjs.* synan'thet'ic; synan'thic, showing synanthy; synan'-thous, synanthic: flowering and leafing simultaneously.—*n.* synan'thy, abnormal fusion of flowers. [Gr. *syn*, together, *anthēsis*, flowering, *anthos*, a flower.]

synaphea, synapheia, *sin-ə-fē'ə, n.* metrical continuity between verses in a system, so that they can be scanned as one verse, as in anapaestics, with possibility of elision at the end of a line. [Gr. *synapheia*—*syn*, together, *haph-*, root of *haptein*, to join.]

synaposematism, *sin-ap-ō-sē'mə-tizm, n.* warning coloration common to a number of dangerous species in the same region.—*adj.* synaposematic (*-mat'ik*). [Gr. *syn*, together, and aposematism.]

synapsis, *sin-aps'is, n.* the pairing of chromosomes of paternal and maternal origin before the reducing division: a synapse.—*ns.* synapse', an interlacing or enveloping connection of a nerve-cell with another; synapt'ase, emulsin; synapte (*sin-ap'tē*), in the Greek Church, a litany.—*adj.* synapt'ic. [Gr. *synapsis*, contact, junction—*syn*, together, *haptein*, to fasten; *synaptē* (*euchē*, a prayer), joined together.]

synarchy, *sin'ər-ki, n.* joint sovereignty. [Gr. *synarchiā*—*syn*, with *archein*, to rule.]

synarthrosis, *sin-ər-thrō'sis, n.* immovable articulation.—*adj.* synarthrō'dial.—*adv.* synarthrō'-dially. [Gr. *synarthrōsis*—*syn*, together, *arthron*, a joint; also *arthrōdiā*, a flattish joint.]

synastry, *sin-as'tri, n.* a coincidence of stellar influences. [Gr. *syn*, together, *astron*, a star.]

synaxis, *si-nak'sis, n.* in the early Church, meeting for worship, esp. for the eucharist.—*n.* synaxā'-rion (Gr. *Ch.*), a lection containing an account of a saint's life. [Gr. *synaxis*, a bringing together—*syn*, together, *agein*, to lead.]

syncarpous, *sin-kär'pəs,* (*bot.*) *adj.* of or having united carpels. [Gr. *syn*, together, *karpos*, a fruit.]

syncategorematic, *sin-kat-i-gor-i-mat'ik, adj.* not able to form a term without other words.—*adv.* syncategoremat'ically. [Gr. *synkatēgorēmatikos*—*syn*, with, *katēgorēma*, predicate.]

synchondrosis, *sing-kon-drō'sis, n.* connection of bones by cartilage. [Gr. *synchondrōsis*—*syn*, with, *chondros*, a cartilage.]

synchoresis, *sing-kō-rē'sis,* (*rhet.*) *n.* a concession, esp. one made for the sake of a more effective retort. [Gr. *synchōrēsis*—*synchōreein*, to agree, yield ground—*syn*, with, *chōros*, space.]

synchrocyclotron, *sing-krō-si'klō-tron,* synchro-tron, *sing'krō-tron.* See accelerator.

synchronal, *sing'krə-nl, adj.* coinciding in time.—*adjs.* synchronic (*-kron'*), -al.—*adv.* synchron'-ically.—*n.* synchronisā'tion, -z-.—*v.i.* syn'chronise, -ize, to coincide or agree in time.—*v.t.* to cause to coincide or agree in time: to time together or to a standard: to represent or identify as contemporary.—*ns.* **synch′roniser, -z-;** **synch′-ronism,** coincidence in time: simultaneity: keeping time together: occurrence of like phrases at the same time: exhibition of contemporary history in one scheme: the bringing together in one picture of different parts of a story.—*adj.* **synchronis′tic.**—*adv.* **synchronis′tically.**—*n.* **synchronol′ogy,** chronological arrangement side by side.—*adj.* **synch′ronous,** simultaneous: contemporary: keeping time together.—*adv.* **synch′-ronously.**—*ns.* **synch′ronousness;** **synch′rony,** simultaneity.—**synchromesh gear,** a gear in which the speeds of the driving and the driven members are automatically synchronised before coupling, so as to avoid shock and noise in gear-changing. [Gr. *syn,* together, *chronos,* time.]

**synchysis,** *sing′ki-sis, n.* confusion of meaning due to unusual arrangement (*rhet.*): fluidity of the vitreous humour of the eye. [Gr. *synchysis—syn,* together, with, *cheein,* to pour.]

**synclastic,** *sin-klas′tik, adj.* having the same kind of curvature in all directions. [Gr. *syn,* together, *klastos,* broken.]

**syncline,** *sin′klin,* (*geol.*) *n.* a fold in which the beds dip downwards towards the axis.—*adj.* **synclin′al.** —*n.* a syncline.—*n.* **synclinorium** (*-kli-nō′ri-əm, -nö′*), a great synclinal structure carrying minor flexures. [Gr. *syn,* together, *klinein,* to cause to lean.]

**syncope,** *sing′kə-pi, n.* a cutting short (*rare*): syncopation (*obs.*): a fainting fit from sudden anaemia of the brain (*med.*).—*adj.* **sync′opal,** of syncope.—*v.t.* **sync′opate,** to shorten by cutting out the middle (of a word): to alter the rhythm of temporarily by transferring the accent to a normally unaccented beat (*mus.*).—*adj.* **sync′-opated.**—*ns.* **syncopa′tion;** **sync′opātor.**—*adjs.* **syncopic** (*sing-kop′ik*); **syncopt′ic.** [Gr. *synkopē,* a cutting up, cutting short, syncope—*syn,* together, *koptein,* to cut off.]

**syncretism,** *sing′kri-tizm,* or *sin′, n.* reconciliation of, or attempt to reconcile, different systems of belief, esp. of different forms of Christianity by Georg Calixtus: fusion or blending of religions, as by identification of gods, taking over of observances, or selection of whatever seems best in each: illogical compromise in religion.—*adj.* **syncretic** (*sin-krē′tik,* or *sing-*).—*v.t.* and *v.i.* **syncretise, -ize** (*sing′kri-tīz*).—*n.* **syn′cretist.**— *adj.* **syncretis′tic.** [Gr. *synkrētismos,* a confederation (orig. app. of *Cretan* communities).]

**syncytium,** *sin-sish′i-əm,* (*biol.*) *n.* a multinucleate cell: a tissue without distinguishable cell-walls. —*adj.* **syncyt′ial.** [Gr. *syn,* together, *kytos,* a vessel.]

**synd, sind,** *sind, v.t.* to rinse: to wash out or down. —*n.* a rinsing: a washing down with liquor.— *n.pl.* **synd′ings, sind′ings.**—Also **syne** (*Burns*). [Origin obscure.]

**syndactyl,** *sin-dak′til, adj.* with fused digits.—*n.* **syndac′tylism.**—*adj.* **syndac′tylous.** [Gr. *syn, daktylos,* finger, toe.]

**synderesis.** See **synteresis.**

**syndesis,** *sin′di-sis, n.* a binding: synapsis (*biol.*). —*adj.* **syndetic** (*-det′ik*), connective.—*adv.* **syndet′ically.** [Gr. *syndesis—syn, deein,* to bind.]

**syndesmosis,** *sin-des-mō′sis, n.* the connection of bones by ligaments.—*adj.* **syndesmotic** (*-mot′ik*). [Gr. *syndesmos—syn, desmos,* a bond.]

**syndet,** *sin′det, n.* synthetic *det*ergent.

**syndic,** *sin′dik, n.* in ancient Greece an advocate, delegate, or judge: at various times and places a magistrate or mayor: a member of a committee of the Senate of Cambridge University: one chosen to transact business for others, esp. the accredited legal representative of a corporation, society, or company.—*adj.* **syn′dical (syndical**

chamber or union, a French trade-union).—*ns.* **syn′dicalism,** a French development of trade-unionism, aiming at putting the means of production in the hands of unions of workers; **syn′dicalist.**—*adj.* **syndicalist′ic.**—*n.* **syn′dicate,** a body of syndics: a council: the office of a syndic: a body of men chosen to watch the interests of a company, or to manage a bankrupt's property: a combination of persons or firms for some common purpose or interest: a combined group of newspapers.—*v.t.* to judge, censure (*obs.*): to control, effect, or publish by means of a syndicate: to sell (as an article) for simultaneous publication in a number of newspapers or periodicals: to join in a syndicate.— *v.i.* to join in a syndicate.—*ns.* **syndicā′tion;** **syn′dicātor.** [Gr. *syndikos—syn,* with, *dikē,* justice.]

**syndrome,** *sin′drōm, sin′drə-mi, -mē,* or *sin′drō-mi, -mē, n.* concurrence, esp. of symptoms: a characteristic pattern or group of symptoms. [Gr. *syndromē.*]

**syndyasmian,** *sin-di-az′mi-ən,* (*anthrop.*) *adj.* pairing, applied to a form of family founded on a loose temporary marriage. [Gr. *syndyasmos,* coupling.]

**syne,** *sin,* (*Scot.*) *adv.* then, next: afterwards, later: ago, since (as in *auld langsyne*). [sithen.]

**synecdoche,** *sin-ek′də-kē, -ki,* (*rhet.*) *n.* the figure of putting part for the whole, or the whole for part.—*adjs.* **synecdochic** (*-dok′*), **-al.**—*adv.* **synecdoch′ically.**—*n.* **synec′dochism,** use of synecdoche: use of part for the whole in sympathetic magic. [Gr. *synekdochē—syn,* together, *ekdechesthai,* to receive.]

**synechia,** *sin-e-ki′ə, sin-ē′ki-ə, n.* morbid adhesion, esp. of iris and cornea. [Gr. *synecheia,* continuity —*syn,* together, *echein,* to hold.]

**synecphonesis,** *sin-ek-fō-nē′sis, n.* synizesis. [Gr. *syn,* together, *ekphōnēsis,* pronunciation—*ek,* out, *phōnē,* voice, utterance.]

**synectics,** *sin-ek′tiks, n.* the study of processes leading to invention, with the end aim of solving practical problems, esp. by a **synectics group,** a miscellaneous group of people of imagination and ability but varied interests. [Gr. *synektikos,* fit for holding together.]

**synedrion,** *sin-ed′ri-on, n.* a judicial assembly: a sanhedrin.—Also **syned′rium**—*pl.* (of both) **syned′ria.**—*adj.* **syned′rial.** [Gr. *syn,* together, *hedrā,* seat.]

**syneidesis,** *sin-i-dē′sis, n.* conscience as passing judgment on past acts—opp. to *synteresis.* [Gr. *syneidēsis,* conscience—*syn,* with, together, *eidenai,* to know.]

**syneresis.** See **synaeresis.**

**synergy,** *sin′ər-ji, n.* combined or co-ordinated action.—*adjs.* **synergetic** (*-jet′ik*), **syner′gic,** working together.—*ns.* **syner′gid** (*bot.*), either of the two cells in the embryo-sac that seem to guide the pollen-tube; **synergism** (*sin′* or *-ûr′*), the doctrine that the human will and the Divine Spirit are two efficient agents that co-operate in regeneration—ascribed to Melanchthon: increased effect of two substances, as drugs, obtained by using them together; **syn′ergist** (or *-ûr′*), a substance which increases the effect of another (e.g. pesticide): a muscle, etc., that acts with another.—*adj.* **synergist′ic.** [Gr. *synergia,* co-operation—*syn,* together, *ergon,* work.]

**synesis,** *sin′ə-sis, n.* syntax having regard to meaning rather than grammatical form. [Gr., sense.]

**syngamy,** *sing′gə-mi, n.* free interbreeding: union of gametes.—*adjs.* **syngamic** (*sin-gam′ik*), **syngamous** (*sing′gə-məs*). [Gr. *syn,* together, *gamos,* marriage.]

**syngenesis,** *sin-jen′i-sis, n.* reproduction by fusion of male and female elements, the offspring being derived from both parents.—*n.pl.* **Syngenesia** (*sin-ji-nē'si-ə*), in the Linnaean system a class of plants with syngenesious stamens, answering to the Compositae.—*adjs.* **syngene'sious,** having the anthers united in a tube about the style, as in Compositae; **syngenetic** (*-net'ik*), of or by syngenesis: of minerals, formed contemporaneously with the enclosing rock. [Gr. *syn*, together, *genesis*, formation, generation.]

**Syngnathidae,** *sin(g)-gnath'i-dē*, or *sing-nath'*, *n.pl.* the pipefish family. [Gr. *syn*, together, *gnathos*, jaw.]

**syngraph,** *sing'gräf*, *n.* a writing signed by both or all of the parties thereto. [Gr. *syn*, together, *graphein*, to write.]

**synizesis,** *sin-i-zē'sis*, *n.* the union into one syllable of two vowels without forming a recognised diphthong: contraction of chromatin towards one side in karyokinesis. [Gr. *synizēsis*, a collapse—*syn*, with, together, and *hizein*, to seat, to sit down.]

**synod,** *sin'əd*, *n.* a meeting: an ecclesiastical council: a Presbyterian church court intermediate between presbytery and the General Assembly: the supreme court of the former United Presbyterian Church: conjunction (*astron.*; *obs.*).—*adj.* **syn'odal,** of, of the nature of, or done in a synod.—*n.* a payment made by a clergyman on the occasion of a synod, or at a visitation.—*adjs.* **synodic** (*-od'ik*), **-al,** synodal: pertaining to conjunction (*astron.*): from conjunction to conjunction (see **month**).—*adv.* **synod'ically.**—**General Synod of the Church of England,** governing body set up in 1970 giving the laity more say in the decisions of the Church. [Gr. *synodos*, a meeting, conjunction—*syn*, together, *hodos*, a way.]

**synoecete,** *sin-ē'sēt*, **sinoekete,** *-kēt*, *n.* a guest tolerated with indifference in an ants' or termites' nest.—*n.* **synoeciosis** (*-si-ō'sis*), the rhetorical figure of coupling opposites.—*adjs* **synoecious** (*-ē'shəs*), **synoicous** (*-oi'kəs*), having antheridia and archegonia in the same group.—*v.t.* and *v.i.* **syn'oecise, -ize** (*-ē-siz*), to unite in one community or city-state.—*ns.* **synoe'cism,** union of communities or cities; **synoecology** (*-kol'ə-ji*), study of plant communities. [Gr. *synoikia*, a living together, community, *synoiketēs*, a housefellow, *synoikizein*, to unite in one community —*syn*, with, *oikeein*, to dwell.]

**synonym,** *sin'ə-nim*, *n.* a word having the same meaning with another (usu. very nearly the same meaning): a systematic name to which another is preferred as valid (*biol.*).—*adjs.* **synonymatic** (*sin-on-i-mat'ik*), **synonym'ic, -al,** of synonyms.— *ns.* **synonym'icon,** a dictionary of synonyms; **synon'ymist,** one who studies synonyms, or the different names of plants and animals; **synonym'ity,** the fact or quality of being synonymous.—*adj.* **synon'ymous,** having the same meaning.—*adv.* **synon'ymously.**—*ns.* **synon'ymousness; synon'ymy,** rhetorical use of synonyms: a setting forth of synonyms: a list of synonyms. [Gr. *synōnymon*—*syn*, with, *onoma*, a name.]

**synopsis,** *sin-op'sis*, *n.* a general view: a summary —*pl.* **synop'sēs.**—*adjs.* **synop'tic, -al,** affording or taking a general view of the whole.—*adv.* **synop'tically.**—*n.* **synop'tist,** one of the writers of the Synoptic Gospels.—*adj.* **synoptis'tic.**—**Synoptic Gospels,** those of Matthew, Mark, and Luke, which readily admit of being brought under one combined view. [Gr. *synopsis*—*syn*, with, together, *opsis*, a view.]

**synostosis,** *sin-os-tō'sis,n.* complete union of bones. [Gr. *syn*, osteon, bone.]

**synovia,** *sin-ō'vi-ə*, *n.* an unctuous fluid in the joints.—*adj.* **syno'vial.**—*n.* **synovi'tis,** inflammation of a synovial membrane.—**synovial membrane,** a membrane of connective tissue that lines tendon sheaths and capsular ligaments and

secretes synovia. [App. an arbitrary coinage of Paracelsus, who applied it more generally.]

**syntan,** *sin'tan*, *n.* a synthetic tanning agent.

**syntax,** *sin'taks*, *n.* grammatical structure in sentences: one of the classes in some R.C. schools. —*adjs.* **syntac'tic, -al.**—*adv.* **syntac'tically.**—*ns.* **syntag'ma,** a systematic body, system, or group: —*pl.* **syntag'mata; syntag'matite,** a kind of hornblende. [Gr. *syntaxis*—*syn*, together— *tassein*, to put in order.]

**syntectic(al).** See **syntexis.**

**syntenosis,** *sin-tə-nō'sis*, *n.* the connection of bones by tendons. [Gr. *syn*, with, *tenōn*, a sinew.]

**synteresis,** *sin-ti-rē'sis*, *n.* conscience as a guide to future action—opp. to *syneidesis.*—Also **synderē'sis** (from the later Gr. pronunciation). [Gr. *syntērēsis*, observation—*syn*, with, *tēreein*, to watch over.]

**syntexis,** *sin-tek'sis*, *n.* liquefaction: melting: wasting.—*adjs.* **syntec'tic, -al.** [Gr. *syntēxis* —*syn*, with, *tēkein*, to melt.]

**synthesis,** *sin'thi-sis*, *n.* building up: putting together: making a whole out of parts: the combination of separate elements of thought into a whole: reasoning from principles to a conclusion:—*pl.* **syn'theses** (*sēz*)—opp. to *analysis.* —*v.t.* **syn'thesise, -ize** (a faulty form for **synthetise**).—*n.* **syn'thesist** (for **synthetist**).—*adjs.* **synthetic** (*-thet'*), **-al,** pertaining to, consisting in, or formed by, synthesis: artificially produced but of like nature with, not a mere substitute for, the natural product: not sincere, sham (*coll.*). —*adv.* **synthet'ically.**—*n.* **synthet'icism,** the principles of synthesis, a synthetic system.— *v.t.* **syn'thetise, -ize,** to put together in synthesis: to form by synthesis.—*ns.* **synthetis'er, -z-, syn'-thetist,** one who makes a synthesis.—**synthetic drug,** a drug made in the laboratory—both those occurring naturally and artificial ones; **synthetic philosophy,** Herbert Spencer's system, a fusion, as he thought, of the different sciences into a whole. [Gr. *synthesis*—*syn*, with, together, *thesis*, a placing.]

**synthronus,** *sin'thrə-nəs*, *n.* the seat of the bishop and his presbyters, behind the altar. [Gr. *syn*, together, *thronos*, a throne.]

**syntony,** *sin-tən-i*, *n.* tuning, or agreement in resonance frequency, of wireless apparatus.— *adj.* **syntonic** (*sin-ton'ik*), tuned together.—*n.* **syn'tonin,** a substance akin to fibrin, found in muscle.—*v.t.* **syn'tonise, -ize** to adjust to agree in frequency.—*adj.* **syn'tonous,** syntonic. [Gr. *syn*, together, *tonos*, tone.]

**sype.** Same as **sipe.**

**syphilis,** *sif'i-lis*, *n.* a contagious venereal disease due to infection with a micro-organism *Spirochaeta pallida.*—*n.* **syphilisā'tion, -z-.**—*v.t.* **syph'-ilise, -ize,** to inoculate or to infect with syphilis. —*adjs.* **syphilit'ic; syph'iloid,** like syphilis.—*ns.* **syphilol'ogist; syphilol'ogy,** the study of syphilis; **syphilō'ma,** a syphilitic tumour; **syphilophō'bia,** a morbid dread of syphilis. [Title of Fracastoro's Latin poem (1530), whose hero *Syphilis* is infected.]

**syphon, syren.** Same as **siphon, siren.**

**Syriac,** *sir'i-ak*, *n.* the ancient Aramaic dialect of *Syria.*—Also *adj.*—*ns.* **Syr'iacism** (*-ə-sizm*), **Syr'ianism, Syr'iasm, Syr'ism,** a Syriac idiom.— *adj.* **Syr'ian,** relating to Syria.—*n.* a native or citizen of Syria.—*ns.* **Syr'iarch** (*-ärk*); *adj.* **Syriarchēs**), the chief priest in Roman Syria; **Syrophoenicia** (*si-rō-fi-nish'yə*), a Roman province between Lebanon and the coast.—*n.* and *adj.* **Syrophoeni'cian.**

**syringa, syringe, etc.** See **syrinx.**

**syrinx,** *sir'ingks*, *n.* Pan-pipes: the vocal organ of birds: a fistula or fistulous opening: a rock-cut tunnel, as in Egyptian tombs:—*pl.* **syringes** (*-in'jēz*) or **syr'inxes.**—*ns.* **syringa** (*-ing'gə*), orig. and still popularly the mock-orange: (*cap.*)

after Linnaeus, the generic name of the lilac; **syr'inge** (-*inj* or *si-rinj'*), an instrument for squirting or injecting.—*v.t.* and *v.i.* to clean, spray, or inject with a syringe.—*adj.* **syringeal** (-*in'ji-əl*).— *n.* **syringitis** (-*ji'tis*), inflammation of the Eustachian tube; **syringotomy** (*sir-ing-got'ə-mi*), cutting for fistula. [Gr. *sȳrinx, -ingos*, Panpipes, gallery.]

**syrlye**, an old form (*Spens.*) of surly.

**Syrophoenicia(n).** See Syriac.

**Syrphus**, *sûr'fəs, n.* a genus of wasp-like flies that hover and dart, giving name to the family **Syr'phidae** (-*fi-dē*).—*n.* and *adj.* **syr'phid.** [Gr. *syrphos*, gnat.]

**syrtis**, *sûr'tis*, (*Milt.*) *n.* a quicksand:—*pl.* **syr'tes** (*tēz*). [L. *Syrtēs*, Gr. *Syrtides* (sing. of each *Syrtis*), name of two sandy bays of N. Africa— Gr. *sȳrein*, to draw, sweep along.]

**syrup**, *sir'əp, n.* a saturated solution of sugar boiled to prevent fermentation: any thick sweet liquid: cloying sweetness (*fig.*; *coll.*).—Also (esp. *U.S.*) **sir'up.**—*adj.* **syr'upy.**—golden syrup, the uncrystallisable part finally separated in manufacture of crystallised sugar. [Fr. *sirop*—Ar. *sharāb*; cf. **shrub, sherbet.**]

**syssarcosis**, *sis-är-kō'sis, n.* the connection of one bone with another by intervening muscle. [Gr. *syn*, together, *sarx*, flesh.]

**syssitia**, *si-sit'i-ə*, or -*sish', n.* the ancient Spartan custom of eating the chief meal together in public. [Gr. *syssitiā*—*syn*, together, *sitos*, food.]

**systaltic**, *sis-tal'tik, adj.* alternately contracting and dilating, pulsatory. [Gr. *systaltikos*, depressing; cf. **systole.**]

**system**, *sis'tim, -təm, n.* anything formed of parts placed together or adjusted into a regular and connected whole: a set of things considered as a connected whole: a group of heavenly bodies moving mainly under the influence of their mutual attraction: a set of bodily organs of like composition or concurring in function: the bodily organism: one of the great divisions of the geological strata, subordinate only to the division into Palaeozoic, Mesozoic, and Cainozoic: a group of (Greek) verses: a body of doctrine: a theory of the universe: a full and connected view of some department of know-

ledge: an explanatory hypothesis: a scheme of classification: a manner of crystallisation: a plan: a method: a method of organisation: methodicalness: a systematic treatise.—*adjs.* **systemat'ic, -al**, pertaining to, or consisting of, for the purpose of, observing, or according to system: methodical: habitual: intentional.— *adv.* **systemat'ically.**—*ns.* **systematician** (-ə-*tish'-ən*); **systemat'ics**, the science of classification: the study of classification of living things in accordance with their natural relationships; **systematisā'tion, -z-, systemisā'tion, -z-.**—*vs.t.* **sys'tematise, -ize, sys'temise, -ize**, to reduce to a system.—*ns.* **sys'tematiser, -z-**; **sys'tematism**; **sys'tematist**; **systematol'ogy.**—*adjs.* **sys'temed**; **systemic** (-*tem'ik*), pertaining to the bodily system or to a system of bodily organs; **sys'temless**, without system: not exhibiting organic structure.—**system building**, building using standardised factory-produced components.— *adj.* **sys'tem-built'.**—**sys'tem-maker, -monger**, one unduly fond of constructing systems; **systems analyst**, one who plans the work of a large organisation so that computers and other equipment are used most efficiently and there are no delays or bottle-necks. [Gr. *systēma*—*sy-, syn-*, together, and the root of *histanai*, to set.]

**systole**, *sis'to-lē, -tə-lē, n.* rhythmical contraction, esp. of the heart—opp. to *diastole*: collapse of the nucleus in mitosis: the shortening of a long syllable (*gram.*).—*adj.* **systolic** (-*tol'ik*). [Gr. *systolē*—*syn*, together, *stellein*, to place.]

**systyle**, *sis'til, (archit.) adj.* having an intercolumniation of two diameters.—*n.* such an arrangement: a building or part so constructed. [Gr. *systȳlos*—*sy-, syn-*, together, *stȳlos*, a column.]

**sythe** (*Spens.*). See **sith** (2).

**syver, siver**, *si'vər*, (*Scot.*) *n.* a drain: a grating over a drain. [Perh. a form of **sewer.**]

**syzygy**, *siz'i-ji, n.* conjunction or opposition: the period of new or full moon: a dipody:—*pl.* **syz'ygies.**—*adj.* **syzyg'ial.** [Gr. *syzygiā*, union, coupling—*sy-, syn-*, with, together, and *zygon*, a yoke.]

**Szekler**, *sek'lər, n.* a Transylvanian Magyar.

Neutral vowels in unaccented syllables: *el'ə-mənt*; for certain sounds in foreign words, see p. viii

# T

**T, t,** *tē, n.* the twentieth letter in our alphabet, eighteenth in the Roman, its usual sound a voiceless stop produced with the tip of the tongue in contact with teeth, gums, or palate: an object or mark in the form of the letter (also͜ tee): as a mediaeval Roman numeral T = 160, T̄ = 160,000. —**T′-band′age,** a bandage composed of two strips fashioned in the shape of the letter T; **T′-bar,** a metal bar with cross-section in the shape of the letter T: a type of ski-lift (also **T′-bar lift**); **T′-cart,** a four-wheeled pleasure-vehicle without top, having a T-shaped body; **T′-cloth,** a plain cotton made for the India and China market—stamped with a T; **T′-cross,** a tau-cross; **T′-junction,** a road junction in the shape of a T; **T′-plate,** a T-shaped plate, as for strengthening a joint in a wooden framework; **T′-rail,** a rail with T-shaped cross-section.—*adj.* **T′-shaped.**—**T′-shirt** (see **tee-shirt**); **T′-square,** a T-shaped ruler.—**marked with a T,** branded as thief; **to a T,** with perfect exactness.

**'t,** a shortened form of **it.**

**t-, t',** an obsolete shortened form of **to** before a vowel, as in Spenser **tadvance,** to advance, **tasswage,** to assuage: in N. of England for **the.**

**ta,** *tä, interj.* (hypocoristic or affected) thank you.

**taal,** *täl, (arch.) n.* Afrikaans or Cape Dutch. [Du., speech.]

**tab,** *tab, n.* a small tag, flap, or strap, forming an appendage: a loop for hanging up by: reckoning, tally, check.—*adj.* **tabbed.**—*v.t.* to fix a tab to: to tabulate.— **keep tabs on** (see **keep**). [Origin unknown.]

**Tabanus,** *tə-bā′nəs, n.* the gadfly genus.—*n.* **tabanid** (*tab′ə-nid*), any member of the genus, or of its family **Tabanidae** (*tə-ban′i-dē*). [L. *tabānus.*]

**tabard,** *tab′ərd, n.* a mediaeval peasant's overcoat: a knight's sleeveless or short-sleeved coat: now, a herald's coat: a woman's outer garment, a sleeveless tunic.—*n.* **tab′erdar,** a scholar of Queen's College, Oxford. [O.Fr. *tabart.*]

**tabaret,** *tab′ə-ret, n.* an upholsterer's silk stuff, with alternate stripes of watered and satin surface.

**tabasco,** *tə-bas′kō, n.* a hot pepper sauce. [From trademark—*Tabasco* state in Mexico.]

**tabasheer, -shir,** *tab-ə-shēr′, n.* a siliceous substance sometimes found in crude form in hollows of bamboos and also prepared by chemical processes. [Hind., Pers., Ar. *tabāshīr.*]

**tabby,** *tab′i, n.* a coarse waved or watered silk: an artificial stone: a tabby-cat: a gossiping, interfering woman (*coll.*).—*adj.* **brindled.**—*v.t.* to water or cause to look wavy:—*pr.p.* **tabb′ying;** *pa.t.* and *pa.p.* **tabb′ied.**—*ns.* **tabb′inet,** a more delicate kind of tabby resembling damask, used for window-curtains; **tabb′yhood.**—**tabb′y-cat,** a brindled cat: hence (or from *Tabitha*) a female cat: an old maid: a spiteful gossiping woman. [Fr. *tabis,* app. from '*Attābiy,* a quarter in Baghdad where it was made.]

**tabellion,** *tə-bel′yən, n.* an official scrivener in the Roman empire and elsewhere. [L.L. *tabelliō, -ōnis*—L. *tabella,* tablet, dim. of *tabula,* a board.]

**taberdar.** See under **tabard.**

**tabernacle,** *tab′ər-nə-kl, n.* a tent or moveable hut: the tent carried by the Jews through the desert and used as a temple: the human body as the temporary abode of the soul: a place of worship, esp. temporary or dissenting: a receptacle for the vessel containing the pyx (*R.C.*): a canopied niche or seat: a canopy: a socket for a mast.—*v.i.* to sojourn.—*v.t.* to put or enshrine in a tabernacle.—*adjs.* **tab′ernacled; tabernacular** (*-nak′ū-lər*).—**tab′ernacle-work,** ornamental work over niches, stalls, etc., with canopies and pinnacles, or any work in which this forms a characteristic feature.—**Feast of Tabernacles,** a Jewish harvest festival, celebrating the sojourn in tents in the wilderness. [L. *tabernāculum,* dim. of *taberna,* a hut.]

**tabes,** *tā′bēz, n.* wasting away.—*n.* **tabefaction** (*tab-i-fak′shən*), wasting away, emaciation.—*v.t.* and *v.i.* **tab′efy.**—*n.* **tabescence** (*tab-es′əns*), wasting: shrivelling.—*adjs.* **tabesc′ent; tab′id.** —**tabes dorsa′lis,** locomotor ataxia. [L. *tābēs, -is.*]

**tabla,** *tab′la, n.* an Indian percussion instrument.

**tablature,** *tab′lə-chər, n.* a tablet: a painting, picture, pictorial representation or work: an old notation for lute music with a line for each string and letters or figures to indicate the stopping, used with modifications for other instruments. [L. *tabula,* a board.]

**table,** *tā′bl, n.* a slab or board: a layer: a flat surface: a board for painting on: a picture: a quadrangular space on the palm of the hand (*Shak.*): a panel: a string-course: a slab with or for an inscription: a slab inscribed with laws: hence, in *pl.,* a code of law (as the Twelve Tables of ancient Rome): a writing tablet (esp. in the obs. phrase *a pair of tables*): a board for a game, e.g. chess: each half of a folding board: hence, in *pl.* (*obs.*), backgammon: a broad flat surface on a cut gem: a tabular crystal: an article of furniture consisting of a flat top on legs, pillar, or trestles, for use at meals, work, play, for holding things, etc.: supply of food, entertainment: the company at a table: a board or committee: a dispensing of the communion: a projecting part of a scarfed joint: a flat gravestone supported on pillars: a condensed statement: a syllabus or index: a compact scheme of numerical information: hence, in *pl.,* a collection of these for reference.—*adj.* of, for, like, or pertaining to a table, or meals.—*v.t.* to tabulate: to lay on the table: to pay down: to put forward for discussion: to shelve: to board.—*v.i.* to board.—*adj.* **tabled** (*tā′bld*), flat-topped: having a smooth sloping surface of dressed stone: having a table or tables.—*n.* **ta′bleful,** as many as a table will hold.—*adj.* and *adv.* **ta′blewise,** in the form or in the manner of a table: of the communion table, not altarwise.—*n.* **ta′bling,** tabulation: backgammon-playing: board: provision of tables: scarfing: a broad hem on the skirt of a sail.—**ta′ble-beer,** light beer for common use; **ta′ble-book,** a book of writing tablets, memorandum book, or notebook: an ornamental book intended to lie on a table: a book of tables; **ta′ble-cloth,** a cloth for covering a table, esp. at meals; **ta′ble-cover,** a cloth for covering a table, esp. at other than meal-times. —*adj.* **ta′ble-cut,** (of gems) cut with a flat top.— **table-d'hôte** (*tä-bl′-dōt;* Fr., host's table), a meal at a fixed price; **ta′ble-knife,** a knife such as one cuts one's own meat, etc., with; **ta′bleland,** an extensive region of elevated land with a flat or undulating surface: a plateau; **ta′ble-leaf,** an extension to a table-top, hinged, drawn out, or inserted; **ta′ble-lin′en,** linen table-cloths, nap-

*fāte, fär; mē, hûr* (her); *mīne; mōte, för; mūte; mōͦn, fōͦot; dhen* (then)

**tableau** 1373 **tack**

kins, etc.; **ta´ble-maid**, a maid-servant who sets the table and waits; **table-manners**, social behaviour during meals; **ta´ble-mat**, a mat placed under dishes on a table; **ta´ble-mon´ey**, an allowance for official entertainment: restaurateur's euphemism for *cover-charge*; **ta´ble-mu´sic**, music in parts that can be read by performers at each side of a table; **ta´ble-nap´kin**, a cloth used at table to protect the clothes and to wipe fingers and lips; **ta´ble-skitt´les**, a game in which a suspended ball is swung to knock down pegs set up on a board; **ta´ble-spoon**, one of the largest spoons used at table; **ta´ble-spoon´ful**, as much as will fill a table-spoon:—*pl.* **ta´ble-spoon´fuls**; **ta´ble-sport** (*Shak.*), the butt of the company at table; **ta´ble-talk**, familiar conversation, as at table, during and after meals; **ta´ble-tenn´is**, a game like lawn-tennis played on a table using celluloid or similar balls; **ta´ble-top**, the top of a table: a flat top.—*adj.* **ta´ble-topped**.—**ta´ble-turn´ing**, movements of tables (or other objects), attributed by spiritualists to the agency of spirits —by the sceptical to collective involuntary muscular action; **ta´ble-ware**, dishes, spoons, knives, forks, etc., for table use; **ta´ble-wa´ter**, a mineral water suitable for the table; **table wine**, an unfortified wine usually drunk with a meal; **ta´ble-work**, the setting of type for tables, columns of figures, etc.—**at table**, at a meal; **fence the tables** (see fence); **lay on the table**, to lay aside for future discussion or indefinitely; **the Lord's table** (see lord); **turn the tables**, to bring about a complete reversal of circumstances, as if the players at backgammon changed sides; **under the table**, not above board: hopelessly drunk. [Partly O.E. *tabule, tabele*, partly O.Fr. (and Fr.) *table*, both—L. *tabula*, a board.]

**tableau**, *tab´lō*, *n.* a picture or vivid pictorial impression: a suddenly created situation that takes all aback:—*pl.* **tableaux** (*tab´lōz*).—**tableau (vivant)**, a 'living picture', a motionless representation by living persons in costume:—*pl.* **tableaux (vivants)** (*tä-blō-vē-vä*). [Fr. dim. of *table*.]

**tablet**, *tab´lit*, *n.* a small slab: a slab or stiff sheet for making notes on: a panel, esp. inscribed or for inscription: an inscribed plate hung up in fulfilment of a vow: a flat confection: a small flat cake of any solid material, often medicinal [O.Fr. *tablete*, dim. of *table*.]

**tabloid**, *tab´loid*, *n.* legally, any product of the chemical manufacturing firm of which the name is a trademark: popularly applied to a drug or anything else in a very concentrated form, e.g. a small, often sensational, newspaper.—*adj.* of, in the form of, tabloids: concentrated.

**taboo, tabu**, *tə-bōō´*, *adj.* subject to taboo: forbidden.—*n.* a Polynesian (or other) system of prohibitions connected with things considered holy or unclean: any one of these prohibitions: any recognised or general prohibition, interdict, restraint, ban, exclusion, ostracism.—*v.t.* to forbid approach to or use of: to place under taboo:—*pr.p.* **taboo´ing**; *pa.t.* and *pa.p.* **tabooed´**. [Tongan *tabu*, pron. *tä´bōō*), holy, unclean.]

**tabor, tabour**, *tā´bər*, *n.* a small drum like a tambourine without jingles, usually played with one stick, along with a pipe: a taborer.—*v.i.* and *v.t.* to play on a tabor: to beat, drum.—*ns.* **tā´borer** (*Spens.* **tabrere**, *ta-brēr´*), one who beats the tabor; **tabo(u)rin** (*tab´ə-rin*, or *-rēn*), a small drum longer in body than the tabor, used in like manner; **tabouret** (*tab´ə-ret*, *tä-bōō-rā*), a stool, orig. drum-shaped; **tabret** (*tab´rit*), a small tabor. [O.Fr. *tabour*; an Oriental word.]

**Taborite**, *tä´bər-it*, *n.* a Hussite of Žižka's party, opposed to the Calixtines or Utraquists.—Also *adj.* [*Tabor* in Bohemia, founded by them as headquarters.]

**tabu.** Same as **taboo.**

**tabula**, *tab´ū-lə*, L. *tab´ōō-la*, *n.* a writing-tablet:

an altar frontal: a flattened structure: a horizontal partition in corals:—*pl.* **tab´ulae** (*-lē*; L. *-lī*). —*adj.* **tab´ular**, of, in the form of, like, according to, a table: laminated: platy: horizontally flattened.—*n.* **tabularisā´tion**.—*v.t.* **tab´ularise**, **-ize**, to tabulate.—*adv.* **tab´ularly**.—*v.t.* **tab´ulate**, to reduce to the form of a table or synopsis.— *adj.* **tabular**: having tabulae.—*ns.* **tabulā´tion**; **tab´ulātor**.—*adj.* **tab´ulatory** (*-lə-tə-ri*).—**tabula rasa** (*tab´ū-lə rā´zə, tab´ōō-la rä´sa*), a smoothed or blank tablet: a mind not yet influenced by outside impressions and experiences. [L. *tabula*, table.]

**tacahout**, *tak´ə-howt*, *n.* a gall on the tamarisk, a source of gallic acid. [From Berber.]

**tacamahac**, *tak´ə-mə-hak*, *n.* a gum-resin yielded by several tropical trees: the balsam poplar. [From Nahuatl.]

**tac-au-tac**, *tak´-ō-tak´*, *n.* in fencing, the parry combined with the riposte: also a series of close attacks and parries between fencers of equal skill. [Fr.]

**tace**, *tā´sē, ta´kä*, *imper.* be silent.—**tacet** (*tā´set, ta´ket*; *mus.*) is silent.—**tace is Latin for a candle**, a phrase understood as requesting or promising silence. [L. *tacē*, imper., *tacet*, 3rd pers. sing. pres. indic., of *tacēre*, to be silent.]

**tace.** Same as **tasse.**

**tach, tache**, *tach*, (*B.*) *n.* a fastening or clasp. [O.Fr. *tache*, cf. **tack, attach.**]

**tach-, tak-, tache-, tachy-, tak´i-**, in composition, speed, speedy.—*ns.* **tacheom´eter, tachym´eter** (*-im´*), a surveying instrument for rapid measurement of distances.—*adjs.* **tacheo-, tachymet´rical.** —*ns.* **tacheo-, tachym´etry**; **tachis´toscope** (Gr. *tachistos*, *superl.* of *tachys*), an instrument which flashes images, sentences, etc., on a screen for very brief, exactly timed, periods, now used esp. to increase reading speed.—*adj.* **tachistoscop´ic.**— *ns.* **tach´ogram**, a record, made by a tachograph; **tach´ograph**, a recording tachometer: a tachogram; **tachom´eter**, a device showing speed of rotation: an instrument for measuring the velocity of machines or currents.—*adj.* **tachomet´rical.**—*ns.* **tachom´etry**; **tachycar´dia** (Gr. *kardiä*, heart), abnormal rapidity of heart-beat; **tach´ygraph, tachyg´rapher, -phist.**—*adjs.* **tachygraph´ic, -ical.**—*ns.* **tachyg´raphy**, shorthand; **tach´ylyte** (also **-lite**; Gr. *lytos*, melted, because easily fused before the blowpipe), a black opaque glass occurring as a thin selvage to intrusive basalt.—*adj.* **tachylytic** (*-lit´ik*).—*ns.* **tachyon** (*tak´i-on*), a theoretical particle moving faster than light; **tachypnoea** (*tak-ip-nē´ə*; Gr. *pnoiä*, breathing), excessive frequency in breathing. [Gr. *tachys*, gen. *-eos*, swift, *tachos*, swiftness.]

**tachism(e)**, *tash´izm*, *n.* a mid-20th-century movement in abstract painting characterised by a clotted laying on of pigment.—*n.* and *adj.* **tach´ist(e).** [Fr. *tache*, blob (of paint).]

**tacit**, *tas´it*, *adj.* unspoken: silent.—*adv.* **tac´itly.** —*n.* **tac´itness.**—*adj.* **tac´iturn**, disinclined to speak.—*n.* **taciturn´ity.**—*adv.* **tac´iturnly.** [L. *tacitus, taciturnus*.]

**tack**, *tak*, *n.* a short, sharp nail with a broad head: a long temporary stitch: a fastening strip: a rope or other fastening for the lower windward corner of a sail: the corner itself: an act of tacking: an alternate course in zigzag: course of action: a change of policy, a strategical move: something tacked on: stickiness: equipment (harness, etc.) needed for horse-riding.—*v.t.* to attach or fasten, esp. in a slight manner, as by tacks or long stitches: to change the course of by a tack.—*v.i.* to change the course or tack of a ship by shifting the position of the sails: to zigzag: to shift one's position, to veer.—*adj.* **tacked.**—*ns.* **tack´er**; **tack´et** (*Scot.*), a hobnail. *adj.* **tack´ety.**—*ns.* **tack´iness**; **tack´ing**, proceeding by tacks: fastening: fastening by tacks:

introducing into a bill (esp. a money bill) provisions beyond its natural scope (*politics*).—*adj.* tack'y, sticky.—*adj.* tack'ed-on. [O.Fr. *taque*, doublet of *tache*.]

tack, *tak*, (*Scot.*) *n.* a tenure: a lease: a leased tenement: a spell: a take or catch.—tacks'man (*Scot.*), a lessee: in the Scottish Highlands, one who holds a lease and sublets. [See tak, take.]

tack, *tak*, (*dial.*) *n.* any distinctive flavour, smack.

tack, *tak*, *n.* food generally, fare, esp. of the bread kind, as *hard tack* (ship's biscuit), *soft tack* (loaves).

tack, *tak*, *n.* the sound of a sharp tap. [Imit.]

tackle, *tak'l*, *n.* the ropes, rigging, etc., of a ship (*naut.*, *tāk'l*): tools, gear, weapons, equipment (for sports, etc.): ropes, etc., for raising heavy weights: a pulley: the act of gripping: an act of tackling (*football*).—*v.t.* to harness: to seize or take hold of: to grapple with: to come to grips with: to begin to deal in earnest with: to confront, encounter, challenge.—*v.i.* (*Rugby football*) to seize and stop or (*association*) intercept a player and get the ball away from him.—*adj.* tackled (*tak'ld*), furnished with harness or tackle: made of ropes (Shak.).—*ns.* tack'ler; tack'ling, furniture or apparatus belonging to the masts, yards, etc., of a ship: harness for drawing a carriage: tackle or instruments: grappling. [Cf. L.G. *takel*.]

tacky, *tak'i*, (*U.S.*) *n.* a poor ill-conditioned horse or person.

tacky. See tack (1).

tact, *takt*, *n.* adroitness in managing the feelings of persons dealt with: nice perception in seeing and doing exactly what is best in the circumstances: the stroke in keeping time (*mus.*).—*adj.* tact'ful.—*adv.* tact'fully.—*adj.* tact'ile (*-īl*), perceptible by touch: pertaining to the sense of touch: concerned in perception by touch: suggestive of touch.—*ns.* tact'ilist (*-il-ist*), a painter who aims at tactile effects; tactil'ity; tac'tion (*rare*), contact.—*adj.* tact'less.—*adv.* tact'lessly.—*n.* tact'lessness.—*adj.* tact'ual, relating to, or derived from, the sense of touch.—*n.* tactual'ity, tactual quality.—*adv.* tact'ually. [L. *tactus, -ūs—tangĕre, tactum*, to touch.]

tactic, *-al*, *tak'tik, -əl*, *adjs.* relating to taxis or tactism, or to tactics.—*n.* tac'tic, a system, or a piece, of tactics.—*adv.* tac'tically.—*ns.* tactician (*-tish'ən*), one skilled in tactics; tactic'ity, stereochemical arrangement of units in the main chain of a polymer (*chem.*).—*n.pl.* (often treated as *sing.*) tac'tics, the science or art of manoeuvring in presence of the enemy: purposeful procedure.—*n.* tac'tism (*biol.*), taxis. [Gr. *taktikos*, fit for arranging, *taktos*, ordered, verbal adj. of *tassein*, to arrange.]

tadpole, *tad'pōl*, *n.* the larva of a toad or frog, rarely of an ascidian.—**Tadpole and Taper**, political hacks, from characters in Disraeli's *Coningsby*. [O.E. *tāde*, toad, and *poll* (head).]

tae, *tā*, a Scots form of toe, to, too (also): also in phrase *the tae* for *that ae*, the one (adjectively). [See tone (2), tother.]

taedium. Same as tedium.—taedium vitae (*tē'di-əm vī'tē, ti'di-ōōm wē'ti*), weariness of life.

tael, *tāl*, *n.* Chinese *liang* or ounce, about 1⅓ oz. avoir. (38 g.): a money of account (not normally a coin) in China, orig. a tael weight of pure silver.—tael bar, a gold bullion measure used in the Far East (1, 5 or 10 tael weight). [Port.,—Malay *taïl*, weight.]

ta'en, *tān*, a contraction of taken.

taenia, *tē'ni-ə*, *n.* a ribbon or fillet: the fillet above the architrave of the Doric order: a ribbon-like structure: (*cap.*) the tapeworm genus:—*pl.* tae'niae (*-ni-ē*).—*n.* taeni'asis, infestation with tapeworm.—*adjs.* tae'niate, tae'nioid, like a ribbon or a tapeworm. [L.,—Gr. *tainiā*, a band.]

tafferel, taffrail, *taf'ril*, *n.* the upper part of a ship's stern timbers. [Du. *tafereel*, a panel—*tafel*, a table—L. *tabula*, a table.]

taffeta, *taf'i-tə*, also taffety, *-ti*, taffetas, *-tas*, *n.* a thin glossy silk-stuff: loosely applied to various similar or mixed fabrics.—*adj.* of taffeta: florid, over-dainty (*Shak.*). [Through Fr. or L.L. from Pers. *tāftah*, woven—*tāftan*, to twist.]

taffy, *taf'i*, (*U.S.*) *n.* Same as toffy: flattery, blarney.

Taffy, *taf'i*, *n.* a Welshman. [Imit. of Welsh pron. of *Davy*.]

tafia, *taf'i-ə*, *n.* a variety of rum. [Perh. a W. Indian name, but cf. Malay *tāfiā*.]

tag, *tag*, *n.* a flap of a slashed garment: a tab: a tie-on label: the point of a lace: any small thing tacked or attached to another: a loose or flapping end: a shred: a stray, matted, or dirty lock: (in *pl.*) a footman's shoulder-knot: the tip of a tail: a trite quotation (esp. Latin): a moral to a story: a refrain: the rabble: anything mean.—*v.t.* to put a tag or tags on: to attach as a tag: to tack, fasten, append: to remove tags from: to dog or follow closely.—*v.i.* to make tags, to string words or ideas together: to go behind as a follower:—*pr.p.* tagg'ing; *pa.t.* and *pa.p.* tagged.—*n.* tagg'er.—*n.pl.* tagg'ers, thin sheet-iron.—tag'-day (*U.S.*), a flag-day; tag'-end, the fag-end; tagged atom, a radioactive isotopic atom of a tracer element; tag'rag, the rabble: a fluttering rag, a tatter.—Also *adj.*—tag'-tail, a worm with a tail like a tag.—tag along (with), to follow; tag, rag, and bobtail, rag-tag and bobtail. [Origin obscure.]

tag, *tag*, *n.* the game of tig.—*v.t.* to tig. [Origin obscure.]

Tagalog, *tä-gä'log*, *n.* a people of the Philippine Islands: their Austronesian language.—Also *adj.*

Tagetes, *tä-jē'tēz*, *n.* a Mexican and S. American genus of composites with yellow and orange flowers. [L. *Tagēs*, an Etruscan god.]

taghairm, *tə-gûrm'*, *n.* in the Scottish Highlands, divination: esp. inspiration sought by lying in a bullock's hide behind a waterfall. [Gael.]

taglioni, *tal-yō'nē*, *n.* an early 19th-century overcoat. [Named after a family of dancers.]

taguan, *ta'gwan, tä'gwän, n.* properly, a large East Indian flying squirrel: applied also to an Australian flying phalanger. [Tagálog.]

taha, *tä'hä*, *n.* a S. African weaver-bird. [Zulu *taka*.]

tahr, tehr, *tär*, *n.* a beardless Himalayan wild goat (*Hemitragus jemlaicus*) that frequents forest precipices. [App. its name in the W. Himalaya, confused with Nepali *thār*; see thar.]

tahsil, *tä(hh)-sēl'*, *n.* in India, a division for revenue and certain other purposes.—*n.* tahsildar', an officer of a tahsil. [Hindi *tahsīl*—Ar.]

tai, *tī*, *n.* a Japanese sea-bream.

T'ai. Same as Thai.

taiga, *tī'ga*, *n.* marshy pine forest. [Russ. *taigá*.]

taigle, *tā'gl*, (*Scot.*) *v.t.* to entangle, hinder.—*v.i.* to linger: to loiter: to trudge. [Cf. Sw. (Bornholm) *taggla*, to disorder.]

tail, *tāl*, *n.* the posterior extremity of an animal, usually a slender prolongation beyond the anus: a bird's train of feathers: a fish's caudal fin: anything of like appearance, position, etc.: the back, lower, hinder, latter, down-stream, or inferior part or prolongation of anything (often opp. to the *head*): the stem of a note in music: a downward extension of a letter: a retinue, suite: a queue: a train: anything long and trailing or hanging, as a catkin, train of a comet, long curl of hair: (usu. in *pl.*) the reverse of a coin: the end of a shoal sloping into deeper water: (often in *pl.*) the skirts of a garment: in Turkey, a horse-tail, formerly a mark of rank: (in *pl.*) a tail-coat: one who follows another and keeps constant watch on him (*coll.*).—*v.t.* to furnish with a tail: to be a tail to: to remove the tail or stalk from: to grip by the tail: to join end to end: to tend (*Austr.*): to dog, shadow (also **tail'-up**).—*v.i.* to straggle: to taper (often with *off* or *away*): to lessen or deteriorate slowly (with *off* or *away*): to show the tail.—*adj.* **tailed.**—*n.* **tail'ing,** inner covered end of a projecting brick or stone in a wall: a winter sport in which a tail-like string of luges is drawn along by a horse-sleigh: (in *pl.*) refuse, dregs.—*adj.* **tail'less,** having no tail.—**tail'-board,** the board at the hinder end of a cart or wagon; **tail'-boom,** a longeron supporting the tail of an aeroplane; **tail'-coat,** a man's formal coat, cutaway at the front and with narrow tails at the back; **tail'-end,** the fag-end: (*pl.*) inferior corn sorted out from better; **tail'-end'er** (*coll.*), one coming at the end; **tail'-feath'er,** one of the rectrices or rudder-feathers of a bird's tail: a feather of the back forming a train, as in the peacock; **tail'-fly** (*fishing*), the fly at the end of the leader; **tail'-gate,** lower gate of a lock: a movable board or flap closing the back end of a wagon, etc.: a jazz style of playing esp. the trombone.—*v.t.* to drive dangerously close behind (another vehicle; *slang*).—Also *v.i.*—**tail'-light,** a light carried at the back of a train, a tram, or other vehicle; **tail'piece,** a piece at the tail or end: an engraving, design, etc., occupying the bottom of a page, as at the end of a chapter: a strip of ebony, etc., to which the ends of the strings are attached in a fiddle; **tail'-pipe,** the suction-pipe in a pump.—*v.t.* to tie a can or the like to the tail of (to annoy a dog—explanation unknown).—**tail'race,** the channel in which water runs away below a mill-wheel; **tail'-rope,** a rope attached to the hinder part of anything; **tail'-spin,** a spiral dive of an aeroplane: a state of great agitation and uncertainty how to act (*fig.*).—**tail of the eye,** the outer corner of the eye: the margin of the field of vision; **turn tail,** to run away; **twist the lion's tail,** to irritate Britain; **with the tail between the legs,** like a beaten cur. [O.E. *tægl, tægel*; Goth. *tagl*, hair.]

**tail,** *tāl, (law) n.* limitation of inheritance to certain heirs.—*adj.* limited.—**tail male,** limitation to male heirs. [Fr. *taille*, cutting.]

**tailor,** *tāl'ər, n.* one whose business is to cut out and make outer garments, esp. for men (*fem.* **tail'oress**).—*v.i.* to work as a tailor.—*v.t.* to make clothes for: to fit with clothes: to fashion by tailor's work: to make or adapt so as to fit a special need exactly (*fig.*).—*n.* **tail'oring.**—**tail'or-bird,** an E. Indian warbler (Sutorius or kindred) that sews leaves together to form a nest. —*adj.* **tail'or-made,** made by a tailor, esp. of plain, close-fitting garments for women: exactly adapted (for a purpose). [A.Fr. *taillour* (Fr. *tailleur*)—L.L. *tāliātor, -ōris—tāliāre*, to cut.]

**tailor,** *tā'lər, (Shak.) interj.* variously explained as referring to the backward fall (opp. to *header*), to the tailor-like squatting position that results, or as the obs. **tailard**, a person with a tail.

**tailzie, tailye, taillie,** *tāl'(y)i, (law) n.* Scots forms of tail (2): entail.

**Taino,** *ti'nō, n.* a member of an extinct Indian tribe of the W. Indies (*pl.* **Tai'nos,** or collectively **Tai'no**): its language.—Also *adj.*

**taint,** *tānt, n.* attaint (*obs.*): a hit in tilting (*obs.*): tint, tinge (*obs.*): a tincture of some evil quality: a stain: a blemish: pollution: infection: a latent or incipient defect or corruption.—*v.t.* to attaint (*obs.*): to touch in tilting (*obs.*): to tint, tinge (*obs.*): to affect or imbue with anything objectionable: to contaminate: to infect: to impart a scent to.—*v.i.* to become infected or corrupted: to go bad: to weaken, wilt, wither. —*adjs.* **taint'ed;** **taint'less.**—*adv.* **taint'lessly.**—*n.* **taint'ure,** defilement.—**taint'-worm** (*Milt.*), some worm supposedly injurious to flocks.

[Partly aphetic for **attaint;** partly O.Fr. *taint* (Fr. *teint*)—L. *tinctus, -ūs—tingĕre, tinctum,* to wet, dye.]

**'taint,** *tānt,* slang or illit. contraction of **it is not.**

**T'ai-p'ing,** *ti-ping', n.* the dynasty that Hung Hsiû-ch'wan sought to found in China: a participator in his rebellion (1851-65). [Chin. *T'âi P'ing,* great peace.]

**taisch, taish,** *tish, n.* in the Scottish Highlands, an apparition or voice of one about to die: second sight. [Gael. *taibhis, taibhse,* apparition.]

**tait.** Same as **tate.**

**tait,** *tāt, n.* the long-snouted phalanger (Tarsipes). [Native Australian name.]

**taiver.** See **taver** (1, 2). **taivert.** See **taver** (2).

**taj,** *tāj, n.* a crown: a dervish's tall conical cap.— **Taj Mahal** (*mə-häl'*), the magnificent mausoleum at Agra erected by Shah Jehan for his wife Mumtāz-i-Mahal (d. 1629). [Ar. and Pers. *tāj,* crown.]

**tak,** *tak, täk,* a Scots form of **take.**

**takahe(a),** *tä'kə-hä, n.* a notornis (q.v.). [Maori.]

**take,** *tāk, v.t.* to lay hold of: to get into one's possession: to seize: to catch: to capture: to captivate: to receive or come to have willingly or by an act of one's own: to appropriate: to assume, adopt: to accept: to receive: to admit: to submerge (*Scot.*): to have normally assigned to one: to find out, come upon, surprise, detect: to swallow or inhale: to apply to oneself: to obtain: to engage, secure: to seek and receive: to have recourse to: to attend a course in: to visit: to call for, necessitate, use up: to remove: to cause to go: to subtract: to convey: to escort: to detract: to derive: to understand: to apprehend: (with *it*) to assume, suppose: to mistake: to conceive: to accept as true: to tolerate: to ascertain: to observe or measure: to ascertain something from: to execute, perform: to set down: to portray: to photograph: to charge oneself with: to asseverate: to strike: to come upon and affect: to bewitch: to blight: to deliver, give (*obs.*): to betake.—*v.i.* to have the intended effect: to be effective, to work: to please the public: to cast a spell (*Shak.*): to betake oneself, begin: to bite (as a fish): to make a capture or acquisition: to admit of being taken: to become, fall, e.g. ill (*coll.*): to freeze (*U.S., Canada*):—*pa.t.* **took;** *pa.p.* **tā'ken.** —*n.* an act of taking: a capture: quantity taken on one occasion: the filming of one scene (*cinematography*): amount of copy set up by a printer at one time.—*adj.* **tā'ken.**—*ns.* **tā'ker;** **tā'king,** action of the verb in any sense: (usu. in *pl.*) that which is taken, receipts: plight (*Spens.*): bewitchment, malignant influence (*Shak.*): agitation, perplexity (*coll.*).—*adj.* captivating: alluring: infectious, catching.—*adv.* **tā'kingly.** —*n.* **tā'kingness.**—*adj.* **tā'ky,** attractive.—**take'-down,** a humiliation; **take'-in',** a deception, fraud, or disappointment of hopes; **take'-leave,** leave-taking; **take'-off,** a burlesque mimicking: a drawback: place, act, or mode of leaving the ground for a jump, dive, or flight; **take'-over,** acquirement of control of a business by purchase of a majority of its shares.—Also *adj.*—**tā'king-off',** removal, assassination.—**take after,** to follow in resemblance; **take down,** to reduce: to lower: to go above in class: to demolish, pull down: to take to pieces: to report or write down to dictation: to escort to the dining-room: (**a peg**) to humiliate in some degree; **take effect,** to come off, succeed: to come into force; **take for,** to suppose to be, esp. wrongly; **take heed,** to be careful; **take-home pay,** pay after deduction of tax, etc.; **take in,** to enclose: to comprise: to annex: to subdue: to receive: to conduct to the dining-room: to subscribe for: to tighten: to furl: to grasp, realise: to accept as true: to cheat; **take in hand,** to undertake; **take into**

one's head, to be seized with a notion; **take in vain**, to use with unbecoming levity; **take it** (*coll.*), to endure punishment or misfortune without giving way; **take it out of**, to exact the utmost from: to exhaust the strength or energy of; **take it out on**, to vent one's ill-temper, anger, etc., on; **take me with you** (*Shak.*), let me understand what you mean; **take notice**, to observe: to show that observation is made: (with *of*) to remark upon; **take off**, to remove: to swallow: to mimic: to leave the ground for a jump or flight; **take on**, to receive aboard: to undertake: to assume: to take into employment: to grieve (*coll.*): to accept a challenge from: (of ideas, etc.) to gain acceptance; **take one up on** (something), to accept (one's challenge or offer): tö put a person's statement to the test; **take out**, to remove from within: to extract: to go out with: to obtain on application: to receive an equivalent for: to copy (*Shak.*); **take over**, to receive by transfer: to convey across: to assume control of; **take-over bid**; **take-over bidder**; **take thought** (*Shak.*), to grieve; **take to**, to betake oneself to: to adapt oneself to: to become fond of; **take to pieces**, to separate into component parts; **take to task**, to call to account, reprove; **take to wife**, to marry; **take up**, to lift, to raise: to pick up for use: to absorb: to accept: to interrupt sharply: to arrest: to adopt the practice, study, etc., of, begin to go in for: to begin to patronise, seek to advance: to resume: to settle, compound (a quarrel; *Shak.*): to reprove (*Shak.*): to cope with (*Shak.*): to buy up: to obtain on credit (*Shak.*): to take in hand: to engross, occupy or fill fully: (usu. in passive) to interest, please (with *about* or *with*; *dial.*): to borrow: to secure, fasten; **take upon oneself**, to assume: to presume: to take responsibility for: to undertake: to feign, make believe (*Shak.*); **take up with**, to begin to associate with, form a connection with. [Late O.E. *tacan* (pa.t. *tōc*), to touch, take—O.N. *taka* (pa.t. *tōk*; pa.p. *tekinn*).]

**takin**, *tä′kin*, *tä-kēn′*, *n.* a large ungulate (*Budorcas taxicolor*) akin to the goats and antelopes. [Tibetan.]

**talapoin**, *tal′ə-poin*, *n.* a Buddhist monk, esp. of Pegu: a small green W. African guenon monkey. [Port. *talapão*—Old Peguan *tala pói*, my lord.]

**tala(u)nt**. Spenserian forms of **talon**.

**talar, talaria**. See under **talus**.

**talayot**, *tä-lä′yot*, *n.* a prehistoric usually unchambered stone monument of the Balearic Islands. [Balearic Sp. for Sp. *atalaya*, an outlook—Ar. *al talā′i*, the vanguard.]

**talbot**, *töl′bət*, *n.* a broad-mouthed large-eared hound, usually white, now extinct. [Poss. from the *Talbot* family.]

**talbotype**, *töl′bə-tīp*, *n.* calotype, invented by William Henry Fox *Talbot* (1800-77).

**talc**, *talk*, *n.* a very soft, pliable, greasy, silvery-white, foliated or compact mineral, acid magnesium silicate: commercially, often muscovite mica.—*adjs.* **talck′y, talc′ose, talc′ous.**—*n.* **talc′um.**—**talc′-schist′**, a schistose rock composed essentially of talc, with accessory minerals. [Fr. *talc* or L.L. *talcum*—Ar. *talq*—Pers. *talk*.]

**tale**, *tāl*, *n.* an act of telling: a narrative, story: a false story: a mere story: (in *pl.*) things told idly or to get others into trouble: number: reckoning.—*adj.* **tale′ful**, abounding in stories.—**tale′bearer**, one who maliciously tells tales or gives information: **tale′bearing.**—Also *adj.*—**tale′-teller**, a teller of stories, narrator: a talebearer.—**be in a** (or **one**) **tale**, to be in full accord; **old wives′ tale**, a marvellous story for the credulous; **tell one′s** (or **its**) **own tale**, to speak for oneself or itself; **tell tales**, to play the informer; **tell tales out of school**, to reveal confidential matters. [O.E. *talu*, story, number; Ger. *zahl*, number.]

**talegalla**, *tal-i-gal′ə*, *n.* the brush-turkey. [Malagasy *talēva*, the purple coot, and L. *gallus*, a cock.]

**talent**, *tal′ənt*, *n.* an ancient unit of weight and of money—60 minas or 6000 drachmas, or about 38 kilograms (Aeginetan talent), 25 (Euboic), 26 (Attic), of gold or silver: hence (from the parable, Matt. xxv. 14-30) faculty: any natural or special gift: special aptitude: eminent ability short of genius: persons of special ability: disposition: (*Shak.* **tallent**) perh. wealth, abundance, or perh. golden tresses.—*adjs.* **tal′ented**, possessing mental gifts; **tal′entless.**—**talent scout**, one whose business is to discover and recruit talented people, esp. on behalf of the entertainment industry. [L. *talentum*—Gr. *talanton*, a balance, a talent.]

**talent**, an old form (*Shak.*, *Scott*, now *dial.*) of **talon**.

**tales**, *tā′lēz*, (orig. *pl.*) *n.* the filling up, from those who are present, of a deficiency in the number of jurymen.—**talesman** (*tā′lēz-mən* or *tālz′*), a bystander so chosen.—**pray a tales**, to plead that the number of jurymen be completed in this way. [From the phrase '*tālēs* de circumstantibus', such of the bystanders: *tālēs*, pl. of L. *tālis*, such.]

**Taliacotian, Tagliacotian**, *tal-yə-kō′shən*, *adj.* pertaining to the Italian surgeon Gasparo *Tagliacozzi* or *Taliacotius* (1546-99), or his rhinoplastic operation.

**talion**, *tal′i-ən*, *n.* like for like: retaliation. [L. *tāliō*, -*ōnis*, like punishment—*tālis*, such.]

**talipes**, *tal′i-pēz*, *n.* club-foot. [L. *tālus*, ankle, *pēs*, foot.]

**talipot, talipat**, *tal′i-pot*, *-pat*, *-put*, *n.* a Ceylon fan-palm (*Corypha*). [Sinh. *talapata*—Sans. *tālī*, palmyra palm, *pattra*, leaf.]

**talisman**, *tal′is-mən*, or *-iz-*, *n.* an object supposed to be indued with magical powers: an amulet, charm:—*pl.* **tal′ismans.**—*adjs.* **talismanic** (*-man′ik*), **-al.** [Ar. *tilsam*—Gr. *telesma*, payment, certificate, later completion, rite, consecrated object—*teleein*, to complete, fulfil, consecrate.]

**talk**, *tök*, *v.i.* to speak, esp. informally or idly: to converse.—*v.t.* to utter: to speak about: to speak in: to bring or render by talking.—*n.* conversation: rumour: discussion: gossip: mention of possibility or proposal: a general theme: utterance: a short informal address.—*adjs.* **talk′able**, easy to converse with: to be talked about; **talk′ative**, given to much talking.—*adv.* **talk′atively.**—*ns.* **talk′ativeness; talk′er; talk′ie** (commonly in *pl.*), a talking film, cinematograph picture accompanied by sound.—*n.* and *adj.* **talk′ing.**—**talk′-back**, a two-way radio system; **talk′ee-talk′ee, talk′y-talk′y**, a corrupt dialect: chatter: a little harangue.—Also *adj.*—**talk′ing-machine′**, a gramophone, phonograph, or the like; **talk′ing-point**, a matter of or for talk; **talk′ing-to**, a reproof; **talk′-you-down′**, an apparatus by means of which instructions are given to the pilot of an aircraft to help him to land.—**talk against time**, to keep on talking merely to fill up time, as often in parliament; **talk at**, to address remarks to indirectly; to talk to incessantly, without waiting for a response. **talk big**, to talk boastfully; **talk down**, to argue down: to talk as to inferiors in intellect or education: to bring (an aircraft) to a landing by radioed instructions from the ground; **talk-down system**; **talking of**, apropos of, now that mention has been made of; **talk into**, to persuade; **talk out**, to defeat (a parliamentary bill or motion) by going on speaking until it is too late to vote on it; **talk over**, to persuade, convince: to discuss, consider together; **talk round**, to talk of all sorts of related matters without coming to the point: to bring to one's way of thinking by persuasive talk; **talk to**, to address: to rebuke:

talk up, to speak boldly: to praise or boost. [M.E. *talken*, freq. of tell.]

tall, *töl*, *adj*. doughty, stout (*obs*.): high in stature: long, esp. in a vertical direction: lofty: great, remarkable: grandiloquent: hardly to be believed.—*n*. tall′ness.—tall′boy, a long narrow top for a smoky chimney: a high chest of drawers, one portion superimposed on another or on a dressing-table: a glass with a long stem; tall copy, a book with ample margins above and below; tall hat, a top hat; tall men, loaded dice; tall order (see order).—a tall man of his hands, a deft worker: a sturdy fighter. [App. O.E. *getæl*, prompt.]

tallage, *tal′ij*, *n*. a tax levied by the Norman and Angevin kings on their demesne lands and towns, or by a feudal lord on his tenants (*hist*.): an aid, toll, or rate.—*v.t.* to lay an impost upon.—*adj*. tall′iable, subject to tallage.—*v.t.* tall′iate, to lay a tallage upon. [O.Fr. *taillage*—*tailler*, to cut, to tax.]

tallat, tallet, tallot, *tal′ət*, (*W. of England*) *n*. a loft. [W. *taflod*—L.L. *tabulāta*, flooring.]

tallith, *tal′ith*, *n*. the Jewish prayer shawl. [Heb. *tallīth*.]

tall-oil, *täl′*, by-product of chemical wood-pulp, used in manufacture of paints, linoleums, soaps, etc. [Sw. *tallolja*—*tall*, pine and *olja*, oil.]

tallow, *tal′ō*, *n*. fat, grease: rendered fat, esp. of ox and sheep: any coarse, hard fat.—*adj*. of, for, or like tallow.—*v.t.* to grease with tallow: to produce tallow.—*adjs*. tall′owish; tall′owy.—tall′ow-can′dle, a candle made of tallow; tall′ow-catch′ (*Shak*.), perh. a receptacle for tallow, or a lump (keech) of tallow; tall′ow-chand′ler, a dealer in tallow candles, etc.: tall′ow-dip′, a candle made by dipping a wick in tallow; tall′ow-face (*Shak*.), a person with a pasty yellow face.—*adj*. tall′ow-faced.—tall′ow-tree, any of various trees (as Sapium, Pentadesma, Aleurites) yielding a thick oil or vegetable tallow, or a substance capable of making candles. [M.E. *talgh*; cf. Ger. *talg*.]

tally, *tal′i*, *n*. a stick notched to mark numbers or keep accounts: half of such a stick split across the notches, serving as receipt or record: anything that answers to a counterpart: a score or account, esp. one kept by notches or marks: credit, tick: a mark made in scoring an account: a distinguishing mark: a label: a plant-label: a tag: a number taken as a unit in computation: a full number: (*pl.* tall′ies).—*adv*. in concubinage.—*v.t.* to notch or mark as a tally: count by tally: reckon: match, adapt.—*v.i.* to correspond, match, agree: deal on credit:—*pr.p.* tall′ying; *pa.t.* and *pa.p.* tall′ied.—tally clerk, a checker of ship's cargoes against a list; tall′y-man, one who keeps a tallyshop: a salesman for a tallyshop: one who lives with a woman without marriage:—*fem*. tall′y-wo′man; tall′yshop, shop where goods are sold to be paid by instalments, the seller having one account-book which tallies with the buyer's; tall′y-sys′tem, -trade, mode of dealing on credit for payment by instalments.—live tally, to cohabit without marriage. [A.Fr. *tallie*—L. *tālea*, a stick.]

tally-ho, *tal-i-hō′*, *interj*. the huntsman's cry betokening that a fox has been sighted.—*n*. cry of tally-ho: a four-in-hand coach.—*v.t.* to greet with tally-ho.—*v.i.* to call tally-ho. [Cf. Fr. *taïaut*.]

talma, *tal′mə*, *n*. a loose cloak or cape. [From F. J. *Talma*, the actor (1763-1826).]

Talmud, *tal′mood*, -mud, *n*. the fundamental code of Jewish civil and canon law, the *Mishna* and the *Gemara*.—*adjs*. Talmud′ic, -al.—*n*. Tal′mudist, one learned in the Talmud.—*adj*. Talmudist′ic. [Heb. *talmūd*, instruction—*lāmad*, to learn.]

talon, *tal′ən*, *n*. a hooked claw or finger: an ogee moulding: cards remaining after the deal, the stock.—*adj*. tal′oned. [Fr. *talon*—L.L. *tālō, -ōnis*—L. *tālus*, the heel.]

Talpa, *tal′pə*, *n*. the mole genus of the family Tal′pidae: (without *cap.*) an encysted tumour on the head, a wen. [L., a mole.]

taluk, *tä-look′*, *n*. a tract of proprietary land: a subdivision of a district, a collectorate.—*n*. taluk′dar, holder of a taluk. [Hind. *ta′alluq*, estate.]

talus, *tä′ləs*, *n*. the ankle-bone or astragalus: a slope (*arch*.): the sloping part of a work (*fort*.): a scree (*geol*.).—*n*. tä′lar, a robe reaching the ankles.—*n.pl.* talaria (*tə-lā′ri-ə*), winged sandals, or wings on the ankles, as of Hermes. [L. *tālus*, ankle.]

talweg. Same as thalweg.

tam. See Tam o' Shanter.

tamale, *tä-mäl′i*, *n*. a highly seasoned Mexican dish of crushed maize, with meat.—Also (more correctly) tamal′. [Sp. *tamal* (pl. *tamales*),—Nahuatl *tamalli*.]

tamandua, *tä-män′dū-ä*, -dwä′, *n*. a S. American ant-eater smaller than the ant-bear.—*n*. tamanoir (*tä-mä-nwär′*), the great ant-bear. [Port. *tamanduá*—Sp. *tamándoa*—Tupi *tamanduá*.]

tamanu, *täm′ä-nōō*, *n*. a lofty gamboge tree of the East Indies and Pacific Islands, its trunk yielding tacamahac. [E. Ind.]

tamara, *tam′ə-rə*, *n*. a mixture of cinnamon, cloves, coriander, etc.

tamarack, *tam′ə-rak*, the American or black larch. [Amer. Ind.]

tamarin, *tam′ə-rin*, *n*. a small S. American squirrel-monkey (Midas). [Fr., from Carib.]

tamarind, *tam′ə-rind*, *n*. a large tropical Caesalpiniaceous tree (*Tamarindus indica*): its pod, filled with a pleasant, acidulous, sweet, reddish-black pulp. [Ar. *tamr-Hindī*, date of India.]

tamarisk, *tam′ər-isk*, *n*. a genus (Tam′arix) giving name to a family (Tamaricä′ceae) of xerophytic plants, one species a naturalised shrub of S. English seashores. [L. *tamariscus, tamarix*.]

tamasha, *tä-mä′shä*, (*Ind*.) *n*. an entertainment, show: fuss. [Ar. and Pers. *tamāshā*.]

tamber, *tam′bər*, *n*. Anglicised form of timbre.

tambour, *tam′bōōr*, *n*. a drum: the bass drum: a frame for embroidery: a rich gold and silver embroidery; embroidery done on a tambour: a cylindrical stone: the drum of a recording instrument: a vestibule in a church porch, etc.: palisading to defend a gate, etc.: a flexible top (as of a desk) or front (as of a cabinet) made of narrow strips of wood fixed closely together on canvas, the whole sliding in grooves.—*v.t.* to embroider on a tambour.—*v.i.* to do tambourwork.—*ns*. tambour′een, an Eastern instrument like a guitar; tambourin (*tä-bōō-rē*), a Provençal dance or dance-tune with drone bass; tambourine (*tam-bə-rēn′*), a shallow single-headed drum with jingles, played on with the hand—(*Spens*.) tam′-burin. [Fr. *tambour*, drum; Pers. *tanbūr*, Ar. *tunbūr*, tamboura.]

tame, *tām*, *adj*. having lost native wildness and shyness: cultivated: domesticated: gentle: spiritless: without vigour: dull, flat, uninspiring: wonted, accustomed (*Shak*.).—*v.t.* to reduce to a domestic state: to make gentle: to subdue: to reclaim.—*v.i.* to become tame.—*n*. tamabil′ity, tameabil′ity.—*adjs*. tam′able, tame′able; tame′-less.—*n*. tame′lessness.—*adv*. tame′ly.—*ns*. tame′ness; ta′mer; tam′ing. [O.E. *tam*; Ger. *zahm*; Gr. *damaein*, L. *domāre*, to tame.]

Tamil, *tam′il*, *n*. a Dravidian language of southeast India and north, east, and central Ceylon: one of the people speaking it.—*adjs*. Tam′il, Tamil′ian, Tamil′ic, Tamūl′ic.

tamin, tamine, *tam′in*, *n*. a thin worsted stuff, highly glazed. [Fr. *étamine*; cf. stammel.]

tamis, *tam′is*, *n*. cloth sieve.—*n*. tamise (*tä-mēz′*), name for various thin woollen fabrics. [Fr.]

Neutral vowels in unaccented syllables: *el′ə-mənt*; for certain sounds in foreign words, see p. viii

**Tammany,** *tam'ə-ni, n.* a society notorious for its corrupt influence in New York city politics.— Also *adj.*—**Tammany Hall,** its building, leased to the Democratic party of New York. [From an Indian chief, *Tammanend,* who is said to have signed the treaty with Penn.]

**Tammie Norie,** *tam'i nō'ri,* (*Scot.*) *n.* the puffin.

**Tammuz,** *tam'ōōz, -uz, n.* a Babylonian sun-god, answering to Adonis: the tenth month of the Jewish civil year, fourth of the ecclesiastical.

**tammy,** *tam'i, n.* à strainer: a glazed woollen or mixed stuff: a Tam o' Shanter. [App. same as **tamis,** or perh. **tamin.**]

**Tam o' Shanter,** *tam-ō-shan'tər, n.* the hero of Burns's poem so entitled: a cap with broad circular flat top—*coll.* **tam, tamm'y.**

**tamp,** *tamp, v.t.* to stop up (a shot hole, with earth, etc., after the explosive has been introduced: to ram down so as to consolidate (as ballast on a railway track): to pack round.—*ns.* **tamp'er; tam'ping,** the act of filling up a hole for blasting: the material used; **tamp'ion, tomp'ion,** a plug: a protective plug placed in the muzzle of a gun when not in use; **tamp'on,** a plug of cotton or other material inserted into a wound or orifice to control haemorrhage, etc.: an inking-pad: a two-headed drumstick.—*v.t.* to plug.—*n.* **tampon-ade',** surgical use of a tampon. [Fr. *tampon.*]

**tamper,** *tam'pər, v.t.* (*obs.*) to temper (as clay).— *v.i.* (usu. with *with*) to work, machinate, practise: to have secret or corrupt dealings: to interfere unwarrantably or vitiatingly: to meddle.—*ns.* **tam'perer; tam'pering.** [A by-form of **temper.**]

**Tampico,** *tam-pē'kō, n.* a port in Mexico.— **Tampico fibre,** ixtle.

**tam-tam,** *tum'-tum, tam'-tam, n.* a gong, esp. one used in an orchestra: esp. formerly, a tom-tom. [**tom-tom.**]

**tan,** *tan, n.* oak bark or other material used for tanning: spent bark: a tawny brown colour.— *adj.* tawny.—*v.t.* to convert into leather by steeping in vegetable solutions containing tannin, or mineral salts, or synthesised chemicals: to treat with tan or tannin: to make brown or tawny: to beat (*coll.*).—*v.i.* to become tanned:—*pr.p.* **tann'ing;** *pa.t.* and *pa.p.* **tanned.** —*n.* **tan'ling** (*Shak.*), one tanned by the sun.— *adj.* **tann'able.**—*ns.* **tann'age,** tanning: that which is tanned; **tann'ate,** a salt of tannic acid.— *adj.* **tanned.**—*ns.* **tann'er; tann'ery,** a place for tanning.—*adj.* **tann'ic** (tannic acid, tannin).—*ns.* **tann'in,** a colourless amorphous substance got from gall-nuts, sumach, and many barks, used in tanning and dyeing; **tann'ing,** the art or act of tanning or converting skins and hides into leather.—Also *adj.*—**tan'-balls,** tanner's spent bark pressed into lumps for fuel; **tan'-bark,** any bark good for tanning; **tan'-bed** (*hort.*), a bark bed.—*adj.* **tan'-coloured.**—**tan'-liq'uor, -ooze, -pickle,** an aqueous extract of tan-bark; **tan'-pit, -vat,** a vat in which hides are steeped with tan; **tan'-ride,** a riding track laid with tan; **tan'yard,** a tannery, or a part of it.—**flowers of tan** (see **flower**). [O.E. *tannian* (found in pa.p. *getanned*), *tannere,* tanner; also O.Fr. *tan*— Bret. *tann,* oak.]

**tan,** *tan,* (*trig.*) *n.* a conventional abbrev. for **tangent.**

**tana, tanna(h), thana(h), thanna(h),** *tä'nə, n.* a military or police station in India.—*n.* **t(h)a'na-dar,** its head. [Hind. *thānā, thāna.*]

**tana,** *tä'nə, n.* a Sumatran and Bornean species of tree-shrew. [Malay (*tūpai*) *tāna,* ground (squirrel).]

**tanager,** *tan'ə-jər, n.* any bird of the S. American family **Tanagridae** (-*ag'*), closely allied to the finches.—*n.* **Tan'agra,** the name-giving genus.— *adj.* **tan'agrine.** [Tupí *tangará.*]

**Tanagra,** *tan'ə-grə, n.* a town of ancient Boeotia: (without *cap*) a terracotta figurine made there.

**tanaiste,** *tön'ish-tä, n.* the deputy prime minister of the Republic of Ireland. [Ir., second, next, deputy; cf. **tanist.**]

**tandem,** *tan'dəm, adv.* in the position of horses harnessed singly one before the other.—*n.* a team (usu. two) so harnessed: a vehicle with such a team: a bicycle, tricycle, etc., for two, one before the other.—Also *adj.*—*adv.* **tan'dem-wise.** [Punning application of L. *tandem,* at length.]

**tane, ta'ne,** obs. spellings (*Spens., Shak.,* etc.) of **ta'en** (**taken**).

**tane,** *tän,* (*Scot.*) one (**the tane,** for *that ane,* the one). [See **tae, tone** (2), **tother.**]

**tang,** *tang, n.* coarse seaweed. [Cf. Norw. and Dan. *tang.*]

**tang,** *tang, n.* a ringing sound: a twang.—*v.t.* to cause to ring: to utter ringingly (*Shak.*).—*v.i.* to ring. [Imit.; influenced by next word.]

**tang,** *tang, n.* a projecting piece or shank: a point, sting, spike: part of a tool that goes into the haft: a prong: a barb: a sea-surgeon: biting, characteristic, or extraneous flavour, after-taste, or smell: a smack, tinge: pungency. —*adj.* **tanged** (*tangd*), with a tang: barbed. [O.N. *tange,* point, tang.]

**tangelo,** *tan'ji-lō, n.* a hybrid between *Tang*erine orange and pom*elo.* [Portmanteau word.]

**tangent,** *tan'jənt, adj.* touching without intersecting.—*n.* a line that touches a curve: the limiting case of a secant when the two points of intersection coincide: (as a function of an angle) the ratio of the side of a right-angled triangle opposite the given angle to the side opposite the other acute angle (*trig.*). (The tangent of an obtuse angle is equal numerically to that of its supplement, but has the negative sign.)—*abbrev.* **tan:** the striking-pin of a clavichord.—*n.* **tan'-gency** (-*jən-si*), fact of being tangent: a contact or touching.—*adj.* **tangential** (-*jen'shal*), of a tangent: in the direction of a tangent.—*n.* **tangentiality** (*tan-jen-shi-al'i-ti*).—*adv.* **tangen'tially,** in the direction of a tangent.—**at a tangent,** in the direction of the tangent: in continuation in the momentary direction instead of following the general course. [L. *tangēns, -entis,* pr.p. of *tangĕre,* to touch.]

**Tangerine,** *tan'jə-rēn,* or -*rēn', adj.* of *Tangier* on the Morocco coast.—*n.* a native of Tangier: **tangerine,** a mandarin or *Tangerine* orange—a small, flattish, loose-skinned variety.

**tanghin,** *tang'gin, n.* a Madagascar poison formerly used for the judicial ordeal: the apocynaceous tree yielding it.—*n.* **tangh'inin,** its active principle. [Malagasy *tangèna.*]

**tangible,** *tan'ji-bl, adj.* perceptible by the touch: capable of being possessed or realised: material, corporeal.—*ns.* **tangibil'ity; tan'gibleness.**—*adv.* **tan'gibly.** [L. *tangibilis*—*tangĕre,* to touch.]

**tangie,** *tang'i, n.* an Orcadian water-spirit, appearing as a seahorse, or man covered with seaweed.

**tangle,** *tang'gl, v.t.* to form into, involve in, or cover with, a confused interwoven mass: to entangle: to hamper or trap (*coll.*).—*v.i.* to become tangled: to become involved in conflict or argument (with) (*coll.*): (with *with*) to embrace (*coll.*).—*n.* a tangled mass or condition: a perplexity, complication: a naturalist's dredge with streamers: involved relations, conflict, argument.—*adj.* **tang'led.**—*ns.* **tang'lement; tang'ler.** —*adj.* **tang'lesome.**—*n.* and *adj.* **tang'ling.**—*adv.* **tang'lingly.**—*adj.* **tang'ly,** tangled: inclined to tangle.—**tang'lefoot** (*U.S.*), whisky, intoxicating liquor. [App. from earlier *tagle*; see **taigle.**]

**tangle,** *tang'gl, n.* coarse seaweed, esp. the edible Laminaria.—*adj.* **tang'ly.** [App. conn. with O.N. *thöngull,* Laminaria stalk—*thang,* bladder-wrack.]

**tangle,** *tang'gl,* (*Scot.*) *n.* any tall and limp person

or thing: an icicle.—*adj.* long and limp.—*adj.*
**tang'ly**. [Origin obscure.]

**tango**, *tang'gō, n.* a dance or dance-tune in 4-4 time, of Argentine Negro origin with Parisian developments.—*v.i.* to dance the tango:—*pa.t.* and *pa.p.* **tang'oed**.—*n.* **tang'oist** [Sp., a S. American Negro festival or dance.]

**tangram**, *tan'gram, n.* a Chinese toy, a square cut into seven pieces that will fit in various forms. [Origin obscure.]

**tangun**, *tang'gun, n.* the Tibetan piebald pony. [Hindi *tāghan*—Tibetan *rtanān.*]

**tanh**, *tansh, than,* a conventional abbreviation for *hyperbolic tangent.*

**tanist**, *tan'ist, n.* a Celtic chief's heir elect.—*n.* **tan'istry**, the system of succession by a previously elected member of the family. [Ir. and Gael. *tànaiste*—*tánaise*, second.]

**tank**, *tangk, n.* a pool, pond, reservoir (*India*): a pond (*U.S.*): a large basin or cistern: a reservoir of water, oil, etc.: an armoured, enclosed, armed vehicle moving on caterpillar wheels.—*v.t.* to store in a tank: to plunge into a tank.—*v.i.* to drink heavily (with *up*): to refuel (often with *up*; *coll.*).—*n.* **tank'age**, storing in tanks: charge for such storage: the capacity of a tank or tanks: residue from tanks.—*adj.* **tanked** (*slang*), drunk. —*ns.* **tank'er**, a ship or heavy vehicle that carries liquids, esp. oil, in bulk: an aircraft that refuels others; **tank'ful:**— *pl.* **tank'fuls. — tank'-car**, **-wag'on**, a railway wagon for carrying oil or other liquid in a large tank; **tank'-engine**, a locomotive that carries its water and coal in itself (without a tender); **tank'-farming**, hydroponics. [Port. *tanque*—L. *stagnum*, a pool.]

**tanka**, *tang'ka, n.* the boat population of Canton, inhabiting **tank'a-boats.**—Also **tan'kia**. [Chin.]

**tanka**, *tang'ka, n.* a Japanese poem of five lines, the first and third lines having five syllables and the others seven. [Jap.]

**tankard**, *tangk'ərd, n.* a large mug-like vessel.— **cool tankard** (see **cool**). [Cf. M. Du. *tanckaert.*]

**tanned, tanner, tannic, tannin, tanning.** See under **tan**.

**tanner**, *tan'ər*, (*slang*) *n.* a sixpence.

**Tannoy**, *tan'oi, n.* a sound-reproducing and amplifying system. [Proprietary name.]

**tanrec**. See **tenrec**.

**tansy**, *tan'zi, n.* a bitter, aromatic roadside composite plant (*Tanacetum vulgare*) with small heads of tubular yellow flowers: extended to other plants, as ragwort, silver-weed, yarrow: a pudding or cake flavoured with tansy, eaten at Easter.—like a tansy, exactly right. [O.Fr. *tanasie*, through L.L. from Gr. *athanasiā*, immortality.]

**Tantalus**, *tan'tə-ləs, n.* a son of Zeus punished in Tartarus for revealing secrets of the gods by having to stand in water that ebbed when he would drink, overhung by grapes that drew back when he reached for them: the wood-ibis genus: (without *cap.*) a case in which decanters are visible but locked up.—*n.* **tan'talate**, a salt of tantalic acid.—*adjs.* **Tantalean** (-*tā'*), **Tanta'lian**, **Tantalic** (-*tal'ik*), of Tantalus; **tantal'ic**, of tantalum (**tantalic acid**, HTaO₃).—*n.* **tantalisā'**-**tion**.—*v.t.* **tan'talise, -ize**, to torment by presenting something to excite desire but keeping it out of reach: torture into unnatural form (*obs.*).—*n.* **tan'taliser**.—*n.* and *adj.* **tan'talising**.—*adv.* **tan'-talisingly**.—*ns.* **tan'talism**, the punishment of Tantalus: a tormenting; **tan'talite** (*min.*), a black mineral, iron tantalate; **tan'talum**, a metallic element (Ta; at. numb. 73) so named from its inability to absorb water.—**tan'talum-lamp**, an electric lamp with tantalum filament; **Tan'talus-cup**, a philosophical toy, with a siphon within the figure of a man whose chin is on a level with its bend.

**tantamount**, *tan'tə-mownt, adj.* amounting to as

much or to the same: equivalent: equal in value or meaning. [A.Fr. *tant amunter*, to amount to as much.]

**tantara**, *tan-tä'rä, n.* a blast of trumpet or horn.— Also **tantara'ra**. [Imit.]

**tanti**, *tan'ti, tan'tē*, (L.) worth while.

**tantivy**, *tan-tiv'i, adv.* at full gallop: headlong.— *n.* a hunting cry: a rapid rush: a Tory High Churchman (*hist.*).—*adj.* headlong: High Church Tory (*hist.*).—*interj.* expressive of galloping or (later) expressive of the sound of the hunting-horn. [Imit.]

**tant mieux**, *tā-myø*, (Fr.) so much the better.

**tanto**, *tan'tō*, (L.) so much.

**tantony**. See **Anthony**.

**tanto uberior**, *tan'tō ū-be'ri-ar, ōō-be'ri-or*, (L.) so much the richer.

**tant pis**, *tä pē*, (Fr.) so much the worse.

**Tantra**, *tun'trə, n.* any of a number of Hindu writings giving religious teaching and ritual instructions (including the use of incantations, diagrams, etc.): the teaching of the Tantras.— *adj.* **Tan'tric.**—*ns.* **Tan'trism**, the teaching of the Tantras; **Tan'trist**. [Sans. *tantra*, thread, fundamental doctrine.]

**tantrum**, *tan'trəm, n.* a capricious fit of ill-temper without adequate cause. [Origin unknown.]

**Tantum ergo**, *tan'təm ûr'gō*, L. *tan'tōōm er'gō*, the fifth stanza of the hymn 'Pange, lingua, gloriosi corporis mysterium', written for the office of the Festival of Corpus Christi, which St Thomas Aquinas drew up in 1263. [From its opening words.]

**taoiseach**, *tē'shohh, n.* the prime minister of the Republic of Ireland. [Ir., chief, leader.]

**Tâoism**, *tä'ō-izm*, or *tow'izm, n.* the religious system founded by the Chinese philosopher Lâo-tsze (b. 604 B.C.), set forth in the *Tâo Teh King.*— *n.* **Tâ'ōist**.—*adj.* **Tâoist'ic**.

**tap**, *tap, n.* a gentle knock or its sound: a shoe sole (*dial.*): a protective piece on a shoe heel: (in *pl.*) a signal for putting lights out (*U.S. mil.*). —*v.t.* and *v.i.* to knock gently.—*v.t.* to furnish or repair with a tap:—*pr.p.* **tapp'ing;** *pa.t.* and *pa.p.* **tapped**.—*n.* **tapp'er**, one who taps: one who soles and heels: an instrument or part that taps: a decoherer.—*n.* and *adj.* **tapp'ing.**—**tap'-dancer**; **tap'-dancing**, dancing with tapping of the feet. [O.Fr. *taper.*]

**tap**, *tap, n.* a peg or stopper: a hole or short pipe with a valve for running off a fluid: a taproom: any particular liquor drawn through a tap: a screw for cutting an internal thread: a tap-root. —*v.t.* to pierce, so as to let out fluid: to broach: to draw off: to draw upon, esp. for the first time (*fig.*): secretly to attach a receiver to a telephone wire in order to overhear a conversation: to get money from (*slang*): to furnish with a tap, or with a screw-thread.—*v.i.* to act as a tapster: —*pr.p.* **tapp'ing;** *pa.t.* and *pa.p.* **tapped**.—*ns.* **tapp'er**, one who taps trees, etc.: a milking-machine; **tapp'ing**, the act or art of drawing out or running off a fluid: an operation for removal of liquid from the body; **tap'ster**, one who draws liquor, a barman.—**tap'-bolt**, a screwed-in bolt; **tap'-cin'der**, slag produced during puddling; **tap'-dress'ing**, well-dressing; **tap'-house**, a tavern; **tap'lash**, poor stale swipes; **tap'room**, a room where beer is served from the tap or cask; **tap'root**, a strong main root striking down vertically; **tap'-wa'ter**, water from a household tap.—**on tap**, kept in cask—opp. to *bottled*: ready to be drawn upon. [O.E. *tæppa*, tap, *tæppestre*, (female) tapster; Du. *tap*, Ger. *zapfen*, tap.]

**tap**, *tap, n.* a Scots form of **top**.—*adj.* **tapp'it**, crested.—**tapp'it-hen'**, a crested hen: a liquor vessel of capacity variously stated at 1, 3, or 6 imperial quarts; **taps'man**, a servant with principal charge: chief of a company of drovers.—

take one's tap in one's lap (*Scot.*), to bundle up (one's tow for the distaff) and go home.

tap, *tap*, *n.* an Indian malarial fever. [Pers.]

tapa, tappa, *tä'pə*, *n.* paper-mulberry bark. [Polynesian generally.]

tapaculo, *tä-pä-kōō'lō*, tapacolo, *-kō'*, *n.* a small S. American bird with tilted tail. [Sp. *tapaculo—tapa*, cover (imper.), *culo*, posterior.]

tapadera, *tä-pä-dä'ra*, tapadero, *-rō*, *n.* the guard in front of a Mexican stirrup. [Sp., lid, cover—*tapar*, to cover.]

tape, *tāp*, *n.* material woven in narrow bands: a strip of such material, used for tying up, connecting, etc.: a ribbon of paper printed by a recording instrument, as in telegraphy: a flexible band that guides the sheets (*print.*): a tape-measure: a tape-recording: liquor (*slang*).—*v.t.* to furnish, fasten, bind, measure with a tape: to get the range or measure of: to deal out, or use, sparingly (*Scot.*): to tape-record.—*adjs.* tape'less; tā'pen, made of tape.—*ns.* tā'per, one who works with tapes; tā'pist, an official formalist.—tape'-grass, Vallisneria; tape'line, -meas'ure, a flexible measuring strip of tape, steel, or other material; tape'-machine, a telegraphic instrument by which messages received are automatically printed on a tape.—*v.t.* tape'-record', to record sound using a tape recorder.—tape'-recorder, an instrument for recording sound on magnetic tape and subsequently reproducing it; tape'-recording, a magnetic tape on which sound has been recorded.—*adj.* tape'-tied, tied up with tape: bound with, or by, red tape (see red).—tape'worm, a ribbon-shaped segmented parasitic worm, any cestode, but esp. of Taenia or kindred genus.—breast the tape, in foot-racing, to touch with the breast the line stretched across the track at the winning-post; have (something or someone) taped, to have a thorough understanding of; magnetic tape (see magnet); red tape (see red). [O.E. *tæppe*, tape, fillet.]

taper, *tā'pər*, *n.* a wax-candle (*obs.*): a long, thin waxed wick or spill: a feeble light: lengthwise diminution in width: gradual leaving off.—*adj.* tapering.—*v.i.* to become gradually smaller towards one end.—*v.t.* to make to taper.—*adj.* ta'pered, tapering: lighted by tapers.—*n.* ta'perer, one who bears a taper.—*n.* and *adj.* ta'pering.—*adv.* ta'peringly.—*n.* ta'perness.—*adv.* ta'perwise. [O.E. *tapor*.]

tapestry, *tap'is-tri*, *n.* an ornamental textile used for the covering of walls and furniture, and for curtains, made by passing coloured threads among fixed warp threads: a machine-made imitation of this.—*adj.* of tapestry (*Milt.* tap'stry).—*v.t.* to hang with tapestry: to work or represent in tapestry.—*adj.* tap'estried. [Fr. *tapisserie—tapis*, a carpet—L.L. *tapĕtium*—Gr. *tapētion*, dim. of *tapēs*, *-ētos*, prob. of Iranian origin.]

tapet, *tap'it*, (*Spens.*) *n.* a piece of tapestry. [L. *tapēte*, perh. through O.E. *tæppet*.]

tapeti, *tap'ə-ti*, *n.* the Brazilian rabbit. [Tupí.]

tapetum, *tə-pē'təm*, *n.* a layer of cells surrounding spore mother-cells (*bot.*): the pigmentary layer of the retina (*zool.*):—*pl.* tape'ta.—*adj.* tape'tal. [L. *tapētum*—Gr. *tapēs*, *-ētos*, carpet.]

taphephobia, tapho-, *taf-ə-fō'bi-ə*, *n.* morbid fear of being buried alive. [Gr. *taphē*, burial, *taphos*, grave, *phobos*, fear.]

tapioca, *tap-i-ō'kə*, *n.* a farinaceous substance got by heating cassava: extended to a kind of sago and a preparation of potato starch: a pudding made from tapioca.—pearl tapioca (see pearl). [Tupí-Guaraní *tipyoca*.]

tapir, *tā'pər*, *n.* a large odd-toed ungulate with short flexible proboscis, of which several species are found in S. America, Malacca, etc. [Tupí *tapira*.]

tapis, *ta'pē*, also *tap'is*, (*obs.*) *n.* a covering,

hanging, etc., of tapestry or the like.—on the tapis, on the table: under consideration. [Fr.]

tapotement, *tä-pōt-mä*, *tä-pōt'mənt*, *n.* percussion in massage. [Fr.]

tappet, *tap'it*, *n.* a projection that transmits motion from one part of a machine to another by tapping.—tapp'et-loom, -mō'tion, -ring, -rod, etc. [tap (1).]

tappice, *tap'is*, *v.i.* to lie low.—*v.t.* to hide. [Fr. *tapir*, *tapiss-*.]

tappit, tappit-hen, tapsman. See tap (3).

tapsalteerie, *tap-sl-tē'ri*, tapsieteerie, *tap-sä-*. Scots forms of topsyturvy.

tapstry, *tap'stri* (*Milt.*). Same as tapestry.

tapu, *tä'pōō*. See taboo.

tar (*Shak.* tarre), *tär*, *v.t.* to set on, incite to fight. [Conn. with O.E. *tergan*, to worry.]

tar, *tär*, *n.* a dark, viscous mixture got by destructive distillation of wood, coal, peat, etc.: a natural bituminous substance of like appearance (*mineral tar*): a sailor (perh. for tarpaulin).—*v.t.* to smear, coat, treat, with tar:—*pr.p.* tarr'ing; *pa.t.* and *pa.p.* tarred.—*n.* tarriness (*tär'i-nis*).—*n.* and *adj.* tarr'ing.—*adj.* tarr'y (*tär'i*), of, like, covered or soiled with, tar.—tar'-box, a shepherd's box for tar as salve for sheep: shepherd; tar'-brush, a brush for applying tar; tar'-heel, North Carolinian; tar-macad'am (also tar'mac, proprietary in *U.S.*), a road surfacing of broken stone covered or mixed with tar: the runways of an aerodrome; tarr'y-breeks (*Scot.*), a sailor. —*adj.* tarr'y-fingered, thievish.—tar'-spot, a black spot of Rhytisma; tar'-wa'ter, a cold infusion of tar in water, once reputed as a medicine; tar'weed, a name for various heavy-scented American composites.—tar and feather, to smear with tar and then cover with feathers; tarred with the same brush, or stick, with the same defects; touch of the tar-brush, (*derog.*) a certain amount of e.g. Negro blood resulting in darkish skin. [O.E. *teru*, *teoro*; Ger. (from L.G.) and Du. *teer*.]

tara, *tä'ra*, *n.* a variety of bracken with edible rhizome.—Also ta'ra-fern.

taradiddle. See tarradiddle.

tarand, *tar'ənd*, (*obs.*) *n.* a northern beast fabled to change colour like the chameleon: a reindeer. [Gr. *tarand(r)os*, a reindeer, or (prob.) elk.]

tarantara. See taratantara.

tarantas(s), *tä-rän-täs'*, *n.* a four-wheeled Russian vehicle mounted on poles. [Russ. *tarantas*.]

tarantella, *tar'ən-tel'a*, *n.* a lively Neapolitan dance—in triplets for one couple—thought a remedy for tarantism: a tune for it.—*ns.* tar'antism, an epidemic dancing mania; tarantūla (*-an'*), a large venomous South European wolf-spider (Lycosa), long supposed to cause tarantism in South Italy: in America applied to large venomous spiders of the bird-catching family (Aviculariidae): in Africa, a biting but not venomous solpugid: in Australia applied to several large harmless laterigrade spiders: (*cap.*) a genus of pedipalps.—tarantula juice (*U.S.*), bad whisky. [It. *tarantella*, *tarantola*—Gr. *Taras*, *-antos*, Tarentum, Taranto.]

taratantara, *tär-ä-tan'tä-rä*, or *-tan-tä'rä*, *n.* the sound of a trumpet.—Also *interj.*, *adj.*, *adv.*, *v.t.*, and *v.i.*—Also taran'tara. [Imit.]

Taraxacum, *tä-raks'ə-kəm*, *n.* the dandelion genus: (without *cap.*) its root and rootstock, a tonic laxative. [App. from Ar. *tarakhshaqōq*— Pers. *talkh chakōk*, assimilated to Gr. *taraxis*, disturbance.]

tarboosh, tarboush, tarbush, *tär-bōōsh'*, *n.* a fez. [Ar. *tarbūsh*.]

tarcel. See tercel.

Tardenoisian, *tär-di-noi'zi-ən*, (*archaeol.*) *adj.* belonging to a stage of culture represented by finds at *Tardenois*, Aisne, France, transitional between Palaeolithic and Neolithic.

tardigrade, *tär'di-grād, adj.* slow-paced.—*n.* a member of the Tardigrada.—*n.pl.* Tardigra'da, formerly the sloths: now, a class of arthropods, the bear-animalcules. [L. *tardus*, slow, *gradī*, to step.]

tardy, *tär'di, adj.* slow: sluggish: behindhand: too long delayed: late: caught at fault (*obs.*).—*v.t.* (*Shak.*) to retard.—*adv.* tar'dily.—*n.* tar'diness.—*adjs.* tar'dive (-*div*), late in development; tar'dy-gait'ed, slow-paced. [Fr. *tardif—tard—*L. *tardus*, slow.]

tare, *tär, n.* a vetch of various kinds, esp. of the lentil-like group: a weed, prob. darnel (*B.*). [Origin obscure.]

tare, *tär, n.* the weight of a vessel, wrapping, or container, which subtracted from the gross weight gives the net weight.—*v.t.* to ascertain or allow for the tare of. [Fr.,—Sp. *tara—*Ar. *tarhah*, thrown away.]

tare, *tär, arch. pa.t.* of tear.

targe, *tärj, n.* a shield, esp. a light shield. [O.Fr. *targe—*O.N. *targe*, shield.]

targe, *tärj*, (*Scot.*) *v.t.* to cross-examine: to supervise strictly: to reprimand: to thrash. [Origin unknown.]

target, *tär'git, n.* a small buckler or round shield: a shield-like or other mark to shoot at for practice or competition: a surface on which electrons impinge: an object aimed at (also *fig.*): a butt: a result to be aimed at: a shooting score: a neck and breast of lamb: a sight on a levelling staff: an American railway signal.—*adj.* tar'geted, provided with a shield.—*n.* targeteer', one armed with a shield, a peltast.—target area, area containing a target. [O.Fr. *targuete*; cf. targe (1).]

Targum, *tär-gōōm', tär'gəm, n.* any Aramaic version or paraphrase of the Old Testament:—*pl.* Targums.—*adj.* Targumic (*tär-gōōm'ik*, -*güm'*, -*gum'*).—*n.* Targum'ist, a writer of a Targum: a student of the Targums.—*adj.* Targumist'ic. [Chaldean *targūm*, interpretation.]

tariff, *tar'if, n.* a list or set of customs duties: a list of charges.—tariff-reform'er, one who favoured the early 20th-century movement for Tariff Reform or Protection opposed to Free Trade. [It. *tariffa—*Ar. *ta'rif*, explanation—'arafa, to explain.]

tarlatan, *tär'lə-tən, n.* an open, transparent muslin. [Fr. *tarlatane*; origin doubtful.]

tarmac(adam). See tar (2).

tarn, *tärn, n.* a small mountain lake. [O.N. *tjörn*.]

tarnal, *tär'nl,* tarnation, *tär-nā'shən,* (*U.S. slang*) *adjs.* and *advs.* softened forms of eternal and damnation, app. influenced by each other.

tarnish, *tär'nish, v.t.* to dull, discolour, render iridescent, diminish the lustre of, by exposure to the air, etc.: to sully.—*v.i.* to become dull: to lose lustre.—*n.* loss of lustre: a surface discoloration or iridescence on metal or mineral: a film of oxide, sulphide, etc.—*adjs.* tar'nishable; tar'-nished.—*n.* tar'nisher. [Fr. *ternir*, *terniss-—terne*, dull, wan; poss. Gmc.]

taro, *tä'rō, n.* a plant (Colocasia) of the arum family, widely cultivated for its edible rootstock in the islands of the Pacific. [Polynesian.]

tarot, (formerly also) tarok, *tar'ō*, -*ok, n.* a card of Italian origin with picture, used in card games and also in fortune-telling: (usu. in *pl.*) a game played with tarots together with cards of the ordinary suits. [Fr. *tarot—*It. *tarocco.*]

tarpan, *tär'pan, n.* a small extinct wild horse of the steppes of S. European Russia, not identical with Przewalski's horse. [Tatar.]

tarpaulin, *tär-pö'lin, n.* strong linen or hempen cloth waterproofed with tar or otherwise: a sheet of it: a sailor's waterproof hat: a sailor (*coll.*): a sea-bred officer (*obs.*).—Also tarpaul'-ing.—Also *adj.* [App. tar, and palling—pall.]

Tarpeian, *tär-pē'ən, adj.* of Tarpeia, said to have betrayed the Capitol at Rome to the Sabines and to have been buried beneath the Tarpeian Rock on the Capitoline Hill, from which criminals were thrown.

tarpon, *tär'pən, n.* a gigantic fish (Megalops) akin to the herring, angled for on the Florida and Gulf coasts. [Origin unknown.]

tar(r)adiddle, *tar-ə-did'l, n.* a fib, a lie. [App. founded on diddle.]

tarragon, *tar'ə-gən, n.* an aromatic Artemisia used for flavouring vinegar, sauces, etc. [Ar. *tarkhūn,* pérh.—Gr. *drakōn,* a dragon.]

Tarragona, *tar-ə-gōn'ə, n.* a port-like Spanish wine. [Province in Catalonia.]

tarras, *tar'əs, n.* an old form (*Spens.*) of terrace. See also trass.

tarre. See tar (1).—Also (*Spens.*) for tar (2).

tarrock, *tar'ək,* (*local*) *n.* a sea-bird of various kinds. [Origin obscure.]

tarry, *tär'i.* See tar.

tarry, *tar'i, v.i.* to linger: to loiter: to delay: to stay behind: to sojourn: to wait.—*v.t.* (*arch.*) to await:—*pr.p.* tarr'ying; *pa.t.* and *pa.p.* tarr'-ied.—*n.* (*arch.*) delay: sojourn, stay.—*ns.* tarr'-iance (*arch.*), tarrying: delay: waiting: a sojourn; tarr'ier, one who tarries or delays.—*v.i.* tarr'ow (*tär'ō*; *Scot.*), to hesitate: to reluct. [History obscure; the form agrees with O.E. *tergan,* to irritate, the meaning with O.Fr. *tarier.*]

tarsal, tarsel, tarcel, *tär'sl.* See tercel.

tarsia, *tär'si-a,* (It. *tär-sē'ä*), *n.* intarsia (*q.v.*).—Also tar'sia-work.

tarsus, *tär'səs, n.* the part of the foot to which the leg is articulated: in birds, sometimes applied to the tarsometatarsus: in insects, the five-jointed foot:—*pl.* tar'si.—*adj.* tar'sal, relating to the tarsus or ankle.—*n.* a bone of the tarsus.—*ns.* tarsalgia (-*sal'ji-ə*), pain in the instep; tar'sier (-*si-ər*), a spectral-looking lemuroid of the East Indies with long tarsal bones.—*adj.* tar'sioid, like the tarsier: of the tarsier family.—*ns.* Tar'sipes (L. *pēs,* foot), the long-snouted honey-mouse, an Australian honey-sucking phalanger with feet like the tarsier; Tarsius, the tarsier genus.—*adj.* tarsometatar'sal.—*n.* tarsometatar'-sus, a bird's shank-bone, the combined metatarsals and distal tarsals. [Gr. *tarsos,* the flat of the foot.]

tart, *tärt, adj.* sharp: biting: acidulous.—*adj.* tart'ish.—*adv.* tart'ly.—*n.* tart'ness. [O.E. *teart.*]

tart, *tärt, n.* a dish of pastry distinguished from a pie either by being uncovered or by containing sweet not savoury materials: a girl (*slang*); often disrespectful): a prostitute (*slang*).—*ns.* tartine (-*ēn;* Fr.), a slice of bread with butter or jam; tart'let, a small tart.—*adj.* tart'y (*slang*).—tart up (*coll.*), to make more showy or striking, esp. in an inartistic way. [O.Fr. *tarte.*]

Tartan, *tär'tən, n.* a material used to lay tracks for athletic events, usable in all weathers. [Trademark.]

tartan, *tär'tən, n.* a woollen (or other) checked stuff: a distinctive checked pattern, as of a Highland clan.—*adj.* of tartan: checked in tartan.—*adj.* tar'taned, clad in tartan. [Origin unknown.]

tartan, tartane, *tär'tən, tär-tän', n.* a Mediterranean vessel with lateen sail. [Fr. *tartane,* poss.—Ar. *taridah,* a small ship.]

tartana, *tär-tä'nə, n.* a little covered wagon. [Sp.]

tartar, *tär'tər, n.* recrystallised and partially purified argol, chiefly acid potassium tartrate (with calcium tartrate, etc.): a deposit of calcium phosphate and other matter on the teeth.—*adjs.* tartareous (-*tä'ri-əs*), of or like tartar: with rough crumbly surface (*bot.*); tartaric (*tär-tar'-ik*), of or got from tartar (tartaric acid, $C_4H_6O_6$, prepared from argol).—*v.t.* tar'tarise, -ize, to treat, mix, or combine with tartar.—*n.* tar'trate, a salt of tartaric acid.—**tartar emetic,** a compound of potassium, antimony, carbon, hydrogen and oxygen.—**cream of tartar,** purified argol. [L.L. *tartarum,* perh. from Ar.]

**Tartar,** tär'tər, *n.* a Tatar: (without *cap.*) a formidable, rough, unmanageable person: (without *cap.*) one who unexpectedly turns the tables on his assailant.—Also *adj.*—*n.* and *adj.* **Tartarian** (-tā'ri-ən), **Tartar,** Tatar.—*adjs.* **Tartaric** ( *tar'ik*), of the Tartars; **tar'tarly,** like a Tartar: ferocious.—**Tartarian lamb,** barometz. [See **Tatar.**]

**tartar(e) (sauce),** tär'tər, tär-tär', *n.* a mayonnaise dressing with chopped pickles, olives, capers, etc., added, usu. served with fish. [Fr. *sauce tartare.*]

**Tartarus,** tär'tə-rəs, *n.* in Homer, a deep and sunless abyss, as far below Hades as earth is below heaven: hell.—Also (*Spens., Shak.*) **Tar'tar,** (*Spens.*) **Tar'tare, Tar'tarie, Tar'tary.**—*adj.* **Tartarean** (-tä'ri-ən). [L.,—Gr. *Tartaros.*]

**Tartuf(f)e,** tär-tüf', *n.* a hypocritical pretender to religion.—*adjs.* **Tartuf(f)'ian, Tartuf(f)'ish.**—*n.* **Tartuf(f)'ism.** [From the character in Molière's *Tartuffe* (3-act version 1664, 5-act 1669).]

**tarwhine,** tär'(h)win, *n.* an Australian sea-bream.

**Tarzan,** tär'zan, *n.* a man of great strength and agility. [From the hero of stories by Edgar Rice Burroughs about a man brought up by apes.]

**tasar,** tus'ər. Same as **tusser.**

**taseometer,** tas-i-om'i-tər, *n.* an instrument for measuring strains in a structure. [Gr. *tasis, -eōs,* a stretching, *metron,* measure.]

**tash,** täsh, (*Scot.*) *v.t.* to soil: to blemish: to disfigure: to disarray. [Fr. *tacher.*]

**tasimeter,** ta-sim'i-tər, *n.* an instrument for measuring changes in pressure, etc., by variations in electrical conductivity. [Gr. *tasis,* a stretch, *metron,* measure.]

**task,** täsk, *task, n.* a piece or amount of work set or undertaken.—*v.t.* to tax (*Shak.*): impose a task on: burden with severe work: employ fully. —*ns.* **task'er,** one who imposes or performs a task: one who does piece-work; **task'ing,** task-work.—**task'-force, task'-group,** a group formed by selection from different branches of the armed services to carry out a specific task: a working party (*q.v.*) for a civilian purpose; **task'master,** one who allots tasks:—*fem.* **task'mistress; task'-work,** work done as a task, or by the job. [O.Fr. *tasque* (Fr. *tâche*)—L.L. *tasca, taxa*—L. *taxāre,* to rate.]

**taslet.** See **tasse.**

**Tasmanian,** tas-, taz-mā'ni-ən, *adj.* of *Tasmania,* discovered in 1642 by Abel Janszoon *Tasman.*—*n.* a native or citizen of Tasmania.—**Tasmanian devil,** a ferocious Tasmanian dasyure; **Tasmanian myrtle,** a Tasmanian and Victorian evergreen beech; **Tasmanian wolf** (or **tiger**), the thylacine, a striped wolf-like dasyure of Tasmania.

**tass,** täs, (*dial.*) *n.* a mow, a heap. [O.Fr. *tas,* poss. from Du.]

**tass,** tas, *n.* a drinking-cup: a small drink.—*n.* **tass'ie** (*Scot.*), a small cup. [Fr. *tasse*—Ar. *tāss,* cup.]

**tasse, tace,** tas, *n.* in plate armour, one of a series of overlapping pieces forming a kind of skirt.—*ns.* **tas'let, tass'et,** a tasse. [O.Fr. *tasse, tasselet, tassete.*]

**tassel,** tas'l, *n.* a clasp or fastening (*Shak.*): an ornamental hanging tuft of threads: an inflorescence of like appearance, esp. of maize: a ribbon book-mark: a gold or silver plate on a vestment. —*v.t.* to furnish with tassels.—*v.i.* to form tassels, flower:—*pr.p.* **tass'elling;** *pa.t.* and *pa.p.* **tass'elled.**—*adj.* **tass'elled.**—*n.* **tass'elling.**—*adj.* **tass'elly.** [O.Fr. *tassel;* origin doubtful.]

**tassel.** See **torsel.**

**tassel, tassel-gent, tassel-gentle.** See **tercel.**

**taste,** tāst, *v.t.* to try, or to perceive, by the sense seated in the tongue and palate: to try by eating a little: to eat a little of: to partake of: to try, test (*obs.*): to relish, enjoy (*arch.*): to experience, perceive: to enjoy carnally (*Shak.*): to give a flavour to (*rare*).—*v.i.* to try or perceive by the mouth: to have a flavour: to act as taster: to have experience.—*n.* the act of tasting: the particular sensation caused by a substance on the tongue: the sense by which we perceive the flavour of a thing: the quality or flavour of anything: a small portion: an experience: discernment of, accordance with, what is socially right: the faculty by which the mind perceives the beautiful: nice perception: choice, predilection, liking.—*adjs.* **tāst'able,** having a taste; **tāst'ed,** having a taste: **taste'ful,** full of taste: having a pleasant or a high relish: showing good taste.—*adv.* **taste'fully,**—*n.* **taste'fulness.**—*adj.* **taste'less,** without taste: without good taste: insipid.—*adv.* **taste'lessly.**—*ns.* **taste'lessness; tāst'er,** one skilful in distinguishing flavours by the taste: one employed to test the innocuousness of food by tasting it before serving it to his master: a publisher's reader (*coll.*).—*adv.* **tāst'ily.**—*n.* **tāst'ing.**—*adj.* **tāst'y,** savoury: tasteful (*coll.*).— **taste'-bud, -bulb,** a group of cells on the tongue sensitive to taste.—**good taste,** intuitive feeling for what is aesthetically or socially right; **to one's taste,** to one's liking. [O.Fr. *taster* (Fr. *tâter*), as if from a L.L. freq. of L. *taxāre,* to touch, handle, estimate—*tangēre,* to touch.]

**tat, tatt,** *tat, v.t.* to make by tatting.—*v.i.* to make tatting.—*n.* **tatt'ing,** knotted lace edging made by hand with a shuttle from sewing-thread: the making of it.

**tat,** tät, *n.* East Indian hempen matting. [Hindi *ṭāṭ.*]

**tat,** *tat, n.* See **tattoo** (3).

**tat,** *tat, n.* a tap.—*v.t.* to touch, tap: to flog. [Cf. **tap,** and see **tit.**]

**ta-ta,** tä-tä', (*childish* and *coll.*) *interj.* good-bye.

**Tatar,** tä'tər, *n.* orig. a member of any of certain Tungusic tribes in Chinese Tartary: extended to any of the Mongol, Turkish, and other warriors who swept over Asia and Europe: loosely, one of the mixed inhabitants of Tartary, Siberia, and the Russian steppes, including Kazan Tartars, Crim Tartars, Kipchaks, Kalmucks, etc.: a speaker of a Turkic language.—Also *adj.*—*adjs.* **Tatarian** (tä-tä'ri-ən), **Tataric** (-tar'ik), of the Tatars: of the Turkic group of languages. [Turk. and Pers. *Tatar;* association with Gr. *Tartaros,* hell, seems to have suggested the form **Tartar.**]

**tate, tait,** tät, (*Scot.*) *n.* a small portion, pinch, tuft.

**tater,** tä'tər, *n.* a colloquial form of **potato.**—Also **tä'tie.**

**tath,** täth, (*dial.*) *n.* cattle dung: coarse tufted grass that grows where it has fallen.—*v.t.* to manure.—*v.i.* to drop dung. [O.N. *tath.*]

**tatler.** See **tattle.**

**tatou,** ta'tōō, or -tōō', *n.* an armadillo, esp. the giant armadillo. [Tupí *tatú.*]

**tatt,** *tat, n.* a rag, esp. an old one: pretentious odds and ends of little real value; e.g. in an antique shop.—*v.t.* to touch up.—*adv.* **tatt'ily.**—*n.* **tatt'iness.**—*adj.* **tatt'y,** (of clothes or ornament) fussy: precious, and often bogus: cheap, of poor quality: untidy: shabby. [**tatter.**]

**tatt.** See **tat** (1), (2).

**tatter,** tat'ər, *n.* a torn shred: a loose hanging rag. —*v.t.* to tear to tatters.—*v.i.* to fall into tatters.— *n.* **tatterdemā'lion** (or -*mal'yən*), a ragged fellow. —*adjs.* **tatt'ered; tatt'ery,** ragged. [Cf. Ice. *tōturr.*]

**Tattersall's,** *tat'ər-sölz, n.* a famous London horse-mart and haunt of racing-men—founded

1766 by Richard *Tattersall* (1724-95): a sweepstake or lottery agency with headquarters at Melbourne, Australia (*coll.* Tatts).

**tattie,** *ta'ti, tä'tä, n.* a Scots form of potato.— **tatt'ie-bo'gle,** a scarecrow; **tatt'ie-claw,** potato soup; **tatt'ie-lift'ing,** potato harvest; **tatt'ie-shaw,** the above-ground parts of a potato plant.

**tatting.** See tat (1).

**tattle,** *tat'l, n.* trifling talk: chatter.—*v.i.* to talk idly or triflingly: to tell tales or secrets.—*v.t.* to tell or utter in tattle.—*n.* **tatt'ler** (form. **tat'ler),** one given to tattling: any (esp. American) bird of the Totaninae, from their giving warning of gunners.—*n.* and *adj.* **tatt'ling,** chattering: tale-telling.—*adv.* **tatt'lingly.** [Used by Caxton to translate M.Du. *tatelen;* imit.]

**tattoo,** *tə-tōō', n.* a beat of drum or other signal calling soldiers to quarters: a drumming: a military fête by night.—**the devil's tattoo,** drumming with the fingers on a table, etc., in absence of mind or impatience. [Du. *taptoe—tap,* tap, *toe,* to, in the sense of shut.]

**tattoo, tatu,** *tə-tōō',* earlier **tatow,** *-tow', n.* a design marked on the skin by pricking in colouring matter.—*v.t.* to mark in this way:—*pa.t.* and *pa.p.* **tattooed'.** [Tahitian *ta'tau,* Marquesan *ta'tu.*]

**tattoo,** *tut'ōō, n.* a native-bred Indian pony.— Abbreviated **tat** (*tat*). [Hind. *ṭaṭṭū.*]

**tatty.** See **tatt** (1); also **tattie;** also **tawtie**—under **taut** (2).

**tatty,** *tat'i, n.* an Indian mat of bamboo, cuscus-grass roots, etc., esp. one kept wet in a doorway or window to cool the air. [Hind. *ṭaṭṭi.*]

**tau,** *tow, n.* the nineteenth letter (Τ, τ) of the Greek alphabet, answering to T: a tau-cross: as a numeral τ' = 300, ͵τ = 300,000.—**tau'-cross,** St Anthony's cross, in the form of a T; **tau'-staff,** a staff with a cross-piece at the top like a crutch. [Gr. *tau,* of Semitic origin.]

**taube,** *tow'ba, n.* a German monoplane with recurved wings. [Ger., dove.]

**taught,** *töt, pa.t.* and *pa.p.* of **teach.**

**tauld,** *töld,* a Scots form of **told** (*pa.t.* and *pa.p.*).

**taunt,** *tönt, v.t.* to reproach stingingly: to censure sarcastically.—*v.i.* to jibe.—*n.* a biting jibe: an object of taunts (*B.*).—*n.* **taunt'er.**—*n.* and *adj.* **taunt'ing.**—*adv.* **taunt'ingly.** [Poss. O.Fr. *tanter* —L. *tentāre,* to tempt; or Fr. *tant pour tant,* tit for tat.]

**taupie.** See **tawpie.**

**Taurus,** *tö'rəs* (or L. *tow'rōōs*), *n.* the Bull, a sign of the zodiac and a constellation formerly coinciding with it.—*adjs.* **tau'ric,** of a bull; **tau'riform,** having the form of a bull; **tau'rine** (or *-in*), of a bull: bull-like.—*ns.* **taurobō'lium** (Gr. *taurobŏlion—bŏlē,* a throw, stroke), the sacrifice of a bull, as in the Mithraic rites: an artistic representation thereof; **tauromachy** (*-om'ə-ki*) Gr. *tauromachiā—machē,* fight), bull-fighting: a bull-fight.—*adj.* **tauromor'phous** (Gr. *morphē,* form), bull-shaped. [L. *taurus* and Gr. *tauros.*]

**taut** (*obs.* **taught**), *töt, adj.* tightly drawn: tense: in good condition.—*v.t.* and *v.i.* **taut'en,** to tighten.—*n.* **taut'ness.** [Prob. conn. with **tow, tight.**]

**taut,** **tawt,** *töt,* (*Scot.*) *v.t.* and *v.i.* to mat, tangle.— *adjs.* **taut'it; tawt'ie, tatt'y.** [Cf. O.E. *tætteca,* rag.]

**taut-, töt-, tauto-, töt'ō-, töt-o'-,** in composition, the same.—*ns.* **taut'ochrone** (*-krŏn;* Gr. *chronos,* time), a curve such that a particle travelling along it under gravity reaches a fixed point in the same time, no matter where it starts; **tautoch'ronism.**—*adjs.* **tautoch'ronous; tautologic** (*-loj'*), **-al.**—*adv.* **tautolog'ically.**—*v.i.* **tautol'ogise, -ize,** to use tautology.—*ns.* **tautol'ogism; tautol'ogist.**—*adj.* **tautol'ogous** (*-ə-gəs*), tautological.—*ns.* **tautol'ogy,** use of words that (esp. needlessly or pointlessly) say the same thing; **taut'omer** (Gr. *meros,* part), a readily interconvertible isomer.— *adj.* **tautomer'ic.**—*n.* **tautom'erism.**—*adjs.* **tautomet'ric, -al,** exactly corresponding in arrangement of syllables.—*n.* **taut'onym,** a binomial name in which the specific name repeats the generic.—*adjs.* **tauton'ymous; tautophon'ical.**— *n.* **tautoph'ony,** repetition of a sound. [Gr. *tauto,* for *to auto,* the same.]

**tautog,** *tö-tog', n.* a labroid fish of the North American Atlantic coast. [Narragansett *tautauog.*]

**taver, taiver,** *tā'vər,* (*Scot.*) *n.* a shred. [Cf. Norw. and Dan. *tave.*]

**taver, taiver,** *tā'vər,* (*Scot.*) *v.i.* to wander: to rave.—*adj.* **ta(i)'vert,** muddled: fuddled: stupid. [Cf. Norw. *tava,* to toil, fumble.]

**tavern,** *tav'ərn, n.* a public-house.—*n.* **tav'erner,** a publican. [O.Fr. (Fr.) *taverne*—L. *taberna,* shed, stall, tavern, from root of *tabula,* a board.]

**taw,** *tö, n.* a large or choice marble: a game at marbles: the line shot from at marbles. [Origin unknown.]

**taw,** *tö, v.t.* to prepare and dress, esp. skins for white leather.—*n.* tawed leather: usu. *pl.* **taws, tawse,** a leather strap, usu. cut in fingers at the end, for corporal punishment.—*ns.* **taw'er,** a maker of white leather; **taw'ery,** a place where skins are dressed.—*adj.* **taw'ie** (*Scot.*), tractable. —*n.* **taw'ing.** [O.E. *tawian,* to prepare; Du. *touwen,* to curry; O.H.G. *zawjan,* to make, prepare.]

**tawdry,** *tö'dri, adj.* showy without taste or worth: gaudily adorned.—*n.* trumpery: a tawdry-lace (*obs.*).—*adv.* **taw'drily.**—*n.* **taw'driness.**—**taw'-dry-lace'** (*obs.*), a woman's silk necktie (in *Spens.* a waist-belt), such as was sold at St Audrey's Fair at Ely (17th October): trumpery adornment. [From *St Audrey* (i.e. Æthelthrȳth, daughter of Anna, King of East Anglia), who thought a tumour in her throat a punishment for having worn jewelled necklaces.]

**tawny,** *tö'ni, adj.* and *n.* yellowish brown.—*n.* **taw'niness.** [Fr. *tanné,* pa.p. of *tanner,* to tan.]

**tawpie, taupie,** *tö'pā,* (*Scot.*) *n.* a clumsy, heedless, or inefficient girl. [Cf. Norw. *taap,* a half-wit.]

**taws, tawse.** See **taw** (2).

**tax,** *taks, v.t.* to lay a tax on: to register or enrol for fiscal purposes (Luke ii. 1-5): to burden: to accuse, censure: to assess: to examine (accounts) in order to allow or disallow items.—*n.* a contribution exacted by the state: anything imposed, exacted, or burdensome: a charge, accusation (*obs.*).—*n.* **taxabil'ity.**—*adj.* **tax'able.**—*adv.* **tax'-ably.**—*n.* **taxā'tion.**—*adj.* **tax'ative,** taxing: of taxing; **taxed.**—*ns.* **tax'er** (also **tax'or); tax'ing,** imposition of taxes: censure, satire (*obs.*).— **tax(ed)'-cart,** a light spring-cart (orig. paying a lower tax, later none); **tax'-collect'or.**—*adj.* and *adv.* **tax'-free,** without payment of tax.—**tax'-gath'erer; tax'ing-mas'ter,** an officer of a court of law who examines bills of costs; **tax'-payer,** one who pays tax or taxes: one who is liable to taxation: a building put up for the express purpose of earning money to pay tax on the land (*U.S.*).—**tax reserve certificate,** a government receipt for money deposited that may later be used, with certain advantages, for payment of tax. [Fr. *taxe,* a tax—L. *taxāre,* to handle, value, charge.]

**taxi,** *tak'si, n.* a taxi-cab: loosely, any motor-car on hire:—*pl.* **tax'is, tax'ies.**—*v.i.* to travel by taxi: of an aeroplane, to run along the ground, or (seaplane) on the surface of water, at low speed under its own power:—*pr.p.* **tax'ying;** *pa.t.* and *pa.p.* **tax'ied;** *3rd pers. pres. indic.* **tax'ies.**—**tax'i-cab,** a cab (now usu. a motor-cab) furnished with a taximeter; **tax'i-dancer,** a girl hirable as a partner, dance by dance, in a dance-hall. [Abbrev. of **taximeter.**]

**taxiarch.** See under **taxis.**

**taxidermy,** *taks'i-dŭr-mi, n.* the art of preparing, stuffing, and mounting skins.—*adjs.* **taxider'mal. taxider'mic.**—*v.t.* **tax'idermise, -ize.**—*n.* **tax'idermist.** [Gr. *taxis,* arrangement, *derma,* a skin.]

**taximeter,** *tak'si-mē-tər, tak-sim'i-tər (obs.* **taxameter),** *n.* an instrument attached to a cab for indicating (distance travelled and) fare due. [Fr. *taxe,* price, Gr. *metron,* measure.]

**taxis,** *tak'sis, n.* arrangement: a division of an ancient Greek army (in Athens the contingent from a phyle): return to position of displaced parts by means of manipulation only (*surg.*): movement of a whole organism in response to stimulus (*biol.*).—*ns.* **tax'iarch** (*-i-ärk*), commander of a taxis; **tax'on,** a biological category (e.g. *species*), or its name:—*pl.* **tax'a.**—*n.* **taxon'omer,** a taxonomist.—*adjs.* **taxonom'ic, -al.** —*adv.* **taxonom'ically.**—*ns.* **taxon'omist; taxon'omy,** classification or its principles: classification of plants or animals (now including study of means by which formation of species, etc., takes place). [Gr.,—*tassein,* to arrange.]

**Taxus,** *tak'səs, n.* the yew genus of conifers, giving name to the family **Taxā'ceae** (*-si-ē*).—*n.* **Taxō'dium** (Gr. *eidos,* form), the swamp-cypress genus. [L. *taxus,* yew.]

**tayra, taira,** *ti'ra, n.* a large South American species of the weasel family. [Tupí *taira.*]

**tazza,** *tat'sa, n.* a shallow vessel mounted on a foot: a saucer-shaped bowl:—*pl.* **taz'ze** (*-sā*), **taz'zas.** [It., cup; cf. **tass** (2).]

**tch-.** For some words see **ch-.**

**tchick,** *chik, ch', n.* a sound made by pressing the tongue against the roof of the mouth and then drawing back one side, as in urging a horse on.—*v.i.* to make such a sound. [Imit.]

**te.** See **ti** (*mus.*).

**tea,** *tē,* formerly *tā, n.* a tree, *Thea sinensis,* close akin to Camellia, cultivated in China, Assam, etc.: its dried and prepared leaves, buds, and shoots: an infusion of the leaves in boiling water: extended to various substitutes (see **Labrador, Paraguay,** etc.): any vegetable infusion as a beverage: rarely, a similar preparation of animal origin (as **beef-tea**): an afternoon meal or light refreshment at which tea is generally served (*slang*).—*v.i.* (*coll.*) to take tea.—*v.t.* (*coll.*) to provide tea for.—**tea'bag,** a bag containing tea-leaves for infusion; **tea'-board,** a tea-tray; **tea'-bread,** light spongy bread or buns to be eaten with tea; **tea'-break,** a break for tea during the working day; **tea'caddy, tea'-can'ister,** an air-tight box or jar for holding tea; **tea'-cake,** a light cake to be eaten with tea; **tea'-chest,** a chest or case in which tea is packed; **tea'-clipper,** a fast sailing-ship in the tea-trade; **tea'-cloth,** a small table-cloth: a cloth used in washing up after tea; **tea'-cosy,** a thick cover for a tea-pot to keep the tea hot; **tea'cup,** a small cup used in drinking tea; **tea'cupful:**—*pl.* **tea'cupfuls; tea'-dealer,** a buyer and seller of tea; **tea'-dish,** an old name for a teacup; **tea'-drinker; tea'-eq'uipage,** apparatus for making and serving tea with all that accompanies it; **tea'-fight** (*slang*), a tea-party; **tea'-gar'den,** a plantation of tea: an open-air restaurant for tea and other refreshments; **tea'-gown,** a loose gown for wearing at afternoon tea at home; **tea'-ho'** (*Austr.*), a tea-break; **tea'-house,** a Chinese or Japanese house for tea, etc.; **tea'kettle,** a kettle for boiling water for tea; **tea'lead,** lead with a little tin for lining tea-chests; **tea'-leaf,** a leaf of tea: a scrap of solid tea in a cup or in the refuse; **tea'-meeting,** a public social meeting at which tea is drunk; **tea'party,** a social gathering at which tea is served: the persons present; **tea'-plant; tea'-planta'tion; tea'-planter,** a cultivator of the tea-plant; **tea'-pot,** a spouted vessel for pouring out tea;

**tea'-room,** a room or restaurant where tea is served; **tea'-rose,** a rose supposed to smell of tea; **tea'-ser'vice, -set,** a set of utensils for a tea-table; **tea'-shop,** a shop where tea is sold: a restaurant in which teas are served; **tea'spoon,** a small spoon used with the teacup; **tea'spoonful:**—*pl.* **tea'spoonfuls; tea'-table,** a table at which tea is drunk: the company at tea; **tea'taster,** an expert who judges tea by tasting it. —*n.pl.* **tea'-things,** the tea-pot, cups, etc.—**tea'(-) time,** the hour of the meal called tea.—Also *adj.* —**tea-towel,** a cloth for drying crockery, etc.; **tea'-tray,** a tray for carrying tea-things; **tea'tree,** the common tea plant or shrub: a name of Australian myrtaceous plants (Melaleuca, Leptospermum) furnishing substitutes for tea: an African solanaceous shrub (Lycium) said to have been labelled by mistake; **tea'-trolley,** a small tiered table on wheels used for serving afternoon tea, etc.; **tea'-urn,** a large closed urn with a tap, often also a heating device, for making tea in quantity.—**another cup of tea,** a very different thing; **black tea,** that which has been fermented between rolling and firing (heating with charcoal in a sieve); (usu. **not**) **for all the tea in China,** (not) for anything whatever; **green tea,** that which is fired immediately after rolling; **high tea,** tea with meat, eggs, fish, or the like; **one's cup of tea** (*slang*), what is to one's taste or appeals to one; **Russian tea,** tea with lemon and no milk usually served in a glass. [South Chinese *te,* the common form being *ch'a* or *ts'a.*]

**teach,** *tēch, v.t.* to show: to direct: to impart knowledge or art to: to guide the studies of: to exhibit so as to impress upon the mind: to impart the knowledge or art of: to accustom: to counsel.—*v.i.* to practise giving instructions: —*pa.t.* and *pa.p.* **taught** (*töt*).—*n.* **teachabil'ity.** —*adj.* **teach'able,** capable of being taught: apt or willing to learn.—*ns.* **teach'ableness; teach'er,** one whose profession is, or whose talent is the ability, to impart knowledge, practical skill, or understanding; **teach'ership; teach'ing,** the act, practice, or profession of giving instruction: doctrine: instruction.—*adj.* occupied with giving instruction: instructive.—*adj.* **teach'less,** incapable of being taught.—**teach'-in,** a long public debate consisting of a succession of speeches by well-informed persons holding different views on a matter of general importance; **teaching machine,** any mechanical device capable of presenting an instructional programme.— **teach school** (*U.S.*), to be a teacher in a school. [O.E. *tǣcan,* to show, teach; cf. Ger. *zeigen,* to show; Gr. *deiknynai,* to show.]

**teachie.** See **tetchy.**

**tead, teade,** *tēd, (Spens.) n.* a torch. [L. *taeda.*]

**teagle,** *tē'gl, (dial.) n.* a hoist or lift: a baited line for catching birds.—*v.t.* to hoist or catch with a teagle. [Prob. a form of **tackle.**]

**Teague,** *tēg, n.* an obs. nickname for an Irishman. [*Tadhg,* an Irish name, Thady.]

**teak,** *tēk, n.* a verbenaceous tree (*Tectona grandis*) of India, Malaya, etc.: its hard and durable wood.—**African teak,** an African euphorbiaceous tree, *Oldfieldia africana;* **bastard teak,** dhak; **white teak,** Flindersia. [Malayalam *tēkka.*]

**teal,** *tēl, n.* any of several kinds of small freshwater duck, esp. of the genus Anas. [M.E. *tēle,* prob. from O.E.; cf. Du. *teling, taling.*]

**team,** *tēm, n.* a brood, a litter (*obs.* or *dial.*): a chain, esp. for hauling a plough, etc. (*dial.*): a set of animals harnessed together: a string of flying ducks, geese, etc.: a set of persons working or playing in combination: a side: a stock of animals: a turn-out (*U.S.*).—*v.t.* to yoke: to join in order to make a team or co-operative effort: to match (clothes, etc.).—*v.i.* to drive a team.—*adj.* **teamed** (*Spens.* **tem'ed, teem'ed),**

harnessed in a team.—*ns.* team′er, a teamster; team′ing, driving a team: work apportioned to a team: transport by team: removal of excavated material from cutting to bank; team′ster, one who drives a team: a truck-driver (*U.S.*). —*adv.* team′wise, harnessed together.—team′- mate, a fellow member of a team; team′-spirit, the spirit of self-suppression in co-operation; team′-work, work done by organised division of labour: co-operation, pulling together, regard to success of the whole rather than personal exploits. —team up with, to join forces with. [O.E. *tēam*, child-bearing, brood, team; in kindred languages a bridle, rope, draught of a net; cf. O.E. *tēon*, to draw.]

teapoy, *tē′poi*, *n.* a small table or tripod: (by confusion with tea) a tea-caddy. [Hind. *tīn*, *tir*-, three, Pers. *pāi*, foot.]

tear, *tēr*, *n.* a drop of liquid secreted by the lachrymal gland: an exuding drop: a blob, bead, pear-shaped drop: a small flaw or cavity as in glass.—*adj.* tear′ful, lachrymose: brimming with, ready to shed, or shedding, tears.—*adv.* tear′- fully.—*n.* tear′fulness.—*adjs.* tear′less, without tears: sorrowless; tear′y, tearful.—tear′-bag, the lachrymal gland: the tear-pit; tear′-bottle (*archaeol.*), a small bottle once thought to contain mourners' tears; tear′-drop, a tear; tear′- duct, the lachrymal duct.—*adj.* tear′-fall′ing (*Shak.*), shedding tears.—tear′-gas, a gas or volatile substance that blinds temporarily by provoking tears; tear′-gland, the lachrymal gland; tear′-jer′ker, an extravagantly sentimental song, book, film, etc., inviting pity, grief, sorrow; tear′-pit, in deer, a gland below the eye secreting a waxy substance; tear′-shell, a shell that disperses tear-gas; tear smoke, a lachrymatory vapour that (as opp. to tear gas) is visible.—*adj.* tear′-stained, stained with tears. —in tears, weeping. [O.E. *tēar*; Goth. *tagr*; Gr. *dakry*.]

tear, *tār*, *v.t.* to draw asunder or separate with violence: to rend: to lacerate: to cause pain, bitterness, etc., to: to make or render by tearing.—*v.i.* to move or act with violence: to rush, move very quickly: to rage: to become torn: —*pa.t.* tōre, *arch.* tāre; *pa.p.* torn.—*n.* tearing: a rent: a rush (*slang*): a spree.—*ns.* tear′er, one who, or that which, tears: a boisterous person (*slang*).—*adj.* tear′ing, great, terrible, rushing.—*adj.* tear′away, impetuous, reckless: pertaining to a tearaway.—*n.* a reckless and (now also) violent young person.—tear′-sheet (*U.S.*), a page torn out for reference; tear web- bing, webbing in which two adhering layers form a fold that will tear apart so as to lessen the violence of a sudden strain.—tear a (the) cat (*obs.*), to rant; tear a strip off (*slang*), to reprimand; tear oneself away, to go off with great unwillingness; tear one's hair, to pull the hair in a frenzy of grief or rage; tear up, to remove from a fixed state by violence: to pull to pieces. [O.E. *teran*; cf. Ger. *zehren*.]

tease, *tēz*, *v.t.* to open out the fibres of: to comb or card, as wool: to scratch, as cloth: to raise a nap on: to vex with importunity, jests, etc.: to plague, irritate, esp. playfully or pleasantly: to tantalise: to banter.—*n.* one who teases: an act of teasing.—*n.* teas′er.—*n.* and *adj.* teas′ing.—*adv.* teas′ingly. [O.E. *tǣsan*, to card.]

teasel, *tēz′l*, *n.* any species of Dipsacus, esp. *D. fullonum*: its head with hooked bracts used in raising a nap on cloth: an artificial substitute for its head.—*v.t.* to raise a nap on with the teasel:—*pr.p.* teas′el(l)ing; *pa.t.* and *pa.p.* teas′el(l)ed.—*ns.* teas′el(l)er; teas′el(l)ing.—Also teazel, teazle, etc. [O.E. *tǣsel*=*tǣsan*; see tease.]

teat, *tēt*, *n.* the small protuberance through which the mammalian young suck the milk: a similar

protuberance through which milk is sucked from a baby's feeding-bottle: a nipple.—*adj.* teat′ed, having a teat or teats. [O.E. *titt*, *tit*; influenced by O.Fr. *tete* (Fr. *tette*).]

teaze, an obs. spelling of tease; teazel, teazle (see teasel).

tebbad, *teb′ad*, *n.* a sandstorm. [Cf. Pers. *tab*, fever, *bād*, wind.]

Tebeth, *teb′eth*, *n.* the tenth month of the Jewish ecclesiastical, and fourth of the secular, year, parts of December and January. [Heb. *Tēbēt*.]

Tebilise, *teb′il-iz*, *v.t.* of cotton and linen fabrics, to treat by a finishing process that prevents shrinking and creasing. [Proprietary name.]

'tec, *tek*, *n.* a slang abbrev. for detective.

technetium, *tek-nē′shi-am*, *n.* the chemical element of atomic number 43 (Tc), the first element to be artificially made. [Gr. *technētos*, artificial—*technē*, art.]

technic, *tek′nik*, *adj.* technical.—*n.* technology: (often in *pl.* form) technicality, technique.—*adj.* tech′nical, pertaining to art, esp. a useful art or applied science: industrial: belonging to, or in the language of, a particular art, department of knowledge or skill, profession: so called in strict legal or technical language.—*n.* techni- cal′ity.—*adv.* tech′nically.—*ns.* tech′nicalness; technician (-*nish′ən*), tech′nicist (-*ni-sist*), one skilled in a practical art; Technicolor, a proprietary name of a process of colour photography in motion-pictures.—*adj.* technicolour (modelled on above), in bright, artificial colours: cheaply romantic.—technique (*tek-nēk*′; Fr.), method of performance, manipulation, esp. everything concerned with the mechanical part of an artistic performance; technoc′racy, government or management by technical experts: a state, etc., so governed: a body of technical experts in governing position; tech′no- crat (Gr. *kratos*, power), a member of a technocracy: a believer in technocracy.—*adj.* tech- nolog′ical.—*adv.* technolog′ically.—*ns.* technol′o- gist; technol′ogy, the practice of any or all of the applied sciences that have practical value and/or industrial use: technical method(s) in a particular field of industry or art: technical nomenclature: technical means and skills characteristic of a particular civilisation, group, or period.—technical chemistry, industrial chemistry; technical knockout, a boxer's defeat on the referee's decision that, though not actually knocked out, he is unable to continue the fight. [Gr. *technē*, art, adj. *technikos*.]

techy. See tetchy.

teckel, *tek′l*, *n.* a dachshund. [Ger.]

tectibranch, *tekt′i-brangk*, *n.* any member of the Tectibranchiā′ta, opisthobranch molluscs with gill covered by the mantle.—*n.* and *adj.* tecti- branch′iate. [L. *tegěre*, *tēctum*, to cover, *branchiae*, gills.]

tectiform, *tekt′i-förm*, *adj.* roof-like: roofing. [L. *tēctum*, a roof, *förma*, shape.]

tectonic, *tek-ton′ik*, *adj.* pertaining to building: structural.—*n.* (*pl.* in form, treated as *sing.*) tectonics, building as an art: the constructive arts: structural features: structural geology.— *adv.* tecton′ically. [Gr. *tektōn*, a builder.]

tectorial, *tek-tō′ri-al*, -*tō′ri-əl*, *adj.* covering. [L. *tēctōrius*—*tegěre*, *tēctum*, to cover.]

tectrix, *tek′triks*, *n.* a covert-feather:—*pl.* tectrices (-*trī′sēz*).—*adj.* tectricial (-*trish′l*). [L. *tēctrix*, -*icis*, fem. of *tēctor*, -*ōris*, a coverer, plasterer— *tegěre*, to cover.]

ted, *ted*, *v.t.* to spread as new-mown grass, for drying:—*pr.p.* tedd′ing; *pa.t.* and *pa.p.* tedd′ed. —*n.* tedd′er, one who teds: an implement for tedding. [Prob. from a lost O.E. *teddan*; cf. Ice. *tethja*, to manure.]

Ted, *ted*, *n.* a Teddy boy.—Teddy boy, an unruly adolescent (1950s) affecting a dandyish garb reminiscent of Edward VII's time; **Teddy girl,** the Teddy boy's female companion and counterpart in conduct; **Teddy suit.** [*Edward.*]

**teddy,** *ted'i,* **teddy-bear** (*-bār'*), *n.* a woolly toy bear. [From Theodore (*Teddy*) Roosevelt, a famous hunter and President of U.S.A. (1901-1909).]

**tedesco,** *te-des'kō, adj.* German:—*pl.* -**deschi** (*-kē*) *fem.* **tedes'ca** (*-ka*), *pl.* -**desche** (*-kā*). [It.]

**Te Deum,** *tē' dē'əm,* L. *tā de'ōōm, n.* a famous Latin hymn of the Western Church: a musical setting of it. [From its first words, *Tē Deum laudāmus,* thee, God, we praise.]

**tedium,** also **taedium,** *tē'di-əm, n.* wearisomeness, esp. owing to length: irksomeness: boredom. —*n.* **tedios'ity.**—*adj.* **te'dious.**—*adv.* **te'diously.** —*n.* **te'diousness.**—*adjs.* (*Scot.*) **te'disome, te'diousome** (*Scott*), **te'dy.** [L. *taedium—taedēre,* to weary.]

**tee,** *tē, n.* the twentieth letter of the alphabet (T, t.); an object or mark of that shape.—**tee'-shirt,** a slip-on shirt usu. with short sleeves, no collar and no buttons; **tee'-square** (see T).

**tee,** *tē, n.* the mark aimed at (*quoits, curling,* etc.): the sand-cone, peg, or other elevation from which the ball is first played at each hole (*golf*): the strip of ground (also **tee'ing-ground**) where this is done.—*v.t.* and *v.i.* to place (the golf-ball) on the tee:—*pr.p.* **tee'ing;** *pa.t.* and *pa.p.* **teed, tee'd.**—**tee up** or **off,** to start (play); **to a tee,** exactly, to a tittle. [Origin unknown.]

**tee,** *tē, n.* the umbrella-shaped finial of a dagoba. [Burmese *h'ti,* umbrella.]

**teem,** *tēm, v.t.* to bring forth.—*v.i.* to bear or be fruitful: to be pregnant: to be full, abound. —*adjs.* **teem'ful; teem'ing; teem'less,** barren. [O.E. *tieman—tēam;* see **team.**]

**teem,** *tēm, v.t.* to pour, empty.—*v.i.* to pour: to flow copiously. [O.N. *tœma,* to empty; cf. **toom.**]

**teen, teene, tene,** *tēn,* (*arch.*) *n.* injury: affliction: grief: anger: pains. [O.E. *tēona,* injury, anger, grief.]

**teen,** *tēn, n.* any number or year of age, etc., from thir*teen* to nine*teen* (usu. in *pl.*).—*adj.* **teen'age,** in the teens; appropriate to one in the teens.—**teen'ager.** [O.E. suffix *-tiene—tien,* ten.]

**teene,** *tēn,* (*Spens.*) *v.t.* app., to allot.

**teeny,** *tē'ni, adj.* a form of tiny.—Also **teen'y-ween'y.**—(*U.S.*) **teen'ty.**

**teepee.** See **tepee.**

**teer,** *tēr, v.t.* to plaster: to daub: to spread. [O.Fr. *terer—terre,* earth.]

**Teeswater,** *tēz'wöt-ər, n.* a shorthorn, originating chiefly from a breed in the *Tees* valley (*water*).

**tee-tee,** *tee'-tee'* (*coll.*) *adj.* teetotal.—*n.* teetotaller. [The abbrev. **t.t.** written out.]

**tee-tee.** Same as **titi.**

**teeter,** *tē'tər, n.* (*U.S.*) see-saw.—*v.t., v.i.* to see-saw: move unsteadily.—**teet'er-board,** a see-saw: (also **teet'er-tott'er**) a board which throws a person into the air when another jumps on the opposite end of it. [*titter* (2).]

**teeth,** *tēth, pl.* of **tooth.**—*v.i.* **teethe** (*tēdh*), to develop or cut teeth.—*v.t.* to furnish with teeth. —*n.* and *adj.* **teething** (*tēdh'ing*).—**teething troubles,** pain and irritation caused by the cutting of teeth: mechanical difficulties encountered on first using a new machine or in the early stages of any undertaking. [O.E. pl. *tēth.*]

**teetotal,** *tē-tō'tl, adj.* abstaining totally from intoxicating drinks: out-and-out (*dial.*).—*n.* a total abstainer: the total abstinence principle, movement, or pledge.—*ns.* **teetō'talism;** **teetō'taller,** a total abstainer from intoxicating drinks.—*adv.* **teetō'tally.** [Said to be from a stammering pronunciation of **total** by Richard Turner of Preston in 1833.]

**teetotum,** *tē-tō'təm, n.* a small top inscribed with letters, or a gambling game decided by the

letter that came uppermost, T standing for L. *tōtum,* all, i.e. take all the stakes: any small top twirled by the fingers:—*pl.* **teeto'tums.**

**tef, teff,** *tef, n.* an Abyssinian cereal grass, *Eragrostis abyssinica.* [Amharic *tēf.*]

**Teflon,** *tef'lon, n.* a trademark for polytetrafluoroethylene.

**teg, tegg,** *teg, n.* a sheep (or *obs.* a doe) in its second year. [Perh. Scand.]

**tegmen,** *teg'mən, n.* a covering: the inner coat of the testa (*bot.*): the leathery fore-wing in Orthoptera:—*pl.* **teg'mina.**—*adj.* **tegmental** (*-ment'al*).— *ns.* **tegment'um,** a bud-scale; **teg'üment,** a covering: an integument.—*adjs.* **tegüment'al, tegüment'ary.** [L. *tēgmen, tēgmentum, tegumentum —tegĕre,* to cover.]

**teguexin,** *te-gwek'sin, n.* a large black and yellow South American lizard. [Aztec *tecoixin.*]

**tegula,** *teg'ū-lə, n.* a flat roofing-tile: a scale at the base of the fore-wing in some insects:—*pl.* **teg'ülae** (*-lē*).—*adj.* **teg'ülar.**—*adv.* **teg'ülarly.**— *adj.* **teg'ülāted,** composed of plates overlapping like tiles. [L. *tegula,* a tile—*tegĕre,* to cover.]

**tehee,** *tē'hē', interj.* expressing derision or merriment.—*n.* a laugh.—*v.i.* to titter. [Imit.]

**tehr,** *tār.* Same as **tahr.**

**Teian, Tean,** *tē'ən, tē'yan, adj.* of Teos in ancient Ionia, or Anacreon, a native. [Gr. *Tēïos,* Teian—*Tēōs,* Teos.]

**teichopsia,** *tī-kops'i-ə, n.* temporary partial blindness with optical illusions, accompanying migraine. [Gr. *teichos,* wall, *opsis,* sight.]

**te igitur,** *tē' ij'i-tər,* L. *tā ig'i-tōōr, n.* the first paragraph of the canon of the mass: a service-book on which oaths were taken. [L. *tē igitur,* thee therefore (the first words).]

**teil,** *tēl, n.* the linden or lime tree.—**teil tree,** the lime: the terebinth (*B.*). [O.Fr. *teil*—L. *tilia.*]

**teind,** *tēnd, n.* in Scotland, a tithe.—*v.t.* to assess or take a tithe on. [A form of **tenth, tithe.**]

**teinoscope,** *tī'nō-skōp, n.* a magnifying and diminishing combination of prisms correcting chromatic aberration. [Gr. *teinein,* to stretch, *skopeein,* to look.]

**teknonymy,** *tek-non'i-mi, n.* the naming of the parent from the child.—*adj.* **teknon'ymous.** [Gr. *teknon,* a child, *onyma, onoma,* a name.]

**tektite,** *tek'tīt, n.* a type of small glassy stone, of uncertain and perh. extra-terrestrial origin, found in certain areas of the earth, including Australia (**australite**). [Gr. *tēktos,* molten.]

**tel.** See **tell** (1).

**tel-.** See **tele-.**

**tela,** *tē'lə,* L. *tā'la, n.* a web, tissue:—*pl.* **tē'lae** (*-lē*; *tā'lī*).—*adj.* **tē'lary,** web-spinning. [L. *tēla.*]

**telaesthesia,** *tel-ēs-thē'zi-ə, -zhi-ə, -zhyə,* or *-is-, n.* an abnormal impression as of sense received from a distance.—*adj.* **teleasthetic** (*-thet'ik*). [tele- (1), Gr. *aisthēsiā,* sensation.]

**Telamon,** *tel'ə-mən,* (*archit.*) *n.* a man's figure as a pillar:—*pl.* **Telamones** (*-mō'nēz*). [Gr. *Telamōn*—the root of *tolmaein,* to endure, dare.]

**telangiectasis,** *tel-an-ji-ek'tə-sis, n.* dilatation of the small arteries or capillaries.—*adj.* **teiangiectatic** (*-tat'ik*). [Gr. *telos,* end, *angeion,* a vessel, *ektasis,* extension.]

**telautograph,** *tel-ö'tə-gräf, n.* a telegraph for reproducing the movement of a pen or pencil and so transmitting writings or drawings: one for transmission of images by electric scanning.— *adj.* **telautographic** (*-graf'ik*).—*n.* **telautography** (*-tog'rə-fi*). [tele- (1), Gr. *autos,* self, *graphein,* to write.]

**teld,** *teld,* (*Spens.*) *pa.t.* and *pa.p.* of **tell.**—(*Scot.*) **teld, tell'd, telt.**

**tele-,** *tel-i,* (also **tel-**), in composition, (1) far, distant; (2) television. [Gr. *tēle,* far.]

**telearchics,** *tel-i-är'kiks.* See **telecontrol.** [tele- (1), Gr. *archein,* to rule.]

*fāte, fär; mē, hûr* (her); *mīne; mōte, fŏr; mūte; mōōn, fŏŏt; dhen* (then)

**telecamera,** *tel'-i-kam-ər-a, n.* television camera (see **camera**).

**telecast,** *tel'i-käst, n. tele*vision broad*cast.*—Also *v.t.*—*n.* **tel'ecaster.**

**telecine,** *tel-i-sin'i, n.* transmission of filmed material by television. [**tele-** (2), **cine.**]

**telecommunication,** *tel-i-kə-mū-ni-kā'shən, n.* communication of information, in verbal, written, coded, or pictorial form, by telephone, telegraph, cable, radio, television: (in *pl.*) the science of such communication. [**tele-** (1), **communication.**]

**telecontrol,** *tel-i-kon-trōl', n.* control of mechanical devices remotely, either by radio (as ships and aircraft), by sound waves, or by beams of light. Also called **telearchics.** [**tele-** (1), **control.**]

**teledu,** *tel'ə-doo, n.* the stinking badger of Java. [Javanese.]

**téléférique,** *tā-lā-fer-ēk,* (Fr.) *n.* a light aerial cable-car, esp. one electrically propelled.

**telefilm,** *tel'i-film, n.* a regular sound-film made specially for subsequent television transmission. [**tele-** (2), **film.**]

**telega,** *tel-eg'ə, tel-yeg'ə, n.* a springless Russian wagon. [Russ.]

**telegenic,** *tel-i-jen'ik, adj.* suitable for television. [**tele-** (2), modelled on **photogenic.**]

**telegony,** *ti-leg'ə-ni, n.* the (imaginary) transmitted influence of a previous mate on the offspring of a female by a later mate. [**tele-** (1), Gr. *gonos,* begetting.]

**telegram,** *tel-i-gram, n.* a message sent by telegraph.—*adjs.* **telegrammat'ic, telegramm'ic,** of or like a telegram. [**tele-** (1), Gr. *gramma,* that which is written—*graphein,* to write.]

**telegraph,** *tel'i-gräf, n.* a combination of apparatus for transmitting messages to a distance, now almost exclusively by electrical impulses: a message so sent (*obs.*): a scoring-board (*cricket,* etc.): often taken as the name of a newspaper.—*v.t.* to convey or announce by telegraph: to signal: to give a premature indication of something to come.—*v.i.* to signal: to send a telegram.—*ns.* **telegrapher** (*ti-leg'rə-fər;* now chiefly *U.S.*), a telegraphist; **tel'egraphese'.** the jargon or contracted idiom used in telegrams.—*adj.* **telegraphic** (*-graf'ik*).—*adv.* **telegraph'ically.**—*ns.* **teleg'raphist,** one who works a telegraph; **teleg'raphy,** the science or art of constructing or using telegraphs.—**telegraph** (**-board**), a scoring-board able to be seen at a distance: a board on which the numbers of the horses and names of jockeys are put up (*racing*); **tel'egraph-ca'ble,** a cable containing wires for transmitting telegraphic messages; **telegraphic address,** a shortened address registered for use in telegraphing; **tel'egraph-plant,** an Indian papilionaceous plant (*Desmodium gyrans*) whose leaflets jerk like semaphore arms; **tel'egraph-pole,** a pole supporting telegraph-wires; **tel'egraph-wire,** a wire for carrying telegraphic messages. [**tele-** (1), Gr. *graphein,* to write.]

**telekinesis,** *tel-i-ki-nē'sis, -ki-, n.* the production of motion at a distance by means beyond the range of the senses.—*adj.* **telekinetic** (*-net'ik*). [**tele-** (1), Gr. *kinēsis,* movement.]

**telemark,** *tel'i-märk, n.* a sudden turn on the outer ski, first practised at *Telemark* in Norway.—*v.i.* to execute a telemark.

**telemeter,** *ti-lem'i-tər, n.* an instrument for measuring distances: a photographer's rangefinder: an instrument for measuring an electrical or other quantity and signalling the measurement to a distant point.—*v.t.* to record and signal by telemeter.—*adj.* **telemetric** (*tel-i-met'rik*).—*n.* **telem'etry.** [**tele-** (1), Gr. *metron,* measure.]

**teleo-,** *tel-i-o-,* in composition, perfect, complete.—*ns.* **Teleosaurus** (*tel-i-o-sö'rəs;* Gr. *sauros,* a lizard), a Jurassic genus of fossil crocodiles;

**tel'eosaur.**—*adj.* and *n.* **teleosau'rian.**—*n.pl.* **Teleostei** (*-os'ti-i;* Gr. *osteon,* bone), the bony fishes with well-developed bones.—*ns.* and *adjs.* **tel'eost, teleos'tean.**—*n.pl.* **Teleostomi** (*-os'tə-mi;* Gr. *stoma,* mouth), fishes with membrane bones in the skull, jaws, etc.—all ordinary fishes except the sharks and rays.—*n.* **tel'eostome** (*-tōm*).—*adj.* **teleos'tomous.** [Gr. *teleios,* perfect, complete.]

**teleology,** *tel-i-ol'ə-ji, n.* the doctrine of the final causes of things: interpretation in terms of purpose.—*adjs.* **teleologic** (*-ə-loj'ik*), **-al.**—*adv.* **teleolog'ically.**—*ns.* **teleol'ogism; teleol'ogist.** [Gr. *telos,* end, purpose, *logos,* a discourse.]

**telepathy,** *ti-lep'ə-thi, n.* communication between mind and mind otherwise than through the known channels of the senses.—*n.* **telepath** (*tel'i-path*), one who practises telepathy.—*v.t.* and *v.i.* to communicate by telepathy.—*adj.* **telepath'ic.**—*adv.* **telepath'ically.**—*v.t.* **telep'athise, -ize,** to affect or act upon through telepathy. —*v.i.* to practise telepathy.—*n.* **telep'athist,** one who believes in or practises telepathy. [**tele-** (1), Gr. *pathos,* feeling.]

**telepheme,** *tel'i-fēm, n.* a telephone message. [**tele-** (1), Gr. *phēmē,* a saying.]

**telephone,** *tel'i-fōn, n.* an instrument for reproducing sound at a distance, esp. by means of electricity.—*v.t.* and *v.i.* to communicate by telephone.—*n.* **tel'ephoner.**—*adj.* **telephonic** (*-fon'ik*).—*adv.* **teleph'onically.**—*ns.* **telephonist** (*ti-lef'ə-nist*), one who works a telephone; **teleph'ony,** telephonic communication. [**tele-** (1), Gr. *phōnē,* a sound.]

**telephotography,** *tel-i-fō-tog'rə-fi, n.* photography of distant objects by means of suitable lenses: wrongly, phototelegraphy.—*n.* **telepho'tograph** (*tel-i-fō'tō-gräf*).—*adj.* **telephotographic** (*-graf'ik*), abbrev. **telepho'to.**—**telephoto lens,** a lens of long focal length for obtaining large images of distant objects. [**tele-** (1), **photography.**]

**teleprinter,** *tel-i-print'ər, n.* a telegraph transmitter with typewriter keyboard. [**tele-** (1), **printer.**]

**teleprompter,** *tel-i-promp'tər, n.* a device by which a television speaker sees a projection of his speech invisible to the audience. [**tele-** (2).]

**telerecording,** *tel-i-ri-kör'ding, n.* recording for broadcasting by television: a television transmission from a recording. [**tele-** (2), **recording.**]

**telergy,** *tel'ər-ji, n.* a physical force assumed to be at work in telepathy.—*adj.* **teler'gic** (*-ûr'jik*), working at a distance, as in telepathy.—*adv.* **teler'gically.** [**tele-** (1), Gr. *ergon,* work.]

**telescope,** *tel'i-skōp, n.* an optical instrument for viewing objects at a distance.—*v.t.* to drive or slide one into another like the movable joints of a spyglass.—*v.i.* to fit or slide in such a way. —*adjs.* **telescopic** (*-skop'ik*), **-al,** of, performed by, or like a telescope: seen only by a telescope: sliding, or arranged, like the joints of a spyglass: capable of retraction and protrusion.—*adv.* **telescop'ically.**—*adj.* **telescop'iform.**—*ns.* **telescopist** (*ti-les'kə-pist*), one who uses the telescope; **Telescopium** (*astron.*), the Telescope, a small southern constellation between Ara and Corona Austrinus; **teles'copy,** the art of constructing or of using the telescope.—**telescope, telescopic sight,** a telescope on a gun used as a sight. [**tele-** (1), Gr. *skopeein,* to see.]

**telescreen,** *tel'i-skrēn, n.* a television screen. [**tele-** (2), **screen.**]

**teleseme,** *tel'i-sēm, n.* a signalling apparatus with an indicator. [**tele-** (1), Gr. *sēma,* a sign.]

**telesm,** *tel'ezm, n.* a talisman.—*adjs.* **telesmat'ic, -al.**—*adv.* **telesmat'ically.** [Gr. *telesma;* see **talisman.**]

**telestic,** *ti-les'tik, adj.* relating to the mysteries. [Gr. *telestikos*—Gr. *teleein,* to fulfil, consummate, initiate, perform—*telos,* end, rite, etc.]

**telestich**, *tel-es'tik*, *tel'es-tik*, *n.* a poem or block of words whose final letters spell a name or word. [Gr. *telos*, end, *stichos*, row.]

**telethon**, *tel'ə-thon*, (*U.S.*) *n.* a very long television programme, esp. one seeking support for e.g. a political candidate, or a charity. [*television* mara*thon*.]

**teletron**, *tel'i-tron*, *n.* a cathode-ray tube for synthesis of television images. [tele- (1), suff. -tron.]

**Teletype**, *tel'i-tīp*, *n.* (proprietary name) a printing telegraph apparatus.—**Teletype'setter** (proprietary name), a telegraphic machine which delivers its message as a perforated roll that can be used to actuate a type-setting machine; **teletype'writer** (*U.S.*), a teleprinter. [tele- (1), Gr. *typos*; see **type**.]

**teleutospore**, *ti-lū'tō-spōr*, *-spör*, *n.* a thick-walled winter-spore of the rust-fungi, producing on germination a promycelium. [Gr. *teleutē*, completion, *sporā*, seed.]

**télévérité**, *tel-i-ver'i-tā*, *n.* the televising of scenes of real life in order to convey a heightened realism.—See also **cinéma vérité**. [tele- (2), modelled on **cinéma vérité**.]

**television**, *tel-i-vizh'ən*, *n.* the viewing of distant objects or events by electrical transmission: the electrical transmission of these: a television receiving set.—Also *adj.*—*v.t.* and *v.i.* **tel'eview**, to view by television.—**tel'eviewer**, a television watcher.—*v.t.* and *v.i.* **tel'evise** (*tel'i-viz*), to transmit by television.—*adjs.* **televi'sional**, **televis'ionary**, of, relating to, television.—*n.* **televi'sor**, a receiver for television.—*adj.* **televi'sual**, **televisional**: **telegenic**. [tele- (1), **vision**.]

**telewriter**, *tel-i-rī'tər*, *n.* telegraph instrument that reproduces writing. [tele- (1), **writer**.]

**telex**, *tel'eks*, *n.* a Post Office service whereby subscribers hire the use of teleprinters. [*tele-* **typewriter** *ex*change.]

**telic**, *tel'ik*, *adj.* expressing purpose: purposive. [Gr. *telikos—telos*, end, purpose.]

**tel(l)**, *tel*, *n.* in Arab lands, a hill, ancient mound. [Ar. *tall*.]

**tell**, *tel*, *v.t.* to count: to count out: to utter: to narrate: to disclose: to inform: to discern: to explain: to order, direct, instruct: to bid (good-bye; *U.S.*).—*v.i.* to give an account: to have an effect (on): to have weight: to make an effective story: to play the informer:—*pa.t.* and *pa.p.* **tōld**.—*adj.* **tell'able**, capable of being told: fit to tell.—*ns.* **tell'er**, one who tells or counts: one who counts votes: a clerk whose duty it is to receive and pay money; **tell'ership**:—*adj.* **tell'ing**, effective.—*n.* numbering: narration: direction, orders.—*adv.* **tell'ingly**.—**tell'ing-off'**, a rating, chiding; **tell'-tale**, one who tells the private concerns or misdeeds of others: a tattler (bird): anything revealing or betraying: an indicator: a recording clock. —*adj.* blabbing: revealing, betraying: indicating.—**take a telling**, to do as one is bid without having to be told again; **tell me another**, you'll have to tell me a more credible story; **tell off**, to count off: to detach on some special duty: to rate, chide; **you're telling me** (*interj.*; *slang*), I know that only too well. [O.E. *tellan*; O.N. *telja*, Ger. *zählen*, to number.]

**tellar, teller**. Same as **tiller** (2).

**Tellus**, *tel'əs*, *n.* the Roman earth-goddess: the earth.—*adj.* **tell'ural**, pertaining to the earth.— *n.* **tell'urate**, a salt of telluric acid.—*adj.* **tell'ūretted**, combined with tellurium; **tellū'rian**, terrestrial.—*n.* an inhabitant of the earth.—*adj.* **tellū'ric**, of or from the earth: of tellurium in higher valency (**telluric acid**, $H_2TeO_4$).—*ns.* **tell'ūride**, a compound of tellurium with another element or radical; **tell'ūrite**, native oxide of tellurium (*min.*): a salt of tellurous acid (*chem.*); **tellū'rium**, the element (Te) of atomic

number 52, app. so named by Klaproth (1798) as the counterpart of his previous discovery of uranium.—*adj.* **tell'ūrous**, of tellurium in lower valency (**tellurous acid**, $H_2TeO_3$). [L. *Tellūs*, *-ūris*.]

**telly**, *tel'i*, (*slang*) *n.* television.

**telophase**, *tel'ō-fāz*, *n.* in mitosis, the stage of reconstruction of nuclei after separation of daughter chromosomes. [Gr. *telos*, completion, *phasis*, phase.]

**telpher**, *tel'fər*, *adj.* pertaining to a system of telpherage.—*n.* a car or carrier in such a system. —*ns.* **tel'pherage**, any system of automatic electric transport: an electric ropeway or cable-way system: overhead traction in general.— **tel'pher-line**; **tel'pherman**; **tel'pherway**. [Irreg. coined by Fleeming Jenkin—Gr. *tēle*, far, *phoros*, bearing—*pherein*, to bear.]

**telson**, *tel'sən*, *n.* the hindermost part of a crustacean or arachnid. [Gr. *telson*, a headland in ploughing; cf. *telos*, end.]

**Telstar**, *tel'stär*, *n.* a satellite launched on 10th July 1962, used to relay television pictures and telephone conversations across the Atlantic.

**Telugu**, *tel'ōō-gōō*, *n.* a Dravidian language of south-east India: one of the people speaking it. —Also *adj.*

**teme**, an old spelling of **team**.

**temenos**, *tem'e-nos*, *n.* a place dedicated to a god, a precinct. [Gr.,—*temnein*, to cut off.]

**temerity**, *ti-mer'i-ti*, *n.* rashness: unreasonable contempt for danger.—*adj.* **temerarious** (*tem-ə-rā'ri-əs*; now *rare*), rash, reckless.—*adv.* **temerā'riously**.—*adj.* **tem'erous**, rash.—*adv.* **tem'erously**. [L. *temeritās*, *-ātis*, and *temerārius— temere*, by chance, rashly.]

**Tempe**, *tem'pē*, *n.* the valley of the Pēneios (Peneus) in Thessaly, praised by the classic poets for its matchless beauty: hence, any place of choice beauty. [Gr. *Tempē (Tempea)*.]

**temper**, *tem'pər*, *v.t.* to mix in due proportion: to modify by blending or mixture: to moderate: to soften: loosely, esp. formerly, to harden (steel) by heating to red heat and quenching: properly, to heat again, less strongly and cool in air: loosely, to carry out both operations: to adjust: to tune: to attune: to adjust to a temperament (*mus.*): to bring to a favourable state of mind.—*v.i.* to tamper, meddle (*Shak.*): to soften (*Shak.*): to become tempered.—*n.* due mixture or balance of different or contrary qualities: state of a metal as to hardness, etc.: constitution of the body: temperament: disposition: habitual or actual frame of mind: mood: composure: self-control: uncontrolled anger: a fit of ill-humour or rage: lime or other substance used to neutralise the acidity of cane-juice.—*n.* **tem'pera**, (*paint.*; It.) distemper.— *adj.* **tem'perable**, capable of being tempered.— *ns.* **temperal'itie** (*Shak.*), Mrs Quickly's elaboration of temper, frame of mind; **tem'perament**, proportioned mixture: state with respect to combination or predominance of qualities (*obs.*): climate (*obs.*): internal constitution or state: combination or predominance of humour (*obs. physiol.*): disposition: type of physical and mental organisation—choleric or bilious, sanguine, melancholy, phlegmatic (*obs. physiol.*): high excitability, nervous instability, and sensitiveness (*coll.*): tempering (*arch.*): compromise (*arch.*): a system of compromise in tuning (*mus.*).—*adjs.* **temperament'al**; **temperament'ful**. —*adv.* **temperament'ally**.—*n.* **tem'perance**, moderation, esp. in the indulgence of the natural appetites and passions—in a narrower sense, moderation in the use of alcoholic liquors, and even entire abstinence from them.—*adj.* advocating or consistent with temperance in or abstinence from alcoholic drinks.—*adj.* **tem'perate**, moderate: self-restrained, esp. in appetites and passions: abstemious: moderate in temperature.—*v.t.* (*obs.* or *rare*) to temper: to moderate: to restrain.—*adv.* **tem′perately.**—*n.* **tem′perateness.**—*adj.* **tem′perative,** having moderating influence.—*n.* **tem′perature,** tempering: tempered condition: mixture: constitution: proportion: degree of hotness: condition determining interchange of heat between bodies: a body temperature above normal (*coll.*).—*adj.* **tem′pered,** having a certain specified disposition or temper: brought to a certain temper, as steel: tuned or adjusted to some mean or to equal, temperament (*mus.*).—*adv.* **tem′peredly.**—*n.* **tem′perer.**—*n.* and *adj.* **tem′pering.**—**temperance hotel,** one which professes to supply no alcoholic liquors; **temperate zones,** the parts of the earth of moderate temperature between the tropics and the polar circles.—**absolute temperature** (see **absolute**); **bad temper,** an angry humour: an inclination to irascibility; **equal temperament,** a compromise in tuning by which the octave is divided into twelve equal intervals; **good temper,** an unruffled humour: good-nature; **keep one's temper,** to restrain oneself from showing, or losing, one's temper; **lose one's temper,** to break out in anger; **out of temper,** in an irritable mood: angry. [L. *temperāre,* to temper, restrain, compound, moderate, partly through O.E. *temprian.*]

**tempest,** *tem′pist, n.* a violent wind storm: a violent commotion or agitation (*fig.*).—*v.t.* (*Milt.*) to stir violently.—*adjs.* **tempestive** (*-pest′*), timely: seasonable; **tempestŭous** (*-pest′*).—*adv.* **tempest′-ŭously.**—*n.* **tempest′ŭousness.**—*adjs.* **tem′pest-beaten, tem′pest-tossed** -**tost,** (*Shak.*) driven about by storms. [O.Fr. *tempeste*—a L.L. form of L. *tempestās,* a season, tempest—*tempus,* time.]

**template.** See **templet.**

**temple,** *tem′pl, n.* a building or place dedicated to, or regarded as the house of, a god: a place of worship: in France, a Protestant church: (*cap.*) the headquarters of the Knights Templars on or near the site of Solomon's temple in Jerusalem: (*cap.*) in London, two inns of court (*Inner* and *Middle Temple*) on the site once occupied by the Knights Templars, with the Knights' church.—*adj.* **tem′plar,** of a temple.—*n.* **Tem′-plar,** a member of a religious and military order (**Knights Templars**) founded in 1119 for the protection of the Holy Sepulchre and pilgrims going thither—extinguished 1307-14: a student or lawyer living in the Temple, London: member of a U.S. order of Freemasons: (see also **good**).—*adj.* **tem′pled.** [L. *templum.*]

**temple,** *tem′pl, n.* flat portion of either side of head above cheekbone. [O.Fr.,—L. *tempus, -oris.*]

**templet, template,** *tem′plit, n.* a mould shaped to required outline from which to execute moulding: a thin plate cut to the shape required, by which a surface of an article being made is marked out. [L. *templum,* a small timber.]

**tempo,** *tem′pō,* (*mus.*) *n.* time: speed and rhythm: —*pl.* **tem′pi** (*-pē*). [It.]

**temporal,** *tem′pər-l, adj.* pertaining to time: pertaining to time in this life or world—opp. to *eternal*: worldly, secular, or civil—opp. to *spiritual, sacred* or *ecclesiastical*: pertaining to tense, or to length of syllable or vowel (*gram.*).—*n.* **temporality** (*-al′i-ti*), state or fact of being temporal: what pertains to temporal welfare: (usu. *pl.*) secular possessions, revenues of an ecclesiastic proceeding from lands, tithes, and the like.—*adv.* **tem′porally.**—*n.* **tem′poralty,** the laity: lay peers: (usu. *pl.*) worldly possessions.—*adj.* **temporā′neous,** temporal.—*adv.* **tem′porarily.**—*n.* **tem′porariness.**—*adj.* **tem′porary,** for a time only: transient.—*n.* a person employed temporarily.—*n.* **temporisā′tion.**—*v.i.* **tem′porise, -ize,** to comply with the time or occasion: to

yield to circumstances: to behave so as to gain time.—*n.* **tem′poriser.**—*n.* and *adj.* **tem′porising.** —*adv.* **tem′porisingly.** [L. *tempus, -oris,* time.]

**temporal,** *tem′pər-l, adj.* of or at the temple (of the head).—*n.* a bone, muscle, or scale in that position. [L. *tempus, -oris;* see **temple** (2).]

**tempore,** *tem′par-ē, tem′por-e,* (L.) in the time of.

**tempt,** *temt, v.t.* to put to trial: to test: to try or tend to persuade, esp. to evil: to entice.—*n.* **temptabil′ity.**—*adj.* **temp′table.**—*ns.* **temp′table-ness; tempta′tion** (*tem-* or *temp-*), act of tempting: state of being tempted: that which tempts enticement to evil: trial.—*adj.* **temptā′tious,** seductive.—*n.* **temp′ter,** one who tempts, esp. the devil:—*fem.* **temp′tress.**—*n.* **temp′ting,** action of the verb.—*adj.* **attractive,** enticing.—*adv.* **temp′tingly.**—*n.* **temp′tingness.** [O.Fr. *tempter* —L. *tentāre,* an intens. of *tendēre,* to stretch.]

**'tempt, tempt,** aphetic for **attempt.**

**temse, tems, tems, temz,** *n.* a sieve.—*v.t.* to sift. [O.E. *temesian,* to sift; cf. Du. *tems.*]

**temulence,** *tem′ū-ləns, n.* intoxication.—Also **tem′-ulency.**—*adj.* **tem′ulent.**—*adv.* **tem′ulently.** [L. *tēmulentus,* drunk.]

**ten, ten,** *n.* the cardinal number next above nine: a symbol representing it (x, etc.): a set of that number of things or persons: used indefinitely, a large number: an article of a size denoted by 10: a card with ten pips: a score of ten points, tricks, etc.: the tenth hour after midday or midnight.—*adj.* of the number ten.—*adj.* and *adv.* **ten′fold,** in ten divisions: ten times as much.—*n.* **tenn′er** (*slang*), a ten-pound note: a ten-dollar bill: ten years.—*adj.* **tenth,** the last of ten: next after the ninth: equal to one of ten equal parts.—*n.* a tenth part: an octave and a third (*mus.*): a note at that interval (*mus.*).—*adv.* **tenth′ly.**—*adj.* **ten′-foot,** measuring ten feet. —**ten′pence,** an amount in money equal to ten pennies.—*adj.* **ten′penny,** offered for, or sold at, tenpence.—**ten′penny nail,** formerly, a nail sold at tenpence a hundred: a large nail; **ten′penny-piece′; ten′pins,** American game like skittles; **ten′-point′er,** a stag of ten points or tines.—*adj.* **ten′-pound,** weighing, worth, sold or offered for, ten pounds.—**ten′-pound′er,** something weighing or worth ten pounds: one who was a voter in virtue of occupying property worth ten pounds a year.—*adj.* **ten′-score,** two hundred.—**long ten,** the ten of trumps in catch-the-ten; **ten-gallon hat** (*U.S.*), cowboy's broad-brimmed hat; **ten minute rule,** parliamentary procedure by which a member makes a short speech (usu. lasting ten minutes) introducing a bill. [O.E. (Anglian) *tēn, tēne* (W.S. *tien, tiene*); Ger. *zehn,* W. *deg,* L. *decem,* Gr. *deka,* Sans. *daśa.*]

**tenable,** *ten′a-bl* (or *tēn′*), *adj.* capable of being retained, kept, or defended.—*ns.* **tenabil′ity, ten′ableness.** [Fr. *tenable*—*tenir,* to hold.]

**tenace,** *ten′ās, -is, n.* the combination in one hand of the cards next above and next below the other side's best in the suit. [Sp. *tenaza,* pincers.]

**tenacious,** *ti-nā′shəs, adj.* retaining or holding fast: sticking stiffly: tough: stubborn.—*adv.* **tenā′-ciously.**—*ns.* **tenā′ciousness, tenacity** (*-nas′i-ti*). [L. *tenāx, -ācis*—*tenēre,* to hold.]

**tenaculum,** *te-nak′ū-ləm, n.* a surgical hook or forceps for picking up blood-vessels. [L. *tenā-culum,* holder, pincers.]

**tenaille,** *te-nāl′,* (*fort.*) *n.* an outwork in the main ditch in front of the curtain.—*n.* **tenaillon** (*te-nal′yən*), a work to strengthen the side of a small ravelin.—Also **tenail′.** [Fr.,—L. *tenā-culum,* pincers—*tenēre,* to hold.]

**tenant,** *ten′ənt, n.* one who holds under another: one who has, on certain conditions, temporary possession of any place: an occupant.—*v.t.* to hold as a tenant: to occupy.—*v.i.* to dwell.— *n.* **ten′ancy,** possession by private ownership: a temporary occupation or holding of land or property by a tenant: time of such holding.— *adj.* **ten´antable,** fit to be tenanted: in a state of repair suitable for a tenant; **ten´antless.**— *ns.* **ten´antry,** the state or time of being a tenant: a set or body of tenants; **ten´antship.**—**tenant-at-will,** one who holds only so long as the proprietor wills; **ten´ant-farm´er,** a farmer who rents a farm; **ten´ant-in-chief´,** one holding lands directly from the sovereign; **ten´ant-right,** the right of a tenant, esp. that of a customary tenant to sit continuously at a reasonable rent, the right to receive compensation for his interest from the incoming tenant, and for all permanent or unexhausted improvements from the landlord. [Fr. *tenant,* pr.p. of *tenir*—L. *tenēre,* to hold.]

**tench,** *tench, -sh, n.* a freshwater fish (*Tinea vulgaris*) of the carp family, very tenacious of life. [O.Fr. *tenche* (Fr. *tanche*)—L. *tinca.*]

**tend,** *tend, v.t.* to attend to: to mind: to watch over or stand by and perform services for or connected with: to minister to, wait upon: to escort (*Shak.*).—*v.i.* (*Shak.*) to attend, hearken: to be in waiting or readiness: to wait, attend.—*n.* **ten´dance,** tending: expectation (*Spens.*): attendants collectively (*Shak.*).—*adj.* **tend´ed.**—*n.* **ten´der,** one who tends: a small craft that attends a larger: a carriage attached to a locomotive to carry fuel and water.—**tend out on** (*U.S.*), to attend or attend to. [Aphetic for **attend.**]

**tend,** *tend, v.i.* to stretch, aim at, move, or incline in some direction: to be directed to any end or purpose: to be apt: to conduce.—*ns.* **ten´dence, tendenz** (*ten-dents´*; Ger.), tendency (esp. in composition, tendentious); **ten´dency,** a trend, drift, inclination: proneness.—*adjs.* **tendential** (*-den´shl*), **tenden´tious, tenden´cious,** purposely tending: with an object: biased.—*adv.* **tenden´tiously.**—*n.* **tenden´tiousness.** [L. *tendēre* and Fr. *tendre,* to stretch.]

**tender.** See under tend (1).

**tender,** *ten´dər, v.t.* to offer for acceptance, esp. to offer in payment: to proffer.—*v.i.* to make a tender.—*n.* an offer or proposal, esp. of some service: the paper containing it: the thing offered: a formal offer to save the consequences of non-payment or non-performance.—*ns.* **ten´derer; ten´dering.**—**legal tender** (see legal). [Fr. *tendre,* to stretch, reach out.]

**tender,** *ten´dər, adj.* soft, delicate: easily chewed, not tough: of porcelain, soft-paste: easily impressed or injured: not hardy: gentle: scrupulous, chary: sensitive, esp. to pain: requiring gentle handling: easily moved to pity, love, etc.: careful not to hurt: considerate, careful (with *of*): pathetic: expressive, or of the nature, affectionate: beloved (*Shak.*): apt to lean over under sail.—*v.t.* to treat with tenderness (*Shak.*): to feel tenderness for (*Shak.*): to cherish: to value, have respect to: to make tender.—*n.* care, regard, concern (*Shak.*): tender feeling, fondness (now usu. in Fr. form tendre, *tädr´*).—*v.t.* ten´derise, -ize, of meat, to break down the connective tissue by pounding or by applying a chemical.—*n.* **ten´derling,** one too much coddled, an effeminate fellow: one of the first horns of a deer.—*adv.* **ten´derly.**—*n.* **ten´derness.**—*adj.* **ten´der-dying** (*Shak.*), dying young.—**ten´derfoot,** one not yet hardened to life in the prairie, mining-camp, etc.: a newcomer: a greenhorn: a boy scout or girl guide who has passed only the first tests (*obs.*):—*pl.* **ten´derfeet.**—*adj.* **ten´derheart´ed,** full of feeling.—*adv.* **ten´der-heart´edly.**—**ten´der-heart´edness.**—*adj.* **ten´der-heft´ed** (*Shak.*), perh. set in a tender haft or frame.—**ten´der-loin,** the tenderest part of the loin of beef, pork, etc., close to the lumbar vertebrae

(*U.S.*): a district juicy with bribes to the police (*U.S. slang*). [Fr. *tendre*—L. *tener.*]

**tendon,** *ten´dən, n.* a cord, band, or sheet of fibrous tissue attaching a muscle to a bone or other structure.—*adj.* **ten´dinous.** [L.L. *tendō, -inis* or *-ōnis,* app.—Gr. *tenōn, -ontos,* sinew, tendon; cf. *teinein,* to stretch; *d* suggested by L. *tendēre.*]

**tendril,** *ten´dril, n.* a plant's coiling threadlike climbing organ (leaf, leaflet, or shoot).—*adjs.* **ten´drillar; ten´drilled.** [Ety. dub.; cf. Fr. *tendrillon, shoot.*]

**tendron,** *ten´drən, n.* a shoot, sprout: (ln *pl.*) cartilages of the ribs. [Fr.]

**tene.** See teen (1).

**tenebrae,** *ten´i-brē,* L. *ten´e-brī, n.pl.* (*R.C.*) matins and lauds in Holy Week with gradual extinction of lights.—*adj.* **tenebrif´ic** (L. *facĕre,* to make), producing darkness.—*n.* **tenebrio** (*tin-eb´ri-ō*), a night-spirit: a night-prowler: (*cap.*) the mealworm genus of beetles, giving name to the family Tenebrionidae (*-on´i-dē*).—*adjs.* **teneb´rious, ten´ebrose, ten´ebrous,** dark.—*ns.* **ten´ebrist,** a painter of the naturalist school of Caravaggio affecting dark colouring; **teneb´rity; tenebros´ity.** [L. *tenebrae,* darkness.]

**tenement,** *ten´i-mənt, n.* a holding, by any tenure: anything held, or that may be held, by a tenant: a dwelling or habitation, or part of it, used by one family: one of a set of apartments in one building, each occupied by a separate family: a building divided into dwellings for a number of families (*Scot.*).—*adjs.* **tenemental** (*-ment´l*); **tenement´ary.** [L.L. *tenementum*—L. *tenēre,* to hold.]

**tenendum,** *ti-nen´dəm, n.* that clause in a deed wherein the tenure of the land is defined and limited. [L. neut. of *tenendus,* ger. of *tenēre,* to hold.]

**tenesmus,** *ti-nes´məs, n.* painful and ineffectual straining to relieve the bowels. [Latinised from Gr. *teinesmos*—*teinein,* to strain.]

**tenet,** *ten´et* (also *tē´nit*), *n.* any opinion, principle, or doctrine which a person holds or maintains as true. [L. *tenet,* (he) holds—*tenēre,* to hold.]

**tenioid, etc.** See Taenia.

**tennantite,** *ten´ənt-it, n.* a mineral composed of sulphur, arsenic, and copper, usu. with iron. [Named after Smithson *Tennant* (1761-1815), English chemist.]

**tenné,** *ten´ā,* (*her.*) *n.* an orange-brown tincture. —Also *adj.* [Obs. Fr.; cf. **tawny.**]

**tennis,** *ten´is, n.* an ancient game played with ball, rackets (orig. palms of the hands), and net, in a specially constructed building or enclosed court (distinguished from lawn-tennis as **close, court, real,** or **royal** tennis): now usu. lawn-tennis.—**tenn´is-ball; tenn´is-court; tennis elbow,** inflammation of the bursa at the elbow, caused by over-exercise; **tenn´is-match; tenn´is-player; tenn´is-racket; tenn´is-shoe.** [Prob. Fr. *tenez,* imper. of *tenir,* to take, receive.]

**tenon,** *ten´ən, n.* a projection at the end of a piece of wood, etc., inserted into the socket or mortise of another, to hold the two together.—*v.t.* to fix or fit with a tenon.—*n.* **ten´oner.**—**ten´on-saw,** a thin back-saw for tenons, etc. [Fr. *tenon*—*tenir,* to hold—L. *tenēre.*]

**tenor,** (*obs.* or *old-fashioned* **tenour**), *ten´ər, n.* continuity of state: general run or course: time of currency: purport: an exact transcript: the higher of the two kinds of voices usu. belonging to adult males (app. because the melody was assigned to it): an instrument, e.g. the viola, of corresponding compass: the part next above the bass in a vocal quartet: one who sings tenor. —Also *adj.*—*ns.* **ten´orist; tenoroon´,** an obsolete tenor oboe.—**ten´or-clef,** the C clef placed on the fourth line. [L. *tenor*—*tenēre,* to hold.]

**tenorite,** *ten´ər-it, n.* melaconite, black copper

ore (CuO), found on Vesuvius. [Named after G. *Tenore*, President of the Naples Academy, 1841.]

**tenotomy,** *tən-ot'əm-i, n.* surgical cutting of a tendon. [Gr. *tenōn,* tendon, *tomē,* a cut.]

**tenrec,** *ten'rek,* **tanrec,** *tan'rek, n.* a large Madagascan insectivore (Centetes). [Malagasy *t(r)àndraka.*]

**tense,** *tens, n.* time in grammar, the form of a verb to indicate the time of the action. [O.Fr. *tens* (Fr. *temps*)—L. *tempus,* time.]

**tense,** *tens, adj.* stretched tight: strained: rigid: pronounced with the tongue tightened or narrowed.—*adv.* **tense'ly.**—*ns.* **tense'ness,** state of being tense; **tensibil'ity.**—*adjs.* **tens'ible,** capable of being stretched; **tens'ile** (*il;* in U.S. *-il, -əl*), tensible: in relation to stretching.—*ns.* **tensility** (*-il'i-ti*); **tension** (*ten'shən*), stretching: a pulling strain: stretched or strained state: strain generally: formerly, pressure in gases or vapours: electromotive force: a state of barely suppressed emotion, as excitement, suspense, anxiety, or hostility: a feeling of strain with resultant symptoms (*psych.*): strained relations (between persons): opposition (between conflicting ideas or forces); **tens'ity,** tenseness.—*adj.* **tens'ive,** giving the sensation of tenseness or stiffness.—*n.* **tens'or,** a muscle that tightens a part: the ratio of lengthening of a vector.—**ten'sion-rod,** a structural member subjected to tensile stress only. [L. *tēnsus,* pa.p. of *tendĕre,* to stretch.]

**tenson,** *ten'sn, n.* a competition in verse between two troubadours before a court of love: a subdivision of the chanson so composed.—Also **ten'zon.** [Fr.,—L. *tēnsiō, -ōnis,* a struggle.]

**tent,** *tent, n.* a portable lodge or shelter, commonly of canvas stretched on poles: a temporary field pulpit: a common shelter spun by a company of caterpillars.—*v.i.* to camp in a tent.—*v.t.* to canopy: to lodge in tents.—*adj.* **ten'ted,** covered with tents: formed like a tent: dwelling in tents.—*ns.* **tent'er,** one who lives in a tent; **tent'ful,** as many as a tent will hold; **tent'ing.**—*adj.* (*Keats*) having the form of a tent.—*adv.* **tent'wise.**—**tent'-bed,** a camp-bed, a bed with a canopy hanging from a central point; **tent'-cloth,** cloth suitable for tents; **tent'-fly,** a flap forming a door to a tent: a subsidiary outer roof to a tent; **tent'-guy,** a stay or guy-rope for a tent; **tent'-maker;** **tent'-peg, -pin,** a strong notched peg driven into the ground to fasten a tent; **tent'-pegging,** the sport of riding at full speed and trying to bear off a tent-peg on the point of a lance; **tent'-pole,** a pole to support a tent; **tent'-preaching;** **tent'-rope,** a rope for securing a tent to a peg. [Fr. *tente*—L. *tendĕre, tentum,* to stretch.]

**tent,** *tent, n.* a probe (*obs.*): a plug or roll of soft material for dilating a wound or keeping open an orifice.—*v.t.* to probe (*obs.*): to dilate or keep open with a tent. [Fr. *tente*—L. *tentāre,* to try.]

**tent,** *tent, n.* a deep-red Spanish wine. [Sp. *tinto*—L. *tinctus,* pa.p. of *tingĕre,* to dye.]

**tent,** *tent,* (*Scot.*) *n.* heed.—*v.t.* to take heed or notice of, attend to.—*n.* **tent'er,** one who tends.—*adj.* **tent'ie, tent'y.** [Aphetic for **attent** and **intent.**]

**tent,** *tent, n.* (*obs.*) an embroidery or tapestry frame.—**tent'-stitch,** an embroidery stitch made in parallel series diagonally to the threads: **tent-work;** **tent'-work,** work in tent-stitch. [Origin obscure; cf. M.E. *tent,* to stretch, **tenter,** and L. *tendĕre, tentum.*]

**tentacle,** *tent'ə-kl, n.* a slender flexible organ for feeling, grasping, etc.: a gland-tipped insect-capturing process in sundew.—Also **tentaculum** (*-ak'ū-ləm; pl.* **tentac'ūla**).—*adjs.* **ten'tacled;** **tentac'ūlar;** **tentac'ūlate;** **tentaculīf'erous.**—*n.*

**tentac'ūlite,** a ringed tapering Silurian and Devonian fossil, app. a pteropod. [L. *tentāre,* to feel.]

**tentation,** *ten-tā'shən, n.* an old form of **temptation:** a method of adjusting by a succession of trials.—*adj.* **tentative** (*ten'tə-tiv*), done or made provisionally and experimentally.—*n.* an experimental attempt.—*adv.* **ten'tatively.** [L. *tentāre,* to try.]

**tenter,** *ten'tər, n.* a frame for stretching cloth: a **tenter-hook:** a hook.—*v.t.* to stretch on hooks.—**ten'ter-hook,** a sharp, hooked nail as on a tenter: a hook.—**on tenter-hooks,** in impatient suspense. [App. conn. with Fr. *tenture,* hangings, and L. *tendĕre,* to stretch.]

**tenter, tentie, tenty.**—See tent (various).

**tentigo,** *ten-tī'gō, n.* priapism: morbid lasciviousness.—*adj.* **tentiginous** (*-tij'i-nəs*). [L. *tentigō, -inis—tendĕre,* to stretch.]

**tentorium,** *ten-tō'ri-əm, -tō', n.* a sheet of the dura mater stretched between the cerebrum and the cerebellum: the internal chitinous skeleton of an insect's head.—*adj.* **tento'rial.** [L. *tentōrium,* a tent—*tendĕre,* to stretch.]

**tenue,** *tə-nü, n.* bearing, carriage: manner of dress. [Fr.]

**tenuis,** *ten'ū-is,* L. *-ōō-is, n.* an unaspirated voiceless stop consonant:—*pl.* **ten'ues** (*-ēz, -ās*).—*adj.* **tenuiros'tral** (L. *rōstrum,* bill), slender billed.—*n.* **tenū'ity,** thinness: slenderness: rarity.—*adj.* **ten'ūous** (*rarely* **tenū'ious**), thin: slender: rarefied. [L. *tenuis,* thin; cf. *tendĕre,* to stretch.]

**tenure,** *ten'yər, n.* holding, occupation: time of holding: conditions on which property is held: a tenant's rights, duties, etc.—*adj.* **tenūr'ial.** [A.Fr. *tenure—tenir,* to hold.]

**tenure,** (*Shak.*) for **tenor.**

**tenuto,** *te-nōō'tō,* (*mus.*) *adj.* sustained. [It., pa.p. of *tenere,* to hold.]

**teocalli,** *tā-, tē-ō-kal'(y)i, n.* a Mexican pyramid temple. [Nahuatl,—*teotl,* god, *calli,* house.]

**tepee, teepee,** *tē'pē, ti-pē', n.* an American Indian tent formed of skins, etc., stretched over a frame of converging poles. [Sioux *tipi,* dwelling.]

**tepefy,** *tep'i-fī, v.t.* and *v.i.* to make or become tepid. [L. *tepefacĕre—tepēre,* to be tepid, *facĕre,* to make.]

**tephigram,** *tē'fi-gram, n.* (*meteor.*) a diagram on which is plotted information about vertical variation of atmospheric conditions. [*t,* for temperature, *phi,* former symbol for entropy.]

**tephrite,** *tef'rīt, n.* a fine-grained basaltic rock containing a feldspathoid as well as feldspar, but no olivine.—*adj.* **tephritic** (*-rit'ik*).—*ns.* **teph'roite** (*-rō-īt*), an ashy-grey or reddish silicate of manganese; **teph'romancy,** divination (Gr. *manteiā*) by ashes, esp. of sacrifice. [Gr. *tephrā,* ashes, *tephros,* ash-coloured.]

**tepid,** *tep'id, adj.* moderately warm: lukewarm.—*ns.* **tepida'rium** (L. *-dä'ri-ōōm*), a warm room between the cold and hot rooms of a Roman bath; **tepid'ity, tep'idness,** lukewarmness. [L. *tepidus—tepēre,* to be warm.]

**tequila, -lla,** *tə-kē'lə, n.* Mexican intoxicating drink made from an agave. [From district of Mexico.]

**ter-,** *tûr-,* in composition, thrice.—*adj.* **tercentenary** (*tûr'sən-tē'nə-ri,* or *-ten'ə-ri,* or *tûr-sen'ti-nə-ri*), of three hundred (usu. years).—*n.* a 300th anniversary.—*adj.* **tercentennial** (*tûr-sen-ten'yəl*), of 300 years.—*n.* a 300th anniversary.—*n.* **tersanctus** (*tûr-sang(k)'təs*), the Sanctus.—*adj.* **tervalent** (*tûr'və-lənt, tər-vā'lənt*), trivalent. [L.] **tera-,** *ter'ə-, pfx.* ten to the twelfth power, formerly **megamega-.**

**terai,** *ter-ī', n.* a wide-brimmed double-crowned ventilated hat, first worn in the *Terai* (Taráí), India.

**teraph,** *ter'əf, n.* in ancient Jewish religion and divination, an image of some sort:—*pl.* **ter'aphim** (also used as *sing.*). [Heb.]

**teras**, *ter'as*, (*med.*) *n.* a monstrosity:—*pl.* **ter'ata**. —*adj.* **teratogenic** (*ter-ə-tō-jen'ik*), producing monsters.—*ns.* **terat'ogen**, an agent that raises the incidence of congenital malformations; **teratogeny** (*-toj'i-ni*), the production of monsters. —*adjs.* **ter'atoid**, monstrous; **teratolog'ic, -al.**— *ns.* **teratol'ogist**; **teratol'ogy**, the study of malformations or abnormal growths, animal or vegetable: a tale of marvels; **teratō'ma**, a tumour, containing tissue from all three germ-layers:—*pl.* **teratō'mata.**—*adj.* **teratō'matous**. [Gr. *teras, -atos*, a monster.]

**terbium**, *tûr'bi-əm*, *n.* a rare metal (Tb; at. numb. 65) found in certain yttrium minerals. —*adj.* **ter'bic.** [From *Ytterby*; see **yttrium.**]

**terce**, *tûrs*, *n.* a widow's right, where she has no conventional provision, to a life-rent of a third of the husband's heritable property (*Scots law*): the office of the third hour (*hist.*). [See **tierce.**]

**tercel**, *tûrs'əl*, **tiercel**, *tēr'səl*, **tarsel**, *tärs'əl*, **tassel(l)**, *tas'əl*, *n.* a male hawk.—*n.* **terc'elet**, a tercel.—**ter'cel-gent'le** (*Scott*), **tass'el-gent'le** (*Shak.*), **tass'ell-gent'** (*Spens.*), a male peregrine falcon; **ter'cel-jer'kin**, a male gerfalcon. [O.Fr. *tercel*—L. *tertius*, third, perh. as being one-third smaller than the female, or as supposed to hatch from the last egg of three.]

**tercet**, *tûr'sit*, *n.* a group of three lines in verse. [It. *terzetto*.]

**tercio**, *tûr'si-ō, -shi-ō* (*Scott* **tertia**), (*hist.*) *n.* an infantry regiment, orig. Spanish. [Sp.]

**terebene**, *ter'i-bēn*, *n.* a light-yellow disinfectant liquid, a mixture of hydrocarbons made from oil of turpentine, used as a solvent for paint.—*n.* **ter'ebinth**, the turpentine-tree (*Pistacia terebinthus*; family Anacardiaceae).—*adj.* **terebinth'ine.** [Gr. *terebinthos*.]

**terebra**, *ter'i-bra*, *n.* a Roman engine for boring walls: a boring instrument: a piercing ovipositor: (*cap.*) a genus of gasteropods with auger-shaped shell.—*adj.* **ter'ebrant**, boring: having a piercing ovipositor.—*n.* (*facet.*) a bore. —*v.t.* and *v.i.* **ter'ebrate**, to bore.—*adj.* having scattered perforations: having a borer.—*ns.* **terebra'tion**; **Terebrat'ūla**, the lamp-shell genus of brachiopods, with perforated beak. [L. *terebra*.]

**Teredo**, *te-rē'dō*, *n.* the ship-worm genus of molluscs. [L. *terēdō, -inis*—Gr. *terēdōn, -onos*, a boring worm—root of *teirein*, to wear away.]

**terefa(h)**, *tə-rä-fä', -rä'*, *adj.* not ritually clean, not kosher. [Heb. *tāraph*, to tear.]

**terek**, *ter'ek*, *n.* a sandpiper of the river *Terek* (Russia).

**Terentian**, *ter-en'shən, -shyən*, *adj.* pertaining to the Roman comic poet *Terence*, P. Terentius Afer (fl. 165 B.C.).

**terete**, *tə-rēt, ter'ēt*, *adj.* smooth and cylindrical. [L. *terēs, terĕtis*, smooth, *terēre*, to rub.]

**terf, terfe**, Milton's spellings of **turf.**

**tergum**, *tûr'gəm*, *n.* the back: the back or back plate of a somite.—*adj.* **ter'gal.**—*n.* **ter'gite** (*-jīt*); the back plate of a somite.—*v.i.* **ter'giversate** (*-ji-*; L. *versārī*, to turn), to turn one's back: to desert, apostatise: to shuffle, shift, use evasions. —*ns.* **tergiversa'tion**; **ter'giversātor.** [L. *tergum*, the back.]

**term**, *tûrm*, *n.* a limit: an end: a term-day: the normal time of child-birth: any limited period: the time for which anything lasts: a division of the academic or school year: a period of sittings: (in *pl.*) conditions, stipulations: (in *pl.*) a footing: (in *pl.*) charge, fee: (in *pl.*) respect (*Shak.*): a quantity added to or subtracted from others in an expression (*alg.*): an item in a series: that which may be subject or predicate of a proposition: a word used in a specially understood or defined sense: an expression generally: a bust in continuity with its pedestal.—*v.t.* to call, designate.—*n.* **term'er**, (*hist.*) one who came

to town in term.—*adj.* **term'less**, endless: inexpressible (*Shak.*): unconditional.—*adj.* and *adv.* **term'ly.**—*n.* a publication appearing once a term.—*n.* **term'or**, one who holds an estate for a term of years or for life.—**term'-day**, a day of the year fixed for some purpose, as payment of rent, beginning or end of a tenancy, hiring of servants, household removals; **term'-time.**—**bring to terms**, to compel to the acceptance of conditions; **come to terms**, to come to an agreement: to submit; **come to terms with** (*fig.*), find a way of living with (some personal trouble or difficulty); **eat one's terms** (see **eat**); **in terms**, in so many words, explicitly: engaged in negotiations; **in terms of**, having or using as unit: in the language peculiar to; **keep a term**, to give the regular attendance during a period of study; **on speaking terms**, friendly enough to speak to each other: well enough acquainted to speak; **on terms**, in friendly relations: on an equal footing; **stand upon terms**, to insist upon conditions; **term of years**, an interest or estate in land for a period; **terms of reference** (see **refer**); **terms of trade**, relation between export and import prices in national accounts. [Fr. *terme*—L. *terminus*, a boundary.]

**termagant**, *tûr'mə-gənt*, *n.* a boisterous brawler or bully, esp. a woman.—*adj.* boisterous: brawling. —*n.* **ter'magancy.**—*adv.* **ter'magantly.** [M.E. *Termagan* or *Tervagant*, a supposed Mohammedan idol, represented in the old plays and moralities as of a violent character.]

**Termes**, *tûr'mēz*, *n.* a genus of termites. [L. *termes, -itis*, a wood-worm.]

**Terminus**, *tûr'min-əs*, *n.* the Roman god of boundaries: (the following meanings without *cap.*) a term (bust) of Terminus, or other: a boundary stone: an end-point, esp. of a route, railway or electric circuit: a railway station at such a point:—*pl.* **ter'mini** (*-ī*).—*n.* **terminabil'ity.** —*adj.* **ter'minable**, that may come or be brought to an end.—*n.* **ter'minableness.**—*adv.* **ter'minably.** —*adj.* **ter'minal**, of, at, forming, or marking, an end, boundary, or terminus: final: of a term: occurring every term.—*n.* an end: an ending: a rail, air, or other terminus: a free end in an open electric circuit.—*n.pl.* **Termina'lia**, an annual Roman festival in honour of Terminus. —*n.sing.* the myrobalan genus of Combretaceae. —*adv.* **ter'minally.**—*v.t.* and *v.i.* **ter'minate.**—*n.* **termina'tion**, ending.—*adjs.* **termina'tional**; **ter'-minative**, tending to terminate or determine: expressive of completion: definitive: absolute. —*adv.* **ter'minatively.**—*n.* **ter'minātor**, one who or that which, terminates: the boundary between the illuminated and dark portions of the moon or of a planet.—*adj.* **ter'minatory.**—*ns.* **ter'miner** (*law*), the act of determining; **ter'-minism**, nominalism (*phil.*): the doctrine that there is a time limit for the operation of grace (*theol.*); **ter'minist.**—*adj.* **terminolog'ical.**—*adv.* **terminolog'ically.**—*n.* **terminol'ogy**, nomenclature: the set of terms used in any art, science, etc.—**terminal illness**, fatal disease in its final stages; **terminal velocity**, speed of object on impact with a target: the greatest speed attained by an object falling or fired through a fluid; **terminological inexactitude** (*facet.*), a lie. [L. *Terminus, terminus*; cf. Gr. *terma*, end.]

**terminus**, *tûr'min-əs*, **ter'min-ōōs**, (L.) the end, limit.—**terminus ad quem** (*ad kwem*), the limit to which: destination; **terminus a quo** (*ä kwō*), the limit from which: starting-point.

**termite**, *tûr'mīt*, *n.* a so-called white ant, a pale-coloured insect of the Isoptera, only superficially like an ant.—*ns.* **termitarium** (*tûr-mi-tā'ri-əm*), **ter'mitary** (*-tər-i-*), a nest or mound of termites. [L. *termes, termitis*, a wood-worm.]

**tern**, *tûrn*, *n.* a long-winged aquatic bird allied to the gulls. [Cf. O.N. *therna*; O.E. *stearn, tearn*.]

**tern,** *túrn, n.* a three, set of three: a prize for drawing three winning numbers.—*adjs.* **ter′nal,** threefold; **ter′nary,** in threes: of three components: based on three: of a third order.—*n.* (*obs.*) a triad.—*adj.* **ter′nate,** with three leaflets (*bot.*): grouped in threes.—*adv.* **ter′nately.**—*n.* **ter′nion,** a triad: a section of paper for a book containing three double leaves or twelve pages. [L. *terni,* three each—*trēs,* three.]

**terne,** *túrn,* **terneplate,** *n.* sheet-iron or steel coated with an alloy, chiefly of lead and tin, known as **terne metal.**—*v.t.* **terne,** to cover with **terne metal.** [Fr. *terne,* dull.]

**Ternstroemiaceae,** *túrn-strēm-i-ā′shi-ē, n.pl.* the Theaceae or tea family of plants. [From a genus *Ternstroemia,* named after Christopher *Ternström,* Swedish naturalist.]

**terpene,** *túr′pēn, n.* any one of a group of hydrocarbons with a composition $C_{10}H_{16}$. [turpentine.]

**Terpsichore,** *tərp-sik′ə-rē, n.* the Muse of choral song and dance.—*adj.* **terpsichorē′an,** relating to dancing. [Gr. *Terpsichorē—terpsis,* delight—*terpein,* to enjoy, *choros,* dance.]

**terra,** *ter′a, n.* the Latin and Italian word for earth.—*n.* **terrā′rium,** vivarium for land animals; **terr′acott′a** (It. *cotta*—L. *cocta,* fem., baked), a composition of clay and sand used for statues, etc., and, esp. formerly, as building material for facings, etc.: an object of art made of it: its colour, a brownish red.—Also *adj.*—*ns.* **terr′a-fir′ma,** properly, mainland: (*coll.* and erroneously) dry land; **terr′a-japon′ica,** pale catechu or gambier; **terr′ama′ra** (*pl.* **-re** *-rā;* It. *dial.* for *terra marna,* marl-earth), a dark earthy deposit formed under prehistoric pile-dwellings in Italy.—*adj.* **terraqueous** (*ter-ā′kwi-əs;* L. *aqua,* water), of land and water.—**terr′a-ross′a** (It. *rossa,* fem., red), a ferruginous red earth, the residue of the weathering of limestone; **terra sigillata** (*sij-i-lā′tə,* L. *sig-i-lä′ta,* sealed earth), Lemnian earth.

**terrace,** *ter′is, n.* a raised level bank or walk: a level stretch along the side or top of a slope: ground or a structure that rises stepwise: a gallery open at the side: a balcony: a flat roof-top: a connected row of houses, properly one overlooking a slope: a defective spot in marble.—*v.t.* to form into a terrace.—*adj.* **terr′aced,** in terraces.—*n.* **terr′acing.** [Fr. *terrasse*—It. *terrazza*—L.L. *terrācea,* an earthen mound—L. *terra,* the earth.]

**terrae filius,** *ter′ē fil′i-əs, ter′i fēl′i-ōōs,* (L.) a son of the soil: a person of humble birth.

**terrain,** *ter′ān,* or *-ān′, n.* ground, a tract, regarded as a field of view or of operations, or as having some sort of unity or prevailing character. [Fr., from a L.L. form of *terrēnum,* terrene.]

**terra incognita** *ter′ə, -a, in-kog′ni-tə, -ta,* (L.) an unknown country.

**Terramycin,** *ter-ə-mi′sin, n.* an antibiotic effective against a wide range of bacteria and a few Rickettsiae, viruses, and protozoan parasites. [Trademark; L. *terra,* the earth, and Gr. *mykēs,* fungus.]

**terrapin,** *ter′ə-pin, n.* an American freshwater or brackish-water tortoise of many kinds: extended to European water tortoises. [Of Algonquin origin.]

**terrazzo,** *ter-rat′sō, -raz′ō, n.* a mosaic covering (sometimes precast) for concrete floors consisting of marble or other chips set in cement and then polished.—Also called **Venetian mosaic.** [It., terrace, balcony.]

**terreen,** an older spelling of **tureen.**

**terrella,** *ter-el′ə, n.* a magnetic model of the earth. [A mod. dim. of L. *terra,* the earth.]

**terremotive,** *ter-i-mō′tiv, adj.* seismic. [L. *terrae motus,* earthquake.]

**terrene,** *ti-rēn′, ter′ēn, adj.* of the earth: earthly: mundane: earthy: terrestrial.—*n.* the world:

a region, terrain.—*adv.* **terrene′ly.** [L. *terrēnus—terra,* the earth.]

**terreplein,** *ter′, tār′plān, n.* orig. the talus on the inner side of a rampart: the top of a rampart, or space behind the parapet. [Fr.,—L. *terra,* earth, *plēnus,* full.]

**terrestrial,** *ti-res′tri-əl, adj.* of, or existing on, the earth: earthly: living or growing on land or on the ground: representing the earth.—*n.* a dweller on earth: a man of the world, layman (*Shak.*).—*adv.* **terres′trially.** [L. *terrestris—terra,* the earth.]

**terret, territ,** *ter′it, n.* a swivel-ring: a ring for fastening a chain to: a ring or loop through which driving reins pass.—Also **torr′et, turr′et.** [O.Fr. *toret,* dim. of *tor, tour,* a round.]

**terre verte,** *ter vert,* green earth (see **green**). [Fr.]

**terrible,** *ter′i-bl, adj.* fitted to excite terror or awe: awful: dreadful: very bad: very notable, exceeding (*coll.*).—*n.* a terrible thing.—*ns.* **terribil′ity** (*rare*); **terr′ibleness.**—*adv.* **terr′ibly,** in a terrible manner: very (*coll.*). [L. *terribilis—terrēre,* to frighten.]

**terricolous,** *ter-ik′ə-ləs, adj.* living in or on the soil.—*n.* **terr′icole** (*-i-kōl*), a land animal or plant: a burrower.—Also *adj.* [L. *terricola,* a dweller upon earth—*terra,* earth, *colēre,* to inhabit.]

**terrier,** *ter′i-ər, n.* a small dog of various breeds orig. one that would follow burrowing animals underground: punningly, a territorial soldier: one who hunts after criminals (*fig.*): a register or roll of a landed estate: an inventory. [O.Fr.,—L.L. *terrārius* (adj.)—*terra,* land.]

**terrify,** *ter′i-fi, v.t.* to cause terror in: to frighten greatly:—*pr.p.* **terr′ifying;** *pa.t.* and *pa.p.* **terr′i-fied.**—*adj.* **terrif′ic,** creating or causing terror: fitted to terrify: dreadful: prodigious (*coll.*): loosely, very good, enjoyable, attractive, etc. (*coll.*).—*adv.* **terrif′ically.** [L. *terrificāre—terrēre,* to terrify, *facēre,* to make.]

**terrigenous,** *te-rij′i-nəs, adj.* earth-born: derived from the land. [L. *terrigenus—terra,* earth, *genēre* (*gignēre*), to produce.]

**terrine,** *te-rēn′, n.* a casserole, etc., orig. of earthenware: a dish of meat or fish, etc., cooked in it: an earthenware jar sold containing a table delicacy: a tureen. [Fr.; see **tureen.**]

**territory,** *ter′i-tər-i, n.* possessions in land: the whole, or a portion, of the land belonging to a state: part of a confederation with an organised government but not yet admitted to statehood: a dependency: region: a jurisdiction: field of activity (*lit.* and *fig.*): domain: area that an animal or bird treats as its own.—*adj.* **territo′rial.**—*n.* soldier in the Territorial and Army Volunteer Reserve.—*v.t.* **territo′rialise, -ize,** to make a territory of: to make territorial: to put on a territorial basis.—*ns.* **territo′rialism,** landlordism organisation on a territorial basis: the theory of church government according to which the civil power is supreme over the church; **territō′rialist; territorial′ity.**—*adv.* **territo′rially.**—*adj.* **terr′itoried,** possessed of territory.—**Territorial Force,** a voluntary military force on a territorial basis, formed in 1908, changed in 1920 into **Territorial Army,** and in 1967 into **Territorial and Army Volunteer Reserve; territorial waters,** that part of the sea reckoned as part of the adjacent state—orig. within three-mile limit. [L. *territōrium,* domain of a town, perh. not orig. conn. with *terra.*]

**terror,** *ter′ər, n.* extreme fear: a time of, or government by, terrorism: an object of dread: one who makes himself a nuisance (*coll.*).—*n.* **terrorisā′tion, -z-.**—*v.t.* **terr′orise, -ize,** to terrify: to govern by terror.—*ns.* **terr′oriser, -z-; terr′orism,** an organised system of intimidation; **terr′-orist.**—*adj.* **terr′orless.**—**terror novel,** a novel full of supernatural horrors.—*adj.* **terr′or-stricken,**

Neutral vowels in unaccented syllables: *el′ə-mənt;* for certain sounds in foreign words, see p. viii

smitten with terror.—**King of Terrors**, death; **Reign of Terror**, or **the Terror**, the period of fever in the first French Revolution when thousands went to the guillotine. [L. *terror—terrēre*, to frighten.]

**terry**, *ter′i*, *n.* a pile fabric with uncut looped pile: one of the loops.—Also *adj.* [Origin unknown.]

**terse**, *tûrs*, *adj.* smooth, clean-cut (*obs.*): compact or concise.—*adv.* **terse′ly**.—*ns.* **terse′ness**; **tersion** (*tûr′shən*), wiping. [L. *tersus—tergēre, tersum, to rub clean*.]

**tertia**. See tercio.

**tertial**, *tûr′shl*, *adj.* of the third rank among flight-feathers of a wing.—*n.* a tertiary flight-feather. —*adj.* **ter′tian** (*-shən*), occurring every other day (i.e. on the *third* day, reckoning both first and last days).—*n.* a fever with paroxysms every other day.—*adj.* **ter′tiary** (*-shər-i*), of the third degree, order, or formation: tertial (*ornith.*): (*cap.*) of the third great division of the geological record and time, including Eocene, Oligocene, Miocene, Pliocene: ranking above secondary (esp. of education).—*n.* the Tertiary period: (without *cap.*) a member of a third order of a monastic order, a layman who may continue to live an ordinary life in the world: a tertiary feather: that which is tertiary. [L. *tertiālis, tertiānus, tertiārius—tertius*, third.]

**tertium quid** (L.), *tûr′sh(y)əm kwid, ter′ti-oōm*, a third something related to two specific known things: something intermediate between opposites: the third person in the eternal triangle.

**tertius**, *tûr′sh(y)əs, ter′ti-oōs*, (L.) third.—**tertius gaudens** (*gö′denz, gow′dāns*), or **gaudet** (*gö′det, gow′*), the third person (who) takes advantage from a dispute between others.

**terts**, *tûrts*, *n.* tetrachlor(o)ethylene, a solvent, used in drycleaning.

**teru-tero**, *ter′oō-ter′o*, *n.* the Cayenne lapwing.

**terza-rima**, *ter′tsa-rē′ma*, *n.* an Italian verse-form in triplets, in which the middle line of each triplet rhymes with the first and third lines of the next with an odd line to end off the canto. [It., third rhyme.]

**terzetta**, *ter-tset′ta*, *n.* a tercet.—*n.* **terzet′to**, a trio. [It.]

**teschenite**, *tesh′ən-īt*, *n.* a coarse-grained basic igneous rock composed essentially of plagioclase and augite, usu. with much analcime. [Found near *Teschen*.]

**tesla**, *tes′lə*, *n.* unit of magnetic flux density, equal to 1 weber per sq. metre. [N. *Tesla*, U.S. inventor.]

**tessara-, tessera-**, *tes′ə-rə-*, in composition, four. —*adj.* **tess′araglot** (Gr. *glōtta*, tongue), in four languages. [Gr. *tessares*, four.]

**tessella**, *tes-el′ə*, *n.* a little tessera:—*pl.* **tessell′ae** (*-ē*; L. *-ī*).—*adj.* **tess′ellar**.—*v.t.* **tessellate** (*tes′i-lāt*) to pave with tesserae: to mark like a mosaic.—*adj.* marked out in little squarish areas. —*adj.* **tess′ellated**.—*n.* **tessellā′tion**. [L. *tessella*, dim. of *tessera*; see next.]

**tessera**, *tes′ə-rə*, *n.* one of the small pieces of which a mosaic is made: a token or ticket: password:—*pl.* **tess′erae** (*-ē*; L. *-i*).—*adj.* **tess′eral**, of tesserae: cubic, isometric (*crystal.*). [L. *tessera*, a die, small cube—Gr. *tessares, tesseres, -a*, four.]

**tessitura**, *tes-i-toō′rə*, *n.* the ordinary compass of a voice. [It., texture.]

**test**, *test*, *n.* a pot or cupel in which metals are tried and refined: any critical trial: means of trial: anything used to distinguish or detect substances, a reagent (*chem.*): a trial of fitness for an examination: an oath or other evidence of religious belief required as a condition of office or exercise of rights: a test-match: a testa.— *v.t.* to put to proof: to try or examine critically. —*n.* **test′a**, a hard shell: a seed-coat, derived

from the ovule integuments.—*adjs.* **test′able**; **testaceous** (*-ā′shəs*), of or having a hard shell: brick-red.—*ns.* **testee′**; **test′er**.—*n.pl.* **Testicar′dines** (*-ēz*), a class of brachiopods with hinged shell and arm skeleton.—*n.* and *adj.* **test′ing**.—**Test Acts**, acts meant to secure that none but rightly affected persons and members of the established religion shall hold office—esp. English act of 1673; **test′-bed**, an iron framework on which a machine is placed for testing; **test′-case**, a law case that may settle similar questions in the future; **test′-flight**, a trial flight of a new aeroplane. *v.t.* **test′-fly**. — **test′-match**, an international cricket match forming one of a series; **test′-paper**, a bibulous paper saturated with some substance that changes colour when exposed to certain chemicals: a paper or questions to test fitness for a more serious examination; **test pilot**, one whose work is testing new aircraft by flying them; **test′-tube**, a glass cylinder closed at one end, used in chemistry, bacteriology, etc.—**test-tube baby**, a child born as the result of artificial insemination: a possible baby of future times, part of whose development takes place in the laboratory. [O.Fr. *test* and *teste*— L. *testa*, an earthen pot, a potsherd, a shell.]

**test**, *test*, *v.t.* to attest legally and date: to authenticate by a testing clause.—*ns.* **test′acy** (*-ə-si*), state of being testate; **testā′mur**, a certificate of having passed an examination.—*adj.* **test′āte**, having made and left a will.—*ns.* **testā′tion**, a witnessing, a giving by will; **testā′tor**, one who leaves a will:—*fem.* **testā′trix**; **testā′tum**, one of the clauses of an English deed, enumerating the operative words of transfer, statement of consideration, money, etc.—**testing clause**, in a Scots deed, the last clause which narrates when and where the parties signed the deed, before what witnesses, by whose hand written, etc. [L. *testārī*, to testify, witness, pa.p. (neut.) *testātum*; 1st pers. pl. *testāmur*; partly through O.Fr. *tester*, to bequeath, partly aphetic for attest.]

**testament**, *tes′tə-mənt*, *n.* that which testifies, or in which an attestation is made: the solemn declaration in writing of one's will: a will: a writing or decree appointing an executor, by the testator (**tes′tament-testament′ar**) or by a court (**tes′tament-dā′tive**) (*Scots law*): (*cap.*) either of the main divisions (**Old** and **New**) of the Bible (a translation of Gr. *diathēkē*, disposition, compact, covenant).—*adjs.* **testamental** (*-ment′*), **testament′ar** (*Scots law*), **testamen′tary**, pertaining to a testament or will: bequeathed or done by will.—*adv.* **testamen′tarily**. [L. *testāmentum*.]

**teste**, *tes′ti, -te*, (L.) witness (so-and-so).

**tester**, *tes′tər*, *n.* a canopy or its support, or both, esp. over a bed. [O.Fr. *testre*, the vertical part of a bed behind the head, and *testiere*, a head-covering—*teste* (Fr. *tête*), head—L. *testa*, an earthen pot, the skull.]

**tester**, *tes′tər*, *n.* **testern**, *tes′tərn*, (*arch.*) *n.* a sixpence.—*v.t.* **tes′tern** (*Shak.*), to present or reward with a sixpence. [See **teston**.]

**testicle**, *tes′ti-kl*, *n.* a male reproductive gland.— *adjs.* **testic′ular**, of or like a testicle; **testic′ulate**, **-d**, like a testicle: in *tes′tis*, a testicle: a rounded body like it:—*pl.* **tes′tes** (*-ēz*). [L. *testis* and its dim. *testiculus*.]

**testify**, *tes′ti-fī*, *v.i.* to bear witness: to make a solemn declaration: to protest or declare a charge (with *against*).—*v.t.* to bear witness to: to affirm or declare solemnly or on oath: to proclaim, declare:—*pr.p.* **tes′tifying**; *pa.t.* and *pa.p.* **tes′tified**.—*ns.* **testif′icate** (*Scots law*), a solemn written assertion; **testificā′tion**, the act of testifying or of bearing witness; **testif′icātor**. —*adjs.* **testif′icatory**; **tes′tified**.—*n.* **tes′tifier**. [L. *testificārī—testis*, a witness, *facēre*, to make.]

**testimony**, *tes′ti-mən-i*, *n.* evidence: declaration

to prove some fact: proof: the two tables of the law (*B.*): divine law: protestation.—*v.t.* (*Shak.*) to test, prove, or judge by evidence.— *adj.* testi´mōnial, of, affording, of the nature of, testimony.—*n.* a written attestation: a writing or certificate bearing testimony to one's character or abilities: a gift or memorial as a token of respect.—*v.t.* testimō´nialise, -ize, to present with a testimonial. [L. *testimōnium*—*testāri*, to witness.]

teston, *tes´tən, n.* a name for various coins, orig. bearing a king's or duke's head: a Henry VIII shilling: later a sixpence.—*n.* testoon´, a Portuguese or Italian teston. [Obs. Fr. *teston*, Port. *testão*, It. *testone*—It. *testa*, head.]

testosterone, *tes-tos´tər-ōn, n.* the chief male sex hormone, a steroid secreted by the testes.

testrill (*Shak.*), testril, *tes´tril, n.* a sixpence. [tester.]

testudo, *tes-tū´dō, n.* a wheeled shelter used by Roman besiegers: a similar shelter made by joining shields: a vaulted roof: an ancient lyre, said to have been first made of a tortoise-shell: (*cap.*) the genus containing the typical land tortoises.—*adj.* testūdin´eous, like a tortoise, tortoise-shell, or a testudo. [L. *testūdō*, *-inis*, tortoise.]

testy, *tes´ti, adj.* irritable.—*adv.* tes´tily.—*n.* tes´tiness. [O.Fr. *testif*, headstrong—*teste* (Fr. *tête*), head—L. *testa*, pot.]

tetanus, *tet´ə-nəs, n.* a disease due to a bacillus, marked by painful tonic spasms of the muscles of the jaw and other parts: the state of prolonged contraction of a muscle under quickly repeated stimuli.—*adj.* tetanic (*ti-tan´ik*).—*n.* tetanisā´tion.—*v.t.* tet´anise, -ize, to produce tetanus or tetanic spasms in.—*n.* tet´any, heightened excitability of the motor nerves with painful muscular cramps. [L.,—Gr. *tetanos*—*teinein*, to stretch.]

tetartohedral, *te-tärt-ō-hē´drəl*, (*crystal.*) *adj.* having one-fourth of the number of faces required for full symmetry. [Gr. *tetartos*, fourth, *hedrā*, seat.]

tetchy, techy, *tech´i, adj.* irritable.—*adv.* tetch´ily. —*n.* tetch´iness. [Origin unknown.]

tête, *tet*, (*obs.*) *n.* an elaborately dressed head of hair: a head-dress. [Fr.]

tête, *tet*, (Fr.) head.—tête-à-tête (*a tet*) a private confidential interview: a sofa for two face to face.—*adj.* confidential, secret.—*adv.* in private conversation: face to face; tête-bêche (*-besh*), head-to-tail; tête-de-pont (*də-põ*), bridgehead; tête folle (*fol*), a scatterbrain.

tether, *tedh´ər, n.* a rope or chain for confining a beast within certain limits.—*v.t.* to confine with a tether: to restrain within certain limits. —at the end of one's tether, desperate, having no further strength, resources, etc. [App. O.N. *tjōthr.*]

Tethys, *tē´this, teth´is, n.* a sea-nymph, wife of Oceanus: a sea that extended in Mesozoic times from Mexico across the middle Atlantic and the Mediterranean into the centre of Asia (*geol.*). [Gr. *Tēthȳs.*]

tetra, *tet´rə, n.* a plant mentioned by Spenser (*The Faerie Queene* II, vii. 52, 4).

tetra-, *tet´rə-*, tetr-, in composition, four.—*ns.pl.* Tetrabranchia, Tetrabranchiata (*-brang´ki-ə, -ki-ā´tə*; Gr. *branchia*, gills), the nautilus subclass of cephalopods, with four gills.—*adj.* tetrabranch´iate, four-gilled.—*n.* tetrachord (*-körd*; Gr. *chordē*, string), a four-stringed instrument: a series of four sounds, forming a scale of two tones and a half.—*adjs.* tetrachord´al; tetract (*tet´rakt*; Gr. *aktis*, *-inos*, ray), four-rayed.—*n.* a four-rayed sponge spicule.—*adjs.* tetract´inal (or *-i´nəl*), tetrac´tine.—*n.pl.* Tetractinell´ida, an order of sponges in which some of the spicules are four-rayed.—*adj.* tetracyclic

(*-si´klik*; Gr. *kyklos*, ring, wheel), of, in, or with four whorls or rings.—*n.* tetrad (*tet´rad*), a group of four: an atom, radical, or element having a combining power of four (*chem.*).— *adjs.* tet´rad, tetrad´ic; tetradactyl (*-dak´til*; Gr. *daktylos*, digit), four-fingered: four-toed.—Also *n.*—*adj.* tetradac´tylous.—*ns.* tetradac´tyly, condition of being tetradactylous; tet´radite, one who attaches mystic properties to the number four: a believer in a godhead of four persons; tetradrachm (*-dram*), an ancient Greek coin worth four drachmas.—*n.pl.* Tetradynamia (*-di-nā´mi-a*), in Linnaeus's system, a class answering to the Cruciferae.—*adjs.* tetradynamous (*-din´ə-məs*; Gr. *dynamis*, power), having four long stamens in pairs and two short, as the Cruciferae; tetraethyl (*-eth´il*), having four ethyl groups as tetraethyl lead or lead tetraethyl, Pb(C₂H₅)₄, used in motor spirit as an antiknock agent.—*n.* tetragon (*-gən*, *-gon*; Gr. *gōniā*, an angle), a plane figure of four angles.—*adj.* tetragonal (*-rag´ə-nəl*), having the form of a tetragon; referable to three axes at right angles, two of them equal (*crystal.*); tetrag´onous (*bot.*), with four angles and convex faces.—*ns.* tetragram (*-gram*; Gr. *gramma*, a letter), a word or inscription of four letters: the tetragrammaton: a (complete) quadrilateral (*geom.*); tetragramm´aton, the name YaHWeH, JeHoVaH, etc., as written with four Hebrew letters, regarded as a mystic symbol: any other sacred word of four letters, as the Latin *Deus*.—*n.pl.* Tetragynia (*-jin´i-ə*; Gr. *gynē*, woman (in the sense of female)), in the Linnaean system an order of plants (in various classes) with four pistils.—*adjs.* tetragyn´ian, tetragynous (*-raj´i-nəs*).—*n.* tetrahedron (*-hē´drən*; Gr. *hedrā*, seat), a solid figure or body with four plane faces.— *adj.* tetrahē´dral.—*ns.* tetrahē´drite, grey copper ore, sulphide of copper and antimony: a mineral of tetrahedral habit; tetrakishexahedron (Gr. *tetrakis*, four times), a figure got by erecting equal pyramids on all the faces of a cube.— *adj.* tetram´eral, four-parted.—*n.* tetram´erism, division into four parts.—*adj.* tetram´erous (Gr. *meros*, part), having four parts, or parts in fours. —*n.* tetrameter (*te-tram´i-ter*; Gr. *metron*, measure), a verse of four measures (dipodies or feet).— Also *adj.*—*adj.* tetramorphic (*-mör´fik*, Gr. *morphē*, form), having four forms.—*n.pl.* Tetran´dria, in Linnaeus's classification, a class of plants with four stamens.—*adjs.* tetran´drian; tetrandrous (*tetran´drəs*; Gr. *anēr*, *andros*, man (in the sense of male)), having four stamens.—*n.* tetrapod (*-pod*; Gr. *pous*, *podos*, foot), a four-footed animal: any vertebrate above the fishes: a reinforced-concrete block laid against a sea-wall to break the force of the waves.—Also *adj.*—*adj.* tetrapodous (*-trap´*). —*ns.* tetrap´ody, a group of four metrical feet; tetrapolis (*te-trap´o-lis*; Gr. *polis*, a city), a group of four towns.—*adjs.* tetrapol´itan (Tetrapolitan Confession, the Confession which the four cities of Strasburg, Constance, Memmingen, and Lindau presented to the Diet of Augsburg (11th July 1530), and, properly speaking, the first Confession of the Reformed); tetrap´teran, tetrapterous (*te-trap´tə-rən*, *-rəs*; Gr. *pteron*, a wing), four-winged.—*ns.* tetraptote (*tet´rap-tōt*; Gr. *ptōsis*, a case), a noun with but four cases; tetrarch (*tet´rärk*, or *tē´trärk*; Gr. *archē*, rule, origin), under the Romans, the ruler of the fourth part of a province: a subordinate prince: the commander of a subdivision of a Greek phalanx.—*adj.* (*bot.*) having four xylem strands.—*n.* tet´rarchy, office, rank, time of office, or jurisdiction of a tetrarch: the fourth part of a province (also tet´rarchate): condition of being tetrarch (*bot.*).—*adj.* tetrasemic (*-sē´mik*; Gr. *sēma*, a sign; *pros.*), equivalent to four short syllables, as a dactyl, anapaest, or spondee —*ns.* tetraspore (*-spōr*, *-spör*; Gr. *sporā*, seed),

Neutral vowels in unaccented syllables: *el´ə-mənt*; for certain sounds in foreign words, see p. viii

a spore formed in groups of four in red seaweeds; **tetrasporangium** (*spor-an'ji-əm*), the sporangium in which they are formed.—*adjs.* **tetrasporic** (*-spor'ik*), **tetrasporous** (*te-tras'pər-əs*, or *tet-rə-spō'rəs*, *-spō'*).—*n.* **tetrastich** (*-stik*; Gr. *stichos*, a row), a stanza or set of four lines.—*adjs.* **tetrastichal** (*ti-tras'ti-kl*), **tetrastichic** (*tet-rə-stik'ik*), of, of the nature of, tetrastichs; **tetras'-tichous**, in four rows.—*n.* **tetrastyle** (*-stil*; Gr. *stylos*, a column), a building or portico with four columns in front: a group of four pillars. —Also *adj.*—*n.* **tetrasyllable** (*-sil'ə-bl*), a word of four syllables.—*adjs.* **tetrasyllabic** (*-ab²k*), **-al.**—*ns.* **tetratheism** (*-thē-izm*; Gr. *Theos*, god), the belief in four elements in the Godhead— the three persons of the Trinity and a divine essence out of which each of these originates; **tetrathlon** (*te-trath'lən*; Gr. *athlon*, contest), a four-event sporting contest.—*adj.* **tetravalent** (*te-trav'ə-lənt*, *tet-rə-vā'lənt*), quadrivalent.—*ns.* **tetraxon** (*te-traks'on*; Gr. *axōn*, *-onos*, an axis), a sponge spicule with four axes; **tetrode** (*tet'rōd*; Gr. *hodos*, a way), a thermionic valve with four electrodes. [Gr. *tetra-*, *tettares*, *tessares*, four.]
**Tetrabranchia** . . . to . . . **tetrachordal.** See **tetra-**.
**tetrachotomy,** *tet-rə-kot'ə-mi*, *n.* division in fours. —*adj.* **tetrachot'omous.** [Gr. *tetracha*, in four parts, *tomē*, a cut—*temnein*, to cut.]
**tetract** . . . to . . . **tetrakishexahedron.** See **tetra-**.
**tetralogy,** *te-tral'ə-ji*, *n.* a group of four dramas, usu. three tragic and one satyric: any series of four related dramatic or operatic works or stories. [Gr. *tetralogiā—logos*, discourse.]
**tetrameral** . . . to . . . **tetrandrous.** See **tetra-**.
**tetrapla,** *tet'rə-pla*, *n.* an edition of four parallel texts, esp. Origen's of the Old Testament.— *adj.* **tetraploid** (*tet'rə-ploid*), having four times the haploid (twice the normal) number of chromosomes.—*n.* **tet'raploidy**, the condition of being tetraploid. [Gr. *tetraploos* (*-plous*, neut.pl. *-pla*), fourfold, *eidos*, form.]
**tetrapod** . . . to . . . **tetrode.** See **tetra-**.
**tetronal,** *tet'rən-əl*, *n.* a hypnotic and sedative drug rarely used because of its high toxicity.
**tetter,** *tet'ər*, (*Shak.*) *n.* a skin eruption.—*v.t.* to affect with a tetter.—*adj.* **tett'erous** (*Shak.*). [O.E. *teter*.]
**tettix,** *tet'iks*, *n.* a cicada: an ornament for the hair of that shape. [Gr.]
**teuch, teugh,** *tūhh*, *adj.* a Scots form of **tough.**
**Teucrian,** *tū'kri-ən*, *n.* and *adj.* Trojan. [Gr. *Teukros*, Teucer, first king of Troy.]
**Teuton,** *tū'tən*, *n.* any speaker of a Germanic language: popularly, a German.—*adj.* **Teutonic** (*-ton'ik*), Germanic—of the linguistic family that includes English, German, Dutch, and the Scandinavian languages: popularly, German in the narrower sense.—*n.* the parent language of the Teutons, primitive Germanic.—*ns.* **Teuton'-icism** (*-i-sizm*), **Teu'tonism,** a Germanism: belief in, enthusiasm for, the Teutons: the study of Germanic philology and culture; **Teutonisā'-tion.**—*v.t.* and *v.i.* **Teu'tonise, -ize,** to make or become Teutonic, Germanic, or German. —*n.* **Teu'tonist.—Teutonic Knights,** a military-religious order founded in 1191-98 to tend wounded Christians and to war on unbelievers, operated first in Palestine and later against the Prussians and Lithuanians. [L. *Teutonus*, from the root of O.E. *thēod*, people, nation; cf. Dutch, Ger. *Deutsch*.]
**tew,** *tū*, *v.t.* to work up: to taw.—*v.i.* to toil, hustle.—*n.* worry: excitement. [Cf. **taw.**]
**tewart.** Same as **tuart.**
**tewel,** *tū'əl*, *n.* the rectum or anus, esp. of a horse (*dial.*): a flue (*obs.*): a tuyère (*dial.*). [O.Fr. *tuel* (Fr. *tuyau*), tube.]
**tewit, tewhit,** *tē'(h)wit* (*Scot.* **teuchat,** *tūhh'ət*), (*dial.*) *n.* a lapwing. [Imit.]
**Texas,** *tek'səs*, *n.* a state of the U.S.A.: (without

*cap.*) an upper structure on a river-steamer.— **Texas fever,** a protozoal cattle-disease transmitted by ticks; **Texas tower,** a radar tower built off-shore as part of an early-warning system.
**text,** *tekst*, *n.* the actual words of a book, poem, etc., in their original form or any form they have been transmitted in or transmuted into: a book of such words: words set to music: the main body of matter in a book, distinguished from notes, commentary, or other subsidiary matter: the Bible (*Shak.*): matter commented on: a short passage from the Bible taken as the ostensible subject of a sermon, quoted in authority, displayed as a motto, etc.: a theme: a copybook heading: text-hand.—*adj.* **textile** (*-il*, in U.S. *-il*), woven: capable of being woven.—*n.* a woven fabric.—*adjs.* **texto'rial,** pertaining to weaving; **tex'tual,** pertaining to, or contained in, the text: serving for a text.—*n.* **text'ualist,** one learned in the text, esp. of the Bible: a literal interpreter: a quoter of texts.— *adv.* **text'ually.**—*n.* **tex'tuary,** a textualist.—*adj.* **text'ural,** pertaining to, in the matter of, texture. —*adv.* **textur'ally.**—*n.* **text'ure,** anything woven, a web: manner of weaving or connecting: disposition of the parts of a body: structural impression resulting from the manner of combining or interrelating the parts of a whole, as in music, art, etc.: the quality conveyed to the touch by woven fabrics.—*v.t.* to give (specified) texture to: to weave.—*adjs.* **text'ured; text'ureless.**— *adj.* **text-book,** (of operation) exactly as planned, in perfect accordance with theory or calculation.—*n.* a book containing the main principles of a subject.—**text'-hand,** a large hand in writing, orig. one suitable for the text of a manuscript book; **text'-man,** a quoter of texts: a textualist; **textual criticism,** critical study directed towards determining the true reading of a text. [L. *texĕre, textum,* to weave.]
**textus receptus,** *teks'təs rə-sep'təs, teks'toōs rekep'toōs,* (L.) the received text (of the Greek New Testament).
**th-** (*obs.*), **th'** (*arch.* or *dial.*), forms of **the,** esp. before a vowel, as in Spenser **thelement,** the element, **thelf,** the elf, **thother,** the other.
**thack,** *thak,* *n.* a Scots form of **thatch.—under thack and rape,** safely secured under thatch and rope, snug generally.
**thae,** *dhā,* (*Scot.*) *pl.* demons. pron. and demons. *adj.* **those.** [O.E. *thā;* see **tho.**]
**Thai,** *tī, tä'ē, adj.* of Thailand.—*n.* a native of (also **Thai'lander**) or the language of Thailand, country of Asia known before 1939 and between 1945 and 1949 as Siam.
**thaim,** *dhām,* Scots form of **them.**
**thairm,** *thärm,* (*Scot.*) *n.* an intestine: catgut, a musical string. [O.E. *tharm, thearm.*]
**thalamus,** *thal'ə-məs, n.* an inner room, nuptial chamber: the receptacle of a flower: part of the mid-brain where the optic nerve emerges (**optic thalamus**):—*pl.* **thal'ami.**—*adj.* **thal'amic** (or *thal-am'ik*), of the thalamus.—*n.pl.* **Thalami-florae** (*-i-flō'rē, -flō'*; L. *flōs, flōris,* flower), in some systems, a subclass of dicotyledons with petals free and stamens hypogynous.—*adj.* **thal-amiflo'ral.** [Gr. *thalamos,* an inner room, bedroom.]
**thalassian,** *tha-las'i-ən, adj.* marine.—*n.* a sea turtle.—*adj.* **thalass'ic,** marine: of the narrow seas.—*ns.* **thalassoc'racy, thalattoc'racy** (Gr. *kratos,* power), sovereignty of the seas; **thalassog'rapher.**—*adj.* **thalassograph'ic.**—*n.* **thalassog'-raphy,** the science of the sea. [Gr. *thalassa, thalatta,* sea.]
**thale-cress,** *thāl'-kres, n.* a cruciferous wall plant with small white flowers (*Sisymbrium thalianum*). [Named after Johann *Thal* (1542-83), German physician.]

*fāte, fär; mē, hûr* (her); *mīne; mōte, för; mūte; mōōn, fŏŏt; dhen* (then)

**thaler**, *tä'lər*, *n.* an obsolete German silver coin. [Ger.; cf. **dollar**.]

**Thalia**, *tha-lī'a*, *n.* the Muse of comedy and pastoral poetry: one of the Graces.—*adj.* **thali'an**. [Gr. *Thaleia*, *Thaliā*—*thallein*, to bloom.]

**Thalictrum**, *thā-lik'trəm*, *n.* the meadow-rue genus. [Gr. *thaliktron*—*thallein*, to bloom.]

**thalidomide**, *thə-lid'ə-mid*, *tha-*, *n.* non-barbiturate sedative drug, withdrawn 1961 because found to cause malformation in the foetus if taken during pregnancy.—**thalidomide baby**, an infant showing the teratogenic effects of thalidomide.

**thallium**, *thal'i-əm*, *n.* a lead-like metal (Tl; at. numb. 81) discovered in 1861.—*adjs.* **thall'ic**, of trivalent thallium; **thall'ous**, of univalent thallium. [Gr. *thallos*, a young shoot, from the bright green line in its spectrum.]

**thallus**, *thal'əs*, *n.* a plant body not differentiated into leaf, stem, and root.—*adjs.* **thall'iform**; **thall'ine**; **thall'oid**.—*n.pl.* **Thallophy'ta** (Gr. *phyton*, plant), the lowest main division of the vegetable kingdom—bacteria, fungi, algae.—*n.* **thall'ophyte**, a member of the Thallophyta. [Gr. *thallos*, a young shoot.]

**thalweg**, *täl'vähh*, *n.* the longitudinal profile of the bottom of a river-bed. [Ger.,—*thal* (now *tal*), valley, *weg*, way.]

**Thammuz**, *tam'ōōz*, *-uz* (*Milt.*). Same as **Tammuz**.

**than**, *dhan*, *dhən*, *conj.* used after a comparative, actual or felt, to introduce that which is in the lower degree.—*prep.* (popularly, and in some authors, e.g. Shelley) in comparison with (esp. with *whom*, as in Milton).—**any more than he could help**, any more than he had to (i.e. could not help). [O.E. *thonne*, *thanne*, *thænne*, than, orig. then.]

**than**, *dhan*, *dhən*, an obs. or dial. form of **then**.

**thana(h)**. See **tana**.

**thanatism**, *than'ə-tizm*, *n.* belief that the soul dies with the body.—*n.* **than'atist**.—*adj.* **thanatog-nomon'ic**, indicating death.—*n.* **thanatog'raphy**, a narrative of a death.—*adj.* **than'atoid**, apparently dead: deathly: deadly.—*ns.* **thanatol'ogy**, the scientific study of death; **thanatophō'bia**, a morbid dread of death; **thanatop'sis**, a view of, or reflection upon, death; **thanatō'sis**, gangrene. [Gr. *thanatos*, death.]

**thane**, *thān*, *n.* in Old English times a king's companion, one who held by service, hence a noble of lower rank than eorl or ealdorman: a hereditary (not military) tenant of the crown (*Scot. hist.*).—*ns.* **thā'nage**, **thane'dom**, **thane'hood**, **thane'ship**. [O.E. *thegn*, servant, follower, courtier, nobleman; cf. O.N. *thegn*, a man, warrior, Ger. *degen*, a soldier, servant, Gr. *teknon*, child.]

**thank**, *thangk*, *n.* (usu. in *pl.*) gratitude: expression of gratitude.—*v.t.* to express gratitude to: ironically, to blame.—*n.* **thank'er**.—*adj.* **thank'ful**, grateful: gladly relieved.—*adv.* **thank'fully**.—*ns.* **thank'fulness**; **thank'ing** (usu. in *pl.*; *Shak.*), thanks.—*adj.* **thank'less**, unthankful: not expressing thanks for favours: not gaining even thanks.—*adv.* **thank'lessly**.—*n.* **thank'lessness**.—**thank'-offering**, an offering made to express thanks; **thanks'giver**; **thanks'giving**, act of giving thanks: a public acknowledgment of divine goodness and mercy: a day (**Thanksgiving Day**) set apart for this, esp. that in the U.S.A. since the time of the Pilgrim Fathers, now fixed as fourth Thursday of November: a form of giving thanks, a grace, that form preceding the last two prayers of morning or evening prayer or of the litany—the *General Thanksgiving*.—Also *adj.*—*adv.* **thank'worthily**.—*n.* **thank'worthiness**.—*adj.* **thank'worthy**, worthy of, or deserving thanks.—**thank'-you-ma'am** (*U.S.*), a ridge or hollow in a road that

causes those who drive over it to bob their heads.—**be thankit** (*Scot.*), thank God; **no thanks to**, not owing to, implying that gratitude is far from being due; **thanks**, **thank you** (old *coll.* **thank'ee**), elliptical forms of thanks be to you, I thank you, or the like; **thanks to**, owing to. [O.E. *thanc*, *thonc*; cog. with Ger. *dank*; from the root of **think**.]

**thanna(h)**. See **tana**.

**thar**, *t'här*, *tär*, *n.* properly the serow: by confusion applied to the tahr. [Nepali (Indic language of Nepal) *thär*.]

**tharborough**. See **farborough**.

**Thargelia**, *thär-gē'li-ə*, or *-jē'*, *n.pl.* an ancient Athenian festival, in honour of Apollo, in the month of *Thargēliōn* (May-June).

**that**, *dhat*, *dhət*, *demons. pron.* and *adj.* (*pl.* **those**) pointing out a person or thing: the former: the more distant: not this but the other: the one to be indicated or defined: such (*obs.*): often indicating an accompanying snap of the fingers (as *I don't care that*, *It wants that*).—*rel. pron.* (*sing.* and *pl.*) who, whom, or which (esp. when defining or limiting, not merely linking on an addition).—*adv.* (chiefly *dial.*) to that extent.—*conj.* used to introduce a noun clause, an adverbial clause of purpose, reason, or consequence, or an expression of a wish in the subjunctive: because (*Shak.*).—*n.* **that'ness**, the quality of being a definite thing, that—**and all that**, and all the rest of that sort of thing—a summary way of dismissing what is vaguely thought of; **and that's that**, and that is the end of that matter: no more of that. [O.E. *thæt*, neut. demons. pron. cog. with Ger. *das*, *dass*; Gr. *to*, Sans. *tad*; see **the**.]

**thatch**, *thach*, *v.t.* to cover, or roof, with straw, reeds, heather, palm-leaves, or the like.—*v.i.* to do thatching.—*n.* a covering or covering material of the kind: thick hair.—*adj.* **thatched** (or **thatcht**).—*ns.* **thatch'er**; **thatch'ing**, the act or art of covering with thatch: materials used for thatching.—Also *adj.*—*adj.* **thatch'less**.—**thatch'-board**, a building-board made of straw. [O.E. *thæc*, covering, thatch, and *theccan*, to cover; cog. with Ger. *decken*, L. *tegēre*, Gr. *stegein*, to cover.]

**thauma-**, *thö'mə-*, **thaumat-**, *-mət-*, in composition, wonder, miracle.—*ns.* **thau'masite**, a mineral, hydrated silicate, carbonate, and sulphate of calcium; **thaumatogeny** (*-toj'*), the doctrine of the miraculous origination of life; **thaumatog'raphy**, description of natural wonders; **thaumatol'atry** (Gr. *latreiā*, worship), wonder-worship; **thau'matrope** (Gr. *tropos*, a turning), an optical toy that combines pictures by persistence of images in the eye; **thaumaturge** (*thö'mə-tûrj*), a wonder-worker.—*adjs.* **thaumatur'gic**, **-al**.—*n.pl.* **thaumatur'gics**, wonderful, esp. magical, performances: feats of legerdemain. — *ns.* **thaumatur'gism**; **thaumatur'gist**; **thaumaturgus** (*-tûr'gəs*), a wonder-worker: a worker of miracles, applied to certain saints. [Gr. *thauma*, *-atos*, wonder, *thaumasios*, wonderful, *thaumatourgos* (—*ergon*, work), a wonder-worker.]

**thaw**, *thö*, *v.i.* to melt or grow liquid, as ice: to become so warm as to melt ice: to become less cold, stiff, or reserved in manner (*fig.*).—*v.t.* to cause to melt.—*n.* the melting of ice or snow by heat: the change of weather that causes it.—Also *fig.*—*n.* **thaw'er**, an ice-melting agent or apparatus.—*n.* and *adj.* **thaw'ing**.—*adjs.* **thaw'less**; **thaw'y**, inclined to thaw.—**thaw out**, to return from frozen to normal condition. [O.E. *thawian*.]

**the**, *dhē* (emphatic), *dhə* (usu.), *dhi*, *dhē* (before vowels), *demons. adj.* called the definite article, used to denote a particular person or thing: also to denote a species: used instead of the pfx.

*to-*, this (*Scot.*; as the day, today, the night, tonight, the morn, tomorrow, the morn's morn, tomorrow morning, the year, this year). [O.E. *the* (supplanting *se*), masc. of *thæt*, that.]

**the,** *dhə, adv.* (with comparatives) by how much: by so much. [O.E. *thý*, by that, by that much, the instrumental case of the def. art.]

**Thea,** *thē'ə, n.* the tea genus of plants (sometimes including Camellia), giving name to the family **Theā'ceae,** akin to the Guttiferae. [From the root of tea, but taken as if from Gr. *theā,* goddess.]

**theandric,** *thē-an'drik, adj.* at once divine and human. [Gr. *theos,* a god, *anēr, andros,* man.]

**theanthropic,** *thē-an-throp'ik, adj.* at once divine and human: embodying deity in human forms. —*ns.* **thean'thropism, thean'thropy,** the ascribing of human qualities to deity, or divine qualities to man: a doctrine of union of divine and human; **thean'thropist.** [Gr. *theos,* a god, *anthrōpos,* man.]

**thearchy,** *thē'ärk-i, n.* a theocracy: a body of divine rulers.—*adj.* **thear'chic.** [Gr. *theos,* a god, *archein,* to rule.]

**Theatine,** *thē'ə-tin, n.* a member of a R.C. religious brotherhood founded in 1524 by John Peter Caraffa, bishop of Chieti (L. *Teāte*), afterwards Pope Paul IV, and others, or of a sisterhood modelled on it.—Also *adj.*

**theatre** (*U.S.* theater), *thē'ə-tər, n.* a structure, orig. in the open-air, for drama or other spectacle: any place backed by a curving hillside or rising by steps like seats of a theatre: a building or room which is adapted for scholastic exercises, anatomical or surgical demonstrations, etc. (see also **operating theatre**): scene of action, field of operations: (with *the*) the social unit comprising actors, producers, etc., or its characteristic environment and conditions: an audience, house: (with *the*) plays or a specified group of plays, collectively: material or method judged by its suitability for a dramatic presentation.—*adjs.* **the'atral;** theatric (-*at'*), **-al,** relating or suitable to, or savouring of, the stage: stagy: histrionic: aiming at or producing dramatic effects.—*v.t.* **theat'ricalise, -ize,** to adapt to dramatic representation: to make stagy.—*v.i.* to act: to attend the theatre.—*ns.* **theat'ricalism,** theatrical'ity, staginess, artificiality.—*adv.* **theat'-rically.**—*n.* **theat'ricalness.**—*n.pl.* **theat'ricals,** dramatic performances: theatrical affairs, properties, or persons.—*v.i.* **theat'ricise, -ize** (*-sīz*), to play a part.—*ns.* **theat'ricism,** theatricality, affectation, staginess; **theat'rics,** the staging of plays, etc., or the art of doing this; **theatromā'nia,** a craze for play-going; **theat'rophone,** a telephone for transmitting stage dialogue from the theatre.— **thē'atre-go'er,** one who habitually goes to the theatre; **theatre-in-the-round,** a theatre with central, or arena, stage and audience on all sides: the style of staging plays in such a theatre; **theatre organ,** a cinema-organ.— **theatre of cruelty,** plays giving an important place to brutal actions; **theatre of fact,** branch of drama using material closely based on real happenings; **theatre of the absurd,** branch of drama dealing with fantastic deliberately unreal situations, in reaction against the tragedy and irrationality of life. [Gr. *theātron*—*theaesthai,* to see.]

**theave,** *thēv,* (*dial.*) *n.* a young ewe, esp. of the first year.

**Thebes,** *thēbz, n.* a city of ancient Boeotia (Greece): a city of ancient Egypt.—*adj.* **Thebaic** (*thē-bā'ik*), of Egyptian Thebes: of opium (as an Egyptian product).—*ns.* **Thebaid** (*thē'bā-id*), a poem on the Seven against Thebes (as that by Statius): the district of Thebes (Egyptian or Greek); **thē'baine** (*-bā-ēn,-bə-ēn*), an alkaloid (C₁₉H₂₁NO₃) got from opium.—*adj.* **Thē'ban,** of Thebes.—*n.*

a native of Thebes: a Boeotian.—**Theban year,** the Egyptian year of 365¼ days. [Gr. *Thēbai,* Thebes.]

**theca,** *thē'kə, n.* a sheath, case, or sac: a spore-case: a lobe or loculus of an anther:—*pl.* **thē'-cae** (*-sē*).—*adjs.* **thē'cal,** of a theca; **thē'cate,** having a theca. [Latinised from Gr. *thēkē,* case, sheath.]

**Thecla,** *thek'lə, n.* the hair-streak genus of butterflies.

**thé dansant,** *tā dā-sā,* (Fr.) tea with dancing.

**thee,** *dhē, pron., dat. and accus,* of **thou:** also (*dial.,* and formerly by Quakers) *nom.*—*v.t.* to use *thee* in speaking to.—*v.i.* to use *thee.* [O.E. *thē, the.*]

**thee,** *thē,* (*Spens.*) *v.i.* to prosper, to thrive. [O.E. *thēon;* cf. Ger. *gedeihen.*]

**theek,** *thēk,* a Scots form of thatch (*vb.*).

**theft,** *theft, n.* act of thieving: a thing stolen.— *adj.* **theft'ūous,** thievish.—*adv.* **theft'ūously.**— **theft'boot, -bote,** illegal compounding of a theft. [O.E. *thēofth, thiefth*—*thēof,* thief.]

**thegither,** *dhə-gidh'ər,* a Scots form of **together.**

**thegn,** *thān,* (*hist.*) *n.* the older form of **thane.**

**theine,** *thē'in, -in, n.* caffeine.—*ns.* **thē'ic,** a tea-drunkard; **thē'ism,** a morbid state resulting from over-much tea-drinking. [**Thea.**]

**their,** *dhār, dhər, pron.* (*gen. pl.*) or *poss. adj.* of or belonging to them.—*pron.* **theirs** (a double genitive), used predicatively or absolutely. [O.N. *theirra,* superseding O.E. *thǣra,* gen. pl. of the def. art.]

**theism,** *thē'izm, n.* belief in the existence of God with or without a belief in a special revelation.— *n.* **thē'ist.**—*adjs.* **thēist'ic, -al.** [Gr. *theos,* God.] **theism.** See **theine.**

**Thelemite,** *thel'ə-mīt, n.* a monk of Rabelais's imaginary abbey of *Thélème,* of an order whose rule was Do as you like.—Also *adj.* [Gr. *thelēma,* will.]

**thelytoky,** *thi-lit'ə-ki, n.* parthenogenetic production of female offspring only.—*adj.* **thelyt'-okous.** [Gr. *thēlys,* female, *tokos,* birth.]

**them,** *dhem, dhəm, pron., dat.* and *accus.* of **they.** [O.N. *theim* or O.E. (Anglian) *thǣm* (dat.).]

**theme,** *thēm, n.* a subject set or proposed for discussion, or spoken or written about: a thesis, a brief essay or exercise: a ground for action: the stem of a word without its inflexions: subject, a short melody developed with variations or otherwise (*mus.*): an administrative division of the Byzantine empire.—*n.* **thē'ma** (or *them'a*), a theme:—*pl.* **them'ata.**—*adj.* **thematic** (*thi-mat'ik*), of, or relating to a theme; (of philately) concerned with collection of sets showing flowers, or birds, etc.—*adv.* **themat'ically.**— **thematic vowel,** a vowel that comes between root and inflexion; **theme song,** a melody that is repeated often in a musical drama, film, or radio or television series, and is associated with a certain character, idea, emotion, etc.: a person's characteristic, often repeated, complaint, etc. [Gr. *thēma, -atos*—root of *tithēnai,* to place, set; partly through O.Fr. *tesme.*]

**Themis,** *them'is, n.* Greek goddess of law and justice. [Gr. *Themis.*]

**themselves,** *dhəm-selvz', pron., pl.* of **himself, herself, itself.** [**them, self.**]

**then,** *dhen, dhən, adv.* at that time: afterward: immediately: at another time: further, again: on the other hand, at the same time: for that reason, therefore: in that case.—*adj.* being at that time.—*n.* that time.—*adv.* **thenabout(s),** about that time.—**by then,** by that time; **then and there,** at once and on the spot. [O.E. *thonne, thanne, thænne.*]

**then,** *dhan,* (*Spens.,* etc.) *conj.* Same as **than.**

**thenar,** *thē'när, n.* the palm: the ball of the thumb: the sole.—Also *adj.* [Gr. *thenär, -äros.*]

**thence,** *dhens, adv.* from that place: from those

premises: from that time: from that cause.—
*advs.* thence′forth, thencefor′ward, from that
time forward: from that place onward. [M.E.
*thennes*—*thenne* (O.E. *thanon*, thence), with adverbial genitive ending; cf. hence, whence.]
theo-, *thē′ō-, -o-,* or *-o′-*, in composition, god.—
*In the following article, strict alphabetical order is
not followed; in each case, the abstract noun in
-y precedes adjectives, etc., dependent on it.*—
*ns.* Theobroma (*brō′mə;* Gr. *brōma,* food),
the chocolate or cocoa genus of Sterculiaceae;
theobrō′mine (*-mēn, -min, -min*), an alkaloid got
from the chocolate nut; theocracy (*thē-ok′rə-si;*
Gr. *theokratiā*—*krateein,* to rule), that constitution of a state in which God, or a god, is
regarded as the sole sovereign, and the laws of
the realm as divine commands rather than
human ordinances—the priesthood necessarily
becoming the officers of the invisible ruler: the
state thus governed; theocrat (*thē′ō-krat*), a
divine or deified ruler.—*adjs.* theocrat′ic, -al.—
*adv.* theocrat′ically.—*ns.* theocrasy (*thē-ok′rə-si,*
or *thē′ō-krā′si;* Gr. *krāsis,* a mixing), a mixture
of religions: the identification or equating of one
god with another or others: a mystic intimacy
with deity reached through profound contemplation; theodicy (*thē-od′i-si;* Gr. *dikē,* justice), a
vindication of the justice of God in establishing
a world in which evil exists.—*n.* and *adj.* theo-
dicē′an.—*n.* theogony (*thē-og′ə-ni;* Gr. *theogoniā*
—*gonē,* birth, generation), the birth and genealogy of the gods.—*adjs.* theogonic (*thē-ə-gon′ik*),
-al.—*ns.* theog′onist, a writer on theogony;
theology (*thē-ol′ə-ji;* Gr. *theologiā*—*logos,*
discourse), the science of God; theologaster
(-*gas′tər*), a shallow theologian; theol′ogate
(-*gāt*), a seminary for R.C. priests; theol′oger
(-*jər*), a theologian; theologian (*thē-ə-lō′jyən*),
one well versed in theology: a divine, a professor of or writer on divinity, esp. in R.C.
usage, a theological lecturer attached to a
cathedral or collegiate church.—*adjs.* theologic
(*thē-ə-loj′ik*), -al.—*adv.* theolog′ically.—*v.t.*
theol′ogise, -ize, to render theological.—*v.i.* to
discourse, speculate, etc., on theology.—*ns.*
theol′ogiser; theol′ogist, a theologian; the′o-
logue (-*log*), a theologian: a theological
student (*U.S.*); theomachy (*thē-om′ə-ki;* Gr.
*theomachiā*—*machē,* a battle), war among or
against the gods, as by the Titans and giants:
opposition to the divine will; theom′achist;
theomancy (*thē′ō-man-si;* Gr. *theomanteiā,*
spirit of prophecy—*manteiā,* divination), divination by means of oracles, or of persons inspired
immediately by some divinity.—*adj.* theoman′tic.
—*ns.* theomania (*-mā′ni-ə;* Gr. *maniā,* madness),
religious madness: belief that one is a god;
theomā′niac.—*adj.* theomorphic (*-mör′fik;* Gr
*theomorphos,* of divine form—*morphē,* form),
having the form or likeness of a god: in the
image of God.—*ns.* theomor′phism; Theo-
paschite (-*pas′kīt;* Gr. *paschein,* to suffer), a
Monophysite, as believing that God had
suffered and been crucified.—*adj.* Theopaschitic
(-*kit′ik*).—*ns.* Theopas′chitism (-*kit-izm*); theo-
pathy (*thē-op′ə-thi;* Gr. *pathos,* experience,
emotion), a religious emotion aroused by
meditation about God.—*adj.* theopathet′ic.—*n.*
theophagy (*thē-of′ə-ji;* Gr. *phagein,* to eat),
the sacramental eating of a god.—*adj.* theoph′-
agous (-*gəs*).—*n.* theophany (*thē-of′ə-ni;* Gr.
*theophaneiā,* a vision of God, exhibition of gods'
statues—*phainein,* to show), a manifestation or
appearance of deity to man.—*adj.* theophanic
(*thē-ō-fan′ik*).—*n.* theophilanthropy (-*fil-an′thrə-
pi;* Fr. *théophilanthropie,* love to God and man;
cf. philanthropy), a deistical system of religion
drawn up under the French Directory in 1796,
and designed to take the place of Christianity.—
*adj.* theophilanthrop′ic.—*ns.* theophilan′thropism;

theophilan′thropist; theophobia (-*fō′bi-ə;* Gr.
*phobos,* fear), morbid fear of God: hatred of
God; theophobist (-*of′ə-bist*).—*adj.* theopneust,
-ic (*thē′op-nūst;* Gr. *theopneustos*—*pneustos,*
inspired—*pneein,* to breathe), divinely inspired.
—*ns.* theopneust′y, divine inspiration; theosophy (*thē-os′ə-fi;* Gr. *theosophos,* wise in
things of God—*sophos,* wise), divine wisdom:
immediate divine illumination or inspiration
claimed to be possessed by specially gifted men,
along with abnormal control over natural
forces; theosoph (*thē′ə-sof*), theos′opher, theos′-
ophist.—*adjs.* theosoph′ic, -al.—*adv.* theosoph′-
ically.—*v.i.* theos′ophise, -ize, to practise theosophy.—*n.* theos′ophism, theosophical tenets.—
*adj.* theosophist′ical, theosophical: sophistical
in theology.—*n.* theotechny (-*tek′ni;* Gr. *technē,*
art), the employment of gods as the machinery
of a poem.—*adj.* theotech′nic.—*n.* theotokos
(*thē-ot′o-kos;* Gr. *theotokos*—*tokos,* birth), the
mother of God, a title of the Virgin Mary
repudiated by Nestorius, accepted by the Council
of Ephesus. [Gr. *theos,* a god.]
Theocritean, *thē-ok-ri-tē′ən, adj.* after the manner
of *Theocritus* (3rd cent. B.C.), the greatest of
Greek pastoral poets: pastoral, idyllic.
theodolite, *thē-od′ə-līt, n.* a surveying instrument
for measuring horizontal and vertical angles.
[Ety. unknown.]
theophylline, *thē-ō-fil′ēn, -in, -in, n.* an isomer
of theobromine found in tea. [Thea, and Gr.
*phyllon,* leaf.]
theorbo, *thē-örb′ō, n.* a large double-necked bass
lute.—*n.* theorb′ist. [It. *tiorba.*]
theorem, *thē′ə-rəm, n.* a demonstrable or established but not self-evident principle: a proposition to be proved.—*adjs.* theoremat′ic, -al.—*adv.*
theoremat′ically.—*n.* theorematist (-*rem′ə-tist*).
—*adjs.* theoret′ic, -al, pertaining, according, or
given to theory: not practical: speculative.—*n.*
(usu. in *pl.*) the speculative parts of a science.—
*adv.* theoret′ically.—*ns.* theoretician (-*et-ish′en*),
one who is concerned chiefly with the theoretical
aspect of a subject; the′oric, the′orique, (*Shak.*)
theory, speculation.—*v.i.* the′orise, -ize, to form a
theory: to form opinions solely by theories: to
speculate.—*ns.* the′oriser; the′orist, a theoriser:
one given to theory and speculation: one who is
expert in the abstract principles of a subject;
the′ory, an explanation or system of anything: an
exposition of the abstract principles of a science or
art: speculation as opposed to practice. [Gr.
*theōrēma, -atos,* spectacle, speculation, theorem,
*theōriā,* view, theory—*theōreein,* to be a spectator,
to view.]
theow, *thāow,* (*O.E. hist.*) *n.* a slave. [O.E. *thēow.*]
theralite, *thēr′ə-līt, n.* a holocrystalline igneous
rock composed essentially of plagioclase,
nepheline, and augite. [Gr. *thēraein,* to hunt,
seek after, *lithos,* stone, because its discovery
was expected.]
Therapeutae, *ther-ə-pū′tē,* L. *ther-a-pū′tī, n.pl.* a
traditional ascetic sect, allied to the Essenes,
living chiefly near Alexandria.—*adj.* therapeu′tic,
pertaining to the healing art: curative.—*adv.*
therapeu′tically.—*n.* (*pl.* in form, treated as *sing.*)
therapeu′tics, that part of medicine concerned
with the treatment and cure of diseases.—*ns.*
therapeu′tist, one versed in therapeutics; ther′-
apist or ther′apy, therapeutics: treatment used to
combat a disease or an abnormal condition:
curative power. [Gr. *therapeutēs,* servant,
worshipper, medical attendant—*therapeuein,* to
take care of, to heal, *therapeiā,* service, treatment.]
there, *dher, dhr, dhār, adv.* in that place: at that
point: to that place: used also (unstressed)
without any meaning of its own to allow the
subject to follow the predicate, and also in
corresponding interrogative sentences, etc.—*n.*

that place.—*interj.* expressing reassurance, finality, accompanying a blow, etc.—*n.* there′ness, the property of having relative situation or existence.—*advs.* there′about, -s (also *-bowts'*), about or near that place: near that number, quantity, or degree; thereaft′er, after or according to that: accordingly; thereagainst′, against that: there-among′, among that or those; thereanent′ (*Scot.*), concerning that matter; thereat′, at that place or occurrence: on that account; there′-away, in that direction: thereabout; thero-beside′, beside that; thereby′, beside that: about that amount: by that means: in consequence of that; therefor′, for that; therefore (*dher′fər*), for that reason: consequently; therefrom′, from that; therein′, in or into that or it: indoors (*Scot.*); thereinaft′er, thereinbefore′, later, earlier, in the same document; therein′to, into that place, thing, matter, etc.; thereof′, of that: from that: thereon′, on that; thereout′, out of that: out of doors (*Scot.*); therethrough′, through that: by that means; thereto′, there-un′to, to that: in addition; there′tofore, before that time; thereun′der, under that; thereupon′, upon that: in consequence of that (*Shak.*): immediately; therewith′, with that: thereupon; there′withal, with that: immediately after: in addition; therewithin′, within that.—there and then, forthwith; there or thereabouts, somewhere near. [O.E. *thǣr*; akin to the, that, etc.]

theriac, *thē′ri-ak*, theriaca, *thē-ri′ə-kə*, (*arch.*) *ns.* an antidote to venomous bites, etc.—*adj.* thēri′-acal. [Gr. *thēriakē—thērion*, a wild beast.]

therio-, theri-, thero-, *thēr′, -i-, -ō-*, in composition, beast, mammal.—*adj.* therianthrop′ic (Gr. *anthrōpos*, man), combining human and animal forms.—*n.* therian′thropism, representation or worship of therianthropic forms or gods.—*n.pl.* Theriodontia (*-ō-don′shyə, -ti-ə*; Gr. *odous, odontos*, a tooth), an extinct order of reptiles with teeth like mammals.—*ns.* theriol′atry (Gr. *latreiā*, worship), animal-worship; ther′iomorph (Gr. *morphē*, form), an animal form in art.—*adj.* theriomorph′ic, beastlike: of theriomorphism.—*n.* theriomorph′ism, belief in gods of the form of beasts.—*n.pl.* Theriomor′pha (Theromor′pha), an extinct order of reptiles with affinities to the labyrinthodont Amphibia and mammals.—*n.* theriomorphō′sis (or *-mōr′*), transformation into a beast.—*adjs.* theriomor′phous, beastlike: mammal-like: of the Theriomorpha; ther′oid, beastlike.—*n.* therol′ogy, the study of mammals. [Gr. *thēr*, and *thērion*, a wild beast.]

therm, *thûrm, n.* hot baths: a bathing establishment (Gr. and *Rom. hist.*): 100,000 British thermal units (used as a unit in reckoning payment for gas).—*n.pl.* thermae (*-ē*), hot springs or baths.—*adj.* therm′al, pertaining to heat: warm.—*n.* an ascending current of warm air.—*adv.* therm′ally.—*adjs.* therm′ic, -al, of heat.—*adv.* therm′ically.—*n.* therm′ion (Gr. *ion* (neut.), going), an electrically charged particle emitted by an incandescent body.—*adj.* thermion′ic (thermionic valve, or tube, a vacuum tube containing a heated cathode from which electrons are emitted, an anode for collecting some or all of these electrons and, generally, additional electrodes for controlling their flow to the anode).—*ns.* thermion′ics (treated as *sing.*), the science of thermions; thermi′stor, a semi-conductor, mixture of certain oxides with finely divided copper, of which the resistance is very sensitive to change of temperature (*thermal* resi*stor*); therm′ite (trademark Thermit), mixture of aluminium powder with oxide of metal (esp. iron), which when ignited evolves great heat, used for local heating and welding; thermobal′ance, a balance for weighing bodies at high temperatures.—*adj.* thermochem′ical.—*ns.* thermochem′ist; thermochem′istry, the study of heat changes

accompanying chemical action; therm o-couple, a pair of metals in contact giving a thermo-electric current.—*adjs.* thermodū′ric, resistant to heat; thermodynam′ic.—*n.* thermodynam′ics, the science of heat as a mechanical agent.—*adj.* thermo-elec′tric.—*ns.* thermo-electric′ity, electricity developed by the unequal heating of bodies, esp. between a junction of metals and another part of a circuit; thermogenesis (*-jen′*), production of heat, esp. in the body by physiological processes.—*adjs.* thermogenet′ic, thermo-gen′ic.—*ns.* therm′ogram, a thermograph record; therm′ograph, a self-registering thermometer; thermog′raphy, any process of writing involving the use of heat: obtaining an image on a small picture-tube by using an infra-red camera: a pictorial record of heat emission from the patient's body used in medical diagnosis.—*adj.* thermolā′bile, readily decomposed by heat.—*ns.* thermol′ogy, the science of heat; thermo-luminesc′ence, release of light by irradiated material upon subsequent heating; thermol′-ysis (Gr. *lysis*, loosing), dissociation or dissolution by heat: loss of body heat.—*adj.* thermo-lyt′ic.—*n.* thermometer (*-om′i-tər*), an instrument for measuring temperature depending on any of several properties of a substance that vary linearly with change of temperature.—*adjs.* thermometric (*-ə-met′rik*), -al.—*adv.* thermomet′-rically.—*ns.* thermomet′rograph, a self-registering thermometer; thermom′etry; therm′onasty, nastic movement in relation to heat.—*adjs.* thermonuc′lear, used of the fusion of nuclei as seen in thermonuclear reaction (thermonuclear reaction, a power reaction produced by the fusion of nuclei at extremely high temperatures, as in the hydrogen bomb); therm′ophil(e) (*-fil*), thermophil′ic, thermoph′ilous, requiring, or thriving best in, a high temperature.—*n.* therm′-opile (*-pil*), an apparatus for the direct conversion of heat into electrical energy.—*adj.* thermoplast′-ic, plastic when heated.—*n.* any resin that can be melted and cooled repeatedly without appreciable change in properties.—*ns.* therm′os, orig. trade-mark for a brand of vacuum or Dewar flask; therm′oscope, an instrument for detecting changes of temperature.—*adj.* thermoscop′ic, indicating, or sensitive to, temperature changes.—*adv.* thermoscop′ically.—*adjs.* thermosett′ing, setting, after melting and moulding with change of properties; thermosta′ble, not readily decomposed by heating.—*n.* therm′ostat (Gr. *statos*, standing), a device for keeping temperature steady.—*adj.* thermostat′ic.—*adv.* thermo-stat′ically.—*adj.* thermotact′ic, of or showing thermotaxis.—*n.* thermotax′is, a taxis towards a position of higher or lower temperature.—*adjs.* thermot′ic, -al, of or due to heat.—*n.* thermot′ics, the science of heat.—*adj.* thermotrop′ic.—*n.* thermot′ropism (Gr. *tropos*, turning), orientation determined by temperature differences.—thermal dissociation, the splitting of certain molecules into simpler molecules by heat, followed by recombination on cooling; thermal springs, natural springs of hot water; thermic lance, a cutting instrument consisting of a steel tube containing metal rods which, with the help of oxygen, are raised to an intense heat. [Gr. *thermos*, hot, *thermē*, heat, *thermotēs*, heat.]

Thermidor, *thûr-mi-dôr′, n.* eleventh month of Fr. Revolutionary calendar, 19th July-17th Aug.—*n.* Thermido′rian, participator in fall of Robespierre. [Gr. *thermē*, heat, *dōron*, gift.]

thero-. See therio-.

Thersitic, *thar-sit′ik, adj.* like Thersitēs, a shameless railer among the Greeks at Troy.

thesaurus, *thi-sö′rəs, n.* a treasury: a storehouse of knowledge, esp. of words, quotations, etc., a dictionary. [L.,—Gr. *thēsauros*.]

these, *dhēz, demons. adj.* and *demons. pron., pl.* of

**this.** [O.E. *thǣs*, a by-form of *thās*, pl. of *thēs*, *thēos*, *this*, this; cf. those.]

**thesis,** *thē′sis*, *thes′is*, *n*. lit. a setting down, a down-beat (*Gr. pros.* and *mus.*): hence the strong position in a bar or foot: understood by the Romans as the weak position: used in English in both senses (opp. to *arsis*): a position or that which is set down or advanced for argument: a subject for a scholastic exercise, esp. one presented for a doctorate: an essay on a theme:— *pl.* **theses** (*thē′sēz*).—*adjs.* **thetic** (*thet′ik*), **-al**, positively asserting: bearing the thesis.—*adv.* **thet′ically.**—**thesis** novel, roman à thèse (see under roman). [Gr. *thĕsis*, from the root of *tithenai*, to put, set.]

**Thesmophoria,** *thes-mō-phō′*, *phŏ′ri-ə*, *n.pl.* an ancient Greek married women's festival in honour of Demeter Thesmophoros (law-giving). [Gr. *thesmophŏria.*]

**thesmothete,** *thes′mō-thēt*, *n.* a law-giver, esp. one of the six junior archons in ancient Athens. [Gr. *thesmothetēs—thesmos*, law, *thetēs*, a placer, setter.]

**Thespian,** *thes′pi-ən*, *adj.* pertaining to tragedy: tragic.—*n.* tragic actor: an actor. [Gr. *Thespis*, founder of Greek tragedy.]

**theta,** *thē′tə*, *thā′tə*, *n.* the eighth (orig. ninth) letter of the Greek alphabet (Θ, θ) transliterated *th*, its sound an aspirated *t*, but in modern Greek like English *th*: as a Greek numeral θ′ = 9, ͵θ = 9000: a mark of condemnation (from the θ for *thanatos*, death, used in balloting). [Gr. *thēta*; Semitic.]

**thetch,** *thech*, (*Spens.*) *v.i.* to thatch. [O.E. *theccan.*]

**thete,** *thēt*, (*Gr. hist.*) *n.* orig. a serf: a poor free-man in Athens under Solon's constitution. [Gr. *thēs*, *thētos.*]

**thetic.** See under thesis.

**theurgy,** *thē′ər-ji*, *n.* magic by the agency of good spirits: miraculous divine action.—*adjs.* **theur′gic, -al.**—*n.* **the′urgist.** [Gr. *theourgiā—theos*, a god, *ergon*, work.]

**thew,** *thū*, (used chiefly in *pl.* **thews, thewes**) *n.* custom: trait: manner: moral quality: later (*Shak.*) bodily quality, muscle or strength.—*adjs.* **thewed,** mannered (*Spens.*): (later) muscular: **thew′less** (see **thowless**); **thew′y,** muscular, strong. [O.E. *thēaw*, manner.]

**they,** *dhā*, *pron.*, *nom. pl.*, used as *pl.* of **he, she, it**: often used as a *sing.* (with *pl. vb.*) of common gender, he or she, people in general, some. [M.E. *thei*—O.N. *theirr*, which supplanted *hi* (O.E. *hīe*).]

**thiamine, thiamin,** *thī′ə-mēn*, **-min**, *n.* vitamin B₁. [Gr. *theion*, sulphur, and amine.]

**thiasus,** *thī′ə-səs*, *n.* a company or troop of wor-shippers, esp. a Bacchic rout. [Gr. *thiasos.*]

**thible,** *thib′l*, *thib′l*, **thivel,** *thiv′l*, (*Northern*) *n.* a porridge-stick. [Origin unknown.]

**thick,** *thik*, *adj.* having a great (or specified) distance in measurement from surface to surface in lesser dimension: deep: dense: viscous: close set or packed: crowded: intimate, in close confidence (*fig.*): abundant: frequent, in quick succession: aboundingly covered or occupied: foggy: opaque: dull: stupid: gross: husky, muffled: indistinctly articulate: exces-sive, approaching the intolerable (*slang*).—*n.* the thickest part of anything: the midst: a stupid person (*slang*): a thicket (*Spens.*).—*adv.* **thickly:** closely: frequently: fast: to a great (or specified) depth.—*v.t.* and *v.i.* (*Spens.*, *Shak.*) to make or become thick.—*v.t.* and *v.i.* **thick′en,** to make or become thick or thicker.— *ns.* **thick′ener;** **thick′ening,** a making or becom-ing thicker: a thickened place: material added to something to thicken it.—Also *adj.*—*n.* **thick′et** (O.E. *thiccet*), a dense mass of trees or shrubs.—*adjs.* **thick′eted;** **thick′ety**—*adj.* **thick′-**

ish, somewhat thick.—*adv.* **thick′ly.**—*n.* **thick′-ness,** quality or degree of being thick: the space between outer surfaces: a layer.—*adjs.* **thick′-and-thin′,** unwavering in devotion to party or principle; **thick′-com′ing** (*Shak.*), coming close upon one another; **thick′-eyed,** dim-sighted; **thick′-grown** (*Shak.*).—**thick′head,** a blockhead: any bird of an Australian family (Pachyce-phalidae) akin to fly-catchers and shrikes.—*adj.* **thick′-head′ed,** having a thick head or skull: stupid.—**thick′-knee,** the stone-curlew (Oedic-nemus), a large plover with thickened knees.— *adj.* **thick′-lipped** (*Shak.*).—**thick′-lips** (*Shak.*), a Negro.—*adjs.* **thick′-pleached** (*Shak.*), closely interwoven; **thick′-ribbed** (*Shak.*); **thick′set,** closely set or planted: having a short thick body. —*n.* a thicket: a stout cotton.—*adj.* **thick-sight′ed** (*Shak.*), dim-sighted.—**thick′skin,** a blockhead. —*adj.* **thick′-skinned′,** having a thick skin: insensitive: indifferent to criticism or insult.— **thick′-skull,** a blockhead.—*adjs.* **thick′-skulled,** having a thick skull: doltish; **thick′-sown,** planted closely: close-set.—**thick′un** (*slang*), a sovereign: a crown.—**a bit thick,** more than one can reasonably be expected to put up with; **a thick ear,** a bruised ear, usually a result of a blow administered as punishment; **lay it on thick,** to praise extravagantly: to exaggerate; **through thick and thin,** in spite of all obstacles: without any wavering. [O.E. *thicce*; Ger. *dick.*]

**thick, thicky,** *dhik*, *dhik′i*. See thilk.

**thief,** *thēf*, *n.* one who takes unlawfully what is not his own, esp. by stealth: a flaw in a candle-wick that causes guttering:—*pl.* **thieves** (*thēvz*).—*adj.* and *adv.* **thief′-like.**—**thief′-catcher, -taker,** one whose business is to arrest thieves: a detective. [O.E. *thēof*: cf. Ger. *dieb.*]

**thieve,** *thēv*, *v.i.* to practise theft: to steal.—*n.* **thiev′ery,** practice of thieving: what is thieved.— *n.* and *adj.* **thiev′ing.**—*adj.* **thiev′ish,** infested by thieves (*Shak.*): given to, or like, theft: thief-like: furtive.—*adv.* **thiev′ishly.**—*n.* **thiev′ish-ness.** [O.E. *thēofian*, to thieve, and *thēof*, thief.]

**thig,** *thig*, (*Scot.*) *v.i.* to beg: to live on alms.—*v.t.* to beg: to get by begging:—*pa.t.* and *pa.p.* **thigg′it.**—*ns.* **thigg′er; thigg′ing.**—**thigging and sorning,** extortionate begging and sponging. [O.N. *thiggja*; cf. O.E. *thicgan*, to take.]

**thigh,** *thī*, *n.* the thick fleshy part of the leg from the knee to the trunk.—**thigh′-bone,** the bone of the leg between the hip-joint and the knee, the femur. [O E. *thēoh* (Anglian *thēh*); O.N. *thjó*; O.H.G. *dioh.*]

**thigmotropism,** *thig-mot′rə-pizm*, (*biol.*) *n.* re-sponse to stimulus of touch.—*adj.* **thigmotropic** (*-mə-trop′ik*). [Gr. *thigma, -atos*, touch, *tropos*, a turning.]

**thilk,** *dhilk*, (*dial.*) *adj.* and *pron.* the same, that same: this.—Also (*S.W. England*) **thick** (*dhik*), **thick′y.** [the ilk.]

**thill,** *thil*, *n.* the shaft of a vehicle.—*ns.* **thill′er,** **thill′-horse,** a shaft-horse, or the last of a team. [Poss. O.E. *thille*, board, plank.]

**thill,** *thil*, (*dial.*) *n.* underclay or floor of a coal-seam: a bed of fireclay. [Origin unknown.]

**thimble,** *thim′bl*, *n.* a cover for the finger, used in sewing: an object of similar form.—*v.i.* to use a thimble.—*v.t.* to use a thimble on.—*n.* **thim′-bleful,** as much as a thimble will hold: a small quantity:—*pl.* **thim′blefuls.**—**thimble-case; thim′-ble-rig,** a sleight-of-hand trick in which the performer conceals, or pretends to conceal, a pea or small ball under one of three thimble-like cups.—*v.i.* to cheat by such means.—*v.t.* to manipulate in this or analogous way; **thimb′le-rigger,** thim′ble-rigging. [O.E. *thýmel*, thumb-stall—*thūma*, thumb.]

**thin,** *thin*, *adj.* (*comp.* **thinn′er**; *superl.* **thinn′est**) having little thickness: slim: lean: freely mobile: watery: dilute: of little density:

rarefied: sparse: slight: flimsy: wanting in body or solidity: meagre: poor: tinkling: too much to the left (golf, etc.).—*n.* that which is thin.—*adv.* thinly.—*v.t.* to make thin or thinner: to make less close or crowded (with *away, out,* etc.).—*v.i.* to grow or become thin or thinner:— *pr.p.* thinn'ing; *pa.t.* and *pa.p.* thinned.—*adv.* thin'ly.—*ns.* thinn'er; thin'ness; thinn'ing.— *adjs.* thinn'ish, somewhat thin.—*adjs.* thin'-belly (*Shak.*), narrow in the belly; thin'-faced (*Shak.*); thin'-skinned, having thin skin: sensitive: irritable.—thin'-skinned'ness.—*adjs.* thin'-sown, sparsely sown; thin'-spun, drawn out fine; thin'-walled.—a thin time, a time of little employment; into, out of, thin air, into, out of, nothing or nothingness; thin on the ground, present in very small, inadequate, quality or numbers; thin on top, balding. [O.E. *thynne*; Ger. *dünn*; O.N. *thunnr.*]

thine, *dhin, pron., gen.* of thou, used predicatively or absolutely, belonging to thee: thy people: that which belongs to thee: adjectively, esp. before a vowel or *h*, thy. [O.E. *thin.*]

thing, *thing, n.* an assembly, parliament, court, council (*hist.*): a matter, affair, problem, point: a circumstance: a fact: an event, happening, action: an entity: that which exists or can be thought of: an inanimate object: a living creature (esp. in pity, tolerant affection, kindly reproach): a possession: a piece of writing, composition, etc.: that which is wanted or is appropriate (*coll.*): a slight obsession or phobia (*coll.*): a liking or dislike (*coll.*): (in *pl.*) clothes, esp. a woman's additional outdoor garments: (in *pl.*) utensils, esp. for the table: (in *pl.*) personal belongings.—*ns.* thing'amy, thing'-ummy, thing'umbob, thing'umajig (*coll.*), what-d'you-call-him (-her, -it): what's-his-name, etc. —used when one cannot or will not recall the name; thing'hood, state or fact of being a thing: substantiality; thing'iness, thing'liness, reality, objectivity: materialistic or matter-of-fact turn of mind; thing'ness, character or fact of being a thing: reality.—*adj.* thing'y, real: actual: objective: matter-of-fact.—thing'-in-itself', a noumenon, the Ger. *ding an sich.*—a stupid, wise, etc., thing to do, a stupid, wise, etc., action; be all things to all men, to meet each on his, her, own ground, accommodate oneself to his, her, circumstances and outlook (1 Cor. ix. 22): loosely, in bad sense, to keep changing one's opinions, etc., so as to suit one's company; do one's (own) thing (*coll.*), to behave as is natural to, characteristic of, oneself: to do something in which one specialises; do the handsome thing by, to treat generously; have a thing about (*coll.*), to have an unaccountable feeling about, as of fear, etc.; know a thing or two, to be shrewd; make a good thing of it, to reap a good advantage from; make a thing of, to make an issue, point of controversy, of: to fuss about; no such thing, something very different: no, not at all; not quite the thing, not in very good health (see also the thing); one of those things, a happening one cannot account for or do anything to prevent; see things, to see something that is not really there; the thing, that which is conventional, fashionable, approved, right, or desirable. [O.E. and O.N. *thing,* parliament, object, etc.: Norw., Sw., Dan. *ting,* parliament; Ger. *ding,* thing.]

think, *thingk, v.i.* to exercise the mind (often with *about, of, on, upon*): to revolve ideas in the mind: to judge: to be of opinion: to consider: to bethink oneself: to conceive or hit on a thought. —*v.t.* to form, conceive, or revolve in the mind: to have as a thought: to aspire or form designs (with *of*): to imagine: to judge: to believe or consider: to expect: to purpose, design: to believe to exist (*Milt.*): to bring by thinking:

—*pa.t.* and *pa.p.* thought, *thöt.*—*n.* (*coll.*) a spell of thinking: a thought.—*adj.* think'able, capable of being thought: conceivably possible. —*n.* think'er.—*n.* and *adj.* think'ing.—*adv.* think'ingly.—I don't think, I disbelieve: a warning that what was said was ironical (*coll.*); I shouldn't think of it, I would not under any conditions; put on one's thinking-cap, to devote some time to thinking about some problem; think aloud, to utter one's thoughts unintentionally; think better of, to change one's mind concerning on reflection; think for, to expect; think little of, to have a poor opinion of—opp. to think much, or well, of; think long, to yearn: to weary (from deferred hopes or boredom); think out, to devise, project completely: to solve by a process of thought; think over, to reconsider at leisure; think shame, to be ashamed; think-tank (*coll.*), a person or a group of people, usu. expert in some field, regarded as a source of ideas and solutions to problems; think up, to find by thinking, devise, concoct. [O.E. *thencan.*]

think, *thingk, v.i.* (*impers., arch.* with *me* or other dat. pron. prefixed; otherwise *obs.*) to seem:— *pa.t.* thought (*thöt*). [O.E. *thyncan,* to seem.]

thio-, *thi'ō-,* in composition, sulphur, indicating in chemistry a compound theoretically derived from another by substituting an atom or more of sulphur for oxygen.—*ns.* thi'o-acid, an acid analogous in constitution to an oxy-acid, sulphur taking the place of oxygen; thiocy'anate, a salt of thiocyan'ic acid, HSCN; thiopent'one, (*U.S.*) thiopent'al (see Pentothal); thi'o-salt, a salt of a thio-acid.—Thiobacillus ferro-oxidans, a rod-shaped bacillus which, in the presence of water, converts copper sulphide ores into copper sulphate (see leaching). [Gr. *theion,* sulphur.]

thir, *dhir,* (*Scot.*) *pl.* demons. pron. and demons. adj. these. [Origin obscure.]

third, *thûrd, adj.* the last of three: equal to one of three equal parts.—*n.* a third part: an interval of two (conventionally called three) diatonic degrees (*mus.*): a note at that interval: a handicap of a stroke at six holes out of eighteen (*golf*). —*adv.* in the third place.—*v.t.* to divide by three: to support after the seconder.—*n.* third'ing, a third part.—*adv.* third'ly, in the third place.— *adj.* third'-class.—*adv.* third'-class'.—third degree (see degree); third force, a group following a middle or uncommitted course between contending extremes.—*adj.* third'-hand'.—third man (*cricket*), a fielder on the offside between point and slip.—*adjs.* third'-party, of a person other than the principals (as insured and insurer); third'-programme, highbrow, in allusion to the Third Programme (1946-70) of the B.B.C.; third'-rate, of the third order.—thirds'man, a mediator.—*adj.* third'-stream, of a style of music, having features of both jazz and classical music.—Third World, the developing countries not aligned politically with the large power blocks.—Picardy third, tierce de Picardie. [O.E. *thridda;* cf. Ger. *dritte,* Gr. *tritos,* L. *tertius.*]

thirdborough, *thûrd'bər-ə,* (*hist.*) an under-constable. [Supposed to be from O.E. *frithborh,* a surety for peace (see under frith).]

thirl, *thûrl,* (*dial.*) *n.* a hole: an opening: a short passage between two headings in a mine.—*v.t.* to pierce: to thrill.—*v.i.* to vibrate, tingle, thrill. [O.E. *thyrel,* hole—*thurh,* through; cf. thrill.]

thirl, *thûrl, n.* a form of thrall: thirlage.—*v.t.* to bind or subject: to confine, restrict.—*n.* thirl'age, a form of servitude by which the grain produced on certain lands had to be ground (or at least paid for) at a certain mill.

thirst, *thûrst, n.* the uneasiness caused by want of drink: vehement desire for drink: eager desire for anything.—*v.i.* to feel thirst.—*n.* thirst'er.— *adj.* thirst'ful.—*adv.* thirst'ily.—*n.* thirst'iness.— *adjs.* thirst'less; thirst'y, suffering from thirst:

dry: parched: vehemently desiring. [O.E. *thurst* (n.), *thyrstan* (vb.); cf. Ger. *durst*, *dürsten*, Gr. *tersesthai*, L. *torrēre*, to dry.]

**thirteen,** *thûr′tēn*, or *-tēn′*, *adj.* and *n.* three and ten.—*adj.* **thir′teenth** (or *-tēnth′*), the last of thirteen: equal to one of thirteen equal parts.— *n.* a thirteenth part.—*adv.* **thirteenth′ly.** [O.E. *thrēotiene, -tēne—thrēo,* three.]

**thirty,** *thûr′ti, adj.* and *n.* three times ten.—*adj.* **thir′tieth,** the last of thirty: equal to one of thirty equal parts.—*n.* a thirtieth part.—*n., adj.,* and *adv.* **thir′tyfold.**—*adjs.* **thir′tyish,** somewhere about the age of thirty; **thirty-two′mo,** (for *tricesimo secundo,* 32mo) in sheets folded to give 32 leaves (64 pages).—*n.* a book so constructed. [O.E. *thrītig—thrēo,* three, *-tig,* suff. denoting ten.]

**this,** *dhis, sing.* demons. *pron.* or *adj.* denoting a person or thing near, topical, just mentioned, or about to be mentioned: the present moment: the place where the speaker is:—*pl.* **these.**—*adv.* (*Shak.*) thus.—*n.* **this′ness,** the quality of being this, not something else, haecceity. [O.E., neut. of *thes, thēos, this* (instrumental *thīs, thȳs*; nom. pl. *thās, thǣs*).]

**thistle,** *this′l, n.* a prickly composite plant (Carduus, Cnicus, Onopordon, etc.)—national emblem of Scotland.—*adj.* **this′tly,** like a thistle: overgrown with thistles.—**this′tle-down,** the tufted feathery parachutes of thistle seeds. [O.E. *thistel.*]

**thither,** *dhidh′ər* (*Spens.* often **thether**), *adv.* to that place: to that end or result.—*adv.* on the far side.—*advs.* **thith′erward, -s,** toward that place. [O.E. *thider.*]

**thivel.** See **thible.**

**thixotropy,** *thiks-ot′rə-pi, n.* the property of showing a temporary reduction in viscosity when shaken or stirred.—*adj.* **thixotropic** (*-trop′ik*) of, or showing, thixotropy: (of paints) non-drip. [Gr. *thixis,* action of touching, *tropos,* a turn.]

**thlipsis,** *thlip′sis, n.* constriction: compression. [Gr. *thlipsis—thlībein,* to press.]

**tho,** *dhō,* (*Spens.*) *pl.* demons. *adj.* those. [O.E. *thā,* pl. of *se, sēo, thæt,* that.]

**tho,** *dhō,* (*Spens.*) *adv.* then. [O.E. (and O.N.) *thā.*]

**tho′.** Same as **though.**

**thoft,** *thoft,* (*dial.*) *n.* a rowing-bench. [O.E. *thofte.*]

**thole,** *thōl, n.* a pin in the side of a boat to keep the oar in place: a peg.—Also **thowl, thowel.**— **thole′-pin,** a peg, thole. [O.E. *thol;* Du. *dol,* O.N. *thollr.*]

**thole,** *thōl,* (now *Scot.*) *v.t.* and *v.i.* to endure. [O.E. *tholian,* to suffer; Goth. *thulan,* O.N. *thola;* O.H.G. *dolên,* Ger. *geduld,* patience, *dulden,* to suffer, L. *tollĕre,* Gr. *tolmaein.*]

**tholus,** *thō′ləs, n.* a round building, dome, cupola, or tomb:—*pl.* **thō′li** (*-lī*).—Also **tholos** (*thol′os; pl.* **thol′oi**).—*n.* **tholobate** (*thol′ō-bāt;* from root of Gr. *bainein,* to go), the substructure of a dome or cupola. [Gr. *tholos.*]

**Thomism,** *tō′mizm, n.* the doctrines of *Thomas* Aquinas (b. prob. 1225; d. 1274).—*n.* and *adj.* **Thō′mist.**—*adjs.* **Thōmist′ic, -al.**

**thon,** *dhon,* **thon′der, -dər,** unexplained modern Scots forms of **yon, yonder** prob. influenced by *this* and *that.*

**thong,** *thong, n.* a strap: a strip: the lash of a whip or crop. [O.E. *thwang.*]

**Thor,** *thōr, n.* the Scandinavian thunder-god, Old English Thunor. [O.N. *Thōrr.*]

**thoracic.** See **thorax.**

**Thorah.** See **Torah.**

**thorax,** *thō′raks, thō′, n.* a corselet (Gr. *ant.*): the part of the body between the head and abdomen, in man the chest, in insects the division that bears legs and wings.—*adj.* **thoracic** (*-ras′*).— **thoracic duct,** the main trunk of the vessels

conveying lymph in the body. [Gr. *thōrax -ākos.*]

**thorium,** *thō′ri-əm, thō′, n.* a radioactive metal (Th; at. numb. 90) resembling aluminium.—*ns.* **thō′rite,** a mineral, thorium silicate, in which it was first discovered, by Berzelius; **thoron** (*thō′- ron, thō′*), the radioactive gas given off by the decomposition of thorium. [*Thor,* the god.]

**thorn,** *thōrn, n.* a sharp hard part (leaf, stem, or root) of a plant: an animal spine: anything prickly: a spiny plant: hawthorn: the Old English and Old Norse letter þ (*th*).—*v.t.* to set with thorns: to prick.—*adj.* **thorned.**—*n.* **thorn′- iness.**—*adjs.* **thorn′less; thorn′set,** set or beset with thorns; **thorn′y,** full of thorns: prickly: troublesome: harassing.—**thorn′-apple,** a poisonous plant (*Datura stramonium,* or other species) of the potato family, with a prickly capsule: a haw; **thorn′back,** a ray with nail-like crooked spines in its back: **thorn′-bush,** any thorny shrub, esp. hawthorn; **thorn′-devil,** the Australian Moloch lizard; **thorn′-hedge,** a hedge of hawthorn; **thorn′tree,** a thorny tree, esp. a hawthorn.— **thorn in the flesh,** any cause of constant irritation, from 2 Cor. xii. 7. [O.E. *thorn;* O.N. *thorn,* Ger. *dorn.*]

**thoron.** See **thorium.**

**thorough,** *thur′ə, adj.* passing or carried through, or to the end: complete: entire: out-and-out: assiduous and scrupulous in completing work.— *prep.*(*obs.*) through.—*n.* that which goes through, a passage: the blind and obstinately tyrannical policy of Strafford and Laud in administering civil and ecclesiastical affairs without regard to opposite convictions.—*adv.* **thor′oughly.** — *n.* **thor′oughness.**—**thor′ough-bass** (*mus.*), a bass part all through a piece, usu. with figures to indicate the chords: loosely, harmony: erron. a deep bass; **thor′oughbrace** (*U.S.*), a leather band supporting the body of a vehicle: a stagecoach.—*adj.* **thor′oughbred,** thoroughly or completely bred or trained: bred from a dam and sire of the best blood, as a horse, and having the qualities supposed to depend thereon. —*n.* an animal, esp. a horse, of pure blood—of race-horses, one all of whose ancestors for seven generations (five in America) are recorded in the stud-book.—**thor′oughfare,** a passage or way through: a road open at both ends: a public way or street: right of passing through. —*adjs.* **thor′ough-go′ing,** going through or to the end: going all lengths: complete: out-and-out; **thor′ough-paced,** thoroughly or perfectly paced or trained: complete.—**thor′oughwax, thor′ow-wax,** the plant hare's-ear, from the stem seeming to grow (wax) through the leaves. [The longer form of **through.**]

**thorp, thorpe,** *thōrp, n.* a hamlet: a village. [O.E. *thorp, throp;* O.N. *thorp,* Goth. *thaurp,* Ger. *dorf.*]

**those,** *dhōz,* demons. *pron.* and *adj., pl.* of **that.** [O.E. *thās,* pl. of *thes,* this.]

**Thoth,** *thōth, thoth, n.* the ancient Egyptian ibis-headed god of art, science, etc. [Gr. *Thōth—* Egypt. *Tehuti.*]

**thou,** *dhow, pron.* of the second person sing., the person addressed (now generally used only in solemn address).—*v.t.* to apply the pronoun *thou* to:—*pa.t.* and *pa.p.* **thou'd.** [O.E. *thū;* Goth. *thu,* Doric Gr. *ty,* L. *tū,* Sans. *tvam.*]

**thou,** *thow,* a coll. abbrev. of **thousand.**

**though,** *dhō, conj.* admitting: allowing: even if: notwithstanding that.—*adv.* nevertheless: however.—**as though,** as if. [O.N. *thauh, thō;* O.E. *thēah, thēh,* Ger. *doch.*]

**thought,** *thöt, pa.t.* and *pa.p.* of **think.** [O.E. *thöhte,* pa.t., (*ge*)*thöht,* pa.p.]

**thought,** *thöt, n.* thinking: mind: consciousness: reasoning: deliberation: that which one thinks: notion: idea: fancy: consideration: opinion:

meditation: design: care: considerateness: purpose: resolution: intention: grief, anxiety (*obs.*): a very slight amount, a 'suspicion'.—*adjs.* **thought′ed**, having thoughts; **thought′en**, (*Shak.*) firm in belief, assured; **thought′ful**, full of thought: employed in meditation: attentive: considerate: expressive of or favourable to meditation.—*adv.* **thought′fully.**—*n.* **thought′-fulness.**—*adj.* **thought′less**, unthinking: incapable of thinking: carefree: careless: inattentive: inconsiderate.—*adv.* thought′leesly.—*n.* **thought′-lessness.**—*adj.* **thought-ex′ecuting**, carrying out the wishes of a master: perh. acting with the speed of thought (*Shak.*).—**thought′-pro′cess**, train of thought: manner of thinking; **thought′-reader**; **thought′-reading**, discerning what is passing in another's mind by any means other than the ordinary and obvious.—*adj.* **thought′-sick** (*Shak.*), sick with the thought.—**thought′-trans′ference**, telepathy; **thought′-wave**, a wave-like progress of a thought among a crowd or a public: a sudden accession of thought in the mind: an impulse in some hypothetical medium assumed to explain telepathy.—**on second thoughts**, on reconsideration; **take thought**, to bethink oneself: to conceive a purpose: to be anxious or grieved (*obs.*); **upon, with, a thought**, (*Shak.*) in a moment: with the speed of thought. [O.E. (*ge*)*thōht*.]

**thous,** *dhowz,* a Northern contracted form of **thou** is, thou art (*Spens.*), and of **thou sal,** thou shalt.

**thousand,** *thow′zand, n.* and *adj.* ten hundred: often used vaguely or hyperbolically.—*adj., adv.,* and *n.* (a) **thou′sandfold,** a thousand times as much.—*adj.* **thou′sandth,** the last of a thousand: equal to one of a thousand equal parts.—*n.* a thousandth part.—**thou′sand-legs,** a centipede or millipede.—*adjs.* **thou′sand-pound′,** weighing, costing, priced at a thousand pounds; **thou′sand-year,** lasting, or coming once in, a thousand years.—**one in (of) a thousand,** anything exceedingly rare or excellent. [O.E. *thūsend;* Ger. *tausend,* Goth. *thūsundi.*]

**thowel, thowl.** See **thole** (1).

**thowless,** *thow′lis,* (*Scot.*) *adj.* pithless: listless: inert. [App. **thewless.**]

**thrae,** *thrā,* another form of Scots **frae.**

**thrall,** *thröl, n.* a slave, serf: slavery, servitude: a stand for barrels, pans, etc.—*adj.* (*arch.*) enslaved.—*v.t.* to enslave.—*n.* **thral′dom** (also **thrall′dom**), slavery: bondage. [O.E. *thræl*—O.N. *thrœll.*]

**thrang,** *thrang,* Scots form of **throng.**

**thrapple,** *thrap′l,* a Scots form of **thropple.**

**thrash,** *thrash, v.t.* to thresh: (with *out*) to discuss exhaustively, or arrive at by debate: to beat soundly: to defeat thoroughly.—*v.i.* to lash out, lay about one: to force one's way (*naut.*).—*n.* an act of threshing or thrashing.—*n.* **thrash′er,** a thresher: a thresher-shark: one who thrashes.—*n.* and *adj.* **thrash′ing,** threshing: beating.—**thrash′ing-floor, -machine, -mill** (see **threshing**). [Orig. a dialect form of **thresh.**]

**thrash,** *thrash,* **thresh,** *thresh,* (*Scot.*) *n.* a rush (plant). [Obscurely conn. with **rush.**]

**thrasher,** *thrash′ər,* **thresher,** *thresh′ər, n.* an American bird akin to the mocking-bird. [Perh. Eng. dial. *thresher,* **thrush.**]

**thrasonic, -al,** *thra-, thrā-son′ik, -l, adjs.* like *Thrasōn,* the bragging soldier, a stock character in Greek New Comedy, or *Thrasō* in Terence's *Eunuchus:* boastful, bragging.—*adv.* **thrason′-ically.**

**thrave,** *thrāv,* **threave,** *thrēv,* (*dial.*) *n.* two stooks of (usu.) twelve sheaves each: two dozen: a good number. [Scand.; cf. Ice. *threfi,* Dan. *trave.*]

**thraw,** *thrö,* a Scots form of **throw** with some old senses preserved; also of **throe,** with senses overlapping **throw.**—*v.t.* to turn: to twist: to wring: to distort: to wrest: to cross, thwart.—*v.i.* to

turn: to twist: to writhe: to sway: to go counter: to be perverse:—*pa.t.* **threw;** *pa.p.* **thrawn.**—*adj.* twisted: distorted: wry.—*n.* a twist: a fit of perversity: a throe.—*adj.* **thrawn,** twisted: wry: cross-grained, perverse.—**dead thraw,** the agony of death; **heads and thraws,** side by side, the head of the one by the feet of another.

**thrawart, thraward,** *thrö′ərt,* (*Scot.*) *adj.* froward: crooked. [M.E. *fraward;* see **froward;** perh. influenced by **thraw;** cf. **thrae.**]

**thread,** *thred, n.* a very thin line of any substance, esp. linen or cotton, twisted or drawn out: a filament: a fibre: the prominent spiral part of a screw: a continuous connecting element.—*v.t.* to pass a thread through: to string on a thread: to pass or pierce through, as a narrow way: to furnish with a thread.—*adj.* made of linen or cotton thread.—*adj.* **thread′en,** (*Shak.*) made of thread.—*ns.* **thread′er; thread′iness.**—*adj.* **thready,** like thread: slender: containing or consisting of thread.—*adj.* **thread′bare,** worn to the bare thread: having the nap worn off: hackneyed: used till its novelty or interest is gone.—**thread′bareness; thread′-cell,** in jellyfishes, etc., a stinging cell that throws out a stinging thread; **thread′-lace,** lace made of linen thread; **thread′-paper,** a piece of thin soft paper for wrapping up a skein of thread; **thread′-worm,** any member of the Nematoda, more or less thread-like worms, many parasitic, others free-living: esp. *Oxyuris vermicularis,* parasitic in the human rectum.—**thread and thrum,** all, the good and bad together; **thread of life,** the thread imagined to be spun and cut by the Fates. [O.E. *thrǣd;* cf. **throw, thraw.**]

**Threadneedle Street,** *thred′nēdl strēt,* a street in the city of London.—**Old Lady, Woman, of Threadneedle Street,** the Bank of England.

**threap, threep,** *thrēp,* (*Scot.* and *Northern*) *v.t.* to rebuke: to maintain persistently: to insist: to urge, to press eagerly.—*v.i.* to dispute:—*pa.t.* and *pa.p.* **threap′it, threep′it.**—*n.* stubborn insistence or assertion: accusation: a traditional belief. [O.E. *thrēapian,* to rebuke.]

**threat,** *thret, n.* declaration or indication of an intention to inflict, punish, or hurt: an appearance of impending evil: a source of danger (to).—*v.t.* and *v.i.* (*Shak., Milt.,* etc.) to threaten.—*v.t.* **threat′en,** to offer a threat of, or against: to intimidate by threats: to seem to impend over: to indicate danger of, or to.—*v.i.* to use threats: to portend evil.—*adj.* **threat′ened.**—*n.* **threat′ener.**—*n.* **threat′ening.**—*adj.* menacing: portending danger or evil: (of sky) heavily clouded over.—*adv.* **threat′eningly.**—*adj.* **threat′-ful,** menacing. [O.E. *thrēat* (n.), *thrēatian,* *thrēatnian* (vbs.); cf. Ger. *verdriessen,* to tremble, L. *trūdere,* to thrust.]

**three,** *thrē, adj.* and *n.* two and one.—*n.* a set of three: a symbol for three: a card with three pips: a score of three points, strokes, etc.: an article of a size denoted by three: the third hour after midnight or midday.—*ns.* **three′ness,** the state of being three; **three′some,** a company of three persons: a game or dance for three.—*adj.* for three: triple.—**three balls,** the pawnbroker's sign.—*adjs.* **three′-bott′le,** able to drink three bottles of wine at a sitting; **three′-card,** played with three cards; **three′-cent′red,** of an arch, composed of circular arcs with three different centres; **three′-cleft,** cut halfway down into three lobes; **three′-colour,** involving or using three colours as primary; **three′-cor′nered,** triangular in form or section: having three competitors or three members; **three′-deck.**—**three′-deck′er,** a ship with three decks or guns on three decks: a building or structure with three floors or tiers: a pulpit with three levels: a three-volume novel: a double sandwich, with two layers of filling, three layers of bread.—*adjs.* **three'-dimen'sional**, having, or seeming to have, three dimensions: giving the effect of being seen or heard in an environment of three dimensions—usu. **3-D**: (of, e.g. a literary work) developed in detail and thus realistic.—**three'-dimensional'ity.** — *adj.* **three-far'thing.** — *n.sing.* **three-far'things**, a silver coin of Queen Elizabeth, distinguished from a penny by a rose behind the queen's head.—*adj.* and *adv.* **three'fold**, in three divisions: three times as much.—**three'foldness.** —*adj.* **three'-foot**, measuring or having three feet.—**three-halfpence** (*thrē-hā'pəns*), a penny and a halfpenny: a coin of that value.—*adj.* **threehalfpenny** (*thrē-hāp'ni*).—**three-halfpennyworth, threeha'porth** (*thrē-hāp'ərth*). — *adjs.* **three'-hand'ed**, having three hands: played by three players; **three'-leaved** (or **-leafed**), having three leaves or leaflets: having leaves in threes; **three'-legged**, having three legs: of a race, run by pairs of runners, each with a leg tied to his partner's; **three'-man** (*Shak.*), worked or performed by three men; **three'-mast'ed.**—**three'-mast'er**, a ship with three masts.—*n.* and *adj.* **three'-month'ly**, quarterly.—*adjs.* **three'-nooked** (*Shak.*), three-cornered; **three'-pair** (**-of-stairs**), on a third floor.—*n.* a room so situated.—*adjs.* **three'-part**, composed in three parts or for three voices; **three'-part'ed**, consisting of three parts: parted in three: divided into three nearly to the base.—*adv.* **three'-parts**, to the extent of three-fourths.—**threepence** (*threp'*, *thrip'*, *thrup'əns*), money, or a coin, of the value of three pence.—*adj.* **threepenny** (*threp'*, *thrip'*, *thrup'ni* or *-ə-ni*), sold or offered at threepence: of little worth: mean, vulgar.—*n.* a coin of the value of threepence (also **threepenny bit**).—**threepennyworth** or **threepenn'orth** (*thrē-pen'i-warth* or *thrē-pen'ərth*), also (chiefly *Scot.*) **threep'enceworth.**—*n.pl.* **three'-per-cents'**, bonds or other securities paying three per cent. interest, esp. a portion of the consolidated debt of Great Britain.—*adj.* **three'-pile**, having loops of three threads.—*n.* (*Shak.*) the finest kind of velvet.—*adjs.* **three'-piled**, three-pile: piled three high; **three'-ply**, having three layers or strands; **three'-pound**, costing or weighing three pounds. —**three-pound'er**, a thing that weighs three pounds: a gun that shoots a three-pound ball; **three'-pricker** (*airman's slang*), a three-point landing: anything right or perfect.—*adj.* and *adv.* **three-quar'ter**, to the amount of three-fourths.—*n.* three-quarter back.—*n.* and *adj.* **three'score**, sixty.—*adjs.* **three'-sid'ed**, having three sides; **three'-square**, equilaterally triangular; **three'-suit'ed** (*Shak.*), allowed three suits of clothes a year as a serving-man; **three'-vol'ume**, in three volumes; **three'-way**, giving connection in three directions from a centre.— **three-card trick**, a card-sharper's ploy in which the victim is invited to wager on which of three cards, turned face-down and deftly manipulated, is the queen (also *find the lady*); **three colour process**, the method of producing colour pictures from three primary originals—yellow, red, blue —prepared by photography; **three-line whip** (see **whip**); **three-point landing** (*aero.*), a landing with all three wheels touching the ground at the same moment—a perfect landing; **three-quarter back**, a player between half-backs and full-backs; **three-quarter face**, an aspect between full face and profile; **three-speed gear**, a gear-changing contrivance with three possibilities; **three times three**, three cheers thrice repeated; **three-went way** (*dial.*), a meeting-place of three roads. [O.E. *thrēo*, fem. and neut. of *thri*; Goth. *threis*, Ger. *drei*, L. *trēs*, *três*, *tria*, Gr. *treis*, *treis*, *tria*, Sans. *tri.*]

**threep.** See **threap.**

**thremmatology**, *threm-ə-tol'ə-ji*, *n.* the science of breeding domestic animals and plants. [Gr. *thremma*, *-atos*, a nurseling, *logos*, discourse.]

**threnody**, *thrēn'*, *thren'ə-di*, *n.* an ode or song of lamentation.—Also **threne** (*thrēn*; *Shak.*), **thren'ode** (*-ōd*), **thren'os** (*Shak.*).—*adjs.* **threnet'ic, -al;** **threnō'dial, threnodic** (*-od'*).—*n.* **thren'odist.** [Gr. *thrēnōidiā, thrēnos*, a lament, *ōidē*, song.]

**thresh**, *thresh*, *v.t.* to beat out, subject to beating out, by trampling, flail, or machinery: to thrash. —*v.t.* to thresh corn: to thrash.—*n.* an act of threshing.—*ns.* **thresh'el**, a flail: a flail-like weapon, the morgenstern; **thresh'er**, one who threshes: a flail: a threshing-machine or a beating part of it: a fox-shark (also **thresh'er-shark'**).—*n.* and *adj.* **thresh'ing.**—**thresh'er-whale'**, a grampus; **thresh'ing-floor**, a surface on which grain is threshed; **thresh'ing-machine, -mill**, one for threshing corn. [O.E. *therscan*; cf. Ger. *derschen*, to thresh; see **thrash**.]

**thresh.** See **thrash** (2).

**thresher.** See **thrasher.**

**threshold**, *thresh'ōld*, *n.* the sill of a house door: the place or point of entering: the outset: the limit of consciousness: the point at which a stimulus begins to bring a response: the smallest dose of radiation which will produce a specified result.—*adj.* at or constituting a threshold.—**threshold lighting**, lights, a line of lights across the ends of a runway or landing area to indicate the usable limits; **threshold of audibility, of sound**, the minimum intensity or pressure of sound wave which the normal human listener can just detect at any given frequency. [O.E. *therscold, therscwald, threscold*, app.—*therscan*, to thrash, thresh, in its older sense of trample, tread.]

**thretty**, *thret'i*, a dial. form of **thirty.**

**threw**, *thrōō*, *pa.t.* of **throw.**

**thrice**, *thris*, *adv.* three times. [M.E. *thriēs*—O.E. *thriwa, thriga*, thrice—*thri*, three, with adverbial gen. ending *-es*.]

**thrid**, *thrid*, (*Spens.*) *n.* a thread.—*v.t.* (*obs.*) to thread. [**thread**.]

**thridace**, *thrid'əs*, *n.* inspissated lettuce juice. [Gr. *thridax*, lettuce.]

**thrift**, *thrift*, *n.* state of thriving: frugality: economy: prosperity (*arch.*): increase of wealth (*arch.*): gain (*arch.*): profitable occupation (*dial.*): savings (*arch.*): sea-pink (Armeria), a seaside and alpine plant of the Plumbaginaceae.—*adv.* **thrift'ily.**—*n.* **thrift'iness.**—*adj.* **thrift'less**, not thrifty: extravagant: not thriving.—*adv.* **thrift'lessly.**—*n.* **thrift'lessness.**—*adj.* **thrift'y**, showing thrift or economy: thriving by frugality: prosperous, in good condition (*U.S.*):—*comp.* **thrift'ier**, *superl.* **thrift'iest.** [**thrive**.]

**thrill**, *thrill*, *v.t.* to pierce: to affect with a strong glow or tingle of sense or emotion.—*v.i.* to pierce, as something sharp: to pass tinglingly: to quiver: to feel a sharp, shivering sensation.—*n.* a tingle: a shivering feeling or emotion.—*adj.* **thrill'ant** (*Spens.*), piercing.—*n.* **thrill'er**, a sensational story.—*adj.* **thrill'ing.**—*adv.* **thrill'ingly.**—*n.* **thrill'ingness.**—*adj.* **thrill'y.** [O.E. *thyrlian*, to bore—*thyrel*, a hole; Ger. *drillen*, to drill a hole.]

**Thrips**, *thrips*, *n.* a genus of Thysanoptera, mostly minute black insects, common in flowers (*erron.* thrip): popularly extended to others of the order, to leaf-hoppers, and to other small insects:—*pl.* **thripses.** [Gr. *thrips, thripos*, a wood-worm.]

**thrissel, thristle**, *thris'l, thrus'l*, Scots forms of **thistle.** [Poss. influenced by *thrist*, to thrust.]

**thrist**, *thrist*, *thrist'y, -i*, old forms (*Spens.*) of **thirst** (*n.* and *vb.*), thirsty.

**thrive**, *thriv*, *v.i.* to grow: to grow healthily and vigorously: to get on, do well: to prosper: to increase in goods: to be successful: to flourish: —*pa.t.* **thrōve**, also **thrived**; *pa.p.* **thriven** (*thriv'n*).

—*adjs.* **thrive'less**, thriftless; **thriven** (*thriv'n*), grown, developed: successful.—*n.* **thri'ver** (*rare*).—*n.* and *adj.* **thri'ving.**—*adv.* **thri'vingly** (*rare*).—*n.* **thri'vingness.** [O.N. *thrifa*, to grasp.]

**thro'**, **thro.** See **through.**

**throat**, *thrōt*, *n.* the passage from mouth to stomach: the forepart of the neck, in which are the gullet and windpipe: voice: a narrow entrance, aperture or passage: the narrow part, as of a vase, a corolla: a groove under a coping or moulding: the end of a gaff next the mast (*naut.*).—*adjs.* **throat'ed**, with a throat; **throat'-full'**, full to the throat.—*adv.* **throat'ily.**—*n.* **throat'iness.**—*adj.* **throat'y**, sounding as from the throat: hoarse: croaking: deep or full-throated: somewhat sore-throated: full or loose-skinned about the throat: potent in swallowing.— **throat'-band, -strap, -latch**, a band about the throat; **throat microphone**, one held directly against the speaker's throat and actuated by vibrations of the larynx; **throat'wort**, the nettle-leaved bellflower (*Campanula trachelium*) once reputed good for throat ailments: the giant bellflower (*C. latifolium*).—**cut the, one's, throat**, usu., to cut the jugular vein: to pursue some course ruinous to one's interests; **give one the lie in his throat**, to accuse one to his face of a lie; **jump down one's throat** (see **jump**); **sore throat**, an inflamed and uncomfortable condition of the tonsils and neighbouring parts; **stick in one's throat**, be more than one can bear: manage; **thrust, ram, down one's throat**, to assert or force upon one insistently without listening to an answer. [O.E. *throte*; cf. **throttle**.]

**throb**, *throb*, *v.i.* to beat strongly, as the heart or pulse:—*pr.p.* **throbb'ing**; *pa.t.* and *pa.p.* **throbbed.**—*n.* a beat or strong pulsation.—*n.* and *adj.* **throbb'ing.**—*adv.* **throbb'ingly.**—*adj.* **throb'less.** [M.E. *throbben*; poss. conn. with L. *trepidus*, trembling.]

**throe**, earlier (*Shak.*, *Spens.*) **throw(e)**, *thrō*, (*Scot.*) **thraw**, *thrō*, *n.* a spasm: a paroxysm: a pang: esp. a birth-pang.—*v.t.* to subject to pangs.—*v.i.* to suffer pangs.—**in the throes**, in travail: in the struggle of composition: in the thick. [M.E. *thrahes, throwes, thrawes*; perh. there have been cross-influences between O.E. *thrawu*, pang, *thrāg*, paroxysm, *thrōwian*, to suffer, *thrāwan*, to twist, throw; see also **thraw**.]

**thrombus**, *throm'bəs*, *n.* a clot of blood in a living vessel.—*ns.* **throm'bin**, an enzyme that causes clotting; **thromboplast'in**, a substance, found esp. in blood-platelets, which participates in clotting.—*v.t.* **thrombose** (*-bōs'*), to cause thrombosis in.—*n.* **thrombō'sis**, clotting in a vessel during life. [Gr. *thrombos*, clot.]

**throne**, *thrōn*, *n.* a king's, pope's, or bishop's chair of state: kingship: an angel of the third order.—*v.t.* to enthrone: to exalt.—*v.i.* to sit in state, as on a throne.—*adjs.* **throned**; **throne'less.**—**throne'-room.** [Gr. *thronos*, a seat.]

**throng**, *throng*, *n.* a crowd: a great multitude: crowding.—*v.t.* and *v.i.* to crowd: to press: to press hard (*Shak.*).—*adj.* (*coll.*) crowded: busy: intimate.—*adjs.* **thronged**, packed, crowded: (with *up*) overpowered (*Shak.*); **throng'ful**, thronged.—*n.* and *adj.* **throng'ing.** [O.E. *gethrang*—*thringan*, to press.]

**thropple**, *throp'l* (*Scots* **thrapple**, *thrap'l*), *n.* the throat: the windpipe, esp. of an animal.—*v.t.* to throttle: to strangle. [Poss. O.E. *throtbolla*, windpipe, gullet—*throte*, throat, *bolla*, boll.]

**throstle**, *thros'l*, *n.* the song-thrush or mavis: a machine for drawing, twisting, and winding fibres (from its sound).—**thros'tle-cock**, a male song-thrush or (*dial.*) missel-thrush. [O.E. *throstle*; Ger. *drossel*, L. *turdus*, thrush.]

**throttle**, *throt'l*, *n.* the throat or windpipe: a throttle-valve: a throttle-lever.—*v.t.* to choke by pressure on the windpipe: to check

the flow of: to cut down the supply of steam, or of gas and air, to or in.—*v.i.* to breathe hard, as when nearly suffocated.—*n.* **thrott'ler.**—*n.* and *adj.* **thrott'ling.**—**thrott'le-lever**, a lever that opens and closes a throttle-valve; **thrott'le-pipe**, the vertical pipe between the throttle-valve and the dry-pipe of a locomotive; **thrott'le-valve**, a valve regulating the supply of steam or of gas and air in an engine.—**throttle down**, to slow down by closing the throttle. [App. dim. of **throat.**]

**through**, *thrōō*, *prep.* from end to end, side to side, or boundary to boundary of, by way of the interior: from place to place within: everywhere within: by way of: along the passage of: clear of: among: from beginning to end of: up to and including, to or until the end of (*U.S.*): by means of: in consequence of.—*adv.* from one end or side to the other: from beginning to end: all the way: clear: into a position of having passed: in connection or communication all the way.—*adj.* passing, or serving for passage, all the way without interruption.—*adv.* **through'ly**, same as **thoroughly** (*obs.*): far through (*arch.*).—*prep.* **throughout'**, in, into, through, during, the whole of.—*adv.* in every part: everywhere.—**through'-bolt**, a bolt that passes through from side to side of what it fastens; **through'fare** (*Shak.*), same as **thoroughfare.**—*adj.* **through'-ganging** (*Scot.*), thorough-going.—**through'-going** (*Scot.* -gaun), a scoiding.—*adj.* passing through: active, energetic.—*adv.* **through'-other** (*Scot.*), in indiscriminate mixture: higgledy-piggledy.—*adj.* (*Scot.*) confusedly mixed: without orderliness.—**through'-put**, amount of material put through a process; **through-stone**, a bonder or bond-stone in building; **through'-tick'et**, a ticket for the whole of a journey; **through'-traff'ic**, the traffic between two centres at a distance from each other: traffic passing straight through an area, as opposed to that travelling within the area; **through'-train**, a train that goes the whole length of a long route; **through'way**, **thruway** (*U.S.*), an expressway.—**be through** (*Shak.*; now chiefly *Scot.* and *U.S.*), to have done: to be at an end: to have no more to do; **through and through**, through the whole thickness: completely: in every point; **through the day**, **night** (*Scot.*), in the daytime, night-time. [O.E. *thurh*; Ger. *durch*.]

**through-stone, -stane**, *thrōōhh'-*, *throhh'-stōn*, *-stān*, (*Scot.*) *n.* a horizontal tombstone on pillars. [O.E. *thrūh*, sarcophagus, and **stone.**]

**throve**, *thrōv*, *pa.t.* of **thrive.**

**throw**, *thrō*, *v.t.* to wind or twist together, as yarn: to form on a wheel, as pottery: to turn, with a lathe: to move (a switch) so as to connect, disconnect: to cast, hurl, fling through the air: to project: to emit: to make a cast of dice amounting to: to dislodge from the saddle: to cast down in wrestling: to defeat, get the better of, or discomfit: to give birth to: to produce: to render suddenly: to cause to be in some place or condition, esp. with suddenness: to put: to execute, perform: to lose (a contest) deliberately, esp. in return for a bribe (*coll.*).—*v.i.* to cast or hurl: to cast dice: to lay about one (*Spens.*):—*pa.t.* **threw**, *thrōō*; *pa.p.* **thrown**, *thrōn.*—*n.* a deflection: amplitude of movement: an act of throwing: a cast, esp. of dice or a fishing-line: a blow (*Spens.*): the distance to which anything may be thrown: the vertical displacement of a fault (*geol.*): a small woollen wrap or rug.—*n.* **throw'er.**—*n.* and *adj.* **throw'ing.**—*adj.* **thrown**, twisted: cast, flung.—*n.* **throw'ster**, one who throws silk: a gambler.—**throw'-away**, an advertisement brochure or handbill freely distributed to the public (*U.S.*): a contest without serious competition: a line, or a joke, that an actor purposely delivers without emphasis, often for the sake of realism.—*adj.* of manner or technique, casual, without attempt at dramatic effect: ridiculously cheap, as if being thrown away.—**throw'-back**, a reversion (e.g. to an earlier developmental type): a set-back; **throw'-down**, a home-made firework, slapbang; **throw'-in**, an act of throwing in: a throw from the touch-line to put the ball back into play (*football*); **throw'ing-stick**, a stick for throwing a spear: a throw-stick; **throw'ing-table**, a potter's wheel; **thrown'-silk**, organzine; **throw'-out**, an act of throwing out: a rejected thing; **throw'-stick**, a weapon thrown whirling from the hand, as the boomerang.—**throw about** (*Spens.*), to cast about or try expedients; **throw a fit** (*coll.*), to have a fit, behave wildly; **throw a party** (*coll.*), to give a party; **throw away**, to reject, toss aside: to squander: to fail to take advantage of: to bestow unworthily; **throw back**, to retort, to refuse: to revert to some ancestral character; **throw down**, to demolish; **throw in**, to interject: to throw the ball in: to add as an extra; **throw in the towel, throw in one's hand**, to give up, surrender; **throw in one's lot** (see **lot**); **throw, fling, mud at**, slander, insult; **throw off**, to divest oneself of: to disengage or release oneself from: to utter or compose off-hand; **throw on**, to put on hastily; **throw oneself at**, to make a determined and obvious attempt to captivate; **throw oneself into**, to engage heartily in: **throw oneself on**, or **upon**, to assail: to entrust oneself to the power of: **throw open**, to cause to swing wide open, to make freely accessible; **throw out**, to cast out: to reject: to expel: to emit: to utter: to cause to project: to disconcert: to distance, leave behind; **throw over**, to discard or desert; **throw up**, to erect hastily: to show prominently: to give up, to resign: to vomit; **throw up (something) against someone**, to reproach him with (something); **throw up the sponge** (see **sponge**). [O.E. *thrāwan*, to turn, to twist; Ger. *drehen*, to twist; see also **thraw, throe**.]

**throw**, *thrō*, (*Spens.*) *n.* a while. [O.E. *thrāg*, *thrāh*.]

**thru.** A U.S. spelling of **through**, alone or in compounds.

**thrum**, *thrum*, *n.* the end of a weaver's thread: any loose thread or fringe: bits of coarse yarn.—*adj.* made of or having thrums.—*v.t.* to furnish, cover, or fringe with thrums:—*pr.p.* **thrumm'ing**; *pa.t.* and *pa.p.* **thrummed**.—*adj.* **thrumm'y**, made of, or like, thrums.—**thrum'-cap**, a cap made of thrums or of coarse, shaggy cloth.—*adj.* **thrum'-eyed**, short-styled with the stamens in the throat of the corolla (esp. of a Primula; opp. to *pin-eyed*).—**thrummed hat** (*Shak.*), a hat made of, fringed with, or covered with thrums. [O.E. *thrum* (found in composition); Ger. *trumm.*]

**thrum**, *thrum*, *v.t.* and *v.i.* to strum: to hum, drone, repeat in sing-song: to drum with the fingers:—*pr.p.* **thrumm'ing**; *pa.t.* and *pa.p.* **thrummed**.—*n.* a strumming: a purring (*dial.*). —*n.* **thrumm'er**.—*n.* and *adj.* **thrumm'ing.**—*adv.* **thrumm'ingly.**

**thruppence, -penny,** coll. for **threepence, -penny.**

**thrush**, *thrush*, *n.* the throstle or mavis (*song-thrush, Turdus musicus*): the storm-cock (*missel-thrush, T. viscivorus*): extended to others of the genus and to birds more or less similar. [O.E. *thrysce.*]

**thrush**, *thrush*, *n.* an inflammation in a horse's frog: a disease, usu. of infants, chiefly affecting the mouth and throat. [Ety. dub.]

**thrust**, *thrust*, *v.t.* and *v.i.* to push: to force: to stab, pierce: to intrude:—*pa.t.* and *pa.p.* **thrust**.—*n.* a push: a pushing force: the force that drives an aircraft forward and its measurement: the horizontal force on the abutment of an arch: a stab.—*n.* **thrust'er**.—*n.* and *adj.* **thrust'ing.** — **thrust'-hoe**, a hoe worked by pushing; **thrust'-plane**, a plane along which a

block of rocks has overridden higher rocks almost horizontally—a reversed fault of very low hade. [O.N. *thrȳsta*, to press.]

**thrust**, *thrust*, (*Spens.*) *v.i.* to thirst.—*n.* thirst.

**thrutch**, *thruch*, (*dial.*) *v.t.* to thrust, press, shove. —*v.i.* to make one's way by great effort.—Also *n.* [O.E. *thrycc(e)an.*]

**thruway.** A U.S. spelling of **throughway.**

**thud**, *thud*, *n.* a dull sound as of a heavy body falling soft.—*v.i.* to make a thud.—*v.t.* to beat. [Perh. O.E. *thyddan*, to strike.]

**thug**, *thug*, properly *t'hug*, *n.* a member of a religious fraternity that murdered stealthily by strangling or poisoning with datura, extirpated 1826-35 (*India*): a cut-throat: a ruffian.—*ns.* **thuggee'** (**thagi'**), **thugg'ery**, **thugg'ism**, the practice and superstition of the thugs. [Hindi *thag*, cheat.]

**Thuja**, *thōō'ja*, -*ya*, *n.* the arbor-vitae genus. [Gr. *thyiā*, a kind of juniper.]

**Thule**, *thū'lē*, *n.* an island six days N. of Orkney discovered by Pytheas (4th cent. B.C.), variously identified as Shetland, Iceland, Norway, Jutland: hence (usu. *ultima Thule*) the extreme limit.—*ns.* **thu'lia**, thulium oxide, separated from erbia by Cleve; **thu'lite**, a red zoisite found in Norway; **thu'lium**, a metallic element (Tm; at. numb. 69). [L. *Thūlē*—Gr. *Thoulē* (understood by Cleve as Scandinavia).]

**thumb**, *thum*, *n.* the short, thick digit, consisting of two phalanges, on the radial side of the human hand: the part of a glove that covers it: in other animals the corresponding digit, or that of the hind foot, esp. when opposable: a thumb's breadth, an inch.—*v.t.* to handle awkwardly: to play, spread, press, touch, wear, or smudge with the thumb: to read assiduously: to turn the pages (of a book) rapidly with the thumb: to signal to with the thumb.—*adj.* **thumbed**, having thumbs: marked by the thumb, worn.—*n.pl.* **thumb'(i)kins** (*Scot.*), the thumbscrew.—*adj.* **thumb'less.**—*n.* **thumb'ling**, a pygmy.—*adj.* **thumb'y**, grubby with thumb-marks: like thumbs, clumsy, awkward.—**thumb'-hole**, a hole to insert the thumb in; **thumb'-index**, one arranged as indentations on the outer margins of the pages of books; **thumb'-latch**, a latch worked by pressure of the thumb; **thumb'-mark**, a mark left by the thumb as on a book: a thumbprint.—*adj.* **thumb'-marked**.—**thumb'nail**, the nail of the thumb: a sketch (**thumb'nail sketch**) as small as a thumbnail; **thumb'piece**, a piece that is pressed by the thumb or receives the thumb; **thumb'pot**, a very small flower-pot; **thumb'print**, an impression of the markings of the thumb, taken as a means of identification; **thumb'-ring**, a ring worn on the thumb (*Shak.*): a ring to protect an archer's thumb; **thumb'-screw**, an old instrument of torture for compressing the thumb by means of a screw; **thumb'-stall**, a covering or sheath for the thumb; **thumb'-tack** (*U.S.*), a drawing-pin.—**bite one's thumb**, to make a sign threatening revenge; **by rule of thumb**, in a rough-and-ready practical manner, found by experience to be convenient; **keep one's thumb on**, to keep secret; **one's fingers all thumbs**, awkward and fumbling; **thumb a lift (ride)** (*coll.*), to beg a lift from passing motorists by signalling from the side of the road with the thumb; **thumb one's nose, cock a snook** (see **snook**); **thumbs down**, a sign indicating disapproval or failure (see **pollice verso**); **thumbs up, a** sign indicating hope of, or wishes for, success; **under one's thumb**, under one's domination. [O.E. *thūma*; Ger. *daumen*.]

**Thummim**, *thum'im*. See **Urim.**

**thump**, *thump*, *n.* a dull heavy blow or its sound.— *v.t.* and *v.i.* to beat with a dull heavy blow: to make such a sound.—*n.* **thump'er**, one who, or that which, thumps: anything very big, a big lie,

# thunder

1408

# tiara

etc. (*coll.*).—*adj.* thump´ing (*coll.*), unusually big. [Prob. imit.]

thunder, *thun´dər, n.* the deep rumbling sound after a flash of lightning: any loud noise: a thunderbolt: vehement denunciation.—*v.i.* to make thunder: to sound as thunder: to inveigh or denounce with vehemence.—*v.t.* to give out with noise or violent denunciation: to deal like thunder.—*ns.* thun´derer, a thunder-god, Zeus, Thor, etc.: a thundering denunciator, inveigher, orator, journalist, or periodical, esp. *The Times* or its leader-writer: a hand who operates stage-thunder: a bull-roarer; thun´dering.—*adj.* discharging thunder: unusually big, tremendous (*coll.*).—Also *n.* and *adv.*—*adv.* thun´deringly.—*adjs.* thun´derless; thun´der-like (*Shak.*); thun´derous (thun´drous), like, threatening, or suggesting thunder.—*adv.* thun´derously.—*adj.* thun´dery, indicative of thunder, or attended by it.—*adj.* thun´der-and-light´ning, in glaring colours.—*n.* a glaringly coloured woollen cloth.—thun´derbearer (*Shak.*), Jove; thun´derbolt, a missile of the thunder-god: a popularly imagined material body seen as lightning: a stone identified therewith, as a belemnite, a stone axe: anything sudden and overwhelming: a fulmination: a violent and irresistible destroyer or hero; thun´der-clap, a sudden crash of thunder; thun´dercloud, a cloud charged with electricity: a black or livid threatening appearance; thun´der-dart, a thunderbolt; thun´der-darter, -master, (both *Shak.*) Jove.—*v.t.* thun´der-drive (*Spens.*), to drive with thunderbolts.—thun´der-god, a god that wields thunder; thun´der-peal, a resounding noise of thunder; thun´der-plump, a heavy fall of rain in a thunder-storm; thun´der-shower, a shower accompanied with thunder, or a short heavy shower from a thunder-cloud; thun´derstone (*Shak.*), a thunderbolt; thun´der-storm, continued discharges of electricity from the clouds, producing lightning and thunder, generally with heavy rain.—*v.t.* thun´der-strike, to strike with, or as with, lightning.—thun´derstroke (*Shak.*), a stroke or blast by lightning.—*adj.* thun´der-struck (also -stricken), struck by lightning: struck dumb with astonishment.—steal one's thunder (see steal). [O.E. *thunor*, thunder, *Thunor*, the thunder-god, Thor; Ger. *donner*, L. *tonāre*; cf. Thor, Thursday.]

thurible, *thū´ri-bl, n.* a censer.—*n.* thu´rifer, an acolyte who carries the thurible.—*adj.* thurif´erous, incense-bearing.—*n.* thurificā´tion.—*v.t.* thū´rify, to cense.—*n.* thus (*thus, thūs*), frankincense. [L. *t(h)ūs, t(h)ūris*, frankincense—Gr. *thyos*, a sacrifice; cf. thyme.]

Thursday, *thûrz´di, n.* the fifth day of the week, originally sacred to Thunor, the English thunder-god. [O.E. *Thunres dæg*, Thunor's day; O.N. *Thōrsdagr*, Thor's day; Ger. *Donnerstag*.]

thus, *dhus, adv.* in this or that manner: to this degree or extent: accordingly, therefore.—*n.* thus´ness, (usu. *facet.*) state of being thus.—*adv.* thus´wise, in this manner. [O.E. *thus*.]

thus. See thurible.

Thuya, a variant of Thuja.

thwack, *thwak, v.t.* to whack.—*n.* a whack.—*n.* thwack´er.—*n.* and *adj.* thwack´ing. [Perh. whack, or O.E. *thaccian*, to smack.]

thwaite, *thwāt, n.* a piece of reclaimed land—common in place-names. [O.N. *thveit*.]

thwart, *thwōrt, adv.* crosswise: from side to side.—*adj.* crosswise, transverse: cross, adverse: cross, perverse, cross-grained.—*prep.* across, athwart.—*v.t.* to cross: to cross the path of: to obstruct: to oppose: to frustrate: to balk: to set crosswise: to plough crosswise.—*v.i.* to cross: to conflict.—*n.* frustration: hindrance: a rower's bench.—*adj.* thwar´ted, frustrated.—*adv.* thwar´tedly.—*n.* thwar´ter.—*n.* and *adj.* thwart´ing.—*advs.* thwart´ingly, perversely; thwart´ly;

thwart´ship(s), across the ship; thwart´ways; thwart´wise.—*adjs.* thwart´ship, thwart´wise. [O.N. *thvert*, neut. of *thverr*, perverse.]

thy, *dhi, poss. pron. or adj.* thine: of thee. [thine.]

Thyestean, *thī-es´ti-ən, -əs-tē´ən, adj.* of Thyestes (Gr. *Thyestēs*), who was made to eat his own sons: cannibal.

thyine, *thī´in, adj.* of a tree supposed to be sandarach (Rev. xviii. 12). [Gr. *thȳinos—thȳon* or *thȳā*, thyine tree.]

thylacine, *thī´lə-sēn, n.* the so-called Tasmanian wolf. [Gr. *thȳlakos*, pouch.]

thylose, thylosis. See tylosis.

thyme, *tim, n.* any member of the labiate genus Thymus, low half-shrubby plants with two-lipped corolla and calyx and four diverging stamens, esp. the fragrant garden thyme (*T. vulgaris*) and wild-thyme (*T. serpyllum*).—*n.* thymol (*thī´mol*), an antiseptic phenol obtained from oil of thyme by distillation.—*adj.* thymy (*tim´i*), like, smelling of, or abounding in, thyme.—basil thyme, a kind of calamint; oil of thyme, a fragrant essential oil got from garden and other thymes; water thyme, Canadian pondweed. [Fr. *thym*—L. *thymum*—Gr. *thȳmon*.]

thymelaeaceous, *thim-, thīm-el-i-ā´sh(y)əs,´adj.* of the Thymelaeā´ceae, the family to which Daphne belongs. [Gr. *thymelaiā*, supposed to be a species of Daphne—*thymos*, thyme, *elaiā*, olive.]

thymus, *thī´məs, n.* a ductless gland near the root of the neck, vestigial in adult man—that of veal and lamb called *neck-sweetbread*.—Also *adj.*—*n.* thymine (*thī´mēn*), one of the four bases in deoxyribonucleic acids, in close association with adenine. [Gr. *thymos*, thymus gland.]

thyratron, *thī´rə-tron, n.* a gas-filled valve with heated cathode, able to carry very high currents —orig. a trademark for one containing mercury vapour.—*n.* thyristor (*thi-ris´tər*), a thyratron-like semiconductor device.

thyroid, *thī´roid*, more correctly but less commonly thyreoid, *-i-oid, adj.* shield-shaped: pertaining to the thyroid gland or the thyroid cartilage.—*n.* the thyroid gland, a ductless gland in the neck whose overactivity may lead to exophthalmic goitre, and defect to cretinism: the principal cartilage of the larynx, forming Adam's apple.—*ns.* thyroidi´tis, inflammation of the thyroid gland; thyrotoxicos´is, hyperthyroidism; thyrox´in(e), an iodine compound, the active principle of the thyroid gland. [Gr. *thȳreoeidēs*, shield-shaped, the thyroid cartilage—*thȳreos*, a (door-shaped) shield—*thȳrā*, a door, *eidos*, form.]

Thyrostraca, *thīr-os´trə-kə, n.pl.* the cirripedes. [Gr. *thȳrā*, door, valve, *ostrakon*, shell.]

thyrsus, *thûr´səs, n.* the wand of Bacchus, a staff wreathed with ivy: a dense panicle broadest in the middle (*bot.*): esp. one whose lateral branches are cymose:—*pl.* thyr´si (*-sī*).—*n.* thyrse (*thûrs*), a thyrsus.—*adjs.* thyr´soid, -al, having the form of a thyrsus. [Gr. *thyrsos*.]

Thysanoptera, *this-ən-op´tə-rə, n.pl.* an order of insects with fringed wings, as Thrips.—*adj.* thysanop´terous.—*n.pl.* Thysanura (-ū´rə), the bristle-tails, an order of small wingless insects with abdominal appendages.—*adj.* thysanū´rous. [Gr. *thysanos*, a fringe, tassel, *pteron*, a wing, *ourā*, a tail.]

thyself, *dhi-self´, pron.* emphatic for, or usually along with, thou or thee: reflexive for thee. [thee (altered to thy) and self.]

ti, *tē,* (*mus.*) *n.* in the tonic sol-fa system a substitute for *si*, to avoid the initial sound of *so* (*sol*).—Also, in anglicised spelling, te.

ti, *tē, n.* a small Pacific liliaceous tree (Cordyline): sometimes also applied (wrongly) to the Australian tea-tree. [Polynesian.]

tiara, *ti-ä´rə, n.* the lofty ornamental head-dress of the ancient Persians: the Jewish high-priest's

*fāte, fär; mē, hûr* (her); *mīne; mōte, fōr; mūte; mōōn, fōōt; dhen* (then) mitre: the pope's triple crown: the papal dignity: a jewelled head-ornament.—*n.* **tiar** (*ti′ər, tir*; *poet.*), a tiara.—*adj.* **tia′ra'd, tia′raed**, wearing a tiara. [Gr. *tiārā*.]

**Tib**, *tib, n.* used as a typical woman's name (*Shak.*): ace of trumps in gleek (*obs.*; *Scott*).— **Tib′-cat**, a she-cat; **Tib(b)'s Eve** (see saint). [**Isabella.**]

**Tibert**, *tib′ərt, tib′ərt, n.* the cat in *Reynard the Fox*: in *Shak.* identified with Tibalt.

**Tibet, Thibet**, *ti-bet′, n.* a country W. of China. **thibet**, a woollen stuff generally printed in colours: a heavy goat's hair fabric used instead of fur—also **Tibet cloth.**—*adj.* **Tibet′an** (or *tib′*), of Tibet.—*n.* the language of Tibet: a native of Tibet.—**Tibetan apso(s)** (same as Lhasa apso(s)).

**tibia**, *tib′i-ə, n.* the shinbone: the fourth joint of an insect's leg: an ancient flute or pipe.—*adj.* **tib′ial.** [L. *tibia*, shinbone, flute.]

**tic**, *tik, n.* a convulsive motion of certain muscles, esp. of the face: an involuntary habitual response (*fig.*).—**tic′-douloureux** (*-dol-ə-rōō′*, Fr. *tēk dōō-lōō-rø*), an affection of the fifth cranial nerve with paroxysms of pain in face and forehead. [Fr.; cf. **tick** (5).]

**tical**, *ti-käl′, tik′l, n.* an obsolete Siamese silver coin, about equal to a rupee: a unit of weight. [Port. *tical*.]

**ticca**, *tik′a, (Ind.) adj.* hired. [Hind. *thikā*, hire.]

**tice**, *tis, v.t.* (*Shak.*) to entice.—*n.* an enticement (*Shak.*): a yorker (*cricket*). [Aphetic for **entice**, or—Fr. *atiser*.]

**tichorrhine**, *ti′kō-rīn, adj.* having an ossified nasal septum, as the fossil woolly rhinoceros. [Gr. *teichos*, wall, *rhis, rhinos*, nose.]

**tick**, *tik, n.* any of the larger blood-sucking acarids: applied also the sheep-ked and similar degenerate bloodsucking Diptera: a small and usu. objectionable person (*coll.*).—**tick fever**, East Coast fever, transmitted by ticks. [O.E. *ticia* (perh. for *tica* or *ticca*); Du. *teek*, Ger. *zecke*.]

**tick**, *tik, n.* the cover of a mattress: ticking.—*ns.* **tick′en, tick′ing**, the cloth of which ticks are made. [L. *thēca*—Gr. *thēkē*, a case; see **theca**.]

**tick**, *tik, n.* a light tap or pat (*obs.*): the game of tig: the sound of a watch, clock, etc.: a beat: a moment: a speck: a small mark, often an angular line, used to indicate or mark off as checked or dealt with.—*v.i.* to tap, pat (*obs.*; **tick and toy**, to dally): make a sound as of a clock: to beat: to work, function (*coll.*).—*v.t.* to mark with a tick: to dot: to measure, record, give out, by ticks.—*adj.* **ticked**, speckled.—*ns.* **tick′er**, anything that ticks, esp. a telegraph instrument that prints signals on a tape, or (*slang*) a watch: the heart (*slang*).—*n. and adj.* **tick′ing**.—**tick′er-tape**, paper ribbon telegraphically printed; **tick′ing-off**, a reprimand; **tick′-tack′**, ticking as of a clock: bookmakers' telegraphy by arm signals: (see also **trick-track**).—Also *adj.—adv.* with recurring ticking.—**tick′-tick**, a ticking: a child's word for a watch; **tick′-tock′**, a ticking, as of a big clock: a tapping.—**in two ticks**, in a moment; **tick off** (*slang*), to reprimand; **tick over**, of an engine, to run gently disconnected: of a person, to lead an inactive, uneventful existence. [M.E. *tek*; cf. Du. *tik*, L.G. *tikk*; prob. imit.]

**tick**, *tik, (slang) n.* credit: trust.—*v.i.* to get or give credit.—**tick′-shop**, a shop where goods are given on credit. [**ticket**.]

**tick**, *tik, n.* crib-biting: a whimsy. [**tic**.]

**ticket**, *tik′it, n.* a card, slip, or placard bearing a notice or serving as a token of any right or debt, as for admission, penalty for some offence (esp. motoring), etc.: a certificate (*slang*): discharge from the army (*slang*): a list of candidates put forward by a party for election (*U.S.*): the principles associated with a particular political party: a visiting-card (*obs.*).—*v.t.* to label: to

designate.—**ticket agent**, agent who sells tickets on behalf of a theatre, or a railway, etc.; **tick′et-collec′tor**; **tick′et-day**, the day before settling day on the Stock Exchange; **tick′et-porter**, a licensed porter: a railway porter who collects tickets; **tick′et-punch**, an instrument for punching holes in used tickets; **tick′et-writer**, an expert in shop-window card and similar lettering; **tick′et-writing.**—**straight ticket**, all the nominees of a political party, and no others; **the ticket** (*slang*), exactly the right thing or the thing to be done; **ticket of leave**, (formerly) a licence to be at large before expiry of sentence; **ticket-of-leave man.** [O.Fr. *estiquet(te)*—*estiquer*, to stick—O.L.G. *stekan*; cf. **stick.**]

**tickey**, *tik′i, (S.Afr.) n.* a former S. Afr. coin, a threepenny-bit. [Origin unknown.]

**tickle**, *tik′l, adj.* unstable, in unstable equilibrium, delicately set, insecure (*Spens., Shak.*): ticklish, nice (*obs.* or *dial.*).—*v.t.* to excite with a pleasant thrill: to affect with a disturbing feeling of a light touch, usually uncomfortable and tending to excite laughter: to amuse: to please: to perplex: to touch lightly: to beat.—*v.i.* to tingle (*Spens.*): to be the seat of a tickling or itching feeling.—*n.* an act or feeling of tickling: a slight touch of the ball with the bat (*cricket*).—*n.* **tick′ler**, one who or that which tickles: a feather-brush: a poker: a cane: a device for reminding: a puzzle: a dram of spirits.—*n. and adj.* **tick′ling**.—*adj.* **tick′lish**, easily tickled: unstable: precarious: easily affected: nice: critical.—*adv.* **tick′lishly.**—*n.* **tick′lishness.**—*adj.* **tick′ly**, tickling: ticklish.— **tick′le-brain** (*Shak.*), strong liquor.—*n.pl.* **tick′ly-bend′ers**, thin ice that bends underfoot: a game played on it.—**tickle pink**, to please or amuse very much. [Perh. a freq. of **tick**; perh. by metathesis from **kittle.**]

**tic-tac.** Same as **tick-tack** (see **tick** (3)).

**tid**, *tid, (Scot.) n.* fit time or condition: a mood.

**tidbit.** Same as **titbit.**

**tiddle**, *tid′l, v.i.* to potter, trifle.

**tiddler**, *tid′lər, n.* a small fish, esp. a stickleback: anything very small. [Perh. **tiddy** (2).]

**tiddley**, *tid′li, (naval coll.) adj.* smart and trim. [Perh. **tiddly.**]

**tiddly**, *tid′li, (slang) n.* drink.—*adj.* slightly drunk. —Also **tiddley.**—**on the tiddly** (*slang*), drunk. [Earlier **titley.**]

**tiddlywink**, *tid′li-wingk, n.* an unlicensed pawnshop or beer-house (*slang*): (in *pl.*; also **tiddledywinks**, *tid′l-di-*), a game in which small disks are flipped into a cup by pressing the edge of the small disk with a bigger one.

**tiddy**, *tid′i, (Scott) n.* the four of trumps at gleek.

**tiddy**, *tid′i, (dial.) adj.* very small. [Origin uncertain.]

**tide**, *tīd, n.* a time: season: festival: opportunity: trend: ebb and flow, esp. of the sea twice daily: time of ebbing, of flowing, of both, or of suitable state for work: sea-water (*poet.*): a flow: river, river-water, or current (*poet.*): flood-tide.—*v.t.* (esp. *fig.*) carry as the tide: effect by means of the tide.—*v.i.* run like a tide: make one's way by taking advantage of the tides (also *v.t.* with *it*). —*adjs.* **tid′al**, of, depending on, regulated by, the tide: flowing and ebbing; **tide′less.**—**tidal wave**, the tide-wave: a great wave caused by the tide: improperly, a great wave started by an earthquake and running on with its own velocity; **tide′-gate**, gate that admits water at flood-tide and retains it at ebb; **tide′-gauge**, instrument for registering the state of the tide continuously; **tide′-lock**, lock by which ships may pass out or in at all times of the tide; **tide′mark**, line on the shore made by the tide: a mark of the limit of washing; **tide′mill**, mill moved by tide-water; **tide′-race**, swift tidal current; **tide′-rip**, disturbed sea due to currents: tidal wave; **tides′-man**, a customs officer who waited the arrival of ships (orig. coming in with the tide); **tide'-table,** a table of times of high-tide; **tide'-waiter,** a tidesman: one who waits to see how things go before acting; **tide'-watership; tide'-water,** water brought by the tide: river water affected by the tide (*U.S.*): seaboard (*U.S.*); **tide'-wave,** the tide regarded as a wave passing round the earth; **tide'-way,** a track followed by the tide: a channel through which there is a stong current or tide.— **tide over,** to carry over, or surmount, difficulties, for the time at least. [O.E. *tíd*; Du. *tijd,* Ger. *zeit.*]

**tide,** *tíd,* (*arch.*) *v.i.* to happen. [O.E. (*ge*)*tídan*; cf. **betide.**]

**tide,** (*Spens.*) for **tied.**

**tidings,** *tī'dingz, n.pl.* news. [Late O.E. *tidung*— O.E. *tídan,* to tide, happen, or—O.N. *títhindi,* events, tidings.]

**tidivate.** Same as **titivate.**

**tidy,** *ti'di, adj.* seasonable (*obs.*): in good condition or order (*dial.*): plump (*dial.*): comely (*dial.*): shapely (*dial.*): fairly good or big (*coll.*): trim: orderly: neat.—*n.* a cover for a chair-back: a receptacle for odd scraps.—*v.t.* to make tidy: to clear away for the sake of tidiness: —*pr.p.* **ti'dying;** *pa.t.* and *pa.p.* **ti'd:ed.**—*adv.* **ti'dily.**—*n.* **ti'diness.** [tide; cf. Ger. *zeitig.*]

**tie,** *tí, v.t.* to bind: to fasten: to knot: to make as a knot: to restrict, restrain: to unite: to mark with a curved line indicating sustentation not repetition (*mus.*): to perform or mark in this way (*mus.*): to limit: to oblige: to subject to bonds: to confirm (*Shak.*): to ligature.— *v.i.* to be equal in votes or score: of dogs, to linger on the scent:—*pr.p.* **ty'ing;** *pa.t.* and *pa.p.* **tied,** *tíd.*—*n.* a knot, bow, etc.: a bond: a string, ribbon, etc., for tying: a necktie: a tie-wig: a shoe (*U.S.*): a member sustaining only a tension: a railway sleeper (*U.S.*): a restraint: an obligation: a mode of tying: an equality in score or votes: a match in any stage of a tournament in which the losers are eliminated: a curved line drawn over notes of the same pitch to be performed as one, sustained not repeated (*mus.*).—*adjs.* **tied;** tie'less.—*n.* **ti'er,** one who ties: a child's apron (*U.S.*).—**tie'-beam,** a beam connecting the lower ends of rafters to prevent moving apart; **tied house,** a public-house whose tenant is bound to get his supplies from one particular brewer or distiller (usually the owner); **tie'-dye'ing,** a method of hand-dying textiles in which parts of the material are bound or knotted so as to resist the dye.—Also **tie-and-dye; tie'-pin,** an ornamental pin stuck in a necktie; **tie'-rod,** a rod serving as a tie; **tie'tack,** ornamental clip attaching tie to shirt; **tie'up,** tape for tying a bookbinding or portfolio: an animal tied up for a bait: a standstill: an entanglement; **tie'-wig,** a wig tied with ribbon at the back.—**tie down,** to fix: to bind by conditions, etc.; **tie in (up) with,** to be closely associated with; **tie up,** to parcel up: to tie so as to remain up: to tether: to secure against squandering, alienation, etc., restrict the use of, by conditions. [O.E. *téah,* band, string, *tígan,* to tie.]

**tier,** *tēr, n.* a row, rank, or layer, esp. one of several placed one above another: a row of guns: a mountain range (*Tasmania*).—*v.t.* to pile in tiers. [O.Fr. *tire,* sequence—*tirer,* to draw.]

**tierce,** *tērs, n.* a third (*obs.*): one-third of a pipe: a cask or vessel of that capacity: (*tûrs*) a sequence of three cards of the same suit: a third (*mus.*): the note two octaves and a third above a given note (*mus.*): a position in fencing: the third hour of the day (ending 9 a.m.): the office of that hour, the terce.—*n.* **tier'ceron** (*archit.*), in vaulting, a subordinate rib springing from the intersection of two other ribs.—**tierce de Picardie** (*tyers də pē-kar-dē*), a major third

closing a piece otherwise in a minor key. [O.Fr. *tiers,* tierce—L. *tertia* (*pars*).]

**tiercel, tiercelet.** See **tercel.**

**tiers état,** *tyer-zā-tā,* (Fr.) the third estate, or commons, formerly in France.

**tiff,** *tif, n.* stale, sour, or thin liquor: a sip: a dram.—*v.i.* to sip: to drink: to lunch.—Also (*Scot.* and *dial.*) **tift.**—*n.* **tiff'ing,** sipping: lunch, a light repast (*India,* etc., **tiff'in**). [Perh. orig. slang.]

**tiff,** *tif,* (*obs.*) *v.t.* and *v.i.* to dress, trick out. [O.Fr. *tiffer* (Fr. *atiffer*), to adorn.]

**tiff,** *tif, n.* a display of irritation, a pet, huff: a slight quarrel.—*v.i.* to be in a huff: to squabble. —Also (esp. *Scot.*) **tift.** [Prob. imit.]

**tiffany,** *tif'ə-ni, n.* a silk-like gauze.—*adj.* of tiffany: transparent. [Gr. *theophaneia,* theophany, or *diaphaneia,* transparency.]

**tig,** *tig, n.* a touch: a twitch: a game in which one who is 'it' seeks to touch another.—*v.t.* to touch, esp. in the game of tig. [Poss. a form of **tick** (3).]

**tig,** *tig, n.* an old drinking-cup with two or more handles.

**tige,** *tēzh, n.* the shaft of a column. [Fr.,—L. *tibia,* a pipe.]

**tiger,** *tí'gər, n.* a fierce striped Asiatic beast, one of the two largest cats (*Felis tigris*): the leopard (*S.Afr.*): the jaguar (*American tiger*) (*U.S.*): the puma (*red tiger*): a boy in livery usually perched behind a vehicle: a ferocious or bloodthirsty person: a flashy vulgarian: a formidable opponent (*slang*): a yell to supplement a cheer (*U.S.*): a tiger-beetle, tiger-moth, tiger-shark, tiger-lily, etc.:—*fem.* **ti'gress.**—*adj.* **ti'gerish** (**ti'grish**), like a tiger in disposition: flashy.—*n.* **ti'gerism,** swagger.—*adjs.* **ti'gerly; ti'gery, ti'grine** (**-grin**), **ti'groid,** like a tiger.—**tiger badge,** a proficiency badge awarded by the Himalayan Club to Sherpas; **ti'ger-bee'tle,** any beetle of the Cicindelidae; **ti'ger-cat,** a general name for a middle-sized striped or spotted wild cat— margay, ocelot, serval, etc.; **ti'ger('s)-eye',** a pseudomorph of quartz after crocidolite; **ti'ger-flower,** a Mexican iridaceous plant (*Tigridia*) with streaked flowers.—*adj.* **ti'ger-foot'ed** (*Shak.*), fiercely swift.—**ti'ger-lil'y,** a lily with black-spotted orange flowers; **ti'ger-moth,** any one of the Arctiidae; **ti'ger-nut,** the edible rhizome of *Cyperus esculentus,* a European sedge: (*U.S.*) the chufa; **ti'ger-shark,** a voracious striped shark of the Indian Ocean; **ti'ger-snake,** the most deadly of Australian snakes (*Notechis scutatus*), brown with black cross-bands; **ti'ger-tail,** type of fast-growing hybrid worm; **ti'ger-wolf,** the spotted hyaena: the thylacine; **ti'ger-wood,** any of several showy black-striped woods. [Fr. *tigre*—L. *tigris*—Gr. *tigris,* prob. from Zend.]

**tight,** *tit, adj.* close: compact: close-fitting: too close-fitting: cramped: allowing little space, or time, for deviation from plan (*fig.*): (of situation) difficult or dangerous: (of contest) close: (of style) concise: taut, not slack: (of, e.g. control) very firm, strict: firmly fixed: impervious, not leaky, proof: trim: neat: snug: competent: hampered or characterised by want of money: (of money) scarce, hard to obtain: unwilling to part with money: intoxicated.—*adv.* **tightly.** —*v.t.* and *v.i.* **tight'en,** to make or grow tight or tighter.—*n.* **tight'ener,** one who, or that which, tightens: a tensor (*anat.*): a heavy meal (*slang*). —*adj.* **tight'ish.**—*adv.* **tight'ishly.**—*adv.* **tight'ly.** — *n.* **tight'ness.** —*n.pl.* **tights,** close-fitting breeches: a close-fitting garment covering the lower part of the body and the legs.—*adj.* **tight'-fisted,** stingy.—*v.t., v.i.,* and *adj.* **tight'-lace'.**— *ns.* **tight'-lā'cer; tight'-lā'cing,** compression of the waist by tight clothes.—*adj.* **tight'-lipped,** uncommunicative.—**tight'-rope,** a taut rope for rope-dancing; **tight'wad,** a skin-flint, miser.

[Earlier *thight*, app. from an older form of O.N. *thēttr*, influenced by various English words of similar meaning; cf. Ger. *dicht*.]

**tight**, *tīt*, (*Spens.*) *pa.t.* and *pa.p.* of tie.

**tigon**, *tī'gon*, *n.* the offspring of a tiger and a lioness. [tig(er) and (li)on.]

**tika**, *tē'ka*, *n.* a red mark on the forehead of Hindu women, formerly of religious significance but now counted as a beauty spot. [Hind.]

**tike**. Same as tyke.

**tiki**, *tī'ki*, *tē'kē*, *n.* an image, often in the form of a small greenstone ornament, representing an ancestor. [Maori.]

**til**, *til*, *tēl*, *n.* sesame.—Also teel.—til'-oil; til'-seed. [Hind. *til*—Sans. *tila*.]

**tilbury**, *til'bər-i*, *n.* a kind of gig for two. [Said to be so named from its first maker.]

**tilde**, *til'dā*, *-di*, *n.* the diacritical sign over *n* in Spanish to indicate the sound *ny*—thus *ñ* (as in *cañon*). [Sp.,—L. *titulus*, a title.]

**tile**, *til*, *n.* a slab of baked clay (or a substitute) for covering roofs, floors, etc.: a tube of baked clay used in drains: a piece for playing mah-jongg: tiling: a top-hat (*slang*).—*v.t.* to cover with tiles: to drain by means of tiles: to secure against intrusion by placing a person at the door: to bind to secrecy.—*adj.* tiled, covered with tiles: imbricated: (of fish) sun dried (*Scott*).—*ns.* ti'ler, a maker or layer of tiles: freemasons' door-keeper—also tyl'er; til'ery, a place where tiles are made; til'ing.—tile'hat; tile'-red, a brownish-red, the colour of baked tiles; tile'-stone, a flat stone used for roofing, esp. a thin-bedded sandstone.—a tile loose (*slang*), a little mad; Dutch tiles, enamelled earthenware tiles, usually blue, with scriptural subjects, for chimney-pieces, etc.; on the tiles, on the loose. [O.E. *tigele*—L. *tēgula*—*tegēre*, to cover.]

**tilefish**, *til'fish*, *n.* an American Atlantic fish noted for the sudden changes in its numbers. [App. from its generic name, Lopholo*til*us, and perh. its tile-like spotted pattern.]

**Tilia**, *til'i-ə*, *n.* the lime or linden genus, giving name to the family Tiliā'ceae, akin to the mallows.—*adj.* tiliā'ceous, belonging to the family. [L. *tilia*, lime-tree.]

**till**, *til*, *n.* a compartment or drawer in a chest, cabinet, etc. (*obs.*): now, a money-drawer or receptacle in or behind a counter. [Cf. M.E. *tillen*, to draw, O.E. *fortyllan*, to draw aside, seduce.]

**till**, *til*, *prep.* to the time of: to (*Scot.*): to, with the infinitive (*Scot.*).—*conj.* to the time when. [O.E. (Northumbrian) *til*—O.N. *til*; cf. O.E. *till*, a fixed point, Ger. *ziel*, end, goal.]

**till**, *til*, *v.t.* to work, cultivate: to set (*obs.* or *dial.*).—*adj.* till'able, arable.—*ns.* till'age, act or practice of tilling: husbandry: a place tilled; till'er; till'ing. [O.E. *tilian*, to aim at, till—*till*, limit; see foregoing word.]

**till**, *til*, *n.* a stiff impervious clay (orig. *Scot.*): boulder-clay (*geol.*): shale (*mining*).—*n.* till'ite, indurated till. [Cf. thill (2).]

**Tillandsia**, *ti-land'zi-ə*, *n.* a mainly epiphytic tropical American genus of the pineapple family. [So called from Finno-Swedish botanist, *Tillands*.]

**tiller**, *til'ər*, *n.* the handle or lever for turning a rudder.—till'er-chain, -rope, the chain or rope connecting the tiller with the steering-wheel. [M.E. *tillen*, to draw (see till (1)), or O.Fr. *telier*, cross-bow stock—L.L. *tēlārium*, a weaver's beam—L. *tēla*, a web.]

**tiller**, *til'ər*, teller, tellar, *tel'ər*, *n.* a sapling: a shoot from a tree stool: a sucker from the base of a stem: a side-shoot from the base as in corn, etc.—*v.i.* to form tillers. [O.E. *telgor*, shoot, twig.]

**tiller**. See till (3).

**tilly-vally**, **-fally**, *til'i-val'i*, *-fal'i*, (*Shak.*) *interj.* of

impatience of what has been said.—Also till'ey-vall'ey.

**tilt**, *tilt*, *n.* a cover, awning, for a wagon, boat, etc.: a tent: a hut.—*v.t.* to cover with a tilt.—*adj.* tilt'ed.—tilt'-boat, a large rowing-boat with a tilt. [O.E. *teld*; cf. Ger. *zelt*.]

**tilt**, *tilt*, *v.i.* to pitch, as a ship: to lean, heel over: to slope: to slant, esp. in a vertical plane: to joust, ride and thrust with a spear: to charge, attack (with *at*): criticise (with *at*): to thrust.—*v.t.* to incline: to tip out: to send by tilting: to forge with a tilt-hammer.—*n.* an act of tilting: a condition of being tilted: a slope: a joust, a course with a lance: an encounter: a duel: a thrust: a tilt-yard.—*ns.* tilt'er; tilt'ing.—tilt'-hammer, a heavy pivoted hammer lifted by a cam; tilt'-yard, a place for tilting.—full tilt, at full speed in a headlong course. [O.E. *tealt*, tottering.]

**tilth**, *tilth*, *n.* cultivation: cultivated land: the depth of soil turned up in cultivation. [From till (3).]

**timariot**, *ti-mä'ri-ot*, (*hist.*) *n.* a Turkish feudal militiaman. [Fr.,—Turk. *timär*.]

**timbal**, **tymbal**, *tim'bl*, (*arch.*) *n.* a kettledrum.—*n.* timbale (*tē-bal*, *tam'bal*, *tim'bl*), a dish cooked in a cup-shaped mould or shell. [Fr. *timbale*; see atabal; app. influenced by L. *tympanum*.]

**timber**, *tim'bər*, *n.* wood suitable for building or carpentry, whether growing or cut: standing trees of oak, ash, elm, or (locally by custom) other kinds, forming part of an inheritance (*English law*): material generally: a beam, or large piece of wood in a framework, as of a house, ship, etc.: familiarly, a wooden object or part: a wooden leg: wood (*dial.*): woodland, forest-land (*U.S.*).—*adj.* of timber: wooden: wooden in tone, unmusical (*Scot.*).—*v.t.* to build (*obs.*): to furnish with timber or beams.—*adj.* tim'bered, built: constructed: built of wood: furnished with timber: app. massive (*Spens.*): wooded.—*n.* tim'bering, timber collectively: work in timber.—tim'ber-line, the upper limit of timber-trees on the mountains, etc.; tim'ber-man, one responsible for the timbers in a mine; tim'ber-toes, a person with a wooden leg; tim'ber-tree, a tree suitable for timber; tim'ber-wolf, an American variety of the common wolf, the grey wolf; tim'ber-yard, a yard or place where timber is stored. [O.E. *timber*, building, wood, *timbrian*, to build; Ger. *zimmer*, room.]

**timbó**, *tim-bō'*, *n.* a South American sapindaceous climber (*Paullinia pinnata*): a fish-poison and insecticide got from its bark. [Guaraní.]

**timbre**, *tēbr*, *tim'bər*, *tam'bər*, *n.* the quality of a sound, tone-colour, distinguished from pitch and loudness. [O.Fr., bell—L. *tympanum*, a drum.]

**timbrel**, *tim'brəl*, *n.* an ancient Oriental tabor or tambourine.—*adj.* tim'brel'd (*Milt.*), sung to the timbrel. [O.Fr. *timbre*—L. *tympanum*, drum.]

**timbrology**, *tim-brol'ə-ji*, **timbromania** (*-brō-mā'ni-ə*), **timbrophily** (*-brof'i-li*), *ns.* outmoded words for stamp-collecting.—*ns.* timbrol'ogist, timbroph'ilist. [Fr. *timbre*, postage-stamp.]

**time**, *tīm*, *n.* concept arising from change experienced and observed: a quantity measured by angle through which earth turns on its axis: a moment at which, or stretch of duration in which, things happen: season: due, appointed, usual time: hour of death or of parturition: spell: a period: actual time of being something or somewhere, as of apprenticeship, residence, sentence, student days, life, etc.: duration of the world: leisure or opportunity long enough for a purpose: a spell of exciting, usually pleasurable, experience: time, or shortest time, of performance, as a race: rhythm, tempo: rate of speed: a unit of duration in metre, a mora: an occasion: an occasion regarded as one of a recurring series:

one of a number of multiplied instances: genera-lised as an indication of multiplication (*so many times* =multiplied by so much): payment for work by the hour, day, etc., back-pay: a reckoning of time: an interval: past time: an allotted period, esp. its completion, as in boxing rounds, permitted drinking hours, etc.: the call, bell, whistle, buzzer, or other signal announcing this: (in *pl.*) the contemporary conditions: (in *pl.*) often the name of a newspaper: (*cap.*) a personification of time, a bald-headed old man with a forelock, a scythe, often an hour-glass.—*v.t.* arrange, fix, choose, a time for: mark, adjust, or observe the rhythm or time of: ascertain the time of: regulate as to time.—*v.i.* keep or beat time.—*adj.* of time: reckoned by time: timed: for a future time.—*interj.* indicating that time is up, or that action is now permitted.—*adjs.* timed; time′less, independent of time: unconnected with the passage of time: ultimately: premature (*Shak.*): ill-timed: eternal: failing to keep time or rhythm.—Also *adv.*—*adv.* time′lessly. — *ns.* time′lessness; time′liness. — *adj.* time′ly, in good time, early: seasonable: well-timed: temporal (*obs.*): of the time of day (*Spens.*): in time, keeping time (*Spens.*).—*adv.* early, soon: in due time or good time.—*adj.* tim(e)ous (*tim′əs*; chiefly *Scot.*), in good time: seasonable.—*adv.* tim(e)′ously, in good time.—*ns.* tim′er, one who or that which times anything: (in composition) one who belongs to, works for, etc., such-and-such a time; tim′ing, fixing, choosing, adjusting, ascertaining, or recording of times: co-ordination in time; tim′ist, a time-server (*obs.*): one who keeps in time: one who times his movements.—time′-ball, a ball arranged to drop at a particular time; time′-bargain, a contract to buy or sell at a certain time in the future.—*adjs.* time′-beguil′ing, making time seem to pass quickly; time′-bett′ering (*Shak.*), in which times are growing better; time′-bewast′ed (*Shak.*), spent by time.—time′-bill, a time-table; time′-bomb, a bomb that explodes by a time-fuze.—*adjs.* time′-consum′ing, requiring much time: wasting time; time′-expired, having completed a term of enlistment.—time′-exposure (*phot.*), an exposure for a time long in comparison with one called instantaneous; time′-fuze, a fuze contrived to act at a definite time; time′-gun, a gun fired to indicate a certain hour.—*adj.* time′-hon′oured, honoured on account of antiquity.—time′-keeper, a clock, watch, or other instrument that measures time: one who keeps account of workmen's hours: one who beats or observes time; time′-killer (*see* kill).—*n.* and *adj.* time′-killing.—time′-lag, the interval of delay between two connected phenomena.—*adj.* time′-lapse, of a motion-picture, taken slowly and projected at a normal speed so that actions are greatly speeded up.—time′-lim′it, a time within which something has to be done.—*adj.* time′ly-part′ed (*Shak.*), having died at a natural time.—time′piece, a piece of machinery for keeping time, esp. one that does not strike but is bigger than a watch; time′-pleas′er (*Shak.*), a time-server.—*n.* and *adj.* time′-saving.—time′-server, one who serves or meanly suits his opinions to the times or those in authority for the time; time′-service.—*n.* and *adj.* time′-serving.—time sharing, the optimum utilisation of a computer and its peripheral devices whereby the differential processing-time of each machine is allowed for, and is used accordingly; time′-signal, an intimation of the exact time given by wireless or otherwise from an observatory; time′-sig′nature (*mus.*), an indication of measure at the beginning of a line or wherever there is a change; time′-spirit, the genius of the age; time′-switch, one working automatically at a set time; time′-table, a table of times, as of classes, etc.; time′-thrust, a

thrust made in fencing at the moment the opponent draws breath for his thrust; time′-work, work paid for by the hour or the day—opp. to *piece-work*.—*adj.* time′-worn, worn or decayed by time.—time zone, one of 24 longitudinal divisions of the globe, each 15° wide, having a standard time throughout its area: a similar zone adapted to a particular country.—against time, with the aim or necessity of finishing by a certain time; all in good time, in due course: soon enough; apparent time, time according to the real sun, without regard to the equation of time—sundial time; astronomical time, till 1925 the time past mean noon, now midnight, reckoned on to twenty-four hours in mean time; at one time, formerly; at the same time, simultaneously: notwithstanding; at times, at distant intervals: occasionally; behind time, late; behind the times, not abreast of changes: between times, in the intervals; by times, betimes; common time, time with two beats or a multiple of two beats to a measure (compound common time where each beat is of three quavers or crotchets); do time, to serve a sentence of imprisonment; for a time, during a time: temporarily; for the time being, at the present time or the actual time in question; from time to time, now and then; have a good time, to enjoy oneself; have little, no, time for, to have little, no, interest in or patience with; in good time, quite early enough: with some time to spare: (ironically; *obs.*) indeed; in no time (at all), within a very short time: in time, after a lapse of time: early enough: keeping rhythm; keep time, to run accurately, as a clock: to move or perform in the same rhythm: to record times of workmen, etc.; know the time of day, to know the state of affairs: to know what one is about, or the best way of doing something; local time, time reckoned from the local meridian; lose time, to fall behindhand: to let time pass without full advantage; make time, to regain advantage of lost time: to find an opportunity; mark time (see mark); mean solar time, time reckoned not by the actual but the mean position of the sun; on, upon, a time, once: at a time in the past (usu. imaginary); on time, up to time: punctually; sidereal time, the portion of a sidereal day that has elapsed since the transit of the first point of Aries; solar time, time reckoned by the sun, real or mean; standard time, a system of time adopted for a wide area instead of local time—usually Greenwich mean time or a time differing from it by a whole number of hours; summer time (see summer); take one's time (*coll.*), not to hurry, dawdle; take Time by the forelock, seize an opportunity before it is too late; take time off (*U.S.* out), to find time to do something, for an activity; time about (chiefly *Scot.*), in turns, alternately; time and again, repeatedly; time and motion study, an investigation of the motions performed and time taken in industrial, etc., work with a view to increased production; time of day, the time by the clock: the point of time reached: a greeting, salutation; time out of mind, during the whole time within human memory, from time immemorial; time-zone disease, symptoms arising from the disturbance of circadian pattern by rapid long-distance flight east or west; triple time, three beats, or three times three beats, to a measure; up to time, punctual, punctually: not later than the due time; what time (*poet.*), when. [O.E. *tima*; O.N. *tími*.]

timenoguy, *tim′an-og-i*, *n.* a rope stretched from place to place in a ship, esp. one to prevent the fore-sheet fouling (*naut.*): a makeshift: a what's-its-name. [Origin obscure.]

timid, *tim′id*, *adj.* inclined to fear: wanting courage: faint-hearted. — *n.* timid′ity. — *adv.* tim′idly.—*n.* tim′idness.—*adj.* tim′orous (*-ər-əs*),

timid.—*adv.* tim'orously.—*n.* tim'orousness.—
*adj.* tim'orsome (*dial.*), easily frightened. [L.
*timidus*, timid, *timor, -ōris*, fear—*timēre*, to fear.]
timocracy, ti-mok'ra-si, *n.* a form of government
in which property is a qualification for office:
one in which ambition or desire of honour is a
ruling principle.—*adjs.* timocratic (*-ō-krat'ik*),
-al. [Gr. *timokratiā—timē*, honour, *krateein*, to
rule.]
timon, ti'mən, (*obs.*) *n.* a helm.—*n.* timoneer', a
helmsman. [Fr.,—L. *tēmō, -ōnis*, a beam.]
Timon, ti'mən, *n.* a famous Athenian misanthrope
(5th cent. B.C.) celebrated by Aristophanes,
Lucian, Plutarch, and Shakespeare: hence, a
misanthrope.—*v.i.* Ti'monise, -ize, to play the
misanthrope.—*ns.* Ti'monism; Ti'monist.
timothy, tim'ə-thi, *n.* (in full timothy-grass) cat's-
tail grass (*Phleum pratense*) much valued for
feeding cattle. [*Timothy* Hanson, who promoted
its cultivation in America about 1720.]
timpano, timp'ə-nō, *n.* an orchestral kettledrum:—
*pl.* tim'pani (*-nē*).—*n.* timp'anist. [It.; see
tympanum.]
tim-whisk(e)y, tim'-(h)wis'ki, *n.* a whisky (gig).
tin, tin, *n.* a silvery-white, easily fusible, malleable
metal (symbol Sn for L. *stannum*; at. numb.
50): money (*slang*): a vessel of tin or tin-plate, a
can, etc.: a tinful.—*adj.* made of tin or tin-plate
or (*coll.*) of corrugated iron: paltry (*coll.*).—*v.t.*
to coat or overlay with tin or tinfoil: to cover
thinly with solder before soldering: to pack in
tins:—*pr.p.* tinn'ing; *pa.t.* and *pa.p.* tinned.—*n.*
tin'ful:—*pl.* tin'fuls.—*adj.* tinned.—*ns.* tinn'er, a
tinsmith: a tin-miner: a canner; tinn'ing.—*adj.*
tinn'y, like tin, esp. in sound.—*n.* (also tinn'ie) a
mug of tin-plate.—tin'-can'; tin'foil, tin or (now)
tin-lead alloy (or aluminium) in thin sheets, as
for wrapping; tin hat (*slang*), a helmet; tin'man,
one who works in tin: a dresser of tin-ore: a
dealer in tinware; tin'-opener, an instrument for
cutting open tins of food, etc.; tin'-plate, thin
sheet-iron or steel coated with tin.—Also *adj.*—
tin'pot, a pot of or for tin or tin-plate.—*adj.*
paltry, rubbishy.—tin'smith, a worker in tin;
tin'stone, cassiterite; tin'-stream'er, one who
washes tin from alluvial deposits; tin'-stream'ing;
tin'-tack', a tack coated with tin; tin'-terne' (see
terne); tin'type, a ferrotype; tin'ware, articles
made of tin.—put the tin hat (lid) on, to finish off,
bring to an end, suppress; tin'-pan alley, the
realm of popular music production. [O.E. *tin*;
O.N. *tin*, Ger. *zinn*.]
tinamou, tin'ə-moō, *n.* a South American part-
ridge-like bird (Tinamus) of or akin to the
Ratitae. [Fr.,—Galibi (Indian language of Fr.
Guiana) *tinamu*.]
tincal, ting'kl, *n.* crude borax. [Malay *tingkal*.]
tinchel, tin'hhyəl, ting'kəl, *n.* a circle of men who
close in round a herd of deer. [Gael. *timchioll*, a
circuit.]
tinct, tingkt, *n.* a tint: a tinge: the alchemist's
elixir (*Shak.*).—*adj.* (*Spens.*) tinged.—*v.t.* (*obs.*)
to tint, tinge, dye: to imbue: to subject to
transmutation.—*adj.* tinctō'rial, of dyeing.—*n.*
tinct'ure, a tinge or shade of colour: a colouring
matter: a metal, colour, or fur (*her.*): a quality
or slight taste added to anything: a principle extracted in solution (*old chem.*): the transmuting elixir or philosopher's stone (*alchemy*):
an alcoholic solution of a drug (*med.*).—*v.t.* to
tinge: to imbue. [L. *tingĕre, tinctum*, to dye; cf.
tint, tinge.]
tind, tind, tind (now *dial.*), teend, tēnd (*Herrick*),
tine, tin (*Milt.*), *v.t.* and *v.i.* to kindle:—*pa.t.* and
*pa.p.* tind'ed, tined (*Spens.* tind, tynd, tynde).
[O.E. *tendan*, and prob. a lost collateral form;
cf. tinder.]
tindal, tin'dəl, *n.* a petty-officer of lascars. [Malay-
alam *tandal*.]
tinder, tin'dər, *n.* dry inflammable matter, esp.

that used for kindling fire from a spark.—*adjs.*
tin'der-like (*Shak.*), inflammable as tinder;
tin'dery, irascible.—tin'der-box, a box for tinder,
and usu. flint and steel. [O.E. *tynder*; O.N.
*tundr*, Ger. *zunder*; O.E. *tendan*, Ger. *zünden*, to
kindle.]
tine, tin, *n.* a spike as of a fork, harrow, or deer's
horn.—*adj.* tined. [O.E. *tind*.]
tine, tyne, tin, (*Scot.*) *v.t.* to lose.—*v.i.* to be lost:
to be painful (*Spens.*): to perish (*Spens.*):—*pa.t.*
and *pa.p.* tint, tint; *Spens.* tyned.—*n.* (*Spens.*)
teen, affliction.—*n.* tinsel (*tin'sl*; *Scot.*), loss.
[O.N. *tỹna*, to destroy, lose, perish; cf. teen.]
tine, tin, (*dial.*) *v.t.* to shut: to enclose. [O.E.
*tỹnan*, to surround; cf. town.]
tine, tin, (*dial.*) *n.* a wild vetch or tare.
tine, tyne, tin, (*Shak.*) *adj.* tiny (always preceded
by little).
tine. See tind.
tinea, tin'i-ə, *n.* ringworm: any of several skin
diseases caused by fungi: (*cap.*) the clothes-moth
genus, giving name to the Tineidae (*ti-nē'i-dē*), a
large family of small moths. [L. *tinea*, moth,
bookworm, etc.]
ting, ting, *v.t.* and *v.i.* to ring.—*n.* the sound of a
small bell.—*n.* ting'-a-ling, a tinkling.—Also
*adv.* [Imit.]
tinge, tinj, *v.t.* to tint or colour: to suffuse: to
impart a slight modification to.—*v.i.* to take on a
tinge:—*pr.p.* ting'ing.—*n.* a slight colouring or
modification. [L. *tingĕre, tinctum*; conn. with
Gr. *tengein*, to wet, to stain.]
tingle, ting'gl, *v.i.* to feel or be the seat of a thrilling sensation: to thrill: to throb: to ring: to
vibrate.—*v.t.* to cause to tingle: to ring.—*n.* a
tingling sensation.—*n.* ting'ler, a stinging blow.
—*n.* and *adj.* ting'ling.—*adjs.* ting'lish, thrilling;
ting'ly, tingling. [M.E. *tinglen*, a variant of
*tinklen*.]
tingle, ting'gl, *n.* a small tack or nail: a clip of
lead: patch over leak in boat's planking. [Cf.
Ger. *zingel*.]
tinguaite, ting'gwa-it, *n.* a fine-grained igneous
rock composed essentially of feldspar, nepheline,
and aegirine. [*Tingua* Mountains in Brazil.]
tink, tingk, *n.* a clear high-pitched short bell-like
sound: a chime of rhyme: a tinker (*coll.* abbrev.,
*Scot.*).—*v.t.* and *v.i.* to sound in this way: to
tinker.—*n.* tink'er, a mender of kettles, pans,
etc.: a botcher or bungler: a slight, temporary,
or unskilful patching-up.—*v.t.* to repair, esp. ineffectually.—*v.i.* to do tinker's work: to botch,
potter, patch up.—*v.i.* tink'le, to make small,
sharp sounds: to jingle: to clink repeatedly
or continuously: to go with tinkling sounds:
to tingle.—*v.t.* to cause to tinkle: to ring: to
make empty sounds or mere sound.—*n.* a sound
of tinkling.—*n.* tink'ler, a small bell: a tinker,
gypsy, or vagrant (*Scot.*).—*n.* and *adj.* tink'ling.
—*adv.* tink'lingly.—*adj.* tink'ly.—give someone a
tinkle, to call someone on the telephone; not to
give a tinker's curse, damn, not to care. [M.E.
*tinken*, to tink, *tinkere*, tinker (perh. unconnected).]
tinnitus, ti-ni'tas, *n.* a ringing in the ears. [L.
*tinnitus, -ūs*, a jingling—*tinnire*, to ring.]
tinsel, tin'sl, *n.* thin glittering metallic sheets or
spangles: anything showy, but of little value.—
*adj.* of or like tinsel: gaudy.—*v.t.* to adorn with,
or as with, tinsel: to make glittering or gaudy:—
*pr.p.* tin'selling; *pa.t.* and *pa.p.* tin'selled.—*adj.*
tin'selly, like tinsel, gaudy, showy.—*n.* tin'selry,
glittering and tawdry material.—*n.* and *adj.* tin'-
sey, (*obs.–dial.*) tinsel.—tin'sel-slipp'er'd (*Milt.*).
[O.Fr. *estincelle*—L. *scintilla*, a spark.]
tinsel. See tine (2).
tint, tint, *n.* a slight tinge distinct from the principal
colour: a hue mixed with white: a series of
parallel lines in engraving, producing a uniform
shading.—*v.t.* to colour slightly: to tinge.—*v.i.*

to take on a tint.—*ns.* **tint′er**, one who, or that which, tints; **tint′iness**; **tint′ing.**—*adjs.* **tint′less**; **tin′ty**, inharmoniously tinted.—*n.* **Tintom′eter**, trademark name for a colorimeter.—**tint′-block**, a block for printing a background; **tint′-tool**, an implement for producing a tint by parallel lines. [L. *tinctus*; cf. **tinct**, **tinge**.]

**tint**, *tint.* See **tine** (2).

**tintinnabulate**, *tin-tin-ab′ū-lāt*, *v.i.* to ring.—*adjs.* **tintinnab′ulant**, **tintinnab′ular**, **tintinnab′ulary.**— *n.* **tintinnabulā′tion**, bell-ringing.—*adj.* **tintinnab′-ulous.**—*n.* **tintinnab′ulum**, a bell: a bell-rattle:— *pl.* **tintinnab′ula.** [L. *tintinnabulum*, a bell— *tintinnāre*, to jingle, reduplicated from *tinnire*, to jingle.]

**tiny** (*slang*), *tī′ni*, *adj.* very small:—*comp.* **ti′nier**, *superl.* **ti′niest.** [Cf. **tine** (5).]

**tip**, *tip*, *n.* a slender extremity: the furthest part. —*v.t.* to put a tip to: to be the tip of: to remove the tip from:—*pr.p.* **tipp′ing**; *pa.t.* and *pa.p.* **tipped**, or **tipt.**—*adj.* **tipped** (tipt).—*n.* **tipp′ing.**— *adj.* (*slang*) topping, ripping, excellent.—*adj.* **tipp′y** (*slang*), in the height of fashion: smart.— *adj.* **tip′-tilt′ed** (*Tennyson*), turned up at the tip.— **on the tip of one's tongue**, on the very point of being spoken. [Cf. O.N. *typpa*, to tip, Du., Norw., Dan. *tip*, Ger. (dim.) *zipfel*.]

**tip**, *tip*, *v.t.* to strike lightly but definitely: to hit glancingly:—*pr.p.* **tipp′ing**; *pa.t.* and *pa.p.* **tipped.**—*n.* a tap.—*n.* **tipp′ing**, a mode of articu-lating with the tongue to give staccato effects on the flute, trumpet, etc.—**tip′-and-run′**, a kind of cricket in which the batsman must run if he hits at all: a raid in which the raiders make off at once. [Cf. Du. and Ger. *tippen*, Sw. *tippa*, to tip.]

**tip**, *tip*, *v.t.* to give, hand, pass, convey: to give a tip to: to indicate.—*v.i.* to give tips:—*pr.p.* **tipp′-ing**; *pa.p.* and *pa.t.* **tipped.**—*n.* a gratuity: a hint or piece of special information supposed to be useful in betting, examinations, etc., a wrinkle.— *ns.* **tipp′er**; **tipp′ing**; **tip′ster**, one whose business it is to furnish tips.—**tip′-off**, a hint or warning in advance.—**tip off**, to give a tip-off to; **tip one the ·wink**, to convey a secret hint. [Orig. rogues' cant.]

**tip**, *tip*, *v.t.* to cast down: to upset: to tilt: to shoot, dump, empty out, by tilting: to toss off. —*v.i.* to topple over: to tilt:—*pr.p.* **tipp′ing**; *pa.p.* and *pa.t.* **tipped.**—*n.* a tilt: a place for tipping rubbish, coal, etc.: a dump: a staith or shoot: a tram for expeditiously transferring coal.—*ns.* **tipp′er**, one who, or that which, tips: a lorry or truck, the main part of which can be tipped up for unloading; **tipp′ing.**—**tip′-cart**, a cart emptied by being canted up: **tip′-cat**, a cat or pointed piece of wood: a game in which the cat is struck with a cat-stick and made to spring up; **tip′-cheese** (*Dickens*), app. tip-cat.—*adj.* **tip′-up**, constructed so as to allow of being tilted.—**tip off liquor**, to turn up the vessel till quite empty; **tip the scale**, to depress one end of the scales. [M.E. *type*; origin obscure.]

**tipper**, *tip′ər*, *n.* a kind of ale—from Thomas *Tipper*, who brewed it in Sussex.

**tippet**, *tip′it*, *n.* a long band of cloth or fur, variously worn, esp. an ecclesiastical scarf (*obs.*): the hangman's rope (*obs.*, *facet.*): a cape: an animal's ruff of hair or feathers: a moth's patagium. [Prob. **tip** (1).]

**tipple**, *tip′l*, *v.t.* and *v.i.* to drink constantly in small quantities: to booze.—*n.* liquor tippled.— *n.* **tipp′ler**—**tipp′ling-house.** [Cf. Norw. dial. *tipla*, to drip slowly.]

**tipstaff**, *tip′stäf*, *n.* a staff tipped with metal: an officer who carries it, a sheriff's officer:—*pl.* **tip′staffs**, **tip′staves** (*-stāvz*). [**tip** (1), **staff.**]

**tipsy**, *tip′si*, *adj.* partially intoxicated.—*v.t.* **tip′-sify**, to fuddle.—*adv.* **tip′sily.**—*n.* **tip′siness.**— **tip′sy-cake**, a cake made of pastry and almonds,

with wine; **tip′sy-key**, a watch-key in which the head is released if an attempt is made to turn it backward. [Prob. **tip** (4).]

**tiptoe**, *tip′tō*, *n.* the end of the toe or toes, more often merely the toes.—*adv.* on tiptoe, literally or figuratively, through excitement, expectation, etc.—*v.i.* to walk on tiptoe, to go lightly and stealthily:—*pr.p.* **tip′toeing**; *pa.t.* and *pa.p.* **tip′toed.** [**tip** (1), **toe.**]

**tiptop**, *tip′top′*, *n.* the extreme top: the height of excellence.—*adj.* of the highest excellence — Also *adv.* [**tip** (1), **top.**]

**Tipula**, *tip′ū-la*, *n.* the daddy-long-legs genus of flies, giving name to the family **Tipū′lidae.** [L. *tippula*, a water-spider.]

**tirade**, *ti-rād′*, *ti-räd′*, *tē-räd′*, *n.* a long vehement harangue: a string of invective: a laisse (*pros.*): a run between two notes (*mus.*). [Fr.,—It. *tirata* —*tirare*, to pull.]

**tirage à part**, *tē-räzh a pär*, (Fr.) an offprint or article reprinted separately from a periodical— the German *abdruck*.

**tirailleur**, *tē-rä-yœr*, *n.* a skirmisher, sharp-shooter. [Fr.]

**tirasse**, *ti-ras′*, *n.* a pedal-coupler in an organ.

**tire**, *tir*, (*arch.*) *n.* equipment, furniture (*Shak.*): attire, apparel: a head-dress: a pinafore (*U.S.*). —*v.t.* to attire: to dress, as the head.—*n.* **tir′ing.** —**tire′-val′iant** (*Shak.*), a kind of fanciful head-dress; **tire′-woman**, a lady's-maid; **tir′ing-glass**; **tir′ing-house**, **-room**, a theatre dressing-room; **tir′ing-woman.** [Short for **attire.**]

**tire**, *tir*, *n.* a metal hoop to bind a wheel: (now usu. **tyre** in Britain) rubber band, cushion, or tube round a wheel-rim.—*v.t.* to put a tire on.— *adjs.* **tired** (tyred); **tire′less** (tyre′less).—*n.* **tir′ing** (tyr′ing).—**tubeless tire** (tyre), a pneumatic tire that has no inner tube and, being self-sealing, deflates only slowly when punctured. [Prob. same word as the foregoing.]

**tire**, *tir*, (*Spens.*) *n.* a train: a tier of guns. [Variant of **tier.**]

**tire**, *tir*, *n.* a volley: a broadside. [Fr. *tir.*]

**tire**, *tir*, (*Shak.*) *v.i.* to tear and tug or feed greedily as a bird of prey: to be intent, occupy oneself, feed one's thoughts or desires. [O.Fr. *tirer.*]

**tire**, *tir*, *v.i.* to weary: to become fatigued: to have interest or patience exhausted or worn down.—*v.t.* to weary: to fatigue: to bore: to wear out.—*adj.* **tired**, fatigued: wearied, bored (with *of*): showing deterioration through time or usage—e.g. limp, grubby, played out.—*n.* **tired′ness.**—*adj.* **tire′less**, untiring.—*adv.* **tire′-lessly.**—*ns.* **tire′lessness**; **tire′ling**, a tired animal.—Also *adj.* (*Spens.* **tyreling jade**).—*adj.* **tire′some**, fatiguing: wearisome: boring: tedious: loosely, irritating, troublesome, irk-some.—*adv.* **tire′somely.**—*n.* **tire′someness.**—**tire down**, hunt to exhaustion. [App. O.E. *tiorian*, to be tired.]

**tirl**, *tirl*, (*Scot.*) *v.t.* and *v.i.* to turn: whirl: rattle. —*n.* a turnstile or the like.—**tirl′ie-wir′lie**, a twirl.—*adj.* twirled: intricate.—**tirl′ing-pin**, pin of a door-latch, rattled to seek admission (*obs.*): now usu. taken to mean a risp. [**trill** (2).]

**tirl**, *tirl*, (*Scot.*) *v.t.* to strip. [Cf. **tirr.**]

**Tir na n-Og**, *tēr-na-nōg′*, *n.* the Irish Elysium. [Ir., land of the young.]

**tiro**, *tī′rō* (also **tyro**), *n.* a beginner: a novice:—*pl.* **ti′ros**, also **ty′roes**, **ti′roes**, **tyrones** (*tī-rō′nēz*).— *n.* **tirocinium** (*-sin′-i-əm*), early training: first experience. [L. *tirō* (L.L. *tȳrō*), *-ōnis*, a recruit, *tīrōcinium*, a first campaign.]

**Tironensian**, *ti-rō-nen′si-ən*, *n.* a Benedictine of a congregation founded (1109) at *Tiron* (Thiron, near Nogent-le-Rotrou), absorbed in 1627 by that of St Maur.—Also *adj.*

**Tironian**, *tī-rō′ni-ən*, *adj.* of *Tirō* (-*ōnis*), Cicero's amanuensis, or of shorthand writing (*Tironian* *notes*) ascribed to him.—**Tironian sign,** ampersand.

**tiros,** *ti'rōs, n.* the name given to one of a series of satellites giving meteorological information from observation of the clouds.

**tirr,** *tir, (Scot.) v.t.* and *v.i.* to strip. [M.E. *tirve*; origin unknown.]

**tirra-lirra, tirra-lyra,** *tir-ə-lir'ə, n.* and *interj.* an old refrain, ascribed by Shakespeare to the lark.

**tirrit,** *tir'it, (Shak.) n.* Mrs Quickly's word for alarm, fright.

**tirrivee, tirrivie,** *tir'i-vi,* or -*vē', (Scot.) n.* a tantrum or fit of passion: a commotion.

**'tis,** *tiz,* a contraction of **it is.**

**tisane,** *ti-zan', n.* a medicinal decoction. [See **ptisan.**]

**tisick,** *tiz'ik, (Shak.) n.* a cough. [**phthisic.**]

**Tisiphone,** *ti-sif'o-nē, n.* one of the Furies. [Gr. *Tisiphonē—tisis,* retribution, *phonos,* murder.]

**'tisn't,** *tiz'nt,* a contraction of **it is not.**

**Tisri,** *tiz'ri, n.* the first month of the Jewish civil year, seventh of the ecclesiastical, usually part of September and October.

**tissue,** *tish'ōō, -ū, tis'ū, n.* anything woven, esp. a rich or gauzy fabric: an aggregate of similar cells (*biol.*): a fabric, mass, or agglomeration, as of lies, nonsense: paper coated with gelatine and pigment (*phot.*): tissue-paper: a handkerchief made of soft, thick, tissue-paper.—*v.t.* to weave or interweave, esp. with gold or silver thread: to clothe, cover, adorn, with tissue: to variegate.— **tissue culture,** growing of detached pieces of tissue, plant or animal, in nutritive fluids: a piece so grown; **tiss'ue-pa'per,** a thin, soft, semitransparent paper (said to have been put between folds of tissue). [Fr. *tissu,* woven, pa.p. of *titre* (O.Fr. *tistre*)—L. *texēre,* to weave.]

**tit,** *tit, n.* a variant of **teat.**

**tit,** *tit, n.* (*dial.*) a tap.—**tit for tat,** a tip for a tap, retaliation: a hat—usu. abbrev. **tit'fer** (cockney rhyming *slang*).

**tit,** *tit, n.* a titmouse (q.v.): a small or inferior horse: a nag: (in real or feigned depreciation) a girl, young woman. [Ice. *tittr,* titmouse.]

**tit,** *tit,* (chiefly *Scot.*) *n.* a twitch: a tug.—*v.t.* and *v.i.* to tug.

**tit.** See **tite.**

**Titan,** *ti'tən, n.* a son or daughter (**Ti'taness**) or other descendant of Uranus and Gaea: one of the elder gods and goddesses overthrown by Zeus: the name of one of them, Hyperion: Helios, the sun-god: the sun personified: Prometheus: Saturn's greatest satellite (*astron.*): (without *cap.*) anything gigantic: (without *cap.*) a man of great intellect but not the highest inspiration.—Also *adj.*—*n.* **Titania** (*ti-tä'ni-ə, ti-tā'ni-ə*), the queen of fairyland, wife of Oberon: a satellite of Uranus.—*adjs.* **Titanesque** (-*esk'*); **Titā'nian; Titantic, titanic,** (*tī-* or *ti-tan'ik*).—*ns.* **Ti'tanism,** the spirit of revolt against the universe; **Titanomachy** (-*om'ə-ki*) Gr. *machē,* fight), the war of the Titans against the Olympian gods; **Titanosau'rus,** a gigantic Cretaceous dinosaur; **Titanothē'rium,** a huge rhinoceros-like American Oligocene fossil ungulate. [Gr. *Titān.*]

**titanium,** *ti-tā'ni-əm, n.* a metallic element (Ti; at. numb. 22) found in ilmenite sphene, rutile, etc.—strong, light and corrosion-resistant.—*n.* **titanate** (*tī'tən-āt*), a salt of titanic acid.—*adjs.* **titanic** (-*tan'ik*), of quadrivalent titanium (**titanic acid,** H₂TiO₃; **titanic iron,** ilmenite); **titanif'erous,** containing titanium.—*n.* **ti'tanite,** sphene, a brown, green, or yellow monoclinic mineral, calcium silicate and titanate.—*adj.* **ti'tanous,** of trivalent titanium.—**titanium white,** titanium oxide used as pigment. [Gr. *Titān,* Titan, on the analogy of **uranium.**]

**titbit,** *tit'bit, n.* a choice delicacy or item.—Also **tid'bit.**

**tite, tyte, tight,** *tīt,* **tit,** *tit,* **titely,** etc., -*li, (obs.) advs.* promptly: at once. [Cf. O.N. *titt,* often.]

**titfer,** *tit'fər.* See **tit** (2).

**tithe,** *tidh, adj.* tenth.—*n.* a tenth part, an indefinitely small part: the tenth of the produce of land and stock allotted originally for church purposes: a rent-charge in commutation of this: any levy of one-tenth.—*v.t.* to take a tithe of or from: to pay a tithe on: to decimate (*obs.*).— *adj.* **tith'able,** subject to the payment of tithes.— *adj.* **tithed.**—*ns.* **tith'er,** one who collects tithes; **tith'ing,** a tithe: exaction or payment of tithes: a district containing ten householders, each responsible for the behaviour of the rest (*hist.*).— **tithe'-barn,** a barn for storing the parson's tithe in corn.—*adj.* **tithe'-free,** exempt from paying tithes. — **tithe'-gatherer.** — *adj.* **tithe'-paying.** — **tithe'-pig,** one pig out of ten paid as a tithe; **tithe'-proctor,** a collector of tithes; **tith'ing-man,** the chief man of a tithing. [O.E. *tēotha,* tenth; cf. **tenth, teind.**]

**titi,** *tee-tee, tē-tē', n.* a small South American monkey (Callithrix).

**Titian, titian,** *tish'ən, -yən, 'n.* a red-yellow colour used by the Venetian painter *Titian* (Tiziano Vecellio, *c.* 1490-1576).—*adj.* (chiefly of hair) of this colour, or (loosely) of other shade of red or reddish-brown.—*adj.* **Titianesque** (-*esk'*), in the manner of Titian, a combination of the richest surface and colour.

**titillate,** *tit'il-lāt, v.t.* to tickle: to stimulate gently. —*ns.* **titillā'tion; tit'illātor.** [L. *titillāre, -ātum.*]

**tit(t)ivate,** *tit'i-vāt,* **tidivate,** *tid', (slang) v.i.* and *v.t.* to smarten up, by dress or otherwise.—*n.* **tit(t)ivā'tion, tidivā'tion.** [Poss. coined from **tidy.**]

**titlark,** *tit'lärk, n.* a pipit. [**tit** (3) and **lark.**]

**title,** *ti'tl, n.* an inscription or descriptive placard: a chapter-heading: a section of a law-book: the name of a book, poem, tale, picture, etc.: a title-page: a book or publication, as an item in a catalogue (*publishers' slang*): a credit title (*cinema*): a subtitle (*cinema*): an appellation of rank or distinction: a right to possession: a ground of claim: evidence of right: a title-deed: a fixed sphere of work, source of maintenance, or a certificate thereof, required as a condition for ordination: a cardinal-priest's parish in Rome: a championship (*sport*).—*v.t.* to designate: to give or attach a title to.—*adjs.* **ti'tled,** having a title; **ti'tleless,** nameless (*Shak.*): untitled.—*ns.* **ti'tler,** a writer of titles: a claimant (*obs.*); **ti'tling,** the giving or attaching of a title. —**ti'tle-deed,** a document that proves right to possession; **ti'tle-leaf,** the leaf on which is the title of a book; **ti'tle-page,** the page of a book containing its title; **ti'tle-poem,** that which gives its title to a book; **ti'tle-role,** the part in a play which gives its name to it; **ti'tle-sheet,** the first sheet of a book as printed, containing title, bastard-title, etc. [O.E. *titul* or *titul* and O.Fr. *title* (Fr. *titre*)—L. *titulus.*]

**titling,** *tit'ling, n.* a small stockfish: the meadowpipit (esp. *Scot.*): also the hedge-sparrow. [Norw. dial. *titling,* small stockfish; O.N. *titlingr,* sparrow; cf. **tit.**]

**titmouse,** *tit'mows* (Spens. **tit'mose,** -*mōs*), *n.* a tit, any of various kinds of little active acrobatic bird of Parus or kindred genus:—*pl.* **titmice** (*tit'mīs*). [**tit** (3), and M.E. *mose,* titmouse—O.E. *māse*; Ger. *meise*; confused with **mouse.**]

**Titoism,** *tē'tō-izm, n.* the communism of Marshal *Tito* (born 1892) of Yugoslavia, adhering to international communism but not at the sacrifice of national independence.— *n.* and *adj.* **Ti'toist.**

**titoki,** *ti-tok'i, tē', n.* a New Zealand tree with reddish paniculate flowers. [Maori.]

**titrate,** *tī'trāt, v.t.* to subject to titration.—*ns.* **titrā'tion,** measurement of the strength of a solution by finding how much of another solution of known strength is required to complete a chemical reaction; **titre** (*U.S.* **titer**; *ti′tər, tē′*), the concentration of a substance in a solution as determined by titration. [Fr. *titre*, standard.]

**ti-tree.** See ti (2).

**titter,** *tit′ər, v.i.* to giggle, snicker, or laugh restrainedly.—*n.* a stifled laugh.—*n.* **titt′erer.**—*n.* and *adj.* **titt′ering.** [Cf. Sw. dial. *tittra.*]

**titter,** *tit′ər, v.i.* to totter, sway. [O.N. *titra*, to shake.]

**tittle,** *tit′l, n.* a dot, stroke, accent, vowel-point, contraction or punctuation mark: the smallest part. [O.Fr. *title*—L. *titulus*, a title.]

**tittle,** *tit′l,* (*dial.*) *v.t.* and *v.i.* to whisper: to tattle.—**titt′le-tatt′le,** idle, empty talk.—*v.i.* to prate idly.—**titt′le-tatt′ler;** **titt′le-tatt′ling.**

**tittlebat,** *tit′l-bat, n.* a childish form of stickleback.

**tittup, titup,** *tit′əp, v.i.* to prance, skip about gaily.—*n.* a light springy step, a canter.—*adj.* **titt′upy,** *tit′upy,* gay, lively: unsteady. [Imit.]

**titty,** *tit′i, n.* a teat: the breast. [Dim. of **tit, teat**.]

**titty,** *tit′i,* (*Scot.*) *n.* sister.

**titubate,** *tit′ū-bāt, v.i.* to stagger, stumble.—*n.* **tit′ūbancy,** staggering.—*adj.* **tit′ūbant.**—*n.* **titūbā′tion.** [L. *titubāre, -ātum,* to stagger.]

**titule,** *tit′ūl, n.* and *v.t.* Same as **title.**—*adj.* **tit′ūlar,** pertaining to title: in name or title only: nominal: having the title without the duties of an office: supplying a title to a cardinal-priest (as a titular church).—*n.* a titled person: one who enjoys the bare title of an office, without actual possession: a person invested with a title in virtue of which he holds a benefice, whether he performs its duties or not: that from which a church takes its name (*patron* if a saint or angel; *R.C.*).—*n.* **titularity** (-*ar′i-ti*).—*adv.* **tit′ularly.**—*adj.* **tit′ularly,** titular.—*n.* one holding a title.—**titular bishop** (*R.C.*), a bishop without a diocese, taking his title from a place where there is no longer a bishop's see—before 1882 bishop in partibus infidelium.—**titular of the teinds** or **tithes,** a layman invested with church lands after the Reformation in Scotland. [L. *titulus.*]

**tityre-tu,** *tit′, tit-i-ri-tōō′, -tū′, n.* a member of a 17th-century fraternity of aristocratic hooligans. [Opening words of Virgil's first eclogue, *Tītyre tū,* Tityrus, thou (lying under the spreading beech), conjectured to indicate the class that had beech trees and leisure to lie under them.]

**Tiw,** *tē′w, n.* the old English war-god. [O.E. *Tīw*; cf. **Tuesday, Tyr.**]

**tizzy,** *tiz′i, n.* a sixpence (*old slang*): state of agitation, nervousness, confusion, or dither over little (*slang*; also tizz).

**tmesis,** *tmē′sis,* (*gram.*) *n.* the separation of the parts of a compound word by a word or words. [Gr. *tmēsis—temnein,* to cut.]

**T.N.T.** Abbrev. for trinitrotoluene, see trinitro-.

**to,** *tōō, tŏŏ, tə, prep.* serving as sign of the infinitive (which is sometimes understood) and forming a substitute for the dative case: in the direction of: as far as: all the way in the direction of: until: into the condition of: towards: beside: near: at: in contact with, close against: before: for: of: with the object or result of: against: in accordance, comparison, or relation with: in honour of, or expressing good wishes for: along with in addition.—*adv.*in one direction, forward: in or into position, contact, closed or harnessed condition.—**to and fro,** alternately this way and that; **toing and froing,** going backwards and forwards in an agitated way, or without achieving anything: also *fig.* [O.E. *tō;* Ger. *zu,* Goth. *du;* Gr. suffix -*de.*]

**toad,** *tōd, n.* a toothless tailless amphibian that walks or crawls instead of jumping like the frog, esp. one of *Bufo* or kindred genus: a hateful or contemptible person or animal: (alchemy) bufo.

—*n.* **toad′y,** a toad-eater, sycophant.—*v.t.* to fawn as a sycophant:—*pr.p.* **toad′ying;** *pa.t.* and *pa.p.* **toad′ied.**—*adj.* **toad′yish.**—*n.* **toad′yism.**—**toad′-eater,** a fawning sycophant—originally a mountebank's assistant, whose duty was to swallow, or pretend to swallow, toads; **toad′-eating,** sycophancy.—*adj.* sycophantic.—**toad′-fish,** a toadlike fish of many kinds; **toad′flax,** any species of Linaria, an genus closely allied to snapdragon with flax-like leaves; **toad′-in-the-hole**, a dish originally of beef, now usu. sausage-meat, cooked in batter; **toad′ rush, -grass,** a low rush (*Juncus bufonius*) with mostly solitary flowers; **toad′-spit,** cuckoo-spit.—*adj.* **toad′-spott′ed,** thickly stained or spotted like a toad.—**toad′-stone,** a stone or concretion formerly believed to be found in a toad's head, and valued as an amulet: a basalt lava or tuff (Derbyshire; supposed to be from its markings; but poss.—Ger. *totes gestein,* dead stone, from the leadminer's point of view); **toad′stool,** any mushroomlike fungus, often excluding the mushroom. [O.E. *tāde, tādige, tādie.*]

**toast,** *tōst, v.t.* to dry and parch: to brown (as bread): to half-melt (as cheese): to warm or heat by rays: to drink to.—*v.i.* to drink toasts: to undergo, or be suitable for, toasting.—*n.* bread toasted: a piece of toasted bread, usu. one put in liquor: the person or thing drunk to, esp. the lady most admired for the moment: a proposal of health.—*adj.* **toast′ed.**—*ns.* **toast′er,** one who toasts: a toasting-fork: an electric apparatus for making toast: that which can be toasted; **toast′ing.**—**toast′ing-fork, -iron,** a long-handled fork for toasting bread: a sword (*facet.*); **toast′-master,** the announcer of toasts at a dinner; **toast′-rack,** a stand with partitions for slices of toast.—**on toast,** served on a slice of toast: swindled: at one's mercy. [O.Fr. *toster*—L. *tostus,* roasted, pa.p. of *torrēre.*]

**toaze,** *tōz* (*Shak.*). See **toze.**

**tobacco,** *tə-bak′ō, n.* an American solanaceous plant, *Nicotiana tabacum,* or other species of the genus: its prepared leaves used for smoking, chewing, or snuffing.—*ns.* **tobaccanā′lian,** a smoker (*facet.*; after **bacchanalian**); **tobacc′-onist,** a smoker (*obs.*): a seller or manufacturer of tobacco.—**tobacc′o-heart,** a functional disorder of the heart due to excessive use of tobacco; **tobacc′o-pipe,** a pipe for smoking tobacco; **tobacc′o-plant; tobacc′o-pouch,** a pouch for holding tobacco; **tobacc′o-stopper,** an instrument for pressing down the tobacco in a pipe. [Sp. *tabaco,* from Haitian.]

**to-be,** *tōō-, tə-bē′, n.* and *adj.* future.

**Tobit,** *tō′bit, n.* an apocryphal Old Testament book, containing the story of *Tobit.*

**toboggan,** *tə-bog′ən, n.* a flat sledge turned up in front.—*v.i.* to slide, coast, travel, on, or as if on, a toboggan.—Earlier also **tobogg′in, tabogg′an, tarbogg′in.**—*ns.* **tobogg′aner; tobogg′aning; tobogg′anist.** [Micmac *tobākun.*]

**to-break,** *tōō-, tə-brāk′,* (*obs.*) *v.t.* to break in pieces:—*pa.t.* (*B., Bunyan*) **to-brake′** (usu. printed *to brake*); *pa.p.* **to-bro′ken.** [O.E. *tōbrecan*—pfx. *tō-,* asunder, and *brecan,* to break.]

**to-bruise,** *tə-brōōz′,* (*obs.*) *v.t.* to bruise severely: to break up:—*pa.p.* (*Spens.*) **to-brusd′.** [O.E. *tō-brȳsan.*]

**Toby,** *tō′bi, n.* a beer-mug shaped like a man with three-cornered hat (also **To′by-jug**): Punch's dog.

**toby,** *tō′bi,* (*thieves' slang*) *n.* the road: robbery on the road.—**high toby,** highway robbery on horseback; **low toby,** footpad robbery. [Shelta *tōbar.*]

**toccata,** *tok′kä′ta,* (*mus.*) *n.* primarily a work intended to display the performer's touch, or in which he seems to try the touch of an instrument in a series of runs and chords before breaking into

*fāte, fär; mē, hûr* (her); *mīne; mōte, fŏr; mūte; mōōn, fŏŏt; dhen* (then)

a fugue: loosely, a sort of fantasia or overture.— *ns.* toccatel′la, toccatina (-*tē′na*), a short toccata. [It.,—*toccare*, to touch.]

toc emma, *tok em′ə,* (*mil. slang*) *n.* a trench mortar.

—Toc H (*ǎch*), a society for handing on the spirit of comradeship of the 1st World War, from its first meetings at Talbot House, at Poperinghe. [Formerly signallers' names of the initial letters T, M and T, H.]

Tocharian, Tokharian, *to-kä′ri-ən,* or *-kä′,* Tocha′rish, Tokha′rish, *-rish, ns.* an extinct Indo-Germanic language, akin to Latin and Celtic, preserved in MSS discovered in the 20th century in Chinese Turkestan. [Gr. *Tocharoi,* a people guessed to be its speakers on the strength of the Uigur (language of Chinese Turkestan) name *Tochri.*]

tocher, *tohh′ər,* (*Scot.*) *n.* a dowry.—*v.t.* to dower. —*adj.* toch′erless.—toch′er-good, property given as tocher. [Ir. *tochar,* Gael. *tochradh.*]

toco, *tō′kō,* (*slang*) *n.* punishment.—Also tō′ko. [Gr. *tokos,* interest.]

tocology, tokology, *tok-ol′ə-ji,* *n.* obstetrics.—*n.* tocoph′erol, vitamin E, whose deficiency causes sterility in some species. [Gr. *tokos,* birth, off-spring, *logos,* discourse, *pherein,* to bring.]

tocsin, *tok′sin, n.* an alarm-bell, or the ringing of it. [Fr. *tocsin*—Prov. *tocasenh*—*tocar,* to touch, strike, *senh*—L. *signum,* sign (L.L. bell).]

tod, *tod,* (*Scot.*) *n.* a fox: a sly person.—Tod-low′rie (i.e. Laurence), Reynard. [Origin unknown.]

tod (*Spens.* todde), *tod, n.* a bush, esp. of ivy: an old wool weight, about 28 lb.: a load.—*v.i.* to yield a tod.—*v.t.* to yield a tod for.

tod, *tod,* in phrase on one's tod, alone. [Rhyming slang *on one's Tod Sloan.*]

today, to-day, *tōō-, tə-dā′, n.* this or the present day.—*adv.* on the present day: nowadays. [O.E. *tōdæg*(e).]

toddle, *tod′l, v.i.* to walk with short feeble steps, as a child: to saunter: to go.—*n.* a toddling gait: an aimless stroll: a toddling child.—*n.* todd′ler, one who toddles, esp. a child.—*adj.* todd′ling.

toddy, *tod′i, n.* fermented palm juice: a mixture of spirits, sugar, and hot water.—todd′y-cat, the palm civet; todd′y-ladle, a small ladle for mixing or serving toddy; todd′y-palm, coconut, borassus, or other palm yielding toddy; todd′y-stick, a stick used in mixing toddy. [Hindi *tāṛī—tāṛ,* a palm-tree.]

to-do, *tə-, tōō-dōō′, n.* bustle: stir: commotion.

tody, *tō′di, n.* a small West Indian insectivorous bird—the *green sparrow, green humming-bird,* etc., akin to the kingfishers. [L. *todus,* a small bird of some kind.]

toe, *tō, n.* one of the five small members at the point of the foot: the front of a hoof: the corresponding part of a shoe, sock, golf-club head, etc.: the lowest part of the front of anything, esp. if it projects.—*v.t.* to stand with the toes against: to kick: to strike with the toe of a club: to nail obliquely through the foot: to perform with the toe: to furnish with a toe, as a stocking.—*v.i.* to place the toes:—*pr.p.* toe′ing; *pa.t.* and *pa.p.* toed.—*adj.* toed (*tōd*), having toes: nailed obliquely.—toe′cap, a cap covering the toe of a shoe; toe′clip, an attachment to a bicycle pedal that receives the toe; toe′-hold, a place to fix the toes in: a small established position: a hold in which the foot is bent back from the toe (*wrestling*); toe′-nail; toe′-piece.—big or great toe, largest of the toes; little toe, smallest of the toes; on one's toes, poised for a quick start, alert, eager; toe the line, stand with toes against a marked line, as in starting a race: conform; tread on the toes of (someone), to offend (someone). [O.E. *tā* (pl. *tān*); O.N. *tā,* Ger. *zehe.*]

to-fall, *tōō′föl,* (*arch.*) *n.* beginning, incidence. [to, fall.]

toff, *tof,* (*slang*) *n.* person of the better classes:

swell: good sort.—*adj.* toff′ish.—*n.* toff′ishness. —*adj.* toff′y. [Perh. tuft.]

toffee, toffy, *tof′i, n.* a hard-baked sweetmeat, made of sugar and butter.—*Earlier* and *U.S.* taff′y.—toff′ee-app′le, a toffee-coated apple on a stick.—*adj.* toff′ee-nose(d) (*slang*), supercilious, conceited. [Ety. unknown.]

tofore, *tōō-, tə-för′, -för′, adv.* (*Shak.*), *prep., conj.* (*obs.*) before. [O.E. *tōforan* (prep.).]

toft, *toft, n.* a homestead (*arch.*): a hillock (*dial.*). [Late O.E. *toft*—O.N. *topt, tupt, toft.*]

tog, *tog,* (*slang*) *n.* a garment—generally in *pl.*—*v.t.* to dress.—*n.* togg′ery, clothes.—long′-togs (*naut.*), shore clothes; tog up, to dress in one's best. [Prob. ultimately L. *toga,* a robe.]

toga, *tō′gə, n.* the mantle or outer garment of a Roman citizen.—Also toge (*tōg; Shak. conjectured*).—*adjs.* to′ga'd, to′gaed, to′gate, -d, toged (*tōgd; Shak.*).—toga praetexta (*prē-, pri-, teks′tə, -ta*), a toga with a deep border of purple, worn by children, magistrates, etc.; toga virilis (*vir-, wir-il′is*), the garb of manhood. [L. *tōga;* cf. *tegēre,* to cover; thatch.]

together, *tə-, tōō-gedh′ər, adv.* in or to the same place: at the same time: in or into connection, company, or concert.—*n.* togetherness, unity: closeness: sense of unity or community with other people. [O.E. *tōgædere—tō,* to, *geador,* together.]

toggle, *tog′l, n.* a cross-piece on a rope, chain, rod, etc., to prevent slipping through a hole, or to allow twisting: an appliance for transmitting force at right angles to its direction.—*v.t.* to hold or furnish with a toggle: to fix fast.—togg′le-iron, a harpoon with a toggle instead of barbs; togg′le-joint, an elbow or knee joint: a mechanism consisting of two levers hinged together, force applied to straighten the hinge producing a considerable force along the levers; togg′le-switch, in telecommunications and electronics, a switch which, in a circuit having two stable or quasi-stable states, produces a transition from one to the other. [App. conn. with tug and tow.]

togue, *tōg, n.* the Great Lake char (or trout), a gigantic salmonid of North America. [From Indian name.]

toheroa, *tō-ə-rō′ə, n.* an edible shellfish found at low tide buried in sandy beaches. [Maori.]

toho, *tō-hō′, interj.* a call to pointers to stop.

tohu bohu, *tō′hōō bō′hōō, n.* chaos. [Heb. *thōhū wa-bhōhū,* emptiness and desolation (Gen. i. 2).]

toil, *toil, v.i.* to struggle hard: to labour hard: to make one's way by strong effort.—*v.t.* to effect or work out with toil: to subject to toil (*arch.* or *dial.*).—*n.* contention (*obs.*): a struggle: hard labour.—*adj.* toiled.—*n.* toil′er.—*adj.* toil′ful.—*n.* and *adj.* toil′ing.—*adjs.* toil′less; toil′some, involving toil: toiling: owing to toil (*Spens.* toylsom, toylesome).—*adv.* toil′somely.—*n.* toil′someness.—*adj.* toil′-worn, worn with toil. [A.Fr. *toiler* (Fr. *touillier*), said to be—L. *tudiculāre,* to stir.]

toil, *toil, n.* a net: a snare.—*ns.* toile (*twäl*), a dress material; toilet (*toil′it*), a cloth for the shoulder during hair-dressing (*arch.*): a toilet-cover: a toilet-table: a dressing-table with a mirror: the articles used in dressing: mode or process of dressing: a reception of visitors during dressing (*arch.*): the whole dress and appearance of a person, any particular costume: a dressing-room, bathroom, or lavatory: the cleansing and dressing of a wound.—*adj.* toil′eted, dressed.—*ns.* toil′etry, any article or preparation used in washing and dressing oneself:—*pl.* toil′etries; toilette (*twä-let′*), toilet; toilinet′ (*toi-*), toilinette (*twäl-i-net′*), a kind of woollen cloth used for waistcoats: silk and cotton warp with woollen weft.—toil′et-cloth, -cover, a dressing-table cover; toil′et-glass, a mirror set on the dressing-table; toil′et-paper, paper for the lavatory;

**toilet-roll**, a roll of toilet-paper; **toil′et-service, -set**, the utensils collectively used in dressing; **toil′et-soap**, soap for personal use; **toil′et-table**, a dressing-table. [Fr. *toile*, dim. *toilette*—L. *tēla*, web.]

**toise**, *toiz*, *n.* an old French lineal measure = 6·395 feet (very nearly 2 metres). [Fr.,—L. *tendēre*, *tēnsum*, to stretch.]

**toisech**, *tō′shehh*, (*hist.*) *n.* an ancient Celtic noble below a mormaor. [Gael. *tòisech*.]

**toison**, *twä-zɔ̃*, (Γr.) a fleece —**toison d′or** (*dor*), the golden fleece.

**to kalon**, *to ka′lon*, (Gr.) the beautiful.

**Tokay**, *tō-kā′*, *n.* a sweetish and heavy wine with an aromatic flavour, produced at *Tokay* (*Hung.* Tokaj, *tō′koi*) in Hungary: the grape that yields it.

**token**, *tō′kn*, *n.* a sign: a symbol: a portent: an indication: an evidence: a plague-spot (*obs.*): an authenticating sign, word, or object: a keepsake: a coin or voucher, issued privately, redeemable in current money or goods (as *gift*, *record*, *token*): in Presbyterian churches a metal voucher admitting to communion (superseded by the communion card): a measure of handpress work, usu. 250 pulls.—*adj.* serving as a symbol: hence, being a mere show or semblance, as *token force*, *token resistance*.—*v.t.* to betoken. —*adj.* **to′ken′d** (*Shak.*), indicated by plaguespots.—**to′ken-money**, money current for more than its intrinsic value as metal: private tokens. —**by the same token**, further in corroboration, or merely by the way; **more by token** (see **more**); **the Lord′s tokens** (*Shak.*), plague-spots. [O.E. *tācen*; Ger. *zeichen*, a mark.]

**toko, tokology.** See **toco, tocology.**

**tola**, *tō′lə*, *n.* an Indian unit of weight = 180 grains troy (11·66 grammes). [Hind.,—Sans. *tulā*, weight.]

**tolbooth.** See **toll.**

**tolbutamide**, *tol-būt′əm-īd*, *n.* a drug taken by mouth in the treatment of diabetes.

**told**, *tōld*, *pa.t.* and *pa.p.* of **tell.**

**tole, toll**, *tōl*, *v.t.* (now *U.S.* and *dial.*) to lure, decoy.—*ns.* **tol′ing, toll′ing** (*U.S.*), the use of tollbait: a method of decoying ducks, etc., by exciting curiosity.—**toll′-bait** (*U.S.*), chopped bait thrown to attract fish. [M.E. *tollen*—root of O.E. (*for*)*tyllan*; see **till** (1).]

**Toledo**, *tō-lē′dō*, *n.* a sword-blade made at *Toledo* (-*lā′*) in Spain.

**tolerate**, *tol′ə-rāt*, *v.t.* to endure: to endure with patience or impunity: to allow, allow to exist.— —*n.* **tolerabil′ity.**—*adj.* **tol′erable**, endurable: passable: fair.—*adv.* **tol′erably.**—*n.* **tol′erance**, ability to endure: disposition or willingness to tolerate or allow: permissible range of variation. —*adj.* **tol′erant**, tolerating: enduring: capable of enduring (e.g. unfavourable conditions, a parasite, a drug) without showing serious effects (*biol.* and *med.*): indulgent: favouring toleration.—*adv.* **tol′erantly.**—*ns.* **tolerā′tion**, act of tolerating: allowance of what is not approved: liberty given to a minority to hold and express their own political or religious opinions; **tolerā′tionist; tol′erator.**—**tolerance dose**, the maximum dose which can be permitted to a specific tissue during radiotherapy involving irradiation of any other adjacent tissue. [L. *tolerāre*, -*ātum*—*tollēre*, to lift up.]

**toll**, *tōl*, *n.* a tax for the liberty of using a bridge or road, selling goods in a market, etc.: a portion of grain kept by a miller in payment for grinding: a place where there is or was or might have been a toll-bar, a road junction (*Scot.*): the cost in damage, injury, or lives (as *toll of the road*): a toll-call.—*v.i.* to take or pay toll.—*v.t.* to take toll of: to take as toll.—*adj.* **toll′able**, subject to toll.—*ns.* **toll′age**, payment of toll: the amount paid as toll; **toll′er**, a toll-gatherer.—**tolbooth**

**tollbooth** (*tōl′* or *tol′booth*, -*boodh*; *Scot.* -*bəth*), an office where tolls are collected: a town-hall: a prison: often a combination of these; **toll′-bar**, a movable bar across a road, etc., to stop passengers liable to toll; **toll′bridge, -gate**, bridge, gate, where toll is taken; **toll′-call**, shortdistance telephone trunk-call: trunk call (*U.S.*, etc.); **toll′dish**, dish for measuring the toll in mills; **toll′-gath′erer.**—*adj.* and *adv.* **toll′-free′.** —**toll′-house**; **toll′man**, the man who collects toll: a toll-gatherer; **tolsel** (*tōl′sel*), **tolzey** (-*zi*), **tolsey** (*tol′si*), local names (app.—O.E. *seld*, seat, or *sæl*, hall) for a tolbooth or exchange.—**take toll of**, to inflict loss, hardship, pain, etc., on. [O.E. *toll*; cf. Du. *tol*, Ger. *zoll*; supposed to be from L.L. *tolōneum*—Gr. *telōnion*, customs—*telos*, fulfilment, tax, etc.; by some connected with **tell, tale**.]

**toll**, *tōl*, *v.i.* to sound, as a large bell, esp. with a measured sound.—*v.t.* to cause to sound, as a bell: to sound, strike, signal, announce, summon, send, by tolling: to toll for the death of.—*n.* the sound of a bell tolling.—*n.* **toll′er.** [Prob. **tole**.]

**toll**, *tōl*, (*law*) *v.t.* to bar: to take away right of. [A.Fr. *toller*—L. *tollēre*, to take away.]

**toll.** Same as **tole.**

**tol-lol**, *tol-lol′*, (*old slang*) *adj.* pretty good.—*adj.* **tol-lol′ish**, tolerable. [**tolerable**.]

**tolt**, *tōlt*, *n.* an old English writ removing a courtbaron cause to a county court. [A.Fr. *tolte*— L.L. *tolta*—L. *tollēre*, to take away.]

**tolter**, *tol′tər*, (*dial.*) *v.i.* to flounder about.

**Tolu**, *tō-lōō′*, *n.* (in full **balsam of Tolu**) a balsam yielded by the South American papilionaceous tree *Myroxylon toluifera.*—*ns.* **toluene** (*tol′ū-ēn*), **tol′uol**, methyl benzene.—*adj.* **tolū′ic.** [From Santiago de *Tolú*, in Colombia.]

**Tom**, *tom*, *n.* short for *Thomas*: (without *cap.*) a male, esp. a cat: (without *cap.*) a name for a big bell.—**Tom′-and-Jerr′y**, hot rum and eggs, spiced and sweetened; **tom′-cat**; **Tom′-nodd′y**, the puffin: a fool; **Tom′-trot**, a kind of toffee.— **Long Tom**, a long gun, esp. one carried amidships on a swivel-carriage; **Old Tom**, gin; **Tom and Tib, Tom, Dick, and Harry**, anybody: people in general; **Tom o′ Bedlam**, formerly, a madman let out with a licence to beg; **Tom Tidd′ler′s ground**, a place where wealth is to be had for the picking up: debatable land: no man′s land (from a children′s game so called).

**tomahawk**, *tom′ə-hök*, *n.* a North American Indian war-axe.—*v.t.* to assail or kill with a tomahawk: to hack, cut up, or slate. [Virginian Indian *tämähāk*.]

**tomalley**, *to-mal′i*, *n.* American lobster fat: extended to tamal. [Said to be Carib.]

**toman**, *tō-män′*, *n.* a myriad, or ten thousand: a former Persian gold coin worth 10,000 dinars. [Pers. *tumān*.]

**tomato**, *tə-mä′tō* (*U.S.* -*mā′*), *n.* the love-apple (*Lycopersicum esculentum* or *Solanum lycopersicum*), a South American plant close akin to the potato: its red or yellow pulpy edible fruit: *pl.* **toma′toes.**—**gooseberry tomato, strawberry tomato**, the Cape gooseberry. [Sp. *tomate*— Mex. *tomatl*.]

**tomb**, *tōōm*, *n.* a grave: a vault for disposal of dead bodies: a sepulchral monument.—*v.t.* to entomb: to bury.—*adjs.* **tombic** (*tōōm′ik*, -*bik*); **tomb′less**—**tomb′stone**, a memorial stone over a tomb. [O.Fr. (Fr.) *tombe*—L. *tumba*—Gr. *tymbos*.]

**tombac, tombak**, *tom′bak*, *n.* an alloy of copper with a little zinc: an alloy of copper and arsenic. [Fr. *tombac*—Malay *tambaga*, copper.]

**tomboc**, *tom′bok*, *n.* a Javanese long-handled weapon.

**tombola**, *tom′bō-lə*, *n.* a kind of lottery (at a fête, etc.): a type of bingo, played esp. in the Services. [It.,—*tombolare*, to tumble.]

*fāte, fär; mē, hûr* (her); *mīne; mōte, för; mūte, mōōn, fōōt; dhen* (then)

**tombolo**, *tom'bə-lō*, *n.* a bar of sand or gravel connecting an island with another or with the mainland. [It.]

**tomboy**, *tom'boi*, *n.* a high-spirited romping girl: formerly, a hoyden: an immodest woman (*Shak.*). [Tom and boy.]

**tome**, *tōm*, *n.* a big book or volume. [Fr.,—L. *tomus*—Gr. *tomos*—*temnein*, to cut.]

**tomentum**, *tō-men'təm*, *n.* a matted cottony pubescence.—*adjs.* **tomentose** (*tō-mən-tōs'*, *tō-men'-tōs*), **tomen'tous.** [L.]

**tomfool**, *tom'fōōl'*, *n.* a great fool: a buffoon: a trifling fellow.—*adj.* extremely foolish.—*v.i.* to play the fool.—*n.* **tomfool'ery,** foolish trifling or jesting: buffoonery.—*adj.* **tom'foolish.** [Tom.]

**tomium**, *tō'mi-əm*, *n.* the cutting edge of a bird's bill.—*adj.* **tō'mial.** [Latinised from Gr. *tomeion*, a knife-edge—*temnein*, to cut.]

**tommy**, *tom'i*, *n.* a penny roll, bread: food: a tommy-shop: the truck system: (sometimes *cap.*) a private in the British army.—*v.t.* to oppress by the truck system.—**Tommy Atkins,** a generic name for the private in the British army; **tomm'y-bar,** a rod for turning a tubular spanner or the like; **tomm'y-gun,** a light machine-gun (after its American inventor, General J. T. *Thompson*); **tomm'y-rot,** absolute nonsense; **tomm'y-shop,** a truck-shop.—**soft tommy,** soft bread, as opposed to hardtack or sea-biscuit. [From the name Thomas.]

**tomography**, *tō-mog'rə-fi*, *n.* radiography of a layer in the body by moving the X-ray tube and photoplate in such a way that only the chosen plane appears in clear detail.—*ns.* **tom'ogram,** a radiogram produced by tomography; **tom'o-graph,** a machine for making tomograms.—*adj.* **tomograph'ic.** [Gr. *tomos,* slice, *graphein,* to draw.]

**tomorrow, to-morrow,** *tə-, tōō-mor'ō, n.* the day after today.—*adv.* on the day after today. [O.E. *tō morgen.*]

**tompion, tompon.** Same as **tampion** (see tamp).

**tompion,** *tom'pi-ən,* (*obs.*) *n.* a watch of the kind made by Thomas *Tompion* (1639-1713).

**tomtit,** *tom'tit',* *n.* the blue or other tit. [Tom, tit (3).]

**tom-tom,** *tom'-tom,* *n.* an Indian drum: any primitive drum or substitute: (esp. formerly) a Chinese gong, tam-tam.—*v.i.* to beat thereon.— Also (esp. formerly) **tam'-tam, tum'-tum.**

**-tomy, -tə-mi,** in composition used to denote surgical incision into an organ. [Gr. adj. *tomos,* cutting, sharp.]

**ton,** *tun,* *n.* a measure of capacity, varying with the substance measured—timber, wheat, etc. (see **tonnage**): a weight =20 cwt. =2240 lb. (2400 lb. was formerly a *long ton*): in U.S. usually = 2000 lb. (*short*), or 2240 lb. (*long*): 100 units of various kinds, e.g. 100 cu. ft in measuring the internal capacity of a ship: £100 (*coll.*): 100 runs (*cricket*; *coll.*): 100 m.p.h. (preceded by *a* or *the*; *slang*): great weight (*coll.*): (in *pl.*) many, a great amount (*coll.*).—*adj.* **ton-up,** orig. of a motor-cyclist, having done a ton: noisy and reckless: travelling at 100 m.p.h.—**metric ton** (see **tonne**). [O.E. *tunne,* a vat, tub; see **tun.**]

**ton,** *tɔ̄,* *n.* fashion: people of fashion.—*adj.* **ton(n)ish** (*ton'ish*), modish, having ton.—*adv.* **ton(n)'ishly.**—*n.* **ton(n)'ishness.** [Fr.]

**tonalite,** *tō'nə-lit,* *n.* a quartz-biotite diorite, found at Monte *Tonale,* Tirol.

**to-name,** *tōō'-nām,* *n.* a byname, nickname: an additional name used to distinguish persons whose names are alike. [O.E. *tōnama*—pfx. *tō-,* meaning in addition to, *nama,* name.]

**tonant,** *tōn'ənt,* *adj.* thundering. [L. *tonāns, -antis,* pr.p. of *tonāre,* to thunder.]

**tondo,** *ton'dō,* *n.* a circular painting or circular carving in relief. [It.]

**tone,** *tōn,* *n.* the character of a sound: quality of

sound: accent: intonation: vocal inflexion, rise or fall in pitch: a sound of definite pitch: a major second, one of the larger intervals between successive notes in the scale, as C and D: a Gregorian psalm-tune: vocal expression: bodily firmness, elasticity, or tension, esp. in muscles: prevailing character or spirit: mood: temper: harmony or general effect of colours: depth or brilliance of colour: a tint or shade.—*v.t.* to intone: to give tone or the desired tone to.—*v.i.* to take a tone: to harmonise (with *in*).—*adjs.* **tōn'al,** of tone: according to key; **tōnal'itive,** of tonality.—*n.* **tōnal'ity,** relation in key: key: rendering of colour relations.—*adjs.* **toned,** having a tone (in compounds): braced up: treated to give tone: slightly tinted; **tone'-less,** soundless: expressionless: dull: relaxed: listless. — *adv.* **tone'lessly.** — *ns.* **tone'lessness;** **toneme,** in a tone language, a phoneme consisting of a particular intonation.—*adjs.* **tonem'ic;** **tonic** (*ton'ik*), relating to tones: producing tension: giving tone and vigour to the system (*med.*): giving or increasing strength.—*n.* a tonic medicine: a keynote (*mus.*): tonic water. —*ns.* **tonicity** (*ton-is'i-ti*), the property or condition of having tone: mode of reaction to stimulus: the healthy state of muscular fibres when at rest; **tōn'us,** tone: tonic spasm.—*adj.* **tōn'(e)y** (*slang*), high-toned: fashionable.—**tonal fugue,** one in which the answer conforms to the tonality of the scale; **tone'-arm,** orig. that part of a gramophone connecting sound-box to horn: the arm that carries an electric pick-up; **tone control,** a manual control in a radio set which adjusts the relative amplitude of high, medium, and low frequencies to obtain clearer reception. —*adj.* **tone'-deaf,** unable to appreciate musical pitch.—**tone language,** a language (e.g. Chinese) in which difference of intonation distinguishes words of different meaning that would otherwise sound the same; **tone picture,** a piece of descriptive music; **tone poem,** a piece of programme music, not divided into movements, conveying or translating a poetic idea or literary theme; **tone row,** in serial music, the basic set of notes in the chosen order; **tonic sol-fa** (*mus.*), a system of notation and teaching devised by Sarah Glover (1785-1867) and developed by John Curwen, using sol-fa syllables (modified) and their initial letters for the notes of the scale with *doh* (*do*) for the tonic, and dividing the bar by colons, dots, and inverted commas; **tonic spasm,** prolonged uniform muscular spasm (opp. to *clonic spasm;* see **clonus**); **tonic water,** aerated quinine water. —**tone down,** to give a lower tone to: to moderate: to soften, to harmonise the colours of as to light and shade, as a painting; **tone up,** to heighten: to intensify. [Gr. *tonos,* pitch, tension, partly through Fr. *ton* and L. *tonus.*]

**tone,** *tōn,* (*obs.* or *dial.*) *pron.* and *adj.* the one.— *Scot.* **tane** (*pron.*), **tae** (*adj.*). [that one; cf. **tother.**]

**tong,** *tong,* *n.* a Chinese guild, association, or secret society. [Chin. *t'ang.*]

**tonga,** *tong'gə,* *n.* a light two-wheeled Indian vehicle. [Hindi *tāṅgā.*]

**tonga,** *tong'gə, n.* a Fijian toothache remedy made from an aroid root (Epipremnum). [Arbitrary invention.]

**tonga-bean.** See **tonka-bean.**

**tongs,** *tongz, n.pl.* a gripping and lifting instrument, consisting of two legs joined by a pivot, hinge, or spring. [O.E. *tang, tange;* O.N. *töng,* Ger. *zange.*]

**tongue,** *tung, n.* the fleshy organ in the mouth, used in tasting, swallowing, and speech: the tongue of an ox, etc., as food: the rasping organ in molluscs: power of speech: manner of speaking: speech: discourse: voice: utterance: a vote (*Shak.*): a language: anything like a tongue in shape: the catch of a buckle: the pointer of a balance: a point of land: a bell clapper: the reed of a musical instrument: a flap in the opening of a shoe or boot: any narrow projection.—*v.i.* to utter: to pronounce (*dial.*): to articulate: to assail with words (*Shak.*): to lick: to touch with the tongue: to furnish with a tongue: to talk, prate (with *it*): to produce or play by tonguing (*mus.*).—*v.i.* to give tongue: to stick out: to practise tonguing (*mus.*).—*adjs.* **tongued**, having a tongue; **tongue'less**, having no tongue: unspoken of (*Shak.*).—*ns.* **tongue'let**, a little tongue; **tongue'ster**, a babbler; **tongu'ing**, articulation to separate the notes in playing wind instruments.—*adj.* **tongue-doubt'ie** (i.e. **doughty**; *Milt.*), bragging.—*adj.* and *adv.* **tongue-in-cheek**, ironical(ly) or whimsical(ly), not sincere(ly) or serious(ly).—*adjs.* **tongue'-tacked**, **-tied**, impeded by a short fraenum: unable to speak out.—**tongue'-twister**, a formula or sequence of words difficult to pronounce without blundering; **tongue'-work**, babble, chatter.—**give tongue**, to give utterance: to give voice as hounds on a scent; **hold one's tongue** (see **hold**); **lose one's tongue**, to become speechless from emotion; **on the tip of one's tongue** (see **tip** (1)); **with (one's) tongue in (one's) cheek**, tongue-in-cheek (*adv.*). [O.E. *tunge*; O.N. *tunga*, Ger. *zunge*, the tongue; L. *lingua* (from *dingua*).]

**tonic, tonicity**. See **tone** (1).

**tonight, to-night**, *tə-*, *tōō-nit'*, *n.* this night: the night of the present day.—*adv.* on this night or the night of today: last night (*obs.*; *Shak.*). [O.E. *tō niht.*]

**tonish**. See **ton** (2).

**tonite**, *tō'nīt*, *n.* a blasting explosive made from guncotton and barium nitrate. [L. *tonāre*, to thunder.]

**tonka-bean**, *tong'kə-bēn'*, *n.* the coumarin-scented seed of a large papilionaceous tree (Dipteryx) of Guiana, used for flavouring snuff, etc.—Also **tonga-** (*tong'gə-*), **tonquin-** (*tong'kēn-*) **bean**. [Said to be the Guiana Negroes' name.]

**tonnag**, *tō'nag*, *n.* a shawl with a shaped neck and side fastening. [Gael.]

**tonnage**, *tun'ij*, *n.* a tax of so much a *tun* on imported wines (sometimes **tunnage**; *hist.*): a charge or payment by the *ton*: carrying capacity of a ship in *tons* (orig. in *tuns* of wine); *register ton* =100 cu. feet, *freight ton* =40 cu. feet, of space for cargo; total amount of shipping so measured: a duty on ships, estimated in tons.—**gross tonnage**, the total space capable of carrying cargo in a ship, measured in register tons; **net register tonnage**, gross tonnage less deducted spaces (those spaces required in running the ship). [See **ton, tun.**]

**tonne, tun** (Fr. pron. *ton*), *n.* preferred name for **metric ton**, equal to 1000 kilograms (0·984 ton). [Fr.]

**tonneau**, *ton'ō*, *n.* the rear part of a motor-car body, orig. opening at the back: tonne. [Fr., cask, tun.]

**tonnell**, obs. form of **tunnel**.

**tonometer**, *tōn-om'ə-tər*, *n.* a device for determining the frequencies of tones (*mus.*): an instrument for measuring fluid pressure within the eyeball, or blood pressure: an instrument for measuring vapour pressure. [Gr. *tonos*, pitch, tension, *metron*, measure.]

**tonquin-bean**. See **tonka-bean**.

**tonsil**, *ton'sl*, *-sil*, *n.* either of two glands at the root of the tongue.—*adj.* **ton'sillar**.—*n.* **tonsillec'-tomy**, surgical removal of a tonsil.—*adj.* **tonsil-lit'ic**.—*ns.* **tonsilli'tis**, inflammation of the tonsils; **tonsillot'omy**, complete or partial removal of a tonsil.—Also **tonsilitis**, etc. [L. *tōnsillae* (pl.).]

**tonsor**, *ton'sər*, *n.* a barber.—*adj.* **tonso'rial**.—*n.* **ton'sure** (*-shər*), act or mode of clipping the hair,

or of shaving the head: in the R.C. and Eastern Churches, the shaving or cutting of part of the hair of the head on entering the priesthood or a monastic order: the shaven part.—*adj.* **ton'-sured**, having the crown of the head shaven as a priest: shaven: bald: clipped. [L. *tōnsor*, barber, *tōnsūra*, a shearing—*tondēre*, *tōnsum*, to clip.]

**tontine**, *ton'tēn*, *ton-tēn'*, *n.* a scheme of life annuity, increasing as the subscribers die.—Also *adj.*—*n.* **tontin'er**. [From Lorenzo *Tonti*, a Neapolitan, its inventor (1653).]

**tonus, tony**. See **tone** (1).

**Tony**, *tō'ni*, (*U.S.*) *n.* award for meritorious work in theatre. [After U.S. actress *Antoinette* Perry.]

**tony**, *tō'ni*, (*obs. slang*) *n.* a simpleton. [**Antony**.]

**too**, *tōō*, *adv.* as well, in addition, also, likewise (never at the beginning of a sentence in English usage): undesirably in excess: so much as to be incompatible with a condition: in affectation, extremely.—**too'-too, too too**, exquisite: extravagantly and affectedly sentimental, gushing.—*adv.* all too: quite too. [Stressed form of **to**.]

**tooart**. Same as **tuart**.

**took**, *tōōk*, *pa.t.* and obsolete *pa.p.* of **take**.

**tool**, *tōōl*, *n.* a working instrument, esp. one used by hand: a weapon: a penis (*Shak.*): one who is used as the mere instrument of another.—*v.t.* to shape or finish with a tool: to mark with a tool, esp. to ornament or imprint designs upon (a book cover), or to chisel the face of (stone): to supply with tools, esp. with machine tools for a particular purpose (also **tool up**): to drive (a coach or other vehicle; *slang*): to carry or draw in a vehicle.—*v.i.* to work with a tool: to provide tools (also **tool up**): to travel (along) in a vehicle, esp. smoothly and skilfully, and usu. at moderate speed: of vehicle, draught animal, to travel (along, etc.).—*n.* **tool'ing**, workmanship done with a tool.—**tool'house**, a shed or outhouse for keeping tools in; **tool'-shed**. [O.E. *tōl*.]

**toom**, *tōōm*, *tüm*, *tim* (now only Scots), *adj.* empty.—*n.* rubbish tip.—*v.t.* to empty. [O.E. *tōm*, clear.]

**toon**, *tōōn*, *n.* Indian tree of the mahogany family, with red wood and astringent bark. [Hind. *tūn*.]

**toorie**, *tōōr'i*, (*Scot.*) *n.* small heap: knob of hair: tuft on a bonnet. [Dim. of *toor*, Scots for **tower**.]

**toot**, *tōōt*, *v.i.* to pry, peer, peep about (*Spens.*): to be prominent (*obs.*).—*n.* a look-out place (*obs.*): a watch-hill (*S.W. England*).—*n.* **toot'er**. [O.E. *tōtian*, to stick out, peep out.]

**toot, tout**, *tōōt*, *v.i.* to make short sounds, as on a flute or horn.—*v.t.* to blow, as a horn, etc.—*n.* a blast as of a horn.—*n.* **toot'er**, one who toots, or his instrument. [Prob. imit.]

**tooth**, *tōōth*, *n.* one of the hard bodies in the mouth, used for biting and chewing: a hard projection of similar use in invertebrates: taste or relish: a tooth-like projection, prong, cog, jag, as on a leaf-margin, comb, saw, or wheel:—*pl.* **teeth**, *tēth*, *q.v.*—*v.t.* to furnish with teeth: to cut into teeth.—*adjs.* **toothed** (*tōōtht*, also *tōōdhd*), having teeth: dentate; **tooth'ful**, full of teeth: toothsome.—*n.* a small drink of spirits, etc.—*adjs.* **tooth'less**; **tooth'some**, palatable.—*n.* **tooth'someness**.—*adj.* **tooth'y**, with prominent teeth: toothsome: biting (*Scot.*).—**tooth'ache**, an ache or pain in a tooth; **tooth'ache-tree**, the prickly ash (Xanthoxylum); **tooth'brush**, a brush for cleaning the teeth; **toothbrush moustache**, a small stiff moustache; **tooth'comb**, a comb with fine teeth placed close together; **tooth'-drawer** (*Shak.*), an extractor of teeth.—*n.* and *adj.* **tooth'-drawing**.—**tooth'-or'nament**, dog-tooth; **tooth'-paste, -pow'der**, a paste, powder, used with a toothbrush; **tooth'-pick**, an instrument for picking shreds of food from between the teeth: a Bowie knife (*U.S. slang*); **tooth'-picker** (*Shak.*), a toothpick: one who picks teeth, as the bird trochilus; **tooth'-shell**, Dentalium; **tooth'wash**, a liquid preparation for cleansing the teeth; **tooth'wort**, a pale fleshy plant (*Lathraea squamaria*) of the broomrape family, parasitic on tree-roots, with tooth-like scale-leaves: the cruciferous coral-root (*Cardamine*, or *Dentaria*, *bulbifera*).—**a colt's tooth**, addiction to youthful pleasures; **armed to the teeth**, armed as completely as possible, from top to toe; **a sweet tooth**, a taste for sweet things; **by the skin of one's teeth** (see **skin**); **cast**, **throw**, **in one's teeth**, to fling at one as a taunt or reproach; **in one's teeth**, to one's face: in direct affront; **in spite of one's teeth**, **in the teeth of**, in direct opposition to; **long in the tooth**, elderly, like a horse whose gums are receding; **set one's teeth on edge** (see **edge**); **take the teeth out of**, to render harmless or powerless; **tooth and nail**, with all possible vigour and fury. [O.E. *tōth* (pl. *tēth*); Goth. *tunthus*, L. *dēns*, *dentis*, Gr. *odous*, *odontos*, Sans. *danta*.]

**tootle**, *tōōt'l*, *v.i.* to make feeble sounds, as on the flute. [Freq. of **toot**.]

**top**, *top*, *n.* the highest part or place: the upper end or surface: a topsail: a top-boot (esp. in *pl.*): a trench parapet: a small platform at the head of the lower mast: a crest or tuft (*naut.*): a handful or bundle of flax, wool, etc., for spinning: the earliest part (as *top of the morning*—a conventional Irishman's greeting): a circus tent (*slang*; **the big top**, the main tent).—*adj.* highest.—*v.t.* to cover on the top: to tip: to rise above: to surpass: to rise to the top of: to surmount: to be on or at the top of: to cover, as a male animal (*Shak.*): to take off the top of: to hit on the upper half (*golf*).—*v.i.* to finish up, round off (with *off* or *up*):—*pr.p.* **topp'ing**; *pa.t.* and *pa.p.* **topped.**—*adjs.* **top'full** (*Shak.*), full to the top or brim; **top'less**, without a top: (of female garb) leaving breasts uncovered: without superior (*Shak.*); **top'most** (*-mōst*, *-məst*), uppermost: highest; **topped.** —*ns.* **topp'er**, one who, or that which, tops in any sense: one who excels (*slang*): a top hat (*coll.*); **topp'ing**, the act of one who tops, that which tops: (*pl.*) pieces cut from the top.—*adj.* surpassing, pre-eminent: arrogant (*U.S.*).—*adv.* **topp'ingly.** —**top'-boot**, a long-legged boot with a showy band of leather round the top.—*adj.* **top'-booted**, wearing top-boots.—**top brass** (see **brass**); **top'-coat**, an overcoat; **top dog**, the winner or dominant person; **top drawer**, the highest level, esp. of society (*out of the top drawer*, belonging to this social rank).—*adj.* **top'-draw'er.**—*v.t.* **top'dress.** —**top'-dress'ing**, surface dressing of manure: the application of it: any superficial covering or treatment (*fig.*).—*adj.* **top-gallant** (*tə-*, *top-gal'ənt*), above the topmast and topsail and below the royal-mast.—**top'-hamp'er**, unnecessary weight on a ship's upper-deck; **top'-hat**, tall cylindrical hat of silk plush.—*adj.* upper class: designed to benefit high executives, or the rich, as *top-hat budget*, *top-hat* (*insurance*) *policy*.—*adjs.* **top'-heav'y**, having the upper part too heavy for the lower: tipsy; **top'-hole** (*slang*), tiptop.—**top'-knot**, a crest, tuft of hair, often a piece of added hair, or knot of ribbons, etc., on the top of the head: the head (*slang*): a small fish (of several species) akin to the turbot.—*adjs.* **top'-knotted**; **top'-level**, at the highest level; **top'-line**, important enough to be mentioned in a headline. —**top-lin'er**, one who is top-line: a principal performer, star.—*adjs.* **top'loftical**, **top'lofty** (*facet.*), high and mighty: stuck-up.—**top'loftiness**; **top'man**, a man stationed in one of the tops: a top-sawyer; **top'mast** (*-mast*, *-mäst*), the second mast, or that immediately above the

lower mast.—*adj.* **top'-notch'** (*slang*), topping.—**topp'ing-out.**—*adjs.* **top'-priority**, very urgent **top'-proud** (*Shak.*), proud in the highest degree. —**top'sail** (*-sl*, *-säl*), a sail across the topmast; **top'-saw'yer**, the upper sawyer in a sawpit: a superior, a person of importance (*coll.*); **top secret**, a profound secret of the highest importance; **top'side**, the upper part: (also in *pl.*) the part of the outer surface of a vessel above the water-line.—Also *adv.*—**tops'man**, a head-drover, a foreman (*Scot.*): a hangman (*slang*); **top'-soil**, the upper part or surface of the soil; **top'-soil'ing**, removal of the top-soil; **top'-stone**, a stone placed on the top, or forming the top; **top table**, the place assigned for those rated of chief importance at a meeting or banquet.—**at the top of one's voice**, at one's loudest; **go over the top**, to go over the front of a trench and attack the enemy: to take sudden action after hesitation; **(in the) top flight** (see **flight**); **on top of the world**, near the North Pole: on a high mountain: revelling in existence; **(the) tops** (*slang*), the very best; **top one's part**, to surpass oneself in playing it; **top out**, to finish (a building) by putting on the top or highest course; **top up**, to fill up, e.g. with fuel oil, alcoholic beverage. [O.E. *top*; Ger. *zopf*.]

**top**, *top*, *n.* a spinning toy: a grooved cone held back between the strands in rope-making: a marine gasteropod of the genus Trochus, with pearly flattish-based conical shell.—**top'-shell.** —**sleep like a top**, to sleep very soundly. [App. late O.E. *top* (but the meaning is doubtful).]

**toparch**, *top'ärk*, *n.* the ruler of a district.—*n.* **top'archy**, a toparch's territory. [Gr. *toparchēs* —*topos*, a place, *archein*, to rule.]

**topaz**, *tō'paz*, *n.* a precious stone, fluoriferous silicate of aluminium, yellow, bluish, colourless, etc.—*adj.* **tō'pazine.**—*n.* **topaz'olite**, a yellow garnet.—**Oriental topaz**, a yellow corundum. [Gr. *topazos*, a green gem.]

**tope**, *tōp*, *v.i.* to drink hard.—*interj.* (*obs.*) used in pledging a health.—*n.* **tō'per**, a drunkard. [Poss. Fr. *toper*, to accept a wager.]

**tope**, *tōp*, *n.* a Buddhist stupa or dome for relics. [Hindi *top*—Sans. *stūpa*, a heap.]

**tope**, *tōp*, *n.* a small species of shark. [Said to be Cornish.]

**topectomy**, *top-ek'tə-mi*, *n.* excision of a part of the cerebral cortex as treatment for certain mental illnesses. [Gr. *topos*, place, *ek*, from, *tomē*, a cut.]

**topek.** Same as **tupik.**

**Tophet**, *tō'fet*, *n.* an ancient place of human sacrifice near Jerusalem, the valley of Hinnom or part of it, later a place of refuse disposal: hence Hell. [Heb. *tōpheth*.]

**tophus**, *tō'fəs*, *n.* a gouty deposit:—*pl.* **tō'phi** (*-fī*). —*adj.* **tophā'ceous.** [L. *tōphus*, *tōfus*, porous stone, tufa.]

**topi**, **topee**, *tō-pē'*, *tō'pē*, (*India*) *n.* a hat, esp. a sola hat, pith-helmet.—**topi-wallah** (*-wo'lə*), a European in India. [Hindi *topī*, hat (perh. from Port. *topo*, top).]

**topiary**, *tō'pi-ə-ri*, *n.* mural decoration in fanciful landscape: a branch of gardening, the clipping of trees into imitative and fantastic shapes.—Also *adj.*—*adj.* **topiā'rian.**—*n.* **to'piarist.** [L. *topiārius*—*topia* (pl.), landscape, landscape gardening—Gr. *topos*, a place.]

**topic**, *top'ik*, *n.* a head under which a rhetorician might look up matter for discourse: a general consideration suitable for argument: a subject of discourse or argument: a matter.—*adj.* **top'ical**, local: relating to a topic or subject: relating to matters of interest of the day.—*n.* **topical'ity**, the quality of being topical: an item or matter possessing that quality.—*adv.* **top'ically.** [Gr. *topikos*, pertaining to place or to commonplaces, *ta topika*, the general principles of argument—*topos*, a place.]

to-pinch, a false emendation of some Shakespeare editors (*Merry Wives* IV, iv. 59), for *to pinch*, the second of two infinitives having *to* where the first is without *to*.

topography, *top-og'rə-fi*, n. detailed study, description, or features of a limited area.—*n.* topog'rapher.—*adjs.* topographic (*top-ə-graf'ik*), -al. —*adv.* topograph'ically. [Gr. *topographiā*— *topos*, a place, *graphein*, to describe.]

topology, *top-ol'ə-ji*, n. topographical study of a particular place: topographical anatomy: a branch of geometry concerned with those properties of a figure which remain unchanged even when the figure is bent, stretched, etc.: the study of limits in sets regarded as consisting of collections of points (*alg.*). [Gr. *topos*, a place, *logos*, a discourse.]

toponymy, *top-on'i-mi*, n. place-name study (also toponym'ics): nomenclature of regions of the body.—*adjs.* topon'ymal, toponymic (-ə-nim'ik), -al. [Gr. *topos*, place, *onyma* (*onoma*), name.]

topple, *top'l*, v.i. to overbalance and fall headlong: to threaten to fall from top-heaviness.—*v.t.* to cause to topple. [top (1).]

to prepon, *to pre'pon*, (Gr.) the fitting: the becoming or seemly.

topsyturvy, *top'si-tûr'vi*, also top'side-tur'v(e)y, *Scot.* tap'salteer'ie, *adv.* bottom upwards.—*adj.* turned upside down.—*n.* confusion.—*v.t.* to turn upside down.—*n.* topsyturvificā'tion, a turning upside down.—*adv.* topsytur'vily.—*ns.* topsytur'viness; topsytur'vydom. [top, and the obs. *terve*, to turn (cf. O.E. *tearflian*, to roll); so, set, and side are only conjectures.]

toque, *tōk*, n. a 16th-century form of cap or turban: a hair-pad (*obs.*): a woman's close-fitting brimless or nearly brimless hat: a macaque (*Macacus pileatus*) of Ceylon. [Fr.]

tor, torr, *tör*, n. a hill, a rocky height. [O.E. *torr*, tor—L. *turris*, tower, or perh. from Celtic.]

Torah, Thorah, *tō'*, *tō'rə*, n. the Mosaic law: the book of the law, the Pentateuch. [Heb. *Tōrāh*.]

toran(a), *tör'*, *tör'ən(-ə)*, n. in India, a type of arched gateway: also a garland of flowers or leaves hung between two points. [Hind.]

torbanite, *tör'ban-it*, n. a shale, almost a coal, once mined for oil at *Torbane* Hill, Bathgate, Scotland.

torbernite, *tör'bərn-it*, n. a bright green radioactive hydrous phosphate of copper and uranium. [After *Torbern* Bergmann (1735-84), Sw. chemist.]

torc. See torque.

torch, *törch*, n. a stick of inflammable material carried or stuck up to give light: a large candle: a portable electric lamp: a glowing flower or inflorescence, as of mullein: a tall cactaceous plant.—*v.t.* to light with torches.—*ns.* torch'er (*Shak.*), a light-giver; torchère (*tor-sher'*; Fr.), a tall ornamental candlestick or lampstand.— torch'-bear'er; torch'-dance; torch'light; torch'-lily, the hot poker (Kniphofia or Tritoma); torch'-race, a race in which the runners carried torches and passed them to others; torch'-singer; torch'-song, a popular song of the 1930s giving lugubrious expression to the pangs of unrequited love; torch'-staff (*pl.* torch'-staves, *Shak.*), a staff for carrying a torch; torch'-thistle, a Cereus.—carry the torch (for), to suffer unrequited love (for). [Fr. *torche*—L. *torquēre*, *tortum*, to twist.]

torchon, *tör-shō̃*, (Fr.) n. a duster or dish-cloth: (in full torchon lace) peasants' bobbin lace of loose texture and geometrical design, or a machine-made imitation: (torchon paper) a rough paper for water-colour drawing. [Fr.,— *torcher*, to wipe.]

torcular, *tör'kū-lər*, n. a tourniquet. [L. *torcular*, *-āris*, a wine-press, oil-press.]

tore, *tōr*, *tör*, *pa.t.* and obs. *pa.p.* of tear.

tore, toric. See torus.

toreador, *tor-i-ə-dōr'*, *-dör'*, n. (before the days of professional bullfighting) name used for a bullfighter, esp. on horseback.—*n.* torero (*tor-ā'rō*), a bullfighter on foot. [Sp.]

to-rend, *ta-*, *tōo-rend'*, (*obs.*) v.t. to rend in pieces: —*pa.p.* (*Spens.*) to-rent'.

toreutic, *tör-ū'tik*, *-ōō'*, *adj.* of chased or embossed metal-work.—*n.* (also in *pl.*, treated as *sing.*) artistic work in metal. [Gr. *toreutikos*, *-ē*, *-on*— *toreuein*, to bore.]

torgoch, *tör'gohh*, n. the red-bellied char. [W.]

toric. See torus.

torii, *tör'ē-ē*, n. a Japanese temple gateway. [Jap.]

torment, *tör'mənt*, n. torture: anguish: a source of distress.—*v.t.* torment (*-ment'*), to torture: to put to extreme pain: to distress: to afflict: to pester: to harass: to agitate, stir violently: to distort, force violently.—*adj.* tormen'ted.— *adv.* torment'edly.—*n.* tor'mentil, a fourpetalled Potentilla with an astringent woody root, growing on heaths.—*n.* and *adj.* torment'ing.—*adv.* tormen'tingly.—*ns.* tormen'tor, one who, or that which, torments: a torturer, an executioner (*B.*): a long meat-fork: a wing in the first groove of a stage; tormen'tum, a Roman machine for hurling missiles. [L. *tormentum*— *torquēre*, to twist.]

tormina, *tör'mi-nə*, *n.pl.* gripes.—*adjs.* tor'minal, tor'minous. [L.,—*torquēre*, to twist.]

torn, *törn*, *törn*, *adj.* and *pa.p.* of tear.—*adj.* torn'-down (*U.S.*), unruly.

tornado, *tör-nā'dō*, n. orig. a violent tropical Atlantic thunderstorm: a very violent whirling wind-storm affecting a narrow strip of country: loosely a hurricane:—*pl.* tornā'does.—*n.* (*poet.*) tornade'.—*adj.* tornadic (*-nad'ik*). [Prob. Sp. *tronada*, thunderstorm, altered as if from Sp. *tornada*, turning.]

toroid, -al. See under torus.

Torpedo, *tör-pē'dō*, n. a genus of cartilaginous fishes with organs on the head that give an electric shock, giving name to the family Torpedin'idae, related to the skates and rays: (without *cap.*) a self-propelled submarine weapon of offence (usually cigar-shaped), carrying an explosive charge which goes off when it hits a ship or other object: (without *cap.*) a bomb, cartridge, case of explosives, or detonator of various kinds, used in warfare, in boring, as a fog-signal, firework, etc.:—*pl.* torpē'does.—*v.t.* to attack, strike, destroy, by torpedo: to wreck (e.g. a plan).—*adj.* torped'inous, benumbing.— *ns.* torpe'doer; torpe'doist.—torpe'do-boat, a small swift warship discharging torpedoes; torpe'do-boom, a spar for carrying a torpedo, projecting from a boat or anchored in a channel; torpe'do-net, a net hung round a ship to intercept torpedoes; torpe'do-tube, a kind of gun from which torpedoes are discharged.—torpe'do-boat destroyer, a swifter, more powerful, type of torpedo-boat (orig. to destroy ordinary torpedoboats; also called destroyer). [L. *torpēdō*, *-inis*, numbness, the torpedo (fish)—*torpēre*, to be stiff.]

torpid, *tör'pid*, *adj.* numb: lethargic: having lost the power of motion and feeling: sluggish: dormant.—*n.* (*Oxford*) orig. a second boat of a college, or its crew: (in *pl.*) the Lent term races of eight-oared clinker-built boats.—*v.t.* tor'pefy, to benumb, paralyse.—*n.* torpesc'ence.—*adj.* torpesc'ent, becoming torpid.—*n.* torpid'ity.—*adv.* tor'pidly.—*ns.* tor'pidness; tor'pitude; tor'por, numbness: inactivity: dullness: stupidity. [L. *torpidus*, *torpefacēre*, *torpēscere*, *torpor*—*torpēre*, to be numb.]

torque, *törk*, n. the turning moment of a tangential force: a necklace in the form of a twisted band (also torc).—*adjs.* torquate, -d (*tör'kwāt*, *-id*), collared; **torqued** (*törkt*), twisted.—**torque-converter** (*mech.*), a device which acts as an infinitely variable gear; **torque'-meter**. [L. *torquēre*, to twist; *torquēs, -is*, a necklace; *torquātus*, wearing a *torquēs*.]

**torr.** See **tor.**

**torr, tör,** *n.* a unit used in expressing very low pressures, 1/760 of a standard atmosphere. [E. *Torricelli*; see **Torricellian.**]

**torrefy,** *tor'i-fī, v.t.* to scorch: to parch:—*pr.p.* **torr'efying;** *pa.t.* and *pa.p.* **torr'efied.**—*n.* **torrefac'tion.** [L. *torrēre*, to parch, roast, *facēre*, to make.]

**torrent,** *tor'ant, n.* a rushing stream: a variable mountain stream: an abounding, strong or turbulent flow.—*adj.* rushing in a stream.—*adj.* **torrential** (*-en'shl*).—*n.* **torrentiality** (*-en-shi-al'i-ti*).—*adv.* **torren'tially.**—*adj.* **torrent'uous.**—**torr'ent-bow,** a bow of prismatic colours formed by the spray of a torrent. [L. *torrēns, -entis*, boiling, pr.p. of *torrēre*, to dry.]

**torret,** *tor'it.* See **terret.**

**Torricellian,** *tor-i-chel'i-ən, adj.* pertaining to the Italian mathematician Evangelista *Torricelli* (1608-47), who discovered in 1643 the principle of the barometer.—**Torricellian tube,** the barometer; **Torricellian vacuum,** the vacuum in the barometer.

**torrid,** *tor'id, adj.* scorching or parching: violently hot: dried with heat.—*ns.* **torrid'ity, torr'idness.** —**torrid zone,** the belt round the earth between the tropics. [L. *torridus*—*torrēre*, to parch, roast.]

**Torridonian,** *tor-i-dō'ni-ən,* (geol.) *n.* and *adj.* Pre-Cambrian of the N.W. Highlands of Scotland, as around Loch *Torridon.*

**torse,** *törs, n.* a heraldic wreath.—*n.* **torsade',** an ornament like a twisted cord. [Fr.,—L. *torquēre*, to twist.]

**torsel,** *tör'sl, n.* a plate in a brick wall to support the end of a beam. Also **tassel.** [L. *taxillus*, a die, It. *tassello*, Fr. *tasseau.*]

**torsion,** *tör'shan, n.* twisting: a twist: the strain produced by twisting: the force with which a thread or wire tends to return when twisted: checking of haemorrhage by twisting the cut end of the artery (*surg.*).—*ns.* **torsibility** (*-si-bil'i-ti*); **tor'siograph,** an instrument for measuring and recording the frequency and amplitude of torsional vibrations in a shaft.—*adjs.* **tor'sional; tor'sive,** twisted spirally.—**tor'sion-bal'ance,** an instrument for measuring very minute forces by a horizontal needle suspended by a very fine filament. [L. *torsiō, -ōnis*—*torquēre, tortum*, to twist.]

**torsk,** *törsk, n.* a North Atlantic fish (*Brosmius brosme*) of the cod family, with long single dorsal fin. [Sw., Norw., Dan. *torsk*—O.N. *thorskr*; cf. Ger. *dorsch*, haddock.]

**torso,** *tör'sō, n.* the trunk of a statue or body, without head or limbs:—*pl.* **tor'sos.**—Also **torse** (Fr.). [It., stalk, core, torso—L. *thyrsus*—Gr. *thyrsos.*]

**tort,** *tört, n.* wrong, injury (*Spens.*): any wrong, not arising out of contract, for which there is a remedy by compensation or damages (*Eng. law*). —*adj.* **tortious** (*tör'shas*), wrongful: of the nature of a tort. [Fr.,—L.L. *tortum*—L. *torquēre, tortum*, to twist.]

**torticollis,** *tör-ti-kol'is,* (*path.*) *n.* wryneck. [L.L., —L. *tortus*, twisted, *collum*, neck.]

**tortile,** *tör'til, adj.* twisted: wreathed: coiled. —*n.* **tortility** (*-til'*).—*adj.* **tor'tive** (*Shak.*), turned awry. [L. *tortilis, tortivus*—*torquēre*, to twist.]

**tortilla,** *tör'tē(l)'ya, n.* a Mexican round flat maize cake. [Sp., dim. of *torta*, cake.]

**tortoise,** *tör'tas, n.* any land or freshwater (rarely marine) chelonian (now, in Britain, usu. restricted to land forms): a testudo (*mil.*).— **tor'toise-plant,** elephant's foot; **tortoise-shell**

(*tör'ta-shel*), the shell of a tortoise: a translucent mottled material, the horny plates (esp. of the back) of the hawk's-bill turtle: a tortoise-shell butterfly or cat.—*adj.* made of, or mottled like, tortoise-shell.—**tortoise-shell butterfly,** a butterfly with orange or reddish wings marked with black and yellow, edged with blue, etc.—*Aglais urticae* (small), *Nymphalis polychlorus* (large tortoise-shell); **tortoise-shell cat,** a domestic cat (nearly always female) mottled in yellow and black. [L.L. *tortuca.*]

**Tortrix,** *tör'triks, n.* the typical genus of **Tortricidae** (*-tris'i-dē*), a large family of small moths whose caterpillars commonly live in rolled-up leaves:—*pl.* **Tortrices** (*-tri'sēz*).—*n.* **tortri'cid,** any moth of the family.—Also *adj.* [Invented L., twister.]

**tortuous,** *tör'tū-as, adj.* full of windings: far from straightforward (*fig.*).—*n.* **tortuos'ity.**—*adv.* **tor'-tuously.**—*n.* **tor'tuousness.** [L. *tortuōsus*—*torquēre, tortum*, to twist.]

**torture,** *tör'char, n.* a putting to the rack or severe pain to extort a confession, or as a punishment: extreme pain: anguish.—*v.t.* to put to torture: to subject to extreme pain: to exact by torture: to distort violently.—*n.* **tor'turer.**—*n.* and *adj.* **tor'turing.**—*adv.* **tor'turingly.**—*adj.* **tor'turous,** causing torture or violent distortion. [Fr.,—L. *tortūra*, torment—*torquēre.*]

**toruffled,** *ta-, too-ruf'ld,* (*arch*) *adj.* (*Milt.* **to ruffl'd**) ruffled up. [Pfx. *to-*, ii.tensive, **ruffle.**]

**torus,** *tō', tö'ras, n.* a large moulding, semicircular or nearly in section, common at the base of a column: a figure generated by the revolution of a circle or other conic section about a straight line in its own plane: the receptacle of a flower: a ridge (*zool.*): a ring-shaped discharge-tube:—*pl.* **tō'ri.**—*n.* **tore** (*tör, tör; archit.* and *geom.*), a torus.—*adjs.* **toric** (*tor', tör', tör'*), of, or having the form of, a torus: a part of a torus; **toroid** (*tor', tör', tör'*), shaped like an anchor-ring.—*n.* a coil or transformer of that shape.—*adj.* **toroid'al.**—*ns.* **Torula** (*tör'ū-la*), a yeast-like micro-organism; **tor'ūlin,** a vitamin in yeast.—*adj.* **tor'ūlose** (*bot.*), with small swellings at intervals.—*ns.* **torūlō'sis,** infection with a Torula affecting the nervous system; **tor'ūlus,** the socket of an insect's antenna. [L. *tōrus*, a bulge, swelling, bed, torus moulding; dim. *tōrūlus.*]

**Tory,** *tō', tö'ri, n.* a Conservative in politics: a bigoted or extreme Conservative: one who sided with the British in the Revolution (*U.S. hist.*).—Also *adj.*—*v.t.* **Tō'rify, Tō'ryfy,** to infect with Tory principles.—*n.* **Tō'ryism,** the principles of the Tories. [Ir. *toiridhe*, a pursuer; first applied to the Irish bog-trotters and robbers; next, about 1680, to the most hot-headed asserters of the royal prerogative.]

**tose.** See **toze.**

**tosh,** *tosh,* (*Scot.*) *adj.* neat, trim: comfortable, friendly, intimate.—Also *adv.*—*v.t.* to trim.

**tosh,** *tosh,* (*slang*) *n.* bosh, twaddle.—*adj.* **tosh'y.**

**tosher,** *tosh'ar,* (*univ. slang*) *n.* a non-collegiate student. [From **unattached.**]

**toss,** *tos, v.t.* to fling, jerk: to fling up, or about, or to and fro: to agitate: to turn the leaves of (*obs.*): to tilt in drinking: to drink.—*v.i.* to be tossed: to be in violent commotion: to tumble about: to fling: to toss up a coin:—*infin., Spens.,* **toss'en;** *pa.t.* and *pa.p.* **tossed, tost,** rarely **tost.**—*n.* . act of throwing upward: a throwing up or back of the head: confusion, commotion: a toss-up.—*n.* **toss'er.**—*adv.* **toss'ily,** pertly. — *n.* and *adj.* **toss'ing.** — *adj.* **toss'y,** pert, contemptuous.—**toss'pot,** a toper, a drunkard; **toss'-up',** the throwing up of a coin to decide anything; an even chance or hazard.— **argue the toss,** to dispute a decision; **toss off,** to drink off: to remark casually: to masturbate (*slang*); **toss out,** to prank up; **toss up,** to throw a coin in order to decide: to cook and serve up hastily. [Origin unknown.]

**tosticated,** *tos'ti-kā-tid, (slang),* adj. fuddled: perplexed—also **toss'icāted.**—*n.* **tosticā'tion,** perplexity. [A mispronunciation of intoxicated, associated with toss.]

**tot,** *tot, n.* anything little, esp. a child, a drinkingcup, or a dram.—*n.* **tott'ie, tott'y** *(dim.).* [Cf. Ice. *tottr,* a dwarf.]

**tot,** *tot, v.t.* and *v.i.* to add up or total (also **tot up**). —*n.* an addition of a long column. [total.]

**tot,** *tot, (slang) n.* a bone: anything retrieved from a dust-bin or the like.—*ns.* **tott'er,** a raker of dust-bins and heaps; **tott'ing.**

**total,** *tō'tl, adj.* whole: complete: ncluding all: co-ordinating everything towards one end.—*n.* the whole: the entire amount.—*v.t.* to bring to a total, add up: to amount to:—*pr.p.* **tō'talling;** *pa.t.* and *pa.p.* **tō'talled.**—*ns.* **totalisā'tion;** **to'talisator, to'taliser** *(familiarly abbrev.* **tote,** *tōt),* an automatic betting-machine, the *pari mutuel.*—*v.t.* **to'talise, -ize,** to find the sum of: to bring to a total.—*v.i.* to use a totalisator.— *adj.* **totalitarian** *(tō-tal-i-tā'ri-ən),* belonging to a form of government that includes control of everything under one authority, and allows no opposition.—Also *n.*—*ns.* **totalitā'rianism;** **totality** *(tō-tal'i-ti),* condition or fact of being total: entirety: completeness: the whole.— *adv.* **to'tally.**—**total abstainer,** one who abstains altogether from all forms of alcohol; **total theatre,** dramatic entertainment comprising in one performance all or most of the following— acting, dancing, gymnastic feats, singing and instrumental music of various kinds, elaborate costumes and other visual effects, sometimes poetry; **total war** (see war). [L.L. *tōtālis*—L. *tōtus,* whole.]

**Totanus,** *tot'ə-nəs, n.* the redshank genus, giving name to the **Totaninae** *(-ni'nē),* the tattler subfamily of sandpipers, with toes webbed at the base. [It. *totano.*]

**tote,** *tōt, (orig. U.S.) v.t.* to carry. [Origin unknown.]

**tote,** *tōt, (slang) v.t.* to add (with *up*). [total.]

**tote.** See total.

**to-tear,** *tə-, tōō-tār',* to tear in pieces:—*pa.p.,* Spens., **to-torne'.** [Pfx. *to-,* asunder, and tear.]

**totem,** *tō'tam, n.* any species of living or inanimate thing regarded by a class or kin within a local tribe with superstitious respect as an outward symbol of an existing intimate unseen relation. —*adj.* **totemic** *(-tem'ik).*—*ns.* **to'temism,** the use of totems as the foundation of a social system of obligation and restriction; **to'temist,** one designated by a totem.—*adj.* **totemist'ic**—**totem pole,** a pole carved and painted with totemic symbols, set up by Indians in the north-west of North America. [From Algonquin.]

**tother,** *t'other, tudh'ər, pron.* and *adj.* the other. [that other; cf. tone (2) and Scots tae, tane.]

**totidem verbis,** *tōt-i'dəm vûr'bis, tot-i'dem ver'-, wer'bēs,* (L.) in just so many words.

**totient,** *tō'shənt, n.* the number of totitives of a number. [L. *totiēs,* so many.]

**toties quoties,** *tō'shi-ēz kwō'shi-ēz, tot'-i-ās kwot'-i-ās,* (L.) as often as.

**totitive,** *tot'i-tiv, n.* a number less than another and prime to it. [L. *tot,* so many.]

**toto caelo,** *tō'tō sē', ki'lō* (L.) by the whole heavens; diametrically opposite.

**to-torne.** See to-tear.

**totter,** *tot'ər, v.i.* to sway: to waver: to rock: to threaten to fall: to reel: to stagger: to be on the verge of ruin.—*n.* **tott'erer.**—*n.* and *adj.* **tott'ering.**—*adv.* **tott'eringly.**—*adj.* **tott'ery,** shaky. [Cf. Norw. dial. *tutra, totra,* to quiver, Sw. dial. *tuttra.*]

**totter, totting.** See tot (3).

**tottered,** *tot'ərd, adj.* a variant of tattered (Shak.):

later (from association with totter) ruinous.— *adj.* **tott'ring** *(Shak.),* hanging in rags.

**totty,** *tot'i, adj.* unsteady: dazed: tipsy. [Cf. **totter.**]

**toucan,** *tōō'kən, -kan, -kän', n.* any member of the Rhamphastidae, large South American picarian birds, with an immense beak.—*n.* **tou'canet,** a smaller kind of toucan. [Fr.,— Tupí *tucana.*]

**touch,** *tuch, v.t.* to come or be in contact with: to cause to be in contact: to meet without cutting, or meet tangentially *(geom.):* to get at: to reach as far as: to attain: to equal, rival, or compare with: to make a light application to: to begin to eat, eat a little of: to affect, esp. injuriously: to impress: to affect with emotion, esp. pity: to have to do with: to concern: to hit, wound, or injure: to strike home to: to play *(mus.):* to call at (as a port): to mark or modify by light strokes: to tinge: to cause to touch the ground behind the goal-line (commonly with *down*; Rugby football): to test as with a touchstone: to receive, draw, pocket: to extract money from *(for* so much): to make some reference to, say something about: to bribe *(obs.):* to cheat *(slang).*—*v.i.* to be or come in contact: to make a passing call at a port: to verge: to make some mention or reference (with *on, upon):* to have reference.— *n.* act, condition, impression, sense, or mode of touching: a feeling: a slight application, modification, stroke: a small quantity: a slight affection of illness: a tinge: a trace: a smack: a trait: a little: a slight hit, wound, blemish, reproach: manner or nicety of producing tone on (now esp.) a keyed instrument: the instrument's response: characteristic manner: a stroke of art: relation of communication, sympathy, harmony: a game in which one has to pursue and touch others: a test, as of a touchstone: a touchstone: a black marble or similar monumental stone *(obs.):* an official stamp of fineness on gold, etc.: fineness: stamp *(fig.):* either side of the field outside the bounds *(football):* theft *(slang):* a sum got by theft or by touching *(slang):* that which will find buyers at such and such a price *(slang).*—*adj.* **touch'able,** capable of being touched: fit to be touched.—*n.* **touch'ableness**—*adj.* **touched,** having been touched: slightly unsound mentally.—*n.* **touch'er.**—*adv.* **touch'ily.**—*n.* **touch'iness.**—*n.* **touch'ing.**—*adj.* affecting: moving: pathetic.— *prep.* concerning.—*adv.* **touch'ingly.**—*n.* **touch'ingness.**—*adjs.* **touch'less,** without sense of touch: intangible; **touch'y,** over-sensitive: irascible.— **touch'-and-go',** a narrow escape: a critical or precariously balanced situation.—*adj.* **precarious:** off-hand.—**touch'-box,** a tinder-box for a matchlock; **touch'-down,** in Rugby football, touching of ball to ground by a player behind the goalline (if his own goal, also called a **touch'-back):** of aircraft, act of alighting; **touch'-hole,** the small hole of a cannon through which the fire is communicated to the charge; **touch'-judge,** an official who marks when and where the ball goes into touch *(Rugby football);* **touch'-line,** the side boundary in football; **touch'-me-not,** the plant balsam (from its explosive fruit): lupus: a forbidden topic.—*adj.* stand-offish.— **touch-me-not'ishness; touch'-paper,** paper steeped in saltpetre for firing a train; **touch'-piece,** a coin or medal formerly given by a king to those he touched for king's evil; **touch'-plate,** one bearing the pewterers' official stamp; **touch'-stone,** Lydian stone, a highly siliceous, usually black stone, or other stone for testing gold or silver by streak, as black marble: any criterion. —*v.t.* and *v.i.* **touch'-type,** to type without looking at the keys of the typewriter.—**touch'-typist; touch'wood,** decayed wood that can be used as tinder.—**in, out of, touch,** in, out of, communication or direct relations; **near touch,** a close shave; **touch down,** of aircraft, to alight; **touch off,** to trigger (also *fig.*); **touch up,** to improve by a series of small touches: to lash lightly, stimulate. [O.Fr. *tuchier* (Fr. *toucher*); origin doubtful.]

**touché,** *tōō´shă, tōō-shă´, interj.* claiming or acknowledging hit in fencing, or a point scored in argument, etc. [Fr., touched, scored against.]

**tough,** *tuf, adj.* stiff and dense: tenacious: hard to cut, chew, break up or penetrate: resistant: viscous, sticky: capable of, or requiring, strenuous effort and endurance: unyielding: robust: laborious: refractory: criminal, ruffianly.—*n.* a rough: a criminal, hooligan (also **tough guy**).—*v.t.* or *v.i.* **tough´en,** to make or become tough.—*n.* **tough´ener.**—*n.* and *adj.* **tough´ening.**—*adj.* **tough´ish,** rather tough.—*adv.* **tough´ly.**—*n.* **tough´ness.**—**tough luck** (see luck). —*adj.* **tough´-mind´ed,** hard-headed, unsentimental, determined. [O.E. *tōh.*]

**toupee,** *tōō-pē´, -pā´,* or *tōō´, n.* a tuft, lock, fringe, or patch, esp. of false hair: a wig with a top-knot.—Also **toupet** (*tōō-pā´, tōō´pä*). [Fr. *toupet.*]

**tour,** *tōōr, n.* a round: a prolonged journey from place to place, esp. for pleasure or for acting: a pleasure trip or outing: a shift or turn of work: a border of false hair (*hist.*).—*v.i.* to make a tour, go on tour.—*v.t.* to make a tour through or of: to tour with (a play).—*n.* **tour´er,** a touring-car: a tourist.—*n.* and *adj.* **tour´ing.** —*ns.* **tour´ism,** the activities of tourists and those who cater for them; **tour´ist,** one who makes a tour, a sight-seeing traveller.—*adj.* **touris´tic.**—**tour´ing-car,** a long motor-car, suitable for touring; **tour´ist class,** the cheapest class of accommodation on a boat or aeroplane. —**Grand Tour,** a journey through Western Europe, once fashionable as completing a youth's education. [Fr.; see turn.]

**touraco,** *tōō´ra-kō,* or *-kō´, n.* an African bird (Turacus) of the plantain-eater family, with a horny shield on the forehead and remarkable pigments in its feathers. [Supposed to be a W. African name.]

**tourbillion,** *tōōr-bil´yan, n.* a swirl: a vortex: a whirlwind: a whirling firework. [Fr. *tourbillon,* whirlwind—L. *turbō, -inis.*]

**tour de force,** *tōōr da fors,* (Fr.) a feat of strength or skill.

**tourmaline,** *tōōr´ma-lēn, n.* a beautiful mineral of complex and varying composition, usually black (schorl) or blackish, strongly pyroelectric and pleochroic. [Fr.,—Sinh. *tōramalli,* carnelian.]

**tournament,** *tōōr´na-mant, n.* a military sport of the Middle Ages in which combatants engaged in single combat or in troops, mainly on horseback, with spear and sword: a military and athletic display: a series of games to determine a winner or winning team by elimination.—*n.* **tourney** (*tōōr´, tûr´, tōr´ni*), a mediaeval tournament.—*v.i.* to ride in tournament.—*n.* **tour´neyer.** [O.Fr. *tournoiement, tornoi—torner*—L. *tornāre,* to turn.]

**tournedos,** *tōōr-na-dō, n.* small beef fillet served with some kind of garnish. [Fr.]

**tourniquet,** *tōōr´ni-ket, -kā, n.* any appliance for compressing an artery: a turnstile (*rare*). [Fr., —L. *tornāre,* to turn.]

**tournure,** *tōōr-nür´, n.* contour, the characteristic turn of line: a bustle or pad worn at the waist. [Fr.]

**touse, touze, towse, towze,** *towz, v.t.* to haul, to pull about: to dishevel, rumple, tumble: to worry: to rack (*obs.*): to tease out (*obs.*).—*v.i.* to touse each other: to be toused: to tussle: to rummage.—*n.* a tousing.—*n.* **tous´er, tows´er,** one who touses: (*cap.*) a common name for a

big dog.—*n.* and *adj.* **tous´ing.**—*v.t.* **tousle, touzle** (*towz´l,* Scot. *tōōz´l*), to disarrange, to tumble: to dishevel.—*v.i.* to tussle: to touse things.—*n.* a tousled mass.—*adj.* **tousy, towsy** (*towz´i,* Scot. *tōōz´i*), shaggy, unkempt, tousled: rough.—**tousy tea** (*Scot.*), high tea. [Prob. from a lost O.E. word answering to Ger. *zausen.*]

**tous-les-mois,** *tōō-la-mwä, n.* the edible starch of the rhizome of a West Indian Canna. [Fr., every month, but perh. really from a native name.]

**toustie,** *tōōs´ti,* (Scott) *adj.* irascible.

**tout,** *towt, v.i.* to look out for custom in an obtrusive way.—*v.t.* to watch or spy on.—*n.* one who touts: a low fellow who hangs about racing-stables, etc., to pick up profitable information.—*n.* **tout´er.** [App. related to toot (1).]

**tout, towt,** *towt,* (Scot.) *v.i.* to pout.—*n.* a pet, a fit of the sulks: a sudden illness.—*adj.* **tout´ie,** petulant.

**tout,** *tōō,* (Fr.) all: every: quite: entirely: the whole.—**tout au contraire** (*tōō tō kõ-trer*), quite the contrary; **tout à fait** (*tōō ta fe*), entirely; **tout à vous** (*tōō ta vōō*), wholly yours; **tout court** (*kōōr*), quite brief(ly), without preface, simply; **tout de même** (*da mĕm*), all the same; **tout de suite** (*swēt*), at once, immediately; **tout ensemble** (see ensemble); **tout le monde** (*la mõd*), all the world, everybody.

**tovarish,** *to-vä´rish, n.* comrade. [Russ. *tovarishch.*]

**tow,** *tō* (Scot. tow), *v.t.* to pull with a rope, primarily by water: to pull along.—*v.i.* to proceed by being towed.—*n.* condition of being towed: act of towing: a tow-rope: that which is towed: a rope, esp. a bell-rope or a hangman's rope (*Scot.*).—*ns.* **tow´age,** act of towing: fee for towing; **tow´er.**—*n.* and *adj.* **tow´ing.**— **tow´ing-bitts,** upright timbers projecting above the deck for fastening tow-lines to; **tow´-iron,** a toggle-iron used in whaling; **tow´line, -rope,** a line used in towing; **tow´-net, tow´ing-net,** a dragnet for collecting objects of natural history, etc.; **tow´path, tow´ing-path,** a path for horses towing barges; **tow´-plane,** an aeroplane which tows gliders.—**have in tow,** to be accompanied by: to have in one's care. [O.E. *togian,* to drag.]

**tow,** *tō, n.* prepared fibres of flax, hemp, or jute: esp. separated shorter fibres.—*adj.* of or like tow.—*adj.* **tow´y.**—**tow´-head,** a person with light-coloured or tousled hair.—*adj.* **tow´headed.** [O.E. *tow-* (in compounds).]

**toward,** *tō´ard, tōrd, adj.* (*arch.*) or (*dial.*) approaching: at hand: impending: getting on: on hand: favourable: well-disposed: apt: ready to do or learn: on the left or near side.—*adv.* in the direction facing one, inward.—*prep.* (now more commonly **towards**) (*ta-, tōō-wôrd´*(*z*), twôrd(*z*), tōrd(*z*), tōrd(*z*)), in the direction of: with a tendency to: for, as a help to: near, a little short of.—*n.* **tow´ardliness.**—*adj.* **tow´ardly** (*arch.*), favourable: promising: well-disposed: tractable.—Also *adv.*—*n.* **tow´ardness.**—*prep.* **tow´ards** (also *ta-wôrdz´*), toward. [O.E. *tōweard,* adj., adv., prep.—*tō,* to, suff. *-weard, -ward.*]

**towel,** *tow´al, n.* a cloth for drying: formerly a cloth for various purposes, as a table-napkin, an altar-cloth.—*v.t.* to rub with a towel: to cudgel: to thrash:—*pr.p.* **tow´elling;** *pa.t.* and *pa.p.* **tow´elled.**—*n.* **tow´elling,** a rubbing with a towel: an absorbent cloth for towels, sometimes used for dressing-gowns, curtains, etc.: a thrashing.—**tow´el-gourd,** the loofah; **tow´el-horse, -rack,** a frame for hanging towels on; **tow´el-rail,** a rod for hanging towels on.—**a lead towel,** a bullet: **an oaken towel,** a cudgel; **throw in the towel** (see throw). [O.Fr. *toaille,* from Germanic; cf. O.H.G. *dwahila—dwahan, twahan,* O.E. *thwēan,* to wash.]

**tower,** *towr, tow´ar, n.* a lofty building, standing alone or forming part of another: a fortress:

(esp. 17th cent.) a woman's high head-dress: a lofty or vertical flight.—*v.i.* to rise into the air: to be lofty: to stand on high.—*v.t.* (*Milt.*) to rise aloft into.—*adjs.* tow'ered; tow'ering, very high, elevated: very violent; tow'erless; tow'ery, having towers: lofty.—tow'er-shell, a gasteropod (Turritella) with elongated manywhorled spiral shell, or its shell.—tower of strength, a stable, reliable person; tower over, to be considerably taller than: to be markedly superior to. [O.Fr. *tur*—L. *turris*, a tower ]

towhee, tow'hē, tō'hē, *n.* an American finch, the chewink, ground-robin, or marsh-robin. [Imit.]

towmont, towmond, towmon, tow'mən(d), -mən(t), (*Scot.* and *N. of Engl.*) *n.* a form of twelvemonth.

town, *town, n.* orig. an enclosure (*obs.*): in Scotland (*Scot.* tōōn) a farmstead or similar group of houses: a populous place bigger or less rural than a village: a municipal or political division (which may include villages and towns in the ordinary sense) of a county (*U.S.*): the principal town of a district: an urban community: the people of a town, esp. fashionable society, tradesmen (distinguished from academic inhabitants), or immoral classes: the business or shopping centre: urban communities generically.—*adj.* of a town: urban.—*n.* townee', a townsman, not a member of the university.—*adj.* town'ish, characteristic of town as opposed to country.—*n.* town'ling, a town-dweller.—*adj.* town'ly, townish.—*ns.* town'ship, a village, a community or local division: a parish (*hist.*): a farm in joint tenancy (*Scot.*): a thirty-six square mile block of public land (*U.S.*): a site for a town (*Austr.*): a small settlement (*Austr.*): the territory or district of a town: the corporation of a town: a subdivision of a county or province (*U.S.*): an administrative district (*U.S.*); town'y, a townsman: a fellow-townsman.—*adj.* townish.—town'-clerk', a secretary and legal adviser of a town; town'-coun'cil, the governing body in a town; town'-coun'cillor; town'-cri'er, one who makes public proclamations in a town; town'-dweller; town'-end', the end of the main street; town (towns) gas, usu. a mixture of coal-gas and carburetted water-gas, made and supplied for domestic or trade use; town'hall', a public hall for the official business of a town: a townhouse; town'house, a house or building for transacting the public business of a town: a house in town; town'land, a township; town'-meet'ing, in New England, a meeting of the voters of a town; town'-plann'ing, deliberate designing in the building and extension of towns to avoid the evils of fortuitous and speculative building; town's'bairn (*Scot.*), a native of a town, esp. one's own; town'scape, a portion of a town which the eye can view at once: a picture of it: the design or building of (part of) a town.—Also *v.t., v.i.*—town'scaping; towns'-folk, the people of a town; town'skip (*Dickens*), a city urchin; towns'man, an inhabitant or fellow-inhabitant of a town:—*fem.* towns'-woman; towns'people (treated as *pl.*), townsfolk; town'-talk', the general talk of a town: the subject of common conversation.—go to town (*slang*), to let oneself go; take to town (*slang*), to mystify, bewilder; town and gown, the general community and the members of the university. [O.E. *tūn*, an enclosure, town; O.N. *tūn*, enclosure, Ger. *zaun*, hedge.]

to-worne, *tə-wörn', -wörn', adj.* (*Spens.*) worn-out. [Pfx. *to-*, inten., worn.]

towse, towze. See touse.

toxic, *toks'ik, adj.* of poison: poisonous: poisoned: due to poison.—*adj.* tox'ical.—*adv.* tox'ically.—*adj.* tox'icant, poisonous.—*n.* poisonous substance.—*ns.* toxicā'tion, toxicity (*is'*), toxic quality; tox'in, a ptomaine: a specific

poison of organic origin; tox'oid, a toxin that has been treated to remove its toxic properties without destroying its ability to stimulate formation of antibodies.—*n.* toxaemia (-*ē'mi-ə*; Gr. *haima*, blood), blood poisoning.—*adjs.* toxaem'ic; toxicolog'ical.—*ns.* toxicol'ogist; toxicol'ogy, the science of poisons; toxicomā'nia, morbid craving for poisons.—*adjs.* toxicoph'agous, toxiph'agous (Gr. *phagein*, to eat), poison-eating.—*ns.* toxicophō'bia, toxiphō'bia (Gr. *phobein*, to fear), morbid fear of poisoning.—*n.* and *adj.* toxiphō'biac.—*n.* toxoplasmos'is, infection of animals and man by micro-organisms, prob. protozoa, of the genus *Toxoplasma*. [Gr. *toxon*, a bow, *toxikos*, for the bow, *toxikon*, arrow-poison.]

toxophilite, *toks-of'i-līt, n.* a lover of archery: an archer.—*n.* toxoph'ily, love of archery: archery. [Gr. *toxon*, a bow, *phileein*, to love.]

toy, *toi, n.* a plaything: a trifle: a thing only for amusement or look: a matter of no importance: a jest, idle tale (*arch.*): a trivial dance-tune, or the like (*arch.*): a whim, crotchet: an old woman's cap with side flaps (*Scot.*): a dwarf breed: amorous sport (*arch.*).—*adj.* made in imitation as a plaything.—*v.i.* to trifle: to sport: to dally amorously.—*n.* toy'er.—*n.* and *adj.* toy'ing.—*adj.* toy'ish, given to toying or trifling: playful: wanton (*obs.*).—*adv.* toy'ishly.—*n.* toy'ishness.—*adj.* toy'some, sportive: playful: whimsical: disposed to toy: wanton (*obs.*).—toy dog, a very small pet dog; toy'man, -woman, a seller of toys; toy'shop, a shop where toys are sold. [Poss. Du. *tuig*, tools; Ger. *zeug*, stuff.]

toze, tose, (*Shak.* toaze), *tōz, v.t.* to tease out, card, comb: to draw out, elicit. [M.E. *tosen*, akin to tease.]

tozie, *tōz'i*, (*Scott*) *n.* a shawl made from a goat's inner coat.

trabeate, -d, *trab', trāb'i-āt, -id, adjs.* built of horizontal beams, not arches and vaults.—*ns.* trabeā'tion, entablature: combination of beams in a structure; trabecula (*trə-bek'ū-lə*), a cell, row of cells, band, or rodlike structure running across a cavity or forming an internal support to an organ:—*pl.* trabec'ūlae (-*lē*).—*adjs.* trabec'-ūlar; trabec'ūlate, -d, having trabeculae: transversely barred. [L. *trabs, trabis*, beam; dim. *trabecula*.]

tracasserie, *tra-kas-(ə)-rē, (*Fr.*) turmoil.

trace, *trās, n.* a way, course (*Spens.*): a beaten path (*U.S.*): a track: a footprint: a vestige: an indication, mark of what is or has been: a small quantity that can just be detected: a tracing: a line marked by a recording instrument: an intersection with or projection on a surface: the ground-plan of a work (*fort.*).—*v.i.* to proceed (*arch.*): to walk (*arch.*): to move (*arch.*): to tread a measure (*obs.*): to be traceable, date back.—*v.t.* to traverse: to track: to follow step by step: to detect: to discover the whereabouts of: to follow or mark the outline of, esp. mechanically or on a translucent paper: to outline, delineate, or write: to produce as tracery: to cover with tracery.—*n.* traceabil'ity.—*adj.* trace'able, that may be traced.—*n.* trace'-ableness.—*adv.* trace'ably.—*adj.* trace'less.—*adv.* trace'lessly.—*ns.* trā'cer, one who traces: an instrument for tracing: a probe for tracing a nerve, etc.: a device by which a projectile leaves a smoke-trail: a projectile equipped with it: a chemical substance used to mark the course followed by a process.—*adj.* tra'ceried.—*ns.* tra'cery, ornamentation in flowing outline: ornamental open-work in Gothic architecture; tra'cing, the act of one who traces: a drawing copied mechanically or on translucent paper laid over the original: an instrumental record.— trace element, a micro-nutrient, a substance (as zinc, copper, molybdenum, etc.) whose presence in the soil in minute quantities is necessary for plant and animal growth; **tracer bullet**; **tracer element** (*physiol.*, etc.), an isotope, often a radio-isotope, used for experiments in which its particular properties enable its position to be kept under observation; **tracer shell**; **tra´cing-paper**, translucent paper for tracing on. [Fr. *trace*— L. *tractus*, pa.p. of *trahĕre*, to draw.]

**trace**, *trās*, *n.* (usu. in *pl.*) a rope, chain, or strap attached to an animal's collar, for drawing a vehicle: a bar for transmitting motion: the vascular tissue branching from the cylinder to pass into a leaf or branch (*bot.*).—*v.t.* to harness in traces.—*n.* **trā´cer**, a trace-horse: a boy who attends a trace-horse.—**trace´-horse**, a horse that draws in traces.—**kick over the traces** (see kick). [O.Fr. *trays*, *trais*, pl. of *trait*, draught; cf. **trait.**]

**trachea**, *trɔ-kē´ɔ*, *U.S.* trā´, *n.* wind-pipe: air-tube in air-breathing arthropods: a conducting tube in xylem (*bot.*):—*pl.* **trachē´ae** (*-ē*).—*adj.* **trachē´al.**—*n.pl.* **Trăcheā´ria**, arachnids with tracheae, but no lung-books.—*ns.* and *adjs.* **trācheā´rian**; **trā´cheary.**—*n.pl.* **Trăcheā´ta**, arthropods with tracheae.—*adjs.* **trā´cheate, -d,** having a trachea.—*ns.* **tracheid(e)** (*trɔ-kē´id*, *-id*, or *trak´i-*), a long tubelike but closed cell in xylem; **tracheitis** (*trak-i-ī´tis*), inflammation of the trachea; **tracheos´copy**, inspection of the trachea; **tracheos´tomy**, surgical formation of an opening into the trachea; **tracheot´omy**, cutting into the trachea; **trachi´tis**, a wrong form of **tracheitis.** [Mediaeval L. *trăchēa* for L. *trăchīa* —Gr. *trăcheia* (*artēriā*), rough (artery).]

**trachelate**, *trak´ɔ-lāt*, *adj.* having a neck. [Gr. *trachēlos*, neck.]

**Trachinus**, *tra-kī´nɔs*, *n.* the weever genus of fishes, giving name to the family **Trachinidae** (*-kin´-i-dē*). [L.L. *trachina*, said to be a local name of a fish.]

**trachoma**, *tra-kō´mɔ*, *n.* a disease of the eye, with hard pustules on the inner surface of the eyelids. [Gr. *trăchōma.*]

**Trachypterus**, *trak-ip´tɔ-rɔs*, *n.* the dealfish genus, giving name to the ribbon-fish family **Trachypteridae** (*-ter´i-dē*). [Gr. *trăchys*, rough, *pteron*, fin.]

**trachyte**, *trak´īt*, *n.* a fine-grained intermediate igneous rock answering to the coarse-grained syenite, commonly porphyritic with sanidine.—*adjs.* **trachytic** (*trɔ-kit´ik*); **trach´ytoid.** [Gr. *trăchys*, rough.]

**tracing.** See under **trace** (1).

**track**, *trak*, *n.* a mark left: a beaten path: a made path: a course, usu. oval-shaped, on which races are run: a railway line, the rails and the space between: the groove cut in a gramophone record by the recording instrument: one out of several items recorded on a disk: in motion-pictures, etc., the sound-track: the endless band on which the wheels of a caterpillar vehicle run (*adj.* **tracked**, equipped with such metal bands).—*v.t.* to follow the track of: to find by so doing: to traverse: to beat, tread (a path, etc.): to follow the movement of (satellite, spacecraft, etc.) by radar, etc., and record its positions.—*v.i.* to follow a trail: to make one's way (*coll.*): to run in alignment: to move a dolly camera in a defined path while taking a shot (**tracking shot**).—*ns.* **track´age**, provision of railway tracks; **track´er**; **track´ing**, the action of the verb: excessive leakage current between two insulated points (*elect.*).—*adj.* **track´less**, without a path: untrodden: leaving no trace: running without rails. — *adv.* **track´lessly.** — *n.* **track´lessness.** — **track event**, in a sports competition, a race of any kind; **track´man** (*U.S.*); **track suit**, a garment worn by athletes before and after, e.g. a race, or when in training; **track´-walker**, one who has charge of a railway track; **track´way**, a beaten track: an ancient road.—**across the**

**tracks, the wrong side of the tracks,** a slum or other socially disadvantageous area; **in one's tracks,** just where one stands; **keep track of,** keep oneself informed about; **make tracks,** to make off: to go quickly; **off the beaten track,** away from frequented roads: out of the usual (*fig.*); **off the track,** off course, in the wrong direction; **the beaten track** (*fig.*), the normal, conventional, routine; **track down,** to find after intensive search; **tracker dog,** one used for tracking, especially in police searches. [Fr. *trac*; prob. Gmc.; cf. next word.]

**track**, *trak*, *v.t.* to tow.—*v.i.* to travel by towing. —*ns.* **track´age**, towing; **track´er**, one who tows: a tug: a pulling part in the action of any organ. —**track´-boat**, a towed boat; **track´road**, a towpath; **track´-scout**, a trekschuit. [See **trek.**]

**tract**, *trakt*, *n.* a stretch or extent of space or time: a region, area: trace, track (*Shak., Spens.*): a tractate: a pamphlet or leaflet, esp. political or (now) religious: a psalm sung instead of the Alleluia in Lent (*R.C.*; also **tract´us**; perh. as drawn out, perh. as sung at a stretch without answers): a region of the body occupied by a particular system (e.g. *the digestive tract*). —*v.t.* (*Spens.*) to trace, track.—*n.* **tractabil´ity.** —*adj.* **tract´able**, easily drawn, managed, or taught: docile.—*ns.* **tract´ableness**; **tractā´rian**, a writer of tracts, esp. (*cap.*) of the *Tracts for the Times* (Oxford, 1833-41—Pusey, Newman, Keble, Hurrell Froude, etc.).—Also *adj.*—*ns.* **Tractār´ianism**, the system of religious opinion promulgated in these, its main aim to assert the authority and dignity of the Anglican Church— —the Oxford movement; **tract´ate**, a treatise, a tract; **tractā´tor**, a tractarian; **traction** (*trak´shɔn*), act of drawing or state of being drawn: pulling on a muscle, organ, etc., by means, e.g. of weights, to correct an abnormal condition (*med.*): propulsion of vehicles.—*adjs.* **trac´tional**; **tract´ive**, pulling.—*ns.* **tract´or**, an aeroplane with screw in front: a traction-engine: a vehicle that propels itself or hauls other vehicles or agricultural implements: a motor-plough: (in *pl.*) bars of different metals which, drawn over diseased parts, were supposed to give relief; **tractorā´tion**, the use of these; **tract´rix**, a curve such that the intercept of a tangent by a fixed straight line is constant.— **trac´tion-engine**, a locomotive for hauling on roads, fields, etc. [L. *tractus*, *-ūs*, a dragging, draught, tract, *tractus*, *tractātus*, pa.ps. of *trahĕre*, *tractāre*, to draw.]

**trad**, *trad*, *adj.* abbreviation of *traditional*, used of style, esp. of a rhythmically monotonous style of jazz which originated in the U.S. in the 1920s.—Also *n.*

**trade**, *trād*, *n.* a track, trail, treading (*Spens.*): a way of traffic: resort (*Shak.*): a way, a course (*obs.*): a practice: an occupation, way of livelihood, esp. skilled but not learned: shop-keeping: commerce: buying and selling: a craft: men engaged in the same occupation, esp. the liquor trade or the book trade: commodities, esp. for barter: a deal: rubbish (*dial.*): medicine: (in *pl.*) the trade-winds.—*v.i.* to tread, go (*obs.*): to resort, esp. for commerce: to ply: to occupy oneself (*obs.*): to have dealings or intercourse: to engage in commerce: to deal: to traffic: to buy and sell: to reckon, count, presume (with *on*), esp. unscrupulously.—*v.t.* to tread (*obs.*): to exchange commercially, to barter.—*adjs.* **trād´ed** (*Shak.*), versed, practised; **trade´ful** (*Spens.*), busy in traffic; **trade´less.**—*n.* **trā´der**, one who trades: a trading ship.—*n.* and *adj.* **trād´ing.**—**trade board**, a council representing employers and employees in a trade; **trade cycle**, the recurring series of conditions in trade from prosperity to depression and back to prosperity.—*adj.* **trade´-fallen (trade-falne;**

*Shak.*), unsuccessful in trade, bankrupt.—**trade'-in**, that which is given in part payment; **trade'-mark**, any name or distinctive device warranting goods for sale as the production of any individual or firm; **trade'-name**, a name serving as a trademark: a name in use in the trade; **trade price**, the price at which goods are sold to members of the same trade, or by wholesale to retail dealers; **trade route**, a route followed by caravans or trading ships; **trade sale**, an auction sale of goods by producers, etc., to persons in the trade; **trades'-folk, -people,** shopkeepers: mechanics: craftsmen: people employed in trade; **trades'man,** a shopkeeper: a craftsman: a mechanic:—*fem.* **trades'woman.** —*adj.* **trades'manlike.**—**trade un'ion,** an organised association of workers of an industry for the protection of their common interests; **trade un'ionism; trade un'ionist; trades union,** an association of trade unions, as the Trades Union Congress (T.U.C.); **trade wind,** a wind blowing toward the thermal equator and deflected westward by the eastward rotation of the earth; **trading estate,** an industrial estate; **trading stamp,** a stamp given to a purchaser of goods who, when he has accumulated a specified number, may exchange them without payment for articles provided by the trading stamp firm.—**Board of Trade,** a department of government for matters of industry and commerce; **trade in,** to give in part payment. [Prob. L.G. *trade;* akin to **tread.**]

**Tradescantia,** *trad-is-kan'shi-ə, n.* the spiderwort genus. [After the English gardener, naturalist, and traveller John *Tradescant* (*c.* 1567-1637).]

**tradition,** *trə-dish'ən, n.* handing over (*law*): oral transmission from generation to generation: a tale, belief or practice thus handed down: anything bound up with or continuing in the life of a family, community, etc.: the continuous development of a body of, e.g. literature, music.— *adjs.* **tradi'tional, tradi'tionary.**—*ns.* **tradi'tionalism; tradi'tionalist; traditional'ity.**—*advs.* **tradi'-tionally, tradi'tionarily.**—*ns.* **tradi'tioner, tradi'-tionist,** one who adheres to tradition.—*adj.* **traditive** (*trad'i-tiv*), traditional.—*n.* **trad'itor,** a traitor, betrayer (*obs.*): one who under persecution gave up sacred books or objects or the names of his fellows (*hist.*).—**traditional jazz** (see **trad**). [L. *trāditiō, -ōnis, trāditor, -ōris—trādĕre,* to give up—*trāns,* over, *dăre,* to give.]

**traduce,** *trə-dūs', in* U.S. *-dōōs', v.t.* to translate (*obs.*): to propagate or transmit (*obs.*): to calumniate: to defame.—*ns.* **traduce'ment; tradū'cer; Tradū'cian** (*-shi-ən*), one who believes that children receive soul as well as body from their parents through natural generation.—Also *adj.—ns.* **Tradū'cianism; Tradū'cianist.**—*n.* and *adj.* **tradū'cing.**—*adv.* **tradū'cingly.**—*n.* **traduction** (*-duk'shən*).—*adj.* **traduc'tive,** transmitted. [L. *trādūcĕre, trāductum—trāns,* across, *dūcĕre,* to bring.]

**traffic,** *traf'ik, n.* commerce, trade: disgraceful trading: dealings: a trading voyage (*obs.*): commodities (*obs.*): transportation of goods and persons on a railway, on an air route, etc.: vehicles, pedestrians, etc. (collectively), using a thoroughfare: passing to and fro.—*v.i.* to trade: to trade disgracefully: to intrigue.—*v.t.* to trade in, or barter:—*pr.p.* **traff'icking;** *pa.t.* and *pa.p.* **traff'icked.**—*ns.* **traff'icātor,** a movable pointer by means of which the driver of a vehicle can give warning of a change of direction; **traff'icker.** —*n.* and *adj.* **traff'icking.**—*adj.* **traff'icless.**— **traffic circle,** a road intersection where traffic circulates in one direction only; **traffic island,** a raised section in the centre of a road to separate lanes, guide traffic, etc.; **traff'ic-lights',** **-sig'nals,** coloured lights to regulate street traffic at crossings; **traff'ic-man'ager,** the manager of the traffic on a railway, etc.; **traff'ic-**

**returns',** statistics of passengers and goods carried and money received in return. [From a Romance language; cf. Fr. *trafic,* It. *traffico,* Sp. *tráfico;* origin obscure.]

**tragacanth,** *trag'ə-kanth, n.* a gum (also gum **tragacanth**) got from several spiny shrubs of the genus Astragalus: the plant yielding it. [Gr. *tragakantha—tragos,* goat, *akantha,* thorn.]

**tragedy,** *traj'i-di, n.* a species of drama in which the action and language are elevated, and the catastrophe usually sad: the art of such drama: any sad story or turn of events: anything with death or killing in it (*journalism*).—*ns.* **tragedian** (*trə-jē'di-ən*), a writer or (usually) an actor of tragedy; **tragedienne** (*trə-jē-di-en';* Fr. **tragé-dienne,** *trä-zhā-di-en'*), an actress of tragic rôles. —*adjs.* **tragic** (*traj'ik*), **-al,** pertaining to, of the nature of, tragedy.—*adv.* **trag'ically.**—*n.* **trag'ic-alness.**—**trag'i-com'edy,** a play (or story) in which grave and comic scenes are blended: a comedy that threatens to be a tragedy.—*adjs.* **trag'i-com'ic, -al.**—*adv.* **trag'i-com'ically.** [L. *tragoedia*—Gr. *tragōidiā,* tragedy, app. lit. goatsong—*tragos,* a he-goat, *ōidē,* song (variously explained).]

**tragelaph,** *trag', traj'i-laf, n.* a fabulous animal, part goat, part stag: a harnessed antelope (Tragelaphus, *-el'ə-fəs*).—*adj.* **tragel'aphine.** [Gr. *tragelaphos—tragos,* a goat, *elaphos,* a deer.]

**tragopan,** *trag'ō-pan, n.* a brilliant Asiatic horned pheasant. [Gr. *tragopān,* hornbill—*tragos,* goat, *Pān,* the god Pan.]

**tragus,** *trā'gəs, n.* a small prominence (bearded in man) at the entrance of the external ear:— *pl.* **tragi** (*-jī*).—*n.* **tragule** (*trag'ūl*), a chevrotain. —*adj.* **trag'uline** (*-īn-*). [Gr. *trăgos,* goat, tragus.]

**trahison,** *tra-ē-zõ,* (Fr.) treason: treachery.— **trahison des clercs** (*dā kler*), the treason of intellectuals, the entry of academics into politics.

**traik,** *trāk,* (*Scot.*) *v.i.* to go wearily or toilsomely: to stray: to get lost: to gad: to decline in health.—*n.* a loss, esp. of sheep: the mutton of sheep that have died of disease or accident.— *adj.* **traik'it,** worn out.—**traik after,** to dangle after.

**trail,** *trāl, v.t.* to draw along or near the surface: to drag wearily: to drag along: to carry (as a weapon) with butt near the ground, or horizontally: to lead on: to quiz (*coll.*): to cover with trailing ornament: to track.—*v.i.* to be drawn out in length: to hang, float, or drag loosely behind: to sprawl over the ground or a support: to straggle: to lag: to move with slow sweeping motion or with dragging drapery: to drag oneself along.—*n.* anything drawn out in length or trailed: a train, tail: the track of a star on a stationary photographic plate: a track, as of game: a beaten path in the wilds: part of a gun-carriage resting on the ground behind: an act or manner of trailing.—*n.* **trail'er,** one who trails: a tracker: a creeping plant: a carriage, car, chair, etc., towed or dragged by a car, bicycle, or tractor: a short motion-picture giving a sample of one that is coming: the blank piece of film at the end of a reel.—**trailing edge,** the rear edge; **trail'-net,** a drag-net.—**trail a pike** (*obs.*), to serve as a soldier; **trail one's coat** (*Ir.*), to invite a quarrel. [Ety. doubtful; O.E. *træglian,* to pluck, pull, and O.Fr. *trailler,* to tow, perh.—L. *tragula,* sledge, dragnet, are possibilities.]

**trail,** *trāl, n.* an aphetic form of **entrail.**

**train,** *trān, v.t.* to draw along (*arch.*): to allure (*obs.*): to draw on (*obs.*): to instruct and discipline: to cause to grow in the desired manner: to prepare for performance by instruction, practice, diet, exercise, or otherwise: to bring up: to direct, aim (as a gun or telescope). —*v.i.* (*Spens.* **trayne**) to trail, drag (*rare*): to prepare oneself by instruction, exercise, diet, or otherwise: to be under drill: to travel by rail. —*n*. that which is dragged along or follows: a tail: tail-feathers or trailing back-feathers: part of a dress that trails: a retinue: a series: a sequence: a number of things in a string, as animals, railway carriages or wagons: process: a line of combustible material to fire a charge: a set of wheels acting on each other, for transmitting motion: artillery and other equipment for a siege or battle: a lure: a thing dragged on the ground to make a scent: a sledge (*Canada*). —*adj*. train'able.—*adj*. trained, having received training: having a train.—*ns*. trainee', one who is under training; train'er, one who prepares men for athletic feats, horses for a race, or the like: an aeroplane with duplicated controls for training pilots; train'ing, practical education in any profession, art, or handicraft: a course of diet and exercise for developing physical strength, endurance, or dexterity.—train'-band (*hist*.), a band of citizens trained to bear arms; train'-bearer, one who holds up a train, as of a robe, or gown; train ferry, a ferry that conveys railway trains; train'ing-college, former name for college of education; train'ing-ship, a ship in which boys are trained for the sea; train mile, a unit of railway traffic, a run of one mile by one train.—in training, undergoing training: physically fit; train fine, to bring body or mind to a high pitch of efficiency. [Mainly O.Fr. traîner, trahiner (Fr. traîner), to drag (nouns traïn, traîne); partly with overlap of meanings, from O.Fr. traïne, guile.]

train, trān, n. (usu. train'-oil') whale-oil extracted from the blubber by boiling. [Du. traen (now traan), tear, exudation.]

traipse, trapes, trāps, v.i. to trail: to trudge: to gad: to go in a slatternly way.—n. a slattern: a trudge.—n. and adj. traips'ing, trapes'ing.— v.i. trape, to traipse. [Origin unknown.]

trait, trā, or trāt, n. a stroke, touch: a characteristic. [Fr.,—L. trahĕre, tractum, to draw.]

traitor, trā'tor, n. a betrayer: one who commits treason (fem. trait'ress).—Also adj.—ns. trai'torhood, trait'orism, trai'torship.—adjs. trait'orly (Shak.); trait'orous. — adv. trait'orously. — n. trait'orousness. [Fr. traître—L. trāditor— trādĕre, to give up.]

traject, trǝ-jekt', v.t. to take across (obs.): to transmit.—n. (traj'ikt) a crossing: a ferry: a transference, transmission (rare).—ns. trajec'tion (-shǝn), passage (obs.): crossing: transmission: transposition: trajectory (traj'ik-tǝr-i, or tra-jekt'ǝr-i), the curve described by a body under the action of given forces. [L. trăjicĕre, -jectum—trāns, across, jacĕre, to throw.]

tralaticious, tralatitious, tral-ǝ-tish'ǝs, adj. transmitted: traditional: handed on, second-hand. [L. trālātīcius—trānslātum, serving as supine to trānsfero; see transfer.]

tram, tram, n. a barrow or car shaft: a vehicle for minerals in mines: a tramway: a tramway-car.—Also adj.—tram'-car, a tramway-car; tram'-conductor; tram'-line, a line of tramway: (in pl.) the lines marking the sides of the court and the lines parallel to them four and a half feet inside the court (lawn-tennis); tram'-road, a track with sunken rails (legally one not running along a road); tram'-stop, a stopping-place for tram-cars; tram'way, a track or system of tracks with sunken rails along a road; tram'way-car, a carriage for conveying passengers on a tramway. [Cf. L.G. traam, beam, shaft, etc.]

tram, tram, n. silk yarn for weft, of two or more strands. [Fr. trame—L. trāma, weft.]

tram, tram. See trammel.

trammel, tram'l, n. a net whose inner fine-meshed layer is carried by the fish through the coarse-meshed outer layer, and encloses it in a pocket:

a fowling net: a hobble: shackles for making a horse amble: anything that confines: an instrument for describing an ellipse (also tram): a contrivance for adjusting a hook in a fire-place: (in pl.) a tress.—v.t. to shackle: to confine: to impede: to entangle:—pr.p. tramm'elling; pa.t. and pa.p. tramm'elled.—n. tramm'eller. —tramm'el-net', a trammel. [O.Fr. tramail, a net—L.L. tramacula, from L. trēs, three, macula, a mesh.]

tramontane, tra-mon'tān, adj. beyond the mountains (the Alps from Rome): foreign: uncivilised.—n. a dweller beyond the mountains: a foreigner: a barbarian.—n. tramontana (trä-mon-tä'na), in Italy, a north wind. [It. tramontana—L. trāns, beyond, mōns, montis, a mountain.]

tramp, tramp, v.i. to tread, esp. heavily or noisily: to walk: to go on a walking tour or long walk: to go about as a vagrant: to go in a tramp steamer.—v.t. to traverse on foot: to trample: to tread in a tub in washing clothes (Scot.).—n. a foot-journey: a vagrant: a plate of iron worn on the sole for pressing a spade or for giving foothold on ice: the footrest of a spade: a cargo-boat with no fixed route: a prostitute, an immoral woman (slang).—adv. with tramping noise.—n. tramp'er. [M.E. trampen; cf. Ger. trampen.]

trample, tramp'l, v.t. to tread roughly under foot: to treat with pride, to insult.—v.i. to tread roughly or in contempt: to tread forcibly and rapidly.—n. a trampling.—ns. tramp'ler; tramp'-ling.—Also adj. [Freq. of tramp.]

trampolin(e), tram'pō-lin, n. a bed-like framework holding a sheet of elastic material for acrobats, gymnasts, diving learners, etc.—n. tram'polinist. [It. trampolino, springboard.]

trance, trăns, n. a dazed, abstracted, ecstatic or exalted state: a deep sleeplike state, profound and prolonged: catalepsy.—v.t. to throw into a trance: to entrance.—adv. tranced (trănst, trăn'sid), in a trance.—adv. tranc'edly. [Fr. transe—transir—L. trānsire, to go across, in L.L. to die.]

trance, trance, trăns, (Scot.) n. a through passage.

tranche, trǎsh, n. a slice: a block, portion, of an issue of shares. [Fr.]

tranect, tran'ekt, (Shak.) n. a ferry. [As if L. trăns, across, nectĕre, to join; but supposed to be a misprint for traject.]

trangam, trang'gam, n. a trumpery gimcrack. [Origin unknown.]

trangle, trang'gl, (her.) n. a diminutive of the fess. [Obs. Fr.]

trankum, trang'kǝm, (Scott) n. a trinket. [trinket.]

tranquil, trangk'wil, adj. calm: peaceful.—n. tranquillisā'tion.—v.t. tranq'uillise, -ize, to make tranquil.—n. tranquilli'ser, that which tranquillises: a sedative drug.—adv. tranquilli'singly. —n. tranquill'ity.—adv. tran'quilly. [L. tranquillus.]

trans-, tranz-, trănz-, trans-, trăns-, pfx. across, beyond, through.—Also tran-, tra-. [L. trāns, across, beyond.]

transact, tranz-, tranz-, -s-akt', v.t. to conduct, negotiate: to perform: to deal with (arch.).— v.i. to negotiate: to have to do.—ns. transac'tion, act of transacting: an agreement: a piece of business performed: (pl.) the reports or publications of certain learned societies; transac'tor. [L. trānsactum, pa.p. of trānsigĕre— agĕre, to carry on.]

transalpine, tranz-al'pin, adj. beyond the Alps (orig. from Rome): crossing the Alps. [L. trānsalpinus—Alpae, Alps.]

transandine, trǝnz-, tranz-an'dīn, adj. beyond, or crossing the Andes.—Also transandē'an (or -an'di-ǝn). [Pfx. trans-.]

transatlantic, tranz-ǝt-lan'tik, adj. beyond the

*Atlantic* Ocean: crossing the Atlantic. [Pfx. **trans-**.]

**transcend**, *tran-send'*, *v.t.* to rise above: to surmount: to surpass: to exceed: to pass or lie beyond the limit of.—*ns.* **transcend'ence**, **transcend'ency**.—*adjs.* **transcend'ent**, transcending: superior or supreme in excellence: surpassing others: as applicable to *being*, relating to the absolute, transcending all limitation—as applicable to *knowledge*, pertaining to what transcends experience, being given *a priori*: beyond human knowledge: abstrusely speculative, fantastic; **transcenden'tal**, transcending: supereminent, surpassing others: concerned with what is independent of experience: vague.—*v.t.* **transcenden'talise**, **-ize**.—*ns.* **transcenden'talism**, the investigation of what is *a priori* in human knowledge, or independent of experience: that which is vague and illusive in philosophy: the American reaction against Puritan prejudices, humdrum orthodoxy, old-fashioned metaphysics, materialistic philistinism, and materialism—best associated with the name of R. W. Emerson (1803-82); **transcenden'talist**.—*advs.* **transcenden'tally**; **transcend'ently**.—*n.* **transcend'entness**. [L. *trānscendĕre—scandĕre*, to climb.]

**transcontinental**, *tranz-kont-i-nent'l*, *adj.* extending or passing across, or belonging to the farther side of, a *continent*. [Pfx. **trans-**.]

**transcribe**, *tran-skrīb'*, *v.t.* to write over from one book into another: to copy: to arrange (a composition) for an instrument, voice, or combination other than that for which it was composed (*mus.*): to record for future broadcasting or the like: to broadcast a transcription of.—*ns.* **transcrib'er**; **transcript** (*tran'skript*), a written or printed copy, esp. a legal or official copy of (sometimes secret) proceedings, testimony, etc.; **transcrip'tion**, the act or result of transcribing.—*adjs.* **transcrip'tional**; **transcrip'tive**.—*adv.* **transcrip'tively**. [L. *trānscrībĕre*, *-scrīptum*.]

**transducer**, *trans-dū'sər*, in U.S. *-dōōs'*, *n.* a device that transfers power from one system to another in the same or in different form.—*ns.* **transduc'-tion**, transfer, esp. transfer of genetic material from one bacterial cell to another by bacteriophage; **transduc'tor**, an arrangement of windings on a laminated core or cores, part of a device for amplifying current. [L. *trānsdūcĕre*, *-ductum*, to lead across.]

**transe**. Same as **trance** (2).

**transect**, *tran'sekt*, *n.* a sample belt of vegetation marked off for study.—Also *v.t.* [**tran**(s)-, **sect** (2).]

**transenna**, *tran-sen'ə*, *n.* a screen enclosing a shrine. [L. *trānsenna*.]

**transept**, *tran'sept*, *n.* part of a church at right angles to the nave, or of another building to the body: either wing of such a part where it runs right across.—*adjs.* **transept'al**, of a transept; **transept'ate**, divided by transverse septa. [L. *saeptum* (used in pl.), fence, enclosure.]

**transfard**, *trans-färd'*, (*Spens.*) transferred (*pa.t.*).

**transfer**, *trans-fûr'*, *v.t.* to carry or bring over: to convey from one place, person, ownership, object, group, football club, etc., to another: to change over: to convey (as a design) to another surface.—*v.i.* to change over, esp. (*U.S.*) from one railway, train, or station, to another: —*pr.p.* **transferr'ing**; *pa.t.* and *pa.p.* **transferred'**.—*ns.* **trans'fer**, the act of transferring: conveyance from one person, place, etc., to another: that which is transferred or is to be transferred (as a picture): a transfer-ticket; **transferabil'ity** (also **transferrabil'ity**, **transferribil'ity**).—*adj.* **trans'ferable** (also **transferr'able**, **transferr'ible**).—*ns.* **transferee͞e**, the person to whom a thing is transferred: one who is transferred; **trans'-ference**, the act of transferring or conveying: passage from place to place: unconscious

transferring of emotion, etc., from one person or object to another (*psych.*); **trans'feror** (*law*), **transferr'er** (*general*), one who transfers.—**transferable vote**, a vote which, if the candidate voted for should be out of the running, is to be transferred to another as second (third, etc.) choice; **trans'fer-book**, a register of the transfer of property, shares, etc.; **trans'fer-day**, a day for registering transfer of bank-stock and government funds at the Bank of England; **trans'fer-paper**, a prepared paper used for transferring impressions with copying-presses, etc.; **trans'fer-ticket**, a ticket for a journey to be resumed on another route. [L. *trānsferre—ferre*, to carry.]

**transfigure**, *trans-fig'ər*, *v.t.* to change the appearance of: to glorify.—*ns.* **transfiguration** (*-ə-* or *-ū-rā'shən*), a transformation or glorification in appearance: (*cap.*) the Christian festival of the transfiguration of Christ (Matt. xvii. 2), celebrated on the 6th of August; **transfig'urement**. [L. *trānsfigūrāre—figūra*, form.]

**transfix**, *trans-fiks'*, *v.t.* to pierce through: to paralyse with sudden emotion.—*n.* **transfixion** (*-fik'shən*). [L. *trānsfīgĕre*, *-fīxum—fīgĕre*, to fix.]

**transform**, *trans-förm'*, *v.t.* to change the shape of: to change to another form, appearance, substance, character: to change the form of (an algebraic expression or geometrical figure).—*v.i.* to be changed in form or substance.—*n.* (*träns'*) expression or figure derived from another: any of a group of linguistic constructions considered as rephrasings of each other.—*adj.* **transform'-able**.—*ns.* **transformā'tion**, change of form, constitution, or substance: metamorphosis: transmutation: a transformed person (*Shak.*): false hair: (in full **transformation scene**) a scene on the stage that changes in presence of the audience or in which the characters of the pantomime were transformed into those of the harlequinade: change from one linguistic transform to another of the group: reflection, rotation, translation, or dilatation (*geom.*).—*adjs.* **transformā'tional**; **transform'ative**; **transformed'**.—*n.* **transform'er**, one who, that which, transforms: an apparatus for obtaining an electric current from another of a different voltage.—*n.* and *adj.* **transfor'ming**.—*ns.* **transform'ism**, the theory of mutability of species; **transform'ist**.—*adj.* **transformis'tic**.—**transformational grammar**, a method of studying a language by considering which elements can be derived by transformation from others.—**conformal transformation**, a change of shape which still preserves a one-to-one matching of points in the original surface with points in the new surface, as in map making. [L. *trānsförmāre—förma*, form.]

**transfuse**, *trans-fūz'*, *v.t.* to pour out into another vessel: to transfer to another's veins: to treat by transfusion: to cause to pass, enter, or diffuse through: to imbue: to instil: to cause to be imbibed.—*n.* **transfū'ser**.—*adj.* **transfū'sible**.—*ns.* **transfū'sion** (*-zhən*), transfusing, esp. of blood; **transfū'sionist**.—*adj.* **transfū'sive** (*-siv*), tending or having power to transfuse.—*adv.* **transfū'sively**. [L. *trānsfundĕre—fundĕre*, *fūsum*, to pour.]

**transgress**, *trans-*, *-z-gres'*, *v.t.* to pass beyond the limit of or set by: to overstep, exceed: to infringe.—*v.i.* to offend by violating a law: to sin.—*n.* **transgression** (*-gresh'ən*), an overstepping: an infringement: sin.—*adjs.* **transgress'-ional**; **transgressive** (*-gres'iv*).—*adv.* **transgress'-ively**.—*n.* **transgress'or**. [L. *trānsgredī*, *-gressum—gradī*, *gressum*, to step.]

**tranship**, **transship**, *tran-*, *tran-ship'*, *v.t.* to transfer from one ship or other conveyance to another.—*v.i.* to change ship, etc.—*ns.* **tran**(s)**ship'ment**; **tran**(s)**shipp'er**; **tran**(s)**shipp'ing**. [Pfx. **tran**(s)-.]

**transhume**, *trans-*, *-z-(h)ūm'*, *v.t.* and *v.i.* to trans-

# transient

fer or pass from summer to winter or from winter to summer pastures.—*n.* **transhu'mance.** —*adj.* **transhu'mant.** [Sp. *trashumar*—L. *trāns, humus,* ground.]

**transient,** *tran'zi-,* *si-ənt, adj.* passing: of short duration: making, or for persons making, only a short stay: passing (*mus.*).—*ns.* **tran'sience,** **tran'siency.**—*adv.* **tran'siently.**—*n.* **tran'sientness.** [L. *trānsiēns, -euntis*—pr.p. of *trānsīre,* to cross —*īre, itum,* to go.]

**transilient,** *tran-, trən-sil'i-ənt, adj.* leaping or passing across.—*n.* **transil'iency.** [L. *trānsilīre* —*salīre,* to leap.]

**transilluminate,** *trænz-, -s-i-lū', -lōō'mi-nāt, v.t.* to throw a strong light through.—*n.* **transillumina'tion.** [Pfx. **trans-.**]

**transire,** *tranz-, -s-i'ri,* (L. *trāns-ē're*), *n.* customs warrant for clearing. [L. *trānsīre;* cf. **transient.**]

**transisthmian,** *tranz-, -s-is(th)'mi-ən, adj.* across an isthmus. [Pfx. **trans-.**]

**transistor,** *tranz-, -s-ist'ər, n.* amplifier with crystal and two cat's whiskers: later development of this, a three-electrode semiconductor device, able to perform many functions of multi-electrode valves.—*n.* **transistorisā'tion.**—*v.t.* **transistorise, -ize,** to fit with a transistor.— **transistor (radio),** small portable radio. [*transfer* and *resistor.*]

**transit,** *tran'zit, -sit, n.* passing or conveyance over, across, or through: the passage of a heavenly body over the meridian: the passage of a smaller body over the disk of a greater: a transit-circle, -instrument, or -theodolite.—*v.i.* to pass across.—*v.t.* to pass across: to reverse.— *n.* **transition** (*-sizh'ən, -zish'ən, -sish'ən*), passage from one place, state, stage, style, subject, or mus. key to another: in archit. esp. the passage from Romanesque or Norman to Gothic.—*adj.* **transitional.**—*adjs.* **transi'tional, transi'tionary.** —*adv.* **transi'tionally.**—*adj.* **trans'itive,** passing over: having the power of passing: taking a direct object (*gram.*).—*adv.* **trans'itively.**—*n.* **trans'itiveness.**—*adv.* **trans'itorily.**—*n.* **trans'itoriness.**—*adj.* **trans'itory,** going or passing away: lasting for a short time: speedily vanishing.— **tran'sit-circle,** a transit-instrument with a graduated circle for declinations; **tran'sit-duty,** a duty chargeable on goods passing through a country; **tran'sit-instrument,** a telescope mounted in the meridian and turned on a fixed east and west axis; **tran'sit-theodolite,** one whose telescope can be reversed; **tran'sit-trade,** the trade of carrying foreign goods through a country.—**in transit,** of goods, in the process of being transported from one place to another. [L. *trānsitus, -ūs, trānsitiō, -ōnis*—*īre, itum,* to go.]

**translate,** *trans-, trəns-, -z-lāt', v.t.* to remove to another place: to remove to heaven, especially without death: to enrapture: to render into another language: to express in another artistic medium: to interpret, put in plainer terms, explain: to transfer from one office (esp. ecclesiastical) to another: to transform: to renovate, make new from old: to perform a translation on (*mech., math.*).—*v.i.* to practise translation: to admit of translation.—*adj.* **translā'table.**—*n.* **translā'tion,** the act of translating: removal to another place, see, etc.: rendering into another language: a version: the working up of new things from old materials: motion, change of place, such that every point moves in the same direction at the same speed: similar change of place of a geometrical figure: an algebraic function obtained by adding the same constant to each value of the variable in a given function, thus moving the graph of this function (or moving the rectangular axes parallel to themselves) while preserving its shape: the automatic retransmission of a telegraphic message.—*adjs.* **translā'tional, trans'latory** (*-lə-*

# transparent

*tər-i,* or *-lā').*—*n.* **translā'tor.** [L. *trānslātum,* used as supine of *trānsferre;* see **transfer.**]

**transleithan,** *tranz-, -s-lī't(h)ən, adj.* beyond the river *Leitha,* once in part the boundary between Austria and Hungary: Hungarian. [Pfx. **trans-.**]

**transliterate,** *tranz-,* or *-s-lit'ə-rāt, v.t.* to write in letters of another alphabet.—*ns.* **transliterā'tion;** **translit'erātor.** [L. *littera,* letter.]

**translocation,** *tranz-,* or *-s-lō-kā'shən, n.* transference from place to place, esp. of materials within body of plant: the transfer of a portion of a chromosome to another part of the same chromosome or to a different chromosome (*genetics*).—*v.t.* **translocate'.** [L. *locus,* place.]

**translucent,** *tranz-,* or *-s-lōō'sənt,* or *-lū', adj.* shining through: imperfectly transparent: clear. —*ns.* **translu'cence, translu'cency.**—*adv.* **translu'cently.**—*adj.* **translu'cid,** translucent.—*n.* **translucid'ity.** [L. *trānslūcēns, -entis*—*lūcēre,* to shine —*lūx, lūcis,* light.]

**translunar,** *tranz-, -s-lōō'nər, adj.* pertaining to the region beyond the moon's orbit round the earth. —*adj.* **translun'ary,** (or *tranz'*), beyond the moon: visionary. [Pfx. **trans-.**]

**transmarine,** *tranz-, -s-mə-rēn', adj.* across or beyond the sea. [L. *trānsmarīnus*—*mare,* sea.]

**transmew,** *tranz-,* or *-s-mū',* (*Spens.*) *v.t.* to transmute. [O.Fr. *transmuer*—L. *transmūtāre;* see **transmute.**]

**transmigrate,** *tranz'-,* or *-s'mi-grāt,* or *-grāt', v.i.* to remove to another place of abode: of the soul, to pass into another body.—*v.t.* to cause to transmigrate.—*n.* **trans'migrant** (or *-mi'*), one who transmigrates: an alien entering a country on his way to another in which he means to settle.—*adj.* **transmigrating.**—*ns.* **transmigrā'-tion; transmigrā'tionism,** belief in the transmigration of souls; **transmigrā'tionist.**—*adj.* **trans'migrative** (*-mi-grā-tiv,* or *-mi'gra-tiv*).—*n.* **transmigrātor.**—*adj.* **transmigratory** (*-grə-tər-i*). [L. *trānsmigrāre, -ātum*—*migrāre,* to migrate.]

**transmit,** *tranz-,* or *-s-mit', v.t.* to send or pass on: to allow to pass through:—*pr.p.* **transmitt'-ing;** *pa.t.* and *pa.p.* **transmitt'ed.**—*n.* **transmissi-bil'ity.**—*adj.* **transmiss'ible** (also **transmitt'able,** less correctly **-ible**).—*n.* **transmission** (*-mish'ən*). —*adjs.* **transmiss'ional; transmiss'ive,** having the quality of transmitting or of being transmitted. —*ns.* **transmissiv'ity; transmitt'al; transmitt'er,** one who or that which transmits: apparatus for sending forth anything, as signals, messages, etc. [L. *trānsmittĕre, -missum*—*mittĕre, missum,* to send.]

**transmogrify,** *tranz-, -s-mog'ri-fī,* (*coll., facet.*) *v.t.* to transform, transmute:—*pr.p.* **transmog'rify-ing;** *pa.t.* and *pa.p.* **transmog'rified.**—*n.* **transmogrifica'tion.** [A grotesque concoction.]

**transmove,** *tranz-, -s-mōōv',* (*Spens.*) *v.t.* to transmute. [App. for **transmew,** remodelled on **move.**]

**transmute,** *tranz-,* or *-s-mūt', v.t.* to change to another form or substance.—*n.* **transmūtabil'ity.** —*adj.* **transmū'table.**—*n.* **transmū'tableness.**— *adv.* **transmū'tably.**—*ns.* **transmūtā'tion,** a changing into a different form, nature, or substance, esp. that of one chemical element into another; **transmūtā'tionist.**—*adj.* **transmū'tative,** serving or tending to transmute.—*n.* **transmū'ter.** [L. *trānsmūtāre*—*mūtāre,* to change.]

**transoceanic,** *tranz-,* or *-s-ō-shi-an'ik, adj.* across or crossing the ocean. [Pfx. **trans-.**]

**transom,** *tran'səm, n.* a cross-piece: a cross-beam: a structure dividing a window horizontally: a lintel. [App. L. *trānstrum,* a cross-beam.]

**transonic.** Common spelling for **trans-sonic.**

**transpadane,** *trans', -z'pə-dān, -pā'dān, adj.* beyond the Po (from Rome). [L. *Padus,* the Po.]

**transparent,** *trans-, trəns-, -z-pār'ənt,* or *-par', adj.* able to be seen through: pellucid: pervious

Neutral vowels in unaccented syllables; *el'ə-mənt;* for certain sounds in foreign words, see p. viii to rays: shining through (*Shak.*): easily detected, understood: obvious, evident: ingenuous.—*ns.* **transpar'ence** (*rare*), **transpar'ency,** the quality of being transparent: that which is transparent: a picture, design, device visible, or to be viewed, by transmitted light: Thackeray's humorous translation of the German title *Durchlaucht.*—*adv.* **transpar'ently.**—*n.* **transpar'entness.** [L.L. *trănspārēns, -entis*—L. *părēre,* to appear.]

**transpicious,** *tran-, trən-spik'ū-əs,* (*Milt.*) *adj.* transparent. [L. *trănspicĕre,* to see through—*specēre,* to look.]

**transpierce,** *trans-pērs',* *v.t.* to pierce through: to permeate. [Pfx. **trans-.**]

**transpire,** *tran-spīr',* *v.t.* to give off as vapour: to exhale: to emit through the skin.—*v.i.* to exhale: to give off water-vapour (as plants) or waste material through the skin (as animals): to become known, come to light: often, wrongly, to happen.—*adj.* **transpir'able.**—*n.* **transpiration** (*tran-spi-rā'shən*), act or process of transpiring: exhalation through the skin: emission of water-vapour through the stomata, etc.—*adj.* **transpir'atory.** [L. *spīrāre,* to breathe.]

**transplant,** *trans-, -z-plänt',* *v.t.* to remove from the ground where it grows and plant in another place: to graft upon another animal or another part of the same: to remove and establish elsewhere.—*v.i.* to bear transplanting.—*n.* a part or organ removed from its normal position and grafted into another position in the same individual or into another individual: the act of transplanting.—*adj.* **transplan'table.**—*ns.* **transplantā'tion; transplan'ter; transplant'ing.** [L. *trănsplantāre*—*plantāre,* to plant.]

**transponder,** *tranz-, -s-pon'dər,* *n.* a radio or radar device which, on receiving a signal, transmits a signal of its own. [*transmitter* res*ponder.*]

**transpontine,** *trans-pon'tīn, adj.* across a bridge: on the Surrey side of the Thames: hence melodramatic. [L. *pōns, pontis,* a bridge.]

**transport,** *trans-, -z-pōrt', -pört',* *v.t.* to carry, convey, remove: to send overseas, as a convict: to translate (as a minister): to put to death (*Shak.*): perh., to carry off (as by the fairies; *Shak.*): to carry away by strong emotion: to throw into an ecstasy.—*ns.* **trans'port,** carriage from one place to another: the conveyance of troops and their necessaries: a ship, wagon, etc., therefor: ecstasy: one who has been transported or sentenced to transportation: **transportabil'ity.**—*adj.* **transport'able,** that may be transported: liable, or rendering liable, to transportation. — *ns.* **transport'al; transport'ance** (*Shak.*), conveyance, transport; **transportā'tion,** removal: removal of offenders beyond seas: means of transport: tickets or passes for transport.—*adj.* **transport'ed.**—*adv.* **transport'edly.**—*ns.* **transport'edness; transport'er.**—*n.* and *adj.* **transport'ing.**—*adv.* **transport'ingly.**—*adj.* **transport'ive,** tending or having power to transport.—**transport café,** a roadside café catering mainly for long-distance lorry drivers; **transporter bridge,** a bridge with a travelling carriage suspended from a girder; **trans'port-rider** (*S.Afr.*), a carrier by wagon; **trans'port-ship,** a ship used for carrying troops, stores, etc. [L. *trănsportāre*—*portāre,* to carry.]

**transpose,** *trans-, -z-pōz',v.t.* to transform (*Shak.*): to transfer: to turn, alter: to change the order of, interchange: to write, perform, or render in another key (*mus.*).—*adj.* **transpōs'able.**—*ns.* **tɩanspōs'al,** a change of place or order; **transpōs'er.**—*n.* and *adj.* **transpōs'ing.**—*n.* **transposition** (*-pō-, -pə-zish'ən*).—*adjs.* **transposi'tional; transpositive** (*-poz'*).—**transposing instrument,** an instrument that by a mechanical device transposes music into another key: one for which music is written in a different key

from the actual sounds. [Fr. *transposer*; see **pose.**]

**transsexual, trans-sexual,** *trans-seks'ū-əl, adj.* and *n.* (a person) apparently normal physically, but having an abnormally strong desire to belong to the opposite sex.—*n.* **transsex'ualism.** [Pfx. **trans-.**]

**trans-shape,** *trans-shăp',* (*Shak.*) *v.t.* to transform.

**trans-ship.** Same as **tranship.**

**trans-sonic,** *trans-son'ik, adj.* designating a narrow zone or region of speed just greater than that of sound.—Often **transonic.** [L. *sonus,* sound.]

**transubstantiate,** *tran-səb-, -zəb-stan'shi-āt, v.t.* to change to another substance.—*ns.* **transubstantiā'-tion,** a change into another substance: the doctrine that, in the consecration of the elements of the eucharist, the whole substance of the bread and wine is converted into Christ's body and blood, only the appearances of bread and wine remaining (cf. **consubstantiation**); **transubstantiā'tion(al)ist, transubstan'tiātor,** one who believes in transubstantiation. [L. *substantia,* substance.]

**transude,** *tran-sūd', -zūd', v.i.* and *v.t.* to ooze out. —*n.* a substance that transudes.—*n.* **transūdā'-tion.**—*adj.* **transū'datory.** [L. *sūdāre,* to sweat.]

**transume,** *tran-sūm', -zūm', v.t.* (*obs.*) to transcribe officially.—*ns.* **transumpt** (*-sumt'*), a copy of a legal writing; **transumption** (*-sum'shən*), transcription: metaphor: transference.—*adj.* **transumptive** (*-sump'tiv*). [L. *trăn(s)sūmēre,* to transcribe—*sūmēre,* to take.]

**transuranic,** *trans-, -z-ū-ran'ik, adj.* of greater atomic number than *uranium.*—Also **transurā'-nium.** [Pfx. **trans-.**]

**transvalue,** *trans-, -z-val'ū, v.t.* to evaluate anew. —*n.* **transvaluā'tion.** [Pfx. **trans-.**]

**transverse,** *tranz'vûrs,* or *-vûrs', adj.* set crosswise. —*adv.* crosswise.—*n.* anything set crosswise.—*v.t.* (*-vûrs'*) to cross: to thwart: to reverse: to transform.—*adj.* **transvers'al,** transverse.—*n.* a line cutting a set of lines.—*n.* **transversal'ity.**—*advs.* **transvers'ally; transverse'ly.**—*n.* **transver'-sion.**—**by transverse** (*Spens.*), awry. [L. *trăns-versus*—*vertēre, versum,* to turn.]

**transverse,** *tranz-vûrs', v.t.* to turn from prose into verse.—*n.* **transver'sion** (*-shən*). [A pun in Buckingham's *Rehearsal.*]

**transvest,** *tranz-vest', v.t.* and *v.i.* to dress oneself in the clothes of another, esp. of the opposite sex.—*adj.* **transvest'ic.**—*n.* and *adj.* **transvestite** (*-vest'-it*), (one) given to this.—*ns.* **transvest'ism; transvest'itism.** [Pfx. **trans-,** and L. *vestis*—*vestīre, vestītum,* to dress; cf. **travesty.**]

**tranter,** *trant'ər,* (*dial.*) *n.* a hawker: a carrier.—*v.t.* and *v.i.* **trant** (back-formation), to hawk. [Cf. L.L. *trăvetārius.*]

**trap,** *trap, n.* a snare, gin: a device for catching: a hidden danger: one who catches offenders (*slang*): trickery (*slang*): a pitfall: a trap-door: a ventilating door in a mine: a lock: a bend in a pipe to stop foul gases: a light carriage: a contrivance for throwing up or releasing a ball or pigeons: the mouth (*slang*).—*v.t.* to catch in a trap: to provide with traps.—*v.i.* to act as a trapper:—*pr.p.* **trapp'ing;** *pa.t.* and *pa.p.* **trapped.**—*ns.* **trapp'er,** one who traps animals for their fur: a boy who minds a mine trap: a horse for a trap; **trapp'iness.**—*n.* and *adj.* **trapp'ing.**—*adj.* **trapp'y,** full of traps, treacherous. —**trap'-ball,** an old game played with a ball, bat, and trap; **trap'-door,** a door in a floor or stage; **trap'-fall,** a trap-door that gives way beneath the feet: a pitfall; **trap'-stick,** a bat for trap-ball. [O.E. *trappe*—*træppe, treppe.*]

**trap,** *trap,* (*geol.: old-fashioned*) *n.* vaguely, a dark fine-grained igneous rock (lying often in steps or terraces).—*adj.* **trapp'ean** (or *-ē'*).—**trap'-rock.** [Sw. *trapp*—*trappa,* a stair.]

**trap,** *trap, n.* a fault (*mining*): a ladder leading to a loft (*Scot.*).—*adj.* **trap'-cut,** of jewellery, cut in steps.—**trap'-ladder, -stair.** [Cf. Du. *trap,* step; cf. foregoing word.]

**trap,** *trap, n.* a horse-cloth (*obs.*): (*pl.*) personal luggage.—*v.t.* to caparison, deck with trappings.
—*adj.* **trapped.**—*n.pl.* **trapp'ings,** gay clothes: ornaments, esp. those put on horses: accompaniments, adornments (of office, etc.). [App. conn. with Fr. *drap,* Sp. and Port. *trapo,* L.L. *drappus* (*trapus*), cloth.]

**trapan.** See **trepan** (1).

**trape, trapes.** See **traipse.**

**trapezium,** *trə-pē'zi-əm, n.* orig., any quadrilateral that is not a parallelogram: one with no sides parallel (*U.S.*): one with only one pair parallel (*Brit.*): a wrist-bone articulating with the thumb metacarpal:—*pl.* **trapē'zia, -ziums.**—*n.* **trapēze** (*trə-pēz'*), a swing of one or more crossbars used in gymnastics.—*v.i.* to perform or go on a trapeze.—*adjs.* **trapē'zial,** pertaining to a trapezium; **trapē'ziform,** having the form of a trapezium.—*ns.* **trapēzohē'dron,** a solid figure whose faces are trapezia or trapezoids; **trapezoid** (*trap'i-zoid,* also *trə-pē'zoid*), a quadrilateral with no sides parallel: one with two sides parallel (*U.S.*): a wrist-bone next the trapezium.—*adj.* **trapezoid'al.** [Latinised from Gr. *trapezion,* dim. of *trapeza,* a table; fit. four-legged—*tetra-,* four-, *peza,* a foot.]

**Trappist,** *trap'ist, n.* a Cistercian of the reformed rule established by De Rancé (1626-1700), abbot of La Trappe in Normandy—austere and silent. —Also *adj.*—*n.* **Trapp'istine** (*-tēn, -tin*), a nun of an affiliated order.

**trash,** *trash, v.t.* (*Shak.*) to check.—*n.* (*dial.*) a leash or other restraint. [Origin obscure.]

**trash,** *trash, n.* broken twigs, hedge-cuttings: sugar-cane refuse: scraps: anything worthless: rubbish: paltry stuff: a worthless person (*Shak.*): worthless people: poor whites (*U.S.*). —*v.t.* to free from trash: to lop the tops from. —*n.* **trash'ery,** trash, rubbish.—*adv.* **trash'ily.** —*ns.* **trash'iness; trash'trie** (*Scot.*), trash.—*adj.* **trash'y,** like trash: worthless.—**trash-can** (*U.S.*), a receptacle for refuse. [Prob. Scand.; cf. Norw. dial. *trask,* trash, O.N. *tros,* fallen twigs.]

**trash,** *trash, v.t.* to wear out, to harass.—*v.i.* to trudge. [Cf. Sw. *traska,* Norw. *traske.*]

**trass,** *tras, n.* an earthy volcanic tuff used as a hydraulic cement.—Also **tarras', terras'.** [Du. *tras.*]

**trattoria,** *trät-tō-rē'a, n.* an Italian restaurant.

**trauchle,** *tröhh'l,* (*Scot.*) *v.t.* to bedraggle: to weary with drudgery or plodding.—*v.i.* to drudge: to trail along. [Cf. Flem. *tragelen,* to go heavily.]

**trauma,** *trö'mə, n.* a wound: an injury: an emotional shock that may be the origin of a neurosis (*psych.*): the state or condition caused by a physical or emotional shock.—*adj.* **traumatic** (*-mat'ik*; often used loosely).—*adv.* **traumat'ically.**—*ns.* **trau'matism** (*-mə-tizm*), condition due to a wound; **traumatous'ty,** a nastic movement after wounding. [Gr. *trauma, -atos,* a wound.]

**travail,** *trav'āl, -əl, n.* excessive labour: toil: labour in childbirth: *obs.* for **travel.**—*v.i.* to labour: to suffer the pains of childbirth: *obs.* for **travel.**—*adj.* **trav'ailed,** toilworn: wearied: experienced: having been in travail.—**trav'ailpain, -pang.** [O.Fr. (Fr.) *travail.*]

**travail.** See **travois.**

**travel,** *trav'l, v.i.* to journey: to go: to walk (*dial.*): to go round soliciting orders: to go on circuit: to move along a course: to go with impetus: to pass: to move: *obs.* for **travail.**—*v.t.* to journey over or through: to conduct or send on a journey (*arch.*):—*pr.p.* **trav'elling;** *pa.t.* and *pa.p.* **trav'elled.**—*n.* journeying: impetus: power of going: range of movement: passage: *obs.* for **travail:** (in *pl.*) an account of journeys.—*adj.* **trav'elled,** having made journeys: transported: not in its original place: experienced: beaten, frequented.—*n.* **trav'eller,** one who travels or has travelled: a wayfarer: one who travels for a mercantile house: a ring that slides along a rope or spar: a piece of mechanism that moves on a gantry, etc.—*n.* and *adj.* **trav'elling.**—*n.* **travelogue** (*trav'ə-log*), a talk, lecture, article, or film on travel.—**travel agency,** an agency which provides information, brochures, tickets, etc., relating to travel; **traveller's cheque,** a cheque which can be cashed at any foreign branch or specified agent of the bank issuing it; **trav'eller's-joy,** the virgin's-bower, *Clematis vitalba;* **traveller's tale,** an astounding lie about what one professes to have seen abroad; **trav'eller's-tree,** a Madagascan tree (Ravenala) of the banana family with great leaves on two sides only, accumulating water in the leafbases. — *adjs.* **trav'el-soiled, -stained, trav'eltaint'ed** (*Shak.*), showing the marks of travel. —**travelling-wave tube,** a device used in communications for increasing signal power, amplification being produced by interaction between a wave of radio frequency travelling on a wire helix and an electron beam travelling at roughly the same velocity inside the helix. [travail.]

**travelator.** Form of **travolator.**

**traverse,** *trav'ûrs, adj.* cross: oblique.—*n.* a crossing or passage across: a straight length in a zigzag course: a passage across the face of a rock in mountaineering: a survey by measuring straight lines from point to point and the angles between: anything set or lying across: an obstruction: adversity: a curtain, screen, partition: a barrier: a parapet: a cross-piece: a gallery from one side of a large building to another: a screened-off compartment: a denial or contradiction: an opposing, counteracting movement (*fencing*).—*v.t.* ((or *-vûrs'*) cross: pass through, across, or over: to move about over: to pass over by traverse: to survey by traverse: to oppose: to thwart: to dispute: to deny, contradict: to turn sideways.—*v.i.* to make a traverse: to move to the side: to direct a gun to the right or left.—*adjs.* **trav'ersable;** **trav'ersed,** crossed, passed over: set crosswise (*Shak.*).—*n.* **trav'erser,** one who traverses: a platform for shifting wagons and carriages sideways. — *n.* and *adj.* **trav'ersing.** — **traversing bridge,** one that can be withdrawn horizontally. [Fr. *travers, traverse, traverser*—L. *trāns, vertère, versum,* to turn.]

**travertine,** *trav'ər-tin, -tēn, -tin, n.* a pale limestone deposited from solution, e.g. from springs.— Also **travertin.** [It. *travertino*—L. *tīburtīnus* (*lapis*), stone of Tibur.]

**travesty,** *trav'is-ti, n.* disguise, esp. of a man as a woman or vice versa: burlesque: ridiculously inadequate representation (of).—*v.t.* to disguise: to burlesque. [Fr. *travesti,* pa.p. of *travestir,* to disguise—L. *trāns, vestire,* to clothe; cf. **transvest.**]

**travis,** *trav'is,* an obs. or dial. form of **traverse.** See also **treviss.**

**travois,** *trä-voi',* **travail,** *trä-vä'i, n.* a North American Indian drag, a pair of trailing poles attached to each side of the saddle, joined by a board or net. [Canadian Fr. pronun. of Fr. *travail.*]

**travolator,** *trav'ō-lā-tər, n.* a moving way for the conveyance of foot-passengers. [From stem of **travel** after **escalator.**]

**trawl,** *tröl, n.* an open-mouthed bag-net for dragging along the bottom: a buoyed line with baited hooks at intervals (*U.S.*).—*v.t.* and *v.i.* to catch or fish with a trawl or (*Scot.* and *U.S.*) a seine-net.—*ns.* **traw'ler,** one who trawls: a trawling vessel; **traw'ling.—trawl'-net.** [Cf. **trail,** and M.Du. *traghel,* drag-net.]

**tray,** *trā, n.* a flat low-rimmed vessel used for carrying articles (as crockery, etc.).—*n.* **tray'ful:** —*pl.* **tray'fuls.—tray'-cloth,** a cloth for covering a tray. [O.E. *trig, trēg,* board.]

**tray,** *trā.* See **trey.**—*n.* **tray'-trip** (*Shak.*), a game played with dice.

**treacher, treachour,** *trech'ər,* (*obs.*) *n.* a deceiver by trickery: a betrayer: a traitor.—Also **treach'-erer.** —*adj* **treach'erous,** ready to betray: not to be trusted: misleadingly inviting in appearance. — *adv.* **treach'erously.** — *ns.* **treach'erous-ness; treach'ery,** betrayal: readiness to betray: falseness: treason; **treach'etour** (*Spens.*), a deceiver: a traitor. [O.Fr. *trecheor,* deceiver—*trechier,* to trick; cf. **trick.**]

**treacle,** *trē'kl, n.* orig. an antidote or prophylactic against bites, hence against poisons, etc.: the dark, viscous uncrystallisable syrup obtained in refining sugar: also molasses, the drainings of crude sugar: blandishments, esp. when suggestive of the cloying and nauseating taste and thickness of treacle.—*v.t.* to dose or smear with treacle.—*v.i.* to treacle trees in order to collect moths.—*n.* **trea'cliness.**—*adj.* **trea'cly,** of, or like, treacle: thick and sweet: unctuously blandishing.—**trea'cle-mustard,** the cruciferous plant *Erysimum cheiranthoides.* [O.Fr. *triacle*—Gr. *thēriakē* (*antidotos,* an antidote to the bites) of beasts—*thērion,* a wild beast.]

**tread,** *tred, v.i.* to set the foot down: to step: to walk: to trample: to copulate, as a cock: same as **trade** (*Scot.*).—*v.t.* to walk on: to press with the foot, as, in threshing, pressing grapes, tramping clothes, packing: to trample: to render by treading: to perform by treading, dance: to copulate with as a cock-bird: to oppress (*fig.*):—*pa.t.* **trod;** *pa.p.* **trodd'en, trod.**—*n.* a footprint: a track: act or manner of treading: a step or tramp: a thing or part trodden on, as of a step: the part that touches the ground, as of a shoe, a wheel: distance between wheels or pedals: the cicatricula, or the chalaza, of an egg: same as **trade** (*Scot.*).—*ns.* **tread'er; tread'ing; tread'le, tredd'le,** a foot-lever for working a machine: a pedal: the chalaza of an egg (once thought to be derived from the cock; *dial.*).—*v.i.* to work a treadle.—*ns.* **tread'ler; tread'ling.—tread'mill,** a cylinder turned by treading on boards on its outside, as formerly by prisoners: a mill so worked: routine drudgery (*fig.*); **tread'-wheel,** a wheel or cylinder turned by treading outside or inside: a treadmill.—**tread water,** to float upright by an action as if of climbing a ladder. [O.E. *tredan;* Ger. *treten;* O.N. *trotha;* cf. **trade.**]

**treague,** *trēg,* (*Spens.*) *n.* a truce. [L.L. *tregua, treuga*—Goth. *triggwa,* treaty.]

**treason,** *trē'zn, n.* betraying of the government or an attempt to overthrow it: treachery: disloyalty.—*adj.* **trea'sonable,** pertaining to, consisting of, or involving treason.—*n.* **trea'sonable-ness.**—*adv.* **trea'sonably.**—*adj.* **trea'sonous.**—**treason felony,** the crime of desiring to depose the sovereign, intimidate parliament, stir up a foreign invasion, etc.—declared by statute in 1848.—**constructive treason,** anything that may be interpreted as equivalent to actual treason by leading naturally to it; **high treason,** offences against the state; **misprision of treason,** knowledge of the principal crime and concealment thereof; **petty treason,** the murder of a husband by a wife, a master by a servant, etc. [A.Fr. *tresun,* O.Fr. *traïson* (Fr. *trahison*)—*traïr* (*trahir*)—L. *tradĕre,* to betray.]

**treasure,** *trezh'ər, n.* wealth stored up: riches: anything much valued.—*v.t.* to hoard up: to collect for future use: to value greatly: to store, enrich.—*ns.* **treas'urer,** one who has the care of a

treasure or treasury: one who has charge of collected funds; **treas'urership; treas'ury,** a place where treasure is deposited: (often *cap.*) a department of a government which has charge of the finances: mistakenly applied to a beehive tomb in prehistoric Greece.—**treas'ure-chest,** a box for keeping articles of value; **treas'ure-city,** a city for stores, magazines, etc.; **treas'ure-house,** a house for holding treasures: a treasury: a store of valuable things; **treasure trove** (*trové* pa.p. of A.Fr. *trover,* to find), ownerless property found hidden (in England gold and silver only), property of the crown; **Treasury bench,** the first row of seats on the Speaker's right hand in the House of Commons, occupied by the members of the government; **Treasury bill,** a security entitling the holder to a stated amount to be paid from the Consolidated Fund at a specified date; **Treasury note,** a currency note issued by the Treasury. [O.Fr. *tresor* (Fr. *trésor*)—L. *thēsaurus*—Gr. *thēsauros.*]

**treat,** *trēt, v.t.* to deal with: to handle: to discuss: to behave towards: to act upon: to deal with the case of: to deal with (disease) by applying remedies: to subject to a process: to stand a drink or other gratification to.—*v.i.* to negotiate: to deal (with *of*): to stand treat.—*n.* a free entertainment, pleasure excursion, or feast: a turn or act of providing and paying: a source of great gratification: negotiation, parley (*Spens.*). —*adj.* **treat'able,** able to be treated: tractable, moderate (*obs.*).—*ns.* **treat'er; treat'ing; treat'ise** (*-iz, -is*), a written composition, esp. one treating a subject formally or systematically; **treat'ment,** act or manner of treating: management: behaviour to anyone: way of applying remedies; **treat'y,** negotiation: a formal agreement, esp. between states: entreaty (*Shak.*).— **treaty port,** a port opened by treaty to foreign trade.—**Dutch treat** (see **Dutch**); **stand treat** (see **stand**). [O.Fr. *traitier*—L. *tractāre,* to manage —*trahĕre, tractum,* to draw.]

**treble,** *treb'l, adj.* triple: threefold: in the treble (*mus.*): high-pitched.—*n.* that which is triple: three times as much: the highest part, soprano (*mus.*): a treble singer, voice, instrument, string, sound, etc.—*v.t.* to make three times as much.— *v.i.* to become threefold.—*n.* **treb'leness.**—*adv.* **treb'ly.—treble chance,** a mode of competing in football pools in which, in a selection of matches made from a list, the aim is to pick all draws, they counting most, the away win and home win chances less; **treble clef,** the G clef on the second line.—*adj.* **treb'le-dated,** living three ages. [O.Fr.,—L. *triplus;* see **triple.**]

**trebuchet,** *treb'ū-shet, trā-bū-shā, n.* a mediaeval military engine for launching stones, etc. [O.Fr.]

**trecento,** *trā'chen'tō, n.* and *adj.* 14th-century (in Italian art, etc.).—*n.* **trecen'tist.** [It., three (for thirteen) hundred.]

**treck.** Same as **trek** (*v.i.* and *n.*).

**tre corde,** *trā kor'dā,* (It.) three strings: a direction to piano players to release the soft pedal.

**treddle.** Same as **treadle.** See **tread.**

**tredrille, tredille,** *tra-d(r)il',* n. a card game for three. [After **quadrille**—L. *trēs,* three.]

**tree,** *trē, n.* a large plant with a single branched woody trunk (sometimes loosely applied): timber: a wooden structure or part of various kinds: a saddle-tree: a boot- or shoe-tree: a gallows: a cross for crucifixion: a branching figure or structure, as an arborescent aggregate of crystals (e.g. *lead tree*) or a pedigree.—*v.t.* to drive into a tree, to corner (also *fig.*): to form on a tree.—*v.i.* to take refuge in a tree.—*adj.* wooden: in composition, inhabiting, frequenting, growing on trees: taking the form of a tree: dendritic.— *adjs.* **tree'less;** tree (*trē'ən*), of a tree (*Spens.*): wooden.—*n.* small articles of wood, esp.

eating and drinking vessels of past times.—*n.* **tree'ship**, existence as a tree.—**tree bicycle**, a mechanical device used for climbing trees; **tree'-bur'ial**, disposal of the dead in the branches of trees; **tree'-calf**, a light-brown calf bookbinding, in conventional imitation of a branching tree; **tree'-creeper**, a little bird (Certhia) that runs up tree-trunks in search of insects; **tree'-fern**, a fern with a tall woody trunk; **tree'-frog**, an arboreal amphibian, esp. one of the family Hylidae, nearer to toads than to frogs; **tree'-kangaroo'**, a tree-climbing kangaroo (Dendrolagus); **tree'-lil'y**, a xerophytic treelike plant of the Brazilian campos (Vellozia); **tree'-mall'ow**, Lavatera; **tree'-moss'**, moss or lichen growing on a tree: a moss like a tiny tree in shape; **treenail, trenail** (*trē'nāl, tren'l*), a long wooden pin or nail to fasten the planks of a ship to the timbers; **tree'-on'ion**, a variety of onion with bulbs in the place of flowers; **tree rings**, annual rings; **tree'-shrew**, a squirrel-shrew, any insectivore of the East Indian family Tupaiidae, squirrel-like animals akin to shrews; **tree'-toma'to**, a South American solanaceous shrub (Cyphomandra) or its tomato-like fruit; **tree'top**, the top of a tree; **tree'-trunk; tree'-wor'ship; tree'-wor'shipper.**—**at the top of the tree**, in the highest position in e.g. a profession; **family tree**, pedigree; **tree of heaven**, ailanto; **tree of lead**, Saturn's tree; **tree of life**, arbor vitae: a tree in the Garden of Eden (Gen. ii. 9); **tree of silver**, Diana's tree, an arborescent deposit of silver; **up a tree**, in a fix. [O.E. *trēow, trēo*; cf. Gr. *drỹs*, oak, *dory*, spear; Sans. *dru*, tree.]

**trefoil**, *trē'foil, tre'foil, n.* a three-lobed form, ornament, or aperture, as in tracery or heraldry: a leaf of three leaflets: a trifoliate plant, esp. of the clover genus (Trifolium).—*adj.* **tre'foiled.**—**bird's-foot trefoil** (see **bird**). [A.Fr. *trifoil*—L. *trifolium*—*trēs*, three, *folium*, a leaf.]

**tregetour**, *trej'ə-tər, n.* a juggler (*obs.*): a trickster: a deceiver. [O.Fr. *tresgetour—tresgeter*—L. *trāns, jactāre*, to throw.]

**trehala**, *tri-hä'la, n.* Turkish manna, cocoons of a beetle. [Turk. *tiqālah*.]

**treille**, *trāl, n.* a trellis.—*n.* **treill'age**, trellis-work: a trellis.—*adj.* **treill'aged.** [Fr.,—L. *trichila*, a bower.]

**trek**, *trek, v.t.* to drag.—*v.i.* to journey by oxwagon: to migrate: to tramp and camp, dragging one's equipment: to make a long hard journey, usu. on foot:—*pr.p.* **trekk'ing**; *pa.t.* and *pa.p.* **trekked.**—*n.* a journey or stage: a migration.—*ns.* **trekk'er.**—**trek'-ox; trek'schuit** (*-s'hhoit, -skoit*), a towed canal-boat. [Du. *trekken*, to draw.]

**trellis**, *trel'is, n.* a structure of cross-barred or lattice work.—*v.t.* to provide with a trellis: to train on a trellis.—*adj.* **trell'ised—trell'is-work**, lattice-work. [O.Fr. *treliz*—L. *trilix, -icis*, woven with triple thread, modified by association with *treille*, q.v.]

**trema**, *trē'mə, n.* an orifice: a diaeresis, two dots placed as a mark of separate pronunciation over a vowel-letter.—*adj.* **trematic** (*tri-mat'ik*), of the gill-slits.—*n.* **trematode** (*trem'ə-tōd*), any member of the **Tremato'da**, a class of parasitic, unsegmented flat-worms with adhesive suckers.—*n.* and *adj.* **trem'atoid.** [Gr. *trēma, -atos*, a hole.]

**tremble**, *trem'bl, v.i.* to shake, as from fear, cold, or weakness: to quiver: to vibrate: to pass tremulously.—*v.t.* to set trembling.—*n.* the act of trembling: tremulousness: a tremulous state: (in *pl.*) a morbid trembling.—*ns.* **trem'blement**; **trem'bler**, one who or that which trembles: any of a number of West Indian birds of the family Mimidae.—*n.* and *adj.* **trem'bling.**—*adv.* **trem'blingly.**—*adj.* **trem'bly**, tremulous.—**trembling poplar**, the aspen. [O.Fr. (Fr.) *trembler*—L. *tremulus*, trembling—*tremĕre*, to shake.]

**Tremella**, *tri-mel'ə, n.* a gelatinous fungus, witches' meat, on decaying wood, etc. [L. *tremulus*, quivering.]

**tremendous**, *tri-men'dəs, adj.* awe-inspiring: huge (*hyperb. coll.*): prodigious, extraordinary, very good (*slang*).—*adv.* **tremen'dously.**—*n.* **tremen'dousness.** [L. *tremendus*, to be trembled at.]

**trémie, tremie**, *trä-mē, trem'i, n.* a hopper-like device for laying concrete under water. [Fr., hopper—L. *trimodia*, a three-peck measure.]

**tremolite**, *trem'ə-lit, n.* a calcium-magnesium amphibole, usually in long prisms, or fibres, pale or colourless.—*adj.* **tremolitic** (*-lit'ik*). [From the Val *Tremola* in the Alps, where the mineral found is not true tremolite.]

**tremolo**, *trem'ō-lō,* (*mus.*) *n.* a tremulous effect as by a rapid succession of interruptions or of up and down bows: a device in an organ for producing this.—Also *adj.*—*n., adj.,* and *adv.* **tremolan'do.**—*n.* and *adj.* **trem'olant**, tremolo. [It. *tremolo, tremolando, tremolante*.]

**tremor**, *trem'ər, n.* a quiver: a quavering: a thrill: an involuntary agitation: a vibration.—*adj.* **trem'orless.** [L. *tremor, -ōris*.]

**tremulous**, *trem'ū-ləs, adj.* trembling: quivering.—*adj.* **trem'ulant**, tremulous.—*n.* tremolant.—*v.i.* and *v.t.* **trem'ūlate.**—*adv.* **trem'ūlously.**—*n.* **trem'ūlousness.** [L. *tremulus*, trembling, and L.L. *tremulāre, -ātum*, to tremble.]

**trenail.** See under **tree**.

**trench**, *trench, trensh, n.* a long narrow cut in the earth, often used in warfare as a cover for troops: a deep wrinkle.—*v.i.* to make trenches: to dig deep with spade or plough: to encroach: to border, verge.—*v.t.* to cut: to make trenches in: to put in a trench: to furnish with a trench: to entrench: to divert by a trench (*Shak.*).—*n.* **trench'ancy**, causticity.—*adj.* **trench'ant** (*Spens.* **trench'and**) cutting: incisive.—*adv.* **trench'antly.**—*n.* **trench'er**, one who trenches.—**trench'-coat**, a short waterproof coat with belt as used in trench warfare: a coat based on this, for man or woman; **trench'-feet'**, a diseased condition of the feet owing to exposure to cold and wet in trench warfare; **trench'-fe'ver**, an infectious disease prevalent among soldiers living in trenches, transmitted by lice; **trench'-mor'tar**, a small smooth-bore gun, throwing large shells short distances, useful in trench warfare; **trench'-plough**, a plough for ploughing more deeply than usual.—*v.t.* to plough with a trench-plough.—**trench warfare**, warfare in which each side entrenches itself in lines facing the enemy. [O.Fr. *trenche*, cut (Fr. *tranche*, slice), *trencher* (Fr. *trancher*, to cut, to slice) to cut, prob.—L. *truncāre* (see **truncate**).]

**trencher**, *tren'char, -shar, n.* a plate or platter: a board.—**tren'cher-cap**, a college-cap, mortarboard.—*adj.* **trench'er-fed**, kept each by his owner, not in a pack.—**tren'cher-friend, -knight** (both *Shak.*), one who frequents the table of another, a parasite; **tren'cher-man** (*Shak.*), a hearty eater. [A.Fr. *trenchour* (Fr. *tranchoir*)—*trencher*, to cut.]

**trend**, *trend, v.i.* to turn, wind: to have a tendency or prevailing direction.—*n.* a bend (*dial.*): general tendency.—*adj.* **tren'dy** (*coll.*), in the forefront of fashion in any sphere.—*n.* **trend'-setter**, one who helps to give a new direction to fashion.—*adj.* **trend'setting.** [O.E. *trendan*.]

**trenise**, *trə-nēz', n.* the fourth movement of a quadrille.—Also **la trenise.**

**trental**, *tren'tl, n.* a series of thirty requiem masses. [L.L. *trentāle*—L. *trigintā*, thirty.]

**trente-et-quarante**, *trät-ā-ka-rät, n.* rouge-et-noir. [Fr., thirty and forty.]

**trepan**, *tri-pan', n.* a decoy: a snare: an entraping.—*v.t.* to ensnare: to lure:—*pr.p.* **trepann'-ing**; *pa.t.* and *pa.p.* **trepanned.**—*n.* **trepann'er.**—

*n.* and *adj.* **trepann'ing.** [Earlier *trapan*; prob. conn. with **trap.**]

**trepan,** *tri-pan'*, *n.* an obsolete cylindrical saw for perforating the skull: a tool for boring shafts. —*v.t.* to remove a piece of the skull from: to cut a cylindrical disk from: to cut an annular groove in.—*ns.* **trepanation** (*trep-ə-nā'shən*); **trepann'er.**—*n.* and *adj.* **trepann'ing.** [Fr. *trépan*—L.L. *trepanum*—Gr. *trȳpanon*—*trȳpaein*, to bore.]

**trepang,** *tri-pang'*, *n.* sea-slug, a holothurian eaten by the Chinese. [Malay *tripang.*]

**trephine,** *tri-fēn'*, *-fīn'*, *n.* an improved trepan.— *v.t.* to perforate with the trephine. [Earlier *trafine*—L. *trēs fīnēs*, three ends, with a suggestion of **trepan.**]

**trepidation,** *trep-i-dā'shən*, *n.* trembling: alarmed agitation: a libration of the celestial sphere assumed to explain a supposed oscillation of the ecliptic (*old astron.*; *Milt.*).—*adjs.* **trep'id,** quaking; **trep'idant; trepid'atory.** [L. *trepidāre, -ātum,* to hurry with alarm—*trepidus,* restless.]

**trespass,** *tres'pəs*, *v.i.* to interfere with another's person or property: to enter unlawfully upon another's land: to encroach: to intrude: to sin.—*n.* act of trespassing: any injury to another's person or property: a sin.—*n.* **tres'-passer.** [O.Fr. *trespasser*—L. *trāns, passus,* a step.]

**tress,** *tres, n.* a plait or braid of the hair of the head: a long lock, braided or not.—*v.t.* to form into tresses.—*adjs.* **tressed,** braided: in tresses: having tresses; **tress'y,** having or like tresses. [Fr. *tresse*—L. *tricia,* perh. Gr. *tricha,* threefold— *treis,* three.]

**tress, tressel.** See **trestle.**

**tressure,** *tresh'ər,* (*her.*) *n.* a subordinary, half the breadth of the orle, and usually borne double, and flowered and counter-flowered with fleurs-de-lis.—*adj.* **tress'ured,** having a tressure. [Fr., from *tresser,* to plait.]

**trestle,** *tres'l, n.* a support composed of a horizontal beam on sloping legs: a braced framework. —Also **tres'el.**—*n.* **tressa,** a trestle.—**trest'le-bridge,** one resting on trestlework; **trest'le-table,** one of boards laid on trestles; **trest'lework,** a braced framework. [O.Fr. *trestel* (Fr. *tréteau*) and *treste, trestre*—L. *trānstrum,* cross-beam.]

**tret,** *tret, n.* an allowance to purchasers of 4 lb. on every 104 lb. for waste. [Poss. A.Fr. *tret,* pull, turn of the scale or Fr. *traite,* transport, both— *traire,* to draw—L. *trahēre, tractum.*]

**trevally,** *tri-val'i, n.* an Australian horse-mackerel (*Caranx*) of various species. [Prob. a modification of **cavally.**]

**treviss, trevis,** *trev'is,* **travis,** *trav'is, trăv'is, n.* forms of **traverse:** a stall partition: a stall.

**trew.** An old spelling of **true.**

**trews,** *trōōz, n.pl.* (orig. *sing.*) trousers, esp. of tartan cloth.—**trews'man,** a wearer of trews. [Ir. *trius,* Gael. *triubhas;* cf. **trouse, trousers.**]

**trey,** *trā, n.* the three in cards and dice: a set of three: the third tine of a deer's horn (in full **trey-ant'ler, -tine;** also **tray, trez, trā, trāz**): a three-penny bit (also **trey'bit, tray, tray'bit;** *slang*). [O.Fr. *treis, trei*—L. *trēs,* three.]

**trez.** See **trey.**

**tri-,** *trī-, tri-,* in composition, three, threefold. [L. *trēs, tria,* and Gr. *treis, tria.*]

**triable.** See **try.**

**triacid,** *tri-as'id, adj.* having three replaceable hydrogen atoms: capable of replacing three hydrogen atoms of an acid. [**tri-.**]

**triaconter,** *tri-ə-kon'tər, n.* an ancient ship, perhaps with thirty men to each group of oars. [Gr. *triākontērēs*—*triākonta,* thirty.]

**triact,** *tri'akt, adj.* three-rayed.—*adjs.* **triact'inal** (*-i-nəl* or *-i'nəl*), **triact'ine** (*-in*). [**tri-** and Gr. *aktis, -inos,* ray.]

**triad,** *tri'ad, -əd, n.* a group or union of three: in Welsh literature, a group of three sayings, stories,

etc., about related subjects: a group of three lines or stanzas in different metres: a chord of three notes, esp. the common chord (*mus.*): an atom, element, or radical with a combining power of three (*chem.*).—*adjs.* **tri'ad, triad'ic.**—*n.* **tri'adist,** a composer of triads. [L. *trias*—Gr. *trias, triados*—*treis,* three.]

**triadelphous,** *trī-ə-del'fəs, adj.* with three bundles of stamens. [**tri-** and Gr. *adelphos,* a brother.]

**triage.** See **try.**

**triakisoctahedron,** *tri-ə-kis-ok-tə-hē'drən, n.* a solid figure like an octahedron with a three faced pyramid on each face. [Gr. *triakis,* three times.]

**trial,** *tri'əl, n.* a trying: examination by a test: examination by a court to determine a question of law or fact, esp. the guilt or innocence of a prisoner: (often in *pl.*) examination, sometimes merely formal, of a candidate: a testing journey, as of motor-cars, motor-cycles: a trial match: suffering: temptation: attempt: a piece used as a test.—*adj.* done, taken, etc., for the sake of trial. —**tri'al-day** (*Shak.*), day of trial; **tri'al-fire** (*Shak.*), a fire for trying or proving; **trial marriage,** for a couple intending matrimony, a period of living together with a view to testing their compatibility; **trial run,** a test drive in a motor vehicle to ascertain its efficiency: any introductory test, rehearsal, etc.; **trial trip,** an experimental trip of a new vessel, to test her sailing-powers, etc.—**by trial and error,** by trying out several methods and discarding those which prove unsuccessful; **on trial,** undergoing proceedings in a court of law: on probation, as an experiment. [A.Fr. *trial*—*trier,* to try.]

**trial,** *trī'əl, adj.* threefold, trinal.—*ns.* **tri'alism,** the doctrine of the existence of body, soul and spirit in man: a scheme for turning the Dual Monarchy into a triple (Austria, Hungary, and a South Slav state; *hist.*); **tri'alist; triality** (*-al'i-ti*). [L. *trēs, tria,* three, after **dual.**]

**trialogue,** *tri'ə-log, n.* a dialogue between three persons. [On false analogy of **dialogue,** as if *dia-* meant two.]

**triandrous,** *tri-an'drəs, adj.* with three stamens.— *n.pl.* **Trian'dria,** in Linnaeus's classification a class of plants with three stamens.—*adj.* **trian'-drian.** [**tri-** and Gr. *anēr, andros,* a man (male).]

**triangle,** *tri'ang-gl* (also *-ang'*), *n.* a plane figure with three angles and three sides (*math.*): part of the surface of a sphere bounded by three arcs of great circles (*spherical triangle*): any mark or thing of that shape: a musical instrument of percussion, formed of a steel rod bent in triangle-form, open at one angle: a tripod, esp. for a pulley for raising weights, or formerly (usu. in *pl.*) for binding soldiers to for flogging.—*adjs.* **tri'-angled; triang'ular,** having three angles: of a number, capable of being represented by dots in a triangle, as 1, 3, 6, 10, etc.: involving three persons or parties.—*n.* **triangular'ity.**—*adv.* **tri-ang'ularly.**—*v.t.* **triang'ūlate,** to survey by means of a series of triangles.—*adj.* with, marked with, made up of, triangles: triangular.—*adv.* **triang'-ūlately.**—*n.* **triangūlā'tion,** act of triangulating: the series of triangles so used.—**the eternal triangle,** an emotional situation involving two men and a woman or two women and a man. [L. *triangulum—angulus,* an angle.]

**triapsidal,** *tri-aps'i-dəl, adj.* with three apses.— Also **triaps'al.** [**tri-.**]

**triarch,** *trī'ärk, adj.* with three xylem strands. [**tri-** and Gr. *archē,* origin.]

**triarchy,** *tri'är-ki, n.* government by three persons: a state governed by a triumvirate. [Gr. *triarchiā* —*archē,* rule.]

**Trias,** *tri'əs,* (*geol.*) *n.* the oldest Mesozoic or Secondary system.—*adj.* **Triassic** (*tri-as'ik*). [Gr. *trias,* triad, from its threefold division in Germany—Bunter, Muschelkalk, Keuper.]

**triatic (stay)**, *trī-at'ik (stā)*, a rope joining adjacent mastheads to which tackle is attached: each of a pair of stays joining the tops of direction-finding masts diagonally and supporting from their points of intersection a vertical aerial. [Origin obscure.]

**triatomic**, *trī-ə-tom'ik, adj.* consisting of three atoms: having three replaceable atoms or groups: trivalent. [tri-.]

**triaxial**, *tri-ak'si-əl, adj.* having three axes.—*n.* a triaxial sponge spicule.—Also **triax'on**. [tri-, Gr. *axōn*, and L. *axis*, axle.]

**tribade**, *trib'ad, n.* a woman homosexualist.—*ns.* **trib'adism, trib'ady**. [Fr. through L. *tribas, -adis*—Gr. *tribas, -ados*—*tribein*, to rub.]

**tribasic**, *tri-bā'sik, adj.* capable of reacting with three equivalents of an acid: (of acids) having three replaceable hydrogen atoms. [tri-, base.]

**tribble**, *trib'l, n.* a horizontal frame with wires stretched across it for drying paper.

**tribe**, *trib, n.* a division of a nation or people for political purposes: a set of people theoretically of common descent: an aggregate of families, forming a community: a race: a breed: a class or set of people: loosely, a classificatory division. —*adj.* **trib'al**.—*n.* **trib'alism**.—*adv.* **trib'ally**.— *adj.* **tribe'less**.—*n.* **tribes'man**. [L. *tribus, -ūs*, one of the divisions of the ancient Roman people: that these were originally three is only a conjecture.]

**triblet**, *trib'lit, n.* a tapering mandrel on which rings, nuts, etc., are forged. [Fr. *triboulet*.]

**tribology**, *trib-, trib-ol'ə-ji, n.* a science and technology embracing all subjects involved when surfaces in contact move in relation to each other. [Gr. *tribein*, to rub, and *logos*, speech, a discourse.]

**tribometer**, *tri-bom'i-tər, n.* a sled-like apparatus for measuring sliding friction. [Gr. *tribein*, to rub, *metron*, measure.]

**tribrach**, *trī'brak, n.* a foot of three short syllables. —*adj.* **tribrach'ic**. [Gr. *tribrachys*—*brachys*, short.]

**tribrom(o)-**, *tri-brōm'(ō)-* in composition, having three atoms of bromine, esp. replacing hydrogen.

**tribulation**, *trib-ū-lā'shən, n.* severe affliction: pawn (*old slang*): a rowdy gang (*Shak.*). [L. *tribulāre, -ātum*, to afflict—*tribulum*, a sledge for separating grain from chaff by rubbing—*terēre*, to rub.]

**tribune**, *trib'ūn, n.* a magistrate elected by the Roman plebeians to defend their rights: a champion of popular rights: a name for a newspaper: a platform for speaking from: a raised area or stand: bishop's stall or throne.— *n.* **tribunal** (*trib-, trib-ū'nl; Spens. trib'*), judgment-seat: court of justice or arbitration: a body appointed to adjudicate in some matter or to enquire into some disputed question: a confessional.—*adj.* of, of the nature of, or authorised by, a tribunal.—*ns.* **trib'unāte, trib'uneship**.—*adjs.* **tribunitial, -icial** (-*ish'l*), **tribunitian, -ician** (-*ish'ən*). [L. *tribūnus*, tribune, *tribūnāl*, tribunal—*tribus*, a tribe.]

**tribute**, *trib'ūt, n.* a payment in acknowledgment of subjection: an act, gift, words, or other expression of approbation: a percentage of ore or its value received by a miner.—*adv.* **trib'u-tarily**.—*n.* **trib'utariness**.—*adj.* **trib'utary**, paying tribute: contributing: paid in tribute.—*n.* a payer of tribute: a stream that runs into another.—*n.* **trib'uter**, a miner paid by tribute. —**trib'ute-mon'ey**, money paid as tribute. [L. *tribūtum*—*tribuĕre*, to assign.]

**tricar**, *trī'kär, n.* a motor-tricycle with a passenger's seat in front: a three-wheeled motor-car. [tri-.]

**tricarpellary**, *tri-kär'pəl-ər-i*, or *-pel'ər-i, adj.* of or with three carpels. [tri-.]

**trice**, *tris, (naut.) v.t.* to haul: to haul and make fast.—*n.* a pulley (*obs.*): a moment (as if the time

of a single tug). [M.Du. *trisen* (Du. *trijsen*), to hoist.]

**tricephalous**, *tri-sef'ə-ləs, adj.* three-headed. [Gr. *trikephalos*—*kephalē*, a head.]

**triceps**, *tri'seps, adj.* three-headed.—*n.* a muscle with three insertions, esp. that at the back of the upper arm. [L. *trīceps, -cipitis*—*caput*, head.]

**Triceratops**, *tri-ser'ə-tops, n.* a gigantic three-horned Cretaceous dinosaur. [tri- and Gr. *keras, -atos*, horn, *ōps*, face.]

**tricerion**, *tri-sē'ri-on, (Gr. Ch.) n.* a three-branched candlestick. [Late Gr.,—Gr. *kēros*, wax.]

**trich-, trik-, tricho-, -ō-**, in composition, hair. [Gr. *thrix*, gen. *trichos*.]

**trichiasis**, *trik-i'ə-sis, n.* turning in of the eyelashes so that they rub against the eye. [L.L.— Gr. *thrix, trichos*, hair.]

**Trichina**, *trik'i-nə, tri-ki'nə*, **Trichinella**, *trik-i-nel'ə, ns.* a nematode worm parasitic in rat, pig, and man, the adult in the small intestine, the larva encysted in muscle.—*r.s.* **trichiniasis** (*trik-i-ni'ə-sis*), **trichinō'sis**, a disease caused by trichinae: **trichinisā'tion, -ization**, infestation with trichinae.—*adjs.* **trich'inised, trich'inosed** (-*nōst*), infested with trichinae: **trichinot'ic, trich'inous**, pertaining to trichinosis. [Gr. *trichinos*, of hair —*thrix, trichos*, hair.]

**trichite**, *trik'it, n.* a hairlike crystallite.—*adj.* **trichitic** (-*it'ik*). [Gr. *thrix, trichos*, hair.]

**Trichiurus**, *trik-i-ū'rəs*, or *-ōō'rəs, n.* a genus of hair-tails, giving name to the family **Trichiu'-ridae**, akin to mackerels and tunnies. [trich- and Gr. *ourā*, tail.]

**trichlor(o)-**, *tri-klōr'(ō)-*, in composition, having three atoms of chlorine, esp. replacing hydrogen. —**trichlorethylene** (*tri-klōr-eth'i-lēn*) an acetylene derivative, used as a solvent, in paint manufacture, and as an analgesic and anaesthetic.

**tricho-. See trich-.**

**trichobacteria**, *trik-ō-bak-tē'ri-ə, n.pl.* filamentous bacteria. [tricho-.]

**trichogyne**, *trik'ō-jin, -jin, n.* in red seaweeds and some fungi, a threadlike prolongation of the female organ. [tricho- and Gr. *gynē*, woman, female.]

**trichoid**, *trik'oid, adj.* hairlike. [Gr. *trichoeidēs*.]

**trichology**, *trik-ol'ə-ji, n.* the scientific study of hair.—*adj.* **tricholog'ical**.—*n.* **trichol'ogist**, one versed in trichology: a name affected by hairdressers. [Gr. *thrix, trichos*, a hair.]

**trichome**, *trik'ōm, trik'ōm, n.* a plant hair or outgrowth from the epidermis. [Gr. *trichōma*, a growth of hair.]

**trichomonad**, *trik-ə-mon'ad, n.* a parasitic protozoon of the genus Trichomonas (*tri-kom'* or *-kə-mon'*).—*n.* **trichomoni'asis** (*-mon-i'*), a sexually-transmitted disease caused by trichomonads, found in human beings and in animals. [Gr. *trichos*, hair, *monas, -ados*, a unit.]

**Trichophyton**, *trik-of'i-tən, n.* a fungus genus causing ringworm.—*n.* **trichophytō'sis**, ringworm caused by Trichophyton. [tricho- and Gr. *phyton*, plant.]

**Trichoptera**, *trik-op'tər-ə, n.pl.* an order of insects with hairy wings, the caddis-flies.—*n.* **trichop'-terist**, a student of the caddis-flies.—*adj.* **trichop'terous**. [tricho- and Gr. *pteron*, wing.]

**trichord**, *trī'körd, adj.* three-stringed: with three strings to one note.—*n.* a three-stringed instrument: a triad. [Gr. *trichordos*—*chordē*, a string.]

**trichosis**, *trik-ō'sis, n.* arrangement, distribution, or morbid condition of hair. [Gr. *trichōsis*, hairiness.]

**trichotomous**, *tri-kot'ə-məs, adj.* divided into three: forking in threes.—*v.t.* and *v.i.* **trichot'omise, -ize**, to divide in three or threes.—*adv.* **trichot'-omously**.—*n.* **trichot'omy**, trichotomous division or forking. [Gr. *tricha*, threefold—*treis*, three, *tomē*, a cutting—*temnein*, to cut.]

**trichroic**, *tri-krō'ik, adj.* having or exhibiting three

colours, esp. when viewed in different directions.—*n*. tri′chroism. [Gr. *trichroos*, three-coloured.]
**trichromatic**, *tri-krō-mat′ik*, *adj*. characterised by three colours: having three fundamental colour-sensations.—*n*. trichro′mat, one who has normal colour vision.—*adjs*. tri′chrome, trichromatic; trichrō′mic, trichromatic.—*n*. one who has three fundamental colour-sensations.—*n*. trichrō′-matism. [Gr. *trichrōmatos—chrōma*, colour.]
**trichronous**, *tri′kro-nəs*, *adj*. trisemic. [Gr. *tri-chronos—chronos*, time.]
**trick**, *trik*, *n*. an artifice: a deceitful device: a deception: a prank: a performance aimed at astonishing, puzzling, or amusing: an expedient: a knack: a characteristic habit, mannerism, trait: a spell or turn, esp. at the helm: a round of play at cards: the cards so played and taken by the winner, forming a unit in scoring: a trinket, toy, or gimcrack: a watch (*slang*): an outline sketch (*her*.).—*v.t.* to deceive, to cheat: to beguile: to deck, prank: to trim: to sketch in outline.—*adj*. of the nature of, for the purpose or performance of, a trick: adroit and trim (*obs*.).—*ns*. trick′er; trick′ery, act or practice of playing tricks: artifice: stratagem: imposition.—*adv*. trick′ily.—*n*. trick′iness.—*n*. and *adj*. trick′ing.—*adj*. trick′-ish, tricky.—*adv*. trick′ishly.—*ns*. trick′ishness; trick′siness.—*n*. trick′some.—*ns*. trick′ster, a cheat: one who practises trickery; trick′-stering, playing the trickster.—*adjs*. tricks′y, pranked up: capricious: sportive: mischievous: tricky: ticklish; trick′y, addicted to trickery: clever in tricks: ticklish: difficult to handle: complicated.—**trick cyclist** (*mil. slang*), a psychiatrist.—**do the trick**, to bring something about. [O.Fr. *trique*, Northern form of *triche*, deceit; perh. in part of other origin.]
**trickle**, *trik′l*, *v.i.* to run in drops or in a small irregular stream.—*v.t.* to emit in a trickle.—*n*. a drop (*obs*.): a succession of drops: a trickling rill.—*n*. trick′let, a little rill.—*n*. and *adj*. trick′-ling.—*adj*. trick′ly, trickling. [M.E. *triklen*, prob. for *striklen*, freq. of **strike**.]
**trickle**, *trik′l*, (*Spens*.) *adj*. ticklish, precarious (another reading **tickle**). [Prob. **trick**.]
**trick-track**, *trik′-trak*, *n*. a form of backgammon in which pegs as well as pieces are used.—Also **tric′-trac, tick′-tack**. [Fr. *tric trac*; imit.]
**triclinic**, *tri-klin′ik*, (*min*.) *adj*. referred to three unequal axes obliquely inclined to each other. [Gr. *treis*, three, *klinein*, to bend.]
**triclinium**, *tri-klin′i-əm*, (*Rom. ant*.) *n*. a couch running round three sides of a table for reclining on at meals: a dining-room. [L. *triclinium*—Gr. *triklinion*—Gr. *treis*, three, *klinē*, a couch.]
**tricolour, tricolor**, *tri′kul-ər*, *adj*. three-coloured.—*n*. (*tri′*) a three-coloured flag, esp. that of France(*trē-kol-or*).—*adj*. tri′coloured. [L. *tricolor* and Fr. *tricolore*.]
**triconsonantal**, *tri-kon-sə-nant′l*, *adj*. having three consonants.—Also **triconsonan′tic**. [tri-.]
**tricorn, tricorne**, *tri′körn*, *adj*. three-horned: three-cornered.—*n*. a three-cornered hat. [L. *tricornis*, three-horned—*cornū*, a horn.]
**tricorporate**, *tri-kör′pə-rāt*, *-rit*, **-d**, *-id*, *adjs*. three-bodied (with one head). [tri- and L. *corpus*, *-oris*, body.]
**tricostate**, *tri-kos′tāt*, *adj*. three-ribbed. [tri- and L. *costa*, rib.]
**tricot**, *trē′kō*, *n*. a hand-knitted woollen fabric, or imitation: a soft, slightly-ribbed cloth for women's garments. [Fr. *tricot*, knitting.]
**tricrotic**, *tri-krot′ik*, *adj*. triple-beating.—*n*. tri′-crotism.—*adj*. tri′crotous. [Gr. *trikrotos*, rowed with triple stroke—*krotos*, a beat.]
**tricuspid, -ate**, *tri-kus′pid*, *-āt*, *adjs*. with three cusps or points. [L. *tricuspis, -idis—cuspis*, a point.]
**tricycle**, *tri′si-kl*, *n*. a three-wheeled cycle.—*v.i.* to ride a tricycle.—*n*. tri′cycler.—*adj*. tricyclic

(*tri-si′klik*), having three whorls or rings.—*ns*. tri′cycling (*-si-*); tri′cyclist.—**tricycle under-carriage, landing-gear**, an aircraft's under-carriage, landing-gear, having three wheels. [tri- and Gr. *kyklos*, circle, wheel.]
**Tridacna**, *tri-dak′nə*, *n*. the giant clam of the Indian Ocean, the greatest known bivalve (more than 200 kg.). [Gr. *tridaknos*, eaten at three bites (applied to a big oyster)—*daknein*, to bite.]
**tridactyl, -ous**, *tri-dak′til*, *-əs*, *adjs*. three-toed: three-fingered. [tri- and Gr. *daktylos*, finger, toe.]
**tride**, an obs. spelling (*Spens*.; *Shak*.) of **tried**. See **try**.
**trident**, *tri′dənt*, *n*. a three-pronged spear, esp. that of the sea-god Poseidon or Neptune: anything of like shape.—*adjs*. tri′dent, tridental (*-dent′*), trident′āte, three-pronged; tridented (*tri-dent′id*), three-pronged: (*tri′dənt-id*) having a trident. [L. *tridēns, -dentis—dēns*, tooth.]
**Tridentine**, *tri-*, *tri-dent′in*, *adj*. of Trent in Southern Tirol, or the Council (1545-63) held there.—*n*. a native of Trent: one who accepts the decrees of the Council, a Roman Catholic. [L. *Tridentum*, Trent.]
**tridimensional**, *tri-di-men′shən-əl*, *adj*. having three dimensions. [tri-.]
**tridominium**, *tri-dō-min′i-əm*, *n*. threefold rule. [tri- and L. *dominium*, lordship.]
**triduum**, *trid′ū-əm*, or *trid′*, *n*. a space of three days: a three days' service.—*adj*. trid′ūan, lasting three days. [L. *triduum—diēs*, day.]
**tridymite**, *trid′i-mit*, *n*. orthorhombic form of silica, in hexagonal scales, often combined in threes. [Gr. *tridymos*, threefold.]
**trie**, an obs. spelling of **try.—tried, tries, trier**. See **try**.
**triennial**, *tri-en′yəl*, *adj*. continuing three years: happening every third year.—*adv*. trienn′ially. [L. *triennis—annus*, a year.]
**trierarch**, *tri′ər-ärk*, (*Gr. hist*.) *n*. the commander of a trireme: one required (alone or with others) to fit out a trireme.—*adj*. tri′erarchal.—*n*. tri′-erarchy, the office of trierarch: the obligation of fitting out ships. [Gr. *triērarchos—triērēs*, a trireme, *archein*, to rule.]
**trieteric**, *tri-i-ter′ik*, *adj*. biennial. [Gr. *trietērikos—trietēris*, a biennial festival—*treis*, three, *etos*, a year (both years being counted).]
**triethyl**, *tri-eth′il*, *adj*. having three ethyl groups.—*n*. triethylamine (*-mēn′*), an oily liquid answer-ing to ammonia with ethyl replacing all the hydrogen. [tri-.]
**trifacial**, *tri-fā′shl*, *adj*. threefold and pertaining to the face, esp. of the trigeminal nerve.—*n*. the trigeminal nerve. [tri- and L. *faciēs*, face.]
**trifarious**, *tri-fā′ri-əs*, *adj*. arranged in three rows: facing three ways. [L. *trifārius*.]
**trifid**, *trif′id*, *tri′fid*, *adj*. three-cleft (about half-way down). [L. *findēre*, to cleave.]
**trifle**, *tri′fl*, *n*. anything of little importance or value: a small amount: a light confection of whipped cream or white of egg, sponge-cake, wine, etc.: a kind of pewter.—*v.i.* to busy oneself idly: to play, toy: to behave without seriousness or respect: to meddle irresponsibly: to sport: to dally.—*v.t.* to spend or pass idly: to play with: to render trivial in comparison (*Shak*.).—*n*. tri′fler.—*adj*. tri′fling, of small value, importance, or amount: trivial.—*adv*. tri′flingly.—*n*. tri′flingness. [O.Fr. *trufle*, mock-ery, deception.]
**trifocal**, *tri-fō′kəl*, *adj*. of a spectacle lens, giving separately near, intermediate, and far vision.—*n.pl.* trifo′cals, spectacles with such lenses. [tri-.]
**trifoliate**, *tri-fō′li-āt*, *adj*. with three leaves or leaflets.—*ns*. Trifō′lium, the clover or trefoil genus; trifoly (*trif′ə-li*; *Browning*), trefoil. [L. *trifolium—folium*, leaf.]
**triforium**, *tri-fō′ri-əm*, *-fō′*, (*archit*.) *n*. a gallery,

storey, or arcade over an aisle:—*pl.* trifo′ria. [L.L.; connection with *trēs*, three, and *foris*, door, does not appear.]

**triform**, *tri′form, adj.* having a triple form—also **tri′formed.** [L. *trifōrmis*—*fōrma*, form.]

**trifurcate**, *tri′fər-kāt*, or *-fûr′, adj.* three-forked.—*v.i.* to divide into three branches.—*adj.* **tri′furcated** (or *-fûr′*).—*n.* **trifurcā′tion.** [L., *trifurcus* —*furca*, a fork.]

**trig**, *trig, adj.* trim, neat: tight, sound.—*v.t.* to make trig: to stuff: to block, hold back with a wedge.—*n.* a block or wedge to stop a wheel.— *adv.* **trig′ly.**—*n.* **trig′ness.** [O.N. *tryggr*, faithful, secure; cf. **true.**]

**trig**, *trig, n.* an abbreviation of **trigonometry.**

**trigamy**, *trig′ə-mi, n.* the having of three legal or supposed husbands or wives at once: a third marriage (*eccl. law*).—*n.* **trig′amist**, one who has committed trigamy.—*adj.* **trig′amous**, of the nature of, involving, living in, trigamy. [Gr. *trigamos*, thrice married—*gamos*, marriage.]

**trigeminal**, *tri-jem′i-nl, adj.* threefold: three-branched.—*n.* the trigeminal, trifacial, or fifth cranial nerve. [L. *trigeminus*, born three at a birth—*geminus*, born at the same birth.]

**trigger**, *trig′ər, n.* a lever that releases a catch so as to fire a gun or set a mechanism going: anything that starts a train of actions.—*v.t.* (often with *off*) to set in action.—*adj.* **trigg′er-happy**, over-ready to shoot (*lit.* and *fig.*): irresponsibly willing to take the risk of beginning a fight or a war.—**trigger-happiness; triggerman**, a gangster's bodyguard: the man who actually fired the shot. [Du. *trekker*—*trekken*, to pull.]

**triglot**, *tri′glot, adj.* in three languages.—*n.* a book which is written in three languages. [tri- and Gr. *glōtta*, tongue.]

**triglyph**, *tri′glif, n.* a three-grooved tablet in the Doric frieze.—*adj.* **triglyph′ic.** [Gr. *triglyphos*—*glyphein*, to carve.]

**trigon**, *tri′gon, n.* a triangle: a set of three signs 120° apart, the zodiac being divided into four trigons—the first or *watery* trigon, Cancer, Scorpio, Pisces; the *earthly*, Taurus, Virgo, Capricornus; the *airy*, Gemini, Libra, Aquarius; the *fiery*, Aries, Leo, Sagittarius (*astrol.*).—*adjs.* **trigonal** (*trig′ə-nl*), of a trigon: triangular: trigonous: bounded by three planes: three-faced, forming half a hexagon in section: of symmetry about an axis, such that a rotation through 120° gives the same figure; **trigonic** (*tri-gon′ik*), of a trigon: triangular; **trigonous** (*trig′ə-nəs*), triangular in section, or nearly so— as with convex (or concave) faces, or rounded angles. [Gr. *trigōnon*—*gōniā*, an angle.]

**trigonometry**, *trig-ə-nom′i-tri, n.* the branch of mathematics that treats of the relations between the sides and angles of triangles.—*n.* **trigonom′-eter**, one versed in or occupied with trigonometry: an instrument for solving triangles.—*adjs.* **trigonometric** (*-nə-met′rik*), **-al.**—*adv.* **trigonomet′rically.** [Gr. *trigōnon*, a triangle, *metron*, a measure.]

**trigram**, *tri′gram, n.* an inscription of three letters: a figure of three lines.—*adjs.* **trigrammat′ic**, **trigramm′ic.** [tri- and Gr. *gramma*, a letter.]

**trigraph**, *tri′gräf, n.* a combination of three letters for one sound. [tri- and Gr. *graphē*, a writing.]

**Trigynia**, *tri-jin′i-ə, n.pl.* in the Linnaean system an order of plants (in various classes) with three pistils.—*adjs.* **trigyn′ian**, **trigynous** (*trij′i-nəs*). [tri- and Gr. *gynē*, a woman, female.]

**trihedral**, *tri-hed′rəl, -hēd′, adj.* three-faced. [tri- and Gr. *hedrā*, a seat.]

**trihybrid**, *tri-hi′brid, n.* a cross between parents differing in three independently heritable characters.—Also *adj.* [tri-.]

**trihydric**, *tri-hi′drik, adj.* having three hydroxyl groups. [tri-.]

**trike**, *trik, n.* and *v.i.* (*coll.*) for **tricycle.**

**trilateral**, *tri-lat′ər-əl, adj.* three-sided.—*n.* a triangle. [tri- and L. *latus, lateris*, side.]

**trilby**, *tril′bi, n.* a soft felt hat.—Also **trilby hat.** [From George du Maurier's novel, *Trilby* (1894).]

**trild**, *trild*, (*Spens.*). See **trill** (2).

**trilemma**, *tri-, tri-lem′ə, n.* a form of argument or a situation differing from a dilemma in that there is a choice of three instead of two. [After **dilemma.**]

**Trilene**, *tri′lēn, n.* trichlorethylene. [Trademark.]

**trilinear**, *tri-lin′i-ər, adj.* consisting of, having, or referred to three lines.—*adj.* **trilin′eate**, marked with three lines. [tri- and L. *linea*, line.]

**trilingual**, *tri-ling′gwəl, adj.* in or using three languages, esp. native or habitual languages. [tri- and L. *lingua*, tongue.]

**triliteral**, *tri-lit′ər-əl, adj.* consisting of three letters.—*n.* **trilit′eralism**, the characteristic (as of Semitic languages) of having roots of three consonants. [tri- and L. *littera*, a letter.]

**trilith**, *tri′lith, n.* a form of megalithic monument consisting of two upright stones supporting another lying crosswise.—Also **trilithon** (*tri′, tri′*).—*adj.* **trilith′ic.** [tri- and Gr. *lithos*, stone.]

**trill**, *tril, n.* a trillo: a tremulous sound: a run or roulade of bird-song: a consonant-sound produced by vibration.—*v.t.* and *v.i.* to play, sing, pronounce, sound, with a trill.—*n.* **trill′o** (*mus.*), a shake. [It. *trillo*; imit.]

**trill**, *tril, v.t.* and *v.i.* to twirl: to roll: to trundle: to pour in a fine stream:—*pa.t.* **trilled** (*Spens.* **trild**). [Cf. Norw. and Sw. *trilla*, to roll.]

**trilling**, *tril′ing, n.* a threefold compound of crystals: one child of triplets. [tri- and -ling; cf. Dan. and Sw. *trilling*; Ger. *drilling*.]

**trillion**, *tril′yən, n.* the cube of a million: cube of ten thousand (*U.S.*, and before 1948 in France).—*n.* and *adj.* **trill′ionth.** [Fr.,—tri-, after **million.**]

**Trillium**, *tril′i-əm, n.* a three-leaved trimerous genus of the lily family. [L. *trēs*, three.]

**trilobate, -d**, *tri-lō′bāt*, or *tri′lō-bāt*, *-id, adjs.* having three lobes.—Also **tri′lobe**, **tri′lobed.** [tri- and Gr. *lobos*, lobe.]

**trilobite**, *tri′lō-bit, tril′ə-bit, n.* any fossil arthropod of a Palaeozoic order (**Trilobi′ta**), with broad head-shield and body longitudinally furrowed into three lobes.—*adj.* **trilobitic** (*-bit′ik*). [tri- and Gr. *lobos*, lobe.]

**trilocular**, *tri-lok′ū-lər, adj.* three-celled. [tri- and L. *loculus*.]

**trilogy**, *tril′ə-ji, n.* a group of three tragedies: any similar group, as of novels: a triad. [Gr. *trilogiā*—*logos*, discourse.]

**trim**, *trim, v.t.* to put in due condition: to fit out: to make ready for sailing: to adjust the balance of (as a boat): to dress, arrange: to set in order: to decorate, as with ribbons: to make tidy or neat: to clip into shape: to make compact: to smooth: to take or put by trimming: to rebuke sharply: to thrash: to cheat (*slang*): to adjust the inclination of a plane to the horizontal.—*v.i.* to balance: to balance or fluctuate between parties:—*pr.p.* **trimm′ing;** *pa.t.* and *pa.p.* **trimmed.**—*adj.* in good order: neat: tidy: well-kept: clean-cut.—*adv.* trimly.—*n.* condition for sailing or flight: balance: condition, order: humour, disposition, temper, way: array: fittings: an act of trimming: window-dressing (*U.S.*): parts trimmed off: adjustment of an aircraft's controls to achieve stability in a desired condition of flight.—*adv.* **trim′ly.**—*ns.* **trimm′er**, one who or that which trims: one who fluctuates between parties: a time-server: a scold: anything trouncing or redoubtable: a small horizontal beam on a floor into which the ends of joists are framed: a float bearing a baited hook and line, used in fishing for pike: a trimming tab; **trimm′ing**, making trim: balancing: clipping: (usu. in *pl.*) ornamental additions: (in *pl.*) accessories: (in *pl.*) fittings:

(in *pl.*) parts trimmed off.—*adj.* that trims.—*adv.* **trimm'ingly.**—*n.* **trim'ness.**—**trimming tab** (*aero.*), a tab which can be adjusted in flight by the pilot to trim out control forces.—**trim one's sails,** to rule one's conduct, principles, etc., to accord with prevailing circumstances. [O.E. *trymman, trymian,* to strengthen, set in order—*trum,* firm.]

**trimaran,** *tri'mə-ran, n.* a boat with three hulls. [tri- and cata*maran.*]

**trimerous,** *trim'ə-rəs, adj.* having three parts, or parts in threes.—*adj.* **trimeric** (*tri-mer'ik*), having the same empirical formula but three times the molecular weight. [tri- and Gr. *meros,* part.]

**trimester,** *tri-mes'tər, n.* three months: an academic term.—*adj.* **trimes'trial.** [L. *trimēstris,* of three months—*mēnsis,* a month.]

**trimeter,** *trim'i-tər, n.* a verse of three measures (dipodies or feet).—*adjs.* **trim'eter, trimetric** (*tri-met'rik*), consisting of three measures, esp. iambic. [Gr. *trimetros—metron,* measure.]

**trimethyl,** *tri-meth'il, adj.* containing three methyl radicals in combination.—*ns.* **trimethylamine** (*-ə-mēn'*), a gas, (CH₃)₃N, which can be got from herring-brine, corresponding to ammonia with methyl replacing all the hydrogen; **trimethylene** (*-ēn*), cyclopropane. [tri-.]

**trimonthly,** *tri-munth'li, adj.* every three months. [tri-.]

**trimorphism,** *tri-mör'fizm, n.* occurrence of three forms in the same species (*biol.*): the property of crystallising in three forms (*chem.*).—*adjs.* **trimor'phic, trimor'phous.** [tri- and Gr. *morphē,* form.]

**Trimurti,** *tri-mŏŏr'ti, n.* the Hindu trinity, Brahma, Vishnu, and Siva. [Sans. *tri,* three, *mūrti,* shape.]

**Trinacrian,** *tri-,* *tri-nā'kri-ən, adj.* Sicilian: (without *cap.*) three-pointed: with three extremities.—*adj.* **trinacriform** (*trin-ak'ri-förm*), three-pronged. [Gr. *Trinakriā,* Sicily, *trinax, -akos,* a three-pronged mattock, *thrinax,* a trident.]

**trindle,** *trin'dl, n.* a piece of wood, etc., laid between the cords and boards of a book to flatten before cutting: a wheel, esp. of a barrow.—*v.t.* and *v.i.* to roll, to trundle.—**trin'dle-tail,** a trundle-tail. [trundle.]

**trine,** *trin, adj.* threefold: 120° apart: hence, benign.—*n.* a triad: the aspect of two planets, as seen from the earth, distant from each other one-third of the zodiac or 120°: a triplet.—*v.t.* to join in trine aspect.—*n.* **trin** (*trin*), a triplet (by birth): a trilling.—*adjs.* **trinal** (*tri'nl*), **tri'nary.** [L. *trinus—trēs, tria,* three.]

**trine,** *trin, v.i.* to go.—**trine to the** (nubbing) **cheat** (*cant*), to go to the gallows.

**tringle,** *tring'gl, n.* a curtain-rod. [Fr.]

**triniscope,** *trin'i-skōp, n.* a cathode-ray tube for colour television. [L. *trinus,* triple, Gr. *skopeein,* to view.]

**trinitro-,** *tri-ni'trō-,* in composition, having three nitro-groups (NO₂), esp. replacing hydrogen.—*ns.* **trinitroben'zene,** C₆H₃(NO₂)₃, answering to benzene C₆H₆; **trinitrophe'nol,** a similar derivative of phenol, esp. picric acid; **trinitrotol'uene,** or **-tol'uol,** a high explosive (familiarly T.N.T.), a trinitro-derivative of toluene. [tri-.]

**trinity,** *trin'i-ti, n.* threefoldness: three in one: a triad: esp. (*cap.*) the triune God of orthodox Christians (Father, Son, Holy Ghost): (*cap.*) any symbolical representation of the persons of the Trinity: (*cap.*) Trinity Sunday: (*cap.*) Trinity term.—*adj.* **Trinitā'rian,** of, in relation to, believing in, the Trinity: of the Trinitarians.—*n.* one who holds the doctrine of the Trinity: a member of a religious order founded at Rome in 1198 to redeem Christian captives from the Mohammedans—also *Mathurins* and *Redemptionists:* a member of Trinity College.—*n.*

**Trinitā'rianism.**—**Trinity House,** a lighthouse and pilot authority for England, and in part Scotland and Northern Ireland, chartered at Deptford in 1514; **Trinity Sunday,** the Sunday after Whitsunday; **Trinity term,** one of the terms of the English law-courts beginning after Trinity Sunday (now **Trinity law sittings**). [L. *trinitās, -ātis—trinus,* threefold.]

**trinket,** *tring'kit, n.* a small ornament or piece of jewellery: any paltry or trumpery object or observance: a delicacy (*obs.*).—*v.i.* (*obs.*) to have traffickings or underhand dealings.—*ns.* **trink'-eter** (*obs.*), an intriguer; **trink'eting; trink'etry,** trinkets collectively. [Poss. O.Fr. *trenquet,* small knife.]

**trinkum,** *tring'kəm.* Same as **trankum.**—Also **trink'um-trank'um.**

**trinomial,** *tri-nō'mi-əl, adj.* consisting of three words: of three terms connected by the sign plus or minus.—*n.* a trinomial name or expression.—*ns.* **trino'mialism,** the system of naming by three words (for genus, species, and subspecies); **trino'mialist.** [After binomial.]

**trio,** *trē'ō, n.* a set of three: a composition for, or combination of, three performers (*mus.*): the second division of a minuet, scherzo, or march (said to have been originally for three instruments), followed by a repetition of the first (*mus.*):—*pl.* **tri'os.** [It.]

**triode,** *tri'ōd, adj.* with three electrodes.—*n.* a three-electrode valve. [tri- and Gr. *hodos,* a path, way.]

**Triodion,** *tri-ō'di-on,* (Gr. *Ch.*) *n.* a service-book for the ten weeks before Easter. [Mod. Gr. *triōdion—ōdē,* hymn.]

**trioecious,** *tri-ē'shəs, adj.* having male, female, and hermaphrodite flowers on different plants. [tri- and Gr. *oikos,* house.]

**triolet,** *tri'ō-lit, trē'ō-lā, -let, n.* an eight-lined poem rhymed *ab aa abab,* lines 4 and 7 repeating 1, and 8 repeating 2. [Fr.]

**triones,** *tri-ō'nēz, n.pl.* the seven stars of the Plough. [L. *triōnēs,* plough-oxen.]

**trionym,** *tri'ə-nim, n.* a trinomial.—*adj.* **trionymal** (*-on'i-məl*). [Gr. *triōnymos—onyma* (*onoma*), name.]

**trior.** See try.

**trioxide,** *tri-oks'īd, n.* a compound with three atoms of oxygen. [tri-.]

**trip,** *trip, v.i.* to move with short, light steps or skips: to stumble: to catch one's foot: to make a slip in chastity, accuracy, etc.: to tip up: to make an excursion.—*v.t.* to cause to stumble or fall by catching the foot (often with *up*): to catch in a fault: to dance trippingly: to trip or dance upon: to loose, as an anchor, from the bottom, by a long rope: to release by striking: to tilt up:—*pr.p.* **tripp'ing;** *pa.t.* and *pa.p.* **tripped.**—*n.* a light, short step or skip: a catching of the foot: a stumble: a point in coursing, when the hare is thrown off its legs: a slip, lapse: a single journey or run, one way or to and fro: a pleasure excursion, jaunt: a specially arranged run at a cheap fare: a company of excursionists: a striking part that releases a catch: a hallucinatory experience under the influence of a drug such as LSD, or a quantity of a drug that will produce such an experience (*slang*).—*adj.* **tripp'ant** (*her.*), tripping, with right foot raised.—*n.* **tripp'er,** one who trips: an excursionist, esp. of the disturbing kind.—*adjs.* **tripp'erish, tripp'ery,** of, like, savouring of, the vulgar or noisy tripper.—*n.* and *adj.* **tripp'ing.**—*adv.* **tripp'ingly.**—**trip'-hammer,** a tilt-hammer; **trip'-hook** (*Browning*), some kind of instrument of torture; **trip'-wire,** a wire which releases some mechanism when pulled, e.g. by being tripped over. [O.Fr. *triper;* of Gmc. origin; cf. O.E. *treppan,* to tread, Ger. *trappe(l)n,* Du. *trippen, trappen, trippelen,* Sw. *trippa.*]

trip, *trip, n.* a small flock of sheep, wildfowl, etc. [Perh. akin to troop.]

tripartite, *tri-pär'tit, adj.* in three parts: cleft in three nearly to the base (*bot.*): relating to three parties.—*n.* tripartition (*-tish'ən*). [L. *trīpartītus* —*partīri*, to divide—*pars*, a part.]

tripe, *trip, n.* entrails: parts of the compound stomach of a ruminant, prepared as food—the paunch or rumen (*plain tripe*), and the smaller reticulum (*honeycomb tripe*): rubbish, poor stuff (*coll.*): claptrap (*coll.*).—*n.* trip'ery, a place for the preparation or sale of tripe.—tripe'man, -wife, -woman, a dresser or seller of tripe; tripe'-shop.—*adj.* tripe'-visag'd (*Shak.*), with a face like tripe.—tripe de roche (*trēp də rosh;* Fr.), rock-tripe. [O.Fr. (Fr.) *tripe;* origin obscure.]

tripedal, *trip'-, trip'i-dl, tri-pē'dl, adj.* three-footed. [tri- and L. *pēs, pedis,* foot.]

tripersonal, *tri-pûr'sən-əl, adj.* consisting of three persons.—*ns.* triper'sonalism; triper'sonalist, a believer in the Trinity; tripersonal'ity. [tri-.]

tripetalous, *tri-pet'əl-əs, adj.* three-petalled. [tri- and Gr. *petalon,* leaf.]

triphenyl- *tri-fē'nil-,* in composition, containing three phenyl radicals in combination.—*n.* triphenylamine (*-mēn'*), a crystalline compound answering to ammonia with all the hydrogen replaced by phenyl. [tri-.]

triphibious, *tri-fib'i-əs, adj.* using the three elements, land, water, air. [tri-, and grotesquely, phibious, after amphibious.]

triphone, *tri'fōn, n.* a shorthand sign representing a triphthongal sound. [tri-, and Gr. *phōnē,* sound.]

triphthong, *trif'thong, n.* a combination of three vowel sounds in one syllable: loosely, a trigraph. —*adj.* triphthongal (*-thong'gl*). [tri- and Gr. *phthongos,* sound.]

triphyllous, *tri-fil'əs, adj.* three-leaved. [tri- and Gr. *phyllon,* a leaf.]

Triphysite, *trif'i-zīt, -sīt, n.* a believer in the existence of three natures in Christ—human, divine, and a third resulting from the union of these. [tri- and Gr. *physis,* nature.]

tripinnate, *tri-pin'āt, -it, adj.* pinnate with the pinnae themselves pinnate, and their pinnae again pinnate. [tri-.]

Tripitaka, *tri-pit'ə-kə, n.* the whole body of the northern Buddhist canonical writings, comprising the three divisions of *Sutras,* or discourses of the Buddha for the laity; *Vinaya,* or discipline for the order; and *Abhidharma,* or metaphysics. [Sans.]

triplane, *tri'plān, n.* an aeroplane with three sets of main planes, one above another. [tri-.]

triple, *trip'l, adj.* threefold: consisting of three: three times as much: third (*Shak.*).—*n.* a quantity three times as much: a thing (e.g. a star) that is triple: a peal of bells interchanging in three sets.—*v.t.* and *v.i.* to treble.—*ns.* trip'leness; trip'let, three of a kind, or three united: three lines rhyming together: a group of three notes occupying the time of two, indicated by a slur and the figure 3 (*mus.*): one of three born at a birth.—*adj.* trip'lex, triple.—*n.* (*Shak.*) triple time.—*adj.* trip'licate, threefold: made thrice as much: as the cubes of the quantities.—*n.* a third copy or thing corresponding to two others of the same kind: the triplicate ratio.—*v.t.* to make threefold.—*ns.* triplicā'tion, the act of triplicating: a reply to a duplication; triplicity (*trip-lis'i-ti*), tripleness: a triad: a trigon (*astrol.*); trip'ling, a making triple: a triplet, trilling or trin.—*adv.* triply (*trip'li*).—*n.* (*tri-plī';* Scots *law*) a pursuer's reply to a defender's duply.— *v.t.* and *v.i.* to reply to a duply.—Triple Alliance, the league of England, Sweden, and the Netherlands formed against France in 1668: the alliance of Britain, France, and Holland against Spain in 1717: the alliance between Germany, Austria, and Italy, 1883-1915, counterbalanced by the

Triple Entente, a friendly understanding (developing into an alliance) between Britain, France, and Russia; triple crown, the pope's tiara: the distinction won by coming out best in a series of matches between England, Scotland, Wales, and Ireland, in which each country plays the other three (*rugby, etc.*).—*adj.* trip'le-crowned, having three crowns or triple crown, as the pope.—triple event, Two Thousand Guineas, St Leger, and Derby.—*adj.* trip'le-head'ed, three-headed.—triple point, the temperature and pressure at which solid, liquid, and gaseous phases of a substance can co-exist, esp. triple point of water, 273·16K; triple time, time or rhythm of three beats, or of three times three beats, in a bar.—*adj.* trip'le-turned (*Shak.*), three times faithless.—Triplex glass (*trademark*), a combination of glass and mica in three layers. [Fr.,—L. *triplus*—Gr. *triploos* (*triplous*); and L. *triplex.*]

triploid, *trip'loid, adj.* having three times the haploid number of chromosomes. [Gr. *triploos,* triple.]

tripod, *tri'pod, trip'od, n.* anything on three feet or legs, esp. a stand for an instrument: the stool on which the priestess sat at Delphi to deliver an oracle.—*adj.* three-legged.—*adj.* tripodal (*trip'-əd-əl*).—*n.* tripody (*trip'ə-di*), a verse or group of three feet. Gr. *tripous, tripodos*—*pous, podos,* foot.]

tripoli, *trip'ə-li, n.* diatomite. [Orig. brought from *Tripoli* in Africa.]

tripos, *tri'pos, n.* a Cambridge honours examination: the list of successful candidates in it: a tripod (*obs.*). [Prob. traceable to the custom by which a B.A., known as Mr *Tripos,* sat on a three-legged stool and disputed in the Philosophy School at Cambridge on Ash Wednesday, his speech being called the Tripos speech.]

trippant, tripper, tripping, etc. See trip.

trippet, *trip'it, n.* a trivet. [Cf. trivet and O.Fr. *trepied.*]

tripple, *trip'l,* (*S.Afr.*) *n.* a horse's ambling canter, between a fast walk and a slow trot.—Also *v.i.*— *n.* tripp'ler. [Du. *trippelen.*]

tripsis, *trip'sis, n.* pulverisation: shampooing: massage. [Gr. *tripsis*—*tribein,* to rub.]

triptane, *trip'tān, n.* trimethyl butane, a powerful aviation fuel. [*trimethyl butane,* with *b* altered to *p.*]

tripterous, *trip'tər-əs, adj.* three-winged. [Gr. *tripteros*—*pteron,* wing.]

triptote, *trip'tōt, adj.* used in three cases only.—*n.* a triptote word. [Gr. *triptōtos*—*ptōsis,* a case, falling.]

triptych, *trip'tik, n.* a set of three tablets, painted panels, etc., hinged together.—*n.* trip'tyque (*trēp-tēk;* Fr.), an international pass for a motor-car. [Gr. *triptychos,* threefold—*ptyx, ptychos,* a fold —*ptyssein,* to fold.]

tripudium, *tri-pū'di-əm, tri-pood'i-oom, n.* an ancient Roman religious dance in triple time, or dance generally: divination from the hopping of birds feeding, or from the dropping of scraps from their bills.—*adj.* tripu'diary.—*v.i.* tripu'-diate, to dance for joy: to exult: to stamp.—*n.* tripudiā'tion. [L. *tripŭdium,* prob. from *trēs,* three, *pēs, pedis,* foot.]

triquetra, *tri-kwet'rə, n.* an ornament consisting of three interlaced arcs, common in early art in northern Europe.—*adjs.* triquet'ral, triquet'rous, triangular: three-edged with concave faces (*bot.*). —*adv.* triquet'rously.—*n.* triquet'rum, a Wormian bone. [L. *triquetrus, -a, -um,* triangular—*trēs,* three.]

triradiate, *tri-rā'di-āt, adj.* three-rayed.—Also trirā'dial. [tri-.]

trireme, *tri'rēm, n.* an ancient galley—esp. a war-galley—with three sets of rowers. [L. *trirēmis*—*rēmus,* an oar.]

**trisaccharide**, *trī-sak'ə-rid, n.* a sugar that hydrolyses into three molecules of simple sugars. [tri-.]

**trisagion**, *tris-ag'i-on, n.* an ancient hymn consisting of the words ' O Holy God, holy and mighty, holy and immortal, have mercy on us ': loosely, the Tersanctus. [Gr. *tris,* thrice, *hagios,* holy.]

**trisect**, *trī-sekt', v.t.* to cut or divide into three (usu. equal) parts.—*ns.* **trisec'tion** (*-shən*); **trisect'or**, one who trisects: esp. one who thinks he can trisect an angle by Euclidean methods (i.e. using straight-edge and compasses) which has been proved to be impossible: a line that trisects; **trisect'rix**, a curve of polar equation *r* = 1 + 2cosθ, by which an angle can be trisected. [tri- and L. *secāre, sectum,* to cut.]

**triseme**, *trī'sēm, adj.* equal to three short syllables. —*n.* a trisemic foot, the tribrach, iamb, trochee. —*adj.* **trisē'mic**. [Gr. *trisēmos—sēma,* a sign.]

**trishaw**, *trī'shö, n.* a three-wheeled light vehicle pedalled by a driver behind the passenger seat. [tri-, rickshaw.]

**triskaidekaphobia**, also -deca-, *tri-ski-dek-ə-fōb'i-ə, n.* fear of the number thirteen. [Gr. *tr(e)iskaideka,* thirteen, *phobos,* fear.]

**triskele**, *tris'kēl, n.* a figure consisting of three radiating curves or legs, as in the arms of the Isle of Man.—Also **triskelion** (*tris-kel'i-on*). [tri- and Gr. *skelos,* a leg.]

**Trismegistus**, *tris-mi-gis'təs, adj.* thrice greatest, an epithet of Thoth, the Egyptian Hermes. [Latinised from Gr. *trismegistos.*]

**trismus**, *triz'məs, n.* tetanic spasm of the muscles of mastication. [Latinised from Gr. *trismos,* a creaking, grating—*trizein,* to grate, gnash.]

**trisoctahedron**, *tris-ok'tə-hē-dron, n.* a solid with twenty-four faces, three for every face of an octahedron. [Gr. *tris,* thrice and **octahedron**.]

**trisomic**, *trī-sōm'ik, adj.* of an otherwise normal diploid organism in which one chromosome type is represented thrice instead of twice. [tri-.]

**trist**, *trist,* (*arch.*) *adj.* sorrowful: dismal.—Also **trist'ful** (*Shak.*). [Fr. *triste*—L. *tristis,* sad.]

**tristich**, *tris'tik, n.* a group of three lines of verse: —*pl.* **tris'tichs** (*-tiks*).—*adj.* **tris'tichous** (*biol.*), in or having three rows. [Gr. *tristichiā,* a triple row, tristich—*stichos,* a row.]

**trisula**, *tri-sōō'la, n.* the trident of Siva.—Also **trisul'**. [Sans. *triśūla.*]

**trisulcate**, *tri-sul'kāt, adj.* having three forks or furrows. [L. *trisulcus—sulcus,* a furrow.]

**trisulphide**, *tri-sul'fīd, n.* a sulphide with three atoms of sulphur to the molecule. [tri-.]

**trisyllable**, *tri-sil'ə-bl,* also *tri-, n.* a word of three syllables.—*adjs.* **trisyllabic** (*-ab'ik*), **-al.**—*adv.* **trisyllab'ically**. [tri-.]

**tritagonist**, *tri-tag'ən-ist, n.* the third actor in the Greek drama. [Gr. *tritagōnistēs—tritos,* third, *agōnistēs,* an actor.]

**trite**, *trīt, adj.* worn: worn out: well-trodden: used till novelty and interest are lost: hackneyed.—*adv.* **trite'ly.**—*n.* **trite'ness**. [L. *trītus,* rubbed, pa.p. of *terēre,* to rub.]

**trite**, *trī'tē,* (*Gr. mus.*) *n.* the third string of the lyre or tone of the tetrachord, reckoned downwards. [Gr. *tritē* (fem.), third.]

**triternate**, *tri-tûr'nāt, adj.* thrice ternate—ternate with each division ternate, and each again ternate.—Also **trip'licate-ter'nate**. [tri-.]

**tritheism**, *tri'thē-izm, n.* belief in three Gods: belief that the Father, Son, and Holy Ghost are actually different beings.—*n.* **tri'theist.**—*adjs.* **tritheis'tic, -al.** [tri- and Gr. *theos,* a god.]

**trithionic**, *tri-thi-on'ik, adj.* containing three sulphur atoms (**trithionic acid**, $H_2S_3O_6$).—*n.* **trithionate** (*tri-thi'ən-āt*), a salt of trithionic acid. [tri- and *theion,* sulphur.]

**tritical**, *trit'i-kl, adj.* trite, common.—*adv.* **trit'ically.** — *ns.* **trit'icalness, trit'icism,** triteness. [Formed from **trite**, in imitation of **critical**, etc.]

**Triticum**, *trit'i-kəm, n.* the wheat genus of grasses. —*adj.* **triticeous** (*-ish'əs*), wheatlike. [L. *triticum,* wheat—*terēre, trītum,* to rub.]

**tritium**, *trish'i-əm, trit', n.* an isotope of hydrogen of triple mass.—*n.* **triton** (*trī'tən*), the nucleus of tritium. [Gr. *tritos,* third.]

**Tritoma**, *trit'ō-mə,* wrongly *trī-tō'mə,* a synonym of Kniphofia. [Gr. *tritŏmos,* thrice cut—*tomē,* a cut (from the splitting capsule).]

**Triton**, *trī'tən, n.* a minor Greek sea-god, son of Poseidon and Amphitrite, represented with a dolphin's tail, sometimes horse's forelegs, blowing a conch: sometimes in *pl.* for the attendants of Poseidon: applied to a seaman or a ship: a genus of large gasteropods with shells that can be used like conchs: a disused generic name for newts. [Gr. *Tritōn, -ōnos.*]

**triton**. See **tritium**.

**tritone**, *trī'tōn,* (*mus.*) *n.* an augmented fourth, an interval of three whole tones. [Gr. *tritŏnos—tonos,* tone.]

**Tritonia**, *tri-tō'ni-ə, n.* the genus commonly called Montbretia.

**tritubercular**, *tri-tū-bûr'kū-lər, adj.* having three tubercles or cusps—also **trituber'culate.**—*ns.* **trituber'culism, trituber'culy**. [tri-.]

**triturate**, *trit'ū-rāt, v.t.* to rub or grind to a fine powder.—*ns.* **tritura'tion; trit'urātor**. [L.L. *triturāre, -ātum*—L. *terēre,* to rub.]

**triumph**, *trī'əmf, n.* in ancient Rome, a solemn procession in honour of a victorious general: a pageant: festivity (*obs.*): pomp, observance (*obs.*): a captive led in triumph (*Milt.*): exultation for success: complete or signal victory or achievement: trump (*obs.*).—*v.i.* to celebrate a victory with pomp: to rejoice for victory: to obtain victory, prevail: to exult, insult (often with *over*): to show in glory (*Shak.*).—*v.t.* (*Milt.*) to triumph over.—*adj.* **triumphal** (*triumf'l*), pertaining to triumph: used in celebrating victory.—*n.* (*Milt.*) a token of victory.—*adj.* **triumph'ant**, celebrating or having achieved a triumph: exultant: transcendent in glory (*Shak.*): triumphal (*Shak.*).—*adv.* **triumph'antly.**—*n.* **tri'umpher.**—*n.* and *adj.* **tri'umphing.**—**triumphal arch**, an arch erected in connection with the triumph of a Roman general: any decorative arch in public rejoicings, etc.—**church triumphant** (see **church**). [L. *triumphus;* akin to Gr. *thriambos,* a hymn to Bacchus.]

**triumvir**, *tri-um'vər, trī-oōm'vir, n.* one of three men in the same office or government: one of three sharing supreme power:—*pl.* **trium'viri, trium'virs.**—*adj.* **trium'viral.**—*n.* **trium'virate** (*obs.* **trium'viry;** *Shak.* **trium'phery**), an association of three men in office or government, or for any political ends—esp. that of Pompey, Crassus, and Caesar (60 B.C.), and that of Octavian (Augustus), Mark Antony, and Lepidus (43 B.C.): any trio or triad. [L. *triumvir,* from the gen. pl. *trium virōrum,* of three men.]

**triune**, *trī'ūn, adj.* three in one.—*n.* a trinity in unity.—*n.* **triū'nity**. [L. *trēs, tria,* three, *ūnus,* one.]

**trivalent**, *tri-vā'lənt, triv'ə-lənt, adj.* having a valency of three.—*ns.* **trivā'lence** (or *triv'əl-*), **trivā'lency** (or *triv'əl-*). [tri- and **valent**.]

**trivalve**, *tri'valv, adj.* three-valved.—*n.* that which is three-valved.—*adjs.* **tri'valved, trival'vūlar**. [tri- and L. *valva,* a door-leaf.]

**trivet**, *triv'it, n.* a tripod, esp. one for a pot or kettle: a bracket with three projections for fixing on the top bar of a grate: a three-legged pot.—**right as a trivet**, perfectly right (from its stability). [O.E. *trefet,* app.—L. *tripēs, tripedis—pēs,* a foot.]

**trivia**, *trī'vi-ə, n.pl.* trifles, trivialities, unimportant details.—*adj.* **trivial** (*triv'i-əl*), of the trivium: to be found anywhere: of little importance: trifling: vernacular (*biol.*): specific, opp. to generic (of a name; *biol.*).—*n.* trivialisā'tion, -z-.—*v.i.* triv'ialise, -ize, to render paltry.—*ns.*

triv'ialism, a trivial matter or remark; triviality (-*al'i-ti*), the state or quality of being trivial: that which is trivial, a trifle.—*adv.* triv'ially.—*ns.*

triv'ialness; triv'ium, in mediaeval schools the group of liberal arts first studied—grammar, rhetoric, and logic: the three anterior radii of an echinoderm. [L. *trivium*, a place where three ways meet—*trēs*, three, *via*, a way.]

tri-weekly, *tri-wēk'li*, *adj.* occurring or appearing once in three weeks or three times a week.—*adv.* once in three weeks: three times a week.—*n.* a periodical appearing three times a week. [tri-.]

trizone, *tri'zōn*, *n.* the area of West Germany comprised in the British, French, and American zones of occupation after World War II.—*adj.* trizō'nal. [tri- and zone.]

troad, troade (*Spens.*). See trod.

troat, *trōt*, *v.i.* to bellow, as a buck.—Also *n.* [O.Fr. *trout, trut*, interj. used to urge on animals.]

trocar, *trō'kär*, *n.* a surgical perforator used with a cannula: sometimes a cannula. [Fr. *trocart*— *trois*, three, *carre*, side.]

trochaic. See trochee. trochal, troche, Tro-chidae, trochisk. See trochus.

trochanter, *trō-kan'tər*, *n.* a rough eminence on the thigh-bone for insertion of muscles: the second joint of an insect's leg.—*adj.* trochanteric (-*ter'ik*). [Gr. *trochantēr*—*trechein*, to run.]

trochee, *trō'kē*, (*pros.*) *n.* a foot of two syllables, a long followed by a short: in English, etc., a stressed followed by an unstressed.—*adj.* trochaic (-*kā'ik*).—*n.* a trochaic verse. [Gr. *trochaios* (*pous*, foot), running, tripping—*trochos*, a running—*trechein*, to run.]

trochilus, *trok'i-ləs*, *n.* a concave moulding: the crocodile bird: (*cap.*) a genus of humming-birds, formerly including all of them, giving name to the humming-bird family Trochil'idae.—*adj.* trochil'ic, pertaining to rotatory motion. [Gr. *trochilos*, a crocodile bird, a wren, a pulley sheaf—*trechein*, to run.]

trochlea, *trok'li-ə*, (*zool.*) *n.* any pulley-like structure, esp. a foramen through which a tendon passes.—*adj.* troch'lear. trochlear nerve, the fourth cranial nerve. [L. *trochlea*—Gr. *trochiliā*, a pulley.]

trochus, *trō'kəs*, *n.* a wheel or hoop (*Gr. ant.*): the inner ring of cilia in a rotifer: (*cap.*) the top genus of molluscs.—*adj.* tro'chal, wheel-like.—*n.* troche (*trōk, trōsh, trōch; trō'kē*, is frowned upon), a round medicinal tablet.—*ns.pl.* Trochel-minthes (*trōk-el-min'thēz*; Gr. *helmins, helmin-thos*, worm), the rotifer phylum of animals; Troch'idae, the top family of molluscs.—*ns.* trochisc'us, troch'isk, a troche; troch'ite, an encrinite joint; troch'oid, the curve traced by a fixed point in the plane of a rolling circle.—*adj.* wheel-like: like a Trochus: trochoidal.—*adj.* trochoid'al, of the nature of a trochoid.—*ns.* trochom'eter or (*ill-formed*) trocheam'eter, a hodometer; troch'otron, *trochoidal* magne*tron*, a high-frequency counting tube which deflects a beam on to radially disposed electrodes. [Gr. *trochos*, a wheel—*trechein*, to run.]

trock (*Scot.*). See truck (1).

troctolite, *trok'tə-lit*, *n.* troutstone, a coarse-grained basic igneous rock composed of feldspar spotted with olivine. [Gr. *trōktēs*, a kind of sea-fish—*trōgein*, to gnaw, nibble, *lithos*, stone.]

trod, *trod* (*Spens.* troad, troade, trode, *trōd*), (*obs.*) *n.* a track: path: footing.—hot trod (*Scott*), the pursuit of moss-troopers. [O.E. *trod, trodu*, track, trace; cf. tread.]

trod, trodden. See tread.

troelie, troely. See troolie.

troggs, *trogz*, (*Scot.*) *n.* and interj. troth.

troglodyte, *trog'lə-dit*, *n.* a cave-dweller: an anthropoid ape (*obs.* and *misapplied*).—Also

*adj.*—*n.* Troglodytes (-*lod'i-tēz*), the wren genus.—*adjs.* troglodytic (-*dit'ik*), -al, cave-dwelling.—*n.* trog'lodytism (-*dit-izm*). [Gr. *trōglodytēs*—*trōglē*, a hole, *dyein*, to get into.]

trogon, *trō'gon*, *n.* any member of a family (Trogon'idae) of tropical and esp. South American birds with brilliant plumage, the first and second toes turned back, including the quetzal. [App. Gr. *trōgōn*, nibbling.]

Troic, *trō'ik*, *adj.* Trojan. [Gr. *Trōikos.*]

troika, *troi'ka*, *n.* a Russian vehicle for three horses abreast: a team of three horses abreast: a team of three men, etc., acting equally as leaders. [Russ.,—*troe*, a set of three.]

troilite, *trō'il-it*, *n.* native ferrous sulphide, found in meteorites. [After Dominico *Troili*, who observed it in the 18th cent.]

Trojan, *trō'jən*, *adj.* of Troy.—*n.* a citizen or inhabitant of Troy: a boon companion: a doughty, trusty, or hard-working person: a good fellow.—**Trojan horse,** the gigantic wooden horse inside which the Greeks entered Troy: a person, organisation, placed within a country, group, etc., with the purpose of destroying it. [L. *Trōjānus*—*Trōja*, Troy.]

troke (*Scot.*). See truck (1).

troll, *trōl*, *n.* in Scandinavian mythology, a goblin or supernatural dwarf (earlier giant). [O.N.]

troll, *trōl*, *v.t.* to roll (*obs.*): to trundle (*arch.*): to spin (*arch.*): to circulate, pass about the table (*arch.*): (*Milt.* troule) to move nimbly, wag (the tongue): to utter fluently, set rolling off the tongue (*obs.*): to sing the parts of in succession, as of a catch or round: to fish for, or in, with a spinning or otherwise moving bait: to allure (*obs.*): to convey by trolley.—*v.i.* to roll (*obs.*): to move or run about (*obs.*): to sing a catch: to stroll, ramble (*obs.*): to fish with revolving or trailing lure: to travel by trolley.—*n.* a moving round, repetition: a round song: trolling: a lure for trolling.—*ns.* troll'er; **trolley** (*trol'i*; sometimes troll'y), a costermonger's cart: a low wheelbarrow: a small truck: a bogie: a pulley, receptacle, or car travelling on an overhead wire or rail: a trolley-wheel: a tram-car (*U.S.*).—*n.* and *adj.* troll'ing (*trōl'*).—troll'ey-bus', a bus that·receives power by a trolley-wheel from an overhead wire; **troll'ey-car'** (*U.S.*), a tram-car so driven; **troll'ey-man,** a man who works a trolley or on a trolley; **troll'ey-ta'ble,** a tiered trolley for a dining-room; **troll'ey-wheel,** a grooved wheel by which a bus, tram-car, etc., obtains current from an overhead wire; **troll'ing-bait, -spoon,** a metallic revolving lure used in trolling. [Cf. O.Fr. *troller* (Fr. *trôler*) to quest, Ger. *trollen*, to roll.]

trolley, trolly, *trol'i*, *n.* lace with pattern outlined with thicker thread or a flat border. [Cf. Flem. *tralje*, trellis.]

troll-my-dame(s), *trōl-mi-dām(z)'*, (*Shak.*) *n.* an old game like bagatelle, in which bullets were trolled into a little arcade.—Also **trou-madame** (*trōō-mä-däm*). [Fr. *trou-madame*—*trou*, hole, associated with troll.]

trollop, *trol'əp*, *n.* a slatternly woman: a draggle-tail: a strumpet.—*v.i.* (*Scot.*) to draggle: to go, dress, or work in a slovenly way.—*n.* trollopee', (18th cent.) a woman's loose dress.—*adjs.* troll'-oping, troll'opish, troll'opy. [Perh. troll (2).]

Trollopean, -pian, *trol-ō-pē'ən*, *adj.* of, in the style of, the novels of Anthony *Trollope* (1815-82).— *n.* an admirer of his novels.

tromba marina, *trom'bə mə-rē'nə*, *n.* an obsolete viol, generally one-stringed, with an irregular bridge, played in harmonics, giving a trumpet-like tone. [It., marine (speaking) trumpet.]

trombone, *trom-bōn'*, *n.* a brass musical wind instrument, consisting of a tube bent twice on itself, with a slide.—*n.* trombōn'ist. [It.; augm. of *tromba*, trumpet.]

**trommel**, *trom'əl*, *n.* a revolving cylindrical sieve for cleaning or sizing minerals. [Ger. *trommel*, drum.]

**tromometer**, *trom-om'i-tər*, *n.* an instrument for measuring slight earthquake shocks.—*adj.* **tromomet'ric**. [Gr. *tromos*, a trembling, *metron*, a measure.]

**trompe, tromp**, *tromp*, *n.* an apparatus for producing a blast of air in a furnace by falling water. [Fr.]

**trompe l'œil**, *trõp lœ y'*, (Fr.) lit 'something that deceives the eye': appearance of reality achieved by use of minute, often trivial, details or of other effects in painting, architecture, etc.

**tron, tron, trone**, *trōn*, (chiefly *Scot.*) *n.* a public weighing machine, used also as a place of punishment as by nailing the ear: the market-place: a system of weights used at the tron. [O.Fr. *trone*—L. *trūtina*—Gr. *trȳtanē*, a pair of scales.]

**-tron**, *-tron*, *suff.* signifying agent, instrument. [Gr.]

**trona**, *trō'nə*, *n.* a native combination of acid and normal sodium carbonate. [Sw.,—Ar. *trōn* for *natrūn*; see **natron**.]

**tronc**, *tronk*, Fr. *trõ*, *n.* a collection of tips to be divided out later, e.g. among waiters: the system by which this is done. [Fr., collecting box.]

**troolie, troelie, troely**, *trōō'li*, *n.* the bussu palm: its leaf. [Tupí *tururi*.]

**troop**, *trōōp*, *n.* a body of soldiers: (in *pl.*) military forces: a band of people: a flock, herd, swarm of animals: (esp. in *pl.*) a great number: a division of a cavalry squadron: a group of (Boy) Scout patrols: a troupe: the command of a troop of horse: a drum signal for assembling.—*v.i.* to assemble: to consort: to pass in a body or in rapid succession: to be off, pack.—*v.t.* to cause to troop: to receive and carry ceremonially along the ranks (as *troop the colour* or *colours*). —*n.* troop'er, a private cavalry soldier (proverbially a swearer): a private soldier in armoured (tank) units: a mounted policeman (*U.S.* and *Austr.*): a cavalry horse: a troop-ship.—**troop'-carrier**, a ship or aeroplane for carrying troops; **troop'-horse**, a cavalry horse; **troop'-ship**, a transport. [Fr. *troupe*—L.L. *troppus*; poss. Gmc.]

**troopial.** Same as **troupial**.

**tropaeolum**, *trop-ē'ə-ləm*, *n.* the Indian cress and Canary creeper genus, South American trailing or climbing plants constituting a family Tropaeolā'ceae, akin to the geraniums—misnamed nasturtium. [Gr. *tropaion*, a trophy (from the shield-shaped leaves and helmet-like flowers).]

**troparion**, *trop-är'i-on*, or *-ar'*, (Gr. *Ch.*) *n.* a stanza or short hymn:—*pl.* **tropar'ia**. [Dim. of Gr. *tropos*, trope.]

**trope**, *trōp*, *n.* a figure of speech, properly one in which a word or expression is used in other than its literal sense—metaphor, metonymy, synecdoche, irony (*rhet.*): a short cadence peculiar to Gregorian melodies: a phrase formerly interpolated in different parts of the mass. [Gr. *tropos*, a turn—*trepein*, to turn.]

**troph-, tropho-**, *trof-*, *-ō-*, *-o'-*, in composition, nutrition.—*ns.* **trophallax'is** (Gr. *allaxis*, exchange), **trophobiō'sis** (Gr. *biōsis*, way of life), mutual exchange of nutriment in symbiosis.—*adjs.* **trophallact'ic, trophobiot'ic; trophesial** (*-ē'zi-əl, -shl*), relating to trophesy.—*n.* **troph'esy, trophoneurō'sis**, a state of deranged nutrition owing to disorder of the trophic action of the nerves.—*n.pl.* **trophi** (*trō'f i*), the mouth-parts of an insect: teeth of the pharynx of a rotifer. —*adj.* **troph'ic**, relating to nutrition.—*ns.* **trophol'-ogy**, the study of nutrition; **trophotax'is**, **trophot'ropism**, chemotaxis, chemotropism, where the stimulating substance is food.—*adjs.* **trophotact'ic, trophotrop'ic.**—**trophic level**, a

division of an ecosystem consisting of all organisms whose food is obtained from plants by the same number of intermediate steps; **trophic structure**, a feature of an ecosystem, measured and described in terms of standing crop per unit area or energy fixed per unit area per unit time. [Gr. *trophē*, food, *trophos*, a feeder; *trephein*, to feed.]

**Trophonian**, *trō-fō'ni-ən*, *adj.* of the deified *Trophōnius* (Gr. *Trophōnios*), or the cave in Boeotia where he delivered oracles and conferred solemnising mystic experiences.

**trophy**, *trō'fi*, *n.* a memorial of victory, orig. arms or other spoils set up on the spot: displayed spoils, as skulls and antlers: a piece of plate or suchlike awarded as a prize: a memorial of success, glory, etc.: an ornamental group of weapons, flags, etc., or a representation of it.—*v.t.* to set with trophies: to bestow trophies on.—*adj.* **trō'phied**. [Fr. *trophée*—L. *trophaeum* (classical *tropaeum*) — Gr. *tropaion* — *tropē*, a turning—*trepein*, to turn.]

**tropic**, *trop'ik*, *n.* an imaginary circle on the celestial sphere about 23° 28' N. (*tropic of Cancer*) or S. (*of Capricorn*) of the equator, where the sun turns on reaching its greatest declination north or south: a corresponding circle on the terrestrial globe: (*pl.*) the part of the earth between the tropics of Cancer and Capricorn: a turning-point or limit.—*adj.* of, relating to, the sun's turning: of the tropics: of, of the nature of, a tropism.—*adj.* **trop'ical**, of, relating to, a tropic or the tropics: found in, characteristic of, the tropics: fervidly hot: luxuriant: of a trope, figurative.—*adv.* **trop'ically**.—*ns.* **trop'-ism** (*biol.*), orientation in response to stimulus: a general term for heliotropism, geotropism, etc.; **tropist** (*trōp'*), a user of tropes: one who understands the Bible as figurative.—*adjs.* **tropistic** (*trop-ist'ik*), of tropism; **tropolog'ic, -al.**—*adv.* **tropolog'ically.**—*ns.* **tropol'ogy**, figurative language: a moral interpretation of the Bible; **trop'opause** (Gr. *pausis*, a ceasing), the boundary between troposphere and stratosphere; **trop'-ophyte** (*-fīt*; Gr. *phyton*, plant), a plant adapted to alterations of moisture and drought.—*adj.* **tropophytic** (*-fit'ik*).—*n.* **trop'osphere**, the lowest layer of the atmosphere in which temperature falls as height increases.—*adj.* **tropospher'ic.**— **tropical month, year** (see **month, year**); **trop'icbird**, a tropical sea-bird (Phaethon) with long tail-feathers. [Gr. *tropos*, a turning.]

**troppo**, *trop'ō*, (It.) in music, too much: excessively.

**trossers**, *tros'ərz*, *n.* an obs. form of **trousers**.

**trot**, *trot*, *n.* a pace between walking and running (in a horse with legs moving together diagonally): an act or spell of trotting: continual activity in moving about: a toddling child: a long line of baited hooks: a crib, literal translation (*U.S.*). —*v.i.* to go, ride, or drive at a trot: to jog: to bustle about: to fish with a trot.—*v.t.* to cause to trot: to conduct around: to bring out for exhibition: to draw out so as to make a butt of: to jog on one's knee: to trot upon: to execute at a trot:—*pr.p.* **trott'ing**; *pa.t.* and *pa.p.* **trott'ed**. —*ns.* **trott'er**, one that trots: a trotting-horse, a pacer: a foot, esp. of a sheep or pig; **trott'ing**, the action of the verb: harness-racing; **trottoir** (*trot-wär*; Fr.), a paved footway at the side of a street.—**trot out**, to exhibit the paces of: to bring forward, adduce, produce for show: to walk out with. [O.Fr. *trot* (n.), *troter* (vb.); perh. Gmc.; cf. O.H.G. *trottōn*, Eng. **tread**.]

**trot**, *trot*, (Shak.) *n.* a beldame, crone. [A.Fr. *trote*.]

**trot-cozy, -cosey**, *trot'-kō'zi*, (Scott) *n.* a riding-hood. [App. **trot** (Jamieson says **throat**) and **cosy**.]

**troth**, *trōth, troth*, (arch.) *n.* a variant of **truth**:

faith, fidelity.—*v.t.* (*Shak.*) to betroth.—*interj.* in truth.—*adjs.* **truth'ful; troth'less.**—**troth'-plight,** a plighting of troth, betrothal.—*v.t.* (*arch.*) to betroth.—*adj.* (*Shak.*) betrothed.—Also **troth'-plighted.**—**troth'-ring,** a betrothal ring.

**Trotskyism,** *trot'ski-izm, n.* the form of Communism associated with Leon *Trotsky* (pseudonym of Lev Davidovich Bronstein, 1879-1940), who advocated world-wide revolution.—*n.* **Trot'skyist.**—Also *adj.*—*n.* **Trot'skyite.**

**troubadour,** *trōō'bə-dōōr, -dōr, -dôr, n.* one of a class of lyric poets of chivalric love, who first appeared in Provence, and flourished from the 11th to the 13th century. [Fr.,—Prov. *trobador* —*trobar* (Fr. *trouver*), to find.]

**trouble,** *trub'l, v.t.* to agitate: to disturb: to muddy: to make turbid: to molest: to afflict: to annoy: to busy or engage overmuch: to put to inconvenience.—*v.i.* to take pains: to put oneself to inconvenience: to be troublesome.— *n.* disturbance: affliction: distress: a scrape: travail: anything amiss: disease: uneasiness: exertion: the taking of pains: a cause of trouble.— *adj.* **troub'led** (*-ld*).—*adv.* **troub'ledly.**—*n.* **troub'ler.** —*adj.* **troub'lesome,** causing or giving trouble or inconvenience: vexatious: importunate.—*adv.* **troub'lesomely.**—*n.* **troub'lesomeness.**—*n.* and *adj.* **troub'ling.**—*adj.* **troub'lous,** full of trouble or disorder: agitated: tumultuous: disturbing.—*adv.* **troub'lously.**—*n.* **troub'lousness.**—**troub'le-house, -state, -town, -world,** one who disturbs the peace of a house, state, etc.; **troub'lemaker,** one who disturbs the peace and (usu.) incites others to do so; **troub'le-mirth,** a kill-joy; **troub'leshooter,** an expert detector and mender of any trouble, mechanical or other.—**ask for trouble,** to behave in such a way as to bring trouble on oneself; **I'll trouble you to,** please; **trouble one for,** ask one to pass. [O.Fr. *trubler* (Fr. *troubler*), from a L.L. freq. of L. *turbāre,* to disturb—*turba,* a crowd.]

**trou-de-loup,** *trōō-də-lōō, n.* a pit with a vertical stake in the middle—a defence against cavalry:— *pl.* **trous-de-loup** (*trōō-*). [Fr., wolf-hole.]

**trough,** *trof, n.* a long, narrow vessel for watering or feeding animals: a vessel for kneading, brewing, washing, tanning, or various domestic and industrial purposes: a vessel for liquid over which gases are collected (*pneumatic trough*): a channel, gutter, or conduit: a long narrow depression: a hollow between wave-crests.— **trough'-fault** (*geol.*), a pair of parallel faults with downthrow between them; **trough'-shell,** a lamellibranch with a somewhat triangular shell fancied to resemble a kneading-trough (Mactra). [O.E. *trog*; Ger. *trog.*]

**trou-madame.** Same as **troll-my-dame(s).**

**trounce,** *trowns, v.t.* to harass (*obs.*): to indict (*dial.*): to punish, beat, rebuke or censure severely.—*ns.* **trounc'er; trounc'ing.** [Origin obscure.]

**trounce,** *trowns, v.i.* to skip, prance, move briskly. —*v.t.* to whisk off, make to skip. [Origin obscure.]

**troupe,** *trōōp, n.* a company, esp. of performers.— —*n.* **troup'er,** a member of a theatrical troupe: an experienced actor. [Fr. See **troop.**]

**troupial, troopial,** *trōō'pi-əl, n.* a bird (*Icterus icterus*) famous for its song: any bird of the Icteridae. [Fr. *troupiale*—*troupe,* troop.]

**trouse,** *trōōz, trowz,* (*hist.*) *n.* Irish close-fitting breeches: trews.—Also in *pl.* (now *vulg.*) trousers. [See **trews.**]

**trousers,** *trow'zərz, obs.* **trossers,** *tros'ərz,* **strossers** *stros', n. pl.* long breeches: a garment worn on the lower part of the body with a loose tubular branch for each leg: any other garment of similar form, as pantalettes. (The sing. is used to form compounds, as **trous'er-butt'on, -clip, -leg', -pock'et, -stretch'er, -suit,** etc.)—*adj.* **trou'-sered,** wearing trousers.—*n.* **trou'sering,** (usu. in

*pl.*) material for trousers.—**wear the trousers,** of a wife, to be the dominant partner in a marriage. [See preceding.]

**trousseau,** *trōō'sō, n.* a bride's outfit: a bundle (*arch.* and *rare*):—*pl.* **trousseaux** (*-sōz*). [Fr., dim. of *trousse,* bundle.]

**trout,** *trowt, n.* a freshwater fish (*Salmo fario*) of the salmon genus, much sought after by anglers: extended to various fishes related or superficially like: an unpleasant, interfering old woman:— *pl.* **trout** (rarely trouts).—*n.* **trout'er,** one who fishes for trout.—*adj.* **trout'ful,** abounding in trout.—*n.* and *adj.* **trout'ing,** trout-fishing.—*adj.* **trout'less.**—*ns.* **trout'let, trout'ling,** a little trout. —*adj.* **trout'y.**—**trout'-bas'ket,** an osier or willow creel for carrying trout.—*adj.* **trout'-coloured,** speckled like a trout: white, with spots of black, bay, or sorrel.—**trout'-farm,** a place where trout are reared artificially; **trout'-rod,** a fishing-rod for trout; **trout'-spoon,** a small revolving spoon used as a lure for trout; **trout'-stone,** troctolite; **trout'-stream,** a stream in which trout are caught. [O.E. *truht*—L. *tructa, tructus*—Gr. *trōktēs,* a sea-fish with sharp teeth —*trōgein,* to gnaw, nibble.]

**trouvaille,** *trōō-vä'ē, n.* a happy find. [Fr.]

**trouvère,** *trōō-ver', n.* one of the mediaeval narrative or epic poets of northern France. [Fr.]

**trove.** See **treasure.**

**trover,** *trō'vər, n.* orig., finding and keeping: hence an action brought to recover goods from a person to whom they do not belong. [O.Fr. *trover* (Fr. *trouver*), to find.]

**trow,** *trō,* (*arch.*) *v.t.* to trust: to believe (often elliptically for *I trow* or *trow you?*). [O.E. *trēowan* (*trēowian, trūwian*); O.N. *trúa,* Ger. *trauen.*]

**trow, trow,** (*Shetland and Orkney*) *n.* a form of **troll** (1).

**trowel,** *trow'əl, n.* a flat or scoop-shaped tool with a short handle, for plastering, gardening, etc.— *v.t.* to dress, apply, move, with or as if with a trowel:—*pr.p.* **trow'elling;** *pa.t.* and *pa.p.* **trow'-elled.**—*n.* **trow'eller.**—**lay on with a trowel,** to spread thickly: to say grossly flattering things. [O.Fr. *truelle*—L.L. *truella* (L. *trulla,* dim. of *trua,* a ladle).]

**trowsers,** an old spelling of **trousers.**

**troy,** *troi, adj.* of a system of weights used for gold, silver, and precious stones, the pound (no longer in legal use) of 5760 grains, being divided into 12 ounces of 20 pennyweight. [*Troyes,* in France.]

**Trojan,** *troi'ən,* (*Shak., Spens.*) *adj.* Trojan.

**truant,** *trōō'ənt, n.* a vagrant (*obs.*): a vague term of reproach (*obs.*): an idler: one who, idly or without excuse, absents himself from school.— Also *adj.*—*v.i.* to play truant.—*ns.* **tru'ancy, tru'antship.**—**play truant,** to stay from school without leave or good reason. [O.Fr. *truant* (Fr. *truand*), prob. from Celtic.]

**Trubenise, -ize,** *trōō'bən-iz, v.t.* to stiffen (a fabric) by binding together two layers by an intermediate layer of cellulose acetate. [Proprietary.]

**trucage, truquage,** *trü-käzh,* (Fr.) faking of works of art.—*n.* **truqueur** (*trü-kœr*), a faker of works of art.

**truce,** *trōōs, n.* a suspension of hostilities: a respite.—*adjs.* **truce'less; trucial** (*trōō'shl, syəl, -shi-əl*), bound by a truce.—*n.* **truce'-break'er.**— **Trucial States,** a group of Arab Sheikdoms, on the S. coast of the Persian Gulf, in treaty with Britain.—**Truce of God,** a cessation of war, decreed by the Church, more or less observed, esp. in the 11th and 12th centuries, in France, Italy, England, etc., from Saturday (afterwards from Wednesday) evening to Monday morning, also during Advent and Lent and on certain holy days. [M.E. *trewes, treowes,* pl. of *trewe*—O.E. *trēow,* truth, pledge, treaty; cf. **true.**]

truchman, *truch'mən*, (*arch.*) *n.* an interpreter. [Ar. *turjamān*; cf. **dragoman.**]

truck, *truk*, *v.t.* to exchange: to barter: to pay in goods.—*v.i.* to traffic: to have dealings or intercourse: to barter: to bargain: to potter about. —*Scot.* **trock** (*trok*), **troke** (*trōk*).—*n.* exchange of goods: barter: payment in goods: (*Scot.* **trock, troke**) dealings, intercourse: a small job, chore: small goods (*coll.*): rubbish: fresh vegetables, market-garden produce (*U.S.*).—*ns.* **truck'age**, barter; **truck'er**, one who trucks: a market-gardener (*U.S.*); **truck'ing.**—**truck'- farm** (*U.S.*), a market-garden; **truck'-farmer**; **truck'-farming**; **truck system**, the practice of paying workmen in goods instead of money, forbidden by the Truck Acts, 1831, etc.—**have no truck with**, to have nothing to do with. [O.Fr. *troquer*, to truck; Sp. *trocar*, to barter, It. *truccare*, to truck.]

truck, *truk*, *n.* a small or solid wheel: an open railway wagon for goods: a trolley: a bogie: a low flat barrow: a small two-wheeled barrow with a turned-up front: a lorry (*U.S.*): a cap at the top of a mast or flagstaff.—*v.t.* to convey by truck: to put on a truck.—*ns.* **truck'age**, carriage by truck: charge for carriage by truck: supply of trucks; **truck'ing.** [L. *trochus*, a wheel—Gr. *trochos*—*trechein*, to run.]

truckle, *truk'l*, *n.* a pulley-wheel: a castor (*obs.*): a truckle-bed.—*v.t.* to move on rollers.—*v.i.* to sleep in a truckle-bed: to behave with servility. —*n.* **truck'ler.**—*n.* and *adj.* **truck'ling.**—**truck'le- bed**, a low bed that may be wheeled under another. [Gr. *trochileiā*, -*iā*, etc., a pulley—*trochos*, a wheel.]

truculent, *truk'-*, *trōōk'ū-lənt*, *adj.* very fierce: cruel: aggressive and discourteous.—*ns.* **truc'- ulence**, **truc'ulency.**—*adv.* **truc'ulently.** [L. *truculentus*—*trux*, wild, fierce.]

trudge, *truj*, *v.i.* to walk with labour or effort: to plod doggedly.—*n.* a heavy or weary walk: a trudger.—*n.* **trudg'er.**—*n.* and *adj.* **trudg'ing.** [Origin obscure.]

trudgen, (incorrectly **trudgeon**), *truj'ən*, *n.* a swimming stroke in which each hand alternately is raised above the surface, thrust forward, and pulled back through the water.—Also *adj.* [John Trudgen, who popularised the stroke in England.]

true, *trōō*, *adj.* faithful: constant: trusty: genuine: properly so called: typical: conformable: accurately adjusted or in tune: straight or flat: agreeing with fact: actual: absolute: corrected: accurate: exact: right: rightful: honest: sincere: truthful.—*adv.* truly: faithfully: honestly: in accurate adjustment: dead in tune: after the ancestral type.—*v.t.* to adjust accurately. —*n.* that which is true, truth: accurate adjustment.—*n.* **true'ness.**—*adv.* **tru'ly.**—**true bill**, a bill of indictment endorsed, after investigation, by a grand jury, as containing a case for the court.—*adj.* and *n.* **true'-blue** (see **blue**).—*adjs.* **true'-born**, of genuine birth: pure-bred: true to the qualities of the breed: legitimate; **true'-bred**, pure-bred: typical: of good breeding; **true'- devot'ed** (*Shak.*), full of honest zeal; **true'- dispos'ing** (*Shak.*), just; **true'-heart'ed**, sincere: faithful.—**true'-heart'edness**; **true'-love**, one truly or really beloved: a sweetheart: a faithful lover: a true-love-knot: a quatrefoil: a four- leaved clover (**true'-love grass**) (*obs.*): herb- Paris.—Also *adj.*—**true'-love-knot**, **true'-lov'er's- knot**, an ornamental or symbolic knot or inter- laced design, as a two-looped bow or a knot with two interlaced loops; **true'man** (*arch.*), an honest man; **true'penny** (*Shak.*), an honest fellow.—*adj.* **true-seem'ing** (*Spens.*), seeming (falsely or truly) to be true.—**out of true**, not straight, not properly balanced, adjusted, or calibrated. [O.E. *trēowe*; O.N. *tryggr*, Ger. *treu.*]

truffle, *truf'l*, *trōōf'l*, *n.* any fungus of the genus Tuber or the family Tuberaceae: its under- ground edible fructification: a rich confection, made with chocolate, butter, etc., usu. shaped into balls.—*adj.* **truff'led**, cooked, stuffed, dres- sed, with truffles.—**truff'le-dog**, **-pig**, one trained to find truffles. [O.Fr. *truffle* (Fr. *truffe*); poss. —L. *tūber*, lump, swelling.]

trug, *trug*, (*dial.*) *n.* a flat wooden fruit-basket. [Prob. **trough.**]

truism, *trōō'izm*, *n.* a self-evident truth: a com- monplace or trite statement.—*adj.* **truist'ic.** [**true.**]

trull, *trul*, *n.* a drab. [Cf. Ger. *trolle.*]

Trullan, *trul'an*, *adj.* held in the domed hall of the palace at Constantinople—applied to the Sixth Ecumenical Council (680-1) and esp. to the Council of 692, not accepted by the Western Church. [L.L. *trullus*, a dome—L. *trulla*, a ladle.]

trumeau, *trōō-mō'*, *n.* a piece of wall or pillar between two openings:—*pl.* **trumeaux** (-*mōz'*). [Fr.]

trump, *trump*, (*obs.*) *v.t.* to deceive.—*n.* **trump'ery**, showy and worthless stuff: rubbish: ritual foolery.—Also *adj.* [Fr. *tromper*, to deceive.]

trump, *trump*, *n.* a trumpet: a blast: a Jew's-harp (now *Scot.*).—*v.t.* and *v.i.* to trumpet.—**trump marine**, the tromba marina. [O.Fr. *trompe.*]

trump, *trump*, *n.* a card of a suit that takes any card of any other suit: ruff, an old card-game like whist: a good, trusty fellow (*coll.*).—Also *adj.*—*v.t.* to play a trump card upon instead of following suit: to take in this way.—*v.i.* to play trumps on another suit.—**trump'-card**, the card turned up to determine the trump suit: any card of that suit: a means of triumph (*fig.*): a vic- torious expedient.—**no'-trumps**, a declaration in bridge whereby no suit is more powerful than the rest.—*adj.* **no'-trump.**—**no'-trump'er**, a hand suitable for no-trumps; **turn up trumps** (*fig.*), to behave in a very helpful or generous way, esp. unexpectedly. [**triumph.**]

trump, *trump*, *n.* (*obs.*) an obstruction cast in one's way.—*v.t.* to cast as an obstruction (*obs.*): to allege (*obs.*): to concoct and put forward unscrupulously (with *up*).—*adj.* **trumped'-up.** [**trump** (3), affected by, or partly from, **trump** (1).]

trumpet, *trum'pit*, *n.* an orchestral, military, and signalling wind instrument of powerful and brilliant tone, in its present form a narrow tube bent twice upon itself, with cupped mouthpiece and flaring bell, giving, by action of the lips and breath-pressure, harmonics of its fundamental, the scale filled up by use of crooks, slides, or valves: applied to other instruments more or less like: a speaking-trumpet: an ear-trumpet: a trumpet-shaped object, as a flared bell or horn, a corolla or corona: a sound of, or as if of, a trumpet: a trumpeter: an organ reed-stop of trumpet-like tone.—*v.t.* to sound or play on a trumpet or with trumpet-like sound: to pro- claim, celebrate, summon, denounce, expel, etc., by trumpet.—*v.i.* to sound a trumpet: to make a sound like a trumpet:—*pr.p.* **trum'peting**; *pa.t.* and *pa.p.* **trum'peted.**—*adj.* **trum'peted**, sounded on a trumpet: loudly extolled: having a trum- pet: funnel-shaped.—*n.* **trum'peter**, one who plays or sounds the trumpet: one who proclaims, praises, or denounces: a loud-voiced crane-like South American bird (Psophia): an American swan: a kind of domestic pigeon: a large New Zealand food-fish (Latris) or other fish that trumpets when caught.—*n.* and *adj.* **trum'peting.** —**trum'pet-call**, a conventional phrase or passage played on the trumpet as a signal: any call to action; **trum'pet-fish**, the snipe-fish or bellows- fish (Macrorhamphosus or Centriscus), a long- snouted fish akin to the pipefish: a flute-mouth, a sea-fish with a tubular muzzle; **trum'pet-**

**flower,** a name for various bignoniaceous, solanaceous, and other plants with large trumpet-shaped flowers; **trum′pet-ma′jor,** a head-trumpeter in a regiment.—*adj.* **trum′pet-shaped,** like the bell of a trumpet.—**trum′pet-shell,** Triton; **trum′pet-tone,** the sound of a trumpet: a loud voice.—*adj.* **trum′pet-tongued,** proclaiming loud as a trumpet.—**trum′pet-tree,** -**wood,** a South American Cecropia whose hollow branches the Indians use as trumpets.— **blow one's own trumpet,** to sound one's own praises; **feast of trumpets,** a Jewish feast in which trumpets played an important part. [Fr. *trompette,* dim. of *trompe,* trump.]

**truncal.** See **trunk.**

**truncate,** *trungk-āt′, v.t.* to cut short: to lop: to delete those digits of a number which are not considered to be significant (*math.*): to maim: to replace (an edge or corner where similar faces meet) by a symmetrically placed face (*crystal.*).— *adjs.* **trunc′ate, -d,** appearing as if squared off at the tip: ending in a transverse line or plane, esp. one parallel to the base.—*adv.* **trun′cately.**—*n.* **truncā′tion.**—**truncation error** (*math.*), one caused by operating with a truncated number or numbers. [L. *truncāre, -ātum—truncus;* cf. **trunk.**]

**truncheon,** *trun′shən, -chən, n.* a broken or cut piece: a length for grafting or planting: a broken spear: a spear-shaft: a short staff: a cudgel: a staff of authority.—*v.t.* to carve (an eel): to beat with a truncheon.—*adj.* **trun′-cheoned,** furnished with a truncheon: armed with a lance.—*n.* **trun′cheoner** (*Shak.*), one armed with a truncheon. [O.Fr. *tronchon* (Fr. *tronçon*) —*tronc;* see **trunk.**]

**trundle,** *trun′dl, n.* a little wheel, castor: a roller: a hoop: a truck (*obs.*): a trundle-bed: a spool of golden thread (*her.*).—*v.t.* and *v.i.* to wheel: to roll: to twirl: to spin: to bowl along. — **trun′dle-bed,** a truckle-bed; **trun′dle-tail, tren′dle-tail, trin′dle-tail,** a curly-tailed dog. [O.E. *trendel.*]

**trunk,** *trungk, n.* the stem of a tree: the body of an animal apart from head and limbs: the body generally: a main line of road, railway, telephone, etc.: a junction circuit between telephone exchanges (*U.S.*): the main body of anything: the shaft of a column: the body of a pedestal: a chest or box, esp. for travelling: a box for fish: a box-like channel, trough, shaft, conduit, or chute: a tube: a speaking-tube: a telescope (*obs.*): a pea-shooter (*obs.*): a large hollow piston: a proboscis: (in *pl.*) the game of trou-madame: (in *pl.*) trunk-hose, also breeches, esp. those worn on the stage over tights, or for sports, swimming, etc: the boot, luggage compartment of an automobile (*U.S.*).—*adjs.* **trunc′al,** pertaining to the trunk: principal; **trunked,** having a trunk: truncated, beheaded (*Spens.*).—*ns.* **trunk′ful,** as much as will fill a trunk'.—*pl.* **trunk′fuls; trunk′ing,** casing.—**trunk′-call′,** a long-distance telephone call, involving connection between two centres; **trunk dialling,** the dialling of trunk telephone calls directly, connections not being made by an operator; **trunk′-fish,** the coffer-fish; **trunk′-hose′, -breech′es,** full breeches reaching from waist to mid-thigh, worn in the 16th and early 17th centuries; **trunk′-line,** the main line of a railway, canal, etc.; **trunk′-mail,** a travelling trunk; **trunk′-maker,** a maker of travelling trunks; **trunk′-road,** a main road, esp. one administered by central authority; **trunk′sleeve** (*Shak.*), a puffed sleeve; **trunk′-work** (*Shak.*), clandestine visiting in a trunk. [Fr. *tronic* and L. *truncus,* a stock, a torso—*truncus,* maimed; with associations of Fr. *trompe,* trump, a proboscis.]

**trunnion,** *trun′yən, n.* either of a pair of side projections on which anything (as formerly a big gun) is pivoted to move in a vertical plane: a

stick, club (*Scott*).—*adj.* **trunn′ioned,** provided with trunnions. [Fr. *trognon,* stump.]

**truquage, truqueur.** See **trucage.**

**truss,** *trus, n.* a bundle, esp. of hay or straw, or a block cut from a stack (esp. 56 lb. of old hay, 60 lb. of new, 36 of straw): a framed structure for supporting a weight: an attachment for holding a yard to the mast: a tuft of flowers at the top of the main stalk or stem: a surgical appliance for retaining a reduced hernia: a close-fitting coat or (in *pl.*) breeches (*hist.*).—*v.t.* to bundle up: to muffle up: to tuck up: to lace up, tie the points of (*hist.*): to string up, hang (*obs.*): to fix for cooking, as with a skewer: to catch in the talons, esp. in the air, and carry off (*arch.*): to furnish with a truss.—*v.i.* to pack up: to make off.—*adj.* **trussed.**—*ns.* **truss′er; truss′ing.** —**truss′-beam,** a wooden beam strengthened by a steel tie-rod: a steel framework acting as a beam. [Fr. *trousse* (n.), *trousser* (vb.).]

**trust,** *trust, n.* worthiness of being relied on: fidelity: confidence in the truth of anything: confident expectation: a resting on the integrity, friendship, etc., of another: faith: hope: credit (esp. sale on credit or on promise to pay): ground of confidence: that which is given or received in confidence: charge: responsibility: anything felt to impose moral obligations: an arrangement by which property is handed to or vested in a person, to use and dispose of it for the benefit of another: an estate so managed for another: an arrangement for the control of several companies under one direction, to cheapen expenses, regulate production, beat down competition, and so obtain a maximum return.—*adj.* held in trust.—*v.t.* to place trust in: to believe: to expect confidently: to hope: to give credit to: to commit to trust.—*v.i.* to have trust: to rely (with *to*).—*ns.* **trustee′,** one to whom anything is entrusted: one to whom the management of a property is committed in trust for the benefit of others; **trustee′ship; trust′er.**—*adj.* **trust′ful,** trusting.—*adv.* **trust′-fully.** — *n.* **trust′fulness.** — *adv.* **trust′ily.** — *n.* **trust′iness.** — *adj.* **trust′ing,** confiding. — *adv.* **trust′ingly.**—*adj.* **trust′less,** not to be trusted: distrustful.— *n.* **trust′lessness.** — *adv.* **trust′-worthily.** — *n.* **trust′worthiness.** — *adjs.* **trust′-worthy,** worthy of trust or confidence: trusty; **trust′y,** to be trusted: deserving confidence: faithful: honest: strong: firm: involving trust (*Shak.*):—*comp.* **trust′ier,** *superl.* **trust′iest.**—*n.* one who can be trusted: a well-conducted convict: a greatcoat (*Ir.*).—**trust′-buster** (*U.S.* and *coll.*), one who works for or achieves the break-up of business trusts, e.g. by legislation; **trust′-deed,** a deed conveying property to a trustee; **trust′-estate′,** an estate held by trustees; **trust′-house,** hotel or tavern owned by a trust company, not privately or by liquor manufacturers; **trust, trustee, stock,** that in which a trustee may legally invest trust funds without being personally liable if it should depreciate in value; **trust territory,** a territory ruled by an administering country under supervision of the Trusteeship Council of the United Nations.— **active,** or **special, trust,** a trust in which the trustee's power of management depends upon his having the right of actual possession; **breach of trust,** a violation of duty by a trustee, etc.; **in trust,** as a charge, for safe-keeping, for management as a trustee; **investment trust,** an organisation which invests in stockholders' money and distributes the net return among them; **Public Trustee,** a government officer (and his department) empowered to act for the state as trustee, executor, etc.; **on trust,** on credit; **split investment trust,** a trust (which must be wound up at a specified date) offering two classes of shares, income and capital, the former earning dividend but to be repaid at par, the latter without dividend but increasing in capital value; **trustee savings bank,** a savings bank statutorily controlled under trustees and having its general fund guaranteed by the state; **unit trust,** type of investment trust in which given amounts of different securities form a unit, choice of a number of differently constituted units being available. [O.N. *traust*, trust; Ger. *trost*, consolation.]

**truth,** *trōōth, n.* faithfulness: constancy: veracity: agreement with reality: fact of being true: actuality: accuracy of adjustment or conformity: in the fine arts, a faithful adherence to nature: that which is true or according to the facts of the case: the true state of things, or facts: a true statement: an established fact: true belief: known facts, knowledge.—*adj.* **truth'ful,** habitually or actually telling what one believes to be true: put forward in good faith as what one believes to be true: conveying the truth.—*adv.* **truth'-fully.** — *n.* **truth'fulness.** — *adj.* **truth'less.** — *n.* **truth'lessness.**—*adjs.* **truth'like; truth'y** (*rare*), true: truthful.—**truth'-teller.**—*adj.* **truth'-telling.** —**truth table,** a Boolean logic table in which the binary digits 0 and 1 are assigned values either 'true' or 'false'; **truth'-value,** in logic, the truth or falsity of a statement.—**God's truth,** a thing or statement absolutely true; **in truth,** truly, in fact; **moment of truth** (see **moment**); **of a truth** (*B.*), truly; **truth drug, truth serum,** scopolamine or pentothal sodium, drugs which make subjects under questioning less wary in their replies. [O.E. *trēowth—trēowe, triewe,* true.]

**try,** *trī, v.t.* to separate out: to sift: to render: to extract: to refine: to purify: to test: to prove by testing (*Shak.*): to use, treat, resort to, experimentally: to put to the test: to strain: to annoy, irritate, afflict: to experience, undergo (*Milt.*): to examine critically: to examine and decide the truth, justice, guilt or innocence, of, as a judge: to conduct in court, as a lawyer (*U.S.*): to attempt, endeavour, essay.—*v.i.* to make an effort: (*Spens.* trie) to turn out, prove: to lie to, keep head to wind (*naut.*; *Shak.*):—*3rd pers. pr.t.* **tries;** *pr.p.* **try'ing;** *pa.t.* and *pa.p.* **tried, trīd.**—*n.* a trial: effort: in Rugby football, the score of three points gained by a player who succeeds in placing the ball with his hand over the goal line.—*adj.* (*Spens.* **trye**) choice, purified.—*adj.* **tri'able,** subject to legal trial: that can be tried.—*ns.* **tri'age,** sorting out: broken coffee-beans; **tri'al** (see separate article). —*adj.* **tried** (*trīd*), proved good by test.—*ns.* **tri'er,** one who tries in any sense: a test—also **tri'or,** in the sense of one appointed to decide on a challenge to a juror, or a peer who is a juror in the trial of a peer; and **try'er** (*cricket*), in the sense of one who is assiduous in trying to win; **try'ing.**—*adj.* making trial or proof: adapted to try: searching, severe: testing: distressing: causing strain.—*adv.* **try'ingly.**—**try'-house,** a place in which oil is extracted from blubber, etc.; **try'-on,** an act of trying on a garment: an attempt at imposition by audacity (*slang*); **try'-out,** a test performance; **trysail** (*trī'sl*), a reduced sail used by small craft, instead of the mainsail, in a storm: a small fore-and-aft sail set with a boom and gaff.—**try and** (*coll.*), try to; **try back,** to revert, hark back; **try for,** make an attempt to reach or gain; **try on,** to put on for trial, as a garment; **try it on,** to attempt to do something risky or audacious to see how far one can go unscathed; **try out,** to test. [O.Fr. *trier,* to pick out.]

**Trygon,** *trī'gon, n.* the sting-ray genus. [Gr. *trygōn,* a sting-ray.]

**trypaflavine,** *trip-ə-flā'vēn, n.* acriflavine.

**trypanosome,** *trip'ən-ə-sōm, n.* a flagellate protozoon (**Trypanoso'ma** of various species) parasitic in the blood of vertebrates.—*adj.* **trypanocidal** (*-sī'dl*).—*ns.* **tryp'anocide** (*-sīd;* L. *caedĕre,* to kill*),* a drug that kills trypanosomes; **trypanosomiasis** (*-sō-mi'ə-sis*), disease caused by a trypanosome, esp. sleeping-sickness. [Gr. *trýpanon,* a borer—*trýpaein,* to bore, *sōma,* body.]

**trypsin,** *trip'sin, n.* a digestive ferment secreted by the pancreas.—*adj.* **tryp'tic.**—*n.* **tryptophan(e)** (*trip'tō-fan, -fān*), an amino-acid obtained e.g. by the cleavage of casein by pancreatic enzymes. [Gr. *tripsis,* rubbing (as first got by rubbing down the pancreas with glycerine), or *trýein,* to wear out, modelled on **pepsin.**]

**trysail.** See **try.**

**tryst,** *trist,* (chiefly *Scot.*) *n.* an appointment to meet: appointed place of meeting: a cattle-fair. —*v.t.* to make an appointment with.—*v.i.* to agree to meet.—*n.* **tryst'er—trys'ting-day, -place, -stile, -tree.**—**bide tryst,** to wait for a person at the appointed place and time. [O.Fr. *triste,* a hunter's station.]

**tsamba,** *tsam'ba, n.* a Tibetan barley dish. [Tibetan.]

**tsar, also czar,** rarely **tzar,** *zär, tsär,* (*hist.*) *n.* the title of the emperors of Russia and of the kings of Bulgaria: a great potentate or despot.—*ns.* **ts-, czar'dom; tsar'evi(t)ch, czar'evi(t)ch** (Russ. *tsär-ye'vĕch*), a son of a tsar; **ts-, czarev'na,** a daughter of a tsar: a wife of a tsarevitch; **czarina** (*-ē'na;* not a Russian form), **czarit'za, tsarit'sa,** a Russian empress; **ts-, czar'ism,** the government of the Russian tsars: absolutism; **tsar'ist, czar'ist,** an upholder of tsarism; **tsesar'evi(t)ch, cesar'evitch, -witch** (Russ. *-ye'vĕch*), the eldest son of a tsar: heir to the tsardom. [Russ. *tsar',* etc.—L. *Caesar,* Caesar.]

**tsetse,** *tset'si, n. Glossina morsitans,* or other species of the African genus Glossina, small flies that transmit trypanosome parasites and cause sleeping-sickness, nagana (**tsetse-fly disease**), etc.—Also **tset'se-fly'.** [Tswana.]

**Tshi,** *ch(w)ē, n.* Same as **Twi.**

**T-shirt.** See **tee-shirt.**

**tsotsi,** *tsot'si, n.* a young coloured South African hooligan or thug. [Corr. of *zoot suit* (q.v.).]

**Tsuga,** *tsōō'gə, n.* the hemlock spruce genus. [Jap. *tsuga,* larch.]

**tsunami,** *tsōō-nä'mē, n.* a very swiftly travelling sea wave that attains great height. [Jap. *tsu,* harbour, *nami,* wave.]

**Tswana,** *(t)swä'na, n.* a Negro people of southern Africa: a member of this people: their language, of the Bantu family:—*pl.* **Tswan'a(s).**—Also *adj.*

**tuan,** *tōō-än', n.* sir: lord: a title of respect. [Malay.]

**Tuareg,** *twä'reg, n.* a nomadic Berber of the Sahara: the language of the Tuaregs. [Ar. *tawāriq.*]

**tuart, tooart.** *tōō'ərt,* **tewart,** *tū', n.* a strong-timbered Eucalyptus (*E. gomphocephala*). [Australian.]

**tuatara,** *tōō-a-tä'ra* (**tuatera,** *-tä'ra*), *n.* a New Zealand lizard-like reptile (Sphenodon or Hatteria), the sole survivor of the class Rhynchocephalia. [Maori, spine on the back.]

**tuath,** *tōō'ə,* (*Ir. hist.*) *n.* a people: an ancient territorial division. [Ir. *tūath.*]

**tub,** *tub, n.* an open wooden vessel made of staves and hoops: a small cask: anything like a tub: a tubful: a pulpit: a clumsy ship or boat: a bath: a pit-shaft casing: a bucket, box, or vehicle for bringing up coal from the mine: a tubfish.—*v.t.* to set, bathe, treat, in a tub: to line with a tub.— *v.i.* to take a bath.—*ns.* **tubb'er; tubb'iness; tubb'ing,** the art of, or material for, making tubs: mine-shaft lining: rowing in clumsy boats: the taking of baths.—*adjs.* **tubb'ish,** round and fat; **tubb'y,** sounding like an empty tub: dull in sound: round like a tub.—*n.* **tub'ful,** as much as a tub will hold:—*pl.* **tub'fuls.—tub'fast** (*Shak.*),

*fāte, fär; mē, hûr* (her)*; mīne, mōte, för; mūte, mōōn, fōōt; dhen* (then) treatment of venereal disease by fasting and sweating in a hot tub; **tub´fish**, the sapphirine (or other) gurnard; **tub´-thump´er**, a declamatory or ranting preacher or public speaker; **tub´-thump´ing**. [Cf. L.G. *tubbe*.]

**tuba**, *tū´bə, tōō´ba, n.* a straight trumpet (*Rom. ant.*): the bombardon (**bass tuba**) or (sometimes) other low-pitched brass instrument of the saxhorn class: a powerful organ reed-stop: a tube (*anat.*):—*pl.* **tu´bas**; L. **tu´bae** (*-bē,-bī*). [L. and It. *tuba.*]

**tube**, *tūb, n.* a pipe: a long hollow body: a telescope or other optical instrument (**optic tube**; *arch.*): a collapsible cylinder from which pasty material can be squeezed out: a thermionic valve: underground railway in tube-shaped tunnel: the united part of calyx, corolla, etc.: any vessel in a plant or animal body.—*v.t.* to furnish with, enclose in, a tube.—*v.i.* to travel by tube.—*n.* **tub´age**, insertion of a tube.—*adjs.* **tub´al**, **tub´ar**; **tubed** (*tūbd*).—*n.* **tube´ful**.—*adjs.* **tube´less**; **tubic´olar**, **tub´icole** (also *n.*), **tubic´olous**, inhabiting a tube; **tubiflo´rous**, having tubular flowers; **tub´iform**, shaped like a tube.—*n.* **tub´ing**, the act of making or supplying tubes: tubes collectively: material for tubes.—*adj.* **tub´ūlar**, having the form of a tube: made of or with tubes: having a sound like that made by the passage of air through a tube.—*n.* **Tubūlā´ria**, a genus of Hydrozoa.—*adj.* and *n.* **tubūlā´rian**.—*n.* **tubūlar´ity**.—*v.t.* **tub´ūlate**, to form into a tube. —*adj.* **tubular**.—*adj.* **tub´ūlated**.—*ns.* **tubūlā´tion**; **tub´ūlature**; **tub´ūle**, a small tube.—*n.pl.* **Tubūliflo´rae**, a section of the Compositae with tubular disk-flowers.—*adjs.* **tubūliflo´ral**; **tub´ūlous**, tubular.—**tube´-foot**, in echinoderms, a tube protruding through a pore, used in locomotion and respiration; **tubeless tire, tyre** (see **tire**); **tube´-skirt**, a very tight skirt; **tube´-well**, a pipe used to obtain water from beneath the ground, with perforations just above its sharp point; **tube´-worm**, a worm that makes a tube to dwell in. [Fr., L. *tubus*, a pipe.]

**tuber**, *tū´bər, n.* a lump: a rounded swelling or knob: a protuberance: a swelling, usually underground, in a plant where reserves are stored up—of stem nature (as in the potato, Jerusalem artichoke, etc.), or of root nature (as in the dahlia): Tuber, the truffle genus of fungi, giving name to the **Tuberā´ceae**, saprophytic Ascomycetes, many with edible underground fructifications (truffles).—*adjs.* **tuberā´ceous**; **tuberif´erous**; **tu´beriform**; **tuberose** (*tū´bə-rōs, -rōz*), tuberous.—*n.* (*tū´bə-rōs, -rōz;* often, by false association with tube and rose, *tūb´rōz*) a Mexican amaryllid (*Polianthes tuberosa*) grown for its fragrant creamy-white flowers, propagated by tubers.—*n.* **tuberosity** (*-ros´i-ti*).—*adj.* **tub´erous**, having tubers: of the nature of, or like, a tuber: knobbed.—**tuberous root**, a fleshy root resembling a tuber but not having buds or eyes. [L. *tŭber*, a swelling, from root of L. *tumēre*, to swell.]

**tubercle**, *tū´bər-kl, n.* a small tuber, protuberance, or swelling: a nodule: a nodule or morbid growth in the lung or elsewhere, in cases of tuberculosis.—*adjs.* **tu´bercled**, having tubercles; **tubercular** (*-būr´*), nodular: having tubercles: affected by, suffering from, tuberculosis; **tuber´culate, -d**, having, covered with, tubercles.—*ns.* **tuberculā´tion**; **tu´bercule**, a tubercle; **tuber´culin**, a preparation from a culture of tubercle bacillus used for testing for tuberculosis; **tuber´culisā´tion**.—*v.t.* **tuber´culise, -ize**, to infect w. tuberculosis.—*n.* **tuberculo´ma**, a slow-growing, circumscribed tuberculous lesion.—*adjs.* **tuber´culose, -d**, tuberculous: tuberculated.—*n.* **tuberculō´sis**, consumption or phthisis, a disease caused by the **tubercle bacillus** (*Bacillus tuberculosis*), characterised by development of

tubercles.—*adj.* **tuber´culous**, of, affected by, tuberculosis: tuberculated (now *rare*).—*n.* **tuber´culum**, a tubercle. [L. *tŭberculum*, dim. of *tŭber.*]

**tuberose.** See under tuber.

**tuchun**, *tōō-chün´, dōō-jün´, n.* a Chinese military governor. [Chin.]

**tuck**, *tuk,* (*Shak.*) *n.* a rapier. [Fr. *estoc*—Ger. *stock*, stick.]

**tuck**, *tuk, Scot.* **touk**, *tōōk, n.* a stroke, tap, beat, esp. of a drum. [O.N.Fr. *toker, toquer* (Fr. *toucher*), to touch.]

**tuck**, *tuk, v.t.* to draw or thrust in or together: to stuff, cram: to fold under: to gather or gird up (often with *up*): to contract (with *up*): to enclose by pressing clothes closely around or under: to put tucks in: to thrust away: to dress, full, or put on tenters: to hamper: to eat (with *in; slang*): to hang (with *up; slang*).—*v.i.* to make an onslaught upon food (usu. with *in* or *into*).—*n.* an act of tucking: a pleat or fold, now one stitched down: the gathering of the bottom planks of a ship at the stern (*naut.*): eatables, esp. delicacies (*slang*).—*n.* **tuck´er**, a piece of cloth tucked or drawn over the bosom: a fuller: food (*slang*).—*v.t.* (*Amer. slang*) to tire exceedingly (often with *out*).—**tuck´-box**, a box of or for tuck, at a boarding school; **tuck´-in´** (*slang*), a hearty feed.—*adj.* contrived for tucking in an edge.—*ns.* **tuck´(ing)-mill**, a fulling-mill; **tuck´-out** (*slang*), a tuck-in; **tuck´-shop** (*slang*), a confectioner's or a pastrycook's shop. [O.E. *tūcian*, to disturb, afflict; cf. Ger. *zucken*, to twitch.]

**tuckahoe**, *tuk´ə-hō, n.* an edible but tasteless underground fungus of the southern United States: the edible rootstock of several American aroids: an inhabitant of eastern Virginia. [From Algonquian.]

**tucket**, *tuk´it,* (*Shak.*) *n.* a flourish on a trumpet. [Cf. tuck (2), and It. *toccata*, a touch.]

**tucutuco**, *tōō-kōō-tōō´kō,* **tucotuco**, *tōō-kō-tōō´kō, n.* a South American rodent of mole-like habits. [From its cry.]

**Tudor**, *tū´dər, adj.* pertaining to the Welsh family of *Tudor,* the time when it held the English throne (1485-1603), or the style of architecture (Late Perpendicular) that prevailed then.—*adj.* **Tudoresque´.—Tudor flower**, a trefoil ornament frequent in Tudor architecture; **Tudor rose, a** red and white rose (combining Lancaster and York) adopted as a badge by Henry VII.

**Tuesday**, *tūz´di, n.* the third day of the week. [O.E. *Tīwes dæg,* the day of *Tīw* (the God of war), translating L. *diēs Martis,* Mars's day; but etymologically, *Tīw,* O.N. *Tȳr,* answers to L. *Jūpiter* (for *Djew pater*), Gr. *Zeus.*]

**tufa**, *tōō´fə, tū´fə, n.* calc-sinter (often *calcareous tufa*): tuff or other porous rock (*obs.*).—*adj.* **tufā´ceous**. [It. *tufa*, a variant of *tufo*—L. *tōfus,* a soft stone.]

**tuff**, *tuf, tōōf, n.* a rock composed of fine volcanic fragments and dust: tufa or other porous rock (*obs.*).—*adj.* **tuffā´ceous**. [Fr. *tuf, tuffe*—It. *tufo*; see tufa.]

**tuffe**, *tuf,* (*Shak.*) *n.* Same as **tuft.**—*n.* **tuff´et**, a tuft: a tussock: a mound.

**tuft**, *tuft, n.* a bunched cluster: a clump: a crest: a separate lock of hair: a goatee or imperial beard: a small tassel: a gold tassel formerly worn on a nobleman's cap in the English universities: hence a titled undergraduate: a person of social consequence.—*v.t.* to separate into tufts: to adorn with tufts: to beat (as a covert): to dislodge.—*adj.* **tuft´ed**.—*ns.* **tuft´er**, a hound that drives deer out of cover; **tuft´ing**.—*adj.* **tuft´y**.—**tuft´-hunt´er**, a toady; **tuft´-hunt´ing**. [Supposed to be—O.Fr. *tuffe* (Fr. *touffe*)—L. *tūfa,* crest—Gmc. (cf. O.L.G. *top, top*); but there are difficulties.]

**tuftaffety,** also **tuff-, tuft-,** *tuf-taf'ə-ti,* and **-taffeta, -ta,** (*arch.*) *n.* a taffeta with tufted pile.— *adj.* of or wearing tuftaffety: richly dressed.

**tug,** *tug, v.t.* to pull forcibly: to haul: to tow: to drag.—*v.i.* to pull forcibly: to strive: to toil: —*pr.p.* **tugg'ing;** *pa.t.* and *pa.p.* **tugged.**—*n.* a forcible or jerking pull: a hard struggle: a rope or chain for pulling: a name for various parts of harness, as a trace, a loop to receive a shaft: a tug-boat: an aeroplane towing a glider.—*n.* **tugg'er,** one who tugs.—*n.* and *adj.* **tugg'ing.** *adv.* **tugg'ingly.**—**tug'-boat,** a towing vessel; **tug-of-war',** a laborious contest: a contest in which opposing teams tug at a rope and strive to pull one another over a line. [M.E. *toggen,* intens. from root of O.E. *tēon;* cf. **tow.**]

**tui,** *tōō'ē, n.* the parson-bird. [Maori.]

**tuille,** *twēl, n.* a steel plate hanging below the tasses.—*n.* **tuillette'** (*dim.*). [Fr.,—L. *tēgula,* a title.]

**tuilyie, tuilzie,** *tül'i, tül'yi,* (*Scot.; obs.*) *n.* a fight, brawl, tussle.—*v.i.* to struggle. [O.Fr. *tooil.*]

**tuism,** *tū'izm, n.* apostrophe: reference to, or regard to the interests of, a second person. [L. *tū,* thou.]

**tuition,** *tū-ish'ən, n.* guardianship (*obs.*): teaching, instruction.—*adjs.* **tui'tional, tui'tionary.** [L. *tuitiō, -ōnis—tuēri, tuitus,* to watch over.]

**tular(a)emia,** *tōō-lə-rē'mi-ə, n.* a disease of rodents caused by a bacterium (*Bacterium tularense,* or *Pasteurella tularensis*), transmitted to man either by insects or directly, causing fever, etc. [*Tulare* county, California, where it was first discovered.]

**tulchan,** *tulhh'ən, n.* a calf's skin set beside a cow to make her give milk freely.—**tulchan bishop** (*Scot. hist.*), a titular bishop appointed to transmit most of the revenues of a diocese to the nobles (1572). [Gael. *tul(a)chan,* a hillock.]

**tule,** *tōō'lā, n.* a large American bulrush (Scirpus). [Sp.,—Nahuatl *tollin.*]

**tulip,** *tū'lip, n.* any plant or flower of the bulbous liliaceous genus **Tu'lipa,** with showy, usually solitary, flowers: a showy person.—*n.* **tulipomā'nia,** a craze for tulip-growing.—*adj.* **tu'lip-eared,** prick-eared, as a dog.—**tu'lip-root,** a disease affecting the stem of oats; **tu'lip-tree,** a North American timber tree (Liriodendron), of the Magnolia family, with tulip-like flowers; **tu'lip-wood,** its wood.—**African tulip tree,** a tree of the genus *Spathodea,* of the *Bignoniaceae.* [O.Fr. *tulipe, tulippe, tulipan—*Turk. *tulbend,* turban.]

**tulle,** *tōōl, tül, tül, n.* a delicate thin silk network fabric. [Fr.; from *Tulle,* in the department of Corrèze.]

**Tullian,** *tul'i-ən, adj.* of or like *Tully,* i.e. Marcus *Tullius* Cicero—Ciceronian.

**tulwar,** *tul'wär, n.* an Indian sabre. [Hind. *talwār.*]

**tum.** See **tummy.**

**tumble,** *tum'bl, v.i.* to roll, wallow, toss about: to perform as a dancer or acrobat: to turn over in flight or fall: to fall headlong, floundering, or revolving: to collapse, fall in a heap: to rush confusedly and hastily: to come by chance.— *v.t.* to send tumbling or headlong: to overthrow: to bundle from one place to another: to jumble: to throw about: to disorder, rumple.—*n.* act of tumbling: a fall: a somersault: a tumbled condition or mass.—*ns.* **tum'bler,** one who tumbles: an acrobat: a large drinking-glass or tall cup, formerly one that could not stand: a tumblerful: a tumbrel: a toy weighted to rock and right itself: a pigeon that turns back-somersaults in the air: a dog that performed antics in catching rabbits (*obs.*): a revolving barrel or cage: part of a lock that holds the bolt in place, till it is moved by the key: part of a firearm lock that receives the thrust of the mainspring and forces the hammer forward: one of a gang of London ruffians who set women on their heads (*early 18th cent.*): a machine which dries (clothes, etc.) by tumbling them in a strong current of hot air (also **tumbler-drier**); **tum'blerful,** as much as will fill a tumbler:—*pl.* **tum'blerfuls.**—*n.* and *adj.* **tum'bling.**—**tum'ble-bug, -dung** (*U.S.*), a dung-beetle (from its rolling pellets of dung); **tum'ble-car, -cart,** a vehicle with wheels and axle in one piece.—*adj.* **tum'bledown,** dilapidated, threatening to fall.—**tum'bler-switch,** a switch that is turned over to put electric current off or on; **tum'ble-weed,** a type of plant that snaps off above the root, curls into a ball, and rolls about in the wind.—**tumble in,** or **home,** to incline inward above the extreme breadth, of a ship's sides: to fit, as a piece of timber into other work: to go to bed; **tumble over,** to toss about carelessly, to upset: to fall over; **tumble to** (*slang*), to comprehend; **tumble up,** to get out of bed: to throw into confusion: to scurry up on deck. [Freq. from O.E. *tumbian;* cf. Ger. *tummeln.*]

**tumbrel, tumbril,** *tum'brəl, -bril, n.* an old instrument of punishment, pillory or cucking-stool (*obs.*): a tip-cart: a two-wheeled military cart (*arch.*): a dung-cart: the name given to the carts that conveyed victims to the guillotine during the French Revolution. [O.Fr. *tomberel* (Fr. *tombereau*)—*tomber,* to fall.]

**tumefy,** *tū'mi-fī, v.t.* and *v.i.* to swell:—*pr.p.* **tu'mefying;** *pa.t.* and *pa.p.* **tu'mefied.**—*ns.* **tumefac'tion: tumescence** (*tū-mes'əns*), a tendency to swell: a swelling.—*adjs.* **tumesc'ent; tu'mid,** swollen or enlarged: inflated: falsely sublime: bombastic.—*n.* **tumid'ity.**—*adv.* **tu'-midly.** — *n.* **tu'midness.** — *adj.* **tu'morous.** — *n.* **tumour, tumor** (*tū'mər*), swelling: turgidity: a morbid swelling or enlargement, now esp. a new growth of cells in the body without inflammation. [L. *tumefacĕre, tumēscĕre, tumidus, tumor—tumēre,* to swell, *facĕre,* to make.]

**tummy,** *tum'i, n.* a childish form of **stomach.**—Also **tum.**

**tump,** *tump,* (*dial.*) *n.* a hillock: a clump.—*v.t.* to make a mound around.—*adj.* **tump'y,** hummocky. [Origin unknown.]

**tump,** *tump,* (*U.S.*) *v.t.* to drag.—**tump'-line,** a strap across the forehead or chest for carrying burdens or hauling. [Prob. from an Indian word.]

**tumphy,** *tum'fi,* (*Scot.*) *n.* a blockhead: coaly fireclay.

**tumult,** *tū'mult, -məlt, n.* violent commotion, usu. with uproar: a riot: a state of violent and confused emotion.—*v.i.* (*Milt.*) to make a tumult.— *v.t.* to put in tumult.—*adj.* **tumultūary** (*-mult'*), acted or acting in tumult: haphazard: chaotic: tumultuous.—*v.i.* **tumult'ūate,** to make a tumult.—*v.t.* to disturb with tumult: to make a tumult in.—*n.* **tumultūā'tion;** *adj.* **tumult'ūous,** full of tumult: disorderly: agitated: noisy.—*adv.* **tumult'ūously.**—*n.* **tumult'ūousness.** [L. *tumultus, -ūs—tumēre,* to swell.]

**tumulus,** *tū'mū-ləs,* L. *tōō'mŏŏ-lŏŏs, n.* a burial mound, a barrow:—*pl.* **tu'muli** (*-lī, -lē*).—*adjs.* **tu'mular, -y.** [L.,—*tumēre,* to swell.]

**tun,** *tun, n.* a large cask: an obsolete liquid measure—216 gallons of ale, 252 of wine: a ton (*obs.*). —*v.t.* to put in a tun.—*ns.* **tunn'age** (see **tonnage**); **tunn'ing.**—*adj.* **tun'bellied.**—**tun'belly,** a potbelly; **tun'-dish** (*Shak.*), a wooden funnel. [O.E. *tunne;* cf. **ton.**]

**tuna,** *tōō'nə, tū'nə, n.* a prickly-pear, plant or fruit. [Haitian.]

**tuna,** *tōō'nə, tū'nə, n.* (California) a tunny. [Sp.]

**tuna,** *tōō'na, n.* a New Zealand eel. [Maori.]

**tund,** *tund, v.t.* and *v.i.* to beat, thump. [L. *tundĕre.*]

**tundra,** *tōōn'-, tun'drə, n.* a frozen Arctic plain, with lichens, mosses, and dwarfed vegetation. [Lapp.]

**tundun.** See **turndun.**

**tune,** *tūn, n.* tone: a melody or air: melodiousness: accurate adjustment in pitch or frequency: harmonious adjustment (*fig.*): frame of mind, temper.—*v.t.* to adjust the tones of: to put in condition for producing tones in tune: to put in smooth working order: to synchronise: to adjust (a radio receiver) so as to produce the optimum response to an incoming signal: to put in accord, bring to a desired state: to begin to play or sing: to start the singing of: to utter, express, or celebrate in music.—*v.i.* to give forth musical sound.—*adj.* **tūn'able,** tuneful: in tune.—Also **tune'able.**—*n.* **tun'ableness.**—*adv.* **tun'ably.**—*adjs.* **tuned** (*tūnd*); **tune'ful,** full of tune: melodious: musical.—*adv.* **tune'fully.**—*n.* **tune'fulness.**—*adj.* **tune'less,** without tune: not melodious or tuneful: unmusical: without sense of tune: silent.—*ns.* **tun'er,** one who tunes instruments or looms: one who makes music, or sings: in organs, an adjustable flap for altering the pitch of the tone; **tun'ing.**—*adj.* **tun'y,** tuneful, esp. in a superficial obvious way.—**tun'ing-fork,** a two-pronged instrument giving a sound of known pitch or vibration; **tun'ing-key,** **tun'ing-hammer,** a key for turning wrest-pins; **tun'ing-peg, -pin,** a peg about which the end of a string is wound and by which it is tuned.—**call the tune** (see **pay the piper,** at **pipe** (1)); **change one's tune,** sing another tune, to alter one's attitude, or way of talking; **in tune,** true in pitch: in accord (*fig.*); **out of tune,** not true in pitch: not agreeing (*fig.*); **to the tune of,** to the amount of; **tune in,** to adjust a wireless receiver for reception; **tune out,** to adjust it so as to eliminate; **tune up,** to put instruments into tune for beginning: to begin to perform, strike up. [A form of **tone.**]

**tung-oil,** *tung'-oil, n.* wood-oil obtained from seeds of the **tung'-tree** or Chinese varnish tree (*Aleurites fordii* or other species). [Chin. *yu-t'ung,* tung-oil.]

**tungsten,** *tung'stən, n.* wolfram, a rare metal (W; atomic number 74) chiefly got from wolframite, used for making lamp filaments and high-speed steel.—*n.* **tung'state,** a salt of **tung'stic acid** ($H_2WO_4$). [Sw., lit. heavy stone—*tung,* heavy, *sten,* stone.]

**Tungus,** *tōōng'gōōs, tōōng-gōōs', -gōōz', n.* a member of an Eastern Siberian people and race, of the type usually called Mongol:—*pl.* **Tungus, Tunguses.**—*adjs.* **Tungus, Tungusian** (*-gōōs'i-ən, -gōōz'*), **Tungus'ic.**—*ns.* their Ural-Altaic language. [Russ. *Tunguz;* Chin. *Tung'hu.*]

**tunic,** *tū'nik, n.* a Roman shirt-like undergarment: applied also to the Greek chiton, and to various similar garments, usually a sort of belted coat and gown, or blouse: a close-fitting soldier's or policeman's coat: a tunicle: an investing layer, membrane, or integument (*biol.*).—*n.pl.* **Tunicā'ta,** the Urochorda, a class or sub-phylum of degenerate Chordata, including the ascidians.—*n.* **tu'nicate,** a member of the Tunicata.—*adjs.* **tu'nicate, -d** (*bot.* and *zool.*), having a tunic: formed in concentric coats: of the Tunicata.—*n.* **tu'nicin** (*-ni-sin*), a gelatinous substance in the tests of tunicates.—*adj.* **tu'nicked.**—*n.* **tu'nicle,** a little tunic: an ecclesiastical vestment like a dalmatic, worn by a sub-deacon at mass. [L. *tunica.*]

**Tunker,** *tungk'ər, n.* See **Dunker.**

**tunnage.** See **tun, ton.**

**tunnel,** *tun'l, n.* a passage cut underground: any tubular passage: an animal's burrow, in earth, wood, etc.: a tunnel-net: a flue, chimney.—*v.t.* to make a passage or passages through: to hollow out: to catch in a tunnel-net.—*v.i.* to make a tunnel:—*pr.p.* **tunn'elling;** *p.a.t.* and *pa.p.* **tunn'elled.**—*n.* **tunn'eller.**—*n.* and *adj.* **tunn'elling.**—**tunn'el-net,** a funnel-shaped net. [O.Fr.

**ton(n)el** (Fr. *tonneau*), cask, and *tonnelle,* vault, tunnel-net, dims. of *tonne,* cask.]

**tunny,** *tun'i, n.* a very large fish akin to the mackerels. [L. *tunnus*—Gr. *thynnos.*]

**tup,** *tup, n.* a ram: paving rammer: pile-driving monkey: striking-face of a steam-hammer.—*v.t.* to copulate with (a ewe): put to the ram.—*v.i.* to copulate (of sheep). [Origin unknown.]

**Tupaia,** *tōō-pī'ə, n.* a genus of insectivores giving name to the tree-shrew family **Tupai'idae.** [Malay *tūpai* (*tāna,* ground), squirrel.]

**tupelo,** *tōō'pə-lō, n.* an American gum-tree (Nyssa). [From an Indian name.]

**Tupi, Tupi,** *tōō-pē', tōō'pē, n.* a S. American Indian of a group of peoples inhabiting the Atlantic coast and the Amazon basin: their language, serving as a lingua franca.—Also *adj.*—*adj.* **Tupi'an.**

**tupik,** *tū'pik,* **tupek, -pek,** *n.* an Eskimo skin tent. [Eskimo.]

**tuppence, tuppenny,** coll. for **twopence, -penny.**

**tuptowing.** See **typto.**

**tuque,** *tūk, n.* a Canadian cap made by tucking in one tapered end of a long cylindrical bag, closed at both ends. [Fr. *toque.*]

**tu quoque,** *tū kwō'kwē, tōō kwok'we,* (L.) you too, you're another.

**turacin,** *tū'rə-sin, n.* the soluble red colouring matter of *touraco* feathers, containing copper.—*n.* **turacoverdin** (*-kō-vûr'din*), a pigment in touraco feathers, the only pure green pigment found in birds.

**Turanian,** *tū-rā'ni-ən, (obs. philol.) adj.* of Asiatic languages, neither Iranian nor Semitic: latterly almost the same as Ural-Altaic.—*n.* a speaker of one of those languages. [Pers. *Turān,* not Iran, applied to those parts of the Sassanian Persian empire beyond the Oxus.]

**turban,** *tûr'bən—obs.* **tulipant', tul'ban;** *Shak.* **tur'band, tur'bond;** *Spens.* **turribant';** *Milt.* **tur'bant,** *n.* a head-covering worn by Eastern nations, consisting of a cap with a sash wound round it: a ladies' headdress of similar appearance.—*adj.* **tur'baned,** wearing a turban. [Turk. *tulbend*—Pers. *dulband;* cf. **tulip.**]

**turbary,** *tûr'bə-ri, n.* the right to take peat from another's ground: a place where peat is dug. [L.L. *turbāria*—*turba,* turf; of Gmc. origin; see **turf.**]

**Turbellaria,** *tûr-bə-lā'ri-ə, n.pl.* a class of ciliated flatworms.—*n.* and *adj.* **turbellā'rian.** [L. *turbellae,* a disturbance.]

**turbid,** *tûr'bid, adj.* disordered: muddy: thick.—*n.* **turbid'ity.**—*adv.* **tur'bidly.**—*n.* **tur'bidness.** [L. *turbidus*—*turba,* tumult.]

**turbinacious,** *tûr-bin-ā'shəs, (Scott) adj.* (of the smell of whisky) peaty. [A blundering form from L.L. *turba,* peat, under the influence of L. *turbō, -inis,* a spinning-top, a swirl.]

**turbine,** *tûr'bin* (sometimes *-bin*), *n.* a rotary motor in which a wheel or drum with curved vanes is driven by reaction or impact or both by a fluid (water in the **water-turbine,** steam in the **steam-turbine,** expanding hot air in the **gas-turbine**) admitted to it and allowed to escape.—*adj.* **tur'binal,** turbinate.—*n.* a scroll-like bone of the nose.—*adjs.* **tur'binate, -d,** shaped like a top or inverted cone: spirally coiled: scroll-like: turbinal.—*n.* a turbinal: a turbinate shell.—*adj.* **tur'bined,** having, driven by, a turbine or turbines.—*n.* **Tur'bo,** a tropical genus of turbinate wide-mouthed gasteropods, large specimens often used as ornaments:—*pl.* **Turbines** (*tûr'binēz*).—**tur'bine-pump,** a contrivance for raising water by the inverted action of a turbine wheel; **turb'ine-steam'er,** a ship driven by steam-turbine; **tur'bo-jet',** a jet-propelled gas-turbine; **turbo-prop,** a jet-engine in which the turbine is coupled to a propeller; **tur'bo-ram'-jet,** an engine consisting of a turbo-jet mounted within the duct of a ram-jet. [L. *turbo*, *-inis*, a whirl, a spinning-top.]

**turbit**, *tûr′bit*, *n.* a domestic pigeon having white body, coloured wings, and short beak. [Ety. dub.]

**Turbo.** See turbine.

**turbot**, *tûr′bət*, *n.* a large, highly-esteemed flatfish (*Psetta maxima*) with bony tubercles: extended to various more or less similar fishes. [O.Fr. *turbot*.]

**turbulent**, *tûr′bū-lənt*, *adj.* tumultuous, violently disturbed: in violent commotion: producing commotion: stormy: of fluid, showing turbulence: insubordinate, unruly: having an exciting, disturbing effect.—*ns.* **tur′bulator**, a device which creates turbulence, e.g. in order to mix or disperse fluids; **tur′bulence**, disturbed state (also, esp. formerly, **tur′bulency**): unruly character or action: irregular eddying motion of particles in a fluid: irregular movement of large volumes of air (also **atmospheric turbulence**).—*adv.* **tur′bulently**. [L. *turbulentus*—*turba*, a crowd.]

**Turco**, *tûr′kō*, (*coll.*) *n.* an Algerian infantryman in the French service. [It., Turk.]

**Turcoman.** Same as Turkoman.

**Turcophil(e)**, *tûr′kō-fil*, *n.* one who favours the Turks (Gr. *phileein*, to love).—Also *adj.*—*ns.* **Turcophilism** (-*kof′il-izm*); **Tur′cophobe** (Gr. *phobeein*, to fear), one who fears or dislikes the Turks.—Also *adj.* [Gr. *Tourkos*, Turk.]

**turcopole**, *tûr′kō-pōl*, *n.* a light-armed soldier of the Knights of St John of Jerusalem.—*n.* **tur′copolier** (-*pō-lēr*), their commander—always an Englishman. [Mod. Gr. *Tourkopoulon*, a Turkish boy.]

**turd**, *tûrd*, *n.* a lump of dung. [O.E. *tord*.]

**Turdus**, *tûr′das*, *n.* the thrush genus.—*adj.* **tur′dine.** [L.]

**tureen**, *tə-rēn′*, *tū-rēn′*, *n.* a large dish for holding soup, etc., at table. [Fr. *terrine*—L. *terra*, earth.]

**turf**, *tûrf*, *n.* the surface of land matted with the roots of grass, etc.: a cake of turf cut off: a sod: peat: horse-racing, the race-course, the racing world:—*pl.* **turfs**, sometimes **turves.**—*v.t.* to cover with turf.—*adjs.* **turfed; tur′fen.**—*ns.* **tur′finess; turf′ing;** **tur′fite** (*slang*), one devoted to horse-racing.—*adj.* **tur′fy,** of, like, or abounding in, turf: pertaining to horse-racing.—**turf′-account′ant,** a euphemism for bookmaker.—*adj.* **turf′-clad,** covered with turf.—**turf′-drain,** one covered with turf; **turf′ing-iron,** an implement for cutting turf; **turf′-spade,** a long narrow spade for digging turf.—**turf out,** forcibly throw out. [O.E. *turf*; O.N. *torf.*]

**turgent**, *tûr′jənt*, *adj.* swelling: dilated: inflated: bombastic.—*adv.* **tur′gently.**—*ns.* **turgescence** (-*jes′əns*), act or process of swelling up: swollenness: distension of cells and tissues with water; **turgesc′ency.**—*adjs.* **turgesc′ent,** swelling: growing big; **tur′gid,** swollen: extended beyond the natural size: pompous: bombastic: firm and tense by distension with water (*bot.*).—*ns.* **turgid′ity, tur′gidness.**—*adv.* **tur′gidly.**—*n.* **turgor** (*tûr′gör*), the state of being full, the normal condition of the capillaries: balance of osmotic pressure and elasticity of cell-wall (*bot.*). [L. *turgēre*, to swell.]

**turion**, *tū′ri-ən*, *n.* an underground bud, growing upward into a new stem. [L. *turiō*, *-ōnis*, a shoot.]

**Turk**, *tûrk*, *n.* a native or citizen of *Turkey*: a Moslem of the former Ottoman empire: any speaker of a Turkic language: a Mohammedan (*obs.*): any one with qualities ascribed to Turks, esp. an unmanageable unruly person: a Turkish horse: a Turkish ship.—*adj.* Turkish.—*adj.* **Turki** (*tōōr′kē*), of the Turkish distinguished from the Tatar branch of Turko-Tatar languages. —*n.* a Turki speaker or language.—*n.* **Turkess** (*tûrk′es; rare*), a Turkish woman.—*adjs.* **Turk′ic,**

**Turko-Ta′tar,** of that branch of the Ural-Altaic languages to which Turkish belongs; **Turk′ish,** of Turkey, the Turks, or their language: Turkic. —*n.* the language of the Turks.—**Turkey carpet,** a soft thick kind of carpet; **Turkey hone,** novaculite; **Turkey merchant,** one trading with the Near East; **Turkey oak,** a Levantine species of oak (*Quercus cerris*); **Turkey red,** a fine durable red dye, obtained from madder, but now mostly chemically; **Turkey stone,** Turkey hone: the turquoise (*rare*); **Turkish bath,** a kind of hot-air bath, the patient being sweated, rubbed down, massaged, and gradually cooled; **Turkish delight,** a gelatinous sweetmeat, orig. Turkish; **Turkish manna,** trehala; **Turk's cap,** the martagon lily (*Lilium martagon*), from the appearance of the rolled-back petals of the nodding flower; **Turk's head,** a kind of knot: a long broom: a figure set up for practice in swordsmanship.— **Grand Turk** (*hist.*), the Ottoman Sultan; **turn Turk,** to become Mohammedan: to be completely reversed.

**turkey**, *tûrk′i*, *n.* formerly, a guinea-fowl (thought to have come from *Turkey*): now, an American genus (Meleagris) of the pheasant family: a domestic breed of that genus: its flesh as food (in *U.S.* also a substitute): extended to various big birds, as bustard, ibis, brush turkey.— **turk′ey-buzz′ard,** an American vulture; **turk′ey-cock,** a male guinea-fowl (*obs.*): a male turkey: a strutting, pompous, vain or gobbling blusterer; **turk′ey-hen,** a guinea-hen (*obs.*): a female turkey; **turk′ey-trot′,** a kind of ragtime dance.— **talk turkey** (*U.S.*), to talk bluntly: to talk business.

**Turki.** See Turk.

**turkis, turkies.** See turquoise.

**Turkoman,** *tûr′kō-man*, *n.* a member of a branch of the Turkish family dwelling north from Persia: —*pl.* **Turk′omans.**—Also *adj.*

**turlough,** *tûr′lohh*, (*Ir.*) *n.* a pond dry in summer. [Ir. *turloch*.]

**turm** (*Milt.* **turme**), *tûrm*, *n.* a troop. [L. *turma*.]

**Turmagant** (*Spens.*). See Termagant.

**turmeric,** *tûr′mər-ik*, *n.* a plant (*Curcuma longa*) of the ginger family: its rootstock, or a powder made from it, used in making curry-powder.— **turmeric paper,** a chemical test-paper impregnated with turmeric, changed from yellow to brown by alkali. [Cf. Fr. *terre-mérite*—as if from L. *terra merita*, deserved earth; origin unknown.]

**turmoil,** *tûr′moil* (*Shak. -moil′*), *n.* commotion: disquiet: tumult.—*v.t.* (formerly *-moil′*) to harass with commotion: to toss about.—*v.i.* (*dial.*) to toil. [Origin unknown.]

**turn,** *tûrn*, *v.i.* to revolve: to rotate, to spin, whirl: to move round: to hinge: to depend: to issue: to change or reverse direction or tendency: to return: to deviate: to direct oneself, face: to shape one's course: to betake oneself: to direct one's attention: to change sides, religion, mode of life: to be fickle: to change: to be transformed, converted: to become: to result, prove or lead in the issue: to be shaped on the lathe: to sour: to change colour: to become giddy: to be nauseated: to bend back, become turned: to beat to windward.—*v.t.* to rotate: to move round: to change the direction of: to deflect: to bend: to bend back the edge of: to reverse: to pass round or beyond: to perform by turning: to wind: to set outside-in, or remake in that form: to set upside-down: to direct: to point: to apply: to send, drive, set: to pour or tumble out: to employ in circulation, pass through one's hands: to translate: to change: to make sour: to nauseate: to make giddy: to infatuate: to transfer, hand over: to convert, make: to make the subject of (with *to* or *into*): to render: to put by turning: to return, give back: to form in a lathe: to shape: to round off, fashion: to have just passed (a certain age, hour, etc.).—*n.* act, occasion, or place of turning: new direction or tendency: a twist: a winding: a complete revolution: a bend: a single traversing of a beat or course: a short walk (or ride or drive): a fit of illness or emotion, esp. an emotional shock, jar, or feeling of faintness: an embellishment in which the principal note is preceded by that next above and followed by that next below (or vice versa in the inverted turn), the whole ending (and sometimes beginning) with the principal note (*mus.*): turning-point: a culmination: a time or moment of change: a crisis: a spell: a recurring opportunity or spell in rotation or alternation: rotation: a trick: a performer's act or the performer: a shift: a bout: fashion: manner: cast of mind: aptitude: bent: occasion, exigency: a vicissitude: a characteristic quality or effect: act of kindness or malice: an inverted type serving for a temporarily missing letter.—*adj.* turned, fashioned: wrought in a lathe: beyond the age (now commonly without *of*): reversed: outside-in: upside-down (esp. of type): soured.—*ns.* turn′er, one who, or that which, turns: one who uses a lathe: a member of a gymnastic club (*U.S.*, from *Ger.*); turn′ery, art of turning in a lathe: turner's work: a turner's shop; turn′ing, rotation: reversal: a bend: the act of making a turn: a winding: deviation: a place where a road strikes off: a shaping, esp. the art of shaping wood, metal, etc., into forms having a curved (generally circular or oval) transverse section, and also of engraving figures composed of curved lines upon a smooth surface, by means of a turning-lathe: (in *pl.*) a shaving from the lathe: in pottery, the shaping of a vase: conversion, transformation.—turn′about, a turning to face the opposite way; turn′again, a refrain; turn′back, a folded-back part: one who abandons an enterprise; turn′broach, a turnspit; turn′buckle, a coupling with screw-threads for adjusting tension; turn′coat, a renegade to his principles or party; turn′cock, valve which by turning regulates flow of water: an official who turns off and on the water for the mains, etc.—*adj.* turn′-down, folded down.—*n.* a turn-down part: a turn-down collar: a turning down, rejection; turn′ing-lathe; turn′ing-point, the point at which anything turns in its course: a maximum or minimum point on a graph: a critical point; turn′ing-saw, a sweep-saw, a thin-bladed saw held taut in a frame, used for cutting in curves; turn′key, an under-jailer: a turncock; turn′-out, a getting out of bed: a coming on duty: a call to come on duty: a siding, passing-place, or turning-place: a movable tapered rail for changing to another track: a muster or assembly: a carriage and its horses, a team: output: get-up: a strike: a striker; turn′over, a turning over: a transference: a part folded over: a newspaper article begun on the front page and continued overleaf: a small pie made by folding over the crust: a small shawl: an apprentice turned over to a new master to complete his apprenticeship: the total amount of money changing hands in a business: the money value of total sales over a period.—*adj.* folded over, or made to fold over.—turnover tax, a tax paid every time goods change hands during manufacture and marketing; turn′-penny, one who is eager for profit; turn′pike, a spiked barrier (*hist.*): a turnstile (*obs.*): a toll-gate: a turnpike-road: a winding stair (also turnpike stair; *Scot.*); turn′pike-man, a toll-gate keeper; turn′-pike-road, a road on which there are or were toll-gates: a main road; turn′-round, a turning round: the whole process of docking, unloading, taking on cargo, passengers, or both, and setting

sail again; turn′-screw, a screw-driver; turn′skin, a werewolf; turn′spit, one who turns a spit: a long-bodied, short-legged dog employed to drive a wheel by which roasting-spits were turned: a roasting-jack; turn′stile, a revolving frame that allows one person to pass at a time; turn′stone, a bird (Strepsilas or Arenaria), intermediate between the true plovers and sandpipers, that turns over pebbles on the beach in search of food; turn′table, a rotating table, platform, or disk, or pair of rings, one rotating within another, as for turning a locomotive, carrying a gramophone record, cementing a microscope slide, turning a camera, etc.; turn′-up (or *tûrn-up′*), a disturbance: a thing or part that is turned up, esp. the cuff at the bottom of a trouser-leg: an unexpected or fortuitous result or occurrence: a piece of good luck.—*adj.* turned up.—a good (bad) turn, a helpful service (a disservice); at every turn, everywhere: incessantly; by turns, one after another: at intervals; not to turn a hair, to be quite undisturbed or unaffected; on the turn, at the turning-point, changing: on the point of turning sour; serve the turn, to answer the purpose: to do well enough; take one's turn, take turns, to participate in rotation; to a turn, exactly, perfectly (as if of the spit); turn about, to face round to the opposite quarter: to spin, rotate; turn about, turn and turn about, alternately: in rotation; turn a deaf ear to, to ignore; turn adrift, to unmoor and let float away: to cast off; turn again, to turn back: to revert; turn against, to use to the injury of: to render hostile: to rebel against; turn an enemy's flank, line, or position, to manoeuvre so as to attack in the rear: to outwit; turn an honest penny (see penny); turn around one's (little) finger, to be able to persuade to anything; turn aside, to avert: to deviate: to avert the face; turn away, to dismiss from service, to discharge: to avert, to look in another direction: to deviate, to depart; turn back, to cause to retreat: to return; turn colour, to change colour; turn down, to bend, double, or fold down: to invert: to lower, as a light: to reject; turn forth, to expel; turn in, to bend inward: to enter: to surrender, hand over voluntarily: to go to bed (*coll.*); turn into, to become by a process of change; turn it up, in, shut up (*imper., coll.*); turn king's (queen's) evidence (see evidence); turn loose, to set at liberty; turn off, to deviate: to dismiss: to divert: to complete, achieve by labour: to shut off: to give in marriage (*coll.*): to hang (*slang*); turn of the century, the period of the end of one century and the beginning of the next; turn on, to set running (as water): to depend on: to turn towards and assail: to give (a person) a sense of heightened awareness and vitality as do psychedelic drugs (*slang*); turn one's hand to, to apply oneself to; turn one's head, or brain, to make one giddy: to infatuate with success; turn out, to bend outwards: to drive out, to expel: to put to pasture (as cattle): to produce and put forth: to prove in the result: to muster: to go on strike: to get out of bed (*coll.*): to go out of doors (*coll.*); turn over, to roll over: to set the other way up: to change sides: to hand over, pass on: to handle or do business to the amount of: to examine by turning the leaves: to rob (*slang*); turn round, to arrive, unload and leave again (*n.* turn′-round): turn the scale, to decide, determine; turn the stomach, to nauseate; turn the tables (see table); turn to, to have recourse to: to point to: to result in: to change or be changed into: to set to work; turn turtle (see turtle); turn up, to point upwards: to fold upwards: to come, or bring, to light: to appear by chance: to set face up: to invert: to grub up: to disturb: to make brighter, as a light (as if by

Neutral vowels in unaccented syllables: *el′ə-mənt*; for certain sounds in foreign words, see p. viii

turning a handle): to refer to, look up: to dis-gust (*coll.*); **turn up for the book**, a totally un-expected occurrence; **turn upon**, to cast back upon, retort: to hinge on. [O.E. *turnian, tyrnan,* and perh. partly O.Fr. *torner* (Fr. *tourner*); all from L. *tornāre,* to turn in a lathe—*tornus,* a turner's wheel—Gr. *tornos,* lathe, compasses.]

**Turnbull's blue,** *tûrn'bəlz blōō,* ferrous ferri-cyanide¹ (or possibly ferric ferrocyanide). [From *Turnbull,* a Glasgow manufacturing chemist (18th cent.), not the discoverer.]

**turndun,** *tûrn'dun,* **tundun,** *tun',* n. an Australian bull-roarer. [Native word.]

**turner,** *tûr'nər,* n. a 17th-century Scots bodle. [Origin doubtful; cf. Fr. *tournois,* coined at *Tours.*]

**Turneresque,** *tûr-nər-esk',* adj. resembling the work of the painter J. M. W. *Turner* (1775-1851). —Also Turnerian (-nē'ri-ən).

**turnip,** *tûr'nip,* n. the swollen edible root of *Brassica rapa* or (*Swedish turnip*) of *B. rutabaga,* cruciferous biennials: the root as food: the plant producing it: extended to more or less similar roots and plants, as the American papilionaceous *prairie turnip* (*Psoralea escu-lenta*): a big watch (*slang*): a dunderhead.—*v.t.* to plant with turnips: to feed on turnips.—**tur'nip-flea',** a leaping beetle that eats young turnip and cabbage plants; **tur'nip-fly',** a fly whose maggots burrow in turnip-roots: the turnip-flea; **tur'nip-lan'tern,** a lantern made by scooping out the flesh of a turnip; **tur'nip-top',** the green sprout of a turnip in its second year, used as a vegetable. [See neep; the first part may be from turn or Fr. *tour,* implying round-ness.]

**turnsole,** *tûrn'sōl,* n. a plant whose flowers are supposed to face the sun, as heliotrope or the euphorbiaceous *Chrozophora tinctoria*: a deep-purple dye got from the latter: litmus. [Fr. *tournesol*—L. *tornāre* (see turn), *sōl,* the sun.]

**turpentine,** *tûr'pən-tin,* n. a balsam, orig. that of the terebinth tree (*Chian turpentine*), now gener-ally of conifers: popularly, oil of turpentine: a tree that yields turpentine, esp. the terebinth.—*v.t.* to treat or smear with turpentine.—*adj.* **tur'pentiny.**—**tur'pentine-tree,** the terebinth-tree. —**oil** (or **spirit**) **of turpentine** (*coll.* **turps**), an oil distilled from turpentine. [O.Fr. *terbentine*—L. *terebinthina* (*rēsina*), terebinth (resin); see **terebinth.**]

**turpeth,** *tûr'pəth,* **turbith,** **-bith,** n. an Oriental Ipomoea or its cathartic root.—**turpeth mineral,** basic mercuric sulphate. [L.L. *turpethum, tur-bithum*—Pers. and Ar. *turbed, turbid.*]

**turpitude,** *tûr'pi-tūd,* n. baseness: depravity: vileness. [L. *turpitūdō*—*turpis,* base.]

**turquoise,** *tûr'kwäz, -k(w)oiz, -kwōz,* formerly **turkis** (*Milt., Tenn.*), **turkies** (*Shak.*), *tûr'kiz, -kis,* n. a massive opaque sky-blue to pale green mineral, a hydrous basic aluminium phosphate, found in Persia: blue colour of the stone.—*adj.* of turquoise: of the colour of turquoise.—*ns.* and *adjs.* **tur'quoise-blue',** turquoise; **tur'quoise-green,** pale bluish green.—**bone,** or **fossil, turquoise,** odontolite. [O.Fr. *turkeis,* and later Fr. *turquoise,* Turkish, as first brought through *Turkey* or from *Turkestan.*]

**turret,** *tur'it,* n. a small tower, usu. attached to a building, often containing a winding stair: a tower, often revolving, carrying a gun: part of a lathe that holds the cutting tool.—*adj.* **turr'eted,** having turrets: formed like a tower or a long spiral.—**turr'et-clock,** a clock for a tower: a large clock with movement quite separate from the dials; **turr'et-gun,** one for use in a revolving turret; **turr'et-ship,** a warship with gun-turrets. [O.Fr. *tourete,* dim. of *tur;* see **tower.**]

**turret.** Same as terret.

**turribant.** See turban.

**turriculated,** *tur-ik'ū-lāt-id,* adj. turreted: formed in a long spiral.—*n.* **Turritell'a,** the tower-shell genus of gasteropods. [L. *turris,* a tower; dim. *turricula.*]

**turtle,** *tûr'tl,* n. a turtle-dove: a constant or demonstrative lover.—**tur'tle-dove,** any dove of the genus Turtur or Streptopelia, a favourite cage-bird, a type of conjugal affection and con-stancy: the mourning dove (*U.S.*). [O.E. *turtla,* turtle—L. *turtur;* cf. Ger. *turtel,* Fr. *tourtereau, tourterelle.*]

**turtle,** *tûr'tl,* n. any marine chelonian: sometimes a freshwater chelonian: esp. in U.S., a terres-trial chelonian: the edible flesh of a turtle, esp. the green turtle: turtle-soup.—*v.i.* to hunt or catch turtles.—*ns.* **tur'tler,** a hunter of turtles; **tur'tling,** the hunting of turtles.—**tur'tleback,** anything arched like a turtle's back, esp. a structure over a ship's bows or stern; **tur'tle neck,** (a garment having) a high close-fitting neckline.—*adj.* **tur'tle-necked.**—**tur'tle-shell,** the shell of the hawk's-bill turtle, commonly called tortoise-shell; **tur'tle-soup,** a soup made from the flesh, fat, and gelatinous tissue of the female green turtle (*Chelone mydas*); **tur'tle-stone',** a septarium.—**mock turtle,** a soup made of calf's head or other meat in lieu of turtle meat; **turn turtle,** to render a turtle helpless by turning it on its back: to turn bottom up. [Fr. *tortue,* Sp. *tortuga,* or Port. *tartaruga,* tortoise, assimilated to foregoing.]

**Tuscan,** *tus'kən,* adj. of Tuscany in Italy: Doric as modified by the Romans, with unfluted columns, and without triglyphs (*archit.*).—*n.* classical Italian as spoken in Tuscany: a native of Tuscany: an ancient Etruscan. [L. *Tuscānus,* Etruscan.]

**tush,** *tush,* (*Shak.*) n. a tusk: a small tusk: a horse's canine tooth. [O.E. *tūsc;* cf. **tusk.**]

**tush,** *tush,* (*arch.*) interj. pshaw: pooh.—Also *v.i.* —*n.* **tush'ery,** word coined by R. L. Stevenson meaning (a style of period novel, etc.) using would-be archaic language.

**tusk.** Same as torsk.

**tusk,** *tusk,* n. a long, protruding tooth: a tush: a sharp projection.—*v.t.* to pierce with the tusks. —*adjs.* **tusked,** **tusk'y.**—*n.* **tusk'er,** a boar, elephant, etc., with tusks.—*adj.* **tusk'less.**— **tusk'-shell,** the mollusc Dentalium or its shell. [O.E. *tūx* (*tūsc*); cf. **tush** (1).]

**tuskar, tusker,** *tus'kər,* **twiscar,** *twis'kər,* (*Orkney* and *Shetland*) n. a peat-spade. [O.N. *torfskeri*— *torf,* turf, *skera,* to cut.]

**tussah,** *tus'ə,* **tusseh, -e,** n. faulty forms of tusser.

**tusser, tussore, tasar,** *tus'ər,* n. a fawn-coloured silk from wild Indian silkworms: its colour: a dress made of it.—Also **tusser-silk.** [Hind. *tasar,* shuttle—Sans. *tasara,* silkworm.]

**tussle,** *tus'l,* n. a sharp struggle.—*v.i.* to struggle. [Freq. of touse; cf. **tousle.**]

**tussock,** *tus'ək,* n. a tuft: a bunchy clump of grass, rushes, etc.: tussock-grass: a tussock-moth.— *adj.* **tuss'ocky.**—**tuss'ock-,** **tuss'ac-grass,** a large grass (*Poa flabellata*) of the Falkland Islands, forming great tufts; **tuss'ock-moth,** any moth of the family Lymantriidae (akin to Lasiocampi-dae), from the tufts of hair on the caterpillars. [Origin obscure.]

**tussore.** Same as tusser.

**tut,** *tut,* interj. an exclamation of rebuke, mild dis-approbation, impatience, etc.—*v.i.* to say 'tut'.— Also **tut'-tut',** *Scot.* toot, toots, tuts.

**tut,** *tut,* n. work paid by measurement or piece.— *v.i.* to do such work.—**tut'work;** **tut'worker;** **tut'(work)man.** [Origin unknown.]

**tutania,** *tū-tā'ni-ə,* n. a kind of Britannia metal. [From W. *Tutin* (c. 1780), its maker or inventor.]

**tutelage,** *tū'ti-lij,* n. guardianship: state of being under a guardian: tuition.—*adjs.* **tu'telar,** **tu'te-lary,** protecting: having the charge of a person or place.—*ns.* a guardian spirit, god, or saint. [L. *tūtēla*, guard—*tūtārī*, to guard—*tuērī*, to look to.]

**tutenag,** *tū'ti-nag, n.* an alloy of zinc, copper, etc.: loosely, zinc. [Marathi *tuttināg*.]

**tutiorism,** *tū'ti-ər-izm, n.* in R.C. moral theology, the doctrine that in a case of doubt between right and wrong one should take the safer course, i.e. the one in verbal accordance with the law.— *n.* and *adj.* **tū'tiorist.** [L. *tūtior, -ōris,* safer, comp. of *tūtus,* safe.]

**tutor,** *tū'tər, n.* a guardian: a guardian of the person and estate of a boy under fourteen, or girl under twelve (*Scots law*): a private instructor: a coach: one who helps a boy or girl with lessons: a college officer who has supervision of an undergraduate: a college teacher who instructs by conference with a small group of students: an instruction-book.—*v.t.* to act as tutor to: to instruct: to coach: to control: to discipline.—*ns.* **tu'torage,** tutorship: tutoring: charge for tutoring: tutelage (*obs.*); **tu'toress, tu'tress** (*obs.* **tu'trix**), a female tutor.—*adj.* **tutorial** (*tū-tō'ri-əl, -tö'*), of a tutor.—*n.* a conference or sitting with a college tutor.—*adv.* **tuto'rially.**—*n.* **tu'toring.**—*v.t.* and *v.i.* **tu'torise, -ize.**—*ns.* **tu'torism, tu'torship.** [L. *tūtor, -ōris,* a guardian—*tuērī,* to look to.]

**tutsan,** *tut'sən, n.* parkleaves, a species of St John's wort (*Hypericum androsaemum*) once regarded as a panacea. [O.Fr. *toutesaine, tout*— L. *tōtus,* all, *sain*—L. *sānus,* sound.]

**tutti,** *toot'(t)ē, (mus.) pl. adj.* all (performers).—*n.* a passage for the whole orchestra or choir, or its rendering. [It., pl. of *tutto*—L. *tōtus,* all.]

**tutti-frutti,** *toot'(t)ē-froot'(t)ē, n.* a confection, esp. ice-cream, flavoured with different kinds of fruit. [It., all fruits.]

**tut-tut,** *tut'-tut'.* Same as **tut** (1).

**tutty,** *tut'i, n.* crude zinc oxide. [O.Fr. *tutie*—L.L. *tutia*—Ar. *tūtiyā*.]

**tutu,** *too'too, n.* a New Zealand shrub (*Coriaria ruscifolia*; fam. Coriariaceae, akin to Empetraceae) whose poisonous black fruit makes a light wine. [Maori.]

**tutu,** *too'too, n.* a ballet dancer's short, stiff, spreading skirt. [Fr.]

**tu-whit tu-whoo,** *too-(h)wit' too-(h)woo', n.* an owl's hoot.—*v.i.* **tu-whoo',** to hoot.

**tuxedo,** *tuk-sē'dō, (U.S.) n.* a dinner-jacket. [From a fashionable club at *Tuxedo* Park, N.Y.]

**tuyère.** See **twyer.**

**tuzz,** *tuz, (Dryden) n.* a tuft.—**tuzz'i-muzzy** (*obs.*), a posy.

**twa,** *twä, twö, twä,* also **twae, tway,** *twä,* Scots forms of **two.**—*adj.* and *adv.* **twa'fald** (*-föld*), twofold: bent double.—*n.* and *adj.* **twa'some** (see **twosome**).—*adj.* **twa'-loft'ed,** two-storied.

**twaddle,** *twod'l, n.* senseless or prosy commonplace talk: a talker of twaddle (*obs.*).—*v.i.* to talk twaddle.—*n.* **twadd'ler.**—*n.* and *adj.* **twadd'ling.**—*adj.* **twadd'ly.** [Perh. **twattle.**]

**twain,** *twān, (arch.) adj.* two.—*n.* a couple, pair.— **in twain,** asunder. [O.E. *twēgen* (masc.), two.]

**twaite,** *twāt, n.* one of the British species of shad. —Also **twaite shad.** [Origin unknown.]

**twal,** *twöl, twäl,* a Scots form of **twelve.**—*ns.* **twal'hours** (*-öōrz*), a noonday meal or refreshment; **twal'penny,** a shilling Scots, a penny (English).—Also **twal'pennies.**

**twang,** *twang, (dial.) n.* a sharp flavour: an aftertaste: a smack, suggestion. [**tang,** affected by next.]

**twang,** *twang, n.* the sound of a plucked string: a nasal tone: a twinge (*dial.*): a local intonation (*coll.*).—*v.t.* and *v.i.* to sound with a twang.—*n.* and *adj.* **twang'ing. — ** *adv.* **twang'ingly. — ** **twangle** (*twang'gl*), a slack or jangly twanging.— *v.t.* and *v.i.* to sound with a twangle.—*n.* and *adj.* **twang'ling** (*-gling*).—*adv.* **twang'lingly** (*-gling-li*).

—*adj.* **twangy** (*twang'i*).—*n.* **twank** (*dial.*), a short twang: a slap. [Imit.]

**twankay,** *twang'kä, n.* a kind of green tea: gin (*slang*). [*Tong-ke* or Tun-chi in China.]

**'twas,** *twoz, twəz,* contraction of **it was.**

**twat,** *twot, n.* vulgarly, the vulva: (blunderingly) part of a nun's dress (*Browning*): a coarse general term of reproach (*slang*). [Origin obscure.]

**twattle,** *twot'l, n.* chatter: babble: twaddle.— *v.t.* and *v.i.* to babble.—*n.* **twatt'ler.**—*n.* and *adj.* **twatt'ling.** [Perh. conn. with **tattle.**]

**tway,** *twä, adj.* and *n.* a form of **twain** (*Spens.*): of **twain,** or of **two** (**twae**) (*Scot.*).—**tway'-blade,** an orchid (Listera) with small green flowers and one pair of leaves: also an American orchid (Liparis).

**tweak,** *twēk, v.t.* to twitch, to pull: to pull with sudden jerks.—*n.* a sharp pinch or twitch: agitation, perplexity (*obs.*). [App. conn. with **twitch.**]

**twee,** *twē, (coll.) adj.* small and sweet: sentimentally pretty. [*tweet* for 'sweet', and later tiny and *wee.*]

**tweed,** *twēd, n.* a rough woollen cloth much used for men's suits: (in *pl.*) clothes of tweed. [Said to be from a happy misreading of **tweel,** the cloth being made in the Tweed basin.]

**tweedle,** *twē'dl, v.i.* to play casually, strum, tootle: to pipe as a bird.—*v.t.* to pipe into acquiescence: to wheedle.—*ns.* **tweedledee', tweedledum',** a fiddler (in conjunction as types of the almost indistinguishable).—*v.i.* to tweedle: to fiddle. [Prob. imit., influenced by **wheedle.**]

**tweel,** *twēl, n.* a Scots form of **twill.**

**'tween,** a contraction of **between.**—*adj.* **'tween'-deck,** lodging between decks.—*n.* and *adv.* **'tween-decks.**—*n.* **tween'y** (*coll.*), a between-maid.

**tweer.** See **twyer.**

**tweet,** *twēt, tweet'-tweet', ns.* the note of a small bird.—*vs.t.* and *vs.i.* to pipe as a small bird.—*n.* **tweet'er,** a loudspeaker used in high-fidelity sound reproduction for the higher frequencies (also (*coll.*) **top tweet**). [Imit.]

**tweezers,** *twēz'ərz, n.pl.* small pincers for pulling out hairs, etc.—**tweez'er-case,** an étui. [Obs. *tweeze,* a surgeon's case of instruments—Fr. *étui.*]

**twelfth,** *twelfth, adj.* last of twelve: equal to one of twelve equal parts.—*n.* a twelfth part: tone eleven (conventionally twelve) diatonic degrees above or below a given tone (*mus.*): an octave and a fifth.—*adv.* **twelfth'ly,** in the twelfth place. —**Twelfth'-cake,** ornamental cake partaken of on Twelfth night; **Twelfth'-day,** twelfth day after Christmas, Epiphany, 6th Jan.; **twelfth man** (*cricket*), a player selected beyond the necessary eleven to play if required as a substitute; **Twelfth'-night,** evening of 6th Jan.: also of 5th Jan.; **Twelfth'-tide,** season of Epiphany. —**the Twelfth,** 12th Aug., opening day of grouse shooting. [O.E. *twelfta*—*twelf.*]

**twelve,** *twelv, adj.* ten and two.—*n.* the cardinal number next above eleven: a set of that number of things or persons: an article of a size denoted by 12: a score of twelve points: the hour of midday or midnight: (in *pl.*) duodecimo.—*adj.* and *adv.* **twelve'fold.**—*ns.* **twelve'mo,** duodecimo, written 12mo; **twelve'month,** a year.—*adj.* **twelve'-penny,** shilling.—**twelve score,** two hundred and forty (yards); **Twelve Tables,** the earliest code of Roman law, civil, criminal, and religious, made by the decemvirs in 451-449 B.C. —*adj.* **twelve-tone** (or -**note**), pertaining to music based on a pattern formed from the twelve notes of the chromatic scale, esp. as developed by Arnold Schönberg (1874-1951) and his pupils: (**twelve-tone, -note, row,** the basic pattern of notes; see also **serial**).—**the Twelve,** the twelve apostles. [O.E. *twelf* (Ger. *zwölf*, and Goth. *twa-lif*), that is, prob. two left; see **eleven**.]

**twenty,** *twen'ti, adj.* twice ten: nineteen and one: an indefinite number.—*n.* the number next above nineteen: a score: an old English division of infantry: (in *pl.*) the years (esp. of age or a century) from the twentieth to the twenty-ninth.—*adj.* **twen'tieth,** next after the nineteenth: equal to one of twenty equal parts.—*n.* a twentieth part.—*n., adj.,* and *adv.* **twen'tyfold,** twenty times as many or much.—*adj.* **twen'tyish,** about twenty.—*adj.* **twen'ty-four',** twenty and four.—*n.* the number made up of four and twenty: a sheet folded into twenty-four leaves (forty-eight pages): a form arranged for printing it.—*n.* **twenty-four'-mo** (written 24mo, for L. *in vicēsimō quārtō*), a book made up of sheets folded in twenty-four leaves (forty-eight pages).—Also *adj.*—**and twenty** (*Shak.*), supposed to be a mere intensive (as *good even and twenty*; *sweet and twenty*; see **sweet**). [O.E. *twēntig,* prob.— *twēgen,* twain, and suff. *-tig* (Goth. *tigjus*), ten; Ger. *zwanzig.*]

**'twere,** contraction of **it were.**

**twerp,** *twûrp,* (*slang*) *n.* a contemptible person, either stupid or a cad, or both.

**twi-, twy-,** *twi, pfx.* two: double.—*adjs.*—**twi'-, twy'fold,** twofold; **twi'-, twy'forked,** bifurcate, **twi'-, twy'formed,** having two forms; **twy'-natured,** of double nature. [O.E. pfx. *twi-.*]

**Twi,** *ch(w)ē, n.* a dialect, and also a literary language of Ghana.—Also **Tshi.**—Also *adj.*

**twibill,** *twi'bil, n.* a double-headed axe. [O.E. *twibill*—pfx. **twi-, bill** (1).]

**twice,** *twis, adv.* two times: doubly: for a second time.—*n.* **twi'cer,** one who is both compositor and pressman: one who habitually goes to church twice on Sunday (*eccles. slang*).—*adjs.* **twice'-born,** born twice, as Bacchus: of high Hindu caste: regenerate (*theol.*); **twice'-laid,** made of old yarns twisted anew; **twice'-told,** counted twice: told twice: hackneyed.—**at twice,** in two stages or operations; **twice over,** twice (emphatically). [Late O.E. *twiges*—*twiga, twiwa, tuwa,* twice, with adverbial gen. ending.]

**twichild,** *twi'child, n.* one who has become a child again. [Pfx. **twi-.**]

**twiddle,** *twid'l, v.t.* to twirl idly: to finger idly, play with.—*v.i.* to twirl: to trifle with something.—*n.* a twirl: a curly mark, ornament.—*n.* **twidd'ler.**—*n., adj.* **twidd'ling.**—*adj.* **twidd'ly.**—*adj.* **twidd'ling-line,** formerly a line for steadying the steering-wheel: a string for setting the compass-card to play freely.—**twiddle one's thumbs,** to rotate the thumbs around each other: to be idle (*fig.*). [Prob. suggested by **twirl, twist,** and **fiddle.**]

**twier.** See **tuyer.**

**twig,** *twig, n.* a small shoot or branch: a divining-rod.—*adj.* made of twigs.—*v.t.* to birch, switch. —*adjs.* **twigg'en** (*Shak.*), covered with, made of, wickerwork; **twigg'y; twig'some.** [O.E. *twig*; cf. Ger. *zweig.*]

**twig,** *twig,* (*slang*) *v.t.* and *v.i.* to observe: to understand. [Poss. Ir. *tuigim,* discern; cf. Gael. *tuig,* understand.]

**twig,** *twig,* (*slang*) *n.* fettle: fashion: recognisable condition.—*v.i.* to act vigorously.—*n.* **twigg'er,** (*obs.*) a vigorous breeder: a wanton. [Origin obscure.]

**twight,** *twit, v.t.* (*Spens.*) for **twit.**

**twilight,** *twi'lit, n.* the faint light after sunset and before sunrise: dim light or partial darkness: period of decay following a period of success, greatness, etc. (*fig.*).—*adj.* of twilight: faintly illuminated: obscure.—*v.t.* to illuminate faintly. —*adjs.* **twi'lighted, twi'lit.**—**twilight sleep,** partial anaesthesia in childbirth by the use of drugs.— **twilight of the Gods** (see **Ragnarök**). [Pfx. **twi-, light.**]

**'twill,** contraction of **it will.**

**twill,** *twil,* or (*Scot.*) **tweel,** *twēl, n.* a woven fabric showing diagonal lines: the appearance so produced.—*v.t.* to weave with a twill. [O.E. *twilic.*]

**twill,** *twil,* **twilt,** *twilt.* Dialect forms of **quill, quilt.**

**twilled,** *twil'id, adj.* prob., protected against floods by plaited osiers (the word so used still at Stratford; *Shak.*): according to some, ridged like twilled cloth: or reedy, from an alleged obs. word *twill,* a reed.

**twilly,** *twil'i, n.* a willowing-machine. [**willow.**]

**twin,** *twin,* **twine, twin,** (*obs.* and *Scot.*) *v.t.* and *v.i.* to separate: to part.—*v.t.* to deprive. [**twin** (2).]

**twin,** *twin, n.* one of two born at a birth: one very like, or closely associated with, another: a counterpart: a pair of twins or pair generally (*obs.*): a combination of two crystals symmetrically united about a plane that is a possible face of each or an axis that is a possible edge of each, or of more than two by repetition.—*adj.* two-fold, double: born two at a birth: forming one, or composed, of two like parts or counterparts: very like another.—*v.t.* to couple, or to produce, like a twin or twins.—*v.i.* to be born at the same birth: to bring forth two at once: to be paired or suited:—*pr.p.* **twinn'ing;** *pa.p.* **twinned.**—*ns.* **twin'er** (*W. de la Mare*), a double limerick; **twin'ling,** a twin.—*adj.* **twinned,** produced at one birth: constituting a twin.—*ns.* **twinn'ing; twin'ship,** condition or relation of a twin or twins.—**twin'-ax'is,** the axis of symmetry of a twin crystal; **twin'-bed,** one of a matching pair of single beds; **twin'-birth,** birth of twins: a twin: a pair of twins.—*adj.* **twin'-born,** born at the same birth.—**twin'-broth'er,** a brother born at the same birth; **twin'-plane',** the plane of symmetry of a twin crystal.—*adj.* **twin'-screw,** with two propellers on separate shafts.—**twin'-set,** a cardigan and jumper made more or less to match; **twin'-sist'er,** a sister born at the same birth.—**the Twins,** Gemini. [O.E. *getwinn* (n.), twin, *twinn* (adj.), double; cf. pfx. **twi-.**]

**twine,** *twin, n.* a twisted cord: string or strong thread: a coil: a twist: a twisted stem or the like: an act of twisting or clasping.—*v.t.* to wind: to coil: to wreathe: to twist: to twist together: to encircle: to make by twisting.—*v.i.* to wind: to coil: to twist: to make turns: to rise or grow in spirals: to wriggle.—*adj.* **twined.**—*n.* **twi'ner,** one who, or that which, twines: a twining plant.—*n.* and *adj.* **twi'ning.**—*adv.* **twi'ningly.**—*adj.* **twi'ny.**—**twining plant,** one that climbs by twining its stem round a support. [O.E. *twin,* double or twisted thread, linen thread; cf. Du. *twijn.*]

**twine,** *twin, n.* a variant of **twin,** to separate.

**twinge,** *twinj, v.t.* to tweak or pinch: to affect with a momentary pain.—*v.i.* to feel or give a momentary pain.—*n.* a tweak, a pinch: a shooting pain. [O.E. *twengan,* to pinch.]

**twink,** *twingk, v.i.* to blink: to twinkle.—*n.* a twinkling, a moment. [Root of **twinkle.**]

**twinkle,** *twing'kl, v.i.* to blink: to quiver the eyelid: to shine by flashes: to glitter: to sparkle: to flicker, vibrate.—*v.t.* to guide by twinkling.— *n.* a blink: a wink: a glitter: a quiver: a flicker: a sparkle: a twinkling: a dance step.—*ns.* **twink'ler; twink'ling,** a quick motion of the eye: the time occupied by a wink: an instant: the scintillation of the fixed stars.—*adj.* **twink'ling,** scintillating: quivering: blinking (*obs.*). [O.E. *twinclian.*]

**twinter,** *twin'tar,* (*Scot.*) *adj.* two years old.—*n.* a two-year-old sheep or other animal. [O.E. *twiwintre,* two-winter.]

**twire,** *twir,* **tweer, twēr,** (*Shak.*) *v.i.* to peer.—*n.* (*obs.*) a glance, leer. [Cf. M.H.G. *zwieren,* to peer.]

**twire.** See **tuyer.**

**twirl,** *twûrl, v.t.* and *v.i.* to spin: to whirl: to twirl.—*n.* a twist: a spin: a whirl: a

whorl: a curly figure.—*n.* twirl′er.—*adj.* twirl′y.
—**twirl one's thumbs,** to twiddle one's thumbs. [Connection with O.E. *thwiril*, churn handle, whisk, doubtful.]

**twiscar.** See **tuskar.**

**twist,** *twist, v.t.* to twine: to unite or form by winding together: to form from several threads: to wind spirally: to form into a spiral: to wring: to wrest: to distort: to entangle: to impart a spin to: to force round: to eat heartily (often with *down*; *old slang*): to pervert, warp.—*v.i.* to twine: to coil: to move spirally or tortuously: to turn aside: to revolve: to writhe.—*n.* that which is twisted: a cord: a strand: thread: silk thread: warp yarn: a twisted part: torsion: act or manner of twisting: a contortion: a wrench: a wresting: a turning aside: a spin, screw, or break: a distortion: a perverted bent or set: a tangle: a twisted roll of tobacco or bread: a spiral ornament in the stem of a glass: a twig (*obs.*): the fork of the body (*obs.*): a mixed drink (*slang*): a good appetite (*slang*).—*adjs.* twist′able; twist′ed.—*n.* twist′er, one who, or that which, twists: a sophistical, slippery, shuffling, or dishonest person: a ball sent with a twist.—*n. and adj.* twist′ing.—*adj.* twist′y.—**the twist,** a dance which became popular in 1962, in which the dancer constantly twists the body. [O.E. *twist*, rope (found in the compound *mæst-twist*, a stay).]

**twit,** *twit, v.t.* to upbraid: to taunt:—*pr.p.* twitt′ing; *pa.t.* and *pa.p.* twitt′ed.—*n.* a reproach.—*v.t.* twitt′er (*Fielding*), to twit.—*n. and adj.* twitt′ing.—*adv.* twitt′ingly. [O.E. *ætwitan*, to reproach—*æt*, against, *witan*, to wite.]

**twit,** *twit,* (*slang*) *n.* a fool.

**twitch,** *twich, v.t.* to jerk: to pluck: to snatch: to steal: to pinch or twinge.—*v.i.* to jerk: to move spasmodically: to carp, sneer.—*n.* a sudden, quick pull: a spasmodic contraction of the muscles: a twinge: a noose: the sudden tapering of a vein of ore.—*n.* twitch′er.—*n. and adj.* twitch′ing.—*adj.* twitch′y. [Related to O.E. *twiccian*, to pluck; Ger. *zwicken*.]

**twitch,** *twich,* twitch′-grass, forms of **quitch,** -grass. See **couch-grass.**

**twite,** *twit, n.* the mountain linnet. [From its note.]

**twitten,** *twit′n,* (*dial.*) *n.* a narrow lane between two walls or hedges.—Also twitt′ing. [Perh. related to L.G. *twiete*, alley, lane.]

**twitter,** *twit′ər, n.* a tremulous feeble chirping: a flutter of the nerves.—*v.i.* to make a succession of small tremulous noises: to palpitate.—*v.t.* to chirp out: to twiddle.—*ns.* twitt′erer.—*n. and adj.* twitt′ering.—*adv.* twitt′eringly.—*adj.* twitt′ery. [Imit.; cf. Ger. *zwitschern*.]

**twitter,** *twit′ər,* twitt′er-bone, *ns.* an excrescence on a horse's hoof.—*adj.* twitt′er-boned. [A form of **quitter.**]

**twitter, twitting.** See **twit** (1).

**'twixt.** Abbreviation for **betwixt.**

**two,** *tōō, adj.* one and one.—*n.* the sum of one and one: a symbol representing two: a pair: a deuce, card with two pips: a score of two points, strokes, etc.: an article of a size denoted by two: the second hour after midnight or midday.—*n.* two′er, anything that counts as, or for, or scores two.—*adj. and adv.* two′fold, in two divisions: twice as much: (esp. *Scot.* twa-fald, *twä, twö-föld*) in a doubled-up position.—*ns.* two′foldness; two′ness, the state of being two: duality; two′some, a company of two: a tête-à-tête: a single (*golf*).—*adj.* consisting of two: performed by two.—**two bits,** twenty-five cents.—*adjs.* two′-bit, paltry; two′-bottle, able to drink two bottles of wine at a sitting.—two′-deck′er, a ship with two decks or with guns on two decks: a bus or tram-car carrying passengers

on a roofed top.—*adj.* two′-dimen′sional.—two′-dimensional′ity, the property of having length and breadth but no depth.—*adjs.* two′-edged, having two cutting edges: capable of being turned against the user; two′-eyed′, having two eyes (**two-eyed steak,** *slang,* a bloater); two′-faced, having two faces: double-dealing, false; two′-fisted, clumsy; two′-foot, measuring, or with, two feet; two′-footed, having two feet.—two′-for-his-heels′, a knave (from the score for turning up a knave in cribbage).—*adjs.* two′-forked, having two prongs or branches; two′-four′ (*mus.*), with two crotchets to the bar; two′-hand (*Shak.*), for two hands; two′-hand′ed, with or for two hands: for two persons: ambidextrous: strapping; two′-head′ed, having two heads: directed by two authorities; two′-horse, for two horses; two′-inch, measuring two inches; two′-leaved, -leafed, with two leaves or leaflets: with leaves in twos; two′-legged, with two legs; two′-line (*print.*), having double depth of body; two′-lipped, having two lips: bilabiate; two′-mast′ed, having two masts.—two′-mast′er, a two-masted ship.—*adj.* two′-pair (-of-stairs), on a second floor.—*n.* a room so situated.—*adjs.* two′-part, composed in two parts or for two voices; two′-part′ed, bipartite: divided into two nearly to the base.—**twopence** (*tup′əns*), the sum of two pennies: a coin worth twopence (*Shak.*).—*adj.* **twopenny** (*tup′ni*), sold or offered at twopence: cheap, worthless.—*n.* ale sold at twopence a quart: in leapfrog, the head.—*adjs.* **twopenny-halfpenny** (*tup′ni-hāp′ni*), twopence-halfpenny, paltry, petty.—*ns.* two-penn′yworth, **two-penn′orth** (*tōō-pen′ərth*), also (chiefly *Scot.*) **twopenceworth** (*tup′*).—*adj.* two′-piece, consisting of two separate parts or pieces; two′-ply, having two layers, or consisting of two strands: woven double; two′-roomed.—*n. and adj.* two′-score, forty.—two′seater, a vehicle or aeroplane seated for two.—*adj.* two′-sid′ed, having two surfaces, aspects, or parties: facing two ways: double-faced: having the two sides different.—two-sid′edness; two′-step, a gliding dance in duple time: a tune for it.—*v.i.* to dance the two-step.—*adjs.* two′-storeyed, -storey; two′stroke, consisting of two piston strokes, as an engine cycle.—*v.t.* two′-time, to deceive: to double-cross.—two-tim′er, one who deceives or double-crosses.—*adjs.* two-tim′ing; two′-tone, having two colours or two shades of the same colour.—two′-up′, an Australian game in which two coins are tossed and bets made on both falling heads up or both tails up.—*adj.* two′-way, permitting passage along either of two ways esp. in opposite directions: able to receive and send signals (*radio*): of communication between two persons, groups, etc., in which both participate equally: involving shared responsibility: able to be used in two ways: having a double mode of variation or two dimensions (*math.*).—*adj.* two′-wheeled. two′-wheel′er, a vehicle with two wheels, esp. a hansom cab.—*adj.* two′-year-old.—*n.* a child, colt, etc., aged two.—**be two,** to be at variance; **in two,** asunder, so as to form two pieces; **in two twos, two ticks** (*slang*), in a moment; **put two and two together** (see **put**); **two or three,** a few; **two-power standard** (*hist.*), the principle that the strength of the British navy must never be less than the combined strength of the navies of any two other powers; **two-speed gear,** a gear-changing contrivance with two possibilities. [O.E. *twā*, fem. and neut., two (masc. *twēgen*); Ger. *zwei*, Goth, *twai*; Gr. *dyo*, L. *duo*, Sans. *dva*, Gael. *dà*.]

**twy-,** *pfx.* See **twi-.**

**twyer, twyere, tweer, twier, twire, tuyère,** *twēr,* also *twir, twē-yer′, n.* a nozzle for a blast of air. [Fr. *tuyère*.]

**Tyburn,** *ti′bərn, n.* the historic place of execution in

London.—**Ty′burn-tick′et**, a certificate of exemption from certain parochial offices formerly granted to the prosecutor of a felon to conviction; **Ty′burn-tipp′et**, a halter; **Ty′burn-tree**, the gallows.

**Tyche**, *ti′kē*, (*Gr. myth.*) *n.* the goddess of fortune. —*n.* **ty′chism**, a theory that accepts pure chance. [Gr. *tўchē*, chance.]

**Tychonic**, *ti-kon′ik*, *adj.* pertaining to the Danish astronomer, *Tycho Brahe* (1546-1601), or his system.

**tycoon**, *ti-kōōn′*, *n.* the title by which the Shoguns of Japan were known to foreigners: a business magnate.—*ns.* **tycoon′ate**, the shogunate; **tycoon′ery**. [Jap. *taikun*, great prince—Chin. *ta*, great, *kiun*, prince.]

**tyde**, a Spenserian spelling of **tied**, *pa.t.* and *pa.p.* of **tie**.

**tye**, *tī*, *n.* an inclined trough for washing ore.—*v.t.* to wash in a tye. [O.E. *tēag*, case, chest.]

**tying**, *ti′ing*, *pr.p.* and *verbal n.* of **tie**.

**tyke**, **tike**, *tik*, (*Shak.*; chiefly *Northern*) *n.* a dog: a cur: a rough-mannered fellow: a Yorkshireman. [O.N. *tik*, bitch.]

**tyler**. See **tile**.

**Tylopoda**, *ti-lop′ə-də*, *n.pl.* a section of the ungulates with padded toes—camels and llamas.—*n.* and *adj.* **ty′lopod**. [Gr. *tўlos*, a knob, callus, *pous, podos*, a foot.]

**tylosis**, *ti-lō′sis*, *n.* an ingrowth from a neighbouring cell through a pit into a vessel (also, perh. orig., **thylose**, *thī′lōs*, **thylosis**, *thi-lō′sis*; *pl.* **thylo′sēs**; perh.—Gr. *thўlakos*, a pocket; *bot.*): an inflammation of the eyelids: callosity:—*pl.* **tylō′sēs**.—*n.* **tylote** (*ti′lōt*), a cylindrical sponge spicule, knobbed at both ends. [Gr. *tўlos*, a knob, callus.]

**tymbal**. Same as **timbal**.

**tymp**, *timp*, *n.* the plate of a blast-furnace opening. [**tympan**.]

**tympan**, *tim′pən*, *n.* any instrument of the drum kind (*arch.*): a tympanum: an ancient Irish stringed instrument played with a bow (Ir. *tiompan*): a frame covered with parchment or cloth, on which sheets are placed for printing (*print.*).—*adjs.* **tym′panal** (*anat., zool.*), of the tympanum; **tympanic** (*-pan′ik*), of or like a drum or tympanum: tympanitic.—*n.* a bone of the ear, supporting the drum-membrane.—*adj.* **tym′paniform** (or *-pan′*), drum-shaped: drum-like.—*ns.* **tym′panist**, a drummer (**tim′panist**, one who plays the timpani); **tympani′tēs**, flatulent distension of the belly.—*adj.* **tympanitic** (*-it′ik*), of, affected with, tympanites.—*ns.* **tympani′tis**, inflammation of the membrane of the ear; **tym′pano** (*pl.* **-i**, *-ē*), a variant of **timpano**; **tym′panum**, a drum: a drum-head: the middle ear: the membrane separating it from the outer ear—the drum: in insects a vibratory membrane in various parts of the body, serving as an ear-drum: in birds the resonating sac of the syrinx: an air-sac in the neck in grouse, etc.: the recessed face of a pediment: a space between a lintel and an arch over it: a wheel for scooping up water: —*pl.* **tym′pana**; **tym′pany**, any swelling, esp. of the abdomen: tympanites: a blowing up as with pride: a drum (*rare*). [L. *tympanum*—Gr. *tympanon*, *typanon*, a kettledrum—*typtein*, to strike.]

**tynd**, **tyn′d**, **tyned**, **tynde**, **tyne** (*Spens.*; *Shak.*). See **tind**, **tine** (various words).

**Tynwald**, *tin′wold*, *n.* the parliament of the Isle of Man. [O.N. *thing-völlr*—*thing*, assembly, *völlr*, field.]

**type**, *tip*, *n.* a mark or stamp: the device on a coin or medal: a distinguishing mark: insignia: a designation: an emblem: a foreshadowing: an anticipation: an exemplar: a model or pattern: a kind: the general character of a class: that which well exemplifies the characteristics of a group: a person of well-marked characteristics: loosely and derogatorily, a person: a simple chemical compound representative of the structure of more complex compounds: the actual specimen on which the description of a new species or genus is based (**type specimen**): a rectangular piece of metal or of wood on one end of which is cast or engraved a character, sign, etc., used in printing: printing types collectively, letter: print: lettering.—*adj.* serving as a type. —*v.t.* to prefigure, foreshadow: to symbolise: to be the type of: to determine the type of (*med.*): to exemplify: to typewrite: to print (*rare*).—*v.i.* to typewrite.—*adjs.* **ty′pal**; **typic** (*tip′-*), typical; **typ′ical**, pertaining to, or constituting, a type: emblematic: figurative: characteristic: representative: typographical (*rare*).—*n.* **typical′ity**.—*adv.* **typ′ically**.—*ns.* **typ′icalness**; **typificā′tion**; **typ′ifier**.—*v.t.* **typify** (*tip′*), to make or be a type of:—*pr.p.* **typ′ifying**; *pa.t.* and *pa.p.* **typ′ified**.—*ns.* **typing** (*tip′ing*); **typist** (*tip′ist*), one who uses a typewriter: one whose occupation is typewriting; **typog′rapher** (*coll.* abbrev. **typo**, *ti′pō*), a compositor; a person engaged in or skilled in typography: a beetle that bores letter-like tunnels in the bark of pine and other trees; **typograph′ia** (*pl.*), matter relating to printers and printing.— *adjs.* **typograph′ic, -al**.—*adv.* **typograph′ically**.— *ns.* **typog′raphist**, one versed in the history or art of printing; **typog′raphy**, art or style of printing. —*adj.* **typolog′ical**.—*ns.* **typol′ogist**; **typol′ogy**, the study of types and their succession in biology, archaeology, etc.: the doctrine that things in the New Testament are foreshadowed symbolically in the Old; **typomā′nia**, a craze for printing one's lucubrations: a craze for finding types in the Old Testament.—**type′-bar**, a line of type cast in one piece: in a typewriter, a lever with a type-face; **type′-body**, measurement of breadth of shank for a size of type.—*v.t.* **type′-cast**, to cast in a rôle that accords with what one is by nature: to cast continually for the same kind of part.—*p.adj.* **type′cast**.—**type′-cutter**, one who engraves dies for printing-types; **type′-cyl′inder**, the cylinder of a rotary printing-machine on which plates are fastened for printing; **type′-face**, the printing surface of a type: manner in which it is cut: a complete range of type cut in a particular style; **type′-founder**, one who founds or casts printers' type; **type′-founding**; **type′-foundry**; **type′-genus**, the genus that gives name to its family.—*adj.* and *adv.* **type′-high**, of or at the standard type height (*c.* 0·918 in.; 23·317 mm.)—measured in the direction of the shank: at the height required for printing—of a woodcut, etc.—**type′-holder**, a bookbinder's pallet or holder for use in hand-stamping; **type locality**, area in which a genus or a geological formation occurs most typically or in which it was classified; **type′-met′al**, metal used for making types: an alloy of lead with antimony and tin, and sometimes copper; **type′-script**, typewritten matter or copy: type in imitation of handwriting or of typewriting.—*adj.* **typewritten**.—**type′-setter**, a compositor: a machine for setting type; **type′-setting**; **type′-species**, a species taken as the one to which the generic name is primarily attached.—*v.t.* and *v.i.* **type′write**, to print or copy with a typewriter.— **type′writer**, a machine, usu. with a keyboard, for printing as a substitute for handwriting: a typist (*rare*); **type′writing**.—*adj.* **type′written**. [L. *tўpus*—Gr. *tўpos*, blow, mark, stamp, model; *typtein*, to strike.]

**-type, -tip**, *suff.* of the same type as: resembling. [**type**.]

**Typha**, *ti′fə*, *n.* the reedmace genus, giving name to a family of monocotyledons, **Typhā′ceae**.— *adj.* **typhā′ceous**. [Gr. *tўphē*, reedmace.]

**typhlitis**, *tif-li'tis, n.* inflammation of the blind-gut. [Gr. *typhlos*, blind.]

**Typhoeus**, *ti-fō'ūs, n.* a monster of Greek mythology buried under Etna.—*adj.* **Typhoean** (*ti-fō'i-ən*). [Gr. *Typhōeus.*]

**typhoid**, *ti'foid, adj.* like typhus.—*n.* (for **typhoid fever**) enteric fever, long confounded with typhus, on account of the characteristic rash of rose-coloured spots.—*adj.* **typhoid'al.** [Gr. *typhōdēs*, delirious—*typhos*, a fever, *eidos*, likeness; cf. **typhus.**]

**Typhon**, *ti'fon, -fən, n.* son of Typhoeus, later identified with him, father of dangerous winds: (without *cap.*) a whirlwind (*obs.*).—*adjs.* **Typhonian** (-*fō'ni-ən*), **Typhonic** (-*fon'ik*; also without *cap.*).—*n.* **typhoon** (-*fōōn'*), a violent cyclonic storm of the China Sea. [Gr. *Typhōn*, Typhon, *typhōn*, a whirlwind; but partly also from Port. *tufāo*—Ar., Pers., Hind. *tūfān*, a hurricane (perh. itself from Gr.), and partly from Chin. *t'ai fung*, a great wind.]

**typhus**, *ti'fəs, n.* a dangerous fever transmitted by lice harbouring a Rickettsia and marked by eruption of red spots.—*adjs.* **ty'phoid** (q.v.); **ty'phous.** [Latinised from Gr. *typhos*, fever, stupor, delusion; cf. *typhein*, to smoke.]

**typical, typify, typist, typography,** etc. See under **type.**

**typto**, *tip'tō, v.i.* to conjugate the Greek verb *typtō*, I strike: to work at Greek grammar:—*pr.p.* (*Scott*) **tup'towing.**

**Tyr**, *tir, tür, n.* the old Norse war-god. [O.N. *Tȳr*; O.E. *Tiw*; cf. **Tuesday.**]

**tyrant**, *ti'rənt, obs.* **tyran**, *ti'ran, n.* in the orig. Greek sense, an absolute ruler, or one whose power has not been constitutionally arrived at: now usu. a ruler who uses his power arbitrarily and oppressively: an oppressor: a bully: a tyrant-bird.—*v.t.* and *v.i.* (*obs.*) **ty'ran(ne),** **ty'rant.**—*n.* **tyr'anness,** a female tyrant.—*adjs.* **tyrannic** (*ti-ran'ik*; sometimes *ti-*), **-al.**—*adv.* **tyrann'ically.**—*n.* **tyrann'icalness.**—*adj.* **tyrannici'dal.**—*n.* **tyrann'icide,** the killing or the killer of a tyrant.—*n.pl.* **Tyrann'idae,** the tyrant-bird family.—*n.* **tyrannis** (*ti-ran'is*; Gr.), a régime illegally set up.—*v.i.* **tyrannise, -ize** (*tir'*), to act as a tyrant: esp. to rule with oppressive severity. —*v.t.* to act the tyrant to.—*adj.* **tyrannous** (*tir'*), despotic: domineering: overpowering: oppressive.—*adv.* **tyr'annously.**—*n.* **tyranny** (*tir'*), absolute or illegally established power: the government or authority of a tyrant: absolute power cruelly administered: oppression: cruelty: harshness.—**ty'rant-bird, ty'rant-fly'catcher,** any member of an American family of birds akin to the pittas and cotingas. [Gr. *tyrannos*, partly through O.Fr. *tirant* (Fr. *tyran*) and L. *tyrannus.*]

**tyre.** Usu. spelling of **tire** (2) in U.K.

**Tyrian**, *tir'i-ən, adj.* of Tyre: red or purple, like the dye formerly prepared at Tyre.—*n.* a native of Tyre.—**Tyrian cynosure,** the north star, a guide to Tyrian mariners.

**tyro.** See **tiro.**

**tyroglyphid**, *ti-rog'li-fid, n.* a mite of the genus **Tyrog'lyphus,** including the cheese-mite and the flour-mite. [Gr. *tyros*, cheese, *glyphein*, to carve.]

**Tyrolese**, *tir-ə-lēz', adj.* relating to *Tyrol* (Tirol), or to its people.—*n.* a native of Tyrol.—*n.* and *adj.* **Tyrolè'an** (or *tir-ō'li-ən*).—*n.* **Tyrolienne** (*ti-rō-li-en'*), a Tyrolese peasants' dance, song, or tune with yodelling.

**Tyronensian.** See **Tironensian.**

**tyrosine**, *ti'rō-sēn, n.* an amino-acid formed by decomposition of proteins, first got from cheese. [Gr. *tyros*, cheese.]

**Tyrrhenian**, *ti-rē'ni-ən, n.* and *adj.* Etruscan.— Also **Tyrrhēne'.**—**Tyrrhenian Sea,** that part of the Mediterranean between Tuscany and Sardinia and Corsica. [Gr. *Tyrrhēnia*, Etruria.]

**Tyrtaean**, *tər-tē'ən, adj.* of or pertaining to *Tyrtaeus* (Gr. *Tyrtaios*), a Greek martial poet of the 7th century B.C.

**tzar.** See **tsar.**

**tzigany**, *tsig'ä-ni, -ə-ni, -ny', n.* a Hungarian gypsy. —Also *adj.*—Also **tsigane** (*tsi-gän'*). [Hung. *cigány*, gypsy; cf. It. *zingano, zingaro,* Ger. *zigeuner.*]

Neutral vowels in accented syllables: *el'ə-mənt*; for certain sounds in foreign words, see p. viii

# U

**U, u, ū, n.** the twenty-first letter in our alphabet, derived from V, a form of Y which the Romans borrowed from the Greeks. From V, the lapidary and capital form, the uncial and cursive forms U and *u* were developed, gradually V (used until modern times initially) becoming appropriated as the symbol for the consonant sound (see V) and the medial form *u* as the symbol for the vowel. In mod. English the vowel has the sounds exemplified in *rule, put, but,* and the diphthongal sound that serves as the name of the letter.—*adj. (cap.*; of words, phrases, customs, etc.) ordinarily used by, found in, the upper classes.—*adj.* **non′-U,** not so used or found (U for *upper* class).—**U′-boat,** a German submarine (Ger. *u*ntersee*boot*); **U′-bolt, U′-trap, U′-tube,** a bolt, drain-trap, tube, bent like the letter U.—*adj.* **U′-shaped.**—**U′-turn,** a turn made by a vehicle which reverses its direction of travel, crossing into the oncoming traffic on the other side of the road.

**uberous,** *ū′bə-rəs, adj.* yielding abundance of milk: abounding.—*n.* **u′berty,** fruitfulness: abundant productiveness. [L. *über,* udder, fruitfulness.]

**ubermensch,** *ü′bər-mensh,* (Ger.) a superman.

**uberrima fides,** *ū-ber′ə-mə fi′dēz, ōō-be-rē′ma fi′däs,* (L.) complete faith.

**ubiety,** *ū-bi′i-ti, n.* the state of being in a definite place, whereness: location. [L. *ubi,* where.]

**ubique,** *ū-bi′kwē, ōō-bē′kwe,* (L.) everywhere.

**ubiquity,** *ū-bik′wi-ti, n.* existence everywhere at the same time: omnipresence.—*adj.* **ubiquā′rian,** found everywhere: ubiquitous.—*n.* **ubiquitā′rian,** one who believes that Christ's body is everywhere, in the Eucharist as elsewhere.—Also *adj.*—*adjs.* **ubiq′uitary,** being everywhere at once; **ubiq′uitous,** to be found everywhere.—*adv.* **ubiq′uitously.** [L. *ubīque,* everywhere—*ubi,* where.]

**ubi supra,** *ū′bī sōō′prə, ōō′bē sōō′prä,* (L.) where mentioned above.

**udal,** *ū′dl, (Orkney* and *Shetland) adj.* allodial: without feudal superior.—*n.* an estate so held.—*n.* **u′daller,** a holder of such an estate. [O.N. *ōthal.*]

**udder,** *ud′ər, n.* the organ containing the mammary glands of the cow, mare, etc.: a dug or teat.—*adjs.* **udd′ered; udd′erful,** with full udder; **udd′erless,** unsuckled. [O.E. *ūder;* Ger. *euter,* L. *über,* Gr. *outhar.*]

**udo,** *ōō′dō, n.* a Japanese species of *Aralia* with edible shoots. [Jap.]

**udometer,** *ū-dom′i-tər, n.* a name for a raingauge, never included in the official glossary of British meteorological terms.—*adj.* **udomet′ric.** [Through Fr.—L. *ūdus,* wet, Gr. *metron,* a measure.]

**uds,** *udz,* in oaths, for God's, or for God save (as in *uds my life*).

**ufology,** *ōō-fol′ə-ji, n.* study of unidentified flying objects, such as flying saucers.—*n.* **ufol′ogist.** [Formed from initials U F O, and **-logy.**]

**ugh,** *uhh, interj.* an exclamation of repugnance.—*n.* used as a representation of a cough or grunt.

**ugli,** *ug′li, n.* a cross between the grapefruit and the tangerine, or its fruit. [ugly; from the fruit's unprepossessing appearance.]

**ugly,** *ug′li, adj.* frightful, horrible (*obs.*): offensive to the sight or other sense, or to refined taste or moral feeling: ill-natured: threatening: disquieting: suggesting suspicion of evil.—*n.* an ugly person (*coll.*): a shade attached to a lady's hat (mid-19th-cent.).—*v.t. (rare)* to make ugly.—*v.t.* **ug** (*obs.* or *dial.* in all meanings), to excite loathing in: to loathe.—*v.i.* to feel loathing.—*n.* **uglificā′tion.**—*v.t.* **ug′lify,** to make ugly.—*adv.* **ug′lily.**—*n.* **ug′liness.**—*adj.* **ug′some,** disgusting: hideous.—*n.* **ug′someness.**—**ugly customer,** a dangerous antagonist; **ugly duckling,** a despised member of a family or group who later proves the most successful; **ugly man,** an actual garrotter, distinguished from his confederates. [O.N. *uggligr,* frightful, *uggr,* fear.]

**Ugrian,** *ū′gri-ən, ōō′, adj.* of that division of the Finno-Ugrian languages and peoples that includes the Magyars, Ostyaks, and Voguls.—Also *n.*—*adjs.* **U′gric; U′gro-Finn′ic,** Finno-Ugrian.

**uh-huh,** *u′hu, m′hm,* a sound used in place of 'yes'.

**uhlan,** *ōō′län, ū′, n.* a light cavalryman in semioriental uniform: a Prussian lancer. [Ger. *uhlan*—Polish *ulan,* orig. a light Tatar horseman—Turk, *oglän,* a young man.]

**uhuru,** *ōō-hōō-rōō, n.* freedom (e.g. from slavery): national independence. [Swahili—*huru,* free.]

**uinta(h)ite,** *ū-int′ä-it, n.* a natural tarlike asphalt found in the *Uinta* valley, Utah.—*n.* **Uintathē′rium,** a gigantic Eocene fossil ungulate from Uinta County, Wyoming.

**uitlander,** *æ′, ä′it-land-ər* (chiefly *hist.*) *n.* a foreigner (orig. a British person in the Transvaal or Orange Free State). [Du. equivalent of **outlander.**]

**ukase,** *ū-kāz′, -kās′, n.* an edict with force of law in Tsarist Russia: an edict with bearing on existing legislation issued by the Presidium of the Supreme Soviet and subject to later ratification by the Supreme Soviet: any arbitrary decree from any source. [Russ. *ukaz.*]

**ukelele.** Common spelling of ukulele.

**Ukrainian,** *ū-krān′i-ən, ōō-krin′i-ən, n.* a native or citizen of (*the*) *Ukraine,* a republic of the U.S.S.R., a rich agricultural region in S.W. Russia: its language, Ruthenian.—Also *adj.*

**ukulele,** *ū-kə-lā′li, ōō-kōō-lä′lä, n.* a small, usually four-stringed, guitar. [Hawaiian, flea, from the movement of the fingers.]

**ulcer,** *ul′sər, n.* an open sore discharging pus: a continuing source of evil, an unsound element (*fig.*).—*v.t.* and *v.i.* to ulcerate.—*v.i.* **ul′cerate,** to form an ulcer.—*v.t.* to cause an ulcer in: to affect with insidious corruption.—*n.* **ulcerā′tion.**—*adjs.* **ul′cerătive; ul′cered; ul′cerous.**—*adv.* **ul′cerously.**—*n.* **ul′cerousness.**—**ulcerative dermal necrosis,** a fungus disease of salmon. [L. *ulcus, ulcēris;* cf. Gr. *helkos.*]

**ule, hule,** *ōō′lä, n.* a Central American rubber tree (*Castilloa*): its crude rubber. [Sp. *hule*—Nahuatl *ulli.*]

**ulema,** *ōō′li-ma, n.* the body of professional theologians, expounders of the law, in a Mohammedan country. [Ar. *'ulema,* pl. of *'ālim,* learned.]

**Ulex,** *ū′leks, n.* the gorse genus. [L. *ūlex, -icis,* a kind of rosemary or the like.]

**ulicon, ulichon, ulikon,** *ōō′li-kən.* Same as eulachon.

**uliginous,** *ū-lij′i-nəs, adj.* slimy: oozy: swampy: growing in swampy places. [L. *ūliginōsus*—*ūligō, -inis,* moisture.]

**ulitis**, *ū-lī′tis*, *n.* inflammation of the gums. [Gr. *oula*, gums, *-itis*.]

**ullage**, *ul′ij*, *n.* the quantity a vessel lacks of being full: loss by evaporation or leakage: dregs (*slang*).—*v.t.* to reckon the ullage of: to affect with ullage: to fill up: to draw off a little from.—*n.* ull′ing, the making good of ullage. [A.Fr. *ulliage*, O.Fr. *eullage—œiller*, to fill up.]

**Ulmus**, *ul′mɔs*, *n.* the elm genus, giving name to the family Ulmā′ceae, akin to the nettles.—*adj.* **ulmā′ceous**, of or like an elm: of its family.—*n.* **ul′min**, a gummy exudation from elms and other trees. [L. *ulmus*, elm.]

**ulna**, *ul′nɔ*, *n.* the inner and larger of the two bones of the forearm:—*pl.* **ul′nae** (*-nē*).—*adj.* **ul′nar**.—*n.* **ulnā′re**, the bone of the carpus opposite the ulna:—*pl.* **ulnā′ria**. [L. *ulna*, elbow, arm; cf. **ell**, and Gr. *ōlenē*, forearm.]

**ulosis**, *ū-lō′sis*, *n.* formation of a scar. [Gr. *oulōsis—oulē*, a scar.]

**Ulothrix**, *ū′lō-thriks*, *n.* a genus of filamentous algae, giving name to the Ulotrichales (*ū-lot-ri-kā′lēz*), an order of multicellular uninucleate green algae, marine and freshwater.—*adj.* **ulotrichous** (*ū-lot′ri-kɔs*), woolly-haired.—*n.* **ulot′-richy** (*-ki*), woolly-hairedness. [Gr. *oulos*, woolly, *thrix*, *trichos*, hair.]

**ulster**, *ul′star*, *n.* a long loose overcoat.—*adj.* **ul′stered**, wearing an ulster.—*n.* **ulsterette′**, a light ulster. [First made in *Ulster*, Ireland.]

**ulterior**, *ul-tē′ri-ɔr*, *adj.* on the further side: beyond: in the future: remoter: (of e.g. motive) beyond what is avowed or apparent.—*adv.* **ulte′riorly**. [L. *ulterior—ultrā* (adv. and prep.), *uls* (prep.), beyond.]

**ultima ratio**, *ul′ta-mɔ rä′shē-ō, ōōl′ti-ma rä′ti-ō*, (L.) the last argument.—**ultima ratio regum** (*rē′gɔm, rä′gōōm*), the last argument of kings (war; once inscribed on French cannon).

**ultimate**, *ul′ti-māt, -mit, adj.* furthest: last: final: limiting.—*n.* a final point: a fundamental.—*n.* **ul′timacy** (*-mɔ-si*).—*adv.* **ul′timately**.—*n.* **ultimā′tum**, final terms: a last offer or demand: a last word: a final point: something fundamental:—*pl.* **ultimā′ta**.—*adj.* **ul′timo** (*contr.* ult.), in the last (month).—*n.* **ultimogeniture** (*-jen′*), succession of the youngest, as in borough-English (*q.v.*)—opp. to *primogeniture*.—the ultimate deterrent, the hydrogen bomb. [L. *ultimus*, last.]

**ultimus haeres**, *ul′ti-mɔs hē′rēz, ōōl′ti-mōōs hi′räs*, (L.) in law, the crown or the state, which succeeds to the property of those who die intestate, or without next of kin; **ultimus Romanorum** (*rō-mɔn-ōr′ɔm, -ōr′, -ōōm*), last of the Romans.

**ultion**, *ul′shɔn*, *n.* revenge: avengement. [L. *ultiō, -ōnis.*]

**Ultonian**, *ul-tō′ni-ɔn*, *adj.* of Ulster.—*n.* an Ulsterman. [L.L. *Ultōnia*, Ulster; O.Ir. *Ult-*, stem of *Ulaid*, Ulster.]

**ultra-**, *ul′trɔ-, pfx.* (1) beyond in place, position (as ultra-Neptunian, beyond the planet Neptune): (2) beyond the limit, range, etc., of (as ultra-microscopic): (3) beyond the ordinary, or excessive(ly) (as ul′tra-Conserv′ative, ul′tra-Conserv′atism, ul′tra-fash′ionable, ul′tra-mod′ern, ul′tra-Prot′estant).—*adj.* **ul′tra**, extreme, esp. in royalism, fashion, or religious or political opinion.—*n.* an extremist.—*ns.* **ultraism** (*ul′trɔ-izm*), extreme principle(s), opinion(s), or measure(s): an attempt to pass beyond the limits of the known; **ul′traist**. [L. *ultrā*, beyond.]

**ultrabasic**, *ul-trɔ-bā′sik*, (*petr.*) *adj.* extremely basic, very poor in silica. [Pfx. ultra- (3).]

**ultracentrifuge**, *ul-trɔ-sen′tri-fūj*, *n.* a very fast-running type of centrifuge. [Pfx. ultra- (2).]

**ultracrepidate**, *ul-trɔ-krep′i-dāt*, *v.i.* to criticise beyond the sphere of one's knowledge.—*n.* and *adj.* **ultracrepidā′rian**. [From Apelles' answer to the cobbler who went on from criticising the

sandals in a picture to finding fault with the leg, *nē sūtor ultrā crepidam*, the cobbler must not go beyond the sandal.]

**ultra-high**, *ul-trɔ-hī′*, *adj.* very high.—**ultra-high frequency** (see frequency). [Pfx. ultra- (3).]

**ultramarine**, *ul-trɔ-mɔ-rēn′*, *adj.* overseas: from overseas: deep-blue.—*n.* a deep-blue pigment, orig. made from lapis-lazuli brought from beyond the sea: its colour. [L. *ultrā*, beyond, *marīnus*, marine.]

**ultramicro-**, *ul-trɔ-mī-krō-*, smaller than, dealing with smaller quantities than, micro-, e.g. *n.* **ultramicrochem′istry**, chemistry concerned with the minutest of quantities, sometimes no greater than one-millionth of a gram.

**ultramicroscope**, *ul-trɔ-mī′krɔ-skōp*, *n.* a microscope with strong illumination from the side, whereby the presence of ultramicroscopic objects can be observed through the scattering of light from them.—*adj.* **ultramicroscopic** (*-skop′ik*), too small to be visible under the ordinary microscope: pertaining to ultramicroscopy.—*n.* **ultramicroscopy** (*-kros′kɔ-pi*). [Pfx. ultra- (2).]

**ultramicrotome**, *ul′trɔ-mī′krɔ-tōm*, *n.* a microtome for cutting ultra-thin sections for examination with the electron microscope. [Pfx. ultra- (2).]

**ultramontane**, *ul-trɔ-mon′tān*, *adj.* beyond the mountains (i.e. the Alps): orig. used in Italy of the French, Germans, etc.; afterwards applied by the northern nations to the Italians: hence, extreme in favouring the Pope's supremacy.—*ns.* **ultramon′tanism** (*-tɔn-izm*); **ultramon′tanist**. [L. *ultra*, beyond, *montānus—mōns, montis*, a mountain.]

**ultramundane**, *ul-trɔ-mun′dān*, *adj.* beyond the world, or beyond the limits of our system. [Pfx. ultra- (1).]

**ultra-rapid**, *ul-trɔ-rap′id*, *adj.* of a motion-picture film, exposed at much greater speed than that at which it is to be exhibited, giving a slow-motion picture. [Pfx. ultra- (3).]

**ultrared**, *ul′trɔ-red′*, *adj.* infra-red. [Pfx. ultra- (1).]

**ultrasensual**, *ul′trɔ-sen′sū-ɔl, -shōō-ɔl, adj.* beyond the reach of the senses. [Pfx. ultra- (2).]

**ultrashort**, *ul′trɔ-shört′*, *adj.* (of electromagnetic waves) of less than ten metres' wavelength. [Pfx. ultra- (3).]

**ultrasonic**, *ul-trɔ-son′ik*, *adj.* pertaining to, or (of instrument or process) using, vibrations of the same nature as audible sound waves but of greater frequency.—*n.* **ultrasonics**, study of such vibrations, used medically for diagnostic and therapeutic purposes.—**ultrasonic communication**, underwater communication using ultrasonic waves. [Pfx. ultra- (2).]

**ultrasound**, *ul-trɔ-sownd′*, *n.* sound vibrations too rapid to be audible. [Pfx. ultra- (2).]

**ultrastructure**, *ul′trɔ-struk′chɔr*, *n.* the ultimate structure of protoplasm at a lower level than can be examined microscopically. [Pfx. ultra- (2).]

**ultra-tropical**, *ul′trɔ-trop′ik-ɔl*, *adj.* beyond the tropics: hotter than the tropics. [Pfx. ultra- (1), (3).]

**ultraviolet**, *ul-trɔ-vī′ɔ-lit*, *adj.* beyond the violet end of the visible spectrum: pertaining to, or using, radiations of wavelengths less than those of visible light.—**ultraviolet star**, one of a class of invisible stars giving out intense ultraviolet radiation. [Pfx. ultra- (1).]

**ultra vires**, *ul′trɔ vī′rēz, ōōl′trä wē′räs*, (L.) beyond one's powers or authority.

**ultra-virtuous**, *ul′trɔ-vûr′tū-ɔs, adj.* prudish. [Pfx. ultra- (3).]

**ultroneous**, *ul-trō′ni-ɔs, adj.* spontaneous, voluntary.—*adv.* **ultrō′neously**.—*n.* **ultrō′neousness**. [L. *ultrōneus—ultrō*, spontaneously.]

**ululate**, *ūl′ū-lāt*, also *ul′*, *v.i.* to hoot or screech.—*adj.* **ul′ulant**.—*n.* **ululā′tion**, howling, wailing. [L. *ūlūlāre, -ātum*, to hoot.]

**ulyie, ulzie,** *ül'(y)i,* obs. Scots forms of oil.

**umbel,** *um'bəl, n.* a flat-topped inflorescence in which the flower stalks all spring from about the same point in an axis (which in a **compound umbel** is grouped in the same way with other axes).—*adjs.* **um'bellate, -d,** constituting an umbel: having umbels.—*adv.* **um'bellately.**—*n.* **umbellifer** (*um-bel'i-fər*), any plant of the Umbelliferae.—*n.pl.* **Umbellif'erae,** the carrot and hemlock family of plants with (usu. compound) umbels, schizocarpic fruit, leaves with sheathing bases.—*adj.* **umbellif'erous.**—*n.* **um'bellule,** a partial umbel. [L. *umbella,* a sunshade, dim. of *umbra,* a shade.]

**umber,** *um'bər, n.* a brown earthy mineral (hydrated oxides of iron and manganese) used as a pigment.—*v.t.* to colour with umber.— brown like umber.—*adjs.* **um'bered, um'bery.**— **um'ber-bird,** the umbrette. [It. *terra d'ombra,* shadow earth, or poss. Umbrian earth.]

**umber,** *um'bər, n.* the grayling. [L. *umbra.*]

**umbilicus,** *um-bil'i-kəs, um-bi-li'kəs, n.* the navel: a depression at the axial base of a spiral shell: a small depression.—*adjs.* **umbilical** (*-bil'*; sometimes *-bi-li'*); **umbil'icate,** navel-like: having a depression like a navel.—**umbilical cord,** the navel-string: an electrical cable or other servicing line attached to a rocket vehicle or spacecraft during preparations for launch: the lifeline of an astronaut outside his vehicle in space by which he receives air and communicates with the vehicle: any similar connection of fundamental importance. [L. *umbilicus,* the navel; Gr. *omphalos.*]

**umbles,** *um'blz, n.pl.* entrails (liver, heart, etc.), esp. of a deer.—Also **hum'bles, num'bles.**— **um'ble-pie'** (see humble-pie). [O.Fr. *nombles,* from *lomble,* loin—L. *lumbulus,* dim. of *lumbus,* loin.]

**umbo,** *um'bō, n.* the boss of a shield: a knob: the protuberant oldest part of a bivalve shell: a knob on a toadstool cap:—*pl.* **umbō'nēs, um'bos.**—*adjs.* **um'bonal** (*-bən-al*); **um'bonate** (*bot.*), having a central boss.—*n.* **umbonā'tion.** [L. *umbō, -ōnis.*]

**umbra,** *um'brə, n.* a shadow: the darker part of the shadow or dark inner cone projected in an eclipse (*astron.*): the darker part of a spot: a shade or ghost: an uninvited guest who comes with an invited.—*adjs.* **umbraculate** (*um-brak'ū-lāt*), overshadowed by an umbraculum; **umbrac'uliform,** umbrella-shaped.—*n.* **umbrac'ulum,** an umbrella-shaped structure.—*adjs.* **um'bral,** of an umbra; **um'brāted** (*her.*), faintly traced; **umbratic** (*-brat'*; *rare*), *-al,* **umbratile** (*um'brə-til, -til*), **umbratilous** (*-brat'i-ləs*), shadowy: shaded: shade-giving: indoor: secluded; **umbrif'erous,** shade-giving; **umbrose** (*-brōs'*), shade-giving: dusky; **um'brous,** shaded. [L. *umbra,* shade, shadow, dim. *umbrāculum,* adj. *umbrātilis.*]

**umbrage,** *um'brij, n.* shade, shadow: that which casts a shade: a shelter: a shadowy appearance: pretext, colour: inkling: suspicion of injury: offence.—*v.t.* to shade: to offend.—*adj.* **umbrā'geous,** shady or forming a shade.—*adv.* **umbrā'geously.**—*n.* **umbrā'geousness.** [Fr. *ombrage*— L. *umbrāticum* (neut. adj.)—*umbra,* a shadow.]

**umbre,** *um'bər.* See umbrette.

**umbrella,** *um-brel'ə, n.* a portable shelter against sun, rain, etc., now usu. with a sliding framework of ribs on a stick: anything of similar form, as a jellyfish disk: a protection, a general cover (as a *fig.*): a cover of fighter aircraft for ground forces (*n.il.*).—Also formerly **ombrell'a,** **umbrell'o.**—*adjs.* **umbrella,** covering many or a variety of things; **umbrell'aed, umbrell'a'd,** with an umbrella.—**umbrell'a-ant,** the sauba ant; **umbrell'a-bird,** any of a number of birds of the *Cotinga* genus with umbrella-like crest and a lappet attached to the throat or breast; **umbrell'a-fir,** a Japanese conifer with radiating tufts of needles; **umbrell'a-stand,** a rack or receptacle for closed umbrellas and walking-sticks; **umbrell'a-tree,** a tree of any kind with leaves or branches arranged umbrella-wise, esp. a small magnolia. [It. *ombrella, ombrello*— *ombra,* a shade—L. *umbra.*]

**umbrette,** *um-bret', n.* the hammerkop, a brown African bird between storks and herons, remarkable for its huge nest.—Also **um'bre** (*-bər*), **umber-bird.** [Fr. *ombrette*—*ombre,* umber.]

**Umbrian,** *um'bri-ən, adj.* of Umbria, in central Italy.—*n.* a native thereof: the old language, Iguvine, akin to Oscan.

**umbriere,** *um'bri-ēr,* (*Spens.*) *n.* a visor.—Also **um'brere, um'bril, um'brel.** [O.Fr. *ombriere, ombrel,* shade.]

**umiak, oomia**(c)**k,** *ōō'mi-ak, ōōm'yak, n.* an open skin boat, manned by women. [Eskimo.]

**umlaut,** *ōōm'lowt, n.* a vowel-change brought about by a vowel or semivowel (esp. i, j) in the following syllable: loosely, the two dots placed over a letter representing an umlauted vowel in German.—*v.t.* to bring about umlaut in. [Ger., —*um,* around, *laut,* sound.]

**umph,** *hm*(*h*). Same as humph.

**umpire,** *um'pīr, n.* a third person called in to decide a dispute or a deadlock: an arbitrator: an impartial person chosen to supervise the game, enforce the rules, and decide disputes (*cricket,* etc.).—Also *v.i.* and *v.t.*—*ns.* **um'pirage, um'pireship.** [M.E. *noumpere, oumper*—O.Fr. *nomper*—*non-,* not, *per, pair,* peer, equal.]

**umpteen,** *um*(*p*)*'tēn,* **umpty,** *um*(*p*)*'ti,* (*slang*) *adjs.* of an indefinite number.—*adjs.* **ump'teenth, ump'tieth,** the *n*th. [*Umpty* in Morse, a dash, from its sound on a telegraph key.]

**umquhile,** *um'hwīl, adv.* and *adj.* a Scots form of **um'while,** formerly, late, whilom. [O.E. *ymb*(*e*) *hwile,* about or at a time.]

**un,** *'un, un, ən,* (*dial.*) *pron.* for one: also for him. [O.E. accus. *hine.*]

*There is hardly a limit to words with prefix* **un-,** *and only a selection is given below. Words from* **unabashed** *to* **unzoned** *are listed continuously, either in the text or at the foot of the page, and words beginning with* **un-** *in which* **un-** *is not a prefix follow after these.*

**un-,** *un-, pfx.* (1) meaning 'not' (in many cases, the resultant word is more than a mere negation; it has a positive force; e.g. **unkind** usu. means 'cruel' rather than just 'not kind'): (2) indicating a reversal of process, removal, or deprivation: (3) merely emphasizing reversal or deprivation already expressed by the simple word, as in **unbare, unloose;** sometimes (in *Shakespeare* and *Milton*) added to a present participle with a passive meaning. The meaning is often ambiguous, esp. in participial adjs. (Partly O.E. *un-,* neg.; cf. Ger. *un-,* L. *in-,* Gr. *an-, a-;* partly O.E. *on-* (or *un-*), the unstressed form of *and-;* cf. Ger. *ent-,* Gr. *anti,* against).— *adjs.* **unaba'ted,** not made less in degree; **una'ble,** not able: not having sufficient strength, power,

---

| | | |
|---|---|---|
| **unabashed',** *adj.* un- (1). | **unab'rogated,** *adj.* un- (1). | **unaccept'able,** *adj.* un- (1). |
| **unabbre'viated,** *adj.* un- (1). | **unabsolved',** *adj.* un- (1). | **unaccept'ableness,** *n.* un- (1). |
| **unabol'ished,** *adj.* un- (1). | **unacadem'ic,** *adj.* un- (1). | **unaccept'ance,** *n.* un- (1). |
| **unabridged',** *adj.* un- (1). | | |

*Words beginning with pfx.* **un-** *are listed first* (pp. 1462 ff.); *other* UN- *words follow* (pp. 1484 ff.).

*fāte, fär; mē, hûr* (her); *mīne, mōte, fŏr; mūte, mōōn, fŏŏt; dhen* (then) or skill (to do): weak, incompetent (*arch*.): ineffectual (*arch*.); **unaccent′ed**, without accent or stress in pronunciation: not marked with an accent; **unaccomm′odated**, unprovided; **unaccomm′odating**, not compliant; **unaccom′panied**, not accompanied, escorted, or attended: having no instrumental accompaniment (*mus*.); **unaccom′plished**, not achieved: lacking accomplishments.—*ns*. **unaccom′plishment**, the fact of not being achieved; **unaccountabil′ity**.—*adj*. **unaccount′able**, difficult or impossible to explain: not answerable (to a higher authority): (of person) puzzling in character.—*n*. **unaccount′ableness**.—*adv*. **unaccount′ably**, inexplicably.—*adjs*. **unaccount′ed for**; **unaccus′tomed**, not customary: not habituated.—*n*. **unaccus′tomedness**.—*adj*. **unacknowl′edged**, not acknowledged, recognised, confessed, or noticed.—*n*. **unacquaint′ance**, want of acquaintance (often with *with*).—*adj*. **unacquaint′ed** (*Scot.* **unacquaint′**), not on a footing of acquaintance: ignorant of (with *with*, or, *Swift*, *in*): uninformed: unknown (*obs*.): unusual (*Spens*.).—*n*. **unacquaint′edness**.—*adjs*. **unact′able**, unfit for the stage; **unact′ed**, not performed; **unac′tive**, inactive; **unadopted**, not adopted: (unadopted road, a road for the repairing, maintenance, etc., of which the Local Authority is not responsible); **unadul′terate, -d**, unmixed, pure, genuine; **unadvis′able**, inadvisable: not prepared to accept advice.—*n*. **unadvis′ableness**.—*adv*. **unadvis′ably**.—*adj*. **unadvised′**, not advised: without advice: not prudent or discreet: ill-judged: inadvertent (*Spens*.).—*adv*. **unadvis′edly**.—*n*. **unadvis′edness**.—*adj*. **unaffect′ed**, not affected or influenced: untouched by emotion: without affectation: not assumed: plain: real: sincere.—*adv*. **unaffect′edly**.—*n*. **unaffect′edness**.—*adjs*. **unaffect′ing**; **unagree′able**, disagreeable: inconsistent (with): discordant; **unāk′ing** (*Shak*.), unaching; **unā′lienable**, inalienable.—*adv*. **una′lienably**.—*adjs*. **unalive′**, not fully aware of (with *to*): lacking in vitality; **unallayed′**, unmixed, unqualified: not diminished, unquenched; **unallied′**, not akin: without allies; **unalloyed′**, not alloyed or mixed (*lit*. and *fig*.); **un-Amer′ican,**

not in accordance with American character, ideas, feeling, or traditions: disloyal, against American interests.—*vs.t*. **un-Amer′icanise, -ize**, to make un-American; **unanch′or**, to loose from anchorage.—*v.i*. to become loose or unattached: to weigh anchor.—*adjs*. **unaneled** (*un-ə-nēld′*; *Shak*., **unnaneld**), without extreme unction; **unan′imated**, not alive: not animated or lively: not actuated (by); **unannealed′**, not annealed (but see also **unaneled**); **unan′swerable**, impossible to answer: not to be refuted, conclusive.—*n*. **unan′swerableness**.—*adv*. **unan′swerably**.—*adj*. **unan′swered**, not answered: unrequited; **unappeal′able**, not admitting of an appeal to a higher court, conclusive, final; **unapplaus′ive**, not applauding; **unappoint′ed**, not appointed: not equipped; **uaapprehend′ed**; **unapprehen′sible**; **unapprehen′sive**, without understanding: without fear.—*n*. **unapprehen′siveness**.—*adjs*. **unapprised′**, not informed; **unapproach′able**, out of reach, inaccessible: stand-offish: inaccessible to advances or intimacy: beyond rivalry.—*n*. **unapproach′ableness**.—*adv*. **unapproach′ably**.—*adjs*. **unapproached′**; **unappro′priate**, unappropriated: inappropriate; **unappro′priated**, not taken possession of: not applied to some purpose: not granted to any person, corporation, etc.; **unapproved′**, untested (*obs*.): unproved: unsanctioned: not approved of; **unapprov′ing**.—*adv*. **unapprov′ingly**.—*adj*. **unapt′**, unfitted: unsuitable: not readily inclined or accustomed (to): lacking in aptitude, slow.—*adv*. **unapt′ly**.—*n*. **unapt′ness**.—*adjs*. **unar′gued** (*Milt*.), undisputed: not debated.—*v.t*. **unarm′**, to help to put off armour: to deprive of arms, to disarm: to make harmless.—*v.i*. to take off one's armour.—*adjs*. **unarmed′**, without weapons: defenceless: unprotected: unaided or without accessory apparatus; **unar′moured**, without armour, armourplating; **unart′ful**, artless, genuine: inartistic: unskilful.—*adv*. **unart′fully**.—*adjs*. **unartic′ulate**, not articulate, **unartic′ulated**, not jointed: not in distinct syllables; **unartist′ic**, not coming within the sphere of art: not concerned with art: inartistic; **unasked′**, not asked: not asked for: uninvited; **unassayed′**, not attempted:

---

**unaccred′ited**, *adj*. un- (1).
**unaccus′able**, *adj*. un- (1).
**unaccus′ably**, *adv*. un- (1).
**unaccused′**, *adj*. un- (1).
**unachiev′able**, *adj*. un- (1).
**unach′ing**, *adj*. un- (1).
**unac′tuated**, *adj*. un- (1).
**unadapt′able**, *adj*. un- (1).
**unadapt′ed**, *adj*. un- (1).
**unaddressed′**, *adj*. un- (1).
**unadjust′ed**, *adj*. un- (1).
**unadmired′**, *adj*. un- (1).
**unadmir′ing**, *adj*. un- (1).
**unadmitt′ed**, *adj*. un- (1).
**unadmon′ished**, *adj*. un- (1).
**unadored′**, *adj*. un- (1).
**unadorned′**, *adj*. un- (1).
**unadvent′urous** (*Milt*.
  **unadvent′rous**), *adj*. un- (1).
**unafraid′**, *adj*. un- (1).
**unaid′able**, *adj*. un- (1).
**unaid′ed**, *adj*. un- (1).
**unaimed′**, *adj*. un- (1).
**unaired′**, *adj*. un- (1).
**unallott′ed**, *adj*. un- (1).
**unallow′able**, *adj*. un- (1).
**unal′terable**, *adj*. un- (1).
**unal′terableness**, *n*. un- (1).
**unal′terably**, *adv*. un- (1).
**unal′tered**, *adj*. un- (1).
**unal′tering**, *adj*. un- (1).

**unambig′uous**, *adj*. un- (1).
**unambig′uously**, *adv*. un- (1).
**unambi′tious**, *adj*. un- (1).
**unambi′tiously**, *adv*. un- (1).
**uname′nable**, *adj*. un- (1).
**unamend′able**, *adj*. un- (1).
**unamend′ed**, *adj*. un- (1).
**unamerced′**, *adj*. un- (1).
**una′miable**, *adj*. un- (1).
**una′miableness**, *n*. un- (1).
**unamu′sable**, *adj*. un- (1).
**unamused′**, *adj*. un- (1).
**unamu′sing**, *adj*. un- (1).
**unamu′singly**, *adv*. un- (1).
**unanalys′able, -z-**, *adj*. un- (1).
**unan′alysed, -z-**, *adj*. un- (1).
**unanalyt′ic, -al**, *adjs*. un- (1).
**unanch′ored**, *adj*. un- (1).
**unann′otated**, *adj*. un- (1).
**unannounced′**, *adj*. un- (1).
**unanx′ious**, *adj*. un- (1).
**unapostol′ic, -al**, *adjs*. un- (1).
**unapostol′ically**, *adv*. un- (1).
**unappalled′**, *adj*. un- (1).
**unappar′el**, *v.t*. un- (2).
**unappar′elled**, *adj*. un- (1).
**unappar′ent**, *adj*. un- (1).
**unappeas′able**, *adj*. un- (1).
**unappeased′**, *adj*. un- (1).
**unapp′etising**, *adj*. un- (1).

**unapplied′**, *adj*. un- (1).
**unappre′ciated**, *adj*. un- (1).
**unappre′ciative**, *adj*. un- (1).
**unar′guable**, *adj*. un- (1).
**unaris′en**, *adj*. un- (1).
**unarranged′**, *adj*. un- (1).
**unartifi′cial**, *adj*. un- (1).
**unartifi′cially**, *adv*. un- (1).
**unart′istlike**, *adj*. un- (1).
**unascend′able, -ible**, *adjs*. un- (1).
**unascend′ed**, *adj*. un- (1).
**unascertain′able**, *adj*. un- (1).
**unascertained′**, *adj*. un- (1).
**unashamed′**, *adj*. un- (1).
**unasham′edly**, *adv*. un- (1).
**unas′pirated**, *adj*. un- (1).
**unaspir′ing**, *adj*. un- (1).
**unaspir′ingly**, *adv*. un- (1).
**unaspir′ingness**, *n*. un- (1).
**unassail′able**, *adj*. un- (1).
**unassailed′**, *adj*. un- (1).
**unasser′tive**, *adj*. un- (1).
**unassign′able**, *adj*. un- (1).
**unassigned′**, *adj*. un- (1).
**unassim′ilable**, *adj*. un- (1).
**unassim′ilated**, *adj*. un- (1).
**unassist′ed**, *adj*. un- (1).
**unassist′edly**, *adv*. un- (1).
**unassist′ing**, *adj*. un- (1).
**unassō′ciated**, *adj*. un- (1).
**unassuage′able**, *adj*. un- (1).

---

*Words beginning with pfx.* **un-** *are listed first* (pp. 1462 ff.); *other* UN- *words follow* (pp. 1484 ff.).

Neutral vowels in unaccented syllables: *el′ə-mənt*; for certain sounds in foreign words, see p. viii

untested; unassumed'; unassum'ing, making no assumption: unpretentious, modest.—*adv.* unassum'ingly.—*n.* unassum'ingness.—*adjs.* unassured', uncertain (of): doubtfully recognised (*Spens.*): insecure: lacking in self-assurance, diffident: not insured against loss; unaton'able, irreconcilable (*arch.*): that cannot be atoned for; unattached', not attached: detached: not arrested: not belonging to a club, party, college, diocese, department, regiment, etc.: not married or about to be; unattaint'ed, not legally attainted: unstained: not blemished by partiality (*Shak.*); unattempt'ed, not attempted: not made the subject of an attempt or attack; unattend'ed, not accompanied or attended: not attended to (*arch.*); unatten'tive, inattentive (the latter being the preferred form); unaugment'ed, not augmented: without the augment (*gram.*); unauspi'cious, inauspicious (*Shak.*); unavail'able, not available: of no avail (*arch.*). — *n.* unavail'ableness.— *adv.* unavail'-ably.—*adj.* unavail'ing, of no avail or effect, useless.—*n.* unavoidabil'ity.—*adj.* unavoid'able, not to be avoided: inevitable: not voidable (*law*).—*n.* unavoid'ableness.—*adv.* unavoid'ably. —*adjs.* unavoid'ed, not avoided: unavoidable, inevitable (*Shak.*); unaware', not aware: unwary (*Shelley*).—*adv.* unawares.—*n.* unaware'-ness.—*adv.* unawares', without being, or making, aware: without being perceived: unexpectedly. —*n.* in the phrase at unawares, unexpectedly, at a sudden disadvantage.

*Words with prefix* un- (*continued*).
*adjs.* unbacked', without a back: without backing or backers: unaided: not moved back: riderless: never yet ridden.—*v.t.* unbag', to let out of a bag.—*adj.* unbaked, not baked: immature.—*n.* unbal'ance, want of balance.—*v.t.* to throw off balance: to derange.—*adjs.* unbal'anced, not in a state of equipoise: without a counterpoise or compensation: without mental balance, erratic or deranged: (of, e.g. a view, judgment) not giving due weight to all features of the situation: not adjusted so as to show balance of debtor and creditor (*book-k.*); unball'asted, without ballast: unsteady, unstable, flighty.—*v.t.* unbar', to remove a bar from or of: to unfasten.—*v.i.* to become unbarred.—*adj.* unbarbed', without barb: without bard, caparison, or armour (so prob. in *Coriolanus*): uncropped, untrimmed.—*vs.t.* unbare', to bare, lay bare; unbark', to strip of bark.—*adjs.* unbarked', not deprived of bark: deprived of bark; unbash'ful, free from bashfulness: shameless (*Shak.*); unba'ted, unblunted (*Shak.*): undiminished.—*v.t.* (*obs.*) unbe', to cause not to

be.—*v.i.* to cease to be, or be non-existent (*Hardy*).—*v.t.* unbear', to free from the bearing-rein.—*adj.* unbear'able, intolerable.—*n.* unbear'-ableness.—*adv.* unbear'ably.—*adjs.* unbear'ing, barren; unbea'vered, without a beaver or hat: having the beaver of the helmet open; unbecom'ing, unsuitable: not suited to the wearer, or not showing her, him to advantage: (of behaviour, etc.) not befitting, unseemly (with *to, in*; *arch.*, without prep. or with *of*).—*n.* the transition from existence to non-existence.—*adv.* unbecom'ingly.—*n.* unbecom'ingness.—*v.t.* unbed', to rouse, remove, dislodge from a bed. —*adj.* unbedd'ed, unstratified: not put to bed; unbedimmed' (*Wordsworth*); unbedinned' (*Leigh Hunt*), not made noisy.—*v.t.* unbeget', to undo the begetting of.—*adjs.* unbegged', (of person) not entreated: not begged for; unbeginn'ing, without beginning; unbegot'; unbegott'en, not yet begotten: existing independent of any generating cause.—*v.t.* unbeguile', to undeceive.—*adjs.* unbeguiled', not deceived; unbegun', not yet begun: without beginning; unbehol'den, unseen: under no obligation of gratitude; unbe'ing, nonexistent.—*n.* nonexistence.—*adjs.* unbeknown', unbeknownst' (*coll.*), unknown.—*advs.* unobserved, without being known.—*n.* un'belief (or -*lēf*'), disbelief, or withholding of belief, esp. in accepted religion.—*adj.* unbeliev'able, incredible.—*adv.* unbeliev'ably.—*v.t.* and *v.i.* unbelieve', to disbelieve: to refrain from believing: to cease to believe.—*adj.* unbelieved'.—*n.* unbeliev'er, one who does not believe, esp. in the prevailing religion: a habitually incredulous person.—*adj.* unbeliev'ing.—*adv.* unbeliev'ingly. —*v.t.* unbelt', to ungird.—*adj.* unbelt'ed, without a belt: freed from a belt.—*v.t.* unbend', to relax from a bending tension, as a bow: to straighten: to undo, unfasten (*naut.*): to relax (the mind): to allow a frown, etc., to disappear from (the brow, etc.).—*v.i.* to become relaxed: to behave with freedom from stiffness, to be affable.—*adjs.* unbend'ed; unbend'ing, not bending: unyielding: resolute.—*n.* a relaxing.—*adv.* unbend'ingly.—*n.* unbend'ingness.—*adj.* unbent', not bent: relaxed: not overcome.—*v.t.* unbeseem', to misbecome: to fail to fulfil (*Byron*). —*adj.* unbeseem'ing.—*adv.* unbeseem'ingly.— *vs.t.* unbespeak', to cancel an order for; unbi'as, to free from bias.—*adj.* unbi'ased (sometimes unbi'assed).—*adv.* unbi'as(s)edly.—*n.* unbi'as(s)-edness.—*adjs.* unbib'lical, contrary to, unwarranted by, the Bible; unbid', not prayed for (*Spens.*): unbidden: not bid; unbidd'en, not bid or commanded: uninvited: spontaneous. —*v.t.* unbind', to remove a band from: to loose: to set free.—*n.* unbind'ing, removal of a band

unassuaged', *adj.* un- (1).
unatoned', *adj.* un- (1).
unattain'able, *adj.* un- (1).
unattain'ableness, *n.* un- (1).
unattain'ably, *adv.* un- (1).
unattained', *adj.* un- (1).
unattend'ing, *adj.* un- (1).
unattest'ed, *adj.* un- (1).
unattired', *adj.* un- (1).
unattract'ive, *adj.* un- (1).
unattract'ively, *adv.* un- (1).
unattract'iveness, *n.* un- (1).
unauthen'tic, *adj.* un- (1).
unauthen'ticated, *adj.* un- (1).
unauthentic'ity, *n.* un- (1).
unau'thorised, *adj.* un- (1).
unauthor'itative, *adj.* un- (1).
unavenged', *adj.* un- (1).
unavert'able, (*rarely*) -ible, *adjs.* un- (1).

unavowed', *adj.* un- (1).
unavow'edly, *adv.* un- (1).
unawak'ened, *adj.* un- (1).
unawak'ening, *adj.* un- (1).
unawed', *adj.* un- (1).
unbaff'led, *adj.* un- (1).
unbail'able, *adj.* un- (1).
unbait'ed, *adj.* un- (1).
unband'ed, *adj.* un- (1).
unbaptise', -ize', *v.t.* un- (2).
unbaptised', -z-, *adj.* un- (1).
unbar'bered, *adj.* un- (1).
unbarred', *adj.* un- (1).
unbarr'icade, *v.t.* un- (2).
unbathed', *adj.* un- (1).
unbatt'ered, *adj.* un- (1).
unbeard'ed, *adj.* un- (1).
unbeat'able, *adj.* un- (1).
unbeat'en, *adj.* un- (1).
unbeaut'iful, *adj.* un- (1).

unbefitt'ing, *adj.* un- (1).
unbefriend'ed, *adj.* un- (1).
unbeloved' (or -*luv'id*), *adj.* un-
    (1).
unben'eficed, *adj.* un- (1).
unbenefi'cial, *adj.* un- (1).
unben'efited, *adj.* un- (1).
unbenight'ed, *adj.* un- (1).
unbenign', *adj.* un- (1).
unbenig'nant, *adj.* un- (1).
unbenig'nly, *adv.* un- (1).
unbereft', *adj.* un- (1).
unbesought', *adj.* un- (1).
unbespok'en, *adj.* un- (1).
unbestowed', *adj.* un- (1).
unbetrayed', *adj.* un- (1).
unbett'erable, *adj.* un- (1).
unbett'ered, *adj.* un- (1).
unbewailed', *adj.* un- (1).

*Words beginning with pfx.* un- *are listed first* (pp. 1462 ff.); *other* UN- *words follow* (pp. 1484 ff.).

fāte, fär; mē, hûr (her); mīne; mōte, för; mūte; mōōn, fŏŏt; dhen (then)

or bond: loosing: setting free.—*adj.* loosening: not binding.—*n.* and *adj.* **unbirth′day** (*Lewis Carroll*), (pertaining to) a day other than one's birthday.—*vs.t.* **unbish′op**, to deprive of the status of bishop; **unbitt′** (*naut.*), to take off from the bitts.—*adj.* **unbitt′ed**, without a bit: unbridled.—*adj.*, *n.*, *adv.* **unblame′able, unblame′-ableness, unblame′ably**, older spellings of un-blamable, etc.—*adj.* **unblenched′** (or *un′*; *Milt.*), unflinching: unstained; **unblench′ing**, unflinching.—*v.t.* **unbless′**, to withhold happiness from: to deprive of blessing.—*adjs.* **unblessed′, unblest′.**—*n.* **unbless′edness.**—*adj.* **unblind′**, not blind.—*v.t.* to free from blindness or from blindfolding.—*adj.* **unblind′ed.**—*v.t.* **unblind′fold** (*pa.p. Spens.* **unblind′fold**).—*adjs.* **unblowed′** (*Shak.*), **un-blown′** (or *un′*), not blown: yet in the bud, not yet having bloomed; **unblush′ing**, not blushing: without shame: impudent.—*adv.* **unblush′ingly.**—*adjs.* **unbod′ied**, disembodied: not having a body or a form; **unbo′ding**, not expecting.—*v.t.* **unbolt′**, to draw back a bolt from.—*v.i.* to become unbolted: to explain, expound (*Shak.*).—*adj.* **unbolt′ed**, unfastened by withdrawing a bolt: not fastened by bolts: not separated by bolting or sifting: coarse.—*v.t.* **unbonn′et**, to remove the bonnet from.—*v.i.* to uncover the head.—*adjs.* **unbonn′eted**, bare-headed: in *Othello*, according to some, without taking off the cap, on equal terms; **unbooked′**, not entered in a book: unreserved: not literary; **unbook′ish**, unlearned: not given to or depending on read-ing: not savouring of books.—*adjs.* **unborn′**, not yet born: non-existent: without beginning; **unborr′owed**, not borrowed: original.—*v.t.* **un-bo′som**, to pour out, tell freely (what is in the mind): to reveal to the eye: (*refl.*) to confide freely (also *v.i.*).—*n.* **unbo′somer.**—*adjs.* **un-bott′omed**, bottomless: having no foundation or support: not founded (in, on); **unbought′**, obtained without buying: not bribed; **unbound′**, not bound: loose: without binding (also *pa.t.* and *pa.p.* of unbind, freed from bonds); **un-bound′ed**, not limited: boundless: having no check or control.—*adv.* **unbound′edly.**—*n.* **un-bound′edness.**—*v.t.* **unbrace′**, to undo the braces, points, or bands of: to loose or relax.—*adjs.* **unbraced′** (*Spens.* **unbraste**), not braced: with clothing unfastened: (of drum) with tension released: relaxed (*lit.* and *fig.*); **unbraid′ed**, not plaited: untarnished, unfaded (*Shak.*); **un-breath′able**, not respirable; **unbreathed′**, not exercised or practised (*Shak.*): out of breath: not out of breath: not breathed: not even whispered; **unbreathed′-on**, untouched by breath, esp. the breath of detraction; **unbreath′ing**, not breathing; **unbred′**, ill-bred: untrained: not yet born (*Shak.*).—*v.t.* **unbreech′**, to remove the

breeches, breech, or breeching from.—*adj.* **un-breeched′**, wearing no breeches.—*v.t.* **unbri′dle**, to free from the bridle: to free from (usu. politic) restraint.—*adj.* **unbri′dled**, not bridled: unrestrained. — *n.* **unbri′dledness.** — *adjs.* **un-Brit′ish**, not in accordance with British character or traditions; **unbrizzed′** (see **unbruised**); **un-broke′** (*arch.*), unbroken; **unbro′ken**, not broken: (of record) not surpassed: uninterrupted: not thrown into disorder: not variegated: not in-fringed.—*adv.* **unbro′kenly.**—*n.* **unbro′kenness.** —*adj.* **unbruised′** (*Shak.* **un′brused**; *Scott* **un-brizzed′**), not bruised or crushed.—*v.t.* **un-buck′le**, to unfasten the buckle(s) of: to un-fasten.—*v.i.* to undo the buckle(s) of a garment, etc.: to unbend (*fig.*).—*adj.* **unbudd′ed**, not yet in bud: not yet having emerged from the bud. —*v.t.* **unbuild′**, to demolish, pull down.—*adjs.* **unbuilt′** (or *un′*), not built: not built upon; **unbuilt′-on.**—*v.t.* **unbur′den**, (*arch.*) **unbur′then**, to free from a burden: to discharge, cast off, as a burden: (*refl.*) to tell one's secrets or anxieties freely.—*adjs.* **unbur′dened**, (*arch.*) **un-bur′thened**, not burdened: relieved of a burden. —*v.t.* and *v.i.* **unburr′ow**, to bring or come out of a burrow.—*v.t.* **unbur′y**, to disinter.—*v.t.* **un-butt′on**, to loose the buttons of.—*v.i.* to loose one's buttons: to unbend and tell one's thoughts. —*adj.* **unbutt′oned**, without a button: with buttons loosed: in a relaxed confidential state.

*Words with prefix un- (continued).*

*adjs.* **uncalled′**, not called or summoned: not invited: not called up for payment; **uncalled′-for** (or **uncalled for**), not required, unnecessary: unprovoked: offensively or aggressively gratui-tous.—*adv.* **uncann′ily.**—*n.* **uncann′iness.**—*adj.* **uncann′y**, weird, supernatural: (of e.g. skill) much greater than one would expect from an ordinary human being: unsafe to associate with: unpleasantly severe (*Scot.*): unsafe (*Scot.*).—*v.t.* **uncap**, to remove a cap from.—*v.i.* to take off one's cap.—*adj.* **uncap′able** (*Shak.*), incapable. —*v.i.* **uncape′** (*Shak.*), prob. a misprint for **un-cope**: some have explained as to uncouple hounds, to unkennel a fox, etc.—*adjs.* **uncared′-for** (**uncared for**), neglected: showing signs of neglect; **uncare′ful**, careless: care-free; **uncar′-ing**, without anxiety, concern, or caution: not caring about (*Burns*).—*v.t.* **uncase′**, to take out of a case: to flay (*obs.*): to undress (*Shak.*): to lay bare.—*v.i.* to strip (*Shak.*).—*adjs.* **un-caused′**, without any precedent cause, self-exis-tent; **unceas′ing**, ceaseless: never-ending.—*adv.* **unceas′ingly.**—*adjs.* **unceremo′nious**, informal: off-hand.—*adv.* **unceremo′niously.**—*n.* **unceremo′-niousness.**—*adj.* **uncer′tain**, not certain (of, about): not definitely known or decided: subject to doubt

| | | |
|---|---|---|
| **unblam′able,** *adj.* un- (1). | **unbowed′,** *adj.* un- (1). | **uncal′culating,** *adj.* un- (1). |
| **unblam′ably,** *adv.* un- (1). | **unbranched′,** *adj.* un- (1). | **uncan′did,** *adj.* un- (1). |
| **unblamed′,** *adj.* un- (1). | **unbreach′able,** *adj.* un- (1). | **uncan′didly,** *adv.* un- (1). |
| **unbleached′,** *adj.* un- (1). | **unbreathed′,** *adj.* un- (1). | **uncan′didness,** *n.* un- (1). |
| **unblem′ished,** *adj.* un- (1). | **unbreak′able,** *adj.* un- (1). | **uncan′dour,** *n.* un- (1). |
| **unblend′ed,** *adj.* un- (1). | **unbrib′able,** *adj.* un- (1). | **uncanon′ic, -al,** *adjs.* un- (1). |
| **unblent′,** *adj.* un- (1). | **unbridged′,** *adj.* un- (1). | **uncanon′icalness,** *n.* un- (1). |
| **unblink′ing,** *adj.* un- (1). | **unbroth′erlike,** *adj.* un- (1). | **uncan′onise, -ize,** *vs.t.* un- (2). |
| **unblink′ingly,** *adv.* un- (1). | **unbroth′erly,** *adj.* un- (1). | **uncan′onised, -z-,** *adj.* un- (1). |
| **unbliss′ful,** *adj.* un- (1). | **unbrushed′,** *adj.* un- (1). | **uncapsiz′able,** *adj.* un- (1). |
| **unblock′,** *v.t.* un- (2). | **unbur′ied,** *adj.* un- (1). | **uncar′peted,** *adj.* un- (1). |
| **unblood′ed,** *adj.* un- (1). | **unburned′, unburnt′** (or *un′*), *adjs.* | **uncart′,** *v.t.* un- (2). |
| **unblood′ied,** *adj.* un- (1). | un- (1). | **uncat′alogued,** *adj.* un- (1). |
| **unblood′y,** *adj.* un- (1). | **unbur′nished,** *adj.* un- (1). | **uncaught′,** *adj.* un- (1). |
| **unblott′ed,** *adj.* un- (1). | **unbus′inesslike,** *adj.* un- (1). | **uncel′ebrated,** *adj.* un- (1). |
| **unblunt′ed,** *adj.* un- (1). | **unbus′y,** *adj.* un- (1). | **uncen′sored,** *adj.* un- (1). |
| **unboast′ful,** *adj.* un- (1). | **unbutt′ered,** *adj.* un- (1). | **uncensor′ious,** *adj.* un- (1). |
| **unbone′,** *v.t.* un- (2). | **uncage′,** *v.t.* un- (2). | **uncen′sured,** *adj.* un- (1). |
| **unboot′,** *v.t.* and *v.i.* un- (2). | **uncal′culated,** *adj.* un- (1). | **uncertif′icated,** *adj.* un- (1). |

*Words beginning with pfx.* un- *are listed first (pp. 1462 ff.); other UN- words follow (pp. 1484 ff.).*

or question (in no uncertain terms, unambiguously): not to be depended upon: subject to vicissitude: hesitant, lacking confidence.—*adv.* uncer'tainly.—*ns.* uncer'tainness; uncer'tainty (uncertainty principle, the principle that it is not possible to measure accurately at the same time both position and velocity).—*adjs.* uncer'tified, not assured, attested, or guaranteed; uncess'ant (*Milt.*), incessant.—*v.t.* unchain', to release from a chain: to remove a chain from: to let loose.—*adjs.* unchained'; unchan'cy (*Scot.*), unlucky: ill-omened: dangerous: ticklish.—*v.t.* uncharge', to unload: to acquit (*Shak.*).—*adj.* uncharged', not charged: not attacked (*Shak.*).—*n.* unchar'ity, want of charity.—*v.t.* uncharm', to free from a spell: to destroy the magical power of.—*adjs.* uncharmed', not affected by a spell: not charmed; unchar'ming, not charming or attractive.—*v.t.* unchar'nel, to take from a charnel.—*adjs.* unchart'ed (*lit.* and *fig.*), not mapped in detail: not shown in a chart; unchart'ered, not holding a charter: unauthorised.—*n.* unchas'tity, lack, or breach, of chastity.—*v.t.* uncheck' (*Shak.*), to fail to check.—*adjs.* uncheck'able; unchecked', not checked or verified: not restrained: not contradicted (*Shak.*).—*v.t.* unchild' (*Shak.*), to make childless: to change from being a child.—*adjs.* unchild'like; unchris'om (*Lamb*), unchristened.—*v.t.* unchrist'en, to annul the christening of: to deprive of a name: to . unchristianise (*Milt.*).—*adjs.* unchrist'ened, unbaptised: without a name; unchris'tian, non-christian (*rare*): against the spirit of Christianity: uncharitable: unreasonable, outrageous (*coll.*).—*v.t.* to unchristianise (*obs.*).—*v.t.* unchris'tianise, -ize, to cause to change from the Christian faith or character.—*adj.* unchris'tianlike.—*adv.* unchris'tianly.—*adj.* unchristianlike.—*vs.t.* unchurch', to deprive of church membership, or of the possession of a church: to take the status of a church from; unci'pher (*obs.*), to decipher.—*adj.* uncir'cumcised, not circumcised: gentile: unpurified (*fig.*).—*n.* uncircumcis'ion, uncircumcised condition: the uncircumcised, the gentiles (*B.*).—*adjs.* unciv'il, not civilised (*Spens.*): discourteous: unseemly: against civic good; unciv'ilised, -ized, not civilised: away from civilised communities.—*adv.* unciv'illy.—*v.t.* unclasp', to loose from a clasp: to relax from clasping: to open.—*v.i.* to close in a clasp.—*adjs.* unclassed', without class divisions: unclassified: not placed in a class; unclass'ified, not classified, esp. of a road: not on the security list; unclean (-*klēn*), not clean: foul: ceremonially impure: lewd; uncleaned',

not cleaned.—*n.* uncleanliness (-*klen*').—*adj.* uncleanly (-*klen*').—*adv.* (-*klēn*').—*n.* uncleanness (-*klēn'nis*).—*adjs.* uncleansed (-*klenzd*'); uncler'ical, not characteristic of, or befitting, a clergyman.—*v.t.* unclew (*arch.*), to unwind, unfold, undo.—*v.t.* uncloak', to divest of a cloak: to show up.—*v.i.* to take one's cloak off.—*v.t.* unclog', to free from a clog or obstruction.—*adj.* unclogged', not clogged.—*v.t.* unclois'ter, to free or remove from the cloister.—*adj.* unclois'tered, not cloistered: without a cloister: freed or taken from a cloister.—*v.t.* and *v.i.* unclose (*un-klōz*'), to open.—*adjs.* unclose (*un-klōs*'), not close; unclosed (*un-klōzd*'), not closed: unenclosed: opened.—*v.t.* unclothe', to take the clothes off: to divest of covering.—*adj.* unclothed'.—*v.t.* and *v.i.* uncloud', to clear of clouds or obscurity.—*adj.* uncloud'ed, free from clouds, obscurity or gloom: calm.—*n.* uncloud'edness.—*adjs.* uncloud'y.—*vs.t.* unclutch', to release from a clutch; uncock', to let down the hammer of: to spread out from a haycock.—*adj.* uncoff'ined, not put into a coffin: removed from a coffin.—*v.t.* and *v.i.* uncoil', to unwind.—*adjs.* uncoined', not coined (*Shak.* uncoyned) variously explained, but prob. meaning 'natural', 'not artificial or counterfeit'.—*v.t.* uncolt' (*Shak.*, punningly; Falstaff has used colt, to cheat), to deprive of a horse.—*v.t.* and *v.i.* uncombine', to separate (*Dickens*).—*adj.* uncom(e)-atable (*un-kum-at'ə-bl*), inaccessible: out of reach.—*n.* uncome'liness.—*adjs.* uncome'ly, not comely: indecent: unseemly; uncom'fortable, feeling, involving, or causing discomfort or disquiet.—*n.* uncom'fortableness.—*adv.* uncom'-fortably.—*adjs.* uncom'forted; uncommitt'ed, not pledged to support any party, policy or action: impartial: not committed; uncomm'on, not common: unusual: remarkably great: strange.—*adv.* (*old slang*) remarkably, very.—*adv.* uncomm'only, rarely (esp. *not uncommonly*, frequently): in an unusually great degree.—*n.* uncomm'onness.—*adjs.* uncom'panied, unaccompanied; uncompan'ionable, unsociable; uncompan'ioned, without a companion or an equal; uncom'plicated, straightforward, not made difficult by the variety of factors involved: (of person) simple in character and outlook; uncompliment'ary, far from complimentary; uncompos'able, incapable of being composed or reconciled; uncompound'ed, not compounded, unmixed; uncomprehen'sive, not comprehensive: incomprehensible (*Shak.*); uncom'promising, refusing to compromise: unyielding: out-and-out.—*adv.* uncom'promisingly.—*n.* uncom'promising-

---

unchall'engeable, *adj.* un- (1).
unchall'engeably, *adv.* un- (1).
unchall'enged, *adj.* un- (1).
unchangeabil'ity, *n.* un- (1).
unchange'able, *adj.* un- (1).
unchange'ableness, *n.* un- (1).
unchange'ably, *adv.* un- (1).
unchanged', *adj.* un- (1).
unchang'ing, *adj.* un- (1).
unchang'ingly, *adv.* un- (1).
unchar'itable, *adj.* un- (1).
unchar'itableness, *n.* un- (1).
unchar'itably, *adv.* un- (1).
uncha'ry, *adj.* un- (1).
unchaste', *adj.* un- (1).
unchaste'ly, *adv.* un- (1).
unchast'ened, *adj.* un- (1).
unchaste'ness, *n.* un- (1).
unchastis'able, -z-, *adj.* un- (1).
unchastised', -z-, *adj.* un- (1).
uncheered', *adj.* un- (1).
uncheer'ful, *adj.* un- (1).

uncheer'fully, *adv.* un- (1).
uncheer'fulness, *n.* un- (1).
unchewed', *adj.* un- (1).
unchos'en, *adj.* un- (1).
unchiv'alrous, *adj.* un- (1).
unchron'icled, *adj.* un- (1).
uncir'cumscribed, *adj.* un- (1).
unclad', *adj.* un- (1).
unclaimed', *adj.* un- (1).
unclass'ical, *adj.* un- (1).
unclear', *adj.* un- (1).
uncleared', *adj.* un- (1).
unclear'ly, *adv.* un- (1).
unclear'ness, *n.* un- (1).
unclench', *v.t.* and *v.i.* un- (2).
unclipped', unclipt', *adjs.* un- (1).
unclub(b)'able, *adj.* un- (1).
uncollect'ed, *adj.* un- (1).
uncol'oured, *adj.* un- (1).
uncombed', *adj.* un- (1).
uncommend'able, *adj.* un- (1).
uncommend'ably, *adv.* un- (1).

uncommend'ed, *adj.* un- (1).
uncommer'cial, *adj.* un- (1).
uncommu'nicable, *adj.* un- (1).
uncommu'nicated, *adj.* un- (1).
uncommu'nicative, *adj.* un- (1).
uncommu'nicativeness, *n.* un- (1).
uncommu'ted, *adj.* un- (1).
uncompact'ed, *adj.* un- (1).
uncompass'ionate, *adj.* un- (1).
uncompelled', *adj.* un- (1).
uncom'pensated, *adj.* un- (1).
uncomplain'ing, *adj.* un- (1).
uncomplain'ingly, *adv.* un- (1).
uncomplais'ant, (or-*kom*'), *adj.* un- (1).
uncomplais'antly, (or *kom*'), *adv.* un- (1).
uncomplet'ed, *adj.* un- (1).
uncomply'ing, *adj.* un- (1).
uncomprehend'ed, *adj.* un- (1).
uncomprehend'ing, *adj.* un- (1).

---

*Words beginning with pfx.* un- *are listed first* (pp. 1462 ff.); *other* UN- *words follow* (pp. 1484 ff.).

fāte, fär; mē, hûr (her); mīne; mōte, för; mūte; mōͦn, fōͦt; dhen (then) ness.—*adj.* unconceiv'able, inconceivable.—*n.* unconceiv'ableness. — *adv.* unconceiv'ably. — *adj.* unconceived'.—*n.* unconcern', want of concern or anxiety: indifference.—*adj.* unconcerned', not concerned, not involved (in): impartial: uninterested: indifferent: untroubled, carelessly secure: sober, unaffected by liquor (*obs.*).—*adv.* unconcern'edly.—*n.* unconcern'edness.—*adj.* unconcern'ing.—*n.* unconcern'ment.—*adjs.* unconclu'sive, inconclusive; unconcoct'ed, not digested: crude: not elaborated or finished (*fig.*); uncondi'tional, not conditional: absolute, unlimited. —*n.* unconditional'ity.—*adv.* uncondi'tionally.— *n.* uncondi'tionalness.—*adjs.* uncondi'tioned, not subject to condition or limitation: infinite, absolute, unknowable: (of person, response) not conditioned by learning or experience: not put into the required state; unconfin'able, not to be confined: unbounded (*Shak.*).—*v.t.* unconfine', to release from restraint: to divulge (*Keats*).—*adj.* unconfined', not confined: not restricted: unlimited: set free.—*adv.* unconfin'edly.—*adjs.* unconfirmed', not confirmed: not yet having received confirmation: uncorroborated: not yet firm or strong: ignorant (*Shak.*); unconform' (*Milt.*), unlike.—*n.* unconformabil'ity, the state or the quality of being unconformable: an unconformity in stratification (*geol.*).—*adj.* unconform'able, not conforming (to e.g., *hist.*, the practices of the Church of England): unwilling to conform: showing an unconformability (*geol.*).—*n.* unconform'ableness. —*adv.* unconform'ably.—*adj.* unconform'ing, not conforming.—*n.* unconform'ity, want of conformity (*arch.*): nonconformity (*obs.*): a breach of continuity in direction, etc. of rock strata (*geol.*). —*v.t.* and *v.i.* uncongeal', to thaw, melt.—*adjs.* uncon'jugal (*Milt.*), not suited to, or fitting in, marriage; unconjunc'tive (*Milt.*), impossible to be joined; unconniv'ing, refusing indulgence (*Milt.*); uncon'scionable, (of person) unscrupulous: not conformable to conscience: outrageous, inordinate.—*n.* uncon'scionableness.— *adv.* uncon'scionably. uncon'scious, without consciousness: unaware (of): not self-conscious. —*n.* (with the) the deepest, inaccessible level of the psyche in which are present in dynamic state repressed impulses and memories.—*adv.* uncon'sciously.—*n.* uncon'sciousness.—*v.t.* uncon'secrate, to deprive of consecrated character. —*adj.* unconsecrated.—*adjs.* uncon'secrated, not consecrated; unconsenta'neous (*Peacock*), not in agreement; unconsid'ered, not esteemed: done without considering; unconsid'ering; uncon'stant (*Shak.*), inconstant; unconstrain'able; un-

constrained'.—*adv.* unconstrain'edly.—*n.* unconstraint', absence of constraint.—*adjs.* uncontemned' (*Shak.*), not despised; uncontest'able, incontestable; uncontest'ed; uncontroll'able, not capable of being controlled: absolute, not controlled (*arch.*): indisputable (*obs.*).—*n.* uncontroll'ableness.—*adv.* uncontroll'ably.—*adj.* uncontrolled', not controlled: not disputed (*obs.*). —*adv.* uncontroll'edly.—*adjs.* uncontrovert'ed, not disputed; uncontrovert'ible; unconven'tional, not conventional: free in one's ways.— *n.* unconventional'ity.—*adj.* unconvers'able, not able or not disposed to converse freely; uncoordinated, not co-ordinated: having clumsy movements, as if muscles were not co-ordinated. —*vs.t.* uncope', to unmuzzle, or unsew the mouth of (a ferret; cf. uncape); uncord', to free (e.g. a trunk) from cords.—*adjs.* uncorrupt', incorrupt; uncorrupt'ed; uncost'ly, inexpensive; uncoun'selled, not given advice: not advised.—*v.t.* uncoup'le, to loose from being coupled: to disjoin. —*v.i.* to uncouple hounds.—*adjs.* uncoup'led, not married: detached; uncour'teous, discourteous; uncouth (un-kōōth'); O.E. *uncūth*, unknown, strange—*un-*, *cūth*, known), unknown (*obs.*): unfamiliar (*arch.*): strange and wild or unattractive: awkward, ungraceful, uncultured, esp. in manners or language.—*adv.* uncouth'ly. — *n.* uncouth'ness. — *adj.* uncov'enanted, not promised or bound by covenant: not included in a covenant: not having subscribed to the Solemn League and Covenant of 1643.—*v.t.* uncov'er, to remove the cover of: to lay open: to expose: to drive out of cover.—*v.i.* to take off the hat.—*adj.* uncov'ered.—*v.t.* uncowl', to withdraw the cowl from.—*adj.* uncowled'.—*v.t.* uncreate', to deprive of existence.—*adj.* uncrea'ted, not (yet) created: not produced by creation (*Milt.*).—*n.* uncreat'edness.—*adjs.* uncrea'ting; uncred'ible (*obs.*), incredible; uncred'itable (*obs.*), discreditable; uncrit'ical, not critical, without discrimination: not in accordance with the principles of criticism.—*adv.* uncrit'ically.—*v.t.* uncross', to change from a crossed position.— *adj.* uncrossed', not crossed—not passed over, marked with a cross, thwarted, etc.: not marked off as paid (*Shak.*).—*v.t.* uncrown', to dethrone: to take the crown off.—*adjs.* uncrowned', not crowned: not yet formally crowned: possessing kingly power without the actual title: unfulfilled; uncrudd'ed (*Spens.*), uncurdled; uncul'tured, not cultured: not cultivated; uncur'able (*Shak.*), incurable; uncu'rious, incurious: not strange.—*v.t.* and *v.i.* uncurl', to take or come out of curl, twist, roll.—*adjs.* uncurled', not

---

unconceal'able, *adj.* un- (1).
unconcealed', *adj.* un- (1).
unconceal'ing, *adj.* un- (1).
unconcert'ed, *adj.* un- (1).
unconcil'iatory, *adj.* un- (1).
unconfed'erated, *adj.* un- (1).
unconfessed', *adj.* un- (1).
unconfused', *adj.* un- (1).
unconfus'edly, *adv.* un- (1).
uncongen'ial, *adj.* un- (1).
uncongenial'ity, *n.* un- (1).
unconject'ured, *adj.* un- (1).
unconnect'ed, *adj.* un- (1).
unconq'uerable, *adj.* un- (1).
unconq'uerableness, *n.* un- (1).
unconq'uerably, *adv.* un- (1).
unconq'uered, *adj.* un- (1).
unconscien'tious, *adj.* un- (1).
unconscien'tiously, *adv.* un- (1).
unconscien'tiousness, *n.* un- (1).
unconsent'ing, *adj.* un- (1).
unconsoled', *adj.* un- (1).

unconsol'idated, *adj.* un- (1).
unconstitu'tional, *adj.* un- (1).
unconstitutional'ity, *n.* un- (1).
unconstitu'tionally, *adv.* un- (1).
unconsumed', *adj.* un- (1).
uncontam'inated, *adj.* un- (1).
uncon'templated, *adj.* un- (1).
unconten'tious, *adj.* un- (1).
uncontradict'ed, *adj.* un- (1).
unconvers'ant, *adj.* un- (1).
unconvert'ed, *adj.* un- (1).
unconvert'ible, *adj.* un- (1).
unconvict'ed, *adj.* un- (1).
unconvinced', *adj.* un- (1).
unconvinc'ing, *adj.* un- (1).
uncooked', *adj.* un- (1).
unco-op'erative, *adj.* un- (1).
unco-op'eratively, *adv.* un- (1).
uncoquett'ish, *adj.* un- (1).
uncor'dial, *adj.* un- (1).
uncork', *v.t.* un- (2).
uncorrect'ed, *adj.* un- (1).

uncorrob'orated, *adj.* un- (1).
uncount'able, *adj.* un- (1).
uncount'ed, *adj.* un- (1).
uncourt'liness, *n.* un- (1).
uncourt'ly, *adj.* un- (1).
uncropped', *adj.* un- (1).
uncrush'able, *adj.* un- (1).
uncrystallis'able, -izable, *adj.* un- (1).
uncrys'tallised, -ized, *adj.* un- (1).
uncuck'olded, *adj.* un- (1).
unculled', *adj.* un- (1).
uncult'ivable, *adj.* un- (1).
uncult'ivated, *adj.* un- (1).
uncum'bered, *adj.* un- (1).
uncurb'able, *adj.* un- (1).
uncurbed', *adj.* un- (1).
uncurd'led, *adj.* un- (1).
uncured', *adj.* un- (1).
uncurr'ent, *adj.* un- (1).
uncurtailed', *adj.* un- (1).

---

*Words beginning with pfx.* un- *are listed first* (pp. 1462 ff.); *other* UN- *words follow* (pp. 1484 ff.).

Neutral vowels in unaccented syllables: *el'ə-mənt*; for certain sounds in foreign words, see p. viii

curled: unrolled, uncoiled; **uncurl'ing.**—*vs.t.* **uncurse'**, to free from a curse, unsay a curse upon; **uncur'tain**, to remove a curtain from. —*adjs.* **uncur'tained**, curtainless; **uncus'tomed**, (of goods) on which customs duty is unpaid, or not payable: unaccustomed (*arch.*): not customary (*arch.*): **uncut'**, not cut: not shaped by cutting: not abridged: of a book, bibliographically, with margins not cut down by the binder (even though opened with a paper-cutter): popularly, unopened.

*Words with prefix un- (continued).*

*adjs.* **undashed'**, undismayed; **undāt'ed**, with no date marked or assigned: unending; **undaunt'ed**, not daunted: bold, intrepid.—*adv.* **undaunt'edly.**—*n.* **undaun'tedness.**—*adj.* **undawn'ing**, not yet dawning or showing light.—*v.i.* **undazz'le**, to recover from a dazed state (*Tennyson*). —*adj.* **undazz'led**, not dazzled.—*v.t.* **undeaf'** (*Shak.*), to free from deafness.—*adj.* **undeceiv'able**, incapable of deceiving (*obs.*), or of being deceived.—*v.t.* **undeceive'**, to free from a mistaken belief, reveal the truth to.—*adjs.* **undeceived'**, not deceived: set free from a delusion; **unde'cent**, indecent (*dial.*): unfitting (*arch.*): unhandsome (*obs.*); **undecid'ed**, not decided or settled: uncertain, irresolute.—*adv.* **undecid'edly.** —*adjs.* **undeci'pherable**, indecipherable; **undeci'sive**, indecisive.—*v.t.* **undeck'**, to divest of ornaments.—*adjs.* **undecked'**, not adorned: having no deck; **undeclin'ing**, unbowed, unsubmissive; **undeed'ed** (*Shak.*), unused in any action; **undefied'** (*Spens.* **undefide'**), not defied or challenged; **undefin'able**; **undefined'**, not defined: indefinite.—*v.t.* **unde'ify**, to deprive of the nature or honour of a god.—*n.* **undelight'**, lack of delight.—*adjs.* **undelight'ed**; **undelight'ful**; **undeni'able**, not to be denied, indisputable: not to be refused: obviously true or excellent.—*n.* **undeni'ableness.**—*adv.* **undeni'ably.**—*adj.* **undenomina'tional**, not confined to or favouring any particular sect.—*n.* **undenomina'tionalism.**—*adj.* **undepend'able** (a word formed irregularly, neither from a noun nor from a transitive verb), not to be depended upon.—*n.* **undepen'dableness.**—*adjs.* **undepen'ding** (*obs.*), independent; **undescri'bable**, indescribable; **undescribed'**; **undescried'.**—*n.* **un'desert**, want of desert, unworthiness.—*v.t.* **undeserve'**, to fail or cease to deserve.—*adj.* **undeserved'**, not deserved.—*adv.*

**undeser'vedly.**—*ns.* **undeser'vedness**; **undeser'ver** (*Shak.*), one who is not deserving or worthy.— *adj.* **undeser'ving.**—*adv.* **undeser'vingly.**—*adj.* **undesigned'.**--*adv.* **undesign'edly.**—*n.* **undesign'edness.**—*adj.* **undesign'ing**, not designing: artless: straightforward: sincere.—*n.* **undesirabil'ity.**— *adj.* **undesi'rable**, not to be wished for.—*n.* an undesirable or objectionable person or thing.—*n.* **undesir'ableness.**—*adv.* **undesir'ably.**—*adjs.* **undesired'**; **undesir'ing**; **undesir'ous**; **undeter'minable**, indeterminable; **undeter'minate**, indeterminate. —*ns.* **undeter'minateness**; **undetermina'tion.**— *adjs.* **undeter'mined**, not settled, not fixed: not ascertained: not limited; **undeterred'**, not discouraged or prevented (from); **undevel'oped**, not developed: of land, not built on or used for public works.—*v.t.* **undid'**, *pa.t.* of undo.—*adjs.* **undiff'erenced** (*her.*), without a modification to distinguish a cadet from the main line; **undifferen'tiated**, not differentiated. —*v.t.* **undight** (*un-dīt'*; *Spens.*), to undo, take off, doff (*pa.t.* and *pa.p.* undight').—*adj.* **undight'**, adorned: not dressed, (of hair) loose (*Spens.*, etc.).—*adj.* **undig'nified.**—*v.t.* **undig'nify**, to deprive of dignity.—*adjs.* **undipped'**, not dipped: unbaptised; **undiscerned'**, unobserved, unperceived.—*adv.* **undiscern'edly.**—*adj.* **undiscern'ible.** —*adv.* **undiscern'ibly.**—*adj.* **undiscern'ing**, showing lack of discernment or discrimination.—*n.* want of discernment.—*adjs.* **undischarged'**, not paid or settled: (of e.g. obligation) not carried out: not released from debt or other liability: (of gun) not fired; **undisc'iplinable.**—*n.* **undisc'ipline**, lack of discipline.—*adjs.* **undisc'iplined**, untrained: unruly; **undiscord'ing** (*Milt.*), not discordant; **undiscrim'inating**, not making distinctions: not showing critical taste or ability; **undiscussed'**, unsettled (*obs.*): not discussed; **undisguis'able**; **undisguised'**, not disguised: frank, open.—*adv.* **undisguis'edly.**—*adjs.* **undisposed'**, not disposed (usu. with -of): disinclined (*Shak.*): disinclined (to); **undissem'bled**, unfeigned: undisguised, unconcealed; **undistem'pered**, not deranged, disturbed, ruffled, or in unhealthy condition; **undistinc'tive**, not distinctive: undistinguishing; **undisting'uishable**, indistinguishable.—*n.* **undisting'uishableness.**— *adv.* **undisting'uishably.**—*adjs.* **undisting'uished**, not distinguished or observed: not marked out by conspicuous qualities, not famous: not having an air of distinction; **undisting'uishing,**

| | | |
|---|---|---|
| **undam'**, *v.t.* un- (2). | **undemocrat'ic**, *adj.* un- (1). | **undirect'ed**, *adj.* un- (1). |
| **undam'aged**, *adj.* un- (1). | **undemon'strable**, *adj.* un- (1). | **undisclosed'**, *adj.* un- (1). |
| **undammed'**, *adj.* un- (1, 2). | **undemon'strative**, *adj.* un- (1). | **undiscom'fited**, *adj.* un- (1). |
| **undamned'**, *adj.* un- (1). | **undemon'strativeness**, *n.* un- (1). | **undiscour'aged**, *adj.* un- (1). |
| **undamped'**, *adj.* un- (1). | **undeplored'**, *adj.* un- (1). | **undiscov'erable**, *adj.* un- (1). |
| **undear'**, *adj.* un- (1). | **undepraved'**, *adj.* un- (1). | **undiscov'erably**, *adv.* un- (1). |
| **undebarred'**, *adj.* un- (1). | **undepre'ciated**, *adj.* un- (1). | **undiscov'ered**, *adj.* un- (1). |
| **undebased'**, *adj.* un- (1). | **undepressed'**, *adj.* un- (1). | **undiscuss'able, -ible**, *adj.* un- (1). |
| **undebauched'**, *adj.* un- (1). | **undeprived'**, *adj.* un- (1). | **undishon'oured**, *adj.* un- (1). |
| **undecayed'**, *adj.* un- (1). | **undescend'ible, -able**, *adj.* un- (1). | **undismant'led**, *adj.* un- (1). |
| **undecid'able**, *adj.* un- (1). | **undescried'**, *adj.* un- (1). | **undismayed'**, *adj.* un- (1). |
| **undeclared'**, *adj.* un- (1). | **undespair'ing**, *adj.* un- (1). | **undisor'dered**, *adj.* un- (1). |
| **undecompos'able**, *adj.* un- (1). | **undespair'ingly**, *adv.* un- (1). | **undispatched'**, *adj.* un- (1). |
| **undecomposed'**, *adj.* un- (1). | **undespoiled'**, *adj.* un- (1). | **undispensed'**, *adj.* un- (1). |
| **undefaced'**, *adj.* un- (1). | **undestroyed'**, *adj.* un- (1). | **undisput'ed**, *adj.* un- (1). |
| **undefeat'ed**, *adj.* un- (1). | **undetect'ed**, *adj.* un- (1). | **undisput'edly**, *adv.* un- (1). |
| **undefend'ed**, *adj.* un- (1). | **unde'viating**, *adj.* un- (1). | **undissolved'**, *adj.* un- (1). |
| **undefiled'**, *adj.* un- (1). | **unde'viatingly**, *adv.* un- (1). | **undissol'ving**, *adj.* un- (1). |
| **undelayed'**, *adj.* un- (1). | **undevout'**, *adj.* un- (1). | **undistilled'**, *adj.* un- (1). |
| **undelect'able**, *adj.* un- (1). | **undigest'ed**, *adj.* un- (1). | **undistort'ed**, *adj.* un- (1). |
| **undel'egated**, *adj.* un- (1). | **undilut'ed**, *adj.* un- (1). | **undistract'ed**, *adj.* un- (1). |
| **undelib'erate**, *adj.* un- (1). | **undimin'ishable**, *adj.* un- (1). | **undistract'edly**, *adv.* un- (1). |
| **undeliv'ered**, *adj.* un- (1). | **undimin'ished**, *adj.* un- (1). | **undistract'edness**, *n.* un- (1). |
| **undelud'ed**, *adj.* un- (1). | **undimmed'**, *adj.* un- (1). | **undistract'ing**, *adj.* un- (1). |
| **undemand'ed**, *adj.* un- (1). | **undint'ed**, *adj.* un- (1). | |

*Words beginning with pfx.* **un-** *are listed first (pp. 1462 ff.); other UN- words follow (pp. 1484 ff.).*

fāte, fär, mē, hûr (her); mīne; mōte, fōr; mūte; mōon, fŏot; dhen (then) not discriminating; **undistrib′uted**, not distributed (**undistributed middle**, the fallacy of reasoning without distributing the middle term, i.e. without making it universal, in at least one premise); **undivert′ed**, not turned away: not amused; **undivert′ing**; **undivest′ed** (*Richardson*), detached.—*adv.* **undivest′edly**.—*adjs.* **undivid′able**, indivisible; **undivi′ded**.—*adv.* **undivi′dedly**. —*n.* **undivi′dedness**.—*v.t.* **undo** (*un-dōō′*), to reverse the doing of: to cancel, annul: to bring to nothing: to unfasten by unbolting, etc.: to open: to unbutton, untie, etc.: to unravel: to solve (problem, riddle; *arch.*): to bring ruin on: to seduce (*arch.*): to prevent the happening or being of (*Shak.*).—*pa.t.* **undid′**; *pa.p.* **undone** (*un-dun′*).—*v.t.* **undock′**, to take (a ship) out of dock.—*adjs.* **undocked′**, not docked or cut short; **undoc′tored**, without a doctor's degree: not patched up, tampered with, or sophisticated.—*ns.* **undoer** (*un-dōō′ər*), one who undoes: one who ruins: a seducer; **undo′ing**, the reversal of what has been done: unfastening: opening: ruin or cause of ruin.—*adj.* **undomes′tic**, not domestic: not content with, adapted to, or relating to, home life: unhomelike (*Coleridge*).—*v.t.* **undomes′ticate**, to make undomestic: to untame.—*adjs.* **undomes′ticated**, not domesticated: not tamed: emancipated from mere domestic interests; **undone** (*un-dun′*), not done: annulled: brought to naught: unfastened: opened: ruined: seduced.—*v.t. and v.i.* **undou′ble**, to unfold, open out.—*adjs.* **undoubt′able**, indubitable; **undoubt′ed**, not doubted: unquestioned: certainly genuine or such as is represented: indubitable.—*adv.* **undoubt′edly**.— *adjs.* **undoubt′ful**; **undoubt′ing**.—*adv.* **undoubt′ingly**.—*adj.* **undraped′**, without drapery: nude. —*v.t. and v.i.* **undraw′**, to draw back.—*adjs.* **undreamed′**, **undreamt′** (also with **-of**), not imagined even in a dream.—*v.t.* **undress′**, to remove the clothes or dressing from.—*v.i.* to take off one's clothes.—*n.* (*un′*) scanty or incomplete dress: ordinary, informal dress: uniform for ordinary occasions.—Also *adj.*—*adj.* **undressed′**, not dressed—not set in order, or made trim, or treated or prepared for use, etc.: divested of clothes.—*n.* **undress′ing**.—*adjs.* **undross′y** (*Pope*), pure; **undue′**, not due or owing: unjustifiable: inappropriate: excessive.—*adv.* **undu′ly**, unjustifiably: more than is right or reasonable, excessively: wrongfully (*arch.*).—

*adjs.* **undu′teous**, undutiful (*poet.*); **undu′tiful**. —*adv.* **undu′tifully**.—*n.* **undu′tifulness**.—*adjs.* **undyed′**, not dyed; **undy′ing**, not dying, immortal: unceasing.—*adv.* **undy′ingly**.—*n.* **undy′ingness**.

*Words with prefix* un- (*continued*).

*adjs.* **uneared′**, not eared: untilled (*Shak.*); **unearned′**, not earned by work: (**unearned income**, income, e.g. dividends, that is not remuneration for work done; **unearned increment**, increase in value of land independent of owner's labour or expenditure): (of something pleasant or unpleasant) unmerited.—*v.t.* **unearth′**, to dig up, disinter: to bring out of obscurity, bring to light: to expel from a burrow.—*adj.* **unearthed′**, not connected to earth electrically: dug up, brought to light, etc.—*n.* **unearth′liness**.—*adj.* **unearth′ly**, celestial: weird, ghostly: unconscionable, absurd (esp. of an early hour).—*n.* **unease′**, lack of ease: discomfort: apprehension.—*adv.* **uneas′ily**.—*n.* **uneas′iness**.—*adjs.* **uneas′y**, not at ease: disquieted: apprehensive: showing troubled restlessness (*lit.* and *fig.*): uncomfortable: (now *rare*) not easy to be done: difficult because of physical obstacles (*obs.*); **uneath** (*un-ēth′*; O.E. *unēathe*; see **eath**; *arch.*), difficult: distressing.—*adv.* with difficulty: in hardship: hardly, scarcely: almost (*Spens.*).—Also (*adv.*) **uneth**, **uneathes**, **unnethes′**.—*adjs.* **uneconom′ic**, not in accordance with sound economics; **uneconom′ical**, not economical.—*v.t.* **unedge′**, to blunt.—*adjs.* **uned′ifying**, not instructing or uplifting morally or aesthetically: morally degrading or degraded; **uned′ited**, never edited, never before published; **unemo′tional**.—*adv.* **unemo′tionally**.—*adjs.* **unemo′tioned**, impassive; **unemploy′able**: **unemployed′**, out of work: not put to use or profit: for or pertaining to those who are out of work.—*n.* the number of people out of work in a given period.—*n.* **unemploy′ment**.— *adjs.* **unenchant′ed** (*Milt.* **uninchant′ed**); **unendeared′** (*Milt.* **unindeared′**), not made precious; **unend′ing**, endless: everlasting: never ceasing, incessant: thorough-going (*Carlyle*).—*adv.* **unen′dingly**.—*n.* **unen′dingness**.—*adjs.* **un-Eng′lish**, not English in character; **un-Eng′lished**, not translated into English; **unen′viable**, not to be envied. —*adv.* **unen′viably**.—*adjs.* **unen′vied**; **unen′vious**; **unen′vying**; **unē′qual**, not equal: not equal (to): inadequate (*obs.*): unjust (*obs.*): excessive (*obs.*): varying, not uniform.—Also *adv.* (*Shak.*).—*n.* one who is not equal in rank,

---

*Words beginning with pfx.* un- *are listed first* (pp. 1462 ff.); *other* UN- *words follow* (pp. 1484 ff.).

Neutral vowels in unaccented syllables: *el′ə-mənt*; for certain sounds in foreign words, see p. viii

ability, etc.—*adj.* unē′qualled, without an equal. —*adv.* unē′qually.—*adjs.* uneq′uitable, inequitable; unequiv′ocal, unambiguous: explicit: clear and emphatic.—*adv.* unequiv′ocally; unerr′ing, making no error, infallible: not, or never, missing the mark (*lit.* and *fig.*).—*adv.* unerr′ingly.— *n.* unerr′ingness.—*v.t.* uness′ence, to deprive of essence or being (*Lamb*).—*adjs.* unessen′tial, without being, immaterial (*Milt.*, etc.): not of the essence: inessential, not necessary, not important; unestab′lished, not established: not on the establishment or permanent staff; unexam′pled, unprecedented, without like or parallel; unexcep′tionable, not liable to objection or criticism, exactly right, excellent: without exception (*Ruskin*).—*n.* unexcep′tionableness.— *adv.* unexcep′tionably.—*adj.* unexcep′tional, not admitting, or forming, an exception: unexceptionable.—*adv.* unexcep′tionally.—*adjs.* unex′ecuted, not executed: not brought into action (*Shak.*); unexpē′rient (*Shak.*), inexperienced; unexpress′ive, not expressive: inexpressible, beyond the power of description (*Shak., Milt.*); unexpug′nable, inexpugnable; unextinct′, not extinguished or dead (*fig.*); uneyed′, unseen, unobserved.

*Words with prefix* un- (*continued*).

*adj.* unfa′bled, not fabled, real.—*n.* un′fact, a fact that must not be acknowledged, or a falsehood that must pass as fact, esp. in international politics.—*adj.* unfail′ing, never failing or giving out: infallible: constant: inexhaustible.—*adv.* unfail′ingly.—*adj.* unfair′, not fair, ugly: inequitable, unjust: involving deception or fraud and leading to undue advantage over business rival(s).—*v.t.* (*Shak.*) to deprive of beauty.—*adv.* unfair′ly.—*ns.* unfair′ness; unfaith′, want of faith or trust.—*adj.* unfaith′ful, not of the approved religion: not faithful, violating trust: untrue to marriage vows: not true to the original. —*adv.* unfaith′fully.—*n.* unfaith′fulness.—*adjs.* unfall′ible (*Shak.*), infallible; unfashionable, not fashionable: incapable of being fashioned (*obs.*): shapeless (*Shak.*).—*n.* unfash′ionableness. —*adv.* unfash′ionably.—*adj.* unfash′ioned, not formed: not shaped: not made polished, elegant, etc. (*obs.*).—*v.t.* unfasten (un-fäs′n), to release from a fastening: to unfix (*Shak.*).—

*v.i.* to become loose or open.—*adjs.* unfas′tened, released from fastening: not fastened; unfa′thered, without a father or acknowledged father: deprived of a father; unfa′therly, unbefitting a father; unfath′omable, not able to be fathomed (*lit.* and *fig.*).—*n.* unfath′omableness.—*adv.* unfath′omably.—*adjs.* unfath′omed, not sounded, of unknown depth: of unascertained meaning (*fig.*); unfeared′, not feared: unafraid (*obs.*); unfear′ful, not afraid.—*adv.* unfear′fully.—*adjs.* unfear′ing; unfeat′ured, without or well-formed features (*lit.* and *fig.*); unfeed′, not retained by a fee: unpaid; unfeel′ing, without feeling: without kind or sympathetic feelings: hard-hearted.—*adv.* unfeel′ingly.—*n.* unfeel′ingness.—*adj.* unfeigned′, not feigned, real: not feigning, sincere.—*adv.* unfeign′edly.—*n.* unfeign′edness.—*adjs.* unfeign′ing; unfell′owed, unmatched; unfelt′, not felt: intangible (*Shak.*).—*v.t.* unfett′er, to free from fetters.—*adjs.* unfett′ered, unrestrained; unfeu′dal, not marked by social attitudes and assumptions like those under the feudal system; unfeud′alise, -ize, to defeudalise.—*adjs.* unfiled′ (*Spens.* unfilde′), not rubbed with a file, unpolished; unfiled′ (now *dial.*), undefiled; unfiled′, not placed ón a file; unfill′eted, not bound with a fillet: not boned; unfil′terable, unfil′trable, unable to pass through a filter (or an ordinary filter); unfine′, not fine; unfin′ished. —*n.* unfin′ishing (*Milt.*), the leaving unfinished. —*adjs.* unfit, not fit: not fitting or suitable: not in fit condition.—*n.* an unfit person.—*v.t.* to make unfit: to make unsuitable (for): to disqualify.—*adv.* unfit′ly, unsuitably, inappropriately.—*n.* unfit′ness.—*adj.* unfitt′ed, not provided (with): without fittings: not made to fit, or fitted for fit: not adapted, qualified, or able.—*n.* unfitt′edness.—*adj.* unfitt′ing, unsuitable.—*adv.* unfitt′ingly.—*v.t.* unfix′, to unfasten, detach: to unsettle (*fig.*).—*v.i.* to become loose. —*adj.* unfixed′.—*ns.* unfix′edness, unfix′ity.— *adj.* unflapp′able (*coll.*), imperturbable, never agitated or alarmed.—*n.* unflappabil′ity.—*adj.* unfledged′, not yet fledged: undeveloped: of early youth.—*v.t.* unflesh′, to remove the flesh from.—*adjs.* unfleshed′, deprived of flesh, reduced to a skeleton: not fleshed, not having tasted blood, uninitiated; unflesh′ly, spiritual:

---

unexact′ing, *adj.* un- (1).
unexagg′erated, *adj.* un- (1).
unexalt′ed, *adj.* un- (1).
unexam′ined, *adj.* un- (1).
unex′cavated, *adj.* un- (1).
unexcelled′, *adj.* un- (1).
unexci′table, *adj.* un- (1).
unexci′ted, *adj.* un- (1).
unexci′ting, *adj.* un- (1).
unexclu′ded, *adj.* un- (1).
unexclu′sive, *adj.* un- (1).
unexclu′sively, *adv.* un- (1).
unexem′plified, *adj.* un- (1).
unex′ercised, *adj.* un- (1).
unexhaus′ted, *adj.* un- (1).
unexpan′ded, *adj.* un- (1).
unexpec′tant, *adj.* un- (1).
unexpec′ted, *adj.* un- (1).
unexpec′tedly, *adv.* un- (1).
unexpec′tedness, *n.* un- (1).
unexpen′sive, *adj.* un- (1).
unexpen′sively, *adv.* un- (1).
unexpē′rienced, *adj.* un- (1).
unexpired′, *adj.* un- (1).
unexplain′able, *adj.* un- (1).
unexplained′, *adj.* un- (1).
unexplored′, *adj.* un- (1).
unexposed′, *adj.* un- (1).

unexpressed′, *adj.* un- (1).
unexpress′ible, *adj.* un- (1).
unex′purgated, *adj.* un- (1).
unexten′ded, *adj.* un- (1).
unexten′uated, *adj.* un- (1).
unexting′uishable, *adj.* un- (1).
unexting′uishably, *adv.* un- (1).
unexting′uished, *adj.* un- (1).
unfa′dable, *adj.* un- (1).
unfa′ded, *adj.* un- (1).
unfa′ding, *adj.* un- (1).
unfa′dingly, *adv.* un- (1).
unfall′en, *adj.* un- (1).
unfal′tering, *adj.* un- (1).
unfal′teringly, *adv.* un- (1).
unfamed′, *adj.* un- (1).
unfamil′iar, *adj.* un- (1).
unfamiliar′ity, *n.* un- (1).
unfamil′iarly, *adv.* un- (1).
unfanned′, *adj.* un- (1).
unfastid′ious, *adj.* un- (1).
unfault′y, *adj.* un- (1).
unfa′vourable, *adj.* un- (1).
unfa′vourableness, *n.* un- (1).
unfa′vourably, *adv.* un- (1).
unfeas′ible, *adj.* un- (1).

unfeath′ered, *adj.* un- (1).
unfed′, *adj.* un- (1).
unfelled′, *adj.* un- (1).
unfem′inine, *adj.* un- (1).
unfenced′, *adj.* un- (1).
unferment′ed, *adj.* un- (1).
unfer′tilised, -z-, *adj.* un- (1).
unfeued′, *adj.* un- (1).
unfig′ured, *adj.* un- (1).
unfil′ial, *adj.* un- (1).
unfil′ially, *adv.* un- (1).
unfill′able, *adj.* un- (1).
unfilled′, *adj.* un- (1).
unfilmed′, *adj.* un- (1).
unfil′tered, *adj.* un- (1).
unfired′, *adj.* un- (1).
unfirm′, *adj.* un- (1).
unfished′, *adj.* un- (1).
unflagg′ing, *adj.* un- (1).
unflagg′ingly, *adv.* un- (1).
unflatt′ering, *adj.* un- (1).
unflatt′eringly, *adv.* un- (1).
unflawed′, *adj.* un- (1).
unflinch′ing, *adj.* un- (1).
unflinch′ingly, *adv.* un- (1).
unfloored′, *adj.* un- (1).
unflus′tered, *adj.* un- (1).

---

*Words beginning with pfx.* un- *are listed first* (pp. 1462 ff.); *other* UN- *words follow* (pp. 1484 ff.).

incorporeal: not carnal.—*v.i.* **unflush´**, to lose a flush of colour (*Arnold*).—*v.t.* **unfold´**, to open the folds of: to spread out: to tell: to disclose, make known: to reveal, display.—*v.i.* to open out, spread open to the view (*lit.* and *fig.*).— *v.t.* **unfold´**, to let out from a sheep-fold.—*adjs.* **unfold´ed**, not folded: opened out from folds; **unfold´ed**, not enclosed in a sheep-fold.—*n.* **unfold´er**.—*n.* and *adj.* **unfold´ing**, opening out from folds: disclosing.—*n.* and *adj.* **unfold´ing**, letting out from a sheep-fold.—*adj.* (of star; *Shak.*) showing the time for unfolding sheep.— *v.t.* **unfool´**, to undo the fooling of.—*adjs.* **unfoot´ed**, untrodden; **unforbid´** (*Milt.*), **unforbidd´en**; **unforced´**.—*adv.* **unfor´cedly.**—*adjs.* **unfor´cible**, without strength (*obs.*): incapable of being forced or (*Milt.*) enforced; **unforebod´ing**, not giving or feeling foreboding; **unfore´skinned** (*Milt.*), circumcised; **unfor´ested**, not wooded: not reckoned as deer-forested: deforested; **unforgott´en** (*arch.* **unforgot´**).—*v.t.* **unform´**, to unmake.—*adjs.* **unfor´mal**, informal; **unfor´malised, -ized**, not made formal; **unformed´**, unmade, uncreated: formless, unshaped: immature, undeveloped; **unfor´tunate**, unlucky: regrettable: of ill omen: (esp. formerly) living by prostitution.—*n.* an unfortunate person.— *adv.* **unfor´tunately.**—*ns.* **unfor´tunateness; unfor´tune** (*arch.*).—*adjs.* **unfor´tuned**; **unfought´** (*arch.* **unfought´en**); **unfound´**, not found; **unfound´ed**, not founded: without foundation, baseless: without bottom, bottomless (*Milt.*). —*adv.* **unfound´edly.**—*adjs.* **unframed´**, not formed or fashioned (*lit.* and *fig.*): not set in a frame; **unfraught´**, not fraught or charged.— *v.t.* to unload, discharge.—*adj.* **unfree´**, not free: in servitude: not free of a corporation.—*n.* **unfree´man**, one who is not free of a corporation.— *v.t.* and *v.i.* **unfreeze´**, to thaw: to free (prices, wages, funds) from the control imposed by a standstill order.—*adj.* **unfrett´ed**, not eaten away or rubbed: not annoyed or worried.—*n.* **unfriend´**, one who is not a friend.—*adj.* **unfriend´ed**, not provided with or supported by friends.— *ns.* **unfriend´edness; unfriend´liness.**—*adj.* **unfriend´ly**, ill-disposed: somewhat hostile.—*adv.* unkindly.—*n.* **unfriend´ship** (*arch.*), unfriendliness.—*adj.* **unfright´ed** (*arch.*), not frightened.— *v.t.* **unfrock´**, to strip of a frock or gown, depose from priesthood: to remove from a comparable position in another sphere of activity.—*adjs.* **unfrocked´**; **unfumed´**, not fumigated: undistilled (*Milt.*); **unfund´ed**, not funded, floating, as a public debt, in the form of exchequer bills

and bonds, to be paid up at certain dates.—*v.t.* **unfurl´**, to release from being furled: to unfold, display.—*v.i.* to spread open.—*v.t.* **unfur´nish**, to deprive (*Shak.*): to deprive of men, defences, or furniture.—*adj.* **unfur´nished**, not furnished: unsupplied.

*Words with prefix* un- (*continued*).

*adjs.* **ungain´** (*obs.*, *arch.*, or *dial.*; from **gain** (2)), indirect: inconvenient: unpleasant: ungainly, awkward: unskilled; **ungain´ful.**—*n.* **ungain´liness.**—*adj.* **ungain´ly**, awkward, clumsy, uncouth.—*adv.* awkwardly.—*adjs.* **ungalled´**, not made painful by rubbing: not irritated or inflamed (*fig.*); **ungazed´**, not gazed (at; also **ungazed´-upon**).—*v.t.* **ungear´**, to unharness (*arch.*): to disconnect a part of a system of moving parts (also *fig.*).—*adjs.* **unge´nial**, not sympathetically cheerful: not comfortably warm, raw: not congenial: not favourable to natural growth; **ungen´itured**, (*Shak.*) without means of generation, or not produced by ordinary generation.— *n.* **ungentil´ity.**—*adjs.* **ungen´tle**, not gentle: not of gentle birth: not of or befitting the gentle; **ungen´tlemanlike**, not like or befitting a gentleman.—Also *adv.*—*n.* **ungen´tlemanliness.**—*adj.* **ungen´tlemanly**, unbecoming a gentleman: not gentlemanlike.—Also *adv.*—*n.* **ungen´tleness.**— *adv.* **ungent´ly.**—*v.t.* **unget´**, to undo the begetting of.—*adjs.* **ungetat´able**, **unget-at´-able**, inaccessible; **unghost´ly**, not pertaining to or like a ghost: not spiritual.—*v.t.* **ungird´**, to free from a girdle or band: to undo the fastening of and take off.—*adj.* **ungirt´** (or **ungird´ed**), not girt: freed from the girdle: not tightened up, not strengthened for action (*fig.*).—*v.t.* **ungirth´**, to remove a girth from: to free from a girth.— *adj.* **ungirthed´.**—*v.t.* **ungod´**, to divest of divinity: to make godless.—*adj.* **ungod´like.**—*adv.* **ungod´lily**, in an ungodly manner.—*n.* **ungod´liness.** —*adjs.* **ungod´ly**, not godly: outrageous, unconscionable (*coll.*); **ungored´** (*Shak.*. **ungord´**; another reading **ungorg´d**) unwounded; **ungorged´**, not gorged or sated; **ungot´**, **ungott´en**, not got or acquired: unbegotten; **ungov´ernable**, uncontrollable: unruly.—*n.* **ungov´ernableness.**—*adv.* **ungov´ernably.**—*adj.* **ungov´erned.**— *v.t.* **ungown´**, to deprive or divest of a gown: to unfrock.—*adjs.* **ungowned´**, not wearing a gown: deprived of one's gown; **ungra´cious**, without grace: graceless: ungraceful: wanting in courtesy, affability or urbanity: behaving with a bad grace: unmannerly: rendering offensive or disagreeable.—*adv.* **ungra´ciously.**

---

unfo´cus(s)ed, *adj.* un- (1).
unford´able, *adj.* un- (1).
unforeknow´able, *adj.* un- (1).
unforeknown´, *adj.* un- (1).
unforesee´able, *adj.* un- (1).
unforesee´ing, *adj.* un- (1).
unforeseen´, *adj.* un- (1).
unforetold´, *adj.* un- (1).
unforewarned´, *adj.* un- (1).
unfor´feited, *adj.* un- (1).
unforged´, *adj.* un- (1).
unforgett´able, *adj.* un- (1).
unforgett´ably, *adv.* un- (1).
unforgiv´able, *adj.* un- (1).
unforgiv´en, *adj.* un- (1).
unforgive´ness, *n.* un- (1).
unforgiv´ing, *adj.* un- (1).
unforgiv´ingness, *n.* un- (1).
unfor´midable, *adj.* un- (1).
unforsa´ken, *adj.* un- (1).
unfor´tified, *adj.* un- (1).
unfossilif´erous, *adj.* un- (1).
unfoss´ilised, -ized, *adj.* un- (1).

unfos´tered, *adj.* un- (1).
unfran´chised, *adj.* un- (1).
unfranked´, *adj.* un- (1).
unfre´quent, *adj.* un- (1).
unfrequen´ted, *adj.* un- (1).
unfre´quentedness, *n.* un- (1).
unfre´quently, *adv.* un- (1).
unfright´ened, *adj.* un- (1).
unfro´zen, *adj.* un- (1).
unfruc´tuous, *adj.* un- (1).
unfruit´ful, *adj.* un- (1).
unfruit´fully, *adv.* un- (1).
unfruit´fulness, *n.* un- (1).
unfu´elled, *adj.* un- (1).
unfulfilled´, *adj.* un- (1).
unfunn´y, *adj.* un- (1).
unfurred´, *adj.* un- (1).
unfurr´owed, *adj.* un- (1).
ungainsaid´, *adj.* un- (1).
ungainsay´able, *adj.* un- (1).
ungall´ant, *adj.* un- (1).
ungall´antly, *adv.* un- (1).
ungar´bled, *adj.* un- (1).

ungar´mented, *adj.* un- (1).
ungar´nered, *adj.* un- (1).
ungar´nished, *adj.* un- (1).
ungar´tered, *adj.* un- (1).
ungath´ered, *adj.* un- (1).
ungauged´, *adj.* un- (1).
ungen´erous, *adj.* un- (1).
ungen´erously, *adv.* un- (1).
ungenteel´, *adj.* un- (1).
ungenteel´ly, *adv.* un- (1).
ungen´uine, *adj.* un- (1).
ungen´uineness, *n.* un- (1).
ungift´ed, *adj.* un- (1).
ungild´, *v.t.* un- (2).
ungild´ed, *adj.* un- (1).
ungilt´, *adj.* un- (1).
ungiv´ing, *adj.* un- (1).
unglad´, *adj.* un- (1).
unglazed´, *adj.* un- (1).
unglossed´, *adj.* un- (1).
unglove´, *v.t.* un- (2).
ungloved´, *adj.* un- (1).
unglue´, *v.t.*, *v.i.* un- (2).

---

*Words beginning with pfx.* un- *are listed first* (pp. 1462 ff.); *other* UN- *words follow* (pp. 1484 ff.).

Neutral vowels in unaccented syllables: *el´ə-mənt*; for certain sounds in foreign words, see p. viii

—*n.* **ungra′ciousness.**—*adjs.* **ungrad′ed,** not classified in grades: not adjusted to easy gradients; **ungrate′ful,** not feeling gratitude: disagreeable, irksome: not repaying one's labour, thankless. —*adv.* **ungrate′fully.**—*n.* **ungrate′fulness.**—*adjs.* **unground′,** not ground; **unground′ed,** not based (with *in*): without basis, unreal, false: without sound fundamental instruction.—*adv.* **unground′edly.**—*n.* **unground′edness.**—*v.t.* **unguard′,** to render, or leave, unguarded.—*adj.* **unguard′ed,** without guard: unprotected: unscreened: incautious: inadvertent.—*adv.* **unguard′edly.**—*n.* **unguard′edness.**—*v.t.* **ungum′,** to free from gum or gummed condition.—*adj.* **ungummed,** not gummed: freed from gum or gumming: (**come ungummed,** of plan, to go amiss; *slang*).

*Words with prefix* un- (*continued*).
*adj.* **unha′ble** (an *obs.* form of **unable**).—*v.t.* **unhair′,** to deprive of hair.—*v.i.* to become free from hair.—*adjs.* **unhaired′,** freed from hair; **unhalsed** (*un-höst′*; *Scott*), unsaluted. —*v.t.* **unhand′,** to take the hands off: to let go.—*adv.* **unhand′ily,** awkwardly.—*n.* **unhand′iness.**—*adjs.* **unhan′dled,** not handled or managed: not broken-in; **unhand′some,** not handsome: unskilful in action (*obs.*): unseemly: ungenerous: ungracious: clumsy, inconvenient (*obs.*).—Also *adv.* (*Spens.*).—*adv.* **unhand′somely.** —*n.* **unhand′someness.**—*adj.* **unhand′y,** not skilful, awkward: not convenient.—*adv.* **unhapp′ily,** in an unhappy manner: unfortunately, regrettably: unsuccessfully: maliciously (*obs.*): unfavourably (*Shak.*): shrewdly (*Shak.*).—*n.* **unhapp′iness.**—*adj.* **unhapp′y,** bringing misfortune: not fortunate: miserable: infelicitous, inapt: mischievous (*obs.*).—*v.t.* (*Shak.*) to make unhappy or unfortunate.—*v.t.* **unhar′bour,** to dislodge from shelter.—*adj.* **unhar′boured,** without a shelter: dislodged from shelter.—*v.t.* **unhar′ness,** to take the armour or the harness off.— *adj.* **unhar′nessed,** not in, or freed from, armour or harness.—*v.t.* **unhasp′,** to unfasten by undoing a hasp.—*v.i.* **unhat′,** to take off the hat from respect.—*adjs.* **unhatched′** (**unhatch′d;** *Shak.*), not out of the egg: not developed: not shaded: **unhacked;** **unhatt′ed,** hatless.—*n.* **unhatt′ing,** lifting of the hat.—*v.t.* **unhead′,** to take the head from; **unheal′** (see **unhele**).—*adjs.* **unheal′able;**

**unhealed′.**—*n.* **unhealth′,** ill-health.—*adj.* **unhealth′ful.**—*adv.* **unhealth′fully.**—*n.* **unhealth′ful-ness.**—*adv.* **unheal′thily.**—*n.* **unheal′thiness.**— *adjs.* **unheal′thy,** not healthy: morbid: unfavourable to health: dangerous (*slang*); **unheard′,** not heard: not granted a hearing: not heard of, unknown to fame: unprecedented (in Shak., *K. John* V, ii. 133, understood by some as unhaired, beardless); **unheard′-of.**—*v.t.* **unhearse′** (used by Spens. in the *pa.t.* **unherst**), app. to remove from a hearse or a stand for candles at a funeral.—*adj.* **unhearsed,** without a hearse. —*vs.t.* **unheart′** (*Shak.*), to dishearten.—*adv.* **unheed′ily,** unheedfully.—*v.t.* **unhele′,** **unheal′,** (*Spens.*) to uncover, disclose; **unhelm′,** to divest of helmet.—*adjs.* **unhelmed′,** **unhel′meted,** without, or divested of, helm or helmet; **unheppen** (*un-ep′n*; *Yorks.*, *Linc.*, *Tennyson*; O.N. *heppinn*, dexterous), clumsy.—*v.t.* (*pa.t.*) **unherst′** (see **unhearse**).—*adj.* **unhes′itating,** not hesitating or doubting: prompt: ready.—*adv.* **unhes′itatingly.**—*adj.* **unhide′bound,** not having a skin confining the body (*Milt.*).—*v.t.* **unhinge′,** to take from the hinges: to derange.—*adj.* **unhinged′.**—*n.* **unhinge′ment.**—*adjs.* **unhistor′ic, -al,** not mentioned in history: not in accordance with history: not having actually existed or happened.—*vs.t.* **unhive′,** to drive from a hive; **unhoard′,** to take from a hoard.—*adv.* **unho′lily.** —*n.* **unho′liness.**—*adjs.* **unhol′pen,** not helped (*arch.*); **unho′ly,** not holy: very wicked: unconscionable, outrageous, unearthly (*coll.*); **unhon′est** (*obs.*), unseemly, indecent, dishonourable: immoral: ′ dishonest.—*v.t.* **unhoop′,** to remove hoops from.—*adjs.* **unhoped′,** unexpected (*obs.*): beyond what was expected with hope (*arch.*; now **unhoped′-for**); **unhope′ful.**— *adv.* **unhope′fully.**—*vs.t.* **unhorse′,** to dislodge or throw from a horse: to take a horse or horses from.—*adj.* **unhos′pitable** (now usu. **inhospitable**). —*v.t.* **unhouse′,** to deprive of or drive from a house or shelter.—*adjs.* **unhoused′,** houseless: deprived of a house; **unhous′eled,** (*Shak.* **unhouzz′led**), not having received the sacrament; **unhung′,** not hung: without hangings: unhanged; **unhus′banded,** uncultivated: without a husband.—*v.t.* **unhusk′,** to strip the husk from.

*Words with prefix* un- (*continued*).
*adj.* **unide′a'd,** without ideas: with unfurnished

---

**ungraced′,** *adj.* un- (1).
**ungrace′ful,** *adj.* un- (1).
**ungrace′fully,** *adv.* un- (1).
**ungrace′fulness,** *n.* un- (1).
**ungrammat′ic, -al,** *adjs.* un- (1).
**ungrammat′ically,** *adv.* un- (1).
**ungrat′ified,** *adj.* un- (1).
**ungrave′ly** (*Shak.*), *adv.* un- (1).
**ungroomed′,** *adj.* un- (1).
**ungrown′,** *adj.* un- (1).
**ungrudged′,** *adj.* un- (1).
**ungrudg′ing,** *adj.* un- (1).
**ungrudg′ingly,** *adv.* un- (1).
**unguer′doned,** *adj.* un- (1).
**unguessed′,** *adj.* un- (1).
**unguid′ed,** *adj.* un- (1).
**unguilt′y,** *adj.* un- (1).
**ungyve′,** *v.t.* un- (2).
**ungyved′,** *adj.* un- (1).
**unhab′itable,** *adj.* un- (1).
**unhabit′uated,** *adj.* un- (1).
**unhacked′,** *adj.* un- (1).
**unhack′neyed,** *adj.* un- (1).
**unhailed′,** *adj.* un- (1).
**unhall′ow,** *v.t.* un- (2).
**unhall′owed,** *adj.* un- (1).
**unhamp′ered,** *adj.* un- (1).

**unhand′seled,** *adj.* un- (1).
**unhang′,** *v.t.* un- (2).
**unhanged′,** *adj.* un- (1).
**unhar′dened,** *adj.* un- (1).
**unhar′dy,** *adj.* un- (1).
**unharmed′,** *adj.* un- (1).
**unharm′ful,** *adj.* un- (1).
**unharm′fully,** *adv.* un- (1).
**unharm′ing,** *adj.* un- (1).
**unharmo′nious,** *adj.* un- (1).
**unhar′vested,** *adj.* un- (1).
**unhast′ing,** *adj.* un- (1).
**unhast′y,** *adj.* un- (1).
**unhatched′,** *adj.* un- (1).
**unhaunt′ed,** *adj.* un- (1).
**unhaz′arded,** *adj.* un- (1).
**unhaz′ardous,** *adj.* un- (1).
**unheat′ed,** *adj.* un- (1).
**unhedged′,** *adj.* un- (1).
**unheed′ed,** *adj.* un- (1).
**unheed′edly,** *adv.* un- (1).
**unheed′ful,** *adj.* un- (1).
**unheed′fully,** *adv.* un- (1).
**unheed′ing,** *adj.* un- (1).
**unheed′ingly,** *adv.* un- (1).
**unheed′y,** *adj.* un- (1).
**unhelped′,** *adj.* un- (1).

**unhelp′ful,** *adj.* un- (1).
**unher′alded,** *adj.* un- (1).
**unhero′ic, -al,** *adjs.* un- (1).
**unhero′ically,** *adv.* un- (1).
**unhewn′,** *adj.* un- (1).
**unhidd′en,** *adj.* un- (1).
**unhired′,** *adj.* un- (1).
**unhitch′,** *v.t.* un- (2).
**unhome′like,** *adj.* un- (1).
**unhome′ly,** *adj.* un- (1).
**unhon′oured,** *adj.* un- (1).
**unhood′,** *v.t.* un- (2).
**unhood′ed,** *adj.* un- (1, 2).
**unhook′,** *v.t.* un- (2).
**unhu′man,** *adj.* un- (1).
**unhu′manise, -ize,** *v.t.* un- (2).
**unhum′bled,** *adj.* un- (1).
**unhunt′ed,** *adj.* un- (1).
**unhurr′ied,** *adj.* un- (1).
**unhurr′iedly,** *adv.* un- (1).
**unhurr′ying,** *adj.* un- (1).
**unhurt′,** *adj.* un- (1).
**unhurt′ful,** *adj.* un- (1).
**unhurt′fully,** *adv.* un- (1).
**unhurt′fulness,** *n.* un- (1).
**unhygien′ic,** *adj.* un- (1).

---

*Words beginning with pfx.* un- *are listed first* (pp. 1462 ff.); *other* UN- *words follow* (pp. 1484 ff.).

fāte, fär; mē, hûr (her); mīne; mōte, fōr; mūte, mōōn, fŏŏt; dhen (then) mind; **unidē′al**, not ideal: not idealistic: conveying no idea (*obs.*): without ideas (*obs.*): without ideals.—*n.* **unidē′alism.**—*adjs.* **unidēal- ist′ic**; **unimag′inable.**—*n.* **unimag′inableness.**— *adv.* **unimag′inably.**—*adj.* **unimag′inative**, not imaginative, prosaic.—*n.* **unimag′inativeness.**— *adjs.* **unimag′ined**; **unimpass′ioned**, not impassioned, calm, tranquil; **unimpeach′able**, not to be impeached: not liable to be accused: free from fault: blameless; **unimpeached′**; **unim′- portuned** (or -*tūnd′*, -*chōōnd′*; often -*pör′*), not persistently begged (to do something); **unim- posed**; **unimpōs′ing**, unimpressive: not burdensome (*Thomson*); **unimproved′**, not made better: not cultivated, cleared, or built upon: not put to use; **unincum′bered**, unencumbered; **unindeared′** (see **unendeared**); **uninformed′**, not having received information: untaught: not imbued with life or activity; **uninform′ing**; **unin′terested**, not personally concerned: not taking an interest; **unin′teresting.**—*adv.* **unin′terestingly.**

*Words with prefix* un- (*continued*).
*v.t.* **unjoint′**, to disjoint.—*adjs.* **unjoint′ed**, disjointed, incoherent: without joints; **unked**, **unket**, **unkid** (*ōōngk′id*, *ungk′id*, -*it*; *N.* and *W. England*; forms of **uncouth**), strange, uncomfortable, lonely, eerie; **unkempt′** (see **kemb**), uncombed: unpolished, rough; **unkenned′**, **unkent′**, unknown.—*v.t.* **unkenn′el**, to dislodge (a fox) from a hole: to let out from a kennel.— *adjs.* **unkept′**, not kept: untended; **unkind′**, unnaturally wicked (*obs.*): wanting in kindness: cruel; **unkin′dled**, not kindled.—*n.* **unkind′liness**, want of kindliness.—*adj.* **unkind′ly**, unnatural: not kind.—*adv.* unnaturally (*Milt.*): against right feeling (*Shak.*): in an unkindly manner: cruelly.—*n.* **unkind′ness**, want of kindness or affection: cruelty: ill-feeling.—*v.t.* **unking′**, to deprive of kingship or of a king.—*adjs.* **unking′- like**; **unking′ly**, unbecoming a king: unlike a king.—*v.t.* **unkiss′** (*Shak.*), to annul by means of a kiss.—*adjs.* **unkissed′**, not kissed; **unknelled** (*un-neld′*), without tolling.—*v.t.* **unknight** (*un- nit′*), to divest of knighthood.—*adj.* **unknight′ed**,

not knighted. —*n.* **unknight′liness.** —*adj.* **un- knightly** (*un-nit′li*), unlike, or unbecoming to, a knight.—*adv.* in an unknightly manner.—*v.t.* **un- knit** (*un-nit′*), to undo the knitting of: to untie: to smooth out from a frown: to relax.—*v.i.* to become unknit.—*adj.* loose, unfirmed.—*v.t.* **un- knot** (*un-not′*), to free from knots: to untie.— *adj.* **unknowable** (*un-nō′ə-bl*), incapable of being known.—*n.* an unknowable thing: the first or original cause: that which is cognisable only in its relations.—*n.* **unknow′ableness.**—*adj.* **un- know′ing**, ignorant, unaware: ignorant (of; *arch.*): not knowing (*arch.* or *poet.*): unwitting: unknown (to; *dial.*).—*adv.* **unknow′ingly.**—*n.* **unknow′ingness.**—*adj.* **unknown** (*un-nōn′*), not known.—*n.* an unknown person or quantity: (with *the*) that which is unknown.—*n.* **unknown′- ness.**

*Words with prefix* un- (*continued*).
*adjs.* **unla′boured**, showing no traces of labour: unworked: unrestrained, easy; **unla′bouring.**— *vs.t.* **unlace′**, to free from being laced: to undo the lacing of: to carve (esp. a rabbit; *obs.*): to undo, destroy (*Shak.*); **unlade′**, to unload.— *adj.* **unla′den**, not laden.—*n.* **unla′ding.**—*adj.* **un- laid′**, not laid.—*vs.t.* **unlash′** (*naut.*), to loose the lashings of; **unlast**, **unlaste** (*un-läst′*, -*läst′*), Spenserian *pa.t.* and *pa.p.* of **unlace**; **unlatch′**, to lift the latch of.—*n.* **un′law**, breach of law (*arch.*): a fine, penalty (*Scots law*; *obs.*).—*v.t.* **unlaw′**, to annul, repeal: to fine (*obs.*).—*adj.* **unlaw′ful**, forbidden by law: illegitimate: illicit: acting illegally.—*adv.* **unlaw′fully.**—*n.* **unlaw′ful- ness.**—*vs.t.* **unlay′** (*naut.*), to untwist; **unlead** (*un-led′*; *print.*), to take the lead or leads from. —*adj.* **unleal′**, unfaithful.—*v.t.* **unlearn′**, to undo the process of learning: to rid one's mind of, eliminate habit(s) of.—*adj.* **unlearned** (-*lûr′nid*; also *poet.* -*lûrnd′*), without learning: (-*lûrnd′*) not learned, got up, acquired: eliminated by unlearning.—*adv.* **unlear′nedly.**—*n.* **unlear′nedness.** —*adj.* and *pa.p.* **unlearnt** (-*lûrnt′*), unlearned. —*v.t.* **unleash′**, to free from a leash, let go.—*adjs.* **unled′**, not led, without guidance;

---

**unident′ified**, *adj.* un- (1).
**unidiomat′ic**, *adj.* un- (1).
**unillumed′**, *adj.* un- (1).
**unillu′minated**, *adj.* un- (1).
**unillu′minating**, *adj.* un- (1).
**unillu′mined**, *adj.* un- (1).
**unill′ustrated**, *adj.* un- (1).
**unimbued′**, *adj.* un- (1).
**unimmor′tal** (*Milt.*), *adj.* un- (1).
**unimpaired′**, *adj.* un- (1).
**unimpart′ed**, *adj.* un- (1).
**unimped′ed**, *adj.* un- (1).
**unimped′edly**, *adv.* un- (1).
**unimplored′**, *adj.* un- (1).
**unimport′ance**, *n.* un- (1).
**unimport′ant**, *adj.* un- (1).
**unimpreg′nated** (or -*im′*), *adj.* un- (1).
**unimpressed′**, *adj.* un- (1).
**unimpress′ible**, *adj.* un- (1).
**unimpress′ionable**, *adj.* un- (1).
**unimpress′ive**, *adj.* un- (1).
**unimpris′oned**, *adj.* un- (1, 2).
**unimpugn′able**, *adj.* un- (1).
**uninclosed′**, *adj.* un- (1).
**uninaug′urated**, *adj.* un- (1).
**unincit′ed**, *adj.* un- (1).
**unincor′porated**, *adj.* un- (1).
**unin′dexed**, *adj.* un- (1).
**uninfect′ed**, *adj.* un- (1).
**uninflamed′**, *adj.* un- (1).
**uninflamm′able**, *adj.* un- (1).

**uninflat′ed**, *adj.* un- (1).
**uninflect′ed**, *adj.* un- (1).
**unin′fluenced**, *adj.* un- (1).
**uninfluen′tial**, *adj.* un- (1).
**uninhab′itable**, *adj.* un- (1).
**uninhab′ited**, *adj.* un- (1).
**uninhib′ited**, *adj.* un- (1).
**unini′tiated**, *adj.* un- (1).
**unin′jured**, *adj.* un- (1).
**uninquir′ing**, *adj.* un- (1).
**uninquis′itive**, *adj.* un- (1).
**uninscribed′**, *adj.* un- (1).
**uninspired′**, *adj.* un- (1).
**uninspir′ing**, *adj.* un- (1).
**uninstruct′ed**, *adj.* un- (1).
**uninstruct′ive**, *adj.* un- (1).
**uninsured′**, *adj.* un- (1).
**unin′tegrated**, *adj.* un- (1).
**unintellect′ual**, *adj.* un- (1).
**unintell′igent**, *adj.* un- (1).
**unintelligibil′ity**, *n.* un- (1).
**unintell′igible**, *adj.* un- (1).
**unintell′igibly**, *adv.* un- (1).
**unintend′ed**, *adj.* un- (1).
**uninten′tional**, *adj.* un- (1).
**unintention′ity**, *n.* un- (1).
**uninten′tionally**, *adv.* un- (1).
**unintermitt′ed**, *adj.* un- (1).
**unintermitt′edly**, *adv.* un- (1).
**unintermitt′ing**, *adj.* un- (1).
**unintermitt′ingly**, *adv.* un- (1).
**uninter′pretable**, *adj.* un- (1).

**uninterrup′ted**, *adj.* un- (1).
**uninterrup′tedly**, *adv.* un- (1).
**unintox′icating**, *adj.* un- (1).
**unintroduced′**, *adj.* un- (1).
**uninured′**, *adj.* un- (1).
**uninven′tive**, *adj.* un- (1).
**uninvest′ed**, *adj.* un- (1).
**uninvid′ious**, *adj.* un- (1).
**uninvi′ted**, *adj.* un- (1).
**uninvi′ting**, *adj.* un- (1).
**uninvolved′**, *adj.* un- (1).
**uni′onised**, -z-, *adj.* un- (1).
**unja′ded**, *adj.* un- (1).
**unjaun′diced**, *adj.* un- (1).
**unjeal′ous**, *adj.* un- (1).
**unjoy′ful**, *adj.* un- (1).
**unjoy′ous**, *adj.* un- (1).
**unjust′**, *adj.* un- (1).
**unjus′tifiable** (or *fī′*), *adj.* un- (1).
**unjus′tifiably** (or *fī′*), *adv.* un- (1).
**unjust′ly**, *adv.* un- (1).
**unjust′ness**, *n.* un- (1).
**unla′belled**, *adj.* un- (1).
**unlabo′rious**, *adj.* un- (1).
**unla′dylike**, *adj.* un- (1).
**unlament′ed**, *adj.* un- (1).
**unleased′**, *adj.* un- (1).
**unleav′ened**, *adj.* un- (1).
**unleis′ured**, *adj.* un- (1).
**unleis′urely**, *adj.* un- (1).
**unlet′**, *adj.* un- (1).

---

*Words beginning with pfx.* un- *are listed first* (pp. 1462 ff.); *other* UN- *words follow* (pp. 1484 ff.).

Neutral vowels in unaccented syllables: *el′ə-mənt*; for certain sounds in foreign words, see p. viii

unless'oned, not instructed; unlett'ered, unlearned: illiterate: without lettering; unli'censed, without a licence: unauthorised; unlich (un-lich'; Spens.), unlike; unlicked', not licked: not licked into shape.—v.t. unlid', to uncover, open.—adjs. unlidd'ed, lidless; unlight'ed; unlight'ened; unlight'some (Milt.), without light.—adj. and adv. (tending to become a prep.) unlike', not like: unlikely (Spens., Shak.).—n. one who c. that which is unlike.—ns. unlike'lihood, unlike'liness, improbability —adj. unlike'ly, not likely: improbable: unpromising (obs.): unprepossessing (obs. or dial.): unsuitable (obs.).—adv. in an unlikely manner, improbably.—n. unlike'ness, want of resemblance.—v.t. unlime', to free from lime.—adj. unlimed', not limed.—v.t. unline', to remove the lining from.—adj. unlined', without lines or lining.—v.t. unlink', to undo the linking or links of.—v.i. to become unlinked.—adjs. unlinked', not linked; unliq'uored (Milt.), not in liquor, sober; unlist'ed, not entered in a list; unlis'tened, not listened to (poet.; also unlistened-to); unlis'tening.—v.t. unlive (un-liv'), to undo the living of: to live in the contrary manner to: to live down: (un-liv') to deprive of life (Shak.).—adjs. unlived'-in, not lived in; unliv'ing.—v.t. unload', to take the load or charge from: to discharge: to disburden: to remove as a load: to get rid of: to dump.—v.i. to discharge freight.—adj. unload'ed, not loaded: discharged.—ns. unload'er; unload'ing.—adj. unloca'ted, not located: not surveyed or marked off (U.S.).—v.t. unlock', to undo the locking of: to free from being locked up: to let loose: to open, make accessible, or disclose.—v.i. to become unlocked.—adjs. unlocked'; unlog'ical, not logical: illogical; unlooked', not looked (at, into); unlooked'-for, unexpected.—vs.t. unloose', unloos'en, to loose; unlord', to strip of the dignity of a lord.—adjs. unlor'ded, deprived of, or not raised to, the rank of lord: not lorded over, without a lord; unlord'ly; unlov'able (also unlove'able).—v.t. unlove', to cease to love: not to love.—n. (un') absence of love.—adjs. unloved'; unlov'erlike; unlov'ing.—adv. unlov'ingly.—n. unlov'ingness.—adv. unluck'ily.—n. unluck'iness.—adj. unluck'y, unfortunate: ill-omened: bringing ill-luck: not praiseworthy (arch.).

Words with prefix un- (continued).

adjs. unmade', not made: self-existent: subjected to unmaking; unmaid'enly, unbecoming a maiden: not like a maiden; unmail'able (U.S.), incapable of being transmitted or delivered by post; unmailed', not clad in mail (mail (1)): not sent by post (mail(2)); unmak'able.—v.t. unmake', to undo the making of: to undo, ruin.—n. unma'king.—v.t. unman', to deprive of the nature, attributes or powers of humanity, manhood, or maleness: to deprive of fortitude: to deprive of men.—adv. unman'fully.—adj. unman'like.—n. unman'liness.—adjs. unman'ly, not becoming a man: unworthy of a noble mind: base: cowardly; unmanned', without a crew: without a garrison: without inhabitants: untamed (esp. of a hawk): deprived of fortitude; unmann'ered, unmannerly: free from mannerism.—n. unmann'erliness.—adj. unmann'erly, not mannerly: ill-bred.—adv. in an unmannerly manner.—v.t. unman'tle, to divest of a mantle: to dismantle (rare).—v.i. to take off one's mantle.—adjs. unmanufac'tured, in a raw state; unmanured', not manured: untilled (obs.); unmarked', bearing no mark: not noticed; unmar'ketable, not suitable for the market, not saleable; unmarred' (Spens.), unmard'), not marred; unmarr'iable (obs.), unmarr'iageable.—n. unmarr'iageableness.—adj. unmarr'ied, not married: usu. never having been married: freed from marriage.—v.t. unmarr'y, to dissolve the marriage of.—v.i. to dissolve one's marriage.—v.t. unmask', to take a mask or a disguise from: to discover the identity of e.g. a thief (fig.): to reveal the place of (gun, battery) by firing: to expose, show up.—v.i. to put off a mask.—adj. unmasked', not wearing a mask: undisguised: divested of mask or disguise: revealed (e.g. identity).—ns. unmask'er; unmask'ing.—adjs. unmas'tered, uncontrolled: not overcome: without a master; unmatch'able; unmatched', matchless: not accompanied by a match or like; unmate'rial, not composed of matter; unmate'rialised, -ized; unmean'ing, meaningless: purposeless: expressionless.—adv. unmean'ingly.—n. unmean'ingness.—adjs. unmeant (un-ment'); unmeas'urable, immeasurable: too great to measure: inordinate: not susceptible of measurement.—adv. unmeas'urably.—adjs. unmeas'ured; unmechan'ic, -al.—v.t. unmech'anise, -ize, to disorganise (Sterne).—adjs. unmech'anised, -z-, disorganised: not mechanised; unmedicinable (un-med'sin-a-bl), incurable: unable to cure; unmed'itated, not meditated, unpremeditated; unmeet', not meet, unfit.—adv. unmeet'ly.—n. unmeet'ness.—adj. unmen'tionable, not fit to be mentioned.—n. unmen'tionableness.—n.pl. unmen'tionables, otherwise inexpressibles, a 19th-cent. would-be humorous name for trousers: now usu. used for articles of underclothing.—adj. unmer'ciful, merciless: excessively and unpleasantly great.—adv. unmer'cifully.—n. unmer'cifulness.—adjs. unmer'itable (Shak.), undeserving; unmer'ited.—adv. unmer'itedly.—adjs. unmer'iting; unme'ted, not meted or measured.—v.t. unmew', to free, release as if from a mew or cage.—adjs. unmind'ed, unheeded; unmind'ful, not keeping in mind, regardless (of).—adv. unmind'fully.—n. unmind'fulness.—adj.

unlibid'inous (Milt.), adj. un-(1).
unlim'ited, adj. un-(1).
unlim'itedly, adv. un-(1).
unlim'itedness, n. un-(1).
unlin'eal, adj. un-(1).
unliq'uefied, adj. un-(1).
unliq'uidated, adj. un-(1).
unlit', adj. un-(1).
unlit'erary, adj. un-(1).
unlive'liness, n. un-(1).
unlive'ly, adj. un-(1).
unlopped', adj. un-(1).
unlos'able, adj. un-(1).
unlost', adj. un-(1).
unlove'liness, n. un-(1).
unlove'ly, adj. un-(1).
unluxur'iant, adj. un-(1).

unluxur'ious, adj. un-(1).
unmacad'amised, -ized, adj. un-(1).
unmaimed', adj. un-(1).
unmali'cious, adj. un-(1).
unmalleabil'ity, n. un-(1).
unmall'eable, adj. un-(1).
unman'acle, v.t. un-(2).
unman'acled, adj. un-(1, 2).
unman'ageable, adj. un-(1).
unman'ageableness, n. un-(1).
unman'ageably, adv. un-(1).
unman'aged, adj. un-(1).
unmas'culine, adj. un-(1).
unma'ted, adj. un-(1).
unmater'nal, adj. un-(1).
unmathemat'ical, adj. un-(1).
unmatric'ulated, adj. un-(1).

unmatured', adj. un-(1).
unmeek', adj. un-(1).
unmell'owed, adj. un-(1).
unmelo'dious, adj. un-(1).
unmelt'ed, adj. un-(1).
unmer'cenary, adj. un-(1).
unmer'chantable, adj. un-(1).
unmet'alled, adj. un-(1).
unmetaphor'ical, adj. un-(1).
unmetaphys'ical, adj. un-(1).
unmethod'ical, adj. un-(1).
unmeth'odised, -ized, adj. un-(1).
unmet'rical, adj. un-(1).
unmil'itary, adj. un-(1).
unmilked', adj. un-(1).
unmilled', adj. un-(1).
unming'led, adj. un-(1).

Words beginning with pfx. un- are listed first (pp. 1462 ff.); other UN- words follow (pp. 1484 ff.).

fāte, fär; mē, hûr (her); mīne; mōte, för; mūte; mōōn, fōōt; dhen (then)

unmit′igable, that cannot be mitigated.—*adv.* unmit′igably.—*adj.* unmit′igated, not mitigated: unqualified, out-and-out.—*adv.* unmit′igatedly. —*adjs.* unmoaned′, not lamented; unmo′dish, unfashionable; unmon′eyed (unmon′ied), without money: not rich.—*v.t.* unmoor′, to loose from moorings.—*v.i.* to cast off moorings.— *adjs.* unmor′al, having no relation to morality: amoral; unmor′alised, -ized, not moralised upon; having no moral attached: without morality; unmoralis′ing.—*n.* unmoral′ity, detachment from questions of morality.—*adjs.* unmor′tised, disjoined from a mortise (*lit.* and *fig.*); un-Mosa′ic, not of or according to *Moses* or the Mosaic law; unmo′tived, without motive: without an artistic motive.—*v.t.* unmould′, to change or destroy the form of.—*adj.* unmould′ed, not moulded.—*v.t.* unmount′, to remove from mountings or mount: to dismount.—*v.i.* to dismount.—*adjs.* unmount′ed, not mounted; unmov′able (also unmove′able), immovable: not movable.—*adv.* unmov(e)′ably.—*adj.* unmoved′, not moved, firm: not touched by emotion, calm.—*adv.* unmov′edly.—*adj.* unmov′ing.—*v.t.* unmuff′le, to take a muffle, muffling, or covering from.—*v.i.* to throw off mufflings.—*v.t.* unmuzz′le, to take a muzzle off.—*adj.* unmuzz′led. —*n.* unmuzz′ling.

*Words with prefix* un- (*continued*).

*v.t.* unnail′ (*un-nāl′*), to free from nails or from being nailed.—*adjs.* unnamable (*un-nām′a-bl*), impossible to name: not to be named; unnamed (*un-nāmd′*); unnative (*un-nā′tiv*), not native; unnatural (*un-nat′ū-ral*), not according to nature: without natural affection: monstrous, heinous. —*v.t.* unnat′uralise, -ize, to make unnatural: to divest of nationality.—*adj.* unnat′uralised, not naturalised.—*adv.* unnat′urally.—*n.* unnat′uralness.—*adjs.* unnavigable (*un-nav′*), not navigable; unnav′igated.—*adv.* unnecessarily (*un-nes′*).—*n.* unnec′essariness.—*adjs.* unnec′essary, not necessary; unneighboured (*un-nā′bard*), without neighbours.—*n.* unneigh′bourliness.—*adj.* unneigh′bourly, not neighbourly, friendly, or social. —*adv.* in an unneighbourly manner.—*v.t.* unnerve (*un-nûrv′*), to deprive of nerve, strength, or vigour: to weaken.—*adjs.* unnerved′; unnerv′ing.—*v.t.* unnest (*un-nest′*), to turn out of a nest (*lit.* and *fig.*).—*adv.* unnethes (see uneath). —*adjs.* unnett′ed, not enclosed in a net; un-

no′ble, not noble: ignoble (*Spens., Shak.*).—*v.t.* to deprive of nobility.—*adjs.* unnumbered (*un-num′bard*), not counted, too many to be numbered: not marked or provided with a number; unnurtured (*un-nûr′chard*), not nurtured or educated: ill-bred.

*Words with prefix* un- (*continued*).

*adjs.* unobe′dient, disobedient; unobeyed′ (*Milt.*); unobserv′able.—*n.* unobser′vance, failure to observe (rules etc.): failure to notice: lack of observing power: inattention.—*adjs.* unobser′vant; unobserved′.—*adv.* unobserv′edly.—*adjs.* unobser′ving; unoffend′ed; unoffend′ing; unoffen′sive, inoffensive; unoff′icered; unoffi′cial, not official.—*adv.* unoffi′cially.—*adj.* unoffi′cious, not officious.—*adv.* unoften (*un-of′n; rare*), seldom (usu. as *not unoften*).—*adjs.* uno′pened, not opened: of a book, not having the leaves cut apart; unop′erative, inoperative.—*v.t.* unor′der, to countermand.—*adjs.* unor′dered, disordered: unarranged, not ordered or commanded; unor′derly, not orderly; unor′dinary, not ordinary; unorig′inal, not original: without origin or birth (*Milt.*).—*n.* unoriginality (-al′).—*adjs.* unorig′inate, -d, not originated; unowed′, not owed or due: unowned (*Shak.*); unowned′, unavowed, unacknowledged: ownerless: (*un-ō′nid*) lost (*Milt.*).

*Words with prefix* un- (*continued*).

*v.t.* unpack′, to undo the packing of: to take out of a pack: to open: to remove a pack from (a pack animal).—*v.i.* to do unpacking. —*adj.* unpacked′, subjected to unpacking: (*un′pakt′*) not packed.—*ns.* unpack′er; unpack′-ing.—*adj.* unpaged′, without numbering of pages. —*v.t.* unpaint′, to free from paint: to paint out. —*adjs.* unpaint′able; unpaint′ed, not painted; unpaired′, not paired: not forming one of a pair; unpal′atable, unpleasant to taste, distasteful, disagreeable (*lit.* and *fig.*).—*adv.* unpal′atably. —*v.t.* unpan′el, (*obs.*; also unpann′el; from panel *n.*, a saddle), to unsaddle.—*adjs.* unpan′-elled, not panelled; unpanged′, without pangs. —*v.t.* unpa′per, to remove paper from.—*adj.* unpa′pered, not papered.—*v.t.* unpar′adise, to turn out of Paradise: to make no longer a paradise.—*adjs.* unpar′agoned, unmatched; unpar′allel, not parallel; unpar′alleled, without parallel or equal; unpared′ (of fruit), not having

unministê′rial, *adj.* un- (1).
unmirac′ulous, *adj.* un- (1).
unmi′ry, *adj.* un- (1).
unmissed′, *adj.* un- (1).
unmistak′able, *adj.* un- (1).
unmistak′ably, *adv.* un- (1).
unmistrust′ful, *adj.* un- (1).
unmixed′, *adj.* un- (1).
unmix′edly, *adv.* un- (1).
unmod′ernised, -ized, *adj.* un-(1).
unmod′ifiable, *adj.* un- (1).
unmod′ifiableness, *n.* un- (1).
unmod′ified, *adj.* un- (1).
unmod′ulated, *adj.* un- (1).
unmois′tened, *adj.* un- (1).
unmolest′ed, *adj.* un- (1).
unmort′gaged, *adj.* un- (1).
unmort′ified, *adj.* un- (1).
unmoth′erly, *adj.* un- (1).
unmown′, *adj.* un- (1).
unmuni′tioned, *adj.* un- (1).
unmur′muring, *adj.* un- (1).
unmur′muringly, *adv.* un- (1).
unmus′ical, *adj.* un- (1).
unmus′ically, *adv.* un- (1).

unmu′tilated, *adj.* un- (1).
unneed′ful, *adj.* un- (1).
unneed′fully, *adv.* un- (1).
unnō′ted, *adj.* un- (1).
unno′ticeable, *adj.* un- (1).
unno′ticed, *adj.* un- (1).
unno′ticing, *adj.* un- (1).
unnour′ished, *adj.* un- (1).
unnour′ishing, *adj.* un- (1).
unobjec′tionable, *adj.* un- (1).
unobjec′tionably, *adv.* un- (1).
unobnox′ious, *adj.* un- (1).
unobscured′, *adj.* un- (1).
unobstruc′ted, *adj.* un- (1).
unobstruc′tive, *adj.* un- (1).
unobtain′able, *adj.* un- (1).
unobtained′, *adj.* un- (1).
unobtru′sive, *adj.* un- (1).
unobtru′sively, *adv.* un- (1).
unobtru′siveness, *n.* un- (1).
unob′vious, *adj.* un- (1).
unocc′upied, *adj.* un- (1).
unoff′ered, *adj.* un- (1).
unoiled′, *adj.* un- (1).
unopposed′, *adj.* un- (1).
unoppress′ive, *adj.* un- (1).

unordained′, *adj.* un- (1).
unor′ganised, -ized, *adj.* un- (1).
unornamen′tal, *adj.* un- (1).
unor′namented (or -ment′), *adj.* un- (1).
unor′thodox, *adj.* un- (1).
unor′thodoxy, *n.* un- (1).
unoss′ified, *adj.* un- (1).
unostentā′tious, *adj.* un- (1).
unostentā′tiously, *adv.* un- (1).
unostentā′tiousness, *n.* un- (1).
unovercome′, *adj.* un- (1).
unoverthrown′, *adj.* un- (1).
unox′idised, -ized, *adj.* un- (1).
unpaid′, *adj.* un- (1).
unpained′, *adj.* un- (1).
unpain′ful, *adj.* un- (1).
unpal′sied, *adj.* un- (1).
unpam′pered, *adj.* un- (1).
unpar′donable, *adj.* un- (1).
unpar′donableness, *n.* un- (1).
unpar′donably, *adv.* un- (1).
unpar′doned, *adj.* un- (1).
unpar′doning, *adj.* un- (1).
unpar′tial, *adj.* un- (1).

*Words beginning with pfx.* un- *are listed first* (pp. 1462 ff.); *other* UN- *words follow* (pp. 1484 ff.).

Neutral vowels in unaccented syllables: *el′a-mant*; for certain sounds in foreign words, see p. viii the skin removed: (of nails) not cut; **unpar-ent′al**, not befitting a parent; **unpa′rented**, without parent or acknowledged parent, or parental care; **unparliament′ary**, contrary to the usages of Parliament: not such as may be spoken, or (of language) used, in Parliament; **unpass′able**, impassable: (of money) not current. —*n.* **unpass′ableness**.—*adjs.* **unpass′ionate**, **unpass′ioned**, without passions: calm: dispassionate; **unpatt′erned**, unexampled, unequalled: without a pattern; **unpaved′**, without pavement: gelded (*Shak.*); **unpavil′ioned**, without a canopy. —*v.t.* **unpay′**, to make good, undo, do away by payment.—*adjs.* **unpay′able**; **unpeeled′**, not peeled: (Shak., *Love's Lab. Lost* II, i. 88) according to some, stripped, desolate (others think it a misprint for **unpeopled**, without servants, the folio reading); **unpeer′able**, not to be matched; **unpeered′**, unequalled.—*v.t.* **unpen′**, to let out from a pen.—*adjs.* **unpenned′**, unwritten: unconfined: let loose; **unpenn′ied**, without pennies; **unpent′**, not penned in.—*v.t.* **unpeo′ple**, to empty of people.—*adjs.* **unpeo′pled**, uninhabited: without servants: depopulated.—*v.t.* **unperch′**, to drive from a perch.—*adj.* **unper′fect** (now *rare*), imperfect: unskilled.—*n.* **unperfec′tion** (*obs.*).—*adv.* **unper′fectly** (*obs.*).— *ns.* **unper′fectness** (*rare*); **un′per′son**, an individual whose influence has ceased so completely that he might never have existed.—*v.t.* **unpervert′**, to reconvert.—*adj.* **unpervert′ed**, not perverted.—*v.t.* **unpick′**, to pick loose, undo by picking.—*adjs.* **unpick′able**, impossible to pick; **unpicked′**, not gathered: not selected: not having had unwanted material removed by picking: picked loose; **unpill′ared**, stripped of pillars: without pillars.—*v.t.* **unpin′**, to free from pins or pinning: to unfasten the dress of by removing pins.—*adj.* **unpinked′**, **unpinkt′** (*Shak.*), not pinked, not adorned with punched holes. —*v.t.* **unplace′**, to displace.—*adj.* **unplaced′**, not assigned to or set in a place: not inducted to a church: not appointed to an office: not among the first three in a race; **unplained′** (*Spens.*), not lamented; **unplau′sible**, implausible.—*adv.* **unplau′sibly**.—*adjs.* **unplau′sive**, not approving; **unpleas′ant**, not pleasant: disagreeable.—*adv.*

**unpleas′antly**. —*ns.* **unpleas′antness**, state or quality of being unpleasant, disagreeableness: a disagreeable incident: disagreement involving open hostility; **unpleas′antry**, want of pleasantness: any unpleasant occurrence, any discomfort.—*adjs.* **unpleased′**; **unpleas′ing**, not pleasing: displeasing.—*adv.* **unpleas′ingly**.—*adj.* **pleas′urable**. — *adv.* **unpleas′urably.** — *v.t.* **unplumb′**, to remove the lead from.—*adj.* **unplumbed′**, unsounded: unfathomed.—*v.t.* **unplume′**, to strip of feathers or plumes (often *fig.*). —*adj.* **unpoint′ed**, not pointed: without point or points: with joints uncemented.—*v.t.* **unpoi′son**, to rid of poison, cure of poisoning.— *adjs.* **unpoi′soned**, not poisoned; **unpol′icied**, without organised political organisation: impolitic; **unpolite′**, unpolished (*obs.*): impolite: inelegant (*obs.*).—*adv.* **unpolite′ly.**—*n.* **unpolite′-ness**.—*adj.* **unpolled′**, not polled: not having voted.—*v.t.* **unpope′**, to divest of popedom.— *adjs.* **unpor′tioned**, without a portion; **unpossessed′**, not possessed: unprejudiced (*obs.*): not in possession; **unpossess′ing** (*Shak.*), without possessions; **unposs′ible** (*Shak.*; *dial.*), impossible; **unpost′ed**, not posted, in any sense: not posted up: without a post; **unpo′table**, undrinkable, unfit to drink; **unprac′ticable** (formerly common), impracticable; **unprac′tised**, having little or no practice or experience, inexpert: not carried out in practice: not yet familiar through practice (*obs.*).—*n.* **unprac′-tisedness**.—*v.t.* **unpraise′**, to dispraise: deprive of praise.—*adjs.* **unpraised′**, not praised; **unpraise′worthy**.—*vs.t.* **unpray′**, to revoke the praying of; **unpreach′**, to recant in preaching: undo the preaching of.—*adjs.* **unpreach′ing**, not preaching; **unprec′edented** (-*pres′*, or -*prēs′*), not warranted by judicial, etc., precedent: of which there has been no previous instance.— *adv.* **unprec′edentedly.**—*v.i.* **unpredict′** (*Milt.*), revoke what has been predicted.—*n.* **unpredict-abil′ity.**—*adj.* **unpredict′able**, that cannot be foretold: (of person, thing) liable to behave in a way that cannot be predicted.—*adjs.* **unpreferred′**, without preferment or advancement; **unpreg′nant** (*Shak.*), slow-witted, unready, ineffective: not quickened by a lively sense (of);

---

---

*Words beginning with pfx.* **un-** *are listed first* (pp. 1462 ff.); *other* UN- *words follow* (pp. 1484 ff.).

unprelat′ical, unbecoming in or to a prelate: not episcopal; unpremed′itable, not to be foreseen; unpremed′itated, not studied or purposed beforehand.—*adv.* unpremed′itatedly.—*ns.* unpremed′itatedness; unpremedita′tion.—*v.t.* unprepare′, to make unprepared.—*adj.* unprepared′, not prepared or ready: not prepared for death: without preparation.—*adv.* unprepa′redly.—*n.* unprepa′redness.—*adjs.* unprepossessed′, not prepossessed or prejudiced; unprepossess′ing, not predisposing others in one's favour, unpleasing; unpresent′able, not fit to be seen; unpretend′ing, not pretending or making pretence: modest.—*adv.* unpreten′dingly.—*adjs.* unprevail′ing, unavailing; unpreven′table.—*n.* unpreven′tableness.—*adjs.* unprevent′ed, not anticipated or preceded (*obs.*): not prevented or obviated; unpriced′, having no fixed or stated price: beyond price, priceless.— *v.t.* unpriest′, to divest of priesthood.—*adjs.* unpriest′ly, unbecoming, unlike, not of the nature of, a priest; unprin′cipled, uninstructed (*Milt.*): without good principles: not based on or in accordance with principles: not restrained by conscience: profligate; unprint′able, not fit to be printed; unprint′ed; unpriz′able (*Shak.*), worthless: beyond price; unprized′, not prized; unprofessed′; unprofess′ional, not of a profession or the profession in question: beyond the limits of one's profession: unbecoming a member of a particular profession.—*adv.* unprofess′ionally. —*adjs.* unprof′ited, without profit or advantage; unprop′er, improper: common, not one's own (*Shak.*).—*adv.* unprop′erly.—*adj.* unpropor′tionable, out of due proportion.—*adv.* unpropor′tionably.—*adj.* unpropor′tionate, out of due proportion.—*adv.* unpropor′tionately.—*adj.* unpropor′tioned, not proportioned.—*v.t.* unprot′estantise, -ize, to transform from Protestantism: to strip of Protestant character.—*adj.* unprotest′ed, not objected to or protested against.— *v.t.* unprovide′ (*Shak.*), to unfurnish, to deprive of what is necessary.—*adj.* unprovi′ded, not furnished, provided, or provided for (also unprovi′ded-for).—*adv.* unprovi′dedly.—*adj.* unprov′ident (*Shak.*), improvident.— *v.t.* un′provoke

(*Shak.*), to counteract provocation of.—*adj.* unprovoked′, not provoked: uncalled for.—*adv.* unprovo′kedly.—*adj.* unprovo′king.—*v.t.* unpurse′, to relax from pursing: to disburse.—*adj.* unpurveyed′ (*Spens.* unpurvaide′), unprovided or unprepared (*obs.*): not provided with (with *of*; *Spens.*): not purveyed.

*Words with prefix* un- (*continued*).

*adjs.* unqual′it(i)ed (*Shak.*), bereft of qualities; unquestionable, not to be questioned, certain, beyond doubt: averse to conversation, or perh. impatient of question (*Shak.*).—*adv.* unques′tionably.—*adjs.* unques′tioned, not called in question: not subjected to questioning: not examined; unques′tioning; unqui′et, disturbed: restless: uneasy.—*n.* disquiet, inquietude.—*v.t.* to disquiet.—*adv.* unqui′etly.—*n.* unqui′etness.—*adj.* unquot′able, unsuitable or unfit for quotation. —*v.i. imper.* unquote′, close inverted commas. —*adj.* unracked′, not drawn off from the lees: not stretched on the rack: not strained.—*v.t.* unrake′, to uncover by raking.—*adj.* unraked′, not raked: uncovering by raking: not banked up, as a fire.—*v.t.* unrav′el, to disentangle: to unknit.—*v.i.* to become disentangled.—*adj.* unrav′elled.—*ns.* unrav′eller; unrav′elling; unrav′elment.—*adjs.* unra′zored, unshaven; unread (*un-red′*), not informed by reading: not perused; unreadable (*un-rēd′a-bl*), indecipherable: too dull or ill-written to be read.—*n.* unrea′dableness.—*adv.* unreadily (*-red′*).—*n.* unread′iness.—*adjs.* unread′y, not ready, prepared, or prompt: hesitating, holding back: (*Shak.*, etc.) undressed or not dressed (make unready, *obs.* to undress): in *Shak.*, etc., redeless; unre′al.—*v.t.* unre′alise, -ize, to divest of reality. —*adj.* unre′alised.—*n.* unre′alism.—*adj.* unrealist′ic.—*n.* unreal′ity, want of reality or existence: an unreal thing.—*adv.* unre′ally.—*n.* unrea′son, lack of reason or reasonableness (see abbot): nonsense: injustice (*obs.*).—*adj.* unrea′sonable, not agreeable to reason: exceeding the bounds of reason, immoderate: not influenced by reason. — *n.* unrea′sonableness. — *adv.* unrea′sonably.

---

unpre′judiced, *adj.* un- (1).
unpreocc′upied, *adj.* un- (1).
unprescribed′, *adj.* un- (1).
unpressed′, *adj.* un- (1).
unpresum′ing, *adj.* un- (1).
unpresump′tuous, *adj.* un- (1).
unpreten′tious, *adj.* un- (1).
unpreten′tiousness, *n.* un- (1).
unprett′iness, *n.* un- (1).
unprett′y, *adj.* un- (1).
unprince′ly, *adj.* un- (1).
unpris′on, *v.t.* un- (2).
unpris′oned, *adj.* un- (1, 2).
unpriv′ileged, *adj.* un- (1).
unproclaimed′, *adj.* un- (1).
unprocur′able, *adj.* un- (1).
unproduced′, *adj.* un- (1).
unproduc′tive, *adj.* un- (1).
unproduc′tively, *adv.* un- (1).
unproduc′tiveness, *n.* un- (1).
unproductiv′ity, *n.* un- (1).
unprofaned′, *adj.* un- (1).
unprof′itable, *adj.* un- (1).
unprof′itableness, *n.* un- (1).
unprof′itably, *adv.* un- (1).
unprof′iting, *adj.* un- (1).
unprogress′ive, *adj.* un- (1).
unprogress′ively, *adv.* un- (1).
unprogress′iveness, *n.* un- (1).
unprohib′ited, *adj.* un- (1).
unprojec′ted, *adj.* un- (1).
unprolif′ic, *adj.* un- (1).

unprom′ised, *adj.* un- (1).
unprom′ising, *adj.* un- (1).
unprom′isingly, *adv.* un- (1).
unpromp′ted, *adj.* un- (1).
unpronounce′able, *adj.* un- (1).
unpronounced′, *adj.* un- (1).
unprop′, *v.t.* un- (2).
unprop′ertied, *adj.* un- (1).
unprophet′ic, -al, *adjs.* un- (1).
unpropi′tious, *adj.* un- (1).
unpropi′tiously, *adv.* un- (1).
unpropi′tiousness, *n.* un- (1).
unproposed′, *adj.* un- (1).
unpropped′, *adj.* un- (1).
unpros′perous, *adj.* un- (1).
unpros′perously, *adv.* un- (1).
unpros′perousness, *n.* un- (1).
unprotec′ted, *adj.* un- (1).
unprotec′tedness, *n.* un- (1).
unprotest′ing, *adj.* un- (1).
unprov′able, *adj.* un- (1).
unprō′ven, *adj.* un- (1).
unproved′, *adj.* un- (1).
unprovis′ioned, *adj.* un- (1).
unprovoc′ative, *adj.* un- (1).
unpruned′, *adj.* un- (1).
unpub′lished, *adj.* un- (1).
unpuck′ered, *adj.* un- (1).
unpulled′, *adj.* un- (1).
unpunct′ual, *adj.* un- (1).
unpunctual′ity, *n.* un- (1).
unpunct′uated, *adj.* un- (1).

unpun′ishable, *adj.* un- (1).
unpun′ishably, *adv.* un- (1).
unpun′ished, *adj.* un- (1).
unpur′chas(e)able, *adj.* un- (1).
unpur′chased, *adj.* un- (1).
unpurged′, *adj.* un- (1).
unpu′rified, *adj.* un- (1).
unpur′posed, *adj.* un- (1).
unpursued′, *adj.* un- (1).
unqual′ified, *adj.* un- (1).
unqual′ifiedly, *adv.* un- (1).
unqual′ifiedness, *n.* un- (1).
unqual′ify, *v.t.* un- (2).
unquanti′fied, *adj.* un- (1).
unquant′ised, -ized, *adj.* un- (1).
unquarr′ied, *adj.* un- (1).
unqueen′ (*Shak.*), *v.t.* un- (2).
unqueened′, *adj.* un- (2).
unqueen′like, *adj.* un- (1).
unqueen′ly, *adj.* un- (1).
unquelled′, *adj.* un- (1).
unquench′able, *adj.* un- (1).
unquench′ably, *adv.* un- (1).
unquenched′, *adj.* un- (1).
unquick′ened, *adj.* un- (1).
unraised′, *adj.* un- (1).
unran′somed, *adj.* un- (1).
unrat′ified, *adj.* un- (1).
unrav′ished, *adj.* un- (1).
unreach′able, *adj.* un- (1).
unreached′, *adj.* un- (1).
unreaped′, *adj.* un- (1).

*Words beginning with pfx.* un- *are listed first* (pp. 1462 ff.); *other UN- words follow* (pp. 1484 ff.).

—*adjs.* **unrea'soned**, not argued out; **unrea'soning**, not reasoning.—*adv.* **unrea'soningly**. —*v.t.* **unreave'** (from *dial.* reeve, reave, to wind or unwind), to unweave (*Spens.*): to unwind (*dial.*).—*adjs.* **unreba'ted**, unblunted: undulled: without rebate; **unrecall'able**; **unrecalled'**; **unrecall'ing** (*Shak.*; *Milt.*), impossible to undo, not to be recalled; **unrecked'**, not regarded or cared about; **unreconciliable** (*Shak.*), **unreconcilable**; **unreconstruct'ed**, not reconstructed: not adjusted or reconciled to reconstruction (*U.S. hist.*); **unrecur'ing** (*Shak.*), incurable; **unred'** (*Spens.*), for unread (unrecounted, untold); **unredeem'able**; **unredeemed'**, not redeemed, esp. spiritually or from pawn: without compensatory quality or circumstance, hence unmitigated, unrelieved; **unredressed'**, **unredrest'**, not redressed: without redress or possibility of escape (*Spens.*).—*vs.t.* **unreeve'**, to withdraw from being reeved; **unrein'**, to relax the rein of, give rein to.—*adjs.* **unreined'**, unchecked; **unrelen'ting**.—*adv.* **unrelen'tingly**. —*ns.* **unrelen'tingness**; **unrelen'tor** (*Keats*), one who does not relent; **unreliabil'ity** (see rely).— *adj.* **unreli'able**, not to be relied upon.—*n.* **unreli'ableness**.—*adjs.* **unrelig'ious**, not connected with religion: not religious without being necessarily contrary or hostile to religion: irreligious; **unremitt'ed**.—*adv.* **unremitt'edly**.—*adj.* **unremitt'ent**.—*adv.* **unremitt'ently**.—*adj.* **unremitt'ing**, not remitting or relaxing: continued: incessant.

—*adv.* **unremitt'ingly**.—*n.* **unremitt'ingness**.— *adj.* **unremorse'ful**, feeling no remorse.—*adv.* **unremorse'fully**.—*adjs.* **unremorse'less** (*obs.*), remorseless; **unremov'able**, not removable: immovable, fixed, constant (*obs.*); **unremoved'**, not removed: fixed, unshaken (*obs.*); **unrepeat'able**, not repeatable: indecent, gross: that cannot be done again; **unrepeat'ed**; **unreprov'able**; **unreproved'** (or -*prōō'vid*), not reproved: not liable to reproof, blameless (*Spens.*, *Milt.*); **unreprov'ing**; **unrequired'**, unasked: unasked-for: unnecessary.—*n.* **unreserve'**, absence of reserve.—*adj.* **unreserved'**, not reserved: without reserve or reservation: unrestricted, unqualified. —*adv.* **unreser'vedly**.—*n.* **unreser'vedness**.—*adjs.* **unresist'ed**; **unresist'ible** (*rare*), irresistible; **unresist'ing**.—*adv.* **unresis'tingly**.—*adjs.* **unresolv'able**; **unresolved'**, not resolved, determined, settled, or solved: irresolute: undecided: not separated into its constituent parts.—*n.* **unresol'vedness**, irresolution.—*adjs.* **unrespect'ed**; **unrespect'ive**, inattentive, unthinking (*Shak.*): undiscriminating (*Shak.*): indiscriminate; **unres'pited** (*Milt.*), without respite or pause.—*n.* **unrest'**, want of rest: disquiet: disturbance: discontent verging on insurrection.—*adj.* **unrest'ful**, not restful: uneasy: full of unrest.—*n.* **unrest'fulness**.—*adj.* **unrest'ing**.—*adv.* **unrest'ingly**.—*n.* **unrest'ingness**.—*adjs.* **unrev'erend**, not reverend: not reverent, irreverent, unreverent (*Shak.*); **unrev'erent**, not reverent; **unrevert'ed**,

---

unrebuked', *adj.* un- (1).
unreceipt'ed, *adj.* un- (1).
unreceived', *adj.* un- (1).
unrecep'tive, *adj.* un- (1).
unreck'oned, *adj.* un- (1).
unreclaim'able, *adj.* un- (1).
unreclaim'ably, *adv.* un- (1).
unreclaim'ed, *adj.* un- (1).
unrec'ognisable, -z- (or -*niz'*), *adj.* un- (1).
unrec'ognisably (or -*niz'*), *adv.* un- (1).
unrec'ognised, *adj.* un- (1).
unrec'ognising, *adj.* un- (1).
unrecollect'ed, *adj.* un- (1).
unrecommend'able, *adj.* un- (1).
unrecommend'ed, *adj.* un- (1).
unrec'ompensed, *adj.* un- (1).
unrec'oncilable (or -*sil'*), *adj.* un- (1).
unreconcil'ableness, *n.* un- (1).
unrec'oncilably (or -*sil'*), *adv.* un- (1).
unrec'onciled (or -*sild'*), *adj.* un- (1).
unrecord'ed, *adj.* un- (1).
unrecount'ed, *adj.* un- (1).
unrecov'erable, *adj.* un- (1).
unrecov'erably, *adv.* un- (1).
unrecov'ered, *adj.* un- (1).
unrect'ified, *adj.* un- (1).
unreduced', *adj.* un- (1).
unreduc'ible, *adj.* un- (1).
unreel', *v.t.* and *v.i.* un- (2).
unrefined', *adj.* un- (1).
unreflect'ed, *adj.* un- (1).
unreflect'ing, *adj.* un- (1).
unreflect'ingly, *adv.* un- (1).
unreform'able, *adj.* un- (1).
unreformed', *adj.* un- (1).
unrefract'ed, *adj.* un- (1).
unrefreshed', *adj.* un- (1).
unrefresh'ing, *adj.* un- (1).
unrefu'ted, *adj.* un- (1).
unregard'ed, *adj.* un- (1).
unregard'ing, *adj.* un- (1).

unregen'eracy, *n.* un- (1).
unregen'erate, -d, *adjs.* un- (1).
unreg'istered, *adj.* un- (1).
unreg'ulated, *adj.* un- (1).
unrehearsed', *adj.* un- (1).
unrejoiced', *adj.* un- (1).
unrejoic'ing, *adj.* un- (1).
unrelat'ed, *adj.* un- (1).
unrel'ative, *adj.* un- (1).
unrelaxed', *adj.* un- (1).
unreliev'able, *adj.* un- (1).
unrelieved', *adj.* un- (1).
unreliev'edly, *adv.* un- (1).
unrel'ished, *adj.* un- (1).
unreluc'tant, *adj.* un- (1).
unremain'ing, *adj.* un- (1).
unremark'able, *adj.* un- (1).
unremarked', *adj.* un- (1).
unrem'edied, *adj.* un- (1).
unremem'bered, *adj.* un- (1).
unremem'bering, *adj.* un- (1).
unremun'erative, *adj.* un- (1).
unrenewed', *adj.* un- (1).
unrent', *adj.* un- (1).
unrepaid', *adj.* un- (1).
unrepair', *n.* un- (1).
unrepair'able, *adj.* un- (1).
unrepaired', *adj.* un- (1).
unrepeal'able, *adj.* un- (1).
unrepealed', *adj.* un- (1).
unrepelled', *adj.* un- (1).
unrepen'tance, *n.* un- (1).
unrepen'tant, *adj.* un- (1).
unrepen'ted, *adj.* un- (1).
unrepen'ting, *adj.* un- (1).
unrepen'tingly, *adv.* un- (1).
unrepi'ning, *adj.* un- (1).
unrepi'ningly, *adv.* un- (1).
unreplace'able, *adj.* un- (1).
unreplen'ished, *adj.* un- (1).
unreport'able, *adj.* un- (1).
unreport'ed, *adj.* un- (1).
unrepose'ful, *adj.* un- (1).
unrepos'ing, *adj.* un- (1).
unrepresent'ed, *adj.* un- (1).
unrepriev'able, *adj.* un- (1).

unreprieved', *adj.* un- (1).
unreproached', *adj.* un- (1).
unreproach'ful, *adj.* un- (1).
unreproach'ing, *adj.* un- (1).
unreproduc'ible, *adj.* un- (1).
unrepug'nant, *adj.* un- (1).
unrepuls'able, *adj.* un- (1).
unreq'uisite, *adj.* un- (1).
unrequit'ed, *adj.* un- (1).
unrequit'edly, *adv.* un- (1).
unrescind'ed, *adj.* un- (1).
unresent'ed, *adj.* un- (1).
unresent'ful, *adj.* un- (1).
unresent'ing, *adj.* un- (1).
unrespon'sive, *adj.* un- (1).
unrespon'sively, *adv.* un- (1).
unrespon'siveness, *n.* un- (1).
unrestored', *adj.* un- (1).
unrestrain'able, *adj.* un- (1).
unrestrained', *adj.* un- (1).
unrestrain'edly, *adv.* un- (1).
unrestraint', *n.* un- (1).
unrestric'ted, *adj.* un- (1).
unrestric'tedly, *adv.* un- (1).
unretard'ed, *adj.* un- (1).
unretent'ive, *adj.* un- (1).
unreturn'able, *adj.* un- (1).
unreturned', *adj.* un- (1).
unreturn'ing, *adj.* un- (1).
unreturn'ingly, *adv.* un- (1).
unreveal'able, *adj.* un- (1).
unrevealed', *adj.* un- (1).
unreveal'ing, *adj.* un- (1).
unrevenged', *adj.* un- (1).
unrevenge'ful, *adj.* un- (1).
unreversed', *adj.* un- (1).
unrevised', *adj.* un- (1).
unrevoked', *adj.* un- (1).
unrewar'ded, *adj.* un- (1).
unrewar'dedly, *adv.* un- (1).
unrewar'ding, *adj.* un- (1).
unrhymed', unrimed', *adj.* un- (1).
unrhyth'mical, *adj.* un- (1).
unrhyth'mically, *adv.* un- (1).

---

*Words beginning with pfx.* un- *are listed first (pp. 1462 ff.); other* UN- *words follow (pp. 1484 ff.).*

fāte, fär; mē, hûr (her); mīne; mōte, för; mūte; mōōn, fŏŏt; dhen (then)

not turned back; unrid', unridden (arch.).—v.t. unridd'le, to read the riddle of: to solve.—adj. unridd'leable.—n. unridd'ler.—v.t. unrig', to strip of rigging, or of clothes, etc.—adj. unrigged', without rigging: stripped of rigging.—n. unright' (arch.), wrong: unfairness, injustice.—adj. (arch.) wrong.—adj. unrigh'teous.—adv. unrigh'teously.—n. unrigh'teousness.—adj. unright'ful.—adv. unright'fully.—n. unright'fulness.—v.t. unrip', to rip up or open: to strip, lay bare: to disclose.—adj. unripped', not ripped: ripped up or open.—n. unripp'ing.—vs.t. unriv'et, to loose from being riveted: to detach (fig.); unrobe', to strip of a robe, to undress.—v.i. to take off a robe, esp. of state.—v.t. unroll', to open out from a rolled state: to strike off the roll (Shak.).—v.i. to become unrolled.—v.t. unroof', to strip the roof from.—adj. unroofed', not roofed: stripped of its roof.—vs.t. unroost' (Shak.), to drive out of a roost; unroot', to tear up by the roots.—adj. unroot'ed, without root: not rooted (out): rooted out.—v.t. unrope', to loose from a rope.—adjs. unrough', not rough: (Shak. unruffe') beardless; unrude', not rude: also (obs., prob. by confusion from obs. unride —O.E. ungerȳde, rough—gerȳde, smooth, easy) rude, uncouth; unruff'able (Dickens), imperturbable.—v.t. unruff'le, to restore or recover from ruffling.—adj. unruff'led, smooth: calm: not disturbed or flustered.—n. unrule', anarchy.—adj. unruled'.—ns. unrul'iment (Spens.), unrul'iness.—adjs. unrul'y, ungovernable: unmanageable: turbulent: stormy.

*Words with prefix* un- (*continued*).

v.t. unsadd'le, to take the saddle from: to dislodge from the saddle.—adj. unsadd'led; unsailed', unnavigated; unsail'orlike; unsained', unblessed.—v.t. unsaint', to divest of saintliness or of the title of saint.—n. unsaint'liness.—adjs. unsaint'ly; unsanc'tified.—v.t. unsanc'tify, to undo the sanctification of: to desecrate.—adjs. unsan'itary, without (regard to) sanitation, unhealthy; unsā'table (Browning), unsā'tiable (now rare), insatiable.—adv. unsa'vourily.—n. unsav'ouriness.—adj. unsa'voury, not savoury, tasteless: of ill savour: offensive.—v.t. unsay', to retract:—pa.t. and pa.p. unsaid'.—adj. unsay'able, that cannot be said.—v.t. unscabb'ard, to unsheathe.—adj. unscal'able, that cannot be

climbed.—v.t. unscale', to remove scales from. —adjs. unscaled', unclimbed: cleared of scales: scaleless; unscanned', not scanned as verse: not scrutinised: (Shak. un'skan'd) unconsidered; unscav'engered (Dickens), not cleared of rubbish; unscep'tred, without a sceptre: deposed; unsciss'-ored, not cut with scissors; unscott'ified, deprived of Scottish qualities or characteristics.— v.t. unscram'ble, to decode from a scrambled state, or to restore to natural sound.—adj. unscreened', not screened: unsifted.—v.t. unscrew', to loose from a state of being screwed: to open, loose, or detach by screwing.—v.i. to admit of unscrewing: to come unscrewed.—adjs. unscrip'ted, not using a script: unrehearsed; unscrip'tural, not in accordance with, or not warranted by, the Bible.—adv. unscrip'turally.— adj. unscru'pled, unscrupulous: not scrupled at. —v.t. unseal', to remove or break the seal of: to free from sealing or closure: to open (sometimes prob. for unseel).—adj. unsealed', not sealed: freed from a seal: opened.—v.t. unseam', to undo a seam of: to rip open (Shak.). —adjs. unseamed',· without seams; unsear'-chable, inscrutable, not possible to be searched into: mysterious.—n. unsear'chableness.—adv. unsear'chably.—adj. unsearched'.—v.t. unsea'son (Spens.), to affect disagreeably.—adj. unsea'son-able, not in season: ill-timed.—n. unsea'sonableness.—adv. unsea'sonably.—adj. unsea'soned, not seasoned: unseasonable (Shak.).—v.t. unseat', to oust, remove, or throw from a seat, esp. on horseback or in Parliament.—adjs. unseat'ed, not seated: ousted, thrown, removed from a seat; unse'cret (Shak.), failing to preserve secrecy; unsee'able, invisible; unseed'ed, not seeded: in lawn-tennis tournaments, etc., not placed in the draw of top players; unsee'ing, not seeing: unobservant: without insight or understanding.—v.t. unseel', to unsew the eyes of, undo the seeling of.—n. unseem'ing (Shak.), not seeming.—adj. (obs.) unbecoming, unseemly. —n. unseem'liness.—adj. unseem'ly, not seemly, becoming, or decent: ill-looking.—adv. in an unseemly manner.—adj. unseen', not seen: invisible: inexperienced, not well up (obs.).—n. an unprepared passage for translation.—adjs. unseiz'able; unseized', not seized: not taken or put in possession.—adv. unsel'dom, not seldom (lit. and rarely): usu., seldom.—n. un'self',

---

*Words beginning with pfx.* un- *are listed first (pp. 1462 ff.); other* UN- *words follow (pp. 1484 ff.).*

Neutral vowels in unaccented syllables: el'ə-mənt; for certain sounds in foreign words, see p. viii

altruism: impersonality.—*v.t.* unself′, to divest of personality, individuality, selfhood, or selfishness.—*adj.* unselfcon′scious.—*adv.* unselfcon′sciously.—*n.* unselfcon′sciousness.—*adj.* unself′ish.—*adv.* unself′ishly.—*n.* unself′ishness.— *adjs.* unsem′inar'd, unsem′inaried (*Shak.*), without means of generation.—*v.t.* unsense′, to deprive of sense or consciousness.—*adjs.* unsensed′, meaningless; unsens′ible (*obs.*or *dial.*), insensible. —*adv.* unsens′ibly (*obs.*), insensibly, imperceptibly: without sense.—*vs.t.* unsens′ualise, -ize, to free from the dominion of the senses; unset′, to undo the setting of.—*adj.* not set: unplanted. —*v.t.* unsett′le, to change from being settled: to make uncertain, unstable, or restless: to unfix.—*v.i.* to become unsettled.—*adj.* unsett′led, not settled, fixed, or determined: changeable: not having the dregs deposited: not yet inhabited and cultivated: turbulent, lawless.—*adv.* unsett′ledly.—*ns.* unsett′ledness; unsett′lement.—*n.* and *adj.* unsett′ling.—*v.t.* unsex′, to divest of sex: to divest of the characteristics or of the qualities expected of one's own sex. —*adjs.* unsexed′; unsex′ual.—*v.t.* unshack′le, to loose from shackles: to remove a shackle from.—*adj.* unshack′led.—*v.t.* unshad′ow, to clear of shadow: to reveal.—*adjs.* unshad′owable, impossible to shadow forth; unshad′owed, not darkened.—*v.t.* unshale′, to shale or shell, strip the husk from: to reveal.—*adj.* unshamed′, not ashamed: not put to shame.—*v.t.* unshape′, to deprive of shape: to undo, destroy, to confound. —*adjs.* unshaped′; unshape′ly; unshap′en.—*v.t.* unsheathe′, to draw from the sheath: to uncover.—*adjs.* unsheathed′, drawn from the sheath: not sheathed; unshed′, not shed: unparted (*Spens.*).—*v.t.* unshell′, to shell, remove the shell from.—*adjs.* unshent′, uninjured: not disgraced.—*v.t.* unship′, to take or put out of a ship or boat, etc.: to remove from a fixed or allotted place (as oars from the rowlocks).— *v.i.* to admit of or undergo unshipping.—*adj.* unshod′, shoeless: with shoe or shoes removed. —*v.t.* unshoe′, to strip of a shoe or shoes; unshout′ (*Shak.* unshoot′), to revoke the shouting of by a contrary shout.—*adj.* unshowered (*unshowrd*, *-show′ərd*), not watered by showers.— *v.t.* unshroud′, to uncover.—*adjs.* unshrubbed′ (*unshrubd*, *Shak.*), without shrubs; unshunn′able; unshunned′ (*unshun'd*, *Shak.*), inevitable.

—*v.t.*, *v.i.*, and *adj.* unshut′, open.—*v.t.* unshutt′er, to open or remove the shutters of.—*adjs.* unsift′ed, not sifted: not critically examined: inexperienced; unsight′ (*obs.*), unsight′ed, not seen: (of gun, etc.) having no sights: fired without use of sights.—*n.* unsight′liness.—*adj.* unsight′ly, displeasing to the eye: ugly.—*v.t.* unsin′ew, to take the strength from.—*adjs.* unsin′ewed (*Shak.* unsinn′owed); unsis′tered, without a sister.—*n.* unsis′terliness.—*adjs.* unsis′terly; unsist′ing (Shak., *Meas. for Meas.*), variously explained as unassisting, unresisting, insisting, unresting; unsiz(e)′able (*obs.*), inordinately big: too little, immature; unsized′, not fitted, adjusted, or sorted in respect of size: not treated with size; unskinned′, skinned: not skinned.—*vs.t.* unsling′, to free from slings or from being slung:—*pa.t.* and *pa.p.* unslung′; unsluice′, to let flow: to open the sluice of.— *adj.* unsmooth′.—*v.t.* to roughen: to wrinkle. —*adjs.* unsmoothed′; unsmote′, unsmitten.—*v.t.* unsnarl′, to disentangle.—*adj.* unsoaped′, not soaped: unwashed.—*n.* unsociabil′ity.—*adj.* unso′ciable, disinclined to associate with others. —*n.* unso′ciableness.—*adv.* unso′ciably.—*adjs.* unso′cial, not social: not regarding or conducing to the good of society: not sociable; unso′cialised, -z-, not socialised, not aware of one's function in, or lacking attributes for living in, society.—*ns.* unso′cialism, unsocial′ity.—*adv.* unso′cially.—*v.t.* unsock′et, to take out of the socket.—*adjs.* unsod′, unsodd′en, unboiled: not soaked or saturated.—*v.t.* unsolder (*un-sod′ər*, or *-sol′*, *-sö′*, *-sö′*, *-sōl′*), to separate from being soldered.—*adjs.* unsol′emn, not solemn: informal; unsolv′able, impossible to solve; unsolved′, not solved; unsoote′ (*Spens.*), unsweet; unsophis′ticate (now *rare*), unsophis′ticated, genuine, unadulterated: unfalsified: free from artificiality: ingenuous: inexperienced in evil. —*ns.* unsophis′ticatedness; unsophistica′tion.— *adjs.* unsort′ed, not sorted or arranged: ill-chosen: unfitting, unsuitable; unsought′, not sought or solicited.—*v.t.* unsoul′, to deprive of soul or spirit.—*adjs.* unsouled′, deprived of, or not endowed with, soul; unsound′, not sound; unsound′able, unfathomable; unsound′ed, not sounded, pronounced, or made to sound: unfathomed, unplumbed.—*adv.* unsound′ly.—*n.* unsound′ness.—*v.t.* unspar′, to withdraw a spar

---

unseg′regated, *adj.* un- (1).
unsensa′tional, *adj.* un- (1).
unsens′itive, *adj.* un- (1).
unsens′itised, -ized, *adj.* un- (1).
unsent′, *adj.* un- (1).
unsent′enced, *adj.* un- (1).
unsentiment′al, *adj.* un- (1).
unsep′arable (*Shak.*), *adj.* un- (1).
unsep′ulchred, *adj.* un- (1).
unser′viceable, *adj.* un- (1).
unsev′ered, *adj.* un- (1).
unsew′, *v.t.* un- (2).
unsewed′, unsewn′, *adjs.* un- (1).
unsha′ded, *adj.* un- (1).
unshak(e)′able, *adj.* un- (1).
unshak(e)′ably, *adv.* un- (1).
unshaked′ (*Shak.*), *adj.* un- (1).
unshak′en, *adj.* un- (1).
unshak′enly, *adv.* un- (1).
unshared′, *adj.* un- (1).
unsharp′ened, *adj.* un- (1).
unshaved′, *adj.* un- (1).
unsha′ven, *adj.* un- (1).
unshel′tered, *adj.* un- (1).
unshield′ed, *adj.* un- (1).
unshift′ing, *adj.* un- (1).

unshing′led, *adj.* un- (1).
unshorn′, *adj.* un- (1).
unshot′, *adj.* un- (1).
unshown′ (unshewn), *adj.* un- (1).
unshrink′able, *adj.* un- (1).
unshrink′ing, *adj.* un- (1).
unshrink′ingly, *adv.* un- (1).
unshrived′, *adj.* un- (1).
unshriv′en, *adj.* un- (1).
unsick′er (*Scot.*), *adj.* un- (1).
unsick′led, *adj.* un- (1).
unsighed′-for, *adj.* un- (1).
unsigh′ing, *adj.* un- (1).
unsigned′, *adj.* un- (1).
unsink′able, *adj.* un- (1).
unskil′ful, *adj.* un- (1).
unskil′fully, *adv.* un- (1).
unskil′fulness, *n.* un- (1).
unskilled′, *adj.* un- (1).
unskimmed′, *adj.* un- (1).
unslain′, *adj.* un- (1).
unslaked′, *adj.* un- (1).
unsleep′ing, *adj.* un- (1).
unslept′-in, *adj.* un- (1).
unslipp′ing, *adj.* un- (1).
unslum′bering, *adj.* un- (1).
unslum′brous, *adj.* un- (1).

unslung′, *adj.* un- (1).
unsmart′, *adj.* un- (1).
unsmiled′-on, *adj.* un- (1).
unsmil′ing, *adj.* un- (1).
unsmil′ingly, *adv.* un- (1).
unsmirched′, *adj.* un- (1).
unsmitt′en, *adj.* un- (1).
unsmoth′erable, *adj.* un- (1).
unsnuffed′, *adj.* un- (1).
unsoft′ (*Spens.*), *adv.* un- (1).
unsoftened (*-sof′(ə)nd*), *adj.* un- (1).
unsoftening (*-sof′(ə)ning*), *adj.* un- (1).
unsoiled′, *adj.* un- (1).
unsol′aced, *adj.* un- (1).
unsol′dierlike, *adj.* un- (1).
unsol′dierly, *adj.* un- (1).
unsolic′ited, *adj.* un- (1).
unsolic′itous, *adj.* un- (1).
unsol′id, *adj.* un- (1).
unsolid′ity, *n.* un- (1).
unsol′idly, *adv.* un- (1).
unsor′sy (*Scot.*), *adj.* un- (1).
unsoured′, *adj.* un- (1).
unsown′, *adj.* un- (1).

---

*Words beginning with pfx.* un- *are listed first* (pp. 1462 ff.); *other* UN- *words follow* (pp. 1484 ff.).

from.—*adjs.* **unspared'**, not spared: unstinted; **unspar'ing**, not sparing, liberal, profuse: unmerciful.—*adv.* **unspar'ingly.**—*n.* **unspar'ingness.** —*v.t.* **unspeak'**, to retract.—*adj.* **unspeak'able**, unutterable: inexpressible, esp. in badness.— *adv.* **unspeak'ably.**—*adjs.* **unspeak'ing**; **unsped'**, without achievement or success: unaccomplished.—*v.t.* **unspell'**, to free from a spell.— *adj.* **unspent'**, not spent.—*v.t.* **unsphere'**, to draw or remove from its sphere.—*adjs.* **unspied'** (*Spens.*, **unspide'**, *Milt.* **unspi'd'**), unobserved; **unspir'ited**; **unspir'itual.**—*v.t.* **unspir'itualise, -ize**, to deprive of spirituality.—*adv.* **unspir'itually.**— *adj.* **unsprung'**, not sprung: without springs.— *v.t.* **unstack'**, to remove from a stack.—*adjs.* **unstanch'able**; **unstanched'** (or *un'*), not stanched: unsated (*Shak.*): leaky, hence incontinent (*Shak.*).—*v.t.* **unstarch'**, to free from starch.— *adj.* **unstarched'**, not starched.—*v.t.* **unstate'** (*Shak.*), to deprive of state or dignity.—*adjs.* **unstat'ed**, not stated; **unstat'utable**, contrary to statute.—*adv.* **unstat'utably.**—*adjs.* **unstayed'**, not stayed or restrained: unsupported: unstable (*Spens.*): without stays; **unstay'ing**, without stop.—*adv.* **unstead'ily.**—*n.* **unstead'iness.**—*adj.* **unstead'y.**—*v.t.* to make unsteady.—*vs.t.* **unsteel'**, to soften, to disarm; **unstep'**, to remove, as a mast, from its place.—*adjs.* **unsterc'orated**, not manured.—*vs.t.* **unstick'**, to free from sticking.—*v.i.* to take off from the surface:—*pa.t.* and *pa.p.* **unstuck'**; **unstitch'**, to take out the stitches of; **unstock'**, to deplete of stock: to remove the stock from: to launch (*obs.*).—*adjs.* **unstocked'**, not stocked: without stock: not wearing a stock; **unstock'inged**, not wearing a stocking or stockings.—*v.t.* **unstop'**, to free from being stopped: to draw out the stop of.—*adj.* **unstopped'**, not stopped: of a consonant, open: without a pause at the end of the line.—*vs.t.* **unstopp'er**, to take the stopper from; **unstow'**, to empty of contents: to take out of stowage. —*adj.* **unstrained'**, not strained or purified by straining: not subjected to strain: not forced, natural.—*v.t.* **unstrap'**, to undo the straps of. —*adj.* **unstri'ated**, not striped.—*v.t.* **unstring'**, to take the strings from: to loose the strings of:

to take from a string: to put out of tone: to disorganise.—*v.i.* to loose the strings of one's purse.—*adj.* **unstringed'**, not stringed, not provided with strings.—*v.t.* **unstrip'** (now *dial.*), to strip.—*adjs.* **unstripped'**, not stripped; **unstrung'**, with strings removed or slacked: not strung: relaxed: disorganised: unnerved; **unstuck'**, detached, loosened from sticking: (**come unstuck**, of plan, to go amiss; *slang*), **unstud'ied**, not studied: not having studied: without premeditation: unlaboured: spontaneous: natural, easy; **un'stuffy** (*fig.*), not stodgy or straightlaced; **unsubstan'tial**, not substantial, real, corporeal, solid, or strong.—*v.t.* **unsubstan'tialise**, **-ize.**—*ns.* **unsubstantial'ity**; **unsubstantia'tion.**— *adj.* **unsucceed'ed**, without a successor.—*n.* **unsuccess'**, want of success: failure.—*adj.* **unsuccess'ful.**—*adv.* **unsuccess'fully.**—*n.* **unsuccess'fulness.**—*adjs.* **unsuccess'ive**, not successive: not in or passing by, succession; **unsuff'erable** (*obs.*), insufferable; **unsuffi'cient** (*obs.*), insufficient.—*v.t.* **unsuit'**, to make unsuitable.—*n.* **unsuitabil'ity** —*adj.* **unsuit'able.**—*n.* **unsuit'ableness.**—*adv.* **unsuit'ably.**—*adjs.* **unsuit'ed**, not suited or adapted; **unsuit'ing**; **unsummed'**, uncounted; **unsumm'ered**, not possessing the characteristics of summer; **unsung'**, not sung: not celebrated in song; **unsunned'**, not exposed to the sun: not lighted, warmed, affected by the sun: not exposed to view; **unsunn'y**; **unsupport'able**, insupportable: indefensible; **unsupport'ed.**—*adv.* **unsupport'edly.**—*adjs.* **unsure** (*un-shōōr'*), insecure: precarious: uncertain: doubtful: not assured: untrustworthy; **unsured'**, not made sure; **unsurmount'able**, insurmountable; **unsuspect'** (*Milt.*), not subject to suspicion; **unsuspec'ted**, not suspected: not known or supposed to exist.—*adv.* **unsuspec'tedly.**—*n.* **unsuspec'tedness.**—*adj.* **unsuspec'ting.**—*adv.* **unsuspec'tingly.** —*ns.* **unsuspec'tingness**; **unsuspi'cion**, absence of suspicion.—*adj.* **unsuspi'cious.**—*adv.* **unsuspi'ciously.**—*n.* **unsuspi'ciousness.**—*vs.t.* **unswadd'le**, to unswathe; **unswathe'**, to take swathings or bandages from.—*adjs.* **unsway'able** (*Shak.*); **unswayed'** (*Shak.* **unswai'd'**), not wielded: not controlled: uninfluenced: not swung.—*v.t.*

---

**unspe'cialised, -ized**, *adj.* un- (1).
**unspec'ified**, *adj.* un- (1).
**unspec'tacled**, *adj.* un- (1).
**unspec'ulative**, *adj.* un- (1).
**unspilled'**, *adj.* un- (1).
**unspilt'**, *adj.* un- (1).
**unsplint'erable**, *adj.* un- (1).
**unspoiled'**, *adj.* un- (1).
**unspoilt'**, *adj.* un- (1).
**unspoke'** (*Shak.*), *adj.* un- (1).
**unspo'ken**, *adj.* un- (1).
**unsport'ing**, *adj.* un- (1).
**unsports'manlike**, *adj.* un- (1).
**unspott'ed**, *adj.* un- (1).
**unspott'edness**, *n.* un- (1).
**unsprink'led**, *adj.* un- (1).
**unspun'**, *adj.* un- (1).
**unsquared'**, *adj.* un- (1).
**unsta'ble**, *adj.* un- (1).
**unsta'bleness**, *n.* un- (1).
**unstaid'**, *adj.* un- (1).
**unstaid'ness**, *n.* un- (1).
**unstain'able**, *adj.* un- (1).
**unstained'**, *adj.* un- (1).
**unstamped'**, *adj.* un- (1).
**unstates'manlike**, *adj.* un- (1).
**unstead'fast**, *adj.* un- (1).
**unstead'fastly**, *adv.* un- (1).
**unstead'fastness**, *n.* un- (1).
**unster'ilised, -ized**, *adj.* un- (1).
**unsti'fled**, *adj.* un- (1).

**unstig'matised, -ized**, *adj.* un- (1).
**unstilled'**, *adj.* un- (1).
**unstim'ulated**, *adj.* un- (1).
**unstint'ed**, *adj.* un- (1).
**unstint'ing**, *adj.* un- (1).
**unstoop'ing**, *adj.* un- (1).
**unstrapped'**, *adj.* un- (1).
**unstrat'ified**, *adj.* un- (1).
**unstrength'ened**, *adj.* un- (1).
**unstressed'**, *adj.* un- (1).
**unstriped'**, *adj.* un- (1).
**unstruck'**, *adj.* un- (1).
**unstruc'tured**, *pa.p.* *adj.* un- (1).
**unstuffed'** (*Shak.* **un'stuft**), *adj.* un- (1).
**unsubdu'able**, *adj.* un- (1).
**unsubdued'**, *adj.* un- (1).
**unsub'ject**, *adj.* un- (1).
**unsubject'ed**, *adj.* un- (1).
**unsub'limated**, *adj.* un- (1).
**unsublimed'**, *adj.* un- (1).
**unsubmerged'**, *adj.* un- (1).
**unsubmiss'ive**, *adj.* un- (1).
**unsubmitt'ing**, *adj.* un- (1).
**unsubscribed'**, *adj.* un- (1).
**unsub'sidised, -ized**, *adj.* un- (1).
**unsubstan'tiated**, *adj.* un- (1).
**unsucc'oured**, *adj.* un- (1).
**unsucked'**, *adj.* un- (1).
**unsued'-for, -to**, *adjs.* un- (1).
**unsull'ied**, *adj.* un- (1).

**unsumm'oned**, *adj.* un- (1).
**unsuper'fluous** (*Milt.*), *adj.* un- (1).
**unsupplied'**, *adj.* un- (1).
**unsuppos'able**, *adj.* un- (1).
**unsuppressed'**, *adj.* un- (1).
**unsurmised'**, **-ized**, *adj.* un- (1).
**unsurpass'able**, *adj.* un- (1).
**unsurpass'ably**, *adv.* un- (1).
**unsurpassed'**, *adj.* un- (1).
**unsurveyed'**, *adj.* un- (1).
**unsuscept'ible**, *adj.* un- (1).
**unsuspend'ed**, *adj.* un- (1).
**unsustain'able**, *adj.* un- (1).
**unsustained'**, *adj.* un- (1).
**unsustain'ing**, *adj.* un- (1).
**unswall'owed**, *adj.* un- (1).
**unsweet'**, *adj.* un- (1).
**unsweet'ened**, *adj.* un- (1).
**unswept'**, *adj.* un- (1).
**unswer'ving**, *adj.* un- (1).
**unswer'vingly**, *adv.* un- (1).
**unsympathet'ic**, *adj.* un- (1).
**unsympathet'ically**, *adv.* un- (1).
**unsym'pathising, -izing**, *adj.* un- (1).
**unsym'pathy**, *n.* un- (1).
**unsystemat'ic, -al**, *adjs.* un- (1).
**unsystemat'ically**, *adv.* un- (1).
**unsys'tematised, -ized**, *adj.* un- (1).

---

*Words beginning with pfx.* **un-** *are listed first* (pp. 1462 ff.); *other UN- words follow* (pp. 1484 ff.).

**unswear'**, to retract the swearing of.—*v.i.* to recall an oath.—*n.* **unswear'ing.**—*adjs.* **unsworn'**, not confirmed, or not bound, by oath; **unsyll'abled**, not syllabled, not articulated; **unsymmet'rical.** —*adv.* **unsymmet'rically.**—*adj.* **unsymm'etrised**, **-ized.**—*n.* **unsymm'etry**, asymmetry.

*Words with prefix* un- *(continued)*.

*vs.t.* **untack'**, to detach from tacking; **untack'le**, to strip of tackle: to free from tackle: to unharness.—*adj.* **untaint'ed**, not tainted: unblemished: not attainted.—*adv.* **untaint'edly.**— *n.* **untaint'edness.**—*adjs.* **untaint'ing**; **untam'able** (also **untame'able**).—*n.* **untam(e)'ableness.**—*adv.* **untam(e)'ably.**—*adj.* **untame'**, not tame.—*v.t.* to make untame, undo the taming of.—*adj.* **untamed'.**—*n.* **untamed'ness.**—*v.t.* **untang'le**, to disentangle.—*adjs.* **untang'led**; **untaught'**, not instructed: not taught or communicated by teaching: spontaneous, native, inborn.—*v.t.* **untax'**, to remit a tax on.—*adj.* **untaxed'**, not taxed: not charged with any fault.—*v.t.* **unteach'**, to undo the teaching of.—*adj.* **unteach'able**, not teachable.—*n.* **unteach'ableness.**—*vs.t.* **unteam'**, to unyoke; **untem'per**, to destroy the temper of, deprive of suitable temper.—*adjs.* **untem'pered**, not tempered: not regulated; **untem'pering** (*Shak.*), unconciliating; **unten'able**, not tenable, not defensible.—*n.* **unten'ableness.**—*v.t.* **unten'ant**, to deprive of a tenant: to dislodge. —*adjs.* **unten'antable**; **unten'anted**, not occupied. —*v.t.* **untent'**, to remove from a tent.—*adjs.* **untent'ed**, having no tents: of a wound, unprobed, undressed, or impossible to treat with a tent: unheeded (*Scot.*); **untent'y**, careless (*Scot.*).—*v.t.* **unteth'er**, to release from a tether. —*adjs.* **unteth'ered**, not tethered.—*v.t.* **unthatch'**, to strip of thatch.—*adj.* **unthatched'**, not thatched. —*v.t.* and *v.i.* **unthaw'**, to thaw.—*adj.* **unthawed'**, not thawed.—*v.t.* and *v.i.* **unthink'**, to think to the contrary, reverse in thought.—*n.* **unthinkabil'ity.**—*adjs.* **unthink'able**, that cannot be thought: outside the realm of thought: beyond the power of thought: inconceivable: unimaginable: utterly impossible (often of things impending but too painful to think about); **unthink'ing**, not thinking: thoughtless.—*adv.* **unthink'ingly.**—*n.* **unthink'ingness.**—*adjs.* **unthought'-of**; **unthought'ful.**—*adv.* **unthought'fully.**—*n.* **unthought'fulness.**—*v.t.* **unthread'**, to take a thread from: to unweave: to loosen:

to find one's way through.—*adj.* **unthread'ed**, not threaded.—*n.* **un'thrift**, a prodigal: a spendthrift: unthriftiness.—*adj.* **prodigal.**—*adv.* **unthrift'ily.**—*n.* **unthrift'iness.**—*adj.* **unthrift'y**, not thrifty; wasteful: prodigal: not thriving: unprofitable.—*n.* **unthrift'yhe(a)d** (*Spens.*), unthriftiness.—*vs.t.* **unthrone'**, to dethrone; **untie'**, to loose from being tied; to unbind: to solve, resolve.—*v.i.* to come loose.—*adj.* **untied'**, not tied: loosed: not loosed, still tied (Shak., *Pericles*). *v.t.* **untilo'**, to strip of tiles.—*adjs.* **untiled'**, not tiled: stripped of tiles; **untim'bered**, not strongly timbered (*Shak.*): unwooded.—*n.* **untime'liness.**—*adj.* **untime'ly**, not timely: before the time, premature: immature: unseasonable, ill-timed: inopportune.—*adv.* at an unsuitable time: too early, prematurely: unseasonably: inopportunely.—*adj.* **untime'ous**, untimely.— *adv.* **untime'ously.**—*v.t.* **untin'**, to take the tin from.—*adjs.* **untinned'**, not tinned; **unti'tled**, having no title: deprived of title; **untoch'ered** (*Scot.*), without tocher; **untold'** (or *un'*), not counted: innumerable: not narrated: not communicated: not informed.—*v.t.* **untomb'**, to disentomb.—*adjs.* **untombed'**, not entombed; **untoned'**, not toned: without tones; **untouch'able**, impossible to touch: not to be equalled or touched.—*n.* one whose excellence in some respect cannot be rivalled: (esp. formerly) Hindu of very low caste, a member of one of the Scheduled Castes.—*adjs.* **untouched'**, not touched: intact: unrivalled; **untoward** (*untō'ərd*), not easily guided: froward: awkward: inconvenient: unlucky: unfavourable: unfitting.—*n.* **unto'wardliness.**—*adv.* **unto'wardly.** —*adj.* **untoward.**—*n.* **unto'wardness.**—*v.t.* **untrace'**, to loose from traces.—*adjs.* **untrace'able**, impossible to trace; **untraced'**; **untra'ded**, unfrequented, as for trade (*obs.*): unhackneyed (*Shak.*).—*vs.t.* **untread'** (*Shak.*), to tread back, to retrace; **untreas'ure**, to despoil (of treasure). —*adjs.* **untreat'able**, intractable (*obs.*): that cannot be treated; **untreat'ed**; **untressed'**, not dressed in tresses; **untried'**, not tried, tested, attempted, experienced, subjected to trial in court: (Shak., *Pericles*, **untride'**) prob. not ventured upon, hence not noticed or dealt with.—*v.t.* **untrim'**, to deprive of trimming or trimness.—*adjs.* **untrimmed'**, not trimmed; **untrod'**, **untrodd'en**, not trodden upon: unfrequented; **untroub'led**, not troubled or disturbed:

---

*Words beginning with pfx.* un- *are listed first* (pp. 1462 ff.); *other* UN- *words follow* (pp. 1484 ff.).

fāte fär; mē, hûr (her); mīne; mōte, fôr; mūte; mōōn, fŏŏt; dhen (then) not turbid; **untrue**', not true: false: not faithful: dishonest: inexact: not in accordance with a standard.—*adv.* (*Shak.*) untruly, untruthfully.—*ns.* **untrue'ness**; **untru'ism**, an untrue platitude. —*adv.* **untru'ly**, falsely.—*v.t.* **untruss**', to unpack: to unfasten: to untie (esp. points): to untie the points of.—*adj.* **untrussed'**, **untrust'**, not trussed: untied: with points untied.—*ns.* **untruss'er**; **untruss'ing**; **untrust'**, distrust.—*adj.* **untrust'ful**, not trusting: not trustworthy: not to be trusted. —*n.* **untrust'iness** (*obs.*).—*adv.* **untrust'worthily.** —*n.* **untrust'worthiness.**—*adjs.* **untrust'worthy**, not worthy of trust; **untrust'y**, not trusty, not deserving trust.—*n.* **untruth'**, unfaithfulness: falseness: falsity: that which is untrue: a lie. —*adj.* **untruth'ful**, not truthful.—*adv.* **untruth'-fully.**—*n.* **untruth'fulness.**—*v.t.* **untuck'**, to unfold or undo from being tucked up or in: to take out tucks from.—*adjs.* **untucked'**, not tucked; **un-tuck'ered**, not having a tucker on; **untun'able** (also **untune'able**), harsh.—*n.* **untun'ableness.**— *adv.* **untun'ably.**—*v.t.* **untune'**, to put out of tune. —*adjs.* **untuned'**, not tuned: put out of tune; **untune'ful.**—*adv.* **untune'fully.**—*n.* **untune'fulness.** —*vs.t.* **unturf'**, to strip of turf; **unturn'**, to turn backwards.—*adjs.* **unturn'able**; **unturned'**, not turned; **unturn'ing**; **untu'tored**, untaught: un-instructed.—*vs.t.* and *vs.i.* **untwine'**, to untwist: to separate by untwisting; **untwist'**, to twist backwards so as to open out: to straighten out from a twist.—*adj.* **untwist'ed**, not twisted: sub-jected to untwisting.—*n.* **untwist'ing.**

*Words with prefix* un- (*continued*).

**adjs. unused** (*un-ūzd'*), not used: (also *un-ūst'*) unaccustomed: unusual (*arch.*); **unuseful** (-*ūs'*). —*adv.* **unuse'fully.**—*n.* **unuse'fulness.**—*adj.* **un-us'ual.**—*adv.* **unus'ually**, more than usually: in an unusual way.—*n.* **unus'ualness.**—*adj.* **un-utt'erable**, beyond utterance, inexpressible: not to be uttered.—*n.* an unutterable thing: (in *pl.*) trousers (*old slang*).—*adv.* **unutt'erably.**—*adjs.* **unutt'ered**; **unval'uable**, not valuable, of little worth: invaluable, priceless (*obs.*); **unval'ued**, not prized or highly esteemed: without having a value assigned: invaluable, priceless (now *rare*); **unvar'nished**, not varnished: not artfully em-bellished or sophisticated.—*v.t.* **unveil'** (*obs.* **un-vail'**, **unvaile'**), to remove or set aside a veil from: to open to public view by ceremonial removal of a covering: to disclose, reveal.—*v.i.* to remove one's veil: to become unveiled, to

reveal oneself.—*adj.* **unveiled'**, without a veil: with veil set aside or removed: unconcealed and undisguised.—*n.* **unveil'er.**—*adjs.* **unvent'ed**, not vented: without a vent; **unvera'cious**, not truthful.—*n.* **unverac'ity.**—*adj.* **unversed'**, not experienced or skilled: not put in verse.—*n.* **unvir'tue**, lack of virtue.—*adj.* **unvir'tuous.**— *adv.* **unvir'tuously.**—*adjs.* **unvis'itable**, unable to visit (*obs.*): unfit to be visited: unsuitable for visiting; **unvis'ited.**—*v.t.* **unvis'or**, **unviz'ard**, to remove or open the visor of.—*v.i.* to unvisor oneself: to unmask.—*v.t.* **unvoice'**, to change to, or utter with, a voiceless sound.—*adj.* **un-voiced'**, not given voice to: without voice.—*n.* **unvoic'ing**, change to a voiceless sound.—*adjs.* **unvoy'ageable**, not navigable, impassable; **un-vulgar.**—*v.t.* **unvul'garise**, -**ize**, to free from vulgarity.

*Words with prefix* un- (*continued*).

**adj. unware'** (O.E. *unwǣr*), unwary (*obs.*): un-aware, without knowing (*Spens.*, *Milt.*): un-expected (*obs.*).—*adv.* unknowingly: unexpect-edly.—*adv.* **unware'ly**, unwarily (*obs.*): suddenly, unexpectedly (*Spens.*).—*n.* **unware'ness** (*arch.*), unwariness.—*advs.* **unwares'**, unawares (*arch.*): unexpectedly, suddenly: unknowingly (*Shak.*); **unwa'rily.**—*n.* **unwa'riness.**—*adjs.* **unwa'ry**, not wary: (*Spens.* **unwarie**) unexpected; **unwashed'** (*B.* **unwash'en**; see **great**).—*v.t.* **unwa'ter**, to drain (esp. a mine).—*adjs.* **unwa'tered**, freed from water: not watered; **unwa'tery**; **unwayed'**, not accustomed to roads: hence, intractable.— *n.* **unweal'**, affliction, ill.—*v.t.* **unweap'on**, to disarm.—*adjs.* **unweap'oned**, unarmed: dis-armed; **unweath'ered**, not worn by the weather or atmospheric agencies.—*v.t.* **unweave'**, to undo from being woven.—*adjs.* **unwedge'able** (**un-wedg'able**; *Shak.*), unable to be split with wedges; **unweened'**, unexpected; **unweet'ing**, unwitting.—*adv.* **unweet'ingly**, unwittingly.— *adjs.* **unweighed'**, not weighed: not pondered: unguarded; **unweigh'ing** (*Shak.*), thoughtless, inconsiderate; **unwept'**, not wept for; **unwhole'-some**, not wholesome: unsound: tainted in health, taste or morals.—*adv.* **unwhole'somely.** —*n.* **unwhole'someness.**—*adv.* **unwiel'dily.**—*n.* **unwiel'diness.**—*adjs.* **unwiel'dy** (*Spens.*, etc., **un-wel'dy**), difficult to wield or move, from bulk or weakness: heavily awkward: unmanageable. —*v.t.* **unwill'**, to will the contrary of: to deprive of will.—*adjs.* **unwilled'**, not willed: involuntary;

| | | |
|---|---|---|
| untum'bled, *adj.* un- (1). | unvit'rifiable, *adj.* un- (1). | unwatch'fulness, *n.* un- (1). |
| untumult'uous, *adj.* un- (1). | unvit'rified, *adj.* un- (1). | unwa'vering, *adj.* un- (1). |
| untur'bid, *adj.* un- (1). | unvo'cal, *adj.* un- (1). | unwa'veringly, *adv.* un- (1). |
| unty'ing, *n.* un- (2). | unvo'calised, -ized, *adj.* un- (1). | unweakened (-wēk'), *adj.* un- (1). |
| unuplift'ed, *adj.* un- (1). | unvul'nerable (*Shak.*), *adj.* un- | unweaned', *adj.* un- (1). |
| unurged', *adj.* un- (1). | (1). | unwearable (-wār'), *adj.* un- (1). |
| unush'ered, *adj.* un- (1). | unwaked', *adj.* un- (1). | unweariable (-wē'), *adj.* un- (1). |
| unvac'cinated, *adj.* un- (1). | unwak'ened, *adj.* un- (1). | unwea'riably, *adv.* un- (1). |
| unvan'quishable, *adj.* un- (1). | unwalled', *adj.* un- (1). | unwea'ried, *adj.* un- (1). |
| unvan'quished, *adj.* un- (1). | unwand'ering, *adj.* un- (1). | unwea'riedly, *adv.* un- (1). |
| unvar'iable, *adj.* un- (1). | unwant'ed, *adj.* un- (1). | unwea'ry, *adj.* un- (1). |
| unvar'ied, *adj.* un- (1). | unward'ed, *adj.* un- (1). | unwea'rying, *adj.* un- (1). |
| unva'riegated, *adj.* un- (1). | unwar'like, *adj.* un- (1). | unwea'ryingly, *adv.* un- (1). |
| unva'rying, *adj.* un- (1). | unwarmed', *adj.* un- (1). | unwebbed', *adj.* un- (1). |
| unvend'ible, *adj.* un- (1). | unwarned', *adj.* un- (1). | unwed', *adj.* un- (1). |
| unven'erable, *adj.* un- (1). | unwarped', *adj.* un- (1). | unwedd'ed, *adj.* un- (1). |
| unvent'ilated, *adj.* un- (1). | unwarr'antable, *adj.* un- (1). | unweed'ed, *adj.* un- (1). |
| unver'ifiable, *adj.* un- (1). | unwarr'antably, *adv.* un- (1). | unwel'come, *adj.* un- (1). |
| unverifiabil'ity, *n.* un- (1). | unwarr'anted, *adj.* un- (1). | unwel'comed, *adj.* un- (1). |
| unver'ified, *adj.* un- (1). | unwarr'antedly, *adv.* un- (1). | unwel'comely, *adv.* un- (1). |
| unvexed', *adj.* un- (1). | unwast'ed, *adj.* un- (1). | unwel'comeness, *n.* un- (1). |
| unviewed', *adj.* un- (1). | unwast'ing, *adj.* un- (1). | unwell', *adj.* un- (1). |
| unvi'olated, *adj.* un- (1). | unwatched', *adj.* un- (1). | unwell'ness, *n.* un- (1). |
| unvi'tal, *adj.* un- (1). | unwatch'ful, *adj.* un- (1). | unwet', *adj.* un- (1). |
| unvi'tiated, *adj.* un- (1). | unwatch'fully, *adv.* un- (1). | unwett'ed, *adj.* un- (1). |

*Words beginning with pfx.* un- *are listed first* (pp. 1462 ff.); *other* UN- *words follow* (pp. 1484 ff.).

unwill'ing, reluctant: done reluctantly: not willed, unintentional (*Shak.*).—*adv.* unwill'ingly. —*n.* unwill'ingness.—*v.t.* unwind (*un-wīnd'*), to undo the winding of: to free from being wound: to wind down or off: to relax (*coll.*).—*v.i.* to become unwound:—*pa.t.* and *pa.p.* unwound (*un-wownd'*).—*n.* and *adj.* unwind'ing, uncoiling.—*adj.* not winding.—*v.t.* unwire', to take the wire from.—*n.* unwis'dom, lack of wisdom: foolishness: injudiciousness.—*adj.* unwise', not wise: injudicious: foolish. *adv.* unwise'ly.—*n.* unwise'ness.—*v.t.* unwish' (*Shak.*), to wish to be away, not to be, to be unfulfilled, or to be undone.—*adjs.* unwished'-for, not wished for: unwish'ful; unwish'ing; unwist', not known (*arch.*; *Spens.*, etc.): unknowing (*Spens.*).—*vs.t.* unwit' (*Shak.*), to deprive of wits; unwitch', to free from witchcraft.—*adj.* unwithdraw'ing, liberal, lavish; unwithhold'en (*Coleridge*), not held back, not restrained; unwithhold'ing, not holding back. —*adv.* unwitt'ily.—*adj.* unwitt'ing, without knowing: unaware: not cognisant: unintentional.—*adv.* unwitt'ingly.—*n.* unwitt'ingness.—*adj.* unwitt'y, foolish: unskilled: without wit.—*v.t.* unwive', to deprive of a wife.—*adj.* unwived', without a wife.—*v.t.* unwo'man, to make unwomanly.—*n.* unwo'manliness.—*adj.* unwomanly, not befitting or becoming a woman: not such as a woman is expected to be.—*adv.* in an unwomanly manner.—*adjs.* unwont' (now *rare*; *Spens.*, etc.), unwont'ed, unaccustomed: unusual.—*adv.* unwont'edly.—*n.* unwont'edness.—*adj.* unword'ed, speechless: not expressed in words.—*v.t.* unwork', to undo.—*adjs.* unwork'-able, not workable: impracticable; unworked', not worked; unwork'ing; unwork'manlike, not like or worthy of a good workman.—*n.* unworld'-liness.—*adjs.* unworld'ly, not of this world: spiritual: above worldly or self-interested motives; unwormed', not worm-eaten: (of a dog) not having had the worm or lytta cut out. —*n.* unworth', lack of worth.—*adj.* unworthy. —*adv.* unwor'thily.—*n.* unwor'thiness.—*adjs.* unwor'thy, not worthy: worthless: unbecoming: discreditable: undeserved; unwound (*unwownd'*), not wound: taken out of winding.—Also *pa.t.*, *pa.p.* of unwind.—*v.t.* unwrap (*un-rap'*), to remove wrappings from: to unroll, unwind. —*v.i.* to become unwrapped.—*adj.* unwreaked (*un-rēkt'*), unrevenged.—*v.t.* unwreathe (*un-rēdh'*), to take out of a wreathed condition.— *v.t.* and *v.i.* unwrink'le, to smooth out from a wrinkled state.—*adj.* unwrink'led, not wrinkled, smooth.—*v.t.* unwrite', to undo the writing of. —*adjs.* unwrit'ing, not writing; unwritt'en, not written or reduced to writing, oral: containing no writing; unwrought (*un-röt'*), not done or worked: not fashioned, formed, composed, or worked up: not mined: not tilled: undone, brought back to an original state; unyeaned', unborn; unyielding', not yielding: stiff: obstinate.—*adv.* unyiel'dingly.—*n.* unyiel'dingness. —*v.t.* unyoke', to loose from a yoke or harness: to disjoin.—*v.i.* to unyoke an animal: to cease work.—*adjs.* unyoked', not yoked or harnessed: freed from yoke or harness: unrestrained (*Shak.*); unzoned', not in zones: ungirt.

una corda, *ūn'ə kör'də, ōōn'ä kör'dä*, (It.; *mus.*) *n.* one string (soft pedal).
unalist, *ū'nəl-ist, n.* a holder of one benefice. [L. *ūnus*, one.]
unanimous, *ū-nan'i-məs, adj.* of one mind: without a dissentient.—*n.* unanimity (*ū-nən-im'i-ti*), agreement without a dissentient.—*adv.* unan'imously. [L. *ūnanimus*—*ūnus*, one, *animus*, mind.]
una voce, *ūn'ə vō'sē, ōōn'ä wō'ke*, (L.) with one voice.
unau, *ū'nö, ōō'now*, *n.* the two-toed sloth. [Fr., from Tupí.]
unberufen, *ōōn-bə-rōōf'ən*, (Ger.) not called for— an exclamation to avert the ill-luck that may possibly follow an over-confident or boastful statement.
uncate, *ung'kāt, adj.* hooked. [L. *uncātus*—*uncus*, a hook.]
unce, *uns, n.* Scots form of ounce.
uncial, *un'shəl, -si-əl, adj.* pertaining to an inch or an ounce: of a form of writing in (usu. large) somewhat rounded characters used in ancient manuscripts.—*n.* an uncial letter: uncial writing: MS written in uncials. [L. *unciālis*—*uncia*, a twelfth.]
unciform, *un'si-förm, adj.* hook-shaped.—*adjs.* un'cinate, -d, hooked at the end.—*n.* unci'nus, a hooklet: a marginal tooth of a mollusc's radula: a hooked chaeta in annelids:—*pl.* unci'ni (*-nī*). [L. *uncīnus*—*uncus*, a hook.]
uncle, *ung'kl, n.* the brother of one's father or mother: an aunt's husband: a great-uncle: an elderly man, esp. a Negro (*U.S.*): a pawnbroker (*slang*).—*v.t.* to address as uncle.—*n.* un'cleship, the state of being an uncle.—Uncle Sam, the United States or its people; Uncle Tom, an old-fashioned American Negro with the outlook and behaviour of the hero of 'Uncle Tom's Cabin'. [O.Fr. *uncle* (Fr. *oncle*)—L. *avunculus*, a maternal uncle.]
unco, *ung'ka, -kō,* (*Scot.*) *adj.* strange, unusual: fearsome: remarkable: great.—*n.* a stranger: a piece of news: a remarkable thing.—*adv.* remarkably, very.—unco guid (*gid*), the obtrusively rigorous in morals. [uncouth.]
uncouth. See un-.
unction, *ungk'shən, n.* an anointing: that which is used for anointing: ointment: that quality in language which raises emotion or devotion: warmth of address: religious glibness: divine or sanctifying grace: gusto.—*n.* unctūos'ity, unctuousness.—*adj.* unc'tūous, oily: greasy: full of unction: offensively suave and smug.—*adv.* unc'tūously.—*n.* unc'tūousness.—extreme unction (*R.C. Church*), the sacrament of anointing with consecrated oil in one's last hours. [L. *unctiō, -ōnis*, unction, besmearing, *ūnctum*, fat.]
uncus, *ung'kəs, n.* a hook or hook-like process:— *pl.* unci (*un'sī*). [L. *uncus*, a hook.]
undate, *un'dāt*, undated, *-id, adjs.* wavy. [L. *unda*, a wave.]
undated. See un-.
undé, unde. See undee.
undecimal, *un-des'i-məl, adj.* based on the number eleven.—*n.* undec'imole (*mus.*), a group of eleven notes in the time of eight. [L. *undecim*, eleven— *ūnus*, one, *decem*, ten.]

---

unwhipped' (unwhipt'), *adj.* un- (1).
unwife'like, *adj.* un- (1).
unwife'ly, *adj.* un- (1).
unwigged', *adj.* un- (1).
unwil'ful, *adj.* un- (1).
unwinged', *adj.* un- (1).
unwink'ing, *adj.* un- (1).
unwink'ingly, *adv.* un- (1).
unwinn'owed, *adj.* un- (1).

unwiped', *adj.* un- (1).
unwith'ered, *adj.* un- (1).
unwith'ering, *adj.* un- (1).
unwithheld', *adj.* un- (1).
unwithstood', *adj.* un- (1).
unwit'nessed, *adj.* un- (1).
unwon', *adj.* un- (1).
unwood'ed, *adj.* un- (1).
unwooed', *adj.* un- (1).
unworn', *adj.* un- (1).

unworr'ied, *adj.* un- (1).
unwor'shipful, *adj.* un- (1).
unwor'shipped, *adj.* un- (1).
unwoundable (*-wōōnd'*), *adj.* un- (1).
unwound'ed, *adj.* un- (1).
unwo'ven, *adj.* un- (1).
unwrung', *adj.* un- (1).
unzeal'ous, *adj.* un- (1).
unzip', *v.t.* un- (2).

*Words beginning with pfx.* un- *are listed firs* (pp. 1462 ff.); *other* UN- *words follow* (pp. 1484 ff.).

**undee, undée, undé,** *un'dā,* (*her.*) *adj.* wavy. [Fr. *ondé*; cf. **oundy, undate.**]

**under,** *un'dər, prep.* beneath: below: in or to a position lower than that of, especially vertically lower: at the foot of: within, on the covered side of: short of: in or into subjection, subordination, obligation, liability, etc., to: in course of: in the state of: (of cultivated land) supporting a specified crop: by the authority or attestation of: in accordance with: in the aspect of: referred to the class, heading, name, etc., of: in the reign or administration of.—*adv.* in or to a lower (esp. vertically lower) position: in or into a lower degree or condition: in or into subjection: in or into a covered, submerged, or hidden state: below.—*adj.* lower: subordinate: falling short.—*n.* **un'derling,** a contemptuous word for a subordinate: a weakling.—*adj.* **un'dermost,** lowest: inmost.—*adv.* in or to the undermost place.—**go, knock, snow under** (see these words); **under age, arms,** etc. (see these words); **under the counter** (see **count** (2)); **under the lee,** to the leeward. [O.E. *under;* Goth. *undar,* O.N. *undir,* Ger. *unter,* L. *infrā.*]

**under-, un-dər-,** *pfx.* (1) below, beneath; (2) lower in position (*lit.*); (3) lower in rank, or subordinate; (4a) too little in quantity, too small, insufficient; (4b) in too small a degree, insufficiently; (5) not coming, or not allowed to come, to the surface or into the open.—*v.t.* and *v.i.* **underact',** to make too little of in acting: to play, for the sake of effect, with little emphasis. —*ns.* **underac'tion,** subordinate action: less than normal or adequate action; **underact'or.**—*adj.* **un'der-age',** not of full age: immature.—*n.* **undera'gent,** a subordinate agent.—*adj.* and *adv.* **underarm',** placed or held under the arm: with the arm below the shoulder.—*v.t.* **underbear'** (*Shak.*), to sustain: (*pa.p.* **underborne,** *Shak.*) perh. to trim (on the lower part), perh. to line or support by a foundation, perh. to have sewn underneath or on strips of tinsel.—*ns.* **un'derbearer** (*dial.*), one who helps to carry a coffin; **underbear'ing.**—*adj.* unassuming.—*n.* **un'derbelly,** the under surface of a body or of something suggesting a body: soft underbelly (q.v.).—*v.t.* **underbid',** to offer at a price lower than that of: to outbid: to bid less than the value of (*bridge*).—*v.i.* to bid unduly low.—*n.* (*bridge*) a bid too low to be valid, or less than the hand is worth.—*n.* **underbidd'er,** one who underbids: the next below the highest bidder.— *v.t.* **un'derbite',** to bite insufficiently with acid, as in etching.—*adj.* **un'derbitt'en.**—*adv.* **un'derboard** (*obs.*), secretly—opp. to *above-board.*—*ns.* **un'derbough,** a lower branch; **un'der-boy,** a boy in the lower school; **un'derbreath,** a subdued voice: rumour.—*adj.* **underbred',** of inferior breeding or manners: not pure-bred.—*ns.* **un'derbridge,** a bridge carrying a road or railway distinguished from one over it; **un'derbrush,** undergrowth of brushwood or shrubs.—*v.t.* to clear of underbrush.—*v.t.* **underbuild',** to build under in support, underpin: build too little upon or in.—*n.* **un'derbuilder,** a subordinate or assistant builder.—*n.* and *v.t.* **un'derbush, underbrush.**—*v.t.* **un'derbuy',** to buy at less than the price paid by, or the value of.—*ns.* **un'dercarriage,** the supporting framework under the body of a carriage or wagon: the landing-gear of an aircraft, or its main part; **un'dercast,** an air-passage crossing under a road in a mine; **un'dercharge,** too small a charge.—*v.t.* **un'dercharge',** to charge too little, or too little for.— *adj.* **underclad',** not wearing clothes enough.—

*ns.* **un'derclay,** a bed of clay underlying a coal-seam representing the soil in which the plants grew; **un'der-clerk,** a subordinate clerk; **un'derclerk'ship;** **un'dercliff,** a terrace of material that has fallen from a cliff.—*v.t.* **un'derclothe,** to provide with underclothing.—*adj.* **un'derclothed,** provided with underclothing: (*-klōdhd'*) underclad.—*n.pl.* **un'derclothes,** and *n.sing.* **un'derclothing,** clothes worn under others, esp. those next the skin.—*ns.* **un'dercoat,** coat worn under another: an underskirt (*obs.*): an underlayer of fur or hair, or of paint.—*v.t.* **un'dercool,** to supercool: to cool insufficiently.—*n.* **un'dercoun'tenance** (*Wordsworth*), that which underlies the superficial aspect of the face.—*adj.* **un'dercover,** working, done, in secret: (**under cover of,** hidden by, using as concealment).—*ns.* **un'dercovert,** a covert of undergrowth; **un'der-craft** (*Sterne*), a sly trick.—*v.t.* **undercrest'** (*Shak.*), to bear like a crest.—*ns.* **un'dercroft** (cf. *krocht,* crypt), a crypt, vault; **un'dercurrent,** a current under the surface.—*adj.* running below or unseen. —*v.t.* **undercut',** to cut under: to cut away under the surface, so as to leave part overhanging: to undermine: to strike with a heavy blow upward: to underbid: to go beyond in lowering prices.— *adj.* made so as to cut from the underside: effected by undercutting: having the parts in relief cut under.—*n.* (*un'*), the act or effect of cutting under: a blow dealt upward: the tenderloin, or fillet, or underside of a sirloin.—*v.t.* **underdevel'op.**—*adj.* **underdevel'oped,** insufficiently developed: of a country, with resources inadequately used, having a low standard of living, and backward in education.—*n.* **underdevel'opment.**—*v.t.* **underdo',** to do, perform, act, or esp. cook, insufficiently or inadequately: —*pa.t.* **underdid';** *pa.p.* **underdone'.**—*ns.* **underdo'er;** **un'derdog,** the dog that gets the worst of it in a fight: any one in adversity.—*adj.* **underdone',** done less than is requisite: insufficiently or slightly cooked.—*vs.t.* **underdrain',** to drain by deep ditches; **un'derdraw,** to draw or describe with moderation or reticence or short of the truth: to cover the underside of with boards or lath and plaster.—*n.* **un'derdress,** underclothing: a dress or part of a dress worn or showing under another.—*v.t.* and *v.i.* **underdress',** to dress too plainly or simply.—*adj.* **underdressed'.**—*n.* **un'derdrive,** a gear which transmits to the driving shaft a speed less than engine speed.—*adjs.* **under-driv'en,** driven from beneath; **un'derearth,** underground.—*ns.* **underemploy'ment,** making too little use (of): the condition of having too large a part of the labour force unemployed: partial employment, or employment on work requiring less skill than the worker has; **un'derespi'al,** a subordinate spy (*Scott*).—*v.t.* **underes'timate,** to estimate or value too low.—*n.* an estimate that falls short of the truth or true quantity.—*v.t.* **underexpose',** to expose too little, esp. (*phot.*) to light.—*ns.* **underexpos'ure;** **un'derfeit,** older term for underlay, usu. of felt.— *v.t.* **un'derfire',** to fire or bake insufficiently.— *adv.* **underfoot',** beneath one's feet.—*v.t.* to underpin.—*adj.* (*un'*) downtrodden.—*ns.* **un'derfur,** short fur hidden by longer hairs; **un'dergarment,** any article of clothing worn under another, esp. that worn next to the skin, underclothing.—*v.t.* **undergird',** to brace with ropes under the bottom.—*adj.* **un'derglaze,** applied or done before glazing (as *underglaze painting* in a vitrifiable pigment before the glaze is applied).— *n.* **undergrad'uate,** a student who has not taken any degree.—*adj.* pertaining to such.—*ns.* **under-**

**undercon'sciousness,** *n.* under- (5).    **un'derdeck,** *n.* under- (2).    **un'derfeed',** *v.t., v.i.* under- (4b).
**un'dercook,** *n.* under- (3).           **underfed',** *adj.* under- (4b).      **un'dergown,** *n.* under- (1).

*Words beginning with pfx.* **un-** *are listed first* (pp. 1462 ff.); *other UN- words follow* (pp. 1484 ff.).

Neutral vowels in unaccented syllables: *el'ə-mənt;* for certain sounds in foreign words, see p. viii

grad′uateship; undergraduette′, a slang feminine of *undergraduate.*—*adj.* un′derground, under the surface of the ground: secret.—*n.* the underworld: an underground place: an underground railway: underlying ground: low ground: a secret resistance movement, or body of people: a group whose activities are partly concerned with resisting things they disapprove of in social, artistic, and political life.—*adv.* underground′, beneath the surface of the earth: secretly.—*ns.* un′dergrove, a grove of low trees under taller trees; un′dergrowth, low plants growing under taller, esp. shrubs under trees: stunted growth.—*adv.* underhand′, surreptitiously: with the hand below the elbow or shoulder.—*adj.* un′derhand, surreptitious, secret: unobtrusive (*Shak.*): not straightforward: delivered underhand.—*n.* an underhand ball: (with *the*) a subordinate position.—*adj.* and *adv.* underhan′ded, underhand: short of hands.—*adv.* underhan′dedly.—*n.* underhan′dedness.—*adjs.* underhon′est (*Shak.*), not quite honest; underhung′ (or *un*′), (of a lower jaw) protruding: having a protruding lower jaw: running on rollers on a rail below.—*n.* un′der-jaw′, the lower jaw.—*adj.* un′derjawed, with a heavy or underhung underjaw.—*v.t.* un′derkeep (*Spens.*), to keep under or in subjection.—*adjs.* underlaid′ (see underlay); underlain (see underlie).—*vs.t.* underlap′, to extend beneath and some way beyond the edge of; underlay′, to support or furnish with something laid under: to lay under: to put down, surpass (*Spens.*): often erroneously for underlie—of which it is the *pa.t.*—*v.i.* (*mining*) to hade:—*pa.t.* and *pa.p.* underlaid′.—*n.* (*un*′) something laid under, e.g. felt or rubber to help preserve carpet, or (*printing*) piece of paper, etc., pasted under to bring to type-height.—*ns.* underlay′er, one who underlays: (*un*′) a lower layer, substratum; un′derlease, a sublease.—*v.t.* and *v.i.* (-*lēs*′) to sublease.—*v.t.* underlet′, to let below the full value: to sublet.—*ns.* underlett′er; underlett′ing.—*v.t.* underlie′, to lie beneath (*lit.* and *fig.*): to undergo: to be subject or liable to:—*pr.p.* underly′ing; *pa.t.* underlay′; *pa.p.* underlain′.—*n.* (*mining*) a hade.—*v.t.* underline′, to draw a line under: to stress.—*n.* (*un*′) a caption, legend.—*ns.* un′derlinen, underclothing, properly of linen; un′derling (see under); un′derlip, a lower lip; un′derlooker, a mine manager's assistant.—*adj.* underly′ing, lying beneath (*lit.* and *fig.*): fundamental: present though not immediately obvious.—*n.* un′derman, an inferior: a subordinate: a man subjected to adverse conditions.—*v.t.* (-*man*), to man with too few.—*adjs.* undermanned′; undermast′ed, with masts too small; undermen′tioned, mentioned underneath or hereafter.—*v.t.* undermine′ (*Spens.* underminde′), to dig beneath (e.g. a wall) in order that it may fall: to wash away, remove by burrowing, etc., the ground from under: to weaken gradually or insidiously (*fig.*): to intrigue against: to tamper with the fidelity of.—*ns.* undermi′ner; undermi′ning.—*adv.* and *prep.* underneath′, beneath, below in position (*lit.* and *fig.*): under the control of (*arch.*).—*n.* the under part or side.—*ns.* un′dernice′ness, want of niceness or delicacy; un′dernote, a subdued note: an undertone.—*adjs.* undernō′ted, noted below; undernour′ished, living on less food than is necessary for satisfac-

tory health and growth.—*ns.* undernour′ishment; un′derpass, a road passing under another road, a railway, etc.; un′derpassion, an underlying or subconscious passion.—*vs.t.* underpeep′ (*Shak.*), to peep under; underpin′, to support by building underneath, or to prop up: to corroborate.—*n.* underpinn′ing.—*v.i.* underplay′, to play a low card while holding up a higher.—*n.* (*un*′) the act of so doing.—*ns.* un′derplot, a subordinate plot in a play or tale: a secret scheme, a trick; un′der-power (*Wordsworth*), an auxiliary power.—*vs.t.* underpraise′, to praise below desert; underprize′ (*obs.* underprise′), to underpraise (*Shak.*): value too little.—*adj.* under-priv′ileged, not enjoying normal social and economic rights.—Also *n.*—*n.* under-produc′tion, too little production: production short of demand.—*adj.* underproof′, (of alcohol) lower or weaker than proof.—*v.t.* underquote′, to offer at a price lower than; underrate′, to rate too low.—*n.* (*un*′) a price less than the worth.—*adj.* inferior (*Swift*).—*adj.* un′der-ripe′, not quite ripe.—*n.* un′der-roof, a roof under another (*Tennyson*).—*v.t.* underrun′, to run or pass beneath: to take aboard on one side (as a cable, line, net, for examination, clearing, baiting) and put overboard on the other.—*v.i.* to move under: to run on the underside.—*ns.* underrunn′ing; un′der-saw′yer, a bottom-sawyer: an inferior, an unimportant person.—*v.t.* undersay′ (*Spens.* undersaye′), to say in answer or contradiction (*obs.*).—*n.* un′der-school, the lower or junior school (*obs.*).—*v.t.* underscore′, to underline.—*n.* un′derscrub, brushwood.—*v.t.* underseal′, to coat exposed parts of underside of (a motor vehicle) with corrosion-resisting substance.—Also *n.*—*ns.* underseal′ing; un′der-sec′retary, a secretary immediately under the principal secretary; under-sec′retaryship; un′derself, the subconscious self.—*v.t.* undersell′, to sell below the price charged by: to sell too cheap.—*ns.* undersell′er; un′dersense, a deeper sense: a secondary sense: a subconscious awareness; un′derset, an undercurrent: a lower vein of ore: a set of underclothing.—*v.t.* (-*set*′) to set under: to prop: to sublet (*obs.*).—*adj.* un′dershapen (*Tennyson*), imperfectly formed.—*v.t.* undershoot′, to fail to reach by falling short.—*n.* (*aero.*) a falling short of the mark in landing.—*n.* un′dershirt, a man's collarless undergarment usu. of woven cotton, which may or may not have sleeves.—*adj.* un′dershot, driven by water passing under: underhung.—*ns.* un′dershrub, a shrubby plant, or a low shrub; un′derside, the lower surface.—*v.t.* undersign′, to sign below.—*adjs.* un′dersigned (or -*sind*′), whose signature is appended; un′dersized, below the usual or desired size.—*ns.* un′derskinker (*Shak.*), an assistant tapster; un′derskirt, a petticoat: a foundation for a dress or skirt; un′dersky, a lower sky (*poet.*).—*adj.* un′derslung, suspended, or supported, from above, or hung so as to extend below a part which, in another arrangement, it might be wholly above.—*n.* un′dersong, a burden, refrain, etc., of song or of sound: an undertone less pleasant in quality (*fig.*).—*adj.* understaffed, having too few members of staff.—*v.t.* understate′, to state more moderately than truth would allow or require: to state or describe, or to use artistically, without emphasis.—*adj.* understat′ed, effective through simplicity,

*Words beginning with pfx.* un- *are listed first* (pp. 1462 ff.); *other UN- words follow* (pp. 1484 ff.).

without embellishment or dramatic emphasis. —*ns.* **understate′ment**; **un′dersteer**, in a motorcar, tendency of car to follow a wider curve than the turning applied by the steering wheel should cause it to follow; **un′derstock** (*arch.*), a stocking.—*vs.t.* **understock′**, to supply with an insufficient amount of stock; **understocd′** (see **understand**).—Also *adj.*—*n.* **un′derstrapper**, an inferior agent, an underling.—*adj.* **un′derstrapping**, subordinate.—*n.* **un′derstratum**, an underlayer:—*pl.* **un′derstrata**.—*v.t.* **un′derstudy**, to study (a part), or to study the part of (an actor or other person) in order to take over in an emergency, or in due course.—Also *v.i.*—*n.* one who understudies.—*n.* **un′derthirst** (*Wordsworth*), an underlying or subconscious thirst.—*adj.* **undertimed′**, (of a photograph) underexposed.— —*ns.* **un′dertint**, a subdued tint: a tint showing through; **un′dertone**, a subdued tone of voice, sound, colour, etc.: a tone felt as if pervading, underlying, or perceptible through others, including (*fig.*) an emotional tone: a difference tone (*q.v.*): a low state of body.—*adj.* **un′dertoned**, in an undertone: (-*tōnd′*) wanting in tone.—*ns.* **un′dertow** (-*tō*), an undercurrent opposed to the surface current: the recoil or back-draught of a wave; **un′der-trick**, a trick short of the number declared; **un′der-turn′key**, an assistant jailer; **undervalua′tion**.—*v.t.* **underval′ue**, to value below the real worth: to rate as inferior (with *to*; *Shak.*): to reduce the value of: to esteem too lightly.—*n.* (*un′*) a value or price under the real worth.—*ns.* **underval′uer**; **un′dervest**, an undershirt, or a similar garment for a woman; **un′derviewer**, an underlooker: **un′dervoice**, a subdued voice; **un′derwater**, underground water: undertow.—*adj.* existing, acting, carried out, etc., below the surface of the water below the water-line.—Also *adv.*—*ns.* **un′derwear**, underclothing; **un′derweight**, shortness of weight: short weight.—*adj.* short in weight.—*n.* **un′derwing**, a wing covered by another, as an insect's hind-wing: a moth (*Catocala*, etc.) with conspicuous hind-wings.—*adj.* and *adv.* under the wing.—*ns.* **un′derwit**, inferior wit: a half-wit; **un′derwood**, undergrowth: a coppice.—*v.t.* **underwork′**, to undermine: to work secretly against (*obs.*; *Shak. pa.t.* **underwrought′**): to employ too little in work: to work for less than the wage of.—*v.i.* to do less work than is desirable. —*n.* (*un′*) a substructure: underhand, inferior, or subordinate work.—*ns.* **un′derworker**; **un′derwork′man**; **un′derworld**, the world beneath the heavens: the world, or a region, beneath the earth: the place of departed souls: the part of the world below the horizon: the antipodes: a submerged, hidden, or secret region or sphere of life, esp. one given to crime, profligacy, or intrigue.—*v.t.* **un′derwrite**, to write (something) beneath: to sign one's name beneath (*obs.*): to subscribe (one's name; *obs.*): to subscribe to (a statement, etc.): to agree to (*Shak.*): to accept the risk of insuring: to guarantee to take, or find others to take (certain shares, under certain conditions): to write too little about: (*refl.*) to write below the level of which one is capable.—*v.i.* to practise as an underwriter.—*ns.* **un′derwriter**, one who practises insurance business, esp. in ships; **un′derwriting**.—*v.t.* **underwrought′** (see **underwork**).

**underact** ... to ... **underfire**. See **under-**.

**underfong**, *un-dər-fong′*, (*Spens.*) *v.t.* to overcome, entrap: to undertake. [O.E. *underfangen*, pa.p. of *underfōn*, to receive, take, steal.]

**underfoot** ... to ... **underglaze**. See **under-**.

**undergo**, *un-dər-gō′*, *v.t.* to be subjected to: to

endure or suffer: to pass through, experience: to enjoy, partake of (*Shak.*): to take in hand (*Shak.*).—*adj.* **undergo′ing** (*Shak.*), enduring. [Late O.E. *undergān*—*gān*, to go.]

**undergraduate** ... to ... **undermining**. See **under-**.

**undern**, *un′dərn*, (*obs.*) *n.* the third hour, about nine in the morning: terce: the forenoon: the afternccn or early evening: a light meal.—*n.* **un′derntime** (*Spens.* **un′deitime**), time of the midday meal. [O.E. *undern*.]

**underneath** ... to ... **understaffed**. See **under-**.

**understand**, *un-dər-stand′*, *v.t.* to comprehend: grasp with the mind: to be able to follow the working, logic, meaning, etc., of: to take the meaning of (a sign, person): to realise: to have a sympathetic, usu. tacit, perception of the character, aims, etc., of (a person) (**understand each other**, to have reached an agreement, sometimes collusive): to know the mcaning of: to be expert in: to have knowledge or information (that), to have been informed: to assume, take to te true: to interpret (as), take to mean: to imply: (*refl.*), to know how to behave (*Shak.*): to stand under (*Shak.*): hence, to support.—*v.i.* to have understanding: to comprehend:—*pa.t.* and *pa.p.* **understood′**.—*adj.* implied but not expressed (usu. *gram.*):—*pa.p* (*arch.*) **understand′ed**.—*adj.* **understand′able**.—*ns.* **understander**, one who understands: a supporter (*Browning*): one who stands in the pit of a theatre (*obs.*); **understand′ing**, the act of comprehending: the power to understand: intellect: an informal agreement: an understood condition (e.g. *on the understanding that*): sympathetic or amicable agreement of minds: (in *pl.*) feet, legs, shoes, boots (*slang*).—*adj.* intelligent: discerning: sympathetic.—*adv.* **understand′ingly**. [O.E. *understandan*—*under*, *standan*, to stand.]

**understate** ... to ... **understudy**. See **under-**.

**undertake**, *un-dar-tāk′*, *v.t.* to receive (*obs.*): to perceive (*Spens.*): to assume (*Shak.*): to be surety for (*Shak.*): to pledge oneself (that): to take upon oneself: to take upon oneself (to deal with, manage, or look after): to set about, engage in: to engage in contest with.—*v.i.* to promise (*arch.*; sometimes with *for*): to become a surety (for): to conduct funerals (*coll.*):—*pa.t.* **undertook′**; *pa.p.* **undertā′ken**, (*Shak.*, etc.) **underta′en**, (*Spens.*) **undertane′**.—*adj.* **underta′kable**.—*ns.* **un′dertaker**, one who takes in hand an enterprise, task, or encounter: one who manages funerals: a projector, entrepreneur: a contractor: a publisher (*obs.*): a stage producer (*obs.*): a compiler or editor (*obs.*): a sponsor or surety (*obs.*): tax-farmer (*obs.*): one of the Fife adventurers who tried to colonise the island of Lewis (*c.* 1600): one of those who undertook to manage the House of Commons for the Stewart kings: one of the English and Scottish settlers on forfeited lands in Ireland; **un′dertaking**, that which is undertaken: any business or project engaged in: the business of conducting funerals. —Also *adj.* [12th cent. *undertaken*, to entrap— O.E. *under*, late O.E. *tacan*; see **take**.]

**undertenancy** ... to ... **underthirst**. See **under-**.

**undertime**. See **underntime** at **undern**.

**undertimed** ... to ... **underwrought**. See **under-**.

**undies**, *un′diz*, (*coll.*) *n.pl.* women's underclothing. [**under**.]

**undine**, *un′dēn*, *un-dēn′* (Ger. *ōōn-dē′nə*), *n.* according to Paracelsus, a water-spirit that can obtain a human soul by bearing a child to a human husband. [L. *unda*, a wave.]

**undulate**, *un′dū-lāt*, *v.t.* and *v.i.* to move like or in waves: to make or be wavy: to vibrate.—*adj.* wavy: with wavy margin, surface, or markings.

---

**un′derten′ancy**, *n.* **under-** (3).     **un′dertenant**, *n.* **under-** (3).     **un′der-tū′nic**, *n.* **under-** (1).

*Words beginning with pfx.* **un-** *are listed first* (pp. 1462 ff.); *other UN- words follow* (pp. 1484 ff.).

Neutral vowels in unaccented syllables: *el′ə-mənt*; for certain sounds in foreign words, see p. viii

—Also un'dulated.—n. un'dulancy.—adj. un'-dulant, undulating: rising and falling.—adv. un'dulately.—adj. un'dulating.—adv. un'dulatingly.—ns. undulā'tion, an undulating, a wave-like motion or form: waviness: a wave; un-dulā'tionist, one who holds the undulatory theory of light.—adjs. un'dulatory, of the nature of undulation: undulating: wavy: referring light to waves in a medium; un'dulose, un'du-lous, (both rare) undulating.—undulant fever, Malta, Mediterranean, Neapolitan, or Rock fever, a remittent fever with swelling of the joints and enlarged spleen, caused by a bacterium (Brucella) transmitted by goat's (or cow's) milk. [L. undulātus, undulated—unda, a wave.]

Unesco, ū-nes'kō, n. the United Nations Educational, Scientific, and Cultural Organisation. [From the initial letters.]

unguent, ung'gwənt, n. ointment.—n. unguentā'-rium, a vessel for holding unguents.—adj. ung'-uentary, of or for unguents.—n. an unguenta-rium: a perfumer, maker of or dealer in unguents. [L. unguentum—unguēre, to anoint.]

unguis, ung'gwis, n. a claw or nail: the claw of an insect's foot: the claw of a petal:—pl. ung'ues (-gwēz).—adjs. ung'ual (-gwal), of or bearing a claw; unguiculate (ung-gwik'ū-lāt), -d, clawed; unguiform (ung'gwi-förm). [L. unguis, a nail.]

ungula, ung'gū-la, n. a hoof (zool.): a section of a cylinder, cone, etc., cut off by a plane oblique to the base (geom.).—adj. ung'ulate, hoofed.—n. a hoofed animal, a member of the order Ungu-lā'ta, hoofed digitigrade mammals, including artiodactyls and perissodactyls.—adjs. unguled (ung'gūld; her.), with claws or hoofs tinctured specially; ung'uligrade, walking on hoofs. [L. ungula, claw, hoof—unguis, nail.]

uni-, ū-ni, in composition, one.—adj. uniax'ial, having one axis, esp. (crystal.) one optic axis or (biol.) one main line of growth or unbranched axis.—adv. uniax'ially.—adj. unicam'eral (L. camera, vault; see chamber), having or con-sisting of but one chamber.—ns. unicam'eralism, the system or principle of having one legislative chamber; unicam'eralist.—adjs. unicell'ular, of or having but one cell; unicen'tral, having a single centre; ū'nicolor (or -kul'), u'nicolour, -ed, unicol'orate, unicol'orous, of one uniform colour.—n. ū'nicorn (L. cornū, a horn), a fabulous animal mentioned by ancient Greek and Roman authors as a native of India, with a body like a horse and one straight horn: an unfortunate translation of the Hebrew re'ēm (Assyr. rímu) anticipated by the monokerōs of the Septuagint—variously understood as the rhino-ceros, wild ox, ox-antelope (B.): applied to various animals with the appearance of a single horn, as the narwhal (also un'icorn-whale), a moth (un'icorn-moth) whose caterpillar has a long process, an American Pacific gasteropod (monoceros, etc.) with a spine on the lip of the shell (un'icorn-shell): a team of two abreast and one in front, or a carriage drawn by it: an old Scottish gold coin bearing a unicorn, worth 18s. Scots: (cap.) one of the Scottish pursuivants.—adj. one-horned.—adv. with two abreast and one in front.—adj. unicos'tate (L. costa, rib), one-ribbed.—n. u'nicycle, an acrobat's one-wheeled cycle.—adjs. unidirec'tional, mainly or wholly in one direction; unifil'ar (L. fīlum, thread), with one thread; uniflōr'ous (L. flōs, flōris, a flower), one-flowered; unifo'liolate (L. foliolum, dim. of folium, leaf; bot.), having a single leaflet, but compound in structure; unilā'biate (L. labium, lip), one-lipped; unilat'-eral (L. latus, lateris, side), one-sided.—n. unilateral'ity.—adv. unilat'erally.—adjs. uniling'-ual (L. lingua, tongue), of, in, using, one tongue, language; unilit'eral (L. littera (lītera), letter), of, or involving, one letter or script; unilō'bar,

unilōbed', having one lobe; unilob'ular, having one lobule; uniloc'ular, having but one loculus or cavity; uninū'clear, with a single nucleus; uninū'cleate; unip'arous (L. parĕre, to bring forth), producing one at a birth: monochasial (bot.); unipar'tite, not divided into parts; u'niped (L. pēs, pedis, foot), one-footed.—n. a one-footed person, animal, or object.—adjs. uniper'sonal, existing as only one person; uniplā'nar, lying in one plane.—n. ū'nipod (Gr. pous, podos, foot), a one-legged support, e.g. for a camera.—adj. unipōlar, of, from, or using one pole: of a nerve cell, having one process only.—n. unipolar'ity.—adj. unisē'rial, in one series or row.—adv. unisē'rially.—adj. unisē'riate, uniserial.—adv. unisē'riately.—adjs. ū'nisex, of a style, esp. in clothes, adopted by both sexes; unisex'ual, of one sex only.—n. unisexual'ity.—adv. unisex'ually.—n. ū'nison (or -zən; L. sonus, sound, sonāre, to sound), identity of pitch: loosely, pitch differing by one or more octaves: a sound of the same pitch: complete agreement. — adj. in unison. — adj. unis'onal.—adv. unis'onally.—n. unis'onance.—adjs. unis'-onant; unis'onous.—ns. univā'lence (or -iv'əl-), univā'lency (or -iv'əl-).—adj. univā'lent (chem.), having a valency of one, capable of combining with one atom of hydrogen or its equivalent.—adj. and n. (pertaining to) one of the single chromosomes which separate in the first meiotic division.—adj. ū'nivalve, having one valve or shell only.—n. a shell of one valve only: a mollusc whose shell is composed of a single piece.—adjs. unival'vular; univā'riant, having one degree of freedom; univā'riate, (of a dis-tribution) having one variate only; univol'tine (It. volta, a turn, winding), of silkworms, having one brood a year. [L. ūnus, one; Gr. oinē, ace (on dice); O.E. ān, one.]

Uniat, ū'ni-at, n. a United Greek, or member of any community of Oriental Christians that acknowledges the papal supremacy, all else—clerical matrimony, communion in both kinds, church discipline, rites, and liturgy—being allowed to remain Greek.—Also U'niate (-āt, -ət). [Russ. uniyat—uniya, union—L. ūnus, one.]

uniaxial . . . to . . . unicameralist. See uni-.

Unicef, ūn'i-sef, n. United Nations International Children's Emergency Fund. [From the initial letters.]

unicellular, unicentral. See uni-.

unicity, u-nis'i-ti, n. oneness: uniqueness. [L. ūnicus, unique.]

unicorn . . . to . . . unifoliolate. See uni-.

uniform, ū'ni-förm, adj. alike: alike all over, throughout, or at all times: unvarying: of a military or other uniform.—n. a distinctive garb for members of a body: a suit of it.—v.t. to make uniform: to clothe in uniform.—adj. u'iformed, wearing uniform.—n. and adj. uniformitā'rian.—ns. uniformitā'rianism, the doctrine that geo-logical changes were brought about not in the main by great convulsions but by such action as may be seen going on now; uniform'ity, state or fact of being uniform: agreement with a pattern or rule: sameness: likeness between parts.—adv. u'niformly.—n. u'niformness. [L. ūniformis —ūnus, one, fōrma, form.]

unify, ū'ni-fi, v.t. to make into one: to consoli-date.—adjs. u'nifiable; unif'ic, making one.—n. unificā'tion.—adj. u'nified.—n. u'nifier.—n. and adj. u'nifying.—unified field, an ultimate basis on which the physicist seeks to bring within a single theory the workings of all natural phenomena; unified scale, the scale of atomic and molecular weights based on the mass of the carbon-12 iso-tope of carbon being taken as 12 exactly. [L.L. ūnificāre—L. ūnus, one, facĕre, to make.]

unigeniture, ū-ni-jen'i-char, n. the state or fact of

being the only begotten.—*n.* Unigen'itus, (from its first word) a bull of Clement XI (1713) condemning 101 propositions of the Jansenist Quesnel. [L.L. *ūnigenitus*, only-begotten.]

**unilabiate ... to ... uninucleate.** See uni-.

**Unio,** *ū'ni-ō, n.* the pearl-mussel genus of fresh-water molluscs, giving name to the family Unionidae (*ū-ni-on'i-dē*).—*n.* union (*ūn'yən; Shak.*), a fine large pearl, a unique or single pearl. [L. *ūniō, -ōnis*, prob.—*ūnus*, one (cf. solitaire as applied to a diamond set by itself).]

**union,** *ūn'yən, n.* a uniting: the state of being united: the state of wedlock: a united whole: combination: a growing together in healing: general concord: incorporation of states in a federation or in a single state: a single state (or sometimes a federation) thus formed: an association or league, esp. a trade union: a student's club: (formerly) a combination of parishes for poor law purposes: its workhouse or poor-house: a connecting part for pipes, etc.: a device emblematic of union borne in the canton of a flag: the same device used separately as a flag, as the Union Jack: a textile fabric of more than one kind of fibre: the set formed from all the elements present in two (or more) sets.—*ns.* ūn'ionism (also *cap.*); ūn'ionist, an advocate or supporter of or believer in union or trade unions: a member of a trade union: (*cap.*) an opponent of Irish Home Rule, esp. a Liberal Unionist (see Liberal)—hence a Conservative: (*cap.*) a supporter of the federal union of the United States, esp. at the time of the Civil War.—Also *adj.*—union flag, a flag symbolising union, esp. the national flag of the United Kingdom, consisting of a union of the crosses of St George, St Andrew, and St Patrick, commonly called the Union Jack; union language, an artificial language formed from related dialects; union list, a list of materials available on a specific subject, in each case naming the library, and locating the material precisely in it; Union Shona (see Shona); union suit, combinations for man or boy.—art union, association aiming at promotion of an interest in the fine arts, esp. by raffling pictures; the Union, the legislative incorporation of England and Scotland in 1707, or of Ireland with both in 1801: the American Union or United States: the Union of South Africa (1910). [Fr. *union*—L. *ūniō, -ōnis*—*ūnus*, one.]

**union.** See Unio.

**unionised.** See un-.

**uniparous ... to ... unipolarity.** See uni-.

**unique,** *ū-nēk', adj.* sole: without a like: often used loosely for unusual, pre-eminent.—*n.* any thing that is unique.—*adv.* unique'ly.—*n.* unique'ness. [Fr.,—L. *ūnicus*—*ūnus.*]

**uniserial ... to ... unisonous.** See uni-.

**unit,** *ū'nit, n.* one: a single thing or person: a single element, section, or item, regarded as the lowest subdivision of a whole: a group of persons forming a subdivision of a larger body: a distinct part within a piece of electrically powered equipment which has its own specific function: a single complete domestic fixture combining what are sometimes separate parts: the least whole number: anything taken as one: a quantity by reference to which others are measured.—*adj.* of the character or value of a unit: individual.—*adj.* u'nital.—*n.* Unitā'rian, one who asserts the unity of the Godhead as opposed to the Trinity, ascribes divinity to God the father only, and who believes that each congregation should have independent authority: one who believes in the unity of God, in freedom of, and tolerance of the differences in, religious beliefs, etc.: member of a particular body holding such doctrines: a monotheist generally: (without *cap.*) a holder of some belief based on unity

or union.—Also *adj.*—*n.* Unitā'rianism.—*adj.* u'nitary, pertaining to unity or to a unit: of the nature of a unit: integral: based on unity.—unit trust (see trust); unity element, an identity element for multiplication (*math.*). [For unity.]

**unite,** *ū-nīt', v.t.* to make one: to join into one: to join: to combine: to clasp: to marry: to have in combination: to make to agree or adhere.—*v.i.* to become one: to combine: to join: to grow or act together.—*n.* (also *ū'*) an English gold coin of James I, worth 20s., later 22s.—*adj.* uni'ted.—*adv.* uni'tedly.—*ns.* uni'tedness; uni'ter.—*n.* and *adj.* uni'ting.—*n.* unition (*ū-nish'ən*), conjunction.—*adj.* unitive (*ūn'i-tiv*), harmonising, uniting.—*adv.* u'nitively.—United Brethren (see Moravian); United Free Church, United Presbyterian Church (see under free, presbyter); United Greeks (see Uniat); United Irishmen, a radical political organisation which, agitating for absolute emancipation, parliamentary reform and universal suffrage, caused the 1798 rising; United Kingdom (of Great Britain and Ireland; from 1922 Northern Ireland), the official title adopted in 1801 for the kingdom consisting of England and Wales, Scotland, and Ireland; United Nations, an association of states that in 1945 undertook many of the functions of the dissolved League of Nations; United Provinces, Holland, Zealand (Zeeland), Utrecht, Gelderland, Groningen, Friesland, and Overyssel, united in 1579 under the Union of Utrecht; United States, a federal union of states, esp. that of (North) America. [L. *ūnītus*, pa.p. of *ūnīre*, to unite—*ūnus*, one.]

**unity,** *ū'ni-ti, n.* oneness: the number one: state or fact of being one or at one: that which has oneness: a single whole: the arrangement of all the parts to one purpose or effect: a unite (*Dickens*).—the unities (of *place, time,* and *action*), the three canons of the classical drama—that the scenes should be at the same place, that all the events should be such as might happen within a single day, and that nothing should be admitted not directly relevant to the development of the plot. [L. *ūnitās, -ātis*—*ūnus*, one.]

**univalency ... to ... univariate.** See uni-.

**universe,** *ū'ni-vərs, n.* all that is: the whole system of things: the cosmos: a system of stars such as the galactic system: the world.—*adj.* univers'al, of the universe: comprehending, affecting, or extending to the whole world or all people: without exception: comprising all the particulars: all-round: unlimited: capable of being applied to a great variety of uses.—*n.* that which is universal: a universal proposition: a general term: a universal concept.—*n.* universalisā'tion, -z-.—*v.t.* univer'salise, -z-.—*ns.* Univer'salism, the doctrine or belief of universal salvation, or the ultimate salvation of all mankind, and even of the fallen angels; Univer'salist, a believer in Universalism.—Also *adj.*—*adj.* universalis'tic.—*n.* universality (-*sal'*), state or quality of being universal.—*adv.* univer'sally.—*n.* univer'salness.—universal beam, a beam made in a standard size; universal donor, one whose blood can be transfused into persons of the other blood groups without causing destruction of their red blood cells; universal joint, one capable of turning all ways; universal second (see universal time); universal time, mean solar time, Greenwich time, in which the value of the second is subject to irregularities which are due to characteristics of the earth's rotation. [L. *ūniversum*, neut. sing. of *ūniversus*, whole, *ūnus*, one, *vertěre, versus*, to turn.]

**university,** *ū-ni-vûr'si-ti, n.* a corporate body (*obs.*): an institution of higher learning with power to grant degrees, its body of teachers, students, graduates, etc., its college or colleges, or its buildings.—*adj.* universitā'rian. [L. *ūniversitās*

-*ātis*, a whole, in L.L. a corporation; see foregoing.]

**univocal**, *ū-niv'ə-kl* (or *ū-ni-vō'kl*), *adj.* of one voice: having one meaning only: unmistakable: unambiguous: of things of the same species (*obs.*).—*n.* a word with but one meaning.—*adv.* **univ'ocally**. [L. *ūnivocus*—*ūnus*, one, *vōx*, *vōcis*, a voice.]

**univoltine**. See uni-.

**unless**, *un-les'*, *ən-les'*, *conj.* (tending to pass into a *prep.*) if not [Earlier followed by *than* or *that*: *on lesse than*, on a less condition than.]

**unneath**, *ə-nēth'*, (*dial.*) *prep.* underneath. [Cf. **aneath, underneath.**]

**uno animo**, *ū'nō*, *ōō'nō*, *an'i-mō*, *adv.* with one mind. [L.]

**until**, *un-til'*, *ən-til'*, *prep.* and *conj.* till. [Pfx. *und-*, as far as; **till**.]

**unto**, *un'tōō*, -*tōō*, (*arch.* or *formal*) *prep.* to.—*conj.* (*obs.*) until. [Pfx. *und-*, as far as; **to**.]

**up**, *up*, *adv.* in, to, toward a higher place, level, or state: aloft: on high: towards a centre (as a capital, great town, university): in residence, at school or college: northward: to windward: in or to a more erect position or more advanced stage of erection: out of bed: on horseback: in an excited state: in revolt: with (increased) vigour, intensity, or loudness: afoot: amiss: into prominence, notice, consideration: forward for sale: in or into court: into custody, keeping, possession: away in a receptacle, place of storage or lodging (as a sheath, purse, stable): ahead in scoring: into closed or compact state, together: to a total: in, near, towards arrival, overtaking, or being abreast: as far as: all the way: to a standstill: at an end: to a finish: thoroughly, completely, fully: well informed, versed.—Also elliptically passing into a verb or interjection by omission of *go, come, put*, etc., often followed by *with*.—*adj.* placed, going, or directed up: top: risen: (of time) ended: having gained (so many) more holes than an opponent (*golf*):—*comp.* **upp'er**: *superls.* **up'-most, upp'ermost** (see below).—*prep.* in an ascent along, through, or by: to or in a higher position on: to or in an inner or more remote part of: along against the current: along: up into (*U.S.*).—*n.* a rise: a high place: a success, spell of prosperity: one who is in prosperity.—*v.t.* to drive up-stream (as swans for owner marking): to lift or haul up.—*v.i.* (*coll.*) to set up: to move up: to intervene boldly, start into activity or speech:—*pr.p.* **upp'ing**; *pa.t.* and *pa.p.* **upped** (*upt*).—*adjs.* **up'most**, uppermost; **upp'er** (see above), higher: superior: higher in rank.—*n.* the part of a boot or shoe above the sole and welt: an upper tooth.—*adj.* **upp'ermost** (see above), highest: first to come into the mind.—*adv.* in the highest place, first.—*n.* **upp'ing**, action of up *v.t.* (*q.v.*).—*adj.* **upp'ish**, assuming, pretentious, snobbish.—*adv.* **upp'ishly**.—*n.* **upp'ishness**.—*adj.* **upp'ity**, uppish.—*advs.* **up'ward** (-*wərd*), upwards, from lower to higher: from outlet towards source: from modern to more ancient: in the upper part (**upward, upwards, of**, more than).—*prep.* **up'ward**, upwards along.—*adj.* **up'ward**, directed upward: ascending: placed high.—*n.* (*Shak.*) top.—*adv.* **up'wardly**.—*n.* **up'wardness**, a rising tendency: a state of being high.—*adjs.* **up'-and-com'ing**, alert and pushful: likely to succeed (in a career, etc.); **up'-and-down'**, undulating: going or working both, or alternately, up and down: downright (*U.S.*).—**up'beat**, an unaccented beat, at which the conductor raises his baton; **up'-bow**, a

movement of the bow from point towards nut over the strings; **up'-current, -draught**, a rising current of air; **up'land**, inland, hilly, or highlying country: upper or high land, as opp. to meadows, river-sides, etc. (*U.S.*).—*adj.* highlying: remote: inland: rural: of the uplands. —**up'lander**.—*adj.* **upland'ish** (*obs.*), rustic: rural: outlandish.—**up-line**, a railway line for upgoing trains (i.e. those going to, not from, e.g. a city); **upper atmosphere**, the region of the atmosphere above about 20 miles from the earth.—*adjs.* **upper-bracket**, in an upper grouping in a list; **upper case** (*print.*), lit. kept in an upper case, capital as opposed to small (of letters). —**upper class(es)**, the people of the highest social rank (*adj.* **upp'er-class'**); **upper crust**, the top of a loaf: the head: a hat: the aristocracy; **upper cut**, an upward short-arm blow; **upper hand**, mastery, advantage; **upper house**, in a bicameral legislature, the house that is the more restricted in membership, e.g. House of Lords, Senate of U.S. and other countries; **Upper Roger**, corruption of Hindi *Yuva-rājā*, young prince; **upper stock** (see **stock**); **upper storey (story)**, any storey above the first floor: the brain (*slang*); **upper ten (thousand)**, the richest or most influential class; **upp'erworks**, the upper part of a structure (of a ship above the load-line): the head (*slang*); **upp'ing-block, -stock, -stone**, a horseblock; **up'side**, the upper side.—*adv.* on the upper side.—*adv.* **up'side-down', up'side down'** (earlier **up so down**; *Spens.* **up'sideowne'**), with the upper part undermost: in or into, complete confusion.—*adj.* turned upside down. —*adv.* **upsides** (with), on a par (with): beside. —**up'-train**, a railway train proceeding towards the chief terminus; **up'trend**.—**be up in**, to have a knowledge of; **it is all up (with)**, there is no hope (for); **on one's uppers**, with soles worn off one's shoes: very short of money; **(on) the up and up**, (in) a state of continuous progress towards ever greater success: honest, on the level; **up against**, face to face with, confronted with (**up against it**, in almost desperate straits); **up and doing**, bestirring oneself; **up and down**, to and fro: here and there through or about: throughout: vertically: out-and-out; **ups and downs**, undulations: vicissitudes; **up to**, as far up as: into the immediate neighbourhood or presence of: immersed in or embedded as far as: about, meditating or engaged in doing (*coll.*): capable of and ready for (*coll.*): incumbent upon (orig. *U.S.*); **up to date**, to the present time or time in question: containing all recent facts, statistics, etc.: knowing the latest developments of fashion, usage, etc.; **up to the minute, moment**, right up to the present time (*adj.* **up-to-the-minute, -moment**, very up to date); **up town**, into town: in or to the residential part of a town (*U.S.*); **up with**, abreast of: even with: to take off, swallow: an exclamation of approbation and partisanship; **what's up (with you)?**, what's the matter, trouble? [O.E. *ūp*, *upp*, up, *uppe*, above, *uppian*, to rise; Ger. *auf*.]

**up-**, in composition, has meanings of *adv.*, *prep.* (and *adj.*; see previous article) **up**. Many of the compounds are *arch.* or *poet.*—*adv.* **up'-along** (*dial.*), up the road: homeward.—*v.i.* **up-anch'or**, to weigh anchor.—*vs.t.* **upbear'**, to raise aloft: to hold up: to sustain; **upbind'**, to bind up:—*pa.p.* **upbound'**, (*Spens.*) also **upbound'en**.—*v.t.* and *v.i.* **upblow'**, to blow up or upward: (of the wind) to spring up.—*adj.* **upblown'** (or *up'*), inflated.—*v.t.* **upbraid** (see separate article).— *vs.t.* **upbrast'** (*Spens.*), *pa.t.* of **upburst**; **upbray'**

**upboil'**, *v.i.*

*Words made with **up** adj. are listed first (p. 1490), then those with **up-** pfx. (pp. 1490 ff.); other UP-words follow (p. 1492).*

(*Spens*; see separate article).—*n.* up′break, a break-up: an outbreak.—*v.t.* (-*brāk*′) to break up or open.—*v.i.* to break out.—*n.* up′bringing, bringing up.—*vs.t.* upbrought′, (*Spens.*) *pa.p.* of *obs.* upbring′, to bring up; upbuild′, to build up. —*n.* upbuild′ing (or *up*′), building up: development: edification.—*adj.* upburn′ing, flaming upwards.—*ns.* upbuoy′ance, buoying up (*rare*); up′burst, a bursting upwards.—*v.t.* and *v.i.* (-*bûrst*′).—*adj.* upburst′ing.—*adv.* upby′, upbye′ (*Scot.*), up the way, a little farther on or up: up there: at the big house.—*n.* up′cast, an upward throw: an upthrow: material thrown up: an upward current of air from a mine: a shaft carrying it (up′cast-shaft): a chance, accident, fluke, or luck.—*v.t.* to some, throw or final throw at bowls (*Shak.*): a reproach (*Scot.*): an upset (*Scot.*).—*adj.* thrown or turned upward.— *vs.t.* (-*käst*′), to cast up; upcatch′, to catch up:— *pa.t.* and *pa.p.* upcaught′.—*adv.* up′-Chann′el, along the English Channel from west to(wards) east (also *adj.*).—*v.t.* upcheer′, to encourage:— *pa.t.* upcheered′, (*Spens.*) upcheard′.—*adj.* up′-coast, up the coast.—*adv.* (-*kōst*′).—*v.i.* upcoil′, to coil upwards: to coil up.—*ns.* up′come, produce, outcome: outward appearance of promise (*Scot.*; *obs.*): decisive movement (*Scot.*); up′-coun′try, the interior, inland part.— *adj.* of or in the interior.—*adv.* (-*kun*′), in or to the interior.—*vs.t.* update′, to bring up to date; up-end′, to set on end.—*v.i.* to rise on end.—*n.* up′flow, an upward flowing.—*v.i.* (-*flō*′), to stream up.—*adj.* up′flung (or -*flung*′), as *pa.p.* of upfling′).—*v.t.* upfoll′ow, to follow (*Keats*).— *n.* up′gang (*Scot.*), ascent.—*v.t.* upgath′er, to gather up or together.—*n.* up′grade, an upward slope or course.—*adj.* and *adv.* uphill.—*v.t.* (-*grād*′) to raise in status.—*v.i.* upgrow′, to grow up:—*pr.p.* upgrow′ing; *pa.t.* upgrew′; *pa.p.* upgrown′.—*n.* and *adj.* up′growing.—*adj.* up′-grown.—*n.* up′growth, process of growing up, development: that which grows up: a structure that has grown upward.—*adj.* up′hand, lifted by hand.—*v.t.* uphaud′, Scots form of uphold.—*n.* upheav′al, a heaving up: the bodily elevation of tracts of country: a profound, thorough, or revolutionary change or movement.—*vs.t.* upheave′:—*pa.t.* and *pa.ps.* upheld′, uphild′ (see uphold).—*adj.* up′hill, ascending: difficult.— Also *n.*—Also *adv.* (-*hil*′).—*adv.* uphill′ward (*Milt.*).—*vs.t.* uphoard′ (*Spens.*, *Shak.* uphoord′), to hoard or heap up; uphold′, to hold up: to sustain: to countenance: to defend: to keep in repair or good condition: (chiefly *Scot.*, uphaud′) to maintain, warrant:—*pa.t.* upheld′; *pa.p.* upheld′, (*Spens.*) uphild′.—*n.* uphold′er, a support or supporter: a dealer in second-hand clothes, furniture, etc. (*obs.*): a funeral undertaker (*obs.*): an upholsterer (*obs.*).—*n.* and *adj.* uphold′ing.— *v.i.* upjet′, to spout up.—*n.* up′keep, maintenance.—*vs.t.* upknit′, to knit up: to bring together, reconcile, or perhaps conclude, explain or sum up (*Spens.*); uplay′, to lay up, to hoard; uplead′, to lead up:—*pa.t.* and *pa.p.* upled′.— *v.i.* uplean′ (*Spens*), to rest one's weight.—*v.t.* uplift′, to lift up, raise: to elevate: to raise to a

higher moral or spiritual level: to elate: to collect (e.g. a parcel), draw (money) (*Scot.*):— *pa.p.* and *adj.* uplift′, -ed.—*n.* (*up*′*lift*′), a lifting up, raising: upheaval: elevation, esp. moral or spiritual, or the feeling thereof.—*adj.* (*up*′), designed to raise higher, usu. of a brassière holding up the breasts.—*n.* uplift′er.—*n.* and *adj.* uplift′ing.—*adv.* uplift′ingly.—*adj.* uplight′ed, lighted up.—*v.t.* uplock′, to lock up.—*adj.* uplock′ed (*Shak.*).—*v.i.* uplook′, to look up.—*n.* up′look, an upward look.—*adj.* up′lying, upland, elevated.—*ns.* up′make, action or mode of making up: constitution (especially mental or moral): slip-proofs arranged in page form; up′-making, filling-up, esp. between bilge-ways and ship's bottom before launching: arrangement of lines into columns or pages (*print.*).—*preps.* upo′ (*ə-pō*′; from *up of*; *arch.* or *dial.*), upon; upon (*ə-pon*′, *ə-pən*), on.—*adv.* thereon, on the surface (*Shak.*): on the person (*arch.*): thereafter (*Shak.*): close in approach (*Shak.*).—*adjs.* upperch′ed (*Keats*), perched aloft; uppiled′, piled up; up-pricked′, pricked up, erected.—*n.* up′-putting (*Scot.*), lodging and entertainment.— *v.t.* upraise′, to raise or lift up: to exalt: to excite, arouse (*Milt.*).—*adj.* upraised′.—*v.t.* uprear′, to raise up: to rear up.—*adj.* upreared′. —*n.* uprest′ (see uprist).—*adj.* up′right (also *up*′*rit*′, *up-rit*′), right or straight up: in an erect position (upright piano, one with the strings in a vertical plane): of habitual rectitude: honest: just: supine (e.g. *lying upright*; *obs.*).—*n.* up′right, an upright post, stone, stroke, or the like: a vertical member of a structure: an upright piano: an elevation (*obs.*): verticality: a basket-maker's tool.—*v.t.* to set erect or right side up.—*adv.* (*up*′*rit*, *up*′*rit*′, *up-rit*′), vertically: honestly.—*advs.* uprigh′teously (*Shak.*), with moral right; up′rightly, in an upright manner: honestly: vertically.—*ns.* up′right-man (*obs. cant*), a sturdy beggar, leader of a gang; up′-rightness; upris′al; uprise′ (or *up*′), rising.—*v.t.* (*riz*′), to rise up, arise:—*pa.t.* uprose′; *pa.p.* upris′en.—*n.* and *adj.* upris′ing.—*n.* uprist′ (*Shelley* uprest′), rising.—*v.i.* uprist′ (*Coleridge*), upryst′ (*Spens.*), an old form of *upriseth*, mistakenly used for a *pa.t.* or *pa.p.* (or perh. from a misunderstanding of the noun).—*n.* up′roar (see separate entry).—*v.t.* and *v.i.* uproll′, to roll up or close: to roll upward.—*v.t.* uproot′, to pull up by the roots: to destroy (*fig.*): to remove forcibly and completely (from, e.g. native land). —*ns.* uproot′al, uprooting; uproot′er; uproot′-ing.—*v.i.* uprose′, *pa.t.* of uprise.—*v.i.* upryst′ (see uprist′).—*v.t.* upset′, to overturn, capsize: to spill or tip out: to interfere with, defeat (a plan): to disconcert: to distress: to disorder (a bodily process or organ): to affect temporarily the health of (a person).—*v.i.* to be upset:—*pa.t.* and *pa.p.* upset′.—*n.* (*up*′*set*′), an overturn or derangement.—*adj.* (*up*′*set*) of a price, the lowest that will be accepted, at which bidding is started. —*n.* upsett′er.—*adj.* upsett′ing, causing upset: conceited, assuming (*Scot.*).—*n.* overturning: overthrow: (*up*′) presumption, overweening assumption (*Scot.*).—*v.t.* and *v.i.* upshoot′, to

---

upclimb′, *v.t.* and *v.i.*
upclose′, *v.t.* and *v.i.*
upcurl′, *v.t.* and *v.i.*
upcurved′, *adj.*
updrag′, *v.t.*
updraw′, *v.t.*
updrawn′, *adj.*
upfill′, *v.t.*
up′filling, *n.*
upflash′ing, *adj.*

upfurl′, *v.t.*
upgaze′, *v.i.*
upgo′, *v.i.*
up′going, *adj.*
upgoing (-*gō*′ or *up*′), *n.*
up′gush, *n.*
upgush′, *v.i.*
up′gushing, *adj.*
uphang′, *v.t.*
upheap′, *v.t.*

upheap′ing, *n.*
uphoist′, *v.t.*
uphurl′, *v.t.*
upleap′, *v.t.*
up′river, *adj.*
uprouse′, *v.t.*
uprun′, *v.i.*
uprush′, *v.i.*
up′rush, *n.*
upsend′, *v.t.*

---

*Words made with* up *adj. are listed first* (p. 1490), *then those with* up- *pfx.* (pp. 1490 ff.); *other* UP- *words follow* (p. 1492).

Neutral vowels in unaccented syllables: *el'ə-mənt*; for certain sounds in foreign words, see p. viii

shoot upward.—*ns.* (*up'*) an upshooting: that which shoots up: upshot (*Shak.*); **up'shot**, the final shot (*archery*): the outcome, final result: the conclusion of an argument: the substance, general effect: aim (*Spens.*): end (*obs.*).—*adj.* (*up'shot'*) shot upward.—Also *pa.t.* and *pa.p.* of **upshoot.**—*n.* **up'sitting**, sitting up, esp. after illness or childbirth (*arch.*): a reception of company on the occasion (*obs.*): sitting up at night as part of courtship (*S.Afr.*): listlessness (*obs. Scot.*).—*adj.* (*obs. Scot.*) listless.—*vs.i.* **upspeak'**, to begin to speak:—*pa.t.* upspoke', (*arch.*) **upspake'**; **upspear'**, (of grass) to shoot up straight like a spear (*Cowper*); **upspring'**, to spring up: to come into being:—*pa.t.* upsprang'; *pa.p.* upsprung'.—*n.* **up'spring** (*Shak.*), a lively dance (acc. to others, *adj.*, newly introduced).—*adv.* **up'stage'**, towards the back of the stage.—*adj.* towards the back of the stage: stand-offish, superior (*slang*).—*v.t.* to treat in a supercilious manner: to move upstage so that (another actor) has to turn his back to the audience, and thus to put him at a disadvantage.—*adv.* **upstairs'**, in or toward a higher storey, or (*fig.*) position.—*adj.* **up'stair(s)**, of or in an upper storey or flat.—*n.* **upstairs'**, the part of a building above the ground floor.—*v.i.* **upstand'** (*Milt.*), to stand up:—*pa.t.* **upstood'.**—*adj.* upstand'ing, erect: on one's feet (*Scot.*): straight and well-built: honest and downright.—*v.i.* **upstare'**, to stare upward: (of hair) to stand up (*Spens.*).—*adj.* upstar'ing.—*n.* **up'start**, one who has suddenly risen to wealth, importance, or power, a parvenu.—*adj.* newly or suddenly come into being: characteristic of a parvenu: pretentious and vulgar: new-fangled: starting on end (*Spens.*).—*v.i.* upstart', to start up.—*v.t.* upstay', to sustain.—*adv.* **up'stream'**, against the current.—*adj.* (*up'*) further up the stream: going against the current.—*v.i.* (-*strēm'*) to stream up.—*n.* up'stroke, an upward stroke: an upward line in writing.—*v.i.* upsurge', to surge up.—*n.* (*up'*) a surging up.—*n.* upsur'gence.—*vs.t.* upswarm' (*Shak.*), to send up in a swarm; **upsway'**, to swing up.—*n.* up'take, the act of lifting up: a pipe or flue with upward current: mental apprehension (orig. *Scot.*; in *Scot.* usu. **up'tak; gleg in, at, the uptak**, quick to understand).—*v.t.* (-*tāk'*) to take up.—*v.t.* upthrow', to throw up.—*n.* (*up'*) an upheaval, uplift: the amount of vertical displacement of the relatively raised strata at a fault.—*v.t.* upthrust', to thrust upward.—*n.* (*up'*).—*v.i.* upthun'der, to send up a noise like thunder (*Coleridge*).—*v.t.* uptie', to tie up: to conclude, wind up (*fig.*)—*adj.* uptight (*coll.*), tense, in a nervy state.—*prep.* up-till' (*obs.* and *Scot.*), up to.—*adj.* up'torn (also **uptorn'**, *pa.p.* of **uptear**).—*adj.* and *adv.* up'town', in or toward the upper part or (*U.S.*) the residential quarters of a town.—*v.t.* and *v.i.* uptrain', to train up, educate (*obs.*).—*n.* up'trend, upward tendency.—*adj.* up'trilled, trilled high (*Coleridge*). —*n.* up'turn, an upheaval: a disturbance: a movement upward, a rise: an upturned part.— *adj.* up'turned.—*n.* and *adj.* upturn'ing.—*v.t.* and *v.i.* upwind (*up-wind'*), to wind up:—*pa.t.* and *pa.p.* upwound'.—*adv.* upwind (*up-wind'*), up-wind, against the wind.—*v.t.* (*pa.p.*) upwrought', wrought up.

**upadaisy.** Same as **ups-a-daisy.**

**upaithric**, *ū-pi'chrik, adj.* from the same root as, and identical in meaning with, **hypaethral** (q.v.).

**Upanis(h)ad**, *ōō-pan'i-shad, ōō-pä'ni-shäd, n.* a

Sanskrit theosophic or philosophical treatise. [Sans. *upa*, near, *ni-shad*, a sitting down.]

**upas**, *ū'pəs, n.* (in full u'pas-tree'), a fabulous Javanese tree that poisoned everything for miles around: Javanese tree (*Antiaris toxicaria*, of the mulberry family): the poison of its latex. [Malay, poison.]

**upbraid**, *up-brād', v.t.* to reproach or chide: to adduce in reproach (against, to, a person; *obs.*). —*v.i.* to utter reproaches.—*n.* (*obs.*) reproach, reproof.—*n.* upbraid'er.—*n.* and *adj.* upbraid'ing. [O.E. *ūpbregdan.*]

**upbray**, *up-brā', (Spens.) v.t.* to upbraid: to bring reproach on.—*n.* (*Spens.*) an upbraiding. [From *upbrayd*, obs. pa.t. of upbraid.]

**upholster**, *up-hōl'stər, v.t.* to furnish with stuffing, springs, covers, etc.: to cushion, be a cover to: to provide with curtains, carpets, etc.—*v.i.* to do upholstery.—*n.* (*obs.*) an upholsterer.—*ns.* uphol'sterer, one who makes or deals in furniture, beds, curtains, etc.:—*fem.* uphol'stress; uphol'stery, upholsterer's work or goods. [Back formation from *upholsterer*—**upholder** in obs. sense (q.v.).]

**upmost.** See up.

**upon.** See up-.

**upper, uppermost.** See up.

**uproar**, *up'rōr, rör, n.* insurrection, commotion and tumult (now *rare*): loud outcry, clamour. —*v.t.* uproar' (*Shak.*), to throw into uproar or confusion.—*v.i.* to make an uproar.—*adj.* uproar'ious.—*adv.* uproar'iously.—*n.* uproar'iousness. [Du. *oproer*—*op*, up, *roeren* (Ger. *rühren*, O.E. *hrēran*), to stir; modified by association with roar.]

**ups-a-daisy**, *ups-ə-dā'zi, interj.* of encouragement in lifting a child or helping to climb.

**upsey, upsee, upsy,** *up'si, (obs.) prep.* in the manner of (e.g. **upsey whore**).—*obs. adv.* (in full **upsey Dutch, English, Friese,** in the German, English, Frisian manner, of drinking) deeply, heavily, heartily.—*n.* a carousal.—*interj.* a Bacchanalian exclamation. [Du. *op zijn*, in his (i.e. the; 'manner' understood).]

**upsilon.** See ypsilon.

**upsy.** Same as upsey.

**uptrain.** See up-; **up-train.** See up.

**ur**, *ûr, interj.* filling a gap in speech, when hesitant.

**ur-**, *ōōr-, pfx.* primitive, original. [Ger.]

**urachus**, *ū'rə-kəs, n.* a ligament connecting the bladder with the umbilicus. [Gr. *ourachos*, the fetal structure from which it is formed.]

**uracil.** See urea.

**uraemia**, *ū-rē'mi-ə, n.* retention of waste materials in the blood.—*adj.* **urae'mic.**—Also **urē'mia**, **urē'mic.** [Gr. *ouron*, urine, *haima*, blood.]

**uraeus**, *ū-rē'əs, n.* the snake symbol on the head-dress of Egyptian gods and kings. [Gr. *ouraios*, a kind of snake; prob. Egyptian.]

**Ural**, *ū'rəl, n.* a river and mountain range of Russia.—*adjs.* **Uralian** (*ū-rā'li-ən*), of the Ural Mountains (**Uralian emerald**, a semi-precious green garnet); **Uralic** (*ū-ral'ik*).—*n.* u'ralite (*ū'rə-līt*), an alteration product, hornblende after augite.—*adj.* uralitic (-*lit'ik*).—*n.* uralitisā'tion, -z-.—*v.t.* u'ralitise, -ize, to turn into uralite.— *adj.* Ural-Altaic (-*al-tā'ik*), of the Ural and Altai Mountains: applied to a family of languages— Finno-Ugrian, Turko-Tatar, Mongolian, Manchu, Tungus, etc., and their speakers.

**urali.** Same as wourali.

**Urania**, *ū-rā'ni-ə, n.* the Muse of astronomy: a name for Aphrodite.—*adjs.* Uranian (also with-

---

---

*Words made with* **up** *adj. are listed first* (p. 1490), *then those with* **up-** *pfx.* (pp. 1490 ff.); *other UP-words follow* (p. 1492).

out *cap.*; *ū-rā'ni-ən*), heavenly: of the heavens: astronomical: of Urania or of Uranus, god or planet; **uranic** (*ū-ran'ik*), of uranium in higher valency: celestial: of the palate.—*ns.* **uranide** (*ū'rən-id*), a transuranium element; **uranin** (*ū'rən-in*), a sodium or potasssium salt of fluorescein (from its fluorescence, like that of uranium glass); **uraninite** (*ū-ran'i-nit*), pitchblende; **uraniscus** (*ū-rən-isk'əs*), the roof of the mouth; **ū'ranism**, a type of male homosexuality; u'ranite, autunite: torbernite.—*adj.* **uranit'ic.**— *ns.* **uranium** (*ū-rā'ni-əm*), a radioactive metal (U; at. numb. 92) named by Klaproth, 1789, after the recently discovered planet (**uranium glass**, a yellow fluorescent glass containing uranium compounds); **uranography** (*ū-rən-og'rə-fi*), descriptive astronomy, esp. of the constellations; **uranol'ogy**, astronomy; **uranom'etry**, astronomical measurement; **u'ranoplasty**, plastic surgery of the palate; **Uranos'copus**, the star-gazer genus of fishes.—*adj.* **u'ranous**, of uranium in lower valency.—*ns.* **U'ranus**, an old Greek god, father of Kronos (Saturn) and the Titans: a planet discovered in 1781 by Herschel; **u'ranyl** (*chem.*), the group $UO_2$. [Gr. *ourānos*, heaven.]

**urao**, *ōō-rä'ō*, *n.* natron. [Sp. *urao*, from Carib.]

**urari.** Same as **wourali.**

**urate**, *ū'rāt.* See **uric.**

**urban**, *ûr'bən*, *adj.* of or belonging to a city.—*adj.* **urbane** (*ûr-bān'*), pertaining to, or influenced by, a city: civilised: refined: courteous: smooth-mannered.—*adv.* **urbāne'ly.**—*n.* **ur'banisation**, -*z*-.—*v.t.* **ur'banise**, **-ize**, to make (a district) town-like, as opposed to rural, in character.—*n.* **urbanity** (-*ban'i-ti*), the quality of being urbane: also townishness, town-life; **urbanol'ogist**, one who studies urban conditions; **urbanol'ogy.**— **urban district**, a thickly-populated district, a subdivision of a county, administered by an **Urban District Council.** [L. *urbānus*—*urbs*, a city.]

**urceolus**, *ûr-sē'ō-ləs*, *n.* a pitcher-shaped structure, with contracted mouth, as the sheath of some rotifers.—*adj.* **ur'ceolate**, having the form of an urceolus. [L. *urceolus*, dim. of *urceus*, a pitcher.]

**urchin**, *ûr'chin*, *n.* a hedgehog: a sea-urchin: a deformed person, hunchback (*obs.* or *dial.*): an elf or imp (*obs.*): a mischievous child, esp. a boy: a child.—*adj.* like, of the nature of, due to, an urchin.—*n.pl.* **ur'chin-shows**, appearances of elves or goblins.—*adj.* **ur'chin-snout'ed**, with snout like a hedgehog. [O.Fr. *herichon*, *heriçon* (Fr. *hérisson*)—L. *ēricius*, a hedgehog.]

**urdé, urdée, urdee, urdy**, *ûr'dā, -dē, -di*, (*her.*) *adj.* pointed: having points. [Origin obscure.]

**Urdú**, *ōōr'dōō, ōōr-dōō'*, *n.* and *adj.* Hindustani: a form of it with many Persian and Arabic words, official literary language of Pakistan. [Hind. *urdū*, camp (language); cf. **horde.**]

**ure**, *ūr*, (*obs.*) *n.* use, practice, operation. [O.Fr. *uevre* (Fr. *œuvre*)—L. *opera*, work, service.]

**ure**, *ūr*, (*obs.*) *n.* the urus. [L. *ūrus.*]

**ure**, *ûr*, (*hist.*; *Orkney and Shetland*) *n.* an eighth of a mark, or land paying so much in feu-duty. [Cf. Norw., Sw., Dan. *öre*—L. *aureus*, a gold solidus.]

**urea**, *ū-rē'ə*, by some *ū'*, *n.* carbamide, $CO(NH_2)_2$, a substance found in mammalian urine, the chief form in which nitrogenous waste is carried off.—*n.* **ūr'acil**, a base in ribonucleic acid.—*adj.* **urē'al** (or *ū'ri-əl*).—**urea resins**, thermosetting resins made by heating urea and an aldehyde, usu. formaldehyde. [Gr. *ouron*, urine.]

**uredo**, *ū-rē'dō*, *n.* rust in plants: a rust-fungus in its summer stage (also **urē'do-stage**):—*pl.* **uredines** (*ū-rē'di-nēz*).—*n.pl.* **Uredinā'lēs**, the Uredineae.—*adj.* **uredine** (*ū'ri-din*).—*n.pl.* **Uredineae** (*ū-ri-din'i-ē*), the rust-fungi, an order of parasitic Basidiomycetes.—*adj.* **uredin'ial** (*U.S.*).—*n.* **uredin'ium** (*U.S.*), a uredosorus.—*adj.*

**urē'dinous.**—*ns.* **urēdoso'rus**, a pustule containing uredospores; **urē'dospore**, a spore produced by rust-fungi in the uredo-stage. [L. *ūrēdō*, -*inis*, blight—*ūrĕre*, to burn.]

**uremia, uremic.** Same as **uraemia, uraemic.**

**Urena**, *ū-rē'nə*, *n.* a tropical genus of the mallow family, yielding a jute substitute. [Malayalam *uren.*]

**urent**, *ū'rənt*, *adj.* burning, stinging. [L. *ūrēns*, -*entis*, pr.p. of *ūrĕre*, to burn.]

**uresis**, *ū-rē'sis*, *n.* urination. [Gr. *ourēsis.*]

**ureter**, *ū-rē'tər*, *n.* a duct that conveys urine from the kidneys to the bladder or cloaca.—*adjs.* **urē'-teral, ureteric** (*ū-ri-ter'ik*).—*n.* **urēteri'tis**, inflammation of a ureter.—*adj.* **uret'ic**, pertaining to, occurring in, urine. [Gr. *ourētēr*, -*ēros*—*ouron*, urine.]

**urethan(e)**, *ū'ri-than*, *-thān*, or *-than'*, *-thān'*, *n.* an anaesthetic, $NH_2 \cdot COOC_2H_5$, prepared from urea and ethyl alcohol.

**urethra**, *ū-rē'thrə*, *n.* the canal by which the urine is discharged from the bladder.—*adjs.* **urē'thral; urēthrit'ic.**—**non-specific urethritis**, disease resembling gonorrhoea, not associated with any identifiable virus.—*n.* **urēthri'tis**, inflammation of the urethra. [Gr. *ourēthrā*—*ouron*, urine.]

**urge**, *ûrj*, *v.t.* to press forward, esp. with earnestness, or insistence (success, an enterprise, etc.; *arch.*): to put forward (an argument, etc.; or in argument, with *that*): to stimulate, excite (*arch.*): to hasten (*arch.*): to incite: to allege earnestly: to advise strongly: to drive, impel.— *v.i.* to press: to be urgent or insistent: to push on.—*n.* an impulse: a prompting.—*ns.* **ur'gence** (*rare*), **ur'gency.**—*adj.* **ur'gent**, urging: pressing: calling for immediate attention.—*adv.* **ur'gently.** —*n.* **ur'ger.**—*n.* and *adj.* **ur'ging.** [L. *urgēre.*]

**urial, oorial**, *ōō'ri-əl*, *n.* a Himalayan wild sheep. [Punjabi *hureāl.*]

**uric**, *ū'rik*, *adj.* of, or got from, or present in, urine.—*ns.* **ū'rate**, a salt of uric acid; **ū'ricase**, an enzyme occurring in the liver and kidneys, which catalyses the oxidation of uric acid.—**uric acid**, an acid, $C_5H_4O_3N_4$, present in urine and blood. [Gr. *ouron*, urine.]

**Uriconian**, *ū-ri-kō'ni-ən*, *adj.* of the Roman station *Uriconium* (*Viroconium*) on the site of Wroxeter in Shropshire: applied to the apparently Pre-Cambrian igneous rocks forming the Wrekin, etc.

**Urim**, *ū'rim*, **Thummim**, *thum'im*, *ns.pl.* first mentioned in Exod. xxviii. 30, apparently a pair of objects used as a kind of traditional oracle. [Heb. *ûrīm*, t(h)*ummîm.*]

**urinant**, *ū'rin-ənt*, (*her.*) *adj.* diving, head downward.—*n.* **u'rinātor**, a diver. [L. *ūrīnārī*, to plunge.]

**urine**, *ū'rin*, *n.* excretory product, usually amber liquid, of the kidneys, chief means of voiding nitrogenous waste.—*v.i.* (*obs.*) to urinate.—*n.* **u'rinal**, a chamber-pot (*arch.*): a vessel for urine, esp. for an incontinent or bed-ridden person: a room or building having fixed receptacle(s) for use in urination.—*adj.* **u'rinary**, pertaining to or like, urine.—*n.* a reservoir for urine.—*v.i.* **u'rinate**, to discharge urine.—*n.* **urinā'tion.**— *adjs.* **u'rinātive; urinif'erous**, conveying urine; **urinip'arous**, producing urine; **urinogen'ital**, pertaining jointly to urinary and genital functions or organs.—*ns.* **urinol'ogy, urinos'copy**, etc., barbarous forms for urology, etc.; **urinom'-eter** (ill-formed), a hydrometer for urine.—*adj.* **u'rinous**, like, or of the nature of, urine. [L. *ūrīna*; cf. Gr. *ouron.*]

**urite**, *ū'rīt*, *n.* an abdominal segment. [Gr. *ourā*, a tail.]

**urman**, *ōōr-män'*, *n.* (swampy) pine forest. [Russ., —Tatar *ūrmān.*]

**urn**, *ûrn*, *n.* a vase with rounded body, usually a narrowed mouth and often a foot: esp. such a vase for ashes of the dead: hence any repository for the dead: a monumental imitation of a burial-urn: a river-source (*poet.*): a vessel for water: a container into which to put voting-tablets, etc. (*Rom. hist.*, etc.): a ballot-box: a closed vessel with a tap and now usu. with heating device inside, for making tea or coffee in quantity: a moss-capsule: an urn-shaped body.—*v.t.* to enclose in an urn.—*adjs.* urn'al; urned.—*n.* urn'ful, as much as an urn will hold:—*pl.* urn'fuls.—*adj.* urn'-shaped, rounded with narrowed mouth. [L. *urna.*]

uro-, *ū-rō-*, *-ro-*, in composition, urine.—*n.* ur'ochrome, the yellow pigment in urine.—*adjs.* urogen'ital; urinogenital; urograph'ic. — *ns.* urog'raphy, radiological examination of the urinary tract; urol'ogy, scientific study of urine; uropoie'sis, formation of urine; uros'copy, diagnostic examination of urine; urō'sis, disease of the urinary organs. [Gr. *ouron*, urine; cf. L. *ūrīna*.]

uro-, *ū-rō-*, *-ro-*, in composition, tail: posterior part.—*n.* u'rochord (*-körd*), a notochord confined to the caudal region, as in larval ascidians: any member of the Urochord'a, a subphylum of Chordata having a urochord in the larva—ascidians and kindred forms.—*adjs.* urochor'dal, urochor'date.—*n.pl.* Urodē'la (Gr. *dēlos*, clear, plain), the (permanently) tailed Amphibia.—*ns.* and *adjs.* urodē'lan, u'rodele.—*adj.* urodē'lous.—*ns.* u'romere (Gr. *meros*, part), an abdominal segment of an arthropod; u'ropod, an abdominal appendage of an arthropod; esp. just before the telson.—*adj.* uropygial (*-pij'i-əl*).—*ns.* uropyg'ium (Gr. *ouropȳgion* or *orropȳgion*—*orros*, tne end of the sacrum, *pȳgē*, buttocks), the rump in birds; u'rosome (Gr. *sōma*, body), the tail region; urostege (*ū'rō-stēj*), urostegite (*ū-ros'ti-jit*; Gr. *stegē*, roof, deck), a snake's ventral tail-plate.—*adj.* urosthen'ic (Gr. *sthenos*, strength), having a tail developed for propulsion.—*n.* u'rostyle (Gr. *stȳlos*, column), a prolongation of the last vertebra. [Gr. *ourā*, tail.]

Ursa, *ûr'sə*, *n.* the Latin name of two constellations, *Ursa Major* and *Ursa Minor*, the Great and the Little Bear.—*adj.* ur'sine, of a bear: bearlike.—*n.* Ur'sus, the bear genus. [L. *ursus, ursa*, bear.].

urson, *ûr'sən*, *n.* the Canadian porcupine. [Fr. *ourson*, dim. of *ours*—L. *ursus*, bear.]

Ursuline, *ûr'sū-lin*, *adj.* of or pertaining to St *Ursula*, esp. of the female teaching order founded by St Angela Merici of Brescia in 1537.—Also *n.*

Urtica, *ûr-ti'kə*, commonly *ûr'ti-kə*, *n.* the nettle genus, giving name to the family Urticaceae (*ûr-ti-kā'si-ē*), akin to (or including) elms and mulberries.—*adjs.* urtica'ceous, like or of the nature of a nettle: of the nettle family; ur'ticant, stinging: irritating.—*n.* urtica'ria, nettle-rash.—*adjs.* urtica'rial, urtica'rious.—*v.t.* ur'ticate, to sting: to flog with nettles.—*n.* urtica'tion. [L. *urtica*, a nettle—*ūrēre*, to burn.]

urubu, *ōō-rōō-bōō'*, *n.* a S. American vulture. [Tupí *urubú*.]

urus, *ū'rəs*, *n.* the aurochs.

urva, *ûr'və*, *n.* the crab-eating mongoose of south-eastern Asia. [Nepali.]

us, *us*, *pron.* the objective (dative and accusative) case of we.—Also in editorial and royal use as a singular.—*adv.* us'ward, toward us.—Also *n.* as in *to usward.* [O.E. *ūs.*]

usage, *ū'zij*, *-sij*, *n.* use: act or mode of using: treatment: practice: custom: interest on money (*obs.*): (in *pl.*, with the) four ceremonies in the celebration of the eucharist, dispute about which caused a separation of the Non-jurors into two groups.—*ns.* u'sager, one of the Non-jurors who maintained 'the usages'; u'sance, usage: interest, or lending at interest (*Shak.*): time allowed for payment of foreign bills of exchange. [O.Fr.,—L. *ūsus*, use.]

use, *ūz*, *v.t.* to put to some purpose: to avail oneself of: to observe, practise, follow (*arch.*): to resort to (a place; *arch.*): to behave, comport (oneself; *arch.*): to habituate (*Scot.*): to treat or behave towards: to make use of (a person; see following article).—*v.i.* to be accustomed (to; used chiefly in the past tense, pronounced in this sense *ūst*; usen't, ūs'nt, for *used not*): to be in the habit of so doing (*arch.*): to accustom oneself (to; *Scot.*): to resort (*arch.*).—*adjs.* u'sable; used (*ūzd*), already made use of: second-hand: accustomed, customary (*obs.*): experienced, expert (*Scot.*).—*n.* u'ser, one who uses: continual enjoyment of a right (cf. **non-user**; Fr. *user*): a right established by long use (*law*).—*adj.* used'-up', exhausted.—use up, to consume: to exhaust: to tire out. [Fr. *user*—L.L. *ūsāre*—L. *ūti, ūsus*, to use.]

use, *ūs*, *n.* act of using: state or fact of being used: advantageous purpose to which a thing can be applied: the fact of serving a purpose: usefulness: employment causing wear: need to use (with *for*): manner of using: power of using (e.g. tongue, limb): habit of using: custom: ordinary experience (*Shak.*): a distinctive form of public worship or service peculiar to a church, diocese, etc.: the profit derived from property: interest for money (*arch.*; also *fig.* in *Shak.*): (in *pl.*) a form of equitable ownership peculiar to English law by which one person enjoys the profit of lands, etc., the legal title to which is vested in another in trust.—*adj.* use'ful, advantageous, serviceable (useful, or applied, arts, those arts with a utilitarian purpose, e.g. weaving, pottery, as opposed to the fine arts (see art)).—*adv.* use'fully.—*n.* use'fulness.—*adj.* use'less, having no use: not answering any good purpose or the end proposed.—*adv.* use'lessly.—*n.* use'-lessness.—have no use for, to have no liking for; in use, in employment or practice; make use of, to use, employ: to take the help, etc., of (a person) in obtaining an end with no intention of repaying him; of no use, useless; of use, useful; out of use, not used or employed; use and wont, the customary practice. [L. *ūsus—ūti*, to use.]

usher, *ush'ər*, *n.* a doorkeeper: one who escorts persons to seats in a hall, etc.: an officer who introduces strangers or walks before a person of rank: an under-teacher or assistant (*hist.*):—*fem.* ush'eress, usherette'.—*v.t.* to conduct: to show (in, out): to introduce, lead up to (now usu. with *in*).—*ns.* ush'ering; ush'ership. [A.Fr. *usser*, O.Fr. *ussier* (Fr. *huissier*)—L. *ostiārius*, a door-keeper—*ostium*, a door.]

Usnea, *us'ni-ə*, *n.* a genus of lichens, tree-moss. [Pers. *ushnah*, moss.]

usque ad nauseam, *us'kwi ad nö'zi-am, ōōs'kwe ad now'se-am*, (L.) to the point of disgust.

usquebaugh, *us'kwi-bö*, *n.* whisky. [Ir. and Gael. *uisgebeatha—uisge*, water, *beatha*, life.]

Ustilago, *us-ti-lā'gō*, *n.* a genus of basidiomycetous fungi, of the family Ustilaginaceae (*-laj-i-nā'si-ē*) and order Ustilaginales (*-laj-i-nā'lēz*) or Ustilagin'eae, the smut-fungi.—*adjs.* ustilagin'eous, ustilag'inous. [L. *ustilāgō, -inis*, a kind of thistle.]

ustion, *us'chən*, (*obs.*) *n.* burning: cauterisation by burning.—*n.* ustulation (*us-tū-lā'shən*), burning: roasting. [L. *ūstiō, -ōnis.*]

usual, *ū'zhōō-əl*, *adj.* occurring in ordinary use: common: customary.—*n.* (*coll.*) normal health: habitual drink, etc.—*adv.* u'sually.—*n.* u'sualness.—as usual, as is or was usual; the usual, menstruation. [L. *ūs.ālis—ūsus*, use.]

usucapion, *ū-zū-kā'pi-ən*, usucaption, *-kap'shən*, (*Rom. law*) *ns.* the acquisition of property by long possession and enjoyment.—*n.* usucā'pient, one who claims or holds by usucapion.—*v.t.* u'sucapt (*-kapt*), to acquire so.—*adj.* usucapt'-

ible. [L. *ūsūcapĕre*—*ūsus*, use, *capĕre*, *captum*, to take.]

usufruct, *ū'zū-frukt*, *n.* the use and profit, but not the property, of a thing: liferent.—*v.t.* to hold in usufruct.—*adj.* usufruc'tūary.—*n.* one who has usufruct [L.L. *ūsūfrūctus*—L. *ūsus* (*et*) *frūctus*, use and fruit.]

usure, usurer, etc. See usury.

usurp, *ū-zûrp'*, *v.t.* to take possession of by force, without right, or unjustly: to assume (the authority, place, etc., of someone, or something, else): to take possession of (the mind): to take or borrow (a name or a word): to supplant (*arch.*).—*v.i.* to practise usurpation: to encroach (on).— *n.* usurpā'tion. — *adj.* usur'patory. — *n.* usurpā'ture (*poet.*), usurpation.—*adj.* usurped'.—*adv.* usur'pedly.—*n.* usur'per.—*n.* and *adj.* usur'-ping.—*adv.* usur'pingly. [Fr. *usurper* and L. *ūsūrpāre*, pern. from *ūsus*, use, *rapĕre*, to seize.]

usury, *ū'zū-ri*, *n.* the taking of (now only in-iquitous or illegal) interest on a loan: interest (*arch.*).—*n.* u'sure (*obs.*), interest: usury.—*n.* (*obs.*) to practise usury.—*n.* u'surer, a money-lender (now for excessive interest):—*fem.* ū'suress.—*adjs.* ū'suring (*Shak.*), taking or expecting usury; usū'rious.—*adv.* usū'riously.—*n.* usū'riousness.—*adj.* u'surous (*obs.*). [L.L. *ūsūria*, L. *ūsūra*—*ūti*, *ūsus*, to use.]

usus loquendi, *ūz'ǝs lo-kwen'dī*, *ōōs'ōōs lo-kwen'dē*, (L.) current usage of speech.

ut, *ōōt*, *n.* a syllable representing the first note of the scale, now generally superseded by *do*. [See Aretinian, gamut.]

ut, *ut*, *ōōt*, (L.) as.—ut infra (*in'frǝ*, *ēn'frä*), as below; ut supra (*sōō'prǝ*, *sōō'prä*), as above.

utas, *ū'tas*, (*obs.*) *n.* the octave of a festival. [M.Fr. *huitaves*—O.Fr. *outaves* (pl.)—L. *octāva*, eight.]

utensil, *ū-ten'sil*, formerly *ū'*, *n.* any useful or ceremonial tool or vessel. [O.Fr. *utensile*—L. *ūtēnsilis*, fit for use—*ūti*, to use.]

uterus, *ū'tǝr-ǝs*, *n.* the womb:—*pl.* ū'teri.—*n.* uterec'tomy, hysterectomy.—*adj.* ū'terine (*-īn*), of, in, or for the uterus: of the same mother by a different father.—*ns.* uteri'tis, inflammation of the womb; u'terogestā'tion, gestation in the womb; uterot'omy, hysterotomy. [L.]

Utgard, *ōōt'gärd*, (*Scand. myth.*) *n.* the abode of the giants. [O.N. *ūt*, out, *garthr*, garth, yard.]

utilise, -ize, *ū'ti-līz*, *v.t.* to make use of, turn to use.—*adj.* u'tilisable, -z-.—*ns.* utilisā'tion, -z-; u'tiliser, -z-; util'ity, usefulness: power to satisfy the wants of people in general (*philos.*): profit (*obs.*): a useful thing: a public utility, public service (esp. *U.S.*): (usu. in *pl.*) stock or bond of public utility.—*adj.* produced or sup-plied primarily for usefulness, esp. provided in order that the public may be supplied in spite of rise of prices.—util'ity-man, an actor of the least important parts: a person who can be used to fill any gap; utility room, a room, esp. in a private house, where things required for the work of running the house are kept. [Fr. *utiliser*, *utilité*—L. *ūtilis*, useful—*ūti*, to use.]

utilitarian, *ū-til-i-tā'ri-ǝn*, *adj.* consisting in, based upon, or pertaining to, utility or to utilitarianism: concerned with, looking to, usefulness alone, without regard to, or without caring about, beauty, pleasantness, etc.—*n.* one who holds utilitarianism: one who looks to usefulness alone.—*v.t.* utilitā'rianise, -ize, to make to serve a utilitarian purpose.—*n.* utilitā'rianism, the ethical theory which finds the basis of moral distinctions in the utility of actions, i.e. their fitness to produce happiness. [Jeremy Bentham's coinage from utility.]

utility. See utilise.

utis, *ū'tis*, (*Shak.*) *n.* clamour, din. [M.E. *ūthēs*, hue and cry, app.—O.E. *ūt*, out, *hǣs*, hest.]

utmost, *ut'mōst*, *-mǝst*, *adj.* outmost: last: in the

greatest degree, extreme.—*n.* the limit: the ex-treme: the most or greatest possible: the end (*Shak.*). [O.E. *ūtemest*, with double superlative suffix *-m-est* from *ūte*, out.]

Utopia, *ū-tō'pi-ǝ*, *n.* an imaginary state described in Sir Thomas More's Latin political romance or satire *Utopia* (1516): any imaginary state of ideal perfection.—*adj.* Uto'pian.—*n.* an inhabi-tant of Utopia: one who imagines or believes in a Utopia: one who advocates impracticable reforms or who expects an impossible state of perfection in society.—*v.t.* and *v.i.* uto'pianise, -ize.—*ns.* uto'pianiser, -z-; uto'pianism; uto'-piast; u'topism (*tap-izm*); u'topist. [Gr. *ou*, not, *topos*, a place.]

Utraquist, *ū'trǝ-kwist*, *n.* a Calixtine, or asserter of the right of the laity to communicate in both kinds (i.e. to take the wine as well as the bread). —Also *adj.*—*n.* U'traquism. [L. *utrāque*—*sub utrāque specié*, under each kind.]

utricle, *ū'tri-kl*, *n.* a little bag, bladder, or cell: a bladder-like envelope of some fruits: a chamber in the inner ear.—*adj.* utric'ular, like or having a utricle.—*ns.* Utricūla'ria, the bladderwort genus of Lentibulariaceae; utric'ūlus, a utricle. [L. *ūtriculus*, a small bag, dim. of *ūter*, *ūtris*, a bag, a bottle.]

utter, *ut'ǝr*, *adj.* outer (*arch.*): extreme: total: out-and-out:—*superl.* utt'erest.—*adv.* utt'erly.—*adj.* and *n.* utt'ermost, utmost.—*n.* utt'erness.—

utter barrister, formerly a barrister of rank next below a bencher: one who pleads without the bar, an ordinary barrister, not a king's or queen's counsel or a serjeant-at-law. [O.E. *ūtor*, outer—*ūt*, out.]

utter, *ut'ǝr*, *v.t.* to put (money) in circulation: to offer for sale (*obs.*): to put out, emit, esp. with force (*lit.* and *fig.*; *arch.*): to speak, pronounce, give voice to.—*v.i.* (*coll.*) to make a remark or express an opinion.—*adj.* utt'erable.—*ns.* utt'erableness; utt'erance, act of uttering: manner of speaking: expression in speech, or in other sound, of a thought or emotion (e.g. gave utterance to): a stretch of speech in some way isolated from, or independent of, what precedes and follows it (*linguistics*); utt'erer; utt'ering, circulation. — *adj.* utt'erless, that cannot be uttered in words. [M.E. *uttren*—O.E. *ūt*, out; and M.Du. *uteren*, to announce.]

utterance, *ut'ǝr-ǝns*, *n.* extremity, the bitter end (*Shak.*): the utmost degree (*obs.*): the utmost effort or force (*arch.*). [Fr. *outrance*—*outre*—L. *ultrā*, beyond.]

utterance. See utter (2).

uva, *ū'vǝ*, *n.* a grape: a grape-like berry, one formed from a superior ovary.—*n.* uvea (*ū'vi-ǝ*), the posterior pigment-bearing layer of the iris of the eye: the iris, ciliary body, and choroid.—*adj.* u'veal, of the uvea.—*n.* uveitis (*ū-vi-i'tis*), inflammation of the iris, ciliary body, and choroid.—u'va-ursi (*ūr'sī*; L. *ursī*, bear's), bear-berry: an infusion of its leaves. [L. *ūva*.]

uvarovite, *ōō-vä'rō-vit*, *n.* a green lime-chrome garnet. [After Count S. S. *Uvarov*, Russian minister of education.]

uvula, *ū'vū-lǝ*, *n.* the fleshy conical body suspended from the palate over the back part of the tongue. —*adj.* u'vular, of, produced by vibration of, the uvula.—*adv.* u'vularly.—*n.* uvuli'tis, inflam-mation of the uvula. [Dim. from L. *ūva*, grape.]

uxorial, *uk-sō'ri-ǝl*, *-sö'*, *-zō'*, *-zö'*, *adj.* of a wife. —*n.* uxo'ricide (*-sīd*), a wife-killer: wife-killing. —*adjs.* uxorilo'cal, matrilocal; uxo'rious, exces-sively or submissively fond of a wife.—*adv.* uxo'-riously.—*n.* uxo'riousness. [L. *uxor*, *-ōris*, a wife.]

Uzbeg, *uz'beg*, Uzbek, *-bek*, *n.* a member of a Turkic people of Turkestan: their language.—Also *adj.*

# V

**V, v,** *vē, n.* the twenty-second letter of our alphabet, a differentiated form of U (q.v.), representing a voiced labiodental sound: an object or mark shaped like the letter: as a Roman numeral V = 5; V = 5000.—**V′-agents,** poisonous gases, less volatile than G-agents: **V′-bomb** (Ger. *vergeltungswaffe,* retaliation weapon), a self-propelled long-range projectile, as a rocket or a flying bomb, made by the Germans in World War II: **V′-day,** Victory day—*specif.* 8th May 1945, when Germany surrendered unconditionally; **V′-neck,** the neck of a garment cut to a point below.—*adjs.* **V′-necked; V′-shaped.**—**V′-sign,** a sign made with the index and middle fingers in the form of a V, with palm turned outwards in token of victory, with palm inwards as a sign of derision.

**vac,** *vak, n.* a colloquial abbreviation of **vacation,** and of **vacuum-cleaner.**—*v.t.* and *v.i.* to clean with a vacuum-cleaner:—*pr.p.* **vack′ing;** *pa.t.* and *pa.p.* **vacked.**

**vacant,** *vā′kənt, adj.* empty: unoccupied: of or at leisure: thoughtless: inane.—*ns.* **vacance** (*vəkans′, -käns′,* or *va′; Scot.*), vacation; **vā′cancy,** emptiness: leisure: idleness: inanity: empty space: a gap: a situation unoccupied — *adv.* **vā′cantly.**—*v.t.* **vacate** (*və-kāt′, U.S. vā′kāt*), to make or leave empty: quit: to annul, to make useless (*obs.*).—*n.* **vacā′tion,** a vacating: a voiding: holidays, esp. of schools, colleges, lawcourts: leisure: intermission.—*v.i.* (*U.S.*) to take a holiday.—*n.* **vacā′tionist,** a holiday-maker.—*adj.* **vacā′tionless.**—*n.* **vacā′tur,** the act of annulling in law. [L. *vacāre, -ātum,* to be empty; pr.p. *vacāns, -antis;* 3rd pers. pr. indic. pass. *vacātur.*]

**vaccine,** *vak′sēn, -sin, adj.* of, derived from, the cow: of vaccinia: of vaccination.—*n.* cowpox virus or lymph containing it: any preparation used to confer immunity to a disease by inoculation.—*adj.* **vac′cinal** (*-sin-*), of or due to vaccine or vaccination.—*v.t.* **vac′cinate,** to inoculate with vaccine.—*ns.* **vaccinā′tion;** **vac′cinātor.**—*adj.* **vac′cinatory.**—*n.* **vaccin′ia,** cowpox.—*adj.* **vaccin′ial.** [L. *vaccinus—vacca,* a cow.]

**Vaccinium,** *vak-sin′i-əm, n.* a genus including cranberry, whortleberry, and cowberry, giving name to a family **Vacciniā′ceae,** or a division **Vaccinioid′eae** of Ericaceae. [L. *vaccinium,* whortleberry.]

**vacillate,** *vas′i-lāt, v.i.* to sway to and fro: to waver: to be unsteady.—*adjs.* **vac′illant,** vacillating; **vac′illāting.**—*adv.* **vac′illātingly.**—*n.* **vacillā′tion.**—*adj.* **vac′illatory,** wavering. [L. *vacillāre, -ātum.*]

**vacuum,** *vak′ū-əm, n.* theoretically, an entirely (in practice, a very nearly completely) empty space (also *fig.*): a vacuum-cleaner (*coll.*):—*pl.* **vac′ūums, vac′ūa.**—*v.t.* and *v.i.* to clean with a vacuum-cleaner.—*adj.* pertaining to a vacuum: containing a vacuum: in which a vacuum is used to carry out a specific operation.—*v.t.* **vac′ūate** (*obs.*), to empty: to evacuate: to annul.—*ns.* **vacūā′tion; vac′ūist,** one who thinks there are empty spaces in nature; **vacū′ity,** emptiness: space unoccupied: idleness, listlessness: vacancy of mind.—*adjs.* **vac′ūolar,** of a vacuole; **vac′-ūolate, -d,** having vacuoles.—*ns.* **vacūolā′tion; vac′ūole,** a very small cavity, esp. in protoplasm; **vacūolisā′tion, -izā′tion,** formation of vacuoles.—*adj.* **vac′ūous,** empty: exhausted of air, etc.:

mentally vacant.—*adv.* **vac′ūously.**—*n.* **vac′-ūousness.**—**vac′ūum-brake′,** a brake in the working of which suction by vacuum(s) supplements the pressure applied by the operator, esp. a braking system of this type applied simultaneously throughout a train.—*v.t.* and *v.i.* **vac′ūum-clean′.**—**vac′ūum-clean′er,** an apparatus for removing dust by suction; **vacuum concrete,** concrete enclosed in special shuttering which enables suction to be applied to remove excess water; **vac′ūum-flask′,** a flask for keeping liquids hot or cold by aid of a vacuum lining.—*adj.* **vac′ūum-packed′,** sealed in a container from which most of the air has been removed.—**vacuum pump,** general term for apparatus which displaces gas against a pressure; **vac′ūum-tube,** a sealed glass tube in which a vacuum has been made, e.g. a thermionic valve.—**ultra-high vacuum,** very close approach to complete vacuum, important for certain work of scientists and technologists. [L. *vacuus,* neut. *vacuum,* empty.]

**vade,** *vād, v.i.* to fade (*Shak.*): to pass away (*Spens.*): to depart (*obs.*). [Partly a form of **fade,** partly from, or associated with, L. *vādēre,* to go.]

**vade-mecum,** *vā′di-mē′kəm, vä′, wä′, mä′kōōm, n.* a handbook, pocket-companion. [L. *vāde,* go (imper. of *vādēre*), *mēcum,* with me.]

**vae, vā.** Same as **voe.**

**vae victis,** *vē vik′tēs, vī, wī vik′, wik′tēs,* (L) woe to the conquered.

**vagabond,** *vag′ə-bond, adj.* roving: without settled home: unsettled.—*n.* one who wanders without settled habitation: an idle wanderer: a vagrant: (often playfully or vaguely) a scamp, a rascal.—*v.t.* to play the vagabond.—*n.* **vag′-abondage.**—*v.t.* **vag′abondise, -ize,** to wander like a vagabond.—*adj.* **vag′abondish.**—*n.* **vag′abondism.** [Fr. *vagabond* and L. *vagābundus—vagārī,* to wander.]

**vagary,** *vā′gə-ri, və-gā′ri, n.* a devious excursion: a digression or rambling: a freakish prank: a caprice:—*pl.* **vagaries.**—*adjs.* **vagā′rious; vagā′rish.** [App. L. *vagārī,* to wander.]

**vagile,** *va′jil, -jil, adj.* having ability to move about.—*n.* **vagil′ity** (*-jil′*), quality of being vagile; hence, the ability to succeed in the struggle for existence. [L. *vagus,* wandering.]

**vagina,** *və-ji′nə, n.* a sheath: a sheathing leaf-base: a female genital passage:—*pl.* **vagi′nae, -nas.**—*adjs.* **vagi′nal** (or *vaj′i-nəl*); **vag′inant,** sheathing; **vag′inate, -d,** sheathed: having a sheath; **vaginic′oline, -olous,** living in a sheath.—*ns.* **vaginis′mus,** spasmodic contraction of the vagina; **vagini′tis,** inflammation of the vagina; **vagin′ūla, vag′inule,** a little sheath, esp. one surrounding the base of a moss seta. [L. *vāgina,* sheath.]

**vagrant,** *vā′grənt, adj.* wandering: without settled dwelling: unsettled: uncertain, erratic.—*n.* one who has no settled home: a tramp.—*n.* **vā′grancy.** [Perh. A.Fr. *wakerant* of Gmc. origin (cf. **walk**), assimilated to L. *vagārī,* to wander.]

**vagrom,** *vā′grəm,* (*Shak.*) Dogberry's perversion of **vagrant.**

**vague,** *vāg, adj.* lacking precision or sharpness of definition: indistinct: blurred: lacking in character and purpose, or addicted to haziness of thought.—*n.* a vague state: an indefinite expanse.—*v.i.* to be vague: to wander (*Scot.;*

*fāte, fär; mē, hûr* (her); *mīne; mōte, för; mūte; mōōn, fŏŏt; dhen* (then)

now *rare*).—*adv.* vague'ly.—*n.* vague'ness. [L. *vagus*, wandering—*vagāri*, to wander.]

vagus, vā'gus, *n.* the tenth cranial nerve, concerned in regulating heart beat, rhythm of breathing, etc.:—*pl.* vagi (jī).—*adj.* vā'gal (gəl). [L., wandering.]

vail, an obs. spelling of veil.

vail, vāl, (*arch.*) *v.t.* to lower, let down: to doff in salutation or submission.—*v.i.* to lower a sail: to lift one's hat: to yield: to do homage (*Shak.*): to go down: to abate.—*n.* (*Shak.*) setting. [O.Fr. *valer*, or aphetic for avale.]

vail, vāl, (*arch.*) *v.i.* and *v.t.* to profit, avail.—*n.* (usu. in *pl.*; also vales) a tip, perquisite, dole, or bribe. [O.Fr. *valoir*, vail, to be worth.]

vain, vān, *adj.* empty, devoid (*obs.*): without real worth: futile: unavailing: thoughtless: empty-minded: pettily self-complacent: valuing oneself inordinately on some trivial personal distinction: conceited.—*n.* vain'esse (*Spens.*), vanity, futility.— *adv.* vain'ly.— *n.* vain'ness, vanity.—*adj.* vainglo'rious, given to, or proceeding from, vainglory.—*adv.* vainglo'riously.— vainglo'riousness; vain'glo'ry, vain or empty glory in one's own performances: idle boastfulness.—*v.i.* to boast vainly.—for vain (*Shak.*), in vain, vainly; in vain, fruitlessly: to no end; take in vain, utter with levity. [Fr. *vain*—L. *vānus*, empty.]

vair, vār, *n.* a kind of squirrel fur, bluish-grey and white, represented heraldically by rows of blue and white shields or bells.—*adjs.* vairé, vairy (vā'ri), charged or variegated with vair. [O.Fr., —L. *varius*, variegated.]

Vaishnava, vish'nä-vä, *n.* a worshipper of *Vishnu*. [Sans.]

Vaisya, Vaishya, vis'yä, *n.* a member of the third caste among the Hindus. [Sans. *vaiçya—viç*, settler.]

vaivode. Same as voivode.

vakass, vä'käs, *n.* an Armenian ephod.

vakil, vakeel, vä-kēl', *n.* an Indian agent, representative, or pleader. [Hind.,—Ar. *vakil*.]

valance, val'əns, *n.* a hanging border of drapery.— Also val'ence.—*adj.* val'anced, furnished with a valance. [Poss. A.Fr. *valer*, to descend.]

Valdenses. Same as Waldenses.

vale, vāl, *n.* a valley (chiefly *poet.*): the world (*fig.*). —vale of years, old age. [Fr. *val*—L. *vallis*, a vale.]

vale, vā'li, L. vä'lā, or wä', *n.* and *interj.* farewell. [L. *valē*, imper. of *valēre*, to be well.]

valediction, val-i-dik'shən, *n.* a bidding farewell: a farewell.—*n.* valedicto'rian (*U.S.*), the speaker of a college valedictory address.—*adj.* valedic'tory, saying farewell: farewell: taking leave.—*n.* (*U.S.*) a farewell oration spoken by a graduand. [L. *valē*, farewell, *dīcēre, dictum*, to say.]

valence, val'əns, *n.* valency (*chem.*): chemical bond (*chem.*).—*n.* vä'lency, combining power: its degree as measured by the number of hydrogen (or equivalent) atoms with which an atom can combine, or by the charge on an ion: numerical arrangement of chromosomes (as single, paired, etc.; *biol.*).—valency electrons, those of the outermost shell of the atom, largely responsible for its chemical and physical properties. [L. *valēre*, to be strong.]

valence. Same as valance.

Valenciennes, val-ən-sēnz', -si-en', vä-lä-syen', *n.* a kind of lace made at *Valenciennes* in France, the design being made at the same time as the ground and with the same thread.

Valentine, val'ən-tīn, *n.* the name of several saints on whose day, 14th February, the birds were fabled to choose their mates: (without *cap.*) a person chosen by lot, or the first of the other sex seen that day, assigned in mock betrothal for a year: an amatory or grotesque missive or a gift sent that day: a bird's love-song (*Tenn.*).

—Saint Val'entide (*Spens.*), the season of St Valentine's Day.

Valentinian, val-ən-tin'i-ən, *n.* a follower of the Gnostic *Valentinus* (died *c.* A.D. 160).—Also *adj.*

valerian, və-lē'ri-ən, *n.* the plant all-heal (*Valeriana officinalis*), or other plant of the genus, which gives name to the family Valerianā'ceae, akin to the teasels: its rhizome and roots which have medicinal properties.—*adj.* valerianā'ceous, of this family.—valerianic (-*an'ik*) or valeric (-*er'ik*) acid, a fatty acid $C_5H_{10}O_2$ (in several isomers).— Greek valerian, Jacob's ladder; red or spur valerian, a plant Centranthus akin to valerian. [Perh. from someone called *Valerius*, or from L. *valēre*, to be strong.]

vales. See vail (3).

valet, val'it (or val'ā), *n.* a man-servant who attends to clothes and toilet.—*v.t.* (*val'it*) to serve or attend to as valet.— *n.* val'eting. — valet de chambre (*də shäbr'*), an attendant: a footman; valet de place (*da plas*), one who serves as a guide, messenger, etc., esp. for strangers. [Fr.]

valeta. Same as veleta.

valetudinarian, val-i-tū-di-nā'ri-ən, *adj.* pertaining to ill-health: sickly: weak: anxious and fanciful about one's own health.—*n.* a valetudinarian person.— *n.* valetūdinā'rianism. — *adj.* and *n.* valetūd'inary (-ə-ri), valetudinarian. [L. *valētūdinārius—valētūdō*, state of health—*valēre*, to be strong.]

valgus, val'gus, *n.* condition of being bow-legged or (sometimes) knock-kneed: (for *tālipēs valgus*) out-turned club-foot. [L., bow-legged.]

Valhalla, val-hal'ə, *n.* the palace of bliss for the souls of slain heroes (*Scand. myth.*): a general burial-place or monument for a nation's great men. [O.N. *Valhöll—valr*, the slain, *höll*, hall.]

vali, vä-lē', *n.* a governor, esp. of a vilayet. [Turk.]

valiant, val'yənt, *adj.* strong (*obs.*): brave: actively courageous: heroic.—*n.* (*obs.*) a valiant person. —*ns.* val'iance, val'iancy, valour: a deed of valour.—*adv.* val'iantly. [Fr. *vaillant*—L. *valēre*, to be strong.]

valid, val'id, *adj.* strong (*arch.*): sound: legally adequate, or efficacious: fulfilling all the necessary conditions: in logic, well based, applicable. —*v.t.* val'idate, to make valid: to ratify: to confirm, substantiate.—*ns.* validā'tion; valid'ity.— *adv.* val'idly.—*n.* val'idness. [L. *validus—valēre*, to be strong.]

valise, və-lēz', (*U.S.*) -lēs', (now *rare* except *U.S.*) *n.* a travelling bag for hand or saddle: a kit-bag. [Fr.; cf. It. *valigia*, Sp. *valija*.]

Valium, val'i-əm, *n.* proprietary name for diazepam, a tranquilliser. [Tradename.]

Valkyrie, val'kir-i, val-kir'i, -kir'i, (*Scand. myth.*) *n.* any one of the minor goddesses who conducted the slain from the battlefield to Valhalla:—*pl.* Valkyries, Valkyr'iur. [O.N. *Valkyrja—valr*, the slain, and the root of *kjósa*, to choose; cf. O.E. *Wælcyrige*, Ger. *Walküre*.]

vallar, vallary. See vallum.

vallecula, va-lek'ū-lə, *n.* a groove or furrow.—*adjs.* vallec'ular, vallec'ulate. [L.L. dim. of L. *vallis*, valley.]

valley, val'i, *n.* an elongated hollow between hills: a stretch of country watered by a river: a trough between ridges: the hollow of an M-shaped roof: —*pl.* vall'eys. [O.Fr. *valee* (Fr. *vallée*)—*val*—L. *vallis*, a valley.]

Vallisneria, val-is-nē'ri-ə, *n.* a tropical and subtropical genus of submerged water-plants of the frogbit family. [After Antonio *Vallisnieri* (1661-1730), Italian naturalist.]

vallum, val'əm, *n.* a rampart: a wall of sods, earth, or other material, esp. of that thrown up from a ditch.—*adjs.* vall'ar, -y, applied to a crown bestowed in ancient Rome on the first to mount an enemy's rampart. [L.]

valonia, vallonia, və-lō'ni-ə, *n.* a tanning material,

acorns of a Levantine oak (valonia oak, *Quercus aegilops*). [It. *vallonea*—Gr. *balanos*, an acorn.]

**valour**, *val'ər*, *n*. intrepidity: courage: bravery: value, worth (*obs.*).—*n*. **valorisā'tion**, -z-, fixing of price.—*v.t*. **val'orise**, **-ize**, to fix the price of.—*adj*. **val'orous**, intrepid: courageous.—*adv*. **val'orously**. [O.Fr. *valour*—L.L. *valor*, *-ōris*—L. *valēre*, to be strong.]

**valse**, *väls*, *n*., *v.i*. and *v.t*. waltz. [Fr.]

**value**, *val'ū*, *n*. worth: a fair equivalent: intrinsic worth or goodness. recognition of such worth: that which renders anything useful or estimable: the degree of this quality: relative worth: high worth: esteem: efficacy: excellence: price: precise meaning: relative duration (*mus.*): relation with reference to light and shade (*paint.*): the special determination of a quantity (*math.*). —*v.t*. to estimate the worth of: to rate at a price: to esteem: to prize.—*v.t*. or *v.i*. (*Shak.*) to be worth.—*adj*. **val'uable**, having value or worth: of high value.—*n*. a thing of value, a choice article—often in *pl.*—*n*. **val'uableness**.—*adv*. **val'uably**.—*v.t*. **val'uate**, to appraise.—*n*. **valuā'tion**, estimation of value.—*adj*. **valuā'tional**.—*n*. **val'uātor**, an appraiser.—*adj*. **val'ued**, that has a value assigned: priced: highly esteemed: prized; **val'ueless**.—*n*. **val'uer**, one who estimates a value: valuator: one who sets a high value.—**valuable consideration** (*law*), a consideration (*q.v.*) having material or monetary value; **valuation roll**, a list of properties and their assessed values for local taxation purposes; **value judgment**, a personal estimate of merit in a particular respect; **value received**, a phrase indicating that a bill of exchange, etc., has been accepted for a valuable consideration. —**good value**, full worth in exchange; **value-added tax**, a tax on the rise in value of a product due to the manufacturing and marketing processes; **value in exchange**, exchange value: amount of other commodities for which a thing can be exchanged in the open market (*econ.*). [O.Fr. *value*, fem. pa.p. of *valoir*, to be worth—L. *valēre*.]

**valuta**, *vä-lū'tə*, *-lōō-*, *n*. the comparative value of a currency: a standard of money. [It.]

**valvassor**. See **vavasour**.

**valve**, *valv*, *n*. a leaf of a folding-door: a single piece forming part or the whole of a shell: one of the parts of a dry fruit separating in dehiscence: a structure or device that regulates flow or passage or allows it in one direction only: a rectifier (*elect.*): loosely, a thermionic valve used in wireless apparatus as rectifier, amplifier, oscillator or otherwise.—*adjs*. **val'val**; **val'var**; **val'vate**, with or having a valve or valves: meeting at the edges without overlapping (*bot.*); **valved**; **valve'less**.—*ns*. **valve'let**, **val'vūla** (in composition, **valvulo-**), **val'vule**, a little valve.—*adj*. **val'vūlar**, of or having a valvule or valve.—*n*. **valvūli'tis**, inflammation of a valve of the heart. [L. *valva*, a folding-door.]

**vambrace**, *vam'brās*, *n*. armour for the forearm.— Also **vant'brace**, (*Milt.*) **vant'-brass**.—*adj*. **vam'-braced**. [A.Fr. *vantbras* for *avant-bras*, forearm.]

**vamoose**, *və-mōōs'*, **vamose**, *-mōs'*, (*slang*) *v.i*. to make off.—*v.t*. to leave. [Sp. *vamos*, let us go.]

**vamp**, *vamp*, *n*. the part of a boot or shoe covering the front of the foot: anything patched up: a simple and uninspired improvised accompaniment.—*v.t*. to provide with a vamp: to repair with a new vamp: to patch up: to give a new face to: to improvise inartistically (*mus.*).—*v.i*. to improvise crude accompaniments: to trudge (now dial.).—*n*. **vam'per**.—*n*. and *adj*. **vamp'ing**. [O.Fr. *avanpié*—*avan* (Fr. *avant*), before, *pié* (Fr. *pied*)—L. *pēs*, *pedis*, foot.]

**vamp**. See **vampire**.

**vampire**, *vam'pīr*, *n*. in eastern European folklore, a dead man that leaves his grave to prey upon

the living: a blood-sucker, a relentless extortionate parasite or blackmailer: adventuress who allures and exploits men (abbrev. **vamp**): a vampire-bat: a stage trap.—*v.t*. to prey upon. —*n*. **vamp** (see above).—*v.t*. to allure.—*v.i*. **vam'pirise**, **-ize**, to play the vampire.—*v.t*. (*lit*. and *fig*.) to suck the blood of.—*n*. **vam'pirism**, belief in human vampires: the actions of a vampire.—*adj*. **vamp'ish**.—**vam'pire-bat'**, a blood-sucking Central and South American bat (as *Desmodus*, *Diphylla*): applied to various bats wrongly supposed to be blood-suckers (as Vampyrus). [Some Slav. languages have *vampir*.]

**vamplate**, *vam'plāt*, *n*. a guard for the hand on a lance. [A.Fr. *van-* for *avant*, before, *plate*, plate.]

**van**, *van*, *n*. a shortened form of **vanguard**.—Also (*Shak.*) **vant**, **vaunt**.

**van**, *van*, (*lawn-tennis*) *n*. short for (ad)**vantage**.

**van**, *van*, *n*. a winnowing basket or shovel: a shovel for testing ore: a test of ore by washing on a shovel: a wing: a windmill sail.—*v.t*. to winnow or test with a van.—*n*. **vann'er**, one who vans: an ore-separator.—*n*. and *adj*. **vann'ing**. [Southern form of **fan**; perh. in part directly from L. *vannus* or O.Fr. *van*.]

**van**, *van*, *n*. a large covered wagon: a light vehicle, whether covered or not, used in transporting goods: a railway carriage or compartment for luggage, the guard, etc.—*v.t*. and *v.i*. to send, convey, confine, travel, or tour in a van:—*pr.p*. **vann'ing**; *pa.t*. and *pa.p*. **vanned**.—*n*. **vann'er**, a horse suitable for a van. [An abbreviated form of **caravan**.]

**vanadium**, *və-nā'di-əm*, *n*. a silvery metallic element (V; at. numb. 23).—*ns*. **vanadate** (*van'ə-dāt*), a salt of vanadic acid.—*adj*. **vanadic** (*və-nad'ik*), of vanadium in higher valency.—*n*. **van'-adinite** (or *-nad'*), a mineral, lead vanadate and chloride. [Named by a Swedish chemist Sefström from O.N. *Vana-dis*, the goddess Freyja.]

**Van Allen radiation belts**, zones of intense particle radiation surrounding the earth at a distance of above 1200 miles (1930 km.) from it. [J. A. *Van Allen*, American physicist, b. 1914.]

**Vandal**, *van'dəl*, *n*. one of a fierce people from north-eastern Germany who overran Gaul, Spain, and North Africa, sacked Rome in 455, destroyed churches, etc.: (usu. without *cap*.) one who destroys what is beautiful: (without *cap*.) one who wantonly damages property.— *adjs*. **Van'dal**; **Vandal'ic**.—*v.t*. **van'dalise**, to inflict wilful and senseless damage on property. —*n*. **Van'dalism** (or **van'-**).

**Vandyke**, *van-dīk'*, or *van'-*, *n*. a painting by the great Flemish artist Anthony *Van Dyck* (1599-1641): (in the following, without *cap*.) deeply-cut collar similar to those seen in his portraits: a point of a deep-cut edging: a short pointed beard (also called **Vandyke beard**).—*v.t*. and *v.i*. to notch or zig-zag.—*adj*. **vandyked'**.—**van'dyke brown**, a deep brown used by Van Dyck: a mixture of lampblack or other material and ochre.

**vane**, *vān*, *n*. a flag: a weathercock or revolving plate, or a streamer, serving to show how the wind blows: a heraldic or ornamental plate fixed on a pinnacle: a blade of a windmill, propeller, revolving fan, or the like: a fin on a bomb or a paravane: a sight on an observing or surveying instrument: the web of a feather.—*adjs*. **vaned**, having a vane or vanes; **vane'less**. [Southern form of **fane**.]

**Vanessa**, *və-nes'ə*, *n*. the red admiral genus of butterflies. [Perh. for *Phanessa*—Gr. *Phanēs*, a mystic divinity.]

**vang**, *vang*, *n*. a guy-rope to steady a gaff. [A form of **fang**.]

**vanguard**, *van'gärd*, *n*. the foremost of an army, etc.: the forefront: those who lead the way or anticipate progress. [Fr. *avant-garde—avant*, before, *garde*, guard.]

**vanilla,** *və-nil'ə, n.* a flavouring substance got from the pods of *Vanilla planifolia,* a Mexican climbing orchid, and other species: the plant yielding it.—*n.* **vanill'in,** its aromatic principle ($C_8H_8O_3$). [Sp. *vainilla—vaina*—L. *vāgīna,* a sheath.]

**vanish,** *van'ish, v.i.* to disappear: to fade out: to cease to exist: to become zero: to exhale, emanate (*Shak.*).—*v.t.* to cause to disappear.— *n.* a vanishing: a glide with which a sound ends. —*n.* **van'isher.**—*n.* and *adj.* **van'ishing.**—*adv.* **van'ishingly.**—*n.* **van'ishment.**—**vanishing cream,** cosmetic cream that, when rubbed over the skin, virtually disappears; **vanishing point,** the point at which parallel lines seen in perspective converge: the verge of disappearance of anything. [Aphetic for **evanish**.]

**Vanitory,** *van'i-tər-i, n.* a unit consisting of a wash-hand basin and a dressing table. [Trademark.]

**vanity,** *van'i-ti, n.* the quality of being vain: that which is vain.—**van'ity-bag, -box, -case,** one containing a mirror and cosmetic appliances.— **Vanity Fair,** the world, or any place or society in it where people are wholly devoted to vanity, triviality, and empty ostentation (from the fair at the town of Vanity, in Bunyan's *Pilgrim's Progress*). [Fr. *vanité*—L. *vānitās, -ātis*; see **vain.**]

**vanner, vanning,** etc. See **van** (2), **van** (3).

**vanquish,** *vangk'wish, v.t.* to conquer: to overcome.—*v.i.* to be victor.—*adj.* **vanq'uishable.**— *ns.* **vanq'uisher; vanq'uishment.** [A.Fr. *venquir,* *venquiss-* (Fr. *vaincre*)—L. *vincĕre,* to conquer.]

**Vansittartism,** *van-sit'ərt-izm, n.* extreme anti-Germanism. [From the British diplomat Lord *Vansittart* (1881-1957).]

**vant, vant,** (*Shak.*) *n.* Same as **van** (1).

**vantage,** *vän'tij, n.* advantage: now less usual form of advantage (*lawn-tennis*): opportunity (*Shak.*): excess, addition (*Shak.*).—*v.i.* (*Spens.*) to benefit, profit.—*adj.* **van'tageless.**—**van'tage-ground, -point,** a favourable or commanding position. [A.Fr. *vantage*; cf. **advantage.**]

**vantbrace, vant-brass.** See as **vambrace.**

**vanward,** *van'wərd, adj.* and *adv.* towards the van or front.

**vapid,** *vap'id, adj.* insipid: dull: flat.—*n.* **vapid'-ity.**—*adv.* **vap'idly.**—*n.* **vap'idness.** [L. *vapidus.*]

**vapour** or (esp. *U.S.*) **vapor,** *vā'pər, n.* a substance in the form of a mist, fume, or smoke, esp. one coming off from a solid or liquid: a gas below its critical temperature, liquefiable by pressure: water in the atmosphere: (in *pl.*) exhalations supposed to arise in the stomach or elsewhere in the body, affecting the health (*old med.*): (in *pl.,* usu. with *the*) low spirits, boredom, nervous disorder: anything insubstantial, vain, or transitory: a fanciful notion: bluster.—*v.i.* to pass off in vapour: to evaporate: to brag: to emit vapour: to bluster.—*v.t.* to make to pass into vapour: to steam: to affect with the vapours: to boast: to drive by bluster.—*adjs.* **vā'porable,** capable of being turned to vapour; **vāporif'ic,** vaporising; **vā'poriform,** existing in the form of vapour.—*n.* **vāporim'eter,** an instrument for measuring vapour pressure or vapour.—*adj.* **vāporis'able, -z-.**—*n.* **vāporisā'-tion, -z-.**—*v.t.* **vā'porise, -z-,** convert into vapour: to spray.—*v.i.* to become vapour.—*ns.* **vāporis'-er, -z-,** apparatus for discharging liquid in a fine spray; **vāporos'ity.**—*adj.* **vā'porous,** of, in the form of, like, or full of vapour: vain: affected with the vapours: unsubstantial: flimsy: vainly fanciful.—*adv.* **vā'porously.**—*n.* **vā'por-ousness.**—*adj.* **vā'poured,** full of vapours: affected with the vapours.—*n.* **vā'pourer,** one who vapours: a moth (Orgyia) of the tussock family.—*n.* and *adj.* **vā'pouring.**—*adv.* **vā'pour-**

**ingly.**—*adj.* **vā'pourish,** vapoury.—*n.* **vā'pourish-ness.**—*adj.* **vā'poury,** full of vapour: affected with the vapours.—**vā'pour-bath,** a bath in vapour: a place or apparatus for the purpose; **vapour trail,** a white trail of condensed vapour left in the sky from the exhaust of an aircraft. [L. *vapor, -ōris.*]

**vapulate,** *vap'ū-lāt, v.t.* to flog.—*v.i.* to be flogged. —*n.* **vapūlā'tion,** a flogging. [L. *vāpulāre, -ātum,* to be flogged.]

**vaquero,** *vä-kā'rō, n.* a herdsman. [Sp.,—L. *vacca,* a cow.]

**vara,** *vä'rä, n.* a Spanish-American linear measure, varying from 33 to 43 inches (*c.* 84-110 cm.). [See **vare.**]

**varactor,** *var-ak'tər, n.* a two-electrode semiconductor device in which capacitance varies with voltage.

**varan,** *var'ən, n.* a monitor lizard.—*n.* **Var'anus,** the monitor genus, constituting the family **Var-anidae** (*-an'*). [Ar. *waran.*]

**Varangian,** *va-ran'ji-ən, n.* a Scandinavian settler in what became Russia: a member of the bodyguard of the Eastern emperors (chiefly Scandinavian): their Scandinavian language (*Scott*). —Also *adj.* [L.L. *Varangus*—Late Gr. *Barangos* —O.N. *Væringi.*]

**vardy,** *vär'di, n.* a once fashionable form of **verdict.**

**vare,** *vär, n.* a vara: a wand of authority. [Sp. *vara,* a rod—L. *vāra,* a trestle, forked stick— *vārus,* crooked.]

**varec, varech,** *var'ek, n.* kelp: wrack. [Fr.; cf. Scand. origin: cf. **wrack, wreck.**]

**vareuse,** *vä-rœz', (southern U.S.) n.* a kind of loose jacket. [Fr.]

**vargueño,** *vär-gän'yō, n.* a cabinet or desk of a kind made at *Vargas* (Bargas) near Toledo.

**variable,** *vā'ri-ə-bl, adj.* that may be varied: changeable: tending or liable to change or vary: showing variations: unsteady: quantitatively indeterminate (*math.*): changing in brightness (*astron.*).—*n.* a quantity subject to continual increase or decrease (*math.*): a quantity which may have an infinite number of values in the same expression (*math.*): a shifting wind.—*ns.* **variabil'ity; vā'riableness.**—*adv.* **vā'ri**' ' *ns.* **vā'riance,** variation: deviation: discrepancy: disagreement: disput the average of the squares of the deviations of a number of observations from the mean; **vā'riant,** a different form of the same thing (esp. a word): a different reading: a specimen slightly differing from the type.—*adj.* changeful: varying: diversified: different: diverging from type.—*n.* **vā'riate,** any one of the observed values of a quantity: a variant: the variable quantity which is being studied (*statistics*).—*v.t.* and *v.i.* to change, vary.—*n.* **vāriā'tion,** a varying: a change: continuous change: difference in structure or character among offspring of the same parents or among members of a related group: departure from the mean or usual character: the extent to which a thing varies: a variant: declination of the compass: an inequality in the moon's motion discovered by Tycho Brahe: a change in the elements of an orbit by the disturbing force of another body: transformation of a theme by means of new figures in counterpoint, florid treatment, changes in tempo, key, and the like (*mus.*): a solo dance (*ballet*).—*adj.* **vāriā'-tional,** pertaining to variation.—*n.* **vāriā'tionist,** a composer of variations: one who attaches importance to variation.—*adj.* **vā'riative,** variational.—**variable gear** (see **gear**).—**at variance,** in disagreement or dissension; **variable-geometry aeroplane,** an aeroplane of varying wing, swept-back for flight, but at right angles for take-off and landing, so removing need for long runways and high landing-speeds. [Partly through O.Fr., from L. *variāre*, *-ātum*, to vary— *varius*; see vary.]

**variae lectiones**, vă'ri-ē lek-shi-ōn'ēz, va', wa'ri-ī lek-ti-ōn'ās, (L.) various readings.

**varicella**, *var-i-sel'ə*, *n.* chickenpox.—*adjs.* **vari- cell'ar**; **varicell'oid**, resembling varicella; **vari- cell'ous**, pertaining to varicella. [Irreg. dim. of **variola**.]

**varices**, *pl.* of **varix**.—**varicocele**, **varicose**. See under **varix**.

**varicoloured**, *va'ri-kul'ərd*, *adj.* diversified in colour. [L. *varius*, various, *color*, colour.]

**Varidase**, *vär'i-dāz*, *n.* proprietary name of a drug used to liquefy, for draining away, clotted blood, thick pus, and dead tissue in deep infections.

**varied**. See **vary**.

**variegate**, *vā'ri-(ə-)gāt*, *v.t.* to diversify, esp. with colours in patches.—*adj.* **vā'riegated.**—*ns.* **varie- gā'tion**; **vā'riegātor**. [L. *variegātus*—*varius*; see **vary**.]

**variety**, *və-rī'ə-ti*, *n.* the quality of being various: diversity: difference: many-sidedness, versatility: a varied set: a kind differing in minor characters: a race not sufficiently distinct to be counted a species: music-hall entertainment, a succession of varied turns:—*pl.* **vari'eties.**—*adj.* of, for, performing in, music-hall entertainment.—*adj.* **vari'etal** (*biol.*), of or having the character of a variety.—*adv.* **vari'etally**. [L. *varietās*, *-ātis*— *varius*, various.]

**variform**. See **various**.

**variola**, *vā'ri-ə-lə*, *n.* smallpox: sheep-pox.—*adj.* **vari'olar.**—*v.t.* **variolate** (*vā'ri-ə-lāt*), to inocu- late with smallpox virus.—*ns.* **văriolā'tion**, in- oculation with smallpox virus; **variole** (*vā'ri-ōl*), a pock-like marking: a spherule in variolite; **vă'riolite** (Gr. *lithos*, stone), a fine-grained basic igneous rock with spherules of radiating feldspar resembling pock-marks.—*adjs.* **văriolit'ic**, of or like variolite; **vă'rioloid**, resembling smallpox. —*n.* modified smallpox occurring in the vac- cinated.—*adj.* **variolous** (*və-rī'ō-ləs*), of, pertain- ing to, suffering from, smallpox: covered with varioles. [L.L. *variola*, pustule, pox—L. *varius*, various, spotted.]

**variometer, variorum**. See **various**.

**various**, *vă'ri-əs*, *adj.* varied, different: several: unlike each other: changeable: uncertain: variegated.—*adj.* **vă'riform**, of various forms.— *n.* **văriom'eter** (Gr. *metron*, measure), an instru- ment for comparing magnetic forces: a variable inductance of two connected coils, one rotating within the other: an instrument that indicates by a needle the rate of climb and descent (*aero.*). —*adj.* **vărio'rum**, with the notes of various commentators or editors (L. *cum notis variōrum*): with the reading of various manuscripts or editions.—*n.* a variorum edition: a succession of changes (*jocular*).—*adv.* **vă'riously.**—*n.* **vă'- riousness**. [L. *varius*; see **vary**.]

**variscite**, *var'i-sīt*, *n.* a greenish mineral, hydrated aluminium phosphate. [L. *Variscia*, Vogtland, in Saxony.]

**varix**, *vā'riks* (L. *va'*, *wa'riks*), *n.* an abnormally dilated, lengthened, and tortuous vein: dilatation: a ridge marking a former position of the mouth of a shell:—*pl.* **varices** (*va'*, *vā'ri-sēz*; L. *va'ri- kās*, *wa'*).—*n.* **varicocele** (*var'i-kō-sēl*; Gr. *kēlē*, tumour), an enlargement of the veins of the spermatic cord or those of the scrotum.—*adj.* **var'icose**, of the nature of, like, pertaining to, affected by, a varix or varices: abnormally dilated or enlarged as a vein: dilated.—*n.* **varicosity** (*var-i-kos'i-ti*), state of being varicose: a distended place. [L. *varix*, *-icis*, a varicose vein.]

**varlet**, *vär'lit*, *n.* an attendant (*arch.*): a municipal officer (*obs.*): a knave (*arch.*):—*fem.* (*rare*) **var'letess.**—*ns.* **var'letry** (*Shak.*), the rabble, the

crowd; **varlett'o** (*Shak.*, *sham* It.), a varlet. [O.Fr. *varlet*; cf. **valet**.]

**varmint, varment**, *vär'mint*, *n.* old variants (now *dial.* or *slang*) of **vermin**: a noxious or trouble- some animal or person: (perh. another word) a skilled amateur sportsman (*obs.*).—*adj.* natty, dashing: sharp, cunning.

**varnish**, *vär'nish*, *n.* a resinous solution that dries to give a glossy coat to a surface: a gloss or glaze: a specious show: an application of varnish.—*v.t.* to coat with varnish: to give a fair show to.—*ns.* **var'nisher**; **var'nishing.**— **var'nishing-day**, a day before the opening of a picture exhibition when exhibitors may varnish or retouch their pictures after they have been hung; **var'nish-tree**, the tung-tree or other tree whose resinous juice is used for varnishing or for lacquering. [Fr. *vernis*; prob.—Medi- aeval L. *veronix*, sandarac.]

**varsal**, *vär'səl*, (*coll.*) *adj.* universal.

**varsity**, *vär'si-ti*, (*coll.*) *n.* and *adj.* university.

**varsovienne**, *vär-sō-vi-en'*, *n.* a dance imitated from the Polish mazurka: a tune for it. [Fr., fem. of *Varsovien*—*Varsovie*, Warsaw.]

**vartabed**, *vär'tə-bed*, *n.* an Armenian order of clergy. [Armenian *vartabet*.]

**Varuna**, *vu'rōō-nä*, *var'*, *vär'*, *n.* an ancient Indian Vedic god of the heavens, later of the waters. [Sans.; cf. Gr. *Ouranos*.]

**varus**, *vā'rəs*, *n.* (for *tālipēs vārus*) in-turned club- foot. [L. *vārus*, bent, knock-kneed.]

**varve**, *värv*, (*geol.*) *n.* a seasonal layer of clay de- posited in still water, of service in fixing Ice Age chronology.—*adj.* **varve(d)**, stratified in distinct layers of annual deposit. [Sw. *varv*, layer.]

**varvel**. Same as **vervel**.

**vary**, *vā'ri*, *v.t.* to make different: to diversify, modify: to alter or embellish (a melody) preserving its identity (*mus.*): to express vari- ously (*Shak.*): to change to something else: to make of different kinds.—*v.i.* to alter or be altered: to be or become different: to change in succession: to deviate: to disagree: to be subject to continuous increase or decrease (*math.*):—*pr.p.* **vā'rying**; *pa.t.* and *pa.p.* **vā'ried.** —*n.* change.—*adj.* **vā'ried.**—*adv.* **vā'riedly.**—*n.* **vā'rier**, one who varies.—*n.* and *adj.* **vā'rying**. For **variance, variation**, etc., see **variable**. [M.E.—(O.) Fr. *varier* or L. *variāre*—L. *varius*, various.]

**vas**, *vas* (L. *väs*, *wäs*,) *n.* a vessel, tube, duct, carrying liquid:—*pl.* **vasa** (*vā'sa*; L. *vä'*, *wä'*).— *adj.* **vā'sal.**—*n.* **vasec'tomy** (Gr. *ek*, out, *tomē*, a cut), excision of the vas deferens, or part of it, esp. in order to produce sterility.—*adjs.* **vas'i- form**, tubular: vase-shaped; **vasomō'tor**, causing constriction or expansion of blood-vessels.— **vas def'erens**, a spermatic duct:—*pl.* **va'sa deferen'tia**. [L. *vās*, *vāsis*, vessel.]

**vas(o)-, vas(-o)**, in composition, vas: vas deferens. —*ns.* **vasoconstric'tion**, narrowing of a blood- vessel; **vasoconstric'tor**, a nerve or drug that causes vasoconstriction.—*adj.* **vasoconstrict'ory.** —*ns.* **vasodilatā'tion**, expansion of a blood-vessel; **vasodilā'tor**, a nerve or drug that causes vasodila- tation.—*adj.* **vasodil(at)ā'tory.**—*ns.* **vasopress'in**, a pituitary hormone that raises blood pressure, regulates kidney secretion, etc.—also prepared synthetically; **vasopress'or**, a substance that causes a rise of blood pressure.

**vasculum**, *vas'kū-lam*, *n.* a botanist's collecting case:—*pl.* **vas'culums**, **vas'cula.**—*adj.* **vas'cular**, relating to, composed of, or provided with con- ducting vessels.—*v.t.* **vas'cularise**, **-ize**, to render vascular.—*n.* **vascular'ity.**—*adv.* **vas'cularly.**— *adj.* **vas'culiform**, vase-shaped.—**vascular bundle**, a strand of conducting tissue in the higher plants, composed of xylem, phloem, and cambium; **vascular cryptogams**, the pteridophytes, or ferns and their allies; **vascular plants**, seed-plants and pteridophytes. [L. *vāsculum*, dim. of *vās*, a vessel.]

**vase,** *vāz*, old-fashioned *vōz*, or (as still *U.S.*) *vās*, *vāz, n.* a vessel, usually tall, round in section, and ornamental, anciently used for domestic purposes: the body of the Corinthian capital (*archit.*).—**vase′-paint′ing,** the decoration of vases with pigments, esp. the decoration of the pottery of the ancient Greeks. [Fr.,—L. *vās.*]

**vasectomy.** See vas.

**Vaseline,** *vaz′* or *vas′i-lēn, n.* a registered trademark name applied to products of a certain firm, consisting in large part, but not solely, of petroleum jelly (*paraffinum molle*) and preparations thereof.—Also *v.t.* [Ger. *wasser*, water, and Gr. *elaion*, oil.]

**vasiform, vasomotor.** See vas.

**vassal,** *vas′əl, n.* one who holds land from, and renders homage to, a superior: a dependant, retainer: a bondman, slave: a low wretch (*Shak.*).—*adj.* in the relation or state of a vassal: subordinate: servile: of a vassal.—*v.t.* to subject.—*ns.* **vass′alage,** prowess, or deeds of prowess (*obs.*): state of being a vassal: dependence: subjection: a fee, fief: vassals collectively; **vass′aless,** a female vassal; **vass′alry,** vassals collectively. [Fr.,—L.L. *vassallus*, servant—Celtic; cf. Bret. *goaz*, W. *gwas.*]

**vast,** *väst, adj.* waste, desert (*obs.*): boundless: huge: exceedingly great: great (18th cent. in hyperbole; e.g. *vast surprise*).—*n.* immensity, an immense tract, boundless or empty expanse of space or time: a waste: a huge quantity, vast amount (*dial.* or *coll.*).—*ns.* **vastid′ity, vast′itude,** **vast′ity,** vastness: a vast extent.—*adv.* vast′ly.—*n.* vast′ness.—*adj.* vast′y, vast.—a vast many (*obs.*), a great many. [L. *vastus*, waste, desolate, huge; cf. waste.]

**vat,** *vat, n.* a large vessel or tank, esp. for fermentation, dyeing, or tanning: dyeing liquor.—*v.t.* to put in a vat.—*n.* **vat′ful,** as much as a vat will hold:—*pl.* vat′fuls. [Southern form of fat (2)—O.E. *fæt*; cf. Du. *vat*, O.N. *fat*, Ger. *fass.*]

**vatic,** *vat′ik, adj.* prophetic: oracular: inspired.—*n.* vat′icide (*-sīd*; L. *caedĕre*, to kill), the killer or killing of a prophet.—*adj.* vaticinal (*-is′i-nl*).—*v.t.* and *v.i.* vati′cinate (chiefly ironical), to prophesy.—*ns.* vaticinā′tion, prophecy; vati′cinator, a prophet. [L. *vātēs*, a prophet, *vāticinārī*, to prophesy.]

**Vatican,** *vat′i-kən, n.* an assemblage of buildings on the Vatican Hill in Rome, including one of the pope's palaces: the papal authority.—*ns.* **Vat′icanism,** the system of theology and ecclesiastical government based on absolute papal authority, ultramontanism; **Vat′icanist,** one who upholds such a system.—**Vatican City,** a small area on the Vatican Hill set up as an independent papal state in 1929; **Vatican Council,** the council that met in St Peter's (1869) and proclaimed papal infallibility (1870). [L. *Mōns Vāticānus*, the Vatican Hill.]

**vau, wow,** *n.* the digamma (see episemon). [L.,—Gr. *wau*—Semitic *wāw.*]

**vaudeville,** *vō′də-vil, vōd′vil, n.* originally a popular song with topical allusions: a play interspersed with dances and songs incidentally introduced and usually comic: variety entertainment.—Also *adj.*—*n.* vau′devillist, a composer of vaudevilles. [From *vau* (*val*) *de Vire*, the valley of the Vire, in Normandy, where they were composed in the 15th century.]

**Vaudois,** *vō-dwä, n.* a native of the Swiss Canton *Vaud* (*pl.* Vaudois): its French.—Also *adj.* [Fr.]

**Vaudois,** *vō-dwä, n.* and *adj.* Waldensian. [Fr.; same root as Waldenses.]

**vaudoo, vaudoux.** See voodoo.

**vault,** *völt,* earlier *vöt, n.* an arched roof or ceiling: a chamber with an arched roof or ceiling, esp. underground: a cellar: a wine-cellar: hence (in *pl.*) a public-house: a burial-chamber: a cavern: anything vault-like.—*v.t.* to shape as a vault: to roof with an arch: to form vaults in.—*v.i.* to curve in a vault.—*n.* **vaul′tage,** an arched cellar (*Shak.*): a range of vaults: vaulted work.—*adj.* vaul′ted, arched: concave overhead: covered with an arch or vault.—*n.* vaul′ting, vaulted work.—*adj.* vaul′ty (*Shak.*), vault-like. [O.Fr. *vaute, vaulte, voute, volte* (Fr. *voûte*)—L. *volvĕre, volūtum*, to roll.]

**vault,** *völt,* earlier *vöt, v.i.* to leap, esp. by resting on the hand or a pole.—*v.t.* to vault over or upon.—*n.* an act of vaulting.—*n.* vault′er.—*n.* and *adj.* vault′ing.—**vault′ing-horse,** a wooden horse for gymnastic exercise; **vault′ing-house** (*obs.*), a brothel. [App. O.Fr. *volter*, to leap.]

**vaunce,** *vöns, v.t.* and *v.i.* obs. aphetic form of advance:—*pr.p.* (*Spens.*) vaunc′ing.

**vaunt,** *vönt* (also *U.S.* vänt), *v.i.* to boast: to behave boastfully or exultingly.—*v.t.* to boast: to boast of: to make known by display (*Spens.*).—*n.* a boast: boastful demeanour.—*adj.* **vaunt′ed.**—*ns.* vaunt′er; vaunt′ery, vaunting.—*adj.* vaunt′ful.—*n.* and *adj.* vaunt′ing.—*adv.* vaunt′ingly. [O.Fr. *vanter*—L.L. *vānitāre*—L. *vānitās*, vanity—*vānus*, vain; partly aphetic for avaunt (2).]

**vaunt,** *vönt,* (*Shak.*) *n.* the first part. [Cf. van (1).]

**vauntage,** *vönt′ij,* (*Spens.*) *n.* Same as (ad)-vantage.

**vaunt-courier,** *vönt-kōō′ri-ər, n.* one sent in advance: a forerunner. [Fr. *avant-courier.*]

**vaurien,** *vō-ryē,* (Fr.) a good-for-nothing.

**vaut, vaute, vawte,** old forms of vault (1 and 2).

**vavasour,** *vav′ə-sōōr,* valvassor, *val′və-sör, n.* one who held his lands of a tenant in chief.—*n.* **vav′asory,** the tenure or the lands of a vavasour. [O.Fr., app.—L.L. *vassus vassōrum*, vassal of vassals—*vassus*, vassal.]

**vaward,** *vö′ərd,* (*Shak.*) *n.* a form of vanguard: forefront.—*adj.* front.

**Veadar,** *vē′ə-där, n.* an intercalary month in the Jewish calendar, following Adar in embolismic years. [Heb. *ve*, and.]

**veal,** *vēl, n.* calf's flesh as food: a calf (*obs.*).—*adj.* of veal.—*adj.* veal′y, like veal or like a calf: immature. [O.Fr. *veël* (Prov. *vedel*)—L. *vitellus*, dim. of *vitulus*; cf. Gr. *italos*, a calf.]

**veale,** *vēl* (*Spens.*). Same as veil.

**vector,** *vek′tor, n.* a directed quantity, as a straight line in space, involving both its direction and magnitude (*math.*): a carrier of disease or infection: the course of an aircraft, missile, etc.—*v.t.* to direct, esp. from the ground (an aircraft in flight) to the required destination.—*adj.* vec′torial.—*ns.* vec′tograph, a picture giving a three-dimensional effect when looked at through special spectacles; **vec′torscope,** an instrument that displays the phase and amplitude of an applied signal, e.g. of the chrominance signal in colour television. [L. *vector, -ōris,* bearer, carrier—*vehĕre, vectum,* to convey.]

**Veda,** *vā′də,* or *vē′, n.* any one of the four holy books of the Hindus:—*pl.* Vedas (*vā′däz*).—*n.* **Vedan′ta,** a system of Hindu philosophy based on the Vedas.—*adjs.* Vedan′tic, Ve′dic.—*ns.* Ve′dism; Ve′dist, one learned in the Vedas. [Sans. *veda*, knowledge; cf. wit, L. *vidēre*, to see, Gr. *oida*, I know; Sans. *Vedānta—anta*, end.]

**Vedda,** *ved′a, n.* (a member of) an aboriginal people of Ceylon.—*adj.* **Veddoid,** of, pertaining to, or resembling, the Veddas: of a S. Asian race, dark-skinned and curly-haired, to which the Veddas belong.—Also *n.*

**vedette,** *vi-det′, n.* a mounted sentry stationed to watch an enemy: a small vessel (**vedette′-boat**) for like purpose: (*və-det*; Fr.) a stage or film star. [Fr.,—It. *vedetta—vedere*—L. *vidēre,* to see.]

**vee,** *vē, n.* the twenty-second letter of the alphabet

(V, v): a mark or object of that shape.—*adj.* shaped like the letter V, as in vee-gutter, vee-joint, etc.—in composition, often V- (*q.v.*).

**veena.** Same as **vina.**

**veer,** *vēr, v.i.* to change direction, esp. (of the wind) clockwise: to change course, esp. away from the wind: to turn, wind: to come round or shift round in mental attitude.—*v.t.* to turn, shift: to turn away from the wind.—*n.* a shifting round.—*n.* and *adj.* **veer′ing.**—*adv.* **veer′ingly.** [Fr. *virer.*]

**veer,** *vēr,* (*naut.*) *v.t.* to pay out: to slack. [M.Du *vieren.*]

**veery,** *vēr′i, n.* the tawny thrush of North America. [Prob. imit.]

**Vega,** *vē′ga, n.* the first-magnitude star α Lyrae. [Ar. *al wāqi′* (*al nasr*), the falling (vulture).]

**vega,** *vā′ga, n.* a low fertile plain: a tobacco-field (*Cuba*). [Sp.]

**Vegan,** *vē′gan, n.* one of a sect of vegetarians using no animal produce at all.—Also *adj.*—*adj.* **vegan′ic,** pertaining to manuring with material which is purely *veg*etable org*anic*.

**vegetable,** *vej′i-tə-bl, n.* an organism belonging to the great division distinguished from animals by being unable to deal with solid food, commonly but not necessarily fixed in position—a plant: a plant or part of one used for food, other than those reckoned fruits.—*adj.* of, for, derived from, composed of, of the nature of, vegetables.—*adv.* **veg′etably,** in the manner of a vegetable.—*adj.* **veg′etal,** vegetable: vegetative: of a level of life below the sensitive.—*n.* (*rare*) a plant, vegetable.—*adj.* **veg′etant,** vegetating.—*n.* **vegetarian** (-*tā′ri-ən*), one who lives wholly on vegetable food, with or without dairy products, honey, and eggs.—Also *adj.*—*n.* **vegetā′rianism,** the theory or practice of a vegetarian.—*v.i.* **veg′etate,** to grow or live as, or like, a vegetable: to increase vegetatively: to live an inactive, almost purely physical, or dull life.—*adj.* **veg′-etāted,** covered with vegetation.—*n.* and *adj.* **veg′etāting.**—*n.* **vegetā′tion,** process of vegetating: vegetable growth: a plant (*obs.*): a plantlike growth: growing plants in mass.—*adj.* **veg′etātive,** growing, as plants: producing growth in plants: concerned with the life of the individual rather than of the race (*biol.*): by means of vegetative organs, not special reproductive structures (*biol.*): pertaining to unconscious or involuntary bodily functions as resembling the process of vegetable growth (*biol.*): without intellectual activity, unprogressive.—*adv.* **veg′etātively.**—*n.* **veg′etātiveness.**—*adj.* **vegete** (*vi-jēt′*), vigorous.—*n.* **veg′etive** (*Shak.*), a vegetable.—*adj.* vegetative.—**vegetable ivory,** corozo-nut; **vegetable kingdom,** that division of natural objects which consists of vegetables or plants; **vegetable marrow,** a variety of pumpkin cooked as a vegetable: the akee fruit; **vegetable mould,** mould consisting mostly of humus; **vegetable parchment,** paper treated with sulphuric acid; **vegetable sheep,** in New Zealand, a dense cushion of composite plants (Raoulia, Haastia) at a distance resembling a sheep; **vegetative nervous system,** the nervous system regulating involuntary bodily activity, as the secretion of the glands, the beating of the heart, etc.; **vegetative organs,** leaves, stems, roots; **vegetative reproduction,** reproduction by detachment of part of the plant-body: budding. [L. *vegetābilis,* animating, *vegetāre,* to quicken, *vegetus,* lively; cf. **vigour.**]

**vehement,** *vē′(h)ə-mənt, adj.* forcible: impetuous: very strong or urgent.—*ns.* **vē′hemence, vē′hemency.**—*adv.* **vē′hemently.** [L. *vehemēns, -entis.*]

**vehicle,** *vē′i-kl, vā′, n.* a means of conveyance or transmission: a medium: a substance with which a medicine, a pigment, etc., is mixed for administration or application: structure in or on

which persons or things are transported, esp. by land: (**space vehicle**), a structure for carrying burdens through air or space or a rocket used to launch a spacecraft.—*adj.* **vehicular** (*vi-hik′ū-lər*).—**vehicle-actuated signals** (see **pad**). [L. *vehiculum*—*vehĕre,* to carry.]

**vehm, fehm,** *fām,* **vehmgericht, fehmgericht,** *-gə-rihht, ns.* a mediaeval German, esp. Westphalian, court in which initiated persons held of the emperor power to try capital cases in public or in secret, their lower officers executing the guilty on the spot or where they could find them:—*pl.* **vehm′e, fehm′e, vehm-, fehmgerichte** (*-ə*).—*adj.* **vehm′ic, vehm′ique, fehm′ic.** [Ger. *vehm,* now *fehm,* criminal court, *gericht,* court, judgment.]

**vehmgericht.** See **vehm.**

**veil,** *vāl, n.* a curtain: a covering: a covering for the head, face, or both, for protection, concealment, or ceremonial reason: a nun's or novice's head-covering: a piece of gauzy drapery worn on the head by a bride: a gauzy face-covering worn by ladies: a humeral: a disguise or concealment: an obstruction of tone in singing: a velum.—*v.t.* to cover with a veil: to cover: to conceal, disguise, or obscure.—*adj.* **veiled.**—*n.* **veil′ing,** the act of concealing with a veil: a veil: material for making veils.—Also *adj.*—*adjs.* **veil′less,** wanting a veil: uncovered; **veil′y,** like a veil, diaphanous.—**eucharistic** or **sacramental veils,** linen or silk covers for eucharistic vessels and elements; **draw a veil over,** to conceal discreetly: to refrain from mentioning; **take the veil,** to become a nun. [O.Fr. *veile* (Fr. *voile*)—L. *vēlum,* a curtain, veil, sail.]

**veilleuse,** *vā-yœz′, n.* a shaded night-lamp. [Fr., —*veiller,* to watch.]

**vein,** *vān, n.* one of the vessels or tubes that convey the blood back to the heart: loosely, any blood vessel: one of the horny tubes forming the framework of an insect's wing: a vascular bundle forming a rib, esp. a small rib, in a leaf: a small intrusion, or a seam of a different mineral running through a rock: a fissure or cavity: a streak in wood, stone, etc.: a streak running through one's nature, a strain of character or ability: a recurrent characteristic streak in manner, style: a mood or humour.—*v.t.* to form veins or the appearance of veins in.—*adj.* **veined,** having veins: streaked, variegated.—*n.* **vein′ing,** formation or disposition of veins: streaking.—*adj.* **vein′ous,** full of veins.—*ns.* **vein′stone, vein′stuff,** gangue. [Fr. *veine*—L. *vēna.* See **vena.**]

**Vela,** *vē′lə, n.* the Sail, a southern constellation: one of the divisions of Argo. [L., *pl.* of *vēlum,* sail.]

**velamen, velar, velarium.** See **velum.**

**velatura,** *vel-ə-tōō′rə, n.* a method of glazing a painting by rubbing with the hand. [It.]

**veld,** also (outside S. Africa) **veldt,** *felt, velt, n.* in South Africa, open, unforested, or thinly-forested grass-country. [Du. *veld* (formerly *veldt*), field.]

**veld(-)schoen** (older form of **veld′skoen**). Same as **velskoen.**

**vele,** *vēl,* (*Spens.*) *n.* Same as **veil.**

**veleta,** *və-lē′tə, n.* a dance or dance-tune in slow waltz time.—Also **valē′ta.** [Sp., weather-cock.]

**veliger.** See **velum.**

**velitation,** *vel-i-tā′shən, n.* a skirmish. [L. *vēlitātiō, -ōnis*—*vēles, -itis,* a light-armed soldier.]

**vell,** *vel, n.* third stomach of a calf, used in making rennet. [Origin unknown.]

**velleity,** *ve-lē′i-ti, n.* volition in its lowest form: mere inclination. [L.L. *velleitās,* irregularly formed from L. *velle,* to wish.]

**vellenage,** *vel′ən-āj* (*Spens.*). Same as **villeinage.**

**vellet,** *vel′it* (*Spens.*). Same as **velvet.**

vellicate, vel'i-kāt, v.t. and v.i. to twitch.—n. vellicā'tion. [L. vellicāre, -ātum, to pluck.]

vellon, ve-lyōn', n. billon: old Spanish copper money. [Sp. vellon—Fr. billon.]

Vellozia, ve-lō'zi-ə, n. the Brazilian tree-lily genus, giving name to an African and S. American family Velloziā'ceae, akin to the amaryllids. [José Vellozo (1742-1811), Brazilian botanist.]

vellum, vel'əm, n. a finer kind of parchment prepared by lime-baths and burnishing from the skins of calves, kids, or lambs. [O.Fr. velin—vel, calf.]

veloce, vā-lō'chā, (mus.) adj. and adv. with great rapidity. [It.]

velocipede, vi-los'i-pēd, n. a dandy-horse, boneshaker, or other early form of bicycle: a swiftfooted person.—adj. swift of foot.—v.i. to ride a velocipede.—n. and adj. velocipē'dean, -ian.—n. veloc'ipēder (or -pēd').—n. and adj. velocipedestrian (-pi-des'tri-ən).—n. veloc'ipēdist (or -pēd'). [Fr. vélocipède—L. vēlōx, -ōcis, swift, pēs, pedis, foot.]

velocity, vi-los'i-ti, n. rate of motion (distance per unit of time) in stated direction: loosely, speed.—velocity-distance law (astron.), the law that the more distant a nebula the greater is its speed of recession. [L. vēlōcitās, -ātis—vēlōx, swift.]

velodrome, vel'ə-drōm, n. a building containing a cycle-racing track. [Fr. vélodrome.]

velour(s), və-lōōr', n. a polishing pad for silk hats: a woollen stuff with velvet-like pile.—Also adj.—ns. veloutine (vel-ōō-tēn'), a velvety corded wool fabric; velure (və-lōōr', -lūr'; Shak.), velvet: a velours.—v.t. to dress with a velours.—adj. velutinous (-lōō', -lū'), velvety. [Fr. velours.]

velouté (sauce), və-lōō-tā, n. a smooth white sauce made with stock. [Fr., velvety.]

velskoen, fel'skōōn, (S.Afr.) n. a shoe made of rawhide. [Du. vel, skin, schoen, shoe.]

velt-mareschal, (Scott) n. Ger. feld-marschall, field marshal.

velum, vē'ləm (L. vā', wā'lōōm), n. veil, integument, or membrane: the membrane joining the rim of a young toadstool with the stalk: the pendulous soft palate: a ciliated disk, a locomotor organ in some molluscan larvae: an in-turned rim in jellyfishes:—pl. vē'la.—n. velamen (vi-lā'men, L. vā-lä'men), a multi-layered sheath of dead cells on some aerial roots:—pl. velā'mina (L. vā-lä'mina).—adj. vē'lar, of the velum: produced by the back of the tongue brought close to the soft palate (phon.).—n. a velar consonant, back consonant.—adj. velar'ic, pertaining to a velar.—v.t. ve'larise, -ize, to pronounce as a velar, esp. through the influence of a vowel sound.—adj. ve'larised.—n. velā'rium (L. vā-lä'ri-ōōm), an awning over an auditorium: in Scyphozoa, the thin marginal region of the umbrella:—pl. velā'ria.—adjs. vē'late, -d, having a velum.—n. vē'liger (-jər), a mollusc larva with a velum. [L. vēlum, a veil, sail, vēlāmen, -inis, a covering, vēlārium, an awning.]

velure. See velour(s).

velvet, vel'vit, n. a silk fabric with soft close short pile: an imitation with silk pile: the velvet-like covering of a growing antler: a velvety surface or skin: gains, winnings (slang).—adj. made of velvet: soft like velvet.—n. vel'veret, a cotton with a silk pile.—adj. vel'veted, clad in velvet.—n. velveteen', a cotton, or mixed cotton and silk, imitation of velvet; vel'vetiness; vel'veting velvet material.—adj. vel'vety, soft and smooth like velvet: deep and soft in colouring.—vel'vet-crab, vel'vet-fidd'ler, a swimming crab with velvety pile; vel'vet-duck, vel'vet-sco'ter, a black duck with a white mark on the wing.—n.pl. vel'vet-guards (Shak.), velvet trimmings, applied metaphorically to the citizens who wore them; vel'vet-leaf, false pareira: tree-mallow; vel'vet-

pa'per, flock paper; vel'vet-pile, material with a soft nap.—on velvet, in a safe or advantageous position: secure against losing, whatever happens; the velvet glove, gentleness, concealing strength (see iron hand at iron). [L.L. velvettum, conn. with L. villus. a tuft.]

vena, vē'nə, L. vā', wā'na, n. vein:—pl. ve'nae.—adj. vē'nal, venous.—n. venation (vi-nā'shən), arrangement of veins or nervures: the veins themselves considered together; venepunc'ture, veni-, puncturing of a vein, esp. with a hypodermic needle; venesec'tion, opening of a vein so as to let blood as a remedial measure.—adj. venose (vē'nōs, -nōs'), veiny: veined: with noticeable veins.—n. venosity (vē-nos'i-ti), the state or quality of being venous, or of having or being like venous blood.—adj. vē'nous, pertaining to, or contained in, veins: of blood, deprived of oxygen and, in man, dark red in colour: veined.—n. venule (ven'ūl), a branch of a vein in an insect's wing: any of the small-calibre blood vessels into which the capillaries empty and which unite to form veins.—vē'na ca'va (L. cāva, hollow), either of two large veins entering the right auricle; vē'na contrac'ta, the point of minimum cross-sectional area in a jet of fluid discharged from an orifice. [L. vēna; see vein.]

venal, vē'nl, adj. for sale: to be bought or bought over: corruptly mercenary.—n. venality (-nal'i-ti).—adv. vē'nally. [L. vēnālis—vēnum, goods for sale; Gr. ōnē, purchase.]

venal. See vena.

venatic, -al, vi-nat'ik, -əl, adjs. pertaining to hunting.—adv. venat'ically.—n. venation (vi-nā'shən; rare), hunting: a hunt.—adj. venatorial (ven-ə-tō'ri-əl, -tō'). [L. vēnāri, to hunt, vēnātiō, hunting, vēnātor, a hunter.]

venation. See vena, venatic.

vend, vend, v.t. to sell or offer for sale, deal in, esp. in a small way: to utter (perh. for vent).—n. a sale: amount sold.—ns. vendee', a buyer; ven'der, -dor, a seller; vendibil'ity.—adj. vend'ible, that may be sold, offered for sale, or readily sold.—n. a thing for sale: a possible object of trade.—n. ven'dibleness.—adv. ven'dibly.—ns. venditā'tion, offering for sale; vendi'tion, sale.—vending machine, a slot-machine. [Fr. vendre or L. vendēre, to sell—vēnum dāre, to offer for sale.]

vendace, ven'dās, n. a whitefish (Coregonus vandesius) found in the Castle Loch and Mill Loch at Lochmaben: another species (C. gracilior) in Derwentwater and Bassenthwaite Lake.—Also ven'dis, ven'diss. [Possibly O.Fr. vendese, vendoise (Fr. vandoise), dace.]

vendage, ven'dij, n. harvest of grapes, vintage. [M.E.—(O.)Fr. vendange; see vintage.]

Vendean, ven-dē'ən, n. an inhabitant of La Vendée, in France: one of those who there resisted the Revolution.—Also adj.

Vendémiaire, vā-dā-myer, n. the first month in the French Revolutionary calendar, about 22nd September to 21st October. [Fr.,—L. vindēmia, vintage—vinum, wine, dēmēre, to take away—dē, from, emēre, to take.]

vendetta, ven-det'ə, n. blood-feud. [It.,—L. vindicta, revenge—vindicāre, to claim.]

vendeuse, vã-dœz, n. a saleswoman. [Fr.]

vendis(s). See vendace.

vendue, ven-dū', (U.S.) n. a public auction sale. [Du. vendu—Fr. vendue.]

veneer, və-nēr', v.t. to overlay or face with a thin sheet of fine wood or other substance: to disguise with superficial refinement.—n. a thin slice for veneering: a specious superficial show: a grass-moth (veneer'-moth, from its markings).—ns. veneer'er; veneer'ing. [Formerly fineer—Ger. furniren—O.Fr. fornir (Fr. fournir), It. fornire, to furnish.]

venefic, -al, vi-nef'ik, -əl, veneficious, ven-ifish'əs, veneficous, vi-nef'i-kəs, adjs. acting by

poison or potions or by sorcery. [L. *veneficus—venenum*, poison, *facere*, to do.]
venepuncture. See vena.
venerate, *ven'ə-rāt, v.t.* to revere.—*adj.* ven'erable, worthy of reverence: hallowed by associations or age: aged-looking: an honorific prefix to the name of an archdeacon, or one in process of canonisation.—*n.* ven'erableness.—*adv.* ven'erably.—*ns.* venerā'tion, the act of venerating: the state of being venerated: awed respect; ven'erātor. [L. *venerāri, -ātus.*]
venery, *ven'ə-ri, n.* sexual indulgence.—*adjs.* venereal (*vi-nē'ri-əl*), pertaining to sexual desire or intercourse: transmitted by sexual intercourse: pertaining to or affected by venereal disease; venē'rean, pertaining to Venus or her service, or to sexual desire or intercourse.—*n.* one addicted to venery.—*ns.* venereology (*vi-nē-ri-ol'ə-ji*), the study of venereal diseases; venereol'ogist.—*adj.* venē'reous, lustful: venereal: aphrodisiac.—venereal disease, a contagious disease characteristically transmitted by sexual intercourse. [L. *venereus*—*Venus, Veneris,* the goddess of love; conn. with L. *venerāri,* to worship.]
venery, *ven'ər-i, n.* hunting: game.—*n.* ven'erer, a gamekeeper: a hunter. [O.Fr. *venerie*—*vener*—L. *vēnāri,* to hunt.]
venesection. See vena.
Venetian, *vi-nē'sh(y)ən, adj.* of Venice.—*n.* a native or inhabitant of Venice: a Venetian blind.—*adj.* Vene'tianed, having Venetian blinds or shutters.—Venetian blind, a window-blind of horizontal slats adjustable to let in or keep out light; Venetian mast, a spirally banded pole for street decoration; Venetian red, ferric oxide as a pigment.
venewe, *ven'ū,* veney, *ven'i.* Shakespearian forms of venue.
venge, *venj, v.t.* (*Shak.*) to avenge.—*adj.* venge'able, revengeful (*Spens.*): destructive (*dial.*): extraordinarily great (*obs.*).—*adv.* venge'ably.—*n.* venge'ance, the infliction of injury in punishment or revenge: retribution: harm, mischief (*Shak.*): a curse (*Shak.*).—*adv.* (*Shak.*) extremely, exceedingly.—*adj.* venge'ful, vindictive, revengeful: retributive.—*adv.* venge'fully.—*ns.* venge'fulness; venge'ment (*Spens.*), vengeance, penal retribution; ven'ger (*Spens.*), an avenger.—what a (or the) vengeance, what the mischief; with a vengeance, orig., with a curse: violently, thoroughly, exceedingly (*coll.*). [O.Fr. *venger*—L. *vindicāre.*]
venial, *vē'ni-əl, adj.* pardonable: excusable: permissible (*Milt.*).—*n.* veniality (*-al'i-ti*).—*adv.* vē'nially.—venial sin, sin other than mortal. [L. *veniālis,* pardonable—*venia,* pardon.]
Venice, *ven'is, n.* a city and former republic of Italy.—*adj.* Venetian.—Venice glass, a fine glass made near Venice, formerly believed to shiver if poison were poured into it; Venice gold (*Shak.*), gold-thread made in Venice; Venice talc, steatite; Venice treacle, a supposed antidote for all poisons, of many ingredients; Venice turpentine, larch turpentine, formerly shipped from Venice. [Fr. *Venise*—L. *Venetia.*]
venire, *ve-nī'rē, ve, we-nē're* (in full venire facias, *fā'shi-as, fa'ki-as; hist.* and *U.S.*) *n.* a writ issued to the sheriff requiring him to cause a certain number of qualified persons to appear in court at a specified time so that jurors may be chosen from them: the persons so caused to appear.—veni'reman (*U.S.*), a juror.
venison, *ven'(i-)zn,* or (esp. in Scotland) *i-sən, n.* a beast of the chase, esp. a deer (*Shak.*): its flesh as food: now deer's flesh. [A.Fr. *venison* (Fr. *venaison*)—L. *vēnātiō, -ōnis,* hunting—*vēnāri,* to hunt.]
venite, *vi-nī'ti* (L. *ve-, we-nē'te*), *n.* the 95th Psalm, beginning *Venīte exultēmus.*
Venn diagram, *ven d'īə-gram,* (*math.*) a diagram in which sets and their relationships are represented, by circles or other figures. [John *Venn,* mathematician.]
vennel, *ven'l,* (*Scot.*) *n.* a lane. [Fr. *venelle*—L. *vēna,* a vein.]
venom, *ven'əm, n.* poison, esp. snake-poison: spite (*fig.*).—*adj.* (*Shak.*) poisonous.—*v.i.* (*obs.*) to poison: to envenom.—*adjs.* ven'omed, venomous: charged with poison, envenomed; ven'omous, poisonous: having power to poison, esp. by bite or sting: malignant, full of spite.—*adv.* ven'omously.—*n.* ven'omousness.—*adj.* ven'om'd-mouth'd' (*Shak.*), having a venomous mouth, slanderous. [O.Fr. *venim* (Fr. *venin*)—L. *venēnum,* poison.]
venose, venous. See under vena.
ven'son. Same as venison.
vent, *vent, n.* a slit in a garment, now in the back of a coat: a crenal (*obs.*). [Fr. *fente*—L. *findēre,* to split; cf. fent.]
vent, *vent, n.* an opening: an aperture: an air-hole or passage: a touch-hole: an outlet: a volcanic orifice: an animal's anus: a chimney (*Scot.*): issue: emission: discharge: escape: passage into notice: publication: utterance: expression: an otter's rise to the surface for breath: the opening in a parachute canopy through which air escapes at a controlled rate.—*v.t.* to give a vent or opening to: to let out, as at a vent: to allow to escape: to publish: to utter: to discharge: to emit: to pour forth: to scent: to sniff at: to lift or open so as to admit air (*Spens.*).—*v.i.* to have or find an outlet: to discharge smoke, to function as a chimney, draw (*Scot.*): to sniff or snuff: to take breath or rise for breath.—*ns.* vent'age, vent'ige (*Shak.*), a finger-hole, as in a flute: a small hole.—*adj.* vent'ed.—*ns.* vent'er, one who utters or publishes; vent'iduct (L. *dūcēre, ductum,* to lead), a ventilating pipe or passage.—*n.* and *adj.* vent'ing.—vent'-hole, a hole for admission or escape of air, fumes, etc., or to admit light; vent'-peg, -plug, a plug for stopping the vent of a barrel; vent'-pipe, an escape-pipe, as for steam or foul gases.—give vent to, to allow to escape or break out: to give, usu. violent, expression to (an emotion). [Fr.,—L. *ventus,* wind; partly Fr. *éventer,* to expose to air; associated with foregoing and following words.]
vent, *vent,* (*obs.*) *n.* sale: market.—*v.t.* (*obs.* or *dial.*) to sell. [O.Fr. *vente*—L. *vendēre, -itum,* to sell.]
ventana, *ven-tä'nä, n.* a window. [Sp.]
ventayle, ventaile, *ven'tāl, n.* (*Spens.*) the movable front of a helmet. [O.Fr. *ventaille.*]
venter, *ven'tər, n.* the belly, abdomen: a womb or mother (*law*): a swelling or protuberance: a medial swelling: the dilated basal part of an archegonium: a shallow concave surface of a bone: the upper side or surface of a leaf, etc.—*adj.* ven'tral, of the belly: on the upper side or towards the axis (*bot.*): on the side normally turned towards the ground—opp. to *dorsal* (*zool.*).—*n.* a ventral fin.—*adv.* ven'trally.—*n.* ven'tricle, a cavity in the body: esp. a cavity in the brain, or a contractile chamber of the heart: the womb (*Shak.*).—*adjs.* ven'tricose, ven'tricous, bellying: swollen in the middle or at one side, or all round at the base: big-bellied; ventric'ular, of, of the nature of, a ventricle: abdominal.—*ns.* ven'tricule, ventric'ulus, a ventricle; ventriculog'raphy, radiography of the brain after the cerebrospinal fluid in the lateral ventricles has been replaced by air or positive contrast medium.—ventral fins the posterior paired fins. [L. *venter, -tris,* dim. *ventriculus.*]
venter, *ven'tər,* an old form (*Milt.*) of venture.
ventifact, *ven'ti-fakt, n.* a stone shaped and/or polished by wind-blown sand. [L. *ventus,* wind, *artifact.*]

*fāte, fär; mē, hûr* (her); *mīne, mōte, för; mūte, mōōn, fŏŏt; dhen* (then)

**ventil**, *ven'til, n.* a valve for giving sounds intermediate between the open harmonics in wind instruments: a valve in an organ for controlling the wind supply to various stops. [Ger.,—L.L. *ventile*, shutter, sluice—*ventus*, wind.]

**ventilate**, *ven'ti-lāt, v.t.* to fan, winnow, blow upon: to open or expose to the free passage of air: to provide with duct(s) for circulating air or for escape of air: to cause (blood) to take up oxygen, by supply of air: to supply air to (lungs): to expose to examination and discussion, to make public.—*adj.* **ven'tilable.**—*n.* **ventilā'tion.**—*adj.* **ven'tilātive.**—*n.* **ven'tilātor,** one who ventilates: a contrivance for introducing fresh air. [L. *ventilāre, -ātum,* to fan, wave, agitate—*ventus,* wind.]

**ventose**, *ven-tōs',* or *ven', adj.* windy: flatulent: puffed up with conceit.—*n.* **Ventôse** (*vā-tōz*), the sixth month of the French Revolutionary calendar, about 19th February to 20th March.—*n.* **ventosity** (*ven-tos'i-ti*), windiness. [L. *ventōsus—ventus,* wind.]

**ventral.** See under **venter** (1).

**ventre,** *ven'tər,* an old form of **venture.**

**ventre à terre,** *vä-tra-ter,* (Fr.) belly to the ground: at high speed.

**ventricle, etc.** See under **venter** (1).

**ventriloquism,** *ven-tril'ə-kwizm, n.* the art of speaking so as to give the illusion that the sound comes from some other source.—*adj.* **ventriloquial** (*-lō'kwi-əl*).—*adv.* **ventrilō'quially.**—*v.i.* **ventril'oquise, -ize,** to practise ventriloquism.—*n.* **ventril'oquist.**—*adjs.* **ventriloquis'tic, ventril'oquous.** — *n.* **ventril'oquy,** ventriloquism. [L. *ventriloquus,* one who speaks by a spirit in the belly—*venter,* the belly, *loquī,* to speak.]

**ventripotent,** *ven-trip'ə-tant,* (*facet.*) *adj.* with great capacity or appetite for food. [After Rabelais—L. *venter,* belly, *potēns,* powerful—*posse,* to be able.]

**venture,** *ven'chər, n.* chance, luck, hazard (*arch.*) that which is put to hazard (esp. goods sent by sea at the sender's risk): an undertaking whose issue is uncertain or dangerous: an attempt: a thing put forward as an attempt: a prostitute (*Shak.*).—*v.t.* to send on a venture: to expose to hazard: to risk: to take the risk of: to dare to put forward.—*v.i.* to make a venture: to run a risk: to dare.—*n.* **ven'turer.**—*adj.* **ven'turesome,** inclined to take risks: involving the taking of risk: risky.—*adv.* **ven'turesomely.**—*n.* **ven'turesomeness.**—*n.* and *adj.* **ven'turing** (*Milt.* **ven'tring**).—*adv.* **ven'turingly.**—*adj.* **ven'turous** (*Spens., Milt.,* etc., **ven'trous, ven't'rous**), adventurous: daring.—*adv.* **ven'turously.**—*n.* **ven'turousness.**—**Venture Scout,** member of senior branch of the Scout organisation, formerly called Rover (Scout); **Venture Air, Sea, Scout.**—**at a venture,** at hazard, random. [For a(d)venture.]

**venturi (tube),** also **Venturi,** *ven-tōōr'ē* (*tūb*), a tube or duct, wasp-waisted and expanding at the ends, used in measuring flow rate of fluids, as a means of accelerating air flow, or to provide a suction source for vacuum-operated instruments. [G.B. *Venturi,* Italian physicist.]

**venue,** *ven'ū, n.* (*Shak.* venewe, veney) a hit in fencing: a bout or match: a lunge, thrust: the place where an action is laid (*law*): the district from which a jury comes to try a question of fact: in England, usually the county where a crime is alleged to have been committed: a scene of action: a meeting-place, esp. for a sport.—**change of venue,** change of place of trial; **lay the venue,** to specify the place where the trial is to be held. [O.Fr. *venue,* arrival—*venir*—L. *venīre,* to come.]

**venule.** See **vena.**

**Venus,** *vē'nəs, n.* the goddess of love, orig. of spring, patron of flower-gardens, later identified with the Greek Aphrodite (*Roman myth.*): an alluring grace (*obs.*): venery (*obs.*): the most brilliant of the planets, second in order from the sun: copper (*alchemy*): a genus of lamellibranch molluscs, including the quahog (**ve'nus-shell',** a shell, or animal, of the genus.).—*ns.* and *adjs.* **Venusian** (*ven-ōō'si-ən, -shi-ən, -shən, ven-ū'*), **Venutian** (*ven-ōō'shi-ən, -shən, ven-ū'*), (inhabitant) of the planet Venus.—**Venus's comb,** an umbelliferous plant (*Scandix pecten-Veneris*) with long-beaked fruits set like comb teeth; **Venus's flower-basket,** a beautiful glass sponge; **Venus's fly-trap,** Dionaea; **Venus's girdle,** a ribbon-like ctenophoran (Cestus); **Venus's looking-glass,** a campanulaceous garden plant (Specularia) with small bright flowers; **mount of Venus,** the elevation at the base of the thumb; (*mons Veneris*) a fatty elevation on the human female pubic symphysis. [L., orig. personified from *venus, -eris,* desire; akin to *venerāri,* to worship.]

**Vera,** *vē'ra, n.* a machine that records television pictures and sound on magnetic tape for almost immediate reproduction. [*vision electronic recording apparatus.*]

**veracious,** *və-rā'shəs, adj.* truthful.—*adv.* **verā'ciously.**—*n.* **veracity** (*-ras'i-ti*), truthfulness. [L *vērāx, -ācis—vērus,* true.]

**veranda, verandah,** *və-ran'də, n.* a roofed gallery, terrace, or open portico along the front or side of a building.—*adj.* **veran'da'd, veran'dahed,** having a veranda. [Hindi *varaṇdā,* app.—Port. *varanda,* a balcony.]

**Veratrum,** *və-rā'trəm, n.* the white hellebore genus.—*n.* **veratrin, -e** (*ver'ə-trin, -trēn*), an alkaloid or mixture of alkaloids got from white hellebore rhizomes, sabadilla, etc. [L. *vērātrum,* hellebore.]

**verb,** *vûrb, n.* (*gram.*) the part of speech which asserts or predicates something.—*adj.* **ver'bal,** of, pertaining to, derived from, a verb or verbs: of, in, of the nature of, in the matter of, or concerned with, words, or words rather than things: word for word: verbose (*Shak.*): oral.—*n.* a word, esp. a noun, derived from a verb.—*n.* **verbalisā'tion, -z-.**—*v.t.* **ver'balise, -z-,** turn into a verb: to put in words.—*v.i.* to use many words.—*ns.* **ver'balism,** an expression: wording: undue attention to words alone: literalism; **ver'balist,** one skilled in words: a literalist: one who looks to words alone; **verbal'ity,** the quality of being verbal or merely verbal: mere words.—*adv.* **ver'bally.**—*n.* **verbā'rian,** a coiner of words.—*adv.* and *adj.* **verbā'tim,** word for word: by word of mouth (*Shak.*).—*n.* **ver'biage,** superfluity of words: wording (*rare*).—*n.* and *adj.* **verb'icide** (*-sīd*), (the quality of) destroying the meaning of a word.—*v.i.* **verbigerate** (*-ij'ə-rāt*).—*n.* **verbigerā'tion,** the morbid and purposeless repetition of certain words and phrases at short intervals.—*adjs.* **verb'less; verbose',** using or containing more words than are desirable: wordy.—*adv.* **verbose'ly.**—*ns.* **verbose'ness, verbosity** (*-bos'*).—**verbal inspiration,** dictation of every word of a book (usu. the Bible) by God; **verbal note,** in diplomacy, an unsigned reminder of a neglected, though perhaps not urgent, matter; **verbal noun,** a form of a verb, e.g. infinitive or gerund, functioning as a noun. [L. *verbum,* word.]

**Verbascum,** *vər-bas'kəm, n.* the mullein (*q.v.*) genus. [L.]

**verbatim,** *vər-bā'tim, -ba'tim,* (L.) word for word. —**verbatim et litteratim** (*-ā'tim, a'tim*), word for word and letter for letter.

**Verbena,** *vûr-bē'nə, n.* the vervain genus, giving name to the family **Verbenaceae** (*vûr-bi-nā'si-ē*), near akin to the labiates.—*adj.* **verbenā'ceous.**—**verbe'na-oil',** an oil got from the kindred plant *Lippia citriodora* (called lemon-scented verbena), or from lemon-grass. [L. *verbēna*, a leafy twig, sacred bough.]

**verberate**, *vŭr'bər-āt*, *v.t.* to beat.—*n.* **verberā'tion.** [L. *verberāre*, *-ātum*, to scourge.]

**verdant**, *vŭr-dənt*, *adj.* green: fresh green or grass-green: green, unsophisticated, raw and gullible. —*n.* **ver'dancy.**—*adv.* **ver'dantly.**—*ns.* **ver'derer**, -or (*hist.*), a forest officer who had charge of the vert and venison; **ver'det**, copper acetate; **ver'-dure**, fresh greenness: greenery: fresh savour (*obs.*).—*adjs.* **ver'dured**, clad with verdure; **ver'dureless**; **ver'durous.** [O.Fr. *verd* (Fr. *vert*) —L. *viridis*, green.]

**verd-antique**, *vŭrd-an-tēk'* (*obs. Fr.*), or **verde-antico**, *ver'dā-än-tē'kō* (*It.*), *n.* a breccia of serpentine containing calcite, etc.—oriental verd-antique, a green porphyry. [Antique green; Fr. now *vert*.]

**verderer.** See **verdant.**

**verdet.** See **verdant.**

**verdict**, *vŭr'dikt*, formerly (*Spens.*, *Milt.*) **verdit**, -dit, *n.* the finding of a jury on a trial: judicial decision or decision generally.—**open verdict** (see **open**); **special verdict**, a verdict in which specific facts are found and put on the record. [O.Fr. *verdit* and L.L. *vērēdictum*—L. *vērē*, truly, *dictum*, said.]

**verdigris**, *vŭr'di-grēs*, *n.* basic cupric acetate: popularly, the green coating of basic cupric carbonate that forms in the atmosphere on copper, brass, or bronze.—*v.t.* to coat with verdigris. [O.Fr. *verd de Grèce*, green of Greece.]

**verdit.** See **verdict.**

**verditer**, *vŭr'di-tər*, *n.* a blue or green pigment, hydrated cupric carbonate. [O.Fr. *verd-de-terre*, earth green.]

**verdoy**, *vŭr'doi*, (*her.*) *adj.* charged with flowers, leaves, or vegetable charges, as a bordure. [Fr. *verdoyé*, pa.p. of *verdoyer*, to become green.]

**verdure.** See **verdant.**

**verecund**, *ver'i-kund*, *adj.* modest. [L. *verēcundus.*]

**verein**, *fər-īn'*, (Ger.) union, association.

**Verey light.** See **Very light.**

**verge**, *vŭrj*, *n.* a rod: a rodlike part: the axis of a clock pallet: a watch with a verge: an intromittent organ: a wand or staff of office: extent of jurisdiction (esp. of the lord-steward of the royal household): a precinct: a pale: a range: scope: jurisdiction: a limit, boundary: a rim: the brink, extreme edge: the horizon: the edge of a roof projecting beyond the gable: a grass edging.—*v.t.* to edge.—*v.i.* to border, be on the edge (with *on*; also *fig.*): to act as verger.—*ns.* **ver'ger**, (see **virger** at **virge**) one who looks after interior of church building, etc.: attendant in a church: a pew-opener (*obs.*); **ver'gership.**— **verge'-board**, a barge board.—**on the verge of** (*fig.*), on the point of: on the brink of. [L. *virga*, a rod; the area of jurisdiction of the holder of the office symbolized by the rod, hence, limit, boundary.]

**verge**, *vŭrj*, *v.i.* to incline: to tend downward: to slope: to tend: to pass gradually, merge.—*n.* **ver'gency.** [L. *vergĕre*, to bend.]

**Vergilian.** Same as **Virgilian.**

**verglas**, *ver-glä*, *n.* a film of ice on rock. [Fr., (*verre*, glass, *glace*, ice) from O.Fr.]

**veridical**, *vi-rid'i-kl*, *adj.* truth-telling: coinciding with fact: (of a dream or vision) corresponding exactly with what has happened or with what happens later: seemingly true to fact.—*n.* **veridicality** (-*kal'i-ti*).—*adv.* **verid'ically.**—*adj.* **verid'icous**, truthful. [L. *vērídicus*—*vērus*, true, *dícĕre*, to say.]

**verier**, **veriest.** See **very.**

**verify**, *ver'i-fī*, *v.t.* to testify: to assert or prove to be true: to ascertain, confirm, or test the truth or accuracy of: to back up (*Shak.*):—*pr.p.* **ver'ifying**; *pa.t.* and *pa.p.* **ver'ified.**—*n.* **verifiabil'ity.**—*adj.* **ver'ifiable.**—*n.* **verificā'tion.**—*adj.*

**ver'ificātory.**—*n.* **ver'ifier.** [L. *vērus*, true, *facĕre*, to make.]

**verily.** See **very.**

**verisimilar**, *ver-i-sim'i-lər*, *adj.* truth-like.—*adv.* **verisim'ilarly.**—*ns.* **verisimil'itude**; **verisimil'ity** (*obs.*).—*adj.* **verisim'ilous.** [L. *vērisimilis*— *vērus*, true, *similis*, like.]

**verism**, *ver'*, *vēr'izm*, *n.* use of everyday contemporary material, including what is ugly or sordid, in the arts, esp. in early 20th-cent. Italian opera (It. *verismo*, *vā-rēs'mō*): the theory supporting this.—*adj.* **ver'ist**—*adj.* **verist'ic.** [L. *vērus*, true.]

**verity**, *ver'i-ti*, *n.* truth: a truth: truthfulness: sincerity: faithfulness:—*pl.* **ver'ities.**—*adj.* **ver'-itable**, true: genuine: real, actual: truly so to be called.—*adv.* **ver'itably.**—**of a verity**, assuredly. [L. *vēritās*, *-ātis*—*vērus*, true.]

**verjuice**, *vŭr'jōōs*, *n.* juice of unripe fruit.—*adj.* sour.—*adj.* **ver'juiced**, soured. [Fr. *verjus*—*vert* (L. *viridis*), green, and *jus*, juice (L. *jūs*, broth).]

**vermeil**, *vŭr'mil*, *-māl*, *n.* and *adj.* bright red, scarlet, vermilion: silver-gilt or gilt bronze.— *v.t.* to colour with vermeil.—Also **ver'mil**, **ver'-meille** (*Spens.* **ver'mell**, **ver'mily**). [O.Fr. and Fr.,—L. *vermiculus*, a little worm, kermes, dim. of *vermis*, worm; cf. **vermilion.**]

**vermes**, *vŭr'mēz*, *n.pl.* worms: (*cap.*) in old classifications a subkingdom of animals, according to Linnaeus including all invertebrates except arthropods, later mainly flat-worms, thread-worms, annelids, now abandoned.—*adjs.* **ver'mian**; **ver'micidal** (L. *caedĕre*, to kill).—*n.* **ver'micide**, a worm-killing agent.—*adjs.* **vermic'-ūlar**, of, like, of the nature of, caused by, a worm: vermiculated: peristaltic; **vermic'ūlate**, **-d**, worm-eaten: marked, inlaid, rusticated, with an appearance of worm-tracks or worms.—*ns.* **vermiculā'tion**; **ver'micule**, a little worm; **vermic'-ūlite**, an altered mica that curls before the blow-pipe flame and expands greatly at high-temperature, forming a water-absorbent substance used in seed-planting, and also used as insulating material.—*adjs.* **vermic'ūlous**, wormy; **ver'-miform**, having the form of a worm; **vermifugal** (-*mif'ū-gl*), expelling worms.—*n.* **ver'mifuge** (-*mi-fūj*), a drug that expels worms.—*adj.* **vermiv'orous**, worm-eating.—**vermiform appendix** (see **appendix**). [L. *vermis*, a worm.]

**vermicelli**, *vŭr-mi-sel'i*, or -*chel'i*, *n.* a very slender macaroni.—Also *adj.* [It., pl. of *vermicello*—L. *vermiculus*, dim. of *vermis*, worm.]

**vermicidal**, etc., **vermiculite**, etc. See **vermes.**

**vermilion**, *vər-mil'yən*, *n.* a bright-red pigment, mercuric sulphide: its bright scarlet colour.—*adj.* bright scarlet.—*v.t.* to colour vermilion. [O.Fr. *vermillon*—*vermeil*; see **vermeil.**]

**vermin**, *vŭr'min*, *n.* a collective name for obnoxious insects, as bugs, fleas, and lice, troublesome animals, such as mice, rats, animals destructive to game, such as weasels, polecats, also hawks and owls, odious, despicable people: any one species or individual of these.—*v.i.* **ver'minate**, to breed vermin.—*n.* **verminā'tion.**—*adj.* **ver'mined**, infested with vermin.—*adjs.* **ver'minous**, **ver'-miny**, infested with vermin: like vermin.—*ver'-min-kill'er.** [Fr. *vermin*—L. *vermis*, a worm.]

**vermis**, *vŭr'mis*, *n.* in lower vertebrates, the main portion of the cerebellum: in mammals, the central lobe of the cerebellum. [L., worm.]

**vermouth**, *vŭr'məth*, *vār'-*, *vŭr'mōōt*, *n.* a drink with white wine base, flavoured with wormwood, etc. [Fr.—Ger. *wermut(h)*, wormwood (O.E. *wermōd*).]

**vernacular**, *vər-nak'ū-lər*, *adj.* (of language) indigenous, native, spoken by the people of the country or of one's own country: of, in, or using the vernacular language: of the jargon or idiom of a particular group: (of other things) native, local, endemic, esp. of architecture or general style of building.—*n.* a native language or dialect: a class jargon: profane language (*facet.*).—*n.* vernacularisā′tion, -z-.—*v.t.* vernac′-ularise, -ize, to make vernacular.—*ns.* vernac′-ularism, a vernacular expression or idiom: the use of the vernacular; vernac′ularist, a user of the vernacular; vernacularity (-*lar′i-ti*).—*adv.* vernac′ularly. [L. *vernăculus*—*verna*, a home-born slave.]

vernal, *vûr′nəl, adj.* of, happening or appearing in spring: springlike: fresh and youthful.—*n.* vernalisā′tion, -z-.—*v.t.* ver′nalise, -ize, make springlike: to freshen: to hasten the develop-ment of (seeds or seedlings) by treating them in various ways before planting, e.g. by subjecting them to a low temperature.—*n.* vernality (-*nal′i-ti*), springlike quality: freshness.—*adv.* ver′nally.—*adj.* ver′nant (*Milt.*), flowering or sprouting in spring.—*n.* vernā′tion, arrangement of leaves in the vegetative bud (rarely that of the individual leaf).—vernal grass, an early-sprouting meadow grass (*Anthoxanthum odoratum*) that gives its scent of coumarin to hay. [L. *vērnālis*, vernal, *vērnāre*, to sprout—*vēr* spring.]

Verner's law. See law.

vernicle, *vûr′ni-kl, n.* a sudarium with the face of Christ, held to have been miraculously impressed on it when St *Veronica* wiped his face: any representation of this: a medal or badge bearing it, worn by pilgrims who had been at Rome.

vernier, *vûr′ni-ər, n.* a short scale sliding on a graduated scale to give fractional readings, invented by the Burgundian P. *Vernier* (*c.* 1580-1637): a small auxiliary device that enables a piece of apparatus to be adjusted very accurately (e.g. a vernier condenser, a condenser of small capacitance connected in parallel with one of larger capacitance): a small rocket engine used to make the movement of a booster rocket, or of a ballistic missile, more precisely as required.—Also *adj.*

vernissage, *ver-nēs-äzh′, n.* varnishing-day. [Fr., varnishing.]

Veronal, *ver′ə-nal, -nəl, n.* a trademark name for barbitone.

Veronica, *və-ron′i-kə, n.* the speedwell genus: (without *cap.*) a vernicle (Sp. *bā-rō′nē-kä*) in bullfighting, the action of a torero when, without moving feet or legs, he swings his open cape to divert the charging bull. [St *Veronica.*]

verquere, *vər-k*(*w*)*ēr′, n.* an obsolete form of back-gammon.—(*Scott*) verquire′. [Du. *verkeeren*, to turn round, to play at backgammon.]

verrel, *ver′l, n.* old (now *dial.*) form of ferrule.

verrey, verry, *ver′i.* Same as vairé.

verruca, *ve-rōō′kə, n.* a wart: a wartlike out-growth:—*pl.* verru′cae (-*sē*; L. -*kī*).—*adjs.* verru′ciform (-*si-förm′*), wartlike; verrucose′ (or *ver′*, or -*rōō′*), verru′cous (or *ver′*), warty.—*n.* verru′ga (Sp.; also *pl.* verru′gas), a fever with warty tumours, endemic in Peru. [L. *verrūca*, a wart.]

vers, *ver,* (*Fr.*) *n.* verse.—*n.* verslibrist (*ver-lē′brist*), a writer of free verse.—vers de société (*də so-syā-tā*), light verse on topics of society; vers d'occasion (*dok-az-yō̃*), occasional verse, pro-duced for a particular event; vers libre (*lē′br′*), free verse. [Fr.]

versability, *vûr-sə-bil′i-ti, n.* aptness to be turned round. [L. *versābilis*—*versāre*, to turn about.]

versal, *vûr′sl,* vär′sl, (*obs. coll.*) *adj.* whole: single, individual. [For universal.]

versal, *vûr′səl, n.* an ornamental letter at the beginning of a section, e.g. in an illuminated manuscript. [verse, -al.]

versant, *vûr′sənt, adj.* versed, conversant: busied, concerned. [L. *versāns, -antis,* pr.p. of *versāre*, to turn over, consider.]

versant, *vûr′sənt, n.* the general slope of surface of

a country. [Fr. *versant*—*verser,* to turn over—L. *versāre.*]

versatile, *vûr′sə-tīl, adj.* turning freely: dangling as an anther attached by the middle of the back (*bot.*): capable of free movement, reversible, as a toe (*zool.*): changeable: unsteady: turning easily from one thing to another: of many-sided ability: capable of many uses.—*adv.* ver′satilely.—*ns.* ver′satileness, versatility (-*til′i-ti*). [L. *versātilis*—*versāre,* freq. of *vertĕre,* to turn.]

verse, *vûrs, n.* a line of metre: metrical composi-tion, form, or work: versification: a stanza: a short division of a chapter, esp. of the Bible: a portion of an anthem to be performed by a single voice to each part: a versicle.—*v.t.* and *v.i.* to versify.—*ns.* verse′let, a little verse: a short poem; ver′ser, a writer of verse; ver′set, a very short organ interlude or prelude: a versicle: a little scrap of verse; ver′sicle, a little verse: in liturgy, the verse said by the officiant.—*adj.* versic′ular, of or in verse.—*ns.* versificā′tion, the making of verse: manner or construction of verse: a turning into verse or its product; ver′-sificâtor, ver′sifier, a maker of verses.—*v.i.* ver′sify, to make verses.—*v.t.* to tell in verse: to turn into verse:—*pr.p.* ver′sifying; *pa.t.* and *pa.p.* ver′sified.—*n.* ver′sing, the composing of verse. — verse′-maker; verse′-making; verse′-man, a writer of verses; verse′-monger, a scribbler of verses; verse′-mongering; verse′-smith, an artificer of verse.—free verse (see free). [O.E. *fers,* reinforced by Fr. *vers,* both—L. *versus, vorsus, -ūs,* a line, row, verse—*vertĕre,* to turn.]

versed, *vûrst, adj.* thoroughly acquainted, skilled. —*v.t.* verse, to make conversant. [L. *versātus,* pa.p. of *versāri,* to busy oneself.]

versed, *vûrst,* (*math.*) *adj.* lit. turned, reversed.—*n.* versine (*vûr′sin*), contracted versin, the versed sine, or one minus the cosine. [L. *versus,* pa.p. of *vertĕre,* to turn.]

versicle. See verse.

versicoloured, *vûr′si-kul-ərd, adj.* diversely or changeably coloured. [L. *versicolor, -ōris*—*vertĕre, versum,* to change, *color,* colour.]

versicular, versification, etc. See verse.

versiform, *vûr′si-förm, adj.* varying in form. [L. *versus,* turned, form.]

versin(e). See versed (2).

version, *vûr′shən, n.* a turning: translation: a Latin prose (*Scot. obs.*): a particular form in which something is embodied, as a particular way of telling a story: a variant.—*adj.* ver′-sional.—*ns.* ver′sioner, ver′sionist, producer of a version. [L. *versiō, -ōnis*—*vertĕre, versum,* to turn.]

verso, *vûr′sō, n.* a left-hand page: the reverse of a coin or medal. [L. *versō* (*foliō*), turned leaf (abl.).]

verst, *vûrst, n.* a Russian measure, almost two-thirds of an English mile (*approx.* 1 km.). [Russ. *versta.*]

versus, *vûr′səs,* (*law, games*) *prep.* against—abbre-viated v. and vs. [L.]

versute, *vər-sūt′, adj.* crafty, wily. [L. *versūtus.*]

vert, *vûrt, n.* in forest law, every green leaf or plant having green leaves that may serve as cover for deer: a power to cut green trees or wood: a green colour, represented by parallel lines sloping diagonally from the dexter chief to the sinister base (*her.*). [Fr. *vert*—L. *viridis,* green.]

vert, *vûrt, n.* a familiar shortening of convert or pervert (esp. to Roman Catholicism).—*v.i.* to become a vert.

vertebra, *vûr′ti-brə, n.* a joint of the backbone:—*pl.* ver′tebrae (-*brē, -bri*).—*adj.* ver′tebral.—*adv.* ver′tebrally.—*n.pl.* Vertebrā′ta, the backboned animals.—*adj.* ver′tebrate, backboned: of the Vertebrata: articulated: firm of character.—*n.*

a backboned animal.—*adj.* **ver'tebrated,** having a backbone: articulated like a backbone.—*n.* **vertebrā'tion,** vertebral structure: backbone (*fig.*).—**vertebral column,** spinal column. [L.,— *vertēre,* to turn.]

**vertex,** *vûr'teks, n.* the top or summit: the zenith (*astron.*): the crown of the head (*anat.*): the point opposite the base (*geom.*): the meeting-point of the lines bounding an angle: the inter-section of a curve with its axis:—*pl.* **ver'tices** (*-ti-sēz*). *adj.* **ver'tical** (*-ti-kl*), of or at the vertex: perpendicular to the plane of the horizon: in the direction of the axis (*bot.*): comprising the various stages in the production of the same goods: in strata: (of mechanism) in which one part is above another.—*n.* a vertical line or position.—*n.* **verticality** (*-kal'i-ti*). —*adv.* **ver'tically.**—*ns.* **ver'ticalness;** **verticity** (*-tis'i-ti*), power of turning; **ver'tiport,** an airport designed for vertical take-off and landing.— **vertical angles,** opposite angles formed by inter-secting lines; **vertical circle,** a great circle of the heavens passing through the zenith and the nadir; **vertical scanning** (*TV*), scanning in which the lines are vertical, not, as normally, horizontal; **vertical take-off** (*aero.*), immediate take-off without preliminary run.—Also as *adj.* [L. *vertex, -icis,* eddy, summit—*vertēre,* to turn.]

**verticil,** *vûr'ti-sil,* (*bot.*) *n.* a whorl.—*n.* **verti-cillas'ter,** an inflorescence so condensed as to look like a whorl.—*adjs.* **verti'cillate, -d,** whorled. [L. *verticillus,* dim. of *vertex.*]

**vertigo,** *vər-tī'gō,* often *vûr'ti-gō,* L. *ver-, wer-tē',* *n.* giddiness: dizziness: a whirling.—*adj.* **ver-tiginous** (*-tij'*), dizzy: giddy: whirling: dizzying. —*adv.* **vertig'inously.**—*n.* **vertig'inousness.** [L. *vertīgō, -inis*—*vertēre,* to turn.]

**vertiport.** See **vertex.**

**Vertoscope,** *vûrt'ō-skōp, n.* proprietary name of a device in which any photographic negative can be viewed immediately as a positive. [L. *vertēre,* to turn, Gr. *skopeein,* to view.]

**vertu,** *vər-tōō', n.* an erroneous form of **virtu:** **ver'tu, ver'tue** (*-tū*), old forms of **virtue.**—*adj.* **ver'tuous** (*Spens.*), possessing virtue or power.

**Verulamian,** *ver-ōō-lā'mi-ən, ver-ū-, adj.* of or pertaining to St Albans, or Francis Bacon, Baron *Verulam,* Viscount St Albans (1561-1626). [L. *Verulāmium,* an ancient British city near the site of St Albans.]

**vervain,** *vûr'vān, n.* a wild verbena, long believed to have great magical and medicinal powers. [O.Fr. *verveine*—L. *verbēna.*]

**verve,** *vûrv, n.* enthusiasm that animates a poet or artist: gusto: spirit: animation: energy. [Fr.]

**vervel,** *vûr'vl,* **varvel,** *vär', n.* a ring for a hawk's jess.—*adj.* **verv'elled, var'velled.** [Fr. *vervelle.*]

**verven.** *vûr'vən,* (*Spens.*) *n.* vervain.

**vervet,** *vûr'vit, n.* an African guenon monkey. [Fr.]

**very,** *ver'i, adj.* true: so called in the true or full sense of the word—that and nothing less, even or exactly that: veritable: actual: mere: precise: extreme:—used, chiefly formerly, in *comp.* **ver'ier,** and also (oftener) in *superl.* **ver'iest,** most truly so called, merest.—*adv.* in high degree: utterly: quite: truly: precisely.—*adv.* **ver'ily,** truly: of a certainty: really.—**in very deed,** of a truth, certainly; **the very thing,** precisely what is wanted or needed; **very high frequency** (see under **frequent**). [Older *verray, veray*—A.Fr. *ver(r)ai* (Fr. *vrai*), from a derivative of L. *vērus,* true; cf. Ger. *wahr.*]

**Very light,** *ver'i līt,* a signalling or illuminating coloured flare fired from a pistol.—Also **Verey.** [Edward W. *Very,* inventor, 1877.]

**vesica,** *ve-, vi-sī'kə,* (*anat.*) *n.* a bladder, sac, esp. the urinary bladder:—*pl.* **vesi'cae** (*-sē*).—*adjs.* **vesical** (*ves'i-kl*), of or pertaining to a vesica; **ves'icant,** blistering.—*n.* anything that causes blisters, including any war 'gas' that blisters and

destroys tissues.—*v.t.* and *v.i.* **ves'icate,** to blister. —*n.* **vesicā'tion.**—*n.* and *adj.* **ves'icatory** (or *-ik'*), vesicant.—*ns.* **ves'icle,** a small globule, bladder, sac, blister, cavity, or swelling: a primary cavity of the vertebrate brain; **vesic'ūla,** a vesicle. —*adjs.* **vesic'ūlar;** **vesic'ūlate, -d.**—*n.* **vesiculā'-tion,** formation of vesicles.—*adj.* **vesic'ūlose.**— **vesica piscis** (*pis'is*; L. *wā-, vä-sē'ka pis'kis*; fish's bladder), a halo in the form of two circular arcs each (properly) passing through the other's centre, enclosing the whole figure. [L. *vēsīca,* bladder, blister.]

**Vespa,** *ves'pə, n.* the common wasp genus, giving name to the family **Ves'pidae.**—*n.* **ves'piary** (modelled on *apiary*), a wasps' nest:—*pl.* **ves'-piaries.**—*adjs.* **ves'pine,** of wasps: wasplike; **ves'poid,** wasplike. [L. *vespa,* wasp.]

**vesper,** *ves'pər, n.* evening: (usu. *pl.*) the last but one of the seven canonical hours: (usu. *pl.*) evensong, evening service generally: a vesper-bell: (*cap.*) Venus as the evening star, Hesperus. —*adjs.* **ves'peral;** **vesperti'nal, ves'pertine,** of or pertaining to the evening: happening, opening, appearing, active, or setting, in the evening.— **ves'per-bell,** the bell that summons to vespers. [L. *vesper;* cf. Gr. *hesperos.*]

**vespiary, vespine, vespoid.** See **Vespa.**

**vessel,** *ves'l, n.* a utensil for holding something: a craft or structure (usually bigger than a boat) for transport by water: a conducting tube for body-fluids in animals, for water in plants: a person regarded as a receptacle, recipient, or embodiment (*B.*): vessels collectively, plate (*Scott* **vessail, vassail**).—**the weaker vessel,** a woman (1 Pet. iii. 7). [O.Fr. *vessel* (Fr. *vaisseau*)—L. *vāscellum,* dim. of *vās, vāsis,* a vessel.]

**vest,** *vest, n.* garb, dress: a garment: a robe: a vestment: a waistcoat: an undershirt: an additional facing to the front of a bodice.—*v.t.* to clothe: to robe: to drape: to put vestments on: to invest: to settle, secure, or put in fixed right of possession (*law*): to endow (*law*).—*v.i.* to descend, devolve, or to take effect, as a right. —*adj.* **vest'ed,** clad: robed: wearing vestments: not contingent or suspended, hence (*law*) already acquired.—*n.* **vest'ing,** the act or fact of clothing, investing, securing legally, etc.: material for waistcoats.—**vested interest,** a particular interest in the continuance of an existing system, institution, etc., for personal reasons, often financial: (in *pl.*) interests already established: (in *pl.*) the class of persons who have acquired rights or powers in any sphere of a country's activities; **vest'-pocket,** waistcoat-pocket. [L. *vestis.*]

**Vesta,** *ves'ta, n.* the Roman goddess of the hearth and household: a minor planet discovered in 1807: (without *cap.*) a wax-stemmed match: a short match with wooden stem:—*pl.* **ves'tas.**— *adj.* **ves'tal,** pertaining or consecrated to Vesta: of or like the Vestal virgins: virgin: chaste.—*n.* one of the Roman patrician virgins consecrated to Vesta: a woman dedicated to celibacy: a nun: a virgin: a woman of spotless chastity. [L.]

**vestiary,** *vest'i-ər-i, n.* a vestry, robing-room, or cloakroom.—*adj.* pertaining to clothes. [L. *vestiārium;* see **vestry.**]

**vestibule,** *ves'ti-būl, n.* a forecourt (*ant.*): an entrance-hall: part of a railway carriage con-necting with and giving access to the next (*U.S.*): a cavity serving as entrance to another, esp. that of the inner ear (*anat.*).—*v.t.* to furnish with a vestibule.—*adj.* **vestib'ular.**—*n.* **vestib'ulum,** a vestibule. [L. *vestibulum.*]

**vestige,** *ves'tij, n.* a footprint: a trace: a surviving trace of what has almost disappeared: a reduced and functionless structure representing what was once useful and developed (*biol.*; also **vestig'-ium**).—*adj.* **vestig'ial.** [L. *vestīgium,* footprint.]

**vestiment,** *ves'ti-mənt,* (*obs.*; *Spens.*) *n.* vestment, garb, garment.—*adjs.* **vestimental** (*-men'tl*), **vestiment'ary.** [L. *vestimentum.*]
**vestiture,** *ves'ti-chər, n.* investiture: clothes: covering, as hair, feathers, scales. [L.L. *vestitūra*—L. *vestis.*]
**vestment,** *vest'mənt, n.* a garment: a ceremonial garment, esp. one worn in religious ceremonies: a covering.—*adj.* **vest'mented.** [L. *vestimentum* —*vestīre,* to clothe, *vestis,* a garment.]
**vestry,** *ves'tri, n.* a room in which vestments are kept and parochial meetings held: a small room attached to a church: in English parishes, a meeting of ratepayers for parish business (later restricted to church affairs): a robing-room: a cloakroom: apparel.—*adj.* **ves'tral.**—**ves'try-clerk,** an officer chosen by the vestry to keep the parish accounts and books; **ves'tryman,** a member of a vestry; **ves'try-room,** a vestry: meeting-place of a vestry.—**common vestry,** an assembly of all the ratepayers; **select vestry,** a board of representatives of the ratepayers. [Prob. through O.Fr.—L. *vestiārium*—*vestis,* a garment.]
**vesture,** *ves'chər, n.* garb: a garment: vegetation clothing the soil.—*v.t.* to cover, clothe.—*adjs.* **vest'ural;** **vest'ured.**—*n.* **vest'urer,** a keeper of vestments. [O.Fr., — L.L. *vestitūra* — *vestis,* garment.]
**Vesuvian,** *vi-sōō'vi-ən,* or *-sū',* *-zōō',* *adj.* of, of the type of, the volcano *Vesuvius.*—*ns.* **vesu'vian,** a smoker's slow-burning match: vesuvianite; **vesu'vianite,** the mineral idocrase, silicate of aluminium and calcium, found in blocks ejected by Vesuvius.
**vet,** *vet, n.* (*coll.*) a veterinary surgeon.—*v.t.* to treat, or examine, medically (animal; also, *facet.,* person): to examine, (e.g. a writing) thoroughly and critically (and pass as sound or correct): —*pr.p.* **vett'ing;** *pa.t.* and *pa.p.* **vett'ed.**
**vet.** See veteran.
**vetch,** *vech, n.* the tare or other species of the papilionaceous genus Vicia: extended to some kindred plants.—*n.* **vetch'ling,** any plant of the sweet-pea genus (Lathyrus).—*adj.* **vetch'y,** abounding with or consisting of vetches.— **bitter vetch,** various species of Vicia and Lathyrus; **kidney vetch,** Anthyllis; **milk vetch,** Astragalus. [O.N.Fr. *veche* (Fr. *vesce*)—L. *vicia.*]
**veteran,** *vet'ə-rən, n.* one who has seen long service: an old and experienced soldier: one old or long experienced in any activity: an ex-serviceman or re-enlisted soldier (*U.S.*; coll. vet).—*adj.* old, experienced: long exercised, esp. in military life.—**veteran car,** an old motor-car, specif. one made before 1916. [L. *veterānus*— *vetus, veteris,* old.]
**veterinary,** *vet'ə-rin-ər-i, adj.* concerned with diseases of animals.—*n.* one skilled in the diseases of domestic animals.—Also **veterinā'-rian,** veterinary surgeon. [L. *veterinārius*— *veterinae,* cattle, beasts of burden.]
**vetiver,** *vet'i-vər, n.* cuscus roots.
**veto,** *vē'to, n.* any authoritative prohibition: the power of rejecting or forbidding: specif., the right of any one of the five permanent members of the Security Council of the United Nations to prevent the Council taking action on any matter other than purely procedural:—*pl.* **vetoes** (*vē'tōz*).—*v.t.* to reject by a veto: to withhold assent to: to forbid.—**local veto,** power of a district to prohibit the liquor trade within its bounds. [L. *vetō* I forbid.]
**vettura,** *vet-tōō'ra, n.* a carriage, cab, or car.—*n.* **vetturino** (*-rē'nō*), its driver or proprietor:—*pl.* **vetturi'ni** (*-nē*). [It.,—L. *vectūra,* a carrying— *vehēre,* to convey.]
**vex,** *veks, v.t.* to harass: to distress: to annoy: to tease: to trouble, agitate, disturb: to discuss

to excess.—*v.i.* (now *rare*) to grieve, fret.—*n.* (*Scot.*) a grief.—*n.* **vexā'tion,** a vexing: state or feeling of being vexed: a source of grief or annoyance.—*adj.* **vexā'tious,** vexing: wantonly troublesome.—*adv.* **vexā'tiously.**—*n.* **vexātious-ness.**—*adjs.* **vex'atory; vexed** (*vekst*).—*adv.* **vex'edly.**—*ns.* **vex'edness;** **vex'er.**—*n.* and *adj.* **vex'ing.**—*adv.* **vex'ingly.**—*n.* **vex'ingness.**—**vexatious suit,** a suit begun without justifiable cause; **vexed question,** a matter greatly debated. [Fr. *vexer*—L. *vexāre,* to shake, annoy.]
**vexata quaestio,** *vek-sä'tə kwēs'ti-ō, vek-,* wek-*sä'ta kwis'ti-ō,* (L.) a disputed question.
**vexillum,** *vek-sil'əm, n.* a Roman standard: a vexillation: a scarf on a pastoral staff: a standard (*bot.*): the series of barbs on the sides of the shaft of a feather:—*pl.* **vexill'a.**—*n.* **vex'illary,** a standard-bearer: one of a company of Roman veterans serving under a special standard.—*adj.* of, pertaining to, under, a vexillum.—*n.* **vexillā'-tion,** a company under one vexillum. [L. *vehēre,* to carry.]
**vezir.** See vizier.
**via, viā,** *vi'a* (L. *vē',* *wē'ä*), *prep.* by way of. [L. *viā,* abl. of *via,* way.]
**via,** *vi'ə, vē'a, wē'a,* (L.) a way, road.—**via crucis** (*krōō'sis, -kis*), way of the Cross (succession of stations of the Cross—see station); **via dolorosa** (*dol-ə-rō'sə, do-lō-rō'sa*), the way to Calvary (lit. mournful way); **Via Lactea** (*lak'-ti-ə, te-a*), Milky Way; **via media** (*mē'di-ə, me'di-a*), a middle course: **via trita, via tuta** (*tri'tə, trē'ta, tūt'ə, tōō'ta*), beaten path, safe path.
**via,** *vē'a,* (*obs.*) *interj.* of dismissal or incitement— come: be off: enough of that. [It.,—L. *via,* way.]
**viable,** *vi'ə-bl, adj.* capable of living, surviving, germinating, or hatching: (of plan, project) of such a kind that it has a prospect of success.—*n.* **viabil'ity.** [Fr.,—*vie*—L. *vita,* life.]
**viaduct,** *vi'ə-dukt, n.* a structure carrying a road or railway over a valley, etc. [After **aqueduct,**— L. *via,* a way.]
**vial,** *vi'əl, n.* same as phial: a spirit-level.—*n.* **vi'alful.**—*adj.* **vi'alled,** put or contained in a vial. —**pour out vials of wrath,** to inflict judgment (Rev. xvi. 1): to storm, rage.
**viameter,** *vi-am'i-tər, n.* a hodometer: a cyclo-meter. [L. *via,* road, Gr. *metron,* measure.]
**viand,** *vi'ənd, n.* an article of food: (usu. in *pl.*) food. [Fr. *viande*—L. *vivenda,* food necessary for life—*vivēre,* to live.]
**viaticum,** *vi-at'ik-əm* (L. *vē-, wē-ä'ti-kōōm*), *n.* money, provisions, etc., for a journey: the eucharist given to persons in danger of death (*R.C. Church*).—*n.pl.* **viat'icals,** baggage. [L. *viāticum*—*via,* way.]
**viator,** *vi-ā'tər* (L. *vē-, wē-ä'tor*), *n.* traveller, way-farer.—*adj.* **viatorial** (*vi-ə-tō'ri-əl, -tö'*). [L. *viātor, -ōris*—*via,* a way.]
**vibe(s),** *vib(z),* (*coll. abbrev.*) *n.* vibraphone.—*n.* **vib'ist.**
**vibex,** *vi'beks, n.* a streak due to extravasation of blood:—*pl.* **vibices** (*vi-, vi-bi'sēz*). [L. *vibīcēs,* weals.]
**vibraculum,** *vi-brak'ū-ləm, n.* a long bristle, a modified zooid, in some Polyzoa:—*pl.* **vibrac'ula.** —Also **vibraculā'rium**:—*pl.* -a. [Coined from L. *vibrāre,* to shake.]
**vibra-.** Variant of vibro-.
**vibraharp.** Same as vibraphone.
**Vibram,** *vē'brəm, n.* tough, heavily-patterned, rubber used, without nails, for the soles of shoes for rock-climbing: Vibram soles.—*n.* **vibs** (*vibz;* coll.), shoes with Vibram soles. [Trademark; *Vitale* and *Bram*ini.]
**vibrancy, vibrant.** See vibrate.
**vibraphone,** *vi'brə-fōn, n.* an instrument having metal bars under which are electrically-operated resonators, played by striking the bars with

small hammers.—Also **vi′braharp** (*U.S.*).—*n.* **vi′braphonist**. [L. *vibrāre*, to shake, Gr. *phōnē*, voice.]

**vibrate**, *vī′brāt*, *-brāt′*, *v.i.* to shake: to tremble: to oscillate: to swing: to change to and fro, esp. rapidly: to resound, ring: to tingle, thrill. —*v.t.* to brandish (*obs.*): to cause to vibrate: to measure by single vibrations: to give off in vibrations.—*n.* **vibrancy** (*vī′brən-si*).—*adjs.* **vi′-brant**, vibrating: thrilling: resonant; **vi′bratile** (*-brə-til*, in U.S. *-til*, *-təl*), vibratory: having or capable of vibratory motion.—*ns.* **vibratility** (*-til′i-ti*); **vibrā′tion**, a vibrating: state of being vibrated: tremulousness: quivering motion: a whole period or movement to and fro of anything vibrating: sometimes a half period or movement one way.—*adjs.* **vibrā′tional**; **vibrā′-tionless**.—*n.* **vibratiuncle** (*vī-brā-shi-ung′kl*), a small vibration.—*adj.* **vi′brative** (*-brə-tiv*), vibrating: consisting in vibrations: causing vibrations. —*n.* **vi′brātor**, that which vibrates: a vibrating part in many appliances: a vibrating tool.— *adj.* **vibratory** (*vī′brə-tər-i*), of, of the nature of, causing, or capable of, vibration. [L. *vibrāre*, *-ātum*, to tremble.]

**vibrato**, *vē-brä′tō*, or *vi-*, *n.* a throbbing effect, without perceptible change of pitch, in singing and in stringed and wind instrument playing. [It.]

**vibrio**, *vib′ri-ō*, or *vīb′*, *n.* a bacterium with a slight spiral curve and usually one flagellum, as that of cholera. [L. *vibrāre*, to shake.]

**vibrissa**, *vī-bris′ə*, *n.* a tactile bristle, as a cat's whisker: a vaneless rictal feather: a bristle, hair, as in the nostril:—*pl.* **vibriss′ae** (*-ē*). [L., a hair in the nostril.]

**vibro-**, *vī′brō-*, in composition, vibration.—*ns.* **vi′broflotation**, a process for compacting sand; **vi′brograph**, **vibrom′eter**, an instrument for recording vibrations. [L. *vibrāre*, *-ātum*, to tremble, to shake.]

**Viburnum**, *vi-bûr′nəm*, *n.* the guelder-rose and wayfaring-tree genus of Caprifoliaceae. [L. *viburnum*, the wayfaring tree.]

**vicar**, *vik′ər*, *n.* one who holds authority as the delegate or substitute of another: a deputy or substitute: a parson of a parish who receives only the smaller tithes or a salary (*Ch. of Eng.*): a bishop's deputy (*R.C.*).—*ns.* **vic′arage**, the benefice or residence of a vicar; **vic′arate**, vicariate; **vic′aress**, an abbess's deputy: a vicar's wife.—*adjs.* **vicarial** (*vī-*, *vi-kā′ri-əl*), delegated: of a vicar or vicars; **vicā′riate**, delegated. —*n.* office, authority, time of office, or sphere of a vicar, in any sense.—*adj.* **vicā′rious**, filling the place of another: exercised, performed or suffered by one person or thing instead of another: (loosely) not experienced personally but imagined through the experience of others.— *adv.* **vicā′riously**.—*ns.* **vicā′riousness**; **vic′arship**, the (time of) office of a vicar; **vic′ary** (*obs.*), a vicarship.—**vic′ar-apostol′ic**, formerly one to whom the pope delegated some remote portion of his jurisdiction: now usu. a titular bishop appointed to a country where there are no sees: one exercising authority in a vacant see or during the bishop's incapacity; **vic′ar-chō′ral**, a cleric or layman who sings in an English cathedral choir; **vic′ar-forane** (*for-ān′*, a form of foreign), a rural dean; **vic′ar-gen′eral**, an official performing the work of an arch-deacon under the bishop (*R.C.*): a lay official representing the bishop, the chancellor of the diocese; **vicarious sacrifice**, the suffering and death of Christ held by orthodox Christians to be accepted by God in lieu of the punishment to which guilty man is liable.—**Vicar of Bray**, one who turns his coat without difficulty to suit the times—from Simon Aleyn, vicar of *Bray* in Berks from 1540 to 1588; **Vicar of Christ** (*R.C.*),

the pope, as representative of Christ on earth. [L. *vicārius*, substituted; see vice-.]

**vice** (in U.S. vise), *vīs*, *n.* a screw (*obs.*): a winding stair or its newel: a tool for gripping an object that is being worked on: a grip (*Shak.*).— *v.t.* to grip, force, jam, strain, as with a vice. [Fr. *vis*, screw—L. *vitis*, a vine.]

**vice**, *vīs*, *n.* a blemish or fault: immorality: depravity: an immoral habit: a bad trick or habit as in a horse: (*cap.*) the personification of a vice in a morality play, usually a farcical part: hence, a buffoon.—*adj.* **vicious** (*vish′əs*), addicted to vice or bad habits: immoral: depraved: bad: faulty: malignant, spiteful: ill-tempered: foul, impure, morbid: impaired, nullified by a flaw: mistaken (*Shak.*).—*adv.* **vic′iously**.—*n.* **vic′iousness**.—**vice squad**, a police squad whose task is to see that the laws dealing with gambling, prostitution, etc., are observed; **vicious circle**, reasoning in a circle, seeking to prove a proposition by means of a conclusion drawn from it: a process in which an evil is aggravated by its own consequences; **vicious intromission** (see under intromit). [Fr.,— L. *vitium*, a blemish; L.L. *viciōsus* for L. *vitiōsus*, faulty, vicious.]

**vice**, *vī′si*, *vī′sē*, *vīs*, *prep.* in place of: in succession to.—**vice versa**, *vûr′sə*, the other way round. [L. *vice*, abl. (nom. not used), turn, place, alteration.]

**vice-**, *vīs-*, in composition, in place of.—*n.* **vice**, place, stead (*rare*): short for **vice-president**, **vice-chancellor**, or the like.—**vice′-ad′miral**, a navy officer ranking next under an admiral; **vice′-ad′miralty**, the office or jurisdiction of a vice-admiral; **vice′-chair′man**, a deputy chairman: a croupier; **vice′-chair′manship**; **vice′-cham′ber-lain**, the Lord Chamberlain's deputy and assistant; **vice′-chan′cellor**, one acting for a chancellor; **vice′-chan′cellorship**; **vice′-con′sul**, a consul's deputy: one who acts as consul in a less important district; **vice′-con′sulate**; **vice′-con′sulship**; **vice′-count′y**, part of a county divided for floristic purposes; **vice′-dean**, a canon chosen to represent an absent dean; **vicegerency** (*-jer′* or *-jēr′ən-si*).—*adj.* **vicegerent** (*-jer′*, *-jēr′*; L. *vicem gerēns*, *-entis*, wielding office), acting in place of another, having delegated authority.—*n.* one ruling or acting in place of a superior.—**vice′-gov′ernor**, deputy governor; **vice′-king**, one who acts in place of a king; **vice′-mar′shal** (see **air-vice-marshal**); **vice′-pres′idency**; **vice′-pres′ident**, a president's deputy or assistant: an officer next below the president.—*adj.* **vice′-presiden′tial**.—**vice′-princ′i-pal**, assistant principal; **vice′-queen**, a woman representing a queen: a viceroy's wife, vicereine. —*adj.* **vice-rē′gal**, of a viceroy.—**vicere′gent**, properly, a substitute for a regent: often blunderingly for vicegerent; **vicereine** (*vis′ren′*, *-rān′*), a viceroy's wife: a vice-queen (*rare*); **vice′roy**, a governor acting in the name of the sovereign; **vice′roy′alty**, **vice′royship**. [See the foregoing article.]

**vicenary**, *vis′i-nər-i*, *adj.* based on the number twenty. [L. *vicēnārius—vicēni*, twenty each— *vigintī*, twenty.]

**vicennial**, *vi-sen′yəl*, *adj.* lasting, or coming at the end of, twenty years. [L. *vicennium—viciēs*, twenty times, *annus*, a year.]

**Vichyite**, *vē′shē-it*, *vish′i-it*, *n.* an adherent of the French Government (1940-42) ruling unoccupied part of France from *Vichy*, and collaborating with the Germans.—Also *adj.*—*adj.* **vichyssois** (*vē-shē-swä*), of the Vichyite government:— *fem.* **vichyssoise** (*-swäz*).—*n.* **vichyssoise**, a cream soup usu. served chilled, with ingredients such as potatoes and leeks.—**Vichy (water)**, mineral water from Vichy springs, containing sodium bicarbonate, etc., or a natural or artificial water resembling it. [*Vichy*, city in central France.]

**vicinage**, *vis'i-nij*, *n.* neighbourhood.—*adj.* **vic'-inal** (or *-in'əl*), neighbouring: local: having substituted groups on adjacent carbon atoms (*org. chem.*): of crystal faces, very nearly in the plane of a normal face.—*n.* **vicin'ity**, neighbourhood: nearness. [L. *vicinus*, neighbour—*vicus*, street, village, district.]

**viciosity.** See **vitiosity** under **vitiate**.

**vicious.** See under **vice** (2).

**vicissitude**, *vi-sis'i-tūd*, *n.* change: alternation: mutation: change of fortune.—*adj.* **vicissitū'din-ous.** [L. *vicissitūdō, -inis*; see **vice** (3).]

**victim**, *vik'tim*, *n.* a living being offered as a sacrifice: one subjected to death, suffering, or ill-treatment: a prey: a sufferer.—*n.* **victimisā'-tiọn, -z-.**—*v.t.* **vic'timise, -ize,** make a victim of: to treat oppressively in revenge: to cheat. —*n.* **vic'timiser, -z-.** [L. *victima*, a beast for sacrifice.]

**victor**, *vik'tər*, *n.* a winner in contest:—*fem.* **vic'toress, vic'tress, vic'trix.**—*adjs.* **vic'tor, victo'rious,** having gained a victory: winning in contest: of, with, marking victory.—*adv.* **victo'riously**—*ns.* **victo'riousness; victory** (*vik'-tər-i*), a contest gained: success against an opponent: (*cap.*) the Greek goddess Nikē.—*adj.* **vic'toryless**—**victory ship,** a successor to the liberty ship. [L. *victor, -ōris*—*vincĕre, victum,* to conquer.]

**Victoria**, *vik-tō'ri-ə, -tö', n.* a Brazilian genus of gigantic water-lilies: a low, light, four-wheeled carriage with a folding hood: a large red plum (**Victoria plum**).—*adj.* **Victo'rian,** of, contemporary with, typical of, the reign (1837-1901) of Queen Victoria: strict but somewhat conventional in morals, inclining to prudery and solemnity: of the state (colony 1851-1901) of Victoria in Australia.—*n.* a contemporary of Queen Victoria: a person of Victorian morality or outlook: a native or inhabitant of Victoria. —*n.pl.* **Victoriana** (*vik-tō-ri-ä'na, -tö', or -ā'na*), bric-à-brac and other characteristic possessions or creations of the Victorian age.—*n.* **Victō'rianism.**—**Victoria Cross,** a bronze Maltese cross, a decoration for conspicuous bravery on the field, founded by Queen Victoria (1856); **Victoria Day,** Empire Day, a holiday on or near Queen Victoria's birthday (24th May).

**victorine**, *vik-tə-rēn', n.* a fur tippet with long ends: a variety of peach. [Woman's name.]

**victress, victrix.** See **victor.**

**victual**, *vit'l, n.* (commonly in *pl.*) food, esp. human food: grain crops, cut or ready for cutting (*Scot.,* in *sing.*).—*v.t.* to supply or store with provision.—*v.i.* to lay in victuals: to feed: —*pr.p.* **victualling** (*vit'l-ing*); *pa.t.* and *pa.p.* **victualled** (*vit'ld*).—*ns.* **vict'uallage,** provisions; **victualler** (*vit'l-ər*), a purveyor of provisions: a victualling ship.—*adj.* **vict'ualless.**—**vict'ualling-bill',** a customs document warranting the captain of an outward-bound vessel to ship bonded stores for the voyage; **vict'ualling-off'ice, -ship,** an office supplying, a ship conveying, provisions to the navy; **vict'ualling-yard',** a public establishment for the collection and supply of provisions to the navy.—**licensed victualler,** an innkeeper licensed to sell spirits, wines, etc. [O.Fr. *vitaille*—L.L. *victuālia*—L. *victuālis,* relating to living—*vivĕre, victum,* to live.]

**vicuña**, *vi-kōō'nyə, n.* a wild species of the llama genus: cloth of its wool, or an imitation. [Sp., from Quechua.]

**vidame**, *vē-däm', n.* in French feudal jurisprudence, the deputy of a bishop in temporal affairs: a minor noble. [Fr.,—L.L. *vicedominus.*]

**vide**, *vī'dē, vē', wē'dā,* L. see.—**vide infra** (*in'frə, ēn'-frä*), see below; **vide supra** (*sū'prə, sōō'prä*), see above.

**videlicet**, *vi-del'i-sit, vi-, wi-dā'li-ket,* L. to wit, namely; usu. shortened to **viz.**

**videndum**, *vi-den'dam, vi-, wi-den'dōōm* (*pl.* **videnda**, *-də, -da*), L. thing(s) to be seen

**video**, *vid'i-ō, n.* (*U.S.*), television.—*adj.* pertaining to the bandwidth and spectrum position of the signal arising from TV scanning, or to the signal, or to the resultant image, or to television. —**video frequency,** that in the range required for a video signal; **vid'eophone, TN** for a telephone with accompanying means of transmitting a picture of each speaker; **video signal,** that part of a TV signal which conveys all the information required for establishing the visual image; **video (tape) recording,** recording both television picture and sound on magnetic tape (**videotape**) so that the programme can be rebroadcast; **video tube,** a television tube. [L. *vidēre,* to see.]

**vidette,** a faulty form of **vedette.**

**Vidicon**, *vid'i-kon, n.* a camera tube operating on the photoconducting principle. [Trademark; *video icon*(oscope).]

**vidimus**, *vī'di-məs* (L. *vē', wē'di-mōōs*), *n.* an attested copy: an inspection, as of accounts, etc. [L. *vidimus,* we have seen—*vidēre,* to see.]

**viduous**, *vid'ū-əs, adj.* widowed: empty.—*n.* **vid'ūage,** widowhood: widows collectively.— *adj.* **vid'ūal.**—*n.* **vidū'ity,** widowhood. [L. *vidua,* a widow, *viduus,* deprived, bereaved.]

**vie**, *vī, v.i.* to make a vie (*obs.*): to contend in rivalry.—*v.t.* to stake (*obs.*): to declare, bid (*obs.; cards*): to put forward in competition or emulation, (*Shak.*) or repeatedly (*Shak.*):— *pr.p.* **vy'ing**; *pa.t.* and *pa.p.* **vied,** *vid.*—*n.* (*obs.*) a bid, challenge, stake.—*adv.* **vy'ingly.** [Fr. *envier*—L. *invitāre,* to challenge, invite.]

**vielle**, *vē-el', n.* a hurdy-gurdy, lute played by a wheel. [Fr.]

**Viennese**, *vē-e-nēz', adj.* of Vienna.—*n. sing.* and *pl.* an inhabitant (*pl.* inhabitants) of Vienna.

**vi et armis,** *vī et är'mis, vē, wē et är'mēs,* L. by force of (lit. and) arms.

**Vietnamese**, *vē-et-nam-ēz', n.* a native or inhabitant, or the language, of Vietnam:—*pl.* as *sing.* —Also *adj.*

**vieux jeu,** *vyə zhə,* Fr. (lit. old game or joke), a subject that has lost all novelty.

**view**, *vū, n.* an act, possibility or opportunity of looking: range or field of sight: whole extent seen: a prospect, wide or distant extent seen: that which is seen: inspection: appearance: aspect: the picture of a scene: general survey of a subject: mode of thinking of something: opinion: intention, purpose: expectation.—*v.t.* to see: to look at: to look at on television: to observe: to consider: to examine intellectually.—*adj.* **view'able,** able to be seen: sufficiently interesting to be looked at or watched.—*ns.* **view'er,** one who views: an inspector: one appointed to examine and report: a colliery superintendent: a television watcher: an apparatus used to project film for purposes of editing and cutting: device with magnifying lens, etc., for viewing transparencies; **view'iness,** character of being viewy; **view'ing.**—*adj.* **view'less,** invisible.—*adv.* **view'lessly.**—*adjs.* **view'ly** (*dial.*), pleasing to look at; **view'y** (*coll.*), holding or expressing opinions vague or purely speculative: inclined to attach undue importance to certain aspects or views: one-sided: cranky.—**view'-finder,** a camera attachment or part for determining the field of view; **view'-halloo',** the huntsman's cry when the fox breaks cover; **view'point,** point of view: standpoint: a selected position for admiring scenery.—**dissolving views,** pictures thrown on a screen and made to pass into one another; **in view,** in sight: in mind: as an aim or prospect; **in view of,** in a position to see or to be seen by: having regard to; **on**

view, open to general inspection: **take a dim view of**, to regard unfavourably; **view away**, to see breaking cover; **with a view to**, having in mind: with a design of. [Fr. *vue—vu*, pa.p. of *voir*—L. *vidēre*, to see.]

**vifda**, *vif'dä*, *n.* See vivda.

**vigesimal**, *vi-jes'i-məl*, *adj.* based on the number twenty.—*adj.* **viges'imo-quar'to**, twenty-four-mo. [L. *vigēsimus* (*vicēsimus*), twentieth—*vīginti*, twenty.]

**vigia**, *vi-jē'ə* (Sp. *vi-hhē'ä*), *n.* a danger warning on a chart. [Sp. *vigia*, look-out—L. *vigilia*.]

**vigil**, *vij'il*, *n.* watching, esp. by night, esp. for religious exercises: the eve of a holy day: a religious service by night: a keeping awake, wakefulness.—*n.* **vig'ilance**, watchfulness: wakefulness: a guard, watch (*Milt.*): a planned effort to uncover and punish corruption and bribery (*India*).—*adj.* **vig'ilant**, watchful.—*n.* **vigilante** (*-an'tä*; originally, *U.S.* from Sp.), a member of an organisation to look after the interests, threatened in some way, of a group: a member of a vigilance committee.—*adv.* **vig'ilantly**.—**vigilance committee** (*U.S.*), an unauthorised body which, in the absence or inefficiency of regular government, exercises powers of arrest, punishment, etc.: any self-appointed association for the compulsory improvement of local morals according to its own standards. [L. *vigilia—vigil*, awake, watchful; cf. *vigēre*, to be lively.]

**vigneron**, *vēn-yə-rõ*, *n.* a vine-grower. [Fr.]

**vignette**, *vēn-yet'*, *n.* orig. a design of vine-leaves and tendrils: a small embellishment without a border, in what would have been a blank space, esp. on a title-page or as a headpiece or tail-piece: a photographic portrait shading off around the head: a character sketch, a word-picture.— *v.t.* to make a vignette of.— *ns.* **vignett'er**; **vignett'ist**. [Fr.,—*vigne*—L. *vinea*, a vine, a vineyard.]

**vigour**, *vig'ər*, *n.* active strength: vital power: forcefulness: activity: energy.—*adj.* **vig'orous**. —*adv.* **vig'orously**.—*n.* **vig'orousness**. [A.Fr. *vigour* (Fr. *vigueur*), and L. *vigor*, *-ōris*—*vigēre*, to be strong.]

**vihara**, *vē-hä'ru*, *n.* a Buddhist or Jain precinct, temple, or monastery. [Sans. *vihāra*.]

**viking**, *vī'king*, *n.* a Scandinavian pirate (8th-10th cent.).—*n.* **vi'kingism**. [O.N. *vikingr*, prob.—O.E. *wīcing*, pirate.]

**vilayet**, *vil-ä'yet*, *n.* a Turkish province. [Turk. *vilāyet*—Ar. *welāyeh*.]

**vild, vilde**, *vild*, *adj.* an old variant (*Spens., Shak.*) of vile.—*adv.* **vild'ly**.—*n.* **vild'ness**.

**vile**, *vil*, *adj.* worthless: mean: paltry: base: detestable: loathsome: foul: depraved: very bad.—*adv.* (*Shak., Spens.*) vilely.—*adv.* **vile'ly**. —*ns.* **vile'ness**; **vilifica'tion** (*vil-*), act of vilifying: defamatory speech: abuse; **vilifier** (*vil'*).—*v.t.* **vilify** (*vil'*), to make vile: to disparage: to defame:—*pr.p.* **vil'ifying**; *pa.t.* and *pa.p.* **vil'ified**. —*v.t.* **vilipend** (*vil'*; L. *vilipendēre*—*pendēre*, to weigh), to despise, make light of: to disparage: to slander, vilify.—*v.i.* to use vilification. [O.Fr. *vil* and L. *vilis*, worthless.]

**vill**, *vil*, *n.* a township, or feudal territorial unit (*hist.*): a manor (*hist.*): a village (*poet.*).—*ns.* **vill'a**, orig., a country house or farmhouse with subsidiary buildings: a country seat, in Italy often a castle: a detached house of some size: a superior middle-class dwelling-house; **vill'a-dom**, villas collectively: the villa-dwelling world. —*adjs.* **vill'ar**, of a vill; **villatic** (*-at'ik*; *Milt.*), farmyard: village. [L. *villa*, a country house, partly through O.Fr. *ville*, farm, village, etc. (Fr., town), and It. *villa*, country house.]

**villa**. See vill.

**village**, *vil'ij*, *n.* a manor, a parish, or an outlying part of a parish: an assemblage of houses

smaller than a town: a small municipality (*U.S.*): the people of a village.—*adj.* of, dwelling in, a village.—*ns.* **vill'ager**, an inhabitant of a village; **villagery** (*vil'ij-ri*; *Shak.* villagree), villages collectively or perh. village people.— **village cart** (see cart). [Fr. *village*, L. *villāticus*.]

**villagio**. See villiago.

**villain**, *vil'ən*, *n.* a villein (*orig.*): a violent, malevolent or unscrupulous evil-doer: playfully, a wretch: the wicked enemy of the hero or heroine in a story or play.—*adj.* low-born: base: villainous.—*ns.* **vill'ainage**, vill'anage, villeinage; **villainess**, a she-villain.—*adj.* **vill'ainous** (or **vill'anous**), of the nature of, like, or suited to a villain: detestable, vile.—*adv.* (*Shak.*) villainously.—*adv.* **vill'ainously** (vill'anously).—*ns.* **vill'ainy** (vill'any), the act (*obs.* the words) of a villain: extreme wickedness: an atrocious crime: disgrace (*obs.*); **vill'an**, a villein. [O.Fr. *villain*—L.L. *villānus*—L. *villa*, a country house.]

**villanelle**, *vil-ə-nel'*, *n.* a poem, on two rhymes, in five tercets and a quatrain, the first line repeated as sixth, twelfth, and eighteenth, the third as ninth, fifteenth, and last. [Fr.,—It. *villanella—villano*, rustic.]

**villanous(ly)**. See under villain.

**Villanovan**, *vil-ə-nō'vən*, *adj.* of an early Iron Age culture of which remains occur at *Villanova*, near Bologna.

**villany**. See under villain.

**villar, villatic**. See vill.

**villeggiatura**, *vi-lej-ə-tōō'ra*, *n.* country retirement or holiday. [It.]

**villein**, *vil'ən*, *-in*, (*hist.*) *n.* orig. app. a free villager: later (13th cent.) a serf, free in relation to all but his lord, and not absolutely a slave: developing later into a copyholder.—*n.* **vill'e(i)nage**, a villein's tenure or status. [A.Fr.; cf. villain.]

**villenage**. See under villein.

**villi**. See villus.

**villiago**, *vil-yä'gõ*, (*Shak.*) *n.* coward.—Also vilia'co (*Scott* villagio). [It. *vigliacco*—L. *vilis*, worthless.]

**villication**, *vil-i-kā'shən*, (*Smollett*) *n.* app. intended as a Scots pronunciation of vellication.

**villus**, *vil'əs*, *n.* a long soft hair: a hair-like process:—*pl.* **vill'i** (*-ī*).—*adjs.* **vill'iform**, having the form of villi; **vill'ose**, **vill'ous**, covered with or formed of villi: like the pile of velvet.—*n.* **villos'ity**. [L. *villus*, wool.]

**vim**, *vim*, (*slang*) *n.* energy, vigour. [App. L. *vim*, accus. of *vis*, force.]

**vimana**, *vi-män'ə*, *n.* the central shrine of an Indian temple with pyramidal roof: a temple gate: an aeroplane. [Sans. *vimāna*, lit. a marking out.]

**vimineous**, *vim-in'i-əs*, *adj.* with long flexible shoots. [L. *vīmineus—vīmen, -inis*, osier, switch.]

**vin**, *vē*, (Fr.) wine.—**vin blanc** (*blā*), white wine; **vin ordinaire** (*ōr-dēn-er*), inexpensive table wine for ordinary use; **vin rosé**, rosé (q.v.).—**les grands vins**, wines from famous vineyards.

**vina**, *vē'nə*, *n.* an Indian stringed instrument with fretted finger-board over two gourds. [Sans. *vīnā*.]

**vinaceous**. See under vine.

**vinaigrette**, *vin-ā-gret'*, *n.* a box or bottle for aromatic vinegar or smelling-salts: a mixture of oil, vinegar and seasoning used as a salad dressing. [Fr.,—*vinaigre*, vinegar.]

**vinal, Vinalia**. See under vine.

**vinasse**, *vi-nas'*, *n.* residue in alcoholic distillation, esp. in beet-sugar-making, a source of potash salts. [Fr.]

**Vinca**, *ving'ka*, *n.* the periwinkle genus. [L. *vinca-pervinca*.]

**Vincentian**, *vin-sen'shən*, *-shyən*, *adj.* pertaining to St *Vincent* de Paul (1576-1660) or to the charitable associations founded by him, or to St Vincent of Lérins (d. 450), or other Vincent.

**vincible**, *vin′si-bl*, *adj.* that may be overcome.—*n.*
**vincibil′ity**. [L. *vincibilis*—*vincĕre, victum,* to conquer.]

**vinculum**, *ving′kū-ləm*, *n.* a bond: a horizontal line placed above, equivalent to brackets (*math.*): a tendinous band (*anat.*):—*pl.* **vinc′ula**. [L., *vincire,* to bind.]

**vindemial**, *vin-dē′mi-əl*, *adj.* pertaining to the vintage.—*v.i.* **vindē′miate**, to gather grapes, or other fruit. [L. *vīndēmia,* vintage; see **vintage**.]

**vindicate**, *vin′di-kāt, v.t.* to justify: to clear from criticism, etc.: to defend with success: to make good a claim to: to lay claim to: to maintain: to avenge (*obs.*): to free (*obs.*).—*n.* **vindicability** (*-kə-bil′i-ti*).—*adj.* **vin′dicable**.—*n.* **vindicā′tion**, act of vindicating: defence: justification: support.—*adj.* **vin′dicātive** (or *vin-dik′ə-tiv*), vindicating: tending to vindicate: revengeful, vindictive (*Shak.*).—*ns.* **vindic′ativeness**, vindictiveness; **vin′dicātor**, one who vindicates:—*fem.* **vin′dicātress.**—*adv.* **vin′dicatorily.**—*adjs.* **vin′dicatory** (*-ə-tər-i,* or *-ā-tər-i*), serving or tending to vindicate: punitive: retributive: avenging: **vindic′tive**, revengeful: pursuing revenge: punitive (as in *vindictive damages*): retributive (as in *vindictive justice*).—*adv.* **vindic′tively.**—*n.* **vindic′tiveness**. [L. *vindicāre, -ātum.*]

**vine**, *vīn, n.* a woody climbing plant (*Vitis vinifera* or other of the genus) that produces grapes: a climbing or trailing stem or (*U.S.*) plant (*hort.*).—*v.t.* to remove vines from, e.g., vines and pods from (peas).—*adjs.* **vinā′ceous**, wine-coloured; **vin′al**, of, due to, wine.—*n.pl.* **Vinā′lia** (L. *vē-nä′li-a*), a Roman wine festival celebrated on 23rd April, when last year's vintage was tasted and offered to Jupiter: also a vintage festival, 19th August.—*ns.* **vi′ner**, a vine-grower; **vinery** (*vīn′ə-ri*), a hot-house for rearing vines; **viniculture** (*vīn′, vin′*), cultivation of the vine, esp. for wine-making; **vin′iculturist.**—*adj.* **vin′olent**, addicted to wine.—*ns.* **vinol′ogist/ vinol′ogy**, scientific study of vines, esp. grape-vine; **vinos′ity**, vinous character: characteristic qualities of a particular wine: addiction to wine.—*adjs.* **vi′nous**, pertaining to wine: like wine: wine-coloured: caused by or indicative of wine; **vi′ny**, pertaining to, like, consisting of, or bearing vines: entwining.—**vine′-branch**, a branch of a vine: a centurion's badge.—*adj.* **vine′-clad**, covered with vines.—**vine′-disease**, a disease affecting the vine; **vine′-dresser**, one who trims and cultivates vines; **vine′-fretter**, a small insect that infests vines, esp. Phylloxera or other greenfly; **vine′-gall**, a gall on a vine, esp. one made by a weevil; **vine′-leaf**, the leaf of a vine; **vine′-mildew**, a disease of vines due to the oidium stage of a mildew fungus, Uncinula; **vine′-prop**, a support for a vine; **vine′-rod**, a Roman centurion's badge; **vine′-stock**, the stock on which a vine of another kind is grafted; **vineyard** (*vin′yərd, -yärd*), a plantation of vines.—**dwell under one's vine and fig-tree**, to live at peace on one's own land. [O.Fr. *vine, vigne*—L. *vinea*, a vineyard, a vine—*vinum*, wine; Gr. *oinos,* wine.]

**vinegar**, *vin′i-gər, n.* a condiment and pickling medium, a dilute impure acetic acid, made from beer, weak wine, etc.—*v.t.* to apply vinegar to.—*n.* **vinegarrette′**, a vinaigrette.—*adjs.* **vin′egar-ish**, sourish; **vin′egary**, like or flavoured with vinegar: sour (also *fig.*).—**vin′egar-eel′**, a minute threadworm that breeds in vinegar; **vin′egar-fly′**, a fruit-fly; **vin′egar-plant′**, a bacterium causing acetic fermentation. [Fr. *vinaigre*—*vin* (L. *vinum*), wine, *aigre,* sour (L. *ācer,* keen, sharp, pungent).]

**vinew**, *vin′ū, v.t.* and *v.i.* to make or become mouldy.—*n.* **mouldiness.**—*adj.* **vin′ewed**, mouldy:

musty. [O.E. *fynegian,* to mould—*fynig,* mouldy —*fyne,* mould.]

**vingt-et-un**, *vē-tā-ü̃, n.* a card game, its object to have a total of pips in one's hand nearest to, but not exceeding, twenty-one.—Also **vingt-un** (*vē-tü̃*). [Fr. *vingt-et-un,* twenty-one.]

**viniculture, -turist.** See **vine.**
**vinolent, vinologist, etc.** See **vine.**

**vint**, *vint, n.* a card game like contract bridge. [Russ.]

**vintage**, *vint′ij, n.* the gathering of grapes and preparation for wine-making: a season's yield of grapes or wine: the time of gathering grapes: wine, esp. of a good year: the product of a particular period: a period of origin.—*adj.* pertaining to the grape vintage: of wine, of a specified year and of good quality: generally, e.g. of a play by an author or of a period, among the best and most characteristic: out of date and no longer admired.—*v.t.* to strip of grapes: to gather (grapes): to make (wine)—esp. of a good year.—*n.* and *v.t.* **vint** (back-formation from **vintage**).—*ns.* **vint′ager**, a worker at the vintage; **vint′aging.—vintage car**, an old fashioned (specif. built between 1916 and 1930) car; **vintage year**, one in which a particular product (usu. wine) reaches an exceptionally high standard. [A.Fr.r. *vintage,* O.Fr. (Fr.) *vendange*—L. *vīndēmia*—*vinum,* wine, grapes, *dēmĕre,* to remove—*dē,* out of or away, *emĕre,* to take; modified by influence of **vintner.**]

**vintner**, *vint′nər, n.* a wine-seller.—*n.* **vint′ry**, a wine-store: a wine-shop. [O.Fr. *vinetier*—L.L. *vinetārius*—L. *vinum,* wine.]

**vinyl**, *vin′il, n.* an organic radical $CH_2CH—$.—*ns.* **vinylidene** (*vin-il′i-dēn*), the bivalent radical $CH_2: C =$ ; **Vinylite** (*vin′il-īt*), proprietary name for a series of vinyl resins.—**vinyl resins**, plastics, thermoplastic resins, polymers or co-polymers of vinyl compounds, e.g. co-polymers of vinyl chloride, $CH_2CHCl$, and vinyl acetate, $CH_3COOCH:CH_2$.

**viol**, *vi′əl, n.* any member of a class of instruments, precursors of the violin class, represented now by the double-bass.—*ns.* **viola** (*vi-ō′lə*), a tenor fiddle, slightly bigger than the violin, tuned a fifth lower; **violer** (*vi′ə-lər*), a viol player: a fiddler; **violin** (*vi-ə-lin′,* or *vi′*), a musical instrument with four strings (E, A, D, G) played with a bow: a violinist; **vi′olinist**, a player on the violin; **violist** (*vi′-əl-ist*), a player on the viol: (*vē-ō′list*), a player on the viola; **violoncellist** (*vē-, vi-ə-lən-chel′ist*), a 'cello-player; **violoncell′o**, a bass instrument of the violin class, commonly called 'cello; **violone** (*vē-ō-lō′nä*), a bass viol, bigger than the viola da gamba—an earlier version of the present double-bass.—**vi′ol-degam′boys** (*Shak.*), the viola da gamba; **violin′-bow**; **violin′-string.—viola da braccio** (*dä brät′chō*; It.), viol for the arm), a tenor viol, held along the arm; **viola da gamba** (*gäm′ba*; It., viol for the leg), a bass viol, resembling the 'cello; **viola d'amore** (*dä-mō′rä*; It., of love), a tenor viol with sympathetic strings under the finger-board; **viola da spalla** (*späl′la*; It., for the shoulder), a bigger form of tenor viol. [Partly **vielle**; partly Fr. *viole* and It. *viola,* dim. *violino,* augmentative *violone,* and its dim. *violoncello*; origin doubtful; cf. L.L. *vitula,* and **fiddle.**]

**viola.** See **viol.**

**Viola**, *vi′ə-lə, n.* the violet and pansy genus of plants, giving name to the family **Violā′ceae,** with spurred zygomorphic flowers.—*adj.* **violā′ceous**, of the Violaceae: violet-coloured. [L. *vīŏla.*]

**violate**, *vi′ə-lāt, v.t.* to do violence to: to fail to observe duly: to abuse: to ravish: to profane.—*adj.* **violated**: defiled.—*adj.* **vi′olable,** that may be violated.—*adv.* **vi′olably.**—*n.* **violā′tion**.

—*adj.* vi'olātive, causing, tending to, or involving violation.—*n.* vi'olātor. [L. *violāre, -ātum* —*vīs,* strength.]

**viold,** (*Milt.*) for **vialled.**

**violent,** *vī'ə-lənt, adj.* intensely forcible: impetuous and unrestrained in action: overmasteringly vehement: due to violence: wrested: expressing violence.—*v.t.* (*obs.*) to force.—*v.i.* (*Shak.*) to rage.—*n.* vi'olence, the state or quality of being violent: excessive, unrestrained, or unjustifiable force: outrage: profanation: injury: rape.—*adv.* vi'olently. [L. *violentus* or *violēns, -entis—vīs.*]

**violet,** *vī'ə-lit, n.* any plant or flower of the genus Viola: extended to unrelated plants, as **dame's violet, water-violet** (see **dame, water**): a bluish purple.—*adj.* bluish purple. [Fr. *violette*—L. *viola.*]

**violin, violist, violoncello,** etc. See **viol.**

**V.I.P.** Abbrev. for **very important person.**

**viper,** *vī'pər, n.* the adder: any member of its genus (**Vi'pera**) or family (**Viperidae,** *vī-per'i-dē*): extended to some other snakes, as the pit-vipers, horned vipers: an ungrateful or treacherous, malignant person (*fig.*).—*adjs.* **viperiform** (*-per'*); **vi'perine** (*-pər-īn*), related to or resembling the viper; **vi'perish,** venomous: spiteful: like a viper; **vi'perous,** having the qualities of a viper: venomous: malignant.—*adv.* **vi'perously.** — **viper's bugloss,** a stiff bristly boraginaceous plant (Echium) of dry places with intensely blue flowers, once thought a remedy or prophylactic for snake-bite; **viper's grass,** black salsify. [L. *vipera—vīvus,* living, *parěre,* to bring forth.]

**virago,** *vi-rä'gō, vi-rä'gō, n.* a heroic or manlike woman: an amazon: a scold: a termagant.—*adjs.* **viraginian** (*vi-rə-jin'i-ən*), **viraginous** (*vi-raj'*), **vira'goish.** [L. *virāgō, -inis—vir,* a man.]

**viral.** See **virus.**

**viranda, virando,** obs. forms of **veranda(h).**

**virelay,** *vir'ə-lā, n.* an old French lyric form in two-rhymed stanzas of short lines, linked by recurrent lines. [Fr. *virelai,* app. from meaningless refrain *vireli,* but associated with *virer,* turn, *lai,* a song.]

**virement,** *vē-rə-mä, n.* authorised transference of a surplus to balance a deficit under another head. [Fr.]

**virent,** *vir'ənt, adj.* verdant: fresh: green.—*n.* **virescence** (*vir-, vir-es'əns*).—*adj.* **viresc'ent,** turning green: inclining to green: fresh: green: abnormally green. [L. *virēns, -entis,* pr.p. of *virēre,* to be green; *virēscēns,* pr.p. of *virēscěre,* to become green.]

**Vireo,** *vir'i-ō, n.* a genus of American singing birds, the greenlets, giving name to the family **Vireonidae** (*-on'i-dē*). [L. *vireō, -ōnis,* perh. **greenfinch.**]

**viretot,** *vir'i-tot,* (Scott after *Chaucer*) *n.* rush, dash, gad. [Origin obscure.]

**virga,** *vûr'gə, n.* trails of water, drops, or ice particles coming from a cloud but not reaching the ground as precipitation. [L., a twig, streak in the sky.]

**virgate,** *vûr'gāt, adj.* rodlike: twiggy.—*n.* an old land measure, commonly 30 acres. [L. *virga,* rod.]

**virge,** *vûrj, n.* obs. Latinised spelling of **verge** (1). —*n.* **virg'er** (*obs.* except in St Paul's Cathedral), **verger.**

**Virgilian, Vergilian,** *vər-jil'i-ən, adj.* of, in the manner of, *Virgil* (*Vergilius*), the Roman poet (70-19 B.C.).

**virgin,** *vûr'jin, n.* a maiden: one (esp. a woman) who has had no sexual intercourse: a madonna, a figure of the Virgin: Virgo, a sign, and a constellation, of the zodiac.—*adj.* in a state of virginity: of a virgin: maidenly: pure: chaste: undefiled: in the original condition—unattained, untouched, unexploited, never scaled, felled,

captured, wrought, used, etc.—*v.t.* (with *it*; *Shak.*) to continue chaste.—*adj.* **vir'ginal,** of or appropriate to a virgin or virginity: in a state of virginity: like a virgin: parthenogenetic.—*adv.* **vir'ginally.** — *ns.* **vir'ginhood, virgin'ity,** state or fact of being a virgin.—*adj.* **vir'ginly,** pure.—*adv.* **chastely.**—*n.* **Vir'gō,** the Virgin, in the zodiac.—*adj.* **virg'in-born,** born of a virgin.— **virgin gold,** gold in the condition in which it is found; **virgin knot,** the fastening of a Greek or Roman woman's girdle, loosed at marriage; **vir'gin's-bow'er,** traveller's-joy (*Clematis vitalba*). —**the (Blessed) Virgin,** Mary the mother of Christ; **the Virgin Queen,** Elizabeth I of England. [Partly through Fr.,—L. *virgō, -inis.*]

**virginal,** *vûr'jin-əl, n.* (often in *pl.,* also *pair of virginals*) an old keyboard instrument, a spinet, esp. a box-shaped spinet.—*v.i.* (*Shak.*) to finger, as on a virginal. [Perh. as played by young ladies; see above.]

**virginal.** See **virgin.**

**Virginia,** *vər-jin'yə, n.* a tobacco grown and manufactured in *Virginia.*—*adj.* **Virgin'ian.**—*n.* a native or citizen of Virginia.—*n.* **virgin'ium** (*chem.*), a name proposed for the element of atomic number 87 (see **francium**).—**Virginia creeper,** an American climbing-plant near akin to the vine, bright red in autumn; **Virginia stock** (see **stock**). [After Elizabeth, the *virgin* queen.]

**virgule,** *vûr'gūl, n.* a slanting line, an old form of comma. [Fr.,—L. *virgula,* dim. of *virga,* a twig.]

**viricide.** See **virus.**

**virid,** *vir'id, adj.* green.—*n.* **viridesc'ence.**—*adj.* **viridesc'ent,** greenish.—*ns.* **virid'ian,** a green pigment, hydrated chromium sesquioxide; **vir'idite,** an indeterminate green decomposition product in rocks; **virid'ity,** verdure: greenness. [L. *viridis,* green—*virēre,* to be green.]

**virile,** *vir'il,* sometimes *vir',* also *-il, adj.* having qualities of a mature male human being: robustly masculine: manly: of a man, sexually potent. —*n.* **virilescence** (*vir-il-es'əns*), development of male character in the female.—*adj.* **virilesc'ent.** —*ns.* **vir'ilism,** presence of male characteristics in the female; **viril'ity,** the state or quality of being a man: the power of a mature male: the power of procreation: manhood: masculinity: vigour, energy. [L. *virilis—vir,* a man; cf. O.E. *wer,* man, and **werwulf.**]

**virl, virl,** (now *Scot.*) *n.* Same as **ferrule.**

**virose,** etc. See under **virus.**

**virtu,** *vûr-tōō', n.* a love of the fine arts: taste for curiosities: objects of art or antiquity.—*adjs.* **virtuose** (*-tū-ōs'*), **virtuō'sic,** exhibiting the qualities of a virtuoso.—*ns.* **virtuosity** (*-os'*), the character of a virtuoso: exceptional technical skill in music or other fine art: interest in or knowledge of articles of virtu; **virtuoso** (*vir-tōō-ō'sō, vûr-tū-ō'sō, -zō*), one skilled or interested in works of art, antiquities, curiosities, and the like: a musician (or other artist) of the highest technical skill:—*pl.* **virtuō'sōs, virtuō'si** (*-sē*):— *fem.* **virtuō'sa,** *pl.* **virtuō'se** (*-sā*); **virtuō'sōship.** [It. *virtù*—L. *virtūs, -ūtis;* see next word.]

**virtual,** etc. See **virtue.**

**virtue,** *vûr'tū, n.* excellence: worth: moral excellence: the practice of duty: a good quality, esp. moral: an accomplishment (*rare*): valour (now *rare*): sexual purity: loosely, virginity: inherent power: efficacy: one of the orders of the celestial hierarchy.—*adj.* **vir'tual,** virtuous (*obs.*): having virtue or efficacy (*arch.*): in effect, though not in fact: not such in fact but capable of being considered as such for some purposes.—*ns.* **vir'tualism,** the doctrine of Christ's virtual presence in the eucharist; **vir'tualist; virtual'ity,** essential nature: potentiality. —*adv.* **vir'tually,** in effect, though not in fact:

loosely, almost, nearly.—*adjs.* vir′tueless; vir′-
tuous, having virtue: morally good: blameless:
righteous: practising duty: according to the
moral law: chaste.—*adv.* vir′tuously.—*n.* vir′-
tuousness.—virtual image (see image).—*adj.*
vir′tue-proof (*Milt.* vertue-), impregnable in
virtue.—by, in, virtue of, through the power,
force, or efficacy of: because of: on account
of; make a virtue of necessity, to do as if from
sense of duty (or with a sense of duty called in
for the occasion) something one must needs do;
seven principal virtues, faith, hope, charity,
justice, prudence, temperance, and fortitude—
the first three the *theological*, the last four the
*moral* virtues; the cardinal virtues (see cardinal).
[O.Fr. *vertu* and L. *virtus*, bravery, moral
excellence—*vir*, a man; cf. Gr. *hērōs*, Sans. *vīra*,
a hero, O.E. *wer*, man.]
virtuose, -osic, etc. See virtu.
virtute officii, vûr-tū′ti of-is′i-ī, vir-, wir-tōō-te
of-ik′i-ē, L. by virtue of office.
virulent, vir′ū-lənt, or -ōō-, *adj.* highly poisonous
or malignant: venomous: acrimonious.—*ns.*
vir′ulence, vir′ulency.—*adv.* vir′ulently. [L.
*virulentus—virus*, see virus.]
virus, vī′rəs, *n.* venom: contagious or poisonous
matter (as of ulcers, etc.): the transmitted cause
of infection: a pathogenic agent, a combination
of chemicals, but capable of increasing rapidly
inside a living cell: any corrupting influence.—
*adj.* vi′ral, pertaining to or caused by a virus.—
*ns.* vir′icide (or vir′), a substance that destroys
or eliminates a virus; virol′ogy, the study of
virus, viruses and virus diseases; virol′ogist.—
*adj.* vi′rose, poisonous: foul.—*n.* viro′sis, a
disease caused by a virus.—*adj.* vi′rous, virose.
—virus disease, a disease caused by a virus. [L.
*virus*, venom; Gr. *īos*, Sans. *viṣa*, poison.]
vis, vis, vēs, wēs, (L.) force, power.—vis comica
(kom′ik-ə, kōm′ik-a), comic power; vis inertiae
(in-ûr′shi-ē, in-ert′i-ī), the power of inertia:
passive resistance; vis major (mā′jər, mä′yor),
superior force; vis mortua (mör′tū-ə, mor′tōō-a),
force of pressure, dead force; vis viva (vī′və,
vē′va, wē′wa), living force, equal to the mass
of a moving body multiplied by the square of
its velocity.—vis a tergo (ā tûr′gō, ä ter′gō),
compulsion from behind.
visa, vē′za, visé, vē′zā, *ns.* an authenticating endorsement on a passport.—*vs.t.* to put a visa
on:—*pa.ts.* and *pa.ps.* vi′saed, vi′séed. [L. *vīsa*,
pa.p. fem. of *vidēre*, to see, and Fr. *visé*, pa.p.
masc. of *viser*, to examine.]
visage, viz′ij, *n.* the face.—*adj.* vis′aged.—*n.* vis-
agiste (vē-zazh-ēst), an expert in facial make-up.
[Fr. *visage*—L. *vīsus*, look.]
vis-à-vis, vē′za-vē, *adv.* face-to-face.—*prep.* face-
to-face with.—*n.* one who faces, or is opposite
to, another: a light carriage with seats facing
each other: an S-shaped couch: opposite number. [Fr. *vis*, face (—L. *vīsus*, look), à, to.]
viscacha, vis-kä′cha, *n.* a S. American burrowing
rodent of heavy build.—Also vizca′cha, bizca′-
cha.—*n.* viscachera (-chä′ra), a settlement of
viscachas. [Sp.,—Quechua *huiscacha*.]
viscera, visceral, viscerate, viscero-. See viscus.
viscid, vis′id, *adj.* semi-fluid, sticky, glutinous,
viscous: of a surface, clammy and covered with
a sticky secretion (*bot.*).—*ns.* viscid′ity; viscin
(vis′in), the sticky substance present in the fruits
of mistletoe. [L.L. *viscidus*—L. *viscum*; see
viscous.]
visco-, visco(si)meter, etc. See viscous.
viscose, vis′kōs, *n.* the sodium salt of cellulose
xanthate, used in the manufacture of viscose
rayon. [See viscous.]
viscount, vī′kownt, *n.* an officer who acted as
administrative deputy to an earl, a sheriff (*hist.*):
a title of nobility next below an earl (first granted
1440): the son or younger brother of a count:

—*fem.* viscountess (vī′kownt-es), the wife of a
viscount: a woman holding a viscounty in her
own right: a size of roofing slate, 18 × 10
inches (457 × 254 mm.).—*ns.* vi′scountcy, vi′-
scountship, a viscounty; vi′scounty, a viscount
(*obs.*): the jurisdiction of, or territory under,
a viscount (*hist.*): the rank or dignity of a
viscount. [O.Fr. *visconte* (Fr. *vicomte*)—*vis-* (L.
*vice*, in place of) *conte*, count, after L.L. *vice-
comes*—L. *comes*, a companion.]
viscous, vis′kəs, *adj.* resistant, or highly resistant,
to flow owing to forces acting between the molecules: tenacious: sticky: viscid.—*n.* vis′cous-
ness.—vis′co-, in composition, viscous, viscosity.
—*n.* viscom′eter, an instrument for measuring
viscosity. — *adjs.* viscomet′ric, -al. — *n.* viscom′-
etry.—Also viscosim′eter, viscosimet′ric, -al,
viscosim′etry.—*n.* viscos′ity.—viscous flow, a
type of fluid flow in which there is a continuous
steady motion of the particles, the motion at a
fixed point always remaining constant; viscous
water, water thickened by addition of chemicals,
used in fighting forest fires. [L.L. *viscōsus*,
sticky—L. *viscum*, bird-lime, mistletoe; cog.
with Gr. *ixos*, mistletoe.]
Viscum, vis′kəm, *n.* a genus of parasitic plants
including the common mistletoe: (without *cap.*)
bird-lime. [L.]
viscus, vis′kəs, (*med.*, *zool.*) *n.* any one of the abdomen—heart, lungs, liver, etc.:—*pl.* viscera
(vis′ər-ə; in common use, esp. the abdominal
organs).—*adj.* visc′eral.—*v.t.* visc′erate, to disembowel.—visc′ero-, in composition, of or pertaining to the viscera or to a viscus.—Also
visc′eri-.—*ns.* visceroptō′sis (Gr. *ptōsis*, a falling),
abnormally low position of the intestines in
the abdominal cavity; viscerotonia (-tōn′), a
pattern of temperament associated with the
endomorphic body type—extravert, sociable,
fond of bodily comforts.—*adj.* visceroton′ic. [L.
*viscus*, pl. *viscera*.]
vise, viz (*obs.*), *v.t.* to advise: to look at.—*v.i.* to
look (with *on*): to consider (with *on*). [Partly
advise; partly Fr. *viser*—L. *vidēre*, *vīsum*, to
see.]
vise. U.S. spelling of vice (1).
visé. See visa.
Vishnu, vish′nōō, *n.* the second god of the Hindu
triad; he became specially the benefactor of
man in his many *avatars* or incarnations. [Sans.]
visible, viz′i-bl, *adj.* that may be seen: in sight:
obvious: (of supplies of a commodity) actually
in store, known to be available: ready or willing
to receive a visitor or visitors.—*n.* a visible thing
(often in *pl.*).—*ns.* visibil′ity, state or quality of
being visible, or perceivable by the eye: clearness of the atmosphere: clarity and range of
vision in the atmospheric conditions, seeing: a
visible thing (usu. in *pl.*): a sight, show place
(*obs.*): appearance (*obs.*): power of seeing,
sight (*obs.*); vis′ibleness.—*adv.* vis′ibly.—Visible
Church, the body of professing Christians, as
opp. to the *Invisible Church*, which consists of
those spiritually minded persons who live up to
the ideals of the Church, together with the departed saints in heaven; visible exports, imports (see exports, imports); visible horizon (see
horizon); visible means, means or resources
which are apparent to or ascertainable by
others; visible speech, a system of phonetic
characters each of which suggests the configuration of the organs in producing the sound.
[Through O.Fr. or direct from L. *vīsibilis*—
*vidēre*; see vision.]
visie. See vision.
Visigoth, viz′i-goth, *n.* one of the Western Goths,
as distinguished from the Ostrogoths or Eastern
Goths; they formed settlements in the south
of France and in Spain, and their kingdom in

the latter lasted into the 8th century.—*adj.*
**Visigoth′ic.** [L.L. *Visigothī*—Gmc. word meaning perh. noble Goths, perh. west Goths.]
**visile,** *viz′il, -il, adj.* of or pertaining to sight: learning by means of visual images and recalling such images readily.—*n.* one whose imagery naturally takes a visual form. [Cn the analogy of **audile,** from L. *vidēre, vīsum,* to see.]
**visiogenic,** *viz-i-ō-jen′ik, adj.* suitable artistically for television transmission. [L. *vidēre, vīsum,* to see, and root of Gr. *gignesthai,* to be produced.]
**vision,** *vizh′ən, n.* the act of seeing: the faculty of sight: anything seen: television, esp. as opposed to sound radio: a look, glance: a vivid concept or mental picture: hence, a person or scene of great beauty (sometimes ironically): a pleasing imaginative plan for, or anticipation of, future events: an apparition: a revelation, esp. divine, in sleep or a trance (sometimes without article): act or power of perceiving imaginative mental images: imaginative perception: foresight: mystical awareness of the supernatural.—*v.t.* to see as a vision, to imagine: to present, or to call up, as in a vision.—*n.* (*Scot.*) visie (*viz′i*), a close or careful look: aim: a sight on the muzzle of a gun.—Also **viz′y, vizz′ie.**—*v.t.* and *v.i.* to look at, or look, closely: to aim.—Also **vizz′ie.**—*adj.* **vis′ional,** of, pertaining to, a vision: derived fiom a vision: visionary, not real: pertaining to sight.—*adv.* **vis′ionally.**—*n.* **vis′ionariness.**—*adj.* **vis′ionary,** capable of seeing visions: apt to see visions: given to reverie or fantasy: out of touch with reality, unpractical: of the nature of, or seen in, a vision, visional: fanciful, not real: impracticable: characterised by visions or fantasy: pertaining to physical or mental vision.—*n.* one who sees visions: one who forms impracticable schemes.—*adj.* **vis′-ioned,** inspired so as to see visions: seen in a vision: produced by, or associated with, a vision.—*ns.* **vis′ioner,** a visionary; **vis′ioning,** seeing visions; **vis′ionist,** one who professes to be a visionary: one who believes that the Biblical details of creation were revealed in vision.—*adj.* **vis′ionless,** destitute of vision.— **beatific vision** (see **beatify**). [Fr.,—L. *visiō, visiōnis—vidēre, vīsum,* to see; cf. Gr. *idein,* Eng. *wit.*]
**visit,** *viz′it, v.t.* (of God or a human being) to come to, or to go to see, in order to succour: to go to with intention of injuring: to go to see professionally: to pay a call upon, or to be in the habit of doing so: to go to stay with: to make a stay in, as migratory birds: to go to for sight-seeing, pleasure, or religious purposes: to examine, inspect, esp. officially: to punish (a person—with *with*; *arch.*): to punish as wrongdoing (*arch.*): (of an idea) to take temporary hold on the mind of: to afflict, trouble, as with disease (*arch.*).—*v.i.* to be in the habit of seeing or meeting each other at home: to make a visit or visits: to chat (*U.S.*).—*n.* act of visiting: a short stay: a sight-seeing excursion: an official or a professional call: a place one visits (*Cowper*): a chat (*U.S.*).—*adjs.* **vis′itable,** subject to official visitation: attractive to visitors; **vis′itant,** paying visits, visiting.—*n.* one who visits: one who is a guest in the house of another: a supernatural visitor: a migratory bird: (*cap.*) one of an order of nuns founded by St Francis de Sales in 1610, also called *Salesians, Order* (or *Nuns*) *of the Visitation.*—*n.* **visitā′tion,** act of visiting: a long and wearisome visit: a formal visit by a superior, esp. ecclesiastical: examination by authority: the act of a naval commander in boarding the vessel of another state to ascertain her character and object: a visit of a herald to a district for the examination of its arms, pedigrees, etc. (*hist.*):

a visit of God, or of a good (or evil) supernatural being: a dispensation of divine favour or displeasure: a sore affliction: the operation of a destructive power, or an instance of it: an influence acting on the mind: the object of a visit (*rare*): an unusual and extensive irruption of a species of animals into a region: (*cap.*) a festival to commemorate the visit of the Virgin Mary to Elizabeth, observed by the Roman and Greek Churches on 2nd July.—*adjs.* **visitā′-tional, vis′itātive.**—*n.* **vis′itātor,** an official visitor. —*adjs.* **visitato′rial, visito′rial.**—*ns.* **visitee′,** the person to whom a visit is paid; **vis′iting,** the act, or an instance, of paying a visit: a visitation, in the senses of divine dispensation, heavy affliction, or influence operating on the mind.—*adj.* that visits: often opp. to *resident*: pertaining to visiting.—*n.* **vis′itor** (now rarely **vis′iter**), one who visits, calls on, or makes a stay with a person: a person authorised to visit for purposes of inspection or supervision:—*fem.* **vis′itress.**—**vis′iting-book,** a book recording the names of persons who have called or are to be called on: a visitors' book (*Thackeray*); **vis′iting-card,** a small card bearing the name and address, or title, left in paying visits, and sometimes sent as an act of courtesy or in token of sympathy; **vis′iting-day,** a day on which one is at home and ready to receive callers; **visitor general** (*hist.*), a personal representative of the King of Spain appointed to investigate affairs, esp. in Spanish America; **visitors′ book,** a book in which visitors write their names and sometimes comments.— **visitation of the sick,** an office in the Anglican Church for use by clergy visiting the sick; **visit with** (*U.S.*), be a guest with: chat with. [Fr. *visiter*—L. *visitāre,* freq. of *visēre,* to go to see, visit—*vidēre,* to see.]
**visite,** *vi-zēt′, n.* a woman's light short cloak worn in mid-19th century. [Fr.]
**visive,** *viz′iv, (rare) adj.* of, pertaining to, sight, visual: able to see: able to be seen. [L.L. *visivus*—L. *vīsus,* sight.]
**visne,** *vē′ni, (law) n.* venue. [O.Fr. *visné,* neighbourhood—L. *vicinus,* neighbour.]
**visnomy,** *viz′nə-mi, (arch.* and *dial.) n.* physiognomy.—Also **vis′nomie.** [Variant of **physiognomy.**]
**vison,** *vī′sən, n.* the American mink. [Fr.; origin unknown.]
**visor,** *vīz′ər, n.* a part of a helmet covering the face, or the upper part of the face, movable, and perforated to allow of seeing and breathing: a mask: disguise, feigning appearance: face, aspect (*obs.*; *lit.* and *fig.*): a hood placed over a signal light: the peak of a cap: a movable flap on a motor-car windscreen, used as a shade against the sun.—Also **viz′or.**—*v.t.* to disguise, or cover with, a visor.—Also **viz′or.**—*adj.* **vis′ored, viz′ored,** having a visor: wearing a visor: masked.—**vis′or-mask,** a vizard-mask. [A.Fr. *viser* (Fr. *visière*)—*vis,* countenance.]
**vista,** *vis′tə, n.* a view or prospect through, or as through, an avenue: an avenue or other long narrow opening or passage: the trees, etc., that form the avenue: a mental view or vision extending far into the past or future, or into any subject engaging the thoughts.—Also **vis′to.**—*v.t.* (*rare*) to make into, or see in, vistas.—*adjs.* **vista′d, vis′taed** (*-təd*), having, or forming, a vista or vistas (*lit.* and *fig.*); **vis′tal; vis′taless** (*-tə-les*). [It. *vista,* sight, view—L. *vidēre, vīsum,* to see.]
**visual,** *vizh′ū-əl, viz′ū-əl, adj.* of, pertaining to, sight: concerned with seeing, or (*fig.*) with mental vision: attained by, or received through, sight: of the nature of, or conveying, a mental vision: visible, having visibility: optic, as in 'visual axis': of the eye (*poet.*): of beams, coming from the eye (*obs.*).—*n.* a visible.—*n.*

**visualisā'tion** -z-.—*v.t.* vis'ualise, -ize-, make visible, externalise to the eye: to call up a clear visual image of.—*v.i.* to call up a clear visual image: become visible (*med.*).—*ns.* vis'ualiser, -z-; vis'ualist, a visualiser: a visile; visual'ity (*Carlyle*), quality or state of being visible to the mind: a mental picture.—*adv.* vis'ually.—visual **aid**, a picture, photograph, film, diagram, etc., used as an aid to teaching; **visual purple** (see **purple**). [L.L. *visuālis*—L. *visus*, sight.]

**visuo-**, in composition, sight. [L. *visus*.]

**vita**, *vī'ta*, *vē'*, *wē'ta*, (L.) life—vita patris ('*tä pat'-ris*), in the father's lifetime.

**Vitaceae.** See Vitis.

**Vita glass**, *vī'ta gläs*, trademark for a glass that transmits ultraviolet rays.

**vital**, *vī'tal*, *adj.* being a manifestation of organic life: supporting, or necessary to, life: life-giving, invigorating: characteristic of life, or of living things: animate, living: full of life: capable of living (*obs.*): pertaining to life, birth, and death: due to living agency: fatal to life: essential, or (loosely) highly important.—*n.* vitalisā'tion, -z-.—*v.t.* vi'talise, -z-, give life to: to stimulate activity in: to give vigour to; to make lifelike.—*n.* vi'taliser, -z-.—*adj.* vi'tal-ising, -z-.—*ns.* vi'talism, doctrine that there is a vital principle (*q.v.*); vi'talist, one who holds this doctrine.—*adj.* vitalis'tic.—*adv.* vitalis'ti-cally.—*n.* vitality (-*tal'*), state or quality of being vital: principle of life, power of living: living-ness: quality of being fully or intensely alive: capacity to endure and flourish: animation, liveliness: a living or vital thing or quality:—*pl.* vital'ities.—*adv.* vi'tally.—*n.pl.* vi'tals (rarely in *sing.*), the interior organs essential for life: the part of any whole necessary for its existence.—*n.* vi'tascope, a form of motion-picture pro-jector.—*adj.* vi'tative, concerned with the pre-servation of life.—*n.* vitativeness (*vī-ta-tiv-*), love of life, assigned by the phrenologists to a pro-tuberance under the ear.—**vital air** (*obs.*), oxygen; **vital force**, the force on which the phenomena of life in animals and plants depends—distinct from chemical and mechanical forces operating in them; **vital functions**, the bodily functions that are essential to life, as the circulation of the blood; **vital principle**, that principle—the *anima mundi*—which, according to the doctrine of vitalism, gives life to all nature: a principle that directs all the actions and functions of living bodies; **vital spark, flame**, the principle of life in man: hence, life or a trace of life; **vital stain** (*bot.*, *zool.*), a stain that can be used on living cells without killing them; **vital statistics**, statistics dealing with the facts of population—births, deaths, etc.: a woman's bust, waist and hip measurements (*facet.*). [L. *vitālis*—*vita*, life—*vīvēre*, to live; cog. with Gr. *bios*, life.]

**vitamin**, *vit'a-min*, *vīt'* (orig. *vitamine*, *-mēn*), *n.* any of numerous organic substances, 'accessory food factors', present in minute quantities in nutritive foods and essential for the health of the animal organism, designated provisionally vitamin A, $B_1$, $B_2$, etc., C, D, $D_1$, etc., E, (F), G (now $B_2$), H, K, $K_1$, etc., L, M (also $B_c$), (P), PP (a vitamin effective against pellagra, as nicotinic acid), X (later P), but later analysed and given names indicating something of their nature; see aneurin (thiamine), riboflavin, panto-thenic acid, nicotinic acid (niacin), pyridoxine (adermin), cyanocobalamine, folic acid, pteroic acid, ascorbic acid, calciferol, tocopherol (linoleic, linolenic, acid), biotin, phylloquinone (phytona-dione), menadione (citrin, bioflavonoid).—*v.t.* vi'taminise, -ize, to add vitamins to (a food).—**vitamin B complex**, a group of vitamins formerly regarded as being a single vitamin. [Coined in 1906 from L. *vita*, life, and (inappropriately) *amine*.]

**vitascope, vitative.** See vital.

**vite**, *vēt*, (*mus.*) *adv.* quickly. [Fr.]

**vitellus**, *vi-*, *vi-tel'as*, *n.* the yolk of an egg:—*pl.* vitell'i.—*adj.* vit'ellary, pertaining to the vitellus: egg-yellow.—*ns.* vitell'in, a phosphoprotein present in yolk of egg; vitell'ine, a vitellus.—*adj.* vitellary.—*n.* vitell'icle, a yolk-sac.—*adj.* vitelligenous (-*ij'*), producing yolk. [L., a yolk; a transferred use of *vitellus*—*vitulus*, a calf.]

**Vitex**, *vī'teks*, *n.* a genus of trees or shrubs, chiefly tropical, of the family Verbenaceae, having a drupe with a four-celled stone; some species yield valuable timber. [L.]

**vitiate**, *vish'i-āt*, *v.t.* to render faulty or defective: to spoil: to make impure: to deprave, corrupt, pervert, debase: to make ineffectual or invalid or inconclusive: to violate, ravish (*obs.*): to adulterate (*obs.*).—Earlier vi'ciate.—*adj.* (*arch.*) vitiated.—*adj.* vi'tiable.—*ns.* vitiā'tion; vi'tiātor; vitios'ity (also vicios'ity), state or quality of being vicious, or (*Scots law*) faulty. [L. *vitiāre*, *-ātum*—*vitium*. See vice (2).]

**viticetum, viticide, viticulture.** See Vitis.

**vitilitigation**, *vit-i-lit-i-gā'shan*, (*rare*) *n.* vexatious wrangling.—*v.i.* (*rare*) vitilit'igate. [Formed from L. *vitilitigāre*, *-ātum*, to quarrel disgrace-fully—*vitium*, a blemish, *litigāre*, to quarrel.]

**vitiligo**, *vit-i-lī'gō*, *-a-lē'gō*, *n.* a skin abnormality in which irregular patches of the skin lose colour and turn white. [L. *vitiligo*, a skin eruption.]

**vitiosity.** See vitiate.

**Vitis**, *vī'tis*, *n.* a genus of plants, including the grape-vines, of the family **Vitaceae** (*vi-tā'sē-ē*) or Ampelidaceae.—*ns.* viticetum (*vit-* or *vit-i-sē'tam*; would-be Latin), a plantation of vines; vit'icide, a vine pest.—*adj.* vitic'olous, living on vines.—*ns.* vit'iculture, cultivation of the vine; viticul'turist.—*adj.* vitif'erous, bearing vines. [L. *vitis*, a vine—*viēre*, to twist.]

**vitrage**, *vē-träzh*, *vit'rij*, *n.* (used also adjectivally) a kind of thin curtain for windows or glazed doors. [Fr., glass window.]

**vitrail**, *vit'rāl*, *vē-trä-ē*, *n.* stained glass:—*pl.* vitraux (*vē-trō*).—*adj.* vitrailled (*vit'rāld*).—*n.* vit'raillist, a maker of glass, esp. stained glass. [Fr.]

**vitrain**, *vit'rān*, *n.* a separable constituent of bright coal, of vitreous appearance. [L. *vitrum*, glass, and suff. -*ain*.]

**vitraux.** See under vitrail.

**Vitreosil.** See under vitreous.

**vitreous**, *vit'ri-as*, *adj.* glassy: pertaining to, con-sisting of, or like glass: glass green in colour: resembling glass in absence of crystalline struc-ture, in lustre, etc. (*geol.*).—*ns.* Vit'reosil, trade mark for vitreous silica used for apparatus which is subject to large temperature variations; vitreos'ity, vit'reousness; vitresc'ence.—*adjs.* vit-resc'ent, tending to become glass, capable of being turned into glass; vitresc'ible.—*ns.* vitres-cibil'ity; vit'reum, the vitreous humour of the eye.—*adj.* vit'ric.—*ns.* vit'rics, glassy materials: glassware: the study of glass and its manufac-ture; vitrifac'tion, vitrifica'tion, act, process, or operation of vitrifying, or converting into glass: the state of being vitrified: a vitrified substance; vitrifac'ture, the manufacture of glass.—*adjs.* vit'rifiable; vit'rified; vit'riform, having the form or appearance of glass.—*v.t.* and *v.i.* vit'rify, to make into, or to become, glass or a glassy substance.—*ns.* Vitri'na, a genus of thin-shelled land molluscs, between slugs and true snails—the glass-snails; vit'rine (-*rēn*, -*rin*), a glass show-case used to protect delicate articles, exhibit specimens, etc.—**vitreous electricity**, old name for positive electricity, because glass becomes positively charged when rubbed with silk; **vitreous humour**, the jelly-like substance filling the posterior chamber of the eye of a vertebrate, between the lens and the retina;

vitrified forts, walls, certain ancient Scottish, French, etc., forts or walls in which the silicious stone has been vitrified by fire, whether by intention or accident is uncertain. [L. *vitrum*, glass.]

vitriol, *vit'ri-əl*, *n*. oil of vitriol (*q.v.*): a hydrous sulphate of a metal, as *blue*, *green*, and *white vitriol*, respectively that of copper (cupric), iron (ferrous), and zinc.—*v.t.* vit'riolate, to convert into, or to treat with, vitriol.—*n*. vitriolā'tion.—*adj.* vitriolic (*-ol'*), pertaining to, or having the qualities of, vitriol: biting, scathing, expressing intense ill-will.—*n*. vitriolisā'tion, -z-.—*v.t.* vit'riolise, -ize, to vitriolate: to injure with vitriol. —elixir of vitriol, aromatic sulphuric acid (i.e. sulphuric acid mixed with certain other substances for use in medicine); oil of vitriol, concentrated sulphuric acid—because formerly prepared from green vitriol. [Fr.,—L.L. *vitriolum* —L. *vitreus*, of glass.]

vitro-, *vit'rō-*, in composition, glass.—*n*. Vitrolite (*-līt*), proprietary name of a kind of opaque glass with a fire-finished surface. [L. *vitrum*, glass.]

vitro-di-trina, *vit'rō-di-trē'nä*, *n*. a Venetian white glass in which fine threads of cane form a lace-like pattern. [It., glass of lace.]

Vitruvian, *vi-trōō'vi-ən*, *adj*. of, or in the style of, *Vitruvius* Pollio, a Roman architect under Augustus: denoting a kind of convoluted scroll-work.

vitta, *vit'a*, *n*. a fillet or band for the head: a strap or sash: a stripe of colour (*bot.* and *zool.*): a thin, elongated cavity containing oil, found in the pericarps of some fruits (*bot.*):—*pl*. vittae (*-ē*).—*adj*. vitt'ate, having vittae: striped length-wise. [L.]

vitular, *vit'ū-lər*, *adj*. pertaining to a calf or to calving.—*adj*. vituline (*vit'ū-līn*), pertaining to a calf or to veal. [L. *vitulus*, a calf.]

vituperate, *vi-tū'pə-rāt*, or *vī-*, *v.t*. to assail with abusive reproaches, revile.—*v.i*. to use abusive language.—*adj*. vitū'perable, deserving vituperation.—*n*. vitūperā'tion, act of vituperating: censure: railing, abuse.—*adj*. vitū'perative (*-rət-* or *-rāt-*), containing vituperation: uttering, or prone to utter, abuse.—*adv*. vitū'peratively.—*n*. vitū'perātor.—*adj*. vitū'peratory, vituperative. [L. *vituperāre*, *-ātum*—*vitium*, a fault, *parāre*, to set in order, prepare.]

Vitus.—St Vitus's dance. See chorea.

viva, *vē'vä*, (It.; Sp.) long live.

vivace, *vē-vä'che*, (*mus.*) *adj*. lively:—*superl*. vivacis'simo. [It.]

vivacious, *vi-vā'shəs*, or *vī-*, *adj*. long-lived, or tenacious of life (*arch.*): lively, full of vitality: sprightly, sportive.—*adv*. vivā'ciously.—*ns*. vivā'ciousness, vivac'ity, state of being vivacious: vitality (*obs.*): tenacity of life, or longevity (*arch.*): vigour: animation: liveliness or sprightliness of temper or behaviour: a vivacious act or saying (*rare*). [L. *vivāx*, *vivācis*—*vivēre*, to live.]

vivandière, *vē-vä-dyer'*, (*hist.*) *n*. in the French and some other Continental armies, a female attendant in a regiment, who sold spirits and provisions:—*masc*. vivandier (*-dyä*). [Fr., fem. of *vivandier*—It. *vivandiere*, a sutler—assumed L.L. *vivanda*, food.]

vivarium, *vī-vā'ri-əm*, *n*. an artificial enclosure for keeping or raising living animals, as a park, a fish-pond: a glass-sided box, etc.:—*pl*. viva'ria, -iums.—Also vī'vary. [L. *vivārium*—*vīvus*, alive —*vīvēre*, to live.]

vivat, *vī'vat*, *vē'*, *wē'wat*, (L.) long live.

viva voce, *vī'və vō'sē*, *vē'vä*, *wē'wä vō'*, *wō'ke*, *adv*. *phrase* by the living voice: by oral testimony.—*n*. (usu. viva alone) an oral examination.—*v.t*. (usu. viva) to examine orally. [L.]

vivda, *viv'dä*, *vev'dä*, *n*. in Shetland, meat hung

and dried without salt.—Also vif'da. [Perh. O.N. *vöthvi*, muscle.]

vive, *viv*, (*Scot.* and *obs.*) *adj*. lively, forcible: vivid.—*adv*. vive'ly.—*n*. viv'ency (*rare*), vitality. [Fr., or L. *vīvus*, alive.]

vive, *vēv*, (Fr.) long live.

viver, *vē'vər*, (*obs.* and *dial.*) *n*. a fish-pond. [A.Fr.,—L. *vivārium*; see vivarium.]

viver, *vī'vər*, (*dial.*) *n*. a fibre, rootlet. [Variant of fibre.]

Viverra, *vi-*, *vī-ver'ə*, *n*. the civet genus, giving name to the family Viverr'idae ( *i dē*), and the subfamily Viverrinae (*-i'nē*).—*n*. any of the Viverridae, esp. one of the Viverrinae.—*adj*. viverr'ine, of or like the ferret or the civet family. [L. *viverra*, a ferret.]

vivers, *vē'vərz*, (*Scot.*) *n.pl*. food, eatables. [Fr. *vivres*—L. *vīvēre*, to live.]

vives, *vīvz*, *n.pl*. a disease of horses, swelling of the submaxillary glands. [O.Fr. *avives*, *vives*— Sp. *avivas*—Ar. *addhiba*—*al*, the, *dhiba*, she-wolf.]

vivi-, *vi'vi-*, in composition, alive, living.—*adj*. viviparous (*vi-vip'ə-rəs*, or *vi-*; L. *parĕre*, to produce), producing living young that have reached an advanced stage of development—opp. to oviparous: germinating from a seed still on the parent plant (*bot.*): producing bulbils or young plants in the flower clusters, etc. (*bot.*).—*ns*. vivip'arism, viviparous reproduction; viviparity (*viv-i-par'i-ti*), vivip'arousness, quality of being viviparous.—*adv*. vivip'arously.—*ns*. vivip'ary, viviparity in plants; vivisection (*-sek'shən*; L. *sectiō*—*secāre*, to cut), the act or practice, or an instance, of making surgical operations on living animals for the purposes of physiological research or demonstration: merciless and minute examination or criticism (*fig.*).—*v.t*. vivisect', to practise vivisection on.—Also *v.i.*—*adj*. vivisec'tional.—*n*. vivisec'tionist, one who practises or defends vivisection.—*adj*. vivisec'tive, practising vivisection.—*ns*. vivisec'tor, one who practises vivisection; vivisecto'rium, a place for vivisection; vivisepulture (*-sep'l-chər*), burial alive. [L. *vīvus*.]

vivianite, *viv'yə-nit*, *n*. ferrous phosphate, blue by oxidation, often found coating fossil fishes and bones. [After J. G. *Vivian*, who first found it crystallised.]

vivid, *viv'id*, *adj*. full of life, vigorous: lively, intense: very bright: presenting a clear and striking picture: forming brilliant mental images. —*adv*. viv'idly.—*ns*. viv'idness, vivid'ity.—*adj*. vivif'ic, vivifying.—*ns*. vivificā'tion; viv'ifier.—*v.t*. viv'ify, to endue with life: to make vivid: to assimilate, convert into living tissue. [L. *vīvidus*—*vīvĕre*, to live.]

vivo, *vē'vō*, (*mus.*) *adj*. lively.—*adv*. vivamente (*vē-vä-men'tā*), in a lively manner. [It.]

vivres. Same as vivers.

vixen, *vik'sn*, *n*. a she-fox: an ill-tempered woman.—*adjs*. vix'en, vix'enish, vix'enly, ill-tempered, snarling. [Southern dialectal form of *fixen*—O.E. *fyxen*, fem. of *fox*.]

vizament, *viz'ə-mənt*, (*Shak.*) *n*. for advisement.

vizard, *viz'ərd*, *n*. a mask (*lit.* and *fig.*).—*v.t*. (*obs.*) to mask: to disguise, conceal.—*adj*. viz'arded, masked: pretended.—viz'ard-mask, a mask: a masked woman: a prostitute. [Variant of visor.]

vizier, vizir, *vi-zēr'*, *viz'yər*, *viz'i-ər*, *n*. a minister or councillor of state in various Mohammedan states.—Also visier', vezir', wizier'.—*ns*. vizier'-ate, vizir'ate, vizier'ship, vizir'ship, the office of a vizier.—*adj*. vizier'ial, vizir'ial.—Grand Vizier, in pre-Republican Turkey, the prime minister, and at one time also commander of the army. [Ar. *wazīr*, a porter—*wazara*, to bear a burden.]

vizor. Same as visor.

vizy, vizzie. Same as visie (under vision).

**Vlach,** *vlak, n.* one of a non-Slav people of south-eastern Europe, found chiefly in Rumania, a Walachian. [O.Slav. *Vlachŭ*—O.H.G. *walh,* a foreigner, esp. a Slav or a Latin.]

**vlei,** *flā, (Afrik.) n.* low-lying ground where a shallow lake forms in the wet season: a swamp (local *U.S.*).—Also **vly.** [Dial. Du.,—Du. *wallei,* valley.]

**voar,** *vōr, vör, n.* in Orkney and Shetland, spring, seed-time. [O.N. *vār,* spring; cf. **ware** (2).]

**vocable,** *vō'kə-bl, n.* that which is sounded with the voice—a word, or a single sound of a word: a term, name (*obs.*).—*adjs.* **vocabular** (*vō-, və-kab'*), of or concerning words; **vocabulār'ian,** of or pertaining to vocabulary.—*n.* a person much, or too much, concerned with words.—*adj.* **vocab'ularied.**—*ns.* **vocab'ulary,** a list of words explained in alphabetical order: a dictionary: any list of words: the words of a language: the words known to and used by, e.g. a particular person: the words used in a (particular) science or art: the signs or symbols used in any non-verbal type of communication, e.g. in computer technology: a collection of forms used in an art or by a particular practitioner of an art; **vocab'ulist,** the maker of a vocabulary: a lexicographer.—*adjs.* **vō'cal,** having a voice: uttered by the voice: oral: sung, or for singing—opp. to *instrumental*: giving forth sound: resounding: talkative: eloquent: concerned in the production of speech: of or pertaining to a vowel: having a vowel function: voiced; **vocal'ic,** containing (esp. many) vowels: of, pertaining to, or of the nature of, a vowel or vowels.—*n.* **vocalisā'tion,** -z-.—*v.t.* **vo'calise,** -ize, to form into voice, to articulate: to sing: to give expression to: to make vocal, endow with power of expression: to convert into a vowel: to insert the vowel points, as in Hebrew. —*v.i.* to sing: to sing on a vowel or vowels.—*ns.* **vō'caliser,** -z-; **vō'calism,** exercise of the vocal organs: the art of using the voice in singing: a vocal sound: system of vowels; **vō'calist,** a singer—esp. opp. to *instrumentalist*; **vōcal'ity, vō'calness.**—*adv.* **vō'cally.**—*adjs.* **vocicul'tural** (*vō-si-*), pertaining to voice-training; **vocūlar** (*vok'*; *rare*), vocal.—*n.* **vocule** (*vok'ūl*), a slight vowel sound completing the articulation of certain consonants.—**vocal c(h)ords,** in air-breathing vertebrates, folds of the lining membrane of the larynx, by the vibration of the edges of which, under the influence of the breath, the voice is produced; **vocal music,** music produced by the human voice alone, as opp. to *instrumental music.* [L. *vocābulum* and *vōcālis*—*vōx, vōcis,* voice.]

**vocal,** etc. See under **vocable.**

**vocalion,** *vō-kā'li-ən, n.* a musical instrument resembling a harmonium, with broad reeds. [**vocal,** and suff. *-ion,* as in **accordion.**]

**vocation,** *vō-kā'shən, n.* a calling, summons (*rare*): a calling by God to his service in special work or in a special position, or to a state of salvation: fitness for God's or other specified work: a way of living or sphere of activity to which one has been called by God, or for which one has a special fitness: one's occupation, business, or profession.—*adj.* **vocā'tional,** pertaining to, concerned with, or in preparation for, a trade or occupation.—*n.* **vocā'tionalism,** the giving of an important place in education to vocational training.—*adv.* **vocā'tionally.**—*adj.* **vocative** (*vok'-ə-tiv*), pertaining to the act of calling: applied to the grammatical case used in direct personal address.—*n.* the case of a word when a person or thing is addressed: a word in that case. [L. *vocātiō, -ōnis,* and *vocātivus*—*vocāre,* to call.]

**vocicultural.** See under **vocable.**

**vociferate,** *vō-sif'ə-rāt, v.i.* to cry with a loud voice, to bawl.—*v.t.* to utter in a loud voice.—*n.*

**vocif'erance,** clamour.—*adj.* **vocif'erant,** clamorous.—*ns.* **vociferā'tion,** act of vociferating: a violent or loud outcry; **vocif'erātor; vociferos'ity** (*rare*).—*adj.* **vocif'erous,** making a loud outcry: noisy.—*adv.* **vocif'erously.**—*n.* **vocif'ercusness.** [L.,—*vōx, vōcis,* voice, *ferre,* to carry.]

**vocular, vocule.** See under **vocable.**

**vodka,** *vod'ka, n.* a Russian spirit, properly distilled from rye, but sometimes from potatoes, etc. [Russ., dim. of *voda,* water.]

**voe,** *vō, n.* in Orkney and Shetland, a bay, creek. [O.N. *vāgr,* a creek.]

**voetganger,** *foot'hhäng-ər, foot'gäng-ər, (S.Afr.) n.* a locust before its wings grow: a pedestrian: an infantryman. [Du. *voet,* foot, *gang,* walk.]

**vogie,** *vō'gi, (Scot.) adj.* vain: merry. [Origin obscure.]

**vogue,** *vōg, n.* the chief place in popular esteem (*obs.*): popularity: a place in popular favour, or the period of it: the mode or fashion at any particular time.—*adj.* in vogue, fashionable.—*v.t.* (*arch.* or *obs.*) to give vogue to, or to repute, reckon.—*adjs.* **vogu'ey, vog'uish.**—**vogue word,** a word much used at a particular time. [Fr. *vogue* (orig. course of a rowing vessel)—*voguer,* to row—It. *vogare;* ety. uncertain.]

**voice,** *vois, n.* sound produced by the vocal organs of living beings, esp. of human beings in speech or song: sound given out by anything: faculty or power of speech or song: ability to sing, esp. well: mode of utterance: quality and range of musical sounds produced by a singer: a singer: a part for a singer, or one of the parts in an instrumental composition: utterance, expression: what one says (*obs.*): expressed wish or opinion: vote, approval: medium of expression: one who speaks: rumour, report, reputation (*obs.*): sound uttered with resonance of the vocal cords (*phon.*): mode of inflecting verbs to indicate whether that represented by the subject acts or is acted upon, or acts so as to affect itself (*gram.*; see **active, passive, middle**).—*v.t.* to utter (*rare*): to give utterance or expression to: to act as mouthpiece of (*rare*): to endow with voice: to rumour or esp. (in impers. construction) to be rumoured or commonly stated (*obs.*): to speak of (*obs.*): to acclaim (*obs.*): to nominate, appoint, elect (*obs.*): to regulate the tone of (*mus.*): to write the voice parts of: to utter with vibration of the vocal cords (*phon.*).—*adjs.* **voiced,** endowed with voice: having a voice of a specified kind: uttered with voice (*phon.*); **voice'ful,** having a voice: vocal (with *with*): full of sound.—*n.* **voice'fulness.**—*adj.* **voice'less,** having no voice: speechless, silent: unspoken: failing to, or unable to, express one's opinion or desire, or to make this felt: having no vote: not voiced (*phon.*).—*ns.* **voice'lessness; voic'er; voic'irg,** the regulation of the tone of organ pipes, ensuring proper power, pitch, and quality.—**voice'-box,** the larynx.—**give voice to,** to express; **in my voice** (*Shak.*), in my name; **in voice,** in good condition for singing or speaking; **with one voice, voice, unanimously.** [A.Fr. *voiz, voice* (Fr. *voix*) —L. *vōx, vōcis;* akin to Gr. *epos,* a word.]

**void,** *void, adj.* containing nothing, empty, deserted: unoccupied, unutilised: having no holder, vacant: devoid, destitute, free (with *of*) worthless (*obs.*): ineffectual, useless: not binding in law, null, invalid.—*n.* an empty space: (with *the*) the expanse of space: emptiness: a lack (*rare*): an emotional lack strongly felt (*fig.*): an unfilled space (*archit.*): in a hand as dealt, total absence of cards of a particular suit (*bridge*).—*v.t.* to make vacant, to empty, clear: to send out, discharge, emit: to send away, dismiss (*obs.*): to remove, clear away (*obs.*) to go away from, withdraw from, quit (*obs.*) to avoid (*obs.*): to lay aside, divest oneself of (*obs.*): to make of no effect, to nullify.—*adj.* **void'able,** that may be voided: that may be either voided or confirmed (*law*).—*n.* **void'ance,** act of voiding or emptying: state of being void: of a benefice, the fact or state of being vacant. —*adj.* **void'ed** (*her.*), having the inner part cut away and showing the tincture of the field— said of a charge.—*ns.* **void'ee** (*hist.*), wine and light food taken before going to bed, or before the departure of guests; **void'er,** (*lit.* and *fig.*) one who empties, or (*hist.*) one who clears a table: a tray for carrying away dirty dishes, crumbs, etc., or a tray, etc., for carrying sweet-meats (*obs.*): a contrivance in armour for cover-ing an unprotected part of the body; **void'ing,** the act of voiding: that which is voided (often in *pl.*); **void'ness.**—**void'ing-lobby** (*obs.*), an ante-room. [O.Fr. *voide*, empty—popular L. *vocitus* —*vocitāre*, to empty—*vocuus*, for L. *vacuus*.]

**voilà, vwä-lä,** (Fr.) behold: there is, or there are. —**voilà tout** (*tōō*), that is all.

**voile, voil,** *n.* a thin semi-transparent material. [Fr., veil.]

**voir dire, vwär dēr** (*law*), an oath administered to a witness. [O.Fr. *voir,* true, truth, *dire,* to say.]

**voisinage, voi'si-nij,** (*obs.*) *n.* neighbourhood, or the neighbourhood. [Fr.]

**voiture, vwä-tür,** *n.* a carriage.—*n.* **voiturier** (*vwä-tür-yā*), the driver of a carriage or coach. [Fr.]

**voivode, voi'vōd, vaivode, vä'vōd,** *n.* orig., the leader of an army: later, in south-east Europe, the title of the head of an administrative division: in Moldavia and Walachia, the former title of the princes: in Turkey, an inferior administrative official.—*n.* **voi'vodeship, vai'vodeship.** [Russ. *voevoda* (Serb. *vojvoda,* Pol. *wojewoda*), a general.]

**voix céleste, vwä sä-lest,** in an organ, a labial stop with a soft, tremulous sound. [Fr., heavenly voice.]

**vol, vol,** (*her.*) *n.* two wings displayed and con-joined in base. [Fr.]

**vola, vō'la,** *n.* the hollow of the hand or foot:— *pl.* **volae** (*vō'lē*).—*adj.* **vo'lar,** pertaining to the palm or to the sole. [L.]

**volable, vol'ə-bl,** (*Shak.*) *adj.* nimble-witted. [L. *volāre,* to fly.]

**volage, vō'läzh,** *adj.* giddy, flighty: fickle.—Also **volageous** (*vō-lā'jəs*). [Fr.]

**Volans, vō'lanz,** *n.* the Flying Fish, a southern constellation. [L. *pr.p.* of *volāre,* to fly.]

**volant, vō'lənt,** *adj.* flying: passing lightly through the air: flying or pertaining to flight (*zool.*): of armed forces, etc., organised for rapid movement (*obs.*): nimble: represented as flying (*her.*).—*adj.* **volante** (*vō-län'tā;* It.; *mus.*), moving lightly and rapidly.—*n.* **vo'lary,** an aviary.—*adj.* **volat'ic,** (now *rare*) flying about; **volatile** (*vol'ə-til,* in U.S. *-til, -təl*), capable of flying: moving lightly and rapidly about: evaporating very quickly: flighty, apt to change. —*n.* a creature capable of flying: a volatile substance.—*ns.* **vol'atileness, volatility** (*-til'*).— *adj.* **vol'atilisable, -z-.**—*n.* **volatilisā'tion, -z-.**— *vb.* **vol'atilise, -ize,** to make or become volatile: to cause to evaporate: to make light, unsubstan-tial, delicate (*fig.*).—*n.* **vol'ery,** a volary: a place for repair, etc., of aircraft.—*adj.* **vol'itant,** flying: flitting: fluttering: moving about: able to fly. —*v.i.* **vol'itate,** to flutter, fly.—*n.* **volitā'tion,** flight: power of flying.—*adjs.* **volitā'tional; volitō'rial,** having the power of flight.—**volatile alkali** (*obs.*), ammonia; **volatile oils** (see **essential oils**). [L. *volāre,* to fly, *volitāre,* to flit, flutter.]

**volante, vō-lan'te,** *n.* a two-wheeled covered vehicle with long shafts, with a chaise-body hung before the axle—the horse, or one of the horses, being ridden by a postillion. [Sp.]

**Volapük, vol', vōl'ə-pük, or -puk, or -pük',** *n.* an

early international language invented about 1879 by Johann Schleyer of Constance, Baden.—*n.* **Volapük'ist,** one versed in Volapük: one who advocates the adoption of Volapük. [Lit. world-speech—*vol,* for Eng. *world, pük,* for Eng. *speak.*]

**volatile, etc.** See **volant.**

**vol-au-vent, vol-ō-vä,** *n.* a kind of pie of light puff pastry filled with meat, or fish, etc. [Fr., lit. flight in the wind.]

**volcano, vol-kā'nō,** *n.* a centre of eruption of sub-terranean matter, typically a more or less conical hill or mountain, built of ash and lava, with a central crater and pipe: a state of affairs, emotional condition, etc., suggestive of a volcano because an upheaval or outburst seems imminent (*fig.*): a form of firework:—*pl.* **volcan'oes.**—*adjs.* **volca'nian** (*Keats*); **volcanic** (*vol-kan'ik*), per-taining to, of the nature of, produced or caused by, a volcano: characterised by the presence of volcanoes.—*adv.* **volcan'ically.**—*ns.* **volcanicity** (*-kə-nis'i-ti*), vulcanicity; **volcanisā'tion, -z-.**—*v.t.* **vol'canise, -ize,** to subject to the action of volcanic heat.—*adj.* **vol'canised.**—*ns.* **vol'canism, vol'canist** (see **Vulcanism, -ist**).—*adj.* **volcanolog'ical.**—*n.* **volcanol'ogy,** vulcanology.—**volcanic ash(es), bomb** (see **ash, bomb**); **volcanic dust,** fine particles of powdered rock blown out from a volcano; **volcanic glass,** rock without crystalline structure, as obsidian, pumice, etc., produced by rapid cooling of molten lava; **volcanic mud, sand,** volcanic ash which has been deposited under water and sorted and stratified; **volcanic rocks,** those formed by volcanic agency. [It. *volcano*—L. *Volcānus, Vulcānus,* god of fire.]

**vole, vōl,** *n.* in certain card games, the winning of) all the tricks in one deal.—*v.i.* to win all the tricks in one deal.—**go the vole,** to risk all for great gain: to try everything. [Fr.,—L. *volāre* to fly.]

**vole, vōl,** *n.* any of numerous blunt-nosed, short-eared, mouselike or ratlike rodents, including the so-called water-rat and some field-mice. [For **vole-mouse,** i.e. field-mouse, of Scand. origin.]

**volente Deo, va-len'tē dē'ō, vō-, wō-len'tä dā'ō,** or **de'ō,** (L.) God willing.

**volery.** See under **volant.**

**volet, vol'ā,** *n.* a short veil worn at the back of the head (*hist.*): one of the wings of a triptych picture. [O.Fr. (mod. Fr., a shutter)—L. *volāre,* to fly.]

**Volga-Baltaic, vol'gä-böl-tā'ik,** *adj.* of, pertaining to, the group of languages to which Estonian, Finnish, and Lapp belong. [*Volga* river, *Baltic* Sea.]

**volitant, volitation, volitate.** See **volant.**

**volition, vō-lish'ən,** *n.* act of willing or choosing: the exercise of the will: the power of determin-ing.—*adjs.* **voli'tient** (*rare*), willing; **voli'tional, voli'tionary.**—*adv.* **voli'tionally.**—*adjs.* **voli'tion-less; vōl'itive,** of, pertaining to, the will: origin-ating in the will: willed, deliberate: expressing a wish (*gram.*).—*n.* a desiderative verb, etc. [Fr.,—L.L. *volitiō*—L. *volō,* pres. indic. of *velle,* to will, be willing.]

**völkerwanderung, fœlk-ər-vän'dər-ōong,** (Ger.) the migration of Germanic and other peoples, chiefly in the 4th to 6th centuries.

**volkslied, folks'lēt,** *n.* a folk-song. [Ger.]

**volksraad, folks'rät,** *n.* a legislative assembly, esp. (*cap.*) that of the Transvaal or the Orange Free State before 1900. [Du. *volk,* people, *raad,* council.]

**volley, vol'i,** *n.* a flight of missiles: the discharge of many missile-throwing weapons (e.g. small arms) at once: a round fired by every gun in a battery: an outburst of many, e.g. words, at once (*fig.*): in tennis, cricket, etc., a return of the ball before it reaches the ground—a *half-volley* is a return by striking the ball as it bounces:

*fāte, fär; mē, húr* (her); *mīne, mōte, för; mūte; mōōn, fŏŏt; dhen* (then) a ball so returned:—*pl.* **voll′eys.**—*v.t.* to discharge in a volley: to return (a ball) before it bounces: to fire a volley or volleys at.—*v.i.* to fly, be discharged, in a volley: to sound, produce sounds, like a volley: to roll, move, be emitted, like a volley: to make a volley at tennis, etc.—*adj.* **voll′eyed.**—**voll′ey-ball,** a game in which a large ball is volleyed by the hand over a high net. [Fr. *volée,* a flight—L. *volāre,* to fly.]

**volost,** *vō′lost, n.* a division for local government in Russia (*hist.*): a soviet of a rural district. [Russ. *volost.*]

**volpino,** *vol-pē′nō, n.* a small Italian dog with long, straight hair and fox-like appearance. [It., —*volpe*—L. *vulpēs,* fox.]

**volplane,** *vol′plān, v.i.* to glide down to earth in an aeroplane with the engine shut off.—*n.* a descent of this kind. [Fr. *vol plané*—*vol,* flight, *plané,* pa.p. of *planer,* to glide.]

**Volscian,** *vol′shan, n.* one of the *Volsci,* an ancient Italian people incessantly at war with the Romans for 200 years previous to 338 B.C.: their Italic language.—*adj.* of, pertaining to, the Volsci.

**Volsungs,** *vol′sōōngz, n.pl.* a famous heroic race in old German legend, its founder *Volsung* being the grandson of Woden or Odin.

**volt, volte,** *vōlt, volt, n.* a sudden movement or leap to avoid a thrust (*fencing*): a gait of a horse going sideways round a centre: a track made by a horse executing this movement.—*n.* **vol′tage.** [Fr. *volte*—It. *volta*—L. *volvĕre, volūtum,* to turn.]

**volt,** *vōlt, n.* the MKSA unit of electromotive force, electric potential, or potential difference, the difference of potential between two points in a conductor carrying a current of one ampere when the power dissipated between them is one watt.—**volta-** (*vol′ta-*), used in composition for *voltaic,* as in **vol′ta-electric′ity, vol′ta-elec′tric.**—*n.* **voltage** (*volt′, vōlt′*), electromotive force in volts.—*adj.* **voltaic** (*vol-tā′ik*), pertaining to Alessandro *Volta,* who constructed the first electrical battery, a **voltaic pile,** and established the science of current electricity: of electricity, generated by chemical action: used in producing such electricity: of, pertaining to, caused by, voltaic electricity.—*ns.* **vol′taism,** the branch of electricity that treats of the production of an electric current from the chemical interaction of two immersed dissimilar metals; **voltam′eter,** an instrument for measuring an electric current by means of the amount of metal deposited, or gas liberated, from an electrolyte in a given time by the passage of the current; **vōlt′meter,** an instrument for measuring electromotive force directly, calibrated in volts. [Alessandro *Volta,* Italian scientist (1745-1827).]

**volta,** *vol′ta, n.* an old dance, the lavolta: turn, time (*mus.*):—*pl.* **vol′te** (-*tā*). [It.]

**Voltairian, Voltairean,** *vol-tār′i-ən, adj.* pertaining to *Voltaire,* French poet, dramatist, historian, and sceptic (1694-1778).—*n.* one who advocates the views and principles of Voltaire.—*ns.* **Voltair′ianism, Voltair′eanism, Voltair′ism,** the spirit of Voltaire—i.e. a sceptical and sarcastic attitude, especially towards Christianity—or a manifestation of it, or adherence to his doctrines.

**volte-face,** *volt-fäs, n.* a turning round: a sudden and complete change in opinion or in views expressed (*fig.*). [Fr.]

**voltigeur,** *vol-ti-zhœr′, n.* a vaulter or tumbler: in the French army, one of a light-armed company of picked men for skirmishing (*hist.*). [Fr., —*voltiger,* to flutter, vault.]

**voltinism,** *vol′tin-izm, n.* breeding rhythm, brood frequency. [It. *volta;* see **volta.**]

**voluble,** *vol′ū-bl, adj.* easy to roll or revolving readily or smoothly (*rare*; *Milt.* **volubil**): flow-

ing smoothly: fluent in speech: too fluent or glib: changeable (*rare*): twining (*bot.*).—*ns.* **volubil′ity, vol′ubleness.**—*adv.* **vol′ubly.** [L. *volūbilis*—*volvĕre, volūtum,* to roll.]

**volucrine,** *vol′ū-krin, -krin, adj.* pertaining to birds, bird-like. [L. *volucris,* a bird—*volāre,* to fly.]

**volume,** *vol′ūm, n.* a roll or scroll, which was the form of ancient books: a book, whether complete in itself or part of a larger work: anything (esp. in the natural world) that may be studied as a book: (often in *pl.*) a rounded mass: a quantity: bulk: cubical content: dimensions: fullness of tone.—*v.i.* to swell, rise, roll.—*v.t.* to send out in volumes, or great quantity: to make into, bind into, a volume.—*adj.* **vol′umed,** having the form of a volume or roll: bulky: consisting of (so-many) volumes.—*ns.* **volum:enom′eter, volumom′eter,** an instrument for measuring the volume of a solid body by the quantity of fluid it displaces; **volu′meter,** an instrument for measuring the volumes of gases.—*adjs.* **volumet′ric, -al.**—*adv.* **volumet′rically.**—*adjs.* **volu′minal,** pertaining to cubical content; **volu′minous,** consisting of many coils, windings, folds: bulky, filling much space: in many volumes: capable of filling many volumes: having written much, as an author.—*adv.* **volu′minously.**—*ns.* **volu′minousness, voluminos′ity; vol′umist** (*rare*), an author.—**volumetric analysis,** the estimation of the amount of a particular constituent present in a compound by determining the quantity of a standard solution required to satisfy a reaction in a known quantity of the compound.—**speak, express,** etc., **volumes,** to mean much, to be very significant. [Fr.,—L. *volūmen, -inis,* a roll—*volvĕre, volūtum,* to roll.]

**voluntary,** *vol′ən-tər-i, adj.* acting by choice, able to will: proceeding from the will: spontaneous, free: done or made without compulsion or legal obligation: designed, intentional: freely given, or given by contributions freely given: free from state control: subject to the will: of or pertaining to voluntaryism.—*n.* one who does anything of his own free-will: a volunteer (*obs.*): a piece of music played at will: a voluntary or extempore composition of any kind: a piece of music played before, during, or after a church service: an unwarranted fall from a horse: an upholder of voluntaryism.—*adv.* **vol′untarily.**—*ns.* **vol′untariness; vol′untaryism, vol′untarism,** the principle or practice of reliance on voluntary action not coercion: the principle or system of maintaining the church by voluntary offerings, instead of by the aid of the state: the principle or system of maintaining voluntary schools; **vol′untaryist.**—*adjs.* **voluntaris′tic; vol′untātive,** voluntary.—**voluntary school,** in England, an elementary school supported by voluntary subscriptions, in many cases controlled by a religious body. [L. *voluntārius*—*voluntās,* choice —*volō,* pres. indic. of *velle,* to will.]

**volunteer,** *vol-ən-tēr′, n.* one who enters any service, esp. military, of his own free choice: a soldier belonging to any body other than the regular army.—*adj.* consisting of, or pertaining to, volunteers: giving voluntary service: given voluntarily: of a plant or plants, growing spontaneously.—*v.t.* to offer voluntarily to give, supply, perform: to give (information) unasked. —*v.i.* to enter into any service of one's own free-will or without being asked. [Fr. *volontaire* —L. *voluntārius.*]

**voluptuary,** *va-lup′tū-ər-i, n.* one excessively given to bodily enjoyments or luxury, a sensualist.— *adj.* promoting, or characterised by, sensual pleasure.—*adj.* **voluptuous** (*va-lup′tū-əs*), full of, or suggestive of, pleasure, esp. sensuous: pertaining to, consisting of, derived from, or ministering to, sensual pleasure: given to excess of pleasure, esp. sensual.—*adv.* volup′tuously.— *ns.* volup′tuousness, voluptuos′ity. [L. *voluptuārius*—*voluptās*, pleasure.]

Völuspa, *vol-us-pa, væl′ōōs-pa, n.* one of the poems of the Elder Edda: (without *cap.*) a sibyl or prophetess—a wrong use, found in Scott's *Pirate.* [O.N. *Völuspā*, the song of the sibyl— *völva*, a wise woman.]

volutation, *vol-ū-tā′shən, (rare or obs.) n.* the action of rolling, turning, wallowing (*lit.* and *fig.*). [L. *volūtātiō, -ōnis*—*volūtāre*—*volvĕre, volūtum*, to roll.]

volute, *və-, vo-lūt′, -lōōt′,* spiral scroll used esp. in Ionic capitals: a spiral form: a thing or part having such a shape: any marine shell of the genus Voluta or kindred genera, allied to the whelks, or the animal itself: a whorl of a spiral shell.—*adj.* rolled up in any direction, having a spiral form.—*adj.* volū′ted, in spiral form: having a volute or volutes.—*ns.* vol′ūtin, a substance found in granular form (volutin granules) in the cytoplasm of various cells, believed to contribute to the formation of chromatin; volū′-tion, a revolving movement: a convolution: a whorl.—*adj.* vol′ūtoid, like a volute. [L. *volvĕre, volūtum,* to roll.]

volva, *vol′və, n.* a sheath enclosing the whole of the fruit body of some agarics.—*adj.* vol′vate, possessing a volva. [L.; see vulva.]

volve, *volv, v.t.* and *v.i.* to turn over (*obs.*): to ponder (*fig.*). [L. *volvĕre.*]

Volvox, *vol′voks, n.* a genus of simple organisms found in ponds, canals, etc., commonly regarded as algae, consisting of green flagellate cells united by protoplasmic bridges in a hollow spherical colony. [Formed from L. *volvĕre.*]

volvulus, *vol′vū-ləs, n.* twisting of an abdominal viscus causing internal obstruction. [Formed from L. *volvĕre.*]

vomer, *vō′mər, n.* a bone of the skull in most vertebrates—in man, a thin flat bone, shaped like a wedge or ploughshare, forming part of the middle partition of the nose.—*adj.* vomerine (*vō′* or *vo′*).—vo′mero-, used in composition, as vomeronas′al, pertaining to the vomer and the nasal cavity. [L. *vōmer*, a ploughshare.]

vomica. See under vomit.

vomit, *vom′it, v.i.* to throw up the contents of the stomach by the mouth, to spew: of an emetic, to cause vomiting: to issue with violence.—*v.t.* to throw out with violence: to cause to vomit:—*pr.p.* vom′iting; *pa.t.* and *pa.p.* vom′ited.—*n.* the act of vomiting: matter ejected from the stomach: vile persons or things (*fig.*): something that excites vomiting, an emetic.— *ns.* vom′ica, a cavity in the lung containing pus; vom′iting.—*adjs.* vom′itive, vom′itory, causing to vomit.—*n.* an emetic.—*ns.* vom′ito, the worst form of yellow fever, usually attended with the black vomit; vom′itory, a door of a large building by which the crowd is let out (also, *Roman hist.*, vomitō′rium): a vent (*lit.* and *fig.*); vomituri′tion, violent retching. [L. *vomĕre, -ĭtum,* to throw up; Gr. *emeein.*]

voodoo, voudou, *vōō′dōō,* or *-dōō′, n.* superstitious beliefs and practices of African origin found among Negroes of the West Indies and southern United States, formerly including serpent-worship, human sacrifice and cannibalism, but now confined to sorcery: any form of magic-working: a Negro sorcerer or witch.—*adj.* of, pertaining to, carrying out, voodoo practices.— *v.t.* to bewitch by voodoo charms.—Also vaudoo′, vaudous (*vō-dōō′*).—*ns.* voo′dooism (or *-dōō′*), voodoo superstitions; voo′dooist (or *-dōō′*).—*adj.* voodooist′ic. [African (Slave Coast) *vodu.*]

voortrekker, *fōr-trek′ər, fōōr′,* or *vōr-, n.* (usu. *cap.*) one of the Dutch farmers from Cape Colony who took part in the Great Trek into the Transvaal in 1836 and following years: (without *cap.*) a pioneer. [Cape Du.,—Du. *voor-*, before, and trek.]

vor, *vör, (King Lear* IV, vi. 247, in dialect passage) *v.t.* perh. means warn.

Vor, *vör, n.* an American aid to aircraft navigation. [*Very*-High-Frequency *O*mni-Directional-*R*ange.]

voracious, *vō-rā′shəs, vö-, adj.* eating greedily or in large quantities: taking in, engulfing, much (*fig.*): very eager, or insatiable (*fig.*): characterised by greediness (*lit.* and *fig.*).—*adv.* vorā′ciously. —*ns.* voracity (*-ras′*), vorā′ciousness. [L. *vorāx, vorācis*—*vorāre*, to devour.]

voraginous, *vō-raj′i-nəs, vö-,* (*obs.* or *rare*) *adj.* pertaining to a whirlpool: voracious.—*n.* vorā′go (*-gō*), a gulf. [L. *vorāgo*—*vorāre.*]

vorant, *vō′rənt, vö′,* (*her.*) *adj.* devouring. [L. *vorāns, -antis,* pr.p. of *vorāre,* to devour.]

vorpal, *vör′pəl, adj.* a nonsense word coined by Lewis Carroll to describe a sword, now used to mean sharp-edged.

vortex, *vör′teks, n.* a whirling motion of a fluid forming a cavity in the centre, a whirlpool, an eddy, a whirlwind: according to a hypothesis of Descartes, etc., a rotary movement of atoms or particles of subtle matter round an axis, or the matter itself in rotation, such phenomena accounting for the formation of the universe and the relative motion of its parts: a pursuit, way of life, situation, etc., that engulfs one irresistibly or remorselessly, taking up all one's attention or energies (*fig.*):—*pl.* vor′tices (*-ti-sēz*), vor′texes. —*adj.* vor′tical, or of pertaining to a vortex: whirling.—*adv.* vor′tically.—*ns.* vor′ticism (*-tis-izm*), a British movement in painting, a development from futurism, blending cubism and expressionism, and emphasising the complications of machinery that characterise modern life; vor′ticist, one who holds the theory of vortices, or who supports vorticism.—*adjs.* vor′ticose, vortic′ūlar, vortiginous (*-ij′*), vortical.—vortex theory, a theory that the material atom consists of a vortically moving frictionless fluid—a conception of Lord Kelvin's. [L. *vortex, vertex, -icis*—*vortĕre, vertĕre,* to turn.]

Vorticella, *vör-ti-səl′a, n.* a genus of ciliated infusorians belonging to the order Peritricha, in which the cilia are restricted to a fringe round the mouth. [Dim., from L. *vortex.*]

Vosgian, *vōzh′i-ən, adj.* of or pertaining to the *Vosges* Mts.—Also Vosgean.

votary, *vō′tə-ri, n.* one devoted as by a vow to some service, worship, or way of life: one enthusiastically addicted to a pursuit, study, etc.: a devoted worshipper or adherent:—*fem.* vō′taress.—*adj.* (*obs.*) consecrated by, or of the nature of, vows: of the nature of a vow.—*n.* vō′tarist, a votary.—*adj.* võt′ive, given, erected, etc., by vow: undertaken or observed in fulfilment of a vow: consisting of, or expressing, a vow or a wish.—votive offering, picture, tablet, one dedicated in fulfilment of a vow. [L.L. *vōtārius*—L. *vovēre, vōtum,* to vow.]

vote, *vōt, n.* an earnest desire (*obs.*): an expression of a wish or opinion in an authorised formal way: collective opinion, decision by a majority: votes or voters of a certain class collectively: a voter: the right to vote: that by which a choice is expressed, as a ballot.—*v.i.* to express choice, esp. at an election, by vote: to declare in favour of, or against (with *for, against*), esp. by vote.— *v.t.* to determine by vote: to grant by vote: to bring about (a specified result or change) by vote: to declare by general consent (*coll.*): to pronounce, adjudge to be (*coll.*): to propose, suggest (*coll.*): to present for voting: to record the votes of.—*adj.* vote′less.—*n.* vō′ter.—voting machine, a machine on which to register votes. —split one's vote(s), to divide one's votes among two or more candidates; **split the vote,** to injure a cause by influencing a body of possible supporters to vote in some other way (**vote'-splitt'-ing**); **vote Conservative, Labour,** etc., to give one's vote, on a particular occasion or habitually, to the Conservative, Labour, etc., candidate or party; **vote down,** to defeat or suppress by vote, or otherwise; **vote in,** to elect; **vote of no confidence,** the legal method of forcing the resignation of a government or governing body; **vote straight,** to give one's vote honestly. [L. *vōtum*, a wish—*vovēre*, *vōtum*, to vow.]

**voteen,** *vō-tēn'*, (*Ir.*) *n.* a devotee. [Perh. **devote**.]

**votive.** See **votary.**

**vouch,** *vowch*, *v.t.* to call upon to witness, esp. to a title to real estate (*arch.*; also **vouch to warrant, vouch to warranty**): to cite as authority: to assert, declare (*obs.*): to assert or guarantee to be true: to support by evidence: to testify (that): to be sponsor for (*rare*): to guarantee legal possession of (*Shak.*): to vouchsafe, condescend to grant (*arch.*): to second, support (*Milt.*).—*v.i.* to bear witness, or be surety (with *for*).—*n.* assertion: attestation.—*ns.* **vouchee'**, the person summoned to witness to a title to real estate: a person quoted as authority or appealed to as witness; **vouch'er** (partly A.Fr. *voucher*, infin.; partly suff. *-er*), the act of vouching to warrant: a piece of evidence, or a written document serving as proof: a paper which confirms the truth of anything, as a receipt, a certificate of correctness: one who vouches or gives witness: a mechanical contrivance used in shops for automatically registering the amount of money drawn. [O.Fr. *voucher, vocher*, to call to defend—L. *vocāre*, to call.]

**vouchsafe,** *vowch-sāf'*, formerly also (*Milt.*) **voutsafe,** *vowt'sāf*, *v.t.* to warrant safe, guarantee (*obs.*): to condescend to grant (*arch.*): to condescend to allow, to accept, or to engage in (*obs.*): to condescend, be graciously willing.—*v.i.* to condescend:—*pr.p.* **vouchsāf'ing**; *pa.t.* and *pa.p.* **vouchsafed'.**—*n.* **vouchsafe'ment.** [Orig. two words, **vouch, safe.**]

**vou(l)ge,** *vōōzh*, *n.* a weapon carried by foot-soldiers in the 14th century, having a blade fixed on a long staff. [Fr.]

**voulu,** *vōō-lü*, *adj.* deliberate, studied. [Fr.]

**voussoir,** *vōō-swär'*, *n.* one of the wedge-like stones that form part of an arch.—*v.t.* to form with voussoirs. [Fr., through L.L., from L. *volūtus* —*volvēre*, to roll.]

**voutsafe.** See **vouchsafe.**

**vow,** *vow*, *n.* a voluntary promise made to God, or to a saint, or to a god or gods: a binding undertaking or resolve: a solemn or formal promise of fidelity or affection: a firm assertion: an earnest wish or prayer.—*v.t.* to give, dedicate, by solemn promise: to promise or threaten solemnly: to maintain solemnly.—*v.i.* to make vows.—*adj.* **vowed,** bound by religious vows (*obs.*): devoted, confirmed, undertaken, etc., by vow, or as by vow.—*n.* **vow'ess** (*hist.*), a woman who has taken a vow: a nun.—**vow'-fellow** (*Shak.*), one bound by the same vow.—**baptismal vows,** the promises made at baptism by the person baptised, or by the sponsors or parents in his name; **solemn,** as opposed to **simple vow,** such a vow as the Church takes under her special charge, solemnly accepts, as those of poverty, obedience, and chastity, involving complete and irrevocable surrender. [O.Fr. *vou* (Fr. *vœu*)—L. *vōtum*—*vovēre*, to vow.]

**vowel,** *vow'əl*, *n.* a speech-sound produced by the unimpeded passage of the breath (modified by the vocal cords into voice) through the mouth, different vowel sounds being made by altering the form and position of the tongue and the lips: a letter (as *a*, *e*, *i*, *o*, *u*) used alone or in combination to represent a vowel sound.—*adj.* vocal: of, representing, of the nature of, a vowel.—*vs.t.* **vow'el, vow'elise, -ize,** to insert vowel signs in (words written primarily with consonants only): to use as a vowel: to modify by vowel sounds.—*adjs.* **vow'elled,** having vowels, esp. in a marked degree: having a vowel or vowels of a specified kind; **vow'elless,** without vowels; **vow'elly,** full of vowels.—**vowel gradation,** ablaut; **vowel mutation,** umlaut; **vowel point,** a mark inserted, e.g. in Hebrew, to indicate a vowel. [Fr. *voyelle*—L. *vōcālis*—*vōx, vōcis,* voice.]

**vox,** *voks,* (L. *vōks, wōks*), *n.* voice:—*pl.* **voces** (*vō'sēz*).—**vox angelica, vox caelestis,** voix céleste; **vox humana,** in organ-building, a reed-stop producing tones resembling those of the human voice; **vox populi, vox Dei** (*voks pop'ū-li, voks dē'ī, vōks, wōks po'pōō-lē, de'ē* or *dā'ē*), the voice of the people is the voice of God. [L. *vōx.*]

**voyage,** *voi'ij,* *n.* a journey of any kind (*arch.*): travel (*obs.*): a military expedition (*obs.*): an enterprise (*obs.*): a passage by water or by air to some place at a considerable distance: a round trip: a cruise: an account of such a journey.—*v.i.* to make a voyage, cruise, journey. —*v.t.* to traverse, pass over.—*adj.* **voy'ageable,** navigable.—*ns.* **voy'ager; voyageur** (*vwä-yä-zher'*), in Canada one who kept up communication by canoe between trading-posts: a boat-man: a trapper. [O.Fr. *veage, voiage,* etc.—L. *viāticum*; see **viaticum.**]

**voyeur,** *vwä-yœr, n.* a sexual pervert who derives gratification from surreptitiously watching sexual acts or objects: a peeping Tom: one who takes a morbid interest in sordid sights.—*n.* **voyeurism.** [Fr., one who sees.]

**vraic,** *vrāk, n.* a Channel Islands name for sea-weed, used for fuel and manure.—*ns.* **vraick'er; vraick'ing.** [Dial. Fr.; see **varec.**]

**vraisemblance,** *vrā-, vre-sä-bläs', n.* verisimilitude, a picture. [Fr. *vrai,* true, *semblance,* appearance.]

**vril,** *vril, n.* electric fluid represented as the common origin of the forces in matter, in E. G. L. Bulwer-Lytton's *The Coming Race,* 1871.

**vrouw,** *vrow, frow, n.* a woman, goodwife, house-wife. [Du.]

**vug,** *vug, n.* a Cornish miner's name for a cavity in a rock, usu. lined with crystals.—*adj.* **vugg'y.**

**Vulcan,** *vul'kən, n.* the god of fire and metal-working (*Roman myth.*): a planet (*intramercurial planet*) once postulated between the sun and Mercury: (without *cap.*) a blacksmith or an iron-worker.—*n.* **Vulcanā'lia,** an ancient Roman festival in honour of Vulcan, held on 23rd August.—*adjs.* **Vulcā'nian,** of, pertaining to, like, related to, sprung from, made by, Vulcan: volcanic; **vulcanic** (*-kan'ik*), volcanic: (*cap.*) of Vulcan.—*n.* **vulcanicity** (*-is'i-ti*), volcanic action or phenomena.—*adj.* **vulcani'sable,** *-z-.*—*n.* **vulcanisā'tion,** *-z-.*—*v.t.* **vul'canise, -ize,** to treat (rubber, etc.) with sulphur or sulphur compounds, etc.—*v.i.* to admit such treatment. —*ns.* **vul'canism,** volcanic activity: (*cap.*) the teaching of the Vulcanists; **Vul'canist** (*hist. of geol.*), a Plutonist, or a follower of James Hutton (1726-97), who asserted the geological importance of subterranean heat and the igneous origin of such rocks as basalt—opp. to *Neptunist*; **vul'canite,** the harder of the two kinds of vulcanised rubber, the softer kind being called *soft rubber*: a general name for any igneous rock of fine grain-size.—*adj.* **vulcanolog'ical.**—*ns.* **vul-canol'ogist; vulcanol'ogy,** the scientific study of volcanoes and volcanic phenomena.—**vulcanised fibre,** a fibre obtained by treating paper pulp with zinc chloride solution, used for low-voltage insulation; **Vulcan's badge,** a cuckold's horns. [L. *Vulcānus.*]

**vulgar**, *vul'gər*, *adj.* pertaining to the common people: plebeian: vernacular: public: common, usual, customary: common to all: prevalent: commonplace: low: unrefined: coarse: spiritually paltry, ignoble, debased, or pretentious.— *n.* the common people: one of the unrefined, of the uneducated, or of those not in good society: a class of inferior persons (*obs.*): the common language of a country.—*n.* vulgā'rian, a vulgar person: a rich unrefined person.—Also *adj.*— *n* vulgarisā'tion, -z-,—*v.t.* vul'garise, -ize-, make common or ordinary: to make unrefined or coarse.—*ns.* vul'garism, a vulgar phrase: coarseness: an instance of this; vulgarity (-*gar'*).— *adv.* vul'garly.—Vulgar era, the Christian era; vulgar fraction, a fraction written in the common way, as opp. to a *decimal fraction*; vulgar tongue, the vernacular. [L. *vulgāris—vulgus*, the people.]

**Vulgate**, *vul'gāt*, or *-git*, *n.* an ancient Latin version of the Scriptures, made by St Jerome and others in the 4th century, and later twice revised—so called from its common use in the R.C. church: (without *cap.*) a comparable accepted text of any other book or author.—*adj.* of or pertaining to the Vulgate: (without *cap.*; of speech, etc.) commonly used or accepted. [L. *vulgāta* (*editio*), popular edition (of the Bible); see **vulgar**.]

**vulgo**, *vul'gō, vōōl', wōōl'gō*, (L.) commonly.

**vulgus**, *vul'gəs*, *n.* the common people: in some public schools, a short verse task in Latin. [L.; see **vulgar**.]

**vulnerable**, *vul'nər-ə-bl*, *adj.* capable of being wounded: liable to injury, or hurt to feelings: open to successful attack: in contract bridge, of a side that has won a game towards the rubber, liable to increased penalties (or premiums) accordingly.—*v.t.* vuln (*vuln*; *her.*), to wound.—

*adj.* vulned (*her.*).—*ns.* vulnerabil'ity, vul'nerableness.—*adj.* vul'nerary, pertaining to wounds: useful in healing wounds.—*n.* anything useful in curing wounds.—*v.t.* vul'nerate (*obs.*), to wound. —*n.* vulnerā'tion (*obs.*). [L. *vulnerāre*, to wound —*vulnus, vulneris*, a wound.]

**Vulpes**, *vul'pēz*, *n.* the genus including the common fox.—*adj.* vulpine (*vul'pin, -pin*), of, pertaining to, or like a fox: cunning.—*ns.* vul'picide, the killing of a fox, except in hunting: a fox-killer; vul'pinism, craftiness.—vulpine opossum, phalanger, the common Australian phalanger (*Trichosurus vulpecula*). [L. *vulpēs*, a fox.]

**vulpinite**, *vul'pin-it*, *n.* a granular scaly form of the mineral anhydrite. [*Vulpino* in Lombardy.]

**vulsella**, *vul-sel'ə*, *n.* a forceps with toothed or clawed blades:—*pl.* vulsell'ae (-*ē*).—Also vulsell'um. [L.]

**vulture**, *vul'chər, -chər*, *n.* any of a number of large rapacious birds of prey, feeding largely on carrion, regarded as forming one, or two, families: one who or that which resembles a vulture.—Also *adj.*—*adjs.* vul'turine, vul'turish; vul'turous, of, pertaining to, or like a vulture: rapacious.—*ns.* vul'turism (*Carlyle*), rapacity; vul'turn (-*túrn*), the Australian brush-turkey. [O.Fr. *voutour, voltour*, etc. (Fr. *vautour*)—L. *vulturius—vultur*.]

**vulva**, *vul'və*, *n.* the external organ of generation of the female mammal, or the orifice of it.—*adjs.* vul'val, vul'var, vul'vate; vul'viform, oval: like a cleft with projecting edges.—*n.* vulvi'tis, inflammation of the vulva.—vul'vo-, used in composition, as vul'vo-ū'terine, pertaining to the vulva and the uterus. [L. *vulva, volva*, wrapping, womb.]

**vum**, *vum*, (*dial. U.S.*) *v.t.* and *v.i.* a corruption of vow, in phrase I vum.

**vying**, *vī'ing*, *pr.p.* of vie.

# W

**W, w,** *dub′l-ū, n.* the twenty-third letter of our alphabet, a 5th-century addition to the Roman alphabet, being a doubled u or v used to express the voiced consonantal sound heard, e.g. in Eng. *way, weak, warrant*; from the 13th century it was regularly used in writing English, superseding the letter wen (q.v.). In mod. Eng. *w* is found as a consonant and also as the second component in certain vowel and diphthong digraphs, i.e. those in *law, few, now.* The unvoiced form of the consonant is written *wh* (corresponding to O.E. *hw*), as in *what, when,* but many English people substitute the voiced sound in pronouncing words spelt *wh,* and Northern speakers insist upon sounding *hw. W* is no longer pronounced in *write, two,* etc., or in *whole* (which represents a dialectal variation of O.E. *hāl*). O.E. *cw* has become *qu,* as in *queen,* from O.E. *cwēn.*

**wa′,** *wö,* Scots form of **wall.**

**Waac,** *wak, n.* the Women's Army Auxiliary Corps (founded 1917), or a member of it, now **WRAC.**
—*n.* **Waaf** (*waf*), the Women's Auxiliary Air Force (1939), or a member, now **WRAF.** [From the initial letters.]

**wabain.** See **ouabain.**

**wabble.** See **wobble.**

**waboom.** See **wagenboom.**

**wabster.** See **webster.**

**wacke,** *wak′ə, n.* an old name for a decomposed basalt. [Ger.,—O.H.G. *wagge,* a pebble; cf. **greywacke.**]

**wacky,** *wak′i,* (*slang*) *adj.* crazy.—*n.* **wack′iness.**

**wad,** *wod, n.* a pad of loose material as hay, tow, etc., thrust in to aid packing, etc.: formerly a little mass of paper, tow, or the like, now a disk of felt or paper, to keep the charge in a gun: a bundle as of hay: a roll or bundle, as of bank notes: a compact mass, often small: a lump of a soft substance (*rare*).—*v.t.* to form into a mass: to pad, stuff out: to stuff a wad into:—*pr.p.* **wadd′ing;** *pa.t.* and *pa.p.* **wadd′ed.**—*n.* **wadd′ing,** a wad, or the materials for wads: sheets of carded cotton for stuffing garments, etc.: cotton-wool. [Origin uncertain; cf. Sw. *vadd,* wadding; Ger. *watte,* Fr. *ouate.*]

**wad, wadd,** *wod, n.* an earthy ore of manganese, mainly hydrated oxide of manganese. [Ety. dub.]

**wad.** See **wed.**

**waddle,** *wod′l, v.i.* to take short steps and sway from side to side in walking, as a duck does: of an inanimate thing, to move in a way suggestive of this: to become a defaulter (*Stock Exchange slang*).—*n.* act of waddling: a clumsy, rocking gait.—*adj.* **wadd′ling.** [Freq. of **wade.**]

**waddy,** *wod′i, n.* a native Australian wooden war-club: a cowboy: a walking-stick.—Also **wadd′ie.**—*v.t.* to strike with a waddy. [Perh. from Eng. **wood.**]

**wade,** *wād, v.i.* to go (*obs.*; *lit.* and *fig.*): to walk through a substance that yields with difficulty to the feet, as water: to go (through) with difficulty or labour (*fig.*).—*v.t.* to cross by wading: to cause to cross thus.—*n.* the act of wading: a ford (*coll.*).—*n.* **wā′der,** one who wades: a bird that wades in search of food, e.g. the heron, snipe, sandpiper: a high waterproof boot.—*n.* and *adj.* **wā′ding.—wade in,** to make a very vigorous attack; **wade into,** to tackle, as a job, energetically: to make a vigorous attack on (*lit.* and *fig.*). [O.E. *wadan,* to go; Ger. *waten.*]

**wadi, wady,** *wod′i, n.* the dry bed of a torrent: a river-valley. [Ar. *wādi.*]

**wadmal,** *wad′* or *wud′məl,* (*hist.*) *n.* a thick or coarse woollen cloth, woven esp. in Orkney and Shetland.—Also **wad′maal, wad′mol(l).** [O.N. *vathmāl—vāth,* cloth, *māl,* measure.]

**wadset,** *wod′set,* (*Scot.*) *n.* a mortgage: something pledged or pawned.—Also **wadsett.**—*v.t.* to mortgage: to pawn.—*n.* **wad′setter,** mortgagee. [wad, which see under wed, and set.]

**wady.** See **wadi.**

**wae,** *wā, n.* (*Spens.*) woe.—*adj.* (*Scot.*) sorrowful. —*adjs.* **wae′ful** (**wae′fu'**), **wae′some** (*Scot.*), woeful, pitiful.—*n.* **wae′ness,** sadness.—*interj.* **wae-sucks′,** alas! [Dial. form of **woe.**]

**Wafd,** *woft, n.* a Nationalist party in Egypt founded in 1918.

**wafer,** *wā′fər, n.* a very thin crisp cake or biscuit baked in **wafer-irons** or **-tongs,** formerly eaten with wine: a similar biscuit eaten with ice-cream, etc.: a thin round cake of unleavened bread, usu. stamped with a cross, an Agnus Dei, the letters I.H.S., etc., used in the Eucharist: a thin leaf of coloured paste for sealing letters, etc.: a thin cake of paste used to form a cachet or wrapping for powders (*med.*): a thin slice of anything.—*v.i.* to close, fasten, stick (as on a wall), with a wafer.—*adj.* **wā′fery,** like a wafer. —**wāf′er-cake,** a wafer. [O.N.Fr. *waufre* (O.Fr. and Fr. *gaufre*)—M.L.G. *wafel,* cake of wax.]

**waff,** *waf, wöf,* (*Scot.*) *adj.* wandering, stray: worthless, paltry: listless.—*n.* a worthless person. [Variant of **waif.**]

**waff,** *waf, n.* (*Scot.*) a waving, or a slight, hasty motion: a signal: a quick light blow: a puff, or a blast: a sudden ailment: a faint, usu. disagreeable, odour: a glimpse: a ghost.—*v.t.* and *v.i.* (*dial.* or *obs.*) to wave, flap, flutter, wave away. [Noun from verb, which is a variant of **wave.**]

**waff,** *waf,* (*dial.*) *v.i.* to bark.—Also **waugh.** [Imit.]

**waffle,** *wof′l, n.* a kind of batter-cake, baked in an iron utensil of hinged halves called a **waff′le-i′ron.** [Du. *wafel,* wafer.]

**waffle,** *wof′l,* (*dial.*) *v.i.* to wave. [Freq. of **waff** (2).]

**waffle,** *wof′l,* (*slang*) *v.i.* to talk incessantly or non-sensically: to waver, vacillate.—Also *n.* [Freq. of **waff** (3).]

**waft,** *wäft, woft, waft, v.t.* to bear, convey, transport, propel, safely or lightly, on the surface of or through a fluid medium, as air or water (*poet.*; also *fig.*): to signal to, beckon (perh. for **waff** (2)): to turn (Shak., *Wint.* I, ii. 372).—*v.i.* to float, sail, pass through the air:—*pa.t.* **waft′ed;** *Spens.* **weft;** *pa.p.* **waft′ed;** *Spens.* **weft.** —*n.* a scent, or sound, or puff of smoke or vapour carried by the air: a rush of air (also *fig.*): a slight taste, esp. an unpleasant one: an act of wafting, or of waving: a waving movement: a passage across the sea or other water (*obs.*): a flag or substitute hoisted as a signal, esp. an ensign, stopped together at the head and middle portions, slightly rolled up lengthwise, and hoisted at different positions at the after-part of a ship (also **weft, wheft**): the act of displaying such a signal.—*ns.* **waft′age,** act of wafting: transportation through air or across water; **waft′er; waft′ing; waft′ure** (Rowe's emendation, *Jul. Caes.* II, i. 246), act of wafting or of waving: waving motion: beckoning: something wafted.

[From obs. *wafter*, a convoying vessel, prob.—
L.G. or Du. *wachter*, guard.]

**wag**, *wag*, *v.i.* to move, or be moved, from side to
side, or to shake to and fro: to oscillate: to
move, or to move one's limbs: to move on, be
off (*arch.*): to play truant (*slang*): of tongue,
chin, beard, etc., to move in light, gossiping or
indiscreet talk: of the world, etc. (in the sense of
human affairs), to go in respect of good fortune
and bad.—*v.t.* to move, shake, wave, to and fro
or up and down: to brandish (*obs.*): to move,
stir a limb, etc.: to move in chatter or indiscreet
talk: to move so as to express reproof or
derision, etc.:—*pr.p.* **wagg′ing**; *pa.t.* and *pa.p.*
**wagged**.—*n.* a shake: an act of wagging: ability
to wag: truant (in **to play the wag**): a droll,
mischievous fellow, a habitual joker, a wit (perh.
from obs. **wag′halter**, one who deserves hanging): a fellow (*obs.*).—*n.* **wagg′ery**, mischievous
merriment or jesting: an instance of such.—*adj.*
**wagg′ish**.—*adv.* **wagg′ishly**.—*n.* **wagg′ishness**.—
**wag′-at-the-wa′′**, **wag′-at**(or -by)**-the-wall′** (*Scot.*
and *Northern*), a hanging clock with exposed
pendulum and weights. [M.E. *waggen*, from
same root as O.E. *wagian*, to shake.]

**wage**, *wāj*, *v.t.* to pledge, offer as a pledge (*obs.*):
to wager (*obs.*): to hazard (*obs.*): to engage in,
to carry on, esp. war: to hire for pay, to pay
wages to, or to bribe (*obs.*): to let out for pay
(*Spens.*).—*v.i.* (*Shak.*) to be equal in value: to
contend, battle.—*n.* a gage or pledge (*obs.*):
payment for services, esp. not professional, or
(*fig.*) reward (both often **wages**, *pl.* in form, but
sometimes construed as *sing.*).—*n.* **wā′ger**, a
pledge (*obs.*): the act of giving a pledge (*obs.*):
something staked on an issue: a bet: that on
which bets are laid: a hazard (*rare*): a contest
for a prize (*rare*): an offer to make oath (*law*).
—*v.t.* to hazard on the issue of anything.—*v.i.*
to lay a wager.—*n.* **wā′gerer**.—**wage′-earn′er**,
one who works for wages: one who earns the
money that supports, or money that helps to
support, the household; **wage′-earn′ing**; **wage′-
freeze**, a fixing of wages at a certain level for
some time ahead; **wage′-packet**, small envelope
in which a worker's wages are issued: loosely,
wages; **wa′ger-boat**, a light boat for a race
between single scullers; **wa′ge(s)-fund**, or
**wa′ges-fund theory**, the theory (now abandoned)
that there is at any given time in a country a
determinate amount of capital available for the
payment of labour, therefore the average wage
depends on the proportion of this fund to the
number of persons who have to share in it;
**wage′-work**, work done for wages.—**living wage**
(see **living**); **wager of battle** (*hist.*), trial by combat, a usage which permitted the accused and
accuser, in defect of sufficient direct evidence, to
challenge each other to mortal combat. [M.E.
*wagen*—O.N.Fr. *wagier* (O.Fr. *gagier*), to pledge
(through popular L. from a Gmc. word).]

**wagenboom**, *vä′gən-bōm*, *-bōōm*, **waboom** (*Afrik.*),
*vä′bōōm*, *n.* a S. African tree (*Protea grandiflora*)
whose wood is used in making wagon wheels.
[Du., wagon-tree.]

**waggle**, *wag′l*, *v.i.* and *v.t.* to wag, esp. in an unsteady manner.—Also *n.*—*adj.* **wagg′ly**. [Freq.
of **wag**.]

**waggon**, etc. See **wagon**.

**wagmoire**, *wag′moir*, (*Spens.*) *n.* a quagmire.

**Wagnerian**, *väg-nē′ri-ən*, *adj.* pertaining to or
characterised by the ideas or style of Richard
*Wagner* (1813-83), German composer of music-
dramas: pertaining to Rudolf *Wagner* (1805-
1864), physiologist.—*n.* a follower or admirer
of Richard Wagner.— *adj.* **Wagneresque′**. — *ns.*
**Wag′nerism**, **Wagne′rianism**, the art theory of
Richard Wagner, its main object being the
freeing of opera from traditional and conventional forms, and its one canon, dramatic fitness;

**Wag′nerist**, **Wag′nerite**, an adherent of Wagner's
musical methods.

**wagon**, **waggon**, *wag′ən*, *n.* a four-wheeled vehicle,
esp. one for carrying heavy goods: an open
railway truck or a closed railway van: a movable
piece of furniture with shelves (see **dinner-wagon**):
a chariot (*obs.*): (*cap.*) Ursa Major.—*v.t.* to
transport by wagon.—*v.i.* to travel in a wagon.
—*ns.* **wag′onage**, conveyance by wagon, or
money paid for it: a collection of wagons
(*Carlyle*); **wag′oner**, **wagg′oner**, one who drives
a wagon: a charioteer (*obs.*): (*cap.*) the constellation Auriga; **wagonette′**, a kind of open
carriage with one or two seats crosswise in
front, and two back seats arranged lengthwise
and facing inwards; **wag′onful**.—**wa′gon-box**,
**-bed**, the carrying part of a wagon; **wag′on-load**,
the load carried by a wagon: a great amount;
**wag′on-lock**, a kind of iron shoe or other device
placed on the rear-wheel of a wagon to retard
motion in going downhill; **wag′on-roof**, **-vault**,
a barrel-vault; **wag′on-train**, a collection or
service of army vehicles for the conveyance of
ammunition, provisions, sick, etc.: a train of
usu. horse-drawn wagons used by pioneer
settlers to travel into new territory; **wag′on-
wright**, a maker of wagons. [Du. *wagen*; cf.
O.E. *wægn*, Eng. **wain**.]

**wagon-lit**, *vä-gō̇-lē*, *n.* a sleeping-carriage on a
continental train:—*pl.* **wagons-lit** (pron. as *sing.*;
sometimes **wagon-lits**). [Fr. *wagon* (—Eng.
**wagon**), *lit*, bed.]

**wagtail**, *wag′tāl*, *n.* any bird of the family *Motacil-
lidae*, so named from their constant wagging of
the tail—the true wagtails, the pipits, etc.:
applied also to other birds, as American water-
thrush and an Australian fly-catcher: contemptuously for a pert, or an obsequious, person
(*obs.*): a harlot (*obs.*).

**Wahabi**, **Wahabee**, *wä-hä′bē*, *n.* one of a sect of
Moslems founded in Central Arabia about 1760
by Abd-el-*Wahhab* (1691-1787), whose aim was
to restore primitive Mohammedanism.—Also
**Waha′b(i)ite**.—*n.* **Waha′bi(i)sm**, the doctrine and
practices of the Wahabis.

**wahine**, *wä-hē′ne*, *n.* a Maori woman. [Maori.]

**wahoo**, *wa-hōō′*, *n.* the burning bush (genus
Euonymus or Evonymus), an ornamental shrub
with scarlet-coated seeds. [Dakota Indian
*wanhu*.]

**wahoo**, *wa-hōō′*, *n.* a Californian buckthorn
(*Rhamnus purshiana*) which yields cascara sagrada: the winged elm, with hard-grained wood:
also the rock-elm. [Creek Indian *ûhawhu*.]

**waid**, **waide**. Old spellings of **weighed**, *pa.t.* and
*pa.p.* or **weigh**: in Shak., *T. of S.* III, ii. 56 or 57
prob. for **swayed** (see **sway**).

**waif**, *wāf*, *n.* a piece of property found ownerless,
as a strayed animal, or goods cast up by the tide
(*Spens.*): **waift**, **weft**; also *fig.*): stolen goods
abandoned by the thief (*obs.*): a homeless
wanderer: a neglected ownerless child.—*adj.*
(*Scot.*) vagabond, neglected.—*v.t.* (*rare*; in *pa.p.*)
to cast up as a waif.—**waif and stray**, strayed
property—same as **waif** alone: (in *pl.*) homeless,
destitute persons. [O.Fr. *waif*; prob.—Scand.;
cf. O.N. *veif*, any flapping or waving thing.]

**waif**, *wāf*, *n.* a streak, puff—same as **waff** (2).

**waift**. See **waif** (1).

**wail**, *wāl*, *v.i.* to lament or sorrow audibly: of
eyes, to weep (*Shak.*).—*v.t.* to bemoan: to
grieve over.—*n.* the action of wailing: a cry of
woe: an animal cry or mechanical sound
suggesting this.—*n.* **wail′er**.—*adj.* **wail′ful**,
sorrowful: expressing woe.—*n.* and *adj.* **wail′ing**.
—*adv.* **wail′ingly**.—**Wailing Wall**, a wall fifty-
nine feet high, part of an enclosed space in
Jerusalem, where Jews traditionally pray on
Fridays and from which they were excluded for a
time. [M.E. *weilen*, *wailen*; cf. O.N. *væla*.]

**wain**, *wān*, *n.* a wagon, esp. for hay or other agricultural produce, or poetically: a chariot (*obs.*): (*cap.*) Charles's Wain or the Lesser Wain.—*v.t.* (*rare*) to carry.—*n.* **wain'age**, the team and implements necessary for the cultivation of land: land under cultivation.—**wain'wright**, a wagonmaker.—**the Lesser Wain**, the constellation Ursa Minor, or seven bright stars in it. [O.E. *wægen*, *wǣn*—*wegen*, to carry; cf. Du. and Ger. *wagen*, Eng. **wagon**.]

**wainscot**, *wān'skot*, *-skət*, or *wen'*, *n.* fine oak for panelling: woodwork, esp. panelled, on an interior wall: similar lining of other material: the lower part of an interior wall when lined with material different from that on the upper part: a collector's name for certain noctuoid moths.—*v.t.* to line with, or as if with, boards or panels: to grain in imitation of oak:—*pr.p.* **wain'scoting**, **wain'scotting**; *pa.t.* and *pa.p.* **wain'scoted**, **wain'scotted**. — *n.* **wain'scoting**, **wain'scotting**, the act of lining with boards or panels: materials for making a wainscot: wainscots collectively. [Orig. perh. wood used for a partition in a wagon—Du. *wagen-schot*, oakwood—*wagen*, wagon, or M.Du. *waeghe*, wave (from the appearance of the grain of the wood), *schot*, partition.]

**waist**, *wāst*, *n.* the smallest part of the human trunk, between the ribs and the hips: a narrow middle part of an insect: the part of a garment that lies round the waist of the body: a woman's blouse or bodice (*U.S.*): the narrow middle part, as of a musical instrument: the middle part of a ship: the middle (of the day or night; *obs.*): something that surrounds, a girdle (*obs.*).—*adj.* **waist'ed**, having a waist, often of specified type.—*n.* **waist'er**, a seaman stationed in the waist, performing menial duties, esp. a green-hand on a whaler.—**waist'-anch'or**, an anchor stowed in the waist of a ship; **waist'band**, part of a garment that fits the waist: a belt or sash; **waist'belt**, a belt for the waist: **waist'boat**, a boat carried in the waist of a vessel; **waist'cloth**, a loin cloth: (in *pl.*) coloured cloths hung about a ship's waist as ceremonial decoration or to conceal the men in a naval action (*obs.*); **waist'coat** (*wās'*, *wāst'kōt*; *arch.*, now *dial.*, *wes'kət*), a garment, plain or ornamental, reaching to or below the waist, and now sleeveless, intended to show partly, worn by men at different periods under doublet, coat, jacket, etc.: a woman's similar garment or front; **waistcoateer'** (*obs.*), a strumpet; **waist'coating**, material for men's waistcoats, esp. of a fancy pattern.—*adjs.* **waist'-deep**, **-high**, as deep, high, as to reach up to the waist.—**waist'line**, a line thought of as marking the waist, but not fixed by anatomy in women's fashions; the measurement of a waist. [M.E. *wast*, from presumed O.E. *wæst*, growth, size; cf. Ice. *vöxtr*, O.E. *wæstm*, growth, Eng. **wax** (2).]

**wait**, *wāt*, *v.i.* to keep watch, be on guard (*Spens.* **waite**; *obs.*): be on the watch for someone, lie in ambush (*obs.*): to be, remain, in expectation or readiness (with *for*): to be, remain, in a place in readiness (also **wait about, around**): to delay action: to be in attendance, or in readiness to carry out orders: to bring food to the table and clear away used dishes.—*v.t.* to watch, watch for, or lie in ambush for (*obs.*): to be, remain, in expectation of, await (*obs.*): to postpone, as a meal, for some purpose (*coll.*): to attend on, attend, escort (*obs.*).—*n.* ambush—now used only in such phrases as **to lie in wait, to lay wait**: a watchman, sentinel, or spy (*obs.*): the act of waiting or of expecting: delay: the period of attendance of a lord-, or lady-in-waiting: (in *pl.*) musicians employed by a town to play on ceremonial occasions (*hist.*): (in *pl.*) persons who welcome in Christmas by playing or singing out-of-doors at night: a member of the town, or of a Christmas, band of waits.—*ns.* **wait'er**, a watchman (*obs.*): a customs officer (*obs.*): one who waits, esp. at table in a hotel dining-room, etc.: an attending servant (*obs.*): a salver or tray: a dumb-waiter (see **dumb**): a uniformed attendant at the London Stock Exchange; **wait'erage** (*rare*), service; **wait'erhood** (*rare*), **wait'ering** (*rare*), the employment of a waiter; **wait'ing**, act of waiting: attendance.—Also *adj.*—*adv.* (*rare*) **wait'ingly**.—*n.* **wait'ress**, a female waiter.—**wait'-a-bit**, (also often *adj.*) a name given to various plants, esp. S. African (*Afrik.* **wag-'n-bietjie**), with thorns that catch the clothing of the passer-by; **wait'-a-while**, a wait-a-bit: an Australian wattle growing in dense thickets; **wait'ing-list**, **wait'-list**, a list of people waiting, as candidates awaiting a vacancy, etc.; **wait'ing-maid**, **-wom'an**, a female attendant; **wait'ing-room**, a room for the use of persons waiting; **wait'ing-vass'al** (obs.), an attendant; **wait'-list** (see **waiting-list**).—*v.t.* to add someone's name to a waiting-list, esp. for a seat on an aircraft.—**lie in wait**, to be in hiding ready to attack or surprise (*lit.* and *fig.*); **lords, and grooms, in waiting**, certain officers in the Lord Chamberlain's department of the royal household; **minority waiter**, meaning uncertain—perh. a waiter, or a tidewaiter, out of employment; **play a waiting game** (*lit.* and *fig.*), to avoid action as far as possible in the hope of having an opportunity later to use one's energies with maximum effect; **wait attendance** (*Shak.*), to remain in attendance; **wait off** (*racing*), to allow oneself to be temporarily outdistanced by other competitors, reserving one's energies for the final stretch; **wait on**, to wait for (*dial.*): to continue to wait (*Scot.*): to wait upon; **wait table**, to wait at table during a meal; **wait up**, to stay out of bed waiting (with *for*); **wait upon, on**, to call upon, visit formally: to accompany: to attend and serve: to be connected with or follow as a consequence: to carry out the duties of (an office; *B.*): to gaze at, keep under observation (*obs.*). [O.N.Fr. *waitier* (O.Fr. *guaitier*, Fr. *guetter*), to watch, attend; of Gmc. origin; cf. O.H.G. *wahta* (Ger. *wacht*), a watchman; cog. with O.E. *wacan*, to watch.]

**waive**, *wāv*, *v.t.* to put away, reject, to abandon, forsake, to vacate, to resign (*obs.*): to outlaw (a woman—her status in the eyes of the law being such that the usual term was not applicable to her; *hist.*): to abandon (stolen goods) (*obs.*): to give up voluntarily, as a claim or a contention (*law*): to refrain from claiming, demanding, taking, or enforcing: to forgo: to evade, avoid (*arch.*): to defer, postpone: to leave out of consideration, disregard (*obs.*).—*n.* **wai'ver**, the act, or an act, of waiving. [A.Fr. *weyver*—O.Fr. *guesver*, to abandon; from same root as **waif**.]

**waivode**, **waivode(ship)**. Same as **voivode**, etc.

**wake**, *wāk*, *v.i.* to be, or to remain, awake, or active or vigilant: to keep watch or vigil, or to pass the night in prayer: to hold a wake: to awake, be roused from, or as from, sleep, from indifference, etc. (often with *up*): to become animated or lively: to be stirred up, aroused: to hold a late revel (*obs.*).—*v.t.* to rouse from sleep: to keep vigil over: to excite, stir up: to disturb with noise: to animate: to reanimate, revive:—*pa.t.* **waked**, *wākt*, or **woke**, *wōk*; *pa.p.* **waked**, **wo'ken**, rare **woke**.—*n.* act or state of waking (*obs.*, except in **sleep and/or wake, wake and/or dream**): a serenade (*James Hogg*): the feast of the dedication of a church, formerly kept by watching all night: a festival: (usu. in *pl.*) an annual holiday (*dial.*): a watch or vigil beside a corpse, sometimes with revelry.—*adj.* **wake'ful**, not asleep: unable, or indisposed, to sleep: vigilant: waking: awakening or rousing (*Milt.*).—*adv.* **wake'fully**.—*n.* **wake'fulness**.—*adj.*

wake'less, sound, undisturbed.—*v.i.* wā'ken, to be, or become, awake: to become active or lively: to remain awake, keep watch (*obs.*).—*v.t.* to rouse from sleep, unconsciousness, inaction: to excite, stir up, evoke.—*adj.* (*Scot.*) waking, awake.—*adj.* wā'kened.—*n.* wā'kener, one who or that which wakens.—*adj.* wā'kening.—*n.* act of one who wakens: revival of an action (*Scots law*).—*ns.* wā'ker, one who wakes; wā'king.—*adj.* that wakes, keeps watch, or is vigilant: that rouses or becomes awake: passed, or experienced, in the waking state.—wake'man (*arch.*), a watchman.—*adj.*, wake'rife (-*rif*, -*rif*; *Scot.*), useful: vigilant. — wake'-robin, cuckoo-pint, *Arum maculatum*: the spotted orchis, *Orchis maculata*: applied to various other flowers, esp. in U.S., to any of the genus Trillium.—wake a night, the night, to remain awake, or be up and about, all night; wake(n) to, wake up to, to become conscious of, alive to. [A combination of an O.E. strong verb *wacan*, to be born, to awake, and an O.E. weak verb *wacian*, to be awake, to watch; cf. watch.]

wake, wāk, *n.* the streak of smooth-looking or foamy water left in the track of a ship: disturbed air behind a flying body: a track on land (*rare*): a trail of light behind a moving body: hence in the wake of (*fig.*), close behind: immediately after (usu. implying consequence). [Of Scand. origin; cf. O.N. *vök*, an ice hole, *vökr*, moist.]

wakiki, wä'kē-kē, *n.* shell money. [Melanesian.]

Walachian. See Vlach.

wald. See weld (1).

Waldenses, wol-den'sēz, *n.pl.* a Christian community of austere morality and devotion to the simplicity of the Gospel, orig. followers of Peter *Waldo*, a merchant of Lyons in the second half of the 12th century; their chief centre was, and is, the Alps in S.E. France and Piedmont (also Valdenses).—*adj.* and *n.* Walden'sian. [Formed from name of Peter *Waldo*, 12-cent. preacher.]

waldflute, wöld'flōot, *n.* an organ flute stop usu. of 4-foot pitch. [Formed after Ger. *waldflöte*, lit. forest flute.]

waldgrave, wöld'grāv, *n.* in mediaeval Germany, a head forest-ranger: an old German title of nobility.— *n.* waldgravine (wöld'grä-vēn), the wife of a waldgrave. [Ger. *waldgraf—wald*, forest, *graf*, count.]

waldhorn, wöld'hörn, *n.* a hunting-horn, a French horn without valves: an organ reed-stop. [Ger.]

wale, wāl, *n.* weal (2): a ridge on the surface of cloth: texture: a vertical ridge in knitted fabrics: a horizontal timber used to bind together piles driven in a row: (in *pl.*) planks all along the outer timbers on a ship's side, bends.—*v.t.* to mark with wales: to make or furnish with, or secure with, wales. [O.E. *walu*; cf. O.N. *völr*, a rod.]

wale, wāl, (*Scot.* and *North.*) *n.* the act of choosing: choice: scope of choice: the pick or best. —*v.t.* and *v.i.* to choose, pick. [O.N. *val*, choice; Ger. *wahl*, choice; from the root of will.]

waler, wā'lər, *n.* in India, a horse imported from New South *Wales*, or from Australia generally.

Walhalla, val-hal'ə, *n.* Same as Valhalla.

wali, wä'lē, *n.* Same as vali.

walise. Scottish form of valise.

walk, wök, *v.i.* to roll, or to toss about (*obs.*): of a biped, to move along leisurely on foot with alternate steps: of a quadruped, to move along in such a way that there are always at least two feet on the ground: to pace: to journey on foot: to ramble, go on foot for pleasure, etc.: of an inanimate object, to be in motion (*obs.*): to make progress (*naut.*): of the tongue, to wag (*obs.*): to make slow progress: to circulate, spread, be rife (*obs.*): to go restlessly about (as a ghost): to move off, depart, withdraw (*obs.* and *coll.*): to conduct oneself, behave: to be associated and in concord (*obs.*).—*v.t.* to pass through or upon, perambulate, traverse: to follow, trace out, on foot: to go through (a dance) at a slow pace: to circulate (*obs.*): to full, as cloth or yarn (*dial.*): to cause to walk, or to move as if walking.—*n.* the action, or an act, of walking: a spell of walking, especially for pleasure: a perambulation in procession: a walking-race: gait: that in or through which one walks: a possible or suitable route or course for walking: a path or place for walking: a tree-bordered avenue: a place for animals, as young hounds, to train or to exercise: a fowl-run: a place where a gamecock is kept: high pasture-ground (*obs.*): a division of a forest: distance as measured by the time taken to walk it: conduct: course of life, sphere of action: a hawker's district or round: a hunting-ground (*obs.*): (in *pl.*) grounds, park (*obs.*): a flock of snipe or of wagtails.—*adj.* walk'able. — *n.* walk'er, one who walks: a colporteur or (*dial.*) a vagrant: a forester (*hist.*): one who trains and walks young hounds: any bird that walks, not hops: a stick-insect.—*interj.* (*cap.*; also Hook'ey Walk'er — *arch. slang*), an exclamation of incredulity (also, as *n.*, humbug).—*n.* walk'ing, the verbal noun of walk: pedestrianism: condition of a surface from the point of view of one who walks on it: the act or process of fulling cloth.—*adj.* that walks, or that moves as if walking: that oscillates: used in or for walking: performed by walking: worked by a person or animal who walks.—*adv.* walk'about (*Austr. slang*), on the move.—*n.* wandering, journey.—walk'-around', a dancing performance by Negroes in which a large circle is described: a march in procession about the stage (*theat.*): the music for either of these; walk'-away (*coll.*), an effortless victory; walk'er-on', one who plays parts in which he has nothing to say; walk'ie-talk'ie, walk'y-talk'y, a portable radiotelephonic transmitting and receiving set; walk'ing-beam, a beam or oscillating lever for transmitting power, as that actuating the cable in cable-drilling for oil; walking case, a patient, but not confined to bed; walk'ing-fish, any of various fishes, mainly Asiatic, which are able to move about on land; walk'ing-gentleman, -lady, an actor or actress playing very small parts for which a good appearance is required; walk'ing-leaf, a leaf-insect; walk'ing-orders, -papers, -ticket (*slang*), dismissal; walk'ing-part, one in which the actor has nothing to say; walk'ing-stick, -cane, -staff, a stick, cane, or staff used in walking; walk'ing-stick, -straw, -twig, a stick-insect; walk'ing-toad, a natterjack; walk'-mill, a fulling-mill: a machine operated by the walking of a horse; walk'-on, a walking-part; walk'-out, the act of walking out, usually to indicate disapproval: a sudden industrial strike; walk'-over, a race where only one competitor appears, and has merely to cover the course to win: an easy or unopposed victory; walk'way, a road, path, etc., constructed for pedestrians only.—walk away from, to outdistance or undo easily; walk away with, to win with ease; walk into (*coll.*), to beat: to storm at: to eat heartily of; walk off, to leave: to depart: to get rid of by walking, as disagreeable feelings or effects; walk off with, to take surreptitiously or feloniously: to win easily; walk on, to walk ahead: to continue to walk: to have a walking part; walk on air, to be exultant or light-hearted; walk one's chalks, to quit, go away without ceremony; walk out, to leave, esp. as a gesture of disapproval: to strike; walk out on (*coll.*), to desert, leave in the lurch; walk out with, to go for walks with as a stage of courtship (also walk with); walk over, to

cross, or traverse: to win an uncontested race: to have an easy victory or easy success (coll.): to disregard rights or feelings of (coll.); walk the chalk, chalkmark, to walk along a chalked line as a test of sobriety: to keep a correct course in manners or morals; walk the hospitals, to be a student under clinical instruction at a general hospital or infirmary; walk the streets, wander about in search of work, or simply aimlessly.
—charity walk, sponsored walk, organised cross-country walk in aid of charity, each participator having obtained from a sponsor or sponsors agreement to contribute according to distance covered. [M.E. walken, walkien, to walk, to full—O.E. wealcan, to roll, revolve, wealcian, to roll up, curl; cog. with Ger. walken, to full cloth.]
Walkyrie, vol'kir-i, wol-kir'i. Same as Valkyrie. [O.E. wælcyri(g)e.]
wall, wöl, n. an erection of brick, stone, etc., for security or to enclose a space such as a piece of land: the side of a building or of a room: (in pl.) fortifications: any bounding surface suggestive of a wall, e.g. the membranous covering or lining of an organ of the body or of a plant or animal cell: the side next the wall: a defence, means of security (fig.): a barrier (fig.): in mah-jongg, the arrangement of the tiles before the hands are drawn: in mining, one of the surfaces of rock enclosing the lode.—In composition, growing on, living in, for hanging on, or otherwise associated with, a wall.—v.t. to enclose with, or as with, a wall: to fortify with, or as with, walls: to divide as by a wall.—adj. walled, enclosed with a wall: fortified.—ns. wall'er, one who builds walls; wall'ing, walls collectively: materials for walls.—adj. wall'-less.—wall'-board, building-board; wall'-cress, rock-cress, any species of Arabis; wall'fish, a snail; wall'-flower, one of the Cruciferae, with fragrant flowers, yellow when wild, found on old walls: any other plant of the same genus (Cheiranthus or Cheirinia): a person who remains a spectator at a dance, usu. a woman who cannot obtain partners (coll.): a yellowish-red colour (also wallflower brown); wall'-fruit, a fruit-tree growing against a wall: its fruit; wall'-game, a variety of football played at Eton against a wall—'at the wall' instead of 'in the field'; wall'-gill'yflower, wallflower; wall'-knot, a nautical method of tying the strands at the end of a rope; wall'-liz'ard, -newt, a common lizard living in the chinks of walls; wall'-moss, a yellow lichen: the common stone-crop; wall'-mustard, a yellow-flowered cruciferous plant (Diplotaxis) of walls, quarries, etc.; wall'-paint'ing, the decoration of walls with ornamental painted designs: a work of art painted on a wall; wall-pa'per, paper, usually coloured or decorated, for pasting on the walls of a room; wall'-pepp'er, the common stone-crop; wall'-plate, a horizontal piece of timber or of rolled steel on a wall, etc., to bear the ends of joists, etc.; wall'-rue, a small fern growing on walls, etc., one of the spleenworts; wall'-space, space on a wall, e.g. on which to hang a picture; Wall Street, a street in New York, the chief financial centre in the United States: hence American financial interests; wall'-tree, a tree trained against a wall; wall'-wort, name applied to various plants growing on walls, as pellitory (Parietaria officinalis), wall-pepper, etc.: see also separate article.—drive to the wall, to push to extremities; go to the wall (obs. walls), to be hard pressed: to be forced to give way: to fail, go under: to give precedence to something else; hang by the wall, to remain unused; push, or thrust, to the wall, to force to give place; the wall, the right of taking the side of the road near the wall when encountering another person, as in the phrase to

give, or take, the wall; turn one's face to the wall, to resign oneself to death or despair; up the wall (coll.), mad, distracted; wall a rope, to make a wall-knot on the end of a rope; walls have ears (see ear); wall up, to block with a wall: to entomb in a wall; with one's back to the wall, in desperate straits: at bay. [O.E. wall (W.S. weall) —L. vallum, a rampart.]
walla. See wallah.
wallaba, wol'ə-ba, n. a valuable caesalpiniaceous tree of the Guianas and Brazil, with durable streaked reddish wood. [Native name.]
wallaby, wol'əb-i, n. any of a number of small kangaroos.—on the wallaby, on the wallaby track (slang; Austr.), travelling through the bush with one's 'swag', looking for work. [Native Austr. wolabā.]
Wallace's line, wol'is-iz līn, a line passing through the East Indian group of islands between Bali and Lombok, roughly separating the very different faunas of the Oriental region and the Australian region, or rather a transitional region. [Alfred Russel Wallace (1823-1913), naturalist.]
Wallachian. Same as Vlach.
wallah, wol'a, n. (often in combination) one employed in, or concerned with, a specific type of work: one who occupies an eminent position in an organization, etc.—Also walla.—competition wallah, a member of the Indian Civil Service who obtained appointment by the competitive system instituted in 1856. [Hindi -wālā, properly an adjectival suffix, in one sense comparable to L. -ārius or Eng. -ar, -er, -or.]
wallaroo, wol-ə-rōō', n. any of various large kangaroos (Macropus). [Native Austr. wolarū.]
wallet, wol'it, n. a bag for carrying necessaries on a journey: a bag with the opening at the middle and a pouch at each end: a pocket-book: a bag for tools: anything protuberant and hanging loosely (Shak.). [M.E. walet, poss.—watel, a bag of woven material; cf. wattle.]
wall-eye, wöl'-ī, n. an eye in which the iris is pale, or the white part is very large or noticeable (e.g. as the result of a squint): the disease of the eye called glaucoma: any of various fishes (U.S.).—adj. wall'-eyed, very light grey in the eyes, or in one eye: having a divergent squint: having a staring or a blank expression or (fig.) appearance: glaring, fierce (Shak.). [The adj. is the earlier; O.N. vagleygr, perh. conn. with mod. Ice. vagl, a film over the eye.]
Walloon, wol-ōōn', adj. of or pertaining to a people living chiefly in southern Belgium and adjacent parts of eastern France, or to their language.—n. a man or woman of this people: their language, a dialect of French. [Fr. Wallon; of Gmc. origin, cog. with Welsh, Walachian.]
wallop, wol'əp, v.i. to gallop (obs.): to move quickly but clumsily, noisily, and with effort: to flounder: to bubble and boil (perh. a different word): to flap about (Scot.).—v.t. (coll.) to beat soundly, thrash: to strike with force.—n. a gallop (obs.): a plunging movement (coll.): a heavy blow (coll.): a flapping rag (Scot.): beer (slang).—adv. with a wallop: heavily or noisily. —ns. wall'oper, one who or that which wallops: something extremely large or big (coll.); wall'op-ing.—adj. that wallops: extremely large or big, bouncing, whopping (coll.).—wallop in a tow, tether (Scot.), to be hanged. [O.N.Fr. waloper (Fr. galoper); cf. gallop.]
wallow, wol'ō, v.i. to roll about in mud, etc., as an animal does (implying enjoyment; lit. and fig.): to flounder: in a bad sense, to live in filth or gross vice: to surge, heave, blow, well up, etc.— v.t. (obs.) to cause to wallow in lit. senses.—n. the act of wallowing: the place, or the filth, an animal wallows in: a hollow or depression suggestive of a wallowing-place: a rolling gait

(*obs.*): the swell of the sea (*poet.*).—*ns.* wall′o-wer; wall′owing, that wallows: very rich (*slang*). [O.E. *wealwian*—L. *volvĕre*.]

wallow, *wol′ō*, (*dial.*) *v.i.* to fade away.—*adj.* wall′-owed, withered, faded. [O.E. *wealwian*.]

wallsend, *wölz′end, n.* orig. coal dug at *Wallsend* (at the *end* of the Roman *Wall*) in Northumberland: later, coal of a certain quality and size.

wallwort, *wöl′wәrt, n.* dwarf elder (also called Danewort, Dane's blood, etc.), a plant with an offensive smell and taste: see also under wall. [O.E. *wealhwyrt, wǣlwyrt*—*wealh*, a foreigner, or (prob. orig., from the belief that it grew on battlefields) *wǣl*, slaughter, and *wyrt*, a root, a plant.]

wally, *wö′li*, (*Scot.*) *adj.* excellent, fine-looking, ample (a general term of commendation).—*adv.* (*obs.*) finely, well.—*n.* an ornament: (in *pl.*) finery: a showy trifle.—Also wa′ly. [Ety. uncertain; perh. wale (2).]

wallydrag, *wol′i-drag*, wallydraigle, *wol′i-drā-gl*, (*Scot.*) *ns.* a person or animal that is feeble, worthless, or slovenly: the youngest of a family. [wally, and drag, draigle (Scots form of draggle).]

walnut, *wöl′nut, n.* a genus (Juglans) of beautiful trees, some yielding valuable furniture wood: their wood: the nut of the Common or English Walnut: walnut-juice.—wal′nut-juice, juice from the husk of walnuts used to stain the skin.—black walnut, a North American walnut, the timber of which is more valuable than that of common walnut, though the fruit is inferior. [O.E. *walhhnutu*—*w(e)alh*, foreigner, *hnutu*, a nut.]

Walpurgis night, *val-pûr′gis nīt*, or *-pōōr′*, the eve of the first of May, when witches, according to German popular superstition, rode on broomsticks and he-goats to hold revel with their master the devil, esp. on the Brocken in the Harz Mountains. [So called because May 1st is the day of St *Walpurga*, abbess of Heidenheim, who died about 778.]

walrus, *wöl′rәs, wöl′rәs, n.* an aquatic, web-footed, carnivorous animal, also called the morse or sea-horse, allied to the seals, having the upper canine teeth developed into enormous tusks: a walrus moustache (*coll.*).—walrus moustache, one with long drooping ends. [Du. *walrus, walros*, lit. whale horse; of Scand. origin.]

Waltonian, *wol-tō′ni-әn, adj.* of or pertaining to Izaak *Walton* (1593-1683), who wrote *The Compleat Angler*.—*n.* a disciple of Walton: an angler.

walty, *wol′ti*, (*naut.*) *adj.* inclined to lean or roll over. [Obs. adj. *walt*, unsteady (—O.E. *wealt*, found only in *unwealt*, steady), and suff. *-y*.]

waltz, *wöl(t)s, n.* orig. a German dance performed by couples with a rapid whirling motion: a slower circling dance, also in triple time: the music for such: a piece of instrumental music in 3-4 time (concert waltz).—*v.i.* to dance a waltz: to move trippingly, to whirl (*slang*; also *v.t.*).—*ns.* waltz′er; waltz′ing.—waltzing mouse (also waltzer), a mouse of a breed that moves forward in small circles not in a straight line.—waltz into, to storm at. [Ger. *walzer*—*walzen*, to roll, dance.]

waly. See wally.

waly, *wā′li*, (*Scot.*) *interj.* alas! [wellaway.]

wamble, *wom′bl*, (*dial.*) *v.i.* of intestines, stomach, to give the feeling of working or rolling: to quake: to twist or wriggle: to move unsteadily. —*v.t.* to turn round, or upside down, or over and over.—*n.* a rolling in the stomach: a feeling of nausea: an unsteady, rolling or staggering movement.—*ns.* wam′bliness; wam′bling.—Also *adj.*—*adv.* wam′blingly.—*adj.* wam′bly, affected with, or causing, sickness: unsteady. — *adj.* wam′ble-cropped, sick at stomach. [Perh. two or more verbs; cf. Dan. *vamle*, to feel sick, conn.

with L. *vomĕre*, to vomit; also Norw. *vamla, vamra*, to stagger.]

wame, *wām*, (*dial.*) *n.* the womb or (more frequently the belly: a protuberant part or a hollow enclosed part. — Also (in 17th-cent. literature) wem(b), weamb.—*adj.* wāmed, having a wame (usu. of a specified kind).—*n.* wāme′ful, a bellyful. [Variant of womb.]

wammus. See wamus.

wampee, *wom-pē′, n.* an edible Asiatic fruit (Clausena; family Rutaceae) about the size of a large grape, with a hard yellow rind. [Chin. *hwang-pi*, lit. yellow skin.]

wampish, *wom′pish*, (*Scott*) *v.t.* to brandish, flourish, wave about.—Also *v.i.* [Origin uncertain.]

wampum, *wom′pәm, wöm′pәm, n.* shortened form of the N. American Indian (Algonquian) name for beads made from shells, used as money, etc. —wam′pumpeag (*-pēg*), the word of which wampum is an abbreviation—lit. white string of beads.—wam′pum-belt, a belt consisting of shell beads so arranged as to convey a message, record a treaty, etc.

wampus. See wamus.

wamus, *wöm′әs, wom′әs*, (*U.S.*) *n.* a kind of cardigan, or a strong jacket, buttoned at neck and wrists.—Also wamm′us, wamp′us. [Du. *wammes*—O.Fr. *wambais*, a military tunic orig. worn under armour.]

wan, *won, adj.* dark, gloomy (*obs.*): wanting colour: pale and sickly: faint.—*n.* (*rare*) wanness.—*v.t.* and *v.i.* to make or to become wan.—wan′d (Shak., *Ant.*, II, i. 21), perh. for *pa.p.* wanned.—*adv.* wan′ly.—*n.* wan′ness.—*adj.* wann′ish, somewhat wan. [O.E. *wann*, dark, lurid; not found in other Gmc. languages.]

wan, *wan*, old *pa.t.* of win: gained, or took (*Spens.*).

wanchancy, wanchancie, *won-chan′si*, (*Scot.*) *adj.* unlucky, dangerous, or uncanny. [O.E. privative or negative pfx. *wan-* (of Gmc. origin; seen in mod. Du. and in Eng. wanton), chance, and suff. *-y*.]

wand, *wond, n.* orig. something slender and supple, as a twig, or a thin stem or branch, or a young shoot of a willow used in basketmaking (now *poet.* and *dial.*): something slender and rigid as a light walking-cane (*obs.*), a rod of authority, a caduceus, a rod used by a fairy, a magician, a conjurer, a conductor, or a diviner. [O.N. *vöndr*, a shoot of a tree; Dan. *vaand*.]

wander, *won′dәr, v.i.* to ramble or move with no definite object, or with no fixed course, or by a round-about way (*lit.* and *fig.*): to go astray, deviate from the right path or course, the subject of discussion, the object of attention, etc. (*lit.* and *fig.*): to lose one's way (*coll.*): to be incoherent in talk, disordered in mind, or delirious.—*v.t.* to traverse: to lead astray, or to bewilder (*coll.*).—*n.* a ramble, stroll.—*adj.* wan′dered, astray: incoherent: bewildered.—*n.* wan′derer, one who or that which wanders, esp. habitually or from inclination: (*cap.*) a Covenanter who left his home to follow a dispossessed minister (*hist.*).—*adj.* and *n.* wan′dering.—*adv.* wan′deringly.—Wandering Jew, a legendary Jew in folklore esp. of north-western Europe who cannot die but must wander till the Day of Judgment, for an insult offered to Christ on the way to the Crucifixion—names given him are *Cartaphilus, Ahasuerus, Buttadeus*, etc.: wandering Jew, any of several trailing or creeping plants (also wandering sailor); wandering nerve, vagus; wanderjahre (*van′dәr-yä-rә*; Ger.), years of journeymanship or of wandering; wanderlust (*won′dәr-lust; van′dәr-loŏst*), an urge to travel or to move from place to place; wander plug, an electrical plug on a flexible wire capable of being inserted in any appropriate socket; wan′der-year, a year spent in travel to complete training before settling down to trade or profession. [O.E. *wandrian*; Ger. *wandern*; allied to wend, and to wind, twist.]

**wanderoo**, *won-də-rōō′*, *n.* usu. applied to the Lion-tailed Macaque, a native of the Malabar coast of India: properly, a langur of Ceylon. [Sinhalese *wanderu*, monkey.]

**wandle**, *won′dl*, (*dial.*) *adj.* supple, pliant, nimble. —Also **wanle**, **wannel**. [Ety. uncertain.]

**wane**, *wān*, *v.i.* to decrease in size, esp. of the moon—opp. to *wax*—or (*obs.*) in volume: to decline in power, prosperity, intensity, brightness, etc.: to draw to a close.—*n.* gradual decrease or decline (esp. in phrases, as **on the wane**, **in wane**, **in the**, **her**, **its wane**), or the time when this is taking place.—*adj.* **waned**, diminished: dying or dead.—*adj.* and *n.* **wan′ing**. [O.E. *wanian*, *wonian*, to lessen (O.N. *vana*)— *wana*, *wona* (also *wan*, *won*), deficient, lacking.]

**wang**, *wang*, (*obs.*) *n.* the cheek: a wang-tooth.— **wang′-tooth**, a molar. [O.E. *wange*.]

**wangan**, **wingun**. See **wanigan**.

**wangle**, *wang′gl*, (*coll.*) *v.t.* to obtain or accomplish by craft: to manipulate.—*v.i.* to use tricky methods to attain one's ends.—*n.* an exercise of such methods.—*ns.* **wang′ler**; **wang′ling**. [Origin uncertain.]

**wanhope**, *won′hōp*, (*obs.*) *n.* despair. [Pfx. *wan-* (see **wanchancy**), hope.]

**wanigan**, *won′i-gən*, *n.* in a lumber camp, a chest for supplies, or a kind of houseboat for loggers and their supplies; also the pay-office.—Also **wan′gan**, **wan′gun**. [Algonkin.]

**wanion**, *won′yən*, (*Shak.*, *Scott*) *n.* found only in phrases—e.g. **with a (wild) wanion**, with a vengeance, vehemently; **with a (wild) wanion to him**, bad luck to him, a curse on him! [Earlier (*in the*) *waniand*, (in the) waning (of the moon), i.e. in an unlucky time.]

**wankle**, *wong′kl*, (*dial.*) *adj.* unstable, unsteady: changeable: not to be depended on. [O.E. *wancol*; of Gmc. origin.]

**wanle**, **wannel**. See **wandle**.

**wannion**. Same as **wanion**.

**wannish**. See **wan**.

**wanrestful**, *won-rest′fōōl*, -*fl*, (*Scot.*) *adj.* restless. [Pfx. *wan-* (see **wanchancy**), and **restful**.]

**want**, *wont*, *n.* state or fact of being without or of having an insufficient quantity: absence or deficiency of necessities: poverty: (in *pl.*) difficult or straitened circumstances (*obs.*): a lack, deficiency: a blemish (*obs.*): a defect, feebleness, in intelligence (**to have a want**; *Scot.*): (in *pl.*) requirements or desires.—*v.t.* to be destitute of or deficient in: to lack, be without (Shak., *Macbeth* III, vi. 8, *who cannot want*, for *who can want, the thought?*): to feel need of, desire: to require, need: to fall short (of something) by (a specified amount): dispense with, do without (now *dial.*). —*v.i.* to be deficient, entirely lacking (*arch.*): to be in need or destitution: to lack (with *for*).—*n.* **want′age** (*U.S.*), deficiency, shortage. — *adj.* **want′ed**, lacking: needed: desired: searched for, esp. by the police.—*n.* **want′er**, one who wants.—*adj.* **want′ing**, absent, missing, lacking: deficient (with *in*, or, *obs.*, with *of*): failing to help, do justice to, come up to (with *to*): slow to (with *infin.*; *obs.*): below the desired or expected standard (in the phrase **found wanting**): defective mentally (*dial.*): poor, needy (*obs.*).—Also *n.*— *prep.* without, lacking, less.—**want′-wit**, a fool, one without sense.—Also *adj.*—**want in**, **out**, **up**, **down**, etc. (*Scot.*), to want to get in, out, etc. [O.N. *vant*, neut. of *vanr*, lacking, and O.N. *vanta*, to lack.]

**want**, *wont*, (*dial.*) *n.* a mole.—**want′-catcher**; **want′hill**. [O.E. *wand*; cf. Norw. *vand*; prob. same root as **wind** (2) and **wend**.]

**wanthriven**, *won-thriv′n*, (*Scot.*) *adj.* stunted: ill-grown: emaciated. [Pfx. *wan-*, wanting, thriven.]

**wanton**, *won′tən*, *adj.* undisciplined, unruly, unmanageable (*obs.*): thoughtlessly cruel: self-indulgent, luxurious (*obs.*): lascivious, or (*obs.*) amorous: insolent, arrogant, merciless in power or prosperity (*obs.*): unprovoked, unjust, merciless: capricious (*arch.*): of persons, jovial (*obs.*): of animals and inanimate things, frisky, gay, moving freely or capriciously (*poet.*): growing luxuriantly (*poet.*): unrestrained, prodigal.—*n.* a spoilt child or pampered, effeminate person (*obs.*): a roguish, sportive child, animal, etc. (*obs.*): a lewd person, esp. a female: a trifler.—*v.i.* to frolic: to play lasciviously, or amorously: to idle, go idly: to trifle: to indulge oneself, run into excesses: to grow luxuriantly, ramble unchecked.—*v.t.* to use wastefully, dissipate (also **wanton away**).—*v.i.* **wan′tonise**, -ize (*arch.*), to play the wanton.—*adv.* **wan′tonly.**—*n.* **wan′tonness.**—**play the wanton**, to trifle, or (*obs.*) to behave lewdly. [M.E. *wantowen*—pfx. *wan-* (prob. akin to **wane**), O.E. *togen*, pa.p. of *tēon*, to draw, lead, educate; cf. Ger. *ungezogen*, ill-bred, rude.]

**wanty**, *won′ti*, *n.* a belt used to secure a load on a pack-horse's back (*obs.*): the belly-band of a shaft-horse (*dial.*): a short rope, esp. one used for binding hay on a cart (*dial.*). [**wame**, and **tie**.]

**wanworth**, *won′wûrth*, (*Scot.*) *n.* a very low price: a bargain.—*adj.* **wanword′y**, worthless: unworthy. [Pfx. *wan-*, wanting, **worth**.]

**wanze**, *wonz*, (*obs.*) *v.i.* to decrease, waste away. [O.E. *wansian.*]

**wap**, *wop*, *v.t.* to throw, pull, quickly or roughly (*dial.*): to strike, drub (*coll.*): to flap (*Scot.*).—*n.* a smart blow: a shake, flap (*Scot.*): a blast, storm (*Scot.*): a fight, quarrel (*Scot.*). [Cf. **whop.**]

**wap**, *wop*, *v.t.* (*obs.*) to wrap, bind.—*n.* (*dial.*) a turn of a string with which anything is tied: a bundle of hay. [Ety. uncertain.]

**wapens(c)haw**. See **wappens(c)haw**.

**wapentake**, *wop′n-tāk*, *n.* a name given in Yorkshire and certain other shires to a territorial division of the county similar to the *hundred* of southern counties. [Late O.E. *wǣpen(ge)tæc*, O.N. *vápnatak*, lit. weapon-taking, assent at a meeting being signified by brandishing a weapon.]

**wapins(c)haw**. See **wappens(c)haw**.

**wapiti**, *wop′i-ti*, *n.* a species (*Cervus canadensis*) of deer of large size, native to N. America. [Algonquian.]

**wappend**, *wop′nd*, *adj.* (Shak., *Timon*, IV, iii. 38) perh. for *wappered* (now *dial.*), fatigued, tired; perh. meaning incontinent, unchaste, and conn. with *obs.* sense of **wap** (1), to copulate.

**wappens(c)haw**, *wop′n-shō*, *wap′*, *n.* in Scottish usage, a periodical gathering of the people within an area for the purpose of seeing that each man was armed in accordance with his rank, and ready to take the field when required (*hist.*): a rifle-shooting competition (in *S.Afr.* equivalent to Du. *wapenschouwing*).—Also **wapens(c)haw**, **wapins(c)haw**, **weapon-s(c)haw**.—*ns.* **wapp′en-s(c)haw** (app. older form than **wappenshaw**), **weap′on-s(c)hawing**. [See **weapon**, **show**.]

**wapper**, *wop′ər*, (*dial.*) *v.i.* to blink: to move tremulously.—*adj.* **wapp′er-eyed**, blinking.—*n.* **wapp′er-jaw**, a projecting under-jaw. — *adj.* **wapp′er-jawed**. [Cf. Du. *wapperen*, to oscillate.]

**war**, *wör*, *n.* a state of conflict: a contest between states, or between parties within a state (**civil war**), carried on by arms: any long-continued struggle, often against or between impersonal forces (*fig.*): fighting (*poet.*): open hostility: the profession of arms: an army, or war-equipment (*rare*; *poet.*).—*v.i.* to make war: to carry on war: to contend:—*pr.p.* warr'ing; *pa.t.* and *pa.p.* warred.—*adj.* war'like, of or pertaining to war: martial, military: equipped for fighting (*obs.*): intended for use in war (*obs.*): fond of war: bellicose.—*ns.* war'likeness; warr'ior, a skilled fighting man (*poet.*, except when used of one at an early stage of civilisation): a redoubtable person:—*fem.* warr'ioress (*rare*).—war baby, a baby born during a war, esp. a soldier's (or other serviceman's) illegitimate child: any discreditable or troublesome result of war; war cloud, a cloud of smoke and dust over a battle field: a sign that war is threatening or impending (*fig.*); war correspondent, a journalist or other person assigned to a seat of war so as to give first-hand reports of events; war crime, one connected with war, esp. one that violates the code of war; war cry, a cry used in battle for encouragement or as a signal: a slogan (*fig.*); war dance, a dance engaged in by some savage tribes before going to war: a dance imitating the actions of a battle; War Department, the name borne from 1784-1857 by what became the War Office—still used in speaking of property, as stores or land; war'dog, a dog used in war: an old warrior: a war hawk; war'-drum, a drum beaten as a summons to war, or during a battle: a sign of impending war (*fig.*); war'fare (from fare, *n.*), an engaging in, waging, or carrying on of war: armed contest: conflict or struggle of any kind (*fig.*).—*v.i.* (*obs.*; *lit.* and *fig.*) to wage war.—*n.* war'farer.—*adj.* and *n.* war'faring.—war game (see kriegspiel); war'-god, -godd'ess, a deity who presides over war, assigning victory or defeat, etc.; war hawk, one who is eager for war; war'head, war'-head, the section of a torpedo or other missile containing the explosive material; war'-horse, a charger, a horse used in battle: an old warrior in any field of conflict; war kettle, among Red Indians, a kettle set on the fire as part of the ceremony of going to war; war loan, a loan raised to pay for a war; war'lord, a commander or commander-in-chief, esp. where and when the military power is great—now usu. derogatory; war'man (*rare*), a warrior; war'-monger, a mercenary soldier (*Spens.*): one who encourages war, esp. for personal gain; war'-mongering; war neurosis, a better term for shell-shock; war note (*poet.*), a summons to war; War Office, a department of the civil government, formerly headed by the Secretary of State for War, since 1964 absorbed in the Ministry of Defence: premises of the department in Whitehall; war paint, paint applied to the face and person by savages, indicating that they are going to war: full-dress, or finery (*coll.*); war'-path, among the Red Indians, the path followed on a military expedition: the expedition itself: in on the warpath (*fig.*), engaged in conflict, in a mood for battle; war'-proof (*rare*), a valour proved in war.—*adj.* able to withstand attack.—war'ship, an armed vessel for use in war; war'song, a song sung by men about to fight: a song celebrating brave deeds in war; war'time, a period during which a war is being fought.—*adj.* of or pertaining to, characteristic of, a time of war.—*adjs.* war'-wast'ed, ravaged by war; war'-wea'ried, -wea'ry, wearied with, or tired of, war. —war'-whoop, a cry uttered by savages on going into battle; war widow, a woman whose husband has been killed in war; war'-wolf, a mediaeval siege engine: a fierce warrior (*Scott*; but see also werewolf).—*adj.* war'-worn, worn, wasted, ravaged, marked, wearied, by war.—carry the war into the enemy's camp, country, to take the offensive boldly (*lit.* and *fig.*); civil war (see civil); cold war, an intense, remorseless struggle for the upper hand by all means short of actual fighting; declare war (on, against), to announce formally that one is about to begin hostilities:

to set oneself to get rid of (*fig.*); go to war, to resort to armed conflict; go to the wars (*arch.*), to go to fight in a foreign country; have been in the wars (*fig.*), to show signs of having been knocked about; holy war (see holy); make, wage, war, to carry on hostilities; private war, warfare between persons in their individual capacity, as by duelling, family feuds, etc.; total war, war with every weapon at the combatant's disposal, sticking at nothing and sparing no one; war of nerves, systematic attempts to undermine morale by means of threats, rumours and counter-rumours, etc [Late O.E. werre—O.N.Fr. werre (O.Fr. and Fr. guerre)—O.H.G. werra, quarrel.]

war, *wär*, *wör*, warre, *adj.* and *adv.* (*Spens.*); now *Scot.* and *North.* waur, *wör*, worse:—*superl.* warst, waurst.—*v.t.* (*Scot.*) to defeat, worst: to excel. [O.N. *verre*.]

waratah, *wor'ə-ta*, *n.* any of a genus of Australian proteaceous shrubs with very showy flowers (Telopea). [Native name.]

warble, *wör'bl*, *v.i.* to sing in a quavering way, or with variations (sometimes used disparagingly): to sing sweetly as birds do: to make, or to be produced as, a sweet quavering sound: to yodel (*U.S.*).—*v.t.* to sing in a vibratory manner, or sweetly: to express, or to extol, in poetry or song: to cause to vibrate or sound musically.—*n.* the action, or an act, of warbling: a quavering modulation of the voice: a song.—*n.* war'bler, one that warbles: a songster: a singing-bird: any bird of the family *Sylviidae*—willow-wren, reed-warbler, whitethroat, blackcap, etc.: any of numerous small, brightly-coloured American birds of a different family: a whistle used in infant classes, etc.: in bagpipe music, an ornamental group of grace-notes.—*n.* and *adj.* war'bling.—*adv.* war'blingly. [O.N.Fr. *werbler* (O.Fr. *guerbler*); of Gmc. origin.]

warble, *wör'bl*, *n.* a small hard swelling on a horse's back, caused by the galling of the saddle, etc.: a swelling caused by a warble-fly or a bot-fly.—war'ble-fly, any of several flies of the same family as bot-flies whose larvae cause painful swellings that spoil the hides of horses, cattle, etc. [Ety. uncertain.]

ward, *wörd*, *v.t.* to watch over, guard (*arch.*): to protect (with *from*; *arch.*): to parry or keep away (now usually ward off): to enclose, as machinery, in order to prevent accidents (*rare*): to place in a ward.—*v.i.* to act on the defensive. —*n.* act of watching or guarding: state of being guarded: look-out, watch: care, protection: guardianship: custody: in feudal times, control of lands of a minor: a person, as a minor, under a guardian: a body of guards: a guarded place, as a court of a castle (inner and outer ward): a means of guarding, as a bolt, bar: a part of a lock of special configuration to prevent its being turned by any except a particular key, or the part of the key of corresponding configuration: a defensive motion or position (*fencing*; also *fig.*): a division of a county (*Scot.* and *North.*): an administrative division of a town or city: a division of an army (*obs.*; *van(t)ward* (vanguard), *middle ward*, *rearward* (rear-guard)): a division or department of a prison: a room with several beds in a hospital, etc.: the patients in a ward collectively.—*n.* ward'en, one who guards or keeps: a gatekeeper or sentinel (*rare*): a regent (*hist.*): the governor of a town, district, etc. (*hist.*): a title of certain officers of the crown: a member of certain governing bodies: a superintendent: the head of certain institutions, as schools, colleges, hostels, etc.: one appointed for duties among the civil population in cases of fire or air-raids or to control traffic circulation and parking of motor vehicles.—*v.t.* (*rare*) to guard as a warden.—*ns.* ward'enry (*rare*), the office of,

*fāte, fär; mē, hûr* (her); *mīne ; mōte, för; mūte; mōōn, fōōt; dhen* (then) or district in charge of, a warden: guardianship (*Thomas Hardy*); **ward'enship**, the office of warden; **ward'er**, one who guards or keeps: one in charge of prisoners in a jail (*fem.* **ward'ress**)—now officially a 'prison officer': a staff, baton, of authority (*hist.*).—*v.t.* to guard as a warder.—*n.* and *adj.* **ward'ing.**—*n.* **ward'ship**, the office of, or the state of being under, a guardian: protection, custody (*fig.*): state of being in guardianship (*fig.*): in English feudal law, the guardianship which the feudal lord had of the land of his vassal while the latter was a minor.—**ward'-corn** (*hist.*), a payment in corn in lieu of military service: misunderstood as the duty of keeping watch in order to give the alarm by blowing a horn; **ward'-mote**, a meeting of a ward, or of a court of a ward; **ward'robe**, a room or a piece of furniture for containing clothes or theatrical costumes: one's stock of wearing apparel: raiment—of colours, flowers, etc. (*fig.*; *Milt.* **ward'rop**): a department of a royal or noble household having charge of robes, wearing apparel, jewels, etc.; **wardrobe mistress**, one who looks after the theatrical costumes of a company or of an individual actor or actresss; **ward'rober** (*hist.*), one in charge of a royal or noble wardrobe; **wardrobe trunk**, a trunk in which clothing may be hung as in a wardróbe; **ward'-room**, the messroom of the officers of a warship: the officers collectively.—**ward in Chancery**, a minor under the protection of the Court of Chancery; **Warden of the Cinque Ports**, or **Lord Warden (of the Cinque Ports)**, the governor of the Cinque Ports, having the authority of an admiral and the power to hold a court of admiralty; **Wardens of the Marches**, officers formerly appointed to keep order in the marches or border districts of England and Scotland. [O.E. *weardian*; cf. Ger. *warten*, to wait, attend, take care of.]

**-ward(s)**, *-wǝrd(z)*, *-wörd(z)*, *suffs.* forming adjs. and advs. with the sense of motion towards. [O.E. *-weard* (gen. *-weardes*), cog. with Ger. *-wörts*; conn. with O.E. *weorthan*, tȯ become, L. *vertĕre*, to turn.]

**warden**, *wör'dn*, *n.* a kind of pear.—**warden pie**, a pie made of warden pears. [Origin uncertain; perh.—A.Fr. *warder* (Fr. *garder*), to keep.]

**warden.** See **ward**.

**Wardian**, *wör'di-ǝn*, *adj.* denoting a kind of glass case for transporting delicate ferns and other such plants, or for keeping them indoors. [Nathaniel Bagshaw *Ward* (1791-1868), the inventor.]

**Wardour Street English**, *wör'dǝr strēt ing'glish*, sham-antique diction, as in some historical novels—from *Wardour Street*, London, once noted for antique and imitation-antique furniture; now given over to business side of entertainment, esp. of films.

**ware**, *wār*, *n.* (now usu. in *pl.*) articles of merchandise collectively: an article of merchandise (*rare*): pottery as Delft ware, Wedgwood ware (see delf, Wedgwood): articles of fine workmanship, as Benares ware, ornamental metal-work from India: in composition, with defining word, as hardware, earthenware.—*n.* **ware'house**, a building or room for storing goods: a shop.—*v.t.* (*-howz*) to deposit in a warehouse, esp. a bonded warehouse: to store up (*fig.*).—*n.* **ware'housing**, the act of depositing goods in a warehouse.—**warehouseman**, a man who keeps, or is employed in, a warehouse or a wholesale store; **warehousing system**, the plan of allowing importers of dutiable goods to store them in a government warehouse without payment of duties until ready to bring the goods into market. [O E. *waru*; cf. Ger. *ware*.]

**ware**, *wār*, (*Scot.* and *dial.*) *n.* springtime. [O.N. *vār*.]

**ware**, *wār*, *adj.* aware (*arch.*): wary, cautious

(*arch.*; sometimes with *of*): prudent (*arch.*; esp. in phrase **ware and wise**).—*v.i.* and *v.t.* (*arch.*; usu. in *imper.*) to beware, beware of: in hunting, to avoid, refrain from riding over, etc. (sometimes *wör*).—*adj.* **ware'less** (*arch.*), incautious: unaware (with *of*).—*adv.* **wār'ily.**—*ns.* **wār'iment** (*Spens.*), wariness; **wār'iness.**—*adj.* **wār'y**, guarding against deception or danger: cautious: circumspect: thrifty (*obs.*).—**be wary of**, to show caution in regard to. [O.E. *wær*; cf. O.N. *varr*. See **aware**.]

**ware**, *wār*, (*Scot.* and *dial.*) *n.* seaware, seaweed. [O.E. *wār*; cf. ore (2).]

**ware**, *wār*, obs. *pa.t.*of **wear**.

**ware**, *wār*, (*Scot.*) *v.t.* to spend. [O.N. *verja*, to clothe, hence to invest: cf. **wear**.]

**warehouse, etc.** See **ware** (1).

**wareless.** See **ware** (3).

**warhable**, *wör-hā'bl*, (*Spens.*) *adj.* fit for war. [**war**, and **able**.]

**warily, wariment, wariness, etc.** See **ware** (3).

**warison, warrison**, *wor'*, *war'i-sǝn*, (*obs.*) *n.* wealth: reward or punishment: used by Scott erroneously for a note of assault. [O.N.Fr. (O.Fr. *guarison*)—*warir*, to guard; cf. **garrison**.]

**wark**, *wörk*, Scots form of **work** (*n.*).

**warling**, *wör'ling*, (*obs.*) *n.* one who is disliked—in proverb 'It is better to be an old man's darling than a young man's warling'. [Prob. formed to rhyme with 'darling'.]

**warlock**, *wör'lok*, *n.* a wizard: a magician (*Scot.*): a demon: a warrior who cannot be wounded with metals (*Dryden* erroneously).—*n.* **war'-lockry**, sorcery. [O.E. *wǣrloga*, a breaker of an agreement—*wǣr*, a compact, *lēogan*, to lie; the ending *-(c)k* appears earliest in Scots.]

**warm**, *wörm*, *adj.* having moderate heat: hot: imparting heat or a sensation of heat: retaining heat: affecting one, pleasantly or unpleasantly, as heat does (*fig.*): strenuous: harassing: characterised by danger or difficulty: passionate: angry: excited: ardent, enthusiastic: lively, glowing: affectionate: amorous: indelicate (*coll.*): comfortable, well-to-do (*coll.*): of a colour, containing red or yellow: esp. in a game, close to discovery or attainment: of a scent or trail, fresh.—*v.t.* to make warmer: to interest: to excite: to impart brightness or suggestion of life to: to beat (*coll.*).—*v.i.* to become warm or ardent.—*n.* a beating (*coll.*): an officer's thick overcoat (also **British warm**).—*adv.* warmly.—*adj.* **warmed.**—*ns.* **war'mer**; **warm'ing**, the action of making or becoming warm: a beating (*slang*).—*adv.* **warm'ly.**—*ns.* **warm'ness**; **warmth.**—*adjs.* **warm'-blood'ed**, homothermous, idiothermous, having bodily temperature constantly maintained at a point usu. above the environmental temperature: ardent, passionate; **warmed'-o'ver** (*U.S.*), **-up'**, heated anew.—**warm front** (*meteor.*), the advancing front of a mass of warm air.—*adj.* **warm'-heart'ed**, affectionate: hearty.—**warm'-heart'edness** (*see* warm'-hearted); **warm'ing-pan**, a covered pan, with a long handle, for holding live coals to warm a bed: a person put into a situation to hold it till another is able to take it; **warm'-up**, a practice exercise before an event.—**a warm reception**, a display of hostility: a vigorous resistance or attack; **keep a place warm**, to occupy or hold it for someone until he is ready to fill it himself; **warm up**, to make or become warm: to heat, as cooked food: to become animated, interested, or eager: to limber up prior to any athletic event contest, etc. [O.E. *wearm*; cf. Ger. *warm*.]

**warn**, *wörn*, *v.t.* to give notice of danger or evil to: to notify in advance: to caution (with *against*): to instruct, command: to summon: to bid, instruct, to go or to keep away (with *off*, *away*, etc.; *lit.* and *fig.*): to admonish: to forbid (*obs.*).—*v.i.* to give warning—specif., of a clock about to strike.—*ns.* **warn'er**; **warn'ing**, caution against danger, etc.: something that gives this: previous notice: notice to quit, of the termination of an engagement, etc.: summons, call: admonition: the sound accompanying the partial unlocking of the striking train, just before a clock strikes.—Also *adj.*—*adv.* **warn'ingly.**— **warning coloration,** aposematic coloration, such as the gaudy colours of some stinging insects. [O.E. *warnian, warenian, wearnian,* to caution (cf. Ger. *warnen*), and perh. in part *wiernan,* to refuse, forbid.]

**warn,** *wörn,* (*Shak.* and *dial.*) *v.t.* to warrant.

**warp,** *wörp, v.t.* to cast, throw (*obs.*): to lay (eggs), or to bring forth (young), esp. prematurely (*dial.*): to twist out of shape: to turn from the right course: to distort: to cause to contract or wrinkle (*Shak.*): to pervert, as the mind or character: to misinterpret, give a deliberately false meaning to: to arrange, as threads, so as to form a warp: to entwine (*obs.*): to move, as a vessel, by hauling on ropes attached to posts on a wharf, etc.: to improve (land) by flooding so that it is covered by a deposit of alluvial mud: to choke, as a channel, with alluvial mud: in rope-making, to stretch into lengths for tarring. —*v.i.* to be twisted out of shape: to become perverted or distorted (*fig.*): to swerve: to move with effort, or on a zigzag course: of cattle, sheep, etc., to miscarry.—*n.* state or fact of being warped: permanent distortion of a timber, etc.: a mental twist or bias (*fig.*): the threads stretched out lengthwise in a loom to be crossed by a woof (also *fig.*): a rope used in towing, one end being fastened to a fixed object: alluvial sediment: a tale of four (herrings, oysters, etc.), thirty-three warps making a long-hundred, and a hundred long-hundreds a mease or maze. —*adj.* **warped,** twisted by shrinking: distorted: perverted: covered or filled with a deposit of alluvial sediment.—*ns.* **war'per; war'ping.** [O.E. *weorpan, werpan;* cf. Ger. *werfen,* O.N. *verpa.*]

**warragal,** *wor'ə-gal, n.* the Australian dingo: a wild Australian horse: an Australian aboriginal. —*adj.* wild, savage.—Also **warr'igal.** [Native word.]

**warran(d).** Obs. forms of **warrant.**

**warrant,** *wor'ənt, v.t.* to protect, defend, keep (*obs.*): to give assurance against danger, etc. (*rare;* with *against, from*): to secure, guarantee the possession of, to: to guarantee to be as specified or alleged: to attest, guarantee, the truth of—(*coll.*) equivalent to 'to be sure, to be convinced', 'to be bound' (also in phrases **I** (**I'll**) **warrant you, I warrant me**): to predict or to presage (*obs.*): to authorise: to justify, be adequate grounds for.—*n.* a defender (*obs.*): a defence (*obs.*): one who or that which vouches, a guaranty: a pledge, assurance: a proof: that which authorises: a writ for arresting a person or for carrying a judgment into execution: in the services, an official certificate inferior to a commission: authorisation: justification: a writing authorising the payment of money: a form of warehouse receipt for goods: a voucher (*obs.*).—*n.* **warr'andice** (-*dis; Scot.; arch.*), a guarantee: a clause in a deed by which the grantor binds himself to make good to the grantee the right conveyed.—*adj.* **warr'antable,** that may be permitted: justifiable: of good warrant, estimable (*obs.*): of sufficient age to be hunted.—*n.* **warr'antableness.**—*adv.* **warr'antably.** —*adj.* **warr'anted.**—*ns.* **warrantee',** one to whom a warranty is given; **warr'anter,** one who authorises or guarantees: a warrantor; **warr'-anting; warr'antise** (-*tīz; obs.* or *arch.*), act of guaranteeing: a guarantee: assurance: authorisation; **warr'antor** (*law*), one who gives warranty: a warranter; **warr'anty** (*law*), an act of warranting, esp. in feudal times, the covenant by which the grantor of land warranted

the security of the title to the recipient (**general warranty,** against the claims of all and every person; **special warranty,** against the claims of the grantor, or others claiming through or by him): an undertaking or assurance expressed or implied in certain contracts: a guarantee: authorisation: justification: evidence.—**warr'-ant-off'icer,** in the services, officer holding a warrant (see **branch-officer**).—**distress warrant,** warrant authorising distraining of goods; **general warrant,** a warrant for the arrest of suspected persons, no specific individual being named or described in it; **of (good) warrant** (*obs.*), esteemed, important; **of warrant** (*obs.*), allowed, warranted; **out of warrant** (*obs.*), not allowed; **take warrant on oneself** (*arch.*), to make oneself responsible; **warrant of attachment,** a writ authorising the seizure of property; **warrant of attorney** (see **attorney**). [O.Fr. *warantir* (*guarantir*); of Gmc. origin.]

**warrant,** *wor'ənt, n.* in coal-mining, under-clay. [Perh. the same as **warrant** (1).]

**warray,** *wŏr-ā', (obs.) v.t.* to make war upon.—*v.i.* to make war.—Also **warrey'.** [O.Fr. *werreier* (*guerreier*).]

**warre.** See **war** (2).

**warren,** *wor'ən, n.* a piece of ground kept for breeding game, esp. hares, rabbits, etc., partridges, etc. (**beasts, fowls, of warren;** *hist.*): the right of keeping or of hunting this (*hist.*): rabbit burrows in waste ground: the rabbits living there: a densely populated slum dwelling or district: a maze of narrow passages.—*n.* **warr'-ener,** the keeper of a warren (*hist.*): one who lives in a warren. [A.Fr. *warenne* (O.Fr. *garenne*), of Gmc. origin.]

**warrigal.** See **warragal.**

**warrior.** See under **war** (1).

**warsle,** *wörs'l.* Scots form of **wrestle.**

**warst.** See **war** (2).

**wart,** *wört, n.* a small, hard excrescence on the skin: a small protuberance.—*adjs.* **wart'ed; wart'less; wart'y,** like a wart: overgrown with warts.—**wart'-cress,** swine's-cress; **wart'-hog,** any of a genus of wild hogs found in Africa, with large wart-like excrescences on their cheeks; **wart'weed,** a kind of spurge (its caustic juice thought to cure warts); **wart'wort,** any of a family of lichens having a warty thallus: a wartweed.—**warts and all,** with none of the blemishes or shortcomings concealed. [O.E. *wearte;* Ger. *warze;* prob. allied to L. *verrūca.*]

**wartime.** See **war** (1).

**warwolf.** See **war** (1), and **werewolf.**

**wary.** See **ware** (3).

**was,** *woz,* used as the *1st* and *3rd pers. sing.* of the *pa.t.* of the verb to be. [O.E. *wæs*—*wesan,* to be; see **wast, were, wert.**]

**wase,** *wāz,* (*dial.*) *n.* a wisp of hay, straw, etc.: a pad on the head to ease the pressure of a burden. [Gmc. word; perh. Scand.]

**wase-goose.** See **wayzgoose.**

**wash,** *wosh, v.t.* to cleanse, or to free from impurities, etc., with water or other liquid: to wet, moisten: to have the property of cleansing: to flow over, past, against: to sweep along, down, etc.: to cover with a thin coat of metal or paint: in mining, to separate from earth by means of water.—*v.i.* to cleanse oneself, clothes, etc., with water: to wash clothes, etc., as one's employment: to stand cleansing (with *well, badly,* etc.): to be swept or carried by water: to stand the test, bear investigation (*coll.*):—*pa.p.* **washed,** *arch.* **wash'en.**—*n.* a washing: the process of washing: a collection of articles for washing: that with which anything is washed: a lotion: the break of waves on the shore: the sound of water breaking, lapping, etc.: the rough water left behind by a boat, etc., or the disturbed air behind an aerofoil, etc. (also *fig.*): the shallow part of a river or arm of the sea: a marsh or fen: alluvial matter: waste liquor, refuse of food, etc.: a watery mixture: a thin, tasteless drink: insipid discourse, in speech or writing: a broad but thin layer of colour put on with a long sweep of the brush: a thin coat of paint, metal, etc.: the blade of an oar.—*adj.* wash′able.— *n.* wash′er, one who washes: a washing-machine: a ring, usu. flat, of metal, rubber, etc., to keep joints or nuts secure, etc. (perh. a different word). —*v.t.* to fit with a washer or washers.—*ns.* wash′- iness, state of being watery: feebleness; wash′- ing, the act of cleansing, wetting, or coating, with liquid: clothes, or other articles, washed, or to be washed: a thin coating: the action of break- ing, lapping, etc.: (usu. in *pl.*) liquid that has been used to wash something, or matter separated or carried away by water or other liquid.—*adj.* that washes: used for washing: washable.—*adj.* wash′y, watery, moist: thin, feeble.—wash′- away, destruction of part of a road, railway, etc., by flooding: the breach so caused; wash′- ball, a ball of toilet-soap; wash′-bã′sin, -bowl, wash′hand bã′sin, a bowl to wash face, hands, etc., in; wash′-board, a washing board: a thin plank on a boat's gunwale to prevent the sea from breaking over: a skirting-board (*dial.*); wash′-bott′le, wash′ing-bott′le, a bottle contain- ing liquid used for purifying gases: a bottle with tubes through the stopper, enabling a stream of cleansing liquid to be directed on a chemical or a piece of apparatus; wash′-cloth, a piece of cloth used in washing; wash′-dirt, earth to be washed for gold.—*adjs.* washed′-out, deprived of colour, as by washing: deprived of energy or animation (*coll.*); washed′-up′, deprived of energy or anima- tion (*coll.*): done for, at the end of one's re- sources (*slang*): finished (with *with*; *slang*).— wash′erman, a man who washes clothes, esp. for hire:—*fem.* wash′erwoman; wash′-gild′ing, a gilding made with an amalgam of gold from which the mercury is driven off by heat, leaving a coating of gold; wash′-house, wash′ing-house, a house or room for washing clothes in; wash′- in, -out, increase, or decrease, in the angle of incidence, i.e. the angle between the chord of a wing and the wind relative to the aeroplane, in approaching the wing-tip along the camber; wash′ing-blue (see blue); wash′ing-board, a corrugated board for rubbing clothes on in washing; wash′ing-day, a day devoted to washing clothes; wash′ing-machine, a machine for washing clothes; wash′ing-powder, a powdered preparation used in washing clothes; wash′ing-soda (see soda); wash′ing-up, cleaning up, esp. of dishes and cutlery after a meal; wash′-leather, split sheep-skin prepared with oil in imitation of chamois: buff leather for regimental belts; wash′-out, an erosion of earth by the action of water: the hole made by such: a complete failure (*coll.*): a useless person (*coll.*): wash′-pot, a vessel for washing; wash′- stand, wash′hand-stand, a piece of furniture for holding ewer, basin, and other requisites for washing the person; wash′-tub, a tub for washing clothes; wash′-up, a washing-up: a washing-up place: anything cast up by the sea, etc.: the washing of ore: a quantity of gold obtained by washing.—come out in the wash, to become clean after washing: of a situation, to work out satis- factorily; wash away, to obliterate; wash down, (of liquid) to carry downward: to help the swallowing or digestion of (a solid food); wash its face (*slang*), of an undertaking, just to pay its way; wash one's brain (*obs. slang*), to drink copiously: (for brainwash see under brain); wash one's hands of (see hand); wash out, to remove by washing: to wash free from dirt, soap, etc.: to disappear or become fainter as a result of washing: to cancel (*coll.*): to

exhaust (*coll.*; esp. in *pass.*): to bring the blade of an oar not cleanly out of the water (*rowing*); wash up, to wash one's hands and face (esp. *U.S.*): to wash the dishes and cutlery after a meal: to sweep up on to the shore: to spoil, finish (*coll.*; esp. in *pass.*). [O.E. *wæscan*, *wascan*; found in other Gmc. languages as O.H.G *wascan* (Ger. *waschen*); same root as water.]

washing, *wosh′ing*, (Shak., *Rom.* I, i. 69) *adj.* for swashing.

Washingtonia, *wosh-ing-tō′ni-ə*, *n.* a genus of ornamental fan palms of California and Mexico: a synonym of Sequoia. [Named after George Washington (1732-99).]

wasp, *wosp*, *n.* any of a large number of insects belonging to the order Hymenoptera and con- stituting many families, including the *Vespidæ*, to which the common wasp (*Vespa vulgaris*) and the European hornet (*Vespa crabro*) belong: a petulant and spiteful person.—*adj.* was′pish, like a wasp: having a slender waist like a wasp: quick to resent an injury: spiteful, virulent.— *adv.* was′pishly.—*n.* was′pishness.—*adj.* was′py, waspish.—*adjs.* was′pish-head′ed (*Shak.*), hot- headed, passionate.—wasp('s) nest, the nest of a wasp: a place very full of enemies or of angry people, or circumstances in which one is assailed indignantly from all sides (*fig.*).—*adjs.* wasp′- tongu'd (Shak., 1 *Hen. IV*, I, iii. 236; 1st quarto wasp-stung, others wasp-tongue), biting in tongue, shrewish; wasp′-waist′ed, very slender waisted: laced tightly. [O.E. *wæsp*, *wæps*; cf. Ger. *wespe*, L. *vespa*.]

wassail, *wos′(ā)l*, *was′l*, *n.* the salutation uttered in drinking a person's health (*hist.*): a liquor in which such healths were drunk, esp. ale with roasted apples, sugar, nutmeg, and toast (*hist.*): a festive occasion: revelry: a drinking-bout: a drinking or festive song.—*v.i.* to hold a wassail or merry drinking-meeting: to sing good wishes, carols, etc., from house to house at Christmas.—*v.t.* to drink to or pour libations for (as fruit-trees).—*ns.* wass′ailer, one who wassails: a reveller; wass′ailing; wass′ailry.— wass′ail-bout, a carouse; wass′ail-bowl, -cup, a cup from which healths were drunk. [O.N. *ves heill*, 'be in health'.]

wasserman, *wos′ər-mən*, (*obs.*) *n.* a sea-monster, shaped like a man. [Ger. *wassermann*—*wasser*, water, *mann*, man.]

Wassermann('s) reaction, test, *väs′ər-man(z) rē-ak′shən*, *test*, a test of the blood serum, or of the cerebrospinal fluid, to determine whether the person from whom it is drawn is suffering from syphilis. [A. von *Wassermann* (1866-1925), Ger- man bacteriologist.]

wast, *wost*, used as *2nd pers. sing. pa.t.* of the verb be. [See was.]

wast, wastfull, wastness, obs. spellings of waste, waist, etc.

waste, *wāst*, *adj.* uncultivated, and at most sparsely inhabited: desolate: lying unused: unproductive: devastated, ruinous (*obs.*): in a devastated condition (to lay waste): empty, unoccupied: refuse, rejected, superfluous: useless, vain (*obs.*).—*v.t.* to devastate: to consume, wear out, impair gradually: to cause to decline, shrink physically, to enfeeble: to put an end to (*obs.*): to impoverish (*obs.*): to expend, spend, consume or pass (*obs.*): to spend, use, occupy, unprofitably: to use, bestow, where due appreciation is lacking (often in passive): to fail to take advantage of: to turn to waste material: to injure (an estate or property; *law*). —*v.i.* to be diminished, used up, or impaired by degrees: to lose strength or flesh or weight (often waste away): of time, to be spent (*obs.*): to be used to no, or little, purpose or effect: to use, consume, spend too lavishly.—*n.* an uncultivated, unproductive, or devasted region: a vast expanse, as of ocean or air: vast (*n.*; Shak., *Ham.* I, ii. 198, quartos 2, 3, 4): a disused working: act or process of wasting: consumption or expenditure (*obs.*): too lavish, or useless, expenditure, or an example of it: squandering: a profusion (*arch.*): superfluous, refuse, or rejected, material: a waste-pipe: gradual decay: destruction: loss: (in *pl.*) ravages (*obs.*): that which is laid waste (*obs.*): injury done to an estate or property by the tenant (*law*).—*n.* wāst′age, loss by use or natural decay, etc.: useless or unprofitable spending: loss, or amount of loss, through this: a devastated or ruined place (*Scot.*): waste ground (*Scot.*).—*adj.* waste′ful, causing devastation, consuming, destructive (*obs.* or *rare*): causing wasting of the body (*rare*): lavish (*obs.*): characterised by, or addicted to, over-lavishness: uninhabited, unfrequented, desolate (*poet.*): vain, profitless (*obs.*).—*adv.* waste′fully.—*ns.* waste′fulness; waste′ness, the state of being waste: a waste place (*obs.*): devastation (*B.*).—*v.t.* wast′er (*Scot.*), to use, spend thriftlessly (whence *adj.* wāst′erful, *adv.* wāst′erfully, *n.* wāst′erfulness).—*n.* one who or that which wastes: a spendthrift: a good-for-nothing (*coll.*): a class of thief (*hist.*): an article spoilt in the making: an animal that is not thriving, or that is not suitable for breeding purposes.—*n.* wāst′ing.—*adj.* that is undergoing waste: destroying, devastating: enfeebling.—*n.* wāst′rel, refuse: a waster, esp. a profligate: a neglected child.— *adj.* waste, refuse: of an animal, feeble: going to waste: spendthrift.—*ns.* wāst′ry, wāst′ery (*Scot.*), prodigality.—*adj.* improvident.—waste′-bas′ket, waste′paper-bas′ket, a basket for holding useless scraps of paper; waste′-book, a day-book or journal, or a rougher record preliminary to it; waste′-gate, a gate for discharging surplus water from a dam, etc.; waste paper, used paper no longer required for its original purpose: paper rejected as spoiled; waste′-pipe, a pipe for carrying off waste or surplus water; waste product, material produced in a process that is discarded on the completion of that process.— *adj.* waste′rife (-*rif*, -*rīf*; *Scot.*), wasteful.—*n.* wastefulness.—go to waste, to be wasted; grow to waste (*obs.*), of a time, to come near an end; in waste (*obs.*), to no effect, in vain; lay waste (see lay); run to waste, orig. of liquids, to be wasted or lost. [O.Fr. *wast* (*guast*)—L. *vāstus*, waste.]

**wastel**, *wos′tl*, **wastel-bread**, (*obs.*) *n.* bread made from the finest of the flour. [O.Fr. *wastel*, a variant of *guastel*, *gastel* (Fr. *gâteau*, cake); of Gmc. origin.]

**waster**, *wäs′tər*, (*obs.*) *n.* a wooden sword for practising fencing with: a cudgel: practice or play with a waster.—play at waster(s), to practise fencing. [Ety. uncertain.]

**waster**, **wasterful.** See **waste.**

**waster**, *wäs′tər*, (*Scot.*) *n.* a four-pronged or five-pronged salmon-spear. [Earlier *wa*(*w*)*sper*—spear, modified after leister; ety. otherwise obscure.]

**wat**, *wot*, (*obs.*) *n.* a hare. [Prob. *Wat*, for Walter.]

**wat**, *wöt*, (*Scot.*) *adj.* wet: drunken. [Variant of wet.]

**wat**, *wöt.* Scots form of **wot.**

**watch**, *woch*, *n.* state of being awake (*obs.*): a religious vigil (*obs.*; survives in watch-night— q.v.): a wake: a flock (of nightingales; *obs.*): a division of the night, of fixed length (*hist.*): (in *pl.*) the period (of the night; *poet.*): act or state of remaining on the alert or of observing vigilantly: the lookout: close observation: act of guarding: surveillance: the office or duty of keeping guard or of being a sentinel (*obs.*; **stand**

upon one's watch (*B.*), to fulfil the duty of watchman): a lying in ambush (*obs.*): one who watches: a watchman, or a body of watchmen, esp. (*hist.*) the body of men who, before the institution of a police force, patrolled the streets at night: a sentinel, or the military guard of a place (*obs.*): in early 18th century, name applied to certain companies of irregular troops in the Highlands: a period, usu. of four hours (see dog-watch) of duty on deck: the part, usu. a half (the *port*—formerly *larboard*—and the *starboard watch*), of the ship's officers and crew who are on duty at the same time: a sailor's turn or period of duty: something that measures or marks time or the passage of time, as a marked candle, the cry of a watchman, a clock (*obs.*): the dial of a clock (*obs.*): a small timepiece for carrying in the pocket, on the wrist, etc.—*v.i.* to remain awake: to keep vigil: to attend the sick by night: to be on the alert: to look out (with *for*): to look with attention: to keep guard: to keep guard over (with *over*).—*v.t.* to keep in view, to follow the motions of with the eyes (*lit.* and *fig.*): to look at, observe, attentively: of a barrister, to attend the trial of (a case) on behalf of a client not directly involved in it: to catch in an act (*Shak.*): to have in keeping: to guard: to tend: to beware of danger to or from, to be on the alert to guard or guard against (*coll.*): to be on the alert to take advantage of, as an opportunity: to wait for (*obs.*): to keep (a hawk) from sleep, in order to tame it (*Shak.*).—*n.* watch′er, one who watches: one of a class of angels.—*adj.* watch′ful, wakeful (*arch.*): spent in watching (*arch.*): habitually on the alert or cautious: watching or observing carefully: characterised by vigilance: requiring vigilance, or in which one must be on the alert. —*adv.* watch′fully.—*n.* watch′fulness.—watch′-bill, a list of the officers and crew of a ship, as divided into watches, with their several stations; watch′-box, a sentry-box; watch′case, the outer case of a watch: a sentry-box (*Shak.*); watch′-clock, a watchman's clock; watch′-committ′ee, a committee of a local governing body exercising supervision over police services, etc.; watch′-crystal (see watch′-glass); watch′-dog, a dog kept to guard premises and property (also *fig.*); watch′-fire, a fire lit at night as a signal: a fire for the use of a watching party, sentinels, scouts, etc.; watch′-glass, a sand-glass: a glass covering for the face of a watch (also watch′-crystal); watch′-guard, a chain, strap, etc., used to attach a watch to the clothing; watch′-house, a house in which a guard is placed: a lock-up, police station; watching brief, instructions to a counsel to watch a legal case; watch′-key, a key for winding a watch; watch′-light, a light used for watching or sitting up in the night; watch′maker, one who makes or repairs watches; watch′-making; watch′man, a man who watches or guards, now usu. a building, formerly the streets of a city, at night; watch′man's clock, a clock recording the times of a watchman's visits; watch′-night, orig. a late service (up to and including midnight) held once a month by Wesleyan Methodists: later a service lasting until midnight held by various denominations on Christmas Eve or New Year's Eve: last night of the year.—Also *adj.*—watch′-officer, the officer in charge of the ship during a watch, also called officer of the watch; watch′-out, a lookout; watch′-paper, a round piece of paper, often decorated, formerly put inside the outer case of a watch to prevent rubbing; watch′-pocket, a small pocket for holding a watch; watch′-spring, the mainspring of a watch; watch′-tower, a tower on which a sentinel is placed to look out for the approach of danger; watch′word, the password to be given to a watch or sentry (*obs.*): any signal: a maxim, rallying-cry.—**be on the watch**, to be on the lookout; **Black Watch**, the 42nd and 73rd Regiments, now the 1st and 2nd Battalions of the Black Watch or Royal Highland Regiment; **watch after** (*Thackeray*), to follow the movements of (with one's eyes); **watch and ward**, the old custom of watching by night and by day in towns and cities: uninterrupted vigilance; **watch in**, to keep awake to welcome (the New Year); **watch one's step**, to step with care: to act warily, be careful not to arouse opposition, give offence, etc. (*fig.*; *coll.*); **watch out** (*coll.*; orig. *U.S.*), to look out, be careful; **watch over**, to guard, take care of; **watch up** (*Thackeray*), to sit up at night. [O.E. *wæcce* (n.), *wæccan*, *wacian* (vb.); cog. with *wacan*, to wake.]

**watchet**, *woch′it*, (*arch.*) *n.* a pale blue: a material of this colour: an angling fly.—*adj.* pale blue. [O.Fr. *wachet*; perh. orig. a material.]

**water**, *wö′tər*, *n.* in a state of purity, at ordinary temperatures, a clear transparent liquid (colourless except in large quantities), perfectly neutral in its reaction, and devoid of taste or smell: extended to the same substance ($H_2O$) in solid or gaseous state (ice, steam): any body of this, as the ocean, a lake, river, etc.: a river valley (*Scot.*): one of the four elements recognised by early natural philosophers: a quantity of the liquid used in any one stage of a washing operation: a liquid resembling or containing water: mineral water: tears: saliva: (usu. in *pl.*) the amniotic fluid, filling the space between the embryo and the amnion: urine: transparency, lustre, as of a diamond: (in *pl.*) waves, moving water, a body of water.—*v.t.* to wet, overflow, irrigate, supply, dilute with water: to soften by soaking (*obs.*): of a river, etc., to surround, as a city (*obs.*); also **water about**: to wet and press so as to give a wavy appearance to: to increase (the nominal capital of a company) by the issue of new shares without a corresponding increase of actual capital.—*v.i.* to fill with, or shed, water: of the mouth (also, *obs.* and *Scot.*, the teeth), to secrete saliva at the sight or thought of food, or (*fig.*) in anticipation of anything delightful: of an animal, to drink: to take in water.—*adj.* pertaining to, or used in, the storage or distribution of water: worked by water: used, living, or operating, on or in water: by way of or across water: made with, or formed by, water.—*n.* wa′terage, conveyance by water: money paid for this.—*adj.* wa′tered, soaked in or with, sprinkled, supplied with, water: having a supply of water in the form of a river, rivers, etc.: periodically flooded: diluted: weakened (*fig.*): marked with a wavy pattern by watering: of capital or stock, increased in nominal value without any corresponding increase in the assets.—*ns.* wa′terer, a vessel for watering with; wa′teriness; wa′tering, the act of one who, or that which, waters: the act of drinking (*obs.*): dilution with water: the art or process of giving a wavy, ornamental appearance: such an appearance.—*adj.* wa′terish, resembling, or abounding in, or charged with, water: dilute, thin, poor.—*n.* wa′terishness.—*adjs.* wa′terless; wa′tery, of or pertaining to water: full of water: moist: consisting of, or containing, water: like water: thin or transparent: tasteless: weak, vapid: associated with, or controlling, the sea, the tides, rain, etc.: watering, eager (Shak., *Troil.* III, ii. 20).—wa′ter-bag, a bag for holding water: a camel's reticulum; wa′ter-bail′iff, a custom-house officer who inspects ships on reaching or leaving port (*obs.*): an official whose duty it is to enforce byelaws relating to fishing, or to prevent poaching in protected waters (also—now *Scot.*— wa′ter-bail′ie); wa′ter-ball′ast, water carried by a

ship to balance or redress change of draught due to consumption of fuel or provisions or discharge of cargo: water carried for purposes of stability: wa′ter-barom′eter, a barometer in which water is substituted for mercury; wa′ter-barr′el, -cask, a barrel, cask, for holding water; wa′ter-bath, a bath composed of water: a vessel of water in which other vessels can be immersed in chemical work; wa′ter-batt′ery, a voltaic battery in which the electrolyte is water: a battery nearly on a level with the water (*fort.*): **Wa′ter-bearer**, Aquarius; wa′ter-bed, a bed whose mattress is a large water-filled plastic bag: a rubber mattress filled with water, sometimes used to prevent bed-sores; wa′ter-beetle, any of a large number of beetles living on or in water, having fringed legs by means of which they swim easily; wa′ter-bell′ows, a form of blower, worked, e.g. by a column of water falling through a vertical tube, formerly used to supply a blast for furnaces; wa′ter-bird, a bird that frequents the water: wa′ter-bis′cuit, a thin plain biscuit made with water; wa′ter-blink, in Arctic regions, a patch of sky reflecting the colour, and hence indicating the presence, of open water: (in *pl.*) the plant blinks (q.v.); wa′ter-bloom, -flow′ers, large masses of algae, chiefly blue-green, which sometimes develop very suddenly in bodies of fresh water; wa′ter-bo′a, the anaconda (*Eunectes murinus*); wa′ter-boat′man, any of a number of aquatic hemipterous insects having one pair of legs suggestive of sculls.—*adj.* wa′ter-borne, floating on water: conveyed by water, esp. in a boat: transmitted by means of water, as a disease. —wa′ter-bott′le, a skin or leather bag, or a glass, rubber, etc., bottle for containing water; wa′ter-bouget (*hist.*), a skin or leather bottle used to carry water, usu. one of a pair hung on opposite ends of a stick.—*adj.* wa′ter-bound, detained by floods: of a macadam road, or road surfacing, formed of broken stone, rolled, and covered with a thin layer of hoggin(g), which is watered in and binds the stones together.—wa′ter-brash, pyrosis, a sudden gush into the mouth of acid fluids from the stomach, accompanied by a burning sensation (heartburn) in the gullet; wa′ter-break, a piece of broken water; wa′ter-breather, any animal that breathes by means of gills.—*adj.* wa′ter-breathing.—wa′ter-brose (*Scot.*), brose made of meal and water alone; wa′ter-buck, any of several antelopes, esp. *Cobus ellipsiprymnus*; wa′ter-buffalo, the common domestic buffalo (Bubalus) of India, etc.; wa′ter-bug, any of a large variety of hemipterous insects, including water-boatmen, etc., found in or beside ponds, etc.; wa′ter-bull, a mythical amphibious animal like a bull; wa′ter-bus, a small boat used to transport passengers on a regular route on an inland waterway; wa′ter-butt, a large barrel for rain-water, usu. kept out of doors; wa′ter-cannon, a high-pressure hose pipe, used to disperse crowds; wa′ter-carriage, conveyance by water: facilities for it; wa′ter-cart, a cart for conveying water, esp. for the purpose of watering streets or roads; wa′ter-cell, one of several cells in a camel's stomach used for storing water; wa′ter-cement, hydraulic cement; wa′ter-chestnut, a water-plant (*Trapa natans*, or other species) of or akin to the Onagraceae: its edible seed; wa′ter-chute (-*shōōt*, -*shŏŏt*), an artificial cascade or slope leading to water, down which boats or toboggans slide for sport; wa′ter-clock, a clock which is made to go by the fall of water: a clepsydra; wa′ter-closet (abbrev. W.C.), a closet used as a lavatory, the discharges being carried off by water; wa′ter-cock, the kora, a large E. Indian gallinule; wa′ter-colour, a pigment diluted with water and gum (or other substance), instead of oil: a painting in such a colour or colours; wa′ter-colourist, a painter in water-colours.—*v.i.* wa′ter-cool, to cool by means of water, esp. circulating water.—*adj.* wa′ter-cooled.—wa′ter-cooler, a machine for cooling by means of water or for keeping water cool.—*adj.* and *n.* wa′ter-cooling.—wa′ter-core, in an apple or other fruit, an abnormality consisting of water-soaked tissue, esp. close to the core: in founding, a hollow core through which water may be passed; wa′tercourse, a channel through which water flows or has flowed: an artificial water-channel; a stream, river: wa′ter-cow, a female water-buffalo or water-bull; wa′ter-craft, a boat: boats collectively: skill in swimming, etc., or in managing boats; wa′ter-crane, an apparatus for supplying water from an elevated tank, esp. to a locomotive tender: a hydraulic crane; wa′ter-cress, (often, esp. formerly, in *pl.*) a perennial cress (*Nasturtium officinale*) growing in watery places, used as a salad; wa′ter-culture, a method of cultivation, often an experimental means of determining the mineral requirements of a plant, the plant being grown with its roots dipping into solutions of known composition; wa′ter-cure, medical treatment by means of water; wa′ter-deck, a decorated canvas cover for a dragoon's saddle; wa′ter-deer, a small Chinese musk-deer of aquatic habits: in Africa, one of the chevrotains; wa′ter-diviner, one who, usu. with the help of a divining-rod, detects, or tries to detect, the presence of underground water; wa′ter-doctor, a hydropathist: formerly, one who divined diseases from the urine: wa′ter-dog, any variety of the dog (formerly a specific variety, a small poodle) valuable to sportsmen in hunting water-fowl on account of its aquatic habits: a water-vole: an otter (*obs.*): also various other animals: an experienced sailor (*coll.*): a good swimmer: a small irregular floating cloud supposed to indicate rain; wa′ter-drinker, a drinker of water: a teetotaler; wa′ter-drop, a drop of water: a tear; wa′ter-dropwort, a genus (Oenanthe) of umbelliferous plants, including the common water-dropwort (*O. fistulosa*) and hemlock water-dropwort, or water-hemlock (*O. crocata*).—*adj.* wa′tered-down, much diluted.—wa′ter-elder, the guelder rose; wa′ter-engine, an engine for raising water: an engine worked by water: an engine for extinguishing fires (*obs.*): wa′ter-equiv′alent, thermal capacity, the product of the specific heat of a body and its mass; wa′terfall, a fall or perpendicular descent of a body of water, a cataract or cascade: a neck-tie (*obs.*): a chignon (*obs.*); wa′ter-fern, any of the Hydropterideae or rhizocarps, water or marsh plants differing from ferns in the narrower sense in being heterosporous, classified in two families, Marsileaceae and Salviniacea; wa′ter-finder, a water-diviner; wa′ter-flag, the yellow iris; wa′ter-flea, the common name for any of numerous minute aquatic crustaceans; wa′ter-flood, an inundation; wa′ter-flow, current of water.—*adj.* wa′ter-flowing, streaming.—wa′ter-fly, an aquatic insect: an insignificant, troublesome person (*Shak.*): wa′ter-fowl, a fowl that frequents water: swimming game-birds collectively; wa′ter-frame, Arkwright's spinning-frame, which was driven by water; wa′terfront, the buildings or part of a town along the edge of and facing the sea, a river etc.; wa′ter-gall (*obs.* and *dial.*), a watery appearance in the sky accompanying the rainbow: also a secondary rainbow; wa′ter-gap, a gap in a mountain range containing a stream; wa′ter-gas, a mixed gas obtained by passing steam (blue water-gas) or steam and air (semi-water-gas) over incandescent coke, or other source of carbon; wa′ter-gate, a floodgate: a gate admitting to a river or other body of water: a street leading to the water (*Scot.*):

wa′ter-gauge, -gage, an instrument for measuring the quantity or height of water: water pressure expressed in inches: an instrument for measuring differences in pressure; wa′ter-gilding, wash-gilding; wa′ter-glass, a water-clock: an instrument for making observations beneath the surface of water: a glass vessel for containing water, as one for keeping plants: a finger-bowl (*obs.*): a tumbler: a concentrated and viscous solution of sodium or potassium silicate in water, used as adhesive, protective covering, etc., and, esp formerly, for preserving eggs.; wa′ter-god, a deity presiding over a tract of water; wa′ter gruel, gruel made with water: anything insipid; wa′ter-guard, river, harbour, or coast police; wa′ter-hammer, the noise made by the sudden stoppage of moving water in a pipe: the concussion so caused: an air vacuum containing some water; wa′ter-head, the source, as of a stream: the region where this is found: a dammed-up body of water, or its quantity, height, or pressure; wa′ter-hemlock, a poisonous plant, *Cicuta virosa*: any other plant of the same genus: water-dropwort (q.v.); wa′ter-hen, any of a number of ralline birds, esp. *Gallinula chloropus*—also called the moorhen; wa′ter-hole, a pool in which water has collected, as a spring in a desert or a pool in the dried-up course of a river; wa′ter-horse, a water-spirit like a horse: a kelpie; wa′ter-hyacinth, a tropical floating aquatic plant (*Eichhornia crassipes*); wa′ter-ice, sweetened fruit juice or a substitute diluted with water, frozen and served with meals as a kind of ice cream; wa′tering-call, a cavalry trumpet-signal to water horses; wa′tering-can, -pot, a vessel used for watering plants; wa′tering-cap (*obs.*), a cavalryman's fatigue cap; wa′tering-house (*obs.*), an inn or other place where horses are watered; wa′tering-place, a place where water may be obtained: a place to which people resort to drink mineral water, or for bathing, etc.; wa′tering-trough, a trough in which horses and cattle drink: a trough between the rails containing water to be scooped up by locomotives; wa′ter-jacket, a casing containing water placed round, e.g. the cylinder-block of an internal-combustion engine, to keep it cool—also wa′ter-box; wa′ter-jet.—*adj.* operated by a jet of water.—wa′ter-joint, a joint in a pavement that is raised to prevent water lying in it: a joint in sheet-metal roofing forming a channel for rain-water; wa′ter-jump, a place where a jump across a stream, etc., has to be made, as in a steeplechase; wa′ter-leaf, any plant of the genus Hydrophyllum or the family Hydrophyllaceae: an ornament used in the capitals of columns, probably representing the leaf of some water plant (*archit.*); wa′ter-lemon, a species of passion-flower, or its edible fruit; wa′ter-lens, a simple lens formed by placing a few drops of water in a vessel, e.g. a small brass cell with blackened sides and a glass bottom; wa′ter-level, the level formed by the surface of still water: an instrument in which water is used for establishing a horizontal line of sight: a water-table (*geol.*): a slightly inclined road to carry off water (*mining*); wa′terlily, a name commonly given to the different species of Nymphaea and Nuphar, and also to other members of the family Nymphaeaceae—the three British species are the white waterlily (*Nymphaea alba*), and the yellow waterlilies (*Nuphar luteum* and *Nuphar minimum*—the latter being rare); wa′ter-line, any of several lines on a ship to which she is submerged under different conditions of loading, e.g. the *light water-line* marking the depth when she is without cargo: in shipbuilding, any of certain lines on a vessel parallel with the water showing the contour of the hull at various heights: the water-level: the outline of a coast:

*fāte, fär; mē, hûr* (her); *mīne; mōte, för; mūte; mōōn, fŏŏt; dhen* (then)

in paper, one of the wider-spaced lines visible by transmitted light (up and down the page in folio, octavo, etc., crosswise in quarto).—*v.t.* wa'terlog, to make unmanageable by flooding with water, as a boat: to saturate with water so as to make heavy or inert, or unfit for use, or to impede life or growth (also *fig.*).—*adj.* wa'terlogged.—wa'ter-lot, a lot of ground which is under water; wa'ter-main, a large subterranean pipe supplying water; wa'terman, a man who plies a boat for hire, a boatman, a ferryman: a good oarsman: one whose employment is supplying water, e.g. (*hist.*) to cab- or coach-horses: an imaginary being living in water; wa'termanship, oarsmanship; wa'termark, the line of the greatest height to which water has risen: a tidemark: a ship's water-line: a distinguishing mark in paper, a design visible by transmitted light, made by the mould or the dandy-roll.—*v.t.* to mark with a watermark: to impress as a watermark.—wa'ter-meadow, a meadow kept fertile by flooding from a stream; wa'ter-measure, measurement formerly used in dealing with goods, as coal, salt, etc., sold on board ship—the standard bushel, etc., being larger than the standard bushel, etc.; wa'ter-melon, a plant (*Citrullus vulgaris*) of the cucumber family, of African origin, having a pulpy, pleasantly flavoured fruit: the fruit itself; wa'ter-me'ter, instrument for measuring the quantity of water passing through a particular outlet; wa'ter-mil'foil (see milfoil); wa'ter-mill, a mill driven by water; wa'ter-moc'assin, a poisonous snake of the southern United States; wa'ter-mole, the desman: the duckbill; wa'ter-monkey, a porous earthenware jar for keeping drinking-water in hot climates, round, with narrow neck—also *monkey-jar*; wa'ter-motor, any water-wheel or turbine, esp. any small motor driven by water under pressure; wa'ter-mouse, the water-vole: any mouse of the genus Hydromys (*Austr.*); wa'ter-music (*hist.*), music performed, or composed for performance, during an excursion by water; wa'ter-nix'ie, a nixie; wa'ter-nymph, a naiad; wa'ter-ouzel (see ouzel); wa'ter-parsnip, any plant of the aquatic genus Sium, esp. the skirret; wa'ter-parting, a watershed, divide; wa'ter-pepper, a very acrid persicaria (*Polygonum hydropiper*) of wet places; wa'ter-pipe, a pipe for conveying water; wa'ter-pistol, a weapon or toy for throwing a jet of water or other liquid; wa'ter-plane, a plane passing through any water-line of a ship: the plane of the surface of water: a canal on the level without locks (*hist.*): a seaplane; wa'ter-plant, a plant that grows in water; wa'ter-plantain, a plant (*Alisma plantago*) having plantain-like leaves: any other plant of the same genus; wa'ter-plate, a plate having a double bottom and a space for hot water, used to keep food warm; wa'ter-poet, a writer of doggerel verse (John Taylor, 1580-1653, a writer of jingling verses, etc., for a time a Thames waterman, called himself 'the Water-poet'); wa'ter-pō'lo, an aquatic game played by swimmers, seven a side: also similar game played by contestants in canoes; wa'ter-pore, a hydathode: a madreporite; wa'ter-pot, a pot or vessel for holding water; wa'ter-power, the power of water, employed to move machinery, etc.: a flow or fall of water which may be so used; wa'ter-pox, varicella; wa'ter-privilege, the right to the use of water, esp. for driving machinery: a place where this right may be exercised.—*adj.* wa'terproof, coated, e.g. with rubber, so as to be impervious to water: so constructed that water cannot enter.—*n.* a material or an outer garment made impervious to water.—*v.t.* and *v.i.* to make, become, or be, impervious to water, esp. by coating with a solution.—wa'terproofing, the act of making any

substance impervious to water: the material with which this is done; wa'ter-pump, a pump for raising water: used humorously of the eyes; wa'ter-purpie (see purpie); wa'terquake, a seismic disturbance affecting the sea; wa'ter-rail, the common rail (*Rallus aquaticus*) of Europe; wa'ter-ram, a hydraulic ram; wa'ter-rat, the popular name of the water-vole: the American musk-rat: a pirate: a sailor or boat-man; wa'ter-rate, a rate or tax for the supply of water.—*adj.* wa'ter-repell'ent, resistant to penetration by water: treated with a substance which is water-resistant.—wa'ter-rice (see Zizania); wa'ter-rug, a kind of water dog—perh. from rug (1) (Shak., *Macb.* III, i. 94); wa'ter-sapphire (trans. of Fr. *saphir d'eau*), an intense blue variety of cordierite used as a gemstone; wa'ter-seal, a seal formed by water in a trap; wa'tershed, the line separating two river-basins: a drainage or a catchment area (*erron.*): a slope or structure down which water flows: a crucial point or dividing line between two phases, conditions etc.; wa'ter-shoot, a channel for the overflow of water: a water-chute.—*adjs.* wa'ter-shot (*rare*), crossed by streams; wa'terside, on the brink of water, shore of a sea, lake, etc.—*n.* the edge of a sea, lake, etc., a shore.—wa'ter-skiing, the sport of being towed at speed on skis behind a motor-boat; wa'tersmeet, a meeting-place of two streams; wa'ter-smoke, water evaporating as visible mist; wa'ter-snake, a snake frequenting the water; wa'ter-softener, a device or substance for removing the causes of hardness in water; wa'ter-soldier, an aquatic plant (*Stratiotes aloides*) common in lakes and ditches in the east of England; wa'ter-souchy (-sōō'chi, -sōō'shi), fish served in the water in which it is boiled (Du. *waterzootje—zootje*, boiling); wa'ter-spaniel (see spaniel); wa'ter-spider, an aquatic spider, esp. *Argyroneta aquatica*, which has a sub-aquatic bell-shaped web inflated with air carried down in bubbles; wa'ter-splash, a shallow stream running across a road; wa'ter-spout, a pipe, etc., from which water spouts: the spout of water: torrential rain: a disturbance like a very small tornado, a revolving column of cloud, mist, spray; wa'ter-spring (*B.*), a spring; wa'ter-sprin'kle (*Spens.*), a spray of water: also a sprinkle; wa'ter-sprite, a spirit inhabiting the water.—*adj.* wa'ter-standing (*Shak.*), brimming with tears.—wa'ter-starwort (see starwort, under star); wa'ter-strider, any long-legged aquatic insect of the family Hydrobatidae; wa'ter-supply', the obtaining and distribution of water, as to a community: the amount of water thus distributed; wa'ter-table, a moulding or other projection in the wall of a building to throw off the water: the level below which fissures and pores in the strata are saturated with water (*geol.*); wa'ter-tap, a tap or cock used for letting out water; wa'ter-ther-mom'eter, a thermometer filled with water instead of mercury, and used for showing the point at which water has its greatest density; wa'ter-thief' (*Shak.*), a pirate.—*adj.* wa'tertight, so tight as not to admit water or let it escape: such that no flaw, weakness, or source of misinterpretation, can be found in it (*fig.*).—watertight compartment, a division of a ship's hull or other underwater structure so formed that water cannot enter it from any other part: a part, esp. of one's thoughts or beliefs, shut off from the influence of other parts (*fig.*); wa'ter-tightness; wa'ter-tower, a tower containing tanks in which water is stored so that it may be delivered at sufficient pressure for distribution to an area: a vertical pipe supplied with water under high pressure, used in fire-fighting; wa'ter-tunnel (*aero.*), a tunnel in which water is circulated instead of air to obtain a visual representation of flow; **wa′ter-twist,** a kind of cotton-yarn, first made by the water-frame: in spinning, more than the usual amount of twist.—*adj.* **wa′ter-vas′cular,** of or pertaining to vessels in certain invertebrates which contain a mixture of water and a nutritive fluid: in echinoderms, of the system of coelomic canals (**water-vascular system**) associated with the ·tube-feet and supplying fluid for their movement.—**wa′ter-vine,** a name for various plants yielding a refreshing watery sap; **wa′ter-violet,** a plant of the genus Hottonia; **wa′ter-vole,** *Arvicola amphibius,* commonly known as the water-rat; **wa′ter-wag′on,** a wagon used to convey water; **wa′ter-wag′tail,** a wagtail, esp. the pied wagtail; **wa′ter-wave,** a wave of water: a wave in the hair made by setting it when wet.—*v.t.* to make such a wave in (hair).—**wa′terway,** a series of pieces of timber, extending round a ship at the junction of the decks with the sides, having a groove connecting with the scuppers to carry off water: any channel for water: a stretch of navigable water: a water-route; **wa′ter-weed,** any plant with very small flowers and leaves growing in ponds, etc., esp. anacharis (q.v.); **wa′ter-wheel,** a wheel moved by water: an engine for raising water; **wa′ter-wings,** a wing-like inflated device for keeping one afloat in water; **wa′ter-work** (usu. in *pl.*), any apparatus or plant by which water is supplied, as to a town, etc.: an ornamental fountain, cascade, etc. (*obs.*): a textile fabric, used like tapestry (*obs.*): used humorously of shedding tears, euphemistically of the human urinary system.—*adj.* **wa′ter-worn,** worn by the action of water.—**wa′ter-yam,** a plant with farinaceous root-stock, the lattice-leaf.—**above water,** out of difficulties, esp. financial; **be, go, on the water-wagon** (*slang*), to abstain from alcoholic liquors; **cast one's water,** to examine one's urine to aid in the diagnosis of disease; **deep water,** or **waters,** water too deep for safety: difficulty or distress (*fig.*); **high′-wa′ter, high′-wa′termark** (see **high**); **hold water,** to be correct or well-grounded, to bear examination; **keep one's head above water** (*fig.*), to keep solvent; **like water,** copiously: extravagantly, recklessly; **low′-wa′ter, low′-wa′termark** (see **low**); **make a hole in the water** (*slang*), to drown oneself; **make the mouth water,** to arouse a delightful feeling of anticipation or desire; **make, pass, water,** to micturate; **oil on troubled waters,** anything that allays or assuages, from the effect of pouring oil on rough water; **still waters run deep,** a quiet exterior often conceals strong emotions, resolution, cunning, etc.; **under water,** below the surface; **water down** (*lit.* and *fig.*), to make less strong; **water of crystallisation, hydration,** the water present in hydrated compounds, which, when crystallised from solution in water, retain a definite amount of water; **water of life,** spiritual refreshment: whisky, brandy, etc.; **water on the brain,** hydrocephalus; **water on the knee,** an accumulation of serous fluid in the knee-joint. [O.E. *wæter;* cf. Du. *water,* Ger. *wasser;* cog. with Gr. *hydōr,* L. *ūdus,* wet, *unda,* a wave, Sans. *udan,* water.]

**Waterloo,** *wö-tər-lōō′,* or *wö′,* n. a final defeat.— **Waterloo cracker** (*obs.*), a kind of firework. [*Waterloo,* near Brussels, where Napoleon was finally defeated in 1815.]

**watertight, waterway.** See **water.**

**Watling Street,** *wot′ling strēt,* n. one of the great Roman highways of Britain, running from near London through St Albans to Wroxeter: often extended at either end to include the roads to Dover and Chester: loosely applied to other Roman roads: the Milky Way (*obs.*). [O.E. *Wæclinga strǣt,* the street of Wæcel's people—of whom nothing is known; the O.E. name of St Albans was *Wæclinga ceaster.*]

**watt,** *wot,* n. the practical and M.K.S. unit of power, equal to a rate of working of one joule per second.—*n.* **watt′age,** amount of power expressed in watts.—**watt′-hour′,** common unit of electrical energy, being the work done by one watt acting for one hour; **watt′meter,** an instrument containing a series (*current*) and a shunt (*voltage*) coil whose combined torque produces a deflection of the needle that is a direct measure of the circuit power in watts. [James *Watt* (1736-1819).]

**Watteau,** *wot′ō, adj.* applied to articles or features of women's dress resembling the costumes in the paintings of Antoine *Watteau* (1684-1721)—as **Watteau bodice,** one with a square opening at the neck and short sleeves.—*adj.* **Watt′eauish.**

**wattle,** *wot′l, n.* a twig or flexible rod (*dial.*): (collective *sing.* or in *pl.*) material for fences, roofs, etc., in the form of rods, branches, etc., either interwoven to form a network or loose: a hurdle (*dial.*): any of various Australian acacias: (perh. a different word) the coloured fleshy excrescence under the throat of some birds, or a similar excrescence or process on any part of the head of a bird, fish, etc.—*v.t.* to bind with wattle or twigs: to form by plaiting twigs.—*adj.* **watt′led.**—*n.* **watt′ling,** the act of making wattles by interweaving twigs, etc.: wattle-work, or the material for it.—**watt′lebark,** bark of various wattles, used for tanning; **watt′le-bird,** any of a number of honey-eaters of Australia that have ear-wattles; **watt′le-work,** wicker-work. —**wattle and daub, dab,** wattle-work plastered with mud and used as a building material. [O.E. *watul, watel;* origin uncertain.]

**wattle,** *wot′l,* (*hist.;* Orkney and Shetland) n. the obligation to entertain the foud on his annual journey, or a tax for which it was later commuted. [Perh. Norw. dial. *veitla*—O.N. *veizla,* entertainment.]

**wauff.** Variant of waff (1 and 2).

**waugh,** *wö, interj.* expressing sorrow, anger, etc.— usu. attributed to North American Indians.

**waught, waucht,** *wöht,* (*Scot.*) n. a large draught. —*v.t.* and *v.i.* to drink in large draughts. [Perh. conn. with quaff.]

**waukrife.** See wake.

**waul, wawl,** *wöl, v.t.* to cry as a cat or a newly-born baby.—Also *n.*—n. and *adj.* **waul′ing, wawl′ing.** [Imit.]

**waul, wawl,** *wöl,* (*Scot.; obs.*) v.i. to roll the eyes. [O.E. *wealwian,* to roll, wallow.]

**waur, waurst.** See war (2).

**wave,** *wāv, n.* a ridge on the surface of a liquid, esp. of the sea: a surge, consisting of vibrating particles of liquid, moving across the surface of a body of liquid such as the sea (*transverse wave*)— the vibrations of the individual particles being at right angles to the line of advance: a unit disturbance in any travelling system of vibrating particles as a light-wave (*transverse wave*) or a sound-wave (*longitudinal wave*—the vibrations of the particles being in the direction of advance): an undulating or vibratory motion (e.g. as a signal), or sound: the sea, or other body of water (*poet.*): curved inequality of surface: a line or streak like a wave: an undulation: an undulating succession of curves in hair, or one of these: a movement of the raised hand expressing greeting, farewell etc.: a swelling up or increase, followed by a subsidence or decline (*fig.*).—*v.i.* to move like a wave: to move backwards and forwards: to float or to hover (*obs.*): to flutter, as a signal: to make a signal in this way: to move the raised hand in greeting, farewell, etc.: to undulate: to waver, vacillate (*obs.*).—*v.t.* to move backwards and forwards: to brandish: to waft or beckon: to express by a wave: to raise into inequalities of surface: to give an undulating appearance to.—*adjs.*

waved, showing a wave-like form or outline: undulating: of hair, artificially made to undulate: indented (*her.*): having on the margin a succession of curved segments or incisions: moved to and fro; wave′less.—*n.* wave′let, a little wave.—*adj.* wave′like.—*v.t.* wāv′er, to move to and fro: to shake, be unsteady, be in danger of falling: to falter, show signs of giving way: to vacillate: to vary, change.—*n.* wāv′erer. —*n.* and *adj.* wāv′ering.—*adv.* wāv′eringly, in a wavering or irresolute manner.—*n.* wāv′eringness.—*adjs.* wāv′erous, wāv′ery, unsteady.—*ns.* wave′son, goods floating on the sea after a shipwreck; wāv′iness, the state or quality of being wavy.—*n.* and *adj.* wāv′ing.—*adj.* wāv′y, full of, or rising in, waves: playing to and fro: undulating.—wave′band, a range of wavelengths occupied by transmission of a particular type; wave′form, wave′shape, graph showing variation of amplitude of electrical signal, or other wave, against time; wave′front, in a propagating vibratory disturbance, the continuous locus of points which are in the same phase of vibration; wave′guide (*electronics*), a hollow metal conductor, usu. rectangular, within which very high-frequency energy can be transmitted efficiently; wave′length, the distance between two successive similar points on an alternating wave, e.g. between successive maxima or between successive minima: the distance, measured radially from the source, between two successive points in free space at which an electromagnetic wave has the same phase; wave mechanics, the part of quantum mechanics dealing with the wave aspect of the behaviour of radiations; wave′-meter, an instrument for measuring wavelengths, directly or indirectly; wave′-mō′tion, undulatory movement: motion in waves, or according to the same laws; wave′-offering, an ancient Jewish custom of moving the hands in succession towards the four points of the compass in presenting certain offerings—opp. to the *heave-offering*, in which the hands were only lifted up and lowered.—on the same wavelength as, in tune with, having the same attitude of mind, background knowledge, etc.; Wavy Navy, the Royal Naval Volunteer Reserve, so-called from the undulating gold braid on officers' sleeves. [O.E. *wafian*, to wave; cf. O.N. *vafra*, to waver.]

wavellite, wā′vəl-īt, *n.* hydrated phosphate of aluminium, occurring commonly in flattened globular aggregates, showing a strongly developed internal radiating structure. [Named after Dr. *Wavel*, who discovered the mineral near Barnstaple.]

wavey, wavy, wā′vi, *n.* the snow-goose. [Cree.]

waw, wö, (*Scott*) *n.* a wave—*Spens.* wawe. [Prob. from a lost O.E. form akin to *wæg*, wave.]

wawl. See waul (1 and 2).

wax, waks, *n.* any of a class of substances of plant or animal origin, usu. consisting of esters of monohydric alcohols, e.g. beeswax, $C_{30}H_{61}O \cdot CO \cdot C_{15}H_{31}$: any of certain hydrocarbons of mineral origin, as ozokerite: any substance like a wax in some respect, as that in the ear: a substance used to seal letters: that used by shoemakers to rub their thread: in mining, puddled clay: a thick sugary substance made by boiling down the sap of the sugar-maple, and cooling by exposure to the air: a person easily influenced (*fig.*): in Shak., *Timon*, I, i. 48, explanation uncertain—according to some, wax tablets, others have thought expansive growth (see wax, 2).—*v.t.* to smear, rub, or (*obs.*) join with wax.—*adj.* wax′en, made of wax: like wax: easily impressed, penetrated, effaced.—*ns.* wax′er, one who or that which waxes; wax′iness; wax′ing.—*adj.* wax′y, resembling wax in texture or appearance: soft: impressible: impressionable (*fig.*): pallid, pasty.—wax′-bill, any of various small seed-eating birds of the weaver-bird family with coloured bills like sealing-wax; wax′-chandler, a maker of, or dealer in, wax candles; wax′-cloth, cloth covered with a coating of wax, used for table-covers, etc.: a popular name for all oil floorcloths; wax′-doll, a child's doll having the head and bust made of hardened beeswax; wax′ed leather, leather finished with a high wax polish on the flesh side; wax′-end, better waxed end, a strong thread having its end stiffened by shoemakers' wax, so as to go easily through the hole made by the awl; wax′-flower, an artificial flower made of wax: any of several plants, as a white-flowered climbing plant of Madagascar, an epiphyte of British Guiana, and plants of the genus Hoya of Australasia; wax′-insect, an insect that secretes wax, as any of several of the Coccidae, etc.; wax′-light, a candle or taper made of wax; wax′-moth, a bee-moth; wax′-myrtle, U.S. candleberry tree; wax′-painting, encaustic painting; wax′-palm, either of two S. American palms yielding wax; wax′-paper, paper spread with a thin coating of white wax and other materials.—*adj.* wax′-red (*Shak.*), bright-red like sealing-wax.—wax′-tree, a tree from which wax is obtained, as a Japanese sumac (*Rhus succedanea*), the wax-myrtle, a privet (*Ligustrum lucidum*), etc.; wax′-wing, a genus of passerine birds (Bombycilla) with small red horny appendages, resembling red sealing-wax, on their wings; wax′work, work made of wax, esp. figures or models formed of wax: (in *pl.*) an exhibition of wax figures; wax′-worker; waxy degeneration, a morbid process in which the healthy tissue of various organs is transformed into a peculiar waxy albuminous substance. [O.E. *weax*; O.N. *vax*, Du. *was*, Ger. *wachs.*]

wax, waks, *v.i.* to grow or increase, esp. of the moon, as opp. to *wane*: to pass into another state, become:—*pa.p.* (*arch.*) wax′en, grown—also (*obs.*) *pa.t. pl.* (as Shak., *M.N.D.*, II, i. 56) and *infin.* [O.E. *weaxan*; O.N. *vaxa*, Ger. *wachsen*, allied to L. *augēre*, to increase, Gr. *auxanein.*]

wax, waks, (*coll.*) *n.* a passion, fit of anger.—*adj.* wax′y (*coll.*), irate, incensed. [Origin uncertain.]

way, wā, (*Spens.*) *v.t.* to weigh, esteem. [Variant of weigh.]

way, wā, *n.* passage: road, street, track: direction of motion: length of space, distance: district: room or opportunity to advance: freedom of action, scope: manner of life: condition, state: advance in life: normal, habitual, course or conduct: (in *pl.*) characteristic conduct, idiosyncrasies: manner, style: method: means: course: respect: will: progress or motion through the water, headway (*naut.*): the direction of the weave, grain, etc.: (in *pl.*) the machined surfaces of the top of a lathe bed on which the carriage slides, shears: (in *pl.*) the framework of timbers on which a ship slides when being launched.—*v.i.* (*Spens.*) to journey.—*adj.* way′less, without a path.—way′bagg′age (*U.S.*), baggage to be laid down at a way-station; way′-bill, list of passengers and goods carried by a public vehicle: a list of places to be visited on a journey: a document giving details regarding goods sent by rail; way′-board, weigh′-board, a thin stratum or seam separating thicker strata; way′bread (*dial.*); O.E. *wegbræde*—*brād*, broad), the common plantain.—*v.i.* way′fāre (*arch.*), to travel, esp. on foot.—*n.* (*arch.*) travel, esp. on foot.—way′fārer, a traveller, esp. on foot.—*n.* and *adj.* way′fāring.—way′fāring-tree, the *Viburnum lantana*, a large shrub common in hedges: way′-freight, freight for a way-station.—*adjs.* way′-going (*Scot.*), departing; way′gone, exhausted by travelling.—*v.t.* waylay′, to lie in ambush for: to attack or seize in the way: to lie in wait for in order to converse with (*fig.*): to obstruct or intercept (*obs.*).—waylay′er; way′-leave, permission to pass over another's ground or property; way′-maker, a pioneer: a precursor; way′mark, a guide-post: something which serves as a guide to a traveller; way′-passenger, one taken up or set down at a way-station or an intermediate point on a coach or bus route; way′-post, a guide-post; way′side, the border of a way, path, or highway.—*adj.* growing or lying near the wayside.—way′-station (*U.S.*), an intermediate station between principal stations; way′-traffic, local traffic, as distinguished from through or express traffic; way′-train (*U.S.*), a train stopping at most of the stations on a line; way′-warden, one elected to supervise the upkeep of roads in a district; way′wiser, an instrument for measuring distance travelled.—*adj.* way′worn, worn-out by travel.—be by way of, to be supposed, alleged (inaccurately) to be, do; by, with, one's way of it (*Scot.*), according to one's belief or assertion; by the way, incidentally: while travelling: beside one's path; by way of, travelling through, via: as if for the purpose of: in character of, as a substitute for; come one's way, to come in the same direction: to come within one's experience or reach, to become attainable (*fig.*); committee of ways and means, the House of Commons when it sits to consider methods of raising supplies; get one's (own) way, to get what one wants; give way (see give); go one's way (see go); go out of the, one's, way, put oneself out of the way, to give oneself trouble: to make a special point of; go the way of all the earth, of all flesh, to die; have a way with one, to have a fascinating personality or persuasive manner; have one's way, to carry one's point, get what one wants; have way (*naut*), to be in motion, as a vessel; in a bad way, in a serious condition: much upset; in a fair way to, likely to succeed in; in a small, big (or large) way, on a petty, or a large or grandiose, scale; in a way, in a state of agitation or distress: to some extent: from one point of view; in the family way (see family); in the way, on the way: in the path (*lit.* and *fig.*): impending, obstructing; in the way of, in a good position for effecting or attaining: in the habit of (*coll.*): in respect of; lead the way, to act as a guide in any movement; make one's way, to push oneself forward (*lit.* and *fig.*); make way, to give place: to advance; on the way, moving towards a destination or event: in progress; out of the way, so as not to hinder or obstruct: lost, hidden (*Shak.*; out-of-the-way, see out-); take one's way, to set out, proceed: to follow one's own inclination or plan; the Way, the Christian Religion (Acts ix. 2, etc.); under way, in motion, as a vessel; Way of the Cross, a series of pictorial representations of the stages of Christ's progress to Calvary: devotions used in connection with these stages; ways and means, resources: methods e.g. of raising money for the carrying on of government. [O.E. *weg*; Ger. *weg*; akin to Sans. *vahati*, he carries, akin to L. *vehĕre*, to carry, draw.]

way, 'way, wā, *adv.*, abbrev. form of away, far: at a considerable distance or interval of time.—*adj.* way-out (*slang*), lost in what one is doing (as, orig., playing avant-garde jazz): excellent, unusual, very satisfying, far-out, eccentric.

wayment, wā-ment′, (*Spens.*) *v.t.* and *v.i.* to lament, grieve.—*n.* lamentation, grief. [O.Fr. *waimenter* —*wai*, alas!]

way-out. See way (3).

wayward, wā′wərd, *adj.* wilful: capricious: irregular.—*adv.* way′wardly.—*n.* way′wardness. [For awayward—away, and suff. -ward.]

wayzgoose, wase-goose, wāz′gōōs, *n.* a printers'

annual dinner or picnic.—Earlier way′goose. [Origin obscure.]

wazir, wä-zēr′, *n.* a vizier. [Ar. *wazîr*.]

we, wē, *pron. pl.* of I: I and others: used for I by monarchs: also by editors, etc. [O.E. *wē*; cog. with Goth. *weis*, Ger. *wir*.]

weak, wēk, *adj.* soft (*obs.*): wanting strength: not able to sustain a great weight: easily overcome: frail: wanting health: feeble of mind: wanting moral or mental force: impressible, easily led: lacking artistic force: unconvincing: inconclusive: inconsiderable (*Shak.*): having little of the important ingredient: of a verb, inflected by regular syllabic addition instead of by change of main vowel: of a Germanic noun or adj., having inflexions in -*n*: of a sound or accent, having little force: of a verse line, having the accent on a normally unstressed syllable: tending downward in price.—*v.t.* weak′en, to make weaker: to reduce in strength or spirit.—*v.i.* to grow weak or weaker: to become less resolute or determined, show signs of giving in.—*ns.* weak′ener; weak′liness; weak′ling, a weak or feeble creature.—*adv.* weak′ly.—*adj.* sickly: not robust: feeble.—*n.* weak′ness, state of being weak: a liking or fondness for.—weaker sex, women; weaker vessel (see vessel).—*adj.* weak′-eyed, having weak eyes or sight.—weak force, interaction, a force involved in radioactive decay, supposed to be one of four forces governing the universe.—*adjs.* weak-handed, powerless; weak′-headed, having a feeble intellect: easily affected by alcoholic liquor; weak′-hearted, of weak spirit: soft-hearted; weak′-hinged, illbalanced; weak′-kneed, having weak knees: weak in will; weak′-minded, having feeble intelligence: having, or showing, lack of resolution: too easily convinced or persuaded.—weak′-mindedness; weak side, point, that side or point in which a person is most easily influenced or most liable to temptation.—*adjs.* weaksighted; weak-spirited, bearing wrong tamely, cowardly. [O.N. *veikr*; allied to O.E. *wāc*, pliant—*wīcan*, to yield; Du. *week*, Ger. *weich*.]

weal, wēl, *n.* state of being well (*arch.*): a sound or prosperous state: welfare: commonwealth (*obs.*).—*adj.* weal′-balanced (Shak., *Meas.*, IV, iii. 108), perh. kept in a state of just proportion by reasons of state, perh. for well-balanced.—weals′man (*Shak.*), a statesman.—the public, general, or common, weal, the well-being, interest, and prosperity of the country. [O.E. *wela, weola*, wealth, bliss; allied to well (2).]

weal, wēl, *n.* a raised streak left by a blow with a lash, etc. [See wale (1).]

weal. Same as weel (1).

weald, wēld, (*poet.*) *n.* open country or wooded country.—*adj.* Weald′en, pertaining to the Weald: of a series of freshwater beds at the base of the Cretaceous, seen in the Weald.— Also *n.*—the Weald, a district, once forested, between the North and South Downs. [O.E. (W.S.) *weald*, a forest, wold; cf. wold.]

wealth, welth, *n.* prosperity, well-being (*arch.*): valuable possessions of any kind: riches: an abundance (*fig.*).—*adv.* wealth′ily.—*n.* wealth′iness.—*adj.* wealth′y, rich: prosperous. [M.E. *welthe—wele*—O.E. *wela*; see weal (1).]

weamb. See wame.

wean, wān, (*Scot.*) *n.* a child. [wee ane.]

wean, wēn, *v.t.* to accustom to nourishment other than the mother's milk: to reconcile to the want of anything: to estrange the affections of from any object or habit.—*n.* wean′el (*Spens.*), a weanling.—*adj.* wean′ling, newly weaned (also *fig.*).—*n.* a child or animal newly weaned.— wean′ing-brash, a severe form of diarrhoea that supervenes, at times, on weaning. [O.E. *wenian*, to accustom; O.N. *venja*, Ger. *gewöhnen*, to accustom, *entwöhnen*, to disuse, wean.]

**weapon**, *wep'n*, *n.* any instrument of offence or defence.—*adjs.* **weap'oned**; **weap'onless**, having no weapons.—*n.* weap'onry, weapons collectively: armament.—**weap'on-salve**, a salve supposed to cure a wound by being applied to the weapon that made it. [O.E. *wǣpen*; Goth. *wēpna*, arms, Ger. *waffe*.]

**weapon-s(c)haw.** See **wappens(c)haw.**

**wear**, *wār*, *v.t.* to be dressed in: to carry on the body: to arrange, as clothes, in a specified way: to display, show: of a ship, to fly (a flag): to consume, waste, damage, by use, time, exposure: to make by friction: to exhaust, to weary: to bring gradually into: to enable to last, endure (*Scot.*; *wēr*): to spend, as a period of· time (*poet.*): to traverse (*Spens.*): to edge, guide, conduct, as sheep into a fold (*Scot.*): to tolerate. —*v.i.* to be wasted by use or time: to consume slowly: of time, to be spent, pass, esp. tediously (*poet.*; usu. in *pa.p.*): to last under use: to resist the ravages of age: stand the test of time: to be in fashion (*Shak.*): to pass into: to become (*obs.*): to go, move, slowly (*Scot.*):— *pa.t.* **wŏre**, *arch.* **wāre**, *pa.p.* **wŏrn.**—*n.* act of wearing: lessening or injury by use or friction: durability: articles worn: fashion.—*adj.* **wear'-able**, fit to be worn.—*n.* **wear'er.**—*adj.* **wear'ing**, made or designed for wear: consuming: exhausting.—*n.* the process of wasting by attrition or time: the action of carrying on the body, or displaying, or flying: durability: passing: that which is worn, clothes (*obs.*).—**wear'ing-apparel**, dress; **wear'-iron**, an iron plate to take the wear due to friction.—**wear and tear**, **tear and wear**, damage by wear or use; **wear away**, to impair, consume, by wear: to decay or fade out: to pass off; **wear down** (*fig.*), to diminish, or overcome, gradually by persistence; **wear off**, to rub off by friction: to diminish by decay: to pass away by degrees; **wear out**, to impair by use: to render, become, useless by decay: to consume tediously: to harass; **(win and) wear**, to (win and) enjoy possession of. [O.E. *werian*, to wear; O.N. *verja*, to clothe, Goth. *wasian*.]

**wear**, *wār*, (*naut.*) *v.t.* and *v.i.* to bring, or be brought, to another course by turning the helm to windward:—*pa.t.* and *pa.p.* **wore.** [Prob. **veer** (1).]

**wear**, *wēr*, *n.* another spelling of **weir**.

**wear**, *wēr*, (*Scot.*) *v.t.* to guard: to ward off. [O.E. *werian*.]

**wearish**, *wēr'ish*, *adj.* tasteless, savourless (*lit.* and *fig.*; *obs.*): feeble, withered, shrunk (*dial.*). [Late M.E. *werische*; cf. **wersh**.]

**weary**, *wē'ri*, *adj.* having the strength or patience exhausted: very tired: causing weariness: tiresome, tedious: puny (*dial.*).—*v.t.* to make weary: to reduce the strength or patience of: to harass.—*v.i.* to become weary or impatient: to long (with *for*; *Scot.*).—*adjs.* **wea'ried**, tired; **wea'riful**, wearisome.—*adv.* **wea'rifully.**—*adj.* **wea'riless**, incessant.—*adv.* **wea'rily.**—*n.* **wea'-riness.**—*adj.* **wea'risome**, causing weariness: tedious.—*adv.* **wea'risomely.**—*n.* **wea'risomeness.** —**Weary Willie** (*slang*), a tramp: a person habitually lackadaisical or deficient in energy.— **weary out**, to exhaust. [O.E. *wērig*, weary.]

**weary**, *wē'ri*, (*Scot.*) *n.* a curse, as in **weary on you**, **weary fall you.** [**weary** (1), prob. with some association with obs. *wary* (O.E. *wiergan*), to curse.]

**weasand**, *wē'zənd*, *n.* the gullet: the windpipe: the throat.—**wea'sand-pipe**, (*Spens.*). [O.E. *wǣsand*; O.S. *wāsend*, O.H.G. *weisant*.]

**weasel**, *wē'zl*, *n.* a small carnivore (*Mustela nivalis*) with long slender body, active, furtive, and bloodthirsty, eating frogs, birds, mice, etc.: person resembling weasel, esp. in bad qualities: small amphibious tank.—*v.t.* to equivocate.—*adj.* **wea'selly.**—**wea'sel-cat**, linsang; **wea'sel-coot**, female or young male of smew.—*adj.* **wea'sel-faced**, with lean sharp face.—**weasel-word**, word, that makes statement evasive or misleading.— **weasel-out**, evade obligation. [O.E. *wesle*.]

**weather**, *wedh'ər*, *n.* atmospheric conditions as to heat or cold, wetness, cloudiness, etc.: type or vicissitude of atmospheric conditions or of fortune: formerly, (*specif.*) storm or adverse weather: the direction in which the wind is blowing (*naut.*): the angle the sail of a windmill makes with the perpendicular to its axis.—*v.t.* to affect by exposing to the air: to sail to the windward of: to gain or pass, as a cape: to come safely through (*lit.* and *fig.*): to shelter from (*obs.*): to set, as the sails of a windmill: to slope, as a roof.—*v.i.* to become discoloured, disintegrated, etc., by exposure.—*adv.* toward the wind, windward.—*adj.* **weath'ered**, having the surface altered in colour, form, texture, or composition by the action of the elements (*geol.*): seasoned by exposure to weather: made slightly sloping so as to throw off water (*archit.*).—*n.* **weath'ering**, weather conditions (*obs.*): the action of the elements in altering the form, colour, texture, or composition of rocks (*geol.*): seasoning by weather: a slight inclination given to the top of a cornice or moulding, to prevent water from lodging on it (*archit.*): the act of passing to windward of (*naut.*).—*v.t.* **weath'erise**, **-ize**, of a fabric, to make weather-proof.—*adjs.* **weath'erly** (*naut.*), making little leeway when close-hauled; **weath'er-most** (*naut.*), furthest to windward.—*n.* **weather-om'eter**, an instrument used to determine the weather-resisting properties of paints.—**weath'er-anchor**, the anchor lying to windward.—*adjs.* **weath'er-beaten**, distressed by, or seasoned by, the weather; **weath'er-bitten**, worn or defaced by exposure to the winds.—**weath'er-board**, the windward side of a ship: a plank in a porthole, etc., of a vessel placed so as to keep off rain, without preventing air from circulating: a board shaped so as to shed water from a building. —*v.t.* to fit with such planks or boards.— **weath'er-boarding**, thin boards placed overlapping to keep out rain: exterior covering of a wall or roof.—*adj.* **weath'er-bound**, detained by bad weather.—**weath'er-bow**, the windward side of the bow; **weath'er-box**, **-house**, a toy constructed on the principle of a barometer, consisting of a house with the figures of a man and wife who come out alternately as the weather is respectively bad or good; **weath'er-cloth**, a protecting tarpaulin on deck; **weath'ercock**, a vane (often in the form of a cock) to show the direction of the wind: one who changes his opinions, allegiance, etc., easily and often.—*v.t.* to act as a weathercock for: to supply with a weathercock: to behave like a weathercock.— *adj.* **weath'er-driven**, driven by winds or storms. —**weath'er-eye**, the eye considered as the means by which one forecasts the weather (also *fig.*).— *v.t.* **weath er-fend** (*Shak.*), to defend from the weather, to shelter.—**weath'er-forecast**, a forecast of the weather based on meteorological observations; **weath'er-ga(u)ge**, position of a ship to the windward of another: advantage of position; **weath'er-gall** (*Scot.* -gaw), an imperfect rainbow, or other supposed sign of coming weather; **weath'er-glass**, a glass or instrument that indicates the changes of the weather: a barometer; **weath'er-gleam** (*dial.*), a bright aspect of the sky at the horizon.—*adj.* **weath'er-headed** (*Scott*), flighty.—**weath'er-helm**, a keeping of the helm somewhat to the weather side when a vessel shows a tendency to come into the wind; **weath'er-map**, a map indicating meteorological conditions over a large tract of country; **weath'er-notation**, a system of abbreviation for meteorological phenomena.—*adj.* **weath'er-proof**, proof

Neutral vowels in unaccented syllables: *el'ə-mənt*; for certain sounds in foreign words, see p. viii

against rough weather.—*n.* weather-proof material.—*v.t.* to make weather-proof.—**weath′er-prophet**, one who foretells weather: a device for foretelling the weather; **weath′er-roll**, the lurch of a vessel to windward when in the trough of the sea; **weath′er-report**, loosely, a weather forecast; **weath′er-satellite**, a satellite used for the study of cloud formations and other meteorological conditions; **weath′er-ship**, a ship engaged on meteorological work; **weath′er-side**, windward side; **weath′er-sign**, a phenomenon indicating change of weather: any prognostic; **weath′er-stain**, discoloration produced by exposure; **weath′er-station**, a station where phenomena of weather are observed; **weath′er-strip**, a thin piece of some material used to keep out wind and cold; **weath′er-symbol**, a conventional sign indicating a meteorological phenomenon.—*adj.* **weath′er-wise**, skilful in foreseeing the changes of the weather (*lit.* and *fig.*): with regard to weather conditions.—**above the weather**, too high in the air to experience the weather conditions on the ground: not, or no longer, under the weather; **keep one's weather eye open**, to be alert: keep a sharp lookout; **keep, have, the weather of**, to be to the windward of: to have the advantage of; **make fair weather** (*Shak.*), to be conciliatory, to flatter; **make good, bad,** etc., **weather of it**, to behave well or badly in a storm (*lit.* and *fig.*); **make heavy weather of**, to find excessive difficulty in; **stress of weather**, violent and unfavourable winds; **under the weather**, indisposed, seedy: drunk; **weather along**, to make headway against adverse weather; **weather a point** (*fig.*), to gain an advantage or accomplish a purpose against opposition; **weather on**, to gain on in a windward direction (*lit.* and *fig.*); **weather out**, to hold out against till the end. [O.E. *weder*; O.N. *vedhr*, Ger. *wetter*.]

**weave**, *wēv*, *v.t.* to make by crossing threads, strands,′ strips, etc., above and below one another: to interlace, as in a loom to form cloth: to work into a fabric, story, etc.: to depict by weaving: to unite, work into a whole: to construct, contrive.—*v.i.* to practise weaving: —*pa.t.* wŏve, rarely weaved; *pa.p.* wŏv′en; cf. wove.—*n.* texture of a woven fabric.—*ns.* **weav′er; weav′ing**, the act or art of forming a web or cloth by the intersecting of two distinct sets of fibres, threads, or yarns—those passing longitudinally from end to end of the web forming the *warp*, those crossing and intersecting the warp at right angles forming the *weft*.—**weav′er-bird**, any bird of a passerine family resembling the finches, so called from their remarkably woven nests. [O.E. *wefan*; O.N. *vefa*, Ger. *weben*; cog. with Gr. *hyphē*, a web, *hyphainein*, to weave.]

**weave**, *wēv*, *v.i.* to move to and fro: to wind in and out: to move back or forward with sinuous movements of the body (*boxing*): to fly with a weaving motion (*aero.*).—*v.t.* to move to and fro or up and down: to make a signal to by waving something.—*n.* and *adj.* **weav′ing**.—**get weaving** (*slang*), get busy, get on the move. [M.E. *weve*; of uncertain origin.]

**weazand**, *wē′zənd*, *n.* Same as **weasand**.

**weazen**, *wē′zn*, *adj.* Variant of **wizen**.

**web**, *web*, *n.* that which is woven: a whole piece of cloth as woven in the loom: a kind of cloth or weave: a thin metal plate or sheet: in paper-making, an endless wire-cloth working on rollers: a large sheet or roll of paper: in birds, the vexillum of a feather: any connective tissue (*anat.*): the fine texture spun by the spider, etc., as a snare: the skin between the toes of water-fowl, etc.: a film over the eye (*obs.*): anything like a cloth web in complication or a spider's web in flimsiness or in power to entangle: a

plot, snare.—*v.t.* to envelop, or to connect, with a web.—*adj.* **webbed**, having the toes united by a web or skin.—*n.* **webb′ing**, a narrow woven fabric of hemp, used for belts, etc., for various purposes in upholstery, and as tapes conducting webs of paper in a printing-machine: state of being palmate (*zool.*): the webs of webbed hands or feet.—*adj.* **webb′y.**—*adj.* **web′-fing′ered.**—**web′-foot**, a foot the toes of which are united with a web or membrane.—*adj.* **web′-foot′ed.**—**web offset**, a method of offset printing using a reel of paper.—*adj.* **web′-toed.**—**web′worm** (*U.S.*), any of a number of caterpillars spinning webs in which they feed or rest.—**web and pin** (*Shak.*), or **pin and web** (see **pin**). [O.E. *webb*; O.N. *vefr*, Ger. *gewebe*; from root of **weave** (1).]

**weber**, *vā′bər*, *wē′bər*, *n.* the M.K.S. unit of magnetic flux. [Wilhelm *Weber*, German physicist (1804-91).]

**webster**, *web′stər*, (*obs.*) *n.* a weaver.—Also (*Scot.*) **wab′ster**. [O.E. *webbestre*, a female weaver—*webban*, to weave.]

**wecht**, *wehht*, (*Scot.*) *n.* an instrument for winnowing or for measuring grain. [Perh. conn. with **weigh**.]

**wed**, *wed* (*Scot.* wad, wŏd), *v.t.* to marry: to join in marriage: to unite closely: to wager (*obs.*).—*v.i.* to marry:—*pr.p.* wedd′ing; *pa.t.* wedd′ed or, *dial.*, wed; *pa.p.* wedd′ed or, *dial.* and *poet.*, wed.—*n.* (*obs.*; Scot. wad) a pledge, security.—*adj.* **wedd′ed**, married: of or pertaining to marriage: closely joined: persistently devoted. —*n.* **wedd′ing**, marriage: marriage ceremony.— **wedd′ing-bed**, the bridal bed; **wedd′ing-breakfast**, a meal served after a wedding; **wedd′ing-cake**, a highly decorated cake served at a wedding, and also divided among absent friends; **wedd′-ing-cards**, cards announcing a wedding, sent to friends; **wedd′ing-day**, day of marriage: its anniversary; **wedd′ing-dower**, marriage portion; **wedd′ing-dress**, a bride's dress; **wedd′ing-favour**, white rosette worn by men at a wedding; **wedd′ing-finger**, the ring-finger; **wedd′ing-garment**, garment worn at a wedding; **wedding-march**, music in march time played at the close of a marriage ceremony; **wedd′ing-ring**, a plain, usu. gold, ring given by the groom to the bride at a wedding.—**penny wedding**, a wedding where the guests paid for the entertainment, and sometimes contributed to the outfit; **silver, golden, diamond wedding**, the celebrations of the 25th, 50th, and 60th anniversaries of a wedding. [O.E. *weddian*, to promise, to marry (Ger. *wetten*, to wager)—*wedd*, a pledge; Goth. *wadi*, Ger. *wette*, a bet.]

**wedge**, *wej*, *n.* a piece of wood or metal, thick at one end and sloping to a thin edge at the other, used in splitting, fixing tightly, etc.: anything shaped more or less like a wedge, as:—an ingot of gold or silver (*obs.*), a formation of troops, the flying formation of geese and other wildfowl, a large piece, e.g. of cake, a stroke in cuneiform characters: a wedge-soled golf-club used for approaching: a shoe in which the heel and sole together form a wedge and there is no gap under the instep (also **wedge-heeled shoe**).—*v.t.* to cleave with a wedge: to force or drive with a wedge: to thrust in tightly: to crowd closely: to fasten or fix with a wedge or wedges: to make into a wedge.—*v.i.* to force one's way like a wedge: to become fixed or jammed by, or as if by, a wedge.—*adj.* **wedged.**—*adv.* **wedge′wise**, in the manner of a wedge.—*n.* **wedg′ing**, a method of joining timbers.—*adjs.* **wedge′-shaped**, shaped like a wedge; **wedge′-tailed**, having the tail wedge-shaped.—**the thin, or small, end of the wedge**, a small beginning that is bound to be followed by a large or significant development; **the (wooden) wedge**, the student lowest on the classical tripos list (on the analogy of wooden spoon, q.v., from Wedgwood the last name on the first list, that of 1824). [O.E. *wecg*; O.N. *veggr*, Ger. *weck*, a wedge.]

**Wedgwood,** *wej'wŏŏd,* ® *n.* a superior kind of pottery, including that lightly glazed with cameo reliefs in white, invented by Josiah *Wedgwood* (1730-1795).

**wedlock,** *wed'lok, n.* matrimony: married state, esp. in the phrase **born in,** or **out of, wedlock,** i.e. legitimate or illegitimate.—**break wedlock,** to commit adultery. [O.E. *wedlāc—wedd,* a pledge, and suff. *-lāc* implying action of some kind.]

**Wednesday,** *wenz'di, wed'nz-di, n.* the fourth day of the week. [O.E. *Wōdnes dæg,* Woden's day.]

**wee,** *wē, (Scot.) n.* a short distance, a short time. —*adj.* tiny.—**Wee Free,** a member of the minority of the Free Church that refused to join with the United Presbyterian Church in 1900. [M.E. *we, wei,* a bit, time, or space, as in phrase a *little wei.*]

**wee,** *wē, interj.* imitating the squeal of a young pig.—Also *v.i.* and *n.*

**weed,** *wēd, n.* any useless plant of small growth: any plant growing where it is not wanted by man: any wild herb: a thick growth of wild herbs: anything useless, troublesome, or obnoxious: a worthless animal: a worthless, contemptible fellow: tobacco, or a cigar or cigarette (*coll.*).—*v.t.* to free from weeds: to remove, uproot (often **weed out**).—*v.i.* to remove weeds.—*adj.* **weed'ed.**—*ns.* **weed'er; weed'ery,** a place full of weeds; **weedicide** (*wēd'i-sīd;* L. *-cida—caedēre,* to kill) a chemical weedkiller; **weed'iness; weed'ing,** the action of the verb to weed: what is weeded out.—*adjs.* **weed'less; weed'y,** weed-like: full of weeds: lanky, ungainly: of worthless character.—*adj.* **weed'-grown,** overgrown with weeds.—**weed'ing chisel, -forceps, -hook, -tongs** (*pl.*), garden implements of varying forms for destroying weeds; **weedkiller,** anything, esp. a chemical preparation, for killing weeds. [O.E. *wēod,* a herb.]

**weed,** *wēd, n.* a garment, or (as collective *sing.*) clothing (*arch.*): armour (*arch.*): (in *pl.*) a widow's mourning apparel.—*adj.* **weed'y,** clad in widow's mourning. [O.E. *wæd, wēde,* clothing; O.H.G. *wāt,* cloth.]

**weed,** *wēd, (Scot.) n.* any sudden illness, cold, or relapse with febrile symptoms, esp. in women after confinement or nursing: a fever in horses, etc.—Also **weid.** [From *wedenonfa*—O.E. *wēden-* (in composition), mad, and Scot. *onfa', onfall.*]

**week,** *wēk, n.* the space of seven days, esp. from Sunday to Saturday (inclusive): the working days of the week: (in *pl.*) an indefinite period.— *adj.* **week'ly,** coming, happening, or done, once a week.—*adv.* once a week: every week.—*n.* a publication appearing once a week.—**week'day,** any day of the week except Sunday; **week'-end** (or *-end'*), **week'end** (or *-end'*), the period from a Friday or Saturday to the Monday or Tuesday following (**long week-end,** a liberal interpretation of this).—*v.i.* to spend a week-end holiday.—**week-end'er; week-end'ing.**—a prophetic week (*B.*), seven years: a **week of Sundays** (*coll.*), seven weeks: a long time; **Feast of Weeks,** Jewish festival 7 weeks after the Passover; **Great Week, Holy Week, Passion Week,** the week preceding Easter Sunday; **in by the week** (*obs.*), trapped, caught; **this day week,** a week from today; **week about,** in alternate periods of seven days; **week in week out,** continuously without a break. [O.E. *wice,* Du. *week,* Ger. *woche.*]

**weeke,** *wēk, (Spens.) n.* Same as **wick.**

**weel,** *wēl, n.* a whirlpool. [O.E. *wǣl.*]

**weel,** *wēl, n.* a trap or snare for fish (*dial.*): a

bearing resembling such (*her.*). [O.E. *wile-* (in composition)—*wilige;* cf. **willy.**]

**weel,** *wēl, adv.* Scots form of **well.**—*adj.* **weel-faur'd, -far'd,** etc. (see **well-favoured**).

**weem,** *wēm, (Scot.) n.* a subterranean dwelling. [Early Gael. *uaim,* cavern.]

**ween,** *wēn, (arch.* or *obs.) v.t.* to think or fancy: to believe: to expect.—*v.i.* (*Shak.*) to imagine expectantly. [O.E. *wēnan;* cog. with *wēn,* expectation, hope.]

**weep,** *wēp, v.i.* to express grief by shedding tears: to wail or lament: to drip, rain: to ooze in drops: to leak: to exude: to be pendent, as a weeping-willow.—*v.t.* to lament: to pour forth: to express while, or by, weeping: to exude:— *pa.t.* and *pa.p.* **wept.**—*n.* **weep'er,** one who weeps: a white border round the sleeve of a mourning dress: a crape hat-band: a widow's crape-veil: anything pendent.—*n.* **weep'ie, weep'y** (*slang*), a highly emotional film, play or book.—*n.* and *adj.* **weep'ing.**—*adv.* **weep'ingly.**—*adj.* **weep'y,** tearful (*coll.*): oozy (*dial.*).—**weep'ing-ash,** a variety of the common European ash, with drooping branches; **weep'ing-birch,** a variety of the white birch, with drooping branches; **Weeping Cross, weep'ing-cross** (*hist.*), a wayside cross where penitents might pray: in phrases as **to come home by weeping cross,** to experience bitter regret, disappointment or failure; **weep'-ing elm,** a variety of wych-elm, with drooping branches.—*adj.* **weep'ing-ripe** (*Shak.*), ripe or ready for tears.—**weep'ing-rock,** a rock through which water percolates slowly; **weep'ing-spring,** a spring from which water escapes slowly; **weep'ing-tree,** a tree with long pendulous branches; **weep'ing-willow,** an ornamental Chinese willow (*Salix babylonica*), with pendent branches. [O.E. *wēpan;* allied to *wōp,* clamour; Goth. *wōpjan.*]

**weet(e), weeting, weetingly, weetless,** obs. forms of **wit** (verb), etc.—*infin.* (*Spens.*) **weeten.**

**weet,** dialectal form of **wet.**—Also *Spens.*

**weever,** *wē'vər, n.* a genus of fishes (Trachinus), of which two species are British, with sharp dorsal and opercular spines capable of inflicting serious wounds. [Prob. O.Fr. *wivre,* serpent, *weever*—L. *vipera;* cf. **wivern, viper.**]

**weevil,** *wēv'l, n.* a popular name for a large number of beetles (the group Rhynchophora, esp. the family Curculionidae) with the anterior part of the head prolonged into a beak or proboscis, which, either in the larval or the adult form, damage fruit, nuts, grain, or trees: any insect injurious to stored grain.—*adjs.* **weev'illed, weev'iled, weev'illy, weev'ily,** infested by weevils. [O.E. *wifel.*]

**weft,** *weft, n.* the threads woven into and crossing the warp: the thread carried by the shuttle (also **woof**): a web: a film, cloud.—*v.i.* (*rare*) to form a weft.—*n.* **weft'age,** texture. [O.E. *weft, wefta;* allied to *wefan;* see **weave.**]

**weft(e),** *weft, (Spens.) n.* a waif, a castaway. [Variant of **waif.**]

**weft(e).** See **waft;** (*Spens.*) *pa.p.* of **waive.**

**wehrmacht,** *vār'mähht, n.* armed forces. [Ger.,— *wehr,* defence, *macht,* force.]

**weid.** See **weed** (3).

**weigh,** *wā, v.t.* to compare with by, or as if by, the balance (with *against*): to find the heaviness of: to be equal to in heaviness: to counterbalance: to raise, as a ship's anchor: to apportion: to hold in the hand(s) in order to, or as if to, estimate the weight: to estimate the value of: to ponder in the mind, consider carefully: to consider worthy of notice: to keep evenly outspread (*Milt.*).—*v.i.* to have weight: to be considered of importance: to balance evenly (*Shak.*): to have value (*Shak.*): to press heavily: to weigh anchor.—*adj.* **weigh'able,** capable of being weighed.—*n.* **weigh'age,** rate paid for the weighing of goods.—*adj.* **weighed,** experienced: considered, balanced.—*ns.* **weigh′er,** an officer who weighs articles or tests weights; **weigh′ing; weight,** the heaviness of a thing, esp. as determined by weighing: quantity as determined in this way: the force with which a body is attracted to the earth, measured by the product of the mass and the acceleration: a mass of metal adjusted to a standard and used for finding weight: a method of estimating, or a unit of, weight; the amount something ought to weigh: a standard amount that a boxer, etc., should weigh: scales (*Spens.*): a heavy object: anything heavy or oppressive: a ponderous mass: pressure: importance: power: impressiveness: the frequency of an item in a frequency distribution or a number indicating this.—*v.t.* to make more heavy (*lit.* and *fig.*): to attach weights to: to hold down in this way: to increase the weight of, as fabrics, by adding chemicals: to assign a handicap weight to (a horse; also *fig.*): to oppress, burden: to attach numbers indicating their relative frequency to (items in a frequency distribution). — *adv.* **weigh′tily.**—*n.* **weigh′tiness.**—*adj.* **weight′less.**—*n.* **weight′lessness,** the condition of a freely falling body at the beginning of the fall when its inertia exactly balances the gravitational force, or that of a space traveller in orbit beyond the earth's atmosphere.—*adj.* **weigh′ty,** heavy: important: having much influence: being the fruit of judicious consideration and hence worthy of attention: severe (Shak., *Tim.,* III, v. 104).—**weigh′-bank** (*Scot.*), the beam of a balance: (in *pl.*) a pair of scales; **weigh′-board** (see **way-board**); **weigh′-bridge,** a machine for weighing vehicles with their loads; **weigh-house,** a public building for weighing goods, ascertaining the tonnage of boats, etc.; **weigh′ing-machine′,** a machine or apparatus for weighing; **weighting allowance,** a salary differential to balance the higher cost of living in a particular area.—**by, in, with, weight** (Shak.), fully: **throw one's weight about,** to over-exercise one's authority: to domineer; **weigh down,** to force down: to depress (*fig.*): to preponderate over, outweigh; **weigh in,** to ascertain one's weight before a fight, or after a horse-race (also *n.* **weigh′-in**): to join in a project (*slang*); **weigh in with** (*fig.*), to produce (a new argument) in a discussion; **weigh out,** to weigh and dispense in portions accordingly: to ascertain one's weight before a horse-race (also *n.* **weigh′-out**); **weight of metal** (now *rare*), the total weight of the projectiles thrown at one discharge from a ship's guns; **weigh to the beam** (Shak.), to outweigh completely; **weigh up,** to force up (*lit.* and *fig.*): to consider carefully and assess the quality of, as a person (*coll.*); **weigh with** (*fig.*), to appear important to, to influence. [O.E. *wegan,* to carry; Ger. *wiegen;* L. *vehĕre,* to carry.]

**weigh, wā,** *n.* a misspelling of **way** in the phrase 'under way', through confusion with the phrase 'to weigh anchor'.

**weil.** Same as **weel** (1).

**Weimar Republic, vī′mär ri-pub′lik,** the federal republic in Germany that was founded in 1919 after the First World War and lasted until 1933.

**weir, wear, wēr,** *n.* a dam across a river: a fence of stakes set in a stream for catching fish. [O.E. *wer,* an enclosure, allied to *werian,* to protect; cf. Ger. *wehr,* a dam, *wehren,* to ward.]

**weird, wērd,** (*arch.* and *Scot.*), *n.* fate: (*cap.*; in *pl.*) the Fates: a witch: one's lot, esp. if evil: a happening, esp. uncanny: a tale of fate: a spell or charm.—*adj.* concerned with, controlling, fate: unearthly, uncanny: peculiar, odd (*coll.*). —*v.t.* (Scot.), to destine, doom: to hand over to as one's fate: to forewarn.—*n.* **weird′ie,** an eccentric: someone unconventional in dress, etc.—*adv.* **weird′ly.**—*n.* **weird′ness.**—**dree one's weird** (see **dree**); **the Weird Sisters,** the Fates: the witches in *Macbeth.* [O.E. *wyrd,* fate; allied to *weorthan,* to become; Ger. *werden.*]

**weise, weize.** See **wise** (2).

**Weismannism, vis′man-izm,** *n.* the doctrine in biology of August *Weismann* (1834-1914), whose central teaching is that acquired characters are not transmitted.

**weka, we′, wä′,** or **wē′ka,** *n.* any of the flightless rails (*Ocydromus*) of New Zealand. [Maori, imit.]

**welaway.** See **welladay.**

**welch, welsh,** an old form of **Welsh** and **welsh.**

**welcome, wel′kam,** *adj.* received with gladness: admitted willingly: causing gladness: free (to): free to take or enjoy.—*n.* the act of welcoming: a kindly reception: a reception.—*v.t.* to greet: to receive with kindness or pleasure: to accept or undergo gladly.—*interj.* expressing pleasure, as to a guest on his arrival.—*ns.* **wel′comeness;** **wel′comer.**—**bid a welcome,** to receive with professions of kindness. [O.E. *wilcuma—wil-* (*willa,* will, pleasure), and *cuma,* guest; O.N. *velkominn.*]

**weld, weld,** *n.* a scentless species of mignonette, also known as dyer's rocket, yielding a yellow dye: the dye itself.—Also (*Scot.*) **wald.** [Cf. Ger. *wau.*]

**weld, weld,** *v.t.* to join (two pieces of metal) by raising the temperature at the joint by means of external heat or (**resistance welding**) of a heavy electric current or (**arc welding**) of an electric arc and then applying pressure, or (**cold welding**) by pressure alone: to join closely.— *v.i.* to undergo welding: to be capable of being welded.—*n.* a welded joint.—*n.* **weldabil′ity.**— *adj.* **weld′able.**—*n.* **weld′er, weld′or.**—*n.* and *adj.* **weld′ing.**—*adj.* **weld′less,** having no welds.—*n.* **weld′ment,** the action or process of welding: a welded assembly. [Same as verb **well;** prob. from pa.p.]

**weld, weld,** (*obs.* and *dial.*) *v.t.* variant of **wield.**

**welfare, wel′fār,** *n.* state of faring or doing well: freedom from calamity, etc.: enjoyment of health, etc.: prosperity: welfare work.—*n.* **wel′farism,** the social policies characteristic of a welfare state.—**welfare state,** a state in which socialist principles have been put into effect with the purpose of ensuring the welfare of all who live in it; **welfare work,** efforts to improve conditions of living for a class, as the very poor, or a group, as employees or workers; hence **welfare worker.** [**well, fare.**]

**welk, welk,** (*obs.*) *v.i.* to wither, shrivel: to wane, decline (*Spens.*) **welke).**—Also *v.t.* [M.E. *welken;* cf. Ger. *welk,* withered.]

**welkin, wel′kin,** *n.* the sky or region of clouds.— *adj.* (Shak.) sky-blue. [O.E. *wolcnu,* pl. of *wolcen,* cloud, air, sky; Ger. *wolke,* cloud.]

**welkt, wealk′d, welkt,** *adj.* (Shak.) twisted—in some mod. edd. **whelk′d.**—*v.i.* **welk** (Scott, founding on Shak.), apparently, to twist about. [**whelk** (1).]

**well, wel,** *n.* a spring: a mineral spring: a source (*fig.*): a lined shaft sunk in the earth whence a supply of water, oil, etc., is obtained: an enclosure in a ship's hold round the pumps: the vertical opening enclosed between the outer ends of the flights in a winding stair: a lift-shaft: the open space in the middle of a court-room: a cavity: an eddy.—*v.i.* to issue forth, as water from the earth (*lit.* and *fig.*).—*v.t.* to pour forth.—*n.* **well′ing,** an outpouring.—**well′-boat,** **-smack,** a fishing-boat having a well for holding live fish; **well′-borer,** a person engaged, or a machine employed, in well-boring; **well′-boring,** sinking wells by drilling through rock; **well′-curb,** the stone ring built round the mouth of a well; **well'-deck,** an enclosed space on the deck of a ship; **well'-drain,** a pit drawing the water from wet land; **well'-dressing,** the festal decoration of wells and springs, as in Derbyshire on Ascension-day, etc.; **well'-head,** the source of a spring: a fountain-head (*fig.*): a spring in a marsh (*Scot.*): the top of a well, or a structure built over it; **well'-hole,** a hole for-a well of any kind: the shaft of a well: a shaft for machinery; **well'-house, well'-room,** a room built over a well; **well'-sinker,** one who digs wells; **well'-sinking; well'-spring,** a fountain.—**the wells,** any place where mineral wells are situated; **well over,** to overflow. [O.E. *wella*; cf. *weallan,* to boil, O.N. *vella,* to boil.]

**well,** *wel* (*comp.* **bett′er;** *superl.* **best**), *adj.* (usu. predicative) good in condition: in health: fortunate: comfortable: satisfactory.—*n.* (*Spens.*) good health or fortune.—*adv.* rightly: skilfully: thoroughly: intimately: favourably, successfully: abundantly: with some degree of luxury: with reason or propriety: conveniently: to a considerable extent: clearly: easily: very, esp. in combination, as (*Shak.*) **well'-accomplisht:** so be it (as a sign of assent).—*interj.* expressing surprise, etc., or introducing resumed narrative.—*adjs.* **well'-acquainted,** having intimate personal knowledge; **well'-advised,** prudent: in one's right mind (*Shak.*).—*interj.* **well′anear** (*Shak.*), welladay.—*adj.* **well'-appointed,** well-equipped.—**well'-appointedness.**—*adjs.* **well'-balanced,** having the parts properly adjusted for smooth working: sane and sensible; **well'-becoming,** befitting well: proper or suitable; **well'-behaved,** behaving or acting in accordance with propriety or with requirements.—**well'-being,** welfare.—*adjs.* **well'-beloved,** very dear; **well'-beseem′ing,** well-becoming; **well'-beseen** (*obs.*), showy in appearance; **well'-born,** born of a good family, not of mean birth; **well'-breathed,** strong of lung: exercised: not out of breath; **well'-bred,** educated to polished manners: of good stock; **well'-built,** (of a building, buildings, a person, a garment, etc.) of strong or well-proportioned make or form; **well'-conditioned,** in a desirable condition; **well'-conducted,** properly managed: acting properly; **well'-derived** (*Shak.*), of good stock or antecedents; **well'-desired** (*Shak.*), much sought after; **well'-directed,** skilfully aimed (*lit.* and *fig.*); **well'-disposed,** healthy (*obs.*): well placed or arranged: inclined to be friendly: favourable.—**well'-doer,** one who lives uprightly or does good: one who thrives and is prosperous (*dial.*).—*n.* and *adj.* **well'-doing.**—*adjs.* **well'-earned,** thoroughly deserved; **well'-educated,** having a good education; **well'-entered** (*Shak.*), instructed, initiated; **well'-famed** (*Shak.*), very famous; **well'-fā′voured** (Scots forms **weel-faird, -faur'd, -far'd, -far't, -faurt**), good-looking; **well'-fed,** plump; **well'-found,** commendable (*obs.*): well provided: fully equipped; **well'-founded,** built on secure foundations: based on solid evidence or sound reasoning; **well'-given** (*obs.*), well disposed, obtained honestly; **well'-graced** (*Shak.*), popular; **well'-grounded,** firmly founded; **well'-heeled,** prosperous; **well'-hung,** hung skilfully: of meat, hung long enough to mature; **well'-informed,** having sound and sufficient information on a particular subject: full of varied information; **well'-intentioned,** having, or arising from, good intentions or purpose; **well'-judged,** correctly calculated, judicious; **well'-judging; well'-knit,** (of a person) strongly built: closely and firmly connected; **well'-known,** fully known: celebrated: notorious; **well'-liking** (*arch.*), in good condition, plump.—*n.* (*obs.*) approbation, fondness.—*adjs.* **well'-lined,** with a good lining: full of money; **well'-looking,** good-looking; **well'-mannered,** polite;

**well'-marked,** obvious, decided; **well'-meaning, well-intentioned;** **well'-meant,** rightly, kindly, intended; **well'-minded,** favourably inclined: well-disposed.—*adv.* **well'-nigh,** nearly, almost.—*adjs.* **well'-off,** in good circumstances; **well'-oiled** (*slang*), drunk; **well'-ordered,** correctly governed: properly arranged; **well'-pleasing,** acceptable; **well'-plighted,** well-folded (see plight, 2); **well'-proportioned,** having correct proportions; **well'-read** (-*red*), of wide reading; **well'-regulated,** well-ordered; **well'-respected,** highly esteemed: given due consideration (Shak., 1 *Hen. IV,* IV, iii. 10); **well'-rounded,** suitably curved: symmetrical: well constructed and complete; **well'-seen** (*arch.*), experienced, skilful; **well'-set,** properly arranged, or well placed: fitly put together: firmly fixed: strongly built; **well'-set-up′** (*coll.*), well-built, shapely; **well'-spoken,** spoken well or fittingly: ready, graceful, or courteous in speech; **well'-tempered,** having a good bodily or mental constitution (*obs.*): good-tempered: of steel, mortar, etc., tempered satisfactorily: tuned in equal temperament (*mus.*); **well'-thewed** (*obs.*), well-mannered, of good disposition: abounding in moral wisdom; **well'-thought-of,** esteemed; **well'-thought-out,** reasoned soundly and arranged with skill; **well'-thumbed,** showing marks of much handling; **well'-timbered,** strongly built of wood: well-built: furnished with much growing timber; **well'-timed,** opportune: keeping accurate time; **well-to-do,** (*Scot.*) **well-to-live** (*Shak.* well to live), prosperous, well-off; **well'-turned,** accurately rounded: shapely: felicitously expressed; **well'-warranted,** having good credit.—**well'-willer,** a well-wisher; **well'-wish** (*rare*), act of wishing well.—*adj.* **well'-wished** (*Shak.*), being the object of good wishes.—**well'-wisher.**—*adj.* and *n.* **well'-wishing.**—*adjs.* **well'-won,** gained honestly or by hard endeavour; **well'-worked-out,** thoroughly or logically planned or developed; **well'-worn,** much worn: trite: becomingly worn (*rare*).—**as well** (see as); **as well as,** in addition to: no less than; **do well** (see do); **very well,** phrase signifying assent, sometimes ironic; **well and good,** phrase signifying acceptance of facts or a situation; **well away,** progressing rapidly: drunk (*slang*); **well done,** (as a word of praise) bravely: nobly; **well enough,** in a moderate but sufficient degree; **well met** (see meet); **well up in** (*coll.*), well versed in, well acquainted with. [O.E. *wel;* cog. with Goth. *waila,* Ger. *wohl;* from the root of will.]

**welladay,** *wel′ə-dā,* **wellaway, welaway,** *wel′ə-wā,* *interjs.* alas. [O.E. *wei lā wei,* woe lo! woe, with *wei* (O.N. *vei*) substituted for the orig. O.E. form *wā.*]

**Wellingtonia,** *wel-ing-tō′ni-ə, n.* a synonym of Sequoia. [Named after the Duke of *Wellington* (1769-1852).]

**wellingtons,** *wel′ing-tənz, n.* a kind of riding-boots covering the knee in front, but cut away behind: shorter closely-fitting boots, worn under the trousers (**half-wellingtons**): rubber boots loosely covering the calves: (in *sing.*) one of a pair of wellingtons. [As previous word.]

**Wellsian,** *wel′zi-ən, adj.* of, pertaining to, or characteristic of, H. G. *Wells* (1866-1946), historian and writer of stories and novels with scientific or social interest.

**welly,** *wel′i,* (*dial.*) *adj.* corr. of **well-nigh.**

**Welsh,** (*obs.*) **Welch,** *welsh, welsh, adj.* pertaining to *Wales* or its inhabitants.—*n.pl.* the inhabitants of Wales: (*sing.*) their language.—**Welsh'-harp,** a large harp with three rows of strings, two tuned in unison and in the diatonic scale, the third in the sharps and flats of the chromatic; **Welsh'-hook,** an old weapon; **Welsh'man,** a native of Wales; **Welsh'-onion,** the cibol; **Welsh'-rabbit** (see rabbit). [O.E. (Angl. and

Kentish) *welisc — wealh*, foreigner; Anglo-Saxons' name for Britons, etc.]

**welsh**, *welsh*, *v.i.* to run off from a race-course without settling or paying one's bets: to dodge fulfilling an obligation.—*v.t.* to cheat in such a way.—Also **welch**.—*n.* **welsh'er, welch'er**. [Of uncertain origin.]

**welt**, *welt*, *n.* a band or strip fastened to an edge to give strength or for ornament: a narrow strip of. leather used in one method of sewing the upper to the sole of a shoe: a weal: a lash, blow.—*v.t.* to furnish with a welt: to lash, beat. [Origin obscure.]

**welt**, *welt*, *v.t.* and *v.i.* to wither, dry. [Perh. **welk**.]

**welt**, *velt*, (Ger.) world; **weltanschauung**, *velt'an-show-ōong*, outlook upon the world, world-philosophy; **weltgeist**, *velt'gist*, the world-spirit; **weltpolitik**, *velt'pol-i-tēk*, world politics: the policy of taking a forceful part in international affairs; **weltschmerz**, *velt'shmerts*, world-sorrow: sympathy with universal misery: thorough-going pessimism.

**welter**, *wel'tər*, *v.i.* to roll or tumble about (*obs.*): to wallow about in dirt or moral degradation, etc. (*rare*): to be, or lie, soaked, as in blood (*poet.*): to be sunk (in; *lit.* and *fig.*): to roll, toss, about in the waves: to roll, surge, as the sea (*poet.*).—*v.t.* (*rare*) to make (one's way) in a weltering manner.—*n.* a state of turmoil or confusion: confusion, agitation: a surging mass.—*adj.* **wel'tering**. [M.Du. *welteren*; cf. O.E. *gewæltan*, to roll.]

**welter-weight**, *wel'tər-wāt*, *n.* a boxer over 9 st. 9 lb. (amateur 10 st.) and not over 10 st. 7 lb. (amateur 10 st. 8 lb.): an unusually heavy weight, carried mostly in steeplechases and hurdle-races.—**wel'ter-race**, a race in which such weights are carried; **wel'ter-stakes**, the stakes in a welter-race.—**light welter-weight**, a boxer, amateur only, whose weight is not over 10 st. [Origin obscure.]

**Welwitschia**, *wel'wich-i-ə*, *n.* a South-west African genus of one species, belonging to the Gnetaceae, with one pair of leaves that grow indefinitely. [After F. *Welwitsch* (1806-72), Austrian traveller.]

**wem(b)**. See **wame**.

**wen**, *wen*, *n.* a sebaceous cyst.—*adjs.* **wenn'ish, wenn'y**, wen-like. [O.E. *wen(n)*, a swelling, a wart; Du. *wen*; origin obscure.]

**wen**, *wen*, *n.* a rune (Ϸ), having the value of modern English *w*, adopted (as þ) into the O.E. alphabet. [O.E., orig. *wynn*, joy (of which *w* is the initial letter).]

**wench**, *wench*, *-sh*, *n.* a child (*obs.*): a damsel, girl: a working-girl, a maid-servant: a mistress (*obs.* or *arch.*): a whore (*obs.* or *arch.*).—*v.i.* to frequent the company of whores: to associate innocently with women (*Scot.* winch): to go courting (*dial.*).—*n.* **wench'er**, one who indulges in lewdness. [O.E. *wencel*, a child.]

**wend**, *wend*, *v.t.* to turn (*obs.*): to turn to the opposite tack (*naut.*): to turn, direct one's course (*obs.*; *refl.*): to change (*obs.*).—*v.i.* to turn (*obs.*): to change (*obs.*): to depart (*arch.*): to make one's way (*arch.*; also *fig.*):—*pa.t.* and *pa.p.* **wend'ed**, (*obs.*) **went** (now used as *pa.t.* of go).—**wend one's way**, to make one's way, follow the road, esp. in a leisurely fashion. [O.E. *wendan*, a common Gmc. verb.]

**Wend**, *wend*, *n.* one of a branch of the Slavs which once occupied the north and east of Germany: one of the Slavic population of Lusatia (part of Brandenburg, Saxony and Silesia) who still speak the Wendish tongue.—*adjs.* **Wend'ic, Wend'ish**.—*ns.* the Wendish language. [Ger. *Wende*; origin obscure.]

**Wenlock**, *wen'lok*, (geol.) *adj.* denoting a group or series of rocks of the Upper Silurian period, consisting of limestone and shale, and largely developed in the neighbourhood of *Wenlock* in Shropshire.

**Wensleydale**, *wenz'li-dāl*, *n.* a breed of long-woolled sheep: a variety of cheese. [*Wensley-dale* in North Riding of Yorks.]

**went**, *went*, properly *pa.t.* of **wend**, but now used as *pa.t.* of **go**.—*n.* (*Spens.*) a path: journey: way: course.

**wentletrap**, *wen'tl-trap*, *n.* a genus (Scalaria) of gasteropod molluscs, having a spiral shell with many deep whorls, crossed by elevated ribs. [Du. *wenteltrap* (Ger. *wendel-treppe*), a winding staircase, a spiral shell.]

**wept**, *wept*, *pa.t.* and *pa.p.* of **weep**.

**were**, *wûr*, *v.i.* the *pl.* of **was**, used as *pa.t.* (*pl.*) and *pa.subj.* (*sing.* and *pl.*) of **be**. [O.E. *wǣron*, subj. *wǣre*; Ger. *waren, wäre*.]

**werewolf**, *wēr'wōōlf*, **werwolf**, *wûr'wōōlf*, *n.* a person supposed to be able to change himself for a time into a wolf: a member of an underground Nazi organisation.—*adjs.* **were'wolfish, wer'wolfish**.—*n.* **were'wolfism**, lycanthropy. [O.E. *werwulf—wer*, man, *wulf*, a wolf.]

**wergild**, *wûr'gild*, **weregild**, *wēr'gild*, *n.* among Teutonic peoples, a fine by which homicide and other heinous crimes against the person were expiated. [O.E. *wergield*, from *wer*, man, *gield* —*gieldan*, to pay.]

**Wernerian**, *vûr-nē'ri-ən*, *adj.* pertaining or according to the opinions or system of A. G. *Werner* (1750-1817), who attributed all geological phenomena to the action of water: Neptunian. — *n.* an upholder of Werner's theories. — *n.* **wer'nerite**, scapolite.

**wersh**, *wersh*, (*Scot.*) *adj.* tasteless, unsalted: sickly, feeble: of weather, raw. [**wearish**.]

**wert**, *wûrt*, used as the *2nd pers. sing.* of the past indicative (for **wast**) and subjunctive of **be**. [**were**, and suff. *-t*.]

**Wertherian**, *vûr-tē'ri-ən*, *adj.* pertaining to or resembling the character of *Werther* in Goethe's romance, 'The Sorrows of Young Werther'—morbidly sentimental.—*n.* **Wer'therism**.

**wesand**, *wē'zənd*, *n.* (*Spens.*). Same as **weasand**.

**Wesleyan**, *wez'*, *wes'li-ən*, *adj.* pertaining to Wesleyanism.—*n.* an adherent of Wesleyanism. —*n.* **Wes'leyanism**, the system of doctrine and church polity of the Wesleyan Methodists—Arminian Methodism. [Named after John *Wesley* (1703-91).]

**west**, *west*, *n.* the quarter where the sun sets: one of the four chief points of the compass: the direction faced when one stands with one's back to the high altar of a church: the regions in the west of any country, esp. (Amer.) those beyond the Appalachian Mts. (see **Middle West**, under **middle**) or those beyond the Mississippi.—*adj.* situated towards, or (of wind) coming from, the west: opposite the high altar of a church.—*adv.* towards the west.—*v.i.* to move towards the west.—*v.i.* **west'er**, to turn westward: to change into the west.—*n.* and *adj.* **west'ering**.—*adj.* **west'erly**, lying or moving towards the west: from the west.—*adv.* towards the west: from the west.—*adj.* **west'ern**, situated in the west: belonging to the west: moving towards, or (of wind) coming from, the west.—*n.* an inhabitant of a western region or country: a film or novel whose scene is the western United States, esp. the former Wild West.—*n.* **west'erner**, a person belonging to the west.—*v.t.* and *v.i.* **west'ernise, -ize**, to make or become like the people of Europe and America in customs, or like their institutions, practices, ideas.—*ns.* **west'ernisa-tion, -z-**; **west'ernism**, idiom or other characteristic of a western people.—*adj.* **west'ernmost**, furthest to the west.—*n.* **west'ing**, space or distance westward: departure westward: direction or course towards the west.—*adjs.* **west'lin** (*Scot.*), western; **west'most**, most westerly.—*adj.* and *adv.* **west′ward,** towards the west.—*advs.* **west′-wardly, west′wards,** towards the west.—*adv.* **west′-about,** towards the west; **west-by-north** (-south), 11¼ degrees north (south) from due west; **West End,** the fashionable quarter in the west of London: a similar district in other large towns; **Western Church,** the Latin Church, as distinguished from the Eastern or Greek Church; **Western Empire,** the western division of the later Roman Empire; **Western Wall (see Wailing Wall); west-north** (or south)-west, 22½ degrees north (south) from the west; **West Saxon,** a southern dialect of Old English, the chief literary dialect before the Norman Conquest.—**go west,** to go to America: to go to the western states or western frontier: to die (with reference to the setting sun, the Islands of the Blest, or Tyburn), or to be destroyed or completely dissipated; **the West,** Europe or Europe and America; **westward ho!** to the west! an old cry of London watermen plying westwards; **Wild West,** the western United States in the days of the first settlers, chiefly cattlemen and goldminers, before the establishment of law and order. [O.E.; a common Gmc. word; cf. L. *vesper.*]

**Westminster,** *west′min-stər, n.* used for Parliament —from the London borough where the Houses of Parliament are situated: Westminster Hall, court of justice: Westminster School, or a past or present pupil of it.

**Westphalian,** *west-fā′li-ən, adj.* pertaining to *Westphalia,* a duchy, a kingdom, a province of Prussia and, since 1946, part of the German land of Nordrhein-Westfalen.—*n.* a native of Westphalia.

**wet,** *wet, adj.* containing, soaked with, covered with, water or other liquid: rainy: bringing or foreboding moisture: tearful: grown in damp soil: using liquid: given to drinking, or tipsy (*slang*): allowing the sale of intoxicating liquors: ineffectual, or crazy (*slang*).—*n.* water, moisture, wetness: the rain: act of wetting: a dram, a debauch.—*v.t.* to make wet: to soak with water: to make (tea) by pouring water on the leaves (*dial.*): to celebrate by drinking (*slang*): —*pr.p.* **wett′ing;** *pa.t.* and *pa.p.* **wet,** or **wett′ed.** —*n.* **wet′ness.**—*adj.* **wett′ish,** somewhat wet.— **wet assay,** use of the processes of solution, flotation, or other liquid means to determine a given constituent in ores, metallurgical residues, and alloys; **wet′back** (*U.S.*), one illegally entering the U.S.A. from Mexico by wading or swimming the Rio Grande; **wet blanket (see blanket); wet bob** (*slang*), a schoolboy at Eton who goes in for rowing; **wet′-dock,** a dock maintaining a level nearly uniform with that of high water; **wet meter,** a gas-meter in which the gas to be measured passes through water; **wet′-nurse,** a nurse who suckles a child for its mother; **wet plate** (*phot.*), a plate coated with collodion and sensitised with a salt of silver.—*adj.* **wet′-shod,** having shoes or feet wet.—**wet suit,** a suit for wearing in cold water, which allows water to pass through but retains body heat; **wetting (out) agent,** a substance that promotes wetting, e.g. a substance, such as an acid, oil, or hydrocarbon, added to a heterogeneous mixture to facilitate the absorption or adhesion between the constituents.—**wet behind the ears,** very young, immature, gullible; **wet bulb thermometer,** a psychrometer; **wet one's whistle** (*coll.*). See under **whistle; wet out,** to wet thoroughly: to cleanse by so doing, as raw material in textile manufacture. [O.E. *wǣt* (noun and adj.), *wǣtan* (verb); the short vowel is from the M.E. pa.t. and pa.p. of the verb.]

**wether,** *weth′ər, n.* a castrated ram. [O.E.; cf. Ger. *widder.*]

**wex(e).** Obs. form of wax.

**wey,** *wāy n.* a measure or weight for dry-goods

differing with different articles as 40 bushels of salt or corn, etc. [Variant of weigh.]

**weyard, weyward.** Spellings of weird in *Macbeth,* older editions.

**wezand.** Obs. form of weasand.

**whack,** (*h*)*wak,* (*coll.*) *v.t.* to strike hard and smartly: to put or take with violence: to beat decisively: to parcel out, share.—*v.i.* to strike: to settle accounts.—*n.* a blow: a share: an attempt.—*adj.* **whacked** (*coll.*), exhausted.—*n.* **whack′er** (*coll.*), something big of its kind: a blatant lie.—*adj.* **whack′ing** (*coll.*), very large, astounding. *n.* a beating (*lit.* and *fig.*). [From— the sound made.]

**whacky.** Same as wacky.

**whaisle, whaizle,** (*h*)*wā′zl,* (*Scot.*) *v.i.* to wheeze. [A form of wheezle; see wheeze.]

**whale,** (*h*)*wāl, n.* any of an order of cetaceous mammals, including the *toothed* whales, such as the sperm whales and the dolphins, and the *whalebone* whales, such as the right whales and the rorquals, in which the teeth are only embryonic: a person with a large appetite (*slang;* *lit.* and *fig.*): something very large of its kind (*slang*); (*cap.*) the constellation Cetus.—*v.i.* to catch whales.—*ns.* **whāl′er,** a whale-boat: a whale-man: something very large of its kind (*slang*); **whāl′ery,** whaling.—*adj.* **whāl′ing,** connected with whale-catching: very large or impressive (also *adv.*).—*n.* the business of catching whales.—**whale′-back,** a turtle-back: a kind of steamboat used on the Great Lakes, to carry grain, etc., having rounded upper deck, etc.: a mound shaped like the back of a whale; **whale′-boat,** a long, narrow boat sharp at both ends once used in the pursuit of whales: a similar boat carried on a large vessel as a life-boat; **whale′bone,** a light flexible substance consisting of the baleen plates of whales: an article made of this.—*adj.* made of whalebone.—**whale′-calf,** a young whale—also **calf whale; whale′-fisher; whale′-fishery; whale′-fishing; whale′-head,** the shoebill; **whale′-line,** strong rope used for harpoon-lines in the whale-fishery; **whale′-louse,** a genus (Cyamus) of amphipod Crustacea parasitic on the skin of cetaceans; **whale′-man,** person or ship employed in whale-fishing; **whale′-oil,** oil got from the blubber of a whale; **whale's bone** (*obs.*), ivory, as from the walrus; **whale(s′) food,** small animals eaten by whales, esp. the Clio genus; **whale′-shark,** a huge but harmless shark of tropical seas; **whāl′ing-gun,** a contrivance for killing whales by means of a projectile; **whāl′ing-master,** the captain of a whaler; **whāl′ing-port,** a port where whalers are registered.—**bull, cow, whale,** an adult male, female, whale. [O.E. *hwæl;* cf. O.N. *hvalr,* Ger. *walfisch.*]

**whale,** (*h*)*wāl,* (*slang*) *v.t.* to thrash: to strike violently.—*n.* **whal′ing,** a thrashing. [Perh. **wale** (1); perh. from *whale*bone whip.]

**whally,** (*h*)*wōl′i,* (*Spens.*) *adj.* wall-eyed: showing much white. [From **wall-eye.**]

**whample,** (*h*)*wŏm′pl,* (*h*)*wam′pl,* (*Scot.*) *n.* a blow, a sudden blow.

**whang,** (*h*)*wang, n.* a leather thong: a thick slice. —*v.t.* to flog: to throw, push, pull, violently: to cut in great slices. [*thwang,* obs. form of thong.]

**whang,** (*h*)*wang, n.* a resounding noise: a blow: —*v.i.* to make the sound of a blow, explosion, etc.—Also used as *adv.* and *interj.* [Imit.]

**whangam,** (*h*)*wang′gam,* (*Goldsmith*) *n.* an imaginary animal.

**whangee,** (*h*)*wang-ē′, n.* any of several grasses of a genus (Phyllostachys) allied to the bamboos, found in China and Japan: a cane made from the stem of one. [Prob. Chin. *huang,* yellow, *li,* bamboo.]

**whap.** Same as whop.

whare, *(h)wör'i*, *(New Zealand)* *n.* a house. [Maori.]

wharf, *(h)wörf*, *n.* a landing-stage, built esp. along the shore, for loading or unloading vessels: the bank of a river *(Shak.)*:—*pl.* wharfs, wharves.—*v.t.* to strengthen or secure by means of a wharf *(obs.)*: to place on, or bring to, a wharf.—*ns.* wharf'age, the dues paid for using a wharf: accommodation at a wharf; wharf'ing, material for making a wharf: wharfs; wharfinger *((h)wörf'in-jər)*, one who has the care of, or owns, a wharf.—wharf'-rat, the common brown rat: a fellow who loafs continually about a wharf. [Late O.E. *hwearf*, bank, shore: allied to *hweorfan*, to turn.]

wharve. See whorl *(spinning)*.

what, *(h)wot*, *interrog. pron.* neuter of who: used to form a question regarding identity, selection from an indefinite number, nature, value, etc.—also used elliptically (as for *what did you say, do you think?* what is it?*): who *(obs.)*.—Also *interrog. adj.—rel. pron.* and *adj.* that which: such . . . as: which *(dial.)*: any (thing) whatever: whoever *(Shak.)*.—*indef. pron.* (or *n.*) something: a portion, bit *(Spens.)*: fare (in phrase such homely what; Spens. *F.Q.* VI, ix. 7, 4).—*adv.* why? *(obs.)*: in what way, how? to what degree?—*conj.* as much as *(dial.)*: that (as in but what, that . . . not).—*interj.* used in summoning, calling attention, expressing surprise, disapprobation, or protest, etc.—*adjs.* what'en, whatt'en *(dial.)*; from *whatkin*, what kind): what kind of; what'na (from *whatkin a*) same as whaten.—*n.* what'ness, what a thing is: essence: quiddity.—*ns.* what'abouts, the things one is occupied about; what'-d'ye-call(-it, -'em, etc.), a word substituted for the name of a thing (or person) in forgetfulness or contempt.—*pron.* whatev'er, whate'er, anything which: no matter what: what? *(coll.)*.—*adj.* any or all that, no matter what.—*n.* what's-his-(her-, its-)name *(coll.)*, that person, or thing, indicated or understood.—*adj.* what'-like *(dial.)*, of what kind, character, or appearance.—*n.* what'not (see separate article).—*adj.* what'so *(arch.)*, of whatever kind.—*pron.* whatever *(arch.)*: whoever *(obs.)*: whosoever *(obs.)*.—*adjs.* whatsoev'er, whatsoe'er', whatever; whatsomev'er *(dial.)*, whatsoever.—know what it is, to know what is involved in an action or experience: to have experienced, suffered, it; so what? what of it; what an if *(Shak.)*, what if, or though; what else, could anything else be the case? what for . . . for what reason, or intended for what purpose *(dial.*; in standard English what . . . for): punishment, esp. a whipping *(slang)*; what for a *(obs.)*, what kind of; what have you *(coll.)*, what not: anything else of the kind; what ho, a loud hail, summons; what if, what would it matter if? what would happen if? what not, elliptical for 'what may I not say?' implying the presence or existence of many other things; what of, what comes of, follows from? what do you think of? what's what, the true position of affairs: the proper, conventional, or profitable way to behave or proceed; what though, what matters it though: notwithstanding the fact that; what time *(arch.)*, at the very time when; what with, by reason of. [O.E. *hwæt*, neut. of *hwā*, who; Ger. *was*, L. *quod*.]

Whatman paper, *(h)wot'mən pā'pər*, fine quality paper used for drawings, engravings, filtering, etc. [Trademark; name of manufacturing firm.]

whatnot, *(h)wot'not*, *n.* a light piece of furniture with shelves for bric-à-brac, etc.: anything, no matter what: a nondescript article. [what, not.]

whaup, *(h)wöp*, *(Scot.)* *n.* a curlew—sometimes great whaup as opp. to little whaup, the whimbrel. [Primarily imit.; history uncertain.]

whaur, *(h)wör*, a Scots form of where.

wheal. Variant of weal (2).

wheal, *(h)wēl*, *n.* a Cornish name for a mine.

whear(e). Obs. spelling of where.

wheat, *(h)wēt*, *n.* any cereal grass of the genus Triticum, or its grain, furnishing a white flour for bread—known as *bearded*, or *beardless* or *bald*, according to the presence or the absence of the awns or beard; as *white*, *red*, or *amber*, according to colour; and as *winter* or *spring* (also *summer*) according to whether it is a type normally sown in autumn or spring.—*adj.* wheat'en, made of wheat: whole-meal.—wheat'-berry, wheat'-corn, the grain of wheat; wheat'-bird, the chaffinch; wheat'-ear, an ear of wheat; wheat'-eel (also wheat'-worm), a small nematode worm that makes its way up wheat stems to the ears: the disease it causes—also *ear-cockle*; wheat'-field; wheat'-fly, the name of several flies that destroy wheat—e.g. the Hessian fly; wheat'-midge, a dipterous insect that lays its eggs in the flowers of wheat-heads, and whose reddish larvae devour the kernels; wheat'-mildew, either of two fungus diseases of wheat; wheat'-moth, any of several small moths whose larvae devour stored wheat.—wheat-ear stitch, a fancy stitch in embroidery. [O.E. *hwǣte*; Ger. *weizen*; allied to white; named from its colour.]

wheatear, *(h)wēt'ēr*, *n.* a bird akin to the chats, a common summer visitant of Britain. [Prob. corr. of white arse.]

Wheatstone('s) bridge, *(h)wēt'stən(z) brij*, an apparatus for measuring electrical resistance, much used, but not invented, by Sir Charles *Wheatstone* (1802-75).

wheedle, *(h)wēd'l*, *v.t.* and *v.i.* to entice by soft words, flatter, cajole: to obtain by coaxing (with *out of*): to cheat by cajolery (with *out of*).—*n.* a piece of wheedling: a coaxing person *(obs.)*. —*n.* wheed'ler.—*adj.* wheed'lesome, coaxing.—*n.* wheed'ling. [Perh. from O.E. *wǣdlian*, (orig.) to be in want, to beg.]

wheel, *(h)wēl*, *n.* a circular frame turning on an axle: an old instrument of torture: a steering-wheel: a potter's wheel: a spinning-wheel: a rotating firework: a bicycle or tricycle *(coll.)*: the wheel of a dog-turned spit *(Shak.)*: the wheel attributed to Fortune personified, the emblem of mutability: hence, the course of events: a celestial sphere *(obs.)*: a disk: a circular design: a circular motion: (in *pl.*) the parts of a machine, esp. fig.: one or more short lines following a bob at the end of a stanza: a refrain: a dollar *(slang)*.—*v.t.* to cause to turn or revolve, esp. round an axis or pivot, as a body of troops: to cause to move in a circular course: to encircle *(Milt.)*: to make wheel-shaped *(rare)*: to put a wheel or wheels on: to form, or treat, on the wheel: to convey on wheels: to propel on wheels.—*v.i.* to turn round or on an axis: to change direction: to move in a circle: to reel, be giddy: to roll forward: to wander, roam *(Shak.)*: to travel in a wheeled vehicle: to ride a bicycle or tricycle *(coll.)*: to be provided with wheels on which to be propelled.—*adj.* wheeled, having wheels: moving on wheels: formed into a wheel *(rare)*.—*ns.* wheel'er, one who makes a cyclist *(coll.)*: a maker of wheels *(dial.)*: in composition, that which wheels, or has such-and-such a kind of or so-many wheels: a wheel-horse; wheel'ing, the act of moving or conveying on wheels: a turning or circular movement: a rather coarse woollen yarn.—*adj.* wheel'y, like a wheel.—wheel'-animal, -animalcule, a rotifer; wheel'barrow, a barrow with one wheel in front and two handles and legs behind: loosely, any other hand-cart; wheel'base, the distance between the front and rear axles of a vehicle: the area enclosed by lines joining the points at which the wheels of a locomotive, etc., touch the rails or the ground, or the length of this area; **wheel'-carriage**, any kind of carriage moved on wheels; **wheel'-chair**, a chair moving on wheels, esp. an invalid's chair.—*adj.* **wheel'-cut**, of glass, cut, or ground and polished, on a wheel.—**wheel'-cutter**, a machine for cutting teeth on wheels; **wheel'-horse**, one of the horses next the wheels in a team; **wheel'-house**, a shelter in which a ship's steering-wheel is placed: a paddle-box: a prehistoric wheel-shaped dwelling; **wheel'-lock**, formerly, a lock for firing a gun by means of a small steel wheel; **wheel'-man**, a steersman: a cyclist; **wheel'-plough**, a plough running on wheels, or the depth of whose furrow is regulated by a wheel; **wheel'-race**, the part of a race in which the water-wheel is fixed; **wheel'-spin**, rotation of the wheels without forward or backward movement of the vehicle; **wheel'-window**, a circular window with radiating tracery; **wheel'work**, a combination of wheels and their connection in machinery; **wheel'-wright**, a wright who makes wheels and wheel-carriages.—**big wheel**, a person of importance or self-importance; **break a butterfly (fly,** etc.) **on the wheel**, to inflict a punishment out of all proportion to the offence: to employ great exertions for insignificant ends; **go on wheels** (*fig.*), to move swiftly, smoothly, and hence pleasantly; **potter's wheel**, a horizontal revolving disk on which clay vessels are shaped; **put a spoke in one's wheel** (see **spoke**); **put one's shoulder to the wheel** (see **shoulder**); **wheel and axle**, one of the mechanical powers, in its primitive form a cylindrical axle, on which a wheel, concentric with the axle, is firmly fastened, the power being applied to the wheel, and the weight attached to the axis; **wheel of fortune**, Fortune's wheel: a gambling device; **wheel of life** (see **zoetrope**); **wheels within wheels**, a situation in which a complication of influences are at work. [O.E. *hwēol*; O.N. *hjōl*.]

**wheen**, (*h*)*wēn*, (*Scot.*) *n.* a few.—*adj.* (*obs.*) few.—**a wheen**, a few: a good many: (used adverbially) a little. [O.E. *hwǣne*—*hwōn*, adv., a little.]

**wheeple**, (*h*)*wē'pl*, (*Scot.*) *v.i.* to make a long drawn-out cry such as that of the curlew: to whistle feebly.—Also *v.t.* and *n.* [Imit.]

**Wheeson**, (Shak., 2 *Hen. IV*, II, i. 99) Whitsun.

**wheeze**, (*h*)*wēz*, *v.i.* to breathe with a hissing sound: to breathe audibly or with difficulty.—*v.t.* to utter with such a sound.—*n.* act, or sound, of wheezing: a gag (*theatrical slang*): a catch-phrase (*slang*): a standard joke (*slang*): a cunning plan (*coll.*).—*adv.* **wheez'ily.**—*ns.* **wheez'iness; wheez'ing.**—*v.i.* **wheez'le** (*Scot.*), to make wheezy sounds.—*adj.* **wheez'y.** [Prob. O.N. *hvǣsa*, to hiss.]

**whelk**, *wilk*, (*h*)*welk*, *n.* a popular name for a number of marine gasteropods, esp. applied to species of the genus Buccinum common on the coasts of northern seas.—*adjs.* **whelked**, ridged like a whelk; **whelk'y**, knobby, rounded: formed in a shell (Spens., *Virg. Gnat.* 105). [Wrong form of *welk*—O.E. *wiloc*, *weoluc*; origin obscure.]

**whelk**, (*h*)*welk*, *n.* a pimple: by confusion with **wale** (1), the mark of a stripe on the body, a wrinkle, an inequality or protuberance. [Late O.E. (W.S.) *hwylca*—*hwelian*, to suppurate.]

**whelk'd.** See **welkt.**

**whelm**, (*h*)*welm*, *v.t.* to turn, as a hollow vessel, upside down, esp. so as to cover something else (now *dial.*): to cover completely, in this way (*obs.*), now with water, etc.: to overturn, overthrow: to plunge deep: to submerge: to overpower: to overburden: to ruin, destroy: to pass over in such a way as to submerge it. [M.E. *whelmen,* to turn over.]

**whelp**, (*h*)*welp*, *n.* the young of the dog kind and of lions, etc.—a puppy, a cub, etc.: contemp-

tuously, a young man: a ridge running longitudinally on the barrel or drum of a capstan or windlass to control the cable: a sprocket on a wheel.—*v.i.* and *v.t.* to bring forth (young). [O.E. *hwelp:* O.N. *hvelpr.*]

**whemmle**, (*h*)*wem'l*, **whomble, whummle**, (*h*)*wum'l*, (*dial.*) *n.* an overthrow, overturn: confusion.—*v.t.* to overturn: to turn upside down: to throw into a state of disorder or agitation: to cover as with an inverted dish.—*v.i.* to capsize. [By metathesis from **whelm.**]

**when**, (*h*)*wen*, *adv.* (*interrog.* and *rel.*) and *conj.* at what time? at which time: at or after the time that: upon or after which: while: although: at which (or *rel. pron.*).—*n.* the time: which time.—*interj.* (*Shak.*) an exclamation of impatience, like *what!*—*conjs.* **when'as'** (*arch.*), when: in as much as: whereas; **whenev'er, whene'er'**, at every time when: as soon as (*Scot.*); **whensoev'er**, at what time soever.—**say when**, tell me when to stop; **seldom when** (*Shak.*), seldom that. [O.E. *hwanne, hwonne* (Ger. *wann, wenn*); from the stem of interrog. pron. *hwā,* who.]

**whence**, (*h*)*wens*, *adv.* and *conj.* (also **from whence**) from what place: from which things: wherefore.—*n.* place of origin: source.—*adv.* **whenceforth** (*Spens.*), whence.—*conj.* **whencesoev'er, whencev'er**, from what place, cause, or source soever. [M.E. *whennes, whannes.*]

**whe'r.** See **whether.**

**where**, (*h*)*wār*, *adv.* (*interrog.* and *rel.*) and *conj.* at or to which place: at what place? to what place? from what source (*lit.* and *fig.*): to a, or the, place in which (*arch.*): in what circumstances or condition: at what point (*fig.*): whereas: wherever: in, at, or to which (or *rel. pron.*).—*n.* the, or a, place: which place.—*n.* **where'ness**, state of having place or position: position, situation.—*adv.* and *conj.* **whereabout'**, about which, about where: near what? on what errand (*Shak.*; *n.* what one is about)—also **where'abouts.**—*n.* **where'about**, now **where'abouts**, situation, esp. approx.—*advs., conjs.* **whereagainst'**, against which; whereas', when in fact: but on the contrary: taking into consideration, in view of, the fact that: where (*obs.*).—*advs.* and *conjs.* **whereat'**, at which: at what? **whereby'**, by which; **wherefor'**, for which; **where'fore** (*-fər*), for which, or what, reason: why?—*n.* the cause.—*advs.* and *conjs.* **wherefrom'**, whence; **wherein'**, in which place or respect: in what?; **whereinsoev'er**, in whatever place or respect; **wherein'to** (or *-in-tōō'*), into which: into what?; **whereof'**, of which: wherewith** (*Shak.*): of what?; **whereon'**, on which: on what?; **whereout'**, out of which; **where'so**, **wheresoe'er', wheresoev'er**, in or to what place soever: whencesoever (*arch.*); **wherethrough'**, through which: through the agency of which; **whereto'**, to which: to what?; **whereun'der**, under which; **whereuntil'** (*Shak.*), to what: whereunto; **whereun'to** (or *-un-tōō'*; *arch.*), whereto: for what purpose?; **whereupon'**, upon or in consequence of which: on what grounds (*Shak.*); **where'er', wherev'er**, at whatever place; **wherewith', wherewithal'**, with which? with what.—*n.* (usu. **wherewithal**) the means.—**from where**, whence: from the, or a, place where; **see, look**, etc., **where**, behold; **where away?** a query as to the direction of an object sighted by the lookout (*naut.*): where are you going? (*dial*); **where it is** (*coll.*), the real situation, point, or explanation; **where you are**, what you are saying or getting at. [O.E. *hwǣr, hwār;* from stem of **who;** cf. **there.**]

**wherret.** See **whirret.**

**wherry**, (*h*)*wer'i*, *n.* a shallow, light boat, sharp at both ends for speed: a kind of barge:—*pl.* **wherr'ies.—wherr'yman**, a man employed in a wherry, esp. one who rows a wherry. [Ety. dub.]

**whet,** (h)wet, v.t. to sharpen by rubbing: to make keen: to excite: to incite (obs.): to preen (obs.; rare):—pr.p. whett'ing; pa.t. and pa.p. whett'ed.—n. act of sharpening: sharpness: a time, occasion (dial.): an incitement or stimulus: something that sharpens the appetite: an appetiser.—n. whett'er.—whet'-slate, novaculite; whet'stone, a stone for sharpening edged instruments: a stimulant.—whet on, or forward (Shak.), to urge on. [O.E. hwettan, cog. with hwæt, sharp; Ger. wetzen.]

**whether,** (h)wedh'ər (Shak., often scanned as one syllable; also spelt whe'r), interrog. and rel. pron. (arch.) which (of two).—conj. introducing the first of two alternative words, phrases, or clauses, the second being introduced by or, or (in the case of clauses) sometimes by or whether: introducing a single dependent question.— whether or no (sometimes not), whether so or not so: in any case, in any event. [O.E. hwæther, from stem of hwā, who, with the old comp. suff. -ther; cog. with Goth. hwathar, Ger. weder; also with L. uter, Ionic Gr. koteros, Sans. katara.]

**whew, wheugh,** hū, (h)wū, interj. expressing wonder or dismay.—n. a whistling sound, esp. one noting astonishment.—v.i. to utter such a sound. [Imit.]

**whew,** (h)wū, (dial.) v.i. to bustle about. [Perh. whew (1).]

**whewellite,** hū'əl-īt, n. calcium oxalate. [Named after William Whewell (1794–1866).]

**whey,** (h)wā, n. the watery part of milk, separated from the curd, esp. in making cheese.—adj. of or containing whey: like whey: whey-coloured. —adjs. whey'ey, whey'ish, of whey: like whey. —n. whey'ishness.—whey'-face, a pale or white face.—adj. whey'-faced, pale, esp. with terror.— whey'-tub. [O.E. hwæg; L.G. wey.]

**which,** (h)wich, interrog. pron. what one of a number? what? (obs.): of what sort or kind? (obs.).—Also used adjectively.—rel. pron. who, whom (obs.): now used chiefly of things, ideas, etc., not persons: that: often having as antecedent a circumstance or statement, being equivalent to 'and that' or 'but that'.—prons. and adjs. whichev'er, whichsoev'er, every one which: any one, no matter which.—the which (obs.), which; which . . . he (obs.), who; which . . . his (obs.), whose; which is which? which is the one, which is the other? [O.E. hwilc, hwelc, from the stem of hwā, who, and līc (from a word meaning body, form), like; Goth. hweileiks, Ger. welch, welcher; L. qualis; cf. such and each.]

**whicker,** (h)wik'ər, (dial.) v.i. to neigh: to bleat: to snigger, titter. [Imit.]

**whid,** (h)wid, (Scot.) n. a rapid noiseless movement.—v.i. to move quickly, to whisk.—v.i. whidd'er, to whiz. [Perh. conn. with O.N. hvitha, a squall, O.E. hwitha, a breeze.]

**whid,** (h)wid, n. a lie (Scot.): a word (obs. slang): a quarrel (dial.).—v.i. to lie.—cut boon whids, to speak good words. [Poss. O.E. cwide, a word—cwethan, to say.]

**whidah-bird.** See widow-bird.

**whiff,** (h)wif, n. a sudden puff of air or smoke from the mouth: a slight inhalation: a puff of smell: a slight blast: a small amount, esp. of something causing or associated with a transient sensation (fig.): a cigarette (slang): a jiffy (coll.): a light kind of outrigger boat: a glimpse (dial.). —v.t. to throw out in whiffs: to puff: to drive or convey by, or as if by, a whiff: to inhale, smell.—v.i. to go out or off in a whiff: to move with, or as with, a puff of air: to blow slightly: to smell.—ns. whiff'er; whiff'et, a whippersnapper.—v.i. whiff'le, to blow in puffs: to

move as if blown by a puff: to talk idly: to make a slight whistling sound: to veer: to vacillate: to prevaricate.—Also v.t.—n. whiff'ler, one who whiffles: a swaggerer: a contemptible person.—n. whiff'lery, levity: trifling.—n. and adj. whiff'ling.—adj. whiff'y.—n. whift (dial.), a breath, snatch. [Prob. partly M.E. weffe; imit.]

**whiff,** (h)wif, n. a fish akin to the turbot. [Ety. unknown.]

**whiff,** (h)wif, v.i. to fish with a hand-line towed behind a boat.—n. whiff'ing. [Perh. whiff (1).]

**whiffler,** (h)wif'lər, (hist.) n. an official who clears the way for a procession. [Perh. wifel, obs. javelin, battle-axe; affected by whiff (1) and whiffle.]

**whiffletree,** (h)wif'l-trē, n. Same as whippletree.

**Whig,** (h)wig, n. a name applied to members of one of the great English political parties— applied in the late 17th century to those upholding popular rights and opposed to the King; after 1830 almost superseded by 'Liberal': a Scottish Presbyterian, first so called in the middle of the 17th century: one of those who in the colonial period were opposed to British rule (U.S.): one of the party formed from the survivors of the old National Republican party and other elements, first so called in 1834—it fell to pieces in the 1850's (U.S.).—adj. of, pertaining to, or composed of, Whigs—also Whigg'ish.— n. Whigg'archy, government by Whigs.—adv. Whigg'ishly.—ns. Whigg'ism, Whigg'ery, Whigg'ishness, Whig'ship, Whig principles. [Prob. short for whiggamore.]

**whig,** (h)wig, (Scot.) v.i. to jog along.—v.t. to urge forward. [Origin uncertain.]

**whig,** (h)wig, (dial.) n. sour milk: whey: buttermilk.—v.t. and v.i. to curdle. [Prob. allied to whey.]

**whiggamore,** (h)wig'ə-mōr, -mör, n. one of the 7000 Western Covenanters who marched on Edinburgh in 1648, sealing the doom of Charles I: a Scottish Presbyterian, a Whig. [Origin disputed; most prob. whig, to urge forward, mere, mare.]

**whigmaleerie, whigmaleery,** (Scot.), (h)wig-mə-lē'ri, n. a trinket, knick-knack: a fantastic ornamentation: a whim. [Origin uncertain.]

**while,** (h)wil, n. a space of time: time and trouble spent.—conj. (also whilst) during the time that: at the same time that: as long as: although: notwithstanding the admitted fact that: until (obs.; North. dial.).—prep. (Shak.; North. dial.) until.—v.t. to pass without irksomeness (with away).—conj. whiles (B.), while, at the same time that: until (Shak.).—adv. (Scot.) at times (orig. gen. of O.E. hwil).—adv. whi'lom, formerly, once.—adj. former (orig. dat. pl. of O.E. hwil, time).—adv. while-ere' (arch.), a little while ago, formerly.—(every) once in a while, now and then; the while (Shak.), at the present time, in the meantime; the whilst (obs.), while: in the meantime. [O.E. hwil; Goth. hweila, Ger. weile.]

**whilk,** (h)wilk, pron., obs. and dial. form of which.

**whilly,** (h)wil'i, whillywha(w), (h)wil'i-(h)wô, -(h)wä, v.t. to wheedle, cajole.—n. cajolery: a coaxing, insinuating, person.—adj. smooth-tongued, wheedling. [Origin obscure.]

**whilom.** See while.

**whim,** (h)wim, n. a fantastic creation of brain or hand (obs.): a whimsical person (obs.): a caprice: a fancy: a vertical rope drum revolved by a horse, used for hoisting from shallow shafts. —v.i. (obs.) of the head, to turn round, swim: to be whimsical.—v.t. to desire as a caprice: to turn aside by a whim (obs.).—adjs. whimm'y, full of whims; whim'sical (-zi-) full of whim: odd, fantastical: delicately fanciful: loosely, expressing gently humorous tolerance.—ns. whimsical'ity, whim'sicalness.—adv. whim'sically.

—*n.* **whim′sy, whim′sey,** a whim, freak: whimsical behaviour: delicate, or affectedly delicate, fantasy.—*adj.* full of whims, changeable.—*adv.* **whim′sily.** — *n.* **whim′siness.** — **whim′-wham,** a ridiculous notion: an odd device: a fanciful trifle. [whim-wham is recorded earlier than whim; cf. O.N. *hvima,* to have the eyes wandering.]

**whimbrel,** (*h*)*wim′brəl, n.* a species of small curlew.—Also **wim′brel.** [Prob. imit. of bird's cry; dim. suff. *-rel.*]

**whimper,** (*h*)*wim′pər, v.i.* to cry feebly, brokenly, and querulously or whiningly: to make a plaintive sound.—*v.t.* to express or utter in a whimper.—*n.* a peevish cry.—*n.* **whim′perer.**—*n.* and *adj.* **whim′pering.**—*adv.* **whim′peringly.** [Imit.; cf. Ger. *wimmern.*]

**whimple,** (*h*)*wim′pl.* Same as **wimple.**

**whin,** (*h*)*win, n.* gorse, furze.—*adj.* **whinn′y,** abounding in whins.—**whin′chat,** a bird that frequents whins, very similar in appearance, esp. when it assumes its duller autumn plumage, to the stonechat, to which it is allied. [Prob. Scand.]

**whin.** See **whinstone.**

**whine,** (*h*)*win, v.i.* to utter a plaintive cry: to complain in an unmanly way.—*v.t.* to express or utter in a whine: to cause to make a whining noise.—*n.* a plaintive cry: an affected nasal tone of utterance.—*ns.* **whi′ner; whi′niness; whi′ning.**—*adv.* **whi′ningly.**—*adj.* **whi′ny.** [O.E. *hwinan,* to whine; O.N. *hvina,* to whistle through the air.]

**whinge,** (*h*)*wēnj,* (*h*)*winj,* (*Scot.*) *v.i.* to whine: to cry fretfully: to complain peevishly.—*n.* **wheenge.** [O.E. *hwinsian,* from root of *hwinan;* see **whine.**]

**whinger,** (*h*)*wing′ər, n.* a dirk.—Also **whin′iard** and **whin′yard.** [Origin obscure.]

**whinid′st,** (Shak., *T. and C.* II, i. 15) folio reading for which Johnson conjectured *vinewd′st.*

**whinny,** (*h*)*win′i, v.i.* to neigh:—*pr.p.* **whinn′ying;** *pa.t.* and *pa.p.* **whinn′ied.**—*n.* a neigh. [Imit.]

**whinstone,** (*h*)*win′stōn, stən, n.* any hard and compact kind of rock, usually basalt or the like: a piece of this.—Also **whin.**—**Whin Sill,** a sheet of intrusive quartz-dolerite or quartz-basalt exposed almost continuously for nearly 200 miles from the Farne Islands to Middleton-in-Teesdale. [*whin* (origin obscure), and **stone.**]

**whinyard.** See **whinger.**

**whip,** (*h*)*wip, n.* a lash with a handle for punishing or driving: a stroke administered as by a whip: a whipping motion: a driver, coachman: one who enforces the attendance of a political party: a call made on members of parliament to be in their places against an important division (called, according to number of times message is underlined as indication of urgency, **three-line whip,** etc.; **five-line whip** is no longer used): a whipper-in, the person who manages the hounds: a simple form of hoisting apparatus, a small tackle consisting of a single rope and block: a preparation of whipped cream, eggs, etc.: a whipping or overcasting: an appeal for contributions (usu. **whip-round**): an individual share in money collected in equal amounts: an instant (*Scot.*): an arm carrying a sail of a windmill: a long twig or slender branch: an arrangement of cars that move with sudden jerks, used for amusement purposes.—*v.t.* to strike with a lash: to drive, or make to move, with lashes: to punish with lashes, or (loosely) by spanking: to strike in a manner suggesting a lash: to lash with sarcasm: to defeat, outdo (*coll.*): to beat into a froth, as eggs, cream, etc.: to keep together, as a party: to fish with fly: to overlay, as one cord with another: to bind round: to sew lightly: to overcast, as a seam: to move quickly, snatch (with *up, away, out,* etc.): to

rouse (with *up*).—*v.i.* to move nimbly: to move in the manner of a whiplash: to make a cast in fishing with fly:—*pr.p.* **whipp′ing;** *pa.t.* and *pa.p.* **whipped, whipt.**—*ns.* **whipp′er,** one who or that which whips: an officer who inflicts the penalty of whipping; **whipp′ing,** act of one who or that which whips: corporal punishment, esp. with the whip or lash: a defeat: a binding of twine, e.g. at the end of a rope: material for binding in this way: overcasting.—*adj.* **whipp′y,** whiplike: pliant: supple.—*n.* **whip′ster,** a term of contempt formerly with various meanings, chiefly remembered for Shak., *Oth.* V, ii. 242, a whippersnapper.—**whip′-and-derr′y,** a hoisting apparatus consisting of a whip and a derrick; **whip′cat,** a tailor; **whip′cord,** cord for making whips: a fabric with a bold steep warp twill, used chiefly for dresses, suitings, and coatings: a whip-like seaweed, as *Chorda filum* or *Chordaria flagelliformis.*—*adjs.* **whip′cord; whip′cordy,** like whipcord.—*v.t.* **whip′-graft,** to graft by fitting a tongue cut on the scion to a slit cut slopingly in the stock.—Also *n.*—*ns.* **whip′-grafting; whip′-hand,** the hand that holds the whip: the advantage; **whip′-handle,** the handle or stock of a whip: an advantage; **whip′jack,** a whining beggar who pretends to be a sailor; whip′lash, the lash of a whip: something resembling the lash of a whip (also *fig.*): a whiplash injury; **whipp′er-in,** one who keeps the hounds from wandering: one who enforces the discipline of a political party: at any moment in a race, the horse in the last place (*slang*); **whipp′ersnapper,** a little or young lively insignificant person; **whipp′ing-boy,** a boy formerly educated along with a prince and punished for the royal pupil's faults: one on whom falls the odium or punishments of the shortcomings of others; **whipp′ing-cheer** (*obs.*), flogging; **whipp′ing-post,** a post to which offenders are tied to be whipped: the punishment itself; **whip(p′ing)-top,** a top kept spinning by means of a whip; **whip-round** (see whip); **whip′-saw,** a narrow saw for dividing timber lengthwise, usu. set in a frame and often worked by two persons.—*v.t.* to cut with a whip-saw: to have the advantage of at every point (*slang*).—**whip′-scorpion,** any arachnid of the order Pedipalpida, slightly resembling true scorpions but being without sting and having usu. a whiplike appendage at the rear of the body; **whip′-snake,** any of various snakes resembling a whiplash, as *Masticophis flagelliformis,* the coach-whip snake, and species of *Philodryas,* etc.; **whip′-socket,** a socket to hold the butt of a whip; **whip′staff,** a former steering device, a vertical wooden lever controlling a ship's rudder; **whip′-stitch,** a small overcasting stitch: a hasty composition: a tailor: a kind of half-ploughing, raftering (*dial.*).—Also *v.t.* and *v.i.*—**whip′-stock,** the rod or handle of a whip.—*adjs.* **whip′-tail, -tailed,** having a long, slender tail.—**whip′worm,** a worm of the genus Trichocephalus, with posterior end thick and anterior long and thin, found parasitic in human intestines.—**whip and spur,** with great haste; **whiplash injury,** a neck injury caused by the sudden jerking forwards and backwards of the head, common in motor-vehicle accidents; **whip the cat,** to practise small economies: to work by the day as a dressmaker, tailor, etc., going from house to house: to idle: to play a practical joke. [M.E. *whippen;* cf. Du. *wippen,* to shake.]

**whippet,** (*h*)*wip′it, n.* a breed developed from a cross between a greyhound and spaniel or terrier: a racing-dog: a small speedy tank.—*n.* **whipp′eting,** training, racing, of whippets. [Partly **whip,** and partly obs. *whippet,* to move briskly.]

**whippletree,** (*h*)*wip′l-trē, n.* the cross-piece of a

carriage, plough, etc., to which the traces of a harnessed animal are fixed. [From whip.]

**whip-poor-will,** (h)wip-pōōr-wil', or -par-, n. a species of goatsucker, a native of N. America. [Imitative of its call.]

**whipstall,** (h)wip'stöl, (aero.) n. a stall as the result of which the nose of the aircraft whips forward and down.—v.i. and v.t. to go, or put, into such a stall. [whip, stall.]

**whir(r),** (h)wûr, n. a sound from rapid whirling or vibratory motion.—v.i. to whirl round with a buzzing noise: to fly, move, with such a sound.—v.t. (Shak.) to hurry away with a whizzing sound:—pr.p. whirr'ing; pa.t. and pa.p. whirred.—n. whirr'ing. [Imit.; cf. Dan. hvirre, to whirl.]

**whirl,** (h)wûrl, n. a turning with rapidity: anything that revolves, esp. rapidly: a great or confusing degree, as of activity or emotion: commotion, agitation: a whorl.—v.i. to revolve rapidly: to move rapidly, esp. in an agitated manner: to turn swiftly round or aside.—v.t. to turn round rapidly: to carry, or move, away rapidly, as on wheels: to throw violently.—n. whirl'er.—n. and adj. whirl'ing.—whirl'-about', act of whirling about: anything that turns round rapidly; whirl'-(whorl'-, hurl'-)bat (obs.), translating L. caestus (see cestus, (2)); whirl'-blast, a whirling blast of wind; whirl'-bone, the round head of a bone turning in a socket: the knee-cap; whirl'igig (-gig), a toy that is spun or whirled rapidly round: a merry-go-round: anything that revolves rapidly (lit. and fig.): an ancient instrument of punishment, consisting of a pivoted wooden cage in which the prisoner was spun round: any water-beetle of the family Gyrinidae, esp. Gyrinus natator (also whirligig beetle); whirl'ing-dervish, one of an order of Mohammedan devotees who dance or spin round, the dancing dervishes, founded in 1273; whirl'ing-table, a machine exhibiting the effects of centripetal and centrifugal forces (also whirl'ing-machine): a potter's wheel; whirl'pool, a circular current in a river or sea, produced by opposing tides, winds, or currents: an eddy: a huge whale-like sea monster (obs.); whirl'-wind, a small rotating wind-storm, which may extend upwards to a height of many hundred feet—a miniature cyclone; whir'lybird (slang), a helicopter. [M.E. whirlen—O.N. hvirfla, freq. of hverfa, to turn round; Ger. wirbeln.]

**whirret,** (h)wir'it, (obs.) n. a blow.—v.t. to give a sharp blow to.—Also wherret. [Poss. imit.]

**whirry,** (h)wûr'i, (Scot.) v.i. and v.t. to move rapidly. [Prob. from whirr.]

**whirtle.** See wortle.

**whish,** (h)wish, v.i. to move with the whizzing sound of rapid motion: to say 'whish'.—interj. asking for silence—hush!—Also whisht.—n. whisht, silence: a whisper.—adj. silent.—v.i. to keep silent.—Also (Scot.) wheesht.—haud, hold, one's wheesht, whisht, to keep silence.

**whisk,** (h)wisk, v.t. to move quickly and lightly: to sweep rapidly: to beat up with a quick, light movement.—v.i. to move nimbly and rapidly.—n. a rapid sweeping motion: a small bunch of anything used for a brush: a small instrument for beating or whisking, esp. eggs: a type of women's neckerchief or large collar worn in the later 17th century (hist.): a hairlike appendage, as on an insect: a tuft: a panicle esp. of millet: the common millet.—ns. whis'ker, he who, or that which, whisks: formerly, hair on the upper lip, now usu. hair on the side of the face, side-whiskers (esp. in pl.): a long bristle on the face of a cat, etc.: a very thin, strong fibre or filament made by growing a crystal, e.g. of silicon carbide, silicon nitride or sapphire: either of two bars extending on each side of the bowsprit (naut.); whiskeran'do, a

whiskered person, in allusion to Don Ferolo Whiskerandos in Sheridan's Critic.—adjs. whiskeran'doed, whis'kered, whis'kery, having whiskers; whis'king, moving briskly.—adj. whis'ky-fris'ky, flighty. [Scand., earliest uses Scot.]

**whisk,** (h)wisk, n. earlier name for whist. [Said to be from whisk (1), from the rapid action of sweeping the cards off the table.]

**whisket,** (h)wis'kit, n. Variant of wisket.

**whisky** (Ir. and U.S. whiskey), (h)wis'ki, n. as legally defined, a spirit obtained by distillation from a mash of cereal grains saccharified by the diastase of malt: formerly applied also to a spirit obtained from potatoes, beetroot, or any starch-yielding material.—adj. whis'key-fied, whis'kified, intoxicated.—whisk(e)y sour, a sour having whisky as its chief ingredient; Whisky Insurrection, an outbreak against the excise regulations which occurred in Western Pennsylvania in 1794; whis'ky-liver, cirrhosis of the liver, from too much whisky; whisky toddy, toddy having whisky for its chief ingredient. [Gael. uisgebeatha—uisge, water, beatha, life; cf. L. vita, life.]

**whisky, whiskey,** (h)wis'ki, n. a light gig. [whisk (1).]

**whisky-john,** (h)wis'ki-jon, n. the grey or Canada jay—Also whis'ky-jack. [From Amer. Indian name of similar sound.]

**whisper,** (h)wis'par, v.i. to speak with a low sound: to speak in a whisper: to speak covertly, spread rumours: to plot secretly: to make a sound like soft speech.—v.t. to utter in a low voice or under the breath, or covertly, or by way of gossip.—n. a low hissing voice or sound: a sound uttered with breath not voice: voiceless speech with narrowed glottis (phon.): a hissing or rustling sound: cautious or timorous speaking: a secret hint: a rumour.—n. whis'perer, one who whispers: a secret informer.—n. and adj. whis'pering. — advs. whis'peringly, in a whisper or low voice; whis'perously, in a whisper.—adj. whis'pery.—whispering campaign, an attack by means of furtively spread rumours; whis'pering-gallery, -dome, a gallery or dome so constructed that a whisper or slight sound is carried to an unusual distance. [O.E. hwisprian; Ger. wispern, O.N. hviskra; allied to whistle.]

**whiss,** (h)wis, v.i. to hiss, whistle, wheeze, etc. [Imit.]

**whist,** (h)wist, interj. hush: silence: be still.—adj. (arch.) hushed, silent: attentive.—v.i. to become silent.—v.t. (Spens.) to hush or silence. [Imit.]

**whist,** (h)wist, n. a card game played by two against two.—whist'-drive, a progressive whist party; whist'-player.—dummy whist, whist played with a dummy hand; long whist, a game of ten points; short whist, a game of five points. [whisk (2); said to be assimilated to whist (1), because of the silence during play.]

**whistle,** (h)wis'l, v.i. to make a shrill sound by forcing the breath through the contracted lips or the teeth: to make such a sound in derision, etc.: of a bird, to pipe, sing: to make a like sound with an instrument: to sound shrill: to make a call or signal by whistling: to whizz through the air: to become informer: to give a landlord information that leads to raising rent (Scott). — v.t. to perform or utter by whistling: to call or bring by a whistle: to send with a whistling sound.—n. an act of whistling: the sound made in whistling, or one like it: a small wind instrument giving a high-pitched sound by air impinging on a sharp edge: an instrument sounded by escaping steam, etc., as on steam locomotives: a summons: the throat (slang).—ns. whis'tler, one who, or that which whistles: large kind of marmot: broken-winded horse: fabulous bird whose whistle was fatal to the hearer (*Spens.*); **whis′tling**.— *adv.* **whis′tlingly**.—*adj.* **whis′tle(d)-drunk** (*obs.*), too drunk to whistle.—**whis′tle-fish**, a rockling; **whis′tle-stop** (*coll.*), small town or railway-station, where trains stop only by signal (**whistle-stop speech**, an electioneering speech made on tour (orig. at railway stations)).—*v.i.* of a political candidate, to make an electioneering tour with many brief personal appearances.—**whis′tling-shop** (*slang*), a place, as a room in a prison, where liquor was sold without a licence.—**boatswain's whistle** (also **pipe, call**), a whistle of special shape used by a boatswain or boatswain's-mate to summon sailors to various duties; **go whistle** (*Shak.*), to go to the deuce; **pay for one's whistle**, to pay highly for one's caprice (from Benjamin Franklin's story of a whistle he, as a boy, bought at an exorbitant price); **penny whistle**, or **tin whistle** (see **flageolet**); **pigs and whistles** (see **pig** (2)); **wet one's whistle** (*coll.*), to take a drink of liquor; **whistle down the wind**, from the practice of casting a hawk off down the wind when turning it loose, to abandon: to talk to no purpose; **whistle for**, to summon by whistling: to ask for in vain (*coll.*); **whistle for a wind**, a superstitious practice of old sailors during a calm; **whistle off, whistle away** (*hawking*), to send off or dismiss by, or as if by, a whistle: to turn loose: to abandon; **worth the whistle**, worth the trouble of calling for. [O.E. *hwistlian*.]

**whit,** (*h*)*wit, n.* the smallest particle imaginable: a bit. [By-form of **wight**, a creature, a thing.]

**white,** (*h*)*wit, adj.* of the colour of pure snow: snowy: of the light complexion characteristic of Europeans: that absorbs the minimum and reflects the maximum of light rays: pale, pallid: bloodless: colourless: pure: unblemished: innocent: purified from sin: bright: burnished, as of steel: unburnished, of silver: light-coloured or golden, as wine: clothed in white: pertaining to the Carmelite monks: in continental Europe, anti-revolutionary (*politics*): auspicious, favourable: reliable, honest: without bloodshed, as a war.—*n.* the colour of snow: anything white, as a white man, a white butterfly, the centre of a target, the albuminous part of an egg, a pigment: a member of a white political party.—*v.t.* to make white.—*adj.* **white′ly** (*obs.* except *Scot.*) whitish, pale.—*v.t.* **whit′en**, to make white: to bleach: to free from guilt, or to make to appear guiltless.—*v.i.* to become or turn white.—*ns.* **whit′ener**; **white′-ness**; **whit′ening**, act or process of making or becoming white: a substance used to make white, whiting; **whites**, leucorrhoea: white attire; **whit′ing**, a small sea-fish allied to the cod, so-called from its white colour: ground chalk free from stony matter and other impurities, extensively used as a size, colour, etc.— (also **white′ning**, **Spanish white** and—the finest quality—**Paris white**).—*adj.* **whit′ish**, somewhat white.—*ns.* **whit′ishness**; **whitster** ((*h*)*wit′star*; *Shak.*), a bleacher of cloth or clothes.—*adj.* **whit′y**, whitish.—**white admiral**, any of a genus of butterflies, of the same family as the red admiral, having white bands on the wings; **white′-ale** (*dial.*), ale brewed or mixed with ingredients, such as flour, eggs, etc., that give it a whitish colour; **white′-ant**, a termite (Isoptera); **white′-arm**, sword, bayonet or lance —a translation of Fr. *arme blanche*; **white arsenic** (see **arsenic**); **white′bait**, the fry of various species of herring, etc.; **white′bass**, a silvery food fish of the American Great Lake region; **white′beam**, a small tree (*Sorbus*, or *Pyrus, aria*) with leaves white and downy on the underside; **white′-bear**, the polar bear; **white′-beard**, an old man.—*adjs.* **white′-bearded**; **white′-bellied**; **white′-billed**;—**white′-bonnet**, one employed to bid at an auction to raise prices;

**white′-bottle**, bladder-campion; **White′boy**, a member of an association of Irish peasants first formed in County Tipperary about 1761 for the purpose of redressing grievances; wearing white shirts, they committed agrarian outrages by night; **white′boyism**, the principles of the White-boys; **white′-brass**, an inferior alloy of copper and zinc.—*adj.* **white′-breasted**.—**white′cap**, the male redstart, or other bird with light-coloured head: a crested wave: a member of a self-constituted vigilance committee who, under the guise of purifying the morals of the community, deal violently with persons of whom they disapprove; **white coal**, water-power (Fr. *houille blanche*).—*adj.* **white′-collar**, pertaining to, or designating, the class of workers, as clerks, etc., who are not engaged in manual labour.—**white copper**, a light-coloured alloy of copper; **white corpuscle**, a leucocyte, one of the colourless amoeba-like cells occurring in suspension in the blood plasma of many animals, in lymph, etc. —*adjs.* **white′-crested, -crowned**, of birds, having the crest or crown white.—**white crops**, grain, as barley, rye, wheat; **white damp**, carbon monoxide; **whited sepulchre**, one professedly righteous but inwardly wicked, a hypocrite (Matt. xxiii. 27); **White Dwarf**, the name given to a small class of stars outside the normal spectral sequence, because their luminosities are extremely low for their spectral type; **white elephant** (see **elephant**); **White Ensign**, a flag with a white field and St George's cross, with the Union Jack in the canton, till 1864 the flag of the White Squadron, now flown by the Royal Navy and the Royal Yacht Squadron.—*adjs.* **white′-faced**, having a face pale with fear or from illness: of animals, having the face, or part of it, white: with white front—also **white′-fronted**; **white′-favoured**, wearing white favours.—**white feather** (see **show the white feather** under **feather**); **white′fish**, a general name for such fish as the whiting, haddock, menhaden, etc.; any species of Coregonus; **white flag**, an emblem of truce or surrender; **White Friar** (also without *caps.*), one of the Carmelite order of friars, so called from their white dress; **white gold**, gold alloyed with nickel or palladium to give it a white colour.—*adj.* **white′-handed**, having white hands or paws: having hands unstained with guilt.— **white′-hass, -hawse** (*Scot.*), a white-pudding; **white′head**, the blue-winged snow-goose: a breed of domestic pigeons.—*adj.* **white′-headed**, of an animal, having the head wholly or partly white: having white hair: favourite, darling, as **white′-headed boy** (*Irish*).—**white heat**, the degree of heat at which bodies become white: an intense state, as of emotion, activity, etc.; **white′-heart**, a cultivated cherry, related to the gean, with soft, tender flesh and pale skin; **white′-herring**, a fresh or uncured herring; **white′-honeysuckle**, an azalea known also as the clammy or swamp azalea; **white′-horse**, a white-topped wave: a figure of a horse on a hillside, formed by removing the turf from the underlying chalk—the most famous in Berkshire, at Uffington.—*adj.* **white′-hot**.—**White House**, the official residence, in Washington, of the President of the U.S.A.; **white iron**, pig-iron or cast-iron in which all the carbon is in chemical combination with the iron; **white′-lady**, a spectral figure said to be associated with the fortunes of a family, as in some German castles; **white lead**, basic lead carbonate used in painting white; **white leather** (see **leather**); **white′-leg**, an ailment of women after parturition—also called milk-leg; **white lie** (see **lie**); **white light**, light containing all wavelengths in the visible range at the same intensity—the term is used, however, to cover a wide range of intensity distribution in the spectrum; **white′-lime** (*obs.*), whitewash;

**white line**, a longitudinal line, either continuous or broken, on a highway to separate lanes of traffic.—*adjs.* **white listed**, having white stripes on a darker ground; **white'-livered**, having a pale look (once thought to be caused by a white liver): cowardly.—**white man**, one of the white race: one assumed to deal fairly with others (*coll.*); **white meat**, food made of milk, butter, eggs, etc.: the flesh of poultry, rabbits, veal, etc.; **white metal**, a tin-base alloy with over 50 per cent. of tin: sometimes, an alloy in which lead is the principal metal; **white night**, a sleepless night; **white noise**, a mixture of sound waves covering a wide frequency range; **white'-out**, a phenomenon in snow regions in fog or overcast conditions in which earth and sky merge in a single whiteness; **white paper**, a statement, printed on white paper, issued by government for the information of parliament; **white'-pot**, a Devonshire dish of sliced rolls, milk, eggs, sugar, etc., baked; **white'-precipitate,** a white mercurial preparation used externally; **white'-pudding**, an oatmeal and suet pudding in a sausage skin; **white pyrites**, marcasite; **white race**, one of the main divisions of mankind, distinguished generally by light complexion and certain types of hair and skull—also known as Caucasian; **white'-rent** (*hist.*), the tinner's poll-tax of eightpence to the Duke of Cornwall: rent paid in silver; **white rhinoceros**, an African two-horned rhinoceros, not much lighter than the black rhinoceros.—*adj.* **white'-rumped.**—**white sale**, a sale of linen goods at reduced prices; **white'-salt**, salt dried and calcined; **white'-seam** (*Scot.*), plain needlework.—*v.i.* to do plain needlework.—**white slave**, a girl procured for prostitution purposes (esp. when exported)—whence **white slaver, white slavery** and **white slave traffic; white'smith**, a worker in tinned or white iron: a tinsmith; **white spirit**, a petroleum distillate used as a substitute for turpentine in mixing paints, and in paint and varnish manufacture; **White Squadron**, one of three divisions of the British Navy in former times: white-painted vessels built in 1883 and following years as part of a strong U.S. Navy; **white squall**, (see **squall**); **white'thorn**, the common hawthorn; **white'throat**, any of several birds of the same genus (Sylvia) as the blackcap, having the breast and belly of a brownish-white; **white vitriol**, zinc sulphate; **white'wash**, a liquid, as lime and water, or whiting, size and water, used for coating walls: a wash for the skin: false colouring: a glass of sherry after other wines. —*v.t.* to cover with whitewash: to give a fair appearance to: to attempt to clear (a stained reputation). — **white'washer**, one who whitewashes; **white'-water**, shoal water near the shore, breakers: the foaming water in rapids, etc.; **white'-wax**, bleached beeswax: Chinese wax; **white whale**, the beluga; **white wine**, yellowish-coloured or uncoloured (as opp. to *red*) wine; **white'wing**, the velvet scoter, or an American scoter closely allied to it: the chaffinch. —*adj.* **white'-winged.**—**white'wood**, a name applied to a large number of trees or their timber—the American tulip-tree, whitewood cedar (*Tecoma*, or *Tabebuia, leucoxylon*; Bignoniaceae), etc.; **whit'ing-pout** (see **pout** (2)); **whit'ing-time** (*Shak.*), bleaching-time. — *adj.* **whit'y-brown**, white with a tinge of brown.— **China white**, a very pure variety of white lead —also silver white and French white; **mark with a white stone** (see **stone**); **white-eyelid monkey**, any of the mangabeys, monkeys with white upper eyelids; **white-footed mouse**, the deer mouse; **white-headed eagle**, the N. American bald eagle; **white man's burden** (*Kipling*), his alleged obligation to govern backward coloured peoples; **white of (an) egg**, the albumen, the

pellucid viscous fluid surrounding the yolk; **white of the eye**, that part of the ball of the eye which surrounds the iris or coloured part; zinc white (see **zinc**). [O.E. *hwit*; O.N. *hvitr*, Ger. *weiss*.]

**Whitechapel**, (*h*)*wit'chap-l*, *n.* a lead from a one-card suit, straightforward leading out of winning cards, or other type of unskilful play (*whist*): intentional pocketing of an opponent's ball (*billiards*).—**Whitechapel cart** (see **cart**). [*Whitechapel* in London.]

**Whitehall**, (*h*)*wit'hōl*, *n.* a street with government offices, in London· the British government or its policy.

**whither**, (*h*)*widh'ər*, *adv.* and *conj.* to what place? to which place: (used relatively) to which: to what: whithersoever.—*adv.* whithersoev'er, to whatever place.—*adv.* **whith'erward(s)**, in what direction, to what point.—**no whither**, to no place. [O.E. *hwider*, allied to **who.**]

**whither.** See **wuther.**

**whiting.** See **white.**

**whiteleather**, (*h*)*wit'ledh-ər*, *n.* leather dressed with alum, white leather: the paxwax of the ox. [**white leather.**]

**Whitley Council**, (*h*)*wit'li kown'səl*, a joint standing industrial council (national or local), composed of representatives of employers and workpeople in an organised trade, to consider and settle conditions of employment, etc. [Recommended (1917) in the 'Whitley Report'—the report of a Reconstruction Sub-committee presided over by Rt. Hon. J. H. *Whitley*.]

**whitling**, (*h*)*wit'ling*, *n.* a kind of trout, probably a young bull-trout. [**white**, and suff. **-ling.**]

**whitlow**, (*h*)*wit'lō*, *n.* a painful inflammation of a finger or toe, esp. near the nail, paronychia.— **whit'low-grass**, any of several plants alleged to cure whitlows, as a small British saxifrage (*Saxifraga tridactylites*), or a small crucifer (*Draba verna*): whitlow-wort; **whit'low-wort**, any of a number of plants of the genus Paronychia. [Perh. a corr. of *whick-flaw*, quick-flaw; cf. **quick** and **flaw.**]

**Whit-Monday**, (*h*)*wit'-mun'dā*, *n.* the Monday following Whitsunday.

**whitret.** See **whit(t)ret.**

**Whitsun**, (*h*)*wit'sn, adj.* pertaining to, or observed at, Whitsuntide.—*n.* Whitsuntide.—**Whit'sun-ale**, a festival formerly held at Whitsuntide; **Whit'sunday**, the seventh Sunday after Easter, commemorating the day of Pentecost, when the converts in the primitive Church wore white robes: in Scotland, one of the term-days (May 15) on which rents, annuities, etc., are payable, the Whitsunday removal terms in towns being fixed as May 28; **Whit'suntide**, the season of Pentecost, comprising **Whit'sun-week, Whit'-week**, the week beginning with Whitsunday. [**white, Sunday.**]

**whittaw**, (*h*)*wit'ō*, (*dial.*) *n.* a saddler.—Also **whitt'awer.** [**white, tawer.**]

**whitterick.** See **whit(t)ret.**

**whittie-whattie**, (*h*)*wit'i-(h)wot'i*, (*Scot.*) *v.i.* to mutter, whisper: to shilly-shally.—*n.* vague language intended to deceive: a frivolous excuse. [Perh. formed from **what.**]

**whittle**, (*h*)*wit'l, v.t.* to pare or cut with a knife: to shape with a knife: to diminish gradually.— *v.i.* to cut wood aimlessly: to peach, or to confess at the gallows (*obs. slang*).—*n.* a large knife, usu. clasp or sheath. [M.E. *thwitel*— O.E. *thwitan*, to cut.]

**whittle**, (*h*)*wit'l*, (*dial.*) *n.* a woollen shawl: a blanket. [O.E. *hwitel*; a white mantle—*hwit*, white.]

**whit(t)ret**, (*h*)*wit'rət*, (*h*)*wut'rət*, **whitterick**, (-ə)*rik*, (*Scot.*) *n.* a weasel.

**whizz, whiz**, (*h*)*wiz, v.i.* to make a hissing sound, like an arrow or ball flying through the air: to move rapidly.—*v.t.* to cause to whizz:—*pr.p.* **whizz′ing**; *pa.t.* and *pa.p.* **whizzed.**—*n.* a hissing sound: a bargain, agreement (*slang*).—*ns.* **whizz′er; whizz′ing.**—*adv.* **whizz′ingly.**—**whizz′-bang** (*slang*), a light shell of high velocity which is heard arriving before the sound of a gun's report: a firework suggestive of this; **whizz′-kid** (*slang*), one who achieves success rapidly: one who has progressive ideas. [Imit.; cf. wheeze, hiss.]

**who,** *hōō, rel.* and *interrog. pron.* what person: which person: he who, the person who: whoever: of what name, standing, etc. (objective case **whom**—O.E. *hwām*, which was orig. dat. of *hwā*, who, and replaced in the 12th and 13th centuries the older accus. *hwone*; possessive case **whose**—M.E. *hwæs*, from O.E. *hwæs*, gen. of *hwā*).—*prons.* **whoev′er, whosoev′er** and **who′so** (*arch.*), every one who: whatever person (objective case **whom′ever, whomsoev′er**; possessive case **whosev′er, whosesoev′er**).—**as who should say,** as if one should say; **know who's who,** to know the position and influence of everyone; **the who** (*Shak.*), who; **who but he,** who else?, he only. [O.E. *hwā*; cog. with Goth. *hwas*, O.H.G. *hwer,* Ger. *wer;* also with Sans. *ka,* L. *quis.*]

**whoa,** (*h*)*wō, interj.* stop.—*interj.* **whoa-ho-ho(a)′** (*obs.*), used to hail a person from a distance.

**who-dun-it, whodunnit,** *hōō-dun′it,* (*coll.*) *n.* a story concerned with the elucidation of a crime mystery. [**who,** done (vulg. pa.t. of **do**), it.]

**whole,** *hōl, adj.* sound in health (*arch.; B.*): uninjured: restored to health: healed: not broken: undamaged: not broken up, or ground, or deprived of any part: containing the total amount, number, etc.: complete: of a sister or brother, full-blooded: in mining, as yet unworked.—*n.* the entire thing: a system or combination of parts.—*adv.* wholly.—*n.* **whole′ness.**—*adj.* **whole′some,** healthy in body, taste, morals or (*Shak.*) condition: indicating health: conducive to bodily or spiritual health: remedial (*obs.*): propitious (*Shak.*): reasonable, sensible (*Shak.*). —*adv.* **whole′somely.**—*n.* **whole′someness.**—*adv.* **wholly** (*hōl′li, hō′li*), completely, altogether.— *adjs.* **whole′-coloured,** all of one colour; **whole′-foot′ed** (*coll.*), unreserved; **whole′-hearted, -souled,** hearty, generous, zealous and sincere.— *adv.* **whole′-heart′edly.**—*adj.* **whole′hog** (*slang*), out-and-out, complete.—**whole′-hogg′er,** one who is inclined to go the whole hog.—*adjs.* **whole′-hoofed,** having undivided hoof; **whole′-length,** giving the whole figure: full-length.— *n.* a portrait, statue giving the whole figure.— **whole′-meal,** meal made from entire grains of wheat; **whole number,** a unit, or a number composed of units, an integral number; **whole′sāle,** sale of goods, usually by the whole piece or large quantity, to a retailer.—*adj.* buying and selling, or concerned with buying and selling, thus: extensive and indiscriminate.—*adv.* **by wholesale:** extensively and indiscriminately.—**whole′-sāler,** one who sells by wholesale.—*adj.* **whole′-skinned,** unhurt: safe in reputation.—**whole′-stitch,** a lace-making stitch used to fill in a pattern.—**go the whole hog,** to do a thing thoroughly or completely: to commit oneself to anything unreservedly; **out of whole cloth,** in a barefaced manner; **the whole,** all the: the complete; **upon, on, the whole,** generally speaking: all things considered; **with whole skin,** safe, unscathed. [O.E. *hāl,* healthy; O.N. *heill,* Ger. *heil;* see hale (1).]

**whom, whomever, whomsoever.** See who.

**whommle, whomble,** (*h*)*wom′l,* (*h*)*wum′l.* Same as whemmle.

**whoobub,** *hōō′bub, n.* (*obs.*). Same as hubbub.

**whoop,** (*h*)*wōōp, n.* a loud eager cry: a N. American Indian war-cry: a form of hide-and-seek: (*hōōp*)

the long noisy inspiration heard in whooping-cough.—*v.i.* to give a loud cry of triumph, eagerness, scorn, etc.: to hoot.—*v.t.* to cheer, or insult, with shouts: to summon, or to urge on, by whooping.—*interj.* (*Shak.*) ho!—*ns.* **whoop′er,** one who whoops: a swan (*Cygnus cygnus, ferus,* or *musicus*) common in north Europe and Asia (also **whoop′ing-swan**).—**whoop′ing-cough, hoop′-ing-cough,** pertussis, an infectious and epidemic disease, mostly attacking children, characterised by catarrh of the respiratory tract and by periodic spasms of the larynx that end in a long crowing inspiration. [O.Fr. *houper,* to shout.]

**whoopee,** (*h*)*wōōp′ē, interj.* an exclamation of delight.—Also *n.*—**make whoopee** (*coll.*), to indulge in hilarious amusements or dissipation. [whoop.]

**whoot.** Obs. variant of **hoot.**

**whop, whap,** (*h*)*wop,* (*coll.* or *dial.*) *v.t.* to whip, thrash: to defeat or surpass: to throw or pull suddenly or violently.—*v.i.* to strike, or to move, quickly: to flop down.—*n.* a blow: a bump: the noise made by either of these.—*n.* **whopp′er,** one who whops: anything very large, esp. a monstrous lie.—*adj.* **whopp′ing,** very large.—*n.* thrashing. [Variant of **wap** (1); origin obscure, prob. partly imitative.]

**whore,** *hōr, hör, n.* a prostitute: any unchaste woman: an allegedly corrupt religious community or practice.—*v.i.* to be, or to have to do with, a whore or whores.—*v.t.* to make a whore of, debauch: to spend in whoring.—*n.* **whore′-dom,** whoring: any illicit sexual intercourse: idolatry.—*adj.* **whō′rish.**—*adv.* **whō′rishly.**—*n.* **whō′rishness.**—**whore′house,** a brothel; **whore′-master** (*obs.*), a whoremonger.—*adj.* **whore′-masterly,** libidinous.—**whore′monger,** a lecher: a pander; **whore′s′-bird,** a whore's child: used as a vulgar term of abuse; **whore′s′-egg,** a sea-urchin; **whore′son** (-*sən*), son of a whore: a bastard: a term of coarse contempt or familiarity.—*adj.* mean, scurvy. [Late O.E. *hōre,* prob. —O.N. *hōra,* adulteress.]

**whorl,** (*h*)*wörl,* (*h*)*wûrl, n.* a group of similar members arising from the same level on a stem, and forming a circle around it: a single turn in a spiral shell: a convolution—e.g. in the ear: a disk on the lower part of a spindle serving as a flywheel (also **wharve;** *spinning*).—*adj.* **whorled,** having whorls: arranged in the form of a whorl or whorls. [Late M.E. *wharwyl,* etc., variants of **whirl.**]

**whorl-bat.** See **whirl-bat.**

**whortleberry,** (*h*)*wör′tl-ber-i, -bər-i, n.* a widely-spread heath plant with a dark blue edible berry, called also the bilberry—in Scotland, blaeberry —sometimes abbreviated to **whort:** extended to certain other plants of the same genus (Vaccinium). [Variant of **hurtleberry.**]

**whose,** *hōōz, pron.* the possessive case of **who** or **which.** See **who.**

**whoso, whosoever.** See who.

**whot,** (*h*)*wot, adj.* (*Spens.*). Obs. variant of **hot.**

**whow,** (*h*)*wow,* (*Scot.*) *interj.* of deploration.— Often **eh whow** (or **aich wow**).

**whummle.** See **whemmle.**

**whunstane.** Scots form of **whinstone.**

**why,** (*h*)*wī, adv.* and *conj.* for what cause or reason, on which account?: therefore: (used relatively) on account of which.—*interj.* expressing sudden realisation, or protest, or marking resumption after a question or a slight pause, or (*Shak.*) to call a person.—*adv.* **whyev′er** (*coll.*), for whatever reason.—**why′-not,** a challenge for reasons: a dilemma (*obs.*); **at a why-not,** at a disadvantage).—**for why** (*arch.* and *dial.*), for what reason: because; **the why and wherefore,** the whole reason; **why, so!** (*Shak.*), so let it be! [O.E. *hwī, hwȳ,* instrumental case of *hwā,* who.]

**whydah-bird.** See **widow-bird.**

**wick,** *wik, (dial.) n.* a creek. [O.N. *vik,* a bay.]
**wick,** *wik, n.* a village or town *(dial.)*: a farm *(dial.):* as suffix *(-ik, -wik,* also *-wich, -ij)* in *Berwick, Greenwich,* etc. [O.E. *wic,* prob. an old Gmc. borrowing from L. *vicus,* a village.]
**wick,** *wik, n.* the twisted threads of cotton or other substance in a candle, lamp, or lighter, which draw up the inflammable liquid to the flame. [O.E. *wēoce, wēoc;* allied to Du. *wick,* a roll of lint, Ger. *wieche.*]
**wick,** *wik, v.t.* and *v.i.* in curling, to strike (a stone) in an oblique direction. [Perh. O.E. *wican,* to bend, yield, give way.]
**wick,** *wik,* (obs. or *dial.) adj.* wicked. [O.E. *wicca* wizard, *wicce,* witch.]
**wicked,** *wik'id, adj.* evil in principle or practice: sinful: ungodly: (of an animal) vicious: cruel: mischievous, spiteful: very bad, harmful, or offensive: roguish *(coll.):* unlucky *(Shak.).—n.* a wicked person *(B.):* (with *the)* wicked persons collectively.—*adv.* wick'edly.—*n.* wick'edness.—**the wicked one,** the devil. [M.E. *wicked, wikked,* prob.—*wicke, wikke,* wicked—O.E. *wicca,* wizard.]
**wicken, wicky.** See **quicken** (1).
**wicker,** *wik'ər, n.* a small pliant twig or osier: wickerwork.—*adj.* made of twigs or osiers: encased in wickerwork.—*adj.* wick'ered, made of wicker: covered with wickerwork.—wick'er-work, basketwork of any kind. [M.E. *wiker,* of Scand. origin; cf. O.E. *wican,* to bend.]
**wicket,** *wik'it, n.* a small gate: a small door in or near a larger one: a grill or loop-hole *(obs.):* an opening or a window with a grille, as at a ticket-office, bank, etc. *(U.S.):* (the following meanings all *cricket),* the upright arrangements of three stumps with two bails on top which the batsman defends against the bowling: a stump: the pitch, esp. in respect of its condition: a batsman's stay at the wicket, or his joint stay there with another: a batsman's innings.—wick'et-door, -gate, a wicket; wick'et-keeper, in cricket, the fieldsman who stands immediately behind the striker's wicket.—get, take, etc., a wicket, to bowl a batsman, or have him put out in any way as a result of one's bowling; keep wicket, to be wicket-keeper; over, round, the wicket, (of bowling) delivered with the hand nearer, farther away from, the wicket; sticky wicket (see stick (1)); throw down the wicket, to put down the wicket in fielding by throw of the ball; win by so-many wickets, to win with so-many wickets still to fall. [O.N.Fr. *wiket* (Fr. *guichet);* of Gmc. origin.]
**widdershins, widershins,** etc. Variants of **withershins.**
**widdy,** *wid'i, (dial.) n.* a rope, esp. one made of osiers: a halter for hanging. [Variant of **withy.**]
**widdy,** *wid'i,* dial. form of **widow.**
**wide,** *wīd, adj.* extending far: having a considerable distance between the sides: broad: of a specified breadth: roomy: expanded: opened as far as possible: far apart: far from the point aimed at, or *(rare)* place mentioned: very different: of large scope, comprehending or considering much *(fig.):* astute, wily *(slang):* lax in morals *(slang):* lax, reverse of *narrow (phon.).* —*n.* wideness: in cricket, a ball bowled out of reach of the batsman: a penalty run allowed for this.—*adv.* (now usu. far and wide) to a great distance, over a large region: at a distance *(Spens.):* far from the point aimed at, the subject under discussion, the truth, etc.: far to one side (with *of*): so that there is a large space or distance between.—*adv.* wide'ly.—*v.t.* and *v.i.* wi'den, to make or grow wide or wider: to throw open *(Shak.).—ns.* wi'dener, one who, or that which, widens: a kind of tool; wide'ness; width *(width),* breadth.—*adjs.* wide'-angle *(phot.),*

pertaining to a lens having an angle of view of 60° or more and a short focal length; wide'-awake, fully awake: on the alert: keen and knowing *(coll.).—n.* a low wide-brimmed soft felt hat.—wide'awakeness.—*adj.* wide'chapped *(Shak.),* open-mouthed.—wide'-gab, the fish known also as the angler.—*adj.* wide'-open, opened wide: open to attack *(coll.):* lax in enforcing laws and regulations *(U.S.).*—wide screen, a wide curved cinema screen designed to give the viewer a greater sense of actuality in the picture.—*adjs.* wide-spectrum, (of antibiotic, etc.) effective against a wide range of micro-organisms; wide'spread, extended or extending widely: found, operative, etc., in many places; wide'-stretched *(Shak.),* large; wide'-watered, bordered or covered by, or having, wide waters.—to the wide, completely: utterly; wide of *(Shak.),* indifferent to, far from observing; wide of the mark, far out, astray from the truth. [O.E. *wīd;* O.N. *vithr,* Ger. *weit.*]
**widgeon, wigeon,** *wij'ən, n.* any duck of the genus Mareca, having the bill shorter than the head, legs short, feet rather small, wings long and pointed, and the tail wedge-shaped: a fool *(obs.).* [Of uncertain origin.]
**widow,** *wid'ō, n.* a woman who has lost her husband by death and has not married again: in the early Church, one of a special class of pious women: an extra hand in some card games.—*v.t.* to bereave of a husband (or wife): to strip of anything valued: to endow with a widow's right *(Shak.):* to be a widow to *(Shak.).—ns.* wid'-ower, *(dial.)* wid'ow-man, a man whose wife is dead; wid'owerhood; wid'owhood, state of being a widow, or *(rarely)* of being a widower: a widow's right *(Shak.).*—wid'ow-bewitched, a grass-widow; wid'ow-bird, any of a group of African birds of the weaver-bird family (genus Vidua, sub-family Viduinae; L. *viduus,* widowed) having much black in the plumage, called also whidah-, whydah-bird, in the belief that they were named from *Whydah* (Ouidah) in Dahomey; wid'ow's-bench *(hist.),* a widow's share of her husband's estate besides her jointure; wid'ow's-chamber, the apparel and bedroom furniture of the widow of a London freeman, to which she was entitled; widow's cruse, a source of supply that never fails (1 Kings xvii. 10-16); widow's man *(naut.),* any of a number of fictitious persons formerly entered as a part of a ship's company in order that the pay allotted to them might be set aside for widow's pensions; widow's mite, a small offering generously given (Mark xii. 42; see also mite); widow's peak, a point of hair over the forehead, like the cusped front of a widow's cap in former days; widow's weeds, the mourning dress formerly worn by all widows; wid'ow-wail, a dwarf shrub (Cneorum) with pink, scented flowers, native to Spain and south France: daphne or mezereon (*Daphne mezereum).*—the Widow, Veuve (Fr. widow) Clicquot, a famous brand of champagne. [O.E. *widewe;* Ger. *witwe,* L. *vidua,* bereft of a husband, Sans. *vidhavā.*]
**width.** See **wide.**
**wiel.** Same as **weel** (1).
**wield,** *wēld, v.t.* to rule *(obs.):* to possess, enjoy, gain *(obs.):* to control, manage: to use with skill: to utter *(obs.).—adj.* wield'able, capable of being wielded.—*ns.* wield'er; wield'iness.—*adjs.* wield'less *(Spens.* weeldlesse), unmanageable; wield'y, easy to wield: manageable: dexterous, active *(obs.).*—wield the sceptre, to have supreme command or control. [O.E. *weldan* (not recorded; W.S. *wealdan);* Goth. *waldan,* Ger. *walten.*]
**wiener schnitzel,** *vē'nər shnit'səl,* (Ger.) a veal cutlet dressed with bread-crumbs and eggs.
**wife,** *wīf, n.* a woman: a married woman: the

woman to whom one is married: the mistress of a house, a hostess (*obs.*)—now often in this sense *good-wife*:—*pl.* **wives.**—*n.* **wife′hood**, the state of being a wife.—*adjs.* **wife′less**, without a wife; **wife′-like**; **wife′ly.**—**take to wife** (see **take**). [O.E. *wīf*; O.N. *vīf*, Ger. *weib*.]

**wig**, *wig*, *n.* an artificial covering of hair for the head worn to conceal baldness, or for fashion's sake, as in the full-dress **full-bottomed wig**, of Queen Anne's time, still worn by the Speaker and by judges, and the smaller **tie-wig**, still represented by the judge's undress wig and the barrister's or advocate's frizzed wig: a judge (*slang*). (For **bag-wig**, see **bag**; **bigwig**, see **big**.)—*adj.* **wigged**, wearing a wig.—*n.* **wigg′ery**, false hair: excess of formality (*Carlyle*).—*adj.* **wig′less**, without a wig.—**wig-block**, a block or shaped piece of wood for fitting a wig on; **wig′maker**, a maker of wigs.—**wigs on the green**, a fray. [Short for **periwig**.]

**wig**, *wig*, (*coll.*) *v.t.* to scold.—*n.* **wigg′ing** (*coll.*), a scolding. [**wig** (1).]

**wigan**, *wig′ən*, *n.* a stiff canvas-like fabric for stiffening garments: a plain grey cloth for boot-linings, etc. [*Wigan*, the town.]

**wigeon.** See **widgeon.**

**wiggle**, *wig′l*, *v.i.* and *v.t.* to waggle, wriggle.—*n.* a wiggling motion.—Also *v.i.*, *v.t.*, and *n.* **wigg′le-wagg′le.**—*n.* **wigg′ler**, one who wriggles.—*adj.* **wigg′ly**, wriggly: much or irregularly waved.—**get a wiggle on** (*slang*), to hurry. [Freq. of verb from which is derived dial. **wig**, to wag; connected with M.L.G. *wiggelen*.]

**wight**, *wīt*, *n.* a creature or a person (*arch.*, *dial.*, or ironically): a supernatural being (*obs.*). [O.E. *wiht*, a creature, thing; Ger. *wicht*; cf. **whit**.]

**wight**, *wīt*, (*arch.* and *dial.*) *adj.* swift, nimble: courageous, strong.—*adv.* **wight′ly.** [O.N. *vīgr*, warlike—*vīg*, war (O.E. *wīg*).]

**wight.** Same as **wite.**

**wigwag**, *wig′wag*, *v.i.* to twist about: to signal by means of flags.—*n.* act of wigwagging: a level-crossing signal which gives its indication, with or without a red light, by swinging about a fixed axis.—*adj.* twisting.—*adv.* to and fro. [Dial. *wig* (from same root as **wiggle**) and **wag** (1).]

**wigwam**, *wig′wom*, *-wam*, *n.* an Indian hut. [Eng. corr. of Algonquian word.]

**wild**, *wīld*, *adj.* being in a state of nature, not tamed or cultivated: of an undomesticated or un-cultivated kind: uncivilised: uninhabited: desolate: tempestuous: violent: fierce: passionate: unrestrained: licentious: agitated: shy: distracted: very angry: very enthusiastic, eager, keen: strong and irrational: fantastic, crazy: disordered: unconsidered: wide of the mark: fresh and natural: (*cap.*) applied to the extreme Evangelical party in the Church of Scotland (*hist.*).—Also *adv.*—*n.* (also in *pl.*) an uncultivated region: a wilderness or desert (also *fig.*): an empty region of air or water (*poet.*).—*n.* **wild′ing**, that which grows wild or without cultivation: a wild crab-apple: a garden plant self-sown, an escape.—*adj.* uncultivated, or wild.—*adv.* **wild′ish**, somewhat wild.—*adv.* **wildly.**—*n.* **wild′ness.**—**wild animals**, undomesticated animals; **wild′-ass**, any of several Asiatic or African asses, as the onager, living naturally in a wild state; **wild birds**, birds not domesticated, esp. those protected at certain seasons under the Acts of 1880 onwards; **wild′-boar**, a wild swine, esp. *Sus scrofa*, from which most domestic swine are derived.—*adj.* **wild′-born**, born in the wild.—**wild′-cat**, an undomesticated cat (*Felis catus*) native to Europe: any of various small wild animals of the cat family: the skins of these: a quick-tempered, fierce person: a speculative or unsound financial scheme (*U.S.*): one who takes part in such a scheme (*U.S.*).—*adj.* (of business,

scheme, etc.), haphazard, reckless, unsound financially: (of strike), unauthorised by union officials.—*v.t.* and *v.i.* (*U.S.*) to drill an experimental well in an area of unknown productivity in search of oil, gas, ore, etc.—**wild′-cherry**, any uncultivated tree bearing cherries, as the gean (*Prunus avium*), or its fruit; **wild′-dog**, any wild species of the dog genus or family, as the dhole, the dingo, etc.; **wild duck**, any duck excepting the domesticated duck; **wild′fire**, a sweeping, destructive fire: a need-fire: a composition of inflammable materials: Greek fire (**like wildfire**, extremely fast): lightning without thunder: a disease of sheep; **wild′-fowl**, the birds of the duck tribe: game-birds; **wild′-fowling**, the pursuit of wild-fowl; **wild′-goose**, a bird of the goose kind that is wild or feral: a flighty or foolish person: (in *pl.*, **Wild-geese**; *hist.*) Irish Jacobites who migrated to the Continent after the abdication of James II; **wild′-grape** a grape-vine (Vitis or Muscadinia) in the wild state, or its fruit: Coccoloba (see **grape-tree**); **wild′-honey**, the honey of wild bees; **Wild Hunt**, in Germanic legend, a host of phantoms rushing along, accompanied by the shouting of hunts-men and the baying of dogs; **Wild Huntsman**, their leader; **wild′-indigo**, any of several plants of different genera belonging to the same family (Papilionaceae) as indigo, as an American tumble-weed (*Baptisia tinctoria*); **wild′-land**, land completely uncultivated; **wild mare**, a see-saw: an instrument of punishment, the horse; **wild′(-)oat**, a tall perennial weed close akin to the cultivated oat; **wild′-olive** (see **oleaster**); **wild rice**, Zizania; **wild silk**, tusser; **wild′-Will′iams** (*dial.*), ragged-Robin; **wild′-wood**, wild uncultivated, or unfrequented, wood.—Also *adj.*—**run wild**, to take to loose living: to live or grow in freedom from constraint or control: to revert to the wild or uncultivated state; **sow one's wild oats** (see **oat**); **wild′-goose chase** (see **chase**). [O.E. *wilde*; common Gmc. word.]

**wild**, *wīld*, obs. variant of **weald, wield.**

**wildebeest**, *vild′i-bāst*, *wild′i-bēst*, *vild′ə-bēst*, (*S.Afr.*) *n.* a gnu. [Du. *wilde*, wild, *beest*, ox.]

**wilderness**, *wil′dər-nəs*, *n.* a region uncultivated and uninhabited: a pathless or desolate tract of any kind, as an extent of sea: a part of a garden or estate allowed to run wild, or cultivated in imitation of natural woodland: conditions of life, or a place, in which the spirit feels desolate (*fig.*): the present world: a large confused or confusing assemblage: wildness (*obs.*).—*v.t.* **wil′der** (prob. formed from *wilderness*; *poet.*) to cause to stray: to bewilder.—*v.i.* to wander wildly or widely.—*adjs.* **wil′dered**; **wil′dering.**—*n.* **wil′derment.** [M.E.,—*wilderne*, wild, wilder-ness—O.E. *wilddēoren*-wild, *dēor*, animal.]

**wildgrave**, *wīld′grāv*, (*obs.*) *n.* a waldgrave. [Ger. *wildgraf—wild* (Eng. adj. **wild**), game, *graf*, count.]

**wile**, *wīl*, *n.* a trick: deceit: a pleasing artifice: (in *pl.*) cajolery.—*v.t.* to beguile, inveigle: coax, cajole: to make to pass easily or pleasantly (with *away*; confused with **while**).—*adj.* **wile′ful**, full of wiles.—*adv.* **wil′ily.**—*n.* **wil′iness.**—*adj.* **wil′y**, full of craft or cunning: using tricks or strata-gem. [O.E. *wīl*, *wīle*; cf. **guile**.]

**Wilhelmstrasse**, *vil′helm-shträ-sə*, *n.* a street in Berlin: formerly, the German Foreign Office.

**will**, *wil*, *n.* power or faculty of choosing or deter-mining: act of using this power: volition: choice or determination: pleasure: inclination: lust: command: arbitrary disposal: feeling towards, as in **good** or **ill will** (see **good, ill**): dis-position of one's effects at death: the written document containing this.—*v.t.* to wish for, desire (*arch.*): to command, order, require (*obs.*): to decree: to seek to force, influence (oneself or another to perform a specified action) by silent exertion of the will: to dispose of by will, to bequeath:—in the foregoing senses, *pa.t.* and *pa.p.* **willed**; *2nd pers. pres. indic.* **will′est**; *3rd pers.* **wills**: used with the infinitive of a verb to form (in sense) a future tense, expressing in the second and third person simple futurity (as **shall** in the first), or custom, or persistent habit, and in the first person promise or determination on the part of the speaker: with ellipsis of verb of motion, as 'I will unto the king' (*arch.*): also, in third person, can: to be likely to:—in these senses, *pa.t.* **would**, *wŏŏd*; no *pa.p.*; *2nd pers. sing. pres. indic.* **wilt**; *3rd pers.* **will**.—*v.i.* to excercise choice, choose, decree: to be willing.—*adj.* **wil′ful**, governed only by one's will, obstinate: done intentionally: willing (*Shak.*).—*adv.* (*Shak.*) **wilfully**.—*adv.* **wil′fully**.—*n.* **wil′fulness**. *adj.* **willed**, having a will: voluntary: given, or disposed of, by will: brought under another's will, as in hypnotism.—*n.* **will′er**, one who wills. —*adj.* **will′ing**, not reluctant: eager: ready and prompt to act: voluntary: chosen: intentional (*rare*): of or pertaining to the will.—*adv.* **will′-ingly**.—*n.* **will′ingness**.—*adj.* **will′ing-heart′ed**, heartily consenting.—**will power**, the ability to control one's actions, emotions, impulses, etc.— **at will**, when or as one chooses; **a will of one's own**, a strong, self-assertive will; **by my will** (*Shak.*), voluntarily: also, with my consent; **conjoint, joint, will**, a testamentary act by two persons jointly in the same instrument; **have one's will**, to obtain what one desires; **tenant at will**, one who holds lands only so long as the owner pleases; **with a will**, heartily and energetically; **work one's will**, to do exactly what one chooses. [O.E. *willa*, will, *willan*, *wyllan* (pa.t. *wolde*, *walde*), to wish; Goth. *wiljan*, Ger. *wollen*, L. *velle*.]

**will, wull**, *wil, wul*, (*Scot.*) *adj* and *adv.* at a loss: astray: bewildered.—*adj.* **will′yard**, **will′yart**, wilful: shy. [O.N. *villr*, astray: cf. **wild**.]

**willemite**, *wil′əm-īt*, *n.* orthosilicate of zinc, $Zn_2SiO_4$, white when pure but commonly red, brown, or green through the presence of manganese or iron—noteworthy as exhibiting an intense bright yellow fluorescence in ultraviolet light. [*Willem* (or William) I of the Netherlands.]

**Willesden paper**, *wilz′dən*, a specially treated paper which keeps out wet and acts as a sound and heat insulator, placed under slates in roofing. [*Willesden*, orig. place of manufacture.]

**willet**, *wil′it*, *n.* a N. American bird of the snipe family, belonging to the tattler group—known locally as the stone-curlew. [Imit.]

**willey.** See willy.

**willies**, *wil′iz*, (*slang*) *n.pl.* the creeps.

**williewaught**, *wil′i-wŏhht*, (*Scot.*) *n.* a deep draught. [From misunderstanding of Burns, *Auld Lang Syne*, iv. 3, 'a right guid willie (or guid-willie) waught' (where 'guid willie' means 'good will'), a generous and friendly draught.]

**Will-o'-the-wisp**, *wil′-ō-dhə-wisp′*, *n.* the ignisfatuus: any elusive and deceptive person or thing:—*pl.* **wills-o′-** or **-wisps**. [Orig. *Will-with-the-wisp*—*Will*, abbrev. of William, and **wisp** (q.v.).]

**willow**, *wil′ō*, *n.* any tree or shrub of the genus Salix, having slender, pliant branches: any of several plants resembling it: the wood of the willow: a cricket-bat or baseball-bat: a willowing-machine.—*v.t.* to clean in a willowing-machine.—*adjs.* **will′owed**, abounding with, or grown with, willows; **will′owish**, like a willow: of the colour of willow leaves: slender and supple; **will′owy**, abounding in willows: flexible: graceful.—**will′ow-grouse**, a species of grouse (*Lagopus albus*) found in northern regions of the world; **will′ow-herb**, a perennial

herb (*Epilobium* or *Chamaenerion*) of the evening primrose family (including rose-bay, bay-willow, French or Persian willow) with willow-like leaves and seeds; **will′owing-machine**, a machine in which a spiked revolving cylinder, usu. contained in a spiked box, loosens or cleans cotton, wool, rags for paper, etc.; **willow pattern**, a blue design of Chinese character but English origin used on china from the late 18th cent. onwards; **will′ow-warbler, -wren**, a small European sylviine bird (*Phylloscopus*, or *Sylvia, trochilus*); **will′ow-weed**, one of various species of Polygonum or knot-weed: the purple loosestrife. [O.E. *welig*; I Ger. *wilge*, Du. *wilg*.]

**will-worship**, *wil′-wûr′ship*, (*B.*) *n.* worship after one's own will or fancy, superstitious observance without divine authority. [**will**, **worship**.]

**willy, willey**, *wil′i*, (*dial.*) *n.* a willow basket: a willowing-machine.—*v.t.* to clean in a willowing-machine. [O.E. *wilige*; allied to **willow**.]

**willy-nilly**, *wil′i-nil′i*, *adv.* willing or unwilling: compulsorily.—*adjs.* having no choice: vacillating (*erron.*). [**will** and **nill**.]

**willy-willy**, *wil′i-wil′i*, (*Austr.*) *n.* a cyclone.

**wilt**, *wilt*, *v.i.* to droop, lose energy: to lose self-confidence or courage (*fig.*).—*v.t.* to render limp, cause to droop: to cause to lose spirit, self-confidence, courage.—*n.* act of wilting: any of various diseases that cause wilting of plants. [Orig. dial.; perh. from **welk**.]

**wilt**, *wilt*, *2nd pers. sing.* of **will**.

**Wilton**, *wil′tən*, *n.* (in full **Wilton carpet**) a carpet differing from a Brussels carpet in having a cut pile, long made at *Wilton*, in Wilts.

**wily, wilily, wiliness.** See **wile**.

**wimble**, *wim′bl*, *n.* an instrument for boring holes, turned by a handle: a gimlet: an auger: a kind of brace: an instrument for boring in soft ground.—*v.t.* to bore through with a wimble. [Through O.Norm.Fr., from M.Du. *wimpel*.]

**wimble**, *wim′bl*, (*Spens.*) *adj.* active, nimble. [A Northern word, now dial.; of Scand. origin.]

**wimple**, *wim′pl*, *n.* a veil folded round the head, neck and cheeks (still part of a nun's dress): a fold, wrinkle, ripple: a turn, wind: a crafty twist (*Scot.*).—*v.t.* to wrap in, or hide with, a wimple: to enwrap, enfold: to blindfold (*Shak.*; in *pa.p.*): to lay in folds.—*v.i.* to meander: to ripple: to lie in folds (*Spens.*).—Also **whimple**. [O.E. *wimpel*, neck-covering; cf. O.H.G. *wimpal*, a light robe, Ger. *wimpel*, a pennon, Fr. *guimpe*, a nun's veil, Eng. *gimp*, a thin cloth for trimming.]

**Wimpy**, *wim′pi*, *n.* a kind of hamburger. [Trademark; orig. name of a hamburger-loving character in a comic strip.]

**win**, *win*, *v.t.* to get by labour: to gain in contest: to secure, to achieve, effect: to reach: to be the victor in: to induce: to gain influence over: to obtain the favour of: to mine (an ore): to open up (a new portion of a coal-seam).—*v.i.* to gain the victory: to gain influence over, (*arch.*) advantage over (with *upon*, etc.): to make one's way (*dial.*): to succeed in getting:—*pr.p.* **winn′-ing**; *pa.t.* and *pa.p.* **won**, *wun*.—*n.* (*coll.*) a victory, success.—*ns.* **winn′er**; **winn′ing**, the act of one who wins: (usu. in *pl.*) that which is won: a shaft or pit to open a bed of coal.—*adj.* that wins: of or pertaining to the act of winning: attractive, prepossessing: persuasive.—*adv.* **winn′ingly**.—*n.* **winn′ingness**—**winn′ing-post**, the goal of a race-course.—**win by a (short) head**, to win very narrowly; **win in a canter**, to win easily; **win of** (*obs.*), to get the better of; **win on, upon**, to gain on: to get the better of: to obtain favour with; **win, or gain, one's spurs**, to earn one's knighthood by valour on the field, hence to gain recognition or reputation by merit of any kind; **win out**, to get out: to be successful (*coll.*); also **win through**); **win over**, to bring over to one's opinion or party. [O.E. *winnan*, to struggle, to suffer; O.N. *vinna*, Ger. *gewinnen*, to win.]

**win**, *win*, (*Scot.*) *v.t.* to dry by exposure to the wind:—*pr.p.* **winning**; *pa.t.* and *pa.p.* **won**. [**win** (1) influenced by **wind** (1).]

**win, winn**, *win*, **wing**, *wing*, (*slang*) *n.* a penny.

**wince**, *wins*, *v.i.* to kick (*obs.* or *dial.*): to shrink or start back: to make an involuntary movement, e.g. in pain: to be affected acutely, as by a sarcasm: to be restive, as a horse uneasy at its rider.—*n.* a kick (*obs.*): an involuntary start back or shrinking.—*n.* **win'cer.**—*n.* and *adj.* **win'cing.** [Cf. O.Fr. *guinchir, ganchir*, to wince —a Gmc. word; cf. O.H.G. *wenkan* (Ger. *wanken*), to wince.]

**wince.** See **winch** (1).

**wincey, winsey**, *win'si*, *n.* a cloth, plain or twilled, usu. with a linen or cotton warp and woollen filling.—*n.* **winceyette'**, a plain cotton cloth of light weight, raised slightly on both sides. [Orig. Scot.—linsey-woolsey.]

**winch**, *winch*, *winsh*, *n.* a reel or roller: the crank of a wheel or axle: a powerful type of hauling or hoisting machine.—Also **wince.**—**winch'-man.** [O.E. *wince*, from a Gmc. and Indo-Gmc. root.]

**winch.** See **wench**.

**Winchester**, *win'chəs-tər*, formerly used attributively of various measures (as 'Winchester bushel'), the standards of which were kept at *Winchester*.

**Winchester** (**rifle**), *win'chəs-tər*, orig. a trademark for a repeating rifle made by Oliver F. *Winchester*, American manufacturer: now a trademark for fire-arms, etc., produced by the makers of the rifle.

**wincopipe.** Obs. form of **wink-a-peep**.

**wind**, *wind* (*poet. wīnd*), *n.* air in motion: a current of air, usually horizontal, either natural or produced by artificial means: any of the directions from which the wind may blow: breath: power of breathing: flatulence: conceit: empty, insignificant words: the wind instruments in an orchestra: their players: air impregnated with scent of game: a hint or suggestion, as of something secret: part of the body covering the stomach (*slang*): a disease of sheep in which the inflamed intestines are distended by gases.—*v.t.* (*wind*) to sound or signal by blowing: (following meanings *wīnd*) to perceive by the scent: to expose to wind: to drive, punch hard, so as to put out of breath: to allow to recover wind:—*pr.p.* **wind'ing, wīnd'ing**; *pa.t.* and *pa.p.* **wind'ed** and (as a horn) **wound** (*wownd*).—*ns.* **wind'age**, the difference between the size of the bore of a gun and that of the ball or shell: the influence of the wind in deflecting a missile, the amount of deflection due to wind, or the allowance made for it: air friction on a moving, esp. revolving, part of a machine; **wind'er**, one who sounds a horn: **wīnd'er** (*slang*), a blow that takes one's breath away.—*adv.* **wind'ily.**—*n.* **wind'iness.**—*adj.* **wind'less**, without wind.—*n.* **wind'ore** (*Ben Jonson*, etc.), a form of **window**, based on false association with **door**.—*adv.* and *adj.* **wind'ward**, towards or on the side the wind blows from.— Also *n.*—*adv.* **wind'wards.**—*adj.* **wind'y**, like, characterised by, exposed to, the wind: moved, played, produced, by wind (*poet.*): controlling the winds (*poet.*): producing, or produced by, flatulence: suggestive of wind, as unsubstantial, changeable, boastful, conceited, wordy (*fig.*): frightened, nervous (*coll.*).—**wind'-bag**, the bellows of a bagpipe, or (*obs.*) organ: the lungs or chest (*facet.*): an inflated bag as a charm to procure a favourable wind: a person of mere words, an excessively talkative person (*slang*). —*adj.* **wind'-bound**, hindered from sailing by contrary wind.— **wind'-break**, a protection against the force of the wind, such as a fence or line of trees.—*adj.* **wind'-broken**, of a horse,

broken-winded.—**wind'burn**, inflammation of the skin due to over-exposure to the wind.—*adj.* **wind'-changing**, fickle.—**wind'-chart**, a chart showing the direction of the wind; **wind'-cheater**, a close-knitted pullover: an anorak; **wind'-chest**, the box or reservoir that supplies compressed air to the pipes or reeds of an organ; **wind'-cone** (*aero.*), a sleeve floating from the top of a mast, its angle with the ground giving a rough conception of the velocity of the wind, and its angle in a horizontal plane the wind direction; **wind'-drop'sy**, tympanites; **wind'-egg**, an addle-egg: one soft-shelled or imperfectly formed; **wind'fall**, fruit blown off a tree by the wind: any unexpected money or other advantage.—*adj.* **wind'fallen**, blown down by wind.—**wind'-flower**, an anemone, esp. the wood-anemone; **wind'-furnace**, any form of furnace using the natural draught of a chimney without aid of a bellows; **wind'-gall**, a puffy swelling about the fetlock joints of a horse; **wind'-gauge**, an instrument for measuring the velocity of the wind: a gauge for measuring pressure of wind in an organ: appliance fixed to a rifle by means of which the force of the wind is ascertained so that allowance may be made for it in sighting; **wind'-gun**, an air-gun; **wind'-hover** (*hov'*, *huv'ər*), the kestrel; **wind'-instrument**, a musical instrument sounded by means of wind, esp. by the breath; **wind'jammer**, a large sailing vessel: a wind-resisting golf blouse (*coll.*); **wind'mill**, a mill in which the motive-power is the wind acting on a set of vanes or sails: a wind-driven set of vanes used to pump water, etc.: any device which is caused to rotate by reason of its being carried through the air, and so develops power (*aero.*); **wind'pipe**, the passage for the breath between the mouth and lungs, the trachea.—*adj.* **wind'-rode** (*naut.*), riding at anchor with head to the wind.—**wind'rose**, a rosette-like diagram showing the relative frequency and strength of winds in a locality for given periods of the year; **wind'row**, a row of hay, etc., raked together to be made into cocks: a row of peats, etc., set up for drying.—*v.t.* to arrange in windrows.— **wind'-sail** (*naut.*), a wide funnel of canvas used to convey a stream of air below deck: a vane of a windmill; **wind'screen**, a shelter against wind, esp. a transparent screen on motor-cars, etc.— *adjs.* **wind'-shak'd, -shaken**, agitated by the wind. —**wind'shield** (*U.S.*), a windscreen; **wind'-side**, the side next the wind; **wind'-sleeve, -sock**, a wind-cone; **wind'-sucker**, (of a horse) a crib-biter.—*adjs.* **wind'swept**, exposed to, or swept by, the wind; **wind'-swift**, swift as the wind; **wind'-tight**, air-tight.—**wind'-tunnel** (*aero.*), an experimental apparatus for producing a uniform steady air-stream past a model for aerodynamic investigation work.—**a capful of wind**, a slight breeze; **before the wind**, carried along by the wind; **between wind and water**, that part of a ship's side which is now in, now out of, the water owing to the fluctuation of the waves: in a vulnerable or precarious place or position; **cast, or lay, an anchor to windward**, to make prudent provision for the future; **cast, fling, throw, to the winds**, to scatter, throw away, recklessly: to throw off all restraint, as of prudence, sense of decorum, etc; **down the wind**, moving with the wind: towards decay (*obs.*; *fig.*); **fight windmills**, to struggle with imaginary opposition, as Don Quixote tilted at the windmill; **get one's wind**, to recover one's breath; **get the wind of**, to get on the windward side of; **get to windward of**, to secure an advantage over; **get the wind up** (*slang*), to become nervous, apprehensive, agitated; **get wind of**, to get a hint or intimation of; **have the wind of**, to be on the trail of; **how the wind blows**, or **lies**, the state of the wind: the position of affairs; **in the wind**, astir, afoot; **in the wind's eye**, **in the teeth of the wind**, right against the wind; **like the wind**, rapidly; **on the windy side** (*Shak.*), on the windward side, from which one cannot be attacked, hence safe, at an advantage; **put the wind up** (*slang*), to make apprehensive or agitated; **raise the wind** (see **raise**); **sail close to the wind**, to keep the boat's head so near to the wind as to fill but not shake the sails: to be in danger of transgressing an approved limit; **second wind**, power of respiration recovered after breathlessness: the energy necessary for a renewal of effort (*fig.*); **sow the wind and reap the whirlwind**, to act wrongly and receive a crushing retribution; **take the wind out of one's sails** (*fig.*), to deprive one of an advantage, to frustrate, discomfit one. [O.E.; allied to O.N. *vindr*, Ger. *wind*, L. *ventus*.]

**wind**, *wīnd*, *v.t.* to turn, to twist, to coil: to encircle: to screw the mechanism of, as a timepiece: to make, direct, as one's way, or to traverse, by turning and twisting: to insinuate (*refl.*): to change the course of, deflect, control (*rare* or *obs.*): to turn to one's left, as a horse: to bring in, involve (*obs.*; also **wind up**), or to extricate, stealthily: to wind up (*arch.*; *fig.*; q.v.): to weave (*Spens.*): to wield (*obs.* and *dial.*): to haul or hoist, as by a winch.—*v.i.* to turn round something: to twist: to move, go, by turns and twists, or (*fig.*) deviously: to meander: to go (*obs.*): to writhe, wriggle (*obs.* and *dial.*): to extricate oneself (with *out*; *obs.*): to be twisted, warped (*dial.*): of a horse, to turn to the left:—*pr.p.* **wind'ing**; *pa.t.* and *pa.p.* **wound**, *wownd*; chiefly *naut.* **wind'ed**; Burns *pa.t.* **win't**.—*n.* a turn, coil, or twist: a turning: a twisted condition.—*n.* **wind'er**, one who winds: an instrument for winding: a clock or watch key: an electrically driven winding-engine for hoisting a cage or cages up a vertical mineshaft: a twisting plant.—*adj.* and *n.* **wind'ing.**—*adv.* **wind'ingly.**—**wind'ing-engine**, a machine for hoisting; **wind'ing-sheet**, a sheet for enwrapping a corpse: the dripping grease that clings to the side of a candle (*dial.*); **wind'ing-stair**, a stair constructed around a solid or hollow newel; **wind'ing-strips**, two pieces of wood with parallel edges, used for testing the parallelism of timber; **wind'-up**, the close, finish.—**turn the wind** (now *rare*), to go, move, or cause to move, from side to side or on a winding course (*lit.* and *fig.*); **wind a ship**, to turn her about end for end; **wind up**, to bring, or come, to a conclusion: to adjust for final settlement: to excite very much (esp. in *pa.p.* **wound up**, excited; *fig.*): to coil completely: to wind the spring or the mechanism of tightly: to furl (*obs.*): to tighten: to hoist, as by a winch: to restore to harmony (*Shak.*); **wind up and down** (*obs.*), to revolve in the mind. [O.E. *windan*; cf. Ger. *winden*, O.N. *vinda*, Goth. *windan*; cf. **wend, wander**.]

**windac.** See **windas**.

**windas**, *wind'as*, (*obs.*) *n.* a windlass: (*R. L. Stevenson*, **wind'ac**) an instrument for bending a cross-bow. [A.Fr. *windas*; cf. O.N. *vindāss*—*vinda*, to wind, *āss*, pole.]

**windlass**, *wind'las*, *n.* any of various modifications of the wheel and axle employing a revolving cylinder, used for hauling or hoisting: a windas for a cross-bow (*obs.*).—*v.i.* to use a windlass. —*v.t.* to hoist by means of such. [Prob. from **windas**.]

**windlass**, *wind'las*, (*obs.*) *n.* a circuitous movement, esp. to intercept game: an indirect, crafty action.—*v.i.* to take a roundabout course. [Prob. from *wanlace*, an earlier A.Fr. form, of unknown origin.]

**windle**, *win'dl*, *n.* an appliance for winding yarn. —(*Scot.*) **winn'le**. [**wind** (2).]

**windlestraw**, *win'dl-strō*, *n.* a thin, dry stalk of

grass: any of various long-stalked species of grass, as rye-grass: anything light or insubstantial: a lanky or feeble person.—Also (*Scot.*) **windlestrae** (*win'l-strā*). [O.E. *windelstrēaw*—*windel*, a woven basket, *strēaw*, straw.]

**window**, *win'dō*, *n.* an opening in the wall of a building, etc., for air and light: the frame in the opening: the space immediately behind the opening: a window-pane: any opening suggesting a window: (in *pl.*) the eyes, or (*Shak.*) the eyelids: strips of metallic foil which when scattered from aircraft derange radar reception: a closed outcrop of strata lying beneath a thrust plane and exposed by denudation (*geol.*).—*v.t.* to furnish with windows: to make rents in (*Shak.*).—*adjs.* **win'dowed**, having a window or windows, or openings or holes resembling these: placed in a window (Shak., *Ant.* IV, xii. 72); **win'dowless**, having no windows.—**win'dow-bar**, a wooden or iron bar between the panes of a window: a bar fitted into a window for security: (*Shak.* **window-barne**, emended *bars*, Timon IV, iii. 116) lattice-work across a woman's stomacher; **win'dow-blind**, a blind or screen for a window; **win'dow-bole** (see **bole**, 1); **win'dow-box**, a box for growing plants on a window-sill; **win'dow-curtain**, a curtain hung over a window, inside a room; **win'dow-dressing**, the arranging of goods in a shop window: the art of doing so effectively: (the art of) presenting a cause, situation, etc., in a favourable light; **window envelope**, an envelope with a transparent panel; **win'dow-frame**, a frame that surrounds a window; **win'dow-gardening**, the cultivation of plants indoors before a window, or in boxes fitted on the outside sill; **win'dow-glass**, glass suitable or used for windows; **win'dow-pane**, a sheet of glass set in a window; **win'dow-sash**, a frame in which panes of glass are set; **win'dow-screen**, any ornamental device for filling the opening of a window; **win'dow-seat**, a seat in the recess of a window; **window-shopping**, gazing in shop windows rather than making actual purchases; **win'dow-sill**, the sill of a window opening; **win'dow-tax**, a tax levied on windows of houses (repealed 1851). [M.E. *windowe*, *windoge*—O.N. *vindauga*—*vindr*, wind, *auga*, eye.]

**windring**, *wind'ring*, *adj.* (Shak., *Temp.* IV, i. 128) perh. for **winding** or **wandering**.

**Windsor**, *win'zər*, *adj.* pertaining to *Windsor*, in Berkshire, as in **Wind'sor-chair**, a kind of strong, plain, polished chair, made entirely of wood; **Wind'sor-soap**, a kind of perfumed toilet-soap (usu. brown).

**wine**, *wīn*, *n.* the fermented juice of grapes: a liquor made from other fruits: intoxication (*fig.*): a wine-drinking, a wine-party: a rich red colour.—Also *adj.*—*v.t.* to supply with wine: to treat with wine.—*v.i.* to take wine, especially at a wine-party.—*adj.* **win(e)'y**, like wine: intoxicated.—*n.* **wino** (*wī'nō*), an alcoholic addicted to wine.—**wine'-bag**, a wine-skin: a tippler; **wine'-berry**, a grape (*obs.*): a red currant, a gooseberry, or a bilberry (*dial.*): a raspberry (*Rubus phoenicolasius*) of China and Japan: the tutu, or another New Zealand tree, the makomako; **wine'-bibber**, a continual drinker of wine: a drunkard; **wine'-bibbing**; **wine'-biscuit**, a biscuit orig. intended to be served with wine; **wine'-cask**, a cask for holding wine; **wine'-cellar**, a cellar for storing wine.—*adj.* **wine'-coloured**, of the colour of red wine.—**wine'-cooler**, a receptacle for cooling wine in bottles about to be served at table; **wine'-glass**, a small glass used in drinking wine; **wine'-glassful**; **wine'-grower**, one who cultivates a vineyard and makes wine.—*n.* and *adj.* **wine'-growing**.—**wine'-meas'ure**, an old English liquid measure, its gallon 5/6ths of the gallon in beer-measure; **wine'-merchant**, a dealer in wine, esp. wholesale; **wine'-palm**, any palm yielding palm-wine (as Borassus, Raphia); **wine'-party**, a drinking-party; **wine'-press**, a machine in which grapes are pressed in the manufacture of wine; **wine'-sap**, a variety of deep-red winter apple; **wine'-skin**, a bag for holding wine, made out of a skin; **wine'-stone**, crude argol; **wine'-taster**, one whose business it is to sample wines; **wine'-vat**, **-fat**, a vat in which grapes are pressed in wine-making; **wine'-vault(s)**, a vaulted wine-cellar: a place where wine is tasted or drunk.—**Adam's wine**, water; **red wine** (see **red**); **Rhine, Rhenish, wine**, wine produced on the banks of the *Rhine*, esp. hock; **spirit of wine**, alcohol; **white wine** (see **white**). [O.E. *win*; Goth. *wein*, Ger. *wein*; all from L. *vinum*; cog. with Gr. *oinos*.]

**wing**, *wing*, *n.* the organ of a bird, insect, or other creature, by which it flies: an animal organ resembling a wing: flight: means of flying: anything resembling a wing: a fan or vane: (usu. in *pl.*) a sail: any side-piece, on a building, etc.: the side of a stage: side scenery: a plane of an aeroplane: the mudguard of a motor vehicle: a similar part of a carriage: a side-piece on the back of an armchair: one of the longer sides of crown-works or horn-works in fortification: the flank corps or division of an army on either side: the ships on either extremity of a fleet ranged in line: a section of a political party: (a player on) either extreme of the forward line in football, etc.: a group of three squadrons in the Royal Air Force: (in *pl.*) a qualified pilot's badge: formerly, the badge of any member of an air-crew other than the pilot: a flock (of plover): means or power of rapid movement (*fig.*): protection (*fig.*).—*v.t.* to furnish, or transport, with wings: to lend speed to: to supply with side-pieces: to bear in flight, to waft: to effect on wings: to traverse by flying: to wound in the wing: to wound in arm or shoulder.—*v.i.* to soar on the wing: to go with speed.—*adj.* **winged** (*wingd* or *wing'id*), furnished with wings: (*wingd*) of a stem, bearing the thin flattened bases of decurrent leaves, of a fruit or seed, having a flattened appendage: (*wingd*) wounded in the wing, shoulder, or arm: swift: lofty, sublime (as **winged words**—Homer *epea pteroenta*): full of flying birds (*Milt.*).—*adv.* **wing'edly**, on or by wings.—*n.* **wing'er**, one who plays in a position on the wing.—*adj.* **wing'less**, without wings.—*n.* **wing'let**, a small wing: a bastard wing: a wing-like appendage.—*adj.* **wing'y**, having, resembling, or soaring on, wings: lofty.—*adv.* **wing'-and-wing'**, in the condition of a ship sailing before the wind with the foresail at one side and the mainsail at the other.—**wing'-case**, the horny case or cover over the wings of some insects, as the beetle; **wing'-commander**, a Royal Air Force officer corresponding in rank to a naval commander or to a lieutenant-colonel; **winged bull**, a common form in Assyrian sculpture, symbolic of domination.—*adjs.* **wing'-footed**, having wings on the feet: aliped; **wing'-led** (Shak., *Cymb.* II, iv. 24, some editions), presumably, led in wings or divisions. —**wing'-loading** (*aero.*), the maximum flying weight of an aeroplane divided by the total area of the main planes, including the ailerons; **wing'-sheath**, a wing-case; **wing'-shell**, a strombus: a mollusc of genus Malleus, or allied genus, or its shell: a wing-snail; **wing'-shoot'ing**, the act or practice of shooting flying birds; **wing'-shot**, a shot at a bird on the wing: one who shoots flying birds.—*adj.* shot in the wing, or while on the wing.—**wing'-snail**, a pteropod; **wing'-spread**, the distance from tip to tip of extended wings.— **birds of one wing** (*obs.*), birds of the same kind; **flying-wing** (see **fly**); **in the wings** (*coll.*), waiting in reserve; **lend wings to**, to give speed to; **make, take, wing**, to begin flight: to depart; **on, upon,**

**the wing**, flying: in motion: departing; **on the wings of the wind**, with the highest speed; **under one's wing**, under one's protection. [O.N. *vængr*, a wing.]

**wing**. See **win** (3).

**winge**, *winj*, (*dial.*) non-Scottish variant of **whinge**.

**wink**, *wingk*, *v.i.* to move the eyelids, or an eyelid, quickly: to give a hint, or convey amused understanding, by a sign of this kind: to shut the eyes (*obs.*): to blink: to seem not to see: to connive (usu. with *at*): to flicker, twinkle.—*v.t.* to close and open quickly: to flicker: to express by flash-lights.—*n.* act of winking: a hint, as by winking: a blink: a closing of the eyes for sleep: a short spell of sleep: a very small time or distance.—*ns.* **wink'er**, one who winks: a horse's blinker (usu. in *pl.*): an eye (*dial.*): nictitating membrane of a bird's eye: a small bellows in an organ, regulated by a spring, controlling variations of wind-pressure: (in *pl.*) direction indicators on a motor vehicle, consisting of flashing lights (*coll.*): **wink'ing**, act of giving a wink.—*adj.* (Shak.) closed, or with eyes shut, or blind.—*adv.* **wink'ingly**.— **wink'-a-peep** (*dial.*), the scarlet pimpernel.—**easy as winking**, very easily indeed; **forty winks** (*coll.*), a short nap; **like winking** (*slang*), very rapidly; **tip one the wink** (see **tip**). [O.E. *wincian*; Ger. *winken*.]

**winkle**, *wing'kl*. Same as **periwinkle** (2).—**winkle-pickers**, shoes with long pointed toes, esp. popular in the early 1960s.—**winkle out** (*fig.*), to force out gradually and with difficulty (perh. derived from Ger. *winkel*, corner).

**winna**, *win'ə*, *wun'ə*, a Scots form of **will not**.

**winner, winning, winningly.** See **win** (1 and 2).

**winnle.** See **windle**.

**winnock**, *win'ək*, **win'dock**, (*Scot.*) *n.* a window. [Scot. development of M.E. *windoge*; see **window**; cf. **warlock**.]

**winnow**, *win'ō*, *v.t.* to separate the chaff from by wind: to fan: to sift: to separate: to blow upon: to waft: to diffuse: to set in motion (*Milt.*): to flap, flutter (*rare*).—*v.i.* to separate chaff from grain: to fly: to blow in gusts.—*n.* a fan for winnowing.—*adj.* **winn'owed** (Shak., *Ham.* V, ii. 201) perh. wise.—*ns.* **winn'ower**; **winn'owing**.— **winn'owing-fan, -machine**, a fan, machine, for winnowing. [O.E. *windwian*, to winnow—*wind*; see **wind** (1).]

**winsey.** Same as **wincey.**

**winsome**, *win'səm*, *adj.* cheerful: pleasant: attractive.—*adv.* **win'somely**.—*n.* **win'someness**. [O.E. *wynsum*, pleasant—*wyn*, joy (Ger. *wonne*)—and *-sum* (see suff. *-some*).]

**winter**, *win'tər*, *n.* the cold season of the year—in northern temperate regions, from November or December to January or February: astronomically, from the winter solstice to the vernal equinox: a year (usu. in *pl.*): any season of cheerlessness.—*adj.* wintry: suitable for wear or use in winter: sown in autumn, as **win'ter-wheat, -barley, win'ter-crop**, etc.—*v.i.* to pass the winter.—*v.t.* to feed and keep through winter.— *adj.* **win'tered**, having seen many winters, aged (*obs.*): exposed to winter: worn in winter (Shak.).—*v.t.* **win'terise, -ize**, to make suitable for use under wintry conditions.—*adj.* **win'terly**, cheerless.—*n.* **win'triness**.—*adj.* **win'try, win'tery**, resembling, or suitable to, winter: stormy: cheerless.—**win'ter-aconite** (see **aconite**); **win'ter-apple**, an apple that keeps well in winter, or that does not ripen till winter.—*adj.* **win'ter-beaten** (*Spens.*), beaten or injured by the cold of winter. —**win'ter-berry**, a name given to several shrubs of the genus Ilex, growing in the eastern parts of N. America; **win'ter-bloom**, the witch-hazel: a species of azalea; **win'ter-bourne**, an intermittent spring of water, as found in the chalk-districts;

---

Neutral vowels in unaccented syllables: *el'ə-mənt*; for certain sounds in foreign words, see p. viii

win'ter-bud, a bud protected by scales in which next year's shoot passes the winter; win'ter-cherry, any species of Physalis, esp. *Physalis alkekengi*: its edible fruit: the balloon-vine, or its fruit.—*adj.* win'ter-clad, warmly clad.—win'ter-clover, the partridge-berry; win'ter-cress, a cruciferous plant (Barbarea) formerly cultivated for winter salad; win'ter-garden, an ornamental garden of evergreens, etc., or a conservatory with flowers, for winter; win'tergreen, a plant of genus Pyrola, also of Chimaphila: a plant of genus Gaultheria, whose oil is an aromatic stimulant, used in flavouring confectionery and in medicine (chickweed-win'tergreen, either of two plants—*Trientalis europaea* or *Trientalis americana*—belonging to the Primulaceae, having white starlike flowers).—*v.t.* win'ter-ground (Shak., *Cymbeline* IV, ii. 229), assumed by Steevens to mean 'to protect, as a plant, from the inclemency of winter'.—win'ter-quarters, the quarters of an army during winter: a winter residence; win'ter-tide (*arch.*), winter; winter sports, open-air sports practised on snow and ice, as skiing, etc.—*adj.* win'ter-weight, of clothes, heavy enough or thick enough to be suitable for cold weather. [O.E.; cf. O.N. *vetr*, Ger. *winter*; from Indo-Gmc. root seen in wet, water.]

winter's-bark, *win'tərz-bärk*, *n.* a stimulant, aromatic, and tonic bark, named from Captain *Winter*, who first brought it from the Strait of Magellan in 1579.

wintle, *win'tl*, (*Scot.*) *v.i.* to stagger.—*n.* a stagger. [Flem. *windtelen—winden*, to wind.]

winy. See wine.

winze, *winz*, (*Scot.*) *n.* a curse. [Flem. *wensch*; from root of wish.]

winze, *winz*, *n.* in mining, a small ventilating shaft between two levels.—Also winds. [Perh. wind (2).]

wipe, *wip*, *v.t.* to clean or dry by rubbing: to clear away (with *away*, *off*, *out*, *up*): to obliterate, annihilate, or abolish (with *out*): to draw across something in order to, or as if to, clean it: to apply solder to with a piece of cloth or leather: to strike (*coll.*).—*n.* act of cleaning by rubbing: a blow: a brand, a scar (Shak., *Lucr.* 537): a handkerchief (*slang*).—*ns.* wi'per, one who wipes, esp. one who is employed in cleaning in certain industrial jobs: that which wipes or is used for wiping: a moving arm or other conducting device for making a selected contact out of a number of possible connections (*elect.*): a moving arm, usu. electrically operated, for removing raindrops, etc., from the windscreen of a motor vehicle; wi'ping, act of one who wipes: a thrashing. [O.E. *wipian*; O.H.G. *wifan*, to wind round, *waif*, bandage, Goth. *weipan*, to crown.]

wire, *wir*, *n.* a thread or rope of metal: a piece of wire, or (in *pl.*) a group or network of wires, used for some purpose: the metal thread used in telegraphy, etc.: a metallic string of a musical instrument: a metal knitting-needle (*Scot.*): a telegram (*coll.*): a clever pickpocket (*slang*): a lash, made of wire (*Shak.*).—*adj.* formed of, pertaining to, or using, wire: running on wire: pertaining to wire-drawing.—*v.t.* to bind, support, protect, snare, or furnish, with wire: to supply, as a building, with wires necessary for carrying an electric current: to send, or to inform, by telegraph: to place (a croquet-ball) where a hoop hampers it.—*v.i.* to telegraph.—*adjs.* wired; wire'less, without a wire or wires: of or pertaining to telegraphy or telephony without wires.—*n.* wireless telegraphy or telephony, radio: a receiving or transmitting set used for this purpose: a message or broadcast so transmitted: broadcast programmes: broadcasting generally.—*v.t.* and *v.i.* to communicate by radio.—*n.* wi'rer, one who wires, or who uses

wire, e.g. to snare animals.—*adv.* wi'rily.—*ns.* wi'riness; wir'ing, the action of the verb: the complex of wires in an electrical system or installation.—*adj.* wi'ry, made of, or like, wire: flexible and strong: of a person, strong and able to endure.—wire'-bridge, a suspension-bridge; wire'-dancer, a performer on a tight wire; wire'-dancing; wired'-glass, glass in which a wire mesh has been incorporated during rolling as a resistance against fire and explosion blast.—*v.t.* wire'-draw, to draw into wire by pulling through successively smaller holes in a hard steel die-block: to throttle a fluid by passing it through a small orifice, thus reducing the pressure: to draw or spin out to a great length: to strain the meaning of.—wire'drawer; wire'drawing.—*adj.* wire'drawn (*fig.*), spun out into needless fine distinctions.—wired wireless, the transmission of signals by means of electromagnetic waves guided by conductors, the frequencies being of the same order as those used for radio communication; wire gauge, any system for designating the diameter of wires by means of a set of numbers: the diameter of a particular piece of wire; wire'-gauze, a kind of stiff close fabric made of fine wire; wire'-grass, a kind of fine meadow-grass (*Poa compressa*): any of various other grasses with wiry stems; wire'-guard, wire-netting placed in front of a fire; wire'-hair, a wire-haired terrier.—*adj.* wire'-haired, having a coat of rather rough, hard hair.—wire'-heel, in horses and cattle, a defect or disease of the foot; wireless station, a station for wireless transmission; wireless telegraphy, telephony, signalling through space, without the use of conducting wires between transmitter and receiver, by means of electromagnetic waves generated by high-frequency alternating currents; wire'-line, one of the close-set white lines in laid paper, perpendicular to the water-lines; wire'-man, one who puts up or who takes care of wires; wire'-nett'ing, a texture of galvanised wire woven in the form of a net; wire'-photo, a photograph sent over a wire circuit by electrical means; wire'-puller, one who exercises an influence felt but not seen: an intriguer; wire'-pulling; wire'-rope, a rope of twisted wire.—*adjs.* wire'-sewed, -stitched, sewed with wire instead of thread; wire'-walker, a wire-dancer; wire'-way, transportation by means of wires; wire wool, a mass of very fine wire for scouring; wire'work, the making of wire, or of objects of wire: articles, or fabric, made of wire; wire'worker; wire'working; wire'-worm, a name given to the larvae of click-beetles, from their slenderness and uncommon hardness.—*adj.* wire'wove, denoting a fine quality of writing-paper (see wove).—give (some-one) the wire (chiefly *mil.*), to give advance information; pull the wires (see wire-puller above); wire away, or in, to act or work with vigour; wire-haired terrier, a type of wire-haired fox-terrier; wire into, to eat vigorously and assiduously. [O.E. *wir*; O.N. *virr* (in composition).]

wis, *wis*, also wist, *Shak.* wish (all *sham arch.*), *v.t.* to know: to believe. [Partly from misunderstanding of the adv. iwis (q.v.) as *I wis*, partly a new present from the pa.t. wist (see wit (1).]

wisard, *wiz'ərd*, *n.* Same as wizard.

wise, *wiz*, *adj.* having knowledge: learned: able to make good use of knowledge: judging rightly: discreet: skilful: dictated by wisdom: containing wisdom: pious, godly: skilled in magic (*dial.*): normal mentally (*dial.*).—*n.* wisdom (*wiz'dəm*), quality of being wise: judgment: ability to make right use of knowledge: a wise course or saying: learning (*hist.*): skilfulness, speculation, spiritual perception (*B.*): sanity (*Shak.*): (*cap.*) the apocryphal Book of the Wisdom of Solomon: Jesus Christ.—*n.* wise'ling, one who pretends to be wise.—*adv.* wise'ly.—*n.* wise'ness.—wis'dom-literature, the book of Job, Proverbs, Ecclesiastes, Wisdom of Solomon, Ecclesiasticus, and the Epistle of James; wis'dom-tooth, any of four double back teeth cut after childhood, usually from the late teens; wise'crack, a lively, pungent retort or comment. —*v.i.* to make such.—*adj.* wise'cracking, making, or addicted to making, wisecracks.—wise guy, a conceited, over-confident person.—*adjs.* wise'-heart'ed, having wisdom: prudent: wise'-like (*Scot.*; *wis*-), sensible, judicious: decent: fitting: looking as if capable of playing one's part well.—wise woman, a witch: a midwife (*Scot.*).—never, none, the wiser, still in ignorance; put one wise (*slang*), to put one in possession of information, make aware; wised up (*slang*), made aware, being in possession of information; wise to (*slang*), aware of. [O.E. *wis*; Ger. *weise*; from root of wit.]

wise, weise, weize, wiz, (*Scot.*) *v.t.* to guide in certain direction. [O.E. *wisian*—*wis*; wise (1).]

wise, wiz, (*arch.*) *n.* way, manner, now chiefly in the phrases in any wise, in no wise, in any way, in no way, on this wise, in this way, and as a *suff.*, meaning in the manner of, e.g. likewise, otherwise, or (*coll.*) in the matter of, e.g. money-wise, business-wise. [O.E. *wise*; Ger. *weise*; akin to wise (1) and wit. Doublet guise.]

wiseacre, wiz'ā-kər, *n.* one who unduly assumes an air of superior wisdom: a simpleton quite unconscious of being such. [M.Du. *wijssegger*—O.H.G. *wizago*, a prophet.]

wish, wish, *v.i.* to have a desire: to long: to be inclined: to express a desire, esp. as part of a superstitious ritual.—*v.t.* to desire or long for: to express a desire for: to ask: to invoke: to bid: to recommend (*obs.*): to foist, palm off (with *on, on to*; *coll.*): to bewitch (*dial.*): to greet, wish (someone) well (*S.Afr.*).—*n.* desire, longing: a thing desired: an expression of desire: (usu. in *pl.*) an expression of desire for good fortune for another: a malediction (*obs.*). —*n.* wish'er.—*adj.* wish'ful, having a wish or desire: eager: desirable, desired (*obs.*).—*adv.* wish'fully.—*n.* wish'fulness.—*n.* and *adj.* wish'ing. —wish fulfilment (*psych.*), the satisfaction of a desire in dreams, day-dreams, etc.; wishful thinking (*psych.*), a type of thinking in which the individual substitutes the phantasy of the fulfilment of the wish for the actual achievement: a belief that a particular thing will happen, or is so, engendered by desire that it should happen, or be so: loosely, thinking about and wishing for an event or turn of fortune that may not take place; wish'ing-bone, wish'-bone, the merrythought; wish'ing-cap, a cap by wearing which one obtains everything one wishes; wish'ing-stone, -tree, -well, etc., a stone, tree, well, etc., supposed to have the power of making a wish expressed at it come true.—wish one further (*slang*), to wish one was in some other place, not present; wish one joy of, to hope possession of may be a benefit to one (usu. *iron.*). [O.E. *wȳscan*, wish; Ger. *wünschen*, Sw. *önska*.]

wishtonwish, wish'tən-wish, *n.* the N. American prairie-dog: the whippoorwill (*Fenimore Cooper*). [Amer. Ind.]

wish-wash, wish'-wosh, (*coll.*) *n.* anything wishywashy.—*adj.* wish'y-wash'y, thin and weak: diluted: feeble: of poor quality. [Formed from wash.]

wisket, wis'kit, (*dial.*) *n.* a basket. [Scand., from same root as whisk (1).]

wisp, wisp, *n.* a small bundle of straw or hay: a tuft, a shred: a thin strand or band: a small broom: a twisted bunch used as a torch: the Will-o'-the-wisp: a flock (of snipe).—*v.t.* to make into a wisp or bundle: to rub down with a wisp.—*adj.* wis'py. [Origin uncertain.]

wist, wist, (*sham arch.*) *v.t.* and *v.i.* to know. [See wis, iwis, wit (1).]

Wistaria, wis-tā'ri-ə, *n.* a genus of papilionaceous plants, some of the species among the most magnificent ornamental climbers known in English gardens, named from the American anatomist Caspar *Wistar* (1761-1818).—Also, wrongly, Wistē'ria (so spelt by Thomas Nuttall, who named it).

wistful, wist'fŏŏl, -fl, *adj.* intent (*obs.*): earnest (*obs.*): longing: yearning with little hope: pensive.—*adv.* wist'fully.—*n.* wist'fulness. [Most prob. for wistly.]

wistiti, wis'ti-ti, *n.* a marmoset. [Fr. *ouistiti*; named from its cry.]

wistly, wist'li, (*Shak.*) *adv.* longingly, earnestly. [Prob. for whistly; see whist (1).]

wit, wit, *v.t.* and *v.i.* (*arch.* except in legal use) to know: to be aware (with *of*): to recognise, discern: to know how:—*infin.* wit, *Spens.*, *Shak.* and others weet(e), wēt; *Spens.* weet'en, also wot, *wot*; *pr.t. 1st pers. sing.* wot, *Scot.* wat, wŏt, wite, wyte, *wit*; *2nd* wost (wott'est); *3rd* wot (wots, wott'eth), *Scot.* wate, wait, wats; *pl. 1st, 2nd, 3rd,* wot; *pa.t.* wist (wott'ed); *pr.p.* witt'ing, weet'ing (wott'ing); *pa.p.* wist.—*n.* witt'ing (*obs.* and *dial.*), knowledge: information. —*adj.* cognisant: conscious: deliberate.—*adv.* witt'ingly, knowingly: by design.—to do wit, to cause to know; to wit, that is to say, namely—the O.E. gerund *tō witanne*. [O.E. *witan*, to know (pres. tense *wāt, wāst, wāt,* pl. *witon*); pa.t. *wiste*, or *wisse,* pl. *wiston,* pa.p. *wist*); Goth. *witan,* to observe, Ger. *wissen*; cf. L. *vidēre,* to see; Gr. *idein*.]

wit, wit, *n.* the mind (*obs.*): the understanding (*arch.*): imagination or invention (*arch.*): ingenuity: intelligence, sense (in phrase have the wit to): a mental faculty (chiefly in *pl.*): the power of combining ideas with a pointed verbal effect: the product of this power: a person endowed with wit: information (*obs.*; in phrase to get wit of).—*adj.* wit'less, lacking wit, wisdom, sense: without intellectual faculties (*obs.*): out of one's mind: stupid, unintelligent: unaware, unconscious.—*adv.* wit'lessly.—*ns.* wit'lessness; wit'ling, one who has little wit: a pretender to wit.—*adj.* witt'ed, having wit or understanding (usu. in composition, as quick-witted).—*n.* witticism (wit'i-sizm), a witty remark: a sentence or phrase affectedly witty: (formerly) a jibe.—*adv.* witt'ily.—*n.* witt'iness.—*adj.* witt'y, possessed of wit: amusing, droll: sarcastic: ingenious (*B.*): wise, discreet, sensible (*obs.*).—wit'-cracker, one who makes witty remarks in a crisp style; wit'-monger, a poor would-be wit; wit'-snapper (*Shak.*), one who affects wit or repartee.—*v.t.* wit'wanton, (with *it; obs.*) to indulge in irreverent wit.—at one's wits' end, utterly perplexed; have one's wits about one, to be alert and resourceful; live by one's wits, to gain a livelihood by ingenious expedients rather than by honest labour; the five wits, the five senses. [O.E. (*ge*)*wit*—wit (1).]

witan, wit'an, *n.pl.* members of the witenagemot: the witenagemot.—*n.* witenagemot (wit'ən-ə-gə-mōt'; popularly -*nag*'), the supreme council of England in Anglo-Saxon times, composed of the bishops, the ealdormen of shires, and a number of the king's friends and dependents. [Pl. of O.E. *wita,* a man of knowledge (*witena,* gen. pl.); *gemōt,* meeting; see preceding words.]

witch, wich, *n.* a woman regarded as having supernatural or magical power and knowledge usu. through compact with the devil or a minor evil spirit: a hag, crone: a fascinating woman (*coll.*): a wizard (now *rare*): the craig-fluke: a curve whose equation is $x^2y = 4a^2(2a - y)$.—*v.t.* to bewitch: to effect, change, transport, etc., by means of witchcraft: to fascinate.—*v.i.* to practise witchcraft or fascination.—*ns.* **witch′ery**, witchcraft: fascination; **witch′ing**, sorcery: enchantment.—*adj.* suited to witchcraft: weird: fascinating.—*adv.* **witch′ingly**.—**witch′craft**, the craft or practice of witches: the black art, sorcery: supernatural power; **witch′-doctor**, among Kaffirs, etc., a magician who detects witches and counteracts evil magical influences: one who professes to heal by means of magic; **witch′es′-broom**, a dense tuft of poorly developed branches formed on a woody plant attacked by a parasite (chiefly fungi and mites); **witch′es′-butter**, nostoc and other gelatinous blue-green algae; **witch′es′-meat**, tremella; **witches′ Sabbath** (see **Sabbath**); **witch′es′-thimble**, a name for various plants with thimble-like flowers, as the foxglove; **witch′-finder**, one whose business was to detect witches: a witch-doctor; **witch hunt** (orig. *U.S.*), the searching out of political opponents for exposure on grounds of alleged disloyalty to the state, etc.: also applied to any similar non-political search; **witch′-knot**, one, esp. in the hair, supposed to be tied by means of witchcraft; **witch′-meal**, the inflammable pollen of the club-moss.—*adj.* **witch′-ridden**, ridden by witches.—**witch′-wife** (*Scot.*), a woman who practises witchcraft. [M.E. *wicche* (both masc. and fem.)—O.E. *wicca* (masc.), *wicce* (fem.), wizard, witch, and verb *wiccian*; ety. dub.]

**witch**, *wich*, *n.* any of several trees with pliant branches, as the wych-elm, the rowan, etc.—*n.* **witch′en**, the mountain ash, the wych-elm.—**witch′-alder**, any of a genus of N. American shrubs related to the witch-hazel—not an alder; **witch′-elm**, the wych-elm; **witch′-hazel**, any of a number of trees, as the wych-elm, the hornbeam, or a N. American shrub (*Hamamelis virginica*) from whose bark is made a supposed remedy for bruises, etc.—a distillate of the bark dissolved in alcohol. [O.E. *wice*; allied to *wican*, to give way.]

**witchetty**, *wich′i-ti*, *n.* edible grubs of species of longicorn beetles. [Austr. native name.]

**wite, wyte**, *wīt*, *v.t.* (*obs.* or *Scot.*) to blame: to lay the blame on.—*n.* (now *dial.*) blame, reproach.—*adj.* **wite′less** (now *dial.*), blameless. [O.E. *wītan*, to see, blame; allied to **wit**.]

**wite.** See **wit** (1).

**witenagemot.** See **witan**.

**with**, *n.* Same as **withe**.

**with**, *widh*, *with*, *prep.* denoting nearness, agreement, or connection: by, beside: among: on the side of: in the company of: in the possession or care of: containing: supplemented by: possessing: characterised by: in the same direction as: at the time of: at the same time as: immediately after: in competition or contest against: in respect of, in the regard of: by means of, through: using: from (as in *to part with*).—*adv.* **withal** (*widh-öl′*), with all or the rest: besides: therewith: thereupon: nevertheless, for all that.—*prep.* an emphatic form of *with*, used after its object.—**feel, or be, or think, with**, to feel as, or be of the same opinion as, the other person specified; **in with** (*coll.*), friendly with; **with it** (*slang*), following current trends in popular taste; **with that**, thereupon. [O.E. *with*, against; O.N. *vith*, Ger. *wider*. It ousted the O.E. *mid*, with (Ger. *mit*).]

**withdraw**, *widh-drö′*, or *with*—, *v.t.* to draw back or away: to take back or away: to take from deposit or investment, as money: to remove (with *from*): to deflect, turn aside (*rare*): to recall, retract, unsay.—*v.i.* to retire: to go away: to take back what one has said, or to recall a motion one has proposed:—*pa.t.* **withdrew** (*-drōō′*); *pa.p.* **withdrawn′**.—*ns.* **withdraw′al**, (*rare*) **withdraw′ment**; **withdraw′er**.—*adj.* **withdrawn′**, (of place) secluded: remote: (of

manner) detached.—**withdraw′ing-room**, a room used to retire into: a drawing-room. [Pfx. *with-*, against, back, and **draw**.]

**withe**, *widh*, *with*, or *widh*, *n.* a flexible twig, esp. o willow: a band of twisted twigs: a halter (*obs.*): an elastic handle to a tool to save the hand from the shock of blows: a boom-iron.—*v.t.* to bind with a withe or withes: to take with a noose of withes.—*adj.* **with′y**, made of withes: like withes, flexible: wiry and agile. [O.E. *withthe*; O.N. *vīthir*, Ger. *weide*, willow; cf. **withy**.]

**wither**, *widh′ər*, *v.i.* to fade or become dry: to lose freshness: to languish, decline: to decay, waste.—*v.t.* to cause to dry up, fade, or decay: to blight (*fig.*): to cause to feel very unimportant or despicable: to dry, as tea.—*adj.* **with′ered**.—*ns.* **with′eredness**; **with′ering**.—*adj.* **with′ering**, fading, becoming dry, etc., or causing to do so: used for drying or curing: blasting, blighting, scorching (*fig.*): snubbing.—*adv.* **with′eringly**.—**with′ering-floor**, the drying-floor of a malthouse. [M.E. *wederen*, to expose to weather.]

**witherite**, *widh′ər-īt*, *n.* the chief source of barium compounds—barium carbonate, occurring as orthorhombic crystals in pseudohexagonal pyramids. [Dr W. *Wither*ing, who first discriminated it from barytes, 1784.]

**withers**, *widh′ərz*, *n.pl.* the ridge between the shoulder-bones of a horse.—*adj.* **with′er-wrung**, injured in the withers.—**one's withers are wrung**, one is wounded by a snub, etc. [O.E. *wither*, against, an extension of *with*, against.]

**withershins**, *widh′*, *wid′ər-shinz*, (*Scot.*) *adv.* in the contrary direction, contrary to the course of the sun: in the wrong way—opp. to *deasil*. [L.G. *weddersins*; cf. O.E. *wither*, against, L.G. *sind*, direction, O.E. *sith*, journey.]

**withhault.** Pseudo-archaic *pa.t.* of **withhold**.

**withhold**, *widh-hōld′*, or *with*—, *v.t.* to hold back, restrain: to keep back: to refuse to give: to keep in bondage or custody (*obs.*).—*v.i.* to refrain (with *from* or infin.; *obs.*): to postpone (*Pope*):—*pa.t.* and *pa.p.* **withheld′** (*arch.* *pa.p.* **withhold′en**).—*ns.* **withhold′er**; **withhold′ment**. [Pfx. *with-*, against, and **hold**.]

**within**, *widh-in′*, *prep.* in or to the inner part of (*arch.*): inside: in the limits of: not going beyond: on the inner side of (*obs.*): entered from: into.—*adv.* in the inner part: inwardly: in the mind, soul, heart: behind the scenes: at home (*arch.*): indoors: in or to an inner room (*arch.*): herein.—**within land** (*obs.*), inland; **within reach**, in a position from which it can be obtained, or attained, without much difficulty, effort, or loss of time. [O.E. *withinnan*—*with*, against, with, *innan*, in.]

**without**, *widh-owt′*, *prep.* outside, or out of (*arch.*): outside the limits of (*arch.*): beyond (*arch.*): not with: in absence of: not having: not using: with no help from: free from.—*adv.* on the outside: outwardly: outside, not members of, a particular group or society: out of doors (*arch.*).—*conj.* (*arch.* or *dial.*) unless, except.—*adj.* **without′-door** (*Shak.*), outward.—*prep.* **without′en** (*arch.*), without.—**from without**, from the outside; **without distinction**, indiscriminately; **without doors**, out of doors: outside the family, nation, etc.: outside Parliament. [O.E. *withūtan*—*with*, against, *ūtan*, outside.]

**withstand**, *widh-stand′*, or *with*—, *v.t.* to stand, maintain one's position, against: to oppose or resist: to hinder (*obs.*):—*pa.t.* and *pa.p.* **withstood′**.—*n.* **withstand′er**. [O.E. *withstandan*—*with*, against; see **stand**.]

**withwind**, *with′wind*, **withywind**, *widh′i-wind*, (*dial.*) *ns.* bindweed, or other climbing plant. [O.E. *withewinde*; cf. **withy**, and **wind** (2).]

**withy**, *widh′i*, *n.* the osier willow: any willow: a flexible twig or branch, esp. one used for binding. [O.E. *withig*, willow; cf. **widdy**, **withe**.]

*fāte, fär; mē, hûr* (her); *mīne; mōte, för; mūte; mōōn, fŏōt; dhen* (then)

**witloof**, *wit'lōf*, *n.* a kind of chicory with large leaves. [Du., lit. white leaves.]

**witness**, *wit'nis*, *n.* knowledge brought in proof: testimony of a fact: that which furnishes proof: one who sees or has personal knowledge of a thing: one who gives evidence: one who or that which attests.—*v.t.* to have direct knowledge of: loosely, to see: to be the scene of: to give testimony to: to attest: to act as legal witness of: to sign: to show: to evince (*arch.*).—*v.i.* to give evidence.—*n.* wit'nesser.—wit'ness-box, the enclosure in which a witness stands when giving evidence in a court of law.—witness, let (such and such) serve as evidence; with a witness (*Shak.*), with a vengeance. [O.E. (*ge*)*witnes*—(*ge*)*wit*; see wit (2).]

**witting**, witty, etc.  See wit (1 and 2).

**wittol**, *wit'əl*, *n.* one who knows his wife's faithlessness, and submits to it.—*adj.* witt'olly (*Shak.*), like a wittol or contented cuckold. [M.E. *wetewold*; associated with cuckold (q.v.), and perh. from witwall, or from wit (1).]

**witwall**, *wit'wöl*, (*dial.*) *n.* the green woodpecker, or the greater spotted woodpecker. [Cf. Ger. *wittewal*, *wiedewall*.]

**wive**, *wiv*, *v.t.* to take for a wife: to provide with a wife: to become the wife of.—*v.i.* to marry a wife.—*n.* wive'hood (*Spens.*), wifehood. [O.E. *wifian*—*wif*, wife.]

**wivern**, *wi'vərn*, (*her.*) *n.* a fictitious monster, winged and two-legged, allied to the dragon and the griffin. [O.N.Fr. *wivre*, a viper—L. *vipera*.]

**wives**, *wivz*, *pl.* of wife.

**wizard**, *wiz'ərd*, *n.* one, usu. a man, who practises witchcraft or magic: one who works wonders: a wise man (*obs.*).—*adj.* with magical powers: wonderful, delightful (*slang*).—*adv.* wiz'ardly, like a wizard.—*n.* wiz'ardry, sorcery. [M.E. *wysar(d)*—*wys*, wise, and noun suff. -*ard*.]

**wizen**, *wiz'n*, *adj.* dried up, thin, shrivelled (also wiz'ened).—*v.i.* and *v.t.* to become, or to make, dry and shrivelled.—*adj.* wiz'en-faced, having a thin, shrivelled face.  Also weazen, etc. [O.E. *wisnian*, to wither; cog. with O.N. *visna*, to wither.]

**wizier**.  Same as vizier.

**wo.**  Same as. woe, or as whoa.—Also wo ha ho.

**woad**, *wōd*, *n.* a genus (Isatis) of cruciferous plants, mostly natives of countries round the Mediterranean—dyer's woad (*Isatis tinctoria*) yielding a good and very permanent dye, largely superseded by indigo: a blue dye.—*adj.* woad'ed, dyed blue with woad. [O.E. *wād*; Ger. *waid*.]

**wobble**, *wob'l*, *v.i.* to move unsteadily or uncertainly from side to side: to move along thus: to quiver: to quaver (*coll.*): to vacillate.—Also *v.t.*—*n.* an unsteady, unequal motion or movement.—*ns.* wobb'ler; wobb'liness; wobb'ling.—*adj.* wobb'ly, shaky: inclined to wobble.—Also wabb'le, wabb'ler, etc.—wobb'le-board, a sheet of hardboard shaken to obtain certain sound-effects. [L.G. *wabbeln*.]

**Woden**, *wō'dən*, *n.* the chief god of the ancient Germanic peoples.—*n.* Wō'denism, the worship of Woden. [O.E. *Wōden*; O.H.G. *Wuotan*; cf. Odin.]

**wodge**, *woj*, (*coll.*) *n.* a large or roughly-cut portion: a lump. [wedge.]

**woe**, wo, *wō*, *n.* grief (*arch.*): misery: (often in *pl.*) a misfortune or calamity: a physical pain (*obs.*): a curse: an exclamation of grief.—*adj.* (*arch.* and *dial.*) sad, wretched, sorry.—*adjs.* woe'ful, wō'ful, woe'some (*Scot.* wae'some), sorrowful or afflicted: bringing misery or calamity: deplorable: wretched, paltry. — *adv.* woe'fully, wō'fully. — *n.* woe'fulness, wō'fulness. — *adjs.* woe'begone, wō'begone (see bego), beset with woe: dismal-looking, suggesting misery; woe'-wea'ried, -worn, wearied, worn with woe.—in weal and woe, in prosperity and adversity; woe

is me (*arch.*), unhappy that I am! cursed am I; woe unto, calamity will befall: may calamity befall; woe worth the day (see worth). [O.E. (*interj.*) *wā*; Ger. *weh*; L. *vae*; cf. wail.]

**wog**, *wog*, *n.* a disrespectful name for an Arab, an Egyptian, etc.: a foreigner generally, usu. coloured. [Perh. from (golly)wog.]

**woggle**, *wog'l*, *n.* the ring a Scout threads his neckerchief through.

**woiwode**.  Same as voivode.

**woke**, woken.  See wake.

**wold**, *wōld*, *n.* an open tract of country, now chiefly upland country. [O.E. (Angl.) *wald*, forest, applied orig. to wooded parts of the country; cf. weald.]

**wolf**, *woolf*, *n.* the common name of certain gregarious and rapacious species of the genus Canis—including the common wolf (*Canis lupus*), the grey or timber wolf, and the coyote: anything very ravenous: a greedy and cunning person: a tuberculous excrescence, or cancerous growth (*obs.*): a dissonance heard in a keyed instrument tuned by unequal temperament (*mus.*): an extraneous non-harmonic note made by the bow on a string of a violin, etc. (*mus.*): a man who pursues women (*slang*):—*pl.* wolves, *woolvz*.—*v.i.* to hunt for wolves.—*v.t.* (*coll.*) to devour ravenously.—*ns.* wolf'er, one who hunts wolves; wolf'ing, the hunting of wolves for their skins.—*adjs.* wolf'ish, wolv'ish, like a wolf: rapacious: ravenous.—*adv.* wolf'ishly.—*ns.* wolf'kin, wolf'ling, a young wolf.—Wolf Cub, one who belonged to the Wolf Cubs, a junior division of the Boy Scouts organisation (now Cub Scouts); wolf'-dog, a dog of large breed formerly used in hunting wolves: a cross between a wolf and a domestic dog; wolf'-fish, any genus of fierce and voracious salt-water fishes—called also sea-wolf; wolf'-hound, a wolf-dog, esp. of large size, as the Russian wolf-hound (see borzoi); wolf'-note (*mus.*), a wolf; wolf'-pack, a pack of wolves: a flotilla of submarines surfacing together for attack; wolf's'-bane, wolfs'bane, an aconite, esp. *Aconitum lycoctonum*; wolf's'-foot, -claw, the club-moss (Lycopodium); wolf'-skin, the skin or pelt of a wolf; wolf's'-peach, the tomato; wolf'-spi'der, any spider of the genus (Lycosa) to which the true tarantula belongs, or of the family Lycosidae; wolf'-tooth, a small supernumerary premolar in a horse; wolf'-whistle, a two-note male whistle excited at sight of a woman.—cry wolf, to give a false alarm—from the story of the boy who cried 'Wolf' when there was none, and was not believed when there was one; have a wolf by the ears, to be in a very difficult situation; have a wolf in the stomach, to be ravenously hungry; keep the wolf from the door, to keep away poverty or hunger; see a wolf, to be tongue-tied (in allusion to an old superstition). [O.E. *wulf*; Ger. *wolf*; L. *vulpēs*, fox, *lupus*, wolf; Gr. *lykos*.]

**Wolffian**, *woōl'fi-ən*, *vol'fi-ən*, *adj.* pertaining to, or associated with, the German embryologist K. F. *Wolff* (1733-94): designating the renal organs in the embryo of vertebrates.

**Wolfian**, *woōl'fi-ən*, *vol'fi-ən*, *adj.* pertaining to the philosophy of Christian *Wolf* (1679-1754), who systematised and popularised the philosophy of Leibniz, and gave a strong impulse to that development of natural theology and rationalism.—Also Wolff'ian.—*n.* Wolf'ianism.

**Wolfian**, *woōl'fi-ən*, *vol'fi-ən*, *adj.* pertaining to, or associated with, Friedrich August *Wolf* (1759-1824)—applied esp. to his theory that the *Odyssey* and *Iliad* are composed of numerous ballads, strung together by subsequent editors.

**wolfram**, *woōlf'rəm*, *n.* (also wolf'ramite) a native compound of tungstate of iron and manganese: tungsten. [Ger.; origin uncertain.]

**wollastonite**, *wŏŏl'əs-tən-īt*, or *-as'*, *n.* a pyroxene of relatively simple composition, silicate of calcium, CaSiO₃—also called *tabular spar.* [After the scientist W. H. *Wollaston* (1766-1828).]

**Wolof,** *wō'lof*, *n.* a tribe living near the Senegal River in western Africa : a member of the tribe : its language.—Also *adj.*

**wolverene, wolverine,** *wŏŏl-və-rēn'*, *n.* the American glutton: its fur. [Extension of **wolf**.]

**woman,** *wŏŏm'ən*, *n.* an adult female of the human race: a wife (now *dial.*): a mistress: the female sex, women collectively: a female attendant: a charwoman or daily domestic help (*coll.*): the reverse or Britannia side of a coin:—*pl.* **women,** *wim'ən.*—Also *adj.*—*v.t.* to cause to act like a woman (*obs.*): (with *it*) to play the part of a woman: to provide or staff with a woman or women: to call a person 'woman' abusively.— *adj.* **wo'man'd** (*Shak.*), accompanied by a woman. —*adv.* **wom'anfully,** like a woman of spirit.— *n.* **wom'anhood,** the state, character, or qualities of a woman: womenkind.—*v.t., v.i.* **wom'anise, -ize,** to make, become, effeminate: (*v.i.*) to consort with women, esp. with prostitutes.— *adj.* **wom'anish,** effeminate: feminine.—*adv.* **wom'anishly.**—*ns.* **wom'anishness; wom'ankind,** a woman (*obs.*): (also **wom'enkind, wom'enfolk, -folks**) a group of women taken together, as the women of a family, or the female sex.—*adj.* and *adv.* **wom'an-like.**—*n.* **wom'anliness.**—*adj.* **wom'anly,** like or becoming a woman: feminine. —*adv.* in the manner of a woman.—**wom'anbod'y** (*Scot.*), a woman.—*adjs.* **wom'an-born,** born of woman; **wom'an-built,** built by women. —**wom'an-child,** a female child:—*pl.* **wom'enchildren.**—*adj.* **wom'an-grown,** grown to womanhood.—**wom'an-hater,** a man who hates women, a misogynist; **wom'an-post** (*Shak.*), a female messenger; **wom'an-quell'er,** a killer of women; **wom'an-suffrage,** possession of the electoral franchise by women.—*adjs.* **wom'an-tired** (*Shak.*), hen-pecked (**tire** (5)); **wom'an-vested,** wearing women's clothes.—**women's rights,** the aim of the movement of women towards equality with men.—**kept woman,** a mistress; **play the woman,** to give way to weakness; **woman of the town,** a whore; **woman of the world,** a woman of fashion, or of worldly wisdom: a woman who knows and makes allowance for, or accepts, the ways of the world: a married woman (*obs.*); **Women's Voluntary Service,** a body (organised in 1938) which participated in civil defence, welfare and other work, in World War II. [O.E. *wimman* —*wifman=wif*, a woman, *man*, man, human being.]

**womb,** *wŏŏm*, *n.* the uterus, the organ in which the young of mammals are developed and kept till birth: the abdomen, or the stomach, or the bowels (*obs.*): the place where anything is produced: any deep cavity.—*v.t.* (*Shak.*) to enclose.—*adj.* **womb'y** (*Shak.*), hollow, capacious. [O.E. *wamb, womb*; Ger. *wamme,* paunch.]

**wombat,** *wom'bət, -bat, n.* a genus (Phascolomys) of Australian marsupial mammals of the same order as opossums. [Native name.]

**womera.** Same as **woomera.**

**won,** *wun, wŏn, v.i.* to dwell, abide (*arch.* and *dial.*): to be, or become, accustomed (*obs.*).—*n.* (*obs.*) a dwelling, an abode: habit, custom.—*n.* **won'ing,** dwelling.—**did won** (*Spens.*), was accustomed. [O.E. *wunian,* Du. *wonen,* Ger. *wohnen,* to dwell.]

**won,** *wun, pa.t.* and *pa.p.* of **win.**

**wonder,** *wun'dər, n.* the state of mind produced by something new, unexpected, or extraordinary: admiration (*obs.*): the quality of being strange or unexpected: a strange, astonishing, admirable, thing or happening: a prodigy: a miracle: a

sweet friedcake, a *cruller* (*U.S.*).—*v.i.* to feel wonder: to be amazed (with *at*): to speculate: to feel doubt.—*v.t.* to speculate, to ask oneself (with noun clause or direct quotation).—*adj.* **won'dered, wond'red** (*obs.*), marvellous: having performed, or able to perform, wonders (*Shak.*). — *n.* **won'derer.** — *adj.* **won'derful,** exciting wonder: strange: expressing vague commendation, admirable, extremely good (*coll.*).—*adv.* **wonderfully.**—*adv.* **won'derfully.**—*n.* **won'derfulness.**—*n.* and *adj.* **won'dering.**—*adv.* **won'deringly.**—*n.* **won'derment,** surprise: an expression of wonder: a wonderful thing: quality of being wonderful.—*adjs.* **won'derous, won'drous,** such as may excite wonder.—Also *adv.*—*adv.* **won'drously.**—*n.* **won'drousness.**—**won'derland,** a land of wonders; **won'der-monger,** a wonder-worker: one who talks much of wonders, esp. incredible ones; **won'der-mongering.**—*adjs.* **won'der-struck, -strick'en,** struck with wonder or astonishment. —**won'der-work,** a prodigy, miracle: thaumaturgy; **won'der-worker; won'der-working.**—*adj.* **won'der-wounded** (*Shak.*), wonder-stricken.—**bird of wonder,** the phoenix; **for a wonder,** by way of an unexpected but pleasant change; **nine days' wonder,** something that astonishes everybody for the moment; **seven wonders of the world** (see **seven**); **to a wonder** (*arch.*), marvellously: extremely well. [O.E. *wundor*; Ger. *wunder,* O.N. *undr.*]

**wonga-wonga,** *wong'(g)a-wong'(g)a, n.* the large Australian white-faced pigeon—a table delicacy. —Also **wong'a.** [Native name.]

**wonky,** *wongk'i,* (*slang*) *adj.* unsound: shaky: amiss: awry. [Cf. **wankle.**]

**wont,** historically *wunt,* commonly *wŏnt, adj.* used or accustomed.—*n.* habit.—*v.i.* to be accustomed. —*adj.* **wont'ed,** accustomed, habituated (*U.S.*): usual (*arch.*).—*n.* **wont'edness.**—*adj.* **wont'less** (*arch.*), unaccustomed. [Orig. pa.p. of **won** (1).]

**won't,** *wŏnt,* will not. [Contr. of M.E. *wol not.*]

**woo,** *wŏŏ, v.t.* to try to win the affection of: to court: to solicit eagerly: to seek to gain.—Also *v.i.:—pa.t.* and *pa.p.* **wooed** (*wŏŏd*).—*n.* **woo'er.** —*n.* and *adj.* **woo'ing.**—*adv.* **woo'ingly.** [O.E. *wōgian,* to woo; origin obscure.]

**woobut.** Same as **woubit.**

**wood,** *wŏŏd, n.* a tree (*obs.*): the Cross (*obs.*): a collection of growing trees (often in *pl.*): wooded country: the hard part of the substance of trees and shrubs, xylem: trees cut or sawed, timber: a kind of timber or wood: firewood: the cask or barrel, as distinguished from the bottle: a woodblock (*print.*): (commonly in *pl.*) the woodwinds of an orchestra: a woodenheaded golf-club: a bowl (*bowls*): an idol made of wood: the pulpit (*slang*).—*v.t.* to cover with trees: to supply or load with wood.—*v.i.* to take in a supply of wood.—*adjs.* **wood'ed,** supplied with wood: covered with trees; **wood'en,** made of, or like, wood: of a golfclub, with head made of wood: hard: dull, insensible: heavy, stupid: lacking animation or grace of manner or execution: clumsy.—*adv.* **wood'enly.**—*ns.* **wood'enness,** wooden quality: want of spirit or expression; **wood'iness,** the state or quality of being woody.—*adj.* **wood'less,** without wood.—*n.* **wood'lessness.**—*adjs.* **wood'sy** (*-zi; U.S.*), pertaining to, or characteristic of, woods; **wood'y,** abounding with woods: inhabiting woods (*Spens.*): situated in a wood: pertaining to wood: consisting wholly or largely of wood: ligneous: like wood in texture, or smell, or taste, etc.—**wood'-acid,** wood-vinegar; **wood'-alcohol,** wood-spirit; **wood'-anemone,** any anemone growing in woods, esp. *Anemone nemorosa,* which has a single whorl of leaves and a white flower; **wood'-ant,** a large forestdwelling ant: a termite infesting the wood of old buildings; **wood'-ash,** (often in *pl.*) ash obtained by burning wood or plants—a source of potassium salts; **wood´bine, wood´bind,** the honeysuckle: applied also to other climbers, such as some kinds of ivy, the Virginia-creeper, etc.: perh. bindweed (Shak., *M.N.D.* IV, i. 48); **wood´block,** a die cut in relief on wood and ready to furnish ink impressions: a woodcut; **wood´-borer,** any of a number of insect larvae, or of molluscs, or of Crustacea, that bore in wood. —*adjs.* **wood´-boring; wood´-born,** born in the woods.—**wood´-carver; wood´-carving,** the process of carving in wood: an object, or part of one, so ornamented or made; **wood´-chat,** a species of shrike; **wood´-coal,** coal like wood in texture, lignite or brown coal: charcoal; **wood´-cock,** a genus (Scolopax) of birds allied to the snipes, but of a more bulky body, and with shorter and stronger legs: a stupid person, a simpleton (*arch.*); **wood´cock's-head** (*obs.*), a tobacco-pipe; **wood´craft,** skill in the chase and everything pertaining to life in the woods: forestry generally; **wood´cut,** an engraving cut on wood: an impression from it; **wood´-cutter,** one who cuts wood: a wood-engraver; **wood´-cutting; wood´-engraver,** one who engraves on wood: any of certain beetles that make a pattern of furrows in the wood of trees; **wood´-engraving,** the art of engraving designs on wood: an engraving on or print from wood; **wood´en-head,** a blockhead, stupid person.—*adj.* **wood´en-headed,** having a head of wood: stupid.—**wood´en-headedness; wooden horse,** the Trojan horse (q.v.): an instrument of punishment (see **horse**): a ship (*arch.*); **wooden leg,** an artificial leg made of wood; **wooden pear,** an Australian tree whose pear-shaped seed-vessels have a woody outside; **wooden spoon,** a spoon of wood presented to the person standing lowest in the mathematical tripos list at Cambridge: a booby prize; **wood´en-tongue,** woody-tongue; **wooden type,** large type cut in wood; **wood´-evil,** diarrhoea of herbivorous animals; **wood´-fibre,** a thick-walled, elongated, dead element found in wood—developed by the elongation and lignification of the wall of a single cell, differing from a tracheide in inability to conduct water; **wood´-flour,** a fine powder, made from sawdust and wood waste, used as a filler in many industries, and in the manufacture of guncotton; **wood´-fretter,** a wood-borer; **wood´-germander,** *Teucrium scorodonia,* which has racemes of yellow flowers; **wood´-grouse,** the capercailzie; **wood´-hole,** a place where wood is stored; **wood´-honey,** wild honey; **wood´-horse,** a saw-horse; **wood´-house,** a house or shed in which wood for fuel is deposited; **wood´-hyacinth,** the wild hyacinth or English bluebell, a flower of the genus Scilla; **wood´-i´bis,** any bird of the family Tantalidae, nearer the storks than the ibises; **wood´land,** land covered with wood (also *adj.*); **wood´lander,** an inhabitant of woodland; **wood´-lark,** a species of lark that perches on trees but sings chiefly on the wing; **wood´-louse** (*pl.* **wood´-lice),** any of numerous isopod crustaceans of family Oniscidae, found in damp places, under stones and bark, in woodwork, among moss, etc.: a book-louse: a termite (*U.S.*); **wood´man,** a man who cuts down trees: a forest officer: a huntsman; **wood´-mite,** any of numerous small mites found in woods; **wood´-naphtha,** the mixture of light hydrocarbons distilled from wood; **wood´-nightshade,** *Solanum dulcamara,* bitter-sweet or woody-nightshade; **wood´-note** (*Milt.*), a wild musical note, like that of a songbird; **wood´-nymph,** a nymph of the woods; **wood´-offering** (*B.*), wood burned on the altar; **wood´-oil,** gurjun balsam: tung-oil: also various other oils obtained from trees; **wood´-opal,** a form of common opal which has replaced pieces of wood entombed as fossils in sediments, in some cases retaining the original structure; **wood´-owl,** European brown owl, or other owl living in woods; **wood´-paper,** paper made from wood-pulp; **wood´pecker,** any of a family (Picidae) or birds in the order Picariae, remarkable for modification of the skull and bill enabling the latter to be used to drill holes, and for the long flexible tongue, used to extract insects from crevices; **wood´-pigeon,** the ringdove, a common species of pigeon (*Columba palumbus*) living in woods; **wood´-pile,** a pile of wood, esp. firewood; **wood´-pulp,** wood mechanically or chemically pulped for paper-making; **wood´-reeve,** overseer of a wood; **wood´ruff** (O.E. *wudurofe*; meaning of second element unknown), a genus of rubiaceous plants with whorled leaves and a funnel-shaped corolla, esp. *sweet woodruff* which has small white flowers and a pleasant scent—(*obs.*) **wood´-roof; wood´-rush,** any plant of the genus Luzula, of the same family as the true rushes, growing in woods; **wood´-sage,** wood-germander; **wood´-sandpiper,** a common European tattler; **wood´-screw,** a screw for fastening pieces of wood or wood and metal; **wood´shed,** a shed for storing firewood; **wood´-shock,** the pekan; **wood´-skin,** an Indian canoe made of bark, or the bark itself; **woods´-man,** a woodman; **wood´-sorrel,** any plant of the genus Oxalis, esp. *Oxalis acetosella,* with trifoliate leaves and white or rose-tinted flowers, which yields potassium binoxalate; **wood´-spirit,** a spirit living among trees: methyl alcohol, methanol; **wood´-spite,** the green woodpecker; **wood´-stamp,** a stamp made of wood, as for stamping fabrics in colours; **wood´-stone,** petrified wood; **wood´-sugar,** xylose; **wood´-swallow,** an Australian name for any of the fly-catching Artamidae, also called swallow-shrikes, the resemblance to shrikes being more fundamental than that to swallows; **wood´-tar,** a product of destructive distillation of wood, containing paraffins, naphthalene, phenols; **wood´thrush,** a singing-thrush common in the woods of the eastern United States, reddish-brown above, olive on the rump, white spotted with black on the breast: locally in Britain, the missel-thrush or the song-thrush; **wood´-tick,** any tick of the family Ixodidae, the young of which are transferred to man and animals from bushes; **wood´-tin,** a botryoidal or reniform variety of cassiterite showing a concentric structure of radiating brown, wood-like fibres; **wood´-vinegar,** crude acetic acid obtained from wood, pyroligneous acid; **wood´wale,** a woodpecker, esp. the green woodpecker; **wood´-warbler,** the yellow willow-warbler or wood-wren: an American warbler, esp. of the genus Dendroeca (or Dendroica); **wood´ward,** an officer to guard the woods; **wood´-wasp,** a large hymenopterous insect (Sirex) that bores wood with its ovipositor; **wood´-wax, -waxen,** dyer's greenweed; **wood´-wind,** a wind-instrument of wood (or sometimes metal, as silver)—flute, oboe, bassoon, clarinet, etc.: (usu. in *pl.*) the section of an orchestra comprising these; **wood´-wool,** fine wood shavings; **wood´work,** a part of any structure made of wood: carpentry; **wood´-worm,** a larva that bores in wood; **wood´-wren,** the willow-warbler or willow-wren (*Phylloscopus trochilus*): the wood-warbler or yellow willow-wren (*Phylloscopus sibilatrix*)—neither being properly a wren; **wood´y-night´shade** (see **wood-nightshade**); **wood´y-tongue,** actinobacillosis, a chronic inflammation of cattle, rarely of sheep and swine, occasionally transmitted to man, due to infection, usu. of the tongue, by the fungus *Actinobacillus ligniersi.*—**cannot see the wood for trees,** cannot grasp the whole because of the superabundance of detail; **Commissioners of Woods and Forests,** a department (1810–1924) having charge of the Crown woods and forests; **out of the wood(s)**, out of difficulty or danger; **something nasty in the woodshed** (*coll.*), an unpleasant or shocking experience in one's past; **wood-wool slabs**, slabs made from long wood shavings with a cementing material, used for linings, partitions, etc. [O.E. *wudu*; cog. with O.N. *vithr*, wood, O.Ir. *fid*, timber.]

**wood**, *wŏŏd*, (*Shak.*; *Scot.* **wud**, *wud*) *adj.* mad: fierce, furious.—*n.* **wood´ness**. [O.E. *wŏd*; O.N. *ōthr*, Ger. *wut*, madness.]

**woodburytype**, *wŏŏd´bar-i-tīp*, *n.* a photo-mechanical process in which an exposed and developed bichromated film is forced into a metal plate by great pressure, and so forms a matrix for subsequent printing. [Named from the inventor.]

**woodchuck**, *wŏŏd´chuk*, *n.* a N. American species of marmot (*Marmota* or *Arctomys monax*). [Corr. of an Amer. Indian name.]

**woodie**, *wŏŏd´i*, -*ē*, (*Scot.*) *n.* the gallows. [widdy (1).]

**wooer**, wooing, etc. See **woo**.

**woof**, *wŏŏf*, *n.* weft: thread for a weft: texture.—*adjs.* **woofed** (*wŏŏft*, *wŏŏf´id*), woven; **woof´y**, dense in texture. [M.E. *oof*, with *w* added by association with **warp**, etc. (*oof* being the normal development of O.E. *ōwef—on*, *wefan*, to weave).]

**woof**, *wŏŏf*, (*N.Eng.*) *n.* cat-fish. [Origin obscure.]

**woofer**, *wŏŏf´ar*, *n.* a large loudspeaker used to reproduce low-frequency sounds only.—Cf. **tweeter**. [Imit. of a dog's bark.]

**wool**, *wŏŏl*, *n.* a modification of hair in which the fibres are shorter, curled, and possess an imbricated surface—the covering of sheep, etc.: short, thick human hair: any light, fleecy substance like wool: any substance with a fibrous texture, resembling wool, e.g. steel-wool: thread or yarn made from animal wool: fabric woven or knitted from it.—*adjs.* **woolled** (*wŏŏld*), bearing wool; **wooll´en**, made of, or pertaining to, wool: clad in, or covered with, wool: rustic (*obs.*).—*n.* cloth made of wool.—*n.* **wooll´iness**.—*adj.* **wooll´y**, consisting of, or like, wool: clothed with wool: lacking in clearness, firmness or definition (*fig.*): having the atmosphere or quality of the Wild West (*coll.*).—*n.* a garment of wool, esp. a knitted one:—*pl.* **woollies**.—*n.* **wool´sey** (*zi*), a fabric of cotton and wool.—*adv.* **wool´ward** (*obs.*), with wool next the skin, esp. as a penance.—**wool´-ball**, a ball of wool, such as is sometimes found in a sheep's stomach.—*adj.* **wool´-bearing**, bearing or yielding wool.—**wool´-card**, **wool´-comb**, a machine for **wool´-carding**, **wool´-combing**, separating the fibres of wool preparatory to spinning; **wool´-carder**, **wool´-comber**; **wool´-clip**, crop of wool; **wool´-driver**, buyer up of wool.—*adj.* **wool´-dyed**, dyed before spinning or weaving.—**wool´fat**, lanolin; **wool´fell**, the skin with the wool still on it; **wool´-gath´ering**, absent-minded dreaming.—*adj.* dreamy: absent-minded.—**wool´-grower**, one who raises sheep for the production of wool; **wool´-growing**. — **wooll´en-dra´per**, one who deals in woollen goods; **wooll´en-dra´pery**; **wooll´en-mill**, a mill where wool is spun and woven into material; **wooll´y-bear**, the hairy caterpillar of a number of moths, including the tiger-moths.—*adjs.* **wooll´y-haired**, -**head´ed**, having the hair like wool.—**wool´man**, a dealer in wool; **wool´-mill**, a woollen-mill; **wool´-oil**, any oil obtained from wool-fat: an oil used to oil wool before spinning; **wool´-pack**, the package in which wool was formerly done up for sale: a bundle weighing 240 lb.: cirrocumulus cloud: the woolsack (*obs.*); **wool´-packer**; **wool´-picker**, a machine for cleaning wool; **wool´sack**, the seat of the Lord Chancellor in the House of Lords, being a large square sack of wool covered with scarlet: the office of Lord Chancellor; **wool´-shears**, shears used in shearing

sheep; **wool´sorter**, one who sorts wool according to quality, etc.; **wool´-staple**, the fibre or pile of wool: a market where wool was sold; **wool´-stapler**, a dealer in wool: a woolsorter; **wool´-winder**, one who packs fleeces; **wool´work**, needlework imitative of tapestry.—**against the wool**, against the texture of the wool, the wrong way; **dye in the wool**, to dye (the wool) before spinning (**dyed-in-the-wool**, out-and-out, complete); **great**, **much**, **cry and little wool**, much palaver and little result; **pull, draw, the wool over one's eyes**, to hoodwink, deceive, one; **woolly-hand crab**, the mitten-crab (q.v.); **woolsorter's disease**, anthrax. [O.E. *wull*, Goth. *wulla*, Ger. *wolle*, L. *vellus*.]

**woold**, *wŏŏld*, *v.t.* to wind a rope or chain round.—*adj.* **woold´ed**.—*ns.* **woold´er**, a stick used in woolding a mast or yard: a pin in a ropemaker's top; **woold´ing**. [Du. *woelen*; Ger. *(be)wuhlen*.]

**woomera**, *wŏŏm´ar-a*, **womera**, *wom´*, **woomerang**, *wŏŏm´ar-ang*, *ns.* throw-stick. [Austr. native.]

**woon**, *wŏŏn*, (*Spens.*) *v.i.* Same as **won** (1).

**woorali**. See **wourali**. **woosel**(l). See **ouzel**.

**woot**, **woo´t**, *wŏŏt*, (*Shak.*) wilt (thou)?—Also **wot**.

**wootz**, *wŏŏts*, *n.* steel made in India, from ancient times, by fusing iron with carbonaceous matter. [For **wook**—Kanarese, *ukku*, steel.]

**woozy**, *wŏŏ´zi*, *adj.* fuddled (with drink, drugs, etc.): dazed, dizzy: blurred, woolly, vague. [Origin obscure.]

**wop**, *wop*, *n.* a derogatory term for an Italian, or other foreigner of olive complexion. [It. (dial.) *guappo*—Sp. *guapo*, bold, handsome.]

**wop**, *wop*, *v.t.* Same as **whop**.

**worcester**, *wŏŏs´tar*, (*hist.*) *n.* fine woollen material made at *Worcester*: **Worcester** (**china**), fine china made there from mid-18th cent.—**worces´terberry**, N. Amer. species of gooseberry (*Ribes divaricatum*), not a hybrid; **Worcester**(**shire**) **sauce**, pungent sauce orig. made in Worcestershire.

**word**, *wûrd*, *n.* a unit of spoken language: a written sign representing such an utterance: (in *pl.*) language: a saying: a brief conversation: a rumour: a hint: a signal or sign: a message: a promise: a declaration: a pass-word: a watch-word: a war-cry: (in *pl.*) verbal contention.—*v.t.* to express in words: to speak to, or of, in words (*obs.*; *rare*): to flatter (*Shak.*).—*v.i.* to speak, talk.—*adj.* **word´ed**, expressed in words.—*adv.* **word´ily**.—*ns.* **word´iness**; **word´ing**, speaking, utterance (*arch.*): act of expressing in words: choice of words, phrasing.—*adj.* **word´ish** (*obs.*), verbose.—*n.* **word´ishness**.—*adjs.* **word´less**, unspoken: silent; **word´y**, using, or containing, too many words: conducted in words.—**word´-blindness**, loss of ability to recognise written words (see **dyslexia**); **word´book**, a book with a collection of words: a dictionary, or vocabulary.—*adj.* **word´bound**, unable to find expression in words: bound by a promise.—**word´-building**, the formation of words from letters or from root words and affixes; **word´-lore**, information about the history, use, etc., of words; **word´-memory**, the power of recalling words to the mind; **word´-painter**; **word´-painting**, the act or art of describing vividly in words.—*adj.* **word´-perfect**, having memorised exactly.—**word´-picture**, a description in words that presents an object, scene, etc., to the mind as if in a picture; **word play**, puns, etc.; **word salad** (*psych.*), a confused outpouring of speech, most often occurring in cases of schizophrenia; **word´-splitting**, hair-splitting.—**a good word**, a recommendation, favourable mention, praise; **at a word**, without more ado, at once: to be brief, in short (*obs.*); **a word in one's ear**, a confidential conversation; **be as good as one's word**

(see good); **break one's word**, to fail to fulfil a promise; **by word of mouth**, orally; **eat one's words**, retract, apologise, usu. under compulsion; **fair words** (*arch.*), pleasant, conciliatory words—usu. implying flattery or deceit; **get a word in edgeways** (see **edge in a word**, under **edge**); **have a word with**, to have some conversation with; **have words (with)**, to quarrel, dispute (with); **in a word, in one word**, in short, to sum up; **in so many words**, explicitly: bluntly; **in word**, in speech only, in profession only; **my word**, mild interj. expressing surprise, annoyance, etc.; **not the word for it**, not a strong enough word to express or describe it; **of few, or many, words**, taciturn, or verbose; **pass one's word**, to make a promise; **take (one) at one's word**, to accept his statements as being literally true; **take (up) the word**, to begin speaking, continue a discourse begun by someone else; **the last word**, the closing remark in an argument, esp. if having an appearance of conclusiveness: the conclusive statement: the ultimate authority: (also **latest word**) the most up-to-date, or the most finished, example; **the Word**, the Scriptures: the gospel message: the second person in the Trinity, the Logos; **word for word**, literally,verbatim. [O.E.; Goth. *waurd*, O.N. *orth*, Ger. *wort*; L. *verbum*, word, Gr. *eirein*, to say, speak.]

**Wordsworthian**, *würdz-wür'thi-ən, adj.* pertaining to the poet William *Wordsworth* (1770-1850) or his style.—*n.* an admirer or imitator of Wordsworth.

**wore**, *wōr, wör₁ pa.t.* of **wear**.

**work**, *würk, n.* effort directed to an end: employment: that on which one works: the product of work, anything made or done: materials for work: needlework: a deed: doings: the result of action: any production of art, as a literary composition: a book: manner of working, workmanship: (in *pl.*) a manufactory, workshop: the act of producing an effect by means of a force (F) whose point of application moves through a distance (s) in its own line of action —measured by the product of the force and the distance (W = Fs; *phys.*): (in *pl.*) walls, trenches, etc. (*fort.*): (usu. in *pl.*) an action in its moral aspect, esp. as tending to justification (*theol.*): (in *pl.*) mechanism, e.g. of a watch: the spin given to a ball by a bowler to cause it to break on pitching (*cricket*): (by confusion with O.E. *wærc*), ache, trouble, fuss (*dial.*).—*v.i.* to make efforts to achieve or attain anything: to be occupied in business or labour: to move, make one's way, slowly and laboriously: to move, become, etc., in a manner not intended or desired: to be in action: to operate, function: to produce effects: to behave in the desired way when worked: to prove practicable: to ache, be painful (*dial.*): to ferment: to be agitated, move convulsively: to strain, labour: to sail in a course, esp. to beat to windward (*naut.*): to contrive, plan (*arch.*).—*v.t.* to make by labour: to bring into any state by action: to effect or strive to effect: to carry on operations in: to keep in operation: to keep employed: to put in motion: to purge (*dial.*): to influence: to affect powerfully: to provoke, excite: to prepare for use by manipulation: to cause to ferment: to fashion, make: to embroider: to make, as one's way, by effort: to solve: to make use of, make profit through (*coll.*): to influence, cajole, or trick (*coll.*):—*pa.t.* and *pa.p.* **worked** or **wrought** (see separate article).—*ns.* **workabil'ity**, **work'ableness**.—*adjs.* **work'able**, that may be worked, esp. practicable; **worked**, that has been treated or fashioned in some way: embroidered: ornamented.—*ns.* **work'er**, one who works: a toiler: one employed in manual work: in social insects, one of a caste of sterile individuals that do all the work of the colony;

**work'ing**, the act or process of shaping, making, effecting, solving, fermenting, etc.: an exposition of the process of calculation: manner of operating or functioning: endeavour (*obs.*): (in *pl.*) deeds (*obs.*): mental or emotional activity (*obs.*): contortion due to agitation: slow and laborious progress: (in *pl.*) the parts of a mine, etc., where work is, or has been, carried on.—*adj.* active: labouring: operational: connected with labour: stirring the emotions (*obs.*).—**work'-aday**, suitable for a work day: toiling: dull, prosaic.—Also *n.*—**work'-bag, -basket, -box**, a bag, basket, for holding materials for work, esp. needlework; **work'-box**, a box for holding instruments or materials for work; **work'-day**, a day for work, a week-day.—*adj.* pertaining to a work-day.—**work'-fellow**, one who is engaged in the same work with another; **work'folk, work'-folks**, work-people.—*adj.* **work'ful**, industrious. —**work'girl**, a girl or young woman employed in manual labour; **work'house** (*hist.*), a house where any work or manufacture is carried on: a house of shelter for the poor, who are given work to do; **work'ing-beam**, a walking-beam; **work'ing-class**, manual workers (often in *pl.*; also *adj.*); **work'ing-day**, a day on which work is done: the period of actual work each day. —*adj.* laborious: plodding: ordinary.—**work'-ing-drawing**, a drawing of the details of a building by which the builders are guided in their work; **work'ing-edge**, an edge of a piece of wood trued square with the working-face to assist in truing the other surfaces square; **work'-ing-face**, that face of a piece of wood which is first trued and then used as a basis for truing the other surfaces; **work'ing-house** (*obs.*), workshop; **working majority**, a majority sufficient to enable the party in office to carry on without accidental defeats; **working man, woman**, a worker, esp. a manual one; **work'ing-model**, a model of a machine that can do, on a smaller scale, the same work as the machine; **work(ing) party**, a group of persons who carry out a specially assigned task: a group appointed to investigate a subject, as methods of attaining maximum efficiency in an industry; **work'man**, a man who works, esp. manually: a skilful artificer.—*adjs.* **work'man-like**, like a workman: becoming a skilful workman: well performed; **work'manly**, becoming a skilful workman.—*adv.* in a manner becoming a skilful workman.— **work'manship**, the skill of a workman: manner of making: that which is made or produced by one's hands (also *fig.*); **work'master**, a master workman, overseer, or employer:—*fem.* **work'mistress**; **work'-mate**, work-fellow: a companion at work; **work'-out**, a practice trial or exercise; **work'-people**, people engaged in manual labour; **work'piece**, a piece of work in progress, being manufactured: something on which a tool or machine works; **work'room**, a room for working in; **works committee, council**, body on which both employer and employees meet to handle labour relations within a business; **work'shop**, a room or shop where work is done. —*adjs.* **work'-shy**, hating, avoiding work, lazy (also used as *n.*); **work'some** (*Carlyle*), industrious.—**work study**, time and motion study; **work'-table**, a table on which work is done, esp., formerly, a small table used by ladies at their needlework; **work'-woman**, a woman who makes her living by manual labour; **work'y-day** (*obs.*), workaday.—**a work of time**, a change, achievement, etc., requiring, or brought about by, time; **give one the works** (*slang*), to inflict punishment on one, or severe pain, in order to coerce in some way; **have one's work cut out**, to have one's work prescribed: to be faced with a difficult task; **make short work of** (see **short**); **Ministry** (formerly **Office**) **of Works**, the body which has the management and control of public works and buildings, of which the expenses are defrayed from public money; **out of work**, without employment (*n.* **out-of-work**, see **out**); **public works**, building, etc., operations financed by the state; **set to work**, to employ in, or to engage energetically in, a piece of work; **Seven Works of Corporal Mercy**, to feed the hungry, give drink to the thirsty, to clothe the naked, visit prisoners, visit the sick, harbour strangers, bury the dead; **Seven Works of Spiritual Mercy**, to convert sinners, instruct the ignorant, counsel the doubtful, console the afflicted, bear wrongs patiently, forgive injuries, pray for the living and the dead; **shoot the works** (see **shoot**); **the works**, the lot, everything; **work double tides** (*naut.*), to work night and day; **work for, against**, to exert oneself in support of, in opposition to; **work in**, to intermix: to introduce carefully and deliberately (*fig.*): to make to penetrate: of workers, to continue at work in protest against, e.g. proposed dismissal (*n.* **work-in**); **working to rule**, observing all the regulations scrupulously for the express purpose of slowing down work; **work into**, to make way gradually into: insinuate: to change, alter, into; **work of art**, a production in one of the fine arts (*lit.* and *fig.*); **work off**, to separate and throw off: to get rid of gradually: to print ready for circulation: to pass, palm, off (*coll.*): to dispose of by hanging (*slang*); **work on, upon**, to act or operate upon: to influence, or try to do so; **work one's passage**, to earn one's passage by services on board (also *fig.*); **work out**, to effect by continued labour: to expiate: to make by cutting, digging, etc. (*obs.*): to exhaust: to solve or calculate: to study fully (*rare*): to develop in detail, elaborate: to come out by degrees: to turn out in the end; **work the oracle** (*slang*), to achieve the desired result by manipulation, intrigue, wire-pulling, favour, etc: to raise money; **work up**, to excite, rouse: to create by slow degrees: to expand, elaborate: to use up, as material: to set at an irksome or needless task (*naut.*): to make one's, its, way gradually upwards: to reach, achieve, by effort and gradually; **work with** (*fig.*), to strive to influence by appeals, etc. [O.E. *weorc*; O.N. *verk*, Ger. *werk*; further conn. with Gr. *ergon.*]

**world**, *wûrld*, *n.* the earth: the earth and its inhabitants: the universe: the system of things: the present state of existence: any analogous state: any planet or heavenly body: public life or society: sphere of interest or activity: environment: the public: the materialistically minded: mundane interests: a secular life: course of life: one of the three kingdoms of nature: a class or division: a very large extent of country, as the 'New World': very much or a great deal, as 'a world of good': a large quantity: time, as in 'world without end', which means 'eternally': possibility, as in 'nothing in the world': the ungodly (*B.*).—*adj.* **world'ed**, containing worlds.—*ns.* **world'liness**; **world'ling**, one who is devoted to worldly pursuits and temporal possessions: a mortal (*obs.*).—*adj.* **world'ly**, pertaining to the world, esp. as distinguished from the world to come: devoted to this life and its enjoyments: bent on gain: mortal (*obs.*).—Also *adv.*—**World Bank**, the popular name of the International Bank for Reconstruction and Development, an agency of the United Nations set up in 1945 to make loans to poorer countries; **World Court**, the popular name of the Permanent Court of International Justice at the Hague, set up under the League of Nations in 1921 to settle or advise on disputes between states; **world language**, a universal language.—*adj.* **world'ly-minded**, having the mind set on the present world.—*n.* **world'ly-**

**mindedness.**—*adjs.* **world'ly-wise**, having the wisdom of those experienced in, and affected by, the ways of the world; **world'-old**, exceedingly ancient.—**world power**, a state, group of states, etc., strong enough to make its influence felt in world politics; **World War**, a war of world-wide scope, esp. the Great War of 1914-1918 (First World War, World War I), 1939-45 (Second World War, World War II).—*adjs.* **world'-wearied, -weary**, tired of the world; **world'-wide**, extending over, or found everywhere in, the world; **world'-without-end**, eternal. —**all the world**, everybody: everything; **all the world and his wife** (*coll.*), everybody: an illassorted assembly; **best, worst, of both worlds**, the advantage, disadvantage, of both alternatives in a choice; **carry the world before one**, to pass through every obstacle to success; **dead to the world** (*coll.*), deeply asleep: in a drunken stupor; **for all the world**, precisely, entirely; **go to the world** (*Shak.*), to get married; **in the world**, an intensive phrase, usu. following an interrogative pronoun or adverb; **next world**, life after death; **on top of the world** (*coll.*), in a state of great elation or happiness; **out of this world**, wonderful, delightful, good beyond all experience; **the New World**, the western hemisphere, the Americas; **the Old World**, the eastern hemisphere, comprising Europe, Africa, and Asia; **the other world**, the non-material sphere, the spiritual world; **the whole world**, the sum of what is contained in the world; **the world is his oyster** (see **oyster**); **the world's end**, the most distant point possible; **think the world of**, to be very fond of. [O.E. *woruld, world, weorold*, orig. meaning age or life of man—*wer*, man, and the root of old; O.N. *veröld*, O.H.G. *weralt* (Ger. *welt*).]

**worm**, *wûrm*, *n.* a snake, a dragon (*arch.*): any creeping or crawling animal (*obs.*): loosely used for any elongate invertebrate lacking appendages, as an earthworm or marine worm (Chaetopoda), a flat-worm (Platyhelminthes), a round-worm (Nematoda): a grub: a maggot: anything spiral: the thread of a screw: the lytta or vermiform cartilage of the tongue of a dog or other carnivorous mammal: a spiral pipe for condensation in distilling: anything that corrupts, gnaws, or torments: remorse: a mean, grovelling creature: (in *pl.*) any intestinal disease arising from the presence of parasitic worms: any ailment supposed to be caused by a worm, as toothache (*obs.*): a tick or mite in the hand, etc., esp. one alleged humorously to infest the hands of idlers (*obs.*).—*v.i.* to seek for or catch worms: to move, make one's way, like a worm, to squirm: to work slowly or secretly.—*v.t.* to cause to be eaten by worms: to treat for, rid of, worms: to work (oneself) slowly or secretly (*refl.*): to elicit by slow and indirect means: to remove the lytta or vermiform cartilage from the tongue of.—*adj.* **wormed**, bored, injured by worms.—*n.* **worm'er.**—*adj.* **worm'y**, like a worm: grovelling: containing a worm: abounding in worms: pertaining to worms: dank-smelling: dismal, like the grave.—**worm'-cast**, the earth voided by the earthworm.—*adjs.* **worm'-eaten**, eaten into by worms: old: worn-out; **worm'-eating**, living habitually on worms.—**worm'-fence**, a zigzag fence formed of stakes crossing at their ends; **worm'-fever**, a feverish condition in children ascribed to intestinal worms; **worm'-gear**, a gear connecting shafts whose axes are at right angles but do not intersect, consisting of a core carrying a single- or multi-start helical thread of special form (the *worm*), meshing in sliding contact with a concave face gear-wheel (the *worm-wheel*); **worm'-gearing**; **worm'-grass**, pinkroot: a kind of stonecrop (*Sedum album*); **worm'-hole**, the hole made by a wood-worm, earthworm, etc.—*adj.* **worm'-holed**, perforated by worm-holes.—**worm'-powder,** a vermifuge; **worm'-seed,** any of a number of plants acting, or reputed to act, as anthelmintics, as species of Artemisia (e.g. *Artemisia santonica*), *Erysimum cheiranthoides* (treacle worm-seed, treacle mustard), *Chenopodium anthelminticum*, etc.: the drug santonica; **worm'-wheel** (see **worm'-gear**). [O.E. *wyrm*, dragon, snake, creeping animal; cog. with Goth. *waurms*, a serpent, O.N. *ormr*, Ger. *wurm*; also with L. *vermis*.]

**Wormian,** *wûrm'i-ən, adj.* associated with the name of the Danish anatomist Olaus Worm (1588-1654), applied esp. to the supernumerary bones developed in the sutures of the skull.

**wormwood,** *wûrm'wōod, n.* the bitter plant *Artemisia absinthium*, formerly used as a vermifuge, with which absinthe is flavoured: bitterness. —cf. **absinthe.** [O.E. *wermōd* (Ger. *wermuth*), wormwood; of doubtful origin, but influenced by **worm** and **wood.**]

**worn,** *wōrn, wörn, pa.p.* of **wear.**—*adj.* that has been worn: showing effects of wear, or (*fig.*) of work, worry, age, etc.: of land, exhausted: hackneyed, trite.—*adj.* **worn'-out,** much injured or rendered useless by wear: wearied: past, gone.

**worral, worrel,** *wur'əl, n.* a monitor lizard. [Ar. *waral,* lizard.]

**worricow, worrycow, wirricow,** *wur'i-kow,* (*Scot.*) *n.* a hobgoblin: the devil: anything frightful or even only grotesque. [**worry** (vb.), and *cow,* a hobgoblin.]

**worrit,** *wur'it, v.t., v.i.,* and *n.* Dial. form of **worry.**

**worry,** *wur'i, v.t.* to tear with the teeth: to devour ravenously (*Scot.*): to harass: to pester: to tease: to make, get, etc., by persistent methods: to choke (*Scot.*).—*v.i.* to trouble oneself: to be unduly anxious: to fret:—*pa.t.* and *pa.p.* **worr'ied.**—*n.* act of worrying: trouble, perplexity, overdue anxiety: a cause of this: the act of injuring by biting and shaking.—*ns.* **worr'ier; worr'iment** (*coll.*), worry, anxiety.— *adj.* **worr'isome,** inclined to worry: causing trouble.—*n.* and *adj.* **worr'ying.**—*adv.* **worr'yingly.**—**worry beads,** a string of beads providing an object for the hands to play with, thus relieving mental tension—esp. popular in Greece.— **I should worry!** it is nothing for me to worry about; **worry down,** to swallow with a strong effort; **worry out,** to find a solution of by intense or anxious effort. [O.E. *wyrgan,* found in compound *āwyrgan,* to harm; cf. Du. *worgen,* Ger. *würgen,* to strangle.]

**worse,** *wûrs, adj.* (used as *comp.* of **bad**) bad or evil in a greater degree: less well than before. —*adv.* badly in a higher degree: less well: with more severity.—*v.t.* (*obs.*) to worst.—*v.i.* and *v.t.* **wors'en,** to grow, or make, worse.—*adv.* **wors'er,** a redundant comparative of *worse.*— **for better or for worse,** whatever may befall of good fortune or bad; **for the worse,** to a worse state; **go by, with, the worse** (*obs.*), to lose, be defeated; **have the worse,** to be at a disadvantage: to be defeated; **none the worse for,** not harmed by; **put to the worse** (*B.*), to defeat; **the worse for,** harmed or impaired by; **worse off,** poorer. [O.E. *wyrsa* (Goth. *wairsiza*), formed with comp. suffix from a Gmc. root *wers,* found in Ger. (*ver*)*wirren,* to confuse, entangle.]

**worship,** *wûr'ship, n.* adoration paid, as to a god: religious service: profound admiration and affection: act of revering or adoring: dignity, reputation, high standing (*arch.*): a position of honour (*obs.*): a title of honour in addressing certain magistrates, etc.—*v.t.* to pay divine honours to: to adore or idolise: to honour, respect, treat with signs of honour (*obs.*).—*v.i.* to perform acts of adoration: to take part in religious service:—*pr.p.* **wor'shipping;** *pa.t.* and

*pa.p.* **wor'shipped.**—*adjs.* **wor'shipable,** capable of being worshipped; **wor'shipful,** worthy of worship or honour: used as a term of respect: worshipping, adoring.—*adv.* **wor'shipfully.**—*n.* **wor'shipfulness.**—*adj.* **wor'shipless,** without worship or worshippers.—*n.* **wor'shipper.**—**house,** or **place, of worship,** a church or chapel, synagogue, mosque, temple; **win (one's) worship** (*obs.*), to gain honour or fame. [O.E. *weorthscipe*— *weorth, wurth,* worth, suff. *-scipe,* -ship.]

**worst,** *wûrst, adj.* (used as *superl.* of **bad**) bad or evil in the highest degree.—*adv.* in the highest degree of badness.—*n.* the highest degree of badness: the most evil state or effect: the least good part.—*v.t.* to get the advantage over in a contest: to defeat: to damage or make worse (*obs.*).—*v.i.* (*obs.*) to grow worse.—**do one's worst,** to do one's utmost in evil or mischief; **get the worst of it,** to be defeated in a contest. [O.E. *wyrst, wyrrest, wyrresta,* from the same source as **worse.**]

**worsted,** *wōost'id,* or *wōōrst'id, n.* orig., a fine wool fabric: twisted thread or yarn spun out of long, combed wool: smooth, closely-woven material made from this: woollen yarn for ornamental needlework.—*adj.* made of worsted yarn. —**worst'ed-work,** needlework done with worsted. [*Worstead,* village near Norwich, England.]

**worsted,** *wûrst'id, pa.t.* and *pa.p.* of **worst.**

**wort,** *wûrt, n.* any herb or vegetable (now *rare* except in composition): specif. a plant of the cabbage kind (*obs.*). [O.E. *wyrt,* a root, herb; Ger. *wurz, wurzel,* a root.]

**wort,** *wûrt, n.* malt unfermented or in the act of fermentation (*sweetwort*): such liquor boiled with hops (*hopped-wort*): malt extract used as a medium for the culture of micro-organisms. [O.E. *wyrt;* allied to **wort** (1).]

**worth,** *wûrth, n.* value: price: that quality which renders a thing valuable: moral excellence: merit: importance: possessions (*obs.*).—*adj.* equal in value to: having a certain value: worth while: having possessions to the value of: deserving of.—*adj.* **worth'ful,** honourable: meritorious: valuable.—*adv.* **worth'ily** (*dh*).—*n.* **worth'iness** (*dh*).—*adj.* **worth'less** (*th*), having no value, virtue, excellence, etc.: useless: unworthy (*obs.*).—*adv.* **worth'lessly.**—*n.* **worth'lessness.**—*adjs.* **worthwhile',** such as to repay trouble and time spent on it (predicatively **worth while;** see **while**): good: estimable; **worth'y** (*dh*), having worth: valuable: estimable (used patronisingly): deserving: deserving of: suited to, in keeping with: of sufficient merit: of high social position (*obs.*).—*n.* a man of eminent worth: a notability, esp. local (sometimes ironical): anything of value, an excellence (*Shak.*):—*pl.* **wor'thies.**—*v.t.* (*obs.*) to make worthy, to honour.—**for all one is worth,** with all one's might or energy; **for what it is worth,** a phrase implying that the speaker is doubtful of the truth of what he has reported or unwilling to be responsible for its accuracy; **nine worthies,** usu. given as Hector, Alexander the Great, Julius Caesar; Joshua, David, Judas Maccabaeus; Arthur, Charlemagne, Godfrey of Bouillon; **worthiest of blood,** in questions of succession, male as opposed to female; **worth it,** worth while. [O.E. *weorth, wurth* (Ger. *wert*), value.]

**worth,** *wûrth, v.i.* to be, become, happen, as in the phrase **woe worth,** woe be (to; with the noun in the dative). [O.E. *weorthan,* to become; cf. Ger. *werden.*]

**wortle,** *wûr'tl, n.* a perforated plate through which wire, tubing, is drawn to make it thinner. —Also **whirtle.** [Ety. uncertain.]

**wosbird,** *wōz'bûrd,* (*dial.*) *n.* form of **whore's-bird.**

**wot, wotteth,** etc. See **wit** (1).

**woubit,** *wōō'bit, n.* (usu. **hairy woubit**) a hairy

Neutral vowels in unaccented syllables: *el'ə-mənt;* for certain sounds in foreign words, see p. viii

caterpillar, esp. one of a tiger-moth: applied derogatorily to a person, often implying smallness and shabbiness.—Also **woo′but, ou′bit, oo′bit.** [M.E. *wolbode, wolbede;* prob.—*wol,* wool; meaning of second element unknown.]
**would,** *wōōd* (formerly, e.g. in *Spens., wōld), pa.t.* of **will.**—*n.* the desired or intended, opp. to *could,* or *should.*—*adj.* **would′-be,** aspiring, or merely professing, to be: meant to be.—*n.* a vain pretender.
**Woulfe-bottle,** *wōōlf′-bot′l, n.* a form of usu. three-necked bottle used for purifying gases, or dissolving them in suitable solvents—from the London chemist Peter *Woulfe* (*c.* 1727-1803).
**wound,** *wownd, pa.t.* and *pa.p.* of **wind** (*wīnd*).
**wound,** *wōōnd, n.* any division of soft parts produced by external mechanical force—whether incised, punctured, contused, lacerated, or poisoned: any cut, bruise, hurt, or injury.— *v.t.* to make a wound in (*lit.* and *fig.*), to injure. —*adj.* **wound′able,** capable of being wounded. —*n.* **wound′er.**—*adv.* **wound′ily** (*arch.*), excessively.—*n.* and *adj.* **wound′ing.**—*adj.* **wound′less,** unwounded: invulnerable (*obs.*): harmless.— *adj.* and *adv.* **wound′y** (*arch.*), excessive(ly).—
**wound′wort,** any of several plants of popular repute as vulneraries, as the kidney-vetch, a number of plants of genus Stachys (marsh or clown's woundwort). [O.E. *wund* (Ger. *wunde,* O.N. *und*); also O.E. *wund,* wounded.]
**wourali, woorali,** *wōō-rä′li,* **woora′ra, oura′li, oura′ri, ura′li, ura′ri,** the plant yielding curare (q.v.).
**wove, woven,** *pa.t.* and *pa.p.* of **weave.**—**wove paper,** paper that shows in its fabric the marks of a fine wire gauze sieve or mould.
**wow,** *wow,* (*Spens.*) *v.i.* to woo.
**wow,** *wow, interj.* an exclamation of wonder, tinged with other emotions as aversion, sorrow, or admiration, pleasure (see **whow**).—*v.i.* to howl.—*n.* a bark: a howl: rhythmic or arrhythmic changes in reproduced sound, fundamentally arising from fluctuation in speed of either reproducer or recorder: anything thrillingly good, successful, or according to one's wishes (*slang*). —*n.* **wow′ser** (-*zər*; perh. not connected with **wow**; *slang*) a puritanical person who tries to interfere with the pleasures of others. [Imit.]
**wowf,** *wowf,* (*Scot.*) *adj.* crazy. [Origin unknown.]
**wow-wow, wou-wou,** *wow′-wow, n.* the silver gibbon of Java: also the agile gibbon of Sumatra. [Imit. of its cry.]
**wox, woxen** (*obs.*), *pa.t.* and *pa.p.* of **wax** (2).
**wrack,** *rak, n.* vengeance, punishment (*obs.*): destruction, devastation.—Cf. **rack** (2).—*adj.* **wrack′ful** (*rare*), destructive. [O.E. *wræc*— *wrecan,* to drive; connected, and confused, with **wrack** (2).]
**wrack,** *rak, n.* a wreck (*dial.*): wreckage: seaweed cast ashore, or growing where it is exposed by the tide (*arch.*): any of the Fucaceae. [M.Du. or M.L.G. *wrak;* cf. **wrack** (1).]
**wraith,** *rāth, n.* a spectre: an apparition, esp. of a living person: a thin, pale person (*fig.*). [Orig. Scot.; perh. O.N. *vörthr,* a guardian.]
**wrangle,** *rang′gl, v.i.* to argue, debate, dispute (*arch.*): to dispute noisily or peevishly.—*v.t.* to obtain, persuade, spend, tire, in wrangling: to debate.—*n.* a noisy dispute: the action of disputing, esp. noisily.—*ns.* **wrang′ler,** one who disputes, esp. angrily: a stubborn foe (*Shak.*): in the University of Cambridge, one of those who attained the first class in the examinations for mathematical honours (**senior wrangler,** the student taking the first place; **second wrangler,** the student next in order of merit, and so on; this method of classification has been abandoned, and since 1909 the first class has been arranged alphabetically): a herdsman, esp. of horses (*Western U.S.*); **wrang′lership.**—*adj.*

**wrang′lesome,** given to wrangling.—*n.* and *adj.* **wrang′ling.** [M.E. *wranglen,* a freq. verb allied to **wring.**]
**wrap,** *rap, v.t.* to roll or fold together: to fold, lap, round something: to enfold, envelop (*lit.* and *fig.*): to embrace: to hide, obscure: to cover by folding or winding something round (often with *up*).—*v.i.* to wind, twine: (with *up*) to put on wraps:—*pr.p.* **wrapp′ing;** *pa.t.* and *pa.p.* **wrapped.**—*n.* a protective covering, for a person or thing, now esp. an outdoor garment: a single turn or fold round.—*ns.* **wrapp′age,** act of wrapping: covering: wrapping materials; **wrapp′er,** one who, or that which, wraps: formerly, a loose outer garment for a woman: a loose paper book cover: a paper band, as on a newspaper for the post.—*v.t.* to cover, or cover up, with a wrapper.—*n.* **wrapp′ing** (also **wrapp′ing-paper**), coarse paper for parcels, etc. —**wrap′-ras′cal,** a loose greatcoat worn in the eighteenth century (a humorous term).—**wrapped up in,** bound up in: comprised in: engrossed in, devoted to; **wrap up** (*slang*), to settle completely: to have completely in hand: (as *interj.*) be quiet! [M.E. *wrappen,* also *wlappen.*]
**wrap, wrapt,** erroneous forms of **rap** (2), **rapt.**
**wrasse,** *ras, n.* a genus (Labrus) of bony fishes representative of the large family Labridae, and including many species on European and N. African coasts. [Cornish *wrach.*]
**wrast.** Obs. Northern form of **wrest,** directly from O.N.
**wrate.** Obs. and Scot. *pa.t.* of **write.**
**wrath,** *röth, roth, Scot. räth, n.* violent anger: an instance, or fit, of this: holy indignation: violence or severity (*fig.*): ardour (*Shak.*).—*adj.* (*arch.*) violently angry.—*v.t.* and *v.i.* (*obs.*) to make, or to become, angry.—*adj.* **wrath′ful,** very angry: springing from, or expressing, or characterised by, wrath.—*adv.* **wrath′fully.**—*n.* **wrath′fulness.**—*adv.* **wrath′ily.**—*n.* **wrath′iness.** —*adjs.* **wrath′less; wrath′y** (chiefly *U.S.*), inclined to wrath: like, expressing, or characterised by, wrath. [O.E. *wrǣththu—wrāth,* adj.; cf. **wroth.**]
**wrawl,** *röl,* (*Spens.*) *v.i.* to cry as a cat, to caterwaul. [Imit.]
**wraxle,** *rak′sl,* (*dial.; S.W. England*) *v.i.* to wrestle.—*n.* **wrax′ling.** [O.E. *wraxlian;* cf. **wrestle.**]
**wreak,** *rēk, v.t.* to drive out (*obs.*): to give expression, vent, free play to: to find expression, outlet, for (*refl.*): to bestow: to punish (*obs.*): to harm (*obs.*): to avenge (*arch.*): to take vengeance on (*obs.*): to revenge (with *of;* *obs.*): to inflict: to effect or bring about:—*pa.t.* **wreaked,** *arch.* **wrōke,** *pa.p.* **wreaked,** *arch.* **wrōk′en,** *Spens.* **wrōke, ywrōke.**—*n.* punishment, vengeance (*arch.*): damage (*obs.*).—*n.* **wreak′er** (*arch.*).—*adjs.* **wreak′ful,** revengeful: avenging; **wreak′less,** unpunished. [O.E. *wrecan;* O.N. *reka,* to drive, pursue, avenge, Ger. *rächen;* conn. with L. *urgēre.*]
**wreak(e),** *rēk,* (*Spens., Shak.*) for **reak,** variant of **reck.**—Also (*Milt.*) **wreck.**
**wreath,** *rēth, n.* a circlet of interwoven materials, esp. flowers, etc.: a single twist or coil in a helical object: a drift or curl of vapour or smoke: a snowdrift: a defect in glass.—*pl.* **wreaths** (*rēdhz*).—*v.t.* **wreathe** (*rēdh*), to form by twisting: to twist together: to form into a wreath: to twine about or encircle: to twist: to cause to twist or contort: of snow, to cover by drifting (*Scot.*).—*v.i.* to be interwoven: to twine: to twist: of snow, to form a drift or wreath (*Scot.*): to turn (*obs.*): to form coils. —*adjs.* **wreathed** (or *rēdh′id*); **wreath′en** (*dh; arch. pa.p.*), wreathed.—*n.* **wreath′er** (*dh*).—*adjs.* **wreath′less; wreath′y** (*th* or *dh*).—**wreath′-filament,** the usual type of filament in large gas-

filled electric lamps, the filament wire being festooned from a horizontal supporting spider. [O.E. *writha*; allied to *writhan*, to writhe.]

**wreck,** *rek, n.* destruction: the act of wrecking or destroying: destruction of a ship: a badly damaged ship: shipwrecked property: remains of anything ruined: a person ruined mentally or physically.—*v.t.* to destroy or disable: to involve in a wreck: to cast up, as on the shore: to ruin.—*v.i.* to suffer wreck or ruin.—*ns.* **wreck′age,** the act of wrecking: wrecked material: a person, or persons, whose life is, or lives are, ruined; **wreck′er,** a person who purposely causes a wreck or who plunders wreckage: one who criminally ruins anything: a person or ship employed in recovering disabled vessels or their cargo: a person, vehicle or ̦rain employed in removing wreckage: a vehicle equipped with a hoisting device, used to tow wrecked or disabled motor vehicles (*U.S.*): a person who is employed in demolishing buildings, etc.—*adj.* **wreck′ful** (*poet.*), causing ruin.—*n.* and *adj.* **wreck′ing.**—wreck commissioners, a tribunal, that inquires into shipping disasters; **wreck′-master,** a person taking charge of a disabled ship or train and its cargo or freight.—**receivers of wrecks,** wreck-masters. [A.Fr. *wrec, wrek,* etc., of Scand. origin; allied to **wreak** (1).]

**wren,** *ren, n.* a genus (Troglodytes) and family (Troglodytidae) of birds, having the wings very short and rounded, and the tail short and carried erect: extended to various very small birds, as the **gold-crested wren** (gold-crest), the **willow wren** (willow warbler).—**wren′-tit,** a Californian bird (*Chamaea fasciata*), resembling the wren and the titmouse. [O.E. *wrenna, wrænna.*]

**Wren,** *ren, n.* a member of the W.R.N.S.

**wrench,** *rench, rensh, v.t.* to wring or pull with a twist: to force by violence: to sprain: to distort.—*v.i.* to perform, or to undergo, a violent wrenching.—*n.* an act or instance of wrenching: a violent twist: a sprain: an instrument for turning nuts, etc.: emotional pain at parting or change: in coursing, bringing the hare round at less than a right angle. [O.E. *wrencan,* to deceive, twist, *wrenc,* deceit, twisting; cf. Ger. *renken,* to twist, *rank,* trick, intrigue.]

**wrenching,** *rensh′ing,* (Shak., *Hen. VIII,* I, i. 167; older editions) *n.* for *renching,* from *dial.* **rench,** to rinse.

**wrest,** *rest, v.t.* to turn, twist, or (*obs.*) screw: to twist, extract, or take away, by force: to get by toil: to misinterpret: to pervert: to derive improperly (*Spens.*): to sprain (*Scot.*).—*v.i.* (*Spens.*) to force a way.—*n.* the act of wresting: violent pulling and twisting: distortion: an instrument, like a wrench, for tuning the piano, etc.—*n.* **wrest′er,**—**wrest′-pin′,** a pin round which the end of a wire (as a piano wire) is wound, turned by the wrest. [O.E. *wrǽstan;* Dan. *vriste.*]

**wrestle,** *res′l, v.i.* to contend by grappling and trying to throw another down: to struggle: to strive: to apply oneself keenly: to pray earnestly: to writhe, wriggle: to proceed with great effort (*lit.* and *fig.*).—*v.t.* to contend with in wrestling: to push with a wriggling or wrestling motion: (with *out*) to go through, carry out, with a great struggle.—*n.* the act, or a bout, of wrestling: a struggle.—*ns.* **wrest′ler; wrest′ling,** the action of the verb to wrestle: a sport or exercise in which two persons struggle to throw each other to the ground, governed by certain fixed rules —catch-hold, ground-wrestling, catch-as-catch-can, back-hold, etc. [O.E. *wrǽstlian;* allied to *wrǽstan,* to wrest.]

**wretch,** *rech, n.* an exile, outcast (*obs.*): a most miserable person: a worthless, or despicable, person: a being, creature (in pity, sometimes

admiration).—*adj.* (*Spens.*) wretched.—*adj.* **wretch′ed** (*-id*), very miserable: distressingly bad: despicable: worthless.—*adv.* **wretch′edly.** —*n.* **wretch′edness.** [O.E. *wrecca,* an outcast— *wrecan;* see **wreak** (1).]

**wrethe,** *rēth,* (*Spens.*) *v.t.* and *v.i.* Same as **wreathe.**

**wrick,** *rik, v.t.* to twist, sprain, strain.—*n.* a sprain, strain. [Allied to L.G. *wrikken,* to turn.]

**wriggle,** *rig′l, v.i.* and *v.t.* to twist to and fro: to move, advance, sinuously (*lit.* and *fig.*): to use evasive tricks.—*n.* the act or motion of wriggling: a sinuous marking, turn, or bend.—*ns.* **wrigg′ler; wrigg′ling.** [L.G. *wriggeln;* cf. Du. *wriggelen,* to wriggle.]

**wright,** *rit* (*Scot. rihht*), *n.* a maker (chiefly used in compounds, as **shipwright,** etc.): a carpenter or joiner (*Scot.*). [O.E. *wyrhta, wryhta,* allied to *wyrht,* a work—*wyrcan,* to work.]

**wring,** *ring, v.t.* to twist: to expel moisture from by hand twisting or by roller pressure: to force out by twisting: to force out: to clasp and shake fervently: to clasp convulsively, as the hands (in grief or agitation): (of a shoe) to pinch: to pain: to distress, afflict: to extort: to subject to extortion: to bend out of its position: to wreathe, coil: to distort.—*v.i.* to writhe: to twist: to feel pain:—*pa.t.* and *pa.p.* **wrung,** *obs.* **wringed.**—*n.* an act or instance of wringing: a cider-, wine-, or cheese-press.—*ns.* **wring′er,** one who wrings: a machine for forcing water from wet clothes (also **wring′ing-machine**); **wring′ing.**—**wring′-bolt,** a bolt with a ring or eye, used to secure a ship's planks against the frame till they are permanently fixed in place. —*adj.* **wring′ing-wet,** so wet that water can be wrung out.—*n.pl.* **wring′-staves** (*sing.* -**staff**), strong pieces of wood used in applying wring-bolts.—**wring from,** to extort from; **wring off,** to force off by wringing; **wring out,** to squeeze out by twisting: to remove from liquid and twist so as to expel the drops. [O.E. *wringan,* to twist; Du. *wringen,* Ger. *ringen.*]

**wrinkle,** *ring′kl,* (*coll.*) *n.* a tip, valuable hint. [Perh. from O.E. *wrenc,* a trick; perh. same as **wrinkle** (2).]

**wrinkle,** *ring′kl, n.* a small crease or furrow on a surface: an unevenness.—*v.t.* to contract into wrinkles or furrows: to make rough.—*v.i.* to shrink into ridges.—*adjs.* **wrinkled; wrink′ly,** full of wrinkles: liable to be wrinkled. [History obscure; adj. **wrinkled** is prob. used earlier than noun and verb.]

**wrist,** *rist, n.* the joint by which the hand is united to the arm, the carpus: the part of the body where that joint is, or the part of a garment covering it: a corresponding part of an animal: a wrist-pin.—*n.* **wrist′let,** a band or strap for the wrist: a bracelet: a watch for wearing on the wrist (also **wrist′-watch,** or **wrist′let-watch**): a handcuff (*slang*).—**wrist′band,** a band or part of a sleeve covering the wrist; **wrist′-drop,** inability to extend the hand, often caused by lead-poisoning; **wrist-pin,** a pin joining the end of a connecting rod to the end of a piston-rod; **wrist′-shot,** in golf, a short stroke from the wrist, usu. played with an iron club. [O.E.; allied to *writhan,* to twist; Ger. *rist.*]

**writ,** *rit,* arch. *pa.t.* and *pa.p.* of **write.**—**writ large,** written in large letters, hence (*fig.*) on a large scale, or very obvious.

**writ,** *rit, n.* a writing (*rare*): a legal or formal document: a written document by which one is summoned or required to do something (*law*). —**Holy Writ,** the Scriptures; **serve a writ on,** to deliver a summons to. [O.E. (*ge*)*writ;* O.N. *rit,* Goth. *writs.*]

**write,** *rit, v.t.* to form (letters or words) with a pen, pencil, or other implement: to express in writing: to compose: to draw, engrave, etc.:

to record: to decree or foretell: to communicate, or to communicate with, by letter.—*v.i.* to perform, or to practise, the act of writing: to be employed as a clerk: to compose, as articles, novels, etc.: to work as an author: to compose, or to send, a letter: to communicate with a person by letter:—*pr.p.* writ′ing; *pa.t.* wrōte, (*arch.*) writ (*rit*); *pa.p.* written (*rit′n*), (*arch.*) writ.—*adjs.* writ′able, capable of being expressed or described in writing: suitable for writing with; writ′ative, inclined, or characterised by inclination, to write.—*ns.* writ′er, one who writes: a professional scribe or clerk: an ordinary legal practitioner in a Scottish country town: an author: his works: one who paints lettering for signs:—*fem.* writ′eress (*rare*); writ′ership, the office of a writer; writ′ing, the act of one who writes: that which is written: (often *pl.*) literary production, or composition: handwriting, penmanship: state of being written.—*adj.* writt′en, reduced to, expressed in, writing—opp. to *oral.*—write′-off, a crashed aircraft (*airmen's slang*): a car so badly damaged that the cost of repair would exceed the car's value: a total loss: see also write off, below; writer's-cramp (see under cramp); write-up (see under write up, below); writ′ing-book, a book of paper for practising penmanship; writ′ing-case, a portable case containing materials for writing; writ′ing-desk, a desk with a sloping top for writing on: a portable writing-case; writ′ing-ink, ink suited for writing with; writ′ing-master, a master who teaches the art of penmanship: the yellow-bunting; writ′ing-paper, paper finished with a smooth surface, for writing on; writ′ing-school (*obs.*), a school for penmanship; writ′ing-table, a table fitted or used for writing on; written law, statute law as distinguished from common law.—*adj.* writt′en-off, (of a person) killed (*airmen's slang*): (of an aircraft) wrecked (*airmen's slang*): (of a car) damaged beyond reasonable repair: completely ruined: see also write off, below.—write down, to put down in written characters: to write in disparagement of: to write so as to be intelligible or attractive to people of lower intelligence or inferior taste: to reduce the book value of an asset; write (in) for, to apply for: to send away for; write off, to cancel, esp., in book-keeping, to take, as a bad debt, off the books: to regard, accept, as an irredeemable loss (*fig.*) (*n.* write′-off; *adj.* writt′en-off); write oneself off (*airmen's slang*), to get killed; write out, to transcribe: to write in full: to exhaust one's mental resources by too much writing (*refl.*); Writer to the Signet, a member of an ancient society of solicitors in Scotland who formerly had the exclusive right to prepare all summonses and other writs pertaining to the supreme court of justice, and still have the exclusive privilege of preparing crown writs; write up, to put a full description of in writing: to write in praise of, esp. to praise above its merits (*n.* write′-up): to bring the writing of up to date; writing on the wall, a happening foreshowing downfall and disaster (Dan. v. 5 ff.). [O.E. *writan*, orig. meaning to scratch; O.N. *rita*.]

**writhe**, *ridh*, *v.t.* to twist: to coil: to wreathe: to twist violently: to contort: to distort (*obs.*).—*v.i.* to twist, esp. in pain.—*n.* (*rare*) a twist or a contortion.—*adj.* writh′en (*ridh′ən*; *arch.*), twisted, convoluted, contorted.—*n.* and *adj.* writh′ing.—*adv.* writh′ingly. [O.E. *writhan*, to twist; O.N. *ritha*; cf. wreath, wrest, wrist.]

**writhled**, *rith′ld*, (*arch.*) *adj.* wrinkled, shrivelled. [Perh. writhe.]

**wrizled**, *riz′ld*, (*Spens.*) *adj.* wrinkled. [Perh. writhled.]

**wroath**, *rōth*, (*Shak.*) *n.* misfortune. [Prob. from ruth.]

**wroke**, *rōk*, obs. *pa.t.*, **wroken**, *rōk′n*, obs. *pa.p.* of wreak.

**wrong**, *rong*, *adj.* crooked, curved, twisted, bent (*obs.*): not according to rule: incorrect: erroneous: not in accordance with moral law: wicked: not that (thing) which is required, intended, advisable, or suitable: amiss, unsatisfactory: mistaken, misinformed: under, inner, reverse.—*n.* whatever is not right or just: any injury done to another: damage, harm (*rare*): wrong-doing: the state or position of being or doing wrong.—*adv.* not correctly: not in the right way: astray.—*v.t.* to do wrong to: to harm physically (*obs.* and *Scot.*): to impair, spoil (*obs.*): to seduce: to deprive of some right: to defraud: to impute fault to unjustly: to dishonour.—*n.* wrong′er, one who wrongs.—*adj.* wrong′ful, wrong: unjust: unlawful: not legitimate: unjustly held (*Spens.*).—*adv.* wrong′fully.—*n.* wrong′fulness.—*adv.* wrong′ly.—*n.* wrong′ness.—*adj.* wrong′ous (-*gəs*, -*əs*), unjust, illegal.—*adv.* wrong′ously.—wrong′-do′er, an offender, transgressor; wrong′-do′ing, evil or wicked action or conduct.—*adj.* wrong′-headed, obstinate and perverse, adhering stubbornly to wrong principles or policy.—*adv.* wrong′-headedly.—wrong′-headedness.—*adj.* wrong′-minded, having erroneous views.—wrong side (see side).—*adj.* wrong′-timed, inopportune.—wrong 'un (*coll.*), a dishonest character, a rogue: in cricket, a googly.—do oneself wrong (*obs.*), to be mistaken; get hold of the wrong end of the stick (see end); get on the wrong side of someone, to arouse dislike or antagonism in someone; get out of bed on the wrong side, to arise in the morning in an ill temper; go wrong, to fail to work properly: to make a mistake or mistakes: to stray from virtue; have wrong (*obs.*), to suffer injustice or injury; in the wrong, holding an erroneous view or unjust position: guilty of error or injustice; private wrong, a violation of the civil or personal rights of an individual; public wrong, a crime which affects the community; put in the wrong, to cause to appear in error, guilty of injustice, etc. [O.E. *wrang*, a wrong; most prob. O.N. *rangr*, unjust; allied to O.E. *wringan*, to wring, like Fr. *tort*, from L. *tortus*, twisted.]

**wroot**. Obs. form of root and wrote.

**wrote**, *rōt*, *pa.t.* of write.

**wroth**, *rōth*, *roth*, *adj.* wrathful: in commotion, stormy. [O.E. *wrāth*, angry; cf. O.N. *reithr*.]

**wrought**, *rōt*, *pa.t.* and *pa.p.* of work, now used chiefly in certain senses:—e.g. fashioned: ornamented: manufactured: beaten into shape, shaped by tools (as metal).—wrought′-iron, malleable iron, iron containing only a very small amount of other elements, but containing slag in the form of particles elongated in one direction, more rust-resistant than steel and welding more easily.—*adj.* wrought′-up, in an agitated condition, over-excited. [O.E. *worhte*, *geworht*, pa.t. and pa.p. of *wyrcan*, *wircan*, to work.]

**wrung**, *rung*, *pa.t.* and *pa.p.* of wring.

**wry**, *ri*, *adj.* twisted or turned to one side: not in the right direction: expressing displeasure or irony (*fig.*): perverse, distorted (*fig.*).—*n.* (*rare*) distortion.—*v.i.* to swerve, to go astray (*obs.*): to be deflected, undergo deflection (*obs.*): to writhe.—*v.t.* to give a twist to: to avert, as the face: to pervert.—*adv.* wryly.—*adv.* wry′ly.—*n.* wry′ness.—wry′bill, a New Zealand bird allied to the plovers with bill bent sideways.—*adj.* wry′-mouthed, having a crooked mouth: unflattering.—wry′-neck, a twisted position of the head on the neck due to disease of the cervical vertebrae or to affections (esp. rheumatic) of the muscles of the neck; wry′neck, a genus of small birds (Jynx) allied to the woodpecker, which twist round their heads strangely when surprised.—*adj.* **wry'-necked**, having a wry neck: played with the head on one side (Shak., *M.* of *V.*, II. v. 30).—**make a wry face**, or **mouth**, to pucker up the face, or mouth, as in tasting anything bitter or astringent, or in sign of disgust or pain. [O.E. *wrigian*, to strive, move, turn.]

**wud.** Scots form of **wood** (1 and 2).

**wulfenite**, *wōōl'fən-it, n.* molybdate of lead, $PbMoO_4$, occurring commonly as yellow crystals in veins with other lead ores, named after an Austrian mineralogist von *Wulfen*.

**wull**, *wul, (Spens.* and *dial.*) *v.i.* Same as **will**.

**wurley**, *wûr'lē, (Austr.) n.* an aborigine's hut, made of branches, leaves and plaited grass: a nest, esp. a rat's nest:—*pl.* **-leys**, or **-lies**. [Native word.]

**Würm**, *vürm, n.* the fourth stage of glaciation in the Alps.—*adjs.* **Würm**, **Würm'ian**. [From a river of Upper Bavaria.]

**wurtzite**, *wûrts'īt, n.* sulphide of zinc, ZnS, of the same composition as sphalerite, but crystallising in the hexagonal system, in black hemimorphic, pyramidal crystals. [From French chemist C. A. *Wurtz*.]

**wuther**, *wudh'ər, (dial.) v.i.* to move swiftly or with force: to make a sullen roaring, as the wind: to throw or beat violently.—*n.* a blow or blast, or the sound of these: a tremble.—*adj.* **wuth'ering**.—Also **whither** ((*h*)*widh'ər*). [From O.N.]

**wuzzle**, *wuz'l, (U.S.) v.t.* to jumble.

**wyandotte**, *wī'an-dot, n.* a useful breed of the domestic fowl, of American origin. [From N. American tribe so called.]

**wych-elm**, *wich'elm, n.* a common wild elm, also called Scotch elm or witch-hazel. [**witch** (2), and **elm**.]

**Wyclifite, Wycliffite**, *wik'lif-it, adj.* pertaining to the English reformer and translator of the Bible, John *Wyclif, Wycliffe* (*c.* 1320-84).—*n.* a follower of Wyclif; a Lollard.

**wye**, *wī, n.* the letter Y (q.v.) or anything shaped like it.

**Wykehamist**, *wik'əm-ist, n.* a pupil, or former pupil, of Winchester College, which was founded by William of *Wykeham*, Bishop of Winchester (1324-1404).

**wylie-coat**, *wī'li-kōt, (Scot.) n.* a flannel undervest or petticoat: a nightdress. [Unknown first element, and prob. **coat**.]

**wynd**, *wīnd, (Scot.) n.* a lane, narrow alley in a town. [Same as **wind** (2).]

**wyte.** See **wit** (1), **wite**.

**wyvern.** Same as **wivern**.

Neutral vowels in unaccented syllables: *el'ə-mənt*; for certain sounds in foreign words, see p. viii

# X

**X, x,** *eks, n.* the twenty-fourth letter in our alphabet, and twenty-first of the Roman alphabet, taken from the Chalcidian Greek, and of the same form, though perhaps not the same origin, as Ionic and classical Greek chi (X, χ; pron. *k-h*, and later *hh*); used in Old English medially and finally as a variant for *cs*. In modern English, medially and finally, it has the value of *ks*, as in *extinct, axe*, and, medially only, of *gz*, as in *exist*, or *gzh*, as usu. in *luxury*, or *gzh*, as in *luxurious*; at the beginning of a word it is pronounced like *z*. As Roman numeral X stands for ten, $\times$ for a thousand, $\bar{X}$ for ten thousand; X (see **chi**) as an abbreviation represents the word Christ—Xian, Xmas; *x* in algebra is the first of the unknown quantities.—**X´-body,** an inclusion in a plant-cell suffering from a virus disease; **X´-chromosome,** a chromosome associated with sex-determination, usually occurring paired in the female zygote and cell, and alone in the male zygote and cell; **X´-particle,** a meson; **X´-rays,** electromagnetic rays of very short wavelength which can penetrate matter opaque to light-rays, produced when cathode rays impinge on matter—discovered by Röntgen in 1895.—*adj.* **X´-ray.**—*n.* a photograph taken by X-rays.—*v.t.* to photograph or treat by, or otherwise expose to, X-rays.—**characteristic X´-rays,** secondary X-rays emitted when X-rays fall on matter, which contain monochromatic radiations that vary in wavelength according to the atoms from which they are scattered; **X-ray crystallography,** the study of crystal structures as shown by their diffraction of X-rays; **X-ray micrography,** the preparation, and study through the microscope, of radiographs obtained by means of X-rays; **X-ray spectrum,** a wavelength or frequency diagram in which a series of lines indicate by their positions the particular X-rays emitted by a body as the result of cathode-ray bombardment; **X-ray therapy,** the use of X-rays for medical treatment; **X-ray tube,** an evacuated tube in which X-rays are emitted from a metal target placed obliquely opposite to an incandescent cathode whose rays impinge on the target.

**xanth-,** *zanth-*, **xantho-,** *zan´thō-, -tho´-*, by some pronounced *gzan-*, in composition, yellow.—*ns.* **xan´thate,** a salt of xanthic acid; **xanthein** (*zan´thē-in*), a soluble yellow colouring matter of flowers; **xanthene** (*zan´thēn*), a white crystalline compound of carbon, hydrogen, and oxygen, from which are derived **xanthene dyestuffs.**—*adj.* **xan´thic,** of a yellow tint, esp. as a description of flowers: pertaining to xanthin or xanthine: designating **xanthic acid,** any of a series of addition compounds of an alcohol with carbon disulphide, esp. ethyl-xanthic acid.—*ns.* **xan´thin,** a name given to the insoluble yellow colouring matter of various flowers: also to a principle in madder: (usu. **xan´thine**) a white substance, closely allied to uric acid, found in muscle tissue, the liver and other organs, urine, etc., leaving a lemon-yellow residue when evaporated with nitric acid; **Xan´thium** (Gr. *xanthion*, a plant used for dyeing the hair yellow), any of a small but widely distributed genus of composite plants whose fruits bear hooked prickles very troublesome to sheep and other animals.—*n.pl.* **Xanthochroi** (*zan-thok´rō-ī*; Gr. *chroā*, or *chroiā*, skin), one of the five groups of men, according to Huxley and other ethnologists, comprising the fair whites.—*n.* **xanthochroia** (*-thō-kroi´ə*), yellowness of the skin.—*adjs.* **xanthochrō´ic, xan´thochroid** (*-kroid*; also used as *n.*).—*n.* **xanthochroism** (*-thok´rō-izm*), a condition in which all pigments other than yellows disappear, as in goldfish, or normal colouring is replaced by yellow.—*adj.* **xanthochroous,** (*-thok´rō-əs*), xanthochroic.—*ns.* **xanthochrō´mia,** any yellowish discoloration, esp. of the cerebrospinal fluid; **xanthoma** (*zan-thō´mə*), a yellow tumour composed of fibrous tissue and of cells containing cholesterol ester, occurring on the skin (e.g. in diabetes) or on the sheaths of tendons, or in any tissue of the body.—*adjs.* **xanthom´atous; xanthomelanous** (*zan-thō-mel´ə-nəs*), applied to a type of men with black hair and yellow or olive skins.—*ns.* **xanthophyll** (*zan´thō-fil*), $C_{40}H_{56}O_2$, one of the two yellow pigments present in the normal chlorophyll mixture of green plants; **xanthop´sia,** the condition in which objects appear yellow to the observer, as in jaundice or after taking santonin; **xanthop´terin(e)** (*-in*), a yellow pigment obtained from the wings of yellow butterflies and the urine of mammals.—*adj.* **xanthous** (*zan´thəs*), yellow.—*ns.* **Xanthoxylum** (*zan-thok´si-ləm*; Gr. *xylon*, wood), a genus of the Rutaceae, comprising over one hundred species, of which many are found in Brazil and the W. Indies, esp. either of two species known respectively as the prickly ash and Hercules club, or their dried bark; **Xanthura, Xanthoura** (*-thū´, -thoō´rə*; Gr. *ourā*, tail), a genus of American jays, with yellow tail. [Gr. *xanthos*, yellow.]

**Xanthian,** *zan´thi-ən, adj.* pertaining to *Xanthus*, capital of ancient Lycia in Asia Minor.

**Xanthium.** See under **xanth-.**

**Xantippe,** *zan-tip´i, n.* a scold, shrew.—Also **Xanthippe** (*-thip´*).—(*Shak.* older editions **Zan´tippe, Zen´tippe**). [Gr. *Xanthippē*, wife of Socrates.]

**xebec,** *zē´bek, n.* a small three-masted vessel much used by the former corsairs of Algiers. [Fr. *chebec*, influenced by Sp. form; perh. from Turkish or Arabic.]

**Xema,** *zē´mə, n.* the genus of fork-tailed gulls. [Arbitrarily invented 1819.]

**xen-, zen-, zēn-, xeno-,** *zen-ō-, zi-no´-*, in composition, strange, foreign, guest.—*n.* **Xenar´thra** (Gr. *arthron*, a joint), a group of American edentates—ant-eaters, sloths, and armadillos—having the dorsolumbar vertebrae jointed in an unusual manner.—*adj.* **xenar´thral,** having additional facets for articulation on the dorso-lumbar vertebrae.—*n.* **xē´nia** (*bot.*), the direct influence of pollen upon endosperm (explained by double fertilisation) or upon the mother-plant of the embryo.—*adj.* **xenial** (*zē´ni-əl*), of or belonging to hospitality, or relations with guests.—*ns.* **xenium** (*zē´ni-əm*), a present made to a guest or an ambassador: an offering, or a compulsory gift, to a ruler, the Church, etc.:—*pl.* **xē´nia; xen´ocryst** (*-krist*), a crystal or mineral grain which has been incorporated by magma during its uprise; **xenodochium** (*zen-o-do-ki´əm*; Gr. *docheion*, a receptacle), a building for the reception of strangers, as a guest-house in a monastery; **xenogamy** (*zen-og´ə-mi*; Gr. *gamos*, marriage; *bot.*), cross-fertilisation; **xenogenesis** (*zen-ō-jen´ə-sis*; Gr. *genesis*, birth), the

*fāte, fär; mē, hûr* (her); *mīne; mōte, för; mūte; mōōn, fŏŏt; dhen* (then)

(imagined) generation of something altogether and permanently unlike the parent.—*adjs.* **xenogenet′ic**; **xenogenous** (*zi-noj′-i-nəs*), due to outside cause.—*ns.* **xenogloss′ia** (Gr. *glōssa*, tongue), in psychical research, knowledge by a person of a language which he has never learned; **xen′ograft**, a graft from a member of a different species; **xen′olith**, a fragment of rock of extraneous origin which has been incorporated in magma; **xenomania** (*-mä′ni-ə*; Gr. *maniā*, madness), an inordinate attachment to things foreign; **xenomenia** (*-mē′ni-ə*; Gr. *mēniaia*, menses), vicarious menstruation, in which, in the absence of normal menstruation, bleeding occurs at regular monthly intervals from other parts of the body (e.g. the nose).—*adj.* **xeno-morphic** (*-mör′fik*; Gr. *morphē*, form), allotrio-morphic.—*ns.* **xenon** (*zen′*, *zēn′on*), a zero-valent element (Xe; at. numb. 54), a heavy gas present in atmosphere in proportion of $1:17 \times 10^7$ by volume, and also a fission product; **xen′ophobe** (*-fōb*; Gr. *phobos*, fear), one who fears or hates foreigners or things foreign; **xenophobia** (*-fō′bi-ə*), **xenoph′oby**, fear of things foreign; **xenophya** (*zen-of′i-ə*; Gr. *xenophyēs*, strange in shape or nature), elements of a shell or skeleton not secreted by the organism itself.—*adj.* **xenoplas′tic**, in experimental zoology, of transplantation in which transplant and host belong to the young germs of different species or genera. —*ns.* **Xenopus**, a genus of African aquatic frog (see **platanna** (frog)); **xenotime** (*zen′ō-tīm*; Gr. *xenos*, strange, in error for *kenos*, empty, vain, and *timē*, honour, in reference to the fact that the mineral was at first supposed to contain a new metal), yttrium phosphate, often containing small quantities of cerium, erbium, and thorium, and an important source of these rare elements; **Xenurus** (*zē-nū′rəs*; Gr. *ourā*, tail), a genus of armadillos in which the tail is almost without plates.—*adj.* **xenū′rine**.—**xenon lamp**, a high-pressure lamp, containing traces of xenon, used in film projectors, high-speed photography, etc. [Gr. *xenos*, (n.) guest, host, stranger, (adj.) strange, foreign.]

**xer-**, **xēr-**, **xero-**, **zē-rō-**, in composition, dry.—*ns.* **xeran′sis**, drying up; **Xeranthemum** (*-an′thi-məm*; Gr. *anthemon*, flower), a genus of plants of southern Europe, belonging to the thistle family: a species of these known as everlastings. —*adjs.* **xeran′tic**, drying up; **xerarch** (*zē′rärk*; Gr. *archē*, beginning), of a plant succession, starting on land where conditions are very dry. —*n.* **xerasia** (*zi-rā′si-ə*), a morbid dryness of the hair.—*adj.* **xē′ric**, dry, lacking in moisture: xerophytic.—*ns.* **xerochasy** (*zi-rok′ə-si*), dehiscence on drying; **xeroderma** (*zē-rō-dûr′mə*; Gr. *derma*, skin), **xeroder′mia**, a disease characterised by abnormal dryness of the skin and by overgrowth of its horny layer.—*adjs.* **xerodermat′ic**, **xeroder′matous**, **xeroder′mic**.—*ns.* **xerog′raphy**, a non-chemical photographic process in which the plate is sensitised electrically and developed by dusting with electrically-charged fine powder; **xeroma** (*-rō′*), xerophthalmia; **xē′romorph** (*-mörf*; Gr. *morphē*, form), a xerophyte.—*adjs.* **xeromor′phic**, **xeromor′phous**, of parts of a plant, protected against excessive loss of water by thick cuticles, coatings of hairs, and similar structural characters.—*n.* **xerophagy** (*zi-rof′ə-ji*; Gr. *phagein*, to eat), the eating of dry food, or of bread, vegetables and water, as a form of fast.—*adj.* **xerophilous** (*-of′il-əs*; Gr. *philos*, loving), of a plant, tolerant of droughty habitat.—*ns.* **xeroph′ily**, adaptation to dry conditions; **xerophthalmia** (*-of-thal′mi-ə*; Gr. *ophthalmos*, eye), a dry lustreless condition of the conjunctiva due to deficiency of vitamin A in the diet; **xē′rophyte** (*-fīt*; Gr. *phyton*, plant), a plant able to inhabit places where the water

supply is scanty, or where conditions, e.g. excess of salts, make it difficult to take in water.—*adj.* **xerophytic** (*-fit′*), able to withstand drought.—*ns.* **xeroradiog′raphy**, X-ray photography by xerography; **xerō′sis**, xerophthalmia; **xerostoma** (*-os′tom-ə*; Gr. *stoma*, mouth), **xerostō′mia**, excessive dryness of the mouth due to insufficiency of the secretions; **xerotes** (*zē′rō-tēz*), a dry habit of body.—*adj.* **xerotic** (*-rot′*).—*ns.* **xerotripsis** (*-trip′sis*; Gr. *tripsis—tribein*, to rub), dry friction; **Xerox**, a registered trademark used in respect of copying machines operating a xerographic method of reproduction. [Gr. *xēros*, dry.]

**xerafin**, **xeraphim**, *sher′ə-fēn*, *-fēm*, (Port.) a silver coin of Goa.

**Xeres**, *hher′es*, (Sp.) wine of Xeres (Jerez), sherry.

**Xhosa**, *kō′sə*, *-zə*, *n.* a group of Bantu-speaking tribes from the Cape district of South Africa, formerly often known as Kaffirs: a member of one of these tribes: the language of these tribes.—Also **Xosa**.—*adj.* **Xho′san**.

**xi**, *zī*, *ksī*, *ksē*, *n.* the fourteenth letter of the Greek alphabet (Ξ, ξ), answering to X: as a numeral ξ′ = 60, ͵ξ = 60,000.

**Xiphias**, *zif′i-as*, *n.* the common swordfish genus, giving name to the family **Xiphi′idae**. [Gr. *xiphias*, swordfish—*xiphos*, sword.]

**xiph-**, **xipho-**, *zif-*, *zif-o-*, *-ō-*, in composition, sword.—*ns.* **xiphihumeralis** (*hū-mər-ā′lis*), in vertebrates, a muscle leading from the xiphoid cartilage to the humerus; **xiphiplas′tron**, in chelonians, one of the plates composing the plastron, lying posterior to the hypoplastron.—*adj.* and *n.* **xiphiplas′tral**.—*n.* **xiphister′num**, a posterior element of the sternum.—*adjs.* **xiph′-oid**, sword-shaped: pertaining to, or designating, the **xiphoid process**, or xiphisternum (also, when cartilaginous, known as **xiphoid cartilage**); **xiphoid′al**.—*n.* **xiphop′agus** (Gr. *pēgnynai*, to fix, fasten together), a monster consisting, as did the Siamese twins, of twins joined in the region of the xiphoid cartilage.—*adjs.* **xiphopagic** (*-paj′ik*), **xiphop′agous**; **xiphophyllus**, (*-o-fil′əs*; Gr. *phyllon*, leaf), with sword-shaped leaves.—*n.* **Xiphosura** (*-ō-sū′rə*; formed irreg. from Gr. *ourā*, tail), an order of Arthropoda of which the only survivors are the king-crabs.—*adj.* and *n.* **xiphosu′ran**. [Gr. *xiphos*, a sword.]

**xoanon**, *zō′ə-non*, *n.* a primitive statue, said to be fallen from heaven, orig. of wood, later overlaid with ivory and gold. [Gr. *xoanon—xeein*, to carve.]

**Xosa.** See **Xhosa.**

**X-rays.** See under **X.**

**xylem**, *zī′lam*, *n.* woody tissue—usu. consisting of vessels, tracheides, and fibres, all with lignified walls, with some more or less lignified parenchyma—concerned in the conduction of aqueous solutions, and with mechanical support. —*ns.* **xy′lene**, $C_6H_4(CH_3)_2$, any of three dimethyl-benzenes, occurring in coal-tar but not separable by fractional distillation; **xy′lenol**, $(CH_3)_2 \cdot C_6H_3 \cdot OH$, any of six monohydric phenols derived from xylenes.—*adj.* **xy′lic**, pertaining to xylem: designating any of six acids, derivatives of xylene.—*ns.* **xylobal′samum** (Gr. *balsamon*, the balsam tree), the dried twigs, or the wood, of the balm of Gilead tree; **xy′locarp**, a hard and woody fruit.—*adj.* **xylocarp′ous**.—*ns.* **xy′lochrome** (Gr. *chrōma*, colour), a mixture of substances to which the colour of heart-wood is due—including tannins, gums, and resins; **xy′logen** (*-jen*), xylem.—*adj.* **xylogenous** (*-loj′ən-əs*; *bot.*), growing on wood.—*ns.* **xylography** (*zi-log′rə-fi*), the art of engraving on wood; **xyl′ograph**, an impression or print from a wood block: an impression of the grain of wood for surface decoration; **xylog′rapher.**—*adjs.* **xylograph′ic**, **-al**; **xy′loid**, woody, ligneous.—

*ns.* **xyloidin, xyloidine** (*zi-loi'din*; Gr. *eidos*, form, appearance), an explosive like gun-cotton, prepared by the action of strong nitric acid on starch or woody fibre—pyroxylin, or similar substance; **xy'lol** (L. *oleum*, oil), xylene; **xylol'ogy**, the study of the structure of wood; **xylō'ma**, in fungi, a sclerotium-like body which forms spores internally and does not put out branches which develop into sporophores; **xylom'eter**, an instrument for determining the specific gravity of wood. —*adj.* **xylon'ic**, designating an acid obtained by oxidising xylose.—*ns.* **Xy'lonite**, a non-thermosetting plastic of the nitrocellulose type, **xylophagan** (*-lof'ə-gən*; Gr. *phagein*, to eat), one of the **Xyloph'aga**, a genus of boring bivalves; **xy'lophage** (*-fāj*), an insect-larva, mollusc, etc., that eats or bores in wood.—*adjs.* **xylophagous** (*-lof'ə-gəs*), wood-eating; **xyloph'ilous**, fond of wood, living upon wood.—*n.* **xy'lophone** (Gr. *phōnē*, voice), a musical instrument consisting of a graduated series of wooden bars, which are rested on straw, etc., and are struck by wooden hammers: an instrument used to measure the elastic properties of wood.—*adj.* **xylophon'ic.**—

*ns.* **xyloph'onist; Xylopia** (*-lōp'i-ə*; Gr. *pikros*, bitter), a genus of trees and shrubs of the custard-apple family, natives of the tropics, chiefly in America; **xylopyrog'raphy**, poker-painting on wood; **xyl'ose**, a pentose found in many plants, also known as wood-sugar.—*adjs.* **xylot'omous** (Gr. *tomē*, a cut), of insects, wood-boring, wood-cutting; **xylotypograph'ic**, pertaining to, or printed from, wooden type.—*ns.* **xylotypog'-raphy; xy'lyl** (*-lil*), any of the univalent radicals, $C_8H_9$, of the xylenes or their derivatives. [Gr. *xylon*, wood.]

**Xyris,** *zi'ris, n.* a genus of sedge-like plants, usu. with yellow flowers, of the family **Xyridaceae** (*zir-i-dā'si-ē*) and order **Xyridā'les**,—*adj.* **xyridā'-ceous** (*-shəs*), of the Xyridaceae. [Gr. *xyris*, a kind of iris.]

**xyster,** *zis'tər, n.* a surgeon's instrument for scraping bones. [Gr. *xystēr*, a graving tool.]

**xystus,** *zis'təs,* (*ant.*) *n.* a covered portico used by athletes for their exercises: an open colonnade: a tree-planted walk.—Also **xyst, xys'tos.** [L.,— Gr. *xystos* or *-on*, perh. orig. a cleared or raked place—*xyein*, to scrape; cf. **xyster.**]

*fāte, fär; mē, hûr* (her); *mīne; mōte, för; mūte; mōon, fōot; dhen* (then)

# Y

**Y, y,** *wī, n.* the twenty-fifth letter of our alphabet, twenty-third of the Roman alphabet, derived, as are also U and V, from Greek upsilon (Υ, υ); it is used to represent a consonant sound as in *year* (*y* = O.E. 3; M.E. 3, yogh), and the vowel and diphthongal sounds, *i,* as in *hymn, folly, ī,* as in *my, pyre, ǝ,* as in *satyr, û,* as in *myrrh*; also in digraphs, as *oy* instead of *oi* when final, e.g. in *toy.* Early printers used *y* as a substitute for thorn (þ), which their founts lacked: hence it came to be so used in MSS. and inscriptions, as *yat* or *yᵗ* for *that, ye* for *the*; cf. ye (2). As a mediaeval numeral, Y = 150; Ȳ = 150,000.— **Y'-alloy,** an aluminium-base alloy of duralumin type, containing copper 4%, magnesium 1.5%, silicon 0.7%, nickel 2%, iron 0.6%, and titanium 0.2%; **Y'-chromosome,** one of a pair of chromosomes associated with sex-determination (the other being the X-chromosome); **Y'-level,** a type of engineers' level whose essential characteristic is the support of the telescope, namely, Y-shaped rests in which it may be rotated, or reversed end-for-end.—Also **wye'-level; Y'-moth,** any of a genus of destructive noctuid moths with a silvery Y-shaped mark on the fore-wings; **Y'-track,** a short track laid at right angles to a railway-line, connected with it by two switches resembling a Y, used for reversing engines.

**y-, i-,** *pfx.* derived from O.E. pfx. *ge-* (3e-), orig. a preposition meaning 'with, together', seen in O.E. nouns and adjectives, as *gefēra,* companion, *getheaht,* counsel, *gelīc,* alike, etc., and in verbs, as *getheodan,* to join together, *gerinnan,* to congeal, but even in O.E. times often used with no very definite meaning: in primitive Germanic *gi-* imparted a perfective meaning to past participles; in O.E. (as *ge-*) and in M.E. (as 3e-, y-, i-, etc.) it was prefixed to past participles, indiscriminately, and it was in this way used freely by Spenser and other archaisers.

**yabber,** *yab'ǝr,* (*Austr.*) *n.* talk, conversation, jabber.—*v.i.* to talk, jabber. [Native word *yabba,* language—perh. modified by **jabber.**]

**yacca,** *yak'ǝ, n.* either of two evergreens (Podocarpus) of the West Indies, or their wood. [Sp. *yaca,* from Taino.]

**yacht,** *yot, n.* orig. a light fast-sailing vessel: a sailing, steam, etc., vessel elegantly fitted up for pleasure-trips or racing.—*v.i.* to sail or race in a yacht.—*n.* **yacht'er,** one engaged in sailing a yacht.—*n.* and *adj.* **yacht'ing.**—*adj.* **yacht'-built,** built on the model of a yacht.—**yacht'-club,** a club of yachtsmen; **yachts'man,** one who keeps or sails a yacht; **yachts'manship,** the art of sailing a yacht.—**land'-, sand'-yacht,** a wheeled boat with sails, for running on land, usu. seabeaches; **land'-, sand'-yachting.** [Du. *jacht* (formerly *jagt*), from *jagen,* to chase; Ger. *jagen,* to hunt.]

**yack,** or **yak,** *yak,* in full **yackety-yak,** *yak'i-ti-yak',* (*slang*) *n.* persistent, often idle or stupid talk.—*v.i.* to talk persistently, esp. in a foolish or gossiping manner. — Also **ya(c)k'ety-ya(c)k', yak'ity-yak'.** [Imit.]

**yacker.** Same as **yakka.**

**yaff,** *yaf,* (*Scot.*) *v.i.* to bark like a snarling dog: to scold, nag. [Imit.]

**yaffle,** (*dial.*), *yaf'l,* **yaffingale** (*Tennyson*), *yaf'ing-gāl, ns.* the green woodpecker. [From its sound; influenced by **nightingale.**]

**yager,** *yä'gǝr, n.* Same as **jäger.**

**yagger,** *yag'ǝr,* (*Scot.*) *n.* a pedlar. [Variant of **jagger** (see **jag,** 2).]

**yah,** *yä.* Variant of **yea.**

**yah,** *yä, interj.* an exclamation of derision, contemptuous defiance, or disgust.

**Yahoo,** *yä-hōō', n.* a name given by Swift in *Gulliver's Travels* to a class of animals with the forms of men but the understanding and passions of brutes: a brutal or boorish lout.

**Yahwe(h),** *yä'wä,* Jehovah (q.v.).—*n.* **Yah'wist,** Jehovist.—Also **Yah've(h), Yah'vist.**

**Yajurveda,** *yuj'ōōr-vä-dǝ,* or *-ve-, n.* one of the four Vedas, the Veda of prayers. [Sans.]

**yak,** *yak, n.* a species of ox found in Tibet, and domesticated there, covered all over with a thick coat of long silky hair, that of the lower parts hanging down almost to the ground.—*n.* **yakh'-dan,** a box which is used for strapping on a yak. [Tibetan.]

**yak, yakety-yak,** etc. See **yack.**

**yakka,** *yak'ǝ,* (*Austr.*) *n.* hard toil.—Also **yacker, yakker.** [Native (Queensland) word.]

**Yakut,** *yä-kōōt', n.* a member of a mixed Turkish race in Siberia, in the Lena district: their Turkic language.

**yald.** See **yauld.**

**Yale lock,** *yāl lok,* trademark for certain kinds of lock. [Linus *Yale* (1821-68), American locksmith.]

**Y-alloy.** See under **Y.**

**yam,** *yam, n.* a large tuberous root like the potato, growing in tropical countries: any plant of the genus Dioscorea, some species of which yield these tubers: a variety of potato (*Scot.*): a sweet-potato (*Southern U.S.*). [Port. *inhame.*]

**Yama,** *yum'ǝ, yam'ǝ, n.* in Hindu mythology, the first mortal. [Sans.]

**yamen,** *yä'men, n.* the offices and residence of a mandarin. [Chin.]

**yammer,** *yam'ǝr,* (*dial.* and *coll.*) *v.i.* to lament, wail: to whine: to make an outcry: to express yearning.—*n.* **yamm'ering.** [O.E. *gēom(e)rian*—*gēomor,* sad; influenced in M.E. by Du. *jammeren.*]

**Yang.** See **Yin.**

**yang,** *yang, n.* various species of Dipterocarpus, valuable timber trees.

**yank,** *yangk, v.t.* (*coll.*) to carry, move, pull with a jerk.—*v.i.* to pull or jerk vigorously (*coll.*): to move actively (*fig.*).—*n.* a blow, buffet (*Scot.*): a strong jerk (*coll.*).—*n.* **yank'er** (*Scot.*), a rap: a big lie.—*adj.* **yank'ing,** active (*Scot.*): pulling, jerking (*coll.*).—*n.* **yank'ie** (*Scot.*), a scold: an impudent woman. [Ety. dub.]

**Yankee,** *yang'ki, n.* in America, a citizen of the New England States, or an inhabitant of the northern United States, as opposed to the southern: in British usage, generally an inhabitant of the United States.—Also *adj.*—Also **Yank** (*coll.*).—*n.* **Yank'eedom,** the land of Yankees: Yankees generally.—Also *adj.*—*adj.* **Yank'eefied.**—*n.* **Yank'eeism,** Yankee characteristics.—**Yank'ee-Doo'dle,** a Yankee (from a popular song). [Prob. *Janke,* a diminutive of Du. *Jan,* John.]

**yaourt,** *yä'ōōrt.* Same as **yoghurt.**

**yap,** *yap, v.i.* to bark sharply or constantly (as a small dog): to speak constantly, esp. in a noisy or foolish manner (*coll.*): to scold (*coll.*).—*n.* a yelp: a cur: incessant, foolish chatter (*coll.*): a fool, bumpkin (*U.S.*): the mouth (*slang*).— *ns.* yapp′er, yap′ster, a dog. [Imit.]

yapok, yapock, *yap′ək, n.* the S. American wateropossum. [From river *Oyapok*, in French Guiana.]

yapon. See yaupon.

yapp, *yap, n.* a limp leather binding in which the cover overlaps the edges of the book. [*Yapp*, a bookseller.]

Yarborough, *yär′bər-ə, n.* a hand containing no card above a nine [From an Earl of *Yarborough*, said to have betted against its occurrence ]

yard, *yärd, n.* a straight thin branch, a wand of authority, a stick for beating as punishment, or a rod for measuring (*obs.*): in English speaking countries, a measure of 3 feet or 36 inches and equivalent to 0.9144 metre: a piece of material this length: a long beam on a mast for spreading square sails: the penis (*arch.*).—*n.* yard′age, the aggregate number of yards: the length, area, or volume measured or estimated in linear, square, or cubic yards: the cutting of coal at so much a yard.—yard′-arm, either half of a ship's yard (right or left) from the centre to the end; yard′land, a virgate, a yard of land; yard′stick, a stick 3 feet long: any standard of measurement (*fig.*).—Also yard′wand. by the yard, sold or measured in yard lengths: in large quantities (*fig.*); yard of ale, etc., a tall slender glass for ale, etc., or its contents; yard of land, a measure of area of land, a virgate. [O.E. *gyrd*, *gierd*, a rod, measure; Du. *garde*, Ger. *gerte*; conn. Goth. *gazds*, a prickle, sting; and prob. L. *hasta*, a spear.]

yard, *yärd, n.* an enclosed place, esp. near a building, often in composition, as 'backyard,' 'courtyard,' 'farmyard,' 'prison-yard,' or where any special work is carried on, as 'brickyard,' 'wood-yard,' 'dockyard,' 'railway-yard': a garden.—*v.t.* to enclose in a yard.—*n.* yard′age, the use of a yard, or the charge made for such.— yard′man, the person having special charge of a farmyard: one employed in a railway-yard in making up trains, etc.; yard′-master, one who has the special oversight of a railway-yard.— the Yard, Scotland Yard, the London Metropolitan Police headquarters. [O.E. *geard*, fence, dwelling, enclosure; Ger. *garten*; conn. with L. *hortus*, Gr. *chortos*.]

yardang, *yär′däng, n.* a ridge formed by wind erosion from sand, silt, etc. and which usu. lies parallel to the prevailing wind direction. [Turk. abl. of *yar*, steep bank, precipice.]

yare, *yär, adj.* (*arch.* and *dial.*) ready, prepared: quick, brisk: easily handled, manageable.—*interj.* (*Shak.*) quick!—*adv.* yare′ly (*arch.* and *dial.*), promptly: skilfully. [O.E. *gearu, gearo*, ready, prompt; Du. *gaar*, done, cooked sufficiently, Ger. *gar*, wholly.]

yarfa. See yarpha.

yarn, *yärn, n.* spun thread: one of the threads of a rope, or these collectively: a sailor's story, spun out to some length, and often having incredible elements: a story generally (*coll.*).— *v.i.* to tell stories. [O.E. *gearn*, thread; O.N. and Ger. *garn*.]

yarpha, yarfa, *yär′fə, n.* peaty soil in Shetland: clayey, sandy, or fibrous peat: a peat-bog. [O.N. *jörfi*, gravel.]

yarr, *yär,* (*dial.*) *n.* the corn spurrey. [Cf. Fris. *jîr.*]

yarrow, *yar′ō, n.* a strong-scented plant, *Achillea millefolium*, or similar species of milfoil. [O.E. *gearwe*; Ger. *garbe*.]

yarta, yarto. See jarta.

yashmak, *yash′mak,* or -*mak′, n.* the double veil worn by Moslem women in public, the eyes only being uncovered. [Ar. *yashmag*.]

yatag(h)an, *yat′ə-gan, n.* a long Turkish dagger, without guard, usu. curved. [Turk. *yātāghan*.]

yate, *yāt,* (*Spens.*) *n.* a gate. [Variant of gate.]

yatter, *yat′ər,* (*Scot.*) *n.* tiresome, importunate or persistent chatter.—*v.i.* to jabber indefatigably. —*n.* and *adj.* yatt′ering.—*adv.* yatt′eringly.

yaud, *yöd, yäd,* (*Scot.*) *n.* a mare: an old mare: an old horse generally. [O.N. *jalda*. Cf. jade (1).]

yauld, yald, *yöld, yäld,* (*Scot.*) *adj.* active, nimble, strong. [Ety. unknown.]

yaup, *yöp,* (*Scot.*) *adj.* hungry. [O.E. *gēap*, shrewd.]

yaupon, *yö′pən, n.* a bushy evergreen shrub of the holly genus, native to the S.E. coasts of the U.S., its leaves yielding the medicinal 'black drink' of the Indians.—Also yapon (*yō′*), yupon (*yōō′*), [Amer. Indian.]

yaw, *yö, v.i.* of a ship, to deviate temporarily from, to turn out of the line of, its course: to move unsteadily or zigzag (*fig.*): to deviate in a horizontal direction from the line of flight (*aero.*).— *v.t.* to cause to deviate from course, zigzag, etc. —*n.* a deviation from the course: the angular motion of an aircraft in a horizontal plane about the normally vertical axis. [Origin uncertain; cf. O.N. *jaga*, to move to and fro, as a door on its hinges.]

yawl, *yöl, v.i.* to howl.—*n.* a howl. [Variant of yowl.]

yawl, *yöl, n.* a ship's small boat, generally with four or six oars: a small fishing-boat: a small sailing-boat with jigger and curtailed mainboom. [Du. *jol.*]

yawn, *yön, v.i.* to take a deep involuntary breath from drowsiness, boredom, etc.: to gape: to gape with astonishment (*Shak.*): to be wide open, as a chasm.—*v.t.* to render, to make, or to effect, by yawning: to utter with a yawn.—*n.* an involuntary deep breath from weariness or boredom: a chasm, opening: dullness (*Shelley*). —*adj.* yawn′ing, gaping, opening wide: drowsy: causing drowsiness or sleep (Shak., *Macb.*, III, ii. 43).—*n.* action of the verb to yawn.—*adv.* yawn′ingly.—*adj.* yawn′y. [O.E. *gānian*, to yawn, and *geonian, ginian* (in composition, *ginan*, pa.t. *gān*), to gape widely; O.N. *gīna*, to gape.]

yaws, *yöz, n.* a tropical epidemic and contagious disease of the skin—also known as framboesia, button scurvy, verruga Peruviana, buba or boba, etc.—*adj.* yaw′(e)y, pertaining to yaws. [Origin uncertain; perh. Amer. Indian.]

ybet, *i-bet′,* obs. *pa.p.* of beat.

yblent, *i-blent′, pa.p.* (*arch.*) of blend, (*obs.*) of blind.

ybore, *i-bōr′, -bör′,* obs. *pa.p.* of bear.

ybrent, *i-brent′,* obs. *pa.p.* of burn.

Y-chromosome. See under Y.

yclad, *i-klad′,* ycled, *i-kled′,* obs. forms of clad, *pa.p.* of clothe.

yclept, *i-klept,* or ycleped (*Milt.* ycleap′d), *i-klēp′id, i-klēpt′.* See clepe.—*infin.* (*Spens.*) ycleepe.

ycond, *i-kond′,* obs. *pa.p.* of con.

ydrad, *i-drad′,* ydred, *i-dred′,* obs. *pa.ps.* of dread.

ye, *yē, yi, pron.* the second person pl. (sometimes sing.) pronoun, now *arch., B., dial., poet.*; cf. you. Formerly, as in the A.V. of the English Bible, *ye* was always used as a nominative, and you as a dative or accusative; later *ye* was sometimes used for all these cases. [M.E. *ye*, nom.; *your*, gen.; *you, yow*, dat. and accus. pl.— O.E. *gē*, nom. ye; *ēower*, gen.; *ēow*, dat. and accus.]

ye, *thē, thi,* archaic script for 'the', arising from the thorn letter, þ. See Y.

yea, *yā, adv.* yes: verily: indeed more than that. —*n.* an affirmative vote or voter. [O.E. *gēa*; Du. and Ger. *ja*, O.N. *jā*; cf. yes.]

yead, yede, yeed, *yēd,* (*Spens.*) *v.i.* to go, proceed: —*pr.p.* yead′ing; *pa.t.* yod (*yod*), yode (*yōd*). [O.E. *ēode*, went, used as pa.t. of *gān*, to go.]

**yeah**, *ye*, *yä*, (*coll.*) *adv.* yes.

**yealdon**, *yel′dən*, (*Scott*, as if Cumberland dialect) *n.* Same as eldin.

**yean**, *yēn*, (*arch.* and *dial.*) *v.t.* and *v.i.* esp. of a sheep, to bring forth (young).—*n.* **yean′ling**, a lamb or a kid.—Also *adj.* [O.E. *ge-*, *eanian*, to bring forth; *ēacen*, increased, pregnant.]

**year**, *yēr*, *yûr*, *n.* a period of time determined by the revolution of the earth in its orbit: the period beginning with 1st January and ending with 31st December, consisting of 365 days, except in 'leap-year', when one day is added to February, making the number 366—the present **legal**, **civil**, or **calendar year**: a space of twelve calendar months: (in *pl.*) period of life, esp. age or old age: (in *pl.*) a very long time:—*pl.* **years** (collective *pl.*, used adjectively with numeral prefixed, **year**, e.g. *a three year period*).—*n.* **year′ling**, an animal a year old.—*adj.* a year old.—*adj.* **year′ly**, happening every year: lasting a year.—*adv.* once a year: from year to year.—**year′-book**, a book published annually, reviewing the events of the past year.—*adj.* **year′long**, lasting a year.—**anomalistic year**, the earth's time of passage from perihelion to perihelion—365 days, 6 hours, 13 minutes, 49 seconds; **astronomical year**, the time of one complete mean apparent circuit of the ecliptic by the sun—365 days, 5 hours, 48 minutes, 46 seconds—called also the **equinoctial**, **natural**, **solar**, or **tropical year**; **canicular year**, the Sothic year (see **Sothic**); **ecclesiastical year**, the year as arranged in the ecclesiastical calendar, with the saints' days, festivals, etc.; **embolismic year**, a year of thirteen lunar months (384 days), occurring in a lunisolar calendar such as that of the Jews; **financial year**, **fiscal year**, a period of twelve months at the end of which accounts are balanced; **Hebrew year**, a lunisolar year, of 12, or 13, months of 29 or 30 days (in every cycle of nineteen years the 6th, 8th, 11th, 14th, 17th, and 19th having thirteen months instead of twelve); **Julian year**, the year according to the Julian calendar (introduced by Julius Caesar, modified by Augustus; superseded by the Gregorian calendar), a period of 365¼ days, longer than astronomical year by about 11 minutes (see **style**); **leap-year** (see above); **legal**, **civil**, or **calendar**, **year**, the year by which dates are reckoned; it has begun on different dates at different periods, and for six centuries before 1752 it began in England on 25th March; since then (earlier in Scotland) it has begun on 1st January; **lunar year**, a period of twelve lunar months or 354 days; **Platonic year**, a cycle of years at the end of which the heavenly bodies were supposed to be again in the same place as at the Creation—also **great**, or **perfect**, **year**; **Sabbatic**, **-al**, **year** (see **Sabbath**); **sidereal year**, the period required by the sun to move from a given star to the same star again—having a mean value of 365 days, 6 hours, 9 minutes, 9·6 seconds; **year in**, **year out**, (happening, done, etc.) every year: with monotonous regularity; **Year of Grace**, or **of our Lord**, date of the Christian era. [O.E. *gēar*; Ger. *jahr*, O.N. *ār*, Gr. *hōrā*, season.]

**yeard**, **yeard-hunger**. See **yird**.

**yearn**, *yûrn*, *v.t.* to desire strongly, feel longing for (*obs.*; also **earn**): to express a desire for, ask for (*obs.*): to cause to mourn (*Shak.*).—*v.i.* to feel earnest desire: to feel compassion, tenderness, grief (also used impersonally, as 'it yearns me'; *obs.*; also **earn**): to express longing, as in sound or appearance.—*n.* a yearning.—*n.* and *adj.* **yearn′ing**.—*adv.* **yearn′ingly**. [O.E. *geornan* (W.S. *giernan*), to desire: allied to *georn*, desirous, eager; cf. Ger. *gern*, willingly.]

**yearn**, *yûrn*, (*obs.* and *dial.*) *v.t.* to earn. [earn (1).]

**yearn**, *yûrn*, *v.i.* to curdle, as milk.—Also **earn**.—*n.*

**yearn′ing**, **earn′ing**, rennet. [earn (2).]

**yeast**, *yēst*, *n.* a substance used in brewing, etc., consisting of minute fungi, which produce zymase, and hence induce the alcoholic fermentation of carbohydrates: the froth on beer (*obs.*): spume or foam of water (*Shak.*): leaven (*fig.*).—*v.i.* (*lit.* and *fig.*) to ferment, or be covered with froth.—*n.* **yeast′iness**.—*adj.* **yeast′y**, like yeast: frothy, foamy: unsubstantial.—**yeast′-plant**, any of the Saccharomycetes; **yeast′-powder**, a baking powder. [O.E. *gist*, *gyst*; Ger. *gäscht*, *gischt*.]

**yede**, **yeed**. See **yead**.

**yegg**, *yeg*, (*U.S.*) *n.* a burglar, esp. a burglar of safes.—Also **yegg′man**. [Poss. the name of an American safe-breaker.]

**yeld**, *yeld*, **yell**, *yel*, (*Scot.*) *adj.* barren: not giving milk: unproductive. [Late O.E. *gelde*; cf. **geld**.]

**yeldring**, *yeld′ring*, *n.* Same as **yoldring**.—Also **yeld′rock**.

**yelk**. Same as **yolk**.

**yell**, *yel*, *v.i.* to howl or cry out with a sharp noise: to scream from pain or terror.—*v.t.* to utter with a yell.—*n.* a sharp outcry: a particular cry affected by an American college: something or someone very funny (*slang*).—*n.* **yell′ing**.—*v.i.* **yell′och** (*-ɲhh*; *Scot.*), to yell.—*n.* a yell. [O.E. (Angl.) *gellan*; Ger. *gellen*; conn. with O.E. *galan*, to sing.]

**yellow**, *yel′ō*, *adj.* of the colour of sulphur or of the primrose: of the colour of gold: of Mongolic race: of mixed black and white race: cowardly, base (*coll.*): sensational (*coll.*).—*n.* the colour of the rainbow between the orange and the green: any dye or pigment producing such a colour: yolk: (in *pl.*) peach-yellows (see **peach**), or other plant disease in which the foliage yellows: jaundice in horses, etc.—*v.t.* and *v.i.* to make, or become, yellow.—*adj.* **yell′owish**, somewhat yellow.—*ns.* **yell′owishness**; **yell′owness**, quality or state of being yellow: jealousy (*obs.*; *fig.*).—*adj.* **yell′owy**, yellowish.—*adjs.* **yell′ow-backed**, **-bellied**, **-billed**, **-breasted**, **-covered**, **-crowned**, **-eyed**, **-footed**, **-fronted**, **-headed**, **-horned**, **-legged**, **-necked**, **-ringed**, **-rumped**, **-shouldered**, **-spotted**, etc.—**yell′owback**, a cheap, sensational novel, specif. one with yellow board or paper covers, common in the 19th cent.; **yellow berries**, Persian berries; **yell′ow-bird**, any of various birds of a yellow colour—the golden oriole, summer-warbler, etc.; **yell′ow-boy** (*slang*), a gold coin: a mulatto or dark quadroon (*fem.* **yell′ow-girl**); **yell′ow-bunting**, the yellow-hammer; **yell′ow-dog**, a mongrel: a cur: a base or cowardly person (also used adjectively); **yell′ow-earth**, yellow ochre; **yell′ow-fever**, an acute disease occurring in tropical America and West Africa, caused by infection with a virus transmitted to man by the bite of a mosquito *Aëdes aegypti* (former name *Stegomyia fasciata*), characterised by high fever, acute nephritis, jaundice, and haemorrhages; **yell′ow-flag**, a flag of a yellow colour, displayed by a vessel in quarantine or over a military hospital or ambulance; **yell′ow-hammer**, **-ammer**, a finch (*Emberiza citrinella*), so named from its yellow colour—also called yellow-bunting; **Yellow Jack** (*slang*), yellow fever; **yell′ow-metal**, a brass consisting of sixty parts copper and forty parts zinc; **yellow pages**, that part of a telephone directory, printed on yellow paper, which classifies participating subscribers alphabetically according to trades, professions, services, etc.; **yellow peril**, the danger that the yellow races may crush the white and overrun the world; **yellow press**, newspapers abounding in exaggerated, sensational articles; **yell′ow-rattle** (see **rattle**);

yell'ow-root, golden-seal; yell'ow-snow, snow sometimes observed in the Alps and in the Antarctic regions, coloured yellow by the growth on it of certain algae; yell'ow-soap, common soap composed of tallow, resin, and soda; yell'ow-spot, macula lutea, the small area at the centre of the retina in vertebrates at which vision is most distinct; yell'ow-wash, a lotion consisting of a mixture of mercuric chloride and lime-water; yell'ow-weed, common ragwort: golden-rod: weld (dial.); yell'ow-wood, any of various woods that are light in colour, as satin-wood, or yield yellow dye, as that of Cladrastis lutea (Southern U.S.): any of the trees that yield these woods: a tree, as a sumach, that gives yellow dye from a part other than the wood; yell'ow-wort, an annual of the gentian family—also yell'ow-cen'taury; yell'ow-yite, -yoldring, -yorling, or -yowley (same as yoldring).—a yellow streak, a tendency to dastardly behaviour; yellow-eyed grass, any plant of the genus Xyris, growing abundantly in the pine-barrens of Southern U.S. [O.E. geolu; Ger. gelb; cog. with L. helvus, light bay.]

yelp, yelp, v.i. to boast (obs.): to utter a sharp bark.—n. a sharp, quick cry or bark.—n. yelp'er. —n. and adj. yelp'ing. [O.E. gielpan, to boast, exult; O.N. gjālpa, to yelp.]

yelt, yelt, (dial.) n. a young sow. [O.E. gilte—M.L.G. gelte, a spayed sow.]

yen, yen, n. formerly a Japanese gold or silver coin: the Japanese monetary unit since 1871:— pl. yen. [Jap.,—Chin. yüan, round, a dollar.]

yen, yen, (slang) n. an intense desire, longing, urge.—v.i. to desire, yearn. [Chin. yeen, craving, addiction.]

yeoman, yō'man, n. a gentleman serving in a royal or noble household, ranking between a sergeant and a groom (hist.): after the fifteenth century, one of a class of small farmers, commonly free-holders, the next grade below gentlemen (often serving as foot soldiers; hist.): a man of small estate, any small farmer or countryman above the grade of labourer: an assistant to an official: a member of the yeomanry cavalry or of the yeomen of the guard: a petty officer on a war vessel whose duties are clerical:—pl. yeo'men. adj. yeo'manly, of yeoman's rank: humble and honest: staunch: brave.—adv. staunchly, bravely.—n. yeo'manry, the collective body of smaller freeholders: a cavalry volunteer force in Great Britain formed during the wars of the French Revolution, later mechanised as part of the Territorials.—yeoman('s) service, powerful aid, such as came from the yeomen in the English armies of early times.—Yeomen of the Guard, a veteran company of picked soldiers, employed in conjunction with the gentlemen-at-arms, on special occasions, as the sovereign's bodyguard—constituted a corps in 1485 by Henry VII, and still wearing the costume of that period. [M.E. yoman, yeman; perh. for young man.]

yep, yep, U.S. dial. and coll. variant of yes.

yerba, yûr'bə, n. a herb, esp. (also yerba mate, yerba de maté), Paraguay tea or maté (q.v.). [Sp.,—L. herba.]

yerd, yerd-hunger. See yird.

yerk, yûrk, (all meanings now dial.) v.t. of a shoemaker, to draw (stitches) tight: to bind or tie with a jerk: to throw or thrust with a sudden, quick motion: to move with a jerk: to lash out with: to utter jerkily: to beat: to rouse, excite (fig.).—v.i. to draw tight, bind, strike, move, rise, with a jerk: to kick: to engage in with energy or eagerness: to gird (1), carp. [Origin obscure; earlier than jerk.]

yes, yes, adv. ay: a word of affirmation or consent: formerly, on the contrary: yea.—yes'-man (coll.), one who agrees with everything that is said to him: an obedient follower with no initiative. [O.E. gēse, gise—gēa, gē, yea, and sī, let it be.]

yest, yesty. Obs. forms of yeast, yeasty.

yester, yes'tər (dial. and arch. yestern), adj. relating to yesterday: last.—adv. yestreen' (contr. of yestereven; Scot. and poet.), yesterday evening. —n. yes'terday, the day last past.—adv. on the day last past.—yestereve'(n), yestereve'ning, yestermorn', yestermorn'ing, the evening, morning, of yesterday; yesternight', last night; yesteryear' (orig. D. G. Rossetti), last year. [O.E. geostran, giestran (always followed by dæg, etc.); Ger. gestern; cf. L. hesternus, Gr. chthes.]

yet, yet, adv. in addition, besides: up to the present time: still: hitherto: at the same time: even: before the affair is finished.—conj. nevertheless: however.—as yet, up to the time under consideration. [O.E. giet, gieta; Ger. jetzt.]

yeti, yet'i, n. the abominable snowman. [Native Tibetan name.]

yett, yet, (Scot.) n. a gate, door—another form of yate (q.v.).

yeuk. See yuke.

yeve, yēv, v.t. to give:—pa.p. (Spens.) yeven (yev'ən). [O.E. giefan; cf. give.]

yew, ū, n. any tree of genus Taxus—family Taxaceae, itself a division of the group Coniferae —widely diffused over the northern parts of the world, with narrow lanceolate or linear leaves, esp. Taxus baccata (in Europe long planted in graveyards) which yields an elastic wood good for bows: its wood: a bow made of its wood: yew twigs regarded as emblematic of grief.—adj. yew'en (arch.), made of yew.—yew'-tree. [O.E. iw, ēow; Ger. eibe.]

yex, yeks, (dial.) v.i. to hiccup, belch, spit.—n. a hiccup, etc.—Also yesk. [O.E. geocsian, to sob.]

Yezidi, ye'zi-di, n. one of a sect in Armenia and the Caucasus believing in a Supreme God but paying respect also to the author of evil and other minor gods.—Also Yez'di, Yez'idee, Zez'idee, etc. [Origin unknown.]

yfere, i-fēr', (obs.) adv. together, in company. [See fere (1), and infere.]

Yggdrasil(l), ig'drə-sil, (Scand. myth.) n. the ash-tree binding together heaven, earth, and hell, and extending its branches over the whole world and above the heavens.—Also Ygdrasil. [O.N.; perh.— Yggr, a surname of Odin, and drasil, horse.]

yglaunst, i-glönst', (Spens.) pa.p. of glance.

ygo, ygoe, i-gō', pa.p. (Spens.) gone: ago. [go.]

Yiddish, yid'ish, n. a compound of very corrupt Hebrew, ancient or provincial German, and other elements, spoken by Jews.—ns. Yid, Yidd'isher, a Jew. [Ger. jüdisch, Jewish.]

yield, yēld, v.t. to pay or repay, or to reward (obs.): to render as due or fitting (arch.): to grant, accord: to admit, concede: to give out: to furnish, afford: to produce: to deliver, surrender, relinquish, resign.—v.i. to submit: to cease fighting or contesting: to give way under pressure: to give place.—n. amount yielded: product: the return of a financial investment, usually calculated with reference to the cost and dividend.—adj. yield'able, that may be yielded: inclined to yield.—ns. yield'ableness; yield'er.—adj. yield'ing, giving, or inclined to give, way: compliant.—n. giving way: compliance.—adv. yield'ingly.—n. yield'ingness.—yield point, in the case of iron and annealed steels, the stress at which a substantial amount of plastic deformation takes place suddenly.—yield up the ghost, give up the ghost (see ghost). [O.E. (W.S.) gieldan, to pay; O.H.G. gelten, O.N. gjalda.]

yill, yil, n. Scots form of ale.

yin, yince. Scots forms of one, once, generally written ane, ance.

Yin, Yang, yin, yang, ns. the two opposing principles of Chinese philosophy and religion influencing destiny, the former negative, feminine and dark, the latter positive, masculine and light.

**yince-errand.** See **errand.**

**yip,** *yip, v.t.* to give a short, sudden cry—esp. of a dog.—Also *n.* [Imit.]

**yippee,** *yip-ē′, interj.* expressing delight, exultation, etc.

**yippy,** *yip′i, n.* one of a group of young people with ideals based on those of the hippies. [From the *Youth International Party* of 1968.]

**yird,** *yûrd, n.* a Scots form of **earth.**—Also **eard, yeard, yerd.**—*v.t.* to bury.—**eard′-, yird′-,** etc., **house** (see **earth-house); eard′-, yeard′-, yerd′-, yird′-hunger,** earth-hunger: the hunger sometimes felt by persons approaching death: voracious hunger.—*adj.* **eard′-,** etc., **hungry.** [**earth.**]

**yirk.** Same as **yerk.**

**yite,** *yit, (dial.) n.* the yellow-hammer. [Origin obscure.]

**ylang-ylang,** *ē′lang-ē′lang, n.* a tree (*Canangium odoratum*) of the Malay Archipelago and Peninsula, the Philippines, etc., or an essence (also **ylang-ylang oil**) distilled from its flowers. [Tagálog.]

**ylem,** *i′lam, n.* the prime substance whence according to some theories, the elements are sprung. [O.Fr. *ilem*—L. *hȳlem,* accus. of *hȳlē*—Gr. *hȳlē,* matter.]

**Y-level, Y-moth.** See **Y.**

**ylike** (*Spens.*). Same as **alike.**

**ylke.** See **ilk.**

**ymolt,** *i-mōlt′,* (*Spens.*) *v.t. pa.p.* of **melt.**

**ympe, ympt** (*Spens.*). Same as **imp, imped.**

**ynambu,** *ē-näm-bōō′, n.* a very large tinamou. [Port. *inambu;* of Tupí origin, related to **tinamou.**]

**Ynd** (*Spens.*). Same as **Ind.**

**yo,** *yō, interj.* calling for, or accompanying, effort, etc.—*interjs.* **yo-ho′,** calling for attention; **yo-heave′-ho′,** formerly, a sailors' chant while hauling on ropes.

**yob,** *yob, (slang) n.* a raw recruit: a teenage loafer: a lout.—Also **yobb′ō.** [Back-slang for **boy.**]

**yod(e).** See **yead.**

**yodel, yodle,** *yō′dl, v.t.* and *v.i.* to sing or shout, changing frequently from the ordinary voice to falsetto and back again after the manner of the mountaineers of the Tirol.—*n.* a song or phrase sung, or a cry made, in this fashion.—Also **jodel** (*yō′dl*). — *n.* **yō′deller, yō′dler.** [Ger. dial. *jodeln.*]

**yoga,** *yō′gə, n.* a system of Hindu philosophy showing the means of emancipation of the soul from further migrations and union with the supreme being: any of a number of systems of physical and mental discipline by means of which such emancipation is attained.—*ns.* **yō′gi (-gē), yō′gin,** a Hindu ascetic who practises the yoga system, consisting in the withdrawal of the senses from external objects, long continuance in unnatural postures, etc.—*adj.* **yō′gic.**—*n.* **yō′gism.** [Sans., union.]

**yogh,** *yohh, n.* the M.E. letter ȝ, derived from O.E. ȝ. [Origin uncertain, but appropriate as exemplifying the two chief sounds of the letter.]

**yoghourt, yoghurt,** *yō′gōort, yog′ərt, n.* a semi-liquid food made from fermented milk.—Also **yaourt** (*yä′ōort*). [Turk. *yōghurt.*]

**yohimbine,** *yo-him′bēn, n.* an alkaloid obtained from the bark of *Corynanthe johimbe.* [Of Bantu origin.]

**yoicks,** *yoiks, interj.* an old fox-hunting cry.—*v.i.* or *v.t.* **yoick(s),** to make, or urge on by, this cry.

**yojan,** *yō′jan,* **yojana,** *yō′ja-nə, ns.* an Indian measure of distance, usu. about five miles. [Hind. *yojan*—Sans. *yojana,* (distance covered in one) yoking.]

**yoke,** *yōk, n.* that which joins together: the frame of wood joining draught oxen: any similar frame, as one for carrying pails: a part of a garment that fits the shoulders (or the hips): a stretch of work, e.g. from meal-time to meal-time (*dial.*): a mark of servitude: slavery: a bond of union: a pair or couple, as of oxen.—*v.t.* to put a yoke on: to join together: to attach a draught-animal to: to enslave: to set to work (*fig.*).—*v.i.* to be joined: to go together: to set to work (*Scot.*).—*n.* **yōk′ing** (*dial.*), as much work as is done at a stretch.—**yoke′-devil** (*Shak.*), a companion devil; **yoke′-fellow, -mate,** an associate, partner, fellow-worker.—*adj.* **yoke′-toed,** zygodactyl. [O.E. *geoc;* Ger. *joch;* L. *jugum,* Gr. *zygon.*]

**yokel,** *yō′kl, n.* a country bumpkin.—*adj.* **yō′kel-ish.** [Ety. dub.]

**yokul.** See **jokol.**

**yold,** obs. *pa.t.* and *pa.p.* of **yield.**

**yoldring,** *yōld′ring, n.* a yellow-hammer. [Variant of dial. *yowlring*—O.E. *geolu;* see **yellow.**]

**yolk,** *yōk, (rare)* **yelk,** *yelk, n.* the yellow part of the egg of a bird or reptile: the nutritive non-living material contained by an ovum.—*adjs.* **yolked, yolk′y,** like yolk.—**yolk′-sac** (*zool.*), the yolk-containing sac which is attached to the embryo by the **yolk′-stalk,** a short stalk by means of which yolk substance may pass into the alimentary canal of the embryo. [O.E. *geolca, geoleca*—*geolu,* yellow.]

**yolk,** *yōk, n.* wool-oil.—*adj.* **yolk′y.**—Cf. **suint.** [O.E. *ēowocig,* yolky.]

**Yom Kippur,** *yōm kip′ōor,* the Day of Atonement, a Jewish fast day.—**Yom Teruah** (*ter′ōō-ä*), the Feast of Trumpets.—**Yom Tob** or **Tov** (*tōb, tōv*), any religious festival. [Heb. *yōm,* day, *kippūr,* atonement, *terū′äh,* blowing (of a trumpet), *tōbh,* good.]

**yon,** *yon,* (now *poet.* or *dial.*) *adj.* that: those: yonder.—Also *pron.* that: the thing you know of.—*adv.* yonder.—*prep.* **yond** (*Scot.* usu. **yont**), across, or through (*obs.*): to, or in, a position beyond.—*adj.* and *pron.* yon.—*adv.* yonder.—*adv.* **yon′der,** to, or at, a distance within view.—*adj.* that, those, at a distance within view (or so conceived).—*pron.* that one, yon.—**hither and yon(d)** (*dial.*), hither and thither; **hither,** or **here, and yonder,** hither and thither; **the yonder,** the farther, more distant. [O.E. *geon* (adj., pron.), *geond* (prep., adv.), and M.E. *yonder.*]

**yond,** *yond,* (*Spens., F.Q.* II, viii. 40, 9) *adj.* furious, mad. [Said to be due to misunderstanding of a passage in an earlier writer: Chaucer's *Clerk's Tale* 1143 has been suggested, but 16th-cent. black-letter Chaucers do not have the word in this line.]

**yongthly.** Same as **youngthly** (see **young).**

**yoni,** *yō′nē, n.* a representation of the female genitals, the symbol under which the Hindu deity Sakti is worshipped.

**yonker,** obs. form of **younker.**

**yoop,** *yōōp, n.* and *interj.* a word imitative of a sobbing sound.

**yore,** *yōr, yör, (obs.) adv.* long ago.—*n.* old time.—Also *adj.*—**of yore,** in times past. [O.E. *gēara,* formerly; app. connected with *gēar,* a year.]

**yorker,** *yörk′ər, (cricket) n.* a ball pitched to a point directly under the bat—formerly called *tice.*—*v.t.* **york,** to bowl someone out with a yorker. [Prob. from *Yorkshire,* but history quite unknown.]

**Yorkish,** *yörk′ish, adj.* pertaining to the county or city of *York:* adhering to the House of York in the Wars of the Roses.—*n.* **York′ist,** one of this party.—Also *adj.*—*adj.* **York′shire,** of or from the county of Yorkshire:—abbrev. **Yorks.**—*n.* one of a breed of animal, esp. pigs, originating in Yorkshire.—**Yorkshire fog,** a tall grass, *Holcus lanatus;* **Yorkshire grit ,**a grit from Yorkshire used for polishing; **Yorkshire pudding,** a pudding made of unsweetened batter, and baked along with meat or in meat dripping—orig. under the spit so as to catch the drippings; **Yorkshire terrier,** a small long-haired kind of terrier.

**Yoruba,** *yo'rōō-ba, yō', n. sing.* and *pl.* a linguistic group of coastal West Africa: a member of the group: the language of the group.—*adjs.* **Yoruba, Yoruban.**

**you,** *ū, pron.* the commonly used second person pronoun (all cases), orig. plural (cf. **thou),** now standard for both singular and plural: (indef. *pron.*) anyone. [O.E. *ēow* (perh. through a later form *eōw*), orig. only dat. and accus.; cf. **ye.]**

**youk.** See **yuke.**

**youghourt,** etc. See **yoghourt.**

**young,** *yung, adj.* not long born: in early life: in the first part of growth: youthful: vigorous: relating to youth: junior, the younger of two persons having the same name: inexperienced: newly arrived—in Australia: miniature (*coll.*).— *n.* the offspring of animals: (with *the*) those who are young.—*adj.* **young'ish,** somewhat young.— *n.* **young'ling,** a young person or animal.—*adj.* youthful, young.—*adv.* **young'ly** (*rare*), in youth: in the manner of youth.—*ns.* **young'ness; young'ster,** a young person, esp. a young man, or formerly, a vigorous young man: a child (*coll.*); **youngth** (*Spens.*), youth.—*adj.* **youngth'ly** (*Spens.*), youthful.—**young blood,** fresh accession of strength; **Young England,** during the Corn-Law struggle (1842-45), a little band of young Tory politicians, who hated Free Trade and Radicalism, and professed a sentimental attachment to earlier forms of social life in England; **Young England, America,** etc., the rising generation in England, America, etc.—*adj.* **young'-eyed** (*Shak.*), with the bright eyes of youth.— **Young Ireland,** a group of Irish politicians who broke away from O'Connell about 1844, because of his rooted aversion to physical force; **Young Italy,** an association of Italian republican agitators, active about 1834, under the lead of Mazzini; **young person,** in Factory Acts, etc., a person who is over eighteen years of age but no longer a child; **Young Turk,** one of a body of Turkish reformers who brought about the revolution of 1908.—**with young,** pregnant. [O.E. *geong*; Ger. *jung*; also conn. with L. *juvenis,* Sans. *yuvan,* young.]

**youngberry,** *yung'ber-i, -bər-i, n.* a large reddish-black fruit, a cross between a variety of blackberry and a variety of dewberry. [B. M. *Young,* an American fruitgrower, and **berry.]**

**Young's modulus,** *yungz mod'ū-las,* the coefficient of elasticity of stretching—for a stretched wire, it is the ratio of the stretching force per unit cross-sectional area to the elongation per unit length.

**younker,** *yung'kər, n.* a young person: a young gentleman or knight (*Spens.*). [Old Du. *jonckher* (Du. *jonker*), from *jong heer,* young master or lord; Ger. *junker.*]

**your,** *ūr, pron.* (*gen. pl.*) or *poss. adj.* of or belonging to you: used to denote a person of a class well known—the ordinary (implying some contempt; *Shak.*).—*prons.* **yourn** (*dial.*), yours; **yours** (a double genitive), used predicatively or absolutely: short for 'your letter':—**you and yours,** you and your family or property; **yours faithfully, sincerely, truly,** etc., **yours to command,** etc., forms used conventionally in letters just before the signature: also sometimes used by a speaker to mean himself (*coll.*). [O.E. *ēower,* gen. of *gē,* ye.]

**yourself,** *ūr-self', pron.* the emphatic form of **you:** in your real character: having command of your facul]ties: sane: in good form: the reflexive form of y ou (objective):—*pl.* **yourselves'.**

**yourt.** See **yurt.**

**youth,** *yōōth, n.* state of being young: early life, the period immediately succeeding childhood: an early period of existence: a young person, esp. a young man (*pl.* **youths,** *yōōdhz*): young persons collectively: recentness, freshness (*Shak.*).—*adj.* **youth'ful,** pertaining to youth or early life: young: suitable to youth: fresh: buoyant, vigorous.—*adv.* **youth'fully.**—*ns.* **youth'-fulness; youth'head, youth'hood** (*obs.*), youth. —*adjs.* **youth'ly** (*Spens.*), young, youthful (also *adv.*); **youth'some,** youthful; **youth'y** (*Scot.*), young.—**youth hostel,** a hostel where hikers, etc., who are members of an organisation find inexpensive and simple accommodation.—*v.i.* to stay in youth hostels.—*n.* **youth hosteller.** [O.E. *geoguth—geong,* young; Ger. *jugend.*]

**yow(e),** *yow,* (*dial.*) *n.* variant of **ewe.**

**yowl,** *yowl, v.i.* to cry mournfully, as a dog: to yell, bawl.—*n.* a distressed cry.—*n.* **yowl'ing,** a howling. [M.E. *youlen*; cf. O.N. *gaula,* to howl.]

**yowley.** Same as **yoldring.**

**Yo-yo,** *yō'-yō, n.* tradename for a toy consisting of a reel attached to, and manoeuvred by, a string which winds and unwinds round it—similar to the 18th-cent. bandalore or quiz.

**ypight,** *i-pīt', obs. pa.p.* of **pitch.**

**yplast,** *i-plāst', obs. pa.p.* of **place.**

**yplight,** *i-plīt', obs. pa.p.* of **plight.**

**ypsilon,** *ip-si'lon, -sē',* or *ip'si-, n.* the twentieth letter of the Greek alphabet (Υ, υ): as a numeral, υ'=400; ͵υ=400,000.—Also **upsilon** (*ūp-si'lon, ūp'si-, up'si-*).—*adjs.* **ypsiliform** (*-sil'*), **ypsiloid** (*ip'sil-oid*), shaped like an ypsilon.

**yrapt,** *i-rapt'* (*Spens.*). Same as **rapt.**

**yravished,** *i-rav'ish-id* (Malone's emendation of Shak. *iranyshed*), *pa.t.* of **ravish.**

**yrent,** *i-rent', obs. pa.p.* of **rend.**

**yrivd,** *i-rīvd', obs. pa.p.* of **rive.**

**ysame,** *i-sām', (Spens.) adv.* together. [Perh. in and **same** (n.).]

**yshend,** *i-shend', (Spens.).* Same as **shend.**

**yslaked,** obs. *pa.p.* of **slake** (Shak., *Pericles* III, line 1, quenched or relaxed the energies of).

**ythundered,** *i-thun'də-rid, (Spens.) v.t., pa.p.* struck by a thunderbolt.

**ytost,** *i-tost', (Spens.) pa.p.* of **toss.**

**Y-track.** See **Y.**

**ytterbium,** *i-tûr'bi-əm, n.* a metallic element (Yb; at. numb. 70), a member of the rare-earth group: name orig. given to a substance later shown to consist of a mixture of this and lutetium. [*Ytterby,* a Swedish quarry.]

**yttrium,** *it'ri-əm, n.* a metallic element (Y; at. numb. 39) in the third group of the periodic system, usu. classed with the rare-earths.—*n.* **ytt'ria,** its oxide, a yellowish-white powder.— *adjs.* **ytt'ric, ytt'rious; yttrif'erous.**—*ns.* **ytt'ro-cē'rite,** a mineral, usu. violet in colour, found embedded in quartz, a fluoride of yttrium, cerium, etc.; **ytt'ro-col'umbite, -tan'talite,** a brownish mineral found at Ytterby, a tantalate of yttrium, iron, calcium, etc. [From *Ytterby*; see **ytterbium.]**

**yu,** *yū, ū, n.* precious jade (nephrite or jadeite).— Also **yu'-stone.** [Chin. *yü, yü-shih.*]

**yuan,** *yü-än, n.* the monetary unit of China:—*pl.* **yuan.** [Chin. *yüan.*]

**yuca** (also **yucca),** *yuk'ə, n.* cassava.—*n.* **Yucc'a** (sometimes **Yuc'a),** a genus of plants of the family Liliaceae, natives of Mexico, New Mexico, etc., some (as *Yucca gloriosa,* the Spanish dagger) cultivated in gardens on account of the singularity and splendour of their appearance. [Of Carib origin.]

**yucker,** *yuk'ər, n.* the American flicker or golden-winged woodpecker. [Imit. of its note.]

**yuft,** *yuft, n.* Russia leather. [Russ. *yuft.*]

**yuga,** *yōō'ga, n.* one of the Hindu ages of the world.—Also **yug.** [Sans.]

*fāte, fär; mē, hûr* (her); *mīne; mōte, fŏr; mūte; mōōn, fōōt; dhen* (then)

**Yugo-Slav, Yugoslav,** *yōō'gō-släv,* or *-släv',* n. a native, citizen, or inhabitant of Yugoslavia, one of the southern group of Slavs consisting of Serbs, Croats, and Slovenes: the Slavonic language (Serbo-Croatian) dominant in Yugoslavia.—Also *adj.—adjs.* and *ns.* **Yugoslav'ian, Yugoslav'ic.**—Also **Jugo-Slav, Jugoslav,** etc. [Serbo-Croatian *jugo-*—*jug,* the south, and Slav.]

**yuke,** *yōōk,* **yuck,** *yuk, (dial.) v.i.* to itch.—*n.* itching: the itch.—Also **youk, yeuk, euk, ewk.**— *adj.* **yuk'y, yuck'y,** itchy. [Same as **itch;** prob. influenced by the M.Du. form, *jeuken.*]

**yulan,** *yōō'lan,* n. a Chinese magnolia, with large white flowers. [Chin.]

**Yule,** *yōōl,* n. the season or feast of Christmas.— **Yule log,** the block of wood cut down in the forest, then dragged to the house, and set alight in celebration of Christmas; **Yule'tide,** the time or season of Yule or Christmas. [O.E. *gēol,* Yule, *se ǣrra gēola,* December; O.N. *jōl.* Not conn. either with O.N. *hjōl,* wheel, or M.E. *youlen, yollen,* to cry out or yawl.]

**yunx,** *yungks,* n. Variant of **Jynx.**

**yupon.** See **yaupon.**

**yurt, yourt,** *yōōrt,* n. a light tent of skins, etc., used by nomads in Siberia. [From Russ.]

**ywis.** Same as **iwis.**

**ywrake,** *i-rāk',* **ywroke,** *i-rōk',* **ywroken,** *i-rō'kən, (Spens.)* obs. *pa.ps.* of **wreak.**

Neutral vowels in unaccented syllables: *el'ə-mənt*; for certain sounds in foreign words, see p. viii

# Z

Z, z, zed, n. the twenty-sixth and last letter in our alphabet, is derived through the Greek zeta (Z, ζ), from zayin, the seventh Semitic letter. Its sound is a voiced sibilant, either voiced s as in 'zeal', or a voiced sh as in 'azure': used in Scots to represent M.E. ʒ (the letter yogh), as in capercailzie: used as a contraction-mark (=;) in viz., sciz., oz., etc.: as a mediaeval Roman numeral, Z = 2000. See also under cedilla, zed and zeta (1).

zabaglione, zä-bäl-yō'ni, n. a frothy custard made from egg yolks, marsala and sugar.—Also zabaione (-bə-yō'ni). [It.]

zabeta, za-bē'ta, (Ar.) a stated tariff.

Zabian, zä'bi-ən, adj. and n. Same as Sabian.

zabra, zä'brä, (hist.) n. a small vessel on the Spanish coast. [Sp.]

zabtieh. Same as zaptieh.

zack, zak, (Austr. slang) n. formerly a sixpenny, now a five-cent, piece.

Zadkiel, zad'ki-əl, n. the name assumed by Richard James Morrison (1794-1874), compiler of a popular astrological almanac.

zaffre, zaffer, zaf'ər, n. the impure oxide obtained by partially roasting cobalt ore previously mixed with two or three times its weight of fine sand. [Fr. zafre, of Ar. origin.]

zakuska, zä-kōōs'ka, n. an hors-d'œuvre: a snack: —pl. zakuski (-kē). [Russ.]

zalambdodont, za-lam'dō-dont, adj. having molar teeth with V-shaped ridges, as some Insectivora. Also n. [Gr. za-, very, lambda, the letter Λ (=L), odous, odontos, a tooth.]

Zalophus, zal'ō-fəs, n. a genus of eared seals. [Gr. za-, intens., lophos, a crest.]

zamarra, zamarro, thä-mär'ä, -ō, (Sp.) a shepherd's sheepskin coat.

zambo, zam'bō, n. the offspring of a Negro man and an American Indian woman: anyone of mixed Negro and Indian blood. [Sp.]

zambomba, thäm-bom'bä, n. a simple Spanish musical instrument, made by stretching a piece of parchment over a wide-mouthed jar and inserting a stick in it, sounded by rubbing the stick with the fingers. [Sp.]

zamboorak. Same as zumbooruk.

Zamia, zä'mi-ə, n. a genus of palm-like trees or low shrubs of the family Cycadaceae, some species of which yield an edible starchy pith. [Named through misreading in Pliny azaniae nuces, pine cones that open on the tree—Gr. azanein, azainein, to dry.]

zamindar. Same as zemindar.

zamouse, za-mōōs', n. the short-horned buffalo of West Africa. [Ar. jāmūs.]

zampogna, tsam-pō'nyä, n. the Italian bagpipe. [It.]

zander, zan'dər, n. Same as sander.

zanella, zə-nel'ə, n. a mixed twilled fabric for covering umbrellas. [Origin uncertain.]

zanja, thäng'hhä, n. an irrigating canal.—n. zanjero (-hhä'rō), one who superintends the distribution of water in irrigation canals. [Sp.]

zante, zan'tē, n. the same as zan'te-wood, the wood of the European smoke-tree, from Zante, one of the principal Ionian Islands: satin-wood. —n. Zan'tiot (-ot), Zan'tiote (-ōt), a native of Zante.—Zante currant, the small seedless fruit of a Zante grape.

Zantedeschia, zan-ti-des'ki-ə, a genus of plants of the Araceae, including Zantedeschia aethio-pica, known as calla lily. [Francesco Zantedeschi, Italian botanist.]

Zanthoxylum. Same as Xanthoxylum.

Zantippe. See Xantippe.

zany, zä'ni, n. an assistant clown or buffoon (hist.): a toady (arch.): a simpleton (dial.): one who plays the fool (coll.).—adj. of, or pertaining to, a zany: crazy, clownish (coll.).—v.t. to play the zany to.—n. zä'nyism, condition or habits of a buffoon. [Fr. zani—It. zanni, a corr. of Giovanni, John.]

zanze, zän'ze, n. an African musical instrument. [Ar. sanj, castanets, cymbals.]

Zanzibari, zan-zib-är'i, n. a native of Zanzibar.

zapateado, thä-pä-te-ädh'ō, n. a lively Spanish dance, for a solo performer, with much clicking and stamping of the heels. [Sp.]

Zapodidae, zä-pod'i-dē, n.pl. the jumping-mouse family. [Formed from Gr. za-, very, pous, podos, foot, and suff. -idae.]

Zaporogian, zä-pō-rō'ji-ən, adj. pertaining to the Little Russian or Ukraine Cossacks dwelling near the Porogi or falls of the Dnieper.—n. one of these people. [Russ. za, beyond, and porogi, rapids.]

zapotilla, zap-ō-til'ə, n. Same as sapodilla.

zaptieh, zap'ti-e, n. a Turkish policeman.—Also zap'tiah, zab'tieh. [From Turk.]

zarape, sä-rä'pe, n. Same as serape.

Zarathustrian, zar-ə-thōōs'tri-ən, adj. and n. Zoroastrian.—Zarathus'trianism, Zarathus'trism, Zoroastrianism; Zarathus'tric, Zoroastrian.

zaratite, zä'rə-tit, n. a hydrous carbonate of nickel, found usually as an incrustation on chromite. [From Zárate, a Spaniard.]

zareba, zə-rē'bä, n. in the Sudan, a stockade, thorn-hedge, etc., against wild animals or enemies: a fortified camp generally.—Also zaree'ba, zarē'ba, zeri'ba. [Ar. zaribah, pen or enclosure for cattle.]

zarf, zärf, n. an ornamental holder for a hot coffee-cup.—Also zurf. [Ar. zarf, a vessel.]

zarnich, zär'nik, n. a native sulphide of arsenic, as orpiment, realgar.—Also zar'nec. [Ar. zarnikh.]

zarzuela, thär-thōō-ā'lä, -thwä', n. a Spanish kind of operetta or vaudeville—named from the royal residence of La Zarzuela.

zastruga, zas-trōō'gä, n. one of a series of long parallel snow-ridges on open wind-swept regions of snow:—pl. -gi (-gē).—Also sastruga. [Russ.]

zati, zä'ti, n. the bonnet-monkey.

zax. Variant of sax (1).

Zea, zē'ə, n. a genus of cereals having monoecious flowers; the only species is Zea mays, maize or Indian corn. [Gr. zeā or zeia, one-seeded wheat.]

zeal, zēl, n. strong feeling, as love, anger, etc., or passionate ardour (B.): intense enthusiasm: activity arising from warm support or enthusiasm: a zealot (obs.).—n. zeal'ant, zeal'ant (Bacon), a zealot.—adjs. zeal'ful; zeal'less.—ns. zealot (zel'ət), an enthusiast: a fanatic: (cap.) one of a fanatical Jewish party whose restless opposition to the Roman domination finally brought about the ruin of Jerusalem in 70 A.D.; zealotism (zel'), the character of a zealot; zealotry (zel').—adj. zealous (zel'), full of zeal: warmly engaged in, or ardent in support of, anything: devoted.—adv. zealously (zel').—n. zealousness (zel'). [O.Fr. zele—L. zēlus—Gr. zēlos—zeein, to boil.]

fāte, fär; mē, hûr (her); mīne; mōte, för; mūte; mōōn, fŏŏt; dhen (then)

**zebec, zebeck.** Variants of xebec.

**zebra,** *zē'brə, ze'brə, n.* any of a group of striped animals of the genus Equus—all of which are peculiar to the African continent : any animal, fish, plant or mineral having stripes reminiscent of a zebra's.—*n.* ze'brass, the offspring of a male zebra and a female ass.—*adjs.* zē'brine, zē'broid. —*ns.* zebrinn'y (cf. hinny), offspring of a male horse and a female zebra; ze'brule, ze'brula, the offspring of a male zebra and a female horse.— **zebra crossing,** stripe-marked street crossing where pedestrians have priority; ze'bra-finch, an Australian weaver-bird striped black and grey; ze'bra-par(r)'akeet, the budgerigar; ze'bra-wood, the hard and beautifully striped wood of a Guiana tree: the tree itself: applied also to various other trees or their wood. [African.]

**zebu,** *zē'bū, n.* a humped domestic ox (*Bos indicus*) very nearly allied to the common ox, diffused over India, China, the east coast of Africa, etc. [Fr. *zébu,* the name taken by Buffon from the exhibitors of one at a French fair in 1752.]

**zebub,** *zē'bub, n.* the zimb. [Ar. (dial.) *zubāb,* a fly.]

**zecchino,** *tsek-kē'nō, n.* a gold coin, the sequin.— Also **zecchine** (zek'in). [See sequin.]

**Zechstein,** *zek'stīn, n.* a deposit of calcareous rock, the higher of the two series into which the Permian System of Germany is divided. [Ger., —*zeche,* mine, *stein,* stone.]

**zed,** *zed,* in U.S. **zee,** *zē, n.* the twenty-sixth letter of the alphabet (Z, z): a bar of metal of form similar to the letter Z. [Fr. *zède*—L. and Gr. *zēta.*]

**zedoary,** *zed'ō-ə-ri, n.* certain species of curcuma, natives of India, China, etc., whose root-stocks are aromatic, bitter, and pungent. [Through mediaeval L.—Ar. *zedwār.*]

**zee,** *zē.* See zed.

**Zeeman effect,** *zā'män ef-ekt', the splitting of a spectral line into several symmetrically disposed components which occurs when the source of light is placed in a strong magnetic field. [Named from Dutch physicist Pieter Zeeman (1865-1943).]

**zein,** *zē'in, n.* a protein found in Indian corn. [Zea.]

**zeitgeist,** *tsīt'gīst,* (Ger.) the spirit of the age. **zeitvertreib,** *tsīt'fər-trīp,* (Ger.) a pastime.

**zel,** *zel, n.* a form of Oriental cymbal. [Turk. *zil.*]

**Zelanian,** *zə-lā'ni-ən, adj.* pertaining to New Zealand.

**zeloso,** *zel-ō'sō,* (mus.) adv. with fervour. [It.]

**zelotypia,** *zel-ō-tip'i-ə, n.* jealousy: morbid zeal in the prosecution of any project or cause. [Gr. *zēlotypiā,* jealousy—*zēlos,* zeal, *typtein,* to strike.]

**zemindar,** *zem-in-där', or zem', n.* under the Mogul emperors of India, the farmer of revenue from land held in common by the cultivators, as responsible for the revenue: later the actual native proprietor paying revenue direct, and not to any intermediate superior.—Also **zamindar.**— *n.* zem'indary, the jurisdiction of a zemindar: the system of land-tenure and taxation under such.—Also **zam'indari, zem'indari,** etc. [Hindi *zamīndār*—Pers. *zamīn,* land, and *-dār,* holder.]

**zemstvo,** *zems'tvō, n.* in Russia, from 1864 until 1917, a district and provincial assembly to which the administration of certain of the affairs of the district and the province was committed. [Russ.]

**Zen,** *zen, n.* a Japanese Buddhist sect which holds that the truth is not in scriptures but in man's own heart if he will but strive to find it by meditation and self-mastery. [Jap.—Chin. *ch'an*— Pali *jhāna,* Sans. *dhyāna,* religious contemplation.]

**zenana,** *ze-nä'nə, n.* in India and Persia, apartments in which women are secluded, correspon-

ding to the harem in Arabic-speaking Moslem lands.—**zenana mission,** a mission to women of the zenanas, necessarily conducted by women. [Pers. *zanāna*—*zan,* a woman.]

**Zend,** *zend, n.* the Avesta or Zend-Avesta: Avestan, the ancient East-Iranian Indo-Germanic language in which the Zend-Avesta was long orally preserved and at last written— closely related to the Vedic Sanskrit.—**Zend-Avesta** (properly meaning the Avesta with the commentary on it), the ancient sacred writings of the Parsees, including works of widely differing character and age, collected into their present canon under Shah-puhar or Shah-pur II (309-338 A.D.). [Pers. *zend, zand,* commentary.]

**zendik,** *zen'dik, n.* an unbeliever in revealed religion in the East: one who practises magic. [Ar. *zendīq.*]

**zenith,** *zen'ith, U.S. zēn', n.* point on the celestial sphere vertically above the observer's head, one of the two poles of the horizon, the other being the nadir: the greatest height (*lit.* and *fig.*).—*adj.* zen'ithal.—**zen'ith-dis'tance,** the angular distance of a heavenly body from the zenith; **zen'ith-sec'tor,** any of several instruments for measuring zenith-distances, used before the invention of the telescope. [O.Fr. *cenit(h),* ultimately from Ar. *samt,* short for *samt-ar-ras,* lit. way, direction, of the head.]

**Zentippe.** See Xantippe.

**zeolite,** *zē'ō-līt, n.* any of a large group of alumino-silicates of sodium, potassium, calcium, and barium, containing very loosely held water.— *adjs.* zeolitic (-lit'); zeolit'iform.—**zeolite process,** a water-softening process using zeolites— formerly zeolites occurring naturally, now synthetic ones. [Gr. *zeein,* to boil (in allusion to the fact that many intumesce under the blowpipe), *lithos,* a stone.]

**zephyr,** *zef'ər, n.* the west wind: a soft, gentle breeze: thin light worsted or woollen yarn: a shawl, jersey, or other garment made of such: any of various types of light-weight material, as a gingham, a flannel with a silk warp, a thin woollen cloth, etc.: anything very light and fine of its kind: (*cap.*) the god of the west wind. [Gr. *Zephyros*; akin to *zophos,* darkness, the west.]

**zeppelin,** *tsep'el-in, tsep', n.* a dirigible, cigar-shaped airship of the type designed by Count Zeppelin (c. 1900).

**zerda,** *zûr'də, n.* a fennec. [Ar. *zardawa.*]

**zereba, zeriba.** Same as zareba.

**Zernebock,** *zûr'nə-bok, n. Czerni Bog,* an evil god of the Slavs, wrongly described by Scott in *Ivanhoe* as a god 'of the ancient Saxons'.

**zero,** *zē'rō, n.* a cipher: nothing: the point from which the reckoning begins on scales, such as those of the barometer, etc.: the lowest point (*fig.*): zero hour.—*adj.* zē'ro-valent (*chem.*), incapable of combining with other atoms.—**ze'ro-grazing,** a system of dairy farming in which the cattle are kept indoors and cut grass is brought to them, thus avoiding the wastage caused by conventional grazing; **zero hour,** the exact time (hour, minute, and second) fixed for launching an attack or beginning an operation.—**absolute zero** (see **absolute**). [Fr. *zéro*—Ar. *sifr*; cf. cipher.]

**zerumbet,** *zə-rum'bet, or ze', n.* an E. Indian drug, allied to cassumunar and zedoary. [Pers. *zerunbād.*]

**zest,** *zest, n.* orange or lemon peel, or the oil squeezed from it, used as a flavouring: anything that gives a relish: piquancy: relish: enthusiasm.—*adj.* zest'ful.—*adv.* zest'fully.—*n.* zest'-fulness. [Fr. *zeste,* orig. the woody thick skin quartering a walnut; origin obscure.]

**zeta,** *zē'tə, n.* the Greek z (Z, ζ): as a numeral ζ' = 7; ‚ζ = 7000.

**zeta,** *zē'tə,* (hist.) *n.* a small room or closet of

some kind, as perh. the sexton's room over a church porch. [Gr. *diaita*, a dwelling.]

**Zeta**, *zē'tə, n.* British equipment for research into fusion reactions and aspects of plasma physics. [*zero energy thermonuclear apparatus.*]

**zetetic**, *zē-tet'ik, adj.* proceeding by inquiry.—*n.* a search, investigation: a seeker, the name taken by some of the Pyrrhonists. [Gr. *zētētikos*—*zēteein*, to seek.]

**Zeuglodon**, *zū'glō-don, n.* a genus of fossil whales, so named from the yoke-like double-rooted formation of their cheek teeth. *adj* and *n.* **zeug'lodont**.—*n.pl.* **Zeuglodon'tia**, a suborder of Cetacea, represented by the zeuglodonts. [Gr. *zeuglē*, the strap or loop of the yoke, *odous*, *-ontos*, a tooth.]

**zeugma**, *zūg'mə, n.* a figure of speech by which an adjective or verb is applied to two nouns, though strictly appropriate to only one of them. —*adj.* **zeugmat'ic**. [Gr.,—*zeugnynai*, to yoke.]

**Zeus**, *zūs, n.* the greatest of the national deities of Greece, son of Kronos (Saturn) and Rhea. His consort was Hera; his supreme seat, Mount Olympus in Thessaly. [Gr.]

**Zeuxian**, *zūk'si-ən, adj.* pertaining to Zeuxis, styled 'of Heraclea' and 'of Ephesus' (*fl. c.* 420-400 B.C.), a Greek painter who excelled in accuracy of imitation of natural objects and in rendering types of sensuous beauty.

**zeuxite**, *zūk'sit, n.* a ferriferous tourmaline. [Gr. *zeuxis*, joining—*zeugnynai*, to join.]

**zho**, *zhō*, one, esp. the male, of a kind of hybrid domestic cattle in parts of the Himalayas—said to be a cross between the male yak and the common horned cow.—Also **zo**, **dso**, and **dzo** (*dzō*).—*ns.* **zhomo** (*zhō'mō*), the female of this cross.—Also **dsō'mo**, **jō'mo**; **zō'bō**, the male of this cross.—Also **zō'bu**, **dsō'bō**. [Tibetan *mdzo*.]

**zibel(l)ine**, *zib'ə-lin, -lin, adj.* pertaining to the sable.—*n.* the fur of the sable: (*zib'ə-lēn*) a soft woollen material with a lustrous pile. [Fr.,— It. *zibellino*, prob. from Slav.; cf. **sable**.]

**zibet**, *zib'it, n.* an Asiatic civet. [It. *zibetto*—Ar. *zabād*; cf. **civet**.]

**ziffius**, *zif'i-əs*, (*Spens*.) *n.* a sea-monster, perh. a swordfish. [Cf. **Xiphias**, **Ziphius**.]

**zigan**, *zi-gan', n.* Variant of **tzigany**.

**ziganka**, *zi-gang'kə, n.* a Russian country-dance: the music for such, usu. quick, with a drone bass. [Russ. *tsyganka*, a gypsy woman.]

**Zigeuner**, *tsi-goi'nər, n.* a gypsy:—*pl.* **Zigeuner**. [Ger.]

**ziggurat**, *zig'ŏŏ-rat, n.* a Babylonian temple-tower, pyramidal in general shape, consisting of a number of storeys each successive one of which was smaller than that below it.—Also **zikkurat** (*zik'*). [Assyrian *ziqquratu*, a pinnacle, top of a mountain.]

**zigzag**, *zig'zag, n.* a short, sharp turning: a line, road, fence, moulding, with sharp angles to right and left alternately.—*adj.* having short, sharp alternate turns: bent from side to side alternately.—*v.t.* to form with short, alternate turns. —*v.i.* to move forward making an alternation of short, sharp turns:—*pr.p.* **zig'zagging**; *pa.t.* and *pa.p.* **zig'zagged**.—*adv.* with frequent sharp turns—also **zig'zaggy**.—*n.* **zigzagg'ery**, angular crookedness.—*adj.* **zig'zaggy**, zigzag. [Fr. *zigzag*; Ger. *zickzack*.]

**zikkurat**. Same as **ziggurat**.

**zillah**, zila, *zil'ə, n.* an administrative district in India. [Ar. *dila* (in Hindi pronunciation, *zila*), a rib, thence a side, a district.]

**zimb**, zimb, *n.* an Abyssinian dipterous insect, like the tsetse, hurtful to cattle. [Amharic, a fly.]

**zimbi**, *zim'bi, n.* a money-cowrie. [Port. *zimbo*; of African origin.]

**zimocca**, *zi-mok'ə, n.* a type of bath-sponge.

**zinc**, zingk, *n.* a bluish-white metallic element (Zn: at. numb. 30), resistant to atmospheric

corrosion.—Also *adj.*—*v.t.* to coat with zinc:— *pr.p.* **zincing**, *zingk'ing*, **zinck'ing**, **zink'ing**; *pa.t.* and *pa.p.* **zinced**, **zingkt**, **zincked**, **zinked**.—*adj.* **zincif'erous** (*zingk-*), **zinkif'erous**, containing or producing zinc.—*ns.* **zincite** (*zingk'it*), a native oxide of zinc, brittle, translucent, deep red; **zinc(k)ificā'tion**, **zinkificā'tion**, the process of coating or impregnating an object with zinc.— *v.t.* **zinc(k)'ify**, **zink'ify**, to cover or impregnate with zinc.—*adj.* **zinc(k)'y**, **zink'y**, pertaining to, containing, or looking like, zinc.—*ns.* **zinco** (*zing'kō*), a line block executed in zinc, i.e. the normal line block; **zinc'ode** (*obs.*), an anode; **zinc'ograph**, a plate or picture produced by zincography; **zincographer** (*-kog'rə-fər*).—*adjs.* **zincograph'ic**, **-al**.—*n.* **zincography** (*-kog'rə-fi*), an engraving process in which zinc is covered with wax and etched: any process in which designs for printing are made on zinc plates. —*adj.* **zinc'oid**, like zinc.—*n.* **zincol'ysis** (*obs.*), electrolysis.—*adj.* **zinc'ous**, pertaining to, or like, zinc.—**zinc'-blende**, sphalerite, native sulphide of zinc; **zinc'-bloom**, basic zinc carbonate, hydrozincite; **zinc'-colic**, a colic caused by the slow poison of zinc oxide; **zinc ointment**, a mixture of zinc oxide and suitable ointment base (wool fat, petroleum jelly, etc.); **zinc oxide**, a whitish solid, much used as a paint pigment in the rubber and other industries; **zinc'-white**, zinc oxide used as a pigment; **zinc'-worker**. [Ger. *zink*; origin unknown.]

**Zincalo**, *zing'kə-lō, n.* a name in Spain for a gypsy:—*fem.* **Zin'cala**, *pl.* **Zin'cali**. [Sp. Romany name.]

**Zingaro**, *zing'gə-rō, n.* a name in Italy for a gypsy:—*pl.* **Zing'ari**; *fem.* **Zing'ara**, *pl.* **Zing'are**. —Also **Zing'ano**, etc. [Cf. **Zincalo**; **Zigeuner**.]

**zingel**, *tsing'əl, zing'əl, n.* a fish of the perch family, found in the Danube. [Ger.]

**Zingiberaceae**, *zin-ji-be-rā'sē-ē, n.pl.* an order of a family of perennial tropical monocotyledonous herbs, with horizontal thickened root-stock and cone-like inflorescence—**Zin'giber**, the typical genus of this family, *Zingiber officinale* being the common ginger.—*adjs.* **zingiberā'ceous**, **zingiberā'ceous**. [L. *zingiber*—Gr. *zingiberis*, ginger.]

**Zinjanthropus**. See **nutcracker man** (at **nut**).

**zinke**, *tsing'kə, n.* an old wind instrument like the cornet. [Ger.]

**zinkenite**, *zingk'ən-it, n.* a steel-grey mineral, essentially sulphide of lead and antimony. [J. K. L. Zincken, a mine director.]

**Zinnia**, *zin'i-ə, n.* a genus of American composite plants. [From J. G. Zinn, botanist (1727-59).]

**Zion**, *zi'ən, n.* Jerusalem: the Israelitish theocracy: the Christian Church: heaven.—*ns.* **Zi'onism**, the movement which secured national privileges and territory in Palestine for the Jews; **Zi'onist**, a supporter of Zionism.—*adv.* **Zi'onward**, heavenward. [Heb. *tsiyōn*, orig. the name of a part of one of the hills of Jerusalem.]

**zip**, zip, *n.* the ping or sound of a bullet striking an object or whizzing through the air: a whizzing sound: a zip-fastener: energy, vigour (*coll.*).— *v.i.* and *v.t.* to whizz: to fasten with a zip: to be full of, act with, proceed with, or (usu. **zip up**) infuse with, life and energy (*coll.*).—*n.* **zipp'er**, a zip-fastener.—*adj.* **zipp'y** (*coll.*), quick, energetic, lively.—**zip-fastener** (*zip-fäs'nər*), a fastening device for clothes, etc., on which two sets of teeth can be opened or interlocked by pulling a slide. [Imit.]

**Ziphius**, *zif'i-əs, n.* a genus of whales, giving name to the family Ziphi'idae, the beaked whales. [Gr. *xiphios*, sword-fish—*xiphos*, sword.]

**zircon**, *zûr'kən, n.* a tetragonal mineral, zirconium silicate, of which jacinth and jargoon are varieties.—*n.* **zircō'nia**, oxide of zirconium.—*adj.* **zirconic** (*-kon'*), of zirconium.—*n.* **zircō'nium**, a metallic element (Zr; at. numb. 40). [Ar. *zarqūn*—Pers. *zargūn*, gold-coloured; cf. jargoon.]

**zither**, *zidh′*, *zith′ər*, *n.* a stringed instrument having a wooden frame and flat sounding-board with from twenty-nine to forty-two metal strings, placed on a table or on the knees, the strings being played by a plectrum on the right thumb.—Also **zith′ern**. [Ger.]

**Zizania**, *zi-* or *zī-zā′ni-ə*, *n.* a genus of tall aquatic grasses, known as wild, water, Indian, or Canada rice (ordinary cultivated rice is of genus *Oryza*). [Gr. *zizanion*, darnel.]

**zizel**, *ziz′əl.* See **suslik**.

**Zizyphus**, *ziz′i-fəs*, *n.* a genus of shrubs of the buckthorn family, the jujube-trees. [L., jujube-tree.]

**zloty**, *zlot′i*, *zwot′ü*, *n.* the monetary unit of Poland.—*pl.* **zloty, zlotys.** [Pol. *zloty*, lit. golden.]

**zo.** See **zho**.

**Zoantharia**, *zō-an-thā′ri-ə*, *n.pl.* an order of Anthozoa the members of which may be either solitary or colonial and possess either six, or more than eight, simple tentacles—including sea-anemones and many corals.—*adj.* and *n.* **zoanthā′rian.** [Mod. L.,—Gr. *zōion*, animal, *anthos*, flower.]

**zoanthropy**, *zō-an′thrō-pi*, *n.* a form of mental delusion in which a man believes himself to be a beast.—*adj.* **zōanthropic** (*-throp′*). [Gr. *zōion*, animal, *anthrōpos*, man.]

**Zoanthus**, *zō-an′thəs*, *n.* the typical genus of **Zoan′thidae** (*-ē*), a family of Anthozoa permanently attached by their bases and having no solid skeleton. [Gr. *zōion*, an animal, *anthos*, a flower.]

**zoarium**, *zō-ā′ri-əm*, *n.* the zooids of a polyzoan colony collectively. [Gr. *zōarion*, dim. of *zōion*, an animal.]

**zobo, zobu.** See **zho**.

**zocco**, *zok′ō*, *n.* a socle.—Also **zocc′olo**. [It. *zocco*, *zoccolo*; see **socle**.]

**zodiac**, *zō′di-ak*, *n.* an imaginary belt in the heavens, about 18° wide, through which the ecliptic passes centrally, and which forms the background of the motions of the sun, moon, and planets; it is divided into twelve equal parts of 30° called **signs of the zodiac**, named from the constellations that once corresponded to them but do so no longer. The constellations, with the appropriate symbols of the corresponding signs, are as follows: Aries (*Ram*), ♈; Taurus (*Bull*), ♉; Gemini (*Twins*), ♊; Cancer (*Crab*), ♋; Leo (*Lion*), ♌; Virgo (*Virgin*), ♍; Libra (*Balance*), ♎; Scorpio (*Scorpion*), ♏; Sagittarius (*Archer*), ♐; Capricornus (*Goat*), ♑; Aquarius (*Water-bearer*), ♒; Pisces (*Fishes*), ♓: a year (*obs.*): a set of twelve, or a recurrent series or course (*fig.*).—*adj.* **zodi′acal.**—**zodiacal light**, a faint illumination of the sky, lenticular in form and elongated in the direction of the ecliptic on either side of the sun, fading away at about 90° from it; best seen after sunset or before sunrise in the tropics. [Fr. *zodiaque*—L. *zōdiacus*—Gr. *zōidiakos*, of figures—*zōidion*, a small carved or painted figure—*zōion*, an animal.]

**zoea**, *zō-ē′ə*, *n.* a larval stage of certain decapod crustaceans, e.g. of crabs.—Also **zooea** (*zō-ē′ə*). —*pl.* **zoë′ae** (also **zoë′as**).—*adjs.* **zoë′al, zooe′al; zo′eform.** [Gr. *zōē*, life.]

**zoechrome.** See **zoetrope**.

**zoetic**, *zō-et′ik*, *adj.* pertaining to life, vital. [Gr. *zōē*, life.]

**zoetrope**, *zō′i-trōp*, *n.* the 'wheel of life', an instrument in which figures on the inside of a rotating cylinder are made visible through slots and provide an illusion of animated motion: (also **zo′ēchrome**) any of several early processes for colour cinematography, using rapidly repeated images of the selected colours in sequence on a screen, the synthesis arising from persistence of vision in the eye.—*adj.* **zoetropic** (*-trop′ik*). [Gr. *zōē*, life, *tropos*, a turning—*trepein*, to turn, *chrōma*, colour.]

**zoiatria**, *zō-i-at′ri-ə*, *zō-i-ə-tri′ə*, **zoiatrics**, *zō-i-at′riks*, *ns.* veterinary surgery. [Gr. *zōion*, an animal, *iātreiā*, healing.]

**zoic**, *zō′ik*, *adj.* pertaining to animals: of rocks, containing evidences of life, in the form of fossils. [Gr. *zōikos*, of animals—*zōion*, an animal.]

**Zoilism**, *zō′i-lizm*, *n.* carping and unjust criticism. —*adj.* **Zoil′ean**, characteristic of *Zoilus*, a Greek grammarian who flourished in the time of Philip of Macedon, and assailed Homer with such asperity that his name became proverbial for a captious and malignant critic.—*n.* **Zō′ilist**, a carping critic.

**zoisite**, *zois′it*, *zō′is-it*, *n.* an orthorhombic mineral closely allied to epidote. [Baron von *Zois*.]

**zoism**, *zō′izm*, *n.* the doctrine that life originates from a specific vital principle.—*n.* **zō′ist**, one who maintains this theory. [Gr. *zōē*, life.]

**Zolaism**, *zō′lä-izm*, *n.* the literary principles and practice of the French novelist Émile *Zola* (1840-1902), who aimed at what he called 'naturalism' (q.v.).

**Zöllner's lines**, *tsœl′nərz linz*, rows of parallel lines appearing to be not parallel through the optical effect of oblique intersecting lines.—Also **Zöllner's illusion, pattern.** [J. K. F. *Zöllner* (1834-82), German physicist.]

**zollverein**, *tsol′fər-in*, *n.* a customs-union: (*cap.*) a union of the German states, under the leadership of Prussia, to enable them to act as one state in their commercial relations with other countries (*hist.*). [Ger., *zoll*, duty, *verein*, union.]

**zombi, zombie**, *zom′bi*, *n.* orig. in Africa, the deity of the python: in American voodooism, the snake deity: a corpse reanimated by sorcery: the power supposed to enter such a body: a stupid or useless person: a very slow-moving, lethargic person.—*n.* **zom′biism**, belief in a zombi, or practice of rites associated with it. [W. African *zumbi*, fetish.]

**zomboruk.** Same as **zumbooruk.**

**zona.** See under **zone.**

**zonda**, *son′də*, *n.* a dry, hot, and dusty wind blowing from the Andes across the Argentine pampas, during July and August. [Sp.; perh. from Amer. Indian.]

**zone**, *zōn*, *n.* a girdle, a belt, an encircling stripe of different colour or substance: one of the five great belts into which the surface of the earth is divided by the tropics and arctic and antarctic circles: any continuous tract with particular characteristics: a region: a group of strata characterised by a distinctive fauna or flora, and bearing the name of one fossil, called the **zonal index** (*geol.*): a set of crystal faces all parallel to the same line (the **zonal axis**).—*v.t.* to encircle, as with a zone: to mark with zones, divide into, or assign to, zones.—*n.* **zō′na** (*pl.* **zō′nae**, *-ē*), a girdle: a zone: an area, patch, strip, or band (*zool.*): herpes zoster.—*adj.* **zō′nal, zō′nary**, like a zone: arranged in zones: pertaining to a zone; **zō′nate(d)**, marked with zones, belted.—*n.* **zonā′tion** (*bot.*), the formation of bands differentiated by colour or other characteristics, or the arrangement of such bands: the occurrence of vegetation in well-marked bands, each band having its characteristic dominant species.—*adjs.* **zoned**, wearing a zone: having zones; **zone′less.** —*n.* **zō′ning**, division into zones: assignment according to zones.—*adj.* **zō′noid**, like a zone. —*ns.* **Zonotrichia** (*zō-nō-trik′i-ə*; Gr. *thrix*, *trichos*, hair), a genus of American finches, the crown-sparrows; **zō'nula**, a small zone. —*adj.* **zō'nular**, like a zone or zonule.—*ns.* **zon'ule, zon'ulet**, a little zone or girdle; **Zonurus** (*zō-nū'rəs*; Gr. *ourā*, tail), a tropical African genus of lizards with tail ringed with spiny scales, giving name to the family **Zonu'ridae.**— **zone'-ticket**, a railway ticket available for a time between any stations of a group. [L. *zōna*—Gr. *zōnē*, a girdle—*zōnnynai*, to gird.]

**zoo-, *zō-o-, zō-o'-*, zō-, zō-,** in zool. terms, etc., animal.—*n.* **zoo** (*zōō*), orig., the Zoological Gardens, London: now any similar collection of animals.—*adj.* **zoobiotic** (*zō-ō-bi-ot'ik*), parasitic on, or living in association with, an animal.—*n.* **zooblast** (*zō'ō-blast*; Gr. *blastos*, a germ), an animal cell.—*adj.* **zōochem'ical.**—*n.* **zōochem'-istry**, the chemistry of the animal body.—*adj.* **zoochorous** (*zō-ō-kōr'əs, -kör'*; Gr. *chōreein*, to spread), of spores or seeds, dispersed by animals. —*ns.* **zō'ochore; zō'ochory**, the condition of being dispersed by animals; **zō'oculture** (*U.S.*), the domestication and control of animals; **zōocytium** (*-sish'i-əm*; Gr. *kytos*, a hollow vessel), a zoothecium:—*pl.* **zōocyt'ia; zōoden'-drium** (*zool.*), the branched stalk connecting the members of the colony in certain colonial Infusoria; **zooecium** (*zō-ē'shi-əm*; Gr. *oikiā*, a house), the body-wall or enclosing chamber of a polyzoan individual:—*pl.* **zooe'cia; zō'ogamete**, a motile gamete.—*adj.* **zoogamous** (*zō-og'ə-məs*; Gr. *gamos*, marriage), pertaining to zoogamy.— *ns.* **zoog'amy**, sexual reproduction of animals; **zoogeny** (*zō-oj'ə-ni*; Gr. *-geneia*, suff. denoting production), the doctrine, or the process, of the origination of living beings—also **zoogony** (*-og'*). —*adj.* **zōogenic** (*-jen'*), **zōog'enous**, produced from animals.—*n.* **zōogeog'rapher.**—*adjs.* **zōo-geograph'ic, -al.**—*ns.* **zōogeog'raphy**, the science of the distribution of animals on the surface of the globe; **zōogloea** (*-glē'ə*; Gr. *gloiā*, glue), a mucilaginous mass of bacteria embedded in slimy material derived from swollen cell walls. —*adjs.* **zōogloe'ic; zōogloe'oid.**—*n.* **zōogonid'-ium**, a swarmspore.—*adj.* **zōog'onous** (*zool.*), viviparous.—*ns.* **zōog'ony**, zoogeny; **zō'ograft** (*-gräft*), a piece of tissue from the living body of an animal grafted on the human body; **zō'ograft-ing; zōog'rapher, zōog'raphist**, one who pursues zōog'raphy, the study or description of animals and their habits: the painting of animals.—*adjs.* **zōograph'ic, -al.**—*ns.* **zooid** (*zō'oid*; Gr. *eidos*, form), earlier, a free-moving cell, as a sperm-cell: in alternation of generations, an individual of an asexually-produced form: usu., an indi-vidual forming part of a colonial organism; **zōol'ater** (Gr. *latreiā*, worship), one who wor-ships animals; **zōolatri'a, zōol'atry**, worship of animals.—*adj.* **zōol'atrous.**—*ns.* **zoolite** (*zō'ō-līt*; Gr. *lithos*, a stone), a fossil animal.—Also **zō'olith.**—*adjs.* **zōolith'ic, zōolit'ic; zoological** (*zō-ō-loj'i-kl*, or *zōō-ō-*; zoological garden, park, a garden or park where living wild animals are kept and exhibited).—*adv.* **zōolog'ically.**—*ns.* **zool'ogist** (*zō-*, or *zōō-*), one versed in zoology (*zō-ol'ə-ji*, or *zōō-ol'*), the science of animal life included along with botany in the science of bio-logy.—*adj.* **zōomagnet'ic.**—*ns.* **zōomag'netism**, animal magnetism; **zoomancy** (*zō'ō-man-si*; Gr. *manteiā*, divination), divination by observation of animals.—*adjs.* **zōoman'tic; zōōmet'ric.**—*ns.* **zoometry** (*-om'ə-tri*; Gr. *metron*, a measure), comparative measurement of the parts of animals; **zō'omorph** (*-mörf*; Gr. *morphē*, form), in art, a representation of an animal form: an image or symbol of a god, etc., who is conceived as having an animal form.—*adj.* **zōōmor'phic**, pertaining to zoomorphism: representing animals in art.—*ns.* **zōōmor'phism**, the represen-tation, or the conception, of a god or a man in an animal form.—Also **zōōmor'phy; zō'on**, a

morphological individual, the total product of a fertilised ovum, or the group of zooids constitu-ting a compound animal:—*pl.* **zō'a, zō'ons.**— *adjs.* **zō'onal**, like a zoon; **zōon'ic**, relating to animals.—*n.* **zō'onite**, one of the segments of an articulated animal.—*adjs.* **zōonit'ic; zōonom'ic.** —*ns.* **zōon'omist; zoonomy** (*zō-on'ə-mi*; Gr. *nomos*, law), animal physiology.—Also **zōonō'-mia; zoonosis** (*zō-on'ə-sis*; Gr. *nosos*, disease), a disease communicated to man from the lower animals, as hydrophobia, etc.: a disease due to animal parasites:—*pl.* **zōon'osēs; zōopathol'ogy**, the study of disease in animals; **zoopathy** (*zō-op'ə-thi*; Gr. *pathos*, suffering), animal pathology. — *adj.* **zōop'eral.** — *ns.* **zōop'erist; zōop'ery** (Gr. *peirā*, experiment), experimenta-tion on animals.—*n.pl.* **Zoophaga** (*zō-of'ə-gə*; Gr. *phagein*, to eat), the carnivorous animals collectively.—*n.* **zōoph'agan**, a carnivorous animal.—*adj.* **zōoph'agous.**—*ns.* **zō'ophile** (*-fil*; Gr. *philos*, loving), a zoophilist: a zoophilous plant; **zōophil'ia, zōoph'ilism, zōoph'ily**, love of animals: a morbid attraction to animals (*psych.*); **zoophilist** (*zō-of'il-ist*), a lover of animals: one suffering from zoophilia (*psych.*). —*adj.* **zōoph'ilous**, loving animals: suffering from zoophilia: pollinated by animals other than insects (*bot.*): of insects, feeding on animals (*zool.*).—*n.* **zōophōb'ia** (Gr. *phobos*, fear), dread of animals, or of animal ghosts.—*adj.* **zōoph'obous.**—*n.* **zōophorus** (*-of'ə-rəs*; Gr. *pherein*, to bear), a continuous frieze sculptured in relief with figures of men and animals.—*adj.* **zōophoric** (*-för'*).—*n.pl.* **Zoophyta** (*zō-of'it-ə*; Gr. *phyton*, plant), in older classifications, a group of invertebrates having no power of locomotion, as sponges, corals, etc.—*n.* **zō'ophyte** (*-fit*), any plant supposed to resemble an animal (*obs.*): (now old-fashioned) any of numerous inverte-brates resembling plants, as sponges, corals, sea-anemones, etc., esp. hydroid colonies of a branched form.—*adjs.* **zōophytic** (*-fit'*), **-al; zōoph'ytoid; zōophytolog'ical** (*-fit'*). — *ns.* **zōophytol'ogist; zōophytol'ogy; zōoplank'ton**, floating and drifting animal life.—*adj.* **zōo-plas'tic** (Gr. *plassein*, to form), pertaining to **zō'oplasty**, the operation of transplanting living tissue from one of the lower animals to man.—*n.* **zoopsychology** (*zō-ō-sī-kol'ə-ji*), the psychology of the lower animals.—*adj.* **zooscop'ic.**—*ns.* **zōos-copy** (*-os'kop-i*; Gr. *skopeein*, to look at), a form of mental delusion in which one sees imaginary animals, esp. snakes; **zō'osperm** (Gr. *sperma*, seed), a spermatozoid: a zoospore.— Also **zōosper'mium.**—*adj.* **zōospermat'ic.**—*ns.* **zōosporan'gium** (*bot.*), a sporangium in which zoospores are formed; **zō'ospore** (Gr. *sporos*, a seed), a swarmspore: an asexual reproductive cell that can swim by means of flagella.—*adjs.* **zōospor'ic; zōos'porous.**—*ns.* **zō'otaxy** (Gr. *taxis*, arrangement), the science of the classifica-tion of animals, systematic zoology; **zōotechnics** (*-tek'niks*; Gr. *technē*, art), **zō'otechny**, the science of the breeding and domestication of animals; **zōothap'sis** (Gr. *thaptein*, to bury), premature burial.—*adj.* **zōothē'cial** (*-shi-*).—*ns.* **zōothecium** (*-thē'shi-əm*, or *-si-*; Gr. *thēkion*, casket, dim. of *thēkē*, box), the tubular sheath of certain social infusorians:—*pl.* **zōothē'cia; zōothē'ism**, the attribution of divine qualities to an animal.—*adj.* **zōotheis'tic.**—*ns.* **zōother'apy** (Gr. *therapeiā*, treatment), veterinary thera-peutics; **zō'othome** (Gr. *thōmos*, heap), a group of zooids, as a mass of coral.—*adjs.* **zōotom'ic, -al.**—*adv.* **zōotom'ically.**—*ns.* **zōot'omist** (Gr. *tomē*, a cut), one who dissects the bodies of animals, an anatomist; **zoot'omy**, the dissection of animals: comparative anatomy; **zōotox'in**, a toxin produced by an animal, as a snake.— *adj.* **zōotrope**, a zoetrope.—*adj.* **zōotrophic** (*-trof'ik*;

Gr. *trophos*, food), pertaining to the nourishment of animals.—*ns.* zöotrophy; zö′otype, an animal serving as a type.—*adj.* zöotypic (*-tip′ik*). [Gr. *zöion*, animal.]

**zooks,** *zōōks, interj.* Same as gadzooks.

**zoom,** *zōōm, v.i.* to make a loud, deep, persistent buzzing noise: to move with this sound: to use the stored energy of the forward motion of an aircraft in order to gain height (*aero.*): to soar (*fig.*).—*v.t.* to cause to zoom.—*n.* the act of zooming: a zooming noise.—**zoom lens,** a lens of variable focal length used, e.g., for bringing television, cinematograph, or cine-camera pictures from distance to close-up without moving the camera: a similar lens used in still cameras and in microscopes. [Imit.]

**zoon politikon,** *zō′on po-lit′i-kon,* (Gr.) a political animal (said of man).

**zoot suit,** *zōōt′ sūt,* a flashy type of man's suit with padded shoulders, fitted waist, knee-length coat, and trousers narrow at the ankles (introduced late 1940s).—*n.* zoot′suiter, one who wears a zoot suit. [Origin unknown; prob. rhyming with **suit** (*U.S. sōōt*).]

**zoozoo,** *zōō′zōō,* (*dial.*) *n.* the wood-pigeon. [From the sound made by it.]

**zopilote,** *sō-pi-lō′te, n.* one of the smaller American vultures—the turkey-buzzard, or the urubu. [Mex. Sp.]

**zoppo,** *tsop′pō,* (*mus.*) *adj.* with syncopation. [It.]

**zorgite,** *zör′git, n.* a metallic copper-lead selenide, found at *Zorge,* in the Harz Mountains.

**zoril, zorille, zorillo, zorino:** See zorro.

**Zoroastrianism,** *zör-,* *zor-ō-as′tri-ən-izm, n.* ancient religion founded or reformed by *Zoroaster*—the Greek pronunciation of Zarathustra—set forth in the Zend-Avesta, and still adhered to by the Guebres and Parsees in India.—*n.* and *adj.* **Zoroas′trian.** [L. *Zōroastrēs*—Gr.]

**zorro,** *sor′ō, n.* a S. American fox or foxlike wild dog.—*ns.* zoril, zorille (*zor′il, -il′*), an African skunklike musteline animal (*Zorilla*); zorillo (*sor-ē′yō,* zor-il′ō), a S. American skunk; zorino (*zor-ēn′ō*), a euphemism for skunk fur used to make garments. [Sp. *zorro, zorra,* fox, *zorilla* (Fr. *zorille*), skunk.]

**zoster,** *zos′tər, n.* an ancient Greek waist-belt for men: herpes zoster or shingles. [Gr. *zōstēr,* a girdle.]

**Zostera,** *zos-tē′rə, n.* the eelgrass or grasswrack genus. [Gr. *zōstēr,* a kind of grasswrack.]

**Zouave,** *zōō-äv′, zwäv, n.* one of a body of French infantry of great dash, orig. Algerians, wearing a quasi-Moorish dress: any of a number of volunteer regiments modelling themselves on the Zouaves who fought on the side of the North in the American Civil War: a woman's short embroidered jacket. [From the *Zouaoua,* an Algerian tribe.]

**zounds,** *zowndz,* (*arch.*) *interj.* an exclamation of anger and astonishment. [A corr. of *God's wounds.*]

**zowie,** *zow′i,* (*U.S.*) *interj.* expressing surprise and pleasure.—*n.* (*cap.*) the slang in use among hippies.

**zucchetto,** *tsōō-ket′ō, n.* the skull-cap of an ecclesiastic, covering the tonsure.—Also zuchetta, -o. [It. dim. of *zucca,* a gourd.]

**zucchini,** *zōō-kē′nē,* (*U.S.*) *n.* a courgette:—*pl.* zucchini, zucchinis. [It.]

**zufolo,** *tsōō′fō-lō, n.* a small flute or flageolet used in training singing-birds.—Also zuff′olo. [It.]

**zugzwang,** *tsōōhh′tsväng,* (Ger.) in chess, a blockade position in which any move is disadvantageous to the blockaded player.

**Zulu,** *zōō′lōō, n.* a branch of the great Bantu family, belonging to S. Africa, conspicuous for physical development: a member thereof: the language of the Zulus.—*adj.* pertaining to the Zulus, their language, etc. [Native name.]

**zum beispiel,** *tsŏŏm bi′shpēl,* (Ger.) for example—often z.B.

**zumbooruk,** *zum′bōō-ruk, or -bōō′, n.* a small cannon mounted on a swivel, carried on the back of a camel.—Also zum′booruck, zom′boruk, zam′boorak. [Hind. *zambūrak;* from Pers.]

**Zuñi,** *zōō′nyē, sōō′nyē, n.* one of a tribe of Pueblo Indians living in large communal houses near the *Zuñi* river in New Mexico.—*adj.* and *n.* Zu′ñian.

**zupa,** *zū′pə, n.* a confederation of village communities governed by a zū′pan, in the early history of Serbia, etc. [Serbian.]

**zurf.** Same as zarf.

**zuz,** *zōōz, n.* a silver coin of ancient Palestine. [Heb.]

**zwanziger,** *tsvan′tsi-gər, n.* an old Austrian silver coin, equivalent to twenty kreutzers. [Ger.,—*zwanzig,* twenty.]

**zwieback,** *tsvē′bäk, or tswē′, n.* biscuit rusk, or a sweet spiced bread toasted. [Ger.]

**Zwinglian,** *zwing′gli-ən, tsving′li-ən, adj.* pertaining to the Swiss reformer Huldreich *Zwingli* (1484-1531), or his doctrines, esp. his divergence from Luther in the doctrine of the Eucharist—Zwingli rejected every form of local or corporeal presence, whether by transubstantiation, impanation, or consubstantiation.—*n.* a follower of Zwingli.

**zwitterion,** *tsvit′ər-i-on, n.* an ion carrying both a positive and a negative charge. [Ger. *zwitter,* hybrid, and ion.]

**Zygaena,** *zi-jē′nə, n.* the burnet-moth genus, typical of the family Zygae′nidae: the hammer-head genus of sharks, now called Sphyrna.—*adjs.* zygae′nid, zygae′nine, zygae′noid. [Gr. *zygaina,* a shark.]

**zygo-,** *zi′gō-, zig′ō-, zyg-, zig-, zig-,* in composition, yoke, union or presence of two similar things.—*adj.* zy′gal, pertaining to a zygon: formed like a letter H.—*n.* zygan′trum (Gr. *antron,* a cave), in snakes and some lizards, an additional vertebral articulation, consisting of a fossa on the posterior surface of the neural arch, into which fits the zygosphene.—*adj.* zygapophyseal, -ial (*-fiz′i-əl*).—*n.* zygapophysis (*-pof′i-sis;* Gr. *apophysis,* process), one of the yoke-pieces or articulations of the vertebrae:—*pl.* zygapoph′ysēs.—*adj.* zygobranchiate (*-brangk′i-āt;* Gr. *branchia,* gills), having paired, symmetrically placed, gills: belonging to the Zygobranchiā′ta, a division of the Gastropoda.—*ns.* and *adjs.* zy′gobranch, zygobranch′iate.—*adjs.* zygocardiac (*-kär′di-ak;* Gr. *kardiā,* heart), a term used to describe certain paired lateral ossicles in the gastric mill of Crustacea; zygodactyl (*-dak′til;* Gr. *daktylos,* toe), having two toes before and behind, as parrots.—Also zygodactyl′ic, zygodac′tylous.—*n.* zygodac′tylism. — *adj.* zy′godont (Gr. *odous, odontos,* tooth), pertaining to molar teeth whose cusps are paired: possessing such molars.—*n.* zygoma (*-gō′mə*), the arch formed by the malar bone and the zygomatic process of the temporal bone of the skull.—*adj.* zygomat′ic, pertaining to the zygoma, or in the region of it (as zygomatic arch; zygomatic fossa, the lower part of the fossa bridged over by the zygomatic arch; zygomatic muscles, two muscles, *major* and *minor,* arising from the zygomatic arch).—*adjs.* zygomor′phic, zygomorphous (*mör′fəs;* Gr. *morphē,* form), yoke-shaped—of flowers symmetrical about one plane only.—*ns.* zygomor′phism, zy′gomorphy.—*n.pl.* Zygomycetes, (*-mi-sē′tēz;* Gr. *mykēs, mykētos,* a mushroom), a group of fungi (moulds, etc.), a division of the Phycomycetes, marked by the production of zygospores.—*n.* zygomycete′.—Also *adj.*—*adj.* zygomyce′tous.—*n.* zy′gon, a connecting bar: an H-shaped fissure of the brain.—*n.pl.* Zygophyllaceae (*-fil-ā′sē-ē;* Gr. *phyllon,* a leaf), the bean-caper family, desert and steppe plants akin to Rutaceae, the typical genus being **Zygophyll'um**.—*n.* **zy'gophyte** (*-fīt*; Gr. *phyton*, a plant), a plant in which reproduction takes place by means of zygospores.—*adjs.* **zygopleural** (*-plōō'rəl*; Gr. *pleurā*, side), bilaterally symmetrical; **zy'gose**, pertaining to zygosis. —*ns.* **zygosis** (*-gō'sis*; *biol.*), conjugation; **zy'gosphene** (*-sfēn*; Gr. *sphēn*, wedge), in snakes and some lizards, an additional vertebral articulation, consisting of a process on the anterior surface of the neural arch, which fits into the zygantrum: **zy'gospore** (Gr. *sporā*, a seed), a spore produced by the union of buds from two adjacent hyphae in the process of conjugation by which some fungi multiply.—Also **zy'gosperm**.—*n.* **zy'gote** (Gr. *zygōtos*, yoked; *bot.* and *zool.*), the product of the union of two gametes: by extension, the individual developing from that product.—*adj.* **zygotic** (*-got'*).— **zygotic number** (*bot.*), the diploid chromosome number. [Gr. *zygon*, yoke.]

**zylonite.** Erroneous spelling of **xylonite**.

**zyme**, *zīm*, *n.* a ferment: a disease-germ.—*n.* **zy'mase**, any of a group of enzymes inducing the alcoholic fermentation of carbohydrates.—*adj.* **zy'mic**, relating to fermentation.—*ns.* **zy'mite**, a priest using leavened bread in the Eucharist; **zy'mogen**, a non-catalytic substance formed by plants and animals as a stage in the development of an enzyme.—*adjs.* **zymogen'ic**; **zy'moid'** like a ferment; **zymolog'ic**, *-al*, pertaining to zymology. — *ns.* **zymol'ogist**, one skilled in zymology; **zymol'ogy**, the science of fermentation; **zymol'ysis**, the action of enzymes; **zymom'eter**, **zymosim'eter**, an instrument for measuring the degree of fermentation; **zymō'sis**, fermentation: the morbid process, thought to be analogous to fermentation, constituting a zymotic disease.—*adjs.* **zymotech'nic**, *-al*, producing and utilising fermentation.—*n.* **zymotech'nics**, the art of managing fermentation.— *adj.* **zymot'ic**, pertaining to fermentation: of the nature of, pertaining to, or causing, an infectious disease.—*n.* an infectious disease.—*adv.* **zymot'ically**. [Gr. *zȳmē*, leaven, *zȳmōsis*, fermentation.]

**zymome**, *zī'mōm*, *n.* an old name for the part of gluten insoluble in alcohol. [Gr. *zȳmōma*, a fermented mixture.]

**zymurgy**, *zī'mûr-ji*, *n.* the department of technological chemistry that treats of wine-making, brewing, distilling, and similar processes involving fermentation. [Gr. *zȳmē*, leaven, *ergon*, work.]

**zythum**, *zī'thəm*, *n.* a kind of beer made by the ancient Egyptians — much commended by Diodorus. [Gr. *zȳthos*.]

**zymo-**, in composition. See **zyme**.

fāte, fär; mē, hûr (her); mīne; mōte, fŏr; mūte, mōōn, fŏŏt; dhen (then)

# Quotations from Latin, Greek and Modern Foreign Languages

*Single foreign words, and certain phrases often used in an English context, are given in the main dictionary*

**abiit, excessit, evasit, erupit** (L.), he is gone, he is off, he has escaped, he has broken away.—Cicero, *In Catilinam*, II. i. 1.

**ab imo pectore** (L.), from the bottom of the heart.

**à bon chat, bon rat** (Fr.), to a good cat, a good rat—well matched: set a thief to catch a thief.

**ab ovo usque ad mala** (L.), from the egg to the apples—of a Roman banquet: from the beginning to the end.

**absens haeres non erit** (L.), the absent one will not be the heir—out of sight, out of mind.

**ab uno disce omnes** (L.), from one (offence) learn all (the race).—Virgil, *Aen.*, II. 65-66: hence, from one example you may know the rest.

**abusus non tollit usum** (L.), abuse does not do away with use—i.e. an abuse is not a reason for giving up the legitimate use of a thing.

**a capite ad calcem** (L.), from head to heel.

**à chaque saint sa chandelle** (Fr.), every saint his candle: to every patron his meed of service.

**Acherontis pabulum** (L.), food for Acheron—of a bad person.—Plautus, *Casina*, II. i. 12.

**actum est de republica** (L.), it is all up with the state.

**actum ne agas** (L.), do not do what is already done —quoted as a proverb by Terence, *Phor.*, II. iii. 72 (or l. 419).

**ad Calendas Graecas** (L.), at the Greek Calends —i.e. never, as the Greeks had no Calends.

**adhuc sub judice lis est** (L.), the dispute is still before the court.—Horace, *A.P.*, 78.

**ad majorem Dei gloriam** (L.), for the greater glory of God—the Jesuit motto.

**adscriptus glebae** (L.), bound to the soil—of serfs.

**ad utrumque paratus** (L), prepared for either case.

**ad vitam aut culpam** (L.), for life or till fault— i.e. till some misconduct is proved.

**advocatus diaboli** (L.), devil's advocate. See Dict.

**aequam memento rebus in arduis servare mentem** (L.), remember to keep a calm mind in difficulties.—Horace, *Od.*, II. iii. 1.

**aequitas sequitur legem** (L.), equity follows law.

**age quod agis** (L.), do what you are doing—i.e. with all your powers.

**aide-toi, le ciel t'aidera** (Fr.), help yourself and Heaven will help you.

**aliquando bonus dormitat Homerus** (L.). See indignor.

**aliquid haeret** (L.), something sticks.

**Allah il Allah**, a corr. of Ar. *lā ilāha illā 'llāh* = there is no God but the God.

**Allahu akbar** (Ar.), God is great.

**alter ipse amicus** (L.), a friend is another self.

**amabilis insania** (L.), a pleasing madness or rapture.—Horace, *Od.*, III. 4. 5-6.

**amantium irae amoris integratio est** (L.), lovers' quarrels are a renewal of love.—Terence, *Andr.*, III. iii. 23.

**amare et sapere vix deo conceditur** (L.), to be in love and to be wise is scarce granted even to a god.—Laberius.

**amari aliquid** (L.), some touch of bitterness.— Lucretius, *De Rer. Nat.*, iv. 1130.

**a mensa et toro** (L.), from bed and board.

**amicus Plato, amicus Socrates, sed magis amica veritas** (L.), Plato is dear to me (or is my friend), Socrates is dear, but truth is dearer still. —L. version of saying attributed to Aristotle.

**amicus usque ad aras** (L.), a friend as far as the altars—i.e. as far as may be without offence to the gods.

**amor sceleratus habendi** (L.), the accursed love of possessing.—Ovid, *Met.*, I. 131.

**amor vincit omnia** (L.). See omnia.

**anathema sit** (L.), let him be accursed.—1 Cor. xvi. 22.

**anch' io son pittore** (It.), I, too, am a painter (said by Correggio on looking at Raphael's 'St Cecilia').

**anērithmon gelasma. See kymatōn anērithmon gelasma.**

**anguis in herba** (L.), a snake in the grass.—Virgil, *Ecl.*, III. 93.

**anima naturaliter Christiana** (L.), a soul naturally Christian, i.e. one who behaves like a Christian without the benefit of Christian revelation. —Tertullian, *Apologia*, xvii.

**animula vagula** (L.), little soul flitting away— beginning of a poem ascribed to the dying Hadrian, translated or paraphrased by Prior, Pope, Byron, and Dean Merivale.

**à nos moutons. See revenons.**

**ante Agamemnona. See vixere fortes.**

**a parte ante** (L.), on the side before, from past eternity—opp. to **a parte post**, in future eternity.

**a posse ad esse** (L.), from the possible to the actual.

**après moi (nous) le déluge** (Fr.), after me (us) the deluge: then the deluge may come when it likes —attributed to Mme. de Pompadour and to Louis XV. Cf. emou thanontos.

**aquila non capit muscas** (L.), an eagle does not catch flies.

**arbiter elegantiae** (L.), judge of good taste—said by Tacitus, *Annals*, XVI. 18, of Gaius Petronius, an exquisite at the court of Nero (prob. same as Petronius Arbiter).—Also quoted as **arbiter elegantiarum.**

**Arcades ambo** (L.), Arcadians both: two of the same stamp.—Virgil, *Ecl.*, VII. 4.—Rendered by Byron blackguards both, *Don Juan*, IV. xciii.

**ariston men hydōr** (Gr.), water is best.—Pindar, *Olympian Odes*, i. 1.

**ars est celare artem** (L.), true art is to conceal art.

**ars longa, vita brevis** (L.), art is long, life short. —Seneca, *De Brevitate Vitae*, 1. Cf. ho bios brachys.

**asbestos gelōs** (Gr.), inextinguishable laughter. —Homer, *Iliad*, I. 599, etc.

**asinus ad lyram** (L.), an ass at the lyre, one ignorant of music or art: one unsuited to an occupation.—From a Greek proverbial expression *onos pros lyran.*

**astra castra, numen lumen** (L.), the stars my camp, God my lamp.

**Athanasius contra mundum** (L.), Athanasius against the world: one resolute man facing universal opposition.

**atra cura** (L.), black care. See post equitem.

**at spes non fracta** (L.), but hope is not yet crushed.

**au bout de son latin** (Fr.), at the end of his Latin, at the end of his knowledge, at his wits' end.

**auctor quae pretiosa facit** (L.), gifts that the giver adds value to.—Ovid, *Her.*, XVII. 71-2.

**audentes fortuna juvat** (L.), fortune favours the daring.—Virgil, *Aen.*, X. 284.

audi alteram partem (L.), hear the other side.— St Augustine, *De Duabus Animabus*, XIV. 2.

auditque vocatus Apollo (L.), and Apollo hears when invoked.—Virgil, *Georg.*, IV. 7.

aufgeschoben ist nicht aufgehoben (Ger.), put off is not given up.

aujourd'hui roi, demain rien (Fr.), king today, nothing tomorrow.

au plaisir de vous revoir (Fr.), till I have the pleasure of seeing you again.

auribus teneo lupum (L.), I am holding a wolf by the ears.—Terence, *Phormio*, III. ii. 21.

auri sacra fames (L.), accursed hunger for gold.— Virgil. *Aen.*, III. 57.

au royaume des aveugles les borgnes sont rois (Fr.), in the kingdom of the blind the one-eyed are kings.—As a Latin proverb, *beati monoculi in regione caecorum.*

aurum omnes, victa jam pietate, colunt (L.), all worship gold, piety being overthrown.— Propertius, III. xiii. 48.

auspicium melioris aevi (L.), augury of a better age.

aussitôt dit, aussitôt fait (Fr.), no sooner said than done.

Austriae est imperare orbi universo (L.), it is Austria's part to command the whole world— often A.E.I.O.U.

aut amat aut odit mulier, nihil est tertium (L.), a woman either loves or hates, there is no third course.—Syrus, 42.

autant d'hommes (or de têtes), autant d'avis (Fr.), so many men, so many minds. Cf. quot homines.

aut Caesar aut nullus, or nihil (L.), either Caesar or nobody (nothing): all or nothing.

aut insanit homo aut versus facit (L.), either the man is mad or he is making verses.—Horace, *Sat.*, II. vii. 117.

aut inveniam viam aut faciam (L.), I shall either find a way or make one.

aut non tentaris aut perfice (L.), either do not attempt or else achieve.—Ovid, *A.A.*, I. 389.

aut prodesse volunt aut delectare poetae (L.), poets seek either to profit or to please.— Horace, *A.P.*, 333.

aut regem aut fatuum nasci oportet (L.), one should be born either king or fool.—Proverb; quoted by Seneca.

autres temps, autres mœurs (Fr.), other times, other manners.

aut vincere aut mori (L.), to conquer or die.

aux absents les os (Fr.), the bones to the absent.

aux grands maux les grands remèdes (Fr.), to desperate evils desperate remedies.

auxilium ab alto (L.), help from on high.

ave, Caesar (or imperator), morituri te salutant (L.), hail, Caesar, men doomed to die salute thee (said by gladiators).

a verbis ad verbera (L.), from words to blows.

à vieux comptes nouvelles disputes (Fr.), old accounts breed new disputes.

a vinculo matrimonii (L.), from the bond of matrimony.

avi numerantur avorum (L.), ancestors of ancestors are counted [to me].

avis au lecteur (Fr.), notice to the reader.

avise la fin (Fr.), weigh well the end.

avito viret honore (L.), he is green with ancestral honours.

avoir la langue déliée (Fr.), to have the tongue unbound, to be glib of speech.

barba tenus sapientes (L.), sages as far as the beard —i.e. with an appearance of wisdom only.

battre la campagne (Fr.), to scour the country, to beat the bush.

bayer aux corneilles (Fr.), to gape at the crows, to stare vacantly.

beatus ille qui procul negotiis . . . paterna rura bobus exercet suis (L.), happy he who, far removed from business . . . tills with his own

oxen the fields that were his father's.—Horace, *Epod.*, ii. 1.

bella gerant alii, tu, felix Austria, nube (L.), let others wage wars; do thou, lucky Austria, make marriages.—Matthias Corvinus of Hungary.

bella, horrida bella (L.), wars, horrid wars.— Virgil, *Aen.*, VI. 86.

bellaque matribus detestata (L.), and wars abhorred by mothers.—Horace, *Od.*, I. i. 24-5.

bellum nec timendum nec provocandum (L.), war is neither to be feared nor provoked (Pliny the Younger, *Panegyricus*, 16, nec times bellum, nec provocas).

belua multorum capitum (L.), monster with many heads—the irrational mob.—Horace, *Epistolae*, I. i. 76.

beneficium accipere libertatem est vendere (L.), to accept a favour is to sell one's liberty.— Syrus, 49.

bene orasse est bene studuisse (L.), to have prayed well is to have endeavoured well.

bene qui latuit bene vixit (L.), he has lived well who has lived obscure.—Ovid, *Trist.*, III. iv. 25.

benigno numine (L.), with favouring godhead.— Horace, *Od.*, III. iv. 74.

bibere venenum in auro (L.), to drink poison from a cup of gold.

biblia abiblia (Gr.), books that are no books.

bis dat qui cito dat (L.), he gives twice who gives promptly.—Proverb; by Bacon.

bis peccare in bello non licet (L.), in war one may not blunder twice.

bis pueri senes (L.), old men are twice boys.

blandae mendacia linguae (L.), falsehoods of a smooth tongue.

bon avocat, mauvais voisin (Fr.), a good lawyer is a bad neighbour.

bon jour, bonne œuvre (Fr.), better day, better deed.

bonnes nouvelles adoucissent le sang (Fr.), good news sweetens the blood.

borgen macht sorgen (Ger.), borrowing makes sorrowing.

boutez en avant (Fr.), push forward.

brevis esse laboro, obscurus fio (L.), I labour to be brief, and I become obscure.—Horace, *A.P.*, 25-26.

briller par son absence (Fr.), to be conspicuous by its absence.

brûler la chandelle par les deux bouts (Fr.), to burn the candle at both ends.

buen principio, la mitad es hecha (Sp.), well begun is half-done.

cadit quaestio (L.), the question drops.

caeca invidia est (L.), envy is blind.—Livy, xxxviii. 49.

caelebs quid agam (L.), (you wonder) what I, a bachelor, am about.—Horace, *Od.*, III. viii. 1.

caelum non animum mutant qui trans mare currunt (L.), they change their sky, not their mind, who scour across the sea.—Horace, *Epist.*, I. xi. 27.

Caesar non supra grammaticos (L.), Caesar has no authority over the grammarians.

ça ira (Fr.), it will go—refrain of a famous song of the French Revolution.

callida junctura (L.), a skilful connection.— Horace, *A.P.*, 47-48.

candida Pax (L.), white-robed Peace.—Tibullus, I. x. 45.

cantabit vacuus coram latrone viator (L.), the empty-handed traveller will sing in presence of the robber.—Juvenal, X. 22.

carent quia vate sacro (L.), because they lack a sacred bard.—Horace, *Od.*, IV. ix. 28.

carpe diem, quam minimum credula postero (L.), enjoy the present day, trust the least possible to the future.—Horace, *Od.*, I. xi. 8.

causa sine qua non (L.), an indispensable cause.

cave quid dicis, quando, et cui (L.), beware what you say, when, and to whom.

cedant arma togae (L.), let arms yield to the gown:

let military authority yield to civil.—Cicero, *De Officiis*, I. xxii. 77.

**cela va sans dire** (Fr.), that goes without saying: of course.

**cela viendra** (Fr.), that will come.

**celui qui veut, peut** (Fr.), who will, can.

**ce monde est plein de fous** (Fr.), this world is full of madmen.

**c'en est fait de lui** (Fr.), it is all up with him.

**ce n'est que le premier pas qui coûte** (Fr.). See **il n'ya.**

**certum est quia impossibile est** (L.), it is certain because it is impossible.—Tertullian.

**c'est-à-dire** (Fr.), that is to say.

**c'est égal** (Fr.), it's all one (to me): it makes no odds.

**c'est le commencement de la fin** (Fr.), it is the beginning of the end.—Attrib. to Talleyrand.

**c'est magnifique, mais ce n'est pas la guerre** (Fr.), it is magnificent, but it is not war (said at Balaklava by a French general watching the charge of the Light Brigade).

**c'est pire (or plus) qu'un crime, c'est une faute** (Fr.), it is worse than a crime, it is a blunder (on the execution of the Duc d'Enghien; attributed to various persons, incl. Boulay de la Meurthe).

**c'est selon** (Fr.), that is according to the circumstances.

**c'est (une) autre chose** (Fr.), that is quite another thing.

**ceterum censeo** (L.), but I think (said of persistent obstruction like that of Cato).

**chacun (à) son goût** (Fr.), everyone to his taste. Also **à chacun son goût.**

**chapeaux bas** (Fr.), hats off.

**cherchez la femme** (Fr.), look for the woman: there's a woman at the bottom of it.—Dumas *père.*

**che sarà sarà** (It.), what will be will be.

**chiesa libera in libero stato** (It.), a free church in a free state (Cavour's ideal for Italy).

**chi tace confessa** (It.), who keeps silence, confesses.

**circulus in probando** (L.), arguing in a circle, using the conclusion as one of the arguments.

**civis Romanus sum** (L.), I am a Roman citizen. —Cicero, *In Verrem*, VI. 57.

**clarior e tenebris** (L.), the brighter from the darkness.

**clarum et venerabile nomen** (L.), an illustrious and venerable name.—Lucan, IX. 202.

**cogito, ergo sum** (L.), I think, therefore I am. (Descartes's fundamental basis of philosophy.)

**comitas inter gentes,** or **comitas gentium** (L.). See comity in Dict.

**conditio sine qua non** (L.), an indispensable condition.

**conjunctis viribus** (L.), with united powers.

**conquiescat in pace** (L.), may he [or she] rest in peace.

**conscia mens recti** (L.), a mind conscious of rectitude.—Ovid, *Fast.*, IV. 311. Cf. **mens sibi.**

**consensus facit legem** (L.), consent makes law or rule.

**consuetudo pro lege servatur** (L.), custom is held as a law.

**consule Planco** (L.), when Plancus was consul, when I was a young man.—Horace, *Od.*, III. xiv. 28.

**contraria contrariis curantur** (L.), opposites are cured by opposites.

**corruptio optimi pessima** (L.), the corruption of the best is the worst of all.

**così fan tutte** (It.), so do they all (of women): they are all like that.

**coûte que coûte** (Fr.), cost what it may.

**crambe repetita** (L.), cauld kale het again—cold cabbage warmed up.—Juvenal, VII. 154.

**credat Judaeus Apella, non ego** (L.), let the Jew Apella believe that, for I don't.—Horace, *Sat.*, I. v. 100.

**credo quia absurdum** (L.), I believe it because it is absurd; —**quia impossibile,** because it is impossible (based on Tertullian; see **certum est quia impossibile est).**

**crescit eundo** (L.), it grows as it goes.—Lucretius VI. 341.

**cucullus non facit monachum** (L.), the cowl does not make the monk.

**cuilibet (or cuicunque) in arte sua (perito) credendum** (L.), every (skilled) person is to be trusted in his own art.—Coke.

**cujus regio, ejus religio** (L.), whose the region, his the religion—the principle that the established religion should be that of the prince in each state.

**curiosa felicitas** (L.), studied felicity of expression —said by Petronius Arbiter, *Saturae* (*Satyricon*), 118, 5 of Horace's style: (*loosely*) curious felicity.

**da dextram misero** (L.), give the right hand to the unhappy.

**da locum melioribus** (L.), give place to your betters.—Terence, *Phormio*, III, ii. 37.

**damnosa haereditas** (L.), an inheritance of debts (*Roman law*): any hurtful inheritance.—Gaius, *Institutes*, ii. 163.

**damnum absque injuria** (L.), loss without legal injury.

**das Ewig-Weibliche zieht uns hinan** (Ger.), the eternal feminine draws us upward.—Goethe, *Faust*, at end.

**data et accepta** (L.), expenditures and receipts.

**date obolum Belisario** (L.), give a penny to Belisarius (ascribed to the great general when reduced to beggary).

**Davus sum, non Oedipus** (L.), I am Davus, not Oedipus—no good at riddles.—Terence, *Andr.*, I. ii. 23.

**de die in diem** (L.), from day to day.

**de gustibus non est disputandum** (L.), there is no disputing about tastes.

**de l'audace, encore de l'audace, et toujours de l'audace** (Fr.), to dare, still to dare, and ever to dare (Danton's famous phrase).

**delenda est Carthago** (L.), Carthage must be wiped out (a saying constantly repeated by Cato).

**de mal en pis** (Fr.), from bad to worse.

**de minimis non curat lex** (L.), the law does not concern itself about very small matters.—Bacon, Letter cclxxxii.

**de mortuis nil nisi bonum** (L.), say nothing but good of the dead.

**de nihilo nihilum.** See gigni.

**de omni re scibili et quibusdam aliis** (L.), about all things knowable, and some others.

**de pis en pis** (Fr.), worse and worse.

**der grosse heide** (Ger.), the great pagan (Heine's name for Goethe).

**desipere in loco.** See dulce.

**desunt cetera** (L.), the rest is wanting.

**de te fabula narratur** (L.), the story is about you.— Horace, *Sat.*, I. i. 69-70.

**detur digniori** (L.), let it be given to the more worthy; **detur pulchriori,** let it be given to the fairer.

**deus nobis haec otia fecit** (L.), it is a god that hath given us this ease.—Virgil, *Ecl.*, I. 6.

**dicamus bona verba** (L.), let us speak words of good omen.—Tibullus, II, ii. 1.

**dichtung und wahrheit** (Ger.), poetry and truth.

**dictum de dicto** (L.), hearsay report.

**dictum sapienti sat est** (L.), a word to the wise is enough (usu. quoted as **verbum).**—Plautus, *Persa*, IV. vii. 19.

**diem perdidi** (L.), I have lost a day (said by the Emperor Titus).

**Dieu défend le droit** (Fr.), God defends the right; **Dieu vous garde,** God keep you.

**Die Wacht am Rhein** (Ger.), the Watch on the Rhine (a famous German patriotic song).

digito monstrari (L.), to be pointed out with the finger: to be famous.—Persius, I. 28.

dignus vindice nodus (L.). See nec deus intersit.

di grado in grado (It.), by degrees.

dis aliter visum (L.), the gods have adjudged otherwise.—Virgil, *Aen.*, II. 428.

disjecta membra (L.), scattered limbs (after Ovid, *Met.*, III. 724); disjecti membra poetae, limbs of the dismembered poet.—Horace, *Sat.*, I. iv. 62.

distinguo (L.), I distinguish.

·divide et impera (L.), divide and rule.

docendo discimus (L.), we learn by teaching.

doctor utriusque legis (L.), doctor of both laws (civil and canon).

doli capax (L.), capable of committing a wrong—opp. to *doli incapax*.

Domine, dirige nos (L.), Lord, direct us (the motto of London).

Dominus illuminatio mea (L.), the Lord is my light.

domus et placens uxor (L.), a home and a pleasing wife.—Horace, *Od.*, II. xiv. 21-22.

dorer la pilule (Fr.), to gild the pill.

dormitat Homerus (L.). See indignor.

dos moi pou stō kai tēn gēn (or tān gān) kinēsō (Gr.), give me where to stand, and I will move the earth (attributed to Archimedes).

do ut des (L.), I give that you may give.

dulce, 'Domum' (L.), sweet strain, 'Homeward' —from a Winchester school song sung before the holidays ; dulce est desipere in loco, it is pleasant to play the fool on occasion.—Horace, *Od.*, IV. xii. 28 ; dulce et decorum est pro patria mori, it is sweet and glorious to die for one's country.—Horace, *Od.*, III. ii. 13.

dum casta (L.), while (she is) chaste.

dum spiro, spero (L.), while I breathe, I hope.

dum vivimus, vivamus (L.), let us live while we live.

dux femina facti (L.), a woman was leader in the deed.—Virgil, *Aen.*, I. 364.

écrasez l'infâme (Fr.), crush the vile thing. Voltaire against the Roman Catholic Church of his time.

edax rerum. See tempus.

ego et rex meus (L.), I and my king.—Cardinal Wolsey.

eheu fugaces . . . labuntur anni (L.), alas! the fleeting years slip away.—Horace, *Od.*, II, xiv. 1-2.

eile mit weile (Ger.), make speed with leisure. Cf. festina lente.

ein mal, kein mal (Ger.), just once counts nothing.

ek parergou (Gr.), as a by-work.

emou thanontos gaia michthētō pyri (Gr.), when I am dead let earth be mingled with fire. Cf. après moi le déluge.

entbehren sollst du, sollst entbehren (Ger.), thou must abstain, abstain thou must.—Goethe, *Faust*, Part I. (Studierzimmer, ii).

en toutōi nika (Gr.), conquer in this (sign). See in hoc (signo) vinces.

epea pteroenta (Gr.), winged words.—Homer (Iliad, I. 201, etc.).

ephphatha (Aramaic), be opened (Mark vii. 34).

e pluribus unum (L.), one out of many—before 1956 regarded as motto of the United States.

eppur si muove (It.), it does move all the same (attrib. to Galileo after he had recanted his doctrine that the earth moves round the sun).

erectos ad sidera tollere vultus (L.). See os homini.

ergo bibamus (L.), therefore let us drink.

Erin go bragh (Ir.), Erin forever.

errare est humanum (L.), to err is human.

es korakas (Gr.), to the ravens: go and be hanged.

esse quam videri (L.), to be, rather than to seem.

est modus in rebus (L.), there is a mean in (all) things.—Horace, *Sat.*, I. i. 106.

esto perpetua (L.), be lasting.

est quaedam flere voluptas (L.), there is in weeping a certain pleasure.—Ovid, *Trist.*, IV. iii. 37.

et hoc (or id) genus omne (L.), and all that sort of thing.

et in Arcadia ego (L.), I, too, lived in Arcadia. (Inscription from tomb, used in Poussin's picture 'The Arcadian Shepherds'.)

et tu, Brute (L.), you too, Brutus. (Caesar's alleged exclamation when he saw Brutus amongst his assassins.)

eventus stultorum magister (L.), the outcome is the schoolmaster of fools.—Livy, XXII, 39.

ex abusu non arguitur ad usum (L.), from the abuse no argument is drawn against the use. cf. abusus non.

exceptio confirmat (or probat) regulam (L.), the exception proves the rule. (See except in Dict.)

exegi monumentum aere perennius (L.), I have reared a monument more lasting than brass.—Horace, *Od.*, III. xxx. l.

exempla sunt odiosa (L.), examples are hateful.

exitus acta probat (L.), the outcome justifies the deed.—Ovid, *Her.*, II. 85.

ex nihilo (or nilo) nihil (or nil) fit (L.), out of nothing nothing comes. See gigni.

ex pede Herculem (L.), (we recognise) Hercules from his foot.

experientia docet stultos (L.), experience teaches fools.

experto crede or (Virgil, *Aen.*, XI. 283) credite (L.), trust one who has tried, or had experience.

expertus metuet, or metuit (L.), he who has experienced it will fear (or fears).—Horace, *Epist.*, I. xviii, 87.

exstinctus amabitur idem (L.), the same man (maligned living) when dead will be loved.—Horace, *Epist.*, II. i. 14.

ex ungue leonem (L.), (judge, or infer) the lion from his claws.

faber est quisque fortunae suae (L.), every man is the fashioner of his own fortunes.—Proverb quoted by Sallust, *De Republica*, I.

fable convenue (Fr.), fable agreed upon—Voltaire's name for history.

facile est inventis addere (L.), it is easy to add to things invented already.

facilis descensus Averno, or Averni (L.), descent to Avernus is easy.—Virgil, *Aen.*, VI. 126.

facinus majoris abollae (L.), the crime of a larger cloak, i.e. of a philosopher.—Juvenal, III. 115.

facit indignatio versum (L.), indignation makes verse.—Juvenal, I. 79.

facta non verba (L.), deeds, not words.

factum est (L.), it is done.

facundi. See facund. faenum. See fenum.

faire bonne mine (Fr.), to put a good face on the matter.

falsus in uno, falsus in omnibus (L.), false in one thing, false in all.

fama nihil est celerius (L.), nothing is swifter than rumour.—Livy.

fama semper vivat (L.), may his (or her) fame live for ever.

far niente (It.), doing nothing.

farrago libelli. See quicquid.

fas est et ab hoste doceri (L.), it is right to learn even from an enemy.—Ovid, *Met.*, IV. 428.

Fata obstant (L.), the Fates oppose.—Virgil, *Aen.*, IV. 440.

Fata viam invenient (L.), the Fates will find out a way.—Virgil, *Aen.*, X. 113.

favete linguis (L.), favour me with your tongues—keep silent to avoid ill omen.—Horace, *Od.*, III. i. 2.

fecundi (or facundi) calices quem non fecere disertum? (L.), whom have not full cups made eloquent?—Horace, *Epist.*, I. v. 19.

felicitas multos habet amicos (L.), prosperity has many friends.

felix qui potuit rerum cognoscere causas (L.), happy is he who has been able to understand the causes of things.—Virgil, *Georg.*, II. 490.

**fendre un cheveu en quatre** (Fr.), to split a hair in four.

**fenum habet in cornu** (L.), he has hay on his horn (sign of a dangerous bull).—Horace, *Sat.*, I. iv. 34.

**festina lente** (L.), hasten gently.

**fiat experimentum in corpore vili** (L.), let experiment be made on a worthless body.

**fiat justitia, ruat caelum** (L.), let justice be done, though the heavens should fall.

**fiat lux** (L.), let there be light.

**fide, sed cui vide** (L.), trust, but take care in whom.

**fidus Achates** (L.), faithful Achates (friend of Aeneas): hence, a close friend.—Virgil.

**finis coronat opus** (L.), the end crowns the work.

**flectere si nequeo superos, Acheronta movebo** (L.), if I can't move the gods, I'll stir up hell.—Virgil, *Aen.*, V.II. 312.

**foenum.** See fenum.

**forsan et haec olim meminisse juvabit** (L.), perhaps some day we shall like to remember even these things.—Virgil, *Aen.*, I. 203.

**Fors Clavigera** (L.), Fortune the club-bearer (used as a title by Ruskin).

**fortes Fortuna adjuvat** (L.), Fortune helps the brave (Terence, *Phorm.*, I. iv. 26); **forti et fideli nihil difficile**, to the brave and faithful nothing is difficult; **fortis cadere, cedere non potest**, the brave man may fall, he cannot yield.

**fortiter in re, suaviter in modo** (L.), forcibly in deed, gentle in manner.

**Fortuna favet fatuis** (L.), Fortune favours fools; **Fortuna favet fortibus**, Fortune favours the bold.

**frangas, non flectes** (L.), you may break, you shall not bend.

**fraus est celare fraudem** (L.), it is a fraud to conceal a fraud.

**frontis nulla fides** (L.), no reliance on the face, no trusting appearances.—Juvenal, II. 8.

**fruges consumere nati** (L.), born to consume the fruits of the soil.—Horace, *Epist.*, I. ii. 27.

**fugit hora** (L.), the hour flies.—Persius, V. 153.

**fuimus Troes; fuit Ilium** (L.), we were Trojans; Troy was.—Virgil, *Aen.*, II. 325.

**fulmen brutum** (L.), a harmless thunderbolt.

**furor arma ministrat** (L.), rage supplies arms. Virgil, *Aen.*, I. 150.

**gaudet tentamine virtus** (L.), virtue rejoices in trial.

**geflügelte worte** (Ger.), winged words. See epea.

**genus irritabile vatum** (L.), the irritable tribe of poets.—Horace, *Epist.*, II. ii. 102.

**gibier de potence** (Fr.), gallows-bird.

**gigni de nihilo nihilum, in nihilum nil posse reverti** (L.), from nothing nothing can come, into nothing nothing can return.—Persius, III. 84.

**giovine santo, diavolo vecchio** (It.), young saint, old devil.

**gli assenti hanno torto** (It.), the absent are in the wrong.

**gloria virtutis umbra** (L.), glory (is) the shadow of virtue.

**glückliche reise** (Ger.), prosperous journey to you.

**Gott mit uns** (Ger.), God with us—Hohenzollern motto.

**gradu diverso, via una** (L.), with different step on the one way.

**gradus ad Parnassum** (L.), a step, or stairs, to Parnassus, a Latin or Greek poetical dictionary.

**Graeculus esuriens** (L.), the hungry Greekling.—Juvenal, III. 78.

**Graecum est: non legitur** (L.), this is Greek; it is not read (placed against a Greek word in mediaeval MSS, a permission to skip the hard words).

**grande chère et beau feu** (Fr.), ample cheer and a fine fire; **grande fortune, grande servitude**, great wealth, great slavery.

**gratia placendi** (L.), the delight of pleasing.

**graviora manent** (L.), greater dangers remain (Virgil, *Aen.*, VI. 84); **graviora quaedam sunt remedia periculis**, some remedies are more grievous than the perils (Syrus).

**gravis ira regum est semper** (L.), the anger of kings is always serious.

**grosse seelen dulden still** (Ger.), great souls suffer in silence.—Schiller, *Don Carlos*, I. iv., end of scene.

**grosse tête et peu de sens** (Fr.), big head and little wit.

**gutta cavat lapidem** (L.), the drop wears away the stone.—Ovid, *Pont.*, IV. x. 5.

**habendum et tenendum** (L.), to have and to hold.

**habent sua fata libelli** (L.), books have their destinies.—Maurus, *De Litteris, Syllabis et Metris*.

**hanc veniam petimusque damusque vicissim** (L.), this liberty we ask and grant in turn.—Horace, *A.P.*, 11.

**Hannibal ad portas** (L.), Hannibal at the gates.—Cicero, *Philippica*, I. v. 11.

**haud longis intervallis** (L.), at no long intervals.

**helluo librorum** (L.), a glutton of books.

**heu pietas! heu prisca fides!** (L.), alas for piety! alas for the ancient faith!—Virgil, *Aen.*, VI. 879.

**hiatus valde deflendus** (L.), a gap deeply to be deplored.

**hic finis fandi** (L.), here (was, or let there be) an end of the speaking.

**hinc illae lacrumae** (L.), hence [came] those tears. —Terence, *Andria*, I. i. 99; also Horace, *Epist.*, I. xix. 41.

**hinc lucem et pocula sacra** (L.), from this source [we draw] light and draughts of sacred learning.

**ho bios brachys, hē de technē makrē** (Gr.), life is short and art is long.—Attributed to Hippocrates.

**hoc age** (L.), this do.

**hoc erat in votis** (L.), this was the very thing I prayed for.—Horace, *Sat.*, II. vi. 1.

**hoc opus, hic labor est** (L.), this is the toil, this the labour.—Virgil, *Aen.*, VI. 129.

**hoc saxum posuit** (L.), placed this stone.

**hoc** (or **sic**) **volo, sic jubeo, sit pro ratione voluntas** (L.), this (thus) I will, thus I command, be my will sufficient reason.—Juvenal, VI. 223.

**hodie mihi, cras tibi** (L.), me today, you tomorrow.

**hominibus plenum, amicis vacuum** (L.), full of men, empty of friends.

**hominis est errare** (L.), it belongs to man to err.

**homo alieni juris** (L.), one under control of another; **homo antiqua virtute ac fide**, a man of the antique virtue and loyalty (Terence, *Adelphi*, III. iii. 88 or l. 442); **homo homini lupus**, man is a wolf to man; **homo multarum litterarum**, a man of many literary accomplishments; **homo nullius coloris**, a man of no colour, one who does not commit himself; **homo sui juris**, one who is his own master; **homo sum: humani nihil a me alienum puto**, I am a man: I count nothing human indifferent to me (Terence, *Heaut.*, I. i. 25); **homo trium litterarum**, man of three letters—i.e. *fur* =thief; **homo unius libri**, a man of one book.

**hon hoi theoi philousi apothnēskei neos** (Gr.), whom the gods love dies young.—Menander. Cf. **quem di diligunt . . .**

**honi soit qui mal y pense** (O.Fr.), the shame be his who thinks ill of it—the motto of the Order of the Garter.

**honneur et patrie** (Fr.), honour and native land.

**honores mutant mores** (L.), honours change manners.

**honor virtutis praemium** (L.), honour is the reward of virtue.

**honos alit artes** (L.), honour nourishes the arts (Cicero, *Tusculanae Disputationes*, I. ii. 4); **honos habet onus**, honour has its burden.

**hora fugit** (L.), the hour flies.

horas non numero nisi serenas (L.), I number none but shining hours. [Common on sun-dials.]

horresco referens (L.), I shudder in relating.—Virgil, *Aen.*, II, 204.

horribile dictu (L.), horrible to relate.

hostis honori invidia (L.), envy is an enemy to honour.

hostis humani generis (L.), enemy of the human race.

humanum est errare (L.), to err is human.

hurtar para dar por Dios (Sp.), to steal in order to give to God.

hypage Satana (Gr.), away Satan.—Mat. iv. 10.

hypotheses non fingo (L.), I do not frame hypotheses (i.e. unverifiable speculations).—Newton.

ich dien (Ger.), I serve.

ici on parle français (Fr.), here French is spoken.

idem velle atque idem nolle ea demum firma amicitia est (L.), to like and to dislike the same things is indeed true friendship.—Sallust, *Catalina*, 20.

Iesus Hominum Salvator (L.), Jesus, Saviour of men.

ignorantia legis neminem excusat (L.), ignorance of the law excuses nobody.

ignoti nulla cupido (L.), for a thing unknown there is no desire.—Ovid, *A.A.*, III. 397.

ignotum per ignotius (L.), the unknown by the still more unknown.

i gran dolori sono muti (It.), great griefs are mute.

il a inventé l'histoire (Fr.), he has invented history.

il a le diable au corps (Fr.), the devil is in him: he is full of devilment, or of vivacity, wit, enthusiasm, etc.: he can't sit still.

il a les défauts de ses qualités (Fr.), he has the defects that answer to his good qualities.

il faut de l'argent (Fr.), money is necessary.

il faut laver son linge sale en famille (Fr.), one should wash one's dirty linen in private.

il gran rifiuto (It.), the great refusal (the abdication of Pope Celestine V).—Dante, *Inferno*, III. 60.

Ilias malorum (L.), an Iliad of woes.

ille crucem sceleris pretium tulit, hic diadema (L.), that man got a cross, this man a crown, as the price of his crime.—Juvenal, XIII. 105.

ille terrarum mihi praeter omnes angulus ridet (L.), that corner of the earth to me smiles sweetest of all.—Horace, *Od.*, II. vi. 13-14.

il meglio è l'inimico del bene (It.), the better is the enemy of the good.

il n'y a pas à dire (Fr.), there is nothing to be said.

il n'y a que le premier pas qui coûte (Fr.), it is only the first step that counts. (Mme du Deffand on St Denis walking after decapitation.)

ils n'ont rien appris ni rien oublié (Fr.), they have learned nothing and forgotten nothing [said of the French *Émigrés*, often of the Bourbons].

impar congressus Achilli (L.), unequally matched against Achilles.—Virgil, *Aen.*, I. 475.

incedis per ignis suppositos cineri doloso (L.), you walk on fires covered with treacherous ash.—Horace, *Od.*, II. i. 7-8.

incidis in Scyllam cupiens vitare Charybdim (L.), you fall into Scylla trying to avoid Charybdis.—Philip Gaultier de Lille.

incredulus odi (L.), I hate and disbelieve.—Horace, *A.P.*, 188.

indignor quandoque bonus dormitat Homerus (L.), I am annoyed whenever good Homer slumbers.—Horace, *A.P.*, 359. Usually cited as aliquando (=sometimes) bonus, etc.

infandum, regina, jubes renovare dolorem (L.), thou bidst me, queen, renew unspeakable woes.—Virgil, *Aen.*, II. 3.

in hoc (signo) vinces (L.), in this sign thou wilt conquer—i.e. in the Cross [the motto of Constantine the Great]. See en toutōi nika.

in magnis et voluisse sat est (L.), in great things even to have wished is enough.—Propertius, II. x. 6.

in meditatione fugae (L.), in contemplation of flight.

inopem me copia fecit (L.), plenty has made me poor.—Ovid, *M.*, III. 466.

integer vitae scelerisque purus (L.), blameless in life and clear of offence.—Horace, *Od.*, I. xxii. 1.

inter arma silent leges (L.), amid wars laws are silent (Cicero); interdum stultus bene loquitur, sometimes a fool speaks aright.

invita Minerva (L.), against the will of Minerva: uninspired.—Horace, *A.P.*, 383.

ira furor brevis est (L.), rage is a brief madness.—Horace, *Epist.*, I. ii. 62.

Italia irredenta (It.), unredeemed Italy—the parts of Italy still under foreign domination after the war of 1866—South Tirol, etc.

jacta est alea (L.), the die is cast (quoted as said by Caesar at the crossing of the Rubicon).

je n'en vois pas la nécessité (Fr.), I don't see the necessity for that [said by the Comte d'Argental in reply to a man who pleaded, 'But one must live somehow'].

joci causa (L.), for the joke.

judex damnatur cum nocens absolvitur (L.), the judge is condemned when the guilty is acquitted.—Syrus, 247.

Jup(p)iter optimus maximus (L.), Jupiter best and greatest; Jup(p)iter Pluvius, rain-bringing Jupiter; Jup(p)iter Tonans, Jupiter the thunderer.

justum et tenacem propositi virum (L.), a man upright and tenacious of purpose.—Horace, *Od.*, III. iii. 1.

j'y suis, j'y reste (Fr.), here I am, here I stay [said by Macmahon at the Malakoff].

kai ta leipomena, kai ta loipa (Gr.), and the rest: and so on.

kalos kagathos, kalokagathos (Gr.), good and honourable: a perfect gentleman.

kat' exochēn (Gr.), pre-eminently: *par excellence.*

keine antwort ist auch eine antwort (Ger.), no answer is still an answer: silence gives consent.

kirche, küche, kinder (Ger.), church, kitchen, children—said, e.g. during the Nazi period, to be the proper interests of a German woman.

ktēma es aei (Gr.), a possession for ever.

kymatōn anērithmon gelasma (Gr.), innumerable smiles of the waves.—Aeschylus, *Prom.*, 89-90.

laborare est orare (L.), work is prayer.

labore et honore (L.), by labour and honour.

labuntur et imputantur (L.), [the moments] slip away and are laid to our account (inscription on sundials). Also pereunt et imputantur (q.v.).

la donna è mobile (It.), woman is changeable.

la garde meurt et ne se rend pas (Fr.), the guard dies, it does not surrender.

la grande nation (Fr.), the great nation—i.e. France.

lā ilāha illā 'llāh (Ar.), there is no god but God.

langage des halles (Fr.), language of the market-place.

l'appétit vient en mangeant (Fr.), appetite comes as you eat.

la propriété c'est le vol (Fr.), property is theft [from Proudhon].

la reyne le veult (s'avisera) (Norm. Fr.). See le roy.

lasciate ogni speranza, voi che'ntrate (It.), abandon all hope ye who enter.—Dante, *Inferno*, III. 9. From the inscription over the gate of hell.

latet anguis in herba (L.), there is a snake hidden in the grass.—Virgil, *Ecl.*, III. 93.

laudator temporis acti (L.), one who praises past times.—Horace, *A.P.*, 173.

le génie n'est qu'une grande aptitude à la patience (Fr.), genius is merely a great aptitude for patience (attributed to Buffon).

**le grand monarque** (Fr.), the great king—i.e. Louis XIV.

**le jeu ne vaut pas la chandelle** (Fr.), the game is not worth the candle.

**l'empire c'est la paix** (Fr.), the empire means peace [said by Louis Napoleon in 1852].

**le roy (or la reyne) le veult** (Norm. Fr.), the king (or queen) wills it—form of royal assent.

**le roy (la reyne) s'avisera** (Norm. Fr.), the king (or queen) will deliberate—form of refusal.

**le style est l'homme (même)** (Fr.), the style is the man himself (from Buffon).

**l'état, c'est moi** (Fr.), I am the state [alleged to have been said by Louis XIV].

**liberté, égalité, fraternité** (Fr.), liberty, equality, fraternity—a slogan of the French Revolution.

**limae labor** (L.), the labour of the file, of polishing. —Horace, *A.P.*, 291.

**littera scripta manet** (L.), what is written down is permanent. See **vox audita.**

**lucri causa** (L.), for the sake of gain.

**lucus a non lucendo** (L.), the grove (*lucus*) (is so named) from its *not* shining (*lucendo*).

**ludere cum sacris** (L.), to trifle with sacred things.

**l'union fait la force** (Fr.), union makes strength.

**lupus in fabula** (L.), the wolf in the fable: talk of the devil.—Terence, *Adel.*, IV. i. 21.

**macte virtute** (L.), be honoured in your valour, virtue—used by Cicero, Virgil, Livy (**macte virtute esto**—Cato to one coming out of a resort of vice, acc. to Horace, *Sat.*, I. ii. 31-32).

**magna est veritas et praevalebit** (L.), truth is great and will prevail (Vulgate, **et prevalet**).

**magni nominis umbra** (L.), the mere shadow of a mighty name.—Lucan, I. 135.

**man spricht deutsch** (Ger.), German spoken here.

**matre pulchra filia pulchrior** (L.), a daughter fairer than her fair mother.—Horace, *Od.*, I. xvi. 1.

**maxima debetur puero reverentia** (L.), the greatest reverence is due to the boy—i.e. to the innocence of his age.—Juvenal, XIV, 47.

**mea virtute me involvo** (L.), I wrap myself in my virtue.—Horace, *Od.*, III. xxix. 54-55.

**mēden agan** (Gr.), [let there be] nothing in excess.

**medio tutissimus ibis** (L.), thou wilt go safest in the middle.—Ovid, *M.*, II. 137.

**mega biblion, mega kakon** (Gr.), big book, great evil.

**mē kinei Kamarinan** (Gr.), do not stir up Kamarina (a pestilent marsh in Sicily): let well alone.

**mens sana in corpore sano** (L.), a sound mind in a sound body.—Juvenal, X. 356.

**mens sibi conscia recti** (L.), a mind conscious of rectitude.—Virgil, *Aen.*, I. 604. Cf. **conscia mens recti.**

**mirabile dictu** (L.), wonderful to tell; **mirabile visu**, wonderful to see.

**mole ruit sua** (L.), falls by its own weight.— Horace, *Od.*, III. iv. 65.

**monstrum horrendum, informe, ingens** (L.), a frightful monster, ill-shapen, huge.—Virgil, *Aen.*, III. 658.

**morituri te salutamus.** See **ave.**

**muet comme un poisson** (Fr.), dumb as a fish.

**natura abhorret vacuum** (L.), nature abhors a vacuum.

**naturam expellas furca, tamen usque recurret** (L.), though you drive out nature with a pitchfork, yet will she always return.—Horace, *Epist.*, I. x. 24.

**natura non facit saltus** (or **saltum**) (L.), nature does not make leaps (or a leap).

**naviget Anticyram** (L.), let him sail to Anticyra [where hellebore could be had, to cure madness]. —Horace, *Sat.*, II. iii. 166.

**nec cupias, nec metuas** (L.), neither desire nor fear.

**nec deus intersit nisi dignus vindice nodus inciderit** (L.), let not a god intervene unless a knot

occur worthy of the untier.—Horace, *A.P.*, 191-2.

**ne cede malis** (L.), yield not to misfortune.— Virgil, *Aen.*, VI. 95.

**necessitas non habet legem** (L.), necessity has no law.

**nec pluribus impar** (L.), no unequal match for several (suns).—Louis XIV's motto.

**nec scire fas est omnia** (L.), it is not permitted to know all things.—Horace, *Od.*, IV. iv. 22.

**ne exeat** (L.), let him not depart.

**negatur** (L.), it is denied.

**nemo me impune lacessit** (L.), no one provokes me with impunity—the motto of the kings of Scotland and of the Order of the Thistle; **nemo repente fuit turpissimus**, no one ever became utterly bad all at once.—Juvenal, II. 83.

**ne obliviscaris** (L.), do not forget.

**neque semper arcum tendit Apollo** (L.), Apollo does not always bend his bow.—Horace, *Od.*, II. x. 19-20.

**ne quid nimis** (L.), [let there be] nothing in excess.

**nescis, mi fili, quantilla prudentia mundus regatur** (L.), you know not, my son, with what a small stock of wisdom the world is governed.— Attributed to Oxenstierna and others.

**nescit vox missa reverti** (L.), a word published cannot be recalled.—Horace, *A.P.*, 390.

**n'est-ce pas?** (Fr.), is it not so?

**ne sutor ultra crepidam** (L.). See **sutor.**

**ne temere** (L.), not rashly—a papal decree of 1907 denying recognition to the marriage of a Catholic unless contracted before a priest.

**nicht wahr?** (Ger.), is it not true? isn't that so?

**nihil tetigit quod non ornavit.** See **nullum.**

**nil actum credens dum quid superesset agendum** (L.), thinking nothing done while anything was yet to do.—Lucan, II. 657; **nil admirari**, to wonder at nothing.—Horace, *Epist.*, I. vi. 1; **nil desperandum**, nothing is to be despaired of. —Horace, *Od.*, I. vii. 27.

**n'importe** (Fr.), no matter.

**nisi Dominus frustra** (L.), except the Lord [keep the city, the watchman waketh but] in vain.— Ps. cxxvii—the motto of Edinburgh.

**nitor in adversum** (L.), I strive in opposition.— Ovid, *M.*, II. 72.

**non amo te, Sabidi, nec possum dicere quare** (L.), I do not love thee, Sabidius, nor can I tell why. —Martial, I. xxxiii.

**non compos mentis** (L.), not of sound mind.

**non est inventus** (L.), he has not been found (he has absconded).

**non licet** (L.), it is not allowed.

**non liquet** (L.), it is not clear.

**non mi ricordo** (It.), I don't remember.

**non multa, sed multum** (L.), not many, but much.

**non nobis, Domine** (L.), not unto us, O Lord.— Psalm cxv.

**non olet pecunia** (L.), the money does not stink.— Attributed to Vespasian, of revenue from an unsavoury source.

**non omnia possumus omnes** (L.), we cannot all do everything.—Virgil, *Ecl.*, viii. 63.

**non omnis moriar** (L.), I shall not wholly die.— Horace, *Od.*, III. xxx. 6.

**non placet** (L.), it does not please—a negative vote.

**non possumus** (L.), we cannot—a form of refusal.

**non tali auxilio nec defensoribus istis tempus eget** (L.), not for such aid nor for these defenders does the time call.—Virgil, *Aen.*, II. 521.

**nonumque prematur in annum** (L.), and let it be kept unpublished till the ninth year.— Horace, *A.P.*, 388.

**non ut edam vivo sed ut vivam edo** (L.), I do not live to eat, but eat to live.—Quintilian.

**nous avons changé tout cela** (Fr.), we have changed all that.—Molière, *Le Médecin malgré lui*, II. iv.

**nous verrons (ce que nous verrons)** (Fr.), we shall see (what we shall see).

**nulla dies sine linea** (L.), no day without a line, without painting (or writing) a little.

**nulla nuova, buona nuova** (It.), no news is good news.

**nullius addictus (or adductus) jurare in verba magistri** (L.), bound to swear to the words of no master, to follow no one blindly or slavishly.—Horace, *Epist.*, I. i. 14.

**nullum (scil. scribendi genus) quod tetigit non ornavit** (L.), he touched no form of literature without adorning it. From Johnson's epitaph on Goldsmith.

**nunc est bibendum** (L.), now is time to drink.—Horace, *Od.*, I. xxxvii. 1.

**obscurum per obscurius** (L.), (explaining) the obscure by means of the more obscure.

**oderint dum metuant** (L.), let them hate so long as they fear.—Accius, *Atreus*, Fragment IV; quoted in Cicero, *Philippic*, I. xiv.

**odi profanum vulgus et arceo** (L.), I loathe and shun the profane rabble.—Horace, *Od.*, iii. i. 1.

**O fortunatos nimium, sua si bona novint, agricolas** (L.), Oh too happy farmers, if they but knew their luck.—Virgil, *Georg.*, II. 458.

**ohe! jam satis** (L.), hold! enough now (a common phrase).

**ohne hast, ohne rast** (Ger.), without haste, without rest.—Goethe's motto.

**olim meminisse juvabit.** See forsan.

**omne ignotum pro magnifico** (L.), everything unknown (is taken to be) magnificent.—Tacitus, *Agric.*, 30.

**omnem crede diem tibi diluxisse supremum** (L.), believe each day to have dawned as your last.—Horace, *Epist.*, I. iv. 13.

**omne tulit punctum qui miscuit utile dulci** (L.), he has carried every vote who has combined the useful with the pleasing.—Horace, *A.P.*, 343.

**omne vivum ex ovo** (L.), every living thing comes from an egg.—Attributed to Harvey.

**omnia mea mecum porto** (L.), all I have I carry with me.

**omnia mutantur.** See tempora mutantur.

**omnia vincit amor, et nos cedamus amori** (L.), love overcomes all things, let us too yield to love.—Virgil, *Ecl.*, X. 69.

**ore rotundo** (L.), with round, full voice (mouth).—Horace, *Ars Poetica*, 323.

**O sancta simplicitas!** (L.), O holy simplicity!

**os homini sublime dedit caelumque tueri jussit et erectos ad sidera tollere vultus** (L.), he gave man an up-turned face and bade contemplate the heavens and raise looks to the stars.—Ovid, *M.*, I. 85.

**O si sic omnia!** (L.), Oh that he had done all things thus, or Oh that all things were thus!

**O tempora! O mores!** (L.), O the times! O the manners! Occurs in Cicero's first speech against Catiline.

**otia dant vitia** (L.), idleness begets vice.

**otium cum dignitate** (L.), dignified leisure.

**ouk esti?** (Gr.), is it not so?

**ovem lupo committere** (L.), to entrust the sheep to the wolf.

**pace tua** (L.), by your leave.

**pallida Mors aequo pulsat pede pauperum tabernas regumque turres** (L.), pale Death knocks with impartial foot at poor men's huts and kings' castles.—Horace, *Od.*, I. iv. 13-14.

**palmam qui meruit ferat** (L.), let him who has won the palm wear it.—Dr Jortin, *Lusus Poetici*, viii, 20.

**panem et circenses** (L.), bread and (Roman) circus-games—food and amusements at public expense.—Juvenal, X. 81.

**panta men kathara tois katharois** (Gr.), all things are pure to the pure.—Titus, I. 15.

**panta rhei** (Gr.), all things are in a flux (a saying of Heraclitus).

**parcere subjectis et debellare superbos** (L.), to spare the vanquished and put down the proud.—Virgil, *Aen.*, VI. 854.

**par nobile fratrum** (L.), a noble pair of brothers.—Horace, *Sat.*, II. iii. 243.

**parturiunt montes, nascetur ridiculus mus** (L.), the mountains are in travail, an absurd mouse will be born.—Horace, *A.P.*, 139.

**parva componere magnis.** See si parva.

**pas op** (Afrik.), look out.

**pathēmata mathēmata** (Gr.), sufferings [are] lessons.

**paulo majora canamus** (L.), let us sing of rather greater things.—Virgil, *Ecl.*, IV. 1.

**pax vobiscum** (L.), peace be with you.

**peccavi** (L.), I have sinned.

**pereant qui ante nos nostra dixerunt** (L.), perish those who have said our good things before us.—Attributed to Donatus and to Augustine.

**pereunt et imputantur** (L.), [the moments, hours] pass away and are reckoned to our account.

**perfervidum ingenium** (L.). See Scotorum.

**per varios casus, per tot discrimina rerum** (L.), through various chances, through so many crises of fortune.—Virgil, *Aen.*, I. 204.

**pleon hēmisy pantos** (Gr.), the half is more than the whole.—Hesiod, *Erga*, 40.

**plus ça change, plus c'est la même chose** (Fr.), the more that changes the more it is the same thing (no superficial or apparent change alters its essential nature).

**poeta nascitur, non fit** (L.), the poet is born, not made.

**pollōn onomatōn mia morphē** (Gr.), one shape of many names.—Aeschylus, *Prometheus*, 210.

**polyphloisboio thalassēs** (Gr.), of the much-sounding sea.—Homer, *Il.*, I. 34; also Hesiod, *Erga*, 648.

**populus vult decipi, ergo decipiatur** (L.), the public wishes to be fooled, therefore let it be fooled.—Ascribed to Cardinal Caraffa.

**poscimur** (L.), we are called on [to sing, etc.].

**post equitem sedet atra cura** (L.), behind the horseman sits black care.—Horace, *Odes*, III. i. 40.

**post hoc, ergo propter hoc** (L.), after this, therefore because of this (a fallacious reasoning).

**pour encourager les autres** (Fr.), to encourage the others (Voltaire, *Candide*, on the shooting of Admiral Byng); **pour faire rire**, to raise a laugh; **pour passer le temps**, to pass away the time; **pour prendre congé**, or **PPC**, to take leave.

**praefervidum.** See Scotorum.

**principiis obsta** (L.), resist the first beginnings.—Ovid, *R.A.*, 91. Cf. venienti, etc.

**probatum est** (L.), it has been proved.

**probitas laudatur et alget** (L.), honesty is commended and left out in the cold.—Juvenal, I. 74.

**procul este, profani** (L.), keep your distance, uninitiated ones.—Virgil, *Aen.*, VI. 258.

**proh pudor!** (L.), oh, for shame!

**proxime accessit** (*pl.* accesserunt) (L.), came next [to the prizeman].

**pulvis et umbra sumus** (L.), we are dust and a shadow.—Horace, *Od.*, IV. vii. 16.

**purpureus pannus** (L.), a purple patch.—From Horace, *A.P.*, 15-16.

**quamdiu se bene gesserit** (L.), during good behaviour.

**quantum mutatus ab illo** (L.), how changed from that (Hector who came back clad in Achilles's spoils).—Virgil, *Aen.*, II. 274.

**que diable allait-il faire dans cette galère?** (Fr.), what the devil was he doing in that galley?—Molière, *Les Fourberies de Scapin*, II. vii.

**quem di diligunt adolescens moritur** (L.), whom the gods love dies young.—Plautus's translation of **hon hoi theoi**....

**quem Iupiter vult perdere dementat prius**, or **quem**

**deus perdere vult, prius dementat** (L.), whom Jupiter (a god) wishes to destroy, he first makes mad.

**que sais-je (sçai-je)?** (Fr.), what do I know?— Montaigne's motto.

**que voulez-vous?** (Fr.), what would you?

**quicquid agunt homines . . . nostri est farrago libelli** (L.), whatever men do is the medley of our little book.—Juvenal, I. 85-86.

**quicquid delirant reges plectuntur Achivi** (L.), whatever madness possesses the chiefs, it is (the common soldiers or people of) the Achaeans who suffer.—Horace, *Epist.*, I. ii. 14.

**quicunque vult salvus esse** (L.), whosoever will be saved (the beginning of the Athanasian creed).

**quid hoc sibi vult?** (L.), what does this mean.

**quid rides? mutato nomine de te fabula narratur** (L.), why do you laugh? with change of name the story is about you.—Horace, *Sat.*, I. i. 69-70.

**quién sabe?** (Sp.), who knows?

**quieta non movere** (L.), not to move things that are at rest—to let sleeping dogs lie.

**qui facit per alium facit per se** (L.), he who acts through another is himself responsible.

**quis custodiet ipsos custodes?** (L.), who will guard the guards themselves?—Juvenal, VI. 347-8.

**quis desiderio sit pudor aut modus tam cari capitis?** (L.), what shame or stint should there be in mourning for one so dear?—Horace, *Od.*, I. xxiv. 1.

**qui s'excuse s'accuse** (Fr.), he who excuses himself accuses himself.

**quis separabit?** (L.), who shall separate [us]?

**qui tacet consentit** (L.), who keeps silence consents.

**qui va là?** (Fr.), who goes there?

**quod avertat Deus** (L.), which may God avert.

**quod bonum, felix, faustumque sit** (L.), may it be right, happy, and of good omen.

**quod erat demonstrandum** (L.), or **Q.E.D.**, which was to be proved or demonstrated; **quod erat faciendum**, or **Q.E.F.**, which was to be done.

**quod ubique, quod semper, quod ab omnibus** (L.), what everywhere, what always, what by all (has been believed).—St Vincent of Lérins's definition of orthodoxy.

**quorum pars magna fui** (L.), in which I bore a great share.—Virgil, *Aen.*, II. 6.

**quot homines, tot sententiae** (L.), as many men, so many minds or opinions.—Terence, *Phormio*, II. iv. 14 (or l. 454).

**quousque tandem abutere, Catilina, patientia nostra?** (L.), how far, O Catiline, will you abuse our patience?—Cicero, *In Catilinam*.

**quo vadis?** (L.), whither goest thou?

**rara avis** (L.), a rare bird, rare person or thing.—Juvenal, VI. 165.

**rari nantes in gurgite vasto** (L.), here and there some swimming in a vast whirlpool.—Virgil, *Aen.*, I. 118.

**reculer pour mieux sauter** (Fr.), to draw back to take a better leap.

**redolet lucerna** (L.), it smells of the lamp.

**re galantuomo** (It.), the honest king—king and gentleman [said of Victor Emmanuel II].

**religio loci** (L.), the religious spirit of the place.—Virgil, *Aen.*, VIII. 349.

**rem acu tetigisti** (L.), you have touched the thing with a needle, hit it exactly.—Proverbial expression used by Plautus.

**remis velisque** (L.), with oars and sails; also **remis ventisque**, with oars and winds (Virgil, etc.): with all vigour.

**res angusta domi** (L.), straitened circumstances at home.—Juvenal, III. 165.

**respice finem** (L.), look to the end.—Playfully perverted into **respice funem**, beware of the (hangman's) rope.

**resurgam** (L.), I shall rise again.

**retro me, satana** (L.) in Vulgate, **vade retro me, satana**, get thee behind me, Satan (Matt. xvi. 23, Mark viii. 33, Luke iv. 8): stop trying to tempt me.

**revenons à nos moutons** (Fr.), let us return to our sheep, i.e. our subject.—From the mediaeval farce, *L'Avocat Pathelin*.

**rhododaktylos Eōs** (Gr.), rosy-fingered Dawn.—Homer, *Odyssey*, II. 1.

**rien ne va plus** (Fr.), lit. nothing goes any more—used by croupiers to indicate that no more bets may be made.

**risum teneatis, amici?** (L.), could you keep from laughing, friends?—Horace, *A.P.*, 5.

**Roma locuta, causa finita** (L.), Rome has spoken, the cause is ended.

**ruat caelum.** See **fiat justitia**.

**rudis indigestaque moles** (L.), a rude and shapeless mass.—Ovid, *M.*, I. 7.

**ruit.** See **mole**.

**rus in urbe** (L.), the country in town.—Martial, XII. 57, 21.

**rusticus expectat dum defluat amnis** (L.), waits like the yokel for the river to run by.—Horace, *Epist.*, I. ii. 42.

**salaam aleikum** (Ar.), peace be upon you.

**salus populi suprema lex esto** (L.), let the welfare of the people be the final law (Cicero, *De Legibus*, III. iii: **suprema est lex**).

**sans peur et sans reproche** (Fr.), without fear and without reproach.

**sapere aude** (L.), dare to be wise.—Horace, *Epist.*, I. ii. 40.

**sartor resartus** (L.), the tailor retailored.

**sauter à pieds joints** (Fr.), to take a standing jump.

**sauve qui peut** (Fr.), save himself who can: every man for himself.

**Scotorum praefervida ingenia** (L.), the ardent tempers of the Scots.—Buchanan, *Hist. Scot.*, XVI. li.

**selon les règles** (Fr.), according to the rules.

**semel insanivimus omnes** (L.), we have all played the fool once.—J. B. Mantuanus, *Ecl.*, i. 217.

**se non è vero, è ben trovato** (It.), if it is not true, it is cleverly invented.

**sero venientibus ossa** (L.), the bones to the late-comers.

**sic itur ad astra** (L.), such is the way to the stars.—Virgil, *Aen.*, IX. 641.

**sic transit gloria mundi** (L.), so passes away earthly glory.

**sic volo.** See **hoc volo**.

**sic vos non vobis** (L.), thus do you, not for yourselves.—Ascribed to Virgil.

**si jeunesse savait, si vieillesse pouvait** (Fr.), if youth but knew, if age but could.

**s'il vous plaît** (Fr.), if you please.

**similia similibus curantur** (L.), likes are cured by likes—a hair of the dog that bit one.

**si monumentum requiris, circumspice** (L.), if you seek (his) monument, look round you (inscription for the architect Christopher Wren's tomb in St Paul's).

**simplex munditiis** (L.), elegant in simplicity.—Horace, *Od.*, I. v. 5.

**sine Cerere et Libero friget Venus** (L.), without Ceres and Bacchus (food and drink) Venus (love) is cold.—Terence, *Eun.*, IV. v. 6.

**sine ira et studio** (L.), without ill-will and without favour.

**sint ut sunt aut non sint** (L.), let them be as they are or not at all.

**si parla Italiano** (It.), Italian spoken.

**si parva licet componere magnis** (L.; Virgil, *Georg.*, IV. 176); **si componere magnis parva mihi fas est** (Ovid, *Metamorphoses*, V. 416-7), if it is permissible to compare small things to great.

**siste, viator** (L.), stop, traveller.

**si vis pacem, para bellum** (L.), if you would have peace, be ready for war.

skias onar anthrōpos (Gr.), man is a dream of a shadow.—Pind., *Pyth.*, VIII. 95.

solitudinem faciunt, pacem appellant (L.), they make a desert and call it peace.—Tacitus, *Agric.*, 30.

solventur risu tabulae: tu missus abibis (L.), the bills will be dismissed with laughter—you will be laughed out of court.—Horace, *Sat.*, II. i. 86.

solvitur ambulando (L.), (the problem of reality of motion) is solved by walking—by practical experiment, by actual performance.

spero meliora (L.), I hope for better things.

splendide mendax (L.), splendidly false, nobly lying.—Horace, *Od.*, III. xi. 35.

spretaeque injuria formae (L.), (and) the insult of beauty slighted.—Virgil, *Aen.*, I. 27.

stans pede in uno (L.), standing on one foot.—Horace, *Sat.*, I. iv. 10.

stat pro ratione voluntas (L.). See hoc volo.

stet fortuna domus (L.), may the fortune of the house last long.

sturm und drang (Ger.), storm and stress.

sua si bona. See O fortunatos....

suaviter in modo, fortiter in re (L.), gentle in manner, resolute in deed.

sunt lacrimae rerum (L.), there are tears for things (unhappy).—Virgil, *Aen.*, I. 462.

suppressio veri suggestio falsi (L.), suppression of truth is suggestion of the false.

sursum corda (L.), lift up your hearts.

surtout, pas de zèle (Fr.), above all, no zeal.

sutor ne supra crepidam judicaret (L.), let not the cobbler criticise (a work of art) above the sandal. See ultracrepidate in Dict.

tacent, satis laudant (L.), their silence is praise enough.—Terence, *Eun.*, III. ii. 23.

tantae molis erat Romanam condere gentem (L.), a task of such difficulty was it to found the Roman race.—Virgil, *Aen.*, I. 33.

tantaene animis caelestibus irae? (L.), are there such violent passions in celestial minds?—Virgil, *Aen.*, I. 11.

tempora (orig. omnia) mutantur, nos et mutamur in illis (L.), the times (all things) change, and we with them.

tempus edax rerum (L.), time consumer of things. —Ovid, *M.*, XV. 234.

tempus fugit (L.), time flies.

thalassa, thalassa! or thalatta thalatta! (Gr.), the sea, the sea! (the exulting cry of Xenophon's men on beholding the sea).—Xenophon, *Anabasis*, IV. 7.

timeo Danaos et dona ferentes (L.), I fear the Greeks, even when bringing gifts.—Virgil, *Aen.*, II. 49.

tiré à quatre épingles (Fr.), as neat as can be.

ton d'apameibomenos prosephē (Gr.), addressed him in reply.—Homer (*passim*).

totus, teres, atque rotundus (L.), complete, smooth, and round.—Horace, *Satires*, II. vii. 86.

toujours perdrix (Fr.), partridge every day—too much of a good thing.

tout comprendre c'est tout pardonner (Fr.), to understand all is to pardon all; tout est perdu fors l'honneur, all is lost but honour [attrib. to Francis I after Pavia]; tout vient (à point) à qui sait attendre, all things come to him who can wait.

traduttore traditore (It.), a translator is a traitor or betrayer:—*pl.* traduttori traditori.

tria juncta in uno (L.), three things in one.

ubi bene, ibi patria (L.), where it goes well with me, there is my fatherland.

ubi saeva indignatio ulterius cor lacerare nequit (L.), where fierce indignation can tear his heart no longer.—Part of Swift's epitaph.

und so weiter (Ger.), or u.s.w., and so forth.

urbi et orbi (L.), to the city (Rome) and to the world, to everyone.

uti possidetis (L.), lit. as you possess—the principle of letting e.g. belligerents keep what they have acquired.

vade in pace (L.), go in peace.

vade retro me, satana. See retro.

varium et mutabile semper femina (L.), woman is ever a fickle and changeable thing.—Virgil, *Aen.*, IV. 569.

vedi Napoli, e poi muori (It.), see Naples, and die.

veni Creator Spiritus (L.), come, Creator Spirit—the beginning of an early Latin hymn.

venienti occurrite morbo (L.), run to meet disease as it comes.—Persius, III. 63.

veni, vidi, vici (L.), I came, I saw, I conquered.—Ascribed to Caesar on his victory over Pharnaces.

vera incessu patuit dea (L.), the true goddess was revealed by her gait.—Virgil, *Aen.*, I. 405.

verbum sapienti sat est (L.), a word to the wise is enough—often abbrev. *verb. sap.* and *verb. sat.* See dictum.

veritas odium parit (L.), truth begets hatred.—Terence, *Andria*, I. i. 41.

vestigia . . . nulla retrorsum (L.), no footprints backwards (at the lion's den): sometimes used to mean no going back.—Horace, *Epist.*, I. i. 74-75.

victrix causa deis placuit, sed victa Catoni (L.), the gods preferred the winning cause, but Cato the losing.—Lucan, I. 128.

video meliora proboque, deteriora sequor (L.), I see the better course and approve it, I follow the worse.—Ovid, *M.*, VII. 20.

vigilate et orate (L.), watch and pray.

viresque acquirit eundo (L.), (Fama, hearsay personified) gains strength as she goes.—Virgil, *Aen.*, IV. 175.

Virgilium vidi tantum (L.), I just saw Virgil [and no more].—Ovid, *Trist.*, IV. x. 51.

virginibus puerisque canto (L.), I sing for maidens and boys—for the young person.—Horace, *Od.*, III. i. 4.

virtus post nummos (L.), virtue after money—i.e. money first.—Horace, *Epist.*, I. i. 54.

vita brevis, ars longa (L.), life is short, art is long (see ho bios....); vita sine litteris mors est, life without literature is death.

vive la bagatelle (quasi-Fr.), long live folly.

vive ut vivas (L.), live that you may live; vive, valeque, life and health to you.

vivit post funera virtus (L.), virtue lives beyond the grave.

vixere fortes ante Agamemnona multi (L.), many brave men lived before Agamemnon.—Horace, *Od.*, IV. ix. 25-26.

vogue la galère! (Fr.), row the boat: row on: come what may!

volenti non fit injuria (L.), no wrong is done to one who consents.

volo, non valeo (L.), I am willing, but unable.

volto sciolto e pensieri stretti (It.), open face, close thoughts.

vous l'avez voulu, George Dandin (Fr.), you would have it so.—Molière, *George Dandin*, Act 1.

vox audita perit, littera scripta manet (L.), the heard word is lost, the written letter abides; vox et praeterea nihil, a voice and nothing more (of a nightingale).

wahrheit und dichtung (Ger.), truth and poetry.

wein, weib, und gesang (Ger.), wine, woman and song.

wer da? (Ger.), who is there?

wie geht's? (Ger.), how are you?

zonam perdidit (L.), he has lost his money-belt: he is in needy circumstances; zonam solvere, to loose the virgin zone, i.e. marry.

# List of abbreviations and symbols

(1) *There is now a tendency to spell abbreviations, esp. of scientific terms and names of international organisations, without stops. In the list below, we have generally left stops out, but it should be understood that in most cases neither method of writing (with or without stops) is wrong.*
(2) *In order to save space, abbreviations for the names of societies and associations are given, but, except for some special reason, abbreviations for the designations of those belonging to any particular organisation—as Associate, Fellow, Associate Fellow, Member, or Associate Member—are not specifically included.*
(3) *The Greek alphabet is given on page 1640.*

**A** Associate . . . See note (2) above; Amateur; Academician; argon; ampere; angstrom; atomic (in **A**-bomb); denoting the first, or a high, class (**A**-road; see Dict.); advanced (in **A**-level); adult—used to mark a motion picture at a showing of which any child under 14 should be accompanied by an adult; Austria (IVR).
**Å** Ångström.
**a** are (metric measure); atto- (see p 1644); accepted; acre; active; afternoon; *annus* year; *ante* before.
**ā, āā** in prescriptions, *ana* (Gr.), i.e. of each a like quantity.
**AA** Automobile Association; Alcoholics Anonymous; anti-aircraft; used to mark motion pictures to which no child under 14 may be admitted.
**AAA** Amateur Athletic Association; American Automobile Association.
**AAM** air-to-air missile.
**A and M** (Hymns) Ancient and Modern.
**AAQMG** Assistant Adjutant and Quartermaster General.
**AAS** *Academiae Americanae Socius* Fellow of the American Academy.
**AB** able-bodied seaman; *Artium Baccalaureus* Bachelor of Arts.
**ABA** Amateur Boxing Association.
**Abb.** Abbess; Abbot; Abbey.
**abbr., abbrev.** abbreviated; abbreviation.
**ABC** Associated British Cinemas; American Broadcasting Corporation.
**abd** abdicated; abridged.
**ABFM** American Board of Foreign Missions.
**ab init.** *ab initio* from the beginning.
**abl.** ablative.
**ABM** anti-ballistic missile.
**Abp** Archbishop.
**abr.** abridged; abridgment.
**ABS** Associate of the Building Societies Institute.
**abs., absol.** absolute(ly).
**abs., abstr.** abstract.
**abs. re.** *absente reo* the accused being absent.
**ABTA** Association of British Travel Agents.
**AC** aircraft(s)man; Aero Club; Alpine Club; *ante Christum* before Christ; (or **ac**) alternating current (*elect.*).
**Ac** actinium.
**a/c** account.
**ACA** Associate of the Institute of Chartered Accountants.
**ACAS** Advisory, Conciliation and Arbitration Service.
**acc.** (or **acct., a/c**) account; accountant; (or **accus.**) accusative; according.
**ACCA** Association of Certified and Corporate Accountants.
**ACGB** Arts Council of Great Britain.
**ACP** African, Caribbean and Pacific.
**ACT** Australian Capital Territory.
**act.** active; acting.
**ACW** aircraft(s)woman.
**AD** *anno Domini* in the year of the Lord.
**ad** (or **advt**) advertisement; after date; *ante diem* before the day.
**ADC** aide-de-camp; (or **AD and C**) advise duration and charge.
**ad fin.** *ad finem* at, towards, or to, the end.

**ad inf.** *ad infinitum* to infinity.
**ad init.** *ad initium* at or to the beginning.
**ad int.** *ad interim* in the meantime.
**adj.** adjective; adjourned; adjustment.
**Adjt.** Adjutant.
**Adjt.-Gen.** Adjutant-General.
**ad lib.** *ad libitum* at pleasure (see Dict.).
**at loc.** *ad locum* at the place.
**Adm.** Admiral.
**admin.** administration.
**ADN** People's Democratic Republic of Yemen (IVR).
**ADP** automatic data processing.
**adv.** advent; adverb; *adversus* against; advocate; advisory.
**ad val.** *ad valorem* according to value.
**advt** advertisement.
**ae., aet.** *aetatis* of his age, aged (so many years).
**AEA** Atomic Energy Authority (UK).
**AEB** Associated Examining Board.
**AEC** Atomic Energy Commission (US).
**AEI** Associated Electrical Industries.
**AERE** Atomic Energy Research Establishment.
**AEU** Amalgamated Engineering Union.
**AF** Associate Fellow . . . See note (2) above; Admiral of the Fleet; audio frequency.
**AFA** Amateur Football Association.
**AFC** Air Force Cross.
**AFG** Afghanistan (IVR).
**AFM** Air Force Medal.
**AG** Adjutant-General; (or **A-G**) Attorney-General; *Aktiengesellschaft* (Ger.) joint stock company.
**Ag** *argentum* silver.
**agm** annual general meeting.
**AGR** advanced gas-cooled reactor.
**agr., agric.** agriculture.
**Agt** Agent.
**AH** *anno Hegirae* in the year of Hegira—i.e. from the flight of Mohammed (AD 622, 13 Sept.).
**Ah** ampere hour.
**ahl** *ad hunc locum* at this place.
**AHS** *anno humanae salutis* in the year of human salvation.
**ahv** *ad hanc vocem* at this word.
**AI** artificial insemination.
**AID** artificial insemination by donor; Agency for International Development (US).
**AIH** artificial insemination by husband.
**AL** Albania (IVR).
**Al** aluminium.
**Al(a).** Alabama.
**Alas.** Alaska.
**Alba.** Alberta.
**Alban.** *Albanensis* of St Albans.
**Alcan** Aluminium Company of Canada.
**Ald.** Alderman.
**alg.** algebra.
**ALGOL, Algol** Algorithmic language.
**alt.** alternate; altitude; alto.
**Alta.** Alberta.
**AM** Associate Member . . . See note (2) above; *Artium Magister* Master of Arts; (or **am**) *ante meridiem* before noon; *Anno Mundi* in the year of the world; *Ave Maria* Hail Mary; amplitude modulation.
**Am** americium.
**Am., Amer.** America; American.

1605

**AMA** Assistant Masters' Association.
**AMC** American Motors Corporation.
**AMDG** *ad majorem Dei gloriam* to the greater glory of God.
**ammo** ammunition.
**amp.** ampere.
**amt** amount; air mail transfer.
**amu** atomic mass unit.
**an.** *anno* in the year; anonymous; *ante* before.
**anal.** analysis; . analogy.
**anat.** anatomy.
**anc.** ancient(ly).
**AND** Andorra (IVR).
**Ang.** *Anglice* in English.
**anme** *anonyme* (Fr.) limited liability.
**anon.** anonymous.
**ans.** answer.
**antiq.** antiquities; antiquarian.
**Anzac** See Dict.
**Anzus** See Dict.
**AO** Army Order.
**AOB** any other business.
**AOCB** any other competent business.
**AOC-in-C** Air Officer Commanding-in-Chief.
**AOF** Ancient Order of Foresters.
**aor.** aorist.
**AP** Associated Press.
**APEX** Association of Professional, Executive, Clerical and Computer Staff.
**apo.** apogee.
**Apoc.** Apocalypse; Apocrypha(l).
**app.** appendix; apparent(ly); apprentice.
**appro.** approval; approbation.
**approx.** approximate(ly).
**Apr.** April.
**APRC** *anno post Romam conditam* in the year after the founding of Rome (753 BC).
**APT** Advanced Passenger Train.
**AQ** achievement quotient.
**aq.** *aqua* water.
**Ar** argon.
**Ar., Arab.** Arabic.
**ar** *anno regni* in the year of the reign.
**ar., arr.** arrive(s); arrival.
**ARA** Associate of the Royal Academy.
**ARAMCO** Arabian-American Oil Company.
**ARC** Agricultural Research Council.
**arccos** inverse cosine.
**arch.** archaic; architecture.
**archaeol.** archaeology.
**Archd.** Archdeacon; Archduke.
**archit.** architecture.
**arcsin** inverse sine.
**arctan** inverse tangent.
**arg.** *argentum* silver.
**arith.** arithmetic(al).
**Ariz.** Arizona.
**Ark.** Arkansas.
**Arm.** Armenian; Armoric.
**ARP** Air Raid Precautions.
**ARR** *anno regni regis* or *reginae* in the year of the king's or the queen's reign.
**arr.** arranged; arrive(s); arrival.
**art.** article; artificial; (or arty.) artillery.
**AS** Anglo-Saxon; *anno salutis* in the year of salvation; Assistant Secretary.
**As** arsenic.
**ASA** Amateur Swimming Association; American Standards Association.
**Asaph** of St Asaph.
**ASC** American Society of Cinematographers.
**Asdic** See Dict.
**ASE** Amalgamated Society of Engineers; Association for Science Education.
**Asean** Association of South-East Asian Nations.
**ASF** Associate of the Institute of Shipping and Forwarding Agents.
**ASH** Action on Smoking and Health.
**ASLEF** Associated Society of Locomotive Engineers and Firemen.
**ASM** air-to-surface missile.
**Ass., Assoc.** Association.

**Asst** Assistant.
**AST** Atlantic Standard Time.
**ASTMS** Association of Scientific, Technical and Managerial Staffs.
**astr., astron.** astronomy.
**astrol.** astrology.
**AT** Alternative Technology.
**At** astatine.
**ATA** Air Transport Auxiliary.
**ATC** Air Training Corps; air traffic control; automatic train control.
**atm.** atmosphere.
**at. no., at. numb.** atomic number.
**ATS** Auxiliary Territorial Service (superseded by WRAC); anti-tetanus serum.
**ats** at suit of (law).
**Att.** Attic (Greek); Attorney.
**Att.-Gen.** Attorney-General.
**attrib.** attribute(d); attributive(ly).
**Atty** Attorney.
**ATV** Associated Television.
**at. wt** atomic weight.
**AU** (or ÅU) Ångström unit (now usu. Ångström; abbrev. Å); astronomical unit.
**Au** *aurum* gold.
**AUC** *anno urbis conditae* or *ab urbe condita* in the year from the building of the city—Rome (753 BC).
**Aufl.** *Auflage* (Ger.) edition.
**Aug.** August.
**aug.** augmentative.
**AUS** Australia, including Papua, New Guinea (IVR).
**AUT** Association of University Teachers.
**aut., auto.** automatic.
**Auth. Ver., AV** Authorised Version.
**AV** audio-visual.
**av** *annos vixit* lived (so many) years.
**av.** (or ave) avenue; average.
**AVM** Air Vice-Marshal.
**avoir., avdp.** avoirdupois.
**AWOL** absent, or absence, without official leave.
**AWRE** Atomic Weapons Research Establishment.
**ax.** axiom.
**az.** azimuth.

**B** Baron; British; Bachelor; boron; bel; black (on lead pencils); Belgium (IVR).
*B* magnetic flux density.
**b** born; book; bowled.
*b* breadth.
**BA** *Baccalaureus Artium* Bachelor of Arts; British America; British Association (for the Advancement of Science); British Academy; Buenos Aires; British Airways; Booksellers' Association (of Great Britain and Ireland).
**Ba** barium.
**BAA** British Airports Authority.
**BABS** beam, or blind, approach beacon system.
**BAC** British Aircraft Corporation.
**Bach.** Bachelor.
**BACIE** British Association for Commercial and Industrial Education.
**BAgr(ic)** Bachelor of Agriculture.
**BAI** *Baccalaureus in Arte Ingeniaria* Bachelor of Engineering.
**bal.** balance.
**BALPA** British Airline Pilots' Association.
**B and B** bed and breakfast.
**B and FBS** British and Foreign Bible Society.
**b and s** brandy and soda.
**BAOR** British Army of the Rhine.
**Bap., Bapt.** Baptist.
**bap., bapt.** baptised.
**Bar.** Barrister.
**bar.** baritone.
**BArch** Bachelor of Architecture.
**Bart** Baronet.
**Bart's** St Bartholomew's Hospital, London.
**BASF** *Badische Anilin und Soda-Fabrik* (German chemical company).

BAT   British-American Tobacco Company.
bat., batt.   battalion; battery.
BB   Boys' Brigade; double, or very, black (on lead pencils).
bb   books.
BBB   triple black, blacker than **BB** (on lead pencils).
BBBC   British Boxing Board of Control.
BBC   British Broadcasting Corporation (orig. Company).
BBFC   British Board of Film Censors.
BC   Before Christ; Board of Control; British Columbia; Battery Commander.
BCAL   British Caledonian (Airways).
bcg   bacillus of Calmette and Guérin, an attenuated strain of the tubercle bacillus, used for inoculation.
BCh   *Baccalaureus Chirurgiae* Bachelor of Surgery.
BCL   Bachelor of Civil Law.
BCom(m)   Bachelor of Commerce.
BCS   British Computer Society.
BD   Bachelor of Divinity.
bd   bound.
BDA   British Dental Association.
Bde   Brigade.
BDH   British Drug Houses.
BDI   *Bundesverband der Deutschen Industrie* (Ger.) Federation of German Industry.
BDS   Bachelor of Dental Surgery; Barbados (IVR).
bds   boards.
BE   Bachelor of Engineering; Board of Education.
Be   beryllium.
be   bill of exchange.
BEA   British European Airways (now incorporated in **BA**).
BEAB   British Electrical Approvals Board.
BEAMA   British Electrical and Allied Manufacturers' Association.
BEd   Bachelor of Education.
Beds   Bedfordshire.
BEF   British Expeditionary Force.
bef.   before.
Belg.   Belgian; Belgium; Belgic.
BEM   British Empire Medal.
Benelux   See Dict.
BEng   Bachelor of Engineering.
Berks   Berkshire.
B ès L   *Bachelier ès Lettres* (Fr.) Bachelor of Letters.
B ès S   *Bachelier ès Sciences* (Fr.) Bachelor of Sciences.
bet.   between.
BeV   billion electron-volt(s) (in USA, where billion means 1000 million, same as GeV).
bf   brought forward; bloody fool.
BFPO   British Forces Post Office.
BG   Bulgaria (IVR).
BH   British Honduras (IVR).
bhp   brake horse-power.
BHS   British Home Stores.
Bi   bismuth.
Bib.   Bible.
Bibl.   Biblical.
bibl.   bibliotheca.
biblio., bibliog.   bibliography.
BICC   British Insulated Callender's Cables.
BIM   British Institute of Management.
biog.   biography.
biol.   biology.
BIPM   *Bureau International des Poids et Mesures* (Fr.) International Bureau of Weights and Measures.
BIR   British Institute of Radiology.
BIS   Bank for International Settlements.
bis.   bissextile.
Bk   berkelium.
bk   book; bank; bark.
bkg   banking.
bkt   basket.

BL   Bachelor of Law; Bachelor of Letters; British Legion; British Library.
bl   barrel; bale; bill of lading.
bldg   building.
BLESMA   British Limbless Ex-Servicemen's Association.
BLit(t)   *Baccalaureus Lit(t)erarum* Bachelor of Literature or Letters.
BLLD   British Library Lending Division.
BLMC   British Leyland Motor Corporation.
BLRD   British Library Reference Division.
Blvd   Boulevard.
BM   Bachelor of Medicine; British Museum; *Beatae Memoriae* of blessed memory; Brigade Major.
BMA   British Medical Association.
BMEWS   ballistic missile early warning system.
BMJ   British Medical Journal.
BML   British Museum Library.
BMus   Bachelor of Music.
BMW   *Bayerische Motoren Werke* (Ger.) Bavarian motor works.
Bn   Baron.
bn   battalion.
BNEC   British National Export Council.
BNFL   British Nuclear Fuels Limited.
BNOC   British National Oil Corporation.
b.o.   branch office; buyer's option; (or **B.O.**) body odour.
BOA   British Optical Association.
BOAC   British Overseas Airways Corporation (now incorporated in **BA**).
BOC   British Oxygen Company.
BOCM   British Oil and Cake Mills.
BOD   biochemical oxygen demand (see Supplement).
Boh.   Bohemia, Bohemian.
Bol.   Bolivia.
bor.   borough.
BoT   Board of Trade (since 1970 incorporated in DTI).
bot.   botany; bought; bottle.
Boul.   Boulevard.
BP   British Pharmacopoeia; British Petroleum; Baden Powell; be prepared.
Bp   Bishop.
bp   boiling-point; bills of parcels; bills payable; (or **b.pl.**) birthplace; *bonum publicum* the public good.
BPC   British Printing Corporation; British Pharmaceutical Codex.
BPharm   Bachelor of Pharmacy.
BPhil   *Baccalaureus Philosophiae* Bachelor of Philosophy.
BQ   *Bene quiescat* may he (or she) rest well.
bque   barque.
BR   British Rail: Brazil (IVR).
Br   bromine.
Br.   Brother.
br   bank rate.
br.   branch; brig; brown; bridge.
Braz.   Brazil; Brazilian.
BRCS   British Red Cross Society.
BRD   *Bundesrepublik Deutschland* (Ger.) German Federal Republic.
b. rec.   bills receivable.
Bret.   Breton.
brev.   brevet; breveted.
Brig.   Brigadier.
Brig.-Gen.   Brigadier-General.
Brit.   Britain; Britannia; British; Briton.
BRN   Bahrein (IVR).
Bro.   Brother.
Bros.   Brothers.
BRS   British Road Services.
BRU   Brunei (IVR).
BS   Bachelor of Science or of Surgery; Blessed Sacrament; Balance Sheet; (or **bs**) Bill of Sale; British Shipbuilders; Bahamas (IVR).
BSA   Building Societies Association; Birmingham Small Arms.
BSAC   British Sub Aqua Club.

**BSC** British Steel Corporation; British Sugar Corporation.

**BSc** Bachelor of Science.

**BSI** British Standards Institution; Building Societies Institute.

**BS(S)** British Standards (Specification).

**BST** British Summer Time; British Standard Time.

**Bt** Baronet.

**Btu** British thermal unit.

**bu.** bushel(s).

**Bucks** Buckinghamshire.

**Bulg.** Bulgaria; Bulgarian.

**BUNAC** British Universities North America Club.

**BUPA** British United Provident Association.

**BUR** Burma (IVR).

**bus., bush.** bushel(s).

**BV** *Beata Virgo* Blessed Virgin; *Bene vale* farewell.

**BVM** The Blessed Virgin Mary.

**BVM(&)S** Bachelor of Veterinary Medicine and Surgery.

**bvt** brevet, breveted.

**BWTA** British Women's Temperance Association.

**BWV** *Bach Werke Verzeichnis* (Ger.) catalogue of Bach's works.

**C** carbon; coulomb; Conservative; Cuba (IVR).

*C* symbol for electrical capacitance.

**°C** degree(s) Celsius, centigrade.

**¢** centi- (see p 1644); *caput* chapter; cent; centime; *circa* about; caught.

**c** cent(s); cedi(s).

**CA** Chartered Accountant (Scotland); County Alderman.

**Ca** calcium.

**ca** *circa* about; cases.

**CAA** Civil Aviation Authority.

**CAB** Civil Aeronautics Board (USA); Citizens' Advice Bureau.

**cad** cash against documents.

**c.-à-d.** *c'est-à-dire* (Fr.) that is to say.

**CAI** computer-aided instruction.

**cal** calorie.

**Cal., Calif.** California.

**Cam., Camb.** Cambridge.

**Cambs** Cambridgeshire.

**CAN** customs assigned number.

**Can.** Canon; Canto.

**C and A** Clemens and August (clothing stores).

**C and G** City and Guilds (of London Institute).

**C & W** country and western.

**Cant.** Canterbury; Canticles.

**Cantab.** *Cantabrigiensis* of Cambridge.

**Cantuar.** *Cantuaria* Canterbury; *Cantuariensis* of Canterbury.

**CAP** Common Agricultural Policy.

**cap.** capital; *caput* chapter; *capitulum* head, chapter; *capiat* let him (or her) take.

**caps** capitals (in printing).

**Capt.** Captain.

**CAR** Central African Republic.

**Car.** *Carolus* Charles.

**car.** carat.

**CARD** Campaign Against Racial Discrimination.

**Card.** Cardinal.

**Cards** Cardiganshire.

**CARE** Co-operative for American Relief to Everywhere.

**carp.** carpentry.

**CASE** Confederation for the Advancement of State Education.

**CAT** College of Advanced Technology; computer-aided typesetting.

**cat.** catechism; catalogue.

**Cath.** Catholic.

**cath.** cathedral.

**CB** Companion of the Order of the Bath;

confined (or confinement) to barracks; Cape Breton; Citizens' Band (radio).

**Cb** columbium (now niobium).

**CBC** Canadian Broadcasting Corporation.

**CBE** Commander of the Order of the British Empire.

**CBI** Confederation of British Industry.

**CBM** Californian Business Machines.

**CBS** Confraternity of the Blessed Sacrament; Columbia Broadcasting System.

**CC** County Council; Cricket Club; closed circuit (transmission).

**cc** cubic centimetre(s); *capita* chapters.

**CCA** current cost accounting.

**CCCP** See USSR.

**CCF** Combined Cadet Force.

**CCPR** Central Council of Physical Recreation.

**CCS** Corporation of Certified Secretaries.

**CD** *Corps Diplomatique* (Fr.) Diplomatic Corps; Civil Defence; contagious disease(s); Canadian Forces Decoration.

**Cd** cadmium.

**cd** candela.

**CDN** Canada (IVR).

**Cdr** Commander.

**CDSO** Companion of the Distinguished Service Order.

**CDV** Civil Defence Volunteers.

**cdv** *carte-de-visite* (Fr.) visiting card.

**CE** Civil Engineer; Christian Endeavour; Council of Europe.

**Ce** cerium.

**CEDO** Centre for Educational Development Overseas (formerly **CREDO**).

**CEF** Canadian Expeditionary Force.

**CEGB** Central Electricity Generating Board.

**CEI** Council of Engineering Institutions.

**cel.** celebrated.

**Celt.** Celtic.

**cen.** central; century.

**CEng** Chartered Engineer.

**cent.** *centum* a hundred; century; central.

**CENTO** Central Treaty Organisation.

**CERN** *Conseil Européen pour la Recherche Nucléaire* (Fr.) European Organisation for Nuclear Research.

**cert.** certainty; (or **certif.**) certificate; certificated; certify.

**Cestr.** *Cestrensis* of Chester.

**CET** Central European Time.

**cet. par.** *ceteris paribus* other things being equal.

**CF** Chaplain to the Forces.

**Cf** californium.

**cf** calf (book-binding).

**cf.** *confer* compare.

**cf (and) i** cost, freight, and insurance.

**cg** centigram(me)(s).

**c.g.** centre of gravity.

**CG(L)I** City and Guilds (of London) Institute.

**CGPM** *Conférence Générale des Poids et Mesures* (Fr.) General Conference of Weights and Measures.

**CGS** (or **cgs**) centimetre-gramme-second (unit or system); Chief of the General Staff.

**CGT** capital gains tax; *Confédération Générale du Travail* (Fr.) General Confederation of Labour.

**CH** Companion of Honour; *Confederatio Helvetica* Switzerland (also IVR).

**Ch.** Chief; China; Church; Champion.

**ch** central heating.

**ch.** chaldron; chapter; child.

**Chal., Chald.** Chaldee; Chaldaic.

**Chamb.** Chamberlain.

**Chanc.** Chancellor; Chancery.

**Chap.** Chaplain; Chapter.

**Chas** Charles.

**ChB** *Chirurgiae Baccalaureus* Bachelor of Surgery.

**chem.** chemistry; chemical.

**Ch. Hist.** Church History.

**Chin.** China; Chinese.

**Ch.J.** Chief-Justice.
**ChM** *Chirurgiae Magister* Master of Surgery.
**choc.** chocolate.
**Chr.** Christ; Christian.
**Chron.** Chronicles.
**chron.** chronicle; chronology; chronological.
**CI** Channel Islands; Ivory Coast (IVR).
**Ci** curie.
**CIA** Central Intelligence Agency (USA).
**Cia** *Compagnia* (It.) Company.
**Cic.** Cicero.
**Cicestr.** *Cicestrensis* of Chichester.
**CID** Criminal Investigation Department; Council of Industrial Design.
**CIE** *Córas Iompair Éireann* (Ir.) Transport Organisation of Ireland.
**Cie** *Compagnie* (Fr.) Company.
**cif** cost, insurance, freight.
**CIGS** Chief of Imperial General Staff (now CGS).
**CII** Chartered Insurance Institute.
**CIM** Commission on Industry and Manpower.
**C-in-C** Commander-in-Chief.
**CIO** Congress of Industrial Organisations.
**CIPM** *Comité International des Poids et Mesures* (Fr.) International Committee of Weights and Measures.
**CIR** Commission on Industrial Relations.
**cir., circ.** *circa, circiter, circum* about.
**circs.** circumstances.
**CIS** Chartered Institute of Secretaries.
**CIT** Chartered Institute of Transport.
**cit.** citation; citizen.
**civ.** civil; civilian.
**CJ** Chief-Justice.
**CL** Sri Lanka (IVR).
**Cl** chlorine.
**cl** centilitre(s); *cum laude* with praise.
**cl.** class; clause.
**class.** classical; classification.
**CLitt** Companion of Literature.
**CLR** computer language recorder.
**CLT** computer language translator.
**CM** Certificated Master: Corresponding Member; Common Metre; *Chirurgiae Magister* Master of Surgery.
**Cm** curium.
**cm** centimetre(s); *carat métrique* (Fr.) metric carat; *causa mortis* by reason of death.
**Cmd** Command Paper (now Cmnd).
**CMG** Companion of the Order of St Michael and St George.
**CMI** computer-managed instruction.
**Cmnd** Command Paper.
**CMRST** Committee on Manpower Resources for Science and Technology.
**CMS** Church Missionary Society.
**CN** Denoting an irritant 'gas' used in the same manner as CS (see below).
**CNAA** Council for National Academic Awards.
**CND** Campaign for Nuclear Disarmament.
**CNR** Canadian National Railway.
**CNS** central nervous system.
**CO** conscientious objector; Colonial Office (before Aug. 1966); Commonwealth Office (from Aug. 1966; see also FCO); Commanding Officer; Criminal Office; Crown Office; Colombia (IVR).
**Co** cobalt.
**Co.** Company; County.
**c/o** care of.
**coad.** coadjutor.
**COBOL, Cobol** See Dict.
**coch., cochl.** *cochleare* a spoon, spoonful.
**coch. amp.,** — *amplum* a tablespoonful. **coch.**
**mag.,** — *magnum* a large spoonful. **coch.**
**med.,** — *medium* a dessertspoonful. **coch.**
**parv.,** — *parvum* a teaspoonful.
**Cod.** Codex.
**c.o.d.** cash (or collect) on delivery.
**co-ed.** co-educational.
**C of A** Certificate of Airworthiness.

**C of E** Church of England; Council of Europe.
**C of I** Church of Ireland.
**C of S** Church of Scotland; Chief of Staff.
**cog.** cognate.
**c.o.g.** centre of gravity.
**COGB** Certified Official Government Business.
**COHSE** Confederation of Health Service Employees.
**COI** Central Office of Information.
**COL** computer-oriented language.
**Col.** Colonel; Colorado; Colossians.
**col.** column.
**coll.** college; colleague; collector; colloquial.
**collat.** collateral(ly).
**colloq.** colloquial(ly).
**Colo.** Colorado.
**Coloss.** Colossians.
**COM** computer output microfilm.
**Com.** Commander; Commodore; Committee; Commissioner; Commonwealth; Communist.
**com.** common; comedy; commerce; committee; commune.
**Comdr** Commander.
**Comdt** Commandant.
**COMECON** Council for Mutual Economic Aid, or Assistance (Communist Nations).
**Comiform, Comintern.** See Dict.
**comm.** commentary; commander; communication.
**Commissr** Commissioner.
**commn** commission.
**Commy** Commissary; Communist.
**comp.** comparative; compositor; compare; compound; compounded.
**compar.** comparative; comparison.
**COMSAT** Communications Satellite (USA).
**Com. Ver.** Common Version.
**Con.** Consul.
**con.** *contra* against; *conju(n)x* consort; conclusion; conversation; convenience.
**conc.** concentrated; concentration.
**Cong.** Congress; Congregation(al).
**conj.** conjunction; conjunctive.
**Conn.** Connecticut.
**conn.** connection; connected; connotation.
**cons.** consonant.
**con. sec.** conic section.
**Consols.** Consolidated Funds.
**cont., contd** continued.
**contr.** contracted; contraction.
**contr. bon. mor.** *contra bonos mores* contrary to good manners or morals.
**conv.** conventional.
**co-op.** co-operative.
**Cop., Copt.** Coptic.
**Cor.** Corinthians; Coroner.
**Cor. Mem.** Corresponding Member.
**Corn.** Cornish; Cornwall.
**corol., coroll.** corollary.
**Corp.** Corporation; Corporal.
**corr.** corrupted; corruption; correspond.
**Cor.Sec.** Corresponding Secretary.
**cos** cosine.
**cosec** cosecant.
**cosech** hyperbolic cosecant.
**cosh** hyperbolic cosine.
**cosmog.** cosmography.
**Coss.** *consules* Consuls.
**cot** cotangent.
**coth** hyperbolic cotangent.
**CP** Clerk of the Peace; Common Pleas; Carriage Paid; College of Preceptors; Communist Party; Cape Province (S. Africa).
**cp** candle-power.
**cp.** compare.
**CPA** Chartered Patent Agent.
**CPAC** Consumer Protection Advisory Committee.
**CPAG** Child Poverty Action Group.
**CPC** Clerk of the Privy Council.
**CPI** consumer price index.
**Cpl** Corporal.

**cpp**  current purchasing power.
**CPR**  Canadian Pacific Railway.
**CPS**  *Custos Privati Sigilli* Keeper of the Privy Seal.
**CPU**  central processing unit.
**CR**  *Carolus rex* King Charles; *civis romanus* a Roman citizen; *Custos Rotulorum* Keeper of the Rolls; Community of the Resurrection (Anglican); Costa Rica (IVR).
**Cr**  chromium.
**cr.**  credit; creditor; crown.
**CRAC**  Careers Research and Advisory Centre.
**cres., cresc.**  crescendo; crescent.
**crim. con.**  criminal conversation (i.e. adultery).
**CRMP**  Corps of Royal Military Police.
**CRO**  cathode-ray oscillograph; Commonwealth Relations Office (until 1966); Criminal Records Office.
**CRT**  cathode-ray tube.
**CS**  Court of Session; Clerk to the Signet; Civil Service; Christian Science; Chemical Society; orthobenzylidene malononitrile, an irritant 'gas' synthesised (1928) by *Corson* and *Stoughton*; Czechoslovakia (IVR).
**Cs**  caesium.
**c/s**  cycles per second (hertz).
**CSA**  Confederate States of America.
**CSE**  Certificate of Secondary Education.
**CSIRO**  Commonwealth Scientific and Industrial Research Organisation.
**CSO**  community service order.
**CSP**  Council for Scientific Policy; Chartered Society of Physiotherapists.
**CST**  Central Standard Time.
**CSV**  community service volunteer.
**CSYS**  Certificate of Sixth Year Studies.
**Ct.**  Connecticut.
**ct**  cent; carat.
**CTC**  Cyclists' Touring Club.
**CTOL**  conventional take-off and landing.
**CTT**  capital transfer tax.
**Cu**  *cuprum* copper.
**cu., cub.**  cubic.
**CUP**  Cambridge University Press.
**cur., curt**  current (this month).
**cusec**  cubic feet per second.
**cv**  *curriculum vitae* (see Dict.), or *cursus vitae* course, progress, of life.
**cva**  cerebrovascular accident (see Dict.).
**CVO**  Commander of the (Royal) Victorian Order.
**cwo**  cash with order.
**cwr**  continuous welded rail.
**CWS**  Co-operative Wholesale Society.
**cwt**  hundredweight(s) — **c** (*centum* a hundred), **wt** (weight).
**CY**  Cyprus (IVR).
**cyc., cyclo.**  cyclopaedia.
**Cym.**  Cymric.

**D**  deuterium; Deutsch (catalogue of Schubert's works); Germany (IVR).
*D*  electric flux (displacement).
**3-D**  three-dimensional (see **three** in Dict.).
**d**  day; diameter; differential operator (for operator, see **operate** in Dict.); deci- (see p 1644); *dele* delete; dead; died; deserted; degree; *denarius* or *denarii* a penny or pence (before 1971); duke.
**DA**  District Attorney; Diploma of Art.
**da**  deca- (see p 1644).
**D(A)AG**  Deputy (Assistant) Adjutant-General.
**daf**  Doorn Automobielfabriek (Netherlands motor factory).
**Dan.**  Daniel; Danish.
**D and C**  dilatation and curettage (*med.*).
**dat.**  dative.
**DATEC**  data and telecommunications.
**dau.**  daughter.
**dB**  decibel.
**DBE**  Dame Commander of the Order of the British Empire.

**DC**  *Da capo* (It.) return to the beginning (*mus.*); District of Columbia; (or **dc**) direct current (*elect.*); District Commissioner.
**DCL**  Doctor of Civil Law; Distillers Company Limited.
**DCM**  Distinguished Conduct Medal.
**DCMG**  Dame Commander of the Order of St Michael and St George.
**DCS**  Deputy Clerk of Session.
**DCVO**  Dame Commander of the (Royal) Victorian Order.
**DD**  *Divinitatis Doctor* Doctor of Divinity; *Deo dedit* gave to God.
**dd, D/D**  days after date; day's date.
**D-day**  See Dict.
**DDD**  *dat, dicat, dedicat* gives, devotes, and dedicates; *dono dedit dedicavit* gave and dedicated as a gift.
**DDR**  *Deutsche Demokratische Republik* (Ger.) German Democratic Republic (also IVR).
**DDS**  Doctor of Dental Surgery.
**DDT**  dichlorodiphenyltrichloroethane (see Dict. at **dichlor(o)-**).
**DE**  Department of Employment.
**DEA**  Department of Economic Affairs.
**Dec.**  December.
**dec.**  deceased.
**dec., decl.**  declaration; declension.
**DEd**  Doctor of Education.
**def.**  definition; (or **deft**) defendant.
**deg.**  degree(s).
**Del.**  Delaware.
**del.**  delegate; (or **delt**) *delineavit* drew it.
**demon., demons.**  demonstrative.
**DEng**  Doctor of Engineering.
**dent.**  dental; dentist; dentistry.
**DEP**  Department of Employment and Productivity.
**Dep., Dept., dep., dept.**  department; deputy.
**dep.**  deposed; depart(s); departure.
**der., deriv.**  derivation; derived.
**derv**  See Dict.
**DES**  Department of Education and Science.
**DesRCA**  Designer of the Royal College of Art.
**Deut.**  Deuteronomy.
**DEW**  distant early warning.
**DF**  Defender of the Faith; Dean of the Faculty.
**DFC**  Distinguished Flying Cross.
**DFM**  Distinguished Flying Medal.
**dft**  defendant; draft.
**DG**  *Dei gratia* by the grace of God.
**dg**  decigram(me)(s).
**d.h.**  *das heisst* (Ger.) that is to say.
**DHSS**  Department of Health and Social Services (formerly Security).
**dial.**  dialect.
**diam.**  diameter.
**DIC**  Diploma of the Imperial College.
**dict.**  dictator; dictionary.
**diff.**  different; difference.
**DIG**  Disabled Income Group.
**DIH**  Diploma in Industrial Health.
**dil.**  dilute.
**DIN**  *Deutsche Industrie Normen* (Ger.) German Industrial Standards.
**DIng**  *Doctor Ingeniariae* Doctor of Engineering.
**Dip.**  Diploma, as e.g. **Dip. Ed.**, Diploma in Education, **Dip. Tech.**, Diploma in Technology.
**Dir.**  Director.
**dis.**  discontinued.
**disc.**  discount; discoverer.
**diss.**  dissertation.
**dist.**  distance; distinguish; district; distilled.
**div.**  divide; division; divine; divorced.
**DIY**  do-it-yourself.
**DJ**  dee-jay, disc-jockey.
**DK**  Denmark (IVR).
**DL**  Deputy Lieutenant.
**dl**  decilitre(s).
**DLit(t)**  *Doctor litterarum* or *litteraturae* Doctor of Letters or Literature.
**DM**  Deutsche Mark (Federal German currency).

**dm** decimetre(s).
**DMus** Doctor of Music.
**DMZ** demilitarised zone.
**DNA** deoxyribonucleic acids (see Dict.).
**DNB** Dictionary of National Biography.
**Dnr** dinar (Yugoslav currency).
**do** *ditto* (It.) the same (aforesaid).
**DOA** dead on arrival.
**d.o.b.** date of birth.
**DOC** District Officer Commanding.
**DOE** Department of the Environment.
**DOG** Directory of Opportunities for Graduates.
**dols** dollars.
**DOM** *Deo optimo maximo* to God, best and greatest; *Dominus Omnium Magister* God the master of all; dirty old man; Dominican Republic (IVR).
**Dom.** *Dominus* Lord; Dominion.
**dom.** domestic.
**DOMS** Diploma in Ophthalmic Medicine and Surgery.
**Dor.** Doric.
**doz.** dozen.
**DP** Displaced Person; data processing; duly performed (the work of the class).
**DPH** Diploma in Public Health.
**DPh, DPhil** *Doctor Philosophiae* Doctor of Philosophy.
**DPM** Diploma in Psychological Medicine.
**dpm** disintegrations per minute.
**DPP** Director of Public Prosecutions.
**dpt** department.
**Dr** Doctor; debtor; Drummer; Driver; drachma (Greek currency).
**dr** dead reckoning.
**dr.** dram; drawer.
**DS** *Dal segno* (It.) from the sign (*mus.*); disseminated sclerosis.
**ds, D/S.** days after sight.
**DSC** Distinguished Service Cross.
**DSc** *Doctor Scientiae* Doctor of Science.
**DSM** Distinguished Service Medal.
**DSO** Distinguished Service Order.
**dsp** *decessit sine prole* died without issue.
**DT** data transmission; (or **dt, DT's, dt's**) delirium tremens.
**DTh** *Doctor Theologiae* Doctor of Theology.
**DTI** Department of Trade and Industry.
**DUKW** See **duck** (4) in Dict.
**Dunelm.** *Dunelmensis* of Durham.
**DV** *Deo volente* God willing.
**dvp** *decessit vita patris* died in father's lifetime.
**dwt** pennyweight — **d** (*denarius* a penny), **wt** (weight).
**DY** Dahomey (IVR).
**Dy** dysprosium.
**dyn** dyne; dynamo; dynamometer.
**DZ** Algeria (IVR).

**E** East; English; exa- (see p 1644); Spain (IVR).
*E* energy.
*e* See pp 1644, 1646.
**EAK** Kenya (IVR).
**E and OE** errors and omissions excepted.
**eaon** except as otherwise noted.
**EAT** Tanzania (IVR).
**EAU** Uganda (IVR).
**EAZ** Tanzania (IVR).
**Ebor.** *Eboracum* York; *Eboracensis* of York.
**EBU** European Broadcasting Union.
**EC** East Central; Established Church; Ecuador (IVR).
**Eccl., Eccles.** Ecclesiastes; Ecclesiastical.
**Ecclesiol.** Ecclesiology.
**Ecclus.** Ecclesiasticus.
**ECE** Economic Commission for Europe.
**ECG** electrocardiogram (-graph).
**ECG(D)** Export Credits Guarantee (Department).
**ECO** English Chamber Orchestra.
**ECSC** European Coal and Steel Community.

**ECT** electroconvulsive therapy.
**ECU** English Church Union.
**Ed.** Editor.
**ed., edit.** edited; edition.
**EdB** Bachelor of Education.
**EDC** European Defence Community.
**Edenburgen.** *Edenburgensis* of Edinburgh.
**EDF** European Development Fund.
**Edin.** Edinburgh.
**edit.** edited; edition.
**EDP** electronic data processing.
**EDS** English Dialect Society.
**EE** errors excepted.
**EEC** European Economic Community.
**EEG** electroencephalogram (-graph).
**EET** Eastern European Time.
**EETS** Early English Text Society.
**EFL** English as a foreign language.
**EFTA** European Free Trade Association.
**e.g., eg, ex. gr.** *exempli gratia* for example.
**EGU** English Golf Union.
**EI** East Indies.
**EIS** Educational Institute of Scotland.
**ejusd.** *ejusdem* of the same.
**EKCO** E. K. Cole (manufacturer of electrical goods).
**El Al** Israeli airline (lit. 'towards the sky').
**ELDO** European Launcher Development Organisation.
**elec., elect.** electric; electricity.
**Elien.** *Eliensis* of Ely.
**ELT** English language teaching.
**EMA** European Monetary Agreement.
**emf** electromotive force.
**EMI** Electric and Musical Industries.
**Emp.** Emperor, Empress.
**emu** electromagnetic unit.
**ency., encyc.** encyclopaedia.
**ENE** east-north-east.
**Eng.** England; English.
**eng.** engineer; engraver; engraving.
**Ens.** Ensign.
**ENSA** Entertainments National Services Association.
**ENT** Ear, Nose and Throat.
**ent., entom.** entomology.
**Ent. Sta. Hall** Entered at Stationers' Hall.
**Env. Ext.** Envoy Extraordinary.
**EOC** Equal Opportunities Commission.
**eod** every other day.
**EP** extended play; electroplated.
**Ep.** Epistle.
**EPA** European Productivity Agency.
**Eph.** Ephesians.
**Epiph.** Epiphany.
**Epis., Episc.** Episcopal.
**EPNS** electroplated nickel silver; English Place-Name Society.
**EPU** European Payments Union.
**ER** *Elisabeth Regina* Elizabeth, Queen.
**Er** erbium.
**ER(I)** *Edwardus Rex* (*Imperator*) Edward, King (and Emperor).
**ERNIE** electronic random number indicator equipment (computer).
**Es** einsteinium.
**Esc.** escudo (Portuguese currency).
**ESE** east-south-east.
**ESL** English as a second language.
**ESN** educationally subnormal.
**ESP** extra-sensory perception.
**esp., espec.** especially.
**Esq., Esqr.** Esquire.
**ESRO** European Space Research Organisation.
**ESSO** Standard Oil.
**EST** Eastern Standard Time.
**est.** established; estimated.
**Esth.** Esther.
**ESU** English-Speaking Union.
**esu** electrostatic unit.
**ET** Arab Republic of Egypt (IVR).

ETA (or D) estimated time of arrival (or departure).

et al. *et alii, aliae,* or *alia* and others; *et alibi* and elsewhere.

etc., &c. *et ceteri* or *cetera* and the others, and so forth.

et seq. or sq. (sing.), *et sequens* et sqq. (pl.) *et sequentes* or *sequentia* and the following.

ETU Electrical Trades Union.

ety., etym. etymology; etymological.

EU Evangelical Union.

Eu europium.

Euratom *European Atom*ic Energy Community.

eV electron-volt.

Ex., Exod. Exodus.

ex. examined; example; exception; excursus; executive; export.

Exc. Excellency.

exc. except; exception.

ex. div. *extra dividendum* without dividend.

ex. gr. *exempli gratia* for the sake of example.

ex lib. *ex libris* from the books (of) — as on bookplates.

Exod. Exodus.

Exon. *Exonia* Exeter; *Exoniensis* of Exeter.

exp. export; exponential.

exr executor.

exrx executrix.

ext. extension; externally; extinct; extra; extract.

Ez. Ezra.

Ezek. Ezekiel.

F Fellow . . . See note (2) p 1605; Fahrenheit; farad; fluorine; France (IVR).

*F* force.

f following; farthing; feminine; fathom; foot; forte; folio; femto- (see p 1644).

*f* frequency.

FA Football Association; Faculty of Actuaries.

Fa. Florida.

fam. familiar; family.

FAO Food and Agriculture Organisation.

FAS Fellow of the Society of Arts; Fellow of the Antiquarian Society.

fas free alongside ship.

FBA Fellow of the British Academy.

FBI Federal Bureau of Investigation.

FCA Fellow of the Institute of Chartered Accountants.

FCO Foreign and Commonwealth Office (FO and CO combined in 1968).

fcp, fcap foolscap.

FD *Fidei Defensor* Defender of the Faith.

Fe *ferrum* iron.

Feb. February.

fec. *fecit* did it, or made it (sing.).

fem. feminine.

FET field-effect transistor.

feud. feudal.

ff *fecerunt* did it, or made it (pl.); folios; following (pl.).

ff fortissimo.

FH fire hydrant.

FIAT *Fabbrica Italiana Automobile Torino* (It.) Italian Motor Works in Turin.

Fid. Def. *Fidei Defensor* Defender of the Faith.

FIDO Fog Investigation and Dispersal Operation; Film Industry Defence Organisation.

fi. fa. *fieri facias* that you cause to be made (a writ of execution).

FIFA *Fédération Internationale de Football Association* (Fr.) International Association Football Federation.

FIFO first in, first out.

fig. figure; figurative(ly).

FIS Family Income Supplement.

FJI Fellow of the Institute of Journalists; Fiji (IVR).

FL Liechtenstein (also IVR).

fl. *floruit* flourished; florin.

Flor., Fla. Florida.

fl. oz. fluid ounce.

FM frequency modulation; Field-Marshal.

Fm fermium.

fm fathom.

FO Foreign Office (see FCO); Field Officer; Flying Officer; Full Organ.

fo., fol. folio.

fob free on board.

FOC father of the chapel.

foc free of charge.

FOE Friends of Europe; Friends of the Earth.

for free on rail.

FORTRAN, Fortran See Dict.

FP fire-plug; former pupil; Free Presbyterian.

fp forte-piano; freezing-point.

FPA Family Planning Association.

FPS foot-pound-second.

Fr francium; franc.

Fr. Father; France; French; Friar; Friday.

fr. fragment; franc; frequently.

frat. fraternise; fraternity.

FRCP Fellow of the Royal College of Physicians (Edin., of Edinburgh; Lond., of London; Irel., of Ireland).

FRCPS Glasg. Fellow of the Royal College of Physicians and Surgeons of Glasgow.

FRCS Fellow of the Royal College of Surgeons (Ed., of Edinburgh; Eng., of England; Irel., of Ireland).

F(R)FPSG (formerly) Fellow of the (Royal) Faculty of Physicians and Surgeons of Glasgow (now FRCPS Glasg.).

FRG Federal Republic of Germany.

FRPS Fellow of the Royal Photographic Society.

FRS Fellow of the Royal Society (E, of Edinburgh).

FSF Fellow of the Institute of Shipping and Forwarding Agents.

FT Financial Times.

ft foot, feet; fort.

fth, fthm fathom.

fur. furlong(s).

fut. future.

fz forzando or forzato (see sforzando in Dict.).

G Gauss; giga- (see p 1644).

*G* constant of gravitation (see gravity in Dict.).

g gram(me).

*g* acceleration of gravity (see gravity in Dict.).

GA General Assembly.

Ga gallium.

Ga. Georgia.

Gael. Gaelic.

Gal. Galatians.

gal., gall. gallon(s).

G. and S. Gilbert and Sullivan.

GATT General Agreement on Tariffs and Trade.

gaz. gazette; gazetteer.

GB Great Britain (also IVR).

GBA Alderney, Channel Islands (IVR).

GBE (Knight or Dame) Grand Cross of the British Empire.

GBG Guernsey, Channel Islands (IVR).

gbh grievous bodily harm.

GBJ Jersey, Channel Islands (IVR).

GBM Isle of Man (IVR).

GBS George Bernard Shaw.

GBZ Gibraltar (IVR).

GC George Cross.

GCA ground control(led) approach system or control apparatus; Guatemala (IVR).

GCB (Knight) Grand Cross of the Bath.

GCE General Certificate of Education.

GCH (Knight) Grand Cross of Hanover.

GCM General Court-martial; (or gcm) greatest common measure.

GCMG (Knight) Grand Cross of the Order of St Michael and St George.

GCVO (Knight or Dame) Grand Cross of the (Royal) Victorian Order.

Gd gadolinium.

Gdns gardens.

**GDR** German Democratic Republic.
**Ge** germanium.
**GEC** General Electric Company.
**Gen.** Genesis; (or **Genl**) General.
**gen.** gender; genitive; genus.
**gent.** gentleman.
**Geo.** Georgia; George.
**geog.** geography.
**geol.** geology.
**geom.** geometry.
**Ger.** German.
**ger.** gerund.
**GeV** giga-electron-volt(s) (see giga- in Dict.; same value in Europe as **BeV** in USA).
**GH** Ghana (IVR).
**GHQ** General Headquarters.
**GI** government (or general) issue (US Army); hence, common soldier.
**Gib.** Gibraltar.
**GIGO** garbage in, garbage out.
**Gk** Greek.
**GKN** Guest, Keen and Nettlefold.
**Gl** glucinum (now beryllium).
**Glam.** Glamorganshire.
**GLC** Greater London Council.
**Gld** guilder (Dutch currency).
**GLORIA** Geological Long Range Asdic.
**Glos.** Gloucestershire.
**GM** George Medal; (or **G-M**) Geiger-Müller counter; General Motors.
**gm** gram(me).
**GmbH** *Gesellschaft mit beschränkter Haftung* (Ger.) limited liability company.
**GMC** General Medical Council.
**GMT** Greenwich Mean Time.
**GNP** gross national product.
**GOC** General Officer Commanding.
**GOM** Grand Old Man (orig. W. E. Gladstone).
**Gov.** Governor; (or **Govt**) Government.
**GP** General Practitioner; Gallup Poll; *Gloria Patri* glory to the Father.
**GPI** general paralysis of the insane.
**GPO** General Post Office.
**GR** Greece (IVR).
**Gr.** Greek.
**gr.** grain; grammar; grouse; gunner.
**GR(I)** *Georgius Rex* (*Imperator*) George, King (and Emperor).
**GS** General Staff; General Service; Geological Society.
**gs** guineas.
**GSM** Guildhall School of Music and Drama; gram(me)s per square metre.
**GSO** General Staff Officer.
**GSP** Good Service Pension.
**GT** *gran turismo* (see gran in Dict.).
**GTC** General Teaching Council (Scotland).
**gu.** guinea; gules.
**guin.** guinea.
**GUM** *Gosudarstvenni Universalni Magazin* (Russ.) State Universal Store.
**GUS** Great Universal Stores.
**GUY** Guyana (IVR).
**GW(R)** Great Western (Railway) (now incorporated in **BR**).

**H** hydrogen; henry; hydrant; hospital; hard (on lead pencils); Hungary (IVR).
**h** hecto- (see p 1644); hour.
*h* height; Planck's constant (see p 1644).
*ħ* Dirac's constant (see p 1644).
**HA** Heavy Artillery.
**Ha** hahnium.
**ha** hectare; *hoc anno* this year.
**Hab.** Habakkuk.
**HAC** Honourable Artillery Company; high-alumina cement.
**Hag.** Haggai.
**h and c** hot and cold (water laid on).
**Hants** Hampshire (*Hantshaving*, orig. name of county).
**HB** hard black (on lead pencils).

**hbar** hectobar.
**HBM** His (or Her) Britannic Majesty.
**HC** Heralds' College; House of Commons; Holy Communion.
**HCF** (or **Hon CF**) Honorary Chaplain to the Forces; (or **hcf**) highest common factor.
**HCM** His (or Her) Catholic Majesty.
**HE** His Excellency; His Eminence; High Explosive; Horizontal Equivalent.
**He** helium.
**Heb., Hebr.** Hebrew; Hebrews.
**HEH** His (or Her) Exalted Highness.
**her.** heraldry; *heres* heir.
**Herts** Hertfordshire.
**HF** high frequency.
**Hf** hafnium.
**hf** half; **hf-bd** half-bound; **hf-cf** half-calf; **hf-mor** half-morocco.
**HG** His (or Her) Grace.
**Hg** *hydrargyrum* mercury.
**HGV** heavy goods vehicle.
**HH** His (or Her) Highness; very hard (on lead pencils).
**hhd** hogshead.
**HIDB** Highlands and Islands Development Board.
**Hi-Fi, hi-fi** high fidelity.
**HIH** His (or Her) Imperial Highness.
**HIM** His (or Her) Imperial Majesty.
**HIS** *hic iacet sepultus* here lies buried.
**hist.** historian; history.
**HJ(S)** *hic jacet* (*sepultus*) here lies (buried).
**HK** House of Keys (Isle of Man); Hong Kong (also IVR).
**HKJ** Jordan (IVR).
**hl** hectolitre(s).
**HLI** Highland Light Infantry (incorporated in Royal Highland Fusiliers).
**HM** His (or Her) Majesty.
**HMAS** His (or Her) Majesty's Australian Ship.
**HMC** His (or Her) Majesty's Customs.
**HMCS** His (or Her) Majesty's Canadian Ship.
**HMG** His (or Her) Majesty's Government.
**HMI** His (or Her) Majesty's Inspector, Inspectorate.
**HMP** *hoc monumentum posuit* erected this monument.
**HMS** His (or Her) Majesty's Ship or Service.
**HMSO** His (or Her) Majesty's Stationery Office.
**HMV** His Master's Voice (gramophone company).
**HNC** Higher National Certificate.
**HND** Higher National Diploma.
**Ho** holmium.
**ho.** house.
**Hon.** Honourable; Honorary.
**Hons** Honours.
**Hon. Sec.** Honorary Secretary.
**hor.** horizon; horology.
**hort., hortic.** horticulture; horticultural.
**Hos.** Hosea.
**HP** hire-purchase; High Priest; half-pay; (or **hp**) horsepower.
**HQ** headquarters.
**HR** House of Representatives; Home Rule.
**Hr** Herr.
**hr** hour.
**HRE** Holy Roman Emperor or Empire.
**HRH** His (or Her) Royal Highness.
**HRIP** *hic requiescit in pace* here rests in peace.
**HS** *hic situs* here is laid.
**HSE** *hic sepultus* (or *situs*) *est* here is buried (or laid).
**HSH** His (or Her) Serene Highness.
**HSS** *Historiae Societatis Socius* Fellow of the Historical Society.
**HT** high tension.
**Hunts** Huntingdonshire.
**HWM** high water mark.
**Hz** hertz (cycles per second).

**I** iodine; Italy (IVR).
*I* electric current.
*i* See p 1646.
**IA** Institute of Actuaries.
**Ia.** Iowa.
**IAEA** International Atomic Energy Agency.
**IAM** Institute of Advanced Motorists.
**IAS** Indian Administrative Service.
**IATA** International Air Transport Association.
**IB** Institute of Bankers.
**IBA** Independent Broadcasting Authority.
**ib., ibid.** *ibidem* in the same place.
**IBM** International Business Machines (computer manufacturers).
**IBRD** International Bank for Reconstruction and Development (World Bank).
**IC** integrated circuit.
**i/c** in charge.
**ICA** Institute of Contemporary Arts.
**ICAO** International Civil Aviation Organisation.
**ICBM** intercontinental ballistic missile.
**ICE** Institution of Civil Engineers; internal combustion engine.
**ICFC** Industrial and Commercial Finance Corporation.
**ich., ichth.** ichthyology.
**IChemE** Institution of Chemical Engineers.
**ICI** Imperial Chemical Industries.
**ICJ** International Court of Justice.
**ICL** International Computers Limited.
**icon.** iconography.
**ICS** Indian Civil Service (in Republic of India, IAS).
**ICWA** Institute of Cost and Works Accountants.
**ID** Intelligence Department; identification; infectious diseases.
**Id.** Idaho.
**id.** *idem* the same.
**IDA** International Development Association.
**IDB** Illicit Diamond Buying (in S. Africa).
**IDN** *in Dei nomine* in the name of God.
**IDV** International Distillers and Vintners.
**i.e., ie** *id est* that is
**IEC** International Electrotechnical Commission.
**IEE** Institution of Electrical Engineers.
**IF** intermediate frequency.
**IFC** International Finance Corporation.
**IFS** Irish Free State (1922-37).
**IHC, IHS,** for the Greek capitals IHC (H, capital eta; C, a form of sigma), first two and last letters of *Iesous* Jesus, often misread as *Jesus Hominum Salvator* Jesus Saviour of Men.
**ihp** indicated horse-power.
**IL** Institute of Linguists; Israel (IVR).
**ILC** irreversible letter of credit.
**ILEA** Inner London Education Authority.
**Ill.** Illinois.
**ill.** illustration; illustrated.
**ILN** Illustrated London News.
**ILO** International Labour Organisation or (its secretariat) International Labour Office.
**ILP** Independent Labour Party.
**IMechE** Institution of Mechanical Engineers.
**IMF** International Monetary Fund.
**imit.** imitative.
**IMM** Institution of Mining and Metallurgy.
**Imp.** Imperial; *Imperator* Emperor.
**imp.** (or **imperf.**) imperfect; (or **imper.**) imperative; *imprimatur* let it be printed; (or **impers.**) impersonal.
**IMunE** Institution of Municipal Engineers.
**In** indium.
**in** inch(es).
**inc., incorp.** incorporated.
**incl.** including; included.
**incog.** *incognito* (It.) unknown, avoiding publicity.
**IND** Same as IDN; India (IVR).
**Ind.** Indiana; Independent.
**ind., indic.** indicative.
**indecl.** indeclinable.
**indef.** indefinite.

**indiv.** individual.
**Ind. Ter.** Indian Territory.
**inf.** *infra* below; infantry; infinitive.
**infra dig.** *infra dignitatem* beneath one's dignity.
**init.** *initio* in the beginning.
**in lim.** *in limine* on the threshold, at the outset.
**in loc.** *in loco* in its place.
**in loc. cit.** *in loco citato* in the place cited.
**in pr.** *in principio* in the beginning.
**INRI** *Jesus Nazarenus Rex Judaeorum* Jesus of Nazareth King of the Jews. (For explanation of I, see J in Dict.)
**Inst.** Institute.
**inst.** instant — the present month; institute.
**Inst. P.** Institute of Physics.
**int.** interest; interior; interpreter; international; integral.
**Interpol** See Dict.
**interrog.** interrogation; interrogative(ly).
**in trans.** *in transitu* in transit.
**intrans.** intransitive.
**intro., introd.** introduction.
**inv.** *invenit* designed it; invented; invoice.
**IOB** Institute of Building.
**IOC** International Olympic Committee.
**IoJ** Institute of Journalists.
**IOM** Isle of Man.
**IOU** I owe you.
**IOW** Isle of Wight.
**IPA** Institute of Practitioners in Advertising; International Publishers' Association; International Phonetic Alphabet.
**IPC** International Publishing Corporation.
**IPD** *in praesentia Dominorum* in presence of the Lords (of Session).
**IQ** Intelligence Quotient.
**iq** *idem quod* the same as.
**IQS** Institute of Quantity Surveyors.
**IR** Iran (IVR).
**Ir** iridium.
**Ir.** Irish.
**IRA** Irish Republican Army.
**IRB** Irish Republican Brotherhood.
**IRBM** intermediate range ballistic missile.
**Irel.** Ireland.
**IRL** Ireland (IVR).
**IRQ** Iraq (IVR).
**IS** Iceland (IVR).
**Is., Isa.** Isaiah.
**ISBN** International Standard Book Number.
**ISCh** Incorporated Society of Chiropodists.
**ISD** international subscriber dialling.
**Is(l).** island.
**ISO** Imperial Service Order; International Organisation for Standardisation.
**ISS** International Social Service.
**ISSN** International Standard Serial Number.
**It.** Italian; Italian vermouth.
**ITA** Independent Television Authority (now IBA).
**ita** initial teaching alphabet.
**ital.** italic; Italian.
**ITN** Independent Television News.
**ITO** International Trade Organisation.
**ITT** International Telephone and Telegraph Corporation.
**ITU** International Telecommunications Union.
**IU** international unit.
**IU(C)D** intra-uterine (contraceptive) device.
**IUPAC** International Union of Pure and Applied Chemistry.
**IUPAP** International Union of Pure and Applied Physics.
**IVR** International Vehicle Registration.
**IW** Isle of Wight.

**J** joule; Japan (IVR).
**J.** Judge; Justice.
**JA** Jamaica (IVR).
**JAL** Japan Air Lines.
**Jan.** January.
**Jas** James.

**JC** *Juris Consultus* Jurisconsult; Jesus Christ; Justice Clerk.
**JCD** *Juris Civilis Doctor* Doctor of Civil Law.
**JCR** junior common room.
**Jer.** Jeremiah.
**JFK** John Fitzgerald Kennedy.
**JHS** Same as IHC.
**JMB** Joint Matriculation Board.
**Jno.** John.
**Jo.** Joel.
**Josh.** Joshua.
**JP** Justice of the Peace.
**Jr, Jun., Junr** Junior.
**JUD** *Juris Utriusque Doctor* Doctor both of Canon and of Civil Law.
**Jud., Judg.** Judges.
**Jul.** July.
**Jun.** June; Junior.
**junc.** junction.
**jurisp.** jurisprudence.

**K** Kelvin (thermometer scale); kelvin; *kalium* potassium; Köchel (catalogue of Mozart's works); Kirkpatrick (catalogue of Domenico Scarlatti's works); Khmer Republic (IVR).
**k** kilo- (see p 1644).
**Kan.** Kansas.
**KB** Knight of the Bath; Knight Bachelor; King's Bench.
**KBE** Knight Commander of the Order of the British Empire.
**KC** King's Counsel; King's College; Kennel Club.
**KCB** Knight Commander of the Bath.
**KCMG** Knight Commander of the Order of St Michael and St George.
**KCVO** Knight Commander of the (Royal) Victorian Order.
**Ken.** Kentucky.
**KG** Knight of the Order of the Garter.
**kg** kilogram(me)(s).
**KGB** *Komitet Gosudarstvennoi Bezopasnosti* (Russ.) Committee of State Security.
**KGCB** Knight of the Grand Cross of the Bath.
**kilo** kilogram(me); kilometre.
**k.k.** *kaiserlich-königlich* (Ger.) Imperial-Royal.
**KKK** Ku Klux Klan.
**KL** Kuala Lumpur.
**KLH** Knight of the Legion of Honour.
**KLM** *Koninklijke Luchtvaart Maatschappij* (Du.) Royal Dutch Airlines.
**KM** Knight of Malta.
**km** kilometre(s).
**kn** knot (nautical, etc., measure).
**KO, ko** knock out; kick off.
**K of L** Knight of Labour.
**Kr** krypton.
**kr** kreutzer; krone.
**Ks.** Kansas.
**KT** Knight of the Thistle.
**Kt** Knight.
**Kt Bach.** Knight Bachelor.
**ktl** *kai ta leipomena* or *kai ta loipa* (Gr.) and the rest, and so forth.
**kW** kilowatt.
**kWh** kilowatt-hour.
**KWT** Kuwait (IVR).
**Ky.** Kentucky.

**L** Lake; Latin; Liberal; lambert; lumen; learner (driver); *libra* pound; Luxembourg (IVR).
*L* symbol for inductance; luminance.
**l** litre (the abbreviation, though the accepted one, is undesirable as liable to be misread); latitude; league; left; long: (or lb) *libra* pound.
*l* length.
**LA** Law Agent; Literate in Arts; Los Angeles; Library Association.
**La** lanthanum.
**La.** Louisiana.
**Lab.** Labour.

**lab.** laboratory.
**LAC** Licentiate of the Apothecaries' Company.
**Lam.** Lamentations.
**LAMDA** London Academy of Music and Dramatic Art.
**Lancs** Lancashire.
**lang.** language.
**LAO** Laos (IVR).
**LAR** Libya (IVR).
**LASER** *light amplification by stimulated emission of radiation.*
**Lat.** Latin.
**lat.** latitude.
**LB** Liberia (IVR).
**lb** *libra* pound.
**lb, lbw** leg before wicket.
**lc** lower-case (in printing); *loco citato* in the place cited; left centre; letter of credit.
**LCC** London County Council (now GLC).
**LCh, LChir** *Licentiatus Chirurgiae* Licentiate in Surgery.
**LCJ** Lord Chief-Justice.
**LCM, lcm** least common multiple.
**LCP** Licentiate of the College of Preceptors.
**LD** Lady Day.
**Ld** Lord.
**Ldp, Lp** Lordship.
**LDS** Licentiate in Dental Surgery.
**LDV** Local Defence Volunteers (later Home Guard).
**LEA** Local Education Authority.
**LEAP** Life Education for the Autistic Person.
**lect.** lecture.
**LED** light emitting diode.
**leg.** legal; legate; legislature.
**Leics** Leicestershire.
**Leip.** Leipzig.
**LEPRA** Leprosy Relief Association.
**Lev., Levit.** Leviticus.
**lex.** lexicon.
**LF** low frequency.
**LGU** Ladies Golf Union.
**lh** left hand.
**LHD** *Litterarum Humaniorum Doctor* Doctor of Letters.
**LI** Long Island; Light Infantry.
**Li** lithium.
**Lib.** Liberal.
**lib.** *liber* book.
**lib. cat.** library catalogue.
**Lieut.** Lieutenant.
**LIFO** last in, first out.
**LILO** last in, last out.
**Lincs** Lincolnshire.
**Linn.** Linnaean, Linnaeus.
**liq.** liquid.
**lit.** literal(ly); literature.
**lith., litho., lithog.** lithograph; lithography.
**Lit. Hum.** *litterae humaniores* humane letters, the humanities.
**Lit(t)D** *Litterarum Doctor* Doctor of Letters.
**LJ** Lord Justice.
**LLB** *Legum Baccalaureus* Bachelor of Laws.
**LLCM** Licentiate of the London College of Music.
**LLD** *Legum Doctor* Doctor of Laws.
**LLM** *Legum Magister* Master of Laws.
**LM** long metre.
**lm** lumen.
**LMS** London Missionary Society; London, Midland and Scottish (Railway) (now incorporated in BR).
**ln** natural logarithm.
**LNE(R)** London and North-Eastern (Railway) (now incorporated in BR).
**LNG** liquefied natural gas.
**LOB** Location of Offices Bureau.
**loc. cit.** *loco citato* at the place quoted.
**L of C** line of communication.
**log** logarithm.
**lon., long.** longitude.
**Lond.** London.

# 1616

**Londin.** *Londiniensis* of London.
**Lonrho** *Lon*don *Rho*desian (industrial conglomerate).
**loq.** *loquitur* speaks.
**LP** long-playing; Lord Provost; low pressure; Labour Party.
**LPG** liquefied petroleum gas.
**LPO** London Philharmonic Orchestra.
**Lr** lawrencium; lira (Italian currency).
**LRAM** Licentiate of the Royal Academy of Music.
**LRCP** Licentiate of the Royal College of Physicians (**Edin.,** of Edinburgh; **Lond.,** of London; **Irel.,** of Ireland).
**LRCS** Licentiate of the Royal College of Surgeons (**Ed.,** of Edinburgh; **Eng.,** of England; **Irel.,** of Ireland).
**LS** Lesotho (IVR); Linnaean Society; *loco sigilli* in the place of the seal.
**LSA** Licentiate of the Society of Apothecaries.
**LSD** lysergic acid diethylamide (see Dict. at lysis).
**L.S.D.** *librae, solidi, denarii* pounds, shillings, pence.
**LSE** London School of Economics.
**LSO** London Symphony Orchestra.
**LT** low tension.
**Lt.** Lieutenant.
**LTA** Lawn Tennis Association.
**Lt.-Col.** Lieutenant-Colonel.
**Ltd** limited liability.
**Lt.-Gen.** Lieutenant-General.
**LTh** Licentiate in Theology.
**Lu** lutetium.
**Lw** (now **Lr**) lawrencium.
**lx** lux.

**M** Member . . . See note (2) p 1605; mega- (see p 1644); Malta (IVR).
**M, m** *mille* a thousand.
**M.** *Monsieur* (Fr.) Mr (pl. **MM.**).
**m** milli- (see p 1644); metre; mile; married; masculine; *meridiem* noon.
*m* mass.
**3M** Minnesota Mining and Manufacturing Company.
**MA** *Magister Artium* Master of Arts; Morocco (IVR).
**Mac., Macc.** Maccabees.
**mach.** machinery.
**MAFF** Ministry of Agriculture, Fisheries and Food.
**mag.** magazine; magnetic.
**Maj.** Major.
**MAL** Malaysia (IVR).
**Mal.** Malachi.
**Man., Manit.** Manitoba.
**Man. Dir.** Managing Director.
**M & B** May and Baker (sulphonamides prepared by this firm and others).
**M & S** Marks & Spencer.
**Mar.** March.
**marg.** margin; marginal; margarine.
**Marq.** Marquis.
**mas., masc.** masculine.
**MASER** *m*icrowave *a*mplification by *s*timulated *e*mission of *r*adiation.
**Mass.** Massachusetts.
**math., maths** mathematics.
**Matt.** Matthew.
**max.** maximum.
**mb** millibar.
**MB** *Medicinae Baccalaureus* Bachelor of Medicine; mark of the Beast.
**MBE** Member of the Order of the British Empire.
**MC** Member of Congress; Master of Ceremonies; Member of Council; Military Cross; Monaco (IVR).
**MCC** Marylebone Cricket Club; Member of the County Council.
**MCh** *Magister Chirurgiae* Master of Surgery.

**MCP** male chauvinist pig.
**MCP(A)** *m*ethyl-*c*hloro-*p*henoxy*a*cetic acid (methoxone; used as selective weedkiller).
**Mc/s** megacycles per second.
**MD** *Medicinae Doctor* Doctor of Medicine; mentally deficient; Managing Director.
**Md** mendelevium.
**Md.** Maryland.
**Mdlle, Mlle** *Mademoiselle* (Fr.) Miss.
**Mdm** Madam.
**MDS** Master of Dental Surgery.
**ME** Methodist Episcopal; Mining or Mechanical Engineer; Most Excellent; Middle English.
**Me.** Maine.
**mech.** mechanic; mechanical.
**med.** medical; medicine; mediaeval; *medius, -a, -um* middle.
**Mem.** Member.
**mem.** memorandum; *memento* remember.
**memo.** memorandum.
**Messrs** *Messieurs* (Fr.) Sirs, Gentlemen; used as pl. of **Mr.**
**met., metaph.** metaphysics; metaphor; metaphorical.
**met., meteor.** meteorology.
**metal., metall.** metallurgy.
**meth(s).** methylated spirits.
**MeV** mega-electron-volt(s).
**MEX** Mexico (IVR).
**Mex.** Mexico; Mexican.
**MEZ** *Mitteleuropäische Zeit* (Ger.) Central European Time.
**mf** mezzo-forte.
**mfd** manufactured.
**MFH** Master of Foxhounds.
**mfrs** manufacturers.
**mft** *mistura* (for classical L. *mixtura*) *fiat* let a mixture be made.
**mfv** motor fleet vessel.
**MG** machine-gun; Morris Garage.
**Mg** magnesium.
**mg** milligram(me)(s).
**Mgr** Monseigneur, Monsignor.
**MHG** Middle High German.
**MHR** Member of the House of Representatives.
**MI** Military Intelligence; **MI5** Security Services, **MI6** Secret Intelligence Service (initials based on wartime Military Intelligence departments).
**Mi.** Mississippi.
**Mic.** Micah.
**Mich.** Michigan.
**MICR** magnetic ink character recognition.
**MIDAS** Missile Defence Alarm System.
**Middx** Middlesex.
**mil., milit.** military.
**Min.** Ministry.
**min.** mineralogy; minimum; minute.
**Minn.** Minnesota.
**MIRV** See Dict.
**misc.** miscellaneous; miscellany.
**Miss.** Mississippi.
**MIT** Massachusetts Institute of Technology.
**MJ** megajoule(s).
**MJI** Member of the Institute of Journalists.
**MK** (on cars) mark.
**Mkk** Markka (Finnish currency).
**MKS** metre-kilogram-second unit, or system.
**MKSA** metre-kilogram-second-ampere unit, or system.
**ml** millilitre(s).
**MLA** Member of Legislative Assembly; Modern Language Association.
**MLC** Member of Legislative Council; Meat and Livestock Commission.
**MLitt** *Magister Litterarum* Master of Letters or Literature.
**Mlle** *Mademoiselle* (Fr.) Miss; — pl. **Mlles** *Mesdemoiselles.*
**MLR** minimum lending rate.
**MM** (Their) Majesties; Martyrs; Military Medal.

**MM.** *Messieurs* (Fr.) Gentlemen, Sirs.
**mm** millimetre(s).
**Mme** *Madame* (Fr.) Mrs; — pl. **Mmes** *Mesdames*.
**mmf** magnetomotive force.
**MN** Merchant Navy.
**Mn** manganese.
**MO** Medical Officer.
**Mo** molybdenum.
**Mo.** Missouri.
**mo.** month.
**MOD** Ministry of Defence.
**mod.** modern; moderato.
**mod. con.** See Dict.
**Mods** moderations.
**MOH** Medical Officer of Health.
**mol** mole (unit).
**mol. wt** molecular weight.
**Mon.** Monmouthshire; Monday.
**Monsig.** Monsignor.
**Mont.** Montana; Montgomeryshire.
**Mor.** Morocco.
**morn.** morning.
**mos** months.
**MOS(T)** metal oxide silicon (transistors).
**MOT** Ministry of Transport (now Transport Industries).
**MP** Member of Parliament; Military Police; Metropolitan Police; Municipal Police (US); mounted police.
**mp** mezzo-piano; melting-point.
**mpg, mph** miles per gallon, hour.
**MPharm** Master of Pharmacy.
**MPS** Member of the Pharmaceutical Society; Member of the Philological Society.
**MR** Master of the Rolls.
**Mr** Mister; Master.
**MRA** Moral Rearmament.
**MRC** Medical Research Council.
**MRCA** multirole combat aircraft.
**MRCP** Member of the Royal College of Physicians.
**MRG** Minority Rights Group.
**Mrs** Mistress (fem. of **Mr**, Mister).
**MS** manuscript; Master of Surgery; *Memoriae Sacrum* Sacred to the Memory; milestone; multiple sclerosis; Mauritius (IVR).
**Ms.** See Supplement.
**ms** millisecond(s); (or **M/S**) months (after) sight.
**MSC** Manpower Services Commission.
**MSc** Master of Science.
**MSF** medium standard frequency.
**msl** mean sea-level.
**MSS** manuscripts.
**MST** mountain standard time.
**MSW** Medical Social Worker.
**MT** Mechanical Transport; mean time.
**Mt, mt** mount.
**MTB** motor torpedo-boat.
**MTh** Master of Theology.
**mth** month.
**Mts, mts** mountains.
**mus.** music; museum.
**MusB(ac)** Bachelor of Music.
**MusD(oc)** Doctor of Music.
**MusM** Master of Music.
**Mv** mendelevium (now **Md**).
**mv** merchant vessel; motor vessel; muzzle velocity; mezza voce.
**MVO** Member of the Royal Victorian Order.
**MW** medium wave; Malawi (IVR).
**MWGM** Most Worshipful (or Worthy) Grand Master (Freemasonry).
**Mx** Middlesex.
**myst.** mysteries.
**myth.** mythology.

**N** nitrogen; newton; Avogadro number; neper; North, Northern; Norway (IVR).
**n** name; noun; *natus* born; neuter; noon; nano- (see p 1644).

**NA** North America; Netherlands Antilles (IVR).
**Na** *natrium* sodium.
**NAAFI** See **Naafi** in Dict.
**Nah.** Nahum.
**NALGO** National and Local Government Officers' Association.
**N and Q** Notes and Queries.
**Nap.** Napoleon.
**NASA** National Aeronautics and Space Administration (USA).
**Nat.** National.
**nat.** *natus* born.
**nat. hist.** natural history.
**NATO** North Atlantic Treaty Organisation.
**nat. ord.** natural order.
**Nat. Phil.** natural philosophy.
**Nat. Sci.** Natural Science(s).
**NATSOPA** National Society of Operative Printers and Assistants (now **SOGAT**).
**Nat. West.** National Westminster Bank.
**naut.** nautical.
**nav.** naval; navigation.
**NAVAR** combined navigation and radar system.
**Nazi** *Nazionale Sozialisten* (Ger.) German National Socialist Party.
**NB** New Brunswick; North Britain; North British; North bag (in postal sorting); (or **nb**) *nota bene* note well, or take notice.
**Nb** niobium.
**NBC** National Broadcasting Company (USA).
**nbg** no bloody good.
**NBL** National Book League.
**NBPI** National Board for Prices and Incomes (usu. **PIB**).
**NBS** National Bureau of Standards (USA).
**NC** New Church; numerical control.
**N.C.** North Carolina.
**NCB** National Coal Board.
**NCCL** National Council for Civil Liberties.
**NCO** non-commissioned officer.
**NCR** National Cash Register Company.
**ncv** no commercial value.
**Nd** neodymium.
**N.D., N.Dak.** North Dakota.
**nd** no date, not dated.
**NDPS** National Data Processing Service.
**NE** north-east; New England.
**Ne** neon.
**NEB** New English Bible; National Enterprise Board.
**Neb., Nebr.** Nebraska.
**NED** New English Dictionary (now **OED**).
**NEDC** National Economic Development Council (Neddy).
**neg.** negative.
**Neh.** Nehemiah.
**NEI** *non est inventus* has not been found.
**nem. con.** *nemine contradicente* no one contradicting.
**nem. diss.** *nemine dissentiente* no one dissenting.
**Nep.** Neptune.
**NERC** Natural Environment Research Council.
**Neth.** Netherlands.
**neut.** neuter.
**Nev.** Nevada.
**New M.** New Mexico.
**NF** Norman French; Northern French.
**N.F., Nfd** Newfoundland.
**NFER** National Foundation for Educational Research.
**NFS** National Fire Service.
**NFU** National Farmers' Union.
**NFWI** National Federation of Women's Institutes.
**NGA** National Graphical Association.
**N.H.** New Hampshire.
**NHBRC** National House-Builders' Registration Council (or Certificate).
**NHI** National Health Insurance.
**NHS** National Health Service.

**NI** Northern Ireland; national insurance.

**Ni** nickel.

**NIBMAR** No Independence Before Majority Rule.

**NIC** National Incomes Commission (Nicky); Nicaragua (IVR).

**ni. pri.** *nisi prius*. See nisi in Dict.

**NIRC** National Industrial Relations Court.

**N.J.** New Jersey.

**NKVD** *Narodny Komitet Vnutrennikh Del* (Russ.) People's Committee of Internal Affairs.

**nl** *non licet* it is not permitted; *non liquet* it is not clear; *non longe* not far.

**NL** Netherlands (IVR).

**NLRB** National Labor Relations Board (USA).

**N.M., N. Mex.** New Mexico.

**n mile** international nautical mile.

**NNE** north-north-east.

**NNI** noise and number index.

**NNW** north-north-west.

**N.O.** New Orleans; natural order.

**No** nobelium.

**no** (or **No**) *numero* (in) number; not out.

**nom., nomin.** nominative.

**Non-Coll.** Non-Collegiate.

**non-com.** non-commissioned.

**Noncon.** Nonconformist.

**non obst.** *non obstante* notwithstanding.

**non pros.** *non prosequitur* does not prosecute.

**non seq.** *non sequitur* (see Dict.).

**non-U** not upper class (see Dict. under U).

**NOP** National Opinion Poll.

**nop** not otherwise provided.

**Northants** Northamptonshire.

**Northumb.** Northumberland.

**Norvic.** *Norvicensis* of Norwich.

**Nos, nos** numbers.

**Notts** Nottinghamshire.

**Nov.** November.

**NP** Notary Public; New Providence; (or **np**) new paragraph.

**Np** neptunium.

**np** no place (of publication).

**NPFA** National Playing Fields Association.

**NPG** National Portrait Gallery.

**NPL** National Physical Laboratory.

**nr** near.

**NRA** National Rifle Association.

**NS** New Style; Nova Scotia.

**ns** nanosecond(s); not specified.

**NSM** New Smoking Material.

**NSPCC** National Society for Prevention of Cruelty to Children.

**NSRA** National Small-bore Rifle Association.

**NSU** non-specific urethritis.

**NSW** New South Wales.

**NT** New Testament; Northern Territory; National Trust.

**ntp** normal temperature and pressure.

**NTS** National Trust for Scotland.

**NU** name unknown.

**NUBE** National Union of Bank Employees.

**NUGMW** National Union of General and Municipal Workers.

**NUI** National University of Ireland.

**NUJ** National Union of Journalists.

**NUM** National Union of Mineworkers.

**Num., Numb.** Numbers.

**NUPE** National Union of Public Employees.

**NUR** National Union of Railwaymen.

**NUS** National Union of Students; National Union of Seamen.

**NUT** National Union of Teachers.

**NV** New Version.

**nvd** no value declared.

**NVM** Nativity of the Virgin Mary.

**NW** north-west.

**NWT** North-west Territory (Canada).

**NY** New York (city or state).

**NYC** New York City.

**NYO** National Youth Orchestra.

**NZ** New Zealand (also IVR).

**O** oxygen.

**O.** Ohio.

**o/a** on account of.

**O&C** Oxford and Cambridge (Schools Examination Board).

**OAP** Old Age Pension or Pensioner.

**OAPEC** Organisation of Arab Petroleum-Exporting Countries.

**OAS** on active service; Organisation of American States.

**OAU** Organisation of African Unity.

**ob.** *obiit* died.

**Ob., Obad.** Obadiah.

**obdt** obedient.

**OBE** Officer of the Order of the British Empire.

**obj.** object; objective.

**obl.** oblique; oblong.

**obs.** obsolete; observation.

**o/c** overcharge.

**OC** Officer Commanding.

**OCF** Officiating Chaplain to the Forces.

**OCR** optical character recognition or reader.

**Oct.** October.

**oct.** octavo.

**OCTU** Officer Cadet Training Unit.

**OD** Ordnance Datum or Data.

**OE** Old English.

**OECD** Organisation for Economic Co-operation and Development.

**OED** Oxford English Dictionary.

**OEEC** Organisation for European Economic Co-operation (now **OECD**).

**OF** Old French; Oddfellow.

**off.** official; officinal.

**OFT** Office of Fair Trading.

**OHMS** On His (or Her) Majesty's Service.

**OIRT** *Organisation Internationale de Radiodiffusion et Télévision* (Fr.) International Organisation of Radio and Television (in East Europe).

**OK** See okay in Dict.

**Okla.** Oklahoma.

**Old Test.** Old Testament.

**OM** Order of Merit; Old Measurement.

**ONC** ordinary national certificate.

**OND** ordinary national diploma.

**ono** or near(est) offer.

**Ont.** Ontario.

**OP** *Ordinis Praedicatorum* of the Order of Preachers (or Dominicans); opposite prompt (*theat.*).

**Op.** Opera; Opus.

**op** out of print.

**op.** opposite; operation.

**op. cit.** *opere citato* in the work cited.

**OPEC** Organisation of Petroleum-Exporting Countries.

**opp.** opposed; opposite.

**Ops** Operations; Operations Officer; Operations room.

**OP's** other people's.

**opt.** optative; *optime* very well indeed.

**OR** other ranks; operations research.

**Or., Ore., Oreg.** Oregon.

**ord.** ordained; order; ordinary; ordnance.

**orig.** origin; original(ly).

**ORTF** *Organisation de Radio et Télévision Française* French Radio and Television Organisation (until 1975).

**OS** Old Style; Ordinary Seaman; outsize; Ordnance Survey.

**Os** osmium.

**OSA** *Ordinis Sancti Augustini* of the Order of St Augustine.

**OSB** *Ordinis Sancti Benedicti* of the Order of St Benedict.

**OSF** *Ordinis Sancti Francisci* of the Order of St Francis.

**osp** *obiit sine prole* died without issue.

**OStJ** Officer of Order of St John of Jerusalem.

**OT** Old Testament; occupational therapy.

**OTC** Officers' Training Corps.

OU   Open University.
OUDS   Oxford University Dramatic Society.
OUP   Oxford University Press.
Oxbridge   *Oxford* and Cam*bridge.*
Oxf.   Oxford.
OXFAM   *Ox*ford Committee for *Fam*ine Relief.
Oxon.   *Oxonia* Oxford; *Oxoniensis* of Oxford.
oz   ounce(s) (15th cent. It. *ōz,* abbreviation of *onza*).

P   phosphorus; poise (cgs unit); parking; President; Prince; pedal; peta- (see p 1644); Portugal (IVR).
*P*   power.
p   new penny; new pence; piano; pico- (see p 1644); page.
p.   participle.
PA   Press Association; Publishers Association; personal assistant; Public Address (system); Panama (IVR).
Pa   protactinium; pascal.
Pa., Penn.   Pennsylvania.
pa.   past.
p.a.   (or pa) per annum; participial adjective.
PA(B)X   Private Automatic (Branch) Exchange.
paint.   painting.
PAK   Pakistan (IVR).
Pal.   Palestine.
pam.   pamphlet.
Pan.   Panama.
Pan Am   Pan-American (World Airways Incorporated).
P and O   Peninsular and Oriental (Steamship Navigation Co.).
pa.p.   past participle.
par.   paragraph; parallel; parish.
pass.   passive.
pa.t.   past tense.
Pat. Off.   Patent Office.
PAYE   Pay As You Earn (Income Tax).
PB   Pharmacopoeia Britannica; Plymouth Brethren.
Pb   *plumbum* lead.
PBX   private branch exchange.
PC   Police Constable; Privy Councillor; *Patres Conscripti* Conscript Fathers.
pc   postcard.
PCM   pulse code modulation.
PCS   Principal Clerk of Session.
Pd   palladium.
pd   paid.
PDI   pre-delivery inspection.
PDSA   People's Dispensary for Sick Animals.
PE   Protestant Episcopal; physical education; Peru (IVR).
p/e   price-earnings ratio.
PEC   photoelectric cell.
ped.   pedal.
PEI   Prince Edward Island.
PEN   Poets, Playwrights, Editors, Essayists, and Novelists.
Pen.   Peninsula.
Penn., Pa.   Pennsylvania.
Pent.   Pentecost.
PEP   Political and Economic Planning.
per.   period; person.
per an.   per annum.
per cent   See Dict.
perf.   perfect.
perh.   perhaps.
per pro.   *per procurationem* by the agency (of).
Pers.   Persian.
pers.   person; personal.
Pes.   peseta (Spanish currency).
Petriburg.   *Petriburgensis* of Peterborough.
PF   Procurator Fiscal.
Pf   pfennig (German currency).
pf   piano-forte.
PFLP   Popular Front for the Liberation of Palestine.
PG   paying guest.
Pg.   Portugal; Portuguese.

PGA   Professional Golfers' Association.
PGM   Past Grand Master.
pH   pH-value (see Dict.).
phar., pharm.   pharmaceutical; pharmacopoeia; pharmacy.
PhB   *Philosophiae Baccalaureus* Bachelor of Philosophy.
PhD   *Philosophiae Doctor* Doctor of Philosophy.
Phil.   Philippians; Philadelphia; philology; philological; philosophy; philosophical.
Philem.   Philemon.
Phil. Trans.   Philosophical Transactions.
phon., phonet.   phonetics.
phonog.   phonography.
phot.   photography.
phr.   phrase.
phys.   physiology; physics; physician.
PIA   Pakistan International Airlines.
PIB   Prices and Incomes Board — National Board for Prices and Incomes.
pinx.   *pinxit* painted it.
PK   psychokinesis.
PL   Primrose League; Poet Laureate; Public Library; Poland (IVR).
PLA   Port of London Authority.
PLO   Palestine Liberation Organisation.
PLP   Parliamentary Labour Party.
PLR   public lending right.
plu., plur.   plural.
plup.   pluperfect.
PLUTO   Pipeline Under the Ocean (1944; later dismantled).
PM   Past Master; (or pm) *post meridiem* after noon; Postmaster; (or pm) *post mortem* after death; Prime Minister; Provost-Marshal.
Pm   promethium.
pm   premium.
PMBX   private manual branch exchange.
PMG   Postmaster-General; Paymaster-General.
PMO   Principal Medical Officer.
Pmr   Paymaster.
PMRAFNS   Princess Mary's Royal Air Force Nursing Service.
pn   promissory note.
PNdB   perceived noise decibel.
PO   Post Office; Petty Officer; Pilot Officer.
Po   polonium.
po   postal order.
po.   pole.
pod   pay on delivery.
Pol. Econ.   Political Economy.
POO   post-office order.
pop.   population; popular.
pos., posit.   positive.
POUNC   Post Office Users' National Council.
POW   prisoner of war.
PP   parish priest; present pupil; past President.
pp   pages; *per procurationem* by proxy (also *per pro* for and on behalf of); pianissimo.
p.p.   past participle.
PPC   *pour prendre congé* (Fr.) to take leave.
ppc   picture post-card.
PPE   Philosophy, Politics and Economics.
PPI   Plan Position Indicator.
ppp   pianississimo.
PPS   *post postscriptum* a later additional postscript; Parliamentary Private Secretary.
PQ   Province of Quebec.
PR   prize ring; Puerto Rico; proportional representation; *Populus Romanus* the Roman people; public relations.
Pr   praseodymium.
Pr.   Prince; priest; Provençal.
pr.   pair; per; present; price.
PRB   Pre-Raphaelite Brotherhood.
Preb.   Prebend; Prebendary.
pref.   preface.
prep.   preparation; preparatory; preposition.
Pres.   President.
pret.   preterite.
Prin.   Principal.
PRN   *pro re nata* for special occasion arising.

**PRO**  Public Relations Officer; Public Record Office.
**pro.**  professional; prostitute; probationary.
**prob.**  probably.
**Prof.**  Professor.
**prop** .  proper(ly); proposition; property.
**Prot.**  Protestant.
**pro tem.**  *pro tempore* for the time being.
**Prov.**  Proverbs; Provincial; Provost.
**prox.**  *proximo* (*mense*) next (month).
**prox. acc.**  *proxime accessit* next (in order of merit) to the winner.
**Pru.**  Prudential Assurance Company.
**PS**  *post scriptum* written after (something), a postscript; Philological Society; Pharmaceutical Society.
**Ps., Psa.**  Psalm(s).
**PSA**  pleasant Sunday afternoon; Property Services Agency; Public Services Authority.
**psc**  passed staff college.
**pseud.**  pseudonym.
**PST**  Pacific Standard. Time.
**PSV**  public service vehicle.
**PT**  physical training; pupil teacher; purchase tax.
**Pt**  platinum.
**pt**  part; pint(s); post-town.
**PTA**  Parent/Teacher Association.
**Pte**  private (military).
**PTFE**  polytetrafluoroethylene (see Dict.).
**PTO**  please turn over.
**pty.**  proprietary.
**PU**  pick-up.
**Pu**  plutonium.
**Pub. Doc.**  public document.
**pulv.**  *pulvis* powder (*pharm.*).
**PVC**  polyvinyl chloride.
**PWD**  Public Works Department.
**pwt**  pennyweight.
**pxt**  *pinxit* painted.
**PY**  Paraguay (IVR).

*Q*  symbol for electric charge; quality (-value).
**Q., Qu.**  query, question; (or Que.) Quebec; Queensland.
**q**  *quadrans* farthing; query; quintal.
**QAB**  Queen Anne's Bounty.
**QARANC**  Queen Alexandra's Royal Army Nursing Corps.
**QARNNS**  Queen Alexandra's Royal Naval Nursing Service.
**QB**  Queen's Bench.
**QC**  Queen's Counsel; Queen's College.
**qd**  *quasi dicat* as if he would say.
**qe**  *quod est* which is.
**QE2**  Queen Elizabeth the Second (liner).
**QED**  *quod erat demonstrandum* which was to be demonstrated.
**QEF**  *quod erat faciendum* which was to be done.
**QEH**  Queen Elizabeth Hall.
**QEI**  *quod erat inveniendum* which was to be found.
**qid**  *quater in die* four times a day.
**ql**  *quantum libet* as much as you please.
**QM**  Quartermaster.
**qm**  *quomodo* in what manner, how.
**QMG**  Quartermaster-General.
**QMS**  Quartermaster-Sergeant.
**QPR**  Queen's Park Rangers Football Club.
**qq**  quartos.
**qqv**  *quae vide* which (pl.) see (sing. qv).
**qr**  quarter.
**QS**  Quarter-Sessions.
**qs, quant. suff.**  *quantum sufficit* a sufficient quantity.
**QSO**  quasi-stellar object (quasar).
**qt**  quantity; quart(s).
**q.t.**  quiet.
**qto**  quarto.
**qty**  quantity.
**Qu.**  Queen; question.
**qu., quar.**  quart; quarter(ly).

**quango**  quasi non-governmental organisation; quasi autonomous national governmental organisation.
**qv**  *quod vide* which (sing.) see (pl. qqv); *quantum vis* as much as you will.

**R**  *rex, regina* King, Queen; rand (S. African currency); Röntgen unit; (or **Réau**) Réaumur's thermometric scale; Romania (IVR).
*R*  symbol for electric resistance.
®  registered trade mark
**r**  right; radius; *recipe* take.
**RA**  Royal Academy or Academician; Royal Artillery; Rear Admiral; Argentina (IVR).
**Ra**  radium.
**RAAF**  Royal Australian Air Force.
**Rabb.**  Rabbinical.
**RAC**  Royal Automobile Club; Royal Armoured Corps; Royal Arch Charter.
**Rad.**  Radical.
**rad**  radian.
**rad.**  *radix* root.
**RADA**  Royal Academy of Dramatic Art.
**RADC**  Royal Army Dental Corps.
**RAEC**  Royal Army Educational Corps.
**RAeS**  Royal Aeronautical Society.
**RAF**  Royal Air Force.
**RAM**  Royal Academy of Music.
**r.a.m.**  relative atomic mass.
**RAMC**  Royal Army Medical Corps.
**RAN**  Royal Australian Navy.
**R and A**  Royal and Ancient (Golf Club) St Andrews.
**R and D**  research and development.
**RAOC**  Royal Army Ordnance Corps.
**RAPC**  Royal Army Pay Corps.
**RAS**  Royal Astronomical Society; Royal Asiatic Society.
**RAVC**  Royal Army Veterinary Corps.
**RAX**  rural automatic exchange.
**RB**  Rifle Brigade; Botswana (IVR).
**Rb**  rubidium.
**RBA**  Royal Society of British Artists.
**RBS**  Royal Society of British Sculptors.
**RC**  Roman Catholic; Red Cross; Royal College of Art; Taiwan (IVR).
**RCA**  Royal Canadian Academy; Radio Corporation of America; Central African Republic (IVR).
**RCAF**  Royal Canadian Air Force.
**RCB**  Congo (IVR).
**RCH**  Chile (IVR).
**RCM**  Royal College of Music; Regimental Court-martial.
**RCMP**  Royal Canadian Mounted Police.
**RCN**  Royal Canadian Navy.
**RCO**  Royal College of Organists.
**RCOG**  Royal College of Obstetricians and Gynaecologists.
**RCP**  Royal College of Physicians; Royal College of Preceptors.
**RCS**  Royal College of Surgeons; Royal Corps of Signals; Royal College of Science.
**RCT**  Royal Corps of Transport.
**RCVS**  Royal College of Veterinary Surgeons.
**RD**  Rural Dean; Naval Reserve Decoration; refer to drawer.
**Rd**  Road; rand (S. African currency).
**rd**  rutherford.
**RDC**  Rural District Council.
**RDS**  Royal Dublin Society.
**RdTh**  radiothorium.
**RE**  Royal Engineers; Royal Society of Etchers and Engravers; Royal Exchange.
**Re**  rhenium.
**Réau**  Réaumur's thermometric scale.
**rec.**  *recipe* take.
**recd**  received.
**REconS**  Royal Economic Society.
**recpt**  receipt.
**Rect.**  Rector; Rectory.
**ref.**  referee; reference.

**Ref. Ch.** Reformed Church.
**Reg. Prof.** Regius Professor.
**regt** regiment.
**rel.** relating; relation; relative.
**rel. d.** relative density.
**REM** rapid eye movement (see **rapid** in Dict.).
**REME** Royal Electrical and Mechanical Engineers.
**rep.** representative; republic; report; reporter.
**rept** receipt; report.
**retd** retired; returned.
**Rev.** revise(d); revision; Revelation; (or **Revd**) Reverend.
**rev** revolution.
**Rev. Ver.** Revised Version.
**RF** *République française* (Fr.) French Republic; radio frequency.
**Rf** rutherfordium.
**RFC** Royal Flying Corps (now **RAF**); Rugby Football Club.
**RFU** Rugby Football Union.
**RGG** Royal Grenadier Guards.
**RGN** Registered General Nurse.
**RGS** Royal Geographical Society.
**Rgt** Regiment.
**RH** Royal Highness; Haiti (IVR).
**Rh** rhodium; rhesus (see Dict.).
**rh** right hand.
**RHA** Royal Horse Artillery; Royal Hibernian Academy; Road Haulage Association.
**rhet.** rhetoric.
**RHF** Royal Highland Fusiliers.
**RHG** Royal Horse Guards.
**RHistS** Royal Historical Society.
**RHM** Rank Hovis McDougall.
**RHS** Royal Humane Society; Royal Horticultural Society; Royal Historical Society; Royal Highland Show.
**RI** Royal Institute of Painters in Water Colours; Rhode Island; religious instruction; Indonesia (IVR).
**RIA** Royal Irish Academy.
**RIAM** Royal Irish Academy of Music.
**RIBA** Royal Institute of British Architects.
**RIC** Royal Irish Constabulary; Royal Institute of Chemistry.
**RICS** Royal Institution of Chartered Surveyors.
**RIGB** Royal Institution of Great Britain.
**RIM** Mauritania (IVR).
**RIP** *requiescat in pace* may he (or she) rest in peace.
**RIPHH** Royal Institute of Public Health and Hygiene.
**RJET** remote job entry terminal.
**RL** Lebanon (IVR).
**RLO** returned letter office.
**RLS** Robert Louis Stevenson.
**Rly, rly** railway.
**RM** Royal Mail; Royal Marines; resident magistrate; riding master; Malagasy Republic (IVR).
**RMA** Royal Military Academy, Sandhurst; Royal Marine Artillery.
**RMetS** Royal Meteorological Society.
**RMM** Mali (IVR).
**RMO** Resident Medical Officer.
**RMP** (Corps of) Royal Military Police.
**RMS** Royal Mail Steamer; Royal Microscopical Society.
**rms** root-mean-square.
**RN** Royal Navy.
**Rn** radon.
**RNA** ribonucleic acids (see **ribose** in Dict.).
**RNAS** Royal Naval Air Service(s).
**RNIB** Royal National Institute for the Blind.
**RNLI** Royal National Lifeboat Institution.
**RNR** Royal Naval Reserve.
**RNVR** Royal Naval Volunteer Reserve.
**RNZAF** Royal New Zealand Air Force.
**RNZN** Royal New Zealand Navy.
**ro** *recto* on the right-hand page.
**ROC** Royal Observer Corps.

**Roffen.** *Roffensis* of Rochester.
**ROI** Royal Institute of Oil Painters.
**ROK** Korea (IVR).
**Rom.** Romans.
**rom.** roman (in printing).
**Rom.Cath.** Roman Catholic.
**Ro-Ro** roll-on-roll-off.
**ROSLA** raising of school leaving age.
**ROSPA** see **RSPA**.
**RP** Reformed Presbyterian; Regius Professor; Received Pronunciation; Royal Society of Portrait Painters.
**RPA** radiation protection adviser.
**RPI** retail price index.
**RPM** retail price maintenance.
**rpm, rps** revolutions per minute, second.
**RPN** reverse Polish notation.
**RPO** Royal Philharmonic Orchestra.
**RPS** Royal Photographic Society.
**RR** Right Reverend.
**RRE** Radar Research Establishment.
**RRP** recommended retail price.
**RS** Royal Society.
**Rs** Rupees.
**RSA** Royal Society of Antiquaries; Royal Society of Arts; Royal Scottish Academy or Academician; Republic of South Africa.
**RSE** Royal Society of Edinburgh.
**RSFSR** Russian Soviet Federated Socialist Republic.
**RSG** Regional Seats of Government.
**RSGS** Royal Scottish Geographical Society.
**RSL** Royal Society of Literature.
**RSLA** raising of school leaving age.
**RSM** Regimental Sergeant-Major; Royal Society of Medicine; Royal School of Music; San Marino (IVR).
**RSO** railway sub-office; railway sorting office; rural sub-office; radiological safety officer; Resident Surgical Officer.
**RSPA, Rospa** Royal Society for the Prevention of Accidents.
**RSPB** Royal Society for the Protection of Birds.
**RSPCA** Royal Society for the Prevention of Cruelty to Animals.
**RSR** Rhodesia (IVR).
**RSS** (or **SRS**) *Regiae Societatis Socius* Fellow of the Royal Society: Royal Statistical Society.
**RSSA** Royal Scottish Society of Arts.
**RSSPCC** Royal Scottish Society for Prevention of Cruelty to Children.
**RSV** Revised Standard Version.
**RSVP** *répondez s'il vous plait* (Fr.) reply, if you please.
**RSW** Royal Scottish Water Colour Society.
**RT** radiotelephone, -phony.
**RTE** *Radio Telefís Éireann* (Ir.) Irish Television.
**Rt Hon.** Right Honourable.
**RTO** Railway Transportation (or Traffic) Officer.
**Rt Rev.** Right Reverend.
**RTZ** Rio Tinto Zinc Corporation Limited.
**RU** Rugby Union; Burundi (IVR).
**Ru** ruthenium.
**RUC** Royal Ulster Constabulary.
**R-unit** Röntgen unit — unit of measurement of X-ray radiation.
**RV** Revised Version.
**RW** Right Worthy.
**RWA** Rwanda (IVR).
**RWS** Royal Society of Painters in Water Colours.
**Ry, ry** railway.
**RYA** Royal Yachting Association.
**RYS** Royal Yacht Squadron.
**RZS** Royal Zoological Society (E, of Edinburgh).

**S** sulphur; square; stokes; Schmieder (catalogue of Bach's works); siemens; South; Sabbath; Saint; society; sun; Sweden (IVR).
**s** second(s).
**$** dollar.

SA  South Africa; South America; South Australia; Salvation Army; sex-appeal; *Société anonyme* (Fr.) limited liability company; Society of Arts; Society of Antiquaries (Scot., of Scotland); *Sturmabteilung* (Ger.) see Dict.

sa  *secundum artem* according to art; *sine anno* without date.

SAA  Small Arms Ammunition; South African Airways; Society of Incorporated Accountants (formerly, and Auditors).

SABENA  *Société anonyme belge d'exploitation de la navigation aérienne* (Fr.) Belgian national airline.

sae  stamped addressed envelope.

Salop  See Dict.

SALT  Strategic Arms Limitation Talks.

SAM  surface-to-air missile.

Sam.  Samuel.

SARAH  Search and Rescue and Homing.

Sarum  *Sarumensis* of Salisbury.

SAS  *Societatis Antiquariorum Socius* Fellow of the Society of Antiquaries; Scandinavian Airlines System; Special Air Service.

Sask.  Saskatchewan.

Sat.  Saturday.

S.A.T.B.  soprano, alto, tenor, bass.

SAYE  save as you earn.

Sb  *stibium* antimony.

SBN  Standard Book Number.

SC  *senatus consultum* a decree of the Roman senate; Special Constable; Supreme Court; Staff College; Staff Corps.

S.C.  South Carolina.

Sc  scandium.

sc  *scilicet* namely; *sculpsit* (he) sculptured (the); (or s. caps, sm. caps) small capitals (in printing).

s/c  self-contained.

ScB  *Scientiae Baccalaureus* Bachelor of Science.

ScD  *Scientiae Doctor* Doctor of Science.

SCDA  Scottish Community Drama Association.

SCE  Scottish Certificate of Education.

SCF  Save the Children Fund.

Sch.  schilling (Austrian currency); school.

sci.fa.  *scire facias* that you cause to know.

sci. fi.  science fiction.

scil., sciz,  *scilicet* namely (cf. viz.).

SCL  Student of Civil Law.

SCM  Student Christian Movement; State Certified Midwife.

Scot.  Scotland; Scottish.

SCR  senior common room.

Script.  Scripture.

SCUBA  self-contained underwater breathing apparatus.

sculp., sculpt.  *sculpsit* (he) sculptured (this); sculpture; sculptor.

SD  Senior Deacon; *salutem dicit* send greeting; standard deviation; Swaziland (IVR).

S.D., S.Dak.  South Dakota.

sd  *sine die* without a day (fixed).

SDA  Scottish Development Agency.

SDC  single data converter.

SDD  Scottish Development Department.

SDLP  Social and Democratic Labour Party.

SDP  social, domestic and pleasure.

SDR  special drawing rights.

SE  south-east; Society of Engineers.

Se  selenium.

SEAC  South-East Asia Command.

SEATO  South-East Asia Treaty Organisation.

Sec., Secy  Secretary.

sec  secant.

sec.  *secundum* in accordance with; second; section.

sech  hyperbolic secant.

sec. leg.  *secundum legem* according to law.

sec. reg.  *secundum regulam* according to rule.

sect.  section.

SED  Scottish Education Department.

Sem.  seminary; Semitic.

SEN  State Enrolled Nurse.

Sen.  Senator; senior.

Sep., Sept.  September; Septuagint.

seq.  *sequens* following (pl. seqq., *sequentes* or *sequentia*).

ser.  series; sermon.

Serg., Sergt  Sergeant.

Serj., Serjt  Serjeant.

Sess.  Session.

SET  Selective Employment Tax.

SF  science fiction; Sinn Fein; signal frequency; Finland (IVR).

SFA  Scottish Football Association; Sweet Fanny Adams.

sfz  sforzando.

SG  Solicitor-General.

sg  specific gravity.

SGF  Scottish Grocers' Federation.

SGHWR  steam-generating heavy water reactor.

SGP  Singapore (IVR).

SHAEF  Supreme Headquarters of the Allied Expeditionary Force.

SHAPE  Supreme Headquarters Allied Powers Europe.

shv  *sub hoc verbo* or *sub hac voce* under this word.

SI  Système International (d'Unités) — see p 1644.

Si  silicon.

sig.  signature.

sin  sine.

sing.  singular.

sinh  hyperbolic sine.

SIPRI  Stockholm International Peace Research Institute.

SIS  Secret Intelligence Service.

SJ  Society of Jesus.

SL  Solicitor at Law; Sergeant-at-Law; (or S Lat.) South latitude.

SLADE  Society of Lithographic Artists, Designers, Engravers and Process Workers.

sld  sailed.

slp  *sine legitima prole* without lawful issue.

SM  Short Metre; Sergeant-Major; *Sa Majesté* (Fr.) His (or Her) Majesty.

Sm  samarium.

SMC  Scottish Mountaineering Club.

SME  Surinam (IVR).

Smith. Inst.  Smithsonian Institution.

SMLondSoc  *Societatis Medicae Londiniensis Socius* Member of the London Medical Society.

SMM  *Sancta Mater Maria* Holy Mother Mary.

SMMT  Society of Motor Manufacturers and Traders.

SMO  Senior Medical Officer.

SMP  School Mathematics Project.

smp  *sine mascula prole* without male issue.

SN  Senegal (IVR).

Sn  *stannum* tin.

sn  *secundum naturam* according to nature.

SNCF  *Société Nationale des Chemins de Fer français* (Fr.) French national railways.

SNO  Scottish National Orchestra.

SNP  Scottish National Party.

SO  Staff Officer; Signal Officer; standing order; special order.

so  seller's option.

s.o.b.  son of a bitch.

Soc.  Society.

SOGAT  Society of Graphical and Allied Trades.

Sol., Solr  Solicitor.

sol.  solution.

Sol.-Gen.  Solicitor-General.

sop.  soprano.

SOS  See Dict.

sp  *sine prole* without issue

sp.  spelling; species (pl. spp.).

SPCK  Society for Promoting Christian Knowledge.

sp.gr.  specific gravity (now relative density).

sport.  sporting.

SPQR  *Senatus Populusque Romanus* the Senate and People of Rome.

## 1623

SPR Society for Psychical Research.
sps *sine prole superstite* without surviving issue.
spt seaport.
sp.vol. specific volume.
sq. (or Sq.) square; *sequens* following (in pl. sqq., *sequentes* or *sequentia*).
sqn squadron.
SR Southern Region; Southern Railway (now incorporated in BR).
Sr senior; Sir; Señor; strontium.
sr steradian.
SRC Science Research Council; Student Representative Council.
SRCh State Registered Chiropodist.
SRI *Sacrum Romanum Imperium* Holy Roman Empire.
SRN State Registered Nurse.
SRS (or RSS) *Societatis Regiae Socius* Fellow of the Royal Society.
SRU Scottish Rugby Union.
SS Saints; *Schutzstaffel* (Ger.) see Dict.
ss steamship; screw steamer.
SSAFA Soldiers', Sailors' and Airmen's Families Association.
SSC Solicitor before the Supreme Court (Scotland); *Societas Sanctae Crucis* Society of the Holy Cross.
SSD *Sanctissimus Dominus* Most Holy Lord (the Pope).
SSE south-south-east.
SSM surface-to-surface missile.
SSN Standard Serial Number.
SSPCA Scottish Society for Prevention of Cruelty to Animals.
SSRC Social Science Research Council.
SST supersonic transport.
SSW south-south-west.
St Saint; Strait; Street; stokes.
st. stone (weight).
Staffs Staffordshire.
STD subscriber trunk dialling.
std standard.
Ste *Sainte* (Fr.) fem. of Saint.
ster., stereo stereophonic; stereotype.
ster., stg sterling.
STOL short take-off and landing.
STP *Sanctae Theologiae Professor* Professor of Theology.
stp standard temperature and pressure.
str steamer.
str. strong.
STS Scottish Text Society.
STUC Scottish Trades Union Congress.
STV Scottish Television.
SU strontium unit — unit of measurement of strontium radiation; Scripture Union; Soviet Union (also IVR).
sub. subject.
subj. subject; subjunctive.
subst. substitute; substantive.
suf., suff. suffix.
sup. superfine; superior; (or superl.) superlative; supreme; *supra* above; supine; supplement.
Sup. Ct Superior Court; Supreme Court.
superl. superlative.
supp., suppl. supplement.
Supr. Supreme.
Supt Superintendent.
Surg. surgeon; surgery.
Surv.-Gen. Surveyor-General.
SV *Sancta Virgo* Holy Virgin; *Sanctitas Vestra* Your Holiness.
sv *sub voce* under that heading; *sub verbo* under the word.
SW south-west; small women('s); short wave.
SWA South West Africa (IVR).
SWALK sealed with a loving kiss.
SWG standard wire gauge.
SY Seychelles (IVR).
SYHA Scottish Youth Hostels Association.
sym. symbol.
syn. synonym.

synop. synopsis.
syr. *syrupus* syrup.
syst. system.

T tritium; tesla; tera- (see p 1644); Thailand (IVR).
t tonne (cf. l, litre).
t time.
TA Territorial Army (from 1967 T and AVR).
Ta tantalum.
tal. qual. *talis qualis* just as they come, average quality.
Tam. Tamil.
tan tangent.
T and AVR Territorial and Army Volunteer Reserve.
tanh hyperbolic tangent.
TASS *Telegrafnoye Agentsvo Sovietskovo Soyuza* (Russ.) telegraph agency of the Soviet Union.
Tb terbium.
TB tuberculosis.
TBD torpedo-boat destroyer.
Tc technetium.
tc tierce.
TCD Trinity College Dublin; Twentieth Century Dictionary.
TCL Trinity College of Music, London.
TCP trichlorophenylmethyliodosalicyl (proprietary germicide).
TD Territorial Decoration; *Teachta Dála* (Ir.) member of the Dail.
Te tellurium.
tech. technical; technology.
TEFL teaching English as a foreign language.
tel. telephone.
tel., teleg. telegram; telegraph.
temp. temporal; *tempore* in the time of; temperature; temporary.
Ten., Tenn. Tennessee.
ten. tenor; tenuto.
Ter., Terr. Territory; terrace.
term. termination.
TES Times Educational Supplement.
TESL teaching English as a second language.
Test. Testament.
Teut. Teutonic.
Tex. Texas.
Text. Rec. *textus receptus* the revised text.
TF Territorial Force.
tf till forbidden.
TFR Territorial Force Reserve.
TG Togo (IVR).
TGWU Transport and General Workers' Union.
Th thorium.
Th. Thursday.
ThD Doctor of Theology.
theat. theatrical.
theol. theology; theologian.
theor. theorem.
THES Times Higher Educational Supplement.
Thess. Thessalonians.
THF Trust Houses Forte.
ThL Theological Licentiate.
Tho., Thos Thomas.
THWM Trinity High-water Mark.
TI Tube Investments.
Ti titanium.
tid *ter in die* thrice a day.
TIF *Transports Internationaux par Chemin de Fer* (Fr.) International Rail Transport.
Tim. Timothy.
TIR *Transports Internationaux Routiers* (Fr.) International Road Transport.
TIROS Television and Infrared Observation Satellite.
Tit. Titus.
Tl thallium.
TLS Times Literary Supplement.
TM transcendental meditation.
Tm thulium.
TN trade name; Tunisia (IVR).
TNT trinitrotoluene.

**TO** turn over; Telegraph-office; Transport Officer.
**Toc H** Talbot House.
**tom.** *tomus* tome or volume.
**tp** township; troop.
**TPI** Town Planning Institute.
**tpr** teleprinter.
**TR** Turkey (IVR).
**tr.** transpose; transactions; translator; trustee.
**trans.** transitive; translated; translation.
**transf.** transferred.
**treas.** treasurer.
**TRH** Their Royal Highnesses.
**trig.** trigonometry.
**Trin.** Trinity.
**Truron.** *Truronensis* of Truro.
**TSB** Trustee Savings Bank.
**TSO** town sub-office.
**TT** teetotal; Tourist Trophy; tuberculin tested; Trinidad and Tobago (IVR).
**TTL** to take leave.
**tty** teletypewriter.
**Tu., Tues.** Tuesday.
**TUC** Trades Union Congress.
**TV** television.
**TVA** Tennessee Valley Authority.
**TVP** texturised vegetable protein.
**TWA** Trans-World Airlines.
**TWI** Training within Industry.
**typ., typo.** typographer; typography.

**U** uranium; universal (motion picture certificate); Unionist; upper-class (see Dict. under U); Uruguay (IVR).
**UAR** United Arab Republic.
**UCAR** Union of Central African Republics.
**UCCA** Universities Central Council on Admissions.
**UDA** Ulster Defence Association.
**UDC** Urban District Council; Universal Decimal Classification.
**UDI** Unilateral Declaration of Independence.
**UDR** Ulster Defence Regiment.
**UDT** United Dominions Trust.
**UEFA** Union of European Football Associations.
**UF** United Free Church (of Scotland).
**UFF** Ulster Freedom Fighters.
**UFO** unidentified flying object.
**UGC** University Grants Committee.
**UHF** ultra high frequency.
**UJD** *Utriusque Juris Doctor* Doctor of both Laws (Canon and Civil).
**UK** United Kingdom.
**UKAEA** United Kingdom Atomic Energy Authority.
**ULCC** ultra large crude carrier.
**ult., ulto** *ultimo* in the last (month), ultimate(ly).
**UMIST** University of Manchester Institute of Science and Technology.
**UN** United Nations.
**UNA** United Nations Association.
**UNCTAD, Unctad** United Nations Commission for Trade and Development.
**UNEP** United Nations Environment Programme.
**UNESCO** United Nations Educational, Scientific and Cultural Organisation.
**UNICEF** United Nations International Children's Emergency Fund — now United Nations Children's Fund.
**UNIDO** United Nations Industrial Development Organisation.
**Unit.** Unitarian.
**Univ.** University; Universalist.
**UNO** United Nations Organisation.
**UNRRA** United Nations Relief and Rehabilitation Administration.
**UP** United Presbyterian; United Press.
**UPU** Universal Postal Union.
**Uru.** Uruguay.
**US** United States; United Service(s); Under-secretary.

**us** *ut supra* as above.
**USA** United States of America (also IVR) United States Army.
**USAF** United States Air Force.
**USCL** United Society for Christian Literature
**USDAW** Union of Shop, Distributive and Allied Workers.
**USIS** United States Information Service.
**USN** United States Navy.
**USPG** United Society for the Propagation of the Gospel.
**USS** United States Ship or Steamer.
**USSR** (also CCCP (Russ.)) Union of Soviet Socialist Republics.
**usu.** usually.
**USW** ultrasonic waves; ultrashort waves.
**usw** *und so weiter* (Ger.) and so forth.
**UT** Universal Time (see Dict.).
**Ut.** Utah.
**ut dict.** *ut dictum* as said.
**ut sup.** *ut supra* as above.
**UU** Ulster Unionist.
**uv** ultraviolet.
**UVF** Ulster Volunteer Force.
**UWIST** University of Wales Institute of Science and Technology.
**ux.** *uxor* wife.

**V** vanadium; volt; Vatican City (IVR).
*V* symbol for electric potential difference.
**v** velocity; *versus* against; *vide* see; verb; verse; volume.
**V1** *Vergeltungswaffe 1* German flying bomb.
**V2** German flying rocket.
**VA** Royal Order of Victoria and Albert; Vicar Apostolic; volt-ampere(s).
**Va.** Virginia.
**vac.** vacuum, vacation.
**VAD** Voluntary Aid Detachment.
**val.** value.
**V and A** Victoria and Albert Museum.
**VAr** volt-ampere(s)-reactive.
**var.** variant; variety; variable.
**var. lect.** *varia lectio* variant reading.
**VAT** Value-added Tax.
**Vat.** Vatican
**vb** verb.
**VC** Victoria Cross; Vice-Chancellor; Vice-Consul.
**VCR** video cassette recorder.
**VD** Venereal Disease(s); Volunteer (Officers') Decoration.
**vd** various dates; vapour density.
**VDC** Volunteer Defence Corps.
**VDM** *Verbi Dei Minister* Preacher of God's Word.
**VDQS** *Vins délimités de qualité supérieure* (Fr.) wines of superior quality from approved vineyards.
**VDU** visual display unit.
**VE** Victory in Europe (1945).
**veg.** vegetable(s).
**vel.** velocity.
**Ven.** Venerable.
**Venet.** Venetian.
**VERA** versatile reactor assembly; vision electronic recording apparatus.
**verb. sap.** *verbum sapienti*, or **verb. sat.**, *verbum sat(is)* a word to the wise is enough (see p 1604).
**Vert.** Vertebrata.
**ves.** vessel.
**Vet., Veter.** Veterinary.
**Vet. Surg.** Veterinary Surgeon.
**VF** voice frequency; video frequency.
**VG** Vicar-General; (or vg) very good.
**vg** *verbi gratia* for example.
**VHF** very high frequency.
**v.i.** verb intransitive.
**Vic.** Vicar; Vicarage.
**Vict.** Victoria; Victoria University.
**vid.** *vide* see.
**vil(l).** village.

VIP   Very Important Person.
VIR   *Victoria Imperatrix Regina.* See **VRI.**
Vis., Visc.   Viscount.
viz   *videlicet* namely (z = mediaeval Latin symbol of contraction).
VJ   Victory over Japan (1945).
vl   *varia lectio* variant reading (pl. **vvll**).
VLCC   very large crude carrier.
VLF   very low frequency.
VMH   Victoria Medal of Honour (of the Royal Horticultural Society).
VN   Vietnam (IVR).
vo   *verso* on the left-hand page.
voc.   vocative.
vocab.   vocabulary.
vol.   volunteer; volume.
VP   Vice-President.
VR   *Victoria Regina* Queen Victoria.
VRD   Volunteer Reserve Decoration.
VRI   *Victoria Regina et Imperatrix* Victoria, Queen and Empress.
VRQ   verbal reasoning quotient.
VS   Veterinary Surgeon; *volti subito* turn quickly.
VSO   Voluntary Service Overseas.
VSOP   very special old pale.
Vt   Vermont.
v.t.   verb transitive.
VTO(L)   vertical take-off (and landing).
VTR   video tape recorder.
Vul., Vulg.   Vulgate.
vul., vulg.   vulgar.
vvll   See **vl.**
VW   *Volkswagen* (Ger.) people's car.
vy   various years.

W   *wolframium* tungsten; watt; West; Welsh; women('s).
w   weak.
WA   West Africa; Western Australia.
WAAC   Women's Army Auxiliary Corps (now **WRAC**).
WAAF   Women's Auxiliary Air Force (earlier and later **WRAF**).
WAG   Gambia (IVR).
WAL   Sierra Leone (IVR).
Wal.   Walloon.
WAN   Nigeria (IVR).
Wash.   Washington.
WASP   White Anglo-Saxon Protestant.
Wb   weber.
WBA   West Bromwich Albion Football Club; World Boxing Association of America.
WBC   World Boxing Council.
WC   water-closet; Western Central; Wesleyan Chapel.
WCC   World Council of Churches.
W/Cdr   Wing-Commander.
WCT   World Championship Tennis.
WD   War Department; Dominica, Windward Islands (IVR).
WEA   Workers' Educational Association.
Wed.   Wednesday.
wef   with effect from.
WEU   Western European Union.
wf   wrong fount (in printing).
WFTU   World Federation of Trade Unions.
WG   Granada, Windward Islands (IVR).
wg   wire gauge.
WHO   World Health Organisation.
WI   West Indies; Women's Institute.
Wigorn.   *Wigorniensis* of Worcester.

Wilts   Wiltshire.
Winton.   *Wintoniensis* of Winchester.
Wis.   Wisconsin.
wk   week.
WL   St Lucia, Windward Islands (IVR).
WLA   Women's Land Army (disbanded 1950).
WLF   Women's Liberal Federation.
Wm   William.
WMO   World Meteorological Organisation.
WNP   Welsh Nationalist Party.
WNW   west-north-west.
WO   War Office (1964 absorbed in Ministry of Defence); Warrant Officer; walk-over.
Worcs   Worcestershire.
Wp, Wpfl   Worshipful.
WP   Warsaw Pact.
wp   weather permitting.
wpb   wastepaper basket.
wpm   words per minute.
WR   Western Region.
WRAC   Women's Royal Army Corps.
WRAF   Women's Royal Air Force.
WRI   Women's Rural Institute.
WRNS   Women's Royal Naval Service.
WRVS   Woman's Royal Voluntary Service (previously **WVS**).
WS   Writer to the Signet; Western Samoa (IVR).
WSW   west-south-west.
wt   weight.
WV   St Vincent, Windward Islands (IVR).
W.Va.   West Virginia.
WVS   Women's Voluntary Service (now **WRVS**).
WWF   World Wildlife Fund.
wx   women's extra.
Wy., Wyo.   Wyoming.

X   Used to mark motion pictures to which persons under eighteen will not be admitted.
X, Xt   Christ. (*X* = Gr. *Ch*)
x   *ex* (L. without), as in **x.d.**, ex dividend.
Xe.   xenon.
Xm., Xmas   Christmas.
Xn, Xtian   Christian.

Y   yttrium; yen (Japanese currency).
y   year; yard.
Yb   ytterbium.
yd   yard.
ye   the (the y not being a y but representing the old letter thorn, þ).
Yeo.   Yeomanry.
YHA   Youth Hostels Association.
YMCA   Young Men's Christian Association.
Yn   yen (Japanese currency).
Yorks.   Yorkshire.
yr   your; younger; year.
yt   that (*y* as in ye above).
YU   Yugoslavia (IVR).
YV   Venezuela (IVR).
YWCA   Young Women's Christian Association.

Z   Zambia (IVR).
ZA   South Africa (IVR).
zB   *zum Beispiel* (Ger.) for example.
Zech.   Zechariah.
Zeph.   Zephaniah.
Zn   zinc.
ZPG   zero population growth.
ZR   Zaire (IVR).
Zr   zirconium.
ZST   Zone Standard Time.

# Musical terms, signs and abbreviations

## Pitch

The **pitch** (high or low) of a musical sound depends on its frequency, i.e. the number of vibrations per second; it is denoted by the position of a note on the staff (see below).

The **staff** (or **stave**) consists of the five horizontal lines and four spaces on which the notes are written. To accommodate notes beyond its compass, short lines (**ledger lines**) may be added.

The **clef**, the sign placed at the beginning of each staff, defines the pitch of a note. There are three clefs in use today. The G (treble) clef and the F (bass) clef are always fixed in the same position on the staff and denote the position of G and F respectively.

G A B C D E F G

G or treble clef

F G A B C D E

F or bass clef

The third, or C clef, is movable and is named the soprano, alto, or tenor clef according as it is placed on the 1st, 3rd, or 4th line of the staff. Middle C is shown in each example:

The **key signature** is the arrangement of sharps or flats at the beginning of a piece or section of a piece, and at the start of each subsequent line, showing in which key the music is to be performed.

## Values of Notes and Rests

In the example below, each note is twice the length of that which follows. The sign to the right of each note is a rest of equal duration:

A **dot** added to a note or rest lengthens it by half its value:

A **double dot** added to a note or rest lengthens it by half as much again as one dot:

Notes of quaver denomination or less are usually joined together to form units of crotchet or minim value:

The staff is divided into **bars**, or measures, with an equal number of beats, by vertical lines (**bar lines**); the most strongly accented beat is usually the first note in each bar:

The main sections of a piece or movement are terminated by a **double bar**, as shown above.

Silence for a complete bar is usually indicated by a semibreve rest, whatever the time value of the bar. A number added above indicates silence for that number of bars.

## Repetition of Passages, Bars or Notes

Repeat the group of notes:

Repeat the bar:

Repeat the bar so many times:

Repeat the note as shown:

## Time Signature

The sign, consisting of a lower and an upper figure, follows the key signature at the beginning of a piece or section of a piece; the lower figure shows the value of the note used as the basic beat (2 = minim, 4 = crotchet, etc.), the upper the number of such beats in the bar:

## Terms, Directions and Signs

**accel., accelerando.** Gradually increasing in speed.

**acciaccatura.** An ornament played as quickly as possible before the principal note to which it is attached:

**accidental.** A sign (sharp ♯, flat ♭, or natural ♮) used to contradict temporarily a key signature by inflecting a note up or down a semitone. Its effect lasts only for the bar in which it appears (and only for that octave), unless the note is tied over into the next bar.

**ad lib., ad libitum.** The performer is at liberty to play the passage freely as regards rhythm or tempo, or to omit the passage, depending on the context.

**alla breve.** Two minims ($\frac{2}{2}$) to the bar, instead of four crotchets ($\frac{4}{4}$), i.e. an indication that the tempo should be doubled:

**anim., animato.** Animatedly.

**appoggiatura.** An ornament that 'leans' on the note to which it is attached. Unlike the acciaccatura, which is virtually timeless, it usually occupies half the time value of the succeeding note:

**arco.** With the bow (cf. **pizzicato**).

**a tem., a tempo.** In time, i.e. reverting to the original speed.

**bind.** See **tie**.

**cal., calando.** Gradually decreasing in speed and volume.

**colla voce.** An instruction to the accompanist to follow the singer closely (lit. 'with the voice').

**col legno.** Strike the strings with the stick of the bow (lit. 'with the wood').

**common time.** Four crotchet beats in the bar, usu. written as:

**con sordino.** Attach mute to instrument.

**cresc., crescendo.** Gradually increasing in volume. Also:

**dash.** When placed over or under a note, implies a very detached staccato style.

**D.C., da capo (al fine, or al segno).** The performer must return to the beginning of the movement (and play to the end, *or* to the sign 𝄋).

**decresc., decrescendo.** Gradually decreasing in volume. Also:

**dim., diminuendo.** Gradually becoming softer.

**dot.** When placed over or under a note, implies a detached, staccato style, but less so than the dash. The dot combined with a slur implies a style midway between the dot and legato, i.e. slightly detached.

**dot, double dot.** See *Values of Notes and Rests*.

**double flat.** ♭♭. Used before a note already flattened to lower it another semitone. It is cancelled by a natural and a flat (♮♭).

**double sharp.** ✗. Used before a note already sharpened to raise it another semitone. It is cancelled by a natural and a sharp (♮♯).

**down bow.** ⊓. Direction for bowing (a stringed instrument) by 'pulling' the bow.

**D.S., dal segno.** The performer must return to and play from the sign 𝄋 (lit. 'from the sign').

**f, forte.** Loud (lit. 'strong').

**ff, fortissimo.** Very loud.

**fff, fortississimo.** As loud as possible.

**figured bass.** A harmonic shorthand to enable keyboard players of the 17th and 18th centuries to accompany chamber and orchestral music without requiring written-out parts. It consists of the bass line, with numerals to indicate the correct chords.

**fine.** End. See under **D.C.**

**flat.** ♭. Sign used in a key signature (see section on *Pitch*) to lower the note in the corresponding position on the staff, and in all octaves throughout the piece, by one semitone, cancelled by a natural sign. See also **accidental**.

**fp, forte-piano.** Loud, then immediately soft.

**fz, forzato.** Accented (lit. 'forced').

**grace note.** An ornament such as an acciaccatura or appoggiatura.

**harmonic.** In string music, a sign placed over a note to indicate that it is to be played as a harmonic by lightly touching the string.

o

**inverted turn.** See **turn**.

**leg., legato.** Smoothly, without a break between the notes; opposite of staccato.

**loco.** Indicating a return to the pitch as printed, after having played an octave higher or lower.

**marc., marcato.** In a marked manner, each note emphasised.

**mf, mezzo-forte.** Moderately loud (lit. 'half-strong').

**M.M.** Maelzel's metronome. Sometimes used to precede the indication of a metronome setting: **M.M.** = 70 means 70 crotchet beats a minute.

**mordent.** An ornament consisting of two auxiliary or grace notes, similar in performance to the acciaccatura in that it is played as quickly as possible before the principal note:

upper mordent      lower mordent

**mp, mezzo-piano.** Moderately soft (lit. 'half-soft').

**natural.** ♮. Restores to its original pitch a note that has been inflected by an accidental.

**ornament.** A melodic embellishment, specifically an auxiliary or grace note such as an acciaccatura, appoggiatura, turn, etc.

**ossia.** Used to propose a usually easier alternative (lit. 'or').

**ottava, 8$^{va}$ or 8.** Indicates that a note or passage is to be played an octave higher or lower depending whether it is written above or below the stave. Col or con 8$^{va}$ means that the printed notes are to be played along with the octave.

**p, piano.** Soft.

**pp, pianissimo.** Very soft.

**ppp, pianississimo.** As soft as possible.

**pause.** ⌒ Placed over a note or rest, to show that it is to be held longer than the indicated time value. Placed over the double bar it indicates the end of the piece.

**ped.** Depress 'loud' pedal on a piano. An asterisk indicates when it is to be released:

**pizz., pizzicato.** Pluck the string with the finger instead of playing it with the bow; cancelled by arco.

**rall., rallentando.** Becoming gradually slower.

**repeat sign.** Placed at the beginning and end of a passage to show that it is to be repeated. The repetition is implied even when the sign is omitted at the beginning.

**rinf., rfz, rf, rinforzato.** Reinforced, suddenly accented.

**rit., ritardando.** Gradually decreasing in speed.

**rubato.** Indicating a certain, limited freedom in performance as regards tempo, the limitation being that the beat should be returned to without an overall loss of time within the phrase so treated.

**segno.** 𝄋. See **D.C.** and **D.S.**

**segue.** Usually to warn that the next movement follows with scarcely a break (lit. 'follows').

**sempre.** Always; as in *sempre legato*, smooth throughout.

**senza sordino.** Remove mute from instrument (lit. 'without mute').

**sf, sfz, sforzando, sforzato.** Forced, strongly accented. Sometimes indicated by >.

**sfp, sforzato-piano.** A strong accent followed immediately by piano.

**shake.** See **trill**.

**sharp.** ♯. Sign used in a key signature (see section on *Pitch*) to raise the note in the corresponding position on the staff, and in all octaves throughout the piece, by one semitone; cancelled by a natural. See also **accidental**.

**simile.** Continue performing in like manner, i.e. as already marked (lit. 'like').

**slur.** Shows that the notes over which it is placed are to be (*a*) performed in a smooth (legato) manner; (*b*) played in one bow (see also **dot**); or (*c*) sung to one syllable. Also used to indicate phrasing.

**smorz., smorzando.** Gradually slower and softer.

**sost., sostenuto.** Sustained.

**sotto voce.** Barely audible (lit. 'under the breath').

**spiritoso.** Spirited, lively.

**staccato.** Detached, i.e. each note shortened; opposite of legato.

**staff, stave.** See section on *Pitch*.

**sul ponticello.** Play with the bow close up to the bridge (lit. 'on the bridge').

**sul tasto.** Play with the bow close up to, or on, the fingerboard (lit. 'on the key', i.e. fingerboard).

**tempo primo, tempo 1mo.** Take up the original tempo.

**ten., tenuto.** Strictly, hold for the full note value, but in practice draw out slightly beyond that.

**tie or bind.** Links a note and its repetition to show that the first note is sustained for the total time value of both notes and not replayed.

**tre corde.** Release soft pedal (lit. 'three strings'): see **una corda**.

**tremolo.** In string music, the rapid repetition of one note (for the time value of that note) by a quick movement at the point of the bow. In piano music a similar effect is achieved by alternating the note with its octave.

**trill or shake.** An alternation, variable in speed, of two notes a tone or a semitone apart, usually ending in a turn, and beginning on the principal note or, in early music, on the note above:

**triplet.** A group of three notes performed in the time of two:

**T.S., tasto solo.** In early music with a figured bass, implies that the bass line should be played without added harmonies (lit. 'one key alone').

**turn.** An ornament of four notes, played differently according to whether the sign is placed above or after the principal note:

The **inverted turn** is played similarly, but begins on the note below the principal note:

**una corda, U.C.** Depress 'soft' pedal, (lit. 'one string'; in a grand piano depressing the 'soft' pedal allows the hammers to strike only one of the three strings).

**up bow.** ⋁. Direction for bowing (a stringed instrument) by 'pushing' the bow.

**V.S., volte subito.** Turn over the page quickly.

# Some English personal names

See especially Miss E. G. Withycombe's *The Oxford Dictionary of English Christian Names*

**Aaron**, *ā′rən, m.* (Heb.) lofty, mountaineer.—Ar. *Harun, Haroun.*
**Abel**, *ā′bl, m.* (Heb.) breath, vanity.
**Abigail**, *ab′i-gāl, f.* (Heb.) father rejoiced, or father of exaltation.—Dims. **Abby, Nabby, Gail.**
**Abner**, *ab′nər, m.* (Heb.) the (divine) father (is) light.
**Abraham**, *ā′brə-həm,* **Abram**, *ā′brəm, m.* (Heb.) perhaps father of a multitude, high father.—Dims. **Abe, Aby, Bram.**
**Absalom**, *ab′sə-ləm, m.* (Heb.) father of peace.
**Ada**, *ā′da, f.* prob. for **Adelaide** or other Gmc. name in Adel-, Adal- (noble).
**Adalbert.** See **Albert.**
**Adam**, *ad′əm, m.* (Heb.) man, earth, red earth.—Scottish dims. **Edie** (*ēd′i*), **Yiddie.**
**Adela**, *ad′i-la, f.* (Gmc.) noble.—Fr. *Adèle.*
**Adelaide**, *ad′i-lād, f.* Fr. *Adélaïde* from Ger. *Adelheid* (from *Adelheidis*), noble, kind (i.e. sort).
**Adeline, Adelina**, *ad′i-lin, -lēn, -līn, -a, f.* (Gmc.) noble.—Dim. **Addy.**
**Adolphus**, *ə-dol′fəs, m.* (Gmc.) noble wolf.—Fr. *Adolphe,* It. and Sp. *Adolfo,* Ger. *Adolf,* O.E. *Æthelwulf.*
**Adrian, Hadrian**, *(h)ā′dri-ən, m.* (L.) of Adria (in Italy).
**Aeneas, Eneas**, *ē-nē′əs, m.* (Gr.) commended.—Fr. *Énée.*—Used for **Angus.**
**Afra**, *af′ra, ā′fra, f.* (Heb.) dust. (Now rare.)
**Agatha**, *ag′ə-tha, f.* (Gr.) good.
**Agnes**, *ag′nis, f.* (Gr.) chaste.—Dims. **Aggie, Aggy, Annis, Annot, Nance, Nancy, Nessa, Nessie, Nesta.**—L. *Agneta,* It. *Agnese,* Fr. *Agnès,* Sp. *Inés.*—Confused with **Ann.**
**Aileen**, *ā′lēn, i′lēn, f.* Anglo-Irish form of **Helen.**
**Ailie**, *ā′li, f.* Scottish dim. of **Alison, Alice,** and **Helen.**
**Alan, Allan, Allen,** *al′ən, m.* (prob. Celt.) harmony.—Fr. *Alain,* W. *Alun.*
**Alaric**, *al′ə-rik, m.* (Gmc.) noble ruler.
**Alasdair, Alastair, Alister**, *al′is-tər, m.* See **Alexander.**
**Alban**, *öl′, al′bən, m.* (L.) of Alba (near Rome).
**Albert**, *al′bərt, m.* (Gmc.) nobly bright.—Dims. **Al, Bert, Bertie.**—Obs. Scot. **Halbert** (dims. **Hab, Habbie, Hob, Hobbie**).—L. *Albertus,* Fr. *Albert,* It. and Sp. *Alberto,* Ger. *Adalbert, Albert, Albrecht,* O.E. *Æthelbeorht.*
**Aldis, Aldous, Aldus,** *öl′dəs, m.* (Gmc.) old.
**Aldred**, *öl′drid, m.* See **Eldred.**
**Alethea**, *al-i-thē′a, f.* (Gr.) truth.
**Alexander**, *al-ig-zan′dər, -zän′, m.* (Gr.) defender of men.—Also (from Gael.) **Alasdair, Alastair, Alister** (*al′is-tər*).—Scot. **Elshender.**—Dims. **Alec(k), Alex, Alick, Eck, Ecky, Sanders, Sandy,** or (as an Englishman's nickname for a Scotsman) **Sawnie.**—Fr. *Alexandre,* It. *Alessandro,* Sp. *Alejandro.*—Fem. **Alexandra, Alexandrina** (*-drē′na, -drīna*).—Dim. **Alexa, Sandra.**
**Alexis**, *ə-lek′sis, m.* (Gr.) help.—Fem. **Alexia.**
**Alfonso.** See **Alphonsus.**
**Alfred**, *al′frid, m.* (Gmc.) elf counsel (good counsellor).—Dims. **Alf, Alfie.**—L. *Alfredus, Aluredus,* O.E. *Ælfred.*
**Algernon**, *al′jər-nən, m.* (O.Fr.) moustached.—Dim. **Algy.**
**Alice**, *al′is,* **Alicia**, *ə-lish′i-a, f.* (Gmc.) from O.Fr. *Aliz* for Gmc. *Adalheidis* (see **Adelaide**).—Dims. **Ailie, Allie, Ally, Ellie, Elsie.** See also **Alison.**
**Aline**, *ə-lēn′,* or *al′ēn, f.* for **Adeline.**

**Alison**, *al′i-sən, f.* a form of **Alice,** mainly Scots, now considered a separate name.—Dims. **Ailie, Elsie.**
**Allan, Allen.** Forms of **Alan.**
**Alma**, *al′ma, f.* (L.) fostering, nourishing, loving.
**Almeric**, *al′mə-rik, m.* See **Emery.**
**Aloys, Aloysius.** See **Lewis.**
**Alphonsus**, *al-fon′səs, m.* (Gmc.) noble ready.—Ger. *Alfons,* Sp. *Alfonso, Alonso,* Port. *Afonso,* Fr. *Alphonse,* It. *Alfonso.*
**Althea**, *al-thē′a, al′, f.* (Gr.) a healer, or wholesome.
**Amabel**, *am′ə-bel, f.* (L.) lovable.—Deriv. **Mabel.**
**Amadeus**, *am-ə-dē′əs, m.* (L.) love God.—Fr. *Amédée.*
**Amalia**, *a-mä′li-a, -mä′.* See **Amelia.**
**Amanda**, *ə-man′da, f.* (L.) lovable.
**Ambrose**, *am′brōz, m.* (Gr.) of the immortals, divine.—L. *Ambrosius,* It. *Ambrogio,* W. *Emrys.*
**Amelia**, *ə-mē′li-a, -mēl′ya, f.* (Gmc.) struggling, labour.—Ger. *Amalia,* Fr. *Amélie,* It. *Amelia, Amalia.*—Dim. **Millie.**
**Amos**, *ā′mos, m.* (Heb.) strong, bearing a burden.
**Amy**, *ā′mi, f.* (Fr.) beloved.—L., It., Sp. *Amata,* Fr. *Aimée.*
**Amyas**, *ām′, am′i-as, m.* prob. for **Amadeus.**
**Anastasia**, *an-ə-stā′zha, -zi-a, f.* (Gr.) resurrection.
**Andrew**, *an′drōō, m.* (Gr.) manly.—Dims. **Andie, Andy, Dandy, Drew.**—Gr., L., Ger. *Andreas,* Fr. *André,* It. *Andrea,* Sp. *Andrés.*—Fem. **Andrea, Andrina.**
**Aneurin, Aneirin**, *a-nā′rin, -nī′, -noi′, m.* (W.) meaning doubtful, perh. for L. *Honorius.*
**Angela**, *an′ji-la, f.* (Gr.) angel, messenger.—Deriv. **Angelica** (*-jel′ik-a*).—Dim. **Angelina** (*an-ji-lē′na, -li′na*).
**Angus**, *ang′gəs, m.* (Celt.) perh. choice.—Gael. *Aonghas.*—**Aeneas** is used as a substitute.
**Ann, Anne** *an,* **Anna,** *an′a,* **Hannah,** *han′a, f.* (Heb.) grace.—Dims. **Anita** (*a-nē′ta,* Sp.), **Annette** (*a-net′,* Fr.), **Annie, Nan, Nana, Nance, Nancy, Nanna, Nannie, Nanny, Nina** (*nē′na, ni′na*), **Ninette** (*nē-net′,* Fr.), **Ninon** (*nē-nɔ̃′,* Fr.).
**Annabel, Annabelle, Annabella,** *an′ə-bel, -bel′-a,* **Annaple,** *an′ə-pl, f.* prob. for **Amabel.**
**Annis, Annot.** Dims. of **Agnes.**
**Anselm**, *an′selm, m.* (Gmc.) god-helmet.
**Anthea**, *an-thē′a, an′, f.* (Gr.) flowery.
**Anthony, Antony,** *an′ta-ni, m.* (L.), from a Roman gentile name, meaning unknown.—Dims. **Tony** (*tō′ni*), **Nanty.**—L. *Antonius,* Fr. *Antoine,* It. and Sp. *Antonio,* Ger. *Antonius, Anton.*—Fem. **Antonia.**—Dims. **Antoinette** (Fr.), **Net, Nettie, Netty.**
**April**, *ā′pril, f.* (L.) from the name of the month.
**Arabella**, *ar-ə-bel′a, f.* origin and meaning doubtful; perh. for **Amabel,** or perh. (L. *orabilis*) easily entreated.—Dims. **Bel, Bell, Bella, Belle.**
**Archibald**, *är′chi-bld, -bōld, m.* (Gmc.) genuine and bold.—Dims. **Arch, Archie, Archy, Baldie.**—L. *Archibaldus,* Fr. *Archembault,* It. *Arcibaldo,* O.E. *Eorconbeald.*
**Arnold**, *är′nld, -nold, m.* (Gmc.) eagle strength.—Fr. *Arnaud, Arnaut.*
**Arthur**, *är′thər, m.* (Celt.) perh. bear, or (Ir.) stone; or from a Roman gentile name *Artorius.*—L. *Arturus,* It. *Arturo.*
**Asa**, *ā′sa, -za, m.* (Heb.) healer.
**Athanasius**, *ath-ə-nā′s(h)i-əs, -z(h)-, m.* (Gr.) undying.
**Athelstan, Athelstane,** *ath′l-stan, -stän, m.* (Gmc.) noble stone.—O.E. *Æthelstān.*

Aubrey, ŏ'bri, m. (Gmc.) elf rule.—Ger. Alberich, O.E. Ælfric.

Audrey, ŏ'dri, f. (Gmc.) noble power.—O.E. Æthelthryth, whence the form Etheldreda (eth-l-drē'da).

Augustine, ŏ'gəs-tēn, ŏ-gus'tin, Austin, ŏs'tin, m. (L.) belonging to Augustus.—L. Augustinus, Ger. and Fr. Augustin, It. Agostino, Sp. Agustín.

Augustus, ŏ-gus'təs, m. (L.) venerable, exalted.— Dims. Gus, Gussie, Gustus.—Ger. August, Fr. Auguste.—Fem. Augusta.

Aurelius, ŏ-rē'li-əs, m. (L.) golden (Roman gentile name).—Fem. Aurelia.—Dim. Aurelian, m.

Aurora, ŏ-rō'ra, -rŏ'ra, f. (L.) dawn.

Ava, ā'va, f. origin and meaning uncertain—perh. Latin.

Averil, av'ə-ril, m. and f. (Gmc.) perh. boar-favour. Associated in people's minds with Avril.

Avice, Avis, ā'vis, av'is, f. origin obscure.

Avril, av'ril, m. and f. (Fr.) April.

Aylmer, āl'mər, Elmer, el'mər, m. (Gmc.) noble, famous.—O.E. Æthelmær. Or from the surname.

Aylwin, āl'win, m. (Gmc.) noble friend.—O.E. Æthelwine.

Baldwin, bŏld'win, m. (Gmc.) bold friend.—L. Balduinus, Fr. Baudouin, It. and Sp. Baldovino, Ger. Balduin.

Balthazar, Balthasar, bal't(h)ə-zär, bal-thā'zər, m. (Babylonian Bal-sarra-uzur, whence Belshazzar) Bel defend the king.—Ger. Balthasar, Fr. Balthazar, It. Baldassare, Sp. Baltasar.

Baptist, bap'ₗist, m. (Gr.) baptiser.—Ger. Baptist, Fr. Baptiste, Batiste, It. Battista, Sp. Bautista.— Fem. Baptista.

Barbara, bär'bə-ra, f. (Gr.) foreign, stranger.— Dims. Bab, Babs, Babbie, (Scot. Baubie), Barbie.

Bardolph, bär'dolf, m. (Gmc.) bright wolf.—Fr. Bardolphe, It. Bardolfo.

Barnabas, Barnaby, bär'nə-bəs, -bi, m. (Heb.) son of exhortation.—Dim. Barney.

Barney, bär'ni, m. See Bernard, Barnabas.

Barry, bar'i, m. (Ir.) spear.

Bartholomew, bär-, bər-thol'ə-mū, Bartlemy, bärt'l-mi, m. (Heb.) son of Talmi.—Dims. Bart, Bat.—L. Bartholomaeus, Fr. Barthélemy, Bartholomé, It. Bartolomeo, Sp. Bártolo, Bartolomé, Bartolomeo, Ger. Bartholomäus, Barthel.

Basil, baz'il, m. (Gr.) kingly.—L. Basilius, Fr. Basile, It. and Sp. Basilio.

Beatrice, Beatrix, bē'ə-tris, -triks, bē-ā'triks, f. (L.) making happy.—Obs. form Bettrice (bet'ris).— Dims. Bee, Beatty, Trix, Trixie.

Beck, Becky, bek('i), f. See Rebecca.

Belinda, bə-lin'da, f. (Gmc.) the second part meaning snake, the first unexplained.—O.H.G. Betlindis.

Bell, Belle, bel, Bella, bel'a, f. See Isabella, also Annabel, Arabella.

Benedict, Benedick, ben'i-dikt, -dik, Bennet, ben'it, m. (L.) blessed.—L. Benedictus, Ger. Benedikt, Fr. Benoit, It. Benedetto, Sp. Benedicto, Benito.—Fem. Benedicta.

Benjamin, ben'jə-min, m. (Heb.) son of the right hand (i.e. of good fortune).—Dims. Ben, Benjie, Bennie.—It. Beniamino, Sp. Benjamín.

Berenice, ber-i-ni'sē, ber-nē'sē, ber'i-nēs, f. (Gr.), a Macedonian form of Phereníkē, victory-bringer. See also Veronica.

Bernard, bûr'nərd, m. (Gmc.) bear-hard.—Dims. Bernie, Barney.—L. Bernardus, Fr. Bernard, Bernardin, It. Bernardo, Bernardino, Sp. Bernardo, Bernal, Ger. Bernhard, Barend, Berend.—Fem. Bernadette.

Bert, bûrt, m. for Albert; Bertie for Albert, Bertram or Herbert.—Both are used for any name ending in -bert, and (f.) for Bertha.

Bertha, bûr'tha, f. (Gmc.) bright.—Dims. Bert,

Bertie.—Ger. Berta, Bertha, Fr. Berthe, It. and Sp. Berta, O.E. Bercta.

Bertram, bûr'trəm, m. (Gmc.) bright raven.— Dims. Bertie, Bert.—Fr. Bertrand, It. Bertrando, Sp. Beltrán.

Beryl, ber'il, f. (Gr.) from the precious stone.

Bess, Bessie, Beth, Betsy, Bettina, Betty. See Elizabeth.

Bevis, bev'is, bēv'is, m. from a French form of the Germanic name Bobo (Frankish), Bobba (O.E.).

Biddy, bid'i, f. See Bridget.

Bill, m. See William.

Blanche, Blanch, blänsh, f. (Fr.—Gmc.) white.— It. Bianca, Sp. Blanca, Ger. Blanka, Fr. Blanche.

Blodwen, blod'win, f. (W.) white flower.

Bob. See Robert.

Boris, bor'is, bŏ', m. (Russ.) fight.

Bram. See Abraham.

Brenda, bren'da, f. perh. a fem. form of the Norse name Brand, brand, or sword, or a fem. form of Brendan; a Shetland name popularised by Scott's Pirate.

Brendan, bren'dən, m. (Ir.) meaning uncertain—stinking hair has been suggested.

Brian, bri'ən, m. (Celt.) meaning doubtful.

Bridget, Brigid, brij'it, f. (Celt.) strength; name of a Celtic fire-goddess, an Irish saint; partly from the Swedish saint Brigitto (prob. a different name).—Dim. Biddy.—Fr. Brigide, Brigitte, Sp. Brígida, It. Brigida, Brigita.

Bronwen, bron'win f. (W.) white breast.

Bruce, brōŏs, m. from the surname.

Bruno, brōŏ'nŏ, m. (Gmc.) brown.

Caleb, kā'lib, m. (Heb.) dog, or bold.

Camilla, kə-mil'a, f. (L.) a free-born attendant at a sacrifice; in Virgil, name of a queen of the Volsci.—Fr. Camille.

Candida, kan'di-da, f. (L.) white.

Carlotta, kär-lot'a, f. See Charles.

Carmen, kär'mən, f. Sp. form of Heb. Carmel, the garden.

Carol, Carola, Carole, Caroline, Carolyn, f. See under Charles.

Casimir, Kasimir, kas'i-mir, m. (Polish) proclamation of peace.

Caspar, Kaspar, kas'pər, m. See Jasper.

Cassandra. See Dict.

Catherine, Catharine, Katherine, Katharine, Kathryn, kath'(ə-)rin, Catherina, -ə-rē'na, -rī'na, Katrine, kat'rin, Katerina, kat-ə-rē'na, Katrina, Kathleen, kath'lēn (Ir. Caitlin), f. from Gr. Aikaterinē, of unknown origin, later assimilated to katharos, pure.—Fr. Catherine, It. Caterina, Sp. Catalina, Ger. Katharina, Dan. Karen, Gael. Catriona.—Dims. Casey, Cathie, Cathy, Kate, Katie, Katy, Kathie, Kathy, Kay, Kit, Kitty.

Catriona, kə-trē'ə-na, kat-ri-ō'na. See Catherine.

Cecil, ses'il, also sēs', sis', m. (L.) the Roman gentile name Caecilius (lit. blind).—Fem. Cecilia (sis'il'ya,-sēl'ya), Cecily (ses'i-li), Cicely (sis'(i-)li), Sisley.—Fr. Cécile, Ger. Cäcilia, Ir. Sile (see Celia).—Dims. Sis, Cis, Sissy, Sissie, Cissy, Cissie.

Cedric, sed'rik, m. prob. a mistake of Scott's for Cerdic (name of the first king of the West Saxons, but apparently not really English—perh. a British name).

Celeste, si-lest', Celestine, si-les'tēn, -tin, -tin, f. (L.) heavenly.

Celia, Caelia, sē'li-a, f. fem. of the Roman gentile name Caelius (poss. heavenly).—Fr. Célie; Ir. Sile (anglicised Sheila, Shelagh, etc.)—Sometimes used for Cecilia.

Charis, kar'is, f. (Gr.) grace.

Charity, char'i-ti, f. (Eng.) charity.—Deriv. Cherry.

Charles, chärlz, m. (Gmc.) manly.—Also Carol, kar'ol.—L. Carolus, Fr. Charles, Ger. Carl, Karl, It. Carlo, Sp. Carlos, Czech Karol, Gael.

*Tearlach.*—Dims. **Charlie, Charley.**—Fem. **Carol, Carole** (*kar'ol*), **Carola** (*-la*), **Caroline** (*kar'ə-lin, -lēn, -lin*), **Carolyn, Carlotta, Charlotte** (*shär'lət*).—Dims. **Caddie, Carrie, Lina** (*lē'na*), **Lottie, Chat** (*shat*), **Chatty, Sharley.**

**Cherry,** *cher'i, f.* from the fruit, or see **Charity.**

**Chloe,** *klō'i, f.* (Gr.) a green shoot, verdure.

**Chloris,** *klō', klō'ris, f.* (Gr.) name of a flower-goddess, also greenfinch or a kind of grape.

**Christabel,** *kris'tə-bel, f.* (L.—Gr.) anointed, or Christ, and (L.) fair.

**Christian,** *kris'ti-ən, -chən, m.,* also *f.* belonging to Christ.—L. *Christianus,* Fr. *Chrétien,* It. and Sp. *Cristiano.*—Dims. **Chris, Christie, Christy.**—Fem. **Christiana** (*-ti-ä'na*), **Christina** (*-tē'na*), **Christine** (*kris'tēn* or *-tēn'*), **Kirsteen** (*kûrs'tēn*).—Dims. **Chris, Chrissie, Kirsty, Teenie, Tina** (*tē'na*).

**Christopher,** *kris'tə-fər, m.* (Gr.) carrying Christ.—L. *Christophorus,* Fr. *Christophe,* It. *Cristoforo,* Sp. *Cristóbal,* Ger. *Christoph.*—Dims. **Chris, Kester, Kit** (Scot. fem. **Crystal, Chrystal**).

**Cicely.** See **Cecilia.**

**Clara,** *klā'ra,* **Clare, Claire,** *klār,* **Clarinda,** *klə-rin'da, f.* (L.) bright.—Fr. *Claire,* Ger. *Klara,* It. *Chiara.*—Derivs. **Clarice** (*klar'is*), **Clarissa.**

**Clarence,** *klar'əns, m.* from the dukedom.

**Claribel,** *klar'i-bel, f.* (L.) brightly fair.

**Claud, Claude,** *klöd,* **Claudius,** *-i-əs, m.* (L.) lame.—Fem. **Claudia** (Fr. *Claude*).

**Clement,** *klem'ənt, m.* (L.) mild, merciful.—Dim. **Clem.**—Fem. **Clemency, Clementina** (*-ē'na*), **Clementine** (*-ēn, -in*).

**Clive,** *klīv, m.* from the surname.

**Clotilda, Clothilda,** *klō-til'da, f.* (Gmc.) famous fighting woman.—Fr. *Clot(h)ilde.*

**Clovis,** *klō'vis, m.* See **Lewis.**

**Colette,** *kol-et', f.* See **Nicholas.**

**Colin,** *kol'in, m.* orig. a dim. of **Nicholas**; used also for **Columba**; now regarded as a separate name.

**Colley,** *kol'i,* orig. dim. of **Nicholas.**

**Connor,** *kon'ər, m.* (Ir.) high desire.—Ir. *Conchob(h)ar,* or *Conchub(h)ar.*—Dims. **Corney, Corny.**—**Cornelius** is used as a substitute.

**Conrad, Conrade, Konrad,** *kon'rad, m.* (Ger.) bold in counsel.—Ger. *Konrad,* It. *Corrado.*

**Constance,** *kon'stəns, f.* (L.) constancy.—L. *Constantia,* Fr. *Constance,* It. *Costanza,* Ger. *Konstanze.*—Dims. **Con, Connie.**—**Constant,** *kon'stənt, m.* firm, faithful.—L. *Constans, Constantius,* It. *Costante, Costanzo,* Ger. *Konstanz.*—Deriv. **Constantine** (*kon'stən-tīn*), *m.*

**Cora,** *kō'ra, kö'ra, f.* a modern name, prob. from Gr. *korē,* girl.

**Coralie,** *kor'ə-li, f.* (Fr.) perh. coral, a modern French invention.

**Cordelia,** *kör-dē'li-a, f.* perh. (L.) warm-hearted.

**Corinne,** *ko-rin', -rēn,* **Corinna,** *-rin'a, f.* (L.—Gr.) maiden.

**Cornelius,** *kör-nē'li-əs, m.* (L.) a Roman gentile name, prob. related to L. *cornu,* horn.—Used for **Connor.**—Dims. **Corney, Corny.**—Fem. **Cornelia.**

**Cosmo,** *koz'mō, m.* (Gr.) order.—It. *Cosimo, Cosmo,* Fr. *Cosme, Côme,* Sp. *Cosme.*

**Craig,** *krāg, m.* from the surname.

**Cressida,** *kres'i-da, f.* (Gr.) English form of *Chryseis,* accus. *Chryseida,* daughter of *Chryses.*

**Crispin,** *kris'pin,* **Crispian,** *-pi-ən,* **Crispinian,** *-pin'i-ən,* **Crispus,** *-pəs, m.* (L.) curly.

**Cuthbert,** *kudh', kuth'bərt, m.* (O.E.) well-known, bright.—Dim. **Cuddie.**

**Cynthia,** *sin'thi-a, f.* (Gr.) of Mount Cynthus, an epithet of Artemis.

**Cyprian,** *sip'ri-ən, m.* (Gr.) of Cyprus.

**Cyril,** *sir'il, m.* (Gr.) lordly.

**Cyrus,** *sī'rəs, m.* (Pers.) throne.—Dim. **Cy.**

**Daisy,** *dā'zi, f.* (Eng.) a translation of Fr. *Marguerite.* See **Margaret.**

**Damian,** *dā'mi-ən, m.* (Gr.) perh. connected with *damaein,* to tame.

**Daniel,** *dan'yəl, m.* (Heb.) the Lord is judge.—Dims. **Dan, Danny.**

**Daphne,** *daf'nē, -ni, f.* (Gr.) laurel.

**David,** *dā'vid, m.* (Heb.) beloved.—Dims. **Dave, Davie, Davy** (obs. **Daw, Dawkin**).—Fem. **Vida,** *vē'da* (Scot. **Davina,** *də-vē'na, -vī'na*).

**Dawn,** *dön, f.* (Eng.) dawn.

**Deborah,** *deb'ə-ra, di-bō'ra, -bö', f.* (Heb.) bee.—Dims. **Deb, Debbie, Debby.**

**Deirdre,** *dēr'dri, f.* (Ir.) meaning doubtful.

**Delia,** *dē'li-a, f.* (Gr.) of the island of Delos.

**Demetrius,** *di-mē'tri-əs, m.* belonging to Demeter.

**Denis, Dennis,** *m.,* **Denise,** *f.* See **Dionysius.**

**Derek, Derrick,** *der'ik, m.* See **Theodoric.**

**Desideratus,** *di-sid-ə-rā'təs,* **Desiderius,** *dez-i-dē'ri-əs, m.* (L.), **Désiré,** *dā-zē-rā', m.* (Fr.), longed for.—Fem. **Desiderata, Désirée.**

**Desmond,** *dez'mond, m.* (Ir.) from the surname or the district.

**Diana,** *dī-a'na, f.* (L.) goddess: the Roman goddess identified with Artemis.—Dims. **Di, Die, Diane.**

**Dick, Dickie, Dickon.** See **Richard.**

**Diggory,** *dig'ə-ri, m.* (Fr.) from *Degarre,* a hero of romance, an exposed child (prob. Fr. *égaré,* astray).

**Dilys,** *dil'is, f.* (W.) sure, constant, genuine.

**Dinah,** *dī'na, f.* (Heb.) judged, or dedicated.

**Dionysius,** *dī-ə-nis'i-əs, -niz', m.* (Gr.), **Denis, Dennis,** *den'is* (Fr.—Gr.), belonging to Dionysos or Bacchus.—Fr. *Denis, Denys,* It. *Dionigi,* Sp. *Dionisio.*—Fem. **Dionysia, Denise** (*di-nēz'*).

**Dod, Doddy.** See **George.**

**Dolores,** *do-lō'rēz, -lö', f.* (Sp.) sorrows.—Dim. **Lola.**

**Dominic(k),** *dom'i-nik, m.* (L.) Sunday.—L. *Dominicus,* It. *Domenico,* Sp. *Domingo,* Fr. *Dominique.*

**Donald,** *don'əld, m.* (Celt.) world chief.—Gael. *Domhnall.*—Dims. **Don, Donnie.**

**Donna,** *don'a, f.* (It.) mistress, lady.

**Dora,** *dō'ra, dö'ra, f.* prob. a dim. of **Dorothy;** used also for **Theodora** and names of like ending.

**Dorcas,** *dör'kəs, f.* (Gr.) gazelle.

**Doreen,** *dō'rēn, dö', dō-rēn', dö-, f.* (Ir.) sullen; or for **Dorothy.**

**Doris,** *dor'is, dō'ris, dö', f.* (Gr.) the name of a sea-nymph; meaning doubtful.

**Dorothy,** *dor'ə-thi,* **Dorothea,** *-thē'a, f.* (Gr.) gift of God.—Fr. *Dorothée, Dorette,* Ger. *Dorothea.*—Dims. **Dol, Doll, Dolly, Dora, Do, Dot.**

**Dougal, Dugald,** *dōō'gəl(d), m.* (Celt.) black stranger.—Gael. *Dùghall.*

**Douglas,** *dug'ləs, m.* (and *f.*) from the surname, or the river.

**Drew.** See **Andrew.**

**Dudley,** *dud'li, m.* from the surname.

**Dulcie,** *dul'si, f.* (L.) sweet—a modern invention.

**Duncan,** *dung'kən, m.* (Celt.) brown head.—Gael. *Donnchadh.*

**Dwight,** *dwīt, m.* from the surname.

**Eamon,** *ā'mən, em'ən, m.* Irish form of **Edmund.**

**Earl, Earle,** *ûrl, m.* (U.S.) from the title.

**Ebenezer,** *eb-i-nē'zər, m.* (Heb.) stone of help.—Dim. **Eben.**

**Ed, Eddie,** dims. of **Edgar, Edmund, Edward, Edwin.**

**Edgar,** *ed'gər, m.* (O.E.) happy spear.—O.E. *Eadgar.*—Dims. **Ed, Eddie, Eddy, Ned, Neddie, Neddy.**

**Edie.** See **Adam, Edith.**

**Edith,** *ē'dith, f.* (O.E.) happy or rich war.—O.E. *Eadgyth.*—Dims. **Edie, Edy.**

**Edmund,** *ed'mənd, m.* (O.E.) happy protection.—Fr. *Edmond,* Ir. *Eamon.*—Dims. **Ed, Eddie, Eddy, Ned, Neddie, Neddy.**

**Edna,** *ed'na, f.* (Heb.) meaning uncertain.

**Edward**, *ed'wərd, m.* (O.E.) rich guard.—Ger. *Eduard*, Fr. *Édouard*, It. *Eduardo, Edoardo, Odoardo.*—Dims. **Ed, Eddie, Eddy, Ned, Neddie, Neddy, Ted, Teddie, Teddy.**

**Edwin**, *ed'win, m.* (O.E.) prosperity or riches, friend.—Dims. **Ed, Eddie, Eddy, Ned, Neddie, Neddy.**

**Effie**, *ef'i, f.* dim. of **Euphemia.**

**Egbert**, *eg'bərt, m.* (O.E.) sword-bright.

**Eileen**, *i'lēn, i-lēn', f.* (Ir.) an old Irish name perh. meaning pleasant; used as a substitute for **Helen.**

**Eirene.** See **Irene.**

**Elaine**, *i-lān', f.* an O.Fr. form of **Helen.**

**Eldred**, *el'drid,* **Aldred,** *öl'drid, m.* (O.E.) old counsel.—O.E. *Ealdred.*

**Eleanor, Eleanore,** *el'i-nər,* **Elinor, Leonora,** *lē-ə-nō'ra, -nō'ra, f.* Same as **Helen.**—It. *Eleonora,* Ger. *Eleonore, Lenore,* Fr. *Éléonore, Aliénor.*—Dims. **Ella, Ellen, Nell, Nellie, Nelly, Nora.**

**Eleazer**, *el-i-ā'zər, m.* (Heb.) God is help.

**Elfleda**, *el-flē'da, f.* (O.E. *Æthelflæd*) noble-clean, and (O.E. *Ælflæd*) elf-clean.

**Elfreda**, *el-frē'da, f.* (O.E.) elf-strength.—O.E. *Ælfthryth.*

**Elgiva**, *el-ji'va, f.* (O.E.) elf-gift—O.E. *Ælfgyfu,* or noble gift (O.E. *Æthelgyfu*).

**Eli**, *ē'lī, m.* (Heb.) height.

**Elias**, *i-lī'əs,* **Elijah,** *i-lī'ja, m.* (Heb.) the Lord is Yah.

**Elizabeth, Elisabeth,** *i-liz'ə-beth,* **Eliza,** *i-lī'za, f.* (Heb.) God an oath.—Fr. *Élizabeth, Élise,* It. *Elisabetta, Elisa,* Ger. *Elisabeth, Elise,* Sp. *Isabel* (q.v.).—Dims. **Bess, Bessie, Bessy, Bet, Beth, Betsy, Bettina, Betty, Elsie, Libby, Lisa, Liza** (*lī'za*), **Lisbeth, Lizbeth, Liz** (*liz*), **Lizzie.**

**Ella**, *el'a, f.* (Gmc.) all.—Also a dim. of **Eleanor** or of **Isabella** or other name in -ella.

**Ellen**, *el'in, f.* a form of **Helen,** also used for **Eleanor.**

**Elma**, *el'ma, f.* for **Wilhelmina,** or a combination of **Elizabeth Mary.**

**Elmer.** See **Aylmer.**

**Eloisa.** See **Heloise.**

**Elsa**, *el'sa,* **Elsie, -si.** See **Elizabeth, Alison, Alice.**

**Elshender.** Scots form of **Alexander.**

**Elspeth**, *el'spəth,* **Elspet,** *el'spət,* Scots forms of **Elizabeth.**

**Elvira**, *el-vē'ra,* or *-vī', f.* (Sp.) prob. of Gmc. origin, elf-counsel.

**Emery, Emory,** *em'ə-ri,* **Almeric,** *al'mə-rik, m.* (Gmc.) work-rule, energetic rule.—L. *Amalricus,* Ger. *Emerich,* It. *Amerigo.*

**Emily**, *em'(i-)li,* **Emilia,** *i-mil'i-a,* fem. of the Roman gentile name *Aemilius.*—L. *Aemilia,* Ger. *Emilie,* Fr. *Émilie,* It. *Emilia.*—Sometimes confused with **Amelia.**

**Emlyn**, *em'lin, m.* (W.) meaning uncertain—L. *Aemilianus,* pertaining to the gens *Aemilius,* has been suggested.

**Emma**, *em'a, f.* (Gmc.) whole, universal.—Also a shortened form of various names beginning Ermin-, Irmin-.—Dims. **Emm, Emmie.**

**Emmanuel, Immanuel,** *i-man'ū-il, m.* (Heb.) God with us.—Sp. *Manuel,* Port. *Manoel.*

**Emmeline, Emeline,** *em'i-lēn, -lin, f.* prob. for **Amelia.**

**Emrys**, *em'ris, m.* Welsh form of **Ambrose.**

**Ena**, *ē'na, f.* (Ir.) fire; or a shortened form of **Eugenia** or other name of similar sound.

**Enid**, *ē'nid, f.* (W.) possibly wood-lark.

**Enoch**, *ē-nək, m.* (Heb.) poss. consecrated, or teaching.

**Ephraim**, *ēf'* or *ef'rā-im, m.* (Heb.) fruitful.

**Erasmus**, *i-raz'məs, m.* (Gr.) lovely, deserving love.—Dim. **Rasmus.**

**Erastus**, *i-ras'təs, m.* (Gr.) lovely.—Dim. **Rastus.**

**Eric**, *er'ik, m.* (Gmc.; O.N. *Eirikr*) perh. sole ruler.—Ger. *Erich,* O.E. *Yric.*—Fem. **Erica,** *er'i-ka* (associated with Gr. *ereikē,* heath).

**Ermentrude, Irmentrude,** *ûr'min-trōōd, f.* (Gmc.) prob. Ermin (the god), and strength.

**Ernest**, *ûr'nist, m.* (Gmc.) earnest.—Ger. *Ernst,* It. and Sp. *Ernesto.*—Dim. **Ernie.**—Fem. **Ernestine.**

**Esau**, *ē'sö, m.* (Heb.) hairy.

**Esme**, *ez'mi, m., f.* (Fr.) beloved (a Scottish name).

**Esmeralda**, *ez-mi-ral'da, f.* (Sp.) emerald.

**Estella**, *es-tel'a,* **Estelle,** *es-tel', f.* See **Stella.** Perh. sometimes for **Esther.**

**Esther**, *es'tər,* **Hester,** *hes'tər, f.* poss. Pers., star; or Babylonian, *Ishtar,* the goddess Astarte.—Dims. **Essie, Hetty.**

**Ethel**, *eth'l, f.* (O.E.) noble (not used uncompounded in O.E.).

**Ethelbert**, *eth'l-bərt, m.* (O.E.) noble-bright.

**Etheldred, -a.** See **Audrey.**

**Ethelind**, *eth'ə-lind,* **Ethelinda,** *-lin'da, f.* (Gmc.) noble snake.

**Etta**, *et'a, f.* See **Henrietta.**

**Eugene**, *ū'jēn, m.* (Gr.) well-born.—L. *Eugenius,* Fr. *Eugène,* Ger. *Eugen.*—Dim. **Gene.**—Fem. **Eugenia.**—Fr. *Eugénie.*—Dims. **Ena, Gene.**

**Eulalia**, *ū-lā'li-a, f.* (Gr.) fair speech.

**Eunice**, *ū-nī'sē, ū'nis, f.* (Gr.) happy victory.

**Euphemia**, *ū-fē'mi-a, f.* (Gr.) of good report.—Dims. **Effie, Euphan, Euphie, Phemie** (*fā'mi*), **Phamie.**

**Eusebius**, *ū-sē'bi-əs, m.* (Gr.) pious.

**Eustace**, *ū'stis,* **Eustachius,** *ū-stā'ki-əs, m.* (Gr.) rich in corn (Gr. *eustachys,* confounded with *eustathēs,* stable).—Ger. *Eustachius,* Fr. *Eustache,* It. *Eustachio,* Sp. *Eustaquio.*—Fem. **Eustacia.**

**Eva**, *ē'va,* **Eve,** *ēv, f.* (Heb.) life.—Fr. *Ève,* Ger. It., Sp. *Eva.*—Dims. **Evie, Evelina** (q.v.), **Eveleen** (Ir.).

**Evan**, *ev'ən, m.* Anglicised Welsh form of **John.**—W. *Ifan.*

**Evangeline**, *i-van'ji-lēn, -lin, -līn, f.* (Gr.) bringer of good news.

**Evelina**, *ev-i-lē'na, -lī'na, f.,* **Eveline,** *ev'i-lēn ēv'lin, f.,* **Evelyn,** *ēv'lin, ev'i-lin, m.* and *f.,* partly dims. of **Eve,** partly from the surname **Evelyn,** partly from Gmc. *Avilina* from *Avi.*

**Everard**, *ev'ə-rärd, m.* (Gmc.) boar-hard.—Ger. *Eberhard, Ebert,* Fr. *Évraud.*

**Ewan, Ewen,** *ū'ən, m.* See **Owen.**

**Ezekiel**, *i-zē'ki-əl, m.* (Heb.) God will strengthen. —Ger. *Ezechiel, Hesechiel,* Fr. *Ézéchiel.*—Dim. **Zeke.**

**Ezra**, *ez'ra, m.* (Heb.) help.—L. *Ezra, Esdras,* Fr. *Esdras,* Ger. *Esra.*

**Fabian**, *fā'bi-ən, m.*—L. *Fabianus,* a deriv. of the gentile name *Fabius,* perh. connected with *faba,* bean.

**Faith**, *fāth, f.* (Eng. or Fr.) faith.

**Fanny**, *fan'i, f.* See **Francis.**

**Farquhar**, *fär'kər, fär'hhar, m.* (Gael.) manly.—Gael. *Fearachar.*

**Faustina**, *fös-ti'na,* **Faustine,** *-tēn', f.* (L.) fortunate.

**Fay**, *fā, f.* (Fr.) perh. faith, perh. fairy.

**Felix**, *fē'liks, m.* (L.) happy.—Fem. **Felicia** (*fi-lish'i-a*), **Felice** (*fi-lēs',* confused with **Phyllis,** happy, **Felicity,** happiness.

**Fenella**, *fin-el'a, f.* anglicisation of Gael. *Fionn-ghuala,* white shoulder.—Ir. *Finola.*

**Ferdinand**, *fûr'di-nənd, m.* (Gmc.) journey-risk.—Ger. *Ferdinand,* Fr. *Ferdinand, Ferrand,* Sp. *Fernando, Hernando,* It. *Ferdinando, Ferrando.*

**Fergus**, *fûr'gəs, m.* (Gael.) supremely choice.—Gael. *Fearghas.*

**Fidelia**, *fi-dē'li-a, f.* (L.) faithful.

**Finlay, Findlay,** *fin'li, -lā, m.* (Gael.) a sunbeam.

**Fiona**, *fē-ō'na, fē'o-na, f.* (Gael.) fair.

**Flavia**, *flā'vi-a, f.* (L.) yellow, fair.

**Fleur**, *flûr, f.* (Fr.) flower.

**Flora**, *flō', flö'ra, f.* (L.) name of the Roman

flower-goddess.—Dims. **Flo, Florrie** (*flor'i*).
**Florence,** *flor'ins, f.* (L.) blooming; also born in Florence.—L. *Florentia* (masc. *Florentius*).— Dims. **Flo, Florrie, Flossie, Floy.**
**Francis,** *frän'sis, m.* (Fr.) Frankish, French.—L. *Franciscus,* Fr. *François,* It. *Francesco,* Sp. *Francisco,* Ger. *Franz, Franziskus.*—Dims. **Frank, Francie, Frankie.**—Fem. **Frances** (*frän'sis, -səz*).—L. *Francisca.* Fr. *Françoise,* It. *Francesca* (dim. *Franceschina*), Sp. *Francisca,* Ger. *Franziska.*—Dims. **Fanny, Frank, Francie, Francine.**
**Freda,** *frē'da, f.* dim. of Winifred, or for Frieda.
**Frederick, Frederic,** *fred'rik, m.* (Gmc.) peace-rule.—L. *Fredericus, Fridericus,* Ger. *Friedrich, Fritz,* Fr. *Frédéric,* It. *Federico, Federigo,* Sp. *Federico.*—Dims. (both genders) **Fred, Freddie, Freddy.**—Fem. **Frederica** (*fred-ə-rē'ka*).—Ger. *Friederike,* Fr. *Frédérique.*
**Frieda,** *frē'da, f.* (Gmc.) peace.—Used as a dim. for any feminine name with the element *fred* or *frid.*
**Fulk, Fulke,** *foolk, m.* (Gmc.) people.

**Gabriel,** *gä'bri-əl, m.* (Heb.) God is mighty, or man of God.—Dims. **Gabe, Gabby** (*gab'i*).—Fem. **Gabrielle.**
**Gail,** *gāl, f.* dim. of Abigail—now regarded as a name in its own right.
**Gareth,** *gar'ith, m.* O.Fr. *Gahariet,* prob. from some W. name.
**Gary, Garry,** *gar'i, m.* perh. a dim. of Gareth; perh. for Garvey (Gmc.) spear-bearer.
**Gaspar,** *gas'pər, m.* See Jasper.
**Gavin,** *gav'in,* **Gawain,** *gä'win, gö'in, m.* (W.) perh. white hawk.
**Gay,** *gā, m.* and *f.* (Eng.) gay.
**Gemma,** *jem'a, f.* (It.) a gem.
**Gene,** *jēn,* for Eugene, Eugenia.
**Genevieve,** *jen'i-vēv, f.* (Fr.—Celt.) meaning obscure.—Fr. *Geneviève.*
**Geoffrey, Jeffrey,** *jef'ri, m.* (Gmc.). Two names have run together—district-peace (O.H.G. *Gaufrid*) and traveller-peace (O.H.G. *Walahfrid*).— L. *Gaufridus, Galfridus,* Sp. *Geofredo,* Fr. *Geoffroi.*—Dim. **Jeff.**—Confounded with Godfrey.
**George,** *jörj, m.* (Gr.) husbandman.—L. *Georgius,* Fr. *Georges, George,* Ger. *Georg,* It. *Giorgio,* Sp. *Jorge,* Gael. *Seòras.*—Dims. **Geordie, Georgie, Georgy, Dod, Doddy.**—Fem. **Georgia, Georgiana** (*-i-ä'na*), **Georgette, Georgina** (*-ē'na*).—Dim. **Georgie.**
**Gerald,** *jer'əld, m.* (Gmc.) spear-wielding.—L. *Geraldus, Giraldus,* Fr. *Géraud, Giraud, Girauld,* It. *Giraldo,* Ger. *Gerold, Gerald.*—Fem. **Geraldine** (*-ēn*).
**Gerard,** *jer'ärd, -ərd, m.* (Gmc.) spear-hard.—L. *Gerardus,* Fr. *Gérard,* It. *Gerardo,* Ger. *Gerhard.*
**Gerda,** *gûr'da, f.* (O.N.) in Norse mythology, the name of the wife of the god Frey.
**German,** *jûr'mən, m.* (L.) German.—Fem. **Germaine** (Fr., *zher-men'*).
**Gertrude,** *gûr'trood, f.* (Gmc.) spear-might.— Dims. **Gert, Gertie, Trudy.**
**Gervase,** *jûr'vis, -väz, m.* (Gmc.) spear-servant.— Also **Gervas, Jervis.**
**Gideon,** *gid'i-ən, m.* (Heb.) hewer.
**Gil.** See Gilbert, Giles.
**Gilbert,** *gil'bərt, m.* (Gmc.) bright hostage.—L. *Gilbertus,* Fr. *Guilbert, Gilbert,* It. and Sp. *Gilberto,* Ger. *Gilbert, Giselbert.*—Dims. **Gib, Gibbie, Gil.**
**Giles,** *jīlz, m.* (Fr.—Gr.) kid.—L. *Aegidius,* Fr. *Gilles,* Ger. *Agidius,* It. *Egidio,* Sp. *Egidio, Gil.*
**Gill, Gillian,** *jil, -i-ən, f.* See Julian.—Also **Jill, Jillian.**
**Gladys,** *glad'is, f.* W. *Gwladys* for Claudia.
**Gloria,** *glō'ri-a, glö', f.* (L.) glory.
**Godfrey,** *god'fri, m.* (Gmc.) God's peace.—L. *Godofridus,* Fr. *Godefroi,* Ger. *Gottfried,* It.

*Goffredo, Godofredo,* Sp. *Godofredo, Gofredo.*— Confused with Geoffrey.
**Godwin,** *god'win, m.* (O.E.) God-friend.
**Gordon,** *gör'dən, m.* from the surname.
**Grace,** *grās, f.* (Fr.) grace.
**Graham,** *grā'əm, m.* from the surname—also sometimes **Graeme.**
**Gregory,** *greg'ə-ri, m.* (Gr.) watcher.—L. *Gregorius,* Ger. *Gregor, Gregorius,* Fr. *Grégoire,* It. and Sp. *Gregorio.*
**Greta,** *grē'ta, gret'a.* See Margaret.
**Griffith,** *grif'ith, m.* (W.) ruddy, rufous.—W. *Gruffydd.*
**Grizel, Grizzel, Grissel, Grisell,** *griz'l,* **Griselda,** *Grizelda, gri-zel'da, f.* (Gmc.) perh. grey war, perh. Christ war.—Ger. *Griseldis,* It. *Griselda.*
**Gustavus,** *gus-tā'vəs, -tä'vəs, m.* (Gmc.) meditation (?) staff.—L. *Gustavus,* Swed. *Gustaf,* Ger. *Gustav,* Fr. *Gustave.*
**Guy,** *gī, m.* (Gmc.) perh. wood, perh. wide.— O.H.G. *Wido, Wito,* L., Ger., It., and Sp. *Guido,* Fr. *Guy, Guyon.*
**Gwendolen,** *gwen'dō-lin, f.* (W.) white (second element obscure).—Dims. **Gwen, Gwenda, Gwennie.**
**Gwillym, Gwilym.** See William.
**Gwyneth,** *gwin'ith, f.* (W.) blessed.

**Hab, Habbie.** See Albert.
**Hadrian.** See Adrian.
**Hal, Hal.** See Henry.
**Halbert,** *hal'bərt, m.* an old Scots form of Albert.
**Hamish,** *hä'mish, m.* See James.
**Hannah,** *han'a, f.* See Ann.
**Harold,** *har'əld, m.* (Gmc.) army rule.
**Harriet, Harriot,** *har'i-ət,* fem. forms of Henry.— Dim. **Hatty.**
**Hartley,** *härt'li, m.* from the surname.
**Hazel,** *hä'zl,* **Heather,** *hedh'ər, f.* from the plants.
**Hector,** *hek'tər, m.* (Gr.) holding fast.—Dim. **Heck.**—Ger. *Hektor,* It. *Ettore,* Sp. *Héctor.*
**Hedwig,** *hed'wig, f.* (Ger.) contention-fight.
**Helen,** *hel'en, -in,* **Helena,** *hel'i-na,* **Ellen,** *el'ən, f.* (Gr.) bright.—L. *Helena,* Fr. *Hélène,* Ger. *Helene,* It. and Sp. *Elena.*—Dims. **Nell, Nellie, Nelly.**
**Helga,** *hel'ga, f.* (Gmc., Norse) holy.
**Heloise, Eloise,** (*h*)*el-ō-ēz',* **Eloisa,** *el-ō-ē'za, f.* (Gmc.) sound or whole, and wide.—Fr. *Héloïse.*
**Henry,** *hen'ri,* **Harry,** *har'i, m.* (Gmc.) house ruler. —L. *Henricus, Enricus,* Fr. *Henri,* It. *Enrico,* Sp. *Enrique,* Ger. *Heinrich* (dims. *Heinz, Heinze, Hinz, Hinze*), Du. *Hendrik.*—Fem. **Henrietta, Harriet, Harriot.**—Fr. *Henriette,* It. *Enrichetta,* Sp. *Enriqueta.*—Dims. **Hatty, Hetty.**
**Herbert,** *hûr'bərt, m.* (Gmc.) army-bright.—Ger. *Herbert,* It. *Erberto,* Sp. *Heriberto.*—Dims. **Bert, Bertie.**
**Hercules,** *hûr'kū-lēz, m.* L. name of the Greek hero Herakles, glory of Hera.—It. *Ercole.*
**Herman, Hermann,** *hûr'mən, m.* (Gmc.) army man, warrior.—Ger. *Hermann.*
**Hermione,** *hər-mī'ə-nē, f.* (Gr.) a derivative of *Hermes* (Greek god).
**Hester.** See Esther.
**Hetty,** *het'i,* dim. of Hester and of Henrietta.
**Hew,** another spelling of Hugh, preferred by certain families.
**Hezekiah,** *hez-i-ki'a, m.* (Heb.) Yah is strength, or has strength.—Fr. *Ézéchias,* Ger. *Hiskia.*
**Hilary,** *hil'ə-ri, m.* and *f.* (L.) cheerful.—L. and Ger. *Hilarius,* Fr. *Hilaire,* It. *Ilario,* Sp. *Hilario.*—Also fem. **Hilaria.**
**Hilda,** *hil'da, f.* (Gmc.) battle.
**Hildebrand,** *hil'di-brand, m.* (Gmc.) battle sword.
**Hildegard,** *hil'di-gärd, f.* (Gmc.) know battle.
**Hiram, Hyram,** *hi'rəm, m.* (Heb.) noble.
**Hob, Hobbie,** *hob, -i, m.* for Halbert, Robert.
**Hodge,** *hoj, m.* for Roger.
**Homer,** *hō'mər, m.* (U.S.) from the name of the poet.

Honor, *on'ər*, Honora, *ho-nō'ra*, -*nö'ra*, Honoria, -*ri-a*, *f.* (L.) honour, honourable.—Dims. Nora, Norah (Ir. Noreen).—Masc. Honorius.
Hope, *hōp*, *m.* and *f.* (Eng.) hope.
Horace, *hor'is*, Horatio, *ho-rā'shō*, *m.* (L.) the Roman gentile name *Horatius*.—Fem. Horatia.
Hortensia, *hör-ten'sya*, *f.* (L.) fem. of a Roman gentile name—gardener.
Hubert, *hū'bərt*, *m.* (Gmc.) mind-bright.
Hugh, Hew, *hū*, Hugo, *hū'gō*, *m.* (Gmc.) mind.—L., Ger., Sp. *Hugo*, Fr. *Hugues*, It. *Ugo*, *Ugone*.—Dims. Huggin, Hughie (obs. Huchon).
Hulda, *hul'da*, *f.* (Gmc.) name of a Germanic goddess—gracious. Also (Norse) covered.
Huldah, *hul'da*, *f.* (Heb.) weasel.
Humbert, *hum'bərt*, *m.* (Gmc.) prob. giant-bright.—It. *Umberto*.
Humphrey, Humphry, *hum'fri*, *m.* (Gmc.) prob. giant-peace.—Ger. *Humfried*, Fr. *Onfroi*, It. *Onofrio*, Sp. *Hunfredo*.—Dims. Humph, Numps, Dump, Dumphy.
Hyacinth, *hī'ə-sinth*, *m.* and *f.* (Gr.) the flower hyacinth (masc. in Greek).
Hyram. See Hiram.

Iain, Ian, *ē'ən*, *m.* Gaelic for John.
Ianthe, *i-an'thē*, *f.* (Gr.) violet flower (name of a sea-nymph).
Ida, *ī'da*, *f.* (Gmc.) labour.
Ifan, *ē'van*, *m.* Welsh form of John.
Ifor, *ē'vor*, *m.* Welsh form of Ivo, Ivor.
Ignatius, *ig-nā'shəs*, *m.* Latinised from a late Greek form of the Roman (perh. orig. Samnite) gentile name *Egnatius* (meaning unknown), assimilated to L. *ignis*, fire.—Fr. *Ignace*, Ger. *Ignaz*, It. *Ignazio*, Sp. *Ignacio*. See Inigo.
Igor, *ē'gör*, *m.* Russian form of the Scandinavian name *Ingvarr*, watchfulness of Ing (the god Frey).
Immanuel. See Emmanuel.
Imogen, *im'ō-jən*, *f.* prob. a misprint in the Folio for *Innogen* (in Shak. *Cymbeline*), poss. O. Ir., a daughter, girl.
Ines, Inez, *i'nez*, *ē'nez*, Sp. *ē-nās'*, *f.* See Agnes.
Ingeborg, *ing'i-börg*, *f.* (Scand.) stronghold of Ing (the god Frey).
Ingram, *ing'(g)rəm*, *m.* raven of Ing (Frey).
Ingrid, *ing'(g)rid*, *f.* (Scand.) ride of Ing (Frey), or maiden of the Ingvaeones.
Inigo, *in'i-gō*, *m.* (Sp.) either a form of Ignatius or another name confused with it.—L. *Enecus*, Sp. *Íñigo*.
Iona, *ī-ō'na*, *f.* from the place-name.
Ira, *ī'ra*, *m.* (Heb.) watchful.
Irene, Eirene, *i-rē'nē*, sometimes *ī-rēn'*, *i'rēn*, *f.* (Gr.) peace.
Iris, *ī'ris*, *f.* (Gr.) rainbow, iris (plant)—name of Hera's messenger.
Irmentrude. See Ermentrude.
Isaac, Izaak, *ī'zək*, *m.* (Heb.) laugh.—Dims. Ik, Ike, Iky.
Isabella, *iz-ə-bel'a*, Isabel, Isobel, *iz'ə-bəl*, -*bel*, or (Scots) Ishbel, *ish'bəl*, Isbel, *iz'bəl*, *f.* (Sp.—Heb.) forms of Elizabeth, now regarded as an independent name.—Sp. *Isabel*, Fr. *Isabelle* (*Isabeau*), It. *Isabella*.—Dims. Bel, Bell, Belle, Bella, Ella, Ib, Ibby, Isa (*i'za*), Tib, Tibbie, Tibby.
Isaiah, *ī-zī'a*, or -*zā'*, *m.* (Heb.) Yahwe helps.—L. *Isaias*, Ger. *Jesaias*, Fr. *Isaïe*, *Esaïe*, Sp. *Isaías*, It. *Isaia*.
Isidor, Isidore, Isadore, *iz'i-dör*, -*dör*, *m.* (Gr.) perh. gift of Isis.—Sp. *Isidro*, *Isidoro*.—Fem. Isidora, Isadora.
Isla, *ī'la*, *f.* from the place-name.
Isold, Isolde, Isolda, *i-zold'*, -*a*, Isolt, *i-zolt'*, *f.* perh. (Gmc.) ice-rule; or a Welsh name.
Israel, *iz'rā-əl*, -*el*, *m.* (Heb.) ruling with the Lord.
Ivan, *i'vən*, *ē-vän'*, *m.* (Russ.). See John.
Ivo, Ivor, *ī'vō*, *i'vər*, or *ē'*, *m.* prob. Celtic, but perh. from a Gmc. root meaning yew.—W. *Ifor*,

Fr. Ives, Yves, Ivon, Yvon; fem. Ivette, Yvette, Ivonne, Yvonne.
Ivy, *ī'vi*, *m.* and *f.* (Eng.) from the plant.

Jabez, *jā'biz*, *m.* (Heb.) perh. sorrow, perh. height.
Jack, *jak*, *m.* See John.
Jacob, *jā'kəb*, *m.* (Heb.) follower, supplanter, or deceiver.—It. *Giacobbe*, Sp. *Jacob*.—Dim. Jake. See also James.
James, *jāmz*, *m.* Same as Jacob.—L. *Jacōbus* (later Jacōbus, Jacōmus, whence the forms with *m*), Fr. *Jacques*, It. *Jacopo*, *Giacomo*, *Iachimo*, Sp. *Jacobo*, *Diego*, *Jaime*, *Jago*, Ger. *Jakob*, Gael. *Seamas*, *Seamus*, *Seumas* (Anglicised vocative Hamish).—Dims. Jim, Jimmie, Jem, Jemmie, Jamie, (*jim'i*, Scot.), Jeames (*jēmz*, Scot. and burlesque).—Fems. Jacoba (*jə-kō'ba*), Jacobina (-*bē'na*), Jacqueline, Jaqueline (*zhak'-(ə)-lin*, -*lēn*), Jacquetta (-*ket'a*), Jamesina (-*si'na*).—Jemima has nothing to do with James.
Jan. See John.
Jane, *jān*, Jean, *jēn*, Joan, *jōn*, Jo(h)anna, *jō-an'a*, Joanne (*jō-an'*), fems. of John.—L. *Johanna*, Fr. *Jeanne* (dim. *Jeannette*), It. *Giovanna*, Sp. *Juana* (dim. *Juanita*), Ger. *Johanna*, Gael. *Seonad* (Anglicised *Shona*), *Sìne* (Anglicised *Sheena*), W. *Sian*.—Dims. Janet (*jan'it*), Janetta, Janey, Janie, Janice, Jeanette, Jeannie, Jen, Jenny, Jennie, Jess, Jessie, Jessy, Netta, Nettie, Nita (*nē'ta*)—some of them regarded as separate names.
Janet, *jan'it*, *f.* a dim. of Jane, regarded as an independent name.
Janice, *jan'is*, *f.* orig. a dim. of Jane, now regarded as a separate name.
Jared, *ja'*, *jā'rid*, *m.* (Heb.) descent.
Jasmine, *jas'min*, *f.* from the flower.—Deriv. Jessamine.
Jason, *jā'sən*, *f.* poss. Gr. rendering of Heb. Joshua or Jesus, or simply (Gr.) a healer.
Jasper, *jas'pər*, Gaspar, *gas'pər*, *m.* prob. Pers. treasure-bringer.—Fr. *Gaspard*, Ger. *Kaspar*.
Jean, *jēn*, *f.* See Jane, etc. For Fr. *m.* (*zhā*), see John.
Jedidiah, Jedediah, *jed-i-dī'a*, *m.* (Heb.) Yah is friend.
Jeffrey, *jef'ri*, *m.* See Geoffrey.
Jem, Jemmie. Dims. of James.
Jemima, *ji-mi'ma*, *f.* (Heb.) meaning unknown (day, dove, pure, fortunate have been suggested).—Not connected with James.—Dim. Mima.
Jennifer, Jenifer, *jen'i-fər*, *f.* (W.) a form of *Guinevere*, perh. white wave, or white phantom.—Dims. Jen, Jennie, Jenny.
Jenny, Jennie, *jen'i*, *jin'i*, *f.* See Jane, Jennifer.
Jeremiah, *jer-i-mi'a*, Jeremias, -*əs*, Jeremy, *jer'i-mi*, *m.* (Heb.) Yah is high, or heals, or founds.—Dim. Jerry (*jer'i*).
Jerome, *jer'ōm*, *ji-rōm'*, *m.* (Gr.) holy name.—L. and Ger. *Hieronymus*, Fr. *Jérôme*, It. *Geronimo*, *Gerolamo*, *Girolamo*, Sp. *Jerónimo*.
Jerry, *jer'i*, *m.* dim. of Jeremy, also of Gerald, Gerard, Jerome.
Jervis, *jûr'vis*, *m.* See Gervase.
Jess, *jes*, Jessie, *f.* forms of Janet, chiefly Scots. See Jane.
Jessamine. See Jasmine.
Jesse, *jes'i*, *m.* (Heb.) Yah is.
Jessica, *jes'i-ka*, *f.* (app. Heb.) perh. Yah is looking.
Jethro, *jeth'rō*, *m.* (Heb.) superiority.
Jill, *jil*, Jillian, -*yən*, *f.* See Julian.
Jim, Jimmie. See James.
Jo, for Joseph, Josepha, Josephine.
Joachim, *jō'ə-kim*, *m.* (Heb.) Yah has set up.—Sp. *Joaquín*, It. *Gioacchino*.
Joan, Jo(h)anna, Joann, Joanne. See Jane.
Joannes. See John.
Job, *jōb*, *m.* (Heb.) perh. pious, or persecuted, afflicted.—Ger. *Hiob*, It. *Giobbe*.
Jocelyn, Jocelin, *jos'(ə)-lin*, *m.* and *f.* perh.

(Gmc.) one of the Geats (a people of southern Sweden), or (L.) connected with **Justin, Justus.** Also fem. **Joceline.**

**Jock,** *jok, m.* See **John.**

**Joe, Jo, Joey,** for **Joseph, Josepha, Josephine.**

**Joel,** *jō'əl, m.* (Heb.) Yah is the Lord.

**John,** *jon, m.* (Heb.) poss. Yah is gracious.—L. *Jo(h)annes,* Fr. *Jean,* It. *Giovanni (Gian, Gianni),* Sp. *Juan,* Port. *Joāo,* Ger. *Johann, Johannes* (dim. *Hans),* Du. *Jan,* Russ. *Ivan,* Ir. *Seán* (Anglicised *Shane, Shawn), Eoin,* Gael. *Iain (Ian),* W. *Ifan.*—Dims. **Johnnie, Jack** (from **Jankin), Jackie,** (Scot. **Jock, Jockie), Jan,** obs. **Jankin.**—Fem. see under **Jane.**

**Jonas,** *jō'nəs,* **Jonah,** *-na, m.* (Heb.) dove.

**Jonathan,** *jon'ə-thən, m.* (Heb.) Yah has given.

**Joseph,** *jō'zif, m.* (Heb.) Yah increases.—L. *Josephus,* Fr. *Joseph,* It. *Giuseppe* (dim. *Beppo),* Sp. *José* (dims. *Pepe, Pepillo, Pepito),* Ger. *Joseph, Josef.*—Dims. **Jo, Joe, Joey, Jos** (*jos*).— Fem. **Josepha** (*-sē'fa, -ze'fa),* **Josephine** (*-zi-fēn*). —Dims. **Jo, Joe, Josie, Jozy.**

**Joshua,** *josh'ū-a, m.* (Heb.) Yah delivers.—L. and Ger. *Josua,* Fr. and Sp. *Josué,* It. *Giosuè.*—Dim. **Josh.**

**Josiah,** *jōz-i'a,* **Josias,** *-əs, m.* (Heb.) Yah supports.

**Joy,** *joi, f.* (Eng.) joy.

**Joyce,** *jois, f.* (Gmc.) a Geat (see Jocelyn).

**Judith,** *joo'dith, f.* (Heb.) Jewess.—Dims. **Judy, Judie.**

**Julian,** *joo'lyən, -li-ən, m., f.* (L.) derived from, belonging to, Julius.—Dim. **Jule.**—Fem. **Juliana** (*-ä'na),* **Jillian, Gillian** (*jil'yən*).—Dim. **Jill.**

**Julius,** *joo'li-əs, m.* (L.) a Roman gentile name, perh. downy-bearded.—Dim. **Jule.**—Fr. *Jules,* It. *Giulio.*—Fem. **Julia.**—Dims. **Julie, Juliet.**

**June,** *joon, f.* (L.) from the month.

**Justus,** *jus'təs, m.* (L.) just.—Derivs. **Justin** (fem. **Justina,** *-ti'na,* **Justine,** *-tēn*) **Justinian** (*-tin'yən, -i-ən*).

**Karen, Karin,** *kä'rən,* **Kate, Katherine, Katharine, Kathryn, Kathleen, Katrine, Katerina, Katrina, Kay.** See **Catherine.**

**Keith,** *kēth, m.* from the surname or place-name.

**Kenelm,** *ken'elm, m.* (O.E. *Cenhelm*) keen helmet.

**Kenneth,** *ken'ith, m.* (Gael.) handsome.—Gael. *Caioneach.*—Dims. **Ken, Kennie, Kenny.**

**Kester,** *kes'tər, m.* See **Christopher.**

**Kevin,** *kev'in, m.* (Ir.) comely birth.

**Keziah,** *ki-zi'a, f.* (Heb.) cassia.

**King,** *king, m.* (U.S.) from the title.

**Kirsty,** *kûr'sti,* **Kirsteen,** *-stēn, f.* See **Christian.**

**Kit.** See **Christopher, Catherine.**—**Kitty.** See **Catherine.**

**Lachlan,** *lahh'lən, m.* (Gael.) warlike.—Dim. **Lachy.**

**Lalage,** *lal'ə-jē, f.* (L.—Gr.) talkative, prattling.— Dim. **Lallie.**

**Lambert,** *lam'bərt, m.* (Gmc.) land-bright.

**Lance,** *läns, m.* (Gmc.) land.—Dims. **Lancelot, Launcelot.**

**Laura,** *lö'ra, f.* (L.) Laurel.—Also **Laurinda, Lorinda.**—Dims. **Lauretta, Lolly.**

**Laurence, Lawrence,** *lo', lö'rəns, m.* (L.) laurel.— L. *Laurentius,* It. *Lorenzo,* Ger. *Lorenz.*— Dims. **Larry** (*lar'i*), **Laurie, Lawrie.**

**Lavinia,** *lə-vin'i-a, f.* (L.) origin unknown (second wife of Aeneas).

**Lazarus,** *laz'ə-rəs, m.* (Gr. *Lazaros* from Heb.) a form of Eleazar.

**Lea, Leah,** *lē'a, f.* (Heb.) a cow.

**Leander,** *li-an'dər, m.* (Gr.) lion man.

**Lee, Leigh,** *lē, m.* and *f.* from the surname.

**Leila,** *lā', lē', li'la, f.* (Pers.) night.

**Lemuel,** *lem'ū-əl, m.* (Heb.) consecrated to God.

**Lena,** *lē'na, f.* See **Helena, Magdalen.**

**Leo,** *lē'ō, m.* (L.) lion.—Fem. **Leonie** (*lē'ə-ni*).

**Leonard,** *len'ərd, m.* (Gmc.) lion-hard.

**Leonora,** *lē-ə-nō'ra, -nö'ra, f.* See **Eleanor.**

**Leopold,** *lē'ō-pōld, m.* (Gmc.) people-bold.—Ger. *Luitpold, Leopold.*

**Leslie,** *m.,* **Lesley,** *f., lez'li,* from the surname or place-name.

**Lettice,** *let'is,* **Letitia, Laetitia,** *li-tish'ya, f.* (L.) gladness.—Dim. **Lettie, Letty.**

**Lewis,** *loo'is,* **Louis,** *loo'is, loo'i,* **Ludovic(k),** *lū', loo'dō-vik,* **Lodowick,** *lō'dō-wik*—also **Aloys,** *al'ō-is, -ois',* **Aloysius,** *-ish'əs, -ē'zi-əs, -is'i-əs, m.* (Gmc.) famous warrior.—L. *Ludovicus, Aloysius,* Fr. *Louis* (from *Chlodowig, Clovis),* Prov. *Aloys,* It. *Ludovico, Luigi, Aloysio,* Sp. *Luis, Aloisio,* Ger. *Ludwig.*—Dims. **Lewie, Louie, Lew.**—Fem. **Louisa** (*loo-ē'za),* **Louise** (*-ēz'*).—Dims. **Lou, Louie.**—Fr. *Louise (Lisette),* It. *Luisa,* Ger. *Luise.*

**Liam,** *lē'əm, m.* Irish form of **William.**

**Libby.** See **Elizabeth.**

**Lily,** *lil'i,* **Lil(l)ian,** *-ən,* **Lil(l)ias,** *-əs, f.* prob. partly from the flower, partly for **Elizabeth.**

**Linda, Lynda,** *lin'da, f.* (Gmc.) short for any feminine name ending in -lind (snake).—Now regarded as a name in its own right.—Dim. **Lindy.**

**Lindsay, Lindsey,** *lin(d)'zi, m.* and *f.* from the surname.

**Lionel,** *li'ə-nəl, m.* (L.) young lion.

**Liz, Lizzie, Lisa, Liza, Lisbeth, Lizbeth.** See **Elizabeth.**

**Llewelyn,** *(h)lē-wel'in, loo-el'in, m.* (W.) meaning doubtful.

**Lloyd,** *loid, m.* (W.) grey.

**Lodowick.** See **Lewis.**

**Lois,** *lō'is, f.* prob. (Gr.) good.

**Lola,** *lō'la, f.* for **Dolores,** or **Carlotta.**

**Lord,** *lörd, m.* (U.S.) from the title.

**Lorenzo,** *lō-ren'zō, lö-, m.* See **Laurence.**

**Lorinda,** *lō-rin'da, lö-, f.* See **Laura.**

**Lorna,** *lör'na, f.* invented by R. D. Blackmore for the heroine of his novel *Lorna Doone.*

**Lorraine,** *lō-, lo-rān', f.* (Fr.) from the region of France so called.

**Lottie,** *lot'i, f.* See under **Charles.**

**Louis,** *m.,* **Louisa, Louise,** *f.* See **Lewis.**

**Lucas,** *loo'kəs, m.* See **Luke.**

**Lucius,** *loo'shi-əs, -shəs, m.* (L.) a Roman name probably connected with L. *lux,* light.—Fem. **Luce, Lucy, Lucinda, Lucilla, Lucil(l)e.**

**Lucretius,** *loo-krē'shəs, -shi-əs, m.* (L.) a Roman name perh. meaning gain.—Fem. **Lucretia, Lucrece** (*-krēs*).

**Ludovic(k).** See **Lewis.**

**Luke,** *look,* **Lucas,** *loo'kəs, m.* (L.) of Lucania (in Italy).

**Luther,** *loo'thər, m.* (Gmc.) famous warrior.—L. *Lutherus,* Fr. *Lothaire,* It. *Lotario.*

**Lydia,** *lid'i-a, f.* (Gr.) Lydian woman.

**Mabel,** *mā'bl, f.* See **Amabel.**

**Madge,** *maj,* **Mag,** *mag,* **Maggie,** *mag'i, f.* See **Margaret.**

**Madoc,** *mad'ək, m.* (W.) fortunate.

**Maeve.** See **Meave.**

**Magdalen(e),** *mag'də-lin, -lēn,* **Madel(e)ine, mad'-** (*ə-*)len, *-lēn, -lin, f.* of Magdala on the Sea of Galilee.—Dims. **Maud, Maude** (*möd*), **Maudlin.**

**Magnus,** *mag'nəs, m.* (L.) great.

**Maida,** *mā'da, f.* origin obscure.

**Màiri,** *mä'ri, f.* See **Mary.**

**Maisie,** *mā'zi, f.* See **Margaret.**

**Malachi,** *mal'ə-ki, m.* (Heb.) messenger of Yah.

**Malcolm,** *mal'kəm, möl', m.* (Gael.) Columba's servant.

**Malise,** *mal'is, m.* (Gael.) servant of Jesus.

**Mamie,** *mā'mi, f.* a chiefly American dim. of **Mary,** used also for **Margaret.**

**Manuel,** *man'ū-əl,* **Manoel.** See **Emmanuel.**

**Marcus,** *mär'kəs.* See **Mark.**

**Margaret,** *mär'gə-rit, f.* (Gr.) pearl.—Fr. *Marguer-*

*ite* (dim. *Margot*), It. *Margherita*, Sp. *Margarita*, Ger. *Margarete* (dims. *Grete, Gretchen*).—Dims.

**Madge, May, Maggie, Margie** (*mär'ji*), **Margery, Marjory, Meg, Meggie, Meta** (*mē'ta*), **Mysie, Peg, Peggie, Peggy, Greta, Rita.**

**Maria, Marie.** See **Mary.**

**Marian, Marion,** *mar'i-ən, mā'ri-ən,* **Marianne,** *mar-i-an', f.* (Fr.) orig. dims. of **Mary;** used also for the combination **Mary Ann.**—Dims. **Maynie, Mysie.**

**Marigold,** *mar'i-gōld, f.* from the flower.

**Marilyn,** *mar'i-lin.* See **Mary.**

**Marina,** *mə-rē'na, f.* (L.) of the sea.

**Marjory, Margery,** *mar'jər-i, f.* orig. a dim. of **Margaret,** now regarded as a name in its own right.

**Mark, märk, Marcus,** *-əs, m.* (L.) a Roman name prob. derived from Mars (the God).—L. *Marcus,* Sp. *Marcos,* Ger. *Markus.*—Derivs. **Marcius** (*mär'shi-əs*; fem. **Marcia**), strictly a Roman gentile name perh. of like origin, **Marcellus** (*-sel'əs*; fem. **Marcella**).

**Marlene,** *mär'lēn, f.* (Gmc.) perh. a compound of **Mary** and **Helena.**

**Marmaduke,** *mär'mə-dūk, m.* prob. (Celt.) servant of Madoc.—Dim. **Duke.**

**Martha,** *mär'tha, f.* (Aramaic) lady, mistress.— Dims. **Mat, Mattie, Matty, Pat, Pattie, Patty.**

**Martin, Martyn,** *mär'tin, m.* (L.) prob. warlike, of Mars.

**Mary,** *mā'ri,* **Maria,** *mə-rī'a, -rē'a,* **Marie,** *mä'ri, mə-rē',* **Miriam,** *mir'i-əm, f.* (Heb.) prob. wished-for child; less probably rebellion.—Gr. *Mariam,* L., It., Ger. *Maria,* Sp. *María,* Fr. *Marie* (dim. *Marion*), Gael. *Màiri.*—Dims. **May, Moll, Molly, Mally, Mamie, Marietta** (*mar-i-et'a*), **Marilyn, Maureen** (*mö-rēn',* or *mö'*), **Minnie, Poll, Polly.**

**Mat, Matty.** See **Martha, Matilda, Matthew.**

**Mat(h)ilda,** *mə-til'da, f.* (Gmc.) battle-might.— Dims. **Mat, Matty, Maud, Maude, Patty, Tilly, Tilda.**

**Matthew,** *math'ū,* **Matthias,** *mə-thī'əs, m.* (Heb.) gift of Yah.—Gr. *Matthaios,* L. *Matthaeus,* Fr. *Matthieu,* It. *Matteo,* Sp. *Mateo,* Ger. *Matthäus.* —Dims. **Mat, Matty.**

**Maud, Maude, möd,** *f.* See **Matilda, Magdalen.**

**Maurice,** *mor'is, mö'ris,* **Morris,** (L.) Moorish, dark-coloured.—L. *Mauritius,* Fr. *Maurice,* It. *Maurizio,* Sp. *Mauricio,* Ger. *Moritz.*

**Mavis,** *mā'vis, f.* (Eng.) thrush.

**Maximilian,** *maks-i-mil'yən, m.* (L.) a combination of *Maximus,* greatest, and *Aemilianus.*—Dim. **Max.**

**Maxwell,** *maks'wəl, m.* from the surname.—Dim. **Max.**

**May, mā,** *f.* partly for **Mary,** partly from the month.—Dim. **Minnie.**

**Meave, Maeve, mäv,** *f.* (Ir.) the goddess, or legendary queen of Connaught, Medb, or Meadhbh.

**Meg.** See **Margaret.**

**Melanie,** *mel'ə-ni, f.* (Gr.) black.

**Melicent.** See **Millicent.**

**Melissa,** *me-lis'a, f.* (Gr.) bee.

**Mercy,** *mûr'si, f.* (Eng.) mercy.—Sp. *Mercedes* (mercies, bounties).

**Meredith,** *mer'i-dith, m.* and *f.* from the surname.

**Meta.** See **Margaret.**

**Mhairi,** *vä'rē, mä'rē, f.* (Gael.) vocative case of **Màiri,** used erroneously as its equivalent. See **Mary.**

**Micah,** *mi'ka, m.* (Heb.) contraction of *Micaiah* —who is like Jehovah?

**Michael,** *mi'kl, m.* (Heb.) who is like the Lord?— Fr. *Michel,* It. *Michele,* Sp. and Port. *Miguel,* Ger. *Michael* (dim. *Michel*).—Dims. **Mick, Micky, Mike.**—Fem. **Michaela, Michelle.**

**Mildred,** *mil'drid, f.* (Gmc.; O.E. *Mildthryth*) mild power.—Dim. **Millie.**

**Miles,** *milz, m.* (Gmc.) meaning doubtful, perh. merciful.

**Millicent,** *mil'i-sənt,* **Melicent,** *mel', f.* (Gmc.) work-strong.—Fr. *Mélisande.*—Dim. **Millie.**

**Millie,** *mil'i, f.* See **Mildred, Millicent, Emilia, Amelia.**

**Mima,** *mi'ma, f.* See **Jemima.**

**Mina,** *mē', mi'na, f.* See **Wilhelmina.**

**Minna,** *min'a, f.* (Gmc.) memory, or love.

**Minnie,** *min'i,* for **Minna, May,** or **Wilhelmina.**

**Mirabel,** *mir'ə-bel, f.* (L.) wonderful.

**Miranda,** *mi-ran'da, f.* (L.) to be admired or wondered at.

**Miriam,** *mir'i-əm.* See **Mary.**

**Moira, Moyra,** *moi'ra, f.* (Ir.) perh. great; (Gr.) a fate.

**Moll, Molly,** *mol'i, f.* See **Mary.**

**Mona,** *mō'na, f.* (Ir.) noble.

**Monica,** *mon'i-ka, f.* the name, possibly African, of St Augustine's mother; sometimes understood as (Gr.) alone, solitary.

**Montagu(e),** *mon'tə-gū, m.* from the surname.— Dim. **Monty.**

**Morag,** *mō'rag, m., f.* (Gael.) great.

**Morgan,** *mör'gən, m.* (W.) sea, sea-shore.—Fem. **Morgan, Morgana** (*-gä'na*).

**Morna,** *mör'na, f.* (Gael.) beloved.

**Morris.** See **Maurice.**

**Mortimer,** *mör'ti-mər, m.* from the surname.

**Morven,** *mör'vən,* **Morwen(n)a,** *mör-wen'a, f.* (Celt.) perh. a wave of the sea.

**Moses,** *mō'ziz, m.* meaning obscure.—Gr. *Mōysēs,* Ger. *Moses,* Fr. *Moïse,* It. *Moisè, Mosè,* Sp. *Moisés.*

**Moyna,** *moi'na, f.* perh. the same as **Mona.**

**Mungo,** *mung'gō, m.* (Gael.) amiable.

**Murdo,** *mûr'dō,* **Murdoch,** *mûr'dəhh, -dək, m.* (Gael.) seaman.

**Muriel,** *mū'ri-əl, f.* (Celt.) perh. sea-bright.

**Murray,** *mur'i, m.* from the surname.

**Myfanwy,** *mi-van'wi, f.* (W.) perh. *mabanwy,* child of water, or *my-manwy,* my fine one.

**Myra,** *mi'ra, f.* app. an arbitrary invention; sometimes used as an anagram of **Mary.**

**Myrtle,** *mûr'tl,* **Myrtilla,** *-til'a, f.* from the shrub.

**Mysie,** *mi'zi, f.* for **Margaret, Marion.**

**Nadine,** *nä'dēn, f.* Fr. form of Russ. *Nadezhda,* hope.

**Nahum,** *nä', nä'(h)əm, m.* (Heb.) consoling.

**Nan, Nana, Nanna, Nannie, Nanny,** *nan, -a, -i, f.* See **Ann.**

**Nance, Nancy,** *nans, -i, f.* See **Ann, Agnes.**

**Nanty,** *nan'ti, m.* dim. of **Anthony.**

**Naomi,** *nā-ō'mi, -mi,* or *nä', f.* (Heb.) pleasant.

**Nat, nat,** for **Nathaniel, Nathan, Natalia.**

**Natalia, Natalie,** (L.). See **Noel.**

**Nathan,** *nä'thən, m.* (Heb.) gift.—Dim. **Nat.**

**Nathaniel,** *nə-than'yəl, m.* (Heb.) gift of God.— Also **Nathanael** (*-ā-əl*).—Dim. **Nat.**

**Ned, Neddie, Neddy,** *ned, -i,* dims. of **Edward;** also of **Edgar, Edmund, Edwin.**

**Nehemiah,** *nē-hi-mi'a, m.* (Heb.) consolation of Yah.

**Neil,** *nēl.* See **Nigel.**

**Nell, Nellie, Nelly,** *nel, -i, f.* dims. of **Helen, Ellen, Eleanor.**

**Nessa, Nessie, Nesta,** dims. of **Agnes.**

**Netta, Nettie,** dims. of **Janet(ta), Henrietta, Antoinette.**

**Neville,** *nev'il, m.* from the surname.

**Niall,** *nēl.* See **Nigel.**

**Nicholas, Nicolas,** *nik'ə-ləs, m.* (Gr.) victory of the people.—Dims. **Nick, Colin** (q.v.), **Colley, Nicol, Nichol.**—Fem. **Nicola** (*nik'ə-la*) **Nicole** (*ni-kōl*).—Dims. **Nicolette, Colette.**

**Nicodemus,** *nik-ə-dē'məs, m.* (Gr.) victory of the people.—Dims. **Nick, Noddy.**

**Nigel,** *ni'jl,* **Neil, Niall,** *nēl, m.* perh. (Ir.) champion, but understood as dim. of L. *niger,* black.

**Nina, Ninette, Ninon.** See **Ann.**

Ninian, *nin'yən, m.* (Celt.) meaning unknown.— Also (Scot.) Ringan (*ring'ən*).

Nita, *nē'ta, f.* for Juanita. See Jane.

Noah, *nō'a, m.* (Heb.) rest.

Noel, *nō'əl, m.* and *f.* (Fr.—L.) birthday, i.e. Christmas.—Fr. *Noël,* It. *Natale.*—Fem. also Noele, Noelle, Natalia (*nə-tä'li-a,* or *-tä',* Natalie (*nat'ə-li.*)

Noll, Nolly, *m.* See Olive.

Nora, Norah, *nō'ra, nö', f.* orig. for Honora, Leonora, Eleanor.—Dim. (Ir.) Noreen (*-rēn'*).

Norma, *nör'ma, f.* (L.) a rule, precept.

Norman, *nör'mən, m.* (Gmc.) Northman.

Norna, *nör'na, f.* (Gmc.) a Norn or Fate.

Obadiah, *ō-bə-dī'a, m.* (Heb.) servant, or worshipper, of the Lord.

Octavius, Octavus, *ok-tā'vi-əs, -vəs, m.* (L.) eighth.—Dims. Tavy (*tā'vi*), Tave.—Fem. Octavia.

Odette, *ō-det', f.* See Ottilia.

Odo, *ō'dō, m.* See Otto.

Olaf, *ō'laf, -ləf, m.* (Scand.) ancestor-relics.

Olga, *ol'ga, f.* (Russ.—Gmc.) holy.

Olive, *ol'iv,* Olivia, *ō-* or *ə-liv'i-a, f.* (L.) olive.— Dim. Livy (*liv'i*).—Oliver, *ol'i-vər, m.* (Fr.) olive-tree (but poss. orig. another name assimilated).—Dims. Noll, Nolly, (*nol, -i*).

Olwen, *ol'wən, f.* (W.) white track.

Olympia, *ō-* or *o-lim'pi-a, f.* (Gr.) Olympian.

Ophelia, *ō-* or *ə-fē'li-a, f.* prob. (Gr.) help.

Orlando, *ör-lan'dō.* See Roland.

Osbert, *oz'bərt, m.* (Gmc.) god-bright.

Oscar, *os'kər, m.* (Gmc.) god-spear.

Osmund, Osmond, *oz'mənd, m.* (Gmc.) god-protection.

Osric, *oz'rik, m.* (Gmc.) god-rule.

Oswald, *oz'wəld, m.* (Gmc.) god-power.

Oswin, *oz'win, m.* (Gmc.) god-friend.

Ottilia, *ot-il'i-a,* Ottilie, *ot'i-li, f.* (Gmc.) heritage (udal).—Dim. Odette (*ō-det'*).

Otto, *ot'ō,* Odo, *ō'dō,* Otho, *ō'thō, m.* (Gmc.) rich. —It. *Ottone.*

Oughtred. See Ughtred.

Owen, *ō'ən, m.* (W.) said to mean youth.—Ir. and Gael. *Ewan, Ewen* (Eoghan).—Used as a substitute for Eugene.

Paddy, *pad'i,* dim. of Patrick, Patricia.

Pamela, *pam'i-la, f.* prob. an invention (as *pam-ē'la*) of Sir Philip Sidney's.

Pansy, *pan'zi, f.* (Fr.) thought; or from the name of the flower.

Parnel, *pär'nel, -nəl, f.* See Petronella.

Pat, dim. of Patrick, Patricia, Martha.

Patience, *pā'shəns, f.* patience.

Patrick, *pat'rik, m.* (L.) nobleman, patrician.— Dims. Pat, Paddy.—Fem. Patricia (*pə-trish'-* (*y*)*a*).—Dims. Pat, Paddy.

Patty, *pat'i, f.* dim. of Martha, Patience.

Paul, Paullus, Paulus, *pöl, -əs, m.* (L.) little.— It. *Paolo,* Sp. *Pablo.*—Deriv. Paulinus (*-i'nəs*).— Fem. Paula, Paulina, Pauline (*-ēn*).

Pearl, *pürl, f.* pearl.

Peg, Peggy, *peg, -i, f.* dims. of Margaret.

Penelope, *pi-nel'o-pi, f.* (Gr.) perh. weaver.—Dims. Pen, Penny.

Pepe, Pepito. See Joseph.

Percival, Perceval, *pûr'si-vl, m.* (Fr.) penetrate the valley.

Percy, *pûr'si, m.* from the surname.

Perdita, *pûr'di-ta, f.* (L.) lost.

Peregrine, *per'i-grin, m.* (L.) wanderer, traveller, pilgrim.—Dim. Perry.

Pernel, *pûr'nəl.* See Petronella.

Persis, *pûr'sis, f.* (Gr.) Persian.

Peter, *pē'tər, m.* (Gr.) rock.—Also Piers, *pērz.*— L. *Petrus,* Fr. *Pierre,* It. *Pietro,* Sp. and Port. *Pedro,* Ger. *Peter, Petrus,* Norw. *Peer.*—Dims. Pete (*pēt*), Peterkin, Perkin (*pûr'kin*).

Petronella, Petronilla, *pet-rə-nel'a, -nil'a, f.* (L.)

from the gentile name *Petrōnius.*—Contracted Parnel (*pär'nəl*), Pernel (*púr'nəl*).

Phelim, *fē'lim, m.* (Ir.) ever good.

Philemon, *fil- fil-ē'mon, m.* (Gr.) affectionate.

Philip, *fil'ip, m.* (Gr.) lover of horses.—L. *Philippus,* Fr. *Philippe,* It. *Filippo,* Sp. *Felipe,* Ger. *Philipp.*—Dims. Phil, Pip.—Fem. Philippa. —Dim. Pippa.

Phillis, Phyllis, *fil'is,* Phillida, Phyllida, *fil'i-da, f.* (Gr.) a leafy shoot.

Philomena, *fil-ō-mēn'a, f.* (Gr.) I am loved, or strong in friendship.

Phineas, Phinehas, *fin'i-əs, m.* (Heb.) meaning obscure—explained as Negro, oracle, serpent's mouth, etc.

Phoebe, *fē'bi, f.* (Gr.) shining, a name of Artemis as moon-goddess.

Piers, *pērz, m.* See Peter.

Pip, *m.,* Pippa, *f.* See Philip.

Polly, *pol'i, f.* See Mary.

Poppy, *pop'i, f.* from the flower.

Primrose, *prim'rōz, f.* from the flower.

Priscilla, *pris-il'a, f.* (L.) dim. of the Roman name *Priscus* (former).

Prudence, *proō'dəns, f.* prudence.—Dim. Prue.

Queenie, *kwēn'i, f.* from *queen.*

Quintin, *kwin'tin,* Quentin, *kwen', m.* (L.) fifth.— L. *Quintianus.*

Rab, Rabbie. See Robert.

Rachel, Rachael, *rā'chl, f.* (Heb.) ewe.—Ger. *Rahel,* Fr. *Rachel,* It. *Rachele,* Sp. *Raquel.*— Dim. Ray.

Ralph, *rāf, ralf, m.* (Gmc.) counsel-wolf.—O.E. *Rædwūlf,* Fr. *Raoul.*

Ranald, *ran'əld, m.* See Reginald.

Randal, *ran'dl,* Randolph, *ran'dolf, m.* (Gmc.) shield-wolf.

Raoul, *rä-ōōl', m.* See Ralph.

Raphael, *raf'ā-el, -əl, m.* (Heb.) God heals.—It. *Raffaele, Raffaello.*

Rasmus, Rastus. See Erasmus, Erastus.

Ray, *rā.* See Rachel, Raymond.—Also used as an independent name, *f.*

Raymond, Raymund, *rā'mənd, m.* (Gmc.) counsel (or might) protector.—Ger. *Raimund,* Sp. *Ramón, Raimundo,* It. *Raimondo.*—Dim. Ray.

Rayner, *rā'nər, m.* (Gmc.) counsel (or might), army (or folk).

Rebecca, Rebekah, *ri-bek'a, f.* (Heb.) noose.— Dims. Beck, Becky.

Reginald, *rej'i-nəld,* Reynold, *ren'əld,* Ronald, *ron',* Ranald, *ran', m.* (Gmc.) counsel (or power) rule. —Ger. *Reinwald, Reinhold, Reinalt,* Fr. *Regnault, Regnauld, Renaud,* It. *Rinaldo, Reinaldo.* —Dims. Reg (*rej*), Reggie (*rej'i*), Rex, Ronnie.

René, *ren'i, rə-nā', m.* (Fr.) Renatus, *ri-nā'təs, m.* (L.) born again.—Fem. Renée, Renata.

Reuben, *roō'bən, m.* (Heb.) behold a son, or renewer.

Rex, *reks, m.* (L.) king.—Also for Reginald.

Reynold, *ren'əld, m.* See Reginald.

Rhoda, *rō'da, f.* (Gr.) rose.

Rhona, Rona, *rō'na, f.* origin and meaning obscure.

Rhys, *rēs, m.* (W.) perh. impetuous man.

Richard, *rich'ərd, m.* (Gmc.) rule-hard.—It. *Riccardo,* Sp. *Ricardo.*—Dims. Dick, Dickie, Dicky, Dicken, Dickon, Rick, Richie (obs. Diccon, Hick).—Fem. Ricarda (*ri-kär'da*).

Ringan, *ring'ən, m.* See Ninian.

Rita, *rē'ta, f.* See Margaret.

Robert, *rob'ərt,* Rupert, *roō'pərt, m.* (Gmc.) fame-bright.—L. *Robertus,* Fr. *Robert,* It. and Sp. *Roberto,* Ger. *Robert, Ruprecht, Rupprecht.*— Dims. Bert, Bertie, Bob, Bobbie, Bobby, Dob, Dobbin, Rob, Robbie, Robin (*rob'in*), Scots Rab, Rabbie.—Fem. Roberta, Robina (*ro-bē'na*).

Roderick, *rod'(ə)-rik, m.* fame-rule.—Ger. *Roderich,* Fr. *Rodrigue,* It. *Rodrigo, Roderico,* Sp. *Rodrigo, Ruy.*—Dim. Roddy.

**Rodney,** *rod'ni, m.* and *f.* from the surname or place-name.

**Rodolph.** See **Rudolf.**

**Roger,** *roj'ər, m.* (Gmc.) fame-spear.—O.E. *Hrōthgār,* Ger. *Rüdiger,* Fr. *Roger,* It. *Ruggero, Ruggiero,* Sp. *Rogerio.*—Dims. **Hodge, Hodgkin** (*hoj'kin*).

**Roland, Rowland,** *rō'lənd, m.* (Gmc.) fame of the land.—Ger., Fr., *Roland,* It. *Orlando,* Sp. *Roldán, Rolando.*

**Rolf,** *rolf, m.* See **Rudolf.**

**Roma,** *rō'ma, f.* from the name of the city.

**Rona.** See **Rhona.**

**Ronald,** *ron'əld, m.* See **Reginald.**

**Rory,** *rō'ri, rō', m.* (Ir.) red.

**Rosalind, Rosaline,** *roz'ə-lind, -lin, -lēn, -lin, f.* (Gmc.) horse-snake, but associated with **Rose** (fair rose).

**Rosamund, Rosamond,** *roz'ə-mənd, f.* (Gmc.) horse protection.—Associated with **Rose** (L. *rosa munda,* fine or pure rose, *rosa mundi,* rose of the world).

**Rose,** *rōz,* **Rosa,** *rō'za, f.* (L.) rose. It may also be sometimes Gmc., horse.—Derivs. **Rosabel** (*roz'ə-bel*), **Rosabella** (*rōz-ə-bel'a*), **Rosalia** (*rō-zā'li-a*), **Rosalie** (*roz'* or *rōz'ə-li*) (L. *rosalia,* the hanging of rose garlands on tombs).—Dims. **Rosetta, Rosie.**

**Roseanna, Rosanna, Roseanne,** *rō-zan'(a),* **Rose-marie,** *rōz-mə-rē', f.* compounds of **Rose** with **Anna, Anne, Marie.**

**Rosemary,** *rōz'mə-ri, f.* from the plant; also for **Rose Mary.**

**Rowena,** *rō-(w)ē'na, f.* perh. Geoffrey of Monmouth's mistake for W. *Rhonwen,* white skirt.

**Roy,** *roi, m.* (Gael.) red.

**Ruby,** *rōō'bi, f.* from the stone.—Also **Rubina** (*-bē'na*).

**Rudolf, Rudolph,** *rōō'dolf,* **Rodolph,** *rō',* **Rolf,** *rolf, m.* (Gmc.) fame-wolf.

**Rufus,** *rōō'fəs, m.* (L.) red.

**Rupert, Rupprecht.** See **Robert.**

**Ruth,** *rōōth, f.* (Heb.) meaning obscure; used sometimes with associations with English *ruth.*

**Sadie,** *sā'di,* **Sal,** *sal,* **Sally.** See **Sarah.**

**Salome,** *sə-lō'mi, f.* (Heb.) perfect, or peace.

**Samantha,** *sa-man'tha, f.* (Heb.) meaning obscure.

**Samson, Sampson,** *sam'sən, m.* (Heb.) of the sun. —Gr. *Sampsōn,* Fr. *Samson,* Ger. *Simson,* It. *Sansone,* Sp. *Sansón,* Port. *Sansão.*

**Samuel,** *sam'ū-əl, m.* (Heb.) heard by God, or name of God.—Dims. **Sam, Sammy.**

**Sancho,** *san'chō, m.* (Sp.) holy.

**Sandra,** *san'dra, f.* It. dim. of **Alessandra;** sometimes used as a diminutive of **Alexandra** but now regarded as a separate name.

**Sandy,** *san'di, m.* See **Alexander.**

**Sarah, Sara,** *sā'ra, f.* (Heb.) princess, queen.— Dims. **Sadie** (*sā'di*), **Sal** (*sal*), **Sally.**

**Saul,** *söl, m.* (Heb.) asked for.

**Seamas, Seamus,** *shā'məs, m.* See **James.**

**Seán,** *shön, m.* See **John.**

**Sebastian,** *si-bas'ti-ən, m.* (Gr.) man of Sebasteia (in Pontus)—Gr. *sebastos,* august, venerable.

**Secundus,** *si-kun'dəs, m.* (L.) second.

**Selina,** *si-lē'na, f.* poss. connected with **Celia,** but associated with Gr. *selēnē,* moon.

**Senga,** *seng'ga, f.* backward spelling of **Agnes.**

**Seonad,** *shē-ō'nat, shō'na, f.* See **Jane.**

**Septimus,** *sep'ti-məs, m.* (L.) seventh.

**Serena,** *si-rē'na, f.* (L.) calm, serene.

**Seth,** *seth, m.* (Heb.) substitute, or compensation.

**Seumas.** See **James.**

**Sextus,** *seks'təs, m.* (L.) sixth.

**Shamus,** for **Seamus** (see **James**).

**Shane, Shawn,** *shān, shön, m.* See **John.**

**Sharon,** *shā'ron, f.* (Heb.) meaning obscure.

**Sheena,** *shē'na, f.* See **Jane.**

**Sheila, Sheelagh,** *shē'la, f.* See **Celia** and **Cecilia.**

**Shirley,** *shûr'li, f.* from the surname or place-name.

**Sholto,** *shol'tō, m.* perh. (Gael.) sower, propagator.

**Shona,** *shō'na,* **Sian,** *shän, f.* See **Jane.**

**Sibyl,** now **Sybil,** *sib'il,* **Sibylla,** *sib-il'a, f.* (L.) a Sibyl.—Dim. **Sib.**

**Sidney, Sydney,** *sid'ni, m.* and *f.,* from the surname.

**Siegfried,** *sēg'frēd,* **Sigurd,** *sē'gōōrd, m.* (Gmc.), victory-peace.

**Sigismund,** *sij'* or *sig'is-mund, -mōōnd,* **Siegmund,** *sēg'mōōnd, m.* (Gmc.) victory-protection.

**Sigrid,** *sēg'rid, f.* (O.N.) prob. victorious (second element obscure).

**Silas,** *si'ləs,* **Silvanus,** *sil-vā'nəs,* **Silvester, Sylvester,** *sil-ves'tər,* **Silvius, Sylvius,** *sil'vi-əs, m.* (L.) living in the woods.—Fem. **Silvia, Sylvia.**

**Simon,** *si'mən,* **Simeon,** *sim'i-ən, m.* (Heb.) perh. hearing; perh. also (Gr.) snub-nosed.—Dims. **Sim, Simmy, Simkin.**

**Solomon,** *sol'ə-mən, m.* (Heb.) peaceable.—Ger. *Salomo,* Fr. *Salomon,* It. *Salomone,* Sp. *Salomón,* Port. *Salomão.*—Dims. **Sol, Solly.**

**Sophia,** *sə-fi'a,* **Sophie, Sophy,** *sō'fi, f.* (Gr.) wisdom. —Russ. (dim.) **Sonia, Sonya** (*son'ya*).

**Sophronia,** *sə-frō'ni-a, f.* (Gr.) prudent, temperate, of sound mind.

**Stanislas,** *stan'is-las,* **Stanislaus,** *-lä'əs, m.* (Pol.) camp-glory.

**Stanley,** *stan'li, m.* from the surname or place-name.

**Stella,** *stel'a, f.* (L.) star.—Also **Estella** (*es-tel'a*), **Estelle** (*-tel'*).

**Stephen,** *stē'vən, m.* (Gr.) crown.—L. *Stephanus,* Fr. *Étienne,* It. *Stefano,* Sp. *Esteban,* Ger. *Stephan.*—Dims. **Steenie, Steve, Stevie.**—Fem. **Stephana** (*stef'ə-na*), **Stephanie** (*-ni*).

**Stewart, Steuart, Stuart,** *stū'art, m.* from the surname.

**Susan,** *sōō'zən, sū'zən,* **Susanna, Susannah,** *-zan'a, f.* (Heb.) lily.—Fr. *Suzanne.*—Dims. **Sue, Suke, Suky, Susie, Susy.**

**Sydney.** See **Sidney.**

**Sylvius, Sylvester, Sylvia.** See **Silas.**

**Tabitha,** *tab'i-tha, f.* (Aramaic) gazelle.

**Taffy,** *taf'i,* Welsh form of **David.**

**Talbot,** *töl'bət, m.* from the surname.

**Tamsin,** *tam'sin, f.* a dim. of **Thomasina,** orig. Cornish. Now regarded as a separate name.

**Tania, Tanya,** *tan'ya, f.* a dim. of Russ. *Tatiana.*

**Terence,** *ter'ins, m.* (L.) the Roman gentile name *Terentius;* used with its dim. **Terry** as a substitute for Ir. *Turlough,* like **Thor.**

**Teresa, Theresa,** *tə-rē'za,* **Theresia,** *-zi-a, f.* (Gr.) origin unknown—more probably connected with the island of Therasia than with reaping.— It. and Sp. *Teresa,* Fr. *Thérèse,* Ger. *Theresia, Therese.*—Dims. **Terry, Tessa, Tracy.**

**Terry,** *ter'i.* See **Terence, Teresa.**

**Tessa,** *tes'a.* See **Teresa.**

**Thaddaeus, Thaddeus,** *thə-dē'əs, thad'i-əs, m.* (Heb.) meaning obscure.—Used with its dims.

**Thaddy, Thady** as a substitute for the Irish name **Tadhgh** (*thēg*), poet, which formerly in the form **Teague** (*tēg*) served as a general nickname for an Irishman, as Pat, Paddy, now.

**Thea,** *thē'a, f.* (Gr.) goddess.

**Thecla,** *thek'la, f.* (Gr.) god-famed.

**Thelma,** *thel'ma, f.* poss. (Gr.) will, popularised by Marie Corelli.

**Theobald,** *thē'ō-böld, tib'əld,* **Tybalt,** *tib'əlt, m.* (Gmc.) people-bold.—Fr. *Thibaut, Thibault,* It. *Tebaldo,* Sp. *Teobaldo.*

**Theodore,** *thē'ō-dōr, -dör, m.* (Gr.) gift of God.— Fem. **Theodora** (*-dō'ra, -dö'ra*).

**Theodoric, Theoderic,** *thē-od'ə-rik, m.* (Gmc.) people-rule—Ger. *Dietrich* (dim. *Dirk*).—Dim. **Derrick, Derek.**

**Theodosius,** *thē-ō-dō'si-əs, m.* (Gr.) gift of God.— Fem. **Theodosia.**

Theophilus, *thē-of'i-ləs, m.* (Gr.) beloved of God (or the gods).—Fem. **Theophila.**

**Theresa, Theresia.** See **Teresa.**

Thomas, *tom'əs, m.* (Heb.) twin.—Fr., Ger. *Thomas,* It. *Tommaso,* Sp. *Tomás.*—Dims. **Tom, Tommy** (Scot. **Tam, Tammie**).—Fem. **Thomasa** (*tom'ə-sa*), **T(h)omasina** (*tom-ə-sē'na*), **Tomina** (*tom-ē'na*).

Thorold, *thor', thur'əld, m.* (Gmc.) Thor-strength.

**Tib, Tibbie,** *tib, -i, f.* dims. of **Isabella,** mainly Scottish.

**Tilly,** *til'i, f.* See **Matilda.**

Timothy, *tim'ə-thi, m.* (Gr.) honoured of God.— Dims. **Tim, Timmie.**

Titus, *ti'təs, m.* (L.) a Roman praenomen—meaning unknown.

Toby, *tō'bi,* **Tobias,** *-bi'əs, m.* (Heb.) Yah is good.

Tony, *tō'ni, m.* Dim. of **Anthony.**

Tracy, *trā'si, m.* and *f.* deriv. of **Teresa;** the masc. form perh. for the surname.

Trevor, *trev'ər, m.* from the surname.

**Tristram, Tristrem,** *tris'trəm,* **Tristan,** *-tən, m.* (Celt.) perh. tumult.

**Trix, Trixy.** See **Beatrice.**

Turlough, *tûr'lō, m.* (Ir. *Toirdhealbhac*) like Thor. —Represented by **Terence, Terry, Charles.**

Tybalt, *tib'əlt, m.* See **Theobald.**


Uchtred, Ughtred, Oughtred, *ū'trid, m.* perh. (O.E.) thought-counsel.

Ulick, *ū'lik, m.* an Irish form of **Ulysses,** but perh. really for a native name.

Ulric, *ul'rik, m.* (Gmc.) wolf-rule.—Ger. *Ulrich.*— Fem. **Ulrica.**—Ger. *Ulrike.*

Ulysses, *ū-lis'ēz, m.* (L. form of Gr.) angry, or hater.—Gr. *Odysseus,* L. *Ulysses, Ulixes.* See **Ulick.**

Una, *ū'na, f.* (L.) one, from Spenser's heroine, personification of truth, but perh. suggested by some Irish name.

Urban, *ûr'bən, m.* (L.) of the town, urbane.

Uriah, *ū-ri'a, m.* (Heb.) perh. Yah is light.

Ursula, *ûr'sū-la, f.* (L.) little she-bear.


Valentine, *val'in-tin, m.* and *f.* (L.) healthy.

Valeria, *və-lē'ri-a, f.* (L.) fem. of a Roman gentile name.—Also **Valerie, Valery** (*val'ə-ri*).—Deriv. **Valerian,** *m.*

Vanessa, *və-nes'a, f.* a name invented by Swift from *Esther Van*homrigh.

Venetia, *vi-nē'sha, f.* (L.) Venetian; perh. also a Latinisation of **Gwyneth.**

Vera, *vē'ra, f.* (L.) true; also (Russ.) faith.

Vere, *vēr, m.* and *f.* from the surname.

Verena, *və-rē'na, f.* the name of a martyr.

Verity, *ver'i-ti, f.* (L.) truth.

Veronica, *vi-ron'i-ka, f.* (L.) true image; or (Gr.) a form of **Berenice.**


Vesta, *ves'ta, f.* (L.) the Roman hearth-goddess.

Victor, *vik'tər, m.* (L.) conqueror.—Dim. **Vic.**— **Victoria,** *vik-tō'ri-a, -tō', f.* victory.—Dim. **Vicky.**

Vida, *vē'da,* a fem. dim. of **David.**

Vincent, *vin'sənt, m.* (L.) conquering.

Viola, *vi'ō-la,* **Violet,** *-lit, f.* (L.) violet (flower).

Virgil, *vûr'jil, m.* (L.) from the Roman gentile name; perh. specif. for the poet Publiu: *Vergilius* Maro.

Virginia, *vər-jin'i-a,* (L.) fem. of a Roman gentile name.

Vivian, *viv'i-ən, m.* and (chiefly in the form **Vivien**) *f.* (L.) lively.—Also **Vyvyen, Vyvian.**


Walter, *wōl'tər, m.* (Gmc.) rule-people (or army). —L. *Gualterus,* Ger. *Walter, Walther,* Fr. *Gautier, Gauthier,* Sp. *Gualterio,* It. *Gualtieri.* —Dims. **Wat, Watty** (*wot, -i*), **Wally, Walt.**

Wanda, *won'da, f.* (Gmc.) stock or stem.

Warren, *wor'ən, m.* (Gmc.) a folk-name—meaning uncertain.

Wendy, *wen'di, f.* an invention of J. M. Barrie's.

**Wilfrid, Wilfred,** *wil'frid, m.* (Gmc.) will-peace.

Wilhelmina, *wil-(h)əl-mē'na* (Ger. *Wilhelmine*), a fem. formed from *Wilhelm* (see **William**).— Dims. **Elma, Wilma, Wilmett, Wilmot, Mina, Minnie, Minella.**

William, *wil'yəm, m.* (Gmc.) will-helmet.—L. *Gulielmus, Guilielmus,* Ger. *Wilhelm,* Fr. *Guillaume,* It. *Guglielmo,* Sp. *Guillermo, Guillelmo,* Ir. *Liam,* W. *Gwillym, Gwilym.*—For fem. see **Wilhelmina.**

Winifred, *win'i-frid, f.* prob. orig. W., the same as *Guinevere* (white-mane), but assimilated to the English masculine name *Winfred, Winfrith* (friend of peace).—Dims. **Win, Winnie, Freda** (*frē'da*).

Winston, *win'stən, m.* (Eng.) from the place name.


Xavier, *zav'i-ər, m.* (Sp.—Ar.) splendid.


Yoland, *yō'lənd, f.* app. a mediaeval form of *Violante,* a deriv. of **Viola.**

Yve, Yves, *ēv,* Yvon, *ē-võ',* Fr. deriv of **Ivo.**— Fem. **Yvonne** (*ē-von'*), **Yvette** (*ē-vet'*).


**Zachariah, Zechariah,** *zak-, zek-ə-ri'a,* **Zachary,** *zak'ə-ri, m.* (Heb.) Yah is renowned.—Dims. **Zach, Zack.**

Zedekiah, *zed-i-ki'a, m.* (Heb.) Yah is might.

Zeke, *zēk, m.,* dim. of **Ezekiel.**

Zena, *zē'na, f.* perh. Pers., a woman.

Zenobia, *zi-nō'bi-a, f.* (Gr.) life from Zeus (but perh. a Semitic name in Greek guise).

Zillah, *zil'a, f.* (Heb.) shade.

Zoe, *zō'ē, f.* (Gr.) life.

# The Greek alphabet

| | | | | | | | | | |
|---|---|---|---|---|---|---|---|---|---|
| A | $\alpha$ | alpha | = | a | N | $\nu$ | nū | = | n |
| B | $\beta$ | bēta | = | b | Ξ | $\xi$ | xī | = | x (ks) |
| Γ | $\gamma$ | gamma | = | g | O | o | omīcron | = | o |
| Δ | $\delta$ | delta | = | d | Π | $\pi$ | pī | = | p |
| E | $\epsilon$ | epsīlon | = | e | P | $\rho$ | rhō | = | r |
| Z | $\zeta$ | zēta | = | z | Σ | $\sigma$ $\varsigma$ | sigma | = | s |
| H | $\eta$ | ēta | = | ē | T | $\tau$ | tau | = | t |
| Θ | $\theta$ $\vartheta$ | thēta | = | th | Υ | $\upsilon$ | upsīlon | = | u |

(often transcribed *y*)

| | | | | | | | | | |
|---|---|---|---|---|---|---|---|---|---|
| I | $\iota$ | iōta | = | i | Φ | $\phi$ | phī | = | ph |
| K | $\kappa$ | kappa | = | k | X | $\chi$ | chī | = | kh |

(often transcribed *ch*, as in Latin)

| | | | | | | | | | |
|---|---|---|---|---|---|---|---|---|---|
| Λ | $\lambda$ | lambda | = | l | Ψ | $\psi$ | psī | = | ps |
| M | $\mu$ | mū | = | m | Ω | $\omega$ | ōmega | = | ō |

The Greek alphabet, apart from its use as the official script in Greek-speaking areas, is of world-wide importance as a source of symbols used in all branches of science and mathematics. The equivalents in our alphabet given above are intended as a guide to transliteration and as indication of the anglicised pronunciation of ancient Greek. We have not attempted to describe modern Greek pronunciation.

For the use of Greek letters as numerals, see the main dictionary under the names of the separate letters.

# The Russian alphabet

| | | | | | | | | |
|---|---|---|---|---|---|---|---|---|
| А | а | = | ä | as in far | С | с | = | s |
| Б | б | = | b | | Т | т | = | t |
| В | в | = | v | | У | у | = | u—o͞o as in fo͞ol |
| Г | г | = | g | as in good | Ф | ф | = | f |
| Д | д | = | d | | Х | х | = | kh—hh as in loch |
| Е | е | = | e—ye as in yet | | Ц | ц | = | ts |
| Ё | ё | = | yo as in yawn | | Ч | ч | = | ch |
| Ж | ж | = | zh | | Ш | ш | = | sh |
| З | з | = | z | | Щ | щ | = | shch |

(pronounced rather as *sh* followed by consonantal *y*)

| | | | | |
|---|---|---|---|---|
| И | и | = | i—ee | as in feed |
| Й | й | = | (consonantal *y* sound; only used as the second letter of a diphthong) |

Ъ

(sign used to separate in pronunciation a following palatalised vowel from a preceding consonant either palatalised or unpalatalised)

| | | | |
|---|---|---|---|
| ы | = | i | as in bit |

| | | | |
|---|---|---|---|
| К | к | = | k |
| Л | л | = | l |
| М | м | = | m |
| Н | н | = | n |

ь

(sign used after a consonant to indicate palatalisation, a sound like consonantal *y*)

| | | | | |
|---|---|---|---|---|
| О | о | = | o | ö as in law |
| Э | э | = | e | as in get |
| П | п | = | p | |
| Ю | ю | = | u—yo͞o | as in universe |
| Р | р | = | r | |
| Я | я | = | yä | as in yard |

# Roman numerals

I = 1    V = 5    X = 10    L = 50    C = 100    D = 500    M = 1000

From the above symbols the numbers are made up as follows:—

| | | | | | | |
|---|---|---|---|---|---|---|
| I | = | 1 | L | | = | 50 |
| II | = | 2 | LI | | = | 51 |
| III | = | 3 | LII, etc. | | = | 52, etc. |
| IV (or IIII, e.g. on clocks) | = | 4 | LX | | = | 60 |
| V | = | 5 | LXI | | = | 61 |
| VI | = | 6 | LXII, etc. | | = | 62, etc. |
| VII | = | 7 | LXX | | = | 70 |
| VIII | = | 8 | LXXI | | = | 71 |
| IX | = | 9 | LXXII, etc. | | = | 72, etc. |
| X | = | 10 | LXXX | | = | 80 |
| XI | = | 11 | LXXXI | | = | 81 |
| XII | = | 12 | LXXXII, etc. | | = | 82, etc. |
| XIII | = | 13 | XC | | = | 90 |
| XIV | = | 14 | XCI | | = | 91 |
| XV | = | 15 | XCII, etc. | | = | 92, etc. |
| XVI | = | 16 | | | | |
| XVII | = | 17 | C | | = | 100 |
| XVIII | = | 18 | CC | | = | 200 |
| XIX | = | 19 | CCC | | = | 300 |
| XX | = | 20 | CCCC or CD | | = | 400 |
| XXI | = | 21 | D (or IↃ) | | = | 500 |
| XXII, etc. | = | 22, etc. | DC (or IↃC) | | = | 600 |
| XXX | = | 30 | DCC (or IↃCC) | | = | 700 |
| XXXI | = | 31 | DCCC (or IↃCCC) | | = | 800 |
| XXXII, etc. | = | 32, etc. | CM (or DCCCC or IↃCCCC) | | = | 900 |
| XL | = | 40 | M | | = | 1000 |
| XLI | = | 41 | MM | | = | 2000 |
| XLII, etc. | = | 42, etc. | V̄[3] (or IↃↃ)[1] | | = | 5000 |

Other letters also were used as numerals in mediaeval times (see Dictionary). For additional information about mediaeval methods of writing numerals, see below.

1. The symbol Ↄ, known as the *apostrophus*, might be repeated one or more times after IↃ, each Ↄ making the number ten times greater, as IↃↃ = 5,000, IↃↃↃ = 500,000. A number of this type might be multiplied by two by adding (in front) as many C's as there were Ↄ's in the number, e.g. CCIↃↃ = 10,000, CCCCIↃↃↃↃ = 1,000,000.

2. The symbols I,V,X,L,D,M are still used today. In the Middle Ages, and also in much later times, methods of writing numerals were common which are found neither in the Roman period nor in the present century. Some are noted below.

3. In the Middle Ages and later, a line was placed above a symbol representing a number 1,000 times greater, as X̄ = 10,000. |X̄| and |X| were variant methods of expressing 1,000,000.

4. In the Middle Ages and later, and still in medical usage, numerals could be written lower case, and j was often substituted for final i.

5. In the Middle Ages and later, Ⅽ appears with the same meaning as D, and there is sometimes a small version of the apostrophus. To take at random an example of the latter, the third volume of John Ray's *Historia Plantarum*, is dated cIↃ Iↄ CCIV—that is 1704.

# Some useful conversion tables

The following tables may be used for conversion from British to metric (SI) units and vice versa.

| in to cm | | cm to in | ft to m | | m to ft | miles to km | | km to miles |
|---|---|---|---|---|---|---|---|---|
| 2·54 | 1 | 0·3937 | 0·3048 | 1 | 3·28084 | 1·60934 | 1 | 0·62137 |
| 5·08 | 2 | 0·7874 | 0·6096 | 2 | 6·562 | 3·219 | 2 | 1·243 |
| 7·62 | 3 | 1·1811 | 0·9144 | 3 | 9·843 | 4·828 | 3 | 1·864 |
| 10·16 | 4 | 1·5748 | 1·2192 | 4 | 13·123 | 6·437 | 4 | 2·485 |
| 12·70 | 5 | 1·9685 | 1·5240 | 5 | 16·404 | 8·047 | 5 | 3·107 |
| 15·24 | 6 | 2·3622 | 1·8288 | 6 | 19·685 | 9·656 | 6 | 3·728 |
| 17·78 | 7 | 2·7559 | 2·1336 | 7 | 22·966 | 11·265 | 7 | 4·350 |
| 20·32 | 8 | 3·1496 | 2·4384 | 8 | 26·247 | 12·875 | 8 | 4·971 |
| 22·86 | 9 | 3·5433 | 2·7432 | 9 | 29·528 | 14·484 | 9 | 5·592 |

| sq in to sq cm | | sq cm to sq in | sq ft to sq m | | sq m to sq ft | sq miles to sq km | | sq km to sq miles |
|---|---|---|---|---|---|---|---|---|
| 6·4516 | 1 | 0·155 | 0·0929 | 1 | 10·764 | 2·58999 | 1 | 0·3861 |
| 12·903 | 2 | 0·310 | 0·1858 | 2 | 21·528 | 5·18 | 2 | 0·772 |
| 19·355 | 3 | 0·465 | 0·2787 | 3 | 32·292 | 7·77 | 3 | 1·158 |
| 25·806 | 4 | 0·620 | 0·3716 | 4 | 43·056 | 10·36 | 4 | 1·544 |
| 32·258 | 5 | 0·775 | 0·4645 | 5 | 53·820 | 12·95 | 5 | 1·931 |
| 38·710 | 6 | 0·930 | 0·5574 | 6 | 64·583 | 15·54 | 6 | 2·317 |
| 45·161 | 7 | 1·085 | 0·6503 | 7 | 75·347 | 18·13 | 7 | 2·703 |
| 51·613 | 8 | 1·240 | 0·7432 | 8 | 86·111 | 20·72 | 8 | 3·089 |
| 58·064 | 9 | 1·395 | 0·8361 | 9 | 96·875 | 23·31 | 9 | 3·475 |

| fl oz to cm³ | | cm³ to fl oz | imp gal to litre | | litre to imp gal | oz to g | | g to oz |
|---|---|---|---|---|---|---|---|---|
| 28·4131 | 1 | 0·03519 | 4·54596 | 1 | 0·21997 | 28·3495 | 1 | 0·03527 |
| 56·826 | 2 | 0·0704 | 9·092 | 2 | 0·4400 | 56·6990 | 2 | 0·07054 |
| 85·239 | 3 | 0·1056 | 13·638 | 3 | 0·6599 | 85·0485 | 3 | 0·10581 |
| 113·652 | 4 | 0·1408 | 18·184 | 4 | 0·8799 | 113·3980 | 4 | 0·14108 |
| 142·065 | 5 | 0·1760 | 22·730 | 5 | 1·0999 | 141·7475 | 5 | 0·17635 |
| 170·478 | 6 | 0·2111 | 27·276 | 6 | 1·3199 | 170·0970 | 6 | 0·21162 |
| 198·891 | 7 | 0·2463 | 31·822 | 7 | 1·5398 | 198·4465 | 7 | 0·24689 |
| 227·304 | 8 | 0·2815 | 36·368 | 8 | 1·7598 | 226·7960 | 8 | 0·28216 |
| 255·717 | 9 | 0·3167 | 40·914 | 9 | 1·9798 | 255·1455 | 9 | 0·31743 |

| lb to kg | | kg to lb | ton to tonne | | tonne to ton | lbf to newton | | newton to lbf |
|---|---|---|---|---|---|---|---|---|
| 0·45359 | 1 | 2·20462 | 1·0160 | 1 | 0·984205 | 4·4482 | 1 | 0·2248 |
| 0·907 | 2 | 4·409 | 2·032 | 2 | 1·9684 | 8·896 | 2 | 0·4496 |
| 1·361 | 3 | 6·614 | 3·048 | 3 | 2·9526 | 13·345 | 3 | 0·6744 |
| 1·814 | 4 | 8·818 | 4·064 | 4 | 3·9368 | 17·793 | 4 | 0·8992 |
| 2·268 | 5 | 11·023 | 5·080 | 5 | 4·9210 | 22·241 | 5 | 1·1240 |
| 2·722 | 6 | 13·228 | 6·096 | 6 | 5·9052 | 26·689 | 6 | 1·3489 |
| 3·175 | 7 | 15·432 | 7·112 | 7 | 6·8894 | 31·138 | 7 | 1·5737 |
| 3·629 | 8 | 17·637 | 8·128 | 8 | 7·8736 | 35·586 | 8 | 1·7985 |
| 4·082 | 9 | 19·842 | 9·144 | 9 | 8·8578 | 40·034 | 9 | 2·0233 |

The table below shows a useful conversion of a non-SI metric unit to an SI metric unit.

| $cal_{IT}$ to J | | J to $cal_{IT}$ |
|---|---|---|
| 4·1868 | 1 | 0·2388 |
| 8·3736 | 2 | 0·4776 |
| 12·5604 | 3 | 0·7164 |
| 16·7472 | 4 | 0·9552 |
| 20·9340 | 5 | 1·1940 |
| 25·1208 | 6 | 1·4328 |
| 29·3076 | 7 | 1·6716 |
| 33·4944 | 8 | 1·9104 |
| 37·6812 | 9 | 2·1492 |

## Examples of use of tables

Reading from line 7 of the first table:

$$7 \text{ in} = 17·78 \text{ cm and } 7 \text{ cm} = 2·7559 \text{ in.}$$

Values above 9 may be obtained by decimal point adjustment and addition. Taking an example based on the third table:

To convert 573 miles to km

| | |
|---|---|
| 500 miles = | 804·7 km |
| 70 miles = | 112·65 km |
| 3 miles = | 4·828 km |
| 573 miles = | 922·178 km |

Such results should be treated as approximations. In the example given the conversion of 500 miles is correct only to the nearest 0·1 km, therefore the final sum can be correct only to the same degree; hence the conversion of 573 miles from the table is correctly stated as '922·2 km to the nearest 0·1 km'. The precise figure for 573 miles is 922·154 112 km.

# Some physical constants

*c*  speed of light in vacuo,
2·997 925 × 10⁸ metres per second.

*e*  electron charge,
1·602 10 × 10⁻¹⁹ coulomb.

*g*  standard acceleration of gravity, 9·806 65 metres per
second per second.  (At Greenwich, *g* = 9·811 83
metres per second per second.)

*G*  gravitational constant,
6·670 × 10⁻¹¹ N m² kg⁻².

*h*  Planck('s) constant, the constant in the expression
for the quantum of energy, 6·625 59 × 10⁻³⁴ joule
seconds.

$\hbar$  *h*-bar, Dirac's constant, $\dfrac{h}{2\pi}$ (Planck's constant divided
by 2π), the unit in which electron spin is measured.

$m_e$  the mass of an electron at rest, 9·109 08 × 10⁻³¹ kg.

$m_p$  the mass of a proton at rest,
1·672 52 × 10⁻²⁷ kg.

$m_n$  the mass of a neutron at rest,
1·674 82 × 10⁻²⁷ kg.

$N_A$  Avogadro('s) number, constant, number of molecules
in a mole of any substance, 6·022 53 × 10²³ per mole.

Speed of sound at sea level at 0°C, 331·7 metres per second.

Standard temperature and pressure (stp), 0°C and 101 325 N m⁻².

Standard volume of ideal gas, 2·241 36 × 10⁻² m³ mol⁻¹ at stp.

Melting point of ice, 0°C or 273·15 K.


# SI metric units of measurement

The Système International d'Unités has been internationally adopted as a coherent system of units for the measurement of all physical quantities.

**Base units**
Seven independent quantities have been chosen which are measured in the *base units* of the system (Table 2).

**Derived units**
To measure any other quantity, a *derived unit* is formed by multiplying or dividing any two or more base units,
or powers of them, together; e.g. speed is measured in metres per second, where the metre and the second are base
units.  The more frequently used derived units have been given names of their own for convenience; e.g. power is
measured in watts, where one watt is derived from one kilogram multiplied by one metre squared divided by one
second cubed.

**Abbreviations**
Each unit name has an agreed abbreviation (column 3 in Table 2).  To abbreviate a unit compounded from more
than one unit name, the abbreviations of the constituent units are written with a small space between them; e.g. a
newton metre is abbreviated N m.  Where a unit is raised to a power, the conventional algebraic indices are used;
e.g. a metre squared, or square metre, is abbreviated m².

**Division of units**
The word *per* indicates division by all succeeding units.  To abbreviate units which are to be divided, negative
indices are preferred, but a solidus (/) may be used; e.g. metre per second is abbreviated m s⁻¹ or m/s, kilogram per
metre cubed is kg m⁻³ or kg/m³.

**Multiples and Submultiples**
To avoid the use of many zeroes in either very large or very small numbers, prefixes indicating multiplication or
division by some power of a thousand (Table 1) can be added to a unit, e.g. mega-: multiply by a million, so a
megawatt (1 MW) is a million watts; milli-: divide by a thousand, so a milliwatt (1 mW) is a thousandth of a watt.

TABLE 1

| prefix | abbrev. | factor | prefix | abbrev. | factor |
|---|---|---|---|---|---|
| exa- | E | 10¹⁸ = million million million | *deci- | d | 10⁻¹ = tenth |
| peta- | P | 10¹⁵ = thousand million million | *centi- | c | 10⁻² = hundredth |
| tera- | T | 10¹² = million million | milli- | m | 10⁻³ = thousandth |
| giga- | G | 10⁹ = thousand million | micro- | μ | 10⁻⁶ = millionth |
| mega- | M | 10⁶ = million | nano- | n | 10⁻⁹ = thousand millionth |
| kilo- | k | 10³ = thousand | pico- | p | 10⁻¹² = million millionth |
| *hecto- | h | 10² = hundred | atto- | a | 10⁻¹⁵ = thousand million millionth |
| *deca-⎱ | da | 10 = ten | femto- | f | 10⁻¹⁸ = million million millionth |
| *deka-⎰ | | | | | |

* These prefixes are used only exceptionally where kilo- or milli- would be impractical; thus a centimetre ($\frac{1}{100}$ metre)
is accepted as an everyday unit of convenient size, but it is not a preferred SI unit.

TABLE 2

Equivalents are given to four significant figures' accuracy, except where they are exact as indicated by bold figures.

| Quantity | SI unit | abbreviation and derivation | equivalent in British units | SI equivalent of one British unit |
|---|---|---|---|---|
| **Base units** | | | | |
| Length | **metre** | m | 3·281 feet | **0·3048** m |
| Mass* | **kilogram** | kg | 2·205 pounds | **0·453 592 37** kg |
| Time | **second** | s | — | — |
| Temperature interval | **kelvin** | K | $\frac{9}{5}$ °Fahrenheit | $\frac{5}{9}$ K |
| Current, electric | **ampere** | A | — | — |
| Amount of substance | **mole** | mol | — | — |
| Luminous intensity | **candela** | cd | 0·9833 candle | 1·017 cd |
| Some derived and additional units | | | | |
| Length | kilometre | km | 0·6214 mile | 1·609 km |
| | centimetre | cm | 0·3937 inch | **2·54** cm |
| *Mass | tonne, metric ton | t = Mg | 0·9842 ton | 1·016 t |
| Area | metre squared | $m^2$ | 10·76 $ft^2$ | 0·092 90 $m^2$ |
| | hectare | ha = 10 000 $m^2$ | 2·471 acres | 0·4047 ha |
| Volume | metre cubed | $m^3$ | 1·308 $yd^3$ | 0·7646 $m^3$ |
| | litre | l = $dm^3$ | 0·2200 gal (UK) | 4·546 litres |
| *Weight; Force | newton | N = kg m $s^{-2}$ | 0·2248 lbf | 4·448 N |
| Energy; Work; Heat | joule | J = m N = kg $m^2$ $s^{-2}$ | $\left\{\begin{array}{l} 0\cdot2388 \text{ calorie} \\ 0\cdot7376 \text{ ft lbf} \\ 1 \text{ kJ} = 0\cdot9478 \text{ Btu} \end{array}\right.$ | 4·1868 J / 1·356 J / 1·055 kJ |
| Power | watt | W = J $s^{-1}$ = kg $m^2$ $s^{-3}$ | 0·001 341 hp | 745·7 W |
| Velocity; Speed | metre per second | m $s^{-1}$ | 3·281 ft/s | **0·3048** m $s^{-1}$ |
| | kilometre per hour | km $h^{-1}$ | 0·6214 mile/h | 1·609 km $h^{-1}$ |
| Pressure; Stress | pascal | Pa = N $m^{-2}$ | 1 kPa = 0·1450 lbf/$in^2$ | 6·895 kPa |
| | bar | bar = $10^5$ Pa | 14·50 lbf/$in^2$ | 0·068 95 bar |
| Frequency | hertz | Hz = $s^{-1}$ | **1** c/s | **1** Hz |
| Angle | radian | rad | 57° 18′ | $\frac{\pi}{180}$ rad |
| Solid angle | steradian | sr | — | — |
| Temperature, absolute | degree Celsius or Centigrade | °C | ($\frac{9}{5}$ **t**°C + **32**) °F | $\frac{5}{9}$ (**t** °F − **32**) °C |
| | kelvin | K | $\frac{9}{5}$ degree Rankine | $\frac{5}{9}$ K |
| Potential difference; Electromotive force | volt | V = kg $m^2$ $s^{-3}$ $A^{-1}$ = W $A^{-1}$ | | |
| Resistance / Reactance }electrical / Impedance | ohm | $\Omega$ = kg $m^2$ $s^{-3}$ $A^{-2}$ = V $A^{-1}$ | | |
| Capacitance, electrical | farad | F = $kg^{-1}$ $m^{-2}$ $s^4$ $A^2$ = A s $V^{-1}$ | | |
| Inductance, magnetic | henry | H = kg $m^2$ $s^{-2}$ $A^{-2}$ = V s $A^{-1}$ | | |

* The mass of a body is the quantity of matter in it; its weight is the force with which the earth attracts it, and is directly proportional to its mass. The use of the term 'weight', where 'mass' is strictly intended, is acceptable in non-technical usage when referring to objects within the earth's atmosphere.

# Mathematical symbols

+ plus

− minus

± plus or minus

× multiply by

÷ divide by

= is equal to

≡ is identically equal to

$\left.\begin{array}{l}\approx \\ \fallingdotseq \\ \risingdotseq\end{array}\right\}$ is approximately equal to

≠ is not equal to

> is greater than

≫ is much greater than

≯ is not greater than

< is less than

≪ is much less than

≮ is not less than

≥ is greater than or equal to

≤ is less than or equal to

∩ intersection

∪ union

∈ is member of set

⊂ is a subset of

∃ there exists

∀ for all values of

∗ denotes an operation

⇔ is equivalent to; if and only if

⇒ implies

$\left.\begin{array}{l}\{\,\} \\ \varnothing\end{array}\right\}$ empty set

$\{x, y\}$ the set whose members are $x$ and $y$

$E$ universal set

$N$ the set of natural numbers

$W$ the set of whole numbers

$Z$ the set of integers

$Q$ the set of rational numbers

$R$ the set of real numbers

$C$ the set of complex numbers

→ maps to

∴ therefore

∵ because

∠ angle

∥ parallel

⊥ perpendicular

$x^n$ $x.x.x \ldots$ to $n$ factors

$x^{-n}$ $\dfrac{1}{x^n}$

$\sqrt{x}$ the square root of $x$

$x^{\frac{1}{n}}, \sqrt[n]{x}$, the $n$th root of $x$

$x^0 = 1$

$x \to a$ $x$ approaches the limit $a$

$x!, \underline{|x}$ factorial $x$

∝ varies directly as

∞ infinity

$i$ or $j$ imaginary square root of $-1$

$\left.\begin{array}{l}\omega, \omega^2 \\ h, h^2\end{array}\right\}$ the complex cube roots of 1, $\frac{1}{2}(-1 \pm \sqrt{3}i)$

$\pi$ pi; the ratio of the circumference of a circle to its diameter, $3 \cdot 14159 \ldots$

$e, \varepsilon$ (1) the base of natural logarithms, $2 \cdot 718\,28 \ldots$
(2) the eccentricity of a conic section

$\log_n x$ log $x$ to the base $n$

$\left.\begin{array}{l}\log_{10} x \\ \lg x\end{array}\right\}$ log $x$ to the base 10, i.e. common logarithm

$\log_e x, \ln x$ log $x$ to the base $e$, i.e. natural or Napierian (q.v.) logarithm

M modulus of common logarithms
$\log_{10} e = 0 \cdot 4343 \ldots$
$(\log_{10} x = \log_e x \times 0 \cdot 4343)$

$\sin \theta = y/r$

$\cos \theta = x/r$

$\tan \theta = y/x$

$\sec \theta = r/x$

$\operatorname{cosec} \theta = r/y$

$\cot \theta = x/y$

$\left.\begin{array}{l}\sin^{-1} x \\ \arcsin x\end{array}\right\}$ the principal value of the angle whose sine is $x$

Similarly $\cos^{-1} x$, arccos $x$, etc.

sh $x$, sinh $x$ (hyperbolic sine of $x$) $\frac{1}{2}(e^x - e^{-x})$

ch $x$, cosh $x$ $\frac{1}{2}(e^x + e^{-x})$

th $x$, tanh $x$ sh $x$/ch $x$

sech $x$, cosech $x$, coth $x$ 1/ch $x$, 1/sh $x$, 1/th $x$

$\Sigma$ the sum of the terms

$\Pi$ the product of the terms

$|x|$ the absolute value of $x$

$\bar{x}$ the mean value of $x$

$\begin{vmatrix} a_1 & b_1 & c_1 \\ a_2 & b_2 & c_2 \\ a_3 & b_3 & c_3 \end{vmatrix}$ a determinant representing $a_1 b_2 c_3 - a_1 b_3 c_2 + a_3 b_1 c_2 - a_2 b_1 c_3 + a_2 b_3 c_1 - a_3 b_2 c_1$

$f(x), F(x), \phi(x)$, etc. function of $x$

$\Delta$ finite difference or increment

$\Delta x, \delta x$ the increment of $x$

$\dfrac{dy}{dx}, D_x y$ the derivative of $y$ with respect to $x$

$F'(x)$ stands for $\dfrac{d(F(x))}{dx}$

$\dfrac{d^n y}{dx^n}$ the $n$th derivative of $y$ with respect to $x$

$\dfrac{\partial y}{\partial u}$ the partial derivative of $y$ with respect to $u$, where $y$ is a function of $u$ and another variable (or variables)

$\nabla$ $\dfrac{\partial}{\partial x} + \dfrac{\partial}{\partial y} + \dfrac{\partial}{\partial z}$ vector derivative

$\nabla^n$ $n$th vector derivative

$\displaystyle\int$ integral

# Supplement

**access broadcasting, access television,** radio or television programmes put out independently by groups of people, not professionally involved in broadcasting, who want to bring their points of view to public notice.

**across the board,** *adv., adj.* of wage increases, etc., applying in all cases. [From a racing term.]

**-aholic, -oholic,** *ə-hol'ik,* (*facet.*) *suffix* having an addiction (to something), as in *workaholic, clothesoholic.*

**alternative,** *adj.* considered by some as preferable to the existing state or form of something, as *alternative society, alternative technology.*

**Ameslan,** *a'mas-lən, n.* American sign language, a means of communication by specified symbols and gestures. [*Ame*rican *s*ign *lan*guage.]

**amniocentesis,** *am-ni-ō-sin-tē'sis, n.* the insertion of a hollow needle into the uterus of a pregnant woman to withdraw a sample of the amniotic fluid to test for foetal abnormalities, etc.

**anabolic steroids,** steroids used to increase the build-up of body tissue, esp. muscle; illegally used by some athletes.

**anti-trust,** *adj.* of legislation, etc., directed against the adverse effects of monopolies on commerce.

**area code,** (*U.S.*) a three-digit number used before the local telephone number when dialling long-distance telephone calls.

**assessment centre,** a place where young offenders are detained to await a decision about their future.

**backpacking,** *n.* hiking from place to place carrying one's food, camping equipment, etc. on one's back in a **backpack.**

**bananas,** *adj., adv.* (*slang*) mad, crazy, wild.

**banding,** *n.* the division of children in the final year of primary school into three groups according to ability, in order to achieve an even spread in the mixed-ability classes usual in comprehensive schools.

**bang,** (*slang*) *v.t.* to have sexual intercourse with.— Also *n.*

**barefoot doctor,** *n.* a Chinese agricultural worker trained in basic first-aid in order to treat his fellow workers.

**base rate,** the rate, determined by a bank, on which it bases its lending rates of interest.

**-bashing,** *n. used as suffix* making malicious attacks, physical or otherwise, on (members of) groups of whom one strongly disapproves, as in *queer-bashing, union-bashing.*

**bed-and-breakfast,** *adj.* of stock exchange deals, in which shares standing at a loss are sold one day and rebought the next to establish a loss for tax purposes.

**Beeb,** *n.* coll. for **BBC** (see List of Abbreviations).

**beefalo,** *bēf'ə-lō, n.* a cross between a cow and a N. American buffalo. [*beef,* buff*alo.*]

**big science,** scientific and technical research that requires large financial resources.

**biochemical oxygen demand,** a measure of the amount of oxygen required by micro-organisms in a volume of water; used as a guide to the state of pollution of the water.

**biofeedback,** *n.* the clinical control of body functions in response to monitoring by electronic instruments such as an electrocardiograph.

**biological clock,** an inherent mechanism which regulates the physiological rhythms and cycles of living organisms.

**biomass,** *bi'ō-mas, n.* the amount of living material (animals, plants, etc.) in a unit of area.

**bionics,** *n.* see under bio- in Dict.: (*loosely*) the replacement of parts of the body with electronic or mechanical devices, such as power-controlled limbs, heart valves, etc.—*adj.* bionic,

relating to, using, etc. bionics: superhuman (*coll.*).

**black hole,** a collapsed star which is invisible because its gravitational field is so strong that matter and energy cannot escape.

**blow-dry,** *v.t.* to arrange (hair) by simultaneously brushing and drying (it) by a hand-held hairdrier.—Also *n.*

**blusher,** *n.* a cosmetic, usu. pinkish, applied to the cheeks to add colour to them.

**bomb,** (*slang*) *v.i.* to be a flop, fail.

**boot boy.** Same as **bovver boy** below.

**boot—put the boot in,** (*slang*) to attack viciously (and unfairly) (*lit.* and *fig.*).

**bottom out,** of prices, etc., to reach and settle at the lowest level, esp. when a rise is expected.

**bovver boy,** *bov'ər,* a member of a gang of hooligans in the habit of engaging in street fights using heavy, hobnailed boots (**bovver boots**) to kick their opponents: a troublemaker, esp. one who uses rough methods. [Prob. Cockney form of *bother.*]

**brain death,** cessation of function of the brain, now thought by some doctors to be the true indication of death, rather than the cessation of the heartbeat.—Also **cerebral death.**

**bunching,** *n.* over-close grouping together, esp. after a long gap, used e.g. of cars on a motorway.

**busing, bussing,** *n.* the transporting by bus of children from one district to school in another, esp. to achieve a more even racial balance.—*v.t.* bus.

**buzz word,** (*coll.*) a hackneyed, impressive-sounding, but often more or less meaningless word, used as part of the jargon of a particular field such as technology.

**cable television,** the transmission of television programmes by cable to individual subscribers.

**cabotage,** *n.* the use of lorries registered in one country to carry goods in another, for the purpose of evading certain taxes and licences.

**cagoule, kagool,** *kə-gōōl', n.* a lightweight weather-proof anorak, often kneelength. [Fr. *cagoule,* a monk's hood.]

**capital transfer tax,** a tax payable on gifts of money or property over a certain value, made either during the lifetime of the giver or after his death.

**card-carrying,** *adj.* openly expressing membership of or support for a party or group: orig. holding a membership card of a party, etc., esp. the Communist party.

**cash flow,** the movement of money in and out of a business.

**Catch 22,** *adj.* of an absurd situation in which one can never win, being constantly balked by a clause, rule, etc. which itself can change to block any change in one's course of action. [Title of novel by J. Heller (1961).]

**cellulite,** *sel'ū-lit, n.* deposits of fat, not responsive to dieting or exercise, which give the skin a dimpled, pitted appearance.

**cerebral death.** See **brain death** above.

**charismatic movement,** a non-denominational religious movement based on a belief in the divinely-inspired gifts of speaking in tongues (see **glossolalia** in Dict.), healing, prophecy, etc.

**charm,** *n.* in particle physics, the quantum number used to account for the unusual behaviour of certain elementary particles.

**chartist,** *n.* one who makes and/or studies charts of past performances, esp. of stocks and shares, with a view to forecasting future trends.—*n.* **chartism.**

**chat-show,** (*coll.*) *n.* a radio or television programme in which invited personalities talk informally with their host.—Also **talk-show.**

**chelation therapy,** *ki-lā'shan*, the treatment of heavy metal (e.g. lead) poisoning or certain other diseases by substances (**chelating agents**) which combine chemically with the toxic substances and render them harmless.

**chevron board,** a road sign consisting of a line of horizontal V-shapes, used to indicate a sharp change in direction.

**childminder,** *n.* a person, usu. with little training, officially recognised as being fit to look after children.

**Chinese restaurant syndrome,** a set of symptoms, including chest pain, dizziness and flushing, attributed to the consumption of too much monosodium glutamate, usu. in Chinese food.

**chip,** *n.* a minute piece of silicon or other semi-conducting material, on which one or more microcircuits can be printed.

**chronobiology,** *krŏn-ō-bī-ol'ə-ji, n.* the science of biological rhythms, esp. where the properties of the rhythms are measured.

**clawback,** *n.* an arrangement by which the financial benefit from family allowances, etc. is partially recouped by the government in extra taxation from the higher-paid; extended to other situations where a seeming financial benefit proves to be almost non-existent.

**cliometrics,** *kli-ō-met'riks, n.* the application of econometrics (q.v. in Dict.) in economic history. [*Clio*, the muse of history, and *econometrics*.]

**clout,** *klowt*, (*coll.*) *n.* influence, power.

**come out,** (*slang*) to declare openly one's homosexuality.

**community council,** a lay body elected to look after local interests.

**community physician,** a physician, appointed by the local health authority, with administrative responsibility for the medical and social welfare of an area.

**complex,** *n.* a collection of interrelated buildings, units, etc. forming a whole, as a *sports complex*.

**conglomerate,** *n.* an industrial group made up of companies which often have diverse and unrelated interests.

**conservation area,** an area, designated as being of special architectural or historic interest, and therefore protected from any alterations which would destroy its character.

**consumerism,** *n.* (the promotion of) the protection of the interests of buyers of goods and services against defective or dangerous goods, etc.: an economic system based on the continued increase in consumer goods.—*n.* **consumerist.**

**control unit,** a section of a prison in which difficult prisoners are detained with much reduced amenities in conditions of near isolation.

**core time.** See flexitime below.

**cot death,** the sudden, unexplained death in sleep of an apparently healthy baby.—Also **sudden infant death syndrome.**

**country rock,** electrically amplified music which combines the influences of rock and roll and country and western music.

**cut-off,** *adj.* of the point at which something ceases to operate or apply.—Also *n.*

**databank, database,** *n.* a large body of information stored in a computer, which can process it and from which particular pieces of information can be retrieved when required.

**day care,** daytime supervision and help given by trained nursing and other staff to a group of pre-school children, or elderly or handicapped people.

**day centre,** a centre which provides social amenities for elderly or handicapped people.

**dedicated,** *adj.* manufactured or set aside for a specific purpose, as a *dedicated calculator*.

**dendrogram,** *den'dra-gram, n.* a diagram with branches indicating the relationships of items in a classification.

**desertisation.** *de-zar-ti-zā'shan, n.* the deterioration

or reversion of land to desert conditions, owing to over-grazing, erosion, etc.

**digital clock, watch,** a clock, watch, without a conventional face, on which the time is indicated directly by numbers.

**digital socks,** socks with individual toe-coverings similar to the fingers of gloves.

**direct drilling,** the ploughing and sowing of a field in one operation.

**disadvantaged,** *adj.* deprived of the resources and privileges, usu. social, enjoyed by the majority of people.

**district,** *n.* the smaller of the two local-government administrative units in Scotland.—**district council,** a council elected to govern the affairs of this. Cf. **region.**

**district heating,** the distribution of heat from a central source to buildings in the surrounding area.

**domino theory,** the theory that one event, e.g. the collapse of a company, will set off a series of similar events: orig. the theory that the fall of one S.E. Asian country to Communism would lead to others following suit.—**domino effect,** the effect resulting from the domino theory. [From the fact that the fall of one domino standing on end causes the whole row to fall in turn.]

**donor card,** *n.* a card carried by one willing to have parts of his body (usu. kidneys) used in transplant surgery in the event of his death.

**doomwatcher,** *n.* a person who is pessimistic in outlook, esp. about the contemporary situation and its future.—Also **doomster.**

**double-bottom,** *n.* an articulated lorry with two trailers.—Also **drawbar outfit.**

**down-market,** *adj.* of (buying, selling or using) commodities relatively low in price, quality or prestige.—Also *adv.*

**drawbar outfit.** See **double-bottom** above.

**dry out,** (*coll.*) *v.i.* to take a course of treatment to cure oneself of alcoholism.—Also *v.t.*

**Dutch elm disease,** a fungal, often fatal, disease of elm trees, spread by bark beetles, and causing the leaves to turn yellow and fall.

**ecocide,** *ek'ō-sid, n.* the destruction of the aspects of the environment which enable it to support life.

**econut,** *ek'ō-nut,* (*slang*) *n.* a person showing extravagant concern for the effects of man's behaviour on the environment.

**effective rate.** See sterling **effective rate** below.

**egg**—to have, get egg on one's face, to be left looking a fool.

**ego-trip,** (*slang*) *n.* an action or experience which inflates one's good opinion of oneself.

**Emi-Scanner,** *em'i-,* ® *n.* a machine which produces X-ray pictures of the head or body with the assistance of a computer. [EMI—see List of Abbreviations.]

**encounter group,** a group which meets with a view to establishing greater self-awareness and greater understanding of others by indulging in unrestrained verbal and physical confrontation and contact.

**enkephalin(e),** *en-kef'ə-lēn, n.* a chemical found in small quantities in the brain, which relieves pain and can now be produced synthetically. [Gr. *en,* in, *kephalē,* head.]

**environics,** *en-vi-ron'iks, n. sing.* the study of methods of influencing behaviour by controlling environmental factors.

**environmental health officer,** a person appointed to investigate and prevent hazards such as pollution, lack of hygiene, etc. which might affect the health of the general public.

**environmentalism,** *n.* concern about the environment and its preservation from the effects of pollution, etc.—*n.* **environmentalist.**

**ethnic,** *adj.* pertaining to the customs, dress, food, etc. of a particular racial group or cult.

**exclusion order,** an order prohibiting the presence

**in,** or entry to, Britain of any person known to be concerned in acts of terrorism.

**exobiology,** *eks-ō-bi-ol'ə-ji, n.* the study of (possible) extra-terrestrial life.

**expo,** *eks'pō, n.* an exhibition or public showing. [*expo*sition.]

**factory-gate price,** the price of goods calculated by the seller exclusive of freight charges to the buyer.

**family income supplement,** a payment by the state to a family whose income is below a certain level.

**fastback,** *n.* a car whose roof slopes smoothly down towards the rear, giving a streamlined effect.

**feedstock,** *n.* raw material used in an industrial process.

**fiscal drag,** the means by which the inland revenue automatically benefits from any increase in earned income without any actual increase in taxation rates.

**flak,** (*fig.*) *n.* adverse criticism: heated disagreement, dissension.

**flexitime, Flextime ®,** *ns.* a system of flexible working hours in which an agreed total of hours may be worked at times to suit the worker often with the proviso that each day certain set hours (**core times**) are included.

**floating currency,** currency whose value is allowed to fluctuate freely against that of other currencies.

**footprint,** *n.* the area surrounding an airport, or the part of an aircraft's flight path, in which the noise level is liable to be above a certain level: the area covered by the down-driven blast of air which supports a hovercraft.

**four-function calculator,** an electronic calculator which can add, subtract, multiply and divide.

**Fourth World,** the poorest of the poor countries of the world.

**fragmentation bomb,** a bomb which shatters into destructive fragments on explosion.

**-freak,** (*slang*) *n.* used as suffix, one who is wildly enthusiastic about something, as in *film-freak, football-freak.*

**fringe,** *adj.* bordering on, or just outside, the recognised or orthodox form, as in *fringe medicine, fringe banks.*

**Frisbee,** *friz'bi, ® n.* a plastic saucer-shaped disk which can be made to skim through the air, used in various catching-games, etc.

**full-frontal,** *adj.* of the front view of a completely naked man or woman: with no detail left unrevealed (*fig.*).

**gang-bang,** (*slang*) *n.* successive sexual intercourse with one, usu. unwilling, female by a group of males. [See **bang** above.]

**gastarbeiter,** *gast'ar-bīt-ər n.* a migrant worker, esp. one who does menial work. [Ger., guestworker.]

**gazump,** *gə-zump', v.t.* to raise the price of property (also extended to wage settlements, etc.) after the acceptance of an offer but before the signing of the contract. [Prob. Yiddish *gezumph*, to swindle.]

**glue-sniffing,** *n.* the practice, sometimes fatal, of inhaling the fumes of certain types of glue to achieve hallucinatory effects, etc.

**grab**—**how does that grab you?** (*slang*) what's your reaction to that?; **up for grabs,** (*slang*)(ready) for the taking, for sale, etc.

**greenfield site,** a site, separate from existing developments, which is to be developed for the first time.

**greenhouse effect,** the progressive warming-up of the earth's surface due to the blanketing effect of man-made carbon dioxide in the atmosphere.

**green paper,** a statement of proposed government policy, intended as a basis for parliamentary discussion.

**green pound,** the agreed value of the pound used to express EEC farm prices in sterling.

**greige,** *grāzh, adj.* of cloth, undyed: of a greyish-beige colour.—Also **grège.** [Fr. (*soie*) *grège*, raw silk.]

**grey area,** an area relatively high in unemployment but not classed as a **development area** (q.v. in Dict.): an area between two extremes, having (mingled) characteristics of both of them: a situation in which there are no clear-cut distinctions.

**groundprox,** *n.* a device, fitted to large passenger aircraft, which gives audible and visible warning to the pilot when altitude falls below a given level. [*ground prox*imity warning system.]

**groupy, groupie,** *grōōp'i,* (*slang*) *n.* a teenage girl who follows pop-groups, or other celebrities, wherever they appear.

**gut,** (*coll.*) *adj.* of feelings or reactions, strong, deeply personal: of issues, etc., having immediate impact, arousing strong feelings.

**hack,** (*slang*) *v.t.* to tolerate, put up with.

**hang-gliding,** *n.* a sport in which one glides from a cliff-top, etc., hanging in a harness from a large kite (**hang-glider**).

**hard rock,** a form of rock and roll, usu. structurally and rhythmically simple and highly amplified.

**hassle,** *has'l,* (*coll.*) *v.t.* to harass, to annoy persistently.—*v.i.* to be involved in a struggle or argument.—*n.* bother, fuss: struggle: argument.

**hatchback,** *n.* car with a sloping rear door which opens upwards.

**headway,** *n.* the time interval between buses, trains, etc. travelling on the same route in the same direction.

**hiding**—**on a hiding to nothing,** in a situation in which one is bound to lose, in spite of all one's efforts.

**high-alumina cement,** a type of quick-hardening cement, made of bauxite and chalk or limestone; found to lose strength through time under certain conditions.

**hit-man,** (*slang*) *n.* one employed to kill or attack others (also *fig.*).

**hydroelastic suspension,** a system of car suspension in which a fluid provides interconnection between the front and rear suspension units.

**hype,** (*slang*) *n.* something intended to stimulate sales, etc.: a publicity stunt: the person or thing promoted by such a stunt.

**hypernatraemia,** *hi-pər-nə-trē'mi-ə, n.* an abnormally high concentration of sodium chloride (salt) in the blood, esp. in infants. [**hyper-**, excessive, **natrium** (see **natron** in Dict.) and Gr. *haima,* blood.]

**immunotherapy,** *n.* the treatment of disease, now esp. cancer, by antigens which stimulate the patient's own natural immunity.

**-in,** *suffix* indicating a (public) gathering of a group of people, orig. as a form of protest (as in *sit-in, work-in*), now for any joint purpose (as in *love-in, teach-in*).

**in-depth,** *adj.* of a survey, research, etc., detailed or penetrating.—Also *adv.*

**indexation,** *n.* a system by which wages, rates of interest, etc. are directly linked (**index-linked**) to changes in the cost-of-living index.

**inertia-reel seat-belt,** a type of self-retracting seat-belt in which the wearer is constrained only when violent deceleration of the vehicle causes the belt to lock.

**informatics.** See **information science** below.

**information science,** the study of processing and communication of data, esp. by means of computerised systems.—Also **informatics.**

**-intensive,** *adj.* used as suffix, having, using, requiring a great deal of something, as in *labour-intensive, capital-intensive.*

**intervention,** *n.* a system of removing surplus produce from the market and storing it until prices rise.

**into,** (*slang*) *prep.* interested in or enthusiastic about.

**jacket,** *n.* a structure fixed to the sea-bed to support an oil production platform.

**jawboning,** *(slang) n.* the urging, by a political leader, of union and industry chiefs, etc. to comply with government policy, e.g. wage restraints.—*v.t.* **jawbone.**

**jitney,** *jit'ni, n.* a passenger vehicle, usu. small, which operates on fixed routes and can be stopped at any point during its journey.

**Jobcentre,** *n.* a government-run employment agency where information about available jobs is displayed.

**jockette,** *jok-et', n.* a female jockey.

**juggernaut,** *n.* a very large lorry, usu. articulated.

**kagool.** See cagoule above.

**kneecapping,** *n.* a form of torture or (terrorist) punishment in which the victim is shot in the kneecap.

**kung fu,** *kung foo,* art of unarmed combat and self-defence developed in ancient China.

**Lassa fever,** *la'sa,* an infectious tropical virus disease, often fatal, transmitted by rodents. [From *Lassa,* in Nigeria, where it was first recognised.]

**law centre,** an office, usu. in a socially deprived area, where free legal advice and assistance are given.—Also **neighbourhood law centre.**

**lifeboat,** *(fig.) adj.* providing emergency rescue, esp. in financial situations.

**life sciences,** the sciences (biology, medicine, etc.) concerned with living organisms.

**life-style,** *n.* the (characteristic) way of life of a group or individual.

**liquid crystal,** a liquid which is anisotropic, like a crystal, over a definite range of temperature above its freezing point.

**liquid crystal display,** a display, esp. in electronic calculators, based on the changes in reflectivity of a liquid crystal cell when an electric field is applied.

**List D schools,** since 1969 the name given in Scotland to community homes (formerly approved schools).

**listed building,** a building which is officially listed as being of special architectural or historic interest and therefore cannot be demolished or altered without the consent of the local planning authority.

**local radio,** radio (programmes) broadcast from a local station to a relatively small area, often on local themes.

**logjam,** *(fig.) n.* congestion of events, etc. leading to complete cessation of action: such cessation of action.

**long-stop,** *(fig.) n.* a person or thing that acts as a final safeguard or check.

**low-key,** *adj.* understated, restrained: of a person, not easily excited, showing no visible reaction.

**low profile,** a manner or attitude revealing very little of one's feelings, intentions, activities, etc.—Also *adj.*

**low-rise,** *adj.* of buildings, having only a few storeys, in contrast to high-rise (q.v. in Dict.).

**machismo.** See macho below.

**macho,** *mach'ō, adj.* exaggeratedly virile, aggressively masculine.—*n.* one displaying these traits: machismo.—*n.* **machismo,** *mak-, mach-ēz'mō,* an exaggerated sense of or assertion of masculinity or virility. (Sp., male.)

**male chauvinist (pig),** *(coll.)* a man who believes in the superiority of men over women and acts accordingly.

**mesothelioma,** *mēz-ō-thēl-i-ō'ma, n.* a rare malignant tumour of the lining of the lung, chest or abdomen, sometimes caused by blue asbestos dust. [**meso-,** middle, **(epi)thelium** (q.v. in Dict.), **-oma,** a tumour.]

**minimum lending rate,** the minimum rate of interest (successor to the **bank rate,** q.v. in Dict.) charged by the Bank of England to the discount market.

**minipill,** *n.* a low-dose oral contraceptive containing no oestrogen.

**mockers—put the mockers on,** *(slang)* put an end to, put paid to.

**modem,** *mō'dəm, n.* an electronic device used to transmit and receive data as a frequency-modulated tone over a communications system. [**modulator,** **demodulator.**]

**monetarist,** *n.* one who advocates an economic policy based chiefly on the control of a country's money supply.—*n.* **monetarism.**

**Ms,** *miz, n.* title substituted for Miss or Mrs before the name of a woman, to avoid distinguishing between the unmarried and the married.

**multinational,** *n.* a large business company which operates in several countries.

**music centre,** a unit consisting of a record player, tape-recorder, and radio, with loudspeakers.

**name—the name of the game,** *(coll.)* what it's all about: the thing that matters.

**neighbourhood law centre.** See law centre above.

**nit-picking,** *(coll.) n.* petty criticism of minor details.—*v.i.* **nit-pick.** [nit (1).]

**nitty-gritty,** *nit'i-grit'i, (coll.) n.* the basic details, the fundamentals.

**no-go area,** orig. in N. Ireland, an area which only certain designated categories of people are allowed to enter (also *fig.*).

**no way,** *(slang)* emphatic expression of disagreement or dissent.

**nuke,** *nūk, (slang) n.* a nuclear weapon.—*v.t.* to attack using nuclear weapons.

**nuts and bolts,** the basic facts, the essential, practical details.

**oil platform,** a steel and/or concrete structure, either fixed or mobile, used in offshore drilling to support the rig and to keep stores.

**oil-rig,** *n.* the complete plant (machinery, structures, etc.) required for oil-well drilling: loosely, a mobile oil platform.

**one-off,** *adj.* made, intended, etc. for one occasion only.—Also *n.*

**on-lend,** *v.t.* to lend money which has already been borrowed from another company, etc.

**on stream,** *adv., adj.* of an industrial plant, etc., in, or going into, operation or production.

**peak,** *v.i.* to reach the height of one's powers, popularity, etc.: of prices, etc., to reach, and remain at, the highest level (sometimes with *out*).

**pelican crossing,** a type of pedestrian street crossing which includes an orange flashing light, during which motorists may move only if the crossing is clear.

**-person,** *n. used as suffix,* as in *chairperson, salesperson,* to avoid illegal or unnecessary discrimination on grounds of sex.

**Peter principle,** the theory that members of an organisation, etc. are promoted to posts one stage above their level of competence.

**petrodollars, petromoney, petropounds,** *ns.* dollars, money, pounds, acquired by the oil-producing countries as profit from the sale of their oil to the consumer countries.

**phone freak, phreak,** *(slang)* one who misuses the telephone, by telephoning (obscene messages) to strangers, or by trying to make free calls, etc.

**phone-in,** *(coll.) n.* a radio programme which consists mainly of telephone calls from listeners on selected topics.

**pixel,** *pik'səl, n.* one of the minute units which make up the picture (e.g. a TV picture) on a cathode-ray tube.

**pneumothorax,** *nüm-ō-thō'raks, n.* lung collapse resulting from the escape of air from the lung into the chest cavity—a potential hazard of working in compressed air, e.g. deep-sea diving.

**pod,** *n.* a protective housing for (external) engineering equipment, e.g. aircraft engines, nuclear reactor, space instruments.

**pole position,** *(fig.)* an advantageous position.

[In racing, the position on the inside of the track.]

**populist**, *n.* one who believes in the right and ability of the common people to play a major part in governing themselves.—*n.* **populism.**

**preservationist**, *n.* one who is interested in preserving traditional and historic things.

**Price Code**, a set of regulations used by the British government to control prices as a measure against inflation.

**Price Commission**, a body set up by the British government to control prices as a measure against inflation.

**prostaglandins**, *pros-tə-gland'inz*, *n.pl.* a group of chemical substances secreted by various parts of the body into the bloodstream and found to have a wide range of effects on the body processes, e.g. on muscle contraction. [*prostate gland*, one of the parts of the body where they are found.]

**Provo**, *prō'vō*, *n.* a member of the Provisional Irish Republican Army, the militant breakaway wing of the Official IRA.

**psych**, **psyche**, *sīk*, (*slang*) *v.t.* to defeat or intimidate by psychological means (sometimes with *out*): to get oneself psychologically prepared for (usu. with *up*): to stimulate (usu. with *up*).

**pulse code modulation**, a system of transmission in which the audio signals are sampled periodically, coded in digital form, and transmitted.

**purpose-built**, *adj.* specially made or designed to meet specific requirements.

**quadraphonics**, **quadrophonics**, *ns.pl.* a system of sound transmission using a minimum of four speakers fed by four, or sometimes three, separate channels.—Also **quadroph'ony, quadraphony.**

**quartz crystal watch**, a watch in which a quartz crystal, energised by a microcircuit, does the work of the hairspring of the traditional watch.

**rabbit on**, (*coll.*) to talk at length and in a rambling fashion.

**rap**, (*slang*) *n.* an informal discussion, chat.—Also *v.i.*

**raunchy**, *rönch'i, ranch'i,* (*slang*) *adj.* coarse, earthy: carelessly untidy, shabby.—*ns.* **raunch**, coarseness, bawdiness; **raunchiness**, state of being raunchy.

**rave-up**, (*slang*) *n.* a lively celebration, party.

**region**, *n.* the larger of the two local-government administrative units in Scotland.—**regional council**, a council elected to govern the affairs of this. Cf. **district.**

**relocate**, *v.t.* to move a firm, workers, etc. to a different area or site.—*v.i.* to move one's place of business or residence.

**ring fence**, the compulsory separation, for tax purposes, of a company's business interests in North Sea oil from their other business interests, to prevent them from paying less tax on their oil profits by setting against these profits any losses made in other businesses.

**rip-off**, (*slang*) *n.* (financial) exploitation: a theft, stealing: a film, etc. that is obviously imitative of another's theme, etc.

**roll**, (*slang*) *v.t.* to attack (and rob).

**roughneck**, *n.* a member of an oil-rig crew employed to deal with equipment on the rig floor.

**roustabout**, *rowst'ə-bowt, n.* a general labourer employed in the maintenance of an oil-rig.

**rumpus room**, a room in a house set aside as a playroom or a recreation room.

**runflat tyre**, a tyre which, after it has been punctured, can be safely driven on for a considerable distance without sustaining further damage.

**safari park**, an enclosed park where wild animals (mostly non-native) are kept uncaged in the open on view to the public.

**salami tactics**, a policy of cutting away, one by one, undesirable elements, e.g. particular people from an organisation.

**salopette**, *sal'ə-pet, n.* a type of ski suit consisting of quilted trousers with a bib and a matching jacket.

**samizdat**, *sam'iz-dat, n.* in the Soviet Union, the secret printing and distribution of government-banned literature. [Russ.]

**scene**, (*slang*) *n.* area of interest or activity.

**sci-fi**, *sī'fī', n.* coll. abbrev. for **science fiction.**

**setting**, *n.* a system of dividing pupils in mixed-ability classes into ability groups for certain subjects only.

**sexism**, *n.* discrimination (orig. against women, now against women or men) on grounds of sex.—*n.* **sexist.**

**sexploitation**, *n.* the exploitation of sex for commercial gain in literature and the performing arts, esp. films. [*sex* ex*ploitation*.]

**shades**, (*slang*) *n.pl.* sunglasses.

**sheltered housing**, housing for the elderly or disabled consisting of separate units with a resident housekeeper or similar person to look after the tenants' well-being.

**sitcom**, *n.* coll. abbrev. for **situation comedy.**

**sit-in**, *n.* occupation of a building, etc. as an organised protest against some (supposed) injustice, etc.

**skateboard**, *n.* a narrow wooden board, mounted on roller-skate wheels, on which one balances.

**skinflick**, (*slang*) *n.* a film in which some of the characters appear in the nude and which usually includes scenes of sexual intercourse.

**sleeping policeman**, a ramp across a road intended to slow down traffic.

**slippage**, *n.* (the extent of) failure to reach a set target.

**slumpflation**, *n.* an economic situation in which there is a marked decline in investment in industry, at the same time as a marked rise in inflation. [*slump*, in*flation*.]

**slush fund**, (*U.S. slang*) a fund of money used, often corruptly, in political campaigning and propaganda, etc.

**Smithsonian parity**, parity agreed for major currencies at an international conference at the Smithsonian Institute, Washington, in 1971.

**snake**, *n.* the band (narrower than the **tunnel** allowed by the IMF on the world market) within which the relative values of certain EEC currencies are allowed to float.

**soft rock**, a form of rock and roll, usu. rhythmically complex, highly melodious and low in volume.

**solar energy**, energy from the sun, esp. when used for home-heating, etc.

**spaghetti western**, an internationally-financed western, filmed in Spain by an Italian producer, characterised by a violent and melodramatic content and a baroque style.

**-speak**, (*coll.*) *n.* used as suffix a particular jargon or style of language, such as *techno-speak*, *doublespeak*, etc.

**spook**, (*slang*) *n.* a spy, an undercover agent.

**squish lip system**, a type of diesel engine combustion chamber designed to lessen fumes and noise pollution.

**stagflation**, *n.* an economic situation in which there is a marked decline in industrial output and consumer demand at the same time as a marked rise in inflation. [*stagnant*, in*flation*.]

**stand-off**, (*coll.*) *n.* deadlock.

**starspot**, *n.* an area of relative darkness on the surface of a star.

**sterling effective rate**, the percentage deviation of sterling from its **Smithsonian parity** (q.v. above) against an average of selected foreign currencies. —Also **effective rate.**

**stick—give someone stick**, (*slang*) to censure, punish.

**streak**, *v.i.* to run naked in public.

**sudden infant death syndrome.** See **cot death** above.

**suss (out)**, (*slang*) *v.t.* to examine, inspect thoroughly, investigate. [*suspect*.]

**swingometer, -om′,** *n.* a device which shows the direction and extent of the current swing of the counted votes in an election.

**tachograph,** *n.* an instrument fitted to commercial vehicles to record mileage, speed, number and location of stops, etc.

**tailback,** *n.* a line of traffic stretching back from anything obstructing or slowing down traffic flow.

**talk-show.** See **chat-show** above.

**tanga,** *tang′ga,* *n.* a brief string-like bikini.

**tank top,** a sleeveless pullover, usu. with a low round neckline, worn over a shirt, etc.

**teeny-bopper,** *(slang)* *n.* a teenager, esp. a teenage girl, who follows enthusiastically the latest trends in pop-music, clothes, etc.

**teleprocessing,** *n.* the use of a computer to process data transmitted from distant points.

**teletext,** *n.* written data, such as business news, etc., transmitted by television companies in the form of coded pulses which can be decoded by a special adaptor for viewing on a regular television.

**terotechnology,** *ter′ō-tek-nol′ə-ji,* *n.* the application of managerial, financial, engineering and other skills to extend the operational life of, and increase the efficiency of, equipment and machinery. [Gr. *tēreō,* to watch, observe, and **technology.**]

**thrift shop,** a shop, usu. run on behalf of a charity, which sells second-hand clothes and other articles.

**tokenism,** *n.* the practice of doing something once to give an impression of doing it regularly, e.g. employing one coloured person to avoid a charge of racialism.

**toxocara,** *toks-ə-kar′ə,* *n.* a parasitic worm found in the intestines of dogs and known to cause disease and eye damage in humans.

**trade-off,** *n.* the giving up of one thing in return for another, usu. as an act of compromise.

**trannie,** *n.* slang abbrev. for **transistor radio.**

**triad,** *trī′ad,* *n.* a Chinese criminal secret society.

**trike,** *trik,* *n.* coll. abbrev. for **trichlorethylene.**

**triticale,** *trī′ti-kāl,* *n.* a hybrid cereal grass, a cross between wheat and rye, grown as a food crop.

**trog,** *(coll.)* *v.i.* to walk, often heavily and wearily.

**tube,** *(slang)* *n.* an aircraft: a television.

**tug of love,** a dispute over the guardianship of a child, e.g. between the natural and the foster parents.

**tunnel.** See **snake** above.

**tunnel vision,** a medical condition in which one is unable to see objects other than those straight ahead: single-minded concentration on one's own pursuits or viewpoints to the total exclusion of those of others.

**unbundling,** *n.* the separation of the costs of the component parts of a package business transaction.

**unit-packaging,** *n.* a method of packaging (pills, etc.) in which the items are individually encased.

**unit-pricing,** *n.* a method of pricing foodstuffs, etc. by showing the cost per agreed unit, e.g. kilogram, pound.

**unsocial hours,** hours worked when the majority of people are at leisure or asleep.

**up-market,** *adj.* of (buying, selling or using) commodities relatively high in price, quality or prestige.—Also *adv.*

**urban guerrilla,** one who is engaged in terrorist activities in towns and cities.

**verbal,** *(slang)* *n.* an oral statement, esp. one of confession (alleged to have been) made, to the police (following arrest).—*v.t.* of the police, to attribute (to a suspect) an (allegedly false) admission.

**vibes,** *vibz,* *(slang)* *n. pl.* feelings or sensations experienced or communicated. [**vibrations.**]

**voice-over,** *n.* background voice of an unseen narrator in a film, etc.

**vote with one's feet,** to indicate one's dissatisfaction with a situation or conditions by leaving.

**walk-on,** *adj.* of an air-service, aeroplane, for which one does not have to purchase a ticket in advance and which is sometimes cheaper than the regular air-service.

**weather window,** a period of time in which the weather is suitable for a particular purpose, e.g. oil-drilling.—Also **window.**

**weeny-bopper,** *(slang)* *n.* a younger version of **teeny-bopper** above.

**wet-look,** *adj.* made of a glossy material, usu. PVC, which gives the appearance of being wet.

**whistle—blow the whistle,** *(slang)* to give information usu. to the authorities, about illegal, underhand practices.—*n.* **whistle-blower.**

**white hole,** a suggested source of the matter and energy observed flowing into the universe. Cf. **black hole** above.

**wholefood,** *n.* unprocessed food produced without any artificial fertilisers, pesticides, etc.

**window.** See **weather window** above.

**workforce,** *n.* the number of workers engaged in a particular industry: the total number of workers potentially available.

**yucky, yukky,** *yuk′i,* *(slang)* *adj.* dirty, unpleasant. —*n.* **yuk.**

**zap,** *(slang)* *v.t.* to hit, strike (also *fig.*): to cause to move quickly.—*v.i.* to go speedily or suddenly. *n.* vitality, force.—*interj.* expressing suddenness. —**zap (it) up,** make (things) livelier.

**zero in (on),** *(slang)* to direct (oneself) straight towards a target: to focus one's attention or energies on, as if on a target.

**zero-rated,** *adj.* of goods on which the purchaser pays no value-added tax but on which the seller can claim back any value-added tax already paid by him.

**zilch,** *zilch,* *(slang)* *n.* zero, nothing.

**zip code,** *(U.S.)* postal code. [**zone i**mprovement **p**lan.]

**zonked,** *zongkt′,* *(slang)* *adj.* utterly exhausted: intoxicated: under the influence of drugs.